INTERNATIONAL
WHO'S WHO IN MUSIC
AND MUSICIANS' DIRECTORY

INTERNATIONAL WHO'S WHO IN MUSIC

EDITOR:
DAVID M. CUMMINGS

PUBLISHER:
Nicholas S. Law

PRODUCTION MANAGER:
Jocelyn Timothy

PRODUCTION ASSISTANTS:
Sheryl Rigby
Rebecca Thompson

All communications to: I. W. M., International Biographical Centre,
Cambridge CB2 3QP, England.

INTERNATIONAL WHO'S WHO IN MUSIC AND MUSICIANS' DIRECTORY

(IN THE CLASSICAL AND LIGHT CLASSICAL FIELDS)

Fourteenth Edition
1994/5

EDITOR
DAVID M. CUMMINGS

INTERNATIONAL WHO'S WHO IN MUSIC
Cambridge, England

ML105.I57+   no.14   1994/95

Distributed exclusively in
the United States and Canada by,
Taylor and Francis International Publication Services
1900 Frost Road
Bristol. PA 19007, USA

First Published
1935
Second Edition
1937
Third Edition
1950
Fourth Edition
1962
Fifth Edition
1969
Sixth Edition
1972
Seventh Edition
1975
Eighth Edition
1977
Ninth Edition
1980
Tenth Edition
1985
Eleventh Edition
1988
Twelfth Edition
1990
Thirteenth Edition
1992
Fourteenth Edition
1994

ISBN 0 948875 71 2

Printed and bound in the United Kingdom by:
The Bath Press, Lower Bristol Road, Bath BA2 3BL

FOREWORD BY THE EDITOR

In the Thirteenth Edition of the International Who's Who in Music (1992) it was my intention to provide a comprehensive record of achievement in the classical and light classical fields. For this, the Fourteenth Edition, I have been responsible for some 2,000 new or largely new entries, while the remaining 6,000 entries have nearly all been revised. The result is a fuller, more accurate and more up-to-date source for contemporary musicians than any other book published so far.

As before, every biographee was sent a typescript of his or her entry for amending and approval, and the necessary corrections and updates have been incorporated in the final copy. Even in a book with such a wide scope as the International Who's Who in Music it is not possible to include in each case all the information which is submitted. If the Honours and Memberships sections have been pruned it will be appreciated that more space is made available to provide essential career information (e.g. works in the case of composers, or repertory for performers). While every care is taken to ensure accuracy, it is inevitable that some detail will have 'fallen under the table'. I must bear the responsibility for such errors but if I am written to care of the publishers I will put matters right in the next edition.

Although I am now solely responsible for the biographical section of the International Who's Who in Music, Professor Dennis McIntire of Indianapolis has continued and developed his invaluable work on the Appendices. Acknowledgements should also be made to various music reference book editors with whom I have worked and who continue to influence me: Michael Kennedy (Oxford Dictionary of Music), Nicolas Slonimsky (who celebrated his 100th birthday last month), Karl-Joseph Kutsch (Grosses Sängerlexikon) and Dr. Stanley Sadie (Grove's Dictionaries). I am also indebted to Alain Pâris, editor of Dictionnaire des Interprètes. Rodney Milnes and Deidre Tilley, through their work at Opera Magazine, have also provided much useful information.

While it is always a pleasure to record the achievement of young musicians, there is also sadness in having to delete those of earlier generations who have died. Perhaps the greatest loss since the last edition is that of Olivier Messiaen; other losses have been sustained by the deaths of such musicians as John Cage, Geraint Evans, Arleen Auger, Nathan Milstein and Tiana Lemnitz.

It only remains for me to thank all those who have helped to produce the Fourteenth Edition: the Publisher Nicholas Law has once again allowed me to act as editor and I am particularly grateful to Production Manager Jocelyn Timothy, and her staff for their patience, cooperation and efficiency.

David Cummings

David Cummings
Editor

May 1994

INTERNATIONAL BIOGRAPHICAL CENTRE
RANGE OF REFERENCE TITLES

From one of the widest ranges of contemporary biographical reference works published under any one imprint, some IBC titles date back to the 1930's. Each edition is compiled from information supplied by those listed, who include leading personalities of particular countries or profession. Information offered usually includes date and place of birth; family details; qualifications; career histories; awards and honours received; books published or other creative work; other relevant information including postal address. Naturally there is no charge or fee for inclusion.

New editions are freshly compiled and contain on average 80-90% new information. New titles are regularly added to the IBC reference library.

Titles include:

Dictionary of International Biography

Who's Who in Australasia and the Far East

Who's Who in Western Europe

Dictionary of Scandinavian Biography

Dictionary of Latin American and Caribbean Biography

International Who's Who in Art and Antiques

International Authors and Writers Who's Who

International Businessmen's Who's Who

International Leaders in Achievement

International Who's Who in Community Service

International Who's Who in Education

International Who's Who in Engineering

International Who's Who in Music and Musicians' Directory

International Who's Who in Poetry

Men of Achievement

The World Who's Who of Women

The World Who's Who of Women in Education

International Youth in Achievement

Foremost Women of the Twentieth Century

Enquiries to:
International Biographical Centre
Cambridge, CB2 3QP
England

CONTENTS

A

AADLAND Eivind, b. 19 Sept 1956, Bergen, Norway. Violinist. *Education:* Norwegian State Music Academy, Oslo with Camilla Wicks; International Menuhin Music Academy, Switzerland with Alberto Lysy and Yehudi Menuhin; Master classes with Sandor Vegh. *Career:* Formerly Concertmaster, Bergen Philharmonic Orchestra; Music Director, European Community Chamber Orchestra, 1988-; Has appeared in major halls nd festivals worldwide including: Musikverein, Vienna; Concertgebouw, Amsterdam; Salle Pleyel, Paris; Gewandhaus, Leipzig. *Recordings:* 12 CDs for various companies. *Address:* Arupsgate 10, 0192 Oslo, Norway.

AAQUIST JOHANSEN Svend, b. 1948, Denmark, Composer; Conductor; Computer Programmer. *Education:* University of Copenhagen; The Royal Danish Academy of Music, Copenhagen; International courses, Teachers Elisabeth Klein, Arne Hammelboe, Michel Tabachnik etc. *Debut:* 1969. *Career:* High School Teacher, 1969-75; Teacher of Conducting, Royal Danish Academy of Music, Copenhagen and State Academy of Music Esbjerg. Has held numerous workshops and seminars for musical and conducting courses; Chief Conductor and Artistic Director, Esbjerg Symphony orchestra; Artistic Adviser, Esbjerg Ensemble, 1984-; Conductor of numerous choirs, chamber ensembles and orchestras, 1969-; Has appeared in many concerts, festivals, radio and television recordings in Denmark, Finland, Iceland, Norway, Sweden, Switzerland, West Berlin, Federal Republic of Germany; Concerts with Danish radio Symphony Orchestra, Odense Symphony Orchestra; Odense Pro Musica; Esbjerg Symphony Orchestra; Stockholm Culture House Orchestra; Concert tours with West German Chamber orchestra, Emsemble Modern, 1981, 1982, 1984; Artistic Director, Lyngby New Music Ensemble and Orchestra, 1970-76; LYT (Listen) Ensemble, 1976-80; DUT, Danish ISCM, Chamber Orchestra, 1980-85; Esbjerg Ensemble Composers Workshop, 1981-; Roskilde Wind Consort, 1980-; The Danish Brass Ensemble, 1982-. *Compositions Include:* Pentagram, 1969; Songs in Between, 1970; Salut-Salut, 1970; Floes (Wintermusic), 1972; Solla famire Dosi, 1972; ke-Tjak, 1973; For Two Pianos, 1974; Unite, 1974; Wiegenleid, 1974; Sinfonia Sisyphus, 1976; The Lilacs Shall Bloom in May, They Shall!, 1978; Sisyphus sings, 1979; Malinche, 1979; Morning, 1979; Sun, 1983; Nocturne, 1983; Malinche, 1984; Hymn with Dances, 1985; Tai-Yang, 1988. *Recordings:* Has made numerous recordings. *Memberships:* Co-Founder, LUT and LYT; Danish State Music council; NOMUS, 1971-76; Nordic Composers' Council, President, 1973-74; Member of Boards of Society for Publication of Danish Music, 1974-84; Danish Composers' Society, Chairman, 1973-74; DUT - Danish ISCM, Chairman, 1980-84. *Address:* Rialtovej 7, DK-2300 Copenhagen, Denmark.

ABAJAN Maria b. 1950, Eriwan, Armenia. Singer. *Education:* Studied at Eriwan and Tchaikovsky Conservatory, Moscow; Further studies, Los Angeles. *Career:* Moved to USA, 1977; Successful at singing competitions, New York, San Francisco, Italy and Mexico; Appeared in Europe, 1985-, notably as Turandot in Liege, as Abigaille in Nabucco, Brussels, 1987, as Aida in Zurich; Has sung the Trovatore Leonora and Elisabeth de Valois in Hamburg, Tosca and Amelia (Ballo in Maschera) in Essen; Appeared as Tosca with Scottish Opera, Glasgow, 1990. *Address:* c/o Scottish Opera, 39 Elmbank Crescent, Glasgow G2 4PT, Scotland.

ABBADO Claudio, b. 26 June 1933, Milan, Italy. Conductor. *Education:* Giuseppe Verdi Conservatory, Milan; Academy of Music, Vienna, with Hans Swarowsky. *Debut:* La Scala, Milan, 1960 in concert celebrating tercentenary of A. Scarlatti; Salzburg Festival 1965, local premiere of G. Manzoni's opera Atomtod. *Career:* Conducted opening of La Scala season, 1967; Music Director La Scala, 1968-86; Covent Garden debut 1968 (Don Carlos); Has conducted the Vienna Philharmonic Orchestra from 1972; Tour of USA, with Cleveland and Philadelphia Orchestras, 1972; Tour with La Scala Company to Munich 1972; USSR 1974; London 1976 (Simon Boccanegra); USA 1976; Japan 1981; Tour with the Vienna Philharmonic to Japan and China 1973; Founder, European Community Youth Orchestra 1978; Musical Director, London Symphony Orchestra 1979-88 (series of concerts, Mahler, Vienna and the 20th Century, 1985); Principal Conductor, Chamber Orchestra of Europe 1981; Founder of La Filharmonica della Scala 1982; Principal Guest Conductor of Chicago Symphony Orchestra 1982-85; Debut at the Vienna State Opera 1984; Director 1986-91; Founder, Gustav Mahler Jugendorchester, Vienna, 1986; Conductor, New Year's Eve Concerts, Vienna, 1988 and 1990; Appointed Musical Director and Principal Conductor Berlin Philharmonic Orchestra 1989; Promenade Concerts, London, 1991, with the Gustav Mahler Jugendorchester (5th Symphony) and the Berlin Philharmonic (Brahms 2nd Piano Concerto and Mahler 4); Conductor, The House of the Dead, Salzburg Festival, 1992; Bruckner's 5th Symphony with the Gustav Mahler Youth Orchestra, Promenade Concerts, 1993; Engaged to return to La Scala, 1994, Il Barbiere di Siviglia; Artistic Director, Salzburg Easter Festival, 1994. *Publications:* La Casa Del Suoni - Book for Children about Music. *Recordings include:* Operas by Rossini and Verdi, Mussorgsky, Berg, Schubert (Fierabras); Music by Berg and Nono; Complete Symphonies of Mahler, Schubert, Mendelssohn, Beethoven and Tchaikovsky; Mozart Piano Concertos with Rudolf Serkin; Brahms Piano Concerto No.1, with Brendel and Vivaldi's Four Seasons, with Viktoria Mullova (Philips); Works of Haydn and Prokofiev, Bartók, Ravel, Debussy; currently working on cycle of complete Bruckner symphonies. *Honours include:* Mozart Medaille; Premio Abbiati; Officier of the French Légion d'Honneur; Koussevitzky Prize (Tanglewood); Winner, Mitropoulos Conducting Competition. *Address:* Harold Holt Ltd, 31 Sinclair Road, London W14 ONS, England.

ABBADO Marcello, b. 7 Oct 1926, Milan, Italy. Musician. *Education:* Diploma in Piano 1944, Diploma inComposition 1947, Milan Conservatory. *Career:* Soloist and Conductor in Europe, America, Africa, Asia, 1944-; Specialised in Debussy and piano concertos of Mozart; Professor of Piano at the Conservatories of Cagliari, Venice, Milan and of Composition at Parma and Bologna, 1950; Director, Liceo Musicale, Piacenza, 1958; Director, Rossini Conservatory, Pesaro, 1966; Director, Verdi Conservatory, Milan, 1972. *Compositions:* Ballet: Scena senza storia; Orchestral: Concerto for orchestra; Variations, theme of Mozart; Hommage à Debussy; Costruzioni, five little orchestras; Double cencerto, violin, piano, double chamber orchestra; Risonanze, two pianos, chamber orchestra; Cantata ebraica, vocal soloists choir, orchestra; Seven ricercari, six intermezzi, violin, orchestra; Ostinato, rhythmus of Sinfonia of Signor Bruschino, Rossini for piano, orchestra; Chamber: 15 Poesie T'ang, voice and 4 instruments; Ciapo for voice, 9 instruments; Cantata for voice and instruments; Three Quatuor; Duo for violin, cello; Fantasian. 2 for 4 instruments, 31 perccussions; Fantasia n. 3 for wind instruments; Riverberazioni for wind instruments, piano; Concertante for piano and instrument; Divertimento for winds and piano; Sonata for flute; For cello; Lento and Rondò, violin and piano; Variations, minuetto of Bach for piano; Lamento for the mother's death for clavicordo; Aus das Klavier for piano; Salmus VIII for choir; Responsorio for choir, organ; Jeux dangereux for harpe; Sarà Sara for guitar; Seven ricercari for violin. *Memberships:* Administrative Council, Teatro alla Scala, Milan; Fondazione Curci, Naples; Fondazione Puccini, Lucca and Verdi Conservatory, Milan; President of juries of national and international competitions of chamber music, composition, conducting, piano and others; Artistic Director of 'Orchestra Sinfonica di Milano Giuseppe Verdi'. *Address:* Via Conservatorio 12, 20122 Milan, Italy.

ABBADO Roberto, b. 1955, Milan, Italy. Conductor. *Education:* Studied at Pesaro and Milan Conservatories, with Franco Ferrara, Rome, and at Teatro La Fenice, Venice. *Debut:* With Orchestra of Accademia Santa Cecilia, 1977. *Career:* Operatic debut, 1978, with new production of Simon Boccanegra at Macerata; Chief Conductor of Munich Radio Orchestra, 1992; Engagements with Staatskapelle Dresden, Bamberg Symphony, Orchestre National De France, Rai Turin, The Orchestra of Saint Luke's, New York, Maggio Musicale Fiorentino Orchestra; opera engagements at La Scala, with world premier of Flavio Testi's Il Sosia and Riccardo III and new production of Don Pasquale; Vienna State Opera, with new production of La Cenerentola, Bayerische Staatsoper, Munich, with new production of La Traviata, 1993 and Adriana Lecouvreur, Manon Lescaut, Don Pasquale; Metropolitan, New York, with Adriana lecouvreur, 1994, San Francisco, with La Forza Del Destino, and Rome, Florence, Bologna, Venice, Berlin Deutsche Oper, Zurich, Barcelona, Tokyo, with Teatro Comunale Bologna, 1993; Festival appearances at Edinburgh, 1982, Israel, 1984, Lille, 1989, Munich. *Recordings:* For RCA Victor. *Address:* c/o Bayerischer Rundfunk, Rundfunkplatz 1, 80300 Munich, Germany.

ABDEL-RAHIM Gamal, b. 25 Nov. 1924, Cairo, Egypt. Composer; Professor. m. Samha El-Kholy, 8 Dec. 1959, 1 daughter. *Education:* BA, History, University of Cairo, 1945; Composition study with H. Genzmer, Staatliche Hochschule für Musik, Freiburg, Federal Republic of Germany, 1950- 57; Diploma, Composition, 1957. *Career:* Assistant Professor, 1959-71, Professor, 1971-84, Vice-Dean, 1978-81, Founder, Chairman of Composition Department (1st in Arab region), 1970s-1984, Professor Emeritus, 1984-, State Conservatory, Cairo; Visiting Professor, University of South Florida, Tampa, Florida, USA, 1987-. *Compositions:* Orchestral: Suite for Orchestra; Baladi, Introduction and Rondo; Symphonic Variation on an Egyptian Theme; Symphonic Poem Isis; Jubiland Dance; March of Amosis; Lotus Pond, flute/oboe, orchestra; Rhapsody for Cello and Orchestra; Echoes, flute, orchestra; Fantasia on an Egyptian Folktune, violin, orchestra; Awakening, cantata for baritone, choir, orchestra; Sinai Epic, cantata for children's and mixed choirs, orchestra; Egyptian Aspects, on 4 Folktunes, choir, orchestra; Kadni'l Hawa, cantata on an ancient Dawr, choir, orchestra; Ballet music: Osiris (5 scenes), percussion, harp, chamber ensemble; Hassan and Naima (3 scenes); Chamber music: Sonata for Violin and Piano; Duet for Violin and Cello; Improvisations for Unaccompanied Cello (both works with microtonal intervals); Lament Conflict, piano; Variations for Piano (Ed.Doblinger, Vienna); Concert Rhumba, trumpet, piano; Many songs; A capella choral works; Incidental music for theatre, film, TV. *Recordings:* All works recorded on Egyptian Radio and Television. *Hobbies:* Anthroposophy and Zen-Buddhism readings; Languages (self-taught). *Address:* 13044 Leverington Street, Tampa, FL 33624, USA.

ABERCROMBY Jillian Dawn, b. 19 Dec 1935, Poole, Dorset, England. Violinist. m. Eric James Abercromby, 20 May 1961, 1 daughter. *Education:* Senior University Scholarship to Royal College of Music, London, 1954-58; ARCM (Piano); ARCM (Violin); GRSM. *Career:* Violin and Piano Teacher, St Helen's, Northwood, 1958-59; Peripatetic Teacher, Oxford, 1959-84; Visiting Teacher, St Helen's, Abingdon, 1964-66; Lecturer, Bulmershe College, 1974-78; Lecturer, King James College of Henley, 1977-87; Private Teacher, Guernsey, 1987-; Freelance Player, Channel Isles, France and England. *Memberships:* Incorporated Society of Musicians; Musicians Union; Royal College of Music Union. *Hobbies:* Conservation; Yoga; Walking; Gardening; Bee-keeping. *Address:* La Primavera, Village de Putron, St Peter Port, Guernsey, Channel Isles.

ABRAHAMSEN Hans, b. 23 Dec. 1952, Copenhagen, Denmark. Composer. *Education:* Studied horn, theory, music history, Royal Danish Conservatory, Copenhagen, 1969-71; Composition with Pelle Gudmundsen-Holmgreen and Per Norgard, Jutland Academy of Music, Arhus. *Compositions:* Orchestral: Foam, 1970; Symphony in C, 1972; Symphony No 1, 1974; Stratifications, 1973-75; Nach und Trompeten, 1981; Marchenbilder for 14 Players, 1984; Cello Concerto, 1987; Chamber: Fantasy Pieces after Hans-Jorgen Nielsen for Flute, Horn, Cello and Piano, 1969,

revised 1976; October for Piano Left Hand, 1969, revised 1976; Round and In Between for Brass Quintet, 1972; 2 woodwind quintets: No 1, Landscapes, 1972; No 2, Walden, 1978; Nocturnes for Flute and Piano, 1972; Flowersongs for 3 Flutes, 1973; Scraps for Cello and Piano, 1973; 2 string quartets: No 1, 10 Preludes, 1973; No 1, 1981; Flush for Saxophone, 1974, revised 1979; Double for Flute and Guitar, 1975; Winternacht for 7 Instruments, 1976-79; Canzone for Accordion, 1978; Geduldspiel for 10 Instruments, 1980; 6 Pieces for Violin, Horn and Piano, 1984; 10 Studies for Piano, 1983-87; Vocal: Herbst for Tenor, Flute, Guitar and Cello, 1970-72, revised 1977; Universe Birds for 10 Sopranos, 1973; Songs of Denmark for Soprano and 5 Instruments, 1974, revised 1976; Aria for Soprano and 4 Instruments, 1979.

ACCARDO Salvatore, b. 26 Sept. 1941, Turin, Italy. Violinist and Conductor. *Education:* Studied with Luigi d'Ambrosio at Naples Conservatory, diploma 1956; Postgraduate study with Yvonne Astruc at the Accademia Chigiana, Sienna. *Career:* Has toured extensively as solo violinist and, latterly, as conductor in Europe and North and South America; Founded the Turin L'Orchestra da Camera Italiana 1968; Soloist with the ensemble I Musici 1972-77 and Semaines Musicales of Chamber Music at Naples; Repertory includes Bach, Vivaldi and Paganini; Works composed for him include Fantasia for violin and orchestra by Walter Piston, Argot for solo violin by Franco Donatoni, Dikhtas by Iannis Xenakis, 1980; Conducted Rossini's opera L'occasione fa il ladro at the 1987 Pesaro Festival; Plays several Stradivarius violins and a Guarnerius del Gesu of 1733; Took part in a performance of Schoenberg's String Trio at the Elizabeth Hall, London, 1990. *Writings:* L'Arte del violino, Milan 1987. *Recordings include:* Paganini's 24 Caprices and the Six Concertos. *Address:* c/o Accademia Musicale Chigiana, Via di Citta n 89, 53100 Sienna, Italy.

ACKER Dieter, b. 3 Nov. 1940, Sibiu, Rumania. Composer; Teacher. *Education:* Studied piano, organ, theory with Franz Dressler, Sibiu, 1950-58; Composition with Sigismund Toduta, Cluj Conservatory, 1959-64. *Career:* Teacher, Theory and Composition, Cluj Conservatory, 1964-69; Teacher, Robert Schumann Conservatory, Dusseldorf, 1969-72; Teacher, Theory and Composition 1972-76, Professor of Composition 1976-, Munich Hochshule fur Musik. *Compositions:* Orchestral: Texturae, 1970; Quodlibet II for Chamber Orchestra, 1975; Symphony No 1, Lebenslaufe, 1977-78; Bassoon Concerto, 1979-80; Violin Concerto, 1981; Symphony No 2, sinfonia Concertante, 1982; Concerto for String Orchestra, 1984; Piano Concerto, 1984; Kammerspiel for 12 Solo Instruments, 1985; Musik for Strings and Harp, 1987; Ballad for violin and Orchhestra, 1989; Music for oboe and strings, 1989; Music for two horns and strings, 1991; Sinfonia concertante Nr. 1 and 2 (violin, viola, cello, piano and orchestra), 1991; Music for viola, harp and strings, 1992; Symphony No. 3, 1992; Chamber: 3 string trios, 1963, 1983, 1987; 4 string quartets, 1964, 1965-66, 1966-68, 1971-75; Clarinet Quintet, 1973; Nachstucke for Winds, 1978; Mörike Sonata for Cello and Piano, 1978; Hölderlin-sonata for piano, 1978; Serenata Notturna for Wind Quintet, 1983; Quibbles for 2 Trumpets, Horn, Trombone and Tuba, 1983; String Sextet, 1983; Rilke Sonata for Violin and Piano, 1983; Eichendorff Sonata for Clarinet and Piano, 1983; Piano Trio No 2, 1984; Sonata for Viola and Piano, 1985; Harp Quartet, 1986; 2 piano quartets, 1986, 1986; Octet No 2 for Flute, Clarinet, 2 Trumpets, 2 Trombones and 2 Bassoons, 1987; Quartet for Violin, Clarinet, Cello and Piano, 1987; Trio for Flute, Viola and Harp, 1987; Sonata for Viola and Harp, 1987; Quartet for Oboe, Violin, Viola and Cello, 1988; Trio for 2 Flutes and Piano, 1988; Octet for clarinet, horn, bassoon, two violins, viola, vcello and double-bass, 1989; Caprice for harp, 1989; String quartet No. 5, 1990; Tro for trumpet, trombone and piano, 1990; Six 'Haiku' for tenor (soprano), violin, vcello and piano, 1990; Piano trio Nr. 3, 1992; Sinfonia brevis for ten brass instruments, 1993; Vocal music; Piano pieces; organ music. *Address:* Kleiststrasse 12, D-8012 Munich-Ottobrunn, Germany.

ACS Janos b. 23 Mar 1952, Hungary. Conductor. div., 1 son, 2 daughters. *Education:* Diplomas, Flute, Pianoforte, Composition, Bratk Bela Institute, F Liszt Academy, Budapest; Organ Diploma, Verdi Conservatorio, Milan. *Debut:* in Fidelio, Teatro Carlo Felice, Genoa, 1979. *Career:* Appearances: Idomeneo, Opera di Roma; Tancredi, La Fenice; Falstaff, I Capuleti, Amico Fritz, Arena di Verona; Offenbach, Comunale di Firenze; La Bohème, Frankfurt; Symphonic programmes, Tokyo; Manon, Pagliacci, La Traviata, Otello, Denver; Carmen, Il Trovatore, Tristan and Isolde, Pretoria; Faust, Hong-Kong; Luciano Pavarotti recital, Budapest; 1 of Luciano Pavarotti's conductors; Principal Conductor, Pact Theater, Pretoria, 1983-88; Principal Conductor, Opera Colorado, Denver, USA, 1985-91. *Recordings:* Bellini symphonies, Donizetti symphonies, Erato; I Puritani, Carmen, videocassette, Pact, Pretoria; Respighi's Gli Uccelli, Trittico Botticelliano, RAI, Rome. *Honours:* Respighi Memorial Concert and Prize, 1985. *Memberships:* Co-Director, Franz Listz Society of Germany, Eschweiger. *Hobbies:* Swimming; Riding. *Address:* Durener str 33/A, 518 Eschweiler, Germany.

ADAM Theo, b. 1 Aug. 1926, Dresden, Germany. Singer (Bass-Baritone); Producer. *Education:* Sang in Dresden Kreuzchor and studied with Rudolf Dietrich, Dresden, and in Weimar. *Debut:* Dresden 1949, as the Hermit in Der Freischütz. *Career:* Berlin State Opera from 1952; Bayreuth debut 1952, as Ortel in Meistersinger; later sang Wotan, Gurnemanz, King Henry, Pogner, Sachs and Amfortas; Covent Garden debut 1967, as Wotan; Metropolitan Opera debut 1969, as Sachs; Guest appearances in Hamburg, Vienna, Moscow, Buenos Aires, Budapest, Chicago and San Francisco; Roles include Don Giovanni, Beethoven's Pizarro, Berg's Wozzeck, Boris Godunov, Verdi's King Philip, and Sarastro in Die Zauberflöte; Sang in and produced the premiere production of Dessau's Einstein at the Berlin State Opera, 1974; Salzburg Festival 1981, 1984 in the premieres of Cerha's Baal and Berio's Un Re in Ascolto; 1985 sang at the reopened Semper Opera House, Dresden, in Der Freischütz and as Ochs in Der Rosenkavalier; Sang Don Alfonso with company of Bavarian State Opera at Tokyo, 1988; La Roche in Capriccio at the Munich Festival, 1990; Has staged Capriccio in Munich, Lohengrin in East Berlin; Graun's Cesare e Cleopatra for the 250th Anniversary of the Berlin State Opera, 1992; Sang Dr Schön in Lulu, Dresden Semper Opera, 1992; Schigolch in Lulu at the Festival Hall, London, 1994. *Publication:* Seht, hier ist Tinte, Feder, Papier....(autobiography) 1983. *Recordings:* Bach cantatas and roles in Freischütz, Parsifal, Meistersinger, Die Zauberflöte, Così fan Tutte, Der Ring des Nibelungen, St Matthew Passion, Fidelio, Krenek's Karl V, Baal, Dantons Tod Rosenkavalier, Die schweigsame Frau; Companies include Eterna, Ariola, Electrola, Deutsche Grammophon, Eurodisc, Philips and Decca. *Address:* Schillerstr. D-8054 Dresden, Germany.

ADAMIS Michael, b. 19 May 1929, Piraeus, Greece. Composer; Choral Director. m. Pany Carella, 30 July 1973, 2 sons. *Education:* Theology Degree, Athens University, 1954; Byzantine Music Degree, Piraeus Conservatory, 1955; Composition Degree, Hellenicon Conservatory, 1959; Graduate studies, Composition, Electronic Music, Byzantine Paleography, Brandeis University, Boston, USA, 1962-65. *Career:* Founder, Director, Hellenic Royal Palace Boys Choir, 1950-67; Athens Chamber Chorus, 1958-61; Taught Byzantine Music, directed Choir, Greek Orthodox College of Theology, Boston, USA, 1961-63; Founder, 1st Electronic Music Studio in Athens, Greece, 1968; Head, Music Department, Choir Director, Pierce College, Athens, 1968-; Many Festival commissions including Hellenic Weeks of Contemporary Music, 1967-72, English Bach Festival, 1971, 1973; Performances of works include: International Festivals worldwide such as ONCE Festival, USA, 1962, ISCM, 1973, 1978, 1979, Europa Cantat, Graz, 1968, 1970, Barcelona, 1973, St Moritz, 1975, Leicester, 1976, Greek Month, London, 1975, 1989, Wittener Tage fur Neue Musik, 1976, Europalia, Brussels, 1982, Art Weeks all over Europe, also Middle East, Japan, Korea, European Broadcasting Stations including 8 on Greek TV, 1962-, WDR, Cologne, SFB, Berlin, France Culture, Greek, Swedish, Hungarian and Bulgarian Radios, 4 programmes on Radio Marseille, 1986; Toured Europe and the Americas with ballet piece Genesis, 1973; Photonymon presented at SIM UNESCO, Paris, 1980; Portrait presentation, Smithsonian Institution, Washington, D.C., USA, 1985. *Compositions:* Published: Epallelon for orchestra; Anakyklesis; Hirmos for voices; Kratema; Recorded: Genessis; Apocalypsis; Minyrismos; Metallic Sculptures; Byzantine Passion; Psalmic Ode. *Memberships:* President, Supreme Council for Music, Ministry of Culture, 1993 . *Address:* Gravias 43, 15342 Ayia Paraskevi, Athens, Greece.

ADAMS Byron, b. 9 Mar. 1955, Atlanta, Georgia, USA. Composer; Conductor; Author; Teacher. *Education:* BM, Jacksonville University, 1977; MM, University of Southern California, 1979; DMA, Cornell University, 1984. *Career:* Composer-in-Residence, Music Center, University of the South, 1979-84; Guest Composer, 26th Warsaw Autumn Festival, 1983, and San Francisco Conservatory, 1986; Lecturer, Cornell University, New York, 1985-87; Assistant Professor, University of California, Riverside. *Compositions:* Quintet for piano and strings, 1979; Concerto for trumpet and string orchestra, 1983; Sonata for trumpet and piano, 1983; Sonata for trumpet and piano, 1983; Concerto for violin and orchestra, 1984; Go Lovely Rose for male chorus, 1984; Missa brevis, 1988; Three Epitaphs, 1988. *Recordings:* Nightingales, 1979; Serenata aestiva, 1986. *Contributions to:* The Instrumentalist; Musical Quarterly; Notes. *Honours:* Grand Prize, Delius Festival Composition Competition, 1977; American Society of Composers, Authors and Publishers - Raymond Hubbell Award, Cornell University, 1984; Medly P Ray Composition Award, 1985; Vaughan Williams Research Fellowship, Carthusian Trust, 1985. *Hobbies:* Reading, traveling, hiking. *Address:* Department of Music, University of California, Riverside, Riverside, CA 92521.

ADAMS Daniel Clifford, b. 28 June 1956, Miami, Florida, USA. Composer. m. Elise Ruth Benjamin, 21 Dec. 1985. *Education:* DMA, University of Illinois, Urbana Champaign, 1985. *Career:* Composer in Residence, Performing and Visual Arts Center, 1985-87; Instructor, University of Miami, Miami Dade Community College, 1986-88; Assistant Professor, Texas Southern University, 1988-; Co-Founder, Director, South Florida Composers Alliance; Freelance Percussionist. *Compositions:* Three Movements for Unaccompanied Marimba, 1980; Mosaics for Clarinet Quartet, 1982; Paradoxical Compression for brass trio, 1985; Stratum for Marimba Quartet, 1986; Five Miniatures for Clarinet and Guitar, 1986; Contrariety for solo clarinet, 1986; Three Subtropical Vistas for mezzo-soprano and percussion, 1988; Twilight Remembered, for flute and Percussion, 1989; Alloy for percussion ensemble, 1990; Elegy for the Concerned for tenor voice with accompaniment, 1990; Impressions of Texas Poem for mixed chorus, 1991; Matecumbe Maelstrom for chamber orchestra, 1992; Confluence for bass clarinet solo, 1993. *Hobbies:* Reading; Fishing; Scuba diving. *Address:* 5026 Kingfisher, Houston, TX 77035, USA.

ADAMS Donald, b. 20 Dec. 1928, Bristol, Avon, England. Opera Singer. m. Muriel Harding, 19 July 1952, 1 daughter. *Education:* Bristol Cathedral School. *Debut:* Embassy Theatre, Swiss Cottage, London, 1949. *Career:* Principal Bass, D'Oyly Carte Opera Company, 1953-69; Co-Founder, Gilbert and Sullivan for All, 1963; Covent Garden Debut, 1983; Frontier Guardsman in Boris Godunov, conducted by Abbado; Has performed with Scottish Opera, Welsh National Opera, Glyndebourne, The English National Opera, Lyric Opera of Chicago, Washington Opera, Los Angeles Opera, Canadian Opera, San Francisco Opera; Netherlands Opera and Geneva Opera; Appearances on stage, TV, Radio and in films; 8 films for TV by Gilbert and Sullivan for All, The Mikado, for Warner Bros.; 3 Brent Walker Gilbert and Sullivan Video films; Monte Carlo Opera, Aix-en-Provence Festival; Other roles include Rossinís

Bartolo; Antonio in Figaro and Dikoy in Katya Kabanova, (Glyndebourne); Falke in Die Fledermaus, at Chicago and San Francisco; Schigolch in Lulu, Canadian Opera Company, 1991; Ochs in Der Rosenkavalier, Welsh National Opera, 1990; Sang Quince in A Midsummer Night's Dream, Aix Festival, 1992. *Recordings:* Numerous for Decca, BASF, Pye, RCA Victor, Pearl, Brookledge Recordings of Hollywood, also Grand Prix du Disque. *Hobbies:* Golf; Walking. *Current Management and Address:* IMG Artists, Media House, 3 Burlington Lane, Chiswick, London W4 2TH, England.

ADAMS John (Coolidge), b. 15 Feb. 1947, Worcester, Massachusetts, USA. Composer; Conductor. *Education:* Studied clarinet with father and Felix Viscuglia; BA 1969, MA 1971, Harvard College; Studied composition with Leon Kirchner, David Del Tredici and Roger Sessions. *Career:* Appearances as Clarinettist and Conductor; Head, Composition Department, San Francisco Conservatory, 1971-81; Adviser on New Music 1978, Composer-in-Residence 1982-85, San Francisco Symphony Orchestra; Conducted Nixon in China at 1988 Edinburgh Festival; Creative Adviser, St Paul (Minnesota) Chamber Orchestra, 1988-89; The Death of Klinghoffer, Premiered at Brussels, Lyon and Vienna, 1991. *Compositions:* Operas: Nixon in China, 1987; The Death of Klinghoffer, 1991; Orchestral: Common Tones in Simple Time, 1979; Harmonium for Chorus and Orchestra, 1980; Grand Pianola Music for 2 Sopranos, 2 Pianos and Small Orchestra, 1981-82; Shaker Loops for String Orchestra, 1983; Harmonielehre, 1984-85; Fearful Symmetries, 1988; The Wound-Dresser for baritone and orchestra, 1989; Eros Piano for Piano and orchestra, 1989; Liszt La lugubre gondola and Wiegenlied arranged for orchestra, 1989; Chamber: Piano quintet, 1970; American Standard for Unspecified Ensemble, 1973; Grounding for 3 Solo Voices, Instruments and Electronics, 1975; Onyx for Tape, 1976; Piano: Ragamarole, 1973; China Gates, 1977; Phrygian Gates, 1977. *Honour:* Guggenheim Fellowship, 1982. *Address:* c/o ASCAP, ASCAP House, One Lincoln Plaza, NY 10023, USA.

ADASKIN Murray, b. 28 Mar 1906, Toronto, Ontario, Canada. Composer. m. (1) Frances James, 16 July 1931, dec. 22 Aug 1988, (2) Asta Dorothea Larsen, 7 May 1989. *Education:* Royal Conservatory of Music, Toronto; Paris, France; Music Academy of the West, California; Aspen School of Music, Colorado; LLD, University of Lethbridge, 1970; DMus, Brandon Univesity, 1972; DMus, University of Windsor, 1977; LLD, University of Saskatchewan, 1984; DMus, Univ of Victoria, 1984. *Career:* Professor, Head, Department of Music, 1952-66, Composer-in-Residence (1st in Canada), 1966-73, University of Saskatchewan; Member, Canada Council, 1966-69; Violinist, Toronto Symphony Orchestra, composer of more than 100 vocal, solo, chamber and orchestral works, 10 years; 2-hour broadcast Profile of Murray Adaskin at 65, CBC, 1971; The Travelling Musicians narrative by P K Page premiered 1984; 6-hour broadcast Murray Adaskin-A Canadian Music Retrospective, CBC, 1989, repeat broadcast, 1990; Premiere, Concerto for Orchestra, commissioned by Victoria Symphony Orchestra (Canada Council grant) dedicated to Myfanwy Pavelic, Canadian Painter, 1990; Murray Adaskin Retrospective week, radio broadcast, CJRT-FM, Toronto, Jan 1993. *Compositions:* Over 100 vocl, solo, chamber and orchestral works including Centennial opera Grant Warden of the Plains; Many commissioned works including: Of Man and the Universe; Coronation Overture; Algonquin Symphony; Concerto for Solo Viola and Orchestra, 1991, dedicated to Rivka Golani, Violist; Woodwind Quintet No 2, 1993, commissioned by CBC Ottawa; Quartet No 2, 1994, La Cadenza, commissioned by Univ of Saskatchewan (Canada Council grant) dedicated to Lafayette String Quartet. *Honours:* Lifetime Award, Excellence in the Arts, Saskatchewan Arts Board, 1991; Honoured by Saskatchewan Music Festival Assoc as distinguished Canadian Composer, 1994. *Address:* 3020 Devon Rd, Victoria, British Columbia, Canada V8R 6C9.

ADDISON John, b. 16 Mar. 1920, West Chobham,

Surrey, England. Composer; Conductor. m. Pamela Druitt, 15 Dec. 1951. 2 sons, 2 daughters. *Education:* Royal College of Music, London, 1938-40 and 1946-50; ARCM. *Career:* Professor of Composition & Theory, Royal College of Music, 1950-56; Conducted: London Symphony, Royal Philharmonic and BBC Symphony Orchestras in performances of own music; Also film music concerts with American orchestras including: San Francisco and Detroit Symphonies; Works commissioned by Sadler's Wells Ballet, English Opera Group, BBC, National Youth Orchestra, Farnham Festival. *Compositions:* Orchestral includes: Three Terpsichorian Studies; Concerto for Trumpet, Strings & Percussion; Carte Blanche, Ballet Suite; Partita for Strings; Wellington Suite; Concertino for Orchestra, 1993. Chamber includes: Serenade for Wind Quintet & Harp; Divertimento for Brass Quartet; Inventions for Oboe and Piano; Conversation Piece for 2 soprano voices, harpsichord/chamber organ & harp; Celebrations for 2 oboes, Bassoon and Harpsichord; Divertimento for Wind Quintet; Bagatelles for Brass Quintette. Theatre music: Cranks, revue; The Entertainer and Luther, John Osborne; St Joan of the Stockyards, Brecht; Hamlet, National Theatre; The Workhouse Donkey, John Arden; Musicals: The Amazons, Nottingham Playhouse; Popkiss, Globe Theatre, London; Films include: Seve Days to Noon; Private's Progress; Reach for the Sky; A Taste of Honey; Tom Jones; The Charge of the Light Brigade; Torn Curtain; Sleuth; The Seven-Per-Cent Solution; A Bridge Too Far; TV includes: Centennial; Pearl; Ellis Island; Beryl Markham-A Shadow on the Sun; Murder, She Wrote; Phantom of the Opera, mini-series. *Recordings:* Numerous. *Hobbies:* Tennis; Skiing; Walking. *Current Management:* Gorfaine & Schwartz Agency. *Address:* c/o Gorfaine & Schwartz Agency, 3301 Barham Boulevard, Suite 201, Los Angeles, CA 90068, USA.

ADEY Christopher, b. 1943, Essex, England. Conductor. *Education:* Royal Academy of Music, London, principally as Violinist with Manoug Parikian. *Career:* Violinist until 1973, primarily with Halle and London Philharmonic Orchestras; Debut as Conductor, 1973; Became Associate Conductor, BBC Scottish Symphony Orchestra, 1973-76; Frequent guest appearances throughout British Isles and with the leading London orchestras; Associate Conductor, Ulster Orchestra, 1981-84; Has worked in most European countries, Middle and Far East, Canada, USA; Frequent broadcasts, BBC and abroad; Extensive repertoire covering symphonic and chamber orchestra works of all periods and including choral works and opera; Professor of Conducting, Royal College of Music, 1979-92; Renowned orchestral trainer in constant demand at conservatoires throughout British Isles and maintaining large commitment to guest conducting with county, national and international youth orchestras; Cycle of the complete Martinů symphonies for BBC, 1992. *Honours include:* ARAM, 1979; FRAM, 1989; Commemorative Medal of the Czech Government, 1986. *Address:* c/o Richard Haigh, Performing Arts, 6 Windmill Street, London W1P 1HF, England.

ADKINS Anthony, b. 14 Jan. 1949, Northampton, England. Concert Pianist; Teacher. m. Kazimiera Brynkus, 13 Oct. 1979, 1 daughter. *Education:* Royal College of Music with Eric Harrison and Bernard Roberts, 1967-72; ARCM, piano performance, 1968; Certificate of Success, advanced pianoforte training, 1972; State Conservatory of Music, Cracow, Poland, 1974-75, with Professor Jan Hoffman. *Debut:* Wigmore Hall, London, 1973. *Career:* Several appearances in London including, Wigmore Hall, South Bank, Fairfield Halls; Extensive tours of England; Engagements in Europe including Holland, Germany and Austria as soloist, accompanist and ensemble player; Teacher of Piano in higher education institutions including, Chiswick Polytechnic, West London Institute and Colchester Institute, 1968-; Recordings for BBC radio and ZDF (Deutsche) Television. *Honours:* Silver Award, Youth of the Year, Harrow, Middlesex, 1965; Nora Naismith Scholarship, Royal Academy of Music, 1967; Foundation Scholarship, Royal College of Music, 1967; Chopin Fellowship, Polish Government, 1974.

Membership: Incorporated Society of Musicians. *Hobby:* The Arts. *Address:* 234 Ashburnham Road, Ham, Richmond, Surrey TW10 7SA, England.

ADKINS Cecil D(ale), b. 30 Jan. 1932, Red Oak, Iowa, USA. Musicologist. *Education:* BFA, University of Omaha, 1953; MM, University of South Dakota, 1959; PhD, University of Iowa, 1963. *Career:* Assistant Conductor and arranger, Fourth Armored Division Band, Fort Hood, Texas, 1954-55; Director of Instrumental Music, Paullina, Iowa, Independent School District, 1955-60; Graduate Assistant, University of Iowa, 1960-63; Instructor, Music Department, Mount Mercy College, Cedar Rapids, Iowa, 1960- 63; Professor of Music, University of North Texas, Denton, 1963-, Regents Professor, 1988-; Chairman, International Musicological Society's Center for Musicological Works in Progress, 1969-; President, American Musical Instrument Society, 1987-91. *Publications:* Edited, Doctoral Dissertations in Musicology, 5th edition 1971, 7th edition 1984, with A Dickinson, 8th edition, 1989; The A. Berg Positive Organ: Basle, Historical Museum 1927-28, Description and Technical Drawing, 1979; A Trumpet by Any Other Name: A History of the Trumpet Marine, with A. Dickinson, 1987; Four Historical Trumpet Marines, Description and Technical Drawings, 1987. *Contributions:* Articles in many journals and reference works. *Memberships:* American Musicological Society; International Musicological Society; American Musical Instrument Society; Dansk Selskab for Musikforskning. *Address:* c/o School of Music, University of North Texas, Denton, TX 76203, USA.

ADLAM Derek Leslie, b. 30 May 1938, Kingston-upon-Thames, Surrey, England. Maker of Historical Keyboard Instruments. *Education:* Guildhall School of Music, 1956-60; AGSM, Piano Performer; GGSM, School Music. *Career:* After 5 years of teaching musical subjects he became involved in restoration of early keyboards, particularly the fortepiano; Curator/Restorer of Colt Collection, 1970; In partnership with pianist Richard Burnett set up the Finchcocks Museum, Goudhurst, Kent, and founded the Adlam Burnett Instrument making workshop; Restored and built many harpsichords, fortepianos, etc. for professional performers and institutions until 1980; Moved to Welbeck, Nottinghamshire with own solo workshop, 1982; Recitals and Broadcasts UK, Germany and USA. *Recordings:* The 6 Partitas for harpsichord, J. S. Bach, Oryx. *Publication:* Chapter: The Anatomy of the Piano in the Book of the Piano, 1981. *Contributions to:* Early Music Magazine; The New Grove. *Honour:* Churchill Memorial Trust Fellowship, 1983. *Hobbies:* Fine Arts; Gardening. *Address:* Rose Cottage, Welbeck, Near Worksop, Nottinghamshire S80 3NB, England.

ADLER Larry (Lawrence Cecil), b. 10 Feb. 1914, Baltimore, Maryland, USA. Harmonica player. m. (1)Eileen Walser, 1938, dissolved 1961, 1 son, 2 daughters. (2)Sally Cline, 1969, dissolved 1977, 1 daughter. *Education:* Baltimore City College. *Career:* First stage appearance, New York, 1928; Appeared in various revues; First solo engagement with Sydney, Australia, Symphony Orchestra, 1939; Command performances for various Heads of State; Tours throughout the USA, Europe and Far East; Radio and television appearances; Nightclub engagements; Recordings; Composer of film scores and other works. *Publication:* Autobiography, It Ain't Necessarily So, 1984. *Honour:* Winner, Maryland Harmonica Championship, 1927. *Address:* c/o Michael Bakewell, 118 Tottenham Court Road, London W1, England.

ADLER Samuel (Hans), b. 4 Mar 1928, Mannheim, Germany. Composer; Conductor; Music Professor. m. Carol Ellen Stalker, 2 daughters. *Education:* BM, Boston University, 1948; MA, Harvard University, 1950; Studied composition with Herbert Fromm, Boston, 1941-46, with Hugo Norden, Walter Piston, Randall Thompson, Paul Hindemith and Aaron Copland; Musicology with Karl Geiringer; Conducting with Serge Koussevitzky, Berkshire Music Center, Tanglewood. *Career:* Founder-1st Conductor, 7th Army Symphony Orchestra, 1952;

Director of Music, Temple Emanu-El, Dallas, 1953-66; Conductor, Dallas Lyric Theater, 1955-57; Professor of Composition, North Texas State Universtiy, Denton, 1957-66; Professor of Composition 1966-, Chairman, Composition Department 1973-, Eastman School of Music, Rochester, New York; Guest Conductor, symphony orchestras and opera companies worldwide; Guest lecturer in USA and other countries. *Compositions:* Operas: The Outcasts of Poker Flat, 1959; The Wrestler, 1971; The Lodge of Shadows, 1973; The Disappointment, 1974; 6 symphonies: 1953, 1957, 1960, revised 1980-81, 1967, 1975, 1985; Orchestral works include: Rhapsody for Violin and Orchestra, 1961; Elegy for String Orchestra, 1962; Requiescat in Pace, in memory of President John F Kennedy, 1963; Song and Dance for Viola and Orchestra, 1965; City by the Lake, 1968; Organ Concerto, 1970; Concerto for Orchestra, 1971; Sinfonietta, 1971; Flute Concerto, 1977; Joi, Amor, Cortezia for Chamber Orchestra, 1982; Piano Concerto, 1983; Pieces for brass; Pieces for wind ensemble or band; Much chamber music including: 7 string quartets, 1945, 1950, 1953 revised 1964, 1963, 1969, 1975, 1981; 4 violin sonatas and other sonatas; 12 pieces entitled Canto, 1970-79; Piano pieces; Sacred vocal music; Secular choral music; Songs; Organ pieces; Concerto for 4 saxophones and Orchestra, 1985; Concerto for Woodwind Quinitet and Orchestra, 1991; 8 String Quartets, 8th 1990. *Publications:* Anthology for the Teaching of Choral Conducting 1971, 2nd edition, 1985; Singing and Hearing, 1979; The Study of Orchestration, 1982, second edition, 1989. *Contributions to:* Numerous journals. *Honours:* Honorary DMus: St Louis Conservatory; Southern Methodist University; Honorary DFM, St Mary's College, Notre Dame; Honorary DFA, Wake Forest University; Guggenheim Fellowship, 1984-85; Numerous commissions; Winner, ASCAP-Deems Taylor Award, 1983; Music Award from the American Academy and Institute of Arts and Letters. *Memberships:* Various professional organizations. *Address:* 54 Railroad Mills Road, Pittsford, NY 14534, USA.

ADNI Daniel, b. 6 Dec 1951, Haifa, Israel. Concert Pianist. *Education:* Haifa School; Tel-Aviv High School, Israel, until 1968; Paris Conservatoire, 1968-69. *Debut:* London, 1970. *Career:* Since debut played as soloist with most orchestras in UK, also Israel, Holland, Germany, USA, Far East, Japan; solo recitals in many major cities and festivals; also chamber music at Festivals, eg Kuhmo, Finland; made over 21 records and countless broadcasts on BBC and other radio services. *Recordings:* All on EMI Label. 2 Chopin records; Debussy record; Complete Songs Without Words by Mendelssohn; Complete Grieg Lyric Pieces; Piano Music by John Ireland and Percy Grainger; Mendelssohn Preludes and Fugues op 35; Schubert Sonatas; Concertos by Saint-Saëns and Mendelssohn; Rhapsody in Blue by Gershwin. *Honours:* First Prizes for Piano, Solfège and Sight Reading, Paris Conservatoire, 1969; Winner, Young Concert Artists, New York, 1976; Winner, Phillip M Fanuett Prize, New York, 1981. *Hobbies:* Cinema; Theatre; Bridge; Walking. *Address:* 64A Menelik Road, London, NW2 3RH, England.

ADOLPHE Bruce, b. 31 May 1955, New York City, New York, USA. Composer. *Education:* Studied at Juilliard School, New York, until 1976. *Career:* Has taught at New York University Tisch School, 1983; Taught at Yale University, 1984-85; Composer-in-Residence: 92nd Street Y School Concert Series, 1988-90, Santa Fe Chamber Music Festival, 1989; His operas performed in Boston and New York. *Compositions include:* The Tell-Tale Heart, 1-act opera after Edgar Allan Poe, 1982; Mikhoels the Wise, opera in 2 acts, 1982; The False Messiah, opera in 2 acts, 1983. *Address:* c/o ASCAP, ASCAP Building, One Lincoln Plaza, New York, NY 10023, USA.

ADORJAN Andras, b. 26 Sept. 1944, Budapest, Hungary. Flautist. *Education:* Studied with Jean-Pierre Rampal and Aurele Nicolet. *Career:* Principal with the orchestra of the Royal Opera, Stockholm, 1970-72; Gurzenich Concerts, Cologne, 1972-73; Sudwestfunk,

Baden-Baden, 1973- 74; Bavarian Radio Symphony Orchestra 1974-88; Teacher at the Nice Summer Academy from 1971; Professor at the Musikhochschule at Freiburg im Brisgau, Germany, from 1988; Revived the Concerto for Two Flutes by Doppler and gave the 1981 premiere of Ground, Concerto for flute and orchestra, by Sven-Erik Werner. *Recordings Include:* Concerto for two flutes and orchestra by Franz Doppler, with Jean-Pierre Rampal. *Address:* Staatliche Hochschule fur Musik, Schwarzwaldstrasse 141, D-7800 Freiburg im Brisgau, Germany.

ADRIANO b. 10 July 1944, Fribourg, Switzerland. Composer; Conductor; Producer. *Education:* Conservatory of Music; Mainly self taught. *Career includes:* Active as stage director and language coach; Performs as concert narrator; Specialised conductor of unknown music and Ottorino Respighi specialist; Writer and Director of classical music videos. *Compositions:* Piano pieces and songs; Orchestrations and editing of many classic film scores by Honegger and of song cycles by Respighi and Mussorgsky; Concertino for Celesta and Strings. *Recordings:* As conductor: 14 recordings of Honegger, Khatchaturian, Bliss, Waxman, Herrmann, Respighi; As producer: 10 items with many world premier recordings. *Publications:* An International Respighi Discography; Liner notes on various labels; Articles on Ottorino Respighi *Honour:* Gold Medal, Italian Respighi Foundation. *Address:* Sihlberg 22, CH-8022, Zurich, Switzerland.

AESCHBACHER Niklaus, b. 30 Apr 1917, Trogen/AR, Switzerland. Conductor. m. Elisabeth Rüetschi, 3 July, 1951. *Education:* Graduated summa cum laude, Zurich Conservatory, 1937. *Debut:* Tonhalle, Zurich, 1938. *Career:* Music Director, Stadttheater, Bern, 1949-54, 1958; Principal Director, NHK Symphony Orchestra, Tokyo, Japan, 1954-56; General Music Director, Kiel, 1959-63, Detmold, 1964-72; Professor, Leiter der Opernschule; NWD Musikakademie, Detmold, 1972-82. *Composition:* Radio Opera, The Red Shoes. *Recordings:* Peter Mieg Concert for 2 pianos; H. Sutermeister's Max & Moritz and The Black Spider. *Publications:* Several musical arrangements. *Honour:* Kulturpreis der Lippischen Landeszeitung, 1973. *Memberships:* Schweiz Tonkünstler; SUISA; Genossenschaft Deutscher Bühnenangehoriger.*Hobbies:* Literature, History.*Current Management:* Konzertgesellschafft Zürich. *Address:* Diesbach-Str. 25, CH-3012 Bern, Switzerland.

AFANASYEVA Veronika, b. 1960, Moscow, Russia. Violinist. *Education:* Studied at Central Music School, Moscow. *Career:* Co-Founder of Quartet Veronique, 1989; Many concerts in former Soviet Union and Russia, notably in the Russian Chamber Music Series and 150th birthday celebrations for Tchaikovsky, 1990; Masterclasses, Aldeburgh Festival, 1991; Concert tour of Britain, season 1992-93; Repertoire includes works by Beethoven, Brahms, Tchaikovsky, Bartok, Shostakovich and Schnittke. *Recordings include:* Schnittke's 3rd Quartet. *Honours include:* With Quartet Veronique: Winner, All-Union String Quartet Competition, St Petersburg, 1990-91; 3rd Place, International Shostakovich Competition, St Petersburg, 1991. *Address:* c/o Sonata (Quartet Veronique), 11 Northgate Street, Glasgow G20 7AA, Scotland.

AGACHE Alexandru, b. 16 Aug 1955, Cluj, Rumania. Singer (Baritone). *Education:* Studied in Cluj. *Debut:* As Silvano in Ballo in Maschera, Cluj, 1979. *Career:* Has sung Sharpless, Don Giovanni, Malatesta, and Verdi's Posa, Luna, Nabucco and Germont at Cluj; Further appearances in Dresden, Budapest and Ankara; Sang Don Giovanni at Livorno and Toulon, 1987, Renato at Covent Garden, followed by Enrico Ashton (Lucia di Lammermoor) and Simon Boccanegra in new production of Verdi's opera, 1991; La Scala debut as Belcore in L'elisir d'amore, 1988; Marquis di Posa in Hamburg, 1988, and La Fenice, Venice, 1992; Sang Renato in Ballo in Maschera in Zurich and Dusseldorf, 1989; Marcello in La Bohème, Lyon Opera, 1991; Renato at Opera Bastille, Paris, 1992. *Recordings include:* Golem

the Rebel by Nicolas Bretan; Video of Covent Garden Simon Boccanegra, conducted by Solti. *Address:* c/o Stafford Law Associates, 26 Mayfield Road, Weybridge, Surrey KT13 8XB, England.

AGAY Karola, b. 30 March 1927, Budapest, Hungary. Singer (Soprano). *Education:* Studied in Budapest. *Career:* Sang first in choir of Hungarian army; stage debut Budapest 1955, as the Queen of Night; Other roles include Gilda, Constanze, Lucia di Lammermoor, Mélisande and Zerbinetta; Metropolitan Opera 1969, Lucia; Guest engagements in Vienna, East Berlin, France, Moscow and Prague; Many song recitals with her husband, the guitarist L. Szendrey-Karper.

AGAZHANOV Artyom Artyomovich, b. 3 Feb 1958, Moscow, USSR. Composer; Pianist. *Education:* Piano and composition, Moscow Central Music School, 1965-76; Further study at Moscow State Chaikovsky Conservatoire. *Career:* Teacher, Moscow Cental Music School, 1983-; Concert appearances as composer and pianist in USSR, Bulgaria, Italy, Germany, including festivals: Moscow 1986, 1987, 1989, Moscow Stars, 1989, International Music Festival, 1988. *Compositions include:* Pax in terra, orchestra, 1983; 6 Japanese hokku, for soprano and piano, 1983 (recorded 1993); Since 3 til 6, for piano, 1984 (recorded 1989); Sonata for violoncello and piano, 1985 (recorded 1989); Soviet composer publisher, 1989; Gust, overture for orchestra, 1987, recorded, 1989; Vision, for violin and piano, 1987 (recorded 1988); Kolobrod, music for film, 1990; Variations on theme by Chopin, for piano, 1991, (recorded 1992); Incute to rebellion the city, music for film, 1992. *Publication:* Without colouring the Truth, 1993. *Honours:* All Union Competition of Young Composers, 1981. *Memberships:* Union of Russian Composers.*Address:* Nezhdanova 8-10, apt 28, Moscow 103009, Russia.

AGNEW Paul, b. 1964, Glasgow, Scotland. Singer (Tenor). *Education:* Chorister at St Chad's Cathedral, Birmingham, Lay-clerkships at Birmingham and Lichfield Cathedrals; Choral Scholar at Magdalen College, Oxford. *Career:* Tours with the Consort of Musicke to Germany, Switzerland, Holland, Italy, Spain, Austria, Sweden and Australia. Handel songs in the National Gallery, London, with the Parley of Instruments; Promenade Concert debut 1989, in The Judgement of Paris; Has sung the Evangelist in the St Matthew Passion for the London Handel Orchestra; South Bank debut at the Purcell Room celebrating the centenary of Ivor Gurney's birth; Engaged for the St John Passion with the Schola Cantorum of Basle and for Les Noces in Zurich; Tour of the United States with the Festival of Voices directed by Paul Hillier; Sang in Monteverdi Madrigals with the Consort of Musicke, Promenade Concerts, 1993. *Recordings include:* Monteverdi Madrigals (Virgin Classics). *Address:* c/o Magenta Music International, 64 Highgate High Street, London N6 5HX, England.

AGOOT Francisco, b.11 Dec 1970, Baguio City, Philippines. Music Teacher. *Education:* BA, Political Science; MEd; Classical Voice, Choral Conducting and Music Theory, Ryan Cayabyab Music Studio. *Debut:* The Voice in the Mountains, 1993. *Career:* Concert, 1985; Music Studio Recitals, 1989, 1990; Messiah Oratorio, 1991; Regional Kundiman Fiesta, 1992; The Voice in the Mountains, 1993; International Choral Workshop, 1993. *Recordings:* This is our Home, in The Voice in the Mountains. *Honours:* Solo Singing Award, 1989; Cultural Competition Award, 1991; Division Kundimah Fiesta, 1992. *Memberships:* Kodaly Society of the Philippines, (Bd); Namcya Foundation Inc. *Hobbies:* Swimming; Tennis. *Address:* 94 Dr Carino Street, Lower Q M, Baguio City, Philippines 2600.

AGUERA Luc-Marie, b. 1960, France, Violinist. *Education:* Studied at the Paris Conservatoire with Jean-Claude Pennetier and with members of the Amadeus and Alban Berg Quartets. *Career:* Member of the Ysaÿe String Quartet from 1985; Many concert performances in France, Europe, America and the Far East; Festival engagements at Salzburg, Tivoli (Copenhagen), Bergen, Lockenhaus, Barcelona and Stresa; Many appearances in Italy, notably with the 'Haydn' Quartets of Mozart; Tours of Japan and the USA 1990 and 1992. *Recordings:* Mozart Quartet K421 and Quintet K516 (Harmonia Mundi); Ravel, Debussy and Mendelssohn Quartets (Decca). *Honours:* Grand Prix Evian International String Quartet Competition, May 1988: special prizes for best performances of a Mozart quartet, the Debussy quartet and a contemporary work; 2nd Prize, Portsmouth International String Quartet Competition, 1988. *Address:* c/o Artist Management International Ltd, 12/13 Richmond Buildings, Dean Street, London W1V 5AF, England.

AGUILAR Maria del Carmen, b. 22 Feb 1945, Buenos Aires, Argentina. Musician. div., 1 son, 1 daughter. *Education:* Graduated in Architecture, University of Buenos Aires; Studied Music Theory, Music Analysis, Choir Conducting, Singing. *Career:* Professor of Music Analysis at the University of Buenos Aire; sPresentations as member of Conjunto Vocal 9 de Camara and Estudio Coral de Buenos Aires in major Argentinian cities including the Colon Theatre, Buenos Aires (choral and opera repertoire). *Recordings:* With Conjunto Vocal 9 de Camara: Renaissance Music; Missa Brevis (Kodaly); With Estudio Coral de Buenos Aires: Works by Zoltan Kodaly; Motets and Missa by Tomas Luis de Victoria; Ziegeunerlieder and Liebeslieder Waltzer by Johannes Brahms. *Publications:* Metodo para leer y escribir musica, 1978; 12 Canciones populares americanas, 1986; Folklore para armar, 1991; Proposal for a Methodology of Rhythmic Analysis (with Francisco Kropfl), 1988. *Membership:* International Society for Music Education. *Hobbies:* Drawing; Trekking. *Address:* Presidente Peron 1547, 6-G, 1037 Buenos Aires, Argentina.

AHLGRIMM Isolde, b. 31 July 1914, Vienna, Austria. Harpsichordist; Professor of Harpsichord, Musikhochschule, Vienna. *Education:* Staatsakademie fur Musik (now called Musikhochschule), Vienna. *Career:* Concerts in most European countries, Teheran, Japan and USA; numerous TV and radio appearances. *Recordings:* complete works for Harpsichord of J S Bach (Philips); Recordings for Amadeo, Belvedere, Deutsche Schallplatten, Tudor and Musical Heritage Society. *Publications:* Reprint of Grundrichtiger...Untericht der Musicalischen Kunst...by Daniel Speer, Ulm, 1687 and 1697, 1974 by Ed Peters, Leipzig; Reprint of Musicus Theoretico-praticus, by Philip Christoph Hartung, Nurnberg, 1749, 1977; Manuale der Orgel-und Cembalotechnik, 1982; Biography, 1992. *Contributor to:* various professional journals. *Honours:* Das goldene Ehrenzeichen für Verdienste um die Republik Österreich, 1975. *Membership:* Wiener Bachgesellschaft (member of honour). *Hobby:* Nature Lover. *Address:* Türkenschanz Platz 2/522, A-1180 Wien, Austria.

AHLSTEDT Douglas, b. 16 Mar 1945, Jamestown, New York, USA. Singer (Tenor). *Education:* Studied at State University, New York and Eastman School, Rochester. *Debut:* As Ramiro in La Cenerentola, Western Opera Theatre, San Francisco, 1971. *Career:* Sang at Metropolitan Opera from season 1974-75, debut as the Italian Singer in Rosenkavalier, then as Fenton in Falstaff; Member of Deutsche Oper Dusseldorf, 1975-84 and guest appearances in Vienna, Hamburg, Zurich and Karlsruhe; Returned to New York, 1983 and sang Iopas in Les Troyens, Almaviva in Barbiere di Siviglia and Debussy's Pelleas, 1988; Salzburg Festival as Anfinoma in the Henze-Monteverdi Ritorno di Ulisse, 1985; Teatro San Carlo, Naples, as Orestes in Ermione by Rossini, 1988; Other engagements in Dallas, Philadelphia, Santiago (as Don Ottavio), Genoa, Avignon and Rome (Idreno in Semiramide, 1982); Other roles include Tamino, Jacquino in Fidelio, Narcisio in Il Turco in Italia, the Fox in The Cunning Little Vixen and Peter Quint in The Turn of the Screw; Sang Dorvil in La Scala di Seta in Stuttgart, 1991; Zurich Opera as Flamand in Capriccio,

1992. *Recordings include:* Video of Il Ritorno di Ulisse, Salzburg, 1985. *Address:* c/o Staatstheater Stuttgart, Oberer Schlossgarten 6, 7000 Stuttgart, Germany.

AHNSJO Claes Haakon, b. 1 Aug 1942, Stockholm, Sweden. Singer (Tenor). m. Helena Jungwirth. *Education:* Studied in Stockholm with Erik Saeden, Askel Schiotz and Max Lorenz. *Debut:* Royal Opera Stockholm 1969, as Tamino. *Career:* Sang in Stockholm until 1973, then with the Munich Opera, notably in operas by Mozart and Rossini; Drottningholm Opera from 1969; Bayreuth Festival 1973; Kennedy Music Center New York 1974, in Die Jahreszeiten by Haydn; Guest appearances in Frankfurt, Cologne, Tokyo, Hamburg, Stuttgart and Nancy; Concert tours of Italy and Spain; Munich 1985, as The Painter in Lulu, and in the premiere of Le Roi Bérenger by Sutermeister; At Berlin in 1987 sang Ramiro in La Cenerentola by Rossini; Sang Wolfgang Capito, Mathis der Maler, and the Abbéin Mathis Adriana Lecouvreur, 1989; Munich Festival, Premiere of Penderecki's Ubu Rex, 1991. *Recordings:* Bastien und Bastienne (BASF); Orlando Paladino, La Vera Costanza and L'Infedeltà delusa by Haydn, Betulia Liberata by Mozart (Philips); Die Lustigen Weiber von Windsor (Decca); Bruckner's Te Deum (Electrola). *Address:* c/o Bayerische Staatsoper, Postbach 745, D-8000 Munich 1, Germany.

AHO Kalevi, b. 9 Mar. 1949, Forssa, Finland. Composer; Teacher; Writer on Music. *Education:* Diploma, Sibelius Academy, Helsinki, 1971; Studied composition with Einojuhani Rautavaara; with Boris Blacher, Staatliche Hochschule für Musik und Darstellende Kunst, Berlin, 1971-72. *Career:* Lecturer on Music, University of Helsinki, 1974-; Author of articles, essays and treatises. *Compositions:* Stage: The Key, dramatic monologue, 1978-79; Insect Life, opera, 1985-87; Orchestral: 7 symphonies: No 1, 1969; No 2, 1970; No 3, Sinfonia concertante, 1971-73; No 4, 1972-73; No 5, 1975-76; No 6, 1979-80; No 7, Insect Symphony, 1988; Chamber Symphony, 1976; Violin Concerto, 1981; Cello Concerto, 1983-84; Piano Concerto, 1988-89; Chamber: 3 string quartets, including Nos 2, 1970 and 3, 1971; Quintet for Oboe and String Quartet, 1973; Sonata for Solo Violin, 1973; Prelude, Toccata, Postlude for Cello and Piano, 1974; Solo I; Tumultos for Violin, 1975; Quintet for Flute, Oboe, Violin, Viola and Cello, 1977; Quintet for Bassoon and String Quartet, 1977; Quartet for Flute, Alto Saxophone, Guitar and Percussion, 1982; Accordion Sonata, 1984; Sonata for Oboe and Piano, 1984-85; Inventions for Oboe and Cello, 1986; Piano pieces; Choral pieces; Songs. *Address:* c/o Music Department, University of Helsinki, Hallituskatu 8, 00 100 Helsinki, Finland.

AHRONOVITCH Yuri, b. 13 May 1933, Leningrad, Russia. Conductor. m. Tamar Sakson, 1973. *Education:* Graduated, Leningrad Conservatory of Music, 1954. *Career:* Debuts with: Leningrad Philharmonic Orchestra; Bolshoi Theatre, Moscow; Professor of Music, 1958-; Principal Conductor and Music Director, Moscow Radio Symphony Orchestra, 1964-72; Guest conductor: London Symphony Orchestra; Vienna Symphony Orchestra; Jerusalem Symphony Orchestra; Rome S Cecilia Orchestra; New York Philarmonic Orchestra; Berlin, Hamburg and Munich Radio Orchestras; Teatro alla Scala, Milan; Opera Guest Conductor with: Royal Opera House, Covent Garden, London; Lyric Opera House, Chicago; Main Italian Opera Houses; Stockholm Royal Opera House; Munich State Opera House; Principal Conductor and Music Director, Cologne Philharmonic orchestra (Gurzenich), 1975-86; Principal Conductor, Stockholm Philharmonic Orchestra, 1982-87. *Recordings:* For RCA; Deutsche Grammomphon, BIS, including Tchaikovsky's Manfred Symphony; Rachmaninov's Piano Concertos, Vasary LSO; Prokofiev's Violin Concertos; Shostakovich's 1st Symphony; Sorochintsy Fair by Mussorgsky. *Honours:* Prize for Best Opera Production, German Music Journal, 1977; Commander, The Royal Order of the Polar Star, by the King of Sweden, 1987; Israeli Etinger Prize for the Arts, 1988. *Membership:* Elected member, Royal Swedish Academy of Music, 1984-. *Address:*

Kunstlersecretariat Schoerke, Mönckebergalle 41, 3000 Hannover 91, Germany.

AINSLEY John Mark, b. 1962, England. Singer (Tenor). *Education:* Studied at Oxford University. *Career:* Many concert performances from 1985 with the Taverner Consort, the New London Consort and London Baroque; Appearances in Mozart Masses at the Vienna Konzerthaus with Heinz Holliger, Handel's Saul at Gottingen with John Eliot Gardiner and the Mozart Requiem under Yehudi Menuhin at Gstaad; Pulcinella at the Barbican under Jeffrey Tate; Other concerts with the Ulster Orchestra and the Bournemouth Sinfonietta; US debut at Lincoln Center in the B minor Mass with Christopher Hogwood; Opera debut at the Innsbruck Festival in Scarlatti's Gli Equivoci nel Sembiante; English National Opera 1989, in The Return of Ulysses; Title role in Méhul's Joseph for Dutch Radio, Handel's Acis in Stuttgart and Solomon for Radio France, under Leopold Hager; Has sung Mozart's Tamino for Opera Northern Ireland and Ferrando for Glyndebourne Touring Opera; Engaged in Falstaff for Scottish Opera and Idomeneo for Welsh National Opera; Sang Ferrando, Glyndebourne Festival, 1992; Haydn's The Seasons with the London Classical Players, Promenade Concerts, London, 1993. *Recordings include:* Handel's Nisi Dominus, under Simon Preston and Purcell's Odes with Trevor Pinnock (Deutsche Grammophon); Mozart's C minor Mass, with Hogwood and Great Baroque Arias with the King's Consort; Acis and Galatea (Hyperion); Saul (Philips). *Address:* Magenta Music International, 64 Highgate High Street, London N6 5HX, England.

AITKEN Hugh, b. 7 Sept. 1924, New York, NY, USA. Composer; Teacher. *Education:* Composition with Wagenaar, Persichetti and Ward at the Juilliard School; MS, 1950 *Career:* Taught privately and at The Juilliard Preparatory Division, 1950-65; Faculty member, Juilliard, 1960-70; Professor, William Paterson College, 1970-. *Compositions:* Stage; FELIPE, opera; FABLES, chamber opera, dance scores; Three violin concertos, 1984, 1988; Oratorio, The Revelation of St John The Divine, 1953-1990; Ten solo cantatas; In Praise of Ockeghem, strings; Rameau Remembered, flute, chamber orchestra; Happy Birthday, overture; Opus 95 Revisited, string quartet; unaccompanied works for vln, vla, vc, cb, fl, ob, cl, bsn, tp, tn; Duo for cello and piano; Trios for eleven players; Quintet, oboe and string quartet. *Publishers:* Theodore Presser Company, Oxford University Press, E.C. Schirmer, G.Schirmer. *Recordings:* Piano Fantasy and 2 cantatas on CRI 365; Other works on New World Recordings, Crystal and Ubris. *Honours:* National Academy of Arts and Letters, 1988; Several grants National Endowment for the Arts. *Address:* Music Department, Wm. Paterson College of New Jersey, Wayne, NJ 07470, USA.

AITKEN Robert (Morris), b. 28 Aug 1939, Kentville, Nova Scotia, Canada. Flautist; Teacher; Composer. m. Marion Isobel Ross. *Education:* Commenced flute lessons as child in Pennsylvania; Studied flute with Nicholas Fiore, Royal Conservatory of Music of Toronto, 1955-59; Composition with Barbara Pentland, University of British Columbia; Electronic music with Myron Schaeffer; Composition with John Weinzweig; Flute with Marcel Moyse, Jean-Pierre Rampal, Severino Gazelloni, Andre Jaunet and Hubert Barwahser, 1964-65; BMus 1961, MMus 1964, University of Toronto. *Career:* Principal Flautist, Vancouver Symphony Orchestra, 1958-59; 2nd Flautist, CBC Symphony orchestra, 1960-64; Principal Flautist, Stratford (Ontario) Festival Orchestra, 1962-64; Co-principal Flautist, Toronto Symphony, 1965-70; Soloist with orchestras and chamber-music player; Many tours abroad; Artistic director, Music Today, Shaw Festival, Niagara-on-the-Lake, 1970-72; New Music Concerts, Toronto, 1971-; Music at Shawnigan, Vancouver Island, 1981-; Advanced studies in music programme 1985-89, Teacher 1977-89, Banff Centre School of Fine Arts, 1985-89; Teacher of Flute, Royal Conservatory of Music of Toronto, 1957-64, 1965-68; Flute and Chamber music 1960-64, 1965-71, Associate Professor 1971-78, University of Toronto; Professor of Flute, Staatliche

Hochschule für Musik, Freiburg im Breisgau, 1988-. *Compositions:* Rhapsody for Orchestra, 1961; Quartet for Flute, Oboe, Viola and Double Bass, 1961; Music for Flute and Electronic Tape, 1963; Noesis for Electronic Tape, 1963; Concerto for 12 Solo Instruments, 1964; Spectra for 4 Chamber Groups, 1969; Kebyar for Flute, Clarinet, 2 Double Basses, Percussion and Tape, 1971; Shadows I: Nekuia for Orchestra, 1971; Shadows II: Lalita for Flute, 3 Cellos, 2 Percussionists and 2 Harps, 1972; Shadows III: Nira for Solo Violin, Flute, Oboe, Viola, Double Bass, Piano and Harpsichord, 1974-88; Spiral for Orchestra with Amplified Flute, Oboe, Clarinet and Bassoon, 1975; Icicle for Solo Flute, 1977; Plainsong for Solo Flute, 1977; Folia for Woodwind Quintet, 1980; Monody for Chorus, 1983. *Recordings:* Various compositions recorded; Many discs as soloist and chamber-music artist. *Address:* 14 Maxwell Avenue, Toronto, Ontario M5P 2B5, Canada.

AJMONE-MARSAN Guido, b. 24 Mar. 1947, Turin, Italy. Orchestral Conductor. m. Helle Winkelhorn, 14 Aug. 1971. *Education:* Bachelor Degree cum laude Conducting and Clarinet, Eastman School of Music, New York, USA, 1968; Study with F. Ferrara, Conservatory of St Cecilia, Rome, Italy, 1968-71. *Career:* Chief Conductor, Gelders Orchestra, Arnhem, Netherlands, 1982-86; Music Advisor and Principal Conductor, Orchestra of Illinois, Chicago, USA, 1982-87; Music Director, Opera House, Essen, Federal Republic of Germany, 1986-90; Guest Conductor with Jerusalem Symphony, Washington Opera, and Miami Opera; Philharmonia, London Symphony, Chicago Symphony, Covent Garden Opera, San Francisco Symphony and Opera, Munich Philharmonic, Amsterdam Philharmonic, Orchestra de Paris, NHK Japan, Sydney and Melbourne Symphonies; Monte Carlo Opera, Welsh National Opera, Spoleto Festival, Italy and USA, National Symphony in Washington, Toronto, Montreal, Cleveland Symphony, St Cecilia in Rome, La Scala Orchestra, BBC Philharmonic, Birmingham, Bournemouth, Stockholm, Oslo, Copenhagen; Metropolitan Opera, New York City Opera and English National Opera. *Recordings:* Many studio recordings for radio broadcast with radio orchestras in Czechoslovakia, UK, Germany, Japan, Australia, Netherlands, Denmark, Italy and France. *Honours:* Many prizes, Cantelli Competition, Milan, 1969; Mitropoulos, New York, 1970; Winner, Rupert Foundation Conducting Competition, with 1 year assistantship to London Symphony, 1973; Winner, G Solti Competition, Chicago, 1973; The Deane Sherman Performing Arts Award, Maryland, USA, 1992. *Current Management:* ICM Artists, New York; Christopher Tennant, London. *Address:* 57 Wood Vale, London N10, England.

AKIYAMA Kazuyoshi, b. 2 Jan 1941, Tokyo, Japan. Conductor. *Education:* Studied conducting with Hideo Saito, Toho School of Music, Tokyo. *Debut:* Tokyo Symphony Orchestra, 1964. *Career:* Music Director, Tokyo Symphony Orchestra, 1964; Conductor, Japanese Orchestras; Music Director, American Symphony Orchestra, New York, 1973-78; Resident Conductor and Music Director, Vancouver (British Columbia) Symphony Orchestra, 1972-85; Music Director, Syracuse (NY) Symphony Orchestra, 1985-. *Recordings:* For CBS; RCA; Turnabout. *Address:* c/o Syracuse Symphony Orchestra, 411 Montgomery Street, Syracuse, NY 13202, USA.

ALAIMO Simone, b. 3 Feb 1950, Villabate, Palermo, Italy. Singer (Bass-Baritone). m. Vittorio Mazzoni, 30 Apr 1988, 1 son, 1 daughter. *Education:* Literary studies, University of Palmermo; Scuola di Perfezionamento Teatro alla Scala di Milano per Giovani Lirici. *Debut:* Role in Don Pasquale, Pavia, 1977. *Career:* Appearances: La Scala, Milan; Teatro dellOpera, Rome; Teatro Comunale, Florence; Teatro San Carlo, Naples; Chicago, San Francisco, Dallas; Vienna, Monaco, Paris, Madrid, Barcelona, Lisbon, Marseilles; Radio and TV appearances: Luisa Miller, Concorso Callas, Cavalleria Rusticana, Zaira; Sang Mustafa in L'Italiana in Algeri at San Francisco, 1992, followed by Dulcamara; Rossini's Don Basilio, Genoa, 1992; Appeared in film,

Il Barbiere di Siviglia. *Recordings:* La Cenerentola, Don Giovanni, Il Turco in Italia, Maria Stuarda, Philips; I Masnadieri, Decca; L'Ebreo, Torquato Tasso, L'Esule di Roma, Convenienze Teatrali, Barbiere di Siviglia, Bongiovanni. *Honours:* Lions Prize, 1977; Voce Verdiane di Busseto International Competition, 1978; Beniamino Gigli di Macerata International Competition, 1978; Maria Callas International Competition, 1980. Hobbies: Antiquities; Gardening; Cookery; Football. *Address:* Via Pacevecchia, Parc Conim, 82100 Benevento, Italy.

ALAIN Marie-Claire, b. 10 Aug 1926, Saint-Germain-en-Laye, France. Organist. m. Jacques Gommier 1950, 1 son, 1 daughter. *Education:* Institut Notre Dame, Saint-Germain-en-Laye, Conservatoire National Supérieur de Musique, Paris. *Career:* Organ Teacher, Conservatoire de Musique de Rueil-Malmaison; Lecturer, Summer Academy for Organists, Haarlem, Netherlands, 1956-72; numerous concerts throughout the world 1955-; lecturer at numerous universities throughout the world; expert on organology to Minister of Culture. *Recordings:* Over 200 records including complete works of J Alain, C P E Bach, J S Bach, C Balbastre, G Böhm, N Bruhns, D Buxtehude, L N Clerambault, F Couperin, L C Daquin, C Franck, N de Grigny, J A Guilain, G F Handel, J Haydn, F Mendelssohn, A Vivaldi etc. *Honours:* Honorary D Hum Lett, Colorado State University; Honorary D Mus, Southern Methodist University, Dallas, numerous prizes for recordings and performances including Buxtehudepreis, Lübeck, Federal Republic of Germany; Leonie Sonning Prize, Copenhagen, Denmark; Prix Franz Liszt, Budapest; Officier de la Légion d'Honneur, Officier des Arts et Lettres, Officier dans l'Ordre du Merite, Chevalier du Daneborg. *Address:* 1 ave Jean-Jaurès, 78580 Maule, France.

ALARIE Pierrette (Marguerite), b. 9 Nov 1921, Montreal, Canada. Soprano; Teacher. m. Leopold Simoneau, 1946. *Education:* Studied voice and acting with Jeanne Maubourg and Albert Roberval; Voice with Salvator Issaurel, 1938-43; With Elisabeth Schumann, Curtis Institute of Music, Philadelphia, 1943-46. *Debut:* Operatic debut, Montreal, 1943. *Career:* Metropolitan Opera debut, New York as Oscar in Un ballo in maschera, 1945; European debut, Paris, 1949; Sang in opera, concert and recital in leading North American and European music centres; Retired from operatic stage, 1966; Farwell appearance as soloist, Handel's Messiah, Montreal Symphony Orchestra, 1970; Taught voice. *Recordings:* Numerous including album of Mozart arias with husband. *Honours:* Won, Metropolitan Opera Auditions of the Air, 1945; Officer of the Order of Canada, 1967; Won, Grand Prix du disque, 1961.

ALBANESE Cecilia, b. 26 Nov 1937, Caracas, Venezuela. Singer (Soprano). *Education:* Studied at Giuseppe Verdi Conservatory, Milan, and with Ettore Campogalliani. *Debut:* Gilda in Rigoletto at Reggio Emilia. *Career:* Many appearances in Italy at La Scala, Milan, Teatro San Carlo, Naples, and in Rome; Overseas engagements, Hamburg, Barcelona, New York City Opera, with Scottish Opera, with Welsh Nationl Opera; Repertoire has included Bellini's Amina, Donizetti's Lucia and Norina, Rosina, the Queen of Night, Verdi's Nanetta and Violetta and Puccini's Musetta. *Honours:* Prizewinner at competitions at Macerate, Vercelli and Parma. *Address:* c/o Teatro la Scala, Via Filodrammatici 2, 20121 Milan, Italy.

ALBANESE Licia, b. 22 July 1913, Bari, Italy. Singer (soprano, retired). m. Joseph Gimma, 7 Apr 1945. *Education:* Studied voice with Emanuel De Rosa, Bari and Giuseppina Baldassare-Tedeschi, Milan. *Debut:* Operatic debut as Butterfly, Teatro Lirico, Milan, 1934. *Career:* Formal operatic debut, Parma, 1935; Sang with Teatro San Carlo, Naples; Teatro alla Scala, Milan; Metropolitan Opera debut, New York as Cio-Cio-San, 1940 and sang there until 1966; Appeared in concerts; Taught; Roles included Butterfly, Violetta, Zerlina, Desdemona, Susanna, Manon, Tosca, Gounod's Marguerite, Mimi. *Recordings:* NBC radio broadcasts under Toscanini. *Honours:* Order of Merit of Italy; Lady

Grand Cross of the Equestrian Order of the Holy Sepulchre. *Address:* Nathan Hale Drive, Wilson Point South, Norwalk, CT 06854, USA.

ALBERMAN David, b. 1959, London, England. Violinist. *Education:* Private tuition with Mary Long, Emanuel Hurwitz, Shelia Nelson, Vera Kantrovich, Igor Ozim, in Cologne; LRAM 1975; MA in Greats, Classical Languages and Literature, from Merton College, Oxford, 1981. *Career:* Leader of the National Youth Orchestra of Great Britain, 1977; Has performed with the London Mozart Players, Royal Philharmonic Orchestra, London Symphony, Associate Member 1983-1985, and the Academy of St.Martin-in-the-Fields; Former leader of the Chamber Orchestra of Europe; Has performed music by Lutoslawski, Penderecki, Osborne and Bainbridge with such groups as the Ballet Rambert and Divertimenti; Member of the Arditti Quartet from Jan 1986; Many performances at festivals across Europe and North America; Resident string tutor at the Darmstadt Ferienkurse for New Music from 1986; Music in camera programme BBC television 1987; Cycle of Schoenberg's Quartets Purcell Room London, Nov 1988; Recital in the Russian Spring Series at South Bank, May 1991; engaged to perform in all the quartets of Berg, Webern and Schoenberg at Antwerp, Cologne, Frankfurt, London and Paris, 1991-1993; Has taken part in the premieres of quartets by Böse, No.3 1989; Bussotti, 1988; John Cage, Music for 4, 1988, 4, 1989; Ferneyhough, Nos.3 and 4; Gubaidulina, No.3, 1987; Harvey, No.2; Kagel, No.3, 1987; Nancarrow, No.3, 1988; Pousseur, No.2, 1989; Rihm, Nos.6 and 8; Xenakis, Akea Piano Quintet, 1986, Tetora 1991, Isang Yun, Flute Quintet, 1987; Premiere of Nono's Hay que caminar sonando for violin Duo, with Irvine Arditti, Violin, 1989; *Recordings include:* CD of Elliott Carter's Quartets, Etcetera, Quartets by Berg, Ferneyhough, Kagel, Rihm, Kurtag, Webern, Cage. *Address:* c/o 57 Rotherwick Road, London NW11 7DD, England.

ALBERT Werner Andreas, b. 1935, Weinheim, Germany. Conductor. *Education:* Studied at the Mannheim Hochschule and at Heidelberg University; Conducting studies with Herbert von Karajan and Hans Rosbaud. *Career:* Conducted the Heidelberg Chamber Orchestra 1961-63; Principal Conductor of the North West German Philharmonic 1963-71; Gulbenkian Orchestra, Lisbon, 1971-74; Musical Director of the Nuremberg Symphony Orchestra and the Bavarian Youth Orchestra, from 1974; Lecturer at Nuremberg Academy of Music 1977-. *Recordings include:* Oboe Concertos by Leclair, Haydn and Dittersdorf; Beethoven Ninth Symphony (Oryx); Rossini Petite Messe Solennelle; Cello Concertos by Sutermeister; Mozart Clarinet Concerto and Horn Concerto K447; Puccini Messa di Gloria.

ALBERY Tim, b. 4 June 1952, Harpenden, England. Stage Director. *Career:* Has produced plays for Liverpool Playhouse, Liverpool Everyman, Contact Theatre, Manchester, The Half Moon, ICA and Almeida Theatres, London; Has directed in Germany and Holland; Was Director of ICA Theatre, London, 1981-82; Has directed Schiller at Greenwich Theatre and at Royal Shakespeare Company; Shakespeare for the Old Vic and Racine at the National Theatre. Debut as opera director with The Turn of the Screw at Batignano, Italy, 1983; Other work includes The Midsummer Marriage, Don Giovanni and La Finta Giardiniera for Opera North; The Trojans for Opera North/Scottish Opera/Welsh National Opera and Opéra de Nice; The Rape of Lucretia at Gothenburg 1987; La Wally at Bregenz, 1990; Billy Budd, Beatrice and Benedict, Peter Grimes and Lohengrin for English National Opera, 1988, 1990, 1991 and 1993; Berlioz's Benvenuto Cellini in Amsterdam, 1991; Don Carlos for Opera North, 1993. *Address:* c/o Harriet Cruikshank, 97 Old Lambeth Road, London SW8 1XU, England.

ALBIN Roger, b. 30 Sept 1920, Beausoleil, France. Conductor; Cellist. *Education:* Studied with Umberto Benedetti at Monte Carlo, from 1926; Paris Conservatoire with Henri Busser, Darius Milhaud and Olivier Messiaen. *Career:* Played cello at Monte Carlo, at the Paris Opera and at the Société des Concerts du Conservatoire; Duo partnership with pianist Claude Helffer 1949-57 ; Studied further with Roger Desormiére, Carl Schuricht and Hans Rosbaud and conducted from 1957 (chorus at the Opéra-Comique, Paris); Musical Director at Nancy 1960-61, Toulouse 1961-66; French Radio Orchestra at Strasbourg 1966-75; Cellist with the French National Orchestra, 1978-81 (also member of the orchestra's String Sextet); Professor of Chamber Music at the Strasbourg Conservatory, 1981-87. *Recordings:* As cellist, Prokofiev's Concerto and Ravel's Trio; Fauré's Fantasie and the Fantasie for piano and orchestra by Debussy; Ibert's Diane Poitiers. *Honours include:* Premier prix (1936) in cello class at the Paris Conservatoire.

ALBRECHT Gerd, b. 19 July 1935, Essen, Germany. Conductor. *Education:* Studied conducting with Wilhelm Bruckner-Ruggeberg, Hamburg Hochschule fur Musik; Musicology, University of Kiel; University of Hamburg. *Career:* Repetiteur and conductor, Wurttemberg State Theater, Stuttgart, 1958-61; First conductor, Mainz, 1961-63; Generalmusikdirektor, Lubeck, 1963-66; Kassel, 1966-72; Chief Conductor, Deutsche Oper, West Berlin, 1972-79; Tonhalle Orchestra, Zurich, 1975-80; Guest Conductor, Vienna State Opera, 1976-, Conducted the premieres of Henze's Telemanniana (Berlin 1967), Fortner's Elisabeth Tudor (Berlin 1972), Henze's Barcarola (Zurich 1980) and Reimann's Troades (Munich 1986); Guest appearances with various European and North American Opera companies and orchestras; Conductor, Der fliegende Holländer at Covent Garden, 1986; Chief Conductor, Hamburg State Opera and Philharmonic State Orchestra, 1988-; Conducted Schreker's Der Schatzgräber at Hamburg 1989-90, followed by Idomeneo and Tannhäuser; Tchaikovsky's Maid of Orleans at the 1990 Munich Festival, with Waltraud Meier; Chief Conductor of the Czech Philharmonic Orchestra from 1992; Season 1992 with Dvořák's Dimitri at Munich, Reimann's Troades at Frankfurt and Tannhäuser at Barcelona. *Recordings:* For Angel-EMI; Deutsche Grammophon; Orfeo; Schwann; Musica Mundi; CD of Der Schatzgräber, Capriccio. *Honours:* Winner, Besançon, 1957; Hilversum, 1958, conducting competitions. *Address:* c/o Hamburg State Opera, Postfach 302448, 2000 Hamburg 36, Germany.

ALBRECHT Theodore John, b. 24 Sept 1945, Jamestown, New York, USA. Orchestra Conductor; Musicologist. m. Carol Padgham, 16 Aug 1976. *Education:* BME, St Mary's University, 1967; MM, 1969, PhD, 1975, North Texas State University. *Career includes:* Assistant Professor, Appalachian State University, 1975-76; Conductor, German Orchestra of Cleveland, 1977-80; Music Director, Northland Symphony Orchestra, Kansas City, Missouri, 1980-87; Professor, Park College, 1980-92; Music Director, Philharmonia of Greater Kansas City, 1987-92; Associate Professor, Kent State University, Kent, Ohio, 1992-; Notable performances include: US premieres of Bruckner Dialog by Gottfried von Einem, 1982; Symphony in C, op 46 by Hans Pfitzner, 1983; Ludi Leopoldini by Gottfried von Einem, 1984; 1st American conductor to conduct all 9 Dvorak symphonies; World premiere of Song of the Prairie by Timothy Corrao, 1987. *Publications:* Dika Newlin, Friend and Mentor: A Birthday Anthology (editor), 1973; Beethoven: A Research Guide, 1994; Translations of Felix Weingartner's On the Performance of the Symphonies of Mozart, 1985, Schubert and Schumann, 1986; Editor: Thayer, Salieri, Rival of Mozart, 1989; Letters to Beethoven and other Correspondence, 1994; Journal of Musicology; Journal of Musicological Research; Beethoven Newsletter; Beethoven Forum. *Contributions to:* Notes; Musical Quarterly; American Choral Review; The Opera Journal; The Clarinet, Symposium. *Hobbies:* Photography; Walking; Cultural geography; Local history. *Address:* 1635 Chadwick Drive, Kent, OH 44240, USA.

ALBRIGHT William (Hugh), b. 20 Oct 1944, Gary, Indiana, USA. Pianist; Organist; Teacher; Composer.

Education: Studied piano with Rosetta Goodkind; theory with Hugh Aitken, Juilliard Preparatory Department, New York, 1959-62; Composition with Ross Lee Finney; Organ with Marilyn Mason, University of Michigan, 1963-70; Composition with George Rochberg, with Olivier Messiaen, Paris Conservatory, 1968. *Career:* Teacher 1970-82, Professor of Music 1982-, Associate Director, Electronic Music Studio, University of Michigan; Concert tours as pianist and organist throughout USA, Canada and Europe. *Compositions:* Multimedia and stage: Tic for Soloist, 2 Jazz-Rock Improvisation Ensembles, Tapes and Films, 1967; Beulahland Rag for Narrator, Jazz Quartet, Improvisation Ensemble, Tape, Film and Slides, 1967-69; Cross of Gold, music theater, 1975; Full Moon in March, incidental music to Yeats's play, 1978; Orchestral: Alliance, suite, 1967-70; Night Procession for Chamber Orchestra, 1972; Gothic Suite for Organ, Strings and Percussion, 1973; Bacchanal for Organ and Orchestra, 1981; Chamber: Amerithon for Variable Ensemble, 1966-67; Marginal Worlds for Ensemble, 1969; Peace Pipe for 2 Bassoons, 1976; Jericho, Battle Music for Trumpet and Organ, 1976; Halo for Organ and Metal Percussion Instruments, 1978; Enigma Syncopations for Flute, Organ, Double Bass and Percussion, 1982; Brass Tacks, rag march for Brass Quintet, 1983; Canon in D (Berimbau!) for Contrabass and Harpsichord, 1984; Piano and Organ music; Vocal: Mass in D for Chorus, Organ, Percussion and Congregation, 1974; Chichester Mass for Chorus, 1974; Pax in Terra for Soprano, Tenor and Chorus, 1981; David's Songs for Chorus, 1982; A Song to David, oratorio, 1983; Sphaera for piano and computer-generated tape, 1985; Take Up the Song for Soprano, Chorus and Piano, 1986; Quintet for Clarinet and string Quartet, 1987; Deum de Deo for choir and organ, 1988; Chasm for orchestra, 1989; Concerto for harpsichord and string orchestra, 1991; Flights of Fancy: Ballet for organ, 1992. *Recordings:* As performer and composer. *Honours:* Guggenheim Fellowship, 1976 and 1987; Composer-in-residence, American Academy, Rome, 1979; Many commissions and awards; Composer of the Year,. American Guild of Organists, 1993. *Current Management:* Karen McFarlane Artists Inc, 12429 Cedar Road, Cleveland, OH 44106, USA. *Address:* c/o Music Department, University of Michigan, Ann Arbor, MI 48109, USA.

ALCANTARA Theo, b. 16 April l941, Cuenca, Spain. Conductor. m. Susan Alcantara. *Education:* Madrid Conservatory and Salzburg Mozarteum. *Career:* Conductor, Frankfurt am Main, 1964-66; director of orchestras, University of Michigan, Ann Arbor, 1968-73; music director, Grand Rapids (Michigan) Symphony Orchestra, 1973-78; music director, 1978-89 Phoenix (Arizona) Symphony Orchestra; artistic director, Music Academy of the West, Santa Barbara, California, 1981-84; principal conductor, Pittsburgh Opera, 1987-; Conducted Elektra at Pittsburgh, November 1989. *Honours:* Silver medal, Mitropoulos Competition, 1966. *Address:* c/o ICM Artists, Ltd, 40 West 57th Street, New York, NY 10019, USA.

ALDEN David, b. 16 Sept 1949, New York City, USA. Stage Director. *Career:* Has directed the premieres of Stephen Burton's The Duchess of Malfi (Wolf Trap, 1978), Pasatieri's Washington Squares and Conrad Susa's Don Perlimpin (San Francisco); Fidelio and Wozzeck at the Metropolitan Opera, Rigoletto, Wozzeck and Mahagonny for Scottish Opera; Productions of The Rake's Progress for Netherlands Opera and at the Israel Festival, Werther at Nancy and the US premiere of Judith by Siegfried Matthus (Santa Fe 1990); English National Opera with Mazeppa, Simon Boccanegra, A Masked Ball and double bill of Oedipus Rex and Duke Bluebeard's Castle (1991); Affiliations with Opera at the Academy, New York (La Calisto) and New Israel Opera (Les Contes d'Hoffmann, La Bohème and the world premiere of Noam Sheriff's The Sorrows of Job). *Address:* c/o English National Opera, St Martin's Lane, London WC2, England.

ALER David, b. 26 Apr 1959, Stockholm, Sweden.

Singer (Baritone). *Education:* Studied in Gothenburg with Jacqueline Delman until 1987; Further studies with Geoffrey Parsons, Janet Baker, Kim Borg and Galina Vishnevskaya. *Career:* Sang at Landestheater Coburg and in Sweden, 1988-, as Don Giovanni, Guglielmo, and Tarquinius in The Rape of Lucretia; Appeared in Vadstena and Reykjavik, 1988-89 in premiere production of Someone I Have Seen by Karolina Eriksdottir; Stora Theater, Gothenburg, as Schaunard in La Boheme, 1989; Concert engagements in Stockholm, with Drottningholm Baroque-Ensemble and Chapelle Royale of Versailles. *Address:* c/o M&M Lyric Artists, 140 Battersea Park Road, London SW11 5NY, England.

ALER John, b. 4 Oct 1949, Baltimore, Maryland, USA. Singer (Tenor). *Education:* Bachelor's and Master's degrees in Voice Performance, School of Music, Catholic University of America, 1972; Juilliard School of Music, American Opera Center and Opera Training Department, 1972-75; Studied with Oren Brown, Martin Isepp. *Career:* Has sung in opera, oratorio, recitals, USA, Canada, UK and most Western European countries; Appearances include Tanglewood, Glyndebourne, Aix-en-Provence Festival, Salzburg Festival, La Scala, London Proms and many more; Has sung with major national and international orchestras; Vienna Staatsoper debut, 1982; Toured Japan with Royal Opera, Covent Garden, 1986; Toured Taiwan with Ludwigsburg Festival Chorus and Orchestra, 1987; Sang Eumolpus in Stravinsky's Persephone at the Promenade Concerts, London, 1993. *Recordings include:* Carmina Burana with London Symphony Orchestra and Chorus, 1980; La Belle Hélène, EMI/Angel, 1984; Berlioz's Requiem, 1985; Liszt songs, Newport Classics, 1986; Così Fan Tutte, EMI/Angel, 1986; Le Comte Ory, Opera de Lyon, Philips, 1988; Handel's Messiah, EMI/Angel, 1986; Bizet's Les pecheurs des Perles, EMI/Angel, 1989; Songs and duos of Saint-Saëns (with John Ostendorf and John Van Buskirk), Newport Classics, 1989; Enesco's Oedipe, EMI/Angel; Semele (with Kathleen Battle), DGG, 1990; Title role in Gazzaniga's Don Giovanni, Orfeo, 1990; Stravinsky works with London Sinfonietta, Sony Classical, 1990; Rossini's Songs of My Old Age, 1991; Handel's Joshua, Newport Classic, 1991; Gounod's Mors et Vita with Orchestre du Capitole de Toulouse (Michel Plasson, conductor), EMI, 1992. Many more. *Current Management:* Herbert Barrett Management, USA. *Address:* c/o Mary Lynn Fixler, Herbert Barrett Management, 1776 Broadway, Suite 1610, New York, NY 10019, USA.

ALEXANDER Carlos, b. 15 Oct 1915, Utica, New York, USA. Singer (Bass-Baritone). *Education:* Studied in Berlin, and with Friedrich Schorr in New York. *Debut:* St Louis 1941, as Masetto. *Career:* Sang widely in North and South America; Founded an opera society at Salt Lake City, 1948; Moved to Germany 1955 and sang first at Munster, Hanover and Krefeld; Cologne 1958-61; Stuttgart Opera from 1961; Glyndebourne Festival 1961, as Gregor Mittenhofer in the first British performance of Henze's Elegy for Young Lovers; Guest appearances in Dusseldorf, and Munich; Maggio Musicale Florence 1961, as Mandryka in Arabella; Bayreuth Festival 1963-65, as Beckmesser in Die Meistersinger; Stuttgart 1968, in the premiere of Prometheus by Orff; Teacher at the Salzburg Mozarteum. *Recordings:* Antigonae by Orff (Deutsche Grammophon); Don Giovanni (Harmonia Mundi).

ALEXANDER Christian David, b. 15 Jan 1964, Liverpool, England. Composer. *Education:* BA Hons, 1986, MMus, 1992, Bristol University; Studied Composition with Robert Saxton; Studied with Maxwell-Davies and Steve Martland, Hoy Summer School, 1990. *Career:* Music written and performed for BBC documentary The Zoo, 1986; Works performed by BBC Singers (op 5 and op 25), Bournemouth Sinfonietta (op 23), Jennifer Stinton (op 36); Works performed at Wigmore Hall (op 36), at Purcell Room (op 21) and at St John's, Smith Square (op 14); Composer-in-Residence, 1991-94. *Compositions:* 6 published works (ensemble, instrumental and vocal music). Other works

include: February Afternoon, Op 5, for choir and vibraphone, 1987; Child of Treblinka, Op 11, for chamber ensemble, 1988; Garden of Love, Op 21, for soprano and piano, 1990; New Earth, Op 23, for chamber orchestra, 1990; Madrigal, Op 25, for choir, 1990; Caol IIa, Op 34, for viola and orchestra, 1992. *Hobbies:* Film; Squash; Cooking; Reading; Malt Whisky. *Address:* Composer-in-Residence, Radley College, Radley, Oxfordshire OX14 2HR, England.

ALEXANDER Haim, b. 9 Aug. 1915, Berlin, Germany. Composer. m. 6 Jan. 1941, 2 sons. *Education:* Sternsches Conservatory, Berlin; Graduated Palestine Conservatory and Academy of Music, 1945; Higher Studies, Freiburg, Germany. *Career:* Teacher of Piano and Theory, 1945-; Associate Professor, Composition and Theory, and Head of Department of Theoretical Subjects, Rubin Academy of Music, Jerusalem, 1972-82; Associate Professor, 1972-76, Full Professorship, 1976-, Theoretical Subjects, Department of Musicology, University of Tel-Aviv; Retired 1982, but continuing part-time work. *Compositions include:* Songs of Love and Expectation for Mezzo-Soprano and Chamber Orchestra, 1985; Miscellaneous works for piano, 2 pianos, chamber music, pieces based on Oriental Folklore, choral music, songs for voice and piano, works for orchestra; Mein blaues Klavier, 8 women voices and percussion, Words: Else Lasker-Schüler, 1990; Metamorphoses on a theme by Mozart, Piano solo, 1990; 4 songs, hebrew, for voice and flute, 2 guitars, percussion and viola. *Publications:* Improvisation am Klavier (two parts and two cassettes), in German, 1986. *Contributions to:* Encyclopedia Hebraica. *Hobbies:* Gymnastics; Swimming; Bridge. *Address:* 55 Tschernichowsky Street, 92587 Jerusalem, Israel.

ALEXANDER Leni, b. 8 June 1924, Breslau, Germany. Composer. m. Ernst Bodenhöfer, 24 Dec. 1941, divorced. 2 sons, 1 daughter. Emigrated to Chile from Hamburg in 1939. *Education:* Real-Gymnasium Hamburg, 1939; Diploma Montessori, University of Chile, 1945; Piano, Violoncello, Composition with Fre Focke; Conservatoire de Paris with Olivier Messiaen and composition studies with René Leibowitz, 1954. *Career:* Public concerts (symphonique works) in: Santiago de Chile, Buenos Aires, Paris, Rome, New York, Cologne (Chamber music) Venice, Toulouse, Tokyo, Stuttgart; Film-music, Ballet music, Santiago; Special broadcast commission, San Francisco. *Compositions include:* Cantata From Death to Morning; Equinoccio; 2..ils se sont perdus dans l'espace etoile.., 1975; Aulicio II, 1985; Cuarteto para Cuerdas 1957; Time and Consumation; Tessimenti; Adras; Par quoi? A quoi? Pour quoi?; Maramoh; Los Disparates; Sous le quotidien, decelez l'inexplicable;...Est-ce donc si doux cette vie?..; Ballet Music: Soon we shall be one, 1959; Les trois visages de la lune, 1966; Un medecin de campagne; Schigan for organ, 1989; Dishona for voice, saxophone and 3 percussions, 1988. *Contributions to:* Music and Psychoanalysis; Alban Berg; The Music Which Freud never heard; Psychoanalytic variations about a theme by Gustav Mahler. *Honours:* Cantata From Death to Morning chosen as best work by RAI Italy, 1960; Festival of the ISMC, Köln, only work played and selected from Latin America; Fellowship of the French government, 1953; Guggenheim Fellowship, 1969; Various commission by the Ministere de la Culture, France and Radio France. *Address:* c/o Beatrice Bodenhofer, Arzobispo Casanova, 24 (Bellavista), Santiago de Chile.

ALEXANDER Roberta, b. 3 Mar 1949, Lynchburg, Virginia, USA. Singer (Soprano). *Education:* Studied at the University of Michigan and with Herman Woltman at the Royal Conservatory, The Hague. *Career:* Sang Mozart's Pamina at Houston in 1980 and Strauss's Daphne at Santa Fe 1981; European debut as Mozart's Pamina, Netherlands Opera, 1979; Covent Garden debut as Mimi in La Bohème, 1981; Metropolitan Opera debut 1983, as Zerlina; returned to New York as Jenůfa, Mimi, Vitellia, Countess and Gershwin's Bess; Netherlands Opera as Vitelia, Fiordiligi and Violetta; Vienna State Opera as Donna Elvira, Jenůfa; Hamburg State Opera as Elletra (Idomeneo), Fiordiligi, Countess;

Glyndebourne debut 1989 as Jenůfa; Sang Mozart's Vitellia at Zurich in 1989, Elettra, Idomeneo, at the Hamburg Staatsoper, 1990. Concert appearances include Strauss Four last songs with Los Angeles Philharmonic (Previn) and San Francisco Symphony; Mahler 4 with Boston Symphony (Ozawa), Concertgebouw (Haitink), Cleveland (Ashkenazy); Mahler 8 at the Salzburg Festval (Maazel); Concerts with Concentus Musicus Wien (Harnoncourt). *Recordings:* Mahler 4, Porgy and Bess excerpts, St John's Passion (Phillips); Giulio Cesare excerpts, Don Giovanni (Elvira); Telemann Cantatas, (Teldec); Songs by Ives, Strauss, Mozart, Bernstein, Barber and Puccini (Et Cetera). *Address:* c/o Harrison/Parrott Ltd, 12 Penzance Place, London W11 4PA, England.

ALEXEEV Dimitri, b. 10 Aug 1947, Moscow, USSR. Pianist. m. Tatiana Sarkissova. *Education:* Piano studies from age 5; Entered Central Music School, Moscow Conservatory, age 6; Postgradute studies, Dimitri Bashkirov, Moscow. *Debuts:* Chicago 1976, New York 1978. *Career includes:* Numerous appearances, great orchestras worldwide. UK recitals include: Major music societies & festivals (Aldeburgh, Edinburgh); Regular performances throughout USSR, Europe, USA, Japan, Australia; Solo appearances; Concerts with soprano Barbara Hendricks (London, Stockholm, Frankfurt, Munich, Milan, Florence & TV, USSR, France); Piano duos, with Tatiana Sarkissova. Recent appearances include: Philharmonia & Royal Philharmonic Orchestras (UK), Berlin Philharmonic debut (Rachmaninov Paganini Variations), Amsterdam Concertgebouw (Prokofiev 3), 1985-86; Berlin Philharmonic (Albrecht), Royal Philhrmonic (Ashkenazy), Orchestre de Paris (Temirkanov), Philharmonia (Bychkov), 1988-89; with Dimitri Sitkovetsky played the Shostakovich Sonata and the Brahms D Minor at St. John's Smith Square, 1991; Prokofiev's 2nd Concerto at the 1991 Promenade Concerts, London; Beethoven's 2nd Concerto, Prom Concerts, 1993. *Recordings include:* Brahms piano works; Prokofiev & Rachmaninov concertos; Shostakovich concertos; Spirituals, with Barbara Hendricks; Chopin waltzes; Chopin preludes; Grieg & Schumann concertos, with Yuri Temirkanov & Royal Philharmonic Orchestra. (USSR & European labels.); CDs of Schumann's Kreisleriana and Etudes Symphoniques, Shostakovich Concertos with the English Chamber Orchestra, Classics for Pleasure. *Current management:* Harold Holt Ltd. *Address:* c/o IMG Artists Europe, Media House, 3 Burlington Lane, Chiswick, London W4 2TH, England.

ALIBERTI Lucia, b. 1957, Mesina, Sicily, Italy. Singer (Soprano). *Education:* Studied at the Messina Conservatory. *Debut:* Teatro Sperimentale Spoleto 1978, as Amina in La Sonnambula. *Career:* Spoleto Festival 1979, as Amina; Wexford Festival 1979, in Crispino e la Comare, by the brothers Ricci; returned 1980, in Un Giorno di Regno, and 1983, as Linda di Chamounix; Piccola Scala Milan 1980, as Elisa in Il re Pastore by Mozart, then in Handel's Ariodante; Glyndebourne Festival 1980, Nannetta; La Scala Milan 1981, Nannetta; At the Teatro Bellini Catania 1982, sang Elvira in I Puritani and Olympia (Les Contes d'Hoffmann); Deutsche Oper Berlin and Munich Opera 1983, as Lucia and Gilda; Cologne and Zurich 1985 and 1986, Violetta; Sang title role in Rossini's La Donna del Lago, followed by Norma at Catania, 1990. *Recordings include:* La buona figliuola by Piccinni (Cetra); CD of L'arte del belcanto, (Capriccio). *Address:* Oper der Stadt Bonn, Am Boselagerhof 1, D-5300 Bonn.

ALLANBROOK Douglas (Phillips), b. 1 Apr 1921, Melrose, Massachusetts, USA. Composer; Teacher. *Education:* Studied with Nadia Boulanger, Longy School of Music, Cambridge, Massachusetts, 1941-42; Paris, 1948-50; BA, Harvard College, 1948; With Walter Piston; Studied harpsichord and early keyboard music with Ruggero Gerlin, Naples, 1950-52. *Career:* Teacher, St John's College, Annapolis. *Compositions:* Operas: Ethan Frome, 1950-52; Nightmare Abbey, 1960-62; Orchestral: 7 symphonies: No 1, 1955; No 2, An Elegy, 1961; No 3, Four Orchestral Landscapes, 1965; No 4,

1968; No 5, 1975; No 6, Five Heroic Attitudes, 1979; No 7, Music from the Country, 1972; Concerto for Harpsichord and Small Orchestra, 1949-50; Violin Concerto, 1959; Serenade for Piano and Orchestra, 1978; Chamber: 4 string quartets, 1955, 1956, 1958, 1972; Fantasy for Violin and Piano, 1956; Concert Music for Cello and Winds, 1958; Partita for Cello, 1958; Night and Morning Music for Brass Quintet, 1978; 5 Marches for the Quick and the Dead for Brass quintet, 1982; Invitation to the Side Show for Brass Quintet, 1985; 25 Building Blocks for Horn and Piano, 1985; 7 for 7 for Brass Quintet, Piano and Percussion, 1987; Piano: 2 sonatas, 1948, 1950; 2 Bagatelles, 1959; 40 Changes, 1967; 12 Preludes for All Seasons, 1970; 5 Transcendental Studies, 1980; 5 Night Pieces, 1986; Harpsichord music; Choral: Ash Wednesday for 2 Soloists, Chorus and Orchestra, 1948; Te Deum for Chorus, Brass, Percussion and Pianos, 1949; The Seven Last Words for 2 Soloists, Chorus and Orchestra, 1968; An English Mass for Chorus and Organ, 1974; An American Miscellany for Chamber Chorus, 1975; 2 Tennyson Settings for Brass and Chorus, 1986; Moon Songs for Children's Chorus and Orchestra, 1986-87; Vocal: Songs to Petrarch Sonnets, 1948; Songs to Shakespeare Sonnets, 1950; 3 Noble Love Songs for Baritone and Orchestra, 1961; 3 Love and Death Songs for High Voice, Oboe, 2 Clarinets and 3 Strings, 1981. *Honour:* Fulbright Fellowship. *Address:* 6 Revell Street, Annapolis, MD 21401, USA.

ALLDIS John, b. 10 Aug 1929, London, England. Conductor. m. Ursula Mason, 23 July 1960, 2 sons. *Education:* Felsted School, 1943-47; Choral Scholar, Kings College, Cambridge, 1949-52; ARCO, 1954; MA, 1957. *Career:* Founder/Conductor, John Alldis Choir, 1962-; Professor, Guildhall School of Music, 1966-77; Founder/Conductor, London Symphony Chorus, 1966-69; Conductor, London Philharmonic Choir, 1969-82; Conductor, Danish Radio Choir, 1972-77; Musical Director, Groupe Vocal de France, 1978-83. *Recordings:* Over 50 various recordings with John Alldis Choir, contemporay music and opera; CD's of Beethoven's Missa Solemnis, Klemperer; Elgar The Dream of Gerontius, Boult; Berlioz Grande Messe des Morts, Colin Davis and L'Enfance du Christ; Ives Symphony No.4, Serebrier; Mozart Die Entführung, Davis; Puccini Turandot, Mehta; Tchaikovsky Eugene Onegin, Solti and Vivaldi Sacred Choral Works, Negri. *Honours:* Various awards and Grammy nominations; Gold Disc with London Philharmonic Choir, 1977; FGSM, 1976; Fellow, Westminster Choir College, Princeton, New Jersey, USA 1978; Chevelier des Arts et des Lettres, 1984. *Current Management:* Allied Artists. *Address:* 3 Wool Road, Wimbledon, London SW20 0HN, England.

ALLEGRETTI John Michael, b. 6 May 1928, San Jose, California, USA. Musician and Manager of Engineers, (retired). m. Shirley Bernal, 4 Nov 1950, 2 sons, 1 daughter. *Education:* Baccalaureate degree, University of San Francisco. *Career:* Formerly: Member, San Jose Symphony Orchestra; Member, San Jose Municipal Band; Leader, US Army Dance Orchestra and Radio Show, Panama Canal Zone, 1946-47; Leader, Johnny Allegretti Orchestra; Trombonist, Buddy King Orchestra. *Memberships:* International Musicians Union; California Pioneers of Santa Clara County. *Hobbies:* Muisc; Family; Gardening. *Address:* 10795 Ridgeview Court, San Jose, CA 95127, USA.

ALLEN Anthony Campbell, b. 6 May 1925, Surrey, England. Composer. m. 1 June 1950. div, 10 July 1979, 1s, 2d. *Education:* Royal Academy of Dramatic Art; Private lessons with Bertie Scott. *Debut:* 5 Nov 1972. *Career:* Teacher of Voice, Royal Academy of Dramatic Art, 1955-56; Director, Racine's Phedre, Theatre in the Round, London, 1957; Lecturer, 1959-61, Director, Love's Labour's Lost, 1961, Bristol, University; Director, Beyreuth-Festspieltreffen, 1962-63; Director, Henry James's The Outcry, London, 1968. *Compositions:* The Wandering Planet, opera: the Hallwyl-Kantate; 3 alphorn concerti; 3 Violin Concerti; Flute Concerto; Piano Concerto; 2 Cello Concerti; Christmas Oratorio for 4 soloists, choir and orchestra; Many songs with orchestra or piano; Chamber music. *Publication:* I Saw In Louisiana, English Poetry and Song Society. *Honours:* Man of the Year. *Memberships:* SUISA; Composers Guild of Great Britain. *Address:* 123 Brauerstrasse, CH-8004, Zurich, Switzerland.

ALLEN Betty, b. 17 Mar. 1930, Campbell, Ohio, USA. Mezzo-soprano; Teacher; Administrator. m. Ritten Edward Lee, III, 17 Oct. 1953. 1 son, 1 daughter. *Education:* Wilberforce University, 1944-46; Certificate, Hartford School of Music, 1953; Private vocal studies with Sarah Peck More, Zinka Milanov, Paul Ulanowsky, Carolina Segrera Holden; Berkshire Music Center, Tanglewood. *Career:* Soloist, Bernstein's Jeremiah Symphony, Tanglewood, 1951; Appeared in Thomson's Four Saints in Three Acts, New York, 1952; Debut, New York City Opera, Kern's Queenie, 1954; Toured Europe under auspices of the US State Department, 1955; New York recital debut, Town Hall, 1958; Formal Operatic debut, Teatro Colon, Buenos Aires, as Jocasta in Oedipus Rex, 1964; USA Operatic debut, San Francisco, 1966; Metropolitan Opera debut, New York, 1973; Appearances with other USA opera companies; Many concert engagements; Teacher, Manhattan School of Music, New York, 1969; North Carolina School of the Arts, Winston-Salem, 1978-87; Philadelphia Musical Academy, 1979; Executive Director, Harlem School of the Arts, 1979-; Teacher of master classes in voice, Inst Teatro Colon, Buenos Aires, 1985-86; Curtis Institute of Music, Philadelphia, 1987-. *Recordings:* Various recordings. *Honours:* Marian Anderson Award, 1953-54; LHD, Wittenberg University, 1971; DMus, Union College, 1981; Doctor Fine Arts, Adelphi University, 1990; American Eagle Award, National Music Council. *Memberships:* NAACP, Urban League; Various musical organizations. *Address:* c/o Harlem School of the Arts, 645 St Nicholas Avenue, New York, NY 10030, USA.

ALLEN Ross Clearman, b. 16 Dec 1921, Kirksville, Missouri, USA. Opera Director; Teacher. *Education:* Studied at Indiana University. *Debut:* Staged the choral sequences in Britten's Billy Budd at its US (student) premiere, 1952. *Career:* Joined faculty of Indiana University, 1953; Has staged more than 150 works, including Candide by Bernstein, 1958; US premieres of Christmas Eve by Rimsky-Korsakov and Martinu's Greek Passion; Staged Aida at the opening of Jones Hall, Houston, 1966; World premiere of John Eaton's Myshkin (after The Idiot by Dostoyevsky), Indiana, 1973; Has also assisted in the direction of 16th century Italian entertainments. *Honours include:* Peabody Award, 1969, for television production of Elegy for Young Lovers by Henze. *Address:* Indiana Universtiy Opera Theater, School of Music, Indiana University, Bloomington, IN 47405, USA.

ALLEN Thomas, b. 10 Sept 1944, Seaham Harbour, County Durham, England. Baritone. m. (1) Margaret Holley, 30 March 1968; (2) Jeannie Lascelles, 12 March 1988. *Education:* Studied at Royal College of Music, London. *Career:* Member, Welsh National Opera, singing many roles, 1969-72; Royal Opera, London 1971-, notably as Mozart's Count and Guglielmo, Rossini's Figaro and Britten's Billy Budd; First appeared at Glyndebourne Festival in 1973 as Papageno and has subsequently sung many roles at this and various other festivals; Has appeared abroad in Paris, Florence, Buenos Aires, Geneva, Metropolitan Opera House, New York; in 1985 sang the title role in Henze's realization of Monteverdi's Il Ritorno d'Ulisse, Salzburg Festival; in 1986 sang title role, first British stage performance of Busoni's Doktor Faust, ENO London Coliseum; 1987 La Scala, Milan, Don Giovanni; Sang Mozart's Count at Los Angeles, 1990, Salzburg, 1991; Malatesta, (Don Pasquale), at Covent Garden, 1990, followed by Forester in a new production of the Cunning Little Vixen; Eisenstein at the Metropolitan; Chicago Lyric Opera debut, 1990, as Rossini's Figaro; Sang Don Giovanni at Covent Garden, 1992; Count Almaviva at the Salzburg Festival, 1993. *Recordings include:* Carmina Burana, Peter Grimes, L'enfance du Christ, Le nozze di Figaro, Il barbiere di Siviglia, King Priam; Don Giovanni;

Iphigénie en Tauride; Eugene Onegin; Werther; Wolf Italian Song Book; War Requiem; Duruflé Requiem; Vaughan Williams Songs of Travel. *Publication:* Foreign Parts, A Sinner's Journal. *Honours:* Honorary MA, University of Newcastle on Tyne, 1984; Honorary DMus, University of Durham, 1988; Honorary FRAM, Royal Academy of Music, 1988; Honorary FRCM, Royal College of Music, 1988; CBE, New Years Honours List, 1989. *Address:* c/o Lies Askonas Ltd, 6 Henrietta Street, London WC2E 8LA, England.

ALLERS Franz, b. 6 Aug. 1905, Czechoslovakia. Orchestra Conductor. m. Janne Furch, 30 May 1963, 1 daughter. *Education:* Diploma in conducting, composition, violin and piano, Academy of Music, Berlin, Germany, 1926; Musicology, University of Berlin, 1926; Member of Berlin Philharmonic, 1924-26. *Debut:* Fledermaus, with Richard Tauber, Carlsbad, Czechoslovakia, 1926. *Career includes:* Conductor, repertoire included Hindemith's Cardillac and Berg's Wozzeck, Wuppertal, Germany; Conductor, Ballet Russe de Monte Carlo, London, England and tours of USA; Soon conducted most major symphony orchestras in USA. *Compositions include:* Innumerable arrangements and transcriptions. *Recordings include:* La Vie Parisienne by Offenbach, prizewinner; Many for CBS, RCA, Capitol New York, Philips etc. *Contributions to:* Music magazines. *Honours:* Grand Cross of Merit 1st Class, in recognition of performing Austrian music with Vienna Tonkuenstler Orchestra on 2 tours in USA, Federal Government of Austria. *Current Management:* Judie Janowski, Columbia Artists Management, New York, USA. *Memberships:* American Conductor's Guild; American Symphony League; Bohemians; New York Musicians Club. *Hobbies:* Reading non-fiction; Hiking; Travelling; Swimming. *Address:* Columbia Artists Management, 165 West 57th Street, New York, NY 10019, USA.

ALLIOT-LUGAZ Colette, b. 20 July 1947, Notre-Dame-de-Bellecombe, France. Singer (Soprano). *Education:* Studied at Bonneville, with Magda Fonay-Besson in Geneva and at the Opera Studio Paris with Rene Koster and Vera Rozsa; Further study at the Lyon Conservatoire. *Career:* Has sung widely in France and elsewhere as Mozart's Pamina, Cherubino and Zerlina; Engagements as Messager's Véronique, Rosina and Weber's Aennchen, and in operas by Monteverdi, Haydn and Rameau; Has often appeared as Debussy's Mélisande, notably at the Lyon Opera in 1980; Festival performances at Aix and Glyndebourne and at the Paris Opéra and the Théâtre de la Monnaie, Brussels; Modern repertory includes La Passion de Gilles by Boesmans (creation 1983) and Berio's Opera; Sang Ascanius in Les Troyens at the opening of the Opéra Bastille, Paris, 1990; appeared as Lully's Alceste at the Théâtre des Champs-Elysées, 1992. *Recordings include:* Pelléas et Mélisande, conducted by Charles Dutoit (Decca); Fragoletto in Les Brigands by Offenbach (EMI); Campra's Tancrède (Erato). *Address:* c/o Opéra de Lyon, 9 Quai Jean Moulin, F-69001 Lyon, France.

ALLISTER Jean Maria, b. 26 Feb. 1932, Northern Ireland. Singer. m. (1) Edgar Fleet, 5 Oct. 1955, 1 son, (2) René Atkinson, 20 Feb. 1974. *Education:* LRAM, 1954, FRAM, 1968, Royal Academy of Music, London; FGSM, 1976; FGSM Emeritus, 1979. *Debut:* Royal Albert Hall, London, 1954. *Career:* Many oratorio and recital appearances, England and abroad, 1954-80; Henry Wood Promenade Concerts, 1959-70; Premiere, In Terra Pax, 1960; Three Choirs Festivals, 1961-77; Appeared as Italian Girl in Algiers, Camden Festival, 1961; Sadler's Wells Opera debut, 1962; Sang at Glyndebourne, 1962-68; British premiere, Henze's Novae de Infinito Laudes, Leeds, 1965; Alexander Nevsky, Festival Hall, 1968; L'Ormindo, Munich, 1969; Covent Garden debut as Page in Salome, 1970; Scipio, Handel Opera Society, Herrenhausen and Drottlingholm, 1970; Premiere, John Gardner's The Visitors, 1972; Delius's Koanga, Sadler's Wells Opera, 1972; British premiere, F Martin's Requiem, 1975; Final appearances before retiring from public performance, Jenůfa, Opera North, 1980. *Recordings:* Stravinsky

Mass (L'Oiseau Lyre), conducted by C Davis; Pirates of Penzance, Ruddigore, D'Oyly Carte; Gilbert and Sullivan Selection, RCA Victor; Koanga, Groves; Cavalli L'Ormindo, Leppard; The Mikado, Sadler's Wells Orchestra. *Publication:* Editor, Sing Solo Soprano, 1985. *Honour:* Minnie Hauk Prize, 1953. *Hobbies:* Cooking; Bridge; Golf. *Address:* 236 Otley Road, Leeds, LS16 5AB, England.

ALLMAN Robert, b. 8 June 1927, Melbourne, Australia. Singer (Baritone). *Education:* Studied with Horace Stevens, at the Melbourne Conservatory, with Marjorie Smith in Sydney and with Dominique Modesti in Paris (1955-57). *Career:* Sang with the Victoria National Opera Company 1952; Royal Opera House, Covent Garden, 1956, as Escamillo; Guest appearances at Sadler's Wells and at the Berlin Staatsoper, Hamburg (as Iago), Frankfurt, Munich and Cologne (until 1967); appearances in Australia from 1960 as Rigoletto, Jochanaan in Salome, Macbeth, Escamillo, Scarpia, Belcore and Valentine; sang Don Giovanni, Iago and Nabucco 1970-71 (with the Elizabethan Opera Company); further guest engagements at Stuttgart, Dusseldorf, Kassel, Zurich and Strasbourg (as Macbeth and Simon Boccanegra); Glyndebourne Festival 1979, as Pizarro; member of the Australian Opera at Sydney from 1971; sang Amonasro in Aida at Brisbane 1988; many concert performances, notably in Messiah. *Address:* c/o Lyric Opera of Queensland, PO Box 677, South Brisbane, Queensland 4101, Australia.

ALMEIDA Antonio Jacques de, b. 20 Jan. 1928, Neuilly-sur-Seine, France. Conductor. 2 sons, 1 daughter. *Education:* BMus. Yale University 1949. *Career:* Portuguese Radio 1957-60; Musical Director, Stuttgart Philharmonic 1962-64; Conductor, Paris Opera 1964-; Guest Conductor: Berlin Philharmonic; Philadelphia Orchestra; LSO; RPO; BBC; Suisse Romande Orchestra; Leningrad Philharmonic etc. Musical Director, Friends of French Opera, New York; Conducted Idomeneo for the English Bach Festival at Covent Garden, 1990. *Publications:* Offrande Musicale Orchestral Series (Heugel), Complete Symphonies of Boccherini (Doblinger), Coppelia (Schott), all Edited; Thematic Catalogue Works by Offenbach (Oxford). *Recordings:* Several Grand Prix du Disques; Repertoire includes Haydn Symphonies, 62-79 and L'infedeltà delusa; Music by Florent Schmitt, Duparc, Chausson and Fauré; Bizet Le Docteur Miracle; Mahler 5th Symphony; Gluck's Iphigénie en Tauride, Lisbon Opera; L'Elisir d'Amore, Philadelphia Opera; Music by Lalo. *Contributions to:* Numerous professional journals, including Opera; Diapason. *Honours:* Officier des Arts et Lettres; Chevalier de la Legion d'Honneur. *Address:* Petite Route des Jardins, 13210 Saint Remy de Provence, France.

ALMEIDA Laurindo, b. 2 Sept 1917, Sao Paulo, Brazil (Naturalized US citizen, 1961). Guitarist; Composer; Music Publisher. m. (1) Maria M. Ferreira, 20 May 1944, deceased 1970; (2) Deltr Eamon, 3 Aug 1971. *Education:* Escola Nacional de Musica do Rio de Janeiro. *Career:* Performed on the radio and led his own orchestra at the Casino da Urca in Rio de Janeiro; settled in the US, 1947; was soloist with Stan Kenton's orchestra, 1947-50; performed in and composed for films; was founder-director, Brazilliance Music Publishing Company, 1952-; toured widely as a recitalist and as a soloist with symphony orchestras; toured Japan for a month as soloist in Concerto de Aranguey with the Modern Jazz Quartet, 1991; performed with the Modern Jazz Quartet, Carnegie Hall, 1991; toured major cities of New Zealand and played with the Symphony in Auckland, 1993; performed as Brazilian Reflection in Wigmore Hall with Deltra Eamon, his wife, 1993. *Compositions:* First Concerto for guitar and orchestra. *Recordings:* First Concerto for guitar and orchestra, (soloist Laurindo Almeida), 1980; Outra Vez, (L Almeida, Trio), 1992. *Address:* 4104 Witzel Drive, Sherman Oaks, California 91423, USA

ALONSO Odon, b. 28 Feb 1925, La Baneza, Leon, Spain. Conductor. *Education:* Studied at the Madrid

Conservatoire and in Siena and Vienna. *Career:* Choral Director of the Madrid Soloists 1952, specializing in music of the Spanish Renaissance and Baroque; Conducted the Spanish National Orchestra 1952-56, Madrid Philharmonic 1956-58; Directed the Zarzuela Theatre at Madrid 1956-57; Conducted the Spanish Radio and Television Orchestra from 1968; Guest engagements at the Vienna Volksoper, New York City Opera, Teatro Liceo Barcelona and the Madrid Opera. *Recordings include:* Guitar concertos by Vivaldi and Rodrigo, with Narcisco Ypes; Turina's Rapsodia Sinfonica (Decca).

ALONSO-CRESPO Eduardo, b. 18 Mar 1956, Tucuman, Argentina. Composer; Conductor. *Education:* Civil Engineer, National University of Tucuman; Professor of Piano, School of Musical Arts, National University of Tucuman; MFA, Conducting, Carnegie Mellon University, Pittsburgh. *Debut:* Conducting: Carnegie Mellon Philharmonic in Ginastera, USA, 1987; Tucuman Symphony in Alonso-Crespo, Mozart, Brahms, Argentina, 1988. *Career:* Assistant Conductor: Pittsburgh Civic Orchestra, 1988-90; Associate Conductor, Carnegie Mellon Philharmonic, 1989-91; Music Director: Tucuman Symphony Orchestra and Carnegie Mellon Contemporary Ensemble, 1989-; Orquesta de Tucuman, seasons 1991, 1992; Carnegie Mellon Wind Ensemble, 1991-92; Conductor-in-Residence, Carnegie Mellon University, 1991-92; Guest conducting, Argentina, USA. *Compositions include:* Gorbachev, 2-act opera; Juana, la loca, 1-act opera; Putzi, 1-act opera; Medea, ballet, for chorus and orchestra; Piano Concerto N 1, Commentaries on three waltzes by Alberdi; Two Stories of Birds for orchestra; Sinfonietta for string orchestra. *Honours include:* 3rd Prize, Viotti-Valsesia International Competition, Italy, 1986; Cristobal Colon International Prize for symphonic composition, 1986; Commission for Symphonic Works, National Endowment for the Arts, Argentina, 1987; Honorary Mention, Secretary of Culture, Argentina, 1987; Musician of Year, Canal 11 Foundation, Salta, Argentina, 1990. *Hobbies:* Books on linguistics and sociology. *Address:* Marcos Paz 250, Tucuman 4000, Argentina.

ALPENHEIM Ilse von, b. 11 Feb 1927, Innsbruck, Austria. Pianist. m. Antal Dorati, 16 Dec 1969, deceased 1988. *Education:* Studied with Franz Ledwinka and Winfried Wolf, Salzburg Mozarteum. *Career:* Soloist with major European and USA orchestras; Many engagements as Recitalist and Chamber-music player. *Recordings:* For Desto; Turnabout; Vox, Philips & Pantheon; Haydn piano music complete, Schubert chamber music with piano complete.

ALPERIN Yoram, b. 1945, Rumania. Cellist. *Education:* Studied with Uzi Wiezel, Rubin Academy of Music, Tel Aviv. *Career:* Member and solo appearances with Israel Philharmonic, 1971-; Co-founded Jerusalem String Trio, 1977, giving many concerts, Israel and Europe, 1981-; Repertoire includes String Trios by Beethoven, Dohnanyi, Mozart, Reger, Schubert and Tanyev, Piano Quartets by Beethoven, Brahms, Dvořák, Mozart and Schumann; concerts with Radu Lupu and Daniel Adni. *Recordings:* Several albums. *Address:* c/o Anglo Swiss Ltd, 3 Primrose Mews, 1a Sharpleshall Street, London NW1 8YW, England.

ALSTED Birgitte, b. 15 June 1942, Odense, Denmark. Composer; Violinist. *Education:* Violin studies, Royal Danish Academy of Music; Music Academy, Warsaw, Poland; Composition Seminars with Per Nørgard, Copenhagen. *Career:* Performer of new music in: Det unge Tonekunstnerselskab; Kvinder i Musik; Danmarks Radio, TV. Acting musician, experimental theatre; Teacher. Compositions performed in DUT, Radio, TV, KIM, Paris, Rome, New York, Mexico City, Berlin, Stockholm, London. Commissions, Contemporary Dance Theatre, London, Nordiske Forum 88, Danmarks Radio. *Compositions include:* Klumpe, 1972; Stykke 2, 1973; 12 toner i Zoo, 1973; Smedierne i Granada, 1976; Strygekvartet i CD, 1977; Konkurrence, 1979; Haiku-Sange, 1979; Solen og jeg, 1981;

Gentagne Gange, 1980; Solen på Møddingen, 1982; Phasing Moon Facing Changing, 1983; Antigone, 1983; Kære Allesammen, 1984; På Afstand af Bølgen, 1984-85; Om Natten, 1985; Skiftetid, 1985; Kindleins Schlaflied, 1986; Frokost i det Grønne, 1985; Nostalgisk Extranummer, 1985; Extra Nostalgisk nr 2, 1986; Espressione Emotionale, 1987; Fatsy, 1987; Drømmespil, 1988; Opbrud, 1988; Vakst, 1989; Lyst, 1990; 2 sange til Døden, 1990; Episoder til Thomas, 1991; Havet ved Forår, 1991; Karcus Å, 1992; Unoder, 1992; Natterdag, 1992; Berceuse Neptunoise, 1993. *Recordings:* Antigone; Frokost i det Grønne. *Honours:* Komponistforemingens Jubilaeumslegat, 1985; Gustav Enna's Mindelegat, 1988; Several grants, Art Foundation of Danish State, including 3 years, 1980-83. *Memberships:* Dansk Komponistforening; Kvinder i Musik; Det Unge Tonekunstnerselskab. *Hobbies:* Tea drinking; Talking; Meditation. *Address:* Dansk Komponistforening, Gråbrødretorv 16, DK-1154 København K, Denmark.

ALTENBURGER Christian, b. 5 Sept 1957, Heidelberg, Germany. Violinist. *Education:* Graduated, Vienna Academy of Music, 1973; Graduated, Juilliard School, New York, 1978; Studied violin with father and Dorothy DeLay. *Debut:* First appearance in 1964, formal debut, Recital, Musikverein, Vienna, 1976. *Career:* Soloist with various major orchestras in Europe and the USA; With Bruno Canino played the Sonata by Strauss, Schoenberg's Fantasy and Bartók's 2nd Sonata, Salzburg Festival, 1990. *Recordings:* For Arabesque; ProArte.

ALTMEYER Jeannine, b. 2 May 1948, La Habra, California, USA. Soprano. *Education:* Studied with Martial Singher and Lotte Lehmann in Santa Barbara, California; attended the Salzburg Mozarteum. *Career:* Operatic debut as the Heavenly Voice in Don Carlos, Metropolitan Opera, N.Y., 25 Sept. 1971; appeared with the Chicago Lyric Opera, 1972, in Salzburg, 1973 and at Bayreuth, 1979; member of the Wurttemberg State Theatre, Stuttgart, 1975-79; then sang throughout Europe, achieving success as a Wagnerian; roles: Elsa, Eva, Sieglinde, Isolde, Elisabeth, Gutrune and Brünnhilde; Sang Isolde at Bayreuth, 1986; Paris Opéra, Los Angeles, 1987, Chrysothemis, Isolde; Brünnhilde in Götterdämmerung at the Zurich Opera, 1989; Sang Leonore, La Scala, 1990. *Recordings:* Sang in the Ring cycles on Philips and Eurodisc; Video of Die Walküre, in production from Bayreuth. *Address:* c/o Theateragentur Dr. Germinal Hilbert, Maximilianstrasse 22, D-8000 Munich 22, Germany.

ALTMEYER Theodor Daniel, b. 16 March 1931, Eschweiler, Aachen, Germany. Singer (Tenor). *Education:* Studied in Cologne with Clemens Glettenberg, 1953-56. *Career:* Sang at the Städtische Oper Berlin 1956-60, notably in the 1958 premiere of Diary of a Madman by Searle; Sang at Hanover from 1960, in operas by Rossini, Lortzing and Mozart, and as Pfitzner's Palestrina; Sang in Stuttgart from 1958, Vienna from 1969; Many concert appearances, often as the Evangelist in the Passions of Bach; Guest engagements in France, Austria, Italy, Belgium, England, Switzerland and Holland; Festivals of Venice, Lucerne, Montreux, Ansbach, Vienna, Florence and Naples; Professor at the Hannover Musikhochschule from 1974. *Recordings:* St Matthew and St John Passions of Bach, Dettinger Te Deum by Handel, Beethoven and Haydn Masses, Bach Cantatas (Electrola); Evangelist in the St Luke Passion by Telemann and the St John Passion by Schütz (Cantate); Schütz St Matthew Passion (Barenreiter). *Address:* Hochschule für Musik und Theater Hannover, Emmichplatz 1, 3 Hannover, Germany.

ALTWEGG Raffaele, b. 17 Nov 1938, Tettenhall, Anglo-Swiss Musician. m. Barbara von Schulthess, 17 Aug 1968, 1 son, 1 daughter. *Education:* MB, St Thomas's Hospital, University of London, 1961; Master Classes with Pablo Casals and Paul Grummer. *Career:* Soloist 1957-; Leader, Cello Section, Tonhalle Orchestra, Zurich, Tonhalle Quartet, 1958-60; Founder Member, Ensemble Die Kammermusiker Zurich, 1960-; Professor, Zurich Academy of Music, 1960-75; Conductor, Master Classes for Cello, 1963-; Called upon by Australian Government to help build up the new National Music School in Canberra, 1968-70; Professor, Basle Academy of Music, 1970-75; State Expert for all Music Diplomas, 1976-; Director, Music School, Zollikon, 1979-; Founder, Conductor, Zollikon Orchestra, 1985-. *Recordings:* A number of recordings. *Honours:* Recipient of many honours and awards. *Memberships:* Schweizerischer Tonkuenstlerverein; Schweizerischer Musikpaedagogischer Verband. *Hobbies:* Reading; Gardening. *Address:* Schlossbergstr 27, CH-8702, Zollikon, Zurich, Switzerland.

ALVA Luigi, b. 10 April 1927, Lima, Peru. Tenor. *Education:* Studied with Roda Morales in Lima and with Emilio Ghiradini and Ettore Campogalliani in Milan. *Debut:* Sang at Lima in the Zarzuela Luisa Fernanada 1949; Beppe in Pagliacci 1950. *Career:* Sang Paolino in Cimarosa's Il matrimonio segreto at La Scala, 1955; Salzburg Festival, 1957-58 as Fenton in Falstaff and Ferrando in Cosi fan Tutte; Sang Rossini's Almaviva more than 300 times, starting with La Scala, 1956; Returned to Milan in 1958 for the local premiere of Janáček's The Cunning Little Vixen and world premieres of Una domanda di matrimonio by Luciano Chailly and Malipiero's La donna e mobile; appeared in the Holland Festival in 1959 in Il mondo della luna by Haydn, and made his Covent Garden debut in 1960; Glyndebourne Festival, 1961-62, as Nemorino in L'elisir d'amore; Aix-en-Provence from 1960, Vienna Staatsoper from 1961; Metropolitan Opera 1964-76 as Ernesto in Don Pasquale, Almaviva, Lindoro in L'Italiana in Algeri and Mozart's Tamino; Other appearances in Hamburg, Berlin, Moscow, Edinburgh, Stockholm, Lisbon, Venice, Florence and Mexico City; Artistic Director of the Fundacion Pro Arte Lirica (FUPAL) in Lima from 1982; Retired as singer 1989. *Recordings include:* Il Barbiere di Siviglia, Il matrimonio segreto and Falstaff (Columbia); La Cenerentola (Deutsche Grammophon); Handel's Alcina, L'Italiana in Algeri and Mozart's Il re pastore (Decca); Haydn's L'Isola disabitata (Philips); Alfonso und Estrella by Schubert (Melodram). *Address:* c/o Allied Artists Agency, 42 Monteplier Square, London SW7 1JX, England.

ALVARES Eduardo, b. 10 June 1947, Rio de Janeiro, Brazil. Singer, (Tenor). *Career:* Started career in Europe, (debut as Don José) Linz, Frankfurt, Vienna and Stuttgart, returned to Brazil and then sang Des Grieux (Manon Lescaut) at Metropolitan, and Netherlands Opera (also Dick Johnson in Fanciulla del West), Manrico in Il Trovatore for Opera North and Calaf in Turandot for Scottish Opera; English National Opera as Radames in Aida, 1985; Teatro Municipal Rio de Janeiro, 1987-88, as Don José and Bacchus; Other roles include Alfredo, Gabriele Adorno, Don Carlos, Faust, Werther and Alva in Lulu; Wexford Festival 1983-84, in Hans Heiling and The Kiss. *Address:* c/o English National Opera, London Coliseum, St Martin's Lane, London WC2, England.

ALVARY Lorenzo, b. 20 Feb 1909, Debrecen, Hungary. (Naturalized US citizen, 1944). Singer (Bass). m. Hallie Carr Fox, 1959. *Education:* Studied law, University of Geneva, BL, 1930, University of Budapest, LLM, 1932; voice in Milan, Berlin. *Career:* Operatic debut, Royal Opera, Budapest, 1934; emigrated to the US, 1938; sang at the San Francisco Opera, 1940, debut in Der Rosenkavalier; regular appearances there until 1979; Metropolitan Opera debut in NY as Zuniga in Carmen; sang 651 performances in 29 seasons, notably in Carmen, La Bohème, Le Nozze di Figaro and Der Rosenkavalier; roles included Benoit, Alcindoro and Antonio; also sang in various US, European and South American cities; host of own radio programme, Opera Topics, WKCR, 1964-86; general manager, Opera Guild of Greater Miami, 1972-73; judge at various international vocal competitions. *Recordings:* For RCA-Victor and Metropolitan Opera private recordings. 2. *Address:* c/o Metropolitan Opera House, Lincoln Center, New York, NY 10023, USA.

ALWYN Kenneth, b. 28 July 1928, Croydon, England. Conductor. m. Mary Law, 2 daughters. *Education:* Graduate, Royal Schools of Music, London, 1951; Associate, Royal Academy of Music, London, 1958. *Debut:* London. *Career:* Conductor: Royal Choral Union, New Zealand; Sadler's Wells Theatre Ballet; Royal Ballet, Royal Opera House, Covent Garden; BBC Staff Conductor; Radio and TV Presenter. *Compositions:* Various TV Signature Tunes and Songs. *Recordings:* Major Recordings with Leading Orchestras; Conductor of 1st Stereophonic Recordings by Decca with London Symphony Orchestra, 1958, Tchaikovsky's 1812 Overture; Complete recording, Hiawatha, with Welsh National Opera for Decca, 1991. *Honour:* Mann's Prize for Conducting, 1951. *Membership:* Incorporated Society of Musicians; Member, BBC's Central Music Advisory Committee. *Hobby:* Flying. *Address:* Horelands, Broadford Bridge, Billingshurst, Sussex RH14 9EA, England.

AM Magnar, b. 9 April, 1952, Trondheim, Norway. Composer. *Education:* Studied Organ and Composition, Bergen Conservatory, 1971; Advanced training in composition, Lidholm, Stockholm, 1971-72. *Compositions:* Prayer for Soprano, Chorus and String Orchestra, 1972; Dawn is Breaking for Chorus and Orchestra, 1972; Song for Brass and Percussion, 1974; Intermezzo for 3 Woodwinds, 1976; Dance for Harp, Guitar and Harpsichord, 1977; Octet, 1977; Point Zero for Soprano, Alto, Chorus, Children's Chorus and Amateur Orchestra, 1979; 2 alternative versions; Agamemnon, choral drama, 1981; Veinje for mixed chorus, Womens Chorus, Men's Chorus, 3 Clarinets, Bass Clarinet and Cello, 1981; Ajar, double-bass concerto, 1981; A Cage-Bird's Dream, Multimedia Piece, 1981; Inconceivable Father for Child Soprano, Children's Chorus, Bass Clarinet, Timpani, Double Bass and Organ, 1982; My Planet, My Soul, symphony, 1982; Piano Pieces; Among Later Works: Like a leaf on the river, for Guitar, 1983; Omen, for violin, horn and piano, 1983; Conqilia, for violin, horn, piano and recitor, 1984; right through all this for orchestra, 1985; Freetonal conversations, for violin, cello and piano, 1986; hovering depths for double bass, 1986; a miracle and a tear, for mixed chorus, 1987; if we lift as one, for orchestra 1988; Tonebath, experience room, 1989; and let the boat slip quietly out, for orchestra, 1989, ... and life, an oratorio, 1990. *Address:* Hagen 18, 6100 Volda, Norway.

AM BACH Rudolf, b. 6 June, 1919, Trogen, Switzerland. Pianist; Professor. m. 2 children. *Education:* Studied, Music Conservatory, 3 years; Private student of Professor Emil Frey, Zurich; Teachers Diploma (piano) 1938; Soloist's Diploma, summa cum laude, 1939; Studies with Professor Frédéric Lamond (student of Franz Liszt), London 1940. *Career:* Teacher of Piano, Collegium, Winterthur, 1939; Piano Recitals, Zurich, 1941-43, 1945, 1948-73; Concert Tours and Recitals, Great Britain, 1951, 1956, 1958, France, Germany, Austria, Spain, Canada (1967); Radio Recitals including Radio London, 1958 (Swiss Compositions); Radio Zurich; Works performed include 3 Siècles de Pianoforte, 47, Concertos and various works by F Busoni, R Strauss, Scriabin, Ravel, Prokofiev. *Recordings include:* Anthologie Schweizer Musik, CTS No 6: Gustav Weber; Idyll on Faust op. 9 pieces for piano, CTS N42: Frank Martin, Petite Symphonie Concertante; Felix Mendelssohn, Songs without works and works by Franz Liszt Années de Pélerinage, Switzerland; Bach, Mozart, Mendelssohn, fantasy op.28, de Falla, 4 prezas espagnolas, Ottorino Respighi piano works. *Hobby:* Playing Chamber Music in Trio. *Address:* Casa Sappho, Via Cantonale, 6967 Dino (TI), Switzerland.

AMADUCCI Bruno, b. 5 Jan 1935 Viganello-Lugano, Switzerland. Conductor. *Education:* Conservatorio Giuseppe Verdi, Milan, Italy; École normale de Musique, Paris, France. *Career:* 1st concert, Mozart Requiem, Swiss Radio Monteceneri, 1951; 1st public concert with Alfred Cortot and Orchestra, Pomeriggi Musicali, Milan, 1951; former Conductor, Metropolitan opera, Vienna State Opera, Vienna Symphony Orchestra, Paris Opera,

Deutsche Oper, Berlin; Member of Jury, Concorso Voci Verdiane, Busseto, Italy and Concours Internationale, Geneva. *Publications:* L'Amfiparnaso de Orazio Vecchi par rapport au développement de l'expression du langage musicale, 1951; La Musica nella Svizzera italiana e la presenzadella Radio-orchestra, 1973; The Puccini Dynasty, 1973. *Address:* Casella postale, Lugano, CH-6901, Switzerland.

AMARA Lucine, b. 1 Mar. 1927, Hartford, Connecticut, USA. Soprano. *Education:* Studied voice with Stella Eisner-Eyn in San Francisco; attended the Music Academy of the West, Santa Barbara, 1947, and the University of Southern California, Los Angeles, 1949-50. *Career:* Member of the San Francisco Opera chorus, 1945-46; concert debut, San Francisco, 1946; sang at the Hollywood Bowl, 1948; Metropolitan Opera debut 1950; regular appearances there in subsequent seasons; also sang at the Glyndebourne Festival 1954-58, as Strauss's Ariadne and Mozart's Donna Elvira; Edinburgh Festival 1954, Vienna State Opera 1960, Russia 1965 and China 1983; major roles: Gluck's Euridice, Mozart's Donna Anna, Verdi's Aida and Leonora (Il Trovatore), Puccini's Mimi and Leoncavallo's Nedda; Sang Mère Marie in Dialogues des Carmélites at the Met, 1987. *Recordings:* Both in operatic and orchestral works. *Memberships:* Sigma Alpha Iota. *Address:* c/o Metropolitan Opera, Lincoln Center for the Performing Arts, New York, NY 10023, USA.

AMBACHE Diana Bella, b. 18 June 1948, Kent, England. Pianist. m. Jeremy Polmear, 12 Feb 1982. *Education:* Bedales School; Royal Academy of Music, 1966-67; Diploma, LRAM Performers, 1967, BA (Honours), 1970, Sheffield University, 1967-70. *Debut:* Purcell Room, 24 Apr 1979. *Career:* Founder and Musical Director, Mozart Chamber Orchestra, 1977-83; Founder and Musical Director, Ambache Chamber Orchestra, 1984-; Concert Tours in India and Nepal, 1977; Malawi, Zambia, Botswana, 1978; Yugoslavia, 1979; China, 1981; Spain, 1982; South East Asia, 1983; Spain and S.E. Asia, 1984; Malaysia, Hong Kong and China, 1985; Thailand, Burma and Nepal, 1987; Italy, Turkey and Malawi, 1988; Oman and Sri Lanka, 1989, Korea and Hong Kong, 1990. First performances, Complete Version In Modern Times of Mozart Rondo in D K386, 1980; Dussek Piano Concerto in G Min op 49, 1981; Fantasy for Piano by Francis Shaw, (Commissioned with funds from Arts Council of Great Britain), 1982, Wigmore Hall, London. UK Premiere of Piano Concerto (1924) by Germaine Tailleferre, 1986, Queen Elizabeth Hall; Kozeluch Piano Concerto in D, 1986, London; Benda Concerto in F; Emilie Candeille Concerto in D; First modern London Performance, Michael Haydn, Concerto for viola and piano. *Recordings:* On Meridian Label, Morceaux De Salon-19th Century Virtuoso oboe/piano collection, 1984; Mozart piano Concertos K449 and K456 with Ambache Chamber Ensemble, 1985; Mozart Quartet in G Minor K478 and Quintet in E Flat K452, with Ambache Chamber Ensemble, 1986; Mozart Quartet K493, Trio K542, Sonata K302; The Other Donizetti, Oboe/Piano Collection; On Pickwick Label: Mozart Piano Concertos K271 and K246, Concert Rondo K386, with Ambache Chamber Orchestra; Mozart piano concertos K467 and K503 on Virgin Classics, 1991; Mozart piano concertos K453 and K459 on Teledisc's Academy Collection; Sweet Melancholy: 20th Century oboe/piano English Collection on Unicorn. *Honours:* Gold Medal, Associated Board, 1966; Scholarship to Royal Academy of Music, 1967; Exhibition from Sheffield University, 1970. *Hobbies:* Travel; Cycling; Walking. *Address:* 9 Beversbrook Road, London N19 4QG, England.

AMBUHL Jane Dutton, b. 31 Dec 1925, Frankfort, Kentucky, USA. Private Music Teacher. m. John C Ambuhl, 16 Feb 1946, dec., 3 sons, 1 daughter. *Education:* BA, Stetson University, DeLand, Florida; MEd, University of Houston, Texas; Graduate study, University of Kentucky, Lexington; Private music study through high school; Piano and Organ study, Bob Jones and Stetson Universities; Private Organ study with Dr Paul Deluney, Ft Myers, Florida; Classical Music

Seminar, Esenstat, Austria. *Career:* Adjudicator for American College of Musicians and other piano and organ contests and auditions; Organist, various churches in Florida, Tennessee and Texas; Private Music Teacher in own studio, Texas, 1958-. *Honours:* Organ and Band Scholarships, Stetson University, 1943-45. *Memberships:* National Guild of Piano Teachers; Keyboard Teachers Association International; Music Teachers National Association; Brazosport Music Teachers Association; Texas Music Teachers Association. *Hobbies:* Gardening; Travel. *Address:* 506 Sycamore, Lake Jackson, TX 77566, USA.

AMECHER Maryanne, b. 25 Feb 1942, Kates, Pennsylvania, USA. Composer; Performer; Mixed-Media Artist. *Education:* Studied composition with George Rochberg at the University of Pennsylvania, BFA 1964; Studies with Karlheinz Stockhausen and at the Universities of Pennsylvania and Illinois (computer science). *Career:* Taught in the experimental music studio at the School of Engineering, University of Illinois, 1964-66; Creative Associate at the Center of Creative and Performing Arts, State University, New York, 1966-67; Fellow at the Massachusetts Institute of Technology, 1972-76; Fellow at Radcliffe College, Harvard, 1978-79; Sound experiments with John Cage and Merce Cunningham; Has initiated various projects with natural sound experiments in the local environment. *Compositions include:* City- Links, performed in New York, Buffalo, Paris and Chicago, 1967-79; Lecture on the Weather, collaboration with Cage, 1975; Remainder, dance music for Merce Cunningham, for tape and electronics, 1976; Mixed media works include Sound-joined Rooms, 1980-82; Close Up; Intelligent Life, 1982; Music for the Webern car. *Honours include:* Multi-media award from New York State Council of Arts, 1978-79; Composition award from the National Endowment of the Arts, 1978-79; Beard Arts Fund, 1980. *Address:* ASCAP, ASCAP Building, One Lincoln Plaza, NY 10023, New York, USA.

AMELING Elly, b. 8 Feb 1938, Rotterdam, Netherlands. Soprano. m. Arnold W Beider, 6 Nov 1964. *Education:* Conservatory of Music, The Hague, 1954-58. *Debut:* Victoria Hall, Geneva, Switzerland. *Career:* Numerous solo recitals also with orchestras throughout the world; Sang Ilia in Idomeneo at the Washington Opera, 1974; Numerous Wigmore Hall Recitals. *Recordings:* Recording artist for Philips, CBS, Decca London, EMI, Angel, RCA, Odeon, Harmonia Mundi, Peters International and Vanguard records, including songs by Duparc and Satie, Debussy's La Demoiselle élue and Ravel's Schéhérazade, Philips; Mozart Requiem, Erato. *Honours:* Order Oranje Nassau, Netherlands, Prize, Deuthschen Schallplattenkritic; Grand Prix du Disque. *Current Management:* Dr G DeKoos & Co Concert Management (London) Ltd, London, England.

AMES Richard, b. 20 Aug 1931, Cleveland, Ohio, USA. Singer (Tenor). *Education:* Studied with Mario Basiola in Milan; Studied with Max Lorenz, 1966-68. *Career:* Sang first as baritone, debut in New Orleans, 1958, as Masetto; Further appearances, Philadelphia and Boston, then sang Don Giovanni in Munster, 1961; Wuppertal, 1962-65, as Iago, Amfortas, and Nick Shadow in The Rake's Progress; Debut as tenor as Siegmund in Die Walkure, Oldenburg, 1967; With Graz Opera, 1968-, notably as Palestrina, Florestan, Otello and Lohengrin; Appeared in premiere of Schwertsik's Der Lange Weg zur grossen Mauer, Lucerne, 1975; Sang as Herod in Salome, in Rome, Monte Carlo and Brussels; Further engagements in Leipzig, Budapest, Zagreb, Dortmund, Mannheim and Basle as Mime, the Captain in Wozeck and Aegisthus in Elektra; Herod at Augsburg, 1988. *Address:* c/o Deutsches Tourneetheater, Dambor strasse 11, 8900 Augsburg, Germany.

AMIRKHANIAN Charles (Benjamin), b. 19 Jan. 1945, Fresno, California, USA. Composer. *Education:* BA, English literature, California State University, Fresno, 1967; MA, interdisciplinary creative arts, San Francisco State University, 1969; MFA, Mills College, Oakland, California, 1980; Studied electronic music and sound recording techniques with David Behrman, Robert Ashley and Paul de Marinis. *Career:* Composer-in-residence, Ann Halprin's Dancers Workshop Company, 1968-69; Music Director, KPFA radio, Berkeley, California, 1969-; Lecturer, San Francisco State University, 1977-80. *Compositions:* Live-Performance: Canticle No 1 for Percussion Quartet, 1963; Canticle No 2 for Flute and Timpani, 1963; Canticle No 3 for Percussion Trio, 1966; Canticle No 4 for Percussion Quartet, 1966; Ode to Gravity, theatre piece, 1967; Spoilt Music, theatre piece, 1979; Text-Sound (Tape): Oratora Konkurso Rezulto: Autoro de la Jara (Portrait of Lou Harrison), 1970; Each'll, 1971; If In Is, 1971; Sound Nutrition, 1972; Heavy Aspirations (Portrait of Nicolas Slonimsky), 1973; Seatbelt Seatbelt, 1973; She She and She, 1974; Mahogany Ballpark, 1976; Dutiful Ducks, 1977; Audience, 1978; Dreams Freud Dreamed, 1979; Hypothetical Moments (in the Intellectual Life of Southern California), 1981; Dog of Stravinsky, 1982; The Real Perpetuum Mobile, 1984. *Address:* c/o ASCAP, One Lincoln Plaza, NY 10023, USA.

AMOYAL Pierre, b. 22 June 1949, Paris, France. Violinist. *Education:* Studied at the Paris Conservatoire and with Jascha Heifetz between 1966 and 1971. *Debut:* Paris 1971, in the Berg Concerto, with the Orchestre de Paris. *Career:* Appearances with the BBC Symphony Orchestra, Hallé Orchestra, London Philharmonic, Philharmonia, Berlin Philharmonic, Boston Symphony, Cleveland Orchestra, Philadelphia Orchestra and orchestras in Canada and France; Conductors include Karajan, Ozawa, Boulez, Dutoit, Sanderling, Maazel, Solti, Prêtre, Masur and Rozhdestvensky; Plays Concertos by Berg, Schoenberg and Dutilleux, in addition to the standard repertory; Played Brahms, Seiber and Beethoven at the Wigmore Hall, 1990; Recital, Bath Festival with Pascal Rogé, playing Fauré, Schubert and Brahms, 1990; Recitals at St John's Smith Square for the BBC; New York Carnegie Hall debut 1985; Professor at the Paris Conservatoire from 1977; Currently Professor at the Lausanne Conservatoire. *Recordings:* Chamber music with Heifetz and Piatigorsky; Concertos by Sibelius and Tchaikovsky; Schoenberg Concerto with the London Symphony Orchestra conducted by Boulez. *Honours include:* Ginette Neveu Prize 1963; Paganini Prize 1964; Enescu Prize 1970. *Address:* c/o Intermusica Artists' Management, 16 Duncan Terrace, London N1 8BZ, England.

AMRAM David, b. 17 Nov 1930, Philadelphia, Pennsylvania, USA. Composer; Conductor; Multi-Instrumentalist. m. Lora Lee, 7 Jan. 1979, 1 son, 2 daughters. *Education:* BA, George Washington University. *Career includes:* Pioneer of the French horn in jazz and Latin music during the late 1940's; World tours as a jazz player, multi-instrumentalist, folklorist, composer and conductor; Director of Music, New York Shakespeare Festival, 1956-67; Director of Music, Lincoln Center Theater, 1963-65; Director, Young Peoples Concerts and Parks Concerts, Brooklyn Philharmonic, 1971-; Guest Conducts annually with 14 orchestras including Montreal, Toronto, Grant Park, and Milwaukee Orchestras. *Compositions:* Over 100 orchestral, choral, operatic and chamber works including American Dance Suite (all published by C F Peters); Composing a commissioned work to celebrate the opening of the Jefferson Wing of the Library of Congress, 1995. *Recordings:* Over 40 recordings of his own compositions; 15 albums as soloist, and as feature performer with Lionel Hampton, Charlie Mingus, Oscar Pettiford, Mary Lou Williams, Kenny Durham. *Publication:* Vibrations: The Musical Times of David Amram, 1968. Symphonic Works performed by New York Philharmonic; Boston Symphony, Philadelphia Orchestras, one of US 20 most performed composers of concert music, since 1974. *Membership:* BMI. *Hobbies:* Farming; Raising his family. *Current Management:* Barnd Ostentag, New York, USA. *Address:* c/o Ostentag, 501 5th Avenue, New York City, NY 10017, USA.

AMY Gilbert, b. 29 Aug 1936, Paris, France. Conductor; Music Educator; Composer. *Education:* Studied piano with Loriod and composition with Milhaud and Messiaen at the Paris Conservatory; attended Boulez's courses in new music at Darmstadt. *Career:* Commenced conducting, 1962; director, Domaine Musical, Paris, 1967-73; founder- conductor, Nouvel Orchestre Philharmonique de Radio France, Paris, I976-81; taught analysis and composition, Yale University, 1982; director, Lyons Conservatory, 1984-. *Compositions:* Orchestral: Mouvements, 1958; Diaphonies, 1962; Antiphonies for 2 orchestras, 1964; Triade, 1965; Chant, 1968-69, revised 1980; Refrains, 1972; Orchestrale, 1985; Chamber: Piano Sonata, 1957-60; Epigrammes for piano, 1961; Inventions for ensemble, 1959-61; Alpha-Beth for wind sextet, 1963-64; Cycle for percussion sextet; 7 Bagatelles for organ, 1975; Quasi scherzando for cello, 1981; Vocal: Cantata breve for soprano and 3 instruments, 1957; D'un Espace deploye for soprano, 2 pianos and 2 orchestral groups, 1973; Strophe for soprano and orchestra, 1965-77; Une saison en enfer for soprano, piano, percussion and tape; Messe for soloists, chorus and orchestra, 1982-3; Ecrits sur toiles for reciter and small ensemble, 1983. *Address:* c/o Conservatoire National superieur de Musique de Lyon, 3 rue de l'Angile, 69005 Lyon, France.

ANDERS Gerald, b. 3 Sept 1943, Jacksonville, Florida, USA. Musician; Teacher; Administrator. *Education:* BA (Hons), Music (Piano, Theory), Carson-Newman College, Jefferson City, Tennessee; MA, Music (History, Piano), Ohio State University, Columbus; Studied piano with Louis Ball and Richard Tetley-Kardos. *Career:* Assistant to Director of Publications, The Cleveland Orchestra, 1968-71; Chairman, Music Department, Columbia Preparatory School, 1972-82; Chairman, Music Department, St Ann's School, 1983-90; Music Director, Organist, Hopewell Reformed Church, Hopewell Junction, New York, 1990-; Chairman of Fine and Performing Arts, Dwight-Englewood School, Englewood, New Jersey, 1992-; Various chamber performances and chamber orchestra conducting. *Publications:* Music: A College Appreciation Text, 1975; Miscellaneous programme notes for The Cleveland Orchestra; Columbia record liner notes: Boulez Conducts Ravel; Szell-Haydn Symphonies 97 and 98; Serkin-Szell-Brahms' Piano Concertos 1 and 2. *Honours:* Pi Kappa Lambda. *Memberships:* Phi Mu Alpha Sinfonia; Sonneck Society for American Music. *Hobbies:* Gardening; Travel; Renovating houses; Cooking. *Address:* 75-34 Bell Boulevard 2G, Bayside, NY 11364, USA.

ANDERSEN Bo, b. 10 Nov 1963, Denmark. Composer; Organist; Musicologist. *Education:* Department of Musicology, University of Copenhagen, 1984-; Composition with Ib Noerholm, Royal Danish Academy of Music, 1988-; Studied organ privately; Exam as Organist, Royal Academy, Copenhgen, 1990. *Career:* Still studying; Numerous concert performances of almost entire output of works as composer, including Tre Pezzi Brevi, 1st performance in Helsinki, 1990; Active as organist and concert arranger, several churches in Copenhagen. *Compositions:* Tre Pezzi Brevi, string quartet, 1989; Cello Sonata, 1990; Violin Sonata, 1990-91; Serenade for three woodwinds, 1991; All My Energy, movement for large chamber orchestra, 1993. *Honours:* Several Danish Composer Association grants; The Astrid nd Aksel Agerby Memorial Grant, 1993. *Memberships:* Danish Composers Association; Young Danish Society of Contemporary Music. *Hobbies:* Modern art exhibitions; Reading poetry; Motorcycles. *Address:* c/o S E Mielche, Frederiksberg Allé 78 1B, DK-1820 Frederiksberg C, Denmark.

ANDERSEN Karsten, b. 16 Feb. 1920, Kristiania (now Oslo), Norway. Conductor; Violinist. *Education:* Studied in Norway and Italy. *Career:* Violinist and Conductor; Music Director, Stavanger Symphony Orchestra, 1945-65; Bergen Symphony Orchestra, 1965-85; Iceland Symphony Orchestra, 1973-80; Guest Conductor of orchestras in Europe and the USA. *Recordings:* For Composers Recordings Inc; Norskkulturrads Klassikerserie; Philipps, including Svendsen's Concertos for violin and cello and Egge's Symphony No 1.

ANDERSON Alexander Cunninghame, b. 18 Mar 1939, Motherwell, Scotland. Organist; Conductor. m. Jennifer Sharon Cosby, 17 Sept 1979, 1 son, 1 daughter. *Education:* Associate, Royal College of Music, 1958; B Mus Honours, University of Glasgow, 1961; Teacher's Certificate, Jordanhill College, 1962; Fellow, Royal College of Organists; Academia Santa Cecilia, Rome, Italy, 1962-63; Academia Chigiana, Siena, 1962-63. *Career:* Assistant Organist, St Giles Cathedral, Edinburgh, Scotland, 1963-66; Staff, Royal Scottish Academy of Music, 1963-69; International Organ Recitalist; Solo recitals, radio and television broadcasts, BBC; Currently Director of Chapel Music, Rollins College, Winter Park, Florida, USA; Currently Conductor, Orlando Chamber Players; Currently Conductor, Central Florida Choral Society. *Recordings:* Solo recording on organ of All Saints Church, Pasadena, California, Crystal; D'Art 12-4, accompanist with choir of St Giles Cathedral, Edinburgh; Recordings with Choir of Paisley Abbey, Crystal and Decca; Rollins Christmas Vespers, non-commercial, 1981. *Honours:* Sir James Caird Scholarship, 1962-63; Italian Government Scholarship, 1962-63; 2nd prize, St Albans International Organ Competition, 1964; Woodrow Wilson Fellowship, 1969; Arthur Vining Davis Fellowship, 1982. *Memberships:* American Guild of Organists; Royal College of Organists; American Association of University Professors; American Choral Directors Association; Pi Kappa Lambda. *Hobbies:* Golf; World affairs; Travel. *Address:* Rollins College, Winter Park, FL 32789, USA.

ANDERSON David Edward, b. 2 Mar 1958, Chicago, Illinois, USA. *Education:* BS summa cum laude, honours in Music, William Jewell College, 1980; MM, Piano Performance and Music History; University of Bayreuth, summer 1983; Currently PhD candidate, Musicology, University of Chicago. *Career:* Editor, University of Chicago Press journals. *Publications:* The Richard Strauss Companion, forthcoming, 1994. *Contributions:* Fritz Busch and Richard Strauss, in The Music Review, 1988; The Original Ending of Die Agyptische Helena; Entries on Henze, Blitzstein, Ebert and 11 more, in The International Dictionary of Opera, 1993; Reviews in Opera Quarterly and Notes; Pfitzner and Our Time, in Notes, 1993. *Membership:* American Musicological Society. *Hobbies:* Cooking; Cinema; European literature. *Address:* 1208 W Montrose No 1, Chicago, IL 60613, USA.

ANDERSON David Maxwell, b. 1964, Scotland. Singer (Tenor). *Education:* Studied at the Glasgow Academy and Queen's College, Cambridge; Royal College of Music from 1986, National Opera Studio 1989. *Debut:* Rinuccio in Gianni Schicchi for Opera North, 1990. *Career:* Has sung Rinuccio for English National Opera; Rodolfo in La bohème for Scottish Opera and Glyndebourne Touring Opera, Pinkerton in Madama Butterly for Opera North, the Duke of Mantua in Rigoletto for Opera North and the Teatro di Pisa, Alfredo in La Traviata for the Teatro di Pisa and Opera North; Other roles include Steva in Jenůfa (English National Opera) and Oronte in I Lombardi (Opera North); Concert engagements include the Verdi Requiem (David Willcocks), Vaughan Williams Serenade to Music (Vernon Handley), Bruckner Te Deum (Alexander Gibson and John Eliot Gardiner), and the Rossini Stabat Mater (Raphael Frühbeck de Burgos). *Address:* 26 Aberdare Gardens, London NW6 3QA, England.

ANDERSON June, b. 30 Dec 1952, Boston, USA. Soprano. *Education:*Won Rockefeller Foundation scholarship to the Metropolitan Opera, New York in 1970. *Career:* New York City Opera 1978-84; Appearances in Italy: Palermo, Florence, La Scala; Milan, Venice, Rome, Bologna, Debut Vienna State Opera, 1987; Naples, 1988. Other European appearances: Hamburg, Geneva, Bordeaux, Paris, Madrid, Nice, Prague Festival, Pesaro, Aix-en-Provence Festival, 1988; Metropolitan Opera, 1989; (debut as

Gilda); Royal Opera House, London (debut 1986); as Semiramide in a concert performance of Rossini's opera; Other roles include Gilda and Giulietta in Bellini's I Capuleti at La Scala; Lucia di Lammermoor and Isabella in Robert le Diable, Paris Opera; Rossini's Armida at Pesaro, and Desdemona at San Francisco; Sang in concert at opening of the Bastille Opera Paris, 1989; Luciano Pavarotti 30th Anniversary Gala at Reggio Emilia, 1991; TV apperances in Beethoven's Ninth Symphony, Berlin, Bernstein, and title role in Luisa Miller, Lyons Opera; Bellini's Elvira in a new production of I Puritani at Covent Garden, May 1992; sang Zoraide in Rossini's Ricciardo e Zoraide at Pesaro, 1990. *Recordings include:* Mosè in Egitto, La Jolie Fille de Perth, Le Postillon de Longjumeau, La Fille du Régiment, Maometto II, La Muette de Portici. *Current Management:* Patricia Greenan Artists Management, 19B Belsize Park, London, NW3. *Address:* c/o Royal Opera House, Covent Garden, London WC2, England.

ANDERSON Laurie, b. 5 June 1947, Chicago, Illinois, USA. Performance Artist; Composer. *Education:* Studied violin; BA, art history, Barnard College, 1969; MFA, Sculpture, Columbia University, 1972; Studied painting with Sol LeWitt. *Career:* Taught Art History, City College of the City University, New York, 1973-75; Performance artist; Composer; Regular tours of the USA and Europe; Created several instruments for own use. *Compositions:* From songs to epic performance-art work, United States, 1983. *Honour:* Guggenheim Fellowship, 1983. *Address:* c/o Liz Rosenberg, Warner Brothers Records, 3 East 54th Street, New York, NY 10022, USA.

ANDERSON Leonard Mark, b. 8 Oct 1963, Eureka, California, USA. Pianist. *Education:* BMus, Honours, San Jose State University, 1987; LRAM, London, 1988; PPRNCM w/distinction, Royal Northern College of Music, Manchester, 1989. *Debut:* New York, 1988; San Francisco, 1988; Toronto, 1993; Tokyo, 1992; London, 1994. *Career:* Performances throughout North America, Japan, Europe and the UK; Appearances with Tokyo Metropolitan Orchestra, City of Birmingham Symphony Orchestra, RTE Symphony Orchestra (Ireland), BBC Welsch Symphony Orchestra, Bournemouth Sinfionetta, Hadyn Chamber Orchestra (Italy), various North American orchestras including l'Orchestra Metropolitain (Quebec), Windsor Symphony (Ontario), Oakland Symphony, San Jose Symphony, California Chamber Orchestra. TV and radio appearances on BBC Radio 3, BBC2 TV, RTE TV, and radio/TV in Italy, Japan, and throughout the US. *Honours:* Winner: Leeds Pianoforte Competition, 1993. *Recordings:* Various solo piano works of Liszt, Brahms and Schumann and the Brahms First Piano Concerto w/the Hungarian State Symphony Orchestra, Adam Fischer cond - Nimbus Records UK. *Address:* 422 St Mary's Street, Pleasanton, CA 94566, USA.

ANDERSON Lorna, b. 1962, Glasgow, Scotland. Singer (Soprano). *Education:* Royal Scottish Academy of Music, with Patricia MacMahon; Royal College of Music, London. *Career:* Concerts with the Bach Choir, the English Concert under Trevor Pinnnock, and the Scottish Chamber Orchestra; Tour of Spain and Poland and appearances at the Kings Lynn, City of London, Brighton, Edinburgh and Aldeburgh Festivals; In 1988 sang with London Baroque under Charles Medlam, with the London Mozart Players under Andrew Parrott and the Bournemouth Sinfonietta under Roger Norrington; Promenade Concert debut 1988; Further concerts with the London Classical Players, the Orchestra of the Age of Enlightenment and the Scottish National Orchestra, under Matthias Bamert; Sang Innocenza in the first modern revival of Marazzoli's La Vita humana, for Scottish Early Music Consort, Glasgow, 1990; The Fairy Queen with the Sixteen at the Elizabeth Hall, 1990; Les Noces with Pierre Boulez and Ensemble Intercontemporain, 1990 and 1992; Morgana in Alcina, Halle Handel Festival and Innsbruck Festival, 1992; Mozart Mass in C minor, with Scottish Chamber Orchestra under Charles Mackerras, 1992; Opera: Clorinda in Il Combattimento di Tancredi e Clorinda,

Netherlands Opera, 1991 and 1993. *Honours:* First Prize in Peter Pears and Royal Overseas League Competition, 1984; Purcell-Britten Prize for Concert Singers, Aldeburgh, 1986. *Major Recordings:* The Fairy Queen with Harry Christophers/The Sixteen, Linley; Shakespeare Ode with The Parley of Instruments. *Address:* c/o Lies Askonas Ltd, 186 Drury Lane, London WC2B 5RY, England.

ANDERSON Robert David, b. 20 Aug 1927, Shillong, Assam, India. Conductor; Writer; Editor. *Education:* MA, Gonville and Caius College, Cambridge, England, 1954. *Career:* Assistant Editor, Record News, 1954-56; Assistant Master and Director of Music, Gordonstoun School, 1956-62; Conductor, Moray Choral Union; Assistant Conductor, Spoleto Festival 1962; Conductor, St Bartholomew's Hospital Choral Society, 1965-90; Associate Editor, The Musical Times, 1967-85; Critic, The Times, 1967-72; Contributor to British Broadcasting Corporation Music Weekly and other programmes; Co-ordinating Editor, Elgar Complete Edition; Television programme on Paganini, BBC2, 1971. *Recordings:* Mozart Sacred Music; Elgar Church Music. *Publications:* Catalogue of Egyptian Antiquities in the British Museum, III, Musical Instruments, 1976; Wagner, 1980; Wagner, in Heritage of Music III, 1989; Elgar in Manuscript, 1990; Elgar, 1993. *Honours:* Liveryman, Worshipful Company of Musicians, 1977; Fellow of the Society of Antiquaries, 1983; D Mus (Hon) City University, 1985. *Memberships:* Egypt Exploration Society; Royal Musical Association. *Hobbies:* Modulating from music to Egyptology. *Address:* 54 Hornton Street, London W8 4NT, England.

ANDERSON (Evelyn) Ruth, b. 21 Mar 1928, Kalispell, Montana, USA. Composer; Flautist. *Education:* Studied at the University of Washington and at Columbia and Princeton Universitites with Earl Kim and Ussachevsky; Further studies with Nadia Boulanger, Darius Milhaud and Jean-Pierre Eampal. *Career:* Flautist with the Totenberg Instrumental Ensemble, the Portland and Seattle Symphony Orchestras and the Boston Pops Orchestra during the 1950s; Orchestrator for NBC television and broadway shows; Teacher of composition and electronic music at Hunter College, NY, from 1966. *Compositions include:* Tape: The Pregnant Dream 1968; DUMP, collage, 1970; 3 Studies 1970; State of the Union Message, collage, 1973; Conversations 1974; Dress Rehearsal 1976; I Come out of your Sleep 1979; Mixed Media: Centering, dance, for 4 performers and live electronics 1979; Sound sculptures: Sound Environment 1975; Time and Tempo 1984. *Honours include:* Five MacDowell Colony Fellowships 1957-73; Fulbright Scholarships 1958, 1959; Martha Baird Rockefeller Fund; Alice M Ditson Fund. *Address:* c/o ASCAP, ASCAP Building, One Lincoln Plaza, New York, NY 10023, USA.

ANDERSON Sylvia, b. 1938, Denver, Colorado, USA. Singer (Mezzo-Soprano). m. Matthias Kuntzsch. *Education:* Studied at the Eastman School with Anna Kaskas and at the Cologne Musikhochschule with Ellen Bosenius. *Debut:* Cologne 1962, as Fyodor in Boris Godunov. *Career:* Sang at the Hamburg Staatsoper 1965-69, notably as Ophelia in the 1968 premiere of Searle's Hamlet; Bayreuth Festival 1970-71; Salzburg Festival 1973, in the premiere of De Temporum fine Comoedia by Orff; Guest appearances in Zurich, Stuttgart, Frankfurt, Dusseldorf, Brussels, Barcelona, Trieste and Amsterdam; US engagements at the Metropolitan and New York City Operas, and in San Francisco, Washington and Santa Fe; repertoire includes operas by Gluck, Purcell, Rossini, Verdi, Wagner and modern composers; Many concert appearances. *Recordings:* Schubert Masses (Vox); De Temporum fine Comoedia (Deutsche Grammophon).

ANDERSON T(homas) J(efferson) Jr, b. 17 Aug. 1928, Coatesville, Pennsylvania, USA. Composer; Music Educator. m. 3 children. *Education:* BMus, West Virginia State College, 1950; MEd, Pennsylvania State University, 1951; Studied composition with Scott Huston, Cincinnati Conservatory of Music, 1954; PhD,

University of Iowa, 1958; With Philip Bezanson and Richard Hervig; With Darius Milhaud, Aspen School of Music, 1964. *Career:* Teacher, Instrumental Music, High Point, North Carolina public schools, 1951-54; Instructor, West Virginia State College, Institute, West Virginia, 1955-56; Professor of Music and Chairman, Music Department, Langston (Okla) University, 1958-63; Professor of Music, Tennessee State University, Nashville, Tennessee, 1963-69; Composer-in-residence, Atlanta (GA) Symphony Orchestra, 1969-71; Danforth Visiting Professor, Morehouse College, Atlanta, Georgia, 1971-72; Professor of Music, Chairman Music Department 1972-80, Chair, Austin Fletcher Professor of Music, 1976-90, Emeritus, 1990, Tufts University, Medford, Massachusetts; Doctor of Music, Honoris Causa, Bridewater State College, 1991. *Compositions:* Stage: The Shell Fairy, operetta, 1976-77; Re-Creation for 3 Speakers, Dancer and 6 Instruments, 1978; Soldier Boy, Soldier, opera, 1982; Orchestral: Pyknon Overture, 1958; Introduction and Allegro, 1959; New Dances, 1960; Classical Symphony, 1961; 6 Pieces for Clarinet and Chamber Orchestra, 1962; Symphony in 3 Movements, 1964; Squares: An Essay for Orchestra, 1965; Chamber Symphony, 1968; Intervals, 1970-71; Messages: A Creole Fantasy, 1979; Concerto for 2 Violins and Chamber Orchestra, 1988; Chamber Concerto: Remembrances, 1988; Band music; Chamber and Vocal music; Songs of Illuminations, Song cycle, for Soprano, Tenor and Piano, 1990; Whatever Happened to the Big Bands?, Alto soprano, Trumpet and Trombone, 1991; Spirit Songs commissioned by Yo Yo Ma, for cello and piano, 1993. *Major recordings:* Chamber symphony: London Philharmonic Orchestra, James Dixon, conductor; Variations on a Theme By M B Talson; Contempory Chamber Ensemble, Arthur Weisberg, conductor; Squares: Baltimore Symphony Orchestra, Paul Freeman, conductor; Intermezzi, Videmus, Vivian Taylor, Artistic Director. *Address:* 111 Cameron Glen Drive, Chapel Hill, NC 27516, USA.

ANDERSSON Einar, b. 13 July 1909, Vasteras, Sweden. Tenor. *Education:* Studied in Stockholm, 1933-38. *Debut:* Stockholm 1938, as Fenton in Die lustigen Weiber von Windsor. *Career:* Sang at the Royal Opera Stockholm until 1963 as Mozart's Ferrando and Tamino; Verdi's Duke of Mantua and Alfredo; Puccini's Cavaradossi and Pinkerton; Vladimir in Prince Igor; Dimitri in Boris Godunov; Faust in the opera by Gounod and Lenski in Tchaikovsky's Eugene Onegin; Sang the title role in the premiere of Aladdin by Atterberg, 1941.

ANDERSSON Laila, b. 30 March 1941, Losen, Blekinge, Sweden. Singer (Soprano). m. Ulf Palme, 1984. *Education:* Studied with Sylvia Mang-Borenberg, Ragnar Hulten, and Hjordis Schymberg in Stockholm. *Career:* Royal Opera Stockholm from 1964, as Susanna, Leonore (Il Trovatore), Mathilde (Guillaume Tell), Madama Butterfly, Jenůfa and Sophie; Sang in the premieres of Herr von Hancken by Blomdahl 1965 and Granskibbutzen by Karkoff 1975; Sang the title role in Berg's Lulu, 1977; Frequent visits to the Drottningholm Festival from 1967 (Gustaf Adolf och Ebba Brahe by the Abbé Vogler, 1973); Guest engagements at the Edinburgh Festival 1974, Copenhagen, Wiesbaden, Helsinki and Oslo; Sang Tosca at Stockholm and Bonn, 1977, Salome at the Metropolitan (debut, 1981), Gelsenkirchen, Vienna, Rio de Janeiro, Berlin and Montreal, 1985; sang Brünnhilde at Arhus, Denmark, 1987; Fidelio at Washington and Montreal, 1988; sang Tiresias in the premiere of Backanterna, by Daniel Börtz, 1992; as Elektra, Stockholm Opera, 1993. Member of the Nya Bjorling Vocal Quartet. *Honours:* Singer of the Royal Court, 1985; Litteris et Artibus, 1992. *Address:* Köpmantorget 10, S-111 31 Stockholm, Sweden.

ANDERSZEWSKI Piotr, b. 4 Apr 1969, Warsaw, Poland. Concert Pianist. *Education:* Studied at the Conservatories of Lyon and Strasbourg, University of Southern California in Los Angeles; Chopin Academy, Warsaw. *Career:* Recitals in Poland, the United States and France; Wigmore Hall, London debut Feb 1991; Further British engagements include the Harrogate Festival (1991) and concerts with the Royal Liverpool Philharmonic and Hallé Orchestras; Festival Hall debut with the London Philharmonic conducted by Franz Welser-Möst; Recordings for Polish radio and television; European recital tour, Autumn, 1992; Regular duo partner with violinist Viktoria Mullova 1992/93 season. *Address:* Harold Holt Ltd, 31 Sinclair Road, London W14 ONS, England.

ANDONIAN Andrea, b. 1950, Colorado, USA. Singer (Mezzo-Soprano). *Education:* Studied at Florida and Ohio Universities and Operastudio in Cologne. *Career:* Sang at Cologne Offenbach Theatre, 1977-78; Engaged at Krefelt-Monchengldbach, 1978-85; Has sung with Deutsche Oper Berlin, 1986-; Guest appearances, Germany and elsewhere in repertory including Cherubino, Dorabella, Ramiro in Mozart's Finta Giardiniera, Idamente in Idomeneo and Annio in La Clemenza di Tito; Humperdinck's Hansel, Siebel in Faust, the Prince in Massenet's Cendrillon, and Britten's Lucretia and Hermia; Sang Urbain in Les Huguenots with Deutsche Oper, 1987, and at Covent Garden, 1991; Paris Opéra-Comique, 1992, in Rossini's L'Occasione fa il Ldro, La Scala di Seta, La Cambiale di Matrimonio and Il Signor Bruschino. *Recordings include:* Schumman's Requiem. *Address:* Deutsche Oper Berlin, Richard Wagnerstrasse 10, 1000 Berlin 10, Germany.

ANDRADE Levine, b. 1954, Bombay, India. Violist. *Education:* Studied violin at the Yehudi Menuhin School with Robert Mastres; also studied with Menuhin and Nadia Boulanger; Viola studies with Patrick Ireland; Royal Academy of Music from 1969, with Frederick Grinke, Max Gilbert, Sidney Griller and Colin Hampton. *Career:* Co-founded the Arditti String Quartet 1974, (member until 1989); Frequent concerts with the London Symphony Orchestra, Royal Philharmonic, Academy of St Martin in the Fields, the London Sinfonietta and the London Mozart Players; Guest professor at the Royal Academy of Music; Many concerts with the Arditti Quartet in Europe and North America; Festival engagements at Aldeburgh, Bath, BBC Proms, Berlin, Budapest, Paris, Venice Biennale, Vienna and Warsaw; Music in Camera programme BBC television 1987; Series of seven recitals Radio 3, 1987; Played in all Schoenberg's quartets in a single recital, Elizabeth Hall London, Nov 1988; Has taken part in the premieres of quartets by Georges Aperghis (1985), Berio (Divertimento for trio 1987), Böse (No 3 1989) Britten (Quartettino, 1983), Gavin Bryars (1985), Bussotti (1988), John Cage (Music for 4, 1988), Davies (1983), Ferneyhough (nos 2,3), Glass (No 2, 1985), Gubaidulina (No 3 1987), Harvey (Nos 1 and 2), Hinemith (Quartet 1915, 1986), Kagel (1987), Nancarrow (No 3, 1988), Ohana (No 2 1982), Pousseur (No 2 1989) Rihm (Nos 5, 6, and 8), Scelsi (No 5 1985), Xenakis (Tetras 1983 and Akea, Piano Quintet 1986); Isang Yun (Flute Quintet, 1987); Has also premiered quartets by Michael Finnissy, Michael Nyman and Tim Souster. *Recordings include:* Henze's Five String Quartets, Wergo; 25 CDs include music by John Cage and the four quartets of Elliott Carter (Etcetera). *Honours include:* Deutsche Schallplattenpreis, (for Henze Quartets, 1987). *Address:* c/o 57 Rotherwick Road, London NW11 7DD, England.

ANDRADE Rosario, b. 6 Apr 1951, Veracruz, Mexico. Singer (Soprano). *Education:* Studied in Veracruz and Accademia di Santa Cecilia, Rome. *Debut:* As Madame Butterfly, Mexico City, 1974. *Career:* Sang at Glyndebourne Festival as Donna Elvira in Don Giovanni, 1977-78; Many guest appearances in Europe and North America: Brussels, 1978, Lyon (in Cavalli's La Calisto), 1979, Warsaw, 1981-82, Connecticut, 1987, Pittsburgh and Mississippi Opera Company, 1988; Metropolitan Opera debut, 1982, as Antonia in Les Contes d'Hoffmann, returning as Manon, 1986; Other roles include Mimi, Micaela, Marguerite, Donna Anna, Aida and Maddalena in Andrea Chenier; Concert repertory includes Marguerite in La Damnation de Faust. *Address:* c/o Metropolitan Opera, Lincoln Center, New York, NY 10023, USA.

ANDRASOVAN Tibor, b. 3 April 1917, Slovenska Lupca, Slovakia. Conductor; Composer. *Education:* Pupil of E Suchon and A Moyzses at the Bratislava Conservatory. *Career:* Repetiteur, Slovak National Theatre, 1946-57; artistic director, Slovak Folk Artistic Ensemble, 1955-58, 1969-74. *Compositions:* Stage: Gelo the Joker, 1957; The Quadrille, operetta, 1960; The White Disease, music drama, 1967; The Gamekeeper's Wife, opera, 1973-74; The King of Fools, musical, 1982; Ballets: Orpheus and Euridice, 1948; The Song of Peace, 1949; The Festival of Solstice, 1985; Orchestral: Little Goral, overture, 1961; Concerto for Cembalo and strings, 1977; Chamber: String Quartet, Folklorica, 1976; Partita romantica for piano, 1983; Vocal: Tokajik, cantata for sopano, chorus and orchestra, 1975; The Echoes of the Uprising Mountains, song cycle for narrator, soprano, tenor and piano, 1979; The Recruit Songs, song cycle, 1973; The Pines Whispered, song cycle for soprano and piano, 1976; The Woman and Muse, song cycle for bass-baritone and piano, 1978; also incidental music, film scores and music for folk ensembles. *Honours:* Numerous awards; made a Merited Artist of the Czechoslovak Socialist Republic, 1971. *Address:* SOZA, Kollarovo nam 20, 813 27 Bratislava, Czech Republic.

ANDRÉ Martin, b. 10 Dec 1960, West Wickam, England. Conductor. *Education:* Studied at the Yehudi Menuhin School, the Royal College of Music and Cambridge University. *Career:* Played with the National Youth Orchestra as percussionist from 1970; Founded the Mozart Chamber Ensemble at Cambridge and was appointed conductor of the University Orchestra and Chorus, and the University Chamber Orchestra; Conducted his edition of Purcell's King Arthur at Cambridge and the Minack Theatre, Cornwall, 1982; Has worked with the Welsh National Orchestra from 1982, leading Aida, Jenůfa, Ernani, Rigoletto, Madame Butterfly, Un Ballo in Maschera, Eugene Onegin and Il Barbiere di Siviglia; Vancouver Opera from season 1986-87 with Janáček's From the House of the Dead and Cunning Little Vixen, Ariadne auf Naxos, La Traviata and La Bohème; Seattle Opera 1987, Carmen; London concert debut Jan. 1987 with the English Chamber Orchestra at the Barbican; Further concerts with the Scottish Chamber Orchestra and the Northern Sinfonia; Scottish Opera from 1989, The Merry Widow and La Clemenza di Tito; Conducted the Love of Three Oranges at the English National Opera, 1990 and at Teatro Sao Carlos, Lisbon, 1991; Madame Butterfly for Opera North; World premiere, The Bacchae by John Butler for ENO, 1992. *Address:* c/o Ingpen and Williams Ltd, 14 Kensington Court, London W8 5DN, England.

ANDRÉ Maurice, b. 21 May 1933, Ales, France. Trumpeter. *Education:* Studied with his father and with Sabarich at the Paris Conservatoire. *Career:* Soloist with the Concerts Lamoureux, 1953-1960, L'Orchestre Philharmonique of ORTF (French Radio), 1953-1962, and the orchestra of the Opéra-Comique, Paris, 1962-1967; Many concert performances in Europe; North American Professor at the Paris Conservatoire, 1967-1978; Composers who have written for him include Boris Blacher (Concerto, 1971), Charles Chaynes, Marcel Landowski, Jean-Claude Eloy, Harald Genzmer, Bernhard Krol, Jean Langlais (Chorals for trumpet and organ), Henri Tomasi and André Jolivet (Arioso barocco, 1968). *Honours:* First prizes at international competitions in Geneva, 1955 and Munich, 1963.

ANDREAE Marc Edouard, b. 8 Nov 1939, Zurich, Switzerland. Conductor. *Education:* Zurich Conservatory; University of Zurich; Study with Nadia Boulanger in Paris, with Franco Ferrara in Rome. *Career:* Chief Conductor, Broadcasting Orchestra of Italian Switzerland, Lugano, 1969-90; Regular guest, numerous European and Japanese, symphony orchestras and at Festivals, Paris, Berlin, Lucerne, Vienna, Salzburg, Ascona, Lugano, Brescia; Numerous concerts and operas for television, including Eurovision. *Recordings:* With NDR Hamburg, Hamburg Philharmonic Orchestra, Munich Philharmonic, Cologne Radio Symphony Orchestra, Bamberg Symphony, National Orchestra of France; Repertoire includes Schubert's Gastein Symphony; Witt's Jena Symphony;

Schumann's G minor Symphony; Schubert Die Verschworenen and many contemporary compositions. *Publications:* Music of Weber, Rossini, Donizetti, Schumann, Lortzing, Tchaikovsky and Liszt, published by C.F.Peters, Frankfurt. *Honours:* 1st Prize, Swiss National Competition, 1966; 2 Grand prix, Italian Record Critics, 1974; L.P. Techo Distinction, Tokyo, 1975. *Memberships:* Swiss Music Edition, President. *Current Management:* Konzertgesellschaft, Steinwiesstrasse 2, 8032 Zurich, Switzerland. *Address:* Via Moretto 6, 6924 Sorengo, Switzerland.

ANDREEV Andrei, b. 1950, Crimea, USSR. Violinist. *Career:* Co-founded Rachmaninov Quartet under auspices of Sochi State Philharmonic Society, Crimea, 1974; Many concerts in former Soviet Union; From season 1975-76 tours to Switzerland, Austria, Bulgaria, Norway and Germany; Participation in Shostakovich Chamber Music Festival, Vilnius, 1976, and festivals in Moscow and St Petersburg; Repertoire has included works by Haydn, Mozart, Beethoven, Bartok, Brahms, Schnittke, Shostakovich, Boris Tchaikovsky, Chalayev and Meyerovich. *Honours include:* With Rachamaninov Quartet: Prizewinner at 1st All-Union Borodin String Quartet Competition, 1987. *Address:* c/o Sonata (Rachmaninov Quartet), 11 Northgate Street, Glasgow G20 7AA, Scotland.

ANDREW Donald, b. 26 May 1920, Barnstaple, North Devon, England. Professional Oboist; Organist. *Education:* The Choristers' School, Exeter, Devon; Exeter Cathedral Choir; Royal Military School of Music, Kneller Hall, Twickenham; Royal Academy of Music, London. *Debut:* BBC Bristol, 1945. *Career:* BBC Soloist, 1945-77; Has played for all leading London orchestras; Principal Oboe: Liverpool Philharmonic Orchestra, Sadler's Wells Opera Orchestra, BBC Revue Orchestra, Leighton Lucas Chamber Orchestra, Ballet Rambert, Old St Paul's Musical Society, Edinburgh; Member, Wind Band, Royal Shakespeare Theatre, Stratford-upon-Avon; Organist, St Margaret's Parish Church, Northam, 1990, 1991; Gave 1st broadcast performance of the Haydn oboe concerto with Reginald Redman and West of England Studio Orchestra, also played the Haydn and Goossens concertos with Sir Malcolm Sargent and Liverpool Philharmonic Orchestra; BBC broadcasts included: Many 9-o'clock recitals and others with piano; Concertos from Bristol, Cardiff, Birmingham, Glasgow and Music at Night, several in Musician in Scotland including 1st broadcast performance of Shaun Dillon's Sonata for oboe and piano and Hans Gal's Sonata for oboe and piano. *Honours:* FIBA, 1978. *Memberships:* Incorporated Society of Musicians; Musicians Union; Royal College of Organists; Lancashire School of Music. *Address:* c/o Girobank Scotland, 93 George Street, Edinburgh EH2 3JL, Scotland.

ANDREW Jon, b. 1936, New Zealand. Singer (Tenor). *Education:* Studied in Auckland. *Debut:* As Don Jose in Carmen, Auckland, 1982. *Career:* Sang with Sadler's Wells Opera, 1963-68, as Riccardo, Radames, Don José, and Agrippa in the British premiere of The Fiery Angel (New Opera Company); Sang in Germany, 1969-, notably in Karlsruhe, Mannhem and Dusseldorf in Wagner roles including Siegmund in Die Walküre; Glyndebourne Festival as the Italian Singer in Rosenkavalier, 1965; Covent Garden, 1967 and 1974, as Froh in Das Rheingold and Dimitri in Boris Godunov; Further appearances with Welsh National Opera, Handel Opera Society, 1967, and at San Diego as Siegmund and Otello, 1975-76; Also sang Siegmund at Madrid, Berlin Staatsoper, and with English National Opera, 1975; Wexford Festival as Pedro in Tiefland, 1978; Further engagements at La Scala, Milan, and Nice and Santiago, 1981; Other roles have included Turiddu, Erik in Fliegende Holländer, Max in Der Freischütz, Laca in Jenůfa, and Bob Boles in Peter Grimes. *Address:* c/o English National Opera, St Martin's Lane, London WC2, England.

ANDREW Ludmilla, b. 1939, Vancouver, Canada. Singer (Soprano). *Debut:* With Vancouver Opera, as Donna Elvira. *Career:* Has sung in San Francisco in Aida

and Der Rosenkavlier; British debut with Sadler's Wells
Opera as Madama Butterfly: later roles have been Senta,
Aida and Tosca; Covent Garden in The Ring and as
Elektra, Leonora (La Forza del Destino), Arabella and
Tosca; Glyndebourne 1968, as Anna Bolena; Scottish
Opera as Donna Anna, and Miss Jessel (The Turn of
the Screw); With Welsh National Opera has sung
Abigaille, Giorgetta (Il Tabarro), Rosalinda, Aida and
Tosa; Venus with Chelsea Opera Group, in a concert
performance of Tannhäuser; Title roles in Donizetti's
Maria di Rudenz and Rosmunda d'Inghilterra, and
Mayr's Medea in Corinto, at the Elizabeth Hall; Other
roles include Ellen Orford (Buenos Aires and Rio de
Janeiro); the Marschallin and Mozart's Electra
(Brussels); Norma (Dublin); Ursula in Mathis der Maler,
Jenůfa, Turandot (New Zealand); Countess Almaviva
(Vancouver); Sieglinde; Sang Anaide in Leoncavallo's
Zazà, Wexford Festival, 1990; Frequent recitals with
Geoffrey Parsons in the French, German and Russian
repertoire; Concert performances with leading British
orchestras in the Requiems of Mozart and Verdi, the
Choral Symphony and Sibelius songs conducted by
Rozhdestvensky. Recordings include: Video of Macbeth
(Glyndebourne); Songs by Bernard Van Dieren. Address:
c/o Korman International Management, 24a Burnaby
Gardens, London W4 3DP, England.

ANDRIESSEN Jurriaan, b. 15 Nov 1925, Haarlem,
the Netherlands. Composer. Education: Studied
composition with father, Hendrik Andrieessen;
Graduated, Utrecht Conservatory, 1947; Studied
conducting with Willem van Otterloo; Film music in
Paris; Composition with Aaron Copland, Berkshire
Music Center, Tanglewood, 1949, 1950. Compositions:
Stage: Kalchas, opera, 1959; The Black Blonde, opera
buffa, 1964; Orchestral: Piano Concertino, 1943;
Symphonietta Concertante for 4 Trumpets and
Orchestra, 1947; Piano Concerto, 1948; 5 symphonies:
No 1, Berkshire Symphonies, 1949, also as the ballet
Jones Beach, 1950; No 2, 1962; No 3, 1963; No 4,
The Birds, 1963; No 5, Time Spirit, 1970; Flute Concerto,
1951; Cymbeline, overture, 1954; Inno della Tecnica,
1957; Tahi, 1960; Omaggio a Sweelinck for Harpsichord
and 24 Strings, 1968; Trelleborg Concerto for
Harpsichord and 3 Orchestral Groups, 1969; Antifona
dell'Aja, 1969; Pasticcio-Finale for Orchestra, Dixieland
Band and Tape, 1974; La celebrazioni, 1977; Les branles
gaulois for Accordion and Chamber Orchestra, 1978;
Monomania e policromia, 1984; Time Suspended, 1984;
Chamber: Hommage a Milhaud for 11 Instruments,
1945, also for Flute and String Quartet, 1948; Violin
Sonata, 1946; Octet Divertissement for Winds, 1948;
Mourning Becomes Electra for 11 Winds and
Percussion, 1954; 5 trios, 1955-59; L'incontro di Cesare
e Cleopatra, sextet for Winds and Piano, 1956; Duo
for 2 Violins, 1958; Movimenti I for Trumpet, Horn,
Trombone, Strings and Timpani, 1965; II for Oboe,
Clarinet, Bassoon, Strings and Percussion, 1972; III for
Violin, Viola, Cello, Winds and Percussion, 1974; Trio
for Clarinet, Cello and Piano, 1965; Entrata festiva for
Brass and Timpani, 1966; Antifono e Fusione for Wind
Quintet, Brass Quartet and Timpani, 1966; In Pompa
Magna for Brass and Percussion, 1966; Summer
Dances for 7 Percussionists, Harp and Guitar, 1966;
Quartetto Buffo for Clarinet and String Trio, 1974; The
Cave for Cello, 12 Winds, 4 Keyboard Instruments and
Electronics, 1976; Perpetual Movement for 13 Strings
and Tape, 1979; Entrata della regina for Brass Ensemble,
1980; Clarinet Quartet, 1984; Sextet, 1985; Cumulus
humulus fumulus for 2 Violins, Viola and Cello, 1985;
Due canzone di Don Chisciotte for Violin and Harp, 1985;
Serenade for Horn, 1985; Music for Harpsichord, 1987;
Piano pieces; Vocal music. 21; Dynamic Overture for
Symfonic Vand, Trio for violin, viola and cello, 1988;
Ballade for guitar and harp, Sonate for bassoon and
piano, Reflections for violin solo, 1990; Divertimento
for 2 oboes and English horn, Aspetti di H.F.A. for organ,
1990; Sonate for 2 harps, violin concerto, 1991; Quartet
for flute, violin, viola and cello, 1992. Address: BUMA,
BUMA/STERMA Huis, Postbus 725, 1180 AS
Amstelveen, Netherlands.

ANDRIESSEN Louis, b. 6 June 1939, Utrecht, The
Netherlands. Composer. Education: Studied with his
father, Hendrik Andriessen, and with Kees van Baaren,
Royal Conservatory of Music, The Hague, 1957-62; with
Luciano Berio, Milan, 1962-63. Compositions: Stage:
Reconstructie, opera, 1968-69, in collaboration with 4
colleagues; Matthew Passion, 1976; Orpheus, 1977;
George Sand, 1980; Orchestral: What it's Like for live
electronic improvisers and 52 strings, 1970; Uproar for
16 winds, 6 percussionists and electronic instruments,
1970; The 9 Symphonies of Beethoven for promenade
orchestra and ice cream bell, 1970; Symphony for Open
Strings,1978; Velocity, 1983; De Stijl, 1985; Chamber:
flute sonata, 1956; Percosse for flute,trumpet, bassoon
and percussion, 1958; A Flower Song I for violin, 1963,
II for oboe, 1963, and III for cello, l964; Double for clarinet
and piano, 1965; Souvenirs d'enfance for piano and
tape, 1966; The Persistence for piano and winds, 1972;
Felicitatie for 3 trumpets, 1979; Disco for violin and
piano, 1982; Overture to Orpheus for harpsichord, 1982;
piano pieces; Vocal: Nocturne for soprano and chamber
orchestra, 1959; Il Principe for 2 choirs, winds, piano
and bass guitar, 1974; The State for 4 Women's Voices
and 27 instruments, 1972-76; Mausoleum for 2
baritones and chamber ensemble, 1979, revised 1981;
Time for choir and orchestra, 1981; Madrigal Concerto
for choir, 1984; Collaboration with Peter Greenaway
in 1991 TV Series Not Mozart: M is for Man, Music
Mozart. Address: c/o BUMA, Postbus 725, 1180 AS
Amstelveen, Netherlands.

ANDSNES Leif Ove, b. 7 April 1970, Karmooy,
Norway. Pianist. Education: Studied at the Music
Conservatory of Bergen with Jiri Hlinka. Debut: Oslo
1987; British debut, Edinburgh Festival with the Oslo
Philharmonic/Mariss Jansons, 1989; US debut,
Cleveland Symphony/Neeme Järvi. Other appearances
include Schleswig-Holstein Festival and with orchestras
such as Los Angeles Philharmonic, Berlin Philharmonic,
London Philharmonic, Leipzig Gewandhaus, City of
Birmingham Symphony Orchestra, Royal Scottish
National Orchestra and BBC Philharmonic Orchestra for
his debut at the Proms, 1992; Recitals at Teatro
Communale, Bologna, Wigmore Hall, London,
Herculesaal, Munich, Concertgebouw, Amsterdam.
Recordings include: Grieg: A minor and Liszt A major
concerti, Janaček: Solo Piano Music (awarded
prestigious Deutschen Schallplaten award); Chopin:
Sonatas and Grieg: Solo Piano Music. Honours: First
prize at the Hindemith Competition in Frankfurt;
Norwegian Critics' Prize; Dorothy Chandler Award in
Los Angeles. Address: c/o Kathryn Enticott, IMG Artists
(Europe), Media House, 3 Burlington Lane, Chiswick,
London W4 2TH, England.

ANGAS Richard, b. 1950, Surrey, England. Singer
(Bass). Education: Studied in Vienna and London. Debut:
With Scottish opera as Fafner in The Ring. Career:
Appearances with the Welsh National Opera and at
Covent Garden; Performances in Germany as King Mark
and King Henry, Baron Ochs, Osmin, Rocco and
Mephistopheles; Engagements throughout Europe,
Israel, Australia and South Ameica in oratorio and
recital; English National Opera as Monteverdi's Seneca
and Pluto, Basilio in Il Barbiere di Siviglia, Pimen (Boris
Godunov), Daland (The Flying Dutchman) and Jupiter
(Orpheus in the Underworld); The Mikado, 1990, and
Bartolo in Figaro; The Doctor in a new production of
Wozzeck, 1990; Has sung in the world premiere of
Birtwistle's The Mask of Orpheus (1986) and the British
premiere of The Making of the Representative for Planet
8 by Philip Glass (1989); Sang in The Love for Three
Oranges with Opera North, Leeds. Address: c/o English
National Opera, St Martins Lane, London, WC2.

ANGEL Marie, b. 3 June 1953, Pinnaroo, South
Australia. Singer (Soprano). m. David Freeman. Career:
Has sung with Opera Factory London and Opera Factory
Zurich in Così fan Tutte (Fiordiligi, also televised); The
Knot Garden (Denise); Birtwistle's Punch and Judy
(Pretty Polly); Aventures by Ligeti; Mahagonny
Songspiel; Gluck's Iphigenia operas (title role); Donna
Anna, and Mozart's Countess 1991; Other roles include
Euridice in Monteverdi's Orfeo and the Oracle of the
Dead in the premiere of The Mask of Orpheus, 1986,

for English National Opera; Mozart's Queen of Night for Welsh National Opera; Musetta for Opera North; Sang Berio's Recital I at South Bank and Jo-Ann for Glyndebourne Touring Opera in Tippett's New Year; Created the role of Morgana Le Fay in the premiere of Birtwistle's Gawain at Covent Garden, May 1991; Sang Monteverdi's Poppea in a new production by Opera Factory, 1992; Has also sung Donna Anna for Victoria State Opera and appeared with Houston Grand Opera and at the New York City Opera. *Address:* c/o Allied Artists Agency, 42 Montpelier Square, London SW7 1JZ, England.

ANGELO Mariana, b. 1954, Sofia, Bulgaria. Singer (Soprano). *Education:* Studied at Conservatoire of Sofia. *Career:* Sang at the Komische Oper Berlin 1978-84; Berne Opera 1984-86; Has appeared at the Nationaltheater Mannheim, 1987- and has sung as guest at Dresden, Karlsruhe, Sofia, Graz, Nancy, Paris, Ghent and Antwerp; Lausanne Opera, 1989, as Liu in Turandot; Other roles include Verdi's Leonora (Il Trovatore and La Forza del Destino), Amelia Boccanegra, Aida, Violetta and Desdemona; Puccini's Mimi, Manon Lescaut and Madame Butterfly; Nedda, Tatiana and Mathilde in Guillaume Tell. *Address:* c/o Music International, 13 Ardilaun Road, London N5 2QR, England.

ANGERDAL Lars Göran, b. 28 Aug 1937, Orebro, Sweden. Organist; Choirmaster. m. Sonja Birgitta Malmström, 1 son, 2 daughters. *Education:* Studied at Universities of Uppsala and Stockholm, Sweden; Studied Chamber Music and Music Education, Royal Academy of Music, Stockholm, 1957-62; Studied at Musikhochschule, Berlin, Germany, 1962-63. *Career:* Organ Concerts, Scandinavia, Germany, Switzerland, France, England, USA; Choir Concerts, Scandinavia, Germany, Australia, Italy; TV and Radio appearances, Sweden and USA; Lecturer, Sweden and USA; Assistant Organist and Choirmaster, Uppsala Cathedral, Sweden, 1967-. *Recording:* Organ and Choir Music, Uppsala Cathedral. *Publications:* Organistpraxis, 1981; Organ Music for Funerals, I & II, 1987, 1990; Organ Music for Weddings, 1993. *Contributions to:* Svensk Kyrkomusik; Sohlmans Musiklexikon, The American Organist. *Memberships:* Member of Professional organisations. *Address:* Fiskgjusevägen 16, S-75756 Uppsala, Sweden.

ANGERER Paul, b. 16 May 1927, Vienna, Austria. Conductor; Violist; Composer. m. Anita Rosser, 18 June 1952, 2 sons, 2 daughters. *Education:* Studied Theory, Piano, Violin and Organ, Hochschule für Musik, Vienna and Vienna Conservatory, 1941-46. *Career:* Violist, 1947, Principal Violist, 1953-56, Vienna Symphony Orchestra; Violist, Zurich Tonhalle Orchestra, 1948, Orchestre de la Suisse Romande, Geneva, 1949-52; Director, Chief Conductor, Vienna Chamber Orchestra, 1956-63; Composer, Conductor, Burgtheater, Vienna, 1960-64; Principal Conductor, Bonn City Theatre, 1964-66; Permanent Guest Conductor, Haydn Symphonic Orchestra of Bolzano and Trento, 1964-; Musical Director (Opera), Ulm Theatre, 1966-68; Salzburg Landestheater, 1968-72; Artistic Director, Hellbrunn Festival, 1970-71; Director, SW German Chamber Orchestra, Pforzheim, 1972-82; Professor, Hochschule für Musik, Vienna, 1983-; Numerous tours as Guest Conductor; Leader of Concilium Musicum; Editor of Baroque and pre-Classical music, and works by Joseph Lanner. *Compositions include:* Orchestral pieces, chamber works, viola and piano concertos, a dramatic cantata, television opera, works for organ, harp, viola, harpsichord. *Recordings:* Numerous recordings for Vox, Pantheon Music, Claves, Amadeo, Orfeo, Carus, Intercord, Pair Music, Dynamic, Metronome, Mediaphon, Kovarik's Musikothek, Christophorus, Darbringhaus und Grimm, as soloist and/or conductor; Works include Concerti Grossi by Handel and Geminiani; Mozart piano concertos K453, K449, K451, K453, K459, K503, K595, with Gulda, Klien and Brendel; Porpora's Cello Concerto; Dvořák Serenade in E and Janáček Idyll. *Honours:* Medal winner, Geneva Music Competition, 1948; 1st Prize for Composition, Organ Competition,

Haarlem, 1954; Austrian State Prize, 1956; Theodor Korner Prize, 1958; 1st Prize, Salzburg Opera Competition, 1959; Vienna Cultural Prize, 1983; Cultural Prize, Lower Austria, 1987. *Hobbies:* Joinery; Masonry. *Address:* Esteplatz 3, A-1030 Vienna, Austria.

ANGERMÜLLER Rudolph Kurt, b. 2 Sept 1940, Bielefeld, Germany. Music Editor; Music Librarian. m. Hannelore Johannböke, 1 son, 1 daughter. *Education:* MA; PhD 1970; Graduate, Försterling Conservatory of Music, Bielefeld. *Career:* Assistant, Musicology Institute, University of Salzburg; Chief Editor, New Mozart Edition, and Librarian, International Mozarteum Foundation 1972-; Chief of Research Department, International Mozarteum Foundation 1981-; General Secretary, International Mozarteum Foundation, 1988; Professor, 1993. *Publications:* Untersuchungen zur Geschichte des Carmen-Stoffes 1967; Antonio Salieri, Sein Leben und seine weltichen Werke unter besonderer Berücksichtigung seiner grossen Opern, 3 volumes, 1971, 1972, 1974; W.A. Mozarts Musikalische Umwelt in Paris (1977-78), Eine Dokumentation 1982; Mozart's Operas, 1988. *Contributions to:* Bulletin of the International Mozarteum Foundation; Mozart-Jahrbuch; Haydn-Jahrbuch; Die Musikforschung; Osterreichische Musikzeitschrift; Wiener Figaro; Musical Times; Deutsches Jahrbuch für Musikwissenschaft; numerous other professional journals and books. *Memberships:* International Musicological Society; Society for Music Research; Austrian Musicological Society. *Hobby:* Collecting Old Books and Copperplate Engravings. *Address:* 92a Moostr, 5020 Salzburg, Austria.

ANHALT Istvan, b. 12 Apr 1919, Budapest, Hungary. Professional Musician; Composer; Author; Educator. *Education:* Royal Hungarian Academy of Music, Conservatoire National de Musique de Paris; Composition Teachers were Zoltán Kodály and Nadia Boulanger; Instruction in Conducting from Louis Fourestier and Piano from Soulima Stravinsky. *Career:* Appointed to Faculty of Music, McGill University, Montreal 1949; Carried out experimentation and compositional work at electronic music laboratory of National Research Centre, Ottawa, Columbia-Princeton Electronic Music Centre and Bell Telephone Laboratories, Anhalt installed electronic music studio and appointed Director and Member of the Senate, McGill University, 1964; Appointed Slee Professorship, New York State University, Buffalo 1969; Head of Music, Queen's University, Kingston, Ontario 1971-81. *Compositions:* Dramatic Works: Arc En Ciel 1951; Winthrop 1983. Orchestral; Interludium 1950; Symphony No 1, 1958; Symphony of Modules (Symphony No 2) 1967; Simulacrum 1987; Sparks-kraps 1988; Sonance Resonance (Welche Töne), 1989. Chorus: The Bell-Man 1954, revised 1980; Cento On Eldon Grier's An Ecstasy (Cantata Urbana) 1967; Three Songs of Death 1954; Three Songs of Love 1951. Solo voices with instruments: Chanson D'Aurore 1955; Comments 1954; Foci 1969; Journey of The Magi 1951; A Little Wedding Music 1963; Psalm XIX, A Benediction 1951; Six Songs from Na Conxy Pan 1948; La Tourangelle 1975. Chamber Music: Funeral Music 1951; Sonata for Violin and Piano 1954; Trio for Violin, Cello and Piano, 1953; Doors . . . Shadows, 1992. Piano: Fantasia for Piano 1954; Sonata for Piano 1951. Electronic Tape: Electronic Composition No 1-4, 1959-62. *Recordings:* Cento; Electronic Composition No 1, 2, 3, 4; Fantasia for Piano; Foci; La Fuite (from La Tourangelle); Sonata for Violin and Piano; La Tourangelle; Trio for Violin, Cello and Piano. *Publication:* Alternative Voices 1984. *Honours:* Doctor of Music, honoris causa, bestowed upon him by McGill University 1982; Professor Emeritus, Queen's University, Kingston, Ontario, 1984; Honorary LLD, Queen's University, 1992. *Address:* 274 Johnson Street, Kingston, Ontario K7L 1Y4, Canada.

ANHORN Carmen, b. 5 Aug 1956, Lucerne, Switzerland. Singer (Mezzo-Soprano). *Education:* Studied at Zurich Musikhochschule, with Brigitte Fassbaender in Munich and Leonore Kirchstein in Augsburg. *Career:* Member of Bayerische Staatsoper,

Munich, 1982-88; Sang first as coloratura soprano, then as mezzo; Guest appearances, Hamburg, Dusseldorf, Frankfurt, Milan, Salzburg, Barcelona and Bordeaux; Appeared in Parsifal at Bayreuth, 1989, as Cherubino at Vienna Volksoper, 1990; Other roles have included Mozart's Zerlina, Despina and Papagena, Woglinde in Das Rheingold, Musetta in La Boheme and Amor in Orfeo ed Euridice; Sang in Wagner's Das Liebesverbot at Palermo, 1991; Concert engagements at the Bach-Wochen in Ansbach and in Leipzig, Munich, Madrid and Vienna. *Recordings include:* Nuri in d'Albert's Tiefland; Iphigenie en Tauride and Egk's Peer Gynt. *Address:* c/o Teatro Massimo di Palermo, Piazza Verdi, 90138 Palermo, Italy.

ANIEVAS Agustin, b. 11 June 1934, New York, NY, USA.Pianist; Teacher. *Education:* Commenced piano lessons at age 4 with his mother; was a pupil of Steuermann, Samaroff and Marcus at the Juilliard School of Music, N.Y. *Career:* Formal debut as soloist with the Little Orchestra Society, N.Y., 1952; later toured North and South America, Australia and the Far East; professor of piano, Brooklyn College of the City University of New York, 1974-. *Recordings:* For Angel-EMI and Seraphim, notably of music by Bartók, Prokofiev, Rachmaninov, Chopin and Liszt. *Honours:* Concert Artists Guild Award,1959; first prize, Dimitri Mitropoulos Competition, 1961. *Address:* c/o Music Department, Brooklyn College of the City University of New York, Brooklyn, NY 11210, USA.

ANISIMOVA Tanya, b. 15 Feb 1966, Grozny, USSR. Musician (Cellist). m. Victor Taratuta, 12 Nov 1989. *Education:* Central Music School, Moscow, 1975-84; Studied Cello with Natalia Shakhovskaya, Igor Gavrysh, Galina Kozolupov, graduated with honours, 1984-89, Assistantship, Cello, String Quartet, Graduate School, 1989-90, Moscow Conservatory; Studied with George Neikrug, Artist's Diploma, Boston University, 1990-92; Graduate studies with Aldo Parisot, Yale University School of Music, 1992-. *Career:* Solo recitals, USSR, Massachusetts, Virginia, Washington DC, and soloist with orchestras, Young Performers Series, Moscow, Minsk, Gorky, Ulianovsk, Lugansk and local philharmonic orchestras, USSR, and Central Massachusetts Symphony, USA, 1985-91; With Clazunov String Quartet, USSR, Poland, Greece, Japan, Germany; Artist-in-Residence, Banff Music Festivl, 1993. *Recordings:* Moscow State Radio, 1987; With Glazunov String Quartet, Athens Radio, Greece, 19899; WBGH Public Radio, Boston, Massachusetts, 1991; WCUW Radio, Worcester, Massachusetts, 1992. *Honours:* 1st Prize, Concertino Praha International Competition, Prague, 1981; 1st Prize, All-Union String Quartet Competition, Voronezh, USSR, 1987. *Hobbies:* Singing (mezzo-soprano); Playing the piano (Bach, Mozart, Chopin). *Address:* 15 Bellvista Road, Boston, MA 02146, USA.

ANNEAR Gwynneth, b. 1939, Tailenbend, South Australia. Singer (Soprano and Mezzo-Soprano). *Education:* Studied at the University of Adelaide and at the Royal College of Music, London. *Debut:* Sang in Amahl and the Night Visitors while at the RCM, 1964. *Career:* Sang the title role in Anna Bolena by Donizetti at the 1965 Glyndebourne Festival; Tour of Italy with Italian company 1968, in Fidelio and Così fan Tutte; Has sung at the Camden Festival and with opera companies in Australia; Frequent broadcasts and concert engagements; Glyndebourne Festival 1970 and 1973, First Lady in Die Zauberflöte. Address: c/o Australian Opera, Sydney Opera House, Sydney, New South Wales, Australia.

ANSELL Gillian, b. 1968, Auckland, New Zealand. Violist. *Education:* Studied at Royal College of Music, London, and with Igor Ozim and the Amadeus Quartet in Cologne. *Career:* Played with Kent Opera Orchestr, Chamber Orchestra of Europe and Philharmonia, 1984-; Co- founded New Zealand String Quartet, under auspices of Music Federation of New Zealand, 1987; Debut concert, Wellington, May 1988; Concerts at Tanglewood School, USA, Banff International Competition, Canada; Performances with Lindsay Quartet at International Festival of the Arts, Wellington, 1990; Soloist with New Zealand Symphony Orchestra; Artist-in-Residence, Victoria University, Wellington; Tour to Australia for Musica Viva Australia, 1990; New Zealand tours, 1992; Concerts in New York, 1993. *Recordings include:* Several albums. *Address:* c/o Ingpen and Williams Ltd, 14 Kensington Court, London W5 5DN, England.

ANTHONY Charles, b. 15 July 1929, New Orleans, Louisiana, USA. Singer (Tenor). *Education:* Studied voice with Dorothy Hulse at Loyola University; continued training with Riccardo Picozzi and Giuseppe Ruisi in Italy. *Career:* Won Metropolitan Opera Auditions of the Air, 1952; Met debut 1954, as Missail in Boris Godunov; later sang Ernesto in Don Pasquale, Almaviva in Il Barbiere di Siviglia, David in Die Meistersinger and Nemorino in L'Elisir d'Amore; sang nearly 2000 performances with Met company; also sang as guest in Dallas, Santa Fe and Boston; Sang Eisslinger in a new production of Die Meistersinger at the Metropolitan, 1993. *Address:* c/o Metropolitan Opera House, Lincoln Center, New York, NY 10023, USA.

ANTHONY James Raymond, b. 18 Feb 1922, Providence, Rhode Island, USA. Professor; Musicologist. m. Louise MacNair, 24 May 1952, 1 son, 2 daughters. *Education:* BS, 1946, MA, 1948, Columbia University, New York; Diploma, Sorbonne, University of Paris, France, 1951; PhD, University of Southern California, USA, 1964. *Career includes:* Professor of Musicology, University of Arizona. *Publications:* French Baroque Music, 1974, 2nd Edition, 1978, Paperback, 1981; Book III of Montéclair's Sonatas (with D Akmajian), 1979; La musique en France à l'époque baroque, 1981; De profundis, M R Delalande, 1981. *Contributor to:* Church Music in France, 1661-1750 (with N Dufourcq) in New Oxford History of Music, 1975; Over 40 articles in New Grove Dictionary of Music and Musicians, 1981; MQ; Journal of the American Musicological Society; Notes; Early Music; Acta Musicologica; Recherches; Others. *Honours:* Grants from ACLS, American Philosophical Society; Festschrift: Studies on Jean-Baptiste Lully and French Baroque Music in honor of James R Anthony, 1987. *Memberships:* American Musicological Society (Council Member 1975-77, 1983-85); Société Française de Musicologie; American Association of University Professors. *Hobbies:* Reading; Travel; Hiking. *Address:* 800 North Wilson Avenue, Tucson, AZ 85719, USA.

ANTOINE Bernadette, b. 8 March 1940, Nancy, France. Singer (Soprano). *Education:* Studied at the Conservatories of Nancy and Paris. *Debut:* Theatre Region Parisienne 1967, as Musetta. *Career:* Has sung at the Grand Opéra and the Opéra-Comique, Paris, and in Lyon, Marseille, Toulouse, Rouen, Hamburg, Brussels, Lisbon and Geneva; ORTF, Radio France, in the 1972 premiere of Don Juan ou l'amour de la geometrie by Semenov; Strasbourg 1974, in the premiere of Les Liaisons Dangereuses by Prey; Repertoire includes works by Gluck, Mozart, Puccini, Berlioz, Debussy, Poulenc, Britten and Prokofiev; Many concert appearances.

ANTOKOLETZ Elliott Maxim, b. 3 Aug 1942, Jersey City, New Jersey, USA. Musicologist. m. Juana Cnabal, 28 May 1972, 1 son. *Education:* Violin, Juilliard School of Music, 1960-65; BA, Musicology, 1968, MA, Musicology, 1970, Hunter College, City University of New York; PhD, Musicology, Graduate Center, City University of New York, 1975. *Career:* Instructor, Violin, Chamber, Brearley School, 1970-76; Lecturer, Ear Training, Chamber Music, Faculty String Quartet, Queens College, City University of New York, 1973-76; Professor, Musicology, University of Texas, Austin, 1976-; Editor, International Journal of Musicology. *Publications:* Books include: The Music of Bela Bartok: A Study of Tonality and Progression in Twentieth-Century Music, 1984; Bela Bartok, A Guide to Research, 1988; Twentieth Century Music, 1992; 3 chapters in The Bartok Companion; In progress: George Perle: A Bio-Bibliography; Stravisky's Les Noces: Genesis and

Structure (with Pieter C van den Toorn). *Contributions to:* Journal of the American Musicological Society; Musica/Realta; Musik und Dichtung; Studia Musicologica; Tempo. *Address:* Department of Music, University of Texas at Austin, Austin, TX 78712, USA.

ANTONACCI Anna Caterina, b. 5 Apr 1961, Ferrara, Italy. Singer (Soprano). *Education:* Studied in Bologna. *Debut:* Sang Rossini's Rosina at Arrezzo, 1986. *Career:* Appeared as Elizabeth I in Maria Stuarda in Bari, 1988, then as Horatia in Cimarosa's Gli Orazi ed i Curiazi in Rome and Lisbon; Further engagements in Venice, Macerata, Catania, Savona and Bergamo as Paisiello's Elfrida, Adalgisa and Fiordiligi; Other roles in Manfroce's Hecuba (Polyxena) and Mayr's La rosa bianca e la rosa rossa; Rossini roles include Dorliska (Torvaldo e Dorliska), Ninetta, Semirmide, and Ermione in British concert premiere of Rossini's Opera, London, 1992; Appeared as Anais in Moise in Bologna, 1991; Rossini's Elisabetta in Naples, 1992, and Elena in La Donna del Lago, Amsterdam Concertgebouw. *Honours include:* Prizewinner at Pavarotti and Callas Competitions. *Address:* c/o Teatro Massimo Bellini, Via Perrotta 12, 95131 Catania, Italy.

ANTONIOU Theodore, b. 10 Feb 1935, Athens, Greece. Composer; Conductor; Teacher. *Education:* Studied violin, voice and theory, National Conservatory, Athens, 1947-58; composition with Yannis Papaioannou, Hellenic Conservatory, 1956-61; composition and conducting with Gunter Bialas, Munich Hochschule für Musik, 1961-65; attended the Darmstadt summer courses, 1963-65. *Career:* Active as a conductor with various contemporary music groups; teacher of composition and orchestration, Stanford University, 1969- 70, University of Utah, 1970, Philadelphia Music Academy, 1970-75, Berkshire Music Center, Tanglewood, 1975, University of Pennsylvania, 1978, Boston University, 1979-. *Compositions:* Stage: Periander, opera, 1977-79; ballets: Bacchae, 1980, and The Magic World, 1984; music theatre pieces; mixed media scores; incidental music to various dramas; film scores; Orchestral: Concerto for clarinet, trumpet, violin and orchestra, 1959; Antithese, 1962; Piano Concertino, 1962; Jeux for cello and strings, 1963; Micrographies, 1964; Violin Concerto, 1965; Kinesis ABCD for 2 string orchestras, 1966; Threnos for wind ensemble, piano, percussion and double bass, 1972; Double Concerto for percussion and orchestra, 1977; The GBYSO Music, 1982; also various choral works, solo vocal pieces and chamber music with tape. *Recordings:* As conductor of his own works and of works by other contemporary composers. *Honours:* Many commissions and awards. *Address:* c/o Music Department, Boston University, Boston, MA 02215, USA.

ANTONSEN Ole Edvard, b. 25 Apr 1961, Furnes, Norway. Trumpeter. *Education:* Studied with Harry Kvaebek at the Norwegian State Academy of Music, diploma 1982. *Career:* Played with the Oslo Philharmonic 1982-90; Solo career from 1990; Concerto appearances with Orchestre de la Suisse Romande, Leipzig Radio Orchestra, Prague Symphony, London Festival Orchestra, Royal Swedish Chamber Orchestra and Cantilena (Scotland); Tour of 15 different countries 1989, including Russia and Brazil; Season 1990 with Paris debut (Oslo Philharmonic) and engagements in Spain, USA (New York and Washington recitals), West Germany and Switzerland; Plays jazz and contemporary music as well as the standard classics. *Recordings include:* Recital with the Norwegian Chamber Orchestra, conducted by Iona Brown; with Wayne Marshall and the ECO, for EMI Classic, 1992. *Honours:* First prize at the 1987 CIEM-competition in Geneva; Laureat of the 1989 UNESCO competition in Bratislava; Norwegian Grammy, Ärets, Spillemann, for his Norwegian recording, Tour de Force, 1992. *Address:* Pro Arte Int, Artists Management, Fosswinckelsgt 9, N-5007 Bergen, Norway.

ANTUNES Jorge, b. 23 Apr 1942, Rio de Janeiro, Brazil. University Professor; Composer; Conductor; Violinist. m. Mariuga Lisboa Antunes, 12 Mar 1969,

3 sons. *Education:* Phys, Master of Composition and Violin, University of Brazil; Master of Composition; Instituto Torcuato di Tella, Buenos Aires; Electronic and electroacoustic music courses; Doctorate, Sorbonne, Paris, France, 1977. *Career:* Professor of Composition, Director, Electronic Music Laboratory and Experimental Music Group, Coordinator of Composition and Conducting, University of Brasilia; General Coordinator of the Nucleus for Studies and Researches in Sonology of University of Brasilia; TV and radio appearances; Numerous recordings. *Compositions:* Cromorfonetica, 1969; Tartinia MCMLXX, 1970; Para Nascer Aqui, 1970-71; Macroformobiles 1, 1972-73; Catastrophe Ultra-Violette, 1974; Plumbea Spes, 1976; Congadasein, 1978; Elegie Violette pour Monseigneur Romero, 1980; Qorpo-Santo, opera, 1983; Sinfonia das Directas, 1984; Dramatic Polimaniquexixe, 1985; Modinha para Mindinha, 1986; Serie Meninos, for young violinist and tape, 1986-87; Amerika 500, 1992; Olga, operra, 1993. *Recordings include:* Jorge Antunes - Musica Electronica, 1975; Jorge Antunes Com A Orquestra Sinfonica Brasileira, 1978; No Se Mata La Justicia - Jorge Antunes, 1981. *Hobby:* Painting. *Address:* University de Brasilia, Depto de Musica, 70910 Brasilia, DF Brazil.

ANTUNES DE OLIVEIRA Glacy, b. 15 Oct 1943, Goiania, Goias, Brazil. Concert Pianist. *Education:* Graduated, Conservatory of Music, Federal University of Goias; Master's degree, National School of Music, Federal University of Rio de Janeiry; PhD, Institute of Arts, Federal University of Goias; Postgraduate work, Rio de Janeiro and USA; Has worked under Professor Jose Kliass, Sao Paulo, and at Brigham Young University, Utah. *Career:* Recitals, solo and chamber music, all over Brazil, North and South America, Germany, Switzerland, Austria; Founder, Director, Musika Centro de Estudos, Goiania; President, National Piano Competition, Coordinator, Postgraduate Diploma Course in Music, Institute of Arts, Federal University. *Recordings:* 3 as Soloist with Orquestra de Camara de Blumenau. *Publications:* Studies and conclusions about Liszt's concept of Piano playing through Martin Krause to Joseph Kliass. *Honours:* Grant to represent Brazil at Sound Celebration II, Louisville, Kentucky, USA, 1993; Bachauer's Representative in South America. *Memberships:* Rodem dos Musicos do Brasil; Advisory Board, Gina Bachauer International Piano Competition; Consultative Committee, Sydney International Piano Competition. *Hobbies:* Poetry; Musicals; Soccer championships. *Address:* Rua 19 No 32 S Oeste, Goiania, Goias 740001-970, Brazil.

ANZAGHI Davide, b. 29 Nov 1936, Milan, Italy. Composer; Teacher. *Education:* Graduated, Milan Conservatory, 1957; Studied composition with E Pozzoli, A Maggioni, G Ghedini and F Donatoni. *Career:* Teacher of composition, Milan Conservatory. *Compositions:* Orchestral: Limbale, 1973; Ausa, 1973; Egophonie, 1974; Aur'ore for Chorus and Orchestra, 1975-76; Ermosonio, 1978; Anco, 1987; First Piano Concerto, 1987-88; Chamber: Limine for string Trio, 1971; Aulografia for Flute, 1975; In-Chiostro for 2 Violins and Viola, 1975, revised 1982; Alena for 10 Wind Instruments, 1976; Remota for 7 Players, 1977; Alia for Bass Clarinet and Piano, 1980; Oiseau triste for Piccolo and Piano, 1980; Soavodia for Clarinet and Piano, 1980; Eco for Cello and Piano, 1980; Onirama for soprano and piano, 1980; Tornelli for Oboe and Piano, 1981; Labia for string Quartet, 1982; Ricrio for Brass Octet, 1982; Soliludio for Flute, Clarinet, Violin, Cello and Piano, 1982; Tremes for Viola; Tremes, for Viola and Piano; Mitofania for Flute, Clarinet, Violin, Cello, Piano and Percussion, 1982; For Four for String Quartet, 1983; Airy for Clarinet, 1983; Halpith for Flute, 1984; Elan for 9 Instruments, 1984; Pri-ter for String Quartet, 1985; Queen That for wind quintet, 1985; Apogeo for 5 Instruments, 1987; Tremes for Viola, 1988; Viol-Once-All, 3 pieces for Cello, 1988; Piano pieces; Second Concerto, for piano and orchestra, 1990-91; Variazioni for piano, Concerto Breve for clarinet and orchestra, 1990-91; Settimino for clarinet, horn, bassoon, piano, violin, viola and cello, 1992; Violin Concert for violin and orchestra, 1992; Third Piano

Concert, for piano and orchestra, 1993. *Address:* Via Previati 37, 20149 Milan, Italy.

APERGHIS Georges, b. 23 Dec 1945, Athens, Greece. Composer. *Education:* Studied with Y Papaioannous, Athens; with I Xenakis, Paris, 1963. *Career:* Founder-director, Atelier Théâtre et Musique, Bagnolet, 1976-91; Nanterre 1992-. *Compositions:* Many musical theatre pieces and operas including: Pandaemonium, opera, 1973; Jacques le Fatalistic, opera, 1974; La Bouteille à la mer for actors, (or amateur musicians) and 4 instruments, 1976; Histoire de loups, opera, 1976; Je vous dis que je suis mort, opera, 1978; Les sept crimes de l'amour, for voice, clarinet and percussion, 1979; Liebestod, opera, 1981; L'écharpe rouge, opera, 1984; Conversations for 2 actors and percussion, 1985; Enumerations for 6 actor-musicians, 1988; Jojo, for 7 actor-musicians, 1990; H, Litanie musicale et égalitaire for 1 soprano, 3 percussions and 4 actors, 1992; Sextuor for 5 female voices and 1 violoncello, 1993. Other works: Vesper, oratorio, 1972; De la nature de l'eau for 6 singers, 2 actors, percussion and piano, 1974; Il Gigante Goglia for soprano and 11 instruments, 1975; 14 recitations for solo voice, 1978; Le corps à corps for solo percussion, 1978; Triangle carré for string quartet and percussion trio, 1989; Tingel-Tangel for voice, accordion and percussion, 1990; Declamations for orchestra, 1990; Ritournelles for 2 baritones, piccolo, clarinet, piano, mandolin, guitar, harp, marimba, violoncello and double-bass, 1992. *Address:* c/o Théâtre des Amandies, 7 av Pablo Picasso, 92022 Nanterre Cedex, France.

APIVOR Denis, b. 14 Apr 1916. Composer. 1 son, 1 daughter. *Education:* Chorister, Christ Church Oxford and Hereford Cathedrals, 1925-30; University College, London, 1934 seq; Studied Pianoforte, Organ, Clarinet; Private Composition pupil, Professor Patrick Hadley and Alan Rawsthorne, 1937-39. *Debut:* 1st London Concert, Wigmore Hall, Apr 1947. *Career:* Works performed: BBC Concert, Broadcasting House, 1950; Royal Ballet, Covent Garden, 1952; Royal Ballet, Sadlers Wells Theatre, 1953; BBC-ICA Concert, 1956; London Proms, 1958; BBC, Camden Theatre, 1960; Dusseldorf and Copenhagen, 1960; Volksoper, Vienna, 1962; Pullitzer Trust, Wigmore Hall, 1967; Cheltenham Festival, 1968; BBC Television, 1968; BBC Invitation Concert, 1973; Royal Northern College, Manchester, 1983; Other occupations, translator of Lorca's verse, sculpture, oriental philosophy. *Compositions:* The Hollow Men, 1951; A Mirror for Witches; Blood Wedding, ballet; Tamar and Amnon for chorus and orchestra; Piano Concerto; Yerma, opera, Sadlers Wells commission; Corporal Jan; Guitar Concerto, 1962; One Man Concert; Triple Concerto for strings; Lorca Songs with guitar, 1972; Neumes, orchestral variations. *Publications include:* Serialism for Guitarists, 1983. *Contributions to:* Setting T S Eliot to Music, (T S Eliot Symposium), 1958; Chapter in Rupert Hart Davis; A Musician's Role in Ballet, to Dancing Times; On Peter Warlock and on Bernard Van Dieren, to Music Review, 1980's. *Memberships:* Composers Guild; Performing Right. *Address:* 9 Ashurst Avenue, Saltdean, East Sussex BN2 8DR, England.

APONTE-LEDÉE Rafael, b. 15 Oct 1938, Guayama, Puerto Rico. Composer; Teacher. *Education:* Took courses in piano, harmony, counterpoint and composition at the Madrid Conservatory, 1957-64, where his principal mentor was Cristobal Halffter; pursued studies with Alberto Ginastera at the Latin American Institute of Higher Musical Studies, Di Tella Institute, Buenos Aires, diploma, 1966. *Career:* Teacher of theory and composition, University of Puerto Rico, 1968-73, and the Puerto Rico Conservatory of Music, 1968-; also promotion of avant-garde music festivals. *Compositions:* Orchestral: Elejia, 1965, revised 1967; Impulsos, in memoriam Julia de Burgos, 1967; Estravagario, in memoriam Salvador Allende, 1973; Dos cuentos para orquesta, 1987; La muchacha de las bragas de oro, 1989; Canción de albada y Epitafio, 1991; Orchestra and Soloist: Cantata, 1988; Chamber Orchestra: a Flor de Piel with two singers; La ventana abierta with two singers; Chamber Opera: El passo de Buster Keaton; Solo Instuments: Tres bagatelas, guitar; Azaleas, clarinet; Tema y seis diferencias, piano; Chamber: Dialogantes for flute and viola, 1965; Epithasis for wind instruments and percussion; piano pieces; many other works for various instruments, tape. *Recordings:* La canción de arte puertorriquena, Margarita Castro, Soprano, 1989; La música de Rafael Aponte Ledée, musica de cámara, 1976. *Publications:* Tema y seis diferencias; Sombras, Zona de Carga y Descarga; La ventana abierta. *Memberships:* Musical Director of Latin American Foundation for Contemporary Music. *Honours:* ASCAP, 1989, 1990, 1991. *Address:* c/o Conservatorio de Musica de Puerto Rico, Apartdo 41227, Minillas Station, Santurce, Puerto Rico 00940.

APPEL Andrew, b. 8 June 1951, New York City, USA. Harpsichordist. *Education:* Duke University, 1969-71; Doctorate, Juilliard School, 1983. *Debut:* Carnegie Recital Hall, 1977. *Career:* Solo Recitals, Europe & USA; Director, Four Nations Ensemble; Festival Participation: Spoleto, Aston Magna; Teaching: Temple University, Juilliard, Princeton; Mostly Mozart. *Recordings:* Bach, Works for Harpsichord, 1983; Couperin Works for Harpsichord, 1989; JB Bach-Bridge, 1987; Couperin, 1991. *Publications:* Gaspard Le Roux - Complete Works, 1989. *Honours:* 1st Prize, Erwin Bodkey Competition, 1977. *Memberships:* American Musical Society; Early Music America; South Eastern Historical Keyboard Society. *Hobbies:* History; Cinema. *Address:* 39 Plaza St, Brooklyn, NY 11217, USA.

APPELGREN Curt, b. 1945, Sweden. Opera Singer (Bass-baritone). *Career:* Began as a violinist and later made his debut as a singer at the Drottningholm Court Theatre, as Dulcamara in L'Elisir d'Amore; Sang Pogner in Götz Friedrich's production of Die Meistersinger at the Royal Opera in Stockholm; other Swedish roles include Cimarosa's Maestro di Capella, Jokanaan in Salome and Leporello in Don Giovanni; Sang Oxenstierna in the premiere of Christina by Hans Gefors, 1986. Perugia Festival, in Spontini's La Vestale; At Glyndebourne he has sung Rocco and Bottom, in Peter Hall's productions of Fidelio and A Midsummer Night's Dream; Bottom at the Hong Kong Festival and Rossini's Basilio at Glyndebourne; Appearances with the London Choral Society and the London Philharmonic Orchestra at the Festival Hall; Sang Johann in a revival of Vogler's Gustaf Adolf och Ebba Braha at Drottningholm, 1990; King Mark in Tristan und Isolde at the Festival Hall, London, 1993. *Address:* c/o Lies Askonas Ltd, 186 Drury Lane, London WC2B 5RY, England.

APPLEBAUM Louis, b. 3 Apr 1918, Toronto, Canada. Composer; Conductor; Administrator; Consultant. m. Janet Hershoff, 19 July 1940, 1 son. *Education:* Harbord Collegiate; University of Toronto; Studied Piano with Boris Berlin, Toronto; Composition with Healey Willan, Sir Ernest MacMillan, Toronto and Roy Harris, Bernard Wagenaar, New York. *Career:* Music Director, National Film Board of Canada, 1940-46; Freelance, Hollywood and New York films, 1946-; Collaborated with Norman McLaren Festival of Britain, 1953; Music Director, Stratford Festival, 1953-60; Consultant and Director, CAPAC/CAB Committee, 1960-70; Adviser, National Arts Centre, 1964-68; Executive Director, Ontario Arts Council, 1970-79; Chairman, Federal Cultural Policy Review Committee, 1979-82; President, CAPAC, 1987-90 (Composers, Authors and Publishers of Canada); President, SOCAN, 1988-92 (Society of Composers, Authors and Music Publishers of Canada). *Compositions include:* Works for orchestra, chorus and orchestra, string quartets, piano, ballet music; Scores for feature films including, Story of GI Joe, Lost Boundaries, Tomorrow the World and scores for several hundred films for National Film Board of Canada, and other producers in Canada, USA and England; Incidental music for over 50 stage productions. *Address:* 1210 Don Mills Road, Apartment 214, Don Mills, Ontario, Canada, M3B 3N9.

APPLETON Jon (Howard), b. 4 Jan 1939, Los Angeles, California, USA. Composer; Teacher.

Education: Studied at Reed College, BA, 1961; privately with Andrew Imbrie in Berkeley, California, 1961-62; with Ussachevsky, Davidovsky and W J Mitchell at the Columbia-Princeton Electronic Music Center, 1965-66. *Career:* Teacher, Oakland University, Rochester, Michigan, I966-67; Dartmouth College, 1967-; founded the Bergman Electronic Music Center there; helped to develop the Dartmouth Digital Synthesizer and the Synclavier. *Publications:* Edited with Perera, The Development and the Practice of Electronic Music, 1975; contributor to many journals.*Honours:* Guggenheim and Fulbright fellowships, 1970. *Compositions:* Orchestral: After Nude Descending a Staircase, 1965; The American Songs for tenor and orchestra, 1966; Chamber: 6 Movements for woodwind quintet, 1964; String Quartet, 1976; piano pieces; Vocal: The Green Waves for chorus, 1964; Ballad of the Soldier for men's voices, 1974; This is America for chorus, 1976; Sonaria for 4 voices and live electronics, 1978; The Lament of Kamuela for 4 voices, electronics, rock band, string quartet, slides, film and video, 1983; many electronic pieces. *Address:* c/o Music Department, Dartmouth College, Hanover, NH 03755, USA.

ARAD Atar, b. 1943, Israel. Violist. *Career:* Member of the Cleveland Quartet, 1980-87; Regular tours of the United States, Canada, Europe, Japan, South America and the Middle East; On faculty of the Indiana University, Bloomington; Concerts in Paris, Lyon, London, Bonn, Prague, Brussels, Houston; Festivals of Salzburg, Edinburgh, Aspen, mostly Mozart and Lucern; In addition to standard repertory, performances of works by John Harbison, Samuel Adler, Christopher Rouse, Toru Takemitsu and Solo Sonata for viola by Atar Arad. *Recordings:* Repertoire from Mozart to Ravel on CBS Masterworks, Pro Arte, RCA Telarc and Teldec; Collaboration Cleveland Quartet, Emanuel Ax and Yo Yo Ma. *Address:* 1657 Bellemeade Avenue, Bloomingotn, IN 47401, USA.

ARAGALL Giacomo, b. 6 June 1939, Barcelona, Spain. Singer (Tenor). *Education:* Studied with Francesco Puig in Barcelona and with Vladimiro Badiali in Milan. *Debut:* La Fenice, Venice, 1963 in the first modern performance of Verdi's Jerusalem. *Career:* La Scala Milan 1963 as Mascagni's Fritz; 1965 sang in Haydn's Le Pescatrici with Netherlands Opera and at the Edinburgh Festival; Vienna Staatsoper debut 1966, as Rodolfo in La Bohème; Covent Garden debut 1966, as the Duke of Mantua; Metropolitan Opera debut 1968; Guest appearances in Berlin, Italy, San Francisco and at the Lyric Opera Chicago; San Carlo Opera Naples 1972, in a revival of Donizetti's Caterina Cornaro; Festivals of Bregenz and Orange 1984, as Cavaradossi and as Don Carlos; Sang Gabriele Adorno at Barcelona, 1990, and Don Carlos at the Orange Festival, 1990; Sang Rodolfo in La Bohème at Barcelona, 1991; Don Carlos at the Deutsche Oper, Berlin, 1992. Other roles include Pinkerton, Romeo (I Capuleti e i Montecchi), Werther and Gennaro (Lucrezia Borgia). *Recordings:* La Traviata, Lucrezia Borgia, (Decca); Faust (RCA); Rigoletto (Eurodisc); Simon Boccanegra, Solti, Decca; Madama Butterfly. *Address:* c/o Stafford Law Associates, 26 Mayfield Road, Weybridge, Surrey KT13 8XB, England.

ARAIZA (Jose) Francisco, b. 4 Oct 1950, Mexico City, Mexico. Opera Singer (Tenor). m. Viviam Jaffray, 30 Sept 1977, 1 son, 1 daughter. *Education:* University of Mexico City; Vocal studies with Irma Gonzalez and Erika Kubacsek (Repertory). *Debut:* In Beethoven's Fidelio (First Prisoner), Mexico City, 1970. *Career:* 1974-78 Karlsruhe Opera, since 1978 fixed member Zurich Opera House; Guest appearances in Vienna, Munich, Hamburg, Berlin, Covent Garden London, Opera Bastille Paris, Scala of Milan, Rome, Parma, Barcelona, Madried, San Francisco, Chicago, Buenos Aires, in Japan and at the International Festivals of Aix-en-Provence, Bayreuth, Salzburg (debut in 1980 under Von Karajan), Edinburgh, Rossini-Festival Pesaro, Schubert-Festival Hohenems; Operatic repertory ranges from Mozart and Rossini to dramatic Italian and French repertory to Wagner roles such as Lohengrin (Venice, 1990) and Walter in Die Meistersinger Von Nünberg (Metropolitan

Opera, New York, 1993), the two highlights of his career. Also famous Lieder and concert singer. *Recordings include:* Tamino in Die Zauberflote; Das Lied von der Erde; Die Schone Mullerin; Il Viaggio a Reims; Così fan Tutte; La Boheme; Faust; Stromminger in La Wally; all the big Mozart roles like Belmonte, Ferrando, Don Ottavio and Idomeneo, Il Barbiere Di Seviglia, Il Viaggio A Reims, Faust, Les Contes D'Hoffmann, La Boheme, Hagenbach in La Wally, Der Freischütz, Das Lied Von Der Erde, Ninth symphony, Die Schöpfung, Mozart Requiem; Arias and Lieder; Several CD-videos including: La Cenerentola; The Abduction from the Seraglio. *Honours:* Deutscher Schallplattenpreis; Orphee d'Or. *Hobbies:* Tennis; Breeding thoroughbreds. *Address:* c/o Kunstlermanagement, M Kursidem, Tal 15, 80331 Munich, Germany.

ARCHER Neill, b. 31 Aug 1961, Northampton, England. Singer (Tenor). *Education:* Studied at the University of East Anglia and the Brevard Music Center in North Carolina. *Career:* Concert engagements with the London Philharmonic, the BBC Symphony, the English Baroque Soloists and the Junge Deutsche Philharmonie; Promenade Concerts debut 1983, with Babylon the Great is Fallen by Alexander Goehr; Festival Hall debut in Mozart's Requiem, followed by Schoenberg's Moses und Aron conducted by John Pritchard; Sang in Bach's St John Passion at the Accademia di Santa Cecilia in Rome, the St Matthew Passion in Stavanger and Schumann's Das Paradies und die Peri at the Paris Opéra; Season 1987-88 with Tamino for Kent Opera, Ferrando for Scottish Opera and Don Ottavio with Welsh National Opera; Teatro Regio Turin 1988, in Testi's Riccardo III: returned to Italy as Andres in Wozzeck at Parma; Buxton Festival 1988 as Ubaldo in Haydn's Armida, followed by Carmina Burana at the Edinburgh Festival; Sang Ferrando in Così fan Tutte for Opera Factory (also televised); Season 1989-90 featured Almaviva in Il Barbiere di Siviglia in Oslo and for Opera North; English National Opera and Covent Garden 1991, as Tamino and Jacquino; Sang Pylade (Iphigénie en Tauride) at Basle, 1991; Season 1991-92 included Don Ottavio in New Zealand and Pelléas with WNO in a Pierre Boulez/Peter Stein presentation of Debussy's opera; Sang the Steersman in a new production of Der fliegende Holländer at Covent Garden, 1992. *Address:* c/o Athole Still Ltd, 113 Church Road, London SE19 2PR, England.

ARCHER Richard Donald, b. 3 July 1947, Leicester, England. Teacher. *Education:* BA, University of Durham; PGCE, Christ's College, University of Liverpool; FRCO (CHM): ADCM, FTCL (Organ); LRAM (Piano accompaniment); ARCM (Organ performing, Honours); MusB, Trinity College, Dublin; MMus, University of Sheffield. *Career:* Organist, recitals at local churches; Solo organist at concerts; Radio broadcasts; Conductor, Hinckley Choral Union; Guest conductor, other societies; Organ and Piano Accompanist for soloists and choirs. *Compositions:* Works for local choirs in manuscript. *Honours:* 1st Prize, Richmond Festival Organ Competition, London, 1972. *Memberships:* Incorporated Society of Musicians; Hymn Society of Great Britain and Ireland; Leicester and District Organists Association, Past President and Secretary; BIOS; Methodist Church Music Society. *Hobbies:* Walking; Reading. *Address:* 11 Frampton Avenue, Leicester LE3 0SG, England.

ARCHER Violet Balestreri, b. 24 Apr 1913, Montreal, Canada. Composer; Teacher; Performer; Adjudicator. *Education:* Teacher's Licence, 1934, BMus 1936, McGill University; Associate, Royal Canadian College of Organists, 1938; BMus 1948, MMus 1949, Yale University, USA. *Debut:* Own composition, Scherzo Sinfonia, Montreal Symphony Orchestra, 1940. *Career:* Faculties: McGill University, 1943-47; North Texas State College, 1950-53; University of Oklahoma, 1953-61; University of Alberta, 1962-78; Visiting Lecturer or Professor, Resident Composer, various other universities & colleges, USA & Canada. *Compositions:* Numerous works, piano, voice, violin, organ, choir, orchestra, harp, trumpet, oboe, saxophone (or combinations). Commissions include: Piano Sonata No. 2, 1979; 4 duets, violin & cello, 1979; Song cycle, 1979; Film score, Whatsoever Things Are True, 1980; Sonata, bassoon & piano, 1980; Psalm 145, a cappella, 1981; Sonata, solo cello, 1981; Sololoquies, B-flat & A clarinets, 1982; 2 Fanfares for a Festive Day, brass quintet, 1989; most published. Performances worldwide; The Owl Queen for High Voice and piano, 1990; Variations for Violin and piano; Improvisation for solo snare drum, 1990. *Recordings:* Numerous & varied. *Honours:* Scholarships, fellowships, awards, honorary degrees. *Hobbies:* Reading; Hiking; Theatre; Films. *Address:* 10805 85th Avenue, Edmonton, Alberta, Canada T6E 2L2.

ARCHIBALD Margaret Helen, b. 3 Feb 1949, London, England. Clarinettist. *Education:* GGSM, Guildhall School of Music and Drama, 1967-70; ARCM, Piano Teachers; Postgraduate certificate of Education, Homerton College, Cambridge, 1971; LRAM, Recital Diploma, Hawkes Prize, Royal Academy of Music, 1972. *Debut:* Wigmore Hall, 1974. *Career:* Appearances at Wigmore Hall, Queen Elizabeth Hall, 1975; member, London Mozart Players, LMP Wind Ensemble, Hanover Band, Sirius Ensemble, Classical Winds; Freelance orchestra work on modern and boxwood clarinets; Clarinet coach, Kent County Youth orchestra; Education and Community Officer to London Mozart Players since 1989, in addition to clarinet work. *Recordings:* With Choir of London Oratory, Missa Scala Aretina, Music for Holy Week; Member of Classical Winds: Mozart Divertimenti for 2 clarinets and bassoon; Beethoven Octet and Sextet; with LMP Wind Ensemble, Mozart 13-wind Serenade. *Contributions to:* Sleeve notes and programme notes. *Hobbies:* Cooking; Walking. *Address:* 17, Hayesford Park Drive, Bromley, Kent, BR2 9DA.

ARDEN-GRIFFITH Paul, b. 18 Jan 1952, Stockport, England. Freelance Opera, Oratorio and Concert Singer (Tenor) in UK and abroad. *Education:* Royal Manchester College of Music; Royal Northern College of Music; GRSM (Teachers), Piano and Singing; ARMCM (Teachers), piano and singing (performers) singing. *Debut:* Puck in Benjamin Britten's A Midsummer Night's Dream, Sadler's Wells Theatre, London, 1973. *Career includes:* Franz Lehar's The Merry Widow etc with English National Opera, London Coliseum; World Premiere of Hans Werner Henze's We Come to the River, Covent Garden, 1976; UK Premiere of Britten's Paul Bunyan, Aldeburgh Festival, 1976; Carlisle Floyd's Of Mice and Men, Wexford Festival, 1980; Carl Orff's Carmina Burana, Singapore Festival of the Arts, 1984; World Concert Tours, 1983, 1985 to Hong Kong, Singapore, Sydney; Greenwich Festival, 1986-87; World Premiere, Andrew Lloyd Webber's The Phantom of The Opera, Her Majesty's Theatre, London, 1986; Mobil Concert Season; Founder Member, Arts Council's Opera 80 UK touring Company; Guest Soloist with Royal Artillery Orchestra; Prokofiev's, The Duenna, Wexford Festival, 1989; Andrew Lloyd Webber, The Great British Musicals, Touring Show, 1990; Wonderful World of Musicals, UK Touring Show, 1991; Count Almaviva in the Rossini Bicentennial UK Tour of The Barber of Seville, 1992; Series of Opera Gala nights aboard Cunard's QE2, 1993. *Recordings:* Debut Record, Paul Arden-Griffith - The Song is You, 1986; The Phantom of The Opera (Original Cast Album), 1987; An Evening with Alan Jay Lerner, 1987; Accolade, 1993; Video Recording: On Stage, Hackney Empire. *Memberships include:* Society of Musicians. *Honours:* Recipient, Gwilym Gwalchmai Jones Scholarship for Singing, RMCM, 1974. *Hobbies:* Travel; Swimming; Painting. *Current Management:* Geoff Stanton Management. *Address:* c/o Ken Spencer Recording Arts, 138 Sandy Hill Road, Woolwich, London SE18 7BA, England.

ARDITTI Irvine, b. 8 Feb 1953, London, England. Violinist. m. Jenny Whitelegg, 3 sons. *Education:* Royal Academy of Music with Clarence Myerscough and Manoug Parikian, 1969-74. *Career:* Concert Violinist; Co-Founder, Leader, Arditti String Quartet, many 20th century music performances, Europe, North America, 1974-; Co-Leader, London Symphony Orchestra, 1976-80; Engagements, major festivals in cities throughout Europe such as Aldeburgh, Bath, BBC Proms, Berlin, Budapest, Paris, Venice Biennale, Vienna and Warsaw, and USA; Resident String Tutor, Darmstadt Ferienkurse for New Music, 1982-; BBC TV Music in Camera, Radio 3 series of 7 recitals, 1987; All Schoenberg's quartets in single recital, Elizabeth Hall, London, Nov 1988; Solo appearances, Turin, Brussels, Berlin, Belgian and Turin Radio Symphony Orchestras, London Sinfonietta, Spectrum and Ensemble Cologne; World premiere, solo works by J Cage (Freeman Etudes), J Dillon, J Harvey, B Ferneyhough, S Gubaidulina, Xenakis; With Arditti Quartet gave complete quartets of Berg, Webern, Schoenberg in Antwerp, Cologne, Frankfurt, Paris, 1991-93; Premieres: Quartets, Georges Aperghis, 1985, Berio Divertimento for Trio, 1987, Bose No 3, 1989, Britten Quartettino, 1983, Gavin Bryars, 1985, Bussotti, 1988, Cage, Music for 4, 1998, Four, 1989; Davies, 1983, Dillon 1, 1982, 2, 1991, Feldman Quintet, 1990, Ferneyhough, Nos 2, 3, 4, Glass, Mishima, 1985, Goehr No 4, 1990, Gubaidulina No 3, 1987, Harvey Nos 1, 2, Hindemith Quartet 1915, 1986, Kagel No 3, 1987, Lachenmann No 2, 1984, Nancarrow No 3, 1988, Ohana No 2, 1982, Pousseur No 2, 1989, Rihm Nos 5,6,8, Roslavetz, 1991; Scelsi No 5, 1985, Trio, 1986, Xenakis Tetras, 1983, Akea Piano Quintet, 1986, Tetora, 1991, Isang Yun Flute Quintet, 1987; Quartets by M Finnissy, M Nyman, T Souster; Rihm's Duomonolog, violin, cello, with R de Saram; Nono's Hay que caminar sognando, 2 violins, with David Alberman, Milan, 1989; Promenade concert debut, 1993, with UK premiere of L Francesconi's Rita Neurali. *Recordings include:* Henze's 5 String Quartets; Ligeti 2 Quartets; Complete Cage music for Quartet; E Carter's Quartets; Bartok Quartets; Complete Quartets of Berg, Webern, Schoenberg; Ferneyhough, Kagel and Nono Quartets; Contemporary solo violin music and Cage Freeman Etudes recital; Premiered new violin and orchestra works by Xenakis, Dox-Orkh, Strasbourg and Lisbon, 1991, Ferneyhough work for violin and ensemble with Asko Ensemble, 1992. *Honours include:* LRAM; Grand Prix du Disque, Paris; Deutsche Schallplattenpreis, 3 times; Chamber Music Award, Royal Philharmonic Society, 1992. *Address:* 57 Rotherwick Rd, London NW11 7DD, England.

ARGENTA Nancy, b. 17 Jan 1957, Nelson, British Columbia, Canada. Singer (Soprano). *Education:* Graduated University of Western Ontario 1980; Vocal study in West Germany and with Peter Pears and Gerard Souzay; Further study with Vera Rosza. *Career:* Appearances at the Vienna and Schwetzingen Festivals with London Baroque; Scarlatti's La Giuditta in Italy; Mozart Mass in C Minor with the English Chamber Orchestra; Handel's Messiah and Giulio Cesare in Canada; Concerts with the Songmakers' Almanac; Opera engagements as Susanna with Welsh National Opera, Haydn's L'Infedeltà Delusa in Paris, Brussels and Cologne, Astreia in Handel's Tamerlano at the Opéra de Lyon, La Chasseuresse in Rameau's Hippolyte et Aricie and Purcell's King Arthur at Aix-en-Provence; Title role in L'Incoronazione di Poppea on South Bank, London; Purcell's Dido in Utrecht, Paris, Beaune and Saintes; Further concerts in the Schoenberg-Reluctant Revolutionary series on South Bank and Cupid in Venus and Adonis by Blow at the 1989 Promenade Concerts; Sang Vespina in Haydn's L'infedeltà delusa, Antwerp 1990; Rossanne in the North American Premiere of Floridante, Toronto, 1990; Sang Clärchen's songs in Beethoven's Egmont at the Festival Hall, 1991; Mozart's Requiem at the 1991 Proms, conducted by Roger Norrington. *Recordings include:* Handel's Solomon and the Magnificat by Bach (Philips); Bach B Minor Mass, St John Passion and Christmas Oratorio, Monteverdi Orfeo (Deutsche Grammophon Archiv); Handel's Tamerlano (Erato); Barbarina in Le Nozze di Figaro (Decca). *Address:* c/o Ron Gonsalves Management, 10 Dagnan Road, London SW12 9LQ, England.

ARGENTO Dominick, b. 27 Oct 1927, York, Pennsylvania, USA. Composer; Teacher. *Education:* Studied with Nicolas Nabokov and Hugo Weisgall at the Peabody Conservatory of Music, Baltimore, B.A. 1951; received training in piano from Pietro Scarpini and in composition from Luigi Dallapiccola at the Florence

Conservatory, 1951-2; studied composition with Bernard Rogers, Howard Hanson and Alan Hovhaness at the Eastman School of Music, Rochester, N.Y. PhD, 1957. *Career:* Teacher of theory and composition, University of Minnesota, 1958-; Regents Professor there, 1979-. *Compositions:* Operas: The Boor, 1957; Colonel Jonathan the Saint, 1958-61; Christopher Sly, 1962-63; The Masque of Angels, 1963; The Shoemaker's Holiday, 1967; Postcard from Morocco, 1971; The Voyage of Edgar Allan Poe, 1975-76; Miss Havisham's Fire,1977-78; Casanova's Homecoming, 1980-84; The Aspern Papers, 1988; Monodramas: A Water Bird Talk, 1974; Miss Havisham's Wedding Night, 1980; Ballets: The Resurrection of Don Juan, 1955; Royal Invitation, or Homage to the Queen of Tonga, 1964; incidental music to plays; Orchestral: Ode to the West Wind, concerto for Soprano and Orchestra, 1956; Variations The Mask of Night, 1965; Bravo Mozart!, 1969; A Ring of Time, Preludes and Pageants, 1972; In Praise of Music, 1977; Fire Variations, 1981; Casa Guidi, 5 Songs for Mezzo-Soprano and Orchestra, 1983; Le Tombeau d'Edgar Poe, 1985; Capriccio: Rossini in Paris for Clarinet and Orchestra, 1986; Chamber: Divertimento for Piano and Strings, 1954; String Quartet, 1956; Vocal: Songs about Spring for Soprano and Piano or Chamber Orchestra, 1954; 6 Elizabethan Songs for High Voice and Piano, 1958; The Relevation of St John the Divine for Tenor, Men's Voices, Brass and Percussion, 1966; A Nation of Cowslips for Chorus, 1968; Letters from Composers for Tenor and Guitar, 1968; Tria carmina paschalia, Easter cantata for Women's Voices, Harp and Guitar, 1970; To be Sung Upon the Water, song cycle for High Voice, Clarinet and Piano, 1972; Jonah and the Whale, oratorio for Tenor, Bass, Narrator, Chorus and Small Ensemble, 1973; From the Diary of Virginia Woolf, song cycle for Mezzo-Soprano and Piano, 1974; Peter Quince at the Clavier for Chorus and Piano, 1979; I Hate and I Love, song cycle for Chorus and Percussion, 1981; The André Expedition, song cycle for Baritone and Piano, 1982; Te Deum for Chorus and Orchestra, 1987. *Honours:* Fulbright Fellowship, 1951-52; Guggenheim Fellowships, 1957, 1964; Pulitzer Prize in Music, 1975; numerous commissions; honorary doctorates. *Memberships:* Institute of the American Academy and Institute of Arts and Letters, 1980.*Address:* c/o School of Music, University of Minnesota, Minneapolis, MN 55455, USA.

ARGERICH Martha, b. 5 June 1941, Buenos Aires, Argentina. Pianist. *Education:* Studied with V. Scaramuzza in Argentine, and with Friedrich Gulda, Madeleine Lipatti, Nikita Magaloff and Michelangeli in Europe. *Debut:* 1946. *Career:* Gave recitals in Buenos Aires 1949, 1952; Moved to Europe 1955; London debut 1964; Soloist with the world's leading orchestras; Often heard in Chopin, Liszt, Schumann, Prokofiev and Bartók; Duo partnership with the violinist Gidon Kremer: London recital 1988, with sonatas by Schumann, Franck and Bartók; Played Beethoven's 3rd Concerto with Chamber Orchestra of Europe, Barbican Hall, London, 1991. *Honours include:* Winner, International Music Competition Geneva 1957; Winner, Busoni Competition Bolzano, 1957; First Prize, Seventh Warsaw International Chopin Competition, 1965; Polish Radio Prize 1965.

ARGIRIS Spiros, b. 24 Aug 1948, Athens, Greece. Conductor. *Education:* Studied piano with Alfons Kontarsky, conducting with Hans Swarowsky; Paris with Nadia Boulanger. *Career:* Conducted at opera houses in Berlin, Hamburg, Cologne and elsewhere in Germany; Has led concerts at the Venice Biennale and at the Maggio Musicale, Florence; Musical Director of the Festival of Two Worlds, Spoleto-Charleston, 1986: conducted Salome 1989; Musical Director of the Trieste Opera 1987, leading The Queen of Spades 1988 and Il Barbiere di Siviglia and Parsifal 1989; Conducted Elektra at the Teatro Nuovo, Spoleto, 1990; Parsifal and Le Nozze di Figaro at Charleston; Modern repertoire includes Henze's El Rey de Harlem (premiere 1980) and Hans Jurgen von Böse's Die Nacht aus Blei (premiere 1981); Appointed Musical Director of the Opera and Orchestre Philharmonique at Nice, 1988. *Address:*

Orchestre Philharmonique de Nice, Opera de Nice, 4 Rue Saint-Francois de Paule, F-06 300 Nice, France.

ARIONDO Nicholas Samuel Jr, b. 10 July 1949, Pittsburgh, Pennsylvania, USA. Musician (Accordionist)/Composer. m. Lorna Teske, 18 Sept 1977. *Education:* BA, Music, 1976, MA, Music, 1980, California State University, Los Angeles. *Career:* Accordionist, symphony orchestras and ensembles; Director, Nick Ariondo Chamber Ensemble; Accompanist, vocalists and instrumentalists; Subject of Accordion Arts cover story, 1978; Music composed for him includes Roy Jelinek's Trepidations for Accordion and Digital Tape, 1990-91; Ross Whitney's TriLucences for Free-Bass Accordion, Piano and Clarinet, 1990; Charles Buel's Works for Accordion and Electronic Keyboards, 1989-90; Radio and Cable TV interviews/concerts: The Art of the Classical Accordion, The Nick Ariondo Chamber Ensemble, The Artistry of Nick Ariondo; Composer, Arranger, Performer, film, TV, studio sessions; Some works in International Museum of Accordions, Italy, 1987, Primose International Viola Archive, Brigham Young University Library, Utah, 1989; Director, Accordion Studies, California State University, Los Angeles, 1990-. *Compositions include:* Kalamatiano for Viola and Free-Bass Accordion, 1983; Arabesque, string sextet, accordion, 1983; Duo for String Bass and Free-Bass Accordion, 1985; Shalakho for Flute, Viola, Harp and Free-Bass Accordion, 1986; Tarantella for Soprano and Free-Bass Accordion, 1987; Matsuri, piano, accordion, 1988; Accordion Concerto in G Minor (with Edward Hosharian), 1991; Acco-sphere, solo accordion, 1993; Publisher, Acco-Music Publishing. *Contributor to:* Journal of the American Viola Society, Keyboard magazine, Arroyo Arts Collective, others. *Honours include:* International Grand Prix, Accordion Federation of North America, 1974, 1978, 1987; Distinguished Music Alumnus Award, Friends of Music, California State University, Los Angeles, 1987; Castelfiardo Prize, International Composers Composition, Italy, 1987; 7 ASCAP Awards, 1987-93; Invited to perform own works, 17th International Viola Congress, Redlands University, California, 1989; Artists Fellowship Grant, California Arts Council, 1990-91. *Memberships include:* Musicians Union Local 47; American Society of Authors, Composers and Publishers; Friends of the Accordion, Past President, Independent Composers Association. *Address:* 4120 W Avenue 41, Los Angeles, CA 90065, USA.

ARISTO Giorgio, b. 28 Dec 1950, New York City, New York, USA. Singer (Tenor). *Education:* Studied at Manhattan School of Music and in Milan and Zurich. *Career:* Sang at Passau, 1979-81, as the Duke in Rigoletto, Rodolfo in La Boheme and Rossini's Count Almaviva; Engaged in Essen, 1981-83, Hanover, 1983-; Guest appearances in Dusseldorf as Don José, Vienna as Massenet's Werther, Munich in The Bartered Bride, and Copenhagen as Cavradossi; Season 1988-89 as Calaf in Nantes and Andrea Chenier in Toulon and Liège; Other roles include Alfredo and Turiddu; Many concert appearances. *Address:* c/o Opera Royale de Wallonie, 4 Leopoldstrasse, B-1000 Brussels, Belgium.

ARKHIPOVA Irina Konstantinova, b. 2 Dec 1925, Moscow, USSR. Singer (Mezzo-Soprano). *Education:* Studied with Leonid Savranski at the Moscow Conservatory. *Career:* Sang at Sverdlovsk 1954-56; Member of the Bolshoi Opera, Moscow from 1956: has sung Azucena, Marina, Marfa (Khovanshchina), Amneris, Eboli and Charlotte; Further Russian repertoire includes Lyubasha (The Tsar's Bride), Polina and Lyubov (The Queen of Spades), and parts in the Bolshoi premieres of War and Peace and The Story of a Real Man by Prokofiev, Khrennikov's The Mother and Shchedrin's Not Love Alone; Teatro San Carlo Naples 1960, as Carmen; La Scala Milan 1964 as Helen in War and Peace (with the Bolshoi Company): 1967-71, as Marfa and Marina; Orange and Covent Garden 1972 and 1975, as Azucena; San Francisco 1972, as Amneris; Savonlinna Festival, Finland, 1989 as Marfa, Khovanshchina; Sang Ulrica at Covent Garden, 1988; Appeared with the Kirov Opera at the Metropolitan, (the

Countess in The Queen of Spades), 1992; and as the Nurse in Eugene Onegin at the Théâtre du Châtelet, 1992. *Recordings:* War and Peace, Khovanshchina, Boris Godunov, The Snow Maiden; The Queen of Spades, Mazeppa (Melodya); Alexander Nevsky by Prokofiev (Decca). *Honours include:* People's Artist of the USSR, 1966. *Address:* c/o Royal Opera House, Covent Garden, London, WC2.

ARMILIATO Fabio, b. 1962, Genoa, Italy. Singer (Tenor). *Education:* Studied at the Paganini Conservatoire of Music and at the Accademia Virgiliana in Mantua. *Debut:* Teatro Pergolesi di Jesi, 1986, as Licinio in La Vestale. *Career:* Appearances throughout Italy and in Lyon, Stuttgart, Graz, Essen, Dublin and Wexford; Other roles have included Alfredo, Edgardo, Gianetto (La Cena delle Beffe), Gabriele Adorno, Manrico, Ernani, Arrigo (I Vespri Siciliani), Riccardo, Turiddu, Don Carlo, Pinkerton, Cavaradossi and Vincent in Mireille. *Honours:* First Prize in the Tito Schipa Competition at Lecce and in the Pavia Lirica Voci Nuove Competition. *Address:* c/o Music International, 13 Ardilaun Road, London N5 2QR, England.

ARMITSTEAD Melanie, b. 1957, England. Singer (Soprano). *Education:* Studied at Guildhall School of Music. *Debut:* Frasquita and Micaela in Carmen for Scottish Opera. *Career:* Appearances with Kent Opera, 1987-, as Venus in Pygmalion, First Lady in The Magic Flute, Minerva in The Return of Ulysses; Scottish Opera debut as Titania in Eugene Onegin, 1988, returning as Fiordiligi; English National Opera and Opera North debuts, 1990, as Nicoletta in The Love for Three Oranges and Melisande in Ariane et Barbe-Bleue; Returned to Leeds as Xenia in Boris Godunov, 1992; Created the Niece in Fenelon's Le Chevalier Imaginaire, Théâtre de Châtelet, Paris, 1992; Concert performances with Liverpool Philharmonic, the Halle and Royal Philharmonic; Season 1989-90 included Vivaldi's Gloria with English Chamber Orchestra, Messiah with Tokyo Philharmonic, St John Passion in Netherlands, and Bach's Magnificat at the Barbican Hall; Recitalist at the Wigmore Hall (debut 1987), Purcell Room and Elizabeth Hall; Appearances with pianist Julian Drake and oboist Nicholas Daniel. *Address:* c/o Opera North, The Grand Theatre, 46 New Briggate, Leeds, Yorkshire LS1 6NU, England.

ARMSTRONG Agnes Rose Fingerlin, b. 9 June 1943, Elizabeth, New Jersey, USA. Organist; Musicologist. m. Ronald William Armstrong, 29 June 1963, 1 son, 2 daughters. *Education:* Hartwick College, Oneona, New York; BA, State University of New York at Albany, 1974; MS, College of Saint Rose, Albany, 1983; MA, New York University, 1993; Piano study with Stanley Hummel; Organ study with Robert Schanck, Pauline Law Mehrtens and Lloyd Cast. *Career:* Organist, Music Director, St John's Lutheran and Helderberg Reformed Churches, Guilderland, New York, and other upstate New York churches; Concerts and lectures specialising in 19th century works for organ; Teacher of Organ, Piano and Music Theory; Scholar and Musicologist. *Compositions:* Tricentennial Hymn of the City of Albany, New York, 1986; Compositions for organ; Children's plays with music. *Publication:* The Wizard of the Organ, 1993. *Contributor to:* Articles and reviews for The American Organist, La Flute Harmonique, The Tracker, The American Music Teacher, Reed Organ Society Bulletin, The New England Organist. *Honours:* Sigma Alpha Iota, 1962; Colleague Certificate, American Guild of Organists, 1978; Delta Epsilon Sigma, 1983; Fellow, American Organ Archive, 1989, 1991; Research Residency, New York State Library, 1993. *Memberships:* District Convener, Past Dean, American Guild of Organists; Vice-President, International Reed Organ Society; Alliance Francaise; Association Cavallie-Coll; Organ Historical Society; American Musicological Society; Music Teachers National Association, New York State Chairman for Organ. *Hobbies:* Travel; Antiques; Cats. *Address:* 168 Main Street, Altamont, NY 12009, USA.

ARMSTRONG Karan, b. 14 Dec 1941, Horne,

Montana, USA. Singer (Soprano). m. Götz Friedrich. *Education:* Studied in Minnesota with Thelma Halverson; California with Lotte Lehmann and Fritz Zweig. *Debut:* Metropolitan Opera 1969, in Hansel and Gretel. *Career:* San Francisco 1970, Musetta in La Bohème; Appearances with opera companies in Houston, Seattle, Cincinnati and Portland: roles include Donizett's Norina and Adina, Puccini's Butterfly and Tosca, Verdi's Alice Ford and Wagner's Eva; New York City Opera 1975-78 as Minnie, Tosca, Concepcion (L'Heure Espagnole) and the Queen of Shemakha; European debut Strasbourg 1976, as Salomé; Guest appearances in Munich, Frankfurt, Geneva, Oslo and Vienna; Bayreuth debut 1979, as Elsa; World premiere performances in Von Einem's Jesu Hochzeit (Vienna 1980), Sinopoli's Lou Salomé (Munich 1981) and Berio's Un Re in Ascolto (Salzburg 1984); Covent Garden 1981, as Lulu in the first British performance of the 3-act version of Berg's opera; Other roles include Debussy's Mélisande (Berlin 1984), Berg's Marie and The Woman in Schoenberg's Erwartung; Sang Katerina Ismailova at Berlin, 1988, Elena Makropoulos and Regina in Mathis der Maler, 1990; Wiesbaden Festival, 1989, as Katya Kabanova; Alice Ford at Los Angeles, 1990, followed by Leonore; sang Wagner's Sieglinde and Gutrune at Covent Garden, 1991; Sang Janáfek's Emilia Marty at Los Angeles, 1992; Megara in the premiere of Desdemona und ihre Schwestern by Siegfried Matthus, Schwetzingen Festival, 1992; Concert appearances in the Four Last Songs of Strauss, Zemlinsky's Lyric Symphony and the Bruchstücke from Wozzeck. *Recordings include:* Elsa in the Bayreuth production of Lohengrin (CBS). *Address:* c/o Harrison/Parrott Ltd, 12 Penzance Place, London W11 4PA, England.

ARMSTRONG Richard, b. 1 July 1943, Leicester, England. Conductor. *Education:* Studied at Cambridge University. *Career:* Member of Music Staff at Royal Opera, Covent Garden, 1966-68; Music Director of Welsh National Opera 1973-86: conducted Elektra, Die Frau ohne Schatten, Wozzeck, operas by Janáfek, The Midsummer Marriage and Peter Grimes; Led the Welsh company in The Ring at Covent Garden 1986; Covent Garden debut 1982, Billy Budd: returned for Andrea Chénier, Un Ballo in Maschera and Don Carlos 1989; Guest engagements with Netherlands Opera (Elektra), Komische Oper Berlin (Peter Grimes), Frankfurt (Der fliegende Holländer); new productions of Elektra and Ariadne auf Naxos; and at Geneva (Don Carlos); Conducted the premiere of John Metcalf's Tornrak for WNO, 1990, followed by Otello and House of the Dead; music director of Scottish Opera; conducted Moses und Aron, and La Voix humaine at the 1992 Edinburgh Festival. *Address:* c/o Ingpen and Williams Ltd, 14 Kensington Court, London W8 5DN, England.

ARMSTRONG Sheila, b. 13 Aug 1942, Ashington, England. Singer (Soprano). *Education:* Royal Academy of Music. *Career:* Sang Despina in Così fan Tutte at Sadler's Wells 1965; Glyndebourne 1966, as Belinda in Dido and Aeneas: returned as Mozart's Pamina and Zerlina and Fiorila in Rossini's Il Turco in Italia; At the 1970 Three Choirs Festival sang in the premiere of John McCabe's Notturni ed Alba; New York debut 1971 with the New York Philharmonic; later sang with the Los Angeles Philharmonic under Mehta; Covent Garden debut 1973, as Marzelline in Fidelio; Donizetti's Norina and Mozart's Donna Elvira for Scottish Opera; Concert enagements include Messiah at the Concertgebouw; Tour of Far East with the Bach Choir; Britten's Spring Symphony conducted by Previn; Strauss's Four Last Songs with the Royal Philharmonic; Also heard in Elgar's Oratorios and the Sea Symphony by Vaughan Williams; Conductors include Barenboim, Bernstein, Boult, Giulini, Haitink, Leppard and Mackerras; Song recitals in the UK and abroad. *Recordings:* Samson, Dido and Aeneas, Deutsche Grammophon; Mozart's Requiem, Carmina Burana, Elgar's Apostles and The Pilgrim's Progress (HMV); Cantatas by Bach; Haydn's Stabat Mater; Beethoven's Ninth Symphony CEMD; Mahler's Fourth, CBS. *Honours:* Won Kathleen Ferrier Memorial Award and Mozart Prize at the RAM. *Address:* c/o

Harrison/Parrott Ltd, 12 Penzance Place, London W11 4PA, England.

ARNAULD Serge, b. 16 Nov 1944, Geneva, Switzerland. Composer; Scholar. m. Christiane Wirz, 16 Jan 1965. 3 sons, 1 daughter. *Education:* Maîtrise, Philosophy Education, supervised by Prof Vladimir Jankelevitch, Sorbonne, Paris, 1973; Studied composition with Darius Milhaud; Marcel Landowski; Adrienne Clostre and Louis Saguer. *Career:* Radio: Swiss selection for Paul Gilson Prize and for Prix Italia with Pugilat, 1979; and miniopera, Masculin-Singulier, 1987; Films: Jean-Luc Godard: Sauve qui peut (la vie) et Passion, participated as actor; Musicology: Les manuscrits de Carpentras, 1979; Scenes de la vie judeo-comtadine, 1980; Founder and Artistic Director: International Music Festival, from the Academies of Rome, 1984-88; Collaborator a la dramaturgie au Grand Théatre de Genève, 1989. *Compositions:* Le Jeu de la Tarasque, Ballet-pantomime, 1985; L'Esprit de Genève, produced by Jean-Louis Martinoty, 1986, performance to commemorate the 450th anniversary of the Reformation in Geneva; Guillaume-Tell en Jacobin, performance to commemorate the bicentenary of the French Revolution and for the 700th anniversary of the Swiss Confederation, 1991. *Recordings:* Cantates Ambivalentes; Requiem de Pâques; L'Amour. *Publications:* La Coronalité and Le Systeme Hexacordal, Paris, 1968-69. *Honour:* Member, Institut Suisse, Rome, 1983. *Hobby:* Travel in Asia. *Address:* 6 rue de la Mairie, 1207 Geneva, Switzerland.

ARNELL Richard Anthony Sayer, b. 15 Sept 1917, Hampstead, London. Composer. m. Joan Heycock, 1992. *Education:* University College School, London; Royal College of Music. *Career:* Music Consultant, BBC North American Service, 1943-46; Lecturer Royal Ballet School, 1958-59; Editor, The Composer, 1961-64; Chairman: Composers' Guild of Great Britain, 1964, 1974-75; Visiting Professor Hofstra University, New York, 1968-70; Music Director and Board Member, London International Film School, 1975-88; Music Director, Ram Filming Ltd 1980; Vice-President, Friends of Trinity College of Music Junior Department, 1987- ; Founder Chairman: Tadcaster Civic Society Arts Committee, 1988-91; Founder Chairman: Saxmundham Music and Arts, 1992. *Compositions:* Operas: Love in Transit; Moonflowers; Ballets: Punch and the Child; Harlequin in April; The Great Detective; The Angels; Orchestral: 6 Symphonies; 2 Concertos for Violin; Concerto for Harpsichord; 2 Concertos for Piano; Symphonic Portrait Lord Byron; Landscapes and Figures; Robert Flauerty: Impression; Ode to Beecham 1986; Chamber: 6 String Quartets; 2 Quintets; Piano Trio; Piano Works; Music for Wind instruments; Brass Instruments; Electronic Music; Song Cycles; Numerous film scores. *Publication:* Technique of Film Music (co-editor). *Memberships:* Composers' Guild of Great Britain; ACTT Union; Savage Club. *Honours:* Tadcaster Town Council Merit Award, 1990. *Address:* c/o Composers Guild of G B, 34 Hanway Street, London W1P 9DE, England.

ARNESTAD Finn (Oluf Bjerke), b. 23 Sept 1915, Kristiania (now Oslo) Norway. Composer; Music Critic. *Education:* Studied violin and piano, Oslo; Studied composition with Bjarne Brustad; African and Oriental Folk Music, Paris, 1952. *Career:* Wrote music criticism, Oslo. *Compositions:* Orchestral: Constellation, 1948; Conversation for Piano and Orchestra, 1950; Meditation, 1952; INRI, 2 suites from a symphonic mystery play, 1952-55; Violin Concerto, 1957; Aria Appassionata, 1962; Cavatina Cambiata, 1965; Overture, 1970; Toccata, 1972; Arabesque, 1975; Piano Concerto, 1976; Mouvement Concertant for Double Bass and Orchestra, 1978; Chamber: String Quartet, 1947; Sextet for Flute, Clarinet, Bassoon, Violin, Cello and Piano, 1959; Quintet for Flute and Strings, 1962; Suite in Old Dance Rhythms for Flute, Oboe, Harpsichord and Strings, 1966; Trombone Sonata, 1971; Solo Violin Sonata, 1980; Solo Double-bass Sonata, 1980; Piano music; Several vocal works.

ARNETOVÁ Renata, b. 22 Sept 1936, Prague, Czechoslovakia. Pianist. *Education:* Conservatory of Music, Prague, 1952-57; Academy of Music, Prague, 1957-61, 1974-75; Conservatory of Music, Moscow, USSR, 1964-65. *Career:* Pedagogue: Popular Conservatory, Prague, 1962-66; Academy of Music, Prague, 1966-69; Pedagogical Faculty, Ceske Budejovice, 1973-78; Soloist, Moravian Philharmonic, Olomouc, 1967-72. *Recordings:* Sonata, Reflections of the Life (Slavicky); Sonatas 1 and 31 (Beethoven). *Publication:* Study of Piano Compositions, 1979; The Book, Meditations, 1992. *Honours:* 1st prize, Czechoslovak Youth Music Competition, 1960; Award, Prague Spring Competition, 1963; 5th prize, M Long/J Thibaud Competition, Paris, 1965. *Membership:* Czech Composers' Association. *Address:* Byt 53 Pofernická 513/56, 108 00 Prague 10 Maleuice, Czech Republic.

ARNOLD Ben, b. 29 Jan 1955, Lancaster, Kentucky, USA. Music Professor. *Education:* BM, 1977, MM, Piano Performance, 1981, PhD, Musicology, 1986, University of Kentucky. *Publications:* Music and War: A Research and Information Guide, 1993. *Contributor to:* The Musical Quarterly; New Grove Dictionary of American Music; Holocaust and Genocide Studies; Journal of the American Liszt Society; International Review of the Aesthetics and Sociology of Music; Biographical Dictionary of Soviet-Russian Music; Encyclopedia of Keyboard Instruments. *Honours:* National Endowment for the Humanities Grant for The Operas of Wagner, Summer Seminar. *Hobbies:* Film; Reading; Book-collecting; Travel. *Address:* 101 Humanities Bldg, Department of Music, Emory University, Atlanta, GA 30322, USA.

ARNOLD David Charles, b. 25 Dec 1943, Atlanta, Georgia, USA. Opera/Concert Singer. *Debut:* Metropolitan Opera, Enrico in Lucia; English National Opera, Escamillo in Carmen; New York City Opera, Zurga in Pêcheurs de Perles. *Career:* Performances of many world premieres, including John Harbison's, Full Moon in March and his Winter's Tale; David Diamond's Ninth Symphony for Baritone and Orchestra, Leonard Bernstein Conducting at Carnegie Hall; Specimen Days by Charles Fussell; Guest appearance at the White House singing Berlioz's L'Enfance du Christ; performances of Amonasro in Aida with Opera Company of Boston, L'Opera de Montréal and Opera Omaha; Le Nozzee Di Figaro with L'Opéra de Québec; Performances with most leading orchestras including, The Boston Symphony (5 seasons), St Louis Symphony, Atlanta Symphony, American Symphony, San Francisco Symphony, Chicago Symphony and with the Spoleto Festivals. *Recordings:* Harbison's Full Moon in March (CRI); Judith Lang Zaimont's Magic World (Leonard Records); Mendelssohn's Walpurgisnacht (Arabesque Records); The Beethoven 9th Symphony, Harvard University, 1993. *Current Management:* William Knight, Grant House, 309 Wood Street, Burlington, NJ 08016, USA.

ARNOLD John Phillip, b. 21 Oct 1944, Hampstead, London, England. Conductor. m. Gillian Rose, 1 son, 1 daughter. *Education:* Licenciate, Cello teacher 1966, Royal Academy of Music. *Debut:* Royal Ballet, 1968. *Career:* Freelance Conductor with Royal Ballet, BBC Welsh, Scottish, Northern Ireland and Studio Strings orchestras, CBSO, London Mozart Players, and with orchestras in America, France, Italy, Poland, Netherlands, Norway and Switzerland. *Compositions:* Short suite for strings, 1962 and 1966; Scherzo for strings, 1964; Cello Concerto, 1966; Compiler of By Command concert programme on Queen Victoria, 1986. *Honour:* 1st Prize, Lugano International Conductors' Competition, Switzerland, 1978. *Memberships:* Incorporated Society of Musicians; Worshipful Company of Painter-Stainers. *Hobbies:* Tennis; Riding; Squash; Gardening. *Address:* 10 Hocroft Avenue, London, NW2 2EH, England.

ARNOLD Malcolm Henry (Sir), b. 21 Oct 1921, Northampton, England. Composer. 2 sons, 1 daughter. *Education:* Studied trumpet with Ernest Hall, piano with

Hurst Bannister, composition with Gordon Jacob, Royal College of Music, London. *Career:* First trumpet player, London Philharmonic Orchestra, 1942-49 (apart from break for military service, and short spell with BBC Symphony Orchestra); numerous appearances on concert platform as soloist in Haydn, Goedicke, Riisager and other concertos; Mendelssohn Scholarship for study in Italy 1948; Composer of wide range of concert music, and nearly 120 film scores; Omnibus - 70th Birthday, 1991. *Compositions include:* Two operas, The Dancing Master, 1951, and The Open Window, 1956; ballets Homage to the Queen, for the 1953 Coronation, Rinaldo and Armida, 1955, and Electra, 1963; Orchestral: 9 Symphonies, 1951, 1953, 1954, 1960, 1961, 1967, 1973, 1979, 1987; 10 overtures, including Beckus the Dandipratt, 1948, and Tam O'Shanter, 1955; Toy Symphony, 1957; Concertos for clarinet, 1951 and 1974, oboe 1952, flute, 1954 and 1972, harmonica, 1954, guitar, 1961, horn, 1947 and 1956, viola, 1971; two violons, 1962; Trumpet Concerto commissioned by the Royal College of Music in celebration of its foundation in 1988; recorder concerto for Michala Petri, 1988; Cello Concerto commissioned by the Royal Philharmonic Society for Julian Lloyd Webber, first performance Royal Festival Hall, London, 1989; Two Brass Quintets 1961 and 1988 and two String Quartets, 1951 and 1975; Children's pieces include music for The Turtle Drum, for BBC Television; Film music includes The Bridge on the River Kwai (awarded Hollywood Oscar, 1958); The Inn of the Sixth Happiness; Whistle Down the Wind; Wind Octet, 1989; Four Welsh Dances, 1989; Flourish for a Battle for RAF Battle of Britian, 1990; Robert Kett Overture, 1990; Manx Suite, 1990; Fantasy for Recorder and String Quartet, 1991. *Recordings:* Chando, string quartets; Film Suites: Conifer Symphonies 6, 7, 8, and Cancenta's; Hyperium, Chamber music; Reference, Ceventuries *Publications:* Music of Malcolm Arnold, Faber; Malcolm Arnold, Introduction to his music, Faber, Hugo Cole, Novello, Lenenick. *Honours:* Commander of the British Empire, 1970; Bard of the Cornish Gorsedd, 1969; W.W. Cobbett Prize, 1941; Honorary Doctorates of Music, Exeter University 1969, Durham University, 1982; Leicester University, 1983; Honorary member, Royal Academy of Music, London; Ivor Novello Award for outstanding services to British music, 1985; Wavendon Allmusic Composer of the Year 1987; Doctor of Arts and Humane Letters, Miami University, Oxford, USA, 1990; FTCL, 1992; Knights Batchelor, 1993. *Current Management:* Anthony Day. *Address:* 26 Springfields, Attleborough, Norfolk NR17 2PA, England.

ARONOFF Josef, b. 13 June 1932, Budapest, Hungary. Violinist; Violist; Conductor. m. Agnes Schreiber, 3 sons, 1 daughter. *Education:* Franz Liszt Academy of Music, Budapest; Guildhall School of Music, London, England; MBC (UK); AGSM; LRAM. *Career:* Radio and TV appearances, Hungary, Austria, UK, Portugal, France, Germany, USA, Hong Kong, Australia; Professor, Royal Manchester College of Music, England, 1965-70; Head of String Department, Queensland Conservatorium of Music, Australia, 1970-75; Musical Director, Conservatorium, Chamber Orchestra, 1970-75; Musical Director, Artemon Ensemble and Orchestra, 1971-; Concertmaster, Director of Instrumental Studies, Darling Downs Institute of Advanced Education, 1975-77; Conductor, Allegri Players, 1975-77; Senior Lecturer, Adelaide College of Arts, 1977-79; Musical Director, South-Western Symphony Orchestra, 1977-79; Professor, Guildhall School of Music and Drama, England, 1979-88; Professor, Birmingham School of Music, 1979-88; Examiner, Australian Music Examination Board, 1988-. *Recordings:* On CD, JCR: Viola Concerto 1989 by C Reichard-Gross; Memories of Sunny Days for Violin and Orchestra by C Reichard-Gross, with Hungarian Northern Symphony Orchestra, soloist Josef Aronoff (viola/violin), conductor Laszlo Kovacs. *Contributions to:* Music and Musicians; Strad Magazine; International Music Magazine. *Honours:* London's Lord Mayor Sheriff Prize, 1959; Alfred Gibson Prize, 1960; Louis Pecskay Prize, 1960. *Memberships:* Incorporated Society of Musicians; Society of Contemporary Music; European String Teachers Association. *Hobbies:* Sailing; Swimming. *Current*

Management: Camerata Artists, UK; Col Robertson Concert Management, Australia. *Address:* 40 Isabella Street, Tarragindi, Brisbane, Queensland 4121, Australia.

ARROYO Martina, b. 2 Feb 1936, Harlem, New York, NY, USA. Soprano. *Education:* Hunter College of the City University of New York, B.A., 1956. *Career:* Sang in the U.S. premiere of Pizzetti's Assassinio nella cattedrale, N.Y.,1958; Metropolitan Opera debut as the Heavenly Voice in Don Carlos, 1959; appeared in Europe from I963, singing at the Vienna State Opera, Berlin State Opera, Zurich Opera, Covent Garden, London, Paris Opera; sang major roles at the Metropolitan Opera from I965, debut as Aida; has sung several Verdi roles as well as Wagner's Elsa and Mozart's Donna Anna; concert perfomances in music by Varèse, Dallapiccola and Stockhausen; Met Opera, Aida, Santuzza, 1986-87; Seattle Opera, 1988, Turandot. *Recordings:* For Angel-EMI, CBS, Desto, Deutsche Grammophon. Nonesuch, Philips, RCA, Turnabout and Wergo. *Honours:* Winner, Metropolitan Opera Auditions of the Air, 1958; honorary D.H.L., Hunter College of the City University of New York, 1987. *Address:* c/o Thea Dispeker, Inc., 59 East 54th Street, New York, NY 10022, USA.

ARTAUD Pierre-Yves, b. 13 July 1946, Paris, France. Flautist. *Education:* Studied at the Paris Conservatoire, graduated 1970. *Career:* Played the piccolo in the Orchestre Philharmonique, Ile-de- France, 1964-68; Flute with the Orchestra Laetitia Musica 1971; Directed contemporary flute studies at Sainte-Baume 1973-80; Visiting Professor at Pecs and Csingrad in Hungary from 1978; Responsible for instrumental research at IRCAM, Paris (electronic music studio) 1981; Professor at Darmstadt 1982; Performer in such recital groups as Arcadie (quartet of flutes) 1964, Wind quintet Da Camera 1970-72 and the Albert Roussel Quintet, 1973-74; Collaboration with Sylvie Beltrando (harp) and Pierre Bouyer (harpsichord); Has premiered works by Brian Ferneyhough, Betsy Jolas, Tristan Murail, Franco Donatoni, Maurice Ohana, and André Boucourechliev; Professor of Chamber Music at the Paris Conservatoire from 1985, of flute from 1987. *Publication:* La Flûte (Paris, 1987). *Honours:* Prix premier at the Conservatoire, 1969 and 1970; Medal of arts, sciences, letters, 1978; Grand Prix of French contemporary music interpretation, 1982; Prix Charles Inos, 1985; Prix de 1Académie du Disque Français, 1984. *Address:* Conservatoire National Superieur de Musique, 209 Avenue, Jean Jaurès, 75079, Paris, France.

ARTHUR Edna M A, b. 25 May 1928, Edinburgh Scotland. Performer; Violin Teacher. m. Bryce Gould, 4 July 1953, 1 son, 1 daughter. *Education:* Waddell School of Music, Edinburgh, 1934-45; Royal College of Music, London, 1945-48; ARCM, 1945. *Career:* Freelance Violinist; Soloist with BBC Scottish Symphony Orchestra; Founder Member, Scottish Baroque Ensemble & Scottish Chamber Orchestra; Member, New Music Group of Scotland; McGibbon Ensemble; Musical Director, Orpheus Caledonius, Edinburgh Festival, 1986; Principal, Waddell School of Music, Edinburgh. *Recordings:* Scots Fiddle High Style; Music of Classical Edinburgh (recorded 1984), Fiddle Pibroch and Other Fancies, 1989. *Honours:* W.H. Reed Prize, 1948; Queen's Silver Jubilee Medal, 1977. *Memberships:* Incorporated Society of Musicians; European String Teachers Association. *Hobbies:* Knitting; Sewing; Reading. *Address:* 2/3 Craufurdland, Braepark Road, Edinburgh EH4 6DL, Scotland.

ARTYOMOV Vyacheslav, b. 29 June 1940, Moscow, USSR. Composer. *Education:* Studied composition with Pirumov; Graduated, Moscow Conservatory, 1968; Studied composition with Sidelnikov. *Compositions:* Piano Concerto, 1961; 2 clarinet sonatas, 1966, 1971; Variations: Nestling Antsali for Flute and Piano, 1974; Capriccio for New Years Eve, 1975 for Soprano Saxophone, Baritone Saxophone and Vibraphone, 1975; Totem for Percussion Group, 1976; A Symphony of Elegies 1977; Way to Olympus for Orchestra, 1984;

In Memoriam, symphony for violin solo and orchestra, 1968-84; Tristia for orchestra, 1983; Invocations for soprano and percussion group, 1981; Moonlight Dreams, a cantata for soprano (mezzo-soprano), alto flute, cello and piano, 1982, Hymns of Sudden Wafts for ensemble, 1985; Gurian Hymns for 3 violins and orchestra, 1986; Requiem for soloists, two choirs and orchestra, 1988; Sola Fiole (By Faith Alone), ballet, 1987; various pieces for different instruments.

ARTZT Alice Josephine, b. 16 Mar 1943, Philadelphia, Pennsylvania, USA. Classical Guitarist. *Education:* BA, Columbia Unviersity, 1966; Studied guitar with Ida Presti and Alexandre Lagoya, France, and with Julian Bream, England; Composition with Darius Milhaud; Graduate work in Composition and Musicology, Columbia University. *Career:* Teacher, Guitar: Mannes College of Music, New York City, 1966-69; Trenton State University, New Jersey, 1977-80; Performer, 1969-; Appearances throughout North America; Many tours, Europe, South and Central America, the Caribbean, Mexico; Performed in Africa, Near East, Japan, Korea, Singapore, Taiwan, Hong Kong, Australia, New Zealand; Soloist with orchestras, Europe, Near East, USA; Premiered 3 new concertos; Duo concerts with harpsichordist Igor Kipnis. *Recordings:* LP albums: Alice Artzt Classic Guitar; Alice Artzt Plays Original Works; Bach and His Friends; Guitar Music by Fernando Sor; Guitar Music by Francisco Tarrega; 20th Century Guitar Music; English Guitar Music; The Music of Manuel Ponce; Virtuoso Romantic Guitar; Musical Tributes; Variations, Passacaglias and Chaconnes; American Music of the Stage and Screen by The Alice Artzt Trio. *Contributor to:* Articles and reviews in numerous magazines. *Honours:* Various Critics Choice awards. *Memberships:* Former Chairman: Board of Directors, Guitar Foundation of America. *Hobbies:* Travel; Hi-Fi; Researching Chaplin films. *Address:* Apt 31, 180 Claremont Avenue, New York, NY 10027, USA.

ARUHN Britt Marie, b. 11 Nov 1943, Motala, Sweden. Singer (Soprano). *Education:* Studied at the Stockholm Academy of Music. *Debut:* Stockholm 1974, in Les Contes d'Hoffmann. *Career:* Has sung at Stocholm and at the Drottningholm Festival as Norina, Zerbinetta, Gilda, Mélisande, Musetta, and Adina; Staatsoper Dresden 1976, as Gilda and Sophie; Covent Garden 1978; Hamburg Staatsoper 1983; Brussels 1984, in Lucio Silla by Mozart; Sandrina in La Finta Giardiniera, Brussels and Gluck's Elena at Drottningholm, 1987; Sang First Lady in a film version of The Magic Flute, arranged by Ingmar Bergman; Frequent concert appearances. *Recordings include:* Brahms Ein Deutsches Requiem, RCA. *Address:* Kungliga Teatern, PO Box 16094, S-103 22 Stockholm, Sweden.

ARVIN Gary, b. 24 May 1954, Alfordsville, Indiana, USA. Pianist; Vocal Coach; Professor of Voice. *Education:* BS, Indiana University; MM, Universlty of Illinois; Diploma, Hochschule für Musik und darstellende Kunst, Vienna; Studies with Elly Ameling, Dalton Baldwin, Elena Nikolaidi, Erik Werba, John Wustman. *Debut:* Carnegie Hall, 1989. *Career:* American Pianist, Vocal Coach; Accompanist for Hans Hotter, Gerard Souzay, Sir Peter Pears; Recitals throughout USA, Europe, Scandinavia; Official Accompanist, International Belvedere Competition, Vienna; Coach/Conductor, Houston Opera, Cincinnati Opera, Santa Fe Opera; Artistic Director of Art Song Festival, Santa Barbara, California, 1990-92; Currently Professor of Voice, Indiana University, Bloomington. *Recordings:* National Public Radio, Hal Leonard, USA; ORF, Austria; Suomen Yleisradio, Finland. *Honours:* Fulbright Scholar, Vienna; ITT International Fellow, Vienna; National Endowment for the Humanities Grant. *Address:* School of Music, Indiana University, Bloomington, IN 47405, USA.

ASAZUMA Fumiki, b. 23 Aug 1931, Tokyo, Japan. Professor of Viola; Conductor; Viola d'amore Player. m. Michiko Nagamatsu, 19 June 1957, 1 son, 2 daughters. *Education:* BMus, Tokyo National University of Fine Arts

and Music, 1956; Viola and Viola d'amore studies, Vienna Academy, 1966-67. *Career:* Violist, NHK, Symphony Orchestra, Tokyo, 1956-62; Professor of Viola, Tokyo National Univrsity of Fine Arts and Music, 1962-; Director and Conductor, Tokio Akademiker Ensemble (Kammerorchester), Tokyo, 1968-; Many TV and radio appearances, NHK and especially FM-Tokyo, 1968-85. *Recordings:* With Tokio Akademiker Ensemble (Kammerorchester): Mozart - 3 Divertimentos, King, 1972; Stamitz, Bach, Mozart, Audio Lab, 1975; Vivaldi - Flute Concertos with Christian Larde, Audio Lab, 1975; Mozart with Christian Larde and Marie Claire Jamet, Denon, 1977; Doppler, Fauré, Gluck, Kreisler, Genin with Paula Robison, CBS, 1984. *Publications:* Translator, The Interpretation of the Music of the XVII and XVIII Centuries (Arnold Dolmetsch), 1966. *Memberships:* President, Japan Viola Research Society; The Dolmetsch Foundation; Japan Musicology Society; Nippon Conductors Association; Rotary Club. *Hobbies:* Painting; Going for a drive. *Address:* 13-17 Hachiyama, Shibuya-ku, Tokyo 150, Japan.

ASCHAFFENBURG Walter, b. 20 May 1927, Essen, Germany. Composer; Educator. m. (1) Nancy Cooper, 14 Aug 1951, 2 daughters; (2) Rayna Barroll, 5 Aug 1987. *Education:* BA, Oberlin College, Ohio, USA, 1951; Diploma, Theory and Composition, Hartford School of Music, 1945; MA, Eastman School of Music, Rochester, New York, 1952. *Career:* Professor of Composition and Music Theory, Oberlin College Conservatory of Music, 1952-87. *Compositions:* Bartleby, opera in a prologue and two acts, Theodore Presser Co; Three Dances for Orchestra; The 23rd Psalm. *Honours:* Guggenheim Fellowship, 1955-56, 1973-74; Award, National Institute of Arts and Letters, 1966; Award, Fromm Music Foundation, 1953; Cleveland, Ohio, Arts Prize in Music, 1980. *Memberships:* American Music Centre; American Society Composers, Authors and Publishers; Society of Composers Inc.; Society for Music Theory. *Address:* 4639 E Monte Way, Phoenix, AZ 85044, USA.

ASHKENASI Shmuel, b. 1940, Israel. Violinist. *Education:* Studied with Ilona Feher in Israel and with Efrem Zimbalist at the Curtis Institute in Philadelphia. *Career:* Concert tours of the United States, Europe, the Soviet Union and Japan; Co-founded the Vermeer String Quartet at the Marlboro Festival in 1970; Performances in all major US centres in Europe, Israel and Australia; Festival engagements at Tanglewood, Aspen, Spoleto, Edinburgh, Mostly Mozart (New York), Aldeburgh, South Bank, Santa Fe, Chamber Music West, and the Casals Festival; Resident quartet for Chamber Music Chicago; Master classes at the Royal Northern College of Music, Manchester; Member of the Resident Artists Faculty of Northern Illinois University. *Recordings:* Paganini Concertos with the Vienna Symphony Orchestra (Deutsche Grammophon); Mozart Concerto K219 and Beethoven Romances (Tudor); Quartets by Beethoven, Dvosák, Verdi and Schubert (Teldec); Brahms Clarinet Quintet, with Carl Leister (Orfeo). *Honours:* Winner, Merriweather Post Contest, Washington DC; Finalist of Queen Elisabeth Competition, Brussels; 2nd Prize, Techaikovsky International Competition, Moscow. *Address:* c/o Allied Artists, 42 Montpelier Square, London SW7 1JZ, England.

ASHKENAZY Vladimir, b. 6 July 1937, Gorky, USSR. Pianist; Conductor. m. Thorunn Sofia Johannsdottir, 25 Feb 1961, 2 sons, 3 daughters. *Education:* Moscow Central Music School, 1945-55; Moscow Conservatory, 1955-63. *Career:* Concert appearances throughout the world, solo recitals and with major orchestras; Conductor of major orchestras especially the Philharmonia, The Concertgebouw (Amsterdam) and the Cleveland Orchestras; Music Director, The Royal Philharmonic Orchestra, 1987; Music Director, The Berlin Radio Symphony Orchestra (now called Deutsches Symphonie Orchester Berlin), 1989-; Conducted at the Prokofiev Centenary Celebrations at the Festival Hall, 1991; Promenade Concerts, London, 1991, with the European Community Youth Orchestra; La Mer, 8th Symphony by Shostakovich, and the Royal Philharmonic, Tippett's Concerto for Double String

Orchestra and Walton's 1st Symphony; conducted works by Walton (Henry V, Cello Concerto and Belshazzar's Feast), at the Festival Hall, London, 1993. *Recordings:* A number of recordings with Decca records including works by Mozart, Prokofikev, Beethoven, Liszt, Chopin, Schumann, and Brahms. *Honours:* 2nd Prize, Chopin International Competition, 1955; 1st Prize, Queen Elisabeth of Belgium Competition, Brussels, 1956 and Tchaikovsky Competition, 1962. *Current Management:* Harrison Parrott Ltd, 12 Penzance Place, London, W11 4PA, England. *Address:* Savinka, Käppelistra, 6045 Meggen, Switzerland.

ASHKENAZY Vovka, b. 1961, Moscow, USSR. Pianist. *Education:* Early piano studies in Iceland with Rögnvaldur Sigurjónsson; moved to England 1977 and completed studies at the Royal Northern College of Music, 1983. *Debut:* Barbican Hall, London, 1983 in the Tchaikovsky 1st Piano Concerto, with the London Symphony Orchestra. *Career:* Concerts in Germany, Italy, Holland, France and Canada; appearances with most London orchestras in concertos by Brahms, Schumann, Grieg, Tchaikovsky and Rachmaninov; US debut with the Los Angeles Philharmonic, at Hollywood Bowl; recital tour of Israel and tours of Australia and Japan. *Current Management:* F.A.M.E. Agency. *Address:* Schlösslistrasse 34, CCH-6045, Meggen, Switzerland.

ASHLEY Robert (Reynolds), b. 28 Mar 1930, Ann Arbor, Michigan, USA. Composer. *Education:* Studied theory at the University of Michigan, Ann Arbor, B.Mus., 1952; piano and composition at the Manhattan School of Music, N.Y., M.Mus.,1952; postgraduate studies in acoustics and composition at the University of Michigan, 1957-60. *Career:* Active with Milton Cohen's Space Theater, 1957-64, the ONCE Festivals and ONCE Group, 1959-69, and the Sonic Arts Union, 1966-76; toured with these groups in the U.S. and Europe; director, Center for Contemporary Music, Mills College, Oakland, California, 1969-81. *Compositions:* Operas: That Morning Thing, 1967; Atalanta (Acts of God), 1982; Now Eleanors Idea; various electronic music theatre pieces, including Heat, 1961; Public Opinion Descends Upon the Demonstrators, 1961; Combination Wedding and Funeral, 1964; Kittyhawk: An Antigravity Piece, 1964; Night Train, 1965; Unmarked Interchange, 1965; The Trial of Anne Opie Wehrer and Unknown Accomplices for Crimes Against Humanity, 1968; Fancy Free, 1970; It's There, 1970; Over the Telephone, 1975; also other electronic works; films; videotapes; Video Operas: Music with Roots in the Aether, 1976; Title Withdrawn, 1976; Perfect Lives (Private Parts), 1977-83; The Lessons, 1981; Atlanta Strategy,1984; instrumental pieces, including Fives for 2 Pianos, 2 Percussion and String Quintet, 1962; In Memoriam....Crazy Horse, symphony for 20 or more String, Wind, or Other Sustaining Instruments, 1963; In Memoriam....Kit Carson, opera,1963; Waiting Room, quartet for Any Number of Winds or Strings, 1965, revised 1978; Odalisque, 1985; Superior Seven, 1988; piano pieces.*Address:* 10 Beach Street, New York, NY 10013, USA.

ASHMAN Mike, b. 16 April 1950, Hertford, England. Stage Director. *Career:* Major producations include Der Fliegende Hollander, 1989 and Das Rheingold (first of full Ring cycle) 1993 for Den Norske Opera, Oslo; Parsifal 1983 and world premiere of John Metcalf's Tornrak, 1990 for Welsh National Opera; Petr Grimes 1991 for Teatro Lirico de la Zarzuela, Madrid; and Der Fliegende Hollander 1986 for Royal Opera, Covent Garden. Has also directed for Scottish Opera Go Round, Dublin Grand Opera, Opera Northern Ireland, Banff Centre Alberta, Opera de Nice, Teatro Regio Turin and Opera Comique, Paris. Since 1988 Associate Producer for Royal College of Music, London, directing 6 producations. Has made performing translations of The Bartered Bride and Weill's Der Jasager. *Address:* Flat C, 20 Denman Street, London W1V 7RJ, England.

ASHWORTH Valerie Grace, b. 12 Sept 1956, Sale, Cheshire, England. Pianist. m. Vincent Pirillo, 2 daughters. *Education:* Chetham's School of Music,

Manchester, 1969-75; Studied with Kendall Taylor at Royal College of Music, London, 1975-79; Master classes in solo repertoire with Sir William Glock, Albert Ferber, Rudolf Firkusny, Hochschule für Musik, Vienna, 1979-81; ARCM, Piano Performer's 1971; LLRAM, Piano Performer's 1974; ARCM, Teacher's Diploma 1977. *Debut:* Radio debut, Young artists, 1969. *Career:* Teaching contract: Coach, String Department 1982-87, Vocal Department 1987-89, Hochschule für Musik und Vienna; Taught piano at University of Osnabrück, 1989-93; Active soloist, chamber musician and accompanist in England, France, Switzerland, Italy, Denmark, Germany, Japan, Hungary and Austria; Television debut, John Amis Music on Two, 1972; American Debut, Carnegie Hall, 1989; Official accompanist, work includes Jacqueline du Pré master classes, England, 1979; Summer Academy, Nice, France, 1980; Irwin Gage in Zurich, 1984-86; Carinthia Summer, 1984 and Summer Academy, Salzburg, 1991, Austria. *Honours:* Finalist, National Junior Piano Playing Competition, 1969; Finalist, Commonwealth Competition, 1972; First Prize, Kathleen Long Chamber Music Competition, 1978; First Prize, Duo Chamber Music Competition, Finale Liguria, Italy, 1985. *Memberships:* ISM; EPTA. *Hobbies:* Languages; Travel; the Arts. *Current Management:* Wilhelm Hansen, Denmark. *Address:* Slukefter Weg 17A, 24955 Harrislee, Germany.

AST Margharete, b. 1932, Guben, Germany. Singer (Mezzo-Soprano). *Education:* Studied at Berlin Musikhochschule. *Career:* Sang in premiere of Krenek's Pallas Atheme weint, Hamburg, 1955; Appeared at Kassel, 1958-, notably in premieres of Barnstable by Francis Burt, 1969, and Ein Menschentraum by P M Hamel, 1981; Guest engagements at Vienna Festival, 1962, Vienna Staatsoper, 1965-68; Elsewhere in Austria and Germany has sung Gluck's Orpheus, Wagner's Magdalene, Erda, Waltraute and Flosshilde, Strauss's Herodias, Composer, Clytemnestra and Adelaide, Verdi's Amneris, Eboli and Mistress Quickly, Marina in Boris Godunov, Tchaikovsky's Maid of Orleans, Kabanicha in Jenvfa, Berg's Countess Geschwitz and Charlotte in Die Soldaten by Zimmermann; Many concert appearances. *Address:* c/o Staatstheater, Freidrichplatz, 3500 Kassel, Germany.

ASTON Peter George, b. 5 Oct 1938, Birmingham, England. Composer; Conductor; University Teacher. m. Elaine Veronica Neale, 13 Aug 1960, 1 son. *Education:* Birmingham School of Music; DPhil, University of York; GBSM; FTCL; FCI; ARCM; Hon RCM; FRSA. *Career:* Lecturer in Music, 1964-72, Senior Lecturer, 1972-74, University of York; Professor, Head of Music, 1974-, Dean, School of Fine Arts and Music, 1981-84, University of East Anglia, Norwich; Director, The Tudor Consort, 1959-65; Conductor, English Baroque Ensemble, 1967-70; Aldeburgh Festival Singers, 1974-88; Series Editor, UEA Recordings, 1979-; Joint Founder, Artistic Director, Norwich Festival of Contemporary Church Music, 1981-. *Compositions:* Chamber music; Opera; Church music; Numerous choral and orchestral works; Editions of baroque music including complete works of George Jeffreys. *Recordings:* Mellers's Life Cycle; Jeffreys's Anthems and Devotional Songs; Choral music by Holst and Britten; Numerous choral and orchestral works. *Publications:* The Music of York Minster, 1972; Co-author: Sound and Silence, 1970, German edition, 1972, Italian edition, 1980, Japanese edition, 1981; Music Theory in Practice, 3 volumes, 1992-93. *Address:* University of East Anglia, School of Music, Music Centre, Norwich NR4 7TJ, England.

ASTRAND (Karl) Hans (Vilhelm), b. 5 Feb 1925, Bredaryd, Sweden. Music Historian; Perpetual Secretary, Royal Swedish Academy of Music. m. Birgitta Helga Margareta Örle, 25 Mar 1972, 1 son. *Education:* Filosofie Licentiatexamen Romance Languages, Lund University, 1958; Studied Organ for 2 years with Gunnar Ek, Double Bass for 4 years with Sune Pettersson and Violoncello for 3 years with Gunnar Berggren. *Debut:* Choir Conductor, Malmö, 1953. *Career:* Perpetual

Secretary, Royal Swedish Academy of Music, 1973-90. *Publications:* Chief Editor, Sohlman's Dictionary of Music, 5 volumes, 1975-79; Bird's Eye Perspectives on American Music Life, 1983; J G Naumann als Opernkomponist - heute, 1991; Joseph Martin Kraus, The Great Exception, 1992. *Contributor to:* Nutida Musik; Artes; Music Critic, Kvällsposten, Malmö, 1950-80; Mientras cantan las cuerdas, on contemporary Spanish music, in Revista de Occidente, 1991. *Memberships:* Royal Swedish Academy of Music; Corresponding member, Real Academia de Bellas Artes de San Fernando, Spain. *Address:* Mästarbacken 145, S-126 57 Hägersten, Sweden.

ATHANASIADES Georges, b. 27 July 1929, Lavey, Switzerland. Catholic Priest; Organist. *Education:* Classical and Theological, Ordination, 1952; Concert Diploma in Organ, 1953, Prix d'excellence, 1954, Conservatory of Lausanne; German Philology and Literature, Universities of Heidelberg and Freiburg, Germany, 1955. *Debut:* Lausanne, 1953. *Career:* Titular Organist, Abbey Church of Saint-Maurice, Switzerland, 1950-; Approximately 20 performances a year with Radio Suisse Romande from the Abbey Church; Concert tours, Europe, Africa, India; USA debut, Lincoln Center, New York, 1979; London debut, 1981; Japan debut, 1990; Member of national and international juries of music competitions; TV Portrait for Television Suisse Romande. *Compositions:* Suite pour un grand orgue (Prélude, Variations, Toccata), 1984; Lisztiana for organ, 1992; Fantasia hellenica, 1992; Choral works. *Publications:* Initiation à la musique par le disque IV - or Das Klingende Buch der Musik, 1956; Translator of books: Le message des Icônes, 1966; Histoire de l'Eglise catholique au Togo, 1968; Mysterium Salutis VII, 1977; Le Psautier (member of official French translation team of Psalms and liturgical texts), 1977; Several publications and translations of theological and artistic articles. *Honours:* Gold Medal, City of Paris, 1980; Rünzi Prize, Valais, Switzerland, 1981; Man of the Year, ABI, 1993. *Memberships:* Association des musiciens suisses; Société suisse de Pédagogie musicale; Consociatio Musicae Sacrae Rom; Beethoven Society, Vienna; Liszt Society, London and Budapest; Paderewski Society, Lausanne; Frank Martin Society, Lausanne; Gesellschaft der Orgelfreunde, Germany. *Current Management:* Interclassica, Box 47, CH-Lausanne 26, Switzerland. *Address:* Abbey of St Maurice, CH-1890 Saint-Maurice, Switzerland.

ATHERTON David, b. 3 Jan. 1944, Blackpool, England. Conductor. m. Ann Gianetta Drake, 1 son, 2 daughters. *Education:* MA, (Cantab); LRAM; LTCL; LGSM. *Debut:* Royal Opera House, Coven Garden, 1968; at Aldeburgh Festival conducted World Premiere of Birtwistle's Punch and Judy, 1968 and Crosse's Grace of Todd, 1969. *Career:* Resident Conductor, Royal Opera House, 1968-80; Il Trovatore, Don Giovanni, The Rake's Progress and Henze's We Come to the River-world premiere; Musical Director and Founder, London Sinfonietta, 1968-73; Principal Conductor, Royal Liverpool Philharmonic Orchestra, 1980-83; Music Director and Principal Conductor, San Diego Symphony, 1980-87; Principal Guest Conductor, Royal Liverpool Philharmonic Orchestra, 1983-86; Principal Guest Conductor, BBC Symphony Orchestra, 1985-90; Music Director, Hong Kong Philharmonic Orchester, 1989-; Music Director, London Sinfonietta, 1989-91; Guest Conductor, Orchestras in Great Britain, Iran, Lebanon, France, Spain, Italy, Portugal, Belgium, Germany, Holland, Iceland, Canada, Russia, Japan, Korea, Hong Kong, USA, Sweden, Finland, Australia, New Zealand, Yugoslavia, Israel and Czechoslovakia; Music Director and founder, Mainly Mozart Festival, Southern California, 1989-; Conducted the 1993 Promenade Concerts; Conducted Wozzeck at Toronto, 1990, Tippett's The Ice Break at the Promenade Concerts, London; New Production of Peter Grimes at the London Coliseum, 1991; Promenade Concerts, 1991, with the National Youth Orchestra of Great Britain, Walton Viola Concerto, 7th Symphony by Shostakovich, and the BBC Symphony, Ravel Piano Concerto and Vaughan Williams 2nd Symphony; New production of Les Huguenots at Covent Garden, 1991; Recordings include: Complete

works for Chamber Ensemble by Schoenberg and Janáfek; works by Mozart, Schubert, Weill and Stravinsky; Numerous recordings with London Symphony Orchestra, London Philharmonic Orchestra, English Chamber Orchestra, London Sinfonietta, Philharmonia, Berlin Radio Symphony Orchestra. *Publications:* Editor, Pandora Suite and Don Quixote Suite, Gerhard; Arranger, Pandora (for Royal Ballet), Gerhard; Editor, The Complete Instrumental and Chamber Music of Arnold Schoenberg and Roberto Gerhard, 1973. *Contributions to:* Revised Musical Companion; Grove's Dictionary of Music and Musicians. *Honours:* Edison Award, Grand Prix du Disque; International Record Critics Award, Cecilia Prize; Special Award, Composers Guild; Conductor of the Year, 1971; Koussevitsky Award. *Membership:* Incorporated Society of Musicians.*Current Management:* Harold Holt Ltd. *Hobbies:* Squash; Reading; Travel. *Address:* c/o Harold Holt Ltd, 31 Sinclair Road, London W14 0NS, England.

ATHERTON Leonard James Archibald, b. 25 Oct 1941, Harrow, Middlesex, England. Conductor. m. Susan Frances Goldie, 26 June 1982, 1 son from former marriage, 1 daughter. *Education:* Holroyd Music Scholar, Keble College, Oxford, 1960-63; Guildhall School of Music, 1963-64; LRAM, 1959; ARCM, 1959; BA, 1963; MA, 1967 (Oxon). *Career:* Music Director, National Symphony Orchestra of Bolivia, 1964-66; Director of Chorus, University of Pennsylvania, USA, 1968-71; Music Director, Niagara Symphony Association, Canada, 1972-80; Music Director, Greater Boston Youth Symphony, USA, 1980-82; Director, Young Artists Vocal Program, 1979-85, Director of Choral Activities, 1986, Boston University, Tanglewood Institute, USA; Director of Orchestras, Professor, Ball State University, USA, 1982-; Music Director, Muncie Symphony Orchestra, USA, 1982-; Guest appearances with Minnesota Orchestra, Baltimore Symphony Orchestra, St Paul Chamber Orchestra, Victoria, Saskatchewan and Kingston Symphony Orchestras, Canada; Rhode Island All-State Orchestra; Sakai Opera Company, Osaka, Japan; Century Orchestra (Osaka), University of Nueva Leon, Monterrey, Mexico. *Recordings:* Various recordings for the Canadian Broadcasting Corporation ranging from Medieval Motets to Premieres. *Hobbies:* Stamp Collecting; Reading; Tennis. *Address:* 704 North Calvert Street, Muncie, IN 47303-3533, USA.

ATKINSON Charles M, b. 15 Aug 1941, Crockett, Texas, USA. Musicologist; Clarinettist. m. Margaret Livingston Atkinson, 1 son, 1 daughter. *Education:* BFA, University of New Mexico, 1963; MMus, University of Michigan, 1965; PhD, University of North Carolina, 1975; Juilliard School of Music, 1967-69. *Career:* Assistant Professor, University of California, 1973-78; Associate Professor, 1978-86, Full Professor 1987-, Ohio State University; Visiting Professor, University of North Carolina, 1987; Performer, 5 compositions from Irvine, recorded. *Publications:* Die einstimmigen Melodien der Sanctus and Agnus Dei mit ihren Tropen; Franco of Cologne on the Rhythm Organum Purum; Early Music History 9, 1989. *Contributor to:* Journal of American Musicological Society; Notes; Handwörterbuch der musikalischen Terminologie; Speculum; Journal of Music Theory; AMS Newsletter; Archiv für Musikwissenschaft; New Grove; Musical Quarterly; Kirchenmusikalisches Jahrbuch; IMS Proceedings, 1977; Liturgische Tropen; IMS Proceedings, 1987; Hermeneutics and Medieval Culture, 1988; The Journal of Musicology. *Hobby:* Spending Time with Wife and Children. *Address:* 372 Fallis Road, Columbus, OH 43214, USA.

ATKINSON Lynton, b. 1962, England. Singer (Tenor). *Education:* Studied under George Guest at Cambridge and in London with David Mason and Gita Denise. *Career:* Concert appearances in festivals at Innsbruck, Utrecht, Malta, Brighton and Edinburgh; Cathedrals of Canterbury, Wells, Durham and Birmingham, King's College, Cambridge and the Sheldonian Theatre, Oxford; Has sung in Bach's St John Passion on tour in Spain, the St Matthew Passion in Bad Homburg and

L'Incoronazione di Poppea at the Spitalfields Festival; Vienna 1989, with Handel's Susanna under Martin Haselbrock; Alfredo in a production of Traviata in Mauritius; Handel's Belshazzar with Concerto Köln in Germany and Italy; Edinburgh Festival and Poland with the City of London Sinfonia under Richard Hickox; Covent Garden 1990-91, as First Prisoner in Fidelio and Ywain in the world premiere of Birtwistle's Gawain; Buxton Festival and Spitalfields 1991, in Il Sogno di Scipione (Mozart) and Acis and Galatea; Season 1992 as Nathaniel in Hoffmann and Zefirino in I Viaggio a Reims at Covent Garden. *Recordings:* Albums for Harmonia Mundia, Virgin Classics and Meridian, including L'Incoronazione di Poppea; Video of Covent Garden Fidelio (First Prisoner) for Virgin Classics. *Honours include:* Prize winner, Alfredo Kraus International Singing Competition, Las Palmas, 1990. *Address:* c/o Magenta Music International, 64 Highgate High Street, London N6 5HX, England.

ATLANTOV Vladimir, b. 19 Feb 1939, Leningrad, USSR. Singer (Tenor). *Education:* Studied with N. Bolotina at the Leningrad Conservatory and at the La Scala opera school, Milan. *Career:* Sang at the Kirov Theatre, Moscow from 1963; Bolshoi Theatre from 1967: roles include Lenski, Hermann, Don Carlos, Radames, Don José, Alfredo, Cavaradossi and Canio; Vienna Staatsoper 1971; Vladimir in Prince Igor with the Bolshoi company at La Scala, 1973; Deutsche Oper Berlin 1974, as Cavaradossi; Has also sung baritone roles from 1977, notably Posa in Don Carlos; Munich 1980, as Otello; Covent Garden 1989, as Canio in Pagliacci (also at Kenwood, Lakeside); Sang Samson at Berlin, Deutsche Opera, 1989; Otello at Covent Garden, 1990, followed by Hermann at La Scala and Canio at the Caracalla Festival, Rome; Sang Samson for Opera Pacific at Costa Mesa, 1992; Concert tours of Canada, Europe and Japan. *Recordings:* Prince Igor, Eugene Onegin, Francesca da Rimini by Rachmaninov, Iolanta by Tchaikovsky, Ruslan and Ludmila, The Stone Guest by Darghomyzhsky. *Honours include:* People's Artist of the RSFSR, 1972. *Address:* c/o Royal Opera House (contract), Covent Garden, London WC2, England.

ATLAS Allan W(arren), b. 19 Feb 1943, New York, USA. Musicologist. *Education:* Hunter College of the City University of New York, BA, 1964; New York University, MA, 1966, PhD, 1971. *Career:* Adjunct lecturer, Hunter College, 1967; research assistant to Gustave Reese, New York University, 1966-68; faculty member, Brooklyn College, 1971-; visiting professor, New York University, 1971, 1984, 1986; Executive Officer, Ph.D. DMA Programs in Music, Graduate School, City University of New York. *Publications:* The Cappella Giulia Chansonnier: Rome, Biblioteca Apostolica Vaticana, C.G. X111.27 - 2 vols, 1975/76; Editor, Robert Morton: The Collected Works, 1981; editor, Aedvardus of Ortona: Missa Sine Nomine, 1985; Editor, Music in the Classic Period: Essays in Honor of Barry S Brook, 1985; Music at the Aragonese Court of Naples, 1985; also articles in the New Grove Dictionary of Music and Musicians and in various journals. *Address:* 945 Cedar Lane, Woodmere, NY 11598, USA.

ATTROT Ingrid, b. 1964, Canada. Singer (Soprano). *Education:* Graduated, Toronto Opera School, 1985; Britten-Pears School at Aldeburgh; National Opera Studio 1986-87. *Career:* Has appeared as Mozart's Countess and Donna Elvira; Purcell's Dido and Meg Page in Sir John in Love by Vaughan Williams; Ibert's Angélique and Respighi's Maria Egiziaca; Sang Madeline in Debussy's Fall of the House of Usher, Elizabeth Hall, 1989; Wigmore Hall and Purcell Room recitals 1989; Handel's Ode to St Cecilia with Charles Dutoit and the Montreal Symphony; Bach's B minor Mass in Montreal; Vivaldi's Gloria in Ottawa and New York, conducted by Trevor Pinnock; Mendelssohn's Midsummer Night's Dream under Neville Marriner at the Festival Hall; Season 1989-90 with Messiah, Carmina Burana and the Petite Messe Solennelle; Szymanowski recital at the Purcell Room; Handel's Floridante in Canada and California; Stravinsky's Les Noces in Antwerp and Elgar's The Kingdom; Tour of

Russia with English National Opera productions of Macbeth and The Turn of the Screw; Season 1992 as Mathilde in Guillaume Tell for Haddo House Opera and the Governess in The Turn of the Screw for Pimlico Opera. *Honours include:* Winner, Eckhardt-Gramatte Competition for Contemporary Music, Canada; Awards from University of Toronto, the Canadian Aldeburgh Foundation and The Friends of Covent Garden. *Address:* c/o Ron Gonsalves Management, 10 Dagnan Road, London SW12 9LQ, England.

ATZMON Moshe, b. 30 July 1931, Budapest, Hungary. Conductor. *Education:* Studied cello in homeland; continued musical training in Israel, where he took lessons in horn and piano; pursued studies at the Tel Aviv Academy of Music (I958-62); studied conducting at the Guildhall School of Music, London. *Career:* Played horn in Israel symphony and opera orchestras; chief conductor, Sydney Symphony Orchestra, 1969-71, Basle Symphony Orchestra, 1972-77, North German Radio Symphony Orchestra, Hamburg, I972-76, and Tokyo Metropolitan Symphony Orchestra, 1978-82; co-principal conductor American Symphony Orchestra, NY, 1982-84; Chief Conductor, Nagoya Philharmonic Orchestra, 1986-92; Director of the Dortmund Opera, 1991; Conducted Siegfried, 1991. *Honours:* First prize, conducting, Guildhall School of Music, London, 1963; first prize, Liverpool International Conductors' Competition, 1964. *Recordings:* For Angel-EMI, Ariola, Decca-London, Denon, Deutsche Grammophon, La Guilde Internationale du Disque; Repertoire includes, Mendelssohn overtures; Liszt's Piano Concertos, (Garrick Ohlsson); Brahms Double Concerto and Serenade Op.11.; Bach's E Major and A Minor violin concertos, Schneiderhan; CD of works for piano and orchestra by Addinsell, Litolff, Gottschalk and Rachmaninov (Ortiz). *Address:* Opernhaus, Kuhstrasse 12, 44137 Dortmund, Germany.

AUBERSON Jean Marie, b. 2 May 1920, Chavorney, Vaud, Switzerland. Conductor. *Education:* Studied at the Lausanne Conservatory; Studied conducting with Van Kampen at Sienna and with Gunther Wand in Cologne, 1950-51. *Career:* Played violin with the Lausanne Chamber Orchestra 1943-46, Suisse Romande Orchestra 1946-49; Conducted the Lausanne Chamber Orchestra, then the Radio Beromunster Orchestra at Zurich, the Suisse Romande Orchestra and the Zurich Tonhalle; Ballet evenings at the Geneva Opera and the Hamburg Staatsoper; Further career with the Orchestra of Radio Basle and of Ville de Saint-Gall; Conducted the premieres of the ballet Paris by Henri Sauguet, 1964, Ginastera's Piano Concerto, 1977 and La Follie de Tristan by Schibler, 1980. *Recordings include:* Mozart C minor Mass, with the Vienna Philharmonic; Handel Organ Concertos with Lionel Rogg and the Geneva Baroque Orchestra; Tchaikovsky Violin Concerto with Tibor Varga; Oboe Concertos by CPE Bach, Marcello and Bellini, with Heinz Holliger. *Address:* c/o Grand Théâtre de Genève, 11 Boulevard du Théâtre, CH-1211 Geneva 11, Switzerland.

AUBERT Laurent, b. 30 July 1949, Neuchatel, Switzerland. Ethnomusicologist. m. Mercedes, 14 July 1981, 1 son, 2 daughters. *Education:* University of Neuchatel; Centre de musique ancienne, Geneva; Tritantri School of Indian Music, Amsterdam. *Debut:* 1973. *Career:* Founder, Director, Geneva Ateliers d'ethnomusicologie, 1974; Ethnomusicologist, Geneva Ethnographic Museum, 1983; Secretary General, International Archives of Folk Music, 1984; Editor, Cahiers de musiques traditionnelles, 1988. *Recordings:* Participation in various recordings of Medieval Music, 1977-84. *Publications:* Cahiers de musiques traditionnelles, annually 1988-; Musiques traditionnelles: Guide di disque, 1991; Planète musicale; Instruments de musique des cinq continents, 1991. *Address:* Musée d'ethnographie, 65-67 boulevard Carl-Vogt, CH-1205 Geneva, Switzerland.

AUDI Pierre, b. 1957, Beirut, Lebanon. Stage Director. *Education:* Studied at Exeter College, Oxford, 1975-78. *Career:* Founded the Almeida Theatre,

Islington, London 1979; Director of theatre and annual contemporary music festival until 1989; Artistic Director of Netherlands Opera from 1988: productions include Schoenberg's Die glückliche Hand, Feldman's Neither and Monteverdi's Il Ritorno di Ulisse - part of a complete cycle; Directed stage works by Wolfgang Rihm, Michael Finnissy (The Undivine Comedy) and John Casken (Golem) for the Almeida Theatre; Opera North 1990 with the British stage premiere of Verdi's Jerusalem; produced Birtwistle's Punch and Judy for Netherlands Opera, 1993. *Honours include:* Lesley Boosey Award, 1990. *Address:* c/o Ingpen and Williams Ltd, 14 Kensington Court, London W8 5DN, England.

AUSTIN Elizabeth Scheidel, b. 15 July 1938, Baltimore, Maryland, USA. Composer. m. (1) Rolf D Scheidel, 2 sons, 1 daughter, (2) Gerhard Austin, 28 Oct 1989. *Education:* Studied with Nadia Boulanger, Conservatoire Americaine, Fontainebleau, France, summer 1958; BA with High Honours, Goucher College, Towson, Maryland, 1960; MMus, Composition, Hartt School of Music, University of Hartford, 1982; PhD, Music, University of Connecticut, 1987. *Career:* Compositions performed in USA and Europe; 2 Portrait Concerts sponsored by Die Staatliche Hochschule fuer Musik, Heidelberg-Mannheim and GEDOK, held in Mannheim, Germany, 1989, 1991; Performed own work, Lighthouse I for harpsichord, American Music Week, Storrs, Connecticut, 1989; Composer-in-Residence, David Lipscomb College, Nov 1992; Currently Assistant Director, Mannheim Programme for Bilingual Careers; Organist, First Church of Christ, Mansfield Center, Connecticut. *Compositions:* Christ Being Raised, SATB, 1959; Klavier Double for piano and tape, 1983; Wilderness Symphony for 2 reciters and orchestra, 1987; Sonnets from the Portuguese for soprano and piano, 1989. *Recordings:* Klavier Double performed by Jerome Reed (Capstone label); Sonate fuer Blockfloete, performed by Stefanie Grundmann, 1991; Sonnets from the Portuguese performed by Melinda Liebermann and Cornelius Witthoeft, 1993; Wilderness Symphony, 1994; CD of Chamber Works, 1994, published by Arsis Press, Peter Toner Verlag. *Honours:* Mention, International League of Women Composers, 1983; Winner, University of Connecticut Composers Competition, 1986; 1st Prize, 1984 for piano and tape, Lipscomb Electronic Composition Competition. *Memberships:* Phi Beta Kappa; Pi Kappa Lambda; Sigma Alpha Iota; Delta Phi Alpha. *Address:* 9 Eastwood Road, Storrs, CT 06268, USA.

AUSTIN Larry (Don), b. 12 Sept 1930, Duncan, Oklahoma, USA. Composer; Music Educator. m. Edna Navarro, 31 Oct 1953. 2 sons, 3 daughters. *Education:* BME 1951, MM 1952, University of North Texas, Denton; Studied with Darius Milhaud, Mills College, Oakland, California, 1955; Seymour Shifrin and Andrew Imbrie, University of California, Berkeley, 1955-58; Computer music workshops, Stanford University, 1969; Massachusetts Institute of Technology, 1978. *Career:* Professor 1958-72, Director of its Bands 1958-72, Co-director, New Music Ensemble 1963-68, University of California, Davis; Publisher-owner, Source and Composer/Performer Edition, 1966-; University of South Florida, Tampa, 1972-78; University of North Texas, 1978-. *Compositions:* Woodwind Quintet, 1949; String Trio, 1952; String Quartet, 1955; Mass for Chorus and Orchestra, 1955-58; In Memoriam JFK for Concert Band, 1964; Roma, theater piece in open style for Improvisation Ensemble and Tape, 1965; Quartet Three, electronic music on tape, 1971; Quadrants, 1-11; Phantasmagoria: Fantasies on Ives' Universe Symphony for Orchestra, Narrator, Tape and Digital Synthesizer, 1977, revised 1981; Catalogo Sonoro-Narcisso for Viola and Tape, 1978; Catalogo Voce, mini-opera, 1979; Protoforms, hybrid musics for 3 Sopranos and Computer, 1980; Ceremony for Organ and Voice, 1980; Protoforms: Fractals for Computer Band, 1980; Euphonia: A Tale of the Future, opera, 1982; art is self-alteration is Cage is..., uni-word omniostic for String Bass Quartet, 1983; Sonata Concertante for Pianist and Computer, 1983-84; Sinfonia Concertante: A Mozartean Episode for Chamber Orchestra and Computer Music Narrative, 1986; Violet's Invention for Piano, 1988; Snare Drum

Cycles for Snare Drum Solo, 1988; A Universe of Symphony: The Earth, Life Pulse and Heavens, 1974-93; La Barbara: The Name/The Sounds/The Music, 1991; Sound Poem Set: Computer Music Tape, 1991; Transmission Two: The Great Excursion, for chorus, computer music ensemble and recodred dialogue, 1989-90; Accidents Two: Sound Projections for Piano with Computer Music, 1992. *Recordings:* Several compositions recorded. *Publication:* Learning to Compose: Modes, Materials and Models of Musical Invention, with Thomas Clark, 1988. *Contributions:* Articles in various publications. *Honours:* Numerous grants and commissions; Several awards. *Address:* 2109 Woodbrook, Denton, TX 76205, USA.

AUSTIN William Weaver, b. 18 Jan 1920, Lawton, Oklahoma, USA. Teacher; Writer; Professor of Musicology. m. Elizabeth Jane Hallstrom, 20 June 1942, 2 daughters. *Education:* AB 1939; AM 1940; PhD 1951; Harvard University. *Career:* Given Foundation Professor, Musicology, Cornell University, USA, Professor Emeritus, 1990. *Publications Include:* Music in the 20th Century, From Debussy Through Stravinsky 1966; New Looks at Italian Opera, Editor 1968; Debussy: Prelude à l'Après-midi d'un faune, Editor 1970; Susanna, Jeanie and The Old Folks at Home: The Songs of Stephen C Foster From His Time To Ours 1975; Translation, Dahlhaus, Esthetics of Music 1982; Susanna, (2nd Edition, 1987). *Contributor to:* Various professional journals and magazines including Musical Quarterly; Articles in Music Review. *Hobbies:* Keyboard practice especially clavichord; Composition of Songs and Choruses. *Address:* Music Faculty, Lincoln Hall, Cornell University, Ithaca, NY 14853, USA.

AVDEYEVA Larisa Ivanova, b.21 June 1925, Moscow, USSR. Mezzo-soprano. m. Evgeny Svetlanov. *Education:* Studied at the Stanislavsky Opera Studio, 1946. *Career:* Sang at the Stanislavsky Music Theatre, Moscow, from 1947 as Offenbach's La Perichole, Suzuki in Madame Butterfly and in Khrennikov's Into the Storm and Molchanov's The Stone Flower; Bolshoy Theatre, Moscow, from 1952 as Olga in Eugene Onegin, Marina in Boris Godunov, Lehl in The Snow Maiden by Rimsky-Korsakov, Konchakovna in Prince Igor, Akhrosimova in Prokofiev's War and Peace, Carmen and the Sorceress in the opera by Tchaikovsky; Has toured as opera and concert singer in Canada, Europe, the USA and the Far East. *Honours include:* People's Artist of the RSFSR, 1964. *Address:* c/o Bolshoy Theatre, Pr Marxa 8/2, 103009 Moscow, Russia.

AVELING Valda b. 16 May 1920, Sydney, Australia. Concert Artist (Piano, Harpsichord and Clavichord). *Education:* Performers and Teachers Diplomas, New South Wales State Conservatorium of Music, 1936. *Debut:* Town Hall, Sydney, with Sir Malcom Sargent, 1938. *Career:* Appearances with all leading orchestras and at all Music Festivals in UK; Frequent concert and record collaboration with Richard Bonynge and Joan Sutherland; Numerous recitals as Duo with Evelyn Barbirolli (oboe); Numerous tours, Europe, Canada and Far East including tour of Germany as joint soloist with Yehudi Menuhin; Performances at Rome Harpsichord Festival, Italy, 1971, 1972; 4 visits to Australia for Australian Broadcasting Commission (latest 1976); Recital, University of Indiana, USA 1976. *Recordings include:* Scarlatti Sonatas for Harpsichord for EMI, issued 1976; Chio Mi Scordi di Te, Mozart; Harpsichord Pieces, Thomas Morley; The Collection of Historic Instruments at the Victoria and Albert Museum, London; Music for Four Harpsichords; Harpsichord Continuo. *Contributor to:* Music and Musicians. *Honours:* Hon FTCL; Awarded OBE in 1982; Elected Honorary Member of the Art Workers Guild, 1985. *Memberships:* Elected Member of Jury, Chairman Sir Yehudi Menuhin, International Violin Competition held in Paris, sponsored by the City of Paris, 1985. *Hobbies:* Cooking; Gardening; Reading. *Address:* 15 Priory Road, London NW6 4NN, England.

AVGERINOS Yannis, b. 30 Apr 1949, Alexandria, Egypt. Music Teacher; Conductor; Composer. *Education:*

Diploma, Department of Ancient Greek Philology, Athens University; Piano, Composition, Athens National Conservatoire; Conducting, Piano, Composition, Trinity College of Music, London. *Debut:* Athens, Greece. *Career:* Conductor, Greek premieres of various 20th century works, theatre music for A Midsummer Night's Dream, music for TV documentary on Concentration Camps; Temporary Orchestrator and Producer, Greek Radio Corporation; Composition Teacher Athinaikon Conservatoire; Founder, Director, Athinaikon Conservatoire; Principal of the Athinaikon Conservatoire. *Compositions:* Several, for piano solo, violoncello solo, voice for Greek and French poetry; Suite for small orchestra; 1-movement sinfonietta; Arrangements of other composers' works for choir, orchestra and different combinations. *Recordings:* Video tapes for Greek Radio and TV: De Falla's Concertino for Harpsichord, Greek premiere; Spiro Mazis' Anaplassis for chamber orchestra, 1st vidoography for TV. *Publications:* Translation, English to Greek: W Lovelock's Two-Part Writing; W Lovelock's Free Counterpoint; E Krenek's Modal Counterpoint. *Contributions to:* Various lectures on music. *Memberships:* Patron, British Music Society, London; Founder member of the Society for Music Analysis (SMA), London. *Hobbies:* Theatre; Cinema; Books; Travel. *Address:* 87 Ionias Avenue, GR-10445 Athens, Greece.

AVIDOM Menahem, b. 6 Jan 1908, Stanislau, Galicia. Composer. m. 31 Jan 1935, 2 daughters. *Education:* BA, American University, Beirut, 1928; Paris, 1934. *Compositions:* 10 Symphonies; 7 Operas; 20 Chamber Music Works; 4 String Quartets; 2 Woodwind Quartets; several vocal works. *Recordings:* Cassettes of all compositions, Israel Broadcasting Authority. *Publications:* Several. *Contributions to:* Music Critic, Jerusalem Post, 1958-72. *Honours:* Recipient, many honours including Hon DMus, London Institute for Appointed Research; Knight of the Lofsenis Ursinos Order. *Memberships:* Hon. President, Israel Composers' League; Israel State Prize Laureate; Qualifying Jury, Leonardo Da Vinci Award, World Cultural Council; Maison International des Intellectuals, Paris. *Hobbies:* Painting; Chess. *Address:* 1 Mazeh St, Herzliya 46408, Israel.

AVNI Tzvi Jacob, b. 2 Sept 1927, Saarbrucken, Germany (lives in Israel since 1935). Composer; Music Educator. m. Hanna Yaddor-Avni, 26 Aug 1979, 1 son, 1 daughter. *Education:* Israel Matriculation Certificate, 1961; Diploma, Theory and Composition, Israel Music Academy, Tel Aviv, 1958; Further studies in USA, 1962-64; Electronic Music, Columbia University; Tanglewood, summer courses. *Career:* Music Teacher, Theory, Schools and Conservatories, 1953-61; Director, AMLI Central Music Library, Tel Aviv, 1961-75; Director, Electronic Music Studio, 1971-, Full Professor, Music Theory and Composition, 1976-, Rubin Academy, Jerusalem, 1971-. *Compositions:* For Orchestra: Meditations on a Drama; By the Rivers of Babylon; Holiday Metaphors; Programme Music, 1980; Metamorphoses on a Bach Chorale; Two String Quartets; Wind Quintet; Five Pantomimes for 8 Players; Two Psalms for Oboe and String Quartet; Michtam for Harp and String Quartet; Vocal: Songs; Works for Choir a Capella; Leda and The Swan, Voice and Clarinet; Various electronic pieces, works for ballet, art films, radio plays; Vitrage for Harp solo, 1990; Saxophone Quartet, 1989; Fagotti Fugati, 2 Bassoons, 1991; Deep Calleth unto Deep, 3 Psalms, for Choir, solo soprano and symphony orchestra, 1988-89. *Recordings:* Numerous. *Publications:* An Orchestra is Born, Editor of The Letters of B.Huberman about the Foundation of the Israel Philharmonic Orchestra, 1969; Bronislaw Huberman, edited by A.Karpinowitz, 1973; Editor of Gittit, Israel Jeunesses Musicales, 1966-80. *Contributions to:* Music in Israel; Dictionary of 20th Century Music; Various other publications. *Hobbies:* Wood carving; Contemporary art. *Current management:* Electronic Music Studio, Rubin Academy of Music, Jerusalem. *Address:* 54 Bourla Str, Tel Aviv 69364, Israel.

AVRIL Franck Thierry Olivier, b. 6 May 1953, Neuilly-Seine, Paris, France. Solo Oboist. *Education:* BA in Music, Yale University, 1970-74; MM in Performance and Literature, Eastman School of Music, 1974-75. *Career:* 7 years as solo oboist with Young Concert Artists: over 80 recitals, (New York, San Francisco, Los Angeles, West Palm Beach, Boston, Geneva, Paris); visiting-artist residencies sponsored by ALCOA General Electric, Exxon, Merrill-Lynch, Arts Alaska; Founding member of Die Serenade Chamber Group; Faculty (Conservatory of) University of Missouri, Kansas City, 1977-82; First Oboe, Long Island, New York, Philharmonic, 1984-88; First Oboe, Concordia: A Chamber Symphony, 1984-90; Oboe section, New York City Opera, 1985 and 1986; Live Recitals on WQXR-FM and WNCN-FM (in NYC), also on group-W TV (NYC), Guest, Dialogues with the New York Philharmonic, Summer Festivals of Sceaux (France), Garth Newel (Virginia) and Cape and Islands (Cape Cod). *Hobbies:* Aikido; Tennis; Photography; Nature and Art. *Address:* University of Alabama, School of Music, Oboe Professor, 175 Moody Music Bldg, Box 870366, Tuscaloosa, Alabama 35487-0366, USA.

AVSHALOMOV Jacob (David), b. 28 Mar 1919, Tsintao, China. Conductor; Composer. *Education:* Studied with father, Aaron Avshalomov, Peking; With Ernst Toch, Los Angeles, 1938; Reed College, Portland, Oregon, 1939-41; With Bernard Rogers, Eastman School of Music, Rochester, New York, 1941-43. *Career:* Teacher 1947-54, Conductor Chorus and Orchestra, Columbia University; Conductor, Portland (Oregon) Junior Symphony Orchestra, 1954-78 and Portland Youth Philharmonic, 1978-. *Compositions:* The Taking of T'ung Kuan for Orchestra, 1943, revised 1953; Slow Dance for Orchestra, 1945; Sinfonietta, 1946; Evocations for Clarinet and Chamber Orchestra, 1947; Sonatine for Viola and Piano, 1947; Prophecy for Cantor, Chorus and Organ, 1948; How Long, O Lord, cantata, 1948-49; Tom O'Bedlam for Chorus, 1953; The Plywood Age for Orchestra, 1955; Psalm 100 for Chorus and Wind Instruments, 1956; Inscriptions at the City of Brass for Female Narrator, Chorus and Orchestra, 1956; Phases of the Great Land for Orchestra, 1959; Symphony: The Oregon, 1959-61; City Upon the Hill for Narrator, Chorus, Orchestra and liberty bell, 1965; The Thirteen Clocks for 2 Storytellers and Orchestra, 1973; Raptures for Orchestra, 1975; Quodlibet Montagna for Brass Sextet, 1975; Praises from the Corners of the Earth for Chorus and Orchestra, 1976; Songs for Alyce, 1976. *Address:* c/o Portland Youth Philharmonic, 1119 S W Park Avenue, Portland, OR 97205 USA.

AX Emanuel b. 8 June 1949, Lwow, Poland. Pianist. m. Yoko Nozaki, 23 Nov 1974, 1 son, 1 daughter. *Education:* BA Columbia University, New York, USA, 1970; Postgraduate Diploma, Juilliard School of Music, 1972. *Career:* Concert Pianist, 1974-; Appearances USA and abroad; Performances with major orchestras including: New York Philharmonic Orchestra, Philadelphia Orchestra; Chicago Symphony Orchestra, Los Angeles Orchestra, London Philharmonic Orchestra; Played Beethoven's 2nd Concerto with the London Philharmonic at the Festival Hall, 1991; Brahms 1st Concerto, Promenade Concerts, London, 1991. *Recordings:* Recording Artist, RCA Victor; With Philadelphia Orchestra, Chicago Symphony, Cleveland Quartet, Guarneri Quartet. *Honours:* 1st prize, Arthur Rubinstein International Piano Master Competition, 1974; Record of the Year Award, Stereo Review, 1977; 1 of 5 Best Records of the Year Award, Time Magazine, 1977; Avery Fisher Award, 1979. *Current Management:* ICM Artists New York City, USA. *Memberships:* Advisory Board, Palm Beach Festival; Chopin Society. *Address:* c/o ICM Artists Ltd, 40 West 57th Street, New York, NY 10019, USA.

AXERLIS Stella, b. 5 March 1944, Alexandria, Greece. Singer (Soprano). *Education:* Studied at the University of Melbourne, Australia. *Debut:* Hagen (Germany) 1968, as Aida. *Career:* Sang at the Deutsche Oper am Rhein Dusseldorf 1970-85, as Leonore,

Elisabeth de Valois, Lady Macbeth, Senta, Venus, Sieglinde, Gutrune, Tatiana, Marina, the Marschallin, Jenvfa, Santuzza and Madama Butterfly; Guest appearances in Hamburg, Cologne, Kassel, Amsterdam, Paris, Sydney and London (Covent Garden); Zurich Opera 1986, as the Kostelnifka in Jenvfa; Sang Ortrud in Lohengrin at Sydney, 1987. *Address:* Deutsche Oper am Rhein, Heinrich Heine Allee, Dusseldorf, Germany.

AYKAL Gurer, b. 1942, Turkey. Music Director; Conductor. widower, 3 sons. *Education:* Degrees in Violin and Composition, Ankara State Conservatory, 1969; Diploma in Conducting, Guildhall School of Music, London, 1971; Resident Conductor under direction of Franco Ferrera, Accademia Santa Cecilia, receiving Diploma in Conducting, Rome, 1973; Studied Gregorian choir music and Renaissance polyphony with Dominico Bartolucci, Pontificial Institute of Sacred Music; Also studied under Andre Previn and George Hurst, London. *Career:* Appointed Permanent Conductor of Presidential Symphony Orchestra, Turkey; Founder, Ankara Chamber Orchestra; Toured Soviet Union as Conductor of Moscow State Symphony Orchestra, 1984; Toured South American and Caribbean Islands as Conductor of English Chamber Orchestra; Music Director, Conductor, Lubbock Symphony Orchestra, Texas, 1987-93; Conducted Istanbul Symphony Orchestra, 1989; Appointed Principal Guest Conductor, Amsterdam Concertgebouw Chamber Orchestra, 1989; Music Director, Conductor, El Paso Symphony Orchestra, Texas, 1992-. *Recordings:* Compact disc of works with London Philharmonic Orchestra. *Honours:* Title of State Artist, Turkish Government, 1981; Selected for National Music Museum, London, for distinguished contributon to the music profession. *Address:* El Paso Symphony Orchestra, 10 Civic Center Plaza, El Paso, TX 79901, USA.

AYRTON Norman Walter, b. 25 Sept 1924, London, England. International Theatre and Opera Director; Dean of British American Drama Academy, London. *Education:* Acting under Michael Saint Denis, Old Vic Theatre School, London, 1947-48. *Career:* War service, RNVR, 1939-45; Member, Old Vic Company, 1949, Festival Season, 1951; Repertory, Farnham and Oxford, 1949-50; Staff Member, Old Vic Theatre School, 1949-52; Opened own teaching studio, 1952; Began dramatic coaching for Royal Opera House, Covent Garden, 1953; Assistant Principal, 1954-66, Principal, 1966-72, London Academy of Music and Dramatic Art; Taught at Shakespeare Festival, Stratford, Ontario, Canada, also Royal Shakespeare Theatre, Stratford-upon-Avon, England, 1959-62; GHQ Drama Adviser to Girl Guide Movement, 1960-74; Dean, World Shakespeare Study Center, Bankside, 1972; Guest Teacher, Loeb Drama Center, Harvard, USA, 1974; Directed: Artaxerxes, for Handel Opera Society, Camden Festival, 1963; La Traviata, Covent Garden, 1963; Manon, Covent Garden, 1964; Sutherland-Williamson Grand Opera Season, Australia, 1965; Twelfth Night, Dallas Theater Center, Texas, 1967; The Way of the World, New York, 1976; Lakmé, Australian Opera, 1976; Der Rosenkavalier, Australian Opera Centre, 1983; Guest Director: Australian Council for Arts, Sydney and Brisbane, 1973; Loeb Drama Center, Harvard, 1974-76; Faculty, Juilliard School of Music, New York, 1974-85; Melbourne Theatre Co, 1974-; National Institute of Dramatic Art, Sydney, 1974-76; Vancouver Opera Association, 1975-83; Sydney Opera House, 1976-81, 1983; Williamstown Festival, USA, 1977; Hartford Stage Company and American Stage Festival, 1978-; Missouri Repertory Theatre, 1980-81; Vassar College, USA, 1990-93; Utah Shakespeare Festival, USA, 1994; National Opera Studio, London, 1980-81; Spoleto Festival, USA, 1984; Resident Stage Director, American Opera Center, New York, 1981-85; Australian Opera, 1981-83; Director of Opera, Royal Academy of Music, 1986-1990. *Hobbies:* Reading; Music; Travel. *Address:* 40A Birchington Road, London NW6, England.

AZKOUL Jad, b. 8 June 1948, New York City, New York, USA. Concert Guitarist. m. Clarissa Whitaker, 27 Dec 1984, 2 sons. *Education:* BA, 1969, MA,

Psychology, 1971, American University, Beirut; Arranging, Composition, Berklee School of Music, Boston, 1971-73; Composition, Analysis with Nadia Boulanger, Pierre Petit, Paris, 1973-75; Guitar with Alberto Ponce, Ecole Normale de Musique, Paris, 1976-78, with Abel Carlevaro, Montevideo, 1978-81; Masterclasses. *Career:* Recitals, chamber music, orchestra soloist, North and South America, Europe, Middle East, including London, Paris, Washington DC, San Francisco, Los Angeles, Montreux, Geneva, Locarno, Warsaw, Budapest, Moscow and many international festivals such as Cracow, Musique en Guyenne, Festival Estival de Paris, Menton, Montreux Guitar Festival Esztergom, Guitar in Russia; Appeared on radio and TV, Switzerland, USA, France, other countries; D'Addario concert series, 1992-93; Acting Assistant Professor, Central Michigan University, 1982; Taught Institut Superieur de Musique, Geneva, 1984-85; Professor, Conservatoire Populaire de Musique, Geneva, 1984-91; Music Faculty, American University, Washington DC since 1993; International workshops, masterclasses, France, Switzerland, Belgium, Spain, Poland, USA, Russia, Hungary; Jury Member, guitar competitions, notably Cracow International, Cracow, annually since 1991, Russia 1994. *Compositions:* Piano pieces; Guitar pieces; Film music. *Recordings:* CD Latin Illustrations for Guitar, Forlane Records, France, 1992. *Publications:* Translator, books by Abel Carlevaro: School of Guitar (into French and English); Master Class, Vol I: Fernando Sor (into French). *Contributor to:* Cahiers de la Guitare; Classical Guitar; American String Teachers Association; Guitar and Lute; Perception and Psychophysics. *Honours include:* Fellowships: French Government, 1974-78, Uruguayan Government, 1979; Winner, Affiliate Artists USA Competition, 1985; Order of the Cedar, Lebanon, 1988. *Memberships:* Societe Suisse de Pedagogie Musicale; Music Esperance; College Music Society; Washington DC Classical Guitar Society; American University of Beirut Alumni Association. *Hobbies:* Reading; Tennis; Theatre; Languages - English, French, Spanish, Arabic. *Address:* 2711 Welcome Drive, Falls Church, VA 22046, USA.

AZUMA Atsuko, b. 11 Dec 1939, Osaka, Japan. Singer (Soprano). *Education:* Studied with Fumiko Yotsuya in Tokyo, Giulia Tess in Milan and Ettore Campogalliani in Parma. *Debut:* Reggio Emilia 1963, as Suzel in L'Amico Fritz. *Career:* Has sung with the Fujiwara Opera Company and at La Scala, Milan; State Operas of Hamburg and Vienna, 1970 and 1971; Metropolitan Opera 1972; State Operas of Dresden and Berlin 1973 and 1976; Further appearances in Buenos Aires, Belgrade, Strasbourg, Washington, Prague, Munich, Copenhagen, Barcelona, Boston, Cincinnati, Miami, Naples and Venice; Other roles include Madama Butterfly, Iris in the opera by Mascagni, Mimi, Micaela, Violetta and parts in operas by Mozart and Strauss.

B

BABAK Renata, b. 4 Feb 1939, Kharkov, Ukraine, USSR. Opera Singer (Mezzo-soprano). *Education:* Rimsky-Korsakov Conservatory, Leningrad, 1955-58; P.I. Tchaikovsky Conservatory, Kiev, Ukraine, 1958-61; Diploma, Opera Singer, 1961. *Debut:* As Princess in Dargomizhsky's The Mermaid, Leningrad State Opera, 1958. *Career:* With Lvov State Opera, Ukraine, 1961-64; With Bolshoi Theatre Opera, Moscow, 1964-73; Roles: Carmen, Amneris, Eboli in Don Carlos, Azucena, Charlotte in Werther, Ortrud in Lohengrin, Marina in Boris Godunov, Marfa in Khovanshchina, Lubasha in Tsar's Bride, Lubov in Mazeppa, Olga in Eugene Onegin, Pauline in The Queen of Spades, Ratmir in Ruslan and Ludmilla, Princess in The Mermaid; Roles in USA, 1973-; Ulrica in Un Ballo in Maschera, Santuzza in Cavalleria Rusticana, Amneris, Azucena, Leonora in La Forza del Destino; Concert tours, North America and Europe; Head, Vocal Department and Opera Workshop, Washington Conservatory of Music, 1983-. *Recordings:* Renata Babak, Golden Age Stereo 1006; Renata Babak Sings Ukrainian Songs and Arias by Puccini and Verdi. *Honours include:* Honorary Degrees: Brandeis University, 1991; Princeton University, 1991; William Schuman Award of Columbia University, 1992. *Address:* PO Box 19645, Washington, DC 20036, USA.

BABBITT Milton (Byron), b. 10 May 1916, Philadelphia, Pennsylvania, USA. Composer; Music Educator; Music Theorist. m. Sylvia Miller, 27 Dec 1939. 1 daughter. *Education:* Studied violin, clarinet and saxophone in childhood; Mathematics, University of Pennsylvania; BA, New York University, 1935; MFA, Princeton University, 1942; Studied music with Marion Bauer and Philip James; Studied privately with Roger Sessions. *Career:* Teacher, Music Faculty 1938-42 and 1948-84, Mathematics Faculty 1942-45, William Shubael Conant Professor 1966-84, Professor Emeritus, Princeton University; Director, Columbia-Princeton Electronic Music Center, 1959-84; Member, composition faculty, Juilliard School, New York, 1973-; Guest lecturer many USA and European colleges and universities; PhD, Princeton University, 1992. *Compositions:* Orchestral: Fabulous Voyage, 1946; Relata I, 1965; II, 1968; Ars combinatoria, 1981; Piano Concerto, 1985; Transfigured Notes for Strings, 1986; Chamber: Composition for 4 Instruments, 1948; Composition for 12 Instruments, 1948, revised 1954; 5 string quartets, 1948, 1954, 1969-70, 1970, 1982; Composition for Viola and Piano, 1950; Woodwind Quartet, 1953; All Set for 8 Instruments, 1957; Sextets for Violin and Piano, 1966; Arie da capo for 6 Instruments, 1973-74; My Ends Are My Beginnings for Clarinet, 1978; Paraphrases for 11 Instruments, 1979; Dual for Cello and Piano, 1980; Melismata for Violin, 1982; Groupwise for 7 Instruments, 1983; Four Play for Clarinet, Violin, Cello and Piano, 1984; Sheer Pluck for Guitar, 1984; The Joy of More Sextets, 1986; Fanfare for Double Brass Sextet, 1987; Homily for Snare Drum, 1987; Whirled Series for Saxophone and Piano, 1987; Beaten Paths for Marimba, 1988; The crowded Air for 11 Instruments, 1988; Consortini for 5 Instruments, 1989; Solo piano pieces; Choruses; Songs; Tape pieces. *Publications:* S Dembski and J Straus, editors, Milton Babbitt: Words about Music (The Madison Lectures), 1987. *Contributions:* Articles in various journals. *Honours:* Joseph A Bearns Prize, 1942; New York Music Critics' Circle citations, 1949, 1964; National Institute of Arts and Letters Award, 1959; Guggenheim Fellowship, 1960-61; Brandeis University Gold Medal, 1970; National Music Award, 1976; Pulitzer Prize Special Citation, 1982; George Peabody Medal, 1983; MacArthur Fellow, 1986-91; American Academy and Institute of Arts and Letters Gold Medal in Music, 1988; Arnold Schoenberg Institute Award, 1988. *Memberships:* International Society of Contemporary Music, president, 1951-52; League of Composers; National Institute and American Academy of Arts and Letters; American Academy of Arts and Sciences; American Institute of Physics; Acoustical Society of America; Audio Engineering Society; Phi Beta Kapa. *Hobbies:* Analytical philosophy; Mathematical studies; Watching football. *Address:* 222 Western Way, Princeton, NJ 08540, USA.

BACH Andreas, b. 29 July 1968, Dennbach-WW, Germany. Pianist. *Education:* 1st music lessons, 1973-80; Studied with Professor Karl-Heinz Kammerlung, Hanover. *Debut:* Alte Opera, Frankfurt, 1984. *Career:* Appearance in Eurovision Competition, 1984; 1st tour to USA, with debuts New York, San Francisco and Washington DC, 1987, to Japan, 1988; Several more tours, USA; Appearances in France, England, Switzerland, Italy and Portugal. *Recordings:* Schumann op 6, op 7, 1989; Beethoven op 7, op 31 no 2, op 126, Novalis, 1990. *Honours:* Winner, several Youth Competitions, 1975-84; Bernhard Sprengel Prize for Music, 1985; Kulturpreis von Rheinland-Pfalz, 1990. *Hobbies:* Reading German literature; Photography; Swimming; Biking. *Current Management:* Concerto Winde-stein, Munich, Germany. *Address:* Ringstrasse 20, 5430 Montabaur, Germany.

BACH Jan Morris, b. 11 Dec 1937, Forrest, Illinois, USA. Composer; Educator. m. Dalia Zakaras, 20 Aug 1971, 2 daughters. *Education:* BMus 1959, MMus 1961, DMA 1971, Composition, University of Illinois, Urbana-Champaign. *Career:* Assistant 1st Horn, United States Army Band, 1962-65; Instructor in Music, University of Tampa, Florida, 1965-66; Professor of Music, Northern Illinois University, Dekalb, 1966-. *Compositions:* Galaxy Music Corporation, New York; Four Two-Bit Contraptions, 1967; Skizzen, 1967; Burgundy Variations, 1968; Woodwork, 1970; Eisteddfod, 1972; The System, 1973; Piano Concerto, 1975; Praetorius Suite, 1977; Hair Today, 1977; Happy Prince, 1978; Gala Fanfare, 1979; The Student from Salamanca, 1979; Rounds and Dances, 1980; Sprint, 1982; Horn Concerto, 1983; Dompes & Jompes, 1986. Associated Music Publishers, New York; Three Bagatelles, 1963 and 1971; Dirge for a Minstrel, 1969; Fanfare and Fugue, 1979; Boosey and Hawkes; My Wilderness, 1974; Carl Fischer: Three Choral Dances, 1969; Mentor Music: Laudes, 1971; M M Cole: Turkish Music, 1967. *Hobbies:* Bicycling; Crossword puzzles; Jigsaw puzzles; Caricature cartooning; Collecting old radio programmes; Playing French horn. *Address:* Music 209, Northern Illinois University, Dekalb, IL 60115, USA.

BACHMANN Rhonda, b. 24 Oct 1952, Chicago, Illinois, USA. Soprano. m. Arthur Hammond, 24 Aug 1986, dec 1991. *Education:* Conservatoire National Superior de Musique de Paris, 1972-76; Concours de Maitres du Chant, Paris, 1973, 1st prize; Institut de Musicologie, Sorbonne, Paris, 1971-72, Licence ès Lettres, 1976; Master of Music in Applied Voice, 1978, Northwestern University, Evanston, Illinois, 1977-78; Further private study with Jan Keizer, Amsterdam, 1983-87. *Career:* Chicago Opera Theatre, 1979-80; Théâtre de la Porte St Martin, Paris, 1981, title role, Rose Marie; Théâtre du Palais Royal, Paris, 1981; Opéra de Lyon, 1981; Opera du Rhin, Strasbourg, 1981-84; Centre France Lyrique, Paris, 1982-83; Concerts include, Radio France, 1980; 1979, 1993 Marie Antoinette Bicentennial, Naantali Festival, Finland, 1981; Salle Gaveau, Paris, 1981; Buffalo, New York, 1985; Royal Opera House, Friends of Covent Garden Christmas Gala, 1985; Institut Français, London, 1986; Pavillon Dauphine, Paris, 1986; Some 40 recitals and chamber music concerts in Paris, Germany, Italy, including the music of Vivaldi, Bach, Handel, Mozart, Schubert, Spohr, Brahms, Schoenberg, Ravel and Dowland; Many appearances in theatres and on television, New York, Paris, Marseilles, etc; Acted in 3 films, 1974-76; Leading role, Harriet Smithson, The Life of Berlioz; Toured extensively with recital in 18th Century Costume as Queen Marie Antoinette, Songs for the Queen, Songs for the Revolution, 150 performances, 5 programmes of which 73 in the Grand Trianon, Versailles, 1988-93; tours to America, England, Scotland, Ireland, Bulgaria, Austria. *Recordings:* Cassettite: Quand tu étais petit, Lieder in French translation by Mozart, Schubert and Brahms; Record, Excerpts from the production of Rose-Marie at the

Théâtre de la Porte St Martin, 1981. *Address:* 47 Floral Street, London, WC2, England.

BACK Andrée, b. 1950, England. Singer (Soprano). *Education:* Studied at the Royal College of Music. *Career:* Has sung in oratorios, recitals and symphony concerts; Appearances in most major European and American cities; Frequent engagements in Switzerland, Norway, Austria, Belgium and the Netherlands (Radio Symphony Orchestra, Rotterdam); Has sung in Carmina Burana at Liège, Siegen and Edinburgh; La Mort de Cléopâtre by Berlioz with the Berlin Symphony Orchestra; Mozart Requiem and Coronation Mass in Marienstatt with the Bonn Bach Choir; Mozart Concert Arias with the Schwabische Symphony Orchestra; Sang in Mahler's 4th Symphony at the Cheltenham Festival and in A Child of our Time at Bury St Edmunds; Telemann Cantatas in Hamburg; Sang Haydn's Berenice and Strauss's Four Last Songs with the Billings Symphony Orchestra, 1989; Other concert repertoire includes Bach's Mass in B Minor, Magnificat, Passions and Christmas Oratorio; Beethoven's Missa Solemnis, Mass in C and Choral Symphony; Requiems by Brahms, Fauré, Britten and Verdi; Handel's Messiah, Judas Maccabeus, Jephtha, Joshua, Acis and Galatea, Hercules, Israel in Egypt, Samson, Saul and Chandos Anthems; Janáček Glagolitic Mass; Mahler 2nd and 8th Symphonies, Rückert Lieder; Schubert Salve Regina, Masses; Vivaldi Gloria and Magnificat; Wagner Wesendonck Lieder. *Address:* Mancroft Towers, Oulton Broad, Lowestoft, Suffolk NR32 3PS, England.

BÄCK Sven-Erik, b. 16 Sept 1919, Stockholm, Sweden. Composer. *Education:* Royal Academy of Music, Stockholm, 1938-43; Composition with Hilding Rosenberg 1940-45; Schola Cantorum Basle 1948-50; Composition with Petrassi in Rome 1951. *Career:* Played violin and viola in various ensembles until 1957; Director, Swedish Radio music school, 1959. *Compositions:* The Crane Feathers, radio opera 1956; A Play about Mary, oratorio 1958; The Feast, chamber opera 1958; The Birds, radio opera 1961; Ikaros, ballet 1963; Movements, ballet 1966; Cat's Journey, ballet 1969; Electronic ballets Wall and Gate and Through the Earth, Through the Sea, 1971; 3 string quartets, 1945, 1947, 1962; String Quintet 1948; Solo Flute Sonata 1949; Sinfonia for Strings 1951; Sinfonia Sacra 1953; String Trio with double bass 1953; Violin Concerto 1957; A Game around a Game for strings and percussion 1959; Intrada for orchestra 1964; Cello Concerto 1965; Humlan for chorus, cello, piano and percussion 1968; String Trio 1970; Aperio for 3 orchestral groups 1973; Decet for wind quintet, string quartet and double bass 1973; Time Present for 2 violins and electronics 1975. *Address:* STIM, Sandhamnsgatan 79, PO Box 27327, S-102 54 Stockholm, Sweden.

BACQUIER Gabriel, b. 17 May 1924, Beziers, France. Singer (Baritone). *Education:* Studied at the Paris Conservatoire. *Debut:* Sang in Landowski's Le Fou at Nice, 1950. *Career:* Sang in Brussels 1953-56 and at the Opéra-Comique, Paris, 1956-58; Appeared at the Paris Opéra from 1958 as Escamillo, Valentin, Rigoletto, Simon Boccanegra and Boris Godunov; Aix-en-Provence 1960, as Don Giovanni, Glyndebourne Festival 1962, as Mozart's Count; Covent Garden 1964; as Riccardo in I Puritani and Scarpia; US debut 1962 at Chicago as the High Priest in Samson et Dalila; Metropolitan Opera 1964-79, as Don Pasquale, the villains in Les Contes d'Hoffmann, Iago, Leporello, Golaud and Rossini's Bartolo; Holland Festival 1972, as Falstaff; Teatro Fenice Venice 1973-74; Teacher at the Paris Conservatoire until 1987; Sang Sancho Panza in Massenet's Don Quichotte at Florence and Monte Carlo, 1992. *Recordings include:* Guillaume Tell, Gounod's Mireille and Roméo et Juliette, La Belle Hélène (HMV); Lakmé, Les Huguenots, Don Giovanni, Les Contes d'Hoffmann, Così fan Tutte, Le nozze di Figaro, Don Quichotte, La Favorite by Donizetti (Decca); Thais by Massenet (RCA); Ariane et Barbe-Bleue by Dukas (Erato).

BADER Hans-Dieter, b. 16 Feb 1938, Stuttgart, Germany. Singer (Tenor). *Education:* Studied with Rudolf Gehrung and in Stuttgart. *Debut:* Stuttgart Staatsoper 1960, as Arturo in Lucia di Lammermoor. *Career:* Sang at Brunswick, Karlsruhe, Essen, Cassel and Mannheim; Appeared in Hannover 1965-84 as Rodolfo (La Bohème), Faust at Nuremberg, Hamburg, Dusseldorf, Strasbourg and Vienna (Volksoper); Other roles include Ferrando (Così fan Tutte) and the Duke of Mantua. *Recordings include:* Reger's Requiem (Schwann); Sly by Wolf-Ferrari and Strauss's Feuersnot (RCA).

BADIAN Maya, b. 18 Apr 1945, Bucharest, Romania. Composer; Doctor of Music. m. Lucian Munteanu, 1 son (deceased). Emigrated to Canada in 1987. *Education:* Master in Music, Composition, Conservatory C Porumbescu, Bucharest, Romania; Doctor in Music, Composition, Faculte de Musique de l'Universite de Montreal, Montreal, Canada. *Debut:* Symphonic Movement, Romania, 1968. *Career:* Musical Director, RTV, Bucharest, Romania 1968-72; Professor of Composition and Keyboard, Bucharest, Romania, 1972-87; currently Professor of Composition and Keyboard, Faculte de Musique de l'Université de Montreal, Montreal, Canada. Lecturer at Conferences and at various contemporary music festivals in Europe and Canada. Performances in Europe, USA and Canada. *Compositions:* Symphonic works for orchestra, including: Holocaust - In Memoriam, symphony; Concertante music for solo instruments and orchestra, including Concertos for Piano, Violin, Guitar, Cello, Marimba and Vibraphone and Timpanis (to Mircea Badian); Vocal-Orchestral works, including Poem for Soprano; Chamber music, including Concerto for Horn and Percussion, solos, duos, trios, and other chamber ensembles. *Recordings:* Numerous radio and disc recordings. *Contributor to:* Different musical periodicals and RTV interviews: Romania, Italy, Hungary, Poland, Canada. *Hobbies:* Reading; Travelling; Films; Fine Arts. *Address:* 3250 Ellendale Avenue 601, Montreal, Quebec, Canada H3S 1W4.

BADINSKI Nikolai I, b. 19 Dec 1937, Sofia, Bulgaria. Composer; Pedagogue. *Education:* Diploma, Academy of Music, Sofia, 1956-61; Masterclass, Composition, Academy of Arts, East Berlin, 1967-70; Scholarship for masterclasses, Accademia Musicale, Siena, Italy, 1975-76. *Career:* Active as Composer, University Teacher in Berlin, Sofia, Halle; Concert Violinist; Concertmaster; Special Advisor for Music Education, String Quartet, German Democratic Republic; Active in the Darmstadt International Courses for New Music, 1974-78; Guest Professor, Universities of Stockholm and Copenhagen; Assistant to Max Deutsch, Sorbonne and Ecole Normale de Musique, Paris, 1982; Living in Paris (Scholar of the French Government), 1985-86; Composer-in-Residence (California); Appearances at various Festivals; Numerous performances, Radio and TV Broadcaster. *Compositions:* Numerous compositions including 3 symphonies, several concertos for instruments and orchestra; Widerspiegelungen der Weisheir for S, B, Choir and orchestra, ballets, music for orchestra, chamber music; 3 Espressioni, for soprano and tape, 1981; Cantico di S Francesco, for baritone and tape, 1981-82; Vocal, Organ Music; Electroacoustic Music; Schwendes Berl Märchen, Traumvisionen, Dostoevsky Reflections, Homage to Kafka, Rotation (in Memory of a Cosmonaut), Phoenixe, Sevtopolis; Watermusic, 1980; Musik mit Papier; Luftmusik, 1980-81; Musicvisuel correspondence P, 1980-82. *Recordings:* 6 LPs with compositions by Aban-Abt and by pro Viva. *Contributor to:* Freelance contributor to the BBC, London. *Address:* Landgrafenstrasse 8, D-1000 Berlin 30, Germany.

BADOREK Wilfried, b. 1936, Germany. Singer (Tenor). *Career:* Sang first in Karlsruhe, 1960-62, then Aachen, Essen and Gartnerplatz, Munich, 1965-67; Later engaged in Mannheim and Cologne, 1977-82; Sang in Innsbruck, 1979-83; Staatsoper Vienna and Bregenz Festival, 1973, as Erik in Fliegende Holländer; Venice as Max in Der Freischütz, 1974, Rome and Lisbon as Florestan, 1977; Further guest appearances in

Teheran, 1976, Ottawa, 1977, and Brussels including as the Drum Major in Wozzeck, 1981; Other roles have included Verdi's Duke and Gabriele Adorno, Pinkerton, Andrea Chenier and Turiddu; Wagner's Lohengrin, Walter and Parsifal; Strauss's Bacchus and Emperor, and title role in La Damnation de Faust. *Recordings include:* Highlights from Die Zauberflöte. *Address:* c/o Theatre Royale de la Monnaie, 4 Rue Leopold, B-1000 Brussels, Belgium.

BADURA-SKODA Eva, b. 15 Jan 1929, Munich, Germany. Musicologist. m. Paul Badura-Skoda, 4 children. *Education:* Universities of Heidelberg, Vienna and Innsbruck; PhD 1953; 3 years study Hochschule für Musik, Vienna. *Career:* Freelance Lecturer and Writer, until 1962; Summer School Lecturer, Mozarteum Salzburg; Professor, University of Wisconsin, 1964-74; Guest Professor, University of Boston, 1976; Queen's University, Kingston, Canada, 1979. *Publications:* Mozart Interpretation 1957; Interpreting Mozart on the Keyboard 1961; Mozart's C minor Piano Concerto 1971; An unknown Singspiel by Joseph Haydn 1972. *Contributions to:* Musical Journals; New Grove Dictionary of Music and Musicians 1980. *Memberships:* International Musicological Society; Haydn Institute, Cologne. *Honours:* 3 University Grants. *Address:* Zuckerkandlgasse 14, 1190 Vienna, Austria.

BADURA-SKODA Paul, b. 6 Oct 1927, Vienna, Austria. Pianist. m. Eva Badura-Skoda, 4 children. *Education:* Studied Conducting and Piano at State Conservatory, Vienna; Master class of Edwin Fischer, Lucerne. *Career:* Concert pianist from 1948, notably in works by Mozart, Beethoven and Schubert; New York debut 1953; Piano duets with Jörg Demus; Held annual master classes, formerly in Edinburgh and Salzburg, latterly at Vienna Festival; Artist-in-residence, University of Wisconsin, 1966-71; Premieres of Martin's 2nd Piano Concerto, 1970 and Fantasie sur des rhythmes flamencos, 1973. *Compositions:* Mass in D; Cadenzas to piano and violin concertos by Mozart and Haydn. *Publications:* Mozart Interpretation 1957 (with wife); The Piano Sonatas of Beethoven (with Jörg Demus) 1970; Bach-Interpretationen, 1988; Editions of works by Schubert, Mozart and Chopin. *Honours include:* Austrian Music Competition 1947. *Address:* c/o Hochschule für Musik und darstellende Kunst, Lothringerstrasse 18, 1037 Vienna, Austria.

BAETEN Herman Jozef Marcel, b. 27 Aug 1948, Peer, Belgium. Musicologist. *Education:* Musicology, Ghent University, 1986-72. *Career:* Belgium Radio and Television, 1972-75; Choir Conductor, 1972-; Teacher, History and Art, public schools, and Tutor, Music History, Musical academy, 1975-86; Conductor, Founding Member, Capilla Flamenca ensemble of Renaissance music, 1978-87; President, 1978-86, Director, 1987-, Founding Member, Musica non-profit organisation centre of early music in Flanders stimulating and coordinating early music in Flanders and maintaining relations with similar organisations abroad; Administrator, Alamire publishing centre for yearbooks, quarterlies, facsimiles, information booklets, miniatures, 1988-; Administrator, Mallemuze, 1989-; Treasurer, Alamire Foundation, International Centre for the Study of Music in the Low Countries, 1991-; Member, Board of Directors, Ruckersgenootschap. *Address:* Musica, PO Box 45, 3990 Peer, Belgium.

BAGINSKI Zbigniew, b. 19 Jan 1949, Stettin, Poland. Composer; Teacher. m. Alicja, 23 Aug 1988, 2 daughters. *Education:* MA, High School of Music, Warsaw, 1972. *Career:* Many performances of compositions in Germany, Great Britain, Denmark, Sweden, USA, USSR, Holland, Hungary, Cuba; Assistant Professor 1978-88, Associate Professor 1988-; Vice-Dean, Faculty of Composition, Conducting and Music Theory, 1987-90, Academy of Music Frederic Chopin, Warsaw. *Compositions:* Sinfonia notturna, 1984; Concerto for Harpsichord and Orchestra, 1985; Oh, Sweet Baroque! suite for string orchestra, 1985; Symphony in Seven Scenes, 1988; Canons, Scherzos and Epigrams, 1987; Nocturne-Berceusee, 1989; Trio

with Coda, 1983; Piano Quartet, 1990; Refrain for 2 Pianos, 1975; Acho for Organ, 1974; Expeditions on the other Side, 1973. *Memberships:* Polish Composers Union, Vice-President of Warsaw Branch 1985-89, General Secretary 1989. *Hobbies:* Tennis; Skiing. *Address:* ul Schillera 8m5, 00-248 Warsaw, Poland.

BAGLIONI Bruna, b. 8 April 1947, Frascati, Italy. Mezzo-soprano. *Education:* Studied with Gina Maria Rebori and Walter Castaldi-Tassoni in Rome. *Debut:* Spoleto 1970, as Maddalena in Rigoletto. *Career:* Has sung at major theatres in Milan, Venice, Naples, Trieste, Rome, Bologna and London (at Covent Garden as Eboli in Don Carlos); Other roles include Verdi's Amneris, Ulrica and Azucena; La Cieca in La Gioconda; Marina in Boris Godunov; Leonore in Donizetti's La Favorite and Giovanna Seymour in Anna Bolena; Charlotte in Werther by Massenet; Sang Amneris at Dallas, Laura in La Gioconda at Rome, 1992; Eboli and Amneris at the Verona Arena, 1992; Many concert appearances. *Recordings include:* Don Carlos from Covent Garden (Thorn-EMI video). *Address:* Arena di Verona, Piazza Bra 28, 37121 Verona, Italy.

BAILES Anthony James, b. 18 June 1947, Bristol, England. Lutenist. m. Anne Van Royen. *Education:* Bulmershe College of Further Education; Studies with Michael Watson (Bristol), Diana Poulton (London), Gusta Goldschmidt (Amsterdam), Eugen M Dombois (Schola Cantorum Basiliensis). *Debut:* Purcell Room, 1971. *Career:* Solo Concerts and Tours throughout Europe and Scandinavia; Many Recordings both solo and in ensemble; Professor of Lute, Sweelinck Conservatorium, Amsterdam, 1979-. *Recordings:* Numerous recordings and Broadcasts. *Publications:* An Introduction to 17th Century Lute Music, 1983; Lessons for the Lute (with A Van Royen), 1983; 32 Easy pieces for baroque lute, 1984. *Contributor To:* Criticism for various journals and magazines and some articles. *Hobby:* Reading. *Address:* Hollenweg 3A, 4144 Arlesheim, Switzerland.

BAILEY Donald Lesley, b. 9 Apr 1956, Nashville, Tennessee, USA. United States Postal Clerk; Amateur Flautist. *Education:* BA, Biology, Fisk University; Meharry Medical School, Nashville, 2 years; Studied Piano formally, 1 year; Clarinet in Band programme, Public School Music System, grades 5-10; Baroque Recorder self-taught; Flute and Piccolo with Ann Richards, 1988-. *Compositions:* Cadenzas for Mozart's Flute Concerto in G major K313, 1991. *Honours:* Honourable Mention, American Recorder Society sponsored Katz Fund Composition Contest, 1986; Winner, Mozart Cadenza Competition, National Flute Association, 1991. *Memberships:* American Recorder Society; National Flute Association. *Hobbies:* Reading about music and musicians; Performing in music ensembles and concert bands. *Address:* 918 38th Avenue North, Nashville, TN 37209-2533, USA.

BAILEY Norman Stanley, b. 23 Mar 1933, Birmingham, England. Operatic and Concert Baritone. m. (1) Doreen Simpson, 1957, divorced 1983, 2 sons, 1 daughter, (2) Kristine Ciesinski, July 1985. *Education:* Rhodes University, Republic of South Africa; BMus, Vienna State Academy, Austria; Performers and Teachers Licenciate in Singing; Diplomas, Opera, Lieder and Oratorio. *Debut:* Linz, 1960. *Career:* Principal Baritone, Sadler's Wells Opera, London, England, 1967-71; Regular engagements at world's major opera houses and festivals including: La Scala, Milan; Royal Opera House, Covent Garden; First British Hans Sachs in Meistersinger 1969, Bayreuth Wagner Festival, he has also sung Amfortas there; Vienna State Opera; Metropolitan Opera, New York; Paris Opera; Edinburgh Festival; Hamburg State Opera; Munich State Opera; English National Opera; Scottish Opera; In 1985 he sang in the world premiere of Goehr's Behold The Sun; Television performances for BBC include: Falstaff, La Traviata, The Flying Dutchman, Macbeth; Sharpless, Scottish Opera, Britten's Theseus, Opera London,

Sadler's Wells, Stromminger, La Wally, Bregenz Festival, 1990; Sang in Reginald Goodall Memorial Concert, Wahnmonolog, Festival Hall, 1991; Season 1992 as Sharpless in Madame Butterfly for ENO and King René in Tchaikovsky's Yolanta for Opera North; Sang Oroveso in Bellini's Norma for Opera North, 1993. *Recordings include:* The Ring, Goodall; Meistersinger and Der fliegende Holländer, Solti; Walküre, Klemperer. *Honours:* Commander of the Order of the British Empire, 1977; Honorary RAM, 1981; Honorary Doctor of Music, 1986. *Membership:* Baha'i World Community. *Hobbies:* Chess; Notaphily; Golf; Microcomputing. *Address:* c/o Music International, 13 Ardilaun Road, Highbury, London N5 2QR, England.

BAILLIE Alexander, b. 6 Jan 1956, Stockport, Lancashire, England. Concert cellist. *Education:* Studied with Jacqueline du Pré, at the Royal College of Music and with André Navarra in Vienna. *Career:* Many performances with leading British orchestras; Concerts in Europe and North America include the first Canadian performance of Penderecki's 2nd Concerto; Tour of Britain with the Budapest String Orchestra 1991, followed by tour of the Far East; Promenade Concert appearances include the premiere of the Concerto by Colin Matthews 1984, Henze's Sieben Liebeslieder, Takemitsu's Orion and Pleiades 1989, Schumann Concerto (1990) and the Delius Concerto (1993); Has premiered works by Lutoslawski (Grave), Schnittke (Sonata for cello and piano), Gordon Crosse (Wave-Songs) and Takemitsu (Orion and Pleiades); Principal Guest Artist with the East of England Orchestra; Concerts with the Villiers Piano Quartet; Recital debut at the Kennedy Center in Washington, 1992; Season 1993 with US concerto debut (Boston Philharmonic) and visits to the Edinburgh and Harrogate Festivals; Professor at the Royal Academy of Music. *Recordings include:* Tippett Triple Concerto (with Ernst Kovacic and Gerard Causse); Concertos by Elgar, Matthews, and Bernard Stevens; Frank Bridge's Oration, the Britten Cello Suites and Sonata; Sonatas by Rachmaninov, Shostakovich, Prokofiev and Schnittke. *Honours:* Prize winner in competitions at Budapest (Casals) and Munich (ARD). *Address:* c/o TBM, 3 Brunswick Place, Julian Road, Bath BA1 2RQ, England.

BAINBRIDGE Elizabeth, b. 28 March 1936, Lancashire, England. Singer (Mezzo-Soprano). *Education:* Studied at Guildhall School with Norman Walker. *Debut:* Glyndebourne 1963 in Die Zauberflöte. *Career:* Sang in British premiere of Rossini's La Pietra del Paragone, London 1963; Member of Covent Garden Opera from 1965, in Butterfly (Suzuki), The Midsummer Marriage, Falstaff (Mistress Quickly), Les Troyens, Un Ballo in Maschera (Amelia), Troilus and Cressida and Lulu, Erda, Rheingold, Siegfried, Otello, Jenufa (Grandmother), Onegin (Nurse), Aida (Amneris); Tours to La Scala Milan 1976; Far East 1979; Los Angeles; Anthens Festival. Guest appearances with English National Opera, Scottish Opera, Welsh National Opera; US debut Chicago 1977, in Peter Grimes; Buenos Aires debut 1979; Covent Garden, First Maid in Elektra, Innkeeper's Wife in The Cunning Little Vixen, 1990; Peter Grimes, Dublin Grand Opera Society; Widow Sweeney in The Rising of the Moon, Wexford Festival; Sang the Hostess in the Covent Garden premiere of Prokofiev's The Fiery Angel, 1992. *Recordings include:* Dido and Aeneas, Sorceress; Sir John in Love, Mistress Ford; The Rape of Lucretia, Bianca; Peter Grimes, Auntie; Cendrillon, Dorothée; Filipyevna in Eugene Onegin for EMI. *Address:* Buckleys, Forestside, Rowlands Castle, Hants, England.

BAINBRIDGE Simon Jeremy, b. 30 Aug 1952, London, England. Composer; Conductor. m. Lynda Richardson, 17 July 1980, 1 daughter. *Education:* Central Tutorial School for Young Musicians (now Purcell School), 1965-66; Highgate School, 1966-69; Royal College of Music, 1969-72; Studied composition with John Lambert at the Berkshire Music Center, Tanglewood, Massachusetts, USA, 1973-74, with Gunther Schuller. *Career:* Freelance Composer, 1972-; His music performed extensively in UK, USA, Europe,

Australia; Has worked as Conductor with BBC Symphony Orchestra, BBC Scottish Symphony Orchestra, Bournemouth Symphony Orchestra, London Sinfonietta, Northern Sinfonia, Nash Ensemble, Composer's Ensemble, Capricorn and Divertimenti; Teaches composition at Royal College of Music and Guildhall School of Music and Drama. *Compositions include:* Wind Quintet; String Quartet; String Sextet; Clarinet Quintet; Works for small and large chamber ensembles, with and without voice; Choral music; Works for large orchestra; Dance score for Rambert Dance Company; Music for 2 Madame Tussaud exhibitions, London and Amsterdam. *Recordings:* Music of Simon Bainbridge: Fantasia for Double orchestra-BBC Symphony Orchestra/composer, Viola Concerto-London Sinfonietta/Michael Tilson Thomas-Walter Trampler viola, Concertante in moto perpetue-composer's ensemble/composer-Nicholas Daniel oboe. *Honours:* Margaret Lee Crofts Fellowship, USA, 1973; Leonard Bernstein Fellowship, USA, 1974; Forman Fellowship, 1976; USA-UK Bicentennial Fellowship, 1978; Published by United Music Publishers, Novello-Music Sales. *Memberships:* Executive Committees: Society for the Promotion of New Music; International Society for Contemporary Music; Association of Professional Composers. *Hobbies:* Cooking; Walking; Swimming; Travel; Movies; Reading. *Address:* 38 Constantine Road, London NW3 2NG, England.

BAIRD Julianne, b. 10 Dec 1952, Statesville, North Carolina, USA. Singer (Soprano). *Education:* Studied at Eastman School with Masako Ono Toribara and at Stanford University; Further study with Walter Berry and Harnoncourt, and at Salzburg Mozarteum. *Career:* Sang in New York with Waverly Consort and Concert Royal; Stage debut in Handel's Il Pastor Fido; Later appearances in Santa Fe, Washington DC, Philadelphia and Los Angeles in operas by Gluck, Mozart, Purcell, Charpentier and Gagliano; Concert engagements in sacred music by Bach and French Baroque music; Sang in Dido and Aeneas with Academy of Ancient Music at the Barbican Hall, London, 1992; Teacher at Rutgers University. *Recordings include:* Handel's Imeneo, Acis and Galatea, Joshua and Siroe; Cantatas by Bach, Telemann and Clerambault; Bach's Magnificat and B minor Mass; J C Bach's Amadis de Gaule; La Serva Padrona by Pergolesi and Monteverdi's Orfeo. *Contributor to:* Journals such as Continuo and Early Music. *Address:* c/o Washington Opera, John F Kennedy Center for the Performing Arts, Washington, DC 20566, USA.

BAKELS Kees, b. 14 Jan. 1945, Holland, Netherlands. Conductor. *Education:* Studied at the Amsterdam Conservatory and at the Accademia Chigiana in Siena with Franco Ferrara and Bruno Rigacci; Further study with Kiril Kondrashin. *Career:* Associate Conductor of the Amsterdam Philharmonic and Principal Guest Conductor of the Netherlands Chamber Orchestra: tours to England, Belgium, Spain and the USA; Has led all the major Dutch orchestras and has guested with the Warsaw Philharmonic, BBC Philharmonics, BBC Welsh, San Diego, Quebec and Oregon Symphony Orchestras; New Belgian Chamber Orchestra; Ulster Orchestra; Scottish Chamber; Bournemouth Sinfonietta; Royal Liverpool Philharmonic; Appeared with the National Youth Orchestra at the 1985 Promenade Concerts; Currently Chief Guest Conductor with the Bournemouth Symphony and Principal Conductor of Netherlands Radio Symphony Orchestra, 1993-; Has worked with the soloists Yehudi Menuhin, Claudio Arrau, Pierre Fournier, Paul Tortelier, David Oistrakh and Ruggiero Ricci; Appearances with Netherlands Opera in Nabucco, Ariadne auf Naxos, Carmen, Lucia di Lammermoor, Idomeneo and I Puritani; San Diego Opera Oberto and Madama Butterfly; Vancouver Opera Carmen, Così fan Tutte, Le Nozze di Figaro and Die Zauberflöte; Conducted the Lyon Opera in Cinderella (also on tour to Poland); Welsh National Opera with Die Zauberflöte, La Bohème and Carmen; At English National Opera has led Aida and Fidelio; Conducted Carmen at San Diego, 1992; Season 1992/1993 with engagements in Britain, the Netherlands and Denmark; US appearances with the

Florida Symphony, Oregon Symphony and Calgary Philharmonic. *Recordings:* Vaughan Williams Symphonies with the Bournemouth Symphony (Naxos). *Address:* Unit 2, 39 Tadema Road, London SW10 0PY, England.

BAKER Gregg, b. 7 Dec 1955, Chicago, Illinois, USA. Singer (Baritone). *Education:* Studied at Northwestern University and with Andrew Smith. *Career:* Sang on Broadway in such musicals as The Wiz, Timbuktu and Raisin; Metropolitan Opera debut, as Crown in Porgy and Bess, 1985, appearing later as Escamillo and the High Priest in Samson and Delilah; Has also sung Crown at Glyndebourne, 1985, and in Helsinki and Tulsa; Concert performance of Porgy and Bess at the Elizabeth Hall, London, 1989; Other roles include Ford in Falstaff, Count Almaviva and Marcello in La Bohème; Old Vic Theatre, London, in Carmen Jones, 1991; Sang Crown in Porgy and Bess at Covent Garden, London, and Savonlinna Festival, Finland, 1992. *Recordings include:* Porgy and Bess. *Address:* c/o Harrison Parrott Ltd, 12 Penzance Place, London W11 4PA, England.

BAKER Israel, b. 11 Feb 1921, Chicago, Illinois, USA. Violinist. *Education:* Studied with Adolph Pick, Chicago Conservatory; Louis Persinger, Juilliard School of Music, New York; Jacques Gordon and Bronislaw Huberman. *Career:* Soloist with various orchestras; Concertmaster; Many chamber-music appearances including 2nd violinist, Heifetz-Piatigorsky Chamber Concerts; Often heard in Schoenberg's Concerto and Berg's Chamber Concerto; Member, Pacific Art Trio; Professor of Music, Scripps College, Claremont, California. *Recordings:* Various recordings as a soloist and chamber-music player, including works by Ives, Antheil, Kubik and Stravinsky. *Address:* c/o Scripps College, Claremont, California, USA.

BAKER Janet Abbott (Dame), b. 21 Aug 1933, Hatfield, Yorkshire, England. Singer (Mezzo-Soprano). m. James Keith Shelley, 1957. *Education:* The College for Girls, York; Vocal studies with Helene Isepp and Meriel St Clair in London. *Debut:* Oxford University Opera Club 1956, as Roza in The Secret by Smetana. *Career:* Sang in concert, and in opera as Gluck's Orpheus, London 1958 and Pippo in La Gazza Ladra at the 1959 Wexford Festival; Sang Eduige in Handel's Rodelinda, London 1959 and the title roles in Tamerlano, Ariodante, Orlando and Admeto, Birmingham, 1962-68; Rameau's Hippolyte et Aricie 1965; Sang in Mahler's Resurrection Symphony at the 1961 Edinburgh Festival; English Opera Group from 1962, as Dido, Polly in The Beggar's Opera and Lucretia; Sang in the premieres of Britten's Owen Wingrave, 1971 and Phaedra, 1976; New York concert debut 1966; Scottish Opera debut 1967, as Dorabella, followed by Dido in The Trojans, Octavian, and the Composer in Ariadne auf Naxos; Glyndebourne Festival 1965-72, as Dido, Diana-Jupiter in La Calisto and Penelope in Il Ritorno d'Ulisse; Covent Garden 1966-74, as Hermia in A Midsummer Night's Dream, Dido, Kate in Owen Wingrave and Vitellia in La Clemenza di Tito; With English National Opera appeared as Poppea, 1971, Mary Stuart, 1973, Charlotte, 1976 and Julius Caesar; Concert repertory includes works by Mahler, Elgar, Britten, Brahms and Bach; Lieder by Schubert and French and English Songs; Retired from opera 1982, singing Gluck's Orpheus at Glyndebourne and Alceste at Covent Garden; Sang Orpheus in a concert performance at Carnegie Hall and retired 1989; Appointed Chancellor of University of York, 1991; Trustee, Foundation for Sport and the Arts, 1991. *Recordings include:* The Angel in The Dream of Gerontius; Dido and Aeneas; La Calisto; Mozart's Requiem; I Capuleti e i Montecchi; Maria Stuarda; The Rape of Lucretia and Owen Wingrave; Duets with Dietrich Fischer-Dieskau; Handel's Messiah, Judas Maccabeus and Ariodante; La Clemenza di Tito; Verdi Requiem; Orfeo ed Euridice; Labels include Erato, Deutsche Grammophon, EMI and Philips. *Publications:* Full Circle, Autobiography, 1982. *Honours include:* CBE 1970; DBE 1976; Shakespeare Prize, Hamburg, 1971; Honorary Fellow, St Anne's College, Oxford, 1975; Copenhagen Sonning Prize, 1979; Honorary DMus from

Birmingham, Leicester, London, Hull, Oxford, Leeds, Lancaster and York Universities; Honorary MusD, Cambridge, 1984; Honorary Fellow, Downing College, Cambridge, 1985; Gold Medal, Royal Philharmonic Society, 1990. *Membership:* Fellow of the Royal Society of Arts, 1979. *Hobbies:* Reading; Walking. *Address:* c/o TRANSART (UK) Ltd, 8 Bristol Gardens, London W9 2JG, England.

BAKER Julius, b. 23 Sept 1915, Cleveland, Ohio, USA. Flautist; Teacher. *Education:* Studied with William Kincaid at the Curtis Institute. *Career:* Member of the Cleveland Orchestra, 1937-41; Principal flautist of the Pittsburgh Symphony Orchestra 1941-43, CBS Symphony Orchestra 1943-50 and the Chicago Symphony Orchestra 1951-53; Performed with the Bach Aria Group 1946-64; Member of faculty, Juilliard School of Music from 1954; Gave the US premieres of the flute concertos by Ibert (1947) and Imbrie (1979); Principal flautist New York Philharmonic Orchestra 1964-83; Joined faculty of the Curtis Institute, Philadelphia, 1980; Graduate of Curtis Institute of Music; Faculty of Carnegre Mellon University since 1991. *Recordings:* RCA Victor, Decca, Vanguard, Vox, Westminster, Cum Laude, Columbia. *Publications include:* Editions of flute solos from sacred music by Bach, 1972. *Address:* c/o Curtis Institute of Music, 1726 Locust Street, Rittenhouse Square, Philadelphia, PA 19103, USA.

BAKER Michael Conway, b. 13 Mar 1937, West Palm Beach, Florida, USA (became Canadian Citizen in 1970). Composer; Lecturer. m. Penny Anne Baker. *Education:* B Mus, University of British Columbia, 1966; MA, Western Washington State College, 1972. *Career:* Active career as film and concert composer; Over period of almost 25 years has taught and developed music programmes for children of all ages, adult education and university students; Currently teaches two courses at University of British Columbia as well as one extension course at Simon Fraser University; Also currently Composer-in-Residence for Vancouver School Board. *Compositions include:* Washington Square: 60 minute ballet for orchestra, 1978; Symphony No 1 Highland, 1977; Capriccio for Clarinet and Orchestra 1991; Through the Lions' Gate: Tone Poems for Orchestra, 1989; Concerto for Piano and Orchestra, 1976; Concerto for Flute and Strings 1974; Counterplay for Viola and Strings, 1971; Seven Wonders: A Song Cycle: Soprano and Piano, 1983; Intermezzo for Flute and Harp 1988; Evocations for Flute, Quartet and Orchestra 1982; Sonata for Piano, 1974; Chanson Joyeuse for Orchestra, 1987. Music for films, such as The Grey Fox, One Magic Christmas and John and the Missus. His Fanfare to Expo 86 opened the proceedings of Expo 86 in Vancouver. *Address:* 2440 Treetop Lane, North Vancouver, BC, Canada V7H 2K5.

BAKER Richard Douglas James, b. 15 June 1925, Willesden, London, England. Radio and Television Broadcaster; Author. m. Margaret Celia Baker, 2 sons. *Education:* MA, Peterhouse, Cambridge. *Debut:* Actor, 1948; As BBC Announcer 1950. *Career:* Actor 1948-49; Teacher 1949-50; BBC TV Newsreader from 1954-82; Panellist on BBC TV's Face the Music, 1964-79; Presenter of TV concerts, 1960-; Presenter of numerous radio programmes including, These you have Loved, Radio 4, 1972-77; Baker's Dozen, Radio 4, 1977-78; Melodies for You, Radio 2, 1988-; Richard Baker Compares notes, Radio 4, 1989-; Music for Awhile, World Service, 1990-91; In Tune, Radio 3, 1992. Numerous concert appearances as narrator and compère. *Recordings:* As Narrator of Peter and the Wolf; Young Person's Guide to the Orchestra; Façade, with Susana Walton. *Publications:* The Magic of Music 1975; Richard Baker's Music Guide, 1979; Mozart, 1982, new illustrated edition, 1991; Richard Baker: Companion to Music, (BBC pubs), 1993. *Memberships:* Garrick; Governor, National Youth Orchestra; Director, Youth and Music; Trustee, D'Oyly Carte Opera. *Honours:* Officer of the Order of the British Empire 1976; Reserve Decoration, 1979; Hon FLCM; Hon RAM. *Hobbies:* Gardening; Sailing. *Management:* Stephannie Williams

Artists, 12 Central Chambers, Wood Street, Stratford upon Avon, CV37 6QJ, England.

BAKHCHIEV Alexander, b. 27 July 1930, Moscow, USSR. Pianist. m. Elena Sorokina, 28 Nov 1962, 1 daughter. *Education:* MA, Performance, 1953, completed postgraduate courses, 1956, Moscow Conservatory. *Debut:* Solo programme, Liszt, Beethoven Hall, Bolshoi Theatre, Moscow, 1954. *Career:* Stage, TV, radio, over 35 years: Solo, with orchestra, in chamber music ensembles, with singers; Regular duo with E Sorokina; Played with orchestras conducted by G Rozhdestvensky, E Svetlanov, K Kondrashin, B Chaikin, with V Popov (bassoon), A Korneyev (flute), etc; Greatest number of radio recordings in USSR; Performed, France, 1954; TV Chamber Music Concerts, 1970s; Many educational TV and radio series; Concerts all over USSR, including Moscow State Conservatory and with Leningrad Philharmonic; Duets, Soviet and British modern music, England, 1989; International Festival dedicated to Mozart in Tokyo, 1991; Participant, International Festivals of Music; Teaching Chamber Ensemble, Moscow State Conservatory, 1990–; Music for him and wife written and dedicated by A Boyarsky, L Lubovsky, G Fried (USSR), T Moore (England); Introitus, concerto for him written and dedicated by S Gubaidulina. *Recordings:* Nearly 70 discs include Solo: Haydn; Liszt, Bach, Handel, etc; Russian music - Rubinstein, Arensky, Liadov, Lyapunov, Mussorgsky, Borodin; Ensembles: All sonatas, flute, harpsichord, Bach, Handel; Vivaldi (with A Korneyev); Czechoslovakian music, bassoon, piano (with V Popov); Series: Early Mozart, solo, ensembles; Duets (with E Sorokina): All Mozart duets; Duet music, Schubert; Music of France; Albums: Music of Old Vienna; J S Bach, his family and pupils; Music for 6 and 8 hands (with E Sorokina, G Rozhdestvensky, V Postnikova); Music and paintings (with E Sorokina, orchestra conducted by G Rozhdestvensky). *Current management:* Soyuzconcert. *Address:* 4-32 Koshkin str, Moscow 115409, Russia.

BAKSA Robert Frank, b. 7 Feb 1938, New York City, USA. Composer. *Education:* BA, composition, University of Arizona, 1969; Studied with Lukas Foss, Berkshire Music Center, Tanglewood. *Career:* Music copyist, New York, 1962-. *Compositions:* Over 500 works including: Operas: Aria da capo, 1969, revised 1975; Red Carnations, 1969; orchestral works; Chamber music; Choral. *Recordings include:* Cadstone Records, Musical Heritage Society. *Address:* ASCAP, ASCAP Building, One Lincoln Plaza, New York, NY 10023, USA.

BAKST Lawrence, b. 1955, Washington, DC, USA. Singer (Tenor). *Education:* Studied in America and Europe. *Career:* Sang Radames with Opera Delaware and Kentucky Opera; Verdi's Don Carlos at several Italian centres; Macduff in New Jersey, Barcelona and Marseilles; Gabriele Adorno, Riccardo, Manrico, Canio, Calaf and Faust in Mefistofeles; Appearances at the New York City Opera, Zagreb, Wexford, Detmold, Wuppertal and the Opera Forum in Holland; Season 1990-91 as Faust, Cavaradossi and Edgar (Lucia di Lammermoor) in Wuppertal; Bob Boles in Peter Grimes at Marseilles and Pylade in Iphigénie en Tauride at the Opéra de Bastille, Paris; Sang Pylade with the Tanztheater of Wuppertal at Rome, 1992. *Honours:* Winner, Metropolitan Opera National Council Auditions Competition; Premier Grand Prix and Best Tenor Award in the Vinas Competition, Barcelona; Concours International de Chant, Toulouse; First Prize, G B Viotti Competition, Vercelli. *Address:* c/o Music International, 13 Ardilaun Road, London N5 2QR, England.

BALADA Leonardo, b. 22 Sept 1933, Barcelona, Spain. Composer; Professor. m. (1) son. (2) Joan Winer, 28 July 1979. *Education:* Studied piano, Barcelona Conservatory; New York College of Music, 1956-57; Juilliard School of Music, 1958-60; Mannes College of Music, 1961-62; Principal teachers: Copland, Tansman and Persichetti for compositions; Markevitch for conducting. *Career:* Teacher, United Nations International School, 1963-70; Faculty Member 1970-75, Professor 1975-, Carnegie-Mellon University.

Compositions: Operas: Hangman, Hangman!, 1982; Zapata!, 1982-84; Christopher Columbus, 1987. Orchestral: Piano Concerto, 1964; Guitar Concerto, 1965; Guernica, 1966; Sinfonia en Negro, 1968; Bandoneon Concerto, 1970; Persistencies: Sinfonia Concertante for Guitar and Orchestra, 1972; Steel Symphony, 1972; Auroris, 1973; Ponce de Leon for Narrator and Orchestra, 1973; Concerto for Piano, Winds and Percussion, 1974; Homage to Casals, 1975; Homage to Sarasate, 1975; Concerto for 4 Guitars and Orchestra, 1976; 3 Anecdotes, concertino for Castanets or Wood Percussion and Chamber Orchestra, 1977; Sardana, 1979; Quasi un Pasodoble, 1981; Violin Concerto, 1982; Fantasias Sonoras, 1987; Alegrias for Flute and String Orchestra, 1988; Symphony No 4, commissioned and premiered by the Lausanne Chamber Orchestra, 1992; Music for Oboe and Orchestra, commissioned and premiered by Lorin Maazel and The Pittsburgh Symphony Orchestra, 1993. Chamber: Violin Sonata, 1960; Concerto for Cello and 9 Players, 1962; Geometrias No 1 for 6 Instrumentalists, 1966, No 2 for String Quartet, 1967; Cuatris for Instrumental Ensemble, 1969; Mosaico for Brass Quintet, 1970; Tresis for Flute, Guitar and Cello, 1973; Apuntes for Guitar Quartet, 1974; Sonata for 10 Winds, 1980; Music for String Quartet and Flute, 1988, also for String Orchestra and Flute; Many solo pieces; Choral works. *Recordings:* Many compositions recorded. *Hobbies:* Theatre; Travel. *Address:* c/o Music Department, Carnegie-Mellon University, Pittsburgh, PA 15213, USA.

BALANCHIVADZE Andrei (Melitonovich), b. 1 June 1906, St Petersburg, Russia. Composer; Teacher. *Education:* Trained with father Meliton Balanchivadze; Studied piano, composition with Ippolitov-Ivanov, Tbilisi Conservatory. *Career:* Staff 1935-, Chairman Composition Department 1962-, Tbilisi Conservatory. *Compositions:* Ballets: The Heart of the Mountains, 1936; Mtsyri, 1964; 23 symphonies: 1944, 1959, 1984; 4 piano concertos: 1944, 1946, 1952, 1968; The Ocean, symphonic poem, 1952; Choral works; Songs. *Address:* Union of Soviet Composers, Moscow, Russia.

BALASSA Sándor b. 20 Jan 1935, Budapest, Hungary. Composer; Teacher of Orchestration. m. Irene Balogh, 18 Aug 1957, 1 son, 1 daughter. *Education:* Studied Choral Leadership, Bela Bartok Conservatory, Budapest; Composer Diploma, Liszt Academy, Budapest. *Debut:* 1965. *Career:* Radio broadcasts including Legend (21 stations), 1971; Requiem for Lajos Kassak (30 stations), 1972-73; Xenia (BBC), 1974; Works performed abroad; Chant of Glarus, full orchestra; compositions on commission from the Koussevitzky Music Foundation, Teacher of Orchestra, Academy of Music, Budapest. *Compositions include:* The Man Outside, opera in 5 movements; Antinomia, trio for Soprano, Clarinet, Cello, recorded; Xenia, nonet, recorded; Motet for mixed choir; Requiem for Lajos Kassak, recorded; Iris, orchestra, recorded; Cantata Y, recorded; Lupercalia, orchestra, recorded; Tabulae, chamber orchestra, recorded; The Island of Everlasting Youth, for orchestra, recorded; Calls and Cries for orchestra commissioned by the Boston Symphonic Orchestra's centennial; The Day Dreamer's Diary for orchestra commissioned by Elizabeth Sprague Coolidge Foundation, Washington; The Last Shepherd for Cello; Quintet for brass; Kyrie for female choir; Three Fantasies for orchestra commissioned by BBC Philharmonic Orchestra; Flowers from Hajta for cimbalom; The Third Planet, opera-cantata text, by the composer commissioned by Hungarian Radio; Damjanich's Prayer, for mixed choir, 1992; Prince Csaba, for string orchestra, 1993; Bölcskei Concerto, for string orchestra, 1993; Szonatina, for harp, 1993; Karl and Anna, opera in three acts, 1988-1992; Tündér Ilonal for orchestra, 1992; Divertimento for two cimbaloms, 1993. *Membership:* Vice-President of the Hungarian Art Academy. *Hobbies:* Nature; Mountains. *Address:* Árnyas út 14, 1121 Budapest, Hungary.

BALATSCH Norbert, b. 10 Mar 1928, Vienna, Austria. Chorus Master. *Education:* Studied at the

Vienna Music Academy; Private studies in cello and piano. *Career:* Sang with the Vienna Boys' Choir as a child, then directed after graduation; Directed the Vienna Mens' Chorus, then from 1952 the chorus of the Vienna Staatsoper (Chorus Master 1978-84); Director of the Bayreuth Festival Chorus from 1972 together with the Philharmonic Chorus, London (1974-79); Chorus of Accademia di Santa Cecilia, Rome, from 1984; Has directed sacred works by Mozart, Haydn and others at the chapel of the Viennese Court; Led the chorus in Der fliegende Holländer at Bayreuth, 1990. *Address:* Festspielhaus, D-8580 Bayreuth, Germany.

BALDWIN Dalton, b. 19 Dec 1931, Summit, New Jersey, USA. Pianist. *Education:* Juilliard School of Music, New York; BM, Oberlin College Conservatory of Music; Studies with Nadia Boulanger, Madeleine Lipatti, Paris; Special coaching from Sibelius, Barber, Poulenc, et al. *Career:* Toured extensively as Accompanist including: Gerard Souzay, Elly Ameling, Marilyn Horne and Jessye Norman; Took part with Souzay in the premiere of Rorem's War Scenes, 1969. *Recordings:* Numerous recordings including the complete songs of Fauré; Debussy; Ravel; Poulenc. *Address:* c/o Columbia Artists Management, 165 West 57th Street, NY 10019, USA.

BALDWYN Rodney Clifford, b. 18 May 1927, London, England. Organist; Harpsichordist. m. Freda Smith, 1 daughter. *Education:* Birmingham School of Music; Licenciate, Royal Academy of Music; Associate, Royal College of Music; Studies with Geraint Jones and André Marchal. *Debut:* Organ Music Society, London. *Career:* Organist, Pershore Abbey, 1951-81; Recitals, major cathedrals and concert halls including Royal Festival Hall and Queen Elizabeth Hall, London, Europe and Scandinavia; Broadcasts, Danish Radio, ORTF Paris, France, KRO Hilversum and Bavarian Radio; Bach Cycle, Milan; Three Choirs Festival; Bruges Organ Week; Director of Music, St Mary's Convent School, Worcester, England. *Composition:* Carol of the Trees. *Publications:* CPE Bach Organ Sonatas; Elgar and the Organ, 1984. *Contributions to:* Music in Education; Organists Review; Elgar Journal. *Hobbies:* Archaeology; Puppetry; Art; Marathon running. *Address:* Stokesay, 6 Church Farm, Wyre Piddle, Pershore, Worcestershire, England.

BALKIND Jonathan Paul Brenner, b. 6 July 1946, Los Angeles, USA. Impresario. *Education:* Cambridge University; Architectural Association, London. *Career:* Historic Buildings Inspector by GLC/English Heritage with special responsibility for Spitalfields, 1974-88; General and Artistic Director, Opera London, 1988-; Director, Songbird Films (Music and Arts); Board Member and Advisor, Endymion Ensemble, 1980-; Artistic Advisor, City of London Sinfonia, 1988-91; Chairman, Collegium Music '90, and Project Director, Bosnia for AIM/UNHCR 1993 (construction of refugee shelters in northern Bosnia); Founder, Spitalfields Festival and Director, 1976-82; Festivals of Handel, 1977, Early Music 1978, English Music, 1979, Young Mozart, 1980; Produced Mozart Lucio Silla, last performances by Dame Janet Baker of Dido and Aeneas and many other concerts and first performances; Produced operas for stage in Spitalfields and other festivals, Barbican, South Bank and Sadler's Wells, including Gluck's Armide 1982, broadcast BBC and recorded EMI, Handel's Alcina, recorded EMI and restaged in Los Angeles, Monteverdi's L'Incoronazione di Poppea, recorded Virgin Classics, and Britten's A Midsummer Night's Dream, recorded Virgin; Also produced extensive music theatre with Endymion Ensemble, including Birtwistle Punch and Judy with Opera Factory, and directed operas by Gluck, Mozart and Mussorksky; Music Advisor for television films Janet Baker - Full Circle BBC 1982 and Jessye Norman - Singer BBC 1986, and various dance documentaries for Channel Four; Beethoven in Love for BBC. *Contributions to:* Frequent contributions and notes for concerts by Endymion Ensemble, City of London Sinfonia and Editor of festival and opera programmes. *Honours:* ABSA/Daily Telegraph Orb Award 1991, Nomination for individual contribution to the arts.

Hobbies: Cooking for friends; Restoring houses; Reading and Travelling. *Address:* 45 Chalcot Road, London NW1 8LS, England.

BALKWILL Bryan Havell, b. 2 July 1922, London, England. Conductor. m. Susan Elizabeth Roberts, 23 July 1949, 1 son, 1 daughter. *Education:* FRAM, Royal Academy of Music. *Debut:* London 1947. *Career:* Conductor, New London Opera, 1947-49, Glyndebourne, 1954-64, Sadler's Wells/English National Opera, Royal Opera House, Covent Garden, 1959-78; Toured USSR and Portugal with the English Opera Group, conducting Albert Herring and A Midsummer Night's Dream; Gave the premiere of Bennett's A Penny for a Song at Sadler's Wells, London, 1967; Musical Director, Welsh National Opera, 1963-67; Freelance, opera and concerts, UK, USA, Canada; Professor of Conducting, Indiana University, USA, 1977-92. *Address:* 8 The Green, Wimbledon Common, London SW19 5AZ, England.

BALL Geoffrey Stewart Morley, b. 26 Aug 1925, Leytonstone, England. Private Music Teacher (Piano and Theory). m. Yvonne Barbara Berthe Kimber, 21 Oct 1965. *Education:* Guildhall School of Music and Drama, 1948-58; LRAM (Harmony and Counterpoint), 1952; LMusTCL, 1954; BMus, Dunelm, 1958. *Career:* Private music teaching, over 40 years; Short periods of teaching, Brentwood School and North East Essex Technical College, Colchester. *Compositions:* Numerous unpublished orchestral and chamber music works. *Membership:* Incorporated Society of Musicians. *Hobbies:* Corresponding in Esperanto; Watching cricket and other sports on television. *Address:* Morley Dene, 107 Ingrave Road, Brentwood, Essex CM15 8BA, England.

BALLARD Louis, b. 8 July 1931, Miami, Oklahoma, USA. Composer. *Education:* Studied at Oklahoma and Tulsa Universities; MM, 1962; Further study with Milhaud, Castelnuovo-Tedesco and Carlos Surinach. *Career:* Programme Director, Bureau of Indian Affairs, Washington, DC, 1970-79. *Compositions include:* Koshare, ballet on Indian themes, 1966; The God will Hear, cantata, 1966; The Four Moons, ballet, 1967; Devil's Promenade for orchestra, 1973; Incident at Wounded Knee for orchestra, 1974; Ritmo Indio for wind instruments, 1968; Katcin Dances for cello and piano, 1970; Desert Trilog for winds, strings and percussion, 1971; Cacega Ayuwipi for percussion ensemble, 1973; Thus Spake Abraham, cantata, 1976; City of Fire for piano; Companion of Talking God for orchestra, 1982; Fantasy Aborigine III for orchestra, 1984. *Publications include:* My Music Reaches to the Sky, 1973; Music of North American Indians, 1974. *Address:* c/o ASCAP, ASCAP Building, One Lincoln Plaza, New York, NY 10023, USA.

BALLEYS Brigitte, b. 18 June 1959, Martigny, Walis, Switzerland. Singer (Mezzo-soprano). *Education:* Studied at the Bern Conservatory, 1978-82 with Jakob Stämpfli; Further study with Elisabeth Schwarzkopf. *Career:* Sang in concert from 1976, notably in sacred music by Bach, the Brahms Alto Rhapsody, Masses by Mozart, Haydn, Schubert, Bruckner, Dvořák and Rossini; Schumann's Paradies und die Peri and Mahler Lieder; Appearances in Switzerland, West Germany, Austria, Italy, France, Portugal, Spain, South America, USA, Chekoslovakia; Festival engagements at Zurich, Lucerne, Florence and Siena; Recitalist in songs by de Falla, Shostakovich, Schoeck and Wolf-Ferrari, as well as French chansons and German songs; Sang in opera at Freiburg, 1985, with guest appearances at Zurich, Geneva, Avignon, Schwetzingen, Lausanne, and Montpellier; Vienna Staatsoper 1987, as Cherubino conducted Leinsdorf; Sang Octavian in Bern, Montpellier, Toulouse, 1990; Season 1992 as Fragoletto in Offenbach's Les Brigands at Amsterdam and Ramiro in Jean-Claude Malgoire's Vivaldi pasticcio Montezuma at Monte Carlo; Other roles include Jocasta in Oedipus Rex (at Palermo), Gluck's Orpheus, Ottavia Coronation of Poppea, Werther of Massenet, Meg Page and Orlofsky. *Recordings include:* La Demoiselle Elue by

Debussy and Janáček's Diary of One who Disappeared (Deutsche Grammophon); Mendelssohn's St Paul and Die Zauberflöte, as Second Lady (Erato); Zelenka's Requiem (Claves). *Honours:* First Prize, Benson and Hedges in London, 1983 and Special Prize for Lied. *Address:* c/o Stadttheater Bern, Mageligasse 1, CH-3011 Bern, Switzerland.

BALLIF Claude (Andre François), b. 22 May 1924, Paris, France. Composer; Teacher; Writer on music. *Education:* Bordeaux Conservatory; courses in composition with Aubin, Galon, and Messiaen, Paris Conservatory, and Blacher and Rufer, Berlin Hochschule für Musik. *Career:* Worked with the Groupe de Recherches Musicales of the French Radio and Television, Paris, 1959-63; Professor, Rheims Conservatory, 1964-71; Professor of analysis, 1971-, and Associate Professor of composition, 1982-, Paris Conservatory; Professor of Analysis and Composition, Sevran Conservatory, October 1990. *Compositions:* Orchestral: Lovecraft, 1955; Voyage de mon oreille, 1957; Fantasio, 1957, revised l962; Ceci et cela, 1959-65; A cor et a cri, 1962; lvre moi immobile for Clarinet and Orchestra, l976; Chamber: pieces for various instruments entitled Imaginaire; 4 quintets, l952-6O; 5 string quartets, 1955, 1958, l959; Violin Sonata, 1957; Quintet for Flute, Oboe, and String Trio, l958; Double Trio for Flute, Oboe and Cello and Violin, Clarinet and Horn, 1961; Poemes de la felicite for 3 Women's Voices, Guitar, and 2 Percussion, l977; Clarinet Sonata, 1978; 5 piano sonatas, 1957-60; 4 organ sonatas, 1956; 15 pieces for various solo instruments entitled Solfeggietto, 1961-82; Choral: Les battentes du coeur de Jesus for Choir, Trumpet and Trombone, 1941; Requiem for 8 Soloists, 5 Choirs and Orchestra, 1953-68; Un coup de des for Choir, Instruments and Tape, 1980; 2 operas: Dracoula, 1984; Il suffit d'un feu d'air, 1991; 4 et 5 string quartet, 1987, 1989; Le livre du Serviteur pour 4 chours grand orchestra, 1985-88-. *Recordings:* Compositions recorded by Adda, Arion, 1991. *Publications:* Introduction à la metatonalite, 1956; Berlioz, 1968; Voyage de mon oreille, 1979; Economie musicale Souhaits entre symboles, 1979; Durand, Paris. *Address:* Conservatoire de SEVRAN, 28 Ave du Génerel Leclerc, Parc Louis Armand, 93270 Sevran, France.

BALLISTA Antonio, b. 30 Mar 1936. Milan, Italy. Pianist. *Education:* Studied piano and composition, Milan Conservatory, graduated 1955. *Career:* Toured widely as a soloist; also many duo recitals with the pianist Bruno Canino; Took part in the premieres of Rapsodia, (1984), by Davidee Anzaghi, Concerto for two pieces by Berio, (1973), Tableaux Vivants, (1964) by Bussotti and Ode, (1966) by Castiglioni; Solo premieres of Wasserklavier and Erdenklavier, (1964, 1970) by Berio, Fogliod'album, (1969) by Bussotti, Couplets, (1979) by Castiglioni, B.A.C.H. (1970) and Piano Concerto, (1976) by Aldo Clementi, Stratto, (1969) by Donatoni and De La Nuit, 1971 by Sciarrino; Professor at Giuseppe Verdi Conservatory from 1964. *Recordings:* Several recordings of contemporary works. *Address:* Conservatorio Giuseppe Verdi, Via Conservatorio 12, 20122 Milan, Italy.

BALOGH Endre, b. 1954, Los Angeles, California, USA. Violinist. *Debut:* New York Town Hall, 1971. *Education:* Attended Yehudi Menuhin's school, England, at age 9; Violin studies with Joseph Piastro, Manuel Compinsky and Mehli Mehta; New York Town Hall, 1971. *Career:* Played 1st concerto with orchestra at age 6; Recital, Los Angeles, at age 15; 1st European tour including concerts in Berlin and London, 1973; Performed in Austria, Netherlands, Italy; Recital for BBC, London, and on-the-air, Amsterdam; Appearances with various orchestras including Los Angeles Philharmonic, and Washington, Seattle, Honolulu and other Symphony Orchestras; Numerous recitals in key US cities; Performed with Berlin Philharmonic, Rotterdam Philharmonic, Frankfurt Symphony, Tonhalle Orchestra of Zurich, Basel Symphony; As soloist with orchestra under conductors Zubin Mehta, Lawrence Foster, Henry Lewis, Vladimir Golschmann, Milton Katims, Hirouko Iwaki, Edo de Waart; Numerous appearances with American Youth Symphony, under Mehli Mehta; Played many benefits for State of Israel, United Nations, Philosophical Research Society and others; Hypnotist and Member of Executive Board of California Hypnotists Examining Council; Uses hypnosis to aid expansion of performers' artistic expression; Violinist, Pacific Trio throughout USA and Canada; Pacific Trio serves as Trio-in-Residence and Chamber Music Faculty for Idyllysild School of Music and The Arts in California. *Recordings:* Pacific Trio, released a new compact disc, 1990; Brahms C Major and Shostakovich E Major Trios. *Hobbies:* Psychology; Comparative religion; Philosophy, Semantics; Designing and executing stained glass windows; Collecting Oriental carpets; Travel; Meeting new people. *Address:* 318 Detroit Street, Los Angeles, CA 90036, USA.

BALSAM Artur, b. 8 Feb 1906, Warsaw, Poland. Concert Pianist; Teacher. m. Ruth Miller, 14 Oct 1933. *Education:* School in Lodz, Poland; University in Warsaw; Conservatory in Lodz; Akademie Hochschule fur Musik, Berlin. *Debut:* In Lodz at age 12. *Career:* Teacher of Piano and Chamber Music, Manhattan School of Music, New York; Teacher of Chamber Music, last 35 years, Summer Sessions Franz Kneisel School of Music, Blue Hill, Maine, USA; Appearances in almost all big cities in Europe, Canada and USA; Recitals in Europe and America; Chamber music concerts with the quartets: Budapest, Juilliard, Kroll; Concerts of solo and chamber music and teaching trio groups, every two years, at the Britten School in Aldeburgh; Several appearances with European and American orchestras as soloist in (mostly) Mozart and Beethoven concertos. *Compositions:* Cadenzas for a dozen Mozart Concertos and for Beethoven Piano Concerto in B Flat, also for the Mozart Bassoon Concerto and for the B Minor Violin Concerto by Paganini; Published: his edition of four Mozart piano concertos (with his cadenzas) for Oxford University and two for the Schirmer Edition in New York. *Recordings:* All 52 Sonatas by Haydn; all piano works bu Mozart; ten Mozart Concertos; Hummel Concerto in A minor; all Beethoven violin sonatas (with Joseph Fuchs); all Beethoven Cello Sonatas (with Zara Nelsova); Rachmaninoff Cello Sonata (with Nelsova); all Mozart violin sonatas (with Oscar Shumsky); all Brahms violin sonatas with Szymon Goldberg; Violin Sonatas by Strauss, Ravel, Debussy, Schubert; two Beethoven violin sonatas (with Nathan Milstein) and Prokofiev violin sonatas; Piano pieces by CPE Bach, Beethoven; Several trios by Beethoven, Mendelssohn; Mendelssohn cello sonata (with Joseph Schuster); Two violin sonatas by Prokofiev with Joseph Szigeti. *Honours:* First Prize in a competition in Berlin (a piano) 1930; the Mendelssohn prize, 1931. *Memberships:* The Bohemians Club, New York. *Hobby:* Stamp collecting. *Address:* 258 Riverside Drive, New York, NY 10025, USA.

BALSLEV Lisbeth, b. 21 Feb 1945, Abenraa, Germany. Singer (Soprano). *Education:* Vestjysk Conservatory in Esbjerg, Denmark; Royal Opera School, Copenhagen. *Debut:* Copenhagen 1976, as Jaroslavna in Prince Igor. *Career:* Sang Mozart's Fiordiligi, Leonora in Il Trovatore and Wagner's Senta in Copenhagen; Bern Opera 1977, as Electra in Idomeneo; Bayreuth from 1978, as Senta in Der fliegende Holländer; Hamburg Opera debut 1979, as Elsa in Lohengrin; Munich Staatsoper 1979, in the title role of Iphigénie en Tauride by Gluck; Guest appearances in Dresden, Amsterdam, Berlin, Stuttgart, Cologne and Frankfurt; La Scala, Milan, 1987, as Salome, Lisbon; and Berne, 1987, Senta and Elisabeth; Turin and Florence, 1988, as Wagner's Isolde; Leonore in Fidelio with Cologne Opera, Hong Kong, 1989; Isolde in a concert performance of Tristan und Isolde with Jutland Opera, Edinburgh Festival, 1990. *Recordings include:* Senta in Der fliegende Holländer from Bayreuth (Philips). *Address:* Ingpen and Williams Ltd, 14 Kensington Court, London W9 2PY, England.

BALTHROP Carmen Arlen, b. 14 May 1948, Washington DC, USA. Singer (Soprano). *Education:* Studied at the University of Maryland, College Park and the Catholic University of America. *Debut:* Washington DC, 1973 as Virtue in L'Incoronazione di Poppea

(Minerva in the US Premiere of Il Ritorno di Ulisse, 1974). *Career:* Sang the title role in Scott Joplin's Treemonisha, Houston Opera, 1975; In 1977 sang in Cavalli's L'Egisto at Wolf Trap and made her Metropolitan Opera debut, as Pamina; New York City Opera 1978, as Roggiero in Rossini's Tancredi; Innsbruck Early Music Festival 1980, as Poppea in Monteverdi's opera, in the edition by Alan Curtis; Sang Poppea at Spoleto, 1979 and Santa Fe, 1986; Venice, as Gluck's Euridice and Poppea in Handel's Agrippina, 1982-83; Michigan Opera, Theater as Treemonisha and Pamina, 1982-84. *Recordings include:* Treemonisha. *Honours include:* Winner, Metropolitan Opera Auditions, 1975.

BALTSA Agnes, b. 19 Nov 1944, Lefkas, Greece. Singer (Mezzo-Soprano). m. Gunter Missenhardt, 1974. *Education:* Study in Athens with Nunuka Fragia-Spilopoulos; Frankfurt with Herbert Champian. *Debut:* Frankfurt Opera 1968, as Cherubino in Figaro. *Career:* Octavian in Der Rosenkavalier at the Vienna Staatsoper, 1969; Guest appearances in Hamburg, Athens, Berlin, Munich, Barcelona and Belgrade; US debut 1971 with Houston Opera, as Carmen; Concert tour of USA, 1976, with Karajan; Salzburg Festival from 1970, in Bastien et Bastienne and as Herodias in Salome, Eboli in Don Carlos and as Octavian; Covent Garden debut, 1976: returned to London as Giulietta in Les Contes d'Hoffmann, Adalgisa in Norma, as Romeo in I Capuleti e i Montecchi 1984, as Isabella in L'Italiana in Algeri, 1987 and as Eboli in Don Carlos, 1989; Metropolitan Opera debut 1979, as Octavian: returned to New York 1987, as Carmen; Sang Santuzza, Vienna Staatsoper, 1989; Cenerentola and Dalila, Covent Garden, 1990-91; Season 1992/93 as Elisabeth in Maria Stuarda at Barcelona and Azucena at the Vienna Staatsoper; Other roles include Berlioz's Dido, Gluck's Orfeo and Mozart's Dorabella. *Recordings:* Roles in: Salome, Don Carlos, Aida (Electola); Orfeo ed Euridice, Così fan Tutte, Les Contes d'Hoffmann, I Capuleti e i Montecchi (HMV); Mitridate, Die Zauberflöte, Rosenkavalier, Don Giovanni (Deutsche Grammophon); Ascanio in Alba, Le Nozze di Figaro (Philips). *Address:* c/o Royal Opera House, Covent Garden, London, WC2, England.

BALTZER Rebecca A, b. 17 June 1940, Memphis, USA. Musicologist; Professor. m. Charles E McCarthy, 17 Mar 1984. *Education:* AB, 1962, MA, 1964, PhD, 1974, Boston University. *Career:* Lecturer, Music, Boston University, 1964-67; Faculty, Music, University of Texas, 1967-, Associate Professor, 1973-, Associate Dean, Graduate School, 1982-86. *Contributions to:* New Grove Dictionary; Musical Quarterly; Notes. *Publications:* Le Judgement du roy de Behaigne; Remede de Fortune, 1988. *Honours:* Recipient, many honours and awards. *Memberships:* American Musicological Society, Vice President 1988-90, Director at Large, 1980-82; Medieval Academy of America; International Machaut Society; College Music Society. *Address:* Dept of Music, University of Texas, Austin, TX 78712, USA.

BALZANI Vincenzo, b. 1965, Milan, Italy. Concert Pianist. *Education:* Studied at the Giuseppe Verdi Conservatory, Milan with Alberto Mozzati. *Debut:* Has performed in public from age of 14. *Career:* Italian engagements at La Fenice Venice, the Comunale of Bologna, the Verdi Theatre in Trieste and the Academia Filarmonica Romana; Further appearances in France, Germany and Spain; London recital debut at the Purcell Room 1989, playing Scarlatti Sonatas, Brahms Paganini Variations, Gaspard de la Nuit, Chopin Etudes Op 10 and Liszt Rigoletto Paraphrase. *Recordings include:* Music by Liszt, Mozart and Hummel; Chopin Etudes Op 10. *Honours include:* Liszt Prize at the Maria Canals Competition, Barcelona.

BAMBERGER David, b. 14 Oct 1940, Albany, New York, USA. Director; Producer. m. Carola Beral, 1 son. *Education:* Yale University School of Drama; Université de Paris, France; BA, Swarthmore College. *Career:* Stage Director/Producer: The Barber of Seville, The Magic Flute, Der Rosenkavalier, New York City Opera; Rigoletto, Lucia di Lammermoor, National Opera,

Santiago, Chile; Madame Butterfly, Don Pasquale, Cincinnati Opera, Don Pasquale, Pittsburgh Opera; The Flying Dutchman, Harford Opera Company; Producer/Director, Don Giovanni, Four Saints in Three Acts, Madame Butterfly; Così Fan Tutte; The Gondoliers, Die Fledermaus, Menotti's Tamu-Tamu (1st production after world premiere), Oberlin Music Theatre, Ohio; General Director, Cleveland Opera, 1976-, 50 productions including La Traviata, La Bohème, Daughter of the Regiment, Tosca, Aida, Faust, Falstaff, The Medium, The Secret Marriage, The Merry Widow, Holy Blood and Crescent Moon (world permiere); Artistic Director, Toledo (Ohio) Opera, 1983-85, staged Faust, Don Pasquale, Aida, Barber of Seville; Non-operatic productions include 1st major New York production of Sophocles Oedipus at Colonus and American tour of Much Ado About Nothing, National Shakespeare Company. *Address:* 1422 Euclid Avenue, Cleveland, OH 44115, USA.

BAMERT Matthias, b. 5 July 1942, Ersigen, Switzerland. Conductor; Composer. *Education:* Studied in Bern and Paris; principall composition teachers: Jean Rivier and Pierre Boulez. *Career:* First oboist, Mozarteum Orchestra, Salzburg, 1965-69; assistant conductor, American Symphony Orchestra, NY, 1970-71; Joined the conducting staff of the Cleveland Orchestra, 1971; music director, Basle Radio Symphony Orchestra, 1977-83; principal guest conductor, Scottish National Orchestra, Glasgow, 1985-; Conducted Schoenberg's Violin Concerto, 1988; Conducted Ulster Orchestra, Belfast, 1991, Nielsen's Helios Overture, Sibelius's 2nd Symphony and works by Sandström and Saariaho; Promenade concerts, London 1991 with BBC Symphony in Liszt's Hunnenschlacht, Alexander Nevsky, Premiere of Martin Butler's O Rio; Conducted the National Youth Orchestra in music by Mussorgsky and Birtwistle (Gawain's Journey) at the 1993 Proms. *Compositions:* Concertino for English Horn, String Orchestra and Piano, 1966; Septuria Lunaris for Orchestra, 1970; Rheology for String Orchestra, 1970; Mantrajana for Orchestra, 1971; Once upon an Orchestra for Narrator, 12 Dancers and Orchestra, 1975; Ol-Okun for String Orchestra, 1976; Keepsake for Orchestra, 1979; Circus Parade for Narrator and Orchestra, 1979. *Honours include:* Received the first George Szell Memorial Award, 1971. *Address:* c/o Scottish National Orchestra, 3 La Belle Place, Glasgow G3 7LH, Scotland.

BAMPTON Rose E, b. 28 Nov 1908, Cleveland, Ohio, USA. Concert & Opera Singer. m. Wilfred Pelletier. *Education:* BMus, Curtis Institute of Music, Philadelphia; LHD, Drake University, Iowa. *Debut:* Metropolitan Opera, New York City, 1932; As Laura, La Gioconda. *Career:* Metropolitan Opera, New York City, 1932-50; Notably as Leonora (Il Trovatore), Sieglinde, Kundry and Donna Anna; Covent Garden, London, UK, 1937; as Amneris, Teatro Colon, Buenos Aires, Argentina, 1945-50; Sang Daphne in the First American Performance of the Opera by Strauss, 1948; Chicago Opera, San Francisco Opera; Voice faculty, Manhattan School of Music 1962-1982, Juilliard School of Music 1974-. *Recordings:* Gurrelieder, Stokowski; Fidelio, Toscanini; Operatic Arias, Wilfred Pelletier. *Honours:* LHD, Holart & William Smith Colleges, Geneva & New York, 1978. *Hobbies:* Tennis; Riding; Swimming; Collecting antique earrings. *Address:* c/o Juilliard School, Vocal Faculty, Lincoln Center, NY 10023, USA.

BANFIELD Stephen David, b. 15 July 1951, Dulwich, London, England. Professor of Music. *Education:* FRCO, 1969; Clare College, Cambridge, 1969-72; BA, Cantab, 1st Class Hons, 1972; St John's College, Oxford, 1972-75; DPhil (Oxon), 1980; Harvard University, 1975-76. *Career:* Lecturer in Music, 1978-88, Senior Lecturer, 1988-92, Keele University; Elgar Professor of Music, Head of School of Performance Studies, University of Birmingham, 1992-. *Publications:* Sensibility and English Song, 1985; Sondheim's Broadway Musicals, 1994; The Blackwell History of Music in Britain, Vol VI (editor), 1994. *Contributions:* Various articles, chapters and reviews. *Memberships:* Royal Musical Association; Sonneck Society for

American Music; Fellow, Royal Society of Arts; Viola da Gamba Society; Kurt Weill Foundation, Member of Kurt Weill Edition Advisory Board; Founder Member, Stephen Sondheim Society. *Hobbies:* Architecture; Literature; Travel. *Address:* 6 King's Court, 108 Livery St, Birmingham B3 1RR, England.

BANIEWICZ Vera, b. 1949, Russia. Singer (Mezzo-Soprano). *Education:* Studied in Warsaw. *Career:* Sang first at chamber operas of Warsaw and Cracow; Engaged at Dortmund, 1976, and sang Flosshilde, Olga in Eugene Onegin, Octavian, Carmen and Concepcion in L'Heure Espgnole; Hannover, 1985-87, notably as Renata in The Fiery Angel; State Operas of Hamburg and Munich as Eboli in Don Carlos; Further guest appearances, Berlin, Stuttgart, Brunswick as Kundry, 1989, and Barcelona as Herodias, 1989; With Deutsche Oper am Rhein Dusseldorf has sung Lady Macbeth, Preziosilla in La Forza del Destino, Azucena, Maddalena, and Brangaene in Tristan und Isolde. *Address:* c/o Deutsche Oper am Rhein, Heinrich Heine Allee 16, 4000 Dusseldorf, Germany.

BANK Jacques, b. 18 Apr 1943, Borne, The Netherlands. Composer. *Education:* Graduated, Amsterdam Conservatory, 1974; Studied with Jos Kunst and Ton de Leeuw. *Compositions:* Opera: Een Tanthologie, 1986-87; Orchestral: Fan It, 1973; Pathetique, 1976; Lost for Wind Orchestra, 1976; Alexandre's Concerto for Piano and Orchestra, 1978; Recorders, concerto for Recorder Player, Strings and Percussion, 1981; Vocal: Emcee, 1969; Song of Sitting Bull for Recorder Player with a Baritone Voice and Organ, 1974; Thomas for recording of Dylan Thomas reading his Lament and 19 Instruments, 1975; Lied, homage to Franz Schubert for Countertenor or Mezzo-soprano, Clavichord or Harpsichord, 2 Percussion Players, 2 Violins, Viola and Cello, 1976; Mesmerized for Mezzo-soprano or Tenor, 3 Trumpets, 3 Percussion Players and Piano, 1977; Muziek voor een slaapstad for Choir and Orchestra, 1979; Minutes of Lives for Soprano, 3 Clarinets and Bas Clarinet, 1982; Coda for Choir and Orchestra, 1983; Moped Song for Mezzo-soprano or Tenor, Accordion and Percussion, 1983; Requiem voor een levende for Reciter, Chorus and Chamber Ensemble, 1985; Chamber: The Memoirs of a Cycklist for 2 Recorders, 1967-70; Last Post for Bass Clarinet and Piano, 1975; Frieze for 1 Percussion Player, 1976; Two for Three for Flute, Bass Clarinet and Piano, 1979; Two for Bass Recorder and Piano, 1979; Two for Four for 4 Pianists Playing 2 Pianos, 1979; Maraens trompetten for 2 Recorder Players and Tape, 1980; 4 Arias for 3 Clarinets and Bass Clarinet, 1982; Solo piano pieces.

BANKS Barry, b. 1960, England. Singer (Tenor). *Education:* Studied at Royal Northern College of Music with Josef Ward. *Career:* Sang Tamino and Don Ottavio at Royal Northern College of Music; Covent Garden debut as Beppe in Pagliacci, 1989; English National Opera as Rossini's Almaviva, Fenton, the Novice in Billy Budd and Brighella in Ariadne auf Naxos; Tamino and Britten's Flute for Glyndebourne Touring Opera; Appearances with Opera North as Mozart's Basilio, Arturo (Lucia di Lammermoor), Topas (Les Troyens) and in the Griffiths/Mozart pasticcio The Jewel Box; Has sung Pedrillo in Die Entführung with Netherlands Opera, performances of Il Signor Bruschino and Peri's Euridice in Paris and Tamino in Leipzig; Concert showings in France, Germany, Italy and Belgium, festivals at Cheltenham, Buxton and Aldeburgh; Messiah with Tokyo Philharmonic and Liverpool Philharmonic; Season 1991 with Tamino in Brussels, debut with BBC Symphony and Mozart's Mitridate with English Chamber Orchestra under Jeffrey Tate at the Barbican; Sang Giannetto in The Thieving Magpie, Opera North, 1992; Tom Rakewell with Glyndebourne Touring Opera. *Honours include:* Peter Moores Foundation Scholarship, 1983. *Address:* c/o Opera North, The Grand Theatre, 46 New Briggate, Leeds, Yorkshire LS1 6NU, England.

BANNATYNE-SCOTT Brian, b. 1955, Edinburgh, Scotland. Singer (Bass). *Education:* Studied at St Andrews University and the Guildhall School of Music; Further study with Norman Bailey. *Career:* Debuts at La Fenice Venice 1981 and the Rome Opera 1982; Scottish Opera from 1982, as Colline, Don Fernando (Fidelio), Nourabad (The Pearl Fishers) and the Speaker in The Magic Flute; English National Opera from 1987 as Monterone (Rigoletto), Pogner and the Commendatore (1991); Varlaam (Boris Godunov) Opera North and BBC Prom, 1992; Banquo, ENO 1993; Sang Fafner and Hagen in the City of Birmingham Touring Opera version of The Ring; Tour of Europe as Cold Genius in Purcell's King Arthur; Salzburg Festival debut 1991, as Polyphemus in Acis and Galatea; Bermuda Festival 1991, as Don Alfonso in Così fan Tutte; Concert engagements with leading British orchestras; Has sung Christus in the St John Passion settings of Bach and Arvo Pärt (in Italy, Germany and Japan); Stravinsky's Les Noces with London Sinfonietta and Simon Rattle, 1993; Aldeburgh: masterclasses with Galina Vishnevskaya (also televised) and recital at 1990 Prom Concert. *Recordings include:* Purcell's King Arthur (Deutsche Grammophon). *Address:* Magenta Music International, 4 Highgate High Street, London N6 5JL, England.

BANSE Juliane, b. 1965, Bavaria, Germany. Singer (Soprano). *Education:* Trained as ballet dancer in Zurich; Vocal studies in Zurich and with Brigitte Fassbaender and Daphne Evangelatos in Munich. *Debut:* Sang Pamina in Harry Kupfer's production of Die Zauberflote at Komische Oper Berlin, 1989. *Career:* Engagements at Komische Oper as Ilia and Susanna, 1991-92; Pamina in Stuttgart and Brussels, Marzelline in Geneva and Hamburg, 1993, Sophie in Rosenkavalier at Landestheater Salzburg and Zerlina at 1994 Glyndebourne Festival; Concert repertoire includes Bach's St John Passion, on European tours with Helmuth Rilling, Mozart Concert Arias with Bamberg Symphony, Lieder recitals in Hohenems, Vienna, Linz and Barcelona. *Recordings include:* Lieder by Schoeck; TV taping of the Christmas Oratorio with the Windsbacher Knabenchor. *Honours include:* Winner, Kultur-Forum Competition, Munich, 1989. *Address:* IMG Artists, Media House, 3 Burlington Lane, London W4 2TH, England.

BÄR Olaf, b. 19 Dec 1957, Dresden, Germany. Singer (Baritone). *Career:* Studied in Dresden, sang in the Dresden Kreuzchor 1966-75 and was a principal member of the Dresden State Opera until 1991; British debut November 1983, at the Wigmore Hall; returned summer 1985; Covent Garden debut 1985, as Harlekin in Ariadne auf Naxos; Aix-en-Provence Festival 1986 in Ariadne; Die Zauberflöte at La Scala; Glyndebourne Festival 1987, as the Count in Capriccio; Aix 1988 as Guglielmo in Così fan Tutte, conducted by Jeffrey Tate; Concert performances in Europe and the USA; US debut 1987, as Christus in the St Matthew Passion with the Chicago Symphony Ochestra conducted by Solti; Tours of Australia and Japan, 1989; Created roles in the premieres of operas by Matthus, 1985 and Mayer, 1989; at Covent Garden Opera sang Papageno, 1991; Glyndebourne as Don Giovanni, 1991; Sang in Britten's War Requiem; Oliver in Capriccio, Opernhaus Zurich, 1992; Marcello in La Bohéme, Staatsoper Dresden, 1992; Tour of Japan; Count in Le Nozze di Figaro, Niederlands Oper Amsterdam, 1993; Tour of Australia. *Recordings:* Schumann Dichterliebe Op 48 and Liederkreis Op 39, Kerner-Lieder Op 35 and Liederkreis Op 24; Schubert: Die Schöne Müllerin, Die Winterreise and Schwanengesang; Wolf Möricke Lieder; Brahms Lieder; Beethoven Lieder; Mozart Arien; Bach Christmas Oratorio with John Eliot Gardiner and the Monteverdi Choir (Deutsche Grammophon); Christus in the St Matthew-Passion (Arias), conductor: John Eliot Gardiner; St Matthew-Passion (Christus), conductor: George Solti; St John-Passion (Arias), conductor: Peter Schreier; Fauré and Duruflé Requiems; Further recordings include Pagageno in Mozart's Die Zauberflöte; Adam in Haydn's Creation and Harlekin in Strauss' Ariadne auf Naxos. *Current Management:* IMG Artists Vocal Division, Media House, 3 Burlington Lane, Chiswick, London W4 2TH, England. *Address:* Olbersdorfer Str 7, 8051 Dresden, Germany.

BAR-ILLAN David (Jacob), b. 7 Feb 1930, Haifa, Palestine (now Israel). Pianist; Teacher. *Education:* Graduate, Haifa Music Institute; Juilliard School of Music; Mannes College of Music. *Debut:* Professional debut, soloist with Palestine Broadcasting Service Orchestra, 1946. *Career:* British debut, Wigmore Hall, London, England, 1953; First USA tour, 1954; Appearances as soloist with many of the world's major orchestras and as a recitalist; Teacher of Piano, Mannes College of Music, 1980-. *Recordings:* For Adiofon; InSync. *Contributions to:* Articles in several journals. *Address:* c/o Mannes College of Music, 150 West 85th Street, New York, NY 10024, USA.

BARAB Seymour, b. 9 Jan 1921, Chicago, Illinois. Composer; Cellist. *Education:* Studied the cello with Gregor Piatigorsky and Edmund Kurtz. *Career:* Performed first as church organist in Chicago; Played the cello in symphony orchestras of Indianapolis, Cleveland, Portland and San Francisco, 1940-60; Assisted in the organization of the Composers Quartet and the New York Pro Musica; Has taught at Rutgers, the State University of New Jersey and the New England Conservatory. *Compositions include:* Operas: Chanticlear, after Chaucer, Aspen, 1956; A Game of Chance, Illinois, 1957; Little Red Riding Hood, New York, 1962; The Toy Shop, New York, 1978; A Piece of String, Colorado, 1985; The Makers of Illusion, New York, 1985; Song settings of The Children's Garden of Verses and Songs of Perfect Propriety. *Address:* c/o ASCAP, ASCAP Building, One Lincoln Plaza, New York, NY 10023, USA.

BARABAS Sari, b. 14 March 1918, Budapest, Hungary. Singer (Soprano). m. Franz Klarwein. *Education:* Studied in Budapest. *Debut:* Budapest 1939, as Gilda in Rigoletto. *Career:* Member of the Hamburg Staatsoper from 1949; San Francisco, 1950, as the Queen of Night; Glyndebourne, 1953-57, as Constanze in Die Entführung, Adèle in Le Comte Ory and Zerbinetta in Ariadne auf Naxos; Florence Maggio Musicale 1955; Guest appearances in Germany and Austria in operettas; London 1969 in The Great Waltz. *Recordings include:* Le Comte Ory from the Glyndebourne Festival, 1956 (HMV); Excerpts from works by Johann Strauss, Gasparone, Telefunken.

BARAN Peter, b. 16 Mar 1950, Bratislava, Czechoslovakia. Musician (Cellist). m. Beata Baranova, 15 Aug 1975, 2 sons. *Education:* Music School, Bratislava, 1956-65; Conservatory, Bratislava, 1965-72; Hochschule fur Musik und Darstellende Kunst, Vienna, 1979-83. *Debut:* Haydn's Cello Concerto in D major, 1972. *Career:* Member: Slovak Philharmonic Orchestra, 1972-; Suchon's Quartet, 1973-77; Bratislava Chamber Harmony, 1973-80; Capella Istropolitana Chamber Orchestra, 1982-89; Bratislava String Trio, 1985-; Kontrapunkte, ensemble of 20th century music, Vienna, 1988-; Concertmaster, Slovak Philharmonic Orchestra, 1989-; Soloist and Member, Orchestra Ensemble Kanazawa, Japan, 1992-; Major performances, solo: Concerto for 2 Celli (Handel) with Slovak Philharmonic Orchestra, 1984; Symphonia Concertante (Haydn) with Slovak Chamber Orchestra, 1985; Cello Concerto op 33 (Saint Saens) with Slovak Philharmonic Orchestra, 1985; Concerto for String Trio and Orchestra (C Stamitz), 1987; Quatuor pour la fin du temps (Messiaen) at BHS Festival, 1987; Concerto in A minor for violin, cello and orchestra, op 102 (Brahms) and Sonata da Camera and Orchestra (Martinu), both with Slovak Philharmonic Orchestra, 1993; Slovak and Austrian Radio performances: Jagdquartet (Haydn); Cello Concerto in C major (Haydn); TV: Sonata in F Major, op 99 (Brahms); String Trio Serenade (Dohnanyi); Divertimento (Mozart); Trio in G major (Hummel); Little Trio (A Moyzes). *Recordings:* Vivaldi: Cello Concerto in A minor, Concerto in G minor for 2 celli; Beethoven: Septet, op 20; String Trio in G major by Hummel. *Memberships:* Slovak Music Union; Musicians Union, Japan. *Hobbies:* Chamber music; Family. *Address:* Medena 35, 81102 Bratislava, Slovak Republic.

BARANTSCHIK Alexander, b. 1953, Leningrad, USSR. Violinist. *Education:* Studied at the Leningrad

Conservatory 1960-72, with Professor Waiman 1972-77. *Career:* Gave concerts in Russia, then emigrated 1979, becoming leader of the Bamberg Symphony Orchestra; Leader of the Radio Philharmonic Orchestra of the Netherlands 1982; Solo engagements with leading orchestras in Germany, Holland, Britain and Hungary; Appearances in Russia with the Kazan Symphony and the Leningrad Philharmonic; Performed the Sibelius Concerto with the London Symphony in Spain, 1987, Prokofiev's 1st in the USA and London 1989-90; Leader of the LSO from 1989, played the Tchaikovsky Concerto with the orchestra March 1991, Bach on tour to the USA, August 1991. *Honours include:* Winner, International Violin Competition at Sion, 1980. *Address:* c/o London Symphony Orchestra, Barbican Centre, London EC2Y 8DS, England.

BARATI George, b. 3 Apr 1913, Gyor, Hungary. Composer; Conductor. m. (1) 1 son, (2) Ruth Carroll, 31 Oct 1948, 2 daughters. *Education:* Cum laude, Gyor Commercial High & Music Schools, 1932; Teacher's & State Artist Diplomas, Franz Liszt Academy of Music, Budapest, 1935; Composition with Roger Sessions, Princeton, 1939-43. *Debut:* Dohnanyi's Cello Concerto, Budapest Symphony, 1938. *Career:* Member, Budapest Symphony, 1933-36; 1st Cellist, Budapest Symphony & Municipal Opera, 1936-38; Cellist, Cello Teacher, Princeton University, 1939-43; Music Director, Alexandria Symphony, 1944; Cellist, San Francisco Symphony & California String Quartet, 1946-50; Music Director: Barati Chamber Orchestra of San Francisco, 1948-52; Honolulu Symphony & Opera, 1950-68; Executive Director, Montalvo Center for the Arts, Saratoga, California, Conductor, Montalvo Chamber Orchestra, 1968-78; Music Director: Santa Cruz Symphony, 1969-80; Barati Ensemble, 1989-92; Touring Conductor, 5 continents. *Compositions include:* Opera: Noelani, 1968; Ballet: The Love of Don Perlimpin, 1947; Film scores: The Ugly Duckling, 1981; What Do Two Rights Make?, 1983; Orchestral: Fever Dreams, 1938; 2 Symphonic Movements, 1941; Lamentoso, 1943; Scherzo, 1946; Configuration, 1947; Chamber Concerto, 1952; Tribute, 1952; Cello Concerto, 1953, revised 1957; The Dragon & the Phoenix, 1960; Symphony, 1963; Polarization, 1965; Baroque Quartet Concerto, 1968; Festival Hula, Symphonic Dance, 1968; Vaudeville, 1968; Piano Concerto, 1973; Guitar Concerto, 1976, revised 1982; Branches of Time, 2 pianos, orchestra, 1981; Confluence, 1982; Violin Concerto, 1986; Serenata Capricciosa, chamber orchestra, 1990; Chant of Darkness, 1993; Chamber: 3 String Quartets, 1944, 1961, 1991; Clarinet Trio; Indiana Triptych; Spring Serenade; Piece for Harp Alone; Trio Profundo & the shadows, 8 instruments; Dialogue for Flute & Piano, 1992; Lumberjack for Trombone & Piano, 1993. *Hobbies:* Swimming; Croquet; Chess; Reading. *Address:* 230 Sunset Lane, Soquel, CA 95073, USA.

BARBAUX Christine, b. 1955, Saint-Mande, France. Singer (Soprano). *Education:* Studied at Paris Conservtory. *Debut:* Strasbourg, as Despina, 1977. *Career:* Sang Barbarina in Le nozze di Figaro in Paris, 1978, Vienna and Salzburg under Karajan; Further engagements in Geneva in The Love of Three Oranges, 1984; Theatre de la Monnaie, Brussels, as Servilia in La Clemenza di Tito and Sophie in Rosenkavalier, 1982, 1986, Aix-en-Provence as Sophie, Amsterdam as Norina, 1988, Salzburg Festival as Servilia, 1988; Other roles include Ophelia in Hamlet by Thomas, Gilda, and Blanche Force in Les Dialogues des Carmélites; Sang Alice Ford in Falstaff in Bonn, 1991. *Recordings include:* Werther and Pelléas et Mélisande; Fauré's Pénélope; Le nozze di Figaro. *Address:* c/o Oper der Stadt Bonn, Am Boselagerhof 1, 5300 Bonn, Germany.

BARBER Graham David, b. 30 Dec 1948, London, England. Musician (Organist). m. Dianne Mackay, 20 July 1990. *Education:* BA 1st Class hons, 1970, MMus, 1971, University of East Anglia; Royal Northern College of Music; ARNCM, Piano, 1974; Piano Accompaniment, distinction, 1975. *Debut:* Royal Festival Hall, London, Nov 1978. *Career:* International Concert Organist;

Musical Director, Chorus Master, Harpsichordist, Piano Accompanist, Coach; Frequent BBC Radio appearances as Organist, mainly featuring German Baroque music and Max Reger; Lecturer in Music, University of Leeds, 1981-; Chorus Master, Leeds Philharmonic Society, 1983-92; Curator, historic Schulze Organ, St Bartholomew's Church, Armley, 1986-; Chorus Master, Sheffield Philharmonic Chorus, 1987-. *Recordings:* Organ Solo, Whitlock Sonata, Coventry Cathedral; Howells Sonata and Partita, Coventry; Karg-Elert Kaleidoscope, Coventry; Reger Inferno Fantasy op 57, 20th Century Music at Bonn-Endenich; Johann Gottfried Walther Organ Works, Reid Concert Hall, Edinburgh; Franz Schmidt: Organ Works; Dupre and Demessieux Organ Works; Max Reger: Introduction, Passacaglias and Fugue op 127; English Romantic at Truro Cathedral; Bolton Town Hall, Rheinberger Sonats, Armley Schulze Organ; Organ works by Karg-Elert, Rheinberger, Reger at St Johanneskirche, Osnabruck; Bach Neumeister Chorales and Early Organ works, Vol 1 and 2; Organ music from Salisbury Cathedral; Organ works, Johann Ludwig Krebs; Georg Bohm, Organist at Luneberg; Dieterich Buxtehude, Organist at Luneberg; The Sandtner Organ at Villingen, Munster; The Klais Organ at Altenberg Dom. *Contributor to:* Musical Times, 1984. *Honours:* Limpus and F J Read Prizes, FRCO Exams, 1969. *Memberships:* Fellow, Royal College of Organists; Trustee, Percy Whitlock Trust; Incorporated Society of Musicians; BIOS; ABC; Karg Elert Society; Incorporated Association of Organists. *Hobbies:* Gardening; 1930's ceramics. *Address:* 37 Chapel Lane, Armley, Leeds LS12 2BY, England.

BARBIERI Fedora, b. 4 June 1920, Trieste, Italy. Opera Singer, Mezzo-Soprano, Stage Director. m. Luigi Barlozzetti 23 Sept 1943 (deceased), 2 sons. *Education:* Conservatory of Trieste. *Debut:* As Fidelma in Matrimonio Segreto and Azucena in Il Trovatore, Nov 1940. *Career:* Appearances in all major opera-houses world wide including: New York Metropolitan; San Francisco Metropolitan; Covent Garden, London; La Scala, Milan; Salzburg Festival and Vienna Staatsoper; Berlin Opera; Geneva Opera; Madrid, Barcelona, Paris, Lisbon, Buenos Aires, Sao Paulo; Her 90 opera roles included: Carmen; L'Italiana in Algieri; Amneris; Eboli in Don Carlo; Ortrud in Lohengrin; Delilah; Film roles in Cavalleria Rusticana with Zeffirelli, Rigoletto with Ponnelle, Il Trovatore with Bastianini and Del Monaco, TV films of Adriana Lecouvreur and Falstaff; Has worked with Toscanini, Bernstein, von Karajan and Serafin, Abbado, and others. *Recordings:* Verdi Requiem; 2 Aida; 2 Ballo in Maschera: 3 Il Trovatore; La Favorita; La Gioconda; Suor Angelica; 2 Medea; Falstaff; Orfeo; Solo album of Arie Antiche; Numerous live recordings; Staged Cavalleria Rusticana at Lodz (Poland), 1991, Norma at Warsaw, 1992. *Honours:* Winner, International Competition, Maggio Musicale, Florence, 1940; Metropolitan Gold Award, 1963; Oscar della Lirica, 1965; La Maschera di Argento di Roma, 1965; Commendation from the Italian President, 1964; San Valentino d'Oro 1972; Trovatore Prize for the Verdi Centennial, 1973; Mario del Monaco Gold Plaque, 1986. *Memberships:* International Juries at Singing Competitions; Amici della Lirica. *Hobbies:* Taking care of her animals and plants; Reading; Cooking. *Address:* Viale Belfiore 9, 50144 Firenze, Italy.

BARBIROLLI Evelyn, b. 24 Jan 1911, Wallingford, England. Musician; Adjudicator; Lecturer; Master Class Giver; Ex-Oboist. m. Sir John Barbirolli, CH, 5 July 1939. *Education:* Downe House School, Nr Newbury, England; Royal College of Music, London. *Career:* Scottish, London Symphony, Glyndebourne Festival Opera Orchestras, 1932-39; Soloist and Chamber Music player later. *Compositions:* Oboe Technique; The Oboist's Companion; (both published by Oxford University Press); many arrangements and editions for oboe published by Oxford University Press, Chester and Boosey and Hawkes. *Recordings:* Many recordings for EMI, some now on CD, including Concertos by Haydn, Mozart, Corelli, Handel, Pergolesi, Cimarosa; also recordings for Pye, Concertos by Albinoni, Marcello. *Publications:* Oboe Technique 1953 (3rd edition 1987) translated into Japanese and Norwegian; The Oboist's Companion, 3 Volumes; A Tune For Oboe; A Book of Scales for The Oboe. All published by Oxford University Press. *Contributions to:* Many articles for various magazines. *Honours:* OBE, 1984; DMus; MA; FRCM; RAM; FRNCM; FTCI. *Membership:* Incorporated Society of Musicians, Ex-President. *Hobbies:* Gardening; Photography. *Address:* 15A Buckland Crescent, London NW3 5DH, England.

BARDON Patricia, b. 1964, Ireland. Singer (Mezzo-soprano). *Career:* Concert engagements have taken her to France, Belgium, Spain, Holland, Hungary, Japan and Switzerland; US debut with the Cincinnati Symphony in Beethoven's Missa Solemnis; Has sung in Verdi's Requiem in Brussels, Mendelssohn's Elijah in Madrid and Janáček's Diary of One who Disappeared in Barcelona; With Welsh National Opera has appeared as Flosshilde in the Ring and Olga in Eugene Onegin; Anna in Les Troyens for Opera North and Scottish Opera (also as guest at Covent Garden, 1990); Other roles include Gluck's Orfeo (Spain and Dublin), Maddalena in Rigoletto R.O.H. and Opera North; Suzuki (Madame Butterfly) Opera North, Edwige (Guillaume Tell and in La Fanciulla, at Covent Garden); Helen (King Priam) Opera North and Third Lady in Die Zauberflöte, Verona 1991; Featured in BBC TV programme on her work; Arsace in Semiramide at La Fenice, Venice; Sang Maddalena in Rigoletto for ENO, 1992. *Recordings include:* Olga in Eugene Onegin for EMI; Giovanna in Rigoletto for Teldec. *Honours include:* Prize winner, 1983, Cardiff Singer of the World Competition. *Address:* 846 Tyrwhitt Road, Brockley, London SEA 1QB, England.

BARENBOIM Daniel, b. 15 Nov 1942, Buenos Aires, Argentina. Pianist; Conductor. m. Jacqueline Du Pre 1967, deceased 1987; (2) Elena Bashkirova, 1988, 2 sons. *Education:* Studied with his father and at the Accademia di Santa Cecilia, Rome; Conducting course at Salzburg, 1954. *Debut:* Buenos Aires, 1949. *Career:* Played at the Salzburg Mozarteum, 1951; Israel Philharmonic Orchestra, 1953-; British debut, 1955; Played a Mozart Concerto at the Festival Hall, 1956, with the Royal Philharmonic; New York debut, 1957, conducted by Stokowski; Berlin Philharmonic Orchestra, 1963-, New York Philharmonic, 1964-; Many appearances with the London Philharmonic and the Chicago Symphony; Conducting debut in Israel, 1962, followed by tour of Australia; Conductor and pianist with the English Chamber Orchestra 1964-: tours of Latin America and the Far East; Directed the South Bank Summer Music festival, London, 1968-70; Gave the premiere of Goehr's Piano Concerto, Brighton 1972; Conducted Don Giovanni and Le Nozze di Figaro at the Edinburgh Festival 1973 and 1975; Music Director of the Orchestre de Paris 1975-89; Conducted Tristan und Isolde at Bayreuth, 1981, Der Ring des Nibelungen, 1988-90; Liszt concert at the Bayreuth Festspielhaus July 31 1986, to commemorate the centenary of the composer's death; Artistic Director of the Mozart Festival in Paris from 1983: Don Giovanni, Così fan Tutte and Le Nozze di Figaro, 1986; Has accompanied Janet Baker and Dietrich Fischer-Dieskau in Lieder and played chamber music with Pinchas Zukerman and Itzhak Perlman; Many complete cycles of the Beethoven Piano Sonatas, notably in a televised series from historic houses in Vienna; Music Director of the Chicago Symphony Orchestra and the Berlin Staatsoper from 1991; Concerts with the Berlin Philharmonic in London, 1990 (Bruckner's 7th symphony, Beethoven's 3rd and Schubert's 8th); Conducted excerpts from Parsifal in Chicago, 1990; Played the Brahms D minor Concerto, Festival Hall, 1991 (Philharmonia Orchestra); Mozart 200 Festival Concert with the ECO, Barbican (K183, K543, K271). *Recordings include:* Cycle of music by Berlioz; Beethoven Concertos as soloist and conductor, formerly with Otto Klemperer and recently with the Berlin Philharmonic; Mozart Concertos with the English Chamber Orchestra; Don Giovanni and Le Nozze di Figaro; Complete Mozart Piano Sonatas; Liszt Cycle on sound and video; Contracted to Warner International to record for Teldec, the whole of the Bruckner Symphonie and to complete the Mozart Piano concerti with the Berlin Philharmonic. *Honours include:* Beethoven Medal 1958; Paderewski Medal 1963;

Beethoven Society Medal 1982. *Address:* 5 place de la Fusterie, 1204 Geneva, Switzerland.

BARGIELSKI Zbigniew, b. 21 Jan 1937, Lomza, Poland. Composer. *Education:* Studied at Warsaw Conservatory with Szeligowski and at Katowice with Boleslaw Szabelski; Further study with Boulanger in Paris and at Graz. *Compositions include:* The Little Prince, musical tale, 1970; Danton, or some scenes from the History of the Great French Revolution, opera, 1968-69; Alice in Wonderland, youth opera, 1972; Phantoms do not Lie, comic opera, 1981; Parades for orchestra, 1965; Percussion Concerto, 1975; Espace etrape for orchestra, 1973; Violin Concerto, 1975; Ballads for wind and percussion, 1976; Three Sonnet-Capricios for clarinet, 1976; Impromptu for percussion, 1976; String Quartet, 1976. *Address:* ZAIKS (Poland), c/o PRS Ltd, Member Registration, 29-33 Berners Street, London W1P 4AA, England.

BARHAM Edmund, b. 1950, England. Singer, Tenor. *Education:* Studied at the Trinity College of Music, London, and the London Opera Centre. *Career:* Sang leading lyric roles in Wuppertal, then became a member of the company of the Theater am Gärtnerplatz, Munich; Many appearances at leading German opera houses; English National Opera from 1985, as Jenik in The Bartered Bride, Turiddu, Narroboth in Salome, Pinkerton, Cavaradossi, Gabriele Adorno, and Vakula in the first British production of Rimsky-Korsakov's Christmas Eve, 1988; Engagements with Opera North as Don José, Boris in Katya Kabanova and Dimitri in Boris Godunov; Sang in the Gounod Grande Messe Solonelle for BBC television; Sang Alfredo, ENO 1990 and Macduff in a new production of Macbeth (also on tour to USSR); Engaged for Manrico, St Gallen, 1991; Don Carlos, ENO 1992; Overseas appearances include The Rise and fall of Mahagonny and Adriana Lecouvreur in Switzerland, Howard Blake's Benedictus in Norway, and Don José at the Bregenz Festival; engaged as Otello for the Victoria State Opera, 1993; Manrico in Il Trovatore for Opera North, 1994. *Recordings:* First Armed Man in Die Zauberflöte (Philips); 18th Century English Songs for orchestra and chorus (Nimbus); Rossini's Petite Messe Solonelle. *Address:* c/o Stafford Law Associates, 26 Mayfield Road, Weybridge, Surrey KT13 8XB, England.

BARK Jan, b. 19 Apr 1934, Harnosand, Sweden. Composer. *Education:* Studied in Stockholm with Larsson, Blomdahl and Ligeti; Further study in Far East. *Career:* Worked at Tape Music Center, San Francisco and with Swedish Broadcasting Service; Co-Founder, Culture Quartet (4 trombones) with Folk Rabe. *Compositions include:* Piano Sonata, 1957; 2 string quartets, 1959, 1962; Metakronismer for orchestra, 1960; Lamento for ensemble, 1962; Boca Chica for chamber ensemble, 1962; Pyknos for orchestra, 1962; Missa Bassa for small orchestra with 7 conductors, 1964; Nota for mixed chorus, 1964; Bar, electronic music; Light Music for chorus a cappella, 1968; Lyndon Bunk Johnson, 1968; Irk-Ork for chamber ensemble, 1970; Memoria in memoria for chamber ensemble, 1974; Utspel for band, 1978; Malumma for tuba and band, 1984; Concerto for orchestra, 1985; Theatre and film music. *Address:* STIM, Sweden, c/o PRS Ltd, Member Registration, 29-33 Berners Street, London W1P 4AA, England.

BARKAUSKAS Vytautas Pranas Marius, b. 25 Mar 1931, Kaunas, Lithuania. Composer; Professor. m. (1) Elena Tverjonaite 27 July 1954 (2) Tiina Vabrit, 20 Dec 1984 (3) Svetlana Cherniavska, 15 Feb 1991, 1 son, 1 daughter. *Education:* Lithuanian State Conservatory, Vilnius, 1953-59. *Career:* Accompanist, Vilnius College of Music, 1954-58; Instructor, House of the People's Creative Work of the Republic, 1958-61; Professor of Theory and composition, Lithuanian State Conservatory, Vilnius, 1961-. *Compositions:* Stage: Conflict, choreographic scene, 1965; Legend About Love, opera, 1975; Orchestral: Tone Poem for Piano and Orchestra, 1960; 5 symphonies, 1962, 1971, 1979, 1984, 1986; Concertino for 4 Chamber Groups, 1966; Expressivistic

Structures for Chamber Orchestra, 1967; 3 Aspects 1969; Overture a priori, 1976; Toccamento, concerto for Chamber Orchestra, 1978; Concerto for Viola and Chamber Orchestra, 1981; The Sun, symphonic picture, 1983; Concerto piccolo for Chamber Orchestra, 1988; Chamber: 2 string quartets, 1972, 1983; 3 sonatas for Violin and Piano: No 1 Sonata subita, 1976; No 2 Dialogue 1978; No 3, 1984; Quintet for 2 Violins, Viola, Cello and Piano, 1980; Rondo capriccioso for Bassoon and Piano, 1981; 2 Monologues for Viola, 1983; Duo Sontata for Violin and Viola, 1984; Sextet for 2 Violins, Viola, Cello, Double Bass and Piano, 1985; Sonata for Double Bass and Piano, 1987; Piano: Sonata for 2 Pianos and 3 Performers, 1984; La poeme de coeur, 1984; Sunday Music for 2 Pianos and 4 Performers, 1985; 13 Pieces, 1986; Vision, 1988; The second Legend of Ciurlionis, 1988; Organ: Gloria Urbi, 1972; Zodiac, 1980; Credo 1989; Vocal: Pathetic Thoughts for Chorus, 1962; Word About Revolution, cantata-poem for Narrator, Men's Chorus and Orchestra, 1967; La vostra nominanza e color d'erba for Chamber Chorus and String Quintet, 1971; Prelude and Fugue for Chorus, 1974; Salute Your Land, oratorio-mystery for 4 Soloists, Women's Chorus and Orchestra, 1976; Open Window for Mezzo-soprano and 5 Instruments, 1978; Cantus Amores, cantata for Soprano, Bass, Chorus and 5 Instruments, 1986; Hope, oratorio for 5 Soloists, 2 Choruses and Organ, 1988. Chamber music, Piano, 'Mirror', 1989; Vivo for 2 Violins, Viola, Cello, Double Bass and Piano, 1990; Trio, Clarinet, Violin and Piano, 1990; 'Lare', Clarinet and Piano, 1991; Concerto for Piano e Orchestra, 1992; Konzertstück für Orchester, 1992; Concert Suite for Cello and Piano, 1993; Reminiscence for Cembals, 1993; Intimate Music for Flute and Percussion, 1993 (op 100); Divertmento for Piano, 6-hands, 1993; The Third Legend of Ciurtionis for Piano, 1993. *Membership:* Union of Composers Lithuania. *Hobbies:* Skiing; Swimming and Lawn tennis. *Address:* Saltiniu Street 11/15 6.44, Vilnius 2006, Lithuania.

BARKER Edwin Bogue, b. 14 Apr 1954, Tucson, Arizona, USA. Musician (Double Bass). m. Pamela Beth Paikin, 28 Sept 1980, 2 daughters. *Education:* BMus, Honours, New England Conservatory of Music. *Career:* Music Academy of West; Blossom Music Festival; Bergen Festival; Tanglewood Music Centre; Carnegie Recital Hall; Substitute member, New York Philharmonic, 1976; Member, Chicago Symphony Orchestra, 1976-77; Principal Bass, Boston Symphony Orchestra & member, Boston Symphony Chamber Players, 1977-; Extensive recital, concerto & chamber music performances; Major recitals, Boston, New York, Amsterdam. Faculties (Double Bass): New England Conservatory, Boston University, Tanglewood Music Centre; Master classes, lectures, clinics, Indiana Univesity, Northwestern University, Oberlin, University of Michigan. *Recordings:* Numerous (most major labels), with Boston Symphony, Boston Symphony Chamber Players, Chicago Symphony. *Hobbies:* Reading; Running; Raising children. *Address:* c/o Boston Symphony Orchestra, Boston, MA 02115, USA.

BARKER Noelle, b. 28 Dec 1928, Aberdeen, Scotland, UK. Soprano. m. Christopher Peake, 3 children. *Education:* MA, Aberdeen University, 1948; Dartington Hall; Amsterdam Conservatory; Munich Academy; studied with Hans Hotter. *Debut:* Royal Festival Hall, London. *Career:* Oratorio, lieder and contemporary music with leading choral societies and ensembles; appearances at 3 Choirs and other festivals; sang with English Opera Group, London Sinfonietta, Dreamtiger ensemble; broadcasts on BBC and European stations; Professor, Guildhall School of Music and Drama, London, 1977-; Consultant Professor, Hong Kong Academy for Performing Arts. *Recordings:* Complete solo vocal works of Messiaen, Argo; jazz songs, Jupiter Records. *Publication:* Co-Editor, Pathodia Sacra e Profana, Constantin Huygens. *Honours:* FGSM, 1974. *Hobbies:* Chamber Music; Skiing; Tennis; Breadmaking; Dressmaking; Swimming. *Address:* Brontë Cottage, 89 South End Road, London, NW3 2RJ.

BARKER Paul Alan, b. 1 July 1956, Cambridge, England. Composer; Conductor; Pianist. m. (1) Christine Susan Barker, 3 Sept 1977, divorced 1991, (2) Maria Huesca, 23 May 1992. *Education:* Guildhall School of Music, 1974-78; GGSM (1st Class); MMus (Dunelm), 1983-85. *Career includes:* Visiting Lecturer, City University, 1978-83; Musical Director, Dancers Anonymous, 1979-86; Artistic Director, Modern Music Theatre Troupe, 1985-; Associate Lecturer, Kingsway-Princeton College, 1984-90; Composer in Residence, West Sussex, 1991-93; Composer in Association, London Mozart Players, 1993-. *Compositions include:* 5 operas: The Marriages Between Zones 3, 4 and 5, The Place, 1985; Phantastes, Camden Festival, 1986; The Pillow Song, London International Opera Festival, 1988; La Malinche, London International Opera Festival, 1989; also Prologue, Festival del Centro Historico, Mexico City, 1992; Albergo Empedocle, London International Opera Festival, 1990; 10 contemporary dance scores for European companies; Orchestral works include Fantasy on Four Notes (1978); instrumental ensemble, vocal, choral and chamber works; music for theatre; children's operas and educational music. *Recordings:* Barbican Fanfare, 1979; The Pied Piper of Hamelin, 1980. *Hobbies:* Literature; Theatre; Travel. *Address:* 8 York Mansions, 84 Chiltern Street, London W1M 1PT, England.

BARKIN Elaine R(adoff), b. 15 Dec 1932, New York City, USA. Composer; Music Educator; Writer on Music. m. George J Barkin, 28 Nov 1957, 3 sons. *Education:* BA, music, Queens College, 1954; MFA, composition 1956, PhD, composition and theory 1971, Brandeis University; Certificate in composition and piano, Berlin Hochschule für Musik, 1957; Studied with Karol Rathaus, Irving Fine, Boris Blacher, Arthur Berger and Harold Shapero. *Career:* Lecturer in Music, Queens College, 1964-70; Sarah Lawrence College, 1969-70; Assistant/Associate Professor of Music Theory, University of Michigan, 1970-74; Visiting Assistant Professor, Princeton University, 1974; Associate Professor 1974-77, Professor 1977, of Composition and Theory, University of California, Los Angeles; Guest Lecturer at various colleges and Universities; Assistant to Co-Editor, Perspectives of New Music, 1963-85. *Compositions:* String Quartet, 1969; Sound Play for Violin, 1974; String Trio, 1976; Plein Chant, alto flute, 1977; Ebb Tide, 2 vibraphones, 1977; '...the supple Suitor...' for Soprano and 5 players, 1978; De Amore, chamber mini-opera, 1980; Impromptu for Violin, Cello and Piano, 1981; Media Speak, theatre piece, 1981; At the Piano, piano, 1982; for String Quartet, 1982; Quilt Piece, graphic score for 7 Instruments, 1984; On the Way to Becoming, for 4-track Tape Collage, 1985; Demeter and Persephone for Violin, Tape, Chamber Ensemble and Dancers, 1986; 3 Rhapsodies, flutes and Clarinet, 1986; Encore for Javanese Gamelan Ensemble, 1988; Out of the Air for Basset Horn and Tape, 1988; To Whom It May Concern, 4-track Tape Collage, Reader and 4 Players, 1989; Legong Dreams, Oboe, 1990 (and, since 1980 many improvised group and duo sessions on tape); Gamélamge, harp and mixed gamelan band, 1992. *Address:* c/o Department of Music, 405 Hilgard Avenue, University of California at Los Angeles, Los Angeles, CA 90024, USA.

BARKL Michael Laurence Gordon, b. 9 Aug 1958, Sydney, New South Wales, Australia. Composer. m. Sharyn Lee, 25 Jan 1986, 1 daughter. *Education:* BMus, New South Wales State Conservatorium of Music, 1981; FTCL, Trinity College of Music, London, 1982; MMus, University of New England, 1986; DipEd, Sydney College of Advanced Education, 1986. *Career:* Freelance Composer, 1981-. *Compositions:* All published by Sounds Australian, Sydney; Major works: Rota, piano trio, 1981; Voce di Testa, for orchestra, 1981; Voce di Petto, for orchestra, 1982; Drumming, solo piano, 1983; Ballade, for flute, clarinet, vibraphone, piano, violin, cello, 1984; Cabaret, for orchestra, 1985; Blues, for contra-alto clarinet and vibraphone/marimba, 1986; Backyard Swing, for concert band, 1986; The Laird of Drumblair, for 7 instruments, 1987; The Animals Noah Forgot, music theatre, for voices, orchestra, rhythm section, 1988; Disco, percussion quartet, 1990.

Honours: Segnalata, International Valentino Bucchi Prize, Italy, 1981; 1st Place, Frank Hutchens Prize, 1982. *Membership:* Writer Full Member, Australian Performing Right Association. *Hobbies:* Visual arts. *Address:* 119 Combermere Street, Goulburn, NSW 2580, Australia.

BARLOW Clara, b. 28 July 1928, Brooklyn, New York, USA. Singer (Soprano). *Education:* Studied with Cecile Jacobson in New York. *Debut:* Berne Opera 1962, as Venus in Tannhauser. *Career:* Sang at Oberhausen 1963-65, Kiel 1965-66; Komische Oper Berlin 1967, as Donna Anna; Engaged at Wiesbaden 1867-69, Zurich 1969-70; Guest appearances at the Spoletto Festival (as Isolde, 1968), San Diego (1969) and the Metropolitan Opera (as Leonore, 1970): returned to New York 1974, as Isolde; Deutsche Oper Berlin 1970, Vienna Staatsoper 1973; Sang Fata Morgana in The Love of Three Oranges at La Scala, 1974; Appearances as Brünnhilde at Seattle (1970-72 and 1976) and Dallas (1981); Scottish Opera 1973, as Isolde; Further appearances at Dresden, Stuttgart, Hamburg, Munich, Chicago (1976-77), Houston, Copenhagen, Toronto, Budapest and Mexico City; Stadttheater Bremen 1985-86, as Elektra and Leonore; Other roles have included the Dyer's Wife (Die Frau ohne Schatten), Agathe, Senta, Elsa, Elisabeth, Ariadne, Salome, Aida, Elisabeth de Valois, Jenůfa, Marina (Boris Godunov) and Giulietta in Les Contes d'Hoffmann. *Address:* c/o Bremer Theater, Postfach 101046, D-2800 Bremen, Germany.

BARLOW Stephen, b. 1954, England. Conductor. *Education:* Studied in Canterbury, at Trinity College, Cambridge, and at the Guildhall School of Music. *Career:* Founded the New London Chamber Group, based at the Riverside Studios in Hammersmith; Guest conductor of opera at the Guildhall School, notably Falstaff and Maw's The Rising of the Moon; Glyndebourne Festival and Tour 1979-85, leading Die schweigsame Frau, Der Rosenkavalier, Arabella, the Oliver Knussen double bill, Così fan Tutte, Gluck's Orfeo, The Rake's Progress and the Love of Three Oranges; For English National Opera has conducted The Flying Dutchman, Carmen, The Abduction from the Seraglio, The Damnation of Faust, La Cenerentola, The Italian Girl in Algiers and The Barber of Seville; Scottish Opera from 1983, with Hansel and Gretel, The Bartered Bride and Intermezzo; Has conducted Opera 80 from its inception, Musical Director from 1987, leading The Marriage of Figaro, The Masked Ball, The Rake's Progress and The Merry Widow, 1989-90; Covent Garden debut 1989, with Turandot, returning for Die Zauberflöte in 1991; San Francisco Opera 1990, Capiccio; Has also worked for Opera North and Vancouver Opera; Australian debut in Melbourne in Die Zauberflöte, 1991; Conducted Faust for Opera Northern Ireland, 1992; Conducted Capiccio in Catonia, Marriage of Figaro at Garsington, and Carmen in Adelaide; Concert engagements with the English Chamber Orchestra, City of London Sinfonia, London Sinfonietta, City of Birmingham Symphony, Royal Liverpool Philharmonic, Scottish Chamber Orchestra, BBC Scottish and the Bournemouth Sinfonietta; Concerts in Spain, Holland and Germany; BBC National Orchestra of Wales; Radio Philharmonic Orchestra, Hilversum; New Zealand Symphony Orchestra; Vancouver Symphony Orchestra; Melbourne Symphony Orchestra; Detroit Symphony Orchestra; BBC Philharmonic. *Address:* c/o Robert Gilder and Co, Enterprise House, 59/65 Upper Ground, London SE1 9PQ, England.

BARLOW Wayne (Brewster), b. 6 Sept 1912, Elyria, Ohio, USA. Composer; Music Educator; Organist; Choirmaster. *Education:* BM, composition and theory 1934, MM, composition 1935, PhD, music (composition) 1937, Eastman School of Music, with Howard Hanson and Bernard Rogers, Rochester, New York; Studied composition with Arnold Schoenberg, University of Southern California, Los Angeles, 1935; Seminar, electronic music with Myron Schaeffer, University of Toronto, 1963-64; Fulbright postdoctoral research grant, Universities of Brussels, Ghent and Utrecht, 1964-65. *Career:* Faculty member 1937-78, Director of Graduate Studies 1955-57, Chairman Composition Department

1968-73, Director, Electronic Music Studio 1968-78, Dean of Graduate Studies 1973-78, Emeritus Professor of Composition 1978-, Eastman School of Music, Rochester, New York; Guest lecturer and composer at various other colleges and universities; Organist and choirmaster, St Thomas Episcopal Church, Rochester, 1946-76; Christ Episcopal Church, Rochester, 1976-78. *Compositions:* Orchestral: De Profundis, 1934; False Faces, ballet suite, 1935; Sinfonietta, 1936; The Winter's Passed for Oboe and Strings, 1938; Lyrical Piece for Clarinet and strings, 1943; Nocturne for Chamber Orchestra, 1946; Rondo-Overture, 1947; Sinfonietta (1950); Lento and Allegro, 1955; Night Song, 1958; Rota for Chamber Orchestra, 1959; Images for Harp and Orchestra, 1961; Sinfonia da Camera for Chamber Orchestra, 1962; Vistas, 1963; Concerto for Saxophone and Band, 1970; Hampton Beach, overture, 1971; Soundscapes for Orchestra and Tape, 1972; Divertissement for Flute and Chamber Orchestra, 1980; Frontiers for Band, 1982; Vocal: Mass for Chorus and Orchestra, 1951; Cantatas Wait for the Promise of the Father and Voices of Faith; Organ music including 4 volumes of Hymn Voluntaries for the Church Year, 1963-81; Oratorio, The Seven Seals, text taken from Bible, Book of Revelations, for large chorus, full symphony, soloists, 1991; Requiem and Alleluia, for ensemble of 100 trombones. *Address:* 95 Elmcroft Road, Rochester, NY 14609, USA.

BARNARD Trevor (John), b. 3 Jan 1938, London, England. Concert Pianist; Lecturer in Music. m. Helen Richmond, 28 Aug 1974. *Education:* Royal Academy of Music, London; Royal College of Music, London; Herbert Fryer; Harold Craxton; Institute of Musical Instrument Technology, London, 1946-60. ARCM 1954; Graduate, MIMIT 1960. *Career:* Pianist-in-Residence, Boston University Radio, 1967-71; Faculty, New England Conservatory of Music, Boston, Massachusetts, USA, 1968-72; Piano tutor, Monash University, Australia, 1972-74; Lecturer in Music, Melbourne College of Advanced Education, 1974-88; Lecturer in Music, University of Melbourne, Examiner, Australian Music Examinations Board, 1989-. Many appearances as pianist, BBC & ABC; Music-in-the-Round chamber music festivals; Many orchestras, music societies. *Recordings:* An Introduction to Piano Music, World Record Club; Bliss Piano Concerto, HMV.*Publications:* Pedalling and Other Reflections on Piano Teaching, University of Melbourne, 1991. *Honour:* Full scholarship, Royal College of Music, 1955. *Membership:* Honorary Secretary, 1982-93, Australian Musicians Guild; President, Camberwell Music Society, 1990-. *Hobbies:* Golf; Swimming; Yoga. *Address:* 10 Grosvenor Road, Glen Iris, Victoria 3146, Australia.

BARNES Ben, b. 28 Mar 1956, Wexford, Ireland. Director. *Education:* BA, Honours, Medieval History, University College, Dublin. *Career:* Teaching Posts: Dublin College of Music; Trinity College Drama Studies, 1983-86; Resident Director, Abbey Theatre, Ireland's National Theatre, 1983-86; Director of Productions, Opera Theatre Company; Director of the Year, Harvey's Theatre Awards, 1987. *Productions include:* Endgame/ Rockaby (Beckett), Dublin, Athens, Tokyo; La Bohème/ Rigoletto, Cork City Opera; Figaro/Così/Irish Premiere of Carmelites, Poulenc; Turn of the Screw, Opera Theatre Company, Inaugural Production, 1986; Les Liaisons Dangereuses; The Field. *Compositions include:* The Field, Dublin, Moscow and Leningrad; Exit Entrance, Dublin, London; The Shadow of a Gunman, Dublin, Glasgow, Adelaide, Perth, Wellington. *Publications:* Editor: The Year of the Hiker; The Field and 3 Plays. *Contributor to:* Music Ireland; Irish University Review. *Hobbies:* Tennis; Reading; Squash; History. *Current Management:* Co-Director; Groundwork. *Address:* Charievire, Killincarrig Road, Greystones, Co Wicklow, Ireland.

BARNES Christopher John, b. 10 Mar 1942, Sheffield, England. University Lecturer. m. Alexa Hilla Dey, 16 July 1975, 2 daughters. *Education:* BA, 1963, MA, 1967, PhD, 1970, Cambridge University; Moscow University, 1963-64; Piano, privately with Stanley Kaye at Sheffield, Phyllis Palmer at Cambridge and Wight Henderson at Glasgow. *Career:* Slavonic Studies (Russian Language and Literature), St Andrews University, 1967-89; University of Toronto, Canada, 1989-; Published on various Russian musical subjects, 1977-; Lecture-recitals, Russian musical subjects; Broadcasts on BBC music and external services, Radio Liberty and Kol Israel; Book on Aleksandr Scriabin in preparation. *Contributions to:* Various articles on musical topics in journals including, Tempo, Performance, La Pensee Russe, Novaya russkaya muzykalnaya gazeta, Slavica Hierosolymitana; Items on Russian literary topics in many academic journals. *Memberships:* Royal Musical Association; British Scriabin Society; Royal Canadian College of Organists. *Hobbies:* Russian Literature; Piano; Musicology. *Address:* Department of Slavic Languages and Literatures, University of Toronto, 21 Sussex Avenue, Toronto M5S 1A1, Canada.

BARNES Milton, b. 16 Dec 1931, Toronto, Canada. Composer; Conductor. *Education:* Studied composition with John Weinzweig and Ernst Krenek; Conducting with Victor Feldbrill, Boyd Neel and Walter Susskind; Piano with Samuel Dolin, Royal Conservatory of Music of Toronto, 1952-55; Studied conducting at: Accademia Musicale Chigiana, Siena, Italy and Berkshire Music Center, Tanglewood, USA; Graduated, Vienna Academy of Music, 1961. *Career:* Music Director and Composer, Crest Theatre, 1961-63; Founder-conductor, Toronto Repertory Orchestra, 1964-73; Conductor, St Catherine's (Ontario) Symphony Orchestra and Chorus, 1964-72; Niagara Falls (NY) Philharmonic and Chorus, 1965-73; Composer and conductor-in-residence, Toronto Dance Theatre, 1968-73. *Compositions:* Many music theatre and multi-media works including: Amber Garden, ballet suite, 1972; The Spiral Stairs for 7 Instruments, 1973; The Dybbuk, masque for Dancing for Tenor and 6 Instruments, 1977; Film and television scores; Orchestral: Divertimento for Harp and String Quartet, 1978; 3 symphonies, 1964, 1973, 1987; The Children's Suite, 1966; Pinocchio, symphonic poem, 1967; Variations for Clarinet and Orchestra, 1968; Concerto for Viola and Orchestra, 1977; Psalms of David for Soprano, Baritone, Chorus and Orchestra, 1973; Shebetim, tableau for String Orchestra, 1975; Song of the Bow: Concerto for String Bass and Orchestra, 1991; Concerto for Violin and Strings, 1975; Chamber Concerto for Wind Quintet and Strings, 1976; Viola Concerto, 1977; Maid of the Mist, symphonic poem, 1977; Concertino No 1 for Flute and String Orchestra, 1978; Serenade for String Quartet and String Orchestra, 1979; Follies Overture, 1983; French Canadian Legends for Orchestra, 1986; Double Concerto for 2 Guitars and String Orchestra, 1986; Chamber: Rhapsody on a Late Afternoon for String Quartet, 1971; Carlebach Variations for Violin, 1972; String Quartet No 2, Scenes from Jewish Life, 1978; Octet for Flute, Piano, Electric Guitar, Violin, Viola, Cello, Double Bass and Trap Drums, 1985; Papageno Variations for String Bass and Piano or string orchestra, 1988; The Odyssey: A Symphonic Tale, 1990; Vocal music. *Recordings:* Lamentations of Jeremiah for Solo Viola or Cello Centrediscs, 1959; Variations for Solo Harp, BIS Records, 1976; Divertimento for Harp and Strings, Musica Viva CBC Records, 1978; Ballade for Solo Viola SNE, Societe Nouvelle D'Enregistrement, 1979; Annexus for Percussion Ensemble, 5 players, Musica Viva CBC Records, 1982. *Membership:* Socan, Canadian Music Centre. *Current Management:* Marilyn Gilbert Artists Management, 516E Wadsworth Avenue, Philadelphia, PA 19119, USA and 18 Bracondale Hill Road, Toronto, Ontario M6G 3P4, Canada. *Address:* 192A Lowther Ave, Toronto, Ontario, M5R 1E8, Canada.

BARNETT John (Manley), b. 3 Sept 1917, New York, USA. Conductor. *Education:* Studied piano and conducting at the Manhattan School of Music; Further studies with Bruno Walter, Nikolai Malko, Felix Weingartner and George Enescu in Europe. *Career:* Worked under Leon Barzin with the National Orchestral Association; Staff Conductor with the WPA Federal Music Project of New York, 1939-42; Assistant to Otto Klemperer with the Federal Knickerbocker Orchestra and worked with the New York Symphony Orchestra and the Stamford Symphony Orchestra; Associate Conductor of the Los Angeles Philharmonic 1946-58, including Far East tour 1956; Organized and trained the Japan-American Philharmonic Orchestra; Musical Director of the National Orchestral Association, 1958-70; Music Director of the Philharmonic Symphony Orchestra of Weschester, New York, 1961-71; Artistic Consultant to the National Endowment of the Arts, 1972-78; Music Director of the Puerto Rico Symphony Orchestra from 1979.

BAROLSKY Michael, b. 19 July 1947, Vilnius, Lithuania. Composer. *Education:* Studied piano, music theory and ethnology in Lithuania; Further studies with Witold Lutoslawski in Warsaw and Edison Denisov and Alfred Schnittke in Moscow. *Career:* Music Adviser to Lithuania Radio, 1969-71; Emigrated to Germany 1971 and attended seminars led by Liget, Stockhausen and Kagel at Darmstadt; Taught in Tel Aviv 1974-77; Settled in Cologne and worked on electronic music with Humpert at the studio there. *Composition include:* Violin Sonata 1964; String Trio 1964; Concertino 1967; Telefonoballade for baritone, 6 narrators and ensemble 1969; Exodus for orchestra 1970; Scriptus after Kafka 1972; Dakar for percussion and electronics 1972; Melos for mezzo-soprano and ensemble 1975; Sublimato for ensemble and tape 1975; Cries and Whispers for ensemble and electronics 1975; Blue Eye, Brown Eye chamber opera 1976; Apocolypse song cycle 1976; Pranah for violin and tape 1976; Sternengesang for chamber orchestra 1977; The Book of Emanations for orchestra 1978; Ein Stuck aus der Nacht for actor and electronics 1978; Tonus for synthesizer 1979; Seelenkalender for mezzo and piano 1982; The Book of Changes for piano 1982; Stuck-Mund-Stuck for trombone and tape 1983; Piccolostuck 1983; Rainbow Music for six recorders 1984; Trioirtrio for violin, cello and tape 1984. *Address:* c/o GEMA, Herzog Wilhelm Strasse 28, 8000 Munich 2, Germany.

BARON Samuel, b. 27 Apr 1925, Brooklyn, New York, USA. Flautist; Conductor. *Education:* Studied at Brooklyn College, 1940-45, and at the Juilliard School with Georges Barrere, Edgar Schenkman and Arthur Lora. *Career:* Played flute in the New York Symphony Orchestra, the orchestra of the New York City Opera and the Minneapolis Symphony (as principal); Founder member of the New York Woodwind Quintet 1949, performing with the ensemble until 1969 and again from 1980; Performances with the American Chamber Orchestra, the New York Brass Ensemble, the Contemporary Chamber Ensemble and the Bach Aria Group (music director from 1980); Has taught at the Yale School of Music, 1965-67, Mannes College, 1969-72 and the Juilliard School, from 1977. *Publications include:* Edition of Bach's Flute sonata in A; Chamber Music for Wind, 1969. *Recordings include:* Many albums with the New York Brass Ensemble; Bach's Art of Fugue arranged for string quartet and five wind instruments. *Address:* c/o Juilliard School of Music, Lincoln Center Plaza, New York, NY 10023, USA.

BARRAUD Henry, b. 23 April 1900, Bordeaux, France. Composer. m. Denise Parly, 3 children. *Education:* Studied Paris Conservatoire, 1926-27; Later study with Dukas and Aubert. *Career:* In charge of music at Paris International Exposition, 1937; Former Musical Director, and Director, National Programme, French Radio, 1944-65. *Compositions:* Finale dans le mode rustique, 1932; Poème for orchestra, 1934; Concerto da Camera, 1936; Le Mystère de Saints Innocents, oratorio, 1944; Le Diable à la Kermesse, ballet, 1943; Piano Concerto, 1946; Offrandre à une Ombre, 1946; La Farce du Maitre Pathelin, 1948; Symphonie de Numance, 1950; Concertino for piano and 4 winds, 1953; Numance, opera, 1955; Te Deum, 1955; Symphony for Strings, 1955; Symphony No.3, 1958; Rapsodie dionysienne, 1961; Lavinia, opera, 1961; Divertimento, 1962; Flute Concerto, 1963; Symphonie Concertante for trumpet and orchestra, 1965; 3 Etudes for orchestra; Une Saison en enfer, symphonic suite after Rimbaud, 1969; La Divine Comedie for 5 solo voices

and orchestra, 1972. *Publications:* La France et La Musique Occidentale; Berlioz 1955, 1966; Pour Comprendre les Musiques d' Aujourd'hui, 1968; Les Cinq Grands Operas, 1972. *Honours:* Legion d'Honneur; Commander, Ordre des Arts et Lettrs; Grand Prix Nationale de la Musique, 1959. *Address:* 20 Rue Jean Daudin, 75015 Paris, France.

BARRERA Giulia, b. 28 April 1942, Brooklyn, New York, USA. Singer (Soprano). *Education:* Studied in New York with Dick Marzollo. *Debut:* New York City Opera 1963, as Aida. *Career:* Sang in Baltimore, New Orleans, Pittsburgh, Washington and Seattle; Member of New York City Opera: roles include Verdi's Amelia and Leonora (Il Trovatore), Santuzza, Don Giovanni, Sieglinde in Die Walküre, Tosca, Manon Lescaut, Venus in Tannhäuser and Monteverdi's Euridice; Guest appearances in Copenhagen, Rome, Parma, Cardiff, Montreal and Nuremburg. *Recordings include:* The Mother in Dallapiccola's Il Prigioniero (Decca). *Address:* c/o New York City Opera, Lincoln Center, New York, NY 10023, USA.

BARRIERE Jean-Baptiste Marie, b. 2 Jan 1958, Paris, France. Composer; Director of Musical Research. m. Kaija Saariaho, 26 May 1984. *Education:* Mathematical Logic (Licence) University of Paris I-Panthéon Sorbonne, 1980; DEA Philosophy, 1981, Philosophy (Doctorate) 1987, University of Paris I-Panthéon Sorbonne. *Career:* Member of the Synthesizer Ensemble of the Sentre Europeen pour la Recherche Musicale of Metz, 1976-77; Researcher/Composer at Institut de Recherche et de Coordination Acoustique Musique of Paris, 1981-84; Director of Musical Research at IRCAM, Paris, 1984-. *Compositions:* Pandemonium: Ville Ouverte, 1975; Pandemonium: Non, Jamais L'Esperance, 1976; Sophistic Variations, 1980; Chreode I 1983; Collisions, 1984; Epigénèse 1986; Hybris, 1987. *Recordings:* Pandemonium: Villa Ouverte 1977 on Atem Record Label No 7003; Pandemonium: Non, Jamais L'Esperance 1978 on Atem No 7004. *Publications:* Le Timbre: Métaphores pour la Composition, et, Christian Bourgois Editions (to be published 1987-88); Actes du Symposium Systèmes Personnels et informatique Musicale et; Publications IRCAM, 1987. *Contributions to:* Chreode I: A Path to a New Music with the Computer in Contemporary Music Review No 1 1984; Mutations de L'Esriture, Mutations du Matériaú in Inharmoniques No 1 1987. *Honour:* Digital Music Prize in the Electro-Acoustic Music Competition in Bourges, France, 1983. *Membership:* Collectif pour La Recherche en Informatique Musicale (CPRIM). *Address:* IRCAM, 31 Rue St Merri, Paris 75004, France.

BARRITT Paul, b. 5 Dec 1953, Belfast, Northern Ireland. Violinist. *Education:* Ulster College of Music, 1965-72; Royal College of Music, 1973-74; Salzburg Mozarteum, 1974-75; Robert Schumann Institut, 1975-76. *Debut:* Wigmore Hall, London, 1981. *Career:* Leader, UK National Youth Orchestra, 1971-73; Leader/Director, Divertmenti; Leader (former), Kent Opera Orchestra; Member, Koenig Ensemble; International Musicians Seminar, Prussia Cove; BBC Recordings; Appearances at Edinburgh, Aldeburgh and Harrogate Festivals; Solo and Chamber music tours to, South-East Asia 1983 and 1985; America 1987 and 1988. Current leader of Northern Sinfonia Orchestra of England. *Recordings:* For BBC, West German, Norwegian, Swedish, Italian and Austrian Radio; Records: Howells and Dyson Quartets; Colin Matthews Chamber Works; Mozart Flute Quartets, Mendelssohn Octet, Rozsa Violin Works, Mozart Clarinet Quintet. *Hobbies:* Birdwatching; Card games; Table-tennis; Cricket. *Address:* 84 Woodbine Road, Gosforth, Newcastle-upon-Tyne NE3 1DE, England.

BARRON Louis, b. 23 Apr 1920, Minneapolis, Minnesota, USA. Composer. m. Bebe (nee Charlotte Wind) Barron, 1947, divorced 1970. *Education:* University of Minnesota; Studies in piano. *Career:* With wife, founded one of the first electro-acoustic music studios in New York, 1948; Los Angeles, 1962.

Compositions: Electronic works in collaboration with wife: Dramatic: Legend, 1955; Ballet, 1958; Incidental music for 4 plays, 1957-62; Tape pieces: Heavenly Menagerie, 1951; For an Elec Nervous System, 1954; Music of Tomorrow, 1960; Spaceboy, 1971, also as a film score, 1973; The Circe Circuit, 1982; Elegy for a Dying Planet, 1982; Film scores: Bells of Atlantis, 1952; Miramagic, 1954; Forbidden Planet, 1956; Jazz of Lights, 1956; Bridges, 1959; Crystal Growing, 1959; The Computer Age, 1968; More than Human, 1974; Cannabis, 1975. *Address:* ASCAP, ASCAP Building, One Lincoln Plaza, New York NY 10023, USA.

BARROSO Sergio, b. 4 Mar 1946, Havana, Cuba. Composer; Synthesist. *Education:* Composition, Piano, Organ, Theory, National Conservatory, Havana, 1950-66; Postgraduate, Prague Superior Academy of Music; Orchestral Conducting, University of Havana; Computer Music, CCRMA, Stanford University, USA. *Career includes:* Professor, Composition, Institute of Arts, Havana; Performances include: Monte Carlo Theatre, 1972; Warsaw Autumn Festivals, 1972, 1985; Budapest Opera, 1976; Teatro de la Zarzuela, Madrid, 1976; MET-Lincoln Center, New York, 1977-78; San Francisco Opera, 1977; Bratislava Philharmonic Hall, 1979; ISCM Festival, Belgium, 1980, Oslo, 1990; IRCMA, Paris, 1980; Array, Toronto, 1981; Utrecht Conservatorium, Netherlands, 1982; Manuel de Falla Festival, Granada, 1985; Wired Society, Toronto, 1986; ACREQ, Montreal, 1987; Museo Tamayo, Mexico City, 1988; National Arts Centre, Ottawa, 1988; South Bank Centre, London, 1989; Toronto New Music Concerts, 1990; Sub-Tropics Festival, Miami, 1991; LIEM, Centro Reina Sofia, Madrid, 1991; ICMC, Montreal, 1991; New Music Across America, Seattle, 1992; Others. *Compositions include:* 2 ballets: Plasmasis, 1970; La Casa de Bernarda Alba, 1975; Oboe Concerto, 1968; Yantra IV, flute, tape, 1975, IX, saxophone, tape, 1979, X, bassoon, tape, 1982; Ireme, voice, percussion, tape, 1985; En Febrero Mueren las Flores, violin, tape, 1987; Tablao, guitar, tape, 1991; Concerto for violin and orchestra, 1992; Synthesizers: Soledad, 1987; Canzona, 1988; La Fiesta, synthesizers, tape, 1989; La Fiesta Grande, synthesizers, orchestra, 1990; Cronicas de Ultrasueno, oboe, synthesizers, 1992; Sonatada, 1992. *Address:* c/o CMC, 200-2021 West Avenue, Vancouver, British Columbia, Canada V6J 1N3.

BARRY Gerald Anthony, b. 28 April 1952, Ennis, Co. Clare, Ireland. Composer. *Education:* MusB, 1973, MA 1975, Diploma in Music Teaching, University College, Dublin; Royal Conservatory, The Hague; State Academy of Music, Cologne with Stockhausen; Vienna Academy of Music with Friedrich Cerha. *Career:* Compositions broadcast throughout Europe and elsewhere under auspices of UNESCO International Rostrum of Composers. *Compositions:* Things that Gain by Being Painted; Decolletage; Mr Volans his Rest; Monocule; Belacquered; Knippenspiel; A Piano Concerto; All the Dead Voices for vocal soloists and orchestra; The Intelligence Park, opera, 1991; The Triumph of Beauty and Deceit, 1992-93. *Memberships:* Founder Member, Association of Irish Composers; PRS; Mechanical Copyright Society. *Honours:* Grants awarded by Dutch, Irish and German Governments. *Hobby:* Belacquering. *Address:* c/o OUP, 3 Park Road, London NW1 6XN, England.

BARSHAI Rudolf, b. 28 Sept 1924, Labinskaya, USSR. Conductor. m. (1) 3 sons, (2) Elena Raskova. *Education:* Leningrad Conducting course under Ilya Musin; Moscow Conservatory violin and viola studies with Lev Zeitlin. *Career:* Solo Violinist, Moscow Philharmonic Quartet, Leader Borodin Quartet, Tchaikovsky Quartet, 1955-77; Founder and Conductor, Moscow Chamber Orchestra, Guest Conductor, Moscow Philharmonic, State Orchestra of USSR, USSR Radio Orchestra, 1955-77; Guest Conductor, Israel Chamber Orchestra, 1977-, LSO, LPO, RPO, BBC, London, Philharmonia, English Chamber Orchestra, Scottish National Orchestra, City of Birmingham Symphony Orchestra, BBC Philharmonic, Vienna Symphony, Orch National de France, Orchestra de Paris,

Mozarteum Salzburg, Yomiuri and NHK Orchestras, Tokyo, RAI, Turin, Pittsburg Symphony, Swiss Radio Orchestra, Basle Symphony Orchestra, Tonhalle Orchestra Zurich; Principal Conductor, Bournemouth Symphony, 1982-88; Music Director, Vancouver Symphony, 1985-88; Principal Guest Conductor, Orchestra National de France, 1987-88. *Compositions:* Arrangements of Bach; Art of the Fugue; Musical Offering; Shostakovich: Chamber Symphony, Symphony, Symphony for Strings, Symphony for Wood Winds and Strings; Prokofiev: Visions Fugitives etc. *Recordings:* Many recordings including, Works by Bach, Vivaldi, Corelli, Mozart, Haydn, Beethoven, Schubert, Stravinsky, Bartók, Shostakovich, Tchaikovsky, Tippett, Prokofiev, for EMI, Decca, Pathé Marconi, Eurodisc, Melodiya etc. *Honours:* Grande Prix du Disque; Honorary Doctorate, University of Southampton, 1985. *Current Management:* Allied Artists, 42 Montpellier Square, London, SW7 1JZ.

BARSTOW Josephine Clare, b. 27 Sept 1940, Sheffield, Yorkshire, England. Opera Singer. m. (1) Terry Hands, (2) Ande Anderson, 25 Oct 1969. *Education:* BA Hons. English, Birmingham University; London Opera Centre (one year). *Debut:* 1964, Opera for All. *Career:* Has appeared with all major British Opera Companies; in world premieres of The Knot Garden and The Ice Break by Tippett and We Come To The River by Henze at Covent Garden, and Story of Vasco at ENO; Summer 1986, at Salzburg Festival in leading role, Penderecki's Die schwarze Maske; has sung in all major houses in USA and in Germany (including Bayreuth), France, Switzerland, Italy, Buenos Aires, in Africa, and in Russia at The Bolshoi; Main Roles: Verdi, Strauss (frequently Salome), Janáček, Mozart, Puccini, Beethoven and Wagner; Role of Kate, Kiss Me Kate; Sang Odabella in a new production of Attila at Covent Garden; Amelia in Un Ballo in Maschera at Salzburg, 1990; Ellen Orford, New production, Peter Grimes, ENO, 1991; Sang Leonora in a new production of La Forza del Destino for ENO, 1992; Chrysothemis in Elektra at Houston, 1993; Elizabeth I in Gloriana for Opera North at Covent Garden, 1994. *Recordings:* The Knot Garden by Michael Tippett; Recital Verdi Arias; Ballo in Maschera (Karajan); Four Opera Finales, Decca; Gloriana for Argo Label (title role). *Honours:* Critics Prize, Berliner Zeitung, Best Debut, Buenos Aires; Honorary doctorate of Music, Birmingham University; CBE, 1985; Fidelio Medal. *Current Management:* John Coast. *Hobbies:* Runs Arabian Stud Farm in Sussex. *Address:* John Coast Ltd, 31 Sinclair Road, London W14 0NS, England.

BARTA Ales, b. 30 Aug 1960, Rychnov, Czechoslovakia. Organist. m. 25 Feb 1984. *Education:* Conservatoire in Brno; Academy of Music, Prague. *Debut:* With Prague Symphony Orchestra, Prague Spring Festival, 1984. *Career:* Foreign tours: Denmark, 1979, Austria, 1983, Hungary, 1984, 1985, Turkey, 1985, Germany, 1986, 1990, France, 1987, USSR, 1988; USA debut, concert of Czech music, New York, 1990; Festival appearances: Recitals, Prague Spring Festival, 1984, 1988, 1991; Avignon Festival, 1987; Istanbul Festival, 1985; Leipzig Festival, 1986; Debut with Prague Radio Symphony Orchestra, Berlin Festival, 1987. *Recordings:* Organ recital, Bach, Reger and Flosman, Panton label, 1986; Organ recital, Bach, Supraphon label, 1991; Organ Recital, Live Recording (Bach, Reger, Sokola), Ultraphon label, 1992. *Honours:* 1st Prize, Anton Bruckner International Organ Competition, Linz, 1982; 1st Prize, Czech Organists Competition, 1984; 1st Prize, Prague Spring International Organ Competition, 1984. *Hobbies:* Football; Driving. *Address:* Nuselska 6, 14000 Prague 4, Czech Republic.

BARTA Jiri, b. 19 June 1935, Sumice, Czechoslovakia. Composer. m. Jindriska Bartova, 1 Feb 1964, 1 daughter. *Education:* Conservatoire; Academy of Musical Arts. *Debut:* Concerto for Orchestra, 1962. *Career:* Master of Conservatoire. *Compositions:* Lyricke variace for violin and piano; Concert da camera per pianoforte ed archi; Relievos for orchestra; Music for

Strings - In memoriam Miloslav Istvan; Concerto grosso per due violini, violoncelle ed archi. *Honours:* Prize, Czech Union of composers, 1987; Prize, Czech Musical Fund, 1991, 1992. *Memberships:* Association of Musicians and Musical Scientists; Formerly The Union of Czech Composers and Concert Artists. *Hobby:* Ornithology. *Address:* Solnicni 5-9, 602 00 Brno, Czech Republic.

BARTA Michael (Mihaly), b. 6 Feb 1954, Budapest, Hungary. Violinist; Conductor. m. Irene Barta, 7 May 1980, 1 son. *Education:* Béla Bartók Conservatory; F Liszt Academy, Budapest. *Career:* Concerts: Wigmore Hall, London; Tokyo, Frankfurt, Carnegie Recital Hall, New York, Detroit Art Institute; Radio: Radio France, Scottish BBC, Radio Bremen, Berlin, Hungarian Radio, WDR Köln, PBS USA. *Recordings:* Goldmark: Suite for Violin & Piano; Prokofiev: Sonata for Two Violins; *Honours:* 2nd Prize, Joseph Szigeti International Competition, Budapest, 1973; Gold Medal, Belgian Eugene Ysaÿe Competition, 1973; Special prize, finals, Tchaikovsky International Competition, Moscow, 1974. *Hobbies:* Travel; Cycling. *Address:* Rt 6 Box 389, Murphysboro, IL 62966, USA.

BARTELINK Bernard G M, b. 24 Nov 1929, Enschede, Netherlands. Musician; Organist; Composer. m. Rina Stolwyk, 23 Apr 1955, 2 sons. *Education:* Diploma (composition), 1955, prix d'excellence (organ), 1954; Amsterdam Conservatory. *Career:* Recitals in major concert halls and cathedrals in UK, Europe and USA; Radio appearances in many countries; Professor of organ at Sweelinck Conservatory, Amsterdam, until 1989; Organist at St Bavo Cathedral, Haarlem; Organist for Concertgebouw Orchestra, Amsterdam. *Compositions:* The Beatitudes, for voice and organ; Works for organ, choir and chamber music, commissioned by Dutch Government, City of Amsterdam, etc. *Recordings:* Several solo LP's and CD's. *Honours:* First Prize, International Organ Improvisation Contest, Haarlem, 1961; Knight in the Papal Order of St Sylvester; Silver Medal of the Academic Society, Arts, Sciences, Letters, Paris. *Address:* Leeghwaterstraat 14, 2012 GD Haarlem, The Netherlands.

BARTHA Clarry, b. 1958, Sweden. Singer (Soprano). *Education:* Studied at the Accadamia di Santa Cecilia Rome, with Maria Teresa Pediconi and Giorgio Favaretto; Further study with Vera Rozsa in London. *Debut:* Donna Anna at Drottningholm, Sweden, 1981. *Career:* Has sung Donna Anna in Catania, at the Montepulciano Festival and at the Brighton Festival with the Drottningholm company; At Marseilles has sung Lisa (The Queen of Spades), Fiordiligi and Margherita in Mefistofele; Basle Opera as Agathe, Tatiana (Eugene Onegin) and Mozart's Countess; Performances of Gluck's La Danza at Bologna, season 1986-87; Frankfurt Opera 1987-88 as Iphigénie (en Tauride), Desdemona and Fiordiligi; She sang Mozart's Countess at Rome in 1989; Sang Katya Kabanova at Basle, 1991; Concert commitments at the Prague Spring, Montreale (Palermo) and Ravello Festivals; Has sung with the Italian Radio (RAI) in Rome, Naples and Milan; Accademia di Santa Cecilia in Rome and the Maggio Musicale in Florence; Mozart's Vespers and Mendelssohn's Elijah in Stockholm; Tour of Israel with Gary Bertini. *Honours include:* Prizewinner at the Beniamino Gigli and Vincenzo Bellini competitions. *Address:* c/o Ingpen and Williams Ltd, 14 Kensington Court, London W11 4PA.

BARTHA Denes, b. 2 Oct 1908, Budapest, Hungary. Musicologist; Music Educator. *Education:* PhD, University of Berlin, 1930; Studied with Wolf, Abert, Blume, Sachs, Hornbostel and Schering. *Career:* Librarian, Music Division, Hungarian National Museum, Budapest, 1930-32; Lecturer, Franz Liszt Academy of Music, Budapest, 1935-; Privatdozent, University of Budapest; Visiting Professor, Smith College, 1964; Harvard University 1964, 1965; Cornell University 1965-66; University of Pittsburgh, 1966-67; Andrew W Mellon Professor, University of Pittsburgh, 1969-78. *Publications:* Benedictus Ducis und Appenzeller, 1930; Das Musklehrbuch einer ungarischen Klosterschule aus 1490, 1934; Lehrbuch der Muskgeschichte, 1935; Franz Liszt, 1936; Die ungarische Musik, with Zoltán Kodály, 1943; Anthologie der Musikgeschichte, 1948; J S Bach 1956, 2nd edition 1960; Beethoven kilenc szimfoniaja 1956, 5th edition revised 1975; Haydn als Opernkapellmeister, with Laszlo Somfai, 1960; Edited Joseph Haydn: Gesammelte Briefe und Aufzeichnungen, 1965; Edited Zenei Lexikon 2nd edition, revised 1965-66. *Address:* Attila ut 87 III 14, H-1012, Budapest, Hungary.

BARTKIEWICZ Urszula, b. 28 Jan 1952, Bielsko-Biala, Poland. Harpsichordist. m. Jerzy Kozub, 13 Sept 1987, 1 son. Certificate of Maturity 1971; Studies at the Academy of Music in Cracow headed by Krzysztof Penderecki 1971-75: graduation with distinction; Studies at Conservatoire National de Bobigny-Paris, 1976-77, Harpsichord Class of Huguette Dreyfus; International Master Courses: with Zuzana Ruzickova, Rafael Puyana, Kenneth Gilbert; Doctor's Thesis in Musicology at Polish Academy of Sciences in preparation. *Career:* Numerous concerts in Poland, eg International Festivals Warsaw Autumn, Wratislavia Cantans, Lancut Chamber Festival; Concerts in France, Czechoslovakia, Germany, Soviet Union, Switzerland, Belgium, Austria, Great Britain, USA; Co-operation with the Polish National Philharmony, Jerzy Maksymiuk's Polish Chamber Orchestra; Several appearances on television and radio in Poland and USA; Master Class and recital for students of Wayne State University, Department of Music, Detroit, Jan 1988. *Recordings:* Regular recordings for Polish Radio 1975-90: International and Polish harpsichord music from XVI-XX centuries (solo and chamber music). Records with Polish National Philharmony and Jerzy Maksymiuk's Polish Chamber Orchestra (basso continuo). *Hobbies:* Philosophy; Literature; Psychology; Sociology; Cycling; Sailing; Walking. *Address:* ul Bacha 10 m 301, 02-743 Warsaw, Poland.

BARTLE Graham Alfred Reginald, b. 6 Nov 1928, Ballarat, Victoria, Australia. University Lecturer. m. Ruth Marian Walker, 11 May 1963, 1 son, 3 daughters. *Education:* Trained Primary Teachers Certificate, 1949; FTCL (organ), 1949; BA, DipEd, 1953, BMus, 1964, MMus, 1971, University of Melbourne. *Career:* Teacher, Yallourn High School, Victoria, 1954-57; Teacher, University High School, Melbourne, Victoria, 1958-61; Lecturer in Music, Secondary Teachers College, Melbourne, 1962-65; Lecturer, then Senior Lecturer, 1966-, Deputy Dean, Deputy Head, 1978-93, Faculty of Music, University of Melbourne, retired 31 Dec 1994. *Publications:* Music in Australian Schools, chapter in The Teacher's Role in Curriculum Design, 1968; International Directoyr of Music Education, 2,800 Institutions in 123 Countries, 1991. *Contributor to:* Australian Journal of Music Education; International Journal of Music Education. *Honours:* Ormond Exhibition, University of Melbourne, 1958; Composition Prize, Faculty of Music, University of Melbourne, 1960. *Memberships:* Australian Society of Music Education; International Society of Music Education; International Kodaly Society; Kodaly Music Education Institute of Australia; Incorporated Society of Musicians; Music Educators National Conference, USA; Victoria Music Teachers Association; Australian National Choral Association. *Hobbies:* Gardening; Walking. *Address:* 10 Chaucer Crescent, Canterbury, Victoria 3126, Australia.

BARTLETT Clifford Alfred James, b. 15 Aug 1939, London, England. Practical Musicologist; Music Writer. m. Elaine King, 16 Aug 1975, 1 son, 1 daughter. *Education:* Dulwich College; Magdalene College, Cambridge University. *Career:* Deputy Music Librarian, BBC, 1970-82; Keyboard Player for Ars Nova, 1969-75; Freelance Writer and Publisher, 1983-; Director, Early Music Centre Festival, 1987-88. *Publications:* Monteverdi, Orfeo, Vespers, Ulisse, Poppea; Blow, Venus and Adonis; Purcell, Dido and Aeneas; Handel, Alcina, Partenope, Scipione, La Resurrezione, Coronation Anthems; Arne, Artaxerxes. *Contributions to:* Monthly surveys in Early Music News, 1977-; Editor, Brio, 1974-85; Contributor of numerous programme notes for major record companies and festivals. *Memberships:* Chairman, Eastern Early Music Forum; Council of Early Music Centre; Committee, Early Music Network. *Address:* Redcroft, Banks End, Wyton, Huntingdon, Cambridgeshire PE17 2AA, England.

BARTLETT Ian James, b. 20 Sept 1934, London, England. Lecturer. m. Anne Verne Lucas, 3 Aug 1960, 1 son, 2 daughters. *Education:* BA, 1956, MA, 1960, Brasenose College, Oxford; ARCM, 1957, LRAM, 1961, Royal Academy of Music; PGCE, Institute of Education, University of London, 1957-58; MMus, 1974, King's College, University of London. *Career:* Director of Music, Bilborough Grammar School, Nottingham, 1958-62; Lecturer in Music, Bretton Hall College of Education, Yorkshire, 1962-65; Director of Music, North Oxon Junior Music School, 1966-70; Director of Music, Banbury School, 1965-70; Senior Lecturer in Music, Goldsmiths' College, University of London, 1970-77; Principal Lecturer, 1977-89, Acting Head of Music, 1980-83; Dean of Faculty of Music, University of London, 1982-86; Freelance Lecturer, Writer, Musician, 1989-. *Compositions:* Arrangements. *Recordings:* BBC, Editor of Works by William Boyce. *Contributor to:* Music Teacher; Education; The Musical Times; Music and Letters. *Hobbies:* Athletics; Theatre. *Address:* 463 Footscray Road, New Eltham, London SE9 3UH, England.

BARTO Tzimon, b. 2 Jan 1963, Eustis, Florida, USA. Pianist; Conductor; Composer. *Education:* Brevard Music Centre, 1978-79; Boston Univesity, Tanglewood Institute, 1980-81; Juilliard School, 1981-84. *Career:* Aarhus Festival, Denmark; Norddeutcher Rundfunk Orchestra, regular Guest conductor; L'orchestre Philharmonie de Monte Carlo; Wiener Symphoniker; Maggio Musicale Orchestra, Florence; Australian Youth Orchestra; Solo Recitals: in every musical capital of the world. *Publications:* Rhapsody Nos: 2 & 6; Harmonies du Soir; 3 Sonetti del Petraca; Consolation No 3. *Honours:* Recipient, various honours & awards. *Address:* c/o Miss Alison Taylor, 16 rue St Sabin, 75011 Paris, France.

BARTOLETTI Bruno, b. 10 June 1926, Sesto Fiorentino, Italy. Conductor. m. Rosanna Bartoletti, 2 children. *Education:* Studied flute at Cherubini Conservatory, Florence; received training in piano and composition. *Career:* Played flute in orchestre of the Teatro Comunale, Florence; assistant conductor from 1949, working with Rodzinski, Mitropoulos, Gui and Serafin; Conducting debut Dec 1953, with Rigoletto; Symphonic debut, Maggio Musicale Fiorentino, 1954 (resident conductor 1957-64); Led the premieres of Rocca's Antiche iscrizioni, 1955 and Malipiero's Il figluol prodigo and Venere prigioniera, 1957 at Florence; Mortari's La scuola delle mogli, (1959) at La Scala and Ginastera's Don Rodrigo at the Teatro Colon Buenos Aires, 1964; Italian premieres of Egk's Der Revisor and The Nose by Shostakovich; Conducted Italian opera at the Royal Opera, Copenhagen, 1957-60; US debut with the Lyric Opera of Chicago, 1956, Resident conductor 1956-63, Co-artistic director 1964-75, Principal Conductor and artistic director, 1975- Artistic Director, Rome Opera 1965-69, artistic adviser 1986-87; Artistic Director, Teatro Comunale Florence, 1987- 92, (conducted Madama Butterfly and I Puritani in Florence 1988-89); Lyric Opera, Chicago 1988-89 with La Traviata and Tancredi; Guest conductor with many opera houses in Europe, the USA and South America; Grand Théâtre Geneva 1991, Peter Grimes; Conducted I Quattro Rusteghi at Geneva, 1992. *Recordings include:* Il Barbiere di Siviglia, Vivaldi's Gloria and Credo (Deutsche Grammophon); Manon Lescaut (EMI); Un Ballo in Maschera (Decca). *Address:* c/o Chicago Lyric Opera, 20 North Wacker Drive, Chicago, IL 60606, USA.

BARTOLI Cecilia, b. 4 June 1966, Rome, Italy. Singer (Mezzo-soprano). *Education:* Studied at the Accademia di Santa Cecilia, Rome. *Career:* Sang in concert at Rome, Florence, Moderna and Bologna; Stage debut at Verona 1987; Appearances at the Staatsoper Berlin, Nantes and Warsaw 1987; Sang Handel arias in the pasticcio Donna

abandonata at Nancy, 1987; Best known as Rossini's Rosina, sung at Cologne, Catania and Schwetzingen (1988); Zurich Opera 1989, as Rosina and Cherubino; Pesaro Festival 1988, in La Scala di Seta; Teatro San Carlo Naples 1990, as Giannetta in Le Cantatrice villane by Fioravanti; Also sings Mozart's Dorabella; Song recital at Wigmore Hall, London, 1989; Featured artist, South Bank Show, London Weekend Television, 1992; Sang Cherubino at Orchestra Hall, Chicago, 1992; Engaged as Elena in La Donna del Lago at Zurich, 1995. *Recordings include:* Il Barbiere di Siviglia and arias by Rossini, conducted by Giuseppe Patanè (Decca); Mozart's Cherubino, Dorabella and Cecilia (Lucio Silla); Concepcion in L'Heure espagnole (Decca). *Address:* c/o Teatro San Carlo, Via San Carlo 98F, I-80132 Naples, Italy.

BARTOLINI Lando, b. 11 Apr 1937, Casale di Prato, Florence, Italy. Opera Singer (Tenor). m. Deanna Mungai, 26 Jan 1966, 2 daughters. *Education:* 5-year scholarship to Academy of Vocal Arts, Philadelphia, USA, 1968-73; Vocal instruction with Nicola Moscona; Graduated, 1973. *Debut:* In Iris of Mascagni, Gran Liceo of Barcelona, Oct 1973. *Career:* American debut in Cavalleria Rusticana, New York City Opera, 1976; Appeared at special events including: Concert with Philadelphia Orchestra, New production of Ernani with Chicago Lyric, Manon Lescaut with Vienna State Opera in Tokyo, Simon Boccanegra at Festival d'Orange, New production of Turandot at Munich State Opera, Turandot with La Scala, Milan, in Seoul during Olympic Games; Has sung in many other major venues around the world including: La Scala, Arena di Verona, Paris Opera, Metropolitan Opera, Covent Garden, Vienna, Budapest, Buenos Aires, Santiago del Chile, South Africa, Canada, Lisbon, Boston and Cleveland with Metropolitan Opera; Wide repertoire, Aida, Tosca, La Bohème, Il Trovatore, Don Carlo, Macbeth, Forza del Destino, Tabarro, Mephistopheles, Rigoletto, Sang Manrico in Il Trovatore at the Orange Festival, 1992. *Recordings:* I Cavalieri Di Ekebù, with director Gian Andrea Gavazzeni; Hungaroton, 1992 Respighi's La Semirama, 1st recording; Hungaroton, 1991 Solo Tenor Arias; Turandot Last Duet Alfano original, first time on record, Decca, 1990. *Publications:* La Follia Di New York, 1989, Orpheus Berlin, 1990; Das Opern Glas Germany, 1990; Opera News New York, 1991-93. *Hobbies:* Pool; Golf; Darts. *Current Management:* ICM Artists, New York. *Address:* Via Bargo 12, 50047 Casale di Prato, (Firenze), Italy.

BARTON Hanus, b. 16 May 1960, Prague, Czechoslovakia. Composer; Pianist. m. Jana Macharackova, 25 June 1988, 1 daughter. *Education:* Composition and Piano studies: Prague Conservatory; Academy of Musical Arts. *Career:* Stage concerts as member of Ars Cameralis ensemble for Gothic and contemporary music; Several radio and TV recordings, mostly with own compositions. *Compositions:* Recorded: Concerto for violin, viola and strings; Golem, opera; The Rhythm of the Street for clarinet and piano (also published); Trio for violin, viola and piano; Return of the Light for symphony orchestra. *Membership:* Society of Composers, Czech Republic. *Hobbies:* Skiing; Motorcycling. *Current Management:* OSA, DILIA, Pragokoncert. *Address:* U Pohadky 356, 164 00 Prague, Czech Republic.

BARTOVA Jindriska, b. 28 Sept 1942, Uherske Hradiste, Czechoslovakia. Musical Publicist. m. Jiri Barta, 1 Feb 1964, 1 daughter. *Education:* Musicology, University Philosophical Faculty. *Career:* Senior Lecturer, Janáček's Academy of Musical Arts. *Publications:* Orientation of opinions of Bohuslav Martinů in initial years of his Paris stay, 1964; Miloslav Istvan. Outline of the composer's profile, 1985; Correspondence Bohuslav Martinů-Vitezslava Kapralova, 1990; Jan Kapr. Transformations of life and creation of Czech composer, 1990, revised edition, 1993. *Contributor to:* Reviews and surveys of musical events in Brno to Hudebni Rozhledy and Opus Musicum magazines, 1964-93, and to newspapers including Rovnost, 1964-93. *Memberships:* Association of

Musicians nd Musical Scientists; Formerly The Union of Czech Composers and Concert Artists. *Hobby:* Genealogy. *Address:* Solnicni 5-9, 602 00 Brno, Czech Republic.

BARTSCHI Werner, b. 1 Jan 1950, Zürich, Switzerland. Musician (Pianist); Composer. *Education:* Volksschule and Gymnasium Zürich. *Career:* Concerts as pianist in over 30 countries in 5 continents; TV appearances in various countries; Film Actor in Justiz by Geissendorfer; Initiation and realisation of the Satie-Saison, 1980-81, and the Ives-Zyklus, 1985-86, both in Zürich; President of Music Committee of City of Zürich, 1990-92; Artistic Advisor of 1991 June Festival in Zürich; Artistic Director of various concert series in Switzerland; Performances of his compositions in over 20 countries, several broadcasts and recordings. *Compositions:* 20 works for various ensembles and instruments: orchestras, chamber music, vocal music, piano music, including: Duett for violin and clarinet; Toccata a due, flute and piano; Partitur (zu einem Teamwork), strings, percussion, soloist ad lib; Die Majestät der Alpen, orchestra. *Recordings:* About 30 recordings including music of over 30 composers; 10 films for Swiss TV. *Publications:* Die unvermeidliche Musik des John Cage, 1969; Musik der Entfremdung-entfremdete Musik, 1981-82; Ratio und Intuition in der Musik, Kunst und Wissenschaft, 1984; Italian translation, 1989, Zu meinem Klavierstück, In Trauer und Prunk, 1989; Leistung und Plausch im Musikuntericht, 1989; German editions of selected writings by Erik Satie, 1980, and Charles Ives, 1985; Music editions of works by Wladimir Vogel, 1989, and Zdenek Fibich, 1988. *Honours:* Grand Prize of Academie du disque francaise, 1983. *Memberships:* Schweizerischer Tonkünstlerverein; Schweizerischer Musikpädagogischer Verband; Others. *Hobby:* Mountain climbing. *Address:* Zollikerstr 97, CH-8702 Zollikon, Switzerland.

BARYLLI Walter, b. 16 June 1921, Vienna, Austria. Violinist. *Education:* Vienna Hochschule; Violin study with F von Reuter, Munich. *Debut:* Munich, 1936. *Career:* Concert tours throughout Europe and overseas; Member, Vienna State Opera Orchestra and Vienna Philharmonic, 1938-; Formerly, leader of both orchestras; Leader Barylli Quartet, 1945-; Professor of violin, Vienna Conservatory, 1969. *Honours include:* Kreisler Prize (twice won). *Address:* Rennweg 4-14, A-1030 Vienna Austria.

BARZUN Jacques, b. 30 Nov 1907, Creteil, Seine, France. Historian; Educator. m. (1) Mariana Lowell, 1936, deceased 1979, 2 sons, 1 daughter; (2) Marguerite Davenport, 1980. *Education:* AB 1927, PhD 1932, Columbia University, New York. *Career:* Lecturer in History 1927, Professor 1945, Dean, Graduate Faculties 1955-58, Dean of Faculties & Provost 1958-67, Seth Low Professor of History 1960-67, Lecturer 1967-75, Columbia University. *Publications:* Darwin, Marx, Wagner: Critique of a Heritage 1941, 2nd edition revised, 1958; Berlioz and the Romantic Century 1950, 3rd edition revised 1969; Clio and the Doctors, 1974; Critical Questions, 1982; The Use and Abuse of Art, 1974; A Word or Two Before You Go, 1986; The Culture We Deserve, 1989; The Forgotten Conditions of Teaching and Learning, 1991; Essay on French Verse for Readers of English Poetry, 1991. *Contributions to:* Articles in various journals. *Honour:* Legion d'honneur. *Memberships:* American Historical Association; American Philosophical Society; American Academy of Arts and Letters, president 1972-75, 1977-78; Phi Beta Kappa; Extraordinary Fellow, Churchill College, Cambridge; Fellow, Royal Society of Arts. *Address:* 1170 Fifth Avenue, New York, NY 10029, USA.

BASELT Franz Bernhard Bernd, b. 13 Sept 1934, Halle (Saale), Germany. Professor of Musicology. m. Elfriede Kalisch, 3 Oct 1962. 1 son, 1 daughter. *Education:* Abitur, 1953; Hochschule fur Musik Halle; Martin-Luther-Universitat Halle (Dipl phil 1958, Dr phil 1963, Dr sc phil 1975). *Career:* Freelance, 1958-59; Assistant Professor, 1959-76, Professor of Musicology,

1977-82, Full Professor of Musicology, 1983-, Chief Editor, Hallische Händel-Ausgabe, 1989; University Halle-Wittenberg; President, Georg-Friedrich-Handel-Gesellschaft, 1991; Editor, Händel-Jahrbuch, 1991. *Publications:* Handel-Handbuch vol I-III, 1978-86; G F Handel, Leipzig, 1988; Editions of operas by G Ph Telemann, Ch W Gluck, G F Handel (1967, 1969, 1970, 1988); editions of Handel's Oreste (Kassel 1991) and Telemann's Don Quichotte (Madison 1991). *Contributions to:* Handel-Jahrbuch; Musical Times; Veroff der Intern; Handel-Akademie Karlsruhe; Music & Letters. *Address:* Reilstrasse 83, D-04020 Halle (Saale), Germany.

BASHMET Yuri, b. 24 Jan 1953, Rostov, USSR. Concert Violist; Conductor. *Education:* Moscow Conservatoire from 1971 with Vadim Borvisovsky and Feodor Druzhinin. *Career:* 1976 won first prize in Munich International Viola Competition; Appearances with the Vienna Symphony, Bavarian Radio and Dresden Staatskapelle orchestras; Conductors include Abbado, Kubelik, Colin Davis, Rozhdestvensky and Mariss Yansons; 1986 formed chamber orchestra Moscow Soloists: Tours to Germany, Italy and France; UK debut tour Oct 1988 Chamber music recitals with Sviatoslav Richter, Oleg Kagan, Natalia Gutman and the Borodin Quartet; Many performances of contemporary music, including the premiere of the Schnittke Concerto with the Concertgebouw Orchestra 1986; Repeated the work with the BBC Philharmonic at the 1987 Lichfield Festival and made a Channel 4 TV programme about it with the London Sinfonietta and Esa-Pekka Salonen; Wigmore Hall debut Jan 1989; Bartók's Concerto at the Barbican Hall, 1989; London Promenade Concert debut 1989; Four concerts at Sydney Opera House, 1990 and at the 1991 Promenade Concerts; Played Walton's Concerto, Festival Hall, 1990; Played Bartók's Concerto and conducted Moscow Soloists, Barbican Hall, 1991; Subject of profile LWT's South Bank Show, 1990; Exclusive Recording Contract with RCA Victor Red Seal; Bartók Concerto at the 1993 Prom Concerts, London. *Address:* c/o Van Walsum Management Ltd, 26 Wadham Road, London, SW15 2LR, England.

BASINSKAS Justinas, b. 22 Jan 1923, Mazoji Trakiske, Lithuania. Composer. m. Vyliute Sofija-Jurate Igno, 12 July 1976, 1 son, 2 daughters. *Education:* Specialized Music School, Kaunas, 1945-50; Lithuanian State Conservatory, Vilnius, 1950-55. *Compositions:* Ballet: The Accursed Monks, 1982; Symphonies: The Bells, 1973; Being, 1977; The Lamentations, 1979; In the Whirlpools, 1983; Chamber Symphony, 1984; The Call of the Earth, 1986; Cantatas: A Tale About Soldier's Bread, 1961; Requiem, 1969; Morning, 1974; Mother's Hands, 1978; Chamber: Piano Sonata, 1979; Sonata for Violin and Piano, 1979; Sonata for Piano, 4-hands, 1979; String Quartet, 1980; Sonata for Solo Viola, 1983; Vocal Cycles for Voice and Piano: The Animals in Winter, 1968; The Autumn, 1969; The Hour of the Eagle-Owl, 1985; Choruses; Solo songs. *Recordings:* Discs of The Bells; Being; The Lamentations; Sonata for Violin and Piano. *Honours:* Lithuanian SSR National Prize, 1983; Received title of Merited Culture Worker of the Lithuanian SSR, 1983. *Membership:* Lithuanian Composers Union. *Hobby:* Enjoying Nature. *Address:* Traidenio Street 34-6, 2004 Vilnius, Lithuania.

BASNEY Nyela, b. 28 Aug 1956, Cuba, New York, US. Conductor. m. Timothy Mueller, 18 Dec 1976. *Education:* Fillmore Central School, Fillmore, New York; Bachelor of Applied Piano, 1978, MMus, 1979, Eastman School of Music. *Debut:* Brooklyn Acdemy of Music, Dec 1992. *Career:* Staff Pianist, Juilliard School, 1982-86; Assistant Conductor, Chorus Master, New York Grand Opera, 1982-86; Conductor, West Side Symphony, 1986-92; Music Director, Roberts Wesleyan College-Community Orchestra, 1986-; Conductor, Western Massachusetts Youth Orchestras, 1987-90; Aspen Music Festival, 1989-90; Sessione Senese per la Musica e l'Arte, 1991; Artistic Director, Premiere Ensemble of New York, 1992-; Fellow, Conductor's Institute, 1992; American Conductors and Composers Forum, 1992; Max Rudolf's Conducting Class, 1992;

Arts America Cultural Specialist with USIA, 1993-; Guest Conductor, Rochester Philharmonic Orchestra Stained Glass Series, April and December 1993. *Contributor to:* 3-part article Progressions, to American Symphony Orchestra League, 1991-92. *Honours:* Alumni Scholarship, Eastman School of Music, 4 years. *Memberships:* American Symphony Orchestra League; Conductors Guild Incorporated; New York Arts Group. *Hobbies:* Racquetball; Foreign languages. *Address:* 90 Park Terrace East, New York, NY 10034, USA.

BASSETT Leslie (Raymond), b. 22 Jan 1923, Hanford, California, USA. Composer. m. Anita Denniston, 21 Aug 1949, 2 sons, 1 daughter. *Education:* BA, Fresno State College (now California State University, Fresno), 1947; MMus, Composition, 1949, AMusD, Composition, 1956, University of Michigan, 1949; Fulbright Fellow, Ecole Normale de Musique, Paris, 1950-51; Pupil of Ross Lee Finney, Nadia Boulanger, Arthur Honegger, Roberto Gerhard. *Career includes:* Henry Russel Lecturer, University of Michigan, 1984; Albert A Stanley Distinguished University Professor of Music Emeritus. *Compositions:* Variations for Orchestra; Echoes from an Invisible World, orchestra; Concerto for Orchestra; From a Source Evolving, orchestra; Concerto Lirico, trombone and orchestra; Fantasy for Clarinet and Wind Ensemble; Sounds, Shapes and Symbols, band; Colors and Contours, band; Sextet for Piano and Strings; Fourth String Quartet; Arias for Clarinet and Piano; Dialogues for Oboe and Piano; Moon Canticle, chorus; Notes in the Silence, choir; Narratives for Guitar Quartet. *Honours:* Pulitzer Prize for Variations for orchestra, 1966; Rome Prize, American Academy in Rome, 1961-63; Koussevitsky Foundation Commissions, 1971, 1990; Guggenheim Fellow, 1973, 1980; Naumberg Recording Award, 1974; Distinguished Artist Award, State of Michigan, 1981. *Membership:* American Academy of Arts and Letters. *Address:* 1618 Harbal Drive, Ann Arbor, MI 48105, USA.

BASTIAN Hanns, b. 30 Jan 1928, Pforzheim, Germany. Singer (Tenor). *Education:* Studied in Karlsruhe with Karl Hartlieb and in Coburg and Pforzheim. *Career:* Sang first in Pforzheim, 1946-53, then at Coburg; Engaged at Basel Opera, 1955-80, notably in premiere of Titus Feuerfuchs by Sutermeister, 1966, and in buffo and character roles; Guest appearances in Zurich, Berne, Darmstadt and Bregenz; Other roles included Florestan, Mozart's Pedrillo and Monostatos, David in Die Meistersinger, and many parts in operetta. *Address:* c/o Theater Basel, Theaterstrasse 7, CH-4010 Basel, Switzerland.

BASTIN Jules, b. 18 March 1933, Pont, Belgium. Singer (Bass-Baritone). *Education:* Brussels Conservatory with Frederic Anspach. *Debut:* As Charon in Monteverdi's Orfeo, Theatre de la Monnaie, Brussels, 1960. *Career:* National Opera of Belgium from 1960; Guest appearances in Geneva, Bonn, Rouen, Amsterdam, Nice, Bucharest, Milan (La Scala), Vienna, Salzburg Festival, Chicago, New York and Toronto; Covent Garden London debut as Ochs in Der Rosenkavalier; Sang The Banker in the first complete performance of Berg's Lulu, Paris Opéra 1979; Repertoire includes operas by Meyerbeer, Offenbach, Berlioz and Massenet as well as Mozart and Wagner; Sang in Benvenuto Cellini at the Maggio Musicale, Florence, 1987; The Love of Three Oranges, Aix-en-Provence, 1989; Sang Grand Inquisitor in Don Carlos at Antwerp, 1990; He also sang Publius in La Clemenza de Tito, Brussels; Other roles include Bartolo (Mozart and Rossini), Osmin, Varlaam, Würfl in The Excursions of Mr Brouček and Graumann in Der ferne Klang; Sang Mozart's Bartolo at Brussels, 1991-92; Concert appearances under Boulez, Prêtre, Barenboim, Colin Davis, Solti, Levine, Karajan and Böhm. *Recordings:* Benvenuto Cellini, La Damnation de Faust, Attila and Der Rosenkavalier (Philips); Così fan Tutte (RCA); Salome, Werther, L'Enfant et les Sortilèges (HMV); Cendrillon (CBS); Lulu (Deutsche Grammophon). *Honours:* Prizes at s'Hertogenbosch Competition Holland 1962 and the Munich Competition 1963.

Address: Ingpen & Williams Ltd, 14 Kensington Court, London W8 5DN, England.

BATE Jennifer Lucy, b. 11 Nov 1944, London, England. Musician (Organist). *Education:* BA (Hons), Music, Bristol University; Early Music with Carl Dolmetsch; Composition with Eric Thiman and Arthur Pritchard; LRAM; ARCM; FRCO. *Career:* Worldwide performing and media appearances; Specialist, 18th century solo and concert repertoire; Represented UK, international festivals worldwide; BBC Proms; Featured in TV recital Great Instrumentalists of the World; Judge, International Organ Festivals, Chartres, Melbourne, and European Organ Competitions; Lecturer, Conductor, master classes; Leading authority on Messiaen; Gave 1st UK performance of his Livre du Saint Sacrement, 1986; Guest artist with Geraint Evans; Consultant, Performer, South Bank Show; Profile, Messiaen, televised Messiaen's Livre du Saint Sacrement and La Nativite; Educational pioneer; Designer of instruments. *Compositions:* Toccata on a Theme of Martin Shaw; Introduction and Variations on an old French carol; 4 Reflections for Organ; Homage to 1685-4 Studies. *Recordings:* Complete Works of Messaien, 7 vols; Complete Works of Franck, 3 vols; Show Pieces for Organ, digital; Jennifer Bate Plays Liszt: An English Choice; Lennox Berkeley, Peter Dickinson, Organ Music; Virtuoso French Organ Music; 2 Centuries of British Organ Music; Panufnik: Metasinfonia; Peter Dickinson Organ Concerto; Vivaldi Double and Triple Concertos; Jennifer Bate Plays Elgar and Schumann; Sounds of the Merry Organ; From Stanley to Wesley, 6 vols; Jennifer Bate and Friends; Jennifer Plays Vierne. *Contributor to:* Grove's Dictionary of Music and Musicians; Musical Times; Organist's Review; Musical Opinion; Times; Independent. *Honours:* J F Reed Prize, Royal College of Organists, 1972; Grand Prix du Disque, World Premiere Recording of Livre du Saint Sacrement; Personnalitee de l'Annee, France, 1990. *Memberships:* Incorporated Society of Music; British Music Society; RPS; North London Organists Association; Royal Society of Musicians; Philatelic Music Circle. *Hobbies:* Reading; Gardening; Cooking; Philately. *Current management:* Bureau de Concerts Maurice Werner. *Address:* 7 Rue Richepance, 75008 Paris, France.

BATIZ Enrique, b. 4 May 1942, Mexico City, Mexico. Pianist; Conductor; m. 1965, div 1982, 1 son, 1 daughter. *Education:* Bachelor's degree, Mexico University Center, 1959; Southern Methodist University, Dallas, USA, 1960-62; Juilliard School of Music, New York, studied piano with Adele Marcus; conducting with Jorge Mester, 1963-66; Postgraduate work, Warsaw Conservatory; studied piano privately with Zbignieg Drzewieckie (1966-70) conducting with Stanislaw Wislocki (1970). *Debut:* Mexico City, 1969. *Career:* Founder-Conductor, Orquesta Sinfónica del Estado de Mexico, 1971-73, 1990- (12 years); Artistic Director, Orquesta Filarmónica de la Ciudad de México, 1983-89 (7 years); Conducted premieres of many contemporary composers for Mexican TV-Radio during 23 years as General Music Director, Mexico; Appointed Guest Conductor, Royal Philharmonic Orchestra, London, England, 1984- (more than 40 concerts in England): Guest conductor with 150 orchestras worldwide; Mtro Batiz has conducted the most important operas in: 1975, 1983, 1984, 1985, 1990; Conductor, Royal Philharmonic Orchestra on Tour in Mexico, 1988. *Recordings:* 107 CD's (40 RPO, 1 LPO, 9 LSO, 2 Philharmonia, 2 Royal LPO, 22 State of Mexico Symphony Orchestra and 19 Mexico City Philharmonic Orchestra) including such labels as worldwide: RPO records, EMI, ASV (Academy Sound and Vision), Naxos, Pickwick, IMG (International Management Group); Europe: Object, Dante, Teldec; Japan: Mitsubishi, Victor JVC; USA: Music Masters, Varese Sarabande, Musical Heritage Society, Sine Qua Non; Mexico: RCA, CBS; His recordings has been received by critics from worldwide with highest price; Recorded the complete works of Bizet, Revueltas, Villa-Lobas Bachianas Brazileiras 1-9, Rodrigo complete works; has recorded with famous soloists: Henryk Szeryng, Francisco Araiza, Aldo Ciccolini, Barbara Hendricks, Alfonso Moreno, Jorge Federico Osorio, Jorge Luis Prats, and Eve Mariz Zuk; Many concerts on Video Alive. *Honours include:*

Symphony No 3 in C minor Op. 78 (organ) - Camille Saint-Saëns: Best Recorded Version; Rossette Penguin Stereo Recording Guide, 1985; Petroushka - Stravinsky. Best Reord of the Year, The Sunday Times, London January 1986; Decoration awarded by Brazilian Government. Order of Rio Branco, Officer Grade 1986; Best Record of the Year - Rachmaninoff Symphonic Dances, Op 45, The Isle of the Dead, Op 29, London, 1992. *Memberships:* IAPA; Club de Clubes, Club Cambridge, Mexico City. *Hobbies:* Swimming; Musical friends. *Current Management:* Joseph Scuro, International Artists Management, 340 West 57th Street, New York, NY 10019, USA. *Address:* Cerrada Rancho Los Colorines, No 11, Col Huipulco Tabla del Llano, Código Postal 14380, Zona Postal 22, Mexico DF.

BATJER Margaret, b. 17 Feb 1959, San Angelo, Texas, USA. Musician (Violinist). m. Joel McNeely, 14 Apr 1985 *Education:* Interlochen Academy; Studied with Ivan Galamian and David Cerone at Curtis Institute of Music. *Debut:* Solo appearance in Violin Concerto by Menotti with Chicago Symphony, aged 15; Appeared as Soloist with Philadelphia Orchestra at Academy of Music, with Dallas and Seattle Symphonies (Mendelssohn's Concerto), St Louis Symphony, Chamber Orchestra of Europe, Prague Chamber Orchestra, Berlin Symphony Orchestra; New York String Orchestra at Carnegie Hall; Radio Telefis Dublin, with Prokofiev's 2nd Concerto; Concerts at the Marlboro Music Festival, Vermont and US tour with Music of Marlboro Ensemble; Tour of Germany, 1984. *Recordings:* Bach Concerto for Two Violins, Salvatore Accardo, Chamber Orchestra of Europe; Mozart Concertone, Salvatore Accordo, Prague Chamber Orchestra; Verdi, Borodin String Quartets; Mozart Complete Viola Quintets. *Honours include:* Winner, G B Dealey Competition, Dallas, 1979. *Current management:* Del Rosenfield Associates, 714 Ladd Road, Bronx, NY 10471, USA. *Address:* 5971 Lubao Ave, Woodland Hills, CA 91367, USA.

BATTEL Giovanni Umberto, b. 11 Dec 1956, Portoguaro, Venice, Italy. Pianist. m. Mariangela Zamper, 15 June 1985. *Education:* Liceo in Classical Studies, 1975; Conservatory Tartini, Trieste, 1977; National Music Academy St Cecilia, Rome, 1984. *Career:* S Remo Theatre, 1980; RAI Radio 3, 1981; Stresa Festival, 1981; With symphony orchestra, Auditorium RAI Rome, 1982; RAI 1, 1982, 1983 and 1984; Alghero Festival, 1983; Mater Festival, 1983; Trondheim Symphony Orchestra, 1983; With Scarlatti Orchestra, Auditorium RAI Naples, 1983; Trieste Theatre, 1985; Auditorium Caglian, 1985; Musik Halle Hamburg, Federal Republic of Germany, 1986; Lubeck, Bonn, 1986; Athens, Salonika, Greece, 1986; San Francisco, Los Angeles, USA; Paris, Nantes, Lille, France, 1987; Todi Festival, 1988; London, 1988. *Recordings:* Miroirs and Valses Nobles et Sentimentales, Ravel; Busoni's Piano Concerto. *Honours:* 1st Prize national competitions: La Spezia, 1975; Trieste, 1978; Taranto, 1979; Albenga, 1979; International competition: 2nd prize, Vercelli, 1978; 2nd prize, Seregno, 1979; 4th prize, Bolzano, 1980; 1st prize, Enna, 1982. *Hobby:* Photography. *Address:* via Valle 23, 30026 Portogruaro, Venice, Italy.

BATTLE Kathleen (Deanna), b. 13 Aug 1948, Portsmouth, Ohio, USA. Soprano. *Education:* BMus 1970, MMus 1971, University of Cincinnati-College Conservatory of Music; Studied with Franklin Bens and Italo Tajo. *Debut:* Professional debut, soloist, Brahms Requiem, Spoleto Festival, 1972. *Career:* Operatic debut as Rosina, Michigan Opera Theatre, Detroit, 1975; Metropolitan Opera, New York, 1978-; Appearances with many other major opera houses of the world, including Covent Garden (debut 1985 as Zerbinetta in Ariadne auf Naxos); Soloist with leading orchestras; Recitalist various music centres; Operatic roles include Susanna, Cleopatra, Zerbinetta, Sophie, Adina, Zerlina, Blonde, Nannetta and Despina; Sang Norina in Don Pasquale, Covent Garden, London, 1990; Contract at NY Met terminated, 1994. *Recordings:* For Deutsche

Grammophon; Angel-EMI; Decca-London; Musicmasters; RCA; Telarc; In Mozart's Requiem, Cosi fan Tutte, Coronation Mass, Don Giovanni and Die Zauberflöte; L'Italiana in Algeri; Ein Deutsches Requiem; Mahler 4th Symphony; Il Barbiere di Siviglia (Abbado); Handel Arias (Marriner); Semele; Videos of Il Barbiere di Siviglia and Die Zauberflöte from the Metropolitan (DGG). *Address:* c/o Columbia Artists Management Inc, 165 West 57th Street, New York, NY 10019, USA.

BATURIN Sergei, b. 1952, Moscow, Russia. Violinist. *Education:* Studied at Moscow Conservatoire with Fjodor Druzhinin. *Career:* Co-founded Amistad Quartet, 1973; Many concerts in former Soviet Union and Russia, with repertoire including works by Haydn, Mozart, Beethoven, Schubert, Brahms, Tchaikovsky, Borodin, Prokofiev, Shostakovich, Bartók, Barber, Bucci, Golovin and Tikhomirov; Recent concert tours to Mexico, Italy and Germany. *Honours include:* With Amistad Quarter: Prizewinner at Bela Bartók Festival, 1976, and Bucchi Competition, Rome, 1990. *Recordings include:* Recitals for US-Russian company Arts and Electronics. *Address:* c/o Sonata (Amistad Quartet), 11 Northgate Street, Glasgow G20 7AA, Scotland.

BAUDO Serge, b. 16 Jul 1927, Marseille, France. Conductor. m. Madelein Reties, 16 Jun 1947, 1 son, 1 daughter. *Education:* Student, Conservatory of Paris. *Career:* Director, Radio Nice, France, 1957-59; Conductor, Paris Orchestra, 1968-70; Music Director, Opéra de Lyon, 1969-71; Music Director, Orchestra of Lyon, 1971-; Conductor of many international Orchestras including Tonhalle Orchestra, Zurich, Orchestra de la Suisse Romande, Berliner Philharmonic, Royal Philharmonic, London Philharmonic, NHR Orchestra, Leningrad Philharmonic, Stockholm Philharmonic, La Scala, Metropolitan Opera, Dallas Orchestra, Deutsche Oper, Berlin; Has conducted premieres at Messiaen's Et expecto, Chartres 1965 and La Transfiguration, Lisbon, 1969; Milhaud's La Mère Coupable, Geneva, 1966; and Dutilleux's Cello Concerto, Aix, 1970; Fastes de l'imaginaire, Nigg, 1974; Ohana's Le Livre des Prodiges, 1979; Daniel-Lesur's Dialogues dans le nuit, 1988; Founder, Berloiz Festival, Lyon, 1979-; Conducted Roméo et Juliette at Zürich, 1990. *Honours:* Decorated, Chevalier Ordre National du Merite; Officer des Arts et des Lettres; Recipient, Grand Prix due Disque, 1976; Chevalier de la Legion D'Honneur Disque D'or. *Address:* Orchestre National de Lyon Hotel de Ville, 69000 Lyon, France.

BAUER-THEUSSL Franz (Ferdinand), b. 25 Sept 1928, Zillingdorf, Austria. Conductor. m. Herta Bauer-Theussl. 1 child. *Education:* Studied piano with Bruno Seidlhofer; Conducting with Clemens Krauss, Vienna Academy of Music. *Career:* Pianist/staff, Baden Municipal Theatre, 1950-52; Conducting debut, Salzburg Landestheater, 1953; Assistant Conductor, Salzburg Festival, 1953-57; Conductor 1957, Principal Conductor, Vienna Volksoper; Principal Conductor, Netherlands Opera, Amsterdam, 1960-64. *Recordings:* For Ariola; Bellaphon; Intercord; Vox. *Honours:* Honorary Professor, Austrian Government; Grosses Ehrenzeichen, Austrian Republic. *Address:* c/o Vienna Volksoper, Vienna, Austria.

BAULD Alison Margaret, b. 7 May 1944, Sydney, New South Wales, Australia. Composer. *Education:* Diploma, National Institute of Dramatic Art, Sydney; BMus, Sydney University; Composition studies with Elisabeth Lutyens and Hans Keller; DPhil, York University, 1974; Studied Piano with Sverjensky, New South Wales Conservatorium. *Career:* Professional actress, Shakespeare and Australian TV; Finalist, Radcliffe Competition, 1973; Musical Director, Laban Centre for Dance, Goldsmiths' College, University of London, 1975-78; Composer-in-Residence, New South Wales Conservatory, Sydney, 1978; Currently teaches part-time, Hollins College, London; Works performed and broadcast, London, also Aldeburgh, York and Edinburgh Festivals, several European countries, Australia. *Compositions:* On the Afternoon of the Pigsty for speaker and ensemble, 1971; Humpty Dumpty for tenor, flute and guitar, 1972; In a Dead Brown Land, music theatre, 1972; Mad Moll for solo soprano, 1973; Dear Emily for soprano and harp, 1973; One Pearl for soprano and string quartet, 1973; Concert for piano and tape, 1974; Exiles, music theatre, 1974; Van Diemen's Land for choir, 1976; One Pearl II for soprano, flute and strings, 1976; I Loved Miss Watson for soprano, piano and tape, 1977; The Busker's Story for ensemble, 1987; Banquo's Buried for soprano and piano, 1982; Richard III for voice and string quartet, 1985; Monody for solo flute, 1985; Copy Cats for violin, cello and piano, 1985; Once Upon a Time, music theatre, 1986; Nell, Ballad opera, 1988; My Own Island for clarinet and piano, 1989; Cry Cock-A-Doodle-Doo and Witches Song for soprano and piano, 1990; Play Your Way, vols I, II, III, A Tutor for Piano/Composition; Farewell Already for string quartet, 1993. *Recordings:* Banquo's Buried, CD; Concert; Farewell Already, CD, NMC. *Membership:* Association of Professional Composers. *Address:* c/o Novello and Company, 8/9 Frith St, London W1V 5TZ, England.

BAUMEL Herbert, b. 30 Sept 1919, New York City, New York, USA. Violinist; Conductor; Composer. m. (1) Rachael Bail, 17 Oct 1949, div Nov 1970, 1 son, 2 daughters (1 dec), (2) Joan Patricia French, 11 July 1971. *Education:* Violin study with Pasquale Pagliucca, Louis Persinger, Paul Stassevitch, Vlado Kolitsch, Lea Luboshutz, Nathan Milstein; Mannes School of Music, 1932-34; Diploma, Curtis Institute of Music, 1942; Santa Cecilia, Accademia Chigiana, Rome & Siena, 1954-56. *Career:* Violinist, Concertmaster, Conductor, orchestras, chamber groups, Broadway shows, jazz ensembles, ballets, operas, worldwide, 1939-; Violin Soloist: Samuel Barber Violin Concerto, Curtis Symphony, Philadelphia Orchestra, 1939-40; New York City Ballet, Fort Wayne Philharmonic, WQXR Orchestra, Radio Italiana, Radio Nacional Venezuela, 1945-; 1st Violin, Philadelphia Orchestra, 1942-45; Member, Baumel-Booth-Smith Trio, 1969-72; Baumel-Booth Duo, 1968-; Violinist/Storyteller, 1969-; Concertmaster: Philadelphia, New York City & San Carlo Operas, Orquesta Sinfonica Venezuela, Broadway musicals including Fiorello, 1959, She Loves Me, 1963, Fiddler on the Roof, 1964, A Little Night Music, 1973; Presidential Gala Orchestra, Washington DC & New York, 1961-65; Conductor: Fort Wayne Civic & Corvallis Symphonies, Chamber Music Associates Orchestra, Alessandro Scarlatti Orchestra (Naples), Oregon State University Chamber Players, 1945-. *Hobbies:* Photography; Tennis; Gardening; Reading; Chess. *Address:* Baumel Associates, 86 Rosedale Road, Yonkers, NY 10710, USA.

BAUMGARTNER Rudolf, b. 14 Sept 1917, Zurich Switzerland. Violinist; Conductor; Administrator. *Education:* University of Zurich; Zurich Conservatory; violin studies with Stefi Geyer, Carl Flesch, Wolfgang Schneiderhan. *Career:* Appearances as a violin soloist and in chamber music ensembles; co-founder with Wolfgang Schneiderhan, Lucerne Festival Strings, 1956; subsequently served as its director; took it on numerous tours abroad; several arrangements, including Bach's Musical Offering and Art of Fugue; appointed director, Lucerne Conservatory, 1960, and Lucerne Festival, 1968. *Recordings:* For Denon, Deutsche Grammophon, Eurodisc, Finlandia, and RCA; notably music by Bach and Mozart; Bach Brandenburg Concertos, Ein musikalisches Opfer, Harpsichord and Violin Concertos; The Four Seasons, Vivaldi with Wolfgang Schneiderhan; Mozart Divertimenti, Piano Concertos with Margit Weber, Clara Haskil and Horsowski; Flute Concertos, Hans-Martin Linde and James Galway; Horn Concertos; Telemann Viola Concerto, Deutsche Grammophon, Archiv. *Address:* c/o Lucerne Conservatory of Music, Lucerne, Switzerland.

BAUMGARTNER Ruth Gabriele, b. 20 Apr 1954, Switzerland. Pianist. *Education:* Diploma, Elementary School Teacher; Conservatory of Berne; Hochschule für Musik Wien. *Career:* Concerts in: Switzerland, Austria, West & East Germany, USSR, South Africa, South West Africa, Namibia, Italy, Spain; Radio & TV in Switzerland.

Compositions: Cadenzas for Mozart & Haydn Piano Concertos. *Contributions to:* Fono Forum; daily newspapers; Complete Janáček Piano Music. *Memberships:* EPTA Switzerland; Swiss Music Pedagogical Society; Frank Martin Society; Leoš Janáček Society. *Hobbies:* Violin Playing; Choir Singing; Reading; Nature; Cookery. *Current Management:* Johannes Klos, Winterthur; EPTA, Swiss music Pedagogic Society. *Address:* Bürglistrasse 39, CH-8400 Winterthur, Switzerland.

BAVERSTAM Asa, b. 1958, Sweden. Singer (Soprano). *Education:* Studied at the Conservatory of Jutland in Aarhus, Denmark and at the Royal Opera Academy, Copenhagen. *Career:* Has performed Susanna and Sophie in Der Rosenkavalier with the Opera Academy; Sang in the premiere of Life is a Bed of Roses by Arne Mellnas, 1989; Debut with the Royal Opera in Copenhagen, 1990, as Despina; Theater Basel from 1990 as Xenia (Boris Godunov), Adina, Zerlina and in Messiah; Sang Zerlina at Basel, 1992; Has sung in masses and oratorios by Bach, Haydn, Handel, Mozart and Schubert in Denmark and Sweden; Concerts with the baroque orchestra La Stravaganza and as a member of the renaissance quartet Ensemble Charneyron. *Honours include:* Fourth round, Cardiff Singer of the World Competition, 1989. *Address:* Kaye Artists Management Ltd, Barratt House, 7 Chertsey Road, Woking, Surrey GU21 5AB, England.

BAVICHI John (Alexander), b. 25 Apr 1922, Boston, Massachusetts, USA. Composer; Conductor; Teacher. *Education:* Studied Business Engineering and Administration, Massachusetts Institute of Technology, 1940-42; Civil Engineering, Newark College of Engineering, 1942-43; Cornell University, 1943; BM, New England Conservatory of Music, 1952; Studied music with Carl McKinley, Francis Judd Cooke; Theory with Archibald T Davison; Composition with Walter Piston; Musicology with Otto Gombosi, Harvard University Graduate School, 1952-55. *Career:* Many teaching positions including: South End Music School, 1950-64; Boston Center for Adult Education, 1952-55; Cape Cod Conservatory of Music, 1956-58; Cambridge Center for Adult Education, 1960-73; Various conducting positions including: American Festival Ballet Company, 1962-65; Arlington Philharmonic Orchestra, 1968-82; Professor of Composition, Berklee College of Music, 1964-. *Compositions:* Orchestral: Concerto for Clarinet and String Orchestra, 1954; Suite No 1, 1955; A Concert Overture, 1957; Fantasy for Harp and Chamber Orchestra, 1959; Concertante for Oboe, Bassoon and String Orchestra, 1961; Fantasia on Korean Folk Tunes, 1966; Caroline's Dance, 1974-75; Mont Blanc, overture, 1976-77; Music for Small Orchestra, 1981; Fusions for Trombone and Orchestra, 1984-85; Pyramid, 1986; Canto I for String Orchestra, 1987; Band: Summer Incident, 1959; Suite No 2, 1961; Festival Symphony, 1965; JDC March, 1967; Spring Festival Overture, 1968; Suite No 3, 1969; Concertante No 2, 1972-75; Band of the Year, 1975; Symphony No 2, 1975-77; Fantasy, 1979; Concord Bridge, 1982-83; Concerto for Clarinet and Wind Ensemble, 1984; Large Ensemble: Suite No 2 for Clarinet Ensemble, 1961; Fireworks, 1962; Music for Mallets and Percussion, 1967; Ceremonial Music, 1978-82; Concerto for 2 Pianos and Percussion, 1985; Chamber music; Piano pieces; Organ music; Choruses; Solo songs. *Address:* 26 Hartford Street, Newton, MA 02161, USA.

BAVOUZET Jean-Efflam, b. 1962, France. Concert Pianist. *Education:* Studied at the Paris Conservatoire with Pierre Sancan; Master classes with Paul Badura-Skoda, Nikita Magaloff, Menahem Pressler and György Sandor. *Career:* Recitals in major concert halls worldwide, including the Kennedy Center, Lincoln Center, Kaufmann Hall, New York and the Salle Gaveau, Paris; Tours of Japan and the USA; British engagements from 1987; Has appeared as concerto soloist with such conductors as Marek Janowski, Andrew Litton, Jorge Meste and Michel Plasson; Engagements in Germany, Holland, Japan, France and the USA; Ravels Left Hand Concerto with the Solingen Philharmonica and the

Bournemouth Symphony, 1991. *Recordings:* Haydn 4 Sonatas and Fantaisie, Harmonic Records HCD 9141. *Contributions to:* Interview with Zoltan Kocsis for Le Monde de la Musique. *Honours include:* Finalist at the 1987 Leeds International Competition; Prize winner at the Young Concert Artists Competition, 1986, (USA); Tomassoni-Beethoven Cologne, 1986; Special Jury Prize, Santander, Spain; Guilde Française des Artistes Soloistes; First prize, Paris Conservatoire, for Piano and Chamber Music; Chamber Music Prize, 1989. *Address:* c/o Robert Gilder and Co. Enterprise House, 59/65 Upper Ground, London SE1 9PQ, England.

BAWDEN Rupert, b. 1958, London. Composer; Conductor; Violinist. *Education:* Studied at Cambridge University with Robin Holloway. *Career:* Plays violin and viola with various ensembles, including London Sinfonietta and the English Concert; Debut as conductor at the 1986 Aldeburgh Festival; Performances of works by Birtwistle, Goehr, Harvey, Weir and Hoyland, including several world premieres; TV recordings of works by Gruber, Holloway and Kagel; Michael Nyman's The Man who Mistook his Wife for a Hat for BBC Radio; Engagements with the Bath, King's Lynn and London International Opera Festivals; BBC Symphony, Scottish Chamber Orchestra; Works have been performed in USA, Australia, Far East, Britain and France; 1989 performances by the London Sinfonietta and at the Promenade Concerts; Ballet commission from Munich Biennale 1990. *Compositions:* Railings for flute and piano 1980; Three-Part Motet for soprano, mezzo, baritone and orchestra 1980; Passamezzo di Battaglia for oboe, horn and harpsichord 1984; Sunless for ensemble 1984; Seven Songs from the House of Sand for brass quintet 1985; Le Livre de Fauvel for soprano, mezzo and ensemble 1986; The Angel and the Ship of Souls for 19 players 1983-87; Souvenirs de Fauvel for 2 pianos 1987; Dramatic Cantata on the Legend of Apollo and Daphne for violin, cello and 13 players 1989; Ultima Scena: Commissioned by Henry Wood Promenade Concerts 1989; Ballet Le Livre de Fauvel 1990. *Address:* c/o Novello & Company, 8 Lower James Street, London W1R 3PL, England.

BAYFORD Frank Raymond, b. 26 Aug 1941, London, England. Composer; Music Critic and Concert Promoter. *Education:* The Grammar School, Enfield; Portsmouth School of Pharmacy, 1961-64. *Career:* Composer, 1960-; Works presented at various music festivals including Greenwich, Bexhill and Enfield; Involved with promotion of new music through COMPASS, including concert organisation and music publication. *Compositions include:* Thaxted Evening; Romney Landscape; Summer Waters; Autumn Changes; The Dances of Winter; In Terra Pax; Dance Elegies; Piano Sonatas No 1 and No 2; An Essex Prelude; Three Downland Sketches; Elegia Atlantica; An Introit for Little Missenden; Choral works: Medieval Carol; Missa Brevis; The Last Rose; Three Motets to words of John Donne; The Starlight Night; Song's for Children's Dreams; The Tapestries of the Sun, for Brass; Wind Quintet - Of Thylacines and Takahes, Impressioni Scozzesi, for Solo Flute; Piano Sonatas Nos 3 and 4; Stanford Bagatelles, for Piano; Variations for Orchestra. *Publications:* The Composer as Critic, chapter in book on the history of the Enfield Choral Society. *Contributions to:* The Enfield Gazette (regular music criticisms), 1969-; Corcy Blyton - a 60th birthday tribute (CASS magazine), 1992. *Hobbies:* Painting; Gardening; Photography; Lecturing on Travels in Scotland. *Address:* Greys Laurel, 21 Canonbury Road, Enfield, Middlesex, England.

BAYLE François, b. 27 Apr 1932, Tamatave, Madagascar. Composer; Music Administrator. *Education:* Studied with Olivier Messiaen, Paris; Pierre Schaeffer, Groupe de Recherches Musicales, Paris, 1958-60; Darmstadt summer courses in new music, Karlheinz Stockhausen, 1959-62. *Career:* Director, Groupe de Recherches Musicales, 1966; Institut National de l'Audiovisuel, 1975. *Compositions:* Principal works include: Trois Portraits d'un Oiseau qui n'existe pas, 1962; l'Archipel, 1963; Pluriel, 1963; Espaces

inhabitables, 1967; Jeita ou Murmure des Eaux, 1969-70; L'Experience Acoustique, 1969-72; Trois Rêves d'Oiseau, 1972; Vibrations Composees, 1973; La Divine Comedie, 1972-74; Grande Polyphonie, 1974; Camera oscura, 1976; Erosphere, 1978-80; Les Couleurs de la Nuit, 1982; Son Vitesse-Lumiere, 1980-83; Aeroformes, 1982-84; Motion-Emotion, 1985-86; Aer, 1987; Théâtre d'Ombres, 1988-89; Fabulae, 1990-91. *Recordings:* Various compositions recorded. *Publications:* Musique Acousmatique. Propositions...positions, Ed. Buchet/ Chastel, 1993. *Contributions to:* Encyclopaedia Universal, 1984, 1990. *Honours:* Ordre du Merite, 1976; Commandeur des Arts et Lettres, 1986; ARS Electronica, 1989; Legion d'Honneur, 1990. *Address:* c/o Institut National de L'Audiovisuel, 116 Avenue du President Kennedy, 75016 Paris, France.

BAYLEY Clive, b. 15 Nov 1960, Manchester, England. Singer (Bass) M. Paula Bradley, 15 July 1989. *Education:* Studied at the Royal Northern College of Music and at the National Opera Studio. *Debut:* with Opera North. *Career:* Sang in The Rape of Lucretia, Il barbiere di Siviglia and Billy Budd (Claggart) while at the RNCM; Professional debut as Schwarz in Die Meistersinger for Opera, followed by the King in Aida, Colline (La Boheme), Don Basilio, Banquo, Bartolo in Le nozze di Figaro and in the British premiere of Verdi's Jerusalem; English National Opera debut 1987, as Pietro in Simon Boccanegra, followed by appearances in Billy Budd, Un ballo in Maschera, Don Giovanni, Doctor Faust and The Return of Ulysses; Netherlands Opera 1989 as Trufaldino in Ariadne auf Naxos; December 1989 in a concert performance of Bernstein's Candide, conducted by the composer; Sang in the premiere of Birtwistle's Gawain at Covent Garden, May 1991; Concert repertory includes the Verdi Requiem, Elgar's Dream of Gerontius and Apostles, the Brahms Requiem, Handel's Messiah and Israel in Egypt, the Choral Symphony, Rossini's Petite Messe Solenelle and Christus in the St Matthew Passion; Roles at ROH, parts in Fidelio, The Fiery Angel, Die Meistersinger, and Colline in La Bohème; Further roles at Opera North include: Sparafucile, The Monk (Don Carlos), Ibn-Hakia (Yolande), Raleigh (Gloriana). *Recordings:* Candide (Deusche Gramaphon). *Honours include:* Curtis Gold Medal for Singing and the Robin Kay Memorial Prize for Opera, RNCM. *Hobbies:* most sport, especially Football; Cricket; Rugby; Weight Training; Walking; Reading; CD Collection, Hi-Fi; and two Persian cats, Boris and Lennie . *Current Management:* Tom Graham, IMG Artists. *Address:* IMG Artists, Media House, 3 Burlington Lane, Chiswick, London W4 2IH, England.

BAZELON Irwin (Allen), b. 4 June 1922, Evanston, Illinois, USA. Composer. *Education:* BA 1944, MA 1945, DePaul University; Composition with Leon Stein, Paul Hindemith, Darius Milhaud. *Compositions:* Orchestral: Symphonies: No 1, 1960; No 2, Short Symphony, 1962; No 3, 1963; No 4, 1964; No 5, 1966; No 6, 1970; No 7, Ballet for Orchestra, 1980; No 8, 1986; No 8-1/2, 1988; Confcert Overture, 1951-52, revised 1960; Adagio and Fugue for Strings, 1952; The Merry Wives of Windsor, suite, 1958; The Taming of the Shrew, overture, 1959; Ballet Centauri 17, 1960; Symphony Concertante for Clarinet, Trumpet, Marimba and Orchestra, 1963; Excursion, 1965; Churchill Downs, chamber concerto, 1970; Dramatic Fanfare, 1970; Concerto for 14 Players, 1971; A Quiet Piece for a Violent Time for Chamber Orchestra, 1975; De-Tonations for Brass Quintet and Orchestra, 1975-76; Junctures for Soprano and Orchestra, 1979; Memories of a Winter Childhood, 1981; Spires for Trumpet and Orchestra, 1981; Tides for Clarinet and Orchestra, 1982; Fusions for Chamber Orchestra, 1983; Trajectories, concerto for Piano with Orchestra, 1984; Motivations for Trombone and Orchestra, 1985; Legends and Love Letters, 5 songs for Soprano and Chamber Orchestra, 1987; Fourscore + 2 for Percussion Quartet and Orchestra, 1988; Chamber music; Phenomena for Soprano and Chamber Ensemble, 1972; Propulsions for 7 Percussionists, 1974. *Recordings:* As composer-conductor for Composers' Recordings, Inc. *Publication:* Knowing the Score: Notes on Film Music, 1975. *Honours:* MacDowell Colony fellowships, 1948, 1950,

1951; Yaddo Festival fellowship, 1969; Composer-in-residence, Wolf Trap Farm Park, 1974; National Endowment for the Arts grant, 1976; Koussevitsky Award, 1982; Various commissions. *Address:* 142 East 71st Street, New York, NY 10021, USA.

BEACH David Williams, b. 5 Sept 1938, Hartford, Connecticut, USA. Professor of Music Theory; Administrator. m. Marcia Francesca Salemme, 20 June 1964, 1 son, 1 daughter. *Education:* BA, Brown University, 1961; MMus, 1964, PhD, 1974, Yale University. *Career:* Academic: Assistant Professor, Yale University, 1964-71; Assistant Professor, Brooklyn College, City University of New York, 1971-72; Associate Professor, 1974-85, Chairman, Theory Department, 1981-90, Professor, 1985-, Eastman School of Music; Chairman, Theory Department, 1981-90; Professor of Music Theory, Eastman School of Music, University Dean of Graduate Studies, University of Rochester, 1991-. *Publications:* The Art of Strict Musical Composition by J P Kirnberger, translated by D Beach and J Thym with introduction and explanatory notes by Beach, 1982; Aspects of Schenkerian Theory, Editor, 1983. *Contributions to:* Acta Musicologica; Music Analysis; Journal of Music Theory; Music Theory Spectrum; Theory and Practice; Journal of Musicological Research Intègral; Journal of Music Theory Pedagogy. *Honour:* Deems Taylor Award (ASCAP), 1983. *Memberships:* Society for Music Theory, Executive Board, 1984-87, Chairman, Publications Committee, 1979-84; American Musicological Society. *Hobby:* Hiking; Running. *Address:* Eastman School of Music, Rochester, NY 14604, USA.

BEAN Hugh Cecil, b. 1929, Beckenham, England. Violinist. m. Mary Harrow. *Education:* Fellow of Royal College of Music; Studies with Albert Sammons and André Gertler. *Career:* Professor, Royal College of Music, 1954; Leader, Philharmonia and New Philharmonia Orchestras, 1957-68; Associate Leader, BBC Symphony Orchestra, 1967; Returned to the Philharmonia as co-leader, 1991. *Recordings include:* Elgar's Violin Concerto and Violin Sonata; Vaughan Williams Lark Ascending; Vivaldi's Concerti Opus 8/1-4; Various recordings with David Parkhouse and Music Group of London. *Honours:* Commander of the British Empire; Cobbett Gold Medal; Double Premier prize, Brussels Conservatory. *Hobbies:* Model Aircraft; Model Railways. *Address:* 30 Stone Park Avenue, Beckenham, Kent, BR3 3LX, England.

BEARDSLEE Bethany, b. 25 Dec 1927, Lansing, Michigan, USA. Singer (Soprano). m. (1) Jacques-Louis Monod, (2) Godfrey Winham, 1956. *Education:* Michigan State University; Juilliard School. *Debut:* New York 1949. *Career:* Concerts with Jacques-Louis Monod, giving the US premieres of works by Berg, Stravinsky, Webern, Krenek and Schoenberg; Concerts of medieval and Renaissance music with the New York Pro Musica, 1957-60; Commissioned and performed Babbitt's Philomel 1964; Performed Schoenberg's Pierrot Lunaire with members of the Cleveland Orchestra 1972; Taught at Westminster Choir College from 1976; Partnership with pianist Richard Goode 1981; Professor of singing at University of Texas, Austin, 1981-82; Brooklyn College, City University of New York, from 1983. *Recordings:* Pierrot Lunaire, conducted by Robert Craft (CBS); Works by Babbitt, George Perle and Mel Powell; Bach, Haydn and Pergolesi. *Honours:* Laurel Leaf from American Composers Alliance 1962; Ford Foundation Grant 1964; Honorary Doctorate, Princeton University, 1977.

BEATTIE Herbert (Wilson), b. 23 Aug 1926, Chicago, Illinois, USA. Opera singer; Music educator. m. (1) Elma Feltner, 11 Jan 1947, divorced 1973, 3 sons, 2 daughters. (2) Laurie Lorck, 15 July 1975. *Education:* BA, Colorado College, 1948; MM, Westminster Choir College, 1950; Salzburg Mozarteum, summer 1955; Voice training with John C Wilcox, American Conservatory of Music, Chicago and Dick Marzzolo, New York. *Debut:* Baron Douphol, La traviata, New York City Opera, 1957. *Career:* New York City Opera, 1957-72

and 1980-84; Appearances with opera companies in: Baltimore, San Francisco, Boston, New Orleans, Amsterdam, Brussels, Rome. Major roles include: Osmin, Leporello, Sarastro, Don Alfonso by Mozart; Bartolo and Mustafa by Rossini; Teacher, Syracuse University, 1950-52; Pennsylvania State University, 1952-53; University of Buffalo, 1953-58; Hofstra University, 1959-82; Broadcaster, 1982-89. *Compositions:* Several published choral pieces. *Recordings:* For Columbia; Desto; Orion. *Address:* 3010 Bonne Vista Drive, Colorado Springs, CO 80906, USA.

BEAUCHAMP Michael John, b, 2 June 1949, London, England. Opera and Theatre Director; Teacher. *Education:* University College, Durham; Trained, Glyndebourne Opera, 1971-74. *Career:* Staff Producer, Sadler's Wells and English National Opera, 1973-75; Resident Producer, Australian Opera, 1975-80; Freelance, 1980-; Productions: Happy End, Adelaide; Simon Boccanegra, HMS Pinafore, La Boheme, Australian Opera; La Bohème, National Opera of New Zealand and Glyndebourne Touring Opera; Rake's Progress, Brisbane and Sydney; Rigoletto, Perth, Western Australia and Melbourne; Lucia di Lammermoor, Songs from Sideshow Alley, Perth; Tancredi, Wexford; Once a Catholic, Whyalla, South Australia; The Happy Prince, Dunstan and the Devil, Morley Opera; Director, gala premieres for Australian Bicentennial, New South Wales Directorate; Teaching: NIDA, Sydney; New South Wales Conservatorium; Flinders University; Elder Conservatorium, Adelaide; Kelvin Grove College of Adult Education, Brisbane; Queensland Conservatorium, Brisbane; Victorian College of Arts; Western Australia Academy of Performing Arts; Guildhall School of Music and Drama, London; Royal Academy of Music, London; Birmingham School of Music; South Warwickshire College; Morley College. *Hobbies:* Cricket; Driving; Wine. *Address:* 40A Regents Park Road, London NW1 7SX, England.

BEAUDRY Jacques, b. 10 Oct 1929, Sorel, Quebec, Canada. Symphony & Opera Conductor. m. Pauline Bonneville. *Education:* BA, University of Montreal; Royal Conservatory of Music, Brussels, Belgium; studied with René Defossez, Paul Van Kempen, Willem Van Otterloo. *Career:* Professor, Orchestral Conducting, University of Montreal; Toured Europe as Conductor, Montreal Symphony, Opéra Comique, Paris Opera House, New York Metropolitan Opera; Radio Performances in Canada, Belgium, Holland, Italy, Czechoslovakia, Norway, Luxembourg, France; Concerts in USSR, Poland, Guatamala, Switzerland, Greece, Monaco, USA; TV appearances in Canada and France. *Honour:* Recipient, Golden Medal of Quebec Lieutenant Governor, 1958. *Current Management:* Beaudry Concerts, Montreal. *Hobbies:* Skiing; Swimming; French wines and Cuisine. *Address:* 235 Sherbrooke O, Montreal, Quebec, Canada H2X 1X8.

BEAUMONT Adrian, b. 1 June 1937, Huddersfield, Yorkshire, England. Lecturer; Composer. m. Janet Price, 25 July 1963. *Education:* BA, Music, 1st Class Honours, 1958, MMus, 1961, DMus, 1972, University College, Cardiff; Associate, Oboe Performance, Royal College of Music, 1961; studied privately with Nadia Boulanger. *Career:* Lecturer, Music, 1961-78, Senior Lecturer, 1978-, University of Bristol; Founder, Conductor, Bristol Bach Choir, 1967-78. *Compositions:* Ortatorio: Now Burn the Bright Redeeming Fire; 3 symphonies, oboe concerto, summea ecstasies, cello sonata, song cycles, two string quartets, A Glimmer of Unshapen Dawn for soprano and string quartet, two trios for flute, oboe and piano. *Publications:* Compositions, Vanderbeell and Imrie Ltd. *Memberships:* Composers Guild; Incorporated Society of Musicians; Musicians Union. *Hobbies:* Fell Walking; Conducting; Gardening. *Address:* 73 Kings Drive, Bishopston, Bristol, Avon BS7 8JQ, England.

BEAVEN Peter Richard, b. 17 Jan 1954, Plymouth, Devon, England. Conductor; Singer; Organist; Arranger and composer. *Education:* Graduate and Licentiate, Trinity College of Music, London; Licentiate, Royal Academy of Music; Associate, Royal College of

Organists. *Debut:* As Conductor at age 17; as Organist and Choirmaster at age 15. *Career:* Founder-Conductor, Feltham Choral Society, 1972-81; Assistant Chorus Master, Hounslow Choral Society, 1973-79; Artistic Director and Principal Conductor, Sunbury Festival Chorus and Orchestra, 1974-84; Director of Music, Sunbury Parish Church, 1973-81; Principal Guest Conductor, The Phoenix Orchestra, 1976-78; Staff, Guildhall School of Music, 1976-89; Musical Director, Putney Operatic Society, 1979-83; Organist and Director of Music, Chiswick Parish Church, 1981-92; Conductor, The Hogarth Singers, 1982-83; Tour of Holland, 1983; Member of Wren Singers of London, 1988-; Inaugural concert of The Peter Beaven Singers and Orchestra, 1984; Research begun for book, Choral Technique, 1985; Appeared at festivals in France, Bath, Royston, 1986-90; Music Director, Ashford Choral Society, 1990-; Appointed Musical Director for 'Wren' - The Musical (Each World Productions), 1992-; Radio debut with The Peter Beaven Singers (with Carlo Curley), 1992; Conductor, Norwood Green Choral Society, 1993; Co-Director, Wren Singers of London; Deputy Vicar-Choral, St Paul's Cathedral, 1993. *Compositions:* Various arrangements, mostly church music; Evening canticles for 8 part choir (first performed St Paul's Cathedral, 1991), Anthems. *Recordings:* Bach, Mass in B Minor; Mozart, Requiem. *Address:* 181 Nursery Road, Sunbury-on-Thames, Middlesex, TW16 6LX, England.

BEBBINGTON Warren Arthur, b. 25 Apr 1952, Melbourne, Australia. Musicologist; Conductor. m. (1) 1981, (div 1990), (2) Barbara neé Watson, 1991, 1 son. *Education:* BMus 1974, MMus 1977, University of Melbourne; MA, Queens College, New York, USA, 1978; MPhil 1979, PhD 1983, City University of New York. *Career:* Tutor, University of Melbourne, 1974-76; Research Assistant to Professor Gustave Reese, 1977; Lecturer, Canberra School of Music, 1979-85; Professor of Music and Dean, Faculty of Music, University of Queensland, 1985-91; Ormond Professor, Head of School of Music, University of Melbourne, 1991-; Conductor, Canberra Chamber Choir & Youth Orchestra, 1981-84; Guest Conductor, Queensland Theatre Orchestra, 1985-86; Director of 2 National Choral Festivals in Australia. *Publications:* Editor, Musicology Australia, 1984-92; Studies in Music, 1988-; Symphonies of J G & C H Graun, 1985; String Trio V 10 of Haydn, 1986; Adviser to Encyclopaedia Britannica; Contributor to Orchestras of the World: Selected Profiles, 1986. *Contributions to:* Various articles in Australian Dictionary of Biography; Journal of the American Musicological Society. *Hobbies:* Swimming; Sailing; Flying. *Address:* School of Music, University of Melbourne, Parkville 3052, Australia.

BECERRA Gustavo, b. 26 Aug 1925, Temuco, Chile. Composer. *Education:* Studied at Santiago Conservatory with Pedro Allende and with Domingo Santa Cruz. *Career:* Cultural Attache to Chilean Embassy in Bonn, 1968-70; Freelance composer. *Compositions include:* La Muerte de Don Rodrigo, opera, 1958; Three Symphonies, 1955, 1958, 1960; La Araucuna and Lord Cochrane, oratorios, 1965, 1967; Violin Concerto, 1950; Flute Concerto, 1957; Piano Concerto, 1958; Four Guitar Concertos, 1964-70; Concerto for oboe, clarinet, bassoon and strings, 1970; Three Violin Sonatas; Viola Sonata; Three Cello Sonatas; Sonata for double bass and piano; Choral music. *Honours include:* Premio Nacional de Arte, 1971. *Address:* SCO (Chile), c/o Member Registration, PRS Ltd, 29-33 Berners Street, London W1P 4AA, England.

BECHLY Daniela, b. 1958, Hamburg, Germany. Singer (Soprano). *Education:* Opera Diploma at the Hamburg Hochschule fur Musik, 1984. *Career:* Sang at Brunswick Opera, 1983-, debut with the Vienna Kammeroper, 1984; Appeared with the Krefeld Mönchengladbach company, 1985-87; Wexford Festival debut 1986 as Humperdinck's Goose Girl (Königskinder); Member of the Deutsche Oper Berlin, 1987-; Has also sung Susanna, Aennchen, Pamina, Anna in Die Lustige Weiber von Windsor, Gretel and Sandrina (Giardiniera) Mozart and Elvira (Don Giovanni)

Bern, 1991; Malwina in Der Vampyr by Marschner, Wexford, 1992; Haydn's L'Incontro Improvviso; Concert engagements in Ireland, Denmark, Norway, France, Italy and Austria. *Recordings:* Blumenmädchen, Parsifal recording Barenboim. *Honours include:* First Prize, Hamburg Singing Contest, 1980; Finals Vienna Belvedere Competition, 1984; Second Prize, Bordeaux Festival International de Jeunes Solistes. *Address:* Music International, 13 Ardilaun Road, London N5 2QR, England.

BECHT Hermann, b. 19 March 1939, Karlsruhe, Germany. Singer (Baritone). *Education:* Studied with E Wolf-Dengel in Karlsruhe and with Josef Greindl. *Career:* Sang at Brunswick and Wiesbaden; Deutsche Oper am Rhein, Dusseldorf, from 1974: roles include Strauss's Mandryka, Falstaff, Amfortas and Pfitzner's Borromeo; Bayreuth Festival from 1979, as Alberich and Kurwenal; Covent Garden Opera in The Ring; Sang Alberich in Festival Hall, London, concert performance of Das Rheingold; Guest appearances in New York, Stuttgart and Vienna; Staatsoper Munich 1986, in the premiere of V D Kirchner's Belshazzar; Waldner in Arabella, Teatro Liceo Barcelona, 1989; Sang Kurwenal at Nantes, 1989; Alberich in Das Rheingold, Bonn, 1990. *Recordings include:* Alberich in Ring cycle from Bayreuth (Philips). *Address:* c/o Ingpen and Williams Ltd, 14 Kensington Court, London W8 5DN, England.

BECKER Günther (Hugo), b. 1 Apr 1924, Forbach, Baden, Germany. Composer; Music Educator. *Education:* Studied conducting with Gerhard Nestler, Badische Hoschschule für Musik, Karlsruhe, 1946-49; Composition with Wolfgang Fortner, 1948-56; Choral conducting with Kurt Thomas 1953-55, North West German Academy of Music, Detmold. *Career:* Music Teacher, Greek National School Anavryta, Athens, 1956-58; Music Advisor, Goethe Institute, Athens, 1957-68; Music Teacher, German Dörpfeld Gymnasium, Athens, 1957-68; Founded Mega-Hertz, live-electronic music group, Germany, 1969; Teacher, International Summer Courses for New Music, Darmstadt, 1967, 1968, 1970; Lecturer, Musikhochschule Rheinland, Robert Schumann Institute, Düsseldorf, 1973; Professor of Composition and live electronics, Hochschule für Musik, Düsseldorf, 1974-89. *Compositions:* Orchestral: Nacht-und Traumgesänge for Chorus and Orchestra, 1964; stabil-instabil, 1965; Correspondances I for Clarinet and Chamber Orchestra, 1966; Griechische Tanzsuite, 1967; Caprices concertans, 1968; Transformationen for Orchestra, Live Electronic Ensemble and Tape, 1970; Attitude, 1972-73; Konzert for Electronic Modulated Oboe and Orchestra, 1973-74; Ihre Bosheit wird die ganze Erde zu einer Wüste machen, sacred concerto for Speaker, Alto, Chorus, Organ, Instrumental Ensemble and Tape, 1978; Magnum Mysterium-Zeugenaussagen zur Auferstehung, scenic oratorio, 1979-80; Pieces for various instruments and electronics; 3 string quartets, 1963, 1967, 1988. *Membership:* International Society for Contemporary Music, president German section, 1971-74. *Address:* Schillerstrasse 46, 40237 Düsseldorf, Germany.

BECKER Heinz, b. 26 June 1922, Berlin, Germany. Musicologist; Music Educator. *Education:* Trained in clarinet, piano, conducting and composition, Berlin Hochschule für Musik; PhD, Humboldt University, Berlin, 1951; Habilitation, University of Hamburg, 1961. *Career:* Assistant Lecturer, Institute of Musicology, University of Hamburg, 1956-66; Professor of Musicology, Ruhr University, Bochum, 1966-87. *Publications:* Der Fall Heine-Meyerbeer, 1958; edited, Giacomo Meyerbeer: Briefwechsel und Tagebucher, 4 volumes, 1960-85; Geschichte der Instrumentation, 1964; Beitrage zur Geschichte der Musikkritik, 1965; Studien zur Entwicklungsgeschichte der antiken und mittelalterlichen Rohrblattinstrumente, 1966; Beitrage zur Geschichte der Oper, 1969; Die Coúleur locale in der Oper des 19 Jahrhunderts, 1976; Giacomo Meyerbeer in Selbstzeugnissen und Bilddokumenten, 1980; Giacomo Meyerbeer: Ein Leben in Briefen, with G Becker, 1983, English Edition with supplements,

1989; Johannes Brahms, 1993. *Contributions to:* Articles in various music journals and other publications; über 400 Einzelveröffentlichungen. *Honours:* Festschrift published in honour of 60th birthday, 1982; Meyerbeeriana, Festschrift in honour of 70th birthday, 1992, ed Sieghart Döhring and Jürgen Schläder. *Membership:* Gesellschaft für Musikforschung since 1951. *Address:* c/o Music Department, Ruhr University, Bochum, Germany.

BECKER-GLAUCH Irmgard, b. 16 Nov 1914, Bochum, Germany. Musicologist. 1 daughter. *Education:* Studied at Universities of Tübingen, Breslau and Heidelberg; PhD, 1941. *Career:* With National Institute for German Musical Research, Berlin, 1942-43; Assistant Seminar Ethnomusicology, Hamburg University, 1943; Lecturer, State College for Music, Weimar, 1944-45 and Peoples College, Hamburg, 1946-55; Director, Music Library and Studio for New Music, British Centre, Die Brücke, Hamburg, 1948-53; Archive Manager, Joseph Haydn-Institute, Cologne, 1955-80; Radio lectures for various stations in Germany. *Publications:* Die Bedeutung der Musik für die Dresdener Hoffeste bis in die Zeit Augusts des Starken, 1951; Editor of several works by J Haydn. *Contributions to:* Various publications. *Memberships:* Member, Board of Directors, Joseph Haydn-Institute, Cologne; Society for Music Research, Kassel; Soroptimist International. *Address:* Wilhelm-Waldeyer-Str 2, D-5000 Cologne 41, Germany.

BECKMANN Judith, b. 10 May 1935, Jamestown, North Dakota, USA. Singer (Soprano). m. Irving Beckmann. *Education:* Studied in Los Angeles and with Lotte Lehmann in Santa Barbara; Further study in Hamburg and Dusseldorf. *Debut:* Brunswick 1962, as Fiordiligi in Così fan Tutte; Sang widely in Germany; Member of Deutsche Oper am Rhein, Dusseldorf, 1964; Hamburg Staatsoper 1967; Guest appearances in Brussels, Nancy, Geneva, Venice, Florence and London; Turin 1986, as the Marschallin in Der Rosenkavalier; Arabella, Munich Staatsoper, 1988; Ariadne, Dortmund Opera, 1988; Sang the Marschallin at Hanover and Munich, 1990; Concert engagements in music by Bach. *Recordings include:* Cantatas by Bach. *Address:* c/o Bayerische Staatsoper, Postfach 745, D-8000 Munich, Germany.

BECKMANN Klaus, b. 6 Dec 1935, Wanne-Eickel, Germany. Teacher of Secondary School. m. Hanne Lintelmann, 1959, 2 sons, 1 daughter. *Education:* Philosophy, Pedagogy, Evangelical Theology, Universities of Cologne and Bonn; Musicology, Universities of Munster and Bochum; Dr phil, 1975; School Music, Music High Schools, Detmold and Cologne. *Career:* Secondary and Grammar School Teacher: Wanne-Eickel, 1960-, Recklinghausen, 1966-, Gelsenkirchen, 1979-; Organist, Choir Director, Wanne-Eickel and Recklinghausen, 1968-. *Publications:* Organ works of M Praetorius, Tunder, Buxtehude, Reincken, Bruhns, Lübeck, Böhm, others. *Contributions:* Articles in Musik und Kirche, Der Kirchenmusiker, Ars organi, Het orgel. *Address:* Weizenkamp 7, D-45701 Herten, Germany.

BECKMANN Thomas (Riemke), b. 18 Apr 1957, Dusseldorf, Germany. Concert Soloist; Cellist. *Education:* Philosophy, Classical Latin and Greek, Universities of Dusseldorf and Cologne; Examination, Music High School, Dusseldorf; Pupil of Pierre Fournier, Geneva, 1980-86. *Debut:* TV concert, ZDF, 1986. *Career:* Over 100 TV appearances; 100 concerts yearly, 1986-; Appearances in all important German concert halls including Berlin Philharmonic, Cologne Philharmonic, Hamburg Musikhalle, Munchen Hosteules-Saal. *Recordings:* OH! That Cello, Play That Cello (Encore), Thomas Beckmann-Charlie Chaplin. *Honours:* Prize, German Record Critics. *Membership:* Violoncello Society, New York. *Hobby:* Jogging. *Current Management:* Jaro, Bremen, Germany. *Address:* c/o Jaro, Bismarkstr 83, 28203 Bremen, Germany.

BECKWITH John, b. 9 Mar 1927, Victoria, British Columbia, Canada. Composer; Teacher; Writer; Pianist. *Education:* MusB, 1947, MusM, 1961, University of Toronto, Faculty of Music; Private piano studies, Alberto Guerrero, Royal Conservatory of Music, Toronto, 1945-50; Private composition studies, Nadia Boulanger, Paris, 1950-51. *Career:* Public Relations Director, Royal Conservatory of Music, Toronto, 1948-50; Staff writer for radio music continuity, Canadian Broadcasting Corporation, Toronto, 1953-55; Freelance Radio programmer and writer, 1955-70; Reviewer and columnist, Toronto Daily Star, 1959-62, 1963-65; Special lecturer, part-time, University of Toronto, 1952-53, Lecturer, 1954-60, Assistant Professor, 1960-66, Associate Professor, 1966-70, Dean, 1970-77, Professor, 1977-90; Director, Institute for Canadian Music, 1984-90. *Compositions:* Night Blooming Cereus, 1958; Concerto Fantasy, 1960; Flower Variations and Wheels, 1962; Canada Dash, Canada Dot, 1967; All the Bees and All the Keys, 1973; The Shivaree, 1978; Keyboard Practice, 1979; A Little Otgan Concert, 1981; Mating Time, 1981; 6 Songs to poems by e e cummings, 1982; A Concert of Myths, 1983; Crazy to Kill, 1988; Peregrine, 1989; Round and Round, 1992. Published Compositions: 4 Songs to Poems of e e cummings, 1950; Fall Scene and Fair Dance, 1956; Jonah, 1963; Sharon Fragments, 1966; Circle, with Tangents, 1967; Gas! 1969; Taking a Stand, 1972; Musical Chairs, 1967; 3 Motets on Swan's 'China', 1981; Sonatina in 2 movements, 1981; Harp of David, 1985. Recorded Compositions: Music for Dancing; The Trumpets of Summer; Sharon Fragments; Circle, with tangents; Quartet; Keyboard Practice; 3 Motets on Swan's 'China'; Etudes; Harp of David; Arctic Dances. *Publications:* The Modern Composer and His World, 1961; Contemporary Canadian Composers, 1975; Canadian Composers Series, 1975-91; Canadian Consultant, The New Grove, London, 1980; The Canadian Musical Heritage, volume 5, 1986; Musical Canada, 1987. *Address:* 121 Howland Avenue, Toronto, Canada M5R 3B4.

BEDFORD David, b. 4 Aug 1937, London, England. Composer. m. (1) Maureen Parsonage, 1958, 2 daughters, (2) Susan Pilgrim, 1969. *Education:* Royal Academy of Music and Trinity College, London, LTCL; ARAM. *Career:* Porter, Guy's Hospital, London, 1956; Teacher, Whitefield School, Hendon, 1965; Teacher, 1968-80, Composer-in-residence, 1969-81, Queen's College, London; Associate Visiting Composer, Gordonstoun, Scotland, 1983-. *Compositions include:* School operas The Rime of the Ancient Mariner, 1975-76, The Death of Baldur, 1979, Fridiof's Saga, 1980, The Ragnarok, 1982-83; Symphony 1981; Sun Paints Rainbows on the Vast Waves, 1982; Snakes and the Giant, 1982; Star Clusters, Nebulae and places in Devon for chorus and orchestra, 1971; Pancakes with Butter, Maple Syrup, and Bacon and the TV Weatherman for brass quintet, 1973; instrumental music; Diafone, flute and vibraphone, 1986; Seascapes, string quintet and voices, 1986; Fortress, brass quintet, 1985; Into thy Wondrous House, sopranom chorus and orchestra, 1987; Gere curam mei finis, vocal soloists and harmonizer, 1987; Erkenne Mich, ensemble, 1988; Odysseus, Children's opera, 1988; The Transfiguration: A Meditation, Chamber orchestra, 1988; Fireworks, 1990; The OCD Band, The Minotaur, soprano and ensemble, 1990. *Recordings:* Numerous. *Memberships:* Executive Committee, Society for the Promotion of New Music; Director, Youth Music English Sinfonia, 1987; Chairman, Association Professional Composers, 1991. *Hobbies:* Squash; Table tennis; Cricket; Astronomy; Ancient history; Philosophy. *Address:* 39 Shakespeare Road, Mill Hill, London NW7 4BA, England.

BEDFORD Steuart John Rudolf, b. 31 July 1939, London, England. Pianist; Conductor. m. (1) Norma Burrowes, 1969, (2) Celia Harding, 1980, 2 daughters. *Education:* BA, Lancing College, Oxford; Royal Academy of Music, FRCO, FRAM. *Debut:* Oxford Chamber Orchestra, 1964. *Career:* Glyndebourne Festival Opera, 1965-67; Debut with The Beggar's Opera, 1967; English Opera Group; English Music Theatre, Aldeburgh and London, 1967-73; at Aldeburgh he conducted the world premieres of Britten's Death in Venice, 1973 and

Phaedra, 1976; Artistic Director and Resident Conductor, English Music Theatre and Aldeburgh Festival, 1975-; Chief Conductor, English Sinfonia Orchestra, 1981-; Freelance conductor at home and abroad, including Metropolitan Opera New York, Santa Fe, Buenos Aires, Rio de Janeiro, Canada, France, Germany, Austria, Australia and New Zealand; Royal Opera House Covent Garden, English National Opera, Welsh National Opera, Opera North. *Recordings include:* Death in Venice; Phaedra; Beggar's Opera; Collins Britten series. *Honours:* Worshipful Company of Musicians, Medal; Organ Scholarship. *Current Management:* Harrison/Parrott, 12 Penzance Place, London W11, England. *Hobbies:* Skiing; Golf. *Address:* 76 Cromwell Avenue, London N6 5HQ, England.

BEECROFT Norma, b. 11 Apr 1934, Oshawa, Ontario, Canada. Composer. *Education:* Studied with John Weinzweg in Toronto, 1952-58, at Tanglewood with Foss and Copland, at Darmstadt with Maderna and in Rome with Petrassi; Further studies in electronic music at the University of Toronto and Columbia-Princeton Electronic Music Center. *Career:* Worked in Toronto, 1965-73, co-founding the New Music Concerts, 1971, president and general manager until 1989. *Compositions include:* Improvvisazioni Concertanti I-III, 1961, 1971, 1973; From Dreams of Brass for narrator, soprano, chorus, orchestra and tape, 1964; Piece concertante for orchestra, 1966; Undersea Fantasy, puppet opera for tape, 1967; The Living Flame of Love for chorus, 1967; Rsasa I-III for chamber ensemble, 1968, 1973, 1974; Collage '76 for ensemble, 1976; Consequences for Five, 1977; Collage '78 for bassoon, piano, 2 percussion and tape; Hedda, ballet for orchestra and tape, 1983; The Dissipation of Purely Sound, radiophonic opera for tape, 1988; Accordion Play, 1989; Requiem Mass for soloists, chorus and orchestra, 1990. *Address:* SOCAN (Canada), c/o Member Registration, PRS Ltd, 29-33 Berners Street, London W1P 4AA.

BEESLEY Mark, b. 1961, Harrogate, Yorkshire, England. Singer (Bass-baritone). *Education:* Studied at Sussex University (MSc) and with Dennis Wicks. *Career:* Appearances with New Sussex Opera, the City of Birmingham Touring Opera, Opera North, Opera 80 and at the Batignano Festival; Member of the Royal Opera Covent Garden, 1989-, in Idomeneo (voice of Neptune), Arabella, Fidelio, Capriccio, Samson et Dalila, Turandot (Timor), La Boheme (Colline), I Capuleti, Otello (Lodovico), and La Damnation de Faust (Brander, 1993); Other engagements in Poppea at the City of London Festival, Tosca (Angelotti) in Hong Kong and Midsummer Night's Dream (Theseus) at Aix-en-Provence; Concert repertoire includes the Verdi Requiem (at Seville) and Beethoven's Ninth (Brussels Philharmonic). *Address:* c/o John Coast Ltd, 31 Sinclair Road, London W14 0NS, England.

BEESON Jack Hamilton, b. 15 July 1921, Muncie, Indiana, USA. Composer; Educator; Writer. m. Nora Beate Sigerist, 1 son (deceased), 1 daughter. *Education:* BMus. 1942; MMus. 1943; Eastman School of Music, Rochester University; Graduate Study, and Columbia University; Studied Piano, Cello and Clarinet and Percussion. *Debut:* As actor in own opera, My Heart's In The Highlands, NET 1970. Over 60 published including: Jonah; Hello Out There; The Sweet Bye and Bye; Lizzie Borden; My Heart's In The Highlands; Captain Jinks of The Horse Marines; Dr Heidegger's Fountain of Youth; Cyrano (Operas); Symphony No 1 in A. *Contributions to:* Journals and Grove's Dictionary, 6th Edition. *Honours:* Rome Prize 1948-50; Fulbright Fellowship 1949; Guggenheim Fellowship 1958-59; Marc Blitzstein Award, National Institute of Arts and Letters 1968; Gold Medal National Arts Club 1976; Great Teacher Award, Columbia University 1978; Alumni Achievement Award, University of Rochester, 1985. *Memberships:* Alice M. Ditson Fund; Music Publishing Committee, Columbia University Press; Co-acting President 1975-76, Honorary Trustee, CRI Inc.; Advisory Board, Composer's Forum; American Academy, Treasurer 1980-83, 1988-91, Vice-President 1984-87, of Arts and Letters; Trustee 1975-84, Trustee

Emeritus 1993-, American Academy in Rome. *Hobby:* Swimming. *Address:* Department of Music, Columbia University, Dodge, New York, NY 10027, USA.

BEGG Heather, b. 1 Dec 1932, Nelson, New Zealand. Opera Singer (Mezzo-Soprano). *Education:* Sydney Conservatorium of Music 1954-56; National School of Opera, London, 1957-59; Pupil of Florence Wiese-Norberg, London. *Debut:* Auckland, New Zealand, 1954, as Azucena in Il Trovatore. *Career:* National Opera of Australia 1954-56; Carl Rosa Company, London, 1960; Sadler's Wells Opera 1961-64; New Zealand Opera Company 1964-66; Royal Opera, Covent Garden, Guest artist, 1959-72, Resident, 1972-76; Australian Opera 1976-; Guest artist in Edinburgh, Salzburg and Orange Festivals, Strasbourg, Bordeaux, Milan, Vancouver, Chicago, San Francisco, San Diego and Barcelona; Concert artist and recitalist for radio and TV in UK, New Zealand and Australia. *Recordings and videos:* Unitel film of Le Nozze di Figaro; Les Troyens, conducted by Colin Davis; Mefistofele; I Puritani; The Little Sweep; Die Fledermaus; Adriana Lecouvreur; Dialogues of the Carmelites; La fille du Régiment; The Mikado; Voss; Gipsy Princess. *Honours:* Sydney Sun Aria Winner 1955; Recipient, New Zealand Government Music Bursary, 1956; Countess of Munster Scholarship, 1959; Order of the British Empire 1978. *Hobbies:* Tapestry; Photography; Painting; Gardening. *Address:* c/o Australian Opera, 480 Elizabeth Street, Surry Hills, NSW 2010, Australia.

BEGLARIAN Eve, b. 22 July 1958, Ann Arbor, Michigan, USA. Composer; Record Producer. *Education:* BA, Princeton University; MA, Columbia University. *Career:* Music performed at Washington Ballet, Kennedy Center, May 1991; Anthony de Hare, Kennedy Center, May 1990; New York New Music Ensemble, June 1988; Dinosaur Annex, Boston, 1989, 1990; Monday Evening Concerts, Los Angeles, 1990, 1991; Weil Recital Hall, April 1987. *Compositions:* Eloise (electric cello and tape); The Beginning of Terror (electronic tape); Making Sense of It (Flute, cello, violin, violoncello, pianoforte, percussion, tape); Miranda's Kiss (piano solo); A Big Enough Umbrella (viola, tape). *Recordings:* Space 1986; Needful Things - Stephen King audio book, 1991; Born Dancin'/Eloise 1991. *Publications:* Mikrokosmos (Bartók) corrected edition 1989 Boosey and Hawkes. *Address:* Suite K114, 496A Hudson Street, New York, NY 10014, USA.

BEGLARIAN Grant, b. 1 Dec 1927, Tiflis, Georgia. Composer; Consultant. m. Joyce Ellyn Heeney, 2 Sept 1950, 1 son, 1 daughter. *Education:* BM, Composition, 1950, MM, Composition, 1961, DMA, 1958, University of Michigan, Ann Arbor, USA; Berkshire Music Center with Aaron Copland, 1960. *Career:* Director, Contemporary Music Project, the Ford Foundation, New York and Washington, 1960-69; Dean, Professor of Music, School of Performing Arts, University of Southern California, Los Angeles, 1969-82; President, National Foundation for Advancement in the Arts, Miami, 1982-91; Consultant in the Arts and Education, 1991-. *Compositions include:* Duets for Violins, 1955; First Portrait For Band, 1959; Sinfonia for Orchestra, 1961; A Short Suite for String Orchestra, 1968; Fables, Foibles and Fancies, for Narrator and Cellist, 1971; Diversions for Viola, Cello and Orchestra, 1972; To Manitou for Soprano and Orchestra, 1976; Partita for Orchestra, 1986. *Publications:* Film-Video as an Artistic Discipline, Editor, 1978; The Arts in Shaping the American Experience, 1979; The Professional Education and Career Entry of Artists, 1982; Fables, Foibles and Fancies, 1992. *Hobby:* Reading; Travel; Amateur Bridge. *Address:* 141 River Road, Scarborough, NY 10510, USA.

BEGLEY Kim, b. 1955, Birkenhead, Merseyside. Singer (Tenor). *Education:* Guildhall School of Music 1980-82; National Opera Studio 1982-83. *Career:* Royal Opera House Covent Garden from 1983 as Andres in Wozzeck; Lysander in A Midsummer Night's Dream; The Prince in Zemlinsky's Florentine Tragedy; Achilles in King Priam and Froh in Das Rheingold. Other appearances include Boris in Katya kabanova, Pellegrin in Tippett's New Year and Laca in Jenůfa for Glyndebourne Festival; Dancing Master in Ariadne and Male Chorus in Rape of Lucretia for ENO; Shuisky in Boris Godunov, Fritz in the British premiere of Der ferne Klang, 1992, and Lohengrin and Alfred, Die Fledermaus in Frankfurt; Narraboth at the 1993 Salzburg Festival; Concert appearances include Die Fledermaus, Alfred, with Andre Previn at the RPO; Elgar's Dream of Gerontius with the Philharmonia under Vernon Handley, Tippett's New Year with the LPO and Janáček's From the House of the Dead with the BBC Symphony Orchestra. *Address:* IMG Artists Europe, Media House, 3 Burlington Lane, Chiswick W4, England.

BEHAGUE Gerard (Henri), b. 2 Nov 1937, Montpellier, France. Musicologist. *Eucation:* Studied piano and composition at the National School of Music, University of Brazil, and at the Brazilian Conservatory of Music, Rio de Janeiro; Studied further at the Institute de Musicologie at the University of Paris, with Chailley; Musicology with Gilbert Chase at Tulane University, PhD 1966. *Career:* Joined faculty of University of Illinois and was appointed professor of music at the University of Texas, 1974; Associate editor of the Yearbook for Inter-American Musical Research, 1969-75; Editor, music section of the Handbook of Latin American Studies, 1970-74; Editor of Ethnomusicology, 1974-78, and Latin American Music Review, from 1980; Editorial adviser and major contributor to the New Grove Dictionary of Music and Musicians, 1970-80. *Publications include:* The Beginnings of Musical Nationalism in Brazil (Detroit 1971); Music in Latin America: an Introduction (Eaglewood Cliffs, New Jersey, 1977).

BEHR Randall, b. 1958, USA. Conductor; Pianist. *Career:* Conducted Peter Hall's production of Salome at Los Angeles Music Center, 1989; Has returned to Los Angeles for La Traviata, Tosca (with Maria Ewing and Placido Domongo) and Peter Hall's production of Die Zauberflote, 1993; Other repertory includes the Oliver Knussen Double Bill, Orfeo ed Euridice, Nixon in China, Così fan Tutte, Die Frau ohne Schatten, La Bohéme and Vivaldi's Orlando Furioso; Music Director of Long Beach Opera, California; Peter Brook's La Tragedie de Carmen on Broadway; Conducted La Traviata at the Liceu, Barcelona, 1992, Die Walküre in Valencia and Tancredi at Bilbao, with Marilyn Horne; Vienna Staatsoper debut, 1993-94, Madama Butterfly; Appearance as pianist with Maria Ewing at Covent Garden and at the Teatro Comunale Florence, Theatre du Chatelet Paris, the Vienna Konzerthaus and the Opera de Lyon. *Address:* c/o Harold Holt Ltd, 31 Sinclair Road, London W14 0NS, England.

BEHRENS Hildegard, b. 9 Feb 1937, Varel, Oldenburg, Germany. Singer (Soprano). m. Seth Scheidman. *Education:* Freiburg Music Academy with Ines Leuwen. *Debut:* Freiburg 1971, as Mozart's Countess. *Career:* Sang in Dusseldorf and Frankfurt as Fiordiligi, Marie (Wozzeck), Agathe (Der Freischütz), Elsa and Katya Kabanova; Covent Garden debut 1976, as Leonore in Fidelio; Metropolitan Opera from 1976, as Giorgetta (Il Tabarro), Donna Anna, Tosca, Mozart's Electra and Wagner's Sieglinde, Isolde and Brünnhilde; Salzburg 1977, Salome; Guest appearances in Munich, Vienna and Lisbon; Bayreuth from 1983: sang Brünnhilde in a new production of The Ring, directed by Harry Kupfer, 1988 and in New York, 1988-90; Marie in Wozzeck, Metropolitan, 1990; Salome at Munich Concert and at Covent Garden, Sept 1990; Sang Elektra at Athens and the New York Metropolitan, 1992. *Recordings include:* Salome, conducted by Karajan (HMV); Fidelio (Decca); Les Nuits d'Éte and Ravel's Shéhérazade (Decca); Tristan und Isolde (Philips); Brünnhilde in The Ring, conducted by James Levine, also on Video; Video of Wozzeck, from Vienna conducted by Abbado (Virgin Classics). *Address:* c/o Royal Opera House, Covent Garden, London WC2, England.

BEHRMAN David, b. 16 Aug 1937, Salzburg, Austria. Composer. *Education:* Studied privately in New York with Wallingford Riegger and at Princeton with Walter Piston; European studies with Henri Pousseur

and Karlheinz Stockhausen. *Career:* From 1966 toured widely in the US with the Sonic Arts Union, giving performances of electronic music; Associated with John Cage, David Tudor and Gordon Mumma at the Merce Cunningham Dance Company, 1970-76; Formerly artist-in-residence at Mills College, Oakland, serving as co-director of the Center for Contemporary Music there. *Compositions include:* Players with Curtains, 1966; Wave Train, 1966; Runthrough, 1967; For Nearly an Hour, 1968; A New Team Takes Over, 1969; Pools of Phase-locked Loops, 1972; Cloud Music, 1974-79; Figure in a Clearing, 1977; On the other Ocean, 1977; Touch Tones, 1979; Indoor Geyser, 1979-81; Singing Stick, 1981; She's Wild, 1981; Sound Fountain, 1982; 6-Circle, 1984; Orchestral Construction Set, 1984; Interspecies Smalltalk, 1984; Installation for La Villett, 1985. *Recordings include:* Many albums of experimental music (Columbia Masterworks). *Address:* c/o ASCAP, ASCAP Building, One Lincoln Plaza, New York, NY 10023, USA.

BEILMAN Douglas, b. 1965, Kansas, USA. Violinist. *Education:* Studied at Juilliard and the New England Conservatory, with Dorothy Delay. *Career:* Co-founded the Sierra Quartet and performed at the Olympic Music Festival; Co-founded the New Zealand String Quartet, 1987, under the auspices of the Music Federation of New Zealand; Debut concert in Wellington, May 1988; Concerts at the Tanglewood School in USA, Banff International Competition in Canada and performances with the Lindsay Quartet at the 1990 International Festival of the Arts, Wellington; Soloist with New Zealand Symphony Orchestra and artist-in-residence at Victoria University, Wellington; Tour to Australia, 1990, for Musica Viva Australia; Tours of New Zealand, 1992, and concerts in New York, 1993. *Recordings include:* Several albums. *Address:* c/o Ingpen and Williams Ltd, 14 Kensington Court, London W5 5DN, England.

BEKKU Sadao, b. 24 May 1922, Tokyo, Japan. Composer. *Education:* Studied with Milhaud, Rivier and Messiaen at the Paris Conservatoire, 1951-54. *Career:* Teacher in Tokyo and president of the Japanese branch of International Society for Contemporary Music, 1968-73. *Compositions:* Operas: A Story of Three Women, Tokyo, 1965; Prince Arima, Tokyo, 1967; Aoi-no-ue, Tokyo, 1981; Two Japanese Suites, 1955, 1958; String Quartet, 1955; Two Prayers for orchestra, 1956; Symphonietta for strings, 1959; 4 Symphonies, 1962, 1977, 1984, 1991; Piano Sonatina, 1965; Kaleidoscope for piano, 1966; Violin Sonata, 1967; Violin Concerto, 1969; Three Paraphrases for piano, 1968; Sonata in Classical Style for piano, 1969; Viola Concerto, 1972; Piano Concerto, 1981. *Publications include:* The Occult in Music, 1972. *Address:* JASRAC (Japan), c/o Member Registration, PRS Ltd, 29-33 Berners Street, London W1P 4AA, England.

BELAMARIC Miro, b. 9 Feb 1935, Sibenik, Dalmatia. Composer; Conductor. *Education:* Studied with Milan Horvat and Stjepan Sulek at the Zagreb Academy of Music, Lovro von Matacic in Salzburg, Sergiu Celibidache in Siena. *Career:* Conductor of the Symphony Orchestra of Zagreb Radio from 1959; Chief Conductor of the Komedija Theatre and from 1978 Chief Conductor of Zagreb Opera; Assistant to Karajan at Salzburg Festival, 1965-68, to Karl Bohn, 1975-77. *Compositions include:* Operas: The Love of Don Perlimplin, Zagreb, 1975, and Don Juan - ein Rebell fur alle Zeiten, 1983. *Honours include:* Winner, Vienna State Opera Competition for Don Juan, 1983. *Address:* c/o Vienna Staatsoper, Opernring 2, A-1010 Vienna, Austria.

BELCOURT Emile, b. 1934, Saskatchewan, Canada. Singer (Tenor). *Education:* Academy of Music, Vienna; Paris with Pierre Bernac and Germaine Lubin. *Career:* Early opera appearances in Germany and France; Paris Opéra Comique as Pelléas; Sang in Debussy's opera for Scottish Opera 1962; Covent Garden 1963, as Gonzalez in L'Heure Espagnole; Sadler's Wells/English National Opera from 1963, in Die Fledermaus, Orpheus in the Underworld, Bluebeard, The Violins of St Jacques,

Patience, Salome and Lucky Peter's Journey; Loge in The Ring; Sang in premières of Bennett's A Penny for a Song, 1967; Hamilton's The Royal Hunt of the Sun, 1977; Blake's Toussaint l'ouverture, 1977; Lead in stage musicals Man of La Mancha and Kiss me Kate; Canadian Opera debut in Heloise and Abelard, 1973; San Francisco, 1982, as Herod in Salome; Sang in the Covent Garden premiere of Berg's Lulu, 1981. *Recordings include:* Loge in The Ring cycle, conducted by Reginald Goodall (EMI). *Address:* c/o English National Opera, London Coliseum, St Martin's Lane, London WC2N 4ES, England.

BELKIN Boris, 26 Jan. 1948, Sverdlovsk, USSR. Violinist. *Education:* Began violin studies aged six; Central Music School Moscow, then Moscow Conservatory with Yankelevitz and Andrievsky. *Career:* Public appearances from 1955; Won Soviet National Competition for violinists 1972 and emigrated 1974; Debut in West,1974 with Zubin Mehta and the Israel Philharmonics; Orchestras with whom he has appeared include Berlin Philharmonic, Concertgebouw, Israel Philharmonic, Los Angeles Philharmonic, Philadelphia and Cleveland; Conductors include Muti, Bernstein, Maazel, Haitink, Mehta, Ashkenazy and Steinberg; Season 1987-88 with London Philharmonic and Cleveland Orchestras and recitals in Spain, Italy, Finland and Portugal. Season 1988-89 with the Pittsburgh, Royal Philharmonic, Concertgebouw and Tokyo Philharmonic orchestras. *Recordings:* Paganini Concerto No.1 with the Israel Philharmonic; Tchaikovsky and Sibelius Concertos with the Philharmonia Orchestra; Prokofiev's Concertos with the London Philharmonic; Brahms Concerto with the London Symphony; Shostakovich Concerto No.1 with the Royal Philharmonic. *Address:* KM Artists (Londin) Ltd, Oxford House, 76 Oxford Street, London W1N 0AX, England.

BELL Christopher, b. 1961, Belfast. Conductor. *Career:* Chorusmaster of the Edinburgh Royal Choral Union 1987-90; Regular concerts with the Scottish Chamber Orchestra from 1988, notably in West Side Story and Porgy and Bess, and a five concert tour of the Highlands; Chorus Master of the Royal Scottish Orchestra Chorus and from 1989 Associate Conductor of the BBC Scottish Symphony; Barbican Hall, London, debut 1989 with the London Concert Orchestra; Has also conducted the Royal Philharmonic, the Basle Symphony, the Brabants Orkest and the Nordhollands Orkest; Gave Tosca with Opera Northern Ireland and Dublin Grand Opera, 1990; Edinburgh Festival 1991 and debut with the City of London Sinfonia; Music in education includes Chorister Training Scheme at Palmerston Place Church Edinburgh (Director of Music); Ulster Orchestra, Royal Scottish National Orchestra, Essex Philharmonic; Associate Conductor BBC, 1989-91; Artistic Director, Edinburgh Royal Choral Union, 1993-. *Current Management:*Robert Gilder & Co. *Address:* Enterprise House, 59-65 Upper Ground, London SE1 9PQ, England.

BELL Donald Munro, b. 19 June 1934, Burnaby, Canada. Associate Professor; Baritone. *Education:* Royal College of Music, 1953-55; Berlin, 1955-60; Oberlin, 1985-; Vocal Enrichment Institute, 1987; Pedagogy, Voice, Style with Dr R Miller, 1989. *Debut:* Wigmore Hall, 1958; Bayreuth, 1958. *Career:* CBC, BBC, NOS TV Holland; Glyndebourne (1963, the Speaker in Die Zauberflöte); Geneva; London Royal Festival Hall; Royal Albert Hall; Opening of Lincoln Center; Carnegie Hall. *Honours:* Recipient, various honours & awards. *Memberships:* Governor-Canada, National Opera Association; National Association of Teachers of Singing; Rotary Club. *Hobby:* Swimming. *Address:* University of Calgary, Dept of Music, 2500 University Drive NW, Calgary, Alberta T2N 1N4, Canada.

BELL Joshua, b. 9 Dec 1967, Bloomington, Indiana, USA. Violinist. *Debut:* Performed with Philadelphia Orchestra 1981, with Riccardo Muti; Carnegie Hall debut 1985, with the St Louis Symphony; made tour of Germany with Indianapolis Symphony in 1987 and later played with the Royal Philharmonic the same year;

Recent and future engagements with orchestras in the USA include the New York Philharmonic, the Chicago and Boston Symphonies, Cleveland Orchestra and Los Angeles Philharmonic and in Europe the Philharmonia, Royal Philharmonic, Orchestre de la Suisse Romande, RAI Rome, Rotterdam Philharmonic, Bamberg Symphony, Orchestre Philharmonique and the CBSO. He collaborates with conductors such as Vladimir Ashkenazy, Paavo Berglund, Charles Dutoit, John Eliot Gardiner, James Levine, Lorin Maazel, André Previn, Esa-Pekka Salonen, Michael Tilson Thomas and Roger Norrington. One of the highlights of the 1993/94 season was premiere of the violin concerto by Nicholas Maw. This was written specially for him and was given its European premiere in October with the Philharmonia Orchestra conducted by Leonard Slatkin. He gave the US premiere with the Orchestra of St Luke's at Avery Fisher Hall conducted by Roger Norrington. *Recordings:* Mendelssohn and Bruch Concertos with the Academy of St Martin-in-the-Fields, the Tchaikovsky and Wieniawski Concertos with the Cleveland Orchestra, Lalo's Symphonie Espagnole, Saint-Saëns's 3rd Concerto, and Mozart Concertos 3 & 5. He has also made threealbums of French repertoire: a recital disc with Jean-Yves Thibaudet, a chamber music disc the the Takacs Quartet and Jean-Yves Thibaudet, and an album of virtuosi pieces with the Royal Philharmonic Orchestra conducted by Andrew Litton. Further recording projects include a Prokofiev recital disc, and his recording of the Prokofiev Violin Concertos released, 1994. *Current Management:* IMG Artists (Europe). *Address:* c/o IMG Artists (Europe), Media House, 3 Burlington Lane, Chiswick, London W4 2TH, England.

BELL Robin McKinlay, b. 9 Sept 1939, Wellington, New Zealand. Singer; Singing Teacher. m. George Gordon, 20 Nov 1971, 1 son, 1 daughter. *Education:* Piano from age 4; All Trinity College grades; Violin, school orchestra; Singing, ATCL and LTCL, 1958, FTCL, 1962; Royal Academy of Music, London, 1960-62; LRAM and ARCM, 1962; Continued privately with Dame Eva Turner, Eduardo Asquez, Gita Denise. *Debut:* Soprano solos, Messiah, Royal Wellington Choral Union, New Zealand; New Zealand representative, Festival of Commonwealth Youth, State Apartments, St James' Palace, London, 1962. *Career:* Sang at Glyndebourne, Camden, Wexford and Aldeburgh Festivals; Opera, oratorio and concert performances throughout Britain; 2 Wigmore Hall recitals for Incorporated Society of Musicians and New Zealand Music Society; Toured with Arts Council's Opera for All, 2 seasons; Sang in Benjamin Britten's Death in Venice at La Fenice, Venice; Still singing oratorio and recitals regularly; Now mainly Registered Private Singing Teacher, Incorporated Society of Musicians, teaching at Carnegie Music Institute, Dumfermline; Conductor, East Fife Ladies Choir, 1985-. *Honours:* New Zealand Government Bursary to study at Royal Academy of Music, 1960; Recital Medal, Royal Academy of Music, 1962. *Memberships:* Incorporated Society of Musicians; British Actors Equity Association. *Hobbies:* Canvas needlework; Reading; Gardening. *Address:* Cramond, 21 Links Rd, Lundin Links, Leven, Fife KY8 6AS, Scotland.

BELLING Susan, b. 3 May 1943, Bronx, New York, USA. Opera Singer; Educator. *Education:* Roslyn High School, Long Island, New York, 1956-60; Chatham Square Music School, 1958-60; Kathryn Long School, 1965-67; Metropolitan Opera Studio, 1964-67; Manhattan School of Music, 1960-63. *Career:* Master Classes and Workshops, Stanford University, California, 1978, University of Houston, 1978, Manhattan School of Music, 1984; Faculty, New School of Social Research, 1986-; Over 100 American and World Premieres; Played title role in Reimann's Melusine for Santa Fe Opera, and Kirchner's Lily with New York City Opera; Performance of Arnold Schoenberg's Second Quartet with Erich Leinsdorf and the Boston Symphony; Belinda in Dido and Aeneas, Metropolitan Opera's Premiere Season of the Forum Opera, Lincoln Center; Performed numerous occasions with conductor James Levine in such roles as Zerlina in Don Giovanni at Hollywood Bowl, Papagena in Magic Flute with Cleveland Concert Associates, as soprano soloist in Midsummer Night's

Dream and the Mahler Fourth Symphony with the Chicago Symphony and with Atlanta Symphony in Marriage of Figaro; Debut in Europe, Baroque Festival of Venetian Music, Castelfranco, Veneto and Teatro Olimico, Italy, 1977; Numerous other performances include, Haydn's Lord Nelson Mass with Minnesota Orchestra, Neville Marriner conducting; Pamina in Magic Flute and numerous others. *Address:* c/o Allied Artists Bureau, Michael Leavitt, 195 Steamboat Road, Great Neck, NY 11024, USA.

BELLUGI Piero, b. 14 July 1924, Florence, Italy. Conductor. m. (1) Ursula Herzberger, 1954 (divorced), (2) Margherita Vivian 1960, five children. *Education:* Conservatorio Cherubini, Florence, Accademia Chigiana, Siena, Akademie des Mozarteums, Salzburg and Tanglewood, Massachusetts, USA. *Career:* Musical Director, Oakland, California and Portland, Oregon Symphony Orchestras, 1955-1961; Permanent Conductor, Radio Symphony Orchestra, Turin, 1967; Professor of courses for orchestral players and conductors, Italian Youth Orchestra, 1981-; Guest Conductor, La Scala, Milan (debut 1961 with Handel's Serse), Vienna State Opera, Rome Opera, Aix-en-Provence Festival, Berlin Radio, Paris, Rome S Cecilia, Chicago, San Francisco Operas etc; his concert repertory includes music by Mahler, Berg, Schoenberg and Webern; Has conducted the premieres of Milhaud's 10th symphony, 1961, and Settimo Concerto by Petrassi, 1965. *Address:* 50027 Strada in Chianti, Florence, Italy.

BELOHLAVEK Jiri, b. 24 Feb 1946, Prague, Czechoslavakia. Conductor. *Education:* Studied at the Prague Academy of Arts with Sergiu Celibidache. *Career:* Assistant Conductor with the Czech Philharmonic; Conductor of the Brno State Philharmonic, 1971-77; Chief Conductor of the Prague Symphony Orchestra 1977-90; Artistic Director and Principal Conductor of the Czech Philharmonic Orchestra from 1990; Extensive tours with the Prague Symphony and the Czech Philharmonic in Europe, the USA and Japan; Guest appearances with the Berlin Philharmonic, New York Philharmonic, the Boston, Toronto and Vienna Symphony Orchestras, Leipzig Gewandhaus, Stockholm Philharmonic, NHK Philharmonic (Tokyo) and the USSR State Symphony Orchestra; Edinburgh Festival 1990, with the Prague Symphony Orchestra; Further British engagements with the City of Birmingham Symphony, the BBC Philharmonic, Scottish National, Royal Liverpool Philharmonic and BBC Welsh Symphony Orchestras; Recent concerts with the Saint Louis, Bavarian Radio, Washington National, Dresden Philharmonic, Deutsche Kammerphilharmonie and Tonhalle (Zurich) Orchestras; Conducted the BBC Philharmonic in music by Brahms, Zemlinsky (Maeterlinck Songs) and Mahler (1st Symphony) at the 1993 Promenade Concerts. *Recordings include:* Works by Martinů and Janáček, with the Czech Philharmonic (Chandos). *Honours include:* Finalist, 1971 Herbert von Karajan International Conducting Competition. *Address:* c/o CPO Korunní Tr 98, Prague 10, Czech Republic.

BELOIU Nicolae, b. 9 May 1927, Ocnita, Romania. Composer; Professor. m. Victoria-Sonia Sabau, 1 Feb 1956. *Education:* Architecture and Mathematics, Bucharest, 1948-51; Academy of Music, Bucharest, 1949-54. *Career:* Musical Director, Radio Bucharest, 1960-72; Professor, Academy of Music, Bucharest, 1970-; Rector of the Academy of Music, Bucharest, 1990-92. *Compositions:* Two symphonies, 1967, 1977; Divertimento per archi, 1953, revised, 1971; Concerto for 18 strings, 1959, revised 1971; Towns Rhythms, 1970; Jubilations and Lamento, 1978; Divertissement for two violas, 1953, revised 1961; Chamber Concerto for two violins and viola, 1959; Settimino Scenico, 1972; String Quartet, 1982; Sonata for solo violin, 1984; Ben Jonson's Volpone, theatre music, 1956; Sonata for Solo Violoncello, 1993. *Recordings:* Symphony in Two Movements (No 1); Symphony No 2. *Honours:* Grand Priz, International Musical Competition, Queen Elisabeth of Belgium, 1969; Prize of the Romanian Academy, 1978; Prizes of the Union of Romanian Composers, 1955, 1972, 1978, 1979, 1985, 1987; Prize of the Romanian Ministry of Culture, 1971. *Membership:* Union of Romanian Composers. *Hobbies:* Sport; Fine arts. *Current Management:*Musical Edition of the Union of Romanian Composers, Calea Victoriei No 141, 71102 Bucharest 1, Romania. *Address:* Strada Olari No 7, 70317 Bucharest II, Romania.

BELSKAYA Nina, b. 1960, Moscow, Russia. Violist. *Eduction:* Studied at Moscow Conservatoire with Professor Strakhovos. *Career:* Member of the Prokofiev Quartet, founded at the Moscow Festival of World Youth and the International Quartet Competition at Budapest; Many concerts in the former Soviet Union and on tour to Czechoslovakia, Germany, Austria, USA, Canada, Spain, Japan and Italy; Repertoire includes works by Haydn, Mozart, Beethoven, Schubert, Debussy, Ravel, Tchaikovsky, Bartok and Shostaskovich. *Address:* c/o Sonata (Prokofiev Quartet), 11 Northgate Street, Glasgow G20 7AA, Scotland.

BELTON Ian, b. 1959, England, Violinist. *Education:* Studied at the Royal Northern College of Music; Diplomas and Degrees, BMus Manchester University; GRNCM and PPRNCM. *Career:* Founder member of the Brodsky String Quartet (name derives from violinist Adolph Brodsky, Principal of the Royal Manchester College of Music, 1895-1929); Resident at Cambridge University for four years and later residencies at Dartington International Summer School, Devon; Concert engagements include the Shostakovich quartets at the Elizabeth Hall, London and performances at the Ludwigsburg and Schleswig-Holstein Festivals; New York debut at the Metropolitan Museum; tours of Italy, North America, Australia, Poland, Czechoslovakia, Istanbul and Japan; Complete quartets of Schoenberg for the BBC; French concerts include visit to the Théâtre du Châtelet, Paris; Concert in Amsterdam; Performances at Berlin Festival, Carnegie Hall; Tour of Australia, 1993. *Recordings include:* Quartets of Elgar and Delius; Schubert A minor and Beethoven Op 74 (Harp); Complete quartets of Shostakovich (Teldec); Borodin quartet No 2 and Tchaikovsky quartet No 3 (Teldec); Collaboration with Elvis Costello entitled, Juliet Letters. *Address:* c/o Brodsky Quartet, 21-22 Old Steine, Brighton BN1 1EG, England.

BELYAEV Yevegeni, b. 1950, Crimea, Russia. Violinist. *Career:* Co-Fdr, the Rachmaninov Quartet, 1974, under the auspices of the Sochi State Philharmonic Society, Crimea; Many concerts in the former Soviet Union and from 1975-76, tours to Switzerland, Austria, Bulgaria, Norway and Germany; Participation in the 1976 Shostakovich Chamber Music Festival at Vilnius, and in festivals in Moscow and St Petersburg; Repertoire has included works by Haydn, Mozart, Beethoven, Bartok, Brahms, Schnittke, Shostakovich, Boris Tchaikovsky, Chalayev and Meyerovich. *Honours include:* (with the Rachmaninov Quarter) Prizewinner, 1st All-Union Borodin String Quarter Competition, 1987. *Address:* c/o Sonata (Rachmaninov Quartet), 11 Northgate Street, Glasgow G20 7AA, Scotland.

BEN-AMOTS Ofer, b. 20 Oct 1955, Haifa, Israel. Composer; Professor of Composition and Theory; Pianist. m. Laura Ben-Amots, 9 Sept 1990. *Education:* Tel-Aviv University, 1978-79; Conservatoire de Musique, Geneva, 1979-80; Nordrhein-Westfalen Hochschule für Musik, Detmold, 1980-86; University of Pennsylvania, 1987-91; PhD, Composition, 1991. *Career:* Story Nr 2, commissioned and performed by Festival de Musique, St Omer, France, 1983; Shtettl Songs, Merkin Hall, New York City, USA, 1988; Psalm 23 for voice, clarinet and percussion performed at Curtis Institute and The Painted Bride, Philadelphia. *Compositions:* Psalm 81 for mixed chorus; Yiddish opera, Fool's Paradise. *Contributions to:* Book reviews in Notes, The Quarterly Journal of the Music Library Association, in field of music theory, analysis and Jewish music, 1991. *Address:* 3802 Lancaster Avenue, Philadelphia, PA 19104, USA.

BEN-YOHANAN Asher, b. 22 May 1929, Kavala, Greece. Composer; Music Educator. m. Shoshana Zwibel, 1 son, 1 daughter. *Education:* Studied Oboe and Piano; Composition studies with Paul Ben-Haim, Israel, Aaron Copland, USA, and Luigi Nono, Italy; Studies with Gustave Reese and Jan La Rue, New York University Music Department, New York, USA; MMus, University of Michigan. *Career:* Compositions performed in Israel, Europe, USA and South America; Published by IMI, Tel Aviv; IMP (Israeli Music Publications), Jerusalem; Head, Music Department, Thelma Yellin Music and Arts School, Tel-Aviv, Israel, 1966-75; Professor of Music, Department of Musicology, Bar-Ilan University. *Compositions include:* Two Movements for Orchestra, 1959; String Quartet, 1962-64; Music for Orchestra, 1967; Chamber Music for 6, 1968; Quartetto Concertato, 1969; Mosaic, 1971; Concerto for String Orchestra, 1973; Four Summer Songs, 1974; Impressions for Piano, 1976; Soliloquy for Violin, 1977; Desert Winds, for Flute, 1979; Three Songs without Titles, 1983; Episode for trombone, 1984; Woodwind Quintet, 1985; Divertimento, for brass Trio, 1988-89; Hidden Feelings, for Harp, 1990. *Publications:* Music in Israel, A Short Survey, 1975; Music Notation, 1983. *Hobby:* Photography. *Address:* 4 Bloch Street, Tel-Aviv 64161, Israel.

BENACKOVA Gabriela, b. 25 March 1944, Bratislava, Czechoslovakia. Singer (Soprano). *Education:* Bratislava Academy with Janko Blaho and Tatiana Kiesakova. *Debut:* Prague National Theatre 1970, as Natasha in War and Peace; returned as Mimi, Marenka (The Bartered Bride), Jenůfa and Libuse in Smetana's opera (1983); Covent Garden 1979, as Tatiana in Eugene Onegin; Cologne Opera 1983, as Maddalena in Andrea Chénier; Vienna Staatsoper 1985, as Marguerite in a new production of Faust directed by Ken Russell; San Francisco 1986 as Jenůfa; Vienna Staatsoper 1987 as Rusalka; Sang Desdemona at Stuttgart, 1990, Leonore at the 1990 Salzburg Festival; Katya Kabanova at the Metropolitan, 1991; Season 1992 as Fidelio at Covent Garden. *Recordings:* Janáček's Jenůfa and The Cunning Little Vixen (Supraphon); The Bartered Bride; Libuse; Rusalka; Soloist in Janáček's Glagolitic Mass and Dvořák's Requiem. *Honours:* Prize winner, Janáček Competition, Luhacovice 1962; Winner, Dvořák Competition, Karlovy Vary 1963; Czech National Artist 1985. *Address:* c/o Lies Askonas Ltd, 186 Drury Lane, London WC2B 5QD, England.

BENARY Barbara, b. 7 Apr 1946, Bay Shore, New York, USA. Composer; Gamelan Performer. *Education:* Studied at Sarah Lawrence College, BA 1968, and at Wesleyan University, PhD in Ethnomusicology, 1973. *Career:* Has played the violin and performs on string instruments of India, China and Bulgaria; In 1974 built the Gamelan Son of Lion, and ensemble of Javanese instruments; Assistant professor at Livingstone College, Rutgers University, New Jersey, 1973-80. *Compositions include:* Music Theatre: Three Sisters who are not Sisters, 1967; The Only Jealousy of Emer, 1970; The Interior Castle, 1973; The Gauntlett, 1976; Sanguine, 1976; The Tempest, 1981; Dance scores Night Thunks, 1980, A New Pantheon, 1981 and Engineering, 1981; Gamelan: Convergance, 1975; Braid, 1975; No Friends in an Auction, 1976; In Time Enough, 1978; Sleeping Braid, 1978; The Zen Story, 1979; In Scroll of Leaves, 1980; Moon Cat Chant, 1980; Singing Braid, 1980; Solkattu, 1980; Sun Square, 1980; Exchanges, 1981; Hot-rolled Steel, 1984. *Address:* c/o ASCAP, ASCAP Building, One Lincoln Plaza, New York, NY 10023, USA.

BENCZÉNÉ MEZÖ, Judit (Dr), b. 16 May 1933, Szeghalom, Hungary. Professor; Teacher. m. Bencze László, 24 Jan 1953, 2 sons, 1 daughter. *Education:* Kossuth Lajos University, Debrecen, Doctorate of Ethnography, 1983; Musical Secondary School of Békés-Tarhos; Liszt Ferenc Academy of Music, Budapest; Choirmaster Diploma as the student of Zoltán Vásárhelyi, 1956. *Career:* Collecting folk music, 1952-following Kodály's, Jardanyi's lead; Learnt notation from Laszlo Lajtha; Broadcast Hungarian Radio for several folk-music, folk-dance groups; Makes folk-music programmes and writes up folk songs; Scientific and educational lectures and gives continuation courses; Professor; Teacher, Conservatoire of Debrecen, 1956-; Professor and Deputy Headmaster of Institute of Debrecen of the Liszt F Academy of Music, 1966-; Professor of the Teacher's Training Institute of Debrecen, 1982-. *Recordings:* Radio lectures about folk-music and 4 folk-song suites for singing voice and folk-music orchestra; 2 records: Hungarian Zither Music, Hungaroton; Hungarian Instrumental Folk Music, Hungaroton. *Publications include:* Dr Nagy József sárreti nepdalgyüjtése, folksongs of Sárrét, 1981; A ladanyi torony tetejebe, folk-songs of Hortobagy, 2nd edition, 1982; Szivarvanyos az eg alja, folksongs of Bihar, 2nd edition, 1982; Folk-music and folkdance in Békés, 1983; The Monograph of Village Csépa, 1984; Barand, 1985. *Contributions to:* Hungarian Academy of Folkmusic Department. *Hobbies:* Travel; Grandchildren.

BENELLI Ugo, b. 20 Jan 1935, Genoa, Italy. Singer (Tenor). *Education:* Studied with assistance of La Scala stipendium. *Debut:* Piccola Scala 1960. *Career:* Guest appearances in Wiesbaden, Buenos Aires, Barcelona, Mexico City and Rio de Janeiro; Wexford Festival, 1966; Glyndebourne Festival, 1970, in Il Turco in Italia; Covent Garden debut 1974, as Ernesto in Don Pasquale; Turin, 1975, in Die Drei Pintos by Weber/Mahler; Further engagements in Edinburgh, Moscow and San Francisco; Théâtre de la Monnaie Brussels, 1986, as Podestà in La Finta Giardiniera; Roles include Rossini's Almaviva, Lindoro, Don Ramiro and Giannetto, Bellini's Elvino, Donizetti's Nemorino and Tonio, Bizet's Nadir and Massenet's Des Grieux and Werther; Season 1992 as Conte Riccardo in I Quattro Rusteghi at Geneva, Don Anchise in La Finta Giardiniera at the Salzburg Festival and Mozart's Basilio at Florence. *Recordings include:* Il Barbiere di Siviglia and La Cenerentola (Decca); Don Pasquale and La Fille du Régiment (Deutsche Grammophon). *Address:* c/o Théâtre Royal de la Monnaie, 4 Léopoldstrasse, B-1000 Brussels, Belgium.

BENES Jiří, b. 24 Sept 1928, Komarno, Czechoslovakia. Viola Player; Musicologist. m. Zdenka Bubenickova, 1 son (by previous marriage), 1 daughter. *Education:* PhD, University of Brno, 1952; Graduate, Conservatory of Brno, 1953; Diploma, Janáček Academy of Musical Arts, 1958. *Debut:* As viola player, Brno, 1952. *Career:* State Philharmonic Orchestra, Brno, 1951-69; as dramaturg, 1992-; Moravian Quartet, 1965-92; Appearances on radio and television with Moravian Quartet, Czechoslovakia, Germany, Sweden, Italy; Tours of most European countries; Teacher, Conservatory of Brno, 1969-82; Janacel Academy, 1968-74. *Recordings:* Numerous chamber music records. *Contributions to:* Professional journals; Radio programme notes; Record sleeve notes; Other publications. *Honours:* Italian Quartet Prize, 1965; Janáček Medal, 1978; Prize of Novecento Musicale Europeo, Naples, 1988. *Memberships:* Czechoslovakian Musical (Janáček) Society. *Hobbies:* Running; Sledging. *Address:* Filipova 19, 635 00 Brno, Czech Republic.

BENES Juraj, b. 2 Mar 1940, Trnava, Czechoslovakia. Composer. *Education:* Piano with R Rychlo, Bratislava Conservatory, 1954-60; Composition under Jan Cikker, Academy of Music, Bratislava, 1960-66. *Career:* Repetiteur, Slovak National Theatre Opera, 1964-74; Lecturer, Music Theory: University of Bratislava, 1974-83; Academy of Music and Theatre, Bratislava, 1984-. *Compositions include:* 3 operas: Emperor's New Clothes, 1969; Petrified, 1974; The Feast, 1980; Orchestral works: Allegro, orchestra, 1974; Memoire, chamber orchestra, 1977; Music for trumpet, percussion, strings, 1978; Music for orchestra, 1982; Preludium, orchestra, 1983; Music for J S for orchestra, 1985; Music for trombone and orchestra, 1989; Chamber works: Divertimento per archi, 1970; Preference, ensemble, 1974; Musique pour Grock Nos 1, flute, guitar, 2, clarinet, violin, trombone, 3, violin, viola, cello, 1975; 3 Marches, wind and brass, 1975; Waltz for Colonel Brumble, ensemble, 1975; Intermezzo Nos 1, 6 flutes, 1976, 2, 12 cellos, 1979, 3, two pianos, 1987; In Memoriam Pavel Raska per 12 archi, 1981;

Events, string quartet, 1977; Canzona, wind quintet, 1977; Quartetto d'archi No 2, 1964; Quartetto d'archi No 3, 1989; Instrumental works: Sonatas Nos 1, 2, 3, 4, for piano, 1971, 1976, 1977, 1978; 1979; 1985. Branched Fingers, compositions for children, 1975; 6 dances, flute, 1975; Septem canones a 2, 1975; Matrimonial music, 2 pianos, 1976; Populacijo Hajkeles, pipe organ, 1976; Sonata, solo violin, 1976; Lamento, solo violin, 1979; Sonata per un clarinetto solo, 1981; Old Boys Anthology, piano suite, 1983; Sonata, solo cello, 1985; Vocal works: Various choral compositions and songs; 14 song cycles eg. Three Monodies, 1979; O Virtú mia, 1983; Il Sogno di Poppea, song cycle, 1984; Requiem, 1986. *Honours:* Prize for Three Monodes, Slovak Music Foundation, 1983; Prize for The Feast, Minister of Culture, 1984; Prize for Quartetto d'archo No 3, Slovak Music Foundation, 1989. *Address:* Palisady 18, 81106 Bratislava, Slovak Republic.

BENESTAD Finn, b. 30 Oct 1929, Kristiansand, Norway. Musicologist; Music Educator. *Education:* Violin lessons with Ernst Glaser, 1947-50; music courses, University of Oslo, MA, 1953, PhD, 1961. *Career:* Teacher, 1950-59, music critic, 1953-61; Professor of musicology, University of Trøndheim, 1961-64, University of Oslo, 1965-; chairman, collected works of Grieg. *Publications:* Johannes Haarklou: mannen og vberket, 1961; Waldemar Thrane: en pioner i norsk musikkliv, 1961; Musikklaere, 1963, 5th edition, 1977; Musikkhistorisk oversikt, 1965, 3rd edition, 1976; edited Norsk musikk: Studier i Norge, volume 6, 1968; edited Skolens visebok, 1972; with D Schjelderup-Ebbe, Edvard Grieg: Mennesket og kunstneren, 1980, English translation, 1987, as Edvard Grieg: The Man and the Artist; with Dag Sckjelderup-Ebbe: Johan Svendsen: Mennesket og kunstneren, 1990. *Contributions to:* Articles in various journals and in other publications. *Honours:* Fulbright scholar, University of California, Los Angeles, 1968-69; made a member, Norwegian Academy of Sciences and Letters, 1979. *Address:* Guldbergs vei 13 B, 0375 Oslo 3, Norway.

BENGL Volker, b. 19 July 1960, Ludwigshafen, Germany. Singer (Tenor). *Education:* Mannheim-Heidelberg Musikhochschule in Munich. *Career:* Sang at Saarbrucken from 1985; Guest appearances in Essen, Brunswick, Karlsruhe and Heidelberg; Sang Hans in The Bartered bride at Kaiserslautern, 1990; Other roles include Max in Der Freischütz, Tamino, Belfiore in La Finta Giardiniera, Don Jose, Pinkerton and parts in operetta; as concert singer appeared in New York, 1989, Berlin (Bruckner F minor Mass and Te Deum) and elsewhere in Europe; Other Repertoire includes Bach Christmas Oratorio and Dvořák Requiem. *Address:* c/o Saarlandisches Stadttheater, Schillerplatz 1, 6600 Saarbrucken, Germany.

BENGTSSON Erling Blondal, b. 1932. Copenhagen, Denmark. Cellist. *Education:* Studied with Piatigorsky, Curtis Institute, USA. *Debut:* First public concert aged 4. *Career:* Played first concerto with Orchestra at age 10; Professor of Cello, Curtis Institute, USA; Played with most of Europe's famous orchestras; Broadcast for the BBC and various European radio stations; Played in North America with distinguished conductors including: Monteux, Kletzki, Schmidt-Isserstedt, Sargent, Lutoslawski, Pritchard, Blomstedt, Dorati, Gibson, Groves, Ehrling and Berglund; Master classes at Aldeburgh and in Switzerland; Professor of Cello, Royal Danish Conservatory and State Academy in Cologne. *Recordings:* Beethoven and Brahms Sonatas, Bach Suites for solo cello, Haydn Concerto in D, Stravinsky Suite Italienne, Vivaldi Concertos (HMV and Danacord).

BENGUEREL Xavier, b. 9 Feb 1931, Barcelona, Spain. Composer. *Education:* Studied in Santiago and in Barcelona with Cristobal Taltabull. *Compositions include:* 2 Violin Sonatas, 1953, 1959; String Quarter, 1955; Concerto for piano and strings, 1955; Concerto for 2 flutes and strings, 1961; Sinfonia contunua, 1962; Successions for wind quintet, 1960; Duo for clarinet and piano, 1963; Nocturno for soprano, chorus and orchestra, 1963; Violin Concerto, 1965; Sinfonia per a un festival, 1966; Sinfonia for small orchestra, 1967; Paraules de Cada Dia for voice and chamber orchestra, 1967; Musica for 3 percussionists, 1967; Sinfonia per a Gran Orquestra, 1969; Dialogue orchestrale, 1969; Musica riservata for strings, 1969; Crescendo for organ, 1970; Organ Concerto, 1971; Arbor, cantata, 1972; Verses for guitar, 1973; Destructio for orchestra, 1973; Capriccio stravagante for ensemble, 1974; Thesis for chamber group; Concerto for percussion and orchestra, 1976. *Honours include:* Winner, Composition prize of the Barcelona Juventudes Musicales, 1955; Represented Spain at ISCM Festival, 1960. *Address:* SGAE (Spain), c/o Member Registration, PRS Ltd 29/33 Berners Street, London W1P 4AA, England.

BENHAM Helen W, b. 4 Dec 1941. Professor of Music. 1 d. *Education:* BA Oberlin College, 1963; BMus, Piano, Oberlin Conservatory of Music, 1962; MS Piano, The Julliard School; Diploma, The Diller Quaile School of Music. *Debut:* Duo at Carnegie Recital Hall, 1980. *Career:* Concert pianist and harpsichordist. Appearances as soloist and in ensembles throughout the US and Europe and in the Far East; Soloist with Hudson Valley Philarmonic and Monmouth Symphony Orchestra. *Publications:* Piano for the Adult Beginner, Book I, 1977, Book II, 1977. *Honours include:* American Keyboard Artists, 1989. *Memberships:* Mu Phi Epsilon; National Guild of Piano Teachers; Music Teachers National Association. *Current Management:* Albert Kay Associates. *Address:* 960 Elberon Avenue, Elberon, NJ 07740, USA.

BENJAMIN George, b. 31 Jan 1960, London, England. Composer; Conductor; Pianist. *Education:* Peter Gellhorn, 1974-76; with Olivier Messiaen at the Paris Conservatoire, 1976-78; with Alexander Goehr at King's College, Cambridge, 1978-82; Research at IRCAM, Paris, 1984-87. *Debut:* Redcliffe Concert, Purcell Room, London, 1979. *Career:* Youngest composer ever played at the BBC Promenade Concerts, 1980; works performed frequently at international festivals and by such orchestras as London Sinfonietta, London Philharmonic, BBC Symphony, Concertgebouw, New York Philharmonic, Toronto Symphony; BBC Television documentary profile, Omnibus, 1987; Artistic Director and Conductor of contemporary music festivals with San Francisco Symphony, 1992; Opera Bastille, 1992; South Bank, 1993; Visiting Professor of composition, Royal College of Music; Principal Guest Artist, Hallé Orchestra, 1993-. *Compositions:* Orchestral: Ringed by the Flat Horizon, 1979-80; A Mind of Winter, 1981; At First Light, 1982; Jubilation, 1985; Antara, (with electronics), 1985-87; Sudden Time, 1989-93; Tribute in Memory of Oliver Messiaen, 1993; Chamber; violin sonata, 1976-77; Octet, 1978; Flight for flute, 1979; Duo for cello and piano, 1980; Piano: Sonata, 1977-78; Sortilèges, 1981; 3 Studies: Fantasy on lambic Rhythm, Meditation on Haydn's Name, Relatively Rag, 1982-85; Upon Silence, mezzo and 5 viols, 1990; Mezzo and string ensemble, 1991. *Recordings:* Orchestral works on CD by Nimbus Records. *Honours:* Lili Boulanger Award, Boston, 1985; Koussevitsky International Record Award, New York, 1987; Grand Prix Charles Cros du Disque, Paris, 1988. *Current Management:* Allied Artists, 42 Montpelier Square, London, SW7 1JZ. *Address:* c/o Faber Music, 3 Queen Square, London, WC1N 3AU.

BENJAMIN Thomas Edward, b. 17 Feb 1940, Bennington, Vermont, USA. Composer; Professor. m. Elizabeth Klein, 15 Aug 1965, 1 son, 1 daughter. *Education:* BA, Bard College; MA, Harvard University; MFA Brandeis University; PhD, Eastman School of Music; studied with Carlos Surinach, Robert Moevs, Arthur Berger, Ernst Krenek, Bernard Rogers. *Career:* Professor of Composition and Theory, School of Music, University of Houston; Teacher of Composition, National Music Camp; Professor of Theory, Composition, Peabody Conservatory of Johns Hopkins University. *Compositions:* 25 published compositions; several recorded. *Recordings include:* Aperitif and Entertainments recorded by Mirecourt Trio on TR Records. *Publications:* The Craft of Modal Counterpoint

Schirmer Books, 1975; Counterpoint in the Style of JS Bach Schirmer Books, 1986; Techniques and Materials of Tonal Music (with Horvit and Nelson), Houghton Mifflin, 1975; Music for Analysis Houghton Mifflin, 1979; Music for Sight Singing Houghton Mifflin, 1985. *Address:* 6305 Blackburn Ct, Baltimore, MD 21212, USA.

BENNETT Elinor, b. 17 Apr 1943, Llanidloes, Wales. Harpist. m. Dafydd Wigley, 26 Aug 1967, 1 s. *Education:* LLB Hons, University College of Wales; Royal Academy of Music, London; Recital Diploma. *Debut:* Wigmore Hall, London. *Career:* Freelance Harpist with London Symphony Orchestra, Philharmonia, English Chamber Orchestra, 1967-71; Soloist and Recitalist, BBC Radio 3; HTV A Week in the Life of Elinor Bennett; BBC At Home (Richard Baker); Teacher and Director of Harp Festival. *Recordings:* Nimbus Records recording artist; Two Harps; With Harp and Voice; The Harp of Wales; Portrait of the Harp, 1988.*Honours:* Countess of Munster Musical Trust, 1964-66; Idloes Owen Prize; Incorporates Society of Musicians Prize, 1982; Churchill Fellow, 1985; Associate of the Royal Academy of Music, 1992. *Memberships:* Incorporated Society of Musicians' Solo Section. *Hobbies:* Politics; Swimming; Cycling; Art Appreciation; Poetry Reading. *Current management:* Caroline Ireland. *Address:* Hen Efail, Bontnewydd, Caernarfon, Gwynedd LL54 7YL, Wales.

BENNETT Richard Rodney, b. 29 Mar 1936, Broadstairs, Kent, England. Composer. *Education:* Leighton Park School, Reading; Royal Academy of Music, London and under Pierre Boulez, Paris. *Career:* Commissioned to write two operas by Sadler's Wells, 1962; Professor of Composition, Royal Academy of Music, 1963-65; Vice-President, Royal College of Music, 1983-. *Compositions:* The Approaches of Sleep, 1959; Journal, Calendar, Winter Music, 1960; The Ledge, Suite Francaise, Oboe Sonata, 1961; Nocturnes, London Pastoral, Fantasy, 1962; Aubade, Jazz Calendar, String Quartet No Four, Five Studies, 1964; Symphony No 1, 1965; Epithalamion, 1966; Symphony No 2, 1967; Wind Quintet, Piano Concerto, 1968; Jazz Pastoral, 1969; Oboe Concerto, 1970; Guitar Concerto, 1971; Viola Concerto, 1973; Commedia I-IV, 1972-73, Spells (choral), 1975; Serenade for Youth Orchestra, 1977; Concerto for Orchestra, 1973; Violin Concerto, 1975; Zodiac for orchestra, 1976; Acteon for horn and orchestra, 1977; Music for Strings, 1977; Double-Bass Concerto, 1978; Sonnets to Orpheus for cello and orchestra, 1979; Harpsichord Concerto, 1980; Anniversaries, 1982; Momento for flute and strings, 1983; Sinfonietta, 1984; Moving into Aquarius; Concerto for Wind Quintet, 1983; Reflections on a Theme of William Walton for 11 solo strings, 1985; Dream Dancing for 13 players, 1986; Symphony No 3, 1987; Clarinet Concerto, 1987; Marimba Concerto, 1988; Saxophone Concerto, 1988; Diversions, 1989; Percussion Concerto, 1990; Five Sonnets for Louise Labé for soprano and 11 players, 1984; Love songs for tenor and orchestra, 1984; Ophelia for countertenor and ensemble, 1987; Chamber and instrumental music. Opera: The Mines of Sulphur, 1964, A Penny for a Song, 1966, Victory, 1969, All the King's Men (childrens opera), 1969; Isadora (ballet), 1981; Film Music; TV music. *Honours:* Arnold Bax Society Prize for Commonwealth Composers, 1964; Anthony Asquith Memorial Award for Murder on the Orient Express film music, Society of Film and TV Awards, 1974. *Membership:* General Council, Performing Rights Society, 1975-. *Hobbies:* Cinema; Modern Jazz. *Address:* c/o London Management, Regent House, 235-241 Regent Street, London W1, England.

BENNETT Stephen Sydney, b. 29 Apr 1945, California, USA. *Education:* Art Centre College of Deisgn, Los Angeles; San Francisco Academy of Art; Private tutors around the world and self taught in music. *Debut:* Wigmore Hall, England, 1980; American Debut, 1976; German Debut, 1977; French Debut, 1978. *Career includes:* Orchestral performances since age 13; Member of professional orchestras in USA Germany, France and England. Solo career began with Nielsen

Concerto, 1966; Principal Clarinettist and Soloist, American Youth Symphony Expo 1967, Montreal, Canada; Founder, Westwind (woodwind quintet), 1966; Alban Trio, (Soprano, clarinet, piano), 1977; Philomela Trio, 1977; Philomela Ensemble, 1980; Concerto and Chamber Music recitals for BBC; Teaches own method of pedagogics. *Compositions:* Film and TV sound tracks. *Publications:* Discovered, edited and published, Dreii Phantasiestucke by August Henrik Winding, Op. 19, 1872; Contributor to: The Clarinet, Clarinet and Saxophone, articles and illustration. *Hobbies:* Painting; Reading; Writing; Photography. *Current Management:* Clarinet Heritage Society, 915 Chula Vista Avenue, Burlingame, CA 94010, USA; J Audrey Ellison International Artists Management, 135 Stevenage Road, London SW6 6PB, England. *Address:* 47 Hambalt Road, London SW4 9EQ, England.

BENNINGSEN Lilian, b. 17 July 1924, Vienna, Austria. Singer (Contralto). *Education:* Studied in Vienna with Anna Bahr-Mildenburg. *Debut:* Salzburg Landestheater, 1948. *Career:* Sang with Cologne Opera, 1950-52; Munich Staatsoper from 1951, as Eboli in Don Carlos, Fricka, Carmen, Amneris, Octavian, Dorabella and Marcellina in Le Nozze di Figaro; Covent Garden, 1953, in the British premiere of Strauss's Die Liebe der Danae, with the Munich company; Salzburg Festival, 1955, in the premiere of Egk's Irische Legende; Schwetzingen Festival, 1961, in the premiere of Henze's Elegie für junge Liebende; Widely heard in recital and concert. *Recordings:* Le Nozze di Figaro; Magdalene in Die Meistersinger conducted by Keilberth; Ariadne auf Naxos; Die tote Stadt by Korngold.

BENOIT Jean-Christophe, b. 18 Mar 1925, Paris, France. Singer (Bass-Baritone). *Education:* Studied at the Paris Conservatoire. *Career:* Sang in the French provinces, thena at the Paris Opera and Opera-Comique; Guest appearances in Geneva for the premieres of Monsieur de Pourceaugnac by Martin, 1963 and Milhaud's La Mere Ccoupable, 1966; Aix-en- Province Festival, 1954-7; Salzburg Festival 1956, La Scala Milan, 1958; Further engagements at the Holland Festival, Monte Carol and Brussels; Best known as Mozart's Guglielmo and Antonio, Rossini's Basilio, Rambaud in Le Comte Ory, Somarone in Beatrice et Benedict, Bonifact in Le Jongleur de notre Dame and Troquemada in L'Heure Espagnole; Professor of Singing at the Paris Conservatoire. *Recordings include:* Carmen; Platee (Pathe); Lakme, Les Contes d'Hoffmann and Il Barbiere di Siviglia (EMI); Les Indes Galantes (CBS); Paer's Le Maitre de Chapelle (Barclay). *Address:* c/o Conservatoire National de Musique, 14 Rue de Madrid, F-75008, Paris, France.

BENOLIEL Bernard, b. 25 Sept 1943, Detroit, USA. Composer. *Education:* University of Michigan, 1961-64; Private Tuition, Stefan Wolpe, 1968-69. *Career:* Administrator, Secretary, Ralph Vaughan Williams Trust, 1978-; Director, RVW Limited, 1983-. *Compositions:* Op I, Eternity Junctions for chorus; Op 2, The Black Tower; Op 3, Two Movements for Piano after Thomas Mann's Doktor Faustus; Op 4, the After-War; The Into Light for chorus & organ; Op 5, Symphony; Op 6 With St Paul in Albion for amplified cello & organ; Op 7, String Quartet; Op 8, Infinity-Edge, amplified violin, organ, chorus and orchestra; Op 9 Three Movements for Piano after Géricault's Fragments Anatomiques; Op 10 Eternity-Junctions second sequence for small chorus and five instruments. *Contributions to:* Tempo; Music & Musicians. *Hobbies:* Psychology; Philosophy; Literature; Visual Arts; Travel. *Address:* Flat 2, 13 Nevern Square, London SW5, England.

BENSON Clifford George, b. 17 Nov 1946, Grays, Essex, England. Concert Pianist. m. 1 Sept 1973, 2 daughters. *Education:* ARCM Performance Diploma, 1964; Studied piano with Lamar Crowson and Cyril Smith, Royal College of Music, London, and privately with George Malcolm, 1964-69; Studied composition with Herbert Howells. *Debut:* Royal Festival Hall, London, 1970. *Career:* Performed, recordings and broadcasts, BBC Radio 3, 1969-; Soloist, Royal Albert Hall Promenade concerts, 1975; Travelled extensively playing at many major music festivals; Numerous recitals, solo and chamber music, also concertos; Duos with Thea King, William Bennett and Levon Chilingirian. *Compositions:* 3 Pieces for Piano, 1983; Mozart Goes to Town (piano duet), 1985. *Recordings:* CRD; Deutsche Grammophon; CBS; Hyperion. *Honours:* Chopin Sonata Prize, Royal College of Music, 1966; Tagore Gold Medal, Royal College of Music, 1969; BBC Beethoven Duo Competition, 1969, Munich International Duo Competition, 1971 (with violinist Levon Chilingirian); Martin Musical Scholarship, NPO, 1968. *Memberships:* Incorporated Society of Musicians; Royal College of Music Union. *Hobbies:* Swimming; Tennis; Snooker; Yoga. *Address:* 76 Quarry Hill Road, Tonbridge, Kent TN9 2PE, England.

BENSON Joan, b. 1935, St Paul, Minnesota, USA. Concert Artist on clavichord and fortepiano; Lecturer. *Education:* Masters of Music, University of Illinois; Performer's Award, University of Indiana; Protegée of Edwin Fischer, Switzerland; Studies in clavichord music with Fritz Neumeyer, Germany, Santiago Kastner, Portugal; Advanced study in Vienna, Paris, Italy and Germany. *Career:* Concerts, lectures and appearances in Festivals and on TV and radio throughout USA, Europe, Near and Far East; Lecturer in Music, Stanford University, 1970-76; Assistant Professor of Music, 1976-82, Adjunct Professor, 1982-87, University of Oregon. *Recordings:* Music by Kuhnau and CPE Bach, clavichord, 1988; Haydn & Pasquini on Boston Museum of Fine Arts clavichords, 1982; CPE Bach on clavichord and fortepiano, 1972; Music for Clavichord, 1962. *Contributions to:* Articles: Haydn and the Clavichord, International Haydn Congress, Vienna, 1982; Gulbenkian Society, Portugal, The Clavichord in 20th Century America, 1989; American Liszt Society Journal, Edwin Fischer, 1985; Clavier Magazine, Bach and the Clavier, 1990. *Hobbies:* Sea; Mountains. *Current Management:* Marla Lowen. *Address:* School of Music, University of Oregon, Eugene, OR 97403, USA.

BENT Ian David, b. 1 Jan 1938, Birmingham, England. University Teacher. m. Caroline Coverdale, 27 Aug 1979, 2 sons, 1 daughter. *Education:* St John's College, Cambridge, 1958-65; BA Music Tripos (1st class), 1961; MusB, 1962; MA, 1965; PhD, 1969; ARCO, 1958. *Career:* Lecturer in Music, King's College, University of London, 1965-75; Senior Consulting Editor, The New Grove Dictionary of Music, 1970-80; Professor of Music, University of Nottingham, 1975-87; Visiting Professor, Harvard University, USA, 1982-83; Visiting Professor, Columbia University, 1986-87; Professor, Columbia University, 1987-. *Publications:* The Early History of the English Chapel Royal, 1066-1327, 1969; Source Materials and the Interpretation of Music: A Memorial Volume to Thurston Dart, 1981; Analysis, 1987; Music Analysis in the Nineteenth Century, 2 vols, 1993-94. *Contributions to:* Journal of the American Musicological Society; Music Analysis; Musical Times; Music and Letters; Proceedings of the Royal Musical Association; Theoria; General Editor: Cambridge Studies in Music Theory and Analysis. *Memberships:* American Musicological Society; Royal Musical Association; Society for Music Theory; International Musicological Society. *Hobbies:* Gardening; Reading. *Address:* Columbia University, New York, NY 10027, USA.

BENT Margaret (Hilda), b. 23 Dec 1940, St Albans, England. Musicologist. m. Ian Bent. *Education:* Studied at Girton College, Cambridge, PhD 1969. *Career:* Taught at Cambridge, King's College London, 1965-75 and Goldsmiths' College, from 1972; Teacher at Brandeis University, 1975-81, and Princeton, from 1981; Researched Old Hall MS under Thurston Dart at Cambridge and published study with Andrew Hughes; President of the American Musicological Society, 1983. *Publications include:* The Old Hall Manuscript in the Corpus Mensurabilis Musicae series, XLVI, (1969-73); Dunstaple, (London, 1981); articles on John Dunstable, Notation, Old Hall MS, Leonel Power and Square in

the New Grove Dictionary of Music and Musicians, 1980.

BENTLEY Andrew, b. 30 June 1952, Fleetwood, England. Composer; Computer Music Researcher. m. Anna-Kaarina Kiviniemi, 9 Aug 1975, 2 sons. *Education:* BA, Honours; DPhil, Composition, University of York, England. *Career:* Designer, Electronic Music Studio, Finnish Radio Experimental Studio, 1976-84; Teacher, Sibelius Academy, Helsinki, 1981-82; Studio Director, Helsinki University, 1982-84; Lecturer, Salford College of Technology, 1985-86; Director, Composers Desktop Project, York, 1986-; Leverhulme Computer Music Fellow, University of Nottingham, 1987-. *Compositions:* Tribal Drum, 1976; Carillon, 1977; Bowing, 1979; Portrait, 1979; Modulo, 1979; Contact with Bronze, 1979; Zoologic, 1980; Winter Winters, 1980; Aerial Views, 1981; Time for Change, 1981; Divertimento, 1983; Small Print, 1983. *Contributions to:* Electronic Music for Schools, 1984; Professional journals. *Honours:* Bourges International EAM Competition, 1979; Luigi Russolo Competition, 1979. *Address:* Leankatu 4 B 13, Helsinki 00240, Finland.

BENTLEY Keith, b. 27 June, 1946, Middlesbrough, England. Pianist; Conductor; Lecturer; m. Julie Andrews, 19 Dec 1970, 2 s. *Education:* Royal Manchester College of Music, 1962-69; ARMCM (Piano): GRSM (Special merit in performance): ARCM (Piano performer): LRAM (Singing teacher). *Debut:* Pianist, BBC Radio, 1962. *Career:* Founder and Conductor, Manchester Opera Company, 1969; Chorusmaster, Yorkshire Opera, 1967-72; Conductor, Cleveland Opera, 1972-77; Senior Lecturer, Cleveland Technical College, 1970; Director, Redcar Junior college of Music, 1976; Adjudicator, major competitive festivals; Toured widely as solo pianist; Conductor, Cleveland Youth Opera, 1985-; Warden, Incorporate Society of Musicians, 1989; Chairman of N Yorkshire Centre, 1990-; Music Director, Cleveland Youth Opera, 1986- . *Address:* 201 Roseberry Road, Redcar, Cleveland TS10 4AP, England.

BENTZON Niels Viggo, b. 24 Aug 1919, Copenhagen, Denmark. Composer. *Education:* Piano tuition from his mother, Karen Bentzon; Royal Danish Conservatoire. *Debut:* Pianist from Soloist Class, Royal Danish Conservatoire, 1943. *Career:* Notable Pianist, performing in Denmark and throughout Europe. *Compositions include:* Opera Faust III, 1964; 7 ballets; Piano Sonatas Numbers 1-22; The Tempered Clavier, numbers 1-6; Toccata, for piano; Woodcuts, for piano; Kaleidoscope, for piano; 10 Small preludes; Paganini Variations, for piano; Prelude, Intermezzo and Fugue, for organ; Mimosas, for organ; Pezzo for 12 pianos; Chamber Music: Sonata for cello solo; Variations of the Volga Boatmen; 11 String Quartets 1940-76; Sonata No 7; Square Root 3, for violin and piano; Maximilian 1, Suite for violin and piano; Suite for cello and piano; Sextet for flute, oboe, clarinet, horn, bassoon and piano; Quartetto Sonare for recorder, oboe, gamba and spinet; Sonata for 12 instruments; In the Zoo, for accordion solo; Orchestra: 15 Symphonies 1942-48; Symphonic Variations; Pezzi Sinfonici; 5 Mobiles; Eastern gasworks No 2; Concertos: 8 for Piano, 1947-82; 4 Violin Concertos, 1951-76; 3 Cello Concertos 1956, 1973, 1982; Flute Concerto, No 2; Oboe Concerto; Clarinet Concerto. *Recordings:* Has had much of his work recorded. *Publications:* Kompositioner, 1980. *Address:* c/o KODA, Rosenvaengets Hovedvej 14, 2100 Copenhagen, Denmark.

BENZI Roberto, b. 12 Dec 1937, Marseilles, France. Conductor. m. Jane Rhodes. *Education:* Studied music from age of 3; Baccalaureat, Sorbonne, Paris; Studied with Andre Cluytens 1947-50. *Debut:* Bayonne, 1948. *Career:* Conducted the Concerts Colonne in Paris, Nov 1948; Appeared in films Prelude à la Gloire, 1949, and L'Appel du Destin, 1950; Debut as opera conductor, 1954; Conducted Carmen at the Paris Opéra, 1959; Tours to Japan (1961), central Europe and North and South America; US debut, 1971; Metropolitan Opera, 1972, Faust; Musical Director of the Orchestre Regional de Bordeaux-Aquitaine, 1973-87. *Compositions:* Orchestrations of the Brahms Variations Op 23 and Op 24, 1970, 1973. *Recordings:* Many works with the London Symphony Orchestra, Lamoureux and Paris Opéra, Hague Philharmonic, Budapest Philharmonic; including Beethoven and Rossini overtures, Chopin's 1st Piano Concerto, Magaloff, Bizet's symphony, Liszt's Faust symphony, Cello Concertos by Lalo and Saint-Saëns, Gendron. *Honours:* Chevalier de l'Ordre National; Chevalier de la Legion d'Honneur. *Hobbies:* Cycling; Zoology.

BERBIÉ Jane, b. 6 May 1934, Ville-franche-de-Lauraguais, Toulouse, France. Singer (Mezzo-Soprano). *Education:* Studied at the Toulouse Conservatory. *Career:* After debut in 1958 sang at La Scala 1960, in L'Enfant et les Sortlièges; Glyndebourne Festival, 1969-71, 1983-84, as Despina in Così fan Tutte; London Coliseum in the British premiere (concert) of Roussel's Padmâvatî; Aix-en-Provence, 1969-70, in operas by Rossini; Salzburg Festival, 1974, as Marcellina in Le Nozze di Figaro; Paris Opéra from 1975, as Zerlina and in Das Rheingold and Jenůfa; Guest appearances in Tokyo, Munich, London, Cologne and Milan (Rosina in Il Barbiere di Siviglia); Other roles include Concepcion in L'Heure Espagnole, Orsini in Lucrezia Borgia, Cherubino and Ascanio in Benvenuto Cellini; Salzburg Festival, 1988 as Mozart's Marcellina; Sang Annina in Der Rosenkavalier at the Théâtre des Champs Elysées, Paris, 1989; Teatro San Carlos, Lisbon, as the Marquise in La Fille du Régiment, 1989. *Recordings include:* Benvenuto Cellini, conducted by Colin Davis (Philips); Così fan Tutte (Decca); L'Enfant et les Sortlièges (Decca); Il Turco in Italia (CBS); Massenet's Cendrillon. *Honours include:* Grand Prix, Toulouse Conservatory. *Address:* c/o Théâtre des Champs Elysées, 15 Avenue Montaigne, F-75008 Paris, France.

BERESFORD Hugh, b. 17 Dec 1925, Birkenhead, England. Singer (Baritone and Tenor). *Education:* Royal College of Music, Manchester; Vienna Music Academy; Studied with Dino Borgioli and Alfred Piccaver. *Debut:* Linz 1953, as Wolfram in Tannhäuser. *Career:* Sang in Graz, Augsburg and Wuppertal; Member of the Deutsche Oper am Rhein Dusseldorf from 1960; Guest appearances at Covent Garden, Vienna, Munich, Stuttgart, Cologne, Brussels and Paris; Holland Festival, 1963, 1966; Venice, 1966, as Mandryka in Arabella; Sang further as Rigoletto, Posa in Don Carlos and Don Giovanni; Later career as tenor: Otello and Florestan at the Vienna Staatsoper, 1973, Tannhäuser at Bayreuth, 1972-73; Cologne Opera, 1981 as Florestan and Erik in Der fliegende Holländer. *Address:* c/o Oper der Stadt Köln, Offenbachplatz, D-5000 Cologne, Germany.

BERG Nathan, b. 1968, Saskatchewan, Canada. Singer (Baritone). *Education:* Augustana University, Alberta; University of Western Ontario; Maitrise Nationale de Versailles; Guildhall School with Vera Rozsa. *Career:* Sang Thesee in Rameau's Hippolyte, Peter Quince, Mr Page, Dr Falke and Eustachio in Donizetti's L'assedio di Calais at the Guildhall, Guglielmo & Figaro (Mozart) with British Youth Opera, various appearances and recordings with William Christie, Colin Davis, Yan Pascal, Tortellier, John Lubbock; Future appearances in Monteverdi's Poppea at the Netherlands Opera, Schaunard at Canadian Opera Company, recital debut at the Wigmore Hall, London, and various Oratorio and recital work. *Honours include:* Prize winner, Peter Pears, Kathleen Ferrier, Walter Gruner and Royal Overseas League competitions. *Address:* IMG Artists, Media House, 3 Burlington Lane, London W4 2TH, England.

BERGANZA Teresa, b. 16 Mar 1935, Madrid, Spain. Opera Singer. m. (1) Felix Lavilla, 1957, (2) Jose Rifa, 1986; 1 son, 2 daughters. *Education:* Bachillerato; Conservatorio, Madrid. *Debut:* Aix-en-Provence, France, 1957, as Mozart's Dorabella. *Career:* Appeared in: Così fan Tutte and Le Nozze di Figaro, Mozart; La Cenerentola, Italiana in Algeri, Barbiere di Siviglia by Rossini; Carmen - Bizet; Werther - Massenet; Orpheo-Gluck; British

debut Glyndebourne, 1958, as Mozart's Cherubino; at Covent Garden she has appeared as Rossini's Rosina and Cinderella and Bizet's Carmen; Sang in the opening concert of Bastille Opera at Paris, 13 July 1989; Carmen at the Palais Omnisports, Paris, 1989; Sang Carmen at Madrid, 1992. Film: Don Giovanni, directed by Losey. *Recordings:* About 120 records by various record companies; including Le Nozze di Figaro, Il Barbiere di Siviglia, Alcina, La Clemenza di Tito and L'Italiana in Algeri (HMV/EMI); La Finta Semplice by Mozart; Don Giovanni (CBS). *Publications:* Meditaciones de Una Cantante, Madrid, 1985. *Honours:* Medalla de Oro Merito Bellas Artes; Commandeur aux Arts et Letres; Grand Prix de Disque, 6 times; Grand Prix Rossini. *Hobbies:* Montañismo; Cycling; Biographical Books; Japanese Culture. *Current Management:* Musiespana, c/Zurbamo, 34, 28101 Madrid, Spain. *Address:* Apdo 137, 28200 SLD Escotial, Madrid, Spain.

BERGE Sigurd, b. 1 July 1929, Vinstra, Norway. Composer. *Education:* Studied with Thor Lief Eken at the Oslo Conservatory and with Finn Mortensen; Course in Electronic Music, in Stockholm and Utrecht. *Career:* Tutor, Sagene College of Education, from 1959. *Compositions include:* Episode for violin and piano, 1958; Divertimento for violin, viola and cello, 1956; Raga, concerto for oboe and orchestra, 1959-76; Sinus for strings and percussion 1961; Pezzo rochestrale 1958; Tamburo piccolo for strings and percussion 1961; Chroma for Orchestra, 1963; A for orchestra, 1965; B for orchestra, 1966; Yang Guan for wind quintet 1967; Ballet for 2 dancers and percussion, 1968; 1970; Horn Call, 1972; Between Mirrors for violin and chamber orchestra, 1977; Juvenes, amateur string orchestra, 1977; Music for orchestra, 1978; Gudbrandsdalsspelet, music drama 1980; Wind ballet, 1981; Music for 4 horns, 1984; Electronic pieces. *Membership:* Chairman, Norwegian Composers Union, 1985-88. *Address:* c/o PRS Ltd 29/33 Berners Street (Member Registration), London W1P 4AA, England

BERGEL Erich, b. 1 June 1930, Rosenau, Romania. Conductor. *Education:* Sibiu and Cluj Consevatorie. *Debut:* US, Houston Symphony Orchestra, 1975. *Career:* Played flute in the Sibiu Philharmonic Orchestra, 1945-48; Studied further in Cluj with Ciolan, 1950-55 and was conductor of the Oradea Philharmonic 1955-59, Cluj Philharmonic, 1959-72; Musical Director of the Nordwestdeutsche Philharmonie, 1972-74; Principal Guest Conductor, Houston Symphony Orchestra, 1979-81; Directed the BBC Welsh Symphony Orchestra at Cardiff and has been Professor of Conducting at the Berlin Hochschule fur Musik. *Publications include:* Bach's Art of Fuge (volume 1), Bonn, 1979. *Address:* c/o BBC Welsh Symphony Orchestra, Broadcasting House, Landaff, Cardiff CF5 2YQ, Wales.

BERGEN Beverly, b. 1950, New Zealand. Singer (Soprano/Mezzo-soprano). *Education:* Studied at London Opera Centre. *Career:* Has appeared as guest artist at the Deutsche Oper Berlin and in Hamburg, Dusseldorf and elsewhere in Germany; Sang in premiere of Maderna's Hyperion at Brussels; Operatic roles include Constanze, Jenůfa, Strauss's Countess, Katerina in Lady Macbeth of Mtsensk, Senta, Luisa Miller, Violetta, Musetta and Lucia di Lammermoor; Has performed throughout Australia in Messiah, Beethoven's Ninth and Das Klagende Lied by Mahler; Other repertoire includes Mozart's Requiem, The Trojans and Bruckner's Te Deum, with the Sydney Symphony Orchestra; Judas Maccabeus with St Hedwig's Cathedral Choir in Berlin; John McCabe's Notturni ed Alba with the Melbourne Symphony Orchestra; Changed to mezzo-soprano repertoire 1989 and appeared as Amneris in Aida; Engagements with Opera Factory, London. *Address:* c/o Opera Factory/London Sinfonietta, 8a The Leather Market, Weston Street, London SE1 3ER, England.

BERGER Arthur Victor, b. 15 May 1912, New York City, USA. Composer; Critic; Educator. m. Ellen Philipsborn Tessman, 8 Dec 1967. *Education:* BS, New York University, 1934; MA, Harvard University, 1936;

Longy School, Cambridge, 1934-36; Ecole Normale de Musique, Boulanger, 1937-39. *Career:* Performances of orchestral works with New York Philharmonic (Mitropoulos), Boston Symphony (Munch, Leinsdorf) and others; I G Fine Professor Emeritus, Brandeis University; member, Composition Faculty, New England Conservatory; Music Critic, NY Herald Tribune, 1946-53; Founding Editor, Perspectives of New Music. *Compositions include:* Published & Recorded: Two Episodes for piano, 1933; Quartet in C Major, for woodwinds, 1941; Partita for piano, 1947; Intermezzo for piano, 1948; Duos for violin and piano, No 1, 1948, No 2, 1950; Duo for Cello and piano, 1951; Polyphony for orchestra, 1956; Chamber Music for Thirteen Players, 1956; String Quartet, 1958; Three Pieces for Two Pianos, 1961; Five Pieces for piano, 1969; Septet, 1966; Trio for guitar, violin and piano, 1972; 5 songs for Tenor, 1979; Trio for violin, cello and piano, 1980; Wind Quintet, 1984; Ode of Ronsard for soprano, 1987; numerous other works published and in manuscript, including: Serenade Cemertaute, 1951; Ideas of Order (for ochestra), 1952; Perspectives II for 15 players, 1985; Diptych (Pierrot ensemble), 1990; Collage III (Pierrot ensemble and percussion), 1992. *Publications:* Author: Aaron Copland, Oxford University Press, 1953. *Contributor to:* The Book of Modern Composers, 1942; Culture for the Millions?; Mass Media in Modern Society, 2nd edition, 1964; Aesthetic Analysis, 1967; Atlantic Brief Lives, 1971; Charles Ives Remembered: An Oral History, 1974; Musical Mercury: Modern Music; Perspectives on Schoenberg and Stravinsky, 1972; numerous professional journals. *Current Management:* Rosalie Calabrese Management, 170 West 74th Street, New York, NY 10023, USA. *Address:* Brandeis University, Music Dept, Waltham, MA 02254, USA.

BERGER Helmut, b. 9 Oct 1941, Vienna, Austria. Singer (Bass). *Education:* Studied at Vienna Conservatory. *Career:* Sang in South America 1967 as Bass-buffo, notably as Falstaff in Die lustigen Weiber von Windsor; Klagenfurt Opera 1968; sung at the Staatsoper, Hanover from 1971; Guest appearances in Hamburg, Stuttgart, Frankfurt, Berlin, Dusseldorf and elsewhere in Germany; Rio de Janeiro, Aarhus (Denmark), Copenhagen, Teheran, Zurich, Graz, Salzburg, Palermo; Repertoire includes Strauss's Waldner, Dr Bartolo (Rossini and Mozart), Wagner's Daland, Varlaam in Boris Godunov, Mozart's Leporello, Commendatore and the Speaker; Don Pasquale, Gianni Schicchi, Dulcamara and Melitone in La Forza del Destino. *Address:* Steinstrasse 10, D-3160 Lehrte, Germany.

BERGER Karol, b. 26 Oct 1947, Bytom, Poland. Musicologist. *Education:* PhD, Yale University, USA, 1975. *Career:* Assistant Professor, Boston University, 1975-82; Associate Professor, Stanford University, 1982-90; Professor, Stanford University, 1990. *Publications:* Theories of Chromatic and Enharmonic Music in Late 16th Century Italy, 1980; Musica Ficta, 1987. *Contributions to:* Shakespeare Studies; Musical Quarterly; Musica Disciplina; The Journal of Musicology; Revue Belge de Musicologie. *Honours:* The Otto Kinkeldey Award of the American Musicological Society, 1988; Research Fellow, Alexander von Humbolt Foundation, 1988-89; Fellow, American Council of Learned Societies, 1992-93. *Memberships:* International Musicological Society; American Musicological Society. *Address:* Department of Music, Stanford University, Stanford, CA 94305, USA.

BERGER Roman, b. 9 Aug 1930, Cieszyn, Poland. Composer. m. Ruth Strbova 6 July 1968. *Education:* Academy of Musical Arts, Katowice, 1949-52; Academy of Musical Arts Bratislava, 1952-56, 1960-65. *Career:* Professor of piano, Conservatoire, Bratislava, 1955-66; Fellow, TV sound laboratory, 1966-67; Secretary, Union of Slovak composers, 1967-69; Lecturer on theory of composition, contemporary music and electronic music, Academy of musical arts, Bratislava, 1969-71, 1983-85; Contracted to Musicological Institute of the Slovak Academy of Sciences, 1977-91. *Compositions:*

Transformations, 4 symphonic pieces, 1965; Memento for orchestra, 1974; Epitaph to Copernicus for electronics, 1973; De Profundis for bass, piano, cello and electronics, 1980; Exodus for organ, 1982. *Publications:* On Music Integration, 1976; System Theory and Musical Communication, 1981; Museum and Utopy, 1985; Theory Wrongly Present, 1989; Velvet Revolution and Music, 1990. *Honours:* Prizes in composition at Bourges, 1974; Herder Prize, 1988; Prize of Czechosl Critics, 1967, 1990. *Address:* Borzovského 11/17, SR 841 01, Bratislava, Slovak Republic.

BERGER Wilhelm Georg, b. 4 Dec 1929, Rupea, Rumania. Composer. *Education:* Bucharest Conservatory, 1948-52. *Career:* Viola player, Bucharest Philharmonic, 1948-57; Secretary, Rumanian Composers Union, 1968. *Compositions include:* Viola sonata, 1953; 15 String Quartets, 1954-83; Oratprio Stefan Furtuna, 1958; Nonet, 1957; Symphonic Variations, 1958; Concerto for String orchestra, 1958; Sonata for solo violin, 1963; 17 symphonies, 1960-86; 2 Viola concertos, 1960-62; Rhapsodic Images for orchestra, 1964; Violin Concerto, 1965; Cello Concerto, 1967; Meditations for chamber orchestra, 1968; Variations for wind orchestra, 1968; Concerto for Two Violas and orchestra, 1968; Concert Music for Fute, strings and percussion, 1972; Quintet for strings and piano, 1968; Concerto for violin, viola and orchestra, 1977; Faust, dramatic symphony, 1981; Concerto for solo organ, 1981; Horia symphonic poem, 1985; 7 Serious Pieces for string quartet, 1986; Songs. *Honours include:* Winner, Concerto Category, Queen Elizabeth of Belgium Composition Contest, 1966. *Address:* c/o Rumanian Composer's Union, Bucharest, Rumania.

BERGER-TUNA Helmut, b. 7 May 1942, Vienna, Austria. Singer (Bass). *Education:* Studied in Vienna with Franz Schuch-Tovini. *Debut:* Linz 1969, as Lodovico in Otello. *Career:* Sang at Graz from 1972; Guest engagements in Vienna, Frankfurt, Karlsruhe and Barcelona; Stuttgart 1981, as Ochs in Der Rosenkavalier; Sang at the Salzburg Festival 1981, in the premiere of Cerha's Baal; Hamburg 1983, in a concert performance of Rudi Stephan's Die ersten Menschen; Paris Opéra 1984, as Ochs; Often herard in operas by Mozart, Rossini, Donizetti, Verdi, Smetana and Strauss; Sang Baron Ochs and Kecal in The Bartered Bride at the Zurich Opera, 1988; Don Magnifico in La Cerentola at Stuttgart, 1989, followed by Kecal in 1990; Sang the Priest in Lady Macbeth of the Mtsensk District, 1992; Other roles include Osmin (La Scala, Paris, Frankfurt and Japan), Hunding (Covent Garden), Rocco, Leporello, Daland and Sarastro, Berlin. *Recordings include:* Zar und Zimmermann (BASF); Die schweigsame Frau (EMI); Baal (Amadeo); Der Corregidor by Wolf (Schwann). *Address:* c/o Staatstheater Stuttgart, Oberer Schlossgarten 6, D-7000 Stuttgart, Germany.

BERGHAUS Ruth, b. 2 July 1927, Dresden, Germany. Stage Director. m. Paul Dessau 1954 (died 1979). *Education:* Studied dance and choreography at the Palucca School, Dresden. *Career:* Choreographer at Dresden from 1950; Production and choreographic assistant with the Berliner Ensemble 1964-71, Director 1971-77; First opera production Dessau's Die Verurteilung des Lukullus, Berlin Staatsoper 1960; also produced Dessau's Puntila and Einstein; Producer at the Frankfurt Opera from 1980, notably with Die Zauberflöte, Die Entführung aus dem Serail (1981), The Makropoulos Case (1982), Parsifal (1982), Les Troyens (1983) and The Ring (1985-87); Other productions have included Elektra and La Clemenza di Tito at Mannheim, Tristan und Isolde at Hamburg and Don Giovanni for Welsh National Opera; produced the premiere of Patmos by Wolfgang von Schweinitz for the 1990 Munich Biennale, later seen at the Kassel Staatstheater; Staged Mahagonny at Stuttgart, 1992. *Address:* c/o Stuttgart Staatsoper, Oberer Schlossgarten 6, 7000 Stuttgart, Germany.

BERGLUND Ingela, b. 1959, Sweden. Singer (Soprano). *Education:* Studied viola at the Stockholm College of Music, 1974-79; State Opera School,

Stockholm, 1985-88, with Kerstin Meyer and Elisabeth Soderstrom. *Debut:* Royal Opera Stockholm, 1988, as Donna Anna. *Career:* Member of Royal Stockholm Philharmonic Orchestra, 1979-84; Sang Mozart's Countess and the woman in La Voix Humaine at Stockholm, 1988; Salzburg Landestheater, 1989-92, as Donna Anna, Musetta, Tatiana, Fiordiligi and Hanna Glawari in Die Lustige Witwe; As Beatrice in Boccaccio of F von Suppè at Royal Opera, Stockholm; Guest appearances at the Semper Opera Dresden and in Austria, USA, Spain and Japan. *Recordings:* Radio and TV in Sweden. *Address:* IM Audio & Music HB, Åsogatan 67 VI 5-118 29 Stockholm, Sweden.

BERGLUND Paavo Allan Englebert, b. 14 April 1929, Helsinki, Finland. Conductor. m. Kirsti Kivekas 1958, 1 son, 2 daughters. *Education:* Sibelius Academy, Helsinki. *Career:* Violinist, Finnish Radio Symphony Orchestra, 1949-56, Conductor, 1956-62, Principal Conductor, 1962-71; British debut, 1965, with the Bournemouth Symphony Orchestra; Principal Conductor, Bournemouth Symphony Orchestra, 1972-79, Helsinki Philharmonic Orchestra, 1975-79; Principal guest conductor Scottish National Orchestra from 1981. *Recordings:* Complete Sibelius symphonies including first recording of Kullervo Symphony, 1971-77, Ma Vlast (Smetana), Shostakovich symphonies 5, 6, 7, 10, 11, and many other recordings including CD of Mozart and Strauss Oboe Concertos with Douglas Boyd and the Chamber Orchestra of Europe (ASV). *Publication:* A Comparative Study of the Printed Score and the Manuscript of the Seventh Symphony of Sibelius 1970. *Address:* Munkkiniemenranta 41, 00330 Helsinki 33, Finland.

BERGMAN Erik Valdemar, b. 24 Nov 1911, Nykarleby. Composer. m. Solveig von Schoultz, 7 July 1961. *Education:* Literature and Esthetics, Musicology, 1931-33 University of Helsinki; Composition Diploma, Sibelius Academy, Helsinki, 1939; Studied Composition in Berlin with Heinz Tiessen and in Switzerland with Wladimir Vogel. *Debut:* Helsinki, 1940. *Career:* Concerts in Washington DC and New York, 1981, 1991, London, 1986, Leningrad, 1989, St Petersburg, 1992, Tokyo, 1994; Works performed at several international festivals; Professor of Composition at the Sibelius Academy, 1963-76; Conductor, Helsinki Univ Chorus, 1950-69. *Compositions:* Opera, The Singing Tree. *Recordings:* The Singing Tree; Concerto for Violin and Orchestra; Birds in the Morning, flute and orchestra; as well as chamberworks and works for piano, guitar, choral and vocal. *Honours:* DPhil, 1978, 1982; Royal Swedish Academy of Music; Hon Member, Soc of Finnish Composers; Comm of the Order of the White Rose of Finland; Comm of the Order of the Lion of Finland; Pro Finlandia Medal, Sibelius Intern Prize, 1965. *Membership:* Academy of Finland, 1982. *Address:* Berggatan 22 C 52, SF-00100 Helsinki, Finland.

BERGMAN Heidi Suzanne, b. 19 July 1958, Hempstead, New York USA. Violinist. *Education:* Juilliard School of Music Pre-College Division, 1974-76; Studies with Zino Francescatti, St Maximin, France, summer 1979; BM, Eastman School of Music, Rochester, NY, 1980; MM, Yale University, New Haven, Connecticut, 1984; Artists Studies, Hochschule für Musik, Vienna, Austria, 1985-88. *Debut:* Volkstheater, Vienna, 1987. *Career:* Violinist: Ariel Trio, USA; Knoxville (Tennessee) Symphony, 1985; Artemis Quartet, Vienna, 1985-88; Erste Frauenkammerorkester von Osterreich, Vienna, 1986-87; Wiener Kammeroper, Vienna, 1987-; Appearances for Connecticut and New Jersey Public TV, UPI Hong Kong, Austrian Radio and Television; Recitalist and soloist with orchestras in USA, Canada, Mexico, France, Austria, Germany, Italy; Faculty, Southeast Missouri State University. *Recordings:* Austrian Radio. *Current Management:* Gildan Associates. *Address:* c/o Southeast Missouri State University, 1 University Plaza, Cape Girardeau, MO 63701, USA.

BERGONZI Carlo, b. 13 July 1924, Busseto, Parma, Italy. Tenor Opera Singer. m. Adele, 2 children. *Education:* Parma Conservatory. *Career:* Debut (as baritone) as Figaro (Il Barbiere di Siviglia) at Lecce 1948; Debut as tenor in title role of Andrea Chénier, Teatro Petruzzelli, Bari, 1951; subsequently appeared at various Italian opera houses including La Scala, Milan; US debut in Il Tabarro and Cavalleria Rusticana, Lyric Opera, Chicago, 1955; Appeared at Metropolitan Opera, New York in Aida (as Radames) and Il Trovatore (as Manrico), 1955-56; London Debut Stoll Theatre, 1953 as Alvaro in La forza del destino; at Covent Garden he has sung Verdi's Riccardo, Radames and Manrico and Puccini's Cavaradossi; now appears at all the major opera houses in Europe and also in USA and South America; repertoire includes many Verdi roles as well as roles in operas by Donizetti, Boito, Leoncavallo and Mascagni. Sang Edgardo at Covent Garden, 1985; Metropolitan Opera 1956-83 in 249 performances of 21 roles, including Canio, Andrea Chénier, Cavaradossi, Riccardo, Nemorino, Macduff, Rodolfo, Alfredo, Pollione, Enzo and Manrico; Metropolitan Gala (25th anniversary), 4 Dec 1981; Sang Edgardo at the Vienna Staatsoper, 1988; Nemorino for New Jersey State Opera, 1989; Farewell Recital at Covent Garden, 1992. *Address:* c/o Royal Opera House (Contracts), Covent Garden, London, WC2.

BERGSMA William Laurence, b. 1 Apr 1921, Oakland, California, USA. Composer; Educator. m. Nancy Jane Nickerson, 1 Sept 1946, 1 son, 1 daughter. *Education:* Stanford University, 1938-40; BA, 1942, MA, 1943, with Howard Hanson and Bernard Rogers, Eastman School of Music. *Career:* Instructor, 1946-63, Chairman Composition Department, Chairman Literature and Materials Music Department and Associate Dean, 1961-63, Juilliard School of Music; Professor, 1963-, Director 1963-71, Music University of Washington, Seattle; Visiting Professor, Brooklyn College, City University New York, 1972-73. *Compositions:* Blatent Hypotheses, trombone and percussion, 1977; Sweet Was the Song the Virgin Sang/Tristan Revisited, Seattle, Washington, 1978; Four All, 3 instruments and percussion, 1979; Quintet for Flute and String Quartet, 1979; The Voice of the Coelacanth, 1980; In Campo Alperto, oboe concertante, 2 bassoons and strings, 1981; Four Songs, medium voice, clarinet, bassoon and piano, 1981; Recordings for Columbia, Decca, Mercury, CRI, Desto and MHS. *Honours:* Society of Publishers of America Music Award, 1945; Guggenheim Fellow, 1946 and 1951; National Endowment for the Arts Fellow, 1979. *Memberships:* American Academy; Institute of Arts and Letters; American Society of Composers, Authors and Publishers; Phi Beta Kappa. *Address:* 2328 Delmar Drive East, Seattle, WA 98102, USA.

BERGSTROM-NIELSEN Carl, b. 28 July 1951, Copenhagen. Composer; Musician; Music Therapist. *Education:* Cand. Phil (Musicology) from University of Copenhagen. *Debut:* Group for Alternative Music, 1971. *Career:* Performances and organisational work, Group for Alternative Music, 1971-77; Member: Group for Intuitive Music, 1975-, Executive Committee of Danish ISCM Section, 1976-63; Commissions for Danish Radio, 1977, 1980, 1983; Performances in most of the western world; Music for TV-Ballet Workshop, with Nanna Nilsson, 1983; Assistant Teacher, Music Therapy, Aalborg University, 1983; Commission from Numus Festival, 1988. *Compositions:* Sonata for Horn Quartet, 1973-74; Numerous compositions for Improvisation including: Postcard Music, Fire-Music, 1976 for unspecified ensemble; 11 September (Tape), 1976-77; Fanfares for Everyday Life, 4 horns, 1977; Minimal Blues (Tape), 1982. *Recordings:* Postcard Music; Nar de Magthavende, solo voice, 1980; Joker-Game/Fire Music/Revision II 1980; Minimal Blues, 1984; Sammenfojninger, 1988 (performance piece); Cassettes: Postcard-Music/Naar de Magthavende (solo voice), 1980; Joker-Game/Fire Music/Revision II, 1980, author; Minimal Blues (Tape), 1984, author; Bumblebee Pieces (tape), 1991. *Publications include:* Cage og Stockhausen. To Musikalske Eventrere, 1986. *Honours:* Danish State Arts Foundation Grants, 1977, 1983; Prizewinner, Young Nordic Music Festival, 1979. *Memberships:* Danish Composers Society; ISCM,

Danish Section. *Address:* Teglgardsvej 649 3 tv, 3050 Humlebaek, Denmark.

BERINI Bianca, b. 20 Dec 1928, Trieste, Italy. Singer (Mezzo-Soprano). *Education:* Studied in Trieste and Milan. *Debut:* Teatro Nuovo Milan 1963, as Suzuki in Madama Butterfly. *Career:* Has sung throughout Italy and in Vienna, Berlin, Amsterdam, Brussels, Marseille, Nice, Toulouse and London; Metropolitan Opera debut 1978, as Amneris: returned to New York as Eboli, Amneris, Santuzza, Dalila, Ulrica, Azucena and Federica in Luisa Miller; Further engagements in Dallas, Philadelphia, Baltimore, San Francisco, Lisbon, Barcelona and Zurich; Other roles include Adalgisa (Norma), Laura (La Gioconda), Ortrud (Lohengrin), Charlotte (Werther) and Jane Seymour in Anna Bolena. *Recordings include:* Verdi Requiem (CBS). *Address:* c/o Metropolitan Opera, Lincoln Center, New York, NY 10023, USA.

BERIO Luciano, b. 24 Oct 1925, Oneglia, Italy. Composer. m. (1) Cathy Berberian 1950 (dissolved 1964) 1 daughter, (2) Susan Oyama 1964 (dissolved 1971), 1 son, 1 daughter, (3) Talia Packer 1977, 1 son. *Education:* Liceo Classico and Conservatorio G. Verdi, Milan; Further study with Dallapiccola in USA. *Career:* Founder of Studio Fonologia Musicale, Italian Radio; Teacher of Composition and Lecturer at Mills College, California, Darmstadt 1954-59 and Harvard University; Professor of Composition at the Juilliard School from 1965; Has worked with Boulez at the studios of IRCAM, Paris. *Compositions:* Dramatic: Allez-Hop mimed story 1959, rev. 1968; Passaggio, mesa in scena, 1963; Laborintus II 1970; Opera 1970, rev. 1979; Recital I (For Cathy) 1972; I Trionfi di Petraca, ballet 1974; Linea, ballet 1974; La Vera Storia, opera 1982; Un Re in Ascolto, opera 1984; Naturale, ballet, 1986. Orchestral: Variazioni 1954; Nones 1954; Divertimento (with Maderna) 1958; Chemins I-IV 1965-75; Tempi Concertati 1959; Bewegung 1971; Concerto for 2 pianos and orchestra 1973; Still 1973; Eindrucke 1974; Points on the curve to find.... for piano and 20 instruments 1974; Il Ritorno degli Snovidenia for cello and orchestra 1977; Piano Concerto 1977; Entrata 1980; Accordo for 4 wind bands 1981; Corale for violin and orchestra 1982; Voci for viola and orchestra 1984; Requiea, 1984; Formazioni 1986; Festum, 1989; Schubert Rendering (sketches) 1989; Brahms/Berio Op 120 No 1, 1986. Vocal: Quattro canzoni Populari 1947; Opus Number Zoo for speaker and wind quintet 1952, rev. 1970; Chamber Music (Joyce) 1953; Circles (Cummings) with harp and 2 percussion 1960; Epifanie for female voice and orchestra 1961; Sinfonia 1968-69; Questo vuol dire che, for solo voices, small chorus, instruments and tape 1969; Ora (Virgil) 1971; Bewegung II for baritone and orchestra 1971; Cries of London for 8 solo voices 1973-73; 11 Folk Songs for mezzo and orchestra 1975; Calmo (In Memoriam Bruno Maderna) for soprano and ensemble 1974; Coro for 40 voices and orchestra 1976; Duo for baritone, 2 violins, chorus and orchestra 1982; Mahler/Berio, Fünf Frühe Lieder and Sechs Frühe Lieder, 1986-87; Ofanim, 1988; Canticum Novissimi Testamenti, 1989. Chamber and Instrumental: Suite for piano 1948; String Quartet 1956; Serenata for flute and 14 instruments 1957; Differences for ensemble 1959; Sincronie for string quartet 1964; Wasserklavier and Erdenklavier for piano 1964, 1970; Memory for 2 pianos and percussion 1970, rev. 1973; Musica Leggera for flute, viola and cello 1974; Sequenze I-XI for solo flute, harp, voice, piano, trombone, viola, oboe, violin, clarinet, trumpet and guitar 1958-88; Duette per due violini 1979-82; Luftklavier, 1985; Ricorrenze per Quintetto a Fiati, 1987; String Quartet, 1986/90; Feuerklavier, 1989. Electronic: Mutazioni 1955; Perspectives 1957; Thema (Omaggio a Joyce) 1958; Momenti 1960; Visage 1961; Chants Paralleles 1975. *Address:* Il Colombaio, Radicondoli, Siena, Italy.

BERKELEY Edward Charles, b. 18 Jan 1945, New York, USA. *Education: Career:* Co-General Director, Aspen Opera Theatre Centre; Faculty, The Julliard School and Director of The Julliard Opera Theatre; Faculty of Circle in the Square Theatre's Professional Workship; co-Founder and Artistic Director, The Willow Cabin Theater Company. Beyond Manhattan, he has seved as Artistic Director of the Musical Theater Lab at the John F Kennedy Center; and has directed at Wolf Trap and The Library of Congress in Washington DC, Opera Festival of New Jersey, Williamstown Theater Festival, Berkshire Theatre Festival, Long Beach Opera, San Diego's Old Globe Theatre, the Eastman School and Brooklyn College. At Aspen usic Festival had directed man unusual and acclaimed productions and co-teaches a unique Opera Scenes master class; Notable productions include the American stage premiere of Milhaud's Christophe Colomb; Macbeth and The Tempest at Lincoln Centre; The American Stage premiere of Mark K Niekrug's Los Alamos; A premiere workshop of Jacob Druckman's Medea, Falla's El Retablo de Maese Pedro, Milhaud's Le Pauvre Matelot and Les Malheurs d'Orphée; The film of Ionesco's Exit the King. *Address:* 1150 Park Avenue, New York, NY 10128, USA.

BERKELEY Michael, b. 29 May 1948, London, England. Composer. *Education:* Westminster Cathedral Choir School; Royal Academy of Music; Further studied with Lennox Berkeley and Richard Rodney Bennett. *Career:* BBC Radio 3 announcer, 1974-79; Presenter of programmes on BBC 2 TV; Composer-in-residence, London College of Music, 1987-88; Opera Baa Baa Black Sheep premiered at the 1992 Cheltenham Festival. *Compositions:* Meditations for strings, 1976; Oboe Concerto, 1977; Fantasia Concertante for chamber orchestra, 1977; String Trio, 1978; The Wild Winds for soprano and chamber orchestra, 1978; Cello Sonata, 1978; Violin Sonata, 1979; Organ Sonata, 1979; At the Round Earth's Imagin'd Corners for soprano, baritone, chorus and organ, 1980; Uprising, symphony, 1980; Chamber Symphony, 1980; String Quartet, 1981; Wessex Graves for tenor and harpsichord, 1981; Flames for orchestra, 1981; Suite, Vision of Piers the Ploughman, 1981; Gregorian Variations for orchestra, 1982; Cello Concerto, 1982; Oratorio, Or Shall we Die?, 1982; Guitar Sonata, 1982; Clarinet Quintet, 1983; Songs of Awakening Love, 1986; Organ Concerto, 1987; Bastet, 1988. Music for a ballet; Keening for saxophone and piano, 1988; Quartet Study, 1988; Coronach for string orchestra, 1988; The Red Macula for chorus and orchestra, 1989; Fierce Tears for solo oboe, 1990; Stupendous Stranger for chorus and brass, 1990; Entertaining Master Punch for chamber orchestra, 1991; Opera, Baa Baa Black Sheep, 1992. *Address:* c/o 49 Blenheim Crescent, London W11 2EF, England.

BERKES Kalman, b. 1952, Budapest, Hungary. Clarinettist. *Education:* Studied Music from the age of 4; Béla Bartók Conservatory, 1966-70; Ferenc Liszt Academy of Music, 1977. *Career:* Principal Clarinettist, Budapest State Opera Orchestra and Budapest Philharmonic, 1972-; Budapest Chamber Ensemble and Jeunesses Musicales Wind Quintet 1973; Extensive Guest Performances throughout Europe including: Austria, France, Federal Republic of Germany, Netherlands, Italy and Switzerland. *Recordings:* Has made a number of records including Bartók's Contrasts. *Honour:* Silver Medal, Geneva International Musical Concours, 1972.

BERKOWITZ Paul, b. 1 Oct 1948, Montreal, Canada. Concert Pianist. *Education:* McGill University, and Curtis Institute with Serkin and Horszowski. *Debut:* London, 1973, (resident from that time); New York solo debut, Alice Tully Hall, 1978. *Career:* Recitalist, Wigmore and Elizabeth Halls, Soloist with major orchestras in Britain and America; Festival engagements in Belgium, Denmark, England, France, Italy and Spain; Barcelona Festival with the Endellion Quartet and the Albion Ensemble; Beethoven duets with Richard Goode at the Wigmore Hall, 1990-91; Appearances with BBC Scottish Symphony and English Sinfonia; Professor, Guildhall Sch, 1975-; Masterclasses at McGill University, elsewhere in Canada and Barcelona. Repretoire includes Sonatas by Beethoven, Brahms, Mozart, Schubert, Chopoina and Bartok; Bach's Italian Concerto, the Brahms Handel Variations and

Schumann's Kreisleriana and C major Fantasy. *Recordings include:* Complete sonatas of Schubert, Schumann's Davidsbundlertänze and Kreisleriana (Meridian). *Address:* c/o Worldwide Artists Ltd, 6 Petersfield Crescent, Coulsdon, Surrey CR5 2JQ, England.

BERL Christine, b. 22 July 1943, New York City, USA. Composer. 2 sons. *Education:* BS, Piano, Mannes College of Music, 1961-64; MA, Composition, Queen's College, 1968-70. *Career:* Performances by Emanuel Ax in Highland Park, Ravinia, 1988; Commissioned by Peter Serkin for 1989-90, The Chamber Music Society of Lincoln Center for their 20th Anniversary Season with Frederica Von Stade as Guest Artist, 1989, Cornell University Chorus 1989; Concert devoted to Berl's works on Distinguished Artists Series of 92nd Street Y, 13 Oct 1990. Commissioned work for Peter Serkin, Emanuel Ax for 2 pianos. Other participants Patricia Spence, Matt Haimovitz, Richard Stoltzman, Luly Stoltzman, Ani Kavafian, Paul Neubauer, Richard Goode, Andre-Michel Schub, 1994; World Premiere by French violinist Pierre Amoyal and Jeremy Menuhin of Masmoudi, violin sonata commissioned by Radio France; New York Premiere of Masmoudi, Merkin Concert Hall, 1994. *Compositions:* Elegy for Piano Solo, 1974; Three Pieces for Chamber Ensemble, 1975; Ab La Dolchor for soprano, female chorus and orchestra, 1979; Sonata for Piano, 1986-7; Dark Summer, for Mezzo-soprano, piano and string trio, The Lord of the Dance (for Peter Serkin), The Violent Bear It Away for orchestra, 1988; Cantilena for Cello and Piano (for Matt Haimovitz). *Recordings:* Three Pieces for Chamber Ensemble, 1975; Advance records; Arthur Weisberg and members of the Contemporary Chamber Ensemble and Speculum Musicae, Ursula Oppens, Piano; Elegy, The Lord of the Dance on CD; Piano Sonata by Edipan. *Address:* 250 West 85 Street, No. 12D, New York, NY 10024, USA.

BERMAN Boris, b. 3 Apr 1948, Moscow, USSR. Concert pianist; Professor of Piano. m. Zina Tabachnikova, 1975, 1 son, 1 daughter. *Education:* BA, MA, 1971, Moscow Tchaikovsky Conservatory. *Debut:* Moscow, 1965. *Career:* Performances in over 30 countries, appeared with Concergebouw, Philharmonia, Royal Scottish, Detroit, Minnesota, Houston, Atlanta, Toronto, Israel Philharmonic, Moscow Philharmonic, St Petersburg Philharmonic and many others; Festivals include Bergen, Ravinia, Israel, Marlboro; Numerous radio and TV appearances around the world; Former Professor of Piano at Tel-Aviv University, Indiana University, Bloomington, Boston University; Currently at Yale School of Music. *Recordings:* All solo piano works by Prokofiev in 9 vols (Chandos), Stravinsky Concerto with Orchestre de la Suisse Romande, N Järvi (Chandos), Prokofiev Concertos 1,4,5 with Concertgebouw Orchestra, N Järvi (Chandos), works by Debussy, Stravinsky, Schnittke (Chandos), Shostakovich (Ottavo), Scriabin all Sonatas in 2 vols (Music and Arts), numerous chamber recordings. *Memberships:* Juror at various national/international piano competitions. *Honours:* Edison Classic Award 1990 (Holland). *Current Management:* Columbia Artists, New York; Lies Asconas-AMI, United Kingdom. *Address:* Yale School of Music, 96 Wall Street, New Haven, CT 06520, USA.

BERMAN Lazar, b. 26 Feb 1930, Leningrad, USSR. Pianist. m. Valentina Berman, 28 Dec 1961, 1 son. *Education:* Graduated, Moscow Conservatory, 1953; Student, master classes, 1953-57. *Debut:* In Concert, 1934. *Career:* Orchestral Debut, Moscow Philharmonic, playing Mozart's C major Concerto K503, 1940; Professional Concert Pianist, 1957-; US Debut, Miami University, Oxford, Ohio, also American Orchestra, 1976; Appearance at Carnegie Hall with New Jersey Symphony Orchestra, 1971; Recording Artist in music by Beethoven, Liszt, Prokofiev, Scriabin and Tchaikovsky (1st Piano Concerto with Karajan 1976). *Honours:* Winner 1st prize, International Youth Festival, East Berlin, 195; 4th place, Queen Elisabeth of Belgium contest, Brussels, 1951. *Memberships:* Philharmonic Society of Moscow; USSR-Belgium Friendship Society, Founder. *Address:* c/o Jacques Leister Artists

Management, Corchester Towers, 155 W 6 Street, New York, NY 10023, USA.

BERMUDEZ Egberto, b. 19 May 1954, Bogotá, Colombia. Musicologist; Musician. *Education:* Los Andes University, Bogotá; Guildhall School of Music and Drama, London, England; King's College, University of London. *Career:* Musicologist, Lecturer, National University, Bogotá; Director, Canto vocal ensemble. *Recordings:* Editing liner notes: Musica Tradicional y Popular Colombiana, 16 records, Bogotá, Procultura, 1987; Latin American Colonial Music, Canto, Bogotá, 1989; Latin American Colonial Music, 1991. *Publications:* Los Instrumientos Musicales en Colombia, 1985; Catalogo Coleccion J I Perdomo Escobar, 1986; Antologia de Música Religiosa Siglos XVI-XVIII, 1988; Compositions, Columbianes of Americanos, 10 cassettes, BogotáBanio de la Republica, 1989-91. *Contributions to:* Numerous articles and reviews in magazines and journals on History of Music in Colombia, Musical Instruments, Colombian Traditional Music. *Address:* PO Box No 91489, Bogotá 8, Colombia, South America.

BERNARD André, b. 6 Apr 1946, Gap, France. Conductor; Trumpet Soloist. *Education:* Diplome Superior of Conducting, Paris; First Price, trumpet, Paris Superior Conservatory; Laureat Concours International, trumpet, Geneva, Switzerland, 1968; Studied German romantic repertory with Carlo Maria Giulini, and Italian opera with Bruno Bartoletti, Sienna, Italy. *Career:* Guest Conductor, London Symphony Orchestra, London Philharmonic Orchestra, Royal Philharmonic Orchestra, Mozarteum Salzburg, Philharmonia Hungarica, Polish Chamber Orchestra, Lyon and Toulouse National Orchestra, Monte Carlo Philharmonic Orchestra, Brno Philharmonie Orchestra; Opera conducting in Strasbourg, Lille, Siena, Geneva, (Suisse Romande); Television in France, Germany, Japan, Italy; Radio appearances in USA, Canada, Japan, Germany, Italy, France; Solo appearances including: Salzburg Festival, Berlin Philharmonie, Carnegie Hall and Lincoln Center in New York, Paris, Tokyo, London, Rome, Prague, Madrid, Vienna, Washington; Appearances with world's most prestigious orchestras; 31 concerts on tour conducting Philharmonia Hungarica, including Carnegie Hall and Los Angeles, USA, 1986; Contract for concerts series in London, tours in France and Italy and recordings, New Symphony Orchestra of London and London Chamber Orchestra, 1982-87. *Recordings:* 20 for Philips, CBS, Decca; Records with Academy of St Martin in the Fields, English Chamber Orchestra, Ensemble Instrumental de France. *Current Management:* Columbia Artists Management, New York, USA. *Hobbies:* Skiing; Tennis. *Address:* 19 rue Joliot Curie, 93100 Montreuil (Paris), France.

BERNARD Annabelle, b. 1938, New Orleans, Louisana, USA. Singer (Soprano). *Education:* Studied at Xavier University, New Orleans, the New England Conservatory. *Debut:* Sang Susanna in Le Nozze di Figaro, conducted by Boris Goldovsky, 1958. *Career:* Appeared as Butterfly in Stuttgart, 1959; Lieder recitals with Hermann Reutter; Vienna Staatsoper debut as Aida, conducted by Karajan; sung at the Deutsche Oper Berlin from 1962, debut as Aida; Salzburg Festival 1973, as Electra in Idomeneo, conducted by Karl Bohm; Visits with the Deutsche Oper to Japan as Fiordiligi and in The Ring, 1987; Washington Opera 1986, as Fiordiligi; New Orleans Opera as Maddalena in Andrea Chénier; Sang in the stage premiere of Musorgsky's Salambo at the San Carlo, Naples; Modern repertory includes the premieres on Montezuma by Sessions, 1964; Dallapiccola's Ulisse, 1968; Concert appearances with the Cleveland Orchestra conducted by Lorin Maazel at Carnegie Hall, the Berlin Philharmonic Orchestra. *Address:* c/o Deutsche Oper Berlin, Richard Wagnerstrasse 10, D-1000 Berlin, Germany.

BERNARDI Mario, b. 20 Aug 1930, Kirkland Lake, Ontario, Canada. Conductor; Pianist. m. Mona Kelly, 12 May 1962, 1 daughter. *Education:* Diplomas in Piano, Organ and Composition, B Marcello Conservatory,

Venice, 1947; Piano with Lubka Kolessa, Toronto. *Career:* Sadler's Wells Opera, 1963-69, with many performances of operas by Verdi; San Francisco Opera, 1967, 1968, 1982; New York City Opera, 1970-86; Metropolitan Opera, 1984; Several major orchestras including Chicago, Pittsburgh, San Francisco, Toronto, Montreal, BBC; 13 years with National Arts Centre Orchestra, Ottawa, 1969-82, giving many premieres of works by Canadian composers; Music Director, Calgary Philharmonic; Season 1987/88 with Cendrillonat Washington and Don Giovanni at Montreal; Conducted Lucia di Lammermoor at Washington, 1989; Gave the Verdi Reqieum at the 1988 Olympic Arts Festival; Conducted Fidelio at Toronto, 1991; Massenet's Chérubin at Covent Garden, 1994. *Recordings:* Numerous recordings for EMI, RCA, CBC with Sadler's Wells Company, National Arts Centre Orchestra, Toronto, Vancouver Symphonies, CBC Radio Orchestra; Works include Hansel and Gretel (with Sadler's Wells Company); Mozart Symphony K551 and Concerto K219 (with Steven Staryk); Haydn arias and symphony No 85; Brahms Serenade Op 11. *Honours:* Companion of the Order of Canada; Several honorary doctorates. *Memberships:* Savage Club, London; Ranchmen's Club, Calgary. *Hobbies:* Chess; Mountain hiking. *Current Management:* Columbia Artists Management, New York. *Address:* 248 Warren Road, Toronto, Ontario M4V 2S8, Canada.

BERNARDINI Alfredo, b. 30 Oct 1961, Rome, Italy. Oboist. 2 sons, 1 daughter. *Education:* Studies, Royal Conservatory, The Hague, Netherlands, 1982-; Soloist diploma, 1987; Diploma, University of Oxford, 1985. *Career:* Performs with major European ensembles: Hesperion XX, Les Arts Florissants, La Petite Bande, Capella Coloniensis, Amsterdam Baroque Orchestra, Collegio Strumentale Italiano, La Grande Ecurie, Concerto Armonico Budapest, Concerto Italiano. *Recordings:* with EMI; D&GM; Astree; Bongioranni; Noralis. *Contributions to:* Articles on Il Flauto Dolce, Early Music, Journal of the American Musical Instruments Society. *Hobbies:* Research on history of woodwind instruments in Italy; Making of 18th century oboes (copies). *Address:* via Sebenico 2, 00198 Roma, Italy.

BERNAS Richard, b. 21 Apr 1950, New York, USA. Conductor. m. (1) Deirdre Busenberg (div); (2)Beatrice Harper. 2 sons. *Debut:* As pianist, Kent University, 1966; As conductor, London, England, 1976; *Career:* Warsaw Autumn Festival, 1977; Vienna Festival, 1984; Opera de Lyons and Paris Opera, 1985; London Sinfonietta, England, 1986; Edinburgh Festival, Scotland, 1986; The Royal Helsinki Philharmonic, 1989; BBC Symphony Orchestra, 1989; Holland Festival, 1989; Aldeburgh Festival Opera, Suffolk, England, 1990; English National Opera, London, 1990; Netherlands Opera, Amsterdam and the Hague, 1991; Ars Musica Festival, Brussels, 1991; Orchestre National de Belgique, Brussels, 1993; Conductor, Saltarello Choir, 1976-80; Conductor, Music Projects, London, 1978-; Conductor in Residence, Sussex University, 1979-82. *Recordings:* Factory Classics, Virgin Classics, Continum, NMC and Decca/ Argo. *Current Management:* Robert Gilder and Co, London, England. *Address:* 73 Avenue Gardens, London W3 8HB, England.

BERNASCONI Silvano, b. 16 Oct 1950, Chiasso, Switzerland. Pianist; Composer. m. Irene Cairoli Alessandra, 20 June 1984, 1 s. *Education:* Conservatoire de Lausanne: Piano with Francesto Zaza; Composition with Andor Kovach; Electronic music with Rainer Bosch; Conservatorio Santa Cecilia in Rome: Composition with Vieri Tosatti, Gregorian song with Domenico Bartolucci; Organ with Ferdinando Germani; Electronic music with Franco Evangelisti. *Debut:* Rome, 1974. *Career:* Pianist composer, 1980-85; Executions of music commissioned by Musica Ticinensis, 1982, and television. *Compositions:* Sounds and Crystals, for two Vibraphones, 1982; Electrons, 1979; Sounds to River, for piano, 1985; Psallite, four lines for organ, 1974; Tourbillon, for violin and Orchestra, 1993. *Recordings:* Sounds and crystals, transparencies for two

vibraphones and piano; Sounds Am Bach, for piano played by the composer. *Publications:* Didactics compositions in the European year of Music, 1985; Contributor to Musica & Teatro magazine. *Honours:* Invitation by UNCM to found a European Composers Union, 1991; Invitation to represent the AMS by the ECU, 1992.*Memberships:* Association of Swiss Musicians; European Composers Union. *Hobbies:* Abstract painting; New fables; Natural sculpture. *Address:* Casa Am Bach, 6803 Camignolo-Lugano, Switzerland.

BERNATHOVA Eva, b. 4 Dec 1922, Budapest, Hungary. Concert Pianist; Senior Lecturer, Trinity College of Music, London. m. Joseph Bernath, 20 Feb 1947. *Education:* Gymnasium, Budapest; Professor Diploma, 1949; Performing Artist Diploma, 1950; Franz Liszt Academy of Music, Budapest.*Debut:* Prague, 1948. *Career:* Has toured in Europe, USA, Canada, Far East, India, Japan, Australia, New Zealand; Soloist with many world famous orchestras, Berlin Philharmonic; Czech Philharmonic; Orchestre de la Suisse Romande; Royal Philharmonic Orchestra, London; Gewandhaus Orchestra. *Recordings:* Solo works by J H Voříšek, F Liszt, M Balakirev, J Suk, Mozart, Janáček: Concertino for Piano and chamber orchestra; C Franck: Symphonic Variations; M Ravel: Concerto in G; B Bartók: Concerto No 3; Chamber Music: A Dvořák: Piano Quintet in A; J Brahms: Piano Quintet in F minor; C Franck: Piano Quintet in F minor; D Shostakovich: Piano Quintet in G minor; numerous gramophone recordings for DGG, Erato, Supraphon. *Hobbies:* Literature; Languages; Table Tennis. *Address:* 8 Purley Avenue, London NW2 1SJ, England.

BERNET Dietfried, b. 14 May 1940, Vienna, Austria. Conductor. *Education:* Studied in Vienna with Hans Swarowsky and Dimitri Mitropoulos. *Career:* Conducted at major opera houses and guested with leading orchestras since 1962; General Director of Music, City of Mainz and Conductor, Vienna State and Volksoper; Appearances with the Vienna and Chicago Symphonies, London Philharmonic and Philharmonia, RAI Orchestras in Italy, Berlin Philharmonic, Municha Raido and Philharmonia Hungarica; Festival engagements at Salzburg, Vienna, Spoleto, Budapest and Turin; Repertoire includes works by Brahms, Bruckner, Mahler, Wagner, Verdi, Puccini and composers of the 20th century, Hindemith, Bartók, Dallapiccola, Penderecki, Ligeti and Shostakovich; Season 1991-92 with Die Meistersinger at Marseille, Don Giovanni at the Schonnbrunnschloss, Vienna; Season 1992-93 with Les contes d'Hoffmann and Der Freischutz at the Volksoper, Les Pecheurs de Perles in Holland and Idomeneo at Pretoria; Engaged at Marseille for La Clemenza di Tito and Der Ring des Nibelungen, 1993-95; Has also conducted opera at Munich, Hamburg, Cologne, Stuttgart, Naples, Barcelona, Venice, Palermo and Trieste. *Recordings:* Almbus for Decca, BASF, Philipps, Teldec and Amadeo. *Honours include:* Winner, International Conductor's Competition at Liverpool, 1962. *Address:* c/o Atholl Still Ltd, Greystoke House, 80-86 Westrow Street, London SE19 3AF, England.

BERNHEIMER Martin, b. 28 Sept 1936, Munich, Germany. Music Critic. m. (1) Lucinda Pearson, 30 Sept 1961, (div 1989), 1 son, 3 daughters, (2) Linda Winer, 27 Sept 1993. *Education:* MusB, Brown University, 1958; Munich Hochschule fur Musik, 1958-59; MA, New York University, 1961; Studied musicology with Gustave Reese. *Career:* Teacher, New York University, 1959-62; Contributing critic, New York Herald-Tribune, 1959-62; Contributing Editor, Musical Courier, 1961-64; Temporary Music Critic, New York Post, 1961-65; Assistant to the music editor, Saturday Review, 1962-65; Managing editor, Philharmonic Hall Programme, New York, 1962-65; New York correspondent 1962-65; Los Angeles Correspondent 1965-, Opera; Music Editor and Chief Music Critic, Los Angeles Times, 1965-; Teacher, University of Southern California, Los Angeles, 1966-71; University of California at Los Angeles, 1969-75; California Institute of the Arts, 1975-82; California State University, Northridge, 1978-81; Member, Pulitzer

Prize Music Jury, 1984, 1986; and 1989. *Contributions to:* Articles in New Grove Dictionary of Music and Musicians; Articles and reviews in various journals; Liner notes for recordings; New Groves Dictionary of American Music; New Grove Dictionary of American Opera. *Address:* c/o Los Angeles Times, Times-Mirror Square, Los Angeles, CA 90053, USA.

BERNSTEIN Elmer, b. 4 Apr 1922, New York City, USA. Composer; Conductor. m. (1) Pearl Glusman, 21 Dec 1946, 2 sons. (2) Eve Adamson, 25 Oct 1965, 2 daughters. *Education:* Studied composition with Israel Citkowitz, Roger Sessions, Ivan Langstroth and Stefan Wolpe; Studied, New York University. *Career:* US Army Air Corps, arranger and composer for the Armed Forces Radio Service; Concert Pianist, 1946-50; Composer and conductor for films; Founder, Film Music Collection, 1974. *Compositions:* How Now, Dow Jones, musical, 1967; 3 orchestral suites; chamber music; Songs; Many film scores including: The Man With the Golden Arm, 1955; The Ten Commandments, 1956; Desire Under the Elms, 1958; The Magnificent Seven, 1960; Walk on the Wild Side, 1963; To Kill a Mockingbird, 1963; Hawaii, 1966; Thoroughly Modern Millie, 1967; The Bridge at Remagen, 1969; The trial of Billy Jack, 1974; Airplane!, 1980; Ghostbusters, 1984. *Recordings:* Many recordings of film scores as both composer and conductor. *Honour:* Academy Award for film score, Thoroughly Modern Millie, 1968. *Memberships:* Academy of Motion Picture Arts and Sciences, first vice president, 1963-; Composers and Lyricists Guild of America, president, 1970-. *Address:* ASCAP Building, One Lincoln Plaza, New York, NY 19923, USA.

BERNSTEIN Jane Agar, b. 23 Mar 1947, New York City, New York, USA. Musicologist. m. James Ladewig, 28 July 1977, 1 daughter. *Education:* BA, City College of New York, 1967; MMus, University of Massachusetts, 1968; PhD, University of California, Berkeley, 1974. *Career:* Assistant Professor, Vassar College, 1974-76; Assistant Professor, 1976-80, Associate Professor, 1980-87, Professor, Chairman, 1987-, Tufts University, Medford, Massachusetts; Fletcher Professor, 1990. *Publications:* French Chansons of the Sixteenth Century, 1985; The Sixteenth-Century Chanson, 30 vols, 1987-; Article in Acta Musicologica. *Contributions to:* Articles and reviews in The New Grove Dictionary, Music and Letters, Musica Disciplina, The Music Review, Journal of the American Music Society. *Honours:* Edward Renson Award; NEH Fellowship; Delmas Fellowship. *Memberships:* American Musicological Society; Board of Directors, Renaissance Society of America; International Musicological Society. *Address:* Department of Music, Tufts University, Medford, MA 02155, USA.

BERNSTEIN Lawrence F, b. 25 Mar 1939, New York City, USA. Musicologist; University Professor. *Education:* BS, Hofstra University, 1960; PhD, New York University, 1969. *Career:* Instructor, 1965-66, Assistant Professor, 1966-70, Music and humanities, University of Chicago; Associate Professor, 1970-81, Chairman Department of Music, 1972-73, 1974-77, Professor of Music, 1981-, University of Pennsylvania; Visiting Lecturer, Columbia University, Graduate School of Arts and Sciences, 1979; Visiting Associate Professor, Princeton University, 1980; Visiting Professor, Rutgers University, 1982-83; Supervising Editor, Masters and Monuments of the Renaissance, 1970-; Editor-in-Chief, Journal of the American Musicological Society, 1975-77. *Publications:* Ihan Gero: Madrigali italiani et canzoni francese a due voci, with James Haar, 1980; La Couronne et fleur des chansons a troys, 1984; The French Secular Chanson in the Sixteenth Century (in preparation). *Contributions to:* Articles in New Grove Dictionary of Music and Musicians, 1980; Articles and reviews in journals and other publications. *Address:* c/o Department of Music, University of Pennsylvania, 201 S 34th Street, Philadelphia, PA 19104-6313, USA.

BÉROFF Michel, b. 9 May 1950, Epinal, France. Pianist. *Education:* Conservatories of Nancy and Paris, with Yvonne Loriod. *Debut:* Paris 1966. *Career:* Has appeared on TV and at Festivals in Portugal and Iran, 1967, also at Royan and Oxford Bach Festivals; Has lectured and given recitals and concerts in various European and South American countries; Appearances with the London Symphony Orchestra, Concerts Colonne, Orchestre de Paris, New York Philharmonic and BBC Symphony Orchestras; Toured Japan and South Africa. *Recordings include:* Prokofiev's Visions Fugitives; Messiaen's Quatuor pour le fin du Temps and Vingt Regards sur L'Enfant Jesus; Debussy's Préludes, Estampes and Pour le Piano; Music by Bartók, Stravinsky and Mozart. *Honours:* First Prize and Excellence Prize, Nancy Conservatory, 1962, 1963; First Prize, Paris Conservatory 1966; First Prize, Olivier Messiaen Competition, Royan. *Address:* 114 rue de Dames, Paris 17, France.

BERRY Walter, b. 8 Apr 1929, Vienna, Austria. Baritone. m. (1) Christa Ludwig, 1957 (divorced 1970) 1 son, (2) Brigitte Hohenecker 1973. *Education:* Vienna School of Engineering and Vienna Music Academy. *Career:* Student Member, Vienna State Opera 1950-53, Ordinary Member 1953-, Roles have included Mozart's Count, Leporello and Papageno; Awarded title Kammersaenger by Austrian Government 1963; Guest singer at openings of opera houses in Vienna, Munich, Berlin, Tokyo, New York (Metropolitan Opera), at festivals in Munich, Aix-en-Provence, Lucerne, Netherlands, Stockholm, Saratoga; Salzburg Festival, from 1952 created roles in the premieres of Liebermann's Penelope, Egk's Irische Legende and Einem's Der Prozess, also frequently appeared as Mozart's Guglielmo; appearances in New York, Chicago, Buenos Aires, Tokyo, London, Paris, Berlin, Munich etc; Covent Garden debut 1976, as Strauss's Barak; other roles include Berg's Wozzeck, Wagner's Telramund and Wotan and Beethoven's Pizarro; sang Waldner in Arabella at Covent Garden 1986, Klingsor at San Francisco 1988; Salzburg Festival 1988, as Don Magnofico in Cenerentola (also on video); Vienna Staatsoper 1990, in Zimmermann's Die Soldaten; Concert artist in works by Bach, Beethoven, Mozart and others. *Honours:* Prizes from Music Concourses in Vienna, Verviers and Geneva. *Hobbies:* Listening to and taping music; Yachting; Swimming; Archaeology; Photography.

BERTINI Gary, b. 1 May 1927, Brichevo, Bessarabia, Russia. Composer; Conductor. m. Rosette Berengole, 21 Oct 1956, 2 children. *Education:* Diploma, Conservatorio Verdi, Milan, 1948; Diploma, Tel Aviv Music College, 1951; Conservatoire National Superieur, Paris, 1954; Ecole Normale de Musique, 1954; Institut de Musicologie, Sorbonne, Paris, 1955. *Career:* Music Director, Rinat Chamber Chorus, 1955-72; Music Director, Israel Chamber Ensemble Orchestra, 1965-75; Principal Guest Conductor, Scottish National Orchestra, 1971-81; Music Director, Jerusalem Symphony Orchestra, 1977-86; Chief Conductor, Cologne Radio-Symphony Orchestra, 1983-91; Intendant and General Music Director, Frankfurt Opera, 1987-91; Guest Conductor, Principal Orchestras and Opera Houses, Europe, USA, Japan; Artistic Advisor, Israel Festival, 1976-83; conducted Dukas' Ariane et Barbebleue at the Paris Opera in 1975; has given the premieres of 3 operas by Josef Tal: Ashmeklai 1971, Masada 1967, 1973 and Die Versuchung 1977; Forthcoming: engaged to conduct Boris Godunov at the opening of the New Israel Opera; Music Director, Israel Opera from 1994; Professor, Tel Aviv University, 1976. *Compositions:* Symphonic, Chamber, Incidental music for theatre and radio. *Publications:* Contributor to musical journals of articles in the field of music. *Honours:* Recipient, Israel State Prize, 1978. *Membership:* Israel League of Composers. *Address:* Concerto Winderstein, Leopoldstr 25, 8000 Munich 40, Germany.

BERTOLINO Mario Ercole, b. 10 Sept 1934, Palermo, Italy. Singer (Bass-Baritone). *Education:* Studied in Palermo and with Mario Basiola in Milan and Giuseppe Danise in New York. *Debut:* Teatro Nuovo

Milan 1955, as Marcello in La Bohème. *Career:* Sang at La Scala, in Rome, Palermo, Munich, Lyon and Mexico City; Moved to Forest Hills, NY, and sang widely in the US: Boston, Cincinnati, Pittsburgh, San Antonio, Washington and the New York City Opera; Roles include Verdi's Amonasro, Renato, Macbeth, Iago, Germont and Luna; Donizetti's Dulcamara, Don Pasquale and Enrico; Gerard in Andrea Chénier; Puccini's Sharpless, Iago, and Lescaut; Also performs in concert.

BERTOLO Aldo, b. 1951, Italy. Singer (Tenor). *Debut:* Sang Mozart's Ferrando at Susa, 1978. *Career:* Many appearances in Italy, South America and Europe in the lyric repertoire; Among his best roles are Donizetti's Edgardo, Tonie and Ernesto, Pylades in Piccinni's Iphigénie en Tauride, Rossini's Lindoro and Adalberto (Adelaide di Borgogna) and Don Ottavio; Season 1985 sang Arturo (I Puritani) at Martina Franca and Ramiro (La Cenerentola) in Santiago; At Valle d'Itria 1986 sang Thoas in the first modern revival of Traetta's Ifigenia en Tauride; Elvino in La Sonnambula at Piacenza, 1986; Teatro Carlo Felice, Genoa 1988, as Narciso in L'Italiana in Algeri; Other roles include the Fisherman in Guillaume Tell, Lorenzo in Fra Diavolo and Verdi's Alfredo; Season 1991 as Ernesto at Pisa and Narciso at Trieste. *Address:* c/o Teatro Carlo Felice, I-16100 Genoa, Italy.

BESCH Anthony John Elwyn, b. 5 Feb 1924, London, England. Opera and Theatre Director. *Education:* Worcester College, Oxford; MA(Oxon); FGSM. *Career:* Director, various operas and theatres, 1950-, produced the world premiere of Birtwistle's Punch and Judy (Aldeburgh 1968) and the British premieres of Shostakovich's The Nose and Ginastera's Bomarzo; Royal Opera House, Covent Garden, London; Glyndebourne Opera; from 1951, produced Mozart's Der Schauspieldirektor there in 1957; English National Opera, London Coliseum; Scottish Opera; New Opera Company, London; Handel Opera Society; Edinburgh Festival; Wexford Festival; Deutsche Oper, Berlin; Royal Netherlands Opera; Théâtre de la Monnaie, Brussels, Belgium; Teatro Colon, Buenos Aires, Argentina; New York City Opera; San Francisco Opera; Canadian Opera Company; National Arts Centre, Canada; Australian Opera; State Opera, South Australia; Victoria State Opera; Head of Opera Studies, Guildhall School of Music & Drama, Barbican, London, Jan. 1987-89; Tosca Scottish Opera 1980; staged Rota's Silent Night for Morley Opera 1990; Other work has included Il Trovatore at Brisbane and Martinů's Julietta for ENO/New Opera Company; Staged Il Barbiere di Siviglia for the Canadian Opera Company at Toronto, 1992. *Hobby:* Gardening. *Address:* 19 Church Lane, Aston Rowant, Oxfordshire, England.

BEST Matthew, b. 6 Feb 1957, Farnborough, Kent, England. Bass Singer; Conductor. m. Rosalind Mayes, 1983. *Education:* Sevenoaks School; Choral Scholar at King's College, Cambridge, MA (Hons) in Music; studied under Otakar Kraus and at National Opera Studio 1979-80, subsequently with Robert Lloyd and Patrick Mcguigan. *Debut:* Seneca in Coronation of Poppaea, Cambridge University Opera Society, 1978. *Career:* Principal Bass, Royal Opera House, 1980-86; Regular guest artist with Welsh National Opera, Opera North, also Alte Oper, Frankfurt and Glyndebourne Touring Opera; Extensive concert career; Founder/Director, Corydon Singers, 1973-. Has also worked frequently (as conductor) with English Chamber Orchestra, also guest appearances with City of London Sinfonia , BBC Singers, London Mozart Players. *Compositions:* Compositions include Opera, Alice, work performed Aldeburgh Festival 1979; sang the Archbishop in a concert performance of Szymanowski's King Roger at the Festival Hall, 1990; Wesver in Milhaud's Les Malheurs d'Orphée at the Elizabeth Hall, 1990; Appearances with Opera North 1992, as Fernando in The Thieving Magpie and as Pimen in Boris Godunov at the London Proms. *Recordings:* as singer: include Rossini Il Barbiere di Siviglia, Stravinsky The Rake's Progress, Verdi Don Carlo (video), Saint-Saëns Samson et Dalila (video). As conductor: Duruflé Requiem,

Bruckner Mass in E Minor, Motets and Requiem, Fauré Requiem, works by Britten, Vaughan Williams, Bernstein, Copland (all with Corydon Singers and English Chamber Orchestra). *Honours:* S.E. Arts Association; Friends of Covent Garden, Bursary 1980; Decca-Kathleen Ferrier Prize 1982. *Address:* c/o Harrison/Parrott Ltd, 12 Penzance Place, London W11 4PA, England.

BEST Roger, b. 28 Sept 1938, Liverpool, England. Violist; College Professor. m. Bronwen Naish, 5 children. *Education:* Royal Manchester College of Music. *Debut:* Manchester 1955. *Career:* With Hallé Orchestra 1958-60; Principal Viola, Northern Sinfonia Orchestra, 1961-73; Gave world premieres of Viola Concertos by Malcolm Arnold, 1972 and Richard Rodney Bennett, 1973; Member, Alberni String Quartet; Professor, Royal College of Music. *Honours:* Open Scholarship, RMCM, 1955; Hiles Gold Meal, 1958; Barber Trust Scholarship to Birmingham University, 1960. *Hobbies:* Painting; Golf. *Address:* 9 Granard Road, Wandsworth Common, London SW12, England.

BESTOR Charles, b. 21 Dec 1924, New York, USA. Composer; Educator. m. Ann N Elder, 1 Nov 1952, 3 s, 3 d. *Education:* BA Swarthmore College, 1948; BMus, Juilliard School of Music, 1951; MMus University of Illinois, 1952; DMA, University of Colorado, 1974. *Career:* Assistant Dean, Juilliard School of Music, 1951-59; Assistant Professor, University of Colorado, 1959-64; Dean, Willmette University, 1964-71; Head of Music, University of Alabama, 1971-73, University of Utah, 1973-77, University of Massachusetts, 1977-88, currently Professor, since 1977. *Compositions:* Chaconne for chamber orchestra; Times Arrow; Incantations and Dances; Soliloquies; In Memoriam Bill Evans; Stations of the Night; Pathways from the Dream Spell Series; Cycles; Overture to a Romantic Comedy; Three Portraits. *Recordings:* JB suite, Suite for Sax and Percuussion, More Sort of Love Songs, Cello Sonata, Lyric Variations (Orion); Piano Sonata (Serenus); Duo Variations, Second Moon of Venus (Capstone). *Hobby:* Bicycling. *Address:* Department of Music and Dance, University of Massachusetts, Amherst MA 01003, USA.

BETHMANN Siegfried, b. 20 July 1915, Bornum, Germany Democractic. Composer. m. Ilse Trippe, 20 July 1948. *Education:* Studied music with Prof Robert Teichmueller and Prof Sigfrit Grundeis, Leipzig, 1935-39. *Career:* Musician in Airforce, 1939-45; Music in Halberstadt, 1945-46; Conductor, theatre, Heidelberg, 1946; Composer and Arranger, Radio Leipzig, Berlin Television, DEFA-Film, 1946-; Installation of professional wind orchestras in former German Democratic Republic (Rundfunkbläsorchester, Leipzig, chief arranger since foundation, 1950). *Compositions:* Haideburger Blasmusik, Volumes I-IV, 1950-70; Unser Kleines Platzkonzert, 1975; Das Kleine Bläsorchester, 1963; More than 1500 compositions for Radio orchestras, Leipzig and Berlin; Symphonies; Overtures; Suites; 114 Marches; Rhapsodies; Many songs; Waltzes. *Recordings:* 25 discs. *Publications:* Author of 30 books and albums including: Teichmueller-Klaviertechnik 1937-50; Books for children: Klingende Operngrüsse, 1952; Lacheude Wiener Operettenwelf, 1953; Frueh uebt sich, 12 volumes 1970-80, *Contributions to:* Articles in magazines and journals. *Honour:* Wilhelm-Mueller-Kunstpreis, 1980. *Hobbies:* Driving good cars; Walking; Nature Conservation. *Address:* Bocksbraendchen 31, Dessau 4500, Germany.

BEUDERT Mark, b. 4 June 1951, New York, USA. Operatic Tenor. m. Jennifer Lynn Knapp, 26 June 1982, 2 daughters. *Education:* BA, Columbia University, New York, 1982; MA, University of Michigan, candidate. *Career:* New York Shakespeare Festival, 1980-82; Teatro Nacional Santo Domingo, 1983; Acapulco International Festival, 1983; Opera Grand Rapids, 1985; Opera Company of Philadelphia, New York City Opera, Glimmerglass Opera and Washington Opera, 1986; Toledo Opera and Queensland State Opera, Australia, 1987; Scottish Opera, Old Vic Theatre (London), 1988; English National Opera, 1989. *Recordings:* Candide (title role), TER Records; Street Scene (Sam Kaplan), TER Records. *Current Management:* Australia: Avene Artists Management; UK & Europe: Music International. *Address:* c/o Avene Artists Management, 52 Comber St, Paddington 2021 Australia.

BEVAN Clifford, b. 25 Jan 1934, Manchester, England. Composer; Author; Organologist. *Education:* Royal Academy of Music, BMus(Hons), FLCM, LRAM, ARCM. *Career:* Freelance trombonist and arranger, 1960-61; Pianist, Chief Arranger and Musical Director, The Temperance Seven, 1961-64; Tuba, Royal Liverpool Philharmonic Orchestra, 1964-71; Orchestra Manager, RPLO, 1966-68; Freelance Tubist, author, composer, 1972-75; Music Officer, Southern Arts Association, 1975-78; Currently freelancing, member of London Serpent Trio, Director of Piccolo Press. *Compositions:* Contributions to several films; Tyne-Tees Television Series; Music for small ensembles, educational purposes and bands. *Publications:* The Tuba Family, 1978; Rhythm; Pitch and Melody; Harmony; Melody and Counterpoint; Form; Terms, Signs and Ornaments, 1983; Musical Instrument Collections in the British Isles, 1990. *Memberships:* Performing Rights Society; Galpin Society. *Hobby:* Walking in cities. *Address:* 10 Clifton Terrace, Winchester, Hants SO22 5BJ, England.

BEVAN Maurice Guy Smalman, b. 10 March 1921, London, England. Singer. m. Anne Alderson, 1 daughter. *Education:* Magdalen College, Oxford; BMus Cantuar, 1990; FTCL; ARCM. *Career:* Vicar Choral, St Paul's Cathedral, 1949-89; Founder Member, The Deller Consort; Oratorio and Recitals, BBC; Soloist in Britain, Europe, USA, Israel and Brazil. *Publications:* Editions of English vocal music of the 17th and 18th Centuries. *Recordings:* Purcell's Faery Queen; Handel's Acis and Galatea; Many recordings for RCA, Vanguard, Abbey and Harmonia Mundi. *Contributions to:* Journal of the American Musicological Society; Die Musik in Geschichte und Gegenwart; Grove's Dictionary of Music and Musicians. *Hobby:* Cooking. *Address:* 45 Court Way, Twickenham, Middlesex, TW2 7SA, England.

BEYER Frank Michael, b. 8 Mar 1928, Berlin, Germany. Composer; Professor. *Education:* Studied sacred music Berlin; Studied composition with Ernst Pepping, Berlin Staatliche Hochschule für Musik. *Career:* Assistant Professor, Berlin Kirchenmusikschule, 1953-62; Assistant Professor 1960-68, Professor of Composition 1968-, Berlin, Hochschule für Musik; Founder-director, musica nova sacra concert series, Berlin; Director, Contemporary Music Section, Berlin Akademie der Kunste. *Compositions:* Ballet: Geburt des Tanzes, 1987; Orchestral: Concerto for Orchestra, 1957; Ode, 1963; Flute Concerto, 1964; Versi for Strings, 1968; Rondeau imaginaire, 1972; Concertino a tre for Chamber Orchestra, 1974; Diaphonie, 1975; Streicherfantasien to a motive by J S Bach, 1977, also for String Quintet, 1978; Griechenland for 3 String Groups, 1981; Deutsche Tänze for Cello, Double Bass and Chamber Orchestra, 1982, arranged from Deutsche Tänze for Cello and Double Bass, 1980; Notre-Dame-Musik, 1983-84; Mysteriensonate for Viola and Orchestra, 1986; Architettura per Musica, 1989; Concerto for Oboe and Strings, 1986; Chamber: 3 string quartets, 1957, 1969, 1985; Concerto for Organ and 7 Instruments, 1966-69, arranged as Concerto for 5 Instruments, 1968; Chaconne for Violin, 1970; Wind Quintet, 1972; Sonata for Violin and Piano, 1977; De lumine for 7 Players, 1978; Trio for Oboe, Viola and Harp, 1980; Fantasia concertante for 2 Violins, 1982; Melos for Viola, 1983; Passacaglia fantastica for Violin, Cello and Piano, 1984; Echo for Bass Flute, 1986; Sinfonien for 8 Players, 1989; Sanctus for Saxophone Quartet, 1989; Organ Music; Piano pieces; Vocal: Maior Angelis for Soprano, Women's Chorus and 6 Instruments, 1970; Canticum Mose et Agni for 8 Voice Double Chorus, 1976. *Recordings:* Several compositions recorded. *Address:* c/o Hochschule der Kunste Berlin, Ernst-Reuter-Platz 10, 1000 Berlin 10, Germany.

BIALAS Gunther, b. 19 July 1907, Bielschowitz, Germany. Composer. *Education:* Studied at the University of Breslau and at the Berlin Academy of Church and School Music. *Career:* Taught at the North-West German Academy of Music in Detmold, 1950-59; Taught at the Munich State Music School, 1959-. *Compositions:* Operas: Hero und Leander, 1966; Die Geschichte von Aucassin und Nicolette, 1967-69; Der gestiefelte Kater, 1973-74; Orchestral: Kleine Konzertmusik, 1935; Viola Concerto, 1940; Violin Concerto, 1949; Sinfonia Piccola, 1960; Cello Concerto, 1962; Chamber: 3 String Quartets, 1936, 1949, 1969; Viola Sonata, 1946; Violin Sonata, 1946; Flute Sonata, 1946; Momemts Musicaux for cello and harp, 1970; Erwartung for organ, 1972; Choral Music. *Honours include:* Music Prize, Bavarian Academy of Fine Arts, 1967; Culture Prize of Upper Silesia, 1971. *Address:* c/o GEMA, Herzog Wilhelm Strasse 28, 8000 Munich 2, Germany.

BIANCHI Lino, b. 14 May 1920, Vedano Olona, Varese, Italy. Musicologist; Composer. m. Gabriella Limentani. *Education:* Diploma in Composition, G Rossini Conservatory, Pesaro, 1945. *Career:* Artistic Director, Centro Oratorio Musicale, Rome, 1949-63; Edition de Santis, Rome, 1960-; GP da Palestrina Foundation, 1973-; Numerous broadcasts on Palestrina, Carissimi and other early composers, Italian Radio and TV, 1952-. *Compositions:* Il Principe Felice, 1-act opera; Uruel, 3-act dramatic commentary. *Recordings:* As conductor, works by Carissimi, Stradella, A Scarlatti and D Scarlatti. *Publications include:* Editions of complete works of G Carissimi and GP da Palestrina; Complete oratorios of A Scarlatti, 1964-, and A Stradella, 1969; A Scarlatti (with R Pagano), 1972. *Contributions to:* Musical encyclopedias and journals. *Address:* Circonvallazione Clodia 82, 00195 Rome, Italy.

BIANCHI Pietro, b. 15 May 1953, Giubiasco, Switzerland. Musician. m. Mireille Ben Haim, 24 Oct 1977, 1 son. *Education:* Licence, Music & Education, University of Paris, France, 1975-79; Doctorate, Musicology (Folk Music in Italian Switzerland). *Debut:* Bellinzona, Switzerland, 1959. *Career includes:* Lyonesse Folk Group, Paris, 1973- (5 LPs). *Compositions:* Cantique, 1975; Quintessence, 1975; Waltz for Ker Is, 1974; Gli Impianti di Valmaggia, 1988. Films: Oreste Zanetti, Liutaio, Autodidatta, 1975; Canti dal Fondo del Sacco, 1986; Bergell, Heimat der Giacometti, 1987. *Recordings:* Lyonesse, 1974; Cantique, 1975; Tristan de Lyonesse, 1976; Musique non Ecrite, 1977; Celtic Legends, 1978; Live in Milan, 1978; Canti e Musiche nel Ticino, 1982; Ballade, with Mireille Ben, 1989. *Contributions:* Editor, L'Almanacco, 1983-86; Musica & Teatro, 1988-89. *Honours:* Musical Prize, Ascona, 1984; Grand Prix du Disque Charles Cros (for Musique Populaire Suisse), 1987. *Memberships:* Committee Chair, International Council for Traditional Music; Swiss Society for Popular Traditions Committee. *Hobbies:* Gardening; Swimming.

BIANCONI Lorenzo Gennaro, b. 14 Jan 1946, Minusio/Muralto, Switzerland. Musicologist. m. Giuseppina La Face, 2 June 1979, 2 sons. *Education:* PhD, University of Heidelberg, Federal Republic of Germany, 1974; Studied Music Theory with Luciano Sgrizzi, Lugano, Switzerland. *Career:* Collaborator, Répertoire International des Sources Musicales, Italy, 1969-70; Member, German Institute, Venice, 1974-76; Guest Assistant, German Historical Institute, Rome, 1976; Guest Professor, Princeton University, USA, 1977; Professor of Musical Dramaturgy, Bologna University, Italy, 1977-; Professor of the History of Music, Siena University, Arezzo, Italy, 1980-83; Co-Editor, Rivista Italiana di Musicologia, 1973-79; Editor, Acta Musicologica, 1987-91; Head of Programme Committee, 14th International Musicological Congress, Bologna, 1987; Co-Editor, Musica e Storia, 1993-. *Publications:* B Marcello, Sonates pour clavecin (editor with Luciano Sgrizzi), 1971; P M Marsolo, Madrigali a 4 voci (1614), 1973; A II Verso, Madrigali a 3 e a 5 voci (1605-19), 1978; Il Seicento, 1982, English Edition, 1987; La Drammaturgia Musicale, 1986; Storia dell'Opera Italiana (editor with G Pestelli), 1987-; I Libretti italiani di G F Händel e le Loro Fonti, 1992-; Il teatro d'opera in Italia, 1993. *Honour:* Dent Medal, Royal Musical Association, 1983. *Memberships:* Council 1982-92, International Musicological Society; American Musicological Society; Council, 1979-82, Società Italiana di Musicologia; Gesellschaft für Musikforschung. *Address:* Via Murri 89, I-40137, Bologna, Italy.

BIBLE Frances, b. 26 Jan 1927, Sacketts Harbour, New York, USA. Singer (Mezzo-Soprano). *Education:* Studied at the Juilliard School with Queena Mario. *Debut:* New York City Center Opera 1948, in Tosca. *Career:* Appeared in New York until 1977 as Adalgisa, Cherubino, Octavian, Nicklausse, Siebel, Amneris and Cenerentola; Glyndebourne 1955, 1962, as Cherubino and in L'Incoronazione di Poppea; Sang in the premieres of The Ballad of Baby Doe (Central City 1956) and Robert Ward's The Crucible (New York 1961); Metropolitan Opera 1967, as Octavian. *Recordings:* L'Incoronazione di Poppea (HMV); Euryanthe (MRV).

BICKERSTAFF Robert, b. 26 July 1932, Sydney, Australia. Singer (Baritone); Teacher (Voice). m. Ann Howard, (writer). *Education:* Studied at the New South Wales Conservatorium with Lyndon Jones; Melbourne Conservatorium with Henry Portnoj; Paris with Dominique Modesti. *Debut:* Marseilles 1962, as Thoas in Iphigénie en Tauride. *Career:* Sang in Nice, Bordeaux and Marseille; Principal Baritone Sadler's Wells/English National Opera 1964-70, Roles include: Amonasro, Escamillo, Macbeth, Boccanegra, Scarpia, Wotan, Mozart's Count and Eugene Onegin; Guest appearances with Pittsburgh Opera, Welsh National Opera and at Covent Garden; over 60 roles in Opera; Other roles include Wagner's Dutchman, Ezio in Attila, Luna, Renato in Un Ballo in Maschera, Enrico in Lucia di Lammermoor and Massenet's Herode; Boris in Lady Macbeth of Mtsensk (Shostakovich) Adelaide Festival; Oratorio and recital performances; Appearances on BBC radio and TV; Previously Professor of singing at the Royal Academy of Music, London and Tutor of Singing, Kings College, Cambridge. *Recordings include:* La Juive (Raritas). *Honour:* ARAM. *Membership:*Member Incorporated Society of Musicians, London. *Hobbies:* Reading; Golf; Outdoor Activities. *Address:* 8 William Street, North Sydney, 2060 Australia.

BIDDINGTON Eric Wilhelm, b. 19 Oct 1953, Timaru, New Zealand. Composer. m. Elizabeth Ann Biddington, 4 July 1989. *Education:* BA, MA (Hons), BSc, MusB, MusB (Hons), ATCL, University of Canterbury, Christchurch. *Debut:* Christchurch Arts Centre, Christchurch. *Career:* Major recitals of chamber music, Christchurch, 1985-93, Lower Hutt, 1988, Hamilton, 1989; Premiere performance of Concerto for Two Violins and String Orchestra at Tempe, Arizona, USA, 1989. *Compositions:* Mainly chamber music and some orchestral works, including: Suite for Violin and Piano, 1985; Three Pieces for Cello and Piano, 1986; Scherzetto, for Clarinet and Piano, 1986; Autumn Music for Viola and Piano, 1987; Music for Friends, for piano trio, 1988; Suite for Oboe and Piano, 1989; Two Dances for Alto Saxophone and Piano, 1989; Four Piano Preludes, 1990; Three Bagatelles for Flute and Piano, 1990; Haere Ra - A Song for 2-part Treble Voices and Piano; Introduction, for Clarinet and Piano, 1993; Concertos for Flute, Oboe, Alto Saxophone, Two Violins; Sinfonietta; Overtures; Sonatinas for Violin and Pianoforte, Tenor Saxophone and Piano, Oboe and Piano, Clarinet and Piano, Treble Recorder and Piano, Flute and Piano, Trumpet and Piano. *Publications:* 10 publications of chamber music with Nota Bene Music; 1 private publication, chamber music. *Honours:* Award, Composers Association of New Zealand Trust Fund, 1989. *Memberships:* Composers Association of New Zealand; New Zealand Composers Foundation; APRA. *Hobbies:* Reading; Gardening. *Address:* 27 Torrens Road, Hillmorton, Christchurch 2, New Zealand.

BIEL Ann-Christin, b. 1958, Sweden. Singer (Soprano). *Education:* Studied at the Royal Music Academy, Stockholm with Birgit Sternberg and with Daniel Ferro, in New York. *Debut:* Drottningholm 1981, as Cherubino. *Career:* Has appeared at the Summer festival at Drottningholm, Stockholm, as Pamina (1982, 1989), Fiordiligi (1984-85) and Ilia (1986, 1991), Susanna (1987) and Serpetta in La Finta Giardiniera (1988, 1990); Royal Opera Stockholm 1985 (L'arbore di Diana by Martin y Soler) and 1986 (as Oscar in Un Ballo in Maschera); Sang Konstanze in the Berne 1986 world premiere of Armin Schibler's Mozart und der graue Bote (Mozart's last days); Toured as Micaela in the Peter Brook version of Carmen, Paris, Hamburg, New York and Tokyo, 1982-86; Théâtre des Champs-Elysées, Paris 1986, as Barbarina in Le Nozze di Figaro; sang Julie in the world premiere of Ms Julie at Stockholm 1990; music by Margareta Hallin, the part of Julie written for Ms Biel; Sang Gluck's Orpheus at Drottningholm, 1992; Concert appearances in Stockholm, New York, Paris, Amsterdam, Parma, Verona, Milano and Copenhagen: repertoire includes Bach's Passions, Die Schöpfung, Mozart's Vespers and Requiem, Monteverdi's Vespers and Ein Deutsches Requiem. *Recordings include:* Videos of Mozart operas from Drottningholm, directed by Göran Järvefelt, conducted by Arnold Östman. *Address:* Drottningholms Slottstheater, PO Box 27050, S-102 51 Stockholm, Sweden.

BIELAWA Herbert, b. 3 Feb 1930, Chicago, IL, USA. Composer. *Education:* BM, MM, and BA at University of Illinois; DMA, University of Southern California; Studied with Gordon Binkerd, Burrill Phillips, Ingolf Dahl, Halsey Stevens and Ellis Kohs. *Career:* Professor of Music and director of Electronic Music Studio at San Francisco State from 1966 to 1991; Now retired. *Compositions:* A Bird in the Bush, Chamber Opera, 1962; Spectrum, for Band and Tape, 1965; Divergents, for Orchestra, 1969; A Dickinson Album for Choir, Synthesized Sound, Piano and Guitar, 1972; Dreams, for SSAA Chorus, 1984; Rants I & II, for SATB and Violin, 1988; Song Cycles, The Snake and Other Creatures, for Soprano and Piano, 1987; Settings of Stone, for Soprano and Piano, 1991; Quodlibet SF42569 for Organ and Tape, 1969; Binaries for French Horn and Tape, 1981; Duo for Violin and Harpsichord, 1984; Ants for soprano, Violin and Piano, 1985; Through Thick and Thin, for Flute, Clarinet, Viola and Piano, 1991; Undertones, for Organ, 1980; Monophonies, for Organ, 1979; Organ Booklet for Organ, 1992; Pentarcs, for Piano, 1982; Expressions, for Piano, 1992. *Address:* c/o ASCAP, ASCAP Building, One Lincoln Plaza, New York, NY 10023, USA.

BIELAWSKI Ludwik Augustyn, b. 27 July 1929, Chojnice, Poland, Ethnomusicologist. m. Krystyna Kowalewska, 6 Dec 1955, 1 son. *Education:* Poznan University; PhD, 1965, Assistant Professor, 1974, Professor, 1987, Polish Academy of Sciences, Warsaw, *Career:* Associate with Action of Gathering Musical Folklore, 1951-55; Research Worker, 1955-69; Head, Study of Documentation of Polish Folklore, Institute of Art, Polish Academy of Sciences, Warsaw, 1969-; Lecturer, Head, Department of Music Theory, 1988-, Music Academy, Warsaw, 1975-; Editor, musical books. *Publications:* Rytmika polskich piesni ludowych, 1970; Strefowa teoria czasu i jej znaczente dla antropologii muzycznej, 1976; Drogi i bezdroza muzykologii polskiej, 1986; Ed, Adolf Chybinski, O polskiej muzyce ludowej, Wybor prac etnograficznych, 1961; Ed, Jadwiga i Marian Sobiescy, Polska muzyka ludowa i jej problemy, Wybor prac, 1973; Ed, Polska piesn i muzyka ludowa - zrodla i materialy, 1974-. *Address:* ul Dluga 24 m 6, 00-238 Warsaw, Poland.

BIERLEY Paul Edmund, b. 3 Feb 1926, Portsmouth, Ohio, USA. Editor; Musician. m. Pauline Jeanette Allison, 17 Sept 1948, 1 son, 1 daughter. *Education:* BAeroEng, Ohio Sate University, 1953. *Career:* Tubist, Columbus Brass quintet, 1964-80; Tubist, Columbus Symphony Orchestra, 1965-81; Tubist, World Symphony Orchestra, 1971; Tubist, Detroit Concert Band, 1973-; Tubist, Brass Band of Columbus, 1984-; Editor, Integrity Press; Board of Directors, the Robert

Hoe Foundation; Board of Advisors, numerous music organisations. *Recordings:* 30 with Detroit Concert Band; numerous freelance groups. *Publications:* John Philip Sousa, A Descriptive Catalog of his Works, 1973; John Philip Sousa American Phenomenon, 1973, 2nd edition 1986; Hallelujah Trombone! the Story of Henry Filmore, 1982; The Works of John Philip Sousa, 1984; The Music of Henry Fillmore and Will Huff, 1982; Editor, The Heritage Encycopeadia of Band Music, 1991. *Address:* 61 Massey Drive, Westerville, OH 43081, USA.

BILASH Olexander Ivanovych, b. 6 Mar 1931, Hraduzk, Ukraine, Russia. Composer. *Education:* Studied at the Kieve Conservatory. *Career:* Freelance composer of songs, choral works, orchestral music and play and film music; Director of the Composers Union of the Ukraine, 1989. *Compositions include:* Stage works Haydamaky, 1965; Ballad of War, 1971; The Clear Well, operetta, 1975; The Legend of Kieve, operetta, 1983; The Russian Bell, operetta, 1984; The Standard Bearers, 1985. *Address:* Composers Union of the Ukraine, Kiev, Ukraine, CIS.

BILINSKA Jolanta, b. 1 Mar 1951, Rzeszów, Poland. Musicologist. *Education:* Diploma with Honours, Musicology Department, Jagiellonian University, Cracow, 1976. *Appointment:* Currently: Festival Secretary, International Festival of Contemporary Music, Warsaw Autumn. *Publications:* Opery Mozarta na scenach polskich w latach 1783-1830 (Mozart's Operas on Polish Stages from 1783-1830), Muzyka 1/1977 p 79-102; Musikbiliothek und Musikleben am Hof der Fuerstin Izabella Lubomirska in Lancut (1791-1816), Musik des Ostens, Bd 11, 1989; Recepcja dziet Mozarta w Polsce (1783-1830), Ruch Muzyczny Nos 1 and 11, 1991 (Reception of Mozart's Works in Poland, 1783-1830); Die Rezeption von Mozarts Opernschaffen in Polen von 1783-1830, Mozart-Jahrbuch, 1992. *Contributions to:* Ruch Muzyczny (bi-weekly music magazine) and Polish Music (quarterly). *Membership:* Polish Composers' Union, Section of Musicology. *Hobbies:* Opera; Theatre; History (Enlightenment). *Address:* Osowska 23 m 5, 04-302 Warsaw, Poland.

BILSON Malcolm, b. 24 Oct 1935, Los Angeles, California, USA. Concert Pianist. *Education:* Studied at Bard College (BA 1957), the Vienna State Academy (Reifezeugnis 1959), Ecole Normale de Musique, Paris (Licence Libre 1960), University of Illinois (MM 1962, DMA 1968). *Career:* Assistant Professor at Cornell Universirty 1968, Associate 1970, Full Professor 1975, Frederick J Whiton Professor of Music, 1990; Acquired five-octave fortepiano by Philip Belt in 1969 and has given many concerts in the USA and abroad with late 18th century keyboard music; Concertos by Mozart and other composers with the Los Angeles Philharmonic, Milwaukee and Chicago Symphony, Vienna Tonkunstler, CBC Vancouver, Smithsonian Chamber Ensemble, Academy of Ancient Music, English Baroque Soloists, Philadelphia Chamber Orchestra and St Paul Chamber Orchestra; Music Director of the series On Original Instruments at Merkin Hall, New York; Recent performances of late 19th century repertoire on historic 6 and 6 1/2 octave Viennese pianos; Solo recitals in season 1990-91 with works by Beethoven, Schubert, Schumann and Chopin, on original 1825 Alois Graf piano; Mozart Bicentennial 1991 with the Mozart piano sonatas in four recitals throughout the USA; European tour with John Eliot Gardiner and the English Baroque Soloists; Orchestra of the 18th Century under Frans Brueggen (also appears with Nicholas McGegan); Co-director of 8 Mozart concerts on original instruments at Lincoln Center 1991-92; Has presented fortepiano workshops and master classes at the University of California, Oberlin, Eastman, Juilliard, the Sibelius Academy in Helsinki, the Utrecht Early Music Festival and the Franz Liszt Academy in Budapest. *Recordings:* Mozart Complete Concertos for fortepiano and orchestra, with the English Baroque Soloists, and the Piano Quartets (Deutsche Grammophon); Mozart Fortepiano-violin sonatas, with Sergiu Luca, Beethoven fortepiano-cello sonatas, with Anner Bylsma, Mozart music for 2 fortepianos and sonatas for fortepiano four

hands (Nonesuch); Haydn English Canzonettas, with Adrienne Csengery (Hungaroton); 7 Haydn sonatas for fortepiano (Titanic). *Address:* c/o Judith Handershott Arts Management, 4 Bennett Park, Blackheath, London SE3 9RB, England.

BIMBERG Siegfried Wolfgang, b. 5 May 1927, Halle, Saale, Germany. Musicologist; Psychologist; Composer; Conductor. m. Ortrud Rummler, PhD, 19 June 1953, 1 son, Dr Guido Bimberg, DSc, Musicologist. *Education:* Studied Musicology and Psychology, Martin Luther University, Halle, Diploma degree, BA; PhD, 1953; DrSc paed, 1956; DrSc phil, 1982. *Debut:* Martin Luther University, Halle. *Career:* Lecturer of Musicology, Halle University, 1952, 1962-; Lecturer of Musicology, Humboldt University, Berlin, 1956-62; Ordinary Professor of Musicology and Music Education, 1964-92; Head od Department for Musikdidaktik, Martin Luther Universität, Halle-Wittenberg. 1962-90; Conductor and Leader, Chamber Choir, Halle University Hallenser Madrigalisten, 1963-80; Concert tours throughout Europe; Records, radio and television; Works: folklore, renaissance, contemporary. *Compositions include:* Opera, The Singing Horse, 1961; Eulenspiegels Brautfahrt, 1987; Cantatas; Songs; Ballads. *Recordings:* Own compositions (choir works); Interpretation of own works and works of other composers. *Publications include:* Einfuehrung in die Musikpsychologie, 1957; Vom Singen zum Musikverstehen, 1957, 1969; Methodisch-didaktische Grundlagen der Musikerziehung, 1968, 1973; Handbuch der Musikästhetik (editor); 1979; Kontrast als musikästhetische Kategorie, 1981; Handbuch der Chorleitung (editor), 1981; Lieder lernen - Lieder singen, 1981; Ferruccio Busoni: von der Macht der Töne (editor), 1983. *Address:* Ernestusstrasse 24, 04020 Halle, Germany.

BING Rudolf, (Sir) b. 9 Jan 1902, Vienna, Austria. Impresario (retired). *Career:* Worked in bookshop in Vienna; Assistant to Carl Ebert at the Hessisches Staatstheater in Darmstadt, 1928-30; Assistant to the Intendant of the Charlottenburg Opera, Berlin, 1930-33; General Manager of Glyndebourne Opera, 1936-49; Co-founder of Edinburgh Festival and artistic director, 1947-49; General Manager of the Metropolitan Opera, New York, 1950-72; Consultant for Special Projects, Columbia Artists Management, 1973. *Honours include:* British Nationality, 1946; Knighted, 1971. *Publications include:* 5000 Nights at the Opera, 1972; A Knight at the Opera 1981.

BINGHAM Judith, b. 21 June 1952, Nottingham, England. Composer; Singer. m. Andrew Petrow, 20 Dec. 1985. *Education:* Royal Academy of Music, London. *Career:* Studied with Hans Keller. Commissions from Peter Pears, King's Singers, BBC Singers, Songmakers' Almanac, Omega Guitar Quartet, New London Consort, TV and Radio scores. Singing debut at penultimate night of the Proms 1984 in Strauss Deutsche Motette. Appearances with Taverner Consort, Combattimento; Member of BBC Singers. *Compositions:* A Divine Image (Harpsichord), 1976; Cocaine Lil (Soprano and Piano), 1975; Chopin (Piano), 1979; A Falling Figure (Baritone, Clarinet and Piano), BBC Commission, 1979; The Ruin (SATB), 1981; Mercutio (Baritone and Piano), 1980; Iago (Bass-baritone and Piano), 1980; Into the Wilderness (Organ), 1982; A Midsummer Night's Dream (Mezzo and Piano), 1981; Clouded Windows (Mezzo and Piano), 1980; Pictured Within (Piano), 1982; Ferrara (Tenor and Piano), 1982; A Hymn Before Sunrise in the Vale of Chamounix (24 SATB-BBC Singers), 1982; Cradle Song of the Blessed Virgin (SSATB), 1983; Mass Setting; Sterna Paradisaea (SATB and Organ), 1984; A Winter Walk at Noon (27 solo voices, BBC Commission), 1984; Just Before Dawn (SSAA), 1986; Chartres (Orchestra), 1987. *Recording:* Cradle Song of the Blessed Virgin on Libra LRS 135. *Honours:* Principals Prize for Composition, 1971; BBC Young Composer, 1976. *Hobbies:* Birdwatching; Photography; Sailing. *Address:* c/o Novello, 8 Lower James Street, London W1, England.

BINI Carlo, b. 1947, Naples, Italy. Singer (Tenor). *Education:* Studied at the Naples Conservatory. *Debut:* Teatro San Carlo Naples, 1969, as Pinkerton. *Career:* Sang in Italy and at the Deutsche Oper Berlin and the State Opera Houses of Munich and Stuttgart; Hamburg Staatsoper 1974, as Alfredo in La Traviata and Rodolfo; Sang further in Brussels, Paris, Marseille, Rio de Janeiro and the New York City Opera; Metropolitan Opera, 1982, as Enzo in La Gioconda; La Scala, 1984, in I Lombardi; sang Arrigo in I Vespri siciliani at Santiago, 1990; Avito in Montemezzi's L'amore dei tre re at Palermo, 1990; Other roles include, Rodolfo in Luisa Miller, Alfredo, Don Carlos, Gabrielle Adorno, Don José, Laca in Jenůfa and Tchaikovsky's Vakula. *Recordings:* Verdi Requeim (Decca); Eine Nacht in Venedig (Hungaroton); Video of I Lombardi. *Address:* c/o Teatro Massimo, 1-90100 Palermo, Italy.

BINKERD Gordon, b. 22 May 1916, Lynch, Nebraska, USA. Composer. *Education:* Studied at the South Dakota Wesleyan University with Gail Kubik, BMus 1937; Eastman School, Rochester, with Bernard Rogers; Harvard University with Walter Piston and Irving Fine, MA, 1952. *Career:* Professor of Music at the University of Illinois, 1949-71; Commissions from the St Louis Symphony Orchestras, the McKim Fund of the Library of Congress and the Ford and Fromm Foundations. *Compositions include:* 3 Symphonies, 1955, 1957, 1959; A Part of Heaven for violin and orchestra, 1972; The Battle for brass and percussion, 1972; Movement for orchestra, 1972; Choral: Autumn Flowers, 1968, To Electra, 1968-73; In a Whispering Gallery, 1969; Nocturne, 1969; A Christmas Caroll, 1970; A Scotch Mist 1976; Sung under the Silver Umbrella, 1977; Requiem for Soldiers lost in Ocean Transports, 1984; Houses at Dusk, 1984; Dakota Day, 1985; Instrumental: Cello sonata, 1952; 4 Piano Sonatas, 1955, 1981-83; 2 String Quartets, 1958, 1961; Violin sonata, 1977; String Trio, 1979; Songs. *Honours include:* Guggenheim Fellowship, 1959; National Institute of Arts and Letters award, 1964. *Address:* c/o ASCAP, ASCAP Building, One Lincoln Plaza, New York, NY 10023, USA.

BINKLEY Thomas, b. 26 Dec 1931, Cleveland, OH, USA. Musician; Teacher. m. Raglind Herrel, 3 sons. *Education:* BMus cum laude, University of Ilinois, 1952-56. *Career:* Director, Studio der Fruhen Musik, Munich, 1957-79; Teacher and Performer, Medieval Program, Schola Cantorum Basiliensis, Switzerland, 1973-77; Visiting Professor, Stanford University, 1977, 1979; Professor of Music and Director, Early Music Institute, Indiana University, 1979-. *Recordings include:* In excess of fifty from 1962, including: Adam de la Hall, Robin et Marion, 1991; Hildegard of Bingen, 1991; Guillaume Dufay, Misse la face ay pale, 1988; Music in Medieval Europe 1&2, 1988; Andalusische Musik, 1984; L'Agonie de Languedoc, 1976; Camino de Santiago I, 1973. *Publications:* Editor: Music: Scholarship and Performance; Publications of the Early Music Institute; Focus Recordings; Collected Articles and Reviews, 1986-89; Translation of Fritz Winckel, Music, Sound and Sensation, 1967; Contributor to: Alte Musik Praxis und Reflection, 1983; Companion to Medieval and Renaissance Music, 1991; Neves Handbuch der Musikwissenschaft, ed Carl Dahlhaus; vol II, Musikalisch & Interpretation: Die Musik des Mittelalters, Laaber, 1992. *Address:* c/o Early Music Institute, School of Music, Indiana University, Bloomington, IN 47405, USA.

BINNS Malcolm, b. 29 Jan 1936, Nottingham, England. Concert Pianist. *Education:* Bradford Grammar School, 1948-52; ARCM, Royal College of Music, 1952-56, Chappell Medal, 1956. *Debuts:* London, 1957; Henry Wood Proms, 1960; Royal Festival Hall, 1961, in the first British performance of Prokofiev 4th Piano Concerto, with the Royal Philharmonic Orchestra. *Career:* Appearances, London Philharmonic Orchestra International series, Royal Festival Hall, 1969-; Concerts, Aldeburgh Festival, Leeds Festival, Three Choirs Festival, 1975; Regular appearances at Promenade concerts; formed a duo partnership with the

violinist Manoug Parikian in 1966; Toured with Scottish National Orchestra and Limbourg Orchestra, 1988. *Recordings:* 1st complete recording of Beethoven piano sonatas on original instruments, 1980; over 30 recordings for Decca, EMI and Chandos; Recordings of four concertos by William Sterndale Bennett with LPO and Philharmonia Orchestra released on Lyrita, 1990. *Honours:* Recipient of Chappel Gold Medal, Medal of Worshipful Company of Musicians, Royal College of Music. *Hobby:* Collecting antique gramophone records. *Current Management:* Melanie Turner Management. *Address:* c/o Melanie Turner Management, 203 Murchison Road, London, E10 6LT.

BIRET Idil, b. 21 Nov 1941, Ankara, Turkey. Concert Pianist. *Education:* Studied at the Paris Conservatoire with Alfred Cortot and Nadia Boulanger; Further studies with Wilhelm Kempff. *Debut:* Played Mozart's Concerto K365 with Kempff in Paris, 1952. *Career:* Worldwide concerts with major orchestras, including the conductors Monteaux, Scherchen, Leinsdorf, Boult, Kempe, Sargent, Rozhdestvensky, Groves, Mackerras, Keilberth and Pritchard; US debut 1962, playing Rachmaninov's 3rd Concerto with the Boston Symphony; London Symphony 1963, under Monteux; Istanbul Festival 1973, playing Beethoven's violin sonatas with Yehudi Menuhin; Frequent tours of the USSR (Leningrad Philharmonic 1984); Tours of Australia 1980 and 1984; 80th birthday celebration concert for Wilhelm Backhaus and 90th birthday for Wilhelm Kempff; Festival engagements at Montreal, Persepolis, Royan, La Rochelle, Athens, Berlin and Gstaad; Symphonies of Beethoven arranged by Liszt at the Montpellier Festival 1987; Ravel Gaspard de la Nuit and Beethoven's 6th Symphony at the Wigmore Hall, 1989; Member of juries at the Queen Elisabeth Competition, Belgium and the Van Cliburn, USA. *Recordings include:* World premiere of Beethoven's Symphonies transcribed by Liszt (EMI, 1986). *Honours include:* Lily Boulanger Memorial Fund, Boston, 1954, 1964; Harriet Cohen/Dini Lipatti Gold Medal, London 1959; Polish Artistic Merit Award 1974; Chevalier de l'Ordre du Merite, France 1976; State Artist of Turkey. *Address:* c/o Wigmore Hall, Wigmore Street, London W1, England.

BIRKS Ronald, b. 1945, England. Violinist. *Education:* Studied with Sidney Griller at the Royal Academy of Music, with Sandor Vegh at the University of Keele and with Vilmos Tatrai in Budapest. *Career:* Member of the Lindsay String Quartet from 1972; Regular tours of Europe, Britain and the United States; From 1974 quartet in residence at Sheffield University, then Manchester University (1979); Premiered the 4th Quartet of Tippett at the 1979 Bath Festival and commissioned Tippett's 5th Quartet, 1992; Chamber Music Festival established at Sheffield, 1984; Regular concerts at the Wigmore Hall, including Haydn series 1987; Plays Campo Selice Stradivarius of 1694. *Recordings include:* Complete cycles of Bartók, Tippett and Beethoven; CDs of Haydn quartets Live from the Wigmore Hall (ASV). *Honours:* Prize winner (with members Lindsay Quartets) at Liège International Competition, 1969; Gramophone Chamber Award for late Beethoven quartets, 1984. *Address:* c/o Ingpen and Williams Ltd, 14 Kensington Court, London W8 5DN, England.

BIRTWISTLE Harrison (Sir), b. 15 July 1934, Accrington, Lancashire, England. Composer. m. Sheila Birtwistle, 3 sons. *Education:* Royal Manchester College of Music and Royal Academy of Music, London. *Career:* Director of Music, Cranborne Chase School 1962-65; Visiting Fellow, Princeton University (Harkness International Fellowship) 1966; Cornell Visiting Professor of Music, Swathmore College, Pennsylvania, 1973-74; Slee Visiting Professor, New York State University, Buffalo, 1975; Associate Director, National Theatre 1975-; Works have been widely performed at the major festivals in Europe including the Venice Biennale, the ISCM Festivals in Vienna and Copenhagen, the Warsaw Autumn Festival and at Cheltenham, Aldeburgh and Edinburgh; With Peter Maxwell Davies founded the Pierrot Players 1967 (later

The Fires of London); The Mask of Orpheus premiered at the London Coliseum 1986, Gawain at Covent Garden 1991; featured composer at the 1991 Aldeburgh Festival. *Compositions include:* Stage: Punch and Judy, 1-act opera 1968; Monodrama for soprano, speaker and ensemble 1967; Down by the Greenwood Side, dramatic pastoral 1969; incidental music for National Theatre productions of Hamlet 1975 and The Oresteia 1981; Ballet Frames, Pulses and Interruptions 1977; Bow Down, music-theatre 1977; The Mask of Orpheus, opera 1973-75, 1981-84; Yan Tan Tethera, TV opera 1986; Gawain, opera 1988-91; King Kong, opera, 1992-94. Orchestral: Chorales 1960-63; 3 Movements with Fanfares 1964; Nomos 1968; An Imaginary Landscape 1971; The Triumph of Time 1972; Grimethorpe Aria for Brass Band 1973, Melencolia I 1976; Silbury Air for small orchestra 1977; Still Movement for 13 solo strings 1984; Earth Dances 1985; Endless Parade for trumpet, vibraphone and strings 1987; Ritual Fragment, 1990; Vocal: Monody for Corpus Christi for Soprano and ensemble 1959; Narration: A Description of the Passing Year for chorus 1963; Entr' actes and Sappho Fragments for soprano and ensemble 1964; Carmen Paschale for chorus and organ 1965; Ring a Dumb Clarion for soprano, clarinet and percussion 1965; Cantata for soprano and ensemble 1969; Nenia on the Death of Orpheus for soprano and ensemble 1970; The Fields of Sorrow for 2 sopranos, chorus and ensemble, 1971-72; Meridian for mezzo, chorus and ensemble 1970-71; Epilogue: Full Fathom Five for baritone and ensemble 1972; ....agm....for 16 solo voices and 3 instruments 1979; On the Sheer Threshold of the Night for 4 solo voices and 12-part chorus; White and Light for soprano and ensemble 1989; Four Poems by Jaan Kaplinski for soprano and ensemble 1991; Instrumental: Refrains and Choruses for wind quintet 1957; The World is Discovered for ensemble 1960; Tragoedia for ensemble 1965; Verses For Ensembles 1969; Ut heremita solus, arr. of Ockeghem 1969; Hoquetus David, arr. of Machaut 1969; Medusa for ensemble 1970, rev. 1980; Chronometer for 8-track tape 1971; Chorales from a Toyshop 1967-74; Carmen Arcadiae Mechanicae Perpetuum for ensemble 1977; For O, For O, the Hobby Horse is Forgot for 6 percussion 1976; Clarinet Quintet 1980; Salford Toccata for brass band and bass drum, 1988; Gawain's Journey for Orchestra, 1991; An Uninterrupted Endless Melody for Oboe and Piano, 1991; Antiphonies for Piano and Orchestra, 1992; Five Distances for Five Instruments, 1992; Tenebrae for Soprano and Ensemble, 1992; Night for Soprano and Ensemble, 1992; Movement for String Quartet, 1992. *Recordings include:* On CD, Punch and Judy, Etcetera, KTC2014; Music for Wind and Pecussion, Etcetera, KTC1130; Earth Dances, Collins Classics 20012; Triumph of Time, Gawain's Journey, Collins Classics, 13872; Melencolia 1. Ritual Fragments, Meridian NMCD009. *Honours include:* Granemyer Award in US for The Mask of Orpheus, 1986; KBE 1987. *Address:* c/o Universal Edition, (London) Ltd., Warwick House, 9 Warwick Street, London W1R 5RA, England.

BISCARDI Chester, b. 19 Oct 1948, Kenosha, Wisconsin, USA. Composer; Teaching. *Education:* BA, English Literature, 1970, MA, Italian Literature, 1972, MM, Composition, 1974, University of Wisconsin at Madison; Studies at Universita di Bologna and the Conservatorio di Musica G. B. Martini; MMA, 1976, DMA, Composition, Yale University School of Music, 1980. *Career:* Music Faculty, Sarah Lawrence College, Bronxville, New York, 1977-; Teacher, University of Wisconsin, 1970-74; Yale University, 1975-76; Presently Chairman of Music Department, Sarah Lawrence College, Bronxville, NY. *Compositions:* Works include, Tenzone for 2 flutes and piano, 1975; Trio for violin, cello and piano, 1976; Mestiere for piano, 1979; At the Still Point for orchestra, 1977; Piano concerto for piano and orchestra, 1983; They Had Ceased to Talk, for violin, viola, horn in f and piano, 1975; Di Vivere, for clarinet in A and piano with flute, violin and cello, 1981; Tight-Rope, a chamber opera in 9 uninterrupted scenes, 1985 and many others. *Publications:* Tight-Rope, a chamber opera in nine uninterrupted scences (1985; libretto, Henry Butler); Piano Sonata (1986; revised 1987); Traverso, for flute and piano (1987); No Feeling

Is The Same As Before, for soprano saxophone in B-flat (1988); Tenzone, two flutes and pano, 1975; Trio, violin, violoncello and piano, 1976; Mestiere, piano, 1979; Traverso, flute and piano, 1987; At The Still Point, orchestra, 1977; Piano Concerto, piano and orchestra, 1983; Tight-Rope, chamber opera in nine uninterrupted scenes, 1985; They Had Ceased to Talk, violin and viola, horn in F and piano, 1975; Di Vivere, clarinet in A and piano with flute, violin and cello, 1981; Piano Sonata, 1986; Incitation To Desire, piano, 1984. *Address:* 542 Avenue of the Americas 4R, New York, NY 10011, USA.

BISCHOF Rainer, b. 20 June 1947, Vienna, Austria. Composer. *Education:* PhD, University of Vienna, 1973; Studied composition privately with Hans Apostel, 1967-72. *Compositions:* Sonatine for Clarinet, 1969; Sonatine for Horn, 1970; Duo for Flute and Clarinet, 1970; Theme and 7 Variations for Oboe and Cello, 1970; Quartet for Flute, Oboe, Horn and Bassoon, 1971; Grave for Violin and Piano, 1970-71; Deduction for Strings, 1973-74; Characteristic Differences for Violin and Piano, 1974; In Memoriam Memoriae, song cycle for Mezzo-soprano, Speaker, Vibraphone, Celesta, Bass Clarinet and Cello, 1975-77; Orchesterstucke, 1976-82; Flute Concerto, 1978-79; Studies from the Flute Concerto for Solo Flute, 1978; Concerto for Violin, Cello and Orchestra, 1979-80; Variations for Organ, 1981; Viola Tricolor, 32 variations for Viola, 1982; Music for 6 Recorders, 1982-83. *Address:* AKM, III Baumstr. 8-10, 1031 Wien, Austria.

BISPO Antonio Alexandre, b. 17 Mar 1949, Sao Paulo, Brazil; came to Germany 1974. *Education:* Licence, music education, Instituto Musical de Sao Paulo, 1972; Licence, conducting, 1973; Diploma, architecture, University of Sao Paulo, 1972; DMusicology, University of Cologne, Germany, 1979. *Career:* Director, Conservatorio Jardim America, Sao Paulo, 1971-72; Lecturer, Ethnomusicology and Aesthetics of Music, 1972-74; Researcher, Institut für Hymnologische und Musikethnologische Studien Maria Laach Germany, 1979-; Director, Musikschule der Stadt Leichlingen, Germany, 1981-84. *Publications:* Die katholische Kirchenmusik in der Provinz Sao Paulo, 1979; Editor Correspondencia Musicológica, 1989-; Author, Collectanea Musicae Sacrae Brasiliensis, 1981; Grundlagen christlicher Musikkultur in der aussereuropäischen Welt der Neuzeit, 1989; Leben und Werk von Martin Braunwieser, 1991. *Contributions to:* Musices Aptatio, 1980-; Editor, Leichlinger Musikforum, 1981-84; Boletim da Sociedade Brasileira de Musicologia, 1981-; Articles, professional journals. *Memberships:* Consociatio Internationalis Musicae Sacrae, Rome, 1979-; Sociedade Brasileira de Musicologia, board, 1981-; Academia Paulistana de Historia, 1981-; Associaçao Brasileira de Folclore, 1981-; Gesellschaft für Musikforschung, 1984-; International Council for Traditional Music, 1984-; Gesellschaft zur Erforschung und Förderung der Blasmusik, 1984-; Ordem Nacional dos Bandeirantes, 1981-; Institut für Studien der Musikkultur des portugisischen Sprachraumes, 1985-. *Address:* Theodor Heuss Ring 14, 50668 Cologne 1, Nordrhein-Westphalen, Germany.

BISSON Yves, b. 31 May 1936, Mostaganem, Algeria. Singer (Baritone). *Education:* Studied at Paris Conservatoire with Renee Gilly-Musy and Louis Noguera. *Career:* sung at the Paris Opera, the Opéra-Comique, notably in Manon, Faust, Platée, Bohème, Werther, Romeo and Juliette, Les Pêcheurs de Perles (all televised); Festival engagements at Aix-en-Provence (Rodolphe in Les Fêtes Vénitiennes by Campra), Avignon, Carpentras and Orange; has sung elsewhere in France and New York, Washington, Amsterdam, Brussels, London (Covent Garden), Lisbon, Geneva, Zurich, Barcelona, Madrid, Vienna, Naples, USSR; Other repertoire includes Lescaut in Auber's Manon Lescaut, Escamillo, Nilakantha (Lakmé), Valentin, Mercutio, Sander in Zemire et Azor by Grétry; Massenet's Lescaut, Albert and Caoudal (Sapho); Mozart's Figaro and Masetto; Rangoni in Boris Godunov; Puccini's Marcello, Schaunard, Sharpless and Lescaut; Rameau's Oromases (Zoroastre) and Citeron (Platée); Verdi's Posa,

Germont and Ford. *Address:* de l'Opéra, 36 Rue Ballu, 75009 Paris, France.

BISWAS Anup Kumar, b. 1957, West Bangal, India. Composer; Concert Cellist. *Education:* Studied in India with Rev T Mathieson, at Royal College of Music; Further study with Pierre Fournier in Geneva and Jacqueline du Pre in London. *Career:* Concerts throughout UK, including St James and Lambeth Palaces, Elizabeth and Wigmore Halls, Grays Inn and Riverside Studios; Festival engagements at Cleveland, Balfast, Greenwich and Hereford; Masterclassed at the Dartington Summer School and concerts in Germany, Finland, Norway; JS Bach Tercentenary concerts in cathedrals and churches in the UK. feauring the suites for unaccompanied cello; Artistic Director of the Dante Alighieri Orchestra, from 1989; Royal Albert Hall, 1992, performing Celebration from his own ballet Ten Guineas under the Banyan Tree; Purcell Room Concert, 1993, playing Beethoven, Shostakovich, Walton and Brahms. *Compositions:* Music for Theatre Taliesin, Wales, 1986 production of Tristan and Essylt, featured by BBC Wales. *Address:* East West Arts Limited, 93b Cambridge Gardens, London W10 6JE, England.

BJONER Ingrid, b. 8 Nov 1927, Kraakstad, Norway. Opera and Concert Singer (Soprano). *Education:* Conservatory of Music, Oslo, with Gudrun Boellemose; Hochschule fur Musik Frankfurt with Paul Lohmann; Further study with Ellen Repp in New York; Graduate pharmacist, University of Oslo, 1951. *Career:* Sang Third Norn and Gutrune in Norwegian radio recording of Götterdämmerung, 1956; Stage debut, Oslo 1957, as Donna Anna; Drottningholm Opera 1957, as Handel's Rodelinda; Member, Wuppertal Opera, Germany 1957-59; Deutsche Oper am Rhein Dusseldorf, 1959-61; Bayreuth Festival 1960, as Freia, Helmvige and Gutrune; Has sung with the Bayerische Staatsoper Munich from 1961, notably as the Empress in Die Frau ohne Schatten 1963 and as Isolde, in the centenary production of Tristan und Isolde 1965; Metropolitan Opera debut 1961, as Elsa in Lohengrin; Covent Garden from 1967, as Senta, Sieglinde and Leonore (Fidelio); Salzburg Festival 1970, Leonore; Sang the Duchess of Parma in the US premiere of Doktor Faust by Busoni, Carnegie Hall 1974; Oslo and Copenhagen 1985-86, as Elektra; Further appearances at La Scala, Vienna, Hollywood Bowl, Hamburg, Deutsche Oper Berlin, Cologne Opera, Warsaw and Vancouver; season 1986/87 sang Isolde at Bayreuth and the Kostelnička in Jenůfa at Karlsruhe; Staatsoper Munich 1988, as the Dyer's Wife in Die Frau ohne Schatten; Oslo Opera 1989, Senta; Concert appearances worldwide, often in the songs of Grieg; Professor at Royal Academy of Music, Copenhagen, 1991; Professor at Royal Academy of Music, Oslo, 1992-. *Recordings include:* Götterdämmerung, conducted by Fjelsted (Decca); Die Frau ohne Schatten (Deutsche Grammophon); Wagner's Wesendonck Lieder; Songs by Sibelius. *Honours include:* Order of St Olav, Norway, 1964; Bavarian Order of Merit. *Address:* Gregers Grams vei 33, 0382-Oslo 3, Norway.

BJORLIN Ulf, b. 21 May 1933, Stockholm, Sweden; Composer; Conductor. *Education:* Studied with Igor Markevitch in Salzburg and Nadia Boulanger in Paris. *Career:* Director of Royal Dramatic Theatre, Stockholm, 1963-68; Freelance Composer; Conductor of leading orchestras in Sweden and elsewhere in Scandanavia. *Compositions include:* Pinocchio, children's musical, 1966; Ekon for orchestra, 1967; In Five years, opera for actors and chamber ensemble, 1967; Epitaph for Lars Gorling, for orchestra 1967; Of Melancholy, choreographic oratoria 1970; The Bit Theatre, opera, 1972; The Ballad of Kasper Rosenrod, opera, 1972; Karlekin till Belisa, radio oepra, 1981; Wind Quintet, 1983; Tillfalle gor Tiufven, opera buffa, 1983; Den Frammande Kvinnan, opera, 1984. *Address:* STIM (Sweden), c/o Member Registration, PRS Ltd 29/33 Berners Street, London W1P 4AA.

BJORLING Rolf, b. 25 Dec 1928, Jonkoping, Sweden. Singer (Tenor). m. Gunnel Eklund. *Education:* Studied at the Stockholm Music Academy 1953-54 and with Dimitri Onofrei in San Francisco. *Debut:* Stockholm 1960, in concert. *Career:* Stage debut Gothenburg 1962, as Pinkerton; Guest appearances in Berlin, Hamburg, Munich, Helsinki, Oslo and San Francisco; Member of the Royal Opera Stockholm from 1969; Appearances at Drottningholm Opera House; Roles include Florestan, Manrico, Cavaradossi, Calaf, Radames and Don José; Founded the Nyla Bjorling Vocal Quartet 1971: tours of Scandinavia and North America.

BLACK Jeffrey, b. 1964, Australia. Singer (Baritone). *Debut:* European, Harlekin in Ariadne auf Naxos at Monte Carlo, 1986. *Career:* Sang with Australian Opera from 1985 as mercutio, Schaunard, papageno, Dr Falke, Dandini, Rossini's Figaro and Ottone in Poppea; Glyndebourne Festival, from 1986, as Sid in Albert Herring, Demetrius and the Count in Figaro and Capriccio; Covent Garden appearances as well as engagements at Los Angeles as Guglielmo and marcello, 1993, Opera Bastille in Paris, Puccini's Lescaut, Geneva Opera, Fieramosca in Benvenuto Cellini, San Francisco, Rossini's Figaro; Lyric Opera of Chicago and 1993 Salzburg Festival as Guglielmo, Teatro Colon Buenos Aires as Dandini, Don Giovanni at Vancouver and Eugene Onegiin at San Diego; Returned to Australia to appear with Lyric Opera of Queensland and Victoria State Opera, Melbourne; Concerts include tour of Australia with Geoffrey Parsons and the ABC orchestras, Carmina Burana with the London Philharmonic and Christus in the St Matthew Passion under Franz Welser-Most. *Recordings include:* Carmina Burana. *Address:* IMG Artists, Media House, 3 Burlington Lane, London W4 2TH, England.

BLACK Robert (Carlisle), b. 28 Apr 1950, Dallas, Texas, USA. Pianist; Conductor. *Education:* Studied at Oberlin College Conservatory and at the Juilliard School with Beveridge Webster, Roger Sessions and Gustave Reese. *Debut:* Carnegie Hall 1976. *Career:* Solo performances of Beethoven, Liszt and contemporary music; Premieres of music by Ralf Shapey, Dane Rudhyar and Stravinsky; Conductor of the New York New Music Ensemble from 1975 and Speculum Musicae from 1978; Founded the orchestra Prism in 1983; Has conducted premieres of works by Shapey, Schwanter and Charles Wuorinen; US first performances of music by Jean Barraque; Teacher at Princeton University 1976-83; University of California at Santa Barbara 1981-82; Columbia University, New York, from 1983. *Address:* c/o Music Faculty, Columbia University, New York, NY 10027, USA.

BLACK Stanley, b. 14 June 1913, London, England. Conductor; Composer; Pianist; Arranger. m. Edna Kaye, 2 children. *Education:* Matthay School of Music. *Career:* Conductor, BBC Dance Orchestra, 1944-52; Musical Director, Associated British Pictures Corporation, Elstree Studios, 1958-63; BBC Television appearances; Guest conductor, New Zealand, Australia, Canada, Japan, Korea, USA, Netherlands, Belgium, UK; Associate Conductor, Royal Philharmonic Orchestra, 1967; Principal Conductor, BBC Northern Ireland Orchestra, 1968-69; Associate Conductor, Osaka Philharmonic Orchestra, 1971; Principal Conductor, New Zealand Proms, 1972 and 1974; Concerts with Royal Philharmonic Orchestra, Bournemouth Symphony Orchestra, English Northern Philharmonia, National Philharmonic Orchestra, BBC Festival of Light Music. *Compositions include:* Over 100 film scores. Numerous recordings. *Contributions to:* Melody Maker; Today's Cinema, and others. *Honours:* Life Fellow, International Institute of Arts and Letters, Zurich, 1962; Joint Novello Award, 1963; Various Gold Records; Order of the British Empire (OBE) in 1986 New Year's Honours List; BASCA (British Academy of Songwriters Composers and Authors), Gold Award, 1987; Freedom of the City of London, December 1988. *Hobbies:* Theatre; Riding. *Address:* 8 Linnell Close, London NW11, England.

BLACK Virginia, b. 1950, England. Harpsichordist. m. Howard Davis. *Career:* London Concerts in the Wigmore Hall, Purcell Room and Queen Elizabeth Hall;

Appearances at major festivals in the United Kingdom; Recordings for the BBC and the Westdeutsche Rundfunk; Television performance of Bach's 5th Brandenburg Concerto, with the English Chamber Orchestra; Tours to Europe, the USA, Australia and New Zealand; Concerts with Howard Davis, violin; Other repertoire includes Sonatas by Soler and Scarlatti; Bach's Chromatic Fantasy and Fugue, Concertos in E and C minor, Fantasie and Fugue in A minor, Toccata in D and Partitas; Pieces by Rameau, Dandrieu, Duphly and Forqueray; Falla's Harpsichord Concerto; Professor of Harpsichord at the Royal Academy of Music. *Address:* Manygate Management, 13 Cotswold Mews, 12-16 Battersea High Street, London SW11 3JB, England.

BLACK William David, b. 23 Feb 1952, Dallas, Texas, USA. Concert Pianist. *Education:* BM, Oberlin College, 1974; MM, 1976, DMA, 1979, The Juilliard School. *Debut:* New York, 1977; London, England, 1979. *Career:* Solo and orchestral engagements across the USA, Canada, England, France, Holland, Belgium, Germany, Iceland, Japan, China and Italy; Television appearances in the USA and numerous USA and European radio broadcasts including worldwide broadcasts over the Voice of America. *Recordings:* Works of David Diamond; World Premiere recordings of the original version of the 4th Piano Concerto of Sergei Rachmaninov; Hunter Johnson Piano Sonata; Gershwin in Rhapsody in Blue. *Contributor to:* Keyboard Classics. *Honours:* Pi Kappa Lambda, 1974; Concert Artists Guild Award; Morris Loeb Award, The Juilliard School; Solo Recitalist Grant, National Endowment for the Arts, 1991. *Memberships:* Bohemians, New York Musicians Club; European Piano Teachers' Association. *Address:* 315 West 106th Street, New York, NY 10025, USA.

BLACKBURN Bonnie J, b. 15 July 1939, Albany, New York, USA. Musicologist. m. (1) Edward E Lowinsky, 10 Sept 1971, deceased 1985, (2) Leofranc Holford-Strevens, 6 Jan 1990. *Education:* BA, Wellesley College, 1961; MA, 1963, PhD, 1970, University of Chicago. *Career:* Research Assistant, Department of Music 1963-76, Visiting Associate Professor 1986, University of Chicago; Lecturer, School of Music, Northwestern University, 1987; Visiting Associate Professor, State University of New York at Buffalo, 1989-90. *Publications:* Music for Treviso Cathedral in the Late Sixteenth Century: A Reconstruction of the Lost Manuscripts 29 and 30, 1987; Josquin des Prez: Proceedings of the International Josquin Festival-Conference, 1976, edited with E Lowinsky; Edited Johannis Lupi Opera omnia, 3 volumes, 1980-89; Edited Music in the Culture of the Renaissance and Other Essays by Edward E Lowinsky, 1989; Editor with E Lowinsky and C A Miller, A Correspondence of Renaissance Musicians, 1991. *Contributions to:* Musical Quarterly; Journal of the American Musicological Society; Musica Disciplina; Early Music History; The New Grove Dictionary of Music and Musicians; Early Music, Studi musicali. *Address:* 115 Kingston Road, Oxford, OX2 6RW, England.

BLACKBURN Olivia, b. 1960, London, England. Singer (Soprano). *Education:* Studied at Trinity College, London, and at the Pears-Britten School. *Career:* Regular concert on South Bank, London, in Die Schöpfung by Haydn, Vivaldi's Magnificat and Handel's Jephtha; German Requiem by Brahms at the Barbican with the Philharmonia and the St Matthew Passion with the Steinitz Bach Players; European performances in the Bach B Minor Mass, Haydn's Paukenmesse (Missa in tempore belli), Messiah and the Mozart Requiem; Opera debut in The Poisoned Kiss by Vaughan Williams at the Bloomsbury Theatre; Wexford Festival 1987; With Cologne Opera has sung Naiad in Ariadne auf Naxos, Siebel in Faust, Sandrina (La Finta Giardiniera), Helena in A Midsummer Night's Dream and Pamina; Song recitals in Paris, Dublin, London, and Cambridge; Appearances with the Songmakers' Almanac in London and at the Nottingham and Buxton Festivals; Season 1989/90 in Ode to the West Wind by Arnell, Acie in Handel's Acie, Galatea e Polifemo with London Baroque at the Beaune Festival, Mendelssohn's Lobgesang

conducted by Richard Hickox and Mozart's C Minor Mass in Scotland and in France with Malgoire and Portugal with Bruggen conducting; Covent Garden debut, 1992, as a Young Nun in The Fiery Angel; TV recording of Handel's Roman Vespers in Vienna. *Recordings include:* Bach B Minor Mass. *Address:* c/o Ron Gonsalves Management, 10 Dagnan Road, London SW12 9LQ, England.

BLACKHAM Joyce, b. 1 Jan 1934, Rotherham, Yorkshire, England. Singer (Soprano). m. Peter Glossop (div). *Education:* Studied at the Guildhall School of Music with Joseph Hislop. *Debut:* Sadler's Wells Opera 1955, as Olga in Eugene Onegin. *Career:* Covent Garden debut as Esmeralda in The Bartered Bride; Best known as Carmen, also sang Dorabella, Mimi, Norina, Mimi, Rosina and roles in operettas by Offenbach, Johann Strauss and Lehar; Guest appearances Berlin, New York and New Zealand, with Welsh National Opera sang Rosina, Amneris and Cherubino; sang Maddalena in Rigoletto at Covent Garden, 1974. *Address:* Royal Opera House, Covent Garden, London, WC2.

BLACKLEY Michael, b. 31 Jan 1935, Kent, England. Tenor; Conductor; Arranger; Teacher; m. Elizabeth Weston, 21 Oct 1961, 1s 2 d. *Education:* Solo Singing, Guildhall School of Music. *Career:* Vicar Choral, St Paul's Cathedral, London; Soloist, most standard oratorio works; Conductor, most standard works, choir and choir and orchestra; Linden Singers; Broadcasts, including Friday Night Music Night; Singing Monk, Film, Martin Luther, London New Music Singers. *Recordings:* Chorus (Pro); Ambrosian Opera Chorus (various). *Honours:* Guildhall School Tenor Prize, 1960; Guildhall Sight Singing Prize, 1960; Queen's Silver Jubilee Medal, 1977. *Memberships:* Equity; ISM; National Early Music Association. *Hobbies:* Table Tennis; Gardening. *Address:* 83 Pendle Road, London SW16 6RX, England.

BLACKWELL Harolyn, b. 1960, Washington DC, USA. Singer (Soprano). *Education:* Studied at the Catholic University of America and with Carlo Bergonzi and Renata Tebaldi in Italy. *Career:* Has sung Jemmy in Guillaume Tell at the San Antonio Festival, Papagena in Cleveland, Oscar in Hamburg, Gilda with the Miami Opera, Sister Constance in Dialogues des Carmélites for Canadian Opera and Clara in Porgy and Bess at the 1986 Glyndebourne Festival; Symphonic engagements with the National Symphony, St Louis Philharmonic, Cincinnati Symphony, Minnesota Orchestra and Buffalo Philharmonic; Carnegie Hall as Xanthe in Die Liebe der Danae by Strauss; Recitals in Buffalo, Denver, Dallas and New York (debut 1987); Season 1986-87 with debuts at Chicago as Oscar (Un Ballo in Maschera) and at the Metropolitan as Pousette in Manon; Xenia in Boris Godunov, conducted by James Conlon; Season 1987-88 with concert performance of Porgy and Bess under Simon Rattle, Nannetta in Falstaff at Nice and the Princess in L'Enfant et les Sortilèges at Glyndebourne; Season 1988-89 included Schubert's A-flat Mass in Detroit, Barbarina and Sophie (Werther) at the Met, Olga in Giordano's Fedora at Carnegie Hall and Zdenka (Arabella) at Glyndebourne; Season 1989-90 with Adele at the Met and Marie (La Fille du Régiment) in Seattle; Blondchen in Die Entführung at Aix-en-Provence; Season 1990-91 highlights were Oscar at the Met, Mahler's 4th Symphony in Florida and Charleston, Bach and Handel with the New York Chamber Symphony, Mozart's Il Re Pastore with the Nice Opera and Le Nozze di Figaro (Susanna) in Toronto. *Recordings include:* Porgy and Bess (EMI). *Address:* c/o Columbia Artists Management Inc, 165 West 57th Street, New York, NY 10019, USA.

BLACKWOOD Easley, b. 21 Apr 1933, Indianapolis, Indiana, USA. Composer; Pianist; Music Educator. *Education:* Received piano training in Indianapolis; studied composition, Berkshire Music Center, Tanglewood, Massachusetts, summers 1948, 1949 (with Messiaen), 1950, with Heiden, Indiana University School of Music, Bloomington; with Hindemith, Yale University, MA 1954 and with Boulanger in Paris, 1954-56. *Career:* Appeared as soloist with the Indianapolis

Symphony Orchestra, 1947; Concerts throughout North America and Europe; Faculty member 1958-68, Professor 1968-, University of Chicago. *Compositions:* Orchestral: 5 symphonies: No 1, 1954-55; No 2, 1960; No 3, 1964; No 4, 1973; No 5, 1978; Chamber Symphony, 1954; Clarinet Concerto, 1964; Symphonic Fantasy, 1965; Oboe Concerto, 1965; Violin Concerto, 1967; Flute Concerto, 1968; Piano Concerto, 1970; Chamber: Viola Sonata, 1953; 2 string quartets, 1957, 1959; Concertino for 5 Instruments, 1959; 2 violin sonatas, 1960, 1973; Fantasy for Cello and Piano, 1960; Pastorale and Variations for Wind Quintet, 1961; Sonata for Flute and Harpsichord, 1962; Fantasy for Flute, Clarinet and Piano, 1965; Symphonic Episode for Organ, 1966; Piano Trio, 1967; 12 Microtonal Etudes for Synthesizer, 1982; Piano pieces; Vocal: Un voyage a Cythere for Soprano and winds, 1966; 4 Letter Scenes from Gulliver's Last Voyage for Mezzo-soprano, Baritone and Tape, 1972. *Publication:* The Structure of Recognizable Diatonic Tunings, 1986. *Honours:* Fulbright Scholarship, 1954-56; First prize, Koussevitzky Music Foundation, 1958; Creative Arts Award, Brandeis University, 1968; Several commissions. *Address:* c/o Music Department, University of Chicago, Chicago, IL 60637, USA.

BLADES James, b. 9 Sept 1901, Peterborough, England. Orchestral Timpanist; Tutor; Lecturer; Author. m. Joan Goossens, 1 child. *Career:* Apprenticed as engineer; Played in orchestras for silent films; Joined London Symphony Orchestra as principal percussionist 1940; Played with most British orchestras and many chamber ensembles; Associated with the English Opera Group in the premieres of Britten's Church Parables; Professor of Timpani and Percussion at the Royal Academy of Music 1960; Many lectures and broadcasts. *Recordings:* Blades on Percussion 1973; Discourses 1974. *Publications:* Percussion Instruments and their History, 1970-75. *Contributions to:* Saturday Book, 1969. *Honours include:* Order of the British Empire 1972. *Hobby:* Mechanics. *Address:* 191 Sandy Lane, Cheam, Surrey SM2 7EU, England.

BLAHA Ivo, b. 14 Mar 1936, Litomysl, Czechoslovakia. Composer; Teacher. *Education:* Pupil of Ridky and Sommer, graduated 1958, Postgraduate studies with Hlobil 1965-70, Prague Academy of Music; Training in electronic music from Kabelac and Herzog, Plzen Radio. *Career:* Teacher 1964-, Docent, Film and Television Department 1967-, Prague Academy of Music. *Compositions:* 3 string quartets, 1957, 1966, 1983; Concerto for Orchestra, 1957; 3 Movements for Violin and Piano, 1961; Spring Plays for Wind Quintet, 1962; Concerto for Percussion and Orchestra, 1964; Solitude, sonata for Solo Violin, 1965; Music for Wind Quintet, 1965; Violin Concerto, 1968; Music to Pictures of a Friend for Flute, Oboe and Clarinet, 1971; Cello Sonata, 1972; 2 Inventions for Solo Flute, 1974; Duo for Bass Clarinet and Piano, 1975; Per archi: Sinfonia, 1977; The Violin for Solo Instrument, 1979; Hymn for Organ, 1980; Sonata transparenta for Flute and Piano, 1982; Cet amour for speaker, wood instruments and tape, 1975; Rays for Piano, 1976; Moravian Lullybies for soprano, flute and piano, 1982; Zoolessons I for guitar, 1984; II, 1987; Vaults for Organ, 1986; Imaginations for violin and piano, 1988; Sonata introspecta for viola, 1989. *Address:* Jablonecká 418, 190 00 Prague 9, Czech Republic.

BLAIR James, b. 1950, Stirling, Scotland. Conductor. *Education:* Studied at Trinity College, London, and with Adrian Boult; won Ricordi Conducting Prize and an Italian Government Scholarship to study with Franco Ferrara in Sienna and Venice. *Career:* Artistic Director and Principal Conductor, Young Musicians Symphony Orchestra, 1971-; many performances of Mahler, Messiaen and Strauss; engagements with all leading British orchestras and works with Opera North, Dublin Grand Opera and Athens Opera; US debut 1984 with the Delaware Symphony; later conducted Colorado Springs and Kansas City Symphony Orchestras; many YMSO concerts given on BBC, including Mahler's 8th Symphony. *Recordings:* Late Romantic repertory with

Philips. *Address:* c/o Anglo-Swiss Artists Management Ltd, 59 St Martin's Lane, London WC2N 4JS, England.

BLAKE David, b. 2 Sept 1936, London, England. Composer; Professor of Music. m. Rita Muir, 24 Sept 1960, 2 s, 1 d. *Education:* BA, MA, Gonville and Caius College, Cambridge, 1957-60; Deutsche Akademie der Künste, 1960-61. *Career includes:* Lecturer in Music, 1964-71, Senior Lecturer, 1971-76, Professor of Music, 1976-, University of York. *Compositions include:* Variations for piano, 1960; Three Choruses to Poems of Robert Frost, 1964; What is the Cause, for chorus, (Fulke Greville, 1967; Nonet for Wind, 1971; Violin Concerto, BBC Proms, 1976; Toussaint (libretto Anthony Ward), premiere London Coliseum, 1977, opera in three acts, 1974-77; Clarinet Quintet, 1980; Scherzi ed Intermezzi for orchestra, 1984; Seasonal Variants for seven players, 1985; Pastoral Paraphrase for bassoon and small orchestra, 1988; The Plumber's Gift, (libretto John Birtwhistle) (premiered at the London Coliseum,) 1989; Night Music for Saxophone Quartet, 1990; Mill Music for brass band, 1990; Cello Concerto, 1992; Three Ritsos Choruses, 1992; *Recordings:* Violin Concerto: In Praise of Krishna: Variations for Piano; The Almanack. *Hobbies:* Golf; Environmental Conversation; Mill Restoration. *Current management:* Novello & Co. *Address:* Mill Gill, Askrigg nr Leyburn, N Yorks, DL8 3HR, England.

BLAKE Howard, b. 1938, London, England. Composer. *Education:* Royal Academy of Music, with Harold Craxton and Howard Ferguson. *Career:* 1960-70 worked in London as pianist, conductor, orchestrator and composer; From 1971 freelance composer: Benedictus performed at Manchester, Llandaff and St Albans Cathedrals, the Perth and Three Choirs Festivals and by the Bach Choir in London (1988) and with the Philharmonia RFH, 1989; Barbican concerts for children; Director of P.R.S. and Executive Director, 1978-87. *Compositions:* Comic opera The Station 1987; Orchestral: Toccata 1976; The Annunciation 1979 (ballet); Concert Dances 1984; Clarinet Concerto 1984; Diversions for cello and orchestra 1985; Vocal: Three Sussex Songs 1973; Two Songs of the Nativity 1976; The Song of St Francis 1976; A Toccata of Galuppi's for baritone and harpsichord 1978; Benedictus, dramatic oratorio 1979; The Snowman for narrator, boy soprano and orchestra 1982; Festival Mass for double choir a capella 1987; Shakespeare Songs for tenor and string quartet 1987; Instrumental: Piano Quartet 1974; The Up and Down Man, children's suite 1974; Penillion for violin and harp 1975; Eight Character Pieces for piano 1976; Dances for 2 pianos 1976; Prelude for solo viola 1979; Sinfonietta for 10 brass 1981; Piano Concerto commissioned by the Philharmmonia to celebrate 30th Birthday of HRH Princess of Wales, 1991; Visiting Professor of Composition at Royal Academy of Music, 1992. *Compositions:* Violin Concerto, world premiere, 1992; Commissioned by Leeds City Council for their Centenary. *Recordings:* Diversions for cello and orchestra, Toccata 1991; Snowman, CBS; Benedictus, CBS; Piano Concerto, Sony; Clarinet Concerto, Hyperion; Granpa, CBS/Sony. *Publications:* Many with Faber Music. *Honours:* Fellow of the Royal Academy of Music, 1989. *Memberships:* APC; ISM; Groucho's.*Address:* c/o Faber Music Ltd, 3 Queen Square, London WC1N 3AU, England.

BLAKE Rockwell (Robert), b. 10 Jan 1951, Plattsburgh, New York, USA. Tenor. m. Deborah Jeanne Bourlier, 25 Aug 1973. *Education:* Studied voice with Renata Booth in high school; Attended, State University of New York, Fredonia; Catholic University of America, Washington, DC. *Career:* Soloist with: US Navy Band; Washington DC, Opera, 1976; Hamburg State Opera, 1977-79; Vienna State Opera, 1978; New York City Opera, 1979-81; Metropolitan Opera, NY, 1981-83, 1986, 1988 as Lindoro in L'Italiana in Algeri, Almaviva, Don Ottavio and Arturo in I Puritani; Chicago Lyric Opera, 1983, 1987; Rossini Opera Festival, Pesaro, 1983-85, 1987-88; San Francisco Opera, 1984; Paris Opera, 1985; Naples San Carlo, 1985-88; Opera-Comique, Paris, 1987; Bavarian State Opera, Munich,

1987; Rome Opera, 1988-89; sang James V in La donna del Lago at Bonn, 1990; Arturo in I Puritani at Barcelona, 1990; Tonio (La Fille du Régiment) at Santiago; Concert performance of Meyebeer's Il Crociato in Egitto at the 1990 Montpellier Festival; Rossini cantatas at Martina Franca; the title role in Il Pirata at Lausanne, 1992; Season 1992 as Rossini's Almaviva at Genoa, Selim in Rossini's Adina at Rome, James V in La Donna del Lago at La Scala, Mozart's Ferrando at Dallas; Almaviva at the 1992 Caracalla Festival; Various concert engagements. *Recordings:* The Rossini Tenor; The Mozart Tenor; Encore Rossini; Alina la Regina di Golconda; Il Barbiere di Siviglia; Video of Rossini's Barber from the Metropolitan, DGG. *Honours:* First winner, Richard Tucker Award, 1978; National Opera Institute Grantee, 1975 and 1976; Honorary Doctorate of Music State orchestra. *Hobbies:* Musicological research; Computers; Designing Jewellery; Making furniture; Woodworking. *Address:* c/o Columbia Artists Management Inc, 165 West 57th Street, New York, NY 10019, USA.

BLANC Ernest Marius Victor, b. 1 Nov 1923, Sanary-sur-Mer, France. Singer (Baritone). m. Eliane Guiraud. *Education:* Studied at the Toulon Conservatory 1946-49. *Debut:* Marseilles 1950, as Tonio in Pagliacci. *Career:* Paris Opera from 1954, debut as Rigoletto; sang in Paris until 1976 in operas by Puccini, Wagner, Offenbach and Verdi; Bayreuth Festival, 1958-59, as Telramund; La Scala Milan, 1960; Glyndebourne, 1960, as Don Giovanni and as Riccardo in I Puritani; Guest appearances in Naples, New York, Barcelona, Lisbon, Tel Aviv, Florence and Amsterdam. *Recordings:* Faust, Carmen, Iphigénie en Tauride, Les Contes d'Hoffmann, Les Pêcheurs de Perles (HMV). *Hobby:* Mechanics.

BLANC Jonny, b. 10 July 1939, Lessebo, Sweden. Singer (Tenor). *Education:* Studied at the Stockholm Conservatory with Kathe Sundstrom and with Clemens Kaiser-Breme in Essen. *Career:* Sang as baritone 1962-67; Tenor debut Stockholm 1967, as Dimitri in Boris Godunov; Sang in the premieres of operas by Braein and Werle and as Florestan, Siegmund, Eisenstein in Die Fledermaus, Don Carlos, Don José, Cavaradossi and Riccardo in Un Ballo in Maschera; Sang in a revival of the Abbé Vogler's Gustaf Adolf och Ebba Brahe at Drottningholm, 1973; Sang Steva in Stockholm Opera producton of Jenůfa at the Edinburgh Festival, 1974; Guest appearances with Scottish Opera and in Malmo, Oslo, Frankfurt, Copenhagen, Miami, Lisbon and Helsinki; Well known as concert singer; Artisitc Manager Malmo City Theatre, 1986; Opera Manager, Royal Opera, Stockholm, 1991-. *Address:* Royal Opera Stockholm, Box 16094, 10322 Stockholm, Sweden.

BLANDFORD Jeremy Richard, b. 23 Apr 1943, Bishop's Stortford, England. Organ Recitalist; Organ, Harpsichord and Pianoforte Accompanist. m. Susan Marsland, 1966, divorced, 1986, 2 sons. *Education:* MA Cantab; GRSM; FRCO; LRAM Organ Performance; ARCM Pianoforte Teaching. *Career includes:* Organist and Master of Music, St Mary's Parish Church, Southampton, 1968-; Director, Mayflower Singers; Visiting Tutor, La Sainte Union College of Higher Education, 1972-; Organist, Southampton Choral Society, 1973-; Music Staff, King Edward VI School, Southampton, 1975-84; Visiting Organ Tutor, University of Southampton, 1977-; Visiting Tutor of Organ, King Alfred's College, Winchester, 1979-; Vaagan Kommune, Norway; Recital tours, USA, France, Switzerland, Norway, West Germany, Austria, Belgium, Denmark, Netherlands; Public performances of Messiaen's major organ suites; Sabbatical Year as organist of Flakstad and Moskenes Churches, Lofoten, Norway, 1990; Recital tour of Guernsey; All EU appointments concluded 1990. *Compositions:* A Prayer of St Francis, anthem for solo soprano, SATB and organ, published 1989. *Recordings:* Carols from Cambridge, Clare College Singers and Orchestra with Organ; The Choir of King Edward VI School, Southampton, with Organ Accompaniment; An evening with Ingegerd Björklund (soprano) and Kaj Nyström (trumpet), pianoforte accompaniments to Rossini, Liszt, Grieg, Sköld, released

by Imogena, 1990. *Honours:* Recipient of Richards' Organ Prize, Royal Academy of Music, 1963. *Hobbies:* Motoring; Theatre; History; Current affairs. *Address:* Postboks 65, 8380 Ramberg, Norway.

BLANK Allan, b. 27 Dec 1925, New York, USA. Composer. *Education:* High School of Music and Art in New York; Juilliard, 1945-47, Washington Square College; MA, University of Minnesota, 1950; University of Iowa. *Career:* Violini, Pittsburgh Symphony Orchestra 1950-52; Teacher, Western Illinois University, 1966-68; Patterson State College, 1968-70, Lehmann College, 1970-77, and Virginia Commonwealth University at Richmond, 1978-; Music Director of the Richmond Community Orchestra, 1986-89; *Compositions include:* Operas Aria da Capo, 1960; Excitement at the Circus, children's opera, Patterson, 1969; The Magic Bonbons, 1983; The Noise, Richmond, 1986; Incidental music for Othello, 1983 and Measure for Measure, 1984; 2 String Quartets, 1958, 1981; Concert Piece for band, 1963; Music for Orchestra 1967; Wind Quintet 1970; An American Medley, 1976; Music for Tubas, 1977; Divertimento for tuba and band, 1979; Kreutzer March for band, 1981; Concertino for bassoon and strings, 1984; Concert for five players, 1986; Concertino for string orchestra, 1987; Forked Paths, suite of 11 miniatures for trumpet, 1988; Songs. *Address:* c/o BMI, 320 W 57th Street, New York 10019, USA.

BLANKENBURG Heinz Horst, b. 15 Oct 1931, New York City, USA. Opera Baritone; Stage Director. m. Gayle Cameron-McComb, 14 Dec 1986. 2 sons, 1 daughter, previous marriage. *Education:* Local universities, Los Angeles. *Debut:* San Francisco Opera, 1955. *Career:* Leading Baritone: Glyndebourne Festival Opera, 1957-70, roles there included Mozart's Papageno and Figaro, Rossini's Raimbaud and Busoni's Arlecchino; Hamburg State Opera, 1959-73, San Francisco Opera, 1955-66; As Beckmesser, Schaunard, Fra Melitone (Forza del Destino) and Paolo in Simon Boccanegra; sang with the Hamburg Staatsoper in the British premiere of Die Frau ohne Schatten, Sadler's Wells theatre, 1966; Guest baritone with opera companies of Munich, Berlin, Vienna, Paris, Frankfurt, Metropolitan, Amsterdam, Rome, Brussels, Lausanne, Basle, Strasbourg, Naples, Venice, New Zealand, St Louis, Portland, Vancouver, Seattle, Los Angeles. *Recordings:* Disc: Decca, Polyphone; TV/Radio: BBC, RAI, ZDF. *Honours:* Kammersaenger, Hamburg State Opera, 1966; Honorary Doctor of Performing Arts, California State University, Los Angeles, 1977, University of California, Los Angeles 1986; Maori Welcome, New Zealand, 1971. *Current management:* Faculty, University of California, Los Angeles; California State University, Los Angeles. *Address:* Opera Theatre, California State University, 5151 State University Drive, Los Angeles, CA 90032, USA.

BLANKENHEIM Toni, b. 12 Dec 1921, Cologne, Germany. Singer (Bass-Baritone). *Education:* Studied with Paul Lohmann in Frankfurt and with Res Fischer in Stuttgart. *Debut:* Frankfurt 1947, as Mozart's Figaro. *Career:* Sang at Frankfurt until 1950, then at Hamburg; Bayreuth Festival 1954-59, as Kothner, Klingsor and Donner; Darmstadt 1965-68; Stuttgart from 1968; Sang at Hamburg in the premieres of operas by Mihalovici, Martinů Henze, Krenek, Von Einem, Goehr, Searle, Kelemen and Constant; Performances of works by Berg, Stravinsky, Liebermann and other modern composers; sang Schigolch at the Paris Opéra in the 1979 premiere of Berg's Lulu; Guest appearances in Vienna, Berlin, Munich, Milan, Paris, Mexico City, San Francisco and New York; Sang in the first local performance of The Birthday by Kalevi, at Hamburg 1982; Many concert appearances. *Recordings:* Bastien et Bastienne by Mozart, Lulu (Deutsche Grammophon); Donner in Das Rheingold, Bayreuth 1957; Klingsor in Parsifal, Bayreuth 1956. *Address:* c/o Hamburgische Staatsoper, Grosse-Theatrestrasse 34, D-200 Hamburg, Germany.

BLANKENSHIP Rebecca, b. 24 Mar 1954, New York. Singer (Soprano). *Education:* Studied voice in New York with Judith Oas. *Career:* Sang two seasons at Ulm as a mezzo-soprano; Sang Ariadne at the Berlin Staatsoper 1986 and appeared in Basle 1986-88 as Mozart's Elettra and First Lady, Leonora (Il Trovatore) and Katharina in Lady Macbeth of Mtsensk; Seasons 1988-90 with Martha in Tiefland in Berlin and at the Vienna Volksoper; Leonore in Fidelio in Stuttgart and with Opera Forum, the Netherlands; Elsa in Liege and Senta at the Bregenz Festival; Marie in Wozzeck with the Vienna Staatsoper, 1990-92; Regular appearances in Vienna 1991-; Other roles include Female Chorus (The Rape of Lucretia), Agathe (Der Freischtz), Hanna Glawari (Die Lustige Wiwe); Sieglinde, San Francisco Opera, 1990; Sieglinde, Wiener Staatsoper, 1991; Wozzeck, Marie, La Fenice, Venice 1992; Lady Macbeth of Mtsensk, Katarina, Wiener Volksoper, 1992-; Erwartung, Schoenberg, for Canadian Opera at Toronto, and Edinburgh Festival, 1993. *Address:* Music International, 13 Ardilaun Road, London N5 2QR, England.

BLASIUS Martin, b. 5 June 1956, Schwelm, Westphalen, Germany. Singer (Bass). *Education:* Studied at the Folkwang-Musikhochschule, Essen. *Career:* Sang at first in concert, notably for Austrian and Italian radio, at the Bach-Woche Ansbach, the Göttingen Handel Festival and at the Frankfurt Festival; Opera debut as Dulcamara, Gelsenkirchen, 1983; moved to Hannover, 1987, Dusseldorf, 1989; Guest appearances in opera and concert throughout Germany; appeared in a new production of Henze's The Bassarids, Duisburg 1991 and sang the Grand Inquisitor in Don Carlos, at Dusseldorf. *Recordings include:* Der Traumgörge by Zemlinsky (Capriccio); Saint-Saens Christmas Oratorio (Concord); Golgotha by Martin (Vengo); Kreutzer: Das Nachtlager von Granada (Capriccio); NoHurui (EMI). *Address:* c/o Deutsche Oper am Rhein, Heinrich-Heine Allee 16, 4000 Dusseldorf, Germany.

BLATNY Pavel, b. 14 Sept 1931, Brno, Czehoslovakia. Composer; conductor. *Education:* Brno Conservatory, 1950-55 and with Borkovec in Prague, 1955-58; Further study in jazz piano at the Berklee College of Music, USA. *Career:* More than 2,000 recitals of piano music, often in a third-stream mode, mixing jazz and classical techniques; Conductor of many concerts in Czechoslovakia; Chief of the music division on Brno television, 1971; Teacher, Janáček Academy of Musical Arts, Brno, 1979-. *Compositions include:* Forest Tales, The Well and Little House, television operas for children, 1975; Cantatas with orchestra, The Willow Tree, 1980; Christmas Eve, 1982 and The Midday Witch, 1982; Third Stream Music; Music for piano and orchestra, 1955; Concerto for Orchestra, 1956; The Bells, symphonic movement, 1981; Hommage a Gustav Mahler for orchestra, 1982; Music for wind instruments; Piano music. *Address:* OSA (Czechoslovakia), c/o Member Registration, PRS Ltd 29/33 Berners Street, London W1P 4AA, England.

BLAUKOPF Kurt, b. 15 Feb 1914, Czernowitz, Austria. Musicologist. *Education:* Studied with Stefan Wolpe and Herman Scherchen in Vienna, 1932-37; Music history at Jerusalem, 1940-42. *Career:* Editor of Phono, 1954-65; Lecturer, music sociology, 1962, Professor, 1968, Vienna Academy of Music; Honorary Professor, Vienna University, 1974; Member, Executive Board of UNESCO, 1972-76; Editor of Hi-Fi Stereophonie, Vienna, from 1965; *Publications:* Muziksoziologie, Cologne, 1952 (in Spanish as Sociologia de la Musica, 1988); 2nd Ed, 1972; Grosse Dirigenten, 1953; Grosse Virtuosen, 1954; Gustav Mahler, order Zeitgenosse der Zukunft, Vienna, 1969 (in English, 1973 and 1985); Die Wiener Philharmoniker: Wesen, Werden, Wirken eines Grossen Orchesters, with H Blaukopf, Vienna, 1986, 2nd Ed, 1992; Edited Gustav Mahler Sein Leben, sein Werk unde seine Welt in zeitgenossischen Bildern und Texten, Vienna, 1976; 2nd Ed, Stuttgart, 1994, in English as Gustav Mahler: A Documentary Study, 1976, 2nd Ed, 1991; Musik im Wandel der Gesellschaft: Grundzuge der Musiksoziologie, Munich 1982; Musical Life in a Changing Society: Aspects of Music Sociology, Portland, Oregon, 1992. *Address:* Institut für Musiksoziologie,

Hochschule für Musik, Schubertring 14, A-1010 Vienna, Austria.

BLAZEKOVIC Zdravko, b. 13 May 1956, Zagreb, Yugoslavia. Musicologist. *Education:* BA, Musicology 1980, MA, Musicology 1983, University of Zagreb. *Career:* Institute for Musicological Research, Yugoslav Academy of Sciences and Arts Zagreb, Assistant 1980-81; Researcher 1984-91; Librarian Croation Music Institute, Zagreb 1985-87; Research Asociate, Research Center for Music Iconography/Répertoire International d'Iconographie Musical (RIdIM), City University of New York, USA 1990-; Associate editor, RILM abstracts of music literature, New York, 1989; Editor RIdIM/RCMI Newsletter, New York, 1989-. *Publications:* Catalogue of music manuscripts and prints in the collections of the Historical Archives and the Museum of the City of Dubrovnik, vol 1 of series, Indices collectiorum musicarum tubulariorumque in SR Croatia, 1988. *Contributions to:* International Review of the Aesthetics and Sociology of Music; Arti musices; Current musicology; Musica periodica; Rad JAZU, Zvuk. *Memberships:* International Musicological Society; Croatian Composers' Society; American Musicological Society; International Council for Traditional Music.

BLECH Harry, b. 2 Mar 1910, London, England. Conductor. m. (1) Enid Lessing 1935, div 1957, 1 son, 2 daughters. (2) Marion Manley 1957, 1 son, 3 daughters. *Education:* Central London Foundation, Trinity College of Music and Manchester College of Music. *Career:* Violin Soloist, 1928-30; with BBC Symphony Orchestra, 1930-36; Founder member, Blech Quartet, 1933-50, London Wind Players, 1942, London Mozart Players, 1949-84, Haydn-Mozart Society, 1949, London Mozart Choir, 1952; Conductor Royal Academy of Music Chamber Orchestra, 1961-65. *Recordings include:* Mozart's mature symphonies, Posthorn Serenade, Sinfonia Concertante (with Norbert Brainin and Peter Schidlof), piano concertos K453 and K503 (Matthews) K491 (Kentner) and K488 (Roll), Bassoon Concerto, Mass K317, Violin Concerto K219 (Milstein) and Divertimento K251. *Honours:* CBE; Honorary Member, Royal Academy of Music; Fellow Royal Manchester College of Music, Trinity College of Music. *Hobby:* Reading. *Address:* The Owls, 70 Leopold Road, Wimbledon, London SW19 7JQ, England.

BLECH Marion Rose (née Manley), b. 7 July 1931, Barrow-in-Furness, Cumbria, England. Former Pianist; Fund-Raising Organiser, Haydn-Mozart Society. m. Harry Blech, 1957, 1 son, 3 daughters. *Education:* Crossland Convent High School, 1936-47; Studied: Privately with Leslie England, 1947-49; Royal Academy of Music, 1949-52; Also with Franz Osborn. *Debut:* London, 1954. *Career:* Appeared in public from age 12; Broadcast at age 14; Gave first public recital at 16; Appeared on ITA, 1955; Concertos and recitals in London and Provinces until marriage in 1957; Secretary of Haydn-Mozart Society, 1964-86. *Honours:* Awarded Lancashire County Music Scholarship, 1950; LRAM (performers), 1953; Won at many music festivals in North of England. *Hobbies:* Environmental and Wildlife Protection; Horses; Dogs; Cookery; Gardening; Music. *Address:* The Owls, 70 Leopold Road, Wimbledon, London SW19 7JQ, England.

BLEGEN Judith, b. 27 Apr 1941, Missoula, Montana, USA. Opera and Concert Singer. m. (1) Peter Singher, 1967 (divorced 1975), 1 son, (2) Raymond Gniewek, 1977. *Education:* Curtis Institute of Music, Philadelphia, Pennsylvania; Music Academy of the West, Santa Barbara, California. *Career:* Leading Soprano, Nuremberg Opera, Federal Republic of Germany, 1965-68, as Donizetti's Lucia and Strauss's Zerbinetta; Staatsoper, Vienna, Austria, 1968-70; Metropolitan Opera, New York, 1970-, debut as Mozart's Papagena; Vienna roles include Zerbinetta (Ariadne auf Naxos), Rosina (The Barber of Seville), Aennchen (Der Freischütz), Norina (Don Pasquale); numerous performances at Metropolitan include Marzelline (Fidelio), Sophie (Werther), Sophie (Der Rosenkavalier), Adina (L'Elisir d'amore), Juliette (Roméo et Juliette);

other appearances include Susanna (The Marriage of Figaro), San Francisco, title role in Manon, Tulsa Opera, Gilda (Rigoletto), Chicago, Despina (Così fan tutte), Covent Garden, Blondchen (Die Entführung), Salzburg Festival, Mélisande (Pelléas et Mélisande), Spoleto Festival, Susanna (The Marriage of Figaro), Edinburgh Festival, Sophie, Paris Opera; Has sung and played the violin in Menotti's Help, Help, the Globolinks!, (premiere Hamburg). *Honours:* Fulbright Scholarship; Grammy Awards. *Recordings:* Numerous recordings including La Bohème (Puccini), Carmina Burana (Orff) Symphony No 4 (Mahler), Harmonienmesse (Haydn), The Marriage of Figaro (Mozart), A Midsummer Night's Dream (Mendelssohn), Lord Nelson Mass (Haydn), Gloria (Poulenc), Peer Gynt Suite (Grieg), Lieder recital (Richard Strauss and Hugo Wolf), Baroque music recital. *Address:* c/o Thea Dispeker, 59 East 54th Street, New York, NY 10022, USA.

BLINKHOF Jan, b. 10 Jul 1940, Leiden, Holland. Singer (Tenor). *Education:* Studied in Amsterdam, with Joseph Metternich in Cologne and with Luigi Ricci in Rome. *Debut:* With Netherlands Opera 1971, as Arturo in Lucia di Lammermoor. *Career:* Holland Festival 1971, in the premiere of Spinoza by Ton de Kruyf; Amsterdam 1974, in the premiere of Dorian Gray by Kox; Geneva Opera 1985, as Tristan; Nice 1986, as Herman in The Queen of Spades; Sang Laca in Jenufa at the Zurich Opera, 1986; Other roles include Ismaele in Nabucco; Boris in Katya Kabanova, and roles in Wozzeck, The Rape of Lucretia, The Gambler by Prokofiev and Henze's Der Junge Lord; sang Tristan at Nice 1986-87, Laca at Covent Garden 1988; Deutsche Oper Berlin 1988, as Sergei in Lady Macbeth of the Mtsensk District; sang Boris in Katya Kabanova at Geneva and Florence 1989; Albert Gregor in The Makropoulos Case at Berlin 1990, followed by Sergei in Hamburg and Laca (Jenůfa) at Barcelona. *Address:* c/o Deutsche Oper Berlin, Richard Wagnerstrasse 10, D-100 Berlin, Germany.

BLISS Anthony, b. 19 Apr 1913, New York, USA. Manager. *Education:* Studied at Harvard University, BA 1936, and the University of Virginia. *Career:* Practised Law on Wall Street; Member of the board of directors of the Metropolitan Opera Association, 1949; President of MOA, 1956-57, Executive Director, 1974-81, General Manager, 1981-85; Established the Metropolitan National Company in 1965; Administrative or board positions with the Joffrey Ballet, the American Arts Alliance, National Endowment of the Arts and the New York Foundation of the Arts. *Address:* c/o Metropolitan Opera, Lincoln Center, New York, NY 10023, USA.

BLOCH Augustyn, b. 13 Aug 1929, Grudziadz, Poland. Composer. *Education:* Studied composition with Tadeusz Szeligowski and organ with Felik Raczkowski at the Warsaw Conservatory. m. Halika Lukomska. *Career:* Music Consultant to the Polish Radio Theatre from 1954. *Compositions include:* Opera-Mystery Ayelet, Jephtha's Daughter, 1968; Children's Opera-Pantomime Sleeping Princess, 1974; musicals Mr Zabloba 1971 and a Tale of the Violin Soul, 1978; Christmas pantomime with the Star in the Stall of Wonder, 1975; Ballets Voci, 1967, The Awaiting, 1964, The Bull, 1965, Gilgamesh 1968, The Looking Glass, 1975; Concertino for violin, strings, piano and percussion, 1958; Meditations for soprano, organ and percussion, 1961; Telegramme for children's chorus, 2 pianos and percussion, 1963; Dialogues for violin and orchestra, 1963; Enfiando for Orchestra, 1970; Salmo gioioso for soprano and 5 wind instruments, 1970; Warsaw for narrator, chorus and orchestra, 1974; Wordsworth Songs for baritone and chamber ensemble, 1976; Clarinetto divertente, 1976; Oratoria for organ, strings and percussion, 1982; Music for clarinet and string quartet, 1985; Abide with us, Lord for orchestra, 1986; For Thy Light is Come for organ, reciter, choir and orchestra, 1937; Exaltabo Te for mixed choir, 1988; Musica per tredici ottoni, 1988; Ostra Brama Litany for choir and orchestra, 1989; Thou Shalt Not Kill, meditations for baritone, cello, choir and orchestra, 1991; Trio per violino, violoncello and pianoforte, 1992;

Upwards for orchestra, 1993; Piano Pieces; Songs. *Address:* Wybieg 14, 00 788 Warsaw, Poland.

BLOCHWITZ Hans Peter, b. 28 Sept 1949, Garmisch-Partenkirchen, Germany. Singer (Tenor). *Education:* Studied at Darmstadt, Mainz and Frankfurt. *Career:* Sang at First in concert, notably as the Evangelist in the St Matthew Passion and in Lieder recitals (Die schöne Müllerin by Schubert); Opera debut Frankfurt 1984, as Lensky; Sang in the Scala-staged version of the St Matthew Passion at San Marco, Milan, 1985; Théâtre de la Monnaie Brussels and Geneva 1986, as Don Ottavio and Lensky; Guest appearances in Hamburg, Amsterdam and London (Ferrando in Cosi fan Tutte 1989); Aix-en-Provence Festival 1987-89, as Belmonte and Ferrando; Sang Idamante in Idomeneo at San Francisco, 1989; Don Ottavio in the Metropolitan Opera, 1990; Sang in the Choral Symphony at the 1993 Prom Concerts, London; Invited to sing Lensky at San Diego, 1994. *Recordings include:* St Matthew Passion (Harmonia Mundi); Mozart Requiem and Schuldigkeit des Ersten Gebotes, Mendelssohn St Paul (Philips); Christmas Oratorio by Bach, Mendelssohn's 2nd Symphony, Così fan Tutte (Deutsche Grammophon); St Matthew Passion (Decca); Die Zauberflöte (Teldec); Davidde Penitente (EMI); Don Giovanni (Teldec). *Address:* c/o Bureau Pieter G Alferink, Apollolaan 181, 1077 Amsterdam, The Netherlands.

BLOMSTEDT Herbert Thorson, b. 11 July 1927, Springfield, Massachusetts, USA (Swedish citizen). Music Director; Conductor. m. Waltraud Regina Petersen, 29 May 1955, 4 daughters. *Education:* Diplomas: Music Education, 1948, Organist/Cantor, 1950, Orchestra Conductor, 1950, Royal Academy of Music, Stockholm; Philosophy candidate, University of Uppsala, Sweden, 1952. *Career:* Music Director, Norrkoping Symphony Orchestra, Sweden, 1954-61; Professor of Conducting, Royal Academy of Music, Stockholm, 1961-70; Permanent Conductor, Oslo Philharmonic, Norway, 1962-68; Music Director: Danish Radio Symphony Orchestra, Copenhagen 1967-77, Dresden Staatskapelle, East Germany, 1975-85, Swedish Radio Symphony, 1977-82, San Francisco Symphony, USA, 1985-; Conducted Nielsen's 4th symphony at the 1990, Edinburgh Festival. *Recordings:* Conductor, over 120 titles, 1955-; including CDs of Bruckner's 4th and 7th Symphonies (Staatskapelle Dresden), Nielsen's 1st, 6th and 4th (San Francisco Symphony); Strauss Ein Heldenleben; Hindemith Mathis der Maler symphony, Trauermusik and Metamorphosis. *Publications:* Author: Till Kannedomen om J C Bach Symfonier, dissertation, 1951; co-author: Lars Erik Larsson och hans Concertinor, book, 1957; Numerous articles. Also editor: Musical score, Franz Berwald's Sinfonie Singulière, 1965. *Honours:* Jenny Lind Scholarship, Royal Academy of Music, Stockholm, 1950; Music Prize, Expressen (daily newspaper), Stockholm, 1964; Knight, Royal Order of North Star, Sweden, 1971; Knight, Royal Order of Dannebrogen, Denmark, 1978; Honorary DMus, Andrews University, Michigan, USA, 1978; Litteris et Artibus Gold Medal, Sweden, 1979. *Membership:* Royal Academy of Music, Stockholm. *Current Management:* Interartists, Keizersgracht 586 I 1017, RK Amsterdam, Netherlands. *Address:* Davies Symphony Hall, San Francisco, California 94102, USA.

BLOOMFIELD Arthur John, b. 3 Jan 1931, San Francisco, California, USA. Music Critic; Food Writer. m. Anne E Buenger, 14 July 1956, 1 son, 2 daughters. *Education:* BA, Music, Stanford University, 1951. *Publications:* Fifty Years of The San Francisco Opera, 1972; The San Francisco Opera 1922-78, 1978; Arthur Bloomfield's Restaurant Book, 1987-; Great Conducting, in progress. *Contributions to:* Music Critic, San Francisco Examiner, 1965-79; San Francisco Correspondent, Opera, 1964-. *Hobbies:* Cooking; Tennis. *Address:* 2229 Webster Street, San Francisco, CA 94115, USA.

BLOOMFIELD Theodore (Robert), b. 14 June 1923, Cleveland, Ohio, USA. Conductor. *Education:* Studied conducting with Maurice Kessler; Piano training, BM 1944, Oberlin College Conservatory of Music;

Conducting with Edgar Schenkman, Juilliard Graduate School, New York; Piano with Claudio Arrau; Conducting with Pierre Monteux. *Debut:* New York Little Symphony Orchestra, 1945. *Career:* Apprentice conductor to George Szell and Cleveland Orchestra, 1946-47; Conductor, Cleveland Little Symphony Orchestra, Cleveland Civic Opera Workshop, 1947-52; Music Director, Portland (Oregon) Symphony Orchestra, 1955-59; Rochester (NY) Philharmonic Orchestra, 1959-63; First conductor, Hamburg State Opera, 1964-66; General Music Director, Franfurt-am-Main, 1966-68; Chief conductor, (West) Berlin Symphony Orchestra, 1975-82. *Recordings:* For Composers Recordings Inc; Everest; MGM. *Address:* c/o Das Sinfonie Orchester Berlin, Kurfurstendamm 225, D-1000 Berlin, Germany.

BLUMENFELD Harold, b. 15 Oct 1923, Seattle, Washington, USA. Composer; Writer; Linguist. *Education:* BM, 1948, MM, 1949, Yale School of Music; Zürich Konservatorium, Winter 1948. *Career:* Professor of Music at Washington University in St Louis, Missouri, 1951-; Director, Opera Theatre of St Louis, 1964-68; Co-Founder, New Music Circle. *Compositions include:* War Lament for chorus after Siegfried Sassoon, 1970; Eroscapes, 1971; Song of Innocence for chorus, soli and orchestra, 1973; Rilke for Voice and Guitar, 1975; Circle of the Eye, Song Cycle, 1975; Starfires, Cantata for Mezzo, Tenor and Orchestra, 1975; La vie antérieure, spatial cantata after Baudelaire, 1976; Voyages, after Hart Crane, 1977; Fritzi, One-Act Bagatelle-Opera, 1979; Silentium, Song Cycle after Mandelstam, 1979; La voix reconnue, Cantata for Tenor, Soprano and Chamber Ensemble after Verlaine, 1980; La face cendrée, Cantata after Rimbaud, 1981; Charioteer of Delphi, after James Merrill, 1985; Fourscore: An Opera of Opposites, 1980-86; Un carnet de damné, cantata after Rimbaud's Season in Hell, 1987, mezzo and eight players; Fields of Emerald and Iron.....Diluvium: Orchestral Evocations of Rimbaud, 1988 (large Orchestra). *Recordings:* Voyages, 1977; Rilke, 1978; War Lament, 1983. *Publications:* English Translation of Michael Praetorius Syntagma Musicum, Volume II, 1980; All musical works published by Magnamusic-Baton Music Corp, St Louis, MO, USA. *Contributions to:* Musical Quarterly; Perspectives of New Music; Opera; Opera Journal. *Honours:* American Academy and Institute of Arts and Letters Composition Award, 1977; National Endowment for Arts Opera Award, 1979. *Memberships:* ASCAP; ASUC; National Opera Association; Fellow of Yaddo; President, River Styx Literary Association, 1987-89.

BLUNT Marcus, b. 31 Dec 1947, Birmingham, England. Composer; Teacher. m. Maureen Ann Marsh, 9 Apr 1988. *Education:* BMus Hons, University College of Wales, Aberystwyth, 1970. *Career:* Composer from age 14 with performances in England, India, Italy, Mallorca, Malta, Netherlands, Saudi Arabia, Scotland, Sri Lanka, Wales; Also on BBC Radio 3; Woodwind Teacher, 1976-. *Compositions:* Symphonies 1 and 2; Two Serenades for Oboe, Bassoon and Piano; Sonatina, for clarinet and piano; Birrens to Burnswark, for clarinet and piano; Lorenzo the much-travelled Clown, for Bassoon and Piano; 3 Contrasts for Two clarinets; Caprice and Scotch Song for Solo Bassoon; The Life Force for Piano. *Memberships:* Composers Guild of Great Britain; Performing Right Society; Incorporated Society of Musicians. *Hobbies:* Photography; Gardening. *Address:* Craigs Cottage, Lochmaben, Lockerbie, Dumfriesshire, Scotland DG11 1RW.

BLY Leon J, b. 13 May 1944, Hampton, Virginia, USA. Music Teacher; Band Director. m. Maria Ilona Tzitschke, 15 June 1968, 2d. *Education:* AB College of William and Mayr, 1966; MMus, 1972, PhD, 1977, University of Miami. *Career:* Band Director, James Monroe High School, Virginia, 1968-71; Band Director, Concord College, Athens, West Virginia, 1974-81; Band Director and Chairman of the Wind Department, Stuttgart Music School, 1981-. *Publications include:* Internationale Festliche Musiktage Uster, 1956-89; Der Status der Musik für sinfonisches Blasorchester im 20 Jahrlundert, 1987; The March in the United States of America, 1985; An Annotated Bibliography of Twentieth Century Symphonies in Print for Wind Ensembles, 1973. *Memberships:* WASBE; CBDNA; IGEB; Phi Mu Alpha Sinfonia. *Hobby:* Philately. *Address:* Graf-von-Galen Strasse 28, D-70565 Stuttgart, Germany.

BLYTH Alan, b. 27 July 1929, London, England. Music Critic and Editor. m. Ursula Zumloh. *Education:* MA, Oxford University. *Career:* Contributor as Critic, The Times, 1963-76; Associate Editor, Opera, 1967-84; Music Editor, Encyclopaedia Britannica, 1971-76; Critic, Daily Telegraph, 1976-89. *Publications:* The Enjoyment of Opera, 1969; Colin Davis, A Short Biography, 1969; Janet Baker, A Short Biography, 1972; Editor, Opera on Record, 1979; Remembering Britten, 1980; Wagner's Ring: An Introduction, 1980; Editor, Opera on Record 2, 1983; Editor, Opera on Record 3, 1984; Editor, Song on Record, Volume 1, 1986; volume 2, 1988; Choral Music on Record, 1990; Opera on CD, 1992. *Contributions to:* Gramophone; BBC; BBC Music Magazine. *Memberships:* Critics Circle; Garrick Club. *Hobbies:* Gardening; Wine; Collecting 78 rpm Vocal Records. *Address:* 22 Shilling Street, Lavenham, Suffolk, CO10 9RH, England.

BLYTON Carey, b. 14 Mar 1932, Beckenham, Kent, England. Composer/Arranger; Author; Music Editor; Lecturer. m. Mary Josephine Mills, 2 sons. *Education:* University College, London University, 1950-51; TCM, 1953-57, AMusTCL, LTCL (TTD), FTCL (Composition), BMus (London); Royal Danish Academy of Music, Copenhagen, 1957-58. *Career:* Music Editor, Mills Music Limited, 1958-63; Freelance Composer/ Arranger, 1963-; Member, Professorial Staff, Trinity College of Music, 1963-73; Music Editor, Faber Music Limited, 1963-74 (Edited work of Benjamin Britten, 1963-70); Professor of Composition for Film, Television and Radio, Guildhall School of Music, 1972-83. *Compositions:* (Published), Numerous Orchestral and Instrumental Works including: Cinque Port, The Hobbit, On Holiday; Music for Solo Guitar; Numerous Vocal works include: Carols, Madrigals, Children's Songs. *Recordings:* Numerous works, mainly for TV plays and documentary films, Wind or Chamber Ensemble. *Publications:* Faber Book of Nursery Songs (with D Mitchell); Bananas in Pyjamas. *Contributions to:* Numerous professional journals. *Honours:* Sir G Bantock Prize for Composition, Trinity College of Music, 1954; Sir W Churchill Endowment Fund Scholarship, 1957. *Memberships Include:* Performing Right Society; Mechanical-Copyright Protection Society; CGGB. *Hobbies:* Reading; Fishing. *Address:* Hawthornden, 55 Goldsel Road, Swanley, Kent BR8 8HA, England.

BOATWRIGHT Helen, b. 17 Nov 1916, Sheboygen, Wisconsin, USA. Soprano; Teacher. m. Howard Boatwright, 1943. *Education:* Pupil of Anna Shram Irving; Studied with Marion Sims, Oberlin College. *Debut:* Ann, Die lustigen Weiber von Windsor, Berkshire Music Center, Tanglewood, Massachusetts, 1942. *Career:* Appeared with Austin (Texas) and San Antonio (Texas) Operas, 1943-45; Sang with many orchestras and choral groups in the USA; Taught voice, New Haven, Connecticut, 1945-64; Adjunct Professor of Voice, Syracuse (NY) University; Professor of Voice, Eastman School of Music, Rochester, 1972-79; Professor of Voice, Peabody Conservatory of Music, Baltimore 1987-89; Professor of Voice, Summers of 1969-88; Masterclass, Glimmerglass Opera; University of Massachusets; University of North Carolina and Washington University, 1989. *Recordings:* Several. *Address:* c/o Music Department, Syracuse University, Syracuse, NY 13210, USA.

BOATWRIGHT Howard (Leake, Jr), b. 16 Mar 1918, Newport News, Virginia, USA. Violinist; Conductor; Music Educator; Composer. m. Helen Boatwright, 1943. *Education:* Studied violin with Israel Feldman, Norfolk, Virginia; Composition with Paul Hindemith, Yale University, 1945-48. *Debut:* Violin soloist, Richmond (Va) Symphony Orchestra, 1935. *Career:* Teacher, University of Texas, Austin, 1943-45; Yale University, 1948-64; Music Director, St Thomas' Church, New

Haven, 1949-64; Concertmaster, New Haven Symphony Orchestra, 1950-52; Dean, School of Music, 1964-72, Teacher 1972-, Syracuse University; Professor Emeritus, 1983-. *Compositions:* Variations for Chamber Orchestra, 1949; Symphony, 1976; 2 string quartets, 1974, 1975; Serenade for 2 String Instruments and 2 Wind Instruments, 1952; Clarinet Quartet, 1958; 12 Pieces for Violin, 1977; Clarinet Sonata, 1980; Mass, 1958; The Passion According to St Matthew for Chorus, 1962; Choral works; Songs. *Address:* c/o School of Music, Syracuse University, Syracuse, NY 13210, USA.

BOATWRIGHT McHenry, b. 29 Feb 1928, Tennille, Georgia, USA. Singer (Bass-Baritone). *Education:* Studied at the New England Conservatory; BM 1950, 1954. *Debut: Jordan Hall, Boston, 1956. Career:* New York Town Hall debut 1958; New England Opera Theater 1958, as Arkel in Pelléas et Mélisande; Concert appearances with Charles Munch, Leonard Bernstein and other leading conductors; Sang with the Hamburg Staatsoper in contemporary works, notably in the 1966 premiere of Schuller's The Visitation (Metropolitan Opera 1967); Concert tour of the Far East and Europe, 1966; Sang at the funeral of Duke Ellington; Well known in Negro Spirituals. *Recordings:* La Damnation de Faust (RCA); Porgy and Bess (Decca). *Honours:* Marian Anderson Awards 1953, 1954; Winner, Arthur Fiedler Voice Contest; Winner, National Federation of Music Clubs Competition, 1957.

BOBOC Nicolae, b. 26 Sept 1920, Ilia, Romania. Conductor; Composer. m. Maria Giurguit, 7 May 1953, 2 daughters. *Education:* Graduate Diploma, Faculty of Philosophy and Letters, Bucharest University, 1946; High School Diploma, Pedagogy, Conducting, Composition, Bucharest Music Academy, 1946. *Career:* Professor, Harmony, Counterpoint, Conservatoire ARAD, Romania, 1947-53; Chief Conductor and Manager, State Philharmonic Orchestra, ARAD, 1948-59; Chief Conductor, State Philharmonic Orchestra, Timisoara, 1959-82; Chief Conductor and Manager, State Opera, Timisoara, 1963-74; Chief Conductor, State Philharmonic Orchestra, ARAD, 1982-; Guest Conductor: Bucharest Festival; Nice Festival; Pleven Festival; Marijanske Lazne Festival; Brasov Festival; Vienna ORF Orchestra; Bucharest Philharmonic; Bucharest RTV Orchestra; Belgrade Symphony Orchestra; Havana, Haiffa, Greensboro (North Carolina), Skopje, Thessaloniki, Wroclaw, Erfurt, Poznan, Rostock, Jena, Schwerin, Cluj, Leeuwarden Iassy, Mulhouse, Lausanne Symphonies (Chamber) Orchestras; Operas in: Cairo, Bonn, Basel, Bucharest, Copenhagen, Plovdiv, Odessa, Bratislava, Gdansk, Sarajevo, Szeged, Klagenfurt, ASO and Ankara; Conductor Opera, Ankara, 1990; Professor History of Music, Academy for Music, Timisoara. *Compositions:* Divertimento in Classical Style (Chamber Orchestra), 1951; Halmagiu Land (Tara Halmagiului), (Great Symphonic Orchestra), 1953; Triptych of Hunedoara (for chorus, soloists and Great Symphonic Orchestra), 1980; Colinde (Winter-Solstice Songs) of Hunedoara (Mixed Chorus and Percussion Instruments), 1979; Ballad (mixed chorus and orchestra), 1989. *Recordings:* 20 Records from 1968-88 including: W A Mozart, Requiem; A Bruckner, Symphony No 1; F. Mendelssohn, Symphony No 3 and 5; Opera Ballet Music, Verdi, Smetana, Ponchielli, Tchaikovsky; Musical Jewels; K D Dittersdorf; Fr Chopin, Concertos No 1 and 2 for piano and orchestra; I Perlea, Symphonic Variations; S V Dragoi, Divertimento; Al Pascanu, The Black Sea; N Boboc, Halmagiu Land, Triptych, Divertimento; Famous choruses, Simeon Opera; R Schumann; Symphony No 2; J Haydn, Symphony no 82 (The Bear) and no 92 (Oxford); Recordings for RTV in Romania, Austria, Czechoslovakia, Cuba, Switzerland, Yugoslavia. *Address:* 3 Mihai Eminescu Boulevard, 1900 Timisoara, Romania.

BODE Hannelore, b. 2 Aug 1941, Berlin, Germany. Singer (Soprano). m. Heinz Feldhoff. *Education:* Studied with Ria Schmitz-Gohr in Berlin, at the Salzburg Mozarteum, Fred Husler, Lugano and Karl-Heinz Jarius, Frankfurt. *Career:* Sang in Bonn from 1964; Basle 1967-

68; Deutsche Oper am Rhein Düsseldorf from 1968, notably as Weber's Agathe, Wagner's Elsa, Eva and Elisabeth, Sieglinde; Kammersängerin, National-Theatre, Mannheim, 1971-; Appearances in London, Beunos Aires, Washington, Vienna, Munich, Berlin; Bayreuth 1969-80, as Elsa, Eva and in The Ring. *Recordings:* Parsifal (Deutsche Grammophon); Die Meistersinger, conducted by Solti (Decca); Die Meistersinger, conducted by Varviso (Philips); Trionfo d'Afrodite by Orff (BASF). *Address:* c/o Nationaltheater Mannheim, Goethestraße, D-68161 Mannheim, Germany.

BODIN Lars-Gunnar, b. 15 July 1935, Stockholm, Sweden. Composer. *Education:* Studied with Lennart Wenstrom 1956-60, and visited Darmstadt, 1962. *Career:* Composer in residence, Mills College, Okland, 1972; Director of the Electronic Music Studio, Stockholm Conservatory, 1978-; Collaborations with Bengt Emil Johnson in Text-Sound compositions. *Compositions include:* Dance pieces Place of Plays, 1967, and ... from one point to any other point, 1968; Music for brass instruments, 1960; Arioso for ensemble, 1962; Semi-Kolon: Dag Knutson in Memoriam for horn and ensemble, 1962; Calendar Music for paino, 1964; My World in Your World for organ and tape, 1966; Primary Structures for bassoon and tape, 1976; Enbart for Kerstin for mezzo and tape, 1979; Anima for soprano, flute and tape, 1984; Diskus for wind quintet and tape, 1987; Electronic: Winter Events, 1967; Toccata, 1969; Traces I and II, 1970-71; Memoires d'un temps avant la destruction, 1982; For Jon II retrospective Episodes, 1986; Text-sound pieces. *Address:* STIM (Sweden), c/o Member Registration, PRS Ltd, 29/33 Berners Street, London W1P 4AA, England.

BODOROVA Sylvie, b. 31 Dec 1954, Ceske Budejovice. Composer. m. Jiri Stilec, 10 Aug 1984, 2 sons. *Education:* Janáček Academy of Arts, Brno, degree in Composition, 1979; PhD, Prague Academy of Arts, Praha, 1982. Composition course in Siena with Franco Donatoni, 1981. *Career:* Performances of works: Gila Rome - Prague Spring, 1981; Planctus - Young Stage, 1983; Sunny Suite - Dresden, 1989; Dignitas homini - London, 1989; Struggle with the Angel, Munchen, 1990. *Compositions:* Planctus, Pontem video, Juniloso, Tre Canzoni da suonare, Musica dedicata, Dignitas homini, Struggle with the Angel. *Recordings:* Pontem video, Planctus (Panton; Tre canzoni da suonare (Supraphon); Dignitas homini (Panton); Jubiloso and many others on Prague Radio. *Honours:* Planctus, Pontem video - Award of Ministry of Culture; The first Prize of Generation Competition - Musica dedicata, Tre canzoni, Two miniatures - Mannheim competition. *Memberships:* Association of Czech Composers and Musicians; Frau and Musik. *Hobbies:* History; Literature; Countryside. *Address:* Valentova 1731, 149 00 Praha 4, Czech Republic.

BOEHMER Konrad, b. 24 May 1941, Berlin, Germany. Composer. *Education:* Studied at cologne University, 1961-66. *Career:* Scientific Assistant, Utrecht University Institute of Sonology, 1966-68; Former Music Editor, Vrij Nederland; Teacher, Royal Conservatory, The Hague, 1971; Director, The Hague Institute of Sociology, 1993. *Compositions include:* Dr Faustus, Paris Opera, 1985; Woutertje Pieterse, Stadsschouwburg Rotterdam, 1988 (premier). *Address:* Royal Conservatory of Music and Drama, Juliana van Stolberglaan 1, 2595 CA The Hague, Netherlands.

BOESCH Christian, b. 27 July 1941, Vienna, Austria. Singer (Baritone). *Education:* Studied at the Vienna Hochschule für Musik. *Debut:* Berne, 1966. *Career:* Sang in Saarbrucken, Lucerne and Kiel; Joined Vienna Volksoper, 1975; Salzburg Festival, 1978, as Papageno in Die Zauberflöte; Metropolitan Opera from 1979, as Papageno, Masetto and Wozzeck; Often heard in modern repertoire; sang Papageno at the Théâtre des Champs Elysées, Paris, 1987; Wolf-Ferrari's Le donne curiose at the Cuvillie's Theatre, Munich, 1989; Wozzeck at Buenos Aires, 1989. *Recordings:* Die Zauberflöte (RCA); Il Prigioniero by Dallapiccola; Haydn's Die Feuersbrunst.

BOESE Ursula, b. 27 July 1928, Hamburg, Germany. Singer (Mezzo-Soprano). *Education:* Studied at the Musikhochschule, Hamburg. *Career:* Began career as concert soloist; Bayreuth Festival, 1958-65, in Parsifal and Der Ring des Nibelungen; Hamburg Opera from 1960, notably in Handel's Giulio Cesare, with Joan Sutherland, 1969; San Francisco, 1968 in Oedipus Rex; Guest appearances in Milan, Rome, Buenos Aires, London, Paris and New York; Opera roles have included Gluck's Orpheus, Handel's Cornelia, Dalila, Gaea in Daphne, Jocasta, Verdi's Ulrica and Azucena and Wagner's Fricka, Erda, Waltraute and Magdalene; Often sang Bach in concert. *Recordings:* Christmas Oratorio by Bach; Der Evangelimann by Kienzl; Salome and Lulu (Deutsche Grammophon); Parsifal and The Devils of Loudun (Philips). *Honour:*Kammersängerin, 1969. *Address:* c/o Hamburgische Staatsoper, Grosse-Theaterstraße 34, D-20354 Hamburg, Germany.

BOESMANS Phillipe, b. 17 May 1936, Tongeren, Belgium. Composer. *Education:* Studied composition with Froidebise and Pousseur at Liège Conservatory, 1954-62. *Career:* Music producer for Belgian radio from l961; worked at Liège electronic music studios, Centre de Recherches Musicales de Wallonie, from 1971; Pianist with the Ensemble Musique Nouvelles. *Compositions:* Etude I for Piano, 1963; Sonance for 2 Pianos, l964; Sonance II for 3 Pianos, 1967; Impromptu for 23 Instruments, 1965; Correlations for Clarinet and 2 Instrumental Groups, 1967; Explosives for Harp and 10 Instrumentalists, 1968; Verticles for Orchestra, 1969; Blocage for Voice, Chorus and Chamber Ensemble, 1970; Upon La, Mi for Voice, Amplified Horn and Instrumental Group, 1970; Fanfare for 2 Pianos, 1971; Intervalles I, 1972, and II, 1973 for Orchestra; and III, 1974, for Voice and Orchestra; Sur Mi for 2 Pianos, Electric Organ, Crotale and Tam-Tam, 1974; Multiples for 2 Pianos and Orchestra, 1974; Element-Extensions for Piano and Chamber Orchestra, 1976; Doublures for Harp, Piano, Percussion and 4 Instrumental Groups, 1977; Attitudes, musical spectacle for Voice, 2 Pianos, Synthesizer and Percussion, l977; Piano Concerto, 1978; Violin Concerto, 1979; Conversions for Orchestra, 1980; La Passion de Gilles, opera, 1983; Ricercar for Organ, 1983. *Honour:* Italia Prize l971. *Address:* SABAM, Rue d'Arlon 75-77, B-1040, Brussels, Belgium.

BOETTCHER Wilfried, b. 11 Aug 1929, Bremen, Germany. Conductor; Professor of Music. m. Ruth Vasicek, 14 Apr 1962. *Education:* Violoncello, Musikhochschule, Hamburg, 1950-55; Studied cello with P Fournier and Pablo Casals, 1955-56. *Career:* Solo Cellist, Hannover Opera, 1956-58; 1958-65; Founder, Musical Director, Wiener Solisten chamber orchestra, Vienna; Chief Conductor, Hamburg Symphony Orchestra, 1967-71; Principal Guest Conductor Rai Torino, Kapellmeister, Hamburg State Opera, Deutsche Oper, Berlin; Vienna State Opera, Principal Guest Conductor, RAI Torino Symphony Orchestra, Italy, 1974-78; Many concerts with leading symphony orchestras in Germany, Austria, Switzerland, Italy, Great Britain, Japan, USA; Festival appearances, Aix-en-Provence, Berlin, Vienna, Salzburg. *Recordings:* Various, including Harpsichord concertos by CPE and J.C. Bach, Telemann's Spring Cantata, Baroque oboe concertos; Early Haydn symphonies; Mozart Piano Concertos K459 and K466 (Brendel), K453 and K491 (Pressler), clarinet and horn concertos, serenades K239, K320 and K203; Beethoven 1st Piano Concerto and Choral Fantasia (Brendel); Cherubini Symphony and Weber's 1st (New Philharmonia, Philips). *Honour:* Professor, Freie und Hansestadt Hamburg, 1971. *Hobby:* Antiquarian books. *Address:* St Alban-Vorstadt, 80, CH 4052, Basel, Switzerland.

BOETTCHER Wolfgang, b. 1940, Berlin, Germany. Cellist. *Education:* Hochschule der Kunste, Berlin. *Career:* Soloist, Berlin Philharmonic until 1976; Co-founder, Brandis String Quartet, 1976, with chamber music appearances in Munich, Hamburg, Milan, Paris, London and Tokyo including concerts with the Wiener Singverein and the Berlin Philharmonic; Festival engagements at Salzburg, Lucerne, Vienna, Florence, Tours, Bergen and Edinburgh; Co-Premiered Helmut Eder's Clarinet Quintet, 1984, the 3rd Quartet of Gottfried von Einem, 1981 and the 3rd Quartet of Giselher Klebe, 1983. Founding member of the Philharmonische Solisten BErlin; Concerto appearances with such conductors as Celibidache, Fischer-Dieskau, Lutoslawski, Karajan and Menuhin; Professor at the Hochschule der Kunst, Berlin. *Recordings include:* Albums in the standard repertoire from 1978, recent releases include quartets by Beethoven, Weill, Schulhoffa and Hindemith and the String Quintet by Schubert. *Honours include:* International ARD Competition prizewinner in Munich. *Address:* c/o Anglo Swiss Ltd, 3 Primrose Mews, 1a Sharpleshall Street, London NW1 8YW, England.

BOGACZ Pavel, b. 6 Mar 1957, Bohumin, Czechoslovakia. Violinist. m. Daniela Kruschberska, 15 Aug 1981, 4 d. *Education:* Ostrava Conservatory; Academy of Music, Prague; Masterclass with N Milstein-Zürich. *Career:* Member of Prague Chamber Soloists, 1978-81; concert Master, Slovak Philharmonic Orchestra, 1981-91, Bratislava; Member and Soloist, Chamber Orchestra Capella Istropolitana; Leader, Bratislava string trio; Teacher of Academy of Music Art, Bratislava; Regular Appearances with various orchestras, foreign concert tours and international festivals to Europe, Japan, Australia and Asia; First Concert Master of Orchestra Ensemble Kanazawa, 1991-. *Recordings:* Bach, Brandenburg Concertos; Romantic Violin Mimiatures; Hummel, String trio G major; Parik, Nocturno; Berger, Violin Sonata Adagio; Schnittke, Concerto Grosso. *Honours:* Best record, Record Acadamey of Japan, 1993. *Address:* Západný Rad 43, 81104 Bratislava, Slovakia.

BOGART John-Paul, b. 17 Sept 1952, USA. Singer (Bass). *Career:* Sang as child in production of Die Zauberflöte at the Metropolitan Opera; Studied at Princeton, Yale and the Juilliard School; Sang at Santa Fe, Miami and Philadelphia; Dallas Opera as First Nazarene in Salome; La Scala Milan as Basilio in Il Barbiere di Siviglia; Staatsoper Vienna as Ramphis, Sarastro, Raimondo, Sparafucile and Colline; Basle Opera, 1984-85, as Mozart's Figaro and La Roche in Capriccio; Paris Opéra-Comique, 1985, in The Stone Guest by Dargomizhsky; Théâtre Châtelet Paris in I Masnadieri by Verdi; Chicago Lyric Opera, as Masetto in Don Giovanni; Baltimore Opera as Gremin in Eugene Onegin; sang in the premiere of Célestine by Maurice Ohana at the Paris Opéra, 1988; Milwaukee, 1989 as Gounod's Mephistopheles; Lodovico in Otello at Lisbon, 1989; Also heard as concert singer. *Recordings:* Zuniga in Carmen (RCA); Turandot, Chichester Psalms (CBS); L'Esule di Roma by Donizetti.

BOGIANCKINO Massimo, b. 10 Nov 1922, Rome, Italy. Opera Director. m. Judith Matthias, 1950. *Education:* Conservatory of Music and Academy Santa Cecilia, Rome; University of Rome; PhD. *Career:* Musicologist and Concert Pianist; Director, Enciclopedia dello Spettacolo, 1957-62; Director, Accademia Filarmonica, Rome, 1960-63; Director, Teatro dell Opera, Rome, 1963-68; Artistic Director, Festival of Two Worlds, Spoleto, 1968-71; Director of Concert Programmes, Accademia Santa Cecilia, Rome, 1970-71; Artistic Director, La Scala, Milan, 1971-74; General manager, Teatro Comunale, Florence, 1974-82; Administration General, Paris Opera, 1982-85, in 1985 became Mayor of Florence; Grosses Bundesverdienstkreuz, Federal Republic of Germany. *Publications:* L'arte clavicembalistica di D. Scarlatti, 1956; Aspetti del Teatro musicale in Italia e in Francia nell eta Barocca, 1968; Le canzonette e i madrigali di V Cossa, 1981. *Address:* Theatre National d'Opera, Paris, France.

BOGIN Abba, b. 24 Nov 1925, New York, USA. Pianist; Conductor. m. Masako Yanagita, 2 children. *Education:* Studied Piano with Isabella Vengerova, Chamber music with William Primrose and Gregor Piatigorsky, Orchestration with Samuel Barber and

Gian-Carlo Menotti; Diploma, Curtis Inst of Music, Philadelphia; Conducting studied with Pierre Monteux, l'Ecole Monteux, Maine. *Debut:* Town Hall, New York City, 1947. *Career:* Pianist, concerts in USA, Canada, Mexico, Europe, Far East; Soloist with New York Philharmonic, Philadelphia, Chicago, San Francisco, Houston, National Buffalo Symphonies; Soloist, Bell Telehone Hour, USA and Coca Cola Hour, Mexico; Conductor: American Symphony Orchestra, Boston Symphony Orchestra Pops, Wiesbaden, FRG, Lake George Opera, NYC Center Light Opera, CBS Symphony; Conductor, Musical Director, 24 Broadway musical theatre productions including: Most Happy Fella; How to Succeed in Business without Really Trying; Consultant, New York State Council on the Arts. *Recordings include:* Complete Sonatas for cello and piano, Beethoven and Brahms, with cellist, Janos Starker; Conductor, cast albums of musicals, Greenwillow and Mrs Patterson. *Address:* 838 West End Avenue, New York, NY 10025, USA.

BOGUSLAWSKI Edward, b. 22 Sept 1940, Chorzow, Poland. Composer; Teacher. *Education:* Studied composition with Szabelski in Katowice and with Haubenstock-Ramati in Vienna. *Career:* Teacher at the State College in Katowice from 1963; currently head of compositon department. *Compositions:* Intonazioni for 9 instruments, 1962; Second String Quartet, 1963; Apocalypse for reciter, choir and ensemble, 1965; Sketch for oboe and piano, 1965; Signals for orchestra, 1966; Intonazioni II for orchestra, 1966; Canti for soprano and orchestra, 1967; Metamarphosis for ensemble, 1967; Oboe Concerto, 1968; Piano Concerto, 1968; Sinfonia for Horn and orchestra, 1969; Musica per ensemble, 1970; Trio for flute, oboe and guitar, 1970; Capriccioso notturno for orchestra, 1972; Impromptu for flute, viola and harp, 1973; L'Etre for soprano and ensemble, 1973; Musica Notturna, 1973; Pro Varsovia for orchestra, 1974; Evocation for baritone and orchestra, 1974; Beelzebub's Sonata, chamber opera, 1977; Prelude and Cadenza for solo violin, 1979; Musica Concertante for alto saxophone and orchestra, 1980; Piano Concerto, 1981; Symphony Concertante for violin and chamber orchestra, 1982; Polonia, symphonic poem for violin and orchestra, 1984; The Game of Dreams, musical drama after Strindberg, 1985; Concerto for accordian, percussion and strings, 1985. *Address:* c/o ZAIKS, 2 rue Hipoteczna, 00 092 Warsaw, Poland.

BOHÁC Josef, b. 25 Mar. 1929, Vienna, Austria. Composer. *Education:* Pupil of Petrzelka, Janacek Academy of Music, Brno, 1951-56. *Career:* Director, Panton publishing concern, 1968-71; Head, Department of Music Broadcasts, Czech Television; Secretary, Union of Czech Composers, 1979-. *Compositions:* Operas: The Wooing, 1967; The Eyes, 1973; Goya, 1971-76; Golden Wedding, 1981; Orchestral: Symphonic Overture, 1964; Fragment, 1969; Elegy for Cello and Chamber Orchestra, 1969; Dramatic Suite for Strings and Kettledrums, 1969-70; Blue and White, suite, 1970; February Overture, 1973; Piano Concerto, 1974; Concerto for Violin and Chamber Orchestra, 1978; Concertino Pastorale for 2 Horns and Orchestra, 1978; Concerto for Orchestra, 1983; Dramatic Variants for Viola and Orchestra, 1983; Chamber: String Trio, 1965; Sonetti per Sonatori for Flute, Bass Clarinet, Harpsichord, Piano and Percussion, 1974; Sonata Giovane for Piano, 1983; Vocal: My Lute Resounds, monodrama for Tenor, Soprano and Nonet or Piano, 1971; 2 cantatas, 1976, 1979; Sonata Lirica for Soprano, Strings and Vibraphone, 1982. *Address:* c/o 14700 Prague 4, Ustavni 39, Czech Republic.

BOHAN Edmund, b. 5 Oct 1935, Christchurch, New Zealand. Singer (Tenor); Writer. m. Gillian Margaret Neason, 18 Nov 1968, 1 s, 1 d. *Education:* Singing with Godfrey Stirling, (Sydney), Eric Green and Gustave Sacher, (London). *Debut:* Oratorio, 1956, Opera, 1962, New Zealand. *Career:* Repertoire of over 170 operas and major works including: Opera, Oratorio, Concerts in England, Europe and Australasia and Brazil; Opera: English Opera Group, Dublin Grand Opera, London Chamber Opera; Wexford Festival, New Zealand International Festival of the Arts, Aldeburgh Festival, Norwich Triennial, Adelaide Festival; Television includes Australian Broadcasting, BBC Proms, ABC, and New Zealand Radio; Film, Barber of Seville. Venues include, Royal Festival Hall, Queen Elizabeth Hall and other major halls with RPO, London Concert, BBC Concert, and Ulster Orchestras; Oratorio soloist with British, Australian and New Zealand choral societies. *Recordings:* A Gilbert and Sullivan Spectacular; When Song is Sweet; Sweet and Low; Gilbert and Sullivan with Band and Voice. *Publications:* The Writ of Green Wax, 1971; The Buckler, 1972; The Opawa Affair, 1994; Edward Stafford: A Superior Man, 1994; Contributor to New Zealand Dictionary of Biography, 1991, 1993. *Memberships:* British Incorporated Society of Musicians; New Zealand Association of Singing Teachers. *Hobbies:* Gardening; Reading. *Address:* 5 Vincent Place, Opawa, Christchurch, New Zealand.

BOHANA Roy, b. 3 June 1938, Caernarfon, Wales. Conductor; Administrator. (1) Mina Bancheva, 16 Nov 1968, (2) Liliana Iabandjieva, 6 Apr 1984, 2 sons, 1 daughter. *Education:* BMus, BA, Celtic Studies, University of Wales. *Career:* Appointed Deputy Director and Music Director, Welsh Arts Council, 1961-; Founder, Conductor, Cardiff Polyphonic Choir, 1964-75; Conductor, Welsh National Choir for Investiture of HRH Prince of Wales, 1969; Guest Conductor: Royal Philharmonic Orchestra, BBC Welsh Symphony Orchestra, Royal Liverpool Philharmonic Orchestra, Svetoslav Obretenov Choir, Sofia, Bulgaria, Romanian National Choir, Bucharest; Tours in USA, Japan, Europe, 1969-; Adjudicator: International competitions in Hiroshima, Varna, Athens, Debrecen, Cork, Arezzo; London Symphony Orchestra Competition, Sainsbury's Choral Competition, BBC Young Musicians; Music Director, Llangollen International Eisteddfod, 1986-. *Recordings:* For two labels. *Publications:* Editor: Composers of Wales Series, 1974-76; John Bird Memorial Lecture, University of Wales, 1986. *Hobbies:* Photography; Gastronomy. *Address:* Welsh Arts Council, 9 Museum Place, Cardiff CF1 3NX, Wales.

BÖHM Ludwig, b. 5 July 1947, Munich, Germany. Music Achivist; Author; Editor. *Education:* University of Munich and Würzburg. *Career:* Teacher (English, French, Spanish) in a Secondary School, Munich, 1981-83; Founder: Theobald Böhm Archives, 1980 and Theobald Böhm Society, 1990; Organizer: Commemorative Concerts, 1981, 1994 and First International Theobald Böhm Flautist Competition, 1994. *Publications:* 1994 - I. Complete Musical Works for Flute by Theobald Böhm in 15 volumes (ed Ludwig Böhm). II. Documentation about Theobald Böhm in 10 volumes: vol 1 - Five Publications on Flute Construction by Th Böhm; vol 2 - Complete Letters and Articles by Th Böhm; vol 3 - Biographies of Th Böhm by Carl von Schafhautl, Marie Böhm and Karl Böhm; vol 4 - Catalogue of the Concerts by and with Th Böhm (ca 120); vol 5 - Catalogue of the Musical Works of Th Böhm (39 works with opus numbers and 46 arrangements without opus numbers); vol 6 - Catalogue of the still existing Flutes of Th Böhm (ca 200); vol 7 - The Estate of Th Böhm in the Munich Municipal Archives; vol 8 - Letters to and Articles about Th Böhm concerning Flute Construction; vol 9 - Letters to and Articles about Th Böhm not concerning Flute Construction; vol 10 - The Musical Works of Th Böhm by Raymond Meylan (Ludwig Böhm is author of vol 4-7 and editor of vol 1-3, 8-10). *Contributions to:* Articles published in flute and music journals worldwide: On the Trail of Th Böhm, 1981; Spelling Th Böhm or Th Boehm, 1984; Th Böhm's Comment on the Closed G Sharp Key, 1984. *Memberships:* President, Theobald Böhm Society; German Flute Society; French Flute Association; British Flute Society; National Flute Association, USA; Honorary Life Member, Victorian Flute Guild, Australia. *Hobbies:* Flute playing; Tennis; Skiing; Mountaineering. *Address:* Asamstrasse 6, D-82166 Grafelfing, Germany.

BOHMAN Gunnel, b. 4 Mar 1959, Stockholm, Sweden. Singer (Soprano). *Education:* Studied at the

Opera School, Stockholm. *Career:* Engaged by Lorin Maazel for the Vienna Staatsoper; Sang at the Mannheim Opera as Pamina, Fiordiligi and Marenka in The Bartered Bride; Sang Pamina at the Bregenz Festival and appeared further in Vienna, Zurich, Houston and Hamburg as Mozart's Countess, Agathe, Micaela, Mimi and Lola; Sang in the Jussi Björling Memorial Concert in Stockholm 1985, with Birgit Nilsson, Elisabeth Söderström, Nicolai Gedda and Robert Merrill; Bregenz Festival 1985-86, as Pamina, Vienna Volksoper from 1987 (as Fiordiligi), Staatsoper from 1988; Zurich and Parma 1987, as Smetana's Marenka and Gluck's Euridice; Glyndebourne Festival 1989, as the Countess in Figaro (also at the Albert Hall); Concert repertoire includes Bach's Passions, B minor Mass and Christmas Oratorio; Ein Deutsches Requiem and Requiems of Mozart and Dvořák; Haydn Die Schöpfung and Die Jahreszeiten; Strauss Vier Letzte Lieder and Wagner Wesendonck Lieder. *Honours include:* Jenny Lind Fellowship, 1978. *Address:* Svenska Konsertbyran AB, Schonfeldts grand 1, Box 2058, S-10312, Stockholm, Sweden.

BOIS Rob du, b. 28 May 1934, Amsterdam, the Netherlands. Composer. *Education:* Received training in piano and jurisprudence; Self-taught in composition. *Compositions:* Orchestral: Piano Concerto, 1960, revised 1968; Cercle for Piano, 9 Winds and Percussion, 1963; Simultaneous, 1965; Breuker Concerto for 2 Clarinets, 4 Saxophones and 21 Strings, 1968; A Flower Given to My Daughter, 1970; Le Concerto pour Hrisanide for Piano and Orchestra, 1971; Allegro for Strings, 1973; 3 Pezzi, 1973; Suite No 1, 1973; Violin Concerto, 1975; Skarabee, 1977; Zodiak, 1977; Concerto for 2 Violins and Orchestra, 1979; Sinfonia da camera for Wind Orchestra, 1980; Chamber: 7 Pastorales, 1960-64; Trio for Flute, Oboe and Clarinet, 1961; Rondeaux pour deux for Piano and Percussion, 1962, 2nd series for Piano 4-hands and Percussion, 1964; Chants et contrepoints for Wind Quintet, 1962; Espaces à remplir for 11 Musicians, 1963; Oboe Quartet, 1964; String Trio, 1967; Symposion for Oboe, Violin, Viola and Cello, 1969; Trio agitate for Horn, Trombone and Tuba, 1969; Reflexions sur le jour ou Perotin le Grand ressuscitera for Wind Quintet, 1969; Fusion pour deux for Bass Clarinet and Piano, 1971; Tracery for Bass Clarinet and 4 Percussionists, 1979; Sonata for Violin and Piano, 1980; Elegia for Oboe d'amore, Violin, Viola and Cello, 1980; String Quartet No 3, 1981l; Sonata for Solo Viola, 1981; Ars aequi for 2 double basses and Piano, 1984; Autumn Leaves for Guitar and Harpsichord, 1984; Hyperion for Clarinet, Horn, Viola and Piano, 1984; Forever Amber for 2 Guitars, 1985; Das Liebesverbot for 4 Wagner Tubas, 1986; On a Lion's Interlude for Alto Flute, 1986; Symphonie for Flute, 1987; String Quartet no 4, (The Independent) 1989-90; Sonata for solo violin, 1992. *Address:* Professor J Bronnerlaan 7, 2012 PM Haaklem, Netherlands.

BOKES Vladimir, b. 11 Jan 1946, Bratislava, Czechoslovakia. Composer. m. Klara Olejárová, 11 July 1970, 2 sons, 1 daughter. *Education:* Middle Music School, Konzervatorium, 1960-65; High Music School, Vysoka skola muzickych umeni, 1965-70. *Career:* Teacher in Conservatory, Bratislava, 1971-75; Assistant, High Music School, Bratislava, 1975-; Docent, 1988. *Compositions:* 5 symphonies: 1st 1970, 2nd 1978, 3rd 1980, 4th 1982, 5th 1987; 2 piano concertos: 1st 1976, 2nd 1984; Chamber and piano works; Vocal cycles Sposob ticha, The way of silence; Na svoj sposob, In its own way; Missa Posoniensis, 1991, for 4 soli, choir, organ and orchestra; 12 preludes and fuges, 1989 for piano. *Recording:* Variations on a Thema from Haydn for Piano/Opus Bratislava 1975, 1st Piano Concerto/Opus 1978; 3rd Symphov/Opus Bratislava, 1989. *Contributions to:* Biennale Zagreb 1977; Hudobny zivot, Bratislava, 1977; Essay/Communicativity in Music, Hudobny zivot, 1988. *Memberships:* Union of Slovak Composers; Slovak Music Society. *Address:* Nesporova 5, 811 03 Bratislava, Slovakia.

BOLCOM William, b. 26 May 1938, Washington,

USA. Composer. m. (1)Fay Levine, div 1967; (2)Katherine Agee Ling, div 1969; (3)Joan Morris, 28 Nov 1975. *Education:* BA University of Washington, 1958; MA, Mills College, 1961; Paris Conservatoire de Musique, 1959-61, 1964-65; DMus Art, Stanford University, 1964; Piano studies with Berthe Poncy Jacobson; Composition studies with John Verrall, Leland Smith, Darius Milhaud, George Rochberg. *Career:* Acting Assistant Professor, Music, University of Washington, 1965-66; Lecturer, Assistant Professor of Music, Queens College, 1966-68; Visiting Critic, Music Theatre Drama School, Yale University, 1968-69; Composer in Residence, New York University, 1969-71; Assistant Professor 1973, Associate Professor, 1977, Professor, 1983-, School of Music, University of Michigan, 1973. *Compositions include:* Five symphonies, 10 string quartets, Décalage for cello and paino, 1961-62, Fantasy Sonata for piano, 1961-62, Spring Concertino, for oboe and chamber orchestra, 1988; Casino Paradise (musical) performed at the American Music Theatre Festival, 1990; 3rd Violin Sonata, 1992; McTeague, (opera), 1992. *Recordings:* Numerous works with various record companies including: Violin Concerto, 5th Symphony; 10th String Quartet; 3rd Symphony. *Publications:* Co-author, Reminiscing with Sissle and Blake, 1973; Contributor to Grove's Dictionary, and Annals of Scholarship (Ed). *Honours include:* Kurt Weill Award for composition, 1962; Guggenheim Fondation Fellow; Rockefeller Foundation Awards; NEA Grants; Pulitzer Price for Music (for the 12 New Etudes), 1988; American Academy of Arts and Letters, 1993. *Memberships:* Board, American Music Center; American Composers' Alliance. *Address:* 3080 Whitmore Lake Road, Ann Arbor, MI 48105, USA.

BOLENS Nicolas, b. 1 Oct 1963, Geneva, Switzerland. Composer; Enseignant. m. 16 Sept 1988. *Education:* Conservatoire Superieur de Geneve; Diplome de Piano, 1988; Diplome de Culture Musicale, 1991. *Career:* Compositions radiodiffusées sur Radio Suisse Romande II 1991 (Octuor a vents), 1993; Musique Orch de Chambre; Sur France Musique, 1993; Professor of Piano, at Institute Jacque Dalcroze, since 1988. *Compositions:* Octuor a vents; Instants Silences, for two pianos; Chamber music for orchestra. *Honours:* Prix du Conseil d'Etat de Geneve 1991; Composition Prize with Distinction, conservatoire de Geneve, 1992; 3rd Prize du Concours de l'OCL Competition, for young composers, 1993. *Address:* 42 rue Maurice-Braillard, 1202 Geneve, Switzerland.

BOLGAN Marina, b. 20 Mar 1957, Mestre, Venice, Italy. Singer (Soprano). *Education:* Studied at Conservatorues in Venice, Siena and Rome. *Debut:* Sang Rosina in various Italian cities, 1981. *Career:* Sang Nannetta in Falstaff at the Teatro della Zarzuela, Madrid, 1982, and Gilda at Toulouse; Adina in L'Elisir d'Amore, Venice, 1984; Bellini's Elvira, Bregnez Festival, 1985; Paisiello's Nina, Catania; Annetta in Crispino e la comare by the brothers Ricci at Teatro La Fenice Venice and Theatre des Champs Elysees, Paris; Elvira and Lucia, Zurich Opera, 1987, 1989; Hamburg Staatsoper, sang Adina and in Donizetti's La Romanziera and Betly; Further appearances at Bologna, Verona and the Vienna Staatsoper (Lucia, 1988); Sang Selinda in Vivaldi's Farnace at the Valle d'Itria Festival, Martina Franca, 1991. *Address:* c/o Hamburgische Staatsoper, Grosse-Theaterstraße 34, 2000 Hamburg 34, Germany.

BOLLER Bettina, b. 19 June 1958, Zurich, Switzerland. Violinist (Solo Concerts and Chamber Music). *Education:* Academy of Music, Zurich; Academy of Music, Berne; Brooklyn College, New York City. *Debut:*Carnegie Hall, New York City, 1990. *Career:* Soloist, many European countries, USA; Leading participant, novel TV music productions including Mozart's violin-concertos; Specialist in 20th century compositions. *Compositions:* Variety of solo cadenzas. *Recordings:* Music videos, TV, 1985-90; Bach, Mozart, Ravel, Laserdiscs, USA; O Schoeck's Concerto for violin and orchestra, Claves, 1991. *Address:* Schickstra 7, CH-8400 Winterthur, Switzerland.

BOLTON Andrea, b. 1960, England. Singer (Soprano). *Education:* Studied at the Royal Northern College of Music and at the National Opera Studio. *Career:* While a student sang Gilda, Rosina, Susanna, Adina (L'elisir d'Amore), Amina (La Sonnambula), Sophie and Zerbinetta; Welsh National Opera from 1985, as Despina, Oscar, Susanna, Adele-Fledermaus, Blondchen (Die Entführung) and Echo in Ariadne auf Naxos; Musica nel Chiostro in Battignano, 1986, as Lisetta in Paisiello's Il re Teodoro in Venezie; Season 1987-88 with debuts at Opera North as Valencienne in The Merry Widow and with Scottish Opera as Cunegonde in Bernstein's Candide; Wexford Festival 1988 as Donna Elvira in Gazzaniga's Don Giovanni, televised by RTE and British Sky Broadcasting; Scottish Opera 1990, as Ascanius in Les Troyens; Concert repertory includes Mendelssohn's A Midsummer Night's Dream (Royal Liverpool Philharmonic); Haydn's Creation (RTE in Ireland); Sacred music by Handel, Caldara and Charpentier (Holst Singers at St John's Smith Square). *Recordings include:* Albums in Opera Rara's One Hundred Years of Italian Opera series. *Address:* c/o Korman International Management, Crunnells Green Cottage, Preston, Herts SG5 7UQ, England.

BOLTON Ivor, b. 17 May 1958, Lancashire, England. Conductor. *Education:* Clare College, Royal College of Music, National Opera Studio. *Career:* Conductor, Schola Cantorum of Oxford; Glyndebourne, 1982-92; Music Director, Glyndebourne Touring Opera, La Clemenza di Tito, 1993-94; Conductor, Gluck's Orfeo, Glyndebourne, 1989, has led Il Barbiere di Siviglia, Die Zauberflöte, The Rake's Progress, and La Bohème for the Touring comapny; Founded St James Baroque Players, 1984, and directs annual Luthansa Festival of Baroque Music at St James, Piccadilly; Music Director of English Touring Opera, 1990-93, leading Don Giovanni, Figaro, Lucia di Lammermor, Così fan tutte, Die Zauberflöte, La Cenerentola and Carmen; Così fan tutte at the Aldeburgh Festival; English National Opera debut, with Xerxes, 1992; La Gazza Ladra for Opera North and Monteverdi's Poppea in Bologna, 1993; Chief Conductor of the Scottish Chamber Orchestra from August 94, regular concerts with the London Mozart Players, English Chamber Orchestra, Scottish Symphony, Bournemouth Sinfonietta and BBC Symphony. *Recordings include:* Bach's concertos for Harpsichord; Purcell's Dido and Aeneas; Brahms and Mendelssohn Violin concertos; Vivaldi's Stabat Mater. *Address:* c/o Ingpen & Williams Ltd, 14 Kensington Court, London W8 5DN, England.

BONAZZI Elaine, b. 1936, Endicott, New York, USA. Singer (Mezzo-Soprano). *Education:* Studied at the Eastman School of Music, Rochester, and at Hunter College, New York. *Career:* Santa Fe Opera from 1959, notably as Meg Page in Falstaff and in the 1961 US premiere of Hindemith's Neues vom Tage; Appearances in Cincinnati, Houston, Dallas, Pittsburgh, Mexico City, Vancouver and New York (City Opera); Caramoor Festival New York in Semele, 1969; Often heard in operas by Rossini and in contemporary music; sang the Marquise in La Fille du Régiment at St Louis, 1990; Many engagements as concert singer; Taught at Peabody Conservatory, Baltimore. *Recordings:* La Pietra del Paragone by Rossini (Vanguard); Le Rossignol by Stravinsky (CBS). *Address:* c/o Opera theater of St Louis, PO Box 13148, St Louis, MO 63119, USA.

BONCOMPAGNI Elio, b. 8 May 1933, Arezzo, Italy. Conductor. *Education:* Violin and Composition, Florence and Padua; Conducting in Perugia and Hilversum. *Debut:* Bologna, 1962, Don Carlos. *Career:* Conductor at opera houses in Europe, including theatre de la Monnaie, Brussels, from 1974; British debut, 1983, Cherubini's Medee at the Barbican Hall, London; Un Ballo in Maschera for Opera Montreal, 1990; Conducted Jose Carreras concert at the Scottish Exhibition Ctr, Glasgow, 1991. *Honours include:* Prize, Italian Radion International Competition, 1961 and Mitropoulos Competition, New York, 1967. *Address:* c/o Opera de Montreal, 1157 Rue Sainte Catherine E, Montreal, Province Quebec H2L 2GB, Canada.

BOND Victoria, b. 6 May 1945, Los Angeles, California, USA. Conductor; Composer; Music Director. m. Stephan Peskin, 27 Jan 1974. *Education:* Rudolf Steiner School (HS); Hollywood (HS) BMA, University of So. California 1968; MMA 1975; DMA 1977; Juilliard School; Teachers include: Conducting: Sixten Ehrling, Herbert Blomstedt, Herbert von Karajan, Leonard Slatkin; Composition: Roger Sessions, Ingolf Dahl, Darius Milhaud, Vincent Persichetti. *Career:* Assistant Conductor: Juilliard Orchestra, Juilliard Contemporary Music Ensemble, American Opera Centre 1972-77; Cabrillo Music Festival, California 1974; White Mountains Music Festival, New Hampshire 1975; Aspen Opera, Colorado 1976; Colorado Philharmonic 1977; Exxon/Arts Endowment Conductor, Pittsburgh Symphony (Previn) 1978-80; Music Director: Pittsburgh Youth Symphony Orchestra 1978-80; New Amsterdam Symphony, 1978-80; Southeastern Music Centre, Georgia 1983-85; Empire State Youth Orchestra, Albany, NY 1982-86; Conducting Staff, Albany Symphony 1983-85; Artistic Director, Bel Canto Opera Company, NYC 1982-88; Music Director, Roanoke Symphony Orchestra, Virginia 1986-; Artistic Director, Opera Roanske, 1989-; National Institute For Music Theatre Grant For Internship With The New York City Opera 1985-86; Guest Conducting: Houston Symphony; Buffalo Philharmonic; Pittsburgh Symphony; Richmond Symphony; Chattanooga, Anchorage (Alaska), Radio Telefis Eireann (Ireland). *Compositions:* Black Light (Piano Concerto); Everyone Is Good For Something (Musical); Great Galloping Gottschalk (Ballet); Equinox (Ballet); Other Selves (Ballet); Frog Prince (Narrator and Orchestra); What's The Point of Counterpoint? (Narrator and Orchestra); Old New Borrowed Blues (Chamber Ensemble); From An Antique Land (Voice and Piano); Molly ManyBloom; Urban Bird (Saxophone Concerto). *Recordings:* Peter Quince At The Clavier; Monologue; Sonata For Cello and Piano; A Mother Goose Primer; Delusion of The Fury; Notes from Underground; An American Collage. *Publications:* The Orchestra At The Time of Mozart, Doctoral Thesis, Juilliard 1977. *Hobbies:* Horseback Riding; Sailing; Hiking. *Address:* 256 W 10th Street, New York City, NY 10014, USA.

BONDARENKO Alexander, b. 1950, Crimea, Russia. Violinist. *Career:* Co-Founder, Rachmaninov Quartet, 1974, under the auspices of the Sochi State Philharmonic Society, Crimea; Concerts in the former Soviet Union and from 1975-76, tours to Switzerland, Austria, Bulgaria, Norway and Germany; Participant in 1976 Schostakovich Chamber Music Festival at Vilnius, and in festivals in Moscow and St Petersburg; Repertoire has included works by Hydn, Mozart, Beethoven, Bartok, Brahms, Schnittke, Shostakovich, Boris Tchaikovsky, Chalayev and Meyerovvich. *Honours include:* Prize, First All-Union Borodin String Quarter Competition, with the Rachamninov Quartet, 1987. *Address:* c/o Sonata (Rachmaninov Quartet), 1 Northgate Street, Glasgow G20 7AA, Scotland.

BONDE Lars Ole, b. 25 Oct 1951, Aarhus, Denmark. Music Producer; University Teacher. 1 d. *Education:* MA Musicology and Scandinavian Literature, Aarhus University, 1979. *Career:* Teacher, part time, Musicology, Aarhus University, 1975-79; High School Teacher, Music and Danish Literature, Skanderborg, 1979-81; Assistant Professor, Musicology, Aalborg University, 1981-87; Music Producer, Danish Broadcasting Corp, 1985-; External Professor, Music Therapy and Musicology, Aalborg University, 1991-; Artistic Director of Ebeltoft Festival with Bent Lorentzen and Gaia Vocal Ensemble with Soren K Hansen. *Recordings:* As Producer: Niels W Gade: The Crusaders; Drommesange. *Publications:* Kunsten Ogrevolutionen, 1979; Man Skal Høre Meget, 1988; Co-Editor of music magazine, Modspil, 1977-87; Various articles and reviews. *Memberships:* Dansk Selskab for Musikforskning. *Hobbies:* Creative writing. *Address:* Kaserneboulevarden 25, DK 8000 Aarhus, Denmark.

BONE Robin, b. 27 Mar 1947, London, England. Composer. *Education:* Dartington College of Arts; Composition privately with Elisabeth Lutyens and Boris Blacher. *Career:* Oboe Quintet, BBC Radio 3; Woman with Camellias for soprano and ensemble, Piccadilly Festival. *Compositions:* Pomes Penyeach for soprano and ensemble, Society for the Promotion of New Music; Duo for 2 Pianos, Society for the Promotion of New Music; Chamber Concerts for 11, Society for the Promotion of New Music; Nocturnii for tenor and ensemble, Society for the Promotion of New Music; String Quartet, Society for the Promotion of New Music; Duo for Clarinet and Piano, Society for the Promotion of New Music; Woman with Camellias for soprano and ensemble; Mario and the Magician, chamber opera; The Past and the Present, chamber opera; Dialogue for Piano; Variations for Piano; Piano Trio; Trio for Clarinet, Violin and Piano; Polyhymnia for orchestra; Far beyond the Stars for orchestra; Concertino I for Six; Concertino II for Six. *Membership:* Performing Rights Society. *Address:* Greentrees, Bishon Lane, Bishopstone, Hereford, England.

BONELL Carlos Antonio, b. 23 July 1949, London, England. Guitarist. m. Pinuccia Rossetti, 2 sons. *Education:* Royal College of Music. *Debut:* Wigmore Hall, London. *Career:* Soloist with all the major British orchestras and many orchestras overseas; Founded, Carlos Bonell Ensemble, 1983; Frequent broadcaster. *Compositions:* Spanish Folk Songs and Dances; 20 First pieces, 1984. *Recordings:* Numerous for various record companies. *Publications:* The Romantic Guitar and The Classical Guitar, 1983; Tarrega: Fantasia and Purcell: 3 Pieces from the Fairy Queen; 3 Spanish Folk Songs for 3 guitars, 1984; Masterclass on Playing the Guitar, 1983; Masterworks of the Classical Guitar, 1984; Airs and Dances of Gasper Sanz, 1977. *Contributions to:* Guitar Magazine. *Honours:* Honorary, Associate, Royal College of Music, 1978; nomination for best chamber music performance for record, John Williams and Friends, American National Academy of Recording Arts and Sciences, 1978. *Membership:* Musicians Union. *Hobbies:* Reading; Walking. *Address:* c/o Harold Holt Ltd, 31 Sinclair Road, London W14 0NS, England.

BONETTI Antoni Robert, b. 6 Nov 1952, London, England. Violinist; conductor. m. Ruth Back, 16 Mar 1974, 3 s. *Education:* AMusA, DSCM, New South Wales Conservatorium, 1973; ARCM, 1978. *Career:* Violinist, Principal 2nd Violin, 1968-72, Australian Youth Orchestra; Tour to Japan, 1970, South East Asia, 1974; Freelance Violinist, London, 1975-76, appearing with RPO, NPO, London Mozart Players; Concert master, Norrlands Opera Orchestra, Sweden, 1976-77; Stockholm Ensemble, 1977-78; Baroque Violin with Gammerith consort, Austria, 1978; Member of Kurpfalzisches Kammerorchester, FRG, 1979-81; Concertmaster: Queensland Theatre Orchestra, 1981-84; Head of Orchestral Studies: St Peters Lutheran College, 1985-; Lecturer: Queensland Conservatorium of Music, 1982-92; Conductor: Baroque Orchestra of Brisbane, Brisbane Christian Chamber Orchestra, 1986-, Concert Society Orchestra, 1987-90; Extensive tours with Divertimento Bonetti ensemble throughout Europe; Music Director and Founder, Brisbane Sinfonia, 1990-; Various conducting engagements with Redcliffe City Choir, Cleveland Symphony Orchestra, Ipswich Youth Orchestra, 1989; Adjudicator, Gold Coast Tropcarnival, Brisbane, 1983. *Composition:* Jacaranda, for orchestra, 1992. *Honours:* Fellowship, Australian Council for the Arts, 1974. *Hobbies:* Philately; Birdwatching; Gardening. *Address:* 17 Allambic Street, The Gap, Queensland 4061, Australia.

BÓNIS Ferenc, b. 17 May 1932, Miskolc, Hungary. Musicologist. m. Terézia Csajbók. *Education:* Doctor of Music, Ferenc Liszt Academy of Music, Budapest. *Career:* Music Producer, Hungarian Radio, 1950-70; Leader, Music Department for Children and Youth, Hungarian Radio, 1970-; Scientific Collaborator, Musicological Institute of Hungarian Academy of Sciences, 1961-73; Professor, Musicological Faculty, Ferenc Liszt Academy of Music, 1972-; Editor, Magyar Zenetudomány (Hungarian Musicology), 1959-; Editor, Magyar Zenetörténeti Tanulmányok (Studies on History of Hungarian Music), 1968-; Editor, Complete Edition of B Szabolcsi's Works, 1977-. *Recordings:* Editor, Early Hungarian Chamber Music; Works by P Wranitzky and L Mozart; Béla Bartók - As We Saw Him (recollections); Zoltán Kodály - As We Saw Him (recollections); Hódolat Bartóknak és Kodálynak, 1992. *Publications:* Mosonyi Mihály, 1960; G Mahler and F Erkel, 1960; Quotations in Bartók's Music, 1963; Die ungarischen Tänze der Handschrift von Appony, 1964 ; Beethoven und die ungarische Musik, 1970; Bartók und der Verbunkos, 1972; Bartók and Wagner, 1979; Így láttuk Kodályt, 1979; Béla Bartok - His Life in Pictures and Documents, (also in German, Hungarian, Russian and Japanese), 1981; Így láttuk Bartókot, 1981; Így láttuk Kodályt (2nd enlarged edition), 1982; Zoltán Kodály, A Hungarian Master of Neoclassicism, 1982; Tizenhárom találkozás Ferencsik Jánossal (Meeting J Ferencsik), 1984; International Kodaly Conference (with E Szönyi and L Vikár), 1986; Zoltán Kodálys Weg zum Psalmus Hungaricus, 1987; Zoltán Kodály's Psalmus Hungaricus - facsimile edition, 1987; Three Days with Sándor Veress the Composer, 1987-88. Mosonyiana, 1989; Mozarts geistige Anwesenheit in der ingarischen Kultur um 1800, 1990; The Miraculous Mandarin: The Birth and Vicissitudes of a Masterpiece, 1991; Harminchárom óra ifjabb Bartok Bélával (33 hours with B Bartók Jr), 1991. *Honour:* Ferenc Erkel Prize, 1973. *Memberships:* Gesellschaft für Musikforschung; President, Hungarian Kodály Society; President, Ferenc Erkel Society. *Address:* Belgrád rakpart 27 1 5, Budapest, H-1056, Hungary.

BONISOLLI Franco, b. 1938, Rovereto, Italy. Singer (Tenor). *Education:* Studied privately. *Career:* Spoleto 1961, as Ruggero in La Rondine. *Career:* Spoleto 1963, in The Love of Three Oranges; Amsterdam 1965, as Des Grieux in Manon Lescaut; US debut San Francisco 1969, as Alfredo; La Scala Milan 1969, in L'Assedio di Corinto by Rossini; Metropolitan Opera from 1971, as Rossini's Almaviva, Nemorino, Faust, the Duke of Mantua, Alfredo and Cavaradossi (1986); Guest appearances in London, Vienna, Rome, Toulouse, Dallas, Philadelphia, Hamburg and Brussels; Other roles include Rodolfo, Alvaro in La Forza del Destino and Pinkerton; Deutsche Oper Berlin 1982, in La Fanciulla del West; Verona Arena 1985, as Manrico; sang Calaf at Covent Garden 1987, Enzo in La Gioconda at the Verona Arena 1988 (Radames 1989). *Recordings:* La Traviata (BASF); Tosca (Deutsche Grammophon); Il Trovatore, Pagliacci (EMI); Rigoletto; Gluck's Iphigénie en Aulide and Paride ed Helena (Orfeo); L'Assedio di Corinto. *Address:* Allied Artists Agency, 42 Montpelier Square, London SW7 1JZ.

BONNEMA Albert, b. 18 Apr 1953, Trummarum, Holland. Singer (Tenor). *Education:* Sweelinck conservatory, Amsterdam and with Nicolai Gedda. *Career:* Chorus, Netherlands Opera, 1985, appearing widely in Holland in operettas as Bettelstudent, Die lustige Witwe and La Belle Helene; Berlin, Theater des Westens, 1988, as Sou-chong in Das Land des Lachelns; Further engagements in Paris (operetta by Offenbach), Wiesbaden, the Landestheater Salzburg, Klagenfurt and Berne; many concert appearances; Sang Jenik in The Bartered Bride, Berne, 1992. *Address:* De Nederlandse Opera, Waterlooplein 22, 1011 PG Amsterdam, Holland.

BONNER Stephen John Levett, b. 3 Feb .1947, Harrow. Music historian. m. Janet Rodgers, 1976, 1 daughter. *Education:* Magdalene College, Cambridge, 1966-70, MA. *Career:* Trustee, Harehills Dance Umbrella, Northern School of Contemporary Dance (Leeds); involved with Community work in the Arts with IBM United Kingdom Limited. *Contributions to:* New Grove, 8 articles, duplicated in New Grove Dictionary of Musical Instruments, Lute Society Journal; Editor of and contributor to Aeolian Harp (4 vols, 1970-74). *Publications:* Angelo Ventura, 1971; The Classic Image, History of the Lyre Guitar, 1972, and various shorter works on musical instruments. *Address:* 2 Knox Gardens, Harrogate, N Yorks, HG1 3AU.

BONNER Tessa, b. 1955, England. Singer (Soprano). *Education:* Studied at Leeds University and the Guildhall School of Music. *Career:* Solo singer and consort member of such groups as the Tallis Scholars, the New London Consort, the Lute Group, Gabrieli Consort, Taverner Consort and the Early Opera Project; Frequent appearances with Musica Secreta, notably at the Early Music Centre Festival, the Lufthansa Festival of Baroque Music, and at the National Gallery; Early Music Network Tour of Britain Nov 1991 with programme Filiae Jerusalem (sacred music for women's voices by Monteverdi, Carissimi, Cavalli, Viadna, Grandi and Marco da Gagliano); Other repertoire includes works by Marenzio, Luzzaschi, Wert, Luigi Rossi and the women composers Francesca Caccini and Barbara Strozzi; Participation in lecture- recitals and workshops on performance practice and ornamentation. *Address:* Robert White Management, 182, Moselle Avenue, London N22 6EX, England.

BONNEY Barbara, b. April 1956, Montclair, New Jersey, USA. Singer (Soprano). m. Håkan Hagegard. *Education:* Studied in Canada and at the Salzburg Mozarteum with Walter Raninger. *Debut:* Darmstadt 1979, in Die Lustigen Weiber von Windsor. *Career:* Sang Blondchen in Die Entführung, Cherubino in Le Nozze di Figaro, Nathali in Henze's Der Prinz von Homburg and Massenet's Manon; Appeared at Frankfurt, Hamburg and Munich 1983-84; Covent Garden 1984, as Sophie in Der Rosenkavalier: returned as Blondchen, 1987; La Scala Milan 1985, as Pamina; Schwetzingen Festival 1985 in Handel's Semele; season 1987-88 as Sophie in Monte Carlo, Pamina at Geneva, Adina at Lausanne and Susanna at Zurich; Metropolitan 1989-90, as Adele in Fledermaus (Sophie in Der Rosenkavalier 1991); Chicago Lyric Opera debut 1989, as Adele; Concert apperances include the Monteverdi Vespers at Copenhagen, 1990; Sang in Mozart Bicentenary Gala at Covent Garden, 1991; Mozart's Coronation Mass and Solemn Vespers at the 1993 Prom Concerts, London. *Recordings:* Moses and Aron by Schoenberg and Haydn's Lord Nelson Mass (Decca); Lortzing's Zar und Zimmermann (EMI); Video of Messiah. *Address:* c/o Metropolitan Opera, Lincoln Center, New York, NY 10023, USA.

BONSAKSEN Per Fridtjov, b. 8 Sept 1946, Trondheim, Norway. Cathedral Organist and Director of Music. m. Randi Nygaard, 17 Aug 1985. *Education:* Trondheim Conservatory of Music majoring in church music; Hochschule fur Musik, (Cologne), organ and harpsichord, (Vienna) organ; Diploma in Solo Performance, 1974; Orchestra Conducting, Hamburg. *Debut:* Organ Diploma Concert, Vienna, 1974. *Career:* Director of Music, Organist and Choir Master, the National Shrine and Nidaros Cathedral of Trondheim, Norway, 1976; Concert tours to Europe and America; Regular performances in Nordic brodcasting and TV; Composer. *Recordings:* Scandinavian Organ Music, 1982; Famous Organ Music from Nidaros Cathedral, 1986; Festival Alleluia (Psalms for choir throughout the centuries), 1986; New Church Music from the Nidaros Cathedral, 1992. *Honours:* First Place, Norwegian Organ Competition, 1974. *Address:* Skogvokterveien 2, N-7018 Trondheim, Norway.

BONSEL Adriaan, b. 4 Aug 1918, Hilversum, the Netherlands. Flautist; Composer. *Education:* Amsterdam Conservatory. *Career:* Soloist with orchestras; chamber-music concerts. *Compositions:* Suite for Flute and String Orchestra, 1946; Folkloristic Suite for Orchestra, 1948; 2 wind quintets, 1949, 1953; Clarinet Concerto, 1950; 2 symphonies, 1956, 1957; Divertimento for Small orchestra, 1957; Minneliederen, 6 love songs for Baritone, Chorus and small Orchestra, 1957; Elegy for Viola, 1961; SOS, overture, 1962; Concert Etudes for Flute, 1963; Musica for Flute, Cello and Piano, 1971; Anthriscus Sylvestris, divertimento for 12 Flutes, 1974; Peace-War-Peace? Moto-perpetuo? for Orchestra, 1975; Octet for Winds, 1975; Intrada for Horn, 2 Trumpets, 2 Trombones and Tuba, 1982. *Address:* c/o BUMA/STERMA Huis, Postbus 725, 1180 AS Amstelveen, Netherlands.

BONYNGE Richard, b. 29 Sept 1930, Sydney, Australia. Opera Conductor. m. Joan Sutherland, 1954, 1 son. *Education:* Trained as a pianist; Specialist in the bel canto repertoire. *Debut:* As Conductor: with Santa Cecilia Orchestra, Rome, 1962. *Career:* Conducted first opera, Faust, Vancouver, 1963; Has conducted in most of the world's leading opera houses and in the Edinburgh Festival, Vienna Festival and Florence Festival; Has been Principal Conductor and Artistic/Musical Director of companies including Sutherland/Williamson International Grand Opera Company, 1965, Vancouver Opera 1974-78, Australian Opera 1975-86; Conducted Les Huguenots for Australian Opera, 1989 (Joan Sutherland's Farewell); Maria Stuarda at Sydney, 1992. *Recordings:* Opera recordings include: Bellini's Beatrice di Tenda, Norma, I Puritani, La Sonnambula; Delibes' Lakmé; Donizetti's L'Elisir d'Amore, La Fille du Régiment, Lucia di Lammermoor, Lucrezia Borgia, Maria Stuarda; Gounod's Faust; Handel's Alcina, Giulio Cesare; Léhar's The Merry Widow; Leoni's L'Oracolo; Massenet's Esclarmonde, Le Roi de Lahore, Thérèse; Meyerbeer's Les Huguenots; Mozart's Don Giovanni; Offenbach's Les Contes d'Hoffmann; Puccini's Suor Angelica; Rossini's Semiramide; Strauss's Die Fledermaus; Thomas' Hamlet; Verdi's I Masnadieri, Rigoletto, La Traviata, Il Trovatore. Ballet recordings include: Adam's Le Diable A Quatre, Giselle; Auber's Marco Spada; Burgmuller's La Péri; Chopin's Les Sylphides; Delibes' Coppelia, Sylvia; Massenet's Le Carillon, La Cigale; Offenbach's Le Papillon; Rossini-Respighi's La Boutique Fantasque; Strauss's Aschenbrödel; Tchaikovsky's The Nutcracker, Sleeping Beauty, Swan Lake. Other recordings include recital discs with Sutherland, Tebaldi, Tourangeau and Pavarotti and many orchestral and ballet anthologies. *Address:* c/o Ingpen and Williams, 14 Kensington Court, London W8, England.

BOOGAARTS Jan, b. 10 May 1934, Helmond, Netherlands. University Lecturer; Docent; Choir Director; Organist; Organ Specialist. m. Dorine Sniedt, 26 Dec 1964, 2 sons, 1 daughter. *Education:* Conservatory Tilburg; Royal Conservatory, The Hague (Piano, organ, direction, schools); Institute of Musicology, University Utrecht. *Career:* Radio Recordings for: BBC England, AVRO NOS KRO NCRV, The Netherlands, Sud Deutscher Rundfunk, ORTF, France; Culture France; Radio DDR, Radio Warsaw, Poland, BRT RTB Belgie; Television: NOS KRO (Holland Festival); Warsaw Poland; Docent Choirdirection, Royal Conservatory, The Hague; Lecturer, University Utrecht; Visiting Professorships throughout Europe & America. *Recordings:* 30 Include: Plainsong; Holy Week, Ordo Missae Instauratus Concilii Vaticani II, Vespers, Compline, Famous Hymni & Sequentiae; etc; Renaissance Music: Madrigals & Chansons with texts Petrach & Ronsard, Works of R White, Josquin, Lasso, Isaak, Senfl, etc. *Publications:* Many articles in period Festschrift and small publications. *Contributions to:* many magazines and journals. *Honours:* Price Radio Warszawa, 1977; Comphaneiro Bandeirante of the Ordem Nacional dos Bandeirantes, Sao Paulo, 1981; Knight, Order of St Gregory, Rome, 1983. *Memberships:* Consociation Internationalis Musicae Sacrae; Vereniging voor Latijnse Liturgie; Advisor to the Monuments Commission of Gelderland on the Restoration of historic organs. *Hobby:* Gardening. *Address:* Haveza The, Die Magerhorst, Duiven, Gelderland, The Netherlands.

BOOKSPAN Martin, b. 30 July 1926, Boston, Massachusetts, USA. Broadcaster; Writer. m. Janet S Sobel, 24 Oct 1954, 1 son, 2 daughters. *Education:* Boston Music School, 1936-42; Harvard College, Class of 1947. *Career:* Host and Commentator, Radio Broadcasts of Boston Symphony Orchestra, 1957-67; Host and Commentator, Radio Broadcasts of Pittsburgh Symphony, National Symphony and American Symphony Orchestra, 1967-69; Host and Commentator, Live from Studio 8H telecasts, 1980-; Radio and Television Voice of the New York Philharmonic, 1975- ; Host and Commentator, Chamber Music Radio Broadcasts Spoleto Festival, USA, 1982-. *Publications:* The New York Times Guide to Recorded Music, 1967;

101 Masterpieces of Music and Their Composers, 1968; Zubin - The Zubin Mehta Story, 1978; André Previn: A Biography, 1981; Consumer Reports Reviews Classical Records, 1971. *Contributions to:* Contributing Editor to Stereo Review Magazine, 1958-74; Record Critic, Consumer Reports, 1962-78; Contributing Editor to Ovation Magazine, 1980-86. *Hobbies:* History; Politics; Spectator Sports. *Current Management:* ICM Artists, 40 West 57th Street, New York, NY 10019, USA. *Address:* c/o ICM Artists, 40 West 57th Street, New York, NY 10019, USA.

BOONE Charles, b. 21 June 1939, Cleveland, Ohio, USA. Composer. *Education:* Pupil of Karl Schiske, Vienna Academy of Music, 1960-61; Received private instruction from Ernst Krenek and Adolph Weiss, Los Angeles, 1961-62; Studied theory at the University of Southern California, Los Angeles, BM, 1963, and composition at San Francisco State College, MA, 1968. *Career:* Chairman, San Francisco Composers' Forum; Coordinator, Mills College Performing Group and Tape Music Center; Composer-in-Residence, Berlin, under the sponsorship of the Deutscher Akademischer Austauchdienst, 1975-77; Writer and Lecturer on contemporary music. *Compositions:* 3 Motets for Chorus, 1962-65; Oblique Formation for Flute and Piano, 1965; Starfish for Flute, Clarinet, 2 Percussion, 2 Violins, and Piano, 1966; A Cool Glow of Radiation for Flute and Tape, 1966; The Edge of the Land for Orchestra, 1968; Not Now for Clarinet, 1969; Zephyrus for Oboe and Piano, 1970; Vermilion for Oboe, 1970; Quartet for Clarinet, Violin, Cello, and Piano, 1970; Chinese Texts for Soprano and Orchestra, 1971; First Landscape for Orchestra, 1971; Vocalise for Soprano, 1972; Second Landscape for Chamber Orchestra, 1973, also for Orchestra, 1979; String Piece for String Orchestra, 1978; Streaming for Flute, 1979; Little Flute Pieces, 1979; Springtime for Oboe, 1980; Winter's End for Soprano, Countertenor, Viola da Gamba, and Harpsichord, 1980; Slant for Percussion, 1980; The Watts Tower for 1 Percussion, 1981; Trace for Flute and 10 Instruments, 1981-83; Solar One for Flute and Trumpet, 1985; The Timberline, and Other Pieces for Carillon, 1987-; Morphosis for Percussion Quartet, 1991. *Honours:* National Endowment for the Arts grants, 1968, 1975, 1983; Commissions. *Address:* 3703 Gravstark Street, Houston, TX 77006, USA.

BOOREN Jo van den, b. 14 Mar 1935, Maastricht, the Netherlands. Trumpeter; Composer. *Education:* Studied trumpet with Marinus Komst; Composition with Kees van Baaren and Klaus Huber. *Career:* Trumpeter in orchestras. *Compositions:* Trio for Oboe, Clarinet and Bassoon, 1960; Sonata for 3 Clarinets, 1962; Suite dionysienne for English Horn and String Orchestra, 1963-64; Estremi for Oboe, Violin, Viola and Cello, 1967; Spectra for Wind Quintet, 1967; Capriccio for Brass Orchestra, 1968; Spiel I for Oboe and Electronic Sound, 1969; Strofa I for Cello, 1969, II for Trumpet, 1970, II for Horn, 1972; Equilibrio for Flute, 1970; Ballade for Oboer, 1971; Intrada Festiva for 4 Horns, 4 Trumpets and 4 Trombones, 1971; Akirob for Flute, Violin and Viola, 1972; Potpourri 1973 for Brass Quintet, 1973; Sinfonia Jubilata for Orchestra, 1975; Birds for 5 Flutes, 1975; Hymn for Organ, 1985; Oblation for Organ, 2 Trumpets, 2 Horns and 2 Trombones, 1985.

BOOTH Juliet, b. 1961, London, England. Singer (Soprano). *Education:* Studied at Bristol University and the Guildhall School of Music. *Career:* Opera North from 1987, Frasquita (debut role), Ninetta (The Love for Three Oranges), Xenia (Boris Godunov); Poussette (Manon), Arminda (La Finta Giardiniera), Norina (Don Pasquale) and Lauretta; Has also sung Mélisande at Aldeburgh, Virtu and Valletto in Opera London's L'Incoronazione di Poppea and Mozart's Countess for Welsh National Opera; Aix-en-Provence 1991, as Helena in A Midsummer Night's Dream; Concert appearances at the South Bank and the Barbican, in France, Belgium and Singapore; Handel's Solomon in Berlin and Carmina Burana at the Edinburgh Festival, under Neeme Järvi; Television appearances include Dennis O'Neill and Friends on BBC2; Season 1990-91 with The Kingdom

(Elgar), Haydn's Nelson Mass and Creation, Salieri's Prima la Musica with the City of London Sinfonia; concert arias with the English Chamber Orchestra; Messiah; Gilda (Rigoletto), Opera North, 1992; Countess (Figaro), Glyndebourne Touring Opera, 1992; Morgana (Alcina), Covent Garden debut, 1992; Musetta and Mimi (La Bohème), Opera North, 1993. *Recordings include:* L'Incoronazione di Poppea conducted by Richard Hickox (Virgin Classics); Bruckner-Mass in F - Hyperion, 1992 . *Honours:* Gold Medal for Singers, the Schubert Prize for Lieder and the Ricordi Opera Prize, at the Guildhall School. *Current management:* IMG Artists, Europe. *Address:* Media House, 3 Burlington Lane, Chiswick, London W4 2TH, England.

BOOTH Philip, b. 6 May 1942, Washington DC, USA. Singer (Bass). *Education:* Sang with US Army Chorus then studied further at the Eastman School of Music, with Julius Huehn, and with Todd Duncan in Washington. *Career:* Kennedy Center Washington 1971, in Ariodante; Many appearances as concert singer; Engagements at the opera houses of San Diego, Houston and San Francisco; Meropolitan Opera from 1973, as Pimen in Boris Godunov, Ramphis, Fasolt and Fafner in Der Ring des Nibelungen, Basilio and Osmin; sang in the US premiere of Mascagni's Le Maschere, with Westchester Opera, 1989. *Address:* c/o Metropolitan Opera, Lincoln Center, New York, NY 10023, USA.

BOOTH-JONES Christopher, b. 1943, Somerset, England. Singer (Baritone). *Education:* Royal Academy of Music, London. *Career:* Toured with Welsh National Opera for All as Mozart's Figaro and Rossini's Bartolo, 1972-73; Welsh National Opera, Figaro in Mozart's Marriage and Bohème; Glyndebourne Festival and Touring Opera; English National Opera from 1982 in Roméo et Juliette, Patience, Così fan Tutte, Pagliacci, La Bohème, War and Peace, Osud, Akhnaten and Xerxes; sang Claudio in a new production of Beatrice and Benedict, 1990; Mr Astley in a revival of The Gambler; English Music Theatre in Tom Jones, La Cenerentola and The Threepenny Opera; Die Zauberflöte; Opera North in Der Freischütz, A Midsummer Night's Dream and Beatrice and Benedict; Kent Opera as Monostatos in Die Zauberflöte; Season 1992 with ENO in the premiere of Bakxai by John Buller and as the Music Master in Ariadne auf Naxos. *Recordings:* Julius Caesar and Pacific Overtures (EMI); Videos of The Gondoliers, Rusalka, Xerxes and Billy Budd. *Address:* c/o Music International, 13 Ardilaun Road, Highbury, London N5 2QR, England.

BOOTHBY Richard, 1955, England. Viola da Gamba player; Cellist. *Career:* Member of the Purcell Quartet, debut concert at St John's Smith Square, London 1984; Extensive tours and broadcasts in France, Belgium, Holland, Germany, Austria, Switzerland, Italy and Spain; Tours of the United States and Japan, 1991-92; British appearances include four Purcell concerts at the Wigmore Hall, 1987, later broadcast on Radio 3; Repertoire includes music on the La Folia theme by Vivaldi, Corelli, CPE Bach, Marais, A Scarlatti, Vitali and Geminiani; instrumental works and songs by Purcell, music by Matthew Locke, John Blow and Fantazias and Airs by William Lawes; 17th Century virtuoso Italian music by Marini, Buonamente, Gabrieli, Fontana, Stradella and Lonati; J S Bach and his forerunners - Biber, Scheidt, Schenk, Reinken and Buxtehude; Member of Fretwork, debut concert at the Wigmore Hall 1986; Appearances in the Renaissance and Baroque repertoire in Sweden, Austria, Belgium, Holland, France and Italy; Tour of Soviet Union Sept 1989, Japan June 1991; Gave George Benjamin's Upon Silence in the Elizabeth Hall, 1990; Wigmore Hall concerts 1990-91 with music by Lawes, Purcell, Locke and Byrd; Other repertory includes In nomines and Fantasias by Tallis and Parsons; Dance music by Holborne and Dowland (including Lachrimae); London Cries by Gibbons and Dering, Resurrection Story and Last Seven Words by Schütz. *Recordings include:* With the Purcell Quartet: Six-record set on the La Folia theme (Hyperion); Purcell Sonatas for two violins, viola da gamba and continuo;

Sonatas by Vivaldi and Corelli (Chandos); Series of ten recordings with Fretwork (Virgin Classics). *Address:* c/o Robert White Management, 182 Moselle Avenue, London N22 6EX, England.

BOOZER Brenda (Lynn), b. 25 Jan 1948, Atlanta, Georgia, USA. Mezzo-soprano. m. Robert Martin Klein, 29 Apr 1973. *Education:* BA, Florida State University, Tallahassee, 1970; Postgraduate studies, Juilliard School, New York, 1974-77. *Career:* Chicago Lyric Opera, 1978; Festival of Two Worlds, Spoleto, Italy, 1978, 1979; Greater Miami Opera, 1979; Houston Grand Opera, 1979; Metropolitan Opera, New York, 1979-83, 1985, as Hänsel, Meg Page, the Composer (Ariadne auf Naxos), Octavian and Orlofsky; Netherlands Opera, Amsterdam, 1981; Paris Opera, 1982-83; Concerts; Television appearances; Falstaff, at Covent Garden, 1983; Spoleto Festival, 1989, as Nicklausse in Les Contes d'Hoffmann. *Honour:* Deutsche Grammophon recording of Falstaff with the Los Angeles Philharmonic was nominated for a Grammy Award in 1984. *Address:* c/o Columbia Artists Management Inc, 165 West 57th Street, New York, NY 10019, USA.

BORETZ Benjamin (Aaron), b. 3 Oct 1934, New York City, USA. Composer; Music Theorist; Teacher; Writer on Music. *Education:* Studied piano and cello; Training in conducting from Julius Rudel; in harpsichord from Erwin Bodky; BA, Brooklyn College, 1954; Manhattan School of Music, New York; MFA, Brandeis University, 1957; Aspen Music School; University of California, Los Angeles; MFA 1960, PhD 1970, Princeton University; Composition teachers included: Irving Fine, Harold Shapero, Arthur Berger, Darius Milhaud, Lukas Foss, Roger Sessions. *Career:* Consultant and writer, Fromm Music Foundation, 1960-70; Founding Co-editor 1961-64, Editor 1964-84, Perspectives of New Music; Music Critic, The Nation, 1962-70; Teacher, various schools including New York University, 1964-69, Columbia University 1969-72, Bard College 1973-; Distinguished Visiting Professor, UCLA, 1991; Visiting Professor, UC Santa Barbara, 1991; Invited Participant, (Interdisciplinary Conference) Calgary, 1991. *Compositions:* Concerto Gross for String Orch, 1956; Violin Concerto, 1956; Divertimento for 5 Instruments, 1957; String Quartet, 1958; Group Variations I for Orchestra 1967, II for Computer 1971; Liebeslied for Piano, 1974; ...my chart shines high where the blue milk's upset... for Piano, 1978, Passage fore Roger Sussions, piano, 1979; recorded on open space CD, 1989; Language, as a Music: Six Marginal Pretexts for Composition for Speaker, Piano and Prerecorded Tape, 1980; Soliloquy I for Piano, 1981; One (an exercise), 1985-88; Series of works in soundscore; Composer, collaborator, recording artist on Inter/Play series, Nos 21-30, 1989; Founder and Director, Music Program Zero, Bard College; A series entitled, Scores for Composing, 1991-93. *Recordings:* One (an excercise) eight pianosolo sound sessions (open space 4CDs,) 1992; An Experiment in Reading, 1981; Open Space CD, 1993. *Publications:* Co-editor with Eward T Cone, Perspectives on Schoenberg and Stravinsky, 1968, 2nd edition revised 1972; Perspectives on American Composers, 1971; Perspectives on Contemporary Music Theory, 1972; Perspectives on Notation and Performance, 1976; If I am a Musical Thinker, 1984; Music Columns from the Nation, 1962-68, Open Space, 1991; Interface, Six sociomusical essays, Perspectives of New Music, 1987-92. *Address:* c/o Music Department, Bard College, Annandale-on-Hudson, NY 12504, USA.

BOREYKO Andrey, b. 22 July 1957, Leningrad, USSR. Conductor; Teacher. m. Julia Wolk, 1 Feb 1990, 1 daughter. *Education:* Choir Conductor, 1979, Symphony Orchestra and Opera Conductor, 1987, Leningrad Conservatory. *Debut:* May 1979. *Career:* Founder, Director, Res Facta early music group, Leningrad, 1977; Founder, Director, Barocco Consert, Leningrad, 1984; Conductor, Leningrad Theatre of Musical Comedy, 1985-86; Conductor, Uljanovsk State Symphony Orchestra, 1986-90; General Musical Director, Ural Philharmonic Orchestra, Sverdlovsk,

1990-; Concerts with Leningrad Philharmonics, Moscow Symphony, RPHO and RSO of NOS (Netherlands); Concerts in Tchaikovsky Hall, Moscow Conservatorium, Schauspielhaus, Berlin, Concertgebouw Amsterdam, Big Hall of Leningrad Philharmonic Society. *Honours:* 3rd Prize, K Kondrashin Competition, Hilversum, Amsterdam, Netherlands, 1989; 4th Prize, XII Fitelberg Competition, Poland, 1987. *Current management:* Benelux countries: Marijke Klinkhamer Artists Management. *Address:* Kultury 22/1 no 122, St Petersburg 194292, Russia.

BORG Kim, b. 7 Aug 1919, Helsinki, Finland. Professor; Singer; Composer. m. Ebon Ringblom, 10 Feb 1950, 1 son, 1 daughter. *Education:* MSc, Chemistry, Institute of Technology, Helsinki; Studied Singing Privately in Finland, Sweden, Denmark, Italy, Austria, USA; Musical Theory and Composition in Finland and Sweden. *Debut:* Helsinki, 1945. *Career:* Professional Singer, 1949-; Opera and Concerts in Europe, North and South America, Asia, Australia and Africa including longer periods with the Metropolitan Opera, (debut 1959 as Mozart's Count); State Opera, Hamburg; Royal Opera, Stockholm; Royal Opera, Copenhagen; National Opera, Helsinki; At Glyndebourne he sang Don Giovanni, 1956, Beethoven's Pizarro, 1959, Tchaikovsky's Gremin, 1968; other roles included Boris Godunov, Hans Sachs and King Philipp; Guest Appearances in Vienna and Moscow; Professor, The Royal Academy of Music, Denmark, 1972-89. *Compositions:* East Karelian Songs; Songs from Saimaa; Concerto for Trombone; 7 Kivi-Songs; Ironical Songs to Fröding Poems; Diatonic Quintet for Wood Winds; Concerto for double bass and strings, Sinfonietta for strings, Symphony for full orchestra; Symphony No 2, Sinfonia da camera, 1992. *Recordings:* German, Scandinavian and Russian Songs, Oratorios and Operas. *Publications:* Suomalainen laulajanaapinen, 1972; many articles in books about music and singing in several countries; Muistelmia (Memoirs), 1992. *Honours:* Decorations: Cross of Liberty Class 4 (Finland); Knight of White Rose Class 1 (Finland); Pro Finlandia-Medaille (Finland); Commander of North Star (Sweden); Knight of Dannebrog (Denmark); Honorary Cross for Arts and Sciences Class 1 (Austria); Commander of Finnish Lion; Finnish Cultural Foundation's Honorary Prize, 1992. *Membership:* Det danske Sangselskab (Chairman), 1972-82. *Current management:* Lies Askonas Ltd, 186 Drury Lane, London WC2, England. *Hobby:* Scandinavian Co-operation. *Address:* Østerbrogade 158, DK 2100 Copenhagen, Denmark.

BORG Matti, b. 1955, Copenhagen, Denmark. Composer; Opera Singer (Baritone). m. Gitta-Maria Sjoberg, 1 July 1989, 1 s. *Education:* Theory of Music, University of Copenhagen, 1974-78; Diploma in Composition, 1983, Diploma in Solo Singing, 1987, Royal Conservatory of Denmark. *Debut:* Copenhagen, 1987. *Career:* Appeared as soloist in concerts in Scandinavia and on TV and Radio; Opera debut in Sweden, Norrlandsoperan; Works performed in Sweden, Norway and Denmark. *Compositions:* Choral works, chamber music and songs, music for theatre, musicals; Symboise for mixed choir and solo instruments, 1979; Thirteen ways of looking at a blackbird, trio for soprano, flute and piano, 1981; Recollection, string quartet, 1983; Musicals: What are we dreaming of, 1986; Irene and her men, 1991. *Membership:* Danish Composers Society. *Hobbies:* Painting. *Address:* Obdams Alle 24, DK 2300 Copenhagen S, Denmark.

BORGIR Tharald, b. 27 Dec 1929, Gjerpen, Norway. Musicologist (Keyboard). m. 5 Sept 1951, 3s, 1 d. *Education:* Music Conservatory, Oslo, 1951; MM, Yale University, USA, 1960; PhD, University of California, Berkeley, 1971. *Debut:* Piano, Oslo, 1957. *Career:* Teaching, 1967-93; Professor, 1987-, Chair, 1987-92, Oregon State University, Corvallis, USA. Numerous appearances on piano, hapsichord, fortepiano. *Publications:* The Performance of the Basso Continuo in Italian Baroque Music, 1987, paperback, 1988. *Memberships:* Greenberg Award Committee, American

Musicology Society; College Music Society; Early Music America. *Address:* Department of Music, Oregon State University, Corvallis, OR 97331, USA.

BORISENKO Vera, b. 16 Jan 1918, Goel, Russia. Singer (Mezzo-soprano). *Education:* Studied in Gomel and at the Minsk Conservatory; Further study in Kiev with Evtushenko and in Moscow and Sverdlovsk. *Career:* Sang at Sverdlovsk, 1941-45, Kiev, 1945-46, Bolshoi Theatre Moscow, 1946-65, notably as Lyubava in Sadko, Lyubasha in The Tsar's Bride and Bonny Spring in The Snow Maiden; Gave concert performances from the 1946-65, notably as Lyubava in Sadko, Lyubasha in The Tsar's Bride and Bonny Spring in The Snow Maiden; Other roles included Marka in Khovanshchina and Carmen; Gave concert performances from the 1960s. *Recordings include:* The Snow Maiden, Prince Igor, Dargomizhsky's Rusalka, Tchaikovsky's The Enchantress, Rimsky's May Night, Carmen (title role) and Rigoletto (Maddalena). *Address:* c/o Bolshoi Theatre, Pr Marxa 8/2, 103009 Moscow, Russia, CIS.

BORISOVA Rosa, b. 1960, Moscow, Russia. Cellist. *Education:* Central Music School, Moscow. *Career:* Co-Founder, Quartet Veronique, 1989; Concerts in Russia, including Russian chamber Music Series and the 150th birthday celebrations for Tchaikovsky, 1990; Masterclasses at the Aldeburgh Festival, 1991; Concert tour of Britain in season, 1992-93; repertoire includes works by Beethoven, Brahms, Tchaikovsky, Bartok, Shostakovich and Schnittke. *Recordings include:* Schnittke's 3rd Quartet. *Honours include:* with the Quartet Veronique: Winner, All-Union String Quartet Competition in St Petersburg, 1990-91; Third place, 1991 International Shostakovich Competition at St Petersburg. *Address:* c/o Sonata (Quartet Veronique), 11 Northgate Street, Glasgow G20 7AA, Scotland.

BORK Hanneke van, b. 1935, Amsterdam, Holland. Singer (Soprano). *Career:* Sang in Solothurn-Biel, 1959-60, Innsbruck, 1960-61, and Brunswick, 1961-62; Member of the Basle Opera, 1962-66; Glyndebourne Festival, 1968-69, in Cavalli's L'Ormindo and as Fiordiligi in Così fan Tutte; Wexford Festival, 1968, Holland Festival, 1971-72; sang with Netherlands Opera, 1972-74 and in 1973 appeared as Elsa in Lohengrin at Mainz; other roles include Mozart's Vitellia and Pamina, Gluck's Euridice, Melisande, Ellen Orford and Sicle in L'Ormindo. *Recordings include:* Die Zauberflöte and L'Ormindo (Decca); Scarlatti's Stabat Mater (EMI). *Address:* c/o Staatstheater, Gutenbergplatz 7, 6500 Mainz, Germany.

BORKH Inge, b. 26 May 1917, Mannheim, Germany. Singer (Soprano). m. Alexander Welitsch. *Education:* Studied first as an actress, in Vienna; Vocal studies with Muratti in Milan, and at the Salzburg Mozarteum. *Debut:* Lucerne 1940, as Agathe. *Career:* Sang in Switzerland until 1952, notably as Magda Sorel in The Consul by Menotti; Bayreuth 1952, as Freia and Sieglinde; US debut San Francisco 1953, Elektra; Guest appearances in Vienna, Hamburg, Stuttgart, Barcelona, Lisbon and Naples; Florence 1954, as Eglantine in Euryanthe; Salzburg Festival, 1955, in the premiere of Irische Legende by Egk; La Scala Milan debut 1955, as Silvana in La Fiamma by Respighi; Cincinnati, 1956, in Britten's Gloriana; Metropolitan Opera, 1958, 1961 as Salome and Elektra; Covent Garden, 1959, 1967 as Salome and as the Dyer's Wife in Die Frau ohne Schatten; Academy of Music, New York, 1968, in the US premiere of Orff's Antigonae; Other roles included Lady Macbeth by Verdi and Bloch, and Turandot; Resumed career as an actress 1977, appearing at the Hamburg Schauspielhaus. *Recordings:* Turandot (Decca); Antigonae, Die Frau ohne Schatten and Elektra (Deutsche Grammophon); Salome; Das Rheingold; Elektra; Euryanthe (Cetra).

BORKOWSKI Marian, b. 17 Aug 1934, Pabianice, Poland. Teacher; Composer. *Education:* MA, Academy of Music, Warsaw, 1959-65; MM, Warsaw University, 1959-66; Postgraduate studies with Nadia Boulanger

and Olivier Messiaen, Paris Conservatory; Musicology with Jacques Chailley and Barry S Brook, Paris University; Philosophy with Jean Hyppolite and Jules Vuillemin, Sorbonne and College de France, 1966-68; Master's courses: International Courses of New Music, Darmstadt, 1972, 1974; Accademia Musicale Chigiana, Siena, 1973, 1975, studied with Franco Donatoni, Diploma with distinction, 1975. *Career:* Assistant Lecturer and Senior Assistant Lecturer, Department of Composition 1967-71, Assistant Professor of Composition, 1971-76, Associate Professor, 1976-, Vice-Dean, Faculty of Composition, Conducting and Music Theory, 1975-78; Vice-Rector, 1978-81 and 1987-; Artistic Director, Laboratory of New Music, 1985-, Chopin Academy of Music, Warsaw; Concert, radio and television performances; Performances at numerous international festivals. *Compositions include:* Spectra, 1980; Dynamics, 1981; Mater mea for mixed choir a capella, to the words by Krzysztof K Baczynski, 1982; Apasionate, 1983; Avante, 1984; Concerto, 1985-86; Pax in terra I, 1987, II, 1988. *Recordings:* Numerous. *Contributions to:* Numerous critiques in magazines and newspapers. *Address:* ul Galczynskiego 5 m 17, 00-362 Warszawa, Poland.

BORNEMANN Barbara, b. 8 Mar 1955, Dingelstadt, Germany. Singer (Mezzo-soprano). *Education:* Studied in Weimar and at the Hans Eisler Musikhochschule Berlin, with Hannelore Kuhse. *Debut:* Halberstadt 1978, as Olga in Eugene Onegin. *Career:* Sang at Halberstadt until 1981, at Schwerin, 1981-86; Member of the Berlin Staatsoper from 1986; Further appearances in Dresden, Leipzig, Czechoslovakia, Poland and Japan; Bayreuth Festival, 1990, as Mary in Der Fliegende Holländer; Genevieve in Pelléas et Mélisande in Berlin, 1991; sang Gaea in Strauss's Daphne, concert performance Rome, 1991; Other roles include Mozart's Marcellina, Verdi's Ulrica and Mistress Quickly, Wagner's Magdalene and Fricka; concert repertoire includes Bach's Christmas Oratorio and St John Passion, the Mozart and Verdi Requiems, Mendelssohn's Elijah and St Paul, Mahler's Kindertotenlieder. *Address:* c/o Deutsche Staatsoper Berlin, Unter den Linden 7, 1087 Berlin, Germany.

BORODINA Olga, b. 1960, St Petersburg, Russia. Singer (Mezzo-Soprano). *Education:* Studied in St Petersburg and San Francisco. *Career:* Tours with the Mariinsky Opera, St Petersburg to Europe and the USA, including Marfa in Khovanshchina and Konchakovna at the 1991 Edinburgh Festival and in Rome 1992; Appearances at the Mariinsky Theatre St Petersburg in Boris Godunov and War and Peace, both televised in the West, as Carmen and as Lyubasha in Rimsky-Korsakov's A Bride for the Tsar; Merida Festival Spain, 1991, in Mussorsky's Salammbo and in the final scene of Carmen, with Placido Domingo; Further engagements at San Francisco, at the Opera Bastille Paris, and in Bologna as Marina; Covent Garden, 1992-93 as Dalila dn Marguerite in La Damnation de Faust; Concert performances of Faust with Valeri Gergiev in St Petersburg; Further engagements in Vienna, Berlin, Edinburgh, and San Francisco. *Recordings:* Songs by Tchaikovsky; Romeo et Juliette; Il Barbiere di Siviglia, La Cenerentola. *Address:* c/o Royal Opera House (Contracts), Covent Garden, London WC2, England.

BORONKAY Antal, b. 5 Feb 1948, Budapest, Hungary. Musicologist; Music Critic. m. Eva Verbenyi, 15 June 1974, 2 sons. *Education:* Conducting and Piano, 1967-69, Diploma in Musicology, 1969-74, Liszt Ferenc Academy of Music, Budapest. *Career:* Music Critic, Muzsika (Hungarian Musical Monthly), 1976-; Editor, Musical book department, 1974-; Deputy Director, Editio Musica Budapest, 1987-; Editor, Hungarian Music Quarterly. *Publications:* Editor: New Liszt Edition, Volume 1/5, 1983; Hungarian Licence edition, Brockhaus-Riemann Dictionary of Music, Volume 1-3, 1983-85. *Honour:* Prize for activities as a music critic, Hungarian Ministry of Culture, 1979. *Memberships:* Association of Hungarian Musicians; Musicologists and Music Critics. *Hobby:* Regatta sailing (Past Hungarian Champion). *Address:* 1114 Budapest, Ulaszlo u 22, Hungary.

BOROWSKA Joanna, b. 1956, Warsaw, Poland. Singer (Soprano). *Education:* Studied in Warsaw, and at the Operastudio of Vienna Staatsoper, 1980-82. *Debut:* Romilda in Serse and Micaela in Carmen at Warsaw, 1980. *Career:* Member of Vienna Staatsoper from 1982, notably as Marenka in The Bartered Bride and as Mozart's Fiordiligi, Susanna and Marzelline, Gluck's Iphigenie en Aulide, (1987), Mimi (1988) and Marguerite in Faust; Further engagements at Klagenfurt (Countess in Figaro), Bregenz (in Zeller's Der Vogelhandler, 1984), Barcelona and Covent Garden, London; Marenka at Bonn, 1981. *Recordings include:* Emma in Khovanshchina, Vienna Staatsoper, 1989 and Maidservant in Elektra, conducted by Abbado (Deutsche Grammophon). *Address:* c/o Oper der Stadt Bonn, Am Boselagerhof 1, 5300 Bonn, Germany.

BORRIS Kaja, b. 8 Jan 1948, Den Haag, Holland. Singer. *Education:* Studied in Cologne and at the Opera Studio of the Deutsche Oper Berlin. *Career:* Member of the Deutsche Oper Berlin from 1973, singing Verdi's Mistress Quickly and Ulrica, Annina in Rosenkavalier, Azucena and Emilia (Othello), Genevieve in Pelléas et Mélisande, 1984 and Marthe in Faust, 1988; Appeared in the premiere of Reimann's Gespenstersonate, 1984; Salzburg Easter Festival, 1982-83, as Mary in Fliegende Holländer; further engagements at Munich, Hamburg, Vienna and Schwetzingen and in the concert hall. *Recordings include:* Dier Fliegende Hollander; Feuersnot by Strauss; Die Lustige Witwe; Der Corregidor by Wolf; Schmidt's Notre Dame and Midwife in Zemlinsky's Der Kreidekreis. *Address:* c/o Deutsche Oper Berlin, Richard Wagnerstrasse 10, 1000 Berlin 10, Germany.

BORROFF Edith, b. 2 Aug 1925, New York, USA. Musicologist; Composer. *Education:* Studied at the Oberlin Conservatory, the American Conservatory of Music in Chicago; PhD, University of Michigan, 1958. *Career:* Teacher at Milwaukee Downer College, 1950-54; Hillsdale College Michigan, 1958-62; University of Wisconsin, 1962-66; Eastern Michigan University, 1966-72, and the State University of of New York at Binghamton, 1973-92. *Compositions include:* String Trio, 1943; Clarinet Quintet, 1948; Sonata for cello and piano, 1949; Spring over Brooklyn, musical, 1954; IONS for flute and piano, 1968; The Sun and the Wind, musical fable, 1976; Game Pieces for woodwind quintet, 1980; Concerto for marimba and small orchestra, 1981; The Elements, sonata for violin and cello, 1987; Music for piano and organ; Choral music; Songs. *Publications include:* Elisabeth Jacquet de la Guerre, 1966; The Music of the Baroque, 1970; Music in Europe and the United States, A History, 1971, 1989; Music in Perspective, 1976; Three American Coomposers, 1986 (co-author). *Address:* 65 Forest at Duke Drive, Durham, NC 27705, USA.

BORST Danielle, b. 27 Jan 1946, Geneva, Switzerland. Singer (Soprano). m. Philippe Huttenlocher. *Education:* Studied at Geneva Conservatoire and with Juliette Bisse and Philippe Huttenlocher. *Career:* Former member of the Ensemble Vocale de Lausanne, under Michel Corboz; Opera appearances in Geneva, Lausanne, Biel-Solothurn, Aix-en-provence, Montpellier and Vienna (Staatsoper); Paris Opera, 1988 as Erydice in Orphee aux Enfers; Mezieres 1988, as Gluck's Euridice; sang Urbain in Les Huguenots at Montpellier, 1990; Hero in Beatrice at Benedict at Toulouse, Pamina at Monte Carlo and Vitellia in Gluck's La Clemenza di Tito at Lausanne, 1991; other roles include Mozart's Despina, Susanna, Sandrina and Illia, Gounods's Juliette, Dalinda (Ariodante), Rameau's Aricie, Micaela and Aennchen in Der Freischutz; Sang Mitrena in Vivaldi's Montezuma (pasticcio) at Monte Carlo, 1992; Concerts include: Haydn's Schopfung and Jahreszeiten, Berlioz L'enfant du Christ, Honegger's Roi David, Passions and Oratorios by Bach, works by Monterverdi, Pergolesi, Handel and Mahler. *Recordings include:* Faure's Pénélope, Armide by Lully, Monteverdi's Orfeo, Dido and Aeneas (Erato); Iphigenie en Tauride (Philips); title role in L'Inncoronazion di Poppea, conducted by Rene Jacobs (Harmonia Mundi).

Address: c/o Opera de Lausanne, PO Box 3972, CH-1002 Lausanne, Switzerland.

BORST Martina, b. 13 Jan 1957, Aachen, Germany. Singer (Mezzo-Soprano). *Education:* Studied with Elsa Cavelti in Frankfurt and with Carla Castellani in Milan. *Career:* Sang at the Nationaltheater Mannheim from 1981, notably as Annius in La Clemenza di Tito, Cherubino, Dorabella, Rosina, Cenerentola, Orpheus, and the Composer in Ariadne auf Naxos; Ludwigsburg Festival 1982, 1985 as Annius and as Juno in Semele; Vienna Volksoper 1987, as Dorabella; Bregenz Festival 1988, Nicklausse in Les Contes d'Hoffmann; Liège and Nantes 1989, as Bersi in Andrea Chénier; sang Octavian at Hanover, 1990; Many concert hall appearances, including Mahler's Kindertotenlieder. *Recordings include:* Così fan Tutte (Harmonia Mundi).

BORTZ Daniel, b. 8 aug 1943, Hasselholm, Sweden. Composer. *Education:* Studied with Hilding Rosenberg, and with Blomdahl and Lidholm at the Stockholm Music Highschool; Electronic music at the University of Utrecht. *Career:* Freelance Composer from 1954; Opera Backenterna performed at the Royal Opera Stockholm in production by Ingmar Begman, 1991. *Compositions include:* Church operas The Wall, the Way and the Word, and The Death of St Bridget and her Acceptance in Heaven, 1971-73; Landscape with a River, chamber opera, 1974; Backenterna opera after Euripides, 1991; Intrada for orchestra, 1964; The Song of Solomon for soprano and instruments, 1965; 3 string quartets, 1966, 1971, 1987; In Memoriam di ... for orchestra, 1969; Voices for 3 voices, tape and orchestra, 1968; Josep K for narrator, 8 solkoists, chorus and orchestra, 1969; Nightflies for mezzo and chamber ensemble, 1973; 8 symphonies, 1973-88; Concerto Grosso No 1 for Orchestra, 1978, No 2 for wind band, 1981; Violin concerto, 1985; Oboe concerto, 1986; Parados for Orchestra, 1987. *Address:* c/o Kungliga Teatern, PO Box 16094, S-103 22 Stockholm, Sweden.

BORUP-JÖRGENSEN Axel, b. 22 Nov 1924, Hjorring, Denmark. Composer. *Education:* Studied Piano with Rachlew and Orchestration with Schierbeck and Jersild, Royal Conservatory, Copenhagen, 1946-51; Darmstadt, 1959, 1962. *Career:* Piano Teacher, Else Printz Music School, Copenhagen, 1950-64, then privately. *Compositions:* Partita viola, 1954; Improvisations quartet, 1955; Music for percussion and viola, 1956; Duino Elegies (Rilke) mezzo, flute violoncello, 1956; Mikroorangisma quarter, 1956; Sommasvit, string orchestra, 1957; Several songs with piano or other instruments, 1957-60; Sonatina, 2 violin 1958; Winter Pieces, piano, 1959; Cretaufoni, Symphony Orchestra, 1961; Mobiles after Alexander Calder, viola, marimba, piano, 1961; Cantala (Rilke Herbsttag) alto, 7 instruments, 1963; many songs for mezzo, piano, also for several voices (mostly Rilke and Th. Storm); Schlusztück (Rilke) choir, 5 instruments, 1964; Nordic Summer pastoral small orchestra, 1964; Torso quartet and tape, 1965; Wintereleige (Hölderlin), 3 voices, 9 instruments; Marin Orchestra, 1970; Mirrors, soprano, marimba, guitar, 1974; Works for speaking choir, 1971-72; Tagebuch im Winter, flute, quarter, piano, 1972; Summer intermezzi piano, 1971; Malinconia quartet, 1974; Ricostruzioni wind quarter, 1974; Praeambula, guitar, 1976; Morceaux, guitar, 1974; Déjà vu, concerto for guitar and string orchestra, 1983; Coast of sirens, 7 instruments and multivoice, tape, 1985; Thalatta, Thalatta, piano, 1988; Several works for recorder instruments (solo or with cembalo). *Address:* Fredsholmvej 11, DK 3460 Birkerod, Denmark.

BOSABALIAN Luisa, b. 24 March 1936, Marseilles, France. Singer (Soprano). *Education:* Studied in Beirut and in Milan with Vittorio Ruffo. *Debut:* Théâtre de la Monnaie Brussels as Micaela, 1964. *Career:* Sang at Brussels as Mimi, Donna Anna, Donna Elvira, Desdemona and Giulietta and Antonia in Les Contes d'Hoffmann; Concert appearances at Edinburgh and th Holland Festival, conducted by Giulini; Member of the Hamburg Staatsoper 1965-73; Metropolitan Opera 1966, as Jenůfa; Guest appearances in London,

Dusseldorf, Frankfurt, Rome, Moscow, Oslo, Milan and Vienna; Strasbourg 1974 in Les Indes Galantes by Rameau; Concert appearances in contemporary works and music by Bach; gave Lieder recital in Stuttgart 1988, concerts for Armenian relief at Munich, 1988-89.

BOSE Hans-Jürgen von, b. 24 Dec l953, Munich, Germany. Composer. *Education:* Hoch Conservatory, Frankfurt am Main, 1969-72; pupil in composition of Hans Ulrich Engelmann and in piano of Klaus Billing, Hochschule fúr Musik, Frankfurt am Main, 1972-75; Opera 63: Dream Palace performed, Munich, 1990. *Compositions:* Stage: Blutbund, chamber opera, 1974; Das Diplom, chamber opera, 1975; Die Nacht aus Blei, kinetic action, 1980-81; Die Leiden des jungen Werthers, lyrical scenes, 1986; Chimera, opera, 1986; 63: Dream Place, 1990; Orchestral: Morphogenesis, 1975; Symphony No 1, 1976; Musik für ein Haus voll Zeit, 1977; 3 Songs for Tenor and Chamber Orchestra, 1977; Travesties in a Sad Landscape for Chamber Orchestra, 1978; Symphonic Fragment for Tenor, Baritone, Bass, Chorus and Orchestra, 1980; Variations for 15 Strings, 1980; Idyllen, 1983; Sappho-Gesänge for Mezzo-Soprano and Chamber Orchestra, 1982-83; Labyrinth I, 1987; Oboe Concerto, 1986-87; Chamber: 3 string quartets, 1973, 1976-77, 1987; 5 Children's Rhymes for Alto and 5 Instrumentalists, 1974; Threnos-Hommage à Bernd Alois Zimmermann for Viola and Cello, l975; Solo Violin Sonata, 1977; Variations for Cello, 1978-79; ...vom Wege abkommen for viola, l982; Guarda el Canto for Soprano and String Quartet, 1982; Studie I for Violin and Piano, 1986; Lorca-Gesänge for Baritone and 10 Instruments, 1986; Wind Sextet, 1986. *Address:* c/o GEMA, Herzog-Wilhelm Strasse 38, 8000 Munich 2, Germany.

BOTES Christine, b. 1964, England. Singer (Mezzo-soprano). *Education:* Studied with Frederic Cox at the Royal Northern College of Music and at the National Opera Studio. *Career:* Sang with Glyndebourne Chorus then with the RSC in The Tempest; Appearances with Scottish Opera as Iolanthe and Second Lady in The Magic Flute; Opera Factory as Diana in La Calisto, Thea (Knot Garden) and Dorabella (also televised); Mozart roles include Cherubino (at Sadler's Wells), Donna Elvira in the Netherlands and Belgium; With English National Opera has sung as Hansel, on tour to the USSR, 1990 and as the Fox in The Cunning Little Vixen, 1991; For ENO Cherubino in Figaro's Wedding, 1991; Pitt. Sang in the Mikado, 1991; Proserpina in Orfeo, 1992; Minerva in the Return of Ulysses, 1992; Concert engagements with the Royal Philharmonic (Elgar's Sea Pictures) and the London Sinfonietta, City of London Sinfonia and the Hanover Band; Bach's B minor Mass in France and Poland and Messiah with the Orchestre de Liège and the City of Birmingham Choir; Concerts in Cologne and Lisbon with the Ensemble Modern of Frankfurt. *Current management:* Robert Gilder and Co, 59-65 Upper Ground, London SE1 9PQ, England. *Address:* Magenta Music International, 64 Highgate High Street, London N6 5HX, England.

BOTT Catherine, b. 11 Sept 1952, Leamington Spa, England. Singer (Soprano). *Career:* Many appearances with leading early music ensembles, notably the New London Consort; Appearances at major concert halls in Europe, Latin America and the USSR; British engagements include Early Music Network Tours; Festival concerts at Bath, Edinburgh and City of London; Medieval Christmas Extravaganza on the South Bank and concerts for the 21st anniversary of the South Bank; Season 1988-89 with visits to Israel, Spain, Holland and Italy; French debut as Salome in Stradella's San Giovanni Battista at Versailles; Solo recitals at the Flanders and Utrecht Festivals, Sadler's Wells Theatre and the Kings Singers Summer Festival at the Barbican; Promenade Concert London 1990 with The Bonfire of the Vanities (Medici Wedding Celebration of 1539); Season 1991 with concerts and recordings in France, recitals in Holland and Belgium and tour of Japan; Sang Mozart's Zaide at the Queen Elizabeth Hall, 1991; Purcell's Dido at the Barbican, 1992. *Recordings include:* Monteverdi Vespers and Orfeo; Virtuoso Italian

Vocal Music: de Rore, Rasi, Cavalieri, Luzzaschi, G and F Caccini, Gagliano, Marini, Rossi, Frescobaldi, Monteverdi, Barnardi and Carissimi (Il Lamento di Maria Stuarda); Cantigas de Amigo by Martin Codax and Cantigas de Santa Maria, anon (all with the New London Consort, Decca Florilegium); Vaughan Williams Sinfonia Antartica, with the LSO; English canzonets and Scotch songs, with Melvyn Tan; English Restoration theatre music: mad songs by Purcell, by Eccles and Weldon; Walton film music, with the Academy of St Martin-in-the Fields. *Address:* c/o Magenta Music International, 4 Highgate High Street, London N6 5JL, England.

BOTTCHER Eberhard, b. 1 Nov 1934, Berlin, Germany. Composer. m. 4 Aug 1959, 2 d. *Education:* Stadt Konservatorium, Berlin, 1952-56. *Debut:* Composer, Sweden, 1960. *Compositions:* Solo sonata for Cello, Berlin; 3 solo pieces for violin; Biciinium for 2 flutes; Fantasia for Saxophone and Piano. *Recordings:* Veni Creator Spiritus for organ; Concerto for horn and strings; Brass quintet; Wind quintet. *Honours:* Carl Maria von Weber Prize, 1957. *Memberships:* Norwegian Society of Composers; Trondheim Composers Group, Leader. *Address:* Ilevolden 2, N 7018 Trondheim, Norway.

BOTTOMLEY Sally Ann, b. 18 May 1959, Yorkshire, England. Concert pianist and teacher. *Education:* Chetham's School of Music, Royal Northern College of Music, PPRNCM. *Debut:* Concert debut with City of Birmingham Symphony, 1980; London recital debut, Purcell Room, 1981. *Career:* Appearances with Royal Philharmonic, London Symphony, City of Birmingham, Halle, RLPO, Scottish National; Conductors include: Skrowaczewski, Järvi, Groves, Downes, Litton; Several TV appearances and advertisements and radio performances; Recently initiated two-piano partnership with John Gough touring Florida in 1991; Lecturer at Huddersfield Polytechnic. *Address:* Dale Cottage, Sheardale Park, Honley, Huddersfield, Yorkshire, HD7 2NH, England.

BOTTONE Bonaventura, b. 19 Sept 1950, England. Singer (Tenor). *Education:* Studied at the Royal Academy of Music with Bruce Boyce. *Career:* Has sung with English National Opera as David in Die Meistersinger, the Duke of Mantua, Beppe, and Nanki Poo in Jonathan Miller's production of The Mikado; invited to return as Sam Kaplan in Weill's Street Scene, Alfredo, and Truffaldino in The Love for Three Oranges, 1989; Alfredo in La Traviata, 1990; Covent Garden debut as the Italian Singer in Der Rosenkavalier, conducted by Haitink; returned in Capriccio by Strauss; Scottish Opera 1989, as the Governor General in Candide and Loge in Das Rheingold; Appearances at the Wexford and Batignano Festivals; US debut as Pedrillo in Die Entführung, at Houston Opera; sang the Italian Tenor in Capriccio at Glyndbourne, 1990; Season 1992 as Verdi's Fenton at the London Coliseum, Conte di Libenskof in Il Viaggio a Reims at Covent Garden; Frequent broadcaster in a wide range of BBC programmes. *Recordings:* The Mikado, and Orpheus in the Underworld. *Address:* c/o Stafford Law Associates, 26 Mayfield Road, Weybridge, Surrey KT13 8XB, England.

BOUCHARD Antoine, b. 22 Mar 1932, St Philippe-de-Neri, PQ, Canada. Organist; Professor of Organ. *Education:* BA, LTh, Laval University, Quebec. *Career:* Concerts, Festivals, Quebec City, Montreal, Paris; Concerts, Canada and USA; Radio performances, CBC and ORTF; Series of concerts on 20 European Historical Organs, Radio Canada; Organ Professor and Director, 1977-80, School of Music, Laval University, Quebec. *Compositions:* Prelude and In Paradisum (for organ), in Le Tombeau de Henri Gagnon. *Recordings:* Music by Dandrieu and Buxtehude; Noels français du 18e Siècle; Bach and Pachelbel; Anthologie de l'organiste, volumes I, II, III; The Early pipe organs of Quebec, volumes II, IV, VII; The 18 Chorals, by J S Bach; Oeuvres de Gaston Litaize, on CD; L'Orgue Français Classique en Nouvelle-France. *Publication:* L'Organiste 3 volumes, 1982. *Contributions to:* The Organ Yearbook (Netherlands); L'Orgue (Paris); Musicanada; L'Encyclopédie de la musique au Canada; Bull des Amis de L'Orgue. *Address:* 908 rue du Belvédère, St-Nicolas-est, QC, Canada G0S 3LO.

BOUCHAUD Dominig Ignace Michel, b. 31 July 1957, Nantes, France. Musician; Harpist (Celtic and early harps). *Education:* Universite de la Sorbonne, Paris; Conservatoire National Superieur de Musique, Paris. *Career* Concerts, Netherlands, Germany, Republic of Ireland, Italy, Austria, Senegal, Algeria; Many TV and radio appearances. *Compositions:* Published: Panorama de la Harpe Celtique, 1983; Pieces classiques pour la Harpe Celtique, 1988; Dialogues 90; Discorde, 1989. *Recordings:* Dïou Dellen, l'art de la Harpe a la Renaissance, Vibrations, Quand la terre etait plate, with Walsingham Ensemble. *Contributions to:* Articles for Harpa magazine. *Address:* Conservatory of Music, Mairie, 29000 Quimper, France.

BOUCHER (Charles) Gene, b. 6 Dec 1933, Tagbilaren, Bohol, Philippines. Baritone. *Education:* BA, Westminster College, Fulton, Missouri, 1955; Diplome de chant, Conservatoire de Lille, 1956. *Debut:* Teatro Nuovo, Milan, Italy, 1958. *Career:* Metropolitan Opera, New York, USA, 1965-85; Guest artist with US opera companies; Concerts. *Honour:* Winner, American Opera Auditions, 1958. *Membership:* President, 1977-82, National executive secretary, 1983-88, American Guild of Musical Artists. *Address:* 235 West 76th Street, New York, NY 10023, USA.

BOUCOURECHLIEV Andre, b. 28 July 1925, Sofia, Bulgaria. Composer; Writer. *Education:* Sofia State Academy, 1946-49; Ecole Normale de Musique, Paris, 1949-51; Saarbrucken Conservatory, 1955, piano with Walter Gieseking. *Career:* French citizen from 1956, resident in Paris from 1949; Assistant at radio stations in Milan and Paris, Teacher of piana at Ecole Normale de Musique, 1954-60; Music critic in France from 1957. *Compositions include:* Piano Sonata 1959; Texte I and II for tape, 1959, 1960; Musique Nocturnes for clarinet, harp and piano, 1960; Archipel Series: No 1 for 2 pianos and 2 percussionists, 1967, No 2 for string quartet 1969, No 3 for piano and 6 percussionists, 1969, No 4 for piano, 1970, No 5 for 6 instruments, 1970; Ombres, Hommage a Beethoven for string orchestra, 1970; Faces for orchestra 1972; Thiene, for tape and 2 speakers, Piano concerto, 1975; Grodek for soprano and 3 percussion groups; Orion series, 1979-83; Lit de Neige, 1984. *Publications:* Biography of Schumann, 1957, Pictorial Biography of Chopin, 1962; Monograph on Beethoven, 1962; Revised Edition of Stravinsky, 1987. *Address:* c/o SACEM (France), PRS Ltd Member Registration, 29/33 Berners Street, London W1P 4AA, England.

BOUE Geori, b. 16 Oct 1918, Toulouse, France. Singer (Soprano). m. Roger Bourdin (dec 1973). *Education:* Studied at the Toulouse Conservatory and in Paris with Henri Busser and Reynaldo Hahn. *Debut:* Toulouse 1935, as Urbain in Les Huguenots. *Career:* Sang at Toulouse as Siebel in Faust, Hilda in Reyer's Sigurd, Mathilde in Guillaume Tell and Bizet's Micaela; Paris Opéra-Comique from 1938, debut as Mireille in the opera by Gounod; Paris Opéra from 1942, notably in Les Indes Galantes by Rameau (1953); Guest appearances in Arles, Brussels, Nice, Barcelona, Germany, Mexico City and Italy; La Scala Milan as Debussy's Mélisande; Tour of Russia as Tatiana in Eugene Onegin and Madama Butterfly; Théâtre de la Monniae Brussels 1960, in La Belle Hélène and Die Lustige Witwe; Appeared as Malibran in the film by Sacha Guitry. *Recordings:* Thais (Urania); Faust conducted by Beecham (HMV); Les Contes d'Hoffmann (Columbia); L'Aiglon by Honegger.

BOUGHTON William Paul, b. 18 Dec 1948, Birmingham, England. Conductor. m. Susan Ann Cullis, 8 Aug 1981. *Education:* Guildhall School of Music, London; Prague Academy; AGSM; Honorary Associate, Janáček Academy. *Career:* Founder, Director, English String Orchestra; Principal Conductor, English

Symphony Orchestra and Jyvaskyla Sinfonia, Finland, 1986-93; Artistic Director, Malvern Festival, 1983-88; Guest conducting with Philharmonia, Royal Philharmonic Orchestra, London Philharmonic Orchestra and London Symphony Orchestra. *Recordings:* Numerous on Nimbus label including 1st recordings of Finzi's Love's Labours Lost and Parry's 1st Symphony and Death to Life. *Honours:* Jyvaskyla City Award; Hon DLitt. *Membership:* Royal Overseas League. *Hobbies:* Reading; Walking; Skiing; Sailing. *Current management:* Anglo-Swiss Artists Management Ltd, England. *Address:* c/o Eleanor Hope, 9 Southwood Hall, Wood Lane, London N6 5UF, England.

BOULAY Laurence, b. 19 Jan. 1925, Boulogne-sur-Seine, France. Professor; Harpsichord Player. *Education:* Dr of Musicology, University of Paris; Conservatory National Supérieur de Musique de Paris. *Career:* Numerous concerts in France; tours of Europe, USA, Canada and Japan; Honorary Professor, Conservatory National Supérieur de Musique de Paris. *Recordings:* More than 40 records. *Publications:* Edited numerous scores of French 18th Century Chamber Music. *Contributions to:* Recherches. *Honours:* Five 1st Prizes from Conservatory National Supérieur de Paris; several Grand Prix du Disque; Distinction honorifique: Chevalier des Arts et Lettres 1985. *Address:* 17 rue Armengaud, 92210 Saint-Cloud, France.

BOULEZ Pierre, b. 26 Mar 1925, Montbrison, France. Composer and Conductor. *Education:* Paris Conservatoire, studied with Messiaen Vaurabourg-Honegger and Leibowitz. *Career:* Director of Music to Jean-Louis Barrault Theatre, 1948; aided by Barrault and Madeleine Renaud Barrault founded the Concerts Marigny which later became the Domaine Musical, Paris; Principal Guest Conductor, Cleveland Symphony Orchestra; Principal Conductor BBC Symphony Orchestra, 1971-75, with the orchestra gave many performances of music by Bartók, Berg, Messiaen, Debussy, Schoenberg and Stravinsky; Musical Director, New York Philharmonic 1971-77; Director, Institute de Recherches et de Co-ordination Acoustique/Musique 1975-91; Conducted the centenary production of Wagner's Ring, Bayreuth 1976-80; Conducted Pelléas et Mélisande for Welsh National Opera, 1992. *Compositions include:* Le Marteau sans Maitre (cantata for voice and instruments to texts by Rene Char); Structures (2 pianos), 1964; Third Piano Sonata, 1957-58; Improvisations sur Mallarmé (soprano and chamber ensemble); Poesie pour Pouvoir (orchestra), 1958; Pli selon Pli, 1958-62; Figures - doubles - prismes, 1964-74, Eclats and Eclats Multiples; Domaines, 1968-69; Cummings ist der Dichter, 1970; Rituel, 1974; Messagesquisse, 1977; Notations, 1980; Repons, 1981; Dialogue, 1984; Derive 1, 1985; Memoriale, 1985; Anthemes for solo violin, 1991; Explosante/Fixe, 1993. *Recordings include:* Video of Bayreuth Centenary Ring (Philips); Bartók The Wooden Prince and Dance Suite (New York Philharmonic); Berg Lulu; Berio Sinfonia and Eindrücke (French National Orchestra); Pli selon Pli (BBC Symphony); Carter Oboe Concerto, Penthode and A Mirror on which to Dwell (Ensemble Intercontemporain); music by Donatoni and Ligeti; Webern's Complete Works with opus numbers; Debussy with Cleveland Orchestra; Stravinsky with New York Philharmonic; Bartok with Chicago Symphony; Video of Pelléas et Mélisande, Welsh National Opera. *Publications:* Releves d'apprenti (essay) 1967; Par volonté et par hasard 1975; Points de repère; Jalons, 1989; Paul Klee, 1989; Correspondence P Boulez/John Cage, 1991. *Honours include:* Honorary Doctorate, Leeds, Oxford, Cambridge, Bristol University of Southern California. *Address:* c/o IRCAM, 1 place Igor-Stravinsky, 75004 Paris, France.

BOULTON Timothy, b. 1960, England. Violist. *Education:*Studied with Nicholas Roth in London. *Career:* Academy of St Martin-in-the-Fields; Teacher at GSM, Junior Department; Member of Domus from 1985; until 1986, performances in a portable white geodesic domus on informal locations in Europe and Australia; public workshops, discussion groups and open rehearsals in a wide repertoire; Frequent performances in London at the Wigmore Hall and on the South Bank, throughout the UK and on Radio 3; Festival engagements at Bath, Cheltenham, Salisbury, Sheffield and the City of London; Tours of South America, Canada, Spain, Italy, Germany, Ireland and Norway; 1991 tours of The Netherlands and New Zealand. *Recordings include:* Piano Quartets by Fauré, Dvořák, Brahms, Mozart and Mendelssohn; Schubert's Trout Quintet and Adagio and Rondo Concertante (with pianist Chi-chi Nwanoku); Works by Martinů, Suk, Kodály and Dohnányi (Hyperion and Virgin Classics). *Honours include:* Deutsche Schallplattenpreis 1986 and Gramophone Magazine award for Best Chamber Music Record of 1986, for Fauré Piano Quartets. *Address:* Christopher Tennant Artists' Management, Unit 2 39 Tadema Road, London SW10 0PY, England.

BOUMAN Hendrik (Henk), b. 29 Sept 1951, Dordrecht, the Netherlands. Harpsichordist; Fortepianist; Conductor; Professor. 1 son. *Education:* Teaching certificate 1977, Harpsichord solo performance diploma, 1978, Sweelinck Conservatorium, Amsterdam. *Career:* Harpsichordist of Musica Antiqua Köln, 1976-83, extensive tours throughout Europe; Festivals in Berlin, London, Holland, Flanders, Besançon and Festival de Paris; World tours of South America, 1980, North America, 1981, Asia, including India and Japan, 1982; Regular radio recordings for all major European stations; Conducting debut, Basilica of Notre Dame, Montreal, Canada, premiere of Tu me cherches by Alain Pierard, mass for orchestra and several hundred choristers, International Year of Youth, 1985; Founder, Director, Ensemble Les nations de Montreal, 1986; Professor, University of Laval, Quebec, 1987-; University of Concordia, 1985-; Master classes and lectures, 1979-. *Compositions:* Several transcriptions for harpsichord duo. *Recordings:* Numerous. *Publications:* Basso Continuo realisations for Marais: Sonnerie, Maresienne; Mancini: Recorder Concerto; Figured Bass and Harpsichord Improvisation. *Honours include:* Diapason d'Or 1982 for Gilles; Diapason d'Or 1982 for Monteverdi; Deutscher Schallplattenpreis, 1982; Early Music Award, 1982. *Membership:* CAPAC. *Hobbies:* Yoga; Childcare; Cartoon making; Travelling.

BOUR Ernest, b. 20 April 1913, Thionville, France. Conductor. *Education:* Studied piano, organ and theory at the Strasbourg Conservatoire, with Fritz Munch; Further study with Hermann Scherchen, 1933-34. *Career:* Chorus master at Radio Geneva; Musical Director of the Radio Strasbourg Orchestra, 1935-39; Professor of piano at the Strasbourg Conservatory, 1940-41; Musical director of the Mulhouse orchestra, 1941-47, director of the Conservatoire there from 1945; Director of the Orchestre Municipal at Strasbourg from 1950; Musical director of the Strasbourg Opera from 1955; Conductor of the South West German Radio Symphony Orchestra at Baden-Baden, 1964-79; Conductor of the Chamber Orchestra of Netherlands Radio at Hilversum from 1979; Conducted the premieres of works by André Jolivet (Cosmogonie, 1947); Jean Rivier (5th Symphony, 1951); György Ligeti (Apparitions, 1960); Jean Claude Eloy (Etude III, 1962); Aribert Reimann (Monumenta, 1963); Isang Yun (Reak, 1966); Wolfgang Fortner (Immagini, 1970); Dieter Schnebel (Diapason), Kazimierz Serocki (Fantasia Elegiaca, 1972); Brian Ferneyhough (Epicycle, 1974); Sylvano Bussotti (Opus Cygne, 1979); Wolfgang Rihm (Endere Schatten, 1985) and Iannis Xenakis (Alax, 1985); Conducted the French premieres of Hindemith's Mathis der Maler, Duke Bluebeard's Castle and The Rake's Progress. *Recordings include:* L'Enfant et les Sortilèges (EMI); Stravinsky's Violin Concerto, with Arthur Grumiaux (Philips); Cello Concertos by Hindemith and B A Zimmermann, with Siegfried Palm; Ligeti's Atmosphères, Lontano and Ramifications; Lutoslawski's 2nd Symphony; Saint-Saëns's 3rd Symphony (Telefunken). *Address:* c/o Radio Kamerorkest, PO Box 10, 1200 JB, Hilversum, Holland.

BOURGE Daniel, b. 12 Jan 1937, Avignon, France.

Horn Player. *Education:* Avignon Conservatoire and Paris Convertoire. *Career:* Concerts with the Musica wind quintet, 1961-67; Horn Soloist, Garde Republicaine Orchestra, 1963, at concerts Pasadeloup, 1964, Opera-Comique, 1967; Paris Opera from 1969 and the Ensemble Intercontemporain and the Ensemble Orchestral de Paris; Member of the Paris Octet, 1965-82. Has premiered works by Messiaen (Appel Interstellaire), Francaix, (Divertimento), Xenakis (Anaktoria, 1965) and Delerue (Concerto); Professor of Chamber Music at the Champigny Conservatoire and teacher in Belgium, Italy and USA. *Recordings include:* Music by Dukas, Chabrier, Corrette, Breval, d'Indy and Gounod. *Address:* c/o Ensemble Orchestral de Paris, Salle Pleyle, 252 Rue du Faubourg St, Honore, F-75008 Paris, France.

BOURGEOIS Derek, b. 16 Oct 1941, Kingston on Thames, England. Director of Music, National Youth Orchestra of GB. m. Jean Berry, 21 Aug 1965. *Education:* Music Degree, (hons), 1962, DMus, 1971, Magdalene College, Cambridge; Royal College of Music, 1963-65. *Career:* Lecturer in Music, Bristol, University, 1971-84; Director of Music, National Youth Orchestra of Great Britain, 1984-93; National Youth Chamber Orchestra of Great Britain, 1989-93; Director of Music, St Paul's Girls' School, London, 1994-. *Compositions include:* Thirteen works including: Six Symphonies: Concertos for double bass, clarinet, trombone, tuba, organ, 8 Euphonium, 3 trombones; 3 Concertos for Brass band; 2 Symphonies for Wind Orchestra; Symphonic Fantasy the Astronauts; 6 works for chorus and orchestra; One Opera. *Memberships:* Composers Guild of Great Britain, Chairman, 1980-83; APC; Royal Society of Musicians. *Hobbies:* Fine Wine; Computing; Golf. *Address:* The Vines, Hewelsfield, Lydney, Glos GL15 6XE, England.

BOVET Guy, b. 22 May 1942, Thun, Switzerland. Organist; Composer; Musicologist. *Education:* Baccalaureate, Gymnase Cantonal Lausanne, 1960; Conservatoire Geneva; 1st Prix de Virtuosité, 1962; Private Instruction with Jeanne Bovet, Marie Dufour, Marie-Claire Alain. *Career:* Concert Artist in Europe, America, Asia, 1962-; Teacher, 1980-; University of Oregon, Southern Methodist University, University of Cincinnati, USA, University of Salamanca, Spain; Music Academy, Basle, Switzerland, 1988-; Organist, The Collégiale Church, Neuchâtel, Swizerland, 1988-. *Compositions:* Organ Music, Chamber and Symphonic Music, Concerti for Organ and Orchestra, Opera, Film and Stage Scores. *Recordings:* Historical Organs of Switzerland, Spain and Mexico. *Current Management:* Murtagh-McFarlane Concert Management, Cleveland, Ohio, USA. *Hobbies:* Swimming; Fishing. *Address:* Maison du Prieur, 1323 Romainmotier, Switzerland.

BOVINO Maria, b. 1960, England. Singer (Soprano). *Education:* Studied at Sheffield University and the Guildhall School of Music and Drama. *Debut:* At King's College, London as Bella in Schubert's Die Verschworenen. *Career:* Sang Fiorella in Offenbach's Les Brigands with the Intermezzi Ensemble; Opera 80 from 1982, as Adele in Die Fledermaus, Despina in Così fan Tutte and Elvira in L'Italiana in Algeri; Season 1984-85 as Emmie in Albert Herring at Glyndebourne and Tytania in A Midsummer Night's Dream for Glyndebourne Tour; Sang First Boy in The Magic Flute for English National Opera in 1986, followed by the Queen of Night (1988); Scottish Opera from 1987, as Blondchen (Die Entführung) and Papagena; English Bach Festival in Gluck's Orfeo and Dido and Aeneas, in London, Granada and Athens; Covent Garden debut 1989, in Albert Herring; Performances with Travelling Opera in season 1990-91, as Mimi and Gilda; Also sings Gilbert and Sullivan with the London Savoyards; Sang Susanna with Crystal Clear Productions, 1991. *Address* c/o English National Opera, St Martin's Lane, London, WC2, England.

BOWDEN Pamela, b. 1934, Lancashire, England. Singer (Contralto). m. Derrick Edwards, 1s, 1d. *Education:* Royal Manchester College of Music. *Career:*

Concert and opera engagements from 1954, throughout United Kingdom and Europe; Tours of West Indies, Middle East and Scandinavia; Festival appearances and seasons with the English Opera Group; Lieder recitals worldwide and concerts with leading orchestra in Britain and Europe, including the Concertgebouw, Suisse Romande and Israel Philharmonic; Conductors include Ansermet, Paul Sacher, Scherchen, Krips, Boult, Boulez, Sargent, Pritchard, Solti, Gui, Mackerras, Rattle and Charles Groves; Many Promenade Concerts and broadcasts: Well known in works of Handel and Bach and as the Angel in The Dream of Gerontius; Premiered works include Malcolm Arnold's Five William Blake Songs; Sang Larina in Eugene Onegin for Glyndebourne Festival Opera, and Royal Opera House, Covent Garden; Head of Singing, London College of Music, Visiting Professor, Royal Scottish Academy of Music and Drama. *Recordings include:* Tippett A Child of Our Time; Berkeley Four Poems of St Teresa; Britten A Charm of Lullabies *Memberships:* President, Incorporated Society of Musicians, 1988; Fellow, RMCM, Hon Fellow, LCM; Fellow, RSA. *Address:* 11 Wickliffe Avenue, London N3, England.

BOWEN Geraint Robert Lewis, b. 11 Jan 1963, London, England. organist. m. Lucy Dennis, 1987, 2 s. *Education:* BA, Cambridge, 1986; MusB, Trinity College, Dublin, 1987; Study with Christopher Herrick, John Scott and Stephen Cleobury. *Career:* Organ Scholar, Jesus College, Cambridge, 1982-85; Assistant Organist: Hampstead Parish Church, St Clement Danes Church, 1985-86, St Patrick's Cathedral, Dublin, 1986-89, Hereford Cathedral, 1989-; Assistant Conductor, Accompanist, Hereford Choral Society, 1989-; Festival Organist, Hereford Three Choirs Festival, 1991. TV and Radio broadcasts as organ accompanist, 1984-. Recital venues include, King's College Cambridge, St John's College, Cambridge, Southwark Cathedral and Three Choirs Festival. *Recordings:* Aeternae laudis lilium; The Psalms of David Vol 1. *Honours:* Selected for Gramophone Magazine's Critics' Choice, 1985. *Memberships:* FRCO, 1987. *Hobbies:* Gardening; Railways; Typography; Walking. *Address:* The Canon's House Flat, The Close, Hereford HR1 2NG, England.

BOWEN Kenneth John, b. 3 Aug 1932, Llanelli, Wales. Singer; Conductor; Teacher; Broadcaster. m. Angela Mary, 31 Mar 1959, 2 s. *Education:* BA, University of Wales, Aberystwyth; MA MusB, St John's College Cambridge; Institute of Education, University of London. *Debut:* Tom Rakewell, New Opera Co, Sadler's Wells, 1957. *Career:* Flying Officer, Education Branch, RAF, 1958-60; Head of Vocal Studies, RAM, 1987-91; (Prof of singing, 1967-); Conductor London Welsh Chorale, 1983-, and London Welsh Festival Chorus; Former concert and operatic tenor (retired 1988); Appeared: Promenade concerts, Aldeburgh, Bath, Swansea, Llandaff and Fishguard Festivals; throughout Europe, Israel, North America and the Far East; Performed at: Royal Opera House, ENO, WNO, Glyndebourne Touring Opera, English Opera Group, English Music Theatre, Kent Opera, Handel Opera Society; Frequent broadcasts; numerous first performances & many recordings. *Honours:* Prizes in Geneva, s'Hertogenbosch, Liverpool & Munich International Competition (1st) & Queens Prize; HonRAM, John Edwards Memorial Award (GPWM). *Memberships:* Fellow, Royal Society of Arts; Vice-President, Guild for the Promotion of Welsh Music; Gorsedd of Bards, Royal National Eisteddfod of Wales; Council, British Youth Opera; Association of Teachers of Singing (Chairman 1990-91); Association of English Singers & Speakers; British Voice Association; Incorporated Society of Musicians; President RAM Club, 1991; Royal Society of Musicians. *Hobbies:* Golf; Cinema; Theatre; Books and Paintings; Walking. *Address:* 12 Steele's Road, London NW3 4SE, England.

BOWER Neville, b. 3 Oct 1934, Allahabad, India. Composer. *Education:* Royal College of Music, pupil of Kendall Taylor and Patrick Hadley; ARCM, 1954; LRAM, 1956; BA, 1985; FTCL, 1987. *Career:* Pianist, Duo-Pianist, Ballet Rambert; Recitals in London, Oxford;

Director of Music, Ealing Grammar School, 1967-74; Conductor, Apollo Singers; Brief appearance, MGM Musical Goodbye Mr Chips, 1969. *Compositions include:* 3 Choral Works; Our Lord and Our Lady; The Coming of Spring; Carillon, Carilla; Piano Sonata, 1959; Escapements, piano; Oboe Sonata, 1966; Concertante, Oboe and Orchestra; Evocation, Clarinet; Glory, Trumpet; Ecstasy, Cello; The Dance of Life, Viola; Eternal, Organ; Fantasie Preludes for Piano; Works for School Use: Processional March: Valse; Spring Dance; Song Cycles; The Dream Follower and The Path of Dreams; Prelude and Threnody for Strings; The Gardens of Villandry for full orchestra; Music for a While for piano Solo; Eternal for Organ; Prism and Colour Studies, both for piano; Music Examiner for University of London Examinations and Assessment Council. *Publications:* The Bells of Rouen, piano; Snowscape, piano. *Honour:* Composition Prize, Waltham Forest Contemporary Music Society, 1966. *Memberships:* PRS; ISM; Composers Guild of Great Britain. *Hobbies:* Golf; Reading; Writing; Painting; Listening. *Address:* 1 Freeford Gardens, Lichfield, Staffs WS14 9RJ, England.

BOWERS-BROADBENT Christopher Joseph, b. 13 Jan 1945, Hemel Hempstead, England. Organist; Composer. m. Deidre Cape, 17 Oct 1970, 1 son, 1 daughter. *Education:* Chorister, King's College, Cambridge, 1954-58; Berkhamsted School, 1958-62; RAM; FRAM, Royal Academy of Music, 1962-66. *Career:* Organ Recitalist; Composer; Organist: West London Synagogue and Gray's Inn; Professor, Organ, Royal Academy of Music, 1976; Professor, organ, Royal Academy of Music, 1976-92. *Compositions include:* The Seacock Bane (teenager's opera); The Last Man (comic opera); Worthy is the Lamb (oratorio); The Hollow Men (Cantata); Te Deum; Collected Church Pieces, 1972. *Recordings:* Passio (ECM 1370), Miserrere (ECM 1430), Trivium, (ECM 1431). *Memberships:* Royal College of Organists. *Hobby:* Painting. *Current management:* Magenta Music International, 64 Highgate High Street, London, N6 5HX. *Address:* 94 Colney Hatch Lane, London N10 1EA, England.

BOWLES Edmund Addison, b. 24 Mar 1925, Cambridge, Massachusetts, USA. Musicologist; Specialist in Medieval Musical Instruments and Performance Practices; Musical Iconography; Timpanist. m. Marianne von Recklinghausen, 1 son, 1 daughter. *Education:* BA, Swarthmore College; PhD, Yale University; Diploma, Berks Music Centre, Tanglewood, Massachusetts. *Career includes:* Instructor, Humanities, Massachusetts Institute of Technology; Publicity Staff, Bell Telephone Laboratories; Senior Programme Administrator, IBM Corporation, 1959-1988; Retired. *Publications include:* Computers in Humanistic Research: Readings and Perspectives, 1967; Musikleben des 15 Jahrhunderts, 1976; Musical Performance in the Late Middle Ages La Pratique Musicale au moyen-âge, 1983; Musical Ensembles in Festival Books: An Iconographical and Documentary Survey, 1988; The Timpani: A History in Pictures and Documents, 1992. *Recording:* Handel's Messiah (Pro Arte), 1984. *Contributions to:* Various professional journals; Dictionary of the Middle Ages; Encyclopeadia Britannica; The New Grove Dictionaries; The New Harvard Dictionary of Music. *Hobbies:* Orchestral Playing; Baroque Timpani. *Address:* 5 Sage Court, White Plains, NY 10605, USA.

BOWLES Garrett H, b. 3 Feb 1938, San Francisco, California, USA. Music Librarian. 1 son, 1 daughter. *Education:* BA, Music, University of California (UC) Davis, 1960; MA, Music Composition, San Jose State University, 1962; MLS, UC Berkeley, 1965; PhD, Musicology, Stanford University, 1978. *Career:* Head Music Cataloguer, Stanford University, 1965-79; Head Music Librarian 1979-, Assistant Adjunct Professor of Music 1980-, UC San Diego; Visiting Lecturer, University of Exeter, UK, 1983. *Compositions include:* Festklang for Ernst Krenek, in Perspectives of New Music, 1985. *Publications:* Directory, Music Library Automation Projects, 1973, 1979; Ernst Krenek, bio-bibliography, 1989; Editor, Ernest Krenek Newsletter,

1990-. *Contributions to:* Journal, Association for Recorded Sound Collectors (ARSC); Notes; Fortes Artis Musicae. *Address:* Music Library 0175-Q, University of California San Diego, 9500 Gilman Drive, La Jolla, CA 92093-0175, USA.

BOWLES Paul Frederick, b. 30 Dec 1910, New York, NY, USA. Composer. m. Jane Auer, 21 Feb 1938. *Education:* Studied Composition with Aaron Copland and Virgil Thomson. *Career includes:* Music Critic, NY Herald-Tribune, 4 years. *Compositions:* Various Chamber Works, Songs and Piano Pieces published and recorded. *Recordings:* Concerto for 2 Pianos, Winds and Percussion; Music for a Farce; The Wind Remains, one act opera excerpts; Scenes d'Anabase; Songs and Piano Music; Sonata for Two Pianos; A Picnic Cantata; Sonata for Flute and Piano. *Honours:* Guggenheim Fellowship, 1941; Rockefeller Grant to record Moroccan Music for the Library of Congress, Washington, 1959. *Membership:* American Society of Composers, Authors and Publishers. *Address:* 2117 Tanger Socco, Tangier, Morocco.

BOWMAN James Thomas, b. 6 Nov 1941. Oxford, England. Counter-tenor. *Education:* Cathedral Choir School Kings School, Ely, Cambridgeshire; New College, Oxford; DipEd, 1964, MA (Oxon), History, 1967. *Career:* School-master, 1965-67; Sang with English Opera Group, 1967-, debut as Britten's Oberon; Early Music Consort, 1967-76; Operatic performances: Sadler's Wells Opera, London, 1970-; Glyndebourne Festival Opera, 1970-; Sydney Opera, Australia, 1978; Opéra Comique, Paris, 1979-; Aix-en-Provence Festival, France, 1979; Le Châtelet, Paris, 1982; Geneva, 1983; Santa Fe and Wolf Trap Festivals, Dallas and San Francisco Operas, USA; Operatic roles include: Oberon in A Midsummer Night's Dream; Endymion in La Calisto, Glyndebourne, 1970-74; The Priest in Taverner, World premiere, Covent Garden, 1972; Polinesso in Ariodante; Apollo in Death in Venice; Astron in The Ice Break, premiere, 1977; Ruggiero in Alcina; Title roles: Handel's Giulio Cesare, Barber Institute; Tamerlano; Xerxes; Scipione; Giustino; Lay Vicar, Westminster Abbey, 1969; sang Ariodante at Santa Fe, 1987; La Scala Milan, 1988, in Jommelli's Fetonte; Amphinomous in The Return of Ulysses for English National opera, 1989; Oberon in A Midsummer Night's Dream for Opera London at Sadler's Wells, 1990; Promenade Concerts, 1991, in Purcell's Ode for St Cecilia's Day; Sang Britten's Oberon at Aix-en-Provence, 1992; Barak in Handel's Deborah at the 1993 Prom Concerts, London; Other roles include Handel's Ptolemy (ENO and San Francisco); Goffredo in Rinaldo (Paris and Reggio Emilia and Orlando (Scottish Opera); Lidio in Cavalli's Egisto at Santa Fe, Theramene in Eritrea at the Camden Festival and Ruggiero in Vivaldi's Orlando Furioso at Dallas and Verona; Sang Herod in Fux's La fede Sacrilega in Vienna and Monteverdi's Ottone (Poppea) at the Spitalfields Festival, London. *Recordings:* Oratorio; Mediaeval and Renaissance vocal music. *Hobbies:* Ecclesiastical architecture; Collecting records. *Address:* 19a Wetherby Gardens, London, SW5 0JP, England.

BOWYER Kevin John, b. 9 Jan 1961, Essex, England. Organist. m. Ursula Steiner, 27 Aug 1981, 2s 2d. *Education:* Royal Academy of Music with Douglas Hawkridge and Christopher Bowers-Broadbent, 1979-82; Also with David Sanger. *Debut:* Royal Festival Hall, 1984. *Career:* Concerts through Europe and North America, specializing in unusual and contemporary repertoire; Performances of Kaikhosru Sorabji's Organ Symphony in London, 1987, Arhus, 1988, and Linz, 1992; Broadcasts for BBC Radio 3 include works by Ligeti, Hugh Wood, Malcolm Williamson, Berio, Henze, Brian Ferneyhough, Charles Camilleri, Niccolo Castiglioni; Numerous broadcasts for other networks. *Recordings:* A late twentieth century Edwardian Bach Recital; Alkan Organ Works, Brahm's Complete Organ Works; Reubke's 94th Psalm Sonata, Schumann's 6 Fugues on BACH, Organ works by Dupre, Langlais, Hindemith, Pepping, Arnold Schoenberg; Complete Organ works of J S Bach; Messiaen Organ Works, 2 vols, and Sorabji Organ Symphony No 1 (Continuum);

Works by Busoni, Ronald Stevenson and Alistair Hinton. *Publications:* Articles on Sorabji for The Organ and Organists Review; *Honours:* Grant, Countess of Munster Musical Trust; First Prize, St Albans International Organ Festival, 1983; First Prizes, International Organ Festivals in Dublin, Paisley, Odense and Calgary, 1990. *Hobbies:* Reading; Malt Whiskeys; Obscure Cinema. *Address:* 2 Kingston Barn College, Kingston Farm, Chesterton, Leamington Spa CV33 9LH, England.

BOYD Anne Elizabeth, b. 10 Apr 1946, Sydney, Australia. Composer; University Music Teacher; Music Critic. 1 daughter. *Education:* BA (1st class Hons), University of Sydney; DPhil, University of York; NSW Conservatorium of Music, Composition Teachers: Peter Sculthorpe, Wilfrid Mellers, Bernard Rands. *Debut:* Adelaide Festival of Arts, 1966. *Career:* Festival Performances include: Adelaide, 1966, 68, 76; Opening Season Festival of Sydney Opera House, 1973; Edinburgh Windsor Festivals, 1974; Aldeburgh Festival, 1980; Hong Kong Arts Festival, 1985; Lecturer in Music, University of Sussex, 1972-77; Founding Head and Reader, Department of Music, University of Hong Kong, 1981-. *Compositions include:* String Quartets I and II; The Voice of the Phoenix, for solo piano, guitar, harp, harpsichord, full orchestra; As It Leaves the Bell, piano, 2 harps and 4 percussion; Goldfish Through Summer Rain, Red Sun, Chill Wind and Cloudy Mountain for flute and piano. *Recordings:* Several recordings. *Contributions to:* Music Now (Founding Managing Editor); Musical Times; Miscellanea Musicologica; Australian Journal of Music Education. *Hobbies:* Swimming; Squash; Photography; Reading; Chinese Calligraphy. *Current management:* Faber Music, London Ltd.

BOYD Douglas, b. 1960, Glasgow, Scotland. Oboist. *Education:* Studied with Janet Craxton at the Royal Academy and with Maurice Bourge in Paris. *Career:* Solo engagements in works by Strauss and Mozart, in Europe, the Far East and the USA: Conductors have included Abbado, Berglund, Menuhin, Alexander Schneider and Michael Tilson Thomas; Co Founder of the Chamber Orchestra of Europe as Principal Oboist and leading member of the Wind Soloists of the Chamber Orchestra of Europe; Played in the Lutoslawski Concert for Oboe and Hapr, Glasgow, 1991. *Recordings:* Bach Concertos, with Salvatore Accardo; Beethoven Music for wind instruments; Dvořák Serenade in D minor; Haydn Sinfonia Concertante, Vivaldi and Strauss Concertos; Mozart Concerto, Concertante K297b. Quartet K370, Serenades in E flat and C minor, Serenade (Gran partita), K361; Schumann recital with Maria Joao Pires. *Address:* c/o Sue Lubbock Concert Management, 25 Courthorpe Road, London NW3 2LE, England.

BOYD James, b. 1960, England. Violist. *Education:* Studied at the Yehudi Menuhin School, Guildhall School of Music and the Menuhin Academy in Gstaad. *Debut:* South Bank, London premiere of Robert Simpson's 13th Quartet; BBC Radio 3 debut, 1991. *Career:* Frequent tours with the Raphael Ensemble; Co-Founder, Vellinger String Quartet, 1990; Participated in master classes with the Borodin Quartet at the Pears-Britten School, 1991; Concerts at the Ferrar Musica Festival, Italy; Season 1992-93 with concerts in London, Glasgow, Cambridge, at the Davos Festival, Switzerland and the Crickdale Ferstival Wiltshire; Wigmore Hall with Haydn, Gubaidulina and Beethoven, Purcell Room with Haydn's Last Seven Words. *Recordings include:* Elgar's Quartet and Quintet, with Piers Lane. *Honours:* Joint winner of the Bernard Shore Viola Prize, 1988. *Address:* Vellinger String Quartet, c/o Georgina Ivor Associates, 66 Alderbrook Road, London SW12 8AB, England.

BOYD Malcolm, b. 24 May 1932. Newcastle-upon-Tyne, England. Lecturer in music. m. Beryl Gowen, 2 sons. *Education:* BMus; MA; ARCO. *Career:* National Service; Teacher; Lecturer; University College, Cardiff; Retired from University College, Cardiff, 1992. *Publications:* Harmonizing Bach Chorales, 1967; Bach's Instrumental Counterpoint, 1967; Palestrina Style,

1973; William Mathias, 1978; Grace Williams, 1980; Bach, 1983; Domenico Scarlatti, Master of Music, 1986; Bach: The Brandenburg Concerto, 1993. *Contributions to:* Musical Times; Music and Letters; The Music Review; Tempo; La Musica; Sohlman's Musiklexikon; The New Grove Dictionary of Music and Musicians. *Memberships:* Royal Musical Association; RCO. *Hobby:* Gardening. *Address:* 211 Fidlas Road, Llanishen, Cardiff CF4 5NA, Wales.

BOYDELL Brian Patrick, b. 17 Mar 1917, Dublin, Ireland. Musicologist; Composer; Retired University Professor of Music. m. Mary Jones, 6 June 1944, 3 sons (1 deceased). *Education:* BA Natural Science, Clare College, Cambridge, England; Royal College of Music, London, 1938-39; BA ad eundem 1939, MusB 1942, MusD 1959, University of Dublin, Republic of Ireland; Licenciate in Singing, Royal Irish Academy of Music, 1941. *Career:* Adjudicator numerous music festivals, including the Canadian Chain and Hong Kong; Over 900 broadcasts on musical subjects; Conductor, Dublin Orchestral Players, 1942-68; Director, Dowland Consort, 1958-69; Guest Conductor, RTE Symphony Orchestra and other orchestras; Professor of Music, University of Dublin, 1962-82. *Compositions include:* Violin Concerto; 3 String Quartets; Orchestral, symphonic, chamber, vocal, choral and film music. *Recordings include:* String Quartet No 1; Symphonic Inscapes; Megalithic Ritual Dances; Dance for an Ancient Ritual. *Publications:* Four Centuries of Music in Ireland (Editor), London, 1979; A Dublin Musical Calendar, 1700-1776, Dublin 1988; Rotunda Music in 18th Century Dublin, 1992. *Contributions to:* New Grove, 1980; New History of Ireland Volume IV, 1986; Proceedings of Royal Musicological Association; Dublin Historical Record. *Hobbies:* Gardening; Fishing; Travel. *Address:* Trinity College, Dublin 2, Republic of Ireland.

BOYKAN Martin, b. 12 Apr 1931, New York, USA. Composer. m. (1) Constance Berke, June 1964 (divorced), (2) Susan Schwalb, Nov 1983, 2 daughters. *Education:* BA, Harvard University, 1951; MM, Yale University, 1953; Berkshire Music Center, Tanglewood, 1949-50; University of Zurich, 1951-52. *Compositions:* String Quartets Nos 1, 2, 3; Concerto for 13 Players, 1971; Piano Trio, 1976; Psalm 128, 1965; Elegy for soprano and six instruments, 1982; Epithalamion, 1985; Shalon Rav, 1987; Fantasy-Sonata for piano, 1987; Symphony No 1, 1989; piano sonata No 2, Nocturne for cello, piano and percussion; Eclogue for 5 instruments, 1991; Echoes of Petrarch, for Flute, Clarinet and piano, 1992; Voyages for Soprano and pf, 1992; Sonata for Cello and Piano, 1992; Sea-Gardems for Soprano and piano, 1993; Impromtu for Violin Solo, 1993; Three Psalms for Soprano and pf, 1993. *Recordings:* String Quartets Nos. 1 and 2; Elegy and Epithalamion; Echoes af Petrarch. *Contributions to:* Perspectives of New Music; Journal of the American Society of University Composers; Musical Quarterly; Notes. *Address:* 10 Winsor Avenue, Watertown, MA 02172, USA.

BOYLAN Patricia, b. 1945, London, England. Singer (Mezzo-soprano). *Education:* Trinity College of Music; National Opera School; London Opera Centre. *Career:* English Opera Group, with tours in Britten's operas under the composer to the former Soviet Union; Appearances with Scottish Opera in Peter Grimes and Die Walkure, concerts and oratorios throughout Britain, including the Aldeburgh and Edinburgh Festivals; Retired to raise a family but returned to the concert hall in such works as Beethoven's Nint and Mass in C, Mozart's C minor Mass and Requiem, the Verdi Requiem and Mahler's Kindertotenlieder; Al Amor Brujo at the Manuel de Falla Festival in Seville; Operatic appearances as Larina in Eugene Onegin in Lisbon, Azucena in Madrid, Orpheus, Carmen and Amneris at Managa; Sang Clytemnestra in Elektra for Welsh National Opera, 1992 and Auntie in Peter Grimes for Scottish Opera, 1993. *Address:* IMG Artists, Media House, 3 Burlington Lane, London W4 2TH, England.

BOZARTH George S, b. 28 Feb 1947, Trenton, New Jersey, USA. Historical Musicologist. *Education:* MFA, 1973, PhD, 1978, Princeton University. *Career:* Associate Professor of Music, University of Washington; Director, Brahms Archive, Seattle, Washington; Director, International Brahms Conference, Washington, DC, 1983; Performer on historical pianos (late 18th through mid-19th centuries); Member of The Classical Consort; Co-Artistic Director of Gallery Concerts (Seattle). *Editions:* Johannes Brahms, Orgelwerke, The Organ Works, Munich, G Henle, 1988; J S Bach, Cantata, Ach Gott vom Himmel sieh darein, BWV2, Neue Bach, Ausgabe, I/16, 1981, 1984. *Publications:* Numerous articles on Brahms's Lieder and duets, the genesis and chronology of Brahms's works, Brahms's piano sonatas and first Piano Concerto, editorial problems and questions of authenticity, Brahms's pianos and piano music; facsimile editions of Brahms manuscripts; Editor of Brahms Studies: Analytical and Historical Perspectives, Oxford University Press, 1990. *Honours:* ACLS Fellowship for Recent Recipient of the PhD, 1982; NEH Research Conference Grant, 1983; Fulbright-Hayes Scholarship to Austria, 1975-77. *Memberships:* American Brahms Society, Executive Director; American Musicological Society; Early Music America. *Address:* School of Music, DN-10, University of Washington, Seattle, WA 98195, USA.

BOZAY Attila, b. 11 Aug 1939, Balatonfüzfö, Hungary. Composer; Teacher. *Education:* Bela Bartók Conservatory, Budapest, 1954-57; pupil of Ferenc Farkas, Budapest Academy of Music, 1957-62. *Career:* Music Producer, Hungarian Radio, 1963-66; teacher of composition and orchestration, Budapest Academy of Music. *Compositions:* Operas: Queen Kungisz, 1968-69; Csongor and Tunde, 1978-84; Hamlet, 1984; Orchestral: Pezzo concertato for Viola and Orchestra, 1965; Pezzo sinfonico, 1967; Pezzo d'archi, 1968-74; Pezzo concertato No 2 for Zither and Orchestra, 1974-75; Pezzo sinfonico No 2, 1975-76; Children's Songs for 18 Strings, 1976; Variazioni, 1977; Chamber Group: Series, 1970, and The Mill, I972-73; Chamber: Duo for 2 Violins, 1958; Episodes for Bassoon and Piano, I959; Trio per archi for Violin, Viola and Cello, 1960, revised I966; Wind Quintet, 1962; 2 string quartets, 1964, 1971; 2 Movements for Oboe and Piano, 1970; Improvisations No 2 for Recorders and String Trio, 1976; Mirror for Zither and Cimbalom, 1977; many pieces for solo instruments; vocal pieces; choruses. *Honours:* Erkel Prize, 1968, 1979; Merited Artist, Hungarian People's Republic, 1984. *Address:* ARTISJUS, Vorosmarty ter I, PB 67, H-1364 Budapest, Hungary.

BOZIC Darijan, b. 29 Apr 1933, Slavonski brod, Croatia. Composer. *Education:* Composition and Conducting, Ljubljana Academy of Music, 1958-61; Further study in London and Paris. *Career:* Conductor and Director of Studies, Slovene Opera, 1968-70; Conductor and Artistic Director, Slovene Philharmonic, 1970-74; Professor, University of Maribor, 1988. *Compositions include:* Stage works: La Boheme, 1957; Opera, 1958; La Putain Respecteuse, opera fater Sartre 1960; Jago, happening for 8 performers and tape after Shakespeare, 1968; Ares-Eros musical drama after Aristophanes 1970; Lizisrata 7 Operatic farce after Aristophanes; Kralj Lear, music drama after Shakespeare, 1985; Telmah, music drama after Shakespeare, Bolt's A Man for all Seasons, 1990. *Address:* c/o Slovensko Narodno Gledaslisce, Zupancicava 1, 61000 Ljubljana, Croatia.

BOZIWICK George E, b. 23 Aug 1954, Rockville Centre, New York, USA. Composer; Librarian. m. Stephanie Doba, 26 July 1986, 2 daughters. *Education:* BA, State University of New York, College at Oneonta, 1976; MA, Composition, Hunter College, 1981; MLS Columbia University School of Library Service, 1987. *Career:* Librarian, Hunter College Music Department, 1978-85; Music Librarian, New York Public Library for the Performing Arts Circulating Music Collection, 1986-88; Music Librarian, The New York Public Library for the Performing Arts Music Division, 1988-91; Curator, American Music Collection, The New York Public Library for the Performing Arts Music Division, 1991-.

Compositions: Flirtations performed by The New York Philharmonic Woodwind Quintet, 1980; Points of Departure, premiered by Orchestra New York, 1992; Third Dance, premiered by the Dorian Wind Quintet, 1993. *Recordings:* Red Skies at Night, recorded by pianist Loretta Goldberg and oboist Brian Charles on Opus One No 135, 1988; First Dance, Beyond the Last Thought, and Boats Against the Current, recorded on Opus One No 162, 1993. *Contributions to:* Journal of the Music Library Association Reviews, 1982-83, 1989. *Address:* 129 - 11th Street, Brooklyn, NY 11215, USA.

BRABEC Jiri, b. 2 July 1940, Prague. Musician and Composer; m. Eva Vavrinova, 18 July 1969, 1s, 1d. *Education:* Prague Conservatory of Music. *Career:* Founded Country Beat, professional country band, 1955; Wembley International Country Music Festival, England, 1973; Nashville Country Music Festival, USA, 1973; Four concerts, Prague's Sport Hall with George Hamilton IV, USA, 1974; Concert Stages in Great Britain, 1975; BBC Country Show with George Hamilton IV, 1976; Cooperation with Moody Brothers, USA, 1988; TV music show, Country Express Prague-Nashville, speaker and author, 1991. *Compositions:* Express, piano instrumental; Shane; One More Country Song; My Little Friend; I'm Jealous; Na Vetvi; Eighteen Wheeler Highway to Somewhere; One Big Honky Tonk; Sorry I'm Fallin'; Straight to the Heart. *Recordings:* Country Beat 1, 1970; Country Beat, 2, Best of Country Beat, 1971; Country Beat 3, 1973; Express, 1974; George Hamilton IV in Prague, 1982; Friends, with Moody Brothers, 1990; Straight from the Heart, Moody Brothers, 1992. *Honours:* Golden Record, 199; CMA Nashville Award, 1978; Golden Record from Artia, 1976; Platinum Record from Artia, 1980 (first in Czechoslovakia); Golden Record From Supraphon, 1982; Golden Reel Award from Ampex, 1991. *Memberships:* CMA Nashville, USA; OSA Prague, author's Organization. *Hobbies:* Sport; Travel. *Address:* 160 00 Praha 6, Na'm Interbrigady 4, Czech Republic.

BRABEC Lubomir, b. 21 May 1953, Pilsen, Czechoslovakia. Guitarist (solo concert guitarist). *Education:* Conservatoire Pilsen, 1968-72; Conservatoire Prague, 1972-74; Royal Academy of Music, 1980-81; Early Music Centre, 1980-81. *Career:* Regular appearances with Prague orchestras; Has performed throughout Europe, USSR, North and Latin America; Many TV and radio appearances, including two one-hour TV recitals. *Recordings:* Baroque Music: Bach, Handel, Weiss, Jelinek (Supraphon); Spanish Music: Torroba, Falla, Albeniz, Turina, Rodrigo (Panton); A Vivaldi - Guitar Concertos with Prague Chamber Orchestra and with violist L Maly and guitarist M Myslivecek (Supraphon); F Tarrega - Guitar Works and Arrangements (Supraphon); H Villa-Lobos - 5 Preludes, 12 Etudes (Panton); J Obrovska - Concerto for Two Guitars with M Zelenka (Panton); S Bodorova - Tre Canzone da Suonare (Supraphon); Transformations I - Bach, Lennon/McCartney, Myers, Satie, Falla, Prokofiev; Transformations II - Bach, Janáček, Musorgsky, Marcello; Lubomir Brabec Live at Prague Spring Festival - Dowland, Bach, Lobos; Viola and Guitar, Italian Music with Lubomir Maly. *Honours:* Title, Laureate of the Concours International de Guitare, Paris, 1974; H Villa-Lobos Medal, 1987, from Brazilian Government. *Membership:* SAI. *Hobbies:* White water canoeing; Trekking. *Current Management:* Pragokoncert. *Address:* Pragokowcert, Maltezske nam 1, 118 13 Praha-1, Czech Republic.

BRACEFIELD Hilary Maxwell, b. 30 June 1938, Dunedin, New Zealand. Lecturer; Critic. *Education:* MA, English and Music, DipMus, University of Otago; DipTchgn, Christchurch Teachers College; LTCL. *Career includes:* Teacher, Bayfield High School, Dunedin; Lecturer, Worcester College of Higher Education; Senior Lecturer, Ulster Polytechnic, Northern Ireland; currently Head of Department of Music, University of Ulster, Jordanstown; Joint Editor, Contact, a journal of contemporary music; Director, Contemporary Music Centre, Dublin, 1985-93. *Publications:* H M Bracefield and J Smyth: Music and the Handicapped in Northern Ireland, 1990. *Contributor to:* ISM Journal; Music and Musicians; Soundpost; Radio Times; BBC Radio Ulster. *Honour:* Awarded Blair Trust Travelling Fellowship, 1970-73. *Memberships:* European Piano Teachers Association; International Federation of University Women; International Society for Music Education; Councillor, 1988-, Convenor, Irish Chapter Member Proceedings Committee, 1987-; Royal Musical Association; Local chapter Treasurer, 1978-, local chapter Secretary, 1985-92, Councillor, 1980-86, Incorporated Society of Musicians; Belfast Musical Society Chairman, 1988-90. *Hobbies:* Films; Theatre; Reading. *Address:* Music Department, University of Ulster, Newtownabbey, Co Antrim, BT37 0QB, Northern Ireland.

BRACHT Roland, b. 1952, Munich. Singer (Bass). *Education:* Studied at the Munich Musikhochschule; Studied at the Munich Music College, under Professor Blaschke. *Career:* Debut at the National Theatre in Verdis Don Carlos; Sang at the Munich Opera Studio from 1971; Member of the Stuttgart Opera from 1973, notably as the Commendatore, in the production of Don Giovanni which reopened the Staatsoper (1984); Ludwigsburg, 1978, as Masetto; Schwetzingen Festival 1983, in the premiere of The English Cat by Henze; San Francisco, 1984-85, in Der Ring des Nibelungen; Debut in the War Memorial Opera House in San Francisco, June 1985; Debut in the Metropolitan Opera in New York, playing the part of King Heinrich, 1986; sang Pogner in Die Meistersinger at the opening of the new Essen opera, 1988; King Heinrich at Pretoria, 1989; Sang Colline in La Bohème at Stuttgart, 1991. *Recordings:* Don Giovanni (Electrola); Die Entführung (Eurodisc); Das Rheingold; Die Zauberflöte; Oedipus Rex; Alceste by Gluck; Die Feen by Wagner; Video of Der Freischütz (Thorn-EMI). *Address:* c/o Staatstheater Stuttgart, Oberer Schlossgarten 6, D-7000 Stuttgart, Germany.

BRADLEY Gwendolyn, b. 12 Dec 1952, New York City, USA. Soprano. *Education:* North Carolina School of the Arts, Winston-Salem, North Carolina; Curtis Institute of Music, Philadelphia; Academy of Vocal Arts, Philadelphia. *Debut:* Nannetta, Falstaff, Lake George Opera, New York, 1976. *Career:* Metropolitan Opera debut, Nightingale, L'Enfant et les Sortilèges, 1981; Appearing as Blondchen, Gilda and Offenbach's Olympia; European debut, Corfu Festival, Greece, 1981; Guest appearances with opera companies in Cleveland, Philadelphia, Central City, Amsterdam, Glyndebourne, Hamburg, Berlin, Monte Carlo, Nice, et al; sang Rodelinda with Netherlands Opera, 1983-84 (also Sophie in Der Rosenkavalier); Paris Opéra 1986, Zerbinetta; Appeared as the Fiakermilli in Arabella at the 1987 Glyndebourne Festival; Deutsche Oper Berlin, 1989, as Musetta; sang Gilda at the Wiesbaden festival, 1990, with the company of the Deutsche Oper; Sang the Heavenly Voice in Don Carlos at the Deutsche Oper, 1992; Many engagements as soloist with leading USA orchestras; recitals. *Address:* c/o Columbia Artists Management Inc, 165 West 57th Street, New York, NY 10019, USA.

BRADSHAW Merrill, b. 18 June 1929, Wyoming, USA. Composer; Teacher. *Education:* Brigham Young University, University of Illinois, DMA, 1962. *Career:* Teacher, Brigham Young University, from 1957; Executive Director, Barlow Endowment for Music Composition. *Compositions:* Dialogue for flute and horn, 1956; 2 string quartets, 1957, 1969; Violin Sonata, 1957; Suite for viola, 1967; Brass Quinted, 1969; 5 symphonies, 1957-79; Piano Concerto, 1955; Faces for orchestra, 1965; Feathers for orchestra, 1968; The Restoration, Oratorio, 1974; Four Mountain Sketches, and Nocturnes and Revels for orchestra, 1974; Nocture for 2 horns and strings, 1977; The Title of Liberty, musical, 1975; Viola Concerto, 1979; Violin Conerto, 1981; Love and Death, 4 Elizabethan Lyrics for viola, soprano and strings, 1982; Christ Metaphors, 1989; Visionscape, 1990; Requiem Music, 1991; Museum Piece, 1993; Double Concerto, 1994; Piano music. *Address:* 248 E 3140 North, Provo, UT 84604, USA.

BRADSHAW Murray Charles, b. 25 Sept 1930, Illinois, USA. Professor of Musicology. m. 2s 1d. *Education:* MMus, American Conservatory of Music, 1955, piano, 1958, Organ; PhD, Musicology, University of Chicago, 1969. *Compositions:* Several organ compositions in The Organists Companion. *Publications:* The Origin of the Toccata, 1972; The Falsobordone, 1978; Francesco Severi, 1981; Girolamo Diruta, Il Transilvano, 1984; Giovanni Luca Conforti, 1985; Gabriele Fattorini, 1986; Emilis de'Cavalier, 1990. *Contributor to:* The Music Quarterly, The Music Review, Studi Musicali, Musica Antiqua, Musica Disciplina, Tijdschriift. *Honours:* American Philsophical Society, 1987. *Memberships:* International and American Musicological Societies; American Guild of Organists. *Hobbies:* Jogging; Bridge; Chess; Yoga; Swimming; Latin (reading). *Address:* Department of Musicology, UCLA, Los Angeles, CA 90024, USA.

BRAEM Thuering L M, b. 10 Apr 1944, Basel, Switzerland. Conductor; Composer. *Education:* Basel University; Heidelberg University; Piano Diploma, degree in Conducting, Academy of Music, Basel; MA, Composition, University of California, Berkeley; Studied Conducting, Curtis Institute of Music, Philadelphia. *Career:* Director, Music School, Basel, 1973-87; Director, Lucerne Conservatory, 1987-; Music Director, Ragio-Choir, Basel and Junge Philharmonie Zentralschweiz; President, Jeunesses Musicales, Switzerland, 1984-90; Principal Guest Conductor, Bohemian Chamber Philharmony Pardubic. *Compositions:* Lettres de Cezanne; Alleluja for Voice; Ara for flute ensemble (all Nepomuk-Verlag, AARAU); Chamber Music, Choral Music; Ombra for VI, Va and string orchestra, 1991; Torrenieri, for horn and strings, 1992; concerto for piano trio and orchestra, 1992. *Recordings:* Children's Songs of the American Indians (Flexagon); Faurés Requiem; Music for violincello and orchestra by Martinů, Fauré, Dvořák and Tchaikovsky; Panton, orch music with Young Philharmonic of Central Switzerland. *Publications:* Musik und Raum, Basel, 1986; series, Information und Versuche, 1975-90, 20 issues; Bewahren and Oeffuen, Aarau, 1992. *Contributions to:* Articles in newspapers and journals. *Honour:* Edwin Fischer Prize, 1992. *Address:* Lerchenstr 56, CH-4059 Basel, Switzerland.

BRAININ Norbert, b. 12 Mar 1923, Vienna, Austria. Violinist. m. Kathe Kottow, 7 Apr 1948, 1 d. *Education:* Studies with Professor Ricardo Odnoposoff, Konservatorium, Vienna; Professor Rosa Hochmann-Rosenfeld, Vienna; Professor Carl Flesch and Professor Max Rostal, London. *Career:* Debut with Amadeus Quartet and for forty years all over the world. *Recordings:* Amadeus Quartet, of almost the entire classical romantic and modern repertoire for string quartet and or strings and piano and strings; Also works with clarinet, oboe and flute. *Honours:* OBE; DHC, University of London; DHC, Oesterreichisches Unterrichtministerium; Das Grosse Verdienstkreuz der Bundesrepublik Deutschlands, First Class. *Memberships:* Royal Academy of Music, London; Hochschule fuer Musik, Cologne. *Address:* 19 Prowse Avenue, Bushey Heath, Herts WD2 1JS, England.

BRAITHWAITE Nicholas Paul Dallon, b. 26 Aug 1939, London, England. Musician; Conductor. m. Gillian Agnes Haggarty, 24 Aug 1985. 1 son, 1 daughter. *Education:* Royal Academy of Music; Festival Masterclasses in Bayreuth and with Hans Swarowsky, Vienna. *Career:* Chief Conductor, Adelaide Symphony Orchestra, 1987-91; Principal Guest Conductor 1977-84, Principal Conductor 1984-91, Manchester Camerata; Chief Conductor, Tasmanian Symphony Orchestra; Permanent Guest Conductor, Norwegian State Radio Orchestra; Associate Conductor to Constantin Silvestri with Bournemouth Symphony Orchestra; Frequent guest conductor for all major orchestras in the UK; Toured Japan and Korea as Associate Conductor to Georg Solti with London Philharmonic orchestra; Appearances with ORTF Orchestra, Paris; Oslo Philharmonic; Bergen Harmonien Symphony Orchestra; Odensee Symphony Orchestra;

New Zealand Symphony Orchestra; Melbourne Symphony Orchestra; Sydney Symphony Orchestra; Danish Radio Orchestra; Bergen Festival; Symphony Nova Scotia, Halifax; Musical Director and Chief Conductor, Stora Teater Opera and Ballet Companies, Gothenberg, 1981-84; Musical Director, Glyndebourne Touring Opera, 1976-80; Associate Principal Conductor, English National Opera Company, 1970-74; Dean of Music, Victorian College of the Arts, 1988-91; conducted Tosca at Elder Park, Adelaide, 1990. *Recordings:* Numerous. *Honour:* FRAM. *Memberships:* ISM; MU. *Hobbies:* Computers; Model aircraft. *Current Management:* Christopher Tennant. *Address:* Taringa Park, Mount Barker Road, Mahndorf, South Australia 5245.

BRAMMA Harry Wakefield, b. 11 Nov 1936, Shipley, Yorkshire, England. Cathedral Organist. *Education:* Bradford Grammar School; Organ Scholar, Pembroke College, Oxford; MA; FRCO (Harding Prize). *Career:* Director of Music, King Edward VI Grammar School, Retford, Nottinghamshire, 1961-63; Assistant Organist, Worcester Cathedral, 1963-76; Director of Music, The Kings School, Worcester, 1965-76; Organist, The Three Choirs Festival, Worcester, 1963-76; Conductor, Kidderminster Choral Society, 1972-79; Organist and Director of Music, Southwark Cathedral, London Bridge, 1976-89; Organ Adviser, Diocese of Southwark, 1976; Hon. Treasurer, Royal College of Organists, 1987-; Director, Royal School of Church Music, 1989-; Organist, All Saints Church, Margaret Street, London, 1989. *Recordings:* As accompanist with Worcester Cathedral Choir on EMI, Polydor and Abbey Labels; As Choral Director with Southwark Cathedral Choir on Abbey Label. *Memberships:* Council Member and Examiner, Royal College of Organists; Liveryman, Worshipful Company of Musicians. *Hobbies:* Walking; Travel. *Address:* Nicholson House, Addington Palace, Croydon, CR9 5AD, Surrey, England.

BRANDIS Thomas, b. 1935, Hamburg, Germany. Violinist. *Education:* Studied with Eva Hauptmann at the Musikhochschule Hamburg, 1952-57 and with Max Rostal in London. *Career:* Leader, Berlin Philharmonic Orchestra, 1962-63; Co Founder, Brandis Quartet, 1976; Many chamber engagements in Europe and Tokyo, with the Wiener Singverein and the Berlin Philharmonic; Festival appearances at Salzburg, Florende, Vienna, Edinburgh, Tours and Bergen; Has co-premiered the clarinet Quintet Helmut Eder, 1984, and the 3rd Quartets of Gottfried von Einem and Giselher Klebe, 1981, 1983. Solo Concerto work under such conductors as Karajan, Bohm, Solti, Abbado, Schmidt-Isserstedt, Keilberth, Jochum, Tennstedt, and Albrecht. *Recordings:* As soloist: Albums with Karajan and Bohm; With the Brandis Quartet: Complete quartets of Schubert and Beethoven with other repertoire for the EMI/Electrola, Teldec, Orfeq, Nimbus and Harmonia Mundi labels. *Honours:* Prize, German Hochschulen Competition, 1946; International ARD Competition in Munich, 1947. *Address:* c/o Anglo Swiss Ltd, 3 Primrose Mews, 1a Sharpleshall Street, London NW1 8YW, England.

BRANDSTETTER John, b. 2 Oct 1949, Wayne, Nebraska, USA. Singer (Baritone). *Education:* Studied at the University of Nebraska and with Richard Hughes in New York. *Debut:* Minnesota Opera, 1976, as Ben in Conrad Susa's Black River. *Career:* Sang at Minneapolis in the premiere of Argento's The Voyage of Edgar Allan Poe, 1976; Has also sung in the premieres of Bernstein's A Quiet Place, 1983, repeated in Vienna, 1986, as Josuke in Miki's Joruri, St Louis, 1985, and in The Balcony by Di Domenica, Boston, 1990; Season 1986-87 appeared as Enrico (Lucia di Lammermoor) at Seattle, Silvio (Pagliacci) in Detroit and as the Beast in the US premiere of Stephen Oliver's Beauty and the Beast, at St Louis; Sang Egberto in Verdi's Stiffelio at Sarasota, 1990, and the High Priest in Alceste at the Chicago Lyric Opera; Other roles include Mozart's Almaviva and Papageno, Figaro, Germont and Falke; Has also appeared at Düsseldorf, the City Opera New York, Miami and Philadelphia.

BRANSCOMBE Peter John, b. 7 Dec 1929, Sittingbourne, Kent, England. University Teacher; Musicologist. m. Marina Elizabeth Riley, 14 Dec 1967, 2 sons, 1 daughter. *Education:* Dulwich College, London, 1944-48; MA, Worcester College, Oxford, 1956; PhD, Bedford College, London, 1977. *Career:* Appearances on BBC radio & television, Austrian Radio; Scottish television; Lecturer, German, 1959-69, Senior Lecturer, 1970-79, Professor of Austrian Studies, 1979-. University of St Andrews. *Publications:* Translator, Mozart & His World in Contemporary Pictures, 1961; Co-translator, Mozart, A Documentary Biography, 1965, revised 1966; revised third edition, 1990; Part-author/co-editor, Schubert Studies: Problems of Style & Chronology, 1982; author Mozart, Die Zauberflöte, 1991. *Contributions to:* New Grove Dictionary of Music & Musicians, (approximately 120 articles), 1980; New Grove Dictionary of Opera, (approximately 120 articles), 1992; Various professional journals. *Honours:* Governor, Royal Scottish Academy of Music, 1967-73; Music Committee, Scottish Arts Council, 1974-81; Scottish Arts Council, 1976-79; Chairman, Conference of University Teachers of German in Scotland, 1983-85. *Memberships:* Advisory committee, Scottish Early Music Consort, 1981-89; Royal Musical Association; Modern Humanities Research Association; English Goethe Society; International Nestroy Society; Schubert Institute, (UK); Haydn Society of Great Britain. *Hobbies:* Walking; Natural history. *Address:* 32 North Street, St Andrews, Fife KY16 9AQ, Scotland.

BRANT Henry (Dreyfuss), b. 15 Sept 1913, Montreal, Quebec, Canada. Composer. *Education:* Studied at the McGill Conservatorium, Montreal, 1926-29, the Institute of Musical Art in New York and the Juilliard School, 1932-34; Private study with Walingford Riegger, Georges Antheil and Fritz Mahler. *Career:* Worked for radio, films, jazz groups and ballets as composer, conductor and arranger; Commercial music in Hollywood and Europe; Teacher at Columbia University, 1945-52, the Juilliard School, 1947-54 and Bennington College, 1957-80; Performer on wind and percussion instruments; Music has employed spatial separation with variously contrasted instrumental groups. *Compositions include:* Antiphony for 5 groups, 1953, revised 1968; Ceremony, triple concerto, 1954; Conclave for mezzo, baritone and ensemble 1955; Labyrinth I and II, 1955; On the Nature of Things, 1956; The Children's Hour for voices, brass, organ and percussion, 1958; Atlantis, antiphonal symphony, 1960; Concerto with Lights, 1961; Fire in Cities, 1961; The Fourth Millenium for brass, 1963; Voyage Four for orchestra, 1963; Odyssey - why not? for 2 flutes and 4 small orchestral groups, 1965; Verticals Ascending for 2 wind ensembles, 1967; Windjammer for wind instruments, 1969; The Immortal Combat for 2 bands, 1972; An American Requiem, 1973; Divinity: Dialogues in the Form of Secret Portraits, 1973; Six Grand Pianos Bash Plus Friends, 1974; Solomon's Gardens for voices, 24 handbells and 3 instruments, 1974; Homage to Ives, 1975; American Commencement for 2 brass and percussion groups; Spatial Concerto, 1976; Antiphonal Responses, 1978; Cerebus, 1978; The $1,000,000 Confessions for 2 trumpets and 3 trombones, 1978; Trinity of Spheres for 3 orchestral groups, 1978; Orbits for 80 trombones, soprano and organ, 1979; The Glass Pyramid, 1980; Inside Track, 1980; The Secret Calendar, 1980; Horizontals Extending, 1982; Desert Forest, 1983; Litany of Tides for violin, 2 orchestras and 4 voices, 1983; Meteor Farm, 1983; Fire under Water, 1983; Burning Brant on the Amstel, 1984; Western Spring for 2 orchestras, 2 choruses and jazz combo, 1984; Prisons of the Mind, Spatial Symphony, 1990. *Address:* c/o ASCAP, ASCAP Building, One Lincoln Plaza, New York, NY 10023, USA.

BRAUCHLI Bernard, b. 5 May 1944, Lausanne, Switzerland. Clavichord Player. *Education:* Piano studies in Lausanne and Vienna, 1963-69; Studied musicology at the New England Conservatory with Julia Sutton; Researched Iberian keyboard music at Lisbon, 1977. *Debut:* Fribourg, Switzerland, 1972; US debut at Marlboro College, Vermont, 1973; Numerous tours of Europe and North America with keyboard works of the 16th-18th centuries, including works by Portuguese and Spanish composers; Has given summer courses in Austria and Spain, 1978-82; Lecturer at the Boston Museum of Fine Arts 1978-83; Professor of clavichord at the New England Conservatory from 1983.

BRAUN Victor, b. 4 Aug 1935, Windsor, Ontario, Canada. Singer (Baritone). *Education:* Studied at the Toronto Conservatory and in Vienna. *Career:* Sang first with the Canadian Opera Company in Montreal and Vancouver; Sang in Germany from 1964, notably at Frankfurt (Escamillo), Cologne, Dusseldorf and Hamburg; Bayerische Staatsoper, Munich, from 1968; La Scala Milan, 1969, as Wolfram in Tannhäuser; Sang Hamlet in the Covent Garden premiere of Searle's opera, and returned to London as Don Giovanni and Mozart's Count, Germont, Posa (Don Carlos) and Eugene Onegin; Salzburg, 1970, as Mozart's Count; Boston, 1977, in the US premiere of Glinka's Ruslan and Ludmilla; Santa Fe, 1983-84, as Mandryka in Arabella by Strauss and in Henze's We Come to the River; Nice, 1986, as Hans Sachs in Die Meistersinger; Maggio Musicale Florence, 1987, in Benvenuto Cellini, Debussy's Golaud, 1989; sang in Doktor Faust by Busoni at Amsterdam, 1987; Chicago Lyric Opera as Wozzeck; Hans Sachs at the opening of the new Essen opera, 1988, Don Alfonso for Netherlands Opera, 1990; sang Holofernes in the US premiere of Judith by Siegfried Matthus, Santa Fe, 1990; engaged for Hans Sachs with the Canadian Opera Company at Toronto, 1992; Sang Gunther in a new production of Götterdämnerung at Brussels, 1991; Amfortas in Parsifal at Essen, 1992. *Recordings include:* Tannhäuser (Decca). *Honours include:* First Prize, International Mozart Competition, Vienna. *Address:* Ingpen & Williams Ltd, 14 Kensington Court, London W8 5DN, England.

BRÄUNINGER Jürgen, b. 13 Sept. 1956, Stuttgart, West Germany. Composer, Electronic Instruments. m. Brigitte Keck, 1985. *Education:* Staatliche Hochschule für Musik und darstellende Kunst, Stuttgart, 1982; MA, San Jose State University, San Jose, California, 1983. *Career:* Tutor, 1977-82; Musical Director, Theatre Tri Buehne, Stuttgart, 1980-82; Member of Musica Nova, Society for New Music and New Jazz, Board of Directors, 1981-85; Co-Organiser, New Music Concert Series, Stuttgart, 1981-82; Courses on Electronic Music/Media, 1984-85; Lecturer, Staatliche Akademie der bildenden Künste, Stuttgart, 1984-85, Staatliche Hochschule für Musik und darstellende Kunst, 1984-85; Lecturer in Composition and Director Electronic Music Studio, University of Natal, 1985-; Distinguished Visiting Composer, San Jose State University, California, 1988-89; Senior Lecturer in Composition, 1991-. *Compositions:* The Tam Tam Tape, Elektronische Musik, Ornament, 1982; Saxomanie, D-Art-S and Bass-Auf, all 1984, on Vibraphony-Saxonomie Ornament; Xherone, 1986; ...anywhere far, 1991. *Recordings:* As a Synthesist, Wir spielen Märchen Otto Maier, Ravensburg, 1980; Traumspiel, Sandra, 1980; Contributing composer and complete score realization motion picture soundtrack: The Lawnmower Man, New Line Cinema Corporation, USA, 1991; Orchestration and additional music motion picture soundtrack: The Dead Pit, Skouras Picture, USA, 1989. *Publications:* As Producer: Mandela Peace Rally, 1990; Music for Liberation, 1990; Celebrating Oral Tradition: Bandlululondini, 1992; Art Gecko, 1993; Old World, New World, Third World Studios, proceedings of the International Computer Music Conference, San Jose, California, 1992. *Address:* University of Natal, Department of Music, King George V Avenue, Durban 4001, RSA.

BRAUS Ira, b. 10 Sept 1951, New York, USA. Musicologist; Psychoacoustic Theorist; Concert Pianist. *Education:* BMus, AB, Oberlin College; MMus, SUNY Stony brook, USA; PhD, Harvard; Piano with Henry Rauch, Jack Radunsky, Gilbert Kalish; Ensemble with Samuel Baron and Bernard Greenhouse. *Debut:* Town Hall, New York City, 1978. *Career:* Pianist, Boston Repertory Ballet Orchestra, 1980; Appearance on WNYC New York, 1978; Lecture-recital on MIT cable TV, 1990;

Concerts on historic pianos, at the EM Frederick Collection, 1991-93. *Publications:* An unwritten Metrical Modulation in Brahms's Op 119, No 2, 1994; Skeptische Beweglichkeit, 1992; Why Doesn't Anyone Play Bars 1-11 of Tristan in tempo? 1991. *Honours:* Wulsin Fellowship, Berkshire Music Centre. *Memberships:* American Brahms Society. *Hobbies:* Hiking; Cycling. *Address:* 142 Nichols St, Lewiston, ME 04240, USA.

BRAUSS Helmut F, b. 19 Oct 1930, Milan, Italy. Concert Pianist. *Education:* German Arbitur, 1950; Handel Conservatory, Munich, Hochschule fur Music, Heidelberg; Private studies with Hans Ehlers, Elly Ney, Edwin Fischer. *Debut:* Munich, 1952. *Career:* Numerous recitals, broadcasts and solo appearances with Orchestras in Europe, USA, Japan, China, and Korea; Appearances in Canada with Saskatchewan Festival Orchestra, Edmonton Symphony, Vancouver and Winnipeg CBC Orchestras, and in most major centres; Initiator and Coordinator, Beethoven Festival, Sasketchewan, 1970; Specialist in music of Beethoven, Brahams and Schumann; Currently, Professor of Music, University of Alberta. *Recordings:* Works by Mozart, Beethoven, Schubert, Schumann, Brahms, Chopin, Pfitzner, Khachaturian on PBS West Germany, and Poulenc, on CBS Canada. *Publications:* Musik Aus Zweiter Hand, (article); Max Reger's Music for Solo Piano, 1993. *Honours:* Killam Professor, University of Alberta, 1993. *Hobbies:* Swimming; Chess. *Address:* Department of Music, University of Alberta, Edmonton, Alberta T6G 2C9, Canada.

BRAY Roger William, b. 29 Mar 1944, Sheffield, Yorkshire, England. University Teacher. m. Juliet A Brown, 8 July 1967, 1 son, 1 daughter. *Education:* King's College Choir School, Cambridge, 1952-57; Chorister, King's College, Cambridge, 1953-57; Academical Clerk, Magdalen College, Oxford, 1962-65; MA, DPhil, Magdalen College, Oxford University, 1970. *Career:* Lecturer, Assistant Professor, 1970, University of Victoria, British Columbia, Canada, 1968-70; Lecturer in Music, University of Manchester, England, 1970-79; Professor of Music, University of Lancaster, 1979-; Dean, Faculty of Humanities, 1992-. *Recordings:* With King's College Choir, Cambridge; Magdalen College, Oxford, Choir; New College Oxford Choir and The Clerkes of Oxenford. *Publications:* John Sheppard: Complete Works II, Hymns, Oxford, Oxenford Imprint (Editor), 1982. *Contributions to:* Articles in Proceedings of RMA; RMA Research Chronical; Music and Letters; Journal of Plainsong and Medieval Music Society, Early Music. *Honour:* Halstead Music prize, Oxford University, 1965-68. *Membership:* Chairman, Board of Governors, Lancaster Royal Grammer School. *Address:* University Music Department, University of Lancaster, Lancaster LA1 4YW, England.

BRAZZI Jean, b. 30 May 1936, Troyes, France. Singer (Tenor). *Education:* Troyes and at the Conservatoire National in Paris. *Debut:* Stage: Besancon 1961, as Alfredo in Traviata. *Career:* Sang in concert from 1961; Appearances in Bordeaux, Rouen, Marseilles, Lyon and Lille; Wexford Festival, 1967, as Gounod's Romeo, Glyndebourne, 1966, 1969, as Werther; Paris Opera 1968 and 1980; Appeared as Charpentier's Julien at Monte Carlo 1970, as Phaedon in the French premiere of Satie's Socrate, Marseilles 1972; Barcelona 1980 as Hoffmann; Other roles include Massenet's Des Grieux and Jean (Herodiade), Don Jose, Turiddu, Cavaradossi, Pinkerton, Maurizio in Adriana Lecouvreur, Steva (Jeúfa) and paco (La Vida Breve). *Recordings include:* Highlights from Werther (Philips); Herodiade (Rodolphe); Les Beatitudes by Franck. *Address:* c/o Gran Teatro del Liceu, Barcelona, Spain.

BREAM Julian, b. 15 July 1933, London. Guitarist and Lutenist. *Education:* Royal College of Music. *Debut:* Began Professional Career Cheltenham 1947; Wigmore Hall, London 1950. *Career:* Tours in Europe, America, Japan, Australia, India and Far East; Appeared at festivals at Aldeburgh, Bath, Edinburgh, Three Choirs, King's Lynn, Holland, Ansbach, Berlin, and Stratford

(Canada); Research into Elizabethan Lute Music which led to revival of interest in that instrument; Has encouraged contemporary English compositions for the guitar (including works by Britten, Walton and Tippett); Henze has composed Royal Winter Music (2 sonatas after Shakespeare) for him; Formed Julian Bream Consort, 1960; Inaugurated Semley Festival of Music and Poetry, 1971; season 1990-91 included concerts with Scottish Chamber Orchestra and tours of Italy and Britain (including 40th anniversary concert at the Wigmore Hall); Spring tours of Germany and the USA; Promenade Concerts, London, with Malcolm Arnold's guitar Concerto, 1991; Season 1992-93 included 60th Birthday Concert at the Wigmore Hall, Summer Festivals and BBC Proms. *Recordings include:* CD of Villa-Lobos Concerto. Five Preludes and 12 Preludes (RCA). *Honours:* DUniv (Surrey), 1968; ARAM, 1969; FRCM, 1981; FRNCM, 1983; Exclusive contract with EMI Classics since 1990; OBE, 1964; Villa-Lobos Gold Medal, 1976; CBE, 1985. *Hobbies:* Playing the Guitar; Cricket; Table Tennis; Gardening; Backgammon. *Address:* c/o Harold Holt Ltd, 31 Sinclair Road, London W14, England.

BRECKNOCK John, b. 29 Nov 1937, Long Eaton, Derbyshire, England. Singer (Tenor). *Education:* Birmingham Music School with Frederic Sharp and Dennis Dowling. *Debut:* Alfred in Die Fledermaus, Sadler's Wells, London, 1967; later repertoire includes Rossini's Almaviva and Comte Ory, Mozart's Belmonte and Ottavio and Verdi's Duke of Mantua; With the English National Opera at the London Coliseum sang in the UK stage premieres of Prokofiev's War and Peace, 1972, and Henze's The Bassarids, 1974, and in the world premiere of Gordon Crosse's The Story of Vasco, 1974; Covent Garden debut 1974, as Fenton in Falstaff; Glydebourne debut 1971; Has sung at the Metropolitan Opera and toured Canada in 1973; At the Teatro Regio Parma, 1985, sang Almaviva in Il Barbiere di Siviglia; Season 1985-86 sang Rossini roles in Paris. *Recordings include:* Alfredo in an English language Traviata, opposite Valerie Masterson. *Address:* c/o English National Opera, St Martin's Lane, London WC2, England.

BREDEMEYER Reiner, b. 2 Feb 1929, Velez, Colombia. Composer. *Education:* Studied with Karl Hoeller in Munich, 1949-53, and with Wagner-Regeny at the Akademie der Kunste in East Berlin, 1955-57. *Career:* Conductor of the German Theatre in East Berlin since 1961; Teacher, Akademie der Kuenste from 1978. *Compositions include:* Leben des Andrea, opera, 1971; Die Galoschenoper, 1978; Orchestral: Integration, 1961; Variante, 1962; Schlagstück, 3 for orchestra and 3 percussion groups; Bagatellen für B, for piano and orchestra, 1970; Piano und ... 1970; Symphony, 1974; Double concerto for harpsichord, oboe and orchestra, 1974; Auftakte for 3 Orchestral groups, 1976; Concerto for oboe and orchestra, 1977; 9 Bagatelles for strings, 1984; Chamber includes: 4 Quintets, 1956, 1958, 1969, 1991; 3 string quartets, 1962, 1968, 1983; 3 Septets, 1980, 1987, 1990; Vocal: Cantata, 1961; Wostock for choir and Orchestra, 1961; Karthago for chorus and chamber ensemble, 1961; Zum 13.7. fur Schoenberg, for female voice and ensemble, 1976; Cantata 2 for 16 voics and 16 instruments, 1977; Das Alltaegliche for soprano, tenor and orchestra, 1980; Die Winterreise for baritone, piano and horn, 1984; Die schoene Muellerin for baritone, string quartet and horn quartet, 1986; Operas: Candide, 1981-82, Der Neinsager, 1990; Songs; Piano music. *Address:* GEMA (Germany), c/o PRS Ltd Member Registration, 29/33 Berners Street, London W1P 4AA, England.

BREHM Alvin, b. 8 Feb 1925, New York, USA. Composer; Conductor; Double Bass Player. *Education:* Studied with Zimmermann and Giannini at Julliard, 1942-43 and with Walingford Reigger at Columbia University, MA, 1951. *Career:* Played double bass with the Pittsburgh SO, 1950-51, the Contemporary Chamber Ensemble, 1969-73, the Group for Contemporary Music, 1971-73, the Philomusica Chamber Music Society, 1973-83, and the Chamber

Music Society of Lincoln Center, 1984-89. Conductor of contemporary music from 1947; Founder-Conductor of the Composers' Theater Orchestra, 1967; Teacher, State University of Stony Brook, 1968-75, Manhattan School of Music, 1969-75, and SUNY at Purchase, from 1982. *Compositions include:* Divertimento for trumpet, horn and trombone, 1962; Dialogies for bassoon and percussion, 1964; Brass Quintet, 1967; Cello Sonata, 1974; Concertino for Violin and Strings, 1975; Quarks for slfuft, bassoon, string quartet and piano, 1976; Sextet for piano and strings, 1976; Piano Concerto, 1977; Double bass Concerto, 1982; Tuba Concerto, 1982; Sextet for Woodwind quintet and piano, 1984; Children's Games for flute, clarinet, string trio and piano, 1985. *Address:* ASCAP, ASCAP Building, 1 Lincoln Plaza, New York, NY 10023, USA.

BRELL Mario, b. 1937, Hamburg, Germany. Singer (Tenor). *Education:* Studied in Hamburg. *Career:* Sang operetta at Hof 1963-65; Lucerne, 1965-67, Oldenburg, 1967-71, Krefeld, 1971-73; At Gelsenkirchen, 1973-82 sang such repertory as Lohengrin, Parsifal, Zemlinsky's Swerg, Hofmann in Les contes d'Hoffmann; Member of the Deutsch Oper am Rhein Dusseldorf from 1982, singing Diomedes in Penthesilea by Schoeck, 1986; Guest appearances in Zurich, Frankfurt, Karlsruhe and Wiesbaden (premiere of Kirchner's Belshazar, 1986); Amsterdam, 1987, as Busoni's Mephisto, Bielefield, 1990, as Bacchus in Ariadne auf Nexos; other roles include the Count in Schreker's Irrelohe and Max in Der Freischutz; Sang the mayor in Einems Besuch der alten Dame, Gelsenkirchen, 1991. *Recordings include:* Der Zar lasst sich photographieren by Weill (Capriccio). *Address:* c/o Deutsche Oper am Rhein, Heinrich-Heine Allee 16, 4000 Dusseldorf, Germany.

BREM Peter, b. 1948, Munich, Germany. Violinist. *Education:* Graduate, Richard Strauss conservatory, Munich, 1970. *Career:* Berlin Philharmonic Orchestra, 1970-76; Co-Founder, Brandis String Quartet, 1976, with concerts in Tokyo, London, Hamburg, Munich, Paris and Milan and engagements with the Wiener Singverein and the Berlin Philharmonic; Festival appearances at Salzburg, Edinburgh, Lucerne, Tours, Bergen, Florence and Vienna; Has Co-premiered the 3rd Quartets of Gottfried von Einem and Giselher Klebe, 1981, 1983, and the Clarinet Quintet of Helmut Eder, 1984; Solo concerts with such orchestras as the Radio-Sinfonieorchester Berlin. *Recordings include:* Albums in the standard repertoire from 1978 with the EMI/Electrola, Teldec, Orfeo and Harmonia Mundi labels; Recent releases of Beethoven, Weill, Schulhoff and Hindemith and the Schubert String Quintet with Nimbus. *Honours:* Prize-winner at the Deutsche Hochschulewettbewerb. *Address:* c/o Anglo Swiss Ltd, 3 Primrose Mews, 1a Sharpelshall Street, London NW1 8YW, England.

BRENDEL Alfred, b. 5 Jan 1931, Wiesenberg, Austria. Pianist and Writer. m. (1) Irish Heymann-Gonzala 1960, divorced, 1972; (2) Irene Semler 1975, 1 son, 3 daughters. *Education:* Studied piano under Sofija Dezelić (Zagreb), Ludovika v. Kaan (Graz), Edwin Fischer (Lucerne), Paul Baumgartner (Basel), Eduard Steuermann (Salzburg); Studied composition under A Michl (Graz) and harmony under Franjo Dugan (Zagreb). *Debut:* First piano recital 1948. *Career:* Concert tours through Europe, Latin America, North America 1963-; Australia 1963, 1966, 1969, 1976; Has appeared at many music festivals, including Salzburg 1960-, Vienna, Edinburgh, Aldeburgh, Athens, Granada, Puerto Rico and has performed with most of the major orchestras of Europe and USA; played the Brahms 2nd Concerto at the 1991 Promenade Concerts, London, with the Berlin Philharmonic. *Recordings:* Numerous recordings, including complete piano works of Beethoven, Schubert's piano works 1822-28 and music by Liszt, Schoenberg, Bartók, Mozart and Stravinsky; CDs of Liszt's B minor Sonata, Haydn Sonatas, Schubert Sonatas D845, D850, D784 and D960; Drei Klavierstücke 946 and Wanderer Fantasy (Philips). *Publications:* Essays on Music and Musicians in Phono,

Fonio Forum, Osterreichische Musikzeitschrift, Music and Musicians, Hi-Fi Stereophonie, High Fidelity, The Gramophone, Die Zeit, New York Review of Books, Neue Zurcher Zeitung; Frankfurter Allgemeine; Musical Thoughts and Afterthoughts, 1976; Music Sounded Out, 1990. *Honours:* Hon RAM; Hon DMus, London, 1978, Oxford, 1983; Hon DLitt, Sussex, 1981; Hon Member, RAM; Commandeur des Arts et des Lettres, 1985; Fellow of Royal Northern College, Manchester, 1988; Academy of Arts and Sciences; Bayer, Akademie der Wissenschaften; Busoni Foundation Award, 1990; Premio Citta de Bolzano, Concorso Busoni, 1949, Grand Prix du Disque, 1965, Edison Prize, 1973, 1981, 1984, Grand Prix des Disquaires de France, 1975, Deutscher Schallplattenpreis, 1976 and 1977, 1982, 1984, Wiener Flötenuhr, 1976, 1977, 1979, Gramophone Award, 1977, 1978, 1981, 1983, Japanese Record Academy Award, 1977, 1978, 1980, 1982, 1984, Franz Liszt Prize, 1979, 1982, 1983, Grand Prix Mondiale du Disque, 1983, Grand Prix du Disque, 1984, Frankfurt Music Prize, 1984; Hon KBE, 1989; Orden pour le Mérite für Wissenschaften und Künste, 1991; Diapason D'Or award, 1992; Hon DMus, Warwick, 1991; Yale, 1992. *Hobbies:* Books; Theatre; Visual Arts; Films; Baroque and Romanesque Architecture; Unintentional Humour; Kitsch. *Address:* c/o Ingpen and Williams, 14 Kensington Court, London W8 5DN, England.

BRENDEL Wolfgang, b. 20 Oct 1947, Munich, Germany. Singer (Baritone). *Education:* Studied in Munich. *Career:* Sang Don Giovani in Kaiserslautern, 1970, then became a member of the Bayersische Staatsoper Munich: roles include Papageno, Germont and Pelléas; Guest appearances in Hamburg, Dusseldorf and Karlsruhe; Metropolitan Opera debut, 1975, as Mozart's Count; Sang Verdi's Miller with the Chicago Lyric Opera, 1983; Bayreuth Festival, 1985, as Wolfram in Tannhäuser; Covent Garden debut, 1985, as Luna in Il Trovatore: Eugene Onegin and Donizetti's Enrico, 1988; Metropolitan Opera and Bayreth Festival, 1989, as Germont and Wolfram; Teatro, San Carlos, Lisbon, 1989, as Amfortas; Chicago, 1990, as Eugene Onegin; Other roles include Puccini's Marcello and Strauss's Mandryka; Season 1991-92 as Amfortas in Parsifal at La Scala and as Count Luna at Munich. *Recordings:* Die Lustigen Weiber von Windsor, Paer's Leonora and Der Freischütz (Decca); Die Zauberflöte, La Bohème and Zar und Zimmermann (HMV); Ein Deutsches Requiem (Deutsche Grammophon). *Address:* c/o Ingpen and Williams Ltd, 14 Kensington Court, London W8 5DN, England.

BRENNEIS Gerd, b. 3 Jan 1936, Nienhegen, Mecklenburg, Germany. Singer (Tenor). *Debut:* Essen, 1960, as Curzio in Figaro. *Career:* Sang at Augsburg from 1965 as Verdi's Manrico and Gabriele Adorno, Idomeneo, Abdre Chenier, Lensky and Dmitri (Boris Godunov) and in operas by Wagner; Bayreuth Festival, 1973-74, as Walther and Siegmund; Deutsche Oper Berlin from 1974 as Wagner's Parsifal, Lohengrin and Tannhauser, Strauss's Bacchus and the Emperor in Die Frau ohne Schatten; Huon in Oberon, 1986; Metropolitan Opera, 1976, as Walther; Has sung Tristan at Pretoria, South Africa, 1985, in Tokyo with the company of the Vienna Staatsoper, 1986, and Turin, 1987; Has also sung in Munich, Cologne, Florence and Milan; New York, 1976-81, as the Emperor; Nice Opera, 1988, as Siegfried; Television appearances include the title role in Wagner's Rienzi, with the Wiesbaden Opera. *Address:* Deutsche Oper Berlin, Richard Wagnerstrasse 10, D-1000 Berlin, Germany.

BRESNICK Martin, b. 13 Nov 1946, New York, USA. Composer. m. Anna Barbara Broell, 21 June 1969, 1 daughter. *Education:* BA, Music Composition, Hartt School of Music, University of Hartford, 1967; MA, 1968, DMA, 1972, Music Composition, Stanford University; Akademie fur Musik, Vienna, Austria, 1969-70. *Compositions:* Introit, 1969; Trio for Two Trumpets and Percussion, 1966; Ocean of Storms, 1970; 3 Intermezzi, 1971; Musica, 1972; B's Garlands, 1973; Wir Weben, Wir Weben, 1978; Conspiracies, 1979; Der Signal, 1982; High Art, 1983; String Quartet 2 Bucephalus,

1984; Bread and Salt, 1984; Tent of Miracles, 1984; Bag o'Tells, 1984; 3 Choral Songs, 1985; Just Time, 1985; One, 1986; Lady Neil's Dumpe, 1987; Trio, 1988; Pontoosuc, 1989; Musica Povera, Nos 1-3, 1991; String Quartet, No 3, 1992. *Recordings:* B's Garlands, on CRI No 336; Conspiracies, 3 Intermezzi, on CRI No 468; String Quartet No 2 Bucephalus, Wir Weben, Wir Weben, Centaur CDCM2; Lady Neils Dumpe (compact disc); piano trio on CRI CD 583; Just Time on New World Records CD 80413. *Publication:* How Music Works. *Contributions to:* Mosaic; Yale Journal of Music Theory. *Address:* Yale School of Music, 96 Wall Street, New Haven, CT 06520, USA.

BRESSLER Charles, b. 1 Apr 1926, Kingston, Pennsylvania, USA. Tenor; Vocal Pedagogue. *Education:* Studied with Lucia Dunham, Sergius Kagen, Marjorie Schloss, Juilliard School of Music, graduated, 1950, postgraduate diploma, 1951. *Career:* Founder-member, New York Pro Musica, toured extensively, 1953-63; Founder-member, New York Chamber Soloists, 1957-; Appeared with: Santa Fe Opera, Washington (DC) Opera Society; Concert tours of Europe; Repertory ranges from medieval to contemporary works; sang at Santa Fe in the US premieres of Henze's Boulevard Solitude, 1967 and The Bassarids, 1968; Vocal teacher, various institutions including Mannes College of Music, 1966-, and Manhattan School of Music, 1978-. *Recordings:* Columbia, Composers Recordings Inc, New World Records, Nonesuch, Vanguard. *Honours include:* Best Male Singer Award at the Théâtre des Nations Festival, Paris, for the play of Daniel, 1963. *Address:* c/o Manhattan School of Music, 120 Claremont Avenue, New York, NY 10027, USA.

BRETT Charles, b. 27 Oct 1941, Maidenhead, England. Countertenor. m. Brigid Barstow, 1 Aug 1973, 1 son, 1 daughter. *Education:* Choral scholar at King's College, Cambridge. *Career:* Leading performer in early and Baroque music ensembles led by Munrow, Harnoncourt, Leonhardt, Hogwood, Gardiner, Herreweghe and Malgoire; Recent engagements in US, France, Switzerland, Germany, Spain and Norway; Handel's Theodora in Oslo and Israel in Egypt in Geneva; Bach's Christmas Oratorio in Versailles; Bach's St John Passion in Cambridge and London and the B Minor Mass with the Collegium Vocale Gent in Lourdes, Paris and Lyon; Many concerts with Le Grande Ecurie et la Chambre du Roy, conducted by Jean-Claude Malgoire; Opera debut, 1984, in Angelica Vincitrice di Alcina by Fux, at Graz; Handel's Semele at Ludwigsburg; Tour of France with La Clemenza di Tito by Gluck; Aachen Opera, 1987, as Oberon in A Midsummer Night's Dream; Founder and Director of the Amaryllis Consort, vocal group specializing in Renaissance repertoire; Professor, Royal Academy of Music; Master Class in Canada, Belgium, Germany, Spain. *Recordings:* Handel's Dixit Dominus, Rinaldo, Messiah, The Triumph of Time and Truth; Bach's B Minor Mass (Virgin Classics); Lambert: Leçons de Ténèbres, Mozart Masses; Bach: Cantatas; Burgon: Canciones od Alma; Italian and English madrigals and madrigals by Demantius (with Amaryllis Consort). *Honour:* Hon RAM, 1991. *Membership:* ISM. *Address:* St Margaret's, St Michael's Road, Winchester, Hampshire SO23 9JE, England.

BRETT Philip, b. 17 Oct 1937, Edwinstowe, England. Musicologist and Conductor. *Education:* Studied at King's College Cambridge, PhD 1965, and the University of California at Berkeley. *Career:* Researched English madrigal composers with Thurston Dart at Cambridge; Fellow, King's College, Cambridge, and Assistant Lecturer, Music 1963-66; Assistant Professor, 1966-71, Associate Professor, 1971-78, Professor, 1978-, University of California, Berkeley; Chairman of Music Department, 1988-90, Professor of Music, University of California, Riverside, 1991-. *Recordings:* Lou Harrison, La Koro Sutro, New Albion; Morton Feldman, Rothko Chapel, New Albion; Handel's, Susanna, Hamonia Mundi (prepared chorus). *Publications include:* Consort Songs, 1969; William Byrd, Consort Songs for Voice and Viols, 1970; William Byrd, Madrigals, Songs and Canons, 1976; William Byrd, The Masses, 1981; William Byrd, Gradualia, 1990-92; Benjamin Britten, Peter Grimes (Cambridge Opera Handbooks, 1983); General Editor, the Byrd Edition. *Contributions to:* Numerous professional journals and Bulletins. *Honours:* Archibald T Davison Medal for Musicology, 1969, Noah Greenberg Award, American Musicological Society, 1980; Grammy Nomination, for Handel's Susanna recording, Choral Class, 1991. *Memberships:* Board Member, American Musicological Society, 1984-86; Royal Musicological Association; Plainsong and Medieval Music Society. *Address:* 17341 Ranchero Road, Riverside, CA 92504, USA.

BREUL Elisabeth, b. 25 Aug 1936, Gea, Germany. Singer (Soprano). *Education:* Studied at the Musikhochschule of Gera and Dresden. *Debut:* Gera 1958, as Donna Anna. *Career:* Member of the Dresden Opera from 1960; Guest appearances in Berlin, Brussels, Brno, Lodz, Budapest, Genoa and Wiesbaden and music centres in Russia, France, Rumania and Spain; Other roles include Tatiana in Eugene Onegin, Natasha in War and Peace, Marguerite, Tosca, Agathe and Mozart's Countess and Susanna; Many appearances in the concert hall, in music by Bach and Handel; Teacher at the Musikhochschule of Dresden and Leipzig.

BREVIG Per, b. 7 Sept 1936, Halden, Norway. Trombonist. *Education:* Studied in Copenhagen, then at Juiliard School, New York: MusB 1968, MusM 1969, DMA 1971; Studied conducting with Stokowski in Sweden, 1966-67. *Career:* Principal Trombonist, Bergen Symphony Orchestra 1957-65; Solo Trombonist with the American Symphony Orchestra 1966-70; Principal Trombonist, Metropolitan Opera Orchestra from 1968; Artist-in-residence, Aspen Music Festival, 1970-; Faculty of Mannes College from 1976; Professor of Trombone, Oberlin College, 1984-88; Manhattan School of Music from 1988; Solo performances and master classes in Europe, USA and Japan; Numerous commissions, recordings, compositions for solo trombone. *Publications:* Avant-Garde Technique in Solo Trombone Music; Problems of Notation and Execution. *Honours include:* XIV International Music Competition in Prague, 1962; Koussevitsky Fellowship, 1960, 1966; Henry B Cabot Award, Boston Symphony Orchestra, 1966.

BREVIK Tor, b. 22 Jan 1932, Oslo, Norway. Composer; Conductor; Music Critic. *Education:* Studied Violin, Viola and Theory, Oslo Conservatory; Also Sweden. *Career:* Founder, Youth Chamber Orchestra, Oslo, 1958; Music critic. *Compositions:* Opera: Da kongen kom til Spilliputt, 1973; Adagio and Fugue for Strings, 1958; Overture, 1958; Serenade for Strings, 1959; Chaconne for Orchestra, 1960; Concertino for Clarinet and Strings, 1961; Music for Violin, 1963; Canto Elegiaco for Orchestra, 1964; Contrasts, chamber ballet, 1964; Elegy for Soprano, Viola, Double Bass and Percussion, 1964; Divertimento for Wind Quintet, 1964; Adagio Religioso for Horn, 1967; String ß/Quartet, 1967; Concertino for Strings, 1967; Music for 4 Strings, 1968; Intrada for Orchestra, 1969; Romance for Violin and Orchestra or Piano, 1972; Andante Cantabile for Violin and Strings, 1975; Septet, 1976; Fantasy for Flute, 1979; Light of Peace, Christmas play for children, 1980; Viola Concerto, 1982; Sinfonietta, 1989; Choral music; Songs; Sinfonia Brevik, 1991. *Recordings:* String Quartet, Divertimento for Wind Quintet, Septet and Elegy for Soprano. *Membership:* The Society of Norwegian Composers. *Address:* Nebbaveien 53, N-1433 Vinterbro, Norway.

BREWER Aline, b. 14 Sept 1963, Shropshire, England. Harpist. *Education:* Royal College of Music with Marisa Robles. *Debut:* Wigmore Hall, 1990. *Career:* Former member of the European Community Orchestra and the Britten-Pears Orchestra; Solo appearances with the London Mozart Players, Primavera and the Britten-Pears Orchestra; Duo recitals with flautist Jennifer Stinton. Member of the Britten-Pears Ensemble, with performances throughout Britain and the USA. *Recordings include:* Romantic music for Flute and Harp;

Mozart's Concerto K299, with Jennifer Stinton and the Philharmonic Orchestra (Collins Classics). *Honours include:* Joint winner, South East Arts Young Artists Platform. *Address:* c/o Owen White Management, 14 Nightingale Lane, London N8 7QU, England.

BREWER Bruce, b. 12 Oct 1941, San Antonio, Texas, USA. Singer (Tenor). m. Joyce Castle. *Education:* Studied with Josephine Lucchese at University of Texas, Austin, and with Richard Bonynge in New York and London; Further study with Nadia Boulanger and Rosalyn Tureck. *Career:* Sang at first in concert, notably in Baroque and early music; Opera debut San Antonio 1970, as Don Ottavio; Camden Festival, London, in Donizetti's Torquato Tasso, 1974; Sang at opera houses in Boston, San Francisco, Berlin, Paris, Toulouse, Spoleto and London, Covent Garden 1979; Aix-en-Provence Festival in revival of music by Campra; La Scala Milan 1980, in L'Enfance du Christ by Berlioz; Rossini's Le Comte Ory, 1991; Often heard in Bach and Mozart; sang Lord Puff in Henze's English Cat in Paris, and in the premieres of Ballif's Dracula and Denison's L'écume des jours; Paris Opéra, 1988, in the premiere of La Célestine by Maurice Ohana; sang Fatty in Weill's Mahagonny at the Maggio Musicale, Florence, 1990; Truffaldino in Busoni's Turandot at Lyon, 1992. *Recordings:* Les Indes galantes by Rameau (CBS); Rameau's Platée and Les Paladins (P Verany); Messiaen's St François d'Assise (KRO); Rameau's Zoroastre (Vox Fono); Boulevard Solitude by Henze (Cascavelle); Beethoven's 9th Symphony (Tempo); Berlioz's Works for Soloists and Chorus (Harmonia Mundi); Donizeth's Teresa e Gianfaldoni, and Les Nuits d'été à Pausilippe (Thesis); Gretry's L'Amant Jaloux (Pathé Marconi); Liszt's Complete Songs for Tenor (Thesis); Lully's Alceste (CBS); Offenbach's Orphee aux Enfers (Pathé Marconi). *Address:* Le Marais, 61370 Planches, France.

BREWER Christine, b. 1960, USA. Singer (Soprano). *Education:* Studies in the USA with Bigit Nilsson. *Career:* Appearances with the Opera Theatre of St Louis as Ellen Orford in Peter Grimes, Ariande, Donna Anna (also for Vancouver Opera, 1994); Sang Sifare in Mozart's Mitridate at the 1992 Mostly Mozart Festival in New York, Lady Billows in Albert Herring at San Diego and Vitellia in La Clemenza di Tito; Concert engagements include Szymanowski's Stabat Mater in Cleveland, the Vaughan Williams Benedicte in Louisville and Poulenc's Stabat Mater with the Leipzig Gewandhaus Orchestra; Beethoven's Ninth Symphony in Colombus and the Missa Solemnis in Washington DC and San Diego; Mendelssohn's Elijah with the Houston and Honolulu Symphonies; Recent engagements include the Mozart and Dvořák Requiems in Toronto, the Janáček Glagolitic Mass in Atlanta and at the Mann Music Center with the Philadelphia Orchestra under Charles Dutoit; Gretchen in Schumann's Faust at the Caramoor Festival. *Honour:* Winner, Metropolital Opera National Council Auditions, 1989. *Address:* c/o IMG Artists, Media House, 3 Burlington Lane, London W4 2TH, England.

BRICCETTI Thomas (Bernard), b. 14 Jan 1936, Mount Kisco, New York, USA. Conductor; Composer. *Education:* Studied piano with Jean Dansereau; Composition with Samuel Barber, Peter Mennin and Alan Hovhaness; Eastman School of Music, Rochester, New York, 1955. *Career:* Music Director, St Petersburg Symphony Orchestra, 1963-68; Florida Sun Coast Opera, 1964-68; Associate Conductor, Indianapolis Symphony Orchestra, 1968-72; Music Director, Fort Wayne Philharmonic Orchestra, 1971-78; Cleveland Institute of Music University Circle Orchestra, 1972-75; Omaha Symphony Orchestra, 1975-83; Nebraska Sinfonia, 1975-83; Principal Guest Conductor, Stavanger Symphony/Radio Orchestra, 1986-87; Artistic Director, Orchestra Stabile, Bergamo, 1988-; Principal Conductor, orchestra Sinfonica Umbria, 1988-; Guest Conductor with various orchestras in North America, South America and Europe. *Compositions:* Opera: Eurydice; Symphony No 1; Violin Concerto; The Fountain of Youth, overture; Illusions, symphonic poem; Some Chamber music including a String Quartet; Flute Sonata; Piano Sonata; Choral pieces; Songs.

Recordings: With the Indiana Chamber Orchestra; Nebraska Sinfonia; Louisville Orchestra. *Honours:* ASCAP Special Awards Grants, 1960-88; Ford Foundation Composers' Fellowships, 1961-63; Yaddo Foundation Residence Grant, 1963; Pulitzer Prize in Music nomination for Illusions, 1985; Various commissions. *Current management:* Columbia Artists Management, New York City. *Address:* VIA Eburnea 1, 06100 Perugia, Italy.

BRIDEOAKE Peter Arthur, b. 23 Apr 1945, Adelaide, South Australia, Australia. Senior Lecturer in Music; Composer. m. Elizabeth Jayne Varnish, 5 July 1980, 1 son. *Education:* Graduated, Adelaide Technical High School, 1962; BMus (Hons), University of Adelaide, 1973. *Career:* Numerous stage and television appearances as member of pop group The Twilights, Australia and New Zealand, 1964-69; Otis '72, ABC TV documentary, 1972; Faculty, 1976, Senior Lecturer, 1990-, University of Adelaide; Composition commissions from The Sydney String Quartet, Australian Chamber Orchestra, The Seymour Group, Victorian String Quartet, Ryszard Pusz, Patrick Brislan. *Compositions:* Solo, chamber and orchestral works including: Gedatsu, pieces for guitar, 1973; Imagery, for string orchestra, 1980; Shifting Reflections, 1981; String Quartet No 2, 1986; Canto for Clarinet Alone, 1987; Dialogue for Three, 1988; Calliope, for recorders, 1989; Concertino da Camera, 1990. *Recordings:* With The Twilights: 13 singles, 2 LPs, EMI; The Way They Played, CD Raven Records. *Honour:* John Bishop Memorial Commission, 1978. *Hobbies:* Chinese music and culture; Reading; Computers; Travel. *Address:* c/o Department of Music Studies, The University of Adelaide, South Australia 5001, Australia.

BRIDGES Althea, b. 11 Jan 1936, Sydney, Australia. Singer (Soprano). *Education:* Studied at the Sydney Conservatory. *Career:* Member of the Australian Opera Company 1961-64; Sang in Europe from 1964, at first in Austria (Graz); Vienna, Theater an der Wien, in the premiere of Hauer's Die Schwarze Spinne, 1966; Stuttgart, 1968, in the premiere of Orff's Prometheus; Landestheater Linz, 1971-83; Sang Tosca at Frankfurt and Donna Anna at the Glyndebourne Festival; Bari, Italy, as Ortrud in Lohengrin; Other roles include Strauss's Elektra and Marschallin, Marguerite in Faust and Azucena in Il Trovatore; sang in the premiere of Michael Kohlhaas by Karl Kögler Linz, 1989. *Address:* c/o Landestheater, Promenade 39, A-4010 Linz, Austria.

BRIGGS Sarah, b. 1972, England. Concert Pianist. *Education:* Studied with Denis Matthews at Newcastle, with John Lill, and at Blonay, Switzerland with Bruno Giuranna (chamber music). *Career:* Many recital and concerto performances throughout England and Scotland; West German and Swiss Performances including television recordings; Chester Summer Festival 1989 with the premiere of posthumous pieces by Benjamin Britten; London concerto debut at the Barbican 1989, playing Mozart K453; also plays Mozart's other 20 original concertos; Further engagements with the Royal Liverpool Philharmonic, Northern Sinfonia, English Chamber Orchestra, Royal Philharmonic, Vester Orchestra, Scottish Chamber Orchestra, Manchester Camerata and the London Soloists Chamber Orchestra; US debut July 1991, in the San Francisco Stern Grove Festival with the Midsummer Mozart Festival Orchestra, conducted by George Cleve; Further visits to US to perform concertos and recitals. *Honours include:* 1st Prize winner, Surrey Young Pianist of the Year Competition; (middle section) Third Prize, 1984 BBC Young Musician of the Year; Hindemith Scholarship 1987; Joint Winner, International Mozart Competition in Salzburg 1988 (leading to engagement with the Austrian Radio Symphony under Michael Gielen). *Address:* 86 The Green, Acomb, York YO2 5LS, England.

BRILIOTH Helge, b. 7 May 1931, Lund, Sweden. Singer (Tenor). *Education:* Studied at the Royal Academy and the Opera School in Stockholm; Academia di Santa

Cecilia Rome; Mozarteum Salzburg. *Career:* In 1960 at Drottningholm sang the baritone role of Bartolo in Paisiello's Il Barbiere di Siviglia; Bielefeld 1962-64; Tenor debut as Don José, Stockholm, 1966; Bayreuth, 1969-75 as Siegmund and Tristan; Salzburg Easter Festival 1970 as Siegfried, under Karajan; Covent Garden 1970- as Siegmund, Siegfried, Tristan and Parsifal; Metropolitan Opera debut 1971, as Parsifal; Glyndebourne 1971, as Bacchus in Ariadne auf Naxos; Drottningholm 1972, in the title role of Cavalli's Scipione Affricano; At the Royal Opera Stockholm 1975 sang the Emperor in the Swedish premiere of Die Frau ohne Schatten; sang at Stockholm in the 1986 premiere of Christina by Hans Gefors. *Recordings include:* Siegfried in Die Götterdämmerung (Deutsche Grammophon). *Address:* Birger Jarlsgatan 79, 11356 Stockholm, Sweden.

BRILOVA Elena, b. 9 Feb 1961, Moscow, Russia. Singer (Soprano). *Education:* Graduate, Moscow Conservatoire, 1986. *Career:* Sang in Concert, 1986-88; Bolshoi Opera Moscow from 1988 as the Queen of Shemakha, Antonida (A Life for the Tsar), Traviata, Rosina and other leading roles; Concert appearances as Constanze, Sophie, Oscar, Norina, Lucia, Amina and Leila (Les Pecheurs de perles); Further engagements as the Queen of Night at Cologne and Vienna, Gilda in Oslo and Vienna dn Palmide in Il Crociato in Egitto at the 1991 Ludwigsburg Festival; British debut, 1992, as the Queen of Shemakha with the London Symphony Orchestra; Season 1993 as Gilda at the Bergen Festival and in concert performances of Rigoletto at Tel Aviv, conducted by Zubin Mehta; Concert engagements at Brussels and Frankfurt and with such conductors as Bashmet, Simonov, Rostropovitch, Rozhdestvensky and Svetlanov. *Address:* c/o Atholl Still Ltd, 80-86 Westrow Street, London SE19 3AF, England.

BRINDUS Nicolae, b. 16 Apr 1935, Bucharest, Romania. Composer. m. Ioana Ieronim, 22 Oct 1982, 2 sons, 1 daughter. *Education:* Graduated in piano 1956, composition 1964, Ciprian Porumbescu Conservatory of Music, Bucharest; DMus, Cluj-Napoca, 1981. *Debut:* Pianist, George Enescu Philharmony of Bucharest, 1955. *Career:* Piano Soloist, 1958-75; Concert performances in Romania and abroad; Soloist, Ploiesti Philharmonic Orchestra, 1959-69; Professor Academy of Music, Bucharest, 1969-81; Editor, Muzica Review, Bucharest, 1981-92; Professor, Academy of Music, Bucharest, 1992-; Compositions printed, recorded, played and broadcast on radio and TV, Bucharest and abroad. *Compositions:* edited and recorded: Pieces for piano, 1966, 1984; 7 Psalms, 1969, 1981; Mamsell Hus, 1977, 1981; edited: 8 Madrigals for choir a capella, 1968; Sonata for 2 pianos, 1978; The Betrothal, opera, 1981; Languir me fais, 1986; Dialo(va)gos, concerto for piano and orchestra, 1988; Rhythmodia, 1989. *Recordings:* Kitsch-N, 1984; Vagues, 1977; Antifonia, 1986; Match II Monody and Polyphony, 1986; Solique I, 1986; Solique IV (Reverberations) 1986; With the Gipsy Girls, opera, 1988. *Publication:* Inter-relations (musical studies), 1984. *Contributions to:* Numerous magazines and journals. *Memberships:* Romanian Composers Union; Societe des Auteurs, Compositeurs et Editeurs de Musique, Paris; President of the Romanian Section of the ISCM (International Society of Contemporary Music); Member of the Executive Committee of the ISCM (1991-93). *Hobbies:* Literature; Theatre. *Address:* Str Dr Felix 101 bl 19, Sc A apt 42 78153, Bucharest, Romania.

BRINGS Allen, b. 24 Feb 1934, New York City, USA. Composer; Pianist; Teacher. m. Genevieve Chinn, 29 Aug 1959, 1 daughter. *Education:* BA, Queens College, City University of New York, 1955; MA, Columbia University, 1957; Mus.AD, Boston University, 1964; Princeton University. *Career:* Professor of Music, Aaron Copland School of Music at Queens College, City University of New York; Associate Director of Weston Music Center and School of Performing Arts, Weston, Connecticut. *Compositions include:* Symphony, sonatas for piano, solo violin, viola (or clarinet) and piano; Chamber concerti for piano and orchestra, violin and

percussion, flute and strings; Quintets for strings and for brass; Essay and Variations for band; Tre Sonetti di Michelangelo Buonarroti; Tre madrigali concertati; Lamentationes Jeremiae Prophetae; Capriccio and Notturno for orchestra; Five Pieces, 1980 for piano; Trio for clarinet, cello and piano; Sonata after Vivaldi for cello with piano; Scherzi musicali for orchestra; Three Holy Sonnets for large chorus & orchestra; Sinfonia da camera for chamber orchestra; Serenade, for orchestra, 1991; Sonata a4, for percussion quartet, 1992; Praetoriana, for band, 1992. *Recordings:* With pianist Genevieve Chinn: 4 sonatas for piano, 4 hands by Muzio Clementi; 2 sonatas for piano, 4 hands, by George Onslow; Antiphonies for piano, 4 hands, and electronic tape by Leo Kraft; Saccade by Robert Helps; Metamorphosis by Thomas Moore; Three Pieces by Raoul Pleskow for piano, 4 hands; Recorded on Centaur compact disc: Eclogue for solo clarinet, Trio for clarinet, cello and piano; Sonata for clarinet & piano, Sonata for solo violin, Sonata for piano, Centaur Compact Disc; Concert Piece for four clarinets; Three Inventions after J S Bach for two clarinets. *Publication:* Co-author of A New Approach to Keyboard Harmony, 1979. *Hobby:* Tennis. *Address:* 199 Mountain Road, Wilton, CT 06897, USA.

BRINKMANN Bodo, b. 7 Dec 1942, Binder, Brunswick, Germany. Singer (Baritone). *Education:* Studied at the Berlin Musikhochschule with Karl-Heinz Lohmann. *Debut:* Kaiserslautern, 1971; Member of the National Theatre Mannheim from 1974; Staatsoper Hamburg in Lohengrin; Munich Staatsoper, notably as Escamillo (1984) and in the 1986 premiere of Reimann's Troades; Guest appearances in Berlin, Paris and Strasbourg; Deutsche Oper an Rhein 1987, as Telramund; Munich Olympia Hall, 1987, as Prince Igor; Bayreuth Festival 1987-90, Kurwenal, Donner and Gunther; sang Jochanaan in Salome at Barcelona 1989; Cologne Opera 1990, as Wotan in Die Walküre; Sang Donner and Gunther in Der Ring des Nibelungen at the 1992 Bayreuth Festival. *Address:* c/o Oper der Stadt Köln, Offenbachplatz, D-5000 Cologne, Germany.

BRITTON David, b. 11 June 1945, Louisville, Kentucky, USA. Singer. m. Kathryn Carter, 26 May 1968, 1 son, 2 daughters. *Education:* BMus, North Texas State University; The Juilliard School of Music; The Manhattan School of Music (Advanced Studies). *Debut:* Metropolitan Opera Mini Met. *Career:* New York Philharmonic, Chicago Symphony, Boston Symphony, Philadelphia Symphony, National Symphony of Washington and Orchestras of Minnesota, St Louis, Detroit, Dallas, Denver, Baltimore, St Paul, Los Angeles, Rochester, Hawaii, Israel, l'Orchestre de France, Montreal, Toronto, Hamburg, Mexico City, New York City Opera, San Francisco Opera, Philadelphia Opera, New Orleans Opera, Dallas Opera, Caracas Festival, Mostly Mozart Festival, Opera de Lyon; Festival of Two Worlds in Spoleto, Italy; Soloist with Bach Aria Group of New York, New York Pro Musica Antiqua, Waverly Consort. *Recordings:* St Matthew Passion, Raymond Leppard Conductor; The Music Master, Gerard Schwarz Conductor. *Current Management:* Colbert Artists Management, New York City. *Address:* Colbert Artists Management, 111 West 57th Street, New York, NY 10019, USA.

BRITTON Rhodri, b. 1961, Hwlfford, Wales. Singer (Bass-baritone). *Education:* Studied at Christ's Hospital, Balliol College, Oxford, and at the Royal Academy of Music. *Career:* While at the RAM sang in The Cunning Little Vixen, Così fan Tutte, Orpheus in the Underworld, Gianni Schicchi and Les Boréades (Adamas in the British stage premiere of Rameau's opera, conducted by Roger Norrington, 1985); Welsh National Opera from 1987 in Les Troyens, Il Barbiere di Siviglia, Salome, Don Giovanni (Masetto) and Tosca (Angelotti); Sang Gremin (Eugene Onegin) and Mozart's Figaro with Opera 80, 1989; Performances of Henze's The English Cat in Gütersloh and Berlin, 1989; Scottish Opera debut 1990, as Gremin; currently principal bass-baritone at the Landestheater, Eisenach; Concert repertory includes Schubert's Winterreise (At Balliol and the RAM, the

Brahms Requiem (Rennes, France) and Bach's St John Passion at Southwell Minster. *Address:* c/o Korman International Management, Crunnells Green Cottage, Preston, Herts SG4 7UQ, England.

BRIZZI Aldo, b. 7 June 1960, Alessandria, Italy. Conductor; Composer. *Education:* Bologna University; Milan Conservatorio. *Debut:* 1st appearance as Conductor, 1978. *Career:* Conducted concerts in Europe, Israel, USA, center and South America; Principal performances with Berlin Philharmonic Chamber Ensemble, The Cluj Philharmonic Orchestra; Santa Cecilia Chamber Orchestra of Rome, The Haydn Orchestra of Bolzano; Musical Conductor of the Ensemble of Ferienkurse, Darmstadt; Permanent Conductor of E M Ferrari Orchestra, Alessandria and Akabthos Ensemble. *Compositions:* Works performed by numerous European orchestras, ensembles and soloists including, Ecyo, Danish Radio Orch, Montepulciano Festival Orch, New Philharmonic Orchestra of Paris, Ens de Cuivres et Percussion de l'InterContemporain; Works broadcast by 21 European radio stations, 2 USA and Israeli State Radio. *Recordings:* Salabert conducting the Arditti String Quartet Consort; Electrecord conducting the Bacau Symphony Orchestra; Edipan with Composition of A Brizzi. *Publications:* Proposte Musicali, 1980; La Musica, Le Idée, Le Cose, 1981. *Contributions to:* To numerous magazines. *Honours:* Venezia Opera Prima, 1981; Stipendiendpzies, Darmstadt, 1984; Young Generation in Europe, Venice, Paris, Cologne, 1985; Franco Evangelisti, Rome, 1986; Young Composers' Forum, Cologne, 1989; Artistic Director of Scelsi Foundation, Rome. *Hobbies:* Walking; Overseas travel; Skiing. *Address:* Via Boves 6, 15100 Alessandria, Italy.

BROADBENT Graeme, b. 1962, Halifax, England. Singer (Bass). *Education:* Studied at the Royal College of Music with Lyndon Vanderpump; Moscow Conservatoire with Evgeny Nesterenko. *Career:* Has sung Thanatos in Gluck's Alceste at Covent Garden, with the English Bach Festival; Monteverdi's Nettuno and Mozart's Osmin and Sarastro for regional companies; English National Opera 1989, as Hans Schwartz in Mastersingers and Ribbing in A Masked Ball; Opera North 1990 as the Emir in the British stage premiere of Verdi's Jerusalem; Don Fernando in Fidelio for Scottish Opera; Concert repertoire includes the Monteverdi Vespers, the Mozart Requiem and Schoenberg's Serenade Op 24; Solo recital at the Rachmaninov Hall, Moscow 1991; English National Opera: Ceprano (Rigoletto), 1992; Guron (Princess Ida), 1993; Opera North: Nikitich (Boris Godunov), also in Promenade Concert, Royal Albert Hall, 1992; Colline (La Bohème), 1993; Engaged to sing Theseus (A Midsummer Night's Dream) in Paris and Bordeaux, 1994. *Current Management:* John Coast. *Address:* c/o John Coast, 31 Sinclair Road, London W14 ONS, England.

BROADSTOCK Brenton Thomas, b. 12 Dec 1952, Melbourne, Australia. Composer. m. 3 children. *Career:* BA, Monash University, 1975; MMus, Memphis State University, USA; Diploma in Composition, University of Sydney, Composition with Peter Sculthorpe; AMus TCL, Trinity College of Music; DMus, University of Melbourne. *Career:* Tutor in Music, 1982-84; Senior Tutor in Music, 1984-87, Faculty of Music, University of Melbourne, Australia; Artistic Director, New Audience Concerts, 1983-87; Inaugural Composer in residence, Melbourne Symphony Orchestra, 1988; Senior Lecturer in Music, University of Melbourne, 1989; *Performances:* Melbourne Summer Music Festival, 1985; Stroud Festival, England, 1985; Adelaide Festival, 1986; Spoleto Festival, Melbourne, 1986; Nova Festival, Brisbane, 1987; Music Today Festival, Tokyo, 1988; ISCM World Music Days, Hong Kong, 1988; ISCM World Music Days, Oslo, 1990. *Compositions:* Symphony No 3; 4 String Quartets; The Mountain for Orchestra; Tuba Concerto; Piano Concerto; Battlements for orchestra; Woodwind Quartet; Aureole 1-4 for flute and piano; Solo Bass Clarinet; Oboe and Piano; Solo Piano; Beast from Air for Trombone and percussion; many works for brass band; Symphony No 1, 1988; Symphony No 2, 1989

(all published by G Schirmer). *Recordings:* Many works performed, recorded and broadcast by ABC; Opera: Fahrenheit 451, 1992. *Hobbies:* Basketball; Reading; Films. *Current management:* G Schirmer (Australia). *Address:* 20 Simmons Street, Box Hill North, Victoria 3129, Australia.

BROADWAY Kenneth, b. 1950, USA. Duo Pianist. *Education:* Studied at the Cleveland Institute of Music with Vronsky and Babin. *Career:* Formed Piano Duo partnership witih Ralph Markham and has given many recitals and concerts in North America and Europe; BBC debut recital 1979 and further broadcasts on CBC TV, Radio France Musique, the Bavarian Radio and Radio Hilversum in Holland; Stravinsky's Three Dances from Petrushka at the Theatre des Champs Elysees, Paris, 1984; Season 1987-88 included 40 North American recitals, concert with the Vancouver Symphony and New York debut on WQXR Radio; Season 1988-89 inlcuded the Concertos for Two Pianos my Mozart and Bruch in Canada and a recital tour of England and Germany; Recent performances of the Bartok Sonata for Two Pianos and Percussion, with Evelyn Gelnnie and a 1990-91 tour of North America, Europe and the Far East; Festival appearances include Newport USA 1988 (releases on CD). *Recordings include:* Duos by Anton Rubenstein; Vaughan Williams Concerto for Two Pianos; Bartok Sonata for Two Pianos and Percussion. *Honours include:* Young Artist of the Year, Musical America Magazine, 1989 (with Ralph Markham). *Address:* c/o Anglo Swiss Ltd, 3 Primrose News, 1a Sharpeleshall St, London NW1 8YW, England.

BROADWAY Michael, b. 5 Dec 1947, London, England. Pianolist. m. Frances Robertson, 20 Oct 1979. *Education:* London College of Music, Organ and Harpsichord with Gordon Phillips, ALCM, 1969, GLCM, 1971. *Debut:* Pianola Concert, Rome, 1990. *Career:* Pianola concert, tour of Rome, Prague, Budapest, 1991; BBC Radio 3 broadcast performance of Herbert Howells Phantasy Minuet for Pianola and Trois Pieces pour Pianola by Alfredo Casella, 1992. *Memberships:* Freeman of the City of London; Liveryman of the Worshipful Company of Glaziers. *Hobbies:* Stained Glass; Croquet. *Address:* 39 Sydner Road, Stoke Newington, London N16 7UF, England.

BRÖCHELER John, b. 21 Feb 1945, Vaals, Limbourg, Holland. Singer (Baritone). *Education:* Studied with Leo Ketelaars in Maastricht and with Pierre Bernac in Paris. *Career:* Sang at first in concert, notably in the Bach Passions, the Choral Symphony and the Brahms Requiem; Berlin Festival in the premieres of Die Erprobung des Petrus Hebraicus by Henri Pousseur 1974 and Mare Nostrum by Kagel 1975; San Diego Opera as Sharpless in Madama Butterfly, Ford in Falstaff, and in the 1979 premiere of Menotti's La Loca, with Beverly Sills; Netherlands Opera as Germont, Don Giovanni and Marcello and in Donizetti's Maria Stuarda with Joan Sutherland; Frankfurt Opera 1983, as Amfortas in Parsifal; Glyndebourne 1984, as Mandryka in Arabella; Los Angeles Opera as Nabucco; La Scala Milan 1985, as Jochanaan in Salome and Golaud in Pelléas et Mélisande; Stuttgart 1985, in Henze's Konig Hirsch; Other appearances in Toronto, New York and Paris, Vienna 1988 - Golaud in Pelléas and Mélisande, Bonn 1989; Wolfram, Tannhäuser, Munich 1989; Mathis der Maler, Hindemith; sang Orestes in Elektra at Barcelona, 1990; Hindemith's Mathis and Von Einem's Danton at the 1990 Munich Festival; Sang Barak in Die Fran ohne Schatten for Netherlands Opera, 1992. *Recordings:* Dichterliebe (Schwann); Handel's Dettinger Te Deum and Judas Maccabeus; Lucrezia Borgia (Decca); Das Paradies und Die Peri (Supraphon). *Address:* c/o Bayerische Staatsoper, Postfach 745, D-8000 Munich 1, Germany.

BROCKLESS Brian, b. 21 Jan 1926, London, England. Conductor; Composer; Organist; Teacher. m. Jennifer Wright, 2 sons (1 by former marriage). *Education:* BMus; ARCM; ARCO; Hon ARAM. *Career:* Concerts with: English Chamber Orchestra, Royal Philharmonic Orchestra; Northern Sinfonia; Italian

Tours with London Schubert Orchestra; Concerts in Romania, Palermo, Stockholm, Brussels, Venezuela, Denmark; Choral & Orchestral Performances for BBC, Belgian, Swedish & Danish Radio; Director, Music, St Bartholomew the Great Priory, London, 1961-71, 1979-; Senior Lecturer, University of Surrey; Festival Adjudicator (retired 1991). *Compositions:* Prelude, Toccata & Chaconne; Introduction, Passacaglia & Coda; Fantasia, Adagio & Fugue, organ; Toccata for an Occasion, 1982, commissioned for Peterborough Organ Festival; English Elegy for String Orchestra; Church Music, Songs & Chamber Music. *Recordings:* English Church Music, ALPHA ACA 522 Elgar, Britten Brochless; Organ Mixtures: PRIORY PRC 239; Darkne, Alcock, Willan, Jackson, Brockless, MSV CD 92002. *Honours:* Conducting Prize, Siena, Italy, 1963; Hon Academician, RAM, 1982. *Memberships:* Director, Dolmetsch Foundation; Herbert Howells Society; Royal Academy of Music Club. *Hobbies:* Reading; Ornithology; Cricket. *Address:* 2 Grove Heath North, Ripley, Surrey GU23 6EN, England.

BRODARD Michael, b. 1 Apr 1946, Fribourg, Switzerland. Singer (Bass-baritone). *Education:* Fribourg Conservatoire, 1965-74. *Career:* Concert Singer in France and Switzerland; Opera Engagements at Geneva, Lusanne, Lucerne, Nancy and Metz; Further concerts at Brussels, Marseilles, Frankfurt, Barcelona, Lisbon, Buenos Aires, Madrid and Warsaw; Repertoire ranges from baroque to modern works. *Recordings include:* L'Enfant et les Sortileges, Pelleas et Melisande, Bach's Christmas Oratorio, Hadyn's St Theresa Mass, Madrigals and Vespers by Monteverdi, Schubert's E-flat Mass and Vivaldi's Psalm 110 (Erato); Stravvinsky's Renard and Les Noces, Masses by Mozart. *Address:* c/o Erato (Contracts), WEA Records, 59 Alperton Lane, Wembley, Middlesex HA0 1FJ, England.

BROIDO Arnold Peace, b. 8 Apr 1920, New York City, USA. Music Publisher. m. Lucille Tarshes, 5 Mar 1944, 3 sons. *Education:* BS, Ithaca College, 1941; MA, Columbia University, 1954; DMus (Hon), Ithaca College, 1990. *Career:* Music Teacher, East Junior High School, Binghamton, NY, USA, 1941-42; Musician First Class, US Coast Guard, 1942-45; Editor and Production Manager, Boosey & Hawkes Inc, 1945-55; Vice-President, Century Music, Heritage Music, and Mercury Music, 1955-57; Education Director, Edward B Marks Music Corp, 1957-62; Director, Publishing and Sales, Frank Music Corp, 1962-69; Vice-President, Boston Music Company, 1968-69; President and Director, Theodore Presser Company, 1969-; Chairman, Elkan-Vogel Inc, 1970-; Chairman, Mercury Music Corp, 1972-. *Publications:* Co-author, Music Dictionary, 1956; co-author, Invitation to the Piano, 1959; Associate Editor, University Society Encyclopedia of Piano Music, 1958; Articles in professional journals. *Address:* 908 Wootton Road, Bryn Mawr, PA 19010, USA.

BROKAW James Albert II, b. 4 Feb 1951, Princeton, New Jersey, USA. Historical Musicologist. m. Mollie Sandock, 27 June 1984. *Education:* BA, German Literature, Kenyon College, 1973; Studies in Music History and Theory, Baldwin Wallace Conservatory, 1977-78; PhD, Musicology, University of Chicago, 1986. *Career:* Assistant Professor of Music, Northeastern Illinois University, 1989-; Lecturer in Music, Chicago State University, 1986-; Lecturer in Music, University of Chicago Open Programme, 1987-; Advisory Board Member, Riemenschneider Bach Institute, 1982-86; Judge, Mu Phi Epsilon Music History Competition, 1988. *Publication:* The Genesis of the Prelude in C Major (BWV 870,1), in Bach Studies, Cambridge University Press, 1989; Techniques of Expansion in the Preludes and Fugues of Johann Sebastian Bach, dissertation; Programme Notes: The Chicago Symphony Orchestra/Performances for Peace, 1984-88; Music of the Baroque, 1984, 1987. *Contributions to:* Reviews of scholarly editions of keyboard music of J S Bach, C P E Bach and Louis Couperin, in Notes, 1985, 1986, 1989; Recent Research on the Genesis and Sources of Bach's Well-Tempered Clavier, II, in Bach: The Quarterly Journal of the Riemenschneider Bach

Institute, 1985. *Honours:* 1st Alternate, Whiting Dissertation Fellowship in the Humanities, 1984; NEH Summer Seminar for College Teachers on Mozart's Operas, Cornell University, 1988. *Memberships:* American Musicological Society; New Bach Society; College Music Society. *Address:* Box 125 Ogden Dunes, Portage, IN 46368, USA.

BROKMEIER Willi, b. 8 April 1928, Bochum, Germany. Singer (Tenor). *Education:* Studied in Mainz. *Debut:* Stadttheater Mainz, 1952. *Career:* Appearances in lighter operatic roles at the Deutsche Oper am Rhein Dusseldorf; Many engagements in operetta, notably at the Theater am Gärtnerplatz, Munich, and elsewhere in Germany; Cologne Opera, 1965, in the premiere of Zimmermann's Die Soldaten; Munich Festival, 1973, as Pedrillo in Die Entführung. *Recordings:* Gräfin Mariza; Czardasfürstin; Die Vierjahrige Posten by Schubert; Lehar's Lustige Witwe and Land des Lächelns; Die Kluge by Orff; Korngold's Die Tote Stadt (RCA); Feuersnot by Strauss (Acanta).

BROMLEY Haworth P, b. 8 May 1947, Washington DC, USA. m. Marilyn Modlin, 7 Nov 1987. *Education:* BMus, Music History, Richmond Professional Institute; Private study in Organ and Violin. *Compositions:* Several hymn tunes, a Mass, and Two Piano Nocturnes. *Memberships:* American Guild of Organists; American Recorder Society. *Hobby:* Sailing. *Address:* 302 Mansion Drive, Alexandria, VA 22302, USA.

BRONDER Peter, b. 1953, England. Singer (Tenor). *Education:* Studied at the Royal Academy of Music with Joy Mammen and at the National Opera Studio. *Career:* Principal tenor with the Welsh National Opera from 1986-90, as Almaviva, Arturo (Puritani), Cassio, Tamino, Edgardo, Rodolfo, Alfred, Narraboth (Salome), Lensky, Alfredo, Elvino (La Sonnambula) and Ferrando; Covent Garden debut 1986, as Arturo in Lucia di Lammermoor and the Major Domo in Der Rosenkavalier; Sang Kudryash in Katya Kabanova with English National Opera 1989, Ernesto with Netherlands Opera and Dr Caius (Falstaff), Mayor (Herring) at Glyndebourne; Further appearances with ENO as Andres in Wozzeck (1990) and Dr Caius and Narraboth on tour with WNO in Japan; Invitations for Falstaff in Paris, Almaviva for ENO and Alfredo and Pylades (Iphigénie en Tauride) with WNO. *Recordings include:* Kiri te Kanawa recital (Phonogram), Osud (EMI), Don Giovanni (Phonogram); Adriana Lecouvreur (Decca). *Address:* Allied Artists, 42 Montpelier Square, London SW7 1JZ, England.

BRONFMAN Yefim, b. 10 Apr 1958, Tashkent, Russia. Pianist. *Education:* Juilliard School of Music, New York, USA; Curtis Institute, Philadelphia, Pennsylvania; Private studies with Rudolf Serkin and Arie Vardi. *Debut:* Israel Philharmonic with Kostalanetz, 1974. *Career:* As Soloist with: Montreal Symphony Orchestra; Philadelphia; Los Angeles Philharmonic; New York Philharmonic; Minnesota Orchestra; Mostly Mozart Orchestra; English Chamber Orchestra; St Louis Symphony Orchestra; Scottish Chamber Orchestra; Vancouver Symphony Orchestra; Pittsburgh Symphony Orchestra; London Philharmonia; St Paul Chamber Orchestra; Houston Symphony Orchestra; Toronto Symphony Orchestra; Goteborg Symphony Orchestra; Royal Philharmonic; San Francisco Symphony Orchestra; Berlin Philharmonic; Chicago Symphony Orchestra; Baltimore Symphony Orchestra; Rotterdam Philharmonic; Bournemouth Symphony Orchestra; Cleveland Orchestra; National Symphony Orchestra; Rochester Philharmonic; Jerusalem Symphony Orchestra; Winnipeg Symphony Orchestra; Richmond Symphony Orchestra; New Jersey Symphony. *Recordings:* Deutsche Grammophon: All Fauré disc and Prokofiev Violin Sonatas with Shlomo Mintz; Musical Heritage, Brahms Sonata in F minor and Scherzo Op 4; Music Masters: Mozart Sonatas for violin and piano with Robert Mann; CBS Masterworks: Prokofiev Piano Sonatas 7 and 8; Sony Classical, 1991, Mussorgsky, Pictures at an Exhibition, Stravinsky, 3 scenes from Petrushka; Rachmaninoff: Piano Concertos 2 and 3, with Esa-Pekka Salonen and Philharmonia Orchestra, Sony

Classical, 1992; Prokofiev: Piano Concertos 1, 3 and 5, with Zubin Mehta and Israel Philharmonic, Sony Classical, 1993. *Honours:* American-Israel Cultural Foundation Scholarship, 1974; Winner of Avery Fisher Prize, 1991. *Current Management:* ICM Artists. *Address:* 40 West 57 Street, New York, NY 10019, USA.

BRONHILL June, b. June 1930, Broken Hill, New South Wales, Australia. Singer (Soprano). m. Richard Finney. *Education:* Studied in London. *Debut:* Adele in Fleldermaus, Sadler's Wells, London, 1954. *Career:* Sang such roles in London as Zerbinetta, Gilda and Norina in Don Pasquale; Successful also as Hanna Glawari in Die Lustige Witwe, the Queen of Night, Lucia (Covent Garden Company) and in the title role of the British premiere of Janáček's Cunning Little Vixen (Sadler's Wells 1961); Blonde in Die Entfuhrung at the Sydney Opera House and Magda in La Rondine with the English Opera Group, 1974. *Honours include:* OBE, 1976. *Address:* c/o Australian Opera, PO Box 291, Strawberry Hills, NSW 2012 Australia.

BROOK Barry, b. 1 Nov 1918, New York, USA. Musicologist. *Education:* MA, Studied at the City College of New York and Columbia University, 1942; Doctorate from the Sorbonne, Paris, 1959. *Career:* On faculty of Queens College New York from 1945; Professor of Music and Executive Officer of the PhD Programme, City University of New York, 1967-89; Director of CUNY Center for Music Research and Documentation from 1989; Has also taught at the Institute de Musicologie at the University of Paris, 1967-68, the Eastman School of Music, 1973, University of Adelaide, 1974, Juilliard from 1977, the Centre National de la Recherche Scientifique in Paris, 1983 and the University of Alabama, 1987. *Publications:* La Symphonie Francaise dans le seconde moitie du XVII siècle, 1962; The Breitkopf Thematic Catalogue, 1762-1787, 1966; Editor in Chief, Repertoire International de Litterature Musicale, Abstracts of Music Literature from 1966; The Symphony 1720-1840, 1979-86; French Opera in the 17th and 18th centuries, 1984-; Joint editor of Giovanni Battista Pergolesi Complete Works, 1986-. Editor: Musicology and the Computer; Musicology 1960-2000: A Practical Program, 1970; Thematic catalogues in Music: An Annotated Bibliography, 1972. *Honours:* Dent Medal, Royal Musical Association, 1965; Chevalier of the Order of Arts and Letters, 1972; Smetana Medal, Czechoslovakia, 1978; Member, Royal Swedish Academy, 1989. *Address:* c/o Royal Swedish Academy of Music, Stockholm, Sweden.

BROOK Peter, b. 21 Mar 1925, London, England. Stage director. *Education:* Studied at Oxford. *Career:* Director of productions at Convent Garden, 1948-50, with Boris Godunov, Salome (designs by Salvador Dali) and the premiere of the Olympians by Bliss, 1949; Filmed The Beggar's Opera by Gay Pepusch with Laurence Olivier, 1953; Metropolitan Opera 1953 and 1957, Faust and Eugene Onegin; His reduction of Carmen, La tragedie de Carmen was produced at the Paris Bouffes du Nord in the season 1981-82 and was seen on tour in Europea and the USA (New York), 1983; a much reduced version of Pelléas et Mélisande (Impressions of Pelléas) was performed in 1992/93. *Address:* c/o Royal Shakespeare Company, Stratford-on-Avon, Warwickshire, England.

BROOKS Richard, b. 26 Dec 1942, Syracuse, New York, USA. Professor of Music. *Education:* BS Music Education, State University College, at Potsdam; MA Composition, SUNY, Binghamton; PhD, Composition, NYU. *Career:* Professor of Music and Chair of Music Department, Nassau community College, New York, USA. *Compositions include:* Moby Dick, opera; Symphony in one movement; String Quartett; Trio for violin, cello and piano; Whitman Choruses; Bachatelles for percussion; Prelude and Lament for wind quintet. *Recordings:* Sonata for violin and piano; Suite for percussion; Prelude and Lament for wind quintet. *Publications:* Layer Dictation, 1978; Structural Functions of Musical Gesture; Articles in Musical American Magazine; Regular reviews for Notes (MLA

journal). *Address:* 252 Dekalb Avenue, Brooklyn, NY 11205, USA

BROPHY Gerard, b. 1953, Sydney, Australia. Composer. *Education:* Master classes with Turibio Santos, 1976; Composition seminar, Mauricio Kagel, Basel, Switzerland; Studied with Richard Toop, BM, Composition, NSW State Conservatorium of Music, 1981; Studied with Franco Donatoni, Italy; Graduated, Accademia Nazionale de Santa Cecilia, Rome, 1983; Composition Course, Accademia Chigiana di Siena, 1983. *Career:* Composer-in-Residence with Musica Viva Australia, 1983; Australian Chamber Orchestra, 1986; Queensland Conservatorium of Music, 1987; Pittsburgh New Music Ensemble, 1988; Queensland Conservatorium of Music, 1989. *Compositions:* Orchestral Works: Salammbo, 1980; Nadja, 1981; Exu, 1982; Orfeo, 1982; Le Reveil de l'Ange, 1987; Matho, 1987. Ensemble Works: Linia, 1980; Ikhos, 1981; Iemenja, 1981; Senso...dopo Skin d'Amourdo, 1982; Sofre, 1983; Breathless, 1983; Cries and Whispers, 1983; Rondino, 1984; Scintille, 1984; Chrome, 1984; Lace, 1985; Mercurio, 1985; Spur, 1988; Head, 1988; Séraphita, 1988; Forbidden Colours, 1988; Frisson, 1989. Instrumental Works: Gheranos, 1980; Axe, 1982; Tres doux tremblement de terre, 1983; Chiarissima, 1987; Nymphe - Echo morphologique; Angelicon. Vocal Works: Flesh, 1987; Shiver, 1989. Stage Works: The Temptation of St Antony, 1985; pink chair light green violet violent FLASH, 1990, for piccolo and persuccion ensemble; Les Roses Sanglantes for bass clarinet and chamber orchestra, 1991; Vorrei Baciarti for baritone and chamber ensemble, 1991; Sanctissima for two sopranos and ensemble, 1990; Tweak for piccolo solo, 1991; Angelicon for solo piano, 1991; Pluck it! for solo guitar; O Dolcezz'amarissime for ensemble, 1992; Spiked Heels for solo piano, 1992; Xanthe for large ensemble, 1992; Glint for percussion sextet, 1992; Lautréamont for flute and chamber orchestra, 1992; Twist for solo clarinet, 1993. *Honours:* Recipient of numerous grants and fellowships including Composer Fellowship, Australia Council Music Board, 1982 and 1983; Italian Government Scholarship. *Address:* 37 Montpelier Street, Wilston, Queensland 4051, Australia.

BROSTER Eileen, b. 23 June, London, England. Pianist. m. R Chaplin, 6 May 1972, 1 son. *Education:* Studied with Frank Merrick and Cyril Smith at the Royal College of Music. *Debut:* Wigmore Hall. *Career:* Performed on BBC Radio and TV; Appeared in all South Bank Halls; Toured extensively as soloist in recitals and concerti; performances, Wigmore Hall. *Memberships:* Incorporated Society of Musicians. *Address:* 199 Beehive Lane, Gants Hill, Ilford, Essex, England.

BROTT Alexander, b. 14 Mar 1915, Montreal, Quebec, Canada. Musical Director; Conductor; Professor of Music. m. Lotte Goetzel, 27 Mar. 1933, 2 sons. *Education:* Lic Mus, McGill University Faculty of Music, 1932; Laureat degree, Quebec Academy of Music, 1933; Postgraduate Diploma, Performer, Composer, Conductor, Juilliard School of Music, New York, USA, 1933-38; D Mus, Chicago University, 1960; LLD, Queen's University, Canada, 1973; Doctor of Music, McGill University, 1979. *Career:* Professor and Conductor-in-residence at McGill University since 1939; Concertmaster, Assistant Conductor, Montreal Symphony Orchestra; Founder, Musical Director, McGill Chamber Orchestra; Conductor, Montreal Pops Concert; Conductor, Musical Director, Kingston Symphony Orchestra and Kingston Pops Concerts. *Compositions:* 18 symphonies (13 commissioned); 25 solo and chamber music (12 commissioned); 8 vocal (5 commissioned), 1938-71; Solo and chamber music, songs and orchestrations (11 commissioned), 1971-78. *Recordings:* 14, many with McGill Chamber Orchestra including own compositions and Mozart, Haydn, Schubert, Bach. *Hobby:* Gemmology. *Address:* 5459 Earnscliffe Avenue, Montreal, Quebec H3X 2P8, Canada.

BROTT Boris, b. 14 Mar 1944, Montreal, Quebec,

Canada. Conductor. m. Ardyth Webster, 2 sons, 1 daughter. *Education:* Conservatoire de Musique, Montreal; McGill University, Montreal; Studied conducting with Pierre Monteux, Igor Markevitch, Leonard Bernstein, Alexander Brott. *Debut:* As violinist with Montreal Symphony, 1949. *Career:* Founder, Conductor, Philharmonic Youth Orchestra, Montreal, 1959-61; Assistant Conductor: Toronto Symphony Orchestra, 1963-65; New York Philharmonic, 1968-69; Music Director: Northern Sinfonia Orchestra, England, 1964-69; Royal Ballet, Covent Garden, 1966-68, including the Covent Garden premiere of Stravinsky's The Soldier's Tale; Lakehead University, Thunder Bay, Ontario, 1967-72; Kitchener Waterloo Symphony, 1970-71; Regina Symphony, 1970-73; Conductor, Music Director: Hamilton Philharmonic Orchestra, 1969-90; Ontario Place Pops Orchestra, 1983-91; Chief Conductor: BBC Welsh Symphony Orchestra, 1972-77; CBC Symphony, 1976-83; President, Great Music Canada, 1977-; Artistic Director, Stratford Summer Music Festival, Ontario, 1982-84; Conductor, McGill Orchestra, Montreal, Quebec, 1989-; Artistic Director, Boris-Brott Summer Music Festival, Hamilton, Ontario, 1988-; Conductor and Music Director, Ventura County Symphony, Ventura, California, 1992-; Guest Conductor, All British orchestras, all major Canadian orchestras, USA, Korea, Japan, Germany, France, Sweden, Israel, Mexico, Salvador, Italy, Denmark; Principal Guest Conductor and Music Advisor, Symphony Nova Scotia, 1981-; Guest Conductor, Sadler's Wells Opera, Canadian Opera Company, Edmonton Opera; Writer, Host, Conductor, over 100 TV programmes, UK, USA, Canada; Appeared in film and radio. *Recordings:* Numerous for CBC, Septre-Mace, Mercury, including suites from operas by Handel; Dvořák's Serenade op 44; Symphonies by Richter, Holzbauer and Cannabich; Sibelius Pelléas; Ravel Le Tombeau de Couperin. *Address:* 301 Bay Street South, Hamilton, Ontario, Canada, L8P 3J7.

BROTT Denis, b. 9 Sept 1950, Quebec, Canada. Cellist. m. 27 Aug 1976, 1s, 3d. *Education:* Studied with Gregor Piatigorsky, University of Southern California, USA. *Career:* Festivals include Marlboro, Aspen, Hampden-Sydney, Orford, and Sitka; Artistic Director, Festival of the Sound, Ontario, 1991; Faculty of the Music Academy of the West, Santa Barbara, 1993 & 1994 summer season, performing chamber music at festivals in Hampden-Sydney, Virginia and Sitka Alaska; Jury member, Evian International String Quartet Competition in France, also recitalist, chamber artist and soloist with orchestra; Currently, Professor of Cello and Chamber Music at Conservatoire de Musique de Montreal, Canada. *Publications include:* Article, Schelome: The Message of King Solomon, Violoncello Society and Canadian Jewish News Viewpoints, 1993. *Recordings include:* 20 chamber music works including the complete string quartets of Beethoven with the Orford String Quartet and Hommage to Piatigorsky, a solo CD; Works of his father, Alexander Brott, featuring Arabesque for Cello & Orchestra, 1993. *Honours:* Two Juno Awards for Best Classical Recording by a Chamber Ensemble; Grand Prix du Disque, 1987; Winner, Munich International Cello Competition. *Hobbies:* Photography; Skiing; Gardening; Swimming. *Current Management:* Davis Joachim, Les Concerts Davis Joachim Inc, 201 Brock Avenue North, Montreal, Quebec H4X 2G1, Canada. *Address:* 201 Brock Avenue North, Montreal, Quebec H4X 2G1, Canada.

BROUWENSTYN Gre, b. 26 Aug 1915, Den Helder, The Netherlands. Opera Singer. *Education:* Amsterdam. *Career:* Joined and subsequently became First Soprano, Amsterdam Opera; Has appeared in London, Berlin, Stuttgart, Brussels, Copenhagen, Paris, Vienna, Bayreuth (1954-56), Barcelona, and Buenos Aires; Covent Garden debut 1951, as Aida, and appeared as Elisabeth de Valois in 1958; Repertoire includes: Forza del Destino; Tosca; Aida; Otello; Un Ballo in Maschera; Tannhäuser ; Die Walküre; Die Meistersinger; Le Nozze de Figaro; Jenůfa; Il Trovatore; Cavalleria Rusticana; Don Carlos; retired in 1971, after singing Beethoven's Leonore with Netherlands Opera. *Honour:* Order of

Orange-Nassau. *Address:* 3 Bachplain, Amsterdam, The Netherlands.

BROWN A Peter, b. 30 Apr 1943, Chicago, Illinois, USA. Professor of Musicology. m. Carol Vanderbilt, 21 Mar 1968, 1 daughter. *Education:* BM 1965, MM 1966, PhD 1970, Northwestern University; Domaine School for Conductors, Hancock, Maine, 1965; Post-doctoral, New York University, 1970. *Career:* Professor of Musicology, University of Hawaii, 1969-74; Professor of Musicology, Indiana University, 1974-. *Publications:* Joseph Haydn in Literature: A Bibliography, 1974; Carlo d'Ordonez: A Thematic Catalogue, 1978; Carlo d'Ordonez 7 Symphonies, 1979; String Quartets Op 1, 1980; Performing Haydn's The Creation, 1986; Joseph Haydn's Keyboard Music: Sources and Style, 1986; The French Music Publishers Guera of Lyon, 1987. *Contributions to:* Journal of American Musicological Society; Music Review; Music and Letters; Musical Times; Haydn Yearbook; Haydn-Studien; Haydn-Studies; Mozart Jahrbuch; Musical Quarterly; Journal of Musicology; The New Grove; The Heritage of Music; Caldana Essays; American Scholar; American Historical Review. *Honours:* Fellow, American Council of Learned Societies, 1972-73; Fellow, John Simon Guggenheim Memorial Foundation, 1978-79; Seminar Director, National Endowment for the Humanities, 1984. *Memberships:* American Musicological Society; International Musicological Society; Music Library Association; National Academy of Recording Arts and Sciences. *Address:* School of Music, Indiana University, Bloomington, IN 47405, USA.

BROWN Christopher Roland, b. 17 June 1943, Tunbridge Wells, Kent, England. Composer. m. (1) Anne Smillie, 29 Mar 1969, 1 son, 1 daughter, (2) Fiona Caithness, 28 Dec 1985, 1 son. *Education:* Westminster Abbey Choir School, 1952-57; Dean Close School, Cheltenham, 1957-62; King's College, Cambridge, 1962-65, BA 1965, MA, 1968; Royal Academy of Music, London, 1965-67; Hochschule für Musik, Berlin, 1967-68. *Career:* Freelance Composer, 1968-; Member, Professorial Staff, Royal Academy of Music, 1969-; Conductor, Huntingdonshire Philharmonic, 1976-91; Composer in Residence, Nene College, Northampton, 1986-88; Conductor, Dorset Bach Cantata Club, 1988-. *Compositions:* Regularly performed worldwide including: Soliloquy, voice & orchestra; Triptych; The Sun: Rising; Organ Concerto; Festive Prelude; Festival Variations; 4 Operas; 2 String Quartets; Chamber Music (5 Instruments); Images; Ruscelli d'oro; La Légende de L'Etoile; Choral Works include: David; A Hymn to the Holy Innocents; Three Medieval Lyrics; Magnificat; Chauntecleer; The Vision of Saul; The Snows of Winter; Hodie Salvator Apparuit; Tres Cantus Sacri; Landscapes; The Circling Year; numerous songs, carols, church music; Mass for 4 voices, 1991; Christmas Cantata, 1992. *Recordings:* Laudate Dominum, Dean Close School Choir; Laudate Dominum, Canterbury Cathedral Choir; Images, Brass Unlimited; A-Courting We Will Go, Livingstone and Mackie; British Chamber Choir: Seascape, Elegy, Lands. *Publications:* Numerous. *Memberships:* Association of Professional Composers; Composers Guild of Great Britain; RAM Club. *Hobbies:* Photography; Games; DIY; Opera; Walking; Making Music. *Current management:* J & W Chester Limited, London. *Address:* 6 Station Road, Catworth, Huntingdon, Cambs, England.

BROWN David, b. 8 July 1929, Gravesend, Kent, England. Professor of Musicology, Southampton University; University Teacher; Writer on Music; Broadcaster. m. Elizabeth Valentine, 24 Dec. 1953, 2 daughters. *Education:* Sheffield University, 1947-52, BA, 1950, BMus, 1951, DipEd, 1952, MA, 1960; PhD, Southampton University, 1971; LTCL. *Career:* Schoolmaster, 1954-59; Music Librarian, London University, 1959-62; Lecturer in Music, Southampton University, 1962-; Professor of Musicology, 1983-89. *Publications:* Thomas Weelkes 1969; Mikhail Glinka, 1973; John Wilbye, 1974; Tchaikovsky, 4 volumes, Vol 1 1840-74, 1978, Vol 2 1874-78, 1982, Vol 3 1878-85, 1986; Vol 4 1885-93, 1991; Tchaikovsky

Remembered, 1993. *Contributions to:* Music and Letters; Musical Times; Music Review; Monthly Musical Record; Listener; Survey. *Honour:* Derek Allen Prize of the British Academy (for Tchaikovsky Vol 2), 1982; Yorkshire Post Music Book Award (for Tchaikovsky Vol 4), 1991. *Memberships:* Royal Musical Association; Royal Society of Arts; Member of Editorial Committee of Musica Britannica. *Hobby:* Walking. *Address:* Braishfield Lodge West, Braishfield, Romsey, Hampshire, SO51 0PS, England.

BROWN Earle, b. 26 Dec 1926, Lunenburg, Massachusetts, USA. Composer. *Education:* Studied at the Schillinger House School of Music, Boston (1946-50) and with Rosalyn Brogue Henning. *Career:* Worked with John Cage on magnetic tape music project in New York, 1952-55; Commissions from Pierre Boulez, Merce Cunningham, Luigi Nono, Lukas Foss and the Rome Radio Orchestra; Teacher at Cologne Conservatory 1966; Guest professor at Basle Conservatory 1975; Visiting Professor at UCLA 1978; Composer-in-residence at the California Institute of the Arts 1974-83. *Compositions:* Perspectives for Piano 1952; Folio 1952-53; 25 Pages, for any number of pianos 1953; Octet I for tapes 1953; Indices for chamber orchestra 1954; Pentathis for ensemble 1957; Hodograph for ensemble 1959; Available Forms 1961; Light Music 1961; Available Forms II for 98 musicians and 2 conductors 1962; Corroboree for 3 pianos 1964; String Quartet 1965; Chef d'Orchestre/Calder Piece 1967; Syntagam for 8 instruments 1970; New Piece Loops 1971; Time Spans for Orchestra 1972; Sign Sounds for ensemble 1972; Centring for violin and ensemble 1973; Cross Sections and Color Fields for orchestra 1975; Patchen for chorus and orchestra 1979; Windsor Jambs for soprano and chamber orchestra; Folio II 1981; Sounder Rounds for orchestra 1982; Tracer for ensemble and 4-track tape 1984. *Honours include:* Guggenheim Fellowship 1965-66; National Institute of Arts and Letters Award 1972; Brandeis University Creative Arts Award 1977. *Address:* c/o ASCAP, ASCAP Building, One Lincoln Plaza, New York, NY 10023; USA.

BROWN Francis, b. 28 Oct 1925, New York, USA. m. Composer; Pianist. m. Mary Gifford, 8 Apr 1983. *Education:* Mannes Music School; Eastman School of Music, 1942-47; Degrees in Piano and Composition. *Compositions:* Have written for film, theatre and ballet as well as operas; The Highboy, opera in two acts; The Jumblies and the Dong with the Luminous Nose, for chorus, soloists chamber group and jazz quintet. *Recordings:* Many songs. *Honours:* Fulbright Scholarship, 1952-53, to study with Lugi Dallapiccola in Florence, Italy. *Memberships:* BMI; American Composers Alliance. *Address:* 15 Maunsel Street, London SW1P 2QL, England.

BROWN Howard Mayer, b. 13 Apr 1930, Los Angeles, California, USA. Professor of Music. *Education:* BA, 1951, MA, 1954, PhD, 1959, Harvard University, USA. *Career:* Instructor, Wellesley College, Wellesley, Massachusetts, USA, 1958-60; King Edward Professor of Music, Kings College, University of London, England, 1972-74; Assistant Associate, then Full Professor, 1960-76, Ferdinand Schevill Distinguished Service Professor, 1976-, University of Chicago, USA. *Publications:* Music in French Secular Theatre, 1400-1550, 1963; Instrumental Music Printed Before 1600, 1965; Music in the Renaissance, 1976; A Florentine Chansonnier From The Time of Lorenzo the Magnificent, 1983. *Contributions to:* Journal of the American Musicological Society; Early Music; The New Grove Dictionary. Fellowships: Naumberg Fellowship, 1951-53; Guggenheim Fellowship, 1963-64; Fellow, Villa I Tatti, Florence, 1969-70; Fellow, American Academy of Arts and Sciences, 1980-. *Memberships:* American Musicological Society, (President, 1978-80); International Musicological Society, (Vice-President, 1982-87). *Honour:* Awarded Galileo Galilez Prize by University of Pisa, 1987, for contribution to the Study of Italian Culture; DMus (hon), Bates College Lewiston, Maine, 1989. *Address:* 1415 East 54th Street, Chicago, IL 60615, USA.

BROWN Iona, b. 7 Jan 1941, Salisbury, Wiltshire, England. Violinist; Conductor. *Education:* Studied in Rome, Brussels, Vienna and Paris, notably with Henryk Szeryng. *Career:* Member of the London Philharmonic Orchestra 1963-66; Solo career from 1966; Violinist and conductor with the Academy of St Martin in the Fields from 1974; Artistic Director of the Norwegian Chamber Orchestra 1981; Director of the City of Birmingham Symphony with reduced size forces 1985; Artistic Director of the Los Angeles Chamber Orchestra 1987-; Played the Beethoven Concerto at the 1988 Schleswig-Holstein Festival; Directed the Norwegian Chamber Orchestra at the 1991 Promenade Concerts: Britten Frank Bridge Variations, Strauss Metamorphosen and the Haffner Serenade. *Recordings include:* CDs with the Academy of St Martin in the Fields of The Lark Ascending by Vaughan Williams and Mozart's Haffner Serenade (as soloist); Poulenc's Organ Concerto and 19th Century Guitar Concertos (as conductor). *Address:* Academy of St Martin in the Fields, 109 Boundary Road, London NW8 0RG, England.

BROWN John, b. 1943, Yorkshire, England. Violinist. *Education:* Royal Manchester College of Music, with Endre Wolf and Gyorgy Pauk, and at Salzburg Mozarteum. *Career:* Co-leader, London Symphony Orchestra, 1968, Leader, 1973; Leader of the Orchestra of the Royal Opera House, Covent Garden, from 1976; Solo appearances with the BBC Scottish, BBC Symphony and London Symphony Orchestras; Plays a Stradivarius violin. *Honours include:* Prizewinner of the 1966 BBC Violin Competition; Order of the British Empire, 1987. *Address:* c/o Royal Opera House, Covent Garden, London WC2, England.

BROWN Rayner, b. 23 Feb 1912, Des Moines, Iowa, USA. Organist; Teacher; Composer. *Education:* BMus 1938, MMus 1947, University of Southern California, Los Angeles; Studied with Ingolf Dahl, Hanns Eisler and Lucien Cailliet. *Career:* Organist, Wilshire Presbyterian Church, Los Angeles, 1941-77; Professor of Music, Biola University, California, 1950-77; Biola University, Professor Emeritus, 1977-; American Guild of Organists, Dean of Los Angeles Chapter, 1961-63. *Compositions:* Orchestral: 6 symphonies: 1952, 1957, 1958, 1980, 1982, 1982; Variations on a Hymn, 1957; 7 organ concertos: 1959, 1966, 1980, 1982, 1983, 1986; Concerto for Organ and Band, 1960; Sinfonietta for Band, 1963; Prelude and Fugue for Brass and Percussion, 1963; Fantasy-Fugue for Brass and Percussion, 1965; Concertino for Piano and Band, 1966; Concerto for 2 Organs, Brass and Percussion, 1967; Symphony for Clarinet Choir, 1968; Concerto for 2 Pianos, Brass and Percussion, 1971; Sinfonietta for Trombone Choir, 1976; Prelude and Fugue for Piano and Clarinet Choir, 1976; Concerto for Clarinet and Wind Orchestra, 1979; Concerto for Flute and Wind Orchestra, 1980; Concerto for Bass Trombone and Wind Orchestra, 1981; Clarinet Concerto, 1984; Concerto for Violin, Harp and Orchestra, 1987; Chamber: 3 sonatas for Flute and Piano, 1944, 1959, 1985; Quartet for Violin, Viola, Cello and Piano, 1947; 3 Fugues for 5 Flutes, 1952; String Quartet, 1953; 4 brass quintets, 1957, 1960, 1981, 1985; Trio for Flute, Clarinet and Viola, 1958; Flute Sonatina, 1961; Concerto for Harp and Brass Quintet, 1962; Variations for Piano and Brass Quintet, 1972; Scherzi for 4 Trombones, 1973; Sonata for Violin and Piano, 1977; Sonata for 2 Bassoons, 1977; Divertimento for Piano 4-hands and Woodwinds, 1978; Sonata for Flute and Clarinet, 1979; Sonata for 6 Trombones, 1980; Tuba Quartet, 1980; Symphony for Flutes, 1983; Sonata for Violin and Harp, 1986; Piano pieces; Concerto for Organ Duet and Orchestra, 1989; Sonata for English Horn and Organ, 1989; Many organ works including 20 sonatas, 1958-87; 35 sonatinas, 1945-80; Sonata for Harp and Organ, 1990; Adagio for organ, Four volumes, 1992; Zymbojk for organ, Two volumes, 1992; pieces for organ and other instruments including sonatas; Several choral works; Owlish Nocturnes for piano, 1992; Cnatata, True Simplicity, 1992. *Honours:* Annual awards, Society of Composers, Authors and Publishers, 1965-. *Memberships:* American Guild of Organists; Society of Composers,

Authors and Publishers. *Address:* 2423 Panorama Terrace, Los Angeles, CA 90039, USA.

BROWN Robert Stephen, b. 11 Feb 1952, Cookeville, Tennessee, USA. Managing Director of Opera Centre. m. Susan Johnson Morse, 24 July 1982, 1 daughter. *Education:* BS, Music Education (Composition and Piano), Tennessee Technological University, Cookeville, 1977; MM, Theory, Opera Conducting, Western Michigan University, Kalamazoo, 1977; Postgraduate study in Opera Stage Direction, School of Music, Indiana University, Bloomington, 1977. *Career:* Freelance director of musical theatre, 1977-; Production Stage Manager and Assistant Director: Fort Worth Opera, 1978-80; New Orleans Opera, 1978-79; San Diego Opera, 1979-81, 1983; Assistant Director and Stage Manager: Opera Theater of St Louis, 1978; Lyric Opera of Chicago, 1980-81; Executive Stage Manager, Lyric Opera of Chicago, 1983-84; Managing Director, 1984-, Stage Director, 1985-, Lyric Opera Center for American Artists, Chicago. *Address:* 1438 Lake Avenue, Wilmette, IL 60091, USA.

BROWNE Sandra, b. 27 July 1947, Point Fortin, Trinidad, West Indies. Singer (Mezzo-Soprano). *Education:* BA Modern Languages, Vassar College, USA; Brussels Conservatory with Mina Bolotine; Royal Manchester College of Music with Frederic Cox. *Debut:* With Welsh National Opera in Nabucco, 1972. *Career:* Sang in the premiere of Alun Hoddinott's The Beach of Falseà, 1974; Kent Opera as Monteverdi's Poppea, English National Opera from 1974, as Octavian, Rosina, Monteverdi's Poppea Dido and Carmen; Guest appearances in Toulouse, Marseille, Nancy and Florence as Carmen; Verona 1978, in a revival of Vivaldi's Orlando Furioso; La Scala Milan 1981 in Ariodante; Aix-en-Provence 1983, in Mozart's Mitridate; Other engagements in Pergolesi's Adriano in Siria (Florence), Dido and Aeneas (New York City Opera), Salome (Welsh National Opera), Radamisto and Ottone (Handel Opera Society); Concerts with most leading British orchestras, and in Norway, Portugal, France, Italy, Latin America and Australia; Regular Prom concert appearances. *Recordings:* Offenbach, Robinson Crusoe; Songs by Barber and Copland; Songs by Falla, Rodrigo, Granados and Montsalvatge; Rossini, Mosè in Egitto (Philips); Albinoni, Il Nascimento dell'Aurora (Erato); Vivaldi, Serenata a tre, Mio Cor Povero Cor (Erato). *Honours:* Kathleen Ferrier Memorial Scholarship 1971; RMCM Gold Medal for Voice 1972; Nominated for Lawrence Olivier Award, 1991. *Hobbies:* Lighting Bonfires; Letter Writing; The Garden; Lying on Tropical Beaches; Good Company. *Address:* New Zealand Cottages, Barnham, Thetford, Norfolk, IP24 2PL, England.

BROWNER Alison, b. 1958, Dublin, Ireland. Singer (Mezzo-soprano). *Education:* BA, Trinity College, Dublin, 1978; Hamburg Music School and the Studio of the Bavarian State Opera, Munich with Hans Hotter. *Career:* Sang in Germany 1983-85, including a Flowermaiden at Bayreuth and Ascanius and Wellgunde at Frankfurt; Darmstadt Opera 1984-87 as Cenerentola, Dorabella, and Charlotte; Mannheim Opera from 1988 as Nicklausse, Cherubino, Rosina the Composer in Ariadne auf Naxos and Octavian; Wexford Festival 1988 as Mathurina in Don Giovanni by Gazzaniga and Adelma in Busoni's Turandot (also televised); Covent Garden debut 1989, as Angelina in La Cenerentola; Oratorio and concert performances in Germany, Spain, Holland, France, Belgium, Italy, Switzerland, Poland, Russia, Hungary and Norway; TV relay of Mozart's La Clemenza di Tito; Wexford Festival 1991, Aurelio in L'Assedio di Calais by Donizetti; Brussels Feb 1992, Rosina; Antwerp, 1991-, La Cenerentola. *Address:* Music International, 13 Ardilaun Road, London N5 2QR, England.

BROWNING John, b. 23 May 1933, Denver, Colorado, USA. Concert Pianist. *Education:* Juilliard School of Music. *Debut:* With New York Philharmonic, Carnegie Hall, New York City, 1956. *Career:* Appearances with numerous orchestras, USA Europe, USSR, Mexico; Recitalist worldwide; Pianist for World Premiere of Samuel Barber's Piano Concerto with Boston Symphony; Pianist with Cleveland Orchestra, State Department; Toured USSR, 1965. *Honours:* Hollywood Bowl Young Artists Competition Award, National Federation of Music Clubs, 1954; Edgar M Leventritt Award, 1955; Queen Elizabeth International Concours Award, 1956; Honorary DMus, Occidental College; Honorary DMus, Ithaca College. *Recordings:* The complete Piano Concertos of Prokofiev, with Erich Leinsdorf and the Boston Symphony Orchestra, and music by Mozart and Rachmaninov; 3 concert length CD's, Rachmaninov, Liszt and Mussorgsky. *Honours:* Grammy Award, Best Instrumental Soloist with Orchestra, 1992. *Current Management:* Laurence Tucker, Coloumbia Artists Management, Incorporated. *Address:* c/o Shirley Kirshblum & Associates, 711 West End Avenue, No 5KN, New York, NY 10025, USA.

BROWNRIDGE Angela Mary, b. 14 Oct 1944, North Humberside, England. Concert Pianist. m. Arthur Johnson, 12 Oct 1968, 1 s. *Education:* Piano Scholar, Edinburgh University Private study with Dorothy Hesse, Guido Agosti and Maria Curcio. *Debut:* Wigmore Hall, London, 1970. *Career:* Appearances in major London concert halls and with major orchestras in Great Britain and Abroad; Regular broadcaster for Radio 3 and stations worldwide; Extensive recital tours in this country, America, Canada, Far East and Europe. *Compositions:* Piano pieces, aged 7. *Recordings:* Solo piano repertoire by Cammilleri, Satie, Barber Tchaikovsky, Scriabin, Schumann and Gershwin; First ever complete collections of solo works by Barber and Gershwin, Barber and Satie voted Records of the month; Concerto with Royal Philharmonic companies. *Honours:* Scholarship to Edinburgh University, 1963; Tovey Prize for Performance, 1965; Frazer Scholarship, 1966; Vaughan Williams Trust Fund, 1972; Arts Council Award, 1972. *Memberships:* Incorporated Society of Musicians; Musicians Union. *Hobbies:* Skiing; Horse Riding; Keeping Fit; Gourmet Cookery. *Current Management:* Karen Durant Management. *Address:* 118 Audley Road, Hendon, London NW4 3HG, England.

BRUCE Margaret, b. 28 June 1943, Vancouver, British Columbia, Canada. Musician; Pianist. m. The Hon H.L.T. Lumley-Savile, 26 July 1972, 3 sons (triplets). *Education:* Bishop Strachan School, Toronto, Canada; ARCM (Performers and Teachers); Royal College of Music, London. *Debut:* Wigmore Hall, 1968. *Career:* Performances at Wigmore Hall, 1968, 1979; Purcell Room, 1970, 1975, 1978, 1980, 1983; Barbican, 1983, 1985; Royal Concert Huddersfield, 1982; Italian Debut, 1983; Czechoslovakian Tour, 1968, 1981; Canadian Tour, 1984, 1987, 1989; Originator new concert series at St Johns, Smith Square, London, Canadians and Classics, 1986, 1988, 1989, 1990; Many other concerts at St John's (solo, duet, etc); With Royal Philharmonic Orchestra, Barbican, 1985; Bulgarian Debut, 1992; Chomé Piano Trio Debut, Barbican; Many concerts and recordings to follow, 1993. *Compositions:* CBC Recordings, Canada, 1969, 1982, 1984. *Recordings:* Premiere recording Dvořák's From the Bohemian Forest Op 68 with Peter Gellhorn; Solo recording, 1983. *Honours:* Royal College of Music, 1962; Sir James Caird Scholarship, 1966. *Hobbies:* Learning Italian, Studying, Art History. *Current Management:* c/o Lyttelton, Via Del Pandolfini 27, Florence 50122, Italy. *Address:* 7 Denbigh Gardens, Richmond, Surrey TW10 6EN, England.

BRUCE Neely, b. 21 Jan 1944, Memphis, Tennessee, USA. Composer; Pianist; Conductor. *Education:* Studied piano with Roy McAllister at the University of Alabama; Piano and Composition studies with Sulma Stravinsky and Ben Johnson at the University of Illinois. *Career:* Teacher at Wesleyan University from 1974 and conductor of the Wesleyan Singers; Founder and director of the American Music/Theater Group; Piano performances of much American music, including the premieres of works by Cage, Duckworth and Farwell; New York debut 1968 at the Electric Circus; European debut Warsaw 1972, in songs by Ives; Directed scenes from American operas at the Holland Festival, 1982. *Memberships include:* Editorial committee New World Records, 1974-78; Chairman, New England Sacred Harp

Singing, 1976, 1979, 1982; Senior Research Fellow at the Institute for Studies in American Music at Brooklyn College, 1980. *Compositions include:* Pyramus and Thisbe, chamber opera, 1965; The Trials of Psyche, opera 1971; Americana, or, A New Tale of the Genii, opera 1983. Instrumental: Fantasy 1967; Percussion concerto 1967; Woodwind quintet 1967; Six piano sonatas 1967-73; Concerto for violin and chamber orchestra 1974. Choral; The Death of a Soldier 1969; Psalm i 1971; 3 Choruses on Poems by Herman Melville 1971; Lines Written on the Roof of 110 Thompson Street 1974; Mass Settings 1959-76; Perfumes and Meanings for 16 solo voices; Solo vocal music. *Address:* c/o ASCAP, ASCAP Building, One Lincoln Plaza, New York, NY 10023, USA.

BRUCK Charles, b. 2 May 1911, Timisora, Rumania. Conductor. *Education:* Studied in Vienna and in Paris with Valdo Perlemuter and Nadia Boulanger. Further study with Pierre Monteux. *Career:* Conducted the Cannes-Deauville Orchestra, 1949-50, Netherlands Opera, 1950-54, Strasbourg Radio Symphony Orchestra, 1955-65, ORTF Philharmonic, 1965-70; Conducted the first performance of Prokofiev's The Fiery Angel, (Paris concert, 1954) and the French premieres of Dallapiccola's Ulisse (Rouen, 1971), The Makropoulos Case, Ligeti's Requiem, Penderecki's St Luke Passion and Dies Irae, and Dallapiccola's Prigionioero; Conducted the premieres of Landowski's 3rd Symphony, Koechlin's 2nd Symphony, 1958, Jerome Bosch Symphonie by Nigg, 1960, Akrata and Nomos Gamma by Xenakis, Martinů's Juliet, 1962 and works by Ohana, Ballif, Martinet, and Tomasi; Music Director of the Pierre Monteux School for Conductors and Orchestra Musicians at Hancock, Maine, from 1970. *Address:* c/o Pierre Monteux School, PO Box 157, Hancock, ME 04640, USA.

BRUDERHANS Zdenek, b. 29 July 1934, Prague, Czechoslovakia. Flautist; University Reader. m. Eva Holubarova, 19 Apr 1962, 1 son, 1 daughter. *Education:* Bacalaureat, Akademicke Gymnasium, Prague; Distinction Diploma, Prague Conservatorium of Music; MMus, Prague Academy of Music. *Debut:* Prague, 1957. *Career:* Assistant Principal Flautist, Prague National Theatre, 1955-59; Principal Flutist, Prague Radio Symphony Orchestra, 1960-68; Flute Professor, Sweden, 1969-73; Lecturer, Senior Lecturer, Reader, Dean of Music, 1987-88, Adelaide University, South Australia, 1973-; Flute Soloist in Czechoslovakia and 12 European Countries, USA, UK, Australia and Asia on Radio and in Festivals. *Recordings:* 10 recordings including 6 LP recitals released by Supraphon, Philips, Panton, Columbia-Nippon, Connoisseur Records, World Record Club and Aquitaine of works by Bach, Mozart, Haydn, Hindemith, Martinů, Messiaen, Berio, Debussy, Varèse, Ravel, and Feld. *Contributions to:* Miscellania Musicologica; The Instrumentalist; Pan and the Flute. *Honour:* Grand Prize, International Competition of Wind Instruments, Prague Spring Festival, 1959. *Hobby:* Swimming. *Address:* 2 McLaughlan Avenue, Brighton 5048, South Australia.

BRUEGGEN Frans, b. 30 Oct 1934, Amsterdam, Netherlands. Recorder Player; Conductor; Musicologist. *Education:* Muzieklyceum Amsterdam, recorder with Kees Otten; awarded recorder diploma; Musicology at University of Amsterdam. *Career:* Many engagements as performer and conductor, in early and modern music; plays original 18th century flutes and recorders or copies; Member of various avant-garde ensembles, including SourCream, and has commissioned many works (Berio's Gesti 1966); 1972-73 Erasmus Professor of late Baroque music at Harvard University; Regent's Professor, University of California, Berkeley, 1974; Professor of recorder and early 18th century music at the Royal Conservatory, The Hague; Frequent concerts with the cellist Anner Bylsma and harpsichordist Gustav Leonhardt; From 1981 has conducted symphonic music; Founder and Conductor of the Orchestra of the Eighteenth Century (concerts with the orchestra and Malcolm Bilson for the Mozart Bicentenary 1991); Conducted Idomeneo for Netherlands Opera, 1991;

Principal Guest Conductor of the Orchestra of the Age of Enlightenment from 1992, leading Orchestra at the 1993 Promendae Concerts in Haydn's London and Beethoven's Ninth Symphonies. *Recordings include:* CDs of Mozart's Piano Concetos K466 and K491 (John Gibbons), Symphony K550 and Beethoven's 1st Symphony; Haydn Symphonies Nos 90 and 93; Rameau Suites from Dardanus and Les Boréades; Vivaldi Flute Concertos. *Publications:* Various editions of early music for Schott (London), Zen-On (Tokyo) and Broekmans & Van Poppel (Amsterdam). *Current Management:* c/o Felix Warnock. *Address:* Orchestra of the Age of Enlightenment, 26 St Anne's Court, Dean Street, London W1V 3AW, England.

BRUHN Siglind, b. 11 Oct 1951, Hamburg, Germany. Concert Pianist; Music Analyst. m. Gerhold Becker, 20 Aug 1985. *Education:* MA, Romance Literature, Philosophy, University of Munich; MA, Piano Performance, Piano Pedagogy, Musikhochschule Hamburg and Stuttgart; Master classes with Wladimir Horbowski, Hans Leygraf, Nikita Magaloff; DrPhil, Music Analysis, Musikhochschule and University of Vienna, 1985. *Debut:* 1965. *Career:* Head of Community Music School, Munich, 1978-82; Head, Institute for Musical Interpretation, 1982-87; Director, Pianists' Academy, Ansbach, 1984-87; Director of Studies, University of Hong Kong, 1987-; Guest Professor, Beijing Central Conservatory of Music, 1990; Visiting scholar, University of Michigan, Ann Arbor, (on sabbatical leave from Hong Kong University), 1993-; Performances in all major West German cities, Zurich, London, Paris, Lisbon, Venice, Athens, Beirut, Rio de Janeiro, Quito, Johannesburg, Cape Town, Hong Kong, Manila, Beijing, Shanghai, Melbourne, Adelaide; TV and radio appearances on most German stations and for British, French, Swiss, Italian, Lebanese and South African, Australian broadcasting corporations; Adjudicator Hong Kong Music Festival 1987; Taiwan International Mozart Competition 1990; Japan Mozart Competition 1991. *Recordings:* Ravel, Moussorgsky, 1984; Dvořák, 1986. *Publications:* Die Kunst musikalischer Gestaltung am Klavier, 1981; Die musikalische Darstellung psychologischer Wirklichkeit in Alban Bergs Wozzeck 1986; Guidelines to Piano Interpretation, 1989; How to Play J S Bach's Little Piano Pieces, 1990; Creative Piano Instruction for Small Children, 1992; Analysis and Interpretation in J S Bach's Well-Tempered Clavier, 1993. *Contributions to:* 10 articles to journals: Kurt Weill's Violin Concerto, 1986, Schoenberg's Wind Quintet - Analysis of the III Movement, 1987; Helmut Eder's Violin Concerto, 1988. *Hobbies:* Romance and South-East Asian languages; Travel. *Address:* The University of Hong Kong, School of Professional and Continuing Education, GPO Box 3783, Hong Kong.

BRUK Fridrich, b. 18 Sept 1937, Kharkov, Ukraine, USSR. Composer. m. Nadezhda Mislavskaya, 10 Sept 1959, 1 son. *Education:* School for Gifted Children, Kharkov; Diploma, Composition, Conservatory Rimsky-Korsakov, Leningrad, 1961. *Debut:* Opera 41, 1961. *Career:* Composer, Music for Theatre and films; popular songs/singers: Arja Saifonmaa, Eino Gron, records. *Compositions include:* String Quartet, 1983; Music for Children; Spring, 1982, Snowdrop, 1983, Sleigh Bells, 1984, Summer, 1985, Golden Autumn, 1988, Winter, 1988, Sunflecks, suite for orchestra, 1987; Five duets for clarinet (B) and violoncello or bassoon, 1983; Lyrical Images, suite for piano, 1985; Variations for Piano on the Karelian Song Strawberry, 1985; The Steppe, suite for woodwind quartet; Variations on a Finnish Shepherd's Song for Young Pianists, 1986; 7 Songs for 3 Voice choir, 1986; Concert Variations on the old Kalevala Song, for violoncello and piano, 1985; Sonata for Cantele, 1986; String Quartet N2 1987; Consertino for two violins and string orchestra 1987; Sonata for two violins, 1988; Sonata for violincello, 1989; Sonatat for two trumpets, 1989; Sonata for piano No2, 1989; Woodwind Quintet, 1989; music to 2 tv-films, 1988, 1989; Sonata for cello (I-II-III); Four pieces for flute and piano (Rose-suite). *Memberships:* Union of Soviet Composers, 1961-; Finnish Composer's Association, 1983-; Decoration of Finnish Lion Knigtage's Cross for Service, from the President of Finland. *Address:*

Nasilinnankatu 42 B 19, Tampere, 33200 Suomi, Finland.

BRUMAIRE Jacqueline, b. 5 Nov 1921, Herbley, France. Singer (Soprano). *Education:* Studied at the Paris Conservatoire. *Debut:* Paris Opéra-Comique 1946, as the Countess in Le Nozze di Figaro. *Career:* Sang in Paris as Mimi in La Bohème, Micaela, Manon, Antonia in Les Contes d'Hoffmann and Fiordiligi; Opéra-Comique 1951, in the premiere of Madame Bovary by Bondeville; Paris Opera 1962, as Donna Elvira in Don Giovanni; Visited Peking 1981, to sing Carmen. *Recordings:* Opera arias (Philips); Milhaud's Les malheurs d'Orphée and Le Pauvre Matelot; Le Roi d'Yvetot by Ibert.

BRUMBY Colin James, b. 18 June 1933, Melbourne, Victoria, Australia. Composer; Lecturer; Conductor. *Education:* Melbourne High School; BMus, 1957; DMus, 1972; Conservatorium of Music, University of Melbourne. *Career:* Lecturer in Music, Kelvin Grove Teachers College, 1960-62; Head of Music Department, Greenford Grammar School, Middlesex, 1962-64; Lecturer in Music, 1964-65; Senior Lecturer, 1966-71; Associate Professor of Music, 1976-; University of Queensland. *Compositions:* Flute Concerto; The Phoenix and The Turtle; Festival Overture On Australian Themes; Charlie Bubbles Book of Hours; Three Italian Songs for High Voice and String Quartet; Guitar Concerto; Violin Concerto 1 and 2; Piano Concerto; South Bank Overture; Symphony No 1 (The Sun); The Vision and The Gap (Cantata); Bassoon Concerto; Bassoon Sonata; Clarinet Sonatina; Flute Sonatina; Haydn Down Under (Bassoon Quintet); Victimae Paschali (SATB and Strings); Stabat Mater (Cantata); Piano Quartet; Christmas Bells, 1986; A Service of Rounds, 1985; Four Australian Christmas Carols, 1986; Operas: Fire on the wind; Summer Carol; Borromeo Suite for flute and guitar; Viola Concerto, Tre aspetti di Roma; Trumpet Concerto; Symphony No 2, Mosaics of Ravenna. *Publications:* Missa Canonica, 1991; Harlequinade, 1987; Oh Come and Worship, 1990. *Honour:* Advance Australia Award (Music), 1981. *Memberships:* University of Queensland Staff Association; Australian Performing Rights Association. *Hobbies:* Reading; Travelling; Eating. *Current Management:* Australia Music Centre, PO Box N690 Grosvenor Place, Sydney, NSW 2000, Australia. *Address:* 9 Teague Street, Indooroopilly, Queensland 4068, Australia.

BRÜN Herbert, b. 9 July 1918, Berlin, Germany. Composer; Professor of Music Composition. m. Marianne Kortner, 2 sons. *Education:* Student Composition with Stefan Wolpe, Jerusalem Conservatory of Music; Columbia University. *Career:* Faculty, University of Illinois, School of Music, Urbana, 1963-; Research in Computer Composition. *Compositions:* Mobile for Orchestra; Sonoriferous Loops; Gestures for Eleven; Non-Seguitur VI; Gesto for Piccolo and Piano; Trio for Flute, Double Bass, Percussion; Trio, Trumpet, Trombone, Percussion; Futility 1964; Mutatis Mutandis: Computer Graphics for Interpreters; Infraudibles; Nonet; Piece of Prose; Three String Quartets; With Computers: Project Sawdust 1976-81. *Recordings:* Compositions. *Publications:* Uber Musik und Zum Computer, 1971; My Words and Where I Want Them, 1986. *Address:* School of Music, University of Illinois, Urbana, IL 61801, USA.

BRUNELLE Philip, b. 1 July 1943, Minnesota, USA. Conductor; Artistic Director. m. Carolyn Olsen, 11 Sept 1965, 2 sons, 1 daughter. *Education:* University of Minnesota. *Debut:* Conducting: Europe, Aldeburgh Music Festival; Sweden, Gothenburg Opera, 1985. *Career:* Artistic Director and Founder, Plymouth Music Series of Minnesota, 1969-; Music Director, Minnesota Opera, 1968-85; Minnesota Orchestra, 1963-68; Guest Conductor of Opera and Orchestra, 1985- present thoroughout the USA and Europe; Organist, Choirmaster, Plymouth Congregational Church, Minneapolis, 1969-. *Recordings:* Virgin Classics: Paul Bunyan, Britten; The Tender Land, Copland; The Company of Heaven, Britten; Mass in D, Smyth; Te Deum and Masque of Night, Argento; Songs of a Cat, Garrison

Keilor; Soliman II, Kraus; Serenade for a Christmas Night, Susa; Pro Arte: In a Winter Garden, Larsen; CRI: Jonah and the Whale, Argento. *Publications:* Monthly column in the American Organist, 1982-; Contributions to the Musical Times. *Honours:* Kodaly medal, 1982; Stikkan Anderson Prize, 1988; Order of the Polar Star, King of Sweden, 1989; Hon PhD, St Olaf college, 1988; Gramophone Prize, Best Opera Recording, 1988; Hon PhD, Gustavus Adolphus College, 1993. *Hobbies:* Tennis; French Cooking; Hiking. *Current Management:* Norman McCann Ltd. *Address:* 4211 Glencrest Road, Golden Valley, MN 55416, USA.

BRUNNER Evelyn, b. 17 Dec 1949, Lausanne, Switzerland. Singer (Soprano). *Education:* Studied at the Lausanne Conservatory with Paul Sandoz, in Milan and with Herbert Graf in Geneva. *Career:* Sang with the Ensemble Vocal de Lausanne under Michel Corboz and with the Orchestre de Chambre de Lausanne under Victor Desrazens; Appearances at the Grand Théâtre de Genève as Micaela in Carmen, Marguerite in Faust and in Cimarosa's Il Matrimonio Segreto (1971); Sang Mozart's Countess at the Paris Opéra and in Hamburg an Berlin; Opéra du Rhin, Strasbourg, as Elsa in Lohengrin, 1986; Engagements at opera houses in Lyons, Toulouse, Avignon and Nantes; Other roles include Mozart's Fiordiligi and Donna Anna, Liu in Turandot, and Verdi's Elisabeth de Valois and Violetta; Many concerts with the Collegium Academicum de Genève. *Recordings include:* Rossini's Il Signor Bruschino, conucted by Robert Dunand. *Address:* c/o Grand Théâtre de Genève, 11 Boulevard du Théâtre, CH-1211 Geneva, Switzerland.

BRUNNER Vladislav, b. 10 Nov 1943, Brno, Czechoslovakia. Flautist. m. E Illesova, 19 Jan 1963, 2 s. *Education:* Music Conservatory, Bratislava. *Debut:* Cimarosa Flute Concerto with Philharmonic Orchestra Ostrava, 1963. *Career:* Solo Flutist Radio Symphony Orchestra Bratislava, 1963; Solo Flutist Slovak Philharmonic Orchestra, Bratislava 1977; Solo Flutist, Radio Symphony Orchestra, Frankfurt, 1978; Major Festivals include Wein, Salzburg, Prague Spring, Jerusalem, European Flutist Festival Frankfurt. *Recordings:* Flute concertos of: Stamitz, Benda, Bach, Romberg, Zimmermann, FX Richter. *Honours:* Honorable mention, Slovakian Ministry of Education; Silver Medal, International Music Competition, Geneva, 1973; Honorary Professor, Music Conservatory, Frankfurt. *Hobby:* Chess. *Current Management:* Radio Symphony Orchestra, Frankfurt. *Address:* LeerbachstraBe 120, D-6000 Frankfurt am Main 1, Germany.

BRUNO Joanna Mary, b. 1944, Orange, New Jersey, USA. Singer (Soprano). *Education:* Studied with Katherine Eastment in New Jersey, at the Juilliard School with Jennie Tourel and with Luigi Ricci in Rome. *Debut:* Spoleto Festival 1969, in The Medium by Menotti. *Career:* Sang in Santa Fe, Houston, Chicago, Fort Worth and at the City Opera, New York, notably in the 1971 premiere of Menotti's The Most Important Man; European engagements in Trieste, Paris, Amsterdam, and with Scottish Opera; Other roles include Mozart's Despina, Susanna and Pamina, Ann Trulove in The Rake's Progress, Micaela, Verdi's Nannetta and Puccini's Butterfly, Musetta and Mimi.

BRUSA Elisabetta Olga Laura, b. 3 Apr 1954, Milan, Italy. Composer; Professor. *Education:* Diploma, Composition, Conservatorio of Milan with Bruno Bettinelli & Azio Corghi, 1980; Further studies with Hans Keller, London. *Debut:* First Composition performed, Piccola Scala, 1982. *Career:* TV Programme on Young Italian Composers, 1983; Various commissions, performances; and Radio and TV broadcasts in Italy, Great Britain, USA, Australia & Albania; Professor, Composition at: Conservatorio of Vicenza, 1980-82; Conservatorio of Mantova, 1982-84; Conservatorio of Brescia, 1984-85; Conservatorio of Milan, 1985-. *Compositions include:* Belsize String Quartet; Marcia Funebre for Piano; Fables for Chamber Orchestra; Nittemero Symphony for Chamber Orchestra;

Symphony No 1 for Large Orchestra; Sonata for Piano; Sonata Rapsodica for violin and piano; La Triade for large orchestra, 1992; Firelights fort large orchestra, 1993. *Recordings:* CD with Edipan Editions. *Publisher:* Edizioni Curci, Edizioni Edipan, Casa Musicale Sonzogno. *Address:* Via Piscane 36, 20129 Milan, Italy.

BRUSCANTINI Sesto, b. 10 Dec 1919, Porto Civitanova, Macerata, Italy. Singer (Bass-Baritone). *Education:* Studied law at first then singing with Luigi Ricci in Rome. *Debut:* As Colline in La Bohème, Civitanova 1946; La Scala Milan from 1949, debut in Cimarosa's Il Matrimonio Segreto; Sang Selim opposite Maria Callas in Il Turco in Italia, Rome 1950; Glyndebourne 1951-60 as Mozart's Guglielmo, Figaro and Leporello, Rossini's Raimbaud, Dandini and Figaro, Strauss's Music Master and Verdi's Ford; US debut 1961, Chicago; At Salzburg, 1953, and Covent Garden, 1974, sang Malatesta in Don Pasquale; sang the Magistrate in Werther at Rome, 1990; Don Alfonso at the 1990 Macerata Festival; Other roles include Verdi's Falstaff, Posa, Germont, Iago, Renato and Rigoletto. *Recordings:* La Fille du Régiment, L'Elisir d'Amore and Don Pasquale (Donizetti); Le Cantatrice villane (Fioravanti); Un Giorno di Regno, La Traviata, I Masnadieri (Verdi); 2 versions of Rossini's La Cenerentola; Orlando Furioso (Vivaldi); Così fan Tutte and Le Nozze di Figaro; La Cecchina (Piccinni); Griselda (A Scarlatti). *Honours include:* Lyons Club Award 1970. *Hobbies:* Photography; Amateur Film Making. *Address:* Via dei Sansovino 6, Rome, Italy.

BRUSILOW (Brusilovsky) Anshel, b. 14 Aug 1928, Philadelphia, Pennsylvania, USA. Violinist; Conductor; Teacher. *Education:* Studied with Efrem Zimbalist, Curtis Institute of Music, Philadelphia, 1943; Jani Szanto, Diploma, Philadelphia Musical Academy, 1947; Conducting, Pierre Monteux, 1944-54. *Debut:* Violinist, Philadelphia Orchestra, 1944. *Career:* Concertmaster, New Orleans Symphony Orchestra, 1954-55; Associate Concertmaster, Cleveland Orchestra, 1955-59; Concertmaster, Philadelphia Orchestra, 1959-66; Founder-Conductor, Philadelphia Chamber Orchestra, 1961-65; Chamber Symphony of Philadelphia, 1966-68; Resident Conductor, 1970-71, Executive Director and Conductor, 1971-73, Dallas Symphony Orchestra; Teacher, Southern Methodist University, Dallas, 1982-89; College of Music, University of North Texas, 1989-. *Recordings:* Columbia; Composers Recordings Inc. *Honours:* Honorary Doctorate of Music, Capitol University, Columbus, Ohio, 1968. *Address:* College of Music, University of North Texas, Denton, TX 76203, USA.

BRUSON Renato, b. 13 Jan 1936, Este, Italy. Baritone. Studied in Padua, Italy. *Debut:* Spoleto Festival, 1961. *Career:* Has appeared at all major Italian Opera Houses including La Scala, Milan (debut 1972) specialising in Verdi and Donizetti operas eg Attila, La Traviata, La Favorita and Lucia di Lammermoor; Other opera houses include: Vienna, Hamburg, Berlin, Paris, Brussels etc; Covent Garden debut 1976, as Renato in Un Ballo in Maschera. Appearances in USA include Chicago, New York Metropolitan Opera, San Francisco; Debut as Enrico at the Metropolitan 1969; has sung at the Verona Arena 1975-76, 1978-82 and 1985; Los Angeles and Covent Garden, 1982, as Falstaff (also at Parma, 1986); Munich, 1985, as Macbeth; sang Iago at La Scala, 1987, and Don Giovanni at the Deutsche Oper Berlin, 1988; Carnegie Hall, New York, 1990, as Montfort in Les Vêpres Siciliennes; sang Carlos in Ernani at Parma, 1990, Germont at Turin and Carlos at La Fenice, Venice; Sang Enrico in Lucia di Lammermoor at La Scala, 1992; Germont at the 1992 Macerata Festival. *Recordings include:* Luisa Miller, Falstaff, Samson and Delilah etc. Films and TV: Don Carlos (La Scala), Luisa Miller (Covent Garden). *Address:* Teatro Alla Scala, Via Filodrammatici 2, Milano, Italy.

BRUYNEL Ton, b. 26 Jan 1934, Utrecht, the Netherlands. Composer. *Education:* Piano, Utrecht Conservatory. *Career:* Associated with Electronic Music Studio, University of Utrecht; Established own electronic music studio, 1957. *Compositions:* Mostly with sound tracks; Resonance I, ballet, 1960-62; Reflexes for Birma Drum, 1961; Resonance II, KXT1963; Relief for Organ, 1964; Mobile, 1965; Milieu, 1965-66; Arc for Organ, 1966-67; Mekaniek for Wind Quintet, 1967; Decor, ballet, 1967; Signs for Wind Quintet and Video Projection, 1969; Ingredients for Piano, 1970; Intra I for Bass Clarinet, 1971; Elegy for Female Voice, 1972; Looking Ears for Bass Clarinet, Grand Piano, 1972; Phases, 1974; Soft Song for Oboe, 1975; Dialogue for Bass Clarinet, 1976; Translucent I, String Quartet, 1977, Translucent II for String Orchestra, 1978; Toccare and Piano, 1979; From the Tripod for Loudspeakers, Women and Listeners, 1981; John's Lullaby for Chorus and Tape, 1985; Continuation for Chorus and Tape, 1985; Rain for four pianists on two pianos, 1982; Adieu petit prince for voice, 1983; Denk Mal das Denkmal, for man's voice, 1984; Chicharres text, 1986; Serène for flute, 1978; Toccare for Clavecimbalo, 1987; Ascolta for chorus and soloist, 1989; Nocturnes en Pedraza for flute and soundtrack, 1988; Kolom for organ, 1987; Non Sono un ucello for tenor bass baritone, La Vertigine, for bass baritone, Save the Whale, for bass contrabass clarinet, La dernière pavane for small mixed choir, 1989; La Cadulta, for tenor bass baritone, Tropico, for tenor bass baritone, 1990; Dust for small organ, 1991; Tarde, for cello, 1992; Le Jardin for alto flute, harpsichord and woman's voice, 1992. *Address:* Fen Have 13, NL 7983 KD, Wapse-Diever, Holland.

BRUZDOWICZ Joanna, b. 17 May 1943, Warsaw, Poland. Composer; Music Critic. *Education:* Piano with Irena Protasewicz and Wanda Losakiewicz; Composition with Kazimierz Sikorski, MA Warsaw Conservatory, 1966; Composition with Nadia Boulanger, Olivier Messiaen, Pierre Schaeffer, Paris, 1968-70. *Career:* Active with: Groupe de Recherches Musicales of the French Radio and Television, Paris; Groupe International de Musique Electroacoustique de Paris; IPEM; Electronic studios, University of Ghent, Belgian Radio and Television; Founder, Jeunesses Musicales of Poland; Founder-president, Frederic Chopin and Karol Szymanowski Society of Belgium; Vice-president, International Federation of Chopin Societies; Writer of music criticism; Advocate of contemporary music. *Compositions:* Operas: In der Strafkolonie or La Colonie Penitentiaire, 1972, revised 1986; Les Troyennes, 1973; The Gates of Paradise, 1987; Tides and Waves, opera-musical, 1992. Ballet: Le Petit Prince, 1976; Many film and theatre scores; Orchestral: Impressions, 1966; Suite in memoriam Serge Prokofiev, 1966-67; Eclairs, 1969; Jour d'ici et d'ailleurs for Vocal Quartet, Chorus, Speaker and Chamber Ensemble, 1971; Piano Concerto, 1974; Symphony, 1975; Violin Concerto, 1975; Aquae sextiae for Winds, 1978; Double-Bass Concerto, 1982; Chamber: Wind Quintet, 1966; Epigrams for Violin, 1966; An der Schönen Blauen Donau for 2 Pianos and Tape, 1973-74; Ette for Clarinet, 1974; Einklang for Harpsichord and Organ, 1975; Trio for Variable Instrumentation, 1975; Trio dei Due Mondi for Violin, Cello and Piano, 1980; Dum Spiro Spero for Flute and Tape, 1981; Para y contra for Double Bass and Tape, 1981; Trio per Trio for Flute, Violin and Harpsichord, 1981; Dreams and Drums for Percussionist, 1982; 2 string quartets: No 1, La Vita, 1983, No 2 with Speaker, Cantus Aeternus, 1988; Oracle for Bassoon and Tape, 1982; Urbi et Orbi, cantata for Tenor, Children's Choir, 2 Trumpets, 2 Trombones and Organ, 1985; Aurora Borealis for Harp and Organ, 1988; Piano pieces, organ music, Electronic and electroacoustic pieces. *Address:* Roelandsheide 38, B-3080 Tervuren, Belgium.

BRYAN John Howard, b. 24 Feb 1952, Ilford, Essex, England. Performer on Early Instruments; Lecturer. 1 son, 2 daughters. *Education:* BA, Honours; BPhil, University of York, 1970-74. *Debut:* 1973. *Career:* Co-director, Landini Consort; Director, Rose Consort of Viols; Artistic Advisor, York Early Music Festival; Principal Lecturer, University of Huddersfield; also plays with Consort of Musicke and Musica Antiqua of London. *Recordings:* Nowell, Landini Consort; Songs and Dances of Fourteenth Century Italy, Landini Consort; The Play of Daniel, Landini Consort and Pro Cantione Antiqua; Elizabethan Christmas Anthems, Rose Consort of Viols;

Dowland, Lachimae, Rose Consort of Viols; Born is the Babe, Ah, Dear Heart, Rose Consort of Viols. *Contributions to:* Music in Education; Compendium of Contemporary Musical Knowledge, Routledge, 1992. *Memberships:* North East Early Music Forum, National Early Music Association. *Hobbies:* Opera; Theatre; Walking.*Current Management:* Karen Durant Management. *Address:* 28 Wentworth Road, Scarcroft Hill, York, YO2 1DG, England.

BRYAN Paul Robey, b. 7 Mar 1920, Pittsburgh, Pennsylvania, USA. Musicologist; Conductor; Teacher. m. 27 Aug 1941, 1 son, 1 daughter. *Education:* BM, MusEd, 1941, MM, Theory, 1948, PhD Music, 1956, University of Michigan. *Career includes:* Conductor, Transylvania Music Camp Band/Orchestra, 1949-57, Duke University Wind Symphony, 1951-; Triangle Symphony Orchestra; Guest Conductor, Wind Bands, USA & Austria; Faculty Member, 1951-, Professor, 1975-, Duke University; Visiting Summer Professor, 1962, Theory Instructor, 1948-51, 1954-55, University of Michigan; Summer Head of Theory, Staff Conductor, 1949-57, Brevard Music Centre, North Carolina; Conductor, Board of Directors, Civic Choral Society, Durham, 1959-67; Conductor, Durham Youth Symphony, 1972-76; Conductor, Summer Sessions and Clinics; Guest Conductor, Wind Ensemble, Hochschule für Musik und Darstellende Kunst, Graz, Austria. *Publications:* The Symphonies of Johann Vanhal (Editor), 1969; Concerto for Trombone & Orchestra by Georg Christoph Wagenseil (Editor), 1969. *Contributions to:* Haydn-Studien; Das Haydn Jahrbuch; Alta Musica; Journal of Band Research (Editorial Board). *Honours:* Research Grants, Duke University, Chapelbrook Foundation, 1967-68; Silver Medal of Honour, mit Dank and Anerkennung für die Forderung der Volksmusik in Niederösstereich, 1978. *Address:* Music Department, Duke University, Box 6695, CS Durham, NC 27701, USA.

BRYARS Richard Gavin, b. 16 Jan 1943, Goole, Yorkshire, England. Composer. *Education:* BA, Honours, Philosophy, Sheffield University, 1964; Northern School of Music, 1964-66; Private Musical Composition Studies with Cyril Ramsey, 1959-61, George Linstead, 1963-66; and Benjamin Johnston, USA, 1968. *Career:* Music Master, Drax Grammar School, 1965-66; Lecturer in Liberal Studies, Northampton College of Technology, 1966-67; Lecturer in Music, Portsmouth College of Art, 1969-70; Senior Lecturer, Music, Leicester Polytechnic, 1970-83, Principal Lecturer, 1983-85, Professor of Music, De Montford University, 1985-. *Compositions:* Opera: Medea, Libretto after Euripides Les Fiancailles, 1982-84; Orchestral, Pico's Flight, 1985-86; Choral and vocal works, Ars Photographica, 1983, Effarene, 1984; Among many chamber pieces are, The Cross-Channel Ferry, 1979, Prolegomenon to Medea, 1981, 3 Studies on Medea, 1983, Les Finncailles, 1983, Eglisak, 1984-85, Hymne a la Rose, 1984, Viennese Dance No 1, 1985 String Quartet No 1, Several pieces for small ensemble include, Ponukelian Melody, 1975, My First Homage, 1978, The English Mail-Coach, 1980, Homage to Vivier, 1985; Various pieces for 2 pianos, solo instruments; By The Vaar, 1987; Invention of Tradition, 1988; Glorious Hill, 1988; Incipit Vita Nova, 1989; Cadman Requiem, 1989; there 3 for Hilliard Ensemble; Alaric I or II for saxaphone quartet, 1989; String Quartet No 2, 1990; The Black River, for organ and soprano, 1991; The Green Ray, for saxaphone and orchestra, 1991. *Recordings:* Obscure, Crepuscule, ECM, Decca, Point Music. *Publication:* Lord Berner's Exhibition Catalogue, Como, 1979. *Contributions to:* Music and Musicians; Studio International; Art and Artists; Contact. *Honour:* British Ambassador for the Foundation Erik Satie; ISCM British representation, 1977 and 1988. *Memberships:* College Pataphysique, 1974-; Oulipopo, 1974-; Association of Professional Composers, 1985-. *Current Management:* Erica Bolton and Jane Quinn Limited. *Address:* 15 Prebend Gardens, London, W4 1TN, England.

BRYDEN John, b. 16 June 1947, Edinburgh, Scotland. Pianist. m. Margaret Greenlaw, 7 Apr 1973,

2 daughters. *Education:* Emmanuel College, Cambridge, 1965-68; Piano Studies with Mary Moore, Peter Katin, Guido Agosti, and Claudio Arrau. *Debut:* Purcell Room, London, 1971. *Career:* Concerts at the Purcell Room and Wigmore Hall (London), and all over the UK as well as France and Italy; Member of the Dartington and Roxburgh Trios, (chamber music); Local TV, Radio 3 and Radio Scotland; Senior Lecturer in Music, Dartington College of Arts, 1982-91; Director of Music, St Matthias Church, Torquay. *Recordings:* Martinů Chamber Music. *Memberships:* National Youth Orchestra of Great Britain, 1963-65; ISM; EPTA. *Hobbies:* Walking; Reading. *Address:* 35 St Marychurch Road, Torquay, Devon TQ1 3JF, England

BRYDON Roderick, b. 1939, Edinburgh, Scotland. Conductor. *Education:* Daniel Stewart's College, Edinburgh; BMus Edinburgh University; Chigiana Academy, Siena. *Career:* Close association with Sadler's Wells Opera and Scottish Opera in operas by Janáček (From the House of the Dead), Stravinsky, Mozart, Puccini, Debussy and Cavalli (L'Egisto); Formerly General Music Director Lucerne Opera, conducting Carmen, Don Giovanni, Albert Herring and Fidelio; Musical Director of Berne Opera, 1988-90, leading A Village Romeo and Juliet, Capriccio and Peter Grimes; Covent Garden debut 1984, with A Midsummer Night's Dream; Guest engagements in Hannover, Copenhagen, Karlsruhe (Handel's Alcina) Bordeaux (Così fan Tutte) and Geneva (Death in Venice, The Rake's Progress and La Clemenza di Tito); Mozart's Mitridate and Rossini's Otello in Venice; Death in Venice at the 1983 Edinburgh Festival; La Traviata and The Rake's Progress with Opera North; Artistic Director of the Scottish Chamber Orchestra for the first 9 years of its existence including concerts at the Aix and Edinburgh Festivals; Promenade Concerts 1982; Further concerts in Munich, Paris and Venice; conducted Parsifal at the City Theatre Berne, 1989, concert performances of The Cunning Little Vixen, 1990; Conducted Albert Herring at Los Angeles, 1992, followed by A Midsummer Night's Dream; The Rake's Progress, at the 1992 Alderburgh Festival. *Address:* c/o Music International, 13 Ardilaun Road, London N5 2QR, England.

BRYMER Jack, b. 27 Jan 1915, South Shields, Co Durham, England. m. 21 Oct 1939, 1s. *Education:* Goldsmith's College, London; Also privately. *Debut:* BBC Recital, 1947. *Career:* Principal Clarinet, Royal Philharmonic, 1947-63; BBC Symphony, 1963-71; London Symphony, 1971-86; Member of Prometheus, Wigmore, London Baroque Ensembles; Directed London Wind Soloists. *Recordings:* Mozart Concerto; Mozart and Brahms Quintets; Siegmeister Concerto; Mozart Trio Complete wind works of Mozart, Haydn, J S Bach, Beethoven, Brahms Sonatas, Weber Duo, Stanford Sonata; Krommer Concerto, Debussy Rhapsody, Weber Concertino and Berman Adogio. *Publications:* The Clarinet; From Where I sat (autobiog); In the Orchestra (autobiog); Regular professional articles in woodwind magazines. *Honours:* OBE, 1960; Hon RAM, 1956; FGSM, 1970; FGCL, 1986; FRNCM, 1989; Hon DMus, Kingston, 1993. *Memberships:* President of ISM and CASS. *Hobbies:* Golf; Swimming; Gardening. *Address:* Underwood, Ballards Farm Road, South Croydon, Surrey CR2 7JA, England.

BRYN-JONES Delme, b. 29 March 1935, Brynamman, Wales. Singer (Baritone). m. Carolyn Bryn-Jones, 1 son, 1 daughter. *Education:* Studied at the Guidhall School of Music and at the Vienna Academy of Music. *Debut:* With the New Opera Company 1959, in The Sofa by Elizabeth Maconchy. *Career:* Sang at Covent Garden from 1963 in operas by Mozart, Verdi, Puccini, Bizet and Britten; Glyndebourne Festival 1963-64, 1972 as the Speaker in Die Zauberflöte, Nick Shadow and Macbeth; Appearances at the Aldeburgh and Edinburgh Festivals, and with the Welsh National Opera and Scottish Opera; US debut San Francisco 1967; Many engagements as concert singer; Broadcasts include British premiere of Henze's The Bassarids and 1-hour documentary on life and career by HTV, 1973. *Recordings include:* Billy Budd by Britten (Decca).

Contributions to: Artists in Wales, 1976. *Membership:* Gorsedd of Bards, Royal National Eisteddod, Wales. *Hobby:* Rugby. *Address:* 57 Elm Avenue, Eastcote, Ruislip, Middlesex HA4 8PE.

BRYN-JULSON Phyllis (Mae), b. 5 Feb 1945, Bowdon, North Dakota, USA. Singer (Soprano). *Education:* Studied singing at the Berkshire Music Center and at Syracuse University. *Debut:* With the Boston Symphony in Berg's Lulu Suite, 1966. *Career:* Has given performances of works by George Crumb, David Del Tredici, Lukas Foss, Ligeti, Berg, Webern and Schoenberg (Pierrot Lunaire); Appearances at the Berlin, Edinburgh, Lucerne and Aldeburgh Festivals; British debut 1975, in Pli selon Pli by Boulez, conducted by the composer; Boulez 60th birthday celebrations at Baden-Baden, 1985; Orchestras with whom she has appeared include the New York Philharmonic, the Boston Symphony, Chicago Symphony and the Berlin Philharmonic under Abbado; First operatic role as Malinche in Montezuma by Roger Sessions (US premiere, Boston 1976); Sang in Stravinsky's Nightingale and Ravel's L'Enfant et les Sortilèges at Covent Garden, season 1986-87; Tours of Australia, New Zealand and the USSR with Boulez and the Ensemble InterContemporain; Tours of the US with the Los Angeles Philharmonic and of Europe with the BBC Symphony; Gave master classes at the Moscow Conservatoire in 1987 and took part in the 80th birthday celebrations for Olivier Messiaen and Elliott Carter, 1988; Sang in Carter's A Mirror on Which to Dwell, at London's Elizabeth Hall, Feb. 1991. *Honours include:* Distinguished Alumni Award, Syracuse University; Amphion Foundation Award. *Recordings include:* A Mirror on which to Dwell; Le Visage Nuptial and Le Soleil des Eaux by Boulez (Erato). *Address:* c/o Ingpen and Williams Ltd, 14 Kensington Court, London W11 4PA, England.

BRYSON Roger, b. 1944, London. Singer (Bass). *Education:* Guildhall School, London; London Opera Centre with Walther Gruner and Otakar Kraus. *Career:* Glyndebourne Festival and Touring Opera from 1978 as Neptune in Il Ritorno di Ulisse, Quince and Bottom in A Midsummer Night's Dream, Osmin in Die Entführung, Rocco in Fidelio and Leporello in Don Giovanni; Kent Opera in Rigoletto, Die Zauberflöte and Don Giovanni; English National Opera in the British premiere of Ligeti's Le Grand Macabre (1982); Opera North in Die Meistersinger, Werther, La Fanciulla del West and L'Amour des Trois Oranges; Scottish Opera as Schigolch in Lulu and Don Alfonso in Così fan Tutte; Sang at Nancy in the French premiere of Tippett's King Priam and on TV in The Midsummer Marriage (1989); Alvise in La Gioconda for the Chelsea Opera Group; Mephistopheles in Faust for New Sussex Opera, 1989; Swallow in Peter Grimes Don Pasquale, for Opera North; Bartered Bride for New Tel Aviv Opera; sang in concert performances of Ligeti's Le Grand Macabre at the Festival Hall, 1989; Don Pasquale for Opera North, 1990, premiere of Europeras 3 and 4 by John Cage at the 1990 Almeida Festival, London; Quince in A Midsummer Night's Dream of Sadler's Wells; Dikoi in Katya Kabanova for Glyndebourne Touring Opera, 1992; Flint in Billy Budd, 1992; Claggart in Billy Budd for Opera de Nancy, 1993. *Address:* c/o Music International, 13 Ardilaun Road, Highbury, London N5 2QR, England.

BUCCI Mark, b. 26 Feb 1924, New York City, USA. Composer. *Education:* St John's University, New York, 1941-42; Composition with Tibor Serly, 1942-45; Frederick Jacobi and Vittorio Giannini, BS, Juilliard School of Music, New York, 1951; Aaron Copland, Berkshire Music Center, Tanglewood. *Compositions:* Operas: The Boor, 1949; The Dress, 1953; Sweet Betsy from Pike, 1953; Tale for a Deaf Ear, 1957; The Hero, 1965; Midas, 1981; Musicals: Caucasian Chalk Circle, 1948; The Thirteen Clocks, 1953; The Adamses, 1956; Time and Again, 1958; The Girl from Outside, 1959; Chain of Jade, 1960; Pink Party Dress, 1960; The Old Lady Shows Her Medals, 1960; Cheaper by the Dozen, 1961; Johnny Mishuga, 1961; Our Miss Brooks, 1961; The Best of Broadway, 1961; Ask any Girl, 1967; Second

Coming, 1976; Incidental music to several plays; Film scores; Concerto for Kazoo and Orchestra, 1959 renamed Concerto for a Singing Instrument; Flute concerto; Choral pieces; Songs. *Honours:* Piatigorsky Award, 1949; MacDowell Colony Fellowships, 1952, 1954; Guggenheim Fellowships, 1953-54 and 1957-58; National Institute of Arts and Letters grant, 1959; Co-winner, Prix Italia, 1966.

BUCHAN Cynthia, b. 1960, Edinburgh, Scotland. Singer, (Mezzo-Soprano). *Education:* Royal Scottish Academy of Music. *Career:* Has appeared widely in Britain and Europe as Mozart's Cherubino and Dorabella, Massenet's Charlotte, Rossini's Rosina, Verdi's Preziosilla, Tchaikovsky's Olga and as Carmen; 1987 in L'Enfant et les Sortilèges at Glyndebourne, Carmen for Opera North and Mistress Quickly in Peter Stein's production of Falstaff for the Welsh National Opera; Guest appearances in Madrid, Munich, Paris, Rosina, Frankfurt, (Babette in Henze's English Cat), Adelaide, Hamburg (Miranda in Cavalli's L'Ormindo) and Amsterdam, (Varvara in Katya Kabanova); Glyndebourne 1989, as Hermia in A Midsummer Night's Dream; Concert appearances in London, Munich, Zurich, Paris and Lyon; Conductors include Gielen, Andrew Davis, Rattle, Ivan Fischer, Knussen, Del Mar, Bernstein and Bertini. *Recordings include:* Video of Bersi in Andrea Chénier, Covent Garden 1985. *Address:* c/o Lies Askonas Ltd, 186 Drury Lane, London WC2B 5RY, England.

BUCHANAN Isobel Wilson, b. 15 Mar 1954, Glasgow, Scotland. Soprano. m. Jonathan King (otherwise Jonathan Hyde, actor, RSC), 1980, 1 daughter. *Education:* Cumbernauld High School; Royal Scottish Academy of Music and Drama (DRSAMD), 1974. *Debut:* Glyndebourne, 1978, as Pamina; Vienna Staatsoper, 1978, as Micaela; Santa Fe, USA, 1979, as Zerlina and Adina; Chicago, 1979; New York, 1979; Cologne, Germany, 1979; Aix-en-Provence, France; 1981. *Career:* Australian Opera Principal Singer, 1975-78; Freelance Singer, 1978-; Performances with Scottish Opera, Covent Garden, Munich Radio, Belgium, Norway, etc; Other roles include Fiordiligi, Susanna and Donna Elvira; sang Dorabella at the 1987 Glyndebourne Festival; in recent years has devoted career to concert appearances. *Recordings:* Various operatic recordings. *Hobbies:* Reading; Gardening; Cooking; Dressmaking; Knitting; Tennis. *Address:* c/o Marks Management Ltd, 14 New Burlington Street, London W1X 1FF, England.

BUCHLA Donald (Frederick), b. 17 Apr 1937, Southgate, California, USA. Electronic Instrument Designer and Builder; Composer; Performer. *Education:* BA, Physics, University of California, Berkeley, 1961. *Career:* Installed first Buchla synthesizer, San Francisco Tape Music Center, 1966; Founded, Buchla Associates, Berkeley, 1966; Designed and manufactured various electronic instruments; Designed electronic music studios including, Royal Academy of Music, Stockholm and IRCAM, Paris; Co-founder, Electric Weasel Ensemble, 1975; Co-director, Artists; Research Collective, Berkeley, 1978-. *Compositions:* Various pieces with electronic instruments including: Cicada music for some 2,500 Cicadas, 1963; 5 Video Mirrors for Audience of 1 or more, 1966; Anagnorisis for 1 Performer and 1 Voice, 1970; Harmonic Pendulum for Buchla Series 200 Synthesizer, 1972; Garden for 3 Performers and 1 Dancer, 1975; Keyboard Encounter for 2 Pianos, 1976; Q for 14 Instruments, 1979; Silicon Cello for Amplified Cello, 1979; Consensus Conduction for Buchla Series 300 Synthesizer and Audience, 1981. *Honours:* Guggenheim Fellowship, 1978; National Ednowment for the Arts grant, 1981. *Address:* Music Department, University of Southern California, Berkeley, California, USA.

BUCHNER Eberhard, b. 6 Nov 1939, Dresden, Germany. Singer (Tenor). *Education:* Studied at the Carl Maria von Weber-Musikhochschule, Dresden, 1959-64. *Debut:* Schwerin 1964, as Tamino. *Career:* Staatsoper Dresden from 1966, Staatsoper Berlin from 1968, notably in operas by Strauss, Mozart and Wagner; Sang

Schubert's Die schöne Mullerin in Vienna, 1972; Appeared at the Vatican, 1973, in a concert conducted by Bernstein; Metropolitan Opera, 1974, Covent Garden, 1975; Hamburg Staatsoper, 1983, in a revival of Amadis de Gaule by J C Bach; Théâtre de la Monnaie, Brussels, and Salzburg Festival, 1985, 1990, as Flamand in Capriccio; Royal Opera Copenhagen, 1986, as Wagner's Lohengrin; Adolar in Euryanthe at the Berlin Staatsoper, 1986; La Scala Milan, 1988, as Erik in Der fliegende Holländer; sang Lohengrin at Lisbon, 1990. *Recordings:* Die schweigsame Frau by Strauss (EMI); Froh in Das Rheingold (Eurodisc); Bach Cantatas (Deutsche Grammophon); B Minor Mass by Bach; Sacred music by Mozart (Philips); Beethoven's 9th Symphony (Capriccio).

BUCHT Gunnar, b. 5 Aug 1927, Stocksund, Sweden. Composer. m. Bergljot Krohn, 12 Apr 1958. *Education:* PhD Musicology; Studied Composition with Karl Birger, Blomdahl, Carl Orff, Geoffredo Petrassi, Max Deutsch, Piano with Yngve Flyckt. *Debut:* Composer and Pianist, 1949. *Career:* Teacher, Stockholm University, 1965-69, cultural attache to the Swedish Embassy at Bonn, 1970-73; Professor of Composition, Stockholm Musikhögskolan, 1975-85, Director, 1987-93. *Compositions:* Opera, The pretenders, after Ibsen, 1966; Opera-Oratorio, The Walls of Jericho, 1967; 10 Symphonies, 1952-93; 2 Cello Concertos, 1955-90; Symphonic Fantasy for Orchestra, 1955; Divertimento 1956; The Day Cools for Soprano and Orchestra, 1956; La fine della diaspora for tenor, chorus and orchestra, 1957; Lutheran mass, 1973; Violin concerto, 1978; En Clairobscur for chamber orchestra, 1981; Tönend bewegte Formen for orchestra, 1987; Chamber music including String Quintet, 1950, 2 String Quartets, 1951, 1959, Sonata for piano and percussion 1955, Symphonie pour la musique libérée for tape, 1969, Blad Från mitt gulsippeänge for clarinet and piano, 1985; Unter Vollem Einsatz for organ and 5 percussion 1987. *Recordings:* Symphony 7, Violin concerto, cantata, Quatre pièces pour le pianiste. *Publications:* Electronic Music in Sweden, 1977; Contributor to the Swedish Journal of Musicology. *Honours:* Litteris et artibus, Royal Medal. *Membership:* Royal Academy of Music. *Address:* Burge Hablingbo, S62011, Havdhem, Sweden.

BUCK Peter, b. 18 May 1937, Stuttgart, Germany. Cellist. *Education:* Stuttgart Conservatory, with Ludwig Hoelscher. *Career:* Former member of Karl Munchinger's Stuttgart Chamber Orchestra in Heilbronn; Co-Founder, Melos Quarter of Stuttgart, 1965; Represented Germany at the Jeunesses Musicales, Paris, 1966; International concert tours from 1967: Bicentenary concerts in the Beethoven Haus at Bonn, 1970; Toured the USSR, Eastern Europe, Africa, North and South America, the Far East and Australia; British concerts and festival appearances from 1974; Cycle of Beethoven quartets at Edinburgh Festival, 1987; Wigmore Hall, St John's Smith Square and Bath Festival, 1990; Associations with Rostropovith in the Schubert Quintet and the Cleveland Quartet in works by Sophr, and Mendelssohn; Teacher at the Stuttgart Musikhochschule. *Recordings include:* Complete quartets of Beethoven, Schubert, Mozart and Brahms; Quintets by Boccherini with Narcisco Ypes and by Mozart with Franz Beyer. *Honours include:* Grand Prix du Disque and Prix Caecilia, from Academie du disque in Brussels, (with Melos Quartet). *Address:* Melos Quartet, c/o Ingpen & Williams Ltd, 14 Kensington Court, London W8 5DN, England.

BUCKEL Ursula, b. 11 Feb 1926, Lauscha, Germany. Singer (Soprano); Teacher. *Education:* Studied with Hans Hoefflin in Freiburg and with Ria Ginster in Zurich. *Career:* Sang in Bach's Johannes Passion at Kreuzlingen, Switzerland; Based in Geneva from 1954; Many performances of cantatas and Passions by Bach, notably at the Bach-Festwochen at Schaffhausen and Ansbach; Tours of Switzerland, England, Finland, Austria, France, Germany and Italy; Far East tour with the Deutsche Bach-Solisten under the direction of Helmut Winschermann; Further tours to Athens and to Israel; Performances of music by Frank Martin;

Teacher of Voice at the Geneva Conservatory from 1971. *Recordings:* Mendelssohn's Elijah (Vox); Bach Cantatas (Deutsche Grammophon); Christmas Oratorio by Schütz; L'Incoronazione di Poppea by Monteverdi (Vox).

BUCKLEY Richard (Edward), b. 1 Sept 1953, New York City, USA. Conductor. *Education:* BM, North Carolina School of the Arts, Winston-Salem, 1973; MMus, Catholic University of America, Washington, DC, 1974; Aspen (Colo) School of Music, 1974; Salzburg Mozarteum, 1977. *Career:* Assistant conductor and chorusmaster, Washington (DC) Opera Society, 1973-74; Assistant Associate, Resident, Principal Guest Conductor, Seattle Opera, 1974-75; Music assistant to Conductor, Seattle Symphony Orchestra, 1974-84; Music Director, Oakland (Calif) Symphony Orchestra, 1983-86; Guest Conductor, New York Philharmonic Orchestra; Philadelphia Orchestra; Houston Symphony Orchestra; San Antonio Symphony Orchestra; Oregon Symphony Orchestra; Los Angeles Philharmonic Orchestra; Minnesota Orchestra; Indianapolis Symphony Orchestra; BBC Symphony Orchestra; Royal Philharmonic Orchestra; Royal Liverpool Philharmonic Orchestra; Chicago Lyric Opera; Los Angeles Opera; New York City Opera; Houston Grand Opera; Canadian Opera; Netherlands Opera; Hamburg State Opera; Recent operatic premieres include Paulus's The Postman always Rings Twice with Miami Opera and The Woodlanders at St Louis; US premiere of Sallinen's The King Goes Forth to France for Santa Fe Opera; other projects include Les Contes d'Hoffmann with Los Angeles Music Center Opera, Aida at Chicago and Rossini's Il Viaggio a Reims at St Louis; conducted Il Barbiere di Siviglia for Miami Opera 1990, Dvořák's The Devil and Kate at St Louis. *Honours:* Prize winner, Besançon Competition, 1979; Rupert Foundation Competition, 1982. *Address:* c/o Herbert Barrett Management Inc, 1776 Broadway, New York, NY 10019, USA.

BUCQUET Marie-Francoise, b. 28 Oct 1937, Montvilliers, France. Pianist; Teacher. *Education:* Studied at the Vienna Music Academy, the Paris Conservatoire and with Wilhelm Kempff, Alfred Brendel and Leon Fleisher. *Debut:* Marguerite Long school, 1948. *Career:* Attended course by Eduard Steuermann at Salzburg, to study the music of Schoenberg, and followed courses by Pierre Boulez at Basle; Sylvano Bussotti, Betsy Jolas and Iannis Xenakis have written for her; Performs Bach, Haydn, Stockhausen, Schoenberg and standard repertory music; Professor of accompaniment at the Paris Conservatoire from 1986. *Address:* c/o Conservatoire National Superieur de Musique, 14 Rue de Madrid, 75008 Paris, France.

BUCZEK (BUCZKÓWNA) Barbara Kazimiera Zofia, b. 9 Jan 1940, Cracow, Poland. Composer. *Education:* Secondary School of Music, Cracow (Secondary School Certificate with distinction, 1959, piano studies with Maria Bilińska-Riegerowa); State College of Music, Cracow, Piano under L. Stefański, Diploma, 1965, Composition under Bogusław Schaeffer, Diploma with distinction, 1974. *Debut:* Performance of Anekumena, Warsaw, 1975. *Career:* Major premieres: Warsaw, 1975; Cracow, 1980; Danzig, 1984; Rome, 1984; Basel, 1984; Salzburg, 1985; Vienna, 1985; Cracow, 1985; Radio Uno, Italy, 1986; Cracow, 1989; Teacher, Music Academy, Cracow, 1972-. *Compositions include:* 2 Impressions, for orchestra; Labyrinth, for orchestra; Anekumena, concerto; Assemblage, alto flute, string orchestra; Concerto for Violin and Orchestra, (also recorded Radio Uno, Italy); Concerto for Cello, Choir and Orchestra; Sextet; Duodecet; Hipostaza; Désunion; Motet; Transgressio, string quartet; primus inter pares; Eidos I for Violin, II for Tuba, III for Bassoon; Vocal Concerto for 12 Solo Voices; Fantasmagorie for Orchestra, 1989, (also 3-part recorded Polskie Nagrania MUZA SK 1314); Music for G Zechberger, 1991. *Recordings:* Transgressio, string quartet - recorded Polskie Nagrania. *Publications:* Wielość Jednośé w Muzyce Sakralnej B Schaeffera; Obeność kompozytora w Tworzonych Przez Niego Dzielach Muzycznych; Uwagi o Warsztacie stwolczesnego kompozytora. *Contributions* to: Artur Malawski: A Drama of Unfulfilment; Of the Way of Existence of a Musical Work; Contemporary Musical Creative Works in the View of Meeting with Art; Bogusław Schaeffer's Creative Works; Polnische, zeitgenössische Komponistin EWA SYNOWIEC - ihre Tätigkeit und Werke; Analyse eigenes Streichquartetts Transgressio. Honours: Award, Fitelberg Composers' Competition, Katowice, 1970; Distinction, Young Composers' Competition, 1976 Warsaw; Distinction, Composers' Competition, Łancut, 1980; Distinction, Concorso Internazionale Niccolo Paganini, Rome, 1982; Award, Internationaler Kompositionswettbewerb, Vienna, 1985; Gold Cross of Merit for 20 years' distinguished service in the field of education, 1985. Memberships: Artistic Society Cracow Group, Art Gallery Krzysztofory; Polish Composers' Union; Internationaler Arbeitskreis Frau und Musik. Hobbies: Nature; Excursions; especially in mountains; Literature; Philosophy of art. Address: Brodowicza 22 m 1, 31-518 Cracow, Poland.

BUCZYNSKI Walter, b. 17 Dec 1933, Toronto, Canada. Composer; Pianist. Education: Studied Composition with Milhaud, 1956, and Nadia Boulanger, 1960-62, Toronto Conservatory. Career: Taught piano and theory at the Royal Conservatory of Toronto, 1962, theory at the University of Toronto from 1970. Compositions include: Children's operas Mr Rhinoceros and his Musicians, 1957 and Do Re Mi, 1967; From the Buczynski Book of the Dea, chamber opera, 1975; Naked at the Opera, 1979; Piano Tri, 1954; Suite for wind Quintet, 1955; Divertimento for violin, cello, clarinet and bassoon, 1957; Squares in a Circle for flute, violin, cello and strings, 1967; Four movements for piano and strings, 1969; Zeroing In, 5 pieces for various vocal and instrumental groups, 1971-72; Three Against Many for flute, clarinet, bassoon and orchestra 1973; Concerto for violin, cello and orchestra, 1975; Olympics '75 for brass quintet: Piano Concerto 1979; Piano Quintet, 1984; The August Collection, 27 preludes, 1987; Litanies for accordian and percussion, 1988; Songs and Piano Music. Address: c/o SOCAN (Canada), PRS Ltd Member Registration, 29/33 Berners Street, London W1P 4AA, England.

BUDAI Livia, b. 23 Jun 1950, Esztergom, Hungary. Singer (Mezzo-Soprano). Education: Franz Liszt Academy Budapest with Olga Revheggi. Debut: Sofia 1973, as Carmen. Career: Member, Hungarian State Opera, 1973-77; Concert appearances with the Hungarian Philharmonic and on Budapest Radio; Guest engagements in Austria, Bulgaria, Finland, France, Germany and the Soviet Union; Member of Gelsenkirchen Opera, 1977; Covent Garden debut, 1978, as Azucena; returned for Eboli in Don Carlos, 1983; US debut San Francisco, 1979, as Eboli; Munich Staatsoper from 1980; Bologna, 1983, as Brangaene in Tristan und Isolde; Appearances in Berlin, Brussels, Vienna, Barcelona, Florence and Madrid as Elisabetta in Maria Sturda, Marguerite in The Damnation of Faust, Wagner's Venus and Fricka, and Verdi's Amneris, Preziosilla and Azucena; Other roles include Gluck's Orfeo, Saint-Saëns's Dalila, Bartók's Judith and the Composer in Ariadne auf Naxos; Aix-en-Provence 1987, as Mistress Quickly, Marseilles 1989, as Cassandre in Les Troyen's; sang Amneris at Bonn 1990, Ortrud at Brussels, and the Princess in Adriana Lecouvreur for L'Opéra de Montréal; Appeared as Marfa in Dvořák's Dimitrij at Munich, 1992; Kundry in Parsifal with RAI at Turin, 1992. Recordings: Cavalleria Rusticana; Liszt's Saint Elizabeth, Stabat Mater and Lange mala umbrae terrores. Address: Ingpen and Williams Ltd, 14 Kensington Court, London W8 5DN, England.

BUDD Harold, b. 24 May 1936, Los Angeles, California, USA. Composer. m. Paula Katzman, 26 June 1960, 2 sons. Education: Los Angeles City College, 1957-59; BA, San Fernando State College, 1963; MM, University of Southern California, 1966. Career: Composition Faculty, California Institute of the Arts, 1971-76. Compositions and Recordings: The Pavilion of Dreams, 1978, Obscure Records/Editions EG; The Plateaux of Mirror (with Brian Eno), 1980, Editions EG;

The Serpent (In Quicksilver), 1981, Cantil Records; The Pearl (with Brian Eno, 1984, Editions EG; Abandoned Cities 1984, Cantil Records; The Moon and the Melodies (with The Cocteau Twins), 1986, 4AD Records; Lovely Thunder 1986, Editions EG; The White Arcades (Opal/ Warner Brothers). Honours: National Endowment for the Arts Composer Fellowship, 1974, 1979. Current Management: Opal Limited, 330 Harrow Road, London W9 2HP. Address: c/o Opal Limited, 330 Harrow Road, London W9 2HP, England.

BUDDEN Julian, b. 9 Apr 1924, Hoylake, Merseyside, England. Musicologist; BBC Producer. Education: MA (Oxon), Queen's College, Oxford, 1942-43; Royal College of Music, London, 1948-50; BMus (London); FBA, 1987. Career: Music Library Clerk, BBC Radio, 1951, became successively Music Presentation Assistant, 1955, Music Producer 1956, Chief Producer Opera, 1970, External Services Music Organiser, 1976, Retired 1983. Publications: The Operas of Verdi, Volume 1, 1973, Volume 2, 1978, Volume 3, 1981; Verdi (The Master Musicians), 1984. Contributions to: Numerous professional journals including Music and Letters; Musical Times; The Listener. Honours: Yorkshire Post Award for best Music Book, 1979; British Academy Derek Allen Prize for work on Verdi, 1980; Premio Diego Fabbri, 1989; OBE, 1991. Membership: Editorial Committee, Critical Edition of the Works of G Verdi. Address: 94 Station Road, Finchley, London N3 2SG, England.

BUFKENS Roland, b. 26 Apr 1936, Ronse, Belgium. Tenor; Singing Professor. m. Simone Deboelpaepe, 25 Apr 1961, 1 daughter. Education: Brussels Conservatoire; Proficiency course in Germany under Clemens Glettenberg. Debut: In Germany. Career: German concerts specializing in Bach tradition and also the St John and St Matthew Passion; Performances with several German Orchestras conducted by Kurt Thomas, Karl Richter, Kurt Redel, Nikolaus Harnoncourt; International career, the heights of which are a performance of Berlioz's Romeo and Juliet in a tour throughout Japan and later in Paris's Théâtre des Champs Elysées, both conducted by Lorin Maazel; Other performances include Stravinsky's Mavra in the Concertgebouw of Amsterdam, Martin's Mystère de la Nativité, Madrid; All these performances were broadcast; Manuel de Falla's Vida Breve conducted by R F de Burgos in Brussels; Participated several times in The Holland Festival, Biennale of Zagreb, Festival of Lourdes, Schwetzinger Festspiele, Festival van Vlaanderen; Professor at Brussels Conservatoire and Lemmens Institute, Leuven. Recordings: Works of Schubert, Grétry, Gossec, Lully, Schütz, Bach, Dumont, Carl Orff, and compositions by Belgian composers Andre Laporte and Willem Kersters. Contributor to: Lemmensinstitute Adem; Articles for Dutch Singers Association ANZ. Honours: First Prize at Brussels Conservatoire, 1959; Chevalier de l'Ordre de la Couronne, 1978; Cecilia Prize Belgium in 1974 for Zemire et Azor, F M Grétry. Hobbies: Connoisseur of Wines; Travelling; Economics. Address: 25 Avenue Georges Leclerq, 1080 Brussels, Belgium.

BUGHICI Dumitru, b. 14 Nov 1921, Iasi, Rumania. Composer; Teacher. Education: Studied with Salmanov, Iasi Conservatory; Schnitke, Leningrad Conservatory, 1950-55. Career: Faculty member, Bucharest Conservatory. Compositions: Orchestral: Symphonies: Simfonie-Poem, 1961; Simfonie coregrafica, 1964, revised 1967; No 3, Ecouri de jazz, 1965-66; Simfonia 1907, 1975-76; Simfonia Bucegilor, 1978-79; Simfonie-balet: Elamuri tineresti, 1983; Simfonie lirico-dramatica-In memoriam for String Orchestra, 1984; Simfonia Romantica, 1984-85; Simfonia aspiratillor, 1985; 2 violin concertos, 1955, 1977; Evocare-Donca Simo, 1956; Poem concertant for Cello and Orchestra, 1957; sinfoniettas: Simfonieta tinertii, 1958; Simfonetia II: Cosmica, 1962; Muzica de concert-Simfonieta III, 1969; Simfonieta for Chamber Orchestra, 1979; 4 Tablouri coregrafice, 1959; Filimon Sarbu, 1959; Poemul primaverii for Violin and Orchestra, 1960; Poemul bucuriei, 1962; Bolero, 1963; Monumentul,

1964; Partita, 1965; Dialoguri dramatice for Flute and String Orchestra, 1967; Omagiu, 1967; Balada concertanta for Violin and Orchestra, 1969; Sonata for String Orchestra, 1979-70; Melodie, Ritm, Culoare, concerto for Orchestra, 1970; Sinfonietta da camera, 1970; Poem iubirii, 1971; File de letopiset, 1970-71; Symphonic Fantasia in Jazz Rhythm, 1973-74; Cello Concerto, 1974; Trumpet Concerto, 1975; 5 Images for Chamber Orchestra, 1976; Tablouri coregrafice, 1978; Sinfonie concertanta No 1, 1979-80 and 2, 1980-81; Jazz Concerto, 1982-83; Chamber: Suite for Violin and Piano, 1953; Scherzo for Cello and Piano, 1954; 5 string quartets, 1954, 1968, 1971, 1976-77, 1978-79; Fantasia for Trumpet and Piano, 1960; Divertimento for Violin, Cello and Piano, 1961; Violin Sonata, 1963; Small Divertissement for Violin, Viola, Cello, Piano, Clarinet and Percussion, 1967; Sonata for Solo Violin, 1968; Fantasia Quartet, 1969; Miniatures for Brass Quintet, 1975; Trio No 2 for Violin, Cello and Piano, 1977; Fantasy for Xylophone and Double Base, 1980; Piano pieces.

BUHLER Philippe Henri, b. 15 May 1919, Lausanne, Switzerland. Composer; Choral Conductor. m. Colette Jeanne Darolle, 5 May 1945, 4 daughters. *Education:* Diploma, Piano, Harmony, Mulhouse Conservatory, 1938; Bachelor's degree, University of Strasbourg, 1939; BM, 1955, MM, 1956, Composition, Universities of Redlands & Southern California, USA. *Career:* Choral Director, Teacher, Mulhouse, France; Teacher: Music, French, Daycroft School, Stamford, Connecticut, USA, 1949-51; Music, French, Desert Sun School, Idyllwild, California, 1951-58; History of Music, Peninsula College, Monterey, California, 1958-61; Music, Gavilan College, Gilroy, California, 1962-65; Professor, Composition, Director, Camerata Singers, North Carolina School of the Arts, Winston Salem, 1965-71; Professor, Music, Colleges de Saussure, Sismondi, Geneva, 1971-84; Composer, Conductor, many concerts, Switzerland, 1971-91; Director: various choirs & choruses, 1973-93; Vocal ensemble for Aucassin & Nicolette, 1989-91. *Compositions include:* Concertino pour piano et orchestre, 1956; Symphony in E, 1962; A Symphonic Essay, 1962; Orchestrographie, orchestra, piano, percussions, 1970; Sonate pour Deux Pianos, 1970; Psaume 148, choir, brass, percussions, 1989; Quatuor pour divers instruments, 1989; Prelude et Allegro, piano, 1989; Dessine moi... un Village, choral suite, 1990; Pot-Pourri du 700eme, choir, 1990; Aucassin et Nicolette, medieval play, solos, ancient instruments, electronic sounds, narrator, 1991. *Recordings:* Symphonic Essay, American League Orchestra, 1960; Six Short Stories for piano, pianist Daisy Bacca, CD, Radio Chablais, 1989; Dors ma colombe, Alsatian Christmas carol, Noels populaires. *Contributions to:* American Choral Directors Association review; A Choeur Joie choral review, Lyon, France. *Honours:* Cadman Scholarship, Composition, 1955-56; Prize-winning composition performed by NCSA Piedmont Orchestra, 1968-69. *Memberships:* American Choral Directors Association; ACJ choral movement, Switzerland & France; International Society of Music Composers. *Hobbies:* Hiking in the mountains; Photography; Travel. *Address:* Route Foule 4, CH-1315 La Sarraz, Switzerland.

BUJARSKI Zbigniew, b. 21 Aug 1933, Muszyna, Poland. composer. *Education:* Studies with Wiechowicz (composition) and Wodiczko (conducting) at the Krakow State college of Music. *Compositions include:* Burning Bushes for soprano and chamber ensemble, 1958; Triptych for string orchestra and percussion 1959; Synchrony I for soprano and chamber ensemble, 1959, and II for soprano, chorus and orchestra, 1960; Zones for chamber ensemble, 1961; Kinoth for orchestra 1963; Chamber Composition for voice and ensemble, 1963; Contraria for Orchestra, 1965; El Hombre vocal soloists, chorus and orchestra, 1969-73; Musica Domestica for 18 strings 1977; Concert for Strings, 1979; Similis Greco, Symphonic cycle, 1979-83; Quartet on the Advent, 1984; Quartet for the Resurrection 1990. *Address:* ZAIKS (Poland), c/o PRS Ltd Member Registration, 29/33 Berners Street, London W1P 4AA, England.

BUJIC Bojan, b. 6 Oct 1937, Sarajevo, Yugoslavia. Musicologist. m. Alison Warwick, 30 June 1979, 1 son, 1 daughter. *Education:* BA English Literature, 1961, BA Musicology, Sarajevo University, Yugoslavia; DPhil, Music, Lincoln College, Oxford University, England, 1967. *Career:* Lecturer in History of Music, Sarajevo Academy of Music, 1968-69; Lecturer in Music, Reading University, England, 1969-78; University Lecturer in Music, Fellow of Magdalen College, Oxford, 1978-; Visiting Fellow, The Society for the Humanities, Cornell University, Ithaca, New York, USA, 1971. *Publications:* Music in European Thought 1851-1912 (Cambridge University Press, 1988). *Contributions to:* Acta Musicologica; Arti Musices; The British Journal of Aesthetics; Erasmus; International Review of the Aesthetics and Sociology of Music; Music and Letters; Early Music History; The Italianist; The New Grove Dictionary; The New Oxford Companion to Music. *Memberships:* Royal Musical Association; British Society of Aesthetics. *Hobbies:* Travel; Photography. *Address:* Magdalen College, Oxford, England.

BUKETOFF Igor, b. 29 May 1915, Hartford, Connecticut, USA. Conductor. *Education:* University of Kansas, 1931-32; BS 1935, MS 1941, Juilliard School of Music, New York; Los Angeles Conservatory. *Career:* Music director, Chautauqua Opera, 1941-47; New York Philharmonic Young People's Concerts, 1948-53; Fort Wayne Philharmonic, 1948-66; Iceland Symphony Orchestra, 1964-65; St Paul (Minnesota) Opera, 1968-74; Texas Chamber Orchestra, 1980-81; Teacher, Juilliard school of Music, 1935-45; Chautauqua School of Music, 1941-47; Columbia University, 1943-47; Butler University, 1953-63; University of Houston, 1977-79; Founder, World Music Bank for International Exchange and Promotion of Contemporary Music, 1957; Director, Contemporary Composers Project, Institute of International Education, 1967-70; conducted the premiere of Rachmaninov's fragmentary opera Mona Vanna, Saratoga Arts Center 1984, with the Philadelphia Orchestra. *Recordings:* Various contemporary works for Composers Recordings Inc; Murray Hill; RCA-Victor; Turnabout. *Honours:* First Alice M Ditson Award for Young Conductors, 1942; Honorary Doctorate, Los Angeles Conservatory. *Address:* c/o Philadelphia Orchestra, Academy of Music, 1420 Locust Street, Suite 400, PA 19102, USA.

BUKOWSKI Miroslaw Andrzej, b. 5 Jan 1936, Warsaw, Poland. Composer; Conductor. m. Hanna Burzynska, 20 Aug 1966, 1 daughter. *Education:* MA, Composition, Academy of Music, Poznan, 1959; MA, Conducting, Academy of Music at Gdansk and Poznan, 1963. *Debut:* Polish Students' Music Festival in Poznan, 1957. *Career:* Assistant, 1963-67, Lecturer, 1967-80, Assistant Professor, 1980-88, Professor, 1988-, Accademy of Music, Poznan; Professor, Pedagogical College in Zielena Gora, 1984-; Conductor, Wielkopolska Symphony Orchestra, 1971-75. *Compositions:* Requiem (based on Akhmatova's poem) for solo voices, mixed choir and orchestra; Pastourelle, Interferances - for symphony orchestra; Concerto for cello and orchestra; Ostinato and Mobile for percussion ensemble; Swinging Concerto, Symphonic Allegro, for symphony orchestra; 3 piano sonatas, sonatina for piano, Expression for piano; Three Sleepy Poems for mixed choir and others. *Memberships:* Association of Polish Composers; Authors' Assoiaction ZAIKS. *Hobbies:* Tinkering; Travel. *Address:* Osiedle Pod Lipami 5/182, 61-632 Poznan, Poland.

BULJUBAŠIĆ Mileva, b. 17 Aug 1937, Sarajevo, Yugoslavia. Singer (Soprano). *Education:* Studies in Sarajevo, Italy and Austria. *Career:* Features as Concert Artist, since 1960-; Stage Career from 1970, with guest appearances in Italy, Germany, England, Russia, Japan and Czechoslovakia; Member of the Deutsche Oper am Rhein, Dusseldorf, from 1979; Sang at Seattle 1975; Roles have included Butterfly, Mimi, Marenka in the Bartered bride, Rusalka, Beethovens's Leonore and Verdi's Amelia (Ballo in maschera) and Trovatore Leonora. *Address:* Sertoriusring 7, 55126 Mainz, Germany.

BULKA Antonia b. 15 Oct 1944, West Bohemia. m. 26 Aug 1967, 1 d. *Education:* High School for Musical Instrument Production and Technology, AMATI Kraslice; Music Conservatory. *Debut:* As Composer, Czech Radio Musical Contest, 1974. *Career:* Recording Director, Czech Radio; Conductor, Pilsen Big Band Orchestra; Professor of Music Theory, Folk Art School. *Compositions:* Brass Music compositions in the area of East-West Folk Music. *Recordings:* Number of works recorded by Czech Radio-TV. *Publications:* Editor, Monitor, Mosch Musik Verlag, Cinerec, Ewoton, Sonoton, Roba, Music Verlag; Numerous songs and compositions. *Honours:* Nominated composer for the 150 anniversary celebrations, Luxembourg; Czech Radio Contest, First Place for Arrangement and 4th Place as Composer. *Memberships:* OSA Prague Society of Authors and Composers; West Bohemia Music Center of Composers, Chairman of the Brass Music Section, 1990-91. *Hobbies:* Out Door Actitivites. *Address:* 31812 Pizen, Vojanova 13, Czechoslovakia.

BULL Edvard Hagerup, b. 10 June 1922, Bergen, Norway. Composer. m. Anna Kvarme, 1955, 2 daughters. *Education:* Examination, Oslo University, 1944; Organ Diploma, Oslo Conservatory, 1947, studying Organ, Composition, Piano, with Sandvold, Irgens Jensen, Brustad, Riefling, Wester; Pupil of Charles koechlin, 1947-49; Composition with Darius Milhaud and Jean Rivier, Analysis with Olivier Messiaen, Diploma, Prize for Musical Composition, Conservatoire National Supérieur de Musique, Paris, 1948-53; Pupil of Boris Blacher and Josef Rufer, Hochschule für Musik, Berlin, 1958-60. *Debut:* Philharmonic Orchestra, Paris. *Career:* Formerly Teacher of Theory, Oslo Klaverakademi and Oslo Musikkonservatorium; Performances in over 30 countries; Many commissions, French Radio and Television, Ministry of Culture, Quatuor Instrumental de Paris, Ensemble Moderne de Paris, Trio Daraux de Paris, Quatuor des Clarinettes de Belgique, Norske Blåse-kvintett. *Compositions:* Numerous including: 5 symphonies, 1955, 1958, 1963-64, 1968, 1972: 6 concertos, 2 for trumpet and orchestra, 1950, 1960, for trombone and chamber orchestra, 1957, for flute and chamber orchestra, 1969, for alto saxophone and orchestra, 1980, for tuba and orchestra, 1992; Other orchestral works; Operas in 1-act: Le Jeu du Feu, 1974; Lamentation pour un Cygne Maudit, Hommage a Israel, 1972-77; Ballets: Le Soldat de Plomb, 1949; Portrait Münchhausen, 1961; Chamber and instrumental works; Vocal works. *Address:* Kringsjavn 6, 1342 Jar, Norway.

BULL Storm, b. 13 Oct 1913, Chicago, Illinois, USA. Professor of Music; Pianist; Musicologist. m. Ellen Cross, 6 Oct 1939, 2 sons, 1 daughter. *Education:* American Conservatory of Music, 1919-31; Chicago Musical College, summers, 1927, 1928, 1930; Sorbonne, Paris, 1931-32; Ecole Normale de Musique, Paris, 1931-32; University of Budapest, Hungary, 1933-35; Liszt Academy of Music, Budapest, 1932-35; Student of Bartók, Percy Grainger, Lazare Levy, Louise Robyn. *Debut:* Soloist, Oslo Philharmonic, 1929; Town Hall, New York, 1939. *Career:* Concert Pianist, 1935-42; Soloist with New York, Chicago, Montreal, Detroit and other synmphonies; US Navy, 1942-45; Assistant Professor of Piano, Baylor University, Texas, 1945-47; Professor of Music, Head of Division of Piano, 1947-77, Visiting Professor of Music, autumn semesters, 1977-83, Professor of Music Emeritus, 1977-, College of Music, University of Colorado, Boulder. *Publications include:* Index to Biographies of Contemporary Composers, 1964, Volume II, 1974, Volume III, 1987; North American Editor: Musikens Verden, Oslo, 1951, revised edition, 1963; Special Consultant, J S Bach, for New Century Cyclopedia of Music, 1954, 3 volumes. *Contributions:* Numerous articles in professional and literary periodicals. *Honours:* Fulbright Guest Professor of Musicology, University of Oslo, Norway, 1956-57. *Memberships:* Member and Officer, several professional organisations. *Hobbies:* Amateur radio; Photography; Golf; Outdoor sports and activities. *Address:* 324 Granite Drive, Sunshine Canyon, Boulder, CO 80302, USA.

BULLER John, b. 7 Feb 1927, London, England. Composer. *Education:* Studied with Anthony Milner from 1959; BMus London University, 1964. *Career:* Joined the McNaughten Concerts Committee, 1965, (Chairman 1971-72); Gained attention in 1970s with series of works based on Finnegans Wake; Proenca and The Theatre of Memory commissioned by the BBC, Promenade Concerts 1977 and 1981; Composer-in-residence University of Edinburgh, 1975-76; Composer-in-residence at Queens University Belfast, 1985-86. *Compositions:* The Cave for ensemble, 1970; 2 Night Pieces from Finnegans Wake for soprano and ensemble, 1970; Scribenery for solo cello, 1970; The Melian Debate for tenor, baritone and ensemble, 1971; Finnegan's Floras for chorus, percussion and piano, 1972; Poor Jenny for flute and percussion, 1973; Le Terraze for 14 instruments and tape, 1974; Familiar for string quartet, 1974; The Mime of Mick, Nick and The Maggies for soprano, tenor, baritone, chorus and orchestra, 1975-76; Proenca for mezzo, electric guitar and orchestra, 1977; Sette Spazi for 2 clarinets, violin, cello and piano, 1978; Music for Film: Correction Please (Arts Council), 1979; The Theatre of Memory for orchestra, 1980-81; Kommos (Aeschylus) for chorus, solists and electronics, 1981; Of Three Shakespeare Sonnets for mezzo, flute, clarinet, harp and string quartet, 1983; Towards Aquarius for 15 players and tape, 1983; A la fontana, for Hilliard Ensemble, 1983; Opera: BAKXAI for English National Opera, 1991-92; Bacchae Metres, BBC Proms, 1993; Mr Purcell's Maggot, for Spitalfields Festival, 1994. *Recordings:* Unicorn Aanchana: Proença, The Theatre of Memory. *Honours include:* Arts Council Bursary 1978; Proenca and The Theatre of Memory selected by the International Rostrum of Composers, Paris. *Membership:* Association of Professional Composers. *Address:* c/o Oxford University Press, Music Department, Walton Street, Oxford OX2 6DP, England.

BUMBRY Grace, b. 4 Jan 1937, St Louis, Missouri, USA. Singer (Soprano and Mezzo-Soprano). *Education:* Boston University; Nortwestern University; Music Academy of the West (under Lotte Lehmann); Paris with Pierre Bernac. *Debut:* Paris Opera, 1960, as Amneris in Aida. *Career:* Sang at the Stadttheater Basle until 1964; Bayreuth Festival, 1961-63, as Venus in Tannhäuser; Brussels Opera, 1961, Carmen; Chicago Lyric Opera, 1963, Ulrica in Un Ballo in Maschera; Covent Garden from 1963, as Eboli, Amneris, Salome and Tosca; Salzburg Festival, 1964-67, Lady Macbeth and Carmen; Metropolitan Opera debut 1965, as Eboli: later sang in New York as Carmen, Tosca, Venus, Gioconda and Gershwin's Bess from 1970: Has sung soprano roles from 1970: Elisabeth de Valois, Santuzza (Vienna 1970), Jenůfa (La Scala 1974) and Ariane in Ariane et Barbe-Bleue by Dukas (Paris Opera 1975); Other mezzo roles include Fricka, Azucena, Orpheus and Dalila; Appearances in Frankfurt, Budapest, Lisbon, Munich, Hamburg and Verona; sang Aida at Luxor and Massenet's Herodiade at Nice, 1987; Marseilles, 1989, as Didon in Les Troyens; sang Cassandre at the opening of the Opéra Bastille, Paris, 1990; Arena di Verona, 1990, as Carmen. *Recordings include:* Israel in Egypt (Westminster); Messiah, Don Carlos (Decca); Tannhäuser (Philips); Aida (RCA); Film of Carmen, 1968. *Honours include:* Richard Wagner Medal, 1963; Honorary Doctorates from Rust College, Holy Spring, Mississippi; Rockhurst College, Kansas City; University of Missouri at St Louis. *Hobbies:* Tennis; Sewing; Body Building; Entertaining. *Address:* c/o Bruce Zemsky, Columbia Artists Management, 165 West 57th Street, New York, NY 10019, USA.

BUNDSCHUH Eva-Maria, b. 16 Oct 1941, Brunswick, Germany. Singer. *Education:* Studied in Chemitz and Leipzig. *Debut:* Bernburg 1967, as Humperdinck's Hansel. *Career:* Sang at Chemnitz, 1969-74, Potsdam, 1974-77; Associated with the Staatsoper Berlin from 1976, the Komische Oper from 1981; Sang first as mezzo, as Dorabella, Carmen and Eboli then soprano repertory from 1978; Olympia and Antonia in Les Contes d'Hoffmann, Wagner's Eva and Freia, Violetta, Mussetta and Donna Anna; recent Berlin Staatsoper roles have included the title part in the premiere of Judith by Siegfried Matthus, 1985, Jenůfa, 1986, and Isolde, 1988; Komische Oper, 1987-88, as Donna Anna and Dalome; Bayreuth Festival, 1988, as Gutrune; further engagements at Amsterdam, Salzburg, Wiesbaden, Bucharest and Moscow; Sang Chrysothemis in a new production of Elektra for Welsh National Opera, 1992. *Address:* c/o Welsh National Opera (Contracts), John Street, Cardiff, Wales CF1 4SP.

BUNIN Victor Vladimirovich, b. 2 Mar 1936, Voroezh, USSR. Pianist; Professor of Music; Writer on Music. m. Svetlana Eruhimovna Beskina, 7 Feb 1958, 1 son. *Education:* Student, 1956-61, postgraduate, 1961-64, Moscow Conservatoire; Study with S E Feinberg and V K Merzhanov. *Career:* Regular appearances with Moscow and provincial orchestras, including Moscow Philharmonic Orchestra, Soviet TV and Radio Large Symphony Orchestra; Participated in: 3 films, Union-TV; Several TV concert programmes; Many radio recordings for Radio Fund, 1967-. *Recordings:* 12 albums including Rubinstein's Concerto No 4, EMI, 1978, 1st performance of A N Alexandrov's Concerto-Symphony, 1981; Feinberg's original compositions, Organisation of his former students, double record, 1981; Feinberg's transcriptions of J S Bach, double record, 1986. *Publications:* Pedagogic Principles of S E Feinberg. *Current management:* Souz-Conzert, Moscow Music Association. *Address:* Prospekt Mira 116 B, apt 105, Moscow 12926, Russia.

BURA Corina, b. 15 Feb 1948, Cluj, Romania. Violinist, Professor. m. Mihai Constantinescu, 17 Apr 1981. *Education:* Bachelorship: Lyceum Emil Racovitza, Cluj, 1967, and Music Lyceum, Cluj, 1967; Diploma, Conservatory of Music, Bucharest, 1973. *Debut:* Soloist with The Philharmonia, Cluj, 1967. *Career:* Recitals and Concerts with Philharmonics in Romania; Recitals in West Germany and GDR; TV Appearances; Radio Recordings: Bach, Handel, Telemann, Corelli, Pergolesi, Rameau, Tchaikovsky, Paganini, Szymanowsky, Bartók and Romanian Music. *Recordings:* 2 Records of Handel. *Contributions to:* Studies About Modern Music and Aesthetics, published in The Conservatory's Publications. *Honours:* Diploma of Chief Promotion of The Music Lyceum, 1965, 1966, 1967; Diploma of Chief Promotion of The Conservatory of Bucharest, 1972. *Membership:* The Professoral Association of The Conservatory of Bucharest. *Hobbies:* Literature; Theatre; Plastic Arts; Animals. *Address:* Str Ecaterina Teodoroiu No 17, 78108 Bucharest I, Romania.

BURCHINAL Frederick, b. 7 Dec 1948, Wichita, Kansas, USA. Singer (Baritone). *Education:* Studied at the Empoira State University and the Juilliard School. *Career:* Worked with the Metropolitan Opera Studio and made European debut in Floyd's of Mice and Men, at Amsterdam, 1976; Sang Scrooge in the 1979 premiere of Musgrave's A Christmas Carol, Virginia Opera; New York City Opera-State Theater, 1978-1988; Metropolitan Opera from 1988, as Macbeth and Rigoletto; Other US appearances for the San Francisco Opera, Miami, Houston, New Orleans and San Diego Opera; Deutsche Oper am Rhein, Dusseldorf from 1988; Title role in Simon Boccanegra with the Cologne Opera, 1990; Has also sung in London, Zürich, Berlin, Frankfurt; Other roles include Rossini's Figaro, Iago, Jack Rance, Tonio, Di Luna, Scarpia, Falstaff and Nick Shadow; Sang Posa in Don Carlos at Düsseldorf, 1991. *Address:* c/o Metropolitan Opera, Lincoln Center, New York, NY 10023, USA.

BURCHULADZE Paata, b. 12 Feb 1951, Tblisi, USSR. Singer (Bass). *Education:* Studied at the Tblisi Conservatory. *Debut:* Tblisi, 1975, as Mephistopheles in Faust. *Career:* Sang in Russia and Milan; Studied further in Italy and began international career after winning competitions 1981-82; Roles include Basilio in Il Barbiere di Siviglia, Leporello, King Rene in Iolanta, Gremin in Eugene Onegin and Boris Godunov; Guest appearacns at the Bolshoy, Moscow; British debut 1983 at the Lichfield Festival, in The Dream of Gerontius by Elgar; Covent Garden debut 1984, as Ramfis in Aida; Salzburg Festival appearances as the Commendatore

in Don Giovanni, conducted by Karajan; sang Rossini's Basilio at the Metropolitan, 1989 and Khan Konchak in a new Production of Prince Igor at Covent Garden, 1990; Boris Godunov in a revival of Mussorgsky's Opera, 1991; the Inquisitor in Prokofiev's The Fiery Angel, 1992. *Recordings include:* Scenes from operas by Mussorgsky and Verdi (Decca); Don Giovanni (Deutsche Grammophon); Fiesco in Simon Boccanegra (Decca); Sparafucile in Rigoletto (Muti); Ramfis in Aida (Maazel); Samson et Dalila (C Davis). *Current Management:* Artist Management International. *Address:* c/o 12/13 Richmond Buildings, London, W1V 5AF, England.

BURDA Pavel, b. 7 Apr 1942, Bohemian Budweis, Czech Republic. University Professor; Conductor; Timpanist; Percussionist. *Education:* Graduate Diploma, Prague Conservatory of Music; MMus, State University of New York, USA; Postgraduate studies, State Academy of Music, Hamburg, Federal Republic of Germany. *Career includes:* Performances in major European cities; Toured Eastern and Western Europe and North Africa; Solo Timpanist with Brazilian Symphony Orchestra, Rio de Janeiro; Principal Timpanist/Percussionist with Orchestra Da Camera, New York; Solo Timpanist with Casals Festival Orchestra and Puerto Rico Symphony Orchestra in San Juan; Conducting includes various ensembles in San Juan, Europe, New York, Milwaukee; Developed The Music-with-Percussion Ensemble, University of Wisconsin-Milwaukee; Founded The Milwaukee 20th Century Ensemble, 1979; TV and radio broadcasts. *Recordings:* Several for major record companies and several films. *Honour:* The Fromm Tanglewood Fellowship, 1970. *Membership:* American Federation of Musicians. *Hobby:* Travel. *Address:* 3003 North Farwell Avenue, Milwaukee, WI 53211, USA.

BUREAU Karen, b. 3 Feb 1951, Glen Ellyn, Illinois, USA. Singer (Soprano). *Education:* Studied at York College, Pennsylvania and at Metropolitan Opera School. *Debut:* Metropolitan, in Macbeth, 1982. *Career:* Sang in various American theatres and in West Germany, 1982- 85; Member of the Hannover Staatstheater from 1985; Roles have included Beethoven's Leonore, Reizia in Oberon, Wagner's Senta, Freia, Elsa and Elisabeth; Leonaor (La Forza del Destino), Maddalena in Andrea (Chenier and Andromache in Reimann's Troades; sang Gutrune at Seattle, 1984-88, Brunnhilde in a new production of Der Ring des Nibelungen at Hannover, 1991-93; Guest Appearances at the Deutsche Oper Berlin, the Staatsoper Berlin, and in Dortmund, Stuttgart, and Victoria, (Australia); Concerts in Hamburg, Barcelona, Toronto and Hong Kong; British debut with the BBC Philharmonic conducted by Jean-Claude Casadesus, 1991. *Address:* c/o Niedersachsische Staatstheater, Opernplatz 1, 3000 Hannover, Germany.

BURGANGER Judith Treer, b. Buffalo, New York, USA. Concert Pianist; Professor of Music. m. 3 daughters. *Education:* Artist Diploma 1961, Graduate Certificate (MM) 1965, State Conservatory of Music, Stuttgart, Germany. *Career:* Early performances 1946-60: Solo recital, debut Buffalo; Orchestral debut, Amherst Symphony; Soloist with: Buffalo Philharmonic, Toronto Symphony, National Symphony, (Washington DC), Marlboro Festival (Vermont). Later performances 1960: Soloist, symphony orchestras throughout USA, Germany, Austria, Netherlands, Scandinavia, Italy, Switzerland, Japan; Conductors include Steinberg, Previn, Commissiona, Dixon, Fiedler, Krips, Solti, Haitink, Tilson-Thomas, Conlon, Akiyama; International guest performances, chamber music; Teaching: Artist Teacher, Cleveland Institute of Music; Associate Professor, Artist-in-Residence, Texas Tech University; Artist Teacher, Carnegie-Mellon University; Associate Professor 1980, Professor 1984-, Florida Atlantic University; Created a Brahms Festival which runs annually; all Chamber Music compositions and works for 4 hand at 1 piano and songs are to be performed. *Address:* Music Department, College of Liberal Arts, Florida Atlantic University, Davie, FL 33314, USA.

BURGER Ernst Manfred, b. 26 Mar 1937, Munich,

Germany. Pianist; Writer on Music; leading researcher for Chopin and Liszt. m. Dorothea Maillinger, 20 Sept 1972, 1 son. *Education:* Liberal Arts High School; Staatliche Hochschule für Musik, Munich; Künstlerische Staatsprüfung, 1964, Paedagogische Staatspruefung 1965. *Publications:* Franz Liszt, A Chronicle of His Life in Pictures and Documents (Munich 1986, Paris 1988, New York 1989); Frédéric Chopin, A Chronicle of His Life in Pictures and Documents (Munich 1990); Carl Tausig (Bonn 1990). *Contributions to:* Die Musik in Geschichte und Gegenwart (MGG); Commentaries for recorded music. *Honours:* Grand Prix de Littérature Musicale, 1988; Order Merite en faveur de la culture polonaise, 1991. *Hobbies:* Reading; Museums; Skiing; Tennis. *Address:* Erhardtstr 6, 80469 München, Germany.

BURGESS Brio, b. 27 Apr 1943, San Francisco, California, USA. Composer; Dramatist. *Education:* Self taught on Recorder, Guitar, Piano, Clarinet and other instruments. *Career:* 3 performances of Sir Real is Blue, Mostly Flowers Gallery, San Francisco, 1973; Selections from Briomindsound included in television show of Voyager II's trip to Saturn, 1980-81; Compositions broadcast on radio in USA, Australia and Netherlands; Live performance of Zen Meditations on electric guitar, State University of NY, Albany, 1987. *Compositions:* Suite for Picasso; Escape, ballet for piano, harp, feet and chains; Girl on a Ball, Childrens Dance and Toys, piano tunes; Sound Dreams, piano music; Space Visions, including The Painter's Song; Hippy Children's Concentration Camp Blues, piano, harp and words; Recordings on tape; Clear, 1978; Briomindsound, 1979; Ulyses Dog No 9, 1980; Gathered Hear, 1980; Still, 1981; Ringade, 1982; Grate, 1982; Ether, 1983; Zen Meditations, 1987. *Contributions to:* The New Penguin Dictionary of Music; The New Penguin Dictionary of Musical Performers. *Address:* c/o ASCAP, ASCAP Building, One Lincoln Plaza, New York, NY 10023, USA.

BURGESS Grayston, b. 7 Apr 1932, Cheriton, Kent, England. Conductor, Countertenor. m. Katherine Mary Bryan, 3 daughters. *Education:* MA King's College, Cambridge. *Career:* Sang with Westminster Abbey Choir, 1955-69; Sang Oberon in Britten's A Midsummer Night's Dream at Covent Garden; Dowland TV programme; Performances with Handel Opera Society and at the Henry Wood Promenade Concerts; Numerous Radio Broadcasts; Founded and directed the Purcell Consort of Voices 1963; Debut as conductor at the 1963 Aldeburgh Festival; Concerts and recordings with the Purcell Instrumental Ensemble, the Elizabeth Consort of Viols, Musica Reservata, the London Sackbut Ensemble, the Philip Jones Brass Ensemble and the Jaye Consort of Viols. *Recordings include:* Josquin's Deploration sur le morte de Johan, Dunstable's Laudi, Ockeghem's Vive le Roy and Ave Maria, Machaut's La Messe de Notre Dame; William Byrd church Music and St Matthew Passion by Richard Davy; Music by Schütz, Schein and Scheidt; Doulce Memoire: 16th Century French Chansons; English Madrigals from the Reign of Queen Elizabeth; English Secular Music of the Late Renaissance; The Eton Choir Book; The Triumphs of Oriana; High Renaissance Music in England.

BURGESS Sally, b. 9 Oct 1953, Durban, South Africa. Singer (Mezzo-Soprano). *Education:* Royal College of Music, with Hervey Alan and Marion Studholm. *Career:* Engaged by English National Opera and sang Zerlina (Don Giovanni), Cherubino, Pamina, Mimi, Micaela, the Composer in Ariadne, Massenet's Charlotte and Mrs Thatcher as Public Opinion in David Poutney's production of Orpheus in the Underworld; Covent Garden debut 1983, as Siebel in Faust; Glyndebourne 1983, in The Love of Three Oranges; 1985 in Cavalli's Eritrea for the Camden Festival; Sang Carmen in a new production by English National Opera 1986; Amneris for Opera North; Other roles include Sextus in Julius Caesar and Orlofski in Die Fledermaus; sang Minerva in The Return of Ulysses at the London Coliseum, 1989; Julie La Verne in Show Boat for RSC/ Opera North (Gluck's Orpheus 1990, Carmen 1991); Fricka in Die Walküre for Scottish Opera, 1991; Annius

in La Clemenza di Tito for Scottish Opera, 1992; sang Judith in a new production of Duke Bluebeard's Castle at the Coliseum, 1991; Sang in the premiere of Paul McCartney's Liverpool Oratorio, written by Carl Davis; Sang Carmen at Bregenz, 1991-92, and at the London Coliseum, 1993; engaged to sing Dalila at Nantes, 1994; Concert appearances in Beethoven's 9th with the Philharmonia, Mozart's C Minor Mass with Charles Mackerras and Handel's Solomon in Stockholm; Wigmore Hall debut 1978; Concerts with the Songmakers' Almanac and performances of Schoenberg's Pierrot Lunaire; Carmen, Portland, Oregan, USA, 1993; Octavian, Der Rosekavalier, ENO, 1994; Delilah, Nante Opera, 1994; Azucena, Il Trovatore, Opera North, 1994; Carmen, New Zealand Opera, 1994; Forthcoming: Carmen (Metropolitan Opera, USA); Forthcoming: The Voyage of Philip Glass (Metropolitan Opera, USA). *Recordings:* Handel's Saul and Alexander's Feast (EMI); Gluck's Armide; Il Barbiere di Siviglia (Phonogram); Mendelssohn's Hymn of Praise, conducted by Chailly; Berlins Songs of Sunset (Chandos); Bluebeard's Castle (BBC); Sally Burgess Sings Jazz (TER); Showboat (TER); West Side Story (TER); 5 Irish Folk Songs, Howarrd Ferguson (Chandos); Ravel 5 Greek Songs (Carla). *Address:* IMG Artists Europe, Media House, 3 Burlington Lane, Chiswick, London W4 2TH, England.

BURGHAUSER Jarmil Michael, b. 21 Oct 1921, Pisek, Southern Bohemia, Czechoslovakia. Composer; Musicologist. *Education:* Prague Conservatory of Music, 1940-44; Master Class of Conducting, 1944-46; Charles University, Prague, 1945-48. *Career:* Choirmaster and Conductor, National Theatre, Prague, 1946-53; Freelance Composer and Musicologist, 1953-; Composer of film, stage and television music, 1945- ; Audiovisual presentations with Scars group, 1969-. *Compositions include:* Operas: The Miser; Karolinka and the Liar; The Bridge; Ballets: The Servant of Two Masters; Tristam and Izalda; Cantatas: In Czech Strain; In The Czech Country; The Mystic Trumpeter; The Pensive Country; Orchestral Works: Seven Reliefs; The Ways; Colours in Time; Ciaconna per il fine d'un tempo; Chamber Music Pieces. *Publications include:* Antonín Dvořak, Thematic Catalogue, 1960 (rev edition in prep); Antonín Dvořak, 1967; Introductions to editions of works of A Dvořak, L Janáček and J B Kittl; Editorial Board Member, Complete editions of A Dvořák, Z Fibich and L Janáček; O Akustische Grundlagen des Orchestrierens, 1967. *Memberships:* Chairman, Composition Section, Guild of Czechoslovakian Composers, 1969; Vice President, Dvořák Society of Great Britain; President, Dvořák Society of Prague, Chairman of the Honorary Troop, Boy Scouts Association of the Czechoslovakia. *Address:* Klidna 25, 162 00 Prague 6, Czech Republic.

BURGON Geoffrey Alan, b. 15 July 1941, Hambledon, Hants., England. Composer. m. (1) Janice Elizabeth Garwood, 1963, marriage dissolved, 1 son, 1 daughter, (2) Jacqueline Krofchak, 1992. *Education:* GGSM. *Career:* Composer, trumpeter, 1964-71; Composer, Conductor, 1971-; As Trumpeter performed: Royal Opera House, Northern Sinfonia Orchestra, Philomusica, London Mozart Players, etc; Session Work Theatres, jazz Bands; As Conductor: Film and TV works. *Compositions include:* Many scores for dance including London Contemporary Dance Theatre, Ballet Rambert, London Festival Ballet and Royal Ballet; Over 40 scores for film, TV and Radio including: Tinker Tailor Soldier Spy; Brideshead Revisited; Bleak House; Life of Brian; Turtle Diary, The Chronicles of Narnia and The Children of The North; Choral and Orchestral Music; Gending; Acquainted with Night; Think on Dredful Domesday; Canciones del Alma; Requiem; Veni Spiritus; The World Again; Revelations; Title Divine; The Trials of Prometheus; Trumpet concerto, 1993; Hard Times, opera. *Recordings:* Requiem; Cathedral Music of Geoffrey Burgon; Brideshead Revisited; Music for counter tenor. *Publications:* Over 30 scores. *Contributions to:* Various professional journals. *Honours:* Prince Pierre of Monaco Award, 1969; Ivor Novello Awards, 1979, 1981; Gold Disc, 1982 (Brideshead Revisited). *Hobbies:* Jazz; Cricket; Old

Bristols; Chopping Wood; Sleeping. *Address:* c/o Chester Music, 8/9 Frith Street, London, W1V 5TZ, England.

BURMESTER Pedro, b. 9 Oct 1963, Oporto, Portugal. Pianist. *Education:* Oporto Musical Conservatory; Private Studies with Helena Costa, Sequeria Costa, Leon Fleisher and Dmitri Paperno; Teaching Oporto High School of Music. *Debut:* 1972. *Career:* Solo Recitalist; Guest Soloist with orchestras in Portugal, Spain, Austria, France, Germany, Italy and USA; TV Appearances in Portugal; various musical festivals in Portugal and Macau; Radio Appearances in Portugal and the USA. *Recordings:* A number of recordings with EMI. *Honours:* Top Prize, 9th International Vianna da Mota Piano Competition, Lisbon, 1983; Jury Discretionary Award, 8th Van Cliburn International Piano Competition, Fort Worth. *Hobby:* Music. *Current Management:* Ingpen & Williams Ltd, 14 Kensington Court, London W8 5DN and Norddeutsche Konzertdirektion Melsine Grevesmühl, Triftstrasse 11, 2850 Bremerhaven 31, GFR. *Address:* Rua do Souto 283, 4470 Porto, Portugal.

BURNSIDE Iain, b. 1950, Glasgow, Scotland. Pianist. *Education:* Studied in Oxford, London and Warsaw. *Career:* Recital accompanist to Margaret Price, Victoria de Los Angeles, Sarah Walker, Nancy Argenta, Thomas Allen and Stephen Varcoe; Chamber music performances with the Brodsky and Delmé Quartets, Douglas Boyd and Shmuel Ashkenasi; Appearances at the major British festivals and recitals in Europe, the USA, Canada and Japan; Devised song series for Schoenberg, The Reluctant Revolutionary concert series on South Bank, London, 1988-89; Further contributions to the French Revolution Festival and Hermann Prey's Schubertiade, 1989; Artistic Director of series of vocal and chamber concerts at St John's Smith Square, London, 1989-; Recitals featuring Karol Szymanowski on South Bank. *Recordings include:* Gurney's Ludlow and Teme, with Adrian Thompson and the Delmé Quartet (Hyperion). *Address:* c/o Ron Gonsalves, 10 Dagnan Road, London SW12 9LQ, England.

BURROUGHS Bruce Douglas, b. 12 Nov 1944, Hagerstown, Maryland, USA. Operatic Baritone; Pedagogue; Writer. *Education:* AB, English Literature, UCLA, 1966; MM, Voice & Vocal Pedagogy, New England Conservatory of Music, 1971. *Debut:* Papageno, in Magic Flute, Los Angeles Guild Opera, 1965; Metropolitan Opera debut: Einstein on the Beach, 1976; more than forty roles, including title roles of Monteverdi's Orfeo, Mozart's Don Giovanni, Busoni's Arlecchino, Menotti's Bishop of Brindisi. *Recordings:* United Artists Records; Columbia Masterworks Recordings; Editor-in-chief, The Opera Quarterly. *Contributions to:* Articles, Features, Reviews, in Music Journal, Opera News; Music Critic, Los Angeles Times. *Honours:* ASCAP - Deems Taylor Award, 1991. *Memberships:* American Guild of Musical Artists. *Address:* c/o The Opera Quarterly, 14832 Hart Street, Van Nuys, CA 91405, USA.

BURROWES Norma Elizabeth, b. 24 Apr 1944, Bangor, County Down, Opera and Concert Singer (soprano). m. Steuart Bedford, 1969, divorced 1980. *Education:* Queen's University, Belfast, Northern Ireland; Royal Academy of Music. *Debut:* Glyndebourne Touring Opera singing Zerlina in Don Giovanni, 1969; debut with Royal Opera House, Fiakermili in Arabella, 1976. *Career:* Roles included Blondchen in The Abduction from the Seraglio; Oscar (Ballo in Maschera) Despina, Così Fan Tutte; Woodbird, Siegfried; Sophie, Der Rosenkavalier; Cunning Little Vixen; Manon, Massenet; Titania, Midsummer Night's Dream; Nannetta, Falstaff; Gilda, Rigoletto; Marie, Daughter of the Regiment; Juliet, Romeo and Juliet; Adina, Elisir d'Amore; Susanna, Nozze di Figaro; Lauretta, Gianni Schicchi; sang regularly with Glyndebourne Opera, Scottish Opera; Aldeburgh Festival; English National Opera; Welsh National Opera and others; Salzburg, Paris, Munich, Aix-en-Provence, Avignon, Ottawa, Montreal, New York, Vienna, Chicago, Buenos Aires; Metropolitan Opera from 1979, as Blondchen, Oscar

and Sophie; sang with all the principal London orchestras and on BBC radio and Television, retired, 1982; made numerous recordings; including Die Schöpfung, The Fairy Queen and Hansel and Gretel (Decca); Acis and Galata (Deutsche Grammophon); Ariodante, Die Entführung and Haydn's Armida (Philips)I Israel in Egypt and Semele (Erato); Riders to the Sea by Vaughan Williams (EMI). *Honours:* DMus Honorary, Queen's University, Belfast; Order of Worshipful Company of Musicians. *Hobbies:* Gardening; Embroidery. *Address:* 56 Rochester Road, London NW1 9JG, England.

BURROWS Donald (Donwald) James, b. 28 Dec 1945, London, England. Lecturer; Conductor; Organist; Harpsichordist. m. Marilyn Jones, 23 July 1971, 3 sons. *Education:* BA, 1968, CertEd, 1969, MA, 1971, Trinity Hall, Cambridge University; PhD, Open University, 1981. *Career:* Director of Music, John Mason School, Abingdon, 1970-82; Lecturer in Music, Open University, 1982-; Senior Lecturer in Music 1989-; Head of Music Department 1991-; Conductor, Abingdon and District Music Society, 1972-83; Conductor, Oxford Holiday Orchestra, 1978-; Organist and Choirmaster, St Nicholas Church, Abingdon, 1972-82; Master of the Music, St Botolph's, Aspley Guise, 1985-; Member, Redaktionskollegium, Hallische Händel-Ausgabe, 1984-; Founder Member, Handel Institute, 1985-; Member of Vorstand, Georg Friedrich Händel-Gesellschaft, 1987-; Member of Advisory Board, Maryland Handel Festival, USA, 1988-. *Recordings:* Insert notes for recordings of Handel; Water Music; Anthems; Utrecht Te Deum; Ode for St Cecilia's Day; Israel in Egypt; Organ Concertos; Messiah. *Publications include:* Handel Alexander's Feast; The Anthem on the Peace; Founding Hospital Anthem, Violin Sonatas, Messiah, As Pants the Hart, Songs for Soprano and Continuo, Belshazzar (all as Editor); A Catalogue of Handel's Musical Autographs, Handel (Master Musicians's Biograpg). Handel's Messiah. *Contributions to:* The Musical Times; Music and Letters; Early Music; Göttingen Händel-Beiträge. *Honours:* Studentship, Merton College, Oxford University, 1979; British Academy Research Grant, 1979. *Memberships:* Royal Musical Association; Royal College of Organists. *Hobbies:* Steam locomotives; Model railways. *Address:* 126 High Street, Cranfield, Bedford MK43 0DG, England.

BURROWS John, b. 3 Aug. 1941, Newcastle-under-Lyme, England. Conductor. m. Rita Sandford, 25 Oct 1968, 1 son, 1 daughter. *Education:* Newcastle High School, 1951-57; GRSM; ARMCM; Royal Manchester College of Music, 1959-62; MusB, Manchester University, 1959-62; London Opera Centre, 1962-64. *Career:* Music Staff, Sadler's Wells (later English National) Opera, 1965-70; Prompter, Ring Cycle (English National Opera), 1970-73; Musical Director, Cowardy Custard, (Mermaid Theatre), 1973-74; Musical Director, Cole, (Mermaid Theatre), 1975-76; Musical Director, A Chorus Line, (Theatre Royal, Drury Lane), 1977-78; Musical Director, London Savoyards (Royal Albert Hall, London, Kennedy Center, Washington, USA, and tours of UK, USA, Canada, Holland, Belgium, Germany), 1979-86; Professor of Opera, Southern Methodist University, (Dallas, Texas), 1980-83; Professor of Opera, Temple University, (Philadelphia), 1983-86; Artistic Director, The Lyric Opera of Dallas, 1983-92; Guest Conductor: National Symphony Orchestra of America, 1986; Opera Theatre of San Antonio, 1988; Shreveport Opera, 1988; Shreveport Opera, 1988-89; Opera Omnia, 1989; Fort Worth Opera, 1991; American Music Theater Festival, 1992; Opera Northeast, 1992-93. Chorus Master: Pennsylvania Opera Theater, 1992; OperaDelaware, 1993; Opera Theatre of Connecticut, 1994; Washington Savoyards, 1994; Faculty, Academy of Vocal Arts (Philadelphia), 1993-94. *Composition:* Composer/Arranger (BBC TV). *Current Management:* Harwood Management Group Inc., 509 West 110th Street, New York, NY 10025, USA. *Address:* 2227 Locust Street, Apt 1B, Philadelphia, PA 19103-5510, USA.

BURROWS Stuart, b. 7 Feb 1933, Pontypridd, Wales. Singer (Tenor). m. Enid Lewis, 1 son, 1 daughter.

Education: Trinity College, Camarthen. *Career:* Sang in concerts at first; Stage debut with Welsh National Opera 1963, as Ismaele in Nabucco; Athens 1965, in Oedipus Rex; Covent Garden from 1967, as Beppe in Pagliacci, Fenton (Falstaff), Elvino (La Sonnambula), Lensky, Don Otttavio and Faust; US debut San Francisco 1967, as Tamino; Vienna Staatsoper 1970, as Tamino and Ottavio; Salzburg Festival from 1970, in Mozart roles; Metropolitan Opera from 1971, as Ottavio, Tamino, Faust, Alfredo and Belmonte; Paris Opéra 1975-76; Appearances at Aix-en-Provence and Orange Festivals, and at Hamburg, Geneva, Houston, Santa Fe and Boston; Other roles include Pinkerton, Berlioz's Faust, Ernesto in Don Pasquale and Des Grieux in Manon; sang the title role in La Clemenza di ́Tito at Covent Garden, 1989; Many concert appearances, notably in music by Bach and Handel; BBC TV films of Faust, La Bohème and Rigoletto. *Recordings:* Maria Stuarda by Donizetti; Die Zauberflöte, Don Giovanni, Beethoven's 9th Symphony, Eugene Onegin (Decca); La Clemenza di Tito, Don Giovanni, Die Entführung (Philips). *Honours include:* Blue Riband, National Eisteddfod of Wales, 1959. *Address:* c/o Harrison/Parrot Ltd, 12 Penzance Place, London W11 4PA.

BURT Francis, b. 28 Apr 1926, London, England. Composer; Professor. m. Lina Burt. *Education:* Royal Academy of Music, 1948-51; Hochschule für Musik, Berlin, 1951-54. *Career:* Professor of Composition, Hochschule für Musik und darstellende Kunst, Vienna 1973-93. *Compositions include:* Iambics (for orchestra), Opus 5; Volpone (opera), Opus 9; Espressione Orchestrale, Opus 10; Der Golem (ballet), Opus 11; Fantasmasgoria (for orchestra), Opus 12; Barnstable (opera), Opus 13; Unter der blanken Hacke des Monds (for baritone and orchestra); Und Gott der Herr sprach (for solo voices, 2 choruses and orchestra); Morgana (for orchestra); Echoes (for 9 players); Hommage à Jean-Henri Fabre (for 5 players); 2 String Quartets. *Recordings:* Classic Amadeo 431 853-2; a CD entitled Francis Burt, with the 4 works: Unter der blanken Hacke des Monds; Echoes; Morgana; Der Golem. *Honours:* Associate Royal Academy of Music, 1957; Mendelssohn Scholarship, 1954, Körner Prize, 1973; Würdigungspreis für Musik, Austrian Federal Ministry of Education and Art, 1978; City of Vienna Prize for Music, 1981; Großes Silbernes Ehrenzeichen für Verdienste um die Republik Österreich, (Great Silver Medal of Honour for services to the Republic of Austria), 1992. *Hobbies:* Reading; Sheep Farming; Eating; Drinking; Good Friends. *Address:* Mayerhofgasse 12/20, A-1040 Vienna, Austria.

BURT Michael, b. 1943, Farnham, Surrey, England. Singer (Bass baritone). *Education:* Studied with Richard Federicks in New York. *Debut:* Caracas, 1977, as Monterone and Sparafucile in the same performance of Rigoletto. *Career:* Concert soloist in North America, including Bach's Christmas Oratorio and B minor Mass at Carnegie Hall; Covent Garden, London, 1979, as Second Armed Man in Die Zauberflöte; Further appearances at Frankfurt as Pizarro in Fidelio and at New Orleans as King Henry in Lohengrin; Zaccaria and the Hoffmann villains at Hannover, 1986-87; King Philip in Don Carlos and Wotan in Der Ring des Nibelungen at Graz, 1988; Adolfo in Schubert's Alfonso und Estrella, 1991; Sang Wagner's Dutchman at Montpellier, 1992, Jochanaan in Salome at Barcelona, 1991. *Address:* c/o Vereinigte Buhnen, Kaiser Josef Platz 10, A-8010 Graz, Austria.

BURT Robert, b. 22 May 1962, England. Singer (Tenor). *Education:* Graduated from the Guildhall School, 1989. *Career:* Appearances with Oper 80 as Monostatos and Don Ottavio at the Wexford Festival as Lysander, Tonio and Fernando in La Favorita, Chelsea Opera Group as Kleontes in Daphne and Mid-Wales Opera as Goro in Butterfly; Sang Don Jerome in the Britain premiere of Prokofiev's The Duenna at the Guildhall School, conducted by Rostropovitch, 1991; Glyndebourne Festival debut, 1992, as Tchaplitsky in The Queen of Spades (repeated at the Promenade concerts, London); Don Curzio in Figaro with

Glyndebourne Touring Opera, 1992 and Janáček's From the House of the Dead at the Barbican Hall, 1993; Recitals and oratorios include Carmina Burana, at Snape, Vaughan Williams Seranade to Music, at the Barbican, and the Easter Oratorio by Bach and Mozart's Requiem in Munich; Festival engagements at Bath, Dijon and Sully-sur-Loire. *Address:* Owen/White Management, 14 Nightingale Lane, Hornsey London N8 7QU, England.

BURT Warren Arnold, b. 10 Oct 1949, Baltimore, Maryland, USA. Composer. *Education:* BA, Music, State University of New York, Albany, 1971; MA, Music, University of California, San Diego, 1975. *Career:* Performances throughout USA, Europe and Australia; Senior Tutor in Music, La Trobe University, Melbourne, 1975-78; Tutor in Music, New South Wales Conservatorium, Sydney, 1979; Part-time Lecturer, La Trobe University, 1981; Music Education Officer, Council of Adult Education, Melbourne, 1982-83; Consultant, Serge Modular Music Systems, San Francisco, 1984; Lecturer, Victorian College of the Arts, Melbourne, 1985; Artist-in-Residence, International Synergy, Los Angeles, 1986; Composer-in-Residence, Australian Broadcasting Corporation, 1987; Composer-in-residence, Monash University Melbourne, 1989-90; Australia Council Composers' Fellowships, 1991, 1992, 1991. *Compositions:* Aardvarks II; Piano Solo, 1971; Nighthawk I, Solo Speaking Voice, 1973; Aardvarks IV, Electronic Tape, 1975; Moods, 1979, Video Synthesis Opera unpublished; Studies for Synthesizer, electronic tape, 1982; 24 Meditations, Video Synthesis/Computer Music, 1986; Samples III for computer processed orchestra, 1987; Soundscape for Sensus Technological Playground, Expo '88, Brisbane, 1988; Chaotic Research Music, 1989-90; Some Kind of Seasoning, live computer music, 1990-91. *Recordings include:* Aardvarks V, 1978; Song Dawn Chords, 1981; Four Pieces for Synthesizer, 1981; Almond Bread Harmonies II, 1985; Chaotic Research Music, 1989-90; Three Inverse Genera, 1990; Parts of Speech, 1992. *Publications:* Music Talks; 24 Pamphlets written or edited, 1982-85, Council of Adult Education, Melbourne. *Hobby:* Nature Studies. *Address:* Flat 18, 102 Park Street, St Kilda West, Victoria 3182, Australia.

BURTON Humphrey McGuire, b. 25 Mar 1931, Trowbridge, England. Television Producer and Presenter, 2 sons, 2 daughters. *Education:* BA, Cantab; Honours Degree (Cambridge) (Music and History). *Career:* Presenter, Aquarius, ITV, 1970-75; Presenter, Concerts, Opera and Ballet, BBC, 1975-93; Presenter, Young Musician of the Year, 1978-92; Head of Music and Arts, BBC TV, 1965-67, 1975-81; Chairman, EBU TV Music Working Party, 1976-86; Artistic Director, Barbican Centre, 1988-90; Director, Tender is the North, Festival of Scandinavian Arts, Barbican Centre, 1992; Artistic Adviser, Barbican Centre; Work in Progress: Authorised biography of Leonard Bernstein. *Recordings:* Mozart Harpsichord Duet K9A, with Erik Smith, Philips. *Contributions to:* The Sunday Times, The Listener; Music and Letters, 1955. *Hobbies:* Tennis; Playing Duets. *Address:* 123 Oakwood Court, London, W14 8LA, England.

BURTON Nigel Mark, b. 9 Apr 1947, Southampton, England. University Lecturer; Conductor; Singer; Pianist; Organist. *Education:* MusB, 1969, MA, 1972, Gonville and Caius College, Cambridge; MusB, 1976, MA, 1977, Trinity College, Dublin; Studied with Bernard Roberts (piano), Gwendoline Hanson (singing), Arnold Richardson (organ); FRCO, 1970. *Debut:* Created the role of Thibaut La Rouge in the premiere of Peter Wishart's opera The Lady of the Inn, Reading, 1983. *Career:* Junior Lecturer in Music, 1974, Director of Church Music, 1975, Lecturer, 1977, Trinity College, Dublin; Lecturer in Music, 1979, Senior Lecturer in Music, 1984-, University of Reading (specialising in 19th Century British Music). *Composition:* Psalm for male voices and organ, Vista Records, 1989. *Publications:* Oratorios and Cantatas 1800-1914 and Opera 1865-1914; Chapters 10 and 15 of The Athlone History of Music in Britain, Volume V: The Romantic Age 1800-

1914, 1981. *Contributions to:* Music and Musicians; Composer Magazine; The Musical Times; Pipers Enzyklopadie des Musiktheaters, 1986; The New Grove Dictionary of Opera, 1992. *Honours:* Vice President, Sir Arthur Sullivan Society, 1990 (GB). *Memberships:* Royal Musical Association. *Hobbies:* Richard III Society; Amateur theatricals; Food; Wine. *Address:* St Patrick's Hall, Reading, Berks RG2 7HB, England.

BURTON Stephen, b. 24 Feb 1943, California, USA. Composer. *Education:* Studied at the Oberlin Conservatory, Vienna Conservatory, 1957-60; Salzburg Mozarteum, 1962-65; Further study with Hans Werner Henze, 1962-66. *Career:* Director of the Munich Kammerspiel, 1963-64; Teacher, George Mason University in Fairfax, Virginia, from 1974. *Compositions include:* No Trifling with Love, opera, 1970; The Duchess of Malfi, opera after Webster, 1978; Aimee, opera, 1983; An American Triptych, 3 1-act operas after Crane's Maggie, Hawthorne's Dr Heidegger's Experiment and Melville's Benito Cereno, 1989; Ballet Finisterre, 1977; Concerto da camera, 1963; Ode to a Nightingale for soprano and ensemble, 1963; Symphony No 1, 1968; Stravinskiana for flute and Orchestra, 1972; Dithyramb, 1972; Symphony No 2 after Sylvia Plath poems, for mezzo, baritone and orchestra, 1979; Variations on a theme of Mahler for chamber orchestra, 1982; Violin Concerto, 1983; String Quarter, 1974; Piano Trio, 1975; 6 Hebrew Melodies after Byron, 1973; Songs of the Tulpehocken for tenor and Orchestra, 1976; Six songs for voice and 13 instruments, 1977; I have a Dream, cantata for narrator, soprano and orchestra, 1987. *Address:* c/o ASCAP, ASCAP Building, One Lincoln Plaza, New York, NY 10023, USA.

BURY Edward, b. 18 Sept 1918, Gniezno, Poland. Composer; Conductor. *Education:* Studied composition with Sikorski, conducting at the Warsaw Conservatory, 1937-44. *Career:* Teacher, Krakow Conservatory, 1945-54; Freelance Composer from 1948. *Compositions include:* Czech Fantasy for piano and orchestra, 1948; Little Suite for Orchestra, 1950; Triptych for Orchestra, 1952; Violin concerto, 1954; Suita Giocosa for Orchestra, 1956; 8 Symphonies, 1960-80; The Millenium Hymn for chorus and orchestra, 1956; Chamber music and piano pieces. *Publications include:* The Principles of Conducting, 1961; The Technique of Reading Scores, 1971. *Address:* c/o PRS Ltd Member Registration, 29-33 Berners Street, London W1P 4AA, England.

BURY Grzegorz Piotr Michal, b. 17 Nov 1961, Katowice, Poland. Composer. *Education:* K Szymanowski Academy of Music in Katowice, Theory of Music, 1981-86, Composition, 1986-89, MA in Art, 1990. *Debut:* Festival of Fascinating Music in Katowice, 13 Dec 1983. *Compositions include:* Pieces for solo instrument include: Suite for flute; Lament Songs (Treny), for piano; Sonata with air-hammer, for piano; Little Prince, suite for piano; Echo, clouds and mountains, for piano; Pieces for solo instrument and piano include: Walo, Lullaby, viola and piano; Gabeag, Folk Dance, for violin and piano; Polonaise, Goliwogs War, Largo cantabile e finale, for bassoon and piano; Sheheresade, for oboe and piano; Dialogues for viola and bassoon; Trio, for clarinet, bassoon and piano; Symphonic compositions include: Crux - for the texts from the Bible, for boy soprano, tenor, bass of a reciter, mixed choir and orchestra; Concerto for piano and orchestra; Symphony for jazz band or soloist improvising and symphonic orchestra; Missa Pro Defunctis (requiem) for voices choir and orchestra. Chamber music pieces include: Imitations for flute, oboe, bassoon, percussion; Oberek for brass quintet; In The Circus, for 2 pianos; Songs on the lapse of time for bass/baritone/oboe and percussion; Classic Quartet, for string; Black and White, for 2 string orchestras; Happy Sorrow, for 5 musicians; Rapsody in suite form, for percussion, piano, and percussion group; Variations for violin and cello; Dialogues for viola and bassoon; Trio, for clarinet, bassoon and piano; Alarm for voice, dock and chamber ensemble; Elegia, for voice and piano, 1993. *Hobbies:* Tourism; Nature; Chess; Tennis; Skiing; Kayaking; Films.

Address: 40-866 ul Piastow 7/3, Osiedle 1000 lecia, Katowice, Poland.

BUSCHING Rainer, b. 1943, Halle, Germany. Singer (Bass). *Education:* Studied at the Mendelssohn Musikhochschule, Leipzig, 1967-71. *Career:* Guest appearances in Germany then engaged at Dessau, 1973-85; Member of the Dresden Staatsoper from 1985, notably as Wagner's Padre, Daland, Landgrave and King Henry; Verdi's Zaccaria, Ramphis and Padre Guardiano, Mozart's Sarastro and Commendatore; Weber's Lysiart and Kaspar, Basilion in Il Barbiere di Siviglia, Handel's Giulio Cesare and Gremin in Eugene Onegin; Guest appearances in Italy, Poland and Russia; Concert repetory includes St John and Matthew Passions by Bach, Messiah, Die Schopfung and Jahreszeiten by Hydn; Schubert's Winterreise. *Address:* c/o Staatsoper, 01069 Dresden, Germany.

BUSH Alan, b. 22 Dec 1900, London, England. Professional Musician; Composer; Conductor; Pianist. m. Nancy Head, 3 daughters (1 deceased). *Education:* Sir Roger Cholmeley's School, Highgate, London, 1912-18; Royal Academy of Music, London, 1918-22; University of Berlin, 1929-31; DMus, London, 1969; DMus, Honoris Causa Dunelm, 1971; FRAM, 1938. Studied composition with John Ireland; piano with Benno Moiseiwitsch, Mabel Lander, Artur Schnabel and Harold Rubens. *Debut:* Concert of Own Compositions, piano recital, Wigmore Hall, London, 1927; as a Conductor, Promenade Concert, Queen's Hall, 1930. *Career:* Professor of Composition, Royal Academy of Music, London, 1925-78; Played solo pianoforte part in Piano Concerto Op 18, BBC Male Voice Choir and Symphony Orchestra conducted by Sir Adrian Boult, London, 1938; World Premiere Operas Wat Tyler, Leipzig Opera House, 1953; Men of Blackmoor, German National Theatre, Weimar, 1956, The Sugar Reapers, Leipzig Opera House, 1966; (libretti Nancy Bush) Joe Hill, the Man who Never Died; (Libretto Barrie Stavis); Deutsche Staatsoper, Berlin, 1970. *Compositions:* Operas; Children's Operas; Orchestral Works; Chamber Music; Pianoforte solos; Songs; Choral works. *Recordings:* Dialectic for String Quartet, Aeolian String Quartet, Decca; Voices of the Prophets, Cantata for Tenor and Piano, Peter Pears and Alan Bush, ARGO; Variations, Nocturne and Finale for Piano and Orchesrtra (Soloist David Wilde), Pye; Violin Concerto, Manoug Parikian, Hyperion; Six Short Pieces for Piano, Alan Bush, Hyperion; 24 Preludes, Nocturne; Letter Gallaird, Corentyne Kwe-Kwo, Peter Jacobs, piano, Altarus Air-2-90004; Full length film, Alan Bush - A Life, shown in National Film Theatre, London, 1983. *Publications:* Strict Counterpoint in Palestrina Style, 1948; In My Eighth Decade and Other Essays, 1980. *Memberships:* Chairman, Composers' Guild of Great Britain, 1948-49; Chairman, Workers' Music Association, 1936-41; President of the same organisation, 1941-; Honorary Member of the Royal Philharmonic Society. *Honours:* Carnegie Hall Award for String Quartet in A Minor, 1924; Arts Council Prize in Festival of Britain Opera Competition for the Opera Wat Tyler, 1951; Handel Prize, City Council of Halle, German Democratic Republic for Byron Symphony, 1962. *Hobbies:* Walking; Foreign travel. *Address:* 25 Christchurch Crescent, Radlett, Hertfordshire, WD7 8AQ, England.

BUSH Geoffrey, b. 23 Mar 1920, London, England. Composer; Pianist; Musicologist; University Lecturer. m. Julie McKenna, 15 Apr 1950, 2 sons. *Education:* Salisbury Cathedral Choir School; Lancing College; Balliol College, Oxford (Nettleship Scholar and Masefield Memorial Student), MA, DMus (Oxon). *Debut:* As composer: Winter Ballet, Bath, 1934. *Career:* Lecturer, Oxford University, 1947-52; Staff Tutor, 1952-64, Senior Staff Tutor, 1964-80, London University; Visiting Professor, King's College, London, 1969-89; Music Adviser, John Ireland Trust, 1969-; Honorary Fellow, University College of Wales, Aberystwyth, 1986-91. *Compositions:* 2 symphonies; Overture Yorick; Christmas Cantata; Summer Serenade; In Praise of Mary; Concertante Works for Trumpet, Piano, Oboe and

Cello; Operas: If the Cap Fits, The Equation, Lord Arthur Savile's Crime; Violin Sonata; Wind Quintet; Trio; Dialogue (Oboe/Piano); 2 Piano Sonatinas; Summmer Serenade, A Menagerie, Farewell Earth's Bliss, Herrick Songs; Song Cycles. *Recordings:* Anthems, Canticles and Carols (Abbey); Symphony No 1, Overture Yorick, Music for Orchestra (Lyrita); A Little Love Music (songs), Quintet, Trio, Dialogue (Chandos); In Praise of Mary (Unicorn-Kanchana); Christmas Cantata (Saydisc); Piano Sonatina No 1; Summer Serenade (Chandos). *Publications:* Musical Creation and the Listener, 1954; Left, Right and Centre 1983; Editor: Musica Britannica vol 37, 1972 vol 43, 1979, vol 49, 1982, vol 52, 1986; An Unsentimental Education, 1990. *Contributions to:* Musical Times; Music and Letters; Music and Musicians; Composer. *Honour:* Philharmonic Prize for Overture Yorick, 1949. *Memberships:* Composers Guild of Great Britain (Chairman 1957); Royal Musical Association; British Academy of Experts; Performing Right Society (Chairman, Members Fund). *Hobbies:* Bridge; Tennis; Detective fiction; Theatre. *Address:* 43 Corringham Road, London NW11 7BS, England.

BUSSE Barry, b. 18 Aug 1946, Gloversville, New York. Singer (Tenor). *Education:* Studied at Oberlin College and the Manhattan School of Music. *Career:* Has sung as tenor from 1977 (Carlisle Floyd's Of Mice and Men, Houston); Created Bothwell in Musgrave's Mary Queen of Scots for Virginia Opera (1977) and repeated the role at the New York City Opera (1980); Santa Fe, 1979, as Alwa in the US premiere of the 3-act version of Lulu; European debut, 1982, as Don José, for Netherlands Opera; Further appearances in Toulouse, San Francisco, Santa Fe and Miami; Seattle Opera, 1985, as Siegmund in Die Walküre; Sang Tichon in Katya Kabanova at Florence in 1988 and Geneva, 1989; Mephistopheles and Agrippa in Prokofiev's Fiery Angel at the Holland Festival, 1990; Other roles include Florestan, Cavaradossi, Canio, Parsifal (Toulouse 1987), Peter Grimes, Narraboth, Apollo in Daphne, Pollione and Massenet's Des Grieux. *Recordings include:* CD of Mary Queen of Scots (Novello Records). *Address:* c/o Seattle Opera Association, PO Box 9248, Seattle, WA 98109, USA.

BUSSI Francesco, b. 14 Sept 1926, Piacenza, Italy. Musician; Musicologist. m. Maria Villa, 20 July 1957. 1 son, 1 daughter. *Education:* Laurea in Lettere Classiche, 1948; Diploma di Pianoforte, 1949; Diploma di Paleografia Musicale, 1953; Diploma di Musica Corale, 1955. *Career:* Docente di Storia ed Estetica Musicale al Conservatorio di Parma, 1955-59; Docente di Storia ed Estetica Musicale al Conservatorio di Piacenza e Bibliotecario dal 1959 a oggi. *Recordings:* Francesco Cavalli, Missa pro Defunctis (Requiem) a 8 voci, con il responsorio Libera me, Domine a 5 voci, 1985. *Publications:* Antifonario-Graduale di S.Antonino in Piacenza; Umanità e arte di G.Parabosco; Catalogo dell' Archivio Musicale del Duomo di Piacenza; La Musica sacra di F.Cavalli in rapporto a Monteverdi; Storia, tradizione e arte nel'Requiem di Cavalli; l'Opera veneziana dalla morte di Monteverdi alla fine del '600. *Contributions to:* Jone di Chio; il cantore spagnolo Pedro Valenzuela; Le'Toscanelle'di Gabriele Villani; La musica strumentale di J Brahms; Altro Cavalli sacro restituito; Moderna Edizione critica di Pezzi di Girolamo Parabosco, del Requiem di Cavalli, delle Toscanelle di Villani, di altri pezzi sacri di Cavalli; Edizione italiana dei voll 2, 4, & 5 della New Oxford History of Music. *Memberships:* SIDM; AIBM; AMS; Membro effettivo della Deputazione di Storia Patria per le Province Parmensi. *Address:* Strada Guastafredda, 45-29100 Piacenza, Italy.

BUSSOTTI Sylvano, b. 1 Oct 1931, Florence, Italy. Composer; Painter; Film Director; Stage Designer. *Education:* Florence Conservatory, 1940-45, with Dallapiccola, Maglioni and Lupi; Independent composition studies, 1949-56; Studied with Deutsch in Paris; Darmstadt courses with Cage; USA, 1964-65, on Rockefeller Foundation Grant. *Career:* Appearances at music festivals from 1958; Co-founder 1962 of the exhibition Musica e Segno: seen in Europe and USA; Exhibited his own paintings in Italy, USA, Japan, France

and Germany; Director and designer of stage works, including his own; 1971-74 Professor of Music Drama at the L'Aquila Academy of Fine Arts Scuola di Musica di Fierole; Bussothoperaballet, Scuola Spattacole, 1984-1992; 1975 Director of the Teatro La Fenice, Venice. *Compositions:* Stage: Tema-variazioni, Geographie Francaise, 1956; La Passion selon Sade, chamber mystery play 1969; Raramente, mystery play 1971; Lorenzaccio, melodrama 1972; Bergkristall, ballet 1974; Syro-Sadun-settimino, ballet 1974; Nottetempo lyric drama 1976; Oggetto amato, ballet 1976; Le Racine 1980; L'Ispirazione, melodramma, 1988; Fedra, lyric tragedy, 1988; Concert works: El Carbonero for 5 voices 1957; Musica per amici for piano 1957-71; Breve for ondes martenot 1958; Due voci for soprano, ondes martenot and orchestra 1958; Sette folgi 1959; Pieces de chair II, including 5 Pieces for David Tudor, 1958-60; Phrase a trois for string trio 1960; Memoria 1962; Torso for solo voices and orchestra 1960-63; Mit einem gewissen sprechenden Ausdruck for chamber orchestra; Rara for guitar and string trio 1964-67; Cinque frammenti all'Italia 1967; Julio organum Julii for speaker and organ 1968; The Rara Requiem 1970; I semi di Gramsci for string quartet and orchestra 1962-71; Novelletta for piano 1962-73; Poesia di De Pisis for soprano and orchestra 1975; Opus Cygne for orchestra, 1979. *Honours include:* First prize Italian section ISCM 1965, 1972; DAAD, Berlin, 1972; Commandeur, l'Ordre des Arts et Les Lettres. *Address:* Via di Colle Marta 1,2, 00030 Genazzano (RM), Italy.

BUSWELL James Oliver (IV), b. 4 Dec 1946, Fort Wayne, Indiana, USA. Violinist; Conductor; Teacher. *Education:* BA, Harvard College, 1970; Studied violin with Ivan Galamian, Juilliard School of Music, New York. *Debut:* Violinist, St Louis, 1963; New York recital debut, Philharmonic Hall, 1967. *Career:* Soloist with orchestras, Recitalist, Chamber-music player; Appearances as Conductor; Visiting Professor, University of Arizona, Tucson, 1972-73; Teacher, Indiana University School of Music, Bloomington, 1974-86; New England Conservatory of Music, Boston, 1986- ; Member, Buswell Parnas Lucisi Trio; TV Host for Stations of Bach on PBS Television. *Recordings:* For Vanguard. *Current Management:* Thea Dispeker, New York. *Address:* c/o New England Conservatory of Music, 290 Huntington Avenue, Boston, MA 02115, USA.

BUTLER Anne Lois, b. 25 May 1912, Texas, USA. Composer; Violinist; Conductor. *Education includes:* BMus, Piano, BMus Violin, Southwestern University, Texas, 1932; Julliard School of Music, 1936-38 (summers); MMus Violin, first woman candidate, Peabody Institute of the Johns Hopkins University, Maryland, 1940; Boston University School of Music, 1947; Berkelee College of Music, Boston, 1949; MMus Composition, Benjamin T Rome School of Music, Catholic University of America, Washington DC, 1972 - Significant Teachers: Cecil Burleigh, Kathleen Parlow and Louise Persinger, Gustav Strube (Composition), Frank Gittelson (violin); Lawrence Berk and Kenneth Mackillop, (Composition), Nicolas Slonimsky, (Composition), Conran Bernier (Composition), G T Jones (Composition); Henry Littleboy (String Instrument Repair); Lloyd Geisler (Conducting); George Bornoff, String Instrument Workshops, Boston University School of Music. *Career includes:* First Violin, Peabody Institute Orchestra, 1st Violin Assistant Concertmaster: WPA Orchestra, 1940-42, Radio Station WBAL Staff Orchestra, 1945-46; Organist, Pilgrims Congregational Church, Cambridge, MA, 1951-55; Studio Accompanist, Jordan Hall Boston, 1946-56; String Instrument Specialist, Composer in Residence, Washington DC Public Schools, 1956-77; First Baptist Church, Silver Spring, MD, 1956-83. *Address:* 1428 Oak Vista Drive, Dallas, TX 75232, USA.

BUTLER Mark, b. 5 Feb 1949, Violinist, Canadian, (British Citizen). *Education:* Studied Royal College of Music with Leonard Hirch. *Career:* Co-Leader Ulster Orchestra, 1970-71; BBC Debut 1971, London debut 1972; Solo Recitals UK and Canada; second violinist of the Chilingirian Quartet, 1971; Resident Quartet of

Liverpool University 1973-76; Resident Quartet of Sussex University, 1978-; Resident Quartet of Royal College of Music, 1986-; Annual series of concerts at the Elizabeth Hall, the Wigmore Hall; Performances at the Edinburgh, Bath, Aldeburgh Festivals; Munich Herkulessaal, Amsterdam Concertgebouw, Zurich Tonhalle, Vienna Konzertaus, Stockholm Konserthuset; New York debut 1976; Annual coast-to-coast tours of the USA and Canada; Represented Britain at the New York International Festival quartet series; Tours of Australia, New Zealand, South America, the Far East; Television and radio throughout Europe, National Public Radio in the USA, and the BBC. *Recordings:* All Great Mozart Quartets; Late Schubert Quartets; Debussy and Ravel Quartets; Elgar Quartet and Piano Quintet; Schubert Cello Quintet and Octet; Mozart Clarinet Quintet; Complete Quartets of Bartók and Dvořák; Bartók Piano Quintet; Labels include EMI, RCA, CRD, Numbus and Chandos. *Address:* c/o Intermusica Artists' Management, 16 Duncan Terrace, London N1 8BZ, England.

BUTLER Martin, b. 1 Mar 1960, Hampshire, England. Lecturer; Composer. *Education:* Winchester School of Art, 1976-78; University of Manchester, 1978-81; Royal Northern College of Music, 1978-82; Princeton University, USA, 1983-87; BMus, (Hons), PPRNCM, MFA. *Publications include:* From an Antique Land for ensemble, 1982; Concertino for chamber orchestra, 1983; Dance Fragments for ensemble, 1984; Cavalcade for orchestra, 1985; Tin Pan Ballet, 1986, arranged as Ballet con Salsa, 1987; Bluegrass Variations for violin, 1987; Piano Piano for 2 pianos and tape, 1988; Graffiti for tape, 1989; Jazz Machines for ensemble, 1990; O Rio, for full orchestra, 1990; Chacnone, for solo oboe, 1991; Down Hollow Winds, for wind quintet, 1991; American Dream, for string quartet and electronic tape, 1991; Going with the grain, for solo marimba and ensemble, 1992; On the Rocks, for solo piano, 1992; Still Breathing, for wind orchestra, 1992. *Address:* Oxford University Press, 3 Park Road, London NW1 6XN, England.

BUTTERLEY Nigel Henry, b. 13 May 1935, Sydney, Australia. Composer; Pianist. *Compositions include:* Chamber Music: String Quartets No.1 1965, No.2 1974, No.3 1979; Trio for clarinet, cello and piano, 1979; Forest I, viola and piano, 1990; Radiophonic: Watershore 1978. Piano: Uttering Joyous Leaves 1981; Lawrence Hargrave Flying Alone 1981; Il Gubbo 1987. Vocal: There Came a Wind Like a Bugle (Emily Dickinson) 1987; The Owl 1983. Orchestral: Meditations of Thomas Traherne 1968; Violin Concerto 1970; Symphony 1980; Goldengrove 1982; In Passing 1982; From Sorrowing Earth, 1991. Opera: Lawrence Hargrave Flying Alone 1988. Compositions recorded: Sometimes With One I Love (Whitman), 1976; Fire in the Heavens, 1973; Laudes, 1963; In the Head the Fire, 1966; Explorations for Piano and Orchestra, 1970; Letter from Hardy's Bay, 1971; First Day Covers (with Barry Humphries), 1973; String Quartet No. 3, 1979, Violin Concerto, 1970. *Honours:* Italia Prize for radiophonic composition for In the Head the Fire, 1966; Appointed Member of the Order of Australia, 1991; Australian Artists Creative Fellowship, 1992-; Sounds Australian Award, Best Work by Australian Composer, 1992. *Address:* 57 Temple Street, Stanmore, New South Wales, Australia 2048.

BUTTERWORTH Arthur, b. 4 Aug 1923, Manchester, England. m. Diana Stewart, 12 July 1952, 2d. *Education:* Royal Manchester College of Music. *Career:* Trumpeter, Scottish National Orchestra, 1949-55, Halle Orchestra, 1955-62; Conductor: Huddersfield Philharmonic Orchestra, 1962-93; Guest conductor to various orchestras from 1965. *Compositions:* Major works include: Symphony 1, 2, 3, 4, 1957, 1965, 1979, and 1986, respectively; Violin Concerto, Organ Concerto, Piano Trio, September Morn, Northern Light (large orchestra), Solent Forts, Viola Concerto, Odin (symphony for Brass). *Recordings:* The Path Across The Moors; Three Impressions for Brass; Caliban, scherzo malevolo. *Hobbies:* Country Living; World Wildlife Fund;

Oil Painting. *Address:* Pohjola, Dales Avenue, Embsay Skipton, N Yorks BD23 6PE, England

BUTTERWORTH David Neil, b. 4 Sept 1934, Streatham, London, England. Composer; Conductor; Writer; Broadcaster. m. Anna Mary Barnes, 23 Apr. 1960, 3 daughters. *Education:* MA, Nottingham University, 1965; BA, Honours, English, 1957, BA, Honours, Music, 1958, London University; Guildhall School of Music, 1960-62. *Career:* Lecturer, Kingston College of Technology, 1960-68; Head of Music Department, Napier College, Edinburgh, Scotland, 1968-87; Conductor, Edinburgh Schools Choir, 1968-72, Glasgow Orchestral Society, 1975-83 and June 1989-, Edinburgh Chamber Orchestra, 1983-85. *Compositions:* Over 300 works including, A Scott Cantata, A Ghost Cantata, Horn Concerto, Rumpelstilzkin, Summer Music for Strings, Sunset Song, Mixed Doubles for Baroque Quartet, Letter to the World (song cycle), 4 Suites for guitar; Count Dracula, opera; Numerous songs, instrumental pieces and arrangements. *Publications:* Haydn, 1976; Dvořák, 1980; 400 Aural Training Exercises, 1970; A Musical Quiz Book, 1974; A Dictionary of American Composers, 1983; Aaron Copland, 1984; Sight-singing Exercises from the Masters, 1984; 20th Century Sight-Singing Exercises, 1984; Vaughan Williams, 1989; Samuel Barber, 1994; Neglected Music, 1991. *Contributions to:* Times Educational Supplement; Sunday Times; Musical Opinion; Music (SMA publication). *Address:* The White House, Inveresk, Musselburgh, Midlothian EH21 7TG, Scotland.

BUTTREY John, b. 16 Aug 1931, Sydney, Australia. Singer. *Education:* MusB, 1962, MA, 1965, PhD, 1967, University of Cambridge, England; Private tuition with Roy Henderson; New South Wales Conservatorium of Music. *Career:* Concert Singer with appearances all over Europe; Former member of Deller Consort, touring USA, South America and Israel; Broadcast talks on English Theatre Music for British Broadcasting Corporation; Devised recordings of music and poetry for Purcell Consort of Voices. *Recordings:* Handel, Acis and Galatea; Purcell, The Fairy Queen; Numerous recordings of madrigals and church music. *Contributions to:* numerous professional magazines, including Musical Times, Music and Letters. *Memberships:* Elgar Society; Royal Musical Association. *Hobbies:* Theatre; Cinema; Gardening. *Address:* 34 Disraeli Gardens, Bective Road, London SW15 2QB, England.

BUUWALDA Sytse, b. 28 Sept 1964, Holland. Singer (Counter-tenor). *Education:* Studied at the Stwelinck Conservatory with Canne-Meyer and Paul Hameleers. *Career:* Appearances throughout Holland and elsewhere in Europe in a repertoire ranging from Montevardi to Britten; Concert performances of Messiah, Handel's Theodora and the Masses of Bach; Engagements with the Netherlands Chamber Choir from 1989, featuring a tour of Europe with music by Bach accompanied by the Orchestra of the Eighteenth ecntury conducted by Frans Bruggen; Opera roles include Gluck's Orpheus. *Recordings include:* Te Deums by Blanchard and Caldara. *Address:* Anglo Swiss Ltd, 3 Primrose Mews, 1a Sharpleshall St, London NW1 8YW, England.

BYCHKOV Semyon, b. 30 Nov 1952, Leningrad, USSR. Conductor. m. Tatiana Rozina, 3 July 1973. 1 son, 1 daughter. *Education:* Diploma of Honour, Glinka Choir School, Leningrad, 1970; Studied with Ilya Musin, graduated 1974, Leningrad Conservatory; Artistic diploma, Mannes College of Music, New York, 1976. *Career:* Music Director, Bonch-Bruyevich Institute Chorus, Leningrad, 1970-72; Conductor, Leningrad Conservatory Symphony and Opera Orchestra, 1972-74; Associate Conductor, Music Director, Mannes College of Music Orchestra, 1976-80; Music Director, Grand Rapids Symphony Orchestra, 1980-85; Associate Conductor 1980-81, Principal Guest Conductor 1981-85, Music Director 1985-89, Buffalo Philharmonic Orchestra; Music Director, Orchestre de Paris, 1987; Music Director of Orchestra de Paris, 1989; Guest Conductor with major world orchestras; Led the

Orchestre de Paris at the 1991 Promenade Concerts, London; Beethoven's 5th Piano Concerto, 10th Symphony of Shostakovich and 2nd by Dutilleux, Dances of Galanta, Also Sprach Zarathustra; Principal Guest Conductor of the Orchestra of the Maggio Musicale Fiorentino, 1992; Conducted Eugene Onegin at the Théâtre du Châtelet, 1992; Principal Guest Conductor of St Petersburg Philharmonic Orchestra, 1992. *Recordings:* For Philips. *Honour:* 1st prize, Rachmaninoff Conducting Competition, 1973. *Address:* c/o Orchestre de Paris, 252 rue du Faubourg St Honore, F-75008 Paris, France.

BYCZEK Lloyd Vincent, b. 12 Dec 1944, Chicago, Illinois, USA. Conductor, Orchestral & Choral Music. *Education:* BMus, DePaul University, 1969; Certificate, Conducting, Hochschule für Musik & Darstellende Kunst Mozarteum, Salzburg, Austria, 1972; Study, conducting, with Dr Walter Duclux, Los Angeles 1978, Henry Lewis, American Symphony Orchestra League workshop 1979, Florida Festival Orchestra workshop 1980, Georg Solti workshop 1981; Master classes, Herbert Blomstedt, 1981-83; etc. Private study, conducting, trombone, piano, violin, cello, clarinet. *Career includes:* Conductor with: DePaul University Concert Band, 1968; DePaul University Military Band, 1966-68; DePaul University Musical Company, 1967-69; Crescent Productions Inc, Chicago, 1969-70; Vincent Ferrer Productions, Illinois, 1975; South Suburban (Chicago) Symphony Orchestra, 1972-73. Music director/conductor, Chicago Symphonic Wind Ensemble, 1974-; Guest conductor, various orchestras. Performer, bass trombone, violoncello, tuba, euphonium, various orchestras. Teaching positions including: Freelance, instrumental, choral, theoretical, historical aspects of music, 1968-; Adult education instructor, Truman College, Chicago, 1975. *Memberships include:* Conductors Guild, American Symphony Orchestra League; Chicago Symphonic Wind Ensemble; Phi Mu Alpha Sinfonia; etc. *Address:* 5751 Higgins Avenue, Chicago, IL 60630, USA.

BYERS Reginald, b. 5 Dec 1934, Sydney, Australia. Singer (Tenor). *Education:* Sydney Conservatory and in Austria. *Debut:* As Cavaradossi with Australian Opera at Sydney. *Career:* Guest appearances in New York (City Opera) and with Scottish Opera in Glasgow; many engagements with opera companies in Australia; Other roles have been Verdi's Radames, Ismaele (Nabucco), Gabriele Adorno, Riccardo, Alfredo and Don Carlos, Faust, Turiddu, Rodolfo, Dick Johnson Calaf, Steva (Jenůfa) and Bacchus in Ariande auf Naxos; After retirement from stage gave concerts and taught in Sydney. *Address:* c/o Sydney Opera House, Sydney, New South Wales, Australia.

BYLES Edward, b. Ebbw Vale, Wales. Tenor. *Career:* Toured with Opera for All and sang with major companies including, Royal Opera and in Europe, USSR, Australia and Ireland; Joined ENO in 1974, varied repertoire including Monostatos, Mime, Missail (Boris Godunov) and Vitek (The Makropoulos Case); He has sung in Tosca, War and Peace, Madama Butterfly, Orpheus in the Underworld and Pacific Overtures. In 1988 took part in the first British performance of Rimsky-Korsakov's Christmas Eve; Season 1992 with ENO as the Broomstick-maker in Königskinder and Trabuco in The Force of Destiny. *Address:* c/o ENO, London Coliseum, St Martin's Lane, London, EC2, England.

BYLSMA Anner, b. 17 Feb 1934, The Hague, the Netherlands. Cellist; Teacher. *Education:* Studied with Carel Boomkamp, Royal Conservatory of Music, The Hague. *Career:* Principal cellist, Concertgebouw Orchestra, Amsterdam, 1962-68; Toured throughout the world as Soloist with orchestras; Recitalist and Chamber-music player; Many trio appearances with Frans Brüggen and Gustav Leonhardt; Teacher, Royal Conservatory of Music, The Hague; Sweelinck Conservatory, Amsterdam; Erasmus Scholar, Harvard University, 1982; Played Cello Suites by Bach, BBC Lunchtime Concert, 1992. *Recordings:* Numerous recordings including Angel-EMI; Das Alte Werk; Decca-

London; Harmonia Mundi; Philips; Pro Arte; RCA; Teldec; Telefunken. *Honours:* Winner, Pablo Casals Competition, Mexico City, 1959; Prix d'excellence, Royal Conservatory of Music, 1957. *Address:* c/o Byers Schwalbe & Associates Inc, One Fifth Avenue, New York, NY 10003, USA.

BYRON Michael, b. 7 Sept 1953, Chicago, Illinois, USA. Composer. *Education:* Studied at the California Institute of the Arts with Mario Guarneri, Thomas Stevens and Joe Higgins; Further studies at York University, Ontario, BA 1974. *Career:* Active on behalf of other US composers; Works in collaboration with the performance art group Maple Sugar. *Honours include:* Grants from York University, the Ontario Arts Council, the National Endowment for the Arts and the New York State Council of the Arts. *Compositions include:* Song of the Lifting up of the Head, for piano, 1972; Starfields, for piano 4 hands, 1974; Morning Glory, for percussion, 1975; Marimbas, 1976; A Living Room at the Bottom of a Lake, for orchestra, 1977; Music for One Piano, 1978; Three Mirrors, for percussion ensemble, 1979; Music of Steady Light: 158 pieces for strings, 1979-82; Tidal, for ensemble, 1981; Double String Quartet, 1984. *Address:* c/o ASCAP, ASCAP Building, One Lincoln Plaza, New York, NY 10023, USA.

C

CAAMANO Roberto, b. 7 July 1923, Buenos Aires, Argentina. Composer; Pianist; Professor. m. Maria Teresa Stafforini, 11 Feb. 1956, 3 sons, 1 daughter. *Education:* National Conservatory, Buenos Aires, 1939-46. *Career:* Piano concerts, Latin America, USA and Europe, 1944-61; Professor of Piano, Universidad Nacional del Litoral, 1949-52; Professor of Piano, National Conservatory, Buenos Aires, 1956-79; Artistic Director, Teatro Colon, 1961-64; Professor of Composition, Orchestration and Harmony, 1964-, Dean, Facultad de Artes y Ciencias Musicales, 1966-, Universidad Catolica, Argentina; Member, Board of Directors of National Arts Fund, 1980-83; Commissioned by Louisville Philharmonic Society, Elizabeth Sprague Coolidge Foundation, Interamerican Music Council, Music Division of Organization American States. *Compositions include:* Works for chorus and orchestra: Magnificat, Cantata de la Paz, Canto a San Martín, Te Deum, etc; Works for soloist and orchestra: 2 piano concerti, guitar concerto, harp concerto; Works for chorus a cappella, chamber music, vocal music. *Publications:* Historia del Teatro Colón, 3 vols, 1969; Apuntes para la Formación del Pianista Profesional, 1978. *Hobby:* Gardening. *Address:* Juan B. Alberdi 1275, 1406 Buenos Aires, Argentina.

CABALLÉ Montserrat, b. 12 Apr. 1933, Barcelona, Spain; Soprano, Opera Singer. m. Bernabé Marti, 1 son. *Education:* Conservatorio del Liceo; Studied under Eugenia Kemeny, Conchita Badia and Maestro Annovazi. *Debut:* Mimi in Bohème, State Opera of Basel, 1956. *Career:* North American Debut, Manon, Mexico City, 1964; US Debut in Lucrezia Borgia, Carnegie Hall, 1965; Appeared in Glyndebourne Festival as the Marschallin in Der Rosenkavalier and as the Countess in The Marriage of Figaro, 1965; Debut, Metropolitan Opera as Marguerite, Faust, 1965; Appears frequently at Metropolitan Opera and numerous other opera houses through out the USA; Has performed in most leading opera houses of Europe, including Gran Teatro del Liceo, Barcelona, La Scala, Milan, Vienna State Opera, Paris and Rome Operas; Bayerische Staatsoper, Munich; Covent Garden debut 1972, as Violetta; also at Teatro Colon, Buenos Aires, Argentina; Repertoire of over 40 roles; Sang Hypermestra in Salieri's Les Danaides at Perugia, 1983; Rome Opera, 1986, title role of Spontini's Agnes di Hohenstaufen; Pesaro and Barcelona, 1987, as Rossini's Ermione and Pacini's Saffo; Vienna Staatsoper, 1988, as Mme Cortese in Il Viaggio a Reims; Barcelona, 1989, in La Fiamma by Respighi and the premiere of Cristobal Colón by Balada; Has also sung Isolde at Barcelona; Sang Mdme Cortese in a new production of Il Viaggio a Reims, Covent Garden, 1992. *Recordings:* Lucrezia Borgia; La Traviata; Salome; Aida. *Honour:* Most Excellent and Illustrious Dobna and Cross of Isabella the Catholic. *Current Management:* Columbia Artists Management Incorporated, NY, USA. *Address:* c/o Columbia Artists Management Incorporated, 165 West 57th Street, New York, NY10019, USA.

CABLE Margaret, b. 1950, England. Singer (Mezzo-Soprano). *Career:* Appearances in Europe, Scandinavia, Israel and the USA; Festival engagements at the Bath and Three Choirs Festivals; Promenade Concerts, London; Performances in Baroque repertoire with ensembles using original instruments: Bach's St Matthew Passion conducted by Andrew Parrott, and Messiah at the 1985 Lucerne Festival, conducted by Christopher Hogwood; Broadcasts include Handel's Belshazzar, Tippett's A Child of our Time; Works with orchestra by Arthur Bliss and Robin Holloway; Stage roles with Kent Opera included Mrs Grose in The Turn of the Screw, Dorabella, and Marcellina in Le Nozze di Figaro (also at the 1986 Vienna International Festival); Sang Juno in Handel's Semele, York Early Music Festival, 1991. *Recordings include:* Haydn Masses with the Academy of Ancient Music, Madrigals directed by Peter Pears; Works by Mozart and Scarlatti directed by George Guest; Glazunov songs and Lux Aetrena by William Mathias with the Bach Choir; Handel's Carmelite Vespers and Messiah with Andrew Parrott and the Taverner Players.

CACHEMAILLE Gilles, b. 25 Nov 1951, Orbe, Switzerland. Singer. (Bass-baritone). *Education:* Studied at the Lausanne Conservatoire with Juliette Bise. *Career:* Concert hall appearances from 1978 at the Aix and Salzburg Festivals, Paris, Lyon, Buenos Aires, Madrid, Strasbourg, Lisbon and Tokyo; Repertoire has included the Passions of Bach, L'Enfance du Christ by Berlioz, Franck's Les Beatitudes, Haydn's Schopfung and Jahreszeiten, works by Monteverdi and songs by Duparc, Poulenc, Schubert and Strauss; Member of the Lyon Opera. Debut: Sang in the stage premiere of Rameau's Les Boréades at Aix, 1982; Lausanne Opera as Guglielmo, Simone in La Finta Semplice, Mozart's Figaro and Papageno, and Belcore in L'Elisir d'Amore, 1988; Mezieres 1988, as Gluck's Orpheus, Leoporello at the Hamburg Staatsoper, 1987 and Vienna, 1989; Sang in Martinů's Les Trois Souhaits at Lyons, 1990 and Leporello at Houston, 1991. *Recordings include:* L'Enfance du Christ, Chausson's Le Roi Arthus, Iphigénie en Aulide, Les Boréades and Gluck's La Rencontre Imprevue (Erato); Dominic in Arabella and Golaud in Pelléas and Mélisande; Guglielmo in Cosi fan Tutte, conducted by Harnoncourt; Claudio in Beatrice et Benedict, *Address:* c/o Balmer & Dixon Management AG, Granitweg 2, CH-8006 Zürich, Switzerland.

CADDY Ian Graham, b. 1 Mar 1947, Southampton, England. Bass-Baritone. m. Kathryn Dorothy Ash, 29 Sept 1979, 1 son, 2 daughters. *Education:* Royal Academy of Music, 1965-70, LRAM, ARCM. *Debut:* London 1974. *Career:* Opera for All; Kent Opera; New Opera Company; Phoenix Opera; Glyndebourne; English National Opera; Nanki-Poo in The Mikado; Scottish Opera; Welsh National Opera; Royal Opera Covent Garden; Opera, oratorio , festivals and recitals throughout Great Britain, also Austria, Canada, Wexford and Versailles Festivals; Denmark, Eire, France, Germany, Hong Kong, Iceland, Italy, Netherlands, Spain, USA, Yugoslavia; numerous TV and Radio broadcasts, in all countries. *Recordings include:* Edited and recorded: Songs and cantatas by Mayr and Donizetti; L'Amor Coniugale, Mayr; Donizetti Songs, Jigs - Reels and Songs of the Bottle, Holbrooke; Vivaldi's Dixit Dominus; Rameau's Princesse de Navarre and Nais; Schoeck: Notturno; Video: Macbeth; The Beggar's Opera; Nais; Castor et Pollux; La Fanciulla del West; Intermezzo. *Honours include:* Ricordi Prize, 1967; Vaughan-Williams Trust Award, 1969; Countess of Munster Musical Trust Award, 1970; Royal Academy of Music President's Prize, 1970; Associate of the Royal Academy of Music, 1984. *Memberships:* Incorporated Society of Musicians; co-founder of The Mayr-Donizetti Collaboration, 1985. *Current Management:* Music International, 13 Ardilaun Road, London N5 2QR. *Address:* c/o English National Opera, St. Martins Lane, London, England, WC2.

CADUFF Sylvia, b. 7 Jan 1937, Chur, Switzerland. Conductor; Professor of Conducting and Orchestral Studies. *Education:* Studied at the Conservatorie of Lucerne; Further studies with Karajan at the Berlin Conservatory and with Kubelik, Matacic and Van Otterloo. *Debut:* With the Tonhalle Orchestra, Zurich. *Career:* Guest conductor in all the European Countries, USA, Japan, South Korea, Appearances with New York Philharmonic, Munich and Berlin Philharmonic, Royal Philharmonic London; Music Director in Solingen, 1977-86; Assistant to Bernstein at the New York Philharmonic, 1966-67; Appearances with the Munich Philharmonic, Radio Orchestra Berlin, Royal Philharmonic Orchestra; Taught conducting at the Berne Conservatory, 1972-77; First Woman to be appointed Music Director in Europe: Solingen, 1977-86. *Memberships:* Swiss Musicians Association; Swiss Conductors Union. *Honours include:* First Prize, Mitropoulos Competition, New York, 1966. *Memberships:*Vice President, Swiss Musicians Association, Swiss Music Council. *Current Management:* Konzertgesellschaft, GmBH, Zurich, Switzerland. *Address:* Belleriverstrasse 31, 6006, Lucerne, Switzerland.

CAGLI Bruno, b. 2 June 1942, Narni, Italy. Administrator; Writer on Music. *Education:* studies at Rome University. *Career:* Writer for the theatre and for broadcasting companies; Music criticism in journals and newspapers; Librettist of L'Ombre di Banquo, 1976 and Le Campanule, 1981 by Renosto; Director of the Fondazione Rossini at Pesaro from 1971, collaborating in the new critical editton of Rossini's wars with Philip Gossett and others; Artistic Director of the Teatro dell'Opera at Rome, 1987-90; Teacher at Naples and Urbino universities and at the Rome Conservatoires; Presidente-Sovriutendente, dal 1990, dell Accademia Nationale diSanta Cecilia. *Publications include:* Studies of Donizetti, Verdi and Rossini (including the literary sources of Rossini's libretti); Storia di San Carlo 1989; Lettere e documenti di G Rossini, 1992. *Address:* c/o Accademia Nationale di Santa Cecilia, via Vittorie 6-00186 Roma, Italy.

CAHILL Teresa Mary, b. 30 July 1944, Maidenhead, Berkshire, England. Singer (Lyric Soprano), divorced. *Education:* Associate, Guildhall School of Music, (Piano); Licentiate, Royal Academy of Music, (Singing). *Debut:* Covent Garden, 1970 and Glyndebourne, 1969. *Career:* Glyndebourne, the English National Opera; Scottish Welsh Opera; Covent Garden; Debut at Santa Fé Opera, 1972; La Scala, Milan, 1976, Philadelphia Opera, 1981 roles include Strauss's Sophie, Verdi's Alice Ford and Mozart's Donna Elvira; Sang at Covent Garden, 1970-77 as Zerlina, Sophie and Barbarina and in the 1976 premiere of Henze's We Come to the River; ENO, 1977, as Pauline Le Clerc in the premiere at Toussaint 1Ouverture by David Blake; Sang the title role in Strauss's Daphne, Chelsea Opera, 1990. *Concerts include:* Edinburgh Festival, Proms, Chicago Symphony Orchestra, Vienna Festival, Berlin Festival, Hallé Orchestra, Frankfurt Radio Orchestra, Danish Radio Orchestra, Stockholm Philharmonic, BBC Orchestras; English Chamber Orchestra; Royal Liverpool Philharmonic Orchestra; all the London orchestras; The West Deutscher Rundfunk; The Rotterdam Philharmonic; Houston Symphony Orchestra; Brussels Radio Orchestra; RAI Turin Orchestra; London Sinfonietta; Hamburg Philharmonie; Numerous television and radio performances; Professor, Royal Northern College of Music, Trinity College and Guildhall School; masterclasses, lecturer and private voice consultant. *Recordings:* King Olaf by Elgar, EMI; Mahler's Eighth Symphony, Denon; Strauss, Lieder Recital, and Spirit of England and Coronation Ode by Elgar, both on Chandos; Elgar War Music on Pearl Label. *Honours:* Silver Medal, Worshipful Company of Musicians, 1966; John Christie Award, Glyndebourne, 1970. *Memberships:* Incorporated Society of Musicians; Equity; Royal Overseas League. *Hobbies:* Photography; Arts; Cooking; Collecting antique furniture. *Address:* 65 Leyland Road, London, SE12 8DW.

CAIRE Patrice, b. 17 June 1949, Lyon, France. Organist. *Education:* Baccalaureat, 1968; Faculty of Law; Lyon Conservatory; Conservatoire National Superieur de Musique, Paris; Licence de Concert, Ecole Normale de Musique, Paris, 1975. *Career:* Organist, Sainte Croix Church, Luon, 1973-83; Organist, St Bonaventure Sanctuary, Lyon, 1983-; Keeper, Grandes Orgues de l'Auditorium Maurice Ravel, Lyon, 1980-; Commissioner, International Improvisation Competition, 1982-83; Teacher, Conservatoire National Superieur de Musique, Lyon, 1979-; Recitals, France, Germany, England, Scotland, Switzerland, Sweden, Spain, Italy, Belgium, USA, Canada; Concert performances: Radio France, France Musique, France Culture, Radio Canado, Radio Suisse Romande, Spanish Radio Television, Sweden Radio; With orchestra under S Baudo, E Krivine, S Skrawaczewski, J Nelson, E Tchakarov, N Corboz, A Siiciliani. *Recordings:* 2 recitals; Ch M Widor, Symphony No 6, extracts from No 7 (REM); A Guilmant, Sonata No 1 (REM); 6 Pieces: Brass, Organ and Percussion, Busser, Litaize, Dupré, Vierne, Gigout (REM); N J Lemmens, Fanfare, Prière, Sonatas No 1, 2, 3, (REM); Lemmens, Lefebure Wely (REM); C Franck et l'orgue du Trocadero (REM); L Vierne, Finales of 6 Symphonies (REM); Ch M Widor, Symphonies No 4, 5 (REM); Ch M Widor, Symphonies No 1, 2 (REM); L Boellmann, Work

for Grand Organ (REM); C Franck, 12 Pieces for Grand Organ (REM); Les Maitres du Trocadero, Guilmant, Widor, Lemmens, Franck, Dubois, Gigouot, Saint-Saëns (REM). *Membership:* Founder/Artistic Director, Les Grandes Orgues de l'Auditorium Maurice Ravel, Lyon. *Current Management:* North America: Ph Truckenbrod, P O Box 69, West Hartford, CT 06107, USA. *Hobbies:* Sport; Cinema; Reading. *Address:* 73 Rue Pierre Corneille 69006, Lyon, France.

CAIRNS Christine, b. 11 Feb 1959, Ayrshire, Scotland. Singer Mezzo-Soprano. *Education:* Royal Scottish Academy of Music and Drama, Glasgow; Further study with Neilson Taylor. *Career:* Concerts with André Previn and the Los Angeles Philharmonic 1985; Prokofiev's Alexander Nevsky in Los Angeles and with the Cleveland and Philadelphia Orchestras; Royal Philharmonic Orchestra 1988, in Mahler's Kindertotenlieder; Tour of the US with Mahler's 4th Symphony; Festival Hall London 1988, in Schoenberg's Songs Op. 22; Promenade Concerts London 1989, in Mozart's Coronation Mass, returned 1990; Guest appearances throughout the British Isles, Athens, Basle, Tokyo, Berlin, San Francisco, Dortmund and touring throughout Spain; Guest engagements in Paris, Madrid, Rome, Zurich, Singapore and Rio de Janiero; Staged performances of Monteverdi's Orfeo in Valencia; Concerts, Ashkenazy, Berlin and London, 1990; Mahler with Simon Rattle and Yuri Temirkanov in LA, 1991. *Recordings:* Mendelssohn's Midsummer Night's Dream, Previn, Vienna; Prokofiev Alexander Nevsky, Previn, LA Philharmonic; Die Erste Walpurgisnacht (Dohnanyi), Cleveland. *Current Management:* c/o Harrison Parrott Ltd, 12 Penzance Place, London W11 4PA, England.

CAIRNS David Adam, b. 8 June 1926, Loughton, Essex. Critic; Writer. *Education:* Oxford University 1945-48; Princeton University 1950-51. *Career:* Co-founded Chelsea Opera Group, 1950; Music Critic, Spectator, 1958-62; Financial Times 1962-67, New Statesman 1967-70, Sunday Times from 1973; succeeded Desmond Shawe-Taylor as chief music critic 1983; Has also written reviews for the Observer, Evening Standard. *Contributions to:* Berlioz in Viking Opera Guide, 1993. *Publications include:* Translation of the Berlioz Memoirs, 1969, revised 1977; Collecton of essays, Responses, 1973-80; First volume of biography of Berlioz, 1989. *Address:* c/o Sunday Times, 1 Pennington Street, London EC2, England.

CAIRNS Janice, b. 1955, Ashington, Northumberland, England. Singer (Soprano). *Education:* Studied at the Royal Scottish Academy, with John Hauxvell and with Titto Gobbi in Rome. *Debut:* Sang Verdi's Desdemona at the Thessaloniki Festival, directed by Gobbi. *Career:* London debut as Odabella in Attila, for University College Opera; Appearances with Kent Opera as Alice Ford, and Donna Anna; Manon Lescaut and Leonora (La Forza del Destino) for Chelsea Opera Group; With English National Opera has sung Musetta, Ariadne, Eva, Maria in Mazeppa, Lisa, Maria Boccanegra, Tosca and Amelia; Scottish Opera as Rezia in Oberon, Leonora (Il Trovatore), Aida and Madama Butterfly; For Opera North has sung Aida, Leonore and Helene in the British stage premiere of Verdi's Jerusalem (1989); Italian debut with Scottish Opera at La Fenice, Venice, as Rezia; Concert engagements include the Verdi Requiem with the LSO, Odabella at the Concertgebouw, Rachmaninov's The Bells at the Proms and Britten's War Requiem at the Norwich Festival; English National Opera, 1992, as Anna in Street Scene and as Ariadne. *Address:* c/o John Coast Ltd, 31 Sinclair Road, London W14 ONS, England.

CALCAFUOCO Angelo, b. 19 May 1957, Ontario, Canada. Concert Violinist. m. Claudia Carolina, 2 sons. *Education:* BMus, Performance, University of Toronto, teachers included Steven Staryk and Sydney Harth. *Debut:* Sault Ste Marie, 1974. *Career:* Concert Master, Canadian Chamber Orchestra; Former Chairman, Royal Conservatory of Music, University of Toronto String Department; Currently Director, Appleby Centre for the Arts; Project Manager, Architect Royal Conservatory

Strings Syllabus and Graded Book Series; Former Director, Algoma Music Camp; Former Director, Founder, Summer Performance Academy, Oakville, Ontario; Formerly on Board of Examiners of RCM; Concert Master, Royal Conservatory Heritage Orchestra; Former Director, Royal Conservatory Chambre Orchestra; Currently, Head of Strings, Appleby College, Ontario, Canada; Director, Appleby Centre for the Arts. *Honours:* Banff Centre, 1980; Scholarships from University of Toronto, 1976-81. *Memberships:* Toronto Musicians Association; Chamber Music America. *Hobbies:* Collecting Ceramics; Carpentry; Gardening. *Address:* 65 Quebec Avenue, Toronto, Ontario M6P 2T3, Canada .

CALDWELL Sarah, b. 6 Mar. 1924, Maryville, USA. Conductor; Opera Impresario; Opera Director. *Education:* University of Arkansas; Hendrix Colelge; Violin with Richard Burgin, New England Conservatory of Music; Viola with Georges Fourel; apprenticeship with Boris Goldovsky. *Career:* Assistant to Boris Goldovsky, Opera Dept., New England Consevatory of Music; Director, Boston University Opera Workshop, 1952-60; Founder, Director, Opera Group, Boston, 1958, which became Opera Company of Boston, 1965; Conducted or Produced, US Premieres, Prokofiev's War and Peace; Nono's Intolleranza, Moses and Aron and Montezuma by Roger Sessions; Producer, original versions, Boris Godunov and Don Carlos. Guest Conductor, various orchestras including: New York Philharmonic; Pittsburgh Symphony; Boston Symphony; Indianapolis Symphony, *Honours:* 1st Woman to appear as a Conductor with the Metropolitan Opera, New York, 1976, (La Traviata). *Address:* c/o Opera Company of Boston, PO Box 50, Boston, MA 02112, USA.

CALLIGARIS Sergio, b. 1941, Rosario, Argentina. Composer; Pianist; Professor of Piano. *Career:* Concerts, Europe, Americas, South Africa, 1954-; Chair, Piano: Cleveland Institute of Music, Ohio, USA; Calfornia State Univeristy, Los Angeles, 1969; Teaching, San Pietro a Majella Conservatory, Naples, A Casella Conservatory, L'Aquila, L D'Annunzio Conservatory, Pescara, Italy, 1974-; Arts Director, American Academy of the Arts in Europe, Verona; Jury, national and international piano competitions, Italy, abroad; Represented Italian National TV-network, Italia International Prize, 1985; Musical profile as Composer and Pianist, Società Aquilana dei Concerti 40th Anniversary concert cycle, 1986; His works performed on TV, Italy and worldwide; Commissioned: Concerto, Istituzione Sinfonica Abruzzese, 1989; Danze Sinfoniche, Omaggio a Bellini, Teatro Massimo Bellini, Catania, 100th Anniversary, 2nd Festival Bellinano, 1990; Continuous and regular performances every week of all his works in the major centers and musical institutions all over the world. *Compositions:* Published, recorded: 24 Studi, 1978, 1979, 1980; Il Quaderno Pianistico di Renzo, 1978; Scene Coreografiche, 1979; Tre Madrigali, 1979; BHS, 1984-85; Published: Scherzo, 1957; Siciliana, 1977; Preludio, Sarabanda e Finale, 1979; Passacaglia, 1983; Preludio, Corale, Doppia Fuga e Finale, 1984; Due Danze Concertanti, 1986; Recorded: Ave Maria, 1978; Sonata, 1978; Suite da Requiem No 2, 1985; Seconda Suite di Danze Sinfoniche, op. 27, for large orchestra, 1990; Suite for solo cello, op 20, 1991; Concerto for piano and orchestra, op. 29, 1992; all published by Nuova Carisch-Time Warner Co., Milan, Italy. *Recordings:* Concerts for Union Europeènne Radiodiffusion, 1977, 1985, 1987; Bis Celebri, EMI; Sergio Calligaris pianoforte; Sergio Calligaris, Contemporanea Vol VI, Classico Records; Calligaris: Quaderni Pianistici, Music by Calligaris, CD Ento dello Spettacolo EDS 1; Stereo Orion: Sergio Callagris, recital; Fantasia Romantica; The Most Beautiful Chopin; Piano Music of Latin America and works by Schumann, Chopin, Ravel; CD dedicated to Sergio Calligaris, Pianist and composer, works by Chopin, Rachmaninoff, Vitalini and Calligaris, 1993. *Address:* Viale Libia 76, 00199 Rome, Italy.

CALM Birgit, b. 1959, Lubeck, Germany. Singer (Mezzo-soprano). *Education:* Studied in Lubeck and Humburg. *Career:* Sang first at the Kiel Opera, then Osnabruck, 1984-85; Appearances at the Bayerische Staatsoper from 1984 have included Humperdinck's Hansel, Alkmene in Die Liebe der Danae and Carlotta in Die Schweigsame Frau; Guest appearances in concert and opera in Germany and abroad. *Recordings include:* Sacred music by Dittersdorf (Harmonia Mundi); Third Maid in Elektra, conducted by Sawallisch. *Address:* c/o Bayerische Staatsoper, Postfach 100148, 8000 Munich 1, Germany.

CAMANI Adrianna, b. 27 March 1936, Padua, Italy. Singer (Mezzo-Soprano). *Education:* Studied at the Padua Conservatory with Sara Sforni Corti. *Debut:* Naples 1968, as the Nurse in L'Incoronazione di Poppea. *Career:* Has sung widely in Italy, notably in Genoa, Turin, Trieste, Venice and Naples; Sang in the Scala premiere of Dallapiccola's Ulisse; Major roles include La Cieca in La Gioconda, Ulrica in Un Ballo in Maschera, Eboli in Don Carlos and parts in Madama Butterfly, Andrea Chénier, Francesca da Rimini and Il Quattro Rusteghi. *Address:* Teatro alla Scala, Via Filodrammatici 2, Milan, Italy.

CAMBRELING Sylvian, b. 2 July 1948, Amiens, France. Conductor. *Education:* Conservatoire National Superieur de Musique de Paris. *Career:* Assistant Conductor, Orchestre de Lyon, 1975-81; First Guest Conductor, Ensemble Intercontemporain, Paris, 1976-81; Musical Director, Théâtre de la Monnaie Bruxelles, 1981-; Guest Conductor: Salzburg and Glyndebourne Festivals; Festival d'Aix-en-Provence; Hamburg Opera; Scala Milan; Paris Opera; Metropolitan Opera, New York; Grand Théâtre, Geneva; Berlin Philharmonic; Munich State Orchestra; Vienna Symphony; Academia Santa Cecilia Rome; Museum Orchestra, Frankfurt; Gurzenich Orchestra Cologne; Cincinnati Symphony; St Paul Chamber Orchestra; Hallé Orchestra; Royal Liverpool Philharmonic; Conducted The Rake's Progess at the 1989 Glyndebourne Festival; Premiere of Des Glas in Kopf Wird Vom Glas by Eugeniusz Knapik at Antwerp, 1990; Lohengrin and From the House of the Dead at Brussels, 1990; New Production of Simon Boccanegra, 1990-1991 season; Director of the Frankfurt Opera from 1993 (Wozzeck, From the House of the Dead and Elektra). *Recordings:* La Clemenza di Tito; Lucio Silla; Louise-Charpentier; Semiramide; The Tales of Hoffmann; Le Sacre du Printemps; Sapho-Gounod; L'Histoire du Soldât, Requiem by Fauré; La Finta Giardiniera. *Management:* DARSA SA Michael Rainer, Paris; Askonas Ltd, London; Concerto Winderstein Munich; ICM New York. *Address:* c/o Théâtre de la Monnaie, 4 Rue Léopold, 1000 Bruxelles, Belgium.

CAMDEN Anthony, b. 26 Apr 1938, London, England. Oboist. m. (1) Diane Camden, (div), 1 son, 1 daughter, (2) Lily Camden. *Career:* Founder Member, London Virtuosi, 1972-; Principal Oboe, London Symphony Orchestra, 1973-88; Chairman, LSO, Board of Directors, 1975-87; Professor, Director and Provost Queensland Conservatorium of Music, 1988-93 (Griffith University); Dean of Music, Academy of Performing Arts, 1993-. *Recordings:* Bach Concerto for Violin and Oboe (with Yehudi Menuhin); Six Albinoni Oboe Concertos for Naxos with London Virtuosi, Grace Williams Oboe Concerto (LSO); Mozart Oboe Quartet, Telemann Concerto for Flute and Oboe (with James Galway). *Hobbies:* Cricket; Swimming. *Address:* c/o Academy of Performing Arts, 1 Gloucester Road, Wanchai, Hong Kong.

CAMERON John, b. 20 Mar 1918, New South Wales, Australia. Lecturer; Teacher; Singer (Baritone). m. 29 Mar 1961 (wife deceased). *Education:* Sydney Technical College; NSW Conservatorium of Music, Australia. *Debut:* Covent Garden, as Germont, 1949. *Career includes:* Sang with Australian Elizabethan Trust Opera, 1949-74, notably as Mozart's Figaro, Guglielmo and Papageno; Glyndebourne Festival, 1953-54; Soloist with Sadler's Wells Opera in premiere of Benjamin's The Tale of Two Cities, 1957, Dallapiccola's Prigioniero and the Premiere of Bennett's The Mines of Suphur, 1965; New Opera Company, 1970, and British premiere of Goehr's Arden must Die, 1974; Concert appearances at the Festival Hall and on tour to India, and throughout Europe; Sang Punch in the premier of Birtwistle's Punch and Judy, Aldeburgh Festival, 1968; BBC engagements include series My Songs go round the world; Principal Lecturer, Fellow, Royal Northern College of Music, 1976-. *Recordings include:* Macheath in The Beggar's Opera, conducted by Sargent; King Arthur and Elijah; Claudio in Beatrice et Benedict; Applausus by Haydn, with Joan Sutherland; Other pressings with Boult, Beecham and Stokowski. *Memberships:* Incorporated Society of Musicians; Australian Musical Symphony. *Address:* c/o Royal Northern College of Music, 124 Oxford Road, Manchester M13 9RD, England.

CAMERON Roderick (Rod), b. 1937, Glasgow, Scotland. Woodwind Maker; Mechanical Engineer; Former Chief Engineer. m. (1) 1 daughter, (2) Kathleen Cameron, 1 daughter. *Education:* Toolmaker's Apprenticeship, Rolls Royce Company, 7 years; 1st degree in Mechanical Engineering through night school; Teacher Training College; Master's degree, Mechanical Engineering, Vancouver; Doctor's degree, Engineering Research, Cambridge University, 1967; Self-taught in woodwind making. *Career:* Began experimental making of early woodwinds (recorders), early 70s; 1st commission, copies of early 17th century Baroque recorders, Early Music Society of Vancouver, Canada, 1974; Began making traversos (baroque flutes), San Francisco, California, USA, 1975; Opened workshop in Scotland, 1984; Moved to Mendocino, California, 1984; Has conducted extensive research trips throughout European capitals, playing and examining important woodwinds using self-designed electronic bore measurer. *Publications:* New method of making complex profile reamers. *Hobbies:* Music; Mountaineering; Kayaking white-water rivers; Skiing; Diving; Other outdoor pursuits; works in Scotland each year from April to Sept. *Address:* PO Box 438, Mendocino, CA 95460, USA and 39 Union Street, Nairn IVI 24PR, Scotland.

CAMILLERI Charles, b. 7 Sept. 1931, Hamrun, Malta. Composer. m. 22 Sept. 1957, 1 son, 1 daughter. *Education:* Lyceum, Malta; Toronto University, Canada. *Career:* Conductor, CBC; Visiting Professor in numerous institutions. *Compositions:* Missa Mundi; Piano Concerto No 1; Stone Island Within; Piano Trio; Taqsim; Piano Concertos Nos 2 and 3; Organ Concerto; Unum Deum, Cantata; Missa Brevis; 3 operas; Oratorio; Chamber works. *Publication:* The Music of the Mediterranean, 1986. *Address:* 24 Orchard Avenue, Finchley, London N3 3NL, England.

CAMPANELLA Bruno, b. 6 Jan 1943, Bari, Italy. Conductor. *Education:* Studied Conducting with Piero Bellugi, Hans Swarowsky and Thomas Schippers; Composition with Dallapiccola. *Debut:*)Spoleto Festival, 1967. *Career:* From 1971, has conducted nineteenth century Italian at La Scala Milan, elsewhere in Italy and in Europe and North America; Conducted Rossini's Le Comte Ory at Montreal 1989, Don Pasquale at Covent Garden and Puccinni's La Cecchina at the 1990 Martina Franca Festival; Conducted L'Italiana in Algeri at the Teatro Regio Turin, 1992; 1992 at La Scala, Le Comte Ory and Fra Diavolo; Direttore stabile, Teatro Regio, Turin, 1992-; Conducted, La Fille du Regiment in San Francisco, 1993; Returned to Covent Garden, 1992 for further Don Pasquale performances and conducts La Cenerentola in 1994. *Recordings include:* Il Barbiere di Siviglia; La Fille du Regiment; DDG recording of bel canto arias with Kathleen Battle. *Address:* c/o Royal Opera House (Contracts), Covent Garden, London WC2, England.

CAMPBELL David, b. 15 Apr 1953, Hemel Hempstead, Hertfordshire, England. Clarinettist. m. 7 Nov. 1981, 1 son. *Education:* Barton Peveril, Hampshire, 1964-71; Royal College of Music, 1971-75; GRSM; ARCM; LRAM. *Debut:* Wigmore Hall, April 1975. *Career:* Solo clarinettist, recitalist and chamber music has played in 36 countries; Concertos with English Chamber Orchestra; City of London Sinfonia; London Mozart Players; BBC Concert; BBC Scottish; Professor, London

College of Music; BBC Welsh; BBC Philharmonic; Bournemouth Sinfonietta; Québèc Symphony; Bilbao Symphony; San Sebastian Symphony. *Recordings:* Mozart Clarinet Concerto with City of London Sinfonia under Hickox - Pickwick; Steptoe Quintet and Complete Chamber Music for Clarinet by Brahms on Phoenix; Ravel Introduction and Allegro, Virgin Classics; Beethoven, Brahms Trios, Pickwick; Schubert Octet, Pickwick. *Publications:* Regular contributor to Allegro magazine published by Boosey and Hawkes. *Honours:* Mozart Memorial Prize, 1976; Martin Musical Scholarship, 1976. *Memberships:* Incorporated Society of Musicians; Clarinet and Saxophone Society. *Hobby:* Walking, Bird Watching. *Current Management:* Janet Hughes, Manager, 76 Cross Oak Road, Berkhamsted, HP4 3HZ, Hertfordshire. *Address:* 83 Woodwarde Road, Dulwich, London, SE22 8UL, England.

CAMPBELL Ian David, b. 21 Dec 1945, Brisbane, Australia. Opera General Director. m. Ann Spira, 1 Sept. 1985, 2 sons. *Education:* BA, University of Sydney, 1967; Voice studies with Godfrey Stirling, Sydney, 1964-72. *Debut:* Australian Opera, Sydney, 1967. *Career:* Principal tenor, Australian Opera, 1967-74; Senior music officer, Australia Council, 1974-76; General Manager, State Opera of South Australia, 1976-82; Assistant Artistic Administrator, Metropolitan Opera, New York, 1982-83; General Director, San Diego Opera, California, USA, July 1983-. *Recording:* War & Peace, television, opening of Sydney Opera House, 1973. *Honour:* Peri Award, services to California opera, 1983. *Memberships:* Associate Fellow, Australian Institute of Management; Member, Kona Kai Club, San Diego; Board Member, Opera America, 1985-. *Hobbies:* Squash; Golf; Surfing. *Address:* San Diego Opera, PO Box 988, San Diego, CA 92112-0988, USA.

CAMPBELL Margaret (Jean), b. 1940, London, England. Author and Lecturer on Musical Subjects. m. Richard Barrington Beare, 2 sons, 1 daughter. *Education:* Art Scholarship, London. *Career:* Talks and interviews on BBC Radio, Cleveland Radio, Voice of America, USA and CBC, Canada; BBC and Southern Television; Lectures at Cornell, Oberlin, Indiana and Oklahoma Universities and Manhattan School of New York; Rice University; University of Texas at Austin; University of Southern California USA; Cambridge, Guildford and Bath Universities, Guildhall School of Music and Drama and Purcell School, England. *Publications:* Dolmetsch: The Man and His Work, London and USA, 1975; The Great Violinists, London, 1980, USA, 1981, Germany, 1982, Japan 1983; The Great Cellists, 1988, Japan due 1994; Henry Purcell: Glory of His Age, London 1993. *Contributions to:* The New Grove Dictionary of Music, 1980; Times Educational Supplement, Daily Telegraph, The Independent, The Strad, Classical Music, The Consort; Early Music and others; Editor of The Journal of British Music Therapy, 1974-1990. *Honours:* Winston Churchill Memorial Travelling Fellowship, 1971; Fellow of the Royal Society of Arts, 1991. *Memberships:* Society of Authors; Royal Society of Literature; Founder Member, Oxford Foundation for Historical Musical Instruments; Committee Member and Governor, Dolmetsch Foundation. *Hobbies:* Swimming, Walking, Reading biography. *Address:* 71 Shrublands Avenue, Berkhamsted, Herts, HP4 3JG, England.

CAMPBELL Richard, b. 1960, England, Viol Player. *Career:* Member of Fretwork, first London concert at the Wigmore Hall, London, July 1986; Appearances in the Renaissance and Baroque repertoire in Sweden, France, Belgium, Holland, Germany, Austria, Switzerland and Italy; Radio broadcasts in Sweden, Holland, Germany and Austria; Televised concert on ZDF, Mainz, Tour of Soviet Union Sept 1989 and Japan, June 1991; Festival engagements in Britain; Repertory includes In Nomines and Fantasias by Tallis, Parsons and Byrd; Dance music by Holborne and Dowland (including Lachrimae); Six-part consorts by Gibbons and William Lawes; Songs and instrumental works by Purcell; Collaborations with vocal group Red Byrd in verse anthems by Byrd and Tomkins, London Cries by

Gibbons and Dering, Resurrection Story and Seven Last Words by Schütz; Gave George Benjamin's Upon Silence at the Elizabeth Hall, Oct 1990; Wigmore Hall concerts 1990-91 with music by Lawes, Purcell, Locke, Dowland and Byrd. *Recordings:* Heart's Ease (late Tudor and early Stuart); Armada (Courts of Philip II and Elizabeth I); Night's Black Bird (Dowland and Byrd); Cries and Fancies (Fantasias, In Nomines and The Cries of London by Gibbons); Go Nightly Cares (Consort songs, dances and In Nomines by Byrd and Dowland): all on Virgin Classics Veritas label. *Address:* Robert White Management, 182 Moselle Avenue, London N22 6EX, England.

CAMPORA Giuseppe, b. 30 Sept. 1923, Tortona, Italy. Singer (Tenor). *Education:* Studied in Genoa and Milan. *Debut:* Bari 1949, as Rodolfo in La Bohème. *Career:* La Scala Milan from 1951; Debut as Maurizio in Adriana Le Couveur; Buenos Aires and Rio de Janeiro 1952; Metropolitan Opera 1954, as Rodolfo; Guest engagements in Verona, Florence, Brussels, Paris, Hamburg, Lisbon, Zurich, Geneva, Monte Carlo, Baltimore and Cincinnati; La Scala 1952 in the premiere of Rocca's Uragano; Bregenz 1964, in Das Land des Lächelns; Italian TV appearances as Radames, Pinkerton, and Enzo in La Gioconda. *Recordings include:* La Forza del Destino; La Gioconda; Madama Butterfly; Zazà by Leoncavallo; Scenes from Conchita by Zandonai. *Address:* Teatro alla Scala, Via Filodrammatici 2, 1-20121 Milan, Italy.

CAMPOS Anisia, Concert Pianist; Pedagogue. m. Rémus Tzincoca. *Education:* Graduate, Ecole Normale de Musique de Paris; Mozarteum Academy of Music, Salzburg. *Career:* Recitals, Soloist, with orchestras in Europe, Canada & South America; Radio & TV Broadcasts; Professor, State Conservatory of Music, Montreal; Master Classes; First auditions, Enesco's Piano Sonata No.1, Europe and North America; Courses at Centre d'Arts d'Orford, Canada; Professor, Ottawa University; Interpretation Course, Ecole Supérieure de Musique Vincent-d'indy, of Montreal; Co-operated with conductor Rémus Tzincoca at reconstitution of Bartok's Original Version of Cantata Profana. *Memberships:* President, Co-Founder, Enesco Foundation, Canada. *Hobbies:* Gardening; Photography; Backgammon. *Address:* 632 Avenue Herve-Beaudry, Laval, Quebec H7E 2X6, Canada.

CANARINA John Baptiste, b. 19 May 1934, New York, USA. Conductor.*Education:* BS, 1957, MS, 1958, Juilliard School; Conducting with Pierre Monteux and Jean Morel, Piano with Arthur Lloyd and Double Bass with Frederick Zimmermann. *Career:* Conductor, 7th US Army Symphony Orchestra, 1959- 60; Assistant conductor, New York Philharmonic, 1961-62; Music Director, Jacksonville Symphony Orchestra, Florida, 1962-69; Director of Orchestral Activities, Drake University, 1973-; Guest Conductor: Royal Philharmonic, Philharmonia Orchestra, Bournemouth Symphony, BBC Welsh and Scottish Symphonies, Belgian Radio Orchestra, Slovak Radio Symphony Bratislava. *Publications:* Contributor to Tempo, High Fidelity, Opus and Keynote. *Honours:* Ford Foundation Grant, 1964; Berkshire Music Centre Fellowship, 1965. *Memberships:* Board, Conductors Guild; Berlioz Society; American Symphony Orchestra League; Leopold Stokowski Society; Delius Association of Florida. *Hobbies:* Films; Baseball; Theatre. *Address:* 3663 Grand Avenue, Apt. 903, Des Moines, IA 50312, USA.

CANELLAKIS Martin, b. 10 Jan 1942, Tientsin, China. Conductor; Music Director; Professor. m. Sheryl Swint, 2 Jan 1968, 1 son, 1 daughter. *Education:* Canterbury Boys' High School, Sydney, Australia, 1952-56; Lycée Carnot, Paris, France, 1956-60; Ecole Normale de Musique (Piano Prize), 1956-60; Bachelor and Master of Science in Piano, Juilliard School of Music, USA, 1965; Professional Diploma, Columbia University Teachers College, 1967; Doctoral Studies, Conducting Program, Peabody Conservatory of Music, 1966-67; Postgraduate Diploma in Conducting, Mannes College of Music, 1968. *Debut:* Alice Tully Hall, Lincoln Center,

New York City, 1978. *Career:* Guest Conductor, Baltimore Symphony Orchestra, 1967; Founder/Conductor, Peabody Chamber Orchestra, 1966-67; Music Director, Brooklyn Symphony Orchestra, 1968-77; Queensborough Orchestra, 1971-; Queens College Orchestral Society, 1975-85; Westchester Symphony Orchestra, 1982-91; Guest Conductor, Southern Vermont Music Festival, 1978, 1979; Guest Conductor, Jerusalem Symphony Orchestra, 1978; Long Island String Festival, 1988; Professor of Music, City University of New York, 1971-. *Honours:* Conducting Fellowships; Meadow Brook Music Festival, 1965, Aspen Music Festival, 1966, 1968, 1969; National Orchestral Association, 1970-71; Perera Award, Mannes College of Music, 1968; Piano Assistantship, Peabody Conservatory, 1966; Congressional Record Tribute and Citation, 1985 and 1991; Laureate Conductor, 1991-. *Address:* 452 Riverside Drive, New York, NY 10027, USA.

CANGALOVIC Miroslav, b. 3 Mar 1921, Glamoc, Yugoslavia. Singer (Bass). *Education:* Studied in Belgrade. *Debut:* Belgrade 1946, as Pimen in Boris Godunov. *Career:* Sang in Belgrade and elsewhere in Yugoslavia as Philip II, Mephistpheles, Leporello, Sarastro and Kecal in The Bartered Bride; Guest appearances in Basel, Zurich and Geneva as Boris; Theatre des Nations Paris, 1957, as Massenet's Don Quichotte; Wiesbaden Festival, 1955-56, as Boris, Dosifey and Prince Igor; Edinburgh Festival, 1962 with the Belgrade Opera and further appearances at Vienna, 1964, La Scala Milan, Brussels, Chicago, Buenos Aires, Leipzig, Berlin and Florence; Other roles have included Konchak and Galitzky in Prince Igor, Gremin and Mefistofele. *Recordings include:* Boris Godunov, Khovanshchina, Prince Igor, Eugene Onegin, The Snow Maiden (Decca); Don Quichotte (Everest). *Address:* Narodno Pozoriste , Francuska 3, 11000 Belgrade, Serbia.

CANIHAC Jean-Pierre, b. 16 Apr 1947, Toulouse, France. Cornet Player. m. Michele Chauzy, 17 Aug 1968, 1 son, 1 daughter. *Education:* Baccalaureat, 1966; Conservatoire de Toulouse; Conservatoire de Versailles; Conservatoire National Superieur de Musique, Paris. *Career:* Founder, Saqueboutiers de Toulouse; Professor, CNR, Toulouse; Professor, Conservatoire National Superior de Musique, Lyon; Member of Hesperion XX, La Grande Ecurie et la Chambre du Roy, La Chapelle Royale, Clemencic Consort. *Recordings:* L'Art de Cornet, Arion; Schütz, Symphoniae Sacrae, Erato; 7 Last Words of Christ, H.Mundi; Siècle d'or à Venise, Adda; Six Marian Vespers of Monteverdi (Malgoire, Parrott, Herreveghe, Corboz, Hennig, Saval). *Contributions to:* Brass Bulletin; Blue Brass. *Honours:* 1st Prize, Conservatoire de Toulouse, 1966; 1st Prize, Conservatoire de Versailles, 1968; 1st Prize, Conservatoire National Superieur, Paris, 1970. *Address:* 8 rue Maran, 31400 Toulouse, France.

CANIN Stuart V., b. 5 Apr. 1926, New York City, USA. Violinist; Educator. m. Virginia Yarkin, m. 8 June 1952, 2 sons. *Education:* Juilliard School of Music, 1946-49. *Career:* Professor, Violin: State University of Iowa, 1953-60, Oberlin Conservatory of Music, 1960-66; Concertmaster, Chamber Symphony of Philadelphia, 1966-68; Concertmaster, San Francisco Symphony, 1970-80; Concertmaster, San Francisco Opera, 1969-72; Artist Faculty, Aspen Colorado Music Festival, 1960-63; Artist Faculty, Music Academy of the West, Santa Barbara, 1983-; Senior Visiting Lecturer, University of California, Santa Barbara, 1983-; Concertmaster: Casals Festival, San Juan, Puerto Rico, 1974-75, Mostly Mozart Festival, New York City, 1980. *Honours:* 1st Prize, Paganini International Violin Competition, Genoa, 1959; Fulbright Professor to Freiburg, Germany Staatliche Hochschule Fur Musik, 1956-57. *Address:* 1302 Holmby Ave., Los Angeles, CA 90024, USA.

CANINO Bruno, b. 30 Dec 1935, Naples, Italy. Pianist; Composer. *Education:* Studied at the Milan Conservatory with Calace and Bettinelli. *Career:* Piano Duo partner from 1953 of Antonio Ballista; Career as soloist from 1956, notably in works by Bussotti, Donatoni and Castiglioni; Played in premieres of Rapsodia, Davide Anzaghi, 1984; Concerto for two pianos, orchestra by Berio, 1973; Tableaux Vivants, Bussotti, 1964, Ode by Castiglioni, 1966; Member of the Trio di Milano; Accompanist to instrumentalists and singers (Cathy Berberian until 1983); Professor of Music at the Milan Conservatory from 1961. *Compositions include:* Chamber and Instrumental music. *Honours:* Prizes at Piano Competitions of Bolzano and Darmstadt, 1956-60. *Address:* Conservatorio Giuseppe Verdi, Via Conservatorio 12, 20122 Milan, Italy.

CANN Claire and Antoinette, (twins). b. 1963, England. Duo- Pianists. *Education:* Studied with Phyllis Sellick at the Royal College of Music, first class honours in solo and duo piano performance. *Debut:* First major concert aged 13.*Career:* Many appearances in Europe, Canada and USA, New Zealand and the Far East: extensive tours of Britain, including concerts at the Festival Hall (local premiere of the Max Bruch Concerto), Fairfield Hall, St David's Hall Cardiff and Glasgow Royal Concert Hall; London orchestras include the Philharmonic, Royal Philharmonic, BBC Concert, Mozart Players and Philomusica; Television engagements in Britain, Japan, and the USA and New Zealand; Season 1992-93, with three concerts at the Festival Hall with the LPO, gala opening of the Ohji Concert Hall Tokyo and recital at St John's Smith Square (Brahms, Lutoslawski, Ravel and Liszt). *Recordings:* Albums titled Gemini, La Danse and Rhapsody. *Honours:* Park Lane Group Series Prize, Countess of Munster Trust Awards, RCM President's Rose Bowl. *Address:* Gwen Howell Management, 7 Gurlings Close, Haverhill, Suffolk CB9 OEG, England.

CANN Roger Bradley, b. 5 Nov 1938, Middlesex, UK. Lecturer; Conductor; Singer. m. Wendy Boswell, 4 Aug 1964, 2 sons. *Education:* BMus, Manchester Univ, 1959-63; GRSM, ARMCM, Royal Manchester College of Music, 1959- 62; MMus, University of East Anglia, 1973-74; LRAM, 1975. *Career:* Lecturer in Music, St Martins College of Higher Education, Lancashire, 1966-92; Head of Music, 1984-92; Voice Tutor, St Martin's College and University of Lancaster, 1992-; Conductor, Haffner Orchestra, Lancaster, 1989- and Eversley Choral Union, 1980-; Tenor Soloist with Choral Societies in North West England. *Memberships:* Incorporated Society of Musicians. *Hobbies:* Composition; Golf; Skiing. *Address:* Greendale, 23 Prospect Drive, Hest Bank, Lancaster LA2 6HZ, England.

CANNAN Phyllis, b. 1945, Paisley, Scotland. Singer (Soprano). *Career:* Sang as soprano with most major companies in Britain; Soprano repertoire from 1983: first major role in Vivaldi's Griselda, Buxton Festival 1983; Sang Gluck's Alceste at the Elizabeth Hall; Kostelnička (Jenůfa) and Katerina (Greek Passion) for Welsh National Opera; Santuzza, Tosca, Rusalka and Goneril in the British premiere of Reimann's Lear, for English National Opera; Appearances in Der Rosenkavalier and King Priam at Covent Garden; Senta in Der fligende Holländer at the 1987 Hong Kong Festival; Gerhilde in Die Walküre at the 1989 Promenade Concerts; Concert engagements include Britten's War Requiem in Belgium; Sang the Overseer in Elektra at the First Night of the 1993 London Proms. *Address:* c/o Lies Askonas Ltd., 186 Drury Lane, London WC2B 5RY, England.

CANNE MEIJER Cora, b. 11 Aug 1929, Amsterdam, The Netherlands. Singer (Mezzo-Soprano); Coach; Voice Teacher. *Education:* Amsterdam Conservatory with Jan Keizer and Re Koster; Studied further with Noëmie Perugia in Paris and Alfred Jerger in Vienna. *Debut:* With Netherlands Opera, Amsterdam, 1951. *Career:* Glyndebourne, 1956, as Cherubino and in Die Zauberflöte and Cenerentola; Salzburg, 1959, in Haydn's Il Mondo della Luna; Zürich Opera, 1960-62; Regular appearances at the Holland Festival; Has sang at many major opera houses including Vienna, Frankfurt, Brussels, Munich and Hamburg; Performed over 65 roles including: Dorabella, Isoliero, Rosina,

Isabella, Octavian, Marina in Boris Godunov, Carmen and in world premiere of Milhaud's La Mere Coupable; Marseille, 1970, title role in world premiere of Mariana Pineda, Louis Saguer composer, Garcia Lorca text; Was also widely demanded as Lied, concert and Oratorio singer, repertory including works by Stravinsky and Berlioz, Bach's St Matthew Passion, Verdi's Requiem; Appeared on TV as Carmen and Rosina; For over 20 years has taught at Amsterdam Sweelinck Conservatorium and giving master classes at home and abroad; Produced and directed open air production of Mozart's Zauberflöte, summer 1989; Frequent Jury Member, international vocal competitions. *Recordings include:* Les Noces by Stravinsky; Der Tag des Gerichts by Telemann; Comte Ory from Glyndebourne; Spanish Folksongs; French and Spanish Songs; Tagebuch eines Verschollenen by Janáček. *Address:* Weteringstraat 48, 1017 SP Amsterdam, The Netherlands.

CANNON Philip, b. 21 Dec 1929, Paris, France. m. Jacqueline Laidlaw, 1950, 1 d. *Education:* Dartington Hall Devon; Royal College of Music, London. *Career:* Lecturer in Music, Sydney University, 1958-60; Professor of Composition, Royal College of Music, 1960- . *Compositions:* 3 Operas, 2 Symphonies (including Son of Man commissioned by the BBC to make Britain's entry to the EC); Choral works (Lord of Light, large scale requiem); Chamber music, all broadcast and performed internationally. *Recordings include:* Commissions: BBC, RF, BBCTV, Three Choirs Festival, Gulbenkian Foundation, Chromaticca USA. *Publications:* Biographical and critical articles in various magazines. *Honours:* Grand Prix, Critics Prize, Paris, 1965; FRCM, 1970; Te Deum, Commissioned by and dedicated to HM The Queen, 1975. *Memberships:* RMA; RPS; ISM; NFMS; PRS; MCPS. *Hobbies:* Meeting people; Philosophy; Art. *Address:* 25 Ansdel Street, London, W8 5BN, England

CANONICI Luca, b. 1961, Tuscany, Italy. Singer (Tenor). *Education:* Studied in Rome with Tito Gobbi and At Pesaro. *Debut:* Teatro Sociale Mantua, 1986, as the Duke of Mantua. *Career:* Sang the Duke in Rome, 1986; Appearances in various Italian theatres, including Bologna and Florence, notably in the Italian premiere of Monteverdi's Ulisse in the version by Henze; Appeared as Rodolfo in the 1987 film version of La Bohème: other roles include Nemorino and Ernesto, Fernando in Donizetti's Il Furioso all isola di San Domingo, Frederico in L'Arlesiana, Almaviva and Werther; Bergamo 1990, in Mayr's La rose bianca e la rosa rossa; Season 1991 as Fenton in Falstaff at Bonn, Pilade in Rossini's Ermione at Rome and leading role in La Cambiale di Matrimonio at the Pesaro Festival; Sang Max in Leoncavallo's La Reginetta della Rose, Palermo, 1992; Idreno in Semiramide at Zurich and Tono in La Fille du Regiment at Rome. *Address:* c/o Teatro dell'Opera, Piazza B Gigli 8, 00184 Rome. Italy.

CANTELO April, b. 2 Apr 1928, Purbrook, Hants, England. Singer (Soprano). *Education:* Studied in London and at Dartington with Imogen Holst. *Debut:* Sang Barbarina in Figaro and Echo in Ariande auf Naxos with the Glyndebourne Company, Edinburgh, 1950. *Career:* Glyndebourne Festivals, 1953, 1963, as Blondchen and Marzelline; English Opera Group, 1960-70, notably as Helena in the premiere of a Midsummer Night's Dream and as Emmeline in Purcell's King Arthur; At Sadler's Wells Theatre, 1962-66 sang in the premieres of Williamson's Our Man in Havana and The Violins of St Jacques and in the British premieres of Henze's Boulevard Solitude and Weill's Aufsteig und Fall der Stadt Mahagonny; Also created roles in Williamson's The Happy Prince, 1965, and Julius Cesar Jones, 1966; Directed Purcell's The Fairy Queen in New Zealand, 1972; Frequent concert appearances. *Recordings:* The Indian Queen, Albert Herring and The Little Sweep; Beatrice et Benedict. *Address:* c/o English National Opera, St Martin's Lane, London WC2, England.

CANTRELL Derrick Edward, b. 2 June 1926, Sheffield, England. Cathedral Organist. m. Nancy Georgina Bland, 4 children. *Education:* MA; BMus,

Oxford University; FRCO. *Career:* Organist, Manchester Cathedral, 1962-77; Lecturer, Royal Northern College of Music. *Recordings:* Manchester Cathedral Organ. *Honours:* Recipient of Sawyer and Limpus Prizes, Royal College of Organists. *Address:* 36 Parsonage Road, Manchester, M20 9PQ, England.

CAPECCHI Renato, b. 6 Nov 1923, Cairo, Egypt. Singer (Baritone); Producer. *Education:* Studied with Ubaldo Carrozzi in Milan. *Debut:* Italian Radio 1948. *Career:* Stage debut 1949, as Amonasro at Reggio Emilia; Sang in the premiere of Ghedini's Billy Budd, 1949, Venice; La Scala Milan from 1950, debut in the premiere of Malipiero's Allegra Brigata; Metropolitan Opera debut 1951, as Germont: returned to New York 1975; Sang at Milan in the premieres of Tosatti's Giudizio Universale, Napoli's Un Curioso accidente, Chailly's Domanda di matrimonio and Malipiero's La Donna e Mobile; Florence 1953, in the stage premiere of Prokofiev's War and Peace; Covent Garden debut 1962, as Melitone in La Forza del Destino; Holland Festival 1970, in Haydn's La Fedeltà Premiata; Schonbrunn, Vienna, in Il Barbiere di Siviglia by Paisiello, 1976; Glyndebourne Festival 1977, 1980, as Falstaff; Sang at Verona Arena, 1953-1983; Genoa Opera, Dulcamera, 1989; Three Week Workshop, Australian Opera, 1989; Production, Il Barbiere di Siviglia; Sang Geronte in Manon Lescaut at Modena, 1990; Guest appearances at Drottningholm, Moscow, the Paris Opéra, Strasbourg, Berlin, Munich, Stuttgart, Montreal and Tel Aviv; Sang Mozart's Don Alfonso at the Metropolitan, 1991. *Recordings:* L'Elisir d'Amore, La Forza del Destino, I Puritani; Rigoletto, Don Pasquale, Gianni Schicchi (Philips); Le Nozze di Figaro, Il Barbiere di Siviglia, La Cenerentola (Deutsche Grammophon); La Bohème (EMI). *Address:* Teatro Carlo Felice, 1-16100 Genoa, Italy.

CAPELLETTI Daniel, b. 20 Sept. 1958, Luxemburg City. Pianist-Composer. *Education:* Studied at Conservatoire Royal de Musique, Brussels; Basic Diplomas: Piano, Chamber Music, Composition. *Career:* Pianist: Concerts in Belgium, France, Grand-Duché of Luxemburg, Germany, Italy and Spain; Radio and Television recordings for Belgium and Grand-Duché; Teaching: Piano at School of Music, Zaventem; Harmony, Pedagogy, Musical Analysis and Chamber Music, Conservatoire Royal de Musique, Brussels; Movie Music, ULB (University of Brussels). *Compositions:* By Jobert, Paris: Suite for Two Harps; Disegni, Cello and Piano; Cariatides, Violin and Piano; Miroirs, Piano Solo; By The CeBeDeM, Brussels: Aquarelles, 3 Symphonic Pieces; Miroirs, Symphonic Version; Concerto for Piano and Orchestra; On One Chord, Oboe and Piano. *Honours:* Sabam Award of International Queen Elisabeth Competition for Piano 1983 and Violin 1985, 1988. *Address:* Avenue Prince Albert, 82, 1410 Waterloo, Belgium.

CAPLAT Moran, b. 1 Oct 1916, Herne Bay, Kent, England. General Administrator. m. Diana Downton, 29 May 1943, 1 sons, 2 daughters. *Education:* Royal Academy of Dramatic Art. *Career:* Actor; Yachtsman; Naval Officer; Opera Administrator; General Administrator, Glyndebourne, 1949-81. *Publication:* Dinghies to Divas, 1985, Autobiography. *Contributions to:* Glyndebourne Programme Book; Sundry articles in professional journals and magazines. *Honour:* Commander of the British Empire, 1968. *Hobbies:* Sailing; Gardening; Conviviality. *Address:* Mermaid Cottage, 6 Church Road, Newick, Lewes, East Sussex BN8 4JU, England.

CAPOBIANCO Tito, b. 28 Aug 1931, La Plata, Argentina. Stage Director; Producer; Set and Lighting Designer; Educator. m. Elena Denda, 2 sons. *Career includes:* Producer and Technical Director 1954, Producing Director, Technical Director and Set Designer 1958, Teatro Colon, Buenos Aires; Artistic Director of Santiago Opera Festival, Stage Director of National Ballet of Chile, Professor of Acting and Interpretation at University of Chile 1956; Stage Director and Lighting Designer of SODRE National Ballet and Opera, Stage Director of SODRE, Montevideo, Uruguay 1957; Artistic Director of Teatro Argentino, Producing Director and Stage Director of National Drama Company of Buenos Aires 1959; Artistic Director, Cincinnati Opera and Summer Festival and Director of Opera Productions throughout USA, 1961-65; Producer and Director, International Opera Festival, Mexico City 1963-65; Founder and General Director of American Opera Centre, Juilliard School of Music, NY 1968-71; Created Opera Department of College of Performing Arts, Philadelphia 1972; Artistic Director 1975, General Director 1977, Created Verdi Festival 1978, Young American Conductors' Programme 1980, San Diego Opera; Vice-President and General Director, Pittsburgh Opera 1983; Professor, Opera Department, Yale University 1983. *Composition:* Libretto of Zapata. *Publication:* The Merry Widow, Franz Lehar (Translation). *Honours:* Cavaliere della Republica, Italy 1979; Officier dans l'Ordre des Arts et Lettres, France 1984; Doctor of Music, Duquesne University, 1988; Doctor of Letters, Indiana University of Pennsylvania, 1988; Doctor of Humane Letters, La Roche College, 1989. *Hobbies:* Reading; Sports. *Address:* Pittsburgh Opera, 711 Penn Avenue, Pittsburgh, PA 15222, USA.

CAPOIANU Dumitru, b. 19 Oct 1929, Bucharest, Romania. Composer. *Education:* Studied at the Bucharest Conservatory 1941-53. *Career:* Manager of the Georges Enescu Philharmonic Orchestra, 1959-73. *Compositions include:* Wind Quintet, 1950; Viola Sonata, 1952; 2 Suites for orchestra, 1953, 1954; 2 String Quartets, 1954, 1959; Divertisement for string orchestra and 2 clarinets, 1956; Violin Concerto 1957; Cosmos 60, ballet scene 1960; Cinematographic Variations for Orchestra 1065; Steel, ballet 1965; String Trio 1968; Curte domneasca (The Princely Countyard, spectacle of sound and light, 1969); Moto perpetuo for violin and Orchestra, 1972; Chemari 77 for orchestra; Muzica de ambianta for orchestra 1980; Valses ignobles et sentimentales du tout for mezzo and strings, 1986; two musicals, Dragostei Printesei, 1982 and Censareasa 1984; Choral music. *Address:* Association of Romanian Composers, Bucharest, Romania

CAPPELLETTI Andrea, b. 21 May 1961, Italy. Violinist. *Education:* Diploma cum laude, Naples Conservatory, Parallel course, Liceo Linguistico. *Career:* 1st Violin, ECYO, 1977; Debut, Israel, 1984; Debut, RFH, 1986; Queen Elizabeth Hall, 1988; Regular appearances with leading orchestras, Italy, France, Germany, Scandinavia. Regular appearances in Europe, Australia, USA. Appointed Art Director, United Nations Concerts for the Disabled, 1990. *Recordings:* Exclusive contract, Koch International, 5 Mozart violin concertos; Italian Baroque Concerti; Respighi Concerti; Tartini sonatas for violin solo; for UNICEF Haydn Concerti. *Honours:* Vittorio Veneto, 1975; Kiefer Hablitzel, 1977-78; Fördergemeinschaft, 1986. *Hobbies:* Archery; Swimming. *Current Management:* Robert Korp Corporation. *Address:* Via della Ripa 77, 50075 Montespertoli, Ripa(FI), Italy.

CAPPUCCILLI Piero, b. 9 Nov 1929, Trieste, Italy. Singer (Baritone). *Education:* Studied in Trieste with Luciano Doaggio. *Debut:* Teatro Nuovo Milan 1957, as Tonio in Pagliacci. Metropolitan Opera debut 1960, as Germont; La Scala Milan from 1964, debut as Ashton in Lucia di Lammermoor; Covent Garden debut 1967, as Germont: returned to London as Iago, Renato in Un Ballo in Maschera and Simon Boccanegra, with the company of La Scala (1976); Verona Arena 1968, 1970, as Posa in Don Calos and as Luna in Il Trovatore; Chicago Lyric Opera 1969, in I Due Foscari; Salzburg Festival 1975-77, as Posa and Boccanegra; Paris Opéra 1978; Arena di Verona, 1988, 1989, Amonasro and Nabucco; Stuttgart Opera, 1990, as Scarpia; Sang Simon Boccanegra at Barcelona, 1990; Luciano Pavarotti 30th Anniversary Gala, Reggio Emilia, 1991; Other roles include Nabucco, Macbeth, Rigoletto and Escamillo. *Recordings:* Lucia di Lammermoor (Columbia); La Wally, I Puritani, Cavalleria Rusticana (Decca); Aida, Don Carlos, Il Pirata (EMI): Macbeth, Nabucco, Rigoletto (Deutsche Grammophon); I Masnadieri, I Due Foscari

(Philips). *Address:* SA Gorlinsky Ltd., 33 Dover Street, London W1X 4NJ, England.

CAPRIOLI Alberto, b. 16 Nov 1956, Bologna, Italy. Composer; Conductor; Musicologist. *Education:* Studied composition with F Margola, C Togni (Parma Conservatory), B Schaeffer (Salzburg, Mozarteum); conducting with O Suitner, (Vienna Academy of Music);humanities with E Raimondi, C, Ginzburg; U Eco (Bologna University). *Career:* Guest Conductor, several European Orchestras and New Music Festivals; Professor, Bologna Conservatory of Music. *Compositions:* Frammenti dal diario, piano, 1974; Abendlied, soprano and orchestra, 1977; Sonata in memoriam Alban Berg, piano, 1982; Canto, orchestra, 1983; Sonetti di Shakespeare, child reciter and 10 instruments, 1983; Trio, piano, violin and cello, 1984; Del celeste confine, string quartet, 1985; Serenata per Francesca, six players, 1985; A la dolce ombra, piano trio, 1985; Dialogue, solo contrabass and 2 string quartets, 1986; Per lo dolce silentio de la notte, piano and computer music tape, 1987; Due Notturni d'oblio, 10 players, 1988; Symphoniae I, II, III, violin, 1988-89; Il vostro pianto aurora o luna, 5 players, 1989; Vor dem singenden Odem, Quintet, 1990; Kyrie per Dino Campana, Soli, Choir and 29 Instruments, 1991; A quinze and, cello, 1992; Anges, G-flute, viola and harp: Folâtre (Notturno di rosa), two guitars, 1993; CD: Pro Viva Munich, 1989; EdiPan, Roma, 1991; Galleria d'Arte Moderna, Bologna, 1992. *Publications:* Sonoton, Munich, 1989; Quaderni Perugini di Musica Contemporanea, 1987, 1990; Comparatistica, Firenze, Olschki, 1989-1991. Bruno Maderna critical edition, Suvini-Zerboni, Milano. *Address:* D. Guglielmini 7, I-40137, Bologna, Italy.

CAPRONI Bruno, b. 1960, England. Singer (Baritone). *Education:* Studied at the Royal Northern College of Music and the National Opera Studio. *Career:* Sang in Menotti's The Consul, Madame Butterfly and Rigoletto while in college; Appearances with Opera Northern Ireland, Dublin Grand Opera and the Wexford and Glyndebourne festivals; Royal Opera House Covent Garden from 1988 in Madame Butterfly, Don Carlos, Rigoletto, Der Freischütz, Otello, Die Meistersinger and Turandot; Sang Ezio in Verdi's Attila in a concert performance conducted by Edward Downes; Other roles include Marcello (La Bohème), Belcore, Ottokar (Der Freischütz) and Verdi's Germont, Posa and Amonasro. *Honours include:* Vaughan Williams/Frederic Cox award 1987; Ricordi Prize for Opera 1988. *Address:* c/o Harrison Parrott Ltd., 12 Penzance Place, London W11 4PA, England.

CARD June, b. 10 Apr 1942, Dunkirk, New York, USA. Singer (Soprano). *Education:* Studied at Mannes College, New York. *Career:* Sang on Broadway from 1959, with New York City Opera from 1963; European engagements at Munich, Gärtnerplatztheater, from 1967; Member of the Frankfurt Opera 1969-; Appearances in Hamburg, London, Paris, Barcelona, Vienna, Cologne, Met, New York; San Carlo, Naples; Roles include Violetta, Jenůfa, Madama Butterfly, Minnie in La Fanciulla del West and Marie in Die Soldaten by Zimmermann; Has sung Janáček's Vixen, Katya and Emilia Marty, Magda in La Rondine, and roles in Schreker's Dre Gezeichneten; Henze's Der Junge Lord and Bassarids; The Rake's Progress, Sieglinde and Katerina Ismailova; Frankfurt, 1988, in Poulenc's La Voix Humaine; Holland Festival in The Orestia by Milhaud; Produced La Clemenza di Tito at Giessen, 1988; Fidelio, in France. *Recordings:* Traviata, Gezeichneten by Schreker. *Current Management:* Agentur Schulz, 8 Munchen 23 Martiustrasse 3, Germany. *Address:* 8 Munich 81, Arabellastrasse 5/1411, Germany.

CARDELL Victor T., b. 31 Oct 1951, Hartford, Connecticut, USA. Music Librarian; Musicologist. *Education:* BA, Music History, Trinity College, 1973; MS, Rare Books, Special Collections, Columbia University, 1975; MA, Musicology, New York University, 1979. *Career:* Assistant to Virgil Thomson, 1974-79; Assistant to Music Librarian, New York University, 1977-78; Assistant Librarian, Music Library, Cornell University, 1979-81, Acting Librarian, 1981-82; Assistant Librarian, Music Library, Yale University, 1982-86; Head, Archive of Popular American Music, University of California, Los Angeles, 1986-; Reviewing Virgil Thomson Reviewing, paper delivered at Sonneck Society Session, University of Kansas, 1982. Papers delivered: Arrangement and Description of Music Archives, 1985; RLG's Preservation Programs for music, 1985; Bibliographic control and access, 1987; all at Music Library Association meetings. The Archive of Popular American Music, 1987, ALA Rare Book and Manuscript Section, pre-conference; Chair, The composing of American Music, I Sonneck Society conference, 1987. *Publication:* John Kirkpatrick, Friend of American Composers, 1985. *Address:* 6320 Green Valley CIR - Apt 200, Culver City, CA 40230, USA.

CARDEN Joan Maralyn,b. 9 Oct 1937, Richmond, Victoria, Australia. Opera and Concert Singer. m. W. Coyne, 31 Aug 1962, (divorced 1980), 2 daughters. *Education:* Trinity College of Music, London, Piano/Theory of music Voice; Thea Phillips, Melbourne; Henry Portnoj, Melbourne; Vida Harford, London, 1961-; London Opera Centre, 1967. *Debut:* New Opera Co in world premiere of Malcolm Williamson's Our Man in Havana, Sadler's Wells Theatre, 1963. *Career:* Australian Opera, 1971; Glyndebourne Opera, 1977; Scottish Opera, 1977; Houston Grand Opera, 1977; Vitellia (Clemenza di Tito), Marschallin (Der Rosenkavalier) Elisabetta (Maria Stuards, Sydney 1992; Metropolitan Opera Tour, 1978; Miami Opera, 1981; Kennedy Center, Washington, 1980; Singapore Festival, 1983; Adelaide Festival, 1984; Sang Tosca at Adelaide in Elder Park, 1990; Other roles include Liu, Fiordiligi, Mozart's Countess, Donna Elvira, Pamina, Violetta, Gilda, Marguerite, Natasha in War and Peace and Leonora, (La Forza del Destino), Sydney, 1988; Sang Gounod's Marguerite at Brisbane, 1991. *Recordings:* Joan Carden Sings Mozart; Stars of Australian Opera Sing Verdi; Music for Australia Day (ABC) CD/Video, Mozart selection (T.A.O.) La Traviata, (T.A.O.) Video. *Honours:* Stuyvesant Scholar, London Opera Centre, 1967; A.O. 1988 (for services to opera); OBE, for services to Opera, 1980; Dame Joan Hammond Award, 1987. *Hobbies:* Walking; Gardening; Knitting; Reading. *Current Management:* J Eddy (opera/classical concert), A. McKinnon, Suite 44, 104 Bathurst St, Sydney 2000, Australia. *Address:* The Australian Opera, PO Box 291, Strawberry Hills, NSW 2012, Australia.

CARDI Mauro, b. 22 July 1955, Rome, Italy. Composer; Teacher, Conservatory of Music. *Education:* Diploma Composition, Diploma, Choral Music & Direction, Rome Conservatory of Music; Diploma, postgraduate composition studies, National Academy, St Cecilia. *Career includes:* Various broadcasts, own works, Italy, France, Holland, Belgium, East Germany, Argentina. *Compositions include:* Melos, soprano & orchestra; Trama, Violin; Les Masques, flute, viola, guitar; String Quartet; Filigrana, 8 performers; Promenade, 7 performers; Bianco, guitar; Texture, 2 guitars; Silete Venti, guitar, 8 performers; R.I.B.E.S. female voice; Trio (le clair sillage). *Recordings:* EdiPan; RCA; Broadcasts. *Contributions to:* Many essays on contemporary music published, newspapers, magazines, reviews. *Honours:* Prizes, international composition competitions: V. Bucchi Prize, 1982; Gaudeamus Prize, 1984. Selection, Gaudeamus Music Week, 1984, 1985, 1986. *Membership:* Nuova Consonanza Association, Rome. *Hobbies:* Photography; Computers. *Address:* Via Latisana 8, 00177 Rome, Italy.

CARDY Patrick Robert Thomas, b. 22 Aug 1953, Toronto, Ontario, Canada. Composer and Professor of Music. *Education:* BMus (Hons.) in Theory and Composition 1975, University of Western Ontario; MMA in Composition 1976; DMus. in Composition 1981, McGill University. *Career:* Professor, School for Studies in Art and Culture, Carleton University, Ottawa, Ontario 1977-; 8 Ontario Arts Council commissions; 7 Canada Council commissions; 2 Canadian Broadcasting Corporation commissions; 9 private commissions; 2

Canada Council Doctoral Fellowships; 3 Canada Council Grants, performances in Canada, USA, Europe. *Compositions include:* Re Atum 1976, organ; Golden Days, Silver Nights 1977, sop, chamber ensemble; Apokalypsis 1978, orch, chorus; Sparkle 1980, flute, piano; Angels 1980, for ensemble; The Snow Queen 1980, string quartet, narrator; The Masks of Astarte 1981, piano; Jeu d'Enfant 1981, SATB, cb;...time presses and night begins to fall...1982, flute, organ; Mirages 1984, sax, piano; Jig 1984, for ensemble; Eclat 1984, org; Outremer: The Land Beyond the Sea 1985, pno duet, Virelai, 1985, cl, string orch; Les Eaux de Tristesse 1986, baritone, pno; Brettl-lieder 1987, arr. of Schoenberg cabaret songs, soprano, chamber ensemble; Mimesis 1987, vln, vla; Qilakitsoq: The Sky Hangs Low 1988, clarinet, bassoon, horn and piano; Tango!, 1989, clarinet, violin, piano; Tombeau 1989, clarinet, cello, piano; The Little Mermaid 1990, narrator, chamber ensemble; Avalon, orchestra, 1991; Serenade 1992, clarinet, bassoon, string orchestra; Chaconne 1992, marimba, orchestra; Autumn 1992, voice, pno; Dulce et decorum est...1993, string quartet; Danses folles et amoureuses, 1993, flute, oboe, violln, cello, hpschd. *Recordings:* All above recorded and broadcast on CBC, Radio Canada, NOS radio, The Netherlands. *Contributions to:* Biographic articles on Bengt Hambraeus in the Encyclopaedia of Music in Canada, 2nd ed., 1992. *Address:* 29 Morgan's Grant Way, Kanata, Ontario, K2K 2G2, Canada.

CAREWE John Maurice Foxall, b. 24 Jan 1933, Derby, England. Conductor. 2 daughters. *Education:* Gresham's School, Holt, Norfolk, England; Guildhall School of Music and Drama, London; Conservatoire National, Paris. *Career:* Founded Music Today, New Music Ensemble, 1958; Principal Conductor BBC Welsh Orchestra 1966-71; Principal Conductor, Fires of London 1980-84; Musical Director, Principal Conductor, Brighton Philharmonic Society 1974-87. *Recordings:* Stravinsky, Histoire du Soldât; Milhaud, Creation du Monde; Bennett, Calendar; Maxwell Davies, Leopardi Fragments; Bedford, Music for Albion Moonlight; Debussy, Ibéria; Falla, Interlude and Dance, La Vida Breve; Bridge Enter Spring and Oration; Colin Matthews, Landscape and Cello Concerto; Muller-Siemens, Under Neon Light I; Leyendecker, Cello Concerto; Debussy, Pelléas et Mélisande; Dvořák, Symphony No.8; Brahms, Tragic Overture. *Honour:* Bablock Prize, 1960. *Hobbies:* Photography; Cooking. *Current Management and Address:* Jürgen Erlebach, Grillparzerstr.24, 2000 Hamburg 76, Germany.

CAREY Thomas, b. 29 Dec. 1931, Bennetsville, Connecticut, USA. Singer (Baritone). *Education:* Studied at the Henry Street Music School New York and with Rose Bampton; Further study at the Stuttgart Musikhochschule and with Hans Hotter. *Debut:* Netherlands Opera, Amsterdam, as Germont, 1964. *Career:* Sang in Lisbon, Nice, Paris, Stockholm, Basle, Zagreb, Venice and Belgrade; Guest singer at the State Operas of Munich, Hamburg, Stuttgart and Berlin; Covent Garden 1970, as Mel in the premiere of Tippett's The Knot Garden; US engagements in Boston, Memphis and New Orleans; Many concert appearances; Teacher of Voice at the University of Oklahoma, Norman. *Recordings include:* The Knot Garden (Philips). *Address:* c/o University of Oklahoma, Catlett Music Center, Norman, OK 73019, USA.

CARIAGA Marvellee, b. 11 Aug 1942, California, USa. Singer (Mezzo-soprano). *Education:* Studied at California State University. *Career:* Sang with San Diego Opera from 1971; Fricka in performances of Der Ring des Nibelungen for Seattle Opera, 1975-81; Guest appearances at San Francisco, 1981, Pittsburgh, Portland, Los Angeles, 1987-88 and Vancouver, 1975-78; Rio de Janeiro, 1979, as Santuzza; Netherlands Opera 1979 and 1982; other roles have included Wagner's Venus, Ortrud, Waltraute, Brünnhilde (Siegfried), Isolde and Magdalene; Donna Anna, Amelia, (Ballo in Maschera), Herodias and Kostelnička in Jenůfa; Colorado 1986, in the premiere of Pasatieri's The Three Sisters; Los Angeles Music Center Opera 1991, as Mrs

Grose in The Turn of the Screw; Mrs Herring at the Dorothy Chandler Pavilion, Los Angeles, 1992. *Recordings include:* The Three Sisters. *Address:* Los Angeles Music Center Opera, 135 North Grand Avenue, Los Angeles, CA 90012, USA.

CARIDIS Miltiades, b. 9 May 1923, Danzig, Gdensk (Greek Citizen). Conductor. m. Dr Sonja Dengel, 1 daughter. *Education:* Diploma in Conducting, Music Academy, Vienna, Austria, 1947. *Career:* Permanent Conductor, Opera in Graz, Cologne, Vienna (State Opera); Permanent Conductor, Danish Radio Symphony Orchestra, Copenhagen, 1962-69; Conductor in Chief, Philharmonia Hungarica, 1960-67; Artistic and Music Director, Philharmonic Society, Oslo, 1969-75; Conductor in Chief, Duisburg Symphony Orchestra, West Germany, 1975-81; Artistic and Music Director, Tonkünstler-Orchester, Vienna, 1979-85, Guest Conductor, more than 100 orchestras, 80 choires. *Address:* Himmelhofgasse 10, A-1130 Vienna, Austria.

CARL Eugene (Gene) Marion, Jr., b. 8 Nov 1953, Los Angeles, California, USA. Composer; Pianist. *Education:* BA cum laude, Pomona College, USA, 1971-75; Freiburg im Breisgau, Germany, 1974; Institute for Sonology, Utrecht State University, Netherlands, 1975-76; Royal Conservatory, The Hague, 1976-81; Piano studies with John Ritter 1971-74, Geoffrey Madge 1976-81, master classes with Padolsky, Voorhies, Kontarsky; Composition with Karl Kohn 1971-75, Konrad Lechner 1974, Jan van Vlymen & Jan Boerman 1976-81, master classes Darmstadt 1976. *Debut:* Beethoven Piano Concerto No 1, with Sepulveda Orchestra, 1968. *Compositions:* Recorded: Gray Matter, Hommage á Tarkovski, Slierten, Leonardo's Doek, Panorama City, Roscoe Boulevard. Compositions: Leonardo, Leonardo, violin, electric guitar, tuba, drum-kit, synthesizers, tape, voice, 1986; Scratch, violin solo, 1985; Gagarin, double orchestra, mixed choir, 2 solo voices, children's choir, synthesizers, tape, 1986-89; Hommage á Tarkovski, 1987, for 2 saxes, violin, synthesizers, percussion and tape; Claremont Concerto, 1987, for Bb. cl., piano and string quartet; Roscoe Boulevard, 1988, for 2 saxes (doubling bass cl. and cl.), and ensemble. *Recordings:* 2 albums as member of Hoketus Ensemble; Pianist: with 5 U U's; Motor Totemist Guild; double LP Balans, Hoketus. *Contributions to:* Co-editor, E 1976-78; Journal, Schoenberg Institute; Key Notes, Amsterdam. *Address:* c/o Donemus, Paulus Potterstraat 14, 1071 CZ Amsterdam, Netherlands.

CARLOS Wendy (Walter), b. 14 Nov 1939, Pawtucket, Rhode Island, USA. Organist; Performer on Electronic Instruments; Composer. *Education:* Pupil, Ron Nelson, Brown University; AB, 1962; MA, 1965. *Career:* Associated with Robert Moog in perfecting the Moog Synthesizer, 1964; Pioneer in utilizing the resources of the synthesizer. *Compositions:* Opera: Noah 1964-65; various pieces for synthesizer & tape or orchestra; film scores; chamber music. *Recordings:* Switched on Bach, 1968; The Well Tempered Synthesizer, 1969; Timesteps, 1970; Pompous Circumstances, 1974-75; Digital Moonscapes, 1985. *Address:* c/o ASCAP, ASCAP Building, One Lincoln Plaza, New York, NY 10023, USA.

CARLSON Claudine, b. 26 Feb 1950, Mulhouse, France. Mezzo-Soprano. *Education:* Vocal Training in California; Pupil of Gertrude Gruenderg, Jennie Tourel & Esther Andreas, Manhattan School of Music, New York. *Career:* Numerous appearances as Soloist with major orchestras, including: Boston Symphony, Detroit Symphony, New York Philharmonic, Minnesota, Los Angeles Philharmonic, St Louis Symphony, National Symphony, London Symphony, L'Orchestre de Paris, Israel Philharmonic; many festival appearances; Recitalist World Wide. *Recordings:* Candide; Orion; RCA; Townhall; Vox Cum Laude. *Honours:* 1st Prize, National Federation of Music Clubs Singing Competition; Martha Baird Rockefeller Award. *Address:* c/o ICM Artists Ltd., 40 West 57th Street, New York, NY 10019, USA.

CARLSON Lenus (Jesse), b. 11 Feb 1945, Jamestown, North Dakota, USA. Baritone; Teacher. m. Linda Kay Jones, 20 Aug 1972. *Education:* BA, 1967; Postgraduate Studies with Oren Brown, Juilliard School, 1970-73. *Career:* Apprentice Artist, Central City (Colo.) Opera, 1965-66; Debut as Demetrius, Midsummer Night's Dream, Minnesota Opera, 1968; sang with opera companies in Dallas, 1972-73, San Antonio 1973, Boston, 1973, Washington DC, 1973, New York (Metropolitan Opera, debut as Purcell's Aeneas, 23 Feb 1973), Amsterdam, 1974; others; British debut, Scottish Opera, Edinburgh Festival, 1975; Covent Garden debut, London, as Valentin, 1976; Sang at the Deutsche Opera Berlin as Paul in Die tote Stadt by Korngold, 1983; Nevers in Les Huguenots, 1987, Arcesias in Die tote Augen by d'Albert, 1987; Premiere of Oedipus by Wolfgang Rihm, 1988; various concert engagements; Teacher, Voice, Minneapolis 1965-70, New York 1970-. *Address:* c/o Columbia Artists Management Inc., 165 West 57th Street, New York, NY 10019, USA.

CARLYLE Joan Hildred, b. 6 April 1931. Wirral, Cheshire, England. Soprano. 2 daughters. *Education:* Howell's School, Denbigh, N. Wales; Studied with Bertha Nicklass Kempner. *Career:* Principal Lyric Soprano, Covent Garden; Major Roles Sung in UK include: Oscar, Ballo in Maschera 1957-58; Sophie, Der Rosenkavalier 1958-59; Nedda, Pagliacci, Zeffirelli production, 1959, Mimi, La Bohème 1960, Titania, Midsummer Night's Dream, Britten (Gielgud Production) 1960, Pamina, Magic Flute 1962, 1966, Countess, Marriage of Figaro 1963, Zdenka, Arabella (Hartmann Production) 1964, Suor Angelica 1965, Desdemona, Othello 1965, Arabella 1967, Marschallin, Der Rosenkavalier 1968, Jenifer, Midsummer Marriage 1969, Donna Anna 1970, Reiza, Oberon 1970, Adrianna Lecouvreur 1970, Russalka, Elisabetta, Don Carlos 1975; Major Roles sung abroad include: Oscar, Nedda, Mimi, Pamina, Zdenka, Micaela, Donna Anna, Arabella, Elisabetta and Desdemona; Debut at Salzburg, Metropolitan Opera, New York and Teatro Colón, Buenos Aires 1968. Currently Teaching and Promoting Young Singers, Opera Afallon Carlyle, Singing. *Recordings:* Several including Von Karajan's production of Pagliacci as Nedda and Midsummer Marriage as Jenifer. *Hobbies:* Gardening; Travel; Preservation of the Countryside; Interior Design; Cooking. *Address:* Laundry Cottage, Hanmer, Clwyd, North Wales, Wales.

CARNEGY Patrick, b. 23 Sept 1940, Leeds, UK. *Education:* Rugby School 1953-58; MA Trinity Hall, Cambridge, 1960-63. *Career:* The Times Educational Supplement 1964-69; Assistant editor (special responsibility for music) The Times Literary Supplement, 1969-78; Editor (music books) Faber and Faber, 1978-88; Director, Faber Music 1979-88; Dramaturg of The Royal Opera House, 1988-92; Writer, lecturer, broadcaster on music, literature; Course director, Bayreuth Youth Festival, from 1968; Founding member, Bayreuth International Arts Centre; Member, BBC Central Music Advisory Committee, 1986-89; Member, BBC General Advisory Council, 1990-. *Publication:* Faust as Musician: A Study of Thomas Mann's novel Doctor Faustus, 1973; Contributions include: The Times and its Supplements; London Review of Books; Opera; The Musical Times; Art International. *Hobbies:* Mountains; Wine. *Address:* 5 The Causeway, Elsworth, Cambridge CB3 8HT, England.

CARNEY Timothy, b. 4 Oct 1956, New York, USA. Choral Conductor. *Education:* ABD, University of Illinois; MMus, University of Tennessee; BA, Hamilton College. *Career:* Director of Choral Music, University of Hawaii; Conductor, Honolulu Symphony Chorus; Conductor, Hawaii Vocal Arts Ensemble; St Olaf College, Ripon College. *Honours:* Knighted, Order of the Holy Sepulchre of Jerusalem, 1989. *Memberships:* American Choral Directors Symphony; Hawaii State President; Chorus America. *Address:* 447 Wyllie Street, Honolulu, HI 96817, USA.

CAROSIO Margherita, b. 7 June 1908, Genoa, Italy. Singer (Soprano). *Education:* Studied with her father, Natale Carosio, and at the Paganini Conservatory, Genoa. *Debut:* Novi Ligure 1927, as Lucia di Lammermoor. *Career:* Covent Garden 1928, as Musetta and as Feodor in Boris Godunov; La Scala Milan 1929-55, notably in the premieres of Mascagni's Nerone (1935) and Wolf-Ferrari's Il Campiello (1936) and in the first local performances of operas by Rimsky-Korsakov, Strauss (Die schweigsame Frau) and Menotti; Buenos Aires 1937, in Le Coq d'Or; Salzburg Festival 1939 as Rosina; Teatro San Carlo Naples 1942, in the premiere of Beatrice Cenci by Pannain; Guest appearances in Barcelona, Antwerp, Vienna, Berlin and Nice; Sang in London 1946 as Violetta (with the San Carlo Company) and in 1950 as Adina in L'Elisir d'Amore, with La Scala. *Recordings include:* L'Elisir d'Amore; Amelia al Ballo by Menotti.

CARR Colin Michael, b. 25 Oct 1957, Liverpool, England. Cellist. *Education:* Yehudi Menuhin School, 1966-74; Associate, Royal College of Music, (Honours), 1972. *Career:* Soloist throughout Europe, North America, Australia and Far East with major orchestras including, The Royal Philharmonic Orchestra, Concertgebouw Orchestra, British Broadcasting Corporation Symphony, Philharmonia, Chicago Symphony, National Symphony Washington, ECO, SCO, CBSO, Philadelphia Orchestra, Montreal Symphony; Recitals, London, Amsterdam, Paris, New York, Washington, Boston, Los Angeles, television and radio recordings, throughout both continents; Faculty Member, New England Conservatory, Boston, USA, 1983-. *Recordings:* For Musical Heritage Society has recorded Sonatas by Debussy and Franck; Elegie, Romance and Papillon by Fauré; Complete Schubert works for Piano Trio (Arabesque label) and complete Mendelssohn works for Piano Trio (Arabesque label) and complete Brahms Trios with Golub, Kaplan, Carr Trio. *Honours:* Martin Musical Scholarship, Gulbenkian Fellowship, Lambeth Music Award, 1st Prize Royal Overseas League Competition, 1974-; Winner, Young Concert Artists Competition, New York, USA, 1978; Piatigorsky Prize, 1981; Naumburg Competition Winner, 1981; Grand Prize Winner Rostropovitch Competition, Paris. *Current management:* Clarion Concert Agency, London, England; Herbert Barrett MGMT, New York, USA. *Hobbies:* Vegetarian and Indian cooking; Soccer; Tennis; Skiing; Squash; Running. *Address:* Rycote Park, Milton Common, Oxford, England.

CARR Paul d'Argaville, b. 13 Aug 1961, Redruth, Cornwall, England. *Career:* Composer/Stage Manager: ASM/DSM, English National Opera 1984-1987, Senior Stage Manager, The Australian Opera 1987-92. *Compositions:* Gloria for mixed voice choir with brass quintet and organ; Brass Bagatelles for brass quintet; Concertino for piano and small orchestra. *Publications:* Three Bagatelles for flute and piano; Dance pieces for clarinet and piano; Divertimento for oboe, bassoon and piano; Sonatina for flute and piano; Sonatina for clarinet and piano; Girl On A Beach Under A Sunshade for bassoon and piano or bassoon and small orchestra; Five English Postcards for wind quintet; Dance Miniatures for wind quintet; Postcards for solo clarinet; Concertino for recorder and string orchestra; Sails and Beach Games for piano solo; Canzonetta for trumpet and organ; The Lamb for mixed choir a cappella; Short For Joy carol for mixed choir a cappella; There Is A Star That Shines So Bright, carol for mixed choir with trumpet and organ, A Quiet Place carol for mixed choir a cappella. *Compositions:* Gloria for mixed voice choir with brass quintet and organ, Brass Bagatelles for brass quintet, Concertino for piano and small orchestra. *Address:* 33 Guildford Street, Brighton, East Sussex BN1 3LS, England.

CARRERAS José, b. 5 Dec 1946, Barcelona, Spain. Tenor. 1 son, 1 daughter. *Debut:* Flavio (Norma) Gennaro (Lucrezia Borgia) Teatro Liceu, 1970-71. *Career:* Appeared in La Bohème, Un Ballo in Maschera and I Lombardi, Teatro Regio Parma, Italy after winning the 1972 Verdi singing competition; American debut as Pinkerton in Madama Butterfly, New York City Opera, 1972; debut Metropolitan Opera House 1974 as

Cavaradossi, debut Teatro alla Scala, Milan, 1975, Riccardo in Un Ballo in Maschera; Appeared in film and video versions of: Don Carlos, Andrea Chenier, I Lombardi, La Bohème, Verdi's Requiem Mass, Stiffelio, My Life (personal life story) Turandot, West Side Story (the making of the record); Other appearances include: Teatro Colón, Buenos Aires, Staatsoper, Vienna, Royal Opera House, Covent Garden, London, Easter and Summer Festival, Salzburg, Austria, Lyric Opera House, Chicago, War Memorial Opera House San Francisco notably as Alfredo (La Traviata) Nemorino (L'Elisir d'amore) Andrea Chénier, Don José (Carmen) Radames (Aida) Werther, Edgardo (Lucia di Lammermoor) Alvaro (La Forza del destino) Manrico (Il Trovatore); Returned to concert and stage after illness, 1987; Open air concert in front of audience of 150,000 people, 1988; Sang with two tenors World Cup finals concert, Rome, Italy, 1990. Recordings: Un Ballo in Maschera, Tosca, Turandot, Werther, Aida, La Bohème, Don Carlo, Requiem Mass (Verdi), West Side Story, South Pacific, La Forza del destino, Carmen, I Pagliacci. Publications: Singing With The Soul, autobiography, 1989. Honours: Winner, Sir L'Olivier Award, 1993. Memberships: President, the Jose Carreras International Leukemia Foundation, established in 1988, head office in Barcelona. Current Management: Carlos Cabelle, Operacaballe. Address: c/o OperaCaballé, Via Augusta 59, Barcelona, Spain.

CARRINGTON Simon Robert, b. 23 Oct 1942, Salisbury, Wiltshire, England. Musician; Teacher; Adjudicator; Bass Player; Director of The King's Singers since 1968. m. Hilary Stott, 2 Aug 1969, 1 son, 1 daughter. Education: Christ Church Cathedral Choir School, Oxford; The King's School, Canterbury; King's College, Cambridge; New College, Oxford; MA (Cantab); Teaching Certificate (Oxon); Choral Scholar, King's College, Cambridge. Career: Director, The King's Singers, 1967-; 62 CD's for EMI and RCA; Tours worldwide; Regular TV appearances worldwide, including Live at The Boston Pops, 1983; BBC TV series, The King's Singers Madrigal History Tour, 1984; On Stage at Wolftrap, PBS TV, USA, 1986; ABCTV (USA) The Sound of Christmas: Salzburg, 1987; Numerous Tonight Show appearances; Festival Director: Summer in the City Festival, The Barbican, 1988, 1989; Major Festival appearances worldwide; Freelance Double Bass Player; Director, Choral Summer Schools, Marlborough College, Wiltshire, and Berwang, Austria. Compositions: Numerous arrangements for The King's Singers, published by Faber Music, Hinshaw Music (USA), Hal Leonard Publishing Corporation (USA). Recordings: Numerous: EMI UK; Intercord, Germany; MMG, USA and Canada; Victor, Japan; EMI, Australia; RCA Victor and Gold Seal. Publications: The King's Singers - A Self Portrait, 1981; Video: The Art of The King's Singers. Honours: Grammy Nomination, 1986; Deutsche Schallplatten Preis, 1978. Current management: IMG Artists, Media House, 3 Burlington Lane, London W4 2TH, England. Hobbies: Vintage Cars; Inland Waterways; Trees; Walking; Books; Jogging. Address: The Old House, Rushall, Pewsey, Wiltshire, SN9 6EN, England.

CARROLI Silvano, b. 22 Feb 1939, Venice, Italy. Singer (Baritone). Education: Studied at the Opera School of La Fenice, Venice. Debut: Venice 1964, as Marcello in La Bohème. Career: Sang widely in Italy and toured North America with the company of La Scala, 1976; Verona Arena from 1973, in Samson et Dalila, as Ezio in Attila (1985) and Renato in Un Ballo in Maschera (1986); Washington Opera 1977-78, as Cavaradossi; London, Covent Garden, as Iago and in La Fanciulla del West; Chicago Lyric Opera 1978; Brussels 1980, in a revival of Donizetti's Il Duca d'Alba; Barcelona 1983, as Escamillo; Paris Opéra 1984, as Nabucco and in Verdi's Jerusalem; Further appearances at the Metropolitan Opera and at the Deutsche Oper Berlin; Amonasro, Luxor, Egypt, 1987; Season 1988-89, Barnaba, Alfio at Verona, Michele in Il Tabarro at Florence, Puccini's Jack Rance at Caracalla Festival, Rome; Iago, Covent Garden, 1990; Scarpia, Arena di Verona; Season 1992 as Gerard in Andrea Chenier at Turin, Scarpia at Covent Garden, Amonasro at the Festival di Caracalla. Recordings include: Video of I

Lombardi (Topaz). Address: c/o Royal Opera House, Covent Garden, London WC2, England.

CARROLL Charles Michael, b. 5 Mar. 1921, Otterbein, Indiana, USA. Professor of Music; Music Critic; Musicologist. m. Mary Lipford Rosenbush, 4 Sept. 1951, 2 sons, 2 daughters. Education: BM, Indiana University, 1949; MM 1951, PhD 1960, Florida State University. Career: Professor of Music, Florida State University, 1950-53; Pensacola Junior College, 1960-64; St Petersburg Junior College, 1964-89; Music Critic, Tallahassee Democrat, 1950-53; St Petersburg Independent, 1976-86. Publications: The Great Chess Automaton, 1975; The Eighteenth Century: A Current Bibliography. Contributions to: Die Musik in Geschichte und Gegenwart; Recherches sur la musique française classique; Music and Letters; Opera Journal; Opera Canada; Studies in Eighteenth-Century Culture; The Opera Quarterly; College Music Symposium; Music Journal. Memberships: College Music Society, (National Council 1977-80, Chairman Southern Chapter 1979-80, Editor 1979-83); South East American Society for Eighteenth-Century Studies, (Executive Board 1974-82, President 1979-80); American Musicological Society, (National Council 1974-77, Chairman Southern Chapter 1974-76); Société d'Etudes Philidoriennes, Conseiller bibliographique, 1988-; American Symphony Orchestra League, (Executive Board 1954-57, Vice President 1955-56). Hobbies: Chess; Gardening. Address: 1701 80th Street North, St Petersburg, FL 33710, USA.

CARROLL Joan, b. 27 July 1932, Philadelphia, USA. Singer (Soprano). Education: Studied in America, then with Margarethe von Winterfeldt in Berlin. Debut: New York Opera Company 1957, as Zerbinetta. Career: Appearances in North America and in Havanna; Santa Fe 1963, as Lulu (US premiere of Berg's opera); European engagements in Belgium, France, Denmark, Switzerland and Holland; Sang Lulu in Hamburg, Munich and Zurich during the 1960s; Member of the Deutsche Oper am Rhein Dusseldorf from 1967; Sang Mozart's Constanze, Donna Anna and Queen of Night, as well as modern repertory, in Hanover, Berlin, Stuttgart, Cologne and Nuremberg. Recordings include: Works by Gorecki and Stravinsky.

CARRON Elizabeth, b. 12 Feb 1933, New York, USA. Singer (Soprano). Education: Studied in New York. Debut: New York City Opera, 1957, as Madame Butterfly. Career: Sang in New York until 1977 and made guest appearances in Cincinnati, Chicago, Pittsburg, San Francisco, and New Orleans; Dallas 1958 as Dirce in Cherubini's Médée, opposite Maria Callas; Edinburgh Festival 1984, with the Washington Opera; other roles have included Mozart's Constanze, Susanna and Zerlina, Violetta, Micaela, Mimi and Liu, Norina, Strauss's Salome and Daphne, Aithra in Die Agyptische Helena and Birdie in Regina by Blitzstein. Recordings include: Regina (Columbia). Address: c/o Washington Opera, Kennedy Center for the Performing Arts, Washington, DC 30566, USA.

CARRUTHERS Glen B., b. 5 July 1954, Manitoba, Canada. Musicologist; Pianist. m. Heather Walker, 17 May 1984. Education: BMus, Brandon University, 1977; ARCT, piano, first class honours, 1982; MA, Canadian Studies, Carleton University, 1981; PhD Musicology, University of Victoria, 1986; Piano studies with Lorne Watson, William Tritt, Elaine Keillor, Bruce Vogt. Career: Associate Professor, Chair Department of Music, Lakehead University. Publications: Subjectivity, Objectivity and Authenticity in 19th century Bach Interpretation, 1992; Contributor: Selected Works of S C Eckhardt-Gramatte, 1984; Encyclopaedia of Music in Canada, 1992. Several conference papers. Memberships: Canadian University Music Society; College Music Society; American Musicological Society; Canadian Society for 18th century Studies; Canadian Music Centre. Hobbies: Collecting autographs, especially of 19th and early 20th century pianists. Address: 140 Ontario Street, Thunder Bay, Ontario P7B 3G3, Canada.

CARSON Clarice, b. 23 Dec 1936, Montreal, Canada. Singer (Soprano). *Education:* Studied with Pauline Donalda and Jacqueline Richard in Montreal, with Julia Drobner in New York. *Debut:* Montreal Opera 1962, in Menotti's Amahl and the Night Visitors. *Career:* Many guest engagements in North America; New York City Opera 1965, as Mozart's Countess; Metropolitan Touring Opera 1967; European engagements in Barcelona, Rouen, Amsterdam and with Scottish Opera, Glasgow, 1969; Schwetzingen 1976, as Paer's Leonora; Other roles include Cassandre in Les Troyens; Mozart's Donna Anna, and Constanze; Verdi's Desdemona, Violetta, Aida, Elisabeth, Amelia and Leonora (II Trovatore); Puccini's Tosca, Mimi, Liu, Butterfly and Musetta; Marguerite in Faust and the title role in Salome; Many concert performances. *Recordings include:* Leonora by Paer (MRF).

CARTER Barbara, b. 1958, Columbus, Ohio, USA. Singer (Soprano). *Education:* Studied at Capital University, at the University of Toronto with Louis Quilico and at the Musical Academy of the West with Martial Singher. *Career:* Sang Violetta and Musetta with the Canadian Opera Company on tour to the USA and Canada; European debut with the Essen Opera, then appeared as the Queen of Night in Die Zauberflöte with the Covent Garden Opera on tour to the Far East; Further appearances in Berlin, Munich, Buenos Aires, Paris, Vienna, Amsterdam, Venice, Barcelona, New York, Ottawa and Bregenz; Roles have included Lucia, Gilda, Marie (La Fille du Régiment), Zerbinetta, Sophie, Constanze, Zerlina, Rosina, Elvira (I Puritani), Amenaide (Tancredi), Olympia, Nannetta and Gretel; Concert appearances in works by Bach, Mozart, Haydn, Handel, Brahms, Orff, Fauré, Schubert and Charpentier; Mahler's Symphonies 2, 4 and 8; Engagements with Giuseppe Sinopoli leading the Czech Philharmonic, the Philharmonia London on tour in Japan, the Accademia di Santa Cecilia in Rome and the Deutsche Oper Berlin (Fiakermilli in Arabella); Recital repertoire includes German Lieder and songs in Russian, French, English, Spanish and Portuguese. *Current Management:* Ilse Zellermayer, Artur. Kutscher, Platz 1, 80802 Munich, Germany. *Address:* Balan Str 82, W. 81541 Munich, Germany.

CARTER Elliott (Cook, Jr), b. 11 Dec 1908, New York City, USA. Composer; Teacher. m. Helen Frost-Jones, 6 July 1939. 1 son. *Education:* Studied piano, Longy School of Music, Cambridge, Massachusetts; MA, Harvard University, 1932; Licence de contrepoint, Ecole Normale de Musique, Paris, France with Nadia Boulanger; Studied literature, languages, harmony and counterpoint with Walter Piston; orchestration with E B Hill. *Career:* Music Director, Ballet Caravan, 1937-39; Teacher of Music, mathematics, physics and Classical Greek, St John's College, Annapolis, Maryland, 1939-41; Faculty Member, Peabody Conservatory of Music, Baltimore, 1946-48; Columbia University, 1948-50; Yale University, 1958-62; Composer-in-residence, American Academy, Rome, 1963; Professor-at-large, Cornell University, 1967-68; Carter Fetival, South Bank, London, 1991, British Premiere of Violin Concerto. *Compositions:* Ballets: Pocahontas, 1936; The Minotaur, 1947; Incidental music to 3 dramas; Orchestral: Symphony No 1, 1942, revised 1954; Holiday Overture, 1944, revised 1961; Elegy for Strings, 1952; Variations for Orchestra, 1954-55; Double Concerto for Harpsichord, Piano and 2 Chamber Orchestras, 1961; Piano Concerto, 1964-65; Concerto for Orchestra, 1968-69; A Symphony of Three Orchestras, 1976; Penthode for 5 Instrumental Quartets, 1984-85; A Celebration of Some 100 x 150 Notes, 1987; Oboe Concerto, 1987; Remembrance, 1988; Violin Concerto, 1990; Anniversary, 1991; Chamber: Elegy for Cello and Piano, 1943, arranged for String Quartet, 1946, for String Orchestra, 1952, for Viola and Piano, 1961; Piano Sonata, 1945-46; Woodwind Quintet, 1948; Sonata for Cello and Piano, 1948; 4 string quartets: 1950-51, 1959, 1971, 1986; Sonata for Flute, Oboe, Cello and Harpsichord, 1952; Canon for 3: In Memoriam Igor Stravinsky for 3 Equal Instruments, 1971; Duo for Violin and Piano, 1973-74; Brass Quintet for 2 Trumpets, Horn and 2 Trombones,

1974; Night Fantasies for Piano, 1980; Triple Duo for Violin, Cello, Flute, Clarinet, Piano and Percussion, 1982-83; Changes for Guitar, 1983; Esprit rude-esprit doux for Flute and Clarinet, 1984; Enchanted Preludes for Flute and Cello, 1988; Con leggerezza pensosa, for clarinet, violin and cello, 1990; Trilogy for Harp and Oboe, 1992; Quintet for Piano and Winds, 1992; Choral music; Solo Vocal; Warble for Lilac-Time for Soprano or Tenor and Piano or Small Orchestra, 1943, revised 1954; Voyage for Mezzo-soprano or Baritone and Piano, 1943, also for Small Orchestra, 1975, revised 1979; A Mirror on Which to Dwell for Soprano and 9 Performers, 1975; Syringa for Mezzo-soprano, Bass and 11 Performers, 1978; In Sleep, in Thunder for Tenor and 14 Performers, 1981. *Recordings:* Various works recorded. *Honours:* Guggenheim Fellowships, 1945, 1950; American Prix de Rome, 1953; Pulitzer Prizes in music, 1960, 1973; Various honorary doctorates including: New England Conservatory of Music, 1961; Princeton University, 1967; Harvard University, 1970; University of Cambridge, 1983; National Medal of Arts, 1985; Chevalier dans l'ordre des Arts et Lettres, 1990; Commendatore in the Order of Merit of the Republic of Italy. *Address:* c/o Boosey & Hawkes Inc, 24 East 21 Street, New York, NY 10010-7200, USA.

CARTER Peter John Burnett, b. 30 Jan 1935, Durban, South Africa. Musician. m. Sally Mackay, 20 Dec 1974, 1 son, 1 daughter. *Education:* Royal College of Music, London, 1952-55; Conservatoire Royale de Musique, Brusselles, 1955-58; ARCM; LCRM; MMus Honoris Causa, University of Hull, 1987. *Career:* 2nd Violin, Dartington String Quartet, 1958-68; Director, Music, Natal Performing Arts Council, 1968-69; 1st Violin, Delmé String Quartet, Member ECO, 1969-74; Senior Lecturer, Cape Town, 1974-77; 1st Violin, Allegri String Quartet, Allegri Robles Ensemble, 1977, Melos Ensemble, 1984. *Recordings:* Complete Schubert Quartets, 1979-81; Brahms Quartets & Quintets; Beethoven Quartets & Quintets; Ravel Septet; Stolen Gems, James Campbell, 1986; Leader Bath International Ensemble, 1988; Brahms Clarinet Quintet (James Campbell); Piano Quintet (Rian de Waal), 1992 CALA. *Memberships:* Musicians Union; Incorporated Society of Musicians. *Hobbies:* Tennis; Bridge; Theatre. *Current Management:* Magenta Music International. *Address:* 35 Gartmoor Gardens, London SW19 6NX, England.

CARTERI Rosanna, b. 14 Dec 1930, Verona, Italy. Singer (Soprano). *Education:* Studied with Cuisnati and Nino Ederle. *Debut:* Rome 1949, as Elsa in Lohengrin. *Career:* La Scala debut 1951, in La Buona Figliuola by Piccinni; Sang in many concerts, notably in Donizetti's Requeim and in the premiere of Pizzetti's Ifigenia (Italian Radio 1950); Salzburg Festival 1952, as Desdemona, conducted by Furtwängler; Florence 1953, as Natasha in the stage premiere of Prokofiev's War and Peace; San Francisco 1954, as Mimi; Chicago Lyric Opera 1955, as Marguerite in Faust; Verona Arena 1958-59; Covent Garden 1960, Mimi; Sang in the premiere of Pizzetti's Calzare d'Argento, Milan 1961; premiere, Gilbert Bécaud's Opéra d'Aran, Theâtre des Champs-Elysées, Paris, 1952. *Recordings include:* La Traviata (RCA); Falstaff, Guillaume Tell, Suor Angelica, La Bohème (Cetra); Solo in the Brahms Requiem, conducted by Bruno Walter.

CARUS Louis, b. 22 Oct 1937, Kasauli, India. Violinist. m. Nancy Reade Noell, 2 sons, 1 daughter. *Education:* Brussels Conservatoire; Peabody Conservatory, Baltimore, USA; LRAM; FRCM. *Debut:* Glasgow, 1952. *Career:* Scottish National Orchestra, 5 years; Solo, Chamber Music and Teaching Career, Scotland; Head, String Department, RSAMD; Member Scottish Trio Scottish Piano Quartet, Clarina Ensemble, New Music Group of Scotland; Leader, Northern Sinfonia Orchestra; Sub-Leader Monteverdi Orchestra; Principal, Birmingham School of Music; Artistic Director, International String Quartet Week; Consultant; Benslow Music Trust. *Recordings:* Shostakovich and Beethoven Piano Trios. *Publications:* Contributor to daily papers, Strad magazine, Incorporated Society of Musicians

Journal. *Honours:* FRSAMD; Hon RAM; FRCM; FBSM and Fellow of the City of Birmingham Polytechnic. *Memberships:* President, Incorporated Society of Musicians, 1986-87; ESTA; Rotary, Royal Society of Musicians. *Hobbies:* Gardening; Sketching; Picture Collection; Travel. *Address:* 15 Kings End Road, Powick, Worcs WR2 4RA, England

CARVALHO Eleazar (de), b. 28 July 1912, Iguatu, Brazil. Conductor; Composer. *Education:* Studied at the National School of Music, Brazil, graduated 1934. *Career:* Played the tuba in the orchestra of the Teatro Municipal in Rio de Janeiro, 1930-40; Conducted the Brazilian Symphony Orchestra from 1941, Conductor for Life 1965; Conducted the Boston Symphony Orchestra 1947; Guest appearances in Europe and the USA; Music Director of the St Louis Symphony Orchestra 1963, Conductor Emeritus 1968; Conductor of the Pro Arte Symphony at Hofstra University, Hempstead, New York, 1968-73; Music Director of the Orquestra Sinfonica Estadual, Sao Paulo, 1973; Taught at the Juilliard School, New York, 1983; Conducted works by Berg, Webern and Schoenberg, as well as the standard repertory. *Address:* c/o Orquestra Sinfonica Estadual de Sao Paulo, Teatro de Cultura Artistica, Rua Nestor Pestona 196, 01303 Sao Paulo, Brazil.

CARY Tristram Ogilvie, b. 14 May 1925, Oxford, England. Composer; Writer; Teacher. m. Doris E Jukes 7 July 1951 (divorced 1978), 2 sons, 1 daughter. *Education:* Dragon School, Oxford, 1929-38; Westminster School, (King's Scholar), 1938-42; Christ Church, Oxford, (Exhibitioner), 1942-43 and 1946-47, interrupted by service in Royal Navy, BA and MA; Trinity College of Music, AMus, TCL., LMus, TCL., 1949-51. *Debut:* Wigmore Hall, London, 12 Dec. 1949. *Career:* Composing from age 14; Record shop assistant, 1951-54; 1st Electronic Music Studio, 1952; Self-employed 1955-; music for concerts, films, radio, TV, theatre, musical directories etc; Founded, Electronic Studio at Royal College of Music, 1967; Senior Lecturer, 1974-then Reader, Dean of Music, 1982, University of Adelaide; Self-employed as Composer, Teacher, Writer, Computer Music Consultant. *Compositions:* 345 Narcissus Trios; Sonata for Guitar Alone; Three Threes and One Make Ten; arrangement of Bach's 6-part Ricercar, Continuum, Contours and Densities at First Hill; Peccata Mundi; Divertimento; The Songs Inside; Romantic Interiors; Steam Music; Two Songs from the Piae Cantiones; Nonet, Soft Walls; I Am Here; Family Conference; Seeds; Trellises; Strands; String Quartet II: Sevens, The Dancing Girls, Black White and Rose, Strange Places, Earth Holds Songs. *Recordings:* Tracks from Divertimento (on Full Spectrum-Move Records MS 3027); Peccata Mundi (BBC Transcription Service); CDs of computer and orchestral music published by Canberra School of Music and Tall Poppies Records; Many radio, film, TV score recordings. *Publication:* Illustrated Compendium of Musical Technology, published in USA as Dictionary of Musical Technology, Faber and Faber, 1992. *Contributions to:* Musical Times; Composer; The Electronic Music Review; The Guardian; Opera Australia, The Australian. *Honours:* Best experimental film of the Year, Venice, 1958, and BFA Award, 1959 for track of The Little Island; Prix Italia, 1962; Hon RCM, Award, 1971; Medal of the Order of Australia, (OAM), 1991. *Memberships:* Council Member, Composers' Guild of Great Britain; Institute of Electrical Engineers (I.Eng). *Hobbies:* Swimming; Sailing; Cycling; Snooker; Cookery; Wine; Good conversation. *Address:* 30 Fowlers Road, Glen Osmond, SA 5064, Australia.

CASADESUS Gaby, b. 9 Aug 1901, Marseilles, France. Concert Pianist; Professor. m. Robert Casadesus (deceased), 16 July 1921, 2 sons, 1 daughter. *Education:* Paris Conservatory. *Career:* Soloist with major orchestras in Europe; Duo piano team with her husband performed worldwide under leading conductors, later joined by their son Jean (deceased); Master classes including Ravel Academy, summer school of Mozarteum in Salzburg, Schola Cantorum in Paris and currently Fontainebleau School; Co-founder with Grant

Johannesen, Martha Joseph and Odette Valabrèque Wurzburger, Robert Casadesus International Piano Competition, Cleveland, Ohio, USA, biannually 1975-; Judge in international piano competitions including Paris, Geneva, Brussels, Montreal, Bolzano, New York, and London; Concert career continues with orchestra and chamber music ensembles. *Recordings:* Numerous recordings of 4 hand, 1, 2 and 3 piano works; Mozart concertos, Fauré, Bach and Saint-Saëns; Compositions of Robert Casadesus for CBS Masterworks; Records issued under Vox, Polydor and CBS. *Publications:* Editor of works of Ravel under Great Performers edition, Schirmer Publishers. *Contributions to:* Clavier; Piano Quarterly; Musique and Concerts. *Honours:* 1st Prize in Piano and Prix Pagès, Paris Conservatory, 1917; French Legion of Honour. *Membership:* Founding member: Robert Casadesus Association. *Current Management:* Maxim Gershunoff, Maxim Gershunoff Attractions Incorporated, 502 Park Avenue, New York, NY 10022, USA. *Address:* 54 Rue Vaneau, 75007 Paris, France.

CASADESUS Jean-Claude, b. 7 Dec 1935, Paris, France. Conductor. m. Anne Sevestre, 2 sons, 1 daughter. *Education:* Harmony, Fugue, Counterpoint, Composition, Percussion, Paris National Conservatory, 1959; Conducting Ecole Normale de Musique, Paris, 1965; with Pierre Dervaux studied with Pierre Boulez, Basle, Switzerland, 1965. *Career:* Solo Timpanist, Concert Colonne, 1959-68; Percussion Soloist, Domaine Musical with P. Boulez; Conductor, Paris Opéra, 1969-71; Co-Director, Orchestra Pays de Loire, 1971-76; Founder, Director, Lille National Orchestra, 1976-; Guest Conductor, USA, Scotland, England, Moscow, Leningrad, Prague, Leipzig, Dresden, Switzerland, Italy, Japan, etc; Conducted, Orchestre National de Lille in the Revolution Revisted series at the South Bank, London, 1989. *Compositions include:* Music for theatre and films. *Recordings include:* 1st Symphony, Dutilleux; Symphonie fantastique, Berlioz; Daphnis and Chloe, Ravel; 2 violin concerti, by Wieniawski, with Gitlis; Bal masqué, Poulenc; Sonata for 2 pianos and percussion, Bartók; Circles, Berio; Préludes, Mephisto Walz, Liszt; 7th Symphony, Beethoven; 3rd piano concerto, violin concerto, Beethoven; Funeral music, clarinet concerto, double concerto for flute and harp, Mozart; 4th Symphony, Kindertotenlieder, Rückertlieder, Des Knaben Wunderhorn, 5th Symphony, Mahler; Petrushka, Firebird, Stravinsky; Cloris et Clothilde, Roma Symphony, Bizet; Carmen Suites, Arlesienne, Bizet; Richard Wagner, Musical Extracts, (José Van Dam); Mahler, 1st, 2nd Symphonies; Ravel, Le Bolero, La Valse, Concertos pour piano; Poulenc, La Voix Humaine; Groupes des Six, Les Mariés de la Tour Eiffel; Debussy, La Mer, La Damoiselle Ellue, Nocturnes. *Honours:* 1st Prize, Percussion, Paris Conservatoire, 1959; 1st Prize, Conducting, Ecole Normale de Musique, 1965; 1st Recording Prize, Academy Charles Cros; Grand Prize for record, European Year of Music, 1985; SACEM Grand Prix, 1985; Advisor to the Prime Minister, 1981-84; General Secretary, Superior Council of Music; Cross of Chevalier, Legion d'Honneur; Cross of Chevalier, Order of Les Palmes Académiques, Cross of Commander, Order of Les Arts et Lettres; Cross of Officer, Leopold Order, Belgium; Commander, Order of Nassau, Netherlands; Commander Merite National. *Hobbies:* Skiing; Sailing; Tennis; Riding. *Current Management:* Anglo-Swiss, 59 St Martin's Lane, London, WC2N 4JS. *Address:* 2 rue de Steinkerque, Paris 75018, France.

CASAPIETRA Celestina, b. 23 Aug 1938, Genoa, Italy. Singer (Soprano). m. Herbert Kegel, (dec 1990). *Education:* Studied at the Milan Conservatory with Gina Cigna. *Debut:* Teatro Nuovo Milan 1961, in Mese Mariano by Giordano. *Career:* Sang in Genoa, San Remo, Pisa, Venice and Lyons; Sang at the Staatsoper Berlin from 1985, notably as Elsa, Constanze, Donna Anna, Agathe, Mimi, Micaela, Tatiana in Eugene Onegin and the title role in Daphne by Strauss; Salzburg Mozartwochen 1984, as Vitellia in La Clemenza di Tito; Las Palmas 1986, as Elisabeth in Tannhäuser; Guest engagements in London, Moscow, Helsinki,

Copenhagen, Vienna and Prague; Zemlinsky's Der Kreidekreis, Hamburg, 1983, Amsterdam, 1989. *Recordings include:* Fiordiligi in Così fan Tutte (Eurodisc); Mozart Masses and Orff's Trionfi (Philips). *Address:* c/o Deutsche Staatsoper, Unter den Linden 7, D-1086 Berlin, Germany.

CASELLATO Renzo, b. 18 Oct 1936, Adria, Rovigo, Italy. Singer (Tenor). *Education:* Studied at the Benedetto Marcello Conservatory Venice and with Maria Carbone. *Debut:* Reggio Emilia 1963, as Nemorino. *Career:* Sang the title role in Mozart's La Clemenza di Tito, La Scala 1966; Guest engagements in Vienna, Rio de Janeiro, Florence, Buenos Aires, Moscow, Copenhagen, Chicago and Dallas; Other roles include Nadir in Les pêcheurs de Perles, Rossini's Almaviva, Alfredo in La Traviata, Fenton in Falstaff and Massenet's Werther. *Recordings include:* Pia de Tolomei by Donizetti; Rossini's Tancredi, with Marilyn Horne. *Address:* c/o Teatro alla Scala, Via Filodrammatici 2, 1-20121 Milan, Italy.

CASEY Graham, b. 12 Jan 1963, Barnet, England. Clarinettist. m. 6 Nov 1988, 1 d. *Education:* Royal College of Music, ARCM, Clarinet Teaching; DipRCM, Performance. *Career:* Freelance clarinettist; Chamber Musician, Recitalist and Soloist; Clarinet Teacher at Anglia Polytechnic University and Homerton College, Cambridge and Oundle School. *Memberships:* Incorporated Society of Musicians. *Hobbies:* Current Affairs; Variety of Sport. *Address:* 29 Langford Road, Old Fletton, Peterborough, Cambs PE2 8EF, England.

CASHMORE John, b. 1960, Birmingham, Singer (Baritone). *Education:* Studied at the Birmingham School of Music and the National Opera Studio, London. *Debut:* Sang Guglielmo with Birmingham Music Theatre. *Career:* Opera engagements with English National Opera, Scottish Opera-Go-Round, Wexford Festival, Batignano and the New D'Oyly Carte Opera Company; Guglielmo for Opera Forum in Holland, 1991, Figaro in a British tour of Mozart's opera, Marullo in Rigoletto for ENO, 1992 and roles from 1992 at Aachen including Lortzing's Zar and Don Giovanni;/ Opera galas at the Albert Hall, Festival Hall and in Glasgow; Oratorio engagements include Carmina Burana in Birmigham and Glasgow, Monteverdi Vespers at Coventry Cathedral and Victory's Ultima Rerum in Dublin. *Address:* Atholl Still Ltd, Greystoke House, 80-86 Westrow Street, London SE19 3AF, England.

CASKEN John, b. 15 July 1949, Barnsley, Yorkshire, England. Composer. *Education:* 1967-71 Birmingham University, with Peter Dickinson and John Joubert; Warsaw 1971-73, with Dobrowolski and Lutoslawski. *Career:* Lecturer at Birmingham University 1973-79; Huddersfield Polytechnic 1979-81; Durham University 1981-; Featured composer at 1980 Bath Festival; Opera, Golem, premiered at 1989 Almeida Festival, London; Professor of Music, University of Manchester, 1992. *Compositions:* Music for cello and piano 1972; Kagura for 13 wind 1973; Jadu for 2 cellos 1973; Fluctus for violin and piano 1974; Music for the Crabbing Sun for quartet 1974; Music for a Tawny-Gold Day for quartet 1976; Arenaria for flute and ensemble 1976; Tableaux des trois ages for orchestra 1977; Amarantos for nonet 1978; Ligatura for organ 1978; la Orana, Gauguin for soprano and piano 1978; Melanos for tuba and nonet 1979; Firewhirl for soprano and septet 1980; A Belle Pavine for violin and tape 1980; Piano Concerto 1980; String Quartet 1982; Masque for oboe and chamber orchestra 1982; Taerset for clarinet and piano 1983; Erin for double-bass and chamber orchestra; To Fields we do not Know for chorus 1984; Orion over Farne for orchestra 1984; Clarion Sea for brass quintet 1985; Vaganza for ensemble 1985; Golem Opera, 1989; Maharal Dreaming, orchestra, 1989; Piano Quartet 1990; Cello Concerto, 1991; A Gathering for unaccompanied chorus, 1991; Sharp Thorne for four solo voices, 1991-92; Still mine for baritone and orchestra, 1991-92. *Honours:* First Britten Award for composition for his opera, Golem, 1990.*Address:* c/o Schott & Co. Ltd., 48 Great Marlborough Street, London W1V 2BN, England.

CASOLLA Giovanna, b. 1953, Italy. Singer (Soprano). *Debut:* Lisbon 1977, as Ebolin Don Carlos. *Career:* Sang at Turin 1978, 1982, Trieste, 1979, Buenos Aires, 1980, Detroit, 1981; San Diego, 1982, in the American premiere of Zandonai's Giulietta e Romeo; Metropolitan Opera 1984, as Zandonai's Francesca da Rimini (returned 1986, as Eboli); La Scala Milan, 1983 and 1986, as Giorgetta in Il Tabarro; Verona Arena 1986 and 1988, as Maddalena in Andrea Chenier and La Gioconda; Caracalla Festival 1987, 1989, as Tosca; Further guest appearances at Vienna dn Miami, 1988, Deutsch Oper Berlin, 1989, Tosca, Stuttgart and Venice, (Eboli, 1991); La Scala and Florence 1991, as Minnie in La Fanciulla del West and Santuzza; Puccini Festival Torre del Lago, 1991, as Giorgetta; other roles include Fedora, Amelia (Ballo in Maschera), Adriana Lecouvreur, Manon Lescaut, Silvana in Resighi's La Fiamma, Bartok's Judith, Maria in Tchaikovsky's Mazeppa and Elena Makropoulos; Many concert appearances. *Address:* c/o Teatro Alla Scala, Via Filodrammatici 2, 20121 Milan, Italy.

CASONI Bianca-Maria, b. 1 Mar 1932, Milan, Italy. Singer (Mezzo-Soprano). *Education:* Studied at the Milan Conservatory with Bruna Jona and Mercedes Llopart. *Debut:* Milan 1956, as Mercedes in Carmen. *Career:* Sang widely in Italy after winning La Scala Competition; Salzburg 1960, as Giacinta in La Finta Semplice, 1960; Glyndebourne 1965, as Cherubino; Concert performance of Bellini's La Straniera, New York 1969; Appearances at Covent Garden and the Festivals of Aix and Edinburgh; Monte Carlo, Geneva, Barcelona, Philadelphia and the Metropolitan Opera; Turin 1975, in the Italian premiere of Die drei Pintos, Mahler/Weber; Berlin Staatsoper 1981, as Cinderella. *Recordings include:* Mozart's Coronation Mass; La Straniera; Preziosilla in La Forza del Destino (EMI). *Address:* c/o Deutsche Staatsoper, Under der Linden 7, D-1086 Berlin, Germany.

CASSEL John Walter, b. 15 May 1910, Council Bluffs, Iowa, USA. Singer (Opera, Recitals, Operetta, Musicals). m. (1) Nadine Blackburn, (2) Gail Manners, 27 Feb 1955, 3 sons, 2 daughters. *Education:* Creighton University, Nebraska; Studied voice privately with Harry Cooper, Council Bluffs; Trumpet, piano and additional voice studies in Council Bluffs; Studied voice with Frank La Forge, New York City, 17 years. *Debut:* Metropolitan Opera, 1943. *Career:* Leads in Broadway musicals, Mason Radio programmes, London Great Waltz, New York City Opera; Created role of Horace Tabor in world premiere, Ballad of Baby Doe, Central City 1956; Leading baritone operatic roles in Europe; With Metropolitan Opera, 1943-74, 203 performances including Strauss's Mandryka and Jochanaan and Wagner's Dutchman, Telramund and Kurwenal; Recitals throughout USA; Sang with all major US orchestras including Philadelphia Orchestra, New York Philharmonic, Boston Symphony, San Francisco Symphony; TV guest; Appeared in Warner Bros films early in career; Noted for acting; Professor of Voice and Drama, Indiana University School of Music, Bloomington, 1974-. *Recordings:* Tosca and Carmen, Metropolitan Opera Guild; Faust and The Ballad of Baby Doe, New York City Opera, MGM Record Co; Belshazzar's Feast, with Philadelphia Orchestra, Columbia Records; Reverence for Life (in honour of Albert Schweizer), Columbia Records; Great Waltz, EMI of London Recordings. *Honour:* Recipient of decoration, New York Society of Voice Teachers, 1957. *Memberships:* Actors Equity; AGMA (1st Vice-President 2 years); AGVA; Screen Actors Guild. *Hobbies:* Horse shoes; Riding; Swimming; Tennis; Travel. *Address:* Studio No 103, Indiana University School of Music, Bloomington, IN 47401, USA.

CASSELLO Kathleen, b. 1958, Delaware, USA. Singer (Soprano). *Education:* Dan Pressley, Delaware, USA; Wilma Lipp, Salzburg, Austria; Sesto Bruscantini, Italy. *Career:* European debut as Queen of the Night in Hamburg, 1985; More than 200 Queen of the Night performances since in Hamburg, 1986-88, Zurich, 1988, Geneva, 1988, Moskow, 1987, Salzburg, 1988,

Stuttgart, 1990, Deutsche Oper and Staatsoper, Berlin, 1986-89; Staatstheater Karlsruhe ensemble, 1987-89; Lucia in Karlsruhe, 1989-92, Sao Paolo, 1989, Marseille, San Sebastian and Zürich, 1990, Malaga, 1992, Treviso, Rome and Palermo, 1993. Traviata in Karlsruhe, 1987-92, Oviedo, 1991, Toulouse, 1992, Festival Orange and Rome, 1993, Tokyo, 1994, Geneva; Elvira in Puritani at Marseille, 1991, Malaga, 1993; Gilda in Rigoletto at Marseille, 1992, Mexico City and Nice, 1993, La Scala with Riccardo Muti, 1994; Konstanze in Entführung in St Gallen, 1986-87, Wien, 1988, Karlsruhe, 1989, Zürich, 1990, München National Theater, 1992, Avignon, 1993, Marseille and Hamburg 1994-; Other roles include: Manon at Met, 1990; Thais at Marseille, 1991; Pamina at Barcelona, 1991; Musetta at the Arena di Verona, 1992; Vitellia in La Clemenza di Tito in Toulouse, 1992; Athens, 1994; Amina in La Sonnambula at Messina, 1993; Elettra in Idomeneo at Venice, 1993; Giulietta in I Capuleti e i Montecchi at Parma, 1994. *Address:* Friedlgasse 57/2, A-1190 Vienna.

CASSIDY Paul, b. 1959, Ireland. Violist. *Education:* Studied at the Royal College of Music; UCLA and Detmold, Germany. *Career:* Founder member of the Brodsky Quartet (name derives from violinist Adolph Brodsky, Principal of the Royal Manchester College of Music (1895-1929); Resident at Cambridge University for four years and later residencies at the Dartington International Summer School, Devon; Concert engagements include the Shostakovich quartets at the Elizabeth Hall, London and performances at the Ludwigsburg and Schleswig-Holstein Festivals; New York debut at the Metropolitan Museum; Further tours of Italy, North America, Australia, Poland, Czechoslovakia and Japan; Complete quartets of Schoenberg for the BBC, 1992; French concerts include visit to the Théâtre du Châtelet, Paris. *Recordings include:* Quartets of Elgar and Delius; Schubert A minor and also Schubert D minor and Crumb, Black Angels; Beethoven Op 74 (Harp); Complete quartets of Shostakovich (Teldec). *Address:* 21-22 Old Steine, Brighton, England.

CASSILLY Richard, b. 14 Dec. 1927, Washington DC, USA, Opera Singer (Tenor). m. Helen Koliopulos, 1951, 4 sons, 3 daughters. *Education:* Peabody Conservatory of Music Baltimore, Maryland. *Career:* New York City Opera, 1955-66; Chicago Lyric, 1959-; San Francisco Opera, 1966-; Deutsche Oper Berlin, 1965-; Hamburgische Staatsoper, 1966-; Covent Garden, 1968-, (debut as Janáček's Laca); La Scala, Milan, Italy, 1970; Wiener Staatsoper, Austria, 1970; Staatsoper München, Federal Republic of Germany, 1970; Paris Opera, France. 1972; Metropolitan Opera, 1973-, as Radames, Tannhäuser, Tristan, Otello, Samson and Captain Vere in Billy Budd; Kammersänger, 1973; Sang Aron in a concert performance of Schoenberg's Moses and Aron, London 1974, conducted by Boulez; Television Performances of Otello, Peter Grimes, St. of Bleecker Street, Fidelio, Wozzeck and Die Meistersinger; Aeneas in concert performance of Les Troyens, Promenade Concerts, London, 1980; Tannhäuser, production of Wagner's opera by Peter Sellars at Chicago, 1988; Herod in Salome, Metropolitan, 1989. *Recordings:* Has made numerous recordings including Aeneas in Les Troyens at Carnegie Hall, (1959-60), Via 1992, and Moses und Aron, Philips. *Current Management:* Robert Lombardo Associates, NY, USA. *Address:* c/o Robert Lombardo Associates, 30 West 60th Street, New York, NY 10023, USA.

CASSIS Alessandro, b. 1949, Italy. Singer (Baritone). *Debut:* Florence 1971, in Un Ballo in Maschera. *Career:* Sang in the Maggio Musicale, Florence 1974 in La Fanciulla del West; Piccola Scala Milan in La Favola d'Orfeo by Casella; Sang Germont at Turin 1977, Amonasro at the Verona Arena 1982; La Scala Milan 1983, as Michele in Il Tabarro, Sharpless in Butterfly 1985; Returned to Verona in 1986 and 1988, As Gerard (Andrea Chenier) and Barnaba (La Gioconda); Further appearances at Naples, Genoa, Geneva, Palermo, Trieste and Lisbon; Baths of Caracalla, Rome, 1991,

as Amonasro; other roles include Carlo in La Forza del Destino and Verdi's Luna, Rigoletto and Renato; High Priest in Samson et Delila. *Recordings include:* I Lutuani by Ponchielli; Nerone by Boito. *Address:* Teatro alla Scala, Via Filodrammatici 2, 20121 Milan, Italy.

CASSUTO Alvaro (Leon), b. 17 Nov 1938, Oporto, Portugal. Conductor; Composer. *Education:* Studied violin and piano as a child; Studied composition with Arthur Santos and Lopes Graca; Courses with Ligeti, Messiaen and Stockhausen, Darmstadt, summers, 1960, 1961; Studied conducting with Karajan, Pedro de Freitas Branco, Lisbon and with Ferrara in Hilversum; PhD, Law, University of Lisbon, 1964; MA, conducting, Vienna Academy of Music, 1965. *Career:* Assistant conductor, Gulbenkian Orchestra, Lisbon, 1965-68; Little Orchestra, New York, 1968-70; Permanent conductor 1970-75, Music Director 1975-, National Radio Orchestra, Lisbon; Lecturer 1974-75, Professor in music, 1975-79, Conductor, Symphony orchestra, University of California, Irvine; Music Director, Rhode Island Philharmonic Orchestra, Providence, 1979-85; National Orchestral Association, New York, 1981-87; Nova Filarmonia Portuguesa. *Compositions:* Opera: In the Name of Peace, 1971; Orchestral: Sinfonia breve No 1, 1959; No 2, 1960; Variations, 1961; Permutations for 2 Orchestras, 1962; Concertino for Piano and Orchestra, 1965; Cro (mo-no)fonia for 20 Strings, 1967; Canticum in Tenebris for Soloists, Chorus and Orchestra, 1968; Evocations, 1969; Circle, 1971; To Love and Peace, symphonic poem, 1973; Homage to My People, suite for Band, 1977; Return to the Future, 1985; The Four Seasons for Piano and Orchestra, 1986; Chamber: String Sextet, 1962; Song of Loneliness for 12 Performers, 1972. *Recordings:* For Imavox; Orion. *Honour:* Koussevitzky prize, Tanglewood, Massachusetts, 1969. *Address:* Rua da Bela Vista 172, 2750 Cascais, Portugal.

CASTEL Nico, b. 1 Aug 1931, Lisbon, Portugal. Singer (Tenor). *Education:* Studied with Carmen Hurtado in Caracas, Mercedes Llopart in Milan and Julia Drobner in New York. *Debut:* Santa Fe 1958, as Fenton in Falstaff. *Career:* New York City Opera 1965, in The Fiery Angel by Prokofiev; Metropolitan Opera from 1970, in Le Nozze di Figaro, Hansel and Gretel and Boris Godunov; Guillot in the Beverly Sills recording of Manon; Appearances in Lisbon, Florence, Chicago, Houston, Baltimore, Philadelphia and Houston; Diction and Phonetics teacher for singers; Staff diction coach, Metropolitan Opera; Adjunct Professor, Boston University; Professor at the Juilliard School. *Recordings include:* La Bohème (RCA); Les Contes d'Hoffmann (EMI). *Publications:* A Singers' Manual of Spanish Lyric Diction, Excalibur Press, New York, 1994; The Complete Puccini Libretti, Translated and Phoneticized, Leyerle Publications, MT Morris, New York, 1994. *Address:* c/o Metropolitan Opera, Lincoln Center, New York, NY 10023, USA.

CASTIGLIONI Nicola, b. 17 July 1932, Milan, Italy. Composer; Writer on Music. *Education:* Studied at the Milan Conservatory with Ghedini, Desderi and Margola; Piano with Friedrich Gulda at the Salzburg Mozarteum; Composition with Blacher. *Career:* Active as a pianist in early career; Composer-in-residence at the State University of New York, Buffalo, 1966; Settled in USA 1967 and became Visiting Professor in Composition at the University of Michigan; Regent Lecturer in Composition at the University of California at San Diego, 1968; Professor of the History of Renaissance Music at the University of Washington at Seattle, 1969. *Compositions:* Opera Uomini e no 1955; Radio opera Through the Looking Glass, 1961; Chamber opera Jabberwocky, 1962; 1 act opera Sweet, 1968; Opera Triptych, 3 Mystery Plays 1968; Concertino per la Notte di natale 1952; 2 Symphonies, 1956-57; Canti for orchestra 1956; Elegia for 19 instruments and soprano 1975; Impromptus for orchestra 1958; Moviemento continuato for piano and 11 instruments; Sequenze for orchestra 1959; Apreslude for orchestra 1959; Disegeni for chamber orchestra 1960; Rondels for orchestra 1961; Concerto for Orchestra 1963; A Solemn Music for soprano and orchestra 1963; Canzoni for soprano and orchestra 1966; The New Melusine for string quartet 1969; La Chant du Cigne for flute and orchestra 1969; Sinfonia in Do, after Jonson, Dante, Shakespeare and Keats, for chorus and orchestra 1969. *Address:* ASCAP, ASCAP House, One Lincoln Plaza, New York, NY 10023, USA.

CASTLE Joyce, b. 17 Jan 1944, Beaumont, TX, USA. Singer (Mezzo- soprano). m. Bruce Brewer. *Education:* Studied at the University of Kansas, the Eastman School and in New York. *Debut:* San Francisco 1970, as Siebel in Faust. *Career:* Many appearances at opera houses in Philadelphia, San Antonio, San Francisco and Washington, as Lola, Mme Flor in The Medium, Elizabeth Proctor in The Crucible, and Zita in Gianni Schicchi; Houston 1989, as the Witch in Hansel and Gretel; Sang Mere Marie in Dialogues des Carmelites at Seattle and in Weill's Street Scene at the New York City Opera, 1990; Santa Fe 1991, as Marcellina in Le nozze di Figaro; Annina in Der Rosenkavalier, 1992. *Recordings include:* Biancofiore in Francesca da Rimini (Rodolphe); Bernstein's Candide (New World). *Address:* c/o Santa Fe Opera, PO Box 248, Santa Fe, NM 87504, USA

CASTLEMAN Charles (Martin), b. 22 May 1941, Quincy, Massachusetts, USA. Violinist; Professor. *Education:* Studied violin with Emanuel Ondricek, 1945; with Ivan Galamian, Curtis Institute of Music, Philadelphia, 1957-63; Private studies with Josef Gingold, Henryk Szeryng and David Oistrakh; Harvard College; A.B. Harvard University; B.M. Curtis Institute of Music; M.A. University of PA. *Career:* Soloist at age 6 with Arthur Fiedler and the Boston Pops Orchestra; Recital debut at age 9, Jordan Hall, Boston; NY Debut, Town Hall, 1964; Founder, Quartet Program, Norton, Massachusets, 1970; Member, New String Trio of New York, 1972-75; Raphael Trio, 1975-; Teacher, Philadelphia Musical Academy; Professor of Violin, Eastman School of Music, Rochester, New York, 1975- ; Festival apperances at Montreux, Vienna, N.Queensland, Spitalfields, Shefield, Marlboro, Saratoga, Great Woods, Newport, Sarasota, Juneau, Bowdoin, Harrisbourg, Deer Valley. *Recordings:* Ysaÿe's 6 Unaccompanied violin sonatas; 20th century violin and Harpsichord music; Reger string trios; Frank Martin string and piano trios; Mendelssohn piano trios; Dvořák piano trios. *Address:* c/o Eastman school of Music, University of Rochester, Rochester, NY 14604, USA.

CASTRO-ALBERTY Margarita, b. Oct 1947, Puerto Rico. Singer (Soprano). *Education:* Studied at the Pablo Casals Conservatory, Puerto Rico, the Accademia di Santa Cecilia Rome and at Juilliard, New York. *Debut:* Santiago 1978, As Amelia in Un Bolla in Maschera. *Career:* Sang at the Teatro Colon, Buenos Aires 1979- 80; European debut 1980, in La Vida Breve by Falla; Carnegie Hall 1981, as Lucrezia in I Due Foscari, Metropolitan debut 1982, as Amelia; Festival d'Orange 1983, as Aida; Guest engagements in Venice, Berlin, Vienna, Nancy, Rome and Toronto; other roles include Donna Anna, Amelia Grimaldi, Nedda, Butterfly, Lucrezia Borgia, Elisabeth de Valois and the Trovatore Leonora; Sang at Marseilles 1987. *Address:* c/o Opéra de Marseille, 2 Rue Moliére, F-13231 Marseille Cedex 01, France.

CATHCART Allen, b. 2 Aug 1938, Baltimore, Maryland, USA. Singer (Tenor). *Education:* Studied at the University of California and with Boris Goldovsky in New York. *Debut:* Metropolitan Opera Studio 1961, as Guglielmo in Così fan Tutte. *Career:* European engagements in Brussels, Rome, Zurich, Cologne, Stuttgart and Kiel; Welsh National Opera in Cardiff; Paris Opéra-Comique, in The Stone Guest by Dargomyzhsky, 1985; Paris Opéra as the Drum Major in Wozzeck; Other roles include Don José, Florestan, Cavaradossi, the Emperor in Die Frau ohne Schatten, Laca in Jenůfa and parts in operas by Wagner. *Recordings include:* Jason in Mayr's Medea in Corinto (Vanguard).

CATHCART David Paul, b. 7 June 1949, Bradford,

England. Conductor. *Education:* Guildhall School of Music, 1968-71; GGSM. *Career:* Conducted several orchestras in UK, Spain, Hungary, West Germany, France. Founded Lambeth Orchestra in London, 1972, Principal Conductor, 1972-82. Currently Guest Conductor, Bombay Philharmonia and Indian National Symphony Orchestra, 1982-; currently conductor of Trinity Sinfonia London, 1985-, and Morley College, London, 1987-. *Recordings:* Schubert Symphony 3 and 8; Bruckner Symphony in F minor. *Publications:* Ed. score Schubert Symphony 8, 1979; completed Tchaikovsky orchestration of Beethoven Kreutzer Sonata, 1983. *Hobbies:* Photography; Cricket. *Address:* 56, Bennerley Road, London SW11 6DS, England.

CAUDLE Mark, b. 1950, England. Bass viol, Bass violin player; Cellist. *Career:* Member of The Parley of Instruments; Frequent tours in Britain and abroad, including the British Early Music Network; Performances in Spain, France, Germany, Holland, Poland and Czechoslovakia; US debut in New York 1988; Many concerts with first modern performances of early music in new editions by Peter Holman; Numerous broadcasts on Radio 3 and elsewhere; Repertoire includes Renaissance Violin Consort Music (Christmas music by Michael Praetorius, Peter Philips, music for Prince Charles I by Orlando Gibbons and Thomas Lupo); Baroque Consort Music by Monteverdi, Matthew Locke (anthems, motets and ceremonial music), Purcell (ayres for the theatre), Georg Muffat (Armonico Tributo sonatas 1682), Heinrich Biber (Sonate tam aris, quam aulis servientes, 1676), Vivaldi (sonatas and concertos for lute and mandolin, concertos for recorders) and J S Bach (Hunt cantata No 208): with Christopher Steele-Perkins, trumpet and Emma Kirkby, soprano, among others. *Recordings:* Many albums on the Hyperion label.

CAVA Carlo, b. 16 Aug. 1928, Ascoli Piceno, Italy. Singer (Bass). *Education:* Studied in Rome. *Debut:* Spoleto 1955, in L'Italiana in Algeri. *Career:* Netherlands Opera, Amsterdam, 1959; Glyndebourne 1961-65, as Seneca in L'Incoronazione di Poppea, as Sarastro, Bartolo in Le Nozze di Figaro, Basilio in Il Barbiere di Siviglia and Henry VIII in Anna Bolena; La Scala 1973, as Boris Godunov; Appearances in Cairo, Amsterdam, Brussels, Frankfurt, Vienna, Munich, Berlin and Paris. *Recordings include:* Oroveso in Norma (Decca); Zaccaria in Nabucco (Decca); L'Incoronazione di Poppea (EMI); Il Barbiere di Siviglia; Linda di Chamounix. *Address:* c/o Teatro alla Scala, Via Filodrammtici, 1-21021 Milan, Italy.

CAVALLIER Nicolas, b. 1964, France. Singer (Bass). *Education:* Studied at Royal Academy of Music and National Opera Studio (1988-89), with Elisabeth Söderström and with Iris dell'Acqua. *Debut:* Nancy Opera 1987 as Cascanda in The Merry Widow; Sang Achilles in Giulio Cesare conducted by Trevor Pinnock at the RAM. *Career:* Season 1988-89 in Massenet's Thais for Chelsea Opera Group and roles in Les Malheurs d'Orphée (Milhaud), Renard (Stravinsky) and Genevieve de Brabant (Satie) at the Elizabeth Hall; Season 1989-90 with Glass's Fall of the House of Usher in Wales, Henze's The English Cat in Berlin, Messiah with the Bournemouth Sinfonietta and John Metcalf's Tornrak at the Banff Centre in Canada; Sarastro in Die Zauberflöte at Glyndebourne; Sang Don Fernando (Fidelio) for the Glyndebourne Tour 1990, Zuniga for Welsh National Opera and in Alcione by Marais for Les Arts Florissants in Paris; Masetto for Nancy Opera; Other roles include Don Giovanni, Narbal in Les Troyens, Don Quichotte, Sparafucile and Mozart's Bartolo and Osmin; Season 1991/92 as Masetto at Nancy, Raleigh in Roberto Devereux at Monte Carlo and Caelnus in Lully's Atys with Les Arts Florissants; 1992/93 in Hamlet by Thomas at Monte Carlo, Leporello at Metz and Mr Flint in Billy Budd at Nancy; Loredano in I Due Foscari by Verdi for Scottish Opera at the 1993 Edinburgh Festival; Concert repertoire includes the Verdi and Mozart Requiems, A Child of our Time, Monteverdi Vespers and Die Schöpfung. *Recording:* Renarad. *Honours include:* Anne Lloyd Exhibition, Helen Eames Prize, Paton Award and Ricordi Award, RAM. *Address:* Robert

Gilder & Co. Enterprise House, 59/65 Upper Ground, London SE1 9PQ, England.

CAVE Penelope, b. 17 Apr 1951, Guildford, Surrey, England. Harpsichordist. m. Michael Heale, 27 July 1974, 1 son, 1 daughter. *Education:* GRSM; Royal Academy of Music, 1969-74; Lessons and Master Classes with Kenneth Gilbert, Colin Tilney, Ton Koopman and Gustav Leonhardt; LRAM. *Debut:* Wigmore Hall, 1980. *Career:* Solo recitals, England and abroad; Purcell Room, Capital Radio, BBC. *Recordings:* Recording with Camerata of London for Hyperion and with Garth Hewitt in settings of the metaphysical poets, on the Eagle label; Harpsichord Tutor, Morley College, 1984-; Kontraste with Flautist Martin Feinstein and violinist Marina Solarek. *Honours:* Raymond Russell Memorial Prize for Harpsichord, 1972; 1st Prize, Southport National Harpsichord Competition, 1976; Laureate Bruges International Harpsichord competition, 1983; ARAM, 1991. *Memberships:* Musicians Union; Committee Chairman, Incorporated Society of Musicians; Arts Centre Group. *Hobby:* Dolls house collection. *Address:* 8 Pit Farm Road, Guildford, Surrey, GU1 2JH, England.

CAVELTI Elsa, b. 4 May 1914, Rorschach, Lake Geneva, Switzerland. Singer (Mezzo-Soprano). *Education:* Studied in Zurich, Frankfurt and Vienna. *Debut:* Katowice 1936. *Career:* Sang first in Dusseldorf and Dresden, then at La Scala and in Vienna; Vicenza and Venice 1949 (L'Incoronazione di Poppea); Paris Opéra and La Scala 1951, as Brangaene and in Honegger's Judith; For Rome Radio sang in the first performance of Berg's Altenberglieder, 1953; Bayreuth Festival 1967; Guest appearances in London, Paris, Chicago and New York; Often heard in music by Bach. *Recordings include:* Fricka in Die Walküre; Brangaene in Tristan und Isolde; Octavian in Der Rosenkavalier.

CAVIC Frank, b. 22 July 1916, Illinois, USA. Sales Engineer. m. Helen Ann Ropac, 3 Sept 1939, 1s. *Education:* Studied with Vincent Kovacic. *Career:* Consultant, Founder and President Emeritus of Tamburitza Association of America, largest oganization in the US and or Canada specifically dedicated to the promotion and preservation of tamburitza music. Appearances on stage during annual concerts in various major cities throughout USA. *Publications:* Contributor to Tamburitza Association of America Times, (quarterly). *Memberships:* Serbian Business and Professional Association; Toast Masters International; American Society of Tool Engineers; Tamburitza Association of America, 1967-; Society of Manufacturing Engineers, 25 years; Life membership, Musicians Guild of American Federation of Musicians, 1992; Interanational Biographical Centre, Who's Who of Intellectuals; Area Governor, President-Vice, President, Secretary, Toastmasters Club: Tyrol: St ,ouis MO; Hall of Fame, Tamburitza Association of America. *Address:* 2 Gandy Drive, St Louis, MO 63146, USA.

CECCARINI Giancarlo, b. 19 July 1951, Pisa, Italy. Singer (Baritone). *Education:* Studied in Pisa and Rome. *Debut:* Spoleto 1975, as Belcore in L'Elisir d'Amore. *Career:* Has appeared widely in Italy as Marcello (La Boheme), Cimarosa's Maestro di Capella and Osmano in L'Ormindo by Cavalli (Venice 1976); Performances of Monteverdi's Combattimento at Terni, Bologna, Zurich, Mantua, Cremona and Frankfurt, 1980. *Recordings:* On Swiss Radio from 1977, including La Gazetta by Rossini and Donizetti's I Pazzi per Progresso; At Geno has sung Podesta in Docteur Miracle by Bizet, and Ggianni Schicchi; San Remo, 1982, as Nabucco; Ping in Turandot at Helsinki, 1991. Records include, I Pazzi per Progresso (UORC); Turandot (Nuova Era). *Address:* c/o Teatro La Fenice, Campo S Fantin 1965, 30124 Venice, Italy.

CECCATO Aldo, b. 18 Feb 1934, Milan, Italy. Conductor. m. Eliana de Sabata, 1966. 2 sons. *Education:* Verdi Conservatory, Milan, 1948-55; Studied conducting with Albert Wolff and Willem van Otterloo, the Netherlands, 1958; Berlin Hochschule für Musik, 1959-62. *Career:* Appearances as jazz and concert pianist; Assistant to Sergiu Celibidache, Accademia Musicale Chigiana, Siena, 1960; Guest conducting engagements throughout Italy and Europe; USA debut, Chicago Lyric Opera, 1969; Music Director, Detroit Symphony Orchestra, 1973-77; Generalmusikdirektor, Hamburg State Philharmonic Orchestra, 1975-83; Chief Conductor, Hannover Radio Orchestra, 1985-; Bergen Symphony Orchestra, 1985-; Conducted Maria Stuarda, Bergamo, 1989. *Recordings:* For ABC; Angel-EMI; Arabesque; Audio Fidelity; Klavier; Philips; Supraphon; La Traviata, Maria Stuarda, The Four Seasons, Mendelssohn's Piano Concertos, (John Ogdon), Music by Ravel and Liszt. *Honour:* 1st prize, RAI conducting competition, 1964. *Address:* c/o Rundfunkorchester Hannover, Rudolf von Bennigsen Ufer 22, D-3000 Hannover, Germany.

CECCHELE Gianfranco, b. 25 June 1940, Galliera Veneta, Italy. Singer (Tenor). *Education:* Studied with Marcello del Monaco in Treviso. *Career:* Sang at Catania from 1964; Many appearances on the major Italian stages; Guest appearances in London, Paris, Barcelona, Hamburg, Munich, Nice, Chicago, Philadelphia and Montreal; Carnegie Hall New York 1968, as Zamoro in a concert performance of Verdi's Alzira; Best known in operas by Puccini and Verdi; Verona between 1967 and 1984; Rio de Janeiro, 1988, as Radames; Mercadante's La Vestale at Split, 1987. *Recordings include:* Aroldo by Verdi (Cetra); Loreley by Catalani (CBS); Alzira; Title role in Rienzi by Wagner; Decio in Mercadante's La Vestale, Bongiovanni. *Address:* c/o Arena di Verona, Piazza Brà 28, 1-3 7121 Verona, Italy.

CECH Vladimir, b. 22 Mar 1944, Brno, Czechoslovakia. Independent Music and Drama Critic. m. Alena Benesova, 29 Aug 1975, 1 son. *Education:* Diploma Engineer, Technical University, Brno, 1970; Graduated, Faculty of Musicology and Theatrology, Brno University, 1974. *Career:* Regular programmes on Musical and Theatre Life, Radio Brno; Author, Speaker, public playbacks of classical. *Contributions:* Regularly to Brno and Prague newspapers, especially Svobodne slovo, Rovnost, Hudobny zivet, Opus musicum, Brnensky vecernik, Lidova demokracie; Regular reports on Brno music life, Prague Spring Festival, Wiener Staatsoper, Bayreuther Festspiele, others; Interviews with Leopold Stokowski, Christa Ludwig, Bernard Haitink, Charles Mackerras, Rudolf Firkusby, Werner Hollweg, Karl Richter, others. *Honours:* Prize, Czech Music Foundation, 1984-90. *Hobbies:* Travel; Sport. *Address:* Drobneho 16, 60200 Brno, Czech Republic.

CEELY Robert Paige, b. 17 Jan 1930, Torrington, Connecticut, USA. Composer. m. Jonatha Kropp, 13 Jan 1962. *Education:* BMus, New England Conservatory, Boston, Massachusetts; MA, Mills College, California; Graduate study, Princeton University, New Jersey; Major composition teachers include Darius Milhaud, Leon Kirchner, Francis Judd Cooke, Roger Sessions, Milton Babbitt. *Career:* Faculty of Composition, Director of Electronic Music at New England Conservatory of Music, Boston, MA, 1967. *Compositions:* String Trio, 1953; Woodwind Quintet, 1954; Composition for Ten Instruments, 1963; Stratti for magnetic tape, 1963; Elegia for magnetic tape, 1964; Vonce for magnetic tape, 1967; Modules for 7 instruments, 1968; Logs for 2 double basses, 1968; Hymn for cello and bass, 1969; Beyond The Ghost Spectrum (ballet), 1969; Mitsyn for computer generated tape, 1971; Slide Music for 4 trombones, 1974; Rituals for 40 flutes, 1978; Frames for computer generated tape, 1978; Lullaby for trombone and soprano, 1979; Flee, Floret, Florens, for 15 solo voices, 1979; Piano Piece, 1980; Bottom Dogs for 4 double basses, 1981; Roundels for large wind ensemble and tape, 1981; Piano Variations, 1982; Totems for Oboe and Tape, 1982; Dialogue for Solo Flute, 1983; Giostra for Oboe and Tape, 1984; Minute Rag for solo piano, 1985; Pitch Dark for Jazz Ensemble, 1985; Synoecy for clarinet and tape, 1986; Timeshares for percussion ensemble, 1988; Special K variations for piano, 1989;

Post hoc, ergo propter hoc for solo bass clarinet, 1989; Harlequin for solo double bass, tape, 1990; Hypallage for solo trumpet and tape, 1990; Asyndeton for piano and tape, 1993. *Address:* 33 Elm Street, Brookline, MA, USA.

CEGOLEA Gabriela, b. 1950, USSR. Singer (Soprano). *Education:* Studied in Bucharest and at the Benedetto Marcello Conservatory Venice; Sang at the Taormina Festival, then studied further at the school of the Royal Opera, Stockholm. *Debut:* Stockholm, 1977, as Tosca. *Career:* Appearances as Tosca at Oslo, and as Manon at Venice; La Scala Milan with Placido Domingo, conducted by Georges Prêtre; Further engagements in New York, Berlin, Stuttgart, San Francisco, Naples and Rome; tours of Australia, Brazil and South Korea; Liège, 1989, as Maddalena in Andrea Chenier.

CELIBIDACHE Sergiu, b. 11 July 1912, Iasi, Romania. Conductor. m. 1 child. *Education:* Hochschule für Musik, Berlin. *Career:* Conductor, Berlin Philharmonic, 1945-52; Artistic Director, Conductor, Radio-Symphony orchestras, Stockholm and Stuttgart; General Music Director, Stadt München, and Chief Director, Munich Philharmonic Orchestra, 1979-; often heard in music by Ravel, Prokofiev, Shostakovich and Beethoven; British debut with London Philharmonic Orchestra 1948; guest conductor with London Symphony Orchestra 1962-63 and from 1977; Conducted the premieres of Henze's Undine, Trois pas de Tritons, 1958; Lamento di Orlando by Gunter Bialas, 1986; 3rd Symphony by Harald Genzmer, 1986; Sinfonie in sechs Teilen by Peter Hamel, 1986. *Compositions:* Symphonies, orchestral suites, piano works. *Honour:* Decorated Knight, Order of Vasa, Sweden. *Address:* Müncher Philharmoniker, Marienplatz 8, D800 Munich 2, Germany.

CELIS Frits, b. 11 Apr 1929, Antwerp, Belgium. Conductor; Writer on Music. Divorced, 2 daughters. *Education:* Studied Greek and Latin at High School; Studied Piano, Harp, Orchestral Direction (conducting), Fugue - Music History, Chamber Music. *Debut:* 1946. *Career:* Harpist, Royal Flemish Opera, Antwerp, 1946-52; Conductor, Royal Opera House, Brussels, 1954-59; Music Director, Royal Flemish Opera, Antwerp, Flanders Opera, Antwerp and Ghent, 1959-88; Guest conductor: Germany, USA, France, Spain, Czechoslovakia, Holland; Professor, Royal Flemish Music Conservatory, Antwerp. *Compositions:* Violin Sonata; Cello Sonata; Intrada and Toccata for oboe or clarinet and piano; Episodes for viola and harpsichord; Nocturno and Danza for 4 flutes - Dreihieder Hymne for Harp. *Recordings:* Elegy for orchestra; Nocturno and Danza for 4 flutes; Hypocritical Funeral Music for Brass Quintet and many other broadcast recordings. *Publication:* A Biography on the Flemish Composers August De Boeck and Edward Kemvacks. *Contributions to:* Many articles on various Flemish composers. *Memberships:* Centre Belge de Documentation Musicale; Union of Belgian Composers. *Hobby:* Study of Nature. *Address:* Zijwegel 28, B- 2920 Kalmthout, Belgium.

CELLI Joseph, b. 19 Mar 1944, Bridgeport, Connecticut, USA. Composer; Oboist. *Education:* Studied at the Hartt School of Music, Northwestern University and Oberlin Conservatory. *Career:* Director of Real Art Ways from 1975, hosted New Music America Festival, 1984; As oboist has given the US premieres of Stockhausen's Spiral and Solo; Has commissioned works for oboe from Fulkerson, Lucier, Cope, Oliveros and Goldstein; Commission from Wesleyan Singers and the Connecticut Council on the Arts for To Be Announced. *Compositions include:* Sky: S for J 1976; Ringing, for antique cymbals, 1978; Improvisations for English horn, 1979-82; Improvisations for oboe and violin 1979-82; Ring Ritual for 2 performers 1981; To Be Announced for 8 groups of voices and 8-track tape, 1981. *Address:* c/o ASCAP, ASCAP Building, One Lincoln Plaza, New York, NY 10023, USA.

CERHA Friedrich, b. 17 Feb 1926, Vienna, Austria. Composer. *Education:* Studied at the Vienna Academy 1946-51, with Vasa Prihoda and Alfred Uhl. *Career:* With Kurt Schwertsik co-founded ensemble Die Reihe 1958: performances of contemporary music and works by the Second Viennese School; Director of the electronic music studio at the Vienna Musikhochschule 1960; Professor 1969; Relazioni fragili performed at the 1960 ISCM Festival; Cycle of 7 Pieces, Spiegel, performed at 1972 ISCM Festival; Completion of Act III of Berg's Lulu performed at the Paris Opéra 1979; Opera Baal premiered at the 1981 Salzburg Festival; Der Rattenfänger at Graz, 1987. *Compositions:* Espressioni fondamentali for orchestra, 1957; Relazioni fragili for harpsichord and chamber orchestra 1957; Enjambements for 6 players 1959; Fasce for orchestra 1959; Spiegel I-VII for various forces, some with tape, 1960-61; Exercises for baritone and chamber ensemble 1962-67; Phantasme 63 for organ and chamber orchestra 1963; Symphonien for winds and timpani 1964; Langegger Nachtmusik I and II for orchestra 1969, 1970; Symphony 1975; Double Concerto, for violin, cello and orchestra 1975; Opera, Baal, 1973-81; Keintate for voice and 11 instruments 1983; Double Concerto for flute, bassoon and orchestra; Opera Der Rattenfänger, 1987. *Address:* c/o AKM, III Baumannstrasse 8-10, Postfach 334-348, 1031 Wien, Austria.

CERNY Florian, b. 1954, Germany. Singer (Baritone). *Education:* Studied in Australia, Vienna and Munich. *Career:* Solo debut with the Israel National Opera; Principal baritone of the Kiel Opera and has sung in Hamburg, Dusseldorf, Hanover and elsewhere in Europe; Geneva Opera as Biterolf in Tannhäuser; Season 1984-85 as Alfio and Tonio (Cav and Pag) with Opera North and Mozart's Figaro with English National Opera; Bayerische Staatsoper Munich 1986-, as Bretigny in Manon, Caliph in Der Barbier von Bagdad, Schaunard, and Dominic in Arabella; Other roles include Wagner's Dutchman and Kothner, Riccardo (I Puritani), Iago and Don Carlos (La Forza del Destino). *Address:* Music International, 13 Ardilaun Road, London N5 2QR, England.

CERONE David P., b. 9 Mar. 1941, Syracuse, New York, USA. Violinist; Educator. m. Linda Sharon, 5 Aug. 1962, 1 son, 1 daughter. *Education:* Student, Juilliard School of Music, 1958; Performance Diploma, Curtis Institute of Music, 1962. *Debut:* Town Hall, 1967. *Career:* Recitalist, Performer, Oberlin Quartet, 1962-71; Professor, Oberlin College Conservatory of Music, 1962-72; Member, Dartmouth Quartet, 1963-66; Concert-Master, Dartmouth Congregation of the Arts Festival Orchestra, 1963-66; Chairman, String Department, Cleveland Institute of Music, 1971-81; Professor, 1975-85, Chairman, Violin Dept. 1981-85, Curtis Institute of Music; Faculty, Meadowmount School of Music, 1966-85; Music Director, Cleveland Chamber Music Seminar, 1974-81; President, Cleveland Institute of Music, 1985-; Director, ENCORE School for Strings, 1985-; The Cleveland Piano Quartet. *Recordings:* Arthur Sheppard, Sonata for Violin and Piano, with Grant Johannesen; Violin Varieties; Dances and Concertos. *Publications:* Mendelssohn Concerto Edition, 1985. *Address:* Cleveland Institute of Music, 11021 East Blvd., Cleveland, OH 44106, USA.

CERQUETTI Anita, b. 13 Mar 1931, Montecorsaro-Macerata, Italy. Singer (Soprano). *Education:* Studied at the Liceo Morlacchi in Perugia. *Debut:* Spoleto 1951, as Aida. *Career:* Sang Aida and the Trovatore Leonora at Verona, 1953; Chicago Lyric Opera 1955-56, debut as Amelia in Un Ballo in Maschera; New York 1957, in Paride ed Elena by Gluck; Milan 1958, as Abigaille in Nabucco; Other roles include Norma, La Gioconda and Elena in I Vespri Siciliani. *Recordings:* La Gioconda (Decca); Reiza in Oberon; Mathilde in Guillaume Tell; Elvira in Verdi's Ernani; Zoraima in Les Abencérages by Cherubini (Cetra). *Address:* c/o Teatro alla Scala, Via Filodrammatici 2, Milan, Italy.

CERVENA Sona, b. 9 Sept 1925, Prague, Czech Republic. Singer (Mezzo-Soprano). *Education:* Studied with Robert Rosner and Lydia Wegener in Prague. *Career:* Janáček Opera Brno, 1952-58, Staatsoper Berlin, 1958-61, Deutsche Oper Berlin, 1962-64, Opera Frankfurt, 1964-90; Title, Kammersaengerin in Berlin and Frankfurt; Guest appearances: Prague, Vienna, Amsterdam, Bruxelles, Geneva, London, Milano, Paris, Barcelona, Lisbon, San Francisco, Los Angeles, Chicago; Festivals: Bayreuth, 1960-66, Salzburg, 1961, Glyndebourne, 1963-64, Edinburgh, 1966-78. *Address:* Thalia Theater, Alstertor, D-20095 Hamburg, Germany.

CERVESATO Michela, b. 29 Sept 1954, Motta di L, Treviso, Italy. Pianist; Singer; Musical Paleographer. m. Walter Durigon, 28 Oct 1989, 1 son. *Education:* Diploma in Musical Paleography and Philology, University of Pavia; Diploma in Piano; Diploma in Singing. *Career:* Many TV and radio appearances; As Pianist and Singer (Italian Renaissance music), concerts in Italy and abroad. *Compositions:* Transcription and revision of Renaissance frottole. *Recordings:* Ascolta, infida, un sogno, LP, Celesta Records, 1986. *Contributions to:* A Collection of 19th Century Musicians' Letters, in La Nuova Rivista Musicale Italiana ERI, 1985. *Honour:* Concorso Kolbe Prize, Naples, 1980. *Hobbies:* Cooking; Basketball; Travel. *Address:* via Corazzin No 14, 31046 Oderzo (TV), Italy.

CERVETTI Sergio, b. 9 Nov 1940, Dolores, Uruguay. Composer; Teacher. *Education:* Pupil, E. Krenek & S. Grove, Peabody Conservatory of Music, Baltimore, USA, 1963-67. *Career:* Composer in Residence, German Artists' Programme, West Berlin, 1969; Faculty, Tisch School of the Arts, New York University, 1970-. *Compositions:* String Trio, 1963; Piano Sonata, 1964; 5 Sequences for Flute, Horn Cello, Electric Guitar, Piano, Percussion, 1966; Orbitas, Orchestra, 1967; El Carro de Heno, 1967; Zinctum, 1968; Peripetia, 1970; Plexus, 1971; Madrigal III, 1976; 4 Fragments of Isadora, 1979; Enclosed Time for Electronics, 1985; Night Trippers, 1986. *Recordings:* Compositions recorded on Composers' Recordings Inc and Periodic Music, Inc. *Honours:* Many commissions; grants for NEA, New York State Council for the Arts, and Meet the Composer. *Membership:* Broadcast Music Inc. *Address:* 96 Park Place, Brooklyn, NY 11217, USA.

CESARINI Franco, b. 18 Apr 1961, Bellinzona, Switzerland. Conductor. *Education:* Conservatory Milan, Italy, Flute and Piano; Academy of Music, Basle, with Peter-Lukas Graf,(Performer's Diploma); Music Theory and Composition with Robert Suter and Wind Band Conducting with Felix Hauswirth. *Debut:* As flutist with the Orchestra della Svizzera Italiana, Marcello Viotti, Conductor; Flute Concerto No 4 from Francois Devienne. *Career:* Has participated in many concerts throughout Europe; Teacher for Wind Band Conducting at the Conservatory of Zurich. *Compositions:* Pastorale d'automne, for symphonic orchestra, 1991; Mosaici Bizantini for symphonic band, 1992; Mexican Pictures, for symphonic band, 1989. *Recordings:* Works recorded by Radio Suisse Romande; Radio Svizzera Italiana and Televisione Svizzera Italiana; Mexican Pictures with the Royal Military Band, Holland; Interlude for Band with the Tokyo Kosey Wind Orchestra; Brass Dynamics with the Desford Colliery Caterpillar Band, England. *Honours:* First place, Swiss Soloist Competition, 1981; Study Award, E Gohner Foundation, 1984. *Memberships:* Schweizer Flotengesellschaft; Schweizer Musikpedagogischer Verband; World Association for Symph Bands and Esembles. *Hobby:* Reading. *Address:* Via Caratti 3, CH-6500 Bellinzona, Switzerland.

CHADWELL Tracey Gillian, b. 9 Mar 1959, Sussex, England. Classical Singer. *Education:* East Sussex Prepatory Music Course, 1977- 78; GGSM Hons, 1978-81; Postgraduate Studies, 1981-82, Guildhall School of Music and Drama; Studies with Dorothy Richardson 1978-82 and Rae Woodland, 1982-86; Rupert Bruce Lockhard, 1987-90; Silvia Beamish, 1987-90; Margaret Hyde, 1991-. *Career:* BBC Singers, 1982-85; Recitals, Wigmore Hall, 1984, 1986, 1989, 1994; Debuts, Queen Elizabeth Hall, Barbican, 1985; Mendelssohn's Midsummer Night's Dream, Promenade Concert debut,

Royal Albert Hall, London 1985; Appearances at Brighton, Aldeburgh, Greenwich and Frankfurt Festivals; 1st BBC recital, Matinee Musicale, 1986; Park Lane group recital, 1986; Work with, Live Music Now, 1987-90; Three Choirs, Hereford Festival, 1988. *Compositions include:* Commissioned Songs from Nicola Lefanu, 1987; Elizabeth Maconchy, 1985; Gillian Whitehead, 1993. *Hobbies:* Reading; Reading; Riding; Swimming; Squash. *Current management:* Quadrivium; Concert Directory International. *Address:* 34 Orchard Way, Hurstpierpoint, Hassocks, W Sussex BN6 9UB, England.

CHADWICK Eric (Bourne), b. 23 Nov 1928, Manchester, England; Musician; Conductor; Chorus Master; Solo Organist; Organ Teacher. *Education:* ARCO, 1946; FRCO, 1948; Royal Manchester College of Music, 1945-50. *Debut:* As Solo Organist, Manchester Town Hall, 1949; As COnductor, City Hall, Sheffield with Halle Orchestra and Sheffield Philharmonic Chorus, 1957. *Career:* Organist, St Luke's Parish Church, Weaste, 1948-; Organist to the Hallé Concerts Society, 1950-63; BBC Recitalist, 1952-76; Organ Professor at the Royal Manchester College of Music, 1954-72; Organist and Musical Advisor, University of Manchester Institute of Science and Technology, 1955; Musical Director, Heaton Hall Chamber Concerts, Manchester, 1955-78; Chorus Master, The Sheffield Philharmonic Chorus, 1955-80; The Hallé Choir, 1956-66; The Huddersfield Choral Society, 1962-69; The Montgomery County Festival Choir, 1955-65; The Welsh National Eisteddfod Choir, 1964-65; The RMC of Music Opera Chorus, 1964-66; Examiner for the Associated Board of the Royal Schools of Music, 1962-74; Senior Lecturer, Organ, Royal Northern College of Music, 1973-89; Guest Conductor with many orchestras. Appearances throughout Europe as well as television appearances. *Honours:* Heywood Silver Medal at the Royal Manchester College of Music, 1950; Hon Fellow, Royal Manchester College of Music, 1962; Recognised Staff member at University of Manchester Institute of Science and Technology in with the Queen's Award for Export Achievement, 1992; Deputy Governor of the ABIRA, (American Biographical Institute Research Association), 1993. *Memberships:* Incorporated Society of Musicians; Incorporated Association of Organists; Musicians' Union. *Hobbies:* Church activities; Sport; Motoring and Cruising. *Address:* 44 Broadway, Fairfield, Droylsden, Manchester M43, 6FE, England

CHAILLEY Jacques, b. 24 Mar 1910, Paris, France. Composer; Musicologist. m. Helene Pompei, 3 Nov 1938, 2 sons, 1 daughter. *Education:* Studies with Nadia Boulanger, Claude Delvincourt, H. Busser, P. Monteux, W. Mengelberg, A. Pirro. *Career:* General Secretary, Paris Conservatoire, later sub Director, 1937, Professor, 1947; Professor, Sorbonne, 1952; Director, Institute of Musicology, General Inspector for Music, 1972-79. *Compositions:* Opera, Thyl De Flandre, 1957; La Dame a La Licorne, 1953; 2 Symphonies; Sonatas. *Publications:* 25 books. *Contributions to:* 250 articles. Many honours and awards. *Address:* 5 rue Remy Dumoncel, F-75014, Paris, France.

CHAILLY Luciano, b. 19 Jan. 1920, Ferrara, Italy. Composer; Administrator; Teacher. m. Anna Maria Motta, 1 son, 2 daughters. *Education:* Violin diploma, Fa, 1941; BA, University of Bologna, 1943; Diploma, Verdi Conservatory, 1945; Studied composition with R Bossi and P Hindemith. *Career:* Director of Music Programming, Italian Radio and Television, 1950-67; Artistic Director 1968-71, General Director 1976-, Teatro alla Scala, Milan; Artistic Director, Teatro Regio, Turin, 1972; Angelicum, Milan, 1973-75; Arena, Verona, 1975-76; Genoa Opera, 1983-85; Teacher of Composition, Perugia Conservatory, Verdi Conservatory, Milan, 1968-83. *Compositions:* Operas: Ferrovia soprelevata, 1955; Una domanda di matrimonio, 1957; Il canto del cigno, 1957; La riva delle Sirti, 1959; Procedura penale, 1959; Il mantello, 1960; Era proibito, 1963; Vassiliev, 1967; Markheim, 1967; L'idiota, 1970; Sogno (ma forse no), 1975; Il libro dei reclami, 1975;

La cantatrice Calva, 1985; Ballets: Fantasmi al Grand-Hotel, 1960; Il cappio, 1962; L'urio, 1967; Shee, 1967; Anna Frank, 1981; Es-Ballet, 1983; Instrumental: Toccata for Orchestra, 1948; 12 Sonate tritematiche: No 1 for Piano, 1951; No 2 for Orchestra, 1952; No 3 for Chamber Orchestra, 1952; No 4 for Orchestra, 1953; No 5 for Cello and Piano, 1954; No 6 for Piano, 1954; No 7 for Strings, 1955; No 8 for Violin and Piano, 1955; No 9 for Orchestra, 1955; No 10 for String Quartet, 1960; No 11 for Piano, 1961; No 12 for Mandolin and Piano, 1961; Sequenze dell'artide for Orchestra, 1961; Piccole serenate for Strings, 1967; Contrappunti a quattro dimensioni for Orchestra, 1973; Newton-Variazioni for Chamber Orchestra, 1979; Es-Konzert for Orchestra, 1980; Psicosi for Instruments and Percussion, 1980; Es-Kammerkonzert for Small Instrumental Group, 1983; Several chamber works; Piano pieces; Choral music; Songs. *Honours:* Le Muse, 1968; Legion d'oro and Rosa del Garda, 1973; Leonardo and S Francesco d'oro, 1977; L'Olifante d'oro, 1978; S Giorgio, 1981; Frescobaldi, 1983; Medaglia d'oro from the President of the Republic, 1984; Accademico di Santa Cecilia, Rome, from 1990. *Hobbies:* Tennis; Skiing; Stamp collecting. *Address:* Viale Bianca Maria 17, 20122 Milan, Italy.

CHAILLY Riccardo, b. 20 Feb 1953, Milan, Italy. Orchestral Conductor. *Education:* Conservatories of Guiseppe Verdi, Milan, and Perugia, and with Piero Guarino, Franco Caracciolo and Franco Ferrara. *Career:* Assistant to Conductor, La Scala, Milan, 1972-74; Debut, Chicago Opera, USA, 1974 with Madama Butterfly; Debut, La Scala, Milan, Italy, 1978; Debut, Covent Garden, London, England, 1979, Don Pasquale; British concert debut, London Symphony, and at Edinburgh Festival, Scotland, 1979; American concert debut, Los Angeles Philharmonic, California, 1980; Metropolitan Opera Debut, New York, 1982, Les Contes d'Hoffmann; Principal Guest Conductor, London Philharmonic, England, 1982-85; Chief Conductor, RSO, Berlin, 1982-90; with the orchestra gave the premiere of Schoenberg's Frühlingstod; Debut, Vienna State Opera, Austria, 1983; Salzburg Festival, 1984, Macbeth, 1985, 1986, 1988, La Cenerentola; Debut, New York Philharmonic, USA, 1985; Exclusive Recording Contract with Decca; Music Director of Bologna, Teatro Comunale, Italy, 1986-89; Principal Conductor, Concertgebouw, Amsterdam, Netherlands, 1988-; Promenade Concerts, 1990, with Beethoven's 1st, Prokofiev's 3rd, Schumann's 4th Symphonies; Conducted The Fiery Angel, Holland Festival, 1990; Rossini's Ricciardo e Zoraide at Pesaro; Concertgebouw, Bruckner's 5th Symphony, Barbican Centre, May 1991. *Recordings include:* Alexander Nevsky; Carmina Burana; Bruckner's Symphonies No. 3 and No 7; Rossini Overtures; William Tell; Andrea Chénier; The Rake's Progress; Tchaikovsky Symphony No 5. *Address:* Thom Van Kleef, Oosteinde 23, 1017 WT Amsterdam, The Netherlands.

CHAITKIN David, b. 16 May 1938, New York City, USA. Composer. m. Carol McCauley, 23 July 1960, 1 son. *Education:* BA, Pomona College, 1959; MA, University of California at Berkeley, 1965; Studied with Luigi Dallapiccola, Seymour Shifrin, Max Deutsch, Andrew Imbrie and Karl Kohn. *Career:* Early experience as a jazz pianist; Composed music for film, The Game; Commissions from Philadelphia Composers' Forum, Sylvan Winds, New Hampshire Music Festival, Da Capo Chamber Players (New York State Council on the Arts), Chamber Music America, Quintet of the Americas; Gordon Gottleib; Pomona College, in honour of its Centennial; Professor of Music, Reed College, 1968-69; New York University, 1969-76. *Compositions:* Symphony; Summersong, for 23 wind instruments; Etudes for Piano; Concerto for Flute and Strings; Seasons Such as These for mixed chorus a cappella; Serenade for 7 players; Scattering Dark and Bright, duo for piano and percussion; Quintet, mixed chamber ensemble; Pacific Images, for chamber orchestra; Music in Five Parts, for septet; Nocturne for Woodwind Quintet; Impromptu for Piano; Song Cycle for soprano and piano, 1992. *Recordings:* Composers Recordings Inc: Etudes for piano, David Burge pianist; Serenade, NY New Music Ensemble, Black; Seasons Such as These, Cantata Singers, Harbison; Summersong, for 23 wind instruments, Sylvan Winds, Weisberg. *Publications:* Etudes for piano, Columbia University Press, 1979; Summersong, GunMar, 1983; Nocturne, Josef Marx, 1991; Impromptu for piano, C.F.Peters, 1993. *Current Management:* Music Publishing Services, 236 West 26th Street, Suite 11-S, New York, NY 10001. *Address:* 160 West 87th Street, New York, NY 10024, USA.

CHALKER Margaret, b. 1958, Waterloo, NY, USA. Singer (Soprano). *Education:* BME, Studied at Baldwin-Wallace College in Ohio; MM, Syracuse University. *Career:* Mostly Mozart Festival New York as Sifare in Mitridate and Giunia in Lucio Silla; Houston Opera as Pamina; Deutsche Oper am Rhein Düsseldorf from 1985, as Oscar (Ballo in Maschera), Gilda, Celia (Haydn's La Fedelta Premiata) and Lauretta in Gianni Schicchi; Zürich Opera from 1987, as Pamina, Gilda, Jemmy in Guillaume Tell, Sophie (Rosenkavalier) and Janáček's Vixen; Other roles include Mozart's Contessa and Donna Anna, Micaela, Antonia in Les contes d'Hoffmann and Helen in Gluck's Paride ed Elena; Many concert appearances, notably in works by Bach and Composers of the 20th Century. *Address:* c/o Opernhaus Zürich, Falkenstrasse 1, CH-8008 Zürich, Switzerland.

CHALLENGER Robert, b. 1967, South Yorkshire, England. Singer (Tenor). *Education:* Studied at the Guildhall School of Music; Schubert Lieder with Martin Isepp and French Melodie with Suzanne Danco and Hugues Cuenod at Aldeburgh. *Career:* Concert appearances as the Evangelist in Bach's Passions; Handel's Messiah and Alexander's Feast; Mozart Requiem and C Minor Mass; Haydn Creation and Mass in Time of War; Britten Rejoice in the Lamb and Cantata Accademica; Other concert repertory includes music by Palestrina, Byrd, Cage and Feldman; Operatic roles include Beppe in Pagliacci, Brack Weaver in Weill's Down in the Valley and parts in La jollie Fille de Perth and Rossini's Il Viaggio a Reims. *Honours include:* Scholarships to Aldeburgh; Winner, Young Songmakers' Almanac Competition (recital at St John's Smith Square); Gramophone prize for recording of Chambermusic, 1992. *Address:* c/o Royal Opera House, Covent Garden, London WC2, England.

CHALLIS Philip, b. 11 Aug. 1929, Huddersfield, Yorkshire, England. Pianist. m. Mary J. White, 19 Nov. 1955. *Education:* Huddersfield College; Royal Manchester College of Music studies with Herbert Fryer, Marguerite Long, Joszef Gat and Ilona Kabos. *Debut:* BBC, London, 1943. *Career:* Many broadcasts and television appearances in the UK, America and Canada; Innumerable concert tours in the UK, America, Canada, Europe, Scandinavia and the Far East. *Recordings:* Mephisto Music, Liszt; Liszt-Beethoven, Piano Transcriptions; Sonatas of John Field; Selected Piano works, Moscheles; Second Piano Concerto, Josef Holbrooke. *Honour:* Fellow of Royal Manchester College of Music, 1972. *Membership:* Incorporated Society of Musicians, Chairman of Brighton Centre, 1983-86. *Hobbies:* Cooking; Travel. *Address:* Balaton, 97 Alinora Crescent, West Worthing, Sussex, BN12 4HH, England.

CHALMERS Penelope, b. 5 Oct 1946, Worcester, England. Singer (Soprano). *Education:* Studied at Bristol University. *Career:* Has sung such roles as the Marschallin (Der Rosenkavalier), Leonora (Trovatore), Turandot and Tosca with fringe opera companies; Title role in the British premiere of Bruch's Lorelei for University College Opera, Fiordiligi for Pavilion Opera and Rezia in Weber's Oberon at Haddo House, Scotland; London debut at the Prom concerts in Lambert's Rio Grande; Recent appearances as the Dyer's Wife in Die Frau ohne Schatten at Geneva, Helmwige and Ortlinde in Die Walküre at Covent Garden and Emilia Marty in The Makropoulos Case at Hagen, Germany; Donna Anna and Lady Billows in Albert Herring for Opera 1980, season, 1991-92; Judith, in Blubeard's Castle, at the English National Opera, April 1993 and Autumn, 1993; Sang title role in Salome with Scottish Opera; National Television debut: as prima donna in major new BBC production of Stendhal's, Le Rouge et le Noir, 1993. *Address:* c/o Atholl Still Ltd, 80-86 Westrow Street, London SE19 3AF, England.

CHAMBERS Martin John, b. 27 Sept 1944, Victoria, Canada. Opera Singer; Professor. m. Elinor Ruth Dandy, 19 Nov 1971, 2 daughters. *Education:* BMus., 1966, MMus, 1969, University of British Columbia. *Debut:* With Vancouver Symphony, 1964. *Career:* Lyric/ Character Tenor with: Vancouver Opera, Vienna Chamber Opera, Hessen State Theatre, Cassel, Lubeck Opera, Dortmund Opera, Essen Opera, Festival Ottawa, Kitchener Opera, Canadian Opera Co., San Diego Opera; Professor, Music, University of Western Ontario; Chairman, Music, San Diego State University, USA. *Recordings:* Poulenc's Dialogues of the Carmelites; Donizetti, Lucia di Lammermoor; Thomas, Hamlet; Monteverdi, Coronation of Poppea. *Honours:* Recipient, various honours & awards. *Memberships:* Canadian Actors Equity Association; Association of Canadian TV & Radio Artists. *Address:* Dept. of Music, San Diego State University, San Diego, CA 92182, USA.

CHAMPNEY Wendy, b. 23 Feb 1958, USA. Violist. *Education:* Studied at Indiana University, the International Menuhin Academy in Gstaad. *Career:* Co-founder and violist of the Carmina Quartet 1984; Appearances from 1987 in Europe, Israel, USA and Japan; Regular concerts at the Wigmore Hall from Oct 1987; Concerts at the South Bank Centre, London, Amsterdam Concertgebouw, the Kleine Philharmonie in Berlin, Konzertverein Vienna; Four engagements in Paris 1990-91, seven in London; Tours in Australasia, USA, Japan; concerts at the Hohenems, Graz, Hong Kong, Montreux, Schleswig-Holstein, Bath, Lucerne and Prague Spring Festivals; Collaborations with Dietrich Fischer-Dieskau, Olaf Bär and Mitsuko Uchida. *Recordings:* Albums for Ex Libris, Bayer, Claves and Denon (from 1991). *Honour:* Joint winner (with members of Carmina Quartet) Paolo Borciani String Quartet Competition in Reggio Emilia, Italy, 1987. *Address:* c/o Intermusica Artists' Management, 16 Duncan Terrace, London N1 8BZ, England.

CHANCE Michael, b. 7 Mar 1955, Penn, Buckinghamshire, England. Singer, Counter-Tenor. *Career:* Choral scholar at King's College Cambridge; Appearances with the English Chamber Orchestra, Academy of Ancient Music, English Concert, Orchestra of St John's, Smith Square and the Bournemouth Sinfonietta; Handel's Messiah at the Alice Tully and Avery Fisher Halls New York; Concerts with John Eliot Gardiner and the Monteverdi Choir in New York and at the Gottingen and Aix-en-Provence Festivals; Operatic roles include Apolllo in Cavalli's Jason (Buxton Festival), 1983; Andronico in Handel's Tamerlano (Lyon Opera), 1985; Otho in Handel's Agrippina (Bath Festival), Ottone in Monteverdi's L'Incoronazione di Poppea and the Military Governor in the world premiere of Judith Weir's A Night at the Chinese Opera (Kent Opera); Britten's Oberon and Voice of Apollo with Glyndebourne Opera; Paris Opéra debut 1988, as Ptolomeo in Handel's Giulio Cesare; Season 1992 as Amphinomous in Monteverdi's Ulisse for ENO, Julius Caesar for Scottish Opera and Britten's Apollo at Glyndebourne; Concerts include Bach cantatas at the Promenade Concerts, London, Messiah at King's College, Cambridge, Royal Albert Hall and in Edinburgh; Handel's Theodora at the Paris Opera 1987; Israel in Egypt in Stuttgart and at La Scala, Milan; Jephtha in London and Göttingen; Bach's St Matthew Passion in Spain and London, B Minor Mass with the Manchester Camerata; World premiere of Bennett's Ophelia 1988; Apollo in Death in Venice with Glyndebourne Touring Opera at Norwich, 1989; The Fairy Queen with the Sixteen, Elizabeth Hall, 1990; Promenade Concerts, London, Britten's Cantata Misericordium, Mozart's Credo Mass, 1991. *Recordings:* Bach's St John Passion, Christmas Oratorio and St Matthew Passion, Handel's Messiah (Deutsche Grammophon); Jephtha (Philips); Cavalli's Giasone (Harmonia Mundi); Bacco and other roles, The Death of Orpheus by Stefano Landi; Handel's Tamerlano, Orfeo settings by Monteverdi and Gluck. *Address:* c/o Lies

Askonas Ltd., 186 Drury Lane, London WC2B 5RY, England.

CHANCE Nancy Laird, b. 19 Mar 1931, Cincinnati, Ohio, USA. Composer. m. 7 Sept 1950 (divorced), 3 sons. *Education:* Magna cum laude, The Foxcroft School, 1945-49; Bryn Mawr College, 1949-50; Columbia University, part-time, 1959-68; Piano with William R Smith and Lilias McKinnon; Theory and Composition with Otto Luening and Vladimir Ussachevsky; Sundance Institute Film Composer Fellow, 1988. *Career:* Performances of her works by Philadelphia Orchestra, St Louis Symphony, The Jupiter Symphony, The American Composers Orchestra, The League ISCM, The Group for Contemporary Music, The New Music Consort, Da Capo Chamber Players, Relache, Continuum, The Goldman Memorial Band and many others. *Compositions:* Odysseus, solo voice, percussion and orchestra; String Quartet No. 1; Liturgy for orchestra; Elegy for String orchestra; Woodwind Quintet; Domine, Dominus: Motet for double chorus a capella; Duos III for violin and cello; Exultation and Lament for alto saxophone and timpani; Ritual Sounds, for brass quintet and percussion; Daysongs for alto flute and percussion; 3 Rilke Songs for soprano, flute, English horn and cello; In Paradisum, solo voice, mixed chorus, orchestra; Rhapsodia for Marimba Quartet; Ceremonial for Percussion Quartet; Planasthai, chamber orchestra, piano and percussion, 1992. *Recordings:* Daysongs, Ritual Sounds, Duos III, Exultation and Lament all recorded on Opus One Records. *Honours:* Winner: ASCAP Rudolph Nissim Prize for Orchestral Compositions, 1982, 1984; NEA Composer Fellowships, 1981, 1983. *Address:* PO Box 96, Austerlitz, New York, NY 12017, USA.

CHANG Debra Wei Kuan, b. 23 Oct 1952, Honolulu, Hawaii, USA. Composer; Multimedia Performance Artist. *Education:* BA, Ethnomusicology, BMus, Composition, University of Hawaii; MMus, North Texas State University; BA, Ethnomusicology, BMUS, Composition, University of Hawaii; MMus, North Texas State University, DMA, University of North Texas. *Career:* Co-Founder, Intermedia Ensemble with Phil Winsor; Guest Composer Residencies at American New Music Festivals and Universities including: New Mexico State University, East Texas State University, Rice University, University of California at San Diego, University of Redlands, San Diego State University, University of New Mexico, Cleveland State University, Bowling Green State University, Del Mar College, Baylor University; Adminstrative Assistant, Teaching Fellow, Centre for Experimental Music & Intermedia, North Texas State University, 1983-86. *Address:* 109 Virginia Street, Bellingham, WA 98225, USA.

CHANNON Michael David Hudleston, b. 3 May 1939, Anniston, Alabama, USA. Musicologist; Harpsichordist; Director, Calistor Concerts Society. *Education:* University of New Mexico; Trinity College, London; Mozarteum, Salzburg. *Career:* United States Navy Security Service 1962-68; BBC Music Division, 1969-. *Publications:* Editor, Two Latin Anthems of Samuel Wesley, 1969; An Evening Service by Richard Portmann, 1970; The Complete Church Music of John Goldwyn, 1986; Co-editor, with Fumiko Matsaga, Glenn Gould-Friend and Colleague, 1988-. *Memberships:* Harpsichordist, Finchley Chamber Orchestra; British Museum Society; Pianist, Hendon Christian Science Church; National Trust; Musical Advisor, Wessex Sinfonia; Musical Advisor, Abbotsbury Festival, 1982-. *Hobby:* Bookbinding. *Address:* 26 Marlborough Road, London N19, England.

CHAPIN Schuyler Garrison, b. 13 Feb 1923, New York City, USA. Music, Arts and Education Administrator. m. 15. Mar 1947, 4 sons. *Education:* Longy School of Music, 1940-41. *Career:* Vice-President, Programs, Lincoln Center, New York, 1963-68; Executive Producer, Amberson Productions, 1968-72; General Manager, Metropolitan Opera, New York, 1972-76; Dean, School of Arts, Columbia University, 1976-87; Dean Emeritus, 1987-; Vice President,

Worldwide Concert and Artist Activities, Steinway and Sons, 1990-92. *Recordings:* Director, Columbia Records, USA, Masterworks and later, Vice-President, Creative Services: Recorded, among others, Bernstein, New York Philharmonic; Ormandy, Philadelphia Orchestra; Szell, Cleveland Orchestra; Stern; Serkin; Francescatti; Casadesus; Fleisher; Tucker; Farrell; Gould; Juilliard Quartet; Budapest Quartet. *Publications:* Musical Chairs, 1978; Leonard Bernstein: Notes From A Friend, 1992. *Contributions to:* New York Times; National Review; Prime Time; Horizons, and others. *Honours:* Gold Medal, National Arts Club; Honorary LHD, New York University, Hobart College, and William Smith College, 1974; Honorary D Litt, Emerson College, 1976; Hon. Mus. D., Mannes College, New School, 1990. *Address:* 901 Lexington Avenue, New York City, NY 10021, USA.

CHAPMAN Janice, b. 1945, Australia. Singer (Soprano); Teacher. *Education:* Studied at the University of Adelaide and at the Royal College of Music in London, and the London Opera Centre. *Career:* Sang leading roles with Sadler's Wells/English National Opera, Welsh and Scottish Operas and in many European houses; Toured Russia with the English Opera Group under Benjamin Britten and worked with the composer on the roles of Miss Jesel and Mrs Grose in The Turn of the Screw; Sang Mrs Julian in the stage premiere of Owen Wingrave at Covent Garden 1973; Other Britten roles have been Ellen Orford and Lady Billows, and she has sung in operas by Mozart, Wagner, Verdi and Puccini; Concert engagements with leading orchestras; Sang with her trio The Alexandra Ensemble at the Women's Music Festival at Beersheba in Israel, 1986; Appeared as Mrs Grose for New Israel Opera, 1990, conducted by Roderick Brydon; Professor of voice at the London College of Music. *Address:* c/o Korman International Management, Crunnells Green, Preston, Herts SG4 7UQ, England.

CHAPPLE Brian b. 24 Mar 1945, London. Composer. *Education:* GRSM, LRAM, Royal Academy of Music, London. *Compositions include:* Scherzos for four pianos, 1970; Trees Revisited, 1970; Praecludiana, 1971; Green and Pleasant, 1973; In Ecclesiis, 1976; Piano Concerto, 1977; Cantica, 1978; Venus Fly Trap, 1979; Little Symphony, 1982; Lamentations of Jeremiah, 1984; Piano Sonata, 1986; Magnificat, 1986; In Memoriam, 1989; Berkeley Tribute, 1989; Frink Tribute, 1990; Requies, 1991; Missa Brevis, 1991; Three Motets, 1992; Anthems, canticles, childrens's songs, piano music. *Honours:* BBC Monarchy 1000 Prize, 1973; UNESCO International Rostrum of Composers, 1976. *Memberships:* PRS: Association of Professional Composers. *Hobbies:* Gardening; Drawing. *Current Management:* Chester Music. *Address:* 31 Warwick Rd, New Barnet, Herts EN5 5EQ, England.

CHARD Geoffrey, b. 9 Aug 1930, Sydney, Australia. Singer (Baritone). *Education:* Studied at the New South Wales Conservatory. *Debut:* Sydney 1951, in Carmen. *Career:* Moved to England and became a member of the English National Opera; Other appearances with Welsh National Opera and the Glyndebourne and Edinburgh Festivals; Aldeburgh Festival 1967, 1968, in the premieres of Berkeley's The Castaway and Birtwistle's Punch and Judy; London Coliseum 1973-83, in the British premiere of Penederecki's The Devils of Loudun; Ginastera's Bomarzo and Ligeti's Le Grand Macabre; Roles in operas by Gluck, Mozart, Wagner, Britten, Orff, Menotti, Shostakovich, Janáček and contemporary British composers; Many engagements as concert singer; Sang Bartolo in Il Barbiere di Siviglia for Victoria State Opera, 1989; Germont in Traviata for the Ballarat Opera Festival, 1992, Balstrode (Peter Grimes) and Pizarro at Sydney. *Address:* Victoria State Opera, 370 Nicholson Street, Fitzroy, VIC 3065, Australia.

CHARLTON David, b. 20 June 1946, London. Musicologist. *Education:* Nottingham University and at Cambridge with Hugh Macdonald, (PhD, 1973). *Career:* Lecturer at the University of East Anglia, 1970, Reader,

1991. *Publications:* Many articles and reference works including entries on French opera of the late 18th and early 19th centuries in the New Grove Dictionary of Music and the New Grove Dictionary of Opera; Chapters on 19th century French Opera in the New Oxford History of Music, 1990; Grétry and the Growth of Opera-Comique, 1986; Edition of ETA Hoffmann's musical writings, 1989; Member, Editorial Boards, Cambridge Opera Journal, New Berlioz Edition; Founder, UEA Opéra-Comique Database. *Address:* School of Music, University of East Anglia, Univerity Plain, Norwich NR4 7TJ, Norfolk, England.

CHARNOCK Helen, b. 1958, England. Singer (Soprano). *Education:* Studied at the University of East Anglia (BA Hons in Music) and at the Guildhall School witn Laura Sarti. *Career:* Many performances with Opera Factory/London Sinfonietta, including the world premieres of Hell's Angels by Nigel Osborne and Birtwistle's Yan Tan Tethera (1986); Weill's Mahagonny Songspiel, Ligeti's Aventures/Nouvelles Aventures and the British premiere of Reimann's Ghost Sonata; Workshops and performances in many venues with the London Sinfonietta's Education Programme, including Holloway Prison and the Huddersfield Contemporary Music Festival; Australian debut 1986, as Clytemnestra in Iphigénie en Tauride; Sang in the premiere of Greek by Mark-Anthony Turnage at the 1988 Munich Biennale, repeated at the Edinburgh Festival 1988 and English National Opera 1990; Has sung Britten's Governess and Mrs Coyle at the Aldeburgh Festival and has appeared elsewhere as Semele, First Lady, Pamina, Micaela, Butterfly, Titania, Gretel, Adele, Despina and Musetta; Television appearances in works by Birtwistle, Ligeti and Turnage; Recorded CD of Greek by Turnage for Decca, 1993. *Honours:* The English Singers and Speakers Prize; 2 Society of Arts Awards; Incorporated Society of Musicians' Young Artists Award; Ian Fleming Bursary. *Address:* 21 Glengall Road, London SE15 6NJ, England.

CHARPENTIER DE CASTRO Eduardo, b. 12 Mar 1927, Panama, Musician. 2 sons. *Education:* Diploma in theory and solfeggio 1946, Diploma in Harmony, 1947, Diploma in Flute summa cum laude 1947, Panama Conservatory of Music; MusB 1950, MusM 1950, Roosevelt University, Chicago, USA; Diploma in chamber music, Marlboro College, Vermont, 1950; Diploma in flute 1951, Diploma in Orchestral Conducting, 1956, National Conservatory of Music, Paris, France; Postgraduate, Eastman School of Music, Rochester, New York, USA, 1957; Doctor of Philosophy in Music and Education, 1985, Columbia Pacific University, San Rafael, California; Diploma in Commerce, Pan-American Institute, Panamá, 1946. *Career:* Flautist, Conductor, Panama National Symphony Orchestra, 1966-; Assessor, Panama Conservatory of Music, 1971-; Director of Department of Music, University of Panama 1972-; Conductor Panama Chamber Music Orchestra, 1976; Guest conductor throughout the world. *Compositions:* Various musical works. *Address:* Apartado 9190, Panama 6, Panama.

CHARTERIS Richard, b. 24 June 1948, Chatham Islands, New Zealand. Musicologist; Writer; Editor. *Education:* BA, Victoria University, Wellington, New Zealand, 1970; MA (with First Class Hons), University of Canterbury, 1972; PhD 1976, Universities of Canterbury and London. *Career:* Rothmans Research Fellowship, University of Sydney, Australia, 1976-78; Research Fellowship, University of Queensland, 1979-80; Australian Research Council Chief Investigator, Music Department, University of Sydney, 1981-90; Australian Research Council Senior Research Fellow, Music Department, University of Sydney, 1991-. *Publications:* Author of over 50 books and editions including: John Coprario Fantasia-Suites; Volume 46 Musica Britannica, 1980; John Coprario: The Five-Part Pieces, No 92, Corpus Mensurabilis Musicae, 1981; Alfonso Ferrabosco I: Pavan and Three in Nomines, a 5, 1990; Giovanni Gabrieli: Audite principles, a 16, 1990, Hic est filius Deï, a 18, 1991, Hodie Christus a mortuïs, a 12, 1991, Miserere mei Deus, a 4; Alfonso

Ferrabosco the Younger: Lamentations for 5 voices, 1982; Thomas Lupo: The Complete Vocal Music, 1982; John Coprario: The Six-part Consorts and Madrigals, 1982; A Catalogue of the Printed Books on Music, Printed Music and Music Manuscripts in Archbishop Marsh's Library, Dublin, 1982; Alfonso Ferrabosco the Elder (1543-1588): Opera omnia, volumes 1-9 in No 96, Corpus Mensurabilis Musicae, 1984-88; John Coprario: A Thematic Catalogue of His Music with a Biographical Introduction, 1977; Alfonso Ferrabosco the Elder (1543-1588): A Thematic Catalogue of His Music with a Biographical Calendar, 1984; Critical Commentary and Additional Material for Volues I, II and II of the opera omnia of Alfonso Ferrabosco the Elder, 1984; Altro Polo: Essays on Italian Music in the Cinquecento, 1990; John Coprario: Twelve Fantasias for Two Bass Viols and Organ and Eleven Pieces for Three Lyra Viols, 1982; Martin Peerson: Anonymous Six-Part Fantasia, 1981; Thomas Lupo: The Four-Part Consort Music, 1983; Thomas Lupo: The Two-and Three-Part Consort Music, 1987; John Coprario: The Five-Part Consort Music I, 1989, II, 1989, III, 1992; Giovanni Gabrieli: Jubilate Deo (8vv), 1989-; Gloria (a 8), 1991;'O Jesu mi dulcissimé (MS version a 8), 1991; Quem vidistis pastores?, (a 14), 1991, 3, 1993; Jubilate Deo, (MS version a 8), 1991; Surrexit Christus (a 16), 1991, 3, 1993; Timor et tremor (a 6), 1991; Canzon XI in echo duodecimi toni (a 10), 1991; Canzon XVII (a 12), 1991; Sonata XX (a 22), 1991; Sonata XXI con tre violini, 1991; John Coprario: The Two-, Three- and Four-Part Consort Music, London, 1991, revised 1993; Giovanni Bassano: The Three-Part Consort Music, 1991; Giovannia Gabrieli: Opera omnia, volumes 1-12 in No. 12, Corpus Mensurabilis Musicae, Volume 7, 1991; Domenico Maria Ferrabosco (1513-1574): Opera omnia, No 102, Corpus Mensurabilis Musicae, 1992. *Contributions to:* Numerous journals and magazines including: Music and Letters; Early Music; Royal Musical Association Research Chronicle. *Honours:* Recipient of honours, awards and grants; elected, Fellow of the Australian Adademy of the Humanities, 1990. *Address:* Music Department, University of Sydney, NSW 2006, Australia.

CHASE Roger, b. 1958, London, England. Concert Violist. *Education:* Studied at the Royal College of Music with Bernard Shore and in Canada with Steven Staryk. *Debut:* Solo, with the English Chamber Orchestra, 1979. *Career:* Performances throughout the world from 1976 with such ensembles as the London Sinfonietta, The Estherhazy Baryton Trio and the Nash Ensemble; Concerts with the chamber ensemble Hausmusik, featuring works by Mendelssohn, Schubert and Hummel; Modern repertoire includes a concerto by Richard Harvey (Premiere at the Exeter Festival 1991); Toured the USA with the Hanover Band, 1992, playing Mozart's Sinfonia Concertante; Professor at the Guildhall School of Music and Drama. *Recordings include:* Works by Mendelssohn, Mozart (Concertante) and Britten (Lachrymae). *Address:* c/o Owen White Management, 14 Nightingale Lane, London N8 7QU, England.

CHATEAUNEUF Paula, b. 1958, USA. Player of Lutes and Early Guitars. *Education:* Studied at University of Connecticut, New England Conservatory and with Patrick O'Brien in New York; Further study as Fulbright Scholar, Guildhall School of Music, London, with Nigel North. *Career:* Moved to London, 1982; Appearances with many early music ensembles, including the New London Consort, Taverner Consort, English Concert, Sinfonye and the Gabrieli Consort; Has worked extensively as continuo player, particularly in Baroque opera; Involved in groups and projects devoted to improvisation and early dance music; Tours of Europe and North America as Soloist and Ensemble Player, performing at major festivals and recording for radio and television. *Recordings:* Various Compositions. *Address:* The Garden Flat, 26 Oliver Grove, London SE25 6EJ, England.

CHATER James Michael, b. 12 June 1951, Henley, England. Musicologist. *Education:* BA in Music, 1973,

DPhil in Music, 1980, Oxford University (Exeter College). *Career:* Fellow, Harvard Center for Italian Renaissance Studies, Florence, Italy, 1981-82; Fellowships and teaching positions: University of Wales, 1982-83; Washington University, St Louis, USA, 1983-84; University of Victoria, Canada, 1984-85; University of British Columbia, 1985-86; English-Language Booklet Editor, Philips Classics Productions, The Netherlands, 1986-. *Publications:* Luca Marenzio and the Italian Madrigal 1577-93, 1981. *Contributions to:* Musical Times; Music and Letters; Journal of the American Musicological Society; Rivista Italiana di Musicologia; Studi Musicali. *Memberships:* .Royal Musical Association; Società Italiana di Musicologia; American Musicological Society. *Hobbies:* Chess; Travel. *Address:* c/o Philips Classics Productions, Postbus 23, 3740 AA, Baarn, The Netherlands.

CHATHAM Stephen, b. 28 Feb 1950, Fairbault, Minnesota, USA. Composer. *Education:* Studied with Joseph Wood at the Oberlin Conservatory and with Ross Lee Finney and William Bolcom at the University of Michigan; Further study in Cologne. *Career:* Teacher at the University of British Columbia from 1976, associate professor 1982. *Compositions Include:* Two Followers of Lien for orchestra 1973; Wild Cat for flute 1975; Whisper, Baby for chorus, piano and percussion 1975; On the Contrary for clarinet and chamber ensemble 1974; Quiet Exchange for clarinet and percussion 1976; Occasions for orchestra 1977; Hesitation for violin and cello 1977; Amusements for piano 1978; Grouse Mountain Lullaby and They all Replied, for orchestra, 1978; Gossamer Leaves for clarinet and piano 1981; Crimson Dream for orchestra, 1983. *Honours include:* Fulbright Scholarship 1974; BMI student composer awards, 1974-76; Ives Award from the American Academy and Institute of Arts and Letters, 1976; Commissions from the Canadian Arts Council, the National Endowment of the Arts and Ontario Arts Council. *Address:* c/o ASCAP, ASCAP Building, One Lincoln Plaza, New York, NY 10023, USA.

CHAUSSON Carlos, b. 17 March 1950, Saragossa, Spain. Singer (Bass-Baritone). *Education:* Studied in Madrid and at the University of Michigan. *Debut:* San Diego, 1977, as Masetto. *Career:* Appearances at Boston, Miami, New York City Opera and Mexico City (as Bartolo in Il Barbiere di Siviglia); Sang at Madrid from 1983, Barcelona from 1985; Vienna Staatsoper from 1986, as Paolo in Simon Boccanegra, and Don Alvaro in Il Viaggio a Reims, conducted by Abbado; Vienna Konzerthaus in Les Danaides by Salieri: Parma 1987, as Falstaff, Bologna, 1988-89, as Michonnet in Adriana Lecouvreur, Pantaleone in Le Maschere by Mascagni and Sharpless in Butterfly; Barcelona 1989, in the premiere of Cristobal Colon by Beladas; returned 1990, as Paolo; Modena 1990 as Geronte in Manon Lescaut; Sang Mozart's Figaro at Madrid, Masetto at the 1990 Vienna Festival; Grand Théâtre de Geneve 1991, as Paolo; Madrid, 1992, as Bartolo in the new production of Il Barbiere di Sigivlia conducted by Alberto Zedda. *Address:* c/o Gran Teatre del Liceu, Barcelona, Spain.

CHAUVET Guy, b. 2 Oct 1933, Montlucon, Tarbes, France. Singer (Tenor). *Education:* Studied with Bernard Baillour in Tarbes. *Career:* After winning prizes at Cannes, Toulouse and Paris sang at the Paris Opéra 1959, as Tamino: returned as Faust, Cavaradossi, Florestan, Aeneas in Les Troyens and Jason in Médée; Holland Festival and Buenos Aires 1961; Covent Garden debut as Cararadossi, 1963; London Coliseum 1969, in a concert performance of Roussel's Padmâvatî; Verona Arena 1971, as Radames; Has sung Parsifal in Brussels, Lohengrin in Berlin and Samson in Geneva; Vienna Staatsoper as Aeneas and Otello; Further appearances in New York, Metropolitan, as John of Leyden, Le Prophète, 1979; Monte Carlo, Lisbon and Dublin; Rio de Janeiro, Don Jose, 1981; San Fransisco, Samson, 1983. *Recordings:* Highlights from Werther and Hérodiade by Massenet; Scenes from Les Troyens; Sigurd by Reyer. *Address:* c/o San Francisco Opera,

War Memorial Opera House, San Francisco CA 94102, USA.

CHEDEL Arlette, b. 25 May 1933, Neuchatel, Switzerland. Singer (Contralto). *Education:* Studied in Neuchatel and at the Vienna Musikakademie with Erik Werba. *Career:* Concert appearances in works by Schutz, Handel, Bach, Kodaly, Frank Martin and Honegger; Radio Lausanne 1974, in the premiere of Trois Visions espagnoles by Gerber; Montreux Festival, 1986, in Folie de Tristan by Schibler; Guest engagements in Vienna, Prague, Berlin, Roma and Besancon; Opera roles include Wagner's Erda, Magadalene and Mary, Mozart's Marcellina, Catherine in Jeanne d'Arc au Bucher, the Nurse in Boris Godunov and Genevieve in Pelléas et Mélisande. *Recordings include:* L'Enfant et les Sortilèges, and Les Noces by Stravinsky (Erato). *Address:* c/o Grand Théâtre de Genève, 11 Blvd du Theatre, CH-1211 Genève 11, Switzerland.

CHEEK John, b. 17 Aug 1948, Greenville, South Carolina, USA. Singer (Bass-Baritone). *Education:* Studied at the North Carolina School of Arts and at the Accademia Chigiana in Siena with Gino Bechi. *Career:* Sang at the Festivals of Ravinia and Tanglewood, and elsewhere in the USA, notably in music by Mozart; Metropolitan Opera debut 1977, as the Doctor in Pelléas et Mélisande: later appeared as Pimen, Ferrando in Il Trovatore, Klingsor, Panthée in Les Troyens, Monterone and Figaro; Teatro La Fenice Venice 1981, in Maria di Rudenz by Donizetti; New York City Opera 1986, as Mephistopheles in Faust; Other roles include Wurm in Luisa Miller; Attila, New York, 1988; Padre Guardiano, Toronto; Metropolitan, La Bohème, 1989; Ramphis in Aida, Cincinnati Opera, 1990; TV Appearances and concerts. *Recordings include:* Tosca (EMI); Maria di Rudenz (Cetra). *Address:* c/o Metropolitan Opera, Lincoln Center, New York, NY 10023, USA.

CHEMPIN Beryl Margaret, b. Birmingham, England. Piano Teacher; Lecturer; Writer. m. (1) Arnold Chempin, deceased, 2 daughters, (2) Bernard While, deceased, (3) Professor Denis Matthews, CBE, deceased, (4) Professor Peter Gilroy Bevan CBE. *Education:* Birmingham Conservatoire; Studied with Harold Craxton and Kendall Taylor; FTCL; LRAM; ARCM; LTCL; ABSM. *Career:* Piano Teacher, Birmingham Conservatoire and Birmingham Junior School of Music; Private Teacher, solo performer and accompanist, Lecturer and adjudicator; Writer of CD Sleeve notes and programme notes; Founder and Chairman, Denis Matthews Memorial Trust; Conducted Master Classes in Australia, Hong Kong, Helsinki and UK. *Publications:* Contributor to magazines and periodicals including Musical Times, Music Teacher, Music Journal, EPTA Journal. *Honours:* Midland Woman of the Year, 1977; National Award for Piano Teaching, 1983. *Memberships:* Lecturing panel, International Piano Teachers Consultants; ISM, (formerly member of National Council and Chairman of Birmingham Centre); ISME; RSM; European Piano Teachers Association; City of Birmingham Symphony Orchestra Society; King Edwards High School Old Edwardians; British Federation of Music Festivals; Birmingham Conservatoire Association. *Hobbies:* Reading; Languages; Art; Cookery. *Address:* 10 Russell Road, Moseley, Birmingham B13 8RD, England.

CHEN Pi-Hsien, b. 1950, Taiwan. Pianist. *Education:* Studied in Taiwan and at the Cologne Musikhochschule, Diploma 1970; Further studies with Hans Leygraf and masterclasses with Wilhelm Kempff, Tatiana Nikolayeva and Geza Anda. *Career:* From 1972 has given performances in London (BBC Proms, South Bank, Barbican), Amsterdam, Zurich, Berlin, Munich, Barcelona and Tokyo; Festival appearances at Huddersfield, Lucerne, Schwetzingen, Hong Kong and Osaka; Orchestras include London Symphony, BBC Symphony, Royal Concertgebouw, Radio orchestras in Austria and Germany, the Zuricher Kammerorchester, Tonhalle Orchestra and the Collegium Musicum Zurich; Conductors include Colin Davis, Bernard Haitink, Jean Martinon, Ferdinand Leitner, Bernhard Klee, Marek Janowski, Paul Sacher, Horst Stein and Peter Eötvös;

Repertory ranges from Scarlatti to Boulez; Piano Duo performances with Pierre-Laurent Aimard. *Honours include:* Prize winner Concours Reine Elisabeth, 1972, Belgium; First prize, competition of the Runfunkanstalten Munich, 1972. *Address:* c/o Ingpen and Williams Ltd., 14 Kensington Court, London W11 4PA, England.

CHEN Xieyang b. 4 May 1939, Shanghai, China. Symphony Orchestra Conductor. m. Jian-Ying Wang, 6 Apr 1973. *Education:* Piano student, Music Middle School, Shanghai Conservatory, 1953-60; Major in Conducting, Shanghai Conservatory, 1960-65; Musical study with Otto Mueller, Yale University, USA, 1981-82. *Debut:* Shanghai. *Career:* Conductor: Shanghai Ballet Orchestra, 1965-81; Aspen Festival, Group for Contemporary Music-New York, Brooklyn Philharmonia, Honolulu Symphony, Philippine State Orchestra, Hong Kong Philharmonic, Shanghai Symphony, Central Philharmonic-Beijing, 1981-83; Vilnius Symphony, Kaunas Symphony, Novosibirsk Symphony- USSR, 1985; Tokyo Symphony, Miyagi Philharmonic, Music Festival-Scotland, 1986-88; Music Director, Principal Conductor, Shanghai Symphony Orchestra; Resident Conductor, Central Philharmonic, Beijing. *Recordings:* Beethoven symphonies and Chinese composition for French Record Co KUKLOS CBE, 1983; Rachmaninov Symphony No 2 and Szymanovski Violin Concerto No 1, 1987; Chen Gang Violin concerto The Butterfly Lovers, Beethoven's 9 symphonies, Shanghai Record Co, 1988. *Address:* 105 Hunan Lu, Shanghai, China.

CHEN Yi, b. 4 Apr 1953, Guangzhou, China. Composer; Violinist. m. 20 July 1983. *Education:* BA, 1983, MA 1986, Central Conservatory of Music, Peking; DMA 1993, Columbia University, New York, USA. *Career:* Concert Mistress, Beijing Opera Troup Orchestra, 1970-78; Composer-Residence, The Women's Philharmonic, Chanticleer, San Francisco, USA, 1993-. *Compositions:* Works performed & broadcast throughout Europe, USA & China, 1984-; Duo Ye No. 2, orchestra; Symphony No. 1; Viola and Orchestra Concerto; Sprout, string orchestra; Three Poems from the Song Dynasty, chorus; Woodwind Quintet; Near Distance, Sextet for chamber ensemble; As in a Dream, for soprano, violin and cello; Overture No.1 and No.2 for Chinese Orchestra; Piano Concerto; Symphony No 2. *Recordings:* Duo ye, a Collection of Orchestral Works by Chen Yi, 1986. *Honours:* Recipient, many honours & awards. *Memberships:* ASCAP; Chinese Musicians' Association; New York Women Composers' Association. *Address:* The Women's Philharmonic, 330 Townsend St, No 218, San Francisco, CA 94107, USA.

CHEN Zuohuang, b. 2 Apr 1947, Shanghai, China. Conductor; Pianist; Music Director. m. Zaiyi Wang, 13 Sept 1969, 1 daughter. *Education:* High School Division, Central Conservatory, Peking, 1960-65; Central Conservatory, Peking, 1977-80; MMus, 1982, DMA Orchestral Conducting, 1985, University of Michigan, USA. *Career:* Conductor, All China Trade Union Music and Dance Troop, 1966-74; Conductor, China Film Philharmonic Orchestra, 1974-76; Associate Professor of Conducting, University of Kansas, USA, 1985-87; Conductor, Central Philharmonic Orchestra, Peking, 1986-, led its US debut tour throughout America, 1987; Conductor of China Youth Symphony Orchestra, 1987-, led its European tour, 1987; Guest conductor in over 15 countries, gave concerts in Amsterdam, Hamburg, Moscow, Lisbon, Budapest, Strasbourg, Leipzig, Mexico City, Basel, Bratislava, Hong Kong, Macau; Music Director/Conductor, Wichita Symphony Orchestra, 1990; Music Director/Conductor, Rhode Island Philharmonic Orchestra, 1992. *Recordings:* Recordings released by China Recording Co., Hong Kong Recording Co., and Opus. *Honours:* Outstanding Educator, March 1986; Hope Award, Feb. 1987; National Arts Associate, May 1987. *Current management:* ICM Artists Ltd., 40 W. 57th Street, New York, NY 10019, USA. *Address:* 1506 E. Kay Street, Derby, KS 67037, USA.

CHENETTE Jonathan Lee, b. 8 May 1954,

Libertyville, Illinois, USA. Composer; Pianist; College Teacher. m. Jeanmarie Kern, 20 May 1978, 2 sons, 1 daughter. *Education:* BA, Mathematics, University of Chicago, 1975; MM, Composition, Butler University, 1980; PhD, Composition, University of Chicago, 1984. *Career:* Performances by St. Paul Chamber Orchestra, Netherlands Radio Chamber Orchestra (1985 ISCM World Music Days), Cedar Rapids Chamber Orchestra, 1994; Dubuque Symphony Orchestra, 1992; Galliano Trio, 1985, Mirecourt Trio, 1985, 1987, members of Canadian National Chamber Orchestra, 1986; Lecturer, Microtonality and the Liberal Arts, 1993, Society of Composers National Convention; Japanese Conceptions of Space and Time in the Music of Toru Takemitsu, 1985 ASUC National Convention. *Compositions:* Jazmines, baritone vioce and chamber ensemble, 1979; Idyll, soprano, flute and harp, 1982; Redolence harp, 1982; Fantasy and Fugue on Bach, piano trio, 1985; Chamber Symphony, 1983; Eric's Salvation, baritone voice and 12 instruments, 1987; Liberty from the Tyranny of 12 Equal Tones, electronic, 1989; Oh Millersville!, soprano and piano, 1990; Oh Millersville!, soprano and orchestra, 1991; Music for Episcopal Worship, 1991; Duo Variations, double bass and harp, 1991; Four Character Pieces, flute and piano, 1992; Eric Hermannson's Soul, chamber opera, 1993. *Publications:* Synthetic Scales, Charles Griffes and the Kairn of Koridwen, PhD Dissertation, 1984; Edited, reorchestrated and conducted world premieres of orientalist works by Charles Griffes, 1985. *Address:* Music Department, Grinnell College, Grinnell, IA 50112-0806, USA.

CHÉREAU Patrice, b. 2 Nov 1944, Lezigne, Maine-et-Loire, France. Opera Producer. *Career:* Co-Director of the Théâtre National Populaire, Paris, 1979-81; Director, Théâtre des Amandiers, Nanterre, from 1982; Opera Productions include Les Contes d'Hoffmann and Lulu, 1979, for the Paris Opéra and Der Ring des Nibelungen, Bayreuth, 1976; Has produced Lucio Silla by Mozart al La Scala, Milan; Engaged for Wozzeck at Paris (Châtelet), Berlin (Staatsoper) and the Lyric Opera, Chicago, 1992-93; Don Giovanni at Salzburg, 1994. *Address:* Festspielhaus, 8580 Bayreuth 1, Germany.

CHERICI Paolo, b. 26 Mar 1952, Naples, Italy. Lute Teacher at Milan Conservatory. *Education:* Classical High School; Milan Conservatoire and Schola Cantorum of Basel. *Career:* Concerts of renaissance and baroque music such as lute soloist and in ensemble in Italy and abroad; Appearances on radio and TV in Italy and Switzerland; Lute Teacher at summer courses in Vicenza and Moneglia. Founder of the lute class at Milan Conservatoire. *Recordings:* Collaborations with several recordings with music of A Vivaldi, G Caccini, P F Cavalli, G A Perti, A.Corelli, Opera Omnia. *Publications:* A Piccinini, Toccata per 2 liuti, Suvini Zerboni, 1977; J S Bach, Opere complete per liuto, Suvini Zerboni 1980; A Vivaldi, Concerto per liuto e archi in D major Suvini Zerboni, 1981. *Contributions to:* Articles and reviews to Il Fronimo. *Honours:* Societá Italiana Del Liuto. *Memberships:* The Lute Society, England; The Lute Society of America.*Address:* Via Abamonti 2, 20129, Milan, Italy.

CHERKASSKY Shura, b. 7 Oct 1911, Odessa, Russia. Concert Pianist. *Education:* Philadelphia division, Curtis Institute of Music, Philadelphia, Pennsylvania, USA, with Josef Hofman. *Career:* First major tour of Europe 1945; often heard in concertos by Liszt and Tchaikovsky; Has played in every continent with all the principal conductors and orchestras of the world; Prokofiev's 2nd Concerto, Russian Spring Series, Festival Hall, May 1991, London Philharmonic; 80th Birthday Concert, Brighton Festival, 1991; Played Gershwin's Concerto at the 1993 Prom Concerts, London. *Recordings:* Numerous, with various record companies, in particular music by Prokofiev and Rachmaninov; CD of Lizst's Fantasia, Hungarian Folk-Themes, Berlin Philharmonic, Conducted by Karajan. *Hobby:* Travel. *Current Management:* Artist Management International Ltd. *Address:* 12/13 Richmond Buildings, London, W1V 5AF, England.

CHERNEY Brian, b. 4 Sept 1942, Canada. Composer, Educator. *Education:* BMus, 1964, MMus, 1967, PhD Musicology, 1974, University of Toronto; ARCT Piano, 1961; Studied composition with Samuel Dolin and John Weinzweig. *Career:* Professor, Faculty of Music, McGill University, Montreal, 1972-. *Compositions:* Chamber Concerto for Viola and 10 players, 1974; String Trio, 1976; Dans le crepuscle du souvenir, 1977-80 for piano; Adieux, for orchestra, 1980; River of Fire, for harp and oboe d'amore, 1983; In the Stillness of the Seventh Autumn, for piano, 1983; Into the Distant Stillness, orchestra, 1984; String Quartet No 3, 1985; In Stillness Ascending for viola and piano, 1986; Illuminations for string orchestra, 1987; Shekhinah, for solo viola, 1988; Oboe Concerto, 1989; Transfiguration for orchestra, 1990; Doppelganger, for 2 flutes, 1991; In the Stillness of September 1942, for English horn and 9 solo strings, 1992. *Recordings include:* Adieux; River of Fire; Into the Distant Stillness; Illuminations. *Publications:* Book, Harry Somers, 1975; Compositions published, 1989- 92. *Honours:* First Place, String Trio, International Rostrum of Composers, 1979; Jules Léger Prize for New Chamber Music, 1985. *Memberships:* Canadian League of Composers; Associate Composer, Canadian Music Center. *Address:* 4362 Hingston Ave, Montreal, Quebec H4A 2J9, Canada.

CHERNOUSHENKO Vladislav, b. 14 Jan. 1936, Leningrad, Russia. Conductor. *Education:* Studied at the Leningrad State Conservatoire. *Career:* Sang with the Boys Choir of the Glinka State Capella from 1944; Conducted the Karelia State Radio Orchestra, then the Leningrad Chamber Choir, 1962-74; Music Director of the Glinka State Capella from 1974; Directed the premiere performance of Rachmaninov's complete Vespers, 1974; Re- established the Symphony Orchestra of the Glinka State Capella, 1988 and has toured with it to Germany, Holland and France in a repertoire including Haydn, Shostakovich, Brahms, Bruckner, Schnittke and Mozart; Rector of the Leningrad/St Petersburg State Conservatoire from 1979. *Recordings include:* A wide repertoire. *Address:* c/o Sonata, 11 Northgate Street, Glasgow G20 7AA, Scotland.

CHERNOV Vladimir, b. 1955, USSR. Singer (Baritone).*Education:* Graduated Moscow Conservatoire 1981; Further study at La Scala, Milan. *Career:* Soloist with the Kirov Theatre, Leningrad, from 1983 as Rossini's Figaro, Germont, Valentine (Faust), Yeletsky (The Queen of Spades), Lefort in Peter the Great and Ryleyev in The Decembrists by Shebalin; Toured Britain and Ireland with the Moscow Radio Symphony Orchestra 1985; US debut 1988 as Marcello in La Bohème with the Opera Company of Boston; Scottish Opera 1990 as Don Carlo in La Forza del Destino; Los Angeles 1990, as Posa in Don Carlo, with Placido Domingo; Covent Garden Nov 1990, as Figaro; engaged as Zurga in Les Pecheurs de Perles, Seattle, 1994; Sang Posa at the Met, 1992, Doge in Due Foscari for the Opera Orchestra of New York, Rossini's Figaro at Seattle and Vienna, Posa at the Verona Arena; Stankar in Verdi's Stiffelio at the Met, 1994. *Honours:* Prize winner at the Tchaikovsky Competition 1982; Competitions in Busseto 1983 and Helsinki 1984 (Tito Gobbi Prize). *Memberships:* Founder Member, World Youth Orchestra Conference, Japan, 1991. *Address:* Allied Artists Ltd, 42 Montpelier Square, London SW7 1JZ, England.

CHERNYKH Pavel, b. 1960, Moscow, Russia. Singer (Baritone). *Education:* Studied at the Tchaikovsky Music School and with Yevgeny Nesterenko at the Moscow Conservatoire. *Debut:* Stage debut in season 1989-90 as Tchaikovsky's Onegin at the Bolshoy. *Career:* Concerts and recordings from 1987 with the Maly State Symphony, the St Petersburg Philharmonic and the Moscow Radio Orchestras; Further performances as Silvio in Pagliacci, Robert in Tchaikovsky's Iolanta, Yeletsky in The Queen of Spades and Renato (Ballo in Maschera); Sang Onegin at the Paris Opéra Comique, 1987 and for the Vlaamse Opera in Antwerp, 1990; Stars of the Bolshoy Theatre concerts in Germany and

Norway, 1990; Toured with the Bolshoy as Onegin to the USA 1990 and sang at the Wolf Trap Theater, Washington DC; Edinburgh Festival 1991, as Onegin. *Address:* c/o Sonata, 11 Northpark Street, Glasgow G20 7AA, Scotland.

CHETINYAN Krikor Hazaros, b. 22 June 1943, Plovdiv, Bulgaria. Conductor. *Education:* Graduated, Bulgarian State Academy of Music, 1970. *Debuts:* Sofia, 1965; Bayreuth, Germany, 1970. Career: Regular concerts with Plovdiv Philharmonic Orchestra and Plovdiv Women's Chamber Choir, Germany, England, USA, Belgium, Russia, Poland, Hungary, Greece, Israel, Netherlands, Italy, Austria, Slovenia, Japan; Numerous recordings for radio and TV, Cologne, Frankfurt, Munich, Berlin, London, Moscow, Milan, Tel-Aviv, Atlanta, Prague, Budapest, Warsaw, Sofia; Head, Conducting Department, Academy of Music and Dance, Plovdiv; Served on international juries, Italy, Netherlands, Hungary, Greece, Bulgaria. *Recordings:* 8 works by Bulgarian and foreign composers, with Bulgarian company Balkanton, Bulgaria and Vivace-Holland. *Publications:* Choir Songs by Bulgarian Composers, 1980; From the Choir Baroque Music, 1985; Songs for a Uniform Choir, 1991. *Hobby:* Football. *Address:* Shesti Septemvri str N158, 4000 Plovdiv, Bulgaria.

CHEW Geoffrey Alexander, b. 23 Apr 1940, South Africa. University Lecturer. m. Jennifer Comrie, 22 July 1967, 1 son, 2 daughters. *Education:* Royal College of Music, 1958-61; Caius College, Cambridge, 1961-64; BA, 1963; Mus.B., 1964; PhD, Manchester University, 1968. *Career:* University Lecturer: Johannesburg, 1968-70, Aberdeen, 1970-77, Royal Holloway College, University of London, 1977-88. *Contributions to:* Music & Letters; Journal of the American Musicological Society; Music Analysis. *Memberships:* Royal Musical Association; American Musicological Society; Gesellschaft für Musikforschung; International Musicological Society. *Address:* The Mount, Malt Hill, Egham, Surrey TW20 9PB, England.

CHIARA Maria, b. 24 Nov 1939, Oderzo, Italy. Singer (Soprano). *Education:* Conservatorio Benedetto Marcello in Venice, with Antonio Cassinelli. *Debut:* Venice Festival 1965, as Desdemona in Otello; Sang widely in Italy 1965-70, notably as Puccini's Liu at Verona, and Verdi's Odabella, Amelia (Ballo in Maschera) and Aida; 1970-71 several debuts in Germany and Austria, including Munich and Vienna as Mimi and Butterfly; La Scala debut 1972, as Micaela in Carmen; Covent Garden debut 1973, as Liu in Turandot; Metropolitan Opera 1977, as Violetta; Chicago Lyric Opera in Manon Lescaut; Appearances in Buenos Aires as Amelia (Simon Boccanegra) and Suor Angelica; Opened the 1985/86 season at La Scala as Aida; Australian Opera, Melbourne, 1986, in Un Ballo in Maschera; Aida at Luxor, Egypt, 1987; Amelia, Ballo in Maschera, at Bologne, Parma and Naples, 1989; Leonora, Forza del Destino, at the 1989, Spoleto and Verona Festivals; Aida at Turin, 1990; Other roles include Donizetti's Anna Bolena and Maria Stuarda, Verdi's Elisabeth de Valois and Giordano's Maddalena; Sang Leonora in Il Trovatore at Turin, 1991. *Recordings include:* Aida (Decca), Madama Butterfly (Eurodisc); Video of the Scala production of Aida. *Address:* c/o S.A. Gorlinsky Ltd., 33 Dover Street, London W1X 4NJ, England.

CHIHARA Paul (Seiko), b. 9 July 1938, Seattle, Washington, USA. Composer. *Education:* Studied with Robert Palmer at Cornell University, with Nadia Boulanger in Paris, Ernst Pepping in Berlin and with Gunther Schuller at the Berkshire Music Center. *Career:* Teacher at University of California, Los Angeles, 1966; Associate Professor at UCLA until 1974; Founded and directed the Twice Ensemble; Andrew Mellon Professor at the California Institute of Technology, 1975; Teacher at the California Institute of the Arts, 1976; Composer-in-residence for the San Francisco Ballet 1980; Commissions from the Boston Symphony Orchestra and the Los Angeles Philharmonic. *Compositions include:* Magnificat for 6 female voices 1965; Driftwood for string quartet 1967; Branches for 2 bassoons and percussion

1968; Forest Music for orchestra 1970; Windsong for cello and orchestra 1971; Grass for double bass and orchestra 1972; Ceremony III for flute and orchestra 1973; Shinju, ballet, 1975; Missa Carminum 1975; The Beauty of the Rose is in its Passing for ensemble 1976; String Quartet (Primavera) 1977; 2 Symphonies 1975 and 1980; Mistletoe Bride, ballet, 1978; Concerto for string quartet and orchestra 1980; Sinfonia Concertante for 9 instruments 1980; The Tempest, ballet, 1980; Saxophone Concerto 1981; Sequoia for string quartet and tape 1984; Film and television scores; Arrangements for musicals. *Address:* ASCAP, ASCAP Building, One Lincoln Plaza, New York, NY 10023, USA.

CHILCOTT Susan b. 1963, England. Singer (Soprano). *Education:* Studied at the Guildhall School, the Banff Centre of Fine Arts in Canada with Mollie Petrie. *Career:* Concer engagements include Mendelssohn's Elijah at the Albert Hall, Haydn's Seasons in Madrid under Neville Marriner and appearances with the Royal Scottish Orchestra and the Scottish CHamber Orchestra; Scottish Opera as Frasquite in Carmen and First Lady in The Magic Flute, 1992; Dona Luisa in the British premiere of Gerhard's The Duenna of Opera North, Ellen Orford in Brussels and Mozart's Countess for Garsington Opera, 1993; Season 1993-94 and Micaela at Barcelona; Lady Rich in Britten's Gloriana for Opera North. *Address:* Ingpen & Williams Ltd, 14 Kensington Court, London W8 5DN, England.

CHILDS Barney Sanford, b. 13 Feb. 1926, Spokane, Washington, USA. Composer; Teacher. m. (divorced), 2 daughters. *Education includes:* BA, University of Nevada, 1949; BA honours, Oxford University, England, 1951; PhD, Stanford University, USA, 1959; Studied with Leonard Ratner, Carlos Chavez, Aaron Copland, Elliott Carter. *Career includes:* Assistant Professor of English, University of Arizona, 1961-65; Dean, Deep Springs College, 1965-69; Composer in Residence, Wisconsin College-Conservatory, 1969-71; Faculty Fellow in Music and Literature, Johnston College, 1971-73; Professor of Composition and Music Literature, University of Redlands, 1973-. *Compositions:* About 80 compositions published, 15 recorded. *Recordings include:* Clay music, A question of summer (tuba and harp); A music, that it might be (2 clarinets); Sonata for solo trombone; Music for two flute players; Mr T his fancy (solo contrabass); The edge of the world (bass clarinet and organ); Variations sur une chanson de canotier (brass quintet), A Box of Views, wind quartet and piano. *Publications:* Contemporary Composers on Contemporary Music (co-editor), 1967; The New Instrumentation (co-editor), 6 volumes. *Contributions to:* Various books and journals. *Hobby:* Reading. *Address:* School of Music, University of Redlands, Redlands, CA 92374, USA.

CHILINGIRIAN Levon, b. 28 May 1948, Cyprus. Violinist. *Education:* Royal College of M usic, London. *Debut:* Purcell Romm, London, 1969. *Career:* Duo with Clifford Benson (Piano), BBC Radio and TV, German and Swiss Radio; Various festivals with Chil. Quartet: Proms; Cheltenham, London, Aldeburgh, Bath, Paris, New York, Berlin and Adelaide Festivals; BBC TV and Radio; Resident Ensemble Liverpool, 1973- 76, Sussex, 1978-93, RCM, 1987- *Recordings:* Quartet: Works by: Arriaga, Berwald, Wilkmanson, Korngold, Mozart, Haydn, Schubert, Beethoven, Schumann, Dvořák, Bartók, Debussy, Ravel, Panufnik; Duo: Schubert, Mathias, Ferguson, Finzi. *Honours:* First Prize: BBC Beethoven Competition, 1969 and Munich Competition, 1971; FRCM, 1989; DMus, Sussex University, 1992. *Memberships:* ISM; Musician's Union; ESTA. *Hobbies:* Table Tennis; Walking. *Current Management:* Intermusica. *Address:* 7 Hollingbourne Road, London , SE24 9NB, England.

CHISSELL Joan Olive, b. 22 May 1919, Cromer, Norfolk, England. Music Critic. *Education:* ARCM; GRSM. *Career:* Lecturer in Music for Extra-Mural Departments, London and Oxford Universities, 1943-48; Piano Teacher, Junior Department, Royal College of Music, 1943-53; Assistant Music Critic, The Times, 1948-79; Regular Broadcaster for BBC and Reviewer for The Gramophone; Jury Member, International piano competitions including, Milan, Leeds, Zwickau, Budapest, Dublin and Sydney (Australia). *Publications:* Schumann, 1948 revised 1989; Chopin, 1965; Schumann's Piano Music, 1972; Brahms, 1977; Clara Schumann, 1983. *Contributions to:* Benjamin Britten (A Symposium); Chamber Music (Pelican); The Concerto (Pelican); The Concerto (Christopher Helm) and many magazines, including Radio Times and The Listener. *Honours:* Awarded the Robert Schumann Prize by the town of Zwickau, 1991. *Memberships:* Critics' Circle; Royal College of Music Society. *Hobby:* Boating on the River Thames. *Address:* Flat D, 7 Abbey Road, London NW8, England.

CHIURCO Erna, b. 21 Sept 1918, Spandau, Germany. Piano Teacher. m. Philip Chiurco, 14 Apr 1943, 1 son, 1 daughter. *Education:* Private lessons with Roslyn Spiro, Miriam Morrison and Dr Albert de Vito. *Career:* Active in church work, over 30 years; Church Piano Accompanist; Accompanist for Philip Chiurco, trumpet player; Soloist; Plays accordion in church orchestra; Arranges hymns to perform with husband; Gives private lessons in Piano. *Publications:* Contributor to Technical Control for the Modern Pianist, Kenyon Publications, 1978. *Contributions to:* Music reviews for Keyboard Teachers Association International Inc. *Memberships:* Piano Teachers Congress of New York Inc; Keybaord Teachers Association International Inc. *Address:* 216 Linden Street, North Massapequa, NY 11758, USA.

CHLOPECKI Andrzej, b. 21 Jan 1950, Bydgoszcz, Poland. Musicologist; Music Critic; Music Publishser. m. Beata, 8 Aug 1978, 2 sons, 1 daughter. *Education:* Music Lyceum, Bydgoszcz, 1969; MA, Warsaw University Institute of Muscology, 1975. *Career:* Head of New Music Department in Polish Radio, Warsaw, 1975-81, 1992-; Promotion Manager, Polish Music Publishers, Warsaw, 1982-92; Assistant Professor, Academy of Music, Cracow, 1982-; Lectures in Poland and throughout Europe on history, theory of aesthetics of new music, modernism and postmodernism, Polish music; Radio and television programmes. *Publications include:* Essays, articles, reviews in books and periodicals; Contributions to magazines and periodicals including: Ruch Muzyczny, Res Publica, Zeitschrift fur Neue Musik, and Polish Music. *Current Management:* Polish Radio, Warsaw. *Address:* Naleczowska 62-64, 02- 922 Warszawa, Poland.

CHMURA Gabriel, b. 7 May 1946, Wroclaw, Poland. Conductor. m. Mareile Chmura. 1 daughter. *Education:* Diploma (Conducting) Vienna Academy of Music; Ecole Normale de Musique, Paris; MA, Piano and Composition, Tel Aviv University. *Career:* Assistant to Karajan, 1971-73; Generalmusikdirektor, Aachen, 1974-82; Bochum Symphony Orchestra, 1982-87; Music Director-Designate 1986-87, Principal Conductor and Music Director 1987-, National Arts Centre Orchestra, Ottawa; Guest Conductor, Berlin Philharmonic Orchestra; Vienna Symphony Orchestra; London Symphony Orchestra; L'Orchestre Nationale de France, Paris; Tonhalle Orchestra, Zurich; North German Radio Symphony Orchestra, Hamburg; Bavarian Radio Symphony Orchestra, Munich; South German Radio Symphony Orchestra, Stuttgart; New York Philharmonic Orchestra; Paris Opera; Bavarian State Opera, Munich; Conducted Werther at Parma, 1990. *Recordings:* For CBS; Deutsche Grammophon; Pro Arte; Mendelssohn Overtures with London Symphony Orchestra. *Honours:* Gold Medal, Guido Cantelli Conducting Competition, Milan, 1971; 1st prize, Herbert von Karajan Conducting Competition, Berlin, 1971; Prix Mondial du Disque de Montreux, 1983. *Address:* c/o National Arts Centre Orchestra, 1 Confederation Square, Ottawa, Ontario K1P 5W1, Canada.

CHODOS Gabriel, b. 7 Feb 1939, White Plains, New York, USA. Pianist; Teacher. *Education:* BA Philosophy, 1959, MA Music, 1964, University of California, Los Angeles; Diploma in Piano, Akademie für Musik, Vienna, Austria, 1966. *Debut:* Carnegie Recital, New York City, 1970. *Career:* Appearances throughout USA; Numerous tours of Europe, Israel, Japan; Solo performances with Chicago Symphony Orchestra, Radio Philharmonic (Holland), Jerusalem Symphony Orchestra; Master classes: Aspen Festival, Rutgers Summer Festival and Chautauqua Festival; Toho Conservatory, Kunitachi Music University, Osaka University of Arts, and elsewhere throughout Japan. *Recordings:* Bartók, Sonata; Bloch, Visions and Prophecies; Franck, Prélude, Aria et Final, Orion; Schubert, Sonata in B-flat major, Op. Posth, Orion; Encore favourites by various composers, Victor (Japan); Berlinsky, Sonata for Violin & Piano (CRI). *Address:* 245 Waban Avenue, Waban, MA 02168, USA.

CHOMINSKI Jozef Michal, b. 24 Aug 1906, Ostrow, Poland. Musicologist; Professor. *Education:* Studied composition with M Soltys; conducting with A Soltys, Lwow Conservatory, 1927-29; Musicology with Chybinski; Ethnography with Adam Fischer; MA 1931 PhD 1936, University of Lwow; Habilitation, University of Poznan, 1949. *Career:* Professor of Music History, Poznan Music School, 1945-48; Lecturer in Music History 1947-51, Senior Lecturer 1951-54, Reader 1954-60, Professor of Music History and Theory 1960-76, University of Warsaw; Chairman, Music Division Art Institute, Polish Academy of Sciences, 1951-63; Editor: Studia Muykologiczne 1953-56, Rocznik Chopinowski, Annales Chopin edited with K.Wilkowska-Chominska 1956-71, Muzyka 1956-71, Monumenta Musicae in Polonia edited with K.Wilkowska-Chominska 1964-71. *Publications:* Preludia Chopina 1950; Music of the Polish Re-naissance 1958; Formy muzyczne edited with K.Wilkowska-Chominska: I. Small instrumental forms 1983; II. Large instrumental forms 1987; III. Song 1974; IV. Opera and Drama 1976; V. Large vocal forms 1984; History of Harmony and Counter-point 3 volume, 1958, 1962, 1988; Sonaty Chopina 1960; A Dictionary of Polish Musicians 2 Volume, 1964-67; Music in the People's Republic of Poland 1968; Studia nad twórczoscia Karola Szymanowskiego 1969; History of Music edited with K.Wilkowska-Chominska 1989; A Catalogue of the works of Frederick Chopin edited with T.D.Turlo 1990. *Address:* Wyszatycka 48, 04-946, Warsaw, Poland.

CHOO David Ik-Sung, b. 10 Sept. 1962, Seoul, Korea. Conductor. *Education:* BMus, California State University, Northridge, 1981-88; MMus, Orchestral Conducting, University of Southern California, 1988-90; Conducting studies with Frederik Prausnitz, Daniel Lewis, Murry Sidlin, Gary Pratt, Jon Robertson, and Lawrence Christiansen; Violin Studies with Manuel Compinsky, Miwako Watanabe, Kathleen Lenski; piano studies with Nobuko Fujimoto. *Debut:* Guest Conductor: Aspen Concert Orchestra, 1988, Central Philharmonic Orchestra of China, Beijing, 1991. *Career:* Conductor: US (Chamber Assistant) and Symphony Orchestras, (Guest); Washington Central Choir and Centrall Orchestra; The Angeles Orchestra; The Central Philharmonic Orchestra of China (guest); The Savaria Symphony Orchestra, (Guest), Hungary, 1992. Concerts include: Central Philharmonic Orchestra of China, Wagner: Die Meistersinger von Nurnberg Overture, Mozart: Clarinet Concerto in A Major, Tchaikovsky: Symphony No 5: Savaria Symphony Orchestra, Ives: Symphony No 4. *Honours:* Nicolai Malko Conducting Competition Prize Winner, Copenhagen, 1992. *Address:* 204 West Fayette St, Baltimore, MD 21201, USA.

CHOOKASIAN Lili, b. 1 Aug 1921, Chicago, Illinois, USA. Singer (Mezzo-Soprano). *Education:* Studied with Philip Manuel in New York and with Rosa Ponselle in Baltimore. *Debut:* With Chicago Symphony Orchestra conducted by Bruno Walter in Mahler 3, 1957. *Career:* Stage debut Little Rock 1959, as Adalgisa in Norma; New York debut 1962, in Prokofiev's Alexander Nevsky; Metropolitan Opera debut 1962, as La Cieca in La Gioconda: returned as Wagner's Erda and in Suor Angelica, Pelléas et Mélisande, Il Tabarro and Falstaff; New York City Opera 1963, The Medium by Menotti;

Appearances at Salzburg, Bayreuth (Erda, 1965), Mexico City, Hamburg and Buenos Aires; Created the Queen in Ines de Castro by Pasatieri (1976); Other roles include Amneris, Azucena, Mary in Der fliegende Holländer, Ulrica, and Madelon in Andrea Chénier; Concert engagements with major US orchestras. *Recordings:* Symphony No.2 by Yardumian and Mahler's Das Lied von der Erde, with the Philadelphia Orchestra; Götterdämmerung (Deutsche Grammophon); Mahler 2 (CBS); Beethoven 9 (BASF)

CHOPARD Patrice, b. 28 Mar 1953, Zurich, Switzerland; Composer Guitarist; Teacher. *Education:* University of Zurich, 1973-82; Classic guitar, 1973-77; Guitar Teacher, 1977; Composition, Zurich, 1980-82. Royal Danish Academy of Music, 1982-83. *Career:* Concerts and compositions; Teacher, Switzerland, 1973-82, University of Bremen, 1984-92; Cultural management and Composer, Bremen, 1990-92; Cultural management, Osnabruck, Germany, 1992-93. *Compositions:* Augenblicke aus dem Fenster, 1982; O Carolan-arrangements, 1984; Waller Gesaenge, 1992. *Recordings:* Land of Erin, Suite, 1984; O'Carolan-arrangements, 1987; Tasten im Raum, 1989. *Memberships:* Swiss Musicians Association; German Composers Society; Swiss Society of Music Education; German Soicety of Musical Educators and Artists. *Hobbies:* Literature; Writing; Nature. *Address:* Lubberstedterstr 34, D-28217 Bremen, Germany.

CHORZEMPA Daniel Walter, b. 7 Dec 1944, Minneapolis, Minnesota, USA. Pianist; Organist; Musicologist; Composer. *Education:* University of Minnesota; Fulbright Scholar, Cologne, Federal Republic of Germany, 1965-66. *Career:* Former Church Organist, USA; Organ Instructor, University of Minnesota, 1962-65; Extensive piano and organ recitals including Germany, Denmark, Italy and UK, 1968-; in 1970 and 1971 played Beethoven's Diabelli Variations in Oxford and London. *Recordings:* For Philips including the major organ works of Liszt. *Hobbies:* Mathematics; Architecture; Poetry; Renaissance history and literature. *Address:* 5000 Cologne 1, Grosse Budengasse 11, Germany.

CHOVEAUX Nicholas, b. 22 Apr 1904, Kent, England. Organist; Teacher; Composer. *Education:* Trent College; Matthay School with R Arnold Grevi. *Career:* Chelsea Old Church; St John's Wimbledon; St Bartholomew the Great, Smithfield, London EC, ENSA Music Adviser (World War 2). *Compositions:* 3 Pieces for Organ; Prelude, improvisation for Organ Variations on Caswall; Communion Service. *Address:* 16 Jubilee Court, Lansbury Road, Halesworth, Suffolk IP19 8SP, England.

CHOWNING John MacLeod, b. 22 Aug 1934, Salem, New Jersey, USA. Composer; Teacher. *Education:* BM, Wittenberg University, Springfield, Ohio, 1959; Studied with Nadia Boulanger, Paris, 1959-62; PhD, Stanford University, 1966. *Career:* Teacher 1966-, Director Computer Music and Acoustics Project 1966-1974, Center for Computer Research in Music and Acoustics (CCRMA) 1975, Professor of Music 1979 at Stanford University; Inventor of FM sound synthesis. *Compositions:* Pieces for computer-generated quadrophonic sound, including Sabelithe, 1971; Turenas, 1972; Stria, 1977; Phone, 1981. *Recordings:* Music with Computers, John Chowing WERGO 2012-50 CD. *Publications:* The Synthesis of Complex Audio Spectra by Means of Frequency Modulation; Journal of the Audio Engineering Society, 1973; The Simulation of Moving Sound Sources; Journal of the Audio Engineering Society, 1972; FM Theoryand Applications; Yamaha Music Foundation, 1986.*Honours:* National Endowment for the Arts grants; Institut de Recherche et de Coordination Acoustique/Musique commissions; Fellow of the American Academy of Arts and Sciences, 1988; Awarded the Hooker Chair by the School of Humanities and Sciences at Stanford, 1993. *Address:* c/o Center for Computer Research in Music and Acoustics, Music Department, Stanford University, Stanford, CA 94305-8180, USA.

CHRISTENSEN Dieter, b. 17 Apr 1932, Berlin, Germany. University Professor of Ethnomusicology. m. Nerthus Karger, 1 son, 1 daughter. *Education:* Study of cello, Berlin State Conservatory; PhD Musicology, Free University, Berlin, 1957. *Debut:* RIAS Radio, Berlin, 1949. *Career:* Taught at University of Berlin, Hamburg, Wesleyan University, City University of New York; Currently Professor and Director, Center for Ethnomusicology, Columbia University, New York. *Recordings:* Lappish folk songs; Kurdish folk music; Yugoslav Folk Music; Traditional Arts of Oman, 1993; A Wedding in Sohar, Oman, 1993. *Publications include:* Die Musik der Kate und Sialum, 1957; Die Musik der Ellice-Inseln (with G. Koch), 1964; Co-Editor, Hornbostel Opera Omnia, 1974; Der Ring des Tlalocan, 1977; Musical Traditions in Oman, 1993. *Contributions to:* German and international professional journals; Book Review Editor, Journal of Society for Ethnomusicology. *Memberships:* Executive Board, Programme Chairman, Edinburgh Conference, 1969, Regensburg Conference, 1975; International Folk Music Council; Secretary General, International Council for Traditional Music; Editor, Yearbook for Traditional Music; Co-Director, UNESCO project The Universe of Music, A History; Member of various committees. *Hobbies:* Agriculture; Electronics. *Address:* Department of Music, Columbia University, New York, NY 10027, USA.

CHRISTENSEN Mogens b. 7 Apr 1955, Laesoe, Denmark. m. Helle Kristensen. *Education:* Diploma in Music history and Music theory, 1983; Teaching Certificate, 1983; Diploma in Composition, studying with Per Norgard and Poul Ruders, 1988; PhD Composition, 1993; MMus, 1992. *Debut:* 1982. *Career:* Teacher, Royal Academies of Music in Copenhagen, Arhus, Aalborg and Esbjerg and at the universities in Arhus and Aalborg; Currently, Ass Professor at the Bergen Academy of Music, (Grieg Academy), 1988-. *Compositions:* Zurvan Akarana, orchestra, 1989; Dreams within Dreams, violin concerto, 1990; A Fancyer's Delight, recorder concerto, 1993; The Khazarian Mirrors, piano, 1992; Hyperions Schicksalslied (sop and ensemble's, orchestra), 1982; Cadenza, violin, 1990; El Mar del tiempo perdido, vlc, 1990. *Recordings:* Mogens Christensen: Vocal and Chamber Music, Vol 1, 1991, Vol 2, 1993; The Lost Poems of Princess Ateh, 1992. *Honours:* Artists Prize of the County of Bergen, 1991; Artist Scholarship, Danish State, 1993-95. *Memberships:* Danish Composers' Society. *Address:* Asylplassen 13, N-5018 Bergen, Norway.

CHRISTESEN Robert b. 15 Feb 1943, Washington DC, USA. Singer (Baritone). *Education:* Studied at the Manhattan School of Music and at Aspen School of Music with Aksel Schiotz and Jennie Tourel. *Debut:* Henrik in Maskarade by Nielsen, at St Paul, 1972. *Career:* Sang with the Frankfurt and Dortmund Operas and appeared as guest Berlin (Komische Oper), Copenhagen, Budapest, Warsaw, Toulouse, Brno, Prague and in North and South America; Other roles have included Mozart's Count and Don Giovanni, Verdi's Ford, Germont and Luna, Eugene Onegin, Jochanaan, Rossini's Figaro, Kaspar in Der Freischütz and Lescaut in Henze's Boulevard Solitude. *Address:* c/o Stadische Buhnen, Untermainanlage 11, 6000 Frankfurt am Main, Germany.

CHRISTIE George (William Langham), (Sir), b. 31 Dec, 1934. Glyndebourne, England. Chairman, Glyndebourne Productions Limited. m. Patricia Mary Nicholson, 1958, 3 sons, 1 daughter. *Education:* Eton. *Career:* Assistant to Secretary of X Calouste Gulbenkian Foundation, 1957-62; Chairman of Glyndebourne Productions, 1956- and of other family companies, has been instrumental in the widening of Glyndebourne Festival repertory to include operas by Henze, Janáček, Stravinsky, Ravel, Strauss and Gershwin; Founder and Chairman, The London Sinfonietta. *Honours:* Knight, 1984; DL, E. Sussex. *Address:* Glyndebourne, Lewes, East Sussex, England.

CHRISTIE Nan, b. 1960, Ayr, Scotland. Singer

(Soprano). *Education:* Royal Scottish Academy of Music; London Opera Centre. *Career:* Repertoire with Scottish Opera includes Britten's Tytania, Rimsky's Queen of Shemakha, the Queen of Night and Zerbinetta, in Ariadne auf Naxos; Tours to Portugal, Poland, Switzerland and Germany; Sang in Mozart's La Finta Giardiniera and the premiere of Oliver's Tom Jones, with English Music Theatre; Tytania with Opera North; Isotta (Die schweigsame Frau) and Despina (Così fan Tutte) at the Glyndeboune Festival; Zdenka (Arabella), the Queen of Night and Offenbach's Eurydice with English National Opera; European engagements with Netherlands Opera (Despina), Opera de Nancy (Pamina), Zurich Opera in the Ponnelle production of Lucio Silla and Frankfurt Opera (Zerbinetta), Marie in Die Soldaten and Susanna, Scottish Opera, 1990 as Despina in a new production of Così Fan Tutte, the Queen of Night at the London Coliseum; Birdie Hubbard in the British premiere of Blitzstein's Regina, Glasgow, 1991; Concerts at the Hong Kong Festival, Hallé Orchestra, BBC Symphony and London Symphony Orchestras, Nash Ensemble and the London Sinfonietta; TV appearances in Mozart's Schauspieldirektor and Ravel's L'Enfant et les Sortilèges; Italian debut: Mitridate by Mozart, La Fenice, Venice, and the Queen of Night in The Magic Flute for ENO, 1992; Premiere of Jonathan Harvey's Inquest of Love, English National Opera, 1993. *Recordings include:* Videos of Glyndebourne Festival Così fan Tutte; The Gondoliers, The Sorcerer and Princess Ida. *Address:* c/o Lies Askonas Ltd., 186 Drury Lane, London WC2B 5RY, England.

CHRISTIE William (Lincoln), b. 19 Dec 1944, Buffalo, New York, USA. Harpsichordist; Conductor; Teacher. *Education:* Studied harpsichord with Igor Kipnis, Berkshire Music Center, Tanglewood; BA, Harvard University, 1966; Harpsichord with Ralph Kirkpatrick; Organ with Charles Kribaum; Musicology with Claude Palisca and Nicholas Temperley; MMus, Yale University, 1970. *Career:* Teacher, Dartmouth College, 1970-71; Member, Five Centuries Ensemble, France, 1971-75; Concerto Vocale, 1972-; Founder-director, Les Arts Florissants, 1978-; Teacher, Innsbruck Summer Academy for Early Music, 1977-83; Professorship, Paris Conservatory, 1982-; Conducted Alcina at the Theâtre de Châtelet, and Geneva, 1990; London debut of Les Arts Florissants at Greenwich, 1990, with Charpentier's Actéon, and Dido and Aeneas; Les Indes Galantes at Aix-en-Provence; Conducted Luigi Rossi's Orfeo at Vienna Konzerthaus, 1990; Season 1992 with Purcell's Fairy Queen at the Barbican Hall, London, Rameau's Castor et Pollux for the Baroque Festival at Versailles and Lully's Atys at Madrid. *Recordings:* Many discs devoted to the masters of the French and Italian Baroque. *Honours:* Numerous awards including a number of Grand Prix du Disque of France and Prix Mondiale du Disque; First American to hold a Professorship at the Paris Conservatory. *Address:* c/o Paris Conservatory, 14 rue de Madrid, 75008 Paris, France.

CHRISTOFF Dimiter, b. 2 Oct 1933, Sofia, Bulgaria. Composer; Professor. *Education:* Studied composition with M Goleminov, State Music Academy, Sofia, 1951-56; Study tour West Germany, USA, France, the Netherlands, 1963; Dr Habil 1975. *Career:* Teacher 1970-76, Professor 1976-, State Music Academy; General Secretary, International Music Council, UNESCO, 1975-79. *Compositions:* Operas: The Game, 1978; The Golden Fish Line, 1984; Orchestral: 2 piano concertos 1954, 1983; Sinfonietta for Strings, 1956; Poem, 1957; 3 Symphonies, 1958, 1964, 1969; Overture, 1961; Symphonic Episodes, 1962; Violin Concerto, 1966; Chamber Suite for Two Piccolo, Piano Percussion and Strings, 1966; Cello Concerto, 1969; Concert Miniatures, 1970; Overture with Fanfares, 1974; Quasi una fantasia-gioco, 1981; Game for Celli and Orchestra, 1983; Perpetui mobili in pianissimi, 1987; Chamber: Suite for Brass Quartet, 1953; 2 Dances for Trumpet and Piano, 1960; Sonata for Solo Cello, 1965; Concerto for 3 Small drums and 5 Instruments, 1967; String Quartet, 1970; Quartet for Flute, Viola, Harp and Harpsichord, 1973; 4 Piano sonatas, 1962, 1974 (three); Also choruses and songs. *Memberships:*

International Society for Music Education; Bulgarian Composers Union, vice-president 1972-85. *Address:* Bou Pentscho Slawejkov 13-a, 1606 Sofia, Bulgaria.

CHRISTOPHERS Harry, b. 26 Dec 1953, Goudhurst, Kent, England. Conductor; Choral Director. *Education:* Studied at Canterbury Cathedral Choir School (Head Chorister), King's School Canterbury and Magdalen College, Oxford, (Academical Clerk). *Career:* Founded the choral group The Sixteen 1977; Tours of Britain, Europe, Brazil and Japan, 1989; BBC debut May 1981; BBC Prom debur, 1990; Has also worked with the Junge Deutsche Philharmonie and with the Turku Philharmonic in Finland; Association with the RTE Concert Orchestra and Chorus (Dublin) with Messiah and Bach's St John Passion and Christmas Oratorio; Concerts in Lahti with Avanti and the Finnish Chamber Choir, in Espoo and Helsinki with the Espoo City Orchestra; Concerts with the Scottish Chamber Orchestra; Appearances with The Sixteen in the premiere of Birtwistle's Gawain at Covent Garden, May 1991; Other 1991 concerts at St John's Smith Square (Poulenc, the Eton Choir Book, Bach's Magnificat and Christmas Concerts); Perpignan, France (Purcell); Cuenca and Madrid (Victoria); Tampere, Finland, and Blythburgh (Taverner); Europalia Festival, Belgium (Teixeira Te Deum); Messiah world tour scheduled 1992, with visits to America, Australia and the Far East. *Recordings include:* Handel's Messiah, Monteverdi Vespers (Hyperion); Handel Chandos Anthems, Bach St John Passion and Tallis Spem in Alium (Chandos); Byrd Mass for 4 Voices and Propers for the Feasts of St Peter and St Paul, Poulenc Figure Humaine (Virgin Classics); Purcell Fairy Queen, Bach Christmas Oratorio; Palestrina Missa Papae Marcelli and Allegri Miserere, Handel Alexander's Feast (Collins Classics); John Sheppard Motets (Hyperion); John Sheppard, Church Music vol. I-IV, Hyperion, Taverner, Festal Mass series; Teixeira Te Deum, music from the Eton Choirbook, vol. I-IV. *Honours include:* Grand Prix du Disque from the Academie Charles Cros, 1988, for Messiah recording; Gramophone, Early Music Award, 1992 for The Rose and the Ostrich Feather; Deutschen Schallplattenkritik, 1992 for Handel Alexander's Feast; Diapason D'Or 1992 for Teixeira Te Deum. *Hobbies include:* Cooking; Football (Arsenal FC). *Address:* c/o Magenta Music International, 64 Highgate High Street, London N6 5HX, England.

CHUNG Kyung-Wha, b. 26 Mar 1948, Seoul, Korea. m. 2 sons. Violinist. *Education:* Studied under Ivan Galamian, Juilliard School of Music, New York, USA. *Debut:* USA. *Career:* European Debut, 1970; Has played under numerous conductors including; Abbado, Barenboim, Davis, Dorati, Dutoit, Giulini, Haitink, Jochum, Kempe, Kondrashin, Leinsdorf, Levine, Maazel, Mehta, Muti, Previn, Rattle, Rozhdestvensky and Solti; Has played with major orchestras including: all London Orchestras, Chicago, Boston and Pittsburgh Symphony Orchestras: New York, Cleveland, Philadelphia, Berlin, Israel and Vienna Philharmonics; Orchestre de Paris; Has toured the world; played at Salzburg Festival, London Symphony Orchestra, 1973; Vienna festival, 1981, 1984; Edinburgh Festival 1981; Played at 80th Birthday Concert of Sir William Walton, 1982; Beethoven's Sonatas Op.30 Nos. 1 and 2, and, Op.96 with Stephen Kovacevich, Barbican Centre, May 1991. *Recordings:* Concertos by Beethoven, Bruch, Mendelssohn, Tchaikovsky, Bartók, Stravinsky, Walton, Vieuxtemps for London/Decca. *Honour:* Winner, Leventritt Competition, 1968. *Hobbies:* Arts. *Current Management:* Columbia Artists Management, Inc, New York. *Address:* c/o Columbia Artists Management, Inc, 165 West 57 Street, New York. NY 10019, USA.

CHUNG Mia, b. 9 Oct 1964, Madison, Wisconsin, USA. Concert Pianist; Assistant Professor of Music. *Education:* BA, magna cum laude, Harvard University, 1986; MM, Yale University, 1988; DMA, Juilliard School of Music, 1991. *Debut:* Hall of the Americas, OAS Building, Washington, DC, 1983. *Career:* Assistant Professor of Music and Artist-in- Residence, Gordon College, 1991-; Appearances with Baltimore Symphony Orchestra, 1977, 1981; Performed with National

Symphony Orchestra, 1983; Performed with National Gallery Orchestra, 1987; Performed with Fort Collins Symphony Orchestra, 1990; Performed with New Haven Symphony, 1989; Solo recitals and chamber performances at OAS, Alice Tully Hall, National Gallery of Art, The Kennedy Center for Performing Arts, American Academy of Arts and Sciences and other venues; Records exclusively for Channel Classics Records. *Honours:* First Prize in 1981 Johann Sebastian Bach International Piano Competition; Selected to be a USIA Artistic Ambassador, performing Internationally, 1993; First Prize in the Concert Artists Guild International Competition in New York City, 1993. *Hobbies:* Long distance swimming; Art history; Cooking. *Address:* Fine Arts Department, Gordon College, Wenham, MA 01984, USA.

CHUNG Myung-Wha, b. 22 Jan 1953, Seoul, Korea. Concert Cellist. *Education:* Studied with Leonard Rose at the Juilliard School and with Gregor Piatigorsky at his University of Southern California master class. *Debut:* Played with the Seoul Philharmonic before study in New York. *Career:* Has appeared widely in Europe and North America from 1971, notably in Britain, Italy, Denmark, Germany, Spain, Holland, Belgium, France, Switzerland, Israel and Mexico; Festival appearances at Lucerne, Flanders, Spoleto, Palma de Majorca, Birmingham, Evian and Dijon; Television programmes in the United States, Britain, West Germany and Switzerland; Season 1988-89 tour of Italy with the London Mozart Players; Chung Trio recitals at Carnegie Hall and in major cities of the United States and Western Europe; Plays a 1731 Stradivarius cello known as Braga. *Recordings include:* Tchaikovsky Rococco Variations with the Los Angeles Philharmonic under Charles Dutoit (Decca); Four piano trio works with the Chung Trio (Decca); Major piano trio repertoire on the EMI label. *Honours include:* First prize, Geneva International Music Competition, 1971. *Address:* c/o Terry Harrison Artists Management, 3 Clarendon Court, Park Street, Charlbury, Oxon OX7 3PS, England.

CHUNG Myung-Whun, b. 22 Jan 1953, Seoul, Korea. Conductor; Pianist. *Education:* Began musical studies as a pianist; Mannes College of Music, New York, with Nadia Rosenberg and Carl Bamburger; Juilliard School 1974-78, with Sixten Ehrling. *Career:* Associate conductor of the Los Angeles Philharmonic Orchestra 1978-81; Moved to Europe 1981 and conducted the Berlin Philharmonic, Munich Philharmonic, Concertgebouw Orchestra, Orchestre de Paris, Israel Philharmonic and the major London orchestras; Music Director and Principal Conductor of the Saarländischer Rundfunk in Saarbrucken, 1984-; On visits to USA has conducted the New York Philharmonic, National Symphony Washington, the Boston Symphony and the Cleveland and Chicago Orchestras; Metropolitan Opera from 1986, debut with Simon Boccanegra; Principal Guest Conductor at the Teatro Comunale in Florence: new productions of Boris Godunov, Simon Boccanegra and Idomeneo; Has worked at opera houses in Monte Carlo and Geneva and conducted a new production of Prokofiev's The Fiery Angel at the Paris Opéra; Appointed Music Director of the Opéra de la Bastille, Paris, 1989; Conducted Les Troyens, first production, 1990; The Legend of the Invisible City of Kitezh, (Rimsky-Korsakov), 1990, Maggio Musicale, Florence; Conducted the Orchestra of the Opéra Bastille de Paris in Symphonie Fantastique at the Spoleto Festival, 1990; Season 1992 with Lady Macbeth of Mtsensk at Paris and Milan, Honegger's Jeanne d'Arc in Paris. *Recordings:* Nielsen Symphonies and Dvořák symphonies 7 and 8 with the Gothenburg Symphony (BIS); Messiaen's Turangalilâ Symphonie; Piano Trios with his sisters Kyung-Wha and Myung-Wha Chung (Decca). *Honours:* Second Prize, Tchaikovsky International Piano Competition, Moscow, 1974; Premio Abbiati for operatic work in season 1987-88. *Address:* Opéra de Paris Bastille, 120 Rue de Lyon, 75012 Paris, France.

CHURGIN Bathia Dina, b. 9 Oct 1928, New York City, New York, USA. Musicologist. *Education:* BA, Hunter College, New York City, 1950; MA, Radcliffe College, 1952; PhD, Harvard University, 1963. *Career:* Instructor to Full Professor, Vassar College, 1952-57, 1959-71; Professor, Founding Head of Department, Bar-Ilan University, Ramat Gan, Israel, 1970-; Visiting Professor: Harvard Summer School, Northwestern University, University of North Carolina, Chapel Hill, CUNY, Queens College and Graduate Center, Tel Aviv University, The Hebrew University, Jerusalem. *Publications:* The Symphonies of G.B. Sammartini, Vol 1: The Early Symphonies, 1968; Thematic Catalogue of the Works of Giovanni Battista Sammartini, Orchestral and Vocal Music (with Newell Jenkins), 1976; Editor, Israel Studies in Musicology, II, 1980; G.B. Sammartini, Sonate a tre stromenti, A New Edition with Historical and Analytical Essays, 1981; G.B. Sammartini: Ten Symphonies, 1984. *Contributions to:* Professional journals Francesco Galeazzi's Description (1796) of Sonata Form, JAMS XXI (1968), 181-99; Beethoven's Sketches for His String Quintet, Op. 29, LaRue Festschrift (1990), 441-79; Harmonic and Tonal Instability in the Second Key Area of Classic Sonata Form, Ratner Festschrift (1992), 23-57. *Address:* Department of Musicology, Bar-Ilan University, Ramat Gan, Israel 52900.

CHUSID Martin, b. 19 Aug 1925, Brooklyn, New York, USA. Musicologist; Professor. m. Anita B Chusid, 1 son. *Education:* BA 1950, MA 1955, PhD 1961, University of California, Berkeley. *Career:* Teaching assistant 1953-55, Associate 1955-57, University of California, Berkeley; Instructor 1959-62, Assistant Professor 1962-63, University of Southern California, Los Angeles; Associate Professor 1963-68, Professor 1968-, Acting Chairman, Music Department 1966-67, 1981, 1986-87, New York University; Chairman, Music Department, Washington Square College of Arts and Sciences, 1967-70; Associate Dean, Graduate School of Arts and Sciences, 1970- 72; Director, American Institute for Verdi Studies, 1976-; Visiting Professor of Music, Boston University, 1975; University of British Columbia, 1979; Southern Methodist University, 1980; Princeton University, 1981; Brigham Young University, 1982; Principal Editor, Verdi Newsletter, 1981-. *Publications:* Schubert's Unfinished Symphony; A Monograph and Edition, 2nd Edition, 1971; A Catalog of Verdi's Operas, 1974; The Verdi Companion, with W Weaver, 1979; Editions of works by Schubert and Verdi. *Address:* 4 Washington Square Village, New York, NY 10012, USA.

CHYLINSKA Teresa Wanda, b. 20 June 1931, Wojciechowice, Poland. Musicologist; Music Editor; Writer on music. m. 1957, divorced 1960, 1 son. *Education:* MA, Musicology, Jagiellonian University, Krakow, 1949-53. *Career:* Chief, Department of Polish Music, Polish Music Publications, Krakow, 1954-89; Lecturer, Jagiellonian University and Academy of Music, 1970's; President, The Karol Szymanowski Music Society, 1979-80; Member, Scientific Board, The Chopin Society, Warsaw, 1982-. *Publications include:* First critical edition of The Complete Works of Karol Szymanowski (26 volumes Polish version, 17 volumes German-English in co-edition with Universal Edition, Vienna; A complete edition of Szymanowski's correspondence, Vol 1, 1982, Vol 2, 1993; Szymanowski's literary writings, 1989; Szymanowski's Days at Zakopane, 1982, 4th edition; Szymanowski and his Music, Popular monograph for young readers, 1990, 3rd edition; Karol Szymanowski, His Life and Works (in English), Publisher: Friends of Polish Music, USC, Los Angeles, 1993. *Contributions to:* New Grove Dictionary of Music and Musicians; Encyclopedia Muzyczna PWM. *Hobbies:* Politics; Architecture; Granddaughter. *Address:* ul Syrokomli 16 m 10, 30-102 Krakow, Poland.

CIANNELLA Giuliano, b. 25 Oct 1943, Palermo, Italy. Singer (Tenor). *Debut:* La Scala 1976, as Cassio in Otello. *Career:* Metropolitan Opera from 1979, as Don Carlos, Des Grieux in Manon Lescaut, Rodolfo, Pinkerton, Alfredo and Macduff; Guest engagements in San Francisco, as Don José 1984 and Munich, Don Carlos 1985; Covent Garden debut 1986, as Manrico in Il

Trovatore; Verona Arena, 1983, 1985 and 1988; Bregenz Festival, 1987, as Ernani; Cologne Opera, 1988, as Don José and Puccini's Des Grieux; Riccardo, Ballo in Maschera, at Parma, 1989. *Address:* c/o Teatro Regio, Via Garibaldi 16, 1-43100 Parma, Italy.

CICCOLINI Aldo, b. 15 Aug 1925, Naples, Italy. Concert Pianist. *Education:* Studied with Paolo Denza at the Naples Conservatory. *Debut:* Naples 1942, in Chopin's F Minor Concerto; Professor at the Naples Conservatory from 1947; Moved to France 1949: Professor at the Paris Conservatoire from 1971; US debut 1950, with the New York Philharmonic, playing Tchaikovsky's 1st Concerto; Many concerts with the world's leading orchestras; Recital programmes include music by Fauré, Ravel, Liszt and Debussy. *Honours:* Santa Cecilia Prize, Rome, 1948; Marguerite Long-Jacques Thibaud Prize, Paris, 1949. *Recordings:* Liszt, Années de Pelerinage and Harmonies poetiques et Religieuses; Complete piano works of Satie; Concertos by Saint-Saëns; Piano Concerto in D by Alexis de Castillon, conducted by Georges Prêtre. *Address:* c/o Conservatoire National Superiuer de Musique, 14 Rue de Madrid, 75008, France.

CIESINSKI Kristine Frances, b. 5 July 1952, Wilmington, Delaware, USA. Soprano. m. Norman Bailey, 1985. *Education:* Temple University, 1970-71; University of Delaware, 1971-72; Boston University, B.A. in voice, 1974. *Career:* New York concert debut, soloist, Handel's Messiah, 1977; European operatic debut, Baroness Freimann, Der Wildschütz, Salzburg Landestheater, 1979, singing there until 1981; member, Bremen State Opera, 1985-88; Guest appearances: Cincinnati Opera, Florentine Opera, Milwaukee, 1983, 1987; Cleveland Opera, 1985, Scottish Opera, 1985, 1989; Canadian Opera 1986; Opera North, Leeds, 1986, 1988; Augsburg Opera, 1986; Mexico City, 1986; Welsh National Opera, 1987, 1989; Bregenz Festival, 1987; Zagreb National Opera, 1988; Wexford Festival, 1988; English National Opera, 1989-93, Munich State Opera, 1989, Baltimore Opera, 1989; Winnipeg Opera, 1989, 1991; Frankfurt State Opera, 1990, 1993, New Orleans Opera, 1992, Leipzig Opera, 1992, La Scala Milan, 1992. Roles include: Medea, La Wally, Eva, Senta, Donna Anna, Tosca, Aida, Ariadne, Salome, Verdi's Lady Macbeth, Shostakovich's Lady Macbeth of Mtsensk, Erwartung, Judith from Bartók's Bluebeard, Berg's Marie, Beethoven's Leonora, Tchaikovsky's Tatiana and Salome, also many concert engagements in a repertory ranging from traditional works to contemporary scores. *Recordings:* Several. *Honours:* Gold Medal, Geneva International Competition, 1977; 1st prize, Salzburg International Competition, 1977; Salzburg International Competition, 1977. *Address:* c/o Trawick Artists Management, Inc., William Guerri, 129 West 72nd Street, New York City, NY 10023-3239, USA.

CIESINSKI Katherine, b. 13 Oct 1950, Newark, Delaware, USA. Mezzo-soprano. *Education:* Studies with Margaret Harshaw at Curtis Institute, Philadelphia. *Career:* Sang in the US premiere of Berg's 3-act Lulu; European debut 1976 at Aix-en-Provence; later sang in Asia, Israel and elsewhere in Europe; In 1988 sang in premiere of Argento's The Aspern Papers (Dallas) and La Celestine by Maurice Ohana (Paris); Metropolitan Opera debut 1988, as Nicklausse in Les contes d'Hoffmann, returning as Judith in Duke Bluebeard's Castle by Bartók; Other roles include Waltraute in Götterdämmerung, Strauss's Composer and Octavian, Brangaene in Tristan and Isolde, Britten's Lucretia, Laura in La Gioconde and Barber's Vanessa; Cassandre in Les Troyens for Scottish Opera and at Covent Garden; La Favorite (title role) in revival of original French Version, 1991. *Recordings include:* War and Peace by Prokofiev, Dukas' Ariane et Barbe Bleue, Sapho by Massenet; Pauline in The Queen of Spades (BMG). *Address:* c/o Metropolitan Opera, Lincoln Center, New York, NY 10023, USA.

CIGNA Gina, b. 6 March 1900, Angere, Paris, France.

Singer (Soprano). *Education:* Studied in Paris with Calvé, Storchio and Darcle. *Debut:* La Scala 1927, as Freia in Das Rheingold. *Career:* Sang at La Scala until 1943, notably as Turandot, La Gioconda and the leading Verdi roles; Covent Garden 1933-39, debut as Marguerite in La Damnation de Faust; Metropolitan Opera 1937-38, as Aida, the Trovatore Leonora, Donna Elvira, Santuzza and Norma; Florence 1933, 1935, 1937, in Nabucco, Alceste and L'Incoronazione di Poppea; Venice 1941, as the Kostelnička in Jenůfa; Guest appearances in Buenos Aires, Paris, Berlin, Vienna, Amsterdam and Brussels; Teacher at Toronto 1953-57 and at the Accademia Chigiana in Siena, 1957-65. *Recordings include:* La Gioconda; Turandot; Norma; Labels include Columbia, Telefunken, Cetra.

CILLARIO Carlo Felice, b. 7 Feb 1915, San Rafael, Argentina. Conductor. *Education:* Studied at the G.B. Martini Conservatory and in Odessa. *Career:* After playing as concert violinist has conducted from 1942; Formed the Orchestra da Camera in Bologna, 1946; Formed the Symphony Orchestra of the University of Tucuman in Argentina, 1948; Resident Conductor of the Orchestra Sinfonica del Estado de Buenos Aires, 1949-51; Conductor of opera seasons at Covent Garden, Glyndebourne (1961-62, L'Elisir d'Amore), Chicago (debut 1961, La Forza del Destino), San Francisco, Buenos Aires, Venice, Paris, Hamburg and Florence; Metropolitan Opera debut 1972, La Sonnambula: conducted Tosca 1985; Royal Opera Stockholm from 1980, with Macbeth, La Bohème, Tosca, Medée and Falstaff; Drottningholm Theatre 1982-84, La Cenerentola and Il Fanatico Burlato by Cimarosa; Performances of La Bohème, Il Trittico, Die Walküre, Tosca, Un Ballo in Maschera, Don Pasquale and Eugene Onegin with Australian Opera; San Francisco 1986, Lucia di Lammermoor; Bi-Centennial concerts at Sydney, 1988; Principal Guest Conductor and Music Consultant to the Australian Opera, 1988; Conducted Maria Stuarda at Stockholm, 1990; Cavalleria Rusticana and Pagliacci at Buenos Aires, 1992. *Recordings include:* Music by Carissimi, Monteverdi's Orfeo, Stradella's San Giovanni Battista, Leo's La Morte di Abele and Rossi's Giuseppe, Figlio di Giacobbe; Handel's Salve Regina and Aci, Galatea e Polifemo, Mozart's Ascanio in Alba, Lucio Silla and La Betulia liberata, with the Angelicum Orchestra of Milan. *Address:* c/o Kungliga Teatern, PO Box 16094, S-10322 Stockholm, Sweden.

CIONI Renato, b. 15 Apr 1929, Portoferraio, Elba. Singer (Tenor). *Education:* Studied at the Florence Conservatory. *Debut:* Spoleto 1956, as Edgardo in Lucia di Lammermoor. *Career:* Italian TV 1957, as Pinkerton; La Scala Milan from 1958; Spoleto 1959, in a revival of Donizetti's Il Duca d'Alba; Appearances in San Francisco and Chicago from 1961; Palermo 1963, in I Capuleti e i Montecchi by Bellini; Covent Garden 1964-65, as Cavaradossi (with Callas), the Duke of Mantua and Gabriele Adorno; Verona Arena 1966, as Cavaradossi; Engagements in Berlin, Prague, Paris, Berlin, Copenhagen, Buenos Aires, Bucharest and Edinburgh; Metropolitan Opera 1969-70. *Recordings include:* Rigoletto and Lucia di Lammermoor, with Joan Sutherland (Decca).

CIUCIURA Leoncjusz, b. 22 July 1930, Grodzisk Mazowiecki, Poland. Composer. m. Sylwia Grelich, 18 June 1967. *Education:* BA, Composition, Theory and Conducting Department, State College of Music, Warsaw, 1960. *Debut:* Concert, State College of Music, Warsaw. *Career:* Initiator and Co-founder, Polish Branch of Jeunesses Musicales movement, 1958-62; Founder, Editor, Carmina Academica musical publication. *Compositions:* Penetrations, for orchestral groups, 4 conductors and composer, 1963; Emergenza, for choirs and orchestra, 3 conductors and composer, 1963; In Infinitum II, for optional instrumental set, 1964-94; Published: Spirale 1 per uno, 1964; Spirale II per uno e piu, 1964; Creatoria I, 1964-94; Creatoria II, 1964-94; Intarsio, 1964-94; Rencontre, 1964-94; In Infinitum, 1964-94 (all with optional instruments and accompaniment). *Recordings:* Spirale I and II. *Hobbies:*

Fishing; Gathering mushrooms. *Address:* Zwirki and Wigury 5, 05-825 Grodzisk Mazowiecki, Poland.

CIVIDINO Ugo Valentino, b. 6 June 1947, Udine, Italy. Pianist; Educator. m. Franca Bertoli, 19 Sept 1981, 1 son, 2 daughters. *Education:* J. Tomadini Conservatory, Udine; Music Academy, Vienna, Austria. *Career:* Solo performances, chamber music, with Klagenfurt Landeskonservatorium String Quartet; Piano duets, with Franca Bertoli; Performances, broadcasts, throughout Europe; Master courses, France, Yugoslavia, Italy, Norway. *Compositions:* Chamber music, Trio Passepied a Quattro, piano, violin, cello (bassoon); Piano solo, in Forma Rapsodica and Competitions for the Childhood. *Recordings:* Brahms, Martinů & Francaix, piano duets with Franca Bertoli. *Contributions to:* Founder & President, Noi e la Musica, music magazine for young people. *Memberships:* Council, Association Internationale d'Education Musicale F Willeme, Lyon, France; Founder & President, Centro Ricerca Divulgazione Musicale; International Society for Music Education; Local President, 1989, Lions Club International. *Hobbies:* Photography; Research & tests, children's musical aptitude. *Address:* Via Mazzini 16, 33030 Maiano, Udine, Italy.

CLAASSEN Rene, b. 1937, Helmond, Netherlands. Singer (Tenor). *Education:* Amsterdam Conservatory, The Hague. *Debut:* Maastricht, 1960. *Career:* Sang at Bremerhaven from 1964, Kassel from 1968 as Wagner's Loge and Mime, Monostatos in Die Zauberflöte, Shuratov (From the House of the Dead) and the villains in Les Contes d'Hoffmann; Appeared in Der Ring des Nibelungen, 1989 and sang Aschenbach in Death in Venice; Amsterdam 1986, in Zemlinsky's Der Kreiderkreis; Loge and Mime at Rotterdam, 1989; Many concert appearances. *Address:* c/o Der Nederlandse Opera, Waterlooplein 22, 1011 P G Amsterdam, Netherlands.

CLAPTON Nicholas, b. 1955, Worcester, England. Singer (Counter-Tenor). *Education:* Studied at Magdalen College Oxford and with David Mason. *Debut:* Wigmore Hall London 1984, with Combattimento. *Career:* 1985 Aldeburgh Festival (Handel's Rodelinda) and Swiss Radio and TV; London recital debut 1986, at the Purcell Room; Handel's Messiah with Trevor Pinnock 1987; 1988: recitals with Combattimento and appearances in France, Germany and Spain, the Brighton Festival, Music at Oxford, and the Flanders Festival; 1989 Handel's Floridante for Cambridge University Opera Society; Towards Bach concert series on South Bank; Recital at Bologna Festival; Premiere of Barry's The Intelligence Park, Almeida; Repertoire now embraces Peri's Euridice and world premieres of operas by LeFanu and Barry; Renaissance Inte-Song and Romantic Lieder. *Recordings:* Purcell: Hail, Bright Cecilia (Unicorn); Duruflé: Requiem (CRD). *Honours:* Winner, English Song Award 1987; Winner, Heart of England International Competition for Singers, 1987. *Current Management:* Magenta (Concerts); Robert Gilder & Co. (Opera). *Address:* 4 Helen Road, Oxford, OX2 ODE, England.

CLARET Lluís, b. 10 Mar 1951, Andorra. Cellist. m. Anna Mora, 1 son. *Education:* Liceo Conservatory, Barceolona; Conservatoire Europeen, Paris; Bloomington School of Music, USA: Teachers include Enric Casals, Radu Aldulescu, Eva Janzer and Gyorgy Sebök. *Debut:* Boccherini Cello Concerto, Barcelona, 1968. *Career:* Soloist concerts with National Symphony of Washington, Moscow Philarmonic, Orchestre National de France, English Chamber Orchestra, Czech Philharmonic, under Rostropovitch, Pierre Boulez, Vaclav Neumann, and Witold Lutoslawski. Played at closing ceremony of Barcelona 92 Olympics. *Recordings include:* Bach: Complete Suites for cello solo, Auvidis Valois, 1993; Schubert: Sonata Arpeggione for cello and piano, Harmonia Mundi, 1992; Chopin: Sonata for cello and piano, Strauss: Sonata for cello and piano, Harmonia Mundi, 1991; Kodály: Sonata for cello, 1990; Schumann: Concerto for cello and orchestra, 1990; Haydn: Concerto No.1 in C minor for cello and orchestra; Boccherini: Concierto No 3 in G minor for cello and

orchestra; Dvorák: Tri, Dumky, op. 90, Trio in F minor, 1992; Other works by Joan Gunjoan, Boulez, Mendelssohn and Ravel. *Honours:* First prize: Rostropovitch Competition, 1977, Casals Competition, 1976, Bolonia Competition, 1975. *Memberships:* Barcelona Trio. *Hobbies:* Family and Friends. *Current management:* Carmen Netzel. *Address:* c/o Netzel, Pasaje Marimon, 10-4, 08021 Barcelona, Spain.

CLAREY Cynthia, b. 25 Apr 1949, Smithfield, Virginia, USA. Singer (Mezzo-soprano). *Education:* Studied at Howard University (Washington DC) and at the Juilliard School. *Career:* Sang first with the Tri-Cities Opera Company; Has sung in The Voice of Ariadne by Thea Musgrave with the New York City Opera; Boston Opera Company in the US premiere of Tippett's The Ice Break (1979) and The Makropoulos Case (1986); Binghamton, New York, 1986 in the premiere of Chinchilla by Myron Fink; UK debut at the Glyndebourne Festival 1984 as Monteverdi's Ottavia, followed by Serena in Porgy and Bess (1986); Wexford Festival 1985 and 1986, as Polinesso in Ariodante and Thomas' Mignon; Has toured with Peter Brook's version of Carmen and appeared in the 1989-90 season in concert versions of Anna Bolena (Concertgebouw, as Jane Seymour), Weill's Lost in the Stars (Almeida Festival, London) and The Ice Break (as Hanna, at the Promenade Concerts, London); Has also sung in operas by Cavalli, Mozart, Verdi, Puccini, Menotti and Offenbach; Other roles include Monteverdi's Penelope, Cavalli's Diana (L'Ormindo), Handel's Rinaldo, Zerlina, Isoletta (La Straniera), Preziosilla, Dalila, Butterfly, Nicklausse and Octavian; Sang Serena in the Covent Garden premiere of Porgy and Bess, 1992, and in Weill/Grosz Concert at the 1993 London Proms; Concert appearances include the premiere of Tippett's The Mask of Time, 1984; 3 roles in Berg's Lulu at the Festival Hall, London, 1994. *Recordings include:* CD of Porgy and Bess (EMI). *Address:* c/o Royal Opera House, (contracts), Covent Garden, London WC2, England.

CLARK Derek J, b. 22 Aug 1955, Glasgow, Scotland. Conductor; Coach; Accompanist. m. Heather Fryer, 26 April 1980, 1 daughter. *Education:* Royal Scottish Academy of Music and Drama 1972-76; Dip.Mus.Ed.(Hons) 1976; Dip.RSAM 1976; B.Mus(Hons) (First Class), University of Durham 1974-78; London Opera Centre 1976-77. *Debut:* Accompanist, Purcell Room 1976; Conductor, Welsh National Opera 1982. *Career:* Repetiteur, Staff Conductor, Welsh National Opera, 1977-; Guest Conductor, Mid Wales Opera 1989- 92; Conductor, Premiere of G Thomas Dagrau Pengwern at 1989 National Eisteddfod; Accompanist many recitals throughout Britain; Member Contemporary Music Ensemble of Wales 1991-; Guest Coach, Conductor, Welsh College of Music 1992-; Composer, Arranger performances throughout Wales, London (Westminster Abbey) and on TV. *Compositions:* Published compositions: musical and 2 one-act operas for young people, all of which have been successfully performed, several other vocal pieces, songs etc; Choral arrangements. *Honour:* Silver Medal, Worshipful Company of Musicians 1976. *Hobbies:* Reading; Origami. *Address:* 23 Baron Road, Penarth, South Glamorgan CF64 3UD, Wales.

CLARK Graham, b. 10 Nov 1941, Littleborough, Lancashire, England. Singer (Tenor). *Education:* Studied with Bruce Boyce in London and in Bologna. *Career:* Debut: with Scottish Opera in 1975; English National Opera from 1978-85; Sang with Welsh National Opera and Opera North in the United Kingdom; Extensive International Career, appearing at the Metropolitan Opera in New York each season from 1985-93; the Bayreuth Festival each season between 1981 and 1992 (where he sang over 100 performances), as well as appearances in Paris, Vienna, Berlin, Chicago, San Francisco, Munich, Zurich, Barcelona, Turin, Nice, Rome, Toronto, Amsterdam, Stockholm, Bonn, Tel Aviv and Vancouver. Has also sung in concert with many of the world's leading orchestras and at the festivals of Lucerne, Edinburgh, Brussels and the London Proms; Recorded with Philips, Decca, EMI, Erato, Teldec, the

Met and the BBC, and appears on several videos including Bayreuth performances of Die Meistersinger, Der Fliegende Holländer, and the 1992 Ring des Nibelungen, as well as the Met's Ghosts of Versailles. *Honours:* Recognized as one of the world's leading singing-actors and has been nominated three times for 'Outstanding Individual Achievement in Opera', including a 1993 Emmy nomination for his role of Bégearss in The Ghosts of Versailles; Won Olivier Award in 1986 for his portrayal of Mephistopheles in Busoni's Doctor Faust. *Address:* c/o Ingpen & Williams Ltd., 14 Kensington Court, London W8 5DN, England.

CLARK J. Bunker, b. 19 Oct 1931, Detroit, Michigan, USA. Musicologist. m. Marilyn Jane Slawson, 3 Aug 1964. *Education:* BMus 1954, MMus 1957, PhD 1964, University of Michigan. *Career:* Instructor of Organ and Theory, Stephens College, Columbia, MO, 1957-59; Lecturer in Music, University of California, Santa Barbara, 1964-65; Professor of Music History, University of Kansas, 1965-93, emeritus, 1993-. *Publications:* Transposition in Seventeenth Century English Organ Accompaniments and the Transposing Organ, 1974; Ed, Anthology of Early American Keyboard Music, 1787-1830, 1977; Ed, Nathaniel Giles: Anthems, 1979; The Dawning of American Keyboard Music, 1988; Editor, American Keyboard Music through 1865, 1990; Series editor, Bibliographies in American Music, 1975-84; Series editor, Detroit Studies in Music Bibliography, 1985-; Series editor, Detroit Monographs in Musicology/Studies in Music, 1990. *Contributions to:* American Organist; The Choral Journal; Music & Letters; Musica Disciplina; Journal of the American Musicological Society; American Music. *Address:* Music Dept, University of Kansas, Lawrence, KS 66045-2279, USA.

CLARK Judith, b. 28 Dec 1943, Washington, DC, United States of America. Executive Director, Opera Roanoke. m. Richard Lee Clark, 1 July 1967. *Education:* BA, Mary Washington College; MMus, Northwestern University; Student of Bernard Lemoine, Pauline Lindsey, Eric Larsen. *Career:* Accompanist for Marilyn Du Bow, Jonathan Mack, Ralph Evans, William Dupré, Nicholas Loren; Rossborough Festival with Nicholas Loren; Coach, Accompanist, Opera Roanoke; Adjunct Professor of Music, Roanoke College and Hollins College; Member of Trittico, Operatic Trio, 1988-91. *Honours:* Affiliate Artists Accompanist 1980; Outstanding Young Women of America 1980; Who's Who in the South and Southwest 1992. *Hobbies:* Swimming; Jogging; Gardening. *Address:* 4529 Royal Oak Drive, Roanoke, VA 24018, USA.

CLARK Richard J., b. 25 Apr 1943, Tucson, Arizona, USA. Singer (Baritone). *Education:* Studied at Academy of Vocal Arts, Philadelphia, and at the Juilliard School, New York. *Debut:* San Francisco, as Monterone in Rigoletto. *Career:* Metropolitan Opera from 1981, as Verdi's Monterone and Di Luna, Wagner's Amfortas and Kurwenal, Barnaba in La Gioconda, Michele in Il Tabarro and Gianciotto in Francesca da Rimini by Zandonai. *Address:* c/o Metropolitan Opera, Lincoln Center, NY 10023, USA.

CLARKE Paul Charles, b. 1965, Liverpool, England, Singer (Tenor). *Education:* Royal College of Music with Neil Mackie. *Career:* Many performances throughout Britain, including concerts with Bournemouth Sinfonietta, London Ensemble and Scottish Chamber Orchestra; Duke (Rigoletto), Ceprano, Fenton, the High priest, Idomeneo and Rodolfo with Welsh National Opera 1990-93; Paris debut 1991 as Fenton at Théâtre des Champs Elysées; Recent engagements as Dimitri in Boris Godunov and Rodolfo for Opera North, Alfredo and Nemorino for Scottish Opera 1993-94. *Honours:* Peter Pears Scholarship and Kathleen Ferrier Memorial Prize. *Address:* c/o John Coast Ltd, 31 Sinclair Road, London W14 ONS, England.

CLARKE Stephen David Justin, b. 21 July 1964, Thame, Oxon, England. Conductor. m. Helen Victoria Morrison. *Education:* New College, Oxford, 1977-82; BA, Music, Honours, Hertford College (organ Scholarship), Oxford University; ARCO; Diploma, Guildhall School of Music and Drama. *Career:* Conductor, Oxford Philharmonia, 1983-85; Founder, St Michael's Sinfonia, 1981; Conductor, Oxford University Opera Club, 1983-85; Conductor, Schola Cantorum of Oxford, 1985-87; Guest Conductor, Oxford Pro Musica, 1985; Guest Conductor, St Endellion Festival Orchestra, 1987; Work with: Kent Opera 1988, Geneva Grand Opera 1988, Royal Scottish Academy of Music & Drama 1988-89, British Youth Opera 1988; Assistant Chorus Master, English National Opera, 1990; Head of Music, Scottish Opera, 1993. *Honours:* Ricordi Conducting Prize, 1985-86; Guildhall Diploma of Conducting, 1986. *Hobbies:* Sailing; Squash; Windsurfing. *Address:* 5 Crown Circus, Glasgow, G12 9HB.

CLARKSON Gustav, b. 20 June 1954, London, England. Musician; Violinist. m. Micaela Comberti, 15 Aug 1980. *Education:* Royal Academy of Music, 1971-76; Mozarteum, 1976-77; Salzburg, Austria. *Career:* As member of the Bochmann Quartet from 1978-83, many appearances on the South Bank, Wigmore Hall, on BBC radio, tours in the UK and abroad; Many solo appearances including Paris and London; past member, the Endymion Ensemble, Schubert Ensemble; member, Arienski Ensemble, Rossignol, Clarkson-Munro Duo. *Recordings:* Clarinet Quintets by Brahms and Steptoe with the Bochmann Quartet and David Campbell; Britten Oboe Fantasy with Robin Canter; Howells and Dyson String Quartets with Divertimenti; Colin Matthews' Octet, Triptych and Oboe Quartet with Divertimenti. *Honours:* Royal Society of Arts Major Award for study abroad, 1976; Awarded A.R.A.M. 1991; Teaches violin at Royal Northern College of Music. *Address:* 15 Elm Park Road, London, N3, England.

CLAUSEN Jeanne, b. 16 October 1944, Los Angeles, California, United States of America. Musician (Violinist). m. John Cleveland, 2 July 1990, 1 d. *Education:* BA, Sarah Lawrence College, New York; MMus, Cleveland Institute of Music, Ohio; Juilliard School of Music, New York; Music Academy of The West, Santa Barbara; Meadowmount School of Music, New York. *Career:* Founder and Leader of Ensemble La Cetra of Milan, Italy; Was Member of Amsterdam Baroque Orchestra, Holland and Los Angeles California New Music Ensemble. *Recordings:* Numerous Recordings. *Honours:* Coleman Chamber Music Auditions in Los Angeles 1959 and 1961. *Membership:* International Lira Society. *Hobbies:* Hiking in Mountains. *Address:* Via Veneto 9/6, 20068 Peschiera Borromeo, Milan, Italy.

CLEGG John, b. 7 Nov 1928, London, England. Concert Pianist. *Education:* Latymer Upper School, London; Jesus College, Cambridge, 1946-49; Royal College of Music, piano studies with Herbert Fryer, 1949-52. *Debut:* London, 1951. *Career:* Has given recitals, concertos and broadcasts in most countries, with frequent tours of Africa, Middle East and Far East, and conserts in principal European centres; Regular performer on BBC radio and television; Pianist-in-Residence, Lancaster University, 1981-93. *Recordings:* 6 LP's for Disques Alpha, of music by British composers and by Fauré, Weber, Scriabin, Reger and Medtner. *Honours:* First Class Honours, Jesus College Cambridge, 1949; Harriet Cohen International Award, 1975; Digital Tapes of music by Ravel, Fauré, Medtner and Poulenc under Sound Steward label. *Membership:* Athenaeum Club, London. *Hobby:* Mathematics. *Current Management:* Lancaster University, Music Department. *Address:* Music Department, Lancaster University, Bailrigg, Lancaster LA1 4YW, England.

CLEMENCIC René, b. 27 Feb 1928, Vienna, Austria. Musician; Composer; Recorder Player; Harpsichordist; Conductor. m. Edda Rischka, 11 Apr 1968, 1 daughter (1 daughter from previous marriage). *Education:* PhD, University of Vienna, 1956; Old Music, J Mertin; Musical Theory, J Polnauer; Recorder with H U Staeps, Vienna and L Höffer V. Winterfeld, Berlin, W Nitschke, Berlin; Harpsichord with Eta Harich-Schneider, Vienna. *Career:*

Founder and Leader of Clemencic Consort, ensemble for early music from 1968; Editor of medieval Carmina Burana; Performances of baroque operas (First modern performances include: Draghi's L'Eternita Soggetta al Tempo, Peri's Euridice and Leopold I's Il lutto dell'universo); TV play; Concerts worldwide. *Compositions:* Maraviglia III; Sesostris II; Sesostris III; Chronos II; Bicinia Nova; Maraviglia V; Music for the Film Moliere of Ariana Mnouchkine; Musik zum Urfaust; Tolldrastische Szenen; Stufen; Musik zum Prinzen von Homburg; Missa Mundi; Unus Mundus; Requiem pro Vivis et Mortuis; Musica Hermetica; Drachenkampf; Strukturen Musica Instrumentalis; Revolution; Opus für Flöte und Streicher, 1991, Kabbala, 1992; Kammeroper, Der Berg. *Recordings:* Over 80 recordings as soloist on recorder and with consort; Numerous flute solos; Josquin Missa Hercules Dux Ferriae, Musica Sacra; Monteverdi Missa da Capella; Medieval Carmina Burana; Dufay missa Ave Regina Coelorum, missa sine Nomine, missa Caput and missa Elle Ancilla; Obrecht missa Fortuna Desperate; Ockeghem Requiem, Monteverdi Il Combattimento and Messa a 4 voce; Marcello, Sonate a Flauto Biber/Fidicinium; Fux/Dafne in Lauro, Carvalho/Testoride, Vivaldi/L'Olimpiade, Pergolesi/Stabat mater. *Publications:* Alte Musikinstrumente, 1968; Carmina Burana, 1979. *Honours:* Edison Award, 1981 (Amsterdam); Accademico della Filarmonica Romana/Ehrenmedaille der Bundeshauptstadt Wien in Gold; Record of the Year (Carmina Burana); Gramophone: Several Grand Prix des disques, Diapason d'or, KMP, Bern. *Current Management:* M Werner, Paris; Kentron Musa Promotion, Bern. *Hobbies:* Italian Literature; Collection of Sculpture; Paintings of Nazarener. *Address:* Reisnerstr. 26/7, A-1030, Vienna, Austria.

CLEMENT Roger, b. 25 July 1950, Manchester, New Hampshire, USA. Editor, Music Publishing. *Education:* BA, MA, Catholic University of America, Washington, DC, 1972; MA, Musicology, New York University, 1975. *Career:* Assistant Editor for Contemporary Music at Musikverlage H. Gerig, Cologne, and Breitkopf & Haertel, Wiesbaden, 1977-80; Chief Editor, Ahn & Simrock, Munich, 1981-87, Freelance Editor 1987-; Style Analysis, Laval University, Quebec City, 1975. *Publications:* 1957-77: Zwanzig Jahre Dokumentation Ueber Auffuehrungen und Realisationen Neuer Musik in der Bundesrepublik Deutschland, in Neue Musik in der Bundesrepublik Deutschland, Vol. 21/22, Bonn, 1980. *Honours:* BA, summa cum laude in Music, Catholic University of America, 1972; Fulbright Fellowship, 1975-76. *Membership:* International Society of Contemporary Music. *Address:* Steinsdorfstrasse 5, D-8000 Munich 22, Germany.

CLEMENTI Aldo, b. 25 May 1925, Catania, Italy. Composer. *Education:* Studied with Pietro Scarpini in Siena, at Catania and with Petrassi in Rome, 1952-54; Summer courses at Darmstadt, 1955-62. *Compositions:* Concertino in forma di variazioni 1956; Tre Studi for chamber orchestra 1957; 7 Scene for chamber orchestra 1961; Informel I-III for various instrumental combinations 1962-63; Collage I-III 1961-67; Variante A for chorus and orchestra and B for orchestra 1964; Silben for female voice, clarinet, violin and 2 pianos 1966; Concerto for wind orchestra and 2 pianos 1967; Reticolo for string quartet 1968; Concerto for piano and 7 instruments 1970; Reticolo for 12 strings 1978; Replica for harpsichord 1972; Blitz, musical action for chamber ensemble 1973; Sinfonia da camera 1974; Concerto for piano, 24 instruments and carillons 1975; Clessidra for 11 instruments 1976; Collage Jesu meine Freude, action for 8 strings, 8 winds and tape 1979; Es, rondeau in one act, produced at Teatro la Fenice, Venice 1981; AEB for 17 instruments 1983; Finale for 4 sopranos and orchestra 1984; O du Selige for orchestra 1985; Concerto for piano and 11 instruments 1986. *Address:* STAE (Italy), c/o PRS Ltd, Member Registration, 29-33 Berners Street, London W1P 4AA, England.

CLEMENTS Joy, b. 1931, Dayton, Ohio, USA. Singer (Soprano). *Education:* Studied at University of Miami and in Philadelphia and New York. *Debut:* Miami Opera 1956 as Musetta in La Bohème. *Career:* Sang 1959-72 at New York City Opera and in Pittsburgh, Cincinnati, Baltimore, San Diego, Fort Worth and Hawaii; Appeared as Mary Warren in premiere of The Crucible by Robert Ward, New York 1961; Appearances at Metropolitan from 1963; Guest engagements at Tel Aviv 1963 and Brussels 1975; Other roles have included Mozart's Despina, Pamina and Susanna, Verdi's Violetta and Gilda, Gounod's Juliette, Manon, Martha and Gershwin's Bess; Many concert appearances. *Address:* c/o Metropolitan Opera, Lincoln Center, New York, NY 10023, USA

CLEOBURY Nicholas Randall, b. 23 June 1950, Bromley, Kent, England. Conductor. m. Heather Kay, 4 Nov 1978, 1 son, 1 daughter. *Education:* Worcester College, Oxford University. *Career:* Assistant Organist, Chichester Cathedral, 1971-72; Assistant Organist, Christ Church, Oxford, 1972-76; Chorus Master, Glyndebourne, 1976-79; Assistant Director, BBC Singers, 1977-80; Freelance Conductor, with all London and BBC orchestras, all major British orchestras; Extensive work in Europe, Scandinavia, USA and Australia, 1980-; Work with English and Welsh National Operas, Opera North and Flanders Opera; Principal Opera Conductor, Royal Academy of Music, 1980-87; Artistic Director Broomhill; Numerous Recordings, Broadcasts, including CD of El Amor Brujo by Falla, with Jill Gomez; Artistic Director, Britten Sinfonia. *Honours:* Fellow, Royal College of Organists, Limpus Prize, 1968; Honorary member, Royal Academy of Music, 1985. *Current Management:* Allied Artists, 42 Montpelier Square, London, SW7 1JZ. *Hobbies:* Reading; Walking; Cricket; Food; Wine. *Address:* c/o Allied Artists, 42 Montpelier Square, London, SW7 1JZ, England.

CLEOBURY Stephen, b. 31 Dec 1948. Musician. 2 daughters. *Education:* King's School, Worcester; St John's College, Cambridge, MA, MusB, FRCM, FRCO. *Career:* Organist, St Matthew's, Northampton, 1971-74; Sub- Organist, Westminster Abbey, 1974-78; Master of Music, Westminster Cathedral, 1979-82; Director of Music, King's College, Cambridge, 1982-; Many Radio and TV appearances in United Kingdom and abroad with King's College Choir. *Recordings:* A wide range of music including that with King's College Choir and as Organist at Westminster Abbey and King's College. *Memberships:* Royal College of Organists, President 1990-92; Incorporated Society of Musicians. *Current Management:* Magenta (UK), McFarlane Artists, (USA). *Address:* King's College, Cambridge CB2 1ST, England.

CLEVE George, b. 9 July 1936, Vienna, Austria. Conductor. *Education:* Studied at Mannes College, New York, and with Pierre Monteux, George Szell, Franco Ferrara and Leonard Bernstein. *Debut:* Salzburg Festival, 1993. *Career:* Appearances with major American orchestras, including the New York Philharmonic and symphony orchestras of Chicago, Boston, Cleveland, Minnesota and San Francisco; Music Director of the San Jose Symphony and founder of the Midsummer Mozart Festival in San Francisco, 1974; Has conducted La Bohème, La Traviata, Le Nozze di Figaro and Oedipus Rex; European engagements with the Northern Sinfonia, the Vienna Symphony Orchestra and the Orchestre National de France; Flanders Festival 1990, Don Giovanni; Tour of Europe with the English Chamber Orchestra; Germany with the Stockholm Chamber Orchestra. *Honours include:* Officier, Order of Arts and Letters, from the French government; Silver Medal of Honour, City of Vienna. *Address:* c/o Van Walsum Management Ltd., 26 Wadham Road, London SW15 2LR, England.

CLIBURN Van (Harvey Lavan), b. 12 July 1934, Shreveport, Louisiana, USA. Pianist. *Education:* Studied with mother Rildia Bee Cliburn, and at Juilliard School of Music. *Debut:* Shreveport, 1940; Houston Symphony Orchestra, 1952. *Career includes:* New York Philharmonic Orchestra, 1954 and 1958; Concert pianist on tour, USA 1955-56, USSR 1958;

Appearances include Brussels, London, Amsterdam and Paris notably in music by Tchaikovsky and Rachmaninov. *Honours include:* Honorary HHD, Baylor University; Winner, 1st International Tchaikovsky Piano Competition, Moscow, USSR, 1958; In 1962 he established a Piano Competition in his name at Fort Worth, Texas. *Current Management:* Shaw Concerts Incorporated, 1995 Broadway, New York, NY 10023, USA. *Address:* 455 Wilder Place, Shreveport, LA 71104, USA.

CLOAD Julia, b. 6 Oct 1946, London, England. Musician (Pianist). *Education:* Royal College of Music, London; Liszt Academy, Budapest, Hungary; Further studies with Maria Curcio and Hans Keller. *Debut:* Wigmore Hall. *Career:* Concerto performances with Royal Philharmonic Orchestra, London Philharmonic Orchestra, Halle Orchestra, Royal Liverpool Philharmonic Orchestra, under conductors including Bernard Haitink, Sir John Pritchard, Sir Adrian Boult, James Loughran, Christopher Seaman; Recitals, Wigmore Hall, Queen Elizabeth Hall, BBC, Budapest Spring Festival; Concertos: Royal Festival Hall and Radio 3. *Recordings:* Haydn Piano Sonatas, 3 CDs, Merriman Records; Schumann Sonatas. *Hobbies:* Walking; Reading. *Address:* 1/6 Colville Houses, Talbot Road, London W11 1JB, England.

CLOZIER Christian Robert Adrien, b. 25 Aug 1945, Compiègne, France. Composer-Director, Groupe de Musique Expérimentale de Bourges. 1 daughter. *Education:* National Conservatory of Music, Paris; Practical School for Higher Studies, Paris. *Career:* Founder/director, GMEB; Director, International Festival of Music, Bourges; Organiser, International Competition of Electro-acoustic Music, Bourges; President, International Confederation of Electro-acoustic Music (ICEM); Conceptor of Music electroacoustic instruments. *Compositions include:* La Discordature; Opéra, A Vie; 22 août; Loin la Lune; Symphonie pour un enfant Seul; A la Prochaine, la Taupe; Quasars; Markarian 205; Par Pangloss Gymnopède; Le Bonheur, une idée neuve en Europe, Mon nom sous le soleil est France, le Temps scintille et le songe est savoir; Eleven spectacles multi-media. *Recordings:* La Discordatura, Pathé Marconi; Lettre à une Demoiselle; Dichotomie, Pathé Marconi; Symphonie pour un Enfant Seul, Edition GMEB; Quasars, Le Chant du Monde. *Contributions to:* Musique en Jeu no. 8, 1970; Faire 2/3, 1974; Faire 4/5, 1975; Poésie Sonore Internationale, Edition J.M. Place. *Honour:* Chevalier des Arts et Lettres, France, 1985. *Memberships:* President, International Confederation of Electroacoustic Music; administrator, Conseil National de la Musique, France. *Current Management:* Groupe de Musique Expérimentale de Bourges. *Address:* GMEB, Place André Malraux, 18000 Bourges, France.

CLURMAN Judith, b. 11 March 1953, Brooklyn, New York, USA. Conductor. m. Bruce Ruben, 15 June 1982, 1 son. *Education:* Oberlin College, 1971-73; BMus 1977, MMus 1978, The Juilliard School. *Career:* Founder, Director, The New York Concert Singers (debut 1988); Appearances on Lincoln Center's Great Performers; PBS television; Merkin Concert Hall series; Lincoln Center's Educational Concerts; Faculty, The Juilliard School, 1989; Choral Director; Chamber Music Coach; Opera Department; Guest appearances: Mostly Mozart, Classical Band, Lincoln Center Salutes the Philharmonic, Mozart Bicentennial, Voice of America, National Public Radio, WQXR Broadcasts; Conducted numerous premieres including Music by Leonard Bernstein, William Bolcoln, John Corigliano, Libby Larsen, David Diamond, Stephen Paulus, Ned Rorem and Ellen Taaffe Zwilich. *Recordings:* Koch International 1994-. *Honour:* New York Concert Singers First Prize in ASCAP-Chorus America Award, 1992. *Hobby:* Reading. *Address:* c/o The Juilliard School, Lincoln Center Plaza, New York, NY 10023, USA.

CLYNES Manfred, b. 14 Aug 1925, Vienna, Austria. Musician; Scientist (Neuroscience). m. Jan 1951, divorced 1972, 3 sons. *Education:* BEngSc, 1946, DSc, 1964, University of Melbourne, Australia; Philosophy, Columbia University, USA, 1948; MS, Piano, Juilliard School of Music, 1949, Psychology of Music, Graduate School, Princeton University, 1952-54; Studied with Olga Samaroff-Stokowski and Sascha Gorodnitzki at Juilliard; Piano, Edwin Fischer's master class, 1953; Pablo Casals, master classes in music. *Debut:* Bach Goldberg Variations, Royal Festival Hall, London, Sept. 1953. *Career:* Concert tours, Europe (Stockholm, Zurich, Copenhagen, Amsterdam, London), Australia; Performed Beethoven 1 Concerto, with orchestra, Berkshire Festival, Tanglewood; Researcher on brain function and central nervous system, regarded as world's foremost researcher of psycho-neurology of music; Inventor of CAT computer for evoked brain potentials, Musical Microstructure, and 40 patents in biomedicine. *Compositions:* 5 Sentone Songs, recorded 1975. *Recordings:* For American Sentic Association: Goldberg Variations, J.S.Bach; Diabelli Variations, Beethoven; Mozart Adagio in B minor and Sonata K 570; Beethoven opus III, Chopin Ballade in A flat, Polonaise in A flat, H Etudes. *Publications:* Sentics, the Touch of Emotion, 1977; Music, Mind and Brain, the Neuropsychology of Music, 1982; Emotions and Psychopathology, 1988. *Current Management:* ICM, 40 West 57th Street, New York, NY 10019, USA. *Address:* 19181 Mesquite Court, Sonoma, California 95476, USA.

COATES Gloria, b. 10 Oct 1938, Wausau, Wisconsin, USA. Composer. *Education:* BMus, Composition, Voice; BA, Art, Theatre; MMus, Composition, Musicology; Studied with Otto Luening and Alexander Tcherepnin, *Career:* Freelance Composer, Munich, Federal Republic of Germany, 1969- ; Organiser of German-American Contemporary Music Series, Munich and Cologne, 1971-84; Demonstrated work in vocal multiphonics, International Summer Course for New Music, Darmstadt, 1972; Compositions widely performed, Europe, USA, India, including Warsaw Autumn Festival, 1978, Musica Viva Series in Munich, East Berlin Festival, 1979, 1st International Festival of New Music in Russia, Moscow, 1981; Radio recordings include BBC-London, Swiss Romande, RAI Rome, Radio Poland, German Radio stations, Radio Johannesburg, Sweden, USA; Additional broadcasts, People's Republic of China, Finland, Spain, Portugal, Brazil, Canada, Belgium, Netherlands; Invited lectures, Harvard University, 1981, Max Mueller Bhavans, India, 1982. *Compositions include:* Music on Open Strings, 1974; String Quartet, commissioned Kronos Quartet; Orchestral piece for Next Wave Festival; Piece for harp, flute and viola for Munich Festival. *Recordings:* Pro Viva ISPV 128: Bielefelder Catalogue, Music on Open Strings, String Quartets I, II and IV. *Honours:* Music on Open Strings cited as 1 of 12 most important recorded works by living composer, International Koussevitzsky Panel, 1986. *Address:* Postfach 0661, 8 Munich 43, Germany.

COATES Leon, b. 15 June 1937, Wolverhampton, England. Lecturer in Music; Musician. m. Heather Johnston, 11 Sept 1976. *Education:* St John's College, Cambridge, 1958-62. *Career:* Broadcast of cantata A Legend's Carol on Radio Eireann, 1964; Lecturer in Music, University of Edinburgh, 1965-; Harpsichordist, Scottish Baroque Ensemble, 1970-76; Conductor, Edinburgh Symphony Orchestra, 1974-85; String quartet, song cycles and video music broadcast on Radio 3 and BBC Scotland; Organist, St Andrew's and St George's Church, Edinburgh, 1981-. *Recordings:* BBC Archive recording of Music for 2 Harpsichords, with Peter Williams. *Contributions to:* Music criticism, Scotsman, 1969-73; Review, Tempo; Article on string bass, Strad, 1986. *Hobbies:* Hill-walking; Reading; Theatre. *Address:* 35 Camely Bank Place, Edinburgh, EH4 1ER, Scotland.

COBB Nancy Goodwin, b. 12 Feb 1919, Hartford, Connecticut, USA. Teacher. m. (1) Harold Ames Dewing Jr, (2) Myron Wright, MD (3) Howard Cobb, 1 son, 1 daughter. *Education:* Milton Academy 1933-37; Smith College 1937-40; Hartt College, Hartford, Connecticut (part-time) 1955-62. *Career:* Tutoring during college years; Teacher, Piano, Hartford, Connecticut; Theory and Composition Courses at Hartt School of University of Hartford; Chair, Theory Department of Junior School of Hartt; Teacher, Piano, Juniors at Hartt. *Honours:* Theory and Composition Prize at Hartt 1961-62; BMu cum laude, 1962. *Membership:* Mu Phi Epsilon. *Hobbies:* Recorder; Gardening; Needlework; Swimming. *Address:* 500 Sea Sage Drive, Delray Beach, FL 33483, USA.

COBBE Hugh Michael Thomas, b. 20 Nov 1942, Farnham, Surrey, England. Music Librarian. m. Katherine Elizabeth Chichester, 16 Jan. 1982, 2 daughters. *Education:* BA, 1965, MA, 1968, Trinity College, Dublin; Corpus Christi College, Oxford; BA(Oxon), 1965; MA(Oxon), 1968. *Career:* Assistant Keeper, Music Manuscripts, British Museum (British Library from 1973), London, 1967-78; Head of Publications, British Library Reference Division, 1978-85; Music Librarian, British Library, 1985-. *Publications:* Edition: Samuel Wesley, Trio in F, 1973; Cook's Voyages and Peoples of the Pacific (editor), 1979. *Contributions to:* Musical Times; Hermathena; British Book News; The Library; The Book Collector; Brio; Fontes Artis Musicae; Harvard Library Bulletin. *Hobbies:* Gardening; Travel; Railways. *Address:* Fox House, North End, Newbury, Berks RG15 0AY, England.

COBOS Henry Diaz, b. 12 Apr 1931, El Paso, Texas, USA. Educator. *Education:* University of Texas, El Paso, 1948-58; BMus 1952, MMus 1955, Eastman School of Music, University of Rochester; Advanced study, University of California, Los Angeles, 1958-61. *Debut:* Ciudad Juarez, Mexico, 1944; Orchestral debut, El Paso Symphony Orchestra, 1953. *Career includes:* Faculty, UCLA summers 1961-63; Visiting Professor, UCLA summer 1988, summer 1989, fall 1989; East Los Angeles College 1969-; Chairman of Department ibid, 1975-85; Chairman and founder of Cultural Arts Committee, ibid, 1988; Programme director, Sinfonia Mexicana concerts, Inland Empire Symphony (San Bernardino, California) 1985-88; Jury, Hispanic, Women's Council Music Scholarships, Los Angeles, 1983-88; Consultant, Latino Arts Festival, UCLA, 1986-87. *Contributions to:* Associate editor, Inter-American Music Review; Contributor, Die Musik in Geschichte und Gegenwart; Notes, Music Library Association; Heterofonìa, Mexico City; Various journals. *Honours:* Award, El Paso City Council, community service, 1982; Award, Mexican Consulate/City of San Bernardino, California, contributions to Inland Empire Symphony, 1986; Award, Student Government Association, East Los Angeles College, Outstanding service, 1987-88; Congressional Award, Certificate for Outstanding Community Contributions, 1991; Certificate of Recognition, City of Monterey Park, 1991; Community Service Award, San Gabriel Valley LULAC Council, 1991; Community Award, Maravilla Area, 1991; Certificate of Recognition, ELAC Faculty Academic Senate Council, 1993. *Memberships:* President, Los Angeles College Teachers' Association, 1975-82; Executive Council, Academic Senate, East Los Angeles College, 1987-88. *Hobby:* Collecting early colonial Spanish paintings. *Address:* 1629 8th Street, Manhattan Beach, CA 90266, USA.

COBURN Pamela, b. 29 March 1955, Dayton, Ohio, USA. Singer (Soprano). *Education:* De Pauw University, Eastman School and Juilliard. *Career:* Has sung at Munich Staatsoper from 1982, Vienna from 1984; Maggio Musicale Florence 1988 as Ellen Orford in Peter Grimes; Los Angeles 1990 as Ilia in Idomeneo; Sang Saffi in Der Zigeunerbaron at Zurich and Alice Ford in Falstaff for Miami Opera 1991; Salzburg and Munich Festivals 1991, as Mozart's Countess; Sang Ellen Orford in a production of Peter Grimes by Tim Albery, Munich 1991; Other roles include Fiordiligi, Rosalinde in Die Fledermaus and Lauretta in Gianni Schicchi. *Recordings:* Honegger's King David; Siebel in Faust, Mozart's L'Ica del Cairo and Mazelline in Fidelio; Zemlinsky's Traumgorge; First Lady in Die Zauberflöte; Flowermaiden in Parsifal conducted by Barenboim. *Honours:* Prizewinner at ARD Competition Munich 1980

and Metropolitan Auditions of the Air 1982. *Address:* c/o Bayerische Staatsoper, Postfach 100148, 8000 Munich 1, Germany.

COBURN Robert James, b. 29 Oct 1949, Montebello, California, USA. Composer; Educator. m. Jeanne N Ashby, 12 May 1974. 1 son. *Education:* MA, Composition, University of California at Berkeley; BMus in Composition, University of the Pacific; PhD in composition (ABD), University of Victoria. *Career:* Composition Commissions: Sun River Music Festival; San Francisco New Music Ensemble; Oregon Coast Music Festival; Sound-Art Environment Comm: Oregon Convention Center (landscape); Henry Gallery, Seattle. Performances: Festival of New Music, Roulette, NY; Forum '82 International Festival, NY; Electronic Music Plus Festival. *Compositions:* Traces (Star Map I) for viola and computer sound; Staursahng for live electronic music & visual images; Cantos for chamber orchestra; Bell Circles II, permanent sound environment, Oregon Convention Center; Luminous Shadows for cello, piano and percussion, 1992-; Songs of Solitude for chorus; Ellipse for solo flute. *Contributions to:* Portland Review; Prologue; Leonardo Music Journal. *Honour:* Oregon Artists Fellowship, 1978. *Memberships:* International Society for the Arts, Sciences and Technology; Computer Music Association. *Hobbies:* Hiking; Cooking; Reading. *Address:* Conservatory of Music, University of the Pacific, Stockton, CA 95211, USA.

COCHRAN James B, b. 11 Feb 1956, DuBois, Pennsylvania, USA. Organist; Conductor. *Education:* BMus (Hons), Susquehanna University, Pennsylvania; MMus and Doctor of Musical Arts, Eastman School of Music of University of Rochester, New York; Architecture and Modern British Literature at University College, Oxford University, England. *Career:* Director of Music at Vanderbilt Presbyterian Church, Naples, Florida where he conducts the 50 voice Chancel Choir, the Handbell Choir and a fully-graded children's choir programme; Coordinator and Performer in church's three concert series which he inaugurated in 1991; Founder-Director of The Philharmonic Center Chorale, an 80 voice auditioned chorus which performs with The Naples Philharmonic and as a separate musical ensemble of the Center; Resident Organist of The Naples Philharmonic and Chairman of the inaugural Naples International Organ Festival in June 1993; Organ recitalist who has performed throughout the United States, Canada, Great Britain and Mexico; Pianist for German baritone Hermann Prey, tenor Seth McCoy, instrumentalists from The Naples Philharmonic anmd local singers; Guest Conductor of The Naples Philharmonic in the December Holiday Pops concerts with The Philharmonic Center Chorale, 1993-94. *Memberships:* American Guild of Organists; Presbyterian Association of Musicians; American Guild of English Handbell Ringers; American Choral Directors Association; Westfield Center for Early Keyboard Studies; Hymn Society of America; Guild of Temple Musicians; Phi Mu Alpha Sinfonia; Phi Sigma Kappa. *Hobbies:* Aerobics; Cooking. *Address:* 2334 Naples Trace Circle No. 7, Naples, FL 33942, USA.

COCHRAN William, b. 23 June 1943, Columbus, Ohio, USA. Singer (Tenor). *Education:* Studied with Martial Singher at the Curtis Institute, Philadelphia, and with Lauritz Melchior and Lotte Lehmann in California. *Career:* Sang Wagner roles in San Francisco and Mexico City; Lieder recitals and concerts in North America; Many appearances in Europe from 1967, notably in Hamburg and Frankfurt: roles include Max in Der Freischütz, Jason in Medée, Otello, Herod in Salome and Dmitri in Boris Godunov; Concert with the New York Philharmonic 1971; Covent Garden debut 1974, as Laca in Jenůfa; San Francisco 1977, as Tichon in Katya Kabanova; Appearances in operas by Busoni, Janáček, Zimmermann, Shostakovich and Stravinsky (Tom Rakewell at Frankfurt 1983); Sang Bacchus in Ariadne auf Naxos at the Metropolitan Opera, 1985; Deutsche Oper Berlin, 1989 Schreker's Die Gezeichneten; Season, 1988-89 at Dusseldorf; Sang Siegfried in Paris and Brussels, 1991; Zimmermann's

Die Soldaten at Strasbourg and Tichon (Katya Kabanova), Los Angeles; The Councillor in The Nose by Shostakovich, Frankfurt City Opera; Title role, Otello for Welsh National Opera, May 1990; Season 1992 as Samson at Amsterdam and Schoenberg's Aron (concert performance) at the Edinburgh Festival; Sang Aegisthus in Elektra at the First Night of the 1993 London Proms. *Recordings:* Mathis der Maler and Act I of Die Walküre (EMI); Doktor Faust by Busoni (Deutsche Grammophon); Mahler's 8th Symphony (Philips). *Address:* c/o Welsh National Opera, John Street, Cardiff, CF1 4SP, Wales.

COECK Louis Jan, b. 19 Sept 1944, Beerzel, Belgium. Violoncellist; Composer. *Education:* Violoncello and General Music Education, Conservatoria: Antwerp, Brussels, Liege, Belgium. *Career:* Violoncellist, Antwerp Opera, 1965-88. *Compositions:* Simphonic Orchestra; 2 Operas, The Fox and Der Schub; Concertos for Clarinet, French Horn, Tuba, Trombone; Lieder; Arrangements for Clarinet-Choir, Chamber Music. *Recordings:* Clarifonia, From J S Bach to L J Coeck, The Walter Bdeykens Clarinet-Choir, 1986 Rene Gailly International Productions. *Honour:* 1988 Chamber Opera Der Schub, Antwerp, Belgium. *Address:* Samadet, F-33 730 Noaillan, France.

COELHO Eliane, b. 1950, Rio de Janeiro, Brazil. Singer (Soprano). *Education:* Studied in Rio and Hanover. *Career:* Sang at Landestheater Detmold from 1974 as Verdi's Violetta and Nannetta, Mozart's Constanze, Zdenka in Arabella and Liu in Turandot; Stadttheater Bremen from 1976, as Norina in Don Pasquale, Mozart's Susanna, Euridice, Fiorilla, Il Turco in Italia and Lulu; Sang at Frankfurt am Main from 1984 and appeared as guest in Turin as Lulu; Further engagements at Aachen, the Vienna Volksoper and the Bregenz Festival, Giulietta in Les Contes d'Hoffmann, 1988; Sang Donna Anna in Don Giovanni at the Teatro Municipal, Rio de Janeiro, 1991; Vienna Volksoper 1992, as Abigaille in Nabucco. *Address:* Stadtische Buhnen, Untermainanlage 11, 6000 Frankfurt am Main, Germany.

COEN Massimo, b. 11 Mar. 1933, Rome, Italy. Violinist; Composer. m. Mirella Thau, 2 sons, 1 daughter. *Education:* Law Degree, Rome University; Violin Diploma, St Cecilia Conservatory, Rome; Private study of chamber music and violin. *Career:* Founder, Chamber Music Groups; 1 Solisti di Roma, 1961 and Quartetto Nuova Musica, 1963, giving concerts & radio performances throughout Europe; Tour of USA and Canada as soloist with Cameristica Italiana, 1969; Founder, Music School, Rome; Teacher, National Academy of Dance; Discoverer, Editor and Performer of numerous ancient Italian musical MSS; Quartetto II, 4 Temperamenti, 1987; Divertimento I, flute and strings, 1988; Divertimento II, La Marsiguese, 1989; Violin-Concerto, Savdades de Rio, 1991. *Compositions:* C'Era una Volta, 1979; Intergrazion, 1980; Dosilado, 1983; Nascite, 1983; Peav Suite, 1983; Didone, 1983; La Donna Senz'ombra, 1984; Il Rovescio della Medaglia, 1984; Sophitour, 1985; Introduzione e Valzer in Do, 1985; Quartetto per Archi No 1, 1986. *Recordings:* of Baroque and Contemporary Music; Massimo Coen works - Edippan Rome (PAN PRC S20-63). *Contributions to:* Mondo Operao. *Memberships:* Professional Associations and Councils. *Honour:* Member, International Jury, Gaudeamus Foundation Competition, Rotterdam, 1976. *Address:* Via Ipponio 8, 00183 Rome, Italy.

COERTSE Mimi, b. 12 June 1932, Durban, South Africa. Singer (Soprano). *Education:* Studied in Johannesburg and in Vienna, with Josef Witt. *Debut:* With the Vienna Staatsoper in Naples, as a Flowermaiden in Parsifal, 1955. *Career:* Basle 1956, as the Queen of Night; Tour of South Africa and appearances at the Salzburg Fesival as Constanze in Die Entführung, 1956; Member of the Vienna Staatsoper from 1957; Glyndebourne Festival 1957, as Zerbinetta; Salzburg 1960, as the Queen of Night and in Mahler's 8th Symphony; Guest appearances in London, Cologne, Brussels, Frankfurt and Munich; Sang

Mozart's Countess in Pretoria, South Africa, 1989. *Recordings include:* Fiakermilli in Arabella (Decca).

COGEN Pierre, b. 2 Oct 1931, Paris, France. Organist; Composer; Music Professor. m. Michele Vermesse, 5 July 1986. *Education:* Baccalaureat, Classical studies, Paris, 1950-51; Higher studies in philosophy, Paris, 1957-59; Cathedral Music School for Children, 1944-51; Organ study with Jean Langlais, Schola Cantorum; Certificate of Competence as Professor of Organ at National Conservatories; CAPES, Music Education (Secondary). *Career:* Liturgical Organist, 1945-; Director of Children's Choir, 1952-65; Concert Organist, 1959-; Professor of Organ and Music Education, 1961-; Assistant to Jean Langlais, Sainte Clotilde and Schola Cantorum, 1972; Organist, Basilique Sainte Clotilde, Paris, 1988-. *Compositions:* Pieces for organ, published in Das neue Orgelalbum II, Universal Edition (Vienna) 1986; Pieces for organ, published in Pedals Only, Universal Edition, 1988; Pieces for organ published by Editions Combre, Paris: Offrande, 1990, Nocturne, 1992, Deux Chorals, 1992; Various unpublished works. *Recordings:* Organ works of Jean Langlais, Tempo FR 760310 and CD Cybelia; Sept Chorals, Soèmes Pour Les Sept Paroles du Christ de Charles Tournemire, (Cybélia, CY 883). *Honours:* Prizes for Organ and for Composition, Schola Cantorum. *Membership:* SACEM. *Address:* 83 Place des Fringilles, Cernay-la-Ville, 78720 Dampierre, France.

COGHILL Harry MacLeod, b. 14 Apr 1944, Edinburgh, Scotland. Opera and Concert Singer (Bass). m. Anna Sweeny, 9 Apr 1970, 1 son, 1 daughter. *Education:* Royal Manchester College of Music, studied singing with Frederick Cox, 1967-71; ARMCM, Teaching and Performing; Studied with Yvonne Rodd-Marling, 1976-82. *Debut:* With English National Opera, Seneca in Monteverdi's L'Incoronazione di Poppea, 1972. *Career:* Concert tour of North America, 1965; Member of Glyndebourne Festival Chorus, 1970, 1971; Principal Bass, English National Opera, 1971-79; Created several roles in contemporary operas; Extensive repertoire in all periods of opera and oratorio; Freelance appearances with English Music Theatre, Handel Opera, Kent Opera, Opera 80 and other English companies, 1979-; Appearances in Festivals at Aldeburgh, Belfast, Dortmund, Exeter, Munich, Vienna; Founder, A Song for Ockenden, concert series for The Ockenden Venture, in aid of refugee children, 1980. *Contributions to:* Educational supplements. *Honours:* Imperial League of Opera Prize and Ricordi Prize, Royal Manchester College of Music, 1970. *Memberships:* Incorporated Society of Musicians; British Actors Equity; Lecturer in Singing School of Music, University of Auckland, New Zealand 1987. *Hobbies:* Golf; Books; Tandem Riding. *Address:* Derryheen, Hook Heath Road, Woking, Surrey GU22 0LB, England.

COHEN Albert, b. 16 Nov 1929, New York City, USA. Professor, Music. m. Betty Joan Berg, 1 son, 1 daughter. *Education:* BS, Juilliard School of Music (Violin), 1951; AM, PhD, Musicology, New York University, 1959; University of Paris, France, 1956-57. *Career:* Professor Theory-Musicology, University of Michigan, 1960-70; Professor, Music, Chairman SUNY, Buffalo, 1970-73; Professor, Music, Chairman, Stanford University, 1973-; Named Wm H. Bonsall Professor of Music, 1974. *Publications:* Translator, Editor, G.G. Nivers, Treatise on the Composition of Music, 1962; Editor, E. Moulinie, Three Fantasies, 1963; Translator, Editor, E. Loulie, Elements on Principles of Music, 1965; Co- Author, Anthology of Music for Analysis, 1965; Editor, J. Millet, La Belle Methode 1973; Author, Music in the French Royal Academy of Sciences, 1981; Co-author, Music in the Royal Society of London 1660-1806, 1987. *Contributions to:* Professional journals. *Memberships include:* Executive Board, Council Member, Chairman, Local Arrangements Committee and Programme Committee, at National meetings, American Musicological Society; Société Française de Musicologie, 1963. *Address:* Department of Music, Stanford University, Stanford, CA 94305, USA.

COHEN Arnaldo, b. 22 Apr 1948, Rio de Janeiro, Brazil. Concert Pianist. 1 son, 2 step children. *Education:* Engineering University of Rio de Janeiro; Graduate in Piano and Violin, School of Music, Federal University of Rio de Janeiro. *Debut:* Royal Festival Hall, London, England, 1977. *Career:* Appearances: Albert Hall, Barbican, and Queen Elizabeth Hall and Wigmore Hall, London; La Scala, Milan, Italy; Concertgebouw, Amsterdam; Musikverein, Vienna; Performed in the Amadeus Piano Trio, 1988-92; Served on the Jury of Busoni Competition, Liszt Competition; Concerts under Menuhin, Tennstedt, Sanderling, Masur; Master classes in Europe, USA and South America. *Recordings:* Chopin Solo (2nd Scherzo, 4th Ballade, Allegro de Concert, Largo, Bolero) for Ricordi, Liszt Solo (B minor Sonata, Dante Sonata, Scherzo and March) for IMP Classics. *Recordings:* TV and Radio recordings: BBC, Dutch, German, Italian and others. *Memberships:* Lectureship as Tutor in Piano, Royal Northern College of Music, 1991. *Honours:* 1st Prize, Beethoven Competition, 1970; 1st Prize, Busoni Piano Competition, Italy, 1972; Appointed to the Broadwood Trust Fellowship, newly established, at the Royal Northern College of Music, 1992. *Current Management:* Anglo Swiss Management. *Hobbies:* Chess; Football. *Address:* 4 Coonnaught Square, London W2 2HG, England.

COHEN Isidore (Leonard), b. 16 Dec 1922, New York City, USA. Violinst; Teacher. m. Judith Goldberg, 1 son, 1 daughter. *Education:* Studied violin with Ivan Galamian; Chamber music with Felix Salmond and Hans Letz; BS, Juilliard School of Music, 1948. *Career:* Member, Schneider String Quartet, 1952-55; Juilliard String Quartet, 1958-66; Beaux Arts Trio, 1968-; Appearances as Soloist with orchestras and as a recitalist; Associated with, Marlboro (Vt) Music School and Festival, 1957-; Teacher, Juilliard School of Music, 1957-65; Mannes College of Music, 1970-88. *Recordings:* Numerous discs as member of Beaux Arts Trio. *Honours:* Various awards as member of Beaux Arts Trio; Career highlighted in N Delblanco's book, The Beaux Arts Trio: A Portrait, 1985. *Address:* c/o Columbia Artists Management Inc, 165 West 57th Street, New York, NY 10019, USA.

COHEN Joel (Israel), b. 23 May 1942, Providence, Rhode Island, USA. Conductor; Lutenist; Writer; Lecturer. *Education:* BA, composition and musicology, Brown University, 1963; MA, Harvard University, 1965; Studied theory and composition with Nadia Boulanger, Paris, 1965-67. *Career:* Director, Boston Camerata, 1968-; Guest conductor at various music festivals, (Aix-en-Provence, Strasbourg, Tanglewood); Lecturer, Early Music Performance at USA and European universities and conservatories; Specialist in medieval, Renaissance and Baroque music. *Recordings:* With Boston Camerata and Cambridge Consort; Grand Prix du Disque, 1989. *Address:* c/o The Aaron Concert Management, 729 Boylston Street Suite 206, Boston, MA 02116, USA.

COHEN Raymond, b. 27 July 1919, Manchester, England. Musician - Violinist. m. 8 Mar. 1953, 1 son, 1 daughter. *Education:* Fellow, Royal Manchester College of Music; Honorary, Royal College of Music. *Debut:* As a child. *Career:* International soloist, having played with major orchestras in many parts of the world; Leader of many orchestras including: Royal Philharmonic Orchestra, 1959-65; Violinist, Cohen Trio; Soloist on BBC radio and television. *Recordings:* Violinist, Delius's Double Concerto, with Royal Philharmonic Orchestra, Pye; Soloist, Robert Farnon's Rhapsody, DeLysé; Saint-Saëns's Introduction and Rondo Capriccioso, RCA; Vivaldi's Concerto for 2 violins and orchestra, RCA. *Honours:* 1st Prizewinner, Carl Flesch International Violin Competition, 1945. *Membership:* Incorporated Society of Musicians. *Hobbies:* Antique furniture; Theatre. *Address:* 6 Alvanley Gardens, London NW6 1JD, England.

COHEN Robert, b. 15 June 1959, London, England. Concert Cellist. m. Rachel Smith, 1 Aug 1987. *Education:* Guildhall School of Music, 1975-77; Cello Studies with William Pleeth, André Navarra, J. Du Pré,

M. Rostropovich. *Career:* Royal Festival Hall Debut, Boccherini Concerto, aged 12; London Recital Debut, Wigmore Hall, aged 17; Invited to Tanglewood Festival, USA, 1978; First Tour of USA, 1979; Concerts in Europe and Eastern Europe, 1979-; Concerts World Wide with major orchestras and eminent conductors, 1980-; many TV appearances and Radio broadcasts; Performs on Bonjour Stradivarius Cello dated 1692. *Recordings:* Elgar Cello Concerto; Dvořák Cello Concerto; Grieg Sonata; Rodrigo Conceirto en modo Galante; Virtuoso Cello Music; Beethoven Triple Concerto; Dvořák Complete Piano Trios with Cohen Trio; Schubert String Quintet with Amadeus Quartet; Tchaikovsky, Rococo Variations; Franck Sonata. *Memberships:* Institute of Advanced Motorists; Incorporated Society of Musicians; Patron, Beauchamp Music Club; Fellow of Purcell School of Music. *Honours:* Suggia Prize 1967-72; Young Concert Artists N.Y. 1978; Piatigorsky Prize 1978; UNESCO Prize Czech, 1980. *Hobbies:* Photography; Squash; Driving Fast Cars; Computers. *Current Management:* Intermusica Artists' Management. *Address:* Intermusica Artists' Management, Grafton House, 2/3 Golden Square, London W1R 3AD, England.

COHN Arthur, b. 6 Nov 1910, Philadelphia, Pennsylvania, USA. Administrator; Conductor; Publishing Executive; Writer on Music; Composer. *Education:* Combs Conservatory of Music, Philadelphia, 1920-28; University of Pennsylvania; Studied Composition with Rubin Goldmark, Juilliard Graduate School, New York, 1933-34; Studied with William F Happich; Violin with Sascha Jacobinoff, 1930-31. *Career:* Director, Edwin A Fleisher Music Collection, Free Library of Philadelphia, 1934-52; Head, Music Department, Free Library of Philadelphia, 1946-52; Executive Director, Philadelphia Settlement Music School, 1952-56; Conductor, Symphony Club of Philadelphia, 1942-65; Haddonfield (NJ) Symphony Orchestra, 1958-92; Head, symphonic and foreign music, Mills Music Company, 1956-66; Director, serious music, MCA Music, 1966-72; Carl Fischer, 1972-; Lecturer music, USA; Wrote music criticism; Appearances on radio and television. *Compositions:* 5 string quartets, 1928-45; 5 Nature Studies for Orchestra, 1932; The Pot-bellied God for Baritone and String Quartet, 1937; Suite for Viola and Orchestra, 1937; Music for Ancient Instruments, 1938; 4 Symphonic Documents, 1939; Quintuple Concerto for 5 Ancient Instruments and Modern Orchestra, 1940; The 12 for Narrator and String Quartet, 1940; Flute Concerto, 1941; Variations for Clarinet, Saxophone and String Orchestra, 1945; Music for Bassoon, 1947; Quotations in Percussion for 103 Percussion Instruments and 6 Players, 1958; Kaddish for Orchestra, 1964; Percussion Concerto, 1970. *Recordings:* Kaddish for Orchestra (Royal Philharmonic Orchestra). *Publications:* The Collector's Twentieth-Century Music in the Western Hemisphere, 1961; Twentieth-Century Music in Western Europe, 1965; Musical Quizzical, 1970; Recorded Classical Music: A Critical Guide to Compositions and Performances, 1981; Encyclopedia of Chamber Music, 2 Vols, 1994; Music Mind-Benders, 1992. *Address:* c/o Carl Fisher Inc, 62 Cooper Square, New York, NY 10003, USA.

COHN James (Myron), b. 12 Feb 1928, Newark, New Jersey, USA. Composer; Musicologist; Inventor. m. Eileen B. Wions, 3 Sept 1979. *Education:* BSc 1949, MSc 1950, Juilliard School of Music; Postgraduate studies in Electronic Music, Hunter College, New York; Study of Musical Composition with Roy Harris, Wayne Barlow, and Bernard Wagenaar. *Career:* Musicologist, American Society of Composers, Authors and Publishers, 1954-84; Inventor of various patented control devices for electronic musical instruments. *Compositions include:* Publications: Symphonies Nos 3-8; A Song of the Waters; Variations on the Wayfaring Stranger; Variations on John Henry; The Little Circus; Sonata for Flute and Piano; Statues in the Park (choral); Concerto for Clarinet and String Orchestra, 1986. *Recordings include:* Concerto da Camera; Quintet for Winds; Little Overture; Sonatina for Clarinet and Piano; Sonata for Flute and Piano; Serenade, for flute, violin and cello; Trio for piano, violin and cello; Mount Gretna

Suite, for chamber orchestra; Recordings for radio, television and films. *Contributions to:* Library Journal (book reviews). *Honours include:* Queen Elisabeth of Belgium Prize, for Symphony No 2, 1953; AIDEM Prize, for Symphony No 4. *Memberships:* American Federation of Musicians; American Society of Composers, Authors and Publishers; Songwriters Guild of America. *Address:* 38-62 240th Street, Little Neck, NY 11363, USA.

COHRS Gunnar, b. 21 Sept 1965, Hameln, Niedersachsen, Germany. Conductor; Flutist; Musicologist. *Education:* Hochschule für Künste Bremen 1989-94. *Debut:* Conductor, orchestra of the Music School for Youth in Hameln, 1984. *Career:* Conductor of Hameln Youth String Orchestra, 1984-90; Assistant to Nicola Samale in performing Bruckner's Ninth in Katovice, Poland with National Broadcasting Orchestra; 1986-93 Co-author of the performing version of the Finale of Bruckner's Ninth; 1991-93 work with Orchestra of Hochschule für Künste, Bremen. *Compositions:* Trois pastorales pour Flute et Clarinette op.3; Choralvorspiel für Orgel op.2; Edition of three unknown works by Arthur Honegger, (Semiramis, The Tempest Suite, La Nuit est si profonde). *Publications:* Bruckner: Performing version of the Finale (IX Symphony) w John Phillips, Nicola Samale and Giuseppe Mazzuca-Adelaide, 1988; Zahlenphänomene in Bruckners Symphonik in: Bruckner-Jahrbuch, 1989/90, Wien, 1993. *Contributions to:* Der musikalische Architekt Anton Bruckner, in: Neue Zeitschrift für Musik, Mainz, 7/8, 1990. *Membership:* Internationale Brucknergesellschaft Wien. *Hobbies:* Sports; Cinema; Chess; Billiards; Books; Collecting unknown orchestral works. *Address:* Hamburger Strasse 250, 28 205 Bremen, Germany.

COKER Paul, b. 1959, London, England. Pianist. *Education:* Began piano studies aged 5 and entered Yehudi Menuhin School 1967, piano with Louis Kentner. *Career:* Won National Federation of Music Societies' Concert Award 1978 and soon gave several London recitals, as well as concerts in France, Germany, Belgium, Holland, the USA, Canada and India; further study at Tanglewood, USA, from 1980; won the Jackson Master Award there; has played with most leading British orchestras and with the Berlin Philharmonic; the Grieg Concerto with the Belgian National Symphony; many recitals with Yehudi Menuhin in Europe, the United States, Far East and Australia. *Address:* c/o Anglo-Swiss Ltd., 4/5 Primrose Mews, 1a Sharpleshall Street, London NW1 8YW, England.

COLANERI Joseph, b. 14 Dec 1955, Jersey City, New Jersey, USA. Chorus Master; Conductor. m. Susan Nelson, 25 Oct 1980. *Education:* BA New York University, 1977; MM, Westminster Choir College, 1980. *Career:* Chorus Master, Conductor, New York City Opera, 1983-; Chorus Master, New Jersey State Opera, 1980-87. *Recordings:* Chorus Preparation, Satyagraha, Philip Glass, CBS label; Chorus Preparation, Candide, Leonard Bernstein, New World Records. *Membership:* Phi Beta Kappa. *Hobby:* Cooking. *Address:* 719 Ridgewood Road, Millburn, NJ 07041, USA.

COLD Ulrik, b. 15 May 1939, Copenhagen, Denmark. Singer (Bass). *Education:* As a Singer, privately educated in Copenhagen & Aarhus; Bachelor of Laws from the Copenhagen University. *Career:* Sang in concert from 1963, then opera in Copenhagen; Engaged at Kassel 1969-71; Komische Oper Berlin 1971, as Massenet's Don Quixote; Sang Sarastro in the Bergman film version of Die Zauberflöte; Intendant of the Royal Opera Copenhagen 1975-77; Baroque repertory concerts in France, Germany, Holland, Switzerland and Scandinavia; Operatic roles include Wagner's Marke, Landgraf and Gurnemanz; Verdi's Padre Guardiano and Zaccharia; Roles in works by Handel, Monteverdi and Rameau; US debut, San Francisco as Sarastro, 1980; Alazim in Zaide, Wexford Festival, 1981; Sang at Teatro Comunale Bologna, 1987; The General in The Gambler by Prokofiev, English National Opera, 1990. *Recordings:* Armide by Lully (Erato); Admeto by Handel (EMI); Rameau's Hippolyte et Aricie and Handel's Xerxes (CBS);

L'Incoronazione di Poppea (Fonit-Cetra); St Matthew Passion by Bach (Harmonia Mundi); Ulrik Cold Sings Carl Nielsen (Amber); Schnittke's Faust-Cantata (BIS). *Address:* c/o Allied Artists Agency, 42 Montpelier Square, London SW7 1JZ, England

COLDING-JØRGENSEN Henrik, b. 21 Mar 1944, Riisskov, Denmark. Composer; Organist; Pedagogue; Choir Leader. m. Birgit Nielsen, 1966-87, Mette Bramsø, 1992, 1 daughter. *Education:* Organist, 1966, Organ Pedagogue, Royal Danish Conservatory. *Career:* Organ teacher; Teacher of Musical Theory; Organist; Choir Leader; Producer of Radio and TV programmes; Composer; Chairman of Board, Holstebro Electronic Music Studio, 1977-85; Member, Musical Committee, Roskilde County, 1979-87; Member of Committee of Representative of State Music Council, 1981-91; Member of Committee of Representatives of State Art Council, 1981-85; Member, Danish Arts Council, 1981-84. *Compositions include:* Ave Maria, 1974; Balances, 1974; To Love Music, 1975; Victoria Through the Forest, 1975; Boast, 1980; Dein Schweigen, 1982; Recitativ and Fuga; An Die Nachgeborenen II, 1984; Du Sollst nicht, 1984; Sic Enim, 1985; Nuup Kangerlua, 1985; Partita, aria e minuetto, 1986; Le Alpi; nel Cuore, 1988; 2 songs by Keats, 1988; Nunc Est, 1989; The Soul and the Butterfly, 1990; Babylon, 1991; As a Traveller, 1992; Krystal. Metamorfose, 1993. *Honours:* Recipient, various bursaries, prizes and commissions; Concours International de Composition Musicale Opera et Ballet, Geneva, 1985. *Memberships:* Danish Composer Society, member of Board, 1981-91; Danish ISCM, Member of Board until 1982; Danish Organist and Cantor Society; Board Member, Danish Organist and Cantor Society, 1992. *Hobby:* Music. *Address:* Rønnevangshusene 71, 2.TH. DK-2630 Taastrup, Denmark.

COLE Hugo, b. 6 July 1917, London, England. Composer; Critic. *Education:* Winchester; King's College, Cambridge; Royal College of Music, with Ivor James, R.O. Morris and Herbert Howells; Further study with Nadia Boulanger in Paris; Freelance composer and music critic for The Guardian from 1964. *Compositions:* Operas: The Tunnel 1959; The Falcon 1968; Children's operas Asses Ears, A Statue for the Mayor, Persephone, Flax into Gold and The Fair Traders; Orchestral: Concerto for flute, viola and strings 1953; Concerto for horn and chamber orchestra 1954; Black Lion Dances 1962; Winter Meetings for chamber orchestra 1975; Choral: A Company of Fools 1954; Of the Nativitie of Christ 1956; Baron Munchausen 1963; Jonah 1965; Chamber music and songs. *Address:* c/o The Guardian, 119 Farringdon Road, London EC1, England.

COLE Maggie, b. 1952, USA. Harpsichordist; Pianist. *Career:* Performed widely in USA, then Europe (from 1974); Gave the 6 Partitas by Bach at the Wigmore Hall, 1985, appeared at Bath, Cheltenham, King's Lynn Festivals; Frequent broadcasts on Radio 3; Overseas engagements at Seattle, Chicago, Bruges, Cologne, Tallinn and Moscow; Collaborations with Lisa Beznosiuk (Flute) in music by Handel, J S Bach, Locatelli, Philidor, Hummel, Clementi and Beethoven; New York debut March 1991; With Simon Standage (Baroque and classical violins) in music by Corelli, J S Bach, Leclair, Mondonville, Mozart, Pinto and Beethoven: the Kreutzer Sonata at the Purcell Room, 1988; With Nigel North (lute and guitar) in music by Weber, Hummel, Diabelli, Beethoven, Guiliani and Sor: Wigmore Hall concerts and tours of Poland, Israel, the USSR; With Steven Isserlis (cello) from 1986, notably in sonatas by Boccherini. *Recordings include:* Scarlatti Sonatas; Poulenc's Concert Champêtre and Bach's Goldberg Variations (Virgin Classics); Boccherini Cello Sonatas; Soler Sonatas on harpsichord and fortepiano. *Address:* c/o Robert White Management, 182, Moselle Avenue, London N22 6EX, England.

COLE Ulric, b. 9 Sept 1905, New York, New York, USA. Composer; Pianist. *Education:* University of California at Los Angeles; Parents both professional musicians and mother first piano teacher, 1910-12;

Studied with Homer Grunn, pianist-composer, 1912-23; Institute of Musical Art, New York, piano with George Boyle, advanced counterpoint with Percy Goetschius, 1923-24; 2 fellowships, Juilliard Graduate School, piano, Josef Lhevinne, composition Rubin Goldmark, 1924-27; 6 months study with Nadia Boulanger in Paris, 1927. *Career:* Appearances with parents as a child; 15 weeks tour of Midwest, 1924; Compositions presented at 1st annual Festival of American Women Composers, Washington, DC, 1925; Radio broadcasts; Many 1st public performances with composer at the piano; 7 appearances with Connecticut String Quartet (Quintet for Piano and Strings), including Kennedy Center, Washington DC, 1974-77; Divertimento for string orchestra and piano, 1939 and Concerto No. 2 for piano and orchestra, 1946 (Cincinnati Symphony, Goossens Conducting). *Compositions include:* For piano: Above the Clouds, 1924; Purple Shadows, 1928; Metropolitones, 1943; Three Vignettes, 1936; For 2 pianos: Man-About-Town, 1947; Divertimento for Two Pianos (commissioned transcription.) Valse, 1943 (transcription of Tchaikovsky's Serenade for Strings); Chamber Music: Sonata for Violin and Piano, 1930; Quintet for Piano and Strings, 1941; For Orchestra: Sunlight Channel (Sydney Symphony); Nevada (Scranton Symphony). *Hobbies:* Swimming; Tennis; Theatre; Languages; Anthropology; News. *Address:* PO Box 284, Southport, CT 06490, USA.

COLE Vinson, b. 21 Nov 1950, Kansas City, USA. Tenor. *Education:* Studied at the Curtis Institute, Philadelphia. *Debut:* Sang Werther in the opera by Massenet while still a student, 1975. *Career:* Sang in the premiere of Jubilee by Ulysses Kay at Jackson, Mississippi, in 1976; European debut 1976 with Welsh National Opera, as Belmonte in Die Entführung aus dem Serail; Later appearances in Stuttgart, Naples, Paris, Salzburg, Paris and Marseilles; St Louis 1976-80 as Tamino and Rossini's Comte Ory; New York City Opera 1981, as Fenton in Die lustigen Weiber von Windsor; Other roles include Gennaro in Lucrezia Borgia, Nadir in Les pecheurs de Perles, Lenski in Eugene Onegin, Gluck's Orfeo and Gounod's Faust; Sang in Mozart's Requiem under Georg Solti at Vienna, 1991; Sang Donizeth's Edgardo at Detroit, Ferrando at Seattle, 1992; engaged as Nadir in Les Pecheurs de Perles in Seattle, 1994. *Address:* c/o Seattle Opera Association, PO Box 9248, Seattle, WA 98109, USA.

COLE-MCCULLOUGH Daniel, b. 22 May 1946, Portland, Oregon, USA. Conductor. m. Maryl M, 21 April 1979, 1 daughter. *Education:* BA, Music, Marylhurst College 1984; MMus, Conducting, University of Portland, 1987. *Debut:* Pacific Crest Wind Ensemble, Portland, Oregon, June 1988. *Career:* Currently Assistant Professor of Music, Director of Bands, Warner Pacific College, Portland, Oregon; Local Public Radio, KBPS, Interviews about Music Concerts. *Memberships:* WASBE; CBDNA; Tuba; MENC; Conductors Guild; ACB; NBA. *Hobbies:* Golf; Horses. *Address:* 17806 N E Edmunds Road, Vancouver, WA 98682-8607, USA.

COLEMAN Tim, b. 30 Oct 1949, Eastbourne, Sussex, England. Stage Director. *Education:* Cambridge and Amsterdam Conservatory, composition. *Career:* Wrote incidental music for over 30 plays, then Chief Dramaturg of The Netherlands Opera; Debut as Director with Opera Northern Ireland in Die Fledermaus, 1990, returned 1991 for Le nozze di Figaro and 1992 Rigoletto;; United States debut with the Beggar's Opera for the Manhattan School of Music; Season 1991/92 Tosca for Minnesota Opera anmd Opera/Omaha, Tamerlano for Dublin Opera Theatre, and The Merry Wives of Windsor for the Guldhall School of Music; Season 1992/3 L'Italiana in Algeri for Dublin Grand Opera/Opera Ireland, Così fan tutte in Oklahoma City; Season 1993/94 Rigoletto in Hong Kong, L'Isola disabitata in New York, Tosca in Indianapolis, Le Nozze di Figaro for the Kirov Opera in the Mariinsky Theatre, St Petersburg. *Address:* c/o Atholl Still Ltd, Greystoke House, 80-86 Westrow Street, London SE19 3AF, England.

COLEMAN-WRIGHT Peter, b. 1958, Australia.

Singer (Baritone). *Education:* Studied in London with Otakar Kraus, Joan Hammond, Paul Hamburger and Geoffrey Parsons. *Career:* Has sung at Glyndebourne as Guglielmo, Demetrius, Dandini, Morales (Carmen) and Sid (Albert Herring); English National Opera as Neils Lynne in Fennimore and Gerda, Rossini's Barber, Schaunard, Billy Budd and Don Giovanni; Australian Opera as Mozart's Count; Covent Garden Dandini, then, Don Alvaro in Rossini's Il Viaggio a Reims and Papageno; Bordeaux Opera - Guglielmo, Masetto, Victoria State Opera - Wolfram, Papageno, Valentin (Faust); Further engagements with Netherlands Opera, the Fenice, Venice and the Australian Opera; Grande Théâtre Genève. Other roles include Eisenstein and Falke in Die Fledermaus, Masetto, Rossini's Figaro, Wolfram in Tannhäuser, Zurga and the Soldier/Brother in Busoni's Doctor Faust; Lieder recitals at the South Bank, Covent Garden, Théâtre du Châtelet in Paris and the Aix and Spoleto Festivals; Brahms Requiem and Mahler Kindertotenlieder in Austria; Concerts in Holland, Spain, Germany and Iceland and for the Australian Broadcasting Commission; premiere of Inquest of Love by Jonathon Harvey, ENO 1993; Wigmore Recital, 1993; Bordeaux Count Almaviva, 1993; Australian Opera, Don Giovanni, 1993; Staatsoper Munich Don Giovanni. *Recordings:* Oedipus Rex by Stravinsky, EMI. *Honours include:* Glyndebourne Touring Prize. *Current Management:* IMG Artists. *Address:* 28 Stanbridge Road, Putney, SW15 1DX, England.

COLES Samuel, b. 1964, England. Flautist. *Education:* Studied with James Galway, at the Guildhall School of Music and at the Paris Conservatoire with Jean-Pierre Rampal. *Career:* Solo and chamber music performances in Britain and Europe in Holland Concertgebouw and The Hague, with the Bordeaux Symphony, the Monte Carlo Orchestra and the London Soloists Chamber Orchestra; Mozart Concerto K313 with the Orchestre de Paris at Rampal's Gala Concert, Paris; Chamber recitals with members of the European Community Youth Orchestra and duet partnership with harpist Isabelle Courret; Concerto engagements with Kenneth Montgomery, Aldo Ceccato and Alain Lombard; As orchestral player has performed under Simon Rattle, Claudio Abbado and Pierre Boulez. *Recordings include:* Mozart Concerti with the English Chamber Orchestra under Yehudi Menuhin. *Honours:* Premier Prix at the Paris Conservatoire 1987; Winner Scheveningen International Flute Competition, Holland, and National Flute Association Young Artists' Competition, San Diego, USA. *Address:* c/o Anglo-Swiss Management, 4-5 Primrose Mews, Sharpeshall Street, London NW1 8YW, England.

COLETTI Paul, b. 1959, Scotland, Concert Violist; Professor. *Education:* Studied at Royal Scottish Academy, International Menuhin Academy, Banff Center and Juilliard School; Teachers included Alberto Lysy, Sandor Vegh and Don McInnes. *Career:* Solo concerts at Elizabeth Hall, Geneva, Buenos Aires, Edinburgh, Assissi, Toulon and Harrogate festivals; Recitals at Toronto, Chicago, Cincinnati, Belgrade and Los Angeles; New York debut recital 1983; Member of the Menuhin Festival Piano Quartet; Chamber performances with Menuhin in Paris, London and Gstaad and member of Chamber Society of Lincoln Center, New York; Further engagements with Camerata Lysy Ensemble and playing Bartók's Viola Concerto in Berlin; Former Professor of Viola and Chamber Music at Menuhin Academy; Head of String Department at University of Washington, Seattle; Currently Head of Viola Department at Peabody Conservatory, Baltimore; Guest conducted the New Japan Philharmonic in Tokyo. *Recordings:* Chamber pieces by Mozart, Strauss and Mendelssohn; 4 Solo CD's, numerous chamber music CD's on Epic, Sony, Hyperion, ARS. *Address:* c/o Peabody Conservatory, Viola Department, 1 East Mount Vernon Place, Baltimore, MD 20742, USA.

COLGRASS Michael (Charles), b. 22 Apr 1932, Chicago, Illinois, USA. Composer. m. Ulla Damgaard, 25 Nov 1966. 1 son. *Education:* MusB, University of Illinois, 1956; Studied composition with Lukas Foss,

Berkshire Music Center, Tanglewood summers 1952, 1954; Darius Milhaud, Aspen, Colorado Music School, summer 1953; Wallingford Riegger, New York, 1958-59; Ben Weber, New York, 1959-62. *Career:* Free-lance solo percussionist with various New York groups, 1956-67; Composer. *Compositions:* Stage: Virgil's Dream, music-theatre, 1967; Nightingale Inc, comic opera, 1971; Percussion, strings, Seventeen, 1960; Something's Gonna Happen, children's musical, 1978; Orchestral: Violin, Clarinet, percussionist and orchestra, Delta, 1979; Divertimento for 8 Drums, Piano and Strings, 1960; Rhapsodic Fantasy for 15 Drums and Orchestra, 1965; Sea Shadow, 1966; As Quiet As...1966; Auras for Harp and Orchestra, 1973; Concertmasters for 3 Violins and Orchestra, 1975; Letter from Mozart, 1976; Déjà vu for 4 Percussionists and Orchestra, 1977; Delta for Clarinet, Violin and Percussion Orchestra, 1979; Memento for 2 Pianos and Orchestra, 1982; Chaconne for Viola and Orchestra, 1984; Demon for Amplified Piano, Percussion, Tape, Radio and Orchestra, 1984; Chamber: Chamber music for 4 Drums and String Quartet, 1954; Percussion Quintet, Invention on a Motive, Michael Colgrass (4) E-57; Chamber Piece: Percussion Quintet, 1954; String Quartet, Folklines, 1987; Flute, Viola, guitar, 2 percussions, Light Spirit, 1962; Variations, Clarinet, Viola and Piano, Strangers, 1986; Variations for 4 Drums and Viola, Three Brothers, 1951, 1957; Rhapsody for Clarinet, Violin and Piano, 1962; Wolf for Cello, 1976; Flashbacks for 5 Brass, 1979; Winds of Nagual-A Musical Fable for Wind Ensemble, 1985; Piano pieces; Choral: Beautiful People, 1976. Vocal: The Earth's a Baked Apple for Chorus and Orchestra, 1969; New People for Mezzo-soprano, Viola and Piano, 1969; Image of Man for 4 Solo Voices, Chorus and Orchestra, 1974; Theatre of the Universe for Solo Voices, Chorus and Orchestra, 1975; Night of the Raccoon, 1979; Mystery Flowers of Spring, 1978; Best Wishes, USA for 4 Solo Voices, Double Chorus, 2 Jazz Bands, Folk Instruments and Orchestra, 1976; For orchestra, The Schubert Birds, 1989; Organ and orchestra, Snow Walker, 1990; Symphonic Band, Arctic Dreams, 1991. *Recordings:* Three Brothers; Variations for Four Drums and Viola; As Quiet As; The Earth's a Baked Apple; New People; Fantasy Variations; Concertmasters; Déjà vu; Light Spirit; Night of the Raccoon; Chaconne, with many other compositions recorded. *Contributions to:* Articles in New York Times. *Honours:* 2 Guggenheim Fellowships, 1964, 1968; Rockefeller grant, 1968; Ford Foundation grant, 1972; Pulitzer Prize in Music, 1978; Emmy Award, the National Association of television Arts, Sciences, 1982 for Soundings: The Music of Michael Colgrass, 1988, Jules Léger Chamber Music Prize. Various awards; Many commissions. *Address:* 583 Palmerston Avenue, Toronto, Ontario M6G 2P6, Canada.

COLIN Georges, b. 15 June 1921, Schaerbeek, Brussels, Belgium. Composer. m. Albertine De Clerck, 17 Mar 1948, 2 sons, 2 daughters. *Education:* Royal Conservatory of Music, Brussels: Harmony 1943, Counterpoint 1948, Fugue, 1949, History of Music, 1959. *Career:* Teacher, Athenee & Ecole Normale de Schaerbeek, 1976; Headmaster, Academy of Music Anderlecht, 1976-81. *Compositions:* Symphonie breve, orchestra, 1950; Cinq poèmes français de R.M. Rilke, voice & piano, 1952; Woodwind Quartet, 1955; Concertstuck La Folia, 1964; Cinq Croquis d'eleves, 1962; Sonatine, violin & piano, 1962; Sonate, flute & piano, 1965; Phantasme, harp, 1977; Sequences, violin & piano, 1978; In Collaboration with Jeanne Colin; Le Tombeau d'André Jolivet, 2 pianos, 1975; Short Pieces for harps, 1976; Flutes Quartet, 1976; Two pieces for Flute & Harp, 1979; Cantate Pour Le Vif Des Temps, (poems d'AndréDoms), tryptique profane pour sprano, et baryton solos, choeurs mixtes et orchestre: La porte de pierre, 1969; Ryoan-Ji, 1986; Corps de feu, 1991. *Publications:* 9 Chants Populaires - Chants & Danses Populaires; Doucle France, flauto dolce; La Flute à bec alto (méthode en 3 volumes). *Honours:* Médaille Commemorative de la Guerre, 1940-45; Prix de Composition de la Province de Brabant, 1964. *Memberships:* SABAM; CeBeDeM. *Address:* Haut du Village 40, B 5600 Sautour-Philippeville, Belgium.

COLIN Jeanne, b. 9 Jan 1924, Brussels, Belgium. Composer. m. Georges Colin, 2 sons, 2 daughters. *Education:* Royal Conservatory of Music, Brussels. *Career:* Teacher, Academy of Music, Anderlecht, until 1976. *Compositions:* String Quartet, 1968; Caprice, violin & piano, 1970; Concertati Movimenti, violin & piano, 1975; Concertos for violin & orchestra, 1974, flute & orchestra, 1972; Fantaisie, 1977; Saxophone quartet, 1977; various pieces for chamber music; flute solo; violin solo; strings, mixed choir, etc; In collaboration with Georges Colin: Le Tombeau d'André Jolivet, 2 pianos, 1975; Short Pieces for Harps, 1976; Flutes Quartet, 1976; Two Pieces for Flute & Harp, 1979; Cantate Pour Le Vif Des Temps, (poems d'André Doms), tryptique profane pour sprano, et baryton solos, choeurs mixtes et orchestre: La porte de pierre, 1969; Ryoan-Ji, 1986; Corps de feu, 1991. *Memberships:* SABAM; CeBeDeM. *Address:* Haut du Village 40, B 5600 Sautour Philippeville, Belgium.

COLLARD Jean-Philippe, b. 27 Jan 1948, Mareuil-sur-Ay, France. Concert Pianist. 3 sons, 1 daughter. *Education:* Studied at the Paris Conservatoire, 1959-64. *Career:* Performances throughout France and in Russia, Japan, Spain, Italy, Germany, Switzerland and the Netherlands; US debut in a series of concerts with the San Francisco Symphony under Seiji Ozawa; Regular appearances with the New York Philharmonic; British engagements with the London Symphony, Royal Philharmonic, Philharmonia, Hallé, City of Birmingham Symphony, Scottish Chamber and BBC Symphony, Welsh and Philharmonic Orchestras; Conductors include Dorati, Previn, Mehta, Lombard, Skrowaczewski, Loughran, Rattle, Maksymiuk, Dutoit and Pritchard; Tour of Britain 1991 with the Orchestre de Paris under Semyon Bychkov; Season 1992/93 included concerts with the New York Philharmonic under Previn, the Philadelphia Orchestra and the Royal Scottish Orchestra; Played Rachmaninov's 1st Concerto at the London Proms, 1993. *Recordings:* Rachmaninov Etudes Tableaux; Brahms Hungarian Dances, with Michel Béroff; Ravel Concertos with the Orchestre National de France; Saint-Saëns Complete Concertos with André Previn and the Royal Philharmonic; Franck and Magnard Violin Sonatas with Augustin Dumay; Chopin Ballades and Third Sonata (EMI). *Honours include:* Premier Prix du Conservatoire de Paris, 1964; Grand Prix du Concours National des Artistes Solistes; Prix Albert Roussel; Grand Prix du Concours International Marguérite Long/Jacques Thibaud; Record of the Year, USA, 1978, 1979; Prize, French Recording Academy, 1978, 1981, 1982; Chevalier des Arts et Lettres. *Hobbies:* Squash; Windsurfing. *Address:* Unit 2, 39 Tadema Road, London SW10 0PY, England.

COLLIER Gilman Frederick, b. 14 Apr 1929, New York City, New York, USA. Composer; Conductor; Pianist; Teacher. *Education:* AB, Harvard University, 1950; Yale School of Music, 1950-51; Mannes Music School, 1951-53; Studied theory and composition with Walter Piston, Paul Hindemith, Bohuslav Martinu, conducting with Carl Bamberger and Pierre Monteux, piano privately with Nadia Reisenberg. *Career:* Music Director, Conductor, The Monmouth Symphony Orchestra, 1964-72; Faculty Member, New School for Social Research, New York City, 1954-60; Faculty Member, Westchester Conservatory of Music, White Plains, New York, 1954-74; Faculty Member, 1969-, Assistant Director, 1975-, Monmouth Conservatory of Music. *Compositions:* 3 piano sonatas and many shorter works for piano solo; Sonata for 1 piano, 4 hands; Duo sonatas for oboe, English horn, clarinet, French horn, trumpet, violin, viola and cello with piano; Trios for flute, violin, piano, violin, cello and oboe, English horn and piano; String quartet; Piano quintet; String Quartet; 4 Chicago Psalms (SSAA); Concerto Grosso for string orchestra and piano; Almande Smedelyn and Divertimento for double reed ensemble; Songs for voice and piano. *Hobbies:* Photography; Horsebreeding. *Address:* 65 Larchwood Avenue, Oakhurst, NJ 07755, USA.

COLLING Norbert Henri, b. 14 Apr 1945, Luxembourg, Grand Duchy. Professor of Music

Education. m. Christiane Laures, 1992, 1 daughter. *Education:* Piano, Organ and Conducting, Conservatory Luxembourg; Musikhochschule, Koln; Musikhochschule Saarbrucken for Conducting. *Career:* Music Teacher at High School in Diekirch, 1968-; Teacher of Piano, Organ, Harmony, Analysis, Composition and Conducting at Conservatory of Diekirch; Conductor of Symphonic Orchestra in Diekirch. *Compositions:* Kantilene for Strings; Sonatine for Piano; Film Music; Stage Music; Partita for Organ; Songs: Der Weg. *Recording:* Partita for Organ. *Publications:* Die Messen von Guillaume Dufay, 1970; Interpretation der Orgelwerke von N Clérambault, 1980; Music Critic for Luxemburger Wort. *Honour:* Officier de L'Ordre de Merite du Grand Duche de Luxembourg, 1989. *Hobbies:* Sailing; Skiing; Photography; Gardening; Teaching; Conducting. *Address:* 21 Rue Laduno, L 9147 Erpeldange, Luxembourg.

COLLINS Anne, b. 29 Aug 1943, Durham, England. Opera and Concert Contralto. *Education:* Royal College of Music, London; ARCM; LRAM. *Debut:* Governess in The Queen of Spades, SWO, Coliseum. *Career:* English National Opera; Covent Garden; Welsh National Opera Company; Glyndebourne Festival; Grand Théâtre Genève; Canadian Opera Company; Roles included, Erda, Waltraute, Mrs Herring and Ulrica; Beroe and Akhrosimova in the UK stage premieres of The Bassarids and War and Peace; Sosostris (Midsummer Marriage) and Anna in Les Troyens, Covent Garden debut, 1977, Scottish Opera, Opera North; BBC Promenade Concerts; Recordings and Song Recitals; Concerts with major orchestras and choral societies in UK and Europe; Toured Australia for ABC; Season 1992 as the Mother Superior in Prokofiev's The Fiery Angel at Covent Garden and Basmanov in Tchaikovsky's The Oprichnik for Scottish Opera at the Edinburgh Festival; Video Films of Gilbert and Sullivan Operas, Gondoliers, Mikado, Iolanthe, Patience and Princess Ida, 1983. *Recordings:* Erda, Rhinegold and Siegfried (ENO, Goodall, EMI); Janáček Glagolitic Mass, Kempe; Vivaldi Cantatas, Phonogram; Elgar Coronation Ode; Third Lady in Die Zauberflöte. *Current Management:* Lies Askonas, 186 Drury Lane, London WC2B.

COLLINS Kenneth, b. 21 Oct 1935, Birmingham, England. Singer (Tenor). *Education:* Studied with Charles Dean, and with Ettore Campogaliani in Mantua. *Debut:* Camden Festival 1970, as Marcello in the British premiere of Leoncavallo's Bohème. *Career:* Welsh National Opera 1971, as Radames; Has appeared with the English National Opera, London, as Nadir (Les Pêcheurs de Perles), Rodolfo, Pinkerton, Cavaradossi, Calaf, Don Carlos, Verdi's Alvaro and Gabriele Adorno and Erik in Der fliegende Holländer; Guest appearances in Strasbourg and elsewhere on the continent; Engagements with Australian Opera, notably as Manrico in Il Trovatore and Cavaradossi in Tosca, 1992; Manrico for Scottish Opera, 1992. *Address:* c/o Scottish Opera, 39 Elmbank Crescent, Glasgow, Scotland, G2 4PT.

COLLINS Michael Augustus, b. 16 Oct 1948, Sydney, Australia. Conductor; Pianist. m. Lynette Kay Jennings, 24 Nov 1971, 2 sons. *Education:* CBHS, St. Mary's Cathedral, Sydney (Leaving Certificate, 1965); Performers and Teachers Diploma in Piano, New South Wales State Conservatorium of Music, 1965-68; Conducting Hochschule für Musik, Vienna, 1973-74. *Career:* Repetiteur and Conductor, Australian Opera, 1970-73; Repetiteur, Vienna Staatsoper, 1974-77; Repetiteur and Conductor, Württembergische Staatsoper, Stuttgart, 1977-79; Musical Director, Stuttgart Ballet, 1979-84; Conductor, Bayerische Staatsoper, Munich, 1984-90; 1 Kapellmeister Staatstheater Braunschweig, Guest Conductor, Deutsche Oper, Berlin, 1990. *Hobbies:* Photography; Stamp Collecting. *Address:* c/o Deutsche Oper Berlin, Richard Wagnerstrasse 10, 1000 Berlin, Germany.

COLLINS Michael, b. 27 Jan 1962, London, England. Clarinettist. *Education:* Began clarinet studies aged 10; Royal College of Music with David Hamilton; Further studies with Thea King. *Career:* BBC TV Young Musician of the Year while still at school; Other awards include Frederick Thurston Prize, First Prize in Leeds National Competition and Concert Artists' Guild of New York Amcon Award 1983; Carnegie Hall debut 1984; BBC Promenade Concert debut 1984, with Thea Musgrave's Concerto; 1985 Proms season played the Copland Concerto and was soloist in Bernstein's Prelude, Fugue and Riffs; 1985 appointed youngest ever Professor at the Royal College of Music; Played the Finzi Concerto with the City of London Sinfonia in 1987; Performances of Weber's 2nd Concerto conducted by Stanislaw Skrowaczewski and Esa Pekka-Salonen; Appointed principal clarinet of the Philharmonia Orchestra 1988; Associated with the Takacs Quartet, the Nash Ensemble and the pianists Noriko Ogawa and Kathryn Stott in chamber music; Recital partnership with Mikhail Pletnev, piano; Played Malcolm Arnold's second concerto at the Last Night of the London Proms, 1993. *Recordings:* Finzi's Concerto (Virgin Classics); Bernstein's Prelude, Fugue and Riffs and Stravinsky's Ebony Concerto (EMI); Quintets by Mozart and Brahms with the Nash Ensemble. *Address:* c/o Clarion/Seven Muses, 64 Whitehall Park, London N19 3TN, England.

COLLINS Michael B., b. 26 July 1930, Turlock, California, USA. Professor of Musicology. *Education:* BA, 1957, MA, 1958, PhD, 1963, Stanford University. *Career:* Eastman School of Music, 1964-68; College of Music, University of North Texas, Denton, 1964-68; School of Music, North Texas State University, Denton, 1968-. *Publications:* Editor, Alessandro Scarlatti's Tigrane, 1983; Co-Editor, Opera and Vivaldi, 1984. *Contributions to:* Dramatic Theory and the Italian Baroque Libretto, Cadential Structures and Accompanimental Practices in Eighteenth-Century Italian Recitative, Brazio Braccioli's Orlando furioso: A History and Synopsis of the Libretto, in Opera and Vivaldi; The Performance of Sesquialtera and Hemiolia in the 16th Century, 1964, The Performance of Triplets in the 17th and 18th Centuries, 1966, A Re-examination of Notes inégales, 1967, In Defence of the French Trill, 1973, The Literary Background of Bellini's I Capuleti ed i Montecchi, 1982, in Journal of the American Musicological Society; A Reconsideration of French Over-dotting, Music and Letters, 1969. *Honour:* Fulbright-Hays Grant for research in Italy, 1963-64. *Membership:* American Musicological Society. *Address:* College of Music, University of North Texas, Denton, TX 76203, USA.

COLLINS Richard L., b. 13 Oct 1927, Louisville, Kentucky, USA. Baritone; Stage Director; Professor. m. Ruth Strittmatter, 25 July 1981, 1 son, 1 daughter. *Education:* BA Chemistry, University of Louisville; BM, Cincinnati Conservatory, Ohio; MA, Columbia University, New York; DM, Indiana University. *Debut:* Punch Opera, New York City, 1952. *Career:* Stage Director, Opera: Birmingham Civic Opera, Alabama, 1963-80; State Opera of Florida, 1964-69; Jacksonville Opera, Florida, 1970-84; Opera Memphis, Tennessee, 1976; Baritone, over 40 roles including: Title roles in Gianni Schicchi and Rigoletto, Ford in Falstaff, Iago in Othello, Amonasro in Aida, with Lake George Opera, Birmingham Civic Opera, and State Opera of Florida; Professor: Auburn University, Florida State University, Millikin University, Memphis State University, and Houston Baptist University. *Publication:* A Study of the Musical and Dramatic Treatment of Five Baritone Roles in Operas by Verdi (doctoral thesis), 1975. *Honour:* Etelka Evans Award, 1948. *Membership:* Vice-President, President, National Opera Association. *Hobby:* Antique phonographs. *Address:* 8722 Reamer Street, Houston, TX 77074, USA.

COLLINS Walter Stowe, b. 12 Jan 1926, West Hartford, Connecticut, USA. University Professor. m. Jane Katherine Reynolds, 21 June 1958, 1 son, 2 daughters. *Education:* AB 1948, BMus 1951, Yale University; MA 1953, PhD 1960, University of Michigan; Oxford University, UK, 1957-58. *Career includes:* Director, choral music, Auburn University 1951-55, University of Minnesota 1958-60; Chairman,

Department of Music, Oakland University, Michigan, 1960-71; Founder, Meadow Brook Festival & School of Music; Professor/associate Dean, University of Colorado, Boulder, 1971-; Professor Emeritus, 1988-. Research interest, editing early choral music; bibliography & literature of choral music. *Publications:* Author & editor, numerous articles & editions of music, 1958-; Co-editor, Thomas Weelkes: Collected Anthems, Musica Britannica, 1966; Co-author, Choral Conducting Symposium, Prentice-Hall, 1973, Second Edition, 1988; Co-Author, Five Centuries of Choral Music; Essays in Honor of Howard Swan, Pendragon Press, 1988; Editor, International Choral Bulletin, International Federation for Choral Music, 1981-89; Familiar Choral Masterworks in Authoritative Editions, Hinshaw Music, 1981-. *Address:* College of Music, University of Colorado, Box 301, Boulder, CO 80309-0301, USA.

COLOMBARA Carlo, b. 1964, Bologna, Italy. Singer (Bass). *Career:* Sang at Teatro Donizetti Bergamo 1985, in a Young Singers Concert; Teatro dell'Opera Rome as Silva in Ernani and Wurm in Luisa Miller; Creon in Oedipus Rex by Stravinsky at Venice, Banquo in Macbeth and Oroveso in Norma in Tokyo; Guest appearances at Vienna Staatsoper, Bolshoi Moscow, London, Berlin, Buenos Aires, Brussels and San Francisco; La Scala debut 1989, as Procida in I Vespri Siciliani, appearances in Moscow with the company of La Scala in Turandot and I Capuleti i Montecchi; Verdi Requiem at Festival Hall, London 1990; Sang Assur in Semiramide at Venice 1990, Rodolfo in La Sonnambula; Engagements with such conductors as Giulini, Colin Davis, Gianandrea Gavazzeni, Maazel, Sawallisch and Solti; Sang Raimondo in Lucia di Lammermoor at Munich 1991, Padre Guardiano at Cremona and Colline at 1992 Verona Arena Festival; Television appearances include Aida and Lucia di Lammermoor from La Scala. *Recordings:* Colline in La Bohème; Verdi Requiem; Handel's Rinaldo. *Honour:* Winner, International Competition G B Viotti, Vercelli 1985. *Address:* c/o Teatro Comunale di Firenze, Via Solferino 15, 50123 Florence, Italy.

COLONELLO Attilio, b. 9 Nov 1930, Milan, Italy. Stage Director and Designer. *Education:* Studied architecture with Gio Ponti and Ernesto Rogers in Milan. *Career:* Designed Traviata for 1956 Florence Festival, Mefistofele at La Scala 1958; Returned to Milan for Don Pasquale, 1965 and 1973 and the premiere of Pizzetti's Clitennestra 1965; United States debut at Dallas 1962, Otello and L'incoronazione di Poppea 1963; Metropolitan Opera New York with designs for Lucia di Lammermoor 1964, Luisa Miller 1968 and Il Trovatore 1969; Designs and productions at San Carlo Naples 1964-88 for Roberto Devereux, Adriana Lecouvreur, Samson et Dalila, Carmen, La Gioconda and I Puritani; Verona Arena 1962-84 with Nabucco, Cavalleria Rusticana, La Bohème, Rigoletto, La Forza del Destino, Aida, Un Ballo in Maschera and I Lombardi; Teatro Margherita Genoa 1991, Andrea Chenier; Directed the Italian premiere of Rossini's Le Siège de Corinthe at Genoa 1992, Turandot at 1992 Caracalla Festival. *Address:* c/o Teatro San Carlo, Via San Carlo, 80132 Naples, Italy.

COLSON Andrée, b. 5 Sept 1924, Paris, France. Violinist; Conductor; Educator; Musical Administrator. m. Charles Meyer, 1 son, 1 daughter. *Education:* National Higher Conservatory of Music, Paris; Chiciana Academy, Siena, Italy. *Career:* Founder, leading violin & soloist, Andree Colson Instrumental Ensemble (chamber orchestra), 1955-; Chamber music concerts, France & abroad; Numerous international tours; TV & radio appearances. Classes & workshops, young instrumentalists (courses, 1-2 years), Vernou; Organiser, International Musical Days, Vernou (festivals, young creative & interpretative artists); Organiser, Club des Jeunes Amis de la Musique among local schoolchildren. Director: Disques Vernou Society; Georges Colson Recording Centre. *Recordings:* Vernou Disques; Nouvel Ensemble Instrumental Andrée Colson - Vallee Des Rois. *Honours:* Chevalier, Arts et Lettres, France; Officer, Arts et Letters. *Hobbies:* Hunting; Riding;

Printing. *Address:* Domaine de Vernou, BP 22, 37130 Langeais, France.

COLVILL Robin, b. 17 Sept 1945, Glasgow, Scotland. Pianist. m. Kim Newman, 22 May 1986, 2 son. *Education:* Diploma, Royal Scottish Academy of Music (with Miles Coverdale and Lawrence Glover); Concert Diploma, Salzburg Mozarteum, Austria (with Hans Leygraf); Licentiate, Royal Academy of Music; Associate, Royal College of Music. *Debut:* Mozart Concerto K459, Gordonstoun School, Scotland, aged 16. *Career:* Recitals and concerto appearances throughout United Kingdom, Austria, France, Spain and Federal Republic of Germany; Chamber concerts throughout UK and Europe, with Bochmann and Coull Quartets, Maggini, Paris and Arpeggione Quartets and Salzburg Residenz Solisten; Permanent duo with French violinist Isabelle Flory entitled The Romantic Violin; Radio and television appearances in Austria, Federal Republic of Germany and Spain. *Recordings:* Elgar Violin Sonata, and favourite encore pieces, with Isabelle Flory. *Hobbies:* Skiing; Tennis; Travel; Laughing. *Address:* 151 The Ridgeway, St. Albans, Herts. AL4 9XD, England.

COLWELL David Bruce, b. 30 May 1959, Kingston, Ontario, Canada. Teacher, Composer; Conductor; Singer; Pianist. m. Jana Milena Skarecky, 6 Aug 1983. *Education:* BMus, Queen's University, Kingston, 1982; MMus 1984, MMA 1985, Yale University School of Music, USA. *Career:* Theory Examiner, Royal Conservatory of Music, Toronto, since 1990; Faculty, Royal Conservatory of Music, Toronto, since 1988; Founding Artistic Director, Contemporary Singers of Sydney, Australia, 1986-87; Teacher of piano and theory, since 1981; Performances as conducot, singer, pianist and trombonist. *Compositions include:* Magnificat, 1989; Arrow to the Sun, 1984; Quadraphon 1, 1983; Sanctus, 1982; Two Scenes from The Fellowship of the Ring, 1981. *Publications:* Thesis, MMA, Questions of Content & Context in Krzysztof Penderecki's Magnificat Including an Analysis of the Relationship Between the Text & the Music, 1985. *Hobbies:* Sports including aquatic & outdoor; Current affairs; Reading; Cinema. *Address:* c/o 2460 Brookhurst Road, Mississauga, Ontario, Canada, L5J 1R3.

COLZANI Anselmo, b. 28 Mar 1918, Budrio, Bologna, Italy. Singer (Baritone). *Education:* Studied with Corrado Zambelli in Bologna. *Debut:* Bologna 1947, as the Herald in Lohengrin; Verona Arena from 1952; La Scala from 1954, notably in the stage premiere of Milhaud's David; US debut 1956, as Count Luna at San Francisco; Metropolitan Opera debut 1960, as Boccanegra; returned to New York for 16 seasons as Verdi's Falstaff and Amonasro, Puccini's Scarpia and Jack Rance, Gerard in Andrea Chénier and Ashton in Lucia di Lammermoor; Sang Amonasro for Houston Grand Opera, 1966. *Recordings:* La Gioconda; La Forza del Destino; Maria di Rohan by Donizetti; Iphigénie en Tauride, with Callas; Agnese di Hohenstaufen by Spontini, Florence 1957; Zandonai's Francesca da Rimini. *Address:* c/o Metropolitan Opera, Lincoln Center, New York, NY 10023, USA.

COMAN Nicolae, b. 23 Feb 1936, Bucharest, Rumania. Composer; Professor of Harmony and Composition. m. Lavinia Tomulescu, 2 July 1966. *Education:* Bacalaureat of Highschool Mihai Eminescu, Bucharest; Ciprian Porumbescu Academy of Music; Diploma in Musical Composition, 1959. *Debut:* Public 1st performance, Piano and Violin Sonata, Athenee, Bucharest, 1957. *Career:* Scientific Researcher, Ethnographical Institute of Rumanian Academy, 1960-63; Professor of Harmony and Composition; Ciprian Porumbescu Academy of Music, 1963-. *Compositions:* Over 60 musical programmes for TV and radio; The Source of the Peace, lyric cantata; Piano concerto with orchestra; 40 piano pieces; 2 piano sonatas; 60 lieder for voice and piano (piano/flute, piano/clarinet, string quartet); Sonata for piano and violin; Réconances mioritiques for violin and piano; 25 songs; Others. *Recordings:* Most compositions recorded; Metamorfozele cerului; Andantine notturne for piano.

Publications: 8 lieder, 1971; 10 pieces for piano, 1978; Sonato for Violin and Piano, 1979; 16 lieders for Voice and Piano, 1987. *Contributions to:* Romania Literara; Contemporanul; Revista Muzica. *Honours:* Prize of the Romanian Composers Union, 1969; Medal, 50 years from liberation of Rumania, 1974. *Membership:* Rumanian Composers Union. *Hobbies:* Poetry; Chess. *Address:* Str Delea Veche nr 45, Sector 2, 73119 Bucharest, Rumania.

COMBOPIANO Charles Angelo, b. 8 Aug 1935, Rome, New York, USA. Artistic Director; General Manager; Conductor; Founder: Whitewater Opera, Sorg Opera. m. Claire Rebecchi, 13 Aug 1967, 2 s, 1 d. *Education:* BMus, magna cum laude, Syracuse University 1957; PhD Musicology (all courses completed) New York University 1970; Private Conducting, Laszlo Halasz, Harpsichord, Cincinnati Conservatory. *Career:* Artistic Director and Conductor for hundreds of performances of operas, ballets and concerts for Whitewater Opera Company and Sorg Opera and for many other organizations including the Peterloon Opera Festival in Cincinnati, Northern Indiana Opera, Southold Dance Theater and others. Debuted as Conductor in a series of opera and orchestral concerts with Orchestra Sinfonica of San Remo, Italy 1985; Leading Arts Administrator serving numerous organizations including the Indiana Arts Commission, National Operas Association and Indiana Presenter's Network as well as Dayton Children's Choir; Artistic and Management Consultant to many performing arts groups; Led a series of workshops for South Carolina Arts Commission; Faculty Member of Earlham College, Indiana University East and State University of New York at Stonybrook; Guest Lecturer at universities, workshop leader, conductor and creator of apprenticeship and foreign study programmes.*Publications:* Author of Surtitles for many operas. *Address:* Whitewater Opera Company, 805 Promenade, PO Box 633, Richmond, IN 47374-0633, USA.

COMES Liviu, b. 13 Dec 1918, Serel-Transylvania, Romania. Composer; Musicologist; Professor. m. (1) Valeria, 13 May 1943, 1 son, 1 daughter; (2) Alice, 22 June 1992. *Education:* Cluj-Napoca Academy of Music, 1946-50; Graduate in Composition, 1950. *Career:* Professor, Harmony, Counterpoint and Musical Forms, 1950-69, Pro-Rector, 1963-65, Rector, 1965-69, Cluj-Napoca Music Academy; Professor, Counterpoint, 1969-81, Pro- Rector, 1971-74, Bucharest Music Academy. *Compositions:* Sonatas for Piano, 1951; For Violin and Piano, 1954; For Clarinet and Piano, 1967; Wind Quintet, 1964; Wind Trio, 1981; A Song in Stone, Oratorio, 1978; Salba, for Orchestra, 1969; Maguri, for Orchestra, 1986; Transylvanian Offer, cantata, 1987; Vocal and Choral Music; String Quartet, 1989; Byzantine Mass, 1990. *Publications:* The Melody of Palestrina, 1971, Italian translation, 1975; Treatise on Counterpoint, 1986; The World of Polyphony, 1984. *Contributions to:* Articles and Papers to Romanian Press. *Address:* Str. Spatarului No. 42, 70241 Bucharest, Romania.

COMISSIONA Sergiu, b. 16 June 1928, Bucharest, Rumania. Conductor. m. Robinne Comissiona, 16 July 1949. *Education:* Studied violin, piano and horn; Studied voice and conducting with Silvestri and Lindenberg, Bucharest Conservatory. *Debut:* Conductor with Gounod's Faust, Sibiu, 1945. *Career:* Violinist, Bucharest Radio Quartet, 1946-47; Violinist 1947-48, Assistant conductor 1948-50, Music Director 1950-55, Rumanian State Ensemble; Principal Conductor, Rumanian State Opera, 1955-59; Music Director, Haifa Symphony Orchestra, 1960-66; Founder-Music Director, Ramat Gan Chamber Orchestra, 1960-67; Music Director, Goteborg Symphony Orchestra, 1966-77; Music Advisor, Northern Ireland Orchestra, Belfast, 1967- 68; Music Director, Baltimore Symphony Orchestra, 1969-84; Chautauqua (NY) Festival Orchestra, 1976-80; Music Advisor, Temple University Festival, 1977-80; American Symphony Orchestra, New York, 1977-82; Artistic Director 1980-83; Music Director-Designate 1983-84, Music Director 1984-88,

Houston Symphony Orchestra; Chief Conductor, Radio Philharmonic Orchestra, Hilversum, 1982-; Music Director, New York City Opera, 1987-88; Chief Conductor, Helsinki Philharmonic Orchestra, 1990; Guest conductor with orchestras and opera companies throughout the world; Music Director, Vancouver Symphony, 1990; Chief Conductor, Orquesta Sinfonica, RTVE, Madrid, 1990. *Recordings:* For Arabesque; Centaur; Composers Recordings Inc; Decca-London; Desto; Deutsche Grammophon; Philips; Pro Arte; Vanguard; Vox/Turnabout; Works include: Roussel's Sinfonietta, Apollon Musagète; Chopin's 2nd Piano Concerto, Nights in the Gardens of Spain, (Alicia de Larrocha); Britten's Les Illuminations and Diversions; Mendelssohn's 3rd symphony. *Honours:* First prize winner, International Competition for Young Conductors, Besançon, France, 1954; Rumanian Order of Merit, 1956; Honorary Doctorate, Peabody Conservatory of Music, 1971; Honorary Doctor of Humane Letters, Loyola College, Baltimore, 1973; Alice M Ditson Award for conductors; Honorary Member, Royal Swedish Academy of Music. *Membership:* Founder member, George Enescu Society of North America. *Hobbies:* Mime; Films. *Address:* c/o Helsinki Philharmonic Orchestra, Karamzininkaktu 4, SF-00100 Helsinki 24, Finland.

COMMAND Michele, b. 27 Nov 1946, Caumont, France. Singer (Soprano). *Education:* Studied at the Conservatories of Grenoble and Paris. *Debut:* Lyons 1967, as Musetta in La Bohème. *Career:* Toulouse 1968, as Fiordiligi; Sang in Paris, at the Opera and the Opéra-Comique, as Mozart's Donna Elvira and Fiordiligi, Gounod's Mireille, Mélisande and Portia in the premiere of Reynaldo Hahn's Le Marchand de Venise; Paris Palais des Sports 1989, as Micaela in Carmen; Sang Gounod's Sapho at Saint-Etienne, 1992. *Recordings include:* Pelléas et Mélisande (Erato); Ariane et Barbe-Bleue and Fauré's Pénélope (Erato); Don Quichotte by Massenet (Decca); Orphée aux Enfers by Offenbach, Siebel in Faust (EMI); Harawi by Messiaen (EMI).

CONANT Robert Scott, b. 6 Jan 1928, Passaic, New Jersey, USA. Harpsichordist. m. Nancy Lydia Jackson, 10 Oct 1959, 1 son, 1 daughter. *Education:* BA, Yale University, 1949; Juilliard School, 1949-50; MM, Yale School of Music, 1956; Piano with Sascha Gorodnitzki; Harpsichord with Ralph Kirkpatrick. *Debut:* Town Hall, New York, 1953; Wigmore Hall, London, England, 1958. *Career:* Major recital series and ensemble engagements in USA and Europe, 1956-; Chicago, Denver and Philadelphia Symphony Orchestras; Founded annual Festival of Baroque Music, now held in Saratoga Springs and Greenfield Center, New York, 1959-; Assistant Professor, Yale School of Music, 1961-66; Associate Professor-Professor 1967-86, Professor Emeritus 1986-, Chicago Musical College, Roosevelt University; Currently harpsichordist with: Viola da Gamba Trio of Basel; The Robert Conant Baroque Trio, with Terry King on baroque cello and Kenneth Goldsmith on baroque violin, 1986-; Nova/Antiqua, with James Ketterer percussion and Brian Cassier on double bass, 1986-. *Recordings:* Solo on old harpsichords, Yale Collection of Musical Instruments, volume 1; Solo CD: Robert Conant, Harpsichord on FBM Records (Fdn for Baroque Music); Ensemble performances on CBS, RCA, Decca, Musurgia Accord and Ex Libris labels. *Publications:* Twentieth Century Harpsichord Music: A Classified Catalog, (with Frances Bedford), 1974. *Contributions to:* The Consort; JAMS; The Music Journal. *Honours:* Lifetime Achievement Award, Saratoga County Arts Council (NY), 1992. *Memberships:* Treasurer 1971-76, College Music Society; American Musical Instrument Society; American Musicological Society. *Hobby:* Photography. *Address:* 163 Wilton Road, Greenfield Center, NY 12833, USA.

CONDO Nucci, b. 1946, Trieste, Italy. Singer (Mezzo-Soprano). *Education:* Studied in Rome. *Career:* Sang in Vivaldi's Juditha Triumphans at the Elizabeth Hall, London, 1972; New York Kennedy Center 1972; Glyndebourne Festival 1972-79, in Le Nozze di Figaro, Falstaff, Il Ritorno d'Ulisse and Der Rosenkavalier;

Cologne 1984, as Lucia in La Gazza Ladra; La Scala 1985, in a revival of Rossi's Orfeo; Guest appearances with Netherlands Opera and at the Prague and Dubrovnik Festivals; Sang, as Ida in Gemma di Vergy, the Teatro Donizetti Bergamo, 1987; Sang Mozart's Marcellina at the Teatro La Fenice, Venice 1991; Concert tours of Yugoslavia, Austria and the USA. *Recordings include:* La Gazza Ladra; Rossini's Otello (Philips); Il Ritorno d'Ulisse (CBS); Mefistofele by Boito (Decca); Video of Le Nozze di Figaro, Glyndebourne 1973. *Address:* c/o Teatro alla Scala, Via Filodrammatici 2, Milan, Italy.

CONE Edward T(oner), b. 4 May 1917, Greensboro, North Carolina, USA. Composer; Pianist; University Professor; Writer. *Education:* AB, 1939, MFA, 1942, Princeton University. *Career:* Assistant Professor, 1947-52, Associate Professor, 1952-60, Professor, 1960-85, Professor Emeritus, 1985-, Princeton University, New Jersey; A.D. White Professor-at-large, Cornell University, 1979-85. *Compositions:* Excursions for unaccompanied chorus, 1955; Silent Noon for soprano, 1964; Numerous unpublished works. *Publications:* Musical Form and Musical Performance, 1968; The Composer's Voice, 1974; Music: A View from Delft, 1989; Editor: Berlioz, Fantastic Symphony, 1971; Roger Sessions on Music, 1979; Co-Editor, Perspectives on Schoenberg and Stravinsky, 1968; Perspectives on American Composers, 1971; Perspectives on Contemporary Music Theory, 1972; Perspectives on Notation and Performance, 1976; Editor, Perspectives of New Music, 1966-68; Advisory Editor, 1968-72. *Contributions to:* Perspectives of New Music; Musical Quarterly. *Honours:* Honorary DMus, University of Rochester, 1973; Honorary DFA, University of North Carolina, 1983; Honorary DMus, New England Conservatory of Music, 1984; Deems Taylor - ASCAP Award, 1975 and 1990. *Memberships:* Club: The Century Association; National Academy of Arts and Sciences; American Philosophical Society. *Address:* 18 College Road West, Princeton, NJ 08540, USA.

CONLON James (Joseph), b. 18 March 1950, New York City, USA. Conductor. *Education:* High School of Music and Art, New York; BM, Juilliard school, New York, 1972; Studied conducting with Jean Morel. *Debut:* Formal debut conducting with Boris Godunov, Spoleto Festival, 1971. *Career:* Conductor, Juilliard School, 1972-75; Youngest conductor to lead a subscription concert, New York Philharmonic Orchestra, 1974; Metropolitan Opera debut, New York with Die Zauberflöte, 1976; Guest conductor with major orchestras and opera companies in USA and Europe, including Chicago, Boston, Philadelphia, Cleveland, Pittsburgh and National Symphony Orchestras; Music Director, Cincinnati May Festival, 1979-; Chief Conductor, Rotterdam Philharmonic Orchestra, 1983-91; Cologne Opera, 1989-; London: Covent Garden Debut with Don Carlo, 1979; Opéra de Paris debut, with Il Tabarro and I Pagliacci in 1982, Maggio Musicale Fiorentino debut with Don Carlo, 1985, Chicago Lyric Opera debut in 1988 with La Forza del Destino, Milano La Scala Debut with Oberon in 1993; General Music Director, City of Cologne, 1991-. *Recordings:* For Erato and EMI. *Address:* c/o Cologne Opera, Buhnen der Stadt Köln, Offenbachplatz, Postfach 18 02 41, 50505 Köln, Germany.

CONNELL Elizabeth, b. 22 Oct 1946, Port Elizabeth, South Africa. Singer (Soprano). *Education:* London Opera Centre with Otakar Kraus; Maggie Teyte Prize 1972. *Debut:* Varvara in Katya Kabanova at the 1972 Wexford Festival; Appeared with Australian Opera and sang mezzo roles with English National Opera 1975-80, notably Verdi's Eboli and Herodias in Salome; Covent Garden debut 1976, as Viclinda in I Lombardi; Bayreuth debut 1980, as Ortrud in Lohengrin; Sang Lady Macbeth in Hamburg, Mozart's Vitellia at Covent Garden and Wagner's Kundry and Venus with Netherlands Opera; Soprano roles from 1983: season 1984-85 as Electra in Idomeneo at Salzburg, Norma in Geneva and Vitellia in a new production of La Clemenza di Tito at the Metropolitan; Season 1985-86 Leonora (Trovatore) and

Beethoven's Leonore at Covent Garden; Electra at Glyndebourne 1985; Appearances at La Scala in Macbeth and I Lombardi; Sang Electra, in new production of Idomeneo, Covent Garden, 1989; Lady Macbeth, Bonn, 1990 and Cologne 1992; Sang Fidelio at Sydney, Odabella in Attila at Geneva, 1992; Senta, Der fliegende Holländer, the Bayreuth Festival; Concert performances of Mendelssohn's 2nd Symphony under Abbado and the Missa Solemnis in Paris; Sang Isolde at the Festival Hall, London, 1993. *Recordings:* I Due Foscari (Philips); Lohengrin (CBS); Video of Covent Garden production of Luisa Miller. *Address:* c/o S.A. Gorlinsky Ltd., 33 Dover Street, London W11 4NJ, England.

CONNELL John, b. 1956, Singer (Bass). *Education:* Studied at the Royal Northern College of Music and at the National Opera Studio. *Debut:* English National Opera; Roles at Royal Opera, Covent Garden: Titutel, Parsifal; Il Frate, Don Carlos; Sparafucile, Rigoletto, 1985, and as Ramphis in Aida. *Career:* With ENO has sung the Commendatore, Colline, the Monk in Don Carlos, Ferrando (Trovatore), Leporello (Stone Guest), Pogner, Basilio, Banquo and Sarastro; Televised appearances in Billy Budd and Lady Macbeth by Shostakovich; Season 1990-91 in new productions of Pelléas et Mélisande and Peter Grimes, as Arkel and Swallow; Sang Banquo in Bolshoi Moscow and Kirov Leningrad 1990, on tour with ENO; Welsh National Opera, Sarastro in The Magic Flute and Silva; Ernani; Opera North in Salome, The Barber of Seville and La Bohème; other engagements as Hunding in Spain and France; Concert engagements in the Verdi Requiem at The Barbican and as Pimen in Boris Godunov; Windsor Festival 1987, in Fidelio; Season 1992 as the Father Superior in The Force of Destiny and as Sarastro for ENO; The Hermit (Der Freischütz) with the New York Philharmonic and Peter Grims with the LSO and Rostropovich. *Recordings include:* Elijah (Philips); Serenade to Music by Vaughan Williams (Hyperion), Szymanowski's Stabat Mater (EMI) and Gremin (Eugene Onegin (EMI) conducted by Mackerras. *Address:* 31 Sinclair Road, London W14 0NS, England.

CONNER Nadine, b. 20 Feb 1913, Compton, California. Singer (Soprano). *Education:* Studied with Horatio Cogswell and Amado Fernandez at the University of Southern California; With Florence Easton in New York. *Debut:* Los Angeles 1940, with the Caifornia Opera Company under Albert Coates, as Marguerite in Faust. *Career:* Metropolitan Opera from 1941, as Mozart's Pamina, Zerlina and Susanna, Verdi's Gilda and Violetta, Marzelline in Fidelio, Mimi, Micaela, Sophie and Rosina; Sang in Europe from 1953, notably in England, France, Belgium and Italy. *Recordings:* Hansel und Gretel (CBS); Soprano solo in the Brahms Requeim, conducted by Bruno Walter.

CONNOLLY Justin Riveagh b. 11 Aug 1933, London, England. Composer. *Education:* Royal College of Music with Peter Racine Fricker and Adrian Boult. *Career:* Harkness Fellowship 1963-65, studying with Mel Powell; Taught at Yale University 1963-66; Professor of Theory and Composition at the Royal College of Music from 1966-89. *Compositions include:* Sonatina in 5 Studies for Piano; Antiphonies for orchestra; Cinquepaces for brass quintet; Poems of Wallace Stevens I and II for soprano and instruments 1967, 1970; Anima for viola and orchestra 1974; Diaphony for organ and orchestra 1977; Chamber music series with titles Obbligati, Triads and Tesserae, 1966-89; Ceilidh for 4 violins 1976; Waka for Mezzo-soprano and piano, 1981; Sestina A and B for ensemble 1978; Verse and Prose for cappella chorus Fourfold, from The Garden of Forking Paths for 2 pianos 1983; Ennead, (Night Thoughts), for piano 1983; Spelt from Sibyl's Leaves, for 6 solo voices and ensemble, 1989; Nocturnal, flutes with piano, percussion, double-bass, 1990; Cantata, Soprano and piano, 1991; Symphony, 1991. *Honours:* Collard Fellowship, The Musicians' Company, 1986. *Memberships:* Association of Professional Composers, Liveryman, Worshipful Company of Musicians. *Address:*

c/o Novello & Co Ltd, Lower James St., London W1, England.

CONRAD Barbara, b. 11 Aug 1945, Pittsburg, Texas, USA. Singer (Mezzo-Soprano). *Education:* Studied at the University of Texas, Austin. *Career:* Metropolitan Opera from 1982, as Verdi's Preziosilla and Maddalena, Annina in Der Rosenkavalier and Maria in Porgy and Bess; European engagements at Frankfurt, Vienna, Brussels and Munich; Other roles include Wagner's Fricka and Verdi's Azucena and Eboli. *Recordings include:* Hamlet, (Thomas) and Porgy and Bess; Sang at Greater Miami Opera, 1989. *Address:* Greater Miami Opera Association, 1200 Coral Way, Miami, FL 33145, USA.

CONSOLI Marc-Antonio, b. 19 May 1941, Italy. Composer; Conductor; Editor. *Education:* BMus., 1966; MMus, 1967; DMA 1976; studied with Ernst Krenek, Gunther Schuller, George Crumb. *Career:* Commissioned by Fromm and Koussevitsky Foundations, the Royan in France, Steirischer Herbst of Austria (Festivals); works performed at International Festivals including ISCM in Helsinki, 1978, Belgium 1981; New York Philharmonic and Los Angeles Philharmonic. *Compositions include:* Greek Lyrics, 1988; Cello Concerto, 1988; Eyes of the Peacock, 1987; The Light Cantata, 1986; Relections, 1986; Musiculi II, 1985/86; Six Ancient Greek Lyrics, 1985; String Quartet, 1983; The Last Unicorn, 1981; Alterimages, 1982; Orpheus Meditation, 1981; Naked Masks, 1980; Vuci Siculani, 1979; Tre Fiori Musicali, 1978; Odefonia, 1976; Tre Canzoni, 1976; Memorie pie, 1976; Canti Trinacriani, 1976; Sciuri Novi II, 1974; Music for Chambers, 1974; Profile, 1973; Lux Aeterna, 1972; Interactions I, II, III, IV, V, 1970-71; Isonic, 1971; Sciuri Novi. *Recordings:* String Quartet; Six Ancient Greek Lyrics; Saxlodie; Afterimages; Fantasia Celeste; Odefonia. *Honours:* Fulbright Scholarship to Poland, 1972-74; National Endowment of the Arts Grants, 1976, 1979; Guggenheim Memorial Fellowships, 1971, 1979; Prize, Competition, Monaco. *Memberships:* Broadcast Music Association; American Composers Alliance. *Address:* 95-27 239th Street, Bellerosse, NY 11426, USA.

CONSTABLE John Robert, b. 5 Oct 1934, Sunbury-on-Thames, Middlesex, England. Piano Accompanist; Harpsichordist. m. Katharine Ingham, 2 daughters. *Education:* Studied with Harold Craxton, Royal Academy of Music, London; Fellow, Royal Academy of Music. *Career:* Repetiteur, Royal Opera House, Covent Garden, London, 1960-72; Principal Keyboard Player, London Sinfonietta, since its formation; Principal Harpsichordist, Academy of St Martin-in-the-Fields, 1984-; Professor, Royal College of Music, 1985-. *Recordings:* Many with London Sinfonietta and Academy of St Martin-in-the-Fields playing Harpsichord continuo for operas and as accompanist on recital records. *Honour:* Fellow, Royal Academy of Music, 1986. *Memberships:* Incorporated Society of Music; Musicians Union. *Hobbies:* Travel; Watching cricket. *Address:* 13 Denbigh Terrace, London W11, England.

CONSTANT Franz, b. 17 Nov 1910, Montignies-le-Tilleul, Belgium. Pianist; Teacher; Composer. m. Jeanne Pellaerts. *Education:* Charleroi Academy of Music; Studied with M Maas, L Jongen, F de Bourguignon and J Absil, Brussels Conservatory; with H Tomasi, Paris. *Career:* Appearances as Pianist; Duo piano recitals with wife; Teacher, Brussels Conservatory, 1947-. *Compositions:* Orchestral: Rhapsodie for Violin and Orchestra, 1962; Saxophone Concerto, 1965; Sinfonietta for Flute, Oboe and String Orchestra, 1968; Fantasia for Saxophone and Orchestra, 1969; Concertino for Flute and String Orchestra, 1970; Violin Concerto, 1971; Rhapsodie, 1973; Expressions for Violin, Piano and Strings, 1973; Clarinet Concertino, 1975; Ballade du sud for 2 Pianos and Orchestra, 1979; Movement rhapsodique for Double Bass and Orchestra, 1980; Preambule, 1980; Musique for Saxophone Quartet and String Orchestra, 1981; Quattro movimenti sinfonici, 1983; Eventail, 1983; Concerto for Accordion and Wind Orchestra, 1985; Concerto for Brass and Wind Orchestra, 1987; Chamber: Sonatine picturale for Clarinet and Piano, 1970; Couleur provencale for Horn and Piano, 1970; 5 Miniatures for Violin, Flute and Piano, 1971; Piano Quartet, 1971; Divertissement for Bassoon and Piano, 1972; Musique à deux for Flute and Guitar, 1973; Maree for Oboe and Piano, 1973; Musica lyrica for Flute, Violin and Piano or Harpsichord, 1976; Suite en trio for Flute, Violin and Piano, 1977; Rhapsodie d'été for Clarinet Octet and Percussion, 1977; Mouvements for Flute, Clarinet, Violin and Piano, 1978; Suite for Violin, Cello and Piano, 1978; Serenade for Violin and Piano, 1980; Odyssée for Cello and Piano, 1982; Movimento for Trumpet and Piano, 1982; Evasion for Clarinet and Piano, 1983; Ballade for Violin and Piano, 1983; Sonate a trois for 2 Violins and Piano, 1983; Triptyque for 2 Pianos and Percussion, 1984; String Quartet, 1985; Episodes for Alto Saxophone and Piano, 1985; Impromptu for Alto Saxophone and Piano, 1987; Piano pieces; Choral works; Songs. *Address:* c/o Conservatoire Royal de Musique, 30 rue de la Regence, Brussels, Belgium.

CONSTANT Marius, b. 7 Feb 1925, Bucharest, Romania. Composer; Conductor. m. Sonia Millian, 1 son. *Education:* Bucharest Conservatory of Music; National Conservatory of Music, Paris. *Career:* Musical Director, French Radio 1953-; Musical Director, Roland Petit Ballet and Paris Opera ballet 1973-78; Conductor, Ars Nova Ensemble; Regular guest conductor of leading orchestras in Europe, Canada, USA and Japan; Teaches composition at Stanford University and conducting at Hilversum, Netherlands. *Compositions:* Operas: Le Souper 1969; Jeu de Sainte Agnes 1974; La Tragedie de Carmen 1981; Impressions de Pelleas, 1992; Oratorio Des Droits de L'Homme 1989; Ballets: Cyrano de Bergerac 1959; Eloge de la Folie 1966; Paradis Perdu 1967; Candide 1970; Septentrion 1975; Nana 1976; L'Ange Bleu 1985; Orchestral: 24 Preludes 1959; Turner; Chants de Maldoror 1962; Twilight Zone, signature tune, 1961; Chaconne et Marche Militaire 1968; 14 Stations for percussion and 6 instruments 1970; Candide for harpsichord and orchestra 1971; Choruses and Interludes for French Horn and Orchestra, 1990; Concerto Gli Elementi for trombone and orchestra 1977; Symphony for Winds 1978; Concertante for alto saxophone and orchestra 1978; Nana- Symphony 1980; 103 Regards dans L'Eau 1981; Pelléas et Mélisande-Symphony 1983; L'Inauguration de la Maison for wind band 1985; Winds 1968; Traits, Cadavre Exquis, aleatoric 1971; Chamber Music. *Recordings:* Music by Satie, Xenakis, Debussy, Varèse, Messiaen and Constant for Erato. *Honours include:* First Prize for composition, Paris Conservatory; Officier, Legion d'Honneur; Prix Italia 1952; Member of the Académie de Beaux-Arts, 1993. *Address:* 16 rue des Fosses St Jacques, 75005 Paris, France.

CONSTANTIN Rudolf, b. 16 Feb 1935, Paris, France. Singer (Baritone). Education: Studied in Paris and Zurich. *Career:* Sang at Rheydt, 1958-59, Aachen, 1959-60, Berne, 1960-63, Graz, 1963-67, Cologns, 1967-69; Frankfurt am Main, 1969-83; Guest appearances at Dresden, Berlin, Amsterdam, Brussels, Vienna (Volksoper), Paris and Copenhagen; Sang Ruprecht in The Fiery Angel at Zurich, Gunther in Götterdämmerung at Covent Garden and the villians in Les Contest d'Hoffmann at the Salzburg Festival; Other roles have included Mozart's Don Giovanni, Count and Guglielmo, Verdi's Amonasro, Luna, Germont, Nabucco, Simon Boccanegra, Rigoletto, Macbeth, Posa and Iago; Wagner's Telramund, Dutchman, Wolfram, Amfortas and Wotan (Die Walküre); Srauss's Orestes, Jochanaan, Mandryka and Faninal; Golaud in Pelléas et Mélisande and Mittenhofer in Elegy for Young Lovers by Henze; Further engagements at Geneva, Marseille, Monte Carlo, Prague and Edinburgh; Many concert appearances. *Address:* c/o Städtische Buhnen, Untermainanlage 11, 6000 Frankfurt am Main, Germany.

CONSTANTINESCU Dan, b. 10 June 1931, Bucharest, Romania. Composer. *Education:* Composer's

Diploma, Bucharest Conservatory of Music. *Debut:* Jassy Philharmonic, 1957. *Career:* Lecturer in Harmony & Composition, Bucharest Conservatory. *Compositions include:* Divertissement for string orchestra; Ballad for orchestra; Chamber Symphony; Symphony Concertante; Concerto for piano & string orchestra; Concerto for 2 pianos & small orchestra; 4 sonatas for 2 Instruments; Trio for violin, clarinet, piano & percussion; 5 Quartets; Symphony for string orchestra; Symphony for wind instruments; Concerto for harpsichord, harp & wind instruments; String sextet; Symphony for 32 voices; 5 cycles of Piano Music. *Recordings:* Piano part, various works. *Honour:* Georges Enesco Prize, Romanian Academy, 1968. *Membership:* Romanian Composers Union. *Address:* Strada Corneliu Botez 3, Bucharest 9, Romania.

CONSTANTINESCU Mihai, b. 22 Aug 1926, Chisinau, USSR. Violinist; Professor. m. Corina Bura, 17 Apr 1981, 1 daughter. *Education:* Bachelorship of the Matei Basarab High School; Diploma, Conservatoire of Music, Bucharest. *Debut:* Radio Bucharest, 1941; Recital Dalles Hall, Bucharest, 1943. *Career:* Soloist, George Enescu Philharmonic, Bucharest; Radio and television appearances; Tours in, USSR, Czechoslovakia, Korea, China, German Democratic Republic, Vietnam, Poland, Bulgaria, France, Belgium, Luxembourg, Hungary, Yugoslavia, German Federal Republic, Italy, Cuba, Spain, Venezuela, Chile, Argentina and Equador etc; Professor, Conservatoire of Music, Bucharest. *Compositions:* Cadenzas for: Mozart's Third Concerto for violin and orchestra and Haydn's First Concerto for violin and orchestra. *Recordings:* Works by, Mozart, Beethoven, Pergolesi, Handel, Sabin Dragoi, Livui Comes, Wilhelm Berger (Romanian music); 2 Handel recordings, and Rameau, 1986. *Address:* Str Ecaterina Teodoriou 17, 78108 Bucharest 1, Romania.

CONTE David, b. 20 Dec 1955, Denver, Colorado, USA. Composer; Teacher. *Education:* DMA, MFA, Cornell University; BM, Bowling Green State University, Ohio; Private Study with Nadia Boulanger for 2 years. *Career:* Faculties, Cornell University, Colgate University, Keuka College, Interlochen Centre for the Arts, San Francisco Conservatory of Music; Conductor, San Francisco Conservatory Chorus. *Compositions:* Invocation and Dance, for male chorus and orchestra; Requiem Triptych (In Memoriam Nadia Boulanger) for Male Chorus and Orchestra; Piano Fantasy; Three Sacred Pieces for Chorus and Piano Four-hands; Of A Summer's Evening, Guitar Duo; Hymn to the Nativity, Chorus & Orchestra; Set Me as a Seal, for chorus & Organ; Pastorale for Organ; Piano Quintet, Praise of Music, (SSA and piano); Ave Maria. *Publications:* All works with E C Schirmer Music Company, Boston. *Honours:* Fulbright Scholarship, 1976; Meet the Composer Grant, 1983, 1986, 1987; Ralph Vaughan Williams Fellowship. *Memberships:* American Society of Composers and Publishers; American Choral Directors Association. *Current Management:* E C Schrner Music Co., 138 Ipswich Street, Boston, MA 02215, USA. *Address:* San Francisco Conservatory of Music, 1201 Ortega Street, San Francisco, CA 94122, USA.

CONTI Nicoletta, b. 12 July 1957, Bologna, Italy; Orchestral Conductor; Teacher. *Education:* Bologna Conservatory of Music; Milan Conservatory. *Debut:* Liszt Academy, Budapest, 1984. *Career:* Aspen Music Festival, 1984; Tanglewood Music Centre, 1985; appearances with; Orchestra Sinfonica di Bari, Orchestra Regionale Toscana, Orchestra Simphonia Perusina, Orchestra Sinfonica Abrudiese, Orchestra Pro Musica Riminia, Danish Radio Orchestra. *Honours:* Concorso Da Camera Stresa, 1981; Malko Competition for Young Conductors, 1986. *Memberships:* American Symphony Orchestra League. *Hobbies:* Skiing; Tennis. *Address:* Via Palestro 7, 40123 Bologna, Italy.

CONTI Paolo, b. 1957, Perugia, Italy. Singer (Baritone). *Education:* Studied in Perugia and with Rodolfo Celletti. *Debut:* Teatro Lirico Milan 1984 as Seid in Verdi's Il Corsaro. *Career:* Guest appearances at Genoa, the Festival of Martina Franca and Bologna, as Henry, Lucia di Lammermoor, Verdi's Germont, Posa Ford and Renato and Riccardo in I Puritani; Metropolitan Opera and Valle d'Itria 1988, as Belcore and as Chevreuse in Donizetti's Maria di Rohan; Further engagements at Cologne, Vienna, London, Covent Garden, Geneva, Florence, Riccardo and Milan, Paolo in Simon Soccanegra; Season 1990-91 as Germont at San Francisco and Naples, Macbeth at Jesi, Posa in Turin, Onegin and Renato at Bologna and the Massenet Lescaut at Parma; Valle d'Itria in Ernani and a Meyerbeer Concert. *Recordings:* Manon Lescaut and Simon Boccanegra; Maria di Rohan; Alina, Regina di Golconda by Donizetti. *Address:* c/o Teatro Comunale di Bologna, Largo Respighi 1, 40126 Bologna, Italy.

CONTIGUGLIA John, b. 13 Apr 1937, Auburn, New York, USA. Pianist. *Education:* Received advice from Percy Grainger; Studied with Jean Wilder and Bruce Simonds, Yale University; Dame Myra Hess, London. *Debut:* Duo recital with brother Richard, at age 6. *Career:* Professional debut, London, 1962; Performed throughout the world as a virtuoso duo; Repertoire includes works from the past to contemporary scores; Special emphasis on the piano transcriptions of Liszt; Premiere of Liszt's Grosses Konzertstuck über Mendelssohn's Lieder ohne Worte, Utrecht, 1986. *Recordings:* Several. *Honour:* Ditson Fellowship. *Address:* c/o ICM Artists, Ltd., 40 West 57th Street, New York 10019, USA.

CONTIGUGLIA Richard, b. 13 Apr 1937, Auburn, New York City, USA. Pianist. *Education:* Received advice from Percy Grainger; Studied with Jean Wilder and Bruce Simonds, Yale University; Dame Myra Hess, London. *Debut:* Playing in a duo with brother John at age 6. *Career:* Professional debut, London, 1962; Toured all over the globe in virtuoso duo. Repertory includes works ranging from traditional to contemporary; Piano transcriptions of Liszt; First performance of Liszt's Grosses Konzertstück über Mendelssohn's Lieder ohne Worte, Utrecht, 1986. *Recordings:* Several. *Honour:* Ditson Fellowship. *Address:* c/o ICM Artists, Ltd, 40 West 57th Street, New York 10019, USA.

CONVERY Robert, b. 4 October 1954, Wichita, Kansas, USA. Composer. *Education:* Studied at Westminster Choir College, Curtis Institute and Juilliard, New York; David Diamond, Vincent Persichetti and Ned Rorem were among his teachers. *Career:* Resident Composer with Philips Exeter Academy, 1988, 91, Dickinson College 1989-90 and the New York Concert Singers 1991-93. *Compositions:* The Lady of Larkspur, opera in one act after Tennessee Williams 1980; Pyramus and Thisbe, two scenes after Shakespeare 1983; The Blanket, opera in one act, produced at Spoleto Festival, Charleston 1986. *Honours:* Charles Miller-Alfredo Casella Award; Charles E Ives Award for The Blanket. *Address:* c/o ASCAP, ASCAP Building, One Lincoln Plaza, New York, NY 10023, USA.

CONWAY Joe, b. 13 Mar 1947, Greenwich, London, England. Music Critic; Composer; Conductor; Pianist. *Education:* Trinity College of Music, London, 1971-72; Huddersfield Polytechnic, 1974-75; Middlesex Polytechnic-London University, 1978-79. *Career:* Conductor, various amateur operatic societies, 1976- ; Pianist with Under the Greenwood Trio, 1990-; Conductor, Lincoln Orpheus Male Voice Choir, 1990- ; Conductor, Cantata Chamber Orchestra, 1992-. *Compositions:* Sonatas Nos. 1, 2, 3 for Folk Fiddle and Piano, 1988-91; Earth Work for Flute, Cello and Piano, 1990; Overture and Incidental Music to Nicholas Nickleby, 1991; 3 Folk Tales for String Orchestra, 1993. *Publications:* Music Critic for Lincolnshire Echo, 1989-93; Classical Music Presenter, BBC Radio Lincolnshire, 1989-; Music Critic for Yorkshire Post, 1990-. *Honours:* B.Ed, 1st class honours, London University 1979; LRAM, LTCL Diplomas 1973; ARCM 1974; Cert.Ed. Huddersfield Polytechnic 1975. *Hobbies:* Cathedral Architecture; Country Walking; Antiquarian Books. *Address:* 22 Cheviot Street, Lincoln LN2 5JD, England.

CONWELL Julia, b. 1954, Philadelphia, Pennsylvania, USA. Singer (Soprano). m. Giancarlo del Monaco. *Education:* Studied at Curtis Institute of Music and with Margaret Harshaw. *Career:* Sang in various United States opera houses, notably as Musetta in La Bohème for Michigan Opera; European debut with Munich Staatsoper as Musetta; Further appearances as Nedda in Pagliacci, Liu in Turandot, Dusseldorf 1982 and Oscar in Ballo in Maschera, Frankfurt 1984; Sang Charpentier's Louise at Nice and Zerlina at Rome 1984; Other roles have included Paolina in Poliuto by Donizetti, Rome 1986; Gilda and Salome at Augsburg 1988 and Diana in Iphigénie en Tauride, Deutsche Oper Berlin; Member of the Stuttgart Staatsoper from 1985. *Recordings:* Sandrina in La Finta Giardiniera; Euridice in Orfeo by Gluck; Works by Henze. *Address:* c/o Stuttgart Staatstheater, Oberer Schlossgarten 6, 7 Stuttgart, Germany.

CONYNGHAM Barry Ernest, b. 27 Aug 1944. Sydney, Australia. Composer; Reader in Music, University of Melbourne. *Education:* MA, University of Sydney; Certificate of Post-doctoral studies, University of California at San Diego; Doctor of Music, University of Melbourne; Profesor Creative Arts, University of Wollongong. *Career:* Part-time Lecturer and Tutor, University of New South Wales and the National Institute of Dramatic Art, 1968-70; Senior Tutor, University of Western Australia, 1971; Post-doctoral appointment, University of California at San Diego, 1972-73; Visiting Fellow, Princeton University, 1973-74; Composer and Researcher in Residence, University of Aix-Marseille, 1974-75; Lecturer 1975-79, Senior Lecturer 1979-84, Reader in Music 1984-, University of Melbourne; Visiting Scholar, University of Minnesota, 1982; Visiting Fellow, Pennsylvania State University, 1982. *Compositions:* Crisis: Thoughts in a City, 1968; The Little Sherriff, 1969; Five Windows, 1969; Three, 1969; Five, 1970; Water..Footsteps..Time, 1970; Ice Carving, 1970; Playback, 1972; Without Gesture, 1973; From Voss, 1973; Edward John Eyre, 1971-73; Snowflake, 1973; Six, 1971; Mirror Images, 1975; Ned, 1974-77; Sky, 1977; Apology of Bony Anderson, 1978; Mirages, 1978; Bony Anderson, 1978; Concerto for Double Bass, 1979; Basho, 1980; Journeys, 1980; Viola, 1981; Imaginary Letters, 1981; Concerto for Orchestra: Horizons; Concerto for Violin and Piano: Southern Cross; Dwellings, 1982; Voicings, 1983; Cello Concerto, 1984; Fly, 1982-84; Preview, 1984; Antipodes, 1984-85; Generations, 1985; The Oath of Bad Brown Bill, 1985; Recurrences, 1986; Diamentina Ghosts, 1986; Vast I the Sea, 1987; II, the Coast 1987, II The Centre 1987, IV The Cities 1987; Glimpses, 1987; Bennelong, 1988; Matilda, 1988; Streams, 1988; Piano Concerto, Monuments, 1989; Viola Concerto, Waterways, 1990; Harp Concerto, Cloudlines, 1990. *Recordings:* Numerous. *Honours:* Churchill Fellowship, 1970; Harkness Fellowship, 1972-74; Australia Council Fellowship, 1975; Fulbright Senior Fellowship, 1982. *Membership:* Board member, Playbox Theatre Company. *Address:* University of Wollongong, Wollongong, Australia.

COOK Brian (Robert) Rayner, b. 17 May 1945, London, England. Singer (baritone) m. Angela Mary Romney, 24 Aug 1974, 1 son, 1 daughter. *Education:* BA, Music, University of Bristol, 1966; Postgraduate studies, Royal College of Music, London; ARCM Hons, Singing Performance; Studied privately with Alexander Young (vocal studies) and Helga Mott (repertoire). *Debuts:* Major conducting debut (opera) 1966; Professional solo singing debut, 1967. *Career:* Church Organist and Choir Master at age of 15; 1st concert at major London venue, Royal Albert Hall (conducted by Sir John Barbirolli) 1969; Appearances as Solo Singer, oratorio, recitals, music-theatre and opera throughout the UK, Western and Eastern Europe, USA, Canada, South America, Middle East, Far East, North Africa; Frequent broadcasts, British and European radio and TV; Many 1st performances and broadcasts particularly of works created for him by various distinguished composers; Visiting Tutor in Vocal Studies: Birmingham Conservatoire, England, 1980-, and formerly Welsh College of Music and Drama, Cardiff;

Has directed a number of Singers' Workshops, taught at summer schools, served on juries of international singing competitions, and given specialist adjudications. *Recordings include:* Opera and oratorio from Schütz, Charpentier, Adam, Fauré, Dvořák, Nielsen and Orff to Parry, Elgar, Delius, Vaughan Williams, Ferguson and Walton; Song recitals including Vaughan Williams, Butterworth, Elgar, Brian, Poston, Coates, Cruft, Holst, Rubbra, Williamson, Plumstead, Camilleri. *Contributor to:* Royal College of Music Magazine. *Hobbies:* Colour photography; 78 rpm recordings; Laurel and Hardy films; Messing about in boats; Conjuring. *Address:* The Quavers, 53 Friars Avenue, Friern Barnet, London N20 0XG, England.

COOK Deborah, b. 6 July 1948, Philadelphia, Pennsylvania, USA. Opera and Concert Singer; Cantor, German Town Jewish Centre, Philadelphia. m. Ronald Marlowe, Concert Pianist, 30 Aug 1985, 1 son. *Education:* Private study with Irene Williams. *Debut:* Operatic-Glyndebourne and Covent Garden; Glyndebourne Touring Opera 1971 as Zerbinetta. *Career:* 3 years principal soprano in Bremen, 2 years Munich National Theatre; Sang in Sydney; Melbourne, Barcelona; Edinburgh; Geneva; Rome; Paris; Los Angeles; San Francisco; Leipzig; East Berlin. Appeared at Covent Garden Opera House; Hamburg State Opera; Deutsche Opera Berlin; Frankfurt Opera; Stuttgart Opera; Deutsche Oper am Rhein; roles incude Verdi's Gilda, Strauss's Zerbinetta, Donizetti's Lucia and Mozart's Queen of Night and Constanze. Created role of Rachel in Henze's We Come to the River, Covent Garden, 1976 and Angel of Bright Future in Rochberg's The Confidence Man; Sang Lucia di Lammermoor at the Buxton Festival, 1979. *Recordings:* Dinorah; Ariadne auf Naxos; L'Étoile du Nord. *Hobbies:* Baking. *Address:* c/o Opera Rara, 25 Compton Tewrrace, London N1 2UN, England.

COOK Donald Frederick, b. 22 May 1937, St John's, Newfoundland, Canada. University Professor. m. Clara June Penney, 27 Dec 1961, 1 son, 2 daughters. *Education:* BMus, Mount Alison University, Canada, 1957; Associate Diploma, (Organ), Royal College of Music, London, England, 1958; Associate Diploma, American Guild of Organists, 1964; Master of Sacred Music, Union Theological Seminary, New York City, 1965; Choirmaster's Diploma, American Guild of Organists, 1965; PhD (musicology), King's College, University of London, England, 1983. *Career:* Organ recitalist and choral director; Joined faculty of Memorial University of Newfoundland, 1968, Head of Music Department, 1975 and to full Professor, 1983, Director of School of Music, 1985-90; Serves concurrently as Organist and Choirmaster, Newfoundland Cathedral in St John's; Left Memorial University and Newfoundland Cathedral in 1992; Principal, Western Ontario Conservatory of Music in London, Ontario, 1992-. *Compositions:* Puer natus (SATB choral), Waterloo Music Co, 1970; Numerous arrangements for choir of Newfoundland Folksongs, Waterloo Music Co, 1977-; all of which have been recorded; Two Miniatures of Sea and Land, 1988. *Recordings:* Conductor of Memorial University Chamber Choir for 2 recordings, Winter's Gone and Past, 1979, At Exeter Cathedral, 1983, Waterloo Music Records; Conductor of The Newfoundland Cathedral Choir for 2 recordings, Christmas at The Newfoundland Cathedral, 1987; Evensong, 1988. *Honours:* Order of Canada, 1993; Donald F Cook Recital Hall, named at Memorial University, 1993. *Hobby:* Sailing. *Address:* Western Ontario Conservatory of Music, 645 Windermere Road, London, Canada N5X 2P1.

COOK Jeff Holland, b. 21 Aug 1940, Chicago, Illinois, USA. Music Director; Conductor; Composer. m. Kate Young, 12 May 1974. 1 daughter. *Education:* BM, Northwestern University, 1962; MA, Ohio State University, 1964; MM, New England Conservatory of Music, 1966; study with Pierre Boulez, Sir John Barbirolli, Jean Fournet, Bruno Maderna, Herbert von Karajan, Erich Leinsdorf, Karlheinz Stockausen, György Ligeti. *Career:* Music Director, Conductor, Wheeling

Symphony Orchestra, 1973-85; Music Director, Conductor, Mansfield Symphony Orchestra, Ohio, 1976-; Conductor, Louisville Ballet, Kentucky, 1990-; Associate Conductor, Pittsburgh Ballet Theatre, 1987-91; Guest Conductor, Anchorage Symphony, Eastern Music Festival, Rhode Island Philharmonic, North Carolina Symphony, Orquesta Sinfonica Nacional (Santa Domingo), Ballet of Ljubljana, Yugoslavia; North Bay Music Festival (Ontario). *Composition:* Euripides Electra, 1972. *Recordings:* Broadcasts on West Virginia Public Radio, Ohio Public Radio, Canadian Broadcasting Corporation. *Hobby:* Travel. *Address:* RD 4 Box 116, Wheeling, WV 26003, USA.

COOK-MACDONALD Linda, b. 22 Sept 1949, Twin Falls, Idaho, USA. Singer (Soprano). *Education:* Studied in Cincinnati and Mainz. *Debut:* Krefeld 1971 as Fiordiligi. *Career:* Sang at such German houses as Krefeld, Wuppertal, Essen and Darmstadt; United States appearances at Memphis, Cincinnati, Pittsburgh and Portland; Sang in New York at City Opera; Roles have included Mozart's Constanze, Pamina Queen of Night and Zerlina, Agathe, Alice Ford, Marguerite, Musetta and Zdenka; Modern repertory has included Thalmar in Leben des Orest by Krenek and Philippe in Penderecki's The Devils of Loudun; Many concert appearances. *Address:* c/o New York City Opera, Lincoln Center, New York, NY 10023, USA.

COOKE Mervyn John, b. 29 Aug 1963, Dover, Kent, England. Composer; Musicologist. *Education:* BA. Hons., 1st Class, 1984, MPhil., 1985, MA, 1987, PhD., 1989; Junior Exhibitioner, Royal Academy of Music; King's College Cambridge. *Career:* Research Fellow, Fitzwilliam College, Cambridge, 1987-93; Lecturer in Music, University of Nottingham, 1993. *Compositions:* Symphonic Poem Messalina, Broadcast, BBC Concert Orchestra, Radio 3, 1980; Horn Sonata, Broadcast, BBC Radio 3, 1986; Compositions performed at Purcell Room, 1979, Royal Festival Hall, 1980, Queen Elizabeth Hall, 1986; Cambridge Greek Plays, Incidental Scores, 1983 and 1989. *Publications:* Britten and the Gamelan, in D. Mitchell, Death in Venice, 1987; Britten: Billy Budd, 1993; Britten: Letters, 1946-56, co-editor with Donald Mitchell, 1994. *Contributions to:* Musical Times; Journal of Musicological Research; Journal of Royal Musical Association, Music and Letters. *Address:* c/o Dept of Music, University of Nottingham NG7 2RD, England.

COOKE Richard, b. 1958, England. Conductor. *Education:* Chorister at St Paul's Cathedral; Choral scholar at King's College, Cambridge, under David Willcocks. *Career:* Conducted various University orchestras; Led the chamber ensemble in the War Requiem at the Festival Hall, 1984; Trained the London Philharmonic Choir in Mahler 8 and for The Kingdom by Elgar; Has conducted concerts at the Albert and Festival Halls and throughout South East England; Gothenburg Symphony Orchestra from 1989 in Belshazzar's Feast, the Glagolitic Mass, Dvořák 6 and the Sea Symphony by Vaughan Williams; Has also conducted the Brahms Requiem, A Child of our Time, Monteverdi's Vespers and St Nicolas in Sweden; Verdi Requiem at the Uppsala International Festival (1990) and in Boulogne and Canterbury; Conductor of the Chalmers Music Weeks in Sweden and Artistic Director of the St Columb Festival in Cornwall. *Recordings include:* Mahler 8th Symphony and The Kingdom, with the London Philharmonic Choir. *Address:* c/o Gothenburg Symphony, Konserthuset, Stenhammarsgaton 1, S-412 56 Gothenburg, Sweden.

COOP Jane Austin, b. 18 Apr 1950, Saint John, New Brunswick, Canada. Concert Pianist. m. George Laverock, 22 Feb 1984. 1 daughter. *Education:* Artist Diploma 1971, MusBac (Performance), 1972, University of Toronto; MM, Peabody Conservatory, Baltimore, 1974. *Debut:* St Lawrence Centre, Toronto, Canada; Wigmore Hall, London, England; Carnegie Recital Hall, New York, USA. *Career:* Soloist with all major Canadian orchestras; Recitals and concerts in Canada, USA, England, France, Poland, Holland, Yugoslavia, Hungary, Czechoslovakia, USSR. *Recordings:* The Romantic

Piano; Beethoven - Eroica variations and Sonatas Op 109 and Op 111; Bach: English Suite No 3 and Partita No 5; Haydn: 4 Sonatas; Mozart: The Piano Quartets, with members of the Orford Quartet; Piano pieces. *Honours:* Finalist, Munich International Competition, 1977; 1st prize, Washington International Piano Competition, 1975; Killam Award for Career Excellence, 1989. *Current Management:* Anglo Swiss Artists Management Ltd, London. *Address:* 3964 West 18th Avenue, Vancouver, British Columbia, Canada V6S 1B7.

COOPER Barry Anthony Raymond, b. 2 May 1949, Westcliff-on-Sea, Essex, England. University Lecturer. m. Susan Catherine Baynes, 7 July 1973, 4 children. *Education:* Gordonstoun School, 1962-66; University College, Oxford, 1966-73; MA, DPhil, FRCO, FRSA, Organ studies with John Webster, Composition with Kenneth Leighton. *Career:* Lecturer in Music, St Andrews University, 1973; Research Officer, 1974, Lecturer in Music, 1978, Senior Lecturer in Music, 1989, University of Aberdeen; Senior Lecturer in Music, University of Manchester, 1990. *Compositions:* Oratorio, The Ascension; Song-Cycle, The Unasked Question; Wind band, Mons Graupius; Choral, Organ and Chamber Music. *Publications:* G B Sammartini - Concerto in G (Editor OUP) 1976; J C Schickhardt - Sonata in D (Ed OUP), 1978; J Stanley - Six Voluntaries (Arranger and Ed, Musica Rara), 1975; Catalogue of Early Printed Music in Aberdeen Libraries, 1978. Englische Musiktheorie im 17 und 18 Jahrhundert (in: Geschichte der Musiktheorie, Band 9, 1986); Beethoven's Symphony No. 10, First Movement (Realisation and Completion), Universal Edition, 1988; English Solo Keyboard Music of the Middle and Late Baroque, 1989; Beethoven and the Creative Process, 1990; L v Beethoven, Three Bagatelles (Ed Novello), 1991; The Beethoven Compendium, (Ed), 1991. *Contributions to:* Musical Times; Music and Letters; Music Review; RMA Research Chronicle; Proceedings of the RMA; Recherches sur la Musique Française Classique; Early Music; Acta Musicologica; Beethoven Newsletter. *Honours:* Osgood Prize, 1972; Halstead Scholarship, 1972-74; RSE Research Fellow (1986-87). *Memberships:* Royal Musical Association; Royal College of Organists. *Hobbies:* Soccer; Drama. *Address:* Department of Music, University of Manchester, Denmark Road, Manchester M15 6HY, England.

COOPER Imogen, b. 28 Aug 1949, London, England. Concert Pianist. m. John Alexander Batten, 18 June 1982. *Education:* Premier Prix Diploma, Paris Conservatoire, 1967; Master classes, Alfred Brendel, Vienna, 1969, 1970. *Career:* TV debut, Promenade Concerts, London, 1973; Prom appearances since; 1st woman pianist (& British artist), South Bank Piano Series, Queen Elizabeth Hall, London; Regular broadcasts, all major British orchestras and festivals; Performances in USA, Australia, Japan and most European Countries. *Recordings:* Schubert: Last 6 Years, 1823-28; Mozart: Concerti for 2 & 3 Pianos, with Alfred Brendel & Sir Neville Marriner, Academy of St Martin-in-the-Fields; Schubert, 3-disc box, 4-hand piano music, with Anne Queffelec. *Honour:* Mozart Memorial Prize, 1969. *Hobbies:* Reading; Walking; Tandem cycling with husband; Visiting art galleries; Eating. *Current Management:* Mebus Artists Management, PO Box 355, 3860 AJ, Nijkerk, Netherlands. *Address:* Mebus Artists Management, PO Box 355, 3860 AJ, Nijkerk, Netherlands.

COOPER Joseph Elliott Needham. b. 7 Oct. 1912, Westbury on Trym, England. Concert Pianist; Lecturer. m. (1) Jean Greig, 1947 (dec 1973) (2) Carol Borg, 1975. *Education:* Organ Scholar, Keble College, Oxford University, MA Oxon; ARCM Solo Piano; Study of piano with Egon Petri. *Debut:* Wigmore Hall 1947 (postponed from 1939 due to WWII). *Career:* Recitals throughout UK and performances with leading orchestras; Presenter of Concert Biographies; Tours of Europe, Africa, India, Canada; Regular Contributor to BBC programmes and Chairman, Face the Music, BBC TV. *Composition:* Arrangement of Vaughan Williams Piano Concerto for 2 pianos. *Recordings:* Standard piano repertoire and Hidden Melodies (own compositions of well-known tunes in styles of classical composers). *Honours:* Ambrose Fleming Award, Royal TV Society, 1961; OBE, 1982. *Memberships:* Liveryman, Worshipful Company of Musicians; Garrick Club; Member, Music Panel, Arts Council & Chairman, Piano Sub-Committee, 1966-71. *Hobbies:* Sailing; Walking. *Address:* Octagon Lodge, Ranmore, Dorking, Surrey RH5 6SX, England.

COOPER Kenneth, b. 31 May 1941, New York City, NY, USA. Harpsichordist; Pianist; Musicologist; Conductor; Educator. m. Josephine Mongiardo, 1 June 1969, 1 son. *Education:* H.S. of Music and Art, NYC; BA 1962; MA Graduate Faculties, 1964, PhD, Graduate Faculties, 1971, Columbia University; Harpsichord Study with Sylvia Marlowe, Mannes College of Music. *Debut:* Wigmore Hall, 1965; Alice Tully Hall, USA, 1973. *Career:* Academic: Instructor, Barnard College, 1965-71; Adjunct Assistant Professor, Brooklyn College, 1971-73; Professor of Harpsichord, Director of Collegium, Mannes College, 1975-; Visiting Specialist in Performance Practice, Montclair State College, 1977-; Artist-in-Residence, Columbia University, 1983-; Graduate Seminars in Baroque Performance Practice, Manhattan School of Music, 1984-; Director, Baroque Orchestra, Manhattan School of Music; Graduate Workshops in Performance Practice, Peabody Conservatory of Music, 1987-; Many residencies and guest appearances and lectures; Performance: Premieres of works by Seymour Barab, Noel Lee, Ferruccio Busoni, Paul Ben-Haim, Ernst Krenek, etc.; Dozens of modern day revivals; Guest appearances and festivals. *Recordings:* Bach Harpsichord Music Vol 1 (Musical Heritage Society); Should Auld Acquaintance Be Forgot; Scarlatti Sonatas Volumes 1 and 2; Handel: Theatre and Outdoor Musick; Handel/Scarlatti Cantatas with Judith Blegen; Bach Gamba-Harpsichord Sonatas with Yo-Yo Ma; Bach/Handel: Flute-Harpsichord Sonatas with Paula Robison; A Musical Celebration with Ani Kavafian, etc; (also as arranger) Silks and Rags with Sam Pilafian etc; Bach: Goldberg Variations. *Publications:* Monteverdi: Tirsi e Clori; Three Centuries of Music in Score. *Contributions to:* Current Musicology; Musical Quarterly; Stagebill; Opus; High Fidelity; MGG; Vanguard. TV: The Adams Chronicles Channel 13; Brandenburg No. 5, Live from Lincoln Center, with Cha. Music Society of Lincoln Center. *Address:* 425 Riverside Drive, New York, NY 10025, USA.

COOPER Paul, b. 19 May 1926, Victoria, Illinois, USA. Composer; Professor. m. Christine Ebert, 30 Apr 1953, 1 son, 1 daughter. *Education:* Studied with Ernest Kanitz, Halsey Stevens, and Roger Sessions, University of Southern California, Los Angeles, BA, 1950, MA, 1953, DMA, 1956, and with Nadia Boulanger, Conservatory and Sorbonne, Paris, 1953-54. *Career:* Teacher, 1955-65, Professor of Music, 1965-68, Chairman of the Theory Department, 1966-68, University of Michigan, Ann Arbor; Professor of Composition, University of Cincinnati College-Conservatory of Music, 1969-74; Shepherd School of Music, Rice University, Houston, Texas, 1974-; Visiting Professor, Royal Academy of Music, Stockholm, 1985, Royal Conservatory of Music, Copenhagen, 1988. *Compositions:* Dramatic: Mysterion for Soprano, Narrator, Chamber Orchestra, and Optional Dancers, 1988; Orchestral: 6 symphonies: No 1, Concertant, 1966, No 2, Antiphons, 1971, No 3, Lamentations, 1971, No 4, Landscape, 1973-75, No 5, Symphony in 2 Movements, 1982-83, No 6, In Memoriam, 1987; 2 violin concertos, 1967, 1980-82; Liturgies for Woodwinds, Brass, and Percussion, 1968; A Shenandoah: For Ives' Birthday for Flute, Trumpet, Viola, and Orchestra, 1974; Descants for Viola and Orchestra, 1975; Homage for Flute, Trumpet, Viola, and Orchestra, 1976; Cello Concerto, 1976-78; Variants, 1978; Flute Concerto, 1980-81; Organ Concerto, 1982; Saxophone Concerto, 1982; Duo Concertante for Violin, Viola, and Orchestra, 1985; Jubilate for Woodwinds, Brass, and Percussion; Double Concerto for Violin, Viola, and Orchestra, 1985-87; Chamber: 6 string quartets, 1952-77; Singforia, solo piano, 1989; John Perry Love Songs, Dances, 1985; Poem, 1990; Cleveland Chamber Orchestra, Last Call; Song Cycle, soprano, flute, clarinet,

piano, violin, viola and cello, premiere, 1990, DA Camera Society, Houston, USA. *Publications:* Perspectives in Music Theory, 1973, 2nd edition, 1981. *Address:* c/o Shepherd School of Music, Rice University, Houston, TX 77251, USA.

COOPERSTOCK Andrew, b. 9 July 1960, Indianapolis, USA. Pianist. *Education:* BM, University of Cincinnati, 1981; MM, Juilliard School, 1983; DMA, Peabody Conservatory, 1988. *Debut:* Weill Hall, New York, May 1989. *Career:* Mozart Bicentennial concerto appearance at Lincoln Center, New York - Alice Tully Hall, Jupiter Symphony Orchestra, Nygaard, May 1991; US Premiere: Twilight Fantasies (Robert Starer) May 1989; Faculty, The University of Oklahoma, Brevard Music Centre, North Carolina; Faculty Inspiration Point Fine Arts Colony (Arkansas); European debut May 1993. *Publication:* The Sports et Divertissements of Erik Satie, (DMA thesis, 1988). *Address:* School of Music, The University of Oklahoma, Norman, OK 73019, USA.

COPE David (Howell), b. 17 May 1941, San Francisco, California, USA. Composer; Writer; Instrument Maker. *Education:* Studied at Arizona State University and with Halsey Stevens, Ingolf Dahl and George Perle at the University of Southern California. *Career:* Teacher at Kansas State College, 1968-9, California Lutheran College, the Cleveland Institute, Miami University of Ohio and the University of California, Santa Cruz, from 1977; Editor of The Composer, 1969-81. *Compositions include:* Tragic Overture 1960; 4 Piano Sonatas 1960-67; 2 String Quartets 1961, 1963; Variations for piano and wind 1965; Contrasts for orchestra 1966; Music for Brass and Strings 1967; Iceberg Meadow for prepared piano 1968; Streams for orchestra 1973; Spirals for tuba and tape 1973; Requiem for Bosque Redondo 1974; Arena for cello and tape 1974; Re-Birth for concertband 1975; Rituals for cello 1976; Vectors for 4 percussion 1976; Tenor Saxophone concerto 1976; Threshold and Visions for orchestra 1977; Glassworks for 2 pianos and tape 1979; Piano Concerto 1980; The Way and Corridors of light, for various instruments, 1981, 1983; Afterlife for orchestra 1983. *Address:* c/o ASCAP, ASCAP Building, One Lincoln Plaza, New York, NY 10023, USA.

COPELAND Robert Marshall, b. 30 Jan 1945, Douglas, Wyoming, USA. Musicologist; Choral Director. m. Louise Margaret Edgar, 10 June 1966, 1 son, 2 daughters. *Education:* BS, Geneva College, 1966; M.Mus., 1970; PhD, 1974, University of Cincinnati, Ohio. *Career:* Assistant, Associate, Professor, Music, Acting Chairman, Fine Arts, Mid America College, Kansas, 1971-81; Visiting Lecturer, Music History, University of Kansas, 1977; Professor, Music, Chairman, Music, Director, Choral Activities, Geneva College, 1981-. *Compositions:* Tunes and Harmonizations; Choral and Chamber Music. *Publications:* Sing Up: Learning Music for Worship 1973; The Book of Psalms for Singing Co-Editor, 1973; Essentials of Canon and Fugue 1979; Spare No Exertions 1986; Editor, Newsletter, American Choral Directors Association of Pennsylvania. *Contributions to:* Musical Quarterly; College Music Symposium; Museums, Humanities and Educated Eyes 1982. *Memberships:* President, Allegheny Chapter, American Musicological Society; Sonneck Society for American Music; College Music Society; American Choral Directors Association; American Association of University Professors. *Hobbies:* Book Collecting; Genealogy; Fiction. *Address:* Department of Music, Geneva College, 3200 College Avenue, Beaver Falls, PA 15010-3599, USA.

COPLEY John (Michael Harold), b. 12 June 1933, Birmingham, England. Opera Director; Producer. *Education:* Sadler's Wells Ballet School; Diploma, honours in theatre design, Central School of Arts and Crafts, London. *Career:* Stage manager, opera and ballet companies, Sadler's Wells in Rosebery Avenue, 1953-57, various musicals, plays, etc., London's West End; Deputy stage manager 1960-63, assistant resident producer 1963-66, associate 1966-72, resident producer 1972-75, principal resident producer 1975-

; Principal Resident Producer, 1975-88, Covent Garden Opera Company. Productions at Covent Garden include: Suor Angelica, 1965; Così fan Tutte, 1968, 1981; Le Nozze di Figaro, 1971; Don Giovanni, 1973; Faust, 1974; Benvenuto Cellini, 1976; Ariadne auf Naxos, 1976; Maria Stuarda, Royal Silver Jubilee Gala, 1977; La Traviata, Lucrezia Borgia, 1980; Semele, 1982; Other productions include: Numerous operas, London Coliseum; Athens Festival; Netherlands Opera; Belgian National Opera; Wexford Festival; Dallas Civic Opera, (US Debut, 1972, Lucia di Lammermoor); Chicago Lyric Opera; Greek National Opera; Australian Opera; English Opera North; Scottish Opera; English Opera Group; Vancouver Opera; Ottawa Festival; San Francisco Opera; Metropolitan Opera, New York; Santa Fe Opera; La Bohème, 1990; Houston Grand Opera; Washington Opera; San Diego Opera; London West End; Dallas production of Hansel and Gretel seen at Los Angeles, 1992; directed the local premiere of Britten's A Midsummer Night's Dream, Houston, 1993. Appearances include: Apprentice, Britten's Peter Grimes, Covent Garden, 1950; Soloist, Bach's St. John Passion, Bremen, Germany 1965; Ferdy, A Patriot for Me, Royal Court Theatre, 1965. Co-director with Patrick Garland, Fanfare for Europe Gala, Covent Garden, 1973. *Address:* 9D Thistle Grove, London, SW10 9RR, England.

CORBELLI Alessandro, b. 21 Sept 1952, Turin, Italy. Singer (Baritone). *Education:* Studied with Giuseppe Valdengo. *Debut:* Bergamo 1974, as Marcello in La Bohème. *Career:* Many appearances in the buffo repertory at opera houses in Italy, Vienna, Paris and Germany; Rossini roles include Pacuvio in La Pietra del paragone (Piccola Scala and Edinburgh 1982), Dandini in La Cenerentola (Glyndebourne 1985) and Gaudenzio in Il Pietra del Paragone (Paris, 1986); Rome Opera 1985-86, as Belcore (L'Elise d'Amore) and Marcello; Covent Garden debut 1988, as Taddeo in L'Italiana in Algeri; Season 1989-90 in Pergolesi's Lo frate 'nnamorato at La Scala, conducted by Muti, as Don Alfonso at the Salzburg Festival and as Germano in La Scala di Seta at Schwetzingen; Other roles include Papageno (Ravenna, 1986), Guglielmo, Escamillo, Malatesta and the Figaros of Mozart, Rossini and Paisiello; Fabrizio in Crispino e la Comare, Pantaleone in The Love of Three Oranges and Monteverdi's Ottone; Season 1992 as Belcore at Parma, Rossini's Martino and Germano at Cologne, the Paris Opéra-Comique and the Schwetzingen Festival. *Recordings include:* La Cenerentola, conducted by Abbado; L'Italiana in Algeri (CBS and Deutsche Grammophon); Paisiello's Barbiere di Siviglia and La Buona Figliuola by Piccinni. *Address:* c/o Teatro alla Scala, Via Filodrammatici 2, I-202121 Milan, Italy.

CORBETT Sidney, b. 26 Apr 1960, Chicago, Illinois, USA. Composer. *Education:* BA with high distinction in Music Composition, 1982, further studies, 1978-82, University of California, San Diego; Studied composition principally with Pauline Oliveros, Bernard Rands, Joji Yuasa, Jean-Charles François; MM, 1984, MMA, 1985, DMA, 1989, Yale School of Music; Principal composition teachers include Jacob Druckman and Martin Bresnick; Thesis on Metaphor Structures in Contemporary Music; DAAD Fellow and member of G. Ligeti Seminar, Hamburg, Germany, 1985-87. *Career:* Compositions performed in USA and Europe, including radio broadcasts; Active as composer in Germany, 1985-. *Compositions:* Arien, violin solo, 1983; Pastel, No 1 & 2, trombone quartet, 1984, 1988; Ghost Reveille, 1984, for orchestra; For Pianos, for 4 pianos, 1984; Bass Animation, for contrabass with 2 percussion, 1985; Arien IV: Solo Music for Guitar, 1986; Kandinsky Romance, for chamber ensemble, 1986; Cactus Flower, for solo flute, 1988; Pianos' Dreams, piano duo (1989); Concerto for trombone and wind orchestra, 1989; Lieder aus der Dunkelkammer, 1990 for soprano, harp and chamber orchestra; Symphony No. 1 Tympan, 1991-92; Hamlet Variations (in memoriam John Coltrane) for solo euphonium, 1992; Gloucester Epiphenies for chamber ensemble, 1993; Music published by Moeck Verlag, Celle, Germany. *Hobbies:* Reading; Sports. *Address:* Vogelsangstr. 55, 70000 Stuttgart 1, Germany.

CORBOZ Michel, b. 14 Feb 1934, Marsens, Switzerland. Conductor. *Education:* Studied at Ecole Normale in Fribourg. *Career:* Chorus Master at Notre-Dame in Lausanne from 1954, leading such works as the Fauré Requiem; Accompanied singers at the organ and worked at various Lausanne churches; Founded the Ensemble Vocal et Instrumental de Lausanne 1961, giving notable performances of Monteverdi's Orfeo; Conductor of the choirs of the Gulbenkian Foundation in Lisbon from 1969, leading works by Bach, Monteverdi and Vivaldi; Conducted Monteverdi's Il Ritorno di Ulisse at Mézières 1989. *Recordings:* Monteverdi's Orfeo and Vespers, Bach's B minor Mass, Cavalli's Ercole Amante, Charpentier's David et Jonathas, works by Vivaldi and Giovanni Gabrieli. *Address:* c/o Erato, WEA Records, PO Box 59, Alperton Lane, Wembley, London HAO 1FJ, England.

CORDERO Roque, b. 16 Aug 1917, Panama. Composer; Conductor; Educator. m. Elizabeth L Johnson, 30 June 1947, 3 sons. *Education:* Mus Ed, University of Minnesota, USA, 1946; BA magna cum laude, Hamline University, 1947; Studied Composition with Ernst Krenek 1943-47, Conducting with Dimitri Mitropoulos 1944-46, Stanley Chapple 1946, and Leon Barzin 1947-49. *Career:* Director/Professor, National Institute of Music, Panama, 1950-64; Conductor, National Orchestra of Panama, 1964-66; Guest Conductor in Colombia, Brazil, Chile, Argentina, Puerto Rico and USA; Professor of Music and Assistant Director, Latin American Music Center, Indiana University, USA, 1966-69; Professor of Music, Illinois State University, 1972-; . *Compositions:* Over 20 published including Cinco Mensajes para Cuatro Amigos (for guitar). *Recordings:* Violin Concerto and 8 Miniatures, Detroit Symphony, Columbia Records; 2nd Symphony, Louisville Editions; Duo 1954, Inter-American Editions. *Publications:* Curso de Solfeo, Argentina 1963, Mexico 1975. *Hobby:* Chess. *Address:* Music Department, Illinois State University, Normal, IL 61790-5660, USA.

CORELLI Franco, b. 8 Apr 1921, Ancona, Italy. Singer (Tenor). *Education:* Liceo Musicale, Pesaro. *Debut:* Spoleto 1951, as Don José in Carmen; La Scala Milan 1954-65, as Licinio in La Vestale, Poliuto, as Raoul in Les Huguenots and as Gualtiero in Il Pirata; Covent Garden debut 1957, as Cavaradossi in Tosca; Metropolitan Opera 1961-74, notably as Puccini's Calaf and Rodolfo, Verdi's Ernani and Manrico, Gounod's Romeo and Massenet's Werther; Guest appearances in Paris, Berlin, Vienna, San Francisco and Florence. *Recordings:* Roles in Aida, Tosca, Carmen, Don Carlos, Les Huguenots, Il Trovatore, Faust and Norma; Companies include Cetra, Columbia, Eurodisc and Decca. 21. *Address:* c/o Teatro alla Scala, Via Filodrammatic 2, Milan, Italy.

CORGHI Azio, b. 9 Mar 1937, Cirie, Turin, Italy. Composer. *Education:* Studied at Turin Conservatory, Piano Diploma 1961 and with Bruno Bettinelli at Milan Conservatory. *Career:* Freelance composer and teacher of composition at Conservatorio Giuseppe Verdi, Milan. *Compositions:* Music theatre pieces, Symbola 1971 and Tactus, 1974; Ballets with voices, Actus III 1978 and Mazapegul, 1986; Opera Gargantua after Rabelais produced at Teatro Regio Turin, 1984; Opera Blimunda produced at Teatro Lirico Milan, 1990; Opera Divara produced at Städtisches Bühnen Münster, 1993. *Publications:* Critical editions of L'Italiana in Algeri and Tosca. *Address:* Conservatorio Giuseppe Verdi, Via del Conservatorio 12, 1-20122 Milan, Italy.

CORIGLIANO John (Paul), b. 16 Feb 1938, New York City, USA. Composer; Teacher. *Education:* BA, Columbia University, 1959; Studied with Otto Luening; Vittorio Giannini, Manhattan School of Music; Privately with Paul Creston. *Career:* Music Programmer, WQXR-FM and WBAI-FM, New York, 1959-64; Associate Producer of Musical Programmes, CBS-TV, 1961-72; Music Director, Morris Theatre, New Jersey, 1962-64; Teacher of Composition, College of Church Musicians, Washington, DC, 1968-71; Manhattan School of Music,

1971-; Lehman College of the City University of New York, 1973-, Distinguished Professor, 1986-; Composer-in-residence, Chicago Symphony Orchestra, 1987-89; Symphony No 1 premiere, performances by Boston Symphony, NY Phil, Chicago Symphony, Seattle Symphony, tour, Chicago symphony; Opera: The Ghosts of Versailles, premiere, 1991 (Metropolitan Opera, NY); Symphony, No 1, 1989-90. *Compositions:* The Naked Carmen, mixed-media opera, 1970; The Ghosts of Versalles, 1991; Incidental music for plays; Film scores; Orchestral: Elegy, 1965; Tournaments Overture, 1966; Piano Concerto, 1968; Creations, 2 scenes from Genesis for Narrator and Chamber Orchestra, 1972; Gazebo Dances for Band, 1973; Aria for Oboe and Strings, 1975; Oboe Concerto, 1975; Voyage for String Orchestra, 1976, also for Flute and String Orchestra, 1983; Clarinet Concerto, 1977; Flute Concerto: Pied Piper Fantasy, 1981; Promenade Overture, 1981; 3 Hallucinations, 1981; Echoes of Forgotten Rites: Summer Fanfare, 1982; Fantasia on an Ostinato, 1985; Chamber: Kaleidoscope for 2 Pianos, 1959; Sonata for Violin and Piano, 1963; Etude Fantasy for Piano, 1976; Vocal: The Cloisters, 4 songs for Voice and Piano, 1965, also for Voice and Orchestra, 1976; Christmas at the Cloisters for Chorus and Organ or Piano, 1966; Poem in October for Tenor and 8 Instruments, 1970 also for Tenor and Orchestra, 1976; Poem on His Birthday for Baritone, Chorus and Orchestra, 1976. *Recordings:* Symphony No. 1, Chicago Symphony/Barenboim, Erato, Pied Piper Fantasy, Fantasia On An Ostinato. *Honours:* Guggenheim Fellowship, 1968-69; National Endowment for the Arts grant, 1976; American Acadamy Award, and Institute of Arts and Letters, 1990; Election to membership, American Academy and Institute of Arts and Letters, 1991. *Memberships:* American Society of Composers, Authors and Publishers; American Academy and Institute of Arts and Letters, 1991. *Current Management:* Michael Mace Associates Ltd; 315 West 57th Street, New York, NY 10019, USA. *Address:* 365 West End Avenue, New York, NY 10024, USA.

CORNWELL Joseph, b. 1959, England. Singer (Tenor). *Career:* Sang originally with such early music groups as the Consort of Musicke and the Taverner Consort; Promenade Concert debut 1982, in Monteverdi's Vespers under Andrew Parrott; Tours of Holland and France in the Bach Passions; Verdi's Requiem at the Albert Hall conducted by David Willcocks; Bruckner's Te Deum at the Festival Hall; Appearances at the Paris, Bruges, Flanders, Three Choirs and Brighton Festivals; Conductors include Trevor Pinnock, Stephen Cleobury, Ton Koopman and Roger Norrington; Bach's B minor Mass with the London Bach Orchestra at the Barbican, Nov 1990; Has sung on ITV, Swiss television and BBC TV; Opera roles include Fenton in Falstaff, Frederic in Mignon, Jove in The Return of Ulysses (Kent Opera) and parts in Mahagonny and Let's Make an Opera; Sang title role in Monteverdi's Orfeo for Oslo Summer Opera, conducted by Andrew Parrott, and in 1993 for Boston Early Music Festival; Also sang Lurcanio in Handel's Ariodante for St Gallen Opera, in Switzerland; Arretro in Peri's Euridice in Rouen, 1992-93. *Recordings include:* Monteverdi Christmas Vespers (EMI); Handel's Messiah (EMI); Albums for Decca, Harmonia Mundi, Gymell and Hyperion; Monteverdi Vespers for EMI, Parrott; Rossini's Petite Messe Sollenelle, Accent label with Jos Van Immerseel. *Honours:* BA Honours in Music, York University. *Address:* c/o Norman McCann International Artists Ltd, The Coach House, 56 Lawrie Park Gardens, London SE26 6XJ, England.

CORP Ronald, b. 1951, England. Conductor. *Career:* Founder Conductor of New London Orchestra 1988 and New London Children's Choir 1991; Chorus Director of London Choral Society and Conductor of Highgate Choral Society; Director of Finchley Children's Music Group 1981-91; Broadcasts for BBC with BBC Singers, BBC Concert Orchestra, Ulster Orchestra, New London Orchestra and New London Children's Choir; Promenade concert debut 1990 with Britten's Noye's Fludde and further Prom with New London Orchestra in 1991. *Compositions:* Andall the Trumpets Sounded,

1989; Laudamus, 1992, other choral works; *Recordings:* Five discs with New London Orchestra -- Poulenc, Satie, Milhaud, Prokofiev and Virgil Thomson. *Publication:* The Choral Singer's Companion, 1987. *Address:* 41 Aberdare Gardens, London NW6 3AL, England.

CORSARO Frank (Andrew), b. 22 Dec 1924, New York, USA. Opera director. *Education:* Studied at the City College of New York, the Yale University School of Drama and the Actors Studio. *Debut:* New York City Opera 1958, Floyd's Susanna. *Career:* City Opera productions have included Rigoletto, La Traviata, Pelléas et Mélisande, Prince Igor, Faust, Don Giovanni, A Village Romeo and Juliet and Janáček's Makropoulos Affair and Cunning Little Vixen, 1981; For Houston Opera has produced premiere productions of Pasatieri's The Seagull, 1974 and Scott Joplin's Treemonisha 1975; Premieres of Floyd's Of Mice and Men (Seattle 1970) and Hoiby's Summer and Smoke (St Paul 1971); At the Glyndebourne Festival has produced Prokofiev's The Love of Three Oranges; Metropolitan Opera 1984, Handel's Rinaldo; Season 1992 with the US Stage premiere of Busoni's Doktor Faust, New York City Opera. *Address:* c/o New York City Opera, Lincoln Center, New York, NY 10023, USA.

CORTES Gardar, b. 1950, Reykjavik, Iceland. Singer (Tenor); Conductor. *Education:* Studied at Royal Academy of Music and Trinity College of Music in London. *Career:* Has conducted choirs in Iceland and founded the Reykjavik Symphony Orchestra 1985, leading it on a tour of Denmark; With Icelandic Opera has conducted Orpheus in the Underworld, Pagliacci and Die Fledermaus, Noye's Fludde at the International Festival in Reykjavik; Appearances as singer with Oslo Opera, Royal Swedish Opera, Seattle Opera, Windsor Festival, Opera North and Belfast Festival; Intendant of the Gothenburg Opera, Sweden; Roles have included Eisenstein, Tamino, Hoffmann, Radames, Cavaradossi, Florestan and Otello. *Address:* c/o John Coast Ltd, 31 Sinclair Road, London W14 ONS, England.

CORTEZ Viorica, b. 22 Dec 1935, Bucium, Rumania. Singer (Mezzo-Soprano). m. Emmanuel Bondeville 1974 (dec 1987). *Education:* Studied at the Iasi and Bucharest Conservatories. *Debut:* Iasi Opera 1960, as Dalila. *Career:* Sang Dalila at Toulouse 1965; Bucharest Opera 1965-70; Covent Garden debut 1968, as Carmen; Italian debut 1969, as Amneris at Naples; La Scala Milan 1970, as Dalila; US debut Seattle Opera 1971; Metropolitan Opera from 1971, as Carmen, Amneris, Giulietta in Les Contes d'Hoffmann, Adalgisa in Norma and Azucena; Chicago debut 1973, in Maria Stuarda; Sang in the premiere of Bondeville's Antoine et Cleopatre, Rouen 1974; Paris Opera 1980, in Bluebeard's Castle, Oedipus Rex and Boris Godunov; Sang La Cieca in La Gioconda at the Verona Arena and Barcelona, 1988; Gertrude in Hamlet, Turin, 1990 and the title role in the premiere of La Lupa by Marco Tutino at Livorno; Season 1992 as Ulrica at Genoa. *Recordings:* Carmen; Aida; Il Trovatore; Verdi's Oberto; Donizetti's Requiem; Rigoletto; Video of Rigoletto. *Address:* c/o S.A. Gorlinsky Ltd., 33 Dover Street, London W1X 4NJ, England.

CORTINAS P, Violinist; Conductor. *Education:* Studied at the Juilliard School of Music, New York; The Musikhochschule Franz Liszt, Germany. *Career:* Concert Choirmaster, the Orchestra Sinfonica de Xalapa, Mexico; The Opéra Royal de Wallonie, Belgium; Royal Winnipeg Ballet, Canada; Guest Leader with the Berner Symphonier Orchestra, Switzerland; Opera comapnies of Cologne and Dusseldorf, Germany; Free-Lance work with New York City; Professor, seven years with Südwestfälische Philharmonie- Has performed new works in Carnegie Hall and Town Hall, New York; Wigmore Hall, London; Isang Yung's University of Berlin, contemporary Music Festival; Invited by Department in Washington, DC, tour all capitals in Latin America; Took part in Festival International Cervantino, 1987; Seminars at the Escuela Nacional de Música in Mexico City; Head of Conducting Department at the National Conservatory; Artistic Director and Conductor of the Orquesta Filarmónica del Conservatorio Nacional.

Publications: Notes on Orchestral Conducting, published by Ed. Rocordi. *Honours:* N Gagliano violin (1740) presented by Mexican President Miguel de la Madrid. *Address:* Herrengasse 9, CH-6430 Schwyz, Schweiz, Switzerland.

COSMA Octavian Lazar, b. 15 Feb 1933, Treznea, Salaj, Romania. Musicologist; Professor. m. Elena, 15 Nov 1958, 1 son, 1 daughter. *Education:* Rimsky-Korsakov Conservatory, St Petersburg, USSR, 1959. *Debut:* Muzica, 1954. *Career:* Counselor, Ministry of Culture and Education, 1959-63; Assistant Lecturer and, Professor, Academy of Music, Bucharest, 1959-; Secretary, 1990 and Vice-President, 1992, Romanian Union of Composers and Musicologists; Editor-in-chief, Journal 'Muzica', 1990. *Publications:* The Romanian Opera, 2 volumes, 1962; Enesco's Oedipus, 1967; The Chronicle of Romanian Music, Volumes I, 1973, II, 1974, III, 1975, IV, 1976, V, 1983, VI, 1984, VII, 1986 VIII, 1988; IX, 1991. *Contributions to:* Various professional journals. *Honours:* Ciprian Porumbescu Prize, Romanian Academy, 1962; Prize, Romanian Union of Composers, 1968. *Memberships:* Romanian Union of Composers; American Musicological Society. *Current Management:* Conservatorul Ciprian Porumbescu, Bucharest. *Hobbies:* Sport; Football; Tourism. *Address:* Cotroceni 5-7, Bucharest 76258, Romania.

COSMA Viorel, b. 30 Mar 1923, Timisoara, Rumania. Musicologist. m. Coralia Cosma. *Education:* Municipal Conservatory, Timisoara; Ciprian Porumbescu Conservatory, Bucharest. *Debut:* As Conductor, 1944. *Career:* Musicologist, 1946-. *Publications:* Ciprian Porumbescu, 1957; Two Thousand Years of Music in Rumania, 1976; Rumanian Performers Lexicn, 1976; Many articles in The New Grove Dictionary of Music and Musicians, 1980. *Contributions to:* International musical journals. *Honours:* Prize, Rumanian Academy of Composers, 1970; Prize, Academy of Rumania, 1971. *Memberships:* International Musicologists Society; Georg Friedrich Handel Society; French Musicological Society; Chopin Society. *Hobby:* Motoring. *Address:* Str Luterana nr 3, Bucharest, Romania.

COSSA Dominic, b. 13 May 1935, Jessup, Pennsylvania, USA. Baritone; Teacher. m. Janet Edgerton, 26 Dec 1957. 1 son, 1 daughter. *Education:* BS, University of Scranton, 1959; MA, University of Detroit, 1961; Detroit Institute of Musical Arts; Philadelphia Academy of Vocal Arts; Principal vocal teachers: Anthony Marlowe, Robert Weede and Armen Boyajian. *Debut:* Operatic debut as Morales, Carmen, New York City Opera, 1961. *Career:* Leading baritone roles, New York City Opera; Metropolitan Opera debut, New York as Silvio in Pagliacci, 1970-76; Guest artist, San Francisco Opera, 1970; Opéra du Rhin, Strasbourg, 1976; Teacher, Manhattan School of Music, New York; University of Maryland, Baltimore. *Recordings:* For Decca-London; New World Records; RCA-Victor including Achilles in Giulio Cesare, conducted by Julius Rudel. *Hobbies:* Antiques; Wine collecting; Jogging; Gardening; Collecting early American pressed glass. *Address:* c/o Metropolitan Opera, Lincoln Center, New York, NY 10023, USA.

COSSOTTO Fiorenza, b. 22 Apr 1935, Crescentino, Italy. Singer (Mezzo-Soprano). m. Ivo Vinco 1958. *Education:* Turin Conservatory; Study with Ettore Campogalliani. *Debut:* La Scala Milan 1957, in the premiere of Poulenc's Les Dialogues des Carmélites; returned to Milan until 1973, notably as Verdi's Eboli, Amneris and Azucena, and La Favorite, Les Huguenots, Il Barbiere di Siviglia and Cavalleria Rusticana; Sang Jane Seymour in Anna Bolena at Wexford in 1958; Covent Garden debut 1959, as Neris in Cherubini's Médée; Chicago Lyric Opera 1964, in La Favorite; Metropolitan Opera debut 1968, as Amneris: returned for Laura in La Gioconda, Adalgisa, Norma, Carmen and Mistress Quickly (Falstaff); Sang, Verona Arena, 1960-89, notably as Amneris, which she sang at the Metropolitan, 1989; Sang Dalila at Newark, New Jersey, 1989, the Princess in Adriana Lecouvreur, Rome; Sang Santuzza, Piacenza, 1990; Ulrica at Lisbon and Amneris

at Buenos Aires; Sang Ulrica at Genoa, 1992. *Recordings:* Roles in Andrea Chénier, Norma, Madama Butterfly, La Sonnambula, Macbeth, Don Carlos, Cavalleria Rusticana, Médée and Il Trovatore; Companies include Decca, HMV, RCA, Columbia and Deutsche Grammophon. *Address:* Teatro Comunale, Via I, Frugoni 15/6 16121 Genoa, Italy.

COSSUTTA Carlo, b. 8 May 1932, Trieste, Italy. Opera Singer (Tenor). m. Nidia Cotic, 29 Apr 1960. *Education:* Vocal Study in Musical Conservatory. *Debut:* Cassio, Otello, at Teatro Colon, Buenos Aires 1958. *Career:* Colon, Covent Garden, Wiener Staatsoper, La Scala, Metropolitan, Lyric Opera Chicago, Opera Paris, Deutsche Oper Berlin, Arena di Verona, Gran Teatro Del Liceo. *Recordings:* Traviata; Trovatore; Samson et Dalila; La Vidabreve; by Falla Messa Da Requiem, Verdi; Otello, Verdi. *Honours:* Grand Officer Italian Republic, 1983; Sigilo Trecentesco di Trieste. *Hobby:* Fishing. *Address:* Devincina 12, Trieste, Italy.

COSTA Mary, b. 5 April 1932, Knoxville, Tennessee, USA. Singer (Soprano). *Education:* Studied with Mario Chamlee at Los Angeles Conservatory and with Ernest St John Metz, *Career:* Sang in concert and took small roles in opera then appeared as Susanna at Glyndebourne 1958; San Francisco Opera from 1959, notably in the United States premiere of A Midsummer Night's Dream, 1961; Royal Opera House 1962, as Concepcion in L'Heure Espagnole and Violetta; Metropolitan Opera from 1964, as Violetta, Vanessa, Gilda, Despina, Alice Ford, Manon, Rosalinde and Musetta; Sang at the Bolshoi Theatre, Moscow 1970 and appeared in the film The Great Waltz 1972; Founded the Knoxville Tennessee Opera Company 1978 and established the Mary Costa Scholarship at the University of Tennessee 1979; Many concert appearances. *Recording:* La Bohème. *Address:* c/o Knoxville Opera Company, PO Box 16, Knoxville, TN 37901, USA.

COSTELLO Marilyn, b. 1924, Cleveland, Ohio, USA. Harpist; Teacher. *Education:* Studied at the Curtis Institute with Leonard Salzedo. *Career:* Played with Philadelphia Orchestra 1945, principal harpist from 1946; Engagements with major orchestras in the USA, recitalist and chamber music performer in North America and Europe; Soloist at the Montreux and Menuhin festivals in Switzerland and recitals with the Radio Suisse Romande, Geneva; Appearances at the Minnesota Orchestra and Vermont Mozart Festivals; Head of the harp department at the Curtis Institute. *Honours include:* Gramophone Critics' Award, Italy, 1965; C Hartmann Kuhn Award, Philadelphia Orchestra, 1973. *Address:* c/o Curtis Institute of Music, 1726 Locust Street, Rittenhouse Square, Philadelphia, PA 19103, USA.

COSTINESCU Gheorghe, b. 12 Dec 1934, Bucharest, Romania. Composer; Conductor; Pianist; Educator. m. Silvelin von Scanzoni, 12 November 1971. *Education:* Masters in Composition, Bucharest Conservatory 1961; Courses in New Music, Darmstadt and Cologne 1968; Postgraduate Diploma, The Juilliard School, 1972; Doctor of Musical Arts, with distinction, Columbia University, 1976. *Positions:* Recent positions include: Professor at Lehman College of the City University of New York; Music Director, Conductor of the Bronx Symphony Orchestra. *Debut:* As Composer Pianist, in his own work. Sonata for Violin and Piano, at Shiraz-Persepolis Festival, Iran 1967; Premieres: Evolving Cycle of Two Part Modal Inventions for Piano, Romanian Broadcast 1964; Past Are The Years for tenor and vocal ensemble with Juilliard Chorus, Lincoln Center, New York City 1970; Premiere of Stage Work The Musical Seminar at Tanglewood Festival 1982; German premiere at the State Opera of Stuttgart, 1989; British premiere with Paragon Opera Project at Royal Academy of Music, Glasgow 1992. *Recordings:* Composers Recordings, Inc., USA. *Publications:* Evolving Cycle for Piano 1964; Song to the Rivers of My Country, (vocall symphonic work), 1967; Sonata for

Violin and Piano 1968. *Honours:* George Enescu Prize of Romanian Academy 1965; Alexandre Gretcheaninoff Prize in Composition, The Juilliard School 1970; Music Award from the American Academy and Institute of Arts and Letters 1985; Winner of League ISCM National Composers Competition 1986; Two Grants from National Endowment for the Arts, as producer 1986 and as composer 1989. *Memberships:* Broadcast Music Inc; American Composers Alliance; American Music Center; Conductors Guild. *Hobbies:* Drawing; Tennis; Downhill Skiing. *Address:* 120 Riverside Drive, Apt 6E, New York, NY 10024, USA.

COTRUBAS Ileana, b. 9 June 1939, Galati, Romania. Opera and Concert Singer. m. Manfred Ramin, 1972. *Education:* Conservatorul Ciprian Porumbescu, Bucharest. *Debut:* Yniold in Pelléas et Mélisande, Bucharest Opera, 1964. *Career:* Frankfurt Opera, 1968-70; Glyndebourne Festival, 1968; Salzburg Festival, 1969; Royal Opera House, Covent Garden, London England, 1971 as Tchaikovsky's Tatiana; Lyric Opera of Chicago, USA, 1973; Paris Opera, France, 1974; La Scala, Milan, Italy, 1975 Metropolitan Opera, New York, USA, 1977 as Mimi in La Bohème; Operatic roles include: Susanna, Pamina, Norina, Gilda, Traviata, Manon, Antonia, Tatiana, Mimi, Mélisande; Concerts with all major European orchestras; Lieder recitals at Musikverein Vienna, Royal Opera House, Covent Garden, Carnegie Hall, New York, La Scala; CD of Manon, 1988; Sang Elisabeth of Valois, Florence, Marguerite at Hamburg, 1985, Amelia Boccanegra, Naples, 1986; Monte Carlo 1987, as Alice Ford, Barcelona, 1988, as Desdemona; Sang Mélisande, Florence, 1989; Retired 1990. *Recordings:* Bach Cantatas; Mozart Masses; Brahms Requiem; Mahler Symphonies 2, 8; Complete Operas including Le Nozze di Figaro, Die Zauberflöte, Hansel und Gretel, Calisto, Louise, L'Elisir d'amore, Les Pecheurs de Perles, La Traviata, Rigoletto, Alzira. *Honours:* 1st Prize, International Singing Competition, Hertogenbosch, The Netherlands, 1965; 1st Prize, Munich Radio Competition, 1966; Austrian Kammersängerin, 1981; Great Officer of the Order Sant Iago da Espada (Portugal), 1990.

COUROUPOS Yorgos, b. 1 Jan 1942, Athens, Greece. Composer. *Education:* Studied the piano at Athens Conservatory, and composition with Messiaen in Paris 1968-72. *Career:* Administrative posts at National Lyric Theatre, Athens; Director of Calamata Municipal Conservatory from 1985. *Compositions:* Music theatre works, notably Dieu le Veut 1975; Grisélidis, 1977; Opera in one act Pylades with libretto G Himonas after Sophocles and Euripides performed at the Athens Concert Hall 1992. *Address:* SACEM (France) and AEPI (Greece), c/o PRS Ltd Member Registration, 29-33 Berners Street, London W1P 4AA, England.

COVELL Roger David, b. 1 Feb 1931, Sydney, New South Wales, Australia. Musicologist; Lecturer; Critic; Conductor. m. (3) Patricia Anne Brown, 3 sons, 1 daughter. *Education:* BA, University of Queensland, 1964; PhD, Music, University of New South Wales, 1976. *Career:* Senior Lecturer, 1966, Associate Professor, 1973, Personal Chair, 1984, Music Department, University of New South Wales; Chief Music Critic, The Sydney Morning Herald, 1960-; Musical Director, University of New South Wales Opera, Grainger Consort; Editor/translator, 17th, 18th and 19th century operas. *Compositions:* Theatre music; Choral pieces. *Recordings:* Barry Conyngham's Edward John Eyre, HMV, 1974. *Publications:* Australia's Music: Themes of a New Society, 1967; Music in Australia: Needs and Prospects, 1970; Editor and arranger, Edward Geoghegan's The Currency Lass, 1976; Folk Songs of Australia, Volume 2 (with J.Meredith and P.Brown), 1987. *Contributions to:* Studies in Music: Australian Journal of Music Education; Quadrant; Australia Encyclopaedia; Miscellanea Musicologica. *Honours:* Fellow, Australian Academy of the Humanities, 1983; Member of Order of Australia, 1986. *Memberships:* The Australia Council, 1977-83; Australian Society for

Music Education, President 1978-81; Musicological Society of Australia, President 1983-84. *Hobbies:* Blackberry cutting; Cycling. *Address:* 9 Kubya Street, Blackheath, New South Wales 2785, Australia.

COVELLI John (Thomas), b. 12 Oct 1936, Chicago, Illinois, USA. Conductor; Pianist. *Education:* Studied at Columbia University. *Debut:* New York Town Hall 1957, as piano soloist. *Career:* Played piano with US army, 1960-62, then assisted Pierre Monteux at the London Symphony Orchestra; Conducted the Harkness Ballet and the New York City Opera in the late 1960s; St Louis Symphony 1970-71, Kansas City Philharmonic 1971-72; Led the Milwaukee Symphony 1974-76 and was music director of the Flint Symphony 1976-82 and the Binghamton Symphony, New York; Has appeared as conductor and pianist with the Boston Pops Orchestra from 1979.

COVEY-CRUMP Rogers, b. 1944, England. Singer (Tenor). *Education:* Studied at the Royal College of Music in London; BMus London University. *Career:* Concert, broadcasting and commercial recording engagements as a solo artist and as a member of the Hilliard Ensemble, Gothic Voices, the Deller and Taverner Consorts and Singcircle (Stockhausen's Stimmung); Promenade Concerts 1984-91, Purcell's Odes, Bach's Matthew Passion; Pärt's Miserere; Turku Festival 1985, with the Sixteen and London Baroque in the Bach B Minor Mass: returned to Finland for Haydn's Creation, Messiah and the St John Passion by Pärt; Bach B Minor Mass in the Netherlands with Ton Koopman and the Amsterdam Baroque Orchestra, 1986; St Matthew Passion in Madrid; Performances of Bach's St John Passion (as Evangelist) in London, Oxford and Cambridge 1987; Arundel Festival 1988, in the Monteverdi Vespers; Tour of Britain 1988 and 1992 with Contemporary Music Network in Pärt's St John Passion and Miserere; Hilliard Summer Schools since 1984; Residences with the Hilliard Ensemble at the University of California at Davis, 1988 and Bucknell University, Pennsylvania, 1992; Summer Schools in Finland; (Lecturer and writer) on aspects of vocal ensemble style; Sang Purcell's Ode for St Cecilia's Day, the 1991 Promenade Concerts, London. *Recordings include:* Lays of Machaut with the Medieval Ensemble of London; Bach's (B Minor Mass and) St John Passion (Evangelist and Arias), Purcell Ode to St Cecilia and Monteverdi Vespers with Andrew Parrott and the Taverner Players (EMI-Reflexe); Purcell's Dioclesian and Timon of Athens (Erato) with John Eliot Gardiner; Pärt's St John Passion and Miserere (ECM); French and English, Lute Songs, with Paul O'Dette (Hyperion) and with Jakob Lindberg (BIS); Stockhausen's Stimmung, with Singcircle (Hyperion). *Address:* Magenta Music International, 64 Highgate High Street, London N6 5JL, England.

COWAN Sigmund, b. 4 Mar 1948, New York, New York, USA. Singer (Baritone). *Education:* University of Miami; University of Florida; New York Institute of Finance; Juilliard School, Scholarship; Manhattan School of Music, Fellowship. *Career:* Appearances: New York City Opera; Deutsche Oper am Rhein; Spoleto Festival; Kennedy Center; Miami Opera, Basel, Essen, Wiesbaden, Vienna Festival, Berlin Staatsheater, Brussels, Amsterdam (Opera and Concertgebouw), Carnegie Hall, Mexico City, Dublin, Calgary and Edmonton, Canada, Rotterdam (TV VARA), Utrecht (Radio KRO), Amsterdam (VARA Radio), Italy (RAI), USA (NBC TV), Austria (TV ORF), Germany (TV 3rd Channel); Rochester Philharmonic; National Symphony; Baltimore Symphony; Flagstaff Festival; National Orchestra Mexico City. Roles in Nabucco, Rigoletto, Macbeth, Il Trovatore, I Due Foscari, Un Ballo in Maschera, La Forza del destino, La Traviata. *Recordings include:* Die Gezeichneten with Edo de Waart; Nabucco for the New Jersey State Opera. *Hobbies:* Cooking; Theatre; Photography. *Current Management:* Athole Still, London; Dorothy Cone, New York. Address: c/o Dorothy Cone, 60E 86th Street, New York, NY 10028, USA.

COWIE Edward, b. 17 Aug 1943, Birmingham, England. m. (3) Stephanie McGrath 1987, 2 sons, 3

daughters. Composer; University Professor; Painter; Film Maker. *Education:* Chorister Gloucester Cathedral 1955-57; Morley College 1961, with Fricker; Alexander Goehr 1964-68; Southhampton University 1970-71; Leeds University 1971-73. *Career:* Worked in Poland 1971; Lecturer, Lancaster University 1973; Guest professor of Music, Kassel University 1979; Professor of creative arts, University of Wollongong, New South Wales, 1983; Composer-in-residence Royal Liverpool Philharmonic Orchestra 1983-86; International recognition as Painter, Conductor, Broadcaster and Public Speaker. *Compositions:* Stage: Commedia 1978; Kelly 1982; Kate Kelly's Roadshow 1982; Orchestral: Concerto for bass clarinet and tape 1969; Leviathan 1975; Clarinet Concerto No.2 1975; Piano Concerto 1977; L'Or de la trompete d'ete 1977; Concerto for Orchestra 1980; Leonardo 1981; 2 Symphonies 1981, 1983; Harp Concerto 1982; Vocal: Dungeness Choruses 1970; Endymion Nocturnes for tenor and string quartet 1973, revised 1981; Leighton Moss for chorus and chamber orchestra 1975; Gesangbuch for 24 voices and 12 instruments 1976; A Charm of Finches for soprano and 3 flutes 1978; Columbine for soprano and chamber orchestra 1979; Kelly Choruses 1981; Choral Symphony, after Turner, 1982; Missa Brevis 1983; Ancient Voices 1983; Chamber: 4 String Quartets 1973, 1977, 1983, 1983; Kelly Passacaglia for string quartet 1980; Harlequin for harp 1980; Commedia Lazzis for guitar 1980; Kelly-Nolan-Kelly for clarinet; Piano music; Music for brass band. *Hobbies:* Painting; Ornithology; Sailing; Reading; Travel. *Address:* Novello & Co Ltd., 8 Lower James Street, London, W1 England.

COX David (Vassall), b. 4 Feb 1916, Broadstairs, Kent, England. Composer; Writer on Music. m. Barbara Ellen Lee Butcher, 2 Jan 1954, 1 son, 2 daughters. *Education:* Royal College of Music, 1938-40; MA, BMus, Oxford University, 1940. *Career:* Music Producer and Organiser, British Broadcasting Corporation; Music Organiser, External Services, British Broadcasting Corporation, 1956-76. *Compositions include:* Opera: The Children in the Forest; Choral: The Summer's Nightingale; Of Beasts; Songs of Earth and Air; This Child of Life; A Greek Cantata; Jubilate Deo; A Warlock Suite; 3 songs from John Donne; 5 songs from John Milton; Mr Playford's Musical Banquet, for flute or recorder and piano. *Recording:* Of Beasts. *Publications:* Debussy's Orchestral Music, 1974; The Henry Wood Proms, 1980. *Contributor to:* The History of Song; The Symphony; Makers of Modern Culture; Makers of 19th Century Culture; Companion to the Symphony; The Musical Times; The Listener. *Hobbies:* Literature; Films; Photography; Swimming. *Address:* 5 Downs View Close, Pratt's Bottom, Orpington, Kent BR6 7SU, England.

COX Geoffrey Arnold, b. 22 Aug 1951, Brisbane, Queensland, Australia. Organist; Musicologist; Choral Conductor. *Education:* Church of England Grammar School, Brisbane, 1963-68; BA, BMus, University of Queensland, 1974; MPhil, 1977, DPhil, 1985, University of Oxford, England; FTCL; ARCO. *Career:* Organ Scholar, New College, Oxford, England, 1975-78; Lecturer in Music, University of Melbourne, Victoria, 1979-84; Senior Lecturer in Music, Australian Catholic University, 1985-92; Head, School of Arts and Sciences (Victoria), Australian Catholic University, 1993-; Organist and Director of Music, St Peter's, Eastern Hill, Melbourne, 1980-. *Publications:* Gazetteer of Queensland Pipe Organs, 1976; Music for An Australian Prayer Book, 1984; Faber Early Organ Series, Volumes 1-3, England, 1986; Organ Music in Restoration: A Study of Sources, Styles and Influences, 1989. *Address:* Australian Catholic University, Mercy Campus, 251 Mount Alexander Road, Ascot Vale, Victoria 3032, Australia.

COX Jean, b. 16 Jan 1922, Gadsen, Alabama, USA. Singer (Tenor). *Education:* University of Alabama and the New England Conservatory; With Wally Kirsamer in Frankfurt, Luigi Ricci in Rome and Max Lorenz in Munich. *Debut:* New England Opera Company 1951, as Lensky in Eugene Onegin. *Career:* Spoleto 1954 as Rodolfo; Sang at Brunswick 1955-59, Mannheim from 1959; Bayreuth Festival 1956-75, as the Steersman, Erik, Lohengrin, Parsifal, Siegfried and Walther; Hamburg Staatsoper 1958-73; Guest appearances in Berlin, Vienna, Munich, Stuttgart and Frankfurt; Bregenz Festival 1961, in Fra Diavolo; Chicago Lyric Opera 1964, 1970, 1973; Paris Opera 1971, as Siegmund; Covent Garden 1975, Siegfried; Metropolitan Opera debut 1976, as Walther; Further engagements in Lisbon, Stockholm, Geneva, Zurich, Mexico City, Houston and Pittsburgh; Other roles include Strauss's Herod and Bacchus; Alvaro in La Forza del Destino, Max in Der Freischütz and the Cardinal in Mathis der Maler by Hindemith; Siegfried and Walter von Stolzing, Bayreuth Festival, 1983-84; Sang Captain Vere in Billy Budd at Mannheim, 1989. *Recordings include:* Die Meistersinger (Philips); Jean Cox sings Wagner (RBM). *Address:* Nationaltheater, Postfach 102362, D-6800 Mannheim, Germany.

COX John, b. 12 Mar 1935, Bristol, England. Opera and Play Producer. *Education:* BA, Oxford University. *Debut:* L'Enfant et les Sortilèges with Sadler's Wells. *Career:* Assisted Gunther Rennert and Carl Ebert at Glyndebourne, Director of Productions, 1971-81; Work has included productions of Arabella, Capriccio and Intermezzo, by Strauss; General Administrator of Scottish Opera 1981-84, Artistic Director 1985-86 (including first local production of Berg's Lulu); Directed Il Barbiere di Siviglia at the Metropolitan 1982 and Midsummer Marriage at San Francisco 1983; Other productions include Le Comte Ory (Nice), Don Carlo and Die Zauberflöte (San Francisco) and Daphne by Strauss (Munich); Also directed at Milan, Stockholm, Brussels, Amsterdam, Sydney, Cologne, Nuremberg, Hanover, Spoleto, Wexford, Houston, Santa Fe (La Calisto), Washington, Honolulu, Salzburg (Il re Pastore) and Florence (Idomeneo); Extensive work in the straight theatre and with television and documentary films; Production Director at Covent Garden 1988-: new productions of Guillaume Tell and Capriccio; directed Die Frau ohne Schatten in London, 1992; Hamlet by Ambroise Thomas at Monte Carlo and Eugene Onegin at Covent Garden, 1993. *Recordings:* Director for stereophonic sound: Coronation of Poppea/Pritchard and Otello/Barbirolli. *Hobbies:* Fine Arts, Gardens. *Address:* Royal Opera House, Covent Garden, London WC2, England.

CRADDOCK Peter Trevor, b. 24 May 1936, Heanor, Derbyshire, England. Lecturer in Music; Professional Conductor/Pianist. m. Sandra Mary Wallbridge, 13 Aug. 1960, 3 daughters. *Education:* ATCL, Piano Teacher, Trinity College of Music, 1953; BMus, 1st Class, Leeds University, 1957; Diploma in Education, Certification of Education, Reading University, 1957-58. *Debut:* Conducting, Guildhall, Portsmouth, 1962. *Career:* Director of Music, Havant Grammar School, 1958-70; Senior Lecturer, Music, Portsmouth Polytechnic, 1970-82; Senior Lecturer, Music, South Downs College of Further Education, 1982-; Founder-Conductor, Havant Symphony Orchestra, 1961-; Conductor, Portsmouth Choral Union, 1962-63; Founder-Conductor, Havant Chamber Orchestra, 1965-; Conductor, Havant Youth Orchestra, 1965-69; Classical records reviewer, BBC Radio Solent, 1973-78; Pianist, Shostakovich Concerto 1 with Ryde Philharmonic, 1972. *Compositions:* 3 Nonsense Songs, 1960; 2 piano trios: Piano quartet; Songs; Piano music. *Hobbies:* Lepidoptera; Tennis. *Address:* 152 West Street, Havant, Hants PO9 1LP, England.

CRAFT Robert (Lawson), b. 20 Oct 1923, Kingston, New York, USA. Conductor; Writer on music. *Education:* BA, Juilliard School of Music, New York, 1946; Berkshire Music Center, Tanglewood; Studied conducting with Pierre Monteux. *Career:* Conductor, Evenings-on-the-Roof and Monday Evening Concerts, Los Angeles, 1950-68; Assistant to, later closest associate of, Igor Stravinsky, 1948-71; Collaborated with Stravinsky in concerts and in preparing several books; Conducted first performances of various later works by Stravinsky; Conducted works ranging from Monteverdi to Boulez; US premiere of Berg's Lulu (2 act version) Santa Fe, 1963. *Recordings:* Many including works of Stravinsky,

Webern, completed works and Schoenberg, several albums for CBS. *Publications:* With Stravinsky: Conversations with Igor Stravinsky, 1959; Memories and Commentaries, 1960; Expositions and Developments, 1962; Dialogues and a Diary, 1963; Themes and Episodes, 1967; Retrospections and Conclusions, 1969; Chronicle of a Friendship, 1972; Prejudices in Disguise, 1974; with Vera Stravinsky, Stravinsky in Photographs and Documents, 1976; Current Convictions: Views and Reviews, 1977; Present Perspectives, 1984; Translator and editor, Stravinsky's Selected Correspondence, 2 volumes, 1982, 1984. *Contributions to:* Articles in various journals and other publications. *Address:* Alf Knopf Inc. 201 East 50th Street, New York, NY 10022, USA.

CRAIG Charles (James), b. 3 Dec 1919, London, England. Opera Singer. m. Dorothy Wilson, 1946, 1 son, 1 daughter. *Education:* In London, protege of Sir Thomas Beecham. *Career:* Principal Tenor with Carl Ross Opera Co, 1953-56; Joined Sadler's Wells Opera Co, 1956; Appears regularly at international opera houses including Covent Garden, Milan, Rome, Vienna, Paris, Berlin, Buenos Aires; Repertoire of 48 roles including: Otello, Radames, Calaf in Turandot, Pollione in Norma, Andrea Chénier, Siegmund in Die Walküre, Siegfried in Götterdämmerung, Lohengrin; Concerts, TV and Radio, and Records; Sang Otello, London Coliseum, 1984. *Honour:* International Opera Medal award, 1962. *Hobbies:* Motoring; Cooking. *Address:* Whitfield Cottage, Whitfield, Brackley, Northants, England.

CRAIG Jon, b. 30 Oct 1923, St Louis, Missouri, USA. Singer (Tenor). *Education:* Studied in Washington, at Juilliard and with Paul Althouse. *Debut:* Sang Pinkerton in 1948. *Career:* Sang at New York City Opera 1952-65, notably in the 1954 premiere of The Tender Land by Copland and in United States premieres of Der Prozess 1953, Der Revisor by Egk 1960 and The Fiery Angel 1965; Metropolitan Opera from 1953, San Francisco from 1957; Further engagements in Pittsburgh, Chicago, Philadelphia, Mexico City and New Orleans; Other roles have included the Duke of Mantua, Fenton and Alfredo by Verdi, Cavaradossi, Don Jose, Turiddu, Rodolfo, Erik in Fliegende Holländer, Dimitri, Boris Godunov and Walton's Troilus. *Recording:* Highlights from Les Contes d'Hoffmann. *Address:* c/o New York City Opera, Lincoln Center, New York, NY 10023, USA.

CRANMER Philip, b. 1 Apr 1918, Birmingham, England. Professor of Music. m. Ruth Loasby, 1 son, 3 daughters. *Education:* BA, BMus, MA, Oxford University; FRCO. *Career:* Staff Accompanist, BBC Midland Region, 1948; Lecturer, Birmingham University, 1950; Professor of Music, The Queen's University, Belfast, 1954; Manchester University, 1970-74; Secretary, Associated Board, Royal Schools of Music, London, 1974-83. *Compositions:* Part-songs; organ compositions; piano duets; Author, The Technique of Accompaniment, 1970; Sight-reading for Young Pianists, 1979; How to follow a score, 1981. *Memberships:* President, Incorporated Society of Musicians, 1971; Council, Royal College of Organists, 1973; Chairman, Musicians Benevolent Fund from 1980. *Honours:* Royal Academy of Music, 1968; MA, Manchester, 1974; FRNCM; FRCM, 1976; Hon. DMus (Belfast) 1985. *Hobbies:* Crossword Puzzles and Handwriting. *Address:* Quince Cottage, Underhill Lane, Clayton, Hassocks, West Sussex, BN6 9PJ, England.

CRASS Franz, b. 9 Dec 1928, Wipperfurth, Germany. Singer (Bass-Baritone). *Education:* Studied at the Cologne Musikhochschule with Clemens Glettenberg. *Debut:* Krefeld 1954, as the King in Aida. *Career:* Sang at Hanover 1956-62; Bayreuth Festival 1959-73, as King Henry, the Dutchman, Fasolt, Wolfram, King Marke and Gurnemanz; La Scala 1960, as Rocco and the Commendatore; Salzburg Festival as Sarastro; London 1960, 1964, in the Missa Solemnis and Mozart's Requiem, conducted by Klemperer; From 1964 sang in Hamburg, Munich, Frankfurt and Vienna; With Hamburg Opera sang Barak in the British premiere of Die Frau

ohne Schatten, Sadler's Wells Theatre, 1966; Other roles include Philip II, Nicolai's Falstaff, Duke Bluebeard and the Hermit in Der Freischütz; Often heard in sacred music by Bach. *Recordings include:* Der fliegende Holländer, Lohengrin, Ein Deutsches Requiem (Philips); Die Zauberflöte, Fidelio, Parsifal, Giulio Cesare by Handel, Der Freischütz (Deutsche Grammophon); Speaker, Second Armed Man and Second Priest in Die Zauberflöte, conducted by Klemperer, EMI: CD issued 1989. *Address:* EMI Classics (Artists' Contracts), 30 Gloucester Place, London W1A 1ES, England.

CRAWFORD Bruce, b. 16 Mar 1929, West Bridgewater, Massachusetts, USA. Manager. m. Christine Crawford, 1958. *Education:* BS, University of Pennsylvania, 1952. *Career:* Entered advertising 1956; Chief Executive Officer of BBDO International 1977-; President of Batten, Barton, Durstine and Osborn 1978-; Joined Board of Metropolitan Opera 1976; Served on Executive Committee 1977-, Vice-President 1981, President May 1984; General Manager, Metropolitan Opera, 1985-89. *Address:* c/o Metropolitan Opera, Lincoln Center, New York, NY 10023, USA.

CRAWFORD David Eugene, b. 16 July 1939, Fort Scott, Kansas, USA. Musicologist. m. Marilyn Opal Shaw, 7 June 1960, 1 son, 1 daughter. *Education:* BA, 1961, MA, 1964, University of Kansas; PhD, University of Illinois, 1967; Studied Musicology, University of Vienna, Austria, also trombone, Vienna Academy of Music, 1961-62. *Career:* Instructor, 1967-69, Assistant Professor, 1969-71, Associate Professor, 1971-77, Professor, 1977-, Department Chairman, 1978-87, Musicology Department, University of Michigan; 1987-, Associate Dean for Undergraduate Studies, University of Michigan. *Publications:* Sixteenth Century Choirbooks in the Archivio Capitolare at Casale Monferatto, 1975; Francesco Cellavenia, Collected Works (in Corpus Mensurabilis Musicae), 1978; The Anonymous Compendium Musices: Venetiis, 1499-1597 (critical edition, Corpus Scriptorum de Musica), 1985. *Contributions to:* Numerous contributions to The Journal of the American Musicological Society, Journal of Musicological Research, Ethnomusicology, Current Musicology, Fontis Artis Musicae, The Musical Quarterly, The Opera Quarterly. *Hobbies:* Skiing; Swimming. *Address:* 1204 Iroquois, Ann Arbor, MI 48104, USA.

CRAWFORD John Charlton, b. 19 Jan 1931, Philadelphia, USA. Composer; Educator. m. Dorothy Lamb, 25 June 1955. 1 son, 1 daughter. *Education:* BMus 1950, MMus 1955, Yale School of Music; PhD, Harvard University, 1963. *Career:* Instructor of Music, Amherst College, 1961-63; Assistant Professor, Wellesley College, 1963-70; Associate Professor of Music 1970-75, Professor of Music 1975-, University of California, Riverside. *Compositions:* Magnificat, 1959; Ash Wednesday, 1968; Three Shakespeare Songs, 1970; Psalm 98, 1971; Don Cristobal and Rosita, 1979; Two Shakespeare Madrigals, 1980. *Publications:* Translator and essayist, Arnold Schoenberg/Wassily Kandinsky: Letters, Pictures and Documents, 1984. *Contributions to:* The Musical Quarterly; Journal of Arnold Schoenberg Inst. *Honour:* Boott Prize in Choral Composition, Harvard University, 1956. *Memberships:* ASCAP; American Musicological Society; American Music Center. *Hobbies:* Tennis; Sailing; Travel. *Address:* 703 11th Street, Santa Monica, CA 90402, USA.

CRAWFORD Timothy Terry, b. 11 July 1948, Farnham, Surrey, England. Lutenist; Musicologist. m. Emilia de Grey, 18 Apr 1975, 1 son, 1 daughter. *Education:* Stonyhurst College 1958-66; University of Sussex 1966-69; Royal College of Music 1971-75; Arts Council Research Grant for Continental Travel 1976. *Career:* Founder Member of Early Music Ensembles: Ars Nova; Parley of Instruments; Frequent appearances with: English Baroque Soloists; London Philharmonic Orchestra; Assistant Editor, Early Music Magazine 1984-85; Music Coordinator for Royal Academy of Arts. *Recordings:* Orfeo (Conductor: J.E. Gardiner); Il Ritorno d'Ulisse (Conductor: R. Leppard); Sacred Music of

Monteverdi (with Parley of Instruments and Emma Kirkby, Ian Partridge and David Thomas). *Publications:* Editor: Lute Society Journal and The Lute 1979-87; Edited Lord Danby's Lute Book (Faber 1987), containing several unknown works by Handel; Editor, Anthology of Renaissance Lute Music (10 Volumes, forthcoming); Editor, Dictionary of Guitar, Lute and Related Instruments (Garland Publishing, Forthcoming). *Contributions to:* Frequent contributor to: The Lute; Early Music; Chelys; Journal of The Lute Society of America. *Memberships:* Lute Society (Committee 1975-87); NEMA (Committee 1985-86); RMA; MU; Early Music Centre Council. *Address:* 40 Albion Drive, Hackney, London E8 4LX, England.

CRAWLEY Clifford, b. 29 Jan 1929, Dagenham, Essex, England. Professor of Composition. m. (1) Ennis Roberts, 6 Aug 1954, 1 son, 1 daughter, (2) Beverley Diamond, 18 Apr 1991. *Education:* Guildhall School of Music; University of Durham; Associate, Royal College of Music, 1954; Fellow, Trinity College London, 1960; BMus, 1963; MMus 1970; Studied privately with Lennox Berkeley. *Career:* School Teacher, 1963; Head of Music Department, College of Education, 1973; Professor of Composition, Queen's University, Kingston, Canada, 1973-93, now Professor Emeritus; Consultant for Canadian Executive Service Overseas in Central America and South East Asia; Examiner, Royal Conservatory of Music. *Compositions include:* Numerous songs and instrumental pieces published in UK and in Canada; Concerto for Piano and Orchestra; Concertino for Piano and Orchestra; Koleda Overture; Tyendinaga for orchestra; Stabat Mater for voice, flute and piano; Nemesis and Childermas for chorus and orchestra; Operas: Barnardo Boy; Slaughter of the Innocents; The Creation; The Trouble With Heroes; Music published by Chappells, Cramer, Curwen and Roberton, UK, Lawson-Gould USA, Frederick Harris, Berandol, Leslie, Canada. *Contributions to:* Reviews in journals including: Queen's Quarterly; Canadian Music Educator. *Membership:* Associate, Canadian Music Centre; Canadian League of Composers. *Address:* 15 Humbercrest Blvd, Toronto, Ontario M6S 4K6, Canada.

CREECH Philip, b. 1 June 1950, Hempstead, New York, USA. Singer (Tenor). *Education:* Studied at Northwestern University. *Career:* Sang with Chicago Symphony Chorus 1973-75; Metropolitan Opera, debut 1979 as Beppe in Pagliacci; Other roles at the Metropolitan have been Mozart's Pedrillo, Edmondo in Manon Lescaut, Brighella in Ariadne auf Naxos, Hylas in Les Troyens and Rinuccio in Gianni Schicchi; Many concert appearances. *Recording:* Carmina Buarana. *Address:* c/o Metropolitan Opera, Lincoln Center, New York, NY 10023, USA.

CREED Kay, b. 19 Aug 1940, Oklahoma City, Oklahoma, USA. Singer; Voice Teacher; Opera Coach; Lecturer. m. Carveth Osterhaus, 5 Oct 1975, 1 daughter. *Education:* BMus, MPA, Oklahoma City University; Study in Munich, Federal Republic of Germany, 1965. *Debut:* New York City Opera, 1965. *Career:* Created role of Fortuna in Don Rodrigo by Ginastera; Mrs Danton in Danton's Death; Opera roles include: Carmen, Cenerentola, Dorabella, Hansel, Giulietta, Sextus in Julius Caesar, Ulrica, Urbain (Les Huguenots); Solo Performances with New York Philharmonic, Chicago Symphony, Philadelphia Orchestra, Carnegie Hall, Les Huguenots; Dallas Symphony; Naumberg Orchestra, Oklahoma City Symphony; Board of Directors, Cimarron Circuit Opera, 1985; Lecturer in Opera and Voice, Cantor classes for Catholic Liturgy; Founding Member, Oklahoma City Guild of Tulsa Opera; Founding Member, Oklahoma Opera and Musical Theater Company; Founding Director, Edmond Central Historical Opera. *Address:* 415 W Eubanks, Oklahoma City, OK 73118, USA.

CREFFELD Rosanna, b. 1945, England. Singer (Mezzo-Soprano). m. Richard Angas. *Education:* Royal College of Music with Flora Nielsen; Paris with Pierre Bernac; Further study with Vera Rosza in London. *Debut:* Glyndebourne 1969, as Second Lady in Die Zauberflöte.

Career: Glyndebourne Touring Opera 1969-70 as Dorabella, and as Olga in Eugene Onegin; Appearances at Aix-en-Provence, Amsterdam, Strasbourg, Lyons and Bremen; Scottish Opera Glasgow as Dorabella and Cherubino; Monteverdi's Orfeo with the English National Opera; Paris Opéra as Cherubino and as Lucretia in The Rape of Lucretia by Britten; Engagements in San Diego, 1984 and Pittsburgh, 1986; Lausanne 1986, in Honegger's Antigone. *Recordings include:* Matilde in Rossini's Elisabetta Regina d'Inghilterra (Philips). *Address:* c/o English National Opera, St Martin's Lane, London, WC2, England.

CRESHEVSKY Noah, b. 13 Jan 1945, Rochester, New York, USA. Composer. *Education:* Studied at the Eastman School, Rochester, 1950-61 and at the Juilliard School with Berio, 1966; Further study with Nadia Boulanger in Paris and with Virgil Thomson. *Career:* Teacher at Juilliard and Hunter College, New York; Brooklyn College from 1969. *Compositions include:* Vier Lieder, stage piece, 1966; Three pieces in the Shape of a Square for 4 performers and tape, 1967; Monogenesis for voices, chamber orchestra and tape 1968; Variations for 4 pianists and tape, 1969; Mirrors for dancers and tape, 1970; Circuit for tape, 1971; Broadcast, 1973; Chaconne for piano or harp, 1974; Guitar, 1975; In Other Words: Portrait of John Cage, 1976; Great Performances for any 2 instruments and tape, 1977; Portrait of Rudy Perez, 1978; Highway, 1979; Sonata, Nightscape and Celebration for tape, 1980-83. *Honours include:* National Endowment of the Arts grant 1981. *Address:* c/o ASCAP, ASCAP Building, One Lincoln Plaza, New York, NY 10023, USA.

CRESPIN Regine, b. 23 Feb 1927, Marseille, France. Singer (Soprano). *Education:* Paris Conservatoire with Suzanne Cesbron-Viseur and Georges Jouatte. *Debut:* Mulhouse 1950, as Elsa. *Career:* Sang Elsa at the Paris Opera 1950: later sang Desdemona, Marguerite, the Prioress in Dialogues des Carmélites and Reiza in Oberon; Paris, Tosca, Ballo in Maschera; Iphigenie; Die Walküre; Tannhaüser; Marschallin; Bayreuth Festival 1958-61, as Kundry and Sieglinde; La Scala Milan 1959, as Pizzetti's Phaedra; Glyndebourne 1959-60, as the Marschallin; Covent Garden from 1960, as Tosca, Elsa and Leonore in Fidelio; US debut Chicago 1962, as Tosca, Marshallin; Metropolitan Opera from 1962, the Marschallin, Senta, Amelia in Un Ballo in Maschera, Sieglinde, Brünnhilde in Die Walküre, Charlotte, Santuzza and Carmen; Teatro Colon Buenos Aires from 1962, as Fauré's Pénélope, Didon and Cassandre in Les Troyens, Gluck's Iphigénie (en Tauride); at the Colon: Parsifal, Der Rosenkavalier; Werther; Damnation de Faust; Carmen; Pique Dame and various concerts and recitals; Salzburg Festival 1967, as Brünnhilde in Die Walküre, conducted by Karajan; Mezzo-Soprano roles from 1971, including title roles, Offenbach's La Grand - Duchesse de Gerolstein and Menotti's The Medium, San Francisco, 1983, 1986; Sang Mme de Croisy at the Metropolitan, Dialogues des Carmélites, 1987; retired 1989 after singing the Countess in The Queen of Spades, Paris; Recitalist in Poulenc, Wolf and Offenbach; Concert repertoire includes Ravel's Shéhérazade and Nuits d'Eté by Berlioz. *Recordings include:* Les Dialogues des Carmélites (EMI); Sieglinde in Die Walküre, Der Rosenkavalier, Don Quichotte by Massenet (Decca); Brünnhilde in Die Walküre (Deutsche Grammophon); Tosca; Iphigénie; Pénélope; Damnation de Faust; Carmen; Les Troyens; La Grande Duchesse de Gérolstein; Le Perichole; La Vie Parisienne; Stabat Mater. *Address:* Music International, 13 Ardilaun Road, London N5 2QR, England.

CRESSWELL Lyell Richard, b. 13 Oct 1944, Wellington, New Zealand. Composer. m. Catherine Mawson, 4 Jan 1972. *Education:* BMus (Hons), Victoria University of Wellington, New Zealand 1968; MusM, University of Toronto, Canada 1970; PhD Aberdeen University 1974. *Career:* Music Organiser, Chapter Arts Centre, Cardiff 1978-80; Forman Fellow in Composition, Edinburgh University 1980-82; Cramb Fellow in Composition 1982-85; Glasgow University 1985-; Freelance Composer. *Compositions:* Ylur, 1990-91;

Voices of Ocean Winds; The Pumpkin Massacre; Il Suono di Enormi Distanze; A Modern Ecstasy; Cello Concerto; O!; Salm; Speak For Us, Great Sea; Passacagli, continuum CCD 1031; O Let The Fire Burn. *Recordings:* Numerous recordings. *Honours:* Ian Whyte Award 1978; APRA Silver Scroll 1980. *Memberships:* APRA; APC, Association of Professional Composers; Composers Guild of Great Britain; Composers Association of New Zealand. *Hobbies:* Chess; Travel. *Address:* 4 Leslie Place, Edinburgh EH4 INQ, Scotland.

CRICHTON Ronald Henry, b. 28 Dec 1913, Scarborough, Yorkshire, England. Writer; Music Critic. *Education:* Radley College 1927-31; BA, MA, Christ Church, Oxford 1932-36. *Career:* Programme Organiser, Anglo-French Art and Travel Society, London 1937-39; Army Service 1940-46; British Council: Greece, Belgium, West Germany, London 1946-67; Music Critic, Financial Times 1967; Freelance 1979; Governing Body, British Institute of Recorded Sound 1973-77; Arts Council Sub-Committees: Dance Theatre 1973-76, Opera 1976-80. *Publications:* Joint Editor, A Dictionary of Modern Ballet 1959; Manuel de Falla: A Descriptive Catalogue of His Works 1976; Falla - BBC Music Guide 1982; The Memoirs of Ethel Smyth, 1987, edited and abridged by Ronald Crichton; . *Contributions to:* The New Grove Dictionary of Music & Musicians; New Grove History of Opera and Dictionary of Opera, Heritage of Music, 1989; contributions to newspapers, reviews, periodicals, in Britain and abroad. *Memberships:* Critics' Circle, Society of Authors. *Address:* c/o David Higham Associates Ltd., 5-8 Lower John Street, London W1R 4HA, England.

CRISPINI Patrick, b. 15 Jan. 1955, Geneva, Switzerland. Conductor; Composer. *Education:* Conservatoire de Musique, Geneva; Accademia Santa Cecilia, Rome. *Debut:* Aged 8. *Career:* Radio & TV Appearances in France & Switzerland, 1963-69; Member, Ensemble Vocal de Lausanne, 1970-78; Assistant Conductor, 1977-85; Founder Director, Ensemble Vocal et Orchestre Elans, Geneva, 1976-; Conductor, Orchestre des Concerts Européens, 1988; Guest Conductor, various orchestras. *Compositions:* 3 Operas; music for films. *Contributions to:* Radio Suisse Romande; Radio France. *Memberships:* International European Musicians Association. *Address:* OCE Production, 6 Rue des Buis, CH-1202 Geneva, Switzerland.

CRIST Richard, b. 21 Oct 1947, Harrisburg, Pennsylvania, USA. Classical Singer (Bass); Vocal Instructor. m. (1) Assunta Ercolano, 3 Aug 1975, divorced, 1 daughter, (2) Yvonne Brennan, 21 Mar 1993, 1 son. *Education:* BS, Music Education, Messiah College, Grantham, Pennsylvania 1970; MM, Voice, New England Conservatory, Boston 1972. *Debut:* Berlioz's Les Troyens, Opera Company of Boston 1972. *Career:* Appearances with Opera Companies including: Santa Fe, Boston, Philadelphia, San Francisco, Memphis, Mobile, Orlando, Lake George and the Virginia and Goldovsky Opera Theatres; European debut with Opera de Lyon in the French Creation under Ken Russell and Serge Baudo; Opera and Oratorio appearances throughout USA and with various orchestras; Canadian debut with Toronto Mendelssohn Choir 1984; Debut with Philippine Philharmonic Orchestra, Internationale Bamboo Organ Festival, Manila 1984; Frequent Soloist with Pro Arte Chorale of New Jersey, Beethoven Society of New York, Rochester Oratorio Society and the Bethlehem Bach Festival; Operatic Repertoire of over 75 roles and nearly 100 Oratorio and Symphonic Works: Opera Performance of Tchaikovsky's The Queen of Spades, filmed for PBS TV, Philadelphia, 1984; Debut in La Traviata, Metropolitan Opera, 1985; Sang in Semiramide, Fidelio, Meistersinger, Der Freishütz and Ballo in Maschera, Hamburg State Opera, 1985; Debut in Contes d'Hoffmann, San Diego Opera, 1985; Debut in Pelléas and Mélisande, Philadelphia Orchestra, 1986; Appearances in Henze's The English Cat, Alte Opera, Frankfurt, Germany and Turin, Italy 1986; First Performance in USA of Mayr's Requiem, Alice Tully Hall

1986; Philadelphia, 1986 as Arkel in Pelléas; Sang with the Company of the Bolshoi, Moscow, at Boston, 1988 in Schedrin's Dead Souls; premiere of The Balcony by Di Domenica, Boston, 1990; other roles include Mozart's Leporello, Osmin, and Sarastro; Rocco in Fidelio, Gremin in Eugene Onegin and Samuel in Un Ballo in Maschera; Season 1991/2 in Gluck's La Rencontre Imprévue at Wexford, as Mozart's Bartolo in Dublin and in the Rossini Birthday Gala at the Barbican Hall; Sang with Bolshoi Opera, Moscow, 1991; Svertlovsk Philharmonic Orchestra, 1993. *Current Management:* Thea SAFIMM, Ludvig Brunner, 250 West 57th Street, New York, NY 10107, USA. *Membership:* American Guild of Musical Artists. *Address:* 484 West 43rd Street, Apartment 9-S, New York, NY 10036, USA.

CRIST Stephen Alan, b. 24 Apr 1957, Winston-Salem, North Carolina, USA. Musicologist; Pianist; Educator. m. Susan Ann Jesitus, 19 Aug. 1978, 2 daughters. *Education:* BA, English and Spanish Literature, Harvard University, 1978; MMus, Music Theory, University of South Florida, Tampa, 1980; PhD, Music History, Brandeis University, 1988. *Career:* Instructor in Musicology, New College, Sarasota, Florida, 1983-86; Assistant Professor of Music, Geneva College, Beaver Falls, Pennsylvania, 1986-90; Assistant Professor of Music, Emery University, Atlanta, Georgia, 1990-; Chamber music performances with principal players of: New York Philharmonic, Los Angeles Philharmonic, Buffalo Philharmonic; Boston, Cincinnati, Pittsburgh and Utah Symphony Orchestras; Cleveland, Minnesota and Florida Orchestras. Member of piano faculty, Sarasota Music Festival, 1986-. *Contributions to:* Articles in: Early Music; Bach Studies; Bach; International Dictionary of Opera; Bach Perspectives; Cambridge Companion to Bach. *Hobby:* Racquetball. *Address:* Department of Music, Emory University, Atlanta, Georgia 30322, USA.

CROCKER Richard L(incoln), b. 17 Feb 1927, Roxbury, Massachusetts, USA. Musicologist; Professor. *Education:* BA 1950, PhD 1957, Yale University. *Career:* Instructor in Music, later Assistant Professor, Yale University, 1955-63; Assistant Professor 1963-67, Associate Professor 1967-71, Professor 1971-, University of California, Berkeley. *Publications:* A History of Musical Style, 1966 reprint, 1986; Listening to Music, with Ann Phillips Basart, 1970; The Early Medieval Sequence, 1977. *Contributions to:* Articles in: Journal of Music Theory; Journal of the American Musicological Society; Journal of Aesthetics and Art Criticism; Rivista Italiana di Musicologica. *Honours:* Alfred Einstein Award, American Musicological Society, 1967; Guggenheim Fellowship, 1969-70; Slee Professorship, State University of New York at Buffalo, 1970; Kinkeldey Award, American Musicological Society, 1978. *Membership:* American Musicological Society. *Address:* 495 Grizzly Peak Boulevard, Berkeley, CA 94708, USA.

CROCKETT Donald, b. 18 Feb 1951, Pasadena, California, USA. Composer; University Professor; Conductor. m. (1) divorced, 1 daughter. (2) Vicki Ray, 6 June 1988. *Education:* BM 1974, MM 1976, University of Southern California; PhD, University of California, Santa Barbara, 1981. *Career:* Conductor, USC Contemporary Music Ensemble, Monday Evening Concerts, regional and national premieres of music by Lutoslawski, Davies, Musgrave, Gruber, Ruders, et.al.; Composer-in-residence, Pasadena Chamber Orchestra (conductor Robert Duerr), 1984-87; Associate Professor, University of Southern California; Composer-in-Residence, Los Angeles Chamber Orchestra (conductor Christof Patrick), 1991-. *Compositions:* Melting Voices (orchestra), Norruth Music Inc, St. Louis, 1986; The 10th Muse (soprano & orchestra), Norruth, 1986; Vox in Rama (double chorus & orchestra), Norruth, 1989; The Pensive Traveller (high voice and piano), Norruth, 1989; Lyrikos (tenor & orchestra), Peer-Southern, New York, 1982; Occhi dell'alma mia (high voice & guitar), Norruth, 1989; Array for String Quartet, commissioned by the Kronos Quartet, 1988; Pilgrimage for piano solo, 1988; Still Life with Bell, 14 players, Commissioned by the Los Angeles Philharmonic, 1989; Celestial Mechanics, oboe and string quartet, 1990. *Recordings:* Melting Voices, orchestra, Orchestra of the Americas, Paul Freeman, conductor, Pro Arte CD. *Publications:* Still Life With Bell, 14 players, Celestial Mechanics, oboe and string quartet; Wedge, orchestra, Norruth Music, Inc, St Louis, 1990; Antiphonies, double reeds, horns, piano and string orchestra, Norruth, 1992, commissioned by the Los Angeles Chamber Orchestra.*Contributions to:* Stucky, Hartke, Crockett: Conversations in Los Angeles, in Contemporary Music Review, 1994. *Hobbies:* Skiing; Backpacking. *Address:* School of Music, University of Southern California, Los Angeles, CA 90089-0851, USA.

CROLL Gerhard, b. 25 May 1927, Dusseldorf, Germany. Musicologist. *Education:* Studied at University of Gottingen, doctorate 1954. *Career:* Assistant lecturer at University of Munster 1958; Chair of Musicology at Salzburg from 1966; President of International Gluck-Gesellschaft from 1987. *Publications:* Editions of Steffani's Tassilone and Die Entfuhrung aus dem Serail; Gluck's Le Cinesi for the complete edition 1958, Editor-in-Chief from 1960 and Alceste 1988; Entries on Gluck and Weerbecke in The New Grove Dictionary of Music; Articles on Mozart discoveries Larghetto and Allegro in E-flat for two pianos and string quartet arrangement of a Bach fugue, K405; Member of Zentralinstitut for Mozart-Forschung and contributor to the Neue-Mozart-Ausgabe. *Address:* c/o Hochschul fur Musik und Darstellende Kunst, 'Mozarteum' Mirabellplatz 1, A-5020 Salzburg, Austria.

CROOM James, b. 1960, North Carolina, USA. Singer (Tenor). *Education:* Studied with James Schwabacher. *Career:* Appeared for two seasons as apprentice artist with Santa Fe Opers; Has sung twenty roles with Scottish Opera, the Glasgow Grand Opera (Calaf, 1990), Western Opera Theatre and San Francisco Opera; Appearances in Simon Boccanegra, Manon Lescaut, Die Zauberflöte (Monostatos) and Die Meistersinger for Scottish Opera; Other roles include Arbace (Idomeneo), Goro (Madame Butterfly) and Mephistopheles in Busoni's Doktor Faust. *Recordings include:* Video of L'Africaine, from San Francisco Opera. *Honours:* Regional finalist, Metropolitan Opera Auditions; Regional winner, National Association of Teachers of Singing Competition. *Address:* c/o Norman McCann International Artists Ltd, The Coach House, 56 Lawrie Park Gardens, London SE26 6XJ, England.

CROPPER Peter, b. 1940, England. Violinist. *Education:* Studied with Sidney Griller at the Royal Academy of Music, with Sandor Vegh at the University of Keele and with Vilmos Tatrai in Budapest. *Career:* Founder member of the Lindsay String Quartet 1986; Regular tours of Europe, Britain and the United States; From 1974 quartet in residence at Sheffield University, then Manchester University (1979); Premiered the 4th Quartet of Tippett at the 1979 Bath festival and commissioned Tippett's 5th Quartet, 1992; Chamber Music Festival established at Sheffield 1984; Regular concerts at the Wigmore Hall, including Haydn series 1987. *Recordings include:* Complete cycles of Bartók, Tippett and Beethoven; CDs of Haydn quartets Live from the Wigmore Hall (ASV). *Honours:* Prize winner (with members Lindsay Quartet) at Liège International Competition 1969; Gramophone Chamber Award for late Beethoven quartets, 1984. Plays Stradivarius from the Golden Period. *Address:* c/o Ingpen and Williams Ltd, 14 Kensington Court, London W8 5DN, England.

CROSBY John (O'Hea), b. 12 July 1926, New York City, USA. Conductor; Opera Impresario; Music Educator. *Education:* BA, Yale University, 1950; Studied composition with Paul Hindemith; Conducting with Rudolph Thomas and Pierre Monteux. *Career:* Accompanist, coach and conductor, New York City Opera, 1951-56; Founder-general Director, Santa Fe (NM) Opera Company, 1957-; Oversaw many USA and world premieres; President, Opera America, 1976-; Manhattan School of Music, 1976-86; Accompanist, Coach and Conductor, New York City, 1951-56; Guest conductor, various opera companies, Canada and USA,

1960-. *Honours:* LittD, University of New Mexico, 1967; MusD, College of Santa Fe, 1968; Cleveland Institute of Music, 1974; LHD, University of Denver, 1977; Yale University, DFA, (Hon), 1991; National Medal of Arts, 1991, USA; Verdienstkreuz First Class Bundesrepublik, Deutschland, 1992. *Address:* PO Box 2408, Santa Fe, NM 87501, USA.

CROSS Lowell (Merlin), b. 24 June 1938, Kingsville, Texas, USA. Composer; Professor. *Education:* Graduated, Texas Tech University; MA, University of Toronto, 1968; Studied electronic music with Myron Schaeffer and Gustav Ciamaga. *Career:* Teacher, Electronic Music and Research Associate, Electronic Music Studio, University of Toronto, 1967-68; Director and Teacher, Mills College Tape Music Center, 1968-69; Consulting Artist and Engineer, Experiments in Art and Technology Inc, 1968-70; Faculty Member 1971, Professor 1981-, University of Iowa. *Compositions:* 4 Random Studies for Tape, 1961; 0.8 Century for Tape, 1962; Eclectic Music for Flute and Piano, 1964; Antiphonies for Tape, 1964; After Long Silence for Soprano and Tape, 1964; 3 Etudes for Tape, 1965; Video I and II for Variable Media, 1965-68; Musica Instrumentalis for Acoustical Instruments, Monochrome and Polychrome Television, 1965-68; Video III for Television and Phase-derived Audio System, 1968; Reunion for Electronic Chessboard, 1968; Electro-Acoustica for Instruments and Variable Media, 1970-71; Video/Laser I-IV for Laser Deflection System, 1969-. *Publications:* A Bibliography of Electronic Music 1967, 3rd edition revised, 1970. *Contributions to:* Articles in journals. *Address:* c/o School of Music, University of Iowa, Iowa City, IA 52242, USA.

CROSS Ronald, b. 18 Feb 1929, Fort Worth, Texas, USA. Musicologist; Keyboard, Wind and String Player; Conductor; Composer. *Education:* Guilmant Organ School, New York; Studied organ with Harold Friedell, New York; Master classes with E Power Biggs and Virgil Fox; BA, Centenary College of Louisiana, 1950; Studied musicology with Gustave Reese and Curt Sachs; Composition with Philip James; MA 1953, PhD 1962, New York University; Studied at: Venice Conservatory; University of Florence; Accademia Chigiana, Siena; University of Siena; University of Vienna, 1955-57. *Career:* Organist and Choirmaster, New York Churches; Concert appearances as keyboard, wind, string player and conductor; Faculty Member, Notre Dame College of Staten Island, 1958-68; Associate Professor 1968-75, Professor 1975-, Director of the Collegium Musicum, Chairman of the Music Department 1981-84, Wagner College, New York. *Compositions:* Many vocal and chamber pieces. *Recordings:* Several discs. *Publications:* Edited Matthaeus Pipelare: Opera omnia, 3 volumes, 1966-67. *Contributions to:* Articles in many journals; Record reviews, Musical Quarterly, 1971-76. *Memberships:* American Musicological Society; International Musicological Society; American Guild of Organists; College Music Society; Society for Ethnomusicology; Lute Society of America; Viola da Gamba Society of America; American Recorder Society; Music Library Association. *Address:* 221 Ward Avenue, Staten Island, NY 10304, USA.

CROSSE Gordon, b. 1 Dec 1937, Bury, Lancashire, England. Composer. *Education:* Oxford University with Wellesz; Accademia di Santa Cecilia, Rome, with Petrassi. *Career:* Birmingham University 1964-69, as tutor in extra mural department and in music department; Fellow in Music, University of Essex, 1969-76; Visiting professor in composition at the University of California, 1977; Freelance composer from 1978; Commissions from the BBC Symphony Orchestra, Royal Philharmonic Orchestra, London Symphony Orchestra and Festivals of Aldeburgh, Cheltenham and Edinburgh; The Story of Vasco premiered at the London Coliseum. *Compositions:* Stage: Purgatory, 1-act opera after Yeats 1966; The Grace of Todd, comedy 1969; Wheel of the World entertainment on Chaucer's The Canterbury Tales 1972; The Story of Vasco, opera in 3 acts 1974; Potter Thompson, 1-act music drama 1975; Orchestral: Elegy 1959; Concerto da Camera 1962; Symphony No.1 1964;

Ceremony 1966; 2 Violin Concertos, 1969, 1970; Some Marches on a Ground 1970; Ariadne for oboe and ensemble 1972; Symphony No.2 1975; Epiphany Variations 1976; Wildboy 1977; Thel for ensemble 1978; Symphony for Chamber Orchestra 1976; Dreamsongs 1979; Cello Concerto 1979; Array for trumpet and orchestra 1986; Vocal: Changes for soprano, baritone, chorus and orchestra 1965; The Covenant of the Rainbow for chorus and organ; For the Unfallen for tenor, horn and strings 1968; Memories of Morning: Night for mezzo and orchestra 1971; The New World, poems by Ted Hughes for voice and piano 1978; Harvest Songs for chorus and orchestra 1980; Dreamcanon I for chorus, 2 pianos and percussion 1981; Chamber: String Quartet 1980; Wave Songs for cello and piano 1983; Meet my Folks 1964, Holly from the Bongs 1974 and Harvest Songs 1980 for children. *Address:* Brants Cottage, Blackheath, Wenhaston, Halesworth, Suffolk, IP19 9EX.

CROSSLAND Anthony, b. 4 Aug 1931, Nottingham, England. Cathedral Organist. m. Barbara Helen Pullar-Strecker, 3 Dec 1960, 1 son, 2 daughters. *Education:* MA; BMus; Christ Church, Oxford; FRCO (CHM); ARCM. *Career:* Assistant Organist, Christ Church Cathedral, Oxford, 1957-61; Assistant Organist, Wells Cathedral, 1961-71; Conductor, Wells Cathedral Oratorio Society, 1965-; Organist and Master of the Choristers, Wells Cathedral, 1971-; Conductor, The Wells Sinfonietta. *Recordings:* As Choir Director: Music from Wells Cathedral, 1980; A Babe Is Born: Christmas Music from Wells Cathedral, 1982; Music for Worship: A Year at Wells Cathedral, 1984; Awake My Soul, 1986; Sunday At Wells, 1989; Love Came Down at Christmas, 1990; The Psalms of David, Vol. 2, 1990; Music for Passiontide and Easter, 1991. *Membership:* President, The Cathedral Organists' Association, 1983-85. *Hobbies:* Reading; Photography. *Address:* 15 Vicars' Close, Wells, Somerset BA5 2UJ, England.

CROSSLEY Paul,b. 17 May 1944, Dewsbury, Yorkshire, England. Pianist. *Education:* Organ scholar at Mansfield College Oxford; Piano with Fanny Waterman; Study with Messiaen and Yvonne Loriod in Paris. *Career:* Won 1968 Messiaen Piano Competition at Royaun; 1973 premiered Tippett's 3rd Sonata (Bath) and Maw's Personae (London); Jan 1985 premiered Tippett's 4th Sonata in Los Angeles; 1986 presented series of six programmes for Channel 4 TV, Sinfonietta, featuring major 20th Century composers; Programmes on Liszt and Ravel for BBC TV and Poulenc for Hessischer Rundfunk, Germany; Piano Soloist in British stage premiere of Janáček's Diary of one who Disappeared, London Coliseum 1986; Season 1988-89 tour of Japan with NHK Symphony Orchestra; Germany and Italy with the Chamber Orchestra of Europe playing the Berg Chamber Concerto; Engagements with the Rotterdam Philharmonic, Swedish Radio and BBC Symphony Orchestras; Joint Artistic Director of the London Sinfonietta 1988-, and played with them in the British premiere of Henze's Requiem at the 1993 London Proms. *Recordings:* Diapason d'Or for the complete solo works of Ravel and Tippett; Prix Caecilia for the Berg Chamber Concerto with the London Sinfonietta; Grand Prix de l'Academie du Disque Française for the Fauré Violin Sonatas, with Arthur Grumiaux; Complete Janáček and Fauré piano works; Messiaen's Turangalîla Symphonie and Poulenc's piano works for CBS Records. *Address:* 26 Wadham Road, London, SW15 2LR, England.

CROSSLEY-HOLLAND Peter Charles, b. 28 Jan 1916, London, England. Composer; Professor; Ethnomusicologist. *Education:* BA, St John's College, Oxford; MA 1941; BMus, 1943; Royal College of Music, London; School of Oriental and African studies, University of London. *Debut:* League of Arts Concerts, London 1938. *Career:* Conductor of own compositions on BBC radio and at UK festivals; Appearances as medieval harpist, TV and radio; Numerous broadcasts and lectures on music of Celts, Tibet and Orient; Assistant director, Institute of Comparative Music Studies, Berlin 1964-66; Visiting Lecturer, University of Ilinois 1966; Visiting Professor of Music, University of Hawaii, 1968-79; Professor of Music, University of California at Los Angeles from 1969. *Compositions:* Cantata The Sacred Dance; 2 Songs for soprano and piano; 24 Rounds of Nature; Cantata The Visions of St Godric; Des Puys d'Amors, songs for string orchestra and harp; Breton Tunes. Field Recordings mainly on Tibetan music. *Publications:* Secular Medieval Music in Wales, 1942; Editor and co-author, Music in Wales, 1948; Music: A Report on Musical Life in England, 1949; The Pelican History of Music, volume 1 part 1, 1960. *Contributions to:* Numerous professional journals. *Address:* 15554 Olden Street, Sylmar, CA 91342, USA.

CROSSMAN Wallace Bruce, b. 2 Nov 1961, Auckland, New Zealand. Composer. m. Colleen Anne Guild, 18 Jan 1986, 1 son. *Education:* MusB (Hons), 1983, MMus with Jack Speirs, 1985, Otago University, Dunedin; MPhil with David Blake, York University, England, 1990. *Career:* New Zealand Queen Elizabeth II Arts Council Grants, 1983-93; Composer-in-Residence, Nelson School of Music, New Zealand, 1987; Fellow in Composition, Pacific Composers Conference, Japan, 1990; Mozart Fellow, Otago University, New Zealand, 1992; Visiting Lecturer in Music, Waikato University, 1994. *Compositions:* Piece Number Two for Orchestra, 1984; Pezzo Languendo for solo piano, 1984; Expression in Blue for violin and piano, 1988; Dual for two violins, 1988; Dialogue for Jerusalem for clarinet and piano, 1989; A Peace in Time for 2 pianos, 1989; City of Broken Dreams for Orchestra, 1989; Timbres for guitar, 1991. *Contributions to :* The 1990 Pacific Composers' Conference, literary article in Canzona Yearbook, New Zealand, 1991. *Honours:* Jennie MacAndrew Prize, Otago University, 1981; New Zealand Emergent Composers Award, Nelson School of Music, 1984; Merit Award, 1985, Commended Prize, 1987, Wellington Youth Orchestra Young Composers Competition; York University Scholarship, British ORS Award, 1987-89; Music Study Grant, New Zealand Queen Elizabeth II Arts Council, 1988. *Membership:* Composers Association of New Zealand. *Address:* "En Hakkore" Sanatorium Road, RD 4 Ranfurly, Central Otago, New Zealand.

CROW Todd, b. 25 July 1945, Santa Barbara, California, USA. Pianist; Music Professor. m. Linda Goolsby, 12 Aug 1967, 1 son, 1 daughter. *Education:* BA, University of California, 1967; MS, Juilliard School, 1968; Music Academy of the West. *Debut:* London, 1975; New York, 1981; London Orchestral debut, LPO, 1986. *Career:* Has given numerous concerts in USA, Europe and South America; Mt Desert Festival of Chamber Music, Maine; Maverick Concerts, Woodstock, New York, Music Mountain, Connecticut; Radio appearances on BBC, National Public Radio, and New York City Stations; Chairman and Professor of Music, Department of Music, Vassar College, Poughkeepsie, New York; New York Orchestral Debut, American Symphony Orchestra, 1992; Additional Festivals: Casals Festival; Bard Music Festival. *Recordings:* Schubert Piano Sonatas, Bridge Records. *Publication:* Bartók Studies, 1976. *Contributions to:* Notes; Journal of the American Liszt Society. *Hobbies:* Golf; Reading. *Address:* Department of Music, Vassar College, Poughkeepsie, NY 12601, USA.

CROXFORD Eileen, b. 21 Mar 1924, Leighton Buzzard, Bucks., England. Cellist. m. Concert pianist, David Parkhouse, (deceased 1989), 2 sons. *Education:* Royal College of Music; Studied with Effie Richardson, Ivor James, Pablo Casals. *Debut:* London: Wigmore Hall; BBC promenade concerts, Royal Albert Hall. *Career:* Recitalist worldwide with husband, David Parkhouse; Concertos with leading orchestras: Trio with David Parkhouse and High Bean; acclaimed in 1987 as world's longest stanging Trio; Tours of East and West Europe, North and South America, Far East, Middle East, China and North Africa. *Recordings:* Beethoven, Ghost and Archduke Trios, Irish Songs; Schubert, Trout Quintet; Trios by Bush, Mendelssohn and Ravel; Cello and piano sonatas by Dohnányi, Barber, Rachmaninov, Kodály, Debussy; Vaughan Williams, 2 Quartets, On Wenlock

Edge, Studies on Folk Songs; Warlock, The Curlew; Lennox Berkeley, Sextet; Elgar, String Quartet. *Honours:* Alexander Prize, 1945; Queen's Prize 1948; Boise Foundation Award, 1949; Fellow of the Royal College of Music, 1983; Cobbett Medal of the Worshipful Co., of Musicians, for services to Chamber Music, 1991; Founder of Parkhouse Award, The International Chamber Music Award for Piano based groups, in memory of David Parkhouse. *Membership:* Founder Member with David Parkhouse of Music Group of London. *Hobbies:* Family; Travelling; Writing; Teaching; Adjudicating. *Address:* 11 Roehampton Ct, Queens Ride, London SW13, England.

CROZIER Eric John, b. 14 Nov 1914, London, England. Writer and Theatrical Producer. m. Nancy Evans. *Education:* University College School, London; Royal Academy of Dramatic Art; British Institute, Paris. *Career:* Play Producer for BBC Television Service, 1936-39, Glyndebourne Opera and other Theatres, 1944-46; Closely associated with Benjamin Britten as Producer or Author of his operas, 1945-51 and was co-founder with him of The English Opera Group, 1947, and the Aldeburgh Festival of Music and the Arts, 1948. *Publications:* Christmas in the Market Place (adapted from French of Henri Ghéon) 1944; The Life and Legends of Saint Nicolas, 1949; Noah Gives Thanks, a play, 1950; (with Benjamin Britten) Albert Herring, a comic opera in three acts, 1947; Saint Nicolas, a cantata, 1948; Let's Make an Opera, an entertainment for children, 1949; (with E M Forster and Benjamin Britten) Billy Budd, an opera in four acts, 1951; Opera translations include, The Bartered Bride, Otello, Falstaff, La Traviata, Idomeneo, Salome, The Woman without a Shadow. *Honour:* OBE 1991. *Hobby:* Listening to Music. *Address:* 4 The Timberyard, Great Glemham, Saxmundham, Suffolk IP17 2DL, England.

CRUMB George, b. 24 Oct 1929, Charleston, West Virginia, USA. Composer; University Professor. m. 2 sons, 1 daughter. *Education:* BM, Mason College of Music, 1950; MMus., University of Illinois, 1952; DMA, University of Michigan, 1959; Hochschule für Musik, Berlin 1955-56. *Career:* Professor, Composition, University of Pennsylvania. *Compositions:* (all Recorded) include 5 Pieces for Piano; Night Music 1; 4 Nocturnes for violin and piano; Echoes of Time and the River; 4 Processionals for orchestra; Night of the 4 Moons; Black Angels for electric string quartet; Makrokosmos Vols 1-IV, 1972-79; Ancient Voices of Children, Soprano and ensemble, 1970; Lux Whale for 3 masked musicians and ensemble, 1971; Dream Sequence, violin, cello, piano and percussion, 1976; Star-Child for soprano, children's chorus and orchestra, 1977; Apparition, Whitman, for soprano and piano, 1979; A Little Suite for Christmas, 1980; Gnomic Variations for piano, 1981; Pastoral Drone for organ, 1982; Processional for piano, 1983; A Haunted Landscape, orchestra, 1984. *Honours:* Pulitzer Prize in Music for Echoes of Time and the River, 1968; Koussevitsky International Recording Award, 1971; International Rostrum of Composers (UNESCO) Award, 1971. *Membership:* Broadcast Music Inc. *Hobby:* Reading. *Address:* 240 Kirk Lane, Media, PA 19063, USA.

CRUZ-ROMO Gilda, b. 12 Feb 1940, Guadalajara, Mexico. Opera Singer (Soprano). *Education:* Mexico City Conservatory, with Angel Esquivel. *Debut:* Mexico City 1962, in Die Walküre. *Career:* Metropolitan Opera from 1970 as Madama Butterfly, Puccini's Tosca, Manon and Suor Angelica; Verdi's Leonora (Trovatore and La Forza del Destino), Elisabeth de Valois, Aida, Amelia (Ballo in Maschera) and Violetta; Season 1972-73 at Covent Garden and La Scala Milan, as Aida; Appearances in Australia, South America and the Soviet Union and at the Vienna State Opera, Rome Opera, Paris Opéra, New York City Opera and Chicago Lyric Opera; Concert appearances in Canada, Mexico, USA, Japan, Israel and Soviet Union; Vienna Staatsoper, 1979, as Leonora in La Forza del Destino; New Jersey and Connecticut, 1988; as Donna Anna and Cherubini's Medea; Ars Musica Chorale and Orchestra, Englewood, New Jersey, as Santuzza and Matilda in the US premiere of

Mascagni's Silvana, 1988-89. *Recordings include:* Rossini's Stabat Mater; video of Aida at 1976 Orange Festival. *Honours include:* First Prize, Metropolitan Opera National Award 1970. *Address:* c/o John Coast Ltd., 31 Sinclair Road, London, W14 0NS, England.

CSAJBÓK Terézia, b. Szajol, Hungary. Singer (Soprano). m. Dr Ferenc Bónis, 1957. *Education:* Ferenc Liszt Academy of Music, Budapest; Accademia Musicale Chigiana, Siena, Italy. *Debut:* Judith in Bluebeard's Castle, by Bartók, National Theatre, Szeged, Hungary. *Career:* Soloist, Hungarian National Philharmony with recitals, Radio and TV appearances throughout Europe, 1969-; Several first performances of compositions by Bartók, Kodály, Farkas, Ránki, Kadosa, Kalabis, Kósa, Suchon, Madarász, Szokolay, Takács, Loránd. *Recordings:* Songs by Bartók and Kodály; Cantatas by Szokolay; Old Hungarian Music, Early Hungarian Love Songs. *Honours:* Merited Artist of the Hungarian Republic, 1985. *Current Management:* Interkoncert, Vörösmarty tér 1, H-1051 Budapest, Hungary. *Address:* Belgrád rakpart 27.1.5., H-1056 Budapest, Hungary.

CSAMMER Alfred, b. 30 Nov 1938, Budweis, Bohemia. Violinist. *Education:* Started to study Violin at age of 5 with his father, Eugen, a former student of Sevcik; Studied at Music Academy in Karlsruhe with Heinz Stanske, Bronislaw Gimpel and Henri Lewkowicz; in Stuttgart with Ricardo Odnoposoff; in Zurich with Nathan Milstein. *Career:* Concerts, radio productions, master classes and recordings in most European countries, in the United States of America and Canada as a Soloist and in chamber music; Artistic Director of Karlsruhe Chamber Orchestra; Teacher of Violin at the Johannes-Gutenberg University, Mainz. *Recordings:* Mendellssohn Sonata in F-major; Dvořák's Romantic Pieces, Strauss Sonata in Eb-major with Pianist Sontraud Speidel. *Hobbies:* Drawing; Filming; Making Cartoons. *Address:* Seegasse 2, D-7500 Karlsruhe 41, Germany.

CSAPÓ Gyula, b. 26 Sept 1955, Pápa, Hungary. Composer. m. Éva Bótai, 10 Oct 1980. 1 son. *Education:* Béla Bartók Conservatory; Diploma in Composition & Music Theory, Franz Liszt Academy of Music, Budapest, 1981; Institute pour la Recherche et Coordination Acoustique/Musique, Paris, 1982; PhD, composition, State University of New York at Buffalo, 1989. *Career:* Member, New Music Studio, Budapest; Extensive concert performances, radio recordings and broadcasts with, or without the Studio in Budapest, Warsaw, Torun (Poland), Vienna, Darmstadt, Milan, Rotterdam, London, Frankfurt am Main, Edmonton (Alberta, Canada), Buffalo, NY, USA, New York City; Film music scores; Associated with Protean Forms Collective, New York City. *Compositions include:* Krapp's Last Tape, After Beckett, 1974-75; Tao Song, 1:1/2, 1974-77; Fanatritraritràna, 1977-81; Handshake After Shot, 1977; Hark, Edward..., 1979-81; Na'Conxypan, 1978-88; Phèdre's Hymn to the Sun, 1981; Yagul, 1987; Infrared Notes, No 1: (Prismed Through Darkness), 1986-88. *Hobbies:* Maya archaeology; Japanese & Indian culture and philosophy; Persian literature; Tennis. *Address:* 182 Graham Avenue Apt No 3, Brooklyn, NY 11206, USA.

CSENGERY Adrienne, b. 1950, Hungary. Singer (Soprano). *Education:* Studied at the Bartók Conservatory in Budapest and with Eva Kutrucz at the Franz Liszt Academy. *Career:* Early engagements at the Budapest State Opera and in Monteverdi's Vespers, conducted by Lovro von Matacic; Engagements in Zagreb, Dubrovnik and Palermo; Marzelline in Fidelio at the 1974 Munich Festival; Hungarian State Opera Budapest as Marguerite, Lulu and Anne Trulove; Mozart roles at Munich: Susanna, Pamina, Fiordiligi and Zerlina; Appearances at Hamburg, Bayreuth, Cologne, Amsterdam and Bern with Sawallisch, Pritchard, Haitink, Lopez-Cobos, Michael Gielen and Roderick Brydon; Glyndebourne Festival 1976-77, as Susanna and Zerlina, in productions directed by Peter Hall; Wigmore Hall recital 1980, with English Canzonettas by Haydn; Gave the world premiere of Kurtag's

Messages of the Late Miss RV Troussova, with the Ensemble Intercontemporain conducted by Boulez, 1981: later performances of the work in La Rochelle, Milan, Venice, Florence, Budapest, Bath, Edinburgh and London; Gave the British premiere of Kafka Fragments by Kurtag at the 1989 Almeida Festival, London. *Recordings include:* Wigmore Hall Recital 1980 (Hungaroton); Messages of the late RV Troussova (Erato). *Honours include:* Gramophone Record Prize 1983; Gramophone Contemporary Music Award 1985. *Address:* c/o Christopher Tennant Artists' Management, 11 Lawrence Street, London SW3 5NB, England.

CSENKI Imre, b. 7 Aug 1912, Puspokladany, Hungary. Composer; Conductor. m. Mária Sándor, 20 Aug 1938, 1 son, 1 daughter. *Education:* Teachers Diploma, 1932; Professor's Diploma, Singing and Music, Franz Liszt Royal Music Academy, 1942. *Debut:* Conductor of the Choir of Debrecen College Concerts in Hungary and Switzerland, 1946. *Career:* Founder, Hungarian State Folk Ensemble, 1950; Artistic Director, Chief Conductor, 1950-70; Conductor, Choir of the Hungarian Radio, 1964-66. *Compositions:* Gypsy Suite; Bagpipe Song; Choral Works; Rhapsody for Violin and Piano; 99 Gypsy Songs; Gypsy Ballads and Laments; Two Operas; Transylvanian Mosaic No 1 and No2 for orchestra; 12 Choral works on poems by Sandor Weores for mixed, female and childrens choir; Cantat 1988 for mixed choir and symphony orchestra; Black Torch, cycle for mixed choir; Rhapsodia Orientale for piano and symphony orchestra. *Recordings:* Works by Bartók, Kodály, Bardos etc; Madrigals, Romantic Composers; Grand Prix du Disques, French Academy for Folklore Records, 1955; Gypsy Rhapsody, Qualiton; Folk Songs, Hungarian, vocal and instrumental arrangements by I Csenki. *Publications:* Gypsy Ballads and Laments; Gypsy Songs and Dances; Hungarian Folk Songs (with Gy Schiffert). *Contributions to:* Music Critic, Tiszantul, prior to 2nd World War. *Honour:* Kossuth Prize, 1952. *Hobbies:* Gardening; Collecting folk songs. *Address:* Parisi utca 6/a, H-1052 Budapest, Hungary.

CSIKY Boldizsar, b. 3 Oct 1937, Targu-Mures, Rumania. Composer; Teacher. *Education:* Studied at Bolyai High School and at the Art School with Sarolta T Erkel; Music Academy, 1955-61, under Sigismund Toduta. *Career:* Music Secretary of Tirgu Mures Philharmonic, 1961-90; Taught chamber music, musical forms, harmony and counterpoint at the Music High Art School, 1986; Director of Tirgu Mures Philharmonic from 1990; His works have been performed several times in Rumania, Hungary, Germany, Italy, USA, England and elsewhere; Initation and organisation of Targu Mures Musical Days, the Musica Sacra Festival and the Constantin Silvestri Festival are connected with his name. *Compositions:* Main works: Two Orchestral Pieces, 1965; Prelude, Fugue and Postlude for orchestra, 1969; Songs of Bravery for chamber orchestra, 1970; Old Transylvanian Songs and Dances for chamber orchestra, 1973; Four Sketches for Strings, 1976; The Mountain, symphonic poem, 1979; Holderlin-Songs for soprano and strings, 1980; Barcsai, ballad for mixed choir and symphonic orchestra, 1981; String quartet, 1988; Divertimento for winds and double-bass, 1989; Cantatas, choral works (especially to poems by Szilagyi, Weores and to folk songs), songs, piano pieces, chamber music, several stage music works for puppet theatre and many folk song adaptations. *Address:* Filarmonica de stat Tirgu Mures, str G Enescu nr 2, 4300 Tirgu Mures, Rumania.

CUBERLI Lella Alice, b. 29 Sept 1945, Austin, Texas, USA. Concert and Opera Singer. m. Luigi Cuberli, 11 Jan 1972. *Education:* B Mus, Southern Methodist University, 1974. *Debut:* European: Violetta in La Traviata in Hungary, 1975. *Career:* Debut at the Sagra Musicale Umbra in the oratorio La Betulia Liberata by Mozart, 1975; Debut at Spoleto Festival concerto da camera with music by Schubert and Beethoven, 1977; Debut at La Scala in Milan in Mozart's Abduction, 1978; since then regular appearances in operas such as Mozart's Re Pastore, 1979, Handel's Ariodante 1981,

opera taken on tour by La Scala to the Edinburgh Fetival, 1982, Mozart's Lucio Silla, 1984; Le Nozze di Figaro, 1987 and Orfeo by Gluck 1989; Debut at Festival Woche in Berlin with the Beethoven Missa Solemnis, conductor Herbert von Karajan, 1985, also performed in the Beethoven 9th, 1986 and the Brahms Requiem, 1987, again with Karajan conducting; 1986 - Debut at Salzburg Festival with Le Nozze di Figaro (role of Countess) with James Levine conducting, with repeats in 1987 and 1988; 1986- debut at the Mozart Festival in Paris again in Figaro with Daniel Barenboim conducting; 1987 - new production of Traviata made especially for her at the Monnaie in Brussels; 1988 - debut at Vienna Staatsoper in Viaggio a Reims, Claudio Abbado conducting; 1989 - concert at Pesaro Opera, Festival of Beethoven's Schottische Lieder, Pianist Maurizio Pollini; Sang Mozart's Countess at Orchestra Hall, Chicago, 1992; Antonia in Les Contes d'Hoffmann at the Opera Bastille, the Countess with the Royal Opera in Japan and at Florence, 1992. *Recordings include:* Beethoven, Missa Solemnis, Deutsche Grammophon (Karajan) 1985; Mozart, Da Ponte operas, Erato (Barenboim) Berlin Philharmonic, 1990. *Honours include:* Franco Abbiati Italian Critics' Award 1981 and Premio Jorio, 1984; Le Grand Prix du Disque conferred by the Academy of France in Paris and Prix Rossini of Paris and the Maschera d'argento award in Campione d'Italia, 1986; Premio Paisiello in Taranto, Italy, 1987. *Address:* c/o Music Centre, Via Ponte Vetero 1, 20121 Milan, Italy.

CUCKSTON Alan, b. 2 July 1940, Horsforth, Yorkshire, England. Harpsichordist; Pianist; Conductor; Lecturer. m. Vivien Broadbent, 16 November 1965, 2 sons, 3 daughters. *Education:* Kings College, Cambridge, BMus 1963, MA 1965. *Debut:* Wigmore Hall 1965. *Career:* BBC recitalist 1964; Solo concerts in Europe, United States; Keyboard Accompanist with Academy of St Martin in the Fields and Pro Cantione Antiqua. *Recordings:* Solo Piano Music of Alan Rawsthorne, William Baines, Eugene Goossens, Edward German, John Field, Sterndale Bennett, Stanford, Corder; Solo Harpsichord Music of Burnett, Kinloch, Farnaby, Tallis, Byrd, Handel, Couperin, Rameau. *Publications:* Reviewer, Music and Letters. *Hobbies:* Gardening; Local History. *Address:* 9 The Crescent, Ripon, North Yorkshire HG3 1ST, England.

CUENOD Hugues, b. 26 June 1902, Corseaux-sur-Vevey, Switzerland. Singer (Tenor). *Education:* Studied at the Conservatories of Geneva and Basle and in Vienna. *Debut:* Paris 1928, in the French premiere of Krenek's Jonny spielt Auf. *Career:* Sang in Geneva 1930-33, Paris 1934- 37; Concert tour of North America with Nadia Boulanger, 1937-39; Professor at the Geneva Conservatory 1940-46; Widely known in French songs and in early music; Lieder recitals with Clara Haskil; Sang in the premiere of Honegger's Le Danse des Morts, Basle 1940; Performances as the Evangelist in Bach's St Matthew Passion; Created Sellem in The Rake's Progress, Venice 1951; Covent Garden 1954, as the Astrologer in The Golden Cockerel; Glyndebourne from 1954, notably as Don Basilio, in Cavalli's L'Ormindo and La Calisto, and in Le Nozze di Figaro (50th Anniversary season, 1984); Metropolitan Opera debut 1987, as the Emperor in Turandot; Geneva Opera 1989, as Monsieur Taupe in Capriccio. *Recordings:* St Matthew Passion (Nixa); L'Enfant et les Sortilèges, Ariadne auf Naxos, Oedipus Rex, Les Contes d'Hoffmann, La Calisto (Decca); Le Nozze di Figaro (EMI); Early music for Erato. *Address:* c/o Glyndebourne Festival Opera, Lewes, Sussex.

CULLELL Agustin, b. 7 June 1928, Barcelona, Spain. Conductor. m. Myrla Montero Raffo, 9 Feb 1953, 1 son, 1 daughter. *Education:* Graduate, Violin & Conducting, National Conservatory of Music, Chile. *Career:* Principal Conductor: National Symphony Orchestra, Philharmonic Orchestra, Chile, 1959-63, 1965-68; Philharmonic Orchestra, Bogota, Colombia, 1978-81; National Symphony Orchestra, Costa Rica, 1980-84; Guest Conductor, National Symphony Orchestra, Buenos Aires, National Symphony Orchestra, Colombia,

National Symphony Orchestra, Dominican Republic; Orchestra of Maracaibo; Orchestra of Mexico State; Currently Titular Conductor, The Valley Symphony Orchestra, Cali, Colombia; Guest Conductor, Symphonic Orchestras of Barcelona, Sevilla and Valladolid, Spain and The South Carolina Symphony Orchestra, EEUU. *Contributions to:* various professional journals. *Honours:* Mesa-Campbell award, Chamber Music, Chile, 1956; Premio De Honor, University Arts Festival, Chile, 1960; National Critics Award, Chile, 1967; Order of Civil Merit, King Juan Carlos of Spain, 1977; *Address:* Victor de la Serna 44, 1 E, Madrid, 28016, Spain.

CULLEN Bernadette, b. 1949, Australia, Singer (Mezzo-soprano). *Career:* Appearances from 1981 with Australian Opera as Maffio Orsini in Lucrezia Borgia, Nicklausse and Giulietta in Hoffmann, Cherubino in Figaro, Angelina in Cenerentola, Ottavia in Poppea, The Secretary in the Consul, Charlotte in Werther and Rosina in Il barbiere di Siviglia; Further performances include Brangaene in a new production of Tristan, Sesto in Clemenza di Tito, Donna Elvira in Don Diovanni, also for Lyric Opera of Queensland; Eboli in Don Carlos and Adalgisa in Norma for the Victoria State Opera; Vitellia in concert under Christopher Hogwood, Gala concert with Joan Sutherland and Richard Bonynge in Perth, Dorabella at Hong Kong and British debut as Isolier in Le Comte Ory for Welsh National Opera; Sang Donna Elvira at the re-opening of the Tyl Theatre, Prague under Charles Mackerras, Leonora in La Favorita for WNO in Cardiff and at Covent Garden, Dido in Dido & Aeneas in Palermo, Cassandre in La Prise de Troie for The Australian Opera; Concert repertoire includes Mahler's 8th under Charles Dutoit, Rossini Stabat Mater and Petite messe Solonelle, Verdi Requiem in Sydney under Carlo Rizzi and with the Hallé Orchestra, Liverpool Oratorio under Carl Davis, Dream of Gerontius with the Ulster Orchestra and Beethoven's Ninth. *Recordings:* Pucinella with the Australian Chamber Orchestra; The Bohemian Girl conducted by Richard Bonynge. *Address:* c/o IMG Artists, Media House, 3 Burlington Lane, London W4 2TH, England.

CULLIS Rita, b. 25 Sept 1952. Ellesmere Port, Cheshire, England. Singer (Soprano). *Education:* Royal Manchester College of Music. *Career:* Joined the chorus Welsh National Opera 1973: Principal on Contract, Welsh National Opera 1976: roles include Leila (Parl Fishers), the Countess (Figaro), Tytania (Midsummer Night's Dream), Pamina (Magic Flute), Ellen (Peter Grimes), Donna Anna (Don Giovanni) and Lenio in Martinů's Greek Passion; Buxton Festival 1981, as Elisetta in Cimarosa's Il Matrimonio Segreto; Opera North 1985, as Jenifer in The Midsummer Marriage and as Christine in Strauss's Intermezzo; Season 1986-87 sang the Countess for Tel-Aviv Opera, Ariadne for Opera Northern Ireland and Donna Anna for her debut at the English National Opera: returned for The Fox in Janáček's Cunning Little Vixen; Concert engagements with RAI Milan, Hallé Orchestra, Ulster Radio, Royal Liverpool Philharmonic and the Bournemouth Symphony; Netherlands Opera, Ariadne auf Naxos, 1988-89; Welsh National Opera, Freishütz, 1989-90; Other engagements as the Composer and Fiordiligi, English National Opera, the Fox in The Cunning Little Vixen, Scottish Opera, and the Countess and Donna Anna, debuts with the Canadian Opera Company and San Diego Opera, 1992; Season 1992/1993 as the composer in Ariadne for ENO and Covent Garden debut as Janáček's Fox. *Address:* c/o Kaye Artists Management, Barratt House, 7 Chertsey Road, Woking GU21 5AB, England.

CULVER (David) Andrew, b. 30 Aug 1953, Morristown, New Jersey, USA. Composer; Performer. *Education:* Studied composition with Bengt Hambaeus, electronic music and sound recording at McGill University, MM 1980. *Career:* Founder member of SONDE, Canadian music design and performance group; Has worked at Yellow Springs Institute for Contemporary Studies, New Music Concerts Toronto, Staten Island Children's Museum 1983 and the Children's Museum of Manhattan 1989-91;

Collaborations with John Cage 1981-92, including computer assistance with the premiere of Europeras 1 and 2 at the Frankfurt Schauspielhaus 1987. *Compositions:* Stage works Viti 1981; Music with Tensegrity Sound Source No 5, 1983; Hard Lake Frozen Moon 1989; Quasicrystals, sound sculpture 1989. *Address:* 127 Willowbrook Road, Clinton Corners, NY 12514, USA.

CUMBERLAND David, b. 1945, Ohio, USA. Singer (Bass-baritone). *Education:* Studied at the Juilliard School New York. *Debut:* Sang Pizarro in a concert performance of Fidelio under Leonard Bernstein at Lincoln Center. *Career:* Has appeared widely at German opera houses, notably in Frankfurt, Gelsenkirchen, Wiesbaden, Cologne, Leipzig and Freiburg; Repertoire has included Hans Sachs, the Landgrave in Tannhäuser, King Phillip in Don Carlo and the Dutchman; Has sung in the opera of Maiseille and appeared in La Serva Padrona and Bastien and Bastienne at Clermont-Ferrand; Linz Opera in Der fliegende Holländer; US engagements at the Kentucky Opera, Philadelphia Opera, National Grand Opera and in Dallas, San Francisco and New York (City Opera); Spoleto Festival as Rodolfo in La Sonnambula; British debut with Opera North, 1988, as the Dutchman; Concert appearances at the Carnegie Hall, in Boston, at the Vienna Musikverein and in Santiago; Cenci in the world premiere of Beatrice Cenci, by Berthold Goldschmidt, 1994. *Address:* Weinmarkt 5, CH 6004, Luzern, Switzerland.

CUMMINGS Claudia, b. 12 Nov 1941, Santa Barbara, California, USA. Opera Singer (Soprano). m. (1) H.W. Cummings, 12 June 1962, (2) Jack Aranson, 26 May 1973, 1 daughter. *Education:* BA, Vocal Performance, San Francisco State University, 1963. *Debut:* San Francisco Opera, 1971. *Appointments:* San Francisco, New York City, Houston, Seattle, San Diego, Minnesota, Miami, Charlotte Opera Companies; Netherlands Opera; Stuttgart Opera; Canadian Opera; Sang Countess de la Roche by B A Zimmermann, 1991 at New York City Opera; other roles have included Violetta, Rosalinda, Lucia di Lammermoor, Lulu, Marguerite, 3 Heroines in the Tales of Hoffmann, Countess in The Marriage of Figaro. *Recordings:* Satyagraha, Philip Glass. *Hobby:* Restoring Historic Houses. *Address:* PO Box 4306, New Windsor, NY 12553, USA.

CUMMINGS Conrad, b. 10 Feb 1948, San Francisco, California, USA. Composer. *Eucation:* Studied with Bulent Arel and Joan Panetti at Yale University and with David Lewin at Stony Brook, New York; Further study with Mario Davidovsky and Ussachevsky at Columbia University; Summer courses at the Berkshire Music Center and Stanford University. *Career:* Teacher at the Columbia-Princeton Electronic Music Center 1974-76; Electronic music coordinator at Brooklyn College 1976-79; Assistant professor at Oberlin College 1980. *Honours include:* MacDowell Colony Fellowships; Grants from the National Endowment of the Arts and the Martha Baird Rockefeller Fund; Commission from the Smithsonian Institution and Oberlin College. *Compositions include:* Operas Eros and Psyche 1983, Cassandra 1985 and Tonkin, 1993; Pere Ubu for Piano and woodwind quintet 1969; Triptych for cello 1971; Divertimento for oboe, cello and guitar 1971; Bone Songs for clarinet, trumpet and double bass 1974; Morning Music for ensemble 1974; Subway Songs for 4- track tape 1974; Movement for orchestra 1975; Composition for orchestra 1977; Endangered Species, dance music 1977; Skin Songs for soprano and ensemble 1978; Tap Dancer for 6 percussion 1978; Beast Songs for soprano and ensemble 1979; Second Bassett for Times Square 1980; Summer air, nonet, 1980; Seven Songs 1981; Dinosaur Music for ten-track tape and 14 loudspeakers 1981; Music for Starlore for stereo tape 1982; Piece for mean-Tone Organ 1982; Zephyr's Lesson for flute, cello, percussion and tape 1985; After Eros and Psyche for chamber orchestra and tape 1985. *Address:* c/o ASCAP, ASCAP Building, One Lincoln Plaza, New York, NY 10023, USA.

CUMMINGS David Michael, b. 10 Oct 1942, London, England. Lexicographer. m. Anne Marie Zammit-Tabona 1970, 2 sons, 1 daughter. *Education:* Dartington Hall School 1953-60; B.Ed.Hons, Sidney Webb College, London, 1971-75. *Career:* Schoolteacher from 1975; Lexicographer, music reference books, 1980-. *Contributions to:* Baker's Biographical Dictionary of Musicians, New York 1984; The Oxford Dictionary of Music, Oxford 1985 and 1994; The Grove Concise Dictionary of Music, London 1988; International Who's Who in Music and Musicians' Directory, 12th Edition, 1990; Penguin Dictionary of Musical Performers, 1990; Grosses Sängerlexikon (Ergänzungsband) Berne, 1991/ 1993; New Grove Dictionary of Opera, 4 Vols, 1992; Articles and reviews in Classical Music, Opera, Music and Musicians, Musical Times, Opera Now. *Publications:* New Everyman Dictionary of Music, 6th edition, London 1988; Editor, International Who's Who in Music, 13th and 14th Editions, 1992-94. *Hobbies:* Armchair Cricket; Casaubonology. *Address:* 7 Gerard Road, Harrow HA1 2ND, England.

CUMMINGS Diana, b. 27 Apr 1941, Amersham, Bucks., England. Violinist. m. Luciano Jorios, 2 sons, 1 daughter. *Education:* Recital Diploma, RAM; ARAM. *Debut:* Wigmore Hall. *Career:* Has toured throughout Britain as soloist and chamber musician; Numerous TV and radio broadcasts; Formerly leader of English Piano Quartet; Member of Cummings String Trio; with Trio gave Haydn's Op 53 No 1, Martinů's trio and Beethoven's Op 9 No 1, for the BBC, 1991. *Recordings include:* Complete String Trios of Beethoven. *Honours include:* Prizewinner, International Paganini Competition, Genoa, 1963; International Competition A. Curci, Naples 1967. *Memberships:* Musicians Union; ISM. *Address:* 2 Fairhazel Mansions, Fairhazel Gadens, London NW6, England.

CUMMINGS Douglas, b. 5 Oct 1946, England. Cellist. m. 2 sons. *Career:* Principal cellist of the London Symphony Orchestra from 1969-92. *Honour:* FRAM 1977. *Recordings:* 2 Bach Suites for unaccompanied cello (Abbey); Swan Lake duet, with Ida Haendl (violin) and the LSO; Schubert Quintet in C, with the Lindsay Quartet. *Address:* 11 St Marks Road, Ealing Common, London W5 3JS, England.

CUNNINGHAM Caroline M, b. 18 Jan 1925, New Haven, Connecticut, USA. Professor of Music History. m. Frederic Cunningham, 25 Aug. 1947. 3 daughters. *Education:* BA 1946, PhD, Musicology 1969, Bryn Mawr College; MA, Wesleyan University, 1960. *Career:* Teacher, Music History: Swarthmore College, 1970; Lafayette College, 1921; Temple University, 1971-72; Manhattan School of Music, 1972-90; Temple University, 1990-. *Publications:* Etienne Du Tertre, savant musicien, Jean d'Estrée and the mid-sixteenth century Chanson and dance. *Contributions to:* 7 articles for the New Grove Dictionary, 1980; Musica Disciplina, 1972 and 1981. *Memberships:* American Musicological Society; Viola da Gamba Society of America; Board Member, Viola da Gamba Society of America, 1987. *Hobbies:* Collecting historical instruments and playing viol consorts and Baroque chamber music. *Address:* 735 Millbrook Lane, Haverford, PA 19041, USA.

CUPERS Jean-Louis (Georges Marie), b. 19 June 1946, Etterbeek, Brussels, Belgium. Philologist; Musicologist; Pianist. m. Michèle Derixhon, 19 Jan 1985, 2 daughters. *Education:* Licentiate, Philosophy and Letters, 1968, B Philosophy, 1971, D Literature, 1978, Licentiate Musicology, 1972, Catholic University, Louvain. *Career:* Performing on 18th and 19th century pianofortes (Musée Instrumental de Bruxelles). *Recording:* Mendelssohn's Piano Concerto No 1 in G minor, 1967. *Contributions to:* Revue des archéologues et historiens d'art de Louvain, 1971; International Review Aesthetics and Sociology Music, 1974; Mélanges de Musicologie, Louvain, 1974; Literature and the Other Arts, 1981; Littérature et musique, 1982; Moderne Encyclopedie van de Wereldliteratuur, 1982; Revue de littérature comparée, 1987. *Publications:* Aldous Huxley and Music, A Little More John Sebastian

Like, 1985; Euterpe and Harpocrates or the Musical Challenge to Literature, 1988; Musico-Poetics Today, co-editor. *Hobbies:* Walking; Dancing; Playing the Piano. *Address:* 10 Avenue Van Crombrugghe, 1150 Brussels, Belgium.

CUPIDO Alberto, b. 19 Mar 1948. Portofino, Italy. Singer (Tenor). *Education:* Studied at the Giuseppe Verdi Conservatory, Milan, and at the Accademia Chigiana in Siena. *Debut:* Geonoa 1977, as Pinkerton. *Career:* Sang widely in Italy and in Strasbourg, Vienna and Frankfurt; Glyndebourne 1978, as Rodolfo; Munich Staatsoper 1982, as Faust; US debut San Francisco 1983; Florence 1983, as Rinuccio in Gianni Schicchi; La Scala debut 1984, as Edgardo in Lucia di Lammermoor: returned 1986, as Orontes in I Lombardi; Wiesbaden 1986 in Giulietta e Romeo by Zandonai; Further appearances in Cologne, Hamburg, Berlin and Montreal; Other roles include Alfredo, Fenton, the Duke of Mantua, Fernando in La Favorita and Rodolfo in Luisa Miller; Sang Edgardo at Monte Carlo, 1987; Faust at Geneva, 1988; Teatro Comunale Florence, 1989, as Faust in Mefistofele, Rodolfo at Rome, 1990; Gabriele Adorno in a new production of Simon Boccanegra at Brussels, 1990; Debut at the Verona Arena as Cavaradossi; Season 1991/92 as Boito's Faust at the Lyric Opera Chicago and as Don Carlo at Verona. Also heard in the concert hall. *Honours:* Prizewinner at Competitions in Parma (1975) and Busseto (1976). *Address:* Lyric Opera, 20 North Wacker Drive, Chicago, IL 60600, USA.

CUPPER Ralph John, b. 9 Aug 1954, Norwich, Norfolk, England. Church Musician; Concert Organist; Composer. m. Karin Suzanne Smith, 2 sons, 1988. *Education:* GRSM, LRAM, Royal Academy of Music, London, 1972-76 and with Susi Jeans and Nicholas Kynaston. *Career:* Numerous organ recitals in UK including Southwark Cathedral; Concert tour, Germany, 1977-78; Organist, Cambridge Lutheran Church, 1978-82; Acting Organist, Choirmaster, Wymondham Abbey, Norfolk, 1981, St Andrew's Church, Trowse, 1983-84; Organist, Director of Music, Christ Church, New Catton, Norwich, 1986-88; Concert Tour, Northern Germany including Ratzeburg International Organ Festival, 1985; Music Tutor for Norfolk Adult Education Service, 1986- ; Director of numerous courses for organists in the county of Norfolk; Organist/Director of Music Nordfjordeid/Stårheim State Lutheran Churches, Norway, Sept. 1988; Numerous concerts, Norway, 1988-91; 1990 Founder of the Nordfordeid Music Festival, annually; Recording of English Organ Music for Norwegian N R K Radio. *Compositions:* Numerous published organ pieces; Preludes and fugues, choral compositions. *Hobbies:* Languages; Theology; Collecting dental equipment/Historic Telephony. *Address:* Prestealleen 33a, 6770 Nordfjordeid, Norway.

CURFMAN David Ralph, b. 2 Jan 1942, Bucyrus, Ohio, USA. Organist; Choirmaster; Neurological Surgeon. m. Blanche Lee Anderson, 6 June 1970. *Education:* AB, 1965; MS, 1967, MD, 1973, George Washington University; Private musical studies of piano & organ. *Career:* Pro Art Music Society, Galion, Ohio, 1959; numerous other recitals throughout the years; Assistant Organist, Peace Lutheran Church, Galion, 1958-61; Choirmaster, Associate Organist, Grace Lutheran Church, Washington DC, 1965-73; Radio Programmes; Dean, District of Columbia Chapter, American Guild of Organists, 1974-76; Washington Program Chairman, International Congress of Organists, 1977; State Chairman, American Guild of Organists, 1983-92; Secretary, District of Columbia, American Guild of Organists Foundation, 1983-87; development committee, National Office American Guild of Organists. *Contributions to:* Lecturer in Music and Liturgy in Judeo-Christian Worship; various professional journals. *Memberships:* American Guild of Organists; Publicity Chairman, National Convention, American Guild of Organists, 1982; Royal School of Church Music; Hymn Society of America; Chairman, Board of Trustees, Cathedral Choral Society, Washington Cathedral, 1984-86; Repertoire Chairman, Cathedral Choral Society; The

Leo Sowerby Foundation. *Address:* 4201 Massachusetts Avenue, NW, Suite 6074-W, Washington DC 20016, USA.

CURLEY Carlo, b. 24 Aug 1952, USA. Concert Organist. *Education:* North Carolina School for the Arts; Privately with Virgil Fox, Robert Elmore (Philadelphia), Arthur Poister (Syracuse University) and Sir George Thalben-Ball (Temple Church, London). *Career:* Organist-Choirmaster and Teacher of Music, Girard College, Philadelphia; Director of Music, Druids Hills Baptist Church, Atlanta, Georgia; Artist-in-Residence, Fountain Street Church, Grand Rapids, Michigan; Organist, Alexandra Palace, London; Performances and Master classes at National Music Camp, Interlochen, Michigan; Frequent appearances on radio and television in USA, UK, Australia, Canada, Japan and Denmark; Organ Consultant and Designer. *Recordings:* CC Plays Virtuoso French Organ Music at the Royal Albert Hall; CC Plays J S Bach; CC Plays Popular Bach; CC Concert Curios (all for RCA); CC goes digital (ASV); Organ Spectacular: CC at the Alexandra Palace (Rediffusion); now records exclusively for Decca International.*Honours:* Patron, Holbrook Music Society, (UK); Patron and Organ Consultant to the City of Melbourne. *Hobbies:* Trains; Reading; Fine Wines. *Current Management:* Paul Vaughan Associates, Alpha Tower, Paradise Circus, Birmingham B1 1TT, England.

CURPHEY Margaret, b. 27 Feb 1938, Douglas, Isle of Man. Singer (Soprano). *Education:* Studied with John Carol Case in Birmingham and with David Galiver and Joan Cross in London. *Debut:* Sadler's Wells Opera 1965, as Micaela in Carmen. *Career:* Sang with Sadler's Wells/English National Opera in operas by Mozart, Wagner, Verdi and Puccini; Sang Eva in new production of The Mastersingers, conducted by Reginald Goodall, Sieglinde in The Valkyrie and Gutrune in The Twilight of the Gods; Camden Theatre 1967, in the British premiere of Mozart's Lucio Silla; Guest engagements in Sofia and elsewhere in Europe; Sang Brünnhilde at the London Coliseum, 1977; Many appearances as concert singer. *Recordings:* The Ring of the Nibelung, conducted by Reginald Goodall (EMI). *Honours include:* Prizewinner at 1970 International Competition, Sofia. *Address:* c/o English National Opera, St Martin's Lane, London, WC2, England.

CURRAN Alvin, b. 13 Dec 1938, Providence, Rhode Island, USA. Composer; Performer. *Education:* BA, Brown University, 1960; Studied composition with Ron Nelson (Brown) and Elliott Carter (Yale), theory with Allen Forte; MMus, Yale University, 1963. *Career:* Co-Founder, Musica Elettronica Viva group, Rome, 1966; Solo performances in major festivals (new music), 1973-; Large-scale environmental works for chorus, orchestra, ship's horns and fog-horns, 1980-. *Compositions:* Songs and Views from the Magnetic Garden; Light Flowers, Dark Flowers; The Works; Canti Illuminati; For Cornelius and Era Ora; Natural History; For Four or More, string quartet. *Contributions to:* EAR magazine; Musics; Almannaco Musicale; Music Works (Toronto). *Honours:* National Endowment for the Arts grants, 1978, 1984; Prix Italia for radio work 1985 - A Piece for Peace; DAAD Resident Composer in Berlin, 1986. *Address:* c/o ASCAP, ASCAP House, One Lincoln Plaza, New York, NY 10023, USA.

CURRIE Russell, b. 3 Apr 1954, North Arlington, New Jersey, USA. Composer. *Education:* Studied composition with Robert Starer at Brooklyn College. *Career:* Founded Orra 1988, promoting a multi-approach to musical performance; Director of the music theatre programme at New York's 3rd Street School; Commissions from the Bronx Arts Ensemble. *Compositions:* The Cask of Amontillado, chamber opera after Poe 1982; A Dream Within a Dream, chamber opera after Poe's The Fall of the House of Usher 1984; Ligeia, operatic fantasy after Poe 1987; Rimshot, music theatre 1990. *Address:* c/o ASCAP, ASCAP Building, One Lincoln Plaza, New York, NY 10023, USA.

CURTI Silvio, b. 16 Mar 1953, St Gallen, Switzerland. Concert pianist. *Education:* Teaching diploma 1973-77, Concert-diploma as soloist 1977-79; Conservatory Winterthur; Master class with Prof Leygraf, Salzburg Mozarteum; Course with N Boulanger, Paris; Studied under Prof H Harry, Luzern 1980-84. *Debut:* St Gallen, 1967. *Career:* Numerous radio recordings, Radio Studio Zurich, 1983; Subscription concert given, Concert Hall, St Gallen, 1987. *Recordings:* Cassette recording from a piano recital, 1986; Cassette recording from Sing with Prof K Pahlen, from the 3rd Ballade-Chopin, 1988. *Contributions to:* Review at the St Gallen Tagblatt for a piano-recital with Mr Roth. *Memberships:* EPTA; Gymnasium Helveticum Association; SMPV, Switzerland. *Hobbies:* Photography; Walking; Swimming. *Address:* Burggraben 25a, CH-9000 St Gallen, Switzerland.

CURTIN Phyllis, b. 3 Dec 1921, Clarksburg, West Virginia, USA. Singer (Soprano). *Education:* Studied at Wellesley College with Olga Avierino; Opera study with Boris Goldovsky at New England Conservatory and Tanglewood. *Debut:* With New England Opera Theater, 1946, as Lisa in The Queen of Spades and Lady Billows in Albert Herring. *Career:* Sang at the New York City Opera from 1953, notably in Von Einem's Der Prozess and in the premieres of Floyd's Susannah, and The Passion of Jonathan Wade; Also took part in Walton's Troilus and Cressida as Cressida, Giannini's The Taming of the Shrew and Poulenc's Les Mamelles de Teresias; Santa Fe 1958, in the premiere of Floyd's Wuthering Heights; Glyndebourne 1959, as Donna Anna; Metropolitan Opera from 1961, as Fiordiligi, Rosalinde, Eva, Mozart's Countess, Violetta and Ellen Orford in Peter Grimes; New York concert performance of Pelléas et Mélisande, 1962; Guest appearances in Vienna, Buenos Aires, Frankfurt, Milan, Glasgow (Scottish Opera), Paris and Trieste; Other roles include Salome and Alice Ford in Falstaff; Sang Rosine in the premiere of Milhaud's La Mère Coupable, Geneva, 1966; Ellen Orford, Edinburgh Festival, 1968; Retired from public singing, 1984; Teacher at the Aspen School of Music and the Berkshire Music Center; recitalist throughout Europe, USA, Australia and New Zealand: Soloist with major USA orchestras and others in Europe, New Zealand, Australia and Israel; Artist-in-residence, Tangelwood Music Center, 1964-. Curently Dean Emerita and Professor of Voice, Artistic Director, Opera Institute in Boston University School for the Arts. *Address:* c/o School of the Arts, Boston University, 855 Commonwealth Avenue, Boston, MA 02215, USA.

CURTIS Alan, b. 17 Nov 1934, Mason, Michigan. Harpsichordist; Conductor; Musicologist. *Education:* Studied at Michigan State University, BM 1955; University of Illinois, PhD 1963; Amsterdam with Gustav Leonhardt, 1957-59. *Career:* Joined faculty of University of California at Berkeley, 1960: Professor from 1970; Active as keyboard player and conductor in the USA and Europe; Productions of L'Incoronazione di Poppea, staged and designed by Filippo Sanjust, in Amsterdam, Brussels, Innsbruck, Spoleto and Venice; Handel's Ariodante at La Scala, 1980: later productions in Innsbruck and Turin; Conducted Rameau's Dardanus at Basle, May 1981; Il Sant'Alessio by Stefano Landi at Rome Opera, June 1981; La Schiava Liberata by Jommelli for Netherlands Opera, Sept. 1982, and at the San Carlo, Naples, 1984; Cesti's Il Tito at Innsbruck, 1983, and Venice and Turin 1984; First production since 1707 of Handel's Rodrigo, Innsbruck, Madeira and Lisbon, 1984; Conducted a new production of Gluck's Armide, to open the restored Bibiena Theatre in Bologna, 1984; Gluck's Paride ed Elena at Vicenza 1988; Conducted Cimarosa's Gli Orazi e i Curiazi at Rome, 1989, to mark the 200th anniversary of the French Revolution; Handel's Floridante with the Tafelmusik Baroque Orchestra at Toronto, 1990; Revival of Gli Orazi at Lisbon, 1990; Collector of early keyboard instruments by Martin Skowroneck. *Publications:* Sweelinck's Keyboard Music: a Study of English Elements in Seventeenth Century Dutch Composition, 1969, 1972; Edition of Jommelli's La Schiava Liberata and L'Incoronazione di Poppea, Novello, 1990. *Recordings:* Cavalli's Erismena; L'Incoronazione di Poppea (Fonit

Cetra); Handel's Admeto and Rodrigo (Erato); La Schiava Liberata (Erato); La Susanna by Stradella; Goldberg Variations by Bach; CPE Bach's Rondos nebst eine Fantasie fürs Fortepiano. *Current management:* Music International, 13 Ardilaun Road, Highbury, London N5 2QR, England.

CURTIS Mark, b. 1958, Hertfordshire, England. Singer (Tenor). *Education:* Studied at the Royal Northern College of Music and at the National Opera Studio; Italy with Maestro Campogalliani. *Career:* Appearances with Glyndebourne Touring Opera in Die Zauberflöte and as Fenton and Jacquino; At Covent Garden in Alceste, Pagliacci (Beppe), Manon Lescaut and Fidelio; Kent Opera as Don Ottavio and Monostatos and in King Priam and Carmen; With Opera North has sung The Steersman, Vasek, Stroh (Intermezzo), Don Basilio (Le Nozze di Figaro) and Arv in the British premiere of Nielsen's Maskarade; English National Opera as Amenophis in Mosè, and Don Ottavio, and in the world premiere of Birtwistle's The Mask of Orpheus, 1986; Other roles include Hylas in Les Troyens, the Madwoman in Curlew River and Nadir in Les Pêcheurs de Perles; Sang in the Mozart pasticcio The Jewel Box and King Priam (Hermes) for Opera North 1991; Has also sung at Bath Abbey and the South Bank Halls, and in Dublin, Brussels, Hanover, Berlin, Rome, Palermo, Seville, Hong Kong, Jerusalem, Helsinki and Edinburgh. Many concert appearances; with English National Opera, Hilarion in Princess Ida and at Théâtre Royal de la Monnaie, Brussels, Der Soldat in World Premiere of Philippe Boesmans, Reigen, 1993. *Recordings include:* Trabuco in La Forza del Destino and Yamadori in Madama Butterfly (Deutsche Grammophon). *Address:* Music International, 13 Ardilaun Road, London N5 2QR, England.

CURTIS-VERNA Mary, b. 9 May 1927, Salem, Massachusets, USA. Singer (Soprano). *Education:* Studied at Hollis College, Virginia, and with Ettore Verna. *Debut:* Teatro Lirico Milan 1949, as Desdemona. *Career:* Appearances in Vienna, Paris, Munich, Stuttgart and Florence; Returned to USA 1951 and sang in Philadelphia; San Francisco 1952, Aida and Donna Anna; New York City Opera 1954, as Donna Anna; La Scala Milan 1954, as Desdemona; Metropolitan Opera, 1968, as the Trovatore Leonora, Tosca, Amelia in Un Ballo in Maschera, Santuzza, Aida, Turandot, Elisabeth de Valois and Violetta; Further engagements in Buenos Aires and at the Verona Arena. *Address:* c/o Metropolitan Opera, Lincoln Center, New York, NY 10023, USA.

CURZI Cesare, b. 14 Oct 1926, San Francisco, USA. Singer (Tenor). *Education:* Studied privately. *Debut:* San Francisco 1947, as Pinkerton. *Career:* Sang in San Francisco and elsewhere in North America; Moved to Europe 1955 and appeared at opera houses in Kiel, Nuremberg and Frankfurt (Alfredo 1957); Salzburg Festival 1959, in II Mondo della Luna by Haydn; Further engagements in Stuttgart, Hamburg, Berlin and Cologne; Maggio Musicale Florence 1959 and 1973-74; Member of the Deutsche Oper am Rhein Dusseldorf from 1965; Other roles include Rodolfo, Ferrando in Così fan Tutte, Ernesto and the Duke of Mantua. *Recordings:* Rigoletto (Electrola); Eine Nacht in Venedig; Die Fledermaus. *Address:* c/o Deutsche Oper am Rheim, Heinrich-Heine Allee 16, D-4000 Düsseldorf, Germany.

CUSTER Laurenz, b. 21 Apr 1930, Frauenfeld, Switzerland. Pianist; Organist. *Education:* Diplomas in Piano and Organ, Winterthur Conservatory, 1952; University studies with Paul Hindemith; Studies with Marguerite Long, Nadia Boulanger, Dupré, Denza. *Career:* Recitals and appearances with orchestras in Switzerland, Germany, France, Italy, South America, South Africa. *Compositions:* 4 Canzone for string orchestra, 1986; Ballad, trumpet and piano, Ed. Marc Reift, Rumikou, Switzerland, 1989. *Recordings:* Schaeuble, Mono Partita (with Rudolf am Bach); Dvořák, Chamber Music (with Ensemble Fauré); Fauré, Piano Quartets (with Ensemble Fauré); Der Virtuose

Kontrabass (with Yoan Goilav); Der Romantische Kontrabass (with Yoan Goilav); Giocoso, with E and R Parolari; Pièces de Concours with K Brunner. *Honours include:* 1st Prize, Rudolf Ganz Competition, 1956; Cultural reward of the town of Frauenfeld, 1993. *Memberships:* Schweizerischer Musikpaedagogischer Verband; Schweizerischer Tonkünstlerverein. *Hobbies:* Painting; Hiking. *Address:* Wielsteinstrasse 56, CH 8500 Frauenfeld, Switzerland.

CVEJIC Biserka, b. 5 Nov 1923, Krilo-Jesenice, Split, Yugoslavia. Singer (Mezzo-soprano). *Education:* Studied at Belgrade Music Academy. *Debut:* Belgrade Opera 1950, as Maddalena in Rigoletto. *Career:* Sang at Belgrade 1954-60, notably as Charlotte in Werther and as Amneris on tour to Vienna 1959; Metropolitan Opera debut 1961, as Amneris; Vienna Staatsoper 1959-79, Zagreb Opera 1975-78; Further appearances at Covent Garden, Verona Arena, La Scala and Buenos Aires; Sang in Massenet's Marie- Magdalene at Paris 1977; Other roles have included Eboli, Azucena, Carmen and Delilah; Retired 1990. *Recordings:* Eugene Onegin, The Queen of Spades. Prince Igor, Boris Godunov, The Snow Maiden; War and Peace; Zigeunerbaron. *Address:* c/o Vienna Staatsoper, Opernring 2, Vienna, Austria.

CYR Gordon Conrad, b. 5 Oct 1925, Oakland, California, USA. Composer; Professor. m. Helen Louise Wheeler, 11 Aug 1951. *Education:* University of California at Berkeley, 1945-46 and 1966-69, AB, 1966, PhD, Music Composition, 1969; studied composition at University of California with Charles Cushing, Joaquin Nin-Culmell, William Denny, Roger Sessions and Edwin Dugger. *Career:* Premiere of 3 Shakespeare Songs and of Lamentations Cabrillo Music Festivals, Aptos, California, 1963 and 1967; Lecturer in Harmony and Counterpoint, University of California, 1969-71; California State University at San Francisco, 1971; Assistant Professor, Associate Professor, and Professor of Theory and Composition, Towson State University, Maryland, 1971-. *Compositions:* String Quartet No. 1, 1969; Sinfonias & Arias, 1972; The Siren Stream to the Outcast, 1980; 2 Songs on Poems of Walt Whitman, 1983; Septem, 1982; String Quartet No. 2, 1983; Elegaie-In Memoriam W. A. Cyr, 1984; From Whitman's, Drum Taps, 1985; Chamber Symphony, 1986. *Recordings:* Tabb Songs (1975) Orion; Tetramusic (1977) Orion; Rhombohedra (1974), ASUC Record Series, No. 10. *Hobbies:* Reading; Films: Shakespearean authorship controversy. *Address:* Music Department, Towson State University, Baltimore, MD 21204, USA.

CZAPO Eva, b. Nov 1944, Budapest, Hungary. Singer (Soprano); Teacher. *Education:* Studied at Bartok Conservatory, Budpest, in Basel and with Elsa Cavelti. *Career:* Sang with Trier Opera 1968-69; Guest appearances in concert and opera at Basel, Zurich, Lucca 1981, Bologna and Spoleto 1981; Appearances at the Salzburg, Lausanne, Lucerne, Lugano, Schwetzingen, Helsinki and Granada festivals; Concert repertoire has included Bach's B minor Mass, Beethoven's Ninth, Messiah, Elijah and St Paul by Mendelssohn, Haydn's Schopfung and Jahreszeiten, Mozart's Requiem and C minor Mass and works by Schoenberg, Nono, Dallapiccola, Stravinsky, Szymanowski, Messiaen and Hindemith; Further engagements at Berlin, Hamburg, Munich, Milan, Rome, Turin, Parma and Lisbon; Voice Teacher in Basel and founded the Divertimento Vocale there in 1987. *Recordings:* Bach Cantatas and Cavalieri's Rappresentazione di anima e di corpo; Schoenberg's Moses und Aron, conducted by Gielen; Schubert Masses; Davidde Penitente by Mozart and Carissimi's Dives malus. *Address:* c/o Musik-Akademie der Stadt Basel, Leonhardsstrasse 6, CH-4501 Basel, Switzerland.

CZERWENKA Oscar, b. 5 July 1924, Vocklabruck, Linz, Austria. Singer (Bass). *Education:* Studied privately and with O. Iro in Vienna. *Debut:* Graz 1947, as the Hermit in Der Freischütz. *Career:* Vienna Staatsoper from 1951, notably as Baron Ochs, Kecal in The Bartered Bride, Osmin, and parts in operas by Lortzing; Salzburg Festival from 1953, in the premieres of Einem's Der

Prozess and Egk's Irische Legende and in Der Rosenkavalier, Ariadne auf Naxos, Haydn's Il Mondo della Luna and Le Nozze di Figaro; Glyndebourne Festival and Metropolitan Opera, 1959 and 1961, as Ochs; Hamburg Staatsoper 1965, in the premiere of Klebe's Jakobowsky und der Oberst; Guest appearances in Cologne, Berlin, Frankfurt, Munich, Lisbon and Stuttgart; Many concert engagements. *Recordings:* Abu Hassan in Der Barbier von Bagdad by Cornelius, conducted by Leinsdorf (Columbia); Tiefland, Salome, Le Nozze di Figaro (Philips); Die Frau ohne Schatten (Decca). *Publication:* Lebenszeiten - Ungebetene Briefe, Vienna, 1987. *Honour:* Vienna Kammersanger 1961. *Address:* c/o Vienna Staatsoper, Opernring 2, A-1010 Vienne, Austria.

CZYZ Henryk, b. 16 June 1923, Grudziadz, Poland. Conductor; Composer. m. Halina Buczacka. *Education:* Studied law and philosophy in Torun; Conducting and Composition at the Music High School, Poznan. *Career:* Conducting debut with Polish National Radio Orchestra 1948; Held posts with the orchestras of Lodz and Krakow, 1957-68; Gave triple bill of works by Debussy, Honegger and Stravinsky at the Warsaw Opera in 1962; Conducted the premieres of Penderecki's St Luke Passion (Munster 1966) and The Devils of Loudun (Hamburg 1969); US debut 1973, with the Minnesota Orchestra; Conducted the Dusseldorf Orchestra 1971-74; Worked at Lodz 1974-80; Professor at Warsaw Academy from 1980. *Compositions:* Etude for orchestra 1949; Symphonic Variations 1952; Comic opera The Dog Lover's Dilemma, 1967. *Recordings include:* St Luke Passion, Dies Irae and other works by Penderecki; Szymanowski's 2nd symphony and excerpts from King Roger; Schumann's Das Paradies and die Peri, EMI. *Address:* Moliera 2-21, Warsaw 00076, Poland.

D

D'ACCONE Frank A(nthony), b. 13 June 1931, Somerville, Massachusetts, USA. Musicologist; Professor. *Education:* BMus 1952, MMus 1953, Boston University; MA 1955, PhD 1960, Harvard University; Studied with Karl Geiringer, Gardner Read, Nino Pirrotta, A Tillman Merritt and Walter Piston. *Career:* Assistant Associate Professor of Music, State University of New York at Buffalo, 1960-68; Visiting Professor 1965-66, Professor of Music 1968-, University of California at Los Angeles; Editor, Music of the Florentine Renaissance, Corpus Mensurabilis Musicae series XXXII, 1966-. *Publication:* Alessandro Scarlatti's Gli equivoci nel sembiante: The History of a Baroque Opera, 1985. *Contributions to:* Articles in many journals and publications including The New Grove Dictionary of Music and Musicians. *Honour:* Guggenheim Fellowship, 1980-81. *Membership:* American Musicological Society. *Address:* c/o Music Department, University of California at Los Angeles, Los Angeles, CA 90024, USA.

D'ALVARENGA Joao Pedro, b. 19 Apr 1961, Lisbon, Portugal. Musicologist. m. Maria Joao Bacelar Begonha, 23 July 1988. *Education:* MA, Musicology, Universidade Nova, Lisbon, 1988; Instituto Gregoriano, Lisbon; PhD candidate, Musicology, Universidade Nova, Lisbon; Scholar, Instituto Nacional de Investigaçao Cientifica (National Institute for Scientific Research), Portugal, 1989-1990. *Career:* Conductor, several amateur choirs; Concerts throughout Portugal. *Recordings:* As Conductor: Collegium Vocale de Lisboa. *Publications:* Música e Músicos Portugueses dos sécs. XVI e XVII, 1988; Música e Músicos Ibéricos dos sécs. XVI e XVII, 1988; A Música Litúrgica na Sé de Braga No séc. XVI, 1988. *Honours:* Research Grant, Archival Research, Braga, 1988. *Memberships:* American Musicological Society; Sociedad Espanola de Musicologia; Associaçao Portuguesa de Educaçao Musical. *Address:* R Guiomar Torresao, 43-c/v Dt, P-1500 Lisboa, Portugal.

D'ANGELO Gianna, b. 18 Nov 1929, Hartford, Connecticut, USA. Singer (Soprano). *Education:* Studied at the Juilliard School, New York, and in Italy with Toti dal Monte. *Debut:* Rome 1954, as Gilda. *Career:* Glyndebourne 1955-56 and 1962, as Rosina, Clorinda in La Cenerentola and Zerbinetta in Ariadne auf Naxos; Brussels Opera 1956; Metropolitan Opera from 1961, as Gilda, Amina in La Sonnambula, Lucia di Lammermoor, Rosina and Zerbinetta; 8 Seasons with 36 Performances in 7 roles; Guest appearances in Milan, Paris and London. *Recordings:* Rigoletto; La Bohème; Il Barbiere di Siviglia; Les Contes d'Hoffmann. *Address:* c/o Metropolitan Opera, Lincoln Center, New York, NY 10023, USA.

D'ANGELO James, b. 17 Mar 1939, Paterson, New Jersey, USA. Teacher; Composer; Pianist. m. Georgina Joysmith, 12 Dec 1970, 2 daughters. *Education:* Columbia University, 1956-57; New York University, 1957- 58; Studies with Gunther Schuller, William Russo, John Lewis (MJQ) and Jan Gorbaty, 1969-75; B Mus, 1961, M Mus, 1966, Manhattan School of Music; PhD, New York University, 1983. *Debut:* Carnegie Recital Hall, New York, 1966. *Career:* As teacher: Professor of Music, City University of New York, 1970-86; Lecturer, Goldsmiths' College and Webster University, London, 1987-; London concerts of own music, 1986-; As composer: Works performed at various colleges in USA 1968-75 and at various London venues, 1985-; Song cycle debuted at Carnegie Recital Hall, 1971. *Compositions to:* Tintinnabulations (song cycle for soprano); Toccata for Solo Percussionist; Songs on poems by E E Cummmings. *Contributions to:* New International Dictionary of Opera, Hindemith Jahrbuch, Kairos Quarterly and Musical Heritage Society. *Address:* 14 Denmark Road, Ealing, London W13 8RG, England.

D'ASCOLI Bernard, b. 18 Nov 1958, Aubagne, France. *Education:* Marseille Conservatoire, 1973-77; Private teachers. *Career:* Paris debut (Salle Cortot) 1981; London debut at QEH and RFH 1982; Australian debut at Sydney Opera House 1983; Amsterdam Concertgebouw, 1984; US début in Houston 1985; Vienna début at Musikverein, 1986; Tokyo début at Casals and Bunka Kaikan Halls, 1988; Orchestral engagements include appearances with Royal Philharmonic Orchestra, London Philharmonic, Philharmonia, BBC SO, Chamber Orchestra of Europe, Amsterdam Phiharmonic, Houston SO, Orchestre National de Toulouse, Boston Symphony Orchestra, under such conductors as Sir John Pritchard, Kurt Sanderling, Yehudi Menuhin, Sergiu Commissiona, Ivan Fischer, Michel Plasson, Otaka Tadaaki. *Recordings:* 1st recording with EMI, 1982; Recent CD recordings include Schumann CD with Nimbus 1989, Chopin CD; Regular television and radio broadcasts. *Honours:* Most talented French artist of the year, Megève, 1976; 1st Prize, Maria Canals Competition, Barcelona, Spain, 1978; 3rd Prize, Leeds International Piano Competition, England, 1981. *Current Management:* c/o TransArt (mc) Ltd, 8 Bristol Gardens, London W9 2JG, England. *Hobbies:* Reading; Literature; Humane sciences; Swimming. *Address:* c/o Van Walsum Management, 40 St Peter's Road, London W6 9BH, England.

D'AVALOS Francesco, b. 11 Apr 1937, Naples, Italy. Teacher; Composer; Conductor. *Education:* Studied classics at college, Naples; Philosophy, Naples University; Started piano study with Vicenzo Vitale at age 12 then orchestration with Renato Parodi; Diploma in Composition, San Pietro a Majella Conservatory, Naples; Accademia Chigiana, Siena, with Franco Ferrare and Sergiu Celibidache. *Debut:* Concert as Conductor, RAI, Rome, 1964. *Career:* Conductor, Teatro Communale, Florence, San Carlo Opera, Naples, RAI Orchestra, Rome, Pomeriggi Musicali, Milan, major symphony orchestras and opera companies throughout Europe; Has appeared with ensembles, Zurich, Lugano, Cologne, Stuttgart, Karlsruhe and Lyon; Conductor with Philharmonia Orchestra, London, 1987-; Has taught at several Italian conservatories; Currently holds Chair of Fugue and Advanced Composition and Chair of Conducting, San Pietro a Majelle Conservatory, Naples. *Compositions:* Symphony for Orchestra and Soprano, premiered at Norddeutsche Rundfunk, Hamburg; Qumran, Study for Orchestra, La Scala with Eliahu Inbal; Forthcoming: Maria di Venosa, music drama in 2 acts, with Philharmonia; Other orchestral works, works for voice, chamber music. *Recordings:* Over 30 including: Brahms: Complete orchestral works, 4 CDs; Martucci: Complete orchestral works, 4 CDs; Clementi: Complete orchestral works, 3 CDs; Wagner: overtures, 4 CDs; Bruckner, Symphony No 7; Mendelssohn: Complete orchestral works, 5 CDs. *Honours:* Premio Marzotto for Composition; Grand Prix International du Disque for Martucci's Symphonies, Academie Charles Cros, 1990; MRA Award for Raff's Symphony No 3, Im Walde, 1993. *Hobby:* Collecting antiques. *Address:* 50 vie dei Mille, Naples, Italy.

D'INTINO Luciana, b. 1959, San vito al Tagliamento, Pordenone, Italy. Singer (Mezzo-soprano). *Education:* Studied at the Benedetto Marcello Conservatory, Venice. *Debut:* Sang Azucena in Il Trovatore, 1983. *Career:* Appearances as Rossini's Rosina in Macerata and Naples, 1984, 1986; Aida at Cagliari and Trieste; La Scala Milan from 1987 in Nabucco, Guillaume Tell; Jommelli's Fetonte, Adriana Lecouvreur and as Luggrezia in Pergolesi's Lo Frate 'Nnamorato; Sang Frederica in Luisa Miller at Rome, 1990 and on Metropolitan Opera Debut, 1991. Turin 1990 as Eboli in Don Carlos and Savona 1991 as Arsace in Rossini's Aureliano in Palmira; Sang Preziosilla in Forza del Destino at Naples, Sara in Roberto Devereux at Bologna, 1992; Preziosilla at the 1992 Maggio Musicale, Florence. *Recordings include:* Lo Frate 'nnamorato, conducted by Riccardo Muti. *Honours include:* Winner, Spoleto Singing Competition, 1983. *Address:* c/o Teatro alla Scala, Via Filodrammatici 2, 20121 Milan, Italy.

DA COSTA Noel (George), b. 24 Dec 1929, Lagos, Nigeria. Composer; Violinist; Conductor. *Education:* Studied at Queens College, Columbia University and with Luigi Dallapiccola in Italy. *Career:* Teacher at Queens and Hunter Colleges, New York, 1963-66;

Rutgers, State University of New Jersey from 1970; Has conducted college orchestras in New York and the Accademia Chigiana; Music director of the Triad Chorale, New York; Violinist with various New York theatre orchestras. *Honours include:* Fulbright Fellowship 1958-60. *Compositions include:* Opera, The Cocktail Sip, 1958; Occurrence for Six, 1965; Verses with Vamps for cello and piano, 1968; The Confession Stone for voices and ensemble, 1969; In the Circle for guitars, 1970; Counterpoint for voices and organ, 1970; November Song, concert scene, 1974; Magnolia Blue for violin and piano, 1975; A Ceremony of Spirituals, 1976; Sermon on the Warpland, 1980; Ukom Memory Songs for organ and percussion, 1981. *Address:* c/o ASCAP, ASCAP Building, One Lincoln Plaza, New York, NY 10023, USA.

DA SILVA Miguel, b. 1960, France. Violist. *Education:* Studied at the Paris Conservatoire with Jean-Claude Pennetier and with members of the Amadeus and Alban Berg Quartets. *Career:* Member of the Ysaye String Quartet from 1984; Many concert performances in France, Europe, America and the Far East; Festival engagements at Salzburg, Tivoli (Copenhagen), Bergen, Lockenhaus, Barcelona and Stresa; Many appearances in Italy, notably with the 'Haydn' Quartets of Mozart; Tours of Japan and the USA 1990 and 1992. *Recordings:* Mozart Quartet K421 and Quintet K516 (Harmonia Mundi); Ravel, Debussy and Mendelssohn Quartets (Decca). *Honours:* Grand Prix Evian International String Quartet Competition, May 1988L special prizes for best performances of a Mozart quartet, the Debussy quartet and a contemporary work; 2nd Prize, Portsmouth International String Quartet Competition, 1988. *Address:* c/o 12/13 Richmond Buildings, Dean Street, London W1V 5AF, England.

DADAK Jaromir, b. 30 May 1930, Znojmo, Czechoslovakia. Composer; Conductor. m. 31 Oct 1981, 1 son, 3 daughters. *Education:* Janacek Academy of Art, Brno, 1956. *Career:* Conductor, Ostrava Radio Orchestra, 1960-63; Secretary, Czechoslovak Composer Federation, 1967-69; Director, Olomous State Symphony Orchestra, 1969-71; Political dissident, 1972-89. *Compositions:* Recorded: Orchestral: Never More, 1959, recorded, 1960; Concerto-Symphony for piano and symphony orchestra, 1959, 1964; Concertino for dulcimer and orchestra, 1965; Concerto for piano 4-hands and symphony orchestra, 1972, 1973; Concerto for viola and small orchestra, 1976, 1988; Sonata concerto for string orchestra, 1977, 1990; Chamber music: 3 studies for piano 4-hands and percussions, 1965, 1969; Partita for violin, clarinet and piano, 1965, 1966; Music to delight for violin, clarinet, violoncello and piano, 1980, 1986; Sonata for dulcimer, 1980, 1989; Published; Perapera ad astra for organ, 1971, 1973; Viola Concerto, 1976, 1983; Recent compositions: Sonata for violin and piano, 1989; Ludi for string quartet and organ or symphony orchestra, 1991; 4 scautry Honours for bassoon and strings, 1991. *Publications:* Our Folk Song, 1991. *Honours:* National Prize, 1960, Prize, CMF, Prague, 1972. *Memberships:* Association of Music Artists and Scientists, Prague; Slovak Music Union, Bratislava; Founder Member, Conrast '91, Ostrava. *Hobby:* National and European folklore. *Address:* Cestmirova 27, 140 00 Prague 4, Czech Republic.

DAGGETT Philip, b. 1962, Chesterfield, England. Singer (Tenor). *Education:* Studied in Chesterfield and at Guildhall School of Music, 1985-. *Career:* Songman at York Minster, 1981-85; Concert appearances include Bach's Actus Tragicus in Paris and the St John Passion throughout Spain; Has sung in Mozart's C minor Mass and Requiem; Mendelssohn's Lobgesang (Elizabeth Hall debut) and Elijah; Britten's Cantata Misericordium and St Nicolas; Operatic roles include Paris in La Belle Hélène, Beppe in Pagliacci and Mozart's Ferrando; Premiere of Birtwistle's Gawain at Covent Garden, May 1991; Also sings Count Almaviva in Il Barbiere di Siviglia; Sang Tamino with Opera Lirica at the Holland Park Theatre, 1992. *Recordings include:* The Fairy Queen with Harry Christophers and The Sixteen; A

Festal Mass at the Imperial Court of Vienna and Charpentier's Vespers for the Feast of St Louis with the Yorkshire Baroque Soloists and Peter Seymour. *Address:* c/o Norman McCann International Artists Ltd, The Coach House, 56 Lawrie Park Gardens, London SE26 6XJ, England.

DAGILAISKAYA Elvira Romanovna, b. 24 Sept 1938, Odessa, USSR. Pianist; Writer on Music. Divorced, 1 son. *Education:* Odessa Conservatoire; Moscow Conservatoire, Doctor of Arts 1977. *Career:* Solo and Camera Pianist; Lecturer of Music, Odessa Conservatoire, Professor, 1961-93; Appearances: TV 1956, 1971-91, Odessa; Moscow Radio 1965-67; Odessa Radio, 1971-91; Stage appearances in Odessa, Moscow, CSFR, Spain, Austria 1992. *Publications:* Respected author of music publications including, Czech and Slovak piano music for Children and teenagers, Kiev, 1993. *Contributions to:* Musical Encyclopaedia, Moscow; Soviet Music, Moscow; Music, Kiev; News of Musical Life, Prague. *Honours:* Honoured cultured artist of Ukraine, 1991. *Hobbies:* Swimming; Tennis; Stamp collecting; Travel. *Address:* 21 Tolstoy str, Apt 19, Odessa 270020, Ukraine.

DAHLBERG Stefan, b. 3 May, 1955, Sweden. Singer (Tenor). *Education:* Studied at the State Academy of Music and the State College of Musical Drama in Stockholm. *Career:* Concerts and broadcasts throughout Scandinavia; Operatic roles include Rustighello in Lucrezia Borgia by Donizetti, Tamino, Beppo, Count Almaviva, King Charles in The Maid of Orleans by Tchaikovsky and Sextus in Giulio Cesare; Royal Opera Stockholm as Tamino, Sextus, Ferrando and Don Ottavio; Drottningholm 1987, as Titus in La Clemenza di Tito: visited Brighton with the Drottningholm company 1987; Season 1988-89 with concert performance of Haydn's Armida in Amsterdam; Grand Théâtre Geneva as Jacquino in Fidelio, conducted by Jeffrey Tate; Gounod's Faust at the Stockholm Opera; Concertgebouw Amsterdam, 1989, as Ubaldo in Rossin's Armida; Drottningholm, 1989, as Tamino; Sang Calaf in Busoni's Turandot at Lyons, 1992; Sang leading tenor role of Vicente Martin y Soler's Una Cosa Rara; Sang Alfredo in Verdi's La Traviata, Stockholm Royal Opera, 1993; Concert repertoire includes Suter's Der Abwesende Gott, Die Schöpfung by Haydn, Le Roi David by Honegger, Messiah, Puccini's Messa di Gloria and works by Thomas Jennefelt and Sven-David Sandstrom. *Recordings:* Videos of La Clemenza di Tito, Die Zauberflöte and Don Giovanni, from Drottningholm. *Address:* Nordk Artist AB, Sveavagen 76, S-11344 Stockholm, Sweden.

DAHLGREN Carl H P, b. 2 July 1929, New York City, USA. Professor; Arts Administrator. m. Ella Kate Bowes, 8 Oct 1961, 3 sons, 1 daughter. *Education:* BM, Westminster Choir College, Princeton, New Jersey, 1954. *Career:* Manager, Princeton Symphony Orchestra, 1956-59; Vice-President, Artistic Manager, Columbia Artists Management Incorporated, partner, Division of Judd, Ries and Dahlgren, 1958-68; Vice-President, Artist Manager, Director of Sales, Sol Hurok Concerts Inc, 1968-70; Executive Director, Central City Opera House Association, General Manager, Central City Opera Company, 1970-72; Associate, Sol Hurok Concerts Inc, 1970-74; President, Dahlgren Arts Management Incorporated, Denver, Colorado, 1970-78; Executive Director-Secretary, Colorado Celebration of the Arts, Denver, 1974-76; Associate Professor, Director of Graduate Studies in Arts Administration, College-Conservatory of Music, University of Cincinnati, 1978-. *Contributions to:* Various magazines and journals. *Hobbies:* Travel; Reading; Family. *Address:* 2216 Bedford Terrace, Cincinnati, OH 45208, USA.

DAKERS Lionel Frederick, b. 24 February 1924, Rochester, England. Church Musician. m. Mary Elisabeth Williams, 21 April 1951, 4d. *Education:* Rochester Cathedral Choir School; Pupil of Sir Edward Bairstow, Organist of York Minster 1943-45; Royal Academy of Music, London 1947-51. *Career:* Assistant Organist, St George's Chapel, Windsor Castle 1950-

54; Organist: Ripon Cathedral 1954-57, Exeter Cathedral 1957-72; Director, Royal School of Church Music 1972-89. *Compositions:* Church Music. *Recordings:* Church Music. *Publications:* Church Music at the Crossroads 1970; Handbook of Parish Music 1979; Church Music in a Changing World 1989; Editor, New Church Anthem Book 1992; Reviews and Articles. *Honours:* DMus, Lambeth 1979; CBE 1983; DMus, Exeter 1993. *Memberships:* Royal College of Organists; Associated Board of Royal Schools of Music. *Hobbies:* Book Collecting; Gardening; Travel; Continental Food. *Address:* 6 Harcourt Terrace, Salisbury, Wiltshire SP2 7SA, England.

DALBERG Evelyn, b. 23 May 1939, Leipzig, Germany. Singer (Mezzo-soprano). *Education:* Studied with Parry Jones at Guildhall School of Music, Annelies Kupper in Munich and with her father, Frederick Dalberg, at Cape Town and Mannheim. *Debut:* Koblenz 1964, as Venus in Tannhäuser. *Career:* Sang at various provincial German opera houses and in South Africa, notably Cape Town and Johannesburg; Other roles have included Verdi's Ulrica, Amneris, Eboli and Mistress Quickly, Nancy in Martha, Giulietta, Les Contes d'Hoffmann, Judith, Bluebeard's Castle, the Witch in Hansel and Gretel and Prince Orlofsky, Die Fledermaus. *Address:* c/o Johannesburg Operatic and Dramatic Society, PO Box 7010, Johannesburg 2000, Transvaal, South Africa.

DALBERTO Michel Jean Jacques, b. 2 June 1955, Paris, France. Pianist. *Education:* Paris National Conservatory, 1972. *Debut:* Paris. *Career:* Appearances, major European Centres; Festivals: Edinburgh, Lucerne, Aix-en-Provence, Montreux; Tours in Japan, Canada; Radio & TV Performances; Paris dubut with the Orchestra de Paris, 1980; Partners with Henryk Szeryng, Augustin Dumay and Viktoria Mullova, Violin, and Nikita Magaloff, Piano. *Recordings:* Works of Schubert, Schumann, Brahms, Beethoven, Mozart. *Honours:* Clara Haskil Prize, 1975; First Prize, Leeds International Competition, 1978; Grand Prix Academie Charles Cros, 1980. *Hobbies:* Skiing; Tennis; Golf. *Management:* Opera Et Concert, Paris, France. *Address:* BD Plumhof 13, 1800 Vevey, Switzerland.

DALBY Martin, b. 25 April 1942, Aberdeen, Scotland. Composer. *Education:* Studied at the Royal College of Music from 1960, with Herbert Howells (composition) and Frederick Riddle (viola); Further study in Italy. *Career:* BBC music producer in London 1965-71; Cramb Research Fellow in composition at Glasgow University 1972; Head of Music, BBC Scotland, 1972-. *Compositions include:* Waltz Overture, 1965; Trio for Piano, Violin and cello, 1967; Oboe Sonatina, 1969; Cantica for high voice, clarinet, viola and piano, 1969; Commedia for clarinet, violin, cello and piano, 1969; Symphony, 1970; Whisper Music, 1971; Concerto Martin Pescatore for strings, 1971; The Keeper of the pass for soprano and instruments, 1971; Cancionero para una Mariposa for 9 instruments, 1971; String Quintet, 1972; Orpheus for chorus, narrator and 11 instruments, 1972; Catigas del Cancionero for 5 solo voices, 1972; The Tower of Victory for orchestra, 1973; Yet Still she is the Moon, brass septet, 1973; Viola Concerto, 1974; El remanso del Pitido for 12 solo voices, 1974; Unicorn for violin and piano, 1975; Aleph for 8 instruments, 1975; Ad Flumina Babiloniae, motet, 1975; Almost a Madrigal for wind and percussion, 1977; El Ruisenor for orchestra, 1979; Coll for the Hazel Tree for chorus and electronics, 1979; Man Walking, octet for wind and strings, 1980; Antoinette Alone for mezzo and piano, 1980; Chamber Symphony, 1982; Nozze di Primavera for orchestra, 1984; A Plain Man's Hammer for symphonic wind ensemble, 1984; Piano Sonata No 1, 1985; De Patre ex Filio octet for wind and strings, 1988; Piano Sonata No 2, 1989. *Hobbies:* Private Pilot's Licence; Railways; Hill Walking; Literature.

DALE Clamma, b. 4 July 1948, Chester, Pennsylvania, USA. Soprano. *Education:* BMus 1970, MS 1975, Juilliard School, New York; Studied voice, Philadelphia Settlement Music School. *Debut:* Operatic

debut as Antonia, Les Contes d'Hoffmann, New York City Opera, 1975. *Career:* Sang with numerous opera companies; Toured as Concert singer; Roles include: Pamina, Countess Almaviva, Nedda, Musetta, Gershwin's Bess at the Theater des Westens, Berlin, 1988; Deutsche Oper Berlin, 1989, as Liù in Turandot. *Recordings:* For Deutsche Grammophon; RCA. *Address:* c/o New York City Opera, Lincoln Center, New York, NY 10023, USA.

DALE Laurence, b. 10 Sept 1957, Pyecombe, Sussex. Singer (Tenor). *Education:* Studied at the Guildhall School of Music (1976-80) and at the Mozarteum, Salzburg. *Debut:* With English National Opera as Camille in The Merry Widow, 1981. *Career:* Covent Garden debut 1982, as Second Noble in Lohengrin; Sang Don Jose in Peter Brook's La tragedie de Carmen in Paris (1981) and on Broadway (1983); in 1983 sang Gounod's Romeo at Basle and Ramiro at Glyndebourne; Visited Los Angeles with the Royal Opera 1984, singing Pong in Turandot; English National Opera 1983, as Monteverdi's Orfeo; For Welsh National Opera has sung Mozart's Ottavio and Ferrando and Eisenstein in Die Fledermaus; With Opera North as Mozart's Tamino and Belmonte and Jenik in The Bartered Bride; Further appearances in Lyons, Paris, Hamburg, Amsterdam, Aix, Geneva, Brussels (Tamino and Idomeneo) and Zurich; Other roles include Tchaikovsky's Lensky, Jacquino in Fidelio, Méhul's Joseph and Gonzalve in L'Heure Espagnole; Concert engagements include Mozart's C minor Mass and Haydn's St Cecilia Mass with the London Philharmonic; Bach's Christmas Oratorio with the Los Angeles Philharmonic; Britten's Spring Symphony at the Festival Hall; The Dream of Gerontius and Liszt's Faust Symphony at the Brighton Festival; Messiah in Vienna, Stravinsky's Pulcinella and Rossini's Stabat Mater; Appearances on television in Britain and Europe; On 27 Jan 1991 sang Tamino in Die Zauberflöte at the Landestheater Salzburg, to inaugurate the Mozart bicentenary; Season 1991/92 as Ferrando at Stuttgart and Belfiore in La Finta Giardiniera at the Salzburg Festival. *Recordings include:* La tragédie de Carmen; videos of Princess Ida, Die Zauberflöte from Aix and Cenerentola from Glyndebourne; Mozart's C minor Mass (EMI). *Address:* c/o Harrison Parrott Ltd, 12 Penzance Place, London W11 4PA, England.

DALIS-LOINAZ Irene, b. 8 Oct 1925, San Jose, California, USA. Executive Director, Opera San Jose; Professor of Music. m. George Loinaz, 16 July 1957, 1 daughter. *Education:* AB, 1946, MS, Honours, 1957, San Jose State University; MA, Columbia University Teachers College, 1947; Studied voice with Edyth Walker, New York City, 1947-50; Paul Althouse, 1950-51; Dr Otto Mueller, Milano, Italy, 1952. *Debut:* Berlin State Opera, 1956; Metropolitan Opera, New York City, 1957. *Career:* Leading Dramatic Mezzo-soprano, Metropolitan Opera, 1957-77 as Eboli, Amneris, Santuzza, Azucena, Lady Macbeth and Dalila, 22 roles in 232 performances; 1st US born Kundry to open Bayreuth Festival, 1963; Opened the Met opera season as Amneris in Aida, 1963; Premiered Dello Joio's Opera, Blood Moon, 1961 and Henderson's Opera, Medea, 1972; in 1966 sang The Nurse in Die Frau ohne Schatten, at Sadler's Wells Theatre; Professor of Music, San Jose State University and Founder and Executive Director, Opera San Jose, from 1984; Hosted Symposium Redrawing the Man at San José, Nov 1989, on behalf of the Music Critics Association. *Recording:* Parsifal, (Wagner) Phillips label. *Honours:* Fulbright Scholar, 1951; Wagner Medallion, 1963; Tower Award, San Jose State University, 1974; Distinguished Service Award, Columbia University, 1961; California Public Educators Hall of Fame, 1985; Award of Merit, People of the City of San Francisco, Honoured Citizen of San Jose, 1986; Honorary Doctor of Music, Santa Clara University, 1987. *Address:* 1731 Cherry Grove Dr, San Jose, CA 95125, USA.

DALLAPOZZA Adolf, b. 14 April 1940, Bozen, Austria. Singer (Tenor). *Education:* Studied with Elisabeth Rado in Vienna. *Career:* Sang in the chorus of the Vienna Volksoper while a student; Solo debut

1962, as Ernesto in Don Pasquale; Sang at the Volksoper until 1972, and guested in Munich, Hamburg, Milan, Brussels and Cologne; Bregenz Festval, 1972-84; Many roles in works by Mozart, Italian opera and in operas of the Baroque; Many appearances in operettas; Wilhelm Meister in Mignon at the Vienna Volksoper, 1988. *Recordings:* Die Fledermaus, Der Vogelhändler; Idomeneo; Intermezzo; Fidelio (Deutsche Grammophon); Die Meistersinger (Decca); Königskinder by Humperdinck. *Address:* c/o Volksoper, Währingertrasse 78, A-1090 Vienna, Austria.

DALLEY John, b. 1 June 1935, Madison, Wisconsin, USA. Violinist. *Education:* Studied at Curtis Institute, Philadelphia, with Ivan Galamian. *Career:* Member of the Oberlin Quartet, formerly teacher at Oberlin Conservatory, Performed in chamber music with Rudolf Serkin at the Marlboro Festival and prompted by Alexander Schneider to co-found the Guarneri String Quartet, 1984; Many tours in America and Europe, notably appearances at the Spoleto Festival, 1965, to Paris with Arthur Rubinstein and London 1970, in the complete quartets of Beethoven; Noted for performances of the Viennese classics, and works by Walton, Bartók and Stravinsky; Season 1987-88 included tour of Japan and concerts at St John's Smith Square and the Elizabeth Hall, London; On faculty of the Curtis Institute, Philadelphia, and at the University of Maryland. *Recordings include:* Mozart's quartets dedicated to Haydn; Complete quartets of Beethoven; With Arthur Rubinstein Piano Quintets of Schumann, Dvořák and Brahms; Piano Quartets by Fauré and Brahms. *Honours include:* Edison Award for Beethoven recordings 1971. *Address:* c/o Curtis Institute of Music, 1726 Locust Street, Philadelphia, PA 19103, USA.

DALTON Andrew, b. 29 Sept 1950, Melbourne, Australia. Singer (Countertenor). *Education:* Studied in Brisbane. *Debut:* Sang at Vadstena, Sweden, in Provenzale's La Stellidaura vendicata. *Career:* Has sung in Baroque opera at Venice, Innsbruck, Munich, Berne and Amsterdam; Appeared with Scottish Opera in Cavalli's Egisto, and at the 1987 Buxton Festival as Fernando in Conti's Don Chisciotte in Sierra Morena; Season 1988-89 in Jommelli's Fetonte at La Scala Milan, in Monteverdi's Ulisse with Opera de Lausanne at Mézières, and as Apollo in Death in Venice with Australian Opera at Sydney; Engagements in Germany and Switzerland as Britten's Oberon, and has sung in Monteverdi's Orfeo, Handel's Agrippina and Ariodante, and Jommelli's La Schiava Liberata. *Address:* Australian Opera, Sydney Opera House, New South Wales, Australia.

DAMARATI Luciano, b. 6 Feb 1942, Lucca, Italy. Musician. *Education:* Diplomas: Piano, 1965; Composition, 1970; Organ, 1971; Orchestral Conducting, 1975; Studies: Organ with Alessandro Esposito and Fernando Germani; Orchestral Conducting with Franco Ferrara; Choral Conducting with Nino Antonellini; Musicology at Chigiana Academy of Music, Siena. *Career:* Many concerts as organist and orchestral conductor; Broadcasts as composer, orchestra conductor and choir conductor on Italian radio and television. *Compositions:* Preghiera Semplice (voice, choir and orchestra); I Due Fanciulli (voice and piano); Vexilla Regis Prodeunt (Choir of 4 mixed voices); Impressioni for viola and piano; Fugue, Prelude, Variations for organ; Meditazione (piano); Contrasti (piano). *Contributions to:* La Provincia di Lucca, 1974; Actum Luce, 1980; Rivista di Archeologia Storia e Costume. *Honour:* 2nd Prize for Composition, Rodolfo del Corona, Leghorn. *Membership:* Italian Society of Musicology. *Address:* Piazza S Francesco 14, 55100 Lucca, Italy.

DAMASE Jean-Michel, b. 27 January 1928, Bordeaux, France. Composer; Pianist. *Education:* Conservatoire National Superieus de Paris. *Career:* United States debut 1954, as pianist and composer in a New York concert. *Compositions:* Quintet for flute, harp and string trio 1947; Interludes for orchestra 1948; Rhapsody for oboe and string orchestra 1948; Trio for flute, harp and cello 1949; Piano Concerto 1950; Ballet La Croquese de Diamants 1950; Violin Concerto 1956; La Tendre Eleonore, opera-bouffe, Marseilles 1962; Colombe, comedie lyrique, Bordeaux 1961; Eugene Le Mysterieux, feuillton musical, Paris 1964; Madame de . . roman musical, Monte Carlo 1970; Eurydice, comedie lyrique, Bordeaux 1972; L'heritiere, opera in 4 acts after Washington Square by Henry James, Nancy 1974; Quatet for flute, clarinette and piano, 1992; Concertos for flute and orchestra, 1993; Variations, Mozart: for piano and orchestra, 1994. *Honour:* Prix de Rome 1947. *Address:* c/o PRS Ltd Member Registration, 29-33 Berners Street, London W1P 4AA, England.

DAMONTE Magali, b. 30 June 1960, Marseilles, France. Singer (Mezzo-soprano). *Education:* Studied in Marseilles. *Debut:* Sang Zulma in L'Italiana in Algeri at Marseilles in 1978. *Career:* Many appearances in France with operas by Rossini, Cimarosa and Gounod; Paris Opera 1980, as Iphise in Rameau's Dardanus; Aix-en-Provence Festival from 1981, as Rosina, Cenerentola and Isaura in Tancredi; At the Opéra de Lyon has sung Aloès in L'Etoile (visit with the company to the Edinburgh Festival, 1985); Marseilles 1987, as Fidalma in Il Matrimonio Segreto, Théâtre des Champs Elysées Paris 1989, as Hedwige in Guillaume Tell; Other Rossini roles include Isabella, Ragonde (Le Comte Ory) and Marie (Moise). *Recordings include:* L'Etoile, conducted by John Eliot Gardiner (EMI/Conifer). *Address:* c/o Opera de Lyon, 9 Quai Jean Moulin, F-69001, France.

DAN Ikuma, b. 7 April 1924, Tokyo, Japan. Composer. *Education:* Studied at Tokyo Music School, graduation 1945 and with Moroi and Yamada. *Career:* Formed Group of Three Composers with Akutagawa and Mayuzumi 1953; Film Music Director and Composer; Presenter of popular music programmes on television from 1967. *Compositions:* Operas The Twilight Heron 1952; The Listening Cap 1955; Yang Kwei-fei 1958; Luminous Moss 1972; Chanchiki 1975; 6 Symphonies 1949-70; Sinfonia Burlesca 1953; The Silken Road, dance suite for orchestra 1954; Japanese Poem for orchestra 1967; Hymn to the Sai-kai for chorus and orchestra 1969; A Letter from Japan for orchestra 1969; Rainbow Tower for orchestra 1970; Chamber: String Trio 1947; String Quartet 1948; Concerto Grosso for harpsichord and strings 1965; Choruses. *Address:* JASRAC (Japan), c/o PRS Ltd Member Registration, 29-33 Berners Street, London W1P 4AA, England.

DANCEANU Liviu, b. 19 July 1954, Romania. Composer. m. Rodica Danceanu, 27 Aug 1976. *Education:* Academy of Music C, Poroumbescu, Bucharest; University Studies, Musical Composition with Stefan Niculescu. *Debut:* Academy of Music, C. Porumbescu, 1978. *Career:* Concerts in Bucharest and other Musical Centres, London, Paris, Rotterdam, Torino, Warsaw, Prague, Moscow, etc; appearances on Romanian Radio and TV, BBC London, Radio France; Recordings with Electrecord Recording House, Bucharest; Leader and Conductor, The Workshop for Contemporary Music Archaeus. *Compositions include:* Les Heros, Op 1, 1978; La Rocade De Janus, Op 2, 1978; Allegorie, Op 3, 1979; Sonate Pour Basson, Op 4, 1980; Archaeus, Op 5, 1981; Angulus Ridet, Op 7, 1981; Ossia, Op 9, 1982; Vers La Paix, Op 10, 1982; Quasifuga, Op 11, 1983; 3 Chansons Infantiles, Op 15, 1984; Florilege, Op 17, 1985; Protocantus, Op 18, 1985; Glass Music, Op 20, 1985; Quasitoccata, Op 21, 1985. *Hobbies:* Philosophy; Arts; Literature; Sport. *Address:* Calea Vacaresti No 276, B1. 63 Sc 2, Apt 44, Sector 4, 75176 Bucharest, Romania.

DANCO Suzanne, b. 22 Jan 1911, Brussels, Belgium. Singer (Soprano). *Education:* Studied at the Brussels Conservatory and with Fernando Carpi in Prague. *Debut:* Genoa Opera 1941, as Fiordiligi in Così fan Tutte. *Career:* Sang at La Scala Milan, notably in the local premieres of Peter Grimes (1947) and Oedipus Rex (1948); Naples 1949, as Marie in Wozzeck; Glyndebourne Festival 1948-51, as Fiordiligi and Donna Anna; Covent Garden 1951, as Mimi in La Bohème;

Broadcasts of Wozzeck and Pélleas et Mélisande; World-wide concert tours in the songs of Debussy, Berlioz and Ravel; Teacher at the Accademia Chigiana in Siena. *Recordings:* Pelléas et Mélisande, conducted by Ansermet; La Damnation de Faust; Le Roi David by Honegger; L'Heure Espagnole; Le Nozze di Figaro; Don Giovanni; Labels include Supraphon, Decca, Philips and RCA.

DANCUO Mirjana, b. 16 January 1929, Karlovac, Croatia. Singer (Soprano). m. Zdenko Peharda. *Education:* Studied in Zagreb. *Debut:* National Opera, Zagreb 1945 as Giannetta in L'Elisir d'amore. *Career:* Sang Belgrade, Sofia, Brno and elsewhere in Eastern Europe; Guest appearances at Teatro Liceo Barcelona, the Vienna Volksoper and Den Norske Opera, Oslo; Other roles have included Mozart's Countess and Donna Anna, Verdi's Amneris, Amelia, Ballo in Maschera and Trovatore Leonora, La Gioconda, Margherita in Mefistofele, Yaroslavna in Prince Igor, Leonore, Fidelio, Marina in Boris Godunov, Wagner's Sieglinde and Elisabeth, the Marschallin in Der Rosenkavalier, Tosca and Desdemona. *Address:* Jerikoveien 89 B, 1052 Oslo, Norway.

DANIEL Nicholas Jeremy Gordon, b. 9 Jan 1962, Liss, Hampshire, England. Solo Oboist; Chamber Musician. m. Joy Farrall, 29 Mar 1986. *Education:* Chorister, Salisbury Cathedral School, 1972-74; Purcell School, London, 1974-80; Royal Academy of Music, 1980-83. *Debut:* South Bank, 1982. *Career:* Concerto and Recital appearances, at home and abroad; Professor, Guildhall School of Music & Drama; Proms Debut, 1990; Founder & Director Haffner Wind Ensemble, 1990; Daniel-Drake Duo 12 years old; Regular broadcasts of wide repertoire; Tours include Hungary, Australia, Scandinavia, Netherlands, Italy, Bulgaria, Spain, France, Switzerland, Germany; Firm dedication to new music, many World & Britain premieres; Played Strauss Concerto at the 1993 Proms. *Recordings:* Virgin Classics, Hyperion, Chandos, Léman Classics; American Gramophone of Alwyn, Belgian music, Albinoni, Strauss, Martinů; Appearances with Lyndsay, Brodsky, Allegri, Van Burgh & Brindisi String Quartets. *Honours:* BBC Young Musician of the Year, 1980; Gillet Young Artists Prize, Graz, 1984 and Munich, 1986; Associate, Royal Academy of Music, 1986; Honorary Fellow, Purcell School, 1988. *Hobbies:* Meditation; Reading; Theatre; Cinema; Walking; Cooking; Wine. *Current Management:* Neil Chaffey; Patrick Garvey. *Address:* 26 Haddon Court, Milton Road, Harpenden, Herts AL5 5NA, England.

DANIEL Paul, b. 1 July 1958, Birmingham, England. Conductor. m. Joan Rodgers. *Education:* Sang in choir of Coventry Cathedral and read music at King's College, Cambridge; Guildhall School, London, with Franco Ferrara in Italy and with Adrian Boult and Edward Downes. *Career:* Engagements with the Royal Philharmonic, City of Birmingham Symphony, Scottish National Orchestra, Rotterdam Philharmonic, London Symphony, London Philharmonic, Minneapolis Orchestra, Rochester Philharmonic, New York, London Sinfonietta and Ensemble Inter Contemporain, Paris and Munich Philharmonic, RSO Berlin, ORF Vienna, Hallé, Manchester; US debut 1988 with the London Sinfonietta at the Pepsico Summer Fare; Music Director of Opera Factory, 1987-90: The Beggar's Opera, Cavalli's La Calisto, Birtwistle's Punch and Judy, Così fan Tutte and a triple bill of works by Maxwell Davies, Ligeti and Weill; productions for English National Opera include Ligeti's Le Grand Macabre, Glass's Akhnaten, Dargomizhsky's Stone Guest, Birtwistle's The Mask of Orpheus and the UK premiere of Reimann's Lear (1989); For Nancy Opera conducted the French premiere of Tippett's King Priam, 1988; Music Director, Opera North, 1990-; Productions include: British Stage Premiere of Jerusalem, Ariane et Barbe-bleue, Dukas; Verdi's Attila, Tippett's King Priam, 1991; British première of Schrecker's Der ferne Klang, Rigoletto, Boris, Don Carlos, Wozzeck; La Gioconda, 1993. *Address:* c/o Harrison Parrott Ltd, 12 Penzance Place, London W11 4PA, England.

DANIEL-LESUR Jean Yves, b. 19 Nov 1908, Paris, France. Composer. m. Simone Lauer, 1943, 1 son, 1 daughter. *Education:* Paris Conservatoire. *Career:* Musical Adviser to radiodiffusion-Television Francaise; Principal Inspector of Music, Ministry of Cultural Affairs; Administrator de la Réunion des Theatres Lyriques nationaux; Inspector-General of Music, Ministry of Cultural Affairs; President, Academy Charles Cros, 1979-84; Honorary President, 1984-; Teacher and Writer of film music; Director Hon Schola Cantorum. *Compositions include:* Suite française pour orchestre, 1935; Passacaille, 1937; pastorale pour petit orchestre, 1938; Ricercare pour orchestre, 1939; Quatre lieder pour chant et orchestre, 1933-39; Trio d'Anches, 1939; Trois poems de Cecile Sauvage, 1939; Quatuor a cordes, 1941; L'enfance de l'art, 1942; Variations pour piano et orchestre a cordes, 1943; Clair comme le jour, 1945; Suite pour trio a cordes et piano, 1943; Suite medievale pour flute harpe et trio a cordes, 1944; Chansons cambodgiennes, 1946; Berceuses a tenir eveille (chant), 1947; Pastorale variee pour piano, 1947; Ballade pour piano, 1948; Andrea del Sarto, (sympohonic poem), 1949; Dix chansons populaires a trois voix egales, 1950; Ouverture pour un festival, 1951; Chansons francaises a quatre voix mixtes, 1951; L'annonciation (cantata), 1952; Cantique des cantiques pour 12 voix mixtes, 1953; Concerto da camera pour piano et orchestre de chambre, 1953; Cantique des colonnes pour ensemble vocal feminin et orchestre, 1954; Serenade pour orchestre a cordes, 1954; Le bal du destin, (ballet); Elégie pour deux guitares, 1956; Symphonie de danses, 1958; Messe du jubile pour choeur mixte, orchestre et orgue, 1960; Fantasie pour deux pianos, Trois etudes pour piano, 1962; Chanson de mariage pour choeur de voix de femmes, 1964; Deux chansons de marins pour choeur d'hommes, 1964; Deux chansons de bord pour choeur mixte, 1964; Andrea del Sarto, (2-act opera), 1968; Symphonie d'ombre et de Lumière, 1975; Ondine (opera in 3 acts), 1982; La reine Morte, (opera in 3 acts), 1987; Dialogues, dans La Nuit, 1988, Soprano, Baritone and Orchestra; Le Voyage D'Automne, 1990, Voices and Orchestra; Permis De Sejour, 1990, Voices and Orchestra; A La Lisiere Du Temps, 1990, Voices and Orchestra; Stele A La Memoire D'Une Jeune Fille, 1991, Flute and á cords; Fantasie Concentante, 1992, violoncello et orchestra; Duo concertant pour flute, harp and orchestra. *Recording:* Integrale Des Oeuvres pour Orgue. *Honours include:* Grand Officer, Legion of Honour; Commander, Ordre nat du Merite; Commander, Ordre des Arts et des Lettres; Grand Prix du Conseil General de la Seine; Grand Prix de Paris; Grand Prix de la Société des Auteurs et Compositeurs de Musique, Membre de l'Institut Académie des Beaux-Arts; Membre associé de l'Académie Royale de Belgium. *Memberships:* Membre de L'Academie européenne des Sciences, des Arts et des Lettres; President honorais, GFASMC. *Address:* 101 rue Sadi Carnot, F-92800 Puteaux, France.

DANIELS Barbara, b. 7 May 1946, Grenville, Ohio, USA. Singer (Soprano). *Education:* Bachelors Degree, Ohio State University; Masters Degree, University of Cincinnati. *Debut:* West Palm Beach, Florida, as Susanna, 1973. *Career:* Sang in Europe from 1974, notably in Innsbruck as Violetta and Cologne as Alice Ford, Rosalinda, Mozart's Countess and Manon Lescaut; Appeared in the Michael Hampe productions and films of Agrippina and Il Matrimonio Segreto; Covent Garden from 1978 as Musetta, Donna Elvira, Rosalinde and Alice Ford; Washington DC 1979, as Donizetti's Norina; San Francisco from 1980, as Zdenka in Arabella and as Violetta, Liu and Micaela; Zurich Opera as the Comtesse, in the Ponnelle production of Le Comte Ory; Metropolitan Opera from 1983, as Musetta, Violetta, Rosalinde, Marguerite and the title role in Les Mamelles de Tiresias; Musetta at Rome, 1987; Teatro Regio Turin, 1988, Violetta; Rosalinde in Fledermaus at the Metropolitan and Chicago, 1990; Jenůfa at Innsbruck, 1990; Minnie in La Fanciulla del West at the Metropolitan, Oct 1991; Concert appearances in Rossini's Mosè at Perugia; Boito's Mefistofele in Zurich Tonhalle, Schumann's Scenes from Faust with the Berlin Philharmonic and the Missa Solemnis under Giulini at the Maggio Musicale Florence. *Recordings* include: La Bohème (EMI); Scenes from Faust (EMI); La Bohème conducted by Bernstein (Deutsche Grammophon). Address: c/o Harrison/Parrott Ltd, 12 Penzance Place, London W11 4PA, England.

DANIELS Claire, b. 1963, England. Singer (Soprano). Education: Studied at Royal Northern College of Music and in Paris with Janine Reiss. Career: Appearances with English National Opera in Street Scene, Rusalka and Peter Grimes; Mozart's Servilia and Susanna for Scottish Opera; Amor in Orfeo ed Euridice for Opera North and Zerlina for Kent Opera; Buxton Festival in King Arthur, Rossini's L'Occasione fa il ladro and L'Italiana in Algeri 1992 and Gretry's Le Huron; Vespina in Haydn's L'Infedelta Delusa for Garsington Opera; Nannetta in Falstaff for Opera Zuid in Holland; Adina in L'Elisir D'Amore for Scottish Opera; Concert appearances throughout Germany, Aix-en-Provence and Gothenburg; Repertoire includes Mozart's Mass in C minor, under Charles Mackerras, Les Nuits d'ete, Perth Festival and Carmina Burana at Valencia; Sang in Peter Grimes with the London Symphony Orchestra under Rostropovitch 1992. Address: c/o IMG Artists, Media House, 3 Burlington Lane, London W4 2TH, England.

DANIELS David, b. 20 Dec 1933, Penn Yan, New York, USA. Conductor; Professor. m. Jimmie Sue Evans, 11 Aug 1956, 2 sons, 1 daughter. Education: Diploma, Eastman School of Music, 1951; AB, 1955, Oberlin College; MA, Boston University, 1956; MFA, PhD, University of Iowa, 1963; Berkshire Music Centre, Tanglewood, 1958, 1959; Institute of Orchestral Studies, 1964, 1966. Career: Assistant Professor, University of Redlands, 1963-64; Assistant Professor, Knox College, 1964-69; Assistant Professor, 1969-71, Associate Professor, 1971-86, Professor, 1986-, Chair, 1982-88, Department of Music Theatre and Dance, Oakland University; Conductor, Warren Symphony, 1974-; Conductor, Pontiac-Oakland Symphony, 1978- . Recordings: Operatic Arias and Art Songs. Publications: Orchestral Music, 1972, 2nd Edition, 1982. Address: Department of Music, Theatre and Dance, Oakland University, Rochester, MI 48309-4401, USA.

DANILEVSKI Alexandre, b. 4 Sept 1957, Leningrad. Composer. m. Emilia, 9 September 1990, 3s, 1d. Education: Composition, Leningrad Conservatoire 1974-80; Lute, Scola Cantorum Basilensis 1991-93. Debut: The I Sonata for Violin, St Petersborug Philharmony 1981 and Luth Recital. Career: 90 solo recitals and concerts throughout Russia; Festivals, recitals and concerts in Europe (early music); Founded Syntagma Musicum (ensemble of early music) with Camille Kerger, tenor and composer from Luxembourg, 1993. Compositions: Sonatas for Violin, Violoncello and Piano; Missa for Choir and Orchestra; Concerto for Organ, Harpsichord and Piano; Quatuors 1-4, Chamber Music. Recordings: Guillaume Defay and Music of His Time, with Ensemble Pro Anima, St Petersburg; Medieval and Renaissance Music with the same; Johannes Ciaconia and His Time; Solo: Francesco da Milano, Fancies and Ricercars, St Petersbourg. Membership: American Lute Society. Hobbies: Literature; Early Instruments. Address: 44 Grand Rue, 57050 Lorry-les-Metz, France.

DANN Steven Arthur, b. 27 Dec 1953, Burnaby, British Columbia, Canada. Musician, Viola Player. m. 2 Aug 1980, 1 son, 1 daughter. Education: Student of: Harry Gomez, Vancouver; Lorand Fenyves, Toronto (University of Toronto); Robert Pikler, Sydney, Australia; Bruno Giuranna, Italy; Hungarian Quartet, Banff. Career: Principal viola: National Arts Centre Orchestra 1977-79; Tonhalle Orchestra, Zurich, Switzerland, 1980; Concertgebouw Orchestra, Holland, 1981-84; Vancouver Symphony Orchestra, Canada, 1984-. Recordings: With various orchestras, as principal viola. Honours: Eaton Award, Kathleen Parlow Award, on graduation, University of Toronto. Current Management: Clive Allen, Toronto. Address: 6450 Vine Street, Vancouver, British Columbia, Canada V6M 4B1.

DANON Oskar, b. 7 February 1913, Sarajevo, Yugoslavia. Conductor; Composer. Education: Studied at Prague Conservatory and University. Career: Conducted opera and concerts in Sarajevo from 1938; Director and Conductor of Belgrade Opera 1945-60; Led performances of The Bartered Bride in Prague, then Prince Igor and Don Quichotte with the Belgrade Company on tour to Paris 1958; Wiesbaden Festival 1959; The Love for Three Oranges, Paris Opera 1960 with Boris Godunov; Edinburgh Festival 1962, leading Don Quichotte, Prince Igor and the British premieres of Prokofiev's The Gambler and The Love for Three Oranges; Prince Igor at the Chicago Lyric Opera 1962; Further engagements with Tristan und Isolde at Barcelona 1969 and Arabella at Amsterdam 1970; Opened the restored National Theatre Belgrade 1990 with The Prince of Zeta by Konjovic. Recordings: Prince Igor and A Life for the Tsar with the Belgrade Company. Address: National Theatre, Belgrade, Croatia.

DAO (Nguyen-Thien-Dao), b. 17 Dec 1940, Hanoi, Vietnam. Composer. m. Helene Latapie, 11 May 1963. Education: Baccalaureat; Olivier Messiaen's class, Paris Conservatory. Debut: Festival de Royan, 1969. Compositions include: Thanh dong to quoc, narrator, soprano, chorus, ondes Martenot, 4 pianos, 6 percussions, 1968; Tuyen Lua, 7 instruments, tape, 1968; The 19, female voices and ensemble, 1969; Nho, soprano, cello, 5 double basses, 1970; Khoc To Nhu, mixed voices; Koskom, orchestra, 1971; Cerf-volant, tape, 1973; Bai tap, ondes Martenot, piano, 1974; Camatithu, 6 percussions, 1974; Framic, bass flute, 1974; Mau va hoa, orchestra, 1974; Bao gio, 2 percussions, 2 pianos, 1975; Mua, harpsichord, 1976; A Mi K giao tranh, double bass, 1976; Giai phong, orchestra, electro-acoustics, 1977; Bay, percussions, 1977; Mai Sau, violin, strings, 1977; Phu Dong II, 4 (2) percussions, 1977; Noi Xa, 2 ondes Martenot, electric guitar, percussion, 1977; My-chau Trong-thuy, opera, 1978; Hoang Hon, soprano, orchestra, 1979; Ecouter/Mourir, opera, 1980; Concerto Ten Do Gu, percussion, orchestra, 1980; Chuong gam song, organ, 1981; Tuon Han, soprano, clarinet, 1982; Than Mong, cello concerto, 1982; Poussiere d'empire, soprano, mixed voices, percussion, 1983; Tay-Son, percussion, 1984; L'Aube est une oeuvre, children's or female choir, string quartet, percussion, 1984; Tay-Son, percussion, 1984; Piano Concerto, 1984; Cimes murmurees, string trio, 1985; La Mer petrifiée, opera, 1986-87; Tim Lua, piano, 1987; Pli-ombre, bass clarinet, 1987; Temps songe, 7 percussionists (165 instruments), 1987; VV2, bassoon, 1987; Concerto, Thien Thai, violin, orchestra, 1988; Concerto l'Envol, flute, strings, 1988; Symphonie pour Pouvoir, symphony orchestra, soprano, 1989; Concerto 1989, string sextet, orchestra, 1989; Voie-Concert, ensemble, 1990; Quatuor A Cordes No 1, 1991; Les Perseides, 1992. Address: 28 rue Madame, 75006 Paris, France.

DARA Enzo, b. 13 Oct 1938, Mantua, Italy. Singer (Bass). Education: Studied with Bruno Sutti in Mantua. Debut: Fano 1960, as Colline in La Bohème. Career: Reggio Emilia 1966, as Dulcamara in L'Elisir d'Amore; La Scala Milan debut 1970, as Bartolo in Il Barbiere di Siviglia; Sang Bartolo on his New York (1982) and Covent Garden (1985) debuts; Pesaro 1984, in a revival of Rossini's Il Viaggio a Reims; Guest appearances in Naples, Bologna, Moscow, Brussels, Venice, Palermo and Rome; returned to Covent Garden 1987, as Dulcamara; Pesaro Festival, 1988, in Il Signor Bruschino; Don Pasquale at Venice, 1990; Teatro de la Zarzuela Madrid, 1990, in Il Turco in Italia. Recordings: Il Barbiere di Siviglia and Il Viaggio a Reims (Deutsche Grammophon); L'Italiana in Algeri; La Buona Figliuola by Piccinni; Donizetti's L'ajo nell' imbarazzo; Il Turco in Italia (CBS).

DARBELLAY Jean-Luc, b. 2 Jul 1946, Berne, Switzerland. Composer; Conductor; Clarinettist. m. Elsbeth Darbellay-Fahrer, 21 Sept 1971, 1 son, 1 daughter. Education: Berne University, Diploma as Physician, 1971; Berne Conservatory 1974-79; Studies in composition with Theo Hirsbrunner, Cristobal Halffter, Dimitri Terzakis; Lucern Conservatory 1991 with Edison

Denisov. Foundation Ludus-Ensemble Berne 1978; Conducting studies with Pierre Dervaux and Franco Ferrara. *Career:* Concerts all over Europe (Germany, France, Austria, Spain, Hungary, Switzerland) as conductor of different orchestras: Ludus-Ensemble, Ensemble 20, Ensemble Denosjours (Paris), Sächsisches Kammerorchester Leipzig, Istvan-Orchestra Budapest, Landesjugenorchester Niedersachsen, Quaderni Perugini di musica contemporanea. *Compositions:* Glanum, 1981; Vestiges, 1982; Amphores, 1983; Sept poèmes Romands, 1986; C'est un peu d'eau qui nous sépare, 1989; Cello Concerto (Radio France recording) in Paris, Ensemble Denosjours dedicated to Siegfried Palm, 1989; Edes (Moskau) 1990; -a- (Madrid) 1991; Interférences, 1991; Before Breakfast (Film-music), 1991; Octuor à vent Command by Swiss Radio, 1991; Andromède (Creation at Paris), 1992; Pranam III (Command of the Quaderni Perugini and Siegfried Palm), 1992; Spectrum for natural horn (Command of Bad Harzburg natural horn competition by Hermann Baumann), 1993; Cantus (Command by the Altenburger Orgelkonzerte), 1993. *Recordings:* Leading the Sächsisches Kammerorchester Leipzig: Mozart, Divertimento KV 251, Violin Concerto KV 218; Haydn: Horn Concerto No 2, Symphony No 1; Mozart: Serenade in c-monor KV 388; Darbellay: Espaces, Sept poèmes Romands, wind octett. *Memberships:* Swiss Tonkünstler; SUISA; Alliance française de Berne. *Address:* Englische Anlagen 6, CH-3005 Bern, Switzerland.

DARGE Moniek, b. 11 May 1952, Bruges, Belgium. Teacher; Concert Organiser; Co-Director of Logos. m. Godfried-Willem Raes, 15 Sept. 1973. *Education:* Music Conservatory, Bruges, 1966; Painting, Ghent Academy of Fine Arts, 1973; Lic. Art History & Kand. Philosophy 1974, Lic. Anthropology 1977, University of Ghent. *Debut:* Logos, 1970. *Career:* Violinist, Organiser, concert tours, all Western European countries 1970-, worldwide 1980-; Radio broadcasts, as above; Television Belgium, France, USA, Japan, Poland, Canada; Cultural radio series (New York City, Africa), Belgian State Radio; Co-Director, Logos Foundation. *Compositions:* Numerous, including: Man-Mo; Stormfugle; Turkish Square; Abbeysounds; Rain; Solstice Sun; Fairy Tale. Also several compositions, Logos Duo. *Recordings:* Integratie, Logos Group; For Grooves, Logos Duo; Composition, Improvisation, Logos Duo; Sounds of Sacred Places, solo album, Moniek Darge. *Publications:* Auto-author, Inter Media Myths, 1986; Logos-Blad, 1977-83; Mixed media Festival, 10 Years, 1980. *Address:* Kongostraat 35, B-9000 Ghent, Belgium.

DARLINGTON Stephen Mark, b. 21 Sept 1952, Lapworth, Warwickshire, England. Organist; Fellow in Music. m. Moira Ellen Hill, 12 July 1975, 3 daughters. *Education:* FRCO; Christ Church, Oxford, 1971-74; MA (Oxon). *Career:* Assistant Organist, Canterbury Cathedral; Several TV and radio appearances as accompanist, soloist and conductor; Organist, Enthronement of Archbishop Coggan, 1975; Concert Organist in most English cathedrals and in Netherlands, Belgium, France, Switzerland, Federal Republic of Germany, Australia, Czechoslovakia; Master of the Music, St Alban's Abbey, Artistic Director, International Organ Festival, St Albans, Conductor, St Albans Bach Choir, until 1985; Fellow in Music, Christ Church and University Lecturer in Music, Oxford, 1985-. *Recordings:* Walton Church Music, ZRG 725; Spirituals and Carols from Canterbury, GRS 1034; French Organ Music, Lammas 071; 20th Century English Church Music, Hyperion; Berkeley and Elgar, Priory; Organ Music by Saint-Saëns and Vierne, Priory; In Honour of St Alban, Priory; Anthems by S.S. Wesley, Meridian; V. Williams Mass NI 5083; Holst/Walton Christmas Music; Palestrina Mass for Pentecost Weelkes Anthems eh. Lassus, Masses & Motets; Vaughan Williams, Oxford Elegy/Flos Campi; Frank Martin & Poulenc, Masses; Byrd-Mass for 3 voices; Mass for 4 voices; Mass for 5 voices; Taverner Motets; Tippett choral music; Taverner to Taverner, NI5328; Vivaldi Glorias (RV588 & RV589), NI5278. *Honour:* Organ Scholar, Christ Church. *Membership:* Council Member, Royal College

of Organists. *Current Management:* Magenta. *Address:* Christ Church, Oxford, OX1 1DP, England.

DARLOW Denys, b. 13 May 1921, London, England. Conductor; Composer; Organist; Professor at Royal College of Music, London. m. Sophy Margaret Guillaume. *Career:* Founder: Tilford Bach Festival 1952, London Handel Festival 1976, BBC Third Programme; Appearances in Sweden, Germany, Austria, Holland, Belgium, France, America, New Zealand; Concerts and Radio. *Compositions:* Te Deum; Stabat Mater; Requiem. *Recordings:* The Triumph of Time and Truth; Oratorio, Handel; Aminta e Fillide; Cantata, Handel. *Honours:* FRCO 1946, FRCM 1984, FLCM 1980. *Membership:* Royal Society of Musicians. *Hobbies:* Gardening; Travel. *Address:* The Coach House, Drury Lane, Redmarley D'Abitot, Gloucestershire GL19 3JX, England.

DATYNER Harry, b. 4 Feb 1923, La Chaux-de-Fonds, Switzerland. Pianist. m. Bluette Blum, 14 June 1954. 1 son. *Education:* Etudes Conservatoire National a Paris with Marguerite Long and after with Edwin Fischer. *Career:* Concerts in Europe, Afrique du Nord et du Sud en Amerique du Nord et du Sud Soloist with orchestras: Suisse Romande, Lausanne, Montreal, Bucarest, Montevideo, Baden-Baden, Madrid, Bruxelles National, London Philharmonic, Prague, Barcelona, Paris; Masterclass, Conservatoire de Musique de Genève; Festival appearances at Montreux, Lausanne, Montevideo, Salzburg, Ascona, Prague, Espagne and Portugal; Member of Jury at International Competitions at Genève, Cologne, Athens, Berlin, Mallorca, Lisbon; Conductors: Ansermet, Prêtre, Dutoit, Sawallisch, Stein, Jordan, Matacic, Carvalho, Dervaux, Groves; Cours d'interpretation: Suisse, Television Suisse, Espagne, Canada. *Honours:* 1st prize a l'unanimite Concours déxécution musicale, Geneva; Prix de l'institut Neuchatelois, 1973. *Hobbies:* Bridge; echecs. *Address:* 1245 Collonge-Bellerive, Switzerland.

DAVELUY Raymond, b. 1926, Victoriaville, Québec, Canada. Organ Virtuoso, Composer and Teacher. m. Hilda Metcalfe. *Education:* Began musical studies under father Lucien Daveluy; Educated at Collège Jean-de-Brébeuf, Montréal; Studied harmony, counterpoint and composition with Gabriel Cusson; Studied organ and harmony under Conrad Letendre 1942, and Hugh Giles, New York. *Career:* Organist, St Jean-Baptiste Church 1946-51, Immaculée-Conception Church 1951-54, St Sixte Church, 1954-59; Principal Titular of Grand Organ at Oratoire Saint-Joseph 1960-61; Concert tours in Canada, Europe, Far-East and USA, performing at various halls and churches including: Royal Festival Hall, London; Kaiser Wilhelm Gedächtnis Church, Berlin; St Germain-des-Prés Church, Paris; Sejong Cultural Centre Hall, Seoul; The Rockefeller Memorial Chapel, Chicago; has also sat on juries of several international competitions including: Munich 1971; Philadelphia 1977; St Albans 1979-83; Frequent performer on CBC Radio; also soloist in Saint-Saëns Organ Symphony, with Orchestre symphonique de Montréal; Played leading part in reform of organ building in Montréal since 1960; Teacher of organ and improvisation at Trois-Rivières and Montréal Conservatories; Director and teacher of organ and improvisation at Montréal Conservatoire; Visiting Lecturer, McGill University. *Recordings:* Recorded works of Bach, Marchand, Corrette, Franck, Liszt on the Oryx, Musical Heritage Society, RCA Victor and Audiorama labels. *Honours:* Winner, Prix d'Europe 1948; Laureate of Haarlem International Competition (The Netherlands) 1959; Member of The Order of Canada 1980.

DAVENPORT Glyn, b. 3 May 1948, Halifax, Yorkshire, England. Singer, Bass/Baritone. m. Jane Keay, 1 Apr 1972, 2 sons. *Education:* Winchester College Choir School, 1958-61; Lancing College, Sussex, 1961-66; Royal College of Music London, 1966-70; ARCM, viola, LRAM, Singing; Staatliche Musikhochschule, Hamburg, Germany, 1970-73. *Debut:* Wigmore Hall, London, England, 1973. *Career:* Opera appearances with English Opera Group, English Music Theatre, Scottish Opera, Royal Opera House, Kent

Opera, Wexford Festival Opera; Recitals for BBC Radio 3, Songmakers' Almanac, British Council in Near/Middle East; Oratorio in major London venues and BBC, Switzerland, Germany and Iceland. *Recordings:* The English Cat, Hans Werner Henze, Wergo Recordings. *Hobbies:* Cricket; Squash; Woodworking. *Current Management:* Concert Directory International: Musicmakers. *Address:* Wendover, Horsell Rise, Horsell, Woking, Surrey GU21 4BD, England.

DAVENPORT (Jack) LaNoue, b. 26 Jan 1922, Dallas, Texas, USA. Recorder Player; Conductor; Teacher; Editor. *Education:* Studied with Erich Katz, New York College of Music. *Career:* Performer on the Recorder and other early instruments, 1949-; Appeared with New York Pro Musica, 1953, 1960-70; Director of the Instrumental Consort and Assistant Director, Renaissance Band; Member, Music for a While Quartet, 1970-; General Editor, Music for Records series; Artist-in-Residence, Sarah Lawrence College. *Recordings:* Numerous discs. *Address:* c/o Music Department, Sarah Lawrence College, Bronxville, NY 10708, USA.

DAVIA Federico, b. 7 July 1933, Genoa, Italy. Singer (Bass-baritone); Opera Director. *Education:* Studied in Genoa with Piero Magenta and Tristan Ilersberg. *Debut:* Dulcamara in L'Elisir d'Amore, 1956; *Career:* Has appeared in many Italian houses from 1959, including La Scala (debut in Gianni Schicchi), Venice, Naples and Rome; has sung in many opera premieres: Nono's Al gran sole carico d'amore, Dallapiccola's Ulisse and the first modern performance of Cavalli's Calisto (Glyndebourne 1970); later British appearances in L'Ormindo, Die schweigsame Frau, La Bohème and L'Amour des Trois Oranges (Glyndebourne), L'Elisir d'Amore (Edinburgh 1980) and Le Nozze di Figaro (Covent Garden 1988); American engagements in San Francisco, Washington, Mexico City and the Metropolitan Opera; Director, Italian Opera Academy, London, and Director of I Commedianti Touring Company; Artistic Director for series of opera telefilms for French TV; Produced L'Elisir d'amore in Geneva, Gianni Schicchi and Rita by Donizetti, in Tel Aviv; Don Pasquale in Avignon, Butterfly and Falstaff in Brighton. *Recordings:* Opera sets for Philips, Decca, RCA and Erato, Alcindoro and Benoît in La Bohème; Le Nozze di Figaro for EMI, 1987. *Address:* c/o Anglo-Swiss Ltd, 4/5 Primrose Mews, 1a Sharpleshall Street, London NW1 8YW, England.

DAVID Avram, b. 30 June 1930, Boston, Massachusetts, USA. Composer; Teacher; Pianist. m. Leslie, 3 Dec 1977. *Education:* BA Music 1955; MA Music 1956; DMA Musical Composition 1964; Boston University; Berkshire Music Center, Tanglewood, Summer 1948; Kranichsteiner Musikinstitut, Darmstadt, West Germany, Summer 1961 and 1966; Private Study of Piano, and Philosophy of Performance and Composition with Margaret Chaloff, and Composition with Francis Cooke, Harold Shapero, Karlheinz Stockhausen, Pierre Boulez. *Career:* Private Teaching 1960-64; Chairman, Composition Department, Composer-in-Residence, Boston Conservatory of Music 1964-73; Director, Avram David Studio 1973-77; Director, Margaret Chaloff Studio 1977-; Lecturer, Harvard University and New England Conservatory of Music; Appearances as Solo Pianist in concert and on TV and Radio. *Compositions:* Composer of 133 works including: 2 Orchestral works including: 1 Symphony; 21 works for chamber ensembles; 6 string quartets; 2 solo violin sonatas; 43 works for solo piano including 5 sonatas; 24 works for solo winds; 8 choral works. *Recordings:* Sonata for Horn Solo, Opus 101, GM Recordings. *Address:* 249 Commonwealth Avenue, Boston, MA 02116, USA.

DAVID Thomas Christian, b. 22 Dec 1925, Wels, Austria. Composer; Conductor. m. Mansoureh Ghassri, 2 sons, 4 daughters. *Education:* Thomasschule, Leipzig Hochschule, Mozarteum, Salzburg. *Career:* Professor of the Hochschule für Musik in Wien; Conductor of numerous orchestras including Riaorchester Berlin, the Munich Philharmonic, Niederosterreichische

Tonkunstlerorchester, Orchester des Osterreichischen Rundfunks, etc. *Compositions:* Bagatellen and Sonata (Piano); Fantasie, Dux Michael, 3 Intermezzi; 3 Canzonen; Concert for 9 solo instruments; Songs based on Chinese stories for voice and piano; Concerto for: Violin and Orchestra, Piano and Orchestra, Oboe and Orchestra, 2 Violins and Orchestra, 3 Violins and Orchestra, Flute and Orchestra, Violin, Clarinet, Piano and Orchestra, 5 Winds and Orchestra, Orchestra, Violoncello and Orchestra; Prolog for Orchestra; Oratorio, The Song of Man; Church Opera, The Way to Emmaus; Choral Works. *Honours:* Austrian State Prize, 1975; Prize of Vienna, 1973; Prize of Niederosterreich, 1986. *Membership:* Chairman, The Austrian Composers Association. *Address:* Fugbachgasse 16/3, 1020, Vienna, Austria.

DAVIDOVICH Bella, b. 16 July 1928, Baku, USSR. Concert Pianist. m. Julian Sitkovetsky (dec), 1 son. *Education:* Moscow Conservatory. *Career:* Recitalist, orchestral soloist, chamber musician, in all major music centres internationally; Duo recitals with son (violinist Dmitry Sitkovetsky). Professor of Piano: Moscow Conservatory (USSR) 16 years, Juilliard School of Music, New York (USA) 1983-. *Honours:* 1st prize, Chopin International Piano Competition, Warsaw, Poland, 1949. *Hobbies:* Opera; Literature; Film. *Address:* c/o Agnes Bruneau, 155 West 68th Street, No 1010, New York, NY 10023, USA.

DAVIDOVICI Robert, b. 1 Oct 1946, Satu-Mare, Romania. Violinist; Professor of Violin. m. Tamara Golan, 8 Mar 1973, 2 sons, 2 daughters. *Education:* School of Music No 1, Bucharest, 1958-62; Conservatorium of Music High School, Sydney, Australia, 1962-63; Performers and Teachers Diploma, 1st Class Honours, 1966; Juilliard School, New York, USA, 1967-73; Postgraduate Diploma, 1970. *Debut:* Alice Tully Hall, New York, USA, 1972. *Recordings:* Recital with Steven DeGroote of works by Copland, Gunther Schuller, Walter Piston, Hugh Aitken and Paul Schonfield. *Honours:* 1st Prize, Carnegie Hall International American Music Competition, 1983; 1st Prize, Naumberg Competition, New York, 1972; Flaggler Award, 1973. *Memberships:* College Music Society; American String Teachers Association; Violin Society of America. *Hobbies:* Chess; Computers; Jogging; Reading spy novels. *Current Management:* Shaw Concerts Incorporated. *Address:* c/o Shaw Concerts Inc, New York, NY, USA.

DAVIDOVSKY Mario, b. 4 Mar 1934, Buenos Aires, Argentina. Composer; Teacher. m. Elaine Davidovsky. *Education:* Received violin lessons in childhood; Studied composition and theory with Guillermo Graetzer, Buenos Aires; Also studied with Teodore Fuchs, Erwin Leuchter, and Ernesto Epstein; Completed training with Milton Babbitt, Berkshire Music Center, Tanglewood, 1958. *Career:* Associated with the Columbia-Princeton Electronic Music Center, 1960-; Teacher, University of Michigan, 1964, Di Tella Institute, 1969-70, City College of the City University of New York, 1968-80, Columbia University, 1981-; Director of the Columbia-Princeton Electronic Music Center. *Compositions:* Synchronisms No 1 for Flute and Electronics, 1963, No 2 for Flute, Clarinet, Violin, Cello, and Electronics, 1964, No 3 for Cello and Electronics, 1965, No 4 for Men's or Mixed Chorus and Electronics, 1967, No 5 for Percussion Ensemble and Electronics, 1969, No 6 for Piano and Electronics, 1970, No 7 for Orchestra and Electronics, 1973, and No 8 for Woodwind Quintet and Electronics, 1974; Orchestral: Concertino for Percussion and Strings, 1954; Suite sinfonica para El payaso, 1955; Serie sinfonica, 1959; Contrastes No 1 for String Orchestra and Electronics, 1960; Planos, 1961; Transientes, 1972; Consorts for Symphonic Band, 1980; Divertimento for Cello and Orchestra, 1984; Chamber: 4 string quartets, 1954, 1958, 1976, 1980; String Trio, 1982; Vocal: Scenes from Shir-ha-shirim for Soprano, 2 Tenors, Bass, and Chamber Orchestra, 1975; Romancero for Soprano, Flute, Clarinet, Violin, and Cello, 1983; Tape: Electronic Study No 1, 1961, No 2, 1962, and No 3, 1965. *Honours:* Koussevitzky Fellowship, 1958; Guggenheim Fellowships, 1960,

1971; Rockefeller Fellowships, 1963, 1964; Brandeis University Creative Arts Award, 1964; American Academy and Institute of Arts and Letters Award, 1965; Pulitzer Prize in Music, 1971; Naumberg Award, 1972; Guggenheim Award, 1982; Various commissions. *Memberships:* Elected to the Institute of the American Academy and Institute of Arts and Letters, 1982. *Address:* c/o Music Department, Columbia University, New York, NY 10027, USA.

DAVIDSON Joy, b. 18 Aug 1940, Fort Collins, Colorado, USA. Singer (Mezzo-Soprano). *Education:* Studied in Los Angeles, at Florida State University and with Daniel Harris. *Debut:* Miami 1965, as Rossini's Cenerentola. *Career:* Sang at the opera houses of Dallas, Houston, New Orleans and San Francisco; Santa Fe 1969, in the US premiere of Penderecki's The Devils of Loudun; Appearances with the Welsh National Opera and at Lisbon, Sofia, Vienna, Munich, Milan and Florence; Other roles include Carmen, Charlotte in Werther, Dalila, Verdi's Eboli and Preziosilla and Gluck's Orpheus; Also heard as concert singer; Sang Baba the Turk in The Rake's Progress at the State Theatre, New York, 1984.

DAVIDSON Tina, b. 30 Dec 1952, Stockholm, Sweden. Composer/Pianist. m. 1 daughter. *Education:* BA in piano and composition, Bennington College 1972-76; Composition studies with Henry Brant, Vivian Fine, Louis Calabro. *Career:* Associate Director, RELACHE, The Ensemble for Contemporary Music 1978-89; Piano Instructor, Drexel University 1981-85; Residencies: Chamber Music Conference and Composers' Forum; Milay Colony for the Arts, October 1981; Yellow Springs Fellowship of the Arts, May 1982; Charles Ives Center 1986. *Compositions:* Inside And Out, piano and 2 players 1974; Recollections of Darkness, string trio 1975; Two Beasts From The Forest Of Imaginary Beings, narrator and orchestra 1975, commissioned by Sage City Symphony, student commission 1976; Five Songs from The Game of Silence, soprano and viola 1976; Piano Concerto, piano and orchestra 1981; Unicorn/Tapestry, mezzo-soprano, violoncello and tape 1982; Other Echoes, 2 violins 1982; Wait For The End Of Dreaming, 2 baritone saxophones, Double Bass 1983-85; Shadow Grief, soprano (or alto saxophone) 1983; Day of Rage, and I Am The Last Witness, piano solo, 1984; Blood Memory: A Long Quiet After The Call, cello and orchestra, commissioned by Sage City Symphony, 1985; Never Love A Wild Thing, variable ensemble, 1986; Descending Figure with Lullaby, variable ensemble and voice, 1986; Star Myths, Solo piano, 1987; Transparent Victims, live & pre-recorded saxophone, 1987; Dark Child Sings, four cellos, 1988; Cassandra Sings, string quartet, 1988; In the Darkness I Find a Face (It Is Mine), orchestra, 1989; Blue Dawn (The Promised Fruit), 3 winds & piano, 1989; Woman Dreaming, 1990; Flute Clarinet, Violin, Violoncello, Percussion, Piano, I Hear The Mermaids Singing, 1990; Viola, Violoncello and Piano, The Selkie Boy, 1991, for Orchestra; For Youth Orchestra Audiences. *Address:* 508 Woodland Terrace, Philadelphia, PA 19104, USA.

DAVIES (Albert) Meredith, b. 30 July 1922, Birkenhead, England. Conductor; Educator. m. Betty Hazel Bates, 1949, 3 sons, 1 daughter. *Education:* Keble College, Oxford; Junior Exhibitioner, Royal College of Music, 1930; Academia di S Cecilia, Rome, Italy. *Career includes:* Principal, Trinity College of Music, 1979-88; Conductor, Royal Choral Society, 1972-85, Leeds Philharmonic Society, 1975-84; President ISM, 1985-86; Conductor, Royal Opera House Covent Garden/Sadlers Wells, also BBC; Organist, Hurstpierpoint College, Sussex, 1939; Served World War II, 1939-45, Royal Artillery 1942-45; Conductor, St Albans Bach Choir, 1947; Organist/Master of Choristers, Cathedral Church of St Alban, 1947-49; Musical Director, St Alban's School, 1948-49; Organist & Choirmaster, Hereford Cathedral/Conductor, 3 Choirs Festival, Hereford, 1949-56; Organist & Supernumerary Fellow, New College, Oxford, 1956; Associate conductor, City of Birmingham Symphony Orchestra, 1957-59; Deputy Musical Director 1959-60; Conductor, City of

Birmingham Choir, 1957-64; Musical Director, English Opera Group, 1963-65, Vancouver Symphony Orchestra, Canada 1964-71; Chief Conductor, BBC Training Orchestra, 1969-72. *Recordings:* Delius: Violin Concerto, Double Concerto; Village Romeo & Juliet; Fennimore & Gerda. Vaughan Williams: Riders to the Sea; Sir John in Love. *Honour:* CBE, 1982. *Address:* 40 Monmouth Street, Bridgwater, Somerset, TA6 5EJ, England.

DAVIES Arthur, b. 11 April 1941, Wrexham, Wales. Singer (Tenor). *Education:* Studied at the Royal Northern Colllge of Music. *Career:* Has sung with Welsh National Opera as Nemorino, Albert Herring, Nadir in Les pêcheurs de Perles, Rodolfo, and Don José; Covent Garden debut 1976, in the world premiere of We Come to the River by Henze; has returned in Lucia di Lammermoor, and as Alfredo, the Italian Tenor in Der Rosenkavalier, Steva in Jenůfa, and Pinkerton; Scottish Opera at the Edinburgh Festival as the Fox in The Cunning Little Vixen, and David in Die Meistersinger; Appearances with English National Opera as the Duke of Mantua, Alfredo, the Gounod Faust, and Werther; Opera North as Jenik in The Bartered Bride, Pinkerton, Don José and Nadir; Foreign engagements in Chicago, Cincinnati, Connecticut, Ghent, Leipzig, Lisbon, New Orleans, Moscow, Santiago and New York (Metropolitan House with the ENO company); Sang Faust with ENO, Jan 1990; Gaston, British stage premiere of Verdi's Jérusalem, Opera North; Cavaradossi and Pinkerton for Scottish Opera; Cincinnati Opera, July 1990 as Faust; Edinburgh Festival, 1990 as Yannakos in the Greek Passion by Martinů; Sang Cavaradossi for Opera Pacific at Costa Mesa, 1992; Don José at San Diego and the Duke of Mantua for ENO; Concerts include the Verdi Requiem at the Festival Hall, London, conducted by Giulini. *Recordings include:* Rigoletto (EMI; also on video); The Dream of Gerontius, with the London Symphony Orchestra (Chandos); Elijah; Rossini's Stabat Mater; The Kingdom by Elgar. *Address:* c/o Stafford Law Associates, 26 Mayfield Road, Weybridge, Surrey KT13 8XB, England.

DAVIES David Somerville, b. 13 June 1954, Dunfermline, Scotland. Conductor; Artistic Director. m. Virginia Henson, 15 Sept 1986. *Education:* Royal Scottish Academy of Music; University of Edinburgh; Salzburg Mozarteum; Conservatoire National De Marseille. *Career:* Assistant Principal Flute, Scottish National Orchestra, 1975-80; Principal Flute, Scottish Opera, 1980-85; Freelance Conductor, 1985-, working with BBC Scottish Symphony Orchestra, Scottish Chamber Orchestra, Royal Scottish National Orchestra, Royal Liverpool Philharmonic Orchestra in Britain; l'Orchestre Philharmonique de Radio France, l'Opéra de Marseille, l'Orchestre Philharmonique de Marseille in France; Ensemble Caput in Iceland and the Stadtorchester Winterthur in Switzerland; Conductor and Artistic Director, Paragon Ensemble, Scotland, Paragon Opera Projects Scotland, 1985-; Lecturer, Royal Scottish Academy of Music and Drama, 1991-. *Recordings:* Two volumes of World premiere recordings of Scottish Contemporary music, 1991 and 1993, Continuum CDs. *Address:* c/o Paragon Ensemble Ltd, 2 Port Dundas Place, Glasgow G2 3LB, Scotland.

DAVIES Dennis Russell, b. 16 Apr 1944, Toledo, Ohio, USA. Conductor; Pianist. *Education:* BMus 1966, MS 1968, DMA 1972, Juilliard School of Music, New York; Studied piano with Lonny Epstein and Sascha Gorodnitzki; Conducting with Jean Morel and Jorge Mester. *Career:* Teacher, Juilliard School of Music, 1968-71; Co-founder (with Luciano Berio) and Conductor, Juilliard Ensemble, 1968-74; Music Director, Norwalk (Conn) Symphony Orchestra, 1968-73; St Paul (Minn) Chamber Orchestra, 1972-80; Cabrillo (Calif) Music Festival, 1974-; American Composers Orchestra, New York, 1977-; Generalmusikdirektor, Wurttemberg State Theater, Stuttgart, 1980-87; Principal Conductor and Director of Classical Music Programming, Saratoga (NY) Performing Arts Center, 1985-88; Generalmusikdirektor, City Theatre and Beethoven Hall Orchestra, Bonn, 1987-;

Guest conductor with various opera companies and orchestras in North America and Europe; Champion of contemporary music; Conducted premieres by Luciano Berio, John Cage, Hans Werner Hanze, Philip Glass, Mauricio Kagel, Heinz Winbeck, William Bolcom, John Tower, Pauline Oliveros; Conducted the premiere of William Bolcom's Songs of Innocence and Experience, Stuttgart 1984; Music Director, Brooklyn Acadmey of Music, 1991; Principal Conductor, Brooklyn Philharmonic, 1991; Conducted the Premiere of Manfred Trojhan's Heinrich IV, Schwetzingen Festival, 1991. *Recordings:* For Musicmasters, CBS, ECM, Composers Recordings, Inc; Louisville; Nonesuch; ProArte. *Honour:* Alice M Ditson Award for Conductors, 1987. *Address:* c/o Columbia Artists Management Inc, 165 West 57th Street, New York, NY 10019, USA.

DAVIES (Doris) Eiluned, b. 5 December 1913, Walthamstow, London, England. Concert Pianist; Composer. *Education:* Royal College of Music with Kathleen Long, Gordon Jacob and C H Kitson, 1929-34; ARCM Diploma 1932; Private study Piano with Frida Kindler. *Debut:* Grotrian Hall, London 1934; Radio debut 1935. *Career:* Concerts with BBC Symphony Orchestra, Liverpool Philharmonic, BBC Welsh Orchestra; Public concerts in Britain, Germany and Holland; Performed many 20th Century British works by Denis Aplvor, Bliss, Lennox Berkeley, Hoddinott, Daniel Jones, Mathias, Rawsthorne, Mervyn Roberts, Bernard Stevens, Grace Williams, David Wynne; Some premieres. *Compositions:* Sociable Pieces for 6 hands at one piano 1969; Glimpses, song cycle for female voices 1993. *Recordings:* Complete piano works of Bernard van Dieren, 1887-1936, for The British Music Society on two audio cassettes, 1982, 1985. *Hobbies:* Foreign Languages, German, French and Spanish. *Address:* 40 The Limes Avenue, New Southgate, London N11 1RH, England.

DAVIES Eirian, b. 1964, Wales. Singer (Soprano). *Education:* Studied at the University College of Wales and the Royal Academy of Music. *Career:* Has sung at the Buxton Festival in Gounod's La Colombe, Vivaldi's Griselda and Conti's Don Quixote; Welsh National Opera as Woglinde and Ortlinde in The Ring (also at Covent Garden, 1986), Lisa (La Sonnambula) and Weber's Aennchen; With Opera North has appeared as Mimi and for English National Opera Venus (Orpheus in the Underworld) and Frasquita; Glyndebourne Touring Opera in the premiere production of Osborne's Electrification of the Soviet Union; Oviedo Festival Spain in Monteverdi's Orfeo and Ligeti's Le Grand Macabre at the Vienna Konzerthaus; Other concert engagements in France and Spain with Vier Letzte Lieder, La Demoiselle Elue and the St Matthew Passion; Appearances with the English Chamber Orchestra, City of Birmingham Symphony, Royal Philharmonic, Scottish National, Bournemouth Symphony and Philharmonia Orchestra; Opera galas at the Barbican, Albert Hall and Festival Hall; Sang lead role for the premiere of Robert Saxton's Caritas, Opera North, 1991; Nathalie in Der Prinz von Homburg, by Henze, for Cologne Opera, 1992; Pamina, Magic Flute for English National Opera, 1993; Countess's Inner Voices in Matthus, Cornet Christoph Rilke's songs of Love & Death for Glyndebourne Tour, 1993. *Recordings include:* Le Grand Macabre; Caritas by Robert Saxton. *Honours:* Catherine and Lady Grace James Award; Winner, Francisco Vinas International Competition, Barcelona, 1984. *Address:* John Coast, 31 Sinclair Road, London W14 0NS, England.

DAVIES Hugh Seymour, b. 23 Apr 1943, Exmouth, Devon, England. Composer; Performer, invented instruments; Musicologist; Specialist in Electronic Music. m. Pamela Judith Bailey, 5 Sept 1981, 1 daughter. *Education:* BA, Music, Oxford University, England, 1964. *Career:* Assistant to K Stockhausen, 1964-66; Director, Electronic Music Studio, University of London Goldsmiths' College, 1967-86, subsequently Consultant Researcher; Consultant, Music Department, Gemeentemuseum, The Hague, 1986-; Over 100 instruments and sound sculptures invented since 1967; performed and broadcast in most of Western Europe,

USA, Canada, Argentina, Cuba, Uruguay, Poland, Hungary, Czechoslovakia, Iran, Japan; Exhibitions including many one-man shows in several Western European countries and USA; Compositions for traditional instruments, invented instruments and electronic music including several music theatre works; Member of now defunct performing groups, Gentle Fire, Music Improvisation Company, Naked Software, many solo performances, 1975-. *Compositions include:* Quintet, 1968; Shozyg I & II, 1968; Shozyg Sequence No 1, 1971, No 2, 1977; Raisonnements, 1973; No 3, 1990-91; The Musical Educator, 1974; Natural Images, 1976; Meldoci Gestures, 1978; Ex Una Voce, 1979; Four Songs, 1979-81; I Have a Dream, 1984-85; Vision, 1987; Strata, 1987. *Recordings:* Shozyg: Music for Invented Instruments, solo performance of own compositions; Mikrophonie I; Sternklang; Gentle Fire; Music Improvisation Company. *Publications:* International Electronic Music Catalog (compiler), 1968; Chapters in Poésie Sonore Internationale, 1979; Electronic Music for Schools, 1981; Chapters in Nuova Atlantide: il Continente della Musica Elettronica, 1900-86; Chapters in Echo: the Images of Sound, 1987; Vitalité et Contradictions de l'Avant-Garde: Italie-France 1909-1924, 1988, Nordic Music Days/100 Years, 1988; Piano, 1988; Musizues Electroniques, 1990, also 300 entries in New Grove Dictionary of Musical Instruments, 1984. *Contributions to:* Numerous professional journals including Source Contact, Musics, EMAS Newsletter/Electro-Acoustic Music; Experimental Musical Instruments. *Address:* 25 Albert Road, London N4 3RR, England.

DAVIES Joan, b. 1940, Swansea, Wales. Singer (Mezzo-soprano). *Education:* Royal College of Music, London. *Career:* Sang with the Glyndebourne Chorus, then with Sadler's Wells until 1969, notably as Offenbach's Hélène and in the premiere of Bennett's A Penny for a Song, 1965; Debut with Welsh National Opera as Meg Page in Falstaff; Sang Meg Page at Covent Garden and appeared in La Traviata and the premiere of Henze's We Come to the River, 1976; Other engagements in Munich and Berlin and with Scottish Opera, Opera North, Phoenix Opera, Basilica Opera and Dublin Grand Opera; New Sadler's Wells Opera from 1983 in The Mikado, The Count of Luxembourg, The Merry Widow and works by Gilbert and Sullivan (also in New York); Appearances at the Wexford Festival in The Devil and Kate and Gazzaniga's Don Giovanni; Other roles include Mme Popova in Walton's The Bear (Lisbon), Auntie in Peter Grimes at the Royal Opera Ghent and Mozart's Marcellina in Bordeaux and Rouen; Television appearances as Meg Page, Marcellina and Mary in Der fliegenda Holländer; Concert engagements with the Royal Liverpool Philharmonic and the Ulster Orchestra. *Address:* Music International, 13 Ardilaun Road, London N5 2QR, England.

DAVIES Peter Maxwell (Sir), b. 8 Sept 1934, Manchester, England. Composer. *Education:* Leigh Grammar School; Manchester College of Music; MusB (honours) Manchester University, 1956; Studied with Goffredo Petrassi in Rome, 1957; Further study with Roger Sessions, Milton Babbitt and Earl Kim, Princeton University, USA, 1962-64. *Career:* Director of Music, Cirencester Grammar School, 1959-62; Lecture tours of Europe, Australia, New Zealand, USA and Canada; Co-founded the Pierrot Players 1967 (later The Fires of London); disbanded 1987: stage works with Fires of London Productions from 1987; Professor of Composition, Royal Northern College of Music, Manchester, until 1980; Artistic Director St Magnus Festival, Orkney Islands, 1977-86; Artistic Director, Dartington Summer School of Music, 1979-84; Associate Composer/Conductor, Scottish Chamber Orchestra, 1985-; Conducted premiere of his 4th Symphony at the 1989 Promenade Concerts, London; 2nd Symphony at the 1993 Proms. *Compositions:* Stage: Operas Taverner 1962-70, The Matryrdom of St Magnus 1976-77, The Two Fiddlers 1978; The Lighthouse 1979; Theatre Pieces: Notre dame des Fleurs 1966; Vesalii Icones 1969; Eight Songs for a Mad King 1969; Nocturnal Dances ballet 1969; Blind Man's Buff 1972; Miss Donnithorne's Maggot 1974; Salome, ballet 1978;

Le Jongleur de Notre dame 1978; Cinderella 1980; The Medium 1981; The No.11 Bus 1983-84; Caroline Mathilde, ballet, 1990; Orchestra and Ensemble: Alma Redemptoris Mater for 6 wind instruments 1957; St Michael, sonata for 17 wind instruments 1957; Prolation 1958; Ricercar and Doubles for 8 instruments 1959; 5 Klee Pictures 1959, rev. 1976; Sinfonia 1962; 2 Fantasias on an In Nomine of John Taverner 1962-64; 7 In Nomine 1963-65; Shakespeare Music 1965; Antechrist 1967; Stedman Caters 1968; St Thomas Wake 1969; Worldes Blis 1969; Renaissance Scotish Dances 1973; Ave Maris Stela 1975; 4 Symphonies 1973-6, 1980, 1984, 1988; Runes from a Holy Island 1977; A Mirror of Whitening Light 1977; Dances from Salome 1979; The Bairns of Brugh 1981; Image Reflection, Shadow 1982; Sinfonia Concertante 1982; Sinfonietta Accademica 1983; Unbroken Circle 1984; An Orkney Wedding, with Sunrise 1985; Jimmack the Postie, overture 1986; Concertos for Violin 1985, Trumpet 1987, Oboe 1988, Clarinet 1990, Violin and Viola 1991, Flute 1991, Doublebass, 1992; Vocal: 5 Motets 1959; O Magnum Mysterium 1960; Te Lucis ante Terminum 1961; Frammenti di Leopardi, cantata 1962; Veni Sancte Spiritus 1963; Revelation and Fall; The Shepherds' Calendar 1965; Missa super L'Homme Arme 1968, rev 1971; From Stone to Thorn 1971; Hymn to St Magnus 1972; Tenebrae super Gesualdo 1972; Stone Litany 1973; Fiddlers at the Wedding 1974; Anakreontika 1976; The Blind Fiddler 1976; Westerlings for chorus 1977; Kirkwall Shopping Songs 1979; Black Pentecost 1979; Solstice of Light 1979; The Yellow Cake Review, 6 cabaret songs 1980; Songs of Hoy 1981; Into the Labyrinth for tenor and orchestra 1983; First Ferry to Hoy 1985; The Peat Cutters 1985; House of Winter 1986; Excuse Me 1986; Sea Runes, vocal sextet 1986; Hymn to the Word of God for tenor and chorus, 1990; The Turn of the Tide for orchestra and children's choir, 1992; Chamber music includes: String Quartet 1961; The Kestrel paced round the Sun 1975; Sonatina 1981; The Pole Star 1982; Sea Eagle 1982; Sonata for violin and cimbalom 1984; Piano Sonata 1981; Organ Sonata 1982. Honours include: CBE, 1981; KBE, 1987. Address: c/o Judy Arnold, 50 Hogarth Road, London SW5 OPU, England.

DAVIES Ryland, b. 9 Feb 1943, Cwym, Ebbw Vale, Wales. Opera and Concert Singer, (Tenor). m. (1) Anne Howells (divorced 1981); (2) Deborah Rees, 1983, 1 daughter. Education: FRMCM, Royal Manchester College of Music, 1971. Debut: Almaviva, Barber of Seville, Welsh National Opera, 1964. Career: Glyndebourne Chorus, 1964-66; Soloist and Freelance, Glyndebourne and Sadler's Wells, Royal Opera House, Covent Garden, Welsh National Opera, Scottish Opera, Opera North, etc; Performances in Salzburg, San Francisco, Chicago, New York, Hollywood Bowl, Paris, Geneva, Brussels, Vienna, Lyon, Amsterdam, Mannheim, Rome, Israel, Buenos Aires, Stuttgart, Berlin, Hamburg, Nice, Nancy, Philadelphia; Sang Lysander in A Midsummer Night's Dream at Glyndebourne 1989; Tichon in Katya Kabanova at the 1990 Festival; Other roles have included Mozart's Ferrando and Don Ottavio, Ernesto, Fenton, Nemorino, Pelléas, (Berlin 1984), Oberon, (Montpellier, 1987); Tamino, Lensky, Belmonte and Enéas in Esclarmonde; Concert Appearances at home and abroad; Radio and TV broadcasts; appeared in films including: Capriccio; Entführung, A Midsummer Night's Dream; Trial by Jury, Don Pasquale, etc. Recordings include: Die Entführung; Les Troyens; Saul; Così fan Tutte; Monteverdi Madrigals, Messiah, Idomeneo, Il Matrimonio, L'Oracolo (Leoni), Lucia Di Lammermoor, Thérèse, Judas Maccabeus, Mozart Requiem, Credo Mass, Mozart Coronation Mass and Vêspres Solenelle. Honours: Boise and Mendelssohn Foundation Scholarship, 1964; Ricordi Prize, 1964; Imperial League of Opera Prize, 1964; John Christie Award, 1965. Hobbies: Antique Art; Cinema; Sport. Address: 71 Fairmile Lane, Cobham, Surrey, KT11 2WG, England.

DAVIES Wyn, b. 8 May 1952, Gowerton, Wales. Conductor. m. Jane Baxendale, 5 July 1975. Education: Gowerton Grammar, Christchurch, Oxford, England. Career: Conductor, Welsh National Opera; Appearances in concert with BBC Welsh Orchestra, BBC Scottish Orchestra, Bournemouth Symphony Orchestra, English Chamber Orchestra; City of Birmingham Symphony Orchestra; Guest Conductor, Opera North, English National Opera, Scottish Opera, New Sadler's Wells Opera, Welsh National Opera; Assistant Conductor, Metropolitan Opera, New York, USA, 1985-86. Membership: Incorporated Society of Musicians. Hobbies: Skiing; Food. Current Management: Performing Arts, 6 Windmill Street, London W1P 1HF, England. Address: 11 Barbauld Road, Stoke Newington, London, N16 0SD, England.

DAVIS Andrew Frank, b. 2 Feb 1944, Ashridge, Hertfordshire, England. Conductor. Education: DMusB, (Organ Scholar), King's College, MA, 1967, Cambridge University, England; student of Franco Ferrara, Rome, 1967-68; DLitt (Honours) York University, Toronto, 1984. Debut: with BBC Symphony Orchestra, 1970. Career: Pianist, Harpsichordist and Organist, Academy of St Martin-in-the-Fields, London, 1966-70; Assistant Conductor BBC Scottish Symphony Orchestra, Glasgow, 1970-72; has appeared with major orchestras and festivals internationally including Berlin, Edinburgh and Flanders; Conductor, Glyndebourne Opera Festival, 1973-; Music Director, Toronto Symphony, Canada, 1975-88; now Conductor, Laureate, 1988-; Conductor, tours in China, US, Japan and Europe, 1983, 1986; Principal Guest Conductor, Royal Liverpool Philharmonic Orchestra, (England), 1974-77; Associate Conductor, New Philharmonic Orchestra, London, 1973-77; conducted at La Scala, Milan, Metropolitan Opera, NY, Covent Garden; Paris Opera; Music Director, Glyndebourne, 1988; Chief Conductor of BBC Symphony Orchestra, 1989; Conducted La Clemenza di Tito at Chicago, Oct 1989; Szymanowski King Roger at the Festival Hall 1990; Katya Kabanova and Tippett's New Year at the 1990 Glyndebourne Festival; Opened 1991 Promenade Concerts, London, with the Dream of Gerontius; Glyndebourne 1992, Gala and The Queen of Spades; Conducted Elektra at the First Night of the 1993 London Proms, Berg's Lulu at the Festival Hall, London, 1994. Compositions: La Serenissima (Inventions on a Theme by Claudio Monteverdi) Chansons Innoccentes. Recordings include: all the Dvořák Symphonies, Mendelssohn Symphonies, and a Borodin Cycle; Enigma Variations, Falstaff by Elgar; Overtures: Coriolan, Leonore No 3, Egmont, Fidelio by Beethoven; Symphony No 10 by Shostakovitch; Concerto No 2 by Rachmaninoff; Cinderella (Excerpts); The Young Person's Guide to the Orchestra; Symphony No 5, Horn Concerto, Piano Concerto No 2 by Hoddinott; Canon (and other digital delights) by Pachelbel; The Planets by Gustav Holst, numerous others. Honours: 2 Grand Prix du Disque Awards for recording of Duruflé's Requiem with Philharmonia Orchestra, Tippett's Mask of Time won Gramophone of Year Award in 1987 and a Grand Prix du Disque in 1988. Hobbies: Medieval stained glass; Fishing; Mycology. Address: c/o Harold Holt Ltd, 31 Sinclair Road, London W14 0NS, England.

DAVIS Anthony, b. 20 February 1951, Paterson, New Jersey, USA. Composer. Education: Studied at Yale University, BA 1975. Career: Appearances in United States of America and abroad in 1970s as Jazz Pianist and Director of Episteme, giving performances of improvised music; Co-founder of Advent 1973 and Trumpeter in Leo Smith's New Delta Ahkri Band 1974-77; Played in New York with violinist Leroy Jenkins 1977-79 and other members of Advancement of Creative Musicians. Compositions: Operas X: The Life and Times of Malcolm X premiered at the New York City Opera 1986 and Under the Double Moon, premiered at Opera Theatre of St Louis 1989; Piano Concerto Wayand V 1985; Notes from the Underground for Orchestra 1988. Recordings: Of Blues and Dreams 1978; Hidden Voices 1979; Under the Double Moon 1982. Address: c/o New York City Opera, Lincoln Center, New York, NY 10023, USA.

DAVIS Colin Rex, Sir, b. 25 Sept 1927, Weybridge, Surrey, England. Conductor. m. (1) April Cantelo, 1949, 1 son. 1 daughter. (2) Ashraf Naini, 1964, 3 son. 2

daughters. *Education:* Christ's Hospital; Royal College of Music. *Debut:* Covent Garden as Music Director of Sadlers Wells Opera (now English National Opera), 1960. *Career:* Performance of Mozart with Chelsea Opera Group in early 1950s and Concert performance of Don Giovanni in London in 1959; Music Director of Royal Opera House, Covent Garden for 15 years until 1986 where he conducted many new productions including world premiere of Tippett's The Knot Garden; First British Conductor to appear at Bayreuth Festival, opening the 1977 season with Wagner's Tannhäuser; Appeared in United States with orchestras of Cleveland, Philadelphia, New York and Los Angeles and was Principal Guest Conductor of Boston Symphony Orchestra from 1972-84; Currently performing and recording in three continents with different orchestras including Dresden Staatskapelle with whom he is Honorary Conductor, the London Symphony Orchestra with whom he is Principal Guest Conductor, the English Chamber Orchestra, Vienna Philharmonic and New York Philharmonic; Principal Conductor and Music Director of the Bavarian Radio Symphony Orchestra, 1984-92; Conductor of new production of Damnation of Faust at Covent Garden early in 1993. *Recordings:* Numerous recordings. *Honours:* International Honours; Bayerischen Verdienstorden in Bavaria; Freedom of the City of London; Order of the Lion of Finland, Commander 1st Class; CBE 1965; Knighthood 1980. *Address:* 39 Cathcart Road, London SW10 9JG, England.

DAVIS Howard, b. 9 Apr 1940, Wolverhampton, England. Musician. m. Virginia Black, 7 Aug 1965, 2 sons. *Education:* Royal Academy of Music. *Career:* Leader, Alberni String Quartet; Worldwide Tours with many broadcasts & TV appearances; Professor, Royal Academy of Music, London. *Recordings:* Many including complete chamber music of Beethoven, Mozart, Schumann and complete quartets of Benjamin Britten. *Honours:* FRAM; FRSAMD: FRSA. *Hobbies:* Water Colour Painting; Photography. *Current Management:* Karen Durant, London. *Address:* Charlotte Cottage, 123 Sheering Road, Harlow, Essex CM17 0JP, England.

DAVIS Nathan Joseph, b. 15 March 1955, Davis, California, USA. Assistant Professor of Cello. m. Elise Midelfort, 13 July 1979, 1s. 1 d. *Education:* BA Manhattan School of Music and New York University; MA Montclair State College; PhD New York University; Cello with Maurice Eisenberg, George Neikrug, David Wells; Ensemble studies with Raphael Bronstin, Juilliard Quartet and Lillian Fuchs. *Career:* Public Radio Broadcasts in New York and Minnesota; Cello Recording for original scoring; Faith Hubley Production, Cannes Award Winner in Animation; Currently Assistant Professor of Cello, Moorhead State University, Minnesota. *Publication:* Dissertation: The Baroque Violoncello and the Unaccompanied Cello Suites of J S Bach, 1986. *Honours:* Graduate Fellowship, Montclair State University; Awarded National and State Grants for String Outreach Projects. *Memberships:* Pi Kappa Lambda; ASTA; Music Educators National Conference; Chamber Music America. *Hobbies:* Golf; Baseball. *Address:* Music Department, Moorhead State University, Moorhead, MN 56563, USA.

DAVIS Richard Beattie, b. 28 August 1922, Croydon, Surrey, England. Chartered Surveyor (Retired). m. Gillian F Wimbourne, 26 March 1983, 1s. (previous marriage). *Education:* Weymouth College, Dorset 1936-40; Piano lessons at school and with James Ching and Deborah Overbeck, otherwise self-taught. *Career:* War Service, WWII, 1941-47; With Knight, Frank and Rutley, International Property Consultants, London, 1948-; Head of Professional Division, 1969-81; Governor, Purcell School, Harrow-on-the-Hill, 1972-83. *Publications:* The Beauty of Belaieff. Catalogue of selected publications 1885-1900 of M P Belaieff, 1987; Adolf von Henselt, 1814-1889, 1989; The Beauty of Belaieff, 1994; Contributor to Music Review and Encyclopedic Dictionary of Russian and Soviet Music, 1994; Lyapunov, 12 studies, Op.11, Malcolm Binns, sleve note, 1992. *Hobbies:* Piano; Collecting Old Music;

Bird Watching. *Address:* Lomas Oast, Sandhurst, Kent, TN18 5PT, England.

DAVISON Nigel St John, b. 1 Dec 1929, Meerut, India. University Lecturer. m. Kirstine Grahame Meikle, 21 August 1965 (divorced), 3s. 1d. *Education:* Wellington, College, Berkshire 1943-47; Royal College of Music 1947-48; Peterhouse, Cambridge University 1950-54 (Organ Scholar); BA 1953; MusB 1954; MA 1957; FRCO 1954; DMus Edinburgh University 1962. *Career:* Assistant Music Master, Oundle School 1954-57; Assistant Director of Music 1957-62, Director of Music 1963-67, Wellington College; Lecturer in Music 1967-71, Senior Lecturer 1971-89, Bristol University; Musical Director, Bristol Opera Company 1967-77; Organist, The Lord Mayor's Chapel, Bristol 1976-79. *Publications:* Editor: Pierre de la Rue (including opera omnia CMM 97,1989-); Tye (EECM 33); Josquin, etc; Contributor to Musical Quarterly, Music and Letters, Music Review, Musical Times, The Organ. *Memberships:* Incorporated Society of Musicians; Royal Musical Association; Royal College of Organists. *Hobby:* Hillwalking. *Address:* 3 South Dene, Stoke Bishop, Bristol BS9 2BW, England.

DAVISON Peter, b. 26 Oct 1948, Los Angeles, California, USA. Composer; Flautist; Synthesist; Conductor. *Education:* BA, composition 1973, MA 1975, California State University, Northridge. *Career:* Conductor, concert of original music, Morgan Theatre, Los Angeles; Conductor, Eagle Springs, Dorothy Chandler Music Pavilion, Los Angeles; Symphony No 1 performed, Immaculate Heart College; Masterclasses and Member of Juries for International Competitions; Numerous film scores. *Compositions include:* Eagle Springs, commissioned, Foundation for New American Music; Symphony No 1, commissioned, National Endowment for the Arts; Poltergeist, Summer's Bittersweet Ending, Cascade, commissioned, California Arts Council; New Commission from the San Luis Obispo Symphony: Double Concerto for Viola, Cello and Strings in 7 Mounts, 1992. *Recordings:* Several, of original music on Avocado Records including: Music On The Way, Glide, Star Gazer, Forest Mountain, Traces; Winds of Space, album on Higher Octave Music. *Hobbies:* Sailing; Swimming; Reading. *Address:* 1924 Euclid, Santa Monica, CA 90404, USA.

DAVY Gloria, b. 29 Mar 1937, Brooklyn, New York, USA. Singer (Soprano); Professor of Voice. *Education:* Studied at the Juilliard School with Belle Julie Soudant and in Milan with Victor de Sabata. *Career:* Sang the Countess in the US premiere of Strauss's Capriccio (Juilliard, 1954); World Tour in Porgy and Bess; Recital and Oratorio appearances before returning to New York in concert performance of Anna Bolena, the Metropolitan as Pamina, Aida, Nedda and Leonora in Trovatore, from 1958; Vienna (Aida-Karajan), Covent Garden debut 1959-60, as Aida, Deutsche Oper Berlin from 1961, with Wieland Wagner and Karl Böhm, as Aida, Amelia, Butterfly, Fiordiligi, Donna Anna, Donna Elvira and Salome; Guest engagements 1963-69 in Hamburg, Munich, Geneva, Paris, Madrid, Brussels, London; Sang in the premiere of Henze's Nachtstücke und Arien, 1957, Stockhausen's Momente, 1972, Vortrag uber Hu, 1974; Concert tours of Germany, Switzerland, Italy, France 1975-85; Debut recital Wigmore Hall, London 1983; Professor of Music in Voice at Indiana University School of Music, Bloomington, from 1985; Sang Berg's Sieben Frühe Lieder, Lulu and Der Wein, with the conductors Otmar Suitner and Kurt Masur, 1981-85; New Year's Eve in Milan, Dortmund, 1988-89. Other repertoire includes Handel's Acis, Gluck's Iphigenie, Mozart's Countess and Pamina; Strauss's Daphne and Anaide in Mose by Rossini; Bach St Matthew Passion; Beethoven Missa Solemnis, Handel Deborah; Schoenberg Erwartung and Shostakovich 14 Symphony. *Recordings include:* Aida, Il Trovatore, Cavalleria Rusticana and Stockhausen's Momente (Deutsche Grammophon); Zandonai's Conchita (Fonit Cetra); Verdi Requiem; Dido and Aeneas. *Address:* Indiana University, School of Music, Bloomington, IN 47405, USA.

DAWSON Anne, b. 8 Dec 1952, Stoke, England. Singer (Soprano). *Education:* Studied at the Royal Northern College of Music. *Career:* Sang Angelica in Handel's Orlando at the Bath Festival 1978, Grenoble Festival 1979; Recital tours throughout Britain; With Glyndebourne Touring Opera has sung Eurydice, Susanna and Micaela; Welsh National Opera as Gilda and Pamina; Marguerite, Gilda and the title role in The Cunning Little Vixen with English National Opera; Covent Garden debut in Don Carlos, 1988; Overseas engagements include Gilda in Frankfurt, the Vixen in Vancouver, and appearances with the Netherlands and Lausanne Operas; Sang Hero in Beatrice and Benedict, London Coliseum 1990; Susanna for Welsh National Opera; Season 1992 as Ninetta in The Thieving Magpie for Opera North, Anne Trulove for Glyndebourne Touring Opera and Chloe in The Queen of Spades at the Festival; Concert repertoire includes Schubert's Fierrabras, at South Bank conducted by Jeffrey Tate, Carmina Burana, and Mozart's Exsultate Jubilate (Fishguard Festival). *Recordings include:* Songs by English composers (Hyperion). *Honours:* John Ireland Festival Centenary Competition and the Gerald Finzi Song Award Competition, 1981; Soprano prize at the l981 International Singing Competition, s'Hertogenbosch; Kathleen Ferrier Memorial Scholarship 1982. *Address:* c/o IMG Artists Europe, Media House, 3 Burlington Lane, Chiswick, London W4 2TH, England.

DAWSON Lynne, b. 3 June 1953, York, England. Singer (Soprano). *Education:* Studied at the Guildhall School of Music, London. *Career:* Appearances from 1985 with Trevor Pinnock and the English Concert; John Eliot Gardiner, the Monteverdi Choir and English Baroque Soloists and Christopher Hogwood and the Academy of Ancient Music; Further concerts with Roger Norrington, Andrew Davis, Simon Rattle, Sir Charles McKerras, Ashkenazy, and Giulini; Tours of Europe and the USA; Opera debut as the Countess with Kent Opera, 1986; Monteverdi's Orfeo at Florence, 1988; Festival engagements at Aldeburgh, Edinburgh, Salzburg, Bruges, Aix-en-Provence (The Fairy Queen, 1989), Paris, Vienna and Promenade Concerts; Opera career includes Zdenka in Arabella at the Châtelet, Pamina for Scottish Opera and in the Mozart Experience at the Queen Elizabeth Hall; Sandrina in a new production of La Finta Giardiniera in Lausanne; Appearances as Fiordiligi at Naples, Constanze Brussels, Teresa in Benvenuto Cellini for Netherlands Opera, 1991; Other roles include, Xiphares in Mitridate (Châtelet, Paris, 1991), Constanze, Brussels, 1990, and Cornelia in Cleopatra & Cesare by Graun at the Berlin Staatsoper, 1992; Soloist in Purcell's Come, Ye Sons of Art Away at the 1993 London Proms. *Recordings include:* Bach B Minor Mass, Monteverdi Orfeo, Purcell, Dido and Aeneas (Deutsche Grammophon Archiv); Messiah (Hyperion); Mozart C Minor Mass; Purcell Timon of Athens and Dioclesian; Iphigénie en Aulide; Jephtha; Vespers by Mozart; Mozart's Requiem; Gluck's La Rencontre Impréuve; Mozart's Elvira and Constanze, Beethoven 9 (Philips), Midsummer Night's Dream, Acis and Galatea. *Address:* IMG Artists, Media House, 3 Burlington Lane, London, W4 2TH, England.

DAWSON Ted, b. 28 April 1951, Victoria, British Columbia, Canada. Composer; Teacher. *Education:* Studied at Victoria School of Music, 1964-68; composition with Brian Cherney and Rudolf Komorous at University of Victoria, BMus, 1972, followed by composition and electronic music with Bengt Hambraeus and Alcides Lanza at McGill University, MMA, 1974; Music and Visual Arts Education at University of Toronto, BED, 1984; compostion, computer music, performance, history, and theory with Charles Wuorinen, Peter Otto, Jan Williams, Jeremy Noble, and Martha Hyde at State University of New York at Buffalo, PhD (ABD), 1994. *Career:* Lecturer at Concordia University, 1974-78 and Vanier College in Montreal, 1978-80; Assistant Professor at Queen's University, Kingston, Ontario, 1987-88; and Assistant Professor at Brock University, St Catharines, Ontario, 1988-90; Founder of the ComPoster Project to promote Canadian music through education; Artistic Director of Canadian Music Days festival of contemporary Canadian music,

held in Estonia, 1993. *Publication:* author of Teachers's Guide to Canadian Music, 1991. *Compositions:* Pentad for string quartet 1971; Concerto Grosso 1 for tape with/ without amplified viola, bassoon, trombone, and percussion 1972-74; Chameleon for amplified flute, 1975; The Land of Nurr, 1975; The Clouds of Magellan for tape and slides, 1976-77; Binaries for 4 dancers, amplified piano, and percussion, 1978-80; Joint Actions for solo female dancer and male double bass player, 1981; Songs from the late T'ang for bass-baritone and piano, 1988; Portraits in a Landscape for tape, 1988; Traces in Glass for orchestra, 1986-92; China Beach for amplified piano and tape, 1992; Symphony 1 for orchestra, 1992-94. *Address:* SOCAN (Canada), c/o PRS Member Registration, 29-33 Berners Street, London W1P 4AA, England.

DAYMOND Karl Morgan, b. 1965, England, Singer (Baritone). *Education:* Studied at Guildhall School with Thomas Hemsley and at National Opera Studio. *Career:* Appeared at Glyndebourne Festival 1992 and sang Valentin in Faust for Opera Northern Ireland; Season 1993 as Schaunard for Welsh National Opera and Mountjoy in Gloriana for Opera North; Has also sung in Rimsky's May Night, La Vida Breve, Angelique by Ibert, Margot-la-Rouge by Delius, Poulenc's Les Mamelles de Tiresias, A Midsummer Night's Dream, Demetrius and the Henze-Paisiello Don Quixote as Sancho Panza. *Honours:* British Song Prize 1987; Polonsky Foundation Award 1989. *Address:* c/o John Coast Ltd, 31 Sinclair Road, London W14 ONS, England.

DAZELEY William, b. 1965, England. Singer (Baritone). *Education:* Studied at Guildhall School, London. *Career:* Season 1991-92 as Schaunard with British Youth Opera and Don Giovanni for Opera North, British premiere of Schreker's Der Ferne Klang 1992; Season 1992-93 with Opera North in Billy Budd and as Mozart's Count and Schaunard; Other roles include Papageno, Marcello, Guglielmo, Eugene Onegin, Pacuvio in La Pietra del Paragone, Harlequin, Ariadne auf Naxos, Demetrius and Billy Budd. *Honours:* 1989 Decaa-Kathleen Ferrier Prize; Richard Tauber Prize 1991; Winner, 1991 Walter Gruner International Lieder Competition. *Address:* c/o John Coast Ltd, 31 Sinclair Road, London W14 ONS, England.

DE ANGELIS Marcello, b. 30 Apr 1941, Milan, Italy. University Professor; Music Critic. *Education:* Laurea in Letters, University of Firenze; Private Study in Music. *Career:* Appeared on Radio and Television in Italy and Switzerland. *Publications:* La musica del Granduca 1978; Le Carte del l'impresario 1982; Le Cifre del Melodramma, 2 volumes 1982; Leopardi e la musica 1987; La felicita in Etruria 1990; Gli scherzi di Saturno. Giannotto Bastianelli, Carteggio 1907-27, 1992; Melodramma Spettacolo e Musica nella Firenze dei Lorena 1991; Contributor to Stabat Mater and various publications. *Honours:* Finalista Premio Viareggio 1978; Cavaliere al merito della Republic Italiana 1989; Critico musicale: Giornale del Mattino, 1963-65; I Unite 1969-88; La Republica dal 1980. *Memberships:* Societa Italiana di Musicologia and several professional organisations. *Address:* Via Giovanni Prati 9, 50124 Firenze, Italy.

DE BEENHOUWER Jozef, b. 26 Mar 1948, Brasschaat, Belgium. Concert Pianist. *Education:* Pharmacy, University of Louvain; Graduate, Chapelle Musicale Reine Elisabeth Argenteuil, 1974; Higher Diploma, Royal Flemish Conservatory, Antwerp, 1975. *Career:* Concert Pianist (with orchestra - solo recitals) Chamber music, Accompanied recitals: Vienna (Musikverein, Konzerthaus with Vienna Symphony), Amsterdam (Concertgebouw), London, Berlin (Schauspielhaus), Dresden (Semper-Oper), Rheinisches Musikfest, Flanders Festival, Festival - Estival de Paris etc; Professor of Piano at the Royal Flemish Conservatory, Antwerp, 1983-. *Recordings include:* Schumann-Fantasiestucke op. 12, Ravel - Gaspard de la Nuit; Peter Benoit - Contes et Ballades & Sonata (Prix Caecilia 1984); Joseph Ryelandt - Piano Works (Prix Caecilia 1986); Clara Schumann, Complete Piano works (3 CD, Partridge Holland, 1991); Rob Schumann (Opus 16, 111, 113), 1993. *Publications:* Concertsatz d-minor, (1839) - Robert Schumann, 1987; Concertsatz f-minor (1847) - Clara Schumann, 1993. *Memberships:* Robert Schumann Gesellschaft Düsseldorf and Zwickau; Felix Mendelssohn - Gesellschaft, Berlin; Kathleen Ferrier Society (England); Peter Benoitfonds, Antwerp. *Address:* Frilinglei 45, 2930 Brasschaat, Belgium.

DE BERNART Massimo, b. 1950, Rome, Italy. Conductor. *Education:* Studied piano, composition and conducting at Conservatories of Florence, Turin and Venice; Further study at Vienna Academy and Accademia Musicale Chigiana. *Career:* Has made many appearances in Italian opera houses, conducting 19th century repertory and reviving neglected works; Conducted Ecuba by Nicola Manfroce and Caterina di Guisa by Carlo Coccia at Savona 1991; Permanent Artistic Director of the Orchestra Giovanile Italiana, from 1977 and of the Orchestra Regionale Toscana 1980; Conducted Traviata at Savona 1991, Leoncavallo's La Reginetta della Rose at Palermo 1992. *Recording:* L'Ebreo by Giuseppe Appolini. *Honours:* Prizewinner, Vittorio Gui International Conducting Competition 1978; Thomas Schippers International Prize 1979. *Address:* c/o Accademia Musicale Chigiana, Via di Citta 89, 1-53100 Siena, Italy.

DE CAPITANI Anna, b. 4 Aug 1961, La Sagne. Pianist. m. Francois de Capitani, 11 Mar 1983. *Education:* Normal schools and high school to final examination; Piano lessons since age of 5; Basic study in Bern Conservatory; Private lessons in Freiburg. *Career:* Accompanist of the masterclass and courses of Professor Igor Ozim and Professor Max Rostal, 1985-90; Tour in Slovenia with Igor Ozim; Further concerts in Germany and Switzerland. *Recordings:* Mythen and Sonata by Szymanowsk (with Sylvia E Viertel and Monika Urbaniak); Brahms Variations op 9; with Igor Ozim 2 CDs with encore pieces, Dvořák 4 Romantic Pieces, Bloch Baal Shem. *Membership:* Schweizerischer Tonkünstlerverein. *Hobbies:* Dance; Gymnastics. *Address:* Viktoriastrasse 45, CH-3013 Bern, Switzerland.

DE CAROLIS Natale, b. 25 July 1957, Anagni, Italy. Opera Singer (Bass-Baritone). *Education:* Pont Institute of Vatican State, studied with Renato Guelfi and Maria Vittoria Romano. *Debut:* 1983. *Career:* La Scala, Milan; Metropolitan Opera, New York; La Fenice, Venice; Maggio Musicale, Florence; Salzburg Festpiele; La Zarzuela, Madrid; Sydney Opera House; Rossini Opera Festival; Pesaro Teatro Comunale; Bologna Opernhaus; Zurich Opera; Teatro Massimo, Palermo; Teatro Bellini, Catania; Colonia; Parigi; Macerata; S Carlo, Napoli and Bonn; Sang Don Parmenione in a Rossini double bill at Cologne and Schwetzingen, 1992; Count Robinson in Il Matrimonico Segreto at the 1992 Ravenna Festival. *Recordings:* Signor Bruschino, Scala di Seta (Rossini); Don Giovanni (Mozart); Rinaldo (Handel); Mozart Recital; L'Occasione Fa Il Ladro and L'Inganno Felice (Rossini); Le Nozze Di Figaro (Mozart); La Ninfa Pazza Per Amore (Paisiello). *Honours:* Spoleto; Baroque Festival Viterbo; Toti Dal Monte (Treviso); Lauri Volpi. *Hobbies:* Tennis; Football. *Current Management:* Fedeli Opera International (Italy), John Coast (Great Britain), Lerin (Spain). *Address:* Bvd de la Suisse 19, Montecarlo, Monaco.

DE CLARA Roberto, b. 30 July 1955, Hamilton, Ontario, Canada. Conductor. m. Anna Colangelo, 1 October 1983. *Education:* BMus, summa cum laude, McMaster University, Canada; Wiener Meisterkurse; Vienna Mozarteum; Salzburg Sommerakademie; Accademia Chigiana, Siena; Aspen Music School; University of Toronto; Royal Conservatory, Toronto. *Debut:* Hamilton Philharmonic 1981. *Career:* Assistant Conductor, Opera Hamilton 1979-84; Assistant Conductor, Hamilton Philharmonic 1981-82; Music Director, Prince George Symphony 1984-87; Artistic Advisor, Symphony Hamilton 1988-90; Music Director, York Symphony 1990-. *Honours:* Heinz Unger Conducting Prize, Toronto 1978; Canada Council

Scholarships 1979, 80; Hans Haring Conducting Prize, Salzburg Mozarteum 1984. *Memberships:* American Federation of Musicians; Opera America. *Current Management:* Conductors Cooperative Management, Cambridge, Massachusetts, United States of America. *Address:* c/o York Symphony, PO Box 355, Richmond Hill, Ontario, Canada L4C 4Y6.

DE CRISTOFARO Joan K Vician, b. 11 August 1947, New York City, USA. Singer (Lyric-classical). Divorced 2d. *Education:* High School of Music and Art (now Juilliard Center), New York City; BA Fredonia State University, SUNY; MMus, Bloomington School of Music, Indiana University. *Debut:* Teatro Sociale, Mantova, Italy, as Musetta from Puccini's La Bohème. *Career:* Teatro alla Scala di Milano tour performances as Rosina, Barber of Seville, Rossini; Appearances in Teatro San Carlo, Napoli; Regio di Torino, Teatro Nazionale di Roma; Sociale di Parma, Giglio di Lucca, Brescia, Bergamo; Liceu di Barcelona. *Recordings:* Radio Free Europe broadcasts of Czechoslovakian arias and songs, New York City; RAI broadcasts, Milano. *Honours:* ASLICO, Milano 1970; Concorso Lirico Internazionale Puccini 1973; Beniamino Gigli, Macerata 1974; Concorso Internazionale, Merano and Parma 1973-74. *Hobbies:* Reading; Languages; Swimming; Yoga. *Address:* Via dei Rospigliosi 1, Milano 20148, Italy.

DE CSILLÉRY Béla, b. 26 Oct 1915, Budapest, Hungary. Naturalised British Subject 1959. Conductor; Violinist. m. Gillian Sansom, 2 June 1965 (dec Aug 1993), 2 sons. *Education:* Reformed Gymnasium, Pázmány Péter University, Budapest, 1936; Liszt Ferenc Music Academy Budapest, Hochschule für Musik Berlin, Accademia di Santa Cecilia, Rome; further studies with Ansermet in Geneva and Hindemith in Zurich. *Career:* Concerts as violinist in Hungary, Denmark, Germany, Holland and Norway; Director Budapest Municipal Symphony Orchestra 1940-44; Nancy Chamber Orchestra 1949-51. Guest Conductor: Austria, France, Germany (Munich Philharmonic SWF etc), Great Britain (BBC Training Orchestra, LMP, LPO, LSO, Scottish National Orchestra), Italy, Spain (Barcelona Symphony, Madrid Philharmonic), Switzerland (Orchestra Suisse Romande, Winterthur Orchestra), among others. Kent County Music Adviser 1962-81, Founder and Musical Director Kent County Youth Orchestra 1962-84, Kent Sinfonia 1963-, Maidstone Symphony Orch 1970-91. Concert tours with KCYOrch: Belgium, (Europalia Festival), Germany, Holland, Italy, Switzerland and USA. *Recordings:* Rossini: Overture Italian Girl In Algiers; Mozart, Piano Concerto No 9, Kent County Youth Orchestra - Andrew Haigh (BBC REB 62S). *Membership:* European String Teachers Association (ESTA). *Hobbies:* Mountaineering; Swimming; Travelling. *Address:* 20 Faraday Road, Maidstone, Kent ME14 2DB, England.

DE FROMENT Louis Georges Francois, b. 5 Dec 1921, Toulouse, France. Conductor. m. Jacqueline Charles, 15 Nov 1952, 1 daughter. *Education:* Lycée et Conservatoire, Toulouse, 1940; Conservatoire, Paris, 1945-48. *Career:* Chief, orchestra, ORTF, Paris, 1949-58; Director of music, Casinos of Cannes & Deauville, 1949-56; Consultant artistic director, Music Casino, Vichy, 1950-69; Chief conductor, Opéra Comique, Paris, 1957-60; Permanent conductor, Orchestre Radio-Tele, Luxembourg, 1958-; Conductor, various recordings. *Honours:* Couronne, Ordre Civil et Militaire, Adolphe de Nassau; Ordre de la Couronne, Belgium; Chevalier, Ordre du Mérite, France; Officier, Ordre Grand Ducal de la Couronne de Chêne, Luxembourg; Chevalier des Arts et Lettres; Commandeur, Ordre Mérite; Grand Prix du Disque; Prix Clemence 1 Saure. *Membership:* Academie du Languedoc. *Address:* Chef d'Orchestre, Radio-Tele, Luxembourg.

DE GEER Ingrid (Baroness), b. 8 Sept 1927, Vastra Eneby, Sweden. Musicologist. m. (1) Frederik van Eck, 5 July 1949, 1 son. (2) Eric, Baron De Geer af Finspong, 21 Mar 1981. *Education:* Candidatsexamen musicology 1972, Doctoraalexamen scientia musices 1975, University of Utrecht; PhD Musicology, University of Uppsala, 1985; Piano studies with Walther Meyer-

Radon, Copenhagen, 1945-52; Everhard van Beijnum, Hague, 1956-59; Iskar Aribo, Leiden, 1959-62; State exam music theory, Hague, 1966. *Career:* Research Assistant, Department of Musicology 1972-75, Faculty Research Associate 1975-78, University of Utrecht; Research Associate, Department of Musicology 1983-89, Docent musicology 1985-, Uppsala University; Teacher of piano and music theory, accompanist, 1947-79; Research Associate, Department of Musicology, Gothenburg University, 1990-93. *Publications include:* Earl, Saint, Bishop, Skald - and Music, 1985; Van Opera danese tot Syngespil, 1973; Music and the Twelfth-Century Orkney Earldom in: St Magnus Cathedral, 1988; Music Archaeology in Music History Writing in: Arch of Early Music Cultures, 1989, *Contributions:* Review editor, Swedish Journal of Musicology, 1980-88; Current contributor to Swedish National Encyclopaedia, Conference and research project reports, reviews. *Hobbies:* Travel; Gardening; Sailing. *Address:* Ritargatan 5, S-75433 Uppsala, Sweden.

DE GRANDIS Renato, b. 24 Oct 1927, Venice, Italy. Composer. *Education:* Studied Musicology and Composition with Malipiero in Venice; Master classes in Siena. *Career:* As composer, has been concerned with dodecaphonic and aleatory techniques; Resident in Darmstadt 1959-81, then Venice. *Compositions:* Unperformed operas, La Fanciulla del Lago, Il Gave and Il Pastore 1951-54; Il Cierco di Hyuga 1959 (Staged Bonn 1969), Gloria al Re 1962 (Staged Kiel 1967), Eduard und Kunigunde, Wiesbaden 1971; Das Wahrhaftige ende des Don Giovanni, Bonn 1973; Die Schule der Kahlen, Karlsruhe 1976. *Honours:* Italian Radio Prize 1945; National First Prize for Composition 1953. *Address:* SIAE (Italy), c/o PRS Ltd Member Registration, 29-33 Berners Street, London W1P 4AA, England.

DE GREY Michael John, b. 6 Sept 1942, Hitchin, England. Music Administrator. m. Charlotte Ashe, 17 June 1989. *Education:* Eton College, 1955-60; Tours University, France, 1960; Pitman Business Course, 1961; Marketing Course, Ashridge Management Centre, 1968; Marketing Strategy Course, Coopers & Lybrand, 1987; Senior Managers Programme, Cranfield School of Management, 1988. *Career:* Concerts Manager, Victor Hochhauser Ltd, 1970-72; General Manager, Administrator of Mozart Prize, London Mozart Players, 1972-81; General Manager, Royal Choral Society, 1976-79; Administrative Director, London Sinfonietta, 1981-88; Administrative Director, Opera Factory, 1984-88; Director, Association of British orchestras, 1984-89; Member, Music Panel, South East Arts, 1987-91; Director, London Philharmonic Orchestra Ltd, 1987-89; General Manager, London Academy of Music and Dramatic Art, 1989; Chief Executive, The National Youth Orchestra of Great Britain, 1991-. *Hobbies:* Travel; Photography; Wine; Reading; Gardening; Carpentry; Visual arts; Theatre; Opera. *Address:* Crooked Cottage, The Hollow, Dunkerton, Bath BA2 8BG, England.

DE GROOTE Philip, b. 25 Dec 1949, South Africa. Cellist. *Career:* Co-founder and cellist of the Chilingirian Quartet, 1971; Resident Quartet of Liverpool University 1973-76; Resident Quartet of Sussex University, 1978-; Resident Quartet of Royal College of Music, 1986-; Annual series of concerts at the Elizabeth Hall and Wigmore Hall; Performances at the Edinburgh, Bath, Aldeburgh Festivals; Munich Herkulessaal, Amsterdam Concertgebouw, Zurich Tonhalle, Vienna Konzerthaus, Stockholm Konserthuset; New York debut 1976; Annual coast-to-coast tours of the USA and Canada; Represented Britain at the New York International Festival quartet series; Tours of Australia, New Zealand, South America, the Far East; Television and radio throughout Europe, National Public Radio in the USA, the BBC. *Recordings:* All Great Mozart Quartets; Late Schubert Quartets; Debussy and Ravel Quartets; Elgar Quartet and Piano Quintet; Schubert Cello Quintet and Octet; Mozart Clarinet Quintet; Complete Quartets of Bartók and Dvořák; Bartók Piano Quintet; Labels include EMI, RCA, CRD, Nimbus and Chandos. *Address:* c/o

Intermusica Artists Management, 16 Duncan Terrace, London N1 8BZ, England.

DE JONG Conrad J(ohn), b. 13 Jan 1934, Hull, Iowa, USA. Composer; Professor. *Education:* BM, music education and trumpet, North Texas State University, Denton, 1954; MM, music theory with B Heiden and brass instruments, Indiana University School of Music, 1959; T de Leeuw, Amsterdam, 1969. *Career:* Professor of Music, University of Wisconsin, River Falls, 1959-. *Compositions:* Prelude and Fugue for Brass Trio, 1958; 3 Studies for Brass Septet, 1960; Music for 2 Tubas, 1961; Essay for brass Quintet, 1963; String Trio, 1964; Fun and Games for Any Woodwind, Brass or String Instrument(s) and Piano, 1966, revised 1970; Peace on Earth for Chorus and Organ, 1969; Aanraking (Contact) for Trombone, 1969; Hist Whist for Voice, Flute, Viola and Percussion, 1969; Grab Bag for Tuba Ensemble, 1970; The Silence of the Sky in My Eyes for 1/2 Track Stereo Tape, Musicians, Light and Optional Dance and Audience Participation, 1973; A Prayer for Chorus, Piano, Brass Wind Chimes and Optional Audience, 1975; Ring! My Chimes for Chimes, 1/2 Track Stereo Tape and Slides, 1977; 3 Short Variation Fanfares for Brass Quintet, 1980; La Dolorosa for English Horn, 1982. *Address:* c/o Music Department, University of Wisconsin at River Falls, River Falls, WI 54022, USA.

DE LA MORA Fernando, b. 1963, Mexico City. Singer (Tenor). *Education:* Studied in Mexico City, New York, Tel Aviv and at North Carolina University. *Debut:* Sang Borsa in Rigoletto at Mexico City. *Career:* Has appeared widely in Mexico as Pinkerton, Cavaradossi and Alfredo; San Francisco Opera 1988-89, as Gounod's Romeo, and Rodolfo; Alfredo at Vienna Staatsoper and the Deutsche Oper Berlin 1989; Faust at Cologne and the Verdi Requiem on tour to Moscow with the ensemble of La Scala; Milan debut 1990, as Alfredo, which he sang also at the Santa Fe Festival 1991; Barcelona 1992 as Nemorino. *Address:* c/o Teatro alla Scala, Via Filodrammatici 2, 20121 Milan, Italy.

DE LA VEGA Aurelio, b. 28 Nov 1925, La Habana, Cuba. Composer; Essayist on Music, Art, Literature; Educator. *Education:* De La Salle College, Havana 1940-44, BA, Humanities, 1944; University of Havana, 1944-46, MA, Diplomacy; MA, Musicology, 1956, PhD, Music (Composition) 1958, Ada Iglesias Music Institute; Private studies in composition with Ernst Toch, Los Angeles, 1947-48. *Career:* Performances of works in the United States, Canada, Latin American countries, Europe, South Africa, Israel, Japan, India, Australia and New Zealand. Numerous works commissioned by orchestras, ensembles, patrons, institutions and music societies; Numerous appearances as lecturer on contemporary music subjects throughout the world. Also lectured on Latin American painting. Distinguished Professor of Music at California State University, Northridge, since 1959, and Director of Electronic Music Studio at the same institution. *Compositions:* Main works: Elegy, for string orchestra, 1954; Intrata for orchestra 1972; Adios for orchestra, 1978; String Quartet in 5 Movements, In Memoriam Alban Berg, 1957; Structures, piano and string quartet, 1962; Septicilium, solo clarinet and chamber ensemble, 1975; Testimonial, mezzo soprano and 5 instruments, 1990; Madrigales de Entonces, a cappella choir, 1991. *Recordings include:* Tangents, violin and piano, 1974, Orion; Para-Tangents, trumpet and piano, 1974, Crystal; Sound Clouds, guitar, 1975, Klavier; Tropimapal for 9 instruments, 1983, Opus One; Inflorescencia, soprano, bass clarinet, tape, 1976, Orion; Antinomies for piano, 1967, Orion; Homenagem for piano, 1987, Viena Modern Masters. *Hobbies:* Painting; Art book collecting; Travelling. *Address:* Music Department, California State University, Northridge, CA 91330, USA.

DE LAET Joris Maurits, b. 12 Jul 1947, Antwerp, Belgium. Professor. m. Maria Vervoort, 11 Aug 1974, 1 daughter. *Education:* Basic music theory, academies of Antwerp; Autodidact in electronic and computer music/recording techniques, computer information/ Composition, first performances in ICC Antwerp

(International Cultural Centre) 1974. *Career:* Tape music composition, Parametric; Live-electronics, video-art at festivals in Europe, Canada, Brazil. Many radio appearances since 1973; International seminars and lectures; Concert organiser of experimental and electronic music and video-art. Director of SEM; Manager of the sound studio activities of the Antwerp Music Conservatory and Professor of Electronic Music Composition; Co-Founder and Vice-President of BeFEM/FeBeMe, Belgian Federation of Electroacoustic Music in 1994. *Compositions include:* Meditatieve Ruimte commissioned 1988; Naderen, commissioned, 1988; Convergencies in Architectuur en Klank, 1989; Metrokunst 1989 Installatie, 1989; Sports in Concert commissioned 1989; Blamis commissioned 1990; Oplichtend Zwart commissioned 1990; Wigwam, commissioned 1991; Transparent Bodies, 1991. *Recordings:* All tape music and video art available on tapes/casettes in all formats by request, including concerts of the SEMensemble. *Publications:* Editor, SEMmagazine, 1975-79; Editor and partly author, Documenta Belgicae II 1985; Author of syllabus in use at Conservatory of Antwerp about Analogue Synthesis-techniques, 1979; Author of articles in newspapers, magazines. *Memberships:* SABAM since 1973; Founder and director of SEM in 1973 (Studio for Experimental Music). *Hobbies:* Sailing; Fencing. *Address:* Scheihagestraat 43, 2550 Kontich-Antwerp, Belgium.

DE LOS ANGELES Victoria, b. 1 Nov 1923, Barcelona, Spain, Soprano, m. Enrique Magrina Mir, 1948, 2 sons. *Education:* University and Conservatory of Barcelona. *Debut:* Barcelona, 1945, *Career:* Paris Opera and La Scala, Milan, 1949; Royal Opera House, Covent Garden, London, England, 1950; Metropolitan Opera House, New York, USA, 1951; Vienna State Opera, 1957; Numerous appearances at other opera houses, concert tours; Roles included Mozart's Countess, Elisabeth in Tannhäuser, Marguerite, Ariadne, Mimi and Carmen (New York City Opera, 1979); Wigmore Hall recitals, 1990. *Recordings:* Has made numerous recordings. *Honours:* Recipient of numerous Orders and decorations including: 1st Prize, Geneva International Competition, 1947; Cross of Lazo de Dama of the Order of Isabel the Catholic; Condecoracion Banda de la Orden Civil de Alfonso X (El Sabio), Spain. *Address:* c/o Wigmore Hall (Artists' Contracts) Wigmore Street, London W1, England.

DE MAEYER Jan Irma Maria, b. 1 Sept 1949, Bornem, Belgium. Musician. m. Godelieve Verstraelen, 3 Aug 1973, 1 son, 1 daughter. *Education:* Licentiate in Classical Philology; Candidate in Ancient History; Higher Diploma, Oboe and Chamber Music; 1st prizes for English Horn, Musical History, Harmony, Counterpoint, Fugue and Composition. *Career:* Formerly Soloist, Antwerp Philharmonic Orchestra and BRT Philharmonic Orchestra; Currently Professor of Oboe and English Horn, Royal Flemish Conservatory, Antwerp, also Director, Municipal Conservatory, Mechelen; Several radio and TV appearances as soloist and chamber music player. *Compositions:* La Gioia, woodwind trio, recorded 1985; Several educational pieces for piano solo, Metropolis, Antwerp, 1985-86; Ritratto di 7 dei Romani, piano solo, Cebedem, 1987; Three educative pieces for guitar, Billaudot, 1987. *Recording:* Musique francaise pour trio d'anches, with Avena woodwind trio, 1985. *Address:* H. Consciencestraat 66, 1800 Vilvoorde, Belgium.

DE MAIN John (Lee), b. 11 Jan 1944, Youngstown, Ohio, USA. Conductor. *Education:* BM 1966, MS 1968, Juilliard School of Music, New York; Studied piano with Adele Marcus; Conducting with Jorge Mester. *Career:* Associate Conductor, St Paul (Minn) Chamber Orchestra, 1972-74; Music Director, Texas Opera Theater, 1974-76; Houston Grand Opera, 1979-94; Opera/Omaha, 1983-; Conducted the local premiere of Britten's A Midsummer Night's Dream, Houston, 1993. *Recordings:* For Composers' Recordings Inc; RCA. *Honours:* Julius Rudel Award, 1971; Grammy Award, 1977; Grand Prix du Disque, 1977. *Address:* c/o Houston Grand Opera, 510 Preston Avenue, Houston, TX 77002, USA.

DE MEY Guy, b. 4 August 1955, Hamme, Belgium. Singer (Tenor). *Education:* Studied at Brussels Conservatory and at Amsterdam with Erna Spoorenberg; Further study with Peter Pears and Eric Tappy. *Career:* Has appeared in Baroque opera at such centres as Berlin, Hamburg, Strasbourg and Spoleto; Lully's Atys under William Christie in Paris, Florence and New York; Alidoro in Cesti's Orontea at Innsbruck 1986, returning for Aegus in Cavalli's Giasone 1988; Rameau's Hippolyte at Regio Emilia and Eurymachus in Il Ritorno di Ulisse at Mézières, 1989, conducted by Michel Corboz; London 1986 as Monteverdi's Orfeo, Brussels 1988, as the Painter in Lulu; Sang Don Polidoro in Mozart's La Finta Semplice at Innsbruck, 1991; Lully's Alceste at Opera Comique, Paris, 1992; Further engagements at Utrecht Early Music Festival, Zurich, Venice anbd Bologna; Concert repertoire includes the Evangelist in Bach's Passions. *Recordings:* Le Cinesi by Gluck; A Scarlatti's La Giuditta; Lully's Atys; Der Geduldige Sokrates by Telemann, Monteverdi's Orfeo and Poppea; Cavalli's Xerse and Giasone, Alessandro by Handel, Orontea and Rameau's Platee. *Address:* Theatre Royale de la Monnaie, 4 Leopoldstrasse, B-1000 Brussels, Belgium.

DE MEZER-LISOWICZ Agata Walentyna, b. 28 May 1965, Warsaw, Poland. Composer, teacher of music. m. Krzysztof Lisowicz, 1 son. *Education:* Master of Art Warsaw Academy of Music, 1988. *Career:* Garden, for symphony orchestra, performed in Warsaw, 1988 and at the Warsaw Autumn Festival, 1993; Rondo, for string orchestra and percussion performed in RAM in London, 1991. *Compositions include:* Orchestral and Chamber Music; Music for Choir; Tape Music; Songs. *Membership:* Polish Society of Composers. *Address:* Dubois 7 m 5 00-182, Warsawa, Poland.

DE MOOR Chris, b. 22 June 1949, Antwerp, Belgium. Vocalist (Bass). m. Michele Bolsaie, 5 Aug 1972, 2 daughters. *Education:* Classical Studies (especially Languages), 1961-69; Degree in Graphic Arts (First Professional Aim - Drawing), 1969-72; Opera, Concert and Chamber Music Diplomas, Brussels Music Conservatoire, 1976-79; STAS Prize for Lied rendering, Brussels, 1980; Private study under Vera Berning, Brussels, 1984. *Debut:* Part of Hagen, Antwerp Opera, 1979. *Career:* Amateur Boy's Choir 1961-73 (Bass Soloist 1965-73); Chorus and small parts, Brussels National Opera, 1973-82; Opera and Concert Performances in Belgium (Flanders and Wallonia Operas and Festivals); Holland (The Hague); France (Paris, Lille, Nancy, Strasbourg, Lyon, Bordeaux, Nice, Cannes); Germany (Berlin, Passau); Italy (Bologna); Spain (Barcelona, San Sebastian); Greece; Radio and TV Appearances in Belgium, France, Germany, Spain and Wales. *Recordings:* Especially Erato Records (Dukas, Chabrier, Schütz) under Armin Jordan, Charles Dutoit, Louis Devos. *Current Management:* Musilyre (Miss V. Reaud), Rue de la Petite Truanderie 2, F-75001, Paris, France. *Address:* Avenue Général Ruquoy 13, B-1420 Braine-L'Alleud, Belgium.

DE PALMA Sandro, b. 14 Feb. 1957, Naples, Italy. Pianist. *Education:* Classical studies in Latin, Greek; Studied piano privately with Vincenzo Vitales, Naples. *Debut:* Naples. *Career:* Appeared O.R.F., Vienna, 1977, Carnegie Hall, New York, 1978; Other appearances include: Dvořák Hall, Prague; Interforum, Budapest; Gewandhaus, Leipzig; Dresden; East Berlin; Performances with major Italian Orchestras: RAI, Rome; San Carlo; Fenice Venice; Milan; Tours, France; Italy, Switzerland, USSR. *Recordings Include:* 1st record at age 15: Liszt; 1st recording of Muzio Clementi's Gradus ad Parnassum, with Fonit Cetra. *Honours:* 1st prize, Casella Competition, Naples, 1976; 1st prize Bruce Hungerford, New York, 1977. *Hobbies:* Computers; Archaeology; Chess. *Current Management:* Patrizia Garrasi, Via Manzoni 31, 20121 Milan, Italy. *Address:* Via del Colosseo 23, Rome, Italy.

DE PAUR Leonard, b. 18 Nov. 1915, Summit, New Jersey, USA. Conductor. *Education:* Studied at the Institute of Musical Art, Columbia University; Private study with Henry Cowell and Pierre Monteux. *Career:* Assistant conductor of the Hall Johnson Choir, 1932-36; Music director of the Federal Theater Project, New York, 1936-39, collaborating with Orson Welles; Toured widely with the De Paur Infantry Chorus of the 372nd Regiment; Founded the De Paur chorus 1963, touring with it until 1969 in the USA and Africa; Conducted the Orchestra of America at the 1964 meeting of the National Association of Negro Musicians; Director of community relations, Lincoln Center, New York; Led the Symphony of the New World until 1973; Conducted William Grant Still's A Bayou Legend for Opera South in Jackson, Mississippi. *Recordings:* Many albums of works by black composers.

DE PEYER Gervase Alan, b. 11 April 1926, London, England. Clarinettist; Conductor. m. (1) Sylvia Southcombe, 1950, divorced 1971, 1 son, 2 daughters, (2) Susan Rosalind Daniel, 1971, divorced 1979, (3) Katia Perret Aubry, 1980. *Education:* Studied with Frederick Thurston at the Royal College of Music and with Louis Cahuzac in Paris. *Career:* International Soloist, 1949-; Co-founded the Melos Ensemble 1950; First clarinet with the London Symphony 1955; Teacher at the Royal Acadedmy of Music from 1959; As soloist has given the premieres of works by Arnold Cooke, Musgrave, Horovitz, Hoddinott and Sebastian Forbes; Joined the Chamber Music Society of the Lincoln Center, New York, 1969: performances with Barenboim, Rostropovitch, Menuhin, Perlman, and the Amadeus Quartet; Has conducted the English Chamber Orchestra, London Symphony and the Melos Sinfonia; Director, London Symphony Wind Ensemble; Associate Conductor, Haydn Orchestra of London; Conductor-in-Residence of the Collegium Musicum, in Assisi and Rome; Tour of the USA 1988, with Quatuor pour le fin du Temps by Messiaen; Gives recitals and master classes throughout the world; Wigmore Hall concert with Gwenneth Pryor and the Allegri Quartet, 1989. *Recordings include:* Many discs with the Melos Ensemble; French, English and German music for clarinet and piano, Brahms Sonatas, with Gwenneth Pryor (Chandos). *Publications include:* Edition of Mendelssohn Sonata in E flat. *Honours include:* Worshipful Company of Musicians Gold Medal, Royal College of Music, 1948; Charles Gros Grand Prix du Disque, 1961, 1962; Plaque of Honour from Academy of Arts and Sciences of America for recording of Mozart Concerto, 1962. *Hobbies:* Theatre; Good Food; Anything Dangerous. *Address:* 16 Langford Place, St. John's Wood, London NW8, England.

DE QUADROS Andre, b. 4 Jan 1953, Bombay, India. Conductor; Music Educator. 1 son, 1 daughter. *Education:* Diploma, Music and Movement Education, Hochschule fur Musik, Mozarteum, Salzburg, Austria, 1980; Graduate Diploma of Music (Orchestral Conducting), Victorian College of the Arts, 1991. *Career:* Pre-school to tertiary teaching including universities and teacher training institutions; Pioneered implementation of post-compulsory courses in Music and Dance; 1 of the most influential music educators, State of Victoria; Was concurrently Member, Accreditation Advisory Group and Field of Study Committee for the Arts, Victorian Curriculum and Assessment; Member, Board of Directors, Australian Music Examination Board; Other consultancy appointments; Community Music Coordinator, 1984-85; Former Acting Director of Music, Presbyterian Ladies College, Conductor, Monash University Choral Society, Freelance Conductor, orchestras and choirs; Conducted choral and orchestral concerts, led workshops; Lectured at in-service courses and major local and national conferences, major Victorian country centres, all Australian states, Finland, Belgium, India, Canada, Austria, USA; Currently: Senior Lecturer in Music, Monash University and Artistic Director, Melbourne International Festival of Choirs. *Publication:* Music of Asia and the Pacific (editor), 1993. *Membership:* Elected Advisor to International Federation of Choral Music. *Hobbies:* Current affairs; Environmental issues; 19th century literature;

Gardening. *Address:* 27 Glen Court, Glen Waverley, Victoria 3150, Australia.

DE SALAS Sergio, b. 1947, Spain. Singer (Bass-baritone). *Education:* Studied in Madrid, Barcelona and Milan. *Career:* Sang at opera houses in Spain from 1971; Appeared as Rigoletto in Valencia and sang in Paris, Marseilles, Bologna and Seville; Liege 1987-88 as the four villains in Les Contes d'Hoffmann; Teatro Real Madrid 1989, as Gerard in Andrea Chenier; Other roles include Wagner's Dutchman, Athanael in Thais, Mephistopheles in La Damnation de Faust and parts in operas by Verdi. *Honours:* Prizewinner at Beniamino Gigli Competition Macerata and the Voci Verdiane at Parma 1974.

DE SARAM Rohan, b. 9 Mar. 1939, Sheffield, Yorkshire, England. Cellist. *Education:* Studied in Ceylon, with Gaspar Cassado in Florence and with Casals in Puerto Rico; Further study with John Barbirolli. *Career:* Gave recitals and concerts in Europe; US debut with New York Philharmonic, Carnegie Hall, 1960; Further concerts in Canada, USSR, Australia and Asia; As a soloist in addition to standard repertoire has worked personally with: Kodály, Walton, Shostakovich; Premieres of works by: Pousseur and composers of the younger generation; Has taught, Trinity College of Music; Member, Arditti Quartet (repertoire includes works by Boulez, Carter, Ferneyhough, Henze, Ligeti and many other living composers); Has also premiered works by Böse, Britten, Bussotti, Cage, Davies, Glass, Gubaidulina, Hindemith, Kagel, Nancarrow, Rihm and Schnittke, with Arditti Quartet; as soloist has premiered Kottos for solo cello by Xenakis, Ligeti's Racine 19 and Berio's Il Ritorno degli Snovidenia, for cello and orchestra; PLayed in the Russian Spring series at South Bank, May 1991, Quartets by Rozlavets, Schnittke and Firsova; Founder, de Saram Clarinet Trio and a duo with his brother Druvi; Interested in the music of his native Sri Lanka and plays the Kandyan drum. *Address:* 20 St Georges Avenue, London, N7.

DE SICA Gennaro, b. 1938, Naples, Italy. Singer (Tenor). *Education:* Studied at Umberto Giordano Conservatory Foggia and with Carlo Tagliabue in Rome. *Debut:* Spoleto 1963 as Ferrando in Cosi Fan Tutte. *Career:* Has sung in such Italian opera centres as Genoa, Milan, Florence and Naples; Guest appearances in Germany at Frankfurt, Karlsruhe, Darmstadt, Nuremberg, Bonn and Kiel; Has also sung at Royal Opera in Copenhagen; Other roles have included Mozart's Don Ottavio and Tamino; Donizetti's Ernesto and Nemorino; Lionel in Martha, Rossini's Almaviva, Comte Ory, Don Ramiro, Lindoro and Narciso, Il Turco in Italia; Verdi's Duke, Alfredo and Fenton, Lensky in Eugene Onegin and David in Die Meistersinger. *Address:* c/o Teatro alla Scala, 12 Via Filodrammatici, 20121 Milan, Italy.

DE SMET Raoul, b. 27 October 1936, Antwerp, Belgium. Professor of Linguistics; Composer. m. Marisa Seys, 26 May 1962, 1s. 3 d. *Education:* M.Phil, Catholic University of Louvain; Postgraduate Diploma, Spanish Literature, University of Salamanca, Spain; Music Academy, Deurne; Composition with A Verbesselt and Ton de Leeuw; Electronic Music with L Goethals, Ipem, Gent. *Debut:* Darmstadt Ferienkurse Neue Musik. *Career:* Founder Orphische Avonden, concerts of new chamber music 1974; Publisher EM-reeks, new music of Flemish Composers 1981; Foundation of Orpheus-Prijs Contest for interpretation of new chamber music 1987; Professor Spanish Linguistics and Translation, Kath. Vlaamse Hogeschool, Antwerp, 1969-. *Compositions:* Chamberopera: Ulrike 1979, 88; Vincent 1990; Concerto for sax alto, strings accordion and percussion 1992; Concerto for violin and symphonic orchestra 1993; 2 string quartets; Clarinet and string quartet; Octopus for 8 Bass clarinets; Track-Sack-Fantasy for 10 accordions; Logbook 1, cello suite; Gnomons 2 for 4 trombones and stereotape; Soledad sonora for Sax Alto Solo. *Recordings:* Numerous recordings. *Memberships:* Sabam; Unie Belgische componisten; Stichting Orpheus; CeBeDeM. *Address:* Ruytenburgstraat 58, B-2600 Berchem, Belgium.

DE VALOIS, Ninette, Dame b. 6 June 1898, Baltiboys, Blessington, County Wicklow, Ireland. Founder, Director, Royal Ballet; Founder, Royal Ballet School. m. Dr A.B. Connell, 1935. *Career:* Prima Ballerina, Royal Opera Season, Covent Garden (International), May to July 1919, again in 1928; Premiere Danseuse, British National Opera Company, 1918; Member, Diaghilev Russian Ballet, 1923-26; Choreographic Director to Old Vic, The Festival Theatre, Cambridge, and The Abbey Theatre, Dublin, 1926-30; Founder, The National School of Ballet, Turkey, 1947; Founder, Director, Royal Ballet (formerly the Sadler's Wells Ballet), Royal Opera House, Covent Garden, and the Sadler's Wells Theatre Ballet, Sadler's Wells Theatre, 1931-63; Founder, Royal Ballet School (formerly the Sadler's Wells School of Ballet). *Compositions:* Principal Choreographic Works: Job; The Rake's Progress; Checkmate; Don Quixote. *Publications:* Invitation to the Ballet, 1937; Come Dance with Me, 1957; Step by Step, 1977. *Honours:* Hon.DFA, Smith College, Massachusetts, USA, 1957; Hon.LLD, Aberdeen, 1958, Sussex 1975; FRAD, 1963; Chevalier of the Legion of Honour, 1950; Gold Albert Medal, RSA, 1964; Jointly, Erasmus Prize Foundation Award (first Woman to receive it), 1974; Irish Community Award, 1980; OM, 1992; CH 1982; DBE 1951; CBE 1947; Hon D. Music, Cambridge University, 1992. *Address:* c/o Royal Ballet School, 153 Talgarth Road, London W14, England.

DE VAUGHN Paulette, b. 8 August 1951, California, USA. Singer (Soprano). *Education:* Studied with Martial Singher at Santa Barbara, at Juilliard School and in Vienna. *Debut:* As Elisabeth de Valois at Paris Opera. *Career:* Appearances at National Theatre Prague from 1980, as Tosca, the Trovatore Leonora, Mimi, Amelia, Bello in Maschera, Lady Macbeth, Turandot, Violetta and Abigaille; Sang Tosca at Stockholm 1988 and in seaon 1989-90 appeared as Savonlinna, as Tosca at Graz as Mozart's Electra at Mannheim, Manon Lescaut, Staatsoper Berlin, Elena in I Vespri Siciliani and Komische Oper Munich, Dresden and Sofia; Saarbrucken as Aida, Salome, Senta, Elsa and Leonore in Fidelio; Sang Aida at Royal Opera Copenhagen 1991 and at Palma and the Montpellier Festival 1992; Concerts and Lieder recitals in Austria, Germany and Sweden. *Address:* c/o Det Kongelige Teater, Box 2185, DK-1017, Copenhagen, Denmark.

DE VITO Gioconda, b. 26 July 1907, Martina Franca, Puglia, Italy. Violinist (Retired). m. David Bicknell, 16 Nov 1949 (deceased). *Education:* Honours, Conservatorio di Musica, Pesaro; Professor, Conservatorio di Bari at age of 17; Professor, Accademia di Santa Cecilia, Rome, 1934. *Debut:* At age of 18. *Career:* International career as Solo Violinist in most European countries (including Russia), Australia, Argentina, Israel; Soloist, Edinburgh International Festival 3 years including inaugural year, Salzburg; Retired 1961. *Recordings:* His Masters Voice - Major works in Violin Repertoire. All recordings issued by Toshiba-Japan recently under title, The Art of Gioconda De Vito. *Honours:* 1st Prize, Vienna Competition, 1932; Diploma di Medaglia d'Oro for Services to Art, 1957; Elected Academician by Accademia di Santa Cecilia, Academician Santa Cecilia since 1961, Roma; Golden Medal Award from Premiere Amadeus, 1991. *Hobby:* Bird Watching. *Address:* Flint Cottage, Loudwater, Rickmansworth, Herts, England.

DE VOL Luana, b. 30 Nov 1942, St Bruno, San Francisco, California, USA. Singer (Soprano). *Education:* San Diego University with Vera Rozsa in London and with Jess Thomas. *Debut:* San Francisco 1983 as Ariadne auf Naxos. *Career:* European debut Stuttgart 1983, as Leonore in Fidelio; Sang the Forza Leonora at Seattle 1983 and appeared at Aachen and Bremerhaven, as Tosca, Dusseldorf as Senta 1985 and Amsterdam; Member of Mannheim Opera from 1986; Appearances in Berlin, Staatsoper and Deutsche Oper from 1986 as Euryanthe, Agathe, Rezia in Oberon, Leonore and Senta; Staatsoper, Hamburg 1989, as Irene in Rienzi, Zurich and Vienna 1989 as Ellen Orford in Peter Grimes and Eva in Schreker's Irrelohe; Further engagements in Bologna, Dortmund, Gelsenkirchen and Frankfurt and at Bregenz and Orange Festivals; Sang Amelia in Ballo in Maschera at Stuttgart and Leonore in a concert performance at Festival Hall 1990; Gutrune in Götterdämmerung Concert in Rome and Elsa in Lohengrin at Taormina, both conducted by Sinopoli 1991; Sang Marina in Dvořák's Dimitrij at Munich, Leonore at Zurich and Andromache in Reimann's Troades at Frankfurt 1992; Other roles include Donna Anna, Isolde, Elisabeth de Valois and Elisabeth in Tannhäuser, Brünnhilde and the Marschallin; Concert repertoire includes the Britten War Requiem and Shostakovich's 14th Symphony. *Address:* c/o Nationaltheater, Am Goetheplatz, 6800 Mannheim, Germany.

DE WAAL Rian, b. 1958, The Netherlands. Concert Pianist. *Education:* Studied at Sweelinck Conservatory Amsterdam; Master classes with Rudolf Serkin and Leon Fleisher. *Career:* Regular concert appearances with the Concertgebouw Orchestra, Rotterdam and Stuttgart Philharmonics, Polish and Radio Chamber Orchestra and the State Orchestra of Lithuania; Further concerts and recitals in Boston, Washington, Atlanta and Montreal and on tour to Poland; Performs works by Godowsky, Balakirev and Tausig, as well as contemporary Dutch composers, in addition to the standard repertoire. *Recordings:* Numerous recordings. *Honours:* Prizewinner at Vianna da Motta Competition, Lisbon 1979 and the Queen Elisabeth in Brussels 1983. *Address:* c/o Robert Gilder and Company, Enterprise House, 59-65 Upper Ground, London SE1 1PQ, England.

DE WAART Edo, b. 1 June 1941, Amsterdam, Holland. Conductor. *Education:* Studied oboe with Haakon Stotijn at the Amsterdam Conservatory; conducting with Franco Ferrara at Hilversum 1964; assistant conductor New York Philharmonic 1965-66. *Career:* Co-principal oboe with Amsterdam Philharmonic 1961 and Concertgebouw Orchestra 1963; Conducted Stravinsky's The Soldier's Tale at the 1965 Spoleto Festival; 1966 Musical Director of the Netherlands Wind Ensemble and assistant conductor Concertgebouw Orchestra; 1969 co-conductor Rotterdam Philharmonic; musical director 1973-79; San Francisco Symphony 1975-83; UK debut 1969, with Royal Philharmonic; Covent Garden debut 1976, Ariadne auf Naxos; Bayreuth 1985; guest conductor with leading orchestras in the US and Europe; recent engagements with the Berlin Philharmonic, Chicago Symphony and Boston Symphony Orchestras; Wagner's Ring cycle at San Francisco 1985; conducted John Adams's Nixon in China in US and for Netherlands Opera, 1987-88; currently Music Director of the Minnesota Orchestra and Artistic Director of the Dutch Radio Organization, Nederlandse Omroep Stichting; Concert performances of Götterdämmerung, Die Gezeichneten by Schreker, 1989; Die Frau ohne Schatten, 1990; Season 1992 with Schreker's Schatzgräber at the Concertgebouw and Don Giovanni at the Santa Fe Festival. *Recordings:* Wide repertoire with the Concertgebouw, Rotterdam, San Francisco and London Philharmonic Orchestras; Mozart with the Netherlands Wind Ensemble. *Address:* c/o Harrison/Parrott Ltd., 12 Penzance Place, London W11 4PA, England.

DEAK Csaba, b. 16 Apr. 1932, Budapest, Hungary. Composer; Teacher. *Education:* Studied clarinet and composition, Bela Bartók Conservatory, Budapest, 1949-55; Composition with Ferenc Farkas, Budapest Academy of Music, 1955-56; with Hilding Rosenberg, Sweden; Composition, clarinet and conducting, Ingesund School of Music, Arvika; Teacher's Certificate, Stockholm Musikhogskolan, 1969. *Career:* Teacher, Swedish State School of the Dance, Stockholm, 1969-; University of Goteborg, 1971-74. *Compositions:* The Fathers, chamber opera, 1968; Lucie's Ascent into Heaven, an astrophonic minimelodrama, 1973; Bye-bye, Earth, A Play About Death, 1976-77; Etude on Spring, ballet, 1970; Jubilemus Salvatori, chamber cantata, 1958; Eden for Symphonic Band, 1978; The Piper's

Wedding for Wind Quintet and Symphonic Band, 1979; Vivax for Orchestra, 1982; 5 Short Pieces for Symphonic Band, 1983; Farina Pagus for Symphonic Band, 1983; 2 string quartets, 1959, 1967; Duo Suite for Flute and Clarinet, 1960; 121 for Winds, Percussion and Double Bass, 1969; Trio for Flute, Cello and Piano, 1971; Andante och Rondo for Wind Quintet, 1973; Verbunk for Brass Sextet, 1976; Hungarian Dances for Wind Quintet, 1977; Octet for Wind Quintet and String Trio, 1977; Herykon for Brass Quintet, 1981; Massallians for Trumpet, Trombone, Brass Ensemble and Percussion, 1985; Saxophone Quartet, 1986; Piano pieces; Choruses; Songs; Quintet for Alto Saxophone and String Quartet, 1988; Concerto Maeutro for Trumpet, Eufonium, Marimba and Symphonic Band, 1989; Quartet for Tubas, 1990; Ad Nordiam Hungarica for Chamber Ensemble, 1991; Concerto for Clarinet and Wind Orchestra, 1992. *Recordings:* Several compositions recorded. *Honour:* Atterberg Music-prize, 1992. *Memberships:* Vice Chairman in Chambermusic Society, Samtida Musik, in Stockholm. *Address:* Gullmarsplan 5, S-121 40 Johanneshov, Stockholm, Sweden.

DEAN Stafford, b. 20 June 1937, Kingswood, Surrey, England. Singer (Bass). *Education:* Epsom College; Opera Scholar, Royal College of Music; Studied with Gordon Clinton and privately with Howell Glynne and Otakar Kraus. *Career:* Toured with Opera for All 1962-63 and 1963-64; Glyndebourne debut as Lictor in L'Incoronazione di Poppea, 1964; Le Bailli in Werther, Rochefort in Anna Bolena, Leporello and Don Alfonso; Sadler's Wells Opera/ENO, 1964-70 (Debut Zuniga); Daland, Sarastro, Padre Guardiano, Sparafucile, Colline, Leporello; Covent Garden, 1969-, (Debut Masetto), Nightwatchman (Meistersinger), Narbal (Trojans), Figaro, Ferrando (Il Trovatore), Publio (Clemenza di Tito), Bottom, Rangoni (Boris Godunov), Leporello, new production of Lucrezia Borgia (Alfonso d'Este), A Midsummer Night's Dream (Bottom), Der Zwerg (Don Estoban), The King goes forth to France (Prime Minister). Guest appearances with: Metropolitan Opera New York, Chicago Lyric, San Francisco, Toronto, Stuttgart, Hamburg, Munich, W Berlin, Cologne, Frankfurt, Vienna, Paris, Aix-en-Provence, Turin, Barcelona, Amsterdam, Geneva, Zurich, Florence and Bonn. Concert appearances in: Beethoven's 9th Symphony, Missa Solemnis, Shostakovich 14th Symphony, Verdi Requiem; Bass Soloist in world premier of Penderecki Requiem (Stuttgart 1984). TV appearances: Rigoletto (Sparafucile), Flying Dutchman (Daland) BBC, Don Giovanni, Così fan Tutte (Glyndebourne), Lucrezia Borgia, Don Giovanni (300th performance as Leporello) Covent Garden; other roles include: Arkel, King Philip, Seneca, Gremin, Kecal and Osmin; Sang Don Pedro in Beatrice and Benedict at the London Coliseum, 1990, Gessler in Guillaume Tell at Covent Garden, 1990, 1992; Melisso in a new production of Handel's Alcina, 1992-93. *Recordings:* Idomeneo, I Lombardi, A Midsummer Marriage, Monteverdi Madrigals, Anna Bolena, Oedipus Rex, The Rake's Progress, The Beggar's Opera (Decca); Monteverdi Orfeo, Beethoven 9th Symphony, L'Enfance du Christ, A Village Romeo and Juliet. *Address:* c/o IMG Media House, 3 Burlington Lane, Chiswick, London, W4 2TH, England.

DEAN Timothy, b. 1955, England. Conductor. *Education:* Studied at Reading University and at the Royal College of Music. *Career:* Has worked with Opera North, the Buxton Festival Opera and the Royal Opera House, Covent Garden; For Kent Opera (1983-90) led Cosi fan Tutte, Agrippina, The Magic Flute, La Traviata, Carmen, Le Comte Ory, and Don Giovanni on the company's visit to the Singapore Festival; Conducted Martin's Le Vin Herbé for the London Music Theatre Group and the British premiere of Legrenzi's Giustino for the Chichester Festival; Vivaldi's Juditha Triumphans at the Camden Festival; Acis and Galatea for the English Bach Festival in Italy; Music Director of British Youth Opera, leading Don Giovanni and The Marriage of Figaro in London and on tour; Music Director of the London Bach Society from 1988, appearing with them at Chichester and City of London Festivals and on the South Bank; Other repertory includes The Burning Fiery Furnace and Peter Grimes. *Address:* c/o Korman International Management, Crunnells Green Cottage, Preston, Herts SG4 7UQ, England.

DEAN Winton Basil, b. 18 Mar 1916, Birkenhead, England. Author; Musicologist. m. Hon Thalia Mary Shaw, 4 Sep. 1939, 1 son, 3 daughters (2 deceased, 1 adopted). *Education:* MA, Classics and English, King's College, Cambridge, 1940. *Career:* Translated Libretto of Weber's Opera Abu Hassan, Arts Theatre, Cambridge, 1938; War Service, Naval Intelligence, 1944-45; Member of Music Panel, Arts Council, 1957-60; Ernest Bloch Professor of Music, University of California, Berkeley, USA, 1964-65; Regent's Lecturer, 1977; Matthew Vassar Lecturer, Vassar College, 1979; Ed. with Sarah Fuller, Handel's Opera Julius Caesar, Birmingham, 1977; Member of Committee, Handel Opera Society, 1955-60; Trustee and Member, Committee The Handel Institute, 1987. *Publications:* The Frogs of Aristophanes, Translation of choruses to music by Walter Leigh, 1937; Bizet, 1948, 3rd Edition revised, 1975; Carmen, 1949; Introduction to the Music of Bizet, 1950; Franck, 1950; Handel's Dramatic Oratorios and Masques, 1959; Shakespeare and Opera, 1964; Georges Bizet, His Life and Work, 1965; Handel and the Opera Seria, 1969; Beethoven and Opera, 1971; Ed., Handel, Three Ornamental Arias, 1976; Ed., E.J. Dent, The Rise of Romantic Opera, 1976; The New Grove Handel, 1982; Handel's Operas 1704-1726 (with J.M. Knapp), 1987; Essays on Opera, 1990. *Contributions to:* Grove's Dictionary of Music and Musicians; Music and Letters; Musical Times Opera. *Honours:* Honorable Member, Royal Academy of Music, 1971; Fellow, British Academy, 1975; Corresponding Member, American Musicological Society, 1989. *Memberships:* Royal Musical Association, Member of Council, 1965-; Vice-President, 1970-; G.F. Händel Gesellschaft, Halle, Member of Vorstand, 1979-, Vice-President, 1991-; Göttinger Händel Gesellschaft, Member of Curatorium, 1981-; International Musicological Society. *Hobbies:* Cricket; Shooting; Naval History. *Address:* Hambledon Hurst, Godalming, Surrey GU8 4HF, England.

DEARNLEY Christopher Hugh, b. 11 Feb 1930, Wolverhampton, England. Organist. m. Bridget Wateridge, 3 sons, 1 daughter. *Education:* MA, Worcester College, Oxford; DMus (Lambeth, 1987) Doctor of Fine Arts (Westminster College, 1989); FRCO. *Career:* Assistant Organist, Salisbury Cathedral, 1954-57; Organist and Master of the Choristers, ibid, 1957-68; Organist and Director of Music, St Paul's Cathedral, 1968-90; Acting Director of Music, Christ Church St Laurence, Sydney, 1990-91; Organist, Locum Tenens, St David's Cathedral, Hobart, 1991; Director of Music, Trinity College, University of Melbourne, 1992-93; Master of Music, St George's Cathedral, Perth, 1993-94. *Compositions:* Various church music; Arrangements and editions of early church music. *Recordings:* EMI Great Cathedral Organ Series, nos, 112 and 17; Organ Music From Salisbury and St Paul's Cathedrals; Numerous choir discs. *Publications:* The Treasury of English Church Music, volume 3; English Church Music, 1650-1750. *Contributions to:* Various Church music journals. *Honour:* LVO, 1990. *Memberships:* President, Incorporated Association of Organists, 1968-71; Chairman, Friends of Cathedral Music, 1971-90, Vice-President, 1991-; Chairman, Percy Whitlock Trust, 1982-89, President, 1989-; Chairman, The Harwich Festival, 1981-89, President, 1989-; Council Member, Royal College of Organists, 1980-89; Director, English Hymnal Company, 1970-; Patron, National Accordion Organisation, 1989-; Honorary Governor, Corporation of the Sons of the Clergy, 1989-; Patron, Organ Historical Trust of Australia, 1990-. *Hobbies:* Sketching; Gardening. *Address:* c/o Cattai PO, NSW 2756, Australia.

DEARS Robert Alan, b. 11 Apr 1948, Pittsburgh, Pennsylvania, USA. Church Musician; Concert Organist; Oratorio Conductor. *Education:* BMus, Duquesne University, 1968; Musikhochschule Lübeck, Germany, 1969-74; Studied Masterclass with Professor Walter Kraft; Orgel, Künstlerische Reifeprufung, Germany,

1971; Kirchenmusikalische A-Prüfung, Germany, 1974. *Career:* Assistant Organist, St. James, Wilkensburgh, USA, 1965-67; Organist and Choir Director, St. Casimir, Pittsburgh, Pennsylvania, 1967-69; Assistant to Professor Kraft, Marienkirche, Lübeck, Germany, 1970-72; 2nd Lübecker Domorganist, Lübeck, Germany, 1975-77; Der Landesbeauftragte für Katholik, Kirchenmusik in Schleswig-Holstein (Diocese of Osnabruck, Germany, 1977-; Kantor and Organist, St. Nikolaus, Kiel, Germany, 1977-; Founder, series of organ concerts at Lübeck Cathedral; Concert Performances in Germany, Denmark, USA. *Honour:* Named Kirchenmusikdirektor (KMD), 1984. *Current Management:* Rathausstrasse 5, 2300 Kiel, Federal Republic of Germany. *Address:* Rathausstrasse 5, 2300 Kiel, Germany.

DEASEY Michael Keith, b. 25 Jan 1947, Sydney, Australia. Cathedral Organist. m. Antonia Harman, 30 Aug 1980, 1 son, 2 daughters. *Education:* Diploma MusEd, New South Wales Conservatorium of Music, 1964-67; Royal School of Church Music, United Kingdom, 1969-71; FTCL, 1969; LRAM, 1970; ARCO, 1971; ARCM, 1969; Bachelor of Education (Music), Sydney, 1984. *Career:* Assistant Organist, St Andrew's Cathedral, Sydney, 1967-69; Organist, Choirmaster, Selsdon Parish Church, Surrey, England, 1969-72; Organist and Choirmaster, St Peter's Brockville, Ontario, Canada, 1973-80; Organist and Master of Choristers, St Andrew's Cathedral, Sydney, 1981-; Director of Music, Cathedral Choir School, Sydney, 1981-; Recitals in Australia, New Zealand, England, Iceland, Canada, USA. *Hobbies:* Tennis; Crosscountry skiing. *Address:* St Andrew's Cathedral, Sydney Square, Sydney, New South Wales 2000, Australia.

DEATHRIDGE John, b. 21 October 1944, Birmingham, England. Musicologist. *Education:* Studied at Oxford University with Egon Wellesz and Frederic Sternfeld. *Career:* Lived in Germany during 1970s, working as Conductor, Organist and Broadcaster; Fellow of King's College, Cambridge 1983; Visiting Professor at Princeton University, 1990-91, University of Chicago, 1992. *Publications:* Study of Wagner's Sketches for Rienzi, 1977; New Grove Wagner, with Carl Dahlhaus, 1984; Verzeichnis der Musikalischen Werke Richard Wagners und ihre Quellen, with Martin Geck and Egon Voss, 1986; Editor, the Wagner Companion, Essays on Wagner's Life and Work, 1986. *Address:* King's College, Music Department, Cambridge, England.

DEAVER John Austin, b. 29 Mar 1952, Staunton, Virginia, USA. Church Musician; Organ Recitalist; Accompanist. *Education:* AB, Davidson College, Davidson, North Carolina; MM, Peabody Conservatory of Music of Johns Hopkins University; DMA, College-Conservatory of Music of University of Cincinnati. *Career:* Director of Music/Organist at Trinity Episcopal Church, Covington, Kentucky, 1980-; Organist-Choirmaster at Convent of the Transfiguration, Cincinnati, Ohio, 1981-; A founder and frequent performer on Midday Musical Menu luncheon concert series, Trinity Church, Covington, Kentucky. *Publication:* The Organ Works of Wilmer Hayden Welsh, 1985. *Honour:* Richard Ross Award, 1974. *Memberships:* Association of Anglican Musicians; Cincinnati Chapter of American Guild of Organists (Subdean 1992-1994); Diocese of Lexington Liturgical Commission. *Hobbies:* Swimming; Golf; Reading. *Address:* 2670 Lehman Road, Apt 705D, Cincinnati, OH 45204, USA.

DECADT Jan, b. 21 June 1914, Ypres, Belgium. Composer; Teacher. *Education:* Studied with J Ryelandt, Ghent Conservatory; with J Absil, Brussels. *Career:* Director, Harelbeke Music School, 1945-57; Professor of Fugue, Antwerp Conservatory, 1957-71; Teacher of Composition, Ghent Conservatory, 1971-. *Compositions:* Variations on Sir Halewijn for Orchestra, 1943; Ballade on a Tree for Soprano, Flute, Oboe and String Trio, 1945; Habanera for Orchestra, 1947; Piano Concerto, 1953; Symphony, 1958; Constant Permeke, cantata, 1963; Monographie musicale d'un grand peintre for Orchestra, 1964; Concerto Overture for Flute,

Oboe and String Orchestra, 1967; Concertante Fantasia for Oboe and Piano, 1970; Saxophone Concerto, 1972; Quartet for Saxophones, 1974; Wens-album for Flute and Clarinet, 1976; Kleine fanfare for Brass Band, 1981; Zomeravond for Medium Voice and Piano, 1986. *Address:* c/o Koninklijk Muziekconservatorium van Ghent, Hoogpoort 64, Ghent, Belgium.

DECKER Franz-Paul, b. 22 June 1928, Cologne, Germany. Conductor. *Education:* Studied with P Jarnach and E Papst, Cologne Hochschule fur Musik; Studied with E Bucken and K Fellerer, University of Cologne. *Career:* Music Director, Krefeld, 1946-50; 1st Conductor, State Opera Wiesbaden, 1950-53, Municipal Music Director 1953-56, Wiesbaden; Generalmusikdirektor, Bochum, 1956-64; Chief Conductor, Rotterdam Philharmonic Orchestra, 1962-68; Music Director, Montreal Symphony Orchestra, 1967-75; Principal Guest Conductor and Music Adviser, Calgary (Alberta) Philharmonic Orchestra, 1975-77; Artistic Adviser, Winnipeg Symphony Orchestra, 1981-82; Principal Guest Conductor, New Zealand Symphony Orchestra, Wellington, 1980-89; Music Director, Barcelona Symphony Orchestra, 1986-; Chief Conductor New Zealand Symphony, 1990-; Principal Guest Conductor, National Arts Centre Orchestra Ottawa, 1991-. *Recordings:* For CBC; Deutsche Grammophon; EMI. *Honours:* Professor D.H.C.; Bundesverdienstkreuz 1st Class Germany; Herscheppend Schep ik Roquette Pinto Medal, Brazil; Medal, Holland; Queen Elizabeth II Jubilee Medal, Canada. *Address:* 486 B Mount Pleasant Avenue, Westmount, Quebec, Canada.

DECKER Willy, b. 1950, Cologne, Germany. Stage Director. *Career:* Produced the world premiere of Henze's Pollicino at Montepulciano, 1980; Wozzeck at Covent Garden and Arabella for the Lyric Opera of Chicago, 1984; Le Nozze di Figaro in Brussels and Così fan Tutte at Drottningholm, 1985; Capriccio for the Maggio Musicale Fiorentino, 1987; Rigoletto, Turandot and Carmen for the Teatro Colon in Bogota; Cologne productions include A Midsummer Night's Dream, Faust, La Finta Giardiniera, Barbe Bleue (1990), Der fliegende Holländer (1991) and Billy Budd (1992); Figaro, Cosi fan Tutte and the world premiere of Macbeth by Antonio Bibalo for the Norwegian Opera; Bonn Opera 1990-91, Il Barbiere di Siviglia and Orfeo ed Euridice; Giulio Cesare by Handel for Scottish Opera, 1992; Other productions (in Germany) include Don Giovanni, Der Freischütz, Cenerentola, Der Rosenkavalier and Ariadne auf Naxos; Also engaged for: Così fan Tutte, Den Norske Opera, Oslo, 1991; Orfeo, Bonn State Theatre, 1991; Macbeth Revival, Den Norske Opera, Dresden, 1992; Das Schloss, Berlin, 1992; Eugene Onegen, Cologne, Wozzeck, Amsterdam, 1993; Barber of Seville, 1993; Peter Grimes, Brussels, 1994; Soldaten, Dresden & Das Schloss, Munich, forthcoming. *Address:* c/o Haydn Rawstron Ltd, PO Box 654, London SE26 4DZ, England.

DECOUST Michel, b. 19 Nov 1936, Paris, France. Composer. m. Irène Jarsky, 1969, 1 daughter. *Education:* Studied Paris Conservatory under Louis Fourestier, Olivier Messiaen, Darius Milhaud; Studies with Stockhausen and Pousseur, Cologne, 1964, 1965, conducting studies with Boulez, Basle, 1965. *Career:* Professor of Composition, Dartington College summer school, England, 1967-69; Set up regional French orchestra, Pays de la Loire, 1967-70; In charge of musical activities, Maisons de la Culture, Rennes and Nevers, 1970-72; Founder, Director, Pantin Conservatory, 1972-76; Head, Education Department, IRCAM, 1976-79; Chief Inspector for Musical Research, Ministry of Culture and Communications, 1979-; His Music performed at various festivals, Europe, Israel, New York, also broadcast on radio, Italy, Germany, Spain, England, Greece, Switzerland, Poland, USA. *Compositions:* Orchestral, small ensemble, wind band and vocal works; instrumental solos and duos, electroacoustic music, etc; Recent works include: Si et Si Seulement, orchestra, 1972; L'application des Lectrices aux Champs, Soprano & orchestra, 1977; Eole, flute quartet, 1985; Figures II, bassoon, double bass,

1986; Marbre, magnetic tape, 1986; Sept Chansons Erotiques, settings of poems for soprano and piano, 1986; Bleus (text Blaise Cendrars), soprano and piano, 1986; De la Gravitation Suspendue des Memoires, orchestra, 1986; Je qui d'Autre, 3 voices & ensemble, 1987; Sonate à quatre, 1987; Sinfonietta, 1983, for 10 instruments; Sonnet, 1985 for 15 instruments; One plus One Equals Four, Piano Percussion, 1988; Spectre for Wind Band, 1978; Interphone, Magnetic Tape; Les Galeries de Pierre, Alto Solo, 1984; Onde, Five Blaser 1982; Olos, Saxo Solo, 1983; le Cygne, flute Solo, 1982; Lierre, 12 Cordes, 1986; Café-theatre, Chant-piano, 1985. *Recording:* Relevé d'Esquisse, le Cygne, sinfonietta, Harmonia Mundi France, HMC 5152 - HM 57. *Publications:* Cahiers Perspectives, 1987. *Membership:* President, ISCM France. *Hobbies:* Nature; Architecture. *Address:* 35 Rue de Clichy, 75009, Paris, France.

DECSENYI Janos, b. 24 Mar 1927, Budapest, Hungary. Composer. *Education:* Studied composition with Rezsö Sugar, Budapest Conservatory, 1948-52; with Endre Szervanszky, Budapest Academy of Music, 1952-56. *Career:* Hungarian Radio, Budapest, 1951-, latterly as Head, Department of Serious Music and Director, Electronic Music Studio. *Compositions:* Stage: An Absurd Story, ballet, 1962; The Nose, pantomime, 1979; Orchestral: Divertimento for Harpsichord and Chamber Orchestra, 1959; Csontvary Pictures, 1967; Melodiae hominis for Chamber Orchestra, 1969; Thoughts-by Day, by Night, 1971; Commentaries on Marcus Aurelius for 16 Solo Strings, 1973; Double for Chamber Orchestra, 1974; Variations for Piano and Orchestra, 1976; Concerto boemo, 1976; Concerto grosso for Chamber Orchestra, 1978; Who Understands the Speech of Crickets? for Chamber Orchestra and Tape, 1983; Cello Concerto, 1984; The Third One for 15 Solo Strings, 1985; I. Symphony, 1986; II. Symphony, 1993; Vocal: Love for Soprano and Orchestra, 1957; Metamorfosi for Soprano and Piano, 1964; Shakespeare Monologues for bass and Piano, 1968; The Plays of Thought, cantata for Soprano and Chamber Orchestra, 1972; Roads, etudes for Soprano and Piano, 1979; Twelfth Symphony of S.W. for Soprano and Percussion, 1980; Chamber: String Trio, 1955; Sonatina pastorale for Flute and Piano, 1956; Sonatina for Piano, 1962; String Quartet, 1978; Old Hungarian Texts, for Soprano, Bass and Chamber Ensemble, 1992; Choral music; Incidental music for theatre, films and radio; Electronic: Stones, 1987; Prospero's Island, 1989; Birds of the Cathedral, 1991, Pedagogical pieces. *Recordings:* Several compositions recorded. *Honour:* Merited Artist, Hungarian Republic. *Address:* c/o Editio Musica Budapest, P O B 322, H-1370 Budapest, Hungary.

DED Jan, b. 22 June 1936, Plzen, Czechoslovakia. Composer. *Education:* Konservator Plzen. *Compositions:* Four songs on the words of folk poetry, chorus, Op.1 1962; Wistful Variationes -- small ballet for 5 dancers, 5 musicians and a reciter, Op.38; Short Czech Mass for combined chorus and symphonic orchestra, Op.42; Chamber compositions, instructive compositions for children and youth; Great Czech-Latin Mass to Our Lady for combined chorus, soloists, symphonic orchestra and organ, Op.44 1992. *Recordings:* Sonatina for soprano recorder and guitar, Op.17 1979; New compositions just recorded. *Memberships:* Music Center of West Bohemia Plzen; Czech Music Society Praha. *Hobby:* Growing Flowers. *Address:* Zelenohorska 2, 31704 Plzen, Czech Republic.

DEDEN Otto, b. 19 Nov 1925, Amsterdam, Netherlands. Composer; Conductor; Organist; Choirmaster. m. S.A.M. van Dijk, 4 children. *Education:* High School of Church Music, Utrecht; Studied composition with Henk Badings. *Career:* Appearances in church services on radio and TV; Choral concerts with various male, female and mixed choirs. *Compositions:* 29 Masses; 50 Motets; Te Deum; Hymns; Ballads; Oratorios; Arrangements of folk songs (commissions); Dirge, Soprano with Organ, 1993; 5 Epigrams, choir, 1992; cinq Aphorismes choir, 1992; two ballards, 1992; Mysteria; Kain; 4 Cantates for mixed choir and orchestra and solo; Magnificat for mixed choir, organ, flute and alto solo; Several cantatas for choir and orchestra preludes and fugas for great organ; Requiem for a Killed Soldier . *Recording:* Raamconcerto, 1973. *Honours:* Ballade v.d. Bezemsteel (male voices), Maastricht, 1958; Requiem for a Killed Soldier. *Memberships:* Royal Order of Knighthood of Oranje Nassau, 1982; Order of Knighthood of Gregorius Magnus, Vatican; Medal of Honour of the City of Dordtecht, Netherlands. *Hobby:* Painting. *Address:* Polluxhof 16, Dordrecht, Netherlands.

DEDIU Constantin, b. 25 Dec 1932, Dragusani, Bacau, Romania. Musicologist; Journalist; Editor; Artistic Director. m. Emilia Babii, 31 July 1966, 1 daughter. *Education:* Iasi Music High School; Cluj G.H. Dima Music Academy. *Career:* Founder, Chief Editor, Music, Iasi RTV Post, 1958-82; Artistic Director, Iasi Romanian Opera, 1982-; Freelance Music Journalist. *Compositions:* About 50 Musical Pieces including Lied, Mass Choruses, Romances, Light Music. *Publications:* Din Culisele Muzicii, 1980; Broadcasting Cycles at Iasi RTV, 1982; Romanian Composers of Yesterday and Today, 60 Broadcasts; The Youth of Music, The Music of the Youth, 50 broadcasts. *Contributions to:* The Music; The Chronicle; Iasi Daily Flame; Columnist various journals. *Honours:* Cultural Merit Award, 1971; The Workers Medal, 1966. *Memberships:* Romanian Society of Composers & Musicologists; Romanian Society of Journalists; Committee, Literature & Art Theory & History, IASI Section, Romanian Academy. *Hobby:* Chess. *Address:* Str. Prof. Tafrali, Nr. 4, Iasi 6600, Romania.

DEDMAN Malcolm John, b. 3 Nov 1948, London, England. Composer; Teacher. m. Janet Dale nee Andrews, 3 Apr 1982, 2s. *Education:* Studied Violin and Singing, Private Tuition; Studied Composition at Guildhall School of Music and Drama with Patric Standford. *Debut:* Performance of 3 Dance Episodes by Andresier Ensemble at Wigmore Hall, London. *Career:* Major First Performances: Christmas Cantata, Birmingham, Birmingham Festival Choral Society; String Quartet, Purcell Room, London, Amsterdam String Quartet; Piano Sonata No.2, Purcell Room, London, Richard Deering; Two Reflections for Piano, Purcell Room, London, Richard Deering. *Compositions:* Prayer for Peace, Guitar Duo; Duo Sonata for Viola and Piano; Concerto for Oboe and Strings; Cantus Conductus for Flute, Vibraphone, Violin and Cello; Sonata for Oboe and Piano. *Recordings:* Record of Mixed Instrumental Music by Malcolm Dedman includes: 6 Dance Episodes for Oboe, Guitar and Piano, Spectrum for Vibraphone, Meditation NoI. for Organ, Piano Sonata No.1. *Publications:* Electronic Instruments for the Serious Musician, Composer Magazine 1984; A Dweller in the Highest Paradise, Composers Forum. *Honours:* First in Brent Music and Dance Festival Piano Sonatina 1970; Second in Stroud International Composers Competition, Duo for Tenor and Guitar 1974; Second in Rencontres Internationales de Chant Choral, Anthem for SATB Choir 1985. *Memberships:* Composers Guild of Great Britain; Incorporated Society of Musicians; Performing Right Society. *Hobbies:* Study World Religions; Use of Music to express need for world peace. *Address:* 27 Pentland Avenue, Thornbury, Bristol BS12 2YB, England.

DEEGAN Robert, b. 2 Oct 1948, Blackburn, Lancashire, England. Harpsichord maker and Restorer. *Education:* Wolverhampton College of Art, BA 1970. *Career:* Apprentice to Robert Davies, Harpsichord-maker, Own Workshop, 1977-; Tutor in Harpsichord making, London College of Furniture, 1980-82; Presented lecture Harpsichord Building, University of W. Australia, 1984; Exhibited, Festival van Vlaanderen, Bruges, Edinburgh International Harpsichord Week, British Crafts Centre; Tage Alter Musik, Herne, Germany; Sunderland Arts Touring Exhibition; Crafts Council Musical Instruments Exhibition, London, 1986; Festival Oude Musick, Utrecht, 1989; Stage, TV and Radio etc, 1983, Woman's Hour, Radio 4; TV Look Northwest, 1985; Radio TV Hong Kong, 1988. Instruments used in several BBC broadcasts. *Honours:*

Toured USA studying collections and makers of Harpsichords. *Memberships:* Member, National Early Music Association. *Address:* Robert Deegan Harpsichords, Tonnage Warehouse, St George's Quay, Lancaster, LA1 1RB, England.

DEERING Richard Jon, b. 15 July 1947, Essex, England. Pianist; Lecturer; Adjudicator. m. Emma Budgen, 4 November 1992, 1s. 1 d. (by previous marriage). *Education:* Trinity College of Music; Guildhall School of Music; Studied with Frank Merrick and Peter Wallfisch. *Debut:* Wigmore Hall, 2 March 1973, works by Bach, Schoenberg, Webern. *Career:* Performances worldwide in over eighty countries; Concerts, Lectures, Seminars, Radio and TV Recordings worldwide specialising in British Music with many premieres; Also performed on music cruises for P & O; Adjudicates at competitions worldwide and similarly examines for ABRSM worldwide. *Recordings:* English Piano Music; Beatles Piano Concerto with Tokyo Symphony Orchestra; Sonatinas of Charles Camilleri; Lutyens Piano Works. *Publications:* Currently engaged on a book for publication in 1995, British and Irish Piano Music since 1950; Regular contributor to ISM Journal and Classical Music Magazine. *Honour:* Elected Member of Royal Philharmonic Society in 1981 for Distinguished Services to British Music. *Memberships:* British Music Society; Incorporated Society of Musicians; British Federation of Music Festivals. *Hobbies:* Cricket; Theatre; Jigsaw Puzzles; Cycling. *Address:* Flat 5, 60 Sinclair Road, London W14 ONH, England.

DEFLO Gilbert, b. 22 September 1944, Menen, Belgium. Stage Director. *Education:* Studied at Brussels and in Milan with Giorgio Strehler. *Debut:* Love of Three Oranges, Frankfurt 1974. *Career:* Staged Boris Godunov at Frankfurt then Pelleas et Melisande and Ligeti's le Grand Macabre at Hamburg; Further productions of Zemlinsky's Der Traumgorge at Nuremberg, World Premiere, 1980, the premiere of Thijl by Gilse at Amsterdam and The Woman Without a Shadow for Welsh National Opera, 1981; At the Theatre de la Monnaie, Brussels from 1981 has staged Idomeneo, Don Carlos, Tristan und Isolde, Der Fliegende Holländer, The Cunning Little Vixen, Cendrillon, Der Rosenkavalier and Simon Boccanegra; Premiere of La Forêt by Liebermann at Geneva 1987; Production of Aida for Scottish Opera seen also at the Royal Opera Copenhagen, 1991; Produced The Queen of Spades at Barcelona, 1992. *Address:* c/o Theatre Royale de la Monnaie, Leopoldstrasse 4, B-1000 Brussels, Belgium.

DEGEN Helmut, b. 14 Jan 1911, Aglasterhausen, Baden, Germany. Composer. m. Maria Hoefer, 1 Mar 1937, 2 sons. *Education:* Music High School, Cologne, Germany, 1930-32; High School for Music, 1932-33; University of Bonn, Musikwissenschaft, 1933-36. *Debut:* Duisburg, 1937. *Career Includes:* Composer, Germany & abroad; Professor, Composition & Theory; Concerts & radio broadcasts. *Compositions Include:* Works for large orchestra, choir, chamber music including string quartet, piano trio & wind quartet; Instrumental music for organ, cello, viola, violin, flute, etc. *Contributions to:* Various professional journals. *Memberships:* Deutscher Komponistenverband; GEMA. *Hobby:* Science of mountains, including book. *Address:* Postfach 1140, D-7218 Trossingen, Germany.

DEGRADA Francesco, b. 23 May 1940, Milan, Italy. Musicologist; Professor; Writer; Music Editor. *Education:* Diploma piano, 1961, composition diploma, 1965, conducting, Milan Conservatory; Arts degree, University of Milan, 1964. *Career:* Teacher, Bolzano Conservatory, Brescia Conservatory; Lecturer, 1964-76, Professor of Music History, 1976-, Director of the Arts Department, 1983-, University of Milan; Teacher, Milan Conservatory, 1966-73; Founder-Director and Harpsichordist, Complesso Barocco di Milano, 1967-76; Consultant to the publisher G Ricordi, 1971-; Member, editorial boards of critical editions of Vivaldi, Pergolesi and Verdi. *Publications:* Al gran sole carico d'amore. Per un nuovo teatro musicale, 1974 2nd edition, 1977; Sylvano Bussotti e il suo teatro, 1976; Antonio Vivaldi da Venezia all'Europa, 1977; Il palazzo incantato. Studi sulla tradizione del melodramma dal Barocco al Romanticismo, 2 volumes, 1979; Vivaldi veneziano europeo, 1980; edited Studi Pergolesiani/Pergolesi Studies, 2 volumes, 1986, 1988; Andrea Gabrieli e il suo tempo, 1988. *Contributions to:* Many articles in scholarly journals. *Membership:* Societa Italiana di Musicologia. *Address:* Via de Amicis 33, 20123 Milan, Italy.

DEHNERT Edmund John, b. 15 Feb. 1931, Chicago, Illinois, USA. Musicologist; Composer; Pianist. m. Donna Marie Wroblewski, 3 sons, 1 daughter. *Education:* BA, St Mary's of the Lake University, Illinois, 1952; BMus 1955, MMus 1956, DePaul University, Chicago; PhD, University of Chicago, 1963. *Career includes:* Pianist/lecturer, public broadcasting system, Chicago, 1967-; Research/scriptwriter, WTTW, WXXW television stations, Chicago, 1969; Radio broadcasts; Fellow, National Humanities Institute, University of Chicago, 1976-77. *Compositions:* For the Dead Children of Auschwitz, 1975; Polonaise, Krakow, 1974; Polonaise for piano, 1975; Pentatonic Sketches for Orchestra, 1975-76; The Consciousness of Music Wrought by Musical Notation, in Beyond the Two Cultures, essays in Science, Literature and Technology; The Myth of Sysiphus: Concerto for Trombone and Orchestra, 1979; Ternion: Trio for Strings, 1980; That Time of Year: Symphonic Poem for Orchestra, 1976. *Publications:* Co-author, Polish Music, The Spirit That Never Dies, 1975; Dialectic of Technology & Culture, in Languages of Creativity, studies in science & culture, volume 2, 1986. *Hobbies:* Chess; Bridge. *Address:* 1121 Harvard Terrace, Evanston, IL 60202, USA.

DEKANY Bela, b. 22 Apr. 1928, Budapest, Hungary. Violinist. m. Dorothy Browning, 22 June 1961, 1 son, 1 daughter. *Education:* Franz Liszt Academy, Budapest, studied with Professor Weiner, Academy for Music, Vienna, Austria, studied with Professor E. Morawec. *Debut:* Budapest, 1947. *Career:* Has given recitals and broadcast performances; Soloist with orchestras in Hungary, Austria, Switzerland, Australia, Great Britain; Formed Dekany String Quartet, Netherlands, 1960-68; Leader, BBC Symphony Orchestra, London, England, 1969-1992. *Recordings:* Haydn String Quartets with Dekany String Quartet. *Hobbies:* Reading; Table tennis; Walking. *Address:* 68 Woodside Avenue, London N6, England.

DEL BIANCO Tito, b. 3 July 1932, Trieste, Italy. Opera Singer (Dramatic Tenor). 1s. 1 d. *Education:* Studied with Augusta Rapetti Bassi in Trieste and with Renata Cotogni in Rome. *Debut:* New York, United States of America in Stabat Mater, G Rossini, Director Thomas Schippers 1965; In Italy as Otello, G Verdi, 8th Festival of Two World, S Poleto, Director T Schippers 1965. *Career:* As Otello in Otello, Teatro Regio Parma 1966-71; Bayerische Staatsoper Munchen 1973; May Festival Wiesbaden 1970; Festival Szeged, Hungary 1971; Festival Varna Bulgaria 1972; Maggio Musicale Florence 1980; As Calaf in Turandot, Naples 1965, Bologna 1969, Parma Regio 1970; Festival Torre del Lago Puccini 1971; As Radames in Aida Naples 1968; As Pollione in Norma, Genoa 1967; As Faone in Saffo Naples 1967; As Ismaele in Nabucco, Trieste 1969; As Canio in Pagliacci, Parma Regio 1969; Director of Studies Centre A Rapetti Bassi, Trieste; Professor, Music Academy, Conservatorio, in Trieste. *Recordings:* Numerous recordings. *Publications:* A Festival for Giuseppe Verdi in Prima Pagina, Parma, Italy, November 1981. *Honours:* Gold Medal Giuseppe Verdi Prize, Parma, 1967. *Hobbies:* Reading; Swimming. *Address:* c/o G Freudlsperger, Eschenweg 8, Elsbethen, Salzburg A-5061, Austria.

DEL GIUDICE Adriana, b. 27 February 1937, Bovino, Foggia, Italy. Teacher. *Education:* State School in Italy, Rome, Diploma in Arte Pubblicitaria; Royal Manchester College of Music, GRSM, ARMCM, Singing and Piano. *Career:* Assistant Music Teacher, Loreto College, Manchester; Music Teacher in Italian State Schools Lecturing on the Art of Teaching Music; Music included in Radio and Television Programmes of RAI. *Compositions:* Momenti Musicali; Il Gatto Che Scopri L'America, Musical for children, performed at Teatro Brancaccio of the Teatro Dell'Opera di Roma. *Publications:* Momenti Musicali 1988; Il Gatto Che Scopri L'America 1993. *Honours:* First Prize National Choral Competition for Schools, 1983, 84, 85; Medal Natale Di Roma 1993; Special Award from the Colombiadi, Genova 1993. *Hobbies:* Painting; Reading; Walking. *Address:* Via Benozzo Gozzoli, 24 00142 Rome, Italy.

DEL MAR Jonathan Rene, b. 7 Jan 1951, London, England. Conductor. *Education:* Scholar, MA, Music, Christ Church, Oxford, 1969-72; ARCM Diploma, Royal College of Music, 1976; Teatro La Fenice, 1976-77; Accademia S. Cecilia, Rome, 1977. *Career:* Conductor, Bournemouth Symphony Orchestra & orchestras in Denmark; Regular Broadcaster, Radio 3, with several of the BBC Orchestras; Performed with London Symphony Orchestra, Royal Philharmonic Orchestra, City of Birmingham Symphony Orchestra, English Northern Philharmonia, Royal Liverpool Philharmonic Orchestra. *Recording:* Urtext Edition of Beethoven Ninth Symphony for Hanover Band (Nimbus). *Publication:* The Text of Beethoven's Ninth Symphony, CUP, 1993. *Honours:* Semi-Finalist, Herbert von Karajan Conducting Competition; Prizes, Imperial Tobacco International Conductors Award, 1978, Nikolai Malko Competition, 1980, First Leeds Conductors Competition, 1984. *Contributions to:* Sunday Times; Tempo; ESTA Magazine. *Memberships:* Incorporated Society of Musicians; Dvořák Society. *Hobbies:* Numismatics; Autonumerology. *Address:* Oakwood, Crescent Lane, London, SW4.

DEL MONACO Giancarlo, b. 27 Dec 1943, Treviso, Italy. Stage Director. *Education:* Studied music and languages at Lausanne. *Debut:* Siracusa 1964, Samson and Dalila. *Career:* Assistant to Gunther Rennert, Wieland Wagner and Walter Felsenstein at Stuttgart 1965-68; Personal Assistant of the General Director of Vienna Staatsoper 1968-70, Principal Stage Director at Ulm 1970-73, Intendant at Kassel 1980-82 and Director of the Macerata Festival 1986-88; Intendant at Bonn from 1992; Staged Les Huguenots at Montpellier 1990 and at Barcelona, Roberto Devereux, the first of a projected trilogy of Donizetti's Tudor Operas; L'Elisir d'Amore at Helsinki 1991, followed by Metropolitan Opera debut with La Fanciulla del West; Further guest engagements at Bayerische Staatsoper, Zurich Opera and Vienna Staatsoper; Staged Montemezzi's L'Amore dei tre re at Kassel, 1992 and Otello at Reggio Emilia; Engaged for Madama Butterfly and Simon Boccanegra at the Metropolitan 1994-95. *Address:* c/o Oper der Stadt Bonn, Am Boselagerhof 1, 5300 Bonn, Germany.

DEL TREDICI David (Walter), b. 16 Mar. 1937, Cloverdale, California, USA. Composer; Teacher. *Education:* Studied piano as a youth; Took courses in composition with Seymour Shifrin, Andrew Imbrie, and Arnold Elston, University of California, Berkeley, BA, 1959, and with Earl Kim and Roger Sessions, Princeton University, MFA, 1963. *Career:* Debut as piano soloist with the San Francisco Symphony Orchestra at age 16; Pianist, Aspen (Colorado) Music Festival, 1958; Berkshire Music Center, Tanglewood, 1964, 1965; Composer-in-residence, Marlboro (Vermont) Music Festival, 1966, 1967; Teacher, Harvard University, 1966-72, State University of New York at Buffalo, 1973, Boston University, 1973-84, City College and Graduate School of the City University of New York, 1984-; Composer-in-residence, New York Philharmonic Orchestra, 1988-. *Compositions:* String Trio, 1959; I hear an Army for Soprano and String Quartet, after James Joyce, 1963-64; Night Conjure-Verse, after James Joyce, 1965; Syzygy for Soprano, Horn, and Chamber Ensemble, after James Joyce, 1966; The Last Gospel for Soprano, Chorus, Rock Group, and Orchestra, 1967, revised 1984; Pop-Pourri for Amplified Soprano, Mezzo-soprano ad libitum, Chorus, Rock Group, and Orchestra, 1968, revised 1973; An Alice Symphony,

after Lewis Carroll, 1969-76; Adventures Underground, after Lewis Carroll, 1971, revised 1977; Vintage Alice: Fantascene on A Mad Tea Party for Amplified Soprano, Folk Group, and Orchestra, after Lewis Carroll, 1972; Final Alice for Amplified Soprano and Orchestra, after Lewis Carroll, 1977-81; March to Tonality for Orchestra, 1983-85; Haddock's Eyes for Soprano and Chamber Ensemble, 1985-86. *Recordings:* Various compositions recorded. *Honours:* Guggenheim Fellowship, 1966; American Academy and Institute of Arts and Letters award, 1968; Naumberg Award, 1972; National Endowment for the Arts grants, 1973, 1974, 1984; Pulitzer Prize in Music, 1980; Friedheim Award, 1982; Various commissions. *Memberships:* Elected a member of the Institute of the American Academy and Institute of Arts and Letters, 1984. *Address:* ASCAP, ASCAP House, One Lincoln Plaza, New York, NY 10023, USA.

DEL VIVO Graziano, b. 1 November 1937, Florence, Italy. Singer (Bass). *Education:* Studied at Florence University and Conservatory. *Debut:* Spoleto 1961, as Ramphis in Aida. *Career:* Teatro Regio Parma, as Onofrio in Galuppi's I tre amantio Ridicoli 1964 and as Achillas in Handel's Giulio Cesare and Sparafucile in Rigoletto; Florence 1965 in Billy Budd and Katerina Ismailova, returning in Robert le Diable by Meyerbeer 1968 and Spontini's La Vestale, 1970; La Scala Milan as Pluto in Casella's Orfeo; Edinburgh Festival, 1969 and 1972; Sang in The Nose by Shostakovich at Rome and at Genoa and Naples in the Verdi Requiem; Pisa, 1973 in a centenary concert for Titta Ruffo. *Address:* c/o Teatro Comunale di Forenze, Via Solferino 15, 50123 Florence, Italy.

DELACÔTE Jacques, b. 16 Aug 1942, Remiremont, Vosges, France. Conductor. m. Maria Lucia Alvarez Machado. *Education:* Paris Conservatory; Studied with Hans Swarowsky, Vienna Academy of Music. *Debut:* New York Philharmonic Orchestra. *Career:* Guest conductor, Cleveland Orchestra, San Francisco Symphony, Orchestre de Paris, Orchestre National de France, London Symphony Orchestra, Scottish National Orchestra, Berlin Radio Symphony Orchestra, Bavarian Radio Orchestra, Cologne Radio Symphony Orchestra, Vienna Philharmonic Orchestra, BBC London, London Philharmonic, Vienna State Opera, Royal Opera House, Covent Garden, London, Paris Opera, Hamburg State Opera, National Orchestra of Belgium, Scottish Chamber Orchestra, English Chamber Orchestra, Danish Royal Orchestra, Copenhagen, Tokyo Philharmonic Orchestra; Bavarian State Opera; Pittsburgh Opera; Israel Philharmonic Orchestra; Teatro Liceo, Barcelona; Teatro Real, Madrid; Teatro Colon, Buenos Aires; Théâtre of La Monnaie Brussels; Opera House, Zürich; Scottish Opera, Glasgow; Welsh National Opera, Cardiff; English National Opera, Coliseum. *Recordings:* For Angel-EMI. *Honour:* 1st prize, Dimitri Mitropoulos Competition, New York, 1971. *Hobby:* Chess. *Address:* Neutorgasse 9/9, 1010 Vienna, Austria.

DELAY Dorothy, b. 31 Mar 1917, Medicine Lodge, Kansas, USA. Teacher of Violin. *Education:* Studied at Oberlin College, 1933-34 then Violin Studies with Michael Press at Michigan State University, Hans Letz and Louis Persinger at Juilliard Graduate School of Music, Diploma, 1941. *Career:* Taught at Juilliard from, 1947; Further posts at Sarah Lawrence College, 1948-87, Meadowmount School of Music, Westport, 1948-70 and Aspen School of Music from 1971; Starling Professor of Violin at University of Cincinnati College-Conservatory of Music from 1974, New England Conservatory of Music at Boston 1978-87; Master classes in the United States of America and abroad; Students have included Shlomo Mintz, Itzhak Perlman, Cho-Liang Lin, Midori, Nigel Kennedy, Kyoko Takezawa, Sarah Chang, Gil Shaham. *Honours:* Artist Teacher Award of American String Teachers Association, 1975; Honorary DMus from Oberlin College, 1981; DMus from Michigan State University, and University of Colorado. *Address:* c/o Juilliard School of Music, Violin Faculty, 60 Lincoln Center Plaza, New York, NY 10023, USA.

DELDEN Lex (Alex) Van, b. 21 June 1947, Amsterdam, Netherlands. Actor; Singer (Tenor). *Education:* Drama School, Amsterdam, 1966-67; Private singing lessons with Jan Keizer, Marianne Blok, and Andrew Field. *Debut:* 1967. *Career includes:* Theatre: The Diary of Anne Frank (F Goodrich and A Hackett); Butterflies Are Free (Leonard Gershe); The Circle (W Somerset Maugham); Journey's End (R C Sheriff); Opera: Gianni Schicchi (G Puccini); Turandot (F Busoni); Die Fledermaus (Johann Strauss); Il Ritorno d'Ulisse (Claudio Monteverdi); Ariadne auf Naxos (Richard Strauss); Television: Small Souls (Louis Couperus); Character (F Bordewijk); Old People And The Things That Pass (Louis Couperus); Saint Joan (George Bernard Shaw); A Kiss, A Fond Embrace (Joan Lingard); Coronation Street (various authors); Unity (John Mortimer); Footsteps of Fate (Louis Couperus); Operation Julie (Gerry O'Hara); Bluebell (Paul Wheeler); Films: Soldier of Orange (director, Paul Verhoeven); Revolution (director, Hugh Hudson); John and Yoko (director, Sandor Stern). *Compositions include:* Active as composer for theatre: Romeo and Juliet (W Shakespeare); Dance of Death (A Strindberg); The Spanish Brabantine (Bredero). *Memberships:* British Actors' Equity Association; The Actors Institute; The Anti-Apartheid Movement; Performers Against Racism; Amnesty International. *Hobbies:* Music; Painting; Sculpture; Architecture; Literature. *Address:* c/o The Spotlight, London, England.

DELLA CASA Lisa, b. 2 Feb 1919, Burgdorf, Switzerland. Singer (Soprano). m. Dragan Debeljevic. *Education:* Studied with Margarete Haeser in Zurich. *Debut:* Solothun-Biel 1941, as Madama Butterfly. *Career:* City Theatre, Zurich, 1943-50, as Pamina, Gilda and Serena in Porgy and Bess, and in the premiere of Willy Burkhard's Die schwarze Spinne; Joined Vienna Staatsoper 1947; Salzburg Festival from 1947, as Zdenka in Arabella, the Countess in Capriccio, Mozart's Donna Elvira, Countess and Pamina, Ariadne, Chrysothemis, Octavian, the Marschallin and in the premiere of Von Einem's Der Prozess, 1953; Glyndebourne Festival, 1951, as the Countess in Le Nozze di Figaro; Bayreuth, 1952, as Eva in Die Meistersinger; Covent Garden and La Scala Milan from 1953; Metropolitan Opera, 1953-68, as Mozart's Countess, Donna Elvira, Arabella, Eva, the Marschallin and Octavian; Sang Arabella in a new production of Strauss's opera at Covent Garden, 1965; Guest appearances at Paris, Chicago, Buenos Aires, Munich and Rome; Retired, 1974. *Recordings:* Le Nozze di Figaro, Don Giovanni, Così fan Tutte, Arabella (Decca); Orfeo ed Euridice (RCA); La Vie Parisienne (Eurodisc). *Hobbies:* Collecting antiques and pictures. *Address:* c/o Staatsoper, Opernring 2, A-1010 Vienna, Austria.

DELLA PERGOLA Edith, b. 12 June 1918, Cluj, Rumania. Professor of Music. m. Luciano Della Pergola, 1 daughter. *Education:* Royal Conservatory of Music, Bucharest. *Debut:* December 1936. *Career:* Leading Soprano, various Roles including: La Bohème, Il Trovatore, Aida, Cavalleria Rusticana, The Queen of Spades, Eugene Onegin, Pagliacci, The Consul, Von Heute auf Morgen, Fledermaus, Zigeunerbaron, Bartered Bride; Appearances at Royal Opera, Bucharest, Cluj, Staatsoper, Vienna; Stadttheater Zurich; Teatro Verdi, Trieste; Teatro S. Carlo, Naples; Theatre Flamand, Brussels, etc; Professor, Music, Director, McGill Opera Studio. *Honours:* Cultural Merit, King Michael I of Roumania, 1945; La Société Des Concerts Des Ecoles Juives Populaires et des Ecoles Peretz, Montreal. *Address:* 2 Westmount Square, Apt 207, Westmount, Quebec H3Z 2S4, Canada.

DELLER Mark Damian, b. 27 Sept 1938, St Leonards-on-Sea, England. Singer (Counter Tenor). m. Shelagh Elizabeth Benson, 3 sons. *Education:* Chorister, Canterbury Cathedral; Choral Scholar, St John's College, Cambridge. *Career:* Lay Vicar, Salisbury Cathedral, 1965-68; Founder and Director, Guildhall Winter Concerts, 1962; Artistic Director, 1st Festival of the Arts, Salisbury, 1967; Vicar-Choral, St Paul's Cathedral 1969-73; Choral Conductor; Began recording

with father Alfred Deller, 1962; Joined Deller Consort in early 1960s; has toured extensively in Europe, USA, Canada and South America, as member of Deller Consort and as solo singer; Director of Deller Consort from 1979; Director of Stour Music and of Canterbury Festival. *Recordings:* As member of Deller Consort, the Accademia Monteverdiana and as solo singer for Vanguard, Argo and Nonesuch labels; Purcell's The Fairy Queen, King Arthur and The Indian Queen (Harmonia Mundi). *Hobbies:* Gardening; Watching Cricket (Kent Supporter); Walking. *Address:* 2, Rural Terrace, Wye, Ashford, Kent, England.

DELLO JOIO Justin Norman, b. 18 Oct 1915, New York City, New York, USA. Composer. *Education:* BM, MM, Doctoral candidate, Juilliard School of Music, New York. *Career:* Currently, Professor of Composition, New York University; Works for orchestra, chamber orchestra, string quartet, vocal music, solo piano; Works performed by Detroit Symphony Orchestra, Juilliard Orchestra with Sixten Ehrling, members of the Mendelssohn String Quartet, and Primavera String Quartet; Piano Sonata premiered in National Gallery of Arts, Washington, District of Columbia, (also broadcast); Collaborated with American novelist John Gardner on opera The Holy Sinner. *Recording:* String Quartet No 1, Primavera String Quartet. *Publications:* Sonata for Piano, Theodore Presser Co, 1986; Musica Humana, Symphonic Poem for Orchestra, G. Schirmer Ass. Music. *Honours:* Charles Ives Scholarship, National Institute and American Academy for the Arts; Grants: New York State Council on the Arts, 1983; National Endowment for the Arts, 1985; New York Foundation for the Arts, 1986. *Address:* c/o Ascap, Ascap House, One Lincoln Plaza, New York, NY 10023, USA.

DELOGU Gaetano, b. 14 Apr 1934, Messina, Italy. Conductor. *Education:* Studied music, University of Catania, Law Degree, 1958; Studied conducting with Franco Ferrara, Rome and Venice. *Career:* Guest conductor, Italian Radio, Rome, Milan, Turin and Naples; New York Philharmonic Orchestra and National Symphony Orchestra, Washington, DC, USA, 1968-69; Conductor, Teatro Massimo, Palermo, Italy, 1975-78; Music Director, Denver Symphony Orchestra, USA, 1979-86; Guest Conductor with various European and USA orchestras and opera companies. *Recordings:* For Classics for Pleasure; Supraphon, including Haydn's Symphonies Nos.83 and 101, Mahler's 1st Symphony and Hindemith's Symphonic Metamorphosis and Nobilissima Visione. *Honours:* 1st prize, Young Conductors' Competition, Florence, 1964; Dimitri Mitropoulos Competition, New York, 1968. *Address:* c/o Harold Holt Ltd, 31 Sinclair Road, London W14 0NS, England.

DELVAUX Albert, b. 31 May 1913, Louvain, Belgium. Director, Professor, Music. m. Fernande Tassignon, 4 Apr 1945, 2 sons, 1 daughter. *Education:* Royal Conservatory, Liège (Diploma of Virtuosity on Violincello); Higher Diploma, Chamber Music; 1st Prize, Harmony, Counterpoint and fugue and history of music. *Career:* Head, Counterpoint, Royal Conservatory, Liège, 1945; Professor, Conservatory of Louvain and Tirlemont Academy until 1945; Honorary Director, St Nicolas Academy, 1945-78; Honorary Professor, Brussels Royal Conservatory until 1978. *Compositions:* Symphony Orchestra: Scherzo, Poème, Symphonique Suite, Variations, Miniatures, Sinfonia II, Sinfonia Burlesa I, Mouvement Symphonique, Sinfonie III, Concerto I and II for violin, Sinfonia IV, Capriccio for Orchestra; Chamber Orchestra: Esquisses, Concerto da Camera I and II, 5 Bagatelles, Introduttione e allegro, Sinfonia Concertaute for Violin and Alto; Concerto for Violin and Violincello, Concerto I and II for Violoncello; Prelude for Flute; Concerto for Viola, etc. *Recordings:* Sinfonia Burlesca; Esquisses; Trio No. 2, Sonata a quattro, Concerto for oboe, clarinet, bassoon and flute. *Hobbies:* Reading; Gardening. *Address:* Kwadeplas 3, 9180 Belsele, Belgium.

DELZ Christoph, b. 3 Jan 1950, Basel, Switzerland. Pianist; Composer. *Education:* Teaching and Concert

Diploma for Piano; Musical Studies in Cologne, Piano with Alois Kontarsky, Composition with Karlheinz Stockhausen and Conducting with Volker Wangenheim; Studied Composition with Henri Pousseur in Liege. *Career:* Worked in Electronic Studio of Cologne Academy of Music 1979-81; Studied German and Philosophy at University of Cologne at same time; Lived in Cologne until 1989 and now living in Riehen near Basle; As Pianist has taken part in many first performances of works by contemporary composers including Klarenz Barlow, Mauricio Kagel and Claude Vivier; His choral works and most of his orchestral pieces have been performed or have received their first performances by BBC Symphony Orchestra and BBC Singers, among others at the Almeida Festival, Donaueschingen Festival and at Concerts by West German Radio in Cologne at Venice Biennial Festival, in Paris with the Ensemble Inter-Contemporain, Lucerne Music Festival, Zurich June Festival and at World Music Festival of International Society of New Music, Graz and Zurich; Repertoire includes music by Bach, Schumann, Liszt, Mussorgsky, Debussy, Janacek, Schonberg and Stockhausen. *Recordings:* Most of Delz's compositions have been recorded. *Address:* Sonneggstrasse 9, CH-4125 Riehen-Basel, Switzerland.

DEMARINIS Paul, b. 8 October 1948, Cleveland, Ohio, USA. Composer. *Education:* Studied at Antioch College, Ohio and with Robert Ashley at Mills College, Oakland. *Career:* Taught composition and computer at Mills College, 1973-78; Wesleyan University, 1979-81, San Francisco State University, 1987-89; Collaborations as a Performer with Robert Ashley and David Tudor in New York and Paris and at New Music America Concerts, 1980-85; Computer audio-graphic systems installed at Museum of Contemporary Art, Chicago and the Wadsworth Atheneum; Audio installations at the Exploratorium San Francisco and the Children's Museum Boston. *Compositions:* Computer-processed speech works Kokole, 1985 and I Want You, 1986; Installations Pygmy Gamelin, Paris, New York and Los Angeles, 1976-80; Music Room, Faultless Jamming, San Francisco and Boston, 1982-; Laser Disk, Eindhoven, Netherlands, 1989. *Address:* c/o San Francisco State University, Music Department, 1600 Holloway Avenue, San Francisco, CA 94132, USA.

DEMBSKI Stephen Michael, b. 13 Dec. 1949, Boston Massachusetts, USA. Composer; Associate Professor, Director, Advanced Composition Programme, University of Wisconsin at Madison, School of Music. *Education:* Diploma, Phillips Academy, Andover 1967; Clifton College, Bristol, England 1967-68; Ecole Normale de Musique, Paris 1971; BA, Antioch College 1973; MA, SUNY, Stony Brook, 1975; MFA 1977, PhD 1980, Princeton University. *Career:* Music Presented by: UNESCO, Denmark, 1978; 5th International Festival of Electronic-Acoustic Music: Bourges, France, 1976; International Society for Contemporary Music Bonn, 1976; New York New Music Ensemble; American Composers' Orchestra; Huddersfield Festival, England; Alan Feinberg; Ursula Oppens; Fred Sherry; Robert Black; Christopher Kendall. *Compositions:* Recorded: Spectra, Orchestra 1985; Stacked Deck, Large Chamber Ensemble 1979; Alta, Piano 1981; Alba, Chamber Ensemble, 1980; Trio, 1977; Digit, Clarinet and computer synthesized tape 1978; Pterodactyl, puo, 1974; Tender Buttons, puo, 1977; Music Published: Sunwood, Guitar 1976; The Show, 1986; Fantasy for solo flute, 1988; Sonata for violin and piano, 1987-88; On Ondine, piano, 1992; Three Scences from Elsaveta, opera, 1992. *Recordings:* Of Mere Being for Soprano & Large Orchestra; Alta, Alba, Digit, Spectra, Trio, Stacked Deck: CRI (CD). *Publications:* International Musical Lexicon, EMT, Paris 1980; Milton Babbitt - Words About Music, with Joseph N. Straus, University of Wisconsin Press. *Contributions to:* Articles: The Context of Composition, Theory & Practice, 1992; Misreading Martino, Perspectives of New Music, 1991. *Address:* 96 Perry Street, B-22, New York, NY 10014, USA.

DEMIDENKO Nikolai, b. 1 July 1955, Aniskino,

Russia. Concert Pianist. *Education:* Studied at Moscow Conservatoire with Dmitri Bashkirov. *Career:* Has performed in Rusia and abroad in concert and recital from 1978; British debut 1985, with Moscow Radio Symphony Orchestra; Frequent tours of Japan and concerts with Bolshoi Symphony, Polish National Radio Orchestra, London Philharmonic, BBC Philaharmonic and BBC Scottish Symphony, London Proms debut 1992 with Rachmaninov's 4th Concerto; Resident in Britain from 1990, teacher at Yehudi Menuhin School; Season, 1992-93 in concerts with the St Petersburg Philharmonic and the Philharmonia Orchestra; Recitals in Paris, Milan and the Concertgebouw, Amsterdam; Two-piano recital with Dmitri Alexeev at Wigmore Hall, March 1993, to mark the 50th anniversary of Rachmaninov's death; Six Piano Masterworks solo recitals at Wigmore Hall, January to June 1993 recreating concerts given by Alkan and Rubinstein in the 19th century: The Classicists, The Age of Beethoven, The Early Romantics, The High Romantics, The Baroque Revival and Legacies and Prophecies, Liszt, Berg, Gubaidulina and Messiaen. *Recordings:* Albums of Bach-Busoni, Chopin and Liszt; Medtner 2nd and 3rd Concertos with BBC Scottish Symphony Orchestra, Medtner and Chopin Concertos with Philharmonia; Live recordings at Wigmore Hall Masterworks series. *Honours:* Medallist, 1976 Concours International de Montreal and 1978 Tchaikovsky International Competition, Moscow. *Address:* c/o Georgina Ivor Associates, 66 Alderbrook Road, London SW12 8AB, England.

DEMIRIS Okan, b. 9 February 1940, Istanbul, Turkey. Composer. *Education:* Studied at Istanbul Municipal Conservatory and the State Conservatory at Ankara. *Career:* Teacher at Istanbul State Conservatory of Turkish Music; Leader of Istanbul State Opera Orchestra, 1969, Conductor, 1980; Director of Istanbul State Opera from 1991. *Compositions:* Operas Murat IV, 1980; Karyagdi Hatun, 1985; Joseph and His Brothers, 1990. *Address:* Istanbul State Opera and Ballet, Ataturk Kultur Merkezi, Taksim, 80124 Istanbul, Turkey.

DEMPSEY Gregory, b. 20 July 1931, Melbourne, Australia. Singer (Tenor). *Education:* Studied in Australia with Mavis Kruger and Annie and Heini Portnoj. *Debut:* National Opera of Victoria 1954, as Don Ottavio. *Career:* Sang with Sadler's Wells/English National Opera from 1962, notably as Wagner's Mime and David, Don José, Peter Grimes, Tom Rakewell, and in the premiere of Bennett's The Mines of Sulphur (1965); Sang in the first local productions of Janáček's The Makropoulos Case (1966) and The Excursions of Mr Brouček (1979); Other roles include the Drum Major in Wozzeck, Dionysus in The Bassarids by Henze (British stage premiere), Aeneas in Les Troyens and the Shepherd in Szymanowski's King Roger (New Opera Company); US debut San Francisco 1966, in The Makropoulos Case; Aldeburgh Festival 1967, in the premiere of Musgrave's The Decision; Covent Garden debut 1972, as Laca in Jenůfa; Sang Bob Boles in Peter Grimes, Sydney, 1986; Prince Populescu in Countess Marita at Melbourne, 1986. *Recordings include:* Billy Budd (Decca); The Ring of the Nibelung (EMI). *Address:* c/o Australian Opera, Sydney Opera House, Sydney, New South Wales, Australia.

DEMPSTER Stuart (Ross), b. 7 July 1936, Berkeley, California, USA. Trombonist; Professor; Composer. m. Renko Ishida, 19 Dec 1964, 2 sons. *Education:* BA, performance 1958, MA composition 1967, San Francisco State College; Private Trombone lessons with AB Moore, Orlando Giosi and John Klock. *Career:* Principal Trombonist, Oakland (Calif) Symphony Orchestra, 1962-66; Member, Performing Group, Mills College, 1963-66; Tours as Soloist, 1962-; Teacher, San Francisco Conservatory of Music, 1961-66; California State College, Hayward, 1963-66; Assistant Professor 1968-78, Associate Professor 1978-85, Professor 1985-, University of Washington, Seattle; Master classes, International Trombone Workshop, 1974-. *Compositions:* Sonata for Bass Trombone and Piano,

1961; Adagio and Canonic Variations for Brass Quintet, 1962; Chamber Music 13 for Voice and Trombones, 1964; The Road Not Taken for Voice, Chorus and Orchestra, 1967; 10 Grand Hosery, mixed media ballet, 1971-72; Pipedream, mixed media piece, 1972; Life Begins at 40, concert series and musical gallery show, 1976; Standing Waves for Trombone, 1976; Didjeridervish for Didjeridu, 1976; Monty for Trombone, 1979; Fog Calling for Trombone and Didjeridu, 1981; Harmonic Tremors for Trombone and Tape, 1982; Hornfinder for Trombone and Audience, 1982; Roulette for Trombones and Audience, 1983; Aix en Providence for Trombones, 1983; JDBBBDJ for Didjeridu and Audience, 1983; Don't Worry, It Will Come for Garden Hoses and Audience, 1983; Sound Massage Parlor for Didjeridu, Garden Hoses, Shell and Audience, 1986; SWAMI (State of Washington as a Musical Instrument), an acoustic guide to the State of Washington for the State's Centennial, 1987-89. *Recordings:* For Columbia; Elektra; Louisville; New Albion; Nonesuch; Orion. *Publications:* The Modern Trombone: A Definition of Its Idioms, 1979. *Address:* c/o School of Music DN-10, University of Washington, Seattle, WA 98195, USA.

DEMUS Jörg Wolfgang, b. 2 Dec. 1928, St. Pölten, Austria. Pianist. *Education:* Vienna State Academy of Music, Austria, 1939-45; Studied Piano with Walter Kerschbaumer, Organ with Karl Walter, Composition with Joseph Marx, Conducting with H. Swarowsky and Joseph Krips; Diploma of the State Academy Vienna Studies with Yves Nat, (Paris), W. Gieseking, W. Kempff, A. Benedetti-Michelangeli, Edwin Fischer. *Compositions:* Franckiana, 6 Little Pieces for Piano. *Recordings:* Has made 350 records, notably of music by Bach, Beethoven and Schubert, often in partnership with pianist Paul Badura-Skoda; accompanist to leading musicians including Dietrich Fischer-Dieskau, Edith Peinemann and the late Antonio Janigro. *Publications:* Abenteuer der Interpretation, Wiesbaden, 1976; Die Klaviersonaten L.v. Beethovens, Wiesbaden, 1974. *Honours:* Hon. Professor of Austria, 1977; Premio Busoni Bolzano, 1956; Edison Prize, Amsterdam; The Harriet Cohen Bach Medal, 1977; Beethoven Ring, Vienna, 1977; Mozart Medal, Vienna Mozartgemeinde, 1979. *Hobbies:* Antiquities; Photography; Natural History. *Current Management:* Mr. Roland Sölder, Döblinger Hauptstrasse 77a, A-1190 Wien, Austria. *Address:* Döblinger Hauptstrasse 77a, A-1190 Vienna, Austria.

DENCH Chris, b. 10 June 1953, London, England. Composer. 1 daughter. *Career:* Commissioned by Elision resulting in Driftglass, 1990-91, which represented Australia at '92 International Rostrum of Composers in Paris; the French Ministry of Culture; the BBC; the Arditti String Quartet; austraLYSIS; Synergy; and others. His works have been performed by Ensemble Accroche Note of Strasbourg, the Berlin Radio Symphony Orchestra, Ensemble Expose, Ensemble InterContemporain, London Sinfonietta, Music Projects-London, the Xenakis Ensemble and such soloists as Andrew Ball, Laura Chislett, James Calpperton, Rolf Hind, Stephanie McCallum, and many others; He has works presented at such events as the Brighton Festival, Darmstadt Ferienkurse für Neue Musik, the Hong Kong ISCM World Music Days, Insel Musik Berlin, many Festivals in France & Italy, the Sydney Spring festival and the Venice Biennale. *Compositions:* Four large-scale solo flute works for Laura Chislett, including Sulle Scale della Fenice; Tilt for solo piano; several large ensemble pieces, including Enoncé and Afterimages, quattro frammenti and planetary allegiances; chamber music: atsiluth, heterotic strings; Current projects include Mentation for flute (Laura Chislett), piano (Stephanie McCallum), and three orchestras; flesh and the mirror for Elision; beyond status geometry for Synergy. *Recordings:* Numerous recordings. *Honour:* Kranichsteiner Musikpreis, 1984. *Hobby:* Popular Musics, especially independents. *Address:* c/o Australian Music Centre, PO Box N690, Grosvenor Place, Sydney 2000, Australia.

DENE Joszef, b. 31 Mar 1938, Budapest, Hungary.

Singer (Bass). *Education:* Studied in Budapest. *Career:* Sang at the Hungarian State Opera, notably as Alberich in Das Rheingold. *Career:* Many performances at the Zurich Opera, in works by Monteverdi, Berg, Verdi, Janáček and Wagner; Berlin Komische Oper, 1975, as Mozart's Figaro; Further engagements at La Scala, Bayreuth, San Francisco and the Metropolitan; Paris Opéra, 1982 and 1985, as Gloucester in Reimann's Lear and as Trithemius in the premiere of Boehmer's Docteur Faustus; Opéra du Rhin Strasborg and Barcelona, 1985-86, as Des Grieux in Manon; Season 1987 at Graz as the Hangman in the premiere of Cerha's Rattenfänger and as Taddeo in L'Italiana in Alegri at the Schwetzingen Festival; Graz Opera, 1988-89, as Alberich in Siegfried and Götterdämmerung; Other roles include Mozart's Alfonso and Papageno, Don Pasquale Pizarro, Kurwenal, Klingsor, Leporello and Handel's Claudius (Agrippina). *Recordings:* Don Giovanni, Boito's Nerone and Juditha Triumphans by Vivaldi (Hungaraton); Il Ritorno di Ulisse, Zurich, 1982 (Telefunken). *Address:* Vereinigte Buhnen, Kaiser Josef Platz 10, A-18010 Graz, Austria.

DENISON John Law, b. 21 Jan. 1911, Reigate, England. Music Administrator. Widower, 1 daughter. *Education:* Chorister, St. George's Chapel, Windsor Castle, 1921-25; Brighton College, 1925-28; Royal College of Music, 1930-32. *Career:* Professional Hornplayer, BBCSO/LPO, CBSO and others, 1932-39; War Service, 1939-46; Commissioned Somerset Light Infantry; DAA & QMG 214 Infantry Brigade, 1945; Music and Theatre Control, Allied Control Commission, Germany; Assistant Music Director, British Council, 1946-48; Music Director, Arts Council of Great Britain, 1948-65; General Manager, Royal Festival Hall, 1965-67; Director, South Bank Concert Halls, 1967-76; Chairman, Cultural Committee, Queen's Silver Jubilee, 1977; Hon. Member, Royal Philharmonic Society, 1989; Trustee Prince Consort, FDN; Royal College of Music; Chairman, Governing Body: Arts Education Schools, 1976-91; Royal Concert in Aid of Musical Charities, 1976-89. *Contributions to:* Various magazines. *Honours:* CBE; FRCM; Hon RAM; Hon GSM; Cdr, Order of Lion, Finland; Chev Ordre des Arts et Lettres, France; FRSA. *Memberships:* Royal Society of Musicians; Garrick Club. *Address:* 9 Hays Park, Shaftesbury, Dorset SP7 9JR, England.

DENISOV Edison, b. 6 April 1929, Tomsk, USSR. Composer. *Education:* Trained in mathematics, then studied with Shebalin at the Moscow Conservatory, 1951-56. *Career:* Teacher at Moscow Conservatory from 1960; an early Soviet exponent of serial music, has also composed in other genres. *Compositions:* Dramatic: Soldier Ivan, opera, 1959; L'Ecume de Jours, lyric drama, 1981; Confession, ballet after Alfred de Musset, 1984; The Four Girls, opera after Picasso, 1986; Orchestral: Peinture, 1970; Cello Concerto, 1972; Bieno Concerto, 1974; Flute Concerto, 1975; Violin Concerto, 1977; Concerto for Flute, Oboe and Orchestra, 1978; Partita for violin and orchestra, 1981; Concerto for bassoon, cello and orchestra, 1982; Tod ist ein langer Schlaf, variations on a theme of Haydn for cello and orchestra, 1982; Chamber Symphony, 1982; Concerto for 2 violas, harpsichord and strings, 1984; Five Paganini Caprices for violin and strings, 1985; Happy End for strings, 1985; Viola Concerto, 1986; Oboe Concerto, 1986; Symphony, 1987; Bells in the Fog, 1988; Clarinet Concerto, 1989; Chamber: Violin Sonata, 1963; String Trio, 1969; Chant des oiseaux for prepared piano and tape, 1969; Piano Trio, 1971; Sonata for solo clarinet, 1972; Aquarelle for 24 strings, 1975; Sonata for solo violin, 1978; Sonata for Guitar, 1981; Sonata for violin and organ, 1982; Three Pictures of Paul Klee for ensemble, 1984; Variations on the Bach choral Es ist genug, for ensemble, 1986; Quintet for clarinet and strings, 1987; Quintet for piano and strings, 1987; Vocal: Canti di Catulli for bass and 3 trombones, 1962; Soleil des Incas for soprano and ensemble, 1964; 5 Geschichten vom Herrn Keuner, to texts by Brecht, for tenor and 7 instruments, 1966; La Vie en rouge, for voice and ensemble, 1973; Requiem, 1980; Ton image charmante for voice and orchestra, to texts by Pushkin, 1982; Au plus haut des cieux for voice and chamber orchestra, 1986; O gladsome light for mixed chorus,

1988; Three Pieces Percussion Instruments, 1989; Legendes de eaux Sontencines for 12 soloists, 1989; Variations on a theme of Mozart for 8 flutes, 1990; Octet, 1992; Dedicare for flute, clarinet and string quartet, 1992; Quintet for four saxophones and piano, 1992; piano music and orchestrations of Mussorgsky and Schubert. *Address:* Moskau 121 165, Studentscheskaia 44/28, kv 35, Russia.

DENIZ Clare Frances, b. 7 Apr 1945, England. Concert Cellist; Teacher. *Education:* Private piano study from age 5; private cello study with Madeleine Mackenzie from age 11; won Junior Exhibition to Royal Academy of Music after only 1 years tuition; teachers were Lilley Phillips and Derek Simpson gained LRAM; further study with Christopher Bunting, Jacqueline Du Pré and Antonia Butler; Master clases with Paul Tortelier, became a pupil. *Debut:* Purcell Room, London, May 1983. *Career:* Former principal cellist Royal Ballet Orchestra, and sub-principal cellist English National Opera; Many recitals specializing in British and French music as well as the standard repertoire; Cambridge Festival; Cheltenham Lunchtime Concerts; Fairfield Hall Centenary Concert for composer Sir Arnold Bax; Bach at the Barbican; Debut at the Concertgebouw Amsterdam, 1987; BBC Radio Oxford recording, 1987; Selected in Spring, 1990 by the Incorporated Society of Musicians to take part in their Counterpoint II recital series; Three concerts of first performances for the Wessex Composers Group, Spring 1990 co-associate concerned by the Incorporated Society of Musicians. Children's Concerts and Workshops; returned to Amsterdam Concertgebouw, June, 1990 to play solo Bach; Haydn C Major Concerto in October, 1990 for the Jacqueline du Pré Appeal Fund. *Hobbies:* Gardening; Badminton; Theology; CS Lewis Society (Oxford University); Lesser Known Music. *Address:* 31 Friday Street, Henley-on-Thames, Oxfordshire RG9 1AN, England.

DENIZE Nadine, b. 6 Nov 1943, Rouen, France. Singer (Mezzo-Soprano). *Education:* Studied with Marie-Louise Christol and Germaine Lubin in Paris. *Debut:* Paris Opéra 1967, as Marguerite in La Damnation de Faust. *Career:* Paris Opéra-Comique, as Charlotte in Werther; Appearances in Marseille, Lyons, Nice and Orange; Member of the Deutsche Oper am Rhein, Dusseldorf, from 1971; Strasbourg 1974-77; Guest engagements at the Hamburg Staatsoper, Vienna Staatsoper and at La Scala Milan; Nancy Opera 1981, as Carmen; Paris Opéra as Octavian and Jenufa; Other roles include Cassandre in Les Troyens, Eboli in Don Carlos, Wagner's Kundry and Honegger's Antigone; Opéra du Rhin Strasbourg, 1986, as Ortrud; Teatro Colon Buenos Aires, 1988, as Marguerite, Berlioz; Opéra-Comique, Paris, 1988, as Marina in Boris Godunov; Sang Brangaene at Nantes, 1989; Anna in Les Troyens, 1990 opening production of Opéra Bastille, Paris. *Recordings:* Carmen, Mireille, Les Pêcheurs de Perles (Columbia); Manon (EMI); Il Barbiere di Siviglia. *Address:* c/o Opéra de Paris Bastille, 12 Rue de Lyon, 75012 Paris, France.

DENLEY Catherine, b. 1954, Northamptonshire, England. Singer (Mezzo Soprano). m. Miles Golding, 3 sons. *Education:* Studied at Trinity College of Music, London. *Career:* Sang 2 years with the BBC Singers; Solo performances with major orchestras and conductors throughout Europe and as far afield as the USA, Canada, China, Japan and the Ukraine; US appearances at the Tanglewood Festival with the Boston Symphony Orchestra; San Francisco concerts with John Eliot Gardiner; Performances of Messiah with the Hallé Orchestra, City of Birmingham Symphony, the English Concert in Belgium and The Sixteen in Finland and Poland; Mozart's Requiem in Salzburg and Innsbruck; Elgar's The Music Makers and the Bliss Pastoral at South Bank; Bach B minor Mass at Aldeburgh and York; Beethoven's Missa Solemnis at the Windsor Festival; Staged performances of L'Incoronazione di Poppea at Spitalfields; Operatic roles include: Olga in Eugene Onegin at the Aldeburgh Festival; Nutrice in Monteverdis Poppea; Handel Operas: Giustino and

Radamisto; Mrs Noah in Noye's Fludde; Radio and TV recordings in Britain and Europe; TV recordings include appearances in Channel 4's Maestro series and Mahler's Eighth Symphony from Dublin; Sang Third Lady in Die Zauberflöte, 1990, Promenade Concerts; Sisera in Handel's Deborah at the 1993 Proms; Mahler 2 in Kiev and Odessa; Tucapsky Stabat Mater in the Czech Republic; Haydn Stabat Master in Madrid and Handel Judas Maccabaeus in Berlin & Halle. *Recordings:* Monteverdi's L'Orfeo and L'Incoronazione di Poppea; Handel's Semele, Hercules, Il Duello Amoroso and Messiah; Vivaldi's Gloria; Requiem by Bruckner; In the Beginning by Copland; Die Zauberflöte. *Honours:* G.T.C.L.; F.T.C.L. *Current Management & Address:* Magenta Music International, 64 Highgate High Street, London, N6 5HX.

DENMAN John Anthony, b. 23 July 1933, London, England. Musician. m. Paula Fan, 6 October 1982. *Education:* Clarke's College, London; Royal Military School of Music, Kneller Hall. *Career:* Principal Clarinet, London Symphony Orchestra, English National Opera and other major British orchestras; BBC soloist, solo tours of Europe, United States of America, Far East and Australia as recitalist, symphony soloist anmd jazz artist; Currently Principal Clarinet, Tucson Symphony, Arizona, United States of America. *Compositions:* Discovery of ms of lost orchestral material to Spohr clarinet concerti, discovery and editing of 3 Caprices by Mozart's clarinettist, Anton Stadler. *Recordings:* Concerti by Spohr, No.2, Stamitz No.3, Finzi, Sonatas by Stanford, Hughes, Bax, Ireland, Benjamin, Alwyn, Brahms, Saint-Saens, Reger, Mendelssohn, Hindemith, Bernstein, Tovey, Bowen. *Publications:* The Kinder-Klari Clarinet Learning System: Tutor and Instrument, a miniature clarinet for small children 1990; Series of Articles, Denmania for International Clarinet Society. *Hobbies:* Golf; Model Railroading. *Current Management:* Albert Kay Associates, New York. *Address:* 1542 E Lester, Tucson, AZ 85719, USA.

DENNISON Robert, b. 10 June 1960, Philadelphia, USA. Concert Pianist. *Education:* Studied in Philadelphia Music Academy, at Temple University and the Peabody Conservatory; further study with claude Frank and Horszowski. *Debut:* Philadelphia 1971, with the Shostakovich Second Concerto. *Career:* Concerts and recitals in Washington, Boston, Cleveland, Los Angeles, St Louis and Chicago; Russian tours 1991-93, with concerts in Kieve, St Petersburg, Vilnius, Moscow and Novosibirsk; further engagements in 1992-93 at Chicago, New Jersey Colorado, San Francisco, Boston, Esssen, Berlin, Hamburg Music Festival, Lucerne Festival and in Hungary, Romania and Czechoslovakia; Repertoire includes contemporary works by American composers as well as the standard classics. *Address:* c/o Sonata, 11 Northgate Street, Glasgow G20 7AA, Scotland.

DENNY Louise Marianne, b. 14 June 1947, London, England. Composer; Pianist. m. Gerald Chatterton (dec), 1 s, 2 d. *Education:* Elmhurst Ballet School, Camberley, Surrey, England. *Debut:* 5 June 1993, Guest conductor, Massed Bands, Fairfield Halls, Croydon. *Compositions:* Atlantis, 1989; The Winged Dagger, 1982; Stirling of Keir, 1987; Theme for Zara, 1982; Utrinque Parafus, 1990; Afore Ye Go, 1991; Halcyon, (25 min ballet), 1992; Handel Festival Fanfare, 255th anniversary of Royal Society of Musicians, 1993; Mulberry Harbours, 1994; The Royal Tournament March. Also songs and music for radio, television and films. *Publications:* The Winged Dagger; Stirling of Keir; Theme for Zara; Atlantis. *Memberships:* Royal Society of Musicians; Composers Guild of Great Britain; BASBWE; PRS. *Address:* Arun House, 58 Sedlescombe Road South, St Leonards on Sea, Sussex TN38 DTJ, England.

DEPLUS Guy Gaston Simon, b. 29 Aug 1924, Vieux Condé, France. Musician; Clarinettist. m. Yvette Vandekerkhove, 3 Aug 1946, 1 son. *Education:* Conservatoire National Superieur du Musique de Paris; 1st Prize, Clarinet and Chamber Music, 1945, 1946. *Career:* Guard Republican Band and Orchestra, 1947;

Concerts Colonne, 1950; Domaine Musical, with Pierre Boulez, 1953; Ars Nova, with Marius Constant, 1963; Paris Octet, 1965; Opéra Comique, 1968; Opera, 1973; Professor, Chamber Music, Paris Conservatory, 1974; Concerts in Berlin, Salzburg, Vienna, 1977; Professor, Clarinet, Paris Conservatory, 1978; Judge, International Competitions; Professor Ecole Normale de Musique de Paris, 1991. *Recordings:* Mozart, Concerto, Trio, Quintet; Weber, 1st Clarinet Concerto, Concertino, Grand Duo; Rossini, Introduction, Theme and Variations; Beethoven Septet. *Contributions to:* The Clarinet, Chairman for France. *Honours:* Quoted by Stravinsky in Memories and Commentaries, 1959; 4 Prix de l'Academie du Disque Francais. *Membership:* International Clarinet Society; French Chairman. *Hobbies:* Reading; Walking. *Address:* 37 Square Saint Charles, 75012 Paris, France.

DEPOLTOVA Eva, b. 5 Aug. 1945, Prague, Czechoslovakia. Singer (Soprano). *Education:* Studied in Prague with Zdenek Otava. *Career:* Sang at Ostrava, Bratislava, Brno and elsewhere in Czechoslovakia; Member of National Theatre Prague from 1979, notably as Dvořák's Rusalka, Smetana's Krasava in Libuse and Mozart's Donna Anna; Tour of Japan with the Czech Philharmonic; Sang Donna Anna in Prague at the 200th Annniversary of the premiere of Don Giovanni, 1987; Other roles include Lady Macbeth, Violetta, Manon Lescaut, Tosca and Turandot. *Recordings:* Dalibor, Libuse and The Kiss, by Smetana; Sarka by Fibich; Eva by Foerster; Martinů's Greek Passion (Supraphon). *Address:* c/o National Theatre, PO Box 865, 11230 Prague 1, Czech Republic.

DEPREIST James (Anderson), b. 21 Nov 1936, Philadelphia, Pennsylvania, USA. Conductor. m. (1) Betty Louise Childress, 10 Aug 1963, 2 daughters. (2) Ginette Grenier, 19 July 1980. *Education:* BS 1958, MA 1961, University of Pennsylvania; Studied with Vincent Persichetti, Philadelphia Conservatory of Music, 1959-61. *Career:* Conductor, Contemporary Music Guild, Philadelphia, 1959-62; Specialist in Music, US State Department, 1962-63; Conductor, Bangkok, Thailand, 1963-64; Assistant Conductor, New York Philharmonic Orchestra, 1965-66; Principal Guest Conductor, Symphony of the New World, 1968-70; European debut, Rotterdam Philharmonic Orchestra, 1969; Associate Conductor 1971-75, Principal Guest Conductor 1975-76, National Symphony Orchestra, Washington, DC; Music Director, L'Orchestre Symphonique de Quebec, 1976-83; Oregon Symphony Orchestra, Portland, 1980-; Malmo Symphony Orchestra, 1991-; Guest conductor with major orchestras in North American and Europe. *Recordings:* For Caprice; Delos. *Publication:* Book of poems, This Precipice Garden, 1987. *Honours:* 1st prize, Dimitri Mitropoulos International Conducting Competition, New York, 1964; Merit Citation, City of Philadelphia, 1969; Medal, City of Quebec, 1983; Honorary LHD, University of Pennsylvania, 1976; Honorary MusD, Laval University, Quebec, 1980; Willamette University, 1987; Honorary DFA, University of Portland, 1983; Pacific University, 1985. *Address:* c/o Malmo Symfonie Orkester, Box 2006, S-200 12 Malmo, Sweden.

DERNESCH Helga, b. 3 Feb. 1939, Vienna, Austria. Singer (Soprano and Mezzo-Soprano). *Education:* Studied at the Vienna Conservatory 1957-61. *Debut:* Berne Opera 1961, as Marina in Boris Godunov. *Career:* Sang Antonia in Les Contes d'Hoffmann, Fiordiligi and Wagner roles; Wiesbaden, 1963-65; Cologne Opera, 1965-69; Bayreuth from 1965, as Freia, Gutrune and Eva; Scottish Opera from 1968, as Gutrune, Leonore, Brünnhilde, Isolde and the Marschallin; Salzburg Easter Festival from 1969, as Brünnhilde, Isolde and Fidelio; Covent Garden debut, 1970 as Sieglinde, followed by Chrysothemis in Elektra, the Dyer's Wife and the Nurse in Die Frau ohne Schatten, and Adelaide in Arabella, 1986; Debuts at Chicago, 1971 and Vienna, 1972 as Leonore in Fidelio; Created Fortner's Elisabeth Tudor, Berlin 1972, Goneril in Reimann's Lear, Munich 1978 and Hecuba in Reimann's Troades, Munich 1986; San Francisco from 1982, as Herodias in Salome, and Erda and Fricka in Der Ring des Nibelungen, 1984-85;

Metropolitan Opera debut 1985, as Marfa in Khovanshchina; Tour of Japan with the Bayreuth ensemble, 1967 and with the Hamburg Staatsoper, 1984; Metropolitan 1989, as Fricka and Waltraute in the Ring and The Nurse in Die Frau ohne Schatten; Sang Mistress Quickly in Falsaff at Los Angeles, 1990; Fricka in the Ring at San Francisco; Covent Garden, in the Ring, 1991; Sang Clytemnestra in Elektra at San Francisco, 1991, and at the Opera Bastille, Paris, 1992; Eletress in Henze's Der Prinz Von Homburg at the 1992 Munich Festival. *Recordings:* Fidelio and Tristan und Isolde (EMI); Der Ring des Nibelungen (Philips and Deutsche Grammophon); Elisabeth in Tannhäuser (Decca). *Address:* Salztorgasse 8/11, A-1013 Wien.

DEROUBAIX Jeanne, b. 16 Feb. 1927, Brussels, Belgium. Singer (Mezzo-Soprano). *Education:* Studied in Brussels. *Career:* Sang in ensemble Pro Musica, under the direction of Safford Cape (1947-53); Toured widely in Europe with repertoire specializing in music of 13th-16th Centuries; Lieder recitals and programmes of French chansons; Often heard in contemporary music: sang in the first performances of Stravinsky's Threni (Venice 1958) and A Sermon, a Narrative and a Prayer (Basle 1962); Also heard in Schoenberg's Pierrot Lunaire and works by Boulez; Professor at the Musikhochschule Detmold from 1957. *Recordings:* Lieder by Brahms; Beethoven's Missa Solemnis; Monteverdi's Orfeo (Deutsche Grammophon); Le Marteau sans Maitre by Boulez (Harmonia Mundi). *Address:* Staatliche Hochscule Für Musik, Westfalen-Lippe Nordwestdeutsche Musikakademie, D-4930 Detmold, Allee 22, Germany.

DES MARAIS Paul (Emile), b. 23 June 1920, Menominee, Michigan, USA. Composer; Professor. *Education:* Studied with Leo Sowerby, Chicago, 1937-41; Nadia Boulanger, Cambridge 1941-42 and Paris 1949; BA 1949, MA 1953, Harvard University. *Career:* Teacher, Harvard University, 1953-56; University of California, Los Angeles, 1956-. *Compositions:* Stage: Epiphanies, chamber opera, 1968; Incidental music to Dryden's A Secular Masque, 1976; Shakespeare's A Midsummer Night's Dream, 1976; Sophocles's Oedipus, 1978; G B Shaw's St Joan, 1980; Dryden's Marriage à la Mode, 1981; Shakespeare's As You Like It, 1983; G Etherege's The Man of Mode, 1984. Dance: Triplum for Organ and Percussion, 1981; Touch for 2 Pianos, 1984. Chamber: 2 piano sonatas, 1947, 1952; Theme and Changes for Harpsichord, 1953; Capriccio for 2 Pianos and Percussion, 1962; 2 Movements for 2 Pianos and Percussion, 1972 revised and enlarged as 3 Movements, 1975; The Baroque Isles for 2 Keyboard Percussionists, 1986; Orpheus, theatre piece for Narrator and Instruments, 1987; The French Park, for two guitars, 1988. Choral: Six-part Mass for double chorus, 1947; Motet for Mixed Voices, Cellos and Double Basses, 1959; Psalm 121, 1959; Organum 1-6 for Chorus, Organ and Percussion, 1972, revised and enlarged, 1980; Brief Mass for Chorus, Organ and Percussion, 1973; Seasons of the Mind for Chorus, Piano 4-hands and Celesta, 1980-81. Vocal: Reflections on Faure for Voice and Piano, 1972; Late Songs for Voice and Piano, 1978; Slowsong for Voice and Piano, 1987; The French Park for two guitars, 1988. *Publication:* Harmony, 1962. *Contributions:* Articles in Perspectives of New Music. *Address:* c/o Music Department, University of California at Los Angeles, Los Angeles, CA 90024, USA.

DESCHÊNES Bruno, b. 12 Oct 1955, Cap-Chat, Quebec, Canada. Composer. m. Shizuko Toguchi, 18 April 1981. *Education:* BMus. Compositions McGill University, Montréal, 1979; Master in Composition, University of Montréal, 1983; Currently doing research on Music Perception, listening and teaching. *Career:* Performing and Conducting on radio and concerts, 1980-; Compositions performed in France, USA, Venezuela, Brazil and Montréal, 1979-; Gives lectures, workshops and writes articles on Music Perception and Music Listening, in Canada, USA and Europe. *Compositions:* Improvised Music: Expansion, Horizon, Pyramide, Chakras; Electronic Music: Murmures for

Tape and Percussion; Different Chamber Groups: Dimension, Innerance, Prisme, Poemes Luminescence, Calme en soi, Double jeu; Choir: Ondes, Ondes et particules. *Contributions to:* The Perceptions of Colour Through Music, Musicwork 26, 1984; Regularly publishes articles in the bulletin of the Centre Québécois de la Couleur. *Hobby:* Computer Programming. *Address:* 5565 Rue Clark, Montréal, Québec H2T 2V5, Canada.

DESDERI Claudio, b. 1945, Alessandria, Italy. Singer (Baritone); Conductor. *Education:* Studied at the Florence Conservatory. *Career:* Sang at first in concert; Opera debut as Gaudenzio in Il Signor Bruschino at the 1969 Edinburgh Festival, with the Maggio Musicale; Has sung widely in Italy and in Munich, Salzburg, Paris, Amsterdam, Chicago, Philadelphia, and Vienna; Best known in operas by Verdi, Berlioz, Monteverdi, Nono, Rossini, Bellini, Mozart, Donizetti and Massenet; Regular appearances in Britan from 1981: Glyndebourne Festival (as Figaro and Alfonso), Promenade and Festival Hall concerts; Covent Garden debut as Mozart's Figaro, 1987; Alfonso in Così fan Tutte, 1989; Conducts Chamber Orchestras in Italy; Master Classes at Musica di Fiesole; Conducted Cosi Fan Tutte and Le Nozze di Figaro at Turin, 1989, Piacenza, 1990, Royal College of Music, London, 1990; Sang Don Magnifico in La Cenerentola at Covent Garden, 1990; Glyndebourne Festival as Falstaff, Maggio Musicale Florence as Leporello. *Recordings include:* Così fan Tutte and Le Nozze di Figaro, conducted by Haitink. *Address:* c/o Royal Opera House, Covent Garden, London, WC2, England.

DESIMONE Robert A., b. 1940. USA. Stage Director; Arts Administrator; Conductor. m. Angela Carol Bonica, 21 July 1974, 1 son, 1 daughter. *Education:* Performance Certificate, Music Academy of the West; BM, MA, University of Southern California; Diploma International Opera Centre, Zurich, Switzerland; DMA, University of Washington, USA. *Debut:* As Stage Director, Rome, Italy. *Career:* Director of Opera, University of Texas, Austin; Director of Opera, College Conservatory of Music, Cincinnati; Assistant Director, School of Music, University of Washington; Executive Director, Visual Arts Center, Anchorage, Alaska; Administrative Coordinator, Music Center Opera Association, Los Angeles; Director: City of the Angels Opera, Los Angeles; John F. Kennedy Center for the Performing Arts, Washington DC; Lincoln Center for the Performing Arts, New York; Seattle Opera Association, Seattle, Washington; Stage Director: Teatro del' Opera, Rome; Teatro Goldoni, Rome; Opernhaus, Zurich, Switzerland; Resident Stage Director, Seattle Opera Association, Seattle, Washington; Guest Director, theatres in Germany, Switzerland, Italy, USA. *Memberships:* National Opera Association; Metropolitan Opera Guild; College Music Society; Central Opera Association. *Address:* 3601 72nd Avenue SE, Mercer Island, WA 98040, USA.

DESJARDINS André Luc, b. 1955, Lévis, Québec, Canada. Composer. *Education:* Studied piano lessons at age of 6 at Saint-Louis-de-Gonzague Boarding School, Québec City; Studied at Conservatoire de Musique de Québec; Studied electroacoustic music with Pierre Genest and Yves Daoust; Composer Degrees from Conservatoire de Musique de Québec and Faculté de Musique de l'Université de Montréal. *Career:* Composer of electroacoustic music. *Compositions Include:* Manu Militari. *Honours:* Won Prize at XIIth Concours International de Musique Electroacoustique de Bourges with his work Manu Militari.

DEUSSEN Nancy Bloomer, b. 1 Feb 1931, New York City, New York, USA. Composer; Teacher. m. (1) Charles J Webster, 1952, (2) John H Bloomer, 1962, (3) Gary R Deussen, 1982, 1 son, 2 daughters. *Education:* Juilliard School of Music, 1949-51; Manhattan School of Music, 1951-1953, BM, Composition, University of Southern California School of Music, 1957-59, BM Music Education; Graduate studies in Composition, University of California, Los Angeles, University of Southern California, Long Beach State University, San

Jose State University. *Career:* Original ballet music The Little Hill performed New York City, 1952; Missa de Angelis premiere, Redlands, California, 1957; Suite for Clarinet and Piano premiere, 1959, Los Angeles, CA; Woodwind Quintet premiere, 1985, TV premiere with interview, Oct 1988; Concert of original chamber music and orchestra premiere of Three Rustic Sketches, 1989. *Compositions:* Little Fugue and Harvest Suite, for recorders, 1956; Missa de Angelis, 1957; Suite for Clarinet and Piano, 1959; The Serpent, cantata, 1965; Woodwind Quintet, 1983; Three Rustic Sketches, for orchestra, 1987; Prelude and Cascades, for piano, 1987; Fanfare and Andante for Winds, 1988; The Long Voyage, for soprano and recorders, 1988; Trio for Violin, Clarinet and Piano, 1988; (on commission) City Festival Overture, for concert band, 1989; Commission from Clara Chorale Canticles of Our Land for SATB, soli and chamber orchestra, World Premiere, 1991; Two pieces for Violin and Piano, 1990; Canticles of Our Land for chorus/ chamber orchestra, premiered by The Santa Clara Chorale, 1992. *Address:* 3065 Greer Road, Palo Alto, CA 94303, USA.

DEUTEKOM Cristina, b. 28 Aug 1932, Amsterdam, Netherlands. Opera Singer (Soprano). 1 daughter. *Debut:* Amsterdam 1962 as the Queen of Night which she sang on her Covent Garden Debut; Appeared at Munich State Opera, 1966. *Career:* Vienna Festwochen, 1966; Sang at Metropolitan Opera, New York, 1967; Has sung in all major opera houses in Europe, especially Italy and also in USA; Specializes in bel canto operas by Rossini, Bellini and Donizetti and the great Verdi operas; among her roles are Mozart's Fiordiligi and Constanze, Bellini's Norma and Elvira, Rossini's Armida and Verdi's Odabella and Giselda. *Recordings:* for EMI, Decca and Philips. *Honours:* Grand Prix du Disque, 1969 and 1972. *Hobbies:* Driving around the world; Singing; Shopping, especially for shoes. *Address:* c/o H.R. Rothenberg, Johannisthaler Chaussee 421, 1 Berlin 47, Germany.

DEVENNEY David Paul, b. 18 Nov 1958, Marshalltown, Iowa, USA. Conductor. *Education:* BM, Iowa State University, 1980; MM, University of Wisconsin, 1982; DMA, University of Cincinnati, 1989. *Career:* Director of Choral Activities: Virginia Technical University, 1982; Otterbein College, Westerville, Ohio, 1983-; Music Director, Vocal Baroque, 1990-. *Publications:* Nineteenth-Century American Choral Music, 1987; Early American Choral Music, 1988; A Conductor's Study of Mass in D by John Knowles Paine, 1989; American Masses and Requiems, 1990; Books: The Chorus in Opera, 1993; American Choral Music since 1920, 1993. *Contributor to:* Articles in The Choral Journal, The American Choral Review, The American Organist, and Research Memorandum Series of The American Choral Foundation. *Memberships:* American Choral Directors Association; International Federation for Choral Music; American Choral Foundation; Sonneck Society; International H.Schutz Society. *Address:* Department of Music, Otterbein College, Westerville, OH 43081, USA.

DEVIA Mariella, b. 1948, Imperia, Italy. Singer (Soprano). *Education:* Studied at the Accademia di Santa Cecilia, Rome. *Debut:* Spoleto 1972, as Despina in Così fan Tutte. *Career:* Rome Opera 1973, as Lucia di Lammermoor; Guest appearances in Italy and at Munich, Hamburg and Berlin; Has sung Donizetti's Adina in Dallas and Verdi's Oscar in Chicago; Metropolitan Opera from 1979, as Gilda, Constanze in Die Entführung, Nannetta in Falstaff, Despina and Constanze, 1990; Concert performance of Lakmé in New York; Sang title role in Donizetti's Elisabeth al castello di Kenilworth at Bergamo, 1989; Elvira in I Puritani at Rome and Madrid, 1990; Maggio Musicale Florence, 1990 as Donizetti's Parisina; Rossini roles include Adele in Le Comte Ory, Amenaide in Tancredi and Semiramide. *Recordings include:* Rossini Adelaide di Borgogna, Donizetti Elisabetta al castello di Kenilworth, Bellini La Sonnambula and I Puritani (Fonit Centra). *Address:* c/ o R Lombardo Inc., One Harkness Plaza, 61 West 62nd Street, Suite 6F, New York, NY 10023, USA.

DEVINU Giusy, b. 1960, Cagliri, Italy. Singer (Soprano). *Education:* Studied at the Cagliari Conservatory. *Debut:* Sang in 1982. *Career:* Has sung Violetta at La Scala under Riccardo Muti and at other Italian Centres; Further engagements in Rigoletto at Bologna, 1990, Rossini's L'Occasione fa il ladro at Pesaro, 1989, and in Don Pasquale and as the Countess in Le nozze di Figaro at the Teatro La Fenice Venice, 1990-91; Sang in the Seven Stars concert at the Baths of Caracalla, 1991; Triests 1991 as Lucieta in Wolf-Ferrari's Il Campiello, Rome 1992 as Marie in La Fille du Regiment; Macerata Festival 1992 as Traviata. *Address:* c/o Teatro La Fenice, Campo S Fantin 1965, 30124 Venice, Italy.

DEVLIN Michael (Coles), b. 27 Nov. 1942, Chicago, Illinois, USA. Bass-baritone. m. Theresa A Padvorac. *Education:* MusB, Louisiana State University, 1965; Vocal training with Treigle, Ferro, and Malas, New York. *Debut:* Operatic debut as Spalanzani, Les Contes d'Hoffmann, New Orleans, 1963. *Career:* First appearance with New York City Opera as the Hermit in USA premiere of Ginastera's Don Rodrigo, 1966; on roster until 1978; British debut as Mozart's Almaviva, Glyndebourne Festival, 1974; Royal Opera Covent Garden, London, 1975, 1977, 1979; European debut, Holland Festival, 1977; Frankfurt Opera and Bavarian State Opera, Munich, 1977; Metropolitan Opera debut in New York as Escamillo, 1978; San Francisco Opera, 1979; Hamburg State Opera and Paris Opera, 1980; Miami Opera and Monte Carlo Opera, 1981; Dallas Opera, 1983; Chicago Lyric Opera, 1984; Los Angeles Opera, 1986; Other roles have been Don Giovanni, Eugene Onegin, Golaud, Escamillo, Don Alfonso, Ford, Wotan and the villains in Les Contes d'Hoffmann; At Santa Fe has sung Altair in Strauss's Die Aegyptische Helena and the Commandant in Friedenstag; Sang Pizarro in Fidelio at Los Angeles, 1990; Jochanaan in Salome at Covent Garden, 1992; Sang Escamillo at Los Angeles, 1992. Numerous appearances as soloist with major orchestras. *Current Management:* New Century Artist Management. *Address:* New Century Artist Management, PO Box 802, Tuxedo Park, NY 10987, USA.

DEVOS Louis, b. 15 June 1926, Brussels, Belgium. Singer (Tenor). *Education:* Vocal studies in Graz, Austria. *Career:* Founded Ensemble Musica Polyphonica 1950, for the performance of early music; Sang in the first performance of Stravinsky's Cantata, Brussels 1952, and in the premiere of the radio opera Orestes by Henk Badings, 1954; Concerts with the Munich Philharmonic from 1956, under the direction of Pierre Boulez and Hermann Scherchen; Sang in the premieres of Martin's Mystère de la Nativité (Geneva 1959) and Pilatus (Rome 1964); Cologne 1972, in Penderecki's Utrejna; Vienna Staatsoper 1974, as Aron in Schoenberg's Moses und Aron; Guest appearances in London, Milan, Amsterdam and Brussels. *Recordings:* Vocal music by Lully (Erato); Der Tod Jesu by Graun; Zelenka's Magnificat; Les Indes Galantes by Rameau; Lutoslawski's Paroles tissées; Moses and Aron (Philips); Rousseau's Le Devin du Village (CBS). *Address:* c/o Staatsoper, Opernring 2, A-1010 Vienna, Austria.

DEVOTO Mark Bernard, b. 11 Jan. 1940, Cambridge, Massachusetts, USA. Professor. m. Deanna Mirsky, 1963 (divorced 1971), 2 daughters. *Education:* AB, Harvard University, 1961; MFA, 1963, PhD, Music, 1967, Princeton University; Longy School of Music, 1946-56. *Career:* Reed College, 1964-68; University of New Hampshire, 1968-81; Professor of Music, Tufts University, 1981-. *Compositions:* Many unpublished. *Publication:* Walter Piston, Harmony, 5th Edition, 1987, Co-author; Editor, An Anthology fot Harmonic Analysis. *Contributions:* Articles on Alban Berg, Debussy, Schubert; Numerous reviews. *Memberships:* AMS; SMT; International Alban Berg Society Limited; Schoenberg Institute; Sonneck Society. *Hobbies:* Writing Fiction; Wiring Houses; Cooking. *Address:* Music Department, Tufts University, Medford, MA 02155, USA.

DEVOYON Pascal, b. 6 Apr 1953, Paris, France. Pianist. m. 29 Feb 1992, 2 sons. *Education:* French Baccalaureat Mathematics Section; Ecole Normale de Musique Conservatoire de Paris. *Career:* Has played with major orchestras including: Philharmonia, Leningrad Philharmonic, NHK Tokyo; Broadcasts over radio and TV with Orchestre de la Suisse Romande, Orchestre National d'Espayne, Rotterdam, Stuttgart Philharmonic and RAI of Milan. *Recordings:* Ravel, Liszt, Tchaikovsky, Bach, Franck, Fauré, Schumann, Grieg, Saint-Saëns. *Honours:* Second Prize, Viotti, 1973; Busoni, 1974; Third Prize, Leeds, 1975; Second Prize, Tchaikovsky, 1978. *Hobbies:* Video; Informatic. *Current Management:* Charles Finch, 11a Queens Road, Wimbledon, London, SW19 8NG, England. *Address:* 50 Avenue de la Paix, 93270 Sevran, France.

DEVREESE Frédéric, b. 2. June 1929, Amsterdam, The Netherlands. Composer; Conductor. *Education:* Malines Conservatory with Father, studied composition with M.Poot; Conducting with R.Defossez, Brussels Conservatory; Composition with I.Pizzetti, Accademia di Santa Cecillia, Rome, 1952-55; Conducting with H.Swarowsky, Staastsakademie, Vienna, 1956. *Career:* Conductor Belgian T.V., Composer of Symphonic music, Opera, Ballet, Chamber music and Film music. *Compositions:* Orchestral: Symphony, 1953; Two Movements for String Orchestra, 1953.63; Mascarade, Ballet, 1955; Divertimento for String Orchestra, 1970; L'Amour de Don Juan, Ballet, 1973; Overture for Orchestra, 1976; Evocation, Suite, 1977; Prelude, 1983; Benvenuta, Suite, 1984; Gemini, 5 Mouvements for orchestra, 1986; l'Oeuvre au Noir, Suite, 1988; Valse Sacrée, 1989; Thème et Danse dun Soir un Train, 1989. Soli and Orchestra: 4 piano concertos, 1949, 1952, 1956, 1983; Violin Concerto, 1951; Recitativo et Allegro for trumpet and orchestra, 1959; Ballade for Harmonica, Strings and Childrens Choir. Chamber: Suite No.1 for Brass quintet, Hommage à J. Ensor, 1970; Suite No.2 for Brass quintet, 1981; Masque for Brass Band, 1989; Divertimenti a Due for Violin and Cello, 1968; 5 Divertimenti for 4 sax, 1985; Benvenuta Suite for violin and piano, 1987; Valse Sacrée for violin, alto and piano, 1989. Piano Solo: Mascarade, 1953; Soundtrack, 1981-1990; prelude, 1982; Black and White, 1983-1990. Two Pianos: Gemini, 1980. Filmmusic, Documentary: Paul Klee, 1957; Les Clefs du Surfealisme, 1966; Breugal, 1969; Evenepoel, 1971; Moi, Ensor, 1972; Dirk Bouts, 1984; François Mitterrand, 1991. Opera: Willem Van Saeftinghe, 1962-63; Le Cavalier Bizarre, 1967. Film music, Fiction: l'Homme au Crâne rasé, 1966; Un SOIR un Train, 1986; Rendez-vous à Braye, 1970; Belle, 1973; Fotormance, 1978; Benvenuta, 1983; Noces Barbares, 1987; l'Oeuvre au Noir, 1988; Il Maestro, 1989; Het Sacrement, 1989; Orchestra, Belle Suite, 1990; Variations and Theme for Strings, 1991; 3 Dances for 10 Wind Instruments, 1992; Piano Wiegelied voor Jesse, 1992. *Address:* c/o Gaillard Edition, Avenue Buysdelle 30, 1180 Brussels, Belgium.

DEW John, b. 1 June 1944, Santiago de Cuba. Stage Director. *Education:* Studied in Germany with Walter Felsenstein and Wieland Wagner. *Debut:* The Rake's; Progress at Ulm, 1971. *Career:* Directed Mozart and Wagner cycles at Krefeld in the 1970's; Head of Production at Bielefeld from 1981, with Maschinist Hopkins by Brand, Schreker's Irrelohe and Der Singende Teufel, Hindmith's Neues vom Tage, Der Sprung uber den Schatten and Zwingburg by Krenek; Bakchantinnen by Wellesz, Fennimore and Gerda, Nixon in China nd Boito's Nerone; Season 1987-88 at the Deutsche Oper Berlin with Les Huguenots and the premiere of Los Alamos by Neikrug; Les Hugenots seen at Covent Garden 1991; Other productions include La Juive, Bielefeld and Nuremburg, Clemenza di tito, Zürich, Death in Venice, Nuremburg, 1992; Aida, Hamburg, 1993; Puritani, Vienna, 1994; Andrea Chenier, Berlin; Leipzig production of Le Nozze di Figaro seen at the Israel Festival, 1992; Forthcoming: Appointed Artistic Director of the Theaters of the city of Dortmund. *Address:* Athol Still Ltd, Greystoke House, 80-86 Westrow Street, London SE19 3AF, England

DEXTER Harold, b. 7 Oct. 1920, Leicester, England. Organist; Teacher; Conductor. m. Faith Grainger, 1 daughter. *Education:* Mus.B; MA, Cambridge University; Fellow, Royal College of Organists; Associate, Royal College of Music; ADCM. *Career:* Organist, Southwark Cathedral 1956-68; Professor, Guildhall School of Music 1956-, Head of General Musicianship Department 1963-85. *Honours:* Fellow, Guildhall School of Music; Fellow, Royal School of Church Music. *Memberships:* Past service on Royal College of Organists, Incorporated Society of Music and IAO Executives; Various associations with Royal School of Church Music. *Address:* 29 Allington Court, Outwood Common Road, Billericay, Essex, CM11 2JB, England.

DI BONAVENTURA Anthony, b. 12 Nov. 1930, Follensbee, West Virginia, USA. Pianist. *Education:* Studied at the Curtis Institute with Vengerova, *Debut:* With the New York Philharmonic in 1943, playing Beethoven's C minor Concerto. *Career:* Beethoven cycle under Otto Klemperer with the London Philharmonic, 1959; Has performed widely in the US with major orchestras in the standard repertory and in works by contemporary composers; Vincent Persichetti, Luciano Berio (Points on a Curve to Find), Alberto Ginastera and Milko Kelemen have written works for him; Teacher at the School of Music, Boston University, from 1973. *Recordings include:* Works by Scarlatti, Chopin, Debussy and Prokofiev (Eighth Sonata).

DI BONAVENTURA Mario, b. 20 Feb. 1924, Follensbee, West Virginia, USA. Conductor. *Education:* Studied conducting with Igor Markevitch in Salzburg and Paris; Studied composition with Nadia Boulanger in Paris, 1947- 53. *Debut:* With the Paris Conservatoire orchestra in the Prix de Paris, 1952. *Career:* Conducted the Fort Lauderdale Symphony, 1959-61, and has appeared as guest in the US and Europe (Warsaw Philharmonic) and as leader of the Juilliard Contemporary Music Ensemble; Has led the premieres of Milhaud's 9th Symphony (1960), Walter Piston's Clarinet Concerto and Malipiero's Endecatode for chamber orchestra; Professor of Music at Dartmouth College 1962-73; Vice President of G Schirmer, New York, 1974-80; Director of the School of Music, Boston University, 1980-82. *Honours include:* Winner, 1952, Besançon International Conducting Competition; Lili Boulanger- Dinu Lipati Memorial Prize in Composition, 1953; Arnold Bax Memorial Award for Conducting, 1968.

DI CESARE Ezio, b. 1939, Rome, Italy. Singer (Tenor). *Education:* Studied in Rome. *Career:* Sang with a Vocal Sextet and made tours of Italy; Stage debut 1975, in Bellini's Beatrice di Tenda; Many appearances in Italy and elsewhere in Europe as Alfredo, Rodolfo, and Tom Rakewell in The Rake's Progress; La Scala Milan, 1980, 1984, in Vivaldi's Tito Manlio and Idomeneo; Arvino, in Verdi's I Lombardi; Appearances in Holland and at the Verona Arena; Sang at Rome 1986 in Spontini's Agnese di Hohenstaufen; Teatro Liceo Barcelona, 1987, in the Spanish premiere of Mozart's Lucio Silla; Pesaro Festival, 1988, as Iago in Rossini's Otello; Sang Carlo in Pergolesi's Lo Frate innamorato at La Scala, 1989; Gabrielle Adorno at Cremona; Rome Opera 1990, in Franco Manninos's Il Principe Felice; Season 1992 as Iarba in Jommelli's Didone abbandonata at the Teatro Rossini, Lugo. *Recordings:* Verdi's Stiffelio (Philips); La Finta Giardiniera (Deutsche Grammophon); Alfano's Cyrano de Bergerac. *Address:* c/o Teatro dellOpera, Piazza Beniamino Gigli 8, 1-00184 Rome, Italy.

DI DOMENICA Robert (Anthony), b. 4 Mar. 1927, New York City, USA. Flautist; Teacher; Composer. *Education:* Studied harmony, counterpoint, fugue and composition with Josef Schmid; BS, music education, New York University, 1951; Flute with Harold Bennett, 1949-55; Composition with Wallingford Riegger. *Career:* New York City Opera Orchestra; New York Philharmonic Orchestra; Various engagements as solo artists; Faculty Member 1969-, Associate Dean 1973-76, Dean 1976-78, New England Conservatory of Music,

Boston. *Compositions:* Operas: The Balcony, 1972; The Scarlet Letter, 1986; Orchestral: Symphony, 1961; Concerto for Violin and Chamber Orchestra, 1962; 2 piano concertos, 1963, 1982; Concerto for Wind Quintet, Strings and Timpani, 1964; Music for Flute and String Orchestra, 1967; The Holy Colophon for Soprano, Tenor, Chorus and Orchestra, 1980; Variations on a Theme by Gunther Schuller for 13 Instruments, 1983; Dream Journeys, 1984; Chamber: Sonata for Flute and Piano, 1957; Sextet for Woodwind Quintet and Piano, 1957; Quartet for Flute, Violin, Horn and Piano, 1959; Quartet for Flute, Violin, Viola and Cello, 1960; String Quartet, 1960; Quintet for Clarinet and String Quartet, 1965; Sonata for Violin and Piano, 1966; Trio for Flute, Bassoon and Piano, 1966; Saeculum aureum for Flute, Piano and Tape, 1967; Sonata for Saxophone and Piano, 1968; Music for Stanzas for Flute, Clarinet, Bassoon, Horn and Tape, 1981; Piano Pieces. Vocal: Wind Quintet for Soprano and Woodwind Quintet, 1963; Songs from Twelfth Night for Tenor, Flute, Viola da Gamba and Harpsichord, 1976; Sonata after Essays for Piano for Soprano, Baritone, Flute and Tape, 1977, alternative version as Concord Revisted for Piano, Soprano, Baritone, Chamber Ensemble and Tape, 1978; Hebrew Melodies for Soprano, Violin and Piano, 1983; Variations and Soliloquies for Orchestra, 1988. *Recording:* Leona Di Domenica in live first performances of the Solo Piano Music of Robert Di Domenica. *Publication:* Dream Journeys for Orchestra, 1984. *Honours:* Guggenheim Fellowship, 1972; Opera The Balcony premiered by the Opera Company of Boston, 1990, repeated at Moscow's Bolshoi Theater, 1991. *Address:* 17 Paul Revere Road, Needham, MA 02194, USA.

DI FRANCO Loretta, b. 28 Oct. 1942, New York City, USA. Singer (Soprano). *Education:* Studied with Maud Webber and Walter Taussig in New York. *Career:* Sang in the chorus of the Metropolitan Opera until 1965; Solo appearances in New York in The Queen of Spades, Don Giovanni (Zerlina), Un Ballo in Maschera (Oscar), Gianni Schicchi (Lauretta), Le Nozze di Figaro (Marcellina) and Lucia di Lammermoor (title role). *Address:* c/o Metropolitan Opera, Lincoln Center, New York, NY 10023, USA.

DI GIUSEPPE Enrico, b. 14 Oct. 1932, Philadelphia, Pennsylvania, USA. Tenor. *Education:* Studied with Richard Bonelli, Curtis Institute of Music, Philadelphia; with Hans Heinz, Juilliard School of Music, New York. *Debut:* Operatic debut as Massenet's Des Grieux, New Orleans, 1959. *Career:* Toured with Metropolitan Opera National Company; New York City Opera debut as Michele, The Saint of Bleecker Street, 1965; On roster 1967-81; Metropolitan Opera debut in NY as Turiddu, 1970; Guest appearances with opera companies in Baltimore, Boston, Cincinnati, Dallas, Houston, Ottawa, Philadelphia, Pittsburgh, San Francisco, Toronto and other cities; Various engagements as Concert Artist. *Recordings:* For Angel-EMI. *Address:* c/o Metropolitan Opera, Lincoln Center, New York, NY 10023, USA.

DI PIANDUNI Oslavio, b. 1939, Montevideo, Uruguay. Singer (Tenor). *Education:* Studied in Montevideo. *Career:* Appeared at Montevideo 1961-65 as Rinuccio in Gianni Schicchi and Lionel in Martha; Sang in Europe from 1968 with Mozart roles at Klagenfurt, 1968-70, and Alfredo, Riccardo, Hoffmann, Don José, Pinkerton and Calaf at Bielefeld, 1970-75; Further engagements at the Theater am Gartnerplatz, Munich, 1975-76, Vienna Volksoper, 1976-78, and Kiel 1979-82; Bremen, 1982-84, Zurich, 1988 as Edmund in Reimann's Lear; Hanover, 1989, as Andrea Chenier; Other roles include Luigi in Il Tabarro, Hermann in The Queen of Spades and Otello, Oslo, 1999; Has also sung in operettas by Lehar, Johann Strauss and Offenbach; Many concert appearances and Lieder recitals. *Address:* c/o Niedersachische Staatstheater, Opernplatz 1, 3000 Hannover, Germany

DI PIETRO Rocco, b. 15 Sept. 1949, Buffalo, New York, USA. Composer. m. Juli Douglass, 28 May 1973, 1 son. *Education:* BPS, State University of New York, 1985; Studied with Hans Hagen, Lukas Foss and Bruno

Maderna. *Career:* Lecturer on modern music; Performances of his compositions have been played in major cities of Europe and USA by such musicians and Ensembles as Christiane Edinger, Christobal Halffter, Lukas Foss, Bruno Maderna, Bavarian Radio Orchestra, Brooklyn Philharmonic, St Paul Chamber Orchestra. *Compositions:* Overture to Combats for History, for percussion orchestra, 1980-81; Melodia Arcana for percussion and tarot cards, 1980-83; Aria Grande for violin and orchestra, 1980; Tratto Bizzaro, opera, 1984; Beauty and the Beast, incidental music for theatre, 1986; Annales after Tasso for madrigal voices and percussion, 1987. *Publications:* Melodia Nera for Timpani, AM Percussion Publications, 1985. *Honours:* ASCAP Fellowship to Berkshire Music Center, Tanglewood; Stipend to Darmstadt Ferienkurse für Neue Musik, Germany; Buffalo Foundation, 1986; Commission from the Kennedy Center for Imagination Celebration, 1986. *Memberships:* Composers' Forum of New York; Electro-Acoustic Society of Great Britain. *Hobby:* Studies in Western history. *Current Management:* Sheldon Soffer, New York. *Address:* c/o American Percussion Publications, PO Box 436, Lancaster, NY 14086, USA.

DI STEFANO Giuseppe, b. 24 July 1921, Motta Santa Anastasia, Italy. Singer (Tenor). *Education:* Studied with Adriano Torchi and Luigi Montesanto in Italy. *Career:* Sang in broadcasts for Swiss Radio 1944-45; Stage debut as Massenet's Des Grieux, Reggio Emilia 1946; La Scala Milan from 1947; Metropolitan Opera 1948-56, as the Duke of Mantua, Rodolfo, Faust, Rossini's Almaviva, Alfredo, Pinkerton, and Don José; Chicago Lyric Opera from 1954, as Edgardo, Arturo in I Puritani, Calaf, Riccardo in Un Ballo in Maschera and Loris in Fedora; Guest appearances in San Francisco, Vienna, Berlin, Paris, Mexico City and Sao Paulo; British debut Edinburgh 1957, as Nemorino; Covent Garden 1961, as Cavaradossi; Other roles include Elvino in La Sonnambula, Fritz in L'Amico Fritz, Radames, Turiddu, Alvaro in La Forza del Destino and Nadir in Les pêcheurs de Perles; Sang with Callas on her farewell tour of 1973-74. *Recordings:* La Gioconda, La Forza del Destino, Lucia di Lammermoor, Manon Lescaut, Un Ballo in Maschera, La Bohème, Madama Butterfly, Rigoletto, Tosca, Werther, Carmen; Labels include HMV, Decca, RCA, Deutsche Grammophon and Cetra. *Address:* c/o Teatro alla Scala, Filodrammatici 2, Milan, Italy.

DI VIRGILIO Nicholas, b. 1937, New York, USA. Singer (Tenor). *Education:* Studied at the Eastman School and in New York. *Debut:* Sang Pinkerton with Chautauqua Opera, 1961. *Career:* Sang at Baltimore from 1956, Cincinnati, New Orleans (1969-70), San Francisco, 1966-67, San Diego, Pittsburgh and the New York City Opera, 1964-71; Metropolitan Opera from 1970, as Pinkerton and as Edgardo in Lucia di Lammermoor; European engagements at Brussels Amsterdam and Lyon, 1968-70; London 1978, in the Verdi Requiem; Other roles have included Mozart's Idomeneo, Don Attavio and Ferrando, Verdi's Alfredo, Fento and Riccardo, Faust, Rodolfo, Hoffmann, Don José, Laca in Jenůfa and Cavaradossi. Voice Teacher at the University of Illinois.

DIAMAND Peter, b. 8 June 1913, Charlottenburg, Germany. Artistic Adviser. 1 son. *Education:* Berlin University, 1931-33. *Career:* Secretary to pianist Artur Schnabel, 1934-39; Director, Holland Festival, 1948-65; Director, Edinburgh Festival, 1965-78; Artistic Adviser, Orchestre de Paris, 1977-; Artistic Adviser, teatro alla Scala, Milan, 1977-78; Director, Mozart Festival, Paris, 1980-87. *Contributor To:* Various magazines, etc. *Honours:* C.B.E.; Officier Arts et Lettres, France; Commendatore della Repubblica, Italy; Offizier Verdienstkreuz, Austria; Knight, Order of Oranje Nassau, Netherlands; Honorary LLD, Edinburgh University, Scotland; Others. *Membership:* Co-Founder, European Association of Music Festivals, Geneva. *Address:* 28 Eton Court, Eton Avenue, London NW3 3HJ, England.

DIAMOND David Leo, b. 9 July 1915, Rochester,

New York, USA. Composer. *Education:* Cleveland Institute of Music, 1927-29; Eastman School of Music, University of Rochester, 1930-34; American Conservatory, Fontainebleau, France, summer 1937, 1938; New Music & Dalcroze Institute, New York City, 1934-36. *Career:* Teacher, composition, Metropolitan Music School, NYC, 1950; Lecturer, American music, Seminar in American Studies, Schloss Leopoldskron, Salzburg, Austria, 1949; Fulbright professor, University of Rome, Italy, 1951-52; Slee professor of music, University of Buffalo, New York, 1961, 1963; Professor/Chairman, Department of Composition, Manhattan School of Music, NYC, 1965-67; Visiting professor, University of Colorado, 1970; Lamont School, University of Denver 1983; Composer-in-residence, American Academy in Rome, 1971-72, Juilliard School of music 1973. *Compositions include:* 11 Symphonies, concertos for violin, flutes, piano & violoncello, 11 string quartets, chamber music, 52 preludes & fugues for piano, sonatas, choral music & songs, scores for motion pictures & other forms of instrumental music. Composer/conductor; original score, Margaret Webster production, The Tempest, 1944-45, Incidental music, Tennessee Williams' Rose Tattoo, 1950; Ballets, Tom, Dream of Audubon; opera, The Noblest Game. *Recordings:* Music for Columbia albums, Romeo & Juliet, The Tempest Overture, 4th Symphony, 4th String Quartet; Delos Int. 1,2,3,4,8 Symphonies. *Memberships:* National Opera Institute; New York State Arts Council; Library of Congress McKim Fund. *Honours include:* Prix de Rome, 1941; Paderewski Award, 1942; Guggenheim Fellowship, 1938; 1941; 1958; Juilliard Publishing Award; Stravinsky Award, ASCAP; Naumberg Records Award Nonet, 9th Quartet Grant, National Endowment for the Arts; William Schuman Lifetime Achievement Ward, 1986; Edward MacDowell Gold Medal Award, 1991. *Publication:* Autobiography, The Midnight Sleep (in progress). *Contributions to:* Modern Music; Decision; New York Herald Tribune. *Membership:* National Academy of Arts & Letters. *Address:* 249 Edgerton Street, Rochester, NY 14607, USA.

DIAZ Joaquin, b. 14 May 1947, Zamora, Spain. Singer; Ethnomusicologist. *Education:* University of Valladolid. *Career:* Concerts, 1964-, Europe & USA; Retired from Concert Circuit, 1974; Founder, Editor, Revista de Folklore, Director, Ethnographic Centre, Spain. *Recordings:* The Music of Spain; Sephardic Ballads & Songs; Songs of Sanabria; Songs of Los Ancares; 30 others. *Publications:* Folkloric Catalog of the Province of Valladolid, 5 volumes, 1978-82; Cancionero de Palencia, 1982-83; Autos de Navidad, 1982; Romances de Castilla y Leon, Wisconsin, 1982; 200 songs for Children, 1983; Traditional Instruments, 1986. *Contributions to:* Numerous journals & magazines. *Honours:* Recipient, various honours & awards. *Membership:* International Council for Traditional Music. *Hobbies:* Collector of Engravings (19th Century). *Address:* San Lorenzo 22, Valladolid 1, 47001 Spain.

DIAZ José Angel, b. 2 Aug. 1955, Chicago, Illinois, USA. Oboist. *Education:* BA, 1977, MM, 1982, DMA, 1989, University of Texas at Austin. *Career:* Oboist, Austin Chamber Players, 1973-83; Principal Oboist, Oboist with Orquesta Sinfonica de Monterrey, Mexico, 1977-78; Inaugural Faculty Member, Escuela Superior de Musica y Danza, Monterrey, 1977- 78; Solo Oboist with Orpheus Chamber Ensemble, 1982-; Assistant Professor of Music, California State University, Fresno, 1982-; Principal Oboist, Fresno Philharmonic Orchestra, 1986-. Lecturer and Guest Performer for inaugural year of California State University Summer Arts Institute, San Lius Obispo, California, 1986; Guest Lecturer on Oboe Pedagogy, California Music Educators Association Conventions, Fresno, 1985, Los Angeles, 1988. *Honours:* 1st Oboe, All American Youth Orchestra, 1971; 2nd Oboe, Bayreuth Jungenfestspiel Orchestra, 1972; Scholarship, Aspen Music Festival, 1974; Guest Artist, Summer Session for Music and the Arts, Siena, Italy, 1989. *Memberships:* International Double Reed Society; California Music Educators' Association; Pi Kappa Lambda; Mu Phi Epsilon. *Address:* California

State University at Fresno, Department of Music, Shaw and Maple, Fresno, CA 93740, USA.

DIAZ Justino, b. 29 Jan. 1939, San Juan, Puerto Rico. Singer (Bass-Baritone). *Education:* Studied at the University of Puerto Rico, at the New England Conservatory and with Ralph Errolle and Frederick Jagel. *Debut:* Puerto Rico 1957, in Menotti's The Telephone. *Career:* Metropolitan Opera from 1963, as Monterone and Sparafucile in Rigoletto, Figaro, Rossini's Maometto II and Colline; Festival Casals, Puerto Rico, 1964-65; Spoleto Festival 1965; Salzburg Festival 1966, as Escamillo; Created Antony in Barber's Antony and Cleopatra, New York Met 1966; La Scala Milan 1969, in Rossini's L'Assedio do Corinto; New York City Opera 1973, in Ginastera's Beatrix Cenci; Covent Garden 1976, as Escamillo; Guest appearances in Hamburg, Vienna, Mexico City, Chicago and San Francisco; San Francisco and Milan 1982, as Scarpia and Asdrubalo in La Pietra del Paragone; Sang Attila at Cincinnati, 1984, Iago at Covent Garden, 1990; Michelle in Il Tabarro at Miami, 1989, Iago and Scarpia at Los Angeles; Sang Escamillo at Rio de Janerio, 1990; Debut as Amonasro at Cincinnati, 1990; Sang Iago in Zeffirelli's film version of Otello, 1987; Greater Miami Opera 1992 as Franchetti's Cristoforo Colombo. *Recordings:* Medea and La Wally (Decca); Thais by Massenet (RCA); L'Assedio di Corinto and Otello (EMI); Semele (Pye); Videos of Zeffirelli's Otello and Meyerbeer's L'Africaine, from San Francisco Opera. *Address:* c/o Stafford Law Associates, 26 Mayfield Road, Weybridge, Surrey KT13 8XB, England.

DIBAK Igor, b. 5 July 1947, Spisska Nova Ves, Czechoslovakia. Composer. m. Katarina Ormisova, 31 Jan 1970. *Education:* Piano study, Conservatorie Zilina, 1962-66; With Professor Jan Cikker, Department of Composition, University of Arts, Bratislava, 1966-71; Magister. *Career:* Editor, Musical Department, Czechoslovak TV, 1969-79; Editor-in-Chief, Musical Department, Czech Radio, Bratislava, 1979-87; Editor-in-Chief, Musical Department, Czech TV, Bratislava, 1987-90; Director of Music School, 1990. *Compositions:* Opera Candlestick; New Year's Eve Part; Ballet Portrait; Symphonic works; Chamber compositions; Compositions for children. *Recordings:* Moments musicaux 1, Fantasy for Viola and Orchestra, Divertimento for Strings, Opera Candlestick, OPUS Bratislava; Opera Candlestick, New Year's Eve Part, Ballet Portrait, Czech TV, Symphonic and Chamber works, Czech Radio Bratislava. *Publications:* Methodics of Piano Improvisation, Slovak Pedagogic Edition, 1981. *Contributions to:* Hudobny zivot (Music Live). *Honours:* Jan Levoslav Bella Award, 1979; Union of Slovak Composers Award, 1987. *Memberships:* Slovak Music Union, Bratislava; Slovak Protective Union of Authors, Bratislava. *Current Management:* Music Information Centre, Fucikova 29, 811 02 Bratislava, Slovak Republic. *Address:* Bajzova 10, 821 08 Bratislava, Slovac Republic.

DICHIERA David, b. 8 Apr. 1937, McKeesport, Pennsylvania, USA. Opera Impresario. m. Karen Vander Kloot, 20 July 1965, 2 daughters. *Education:* BA summa cum laude, Music, 1956, MA Composition, 1958, PhD Musicology, 1962, University of California, Los Angeles; Certificate in Composition and Piano (Fulbright Research Guarantee), Naples Conservatory of Music, 1959. *Career:* Assistant Professor, University of California, Los Angeles, 1960-61; Assistant Professor of Music, 1962-65, Chairman, Music Department, 1966-73, Oakland University, Rochester, Michigan; Producer, Director, Overture to Opera Series, Detroit Grand Opera Series, 1963-71; Founder, General Director, Michigan Opera Theatre, Detroit, 1971-; Founding Director, Music Hall for the Performing Arts, Detroit, 1973-85; Artistic Advisor to President of Oakland University; Artistic Director, Dayton Opera Association, 1981-; General Director, Opera Pacific, California, 1984-. *Compositions:* Various works for piano, violin, voice, orchestra. *Address:* 6519 Second Avenue, Detroit, MI 48202, USA.

DICHTER Misha, b. 27 Sep. 1945, Shanghai, China. Concert Pianist. m. Cipa Dichter, 21 Jan. 1968, 2 sons. *Education:* BSc., Juilliard School of Music, USA. *Career:* Performs in Recital and with major orchestras and in chamber music concerts world-wide; Performances with Chicago Symphony, Los Angeles Philharmonic, Philadelphia Orchestra, etc; Performs in duo-piano programmes with wife, Cipa Dichter. *Recordings include:* Beethoven: Sonatas No. 14 in C Sharp Minor, Op 27 No 2, Moonlight; No 8 in C Minor, Op 13, Pathetique; No 28 in A Major, Op 101; Brahms Piano Concerto No 1 in D Minor; Brahms Piano Concerto No 2 in B Flat Major Op 83; Gershwin Rhapsody in Blue; Addinsell Warsaw Concerto; Litolff, Scherzo from Concerto Symphonique Op 102; Works by Liszt, including: Liszt complete Hungarian Rhapsodies; Fantasy on the Waltz from Gounod's Faust; Etudes de Concert; Schumann Symphonic Studies, Op 13 and Fantasie in C Major. *Contributions to:* New York Times; Ovation; Contemporary Keyboard. *Honours:* Silver Medal, International Tchaikovsky Competition, Moscow, 1966. *Hobbies:* Tennis; Jogging; Drawing; Sketching. *Address:* Shuman Associates, 120 West 58 Street, New York, NY 10019, USA.

DICK Eleanor, b. 12 Apr. 1918, New York City, USA. Teacher of Piano and Theory; Adjudicator. m. Franklin Dick, 3 sons, (1 deceased). *Education:* BS, Brooklyn College; MS, Columbia University; Student of A. K. Virgil, Alexander Bartnowksy, and Joseph Fidelman; Faculty Member, American College of Musicians; Master Class of Artur Schnabel; Graduate Studies at Hunter College, New York. *Career:* 40 years teaching experience presenting annual student recitals of solo and ensemble works at Carnegie Recital Hall, New York City; Solo students presented in recital at Judson Hall, Town Hall, CAMI Hall and the Young American Artists of the Municipal Broadcasting System, New York; Her musical transcriptions for one hand for handicapped students (Baroque-Contemporary), played by students in recitals and competitions and many students have won piano scholarships for colleges throughout the USA. *Memberships:* Piano Guild Hall of Fame; State and National Federation of Music Clubs; Music Teachers' National Association; New York State Music Teachers' Association; Piano Teachers' Congress; Chairman of Scholarship Awards and Auditions, Associated Music Teachers' League of New York City; Chairman of Young Musicians Concerts; Member of National Roster of Judges for the Music Teachers National Association. *Hobbies:* Reading; Travel. *Address:* 530 Valley Road, Upper Montclair, NJ 07043, USA.

DICKENSON James William, b. 20 Oct 1940, Cheshire, England. Musician. m. Gjertrud B Furuseth, 1989, 1 daughter. *Education:* Music Scholar, Canford School, Dorset, 1954-58; organ and piano with Antony Brown; LLB (Bristol), 1962; MusB (Manchester), 1974; GRSM, ARMCM, Royal Manchester College of Music, 1974; harpsichord with Robert Elliott, piano accompaniment with Clifton Helliwell; Private organ study with Roger Fisher and Graham Barber. *Debut:* BBC Radio 3, 1972. *Career:* Schoolmaster, 1966-70, 1974-78; Own piano teaching practice, 1978-83; Professional Keyboard Player, 1972-; Lecturer in Jazz Piano, Salford College of Technology, 1983-88; Examiner, Associated Board, Royal Schools of Music, 1979-; Resident in Norway, 1988-; Regular broadcasts on Norwegian Radio and concerts as organist and pianist; Organist, Resident Music Leader, South Fron Kommune, Gudbrandsdalen, Norway, 1990-. *Address:* N-2647 Hundorp, Gudbrandsdalen, Norway.

DICKERSON Roger Donald, b. 24 Aug. 1934, New Orleans, Louisiana, USA. Composer. *Eucation:* Studied at Dillard University, New Orleans and with Bernard Heiden at Indiana University, Bloomington; Further study at the Akademie für Musik und Darstellende Kunst, Vienna. *Career:* Played double bass while in military service; Has taught and performed in the New Orleans area; Co-founder of the Creative Arts Alliance, 1975; Subject of PBS programme, New Orleans Concert. *Honours include:* Fulbright scholarship, 1959-62; John Hay Whitney Fellowship 1964; Louis Armstrong Memorial Award. *Compositions Include:* Perkussion

1954; Variations for woodwind trio 1955; Sonatina for piano 1956; String Quartet 1956; Music I Hears for soprano and piano 1956; Chorale prelude for organ 1957; Music for String Trio 1957; Concert Overture 1957; Essay for band 1958; Fugue 'n' Blues for band 1959; Clarinet Sonata 1960; Wind Quintet 1961; A Musical Service for Louis 1972; Orpheus an'his Slide Trombone 1975; New Orleans Concerto for piano and orchestra 1976; Psalm XLIX 1979. *Address:* c/o ASCAP, ASCAP Building, One Lincoln Plaza, New York, NY 10023, USA.

DICKIE Brian, b. 23 July 1941. m. (1) Victoria Teresa Sheldon (nee Price), 1968, 2s 1d; (2) Nancy Gustafson, 1989. *Education:* Haileybury; Trinity College, Dublin. *Career:* Admin Assistant, Glyndebourne Opera, 1962-66; Administrator, Glyndebourne Touring Opera, 1967-81; Glyndebourne Festival Opera: Opera Manager, 1970-81, Gen Administrator, 1981-89; Artistic Director, Wexford Festival, 1967-73; Artistic Advisor, Theatre Musical de Paris, 1981- 87; Chairman, London Choral Society, 1978-85; Vice-Chairman, TNC, 1980-85 (Chairman, TNCC Opera Committee, 1976-85); Vice President, Theatrical Management Association, 1983-85; General Director, Canadian Opera Company, 1989-93. *Address:* 405 Edgemere Way, North, Naples, FL 33999, USA.

DICKIE John, b. 5 Sept. 1953, London, England. Singer (Tenor). *Education:* Studied with Luise Scheidt and with Hilde Zadek at the Vienna Conservatory. *Career:* Sang at Wuppertal 1979-82, Mannheim 1982-85; Hamburg Staatsoper from 1985; Bregenz Festival 1981-86, in L'Incontro Improvviso, Lucia di Lammermoor, Der Vogelhändler and Die Zauberflöte; Guest appearances in London, Geneva, Dusseldorf, Berlin and Vienna; Other roles include Mozart's Belmonte, Don Ottavio, Ferrando and Belfiore, Lionel in Martha, Nemorino in L'Elisir d'Amore, Berlioz's Benedict, Lensky in Eugene Onegin and Wagner's Steuermann and Froh; Also heard as concert singer. *Address:* c/o Hamburgsche Staatsoper, Grosse Theaterstrasse 34, D-2000 Hamburg, Germany.

DICKIE Murray, b. 3 April 1924, Bishopton, Glasgow, Scotland. Singer (Tenor). *Education:* Studied with Dino Borgioli in London, Stefan Pollmann in Vienna and Guido Farinelli in Milan. *Career:* Sang at the Cambridge Theatre, London, 1947-49; Covent Garden 1949-52, notably in the premiere of The Olympians by Bliss; Glyndebourne Festival 1950-54, in Die Entführung, Le Nozze di Figaro, Ariadne auf Naxos, The Rake's Progress and Arlecchino; Vienna Staatsoper from 1951, notably in the 1956 premiere of Frank Martin's The Tempest; Salzburg Festival from 1955, as Pedrillo in Die Entführung and in Martin's Mystère sur la Nativité; Guest appearances in Milan, Barcelona, Paris and Munich; Metropolitan Opera 1962, as Don Ottavio; Produced Eine Nacht in Venedig at the London Coliseum, 1976. *Recordings:* Arlecchino by Busoni; Die Frau ohne Schatten (Decca); Salome; Der Rosenkavalier; Ariadne auf Naxos; Fidelio (Deutsche Grammophon). *Address:* c/o Staatsoper, Opernring 2, A-1010 Vienna, Austria.

DICKINSON Meriel, b. 8 April 1940, Lytham St Annes, England. Singer (Mezzo-Soprano). *Education:* GRSM; ARMCM; Piano and Singing Performer's Diploma with Honours; Vienna Academy, Austria. *Debut:* London 1964. *Career:* Frequent radio programmes; 2 BBC TV Documentary films; Recital programmes with composer Peter Dickinson (brother) throughout Europe. *Recordings:* Contemporary British Composers (Crosse, Berkeley, Dickinson); Erik Satie Songs and Piano Music; Brecht-Weill series with London Sinfonietta. *Honours:* Countess of Munster Musical Trust Scholarship, 1964-66. *Memberships:* Society for Promotion of New Music; Park Lane Group; ISM. *Hobbies:* Listening to Jazz; Entertaining. *Address* c/o Music International, 13 Ardilaun Road, London, N5 2QR, England.

DICKINSON Peter, b. 15 Nov. 1934, Lytham, Lancashire, England. Composer; Pianist; Emeritus Professor of Music. m. Bridget Jane Tomkinson, 2 sons. *Education:* Queens' College, Cambridge; MA, Music; LRAM; ARCM, Piano Performance; ARCO, Sawyer Prize; FRCO; DMus; Hon FTCL; Juilliard School of Music, New York, USA. *Career:* Various teaching posts in New York, London and Birmingham; First Professor of Music, Keele University, 1974-84; now Emeritus; Professor, Goldsmiths' College, University of London, 1991-; Regular Performances as Pianist most with sister Meriel Dickinson (mezzo), radio and television in Great Britain and abroad. *Compositions include:* Orchestral works; Concertos; Chamber music; Choral works; keyboard music; Church music (all Novello). *Recordings:* Piano Concerto; Organ Concerto; Outcry; A Mass of the Apocalypse; Winter Afternoons; Recorder Music; Extravaganzas; Surrealist Landscape; The Unicorns; Organ Music; Piano Music and Songs; Has recorded on Argo, Unicorn, Hyperion, Conifer and EMI labels. *Publications:* Editor, 20 British Composers, 1975; The Complete Songs and Piano Music of Lord Berners, 1982; The Music of Lennox Berkeley, 1989. *Contributions to:* Various books and journals to include book chapters and Dictionaries. *Honours:* Recipient of various honours including, Fellowship of the Royal Society of Arts, (FRSA). *Memberships include:* PRS; Association of Professional Composers; Sonneck Society; Royal Musical Association; Board, Trinity College of Music, 1985-; President, London Concert Choir, 1985-. *Hobby:* Books. *Address:* Goldsmiths' College, New Cross, London SE14 6NW, England.

DICKMAN Stephen (Allen), b. 2 Mar 1943, Chicago, Illinois, USA. Composer. *Education:* Studied composition with Jacob Druckman at Bard College, and theory and composition with Arthur Berger and Harold Shapero at Bandeis University; Further study with Ernst Krenek at the Berkshire Music Center and with Goffredo Petrassi in Rome. *Career:* Has travelled widely, in order to study the music of Asia and the Middle East; Teacher at the Tape Music Center, Mills College, 1976-81. *Compositions include:* 2 String Trios 1965, 1971; The Snow Man for soprano and ensemble 1966; Frei for tape 1966; Lacerations for tape 1966; 4 String Quartets 1967-78; Damsel for 16 instruments 1968; Violoncello 1969; 2 Violins 1969; Real Magic in New York, opera 1971; Song Cycle 1975-80; Musical Journeys 1-1V 1972-76; 10 Not Long Songs 1977; Magic Circle for chorus and ensemble 1980; String Trio: Dance 1980; Influence of India for ensemble 1980; Everything and Everything for 3 trumpets and strings 1982; Orchestra by the Sea for 4 sopranos and orchestra 1983; Trees and other Inclinations for piano 1983. *Address:* c/o ASCAP, ASCAP Building, One Lincoln Plaza, New York, NY 10023, USA.

DICKSON Joan, b. 21 Dec. 1921, Edinburgh, Scotland. Cellist; Teacher. *Education:* LRAM; ARCM; Studied in Paris and Rome. *Career:* Solo Cellist with major British orchestras; Appearances at the London Promenade Concerts, Cheltenham Festival, Edinburgh Festival; Tours abroad; Regular Broadcaster; TV appearances; Professor of Cello, Royal College of Music, London; Teacher of Cello, Royal Scottish Academy of Music, Glasgow; Short Talks, BBC Radio. *Recordings:* Iain Hamilton Cello Sonata; Tam O'Bedlam's Song; Cesar Franck Sonata. *Contributions to:* Incorporated Society of Musicians Magazine. *Honours:* FRCM; FRSAMD; Cobbett Gold Medal for services to Chamber Music. *Hobbies:* Gardening; Philately; Painting. *Address:* 4 Great Stuart Street, Edinburgh EH3 6AW, Scotland.

DICTEROW Glenn (Eugene), b. 23 Dec. 1948, Los Angeles, California, USA. Violinist; Teacher. m. Georgeann Tobin, 27 June 1980, 2 daughters. *Education:* BMus, Juilliard School of Music, New York, 1970. *Career:* Associate Concertmaster then Concertmaster, Los Angeles Philharmonic Orchestra, 1972-79; Concertmaster, New York Philharmonic Orchestra, 1980-; Soloist with various USA Orchestras; Engaged in private teaching; Teacher, University of Southern California, Los Angeles and Manhattan School of Music, New York. *Honours:* 1st prize, Young Musicians Foundation, 1962; 3rd prize, Merriweather Post Competition, 1963; Bronze Medal, Tchaikovsky International Competition, 1970. *Address:* c/o New York Philharmonic Orchestra, Lincoln Center, New York, NY 10023, USA.

DIDONE Rosanna, b. 13 Feb 1952, Veneta, Italy. Singer (Soprano). *Education:* Studied at the Benedetto Marcello Conservatory Venice. *Debut:* Padua 1978, as Serpina in La Serva Padrona. *Career:* Appearances at Venice in Idomeneo, as Rosette in Manon and Bianca in La Rondine; Clarice in Il Mondo Della Luna at Turin and Frasquita in Carmen at Padua, 1982; At Trieste (from 1982) has sung Gnese in Il Campiello, Amor (Orpheus ed Euridice), Barbarina, and a Naiad in Aridne auf Naxos; Rome Opera 1982 and 1988 in Don Carlos and as Mme Silberklang in Der Schauspieldirektor by Mozart; Other roles include Musetta, Marie-Louise in Kodaly's Hary Janos, Biancofiore in Francesca and Rimini, Gilda, Susanna, Carolina (Il matrimonio segreto), Norina (Don Pasquale), Oscar, Nannetta, Laura and Despina; Guest appearances in Holland and Bulgaria. *Recordings include:* Egloge in Mascagni's Nerone, and Francesca da Rimini (Bongiovanni).

DIEMECKE Paulo Roberto, b. 1 Dec. 1950, Xalapa, Veracruz, Mexico. Violinist. m. Joan King, 19 Sept. 1979. *Education:* Diemecke Academy; Mexico City Conservatory; Studies with Enrique Espin Yepez, Henryk Szeryng, Emilio Diemeck, Robert Gerle, Daniel Majeske. *Debut:* Carnegie Hall, New York, 1977. *Career:* Concertmaster, Guanajuato Symphony, 1968-71; Concertmaster, Mexico State Symphony, 1975-79; 2nd Concertmaster, National Symphony of Mexico, 1977-79; Assistant Concertmaster, Filarmónica de las Americas, 1979, 1980; Assistant Concertmaster, Washingtom Chamber Orchestra, National Gallery, and Washington Ballet Orchestra, 1979-80; Concertmaster, Xalapa Symphony, 1980-86; Concertmaster, Victoria Symphony, 1986-; Recitals, Mexico and USA, 19601; Solo performances, with major Mexican orchestras, Mexico, USA, with Victoria Symphony, Canada, 1969-. *Honour:* Golden Lyre, 1983. *Current Management:* Associacion Daniel, Mexico City. *Address:* Cerrada de los Naranjos apt 26, Jardines de las Animas, Zalapa, Veracruz 91190, Mexico.

DIEMER Emma Lou, b. 24 Nov 1927, Kansas City, Missouri, USA. Composer; Musician; University Professor. *Education:* BM, 1949, MM, 1950, Yale School of Music; PhD, Eastman School of Music, 1960. *Career:* Pianist; Organist; Composer-in-Residence, Santa Barbara Symphony, 1990-; Professor of Composition, University of California, Santa Barbara, 1971-91; Organist, first Presbyterian Church, Santa Barbara, 1984-. *Compositions:* Over 100 published compositions; 10 listings in Schwann Catalogue, 17 works recorded; Concerto for Marimba, 1990; Concerto for Piano, 1953-91; Sextet, 1992; Four Biblical Settings for organ, 1992. *Recordings:* 10 including Declarations for Organ; Toccata & Fugue for Organ; Toccata for Piano; Summer of 82 for Cello and Piano; Quartet for Piano, Violin, Viola and Cello; Sextet for Woodwind Quintet and Piano; Youth Overture; Encore for Piano, 1991; Sextet, 1993. *Publications:* Over 100 including, Toccata for Marimba, 1956; Sonata for Violin and Piano, 1968; Sextet for Woodwind Quintet and Piano, 1968; Concerto for Flute, 1973; Symphony No 2, 1976; Toccata for Piano, 1979; Anniversary Choruses for Chorus and Orchestra, 1970; Suite of Homages for orchestra, 1985; String Quartet No. 1, 1987; Choral - A Feast for Christmas, 1992; Organ Works, 1957-1993. *Address:* 2249 Vista del Campo, Santa Barbara, CA 93101, USA.

DIENER Betty Sue, b. 18 Aug 1959, Maryland, USA. Musicologist. *Education:* BA, Goucher College, 1981; MA, Mus, 1985; MPhil Music, 1987; PhD Music, Columbia University, 1992; Piano Graduate, Peabody Institute, Johns Hopkins University, 1976; Private studies with Julio Esteban, 1976-77. *Career:* Tutor, Music Humanities, Columbia University, 1983-89, 1991; Administrative Research, 1983-84; 1991-92, Columbia University, New York City; Part-time Faculty, Peabody Elderhostel, Peabody Institute, Johns Hopkins University, Baltimore, Maryland, 1993-94; Faculty Associate, School of Continuing Studies, Johns Hopkins University, Baltimore, 1994; Mozart Akademie Lecturer, 1993; Lectured at Annual Meeting of American Musicological Society in Chicago, Ilinois, USA, 1991. *Publications:* Editorial Board, Current Musicology, 1985; Irony in Mozart's Operas, doctoral dissertation. *Honours:* Two Travel Grants, 1989, 1991, 5 President's Fellowships, 1987-91, 1992, Columbia University; German Academic Exchange Service Scholarship, 1989; General Honours and Honours in Music, 1981, Ruth Blaustein Rosenberg Prize in Music, 1981, Henry and Ruth Blaustein Rosenberg Scholarship in Music, 1977-79, 2 Goucher Scholarships, 1979-81, Goucher College. *Memberships:* American Musicological Society. *Hobbies:* Painting; Travel. *Address:* 15 Farmhouse Ct, Baltimore, MD 21208, USA.

DIESSELHORST Jan, b. 1956, Marburg, Germany. Cellist. *Education:* Studied in Frankfurt and with Wolfgang Boettcher in Berlin. *Career:* Joined the Berlin Philharmonic Orchestra 1979; Co-founded the Philharmonic Quartet Berlin, giving concerts throughout Europe the USA and Japan; British debut 1987, playing Haydn, Szymanowski and Beethoven at Wigmore Hall; Bath Festival, 1987, playing Mozart, Schumann and Beethoven (Op. 127); Other repertoire includes quartets by Bartok, Mendelssohn, Nicolai, Ravel and Schubert; Quintets by Brahms, Weber, Reger and Schumann. *Address:* Philharmonia Quartet Berlin, Anglo Swiss Ltd, 3 Primrose Mews, 1a Sharpleshall St, London NW1 8YW, England.

DIETHELM J Caspar, b. 31 Mar 1926, Lucerne, Switzerland. Composer; Conductor; Professor; Author. m. Brigitte Ullrich, 8 Aug 1960, 3 daughters. *Education:* Diploma in Theory of Music, Academy of Music, Lucerne. *Debut:* Tonhalle, Zurich, 1948. *Career:* Professor of History of Music, Professor of Theory of Music, Professor of Composition, Chamber Music, Academy of Music, Lucerne, 1963-93. *Compositions:* 300 works including 2 oratorios, 9 symphonies, 40 concertos, cantatas, chamber music and one ballet. *Recordings:* String quartet No 3; Piano Sonatas No 7, 9, 20; Sonata for Violin; Sonata Nos 1, 2 for Guitar; Pan for flute; Menhir for Violin Solo and String-Orchestra. *Publication:* Editor, Amadeus Winterthur. *Honours:* Creative Arts Award, Canton of Obwalden, 1968; Creative Arts Award, City of Lucerne, 1986. *Hobbies:* Mineralogy; Philosophy; Painting; Writing. *Address:* Rebstockhalde 4, CH-6006 Lucerne, Switzerland.

DIETRICH Karl, b. 9 Jul. 1927, Wachstedt, Eichsfeld, Germany. Composer; Teacher .m. Gerda Lins, 29 Apr. 1952, 2 daughters. *Education:* Matriculation and Study, University Jena and High School of Music, Franz Liszt, Weimar, State examination for Music Teachers. *Career:* Professor for composition in the High School of Music, Franz Liszt, Weimar. *Compositions:* Numerous compositions including: 7 Symphonies, 2 Operas, 1 Piano Concerto, 1 Violoncello Concerto, Dramatic Szenes for 3 flutes, 1 soloist, and large Orchestra, 2 Concertos for string orchestra, Symphonic Choral Works, Chamber Music, Songs; O vos omnes, aus den Klageliedern des Jeremias, in memoriam G. P. Palestrina, für Sopran und Streichquartett, 1991; Lobpreis und Bitte, für 4-6 voice mixed choir, Hymnus mit Orgelbegleitung, 1991, Kirchenmusik; Memorial für Streichorchester nach dem Bach-Choral, Vergiß mein nicht, 1993. *Recordings include:* Nova 1985, VEB Deutsche Schallplatten Berlin: Symphony Nr.4-contra bellum- (Staatliches Sinfonieorchester Thüringen, Sitz Gotha, Conductor Lothar Seyfarth) and Dramatische Szenen for 3 flutes (1 soloist) and large Orchestra, Rundfunk-Sinfonie Orchester Leipzig, (Conductor Herbert Kegel) *Publications:* Komische Oper, Pervonte, Berlin; Symphony Nr.4 - contra bellum - Leipzig; Violoncello Concerto - Leipzig; Vision for Flute and Organ - Leipzig; Konzertsuite for String Orchestra - Berlin; Concertino giocoso for string orchestra, Leipzig;

Dramatische Szenen, Berlin, Prokofiev, Variationen für Klavier zu 4 Händen, Berlin; Aus Ellens Blockflötenalbum für Blockflöte u.Klavier, Leipzig; Three Cheerful Stories (a cappella choir), Leipzig. *Honours:* Kunstpreis des FDGB, 1971; Kunstpreis der DDR, 1975; Literatur-und Kunstpreis der Stadt Weimar, 1983. *Memberships:* Komponistenverband, Landesverband Thüringen; Mitglied Deutscher Komponisten-Verband. *Address:* Zum Wilden Graben 24, 99425 Weimar, Germany.

DIETRICHS Marilyn Dixon Altrock, b. 5 Nov. 1927, Hartford, USA. Concert Artist; Founder/Artistic Director (1978) of the Atlanta Repertory Opera Company (Georgia, USA). m. Donald Dietrichs, 3 sons. *Education:* AA, Music Lasell Junior College; Credits, Boston University, Juillard School of Music, Brevard Summer Music Camp. *Career:* Accomplished soprano of Opera & Concert Stage throughout the Southeast for 36 years under management of Alkahest Attractions Inc. & The Charlotte Gaines Productions: In 1978, became Founder/Artistic Director of Atlanta Repertory Opera Company serving as President of Board of Directors for four years. In 1980, President of The Pro-Mozart Society after previously serving 6 years as Vice President of Membership & Publicity. Radio & TV Club Engagements; Soloist, Churches of Christ Scientists; Music Director, 2nd Church, Christ Scientist, Atlanta, 1980-89. *Address:* 9035 Niblick Drive, Alpharetta, GA 30201, USA.

DIETSCH James William, b. 21 Mar. 1950, Kansas City, Missouri, USA. Opera Singer, Baritone. m. Susan Kay Schell, 23 Aug. 1980. 1 son. *Education:* BME 1972, MMus Voice 1975, University of Missouri, Kansas City; Juilliard School of Music American Opera Center, 1979-82; Vienna Academy of Music, Austria. *Debut:* Fargo-Moorhead Civic Opera, 1975; New York Town Hall, 1981; Carnegie Hall, 1982. *Career:* Leading artist with numerous opera companies and concert appearances in USA and abroad including: San Francisco Opera, New York City Opera, English Opera North, Karlsruhe Badisches Staatstheater; Saarbrucken Saarländiches Staatstheater; Michigan Opera, Milwaukee Opera, Dusseldorf Oper am Rhine, Minnesota Opera, Hawaii Opera, Staatstheater Essen, Santa Fe Opera, Spoleto Festival USA, New York Philharmonic, Mexico City Philharmonica; Season 1992 as Scarpia at Costa Mesa, (Opera Pacific) and Nabucco at Montreal. *Recording:* Il Corsaro by Verdi, Historical Recording Incorporate, 1981. *Hobbies:* Golf; Skiing; Swimming; Basketball; Electric trains; Coin collections; Biking. *Address:* c/o Robert Lombardo Associates, 62 West 62nd Street Suite 6F, New York, NY 10023, USA.

DIGGER Anthony M., b. 5 July 1938, Hereford, England. Pianist; Teacher. m. Margaret Munday, 13 Aug 1966, 3s. *Education:* Guildhall School of Music; Trinity College of Music, London; Studied with Frank Laffitte, Frank Merrick, Sidney Harrison and Kendall Taylor. *Career:* Assistant Director of Music, Ifield Grammar School, Sussex, 1963-65; Director of Music, Kingsbury School, Dunstable, 1965-67; Director of Music, City of Worcester Grammar School for Girls, 1967-84; Director of Music, Worcester Sixth Form College, 1984-89; Examiner, Associated Board of The Royal Schools of Music, 1981-. *Memberships:* Incorporated Society of Musicians; European Piano Teachers' Association. *Hobbies:* Calligraphy. *Address:* 15 Wykewane, Malvern, Worcs WR14 2SU, England.

DIJKSTRA Hebe, b. 1952, Holland. Singer (Mezzo-soprano); m. Jan Alofs. *Education:* Studied at the Hague Conservatory. *Debut:* Sang Gluck's Orpheus at Enschede, 1975. *Career:* Sang Mistress Quickly at Enschede, and appeared in Rimsky's Sadko at Bonn, 1976; Engaged at Detmold, 1976-79, Saarbrucken 1979-80, Freiburg, 1981-83; Krefeld, 1982-85, Wuppertal, 1987-89; Amsterdam, 1989, in Der Kreidekreis by Zemlinsky; Member of the Staatstheater am Gartnerplatz, Munich, from 1989; Sang Rossweise in Die Walkure at Bayreuth, 1988-91; Ulrica at Amsterdam 1992; Mary in Fliegende Hollander at the 1992 Bayreuth Festival; Other roles include Carmen, Fricka, Waltraute, the Nurse in Boris Godunov, and La Comandante in I Cavalieri di Ekebu by Zandonai. *Address:* c/o Staatstheater am Gärtnerplatz, Gärtnerplatz 3, 8000 Munich, Germany.

DILLON James, b. 29 Oct. 1950, Glasgow, Scotland. Composer. *Education:* Glasgow School of Art, 1967-68; Polytechnic of Central London, 1972-73; Polytechnic of North London, 1973-76. *Career:* Works performed and featured at festivals throughout the world including: Antidogma (Turin), Bath, Darmstadt, Gulbenkian (Lisbon), Huddersfield, ISCM (Toronto), La Rochelle, Musica Nel Nostro Tempo (Milan), Music of Eight Decades (London), Paris d'Automne, Warsaw, Zig-Zag (Paris), Ars Musica (Brussels), Musica (Strasbourg), Chatalet (Paris), Donauerchingen (Germany); Guest Lecturer at the Universities of Keele, London, New York, Nottingham, Oxford also Universities of Central England and Gothenburg; Guest Composer at the 1982, 1984 and 1986 Darmstadt Fierenkurse. *Compositions:* Spleen, 1980; Once Upon a Time, 1980; Come Live With Me, 1981; Parjanya-Vata, 1981; East 11th Street, 1982; String Quartet, 1983; Le Rivage, 1984; Sgothan, 1984; Diffraction, 1984; Windows and Canopies, 1985; Uberschreiten, 1986; La Coupure, 1986; helle Nacht, 1987; Works recorded and broadcast throughout the world; Del Cuarto Elemento, 1988; L'Eclan Parfum, 1988; Shrouded Mirrors, 1988; La Femme Invisible, 1989; L'Oeuvrs Au Noir, 1990; Eileadh Sguaibe, 1990; String Trio, 1990-91; Blitzschlag, 1991; String Quartet No.2. 1991; Nuée, 1991; Ignis Noster, 1991-92; Siorram, 1992; Lumen Naturae, 1992; Vernal Showers, 1992; L'Evolution Du Vol, 1993; Viriditas, 1993. *Recordings:* Sgothan, AMI 861-862; Del Cuarto Elemento; La Femme Invisible; East 11th Street, NY 10003; Windows and Canopies; Dillug-Kefitsah; Evening Rain; Come Live With Me. *Publications:* Problemas Discursivos en La Muska Contemporanea, Valencia, 1989; Speculative Instruments: Timbre, Métaphore pour La Composition, 1991. *Honour:* Kranichsteiner Musikpreis, Federal Republic of Germany, 1982; Classical Music Personality of the Year, London Times, 1989. *Current Management:* c/o Peters Edition Ltd. *Address:* c/o Peters Edition Ltd, 10-12 Baches Street, London M6DN, England.

DILWORTH-LESLIE Samuel, b. 17 Sept. 1937, Savannah, Georgia, USA. Concert Pianist; Teacher. *Education:* Graduated, New York City High School of Music and Art, 1951; BMus, MMus, Manhattan School of Music, 1951-56; Studies with N Boulanger, M Munz, D Zaslavsky; MA, Columbia University, New York City, 1956; Master classes with A Rubinstein, C Curzon, R and G Casadesus, N Magaloff. *Debut:* Carnegie Recital Hall, New York City, 1954. *Career:* Performed throughout Europe and USA; Participated in TV film Finding True Freedom, 1971; 1st public performance of complete piano works of Gabriel Fauré, Paris, 1974, New Brunswick, New Jersey, 1973-74, London, 1984; Organiser, Participant, 1st Chopin Festival, Rutgers University, New Brunswick, 1977; Gave 1st performance outside USSR of Estonian Arthur Lemba's Concerto No 1 with Swedish National Orchestra of Gothenburg, 1982, also American premiere with same orchestra, conductor Neeme Järvi, 1983; Professor of Piano, Mason Gross School of the Arts, Rutgers University. *Recording:* Fauré, CRS, 1985. *Address:* Mason Gross School of the Arts, Department of Music, Rutgers University, New Brunswick, NJ 08903, USA.

DIMEDIO Annette Maria, b. 22 Aug. 1958, Camden New Jersey, USA. Concert Pianist; College Professor; Researcher. *Education:* BA, Sociology, Anthropology, BA, Music, Swarthmore College; MM, Music History, Temple University; PhD, Musicology, Bryn Mawr, 1984. *Debut:* Soloist at age 9, Philadelphia Orchestra. *Career:* Piano Soloist with Toulouse Orchestra, under Michel Plasson, St Jean de Luz, France; Colombian Philharmonic, under Jaime Leon; Recitalist for Cardinal Keals Anniversary Celebration, Rome; Invitation to compete in Tchaikovsky Competition, Moscow; Director, Department of Defence Tour to Germany and Siam;

Appearances on TV including Crystal Cathedral and Fantasy; Radio broadcasts including Young Artists Showcase; Talent Co-ordinator, Community Arts Alliance, Philadelphia. *Composition:* Recorded: Outside My Door. *Recording:* Annette DiMedio in Recital. *Publication:* Frances McCollin, Unsung Heroine of Philadelphia, 1984. *Address:* 474 Loucroft Road, Haddonfield, NJ 08033, USA.

DIMITROVA Anastasia, b. 16 Nov 1940, Pernik, Bulgaria. Singer (Soprano). *Education:* Studied at the State Conservatory, Sofia and in Zagreb. *Debut:* Sang in Nabucco at Skopje, 1965. *Career:* Many appearances at opera houses in Bulgaria and Yugoslavia, notably Belgrade, Sofia, Zagreb and Rijeka; Roles have included Verdi's Elisabetta and Leonora (Trovatore), Mimi, Yaroslavna (Prince Igor), Tataiana in Eugene Onegin, Marenka (Bartéred Bride), Rusalka, Micaela, Euridice and Marguerite. *Honours:* Winner, Francisco Vinas (Barcelona 1969) and Bussetto Competitions. *Address:* c/o Sofia State Opera, Boulevard Dondoukov 58, 1000 Sofia, Bulgaria.

DIMITROVA Ghena, b. 6 May 1941, Beglej, Bulgaria. Singer (Soprano). *Education:* Studied with Professor Christo Brumbarov in Sofia. *Debut:* Sofia, as Abigaille in Nabucco. *Career:* Sang widely in Bulgaria and Yugoslavia; From 1970 sang in Italy and at Strasbourg, Karlsruhe, Mannheim and Stuttgart; US debut 1981, as Elvira in Ernani at Dallas; Verona Arena and La Scala Milan 1982, 1983, as Turandot; Barcelona 1984, as Verdi's Odabella; Salzburg Festival 1984, as Lady Macbeth; Covent Garden debut 1984, Turandot, returned 1990; New York debut as Abigaille, 1984; Guest appearances in Buenos Aires, Vienna, Paris, Dusseldorf and Berlin; Other roles include Aida, Norma, Leonora in Il Trovatore and La Gioconda; Sang Norma at Houston, 1987 and Paris; Aida at Luxor, Egypt, 1987; Verona Arena, 1988, as Turandot; Sang Santuzza at Covent Garden and the Metropolitan, 1989; Season 1992 as the Forza Leonora at Naples, Gioconda at Rome, Turandot at the Festival of Caracalla and Tosca at Torre del Lago. *Recordings:* Nabucco (Deutsche Grammophon); Aida; La Gioconda; I Lombardi and Oberto by Verdi; Video of Turandot (Thorn-EMI). *Address:* (Except for UK Engagements), Marks Management Ltd, 14 New Burlington Street, London W1X 1FF, England.

DINESCU Violeta, b. 13 July 1953, Bucharest, Romania. *Education:* Bachelor's Degree, College Georghe Lazar, Bucharest, 1972; Master's Degree 1977, Special diploma and study year for composition 1978, Conservatory Ciprian Porumbescu. *Career:* Instructor George Enescu Music School, Bucharest, 1978-82; Instructor, Conservatory for Church Music, Heidelberg, West Germany, 1986-1990; Lecturer, various Universities in West Germany, RSA, USA, 1986; Instructor for harmony/counterpoint in Hochschule, Frankfurt, 1989; Professor for theory/harmony and counterpoint at the Academy of church music, Bayreuth. *Compositions:* Orchestral compositions; Vocal compositions; Chamber music; Solos; Duos; Trios; Quartets; Quintets; Sextets; Septets; Chamber ensemble; Operas; Chamber opera; Children's opera; Ballet music; Film music; Experimental music. *Recordings:* Numerous radio recordings. *Honours:* Recipient of over 40 international prizes, distinctions and selections from several countries including: Romania, West Germany, Canada, USA, Italy, England, Columbia, RSA, Hungary, Poland, GDR and Austria. *Address:* Buttenstrasse 15, 76530 Baden-Baden, BP 140207, Germany.

DINGSTAD Tore, b. 8 Apr 1951, Oslo, Norway. Pianist and Conductor. m. Martina, 9 July 1976, 2 sons, 1 daughter. *Education:* Piano and Organ Diploma, Oslo Conservatory, 1973; Piano and Harpsichord Diploma, Musikhochschule Hannover, 1976. *Debut:* 1972. *Career:* Appearances with Norwegian orchestras, radio recordings NRK, Regular guest of the Bergen International Festival, one of the best known chamber musicians and accompanists in Norway; Working as Repetiteur and Conductor at the Norwegian State Opera, 1979-. *Recordings:* Works of Morten Gaathaug, Piano and Flute (Victoria) (VCD 19073) with Martina Dingstad. *Honours:* Debut Prize from Rikskonsertene, 1972; Scholarship from the Norwegian State, 1976-79; Klaestad Legat, 1975; Klaveness Legat, 1989. *Membership:* Norsk Tonekunstnersamfund. *Address:* Johan Svendsens vei 13, N-1410 Kolbotn, Norway.

DIVALL Richard S, b. 9 Sept. 1945, Sydney, New South Wales, Australia. Opera Conductor, General Music Director. *Debut:* Sydney, Australia. *Career:* Producer, Australian Broadcasting Commission 1962-70; Musical Director, Queensland Opera Company 1971-; Victoria State Opera 1972-; Associate, Faculty of Music, University of Melbourne; Artist in Residence, Queen's College, University of Melbourne; Numerous recordings for ABC. *Publications:* Complete works of Carl Linger, 1971; Numerous Colonial Australian works; Symphonies, Cipriani Potter, Samuel Wesley, 1980; Edited works by Gluck, Rameau, Handel, Wesley, Bellini, Verdi; Associate Professor, Faculty of Music, University of Melbourne, 1991. *Hobbies:* History; Historical cooking; Pewter collecting. *Current Management:* Jennifer Eddy. *Address:* East Wing Flat, Queen's College, University of Melbourne, Parkville, NSW 3053, Australia.

DIVOKY Zdenek, b. 1954, Brno, Czechoslovakia. Horn Player. *Education:* Studied at the Janacek Academy in Brno with Frantisek Solc. *Career:* Wind section of the State Philharmonic Orchestra in Brno; Czech Philharmonic 1979; Solo performer in concert and member of such chamber ensembles as the Prague Brass Trio, the Horn Quartet of the Czech Philharmonic, the Collegium Musicum Pragense and the Stamic Quartet; Solo engagements in Germany, Austraia, England, Spain and Canada; Repertoire includes concertos by M and J Haydn, Telemann, Mozart, Punto, Rosetti, Schumann, Weber and Strauss; Recitalist in Beethoven, Mozart, Reicha, Brahms, Britten, Hindemith and Burghauser; Tours with the Czech Philharmonic and with various chamber ensembles to Europe, the USA and Japan. *Honours include:* Prizewinner at Prague Spring International Festival and competitions in Munich and Markneukirchen. *Address:* c/o Anglo Swiss Ltd, 3 Primrose Mews, 1a Sharpleshall St, London NW1 8YW, England.

DIXON James, b. 26 April 1928, Estherville, Iowa, USA. Conductor. *Education:* Studied at the University of Iowa and with Dimitri Mitropoulos, 1949-60. *Career:* Conducted the US 7th Army Band in Germany; Led the University of Iowa Symphony 1954-59; New England Conservatory Symphony in Boston 1969-61; Conductor of the Tri-City Symphony in Davenport, Iowa, and Rock Island, Illinois; Associate conductor of the Minneapolis Symphony 1961-62; Guest conductor with the National Orchestra of Greece in Athens, the Norddeutscher Rundfunk, Hamburg, the Westdeutscher Rundfunk, Cologne, the Tanglewood orchestra, the Chicago Civic Symphony and the Chicago Symphony (1972); Conducted a student group at the International Society for Contemporary Music Festival in Boston, 1976; Has led the premieres of Charles Wuorinen's Piano Concerto and works by T J Anderson and William Matthews. *Honours include:* Gustav Mahler Medal, 1963.

DLUGONSKA Barbara, b. 28 Jan 1944, Grudziadz, Poland. Teacher; Music Theorist. *Education:* MA, Theory of Music; Lyceum of Music, Bydgoszcz, 1958-63; Diploma, Academy of Music, Gdansk, 1968. *Career:* Teacher, Theory of Music, Editor, Gdansk Music Academy, 1974-, *Publications include:* Bibliography of Polish Manuals and Papers for Educating an ear for Music, musical Forms and Counter Point of XIX and XX centuries, co-author, 1975; Piano Concerto in Polish Music of the XX century, 1976; Piotr Rytel's Views on Beauty and Want of Beauty in Music, 1983; Piotr Rytel 1884-1970, 1984; Piotr Rytel about Chopin and Moniuszko, 1989; Remarks from Piotr Rytel on Polish Pianists and Pianist Art, 1989; Piotr Rytel, Composer, 1991; Biography of Piotr Rytel, 1992; Contributor to

Polish Biographical Dictionary and National Library at Warsaw Institute of Music Collection. *Honours:* Minister of Culture Prize, 1977; Rector's Music Prizes, Academy, Gdansk, 1974-89. *Memberships:* Scientific Society of Gdansk. *Hobbies:* History; History of Culture. *Address:* Malczewskiego 78m 187, 80-107 Gdansk, Poland.

DLUGOSZEWSKI Lucia, b. 16 June 1934, Detroit, Michigan, USA. Composer. *Education:* Studied piano with Grete Sultan, music analysis at Mannes College and composition with Edgard Varese. *Career:* Devised the timbe piano 1951; Association with Erick Hawkins Dance Company; Commissions from the New York Philharmonic, the Music Society of Lincoln Center, the American Composers Orchestra and the Louisville Orchestra. *Compositions include:* Arithmetic Progressions for orchestra 1954; Orchestral Radiant Ground 1955; Here and Now with Watchers, dance 1954-57; Naked Wabin for flute and ensemble 1956; Suchness Concert for large percussion ensemble 1958; Clear Places, ballet 1958-60; Beauty Music 1965; Naked Flight Nageire for chamber orchestra 1966; Lords of Persia, ballet 1966-68; Balance Naked Flung for clarinet and ensemble 1966; Naked Quintet for brass 1967; Blake Lake ballet 1970; Space is a Diamond for trumpet 1970; Angels of the Inmost Heaven, ballet 1972; Strange Tenderness of Naked Leaping for orchestra 1977; Amor now Titling Night for orchestra 1978; Almost Elusive Empty August, woodwind quintet 1979; Cicada Terrible Freedom for flute and ensemble 1981; Startle Transparent Terrible Freedom for orchestra 1981; Avanti, ballet 1983; Duende Amor for orchestra 1983; Quidditas Sorrow Terrible Freedom for orchestra 1983; This Woman Duende Amor, ballet 1984; Quidditas, string quartet 1984. *Honours include:* Guggenheim Fellowship; Grant from the Martha Baird Rockefeller Fund; Koussevitsky International Recording Award 1977 for Fire Fragile Light. *Address:* c/o ASCAP, ASCAP Building, One Lincoln Plaza, New York, NY 10023, USA.

DMITRIEV Aleksander, b. 1935, Leningrad, USSR. Conductor. *Education:* Leningrad Conservatory, under Kudriavtseva, Tiulin, Rabinovitch. *Career:* Conductor Karelian Radio & TV Symphony Orchestra, 1961, principal conductor 1962-73; Princicpal conductor, Maly Opera & Ballet Theatre, Leningrad, 1973-77, Symphony Orchestra, Leningrad Philharmoniya, 1977-. *Recordings include:* Miaskovsky's Violin Concerto; Balakirev's Piano Concerto; Medtner's Piano Concerto No 1. *Honour:* Prize, 2nd USSR Competition for Conductors, 1966. *Address:* c/o Symphony Orchestra, Leningrad Philharmoniya, U1 Brokskogo 2, St Petersburg, Russia.

DOBBINS Frank, b. 6 Apr 1943, Dublin, Ireland. Musicologist; Lecturer. m. 3 sons. *Education:* Oxford University; Centre National de la Recherce Scientifique, Paris. *Career:* Lecturer, King's College, London, 1969-73; Senior Lecturer, Goldsmith's College, London, 1973-92, Reader, 1993-; Music Critic to The Financial times, 1970-73, The Times, 1974- 80, The Musical Times, 1971-85. *Publications:* Ed, Oxford Book of Chansons, 1987; Sonets de P de Ronsard mis en musique par G Boni, 1987; Music in Renaissance Lyons, 1992; Contributor to Doulce Memoire, Proceedings Royal Musical Association, 1970. *Honours:* Malin Memorial Award, 1990 for Oxford Book of Chansons. *Memberships:* Royal Musical Association; American Musicological Society. *Hobbies:* Bridge; Travel. *Address:* 62 Manor Avenue, London SE4 1TE, England.

DOBBS Jack, b. 22 July 1922, Gloucestershire, England. m. Ruth Astrid Heaton, 16 July 1960, 2s. *Education:* BA Hons Music, 1943; Dip. Ed, 1944, University of Wales; MEd, University of Durham, 1954; MPhil, London University, 1972; LRAM, 1944; LTCL, 1950; FRSA, 1974; FRAS, 1983; Diploma in Theology, University of Oxford, 1988. *Career:* Music Master, Stanley Grammar School, 1944-47; Music Advisor for County Durham, 1947-51; Staff Tutor and Research Fellow, Durham University Institute of Education, 1952-54; Director of Music, Malayan Teachers College, Brinsford Lodge, 1955-59; Lecturer, University of London Institute of Education, 1959-67; Head of Music

and Deputy Principal, Dartington College of Arts, 1967-87. *Compositions:* Songs; Anthems; Hymn Tunes; String Suite. *Publications include:* The Oxford School Music Books, 1954-61; Ears and Eyes, 1974, 1979, 1980; Editor: International Society of Music Education Year Books, 1982-88; Music Education: Facing the Future, 1990; Co- Editor, International Journal of Music Education, 1985-. Contributor to professional journals as well as: The New Grove Dictionaries of Music and Musical Instruments, 1981, 1984; Folk Music in Schools, 1978; Curriculum Opportunities in a Multicultural Society, 1984. *Hobby:* Fell Walking. *Address:* 8 Haytor Vale, Newton Abbot, Devon TQ13 9XP, England.

DOBBS Mattiwilda, b. 11 July 1925, Atlanta, Georgia, USA. Opera Singer (coloratura soprano); Professor. m. Bengt Janzon. *Education:* BA, Spelman College, USA; MA, Columbia University, USA; Studied voice, New York with Lotte Leonard, 1946-50; Special coaching in Paris with Pierre Bernac, 1950-52. *Career:* Appeared in Royal Dutch Opera, Holland Festival, 1952; Recitals, Sweden, Paris, Holland, 1952; Appeared in Opera, La Scala, Milan, 1953; Concerts in England and Continent, 1953; Glyndebourne Opera, 1953-54, 1956, 1961; Covent Garden Opera, 1953, 1954, 1956, 1958; Command Performance, Covent Garden, 1954; Annual Concert Tours, USA, 1954-; Australia and New Zealand, 1955, 1959, 1968; Australia, 1972, 1977; Israel, 1957 and 1959; USSR concerts and opera (Bolshoi Theatre), 1959; San Francisco Opera, 1955; Debut at Metropolitan Opera, 1956, there annually, 1956-; Appearances, Hamburg State Opera, 1961-63; Royal Swedish Opera, 1957 and then annually; Norwegian and Finnish Operas, 1957-64; Visiting Professor, University of Texas at Austin, 1973-74; Professor, University of Illinois, 1975-76; University of Georgia, 1976-77; Professor, Howard University, Washington, DC, 1977-. *Address:* 1101 South Arlington Ridge Road, Arlington, VA 22202, USA.

DOBIASOVA Marica, b. 1 Apr 1951, Bratislava, Czechoslovakia. Harpsichordist. m. Viliam Dobias, 9 Nov 1974, 2 daughters. *Education:* Bratislava Conservatoire, 1972; MA, Academy of Art, 1976. *Debut:* Summer Festival, Bratislava, 1976. *Career:* Member, Music Aeterna chamber orchestra, 1974-; Teacher, Commenius University, 1976-79; Teacher, Academy of Art, 1985-88; Member, Slovak Philharmony, 1986-; Regular TV and radio appearances; Participant, Bratislava Music Festival (AEFM); 1st performances of compositions by Santroch, Roskovsky, Speer, Zimmermann, Hrusovsky. *Recordings:* F P Riegler: Sonatas, world premiere; V Kubicka: Concerto for harpsichord, world premiere; Ch W Gluck: Trio sonatas; Continuo recordings with Musica Aeterna. *Honours:* Laureat, Beethoven's Hradec, 1975. *Hobbies:* Fine art; Swimming. *Address:* Gessayova 17, 85103 Bratislava, Czech Republic.

DOBREE Georgina, b. 8 Jan 1930, London, England. Clarinet and basset horn soloist; Teacher. Editor. *Education:* Royal Academy of Music, 1946-48; studied with Gaston Hemelin, Paris, 1949. *Career:* Member of chamber music ensembles; Recitals, broadcasts, lecture recitals and masterclasses in Europe and USA; many premières and recipient of numerous dedications; Professor, Royal Academy of Music, 1967-86; Director, Chantry Records, formed, 1975, mainly of 19th/20th Century works and own performances. *Publications:* Chantry Publications, 1988, eds. of 19th Century music for clarinet and/or basset horn; Chantry Publications, 1988; Editions of other works with clarinet for MR, OUP, Schott, Chester & Nova. *Honours:* French Government Scholarship, 1949; First Prize, Darmstadt, 1953; Fellow, RAM, 1982. *Memberships:* RMA; International Clarinet Association; CASS; RAM Club; Royal Society of Musicians. *Address:* 109 Friern Park, London N12 9LH, England.

DOBSON John, b. 1930, Derby, England. Singer (Tenor). *Education:* Guildhall School of Music, with Norman Walker; Study in Italy with Giovanni Inghilleri.

Debut: Bergamo 1957, as Pinkerton. *Career:* New Opera Company 1958, in Sir John in Love and A Tale of Two Cities; Glyndebourne Festival 1959, in Der Rosenkavalier; Engagements with English National Opera, Welsh National Opera and Scottish Opera; Deutsche Oper am Rhein, Dusseldorf, Orange Festival and Maggio Musicale, Florence; Covent Garden from 1959, in 95 roles and 1900 performances: roles include Wagner's David, Mime, Loge and Melot, Beethoven's Jacquino and Mussorgsky's Shuisky; Sang Paris in the premiere of Tippett's King Priam, Coventry, 1962; Sang Luke in the 1977 premiere of Tippett's The Ice Break; With the Royal Opera at La Scala Milan, 1976 and the Far East, 1979, 1986 & 1992; Sang Mime in the first Japanese performances of Wagner's Ring, with the Deutsche Oper, 1987; Sang in the British Premiere of Berio's Un Re in Ascolto, 1989; Borsa in Rigoletto; InnKeeper in a new production of the Cunning Little Vixen, 1990, The Emperor in Turandot; Director of Young Singers Ensemble at Covent Garden; Sang Mime in Siegfried, 1991, Jakob Glock in a new production of Prokofiev's Fiery Angel, 1992. *Recordings include:* Videos of Peter Grimes, Otello, Samson et Dalila and La Fanciulla del West. *Honour:* OBE, 1985. *Address:* c/o Royal Opera House, Covent Garden, London, WC2.

DODERER Gerhard, b. 25 Mar 1944, Kitzingen, Germany. Musicologist; Organist. m. C Rosado Fernandes, 11 Sept 1970. *Education:* PhD, University of Würzburg; Bay. Staatskonservatorium of Würzburg. *Career:* Organ recitals, since 1970, in many European and and Extraeuropean countries. *Recordings:* Longplays and CDs on historical Portuguese organs. *Publications:* Portuguese Clavichords of 18th Century, 1971; Orgelmusik und Orgelban in Portugal, 1976; Organa Hispanica, 1971-84, 9 vols; The Organs at Braga Cathedral, 1992; Demenico Scarlatti: Libro di Tocate, 1991. *Memberships:* American, Spanish, Portuguese and German Musicological Societies. *Hobbies:* Travelling. *Address:* Alam D Afonso, Henriques 48-5 DT, 1900 Lisbon, Portugal.

DODGE Charles, b. 5 June 1942, Ames, Iowa, USA. Composer. m. Katharine Schlefer, 1 July 1978. 1 son, 1 daughter. *Education:* BA, University of Iowa; MA, DMA, Columbia University; Studied composition with Richard Hervig, Darius Milhaud, Philip Bezanson, Gunther Schuller, Otto Luening, computer music with Godfrey Winham. *Career:* Major performances: Tanglewood, 1965, 1973, 1986; Warsaw Autumn Festival, Poland, 1978, 1985, 1986; New Music, New York Festival, USA, 1979; Stockholm Festival of Electronic Music, Sweden, 1980, 1982; Venice Biennale, Italy, 1981; Calarts Festival, USA, 1983; Olympic Arts Festival, Los Angeles, 1984; New York Philharmonic, 1984; Los Angeles Philharmonic, 1984. *Compositions:* Folia; Changes; Earth's Magnetic Field; Speech Songs; Extensions; The Story of Our Lives; In Celebration; Cascando; Any Resemblance Is Purely Coincidental; The Waves. *Recordings:* Earth's Magnetic Field, Nonesuch; Charles Dodge-Synthetic Speech Music. *Publication:* Computer Music; Synthesis, Composition and Performance (with Thomas A Jerse), 1985. *Contributions to:* Musical Fractals, Byte Magazine, 1986. *Honours:* BMI Student Composers Awards, 1963, 1964, 1966, 1967; Joseph H Bearns Award, 1964, 1967; Margaret Lee Crofts Fellowship, 1964; Woodrow Wilson National Fellowship, 1964; Guggenheim Fellowships, 1972, 1975. *Memberships:* American Music Center (President 1979-82); American Composers Alliance (President 1971-75). *Address:* Conservatory of Music, Brooklyn College, City University of New York, Brooklyn, NY 11210, USA.

DODGSON Stephen (Cuthbert Vivian), b. 17 March 1924, London, England. Composer. *Education:* Studied at the Royal College of Music with R.O. Morris and others. *Career:* Teacher at the RCM from 1964; Frequent broadcaster on BBC, Radio 3 (Record Review, Mainly for Pleasure etc). *Compositions:* A Bag of Winds for 5 string quartets and narrator; A Hymn to Harmony for chorus and strings; Bassoon Concerto; Cadilly for 4 vocal soloists and wind quintet; Concerto da Camera 1-3; Five

Occasional Pieces for cello and piano; Four Fables for chorus and orchestra; 2 Guitar Concertos; 5 operas for children: Lammas Fair, The Miller's Secret, The Old Master, Strong Drink, and Threadneedle Street; Magnificat for soloists, chorus and orchestra; Methought this other Night, piano trio; The Old Cigarette Lighter for flute, oboe, piano and narrator; Quintet for guitar and strings; Quintet in C for piano and strings; Serenade for oboe, clarinet and bassoon; 3 Sets of Six Inventions for Harpsichord; 2 String Trios; Sonata for cello and piano; 2 Suites for Clavichord; Suite for Wind Quintet; Te Deum for soloists, chorus and orchestra; Three Winter Songs for voice, oboe and piano; Trio in One Movement, piano trio; Warbeck Dances for recorder and harpsichord; Wind Symphony for Symphonic Band; Music for Anthony Rooley and the Consort of Musicke. *Address:* c/o Chappell & Co., 129 Park Street, London W1, England.

DOESE Helena, b. 13 Aug. 1946, Göteborg, Sweden. Singer Soprano. *Education:* Studied in Göteborg, with Luigi Ricci in Rome and with Erik Werba and Gerald Moore in Vienna. *Debut:* Göteborg 1971, as Aida. *Career:* Bern Opera 1972-75, as Jenůfa, Micaela and Donna Anna; Royal Opera Stockholm from 1973 as Liu in Turandot, Mimi, Katya Kabanova and Eva in the Friedrich production of Die Meistersinger; Glyndebourne debut 1974, as Mozart's Countess: Fiordiligi 1975; Covent Garden from 1974 as Mimi, Gutrune in Götterdämmerung, Agathe in Der Freischütz and Amelia in Simon Boccanegra; Tatiana in Eugene Onegin for Scottish Opera; Guest appearances in Marseilles (Elisabeth de Valois), Sydney, (Aida), Paris Opéra, (Fiordiligi), Hamburg, (Agathe), San Francisco, (Countess) and Zürich (Sieglinde); Currently a member of Frankfurt Opera: has sung title roles in Ariadne auf Naxos, Jenůfa and Iphigénie en Tauride, Countess in Capriccio, the Marschallin, and Chrysothemis in Elektra; Deutsche Oper Berlin, 1987, as Agathe followed by the Marschallin at Copenhagen; Sydney, 1988, as Eva in Die Meistersinger; Sang Rosalinde at Oslo, 1988, Tosca 1989; Season 1991/92 as Fidelio at Toronto, Elsa at Frankfurt and Ariadne at Stuttgart. *Recordings include:* Videos of Glyndebourne Così fan Tutte and Covent Garden Bohème. *Address:* c/o Lies Askonas Ltd., 186 Drury Lane, London WC2B 5RY, England.

DOGHAN Philip, b. 1949, England. Singer (Tenor). *Education:* BA, Durham University. *Career:* Sang as a boy in premiere of Tippett's King Priam, 1962; Sang in chorus at Glyndebourne and with the English Opera Group and English Music Theatre; English National Opera in Orfeo, the premiere of The Plumber's Gift and The Return of Ulysses; Has sung with Opera Factory in the premiere of Birtwistle's Yan Tan Tethera, 1986, La Calisto, The Knot Garden and Reimann's The Ghost Sonata; Appearances in Il Matrimomio Segreto and Les Pêcheurs de Perles in Rennes; Tom Rakewell at Cologne Opera, Alessandro in Il Re Pastore at The Théâtre des Champs Elysées; Mignon, La Straniera, La Cena delle Beffe, Elisa e Claudio and Gazzaniga's Don Giovanni at the Wexford Festival; Don Juan in The Stone Guest for the Berlin Kammeroper; Così fan Tutte in Tours and Idomeneo in Metz; Concert engagements include Stravinsky's Threni for Italian Radio and appearances with Janowski, Hager, Rattle, Malgoire and Hogwood in Holland, Germany, Italy, Belgium and France; Sang several roles in the ENO revival of Busoni's Doctor Faust, 1990; Regular broadcasts for the BBC, Radio France and RAI; Orphew in Lord's Masque by Castiglioni at La Fenice; Paris Opera Debut as Le Duc in Offenbach's, Les Brigands, 1993; Royal Opera House, Basilo in Figaro, 1994. *Honour:* Winner, Premier Grand Prix at Toulouse, 1980.*Address:* English National Opera, St Martin's Lane, London WC2N 4AP, England.

DOHMEN Albert, b. 1955, Krefeld, Germany. Singer (Bass-baritone). *Education:* Studied in Cologne and with Gladys Kuchta, 1977-84. *Career:* Sang at the Deutsche Oper am Rhein Dusseldorf, 1983-85; Wiesbaden from 1986, Hamburg, 1986-87, Vienna Volsoper, 1987-90; Guest appearances at Stockholm (Assur in Semiramide, 1988), Catania (Kaspar in Der Freischutz) and Cairo, in Haydn's La Vera Costanza; Sang in the premiere of Bose's Die Leiden des Jungen Werthers at Ludwigsburg, 1986 and in the German premiere of La Princesse de Cleve by Jean Francaix; Sang Don Giovanni in festivals at Prague and Macerata, 1991; Returned to Macerata 1992, as Don Parmenione in Rossini's L'Occasione fa il ladro. Other roles include Mozart's Count and Alfonso, Don Magnifico, the Grand Inquisitor and Verdi's Procida and Paolo, Scarpia and Gianni Schicchi; Wagner's King Henry, Biterolf, Wotan, Donner, Gunther and Amfortas; Concert repertoire includes the Verdi Requiem and Zemlinsky's Sieben Sinfonische Gesange. *Recordings:* Spirit Messenger in Die Frau ohne Schatten, conducted by Solti. *Address:* c/o Volksoper, Wahringerstrasse 78, A-1090 Vienna, Austria.

DOHNÁNYI Christoph von, b. 8 Sept 1929, Berlin, Germany. Conductor. m. Anja Silja. *Education:* Studied at the Munich Musikhochschule; Further study in the USA with his grandfather, Erno von Dohnányi, and Leonard Bernstein. *Career:* Assistant to Solti at the Frankfurt Opera 1952-56; Music Director at Lubeck 1957-63; Kassel 1963-66; London debut 1965, with the London Philharmonic; Chief Conductor Cologne Radio Symphony Orchestra 1964-70; Conducted the premieres of Henze's Der junge Lord (Berlin 1965) and Die Bassariden (Salzburg l966); Music Director Frankfurt Opera 1968-75, Hamburg Staatsoper 1977-84; Has conducted Schoenberg's Moses und Aron at Frankfurt, Vienna, and elsewhere in Europe; Conducted Salome at Covent Garden 1974: later directed Wozzeck; returned for Die Meistersinger and Fidelio, 1990; Opera engagements at the Metropolitan, Falstaff and Der Rosenkavalier, La Scala Milan, Chicago (debut 1969, Der fliegende Holländer), Berlin, Paris, Munich, Salzburg and San Francisco (Die Frau ohne Schatten, 1989); Guest appearances with the BBC Symphony, New York Philharmonic, Zurich Tonhalle, Philadelphia Orchestra, Israel Philharmonic, Vienna Philharmonic and the Orchestre de Paris; Music Director of the Cleveland Orchestra from 1984: visited London, 1980, 1989, 1990 and 1992; conducted a new production of Der Ring des Nibelungen at the Vienna Staatsoper, 1992-93; Salome at the 1992 and 1993 Salzburg Festival and Cosi Fan Tutte at the 1993 Salzburg Festival. *Recordings include:* with The Cleveland Orchestra: complete Symphonies of Brahms, Schumann and Beethoven; Works by Bartók, Schubert, Dvořák, Mahler, Busoni (Piano Concerto), Berg and Schoenberg; Der Ring des Nibelungen. *Honours:* Bartók Prize of Hungary; Goethe Medal of the City of Frankfurt; Arts and Sciences Prize of the City of Hamburg; Commander de L'Ordre des Arts et des Lettres of the Republic of France, 1988; Commander's Cross of the Republic of Austria and Germany's Commander's Cross of the Order of Merit; Abraham Lincoln Award, from the Magyar Club of Cleveland and the American Hungarian Foundation, 1988; Honorary Doctorate, Cleveland Institute of Music, 1988. *Address:* Harrison/Parrott Ltd., 12 Penzance Place, London W11 4PA, England.

DOHNANYI Oliver, b. 1955, Czechoslovakia. Conductor.*Education:* Composition, Conducting, Violin playing, Bratislava Conservatory; Conducting, Academy of Music and Drama, Prague; Hochschule für Musik und darstellende Kunst, Vienna, Austria, 1980. *Career:* Artistic Director, University Artistic Ensemble, Prague, Conductor of Prague Choir, Canticorum jublio, 1977-; Has toured USSR, Spain, Belgium and Sweden with Canticorum jublio; Bratislava Radio Symphony Orchestra, 1979; Opera of the National Theatre and Slovak Philharmonic Orchestra, 1984-; Regular appearances as Conductor with numerous orchestras. *Recordings:* Has recorded over 100 compositions. *Honours:* 1st Prize, Canticorum jublio, International Contest of Choirs, Varna, Bulgaria, 1985; 3rd prize for Competition of Conductors, Italy, 1976; Titles of Laureate, International Competition of Hungarian radio and television, Budapest 1983; 37th International Contest, Prague Spring.

DOIG Christopher, b. 4 Apr 1948, New Zealand. Singer (Tenor). *Education:* Studied in New Zealand and with Anton Dermota at the Vienna Music Academy. *Career:* Sang at the Vienna Staatsoper from 1976 as David, Jacquino, Steuermann, Dr Caius and Remendado (Carmen); Linz Opera from 1980 as Don Ottavio, Tamino, Lionel (Martha), Fenton, Nemorino and the Duke of Mantua; Guest engagements in Vienna and at La Scala and the Salzburg Festival; Debut with Australian Opera 1988, as Nerone in L'Incoronazione di Poppea; Sang David in Die Meistersinger at Sydney, conducted by Charles Mackerras; Hamburg Opera 1991, as Elemer in Arabella; Director of the New Zealand International Festival of the Arts; also sang: Jenůfa, Sydney, 1992; Adriana Lecouvreur, Sydney, 1992; Carmen and Fliegende Holländer, Cologne, 1992; Wozzeck, Stuttgart; Salome, Melbourne and Don José in Barcelona; Will sing Walther van Stokingin, Sydney, 1994. *Address:* c/o Haydn Rawstron Ltd, PO Box 654, London SE26 4DZ, England.

DOIG John, b. 2 Aug. 1958, Helensburgh, Scotland. Violinist. *Education:* Holyrood School, Glasgow, Scotland; First enrolled pupil, St Mary's Music School, Edinburgh. *Career:* BBC Symphony Orchestra, 1975-78; Principal 1st Violin, BBC Philharmonic Orchestra, 1979-81; Co-Leader, Scottish Opera Orchestra, 1981-83; Co-Leader 1986-88, Guest Leader 1988-90, Scottish Chamber Orchestra. *Hobbies:* Horse riding; Country walks. *Address:* International Celebrities Management, 13-17 Longlane, Barbican, London EC1A 9PN, England.

DOLEZAL Karel, b. 16 Jan. 1948, Prague, Czechoslovakia. Musician; Viola Player. m. 18 June 1974. 2 sons. *Debut:* Knighthall of The Waldstein Palacve, Prague 1973. *Career:* Solo Only: Prague Spring Festival, 1976; Bratislava Music Festival, 1977; Music Festivals: Brno, Karlovy Vary, T Teplice, Poland, GDR, Rumania; 1 Solo Concert, BBC, TV Prague and 12 Concerts for Radio Prague; With The Dolezal String Quartet Biographical film for Czech Film Corporation; Evening Programme for TV Prague, One hour-long programme for Radio NY 1981; Major Stage: Wigmore Hall, London; Birmingham; Dublin; Prague Spring Festival; Paris Festival; Bretagne; Tonhalle Zurich; Berlin; Halle; Concert Tours of Austria, Spain, Scandinavia, Hungary, Tunisia etc. Radio and TV Programmes for Hamburg, Bremen, Frankfurt, Wiesbaden, Saarbrucken; The Quartet was invited for a concert tour of USA 1980. *Recordings:* 2 String Quartets by Antonin Dvořák 1983; 2 String Quartets by Leoš Janáček 1984; 5 LP records by Mozart, Dvořák, Janáček, Martinů, Shostakovich, Flosman and others. *Honours:* Silver Medal, International Festival at Bordeaux 1977; Honorary Diploma of The Performing Arts Competition organized by The Czech Ministry of Culture 1974; 3rd Prize of The Prague Spring International Competition (1st Prize was not awarded), 1975. *Membership:* The Union of Czech Composers and Musicians. *Address:* Milešovska Street 6, Prague 3, 130 00, Czech Republic.

DOLIN Samuel, b. 22 Aug. 1917, Montreal, Canada. Composer. *Education:* Studied under Tania and Vladimir Elgart, Stanley Gardiner and Vladimir Emenitov (piano and theory); Studied at Royal Conservatory of Music, Toronto; BMus, Doctor of Music Degree 1958, University of Toronto; Studied Composition under John Weinzweig; Weldon Kilburn and E Robert Schmitz (piano) and Ernst Krenek (composition). *Career:* Teacher, Composition and Theory Department, Royal Conservatory of Music; Serves on the Board of Examiners; Founder, Electronic Music Studio 1966; Revived and brought up-to-date ARCT Diploma Course in Composition and Theory; Artistic Director of Canadian Contemporary Music Workshop, 1984. *Compositions:* Opera: Casino 1966-67, Orchestral Scherzo 1950; Serenade for Strings 1951; Sinfonietta 1950; Sonata for String Orchestra 1962; Symphony No 1 (Elk Falls) 1956; Symphony No 2 1957; Symphony No 3 1976, Soloists with Orchestra; Concerto for Accordion and Orchestra 1984; Concerto for Piano and Orchestra 1984; Drakkar 1972; Fantasy for Piano and Chamber Orchestra 1967; Golden Section: The Biography of A Woman 1981; Hero of Our Time

1985; Isometric Variables 1957. Instrumental Ensemble: Adikia 1975; Barcarolle 1962; Blago's Trio 1980; Concerto Grosso (Georgian Bay) 1970; Duo Concertante 1977; Kinesis I and Kinesis II 1981; Little Sombrero 1964; Portrait 1961; Quintet for Brass 1981; Sonata 1960; Sonata 1978; Sonata Fantasia 1980; Sonatina 1954; Trio for Violin, Cello and Piano 1980; Instrumental Solo: Little Toccata 1959; Prelude, Interlude and Fantasy 1976; Psalmody for Solo Oboe 1982; Ricercar and Fantasy 1975; Sonata 1970; Three Sonatas 1973; Stelcel 1978. Voice: Bird of Time 1979; Chloris 1951; Deuteronomy XXXII, 1977; Julia 1951; Ozymandias 1951. Chorus: The Hills of Hebron 1954; Marchbankantata 1971; Mass 1972; Piano Music. *Address:* c/o Canadian Music Centre, Chalmers House, 20 St Joseph Street,, Toronto, Ontario, M4X 1J9, Canada.

DOLMETSCH Carl Frederick, b. 23 Aug. 1911, Fontenay-sous-Bois, France. Musician (Specalist and Authority on early music and instruments). m. divorced, 2 sons (1 deceased), 2 daughters. *Debut:* First Concert Performance, aged 7; First Concert tour aged 8. *Career:* Director, Society of Recorder Players, 1937-; Frequent tours as recorder player throughout Europe and North and South America; Works written for him by Gál, Maw, Cooke, Berkeley, Chagrin and Rubbra; Director, Haslemere Festival of Early Music & Instruments, 1940-, Dolmetsch International Summer School, 1971-; Managing Director, Arnold Dolmetsch Ltd., 1940-76, Chairman 1963-78; Chairman, Dolmetsch Musical Instruments, 1982-. *Publications:* Many editions of recorder music. *Honours:* Hon. Fellow, Trinity College of Music, London, London College of Music; Hon.D.Litt., Exeter; CBE. *Memberships:* Art Workers Guild. *Hobbies:* Ornithology; Natural History. *Address:* Jesses, Haslemere, Surrey GU27 2BS, England.

DOLMETSCH Jeanne-Marie, b. 15 Aug 1942, Hindhead, Surrey, England. Concert artist (Recorder, Treble Viol). *Education:* Royal Academy of Music, violin and piano, 1961-64; LRAM (piano teacher). *Debut:* Elizabeth Hall, London, 1973. *Career:* Toured America, France, Ireland and Sweden with the Dolmetsch Ensemble; Recorder soloist and Assistant Director, Haslemere Festival; Appearances at Bath Festival, English Bach Festival; Numerous radio broacasts and TV programmes. *Recordings:* Collections of early music with the Dolmetsch Ensemble. *Hobbies:* Painting; Gardening. *Address:* Jesses, Grayswood Road, Haslemere, Surrey, England.

DOLMETSCH Marguerite Mabel, b. 15 Aug. 1942, Hindhead, Surrey, England. Recorder and Viola da Gamba Player. m. Brian E. Blood. *Education:* LRAM. *Career:* Travelled widely with the Dolmetsch Ensemble and the Dolmetsch Concertante, touring America, France, Germany, Sweden; Has performed at the Three Choirs Festival, Bath Festival and Haslemere Festival; Has also appeared at Elizabeth Hall, Purcell Room and Wigmore Hall; Radio broadcasts and TV programmes in Britain and Germany. *Recitals:* Various recitals with the Dolmetsch Ensemble; Director of the Dolmetsch Summer School and Partner in Dolmetsch Instruments Workshop. *Recordings:* CD, Cassette, Choice Consorts for Recorders; A Christmas Tapestry, in Words and Music; A Chest of Viols. *Honour:* LR.A.M. *Memberships:* National Federation of Decorative and Fine Arts Societies, NADFAS. *Hobbies:* Gardening; Dressmaking; Cooking. *Address:* Heartsease, Grayswood Road, Haslemere, Surrey, England.

DOLSKAYA Olga, b. 10 Jan 1948, Paris, France. Professor. 1 daughter. *Education:* Conservatoire S Rachmanioff, Paris; High School of Performing Arts, New York, 1965; BM, Piano, 1969, MM, Musicology, 1970, Manhattan School of Music; MA, Slavic and Soviet Studies, PhD, Musicology, University of Kansas, 1983. *Career:* Faculty, University of Missouri Conservatory, Kansas City, 1983-; Radio programme (3 broadcasts) on Russian vocal music, KCUR FM, 1984; Narrator for history of Russian opera, choral and art songs programmes; Research on 17th-century Russian vocal music and Muscovite Baroque; Worked on manuscripts, State Historical Museum and Glinka Museum, Moscow, and Manuscript Division, University Library, Kiev, USSR; Lecturer, Speaker, various universities, USA and Conservatoire S Rachmaninoff, Paris, and professional music and Slavic conference; Historical Consultant for Russian Baroque and choral music. *Publications:* One Thousand Years of Russian Sacred Music (co-editor), 1991; Osobennosti ispolneniia kontsertov Vasilia Titova, 1991; German Voskresenskii: A Seventeenth-Century Poet Musician, 1991; Transcriptions: choral works by 17th-century Russian Baroque composer Vasilii Titov, 1993 and Musica Russica, 1994. *Address:* The Conservatory, University of Missouri at Kansas City, 4949 Cherry, Kansas City, MO 64110, USA.

DOLTON Geoffrey, b. 1958, England. Singer (Baritone). *Education:* Studied at the Royal Academy of Music with Joy Mammen. *Debut:* With Opera North, as Guglielmo in Cosi fan Tutte. *Career:* Further roles with Opera North as Mozart's Count, Lescaut in Manon Lescaut and Henrik in the British premiere of Nielsen's Maskarade; With Opera Factory has sung Guglielmo (also televised) and Orestes in Gluck's Iphigenia operas; Manoel Theatre Malta, Figaro in Il Barbiere di Siviglia; Season 1992 as Hector in Tippett's King Priam at Antwerp, Monteverdi's Otho for Opera Factory, in Krenek's What Price Confidence? at the Almeida Festival and as Alan in Birtwistle's Yan Tan Tethera; Other roles include Papageno for Welsh National Opera and Opera Northern Ireland; Schaunard in La Bohème for Scottish Opera; Hector in King Priam for Opera North, Malatesta in Don Pasquale for New Israeli Opera and the leading role in Gretry's Le Huron at the Buxton Festival, 1990; Sang Guglielmo in Cosi fan Tutte for ENO, 1990; Recitals with the pianist Nicholas Bosworth. *Honours include:* Peter Pears Prize for Recital Singing at the RAM; Honorary ARAM, 1992. *Recording:* Donizetti's Emilia di Liverpool, with the Philharmonia Orchestra (Opera Rara). *Address:* Allied Artists Agency, 42 Montpelier Square, London SW7 1JZ, England.

DOMANINSKA Libuse, b. 4 July 1924, Brno, Czechoslovakia. Singer (Soprano). *Education:* Studied at the Prague Conservatory with Hana Pirkova and Bohuslav Sobesky. *Debut:* Brno 1946, as Vendulka in The Kiss by Smetana. *Career:* Sang at Brno in operas by Smetana and Janáček (Jenůfa, Katya Kabanova and the Vixen); Prague National Opera 1955-85: visited Edinburgh with the company in 1964, as Milada in Dalibor; Komische Oper Brelin 1956, Vienna Staatsoper 1958-68; Holland Festival 1959, as Katya Kabanova; Roles in Russian and Soviet operas and in Mozart, Puccini and Verdi; Marenka in The Bartered Bride, Smetana's Libuse, Jenůfa, Aida, Elisabeth de Valois, Euridice and Foerster's Eva; Many concert appearances, notably in Janáček's Glagolitic Mass at La Scala. *Recordings:* Glagolitic Mass, The Cunning Little Vixen, The Devil's Wall by Smetana (Supraphon). *Honours:* Artist of Merit 1966; National Artist 1974. *Address:* c/o National Theatre, PO Box 865, 11230 Prague 1, Czech Republic.

DOMANSKY Hanus, b. 1 Mar. 1944, Novy Hrozenkov, Slovakia. Composer. *Education:* Studied piano with Jaroslav Shanel; Composition with Jan Duchan, Brno Conservatory; Composition with Dezider Kardos, graduated 1970, Bratislava Academy of Musical Arts. *Career:* Associated with Czech Radio, Bratislava. *Compositions:* Concerto piccolo for Orchestra, 1970; Symphony, 1980; Piano Concerto, 1984; Music for Trumpet, Flute and Bass Clarinet, 1966; Musica giocosa for Violin and Piano, 1971; Dianoia for Violin, 1976; Piano pieces; Organ music; About Winter, cantata for Narrator, Children's Choir and Orchestra, 1968; Fiat lux, oratorio for Narrator, Soprano, Chorus and Orchestra, 1970; Versifying for Chorus and Percussion, 1972; Recruiting Songs for Men's Chorus, 1978; Solo Songs. *Honour:* Slovak Composers Award, 1983. *Address:* c/o Czech Radio, Bratislava, Slovak Republic.

DOMINGO Placido, b. 21 Jan. 1941, Madrid, Spain.

Opera Singer (Tenor). m. Marta Ornelas, 3 sons. *Education:* National Conservatory of Music, Mexico City. *Debut:* Monterrary, Mexico, 1961; Metropolitan Opera, New York, USA, 1968; British Debut, Verdi's Requiem, Festival Hall, 1969; Covent Garden, Tosca, 1971. *Career:* Aida, Carmen, 1973; Bohème, 1974; Un ballo in maschera, 1975; La Fanciulla del West; Has sung leading roles in approximately 50 operas; Recent engagements include: Tosca (conducting), Romeo and Juliet, Metropolitan Opera, New York, USA; Aida; Il Trovatore, Hamburg, Federal Republic of Germany; Don Carlos, Salzburg; Vespri siciliani and La Forza del destino, Paris, France; Turandot, Barcelona; Otello, Paris, London, Hamburg; Carmen, Edinburgh; Film, Madama Butterfly with Von Karajan; La Traviata, 1982; Sang Luigi at the Met, 1989 in Il Tabarro; Othello at Covent Garden, 1990, Lohengrin at the Vienna Staatsoper, Don José at Rio de Janeiro, Otello at the Met and Barcelona; Sang Don Carlos at Los Angeles, Dick Johnson at Chicago; Riccardo in Un Ballo in Maschera at the 1990 Salzburg Festival; Debut as Parsifal at the Met, 1991; Sang Otello at Covent Garden 1992, (also televised), Siegmund in Die Walküre at the Vienna Staatsoper, 1992; Metropolitan Opera, 1992, Hoffmann. *Recordings:* Most recent include: Aida; Un ballo in maschera; Tosca; Tannhäuser (1989); Video of Lohengrin, from Vienna, issued 1991. *Publication:* My First Forty Years, autobiography, 1984. *Honours:* Doctor Honoris Causa, Royal College of Music, 1982; Chevalier, Legion d'Honneur. *Current Management:* Metropolitan Opera Company, NY, USA. *Address:* c/o Metropolitan Opera Company, Lincoln Center Plaza, New York, NY 10023, USA.

DOMINGUEZ Guillermo, b. 1961, Caracas, Venezuela. Singer (Tenor). *Education:* Studied with Jose Castro in Caracas, then at Rome and Turin. *Debut:* Treviso, 1984, as Rodolfo. *Career:* Sang Rodolfo at Prias, Amiens and Munich; Zurich Opera as Don Ottavio and Ferrando and in Guillaume Tell; appearances at Monte Carlo as Edgardo in Lucia di Lammermoor and at Innsbruck as Cavaradossi and the Duke of Mantua, 1988; National Theatre Mannheim as Alfredo and Puccini's Edgar with the Dresden Staatskapelle; Engagements in Spain as the Duke; Many concert appearances. *Address:* c/o Nationaltheater , Am Goetheplatz, 6800 Mannheim, Germany.

DOMINGUEZ Oralia, b. 15 Oct. 1927, San Luis Potosi, Mexico. Singer (Contralto). *Education:* Studied at the Mexican National Conservatory. *Career:* Sang in Debussy's La Demoiselle Elue while a student; Stage debut Mexico City 1950, appeared as Amneris in 1951; Sang in Eurpe from 1953, London debut at the Wigmore Hall; La Scala Milan 1953, in Adriana Lecouvreur; Covent Garden 1955, as Sosostris in the premiere of The Midsummer Marriage by Tippett; Glyndebourne Festival 1955-64, as Mistress Quickly, Isabella, and Arnalta in the Leppard-Monteverdi L'Incoronazione di Poppea; Venice 1960, in Alcina, with Joan Sutherland; Sang at the Deutsche Oper am Rhein Dusseldorf from 1960; Guest appearances in Buenos Aires, Vienna, Frankfurt, Paris, Rome, Naples, Florence, Chicago, Dallas and New Orleans. *Recordings:* Erda in The Ring, Mozart's Coronation Mass, Verdi Requeim (Deutsche Grammophon); Il Tabarro, La Gioconda (Decca). *Address:* c/o Deutsch Oper am Rhein, Heinrich-Heine Allee 16, D-4000 Dusseldorf, Germany.

DONAKOWSKI Conrad Louis, b. 13 Mar. 1936, Detroit, Michigan, USA. Professor of Cultural History of Music. m. Judith Wharton, 1 July 1960. 1 son, 1 daughter. *Education:* PhD, distinction, Columbia University, New York, 1969; MA, Xavier University, Cincinnati, 1957; Diploma, First in Class, Palestrina Institute of Music, 1956. *Career:* Director of Music, St Hugo of the Hills Church, Bloomfield Hills, Michigan, 1960-66; Instructor, Humanities, Michigan State University, 1966-69; Assistant Professor 1969-72, Associate Professor 1973-75, Professor of Humanities 1975-, Assistant Dean, Arts and Letters 1979, Professor of Music 1981-, Michigan State University; Director of Music, St Thomas Aquinas Church, East Lansing, 1974-

. *Publication:* A Muse for the Masses: Ritual and Music in an Age of Democratic Revolution 1770-1870, 1977. *Address:* School of Music, Michigan State University, East Lansing, MI 48824-1043, USA.

DONAT Zdislava, b. 4 July 1939, Poznan, Poland. Soprano coloratura. *Education:* Studied with Zofia Bregy in Warsaw and Gino Bechi in Siena, Italy. *Debut:* Poznan 1964, as Gilda from 1971 in Teatr Wielki, Warsaw. *Career:* Theater am Gärtnerplatz, Munich, as Queen of the Night; Bayerische Staatsoper Munich, Hamburg; Vienna Staatsoper; London Covent Garden; La Scala, Milan; Met-Opera, New York; Teatro Colon Buenos Aires; Deutsche Oper, Berlin; SSan Francisco Opera; Opera in Moscow, Napoli, Zurich, Frankfurt, many others Festivals: in Salzburg, 1979-87; Bregenz, Orange, Munich, Tokyo, Athens, Wroclaw and others. Roles include: Lucia di Lammermoor, La Sonnambula, Julia, Capuletti, Norina, Konstanze, Blonde, Zerlina, Olympia, Gilda, Violetta, Manon, Massenet, Martha, Flotow, Queen in Golden Cockerel, La Princess and Le Feu, L'Enfant et Les sortileges - Ravel, Hanna, Moniuszko, Marzelline, Beethoven, Adele, Johann Strauss and others. TV Productions, recitals and appearances with symphony orchestras. *Recordings include:* Die Zauberflöte, RCA, conductor J Levine; Operatic Arias, Polskie Nagrania, conductor J Dobrzański; Requiem by R Maciejewski, conductor, T Strugała. *Honours:* Awards: Grand Prix in Toulouse; Kammersängerin, Munich, 1977. *Address:* Teatr Wiekli, Moliera 3, 00 076 Warsaw, Poland.

DONATH Helen, b. 10 July 1940, Corpus Christi, Texas, USA. Soprano. m. Klaus Donath, 10 July 1965. 1 son. *Education:* Del Mar College, Corpus Christi, Texas; Paola Novikova; Maria Berini. *Debut:* Cologne Opera as Inez in Il Trovatore, 1960. *Career:* Hannover Opera; Bavarian State Opera, Munich; Salzburg Festival; Vienna State Opera; Deutsche Oper, Berlin; La Scala, Milan; Royal Opera, Covent Garden; Lisbon; Hamburg; Bayreuth Festival, San Francisco Opera, Paris Opéra; Sang Pamina at the 1970 Salzburg Festival; US debut as Sophie at San Francisco, 1971; Covent Garden debut as Anne Trulove, The Rake's Progress, 1979; Other roles include: Mozart's Zerlina, Ilia and Susanna, Micaela, Mélisande, Mimi, Oscar and Aennchen; Sang Eva in Die Meistersinger at Seattle, 1989; Season 1993/94 as Eva in Dresden and Agathe at the Berlin Staatsoper. *Recordings:* Beethoven, Fidelio (Angel); Britten, Turn of the Screw (Philips); Handel, Messiah (Deutsche Grammophon); Mozart, Requiem (Angel and Philips); Pfitzner, Palestrina (Deutsche Grammophon); Strauss, Arabella (Angel); Strauss, Der Rosenkavalier (London). *Honours:* Pope Paul Medal, 1967; Grand Prix du Disque, Deutsche Schallplatten Preis; 1990, Bavarian Kammersängerin; Culture Prize of Lower Saxony. *Current Management:* Shaw Concerts, 1900 Broadway, New York, NY 10023. *Address:* Bergstrasse 5, D-3002 Wedemark 1, Germany.

DONATONI Franco, b. 9 June 1927, Verona, Italy. Composer; Professor of Musical Composition. m. Susan Park, 1958. 2 sons. *Education:* Bologna and Rome. *Career:* Professor of Composition, Bologna, 1953-55; Milan, 1969; Docente, Advanced course in Composition, Academy Chigiana di Siena, 1970. *Compositions include:* Puppenspiel, 1951; 4 String Quartets, 1950-60; Serenata for soprano and 16 instruments; Sezioni, 1960; Per Ochestra, 1962; Asar, 1964; Puppenspiel (2), 1965; Souvenir, 1967; Etwas ruhiger im Ausdruck, 1967; Doubles II, 1969-70; Questo, 1970; Atem, theatre piece, 1984; Ecco for chamber orchestra, 1991 *Honours:* Marzotto Prize, 1966; Koussevitsky Prize, 1968, many other prizes for composition. *Address:* Via Giovanni Milani, 1 Milano, Italy.

DÖNCH Karl, b. 8 Jan 1915, Hagen, Westphalian, Germany. Singer (Bass-Baritone). *Education:* Studied at the Dresden Conservatory. *Career:* Sang in Gorlitz from 1936, followed by engagements in Reichenberg, Bonn and Salzburg; Vienna Staatsoper from 1947, notably in the 1956 premiere of Der Sturm by Frank Martin; Salzburg Festival until 1965, as Don Alfonso, the Doctor in Wozzeck, and Malatesta, and in the 1954 premiere of Penelope by Liebermann; Bregenz Festival 1955-84; Guest appearances in Milan, Dusseldorf and Berlin; Buenos Aires 1952-53; Holland Festival 1958; Metropolitan Opera 1959-60, 1966-67, notably as the Witch in Hansel and Gretel; Director of the Vienna Volksoper from 1973-86; appeared as Jupiter in Orpheus in the Underworld 1985. *Recordings:* Beckmesser in Die Meistersinger, Der Freischutz, Ariadne auf Naxos (Decca); Die Fledermaus, Wiener Blut, Eine Nacht in Venedig (Columbia); Der Vogelhändler (Electrola); Wozzeck (CBS); Die Zauberflöte; La Forza del Destino; Der Rosenkavalier. *Address:* c/o Volksoper, Währingerstrasse 78, A-1090 Vienna, Austria.

DONGEN Maria van, b. 23 Mar 1928, Holland. Singer, (Soprano). *Career:* Sang Mozart's Countess and Pamina at Amsterdam; Member of the Zurich Opera, 1959-65, debut as the Forza Leonora; Guest appearances at Frankfurt, London, (Countess at the Albert Hall), Bologna, Parma (Elisabeth, 1963), and isa (Elsa); Amsterdam 1963-67, as Donna Elvira; Munich from 1964, Vienne from 1967 as Ariadne, Fiordiligi, Senta and Desdemona; Munich Opera 1967, as Strauss's Danae, and as Irene in Rienzi; Further engagements at Barcelona and Hamburg (as Leonora in Fidelio), Graz, the Deutsche Oper Berlin, Piccola Scala Milan and the Salzburg Festival (First lady in Die Zauberflöte, 1963-64); Sang Leonore at the Landestheater Salzburg, 1971; Frequent concert engagements. *Address:* c/o Tiroler Landestheater, Rennweg 2, A-6020 Innsbruck, Austria.

DONNELLY Malcolm Douglas, b. 8 Feb. 1943, Sydney, Australia. Opera Singer (Baritone). m. Dolores Ryles. *Education:* Sydney Conservatory and Opera School; London Opera Centre. *Debut:* Australian Opera, 1966. *Career:* Australian Opera, Scottish Opera, English National Opera, Opera North, Netherlands Opera, Victoria State Opera, State Opera South Australia, Welsh National Opera, Royal Opera house, Covent Garden, English National Opera Tour, Moscow Leningrad 1991, Adelaide Festival 1991; Appearances at Edinburgh Festival, 1975, 1976; Wexford Festival, 1977, 1978; Glyndebourne, 1979, 1981, 1985; Hong Kong Festival, 1987; Brighton International Festival, 1988; Roles include: Macbeth, Simon Boccanegra, Rigoletto, Pizarro (Fidelio); Sang Kurwenal in Tristan und Isolde for Australian Opera, 1990, Macbeth with ENO on tour to Russia, Scarpia with Scottish Opera and Shishkov in From the House of the Dead for Welsh National Opera, 1990; Season 1992 in Ovations concert by ENO at the Barbican Hall, Don Carlos in Ernani for Welsh National Opera and Ford in Falstaff at the Coliseum; Boccanegra and Iago in Australia; Sharpless, Royal Opera House, Covent Garden. *Honours:* Sydney Sun Aria competition, 1969; Australian Opera Auditions Scholarship, 1970. *Hobbies:* Philately; Gardening. *Current management:* Ingpen & Williams Ltd, London. *Address:* 60 Nightingale Road, Carshalton, Surrey SM5 2EN, England.

DONNELLY Patrick, b. 1958, Sydney, Australia. Singer (Bass-baritone). *Education:* Studied at the Conservatorium of Music, Sydney and at the Guildhall School of Music, London. *Career:* Concert debut at Sydney Opera House in Belshazzar's Feast by Walton; Also appeared as Tiresias (Oedipus Rex) and in the Monteverdi Vespers; Sang with Glyndebourne Chorus on the 1983 Tour, solo debut as Theseus in A Midsummer Night's Dream, 1985; Festival and Tour appearances in Idomeneo (Neptune), Don Giovanni (Masetto), La Traviata, Le Nozze di Figaro (Bartolo) and L'Incoronazione di Poppea. Other roles include Mozart's Figaro for Opera 80, First Minister in Cendrillon at the Wexford Festival and Bartók's Bluebeard at the Barbican; Sang Polyphemus in Acis and Galatea on tour in France, Hayden in the premiere of 63 Dream Palace by Jurgen Böse in Berlin, 1990, and the Herald in Lohengrin for Australian Opera, Oct 1990; Licone and Caronte in Haydn's Orlando Paladino at Oxford; Concerts at most major London centres, including Stravinsky's

Renard at the Elizabeth Hall. *Recordings include:* Renard with the Matrix Ensemble; Pergolesi's La Serva Padrona (Meridian). *Address:* c/o Ron Gonsalves Management, 10 Dagnan Road, London SW12 9LQ, England.

DONOHOE Peter Howard, b. 18 June 1953, Manchester, England. Pianist; Conductor. m. Elaine Margaret Burns, 23 Aug 1980, 1 daughter. *Education:* Chethams School of Music, Manchester, 1961-71; Leeds University, 1971-72; Royal Manchester College of Music, 1972-73; Royal Northern College of Music, 1973-76; Paris Conservatoire, 1976-77; Diplomas: ARCM; GRNCM; BMus. *Career:* Concert appearances throughout the world as Recitalist, Soloist with major orchestras and Chamber Musician, including USA, Canada, Japan, Australia, USSR, Continental Europe, UK; Annual appearances at Henry Wood Promenade Concerts, 1979-; Regular appearances at South Bank, London, broadcasts on TV and radio; Appearances at several major festivals including Edinburgh, Cheltenham, Bath, Hollywood Bowl, La Roche d'Arraignon, Prague; Guest Conductor including Ulster Orchestra, City of Birmingham Symphony Orchestra, Royal Liverpool Philharmonic Orchestra, Halle Orchestra, Moscow Chamber Orchestra; Played Tippett's Piano Concerto at the 1991 Promenade Concerts, London; Tchaikovsky's Second Concerto at the 1993 Proms. *Recordings:* Numerous including: Stravinsky, Three Movements from Petrushka; Prokofiev, Sonata No 6; Tchaikovsky, Complete Works for Piano and Orchestra; Messiaen, Turangalila Symphony; Rachmaninov Concerto No 3 and Etudes Tableaux and Preludes; Muldowney Concerto; Gershwin Rhapsody in Blue on The Jazz Album, with Simon Rattle; Benjamin, Early Works for Piano and Orchestra. *Honours:* Dayas Gold Medal, Royal Manchester College of Music, 1977; Finalist: British Liszt Competition, 1976; Liszt-Bartok Competition, Budapest, 1976; Leeds International Piano Competition, 1981; Winner, 7th International Tchaikovsky Competition, Moscow, 1982; Honorary Fellow, Royal Northern College of Music, 1983.

DOOLEY Jeffrey Michael, b. 7 Oct 1945, Milwaukee, Wisconsin, USA. Singer (Counter-Tenor); Choral Conductor. *Education:* Milton College, Milton, Wisconsin; BA, Wisconsin Conservatory, 1968; Apprenticeship with Mark Deller, Deller Consort, Canterbury, England, 1974. *Debut:* Carnegie Hall, 1977. *Career:* Regular appearances in Early Music scene, New York: Basically Bach (Lincoln Centre), Clarion Concerts, Amor Artis Ensemble, Waverly Consort, Boston Early Music Festival Orchestra, Milwaukee Symphony Orchestra, Connecticut Symphony; Recital-lecture presentations, The Art of the Counter-Tenor, duo with Richard Kolb, lutenist, founder of The Gotham Consort; Founder, Director, The Stuyvesant Singers, Toronto, Canada; Ongoing appearances with the following Baroque Orchestras: Tafel Musik, Toronto, Ars Musica, Michigan, Levin Baroque Ensemble, Amor Artis Ensemble, Concert Royal, ARTEC Ensemble, New York; European appearances, Madeira Bach Festival, 1981; Stour Music, England, 1985, 1985, Amor Artis tour, Switzerland and Italy, 1991; Specialist in the Handel Oratorio, frequently giving masterclasses in interpretation of the arias, and performing. *Recordings:* Henry Purcell: Airs and Duets, Nonesuch; J S Bach: Mass in B Minor, Nonesuch; Johannes Ockeghem: Masses, Nonesuch; G Dufay: Masses, Nonesuch; J S Bach: St John Passion, Newport Classic; G F Handel: Acis and Galatea, Newport; H Schütz: St Matthew Passion, Newport. *Contributions to:* The Counter-Tenor Voice Defined, in the American Recorder, 1977; The Counter-Tenor's Roles in Music, in Continuo Magazine, Toronto, 1982. *Memberships:* Founding Member, Early Music America; International Society of Early Music Singers. *Hobbies:* Avid mystery reader; Gourmet cooking; Gardening. *Current management:* Melody Bunting International, 127 West 72nd Street, Suite 2-R, New York, NY 10023, USA. *Address:* 229 East 11th Street, New York, NY 10003, USA.

DOOLEY William, b. 9 Sept. 1932, Modesto,

California, USA. Singer (Baritone). *Education:* Studied at the Eastman School of Music and in Munich with Viktoria Prestel and Hedwig Fichtmuller. *Debut:* Heidelberg 1957, as Posa in Don Carlos. *Career:* Sang at Bielefeld 1959-62; member of the Deutsche Oper Berlin from 1962, notably in the premieres of Montezuma by Sessions (1964), Gespenstersonate by Reimann (1984) and Rihm's Oedipus, 1987; Salzburg Festival 1964, as Lucio Silla and 1966, in the premiere of The Bassarids by Henze; Metropolitan Opera from 1964, as Amonasro, Eugene Onegin, the villains in Les Contes d'Hoffmann, Telramund, Orestes (Elektra), and Mandryka; Hamburg Staatsoper 1967 as Iago, and 1979 in the premiere of Jakob Lenz by Wolfgang Rihm; Guest appearances at the Royal Opera Stockholm from 1967; Other Roles include: Berg's Wozzeck and Dr. Schön, Pizarro, Kothner, Macbeth, Escamillo, Nick Shadow, Captain Mary (Die Soldaten) and Goryanchikov in From the House of the Dead; Sang Eagle in the premiere of Los Alamos by Marc Neikrug at Berlin, 1989. *Recordings include:* Telramund in Lohengrin (RCA); Jakob Lenz (Harmonia Mundi). *Address:* c/o Deutsch Oper Berlin, Richard Wagnerstrasse 10, D-100 Berlin, Germany.

DORAN Matt (Higgins), b. 1 Sept. 1921, Covington, Kentucky, USA. Composer; Flute Teacher. *Education:* Los Angeles City College; Studied composition with Toch, Kubik and Eisler, BM 1947, DMA 1953, University of Southern California, Los Angeles; Training in flute from Ary Van Leeuwen, Archie Wade, Jules Furman and William Hullinger. *Career:* Orchestral Flautist; Teacher, Del Mar College, Corpus Christi, Texas, 1953-55; Ball State University, Munci, Ind, 1956-57; Instructor 1957-66, Professor 1966-, Mount Saint Mary's College, Los Angeles. *Compositions:* 10 operas, including: The Committee, 1953; The Marriage Counselor, 1977; 4 symphonies, 1946, 1959, 1977, 1979; Flute Concerto, 1953; Horn Concerto, 1954; Piano Concerto, 1975; Cello Concerto, 1976; Double Concerto for Flute, Guitar and Strings, 1976; Eskaton, oratorio for Soloists, Chorus and Orchestra, 1976; Poem for Flute and Piano, 1965; Clarinet Sonata, 1967; Sonatina for Flute and Cello, 1968; Quartet for Oboe, Clarinet, Bassoon and Viola, 1970; Trio for Flute, Clarinet and Piano, 1979-80; Numerous flute pieces; Piano music; Songs. *Honours:* MacDowell Colony Fellowship, 1954; Huntington Hartford Foundation Awards, 1956, 1964. *Address:* c/o Music Department, Mount Saint Mary's College, Los Angeles, CA 90049, USA.

DORFMULLER Kurt, b. 28 Apr. 1922, Munich, Germany. Musicologist; Librarian. m. Liselotte Laubmann, 2 sons. *Education:* Training & state examination, library science; Musicology, University of Munich, 1946-52; Dr phil. *Career:* Bavarian State Library 1954-84, including: Head, Music Collection, 1963; Head, Acquisitions Division, 1969-, Vice-Director 1972. *Publications:* Studien zur Lautenmusik in der ersten Halfte des 16 Jahrhunderts, 1967; Beiträge zur Beethoven-Bibliographie, 1977; Bestandsaufbau an wissenschaftlichen Bibliotheken, 1989. *Contributions to:* Journals, Festschriften and Library Exhibition Catalogues (Musicology and Library Science). *Honours:* Ars Jocundissima, Festschrift für Kurt Dorfmülier, 1984. *Memberships include:* International Association of Music Libraries; Member of the board, International Inventory of Musical Sources. *Hobby:* Puns. *Address:* D-82031 Grunwald, Gabriel-von-Seidl-Strasse 39, Germany.

DORN Reinhard, b. 18 Feb. 1957. Singer (Bass). *Education:* Studied at the Cologne Musikhochschule. *Career:* Sang at Krefeld/Mönchengladbach from 1983 as Moruccio in Tiefland, Nicolai's Dr Caius, Alcindoro in La Bohème and Dr Bartolo in Il Barbiere di Siviglia; Has sung at Karlsruhe as Baculus in Der Wildschutz, Geronimo (Il Matrimonio Segreto), Mamma Agatha (Donizetti's Viva la Mamma) and Leporello; Cologne Opera from 1987 as Britten's Bottom, Dr Bartolo, Frank (Die Fledermaus), Papageno, Nardo (La Finta Giardiniera), Kezal and Don Pasquale; French debut at Toulouse 1990, as Leporello; Guest appearances in

Germany and Brussels; Also engaged for season 1991-92 in: Die Zauberflöten and La Finta Gardiniera, Cologne Opera; in Prague Don Giovanni, Cologne Opera; Meister and Margarita, Die Zauberflöte, Julius Caesar, Scottish Opera; Recent and forthcoming engagements include: Kezal and Leporello, Cologne; Don Alfonso in Cologne in 1993/94; Season as Samuel in Ballo at Dresden. *Address:* c/o Haydn Rawstron Ltd, PO Box 654, London SE26 4DZ, England.

DORNBUSCH Hans, b. 1946, Sweden. Singer (Tenor). *Education:* Studied at the Stockholm Academy and at the School of the Royal Opera. *Debut:* Stockholm, 1969, as Calaf. *Career:* Member of the Royal Opera Stockholm from 1970, notably as Manrico, Otello, Pinkerton, Turiddu, Andres in Wozzeck and the Steuermann in Fliegende Hollnder: Sang Pope Alexander VII in the premiere of Chriatina, by Hans Gefors, 1986; Character roles in Albert Herring and Hansel und Gretel; Guest appearances in England and Germany; Frequent concert engagements. *Address:* c/o Kungliga Teatern, PO Box 10694, S-103 22 Stockholm, Sweden.

DOROW Dorothy, b. 1930, London, England. Singer (Soprano). *Education:* Studied at Trinity College, London. *Career:* Sang in London from 1958, notably in BBC Invitation Concerts (Webern conducted by John Carewe, and the British premiere of Herzgewäcshe by Schoenberg, 1960); Has sung in the premieres of works by Birtwistle, Nono, Maderna, Dallapiccola, Bussotti, Ligeti, Boulez, Goehr and Bennett (The Ledge, Sadler's Wells, 1961); Sang Hilda Mack in the British premiere of Henze's Elegy for Young Lovers, Glyndebourne 1961; Lived in Sweden 1963-77, Holland from 1977: Professor of Voice at the Conservatories of Amsterdam and The Hague; Master Classes in Europe and Scandinavia; Concerts and opera in Italy, at La Scala, Venice, Rome, Florence and Bologna (Le Grand Macabre by Ligeti); Repertoire from Monteverdi to the 20th Century; Covent Garden debut 1983, as Stravinsky's Nightingale.

DOSSOR Harry Lancelot, b. 14 May 1916, Weston-super-Mare, Somerset, England. Musician (Concert Pianist and Teacher). m. Diana Isobel Levinson, 30 Nov 1940, 1 son, 2 daughters. *Education:* Seaford College, Sussex, 1930-32; Studied Piano with Herber Fryer, Composition with Herbert Howells, Royal College of Music, London, 1932-37. *Debut:* Aeolian Hall, London, 1937. *Career:* Solo recitals, concertos and chamber music for BBC; Soloist for Royal Philharmonic Society, Henry Wood Promenade Concerts, and with main English orchestras; Concertos with Wood, Boult, Barbirolli, Sargent, Kubelik, Galliera, Malko; Guest Soloist with Israel Philharmonic Orchestra in Israel, 1950; Member of Staff, Royal College of Music, 1946-53; Principal Teacher of Piano, Elder Conservatorium of Music, University of Adelaide, South Australia, 1953-79. *Address:* 48 Dashwood Road, Beaumont, South Australia 5066, Australia.

DOUGLAS Barry, b. 23 Apr 1960, Belfast, Northern Ireland. Pianist. *Education:* Belfast School of Music; Royal College of Music, London, 1978-82; Diploma RCM (Performance); ARCM; LRAM. *Debut:* Wigmore Hall, London, 1981; Carnegie Recital Hall, New York, 1982; Royal Festival Hall with London Philharmonic Orchestra, 1983. *Career:* Subject of BBC Documentary Film, Rhapsody in Belfast and also film entitled After the Gold; Appeared in Madame Sousatska, a film by John Schlesinger; television series Concerto in which he played Rachmaninov 2 with the LSO and Michael Tilson-Thomas; Broadcasts for BBC Radio 3 and Radio Ulster, Radio London and BBC TV; Live performances with orchestras and recorded concerts; Performances for Thames TV; Concerts given in USA, Japan, France, Germany, UK, Denmark, Sweden, Holland, Italy, Greece, Ireland, USSR, Australia and New Zealand. Played at British Embassy in Washington, USA, 1982; Performed with major British orchestras; Played the Brahms Piano Quintet with the Tokyo Quartet at the Elizabeth Hall, 1991; Beethoven's Fourth Concerto at the 1993 London Proms. *Recordings:* RCA contract; Tchaikovsky Concerto

No 1 with LSO/Slatkin, Brahms Concerto No.1 with LSO; Mussorgsky, Liszt and Beethoven solo works; Liszt Concertos 1 & 2 and Hungarian Fantasy with LSO/Hirokami; Prokofiev Solo Sonatas 2, 7 and Cinderella; Berg and Liszt Sonatas; Brahms Quintet with Tokyo Quartet; Tchaikovsky 2, 3 & the Concert Fantasy; Rachmaninov 2 coupled with some Rachmaninov Preludes. *Honours:* Worshipful Company of Musicians Medal; Boise Award, 1st Prize, classified, Paloma O'Shea Piano Competition, Spain, 1980; Concert Artists Guild Award of New York, 1982; Silver Medallist, Arthur Rubinstein Piano Master Competition, Israel, 1983; Hon. D Mus, Queens, Belfast, 1987; Gold Medal, Tchaikovsky Competition, Moscow, 1986. *Hobbies:* Driving; Reading; Food and wine. *Address:* c/o Terry Harrison Artists, 3 Clarendon Court, Park Street, Charlbury, OX7 3PA, England.

DOUGLAS James, b. 1932, Dumbarton, Scotland. Composer. m. Helen Torrance Fairweather, 16 Apr 1968, 2s, 1d. *Education:* Heriot Watt College, Edinburgh; Conservatoire, Paris; Hochschule, Munich; Mozarteum, Salzburg. *Career:* Director: Eschenbach Editions, Caritas Records, Caritas Voices and Caritas Ensemble. Professor, L'Academie des Sciences Universelles, Paris, 1992-. *Compositions:* 10 symphonies, 11 string quartets, 22 orchestral works 200 songs, organ works, chamebr and instrumental works, piano works, 3 operas: Mask, Molière, Cuthbert; 3 ballet scores. *Recordings:* Visions of Glory; Symphony (A Cloud of Unknowing) for organ; The Complete organ Music of James Douglas - 3 vols. *Memberships:* Royal College of Organists; Incorporated Society of Musicians. *Hobbies:* Literature; Art. *Address:* c/o Eschenbach Edition, 28 Dalrymple Crescent, Edinburgh EH9 2NX, Scotland.

DOUGLAS Nigel, b. 9 May 1929, Lenham, Kent, England. Operatic Tenor; Director; Writer. m. Alexandra Roper, 21 July 1973, 1 son, 2 daughters. *Education:* Eton College; Magdalen College, Oxford University; Musikakademie, Vienna, Austria. *Debut:* Rodolpho in La Bohème, Vienna, Kammeroper, 1959. *Career:* Leading Roles in Opera Houses and Festivals; Aldeburgh, Antwerp, Barcelona, Basel, Berne, Brussels, Covent Garden, Dusseldorf, Duisburg, Edinburgh, English National Opera, Sadler's Wells, Scottish Opera, Venice, Lisbon, Vienna Volksoper, Welsh National Opera, Wexford, Zurich, Tokyo, Catania and others; Repertoire of 80 roles include, Peter Grimes, Captain Vere (Billy Budd), Aschenbach (Death in Venice), Eisenstein (Fledermaus), Danilo (Merry Widow), Loge (Rheingold), Herod (Salome), Captain (Wozzeck); Director of Viennese Operettas for New Sadler's Wells Opera; Royal Flemish Opera, Australian Opera, and Buenos Aires Opera; Has written and presented over 300 programmes on Opera and operetta for BBC radio 2,3,4 and World Service; Regular television appearances in UK and Europe. *Recordings:* Opera and Operetta; Numerous recordings for HMV, Decca, Philips. *Publications:* English versions of, Die Csardasfürstin (Kalman), 1982; Gräfin Mariza, (Kalman), 1983; Merry Widow (Lehar), 1983; Legendary Voices, 1992. *Honour:* Nominated for Royal Philharmonic Society Book Prize, 1993. *Current Management:* Music International UK; Thea Dispecker, USA. *Hobbies:* Gardening; Bee-keeping; Fishing. *Address:* Eythorne House, Eythorne, Dover, Kent, CT15 4BE, England.

DOUSA Eduard, b. 31 Aug 1951, Prague, Czechoslovakia. Composer; Teacher. m. 21 Oct 1976, 2 sons. *Education:* Graduated, Gymnasium, 1969; Studied Musicology, Charles University, Prague, to 1972; Graduated in Composition, Theory of Music, Academy of Musical Arts, Prague, 1977. *Career:* Teacher, Theory of Music, Conservatoire, Prague, 1977-86; Teacher, Theory of Music, Philosophical Faculty, Prague, 1986-. *Compositions:* Published compositions: Sonata for organ; Variations on a baroque theme for strings; Miniatures for piano (for children); Sonatine for clarinet and piano (for children); Rhapsody for clarinet and piano; Three short suites for guitar (for children). *Recordings:* Rhapsody for clarinet and piano (Supraphon, Prague) 1989; Variations on a baroque

theme for strings (Supraphon) 1988; Miniatures for flute, violin, violoncello and harpsichord (Bonton, Prague) 1990; Many compositions were recorded for Czechoslovak Radio - Concertino for trumpet and orchestra, Sonata for piano, String-quartet, Romantic Phantasy for violin and piano, Rhapsody for clarinet and piano and many compositions for children - musical fairy tales, songs, choirs etc. *Membership:* Society of Czech Composers. *Hobbies:* History; Literature; Sport - tennis, swimming. *Address:* Tenisova 9, 102-00 Prague 10, Czech Republic.

DOW Dorothy, b. 8 Oct 1920, Houston, Texas, USA. Singer (Soprano). *Education:* Juilliard School, New York. *Career:* Sang in and directed various choirs in New York, 1938-44; Sang Santuzza in a concert performance of Cavalleria Rusticana, Buffalo 1944; Columbia University, New York, in the premiere of The Mother of us All, by Thomson (1947); Sang with the Zurich Opera 1948-50; La Scala from 1950, as Elisabeth, Marie (Wozzeck), Danae by Strauss, Chrysothemis, Gioconda and Walton's Cressida; Sang Erwartung in the US premiere of Schoenberg's monodrama, with the New York Philharmonic, 1951; Glyndebourne Festival 1952-53, Lady Macbeth and Ariadne; Carnegie Hall New York 1952, in the US premiere of Christophe Colombe by Milhaud; Florence 1953, Agnese di Hohenstaufen by Spontini; Sang Renata in the stage premiere of Prokofiev's Fiery Angel, Venice 1955.

DOWER Catherine A, b. 19 May 1924, South Hadley, Massachussetts, USA. Professor of Music History. *Education:* AB, Hamline University, 1945; MA, Smith College, 1948; PhD, Catholic University of America, 1968; Pius X School of Liturgical Music 1945-46; University of Innsbruck, 1950; Solesmes Abbey, 1950. *Compositions:* Editions of choral music published by Broude (Alexander Broude) New York City. *Recordings:* College Glee Club recordings. *Publications:* Puerto Rican Music Following the Spanish American War 1983; Alfred Einstein on Music, 1991; Yella Pessl, First Lady of the Harpsichord, 1993. *Contributions to:* Musart; Music Journal; NOTES; Inter American Review; Groves 6; MGG; Boletin de la Academia des Artes y Ciencias de Puerto Rico; Sacred Music; Orchestras of the World; Orchestras of the United States. *Hobby:* Walking. *Address:* 60 Madison Avenue, Holyoke, MA 01040, USA.

DOWLING Richard William, b. 6 Sept 1962, Houston, Texas, USA. Concert Pianist. *Education:* BM summa cum laude, University of Houston, 1985; MM, Yale University, 1987; DMA, Piano Performance, University of Texas, Austin, 1990; Principal Teacher, Abbey Simon; Additional studies: Le Conservatoire de Musique, Nice, France; Yale Norfolk Summer School and Music Festival, Connecticut, USA. *Debut:* With Fort Worth Symphony, Texas, 1981. *Career:* Solo recitals throughout USA; PBS television solo recital programme debut aired nationally, 1986; Recital tour, France, 1991; Concerto appearances with Oklahoma Symphony, Houston Civic Symphony, Shreveport (Louisiana) Symphony, Midland-Odessa (Texas) Symphony, Brazos Valley (Texas) Symphony, Yale Trumbull Symphony, Arkansas Symphony; Concerto appearances with Jupiter Symphony, Tully Hall, Lincoln Center, New York City, 1992; 1st Holder of Walles Chair in the Performing Arts, Lamar University, 1989-90; Artist Faculty (Piano) at The Harid Conservatory of Music, Boca Raton, Florida, USA; Recitals: Austria, Australia, South Africa, 1992; 2nd tour of France, 1992; Gina Bachaeur Festival, Salt Lake City, Utah, 1993; Paris Recital Debut: Salle Cortot, 1994. *Recordings:* Rachmaninoff: Piano Concerto No 1 with Brazos Valley (Texas) Symphony, Franz Krager, conductor, 1988; Concerto Appearances: Lawton Philharmonic (Oklahoma), 1993; Abilene Philharmonic (Texas), 1992; Laredo Philharmonic (Texas), 1992; Amarillo Symphony (Texas), 1994. *Publication:* New critical edition of Maurice Ravel's Trio for Piano, Violin and Cello, 1990. *Current Management:* LA Artists Managements, 21346 St Andrew's Blvd, Suite 260-207, Boca Raton, FL 33433, USA. *Address:* 261 West 71st Street, No 3, New York, NY 10023, USA.

DOWNES Andrew, b. 20 Aug 1950, Handsworth, Birmingham, England. Composer; Lecturer. m. Cynthia, 9 Aug 1975, 2 daughters. *Education:* Aldridge Grammar School, 1961-68; BA Hons, 1972; MA Cantab, 1975; Choral Scholar, St. John's College, Cambridge, 1969-72; Royal College of Music, 1972-74; Studied Singing with Gordon Clinton; Composition with Herbert Howells; later studied with Sir Lennox Berkeley. *Career:* Appointed Tutor in Composition, Birmingham School of Music, 1975; Performances in Britain and Europe including Vienna, Salzburg, Berlin, Amsterdam, Wigmore Hall, Festival Hall and many Cathedrals and leading concert halls; several works broadcast on TV and radio, home and abroad, including a series on Central Peking Radio; performances in Britain, Europe, USA, Australia, Israel and China. *Compositions:* Temple of Solomon, opus 19, 1980; O Vos Omnes, opus 23, 1981; Odysseus and the Cyclops, opus 25, 1981; Symphony No. 1, opus 27, 1982; Suite for Brass Quintet, opus 28, 1983; Old Love's Domain, opus 29 (commissioned, John Mitchinson), 1983, Broadcast BBC Radio 3, 1985; Symphony No. 2, opus 30, 1984; 3 Anthems, opus 31 (commissioned, BBC Daily Service) 1984; Prelude, Fanfare and Postlude for Organ, opus 9, 1975, Broadcast 1979, BBC Radio 3; Piano, Opus 32, 1985, Broadcast BBC Radio 3, 1987; I Will Lift Up Mine Eyes (Commissioned for Shakespeare's Birthday), 1985; In The Cotswolds (Commissioned for Three Choirs Festival), 1986; Songs from Spoon River, opus 39 (Commissioned, Sarah Walker), 1986, performed BBC Radio 3 1989; Sonata for 2 pianos (Commissioned Society for Russian Jewry), 1987; Firedances, commisioned for the centenary of the City of Birmingham, 1989, and performed to an audience of 20,000 with a massive fireworks display, 1989 and 1991; Song of the Prairies commisioned by Shrewsbury Choral Festival, conducted by John Rutter, 1989; The Last Trumpet, 1991 (commissioned BBC Radio 3); The Dancers of Huai-Nan (commissioned Cantamus) 1991; Symphony No.3 Completed 1991; A St Luke Passion (commissioned Wolverhampton Civic Choir, Brian Raynor, 2nd performance Crane School of Music, USA), 1992; Ballards for Christmas (commissioned Hillcrest School Chamber Choir, Robert Johnston-Harp), 1992. *Recordings:* The Marshes of Glynn, Cantata commissioned for Royal opening of Sir Adrian Boult Hall, Birmingham 1986, (Centenary); O Vos Omnes, Motet, commissioned by Cantamus; Fanfare for a Ceremony, commissioned for Open University (Cassette); Firedances. *Publications:* 51 Works published by Lynwood Music. *Honours:* Prizewinner, Stroud International Composition Competition, 1980; Trees planted in Israel in his name by Interdenominational Society for Soviet Jewry in recognition of his composition, Sonata for 2 pianos, written for their cause. *Memberships:* ISM; PRS; MCPS; Adviser to West Midlands Arts; Advisor to Live Music Now; Member of Committee for Indian Classic Music at Nottingham University; Fellow of IBA; Executive Member of Composers Guild. *Hobbies:* Walking; Camping; Reading. *Current Management:* Publisher: Lynwood Music, West Hagley, West Midlands, England. *Address:* Lynwood Music, 2 Church Street, West Hagley, West Midlands, DY9 0NA, England.

DOWNES Edward O(lin) D(avenport), b. 12 Aug 1911, Boston, Massachusetts, USA. Music Critic; Musicologist; Broadcaster; Teacher; Writer. *Education:* Columbia University, 1929-30; University of Paris, 1932-33; University of Munich, 1934-36 and 1938; PhD, Harvard University, 1958. *Career:* Wrote music criticism for New York Post, 1935-38; Boston Transcript, 1939-41; New York Times, 1955-58; Program Annotator, New York Philharmonic Orchestra, 1960-; Teacher, Wellesley College, 1948-49; Harvard University, 1949-50; University of Minnesota, 1950-55; Musicologist-in- Residence, Bayreuth master classes, 1959-65; Professor of Music History, Queens College of the City University of New York, 1966-81, NYU 1981-86; Professor of Music, Juilliard School of Music, 1986-; Quizmaster, Metropolitan Opera Saturday afternoon radio broadcast intermission feature, 1958-; Regular music critic panellist, syndicated radio programme, First Hearing. *Publications:* Translated Werfel and Stefan's Giuseppe Verdis Briefe as Verdi: The Man in his Letters, 1942; Adventures in Symphonic Music, 1943; Perspectives in Musicology, edited with Brook and van Solkema, 1972; The New York Philharmonic Guide to the Symphony 1976, 2nd edition 1981 as Guide to Symphonic Music. *Contributions to:* Articles in various journals and other publications. *Membership:* American Musicological Society. *Address:* 1 West 72nd Street, New York, NY 10023, USA.

DOWNES Edward (Thomas), (Sir) b. 17 June 1924, Birmingham, England. Conductor. *Education:* Studied at the University of Birmingham and the Royal College of Music (composition and horn); Further study with Hermann Scherchen. *Career:* Worked for Carl Rosa Opera 1950-52; Covent Garden from 1952, notably Der Freischütz (1954), Les Contes d'Hoffmann, Katerina Ismailova (1963), Der Ring des Nibelungen (1967), Hamlet by Searle 1969, Victory (1970) and Taverner (1972); Many performances of operas by Verdi; British premiere of The Bassarids by Henze, BBC 1968; Conducted the premieres of Birtwistle's Chorales 1967, and Brian's Symphonies Nos 14 and 21, 1970; Musical Director of Australian Opera 1972-76, conducting Prokofiev's War and Peace at the opening of the Sydney Opera House (1973); Welsh National Opera 1975, Der fliegende Holländer; Conducted the first performance of Prokofiev's opera Maddalena (BBC, 1979; also prepared edition); Conducted the first modern performance of Tchaikovsky's Vakula the Smith, BBC 1989; Led Revivals of Othello and Il Trovatore at Covent Garden, 1990, new production of Attila; Principal Conductor, BBC Philharmonic, from 1980: with the orchestra recorded a studio performance of Jerusalem by Verdi; Promenade Concerts 1989, with music by Bax, Walton, Strauss, John McCabe and Sibelius; Prokofiev's Symphonies in the Russian Spring series at the Festival Hall, 1991; Promenade Concerts, 1991, with the first Russian language performance of Prokofiev's Fiery Angel in Britain; Appointed Associate Music Director and Principal Conductor at Covent Garden, 1991; New Produciton of Verdi's Stiffelio, 1993. *Publications:* Translations of Jenûfa, Katerina Ismailova and Khovanshchina. *Honours include:* Commander of the British Empire, 1986; Knight of the British Empire, 1991. *Address:* Ingpen & Williams Ltd, 14 Kensington Court, London W8 5DN, England.

DOWNES Ralph William, b. 16 Aug 1904, Derby, England. Organist; Choral Conductor; Organ Consultant; Writer. m. Agnes Mary Rix, 17 Aug 1929, 1 son, deceased 20 September 1980. *Education:* Derby Municipal Secondary School, 1915-20; Oxford University, 1925-28; BA, 1928; MA, 1931; B.Mus, 1935; Royal College of Music, London, 1922-25; ARCM, 1925; Organ Scholar, Keble College, Oxford, 1925-28 (Conductor of Musical Society). *Debut:* Organ, London, 1925. *Career:* Assistant Organist, Southwark Cathedral, 1923-25; Director of Chapel Music and Lecturer in Music, Princeton University, NJ, USA, 1928-35; Summer School Lecturer, Pius X School of Liturgical Music, NY, 1931-32; Organist, The London Oratory, 1936-77; Now Emeritus; Many Recitals and Broadcasts, UK and abroad, important premieres, 1937-79, including TV; Designed famous organs especially London Royal Festival Hall; Professor of Organ, Royal College of Music, 1954-75. *Compositions:* Short works for piano and organ. *Recordings:* Bach and Widor (Royal Festival Hall); Bach Klavierübung Pt. 3, 18 chorales, Schübler Preludes (Festival Hall); 75th Birthday Recital (Bach, Franck, Karg-Elert and Dupré - Festival Hall); César Franck and His Pupils (London Oratory); Four Handel Concertos (Festival Hall, with London Chamber Orchestra, Conductor, A. Bernard). *Publications:* Essay On Purcell's Organ Music, in Symposium Henry Purcell (edited by Imogen Holst) 1959; Baroque Tricks - Adventures With The Organ- Builders, 1985. *Contributions to:* Musical Times (passim); The Organ (passim); The Consort, 1948; Organists' Review, 1984, 1985. *Honours:* Hon RAM, 1965; Hon FRCO, 1966; CBE, 1969; FRCM, 1970; Knight of St Gregory, 1970. *Memberships:* Dolmetsch Foundation, Life Member; Association Cavaillé-Coll, Paris, Comité d'Honneur;

RCM Union, Life Member; ISM. *Address:* c/o The Oratory, London SW7, England.

DOWNEY John (Wilham), b. 5 Oct 1927, Chicago, Illinois, USA. Composer; Professor. *Education:* BM, De Paul University, 1949; MM, Chicago Musical College, 1951; Paris Conservatoire, 1956; Doctor des lettres, Sorbonne, Paris, 1957. *Career:* Teacher, De Paul University; Chicago City College; Roosevelt University; Professor of Composition and Composer-in-Residence, University of Wisconsin, 1964-; Founder, Wisconsin Contemporary Music Forum. *Compositions:* Ageistics, ballet, 1967; Incidental music to Shakespeare's Twelfth Night, 1971; Orchestral: La Joie de la paix, 1956; Chant to Michelangelo, 1958; Concerto for Harp and Chamber Orchestra, 1964; Jingalodeon, 1968; Prospectations III-II-I for 3 Orchestras, 1970; Symphonic Modules, 1972; Tooter's Suite for Youth Orchestra, 1973; The Edge of Space for Bassoon and Orchestra, 1978, Discourse for Oboe, Harpsichord and Strings, 1984; Double Bass Concerto, 1987; Declamations, 1985; Chamber: String Trio, 1953; Violin Sonata, 1954; Wind Octet, 1954; 2 string quartets, 1964, 1976; Cello Sonata, 1966; Crescendo for 13 Percussionists, 1977; Agort for Woodwind Quintet, 1967; Almost 12 for Wind Quintet, String Quintet and Percussion, 1970; Ambivaliences I for Any Chamber Combination, 1972; High Clouds and Soft Rain for 24 Flutes, 1977; Duo for Oboe and Harpsichord, 1981; Portrait No 2 for Clarinet and Bassoon, 1983 and No 3 for Flute and Piano, 1984; Piano Trio, 1984; Prayer for Violin, Viola and Cello, 1984; Recombinance for Double Bass and Piano, 1985; Solo Pieces: Tabu for Tuba, 1967; Lydian Suite for Cello, 1975; Silhouette for Double Bass, 1980; Piano pieces; Vocal music, including Tangents, jazz oratorio, 1981; Choral works; What If? for choir, brass octet and solo timpany, 1973; Suite of Psalms for a cappella choir, 1989. *Recordings:* The Edge of Space on Chandos Records; Cello Sonata on PRI; String Quartet No.2 on Gasparo records; John Downey Plays John Downey on Gasparo records. *Publication:* La musique populaire dans l'oeuvre de Bela Bartók, 1966. *Address:* 4413 North Prospect Avenue, Shorewood, WI 53211, USA.

DOWNEY Peter, b. 14 Feb 1956, Belfast, Northern Ireland. Music Lecturer; Organist and Choirmaster. m. Una Feeney, 3 Aug 1985, 1 son, 1 daughter. *Education:* BSc (Hons), Physics, The Queen's University of Belfast, 1977; LTCL in Trumpet teaching, 1976; Diploma in Musical Education, 1978; PhD, The Queen's University of Belfast, 1983. *Career:* Music Teacher; Organist and Choirmaster, Clonard Monastery, Belfast; Senior Lecturer, St Mary's College, Belfast. *Compositions:* Sacred choral music. *Recordings:* Festal Mass at the Court of Vienna, 1648. *Contributions to:* Dansk Arbog for Musikforskning; Irish Musical Studies; Early Music Journal. *Honour:* Winner of Danish Government Scholarship to undertake musical research in Copenhagen, 1978. *Memberships:* Royal Musical Association; Historic Brass Society. *Hobbies:* Squash; Swimming; Archaeology; European Languages and History. *Address:* 56 Oakhurst Avenue, Black's Road, Belfast BT10 0PE, Northern Ireland.

DRAGONI Maria, b. 1958, Procida, Naples, Italy. Singer (Soprano). *Education:* Studied in Naples. *Debut:* Sang Imogene in Il Pirata at Naples, 1984 (Teatro di Jesi). *Career:* Appeared in the title role of Pergolesi's Il Flamino at the Teatro San Carlo Naples, 1984; Season 1988- 89, as Fenena in Nabucco at La Scala, Turandot at Nancy and Revenna and Aida at Macerata; Mathilde in Guillaume Tell and Bellini's Norma at the Theatre des Champs Elysées and Mulhouse, 1989. Season 1990-91, as Elisabeth de Valois at Turin and Donna anna at the Teatro dell'Opera at Rome; Sang Mimi at Naples and Elisabeth de Valois at the Verona Arena, 1992. Other roles include Paolina in Poliuto by Donizetti, Donna Anna, and La Gioconda. *Address:* c/o Teatro dell'Opera, Piazza B Gigli 8, 00184 Rome, Italy.

DRAHEIM Joachim, b. 26 July 1950, Berlin-Schmargendorf, Germany. Musicologist; Pianist; Teacher of Latin and Music. *Education:* 1st State examination, 1974, 2nd State examination, 1978, promoted to PhD, Latin, Greek, Musicology, 1978, University of Heidelberg; Studied Piano with Ursula Draheim, 1955-68, Violoncello with Annlies Schmidt-de Neveu, 1963-68. *Career:* Concerts as solo, chamber music and lieder pianist in Germany and Switzerland; Freelance, many radio recordings of lieder and piano pieces, Süddeutscher Rundfunk Karlsruhe and Heidelberg, 1973-; Freelance, several German and foreign music publishers including Breitkopf and Härtel, Wiesbaden and Wiener Urtext Edition, and recording companies, 1974-; Numerous editions including Brahms und seine Freunde-works for piano, works by Mozart, Beethoven, Loewe, Fanny Hensel, Liszt, Mendelssohn, Robert and Clara Schumann, Chopin, Brahms, Busoni, others, and first editions: Mendelssohn: Albumblatt in A major; Brahms: Die Müllerin; Schumann: Der Korsar, Piano accompaniment to Bach's Suite in C major for solo cello, Violin setting of Cello Concerto in A minor op 129, others; Has taught at Lessing Gymnasium, Karlsruhe, 1978-; Works for Neuen Schumann-Gesamtausgabe and the new MGG. *Hobbies:* Music and playing the piano; Collecting autographs, scores and books. *Address:* Sophienstr 165, D-76185 Karlsruhe, Germany.

DRAHOS Bela, b. 1955, Kaposvar, Hungary. Flautist; Conductor. *Education:* Studied with Henrik Prohle at the Gyor Conservatory and with Larant Kovacs at the Franz Liszt Academy, Budapest, graduated 1978; From 1978 studied Conducting with Prof Carl Österreicher in Wien. *Career:* Solo flautist with the Budapest Symphony Orchestra from 1976, including many foreign tours; Solo flautist with the Hungarian State Orchestra, 1990; Solo career in Austria, Bulgaria, Belgium, Czechoslovakia, England, Finland, France, the Soviet Union, Switzerland and Germany; Concerts with the New Zealand Symphony Orchestra 1988, West Berlin Philharmonie 1989; Leader and founding member of the Hungarian Radio Wind Quintet; Music Director, Kaposvár Symphony Orchestra, 1990; Assistant Conductor, Hungarian State Symphony Orchestra, 1993; Guest Conductor of leading orchestras in Hungary; Conducts operas and concerts in Austria and Germany. *Recordings:* Mozart Concerto K314; Paganini 24 Caprices; Bach 4th Brandenburg Concerto and Concerto for Two Flutes in F; Vivaldi Concertos (Hungaroton). *Honours:* First Prize, Concerto Praha, 71; Second Prize at the Prague Spring International Competition 1975; Grand Prize of UNESCO at the Bratislava Interpodium 1979; Ferenc Liszt Prize 1985; Artist of the Year 1986; Bartók-Pastory Prize 1988. *Address:* Co-Nexus Concert Ltd, Budapest 1, Roham U 1, PO Box 437, H-1371 Budapest, Hungary.

DRAKE Bryan Ernest Hare, b. 7 Oct 1925, Dunedin, New Zealand. Director of Opera; Baritone Singer. m. Jean Margaret Keen, 18 Apr 1949, 2 sons, 1 daughter. *Education:* BA, University of Otago, New Zealand, 1946; Studied with Ernest Drake, New Zealand, Dawson Freer, London. *Debut:* Escamillo, Carmen, 1948, New Zealand. *Career:* Created roles in Benjamin Britten's Billy Budd, Curlew River, Burning Fiery Furnace, Prodigal Son; TV, Billy Budd, Peter Grimes; Royal Opera, English National Opera, Welsh National Opera; English Opera Group, English Music Theatre; Recitals, Curlew River, Burning Fiery Furnace, Prodigal Son, Billy Budd, Rape of Lucretia; Professor, Guildhall School of Music and Drama, 1971-81; Director of Opera, Royal College of Music, 1981-85; Voice Consultant, Britten-Pears School for Advanced Musical Studies at Snape, 1987-. *Recordings:* Numerous including, Curlew River, Burning Fiery Furnace, Prodigal Son, Billy Budd, etc. *Honour:* Fellow, Royal College of Music, 1983. *Hobbies:* Gardening; Camping; Sailing. *Address:* 2 Fen Cottages, Aldringham, Leiston, Suffolk, IP16 4QR, England.

DRAKE George Warren James, b. 4 Aug 1939, Auckland, New Zealand. Lecturer in Music and Musicologist. m. Carla Maria Driessen, 1 son, 1 daughter. *Education:* BA, 1961, MA, 1963, University of Auckland, New Zealand; PhD, University of Illinois, USA, 1972. *Career:* Senior Lecturer, University of

Auckland, New Zealand; Dean, Faculty of Music, 1985-1988, Head of the School of Music, 1988-1991. *Publications:* The First Printed Books of Motets, Petrucci's Motetti a Numero Trentatre (Venice, 1502) and Motetti de Passione, de Cruce, de Sacramento, de Beata Virgine, de Huiusmodi (Venice 1503): A Critical Study and Complete Edition, 1972. *Memberships:* President, New Zealand Musicological Society, 1982-85; American Musicological Society; Musicological Society of Australia; Australia and New Zealand Association for Mediaeval and Renaissance Studies. *Address:* c/o School of Music, University of Auckland, Auckland, New Zealand.

DRAN Thierry, b. 1953, Bordeaux, France. Singer (Tenor). *Education:* Studied at the Bordeaux Conservatory and in Paris with Michel Senechal. *Career:* Appearances at the Paris Obera-Comique, the Berlioz Festival at Lyon (as Benedict), Rouen (Nadir and in Les Indes Galantes), Marseille (in Capuleti e i Montecchi) and Lyon, as Fenton in Falstaff; Grand Theatre Geneva, in Offenbach's Les Brigands and Barbe Bleue; Sang in the Ravel Double Bill at Glyndebourne, 1987-88; Paris Opera as Don Ottavio and as Mercure in Orphée aux Enfers; Guest appearances at Bordeaux, as Jena in Le Jongleur de Notre Dame, Liège (Ernesto, the Duke of Manuta and Rossini's Count Almaviva); Frequent concert engagements. *Recordings:* Messager's Fortunio, and Duc de Mantoue in Les Brigands. *Address:* c/o Opera de Lyon, 9 Quai Jean Moulin, F-69001 Lyon, France.

DRATH Jan Bogdan, b. 29 May 1923, Torun, Poland. Concert Pianist; Pedagogue; Editor of Music. m. Helene Marta Golikowna, 30 June 1951, 1 daughter. *Education:* State College of Music, Katowice, 1945-48; MA, Artist's Diploma; Doctoral studies, State College of Music, Cracow, 1956-58; Docent degree (habilitation), Warsaw Academy of Music, 1966; DMA, North Texas State University, USA, 1969. *Debut:* Bydgoszcz, 1939. *Career:* Concert appearances, Poland, Albania, Czechoslovakia, Hungary, Bulgaria, Iraq, USA, in recitals, radio and TV recordings, symphony concerts; World premiere of L Nikolov's Concerto for Piano and Orchestra, Sofia, 1961; Artist-Teacher, State Colleges of Music, Katowice and Wroclaw, Poland, Fine Arts Institute in Baghdad, Iraq, and New Mexico State University, North Texas State University and Texas A&I University, USA; Founder, Director, Annual Chopin Workshops, Texas A&I University, 1980. *Publications:* A Scriabin Selected Preludes, 1959; G J Vogler Concerto In C, 1959; Etudes Op 33 Karol Szymanowski's, 1963; A Skriabin Prelude for the Left Hand, 1963; Old English Music (XVI & XVII century), 1966; H Purcell Selected Pieces, 1966; D Scarlatti 60 sonatas (Excerpts from the Preface) by Ralph Kirkpatrick, translation, 1967; Waltzes of Fryderyk Chopin: Sources: Volume I, 1980. *Current Management:* Irene Neidich, Las Cruces, New Mexico, USA. *Address:* 4610 Abner Drive, Corpus Christi, TX 78411, USA.

DRATH Nina (Drath-Nowicka, Janina Irena), b. 14 Oct 1954, Katowice, Poland. Solo Concert Pianist. m. Jerzy Bogdan Nowicki, 25 Oct 1981, 1 son. *Education:* Academy of Music, Warsaw; MA, Artist's Diploma. *Debut:* With Silesian Philharmonic Orchestra, 1968; With WOSPRIT (Great Symphony Orchestra of Radio and Television), 1968. *Career:* 1st recital, Katowice, 1963; 1st recital abroad, Ostrava, Czechoslovakia, 1965; Regular concert appearances, solo and with orchestra, from age 14; Concert tours and performances, Poland, Spain, Italy, Germany, USA, Czechoslovakia; Many radio and TV performances; Guest Artist, Annual Chopin Workshops, Texas A&I University, USA, 1981-94; Artist-in-Residence, Central State University, Oklahoma, 1985-87. *Recordings:* On Muza, Vandor Music Group and PML TEX labels: J Haydn, P Petrof, F Chopin. *Honours:* 1st prize, WOSPRIT Radio and Television Contest, Katowice, 1968; Bacewicz Sonata, Weimar, 1975; Bronze Medal and 4th Prize, Paloma O'Shea International Piano Competition, Santander, 1976; Beethoven Concerto No 4, Frankfurt, 1978; Finalist, Senigallia International Piano Competition, Italy, 1979; Prizewinner, Slupsk National Piano Competition,

Poland, 1979. *Memberships:* Stowarzyszenie Polskich Artystów Muzyków; American Music Teachers Association; Regional Chairman, American Music Scholarship Association; President, Fryderyk Chopin Society of Texas; President of Ne Plus Ultra Club since 1991; President Founder of International Chopin Piano Competition and Sonatina and Sonata International Youth Piano Competition, 1993, 1994. *Hobby:* Antiques especially Louis XV. *Current Management:* Sue Keenon Artist Management. *Address:* 4610 Abner Drive, Corpus Christi, TX 78411, USA.

DRAZINIC Ivan Ivo, b. 3 July 1942, Lastovo, Dalmatia, Yugoslavia. Conductor. 1 son, 1 daughter. *Education:* Academy of Music, Belgrade. *Debut:* Belgrade. *Career:* Conductor/musical director, Abrasevic Choir, 1963-66; Conductor, Yugoslav Army Mixed Chorus, 1965-71; Chief conductor, Yugoslav Army Artistic Ensemble, 1971-80; Conductor/musical director, Ivo Lola Ribar Choir, 1970-80; Chief conductor, Dubrovnik City Orchestra, Libertas Symphony Choir, 1980-86; Artistic director, Dubrovnik Festival, 1986-; Conductor, Dubrovnik Festival Symphony Orchestra, 1986-. *Recordings:* 4 LP records, Yugoslav classical vocal, instrumental & vocal-instrumental works; Numerous recordings, radio & television, North German Radio, WDR, Swedish TV, etc. *Honours:* Winner, BBC, Let The People Sing, 1975; Decoration of Merit, President Tito, 1968; Winner, All-Yugoslav Choir Competition, Dubrovnik City Award, 1986; Luka Sorkocevic Prize, 1986. *Address:* Festival Dubrovnik, Od Sigurate 1, 50 000 Dubrovnik, Croatia.

DRESEN Adolf, b. 31 Mar 1935, Pomerania, Germany. Stage Director. *Education:* Studied at the Karl Marx University, Leipzig. *Career:* Emigrated to Vienna 1977 and produced Eugene Onegin at Hamburg, 1978; Zemlinsky's Der Zwerg and Eine Florentinische Tragodie staged 1981 and seen at Edinburgh 1983, Covent Garden, 1985 and the Vienna Volksoper 1990; Boris Godunov at Brussels 1986, followed by Fidelio 1988 (staged at Covent Garden 1990); Directed the three-act version of Lulu at the Châtelet, Paris, 1991. *Address:* c/o Royal Opera House (Contracts), Covent Garden, London WC2, England.

DRESHER Paul Joseph, b. 8 Jan 1951, Los Angeles, California, USA. Composer. m. 8 Mar 1986. *Education:* BA Music, University of California, Berkeley, 1977; MA Composition, University of California, San Diego, 1979; Private studies of North Indian classical music with Nikhil Banerjee, 1974-77, Ghanaian drumming with C K and Kobla Ladzekpo, 1975-79; Also studies Javanese and Balinese Gamelan. *Career:* Participated as composer and performer, throughout USA, Canada, Europe; Works performed at New York Philharmonic, San Francisco Symphony, Minnesota Opera, Brooklyn Academy of Music, Cal Arts Festival, New Music America, 1981, 1983, 1985, London International Festival of Theatre, Munich State Opera, Festival d'autumne in Paris; Various commissions including Nonsuch Commission Award from American Music Center, and radio composition for Olympic Arts Festival. *Compositions:* This Same Temple, 1977; Channels Passing, 1981; Night Songs, 1981; Liquid and Stellar Music, 1981; The Way of How, opera, 1981; ave ave, opera, 1983; Dark Blue Circumstance, electronic, 1982-84; re:act:ion, 1984; See hear, opera, 1984; Other Fire, electronic, 1984; Slow Fire, opera, 1985-86; Water Dreams, electronic, 1986; Power Failure, opera, 1989; Double Ikat, trio, 1989. *Recordings:* Liquid and Stellar Music/This Same Temple, Lovely Records; Channels Passing/Night Songs, New Albion Records; Dark Blue Circumstance/Water Dreams/Destiny, MinMax Music; Slow Fire, Act I, MinMax Music. *Contributions to:* Sounding Eleven. *Address:* 1937 Carleton Street, Berkeley, CA 94704, USA.

DREW David, b. 1930, England. Writer on Music; Publisher, Producer and Editor. m. Judith Sutherland. *Education:* Cambridge University. *Career:* Publicity Consultant and Writer, The Decca Record Company, 1955-59; Producer, BBC Music Department, 1960;

Music Critic, New Statesman, 1960-67; Musical Consultant to the Calouste Gulbenkian Foundation, UK branch, and Artistic Director of the Foundation's recording series Music Today, EMI/Argo, 1961-75; European Representative and Advisor, The Kurt Weill Foundation for Music, 1971-76; Editor, later Advisory Editor, of Tempo, 1971-92; BBC Music Advisory Committee and Arts Council Music Panel, 1971-80; Advisor to the Holland Festival, 1971, Berlin Festival, 1974-75; Director of Contemporary Music, Boosey & Hawkes Music Publishers from 1975 until resignation in 1992; Programme Committee of Mürztal Music Workshop, Austria, 1983-91; Executive Committee of Les amis du compositeur Igor Markevitch, Lausanne and London, 1988-; Trustee, Britten-Pears Foundation, 1989-; Director of Recordings, Largo Records, Cologne, and Supervisory Editor, The Kurt Weill Edition, 1992-; Editions of many stage and concert works by Kurt Weill, notably Cry the Beloved Country, Carnegie Hall, 1988; Performing Edition of Roberto Gerhard's opera The Duenna, Madrid, Barcelona, Opera North, 1992. *Publications:* Über Kurt Weill, and Weill, Ausgewählte Schriften, 1975; Introduction to Ernst Bloch Essays on the Philosophy of Music, 1985; The Kurt Weill Handbook, 1987. *Contributions:* numerous articles on 20th-century composers such as Stravinsky, Messiaen, Gerhard, Spinner, Górecki. *Address:* 12 Favart Road, London SW6 4AZ, England.

DREW James, b. 9 Feb 1929, St Paul, Minnesota, USA. Composer; Playwright; Pianist; Director. m. Gloria Kelly, 26 Mar. 1960, 1 son, 1 daughter. *Education:* Certificate, New York School of Music, 1956; MA, Tulane University, 1964; Private study with Wallingford Riegger, 1956-69, and Edgard Varèse, 1956. *Career:* Composer, concert hall, theatre, film; Composer: Northwestern University, 1964-66; Yale University, 1966-73; Tanglewood, Lennox, Massachusetts, summer 1973; LSU, 1973-75; Visiting Composer, California State University, 1976-77; Visiting Composer, University of California, Los Angeles, 1977-78; Director, American Music Theatre, 1978-; Director, Mysterious Travelling Cabaret, 1980-; Director, No Sleep Theatre, 1984-. *Compositions include:* The Lute in the Attic; Symphonies; October Lights; Lux Incognitus; Concerto for Small Percussion Orchestra; West Indian Lights; Mysterium (opera); Songs of Death and Bluelight Dancing; Trinity; American Elegy; Faustus - an Epilogue for 2 pianos, solo viola and chamber ensemble; The Orangethorpe Aria; Five O'Clock Ladies (stage work); Last Dance (video work); Whisper (video); Cantobosolo (contrabass solo); Cantobosolo for percussion and orchestra; Live from the Black Eagle (video work); Cello Concerto; In this Place of Half Lights, Gloria...Sotto Voce, a monodrama: In Memory of Gloria Kelly Drew, 1990; Piano Concerto, Formingreforming, 1991; Donaldsonville: Whistles, Steeples, Fog, 1990; Sacred Stones Resonating Under Fog, 1991; Inaudible Answers, 1992; Theater of Phantom Sounds, 1992; Easter Concerto, for violino Grand & Orchestra, 1992; Book of Lights, Clarinet and Piano Trio, 1993; Antitangos, Alto Flute, Contrabass, 1993. *Current Management:* Cooke Associates, Nicolaistraat 17, 2517 SX Den Haag, Netherlands. *Address:* c/o Theodore Presser Company, Presser Place, Bryn Mawr, PA 19010, USA.

DREYFUS George, b. 22 July 1928, Wuppertal, Germany. Musician; Composer. m. Francis Kay Lucas, 4 Nov. 1968. *Education:* Vienna Academy of Music, Austria, 1955-56. *Career Includes:* Orchestral Musician, Australian Broadcasting Commission, 1953; Formed New Music Ensemble, Melbourne, 1958; Freelance Composer, 1965-; Foundation member, Musical Director, ISCM, Melbourne, 1965; Formed George Dreyfus Chamber Orchestra, Melbourne, 1970; Musica Viva Outback Tour, 1974; 1-man Show, Melbourne, Sydney and various country centres, 1977-78; Composer in residence Rome 1976, Jerusalem 1980, Tienjin 1983, Shanghai 1986 and Nanjing 1991. *Compositions include:* Galgenlieder, 1957; Songs, Comic and Curious, 1959; Music in the Air, 1961; The Seasons, 1963; Quintet for Wind Instruments, 1965; Garni Sands, 2 act opera by Frank Kellaway, 1965-66;

Symphony No 1, 1967; Reflections in a Glasshouse, 1969; The Gilt-Edged Kid, 1 act opera by Lynne Strahan, 1970; Sextet for Didjeridu and Wind Instruments, 1971; The Lamentable Reign of Charles the Last, 1 act pantopera by Tim Robertson, 1975; 1976; Symphony No 2, 1976; Symphonie Concertante, 1978; An Australian Folk Mass, 1979; The Ballad of Charles Rasp; The Sentimental Bloke, 1985; Rathenau, 1993; Film and television scores; Several recorded including From Within Looking Out, conducted by composer. *Recordings:* As musician: George Dreyfus-Live!; Rush, Sebastian the Fox and other goodies. *Publication:* The Last Frivolous Book, autobiography, 1984. *Address:* 3 Grace Street, Camberwell, Victoria 3124, Australia.

DREYFUS Huguette Pauline, b. 30 Nov 1928, Mulhouse, France. Harpsichordist. *Education:* Diplomas, Piano, Harmony, Counterpoint, Ecole Normale de Musique, Paris; Conservatoire National Supérieur de Musique, Paris; Advance studies, harpsichord, Chigiana Academy, Siena, Italy. *Career:* Soloist, ORTF and numerous other Radio and TV networks in France, South Africa, Germany, Belgium, Canada, UK, Switzerland, Austria, Brasil, Colombia, Denmark, Equador, Italy, Luxembourg, Peru, Sweden, Czechoslovakia, Yugoslavia, Japan and USA; Harpsichord teacher, Conservatoire National Supérieur de Musique de Lyon; Harpsichord teacher, Conservatoire National de Régioin de Rueil-Malmaison. *Recordings:* JS Bach 6 English Suites, 6 French Suites; Rameau Pieces de Clavecin; Couperin Pieces de Clavecin; Scarlatti, Chronological Anthology of 70 Sonatas; Seixas, 14 Sonatas; Bartók, Pieces from Mikrokosmos; Chamber music by J S Bach, Leclair, Rameau, Haydn, Vivaldi, Corelli, C P E Bach and W A Mozart; J S Bach, Italian Concerto, Chromatic Fantasy and Fugue, Inventions and Sinfonias, 6 Partitas, French Overture, 4 Duetti, Praeludium, Fuga and Allegro in E flat major Goldberg variations; Wilhelm-Friedemann Bach, 9 Fantasien; J S Bach: Harpsichord Transcriptions of 16 Concerti by various composers (B W V 972/987/) W A Mozart: Sonatas and fantasias for fortepiano; J S Bach: The Well Tempered Clavier, volume I, Denon-Nippon Columbia. *Honours:* 1st Medal, Harpsichord, International Competition Geneva 1958; Officier de l'Ordre National du Merite, 1987; Numerous Grand Prix for her recordings; Prix du Président de la République de l'Académie Charles Cros in 1985. *Address:* 91 Quai d'Orsay, 75007 Paris, France.

DRISCOLL Loren, b. 14 April 1928, Midwest, Wyoming, USA. Singer (Tenor). *Education:* Studied at Syracuse and Boston University. *Debut:* As Caius in Falstaff, Boston 1954; New York City Opera debut 1957, as Timur in Turandot; sang Tom Rakewell in The Rake's Progress at Santa Fe, 1957; Deutsche Oper Berlin from 1962, notably as Fenton, Pinkerton, Flamand (Capriccio), Don Ottavio and The Painter in Lulu; Sang in the premieres of Henze's Der junge Lord (1965) and Ulisse by Dallapiccola (1968); Glyndebourne Festival 1962, Ferrando; Salzburg Festival 1966, as Dionysos in the premiere of The Bassarids by Henze: repeated the role at La Scala and Santa Fe, 1968; Metropolitan Opera from 1966, as David, and Alfred in Die Fledermaus; Schwetzingen Festival 1971, as the Architect in the premiere of Reimann's Melusine, repeated at Edinburgh; Brussels, 1973, in the premiere of Love's Labour Lost by Nabokov; Santa Fe 1967, in the US premiere of Boulevard Solitude by Henze; Rome 1982, with the company of the Deutsche Oper, in Undine by Lortzing; Further appearances in Hamburg, Cologne and Edinburgh. *Recordings:* Der junge Lord and Lulu (Deutsche Grammophon); Oedipus Rex, Renard and The Nightingale, conducted by Stravinsky (CBS). *Address:* c/o Deutsche Oper Berlin, Richard Wagner Strasse 10, 1000-Berlin, Germany.

DROWER Meryl, b. 1955, Wales. Singer (Soprano). *Education:* Studied at the Royal College of Music and in Italy. *Career:* Joined English Music Theatre 1976 and sang Clorinda in La Cenerentola, Serpetta (La Finta Giardiniera), Miss Wordsworth (Albert Herring) and Papagena; Appearances with Kent Opera as Gilda, the Governess (Turn of the Screw), Susanna, Nannetta,

Zerlina and Marzelline (Fidelio), Donna Elvira and Ellen Orford; Has sung Despina for English National Opera and Papagena at Glyndebourne; Scottish Opera as Tytania in A Midsummer Night's Dream and in a Rossini double bill; Covent Garden as Barbarina (Le Nozze di Figaro) and in Lulu and L'Enfant et les Sortilèges; Appeared with the Royal Opera in Los Angeles (1984) as Papagena and in Peter Grimes; European engagements as Poppea in Agrippina (La Fenice, Venice), Serpetta (Bordeaux), Susanna (Vienna) and Donna Elvira and Marzelline (Valencia); Concert repertoire includes African Sanctus by David Fanshawe (premiere, London, 1972), and works by Britten, Vaughan Williams, Brahms, Beethoven, Bach, Handel and Haydn. *Recordings include:* Rossini double bill and A Night at the Chinese Opera (Kent Opera) for television. *Address:* c/o Korman International Management, Crunnells Green Cottage, Preston, Herts SG4 7UQ, England.

DROZDZEWSKI Piotr Michal, b. 30 Nov 1948, Zbaszyn, Poland. Composer; Chemist. m. Marta Kurek, 18 Oct 1975, 2 daughters. *Education:* Diploma, Violin, Secondary Music School, Wroclaw, 1970; MA, Chemistry, 1971; PhD, Chemistry, 1976; MA, Composition, Academy of Music, Wroclaw, 1977; DSc, Chemistry, 1990. *Compositions include:* Symphonic works: Dance for Strings, 1979; Sinfonia da Camera, 1980; Expansion, 1980-86; Choral work: Salve Regina; Chamber works: 3 String Quartets, 1976, 1978, 1981; Sonata a due violini, 1983; Several solo selections for violin, piano (harpsichord) and organ. *Recordings:* For Polish Radio: Cadenza; Dance for Strings; Expansion. *Honours:* Polish Radio Composers Competition, 1979; XXIII Young Composers Competition, Polish Composers Union, 1980; K Lipinski Composers Competition, Wroclaw, 1990. *Memberships:* Polish Composers Union. *Hobbies:* Electonics; Astronomy; All kinds of tinkering; Skiing. *Address:* Arctowskiego 24, 53211 Wroclaw, Poland.

DRUCKER Eugene, b. 17 May 1952, Coral Gables, Florida, USA. Violinist. *Career:* Co-leader of the Emerson String Quartet from its foundation in 1978; Public debut at Alice Tully Hall, New York, in March 1979, playing works by Mozart and Bartók; Quartet-in-residence at the Smithsonian Institute, Washington, from 1980 and the Hartt School of Music and the Aspen Music Festival from 1981; European debut at the Spoleto Festival, 1981; Noted for performances of the quartets of Bartók, including all six works in a single evening; Has given the premieres of works by Mario Davidovsky, and Maurice Wright; With Emerson Quartet 120 concerts annually in major musical capitals of Europe, US and Canada; Tours of Japan and Australia; Resident Quartet of Chamber Music Society of Lincoln Center, 1982-89. *Recordings include:* Bartók complete Quartets, Mozart 6 Quartets dedicated to Haydn, Schubert Cello Quintet with Rostropovich, Ives and Barber Quartets, Prokofiev Quartets & Sonata for 2 violins; As soloist: Bach Sonatas amd Partitas for violin. *Honours include:* Naumburg Award for Chamber Music, 1978; Gramophone Magzine: Best Chamber Music Record and Record of the Year for Bartók Quartets, 1989; Grammy for Best Chamber Music and Classical Record of the Year, also for Bartók, 1990. *Current Management:* IMG Artists. *Address:* c/o IMG Artists, 22 East 71 Street, New York, NY 10021, USA.

DRUCKER Stanley, b. 4 Feb 1929, New York City, USA. Clarinetist; Teacher. *Education:* Studied with Leon Russianoff. *Career:* Commenced performing at age 10; 1st Clarinetist, Indianapolis Symphony Orchestra, 1945-48; Member 1948-60, 1st Clarinetist 1960-, New York Philharmonic Orchestra; Various solo engagements; Teacher, Juilliard School, New York, 1968-; Commissioned works for the clarinet; Edited clarinet music. *Address:* c/o New York Philharmonic Orchestra, Lincoln Center, New York, NY 10023, USA.

DRUCKMAN Jacob, b. 26 June 1928, Pennsylvania, USA. Composer. m. Muriel Topaz, 5 June 1954, 1s, 1d. *Education:* BS 1954, MS 1956, Julliard of School

of Music, New York. Private study with Renee Longy, Aaron Copland and Tony Aubin. *Career:* Composer in Residence, NY Phil and Artistic Director of NYP Horizons Festivals, 1984-86; Guest conductor with many orchestras including New York and LA Philharmonics, Buffalo, New Orleans, Akron Symphonies, BBC Philharmonic, Netherlands Radio Orchestra and Krakow Radio and TV Orchestra. *Compositions include:* Seraphic Games, 1991; Demos, 1992; Sumemr Lightining, 1991; Nor Spell Nor charm, 1990. *Recordings include:* Aureol, St Louis Symphony; Prism, NY Philharmonic; Lamia, Louisville Orchestra; Nor Spell Nor Charm, Orpheus Chamber Orchestra; Reflections on the Nature of Water. *Publications:* Aureole, 1979; Brangle, 1991; Animus III, 1978; Delizie contente che l'Alme Beate, 1978; Lamia, 1978; Prism, 1981; The Seven Deadly Sins, 1980; Viola Concerto, 1978; Windows, 1973; Animus II, 1973; Valentine, 1970. *Honours include:* Pulitzer Prize, 1972; Society for Publication of American Music Award, 1967; American Academy and Nat Inst Arts and Letters Award, 1969. Guggenheim Fellow, 1957, 1968. *Memberships:* American Academy of Arts and Letters; Board, American Composers Orch; President, Koussevitsky Music Foundation and Chairman of the Kousssevitzky Foundation in the Library of Congress, 1980-; President, Aaron Copland Fund for Music, 1991-. *Address:* Yale University School of Music, PO Box 2014A, Yale Station, New Haven CT 06520-7440, USA.

DRUIAN Rafael, b. 20 Jan 1922, Vologda, Russia. Violinist; Teacher. *Education:* Studied at the Curtis Institute, Philadelphia, with Lea Luboshutz and Efrem Zimbalist. *Career:* Appointed leader of the Dallas Symphony 1947; Later positions with the Minneapolis Symphony, the Cleveland Orchestra, 1960-69, and the New York Philharmonic 1970-73; Has appeared widely as concert soloist and as recitalist; Teacher at the University of Minnesota, 1949-60, the Cleveland Institute, the University of California at San Diego and Boston University, from 1982. *Recordings include:* Sonatas by Bloch, Mozart, Bartók and Charles Ives. *Address:* Music Dept, Boston University, Commonwealth Avenue, Boston, MA 02215, USA.

DRUIETT Michael, b. 1967. Singer (Bass-Baritone). *Education:* Studied at the European Opera Centre in Belgium, the Scola Superiore in Italy, and the National Opera Studio, London. *Career:* Appearances with English National Opera in The Love for Three Oranges, Wozzeck, Gianni Schicchi, Salome, Cunning Little Vixen, Rigoletto (Sparafucile), Ariodante (King), Don Carlos, (Monk), A Masked Ball, Monteverdi's Orfeo and Lohengrin (Henry The Fowler); Sang in Wozzeck under Barenboim in Paris and appeared as Raimondo in Lucia di Lammermoor with Welsh National Opera; Principal bass with the Royal Opera, Covent Garden, from 1993-94; concert repertoire includes Elijah, St John Passion, Puccini's Messa di Gloria, Haydn's Nelson mass, Mozart's Requiem, Mahler's 8th with the CBSO/Elder, Messiah and Beethoven's Ninth, with the LSO under Libor Pesek. *Recordings:* Floyd's Susannah, with the Oper de Lyon. *Address:* c/o John Coast Ltd, 31 Sinclair Road, London W14 ONS, England.

DRUMMOND John Dodds, b. 11 Sept 1944, Lancaster, England. Music Educator; Composer; Musicologist; Opera Director; Broadcaster. m. Louise Isabel Benny, 28 Jan 1984, 1 son, 1 daughter. *Education:* Bootham School, York; Universities of Leeds and Birmingham; BA, Hons. Music; MusB, University of Leeds; PhD, University of Birmingham. *Career:* Haywood Research Fellow, Lecturer in Music, University of Birmingham, 1969-76; Blair Professor of Music, University of Otago, 1976-. *Composition:* Plague Upon Eyam, opera in three acts, University of Otago Press, 1984. *Publication:* Opera in Perspective, London and Minneapolis, 1980. *Memberships:* National Music Council of New Zealand; New Zealand Society for Music Education; Composers' Association of New Zealand. *Hobbies:* Walking; Science Fiction; Good Company. *Address:* Department of Music, University of Otago, PO Box 56, Dunedin, New Zealand.

DRUMMOND John Richard Gray, b. 25 Nov 1934, London, England. Arts Administrator. *Education:* Trinity College, Cambridge; MA Cantab. *Career:* BBC Radio and TV, 1958-78, as writer, director, producer and editor; Member, Music Panel, Arts Council, 1974-78; Member, Dance Committee, Arts Council, from 1974; Director, Edinburgh International Festival, 1978-83; Controller, BBC Music from 1985, BBC Radio 3, 1987-91; Director, Promenade Concerts, 1992-. *Membership:* Scottish Arts Club. *Hobbies:* Architecture; Conversation. *Address:* c/o BBC Radio 3, Broadcasting House, Portland Place, London W1, England.

DU Mingxin, b. 19 Aug 1928, Qian Jiang County, Hubei Province, China. Composer; Music Educator. m. 1 Sept 1966. 1 son, 1 daughter. *Education:* Yu Cai Music School, 1939; Tchaikovsky Music Conservatory, 1954-58. *Debut:* Piano solo concert, Shanghai, 1948. *Career:* Participated in the Asian Composers Conference & Music Festival, Hong Kong, 1981; Two concerts, Hong Kong Philharmonic Orchestra of works by Du Mingxin, 1982, 1988, composed for the movie Wonderful China; Travelled to USA in 1986 for performance of Violin Concerto in John F Kennedy Center and gave lectures in some famous music institutes. *Compositions:* Ballet suite, The Mermaid; The Red Detachment of Women; Symphonic Picture, The South Sea of My Mother Land; Symphonic fantasia, The Goddess of the River Luo; Symphony, Youth; Violin Concerto, Piano Concerto, Great Wall Symphony; Flapping! the Flags of Army. *Recordings:* The Mermaid; The Red Detachment of Women; The South Sea of My Mother Land; The Goddess of the River Luo; Youth; Great Wall Symphony. *Membership:* Executive Director and General Secretary, Chinese Musicians Association. *Hobbies:* Watching football and sports competition. *Address:* Central Conservatory of Music, 43 Bao Jia Street, Beijing 100031, China.

DU PLESSIS Christian, b. 2 July 1944, Vryheid, South Africa. Singer (Baritone). *Education:* Studied with Teasdale Griffiths and Esme Webb in South Africa and Otakar Kraus in London. *Debut:* With the PACT Opera in Johannesburg, as Yamadori in Madame Butterfly, 1967. *Career:* Sang in a 1970 concert performance of Andrea Chenier in London and appeared as Valentin in Faust at Barcelona, 1971; Member of the Sadler's Wells/English National Opera 1973-81, notably as Cecil in Maria Stuarda, and Verdi's Germont and Posa; Guest appearances in Barcelona, Johannesburg and elsewhere; Concert performances for London Opera Society and Opera Rara in L'Etoile du Nord by Meyerbeer, Gli Orazi ed i Curiazi by Mercadante, Donizetti's Torquato Tasso, Maria di Rudenz, Rosmonda d'Inhilterra and Maria Padilla, and Bellini's Il Pirata; Retired 1988. *Recordings include:* Germont in an English-language Traviata conducted by Charles Mackerras; Maria Stuarda (Decca); Meyerbeer's Dinorah; L'Assedio di Calais by Donizetti (Opera Rara).

DUBAL David, b. Cleveland, Ohio, USA, 1940. Pianist; Teacher; Writer on music. *Education:* Ohio State University; Juilliard School, New York; Piano studies with Arthur Loesser, Cleveland. *Career:* Piano Faculty, The New York Institute for the Education of the Blind, 1966-67; Music Director 1967-, Host of daily programme A Musical Offering 1975-76, Host of weekly radio programme For the Love of Music 1979-, Interviewer-Producer 6-part series Conversations with Horowitz, many other programmes, WNCN Classical Music Radio Station, New York; Extension Division, Manhattan School of Music, 1975-80; Faculty, The Juilliard School, 1983-; Performances and master classes in South Korea, 1986; Piano recitals and lecture recitals throughout USA; Lectures at New School for Social Research and The Metropolitan Museum; Adjudicator of leading piano competitions including Busoni Competition, Bolzano, Italy, 1984; Cassagrande, Termi, Italy, 1986. *Recordings:* Piano Music of Khachaturian; The Piano in America; The Music of the Romantic Pianist Composer; Invitation to the Waltz; Over 30 composers recorded. *Publications:* Reflections From the Keyboard; Summit Books, In England, The World

of The Concert Pianists, Gollancz; The Art of The Piano, 1990; Conversations with Menuhin, 1991; Evenings with Horowitz, 1991. *Address:* The Julliard School, 60 Lincoln Center Plaza, New York, NY 10025, USA.

DUBINBAUM Gail, b. 1958, New York, USA. Singer (Mezzo-soprano). *Education:* Studied with Herta Glaz and with the Metropolitan Young Artists Program. *Career:* Sang at the Metropolitan from 1982, debut in L'Enfant et les Sortileges; Appearances in New York and elsewhere in the USA as Rossini's Rosina and Isabella and as Mozart's Dorabella; Engagements at the Vienna Staatsoper 1986-88; Suzuki in Butterfly for Opera Pacific at Costa Mesa and again at Detroit, 1991; Sang Jeremiah, Symphony with Leonard Bernstein conducting Boston Symphony, Los Angeles Philharmonic and the Pittsburgh Symphony (40th Anniversary of premiere), sang Suzuki and Bach Magnificat with Zubin Mehta and Israel Philharmonic. *Address:* 6614 W Kingston Lane, Glendale, AZ 85306, USA.

DUBOIS Jocelyne, b. 20 Feb 1965, Douai, France. Director, School of Music, Dance and Theatre; Dancer; Singer. m. Jean-Marie Adrien, 23 May 1990. *Education:* National Conservatory of Douai, 1976-84; Lille University, 1982-84; National High Conservatory of Paris, 1983-91; National Conservatory of Amiens, 1985-87; Maîtrise de musique, 1988, Agrégation, Musical Educational, 1989, Paris-Sorbonne University; Tours University, 1990-93. *Career:* Dancer, Compagnie Lyrique de France, 1979-82; Violinist, Jeune Orchestre Symphnique de Douai et des Hauts de France, 1979-82; Singer, Ensemble BWV, 1983-91; Director, Municipal School of Music and Dance, Houilles, 1989-90; Currently Director, National School of Music, Dance and Theatre, Marne-la-Vallee. *Composition:* Cinq variations, for violins, 1991. *Recording:* Honegger's La Danse des morts, as Violinist, Jeune Orchestre Symphnique de Douai et des Hauts de France, 1981. *Publication:* 1913: Le Festin de l'Araignée, 1989. *Contributions to:* La Musique de Chambre avec piano et les oeuvres pour harmonica de verre, in new edition of Mozart, 1991. *Hobby:* Oriental philosophy. *Address:* 2 Rue Boutarel, 75004 Paris, France.

DUBOSC Catherine, b. 12 Mar 1959, Lille, France. Singer (Soprano). *Education:* Studied at the Strasbourg Conservatory, Ecole Natatione in Paris from 1980 with Denise Dupleix and Hans Hotter; Further study with Eric Tappy at Lyons. *Career:* Sang at Lyon Opera, 1985-87; As Mozart's Despina, Pamina and Susanna, Nannetta, Blanche in Dialogues des Carmelites and Marzelline (Fidelio); San Gretel at Geneva 1987 and Isipile in Cavalli's Giasone at Utrecht, 1988, and the Theatre des Champs Elysées, Paris, 1990; Appearances at Montpellier (Pamina, 1991), Avignon, Nancy, Edinburgh, and Strasbourg; Sang Mélisande at Lausanne, 1992; *Recordings include* Giasone, The Love for Three Oranges, Campra's Tancrède, Sylla et Glaucus by Leclair and Darande in Gluck's La Rencontre Imprevue (Erato).

DUBROVAY Laszlo, b. 23 Mar 1943, Budapest, Hungary. Composer; Teacher. *Education:* Bartók Conservatory, Budapest; Graduated, Academy of Music, Budapest, 1966; Principal teachers: Istvan Szelenyi, Ferenc Szabo, Imre Vincze; Completed training in Germany with Karlheinz Stockhausen, composition and electronic music from Hans-Ulrich Rumpert, 1972-74. *Career:* Teacher of music theory, Budapest Academy of Music, 1976-; Residence in Berlin, 1985. *Compositions:* Orchestral: Verificazione, 1970; Succession, 1974; Concerto for 11 Strings, 1979; Concerto for Flute and 45 Strings, 1981; Concerto for Trumpet and 15 Strings, 1981; Concerto for Piano, orchestra and Synthesizer, 1982; Piano Concerto, 1984; Variations on an Oscillating Line, 1987; Concerts romantico for piano 1990; Tripleconcert for trumpet, trombone, tuba 1989; Psychodramatic for brass 1989; March for winds 1990; Il ricatto opera 1991; Chamber: Stigmata for Tenor and Piano, 1969; 2 brass quintets, 1971, 1980; 2 wind quintets, 1972, 1983; Magic Squares for Violin and Cimbalom, 1975; Matuziada Nos

1 to 5 for 4 Flutes, 1975-76; Geometrum II: String Quartet No 2, 1976; Numberplay No 1 for 20 Players, 1976; Interferences No 1 for 2 Cimbaloms, 1976; Music for 2 Cimbaloms, 1977; Brass Septet for 3 Trumpets, Horn, 2 Trombones and Tuba, 1980; String Quartet No 3, 1983; Octet for Clarinet, Bassoon, Horn and String Quintet, 1985-87; Pieces for solo instrument; Choruses; Live electronic works; Tape pieces; Computer music; Deserts for brass orchestra, 1987; Recitativo and aria for soprano and chamber ensemble, 1988; The sculptor dance-play in one act, 1993. *Address:* H-1026 Budapest,Gárdonyi G.u. 45/b, Hungary.

DUCLOUX Walter Ernest, b. 17 Apr. 1913, Kriens, Lucerne, Switzerland. Opera, Symphony and Ballet Conductor; Opera Director. m. Gina Rifino, 29 Nov. 1943, 2 sons, 1 daughter. *Education:* PhD, Philosophy, Music History, University of Munich, Federal Republic of Germany, 1935; Conducting Diploma, Academy of Vienna, Austria, 1937. *Debut:* Casino Lucerne, 1937. *Career:* Symphony and Opera Conductor, Lucerne, 1937-39; Assistant, Metropolitan Opera, New York, 1939, 1941; Guest Conductor, USA, France, Federal Republic of Germany, etc. 1945-49; Conductor, Prague National Opera and Radio, Czechoslovakia, 1945-48; Conductor, Ballet Russe, 1948; Musical Director, Voice of America, 1950, 1953; Professor of Opera and Conducting, University of Southern California, 1953-68; Professor of Opera and Conducting, University of Texas, Austin, 1968-; Artistic and Musical Director, Austin Lyric Opera, 1986-. *Recordings:* Sound track of Metro-Goldwyn-Mayer's Interrupted Melody. *Publications:* Opera translations into English including: All late works of Verdi; Many late works of Strauss, Hindemith, Prokofiev, Dvořák. *Contributions to:* Opera News; Other musical publications. *Address:* 2 Wildwind Point, Austin, TX 78746, USA.

DUDAROVA Veronika, b. 1916, Baku, Azerbaidjan. Conductor. *Education:* Studied in Baku and at the Leningrad and Moscow Conservatories. *Career:* Artistic Director and Chief Conductor of the Moscow State Symphony Orchestra from 1960 (first woman in Russia to hold such a post); tours with the Orchestra to venues throughout Europe and South America; Left Moscow 1989, to conduct in Istanbul; Returned to Russia in 1991 and established the Symphony Orchestra of Russia; Repertoire has included music by Brahms, Beethoven, Schumann, Wagner, Scriabin, Tchaikovsly and contemporary Western and Russian works. *Recordings include:* Music by Gershwin, Bizet, Myaskovsky and Strauss. *Honours:* Glinka Award and Peoples Artist of the USSR. *Address:* c/o Sonata, 11 Northpark Street, Glasgow G20 7AA, Scotland.

DUDGEON Ralph T, b. 8 Nov 1948, Pennsylvania, USA. Professor of Music; Trumpeter. m. Virginia Britten, 14 Apr 1974, 2s. *Education:* BA, MA, San Diego State University; PhD Musicology, University of California. *Career:* Acting Director, Streitwieser Foundation Trumpet Museum, 1983- 94; Professor of Music, SUNY Cortland; Formerly at University of Texas, Dallas. *Recordings:* Time Stands Still; Listen to the Mockingbord; The Music of Francis Johnson; Music for Keyed Bugle. *Publications:* The Keyed Bugle, 1993; Articles in the New Grove Dictionary of Music and Musicians; also the Historic Brass Society and American Musical Inst Journals. *Memberships:* International Trumpet Guild; American Musical Inst Soc; Sonneck Society; Historic Bass Society; American Musicological Society. *Hobbies:* Collecting antique musical instruments. *Current Management* Spring Tree Enterprises. *Address:* 5745 US Route 11, Homer, NY 13077, USA.

DUESING Dale, b. 26 Sept 1947, Milwaukee, USA. Singer (Baritone). *Education:* Began studies in Milwaukee as a pianist; Vocal studies at Lawrence University in Wisconsin. *Career:* San Francisco Opera as Britten's Bily Budd and Donizetti's Belcore; Seattle Opera as Wagner's Wolfram and Tchaikovsky's Eugene Onegin; Glyndebourne debut 1976, as Olivier in Capriccio; later sang Guglielmo in Così fan Tutte,

conducted by Bernard Haitink; Ottone in L'Incoronazione di Poppea, Lysander in A Midsummer Night's Dream, 1989, and Figaro, 1989; Metropolitan Opera debut 1979, as Harlekin in Ariadne auf Naxos; Concert engagements with the New York Philharmonic, Berlin Philharmonic, Boston Symphony, Concertgebouw Orchestra, BBC Symphony and Santa Cecilia of Rome; Conductors include Giulini, Levine, Leppard, Ozawa, Sawallisch, Dohnanyi and Previn; Recent opera engagements include Ariadne at La Scala, Billy Budd and Peter Grimes at the Metropolitan, Die Meistersinger in Brussels and Così fan Tutte at Santa Fe; Sang Figaro at Seattle, 1989, Goryanchikov in From the House of the Dead, at Brussels, 1990; Guglielmo at Barcelona and Olivier at the 1990 Glyndebourne Festival; Solo recitalist in the USA and Europe; World Premiere: Wade in Johnathan Wade by Carlyle Floyd, Houston Opera; Cosi at Liceo, Barcelona; Marriage of Figaro, Glyndebourne Opera under Rattle; Metropolitan Opera, New York, Pelléas and Papageno; Season 1991/92 as Mozart's Count at Brussels, 'I' in the premiere of Schnittke's Life with ann Idiot at Amsterdam and Nardo in La Finta Giardiniera at the Salzburg Festival. *Recordings include:* Don Giovanni and Zemlinsky's Lyric Symphony; Così fan Tutte; Arias and Barcaroles, Leonard Bernstein. *Address:* c/o Lies Askonas Ltd., 186 Drury Lane, London WC2B 5RY, England.

DUFALLO Richard John, b. 30 Jan 1933, East Chicago, Indiana, USA. Conductor. m.(1) Zaidee Parkinson, 15 Oct 1966, 2 sons. m.(2) Parela Mia Paul, 19 June 1988. *Education:* BMus, American Conservatory of Music, Chicago, 1953; BA 1956, MA 1957, University of California; Studies with William Steinberg and Pierre Boulez. *Debut:* European debut with Paris Radio Orchestra, 1971. *Career includes:* Associate Conductor, Buffalo Philharmonic Orchestra, New York, 1962-67; Faculty, State University of New York, Buffalo, 1963-67; Conductor, Center of Creative and Performing Arts, Buffalo, 1964-67; Assistant Tour Conductor, New York Philharmonic tour of Japan and other Asian countries, 1967; Artistic Director, Aspen Music Festival's Conference on Contemporary Music, 1970-; Conductor, Mini-Met, adjunct to Metropolitan Opera, New York, 1972-74; Director and Conductor, 20th Century Music Series, Juilliard School of Music, New York, 1972-79; Artistic Adviser, Het Gelders Orkest, Arnhem, Netherlands, 1980-; Guest appearances internationally including: Concertgebouw Orchestra of Amsterdam, London Symphony, Chicago Symphony, Berlin Philharmonic, Pittsburgh Symphony, Royal Philharmonic, BBC Symphony and Philadelphia Orchestra; Conductor at festivals in 10 countries; Television performances; Operas including Cincinnati Opera; Bath and Aldershot Festivals, New York Mini-Met and City Operas, Edinburgh, Saratoga and Holland Festivals. *Recordings include:* Mozart's Concerto for Two Pianos with National Philharmonic Orchestra; Escher's Symphony with Rotterdam Philharmonic; Peter Maxwell Davies' St Thomas Wake; Willem Pijper - Symphonies No 1 & 3; Composers Voice Special 1987; Rotterdam Philharmonic.*Publications:* Trackings - composers speak with Richard Dufallo, Oxford Press.*Current Management:* Schofer/Gold, New York City. *Address:* c/o Het Gelders Orkest, PO Box 1180, Jans Buiten Singel 29-111, 6801 Arnhem, Holland.

DUFFIE Bruce, b. 11 Mar 1951, Evanston, Illinois, USA. Radio Announcer/Producer; Interviewer; Writer on Music. *Education:* BME, Illinois Wesleyan University, 1972; MM, Northwestern University, 1973. *Career:* Teacher of Instrumental Music and Conductor of Ensembles, Evanston Public Schools, 1973-75; Adult Education Lecturer, Opera, City Colleges of Chicago, Central YMCA College, Latin School of Chicago, etc, 1974-; Announcer, 1975-, Producer, Interviews, Special Features, 1978-, WNIB, Classical 97, Chicago; Lecturer, Lyric Opera of Chicago, 1979-; Announcer/Programmer/Interviewer, Music in the Air Corporation, 1988-89, Classical Music programs aboard United, Delta, Northwest, Eastern Airlines, and Air Force One, the Presidential Airliner; Convocation Address, School of Music, Northwestern University, June 1990. *Publications:* Creator, Editor, Opera Scene, 1982-83.

Contributions to: Wagner News, 1980-92; Massenet Newsletter, 1982-; Nit & Wit, 1984-87, Music Editor, 1986; The Opera Journal, 1985-; Opera Canada; Avenue M Magazine; Sonus. Copies of recorded interviews placed in the Archive of Contemporary Music, Music Library, Northwestern University; Spaulding Library, New England Conservatory of Music; School of Music, De Paul University. *Honour:* ASCAP/Deems Taylor Broadcast Award, 1991. *Address:* c/o WNIB, 1140 West Erie Street, Chicago, IL 60622, USA.

DUFFUS John Logie Lyall, b. 12 Feb 1946, Aberdeen, Scotland. Arts Administrator. *Education:* University of Aberdeen 1964-69; MA (First Class Hons. in Music) University of Aberdeen 1969. *Career:* Programme Operations Assistant, BBC London 1969-70; Assistant General Administrator 1971-73, Personal Assistant to General Administrator 1973-76, Scottish Opera; Technical Controller, Scottish Opera 1976-78; General Manager, Hong Kong Philharmonic Orchestra 1979-86; Chairman and Managing Director, Pacific Images Ltd, 1986-; Chairman, City Contemporary Dance Co. 1985- ; Secretary General, Federation for Asian Cultural Promotion, 1986-. *Contributor To:* Asian Wall Street Journal; South China Morning Post; Radio Television Hong Kong. *Hobbies:* Theatre; Opera; Swimming. *Address:* Pacific Images Ltd, 403 D'Aguilar Place, 7 D'Aguilar Street, Hong Kong.

DUGDALE Sandra, b. Pudsey, Yorkshire, England, 1950. *Education:* Studied in Leeds and at the Guildhall School, London. *Debut:* With Glynebourne Touring Opera as Despina in Così fan Tutte. *Career:* Has sung with English National Opera in operas by Mozart, Janáček and Strauss; Welsh National Opera in The Greek Passion by Martinů; Four principal roles with the Handel Opera Society; Handel roles with the English Bach Festival; Covent Garden debut 1983 as Fire and The Nightingale in the Ravel/Stravinsky double bill; returned 1985, as Adele in Die Fledermaus; Festival appearances include Hong Kong, Camden, Batignano, Wexford and Vienna; Frequent broadcasts with the BBC, including the Much Loved Music Show and Lo Speziale by Haydn (ITV); sang Adele for Opera Northern Ireland at the Grand Opera House, Belfast, 1990; Sullivan's Angelina for D'Oyly Carte at Bournemouth, 1990; Concert engagements with most major British orchestras, under the batons of Charles Mackerras, Roderick Brydon, Charles Groves, David Atherton, Philip Ledger, Mark Elder, John Eliot Gardiner and Vernon Handley; Regular visits to the USA. *Recordings include:* Videos of operettas by Gilbert and Sullivan; Series, 100 Years of Italian Opera, with the Philharmonia Orchestra. *Address:* c/o Korman International Management, 24a Burnaby Gardens, London W4 3DP, England.

DUGGAN Mary Kay, b. 18 Nov 1938, Peru, Indiana, USA. Professor. 2 daughters. *Education:* BMus, 1960, MA, 1962, Ohio State University; MLA, 1975, PhD, 1981, University of California, Berkeley. *Career:* Assoc. Professor, School of Library and Information Studies, University of California, Berkeley, 1987-; Associate Director, University of California Study Centre, London, 1991-1993. *Publications:* Queen Joanna and her Musicians, Musica Disciplina, XXX, 1976; Early Music Printing in the Music Library of the University of California, Berkeley, 1977; Music Publishing and Printing in San Francisco. The Kemble Occasional No. 24, 1980 and No. 30, 1983; A System for Describing Fifteenth Century Music Type, Gutenberg-Jahrbuch, 1984;. The Music Type of the Second Dated Printed Music Book, the 1477 Graduale Romanum, La Bibliofilia, 1987; Italian Music Incunabula, 1992.*Contributions to:* Fontes Artis Musicae; Electronic Information and Applications in Musicology and Music Theory, Library Trends, 1992. *Honours:* Martha Baird Rockefeller Fund for Music, Venice, 1978-79; Fulbright Grant, Paris, 1962-63. *Address:* 2229 Marin Avenue, Berkeley, CA 94707, USA.

DUHAMEL Antoine, b. 30 July 1925, Valmondois, France. Composer. *Education:* Studied with Messiaen and Liebowitz in Paris. *Career:* Wrote for the Club d'Essai 1951-52 and later wrote film music for such directors as Truffaut and Godard; Staged performances of operas by Rameau (Pygmalion and Scarlatti, Il Triofo d'Amore); *Compositions:* Operas and other works for stage L'Ivrogne, 1952; staged Tours, 1984; Gala de cirque, Strasbourg 1965; Lundi, Monseir, vous serez riche, Paris 1969; L'Opera des Oiseaux, Lyons, 1971; Ubu a L'Opera, Avignon, 1974; Gambara, Lyons, 1978; Le Cirque Imperial, Avignon, 1979; Les Travaux d'Hercule, Vaise 1981; Le Transsiberien, Paris, 1983; Le Scieur de Long, Tours, 1984; Quatre-vingt- trieze, Fourvieres, 1989; Les Aventures de Sinbad le Marin, Colmar, 1991. *Address:* SACEM France, c/o PRS Ltd Member Registration, 29-33 Berners Street, London W1P 4AA, England.

DUMAY Augustin, b. 17 Jan 1949, Paris, France. Concert Violinist. *Education:* Studied at the Paris Conservatoire from 1959 with Roland Charmy. *Debut:* Théâtre des Champs Elysées, Paris, 1963, *Career:* Studied further with Arthur Grumiaux 1962-67, then played regularly in public; Partnerships with Jean-Philippe Collard and Michel Beroff; Concert with Karajan and the Berlin Philharmonic 1979 followed by Bartók's 2nd Concerto conducted by Colin Davis; Further engagements with L'Orchestre National de France, Suisse Romande Orchestra, London Symphony and English Chamber, and at the Montreux, Bath, Berlin, Lucerne, Monaco, Aix, Leipzig and Montpellier festivals; Other conductors include Ozawa, Dutoit, Sanderling, Sawallisch, Fruhbeck de Burgos and Skrowaczewski; Chamber music collaborations with Maria Joao Pires, Michel Dalberto, Lynn Harrell, Jean-Bernard Pommier, Yo Yo Ma and Richard Stoltzmann; Gave the premiere of Berio's Sequenza 9, for solo violin, and the premieres of the concertos by Marius Constant and Isang Yun; Director of the National Chamber Orchestra of Toulouse from 1988; Plays a 1721 Stradivarius, formerly belonging to Fritz Kreisler. *Recordings include:* Lalo's Symphonie Espagnole, conducted by Michel Plasson, and Chausson's Concerto for piano, violin and string quartet, with Collard and the Muir Quartet; Mozart, Complete Violin Concertos; Tchaikovsky & Mendelssohn, Violin Concertos, London Symphony Orchestra; Mozart, Piano & Violin Sonatas; Brahms, Complete Violin & Piano Sonatas with Maria Joao Pires. *Current Management:* Transart, London; Valmalette, Paris; CAYI, New York City. *Address:* Granjinha Do Meio, Excalos De Baixo, 6005 Alcains, Portugal.

DUMITRESCU Iancu Ioan, b. 15 July 1944, Sibiu, Romania. Composer; Music Critic; Conductor; Pianist. m. Cristina, 10 May 1979. *Education:* Piano with Cici Manta; Composition with Alfred Mendelssohn, Stefan Niculescu and Aurel Stroe and with Sergiu Celibidache, Trier, Federal Republic of Germany. *Career:* Founder, chamber music ensemble Hyperion; Pianist specializing in avant garde music; Compositions performed on television and radio in Romania, Austria, Netherlands, France and Italy, 1970-. *Compositions Include:* Diachronies II and III for piano; Metamorphoses for clarinet; Eco I and II for flute and percussion; Apogeum for orchestra; Reliefs for 2 orchestras and piano; Pasarea Maiastra for undertermined ensemble; Jeu de la Génesse for 2 pianos; Movemur II, III, IV and V for strings; Movemur et Sumus for strings; Basoreliefs Simphonique for orchestra; Sursum Corda II for choir; Orion I and II for percussion; Mendium II for Fernando Grillo for double-bass; Alfa Centaori for ensemble; Cogito-trompe L'Oeil for chamber ensemble; Ursa Mare for 2 moog synthesizers and instruments; A Doua Moira for traditional instruments, percussion, 2 double basses, 2 cellos and tape; Panta Rhei for artisanal abjects and rtape; Orfice for artisanal objects and synthesizer. Recorded by: Electrecord and RTV, Bucharest; Westdeutscher Rundfunk-Cologne and Sudwestfunk, Germany; CBS-Escargot, Paris, France; Au-dela de Movemur for string orchestra, Profondis for clarinet, bass clarinet and orchestra, Pièrres Sacrées for ensemble; Multiples for 3 groups of percussion, 1972; Zenith for percussion, 1980; Alternances I & II for string quartet, 1968; Aulodie Mioritica for doublebass and orchestra, 1984: Perspectives au Movemur, 1979; for String Quartet: Nimbus for 3 trombones, percussion and tape music, 1980; Harryphonies, (alpha, beta, gamma), for double bass, percussion, harryphono and piano préparé, 1985; Holzwege for viola solo, 1986; L'Orbite D'Uranus for flute, oboe, bass, clarinet, piano préparé and percussion; Harryphonies (epsilon), for large orchestra, 1986: Astrée Lointaine for bass saxophone and orchestra, 1991; L'Empire des Signes, 1992; Clusterum for percussion, 1993. *Recordings:* Edited by Editions Salabert, Paris; Edition RZ, Berlin, Generations Unlimited, New York. *Address:* 16 dr Draghiescu sect 5, 76224 Bucarest, Romania.

DUNHAM Benjamin Starr, b. 19 Sept 1944, New York City, Editor, American Recorder, American Recorder Society. m. Wendy Rolfe-Dunham, 12 Apr 1986, 1 son. *Education:* BA English Literature, Harvard College, 1966; Musicology, Boston University, 1970; Musicology, Catholic University, Washington DC, 1971-74. *Career:* Copywriter, Batten Barton Durstine and Osborn, Boston, 1966-67; Assistant Editor, Music Educators Journal, Music Educators National Conference, Washington DC, 1967-70; Director Public Relations and Publications, Editor Symphony News, American Symphony Orchestra League, Vienna, Virginia, 1971-78; Recorder teacher, 1971-78 and 1986-; Music Faculty, Trinity College, Washington DC, 1973-75; Washington Consort, 1973-78; Principal Recorder, Handel Festival Orchestra, 1977-78; Executive Director, Editor American Ensemble, Chamber Music America Incorporated, New York, 1978-82; Executive Director, American Symphony Orchestra, 1982-84; Executive Vice-President, National Music Council, 1984-90; Performing member, Cranberry Concerts, 1985-. *Contributions to:* Musical America; American Arts; The Washington Post. *Address:* 472 Point Road, Marion, MA 02738, USA.

DUNN Mignon, b. 176 June 1931, Memphis, Tennessee, USA. Opera Singer. m. 24 July 1972. *Education:* Southwestern University; Private study with Lorin Branzell, K Johnson and A Baojan. *Debut:* New Orleans Opera, 1954. *Career includes:* Metropolitan Opera, leading mezzo, 1958-; Performances at Teatro Collon, Buenos Aires, La Scala Milan; Covent Garden; Vienna Staatsoper; Teatre Wielki, Warsaw; Bolshoi Moscow; National Opera Mexico; Staatsoper Hamburg; Deutsche Oper Berlin; Opera du Rhin; Maggio Musicale Fiorentino; Festival de Due mondi, Charleston, Spoleto; L'Arena d'Orange; Arena di Verona, as well as at San Francisco, Chicago and Boston; Major Symphony Orchestras include: Chicago, New York, Boston, Detroit, Philadelphia, St Louis, Houston, Los Angeles, Vienna, Hamburg, Munich, Lisboa and Barcelona. *Recordings:* Rigoletto; Mother of us All; Salome; Verdi Requiem. *Honours:* HonD, Rhodes College, Memphis; Tampa (Mignon Dunn Day); Hall of Fame, (AVA Philadelphia). *Memberships:* NATS; Faculty of University of Ilinois, Manhattan School of Music, Israel Vocal Arts Institute. *Current Management* Columbia (CAMI). *Address:* 1204 Theodore Drive, Champaign, IL 61821, USA.

DUNN Susan, b. 23 July 1954, Malvern, Arkansas, USA. Singer (Soprano). *Education:* Studied at Hendrix College, Arkansas and at Indiana University, Bloomington. *Debut:* Peoria Illinois 1982, as Aida. *Career:* Sang Sieglinde in Act 1 of Die Walküre at Carnegie Hall, 1985; Appearances at the Lyric Opera, Chicago, 1986-88, and at San Francisco, Houston and Washington, notably in operas by Verdi; Teatro Communale Bologna 1986, 1988, as Elena in I Vespri Siciliani and Elisabeth de Valois in Don Carlo; Season 1988 as Leonora (La Forza del Destino) at Chicago, the Trovatore Leonora at San Diego and Amelia (Un Ballo in Maschera) at the Vienna Staatsoper; La Scala Milan, as Aida; Metropolitan Opera debut 1990, as Leonora in Il Trovatore. *Recordings include:* Beethoven Mass in C and arias from Die Walküre, Tannhäuser, Un Ballo in Maschera, Vêpres Siciliennes, La Forza del Destino and Il Trovatore (Decca); Verdi Requiem (Telarc); Das klagende Lied; Gurrelieder. *Current Management:* Herbert H Breslin, Inc. *Address:* Metropolitan Opera, Lincoln Center, New York, NY 10023, USA.

DUNSBY Jonathan Mark, b. 16 Mar 1953,

Wakefield, Yorkshire, England. Musician; Professor of Music, University of Reading. m. (1) Anne Davies 7 Sept. 1974, 1 daughter; (2) Esther Cavett, 25 May 1983, 1 daughter. *Education:* ARCM 1968; BA, Hons. New College, Oxford 1973; PhD, Leeds University 1976; Harkness Fellow 1976. *Debut:* Wigmore Hall 1972, piano. *Career:* Bronze Medal, Geneva International Competition 1970; Jury Prize, Munich International Competition 1970; Winner, Commonwealth Competition 1974; Regular appearances with violinist, Vanya Milanova; Professor of Music, University of Reading. *Publications:* Structural Ambiguity in Brahms 1981; Founding Editor of Journal of Music Analysis 1981; Music Analysis in Theory and Practice (with Arnold Whittall: Faber, March 1987); Schoenberg, Pierrot Lunaire, 1992. *Contributions to:* Music and Letters; The Musical Quarterly; Journal of Music Theory; Perspectives of New Music; Journal of the Arnold Schoenberg Institute. *Address:* University of Reading, Department of Music, 35 Upper Redlands Road, Reading, Berkshire, RG1 5JE, England.

DUPRÉ Heather, b. 30 Mar 1949, Channel Islands. Pianist. *Education:* Licenciate, Recital Diploma, Royal Academy of Music, 1967-72. *Debut:* Wigmore Hall, 1976. *Career:* Solo Pianist, Recitals in Britain including several appearances at Edinburgh Festival Fringe, Wigmore Hall and Purcell Room; Broadcast on Radio London, 1974; Junior Professor, Royal Academy of Music, 1973-76; Examiner, Associated Board of Royal Schools of Music, 1979-. *Membership:* Solo Performers Section, Incorporated Society of Musicians. *Hobbies:* Reading; Walking. *Address:* 19c Abercorn Place, St Johns Wood, London NW8 9DX, England.

DUPUY Martine, b. 1952, France. Singer (Mezzo-soprano). *Debut:* Aix-en-Provence 1975, as Eurydice in Campra's Le Carnaval de Venise. *Career:* Has sung in the coloratura mezzo repertoire in Europe and North and South America; Marseilles Opera 1985, as Bellini's Romeo and as Isabella in L'Italiana in Algeri; Paris Opera 1985, as Neocles in Le Siège de Corinth; Other Rossini roles include Malcolm (La Donna del Lago) at Nice 1985 and Bonn 1990, Cenerentola (Lausanne) and Arsace in Semiramide at Valle d'Itria and Nice, 1985; Metropolitan Opera debut 1988, as Sextus in Giulio Cesare; Sang in the opening concert at the Bastille Opera, Paris, 13 July 1989; Season 1990-91 as Mêre Marie in Les Dialogues des Carmélites for Lyon Opera, Jane Seymour (Anna Bolena) at Marseilles and Madrid and Armando in a concert perfromance of Meyerbeer's Il Crociato in Egitto at Montpellier; Other roles include Monteverdi's Nero and Penelope, Mozart's Cecilio (Lucio Silla) and Sextus (La Clemenza di Tito); Adalgisa in Norma and Donizetti's Maffeo Orsini (Lucrezia Borgia) and Ada (Il Diluvio Universale); Has also sung in Buenos Aires, Salzburg and Lausanne. *Honours include:* Winner, International Singing Competition, Peschiera del Garda, 1975; Grand Prix 1985 from Opera International, France. *Address:* c/o Opéra de Lyon, 9 Quai Jean Moulin, F-69001 Lyon, France.

DURKÓ Zsolt, b. 10 Apr 1934, Szeged, Hungary. Composer. m. Rita Geremcsér, 1970, 2 sons. *Education:* Music Academy of Budapest under F Farkasl Academy Santa Cecilia, Rome under G Petrassi. *Career:* Professor of 20th Century composition, Music Academy of Budapest, 1970-80; Supervisor of classical and contemporary music, Hungarian Radio, Budapest, 1982-. *Compositions:* Vocal, Altamira, 1968, Kolliodok, 1969, two Cantatas, 1971, 1972, Halotti (Funeral Sermon), 1972, Moses (Opera), 1977; Instrumental, Organismi, 1964, Una Rapsodia ungherese, 1965, Fioriture, 1966, String Quartets, no I, 1966, no 2, 1970, Iconographies, no 1, 1970, no 2, 1971, Chamber Music, 1973, Fire Music, Turner Illustrations, 1976, Refrains, 1978, Quattro Dialoghi, 1979, Son et Lumiere, 1980, Andromeda, 1980, Piano Concerto, 1981, Essay for Clarinet and Piano, 1983, Psicogramma for piano, 1984; Ornaments for Orchestra, 1987; 3 English Verses for Mezzosoprano and 12 instruments 1991; The Story of the Spheres, 60 pieces, 1990-91; Violin Concerto, 1992-93. *Honours:* Premio d'Atri, Rome, 1963; First Prize,

International Tribune of Composers, Paris, 1975; Critics' Prize, Hungarian Radio, twice; Listeners' Prize, Hungarian Radio, twice; Special Citation of International Koussevitzky Award, Kossuth Prize, 1978. *Memberships:* Board, Federation of Hungarian Musicians, 1969-; President of the Hungarian Music Society, 1987-. *Address:* Edito Musica Budapest, Boosey and Hawkes, London, Chester Music Publishers, London, England.

DURMULLER Jorg, b. 28 Aug 1959, Berne, Switzerland. Singer (Tenor). *Education:* Studied at Winther and Hamburg and with Christa Ludwig and Hermann Prey. *Career:* Appeared with the company of the Hamburg Staatsoper at the 1986 Schwetzingen Festival, in the premiere of Die Lieden des Jungen Werthers by Hans-Jurgen von Bose; Member of the Bielefeld Opera from 1987, notably as Mozart's Ferrando and Tamino, Verdi's and Nicolai's Fenton, and Chateauneuf in Zar und Zimmermann; Sang Ramiro in Cenerentola 1989; Tour of Russia and Spain, 1989, guest appearances in concert and opera in Brussels, Paris, Pesaro, Geneva and Mannheim; Innsbruck Early Music Festival 1991, as Fracasso in Mozart's La Finta Semplice, conducted by Rene Jacobs. *Recordings:* Bruckner's Missa Solemnis in F. *Address:* Stadtisches Buhnen, Brunnenstrasse 3, 4800 Bielfeld 1, Germany

DURR Alfred, b. 3 Mar. 1918, Charlottenburg, Germany. Musicologist; Writer on Music; Editor. *Education:* PhD, Musicology, University of Göttingen, 1950. *Career:* Member 1951-83, Assistant Director 1962- 81, Johann-Sebastian-Bach-Institute, Göttingen; Editor, Bach-Jahrbuch, 1953-74; Editor of works for Bach Neue Ausgabe sämtlicher Werke. *Publications:* Studien über die frühen Kantaten Johann Sebastian Bachs, 1951, 2nd Edition, revised 1977; Zur Chronolgie der Leipzigir Vokalwerke J. Bachs (revised reprint from Bach-Jahr-buch 1957), 1976; Johann Sebastian Bach, Weihnachts Oratorium, 1967; Die Kantaten von Johann Sebastian Bach, 1971, 5th edition, revised, 1985; Johann Sebastian Bach: Seine Handschrift-Abbild seines Schaffens, 1984; Im Mittelpunkt Bach: Ausgewählte Aufsätze und Vorträge, 1988; Die Johannes-Passion von Johann Sebastian Bach: Entstehung, Überlieferung, Werkeinführung, 1988; Bachs Werk vom Einfall bis zur Drucklegung, 1989. *Contributions to:* Articles in scholarly journals. *Honours:* Honorary doctorate, Baldwin-Wallace College, Berea, Ohio, 1982; Festschrift published in honour of 65th birthday, 1983; Member, Akademie der Wissenschaften, Göttingen, 1976-; Corresponding member, American Musicological Society, 1988-. *Address:* Leipziger Strasse 20, D-37120 Bovenden, Germany.

DÜRR Karl Friedrich. b. 1949, Stuttgart, Germany. Singer (Bass-baritone). *Education:* Studied German Literature and Political Science and received his PhD in 1978. *Debut:* Sang Antonio in Le Nozze di Figaro at Ludwigsburg. *Career:* Studied further with Gunther Reich and sang with the Stuttgart Staatsoper from 1980, notably as Rihm's Jakob Lenz, Mozart's Figaro (production by Peter Zadek), Leporello, Don Alfonso, Klingsor (Parsifal) and Biterolf (Tannhäuser), Alfio (Cavalleria), Monterone, Zuniga in Carmen, Krishna in Satyagraha by Philip Glass, Faninal (Rosenkavalier) since 1994; Appearances at the Ludwisburgh and Schwetzingen Festivals and with the ensemble of the Stuttgart Staatsoper on tour to Russia (Zimmermann's Die Soldaten); Further engagements as Kaspar in Der Freischütz, Kurwenal, and Wozzeck (Kiel 1985); Concerts in Kassel, Trieste, Berlin and New York, 1989; Vienna Festival 1990, as Krenek's Diktator and as the Boxer in Schwergewicht; Sang Don Alfonso at Stuttgart, 1991; Also in Paris, Bastille Opera (Die Soldaten) and Semper-Oper, Dresden (Leporello). *Recordings:* Eisenhardt in Die Soldaten. *Address:* c/o Staatstheater Stuttgart, Oberer Schlossgarten 6, 7000 Stuttgart, Germany

DÜRR Walther, b. 27 Apr 1932, Berlin, Germany. Musicologist. m. Vittoria Bortolotti, 25 June 1960, 2 daughters. *Education:* PhD, Tübingen University, 1956. *Career:* Lecturer, Bologna University, 1957; Assistant, Tübingen University, 1962; General Editor, Neue Schubert-Ausgabe, 1965; Honorary Professor, Tubingen University, 1977; Broadcasts for Radio Stations, Deutsche Welle, Cologne Südwestfunk, Baden-Baden. *Publications:* Kleine Deutsch (with Werner Aderhold and Arnold Feil), 1983; Das Deutsche Sololied im 19 Jahrhundert, 1984. Franz Schubert, 1991, with Arnold Feil; Rhythmus und Metrum im Italienischen Madrigal insbesondere bei Luca Marenzio, 1956; Serie IV (Lieder) of Neue Schubert Ausgabe, 1966. Franz Schuberts Werke in Abschriften; Liederalben und Sammlungen, 1975; Zeichen-Setzung Aufsätse zur Musikalischen Poetik, 1992. *Contributions to:* Die Musikforschung; Archiv für Musikwissenschaft; Österreichische Musikzeitschrift; 19th Century Music; MGG; New Grove Dictionary of Music & Musicians; numerous anniversary honorary works and reviews. *Memberships:* Society for Musical Research; International Musicological Society. *Address:* Hausserstr. 140, D-7400 Tübingen, Germany.

DUSSEK Michael, b. 1958, England. Concert Pianist. *Career:* Chamber musician throughout Europe, Japan and Australia, and Canada, notably with such soloists as Cho-Liang Lin, Anne Akiko Meyers, Kurt Nikkanen and Ofra Harnoy; Recent recitals in the Amsterdam Concertgebouw, Tokyo, Madrid, Milan and Vienna; Engagements throughout Britain with the cellist Alexander Baillie, oboist Douglas Boyd and violinist Lorraine McAslan; Concerto soloist with the London Mozart Players at the Festival Hall and work for BBC Radio 3 as chamber musician and accompanist; Purcell Room recital 1993 with Markus Stocker, featuring music by Schumann, Brahms, Liszt and Martinu. *Recordings include:* Brahms Piano Trios and Horn Trio with the Dussek Trio, contemporary Finnish music with the Edoymion Ensemble, cello sonatas with Ofra Harnoy and cello sonatas by Reger; Professor, Royal Academy of Music.

DUTILLEUX Henri, b. 22 Jan. 1916, Angers, France. Composer. m. Genevieve Joy, 1946. *Education:* Conservatoire National de Musique, Paris. *Career:* Devoted to Music, 1945-; Director, service Creations Musicales Radiodiffusion Française, 1945-63; Professor of Composition, Ecole Normale de Musique, Paris, 1961- ; President, 1969-; Associate Professor, Conservatoire National Superieur Musique, Paris, 1970-71; Former Member, UNESCO Music Council; Honorary Member, American Academy and Institute of Arts and Letters, New York, USA; Honorary Member Accademia di Santa Cecilia Rome; Associate Member Royal Academy of Belgium. *Compositions:* Sonata for piano, 1948; First Symphony, 1951; Le Loup, ballet, 1953; 2nd Symphony, Le Double, 1959; Metaboles for orchestra, 1964; Cello Concerto; Tout un monde lointain, 1970; Figures de Resonances for 2 pianos, 1971; Preludes for Piano, 1974; Ainsi la Nuit, for string quartet, 1976; Timbres Espace, Mouvement for orchestra, 1978; 3 strophes sur le nom de Sacher, for cello, 1981; Violin Concerto, 1985; Mystère de L'instant, for string orchestra, 1988; Les Citations for Oboe, Harpsichord Double-Boss and Perc, 1991. *Honours:* Grand Prix de Rome, 1938, Grand Prix du Disque, 1957, 1958, 1966, 1968, 1976, 1978, 1984; Grand Prix National de la Musique, 1967; Prix de la Ville de Paris, 1974; Koussevitzky International Recording Award, 1976; World Record Award, Montreux, 1983; Prix International Maurice Ravel 1987; Prix UNESCO-International Music Council, 1987; Grand-Officier, Legion of Honour. *Address:* 12 rue Saint-Louise en l'Ile, 75004 Paris, France.

DUTOIT Charles, b. 7 Oct 1936, Lausanne, Switzerland. Conductor. *Education:* Studied at the Lausanne Conservatory with Wachsmuth, Mermoud and Hans Haug; Further study at the Geneva Academy, the Accademia Musicale in Siena and at the Benedetto Marcello Conservatory in Venice; Courses with Charles Munch at Tanglewood. *Career:* Conducted an amateur orchestra in Renanas, 1957-58; Conducted the choir of the University of Lausanne 1959, and the Lausanne

Bach Choir 1963; Second Conductor of the Berne Symphony 1964, principal from 1967; Conductor and Artistic Director of the Zurich Radio Orchestra 1967: tours of South America, Australia, Japan, Israel and Egypt; Conductor of the Gothenburg Symphony 1975; Music Director of the Montreal Symphony 1977: repertoire includes Haydn, Stravinsky, Beethoven and Mozart, and much French and Canadian music; Principal Guest Conductor, Minnesota Orchestra, from 1983; Falla's Three Cornered Hat and El amor Brujo; The Planets by Holst; Tchaikovsky's 1st Piano Concerto, Argerich; Ravel Daphnis et Chloe; Saint-Saëns 3rd Symphony; Bizet L'Arlesienne and Carmen Suites; Gubaidulina Offertorium, Boston Symphony; Symphonies by Honegger, 1,2 and 4; Roussel's Symphonies, French National Orchestra; Saint-Saëns Piano Concertos, Pascal Rogé; Suppé Overtures. *Address:* Orchestre Symphonique de Montréal, Salle Winifred-Pelletier, Place des Arts, 200 West de Maisonneuve, Montréal, Province Québec, H2X 1Y9, Canada.

DUTT Hank, b. 4 Nov 1952, Muscatine, Iowa, USA. Violist. *Career:* Joined the Kronos String Quartet 1977; Many performances of contemporary music, including the premieres of works by John Cage (30 Pieces for String Quartet), Pauline Oliveros (The Wheel of Time) and Terry Riley (G-Song, Sunrise of the Planetary Dream Collector and Cadenzas on the Night Plain); Formerly quartet-in-residence at Mills College, Oakland; From 1982 resident quartet at the University of Southern California; Appearances at the Monterrey Jazz Festival, Carnegie Recital Hall, San Quentin Prison and London's South Bank; New York debut 1984; Noted for 'cross-over' performances of jazz and popular music in arrangement. *Address:* c/o UCLA Music Dept, University Park, Los Angeles, CA 90089, USA.

DUTTON Brenton Price, b. 20 Mar 1950, Sakatoon, Canada. Composer; Tubist. 2 sons, 1 daughter. *Education:* BM, MM, Oberlin Conservatory of Music. *Career:* Tubist with: Cleveland Orchestra, 1968-74, L'Orchestre Symphonique de Quebec, 1971-74, San Diego Symphony, 1980-; Solo Recital appearances throughout Canada, USA, Europe; Professor of Music, San Diego State University, 1980-, California Institute of the Arts, 1981-84; Brass Coach for the Jennesses Musicales World Orchestra, in Europe, North and South America, 1986-. *Compositions:* Over 100 including Symphony No 2, 1972; Symphony No. 3, 1974; Song of the Moon, solo flute; On Looking Back, Brass Quintet; December Set, Woodwind Quintet; Dialogues of the sybarites, 3 trumpets & organ; Circles; Chineese Reflections; A Rolling Silence; Songs of Love, all song cycles for baritone and chamber ensemble; Additional Works: Ecq theow Variants, Brass Quintet; On A Darkling Plain, Brass Quintet; Song of the Sun, solo viola; Hotel Europejski Suite, violin, piano; Gilgamesh, opera in 3 acts, 1977-78. *Recordings:* Symphony No 5 Dark Spirals, 1985; Character Dances & proud Music of the Storm, 1986; Carnival of Venice, brass Quintet, 1983; Olympic Entrance, Tuba Suite, 1984; many radio & TV broadcasts; Krakow, Summer; Quebec, Spring, both for string orchestra. *Publications:* Sonata In Fact for Trumpet, Piano; Resonances for Tuba Quartet. *Hobbies:* Woodwork; Long Distance Running. *Address:* Department of Music, San Diego State University, San Diego, CA 92182, USA.

DUTTON Lawrence, b. 9 May 1954, New York, USA. Violist. *Career:* Member, Emerson String Quartet 1976-; Premiere concert at Alice Tully Hall, New York, 1977, with works by Mozart, Smetana and Bartók; European debut at Spoleto, Italy, in 1981; Quartet-in-residence at Smithsonian Institute, Washington 1980-, at the Hartt School 1981- and at Spoleto and Aspen Festivals 1981-; First resident quartet at Chamber Music Society of Lincoln Center, season 1982-83; Tour of Japan and Australia 1987; Many performances of works by Bartók, including all six quartets in a single evening, and contemporary works; Premieres include Mario Davidovsky's 4th Quartet and works by Maurice Wright and George Tsontakis. *Recordings include:* Walter

Piston's Concerto for string quartet, winds and percussion (CRI); Works by Andrew Imbrie, Henry Howell, Roy Harris and Gunther Schuller (New World); Bartók's Six Quartets (Deutsche Grammophon). *Hobbies:* Backpacking; Tennis. *Address:* 60 West 76th Street, Apt 5E, New York, NY 10023, USA.

DUVAL Denise, b. 23 Oct 1921, Paris, France. Singer (Soprano). *Education:* Studued at the Bordeaux Conservatory. *Debut:* Bordeaux 1943, as Lola in Cavalleria Rusticana. *Career:* sang at the Folies Bergères, Paris, 1944; Paris Opéra from 1947, notably as Salome in Herodiade by Massenet, and as Blanche in the French premiere of Dialogues des Carmelites, 1947; Sang at the Opéra-Comique Paris in the 1947 premiere of Poulenc's Les mamelles de Tiresias: returned 1959 for the premiere of La Voix Humaine (repeated at La Scala 1960); Paris 1949, in the premiere of Le oui des jeunes Filles, by Hahn-Busser; Other roles were Thais, the Princess in Marouf by Rabaud, Concepcion, and Portia in La Marchande de Venise by Hahn; Edinburgh Festival with the Glyndebourne company in 1960, as Elle in La Voix Humaine; Glyndebourne Festival 1962-63, as Mélisande; Guest appearances in Milan, Vienna, Brussels, Amsterdam and Buenos Aires; Retired 1965 and became Professor at the Ecole Française de Musique in Paris. *Recordings:* L'Heure Espagnole, Les mamelles de Tiresias (Columbia); Dialogues des Carmélites (HMV).

DVORACEK Jiri, b. 8 June 1928, Vamberk, Czechoslovakia. Composer; Professor; Music Administrator. *Education:* Studied organ, Prague Conservatory, 1943-47; Studied composition with Ridky and Dobias, Prague Academy of Music, 1949-53. *Career:* Teacher 1953-67, Senior Lecturer 1967-79, Professor of Composition and Head, Composition Department, 1979-1990, Prague Academy of Music; President, Union of Czech Composers and Concert Artists, 1987-1989. *Compositions:* Opera: Aphrodite's Island, 1967; Orchestral: 2 symphonies, 1953, 1985; Symphonic Suite, 1958; Overture, 1958; Concertante Suite, 1962; Ex Post for Piano and Orchestra, 1963; Quattro Episodi, 1971; I am Living and Singing, cantata for Soloists, Choir, Reciter, Children's Choir and Orchestra, 1978; Giubilo, 1983; Concert for Violin and Orchestra, 1989; Chamber: Sonata Capricciosa for Violin and Piano, 1956; Invention for Trombone and Piano or Small Orchestra, 1961; Meditations for Clarinet and Percussion, 1964; Music for Harp, 1970; Due per duo for Horn and Piano, 1970; Dialogues for Flute and Piano, 1973; Brass Quintet, 1973; Music for Viola and Piano, 1976; Sonata for Trumpet and Piano, 1977; Organ Sonata, 1979; Accordion Sonata, 1979; Theme and Variations for Trombone and Piano, 1980; Prague Transformations for Wind Quintet, 1981; Clarinet and Piano Play, 1982; Violin and Organ Play, 1984; Partita for Oboe and Bassoon, 1986; Partita Piccola for Violin, Guitar and Harmonica, 1987; Three Movements for String Quartet, 1990; Choral music; Songs. *Recordings:* Various compositions recorded. *Address:* Antala Staska 1015/43, 140 00 Prague 4, Czech Republic.

DVORAKOVA Ludmila, b. 11 July 1923, Kolin, Czechoslovakia. Singer (Soprano). m. Rudolf Vasata (died 1982). *Education:* Studied with Jarmila Vavrdova at the Prague Conservatory. *Debut:* Ostrava 1949, as Katya Kabanova. *Career:* Sang Rusalka, Elisabeth Valois, Countess Almaviva and Aida in Ostrava; Sang in Bratislava and at the Smetana Theatre Prague from 1952; Member of the Prague National Opera 1954-57, as Milada in Dalibor, Elisabeth, Leonore and Senta and Czech Operas; Vienna Staatsoper 1956, Leonore; Sang at the Berlin Staatsoper from 1960-84, as Brünnhilde, Venus, Elisabeth Valois, Kundry, Isolde, Ortrud, Tosca and the Marschallin; Karlsruhe 1964, as Isolde; Bayreuth Festival 1965-71, as Gutrune, Brünnhilde, Venus, Ortrud and Kundry; Covent Garden 1966-71, Brünnhilde, Isolde and Leonore; Metropolitan Opera 1965-68; Paris Opera 1966; Opera München, La Scalla, Opera Roma, San Francisco, Buenos Aires, Deutsche Oper am Rhein Dusseldorf 1973-74; Vienna Staatsoper, 1964-85; Visited Japan 1983 and 1984, with the State

Operas of Berlin and Hamburg; Other roles included Katerina Ismailova - Elektra (Vienna 1965), Ariadne, The Dyer's Wife in Die Frau ohne Schatten. *Recordings:* Gutrune in Götterdämmerung, from Bayreuth (Philips); Wagner Recital Supraphon. *Address:* 16200 Praha 6, Na Orechovce 14, Czech Republic.

DVORSKY Peter, b. 25 Sept 1951, Partizánske, Czechoslovakia. Opera Singer (Tenor). m. Marta Varsová, 19 July 1975, 2 daughters. *Education:* Basic Nine Year School; Graduated Conservatory Bratislava 1973. *Debut:* Slovak National Theatre, Bratislava in Onegin 1973. *Career:* 5th Prize, Tchaikovsky Competition (Laureate), Moscow 1974; 1st Prize, Geneva 1975; Regular appearances in: Bratislava, Prague, Budapest, Moscow, Vienna, Milan, London, New York, Munich, San Francisco, Chicago, Frankfurt, etc; Sang at Covent Garden from 1978, as Alfredo, 1986, and Lensky and Riccardo, 1988; Metropolitan New York and Barcelona, 1987, as Rodolfo and Edgardo; Salzburg Festival, 1989, as Cavaradossi; Sang Massenet's Des Grieux at Modena and Barcelona, 1990; Maggio Musica Florence, 1992, as Don Alvaro in La Forza del Destino. *Recordings:* Janáček: Makropulos Case, Jenůfa, Kata Kabanova, all with Charles Mackerras; Verdi: Otello, Cassio with Georg Solti, La Bohème, Bartered Bride, Madame Butterfly, Elisir d'amore; Dvořák: Stabat Mater, Requiem; Recital 1, 2, 3; Folk Songs; Dusik: The Blue Rose, Operetta; Peter Dvorský in Concert/live rec./- for OPUS Arias - for Acanta; G. Puccini: La Bohéme; Gounod: Faust; E.Suchon: Katrena; P.Mascagni: Cavalleria Rusticana; J.Massenet: Werther; G.Donizetti: Elisir d'amore; G.Verdi: Requiem for OPUS, Supraphon, Ariola and Balcanton. *Honours:* People Artist, CSSR 1984; Kammersänger, Austria, 1986. *Hobbies:* Hunting; Music-Piano; Family. *Current Management:* Slovkoncert, Slovak Artistic Agency, Bratislava, Slovakia. *Address:* Slovak National Theatre/Slovenske národńe divadlo, Gorkeho 2, Bratislava, Slovakia.

DYSON Ruth, b. 28 Mar 1917, London, England. Musician. *Education:* Private ARCM Piano, 1936; ARCM Violin, 1939, Royal College of Music, 1935-1939. *Debut:* Wigmore Hall, London, 1941. *Career:* BBC: Solo recitals since 1951; Concertos with London Philaharmonic, Royal Philharmonic, Mozart Players, London Studio Strings, Liverpool Philharmonic; Professor of Harpsichord and Piano, Royal College of Music, 1964-87; Tours in Scandinavia for British Council, lectures and broadcasts, 1950-1956; Adjudicator, Bruges International Fortnight, 1972. *Recordings:* English Harpsichord Music, 1991; Howells and the Clavichord, 1983; For Two to Play, 1987. *Publications:* Articles on the Piano, New Oxford Companion. *Honours:* FRCM, 1980. *Memberships:* Galpin Society (Committee); Royal Musical Association. *Hobbies:* Ornithology. *Address:* 2 St Mary's Garden, Chichester, W Sussex PO19 1NY, England.

DZEMJANOVA Emilia, b. 20 May 1959, Snina, Slovakia. Professor; Concert Organist. *Education:* Conservatory Košice, Slovakia; Academy of Music, Bratislava, Slovakia, Masterclass Flor Peeters at Mechelen, Belgium. *Career:* Recitals, Concerts with Orchestra, recordings for Radio and TV; Appearances in major European cities, including Music Festivals, Organ Festivals; Professor at the Conservatory in Kosice 1982-. *Recordings:* Contemporary Czechoslovak composers, including Eben, Suchon and Burlas. *Publications:* Organ Works of Eugen Suchon (revised edition) HF Bratislava, 1989; Organ School, 1991. *Honours:* Prizes in National Competitions, 1983. *Membership:* Neue Bachgesellschaft. *Current Management:* Slovkoncert, Bratislava, Slovakia. *Address:* Huskova 31, 040 11 Košice, Slovakia.

E

EAGLE David Malcolm, b. 21 Dec 1955, Montreal, Quebec, Canada. Composer; Flautist; Teacher. m. Hope Lee, 23 Aug 1980. *Education:* BMus, 1979, MMus, 1982, McGill University; Studied Flute with Cindy Shuter, Composition with Bengt Hambraeus and Donald Steven; Composition with Klaus Huber and Brian Ferneyhough, Hochschule fur Musik, Freiburg, 1981-83; PhD, University of California at Berkeley, 1992. *Career:* Freelance Composer; Works played, Canada, Holland Festival, 1985, Germany, Switzerland; Broadcasts on CBC Radio Canada, BBC, Hessischer Rundfunk, Swiss Radio, KRO (Netherlands); Invited Guest Composer, Boswil Kunstlerhaus, Switzerland, 1985; Commissions from Montreal Chamber Orchestra, Array-Music, Toronto Consort, many individuals; Coordinator, Electroacoustic Music Studio, Assistant Professor, Composition, Theory, University of Calgary, 1990-. *Compositions include:* Zhu Fong, string quartet, 1978; Strata-Vari for 14 strings, 1980; Within for solo cello, 1982; Strahlen for organ, 1983; Aura for septet, 1984; Renew'd at ev'ry glance for variable instruments, 1985; Toccare for harpsichord, 1986; Luminous Voices for early music ensemble and tape, 1987-88; Crossing Currents for orchestra, 1991; Hsuan for guzheng and tape, 1992; Nohocki for flute and cello, 1993; Music for AXIO, Open This Door, for AXIO (midi-controller), 1993; Sounding after Time for violin, cello, piano, computer, synthesizer, 1993. *Address:* 27 Stradwick Rise SW, Calgary, Alberta, Canada T3H 1G6.

EAGLEN Jane, b. 4 Apr 1960, Lincoln, England. Singer (Soprano). *Education:* Royal Northern College of Music; Study with Joseph Ward. *Career:* Engagements with English National Opera as Leonora (Il Trovatore), Elizabeth I (Mary Stuart), Sinaida (Moses), Donna Elvira, Micaela, Santuzza; Royal Opera Covent Garden in Die Zauberflöte and Il Barbiere di Siviglia; Western Australia Opera, Perth, as Tosca; Lyric Opera of Queensland, Brisbane, as Madama Butterfly; Scottish Opera as Mimi, Donna Anna; Sang Eva in The Mastersingers at the London Coliseum, 1989; London Promenade Concert debut 1989, as Sieglinde in Act III of Die Walküre; Sang Fata Morgana in the Love for Three Oranges, Coliseum, Dec 1989, Fiordilgi for Scottish Opera, 1990, Brünnhilde, 1991; Tosca for ENO, 1990; Donna Anna & Amelia (Ballo), Bologne, 1991; Sang Mathilde in Guillaume Tell at Covent Garden, Geneva, 1992; Scottish Opera as Norma in a new production of Bellini's Opera; Tosca, Buenos Aires, 1993. Concert appearances at the Wigmore Hall, Festival Hall and the Barbican Centre; Verdi Requiem and Mahler 8 Symphony; Recitals for the Wagner Societies of London, New York & Buenos Aires. *Honours include:* Peter Moores Foundation Scholarship; Countess of Munster Award; Carl Rosa Trust Award. *Address:* c/o IMG Artists, Media House, 3 Burlington Lane, London, W4 2TH, England.

EARLE Roderick, b. 29 Jan 1952, Winchester, England. Singer (Bass-Baritone). *Education:* Chorister at Winchester Cathedral; St John's College, Cambridge; Royal College of Music London; Further study with Otakar Kraus. *Career:* Has sung with English National Opera in Gianni Schicchi, Carmen, Aida, The Force of Destiny, Tosca and The Damnation of Faust; Principal Singer with the Royal Opera Covent Garden, in Le Nozze di Figaro, Un Ballo in Maschera, Don Giovanni, Siegfried, Götterdämmerung, Butterfly, Turandot, Elektra and Peter Grimes, Tosca, Carmen, Samson et Dalila, La Bohème; Visited Japan and Korea with the Royal Opera; Appearances with Opera North as Leporello and in I Puritani and The Midsummer Marriage; Welsh National Opera as Fafner and Hunding in The Ring; Athens Festival as Jupiter in Castor et Pollux by Rameau; Israel Festival in Renard by Stravinsky; Buxton Festival from 1986, as Orestes in Giasone (Cavalli-Leppard) and in Ariodante; Performances in Poland and Italy as Mephistopheles in La Damnation de Faust; Sang Monterone in Rigoletto, Covent Garden, 1989, Leuthold in a new production of Guillaume Tell, 1990 and Schaunard in a revival of La Bohème. Concert engagements with the Academy of St Martin in the Fields and the Monteverdi Choir; Performances of Messiah in Stuttgart and Stravinsky's Les Noces in Tel Aviv; Edinburgh Festival with the Scottish National Orchestra conducted by Neeme Järvi; Verdi Requiem in Southampton and Oxford, with the City of Birmingham Symphony. *Recordings:* Dinorah (Meyerbeer); La Traviata, Il Trovatore; Brahms Requiem and Delius Mass of Life with the CBSO, Damnation de Faust with the Philharmonia under Dutoit, Bach Christmas Oratorio in Denmark; Maria Padilla (Donizetti); Videos of Covent Garden productions of La fanciulla del West, Manon Lescaut, Der Rosenkavalier, Salome, Carmen and Andrea Chénier. *Address:* Athole Still Ltd, Greystoke House, 80-86 Westow St, London, SE19 3AF, England.

EARLS Paul, b. 9 June 1934, Springfield, Missouri, USA. Composer. m. Zeren Barutcuoglu, 13 Aug 1960, 1 son. *Education:* B.Mus., cum laude, Eastman School of Music, 1955; MM, 1956; PhD, University of Rochester, 1960. *Career:* Instructor: S.W.Mo. State, 1955-56, Duke University, 1959-60; Assistant Professor, University of Oregon, 1962-65; Chairman, Music, Chabot College, 1961-62; Associate Professor: Duke University, 1964-72, MIT, 1971-; Visiting Professor: University of California, 1972, University of Lowell, 1976-77, UNIH, Helsinki, 1992; Instructor, Massachusetts College of Art, 1972-78. *Compositions include:* And on the Seventh Day, orchestra, 1955; Flight, opera, 1964; Incidental Music for Love Suicide at Schofield Barracks, 1971; The Death of King Phillip, Opera, 1975; Icarus/Ikarus, Sky Opera, 1982-84; The Building of the Universe, 1983; Augenmusrk, 1986; Eliotime, 1989; Mozart and Cosmology, 1991; *Recordings:* And on the Seventh Day; 2 Wedding Songs. *Publications:* Music, Choral Works & Organ Works by Ione Press. *Contributions to:* Groves Dictionary; Perspectives of New Music. *Address:* Center for Advanced Visual Studies/MIT, 265 Massachusetts Avenue, Cambridge, MA 02139, USA.

EASTWOOD Thomas Hugh, b. 12 Mar 1922, Hawley, Hampshire, England. Composer. m. Cristina Carneiro de Mendoncça Avelino, 4 June 1974, 2 sons, 2 daughters. *Education:* Eton College, Windsor; Trinity College, Cambridge; Studied Composition with Necil Kazim Akses (Turkey), Boris Blacher (West Berlin), Erwin Stein (London). *Career:* Organiser, 4 Anglo-Turkish Music Festivals, British Council, Turkey 1948-51; Director of British Council, West Berlin 1951-54; Music Director of Save The Titian Gala Evening at London Coliseum 1972; Artistic Director, Andover Festival 1985, 1986; Music Director, Latin American Arts Association, organising Villa-Lobos Centenary 1986. *Compositions:* Operas: Christopher Sly (for English Opera Group); The Rebel (for BBC TV); The Beach of Aurora (for English National Opera); Love In A Village (new realization for BBC Radio); Orchestral Works: Music To Celebrate; Hymn to Pan; Concerto for flute and strings; Chamber Works: Solitudes for tenor voice, guitar, flute, string quartet, Uirapuru for flute or oboe and guitar; Ballade-Phantasy; Amphora; Romance et Plainte for solo guitar; Song Cycles for voice and string orchestra, voice and piano; choral works; numerous other pieces for theatre, television and radio. *Recordings:* Ballade-Phantasy (solo guitar) 2 commercial recordings. *Publications:* Disasters In Concert 1986. *Contributions to:* Musical Opinion; Music and Musicians; Composer; Musical Times; Sleeve Notes for RCA, Virgin Classics and Decca; Twice nominated for Grammy Awards 1972, 1973. *Hobby:* Travelling. *Address:* c/o Faber Music, 3 Queen Square, London WC1N 3AU, England.

EATHORNE Wendy, b. 25 Sept 1939, Four Lanes, Cornwall, England. Singer (Soprano); Teacher. 1 daughter. *Education:* Studied at the Royal Academy of Music, 1959-65; ARAM; LRAM; ARCM. *Career:* West End production, Robert and Elizabeth, 1965-67; Numerous concert appearances, including Promenade Concerts, London; Engagements with the London Bach Choir, London Symphony Orchestra, Hallé Orchestra and other leading British orchestras; Repertoire includes works by Handel (Susanna and Belshazzar), Liszt (Missa Solemnis) and Haydn (The Creation); Appearances with

Welsh National Opera, English National Opera and Royal Opera Covent Garden; Glyndebourne 1969-71, as Sophie in Werther, First Boy in Die Zauberflöte and Atalanta in The Rising of the Moon; Italian debut in Ariadne auf Naxos; Repertoire also includes Julia in La Vestale by Spontini and Marguerite in Faust; Festival adjudicator; Professor, Trinity College of Music; Many recitals with the pianist Geoffrey Pratley: programmes include groups of songs by Purcell to modern pieces. *Recordings:* Masses by Bach (Argo); A Village Romeo and Juliet (EMI); Monteverdi Madrigals Libro IV (Philips); A. Scarlatti Clori e Zeffiro and St Cecilia Mass, Schubert Mass in A flat (Argo); Vaughan Williams The Pilgrim's Progress and Sir John in Love (EMI); Bridge, The Christmas Rose (Pavilion). *Honours:* Numerous Prizes, Royal Academy of Music; Winner, Kathleen Ferrier Competition, 1965; Award, Gulbenkian Foundation, 1967, J P Aram Lrannarcnn; JP, 1988; FRSA, 1990. *Hobbies:* Cooking; Dressmaking; Swimming; Gardening; Rambling. *Current Management:* Head of Vocal Dept, Trinity College of Music. *Address:* 23 King Edward's Road, Ruislip, Middlesex HA4 7AQ, England.

EATON John C, b. 30 Mar 1935, Bryn Mawr, USA. Composer. m. Nelda Nelson, 31 May 1973, 1 son, 1 daughter. *Education:* AB, MFA, Princeton University. *Career:* Concerts: Columbia Artists in USA, Hamburg Opera, Maggio Musicale, Venice Festival, Los Angeles Philharmonic, Tanglewood, many more; Operas performed: The Tempest, 1985; The Cry of Clytaemnestra, 1980; Danton and Robespierre; The Lion and Androcles; Myshkin; Herakles. *Compositions:* The Tempest; The Cry of Clytaemnestra; Danton and Robespierre; The Lion and Androcles; Myshkin; Herakles; 2 Symphonies; Duo, mixed chorus; Mass; Blind Man's Cry; Concert Music for Solo Clarinet; Piano Variations; Microtonal Fantasy; Piano Trio; Concert Piece. *Recordings:* Danton and Robespierre; The Music of John Eaton; Microtonal Fantasy; Electro Vibrations. *Publications:* New Music Since 1950, 1974. His work was reviewed in, Time; New Yorker; London Financial Times; New York Times; High Fidelity; Opera News. *Honours include:* Priz de Rome, 1959-61; Guggenheim, 1962, 1965; Fromm Commission, 1966; Koussevitzky Commission, 1970; Citation, NIAL, 1972; Composer in Residence, AAR, 1975; PBC Commission, 1970; Peabody Award, 1973; National Music Theater Award, 1988; MacArthur Fellow, 1990, numerous other commissions and awards. *Address:* ASCAP, ASCAP House, One Lincoln Plaza, New York, NY, USA.

EBBECKE Michael, b. 8 Dec 1955, Wiesbaden, Germany. Singer (Baritone). *Education:* Studied at the Richard Strauss Conservatory Munich and with Josef Metternich in Cologne. *Debut:* Stuttgart 1982, as Mozart's Figaro. *Career:* Member of the Stuttgart Staatsoper from 1982, notably as Belcore, Giulio Cesare, Eugene Onegin, Silvio, and Don Fernando in Fidelio; Guest appearances at the Berlin Komische Oper (Guglielmo, 1984) and Deutsche Oper (Orestes in Iphigénie en Tauride, 1988); Appearances at Karlsruhe, Paris, Lyon (Wolfram in Tannhäuser) and La Scala Milan (Scherasmin in Oberon, 1989); Sang Stolzius in Die Soldaten at Stuttgart, 1987, Papageno and Escamillo in Season, 1990-91, Guglielmo, 1991-92; Concert engagements include Bach's St John Passion at Amsterdam, 1987. *Recordings include:* Die Soldaten. *Address:* c/o Stuttgart Staatsoper, Oberer Schlossgarten 6, 7000 Stuttgart, Germany.

EBEL Gudrun, b. 1948, Hamburg, Germany. Singer (Soprano). *Education:* Studied with Fred Husler in Lugano and Erna Berger in Hamburg. *Career:* Sang at first in Coburg, Bielfeld and Nuremberg; Guest appearances in Dusseldorf, Berlin, Vienna, Munich and Hamburg; Cologne 1982, as Aennchen in Der Freischütz; Other roles include Mozart's Blondchen, Queen of Night and Zerlina; Zerbinetta and Sophie; Carlotta in Il Matrimonio Segreto; Lucia di Lammermoor and Gilda; Frau Fluth in Die Lustigen Weiber von Windsor; Many concert appearances. *Recordings include:* Die Entführung aus dem Serail (Eurodisc).

Address: c/o Oper der Stadt Köln, Offenbachplatz, D-5000 Cologne, Germany.

EBEN Petr, b. 22 Jan 1929, Zamberk, Czechoslovakia. Composer; Pianist; Lecturer. m. Sárka Hurniková-Ebenová, 3 children. *Education:* Academy of Music, Prague. *Debut:* Pianist, Prague 1952; Composer, Concerto for organ & orchestra, Prague 1954. *Career:* Music director, TV, Prague, 1954; Lecturer, Institute for Musicology, Charles University, Prague, 1955-. *Compositions Include:* Sunday Music for Organ; Concerto, piano & orchestra; Apologia Sokratus, oratorio; Vox Clamantis, orchestra; Maidens & Swallows, female choir; Unkind Songs; Vespers, choir & organ; Pragensia, cantata; Greek Dictionary, cycle, female choir & harp; Nachtstunden (Night Hours), symphony, wind quintet & chamber orchestra; Faust, organ; Windows After Chagall, trumpet & organ; Mutationes, commissioned, Cardiff Festival; String Quartet; II Concerto, organ & Orchestra, commissioned, ORF, Vienna; Ballet, Curses & Blessings, commissioned, Nederlands Dans Theater; Prague Nocturne, orchestra; Tabulatura nova, guitar; Cantata, In Honorem Caroli, men's choir & orchestra. *Recordings:* Most compositions recorded, plus: Missa Adventus; Vespers. *Publication:* Cteni a hra partitur, co-author. *Contributions to:* Various journals. *Honours:* 1st prize, Gold Medal, 6 love songs, Moscow 1957; 1st prize, The Lovers Magic Spell, cantata, Jihlava Vocal Festival, 1959; 1st prize, 10 children's duets, Jirkov, 1966; 2 prizes, Laudes, Kassel, 1965. *Current Management:* Pragokoncert, Prague 1. *Memberships:* Union of Composers, Prague; Chairman, Creative Section, Czechoslovakian Music Society. *Address:* Union of Czech Composers, Prague 5, Czech Republic.

EBERHARDT Cornelius, b. 3 Jan 1932, Oberaudorf, Federal Republic of Germany. Conductor. m. Ursula Schade, 7 Aug 1957, 1 daughter. *Education:* Universities of Munich and Hamburg, 1950-53; State Academy of Music, Munich, 1953-56; Accademia Chigiana, Siena, Italy, 1958. *Career:* Chorus Master, Municipal Opera, Ulm, Germany, 1956-60; Associate Conductor, Munich State Theatre, 1960-69; Music Director, Regensburg Symphony and Opera, 1969-77; Founder, Regensburg Music School; Co-Founder, Bavarian Festival of Modern Composers, 1973; Music Director, Corpus Christi Symphony, Texas, USA, 1975-; Professor of Opera, Conductor, State Academy of Music, Munich, Federal Republic of Germany, 1977-; Music Director, American Institute of Musical Studies, Dallas, Texas, USA, 1978-; Visiting Professor 1979-80, Professor and Music Director 1984-87, University of Texas, Austin; Visiting Professor, Corpus Christi State University, 1981-82; Guest Conductor, Europe, North and South America; Music Director, Mozart Festival International, 1991; President, State Academy of Music, 1991. *Publications:* Das Regensburger Orchester, 1972; Volksmusik und Kunstmusik in Südosteuropa, 1988; Der Dirigent in Handbuch der Musikberufe, 1987. *Hobbies:* Astronomy; History of Art. *Address:* Darmstaedterstraße 11/7, D-80992 Muenchen, Germany.

EBERS Clara, b. 26 Dec 1902, Karlsruhe, Germany. Singer (Soprano). *Education:* Studied with Eduard Erhard in Karlsruhe. *Career:* Sang at Karlsruhe, Mönchengladbach, and Dusseldorf, 1924-28; Frankfurt Opera, 1928-44, notably as Olympia and Sophie and in the premieres of Carmina Burana, 1937 and Egk's Columbus, 1942; Guest appearances with the Frankfurt Company, 1938-41, in Bucharest, Sofia, Athens, Belgrade, Zagreb and Barcelona; Sang at Hamburg, 1945-65; Glyndebourne, 1950, as Mozart's Countess; Guest engagements in Milan, Berlin, Brussels and Munich; Other roles included Violetta, Rosina, Zerbinetta, Fiordiligi, the Marschallin and Elisabeth de Valois. *Recordings include:* Soprano solo in Ein Deutsches Requiem by Brahms.

EBERT Peter, b. 6 Apr 1918, Frankfurt, Germany. Director and Administrator. m. Silvia Ashmole, 10 Mar 1951, 5 sons, 5 daughters. *Education:* Salem School, Germany; Gordonstoun School, Scotland. *Career:*

Directed about 100 different operas in many countries and venues including international festivals; Taught at academies of music in Germany, Canada and Scotland; Directed many television operas from theatres and in studios; Administrator and Executive Director of theatres in Germany and Scotland, director of productions Scottish Opera, 1965-75; general administrator, 1977-80; University lecturer. *Contributions to:* Numerous publications. *Honour:* Honorary Doctorate of Music, St Andrew's University, Scotland, 1979. *Hobbies:* Travel; Family. *Address:* c/o Scottish Opera, 39 Elmbank Crescent, Glasgow, Scotland, G2 APT.

EBRAHIM Omar, b. 6 Sept 1956, England. Singer (Baritone). *Education:* Studied at the Guildhall School of Music, London. *Career:* Appearances with the Opera Factory in Punch and Judy, The Beggar's Opera, The Knot Garden, and La Calisto; Sang in the premieres of Birtwistle's Yan Tan Tethera, South Bank, 1986 and Nigel Osborne's The Electrification of the Soviet Union, Glyndebourne, 1986; Glyndebourne Touring Opera in Il Barbiere di Siviglia and La Bohème; Has sung Hector in King Priam for Kent Opera; With Scottish Opera has appeared in Mahoganny, Die Fledermaus and Iolanthe; Covent Garden, 1989, in the British premiere of Un Re in Ascolto by Berio; Sang Don Giovanni with Opera Factory, The Elizabeth Hall, 1990, Parkhearst in the premiere of Böse's 63: Dream Palace at the 1990 Munich Biennale; The Fool in the premiere of Birtwistle's Gawain, Covent Garden, May 1991; Sang the Voice of Goya in the premiere of Osborne's Terrible Mouth, Almeida Festival, 1992; Television appearances include Yan Tan Tethera, The Kiss by Michael Nyman and the title role in a BBC version of Marschner's Vampyr, 1992; Concert repertoire includes Eight Songs for a Mad King (Maxwell Davies), Aventures, Nouvelles Aventures (Ligeti), Enoch Arden (Strauss) and Ode to Napoleon Bonaparte (Schoenberg). *Address:* c/o Allied Artists, 42 Montpelier Square, London SW7 1JZ, England.

ECHOLS Paul Clinton, b. 13 Feb 1944, Santa Monica, California, USA. Opera Director; Musicologist; Editor. *Education:* BA, Magna cum laude, Duke University, Durham, North Carolina, 1966; MA, Musicology, New York University, 1968. *Career:* Deputy Chairman, 1971-75, Assistant Professor of Music, 1971-75, Department of Music, Brooklyn College, NY; Editorial Coordinator, The Charles Ives Society, 1976-82; International Director, Concert Music Division, Peer Southern Music Publishers, NY, 1982-85; Director, Historical Performance Programme, 1980-84, Director, Opera Program, 1988-, The Mannes College of Music, NY; Vice-President and Director of Publishing, G Schirmer/Associated Music Publishers Inc, NY, 1986-87; Editor, Historical Performance; The Journal of Early Music America, 1987-. *Publications:* Numerous articles for scholarly journals and other publications including New Grove Dictionary of Music in America; Numerous editions of music including Renaissance and Baroque Choral Music and The Orchestral Works of Charles E Ives. *Memberships:* Board of Directors, The Charles Ives Society, Inc; Early Music America, Inc; American Musicological Society; Sonneck Society, and others. *Address:* The Mannes College of Music, 150 West 85th Street, New York, NY 10024, USA.

ECKHARDT Andreas, b. 6 Dec 1943, Marienberg, Germany. Secretary General of the German Music Council. m. Edda Lusse, 1968, 2 sons. *Education:* State examinations for Arts and Higher Education (Music and History); Graduate, Musicology. *Career:* Director of Production, B Schott's Sohne, Mainz (Music Publisher), 1980-; Secretary General, German Music Council, Bonn. Professor in Studiengang fur Kulturmanagement an der Musikhochschule Hamburg. *Publications:* Mannerchor; organisation and Chorliteratur after 1945, 1977; Editor, Musikforum Referate und Informationen des Deutschen Musikrates; Editor, Musik-Almanach Musikleben in der Bundesrepublik Deutschland. *Address:* German Music Council, Am Michaelshof 4a, 5300 Bonn, Germany.

ECKHARDT Mária, b. 26 Sept 1943, Budapest, Hungary. Musicologist, Choral Conductor. *Education:* Diploma, Liszt Ferenc Academy of Music, Budapest, 1966. *Career:* Librarian and Research Worker, Music Department, National Széchényi Library, Budapest, 1966-73; Research Worker, Institute for Musicology, Hungarian Academy of Sciences, Budapest, 1973-87; Director, Liszt Ferenc Memorial Museum and Research Centre, Liszt Ferenc Academy of Music, Budapest, 1986- . *Publications:* Franz Liszt und sein Kreis in Briefen und Dokumenten aus den Beständen des Burgenländischen Landesmuseums (with Cornelia Knotik), 1983; Liszt Ferenc Memorial Museum Catalogue, 1986; Franz Liszt's Estate at the Budapest Academy of Music, I Books, 1986; Franz Liszt's Music Manuscripts in the National Széchényi Library, Budapest, 1986; Liszt Ferenc válogatott levelei 1824-1861 (selected letters of F.L. 1824-1861), Budapest, 1989; Franz List's Estate at the Budapest Academy of Music, II, Music, 1993. *Contributions to:* Studies on Liszt in: Studia Musicologica; Magyar Zene; The New Hungarian Quarterly; Journal of the American Liszt Society; Muzsika; and others. *Honours:* Award of Excellence, American Liszt Society, 1985; Erkel Prize, 1987. *Address:* Ruszti ut 11, H-1022 Budapest, Hungary.

ECKHART Janis Gail, b. 21 July 1952, California, USA. Opera singer; Mezzo soprano. m. Harry Dworchak, 1990. *Education:* BA, Magna cum laude, 1973, Sec Teaching Credential, 1974, University of California, Los Angeles; Academia Real de Musica, Madrid, Spain, 1974. *Debut:* New York City Opera, 1981. *Career:* Numerous roles, New York City Opera including: Carmen, 1986, 1988; Rigoletto, 1981, 1984, 1988, 1989; Nabucco, 1981; Rigoletto, Opera de Monte Carlo, 1983; Aida, Opera Delaware, 1984; Il Trovatore, National Grand Opera, 1986; Un Ballo in Maschera, National Grand Opera, 1985; Carmen, Seattle Opera, 1982; Greater Miami Opera, 1981; Cincinnati Opera, 1980; Nabucco, Teatro de Opera, Puerto Rico, 1988; Carmen, Theater Oberhausen, West Germany, 1979; Les Contes D'Hoffmann, Opera Metropolitana, Caracas, 1981; Samson et Dalila, National Philharmonic of the Philippines, 1980; Die Walküre, Teatro Lirico di Cagliari (Italy), 1983; Opera Carolina, Rigoletto, 1990, Cavalleria Rusticana, NYCO, 1987, 1988; Carmen, Metro Lyric Opera, 1992; Carmen, Cairo Opera, Egypt, 1992; Concerts: Mahler: Kindertotenlieder, Maracaibo Symphony; Songs of a Wayfarer, Nashville Symphony; Verdi: Requiem, Plymouth Church of the Pilgrims; Concert Tour, Instituto Tecnológico de México, 1992; Kismet, Tapei Symphony, 1993; Ambassadors of Opera, Far East Concert Tour, 1993; Mid-East Concert Tour, 1993. *Current Management:* USA: Robert Lombardo Associates. Eur: Dr Rudolph Raab. *Address:* 15 West 72nd Street, New York, NY 10023, USA.

ECKSTEIN Pavel, b. 27 Apr 1911, Opava, Czechoslovakia. Music Writer; Critic; Commentator; Organiser. m. Anna Gerberova. 1 daughter. *Education:* PhD, Prague University. *Career:* Music Critic; Lecturer, Germany, Holland, England, USSR, Australia, USA; General Secretary, International Musical Festival, Prague, Spring, 1948-52; Secretary, Czechoslovakian Composers Guild, 1952-71; Artistic Adviser, National Theatre, Prague, 1969-92, Chief Drama, State Opera, Prague, 1992; Member of the Board, Czech Music Council, 1993. *Publications:* David Oistrakh, 1959; Czechoslovak Opera, 1964; Czechoslovak Contemporary Opera, 1967. *Contributions to:* Encyclopaedias and journals in Czechoslovakia, England, USA, Canada, Germany, Denmark, USSR. *Hobbies:* Reading; Theatre; Wandering. *Address:* Srobarova 23, 130 00 Prague, Czech Republic.

EDA-PIERRE Christiane, b. 24 Mar 1932, Fort de France, Martinique. Singer (Soprano). m. René Lacaze. *Education:* Studied at the Paris Conservatoire. *Debut:* Nice 1958, as Leila in Les pêcheurs de Perles. *Career:* Aix-en-Provence, 1959, as Pamina in Die Zauberflöte; Opéra-Comique Paris, 1961, as Lakmé; Paris Opéra from, 1962, as Lucia di Lammermoor, Constanze and in Milhaud's Médée and Rameau's Dardanus, 1980;

Covent Garden, 1966, as Teresa in Benvenuto Cellini; Wexford Festival, 1976, as Imogene in Il Pirata; Metropolitan Opera with Paris Opéra Company, 1976, as Mozart's Countess: returned to New York from 1980 as Constanze, Antonia in Les Contes d'Hoffmann and Gilda; Guest appearances in Strasbourg, Lyons, Amsterdam, Barcelona, Chicago, Miami, Brussels (Vitellia in La Clemenza de Tito) and Moscow; Other roles include the Queen of Night and Zerbinetta; Sang in the premieres of D'Une Espace Deployé by Gilbert Amy (1973) and Erzsebet by Charles Chaynes (Paris Opéra 1983); Created the Angel in the premiere of Messiaen's François d'Assise, Palais Garnier Paris, 1983; Professor at the Paris Conservatoire from 1977. *Recordings include:* Benvenuto Cellini, conducted by Colin Davis (Philips); Hero in Béatrice et Bénédict; Die Entführung; Arias by Grétry and Philidor; Dardanus (Erato). *Address:* c/o Conservatoire National, 14 Rue de Madrid, 75008 Paris, France.

EDDY Jennifer, b. 1933, Melbourne, Australia. Singer (Colorature Soprano). *Education:* Studied in Melbourne with Henry Portnoj and in London with Bertha Nicklauss Kampner and Roy Henderson. *Career:* Frequent guest soloist with Australian Broadcasting Corporation in concerts, studio broadcasts and on television and major choral groups, 1953-58; Elizabethan Opera Company, 1956-57 as Mozart's Susanna, Despina, Papagena and as Polly Peachum, Beggar's Opera; Covent Garden, 1959-69, roles including Xenia (Boris Godunov), Amor (Gluck's Orpheus), Fiakermilli (Arabella), Olympia (Tales of Hoffmann), Sophie (Der Rosenkavalier), Tytania (A Midsummer Night's Dream); Guest apperances with Sadler's Wells Opera, English National Opera, Welsh National Opera, Scottish Opera, English Opera Group, Bordeaux Opera, Maggio Musicale, Edinburgh, Bath and Schwetzigen Festivals; Roles include Despina, Rosina, Norina, Blondchen, Madame Herz (The Impressario), Musetta, Zerbinetta, Adele (Die Fledermaus); Appearances for BBC on radio, television and in concert; Managing Director, Jenifer Eddy Artists' Management, Melbourne, 1975-; Director, Lies Askonas Ltd, London, 1982-. *Recordings include:* Il Seraglio, Gypsy Baron, Hansel and Gretel. *Address:* Jenifer Eddy Artists' Management, Suite 11, The Clivedon, 596 St Kilda Road, Melbourne, 3004, Victoria, Australia.

EDDY Timothy, b. 1965, USA. Cellist. *Career:* Recitalist at Lincoln Center's Alice Tully Hall, the 92nd Street 'Y' and appearances with major orchestras; Chamber musician at the Santa Fe Festival, Spoleto Festival the Lockenhaus Kammnmermusikfest and the International Musicians Seminar in Prussia Cove; Fo-Founder, Orian Quartet and has given concerts at Washington DC, Kennedy Center, at Boston's Gardner Museum and throughout the USA: Carnegie Hall recital 1991 as part of the Centennial Celebration tribute to the next 100 years of music making; Concerts at the Turku Festival in Finland. *Address:* Orian Quartet, Ingpen & Williams Ltd, 14 Kensington Court, London W8 5DN, England.

EDELMANN Otto Karl, b. 5 Feb 1917, Vienna, Austria. Opera Singer (Bass). m. Isle-Maria Straub, 1960. 2 sons, 1 daughter. *Education:* Realgymnasium and State Academy of Music, Vienna. *Debut:* Opera Appearances, 1938. *Career:* POW in USSR for 2 years during 2nd World War; Member, Vienna State Opera, 1948-; with Salzburg Festival, 1948, sang Baron Ochs (Rosenkavalier) in first opera performance in the Festspielhaus 1960 (also filmed); Permanent Member, Metropolitan Opera, New York, 1954-; Took part in first post-war Bayreuth Festival, 1951; World famous as Sachs in Die Meistersinger; also well known as Mozart's Leporello, Beethoven's Rocco and Wagner's Amfortas and Gurnemanz. *Honours:* Knight, Order of Dannenbrog; Austrian Gold Cross of Honour for Sciences and Arts. *Hobbies:* Painting; Boxing. *Address:* Wien-Kalksburg 1238, Breitenfurterstrasse 547, Austria.

EDELMANN Peter, b. 1962, Vienna, Austria. Singer (Baritone). *Education:* Studied with his father (Otto) and at the Vienna Musikhochschule. *Career:* Sang Mozart's Figaro on tour in Europe; Member of the Koblenz Opera from 1985, notably in the title role at the premiere of Odysseus by Klaus Arp, 1989; Guest appearances in Mannheim, Dortmund, Wuppertal and Krefeld, as Mozart's Don Giovanni and Guglielmo, Marcello, the Forester in Cunning Little Vixen, Rossini's Figaro, Posa and Lord Tristan in Martha; Lieder recitals and concerts in Vienna, Budapest, Salzburg and Wexford; Member of the Deutsche Oper Berlin from 1990 (Papageno 1991); Sang in the premiere of Desdemona und ihre Schwestern by Siegfried Matthus, Schwetzingen 1991. *Honours:* Winner, 1989 Belvedere Competition, Vienna. *Address:* c/o Deutsche Oper Berlin, 10 Richard Wagnerstrasse, 1000 Berlin, Germany.

EDELMANN Sergei, b. 22 July 1960, Lvov, Russia. Pianist. *Education:* Studied with father, Head piano department, Lvov Conservatory; Studied with Rudolf Firkusny, Juilliard School, New York, 1979 and Claude Frank, Aspen (Colorado) Music School. *Debut:* First public appearance as soloist, Beethoven Piano Concerto No 1 with Lvov Philharmonic Orchestra, 1970. *Career:* More than 50 concerts throughout the Soviet Union; Toured widely in Europe and North America as soloist with leading orchestras and as a Recitalist. *Recordings:* For RCA. *Honour:* Gina Bachauer Memorial Scholarship Award, 1979. *Address:* c/o Shaw Concerts Inc, 1900 Broadway, New York, NY 10023, USA.

EDELSTEIN Stefan, b. 28 Dec 1931, Freiburg, Germany. Director. m. (1) Anne Marie Egloff, 7 July 1961, div. Mar 1980, (2) Johanna Lovdahl, 17 Aug 1991, 2 sons, 1 daughter. *Education:* Degree in Electronic Engineering, University of Southampton, England; Conservatory of Music, Reykjavik, age 10-16; School Music for Secondary Schools, Piano major, Staatliche Hochschule fur Musik, Freiburg, 1958-62. *Debut:* With Icelandic Symphony Orchestra, 1965. *Career:* Appearances as piano soloist and with partner in 2-piano performances, in concerts, on radio and TV, Reykjavik, Iceland, 1965-71; Director, Reykjavik Children's Music School, 1962-; Head, Department of Music Education, College of Music, Reykjavik, 1965-. *Publication:* Creating Curriculum in Music (co-author), 1980. *Contributions to:* Several articles to Icelandic, British and German professional magazines. *Honours:* Prize for Talent in Performance, Freiburg Musikhochschule, 1961; Prize for Young Musicians (Performers), German Radio Broadcasting Stations, 1962. *Memberships:* International Society of Music Education; Music Educators National Conference. *Hobbies:* Travel; Highland trekking. *Address:* Laugateigur 18, PO Box 5171, 125 Reykjavik, Iceland.

EDEN Danielle, b. 17 Sept 1964, Sydney, Australia. Piccoloist; Flautist. *Education:* Bachelor of Music from the Sydney Conservatorium; Advanced Performers Course at the Royal Academy of Music; Master of Music from London University; Currently completing a Doctorate at London University; Studied flute with Sebastian Bell and piccolo with Francis Nolan. *Career:* Toured the USA with Sydney Conservertorium Symphony Orchestra; Past member of the Australian Youth Orchestra; Performances with the Australian Chamber Orchestra, BBC Welsh Symphony Orchestra, Glynbourne Touring Opera and D'Oyly Carte Opera; Presented the first solo piccolo recital at London's Southbank Centre, 1993, including World premiere of Sarab by Malcolm Hill and UK premiere of Piccolo Play by Thea Musgrave; Tutor Piccolo!, Piccolo!, 1994; Repertoire includes compositions by Donatoni, Ferneyhough, Persichetti, Musgrave, Damaré, Harrington-Young and Vivaldi. *Current Management:* Morgenstern's UK.

EDER Helmut, b. 26 Dec 1916, Linz, Austria. Composer; Teacher. *Education:* Studied at the Linz Conservatory; Received training in composition from Hindemith in Salzburg, 1949, Orff in Munich, 1953-54, and J.N.David in Stuttgart, 1954. *Career:* Teacher, Linz Conservatory, 1950-; Co-founder of its electronic music studio, 1959; Teacher, Salzburg Mozarteum, 1967-; em. H Prof Mozarteum Salzburg, Komponist. *Compositions:* Operas: Oedipus, 1958; Der Kardinal, 1962; Die weisse Frau, 1968; Konjugationen 3, 1969; Der Aufstand, 1975; Georges Dandin oder Der betrogne Ehemann, 1978-79; Ballets: Moderner Traum, 1957; Anamorphose, 1963; Die Irrfahrten des Odysseus, 1964-65; Orchestral: 5 symphonies: No 1, 1950; No 2, 1962; No 3, 1959; No 4, Choral Symphony, 1973-75; No 5, Organ Symphony, 1979-80; Musica semplice for Flute, Harpsichord, and Strings, 1953; Musik for 2 Trumpets and Strings, 1955; Concerto for Piano, 15 Wind Instruments, Double Basses, and Percussion, 1956; Pezzo Sereno, 1958; Concerto semiserio for 2 Pianos and Orchestra, 1960; Oboe Concerto, 1962; 2 violin concertos, 1963, 1964; Danza a solatio, 1963; Concerto a dodici per archi, 1963; Nil admirari, 1966; Syntagma, 1967; Concerto for Bassoon and Chamber Orchestra, 1968; L'Homme arme, concerto for Organ and Orchestra, 1968- 69; Metamorphosen for Flute, Oboe, String Quartet, and Orchestra, 1970; Melodia-ritmica for Strings, 1973; Pastorale for Strings, 1974; Divertimento for Soprano and Orchestral Group, 1976; Jubilato for Chamber Orchestra, 1976; Serenade for 6 Horns and 46 Strings, 1977; Double Concerto for Cello, Double Bass, and Orchestra, 1977-78; Cello Concerto, 1981; Concerto No 3 for Violin and Orchestra, 1981-82; Concerto A.B. for Chamber Orchestra, 1982; Notturni for Flute, Oboe, and Strings, 1983, revised 1984; Haffner Concerto for Flute and Orchestra, 1984; Concertino for Classical Orchestra, 1984; Piece de concert for Strings, 1984; Chamber: String Quartet, 1948; Szene for 6 Horns, 1977; Suite with Intermezzo for 11 Winds, 1979; Quintet for Clarinet, 2 Violins, Viola, and Cello, 1982; Quartet for Flute and String Trio, 1983; Duetto-Concerto für 2 Flöten u. Orchester, op. 95; 4. Streichquartett, op, 94; Mozart in New York, Oper in 3 Akten, UA, Salzburger Festspiele, 1991. Piano pieces; Organ music; Choral works. *Recordings:* Compositions recorded on Amadeo, Deutsche Grammophon, Deutscher Musikrat, Telefunken, et al. *Honours:* Several prizes; Various commissions. *Memberships:* Programmgestalter der Internationalen Stiftung Mozarteum Mitglied des Rorary Clubs Salzburg-Nurd. *Address:* c/o Hochschule fur Musik und darstellende Kunst Mozarteum, Schwarzstrasse 26, A-5020 Salzburg, Austria.

EDGAR-WILSON Richard. b. 1963, Ipswich, Suffolk, England. Singer (Tenor). *Education:* Studied at Christ's College, Cambridge (choral exhibition); the Royal College of Music with Edward Brooks. *Career:* Has sung with vocal groups including Tallis Scholars, the Consort of Musicke, Combattimento and The Scholars; Concert repertoire includes Messiah, Bach's B minor Mass, the Monteverdi Vespers, Mozart's Coronation and C minor Masses and Carissimi's Jephtha; Works by Kodály, Stainer, Vaughan Williams, Berio and Britten; Solo appearances all over the UK and in North America, France, Norway and Germany; Operatic roles include Handel's Acis and The Mad Woman in Britten's Curlew River. *Address:* Ron Gonsalves Management, 10 Dagnan Road, London SW12 9LQ, England.

EDLUND Mikael, b. 19 Jan 1950, Tranas, Sweden. Composer. 1 daughter. *Education:* Musicology, University of Uppsala, 1970-72; Composition with I Lidholm and A Mallnas, State College of Music, Stockholm, 1972-75. *Career:* Producer at Fylkingen, Stockholm, 1979; Teacher in composition, State College of Music, Gothenburg, 1985-87. *Compositions:* The Lost Jugglery for mezzo soprano, cello, piano and two percussionists, 1974-77; Trio Sun, for clarinet, bassoon and piano, 1980; Leaves for eight female voices, accoustic piano, electric piano, harp and seven percussionists, 1977-81; Brains and Dancin' for string quartet, 1981; Jord for five percussionists, 1982; Sma Fotter, a miniature for guitar, 1982; Music for Double wind quintet, 1984; Fantasia on a City for piano, 1981-86; Orchids in the embers, for piano, 1984; Dissolved Window for 21 strings (in progress), Ajar for Orchestra, 1988-91; Blue Garden for piano trio, 1991-93. *Recordings:* Brains and Dancin-Trio Sun-orchids in the embers-Små Fötter-Leaves-Fantasia on a city, Phono

Suecia, PSCD20 and other. *Honour:* Christ Johnson, 1985. *Memberships:* Society of Swedish Composers; Swedish Performing Rights Society (STIM); ISCM (Swedish Section); Fylkingen. *Address:* Backvagen 2, S-19145 Sollentuna, Sweden.

EDWARDS George (Harrison), b. 11 May 1943, Boston, Massachusetts, USA. Composer. m. Rachel Hadas, 22 July 1978. *Education:* BA, Oberlin College, 1965; MFA, Princeton University, 1967. *Career:* Theory Faculty, New England Conservatory of Music, 1968-76; Assistant Professor of Music, 1976-86, Associate Professor of Music, 1986-93, Professor, 1993, Columbia University. *Compositions:* String Quartet, 1967; Kreuz und Quer, 1971; Monopoly, 1972; Giro, 1974; Exchange-Misere, 1974; Draconian Measures, 1976; Gyromancy, 1977; Veined Variety, 1978; Northern Spy, 1980; String Quartet 2, 1982; Moneta's Mourn, 1983; Suave Mari Magno, 1984; A Mirth but Open'd, 1986. *Recordings:* CRI and Opus One records. *Hobbies:* Tennis; Chess. *Address:* 838 West End Avenue Apt 3A, New York, NY 10025, USA.

EDWARDS Joan, b. 1954, London, England. Singer (Mezzo-soprano). *Education:* Studied at the London Opera Centre. *Debut:* Schwertleite in Die Walküre at Covent Garden. *Career:* Sang with the English Opera Group in Britain and abroad, often with Benjamin Britten conducting; Opera North from 1978 as Marcellina in Le Nozze di Figaro, Third Lady (Magic Flute), Mother in Hansel and Gretel, Juno and Minerva in Orpheus in the Underworld, Berta in Il Barbiere di Siviglia and Mary in The Flying Dutchman; Many concert performances; appeared on BBC TV in La Traviata. *Address:* Norman McCann International Artists Ltd, The Coach House, Lawrie Park Gardens, London SE26 6XJ, England.

EDWARDS Owain Tudor, b. 10 Nov 1940, Ruabon, Wales. Musicologist. m. Grete Strand, 1965. 1 son, 2 daughters. *Education:* BMus 1962, MMus 1964, PhD 1967, University College of North Wales, Bangor. *Career:* Assistant Lecturer 1965, Lecturer 1967, Music Department, University College of Wales, Aberystwyth; Lecturer in Music, Liverpool University, 1970; Lecturer in Music, Open University, 1973; Reader and Head of Music History 1974, Professor 1985, Norges Musikkhøgskole, Oslo, Norway; Organist; Kroer church, 1980-. *Compositions:* Adventsgudstjeneste, 1986; 155 orgelsatser til gudstjeneste bruk, 1992. *Publications:* Joseph Parry 1841-1903, 1970; Beethoven, 1972; People, Instruments and the Continuo, 1974; Suite, Sonata and Concerto, 1974; Matins, Lauds and Vespers for St David's Day, 1990. *Contributions to:* New Grove Dictionary of Music and Musicians; The Music Review; The Musical Quarterly; Proceedings of the Royal Musical Association; Modern Asian Studies; Norsk Musikk Tidsskrift; Svensk tidskrift for musikforskning; Studia Musicologica Norvegica; History Today; Welsh Music; National Library of Wales Journal; Die Musik in Geschichte und Gegenwart; Journal of the Plainsong & Medieval Music Society; Welsh History Review; Revue Bénédictine; Cantus Planus. *Hobbies:* Fishing; Golf; Skiing. *Address:* Norges Musikkhøgskole, Gydasv.6, Postboks 5190, Majorstua, 0302 Oslo 3, Norway.

EDWARDS Ross, b. 23 Dec 1943, Sydney, New South Wales, Australia. Composer. m. Helen Hopkins, 7 Aug 1974, 1 son, 1 daughter. *Education:* New South Wales State Conservatory of Music, University of sydney; MMus, University of Adelaide, 1970. *Career:* International Society of Contemporary Music Festivals, Stockholm, 1966, Basel, 1970. *Compositions:* Sonata for 9 instruments, Quem Quaeritis (Children's Nativity Play), 1967; Etude for Orchestra, 1969; Monos I, cello solo, Monos II, piano solo, 1970; Chorus for piano and orchestra, 1972; Mountain Village in a Clearing Mist, for orchestra; Antifon for Voices, brass ensemble, organ and percussion; 5 little piano pieces; the Tower of Remoteness; Concerto for Piano and Orchestra; Christina;s World, Concerto, chamber opera; Maninya II for String Quartet; Kumari, solo piano; Laikan I; Laikan II; the Hermit of Green Light, 1979; Maninya I, 1981;

Maninya V, 1986; Ab Estasis Foribus, 1980; Flower Songs, 1986-7; Ten Little Duets, 1982; Marimba Dances, 1982; Etymalong, 1984; Shadow D-Zone, 1977; Reflections, 1985; Maninya III, 1985; Maninya IV, 1985-86; Maninyas for Violin and orchestra, 1988; Varrageh for solo percussion and orchestra, 1989; Aria and Transcendental Dance for horn and string orchestra, 1990. *Contributor to:* Music Now; Australian Contemporary Music Quarterly. *Memberships:* Member of numerous professional organisations. *Hobbies:* Prospecting; Mountaineering. *Address:* 2 Diamond Road, Pearl Beach 2256, Australia.

EDWARDS Sian, b. 27 May 1959, West Chiltington, Sussex, England. Conductor. *Education:* Studied at the Royal Northern College of Music and with Charles Groves, Norman Del Mar and Neeme Järvi; Further study with Ilya Alexandrovitch Musin at the Leningrad Conservatoire, 1983-85. *Career:* Concert engagements with the London Philharmonic, Royal Philharmonic, London Sinfonietta, Scottish National Orchestra, City of Birmingham Symphony, Hallé, BBC Philharmonic, BBC Scottish Symphony and the Royal Liverpool Philharmonic; Opera debut with Scottish Opera 1986, Mahagonny by Weill; Glyndebourne Festival 1987, La Traviata, L'Heure Espagnole and L'Enfant et les Sortilèges; Katya Kabanova with Glyndebourne Touring Opera 1988; Covent Garden 1988, as the first woman to conduct opera there (The Knot Garden by Tippett); Conducted the world premiere of Greek by Mark Anthony Turnage at the 1988 Munich Biennale (repeated at the Edinburgh Festival); Season 1989-90 included concerts with the London Philharmonic and the BBC Symphony at the Festival Hall; Rigoletto at Covent Garden; French debut with the Orchestre de Paris and US concerts with the San Francisco Symphony; The Gambler by Prokofiev for English National Opera; Conducted Il Trovatore at Covent Garden, 1990, Carmen, 1991; Music Director of English National Opera from 1993; Led the Docklands Sinfonietta in London Proms debut 1993, with music by Britten, Dallapiccola and Mozart (K551). *Honours include:* British Council Scholarship 1983; Winner, Leeds Conductors' Competition 1984. *Address:* c/o Ingpen & Williams Ltd, 14 Kensington Court, London W8 5DN.

EDWARDS Terry, b. 1939, London, England. Choral Director. *Career:* Has formed and directed such groups as London Sinfonietta Voices, Electric Phoenix and London Voices; Concerts and recordings with radio choirs, choral societies and choruses the world over; Season 1988 with the BBC Singers and Choral Society at the Festival Hall, Bach's B minor Mass at Glasgow; Concerts with the London Sinfonietta, in the Promenades and festival appearances in Berlin, Geneva and Turin; Chorus Master for Georg Solti in three Verdi concerts in Chicago; Directed the chorus at the Michael Vyner Memorial at Covent Garden, 1990; Chorus Director at the Royal Opera House, Covent Garden, 1992-; Concerts with the Danish Radio Choir 1991 and works by Erik Bergmann in Finland. *Recordings include:* Messiaen Cinq Rechants, Rachmaninov and Tchaikovsky Vespers, Britten was born (Virgin Classics); Verdi Choruses, A Boy and Otello, (Decca). *Address:* Magenta Music International, 64 Highgate High Street, London NW1 8YW, England.

EDWARDS Warwick Anthony, b. 22 Apr 1944, Dewsbury, England. University Lecturer; Performer on early instruments. m. Jacqueline Freeman, 2 daughters. *Education:* King's College, University of Cambridge; MA, BMus; PhD. *Career:* Lecturer 1971-, Senior Lecturer 1986-, Glasgow University; Director, Scottish Early Music Consort, 1976-; Director, Glasgow International Early Music Festival, 1990-. *Recordings:* Mary's Music: Songs and Dances from the time of Mary Queen of Scots, Scottish Early Music Consort, W Edwards Director, Chandos, 1984. *Publications:* Editor, Music for Mixed Consort (Musica Britannica 40), 1977; Editor, W Byrd; Latin Motets (from manuscript scores) (The Byrd Edition 8), 1984. *Contributions to:* Grove's Dictionary, 6th edition; Music and Letters; Proceedings of the Royal Music Association; Early Music; The Consort; British Book News. *Hobby:* Hill walking. *Address:* 22 Falkland Street, Glasgow G12 9PR, Scotland.

EEROLA Lasse Olavi, b. 24 Sept 1945, Kuusankoski, Finland. Composer; Music Teacher. m. Paivi Irmeli Eerola, 27 Aug 1983. 1 son. *Education:* Sibelius Academy, Helsinki, 1970-77. *Career:* Clarinet and saxophone player, 1967-74; Teacher of theory and clarinet 1969-; Composer, 1974-. *Compositions:* Variations for Wind Orchestra, 1974, recorded 1980; Variations for Orchestra, 1977; Metamorphoses for Orchestra, 1979; Suite for Orchestra, 1980-81; Music for Clarinet and Piano, 1980-82; Miniature for Orchestra, 1982; Chamber Music, 1983-84; Aino, 1984-85; Ceremonial Fanfare for Kouvola, 1984, recorded 1986; Fantasy for Orchestra, 1985; Two Pieces for Orchestra, 1985-86; Syksyisia Kuvia, 1985; Fantasia for Clarinet and Wind Orchestra, 1986; Brass Quintet, 1987. *Honour:* Province of North Karelia Art Prize, 1986. *Memberships:* Society of Finnish Composers; The Finnish Clarinet Society. *Hobbies:* Music; Reading. *Address:* Kauppakatu 2B, 80110 Joensuu, Finland.

EETVELT Francois van, b. 23 May 1946, Bornem, Belgium. Singer (Bass-baritone). *Education:* Studied at the Brussels and Antwerp Conservatories and in Italy and Germany. *Career:* Sang Amfortas in Parsifal at Antwerp, 1976 and has sung there and in Brussels, Prague, Leipzig, Bratislava, Dresden and Helsinki as Don Giovanni, Wagner's Donner, Gunther, Wolfran and Kurwenal; Appolo in Monteverdi's Orfeo, Jochanaan and Tarquinius in The Rape of Lucretia; Sang in the premiere of Das Scloss by Andre Laporte at Brussels, 1986; Festival engagements at Flanders and Aldeburgh; Television include the Monteverdi Orfeo. *Honours include:* Winner, Belcanto Competition, Ostend, 1978. *Address:* Theatre Royal de la Monnaie, 4 Leopoldstrasse, B-1000 Brussels, Belgium.

EGEL Martin, b. 1949, Freiburg, Germany. Singer (Bass-Baritone). *Education:* Studied with his mother, Marga Höffgen, and in Frankfurt and Basle. *Career:* Sang at first in Basle; Salzburg Easter and Summer Festivals from 1974; Bayreuth Festival 1975-84, in Lohengrin, Die Meistersinger and Parsifal, and as Donner in Das Rheingold; Guest appearances in Hamburg, Berlin, Paris, Milan, Brussels, Paris and London; Barcelona 1984, as Mozart's Figaro; Opéra du Rhin Strasbourg 1985; Sang in Dallapiccola's Ulisse at Turin, 1987, the Music Master in Ariadne at Trieste, 1988; Nice, 1990, as the Herald in Lohengrin. *Recordings:* Lohengrin (CBS); Der Vampyr by Marschner (Fonit-Cetra); Armide by Gluck (RCA); Winterreise; Bach Cantatas. *Address:* c/o Théâtre de l'Opéra de Nice, 4&6 rue St Françoise de Paule, F-06300 Nice, France.

EGERTON Francis, b. 14 July 1930, Limerick, Eire. Singer (Tenor). *Career:* Early appearances with Scottish Opera, the Glyndebourne Festival and at Sadler's Wells; Covent Garden from 1972 as Iopas (Les Troyens), Beppe, Flute, the Captain in Wozzeck and roles in Carmen, Les Contes d'Hoffmann and La Fanciulla del West; Has sung Mime in Siegfried for Scottish Opera and in San Francisco; Other roles include Pedrillo (Die Entführung, in Palermo); Strauss's Scaramuccio (Nice), Italian Tenor (Glasgow) and Monsieur Taupe (in Capriccio, at Glyndebourne); Bardolfo in Falstaff at San Francisco, Chicago (concert) and Los Angeles, conducted by Giulini; Il Conte in Cimarosa's Il Fanatico Burlato at Drottningholm; the Captain in Wozzeck (Edinburgh and Los Angeles); Season 1990-91 with Mr Upfold in Albert Herring at San Diego, The Four Tenor Roles in Hoffmann in Paris; Goro (Madame Butterfly) and Eumaus (Il Ritorno di Ulisse) in Los Angeles; appearances in Prokofiev's The Fiery Angel at the Proms and Covent Garden, 1991/92 (as the Doctor). *Address:* c/o Athole Still Ltd, 113 Church Road, London SE19 2PR.

EGMOND Max van, b. 1 Feb 1936, Semarang, Indonesia. Singer (Baritone). *Education:* Studied in Holland with Tine van Willigen-de Lorme. *Career:* After winning prizes in Holland, Brussels and Munich made many appearances as concert singer, notably in Baroque music: Holland, England, Brasil, Germany, Austria, Italy, Poland, Belgium, USA and Canada; Engagements at most leading music festivals and centres; Radio and TV broadcasts; Teacher of singing at the Amsterdam Musieklyceum from 1973. *Recordings:* St Matthew and St John Passions by Bach (Telefunken); Bach Cantatas conducted by Gustav Leonhardt and Nikolaus Harnoncourt; Der Tag des Gerichts by Telemann; Reger's Requiem; Il Ritorno d'Ulisse, Orfeo and Il Combattimento by Monteverdi; St Luke Passion by Schütz; Schubert's Schwanengesang; Lully's Alceste (CBS). *Honours include:* Winner, 's-Hertogenbosch Competition 1959; Edison Awards for Gramophone Recordings, 1969, 1971. *Hobbies include:* Theatre. *Address:* Willemsprarkweg 150-1, Amsterdam 1007, Netherlands.

EHDE John Martin, b. 25 Apr 1962, Stockholm, Sweden. Solo Cellist. *Education:* Royal Academy of Music, Aarhus, Denmark, 1979-85, 1986-87; Diploma, 1984; Soloist Diploma with debut, 1987; Hochschule fur Musik, Vienna, 1985-86, 1987-89. *Debut:* Recital, Royal Academy, Copenhagen, 1987. *Career:* First appeared on Swedish Radio aged 11; Recitals and concertos with orchestras in all Scandinavian countries, Iceland, England, Scotland, Austria, Canada and USSR; Radio and TV appearances in Scandinavia, Iceland, Italy; Solo Cellist, Helsingborg Symphony Orchestra, Sweden, 1989-; Speciality: Performing the music by Frederick Delius; Cello Concerto, sonata. *Honours:* 1st Prize in many Swedish Youth Competitions; Cultural Grant, Malmo Lions Club, 1974; 1-year Grant for studies in Vienna, Swedish Institute for Science and Art, 1987; Awarded Scholarship from Foundation of legendary Swedish conductor Sten Frykberg, 1990. *Membership:* Leopold Stokowski Society, London. *Hobbies:* Performing magic; Record collecting. *Address:* Mandelpilsgatan 16, S- 212 31 Malmo, Sweden.

EHRLICH Abel, b. 3 Sept 1915, Cranz, East Prussia (then in Germany). Composer. m. Lea Klauber, 1 Apr 1947, 1 son, 1 daughter. *Education:* Violin studies since 6th year, music academies in Zagreb, Yugoslavia until 1938, Jerusalem, Israel until 1944. *Career includes:* Teacher, music academies, conservatories, music teachers' colleges in Israel; Teacher, composition, Academy of Tel-Aviv University, 1966-. Professor of Music, now Professor Emeritus, 1982-. Compositions performed in Israel, Europe, USA. *Compositions:* Over 2100 works to date, composed since age 11. Works include: Opera: Dead Souls; Oratorio, Let Us Proclaim; Oratorio Hiov, (Job). Numerous orchestral scores, choral works, chamber music, songs. *Recordings:* The Writing of Hiskia; Bashrav; Do Not Be As Your Fathers. *Honours:* 7 AKUM awards; 3 Liberson Prizes; Boswil performance prize 1972; Rinath Prize, 1964; Prize of the Head of Government, 1989, 7th time AKUM award, 1990. *Address:* 6/3 Refidim Street, Maoz Aviv, Tel-Aviv 69982, Israel.

EHRLICH Cyril, b. 13 Sept 1925, London, England. Emeritus Professor of Economic and Social History. m. Felicity Bell-Bonnet, 1 May 1954, 2 sons, 1 daughter. *Education:* BSc Economics, PhD, London School of Economics, 1947-52. *Career:* Lecturer, Makerere College, Uganda, 1952-61; Lecturer - Emeritus Professor, Queen's University, Belfast, Northern Ireland. *Publications:* The Piano, A History, 1976; The Music Profession in Britain Since the Eighteenth Century, 1986; Harmonious Alliance: A History of the Performing Right Society, 1989. *Contributions to:* The New Grove Dictionary of Music and Musicians; Reviews of books and recordings in Musical Times and Times Literary Supplement. *Memberships:* Royal Musical Association; Economic History Society. *Hobbies:* Piano; Clavichord. *Address:* 8 Chilswell Road, Grandpont, Oxford OX1 4PJ, England.

EHRLING Sixten, b. 3 Apr 1918, Malmo, Sweden. Conductor. m. Gunnel Lindgren, 2 daughters. *Education:* Studied at the Royal Academy of Music, Stockholm.

Debut: Royal Opera Stockholm 1940. *Career:* Assistant to Karl Böhm at Dresden, 1941; Music Director of the Royal Opera Stockholm, 1953-60: visited Edinburgh and London with the premiere production of Blomdahl's Aniara, 1959; Director of Salzburg Mozarteum course for conductors, 1954; Music Director, Detroit Symphony Orchestra 1963-73; Head of the conducting department at the Juilliard School, New York, from, 1973; Metropolitan Opera, 1973-77, Peter Grimes, Der Ring des Nibelungen, Il Trittico, Simon Boccanegra, Bluebeard's Castle; Principal Guest Conductor, Denver Symphony Orchestra from 1979. *Recordings include:* Symphonies by Berwald with the London Symphony Orchestra; Music by Blomdahl with the Stockholm Philharmonic. *Honours include:* Knight Commander, Order of the White Rose, Finland (for championing the works of Sibelius). *Address:* c/o Juilliard School Lincoln Plaza, NY 10023, New York, USA.

EINEM Gottfried von, b. 24 Jan 1918, Berne, Switzerland, Professor and Composer. m. Lotte Ingrisch, 1 son. *Education:* Gymnasium at Ratzeburg and musical studies with Boris Blacher. *Career:* Coach, State Opera in Berlin, 1939-44; Musical Adviser to Director of Dresden State Opera, Coach Bayreuth Festival, 1938-39; Member of Board of Salzburg Festival 1948-51; Member, Academy of Arts, Berlin (West and East), Vienna Konzerthaus Gesellschaft, 1963-; Emeritus Professor, Hochschule fur Musik, Vienna. *Compositions:* Operas: Death of Danton (Büchner), The Trial, (Kafka), Der Zerrissene (Nestroy), Visit of the Old Lady (Dürrenmatt), Kabale und Liebe (Schiller), Jesu Hochzeit; Der Tulifant (Ingrisch); Cantatas: Stundenlied (Brecht), An die Nachgeborenen (various poets); also five ballets, four symphonies and various other works for orchestra including two piano concertos, a violin concerto, 100 songs, four string quartets, one string trio. *Honours:* Numerous awards and prizes including the Austrian State Prize, 1965. *Address:* Vienna-Hofburg, Vienna A1010, Austria.

EIPPERLE Trude, b. 12 Aug 1910, Stuttgart, Germany. Singer (Soprano). *Education:* Studied at the Musikhochschule Stuttgart. *Career:* Sang at Wiesbaden from 1930, Brunswick, Nuremberg and Munich until 1944; Salzburg Festival, 1942, Zdenka in Arabella; Cologne Opera, 1945-51, notably in the 1948 premiere of Die Verkundigung by Walter Braunfels; Bayreuth Festival 1952, as Eva in Die Meistersinger; Other roles included Desdemona, Elsa, Elisabeth, Pamina and Mozart's Countess, Madama Butterfly. *Recordings include:* Tannhäuser (Deutsche Grammophon); Die Schöpfung; Die Rose vom Liebesgarten by Pfitzner.

EIRIKSDOTTIR Karolina, b. 10 Jan 1951, Reykjavik, Iceland. Composer. m. Thorsteinn Hannesson, 1 Aug 1974, 1 daughter. *Education:* Graduated, Reykjavik College, 1971, Reykjavik College of Music, 1974; MMus, Music History & Musicology 1976, MMus Composition 1978, University of Michigan, USA. *Career includes:* Major performances of works: Iceland Symphony Orchestra (4 works), at Nordic Music Days in Helsinki 1980, Oslo 1982, Copenhagen 1984; at Scandinavia Today, Washington DC, 1982; Opera, Någon har jag sett in Vadstena in Sweden, 1988, Reykjavík, 1989; Sinfonietta performed by the BBC Scottish Symphony Orchestra during Breaking The Ice Festival in Glasgow, 1992; Six Movements for String quartett performed by The Arditti String Quartet, London, 1992; Three Paragraphs for Orchestra performed by the Malmö Symphony Orchestra at Stockholm New Music Festival, Stockholm, 1993; Performances at Nordic Music Festival, Göteborg, 1991; Dark Music Days Festival in Reykjavík, 1993 & Kuhmo Festival in Finnland, 1993; Commission, Icelandic State TV, work for symphony orchestra, 1985; Several performances, Iceland & abroad. *Compositions include:* Notes, Sonans, Sinfonietta, for Orchestra; 5 pieces for chamber orchestra; 6 movements for string quartet; Rondo & Rhapsody for Piano; In Vultu Solis, violin; Trio, violin, cello, piano; 6 poems from the Japanese, & Some Days, voice & instruments; All pieces in manuscript at Iceland Music Information Centre, Reykjavik; orchestral pieces:

Notes, Sonans, Sinfonietta, Klifur, Three Paragraphs, opera: Någon har jag sett, chamber orchestra: Five pieces and Rhapsody in C; Land posessed by poems for baritone and piano, solo pieces for clarinet, harpsichord and guitar and chamber music. *Recordings:* In Vultu Solis, with Gudny Gudmundsdottir, violin; Sinfonietta, Iceland Symphony Orchestra, conductor Paul Zukofsky; Other works recorded by Iceland State Broadcasting Service. *Address:* Njardargata 31, 101 Reykjavik, Iceland.

EISENFELD Brigitte, b. 19 Sept 1945, Fralkenstein, Germany. Singer (Soprano). *Education:* Studied at the Berlin Musikhochschule. *Debut:* Chemnitz 1970, as Papagena. *Career:* Engaged at Chemnitz, 1970-74, Staatsoper Berlin from 1974, notably in the premiere of Graf Mirabeau by Matthus and as Constanze in Die Entführung, 1989; Guest appearances with the Staatsoper ensemble in Tokyo, Moscow, Bologna and Lucerne; Schwetzingen Festival, 1989, as Zerbinetta in Ariadne auf Naxos; Other roles have included Bondchen, Zerlina, Aennchen in Der Freischutz, Rosina and Norina. *Address:* c/o Berlin Deutsche Stattsopher, Unter den Linden 7, 1086 Berlin, Germany.

EISENSTEIN Alfred, b. 14 Nov 1899, Brody, previously Galicia. Consulting Professional Engineer and Builder; Composer of Classical Music. m. (1) Marya Brettler, 14 May 1933 (deceased). (2) Mercedes Malespin-Felix, 21 Feb 1952, deceased 19 Dec 1987. *Education:* Vienna Technical College, Graduated, 1928; Diploma, Civil Engineering, Berlin, 1929; Piano studies with Professor Anton Trost, Vienna, Austria. *Debut:* Berlin, 1929. *Compositions:* Numerous including, Memento; Melody in E Major; Nostalgic Rhapsody for piano, also performed as Orchestral work 10 Jan 1988; Adagio Lamentose, Symphonic Tone Poem; Melodic Reflections for cello and orchestra; Romance and Souvenir for violin and orchestra; Tango of Love, for orchestra; Impromptu, Symphonic Tone Poem; Epilogue for piano, also orchestrated, and performed in a special Holocaust Concert; Dedication for piano; Elegy, world premiere performance, 1992; Requiem to my Beloved, world premiere, 1990; Piano Works: Rhapsodic Feelings, 1993; Trubbing Threnody, 1994. *Recordings:* 2 LP Record Albums, Relax and Enjoy, the music of Alfred Eisenstein, containing 16 works, 2 symphonic tone poems, 3 instrumentals, 1 ballet suite in 4 movements: Petite Suite, 3 orchestral works including a new symphonic work: Requiem to My Beloved, In Memoriam of his wife who died in 1987, 3 symphonic works and 8 songs with orchestra. *Honours:* 24 Special Standard Awards from American Society of Composers, Authors and Publishers, every year since 1966; Honorary (Doctor Degrees) Plaques by the Variety Club of Greater Miami, 1974 and Audio Society, New York, 1967; Honorary DFA, 1984; Special Citation as Composer by Alexander von Humboldt Society, 1986. *Memberships:* American Society of Composers, Authors and Publishers; (Past): International Platform Association; Institute of Polish Culture. *Hobbies:* Improvising; Chess; Swimming; Exploring Engineering sciences. *Address:* 18900 NE 14th Avenue, North Miami Beach, FL 33179, USA.

EISINGER Irene, b. 8 Dec 1903, Kosel, Germany. Singer (Soprano). *Education:* Studied with Paula Mark-Neusser in Vienna. *Debut:* Basle 1926. *Career:* Berlin Städtische Oper, 1928-31; Sang under the direction of Otto Klemperer at the Kroll Opera, Berlin, notably as Susanna in Le Nozze di Figaro; Vienna Staatsoper, 1930-31; Mozart roles at Salzburg, 1930-33; German Opera Prague, 1933-37; Covent Garden, 1936, as Gretel (with Maggie Teyte as Hansel); Glyndebourne Festival, 1935-49, as Despina, Blondchen, Papagena, Susanna and Polly Peachum; Resident in England from 1938. *Address:* 5 Lime Court, Gipsy Lane, London SW15, England.

EISMA Will Leendert, b. 13 May 1929, Sungailiat, Indonesia. Composer; Violinist; m. Wilhelmina A. Reeser, 30 Nov 1960, 1 son, 1 daughter. *Education:* Conservatory of Rotterdam; Composition, Accademia di Santa Cecilia, Rome; Institute for Sonology, Utrecht.

Career: Violinist, Rotterdam Philharmonic, 1953-59, Chamber Orchestra, Società Corelli, 1960-61, Chamber Orchestra, Radio Hilversum, 1961-89; Member of electro instrumental group ICE; Director, Studio for Electronic Music, Five Roses. *Compositions:* 3 Concerti for orchestra, 1 for 2 violins and orchestra; Taurus-A, Volumina for orchestra; Concerti for oboe, horn; chamber and electronic music; Concerto for String Trio & Orchestra; Concerto for English Horn, 1981; Concerto for Percussion, 1979; Concerto for 5 violas, 1982; Du dehors - Du dedans, 1983; Silver Plated Bronze, 1986, Te Deum, 1988; Passo del Diavolo, 1988. *Hobby:* Photography. *Address:* Oude Amersfoortsweg 206, Hilversum, 1212 AL, Holland.

EK Harald, b. 1936, Jonkoping, Sweden. Singer (Tenor). *Education:* Studied in Gothenburg with G. Kjellertz and R. Jacobson. *Debut:* Gothenburg 1966 in Die Lustige Witwe. *Career:* Drottningholm 1967, as Almaviva in Paisiello's Il Barbiere di Siviglia; Stadtstheater Berne, 1969-72; Bayreuth Festival, 1971 in Der fliegende Holländer and Das Rheingold; Member of the Staatsoper Hamburg, 1972-75, Zurich Opera from 1975; Other roles include Don Ottavio, Tamino, Hoffmann, Comte Ory, Cavaradossi, Tom Rakewell and Alfred in Die Fledermaus. *Recordings include:* Der fliegende Holländer (Deutsche Grammophon); Sang Don José at Gothenburg, 1988. *Address:* Stora Teatern, Box 53116, S-40015 Göteborg, Sweden.

EKLUND Anna, b. 1964, Sweden. Singer (Soprano). *Education:* Studied at the Stockholm College of Music and the State Opera School. *Debut:* Stockholm Royal Opera as Papagena. *Career:* Sang in staged version of Carmina Burana at Stockholm, 1991; Other roles have included Ismene in Haeffner's Elektra (at Drottningholm); Novis Elisabeth in Forsell's Riket ar ditt, the Queen of Night and Serpetta in La Finta Giardiniera; Season 1991-92, in the St Matthew Passion under Philippe Herreweghe in Sweden, Barcelona and Madrid, Betty in Salieri's Falstaff at Drottningholm; Season 1992-93 as Zemir in Gretry's Zemire et Azor at Drottningholm and the leading female role in the premiere of Amorina by Iars Runsten at the Royal Opera Stockholm. *Address:* Nordic Artists Management, Sveavagen 76, S-11359 Stockholm, Sweden.

EKLUND Hans, b. 1 July 1927, Sandviken, Sweden. Composer; Professor. *Education:* Studied with Lars-Erik Larsson, Stockholm Musikhogskolan, 1949-52; Ernst Pepping, Berlin, 1954; Rome, 1957. *Career:* Professor of Harmony and Counterpoint, Stockholm Musikhogskolan, 1964-. *Compositions:* Opera: Mother Svea, 1972; Orchestral: Symphonic Dances, 1954; Musica da camera No 1 for Cello and Chamber Orchestra, 1955, No 2 for Trumpet, Piano, Percussion and Strings, 1956, No 3 for Violin and Chamber Orchestra, 1957, No 4 for Piano and Orchestra, 1959, No 5 for Cello and Strings, 1970, No 6 for Oboe and Chamber Orchestra, 1970; 9 symphonies: No 1, Sinfonia seria, 1958; No 2, Sinfonia breve, 1964; No 3, Sinfonia rustica, 1967-68; No 4, Hjalmar Branting in memoriam, 1973-74; No 5, Quadri, 1978; No 6, Sinfonia senza speranza, 1983; No 7, La Serenata, 1984; No 8, Sinfonia Grave, 1985; Symphony No 9; Sinfonia Introvertita, 1992; Toccata, 1966. Primavera for Strings, 1967; Concerto for Trombone, Winds and Percussion, 1972; Little Serenade for Wind Orchestra, 1976; Requiem per Soli Coro Ed Orchesta, 1977-78; Chamber Concerto for Violin and Strings, 1977; Horn Concerto, 1979; Concerto for Clarinet and Strings, 1980; Concerto for Tuba and Brass Orchestra, 1980; Concerto for Clarinet, Cello and Orchestra, 1983; Divertimento, 1986; Concerto Grosso for String Quartet and String Orchestra, 1987; Chamber: 4 string quartets, 1954-62; 2 sonatas for Solo Violin, 1956, 1982; Piano Trio, 1963; L'Estate per Archi, 1985; 3 preludes for the piano, Serenata per Flauto e pianoforte, 1990; Mesto per Archi, 1990; Apertura per Orchestra, 1990; 3 Impromptus for Agneta Pianosoco, 1993; 2 Pastoral Songs (Choir), 1993. Various solo pieces; Piano music; organ works; Choruses. *Honours:* Member, Royal Swedish Academy of Music, 1975-; Awarded degree, Litteris et Artibus from the King of

Sweden, 1985; Christ Johnson Fund Music Prize, 1989. *Address:* Bjornskogsgrand 63, 162 46 Vallingby, Sweden.

EKSTROM Robert Carl, b. 26 Mar 1917, Duluth, USA. Music Educator; Choral Conductor; Singer. m. Charlotte Virginia Tuttle, 28 Dec 1940, 2 sons, 4 daughters. *Education:* BS, 1940, MEd., 1946, Music Ed., University of Minnessota; Ed.D., University of Southern California, 1959. *Debut:* Tenor Soloist, Duluth Symphony Orchestra. *Career includes:* Head, Vocal Dept., Sherburn, 1940-41; Instructor, Music, Duluth Public Schools, 1941-52, 1954-64; Professor, Music, Pasadena City College, 1942-54; Head, Music, Lindblom Technical High School, Chicago, 1964-; Director, Soloist, Chicago Choral Society, 1970; Numerous radio, tv & film appearances. *Publications:* Bearing the Cross; You Need the Cross; On the Cross He Died to Save; Don't Deny the Lord; The Lord is Risen; Mother; The Male Voice, 1945; Correlation of Music Talent with Intelligence, 1946; Development of the Madrigal, 1947; Comparison of the Male Voice, 1959. *Recordings:* Capitol; Laos. *Contributions to:* Journals & Magazines. *Honours:* Recipient, many honours & awards.*Memberships Include:* National Director, American Union of Swedish Singers; National Director, Norwegian Singers League; Associated Male Choruses of America. *Hobbies:* Composing; Writing Books. *Address:* 2321 West 110th Place, Chicago, IL 60643, USA.

EL SISI Yousef Ibrahim, b. 19 Mar 1935, Shebin El Kom, Egypt. Conductor; Composer; Teacher. m. Nadia El Sisi, 12 July 1958, 2 sons. *Education:* Diploma, major Piano, Higher Institute of Music, Cairo, 1956; BA, English Literature, Faculty of Arts, Cairo University, 1959; Artistic Maturity degree (Kunsteerische Reife Prufung), Conducting and Composition, Vienna Music Academy, 1965. *Debut:* Cairo, 13 Nov 1965. *Career:* Conductor, Artistic Director, Principal Conductor, Cairo Symphony Orchestra and Cairo Opera Troupe, 1965-; Guest Conductor, major orchestras of Albania, Austria, Bulgaria, Czechoslovakia, China, England, Germany, Italy, France, North and South Korea, Poland, USA; Visiting Professor for Postgraduates, most music institutions, Egypt; Managing Director, El Magalla El Mousikeya monthly musical magazine, 1973-77; Egyptian Under Secretary for Music and Opera, Ministry of Culture. *Compositions:* 33 radio drama music works; 170 songs for children's choir; Suite for Brass Band; Variations on Sayed Darwish Theme for Soli Choir and Orchestra; 7 compositions based on classical Arabic music forms. *Recordings:* Mozart: 3 complete operas in Arabic; Digital recording: Le Nozze di Figaro, Don Giovanni, Cosi Fan Tutte with Polish National Radio Orchestra, OIA London. Over 200 recordings in films, TV and radio, live concerts, Cairo, Tirana, Peking and Pyong Yang; Carmina, Beethoven's Fantasia Burana and Adagio (Albinoni) on documentary film. *Publications:* Invitation to Music (in Arabic), 1981. *Current Management:* Go Management, 1725 York Avenue, suite 27b, New York, NY 10128, USA. *Address:* 59 Medinet El-Alaam, Agouza, Cairo, Egypt.

EL-DABH Halim (Abdul Messieh), b. 4 Mar 1921, Cairo, Egypt. Composer; Teacher. *Education:* Studied piano and Western music, Sulcz Conservatory, Cairo, 1941-44; Graduated, agricultural engineering, University of Cairo, 1945; Composition with Aaron Copland and Irving Fine, Berkshire Music Center, Tangelwood; MM, New England Conservatory of Music, Boston; MFA, Brandeis University. *Career:* Teacher, Haile Selassie University, Addis Ababa, 1962-65; Howard University, 1966-69; Teacher 1969-, Co-director, Center for the Study of World Musics, 1979-, Kent State University. *Compositions:* Black Epic, opera-pageant, 1968; Opera Flies, 1971; Ptahmose and the Magic Spell, opera trilogy, 1972-73; Drink of Eternity, opera-pageant, 1981; Clytemnestra, epic dance-drama, 1958; 3 symphonies, 1950, 1952, 1956; Concerto for Darabukka or Timpani and Strings, 1954; Fantasia-Tahmeel for Darabukka or Timpani and Strings, 1954; Bacchanalia for Orchestra, 1958; Tahmeela for Flute and Chamber Orchestra, 1958-59; Concerto for Darabukka, Clarinet and Strings, 1981; Rhapsodia Egyptia-Brasileira for Orchestra, 1985; String Quartet, 1951; Thumaniya, octet, 1952; Juxtaposition No 1 for Percussion Ensemble, 1959; Tonography for Clarinet, 1980; Tonography III for 5 Wind Instruments, 1984; Piano pieces; Choruses. *Publications:* The Derabucca: Hand Techniques in the Art of Drumming, 1965. *Honours:* Fulbright Scholarship; 2 Guggenheim Fellowships; Commissions. *Address:* c/o Center for the Study of World Musics, Kent State University, Kent, OH 44242, USA.

EL-KHOLY Samha, b. 27 July 1925, Cairo, Egypt. Musicologist; Educator. m. Gamal Abdel-Rahim, 8 Dec 1959, 1 daughter. *Education:* Diploma, Higher Institute for Music Education, Cairo, 1951; Licentiate, Royal Academy of Music, London (Piano Performance), 1954; PhD, Edinburgh University, 1954. *Career:* Teacher, Founding Committee Member, 1959-62, Professor, History of Music, Analysis, 1968-85, Dean, 1972-81, Professor Emeritus, 1985-, Cairo Conservatoire; President, Academy of Arts (7 art colleges including Cairo Conservatoire); Fulbright Professor, University of South Florida, Tampa, Florida, USA, 1987-; Presented weekly musical programme on TV, Egypt, 13 years; Currently Professor Emerita, Dept of Musicology, Cairo; Founder, 1985, and present Chair, Egyptian Jeunesses Musicales, 1990. *Publications:* The Function of Music in Islamic Culture (English); Music Education, teachers' manual (co-author), 1958; European Music in the 17th and 18th centuries, in The Compendium of the Arts (Arabic), 1971; Traditions of Improvisation in Arab Music, Past and Present; Nationalism in the 20th century (Arabic), 1987; Translations into Arabic: Our Musical Heritage (Curt Sachs), 1965; Musical Structure and Design (C.T.Davie), 1970; A History of Music (T.Finney) (with G.Abdel-Rahim), 1975; Nationalism in Music of the 20th Century in Arabic, to appear, 1992. *Contributions to:* Major Arabic periodicals, Cairo, Kuwait; Major Cairo newspapers: Al Ahram, Al Akhbar, Al Goumhuriya; 13 articles on Egyptian Musicians for Grove's Dictionary of Music, 1980; The New Grove Opera Dictionary, 1992. *Address:* 2/4 Lasilky Str. New Maadi, Cairo 11742, Egypt.

ELCHLEPP Isolde, b. 1958, Strasbourg, France. Singer (Mezzo-soprano). *Education:* Studied at the Opera School of the Bavarian State Opera. *Career:* Sang first at Bremen, notably as The Woman in Schoenberg's Erwartung, 1985; Wiesbaden from 1986 as Wagner's Venus, Fricka and Waltraute, and Azucena in Il Trovatore; Hanover Opera as Carmen, Ortrud, Santuzza, Octavian, the Composer, Amneris and Kundry; Deutsche Oper Berlin 1990, as Ortrud; Guest appearances in Dusseldorf, Mannheim, Brunswick, Karlsruhe, Basle (Herodias in Salome) and Brussels; Concert repertory includes Schoenberg's Pierrot Lunaire, which she has sung in Paris and Nuremberg; Guest in Tokyo in Erwartung; also sang Elektra, Oslo Philharmonic; Troades, Franfurt Opera; Fricka in Das Rheingold and Die Walküre at Hanover, 1992 as well as Hostess in the premiere of Reimann's Das Schloss, Deutsche Oper Berlin; Made debut at The Bayreuth Festival as Ortrud in 1993. *Address:* c/o Haydn Rawstron Ltd, PO Box 654, London SE26 4DZ, England.

ELDER Mark Philip, b. 2 June 1947, Hexham, England. Conductor. m. Amanda Jane Stein, 1980. *Education:* BA Honours, MA, Cambridge University; CBE, June 1989. *Career:* Music staff, Wexford Festival, 1969-70; Chorus master, assistant conductor, Glyndebourne, 1970-71; Music staff, Covent Garden, Royal Opera House, London, 1970-72; Conducted Rigoletto, 1976; Staff conductor, Australian Opera, 1972-74; English National Opera 1974-77; Associate Conductor 1977-79, Music Director, 1979-92, English National Opera; conducted world premiere of Blake's Toussaint 1977 and the British premiere of Busoni's Doktor Faust 1986; Hansel and Gretel, 1989; New production of Beatrice and Benedict - Macbeth and Wozzeck, 1990; Led ENO on tour to Russia, 1990; Conducted Reginald Goodall Memorial Concert, Festival

Hall, June 1991; New production of the Force of Destiny at the Coliseum, 1992 and the British premiere of Rossini's Ermione, with the Orchestra of the Age of Enlightenment at the Elizabeth Hall; Conducted Die Meistersinger at Bayreuth 1981. Principal guest conductor, BBC Symphony Orchestra, London, 1982-85, London Mozart Players 1980-83; Music Director, Rochester Philharmonic Orchestra, New York, USA, 1989-; Principal Guest Conductor of the City of Birmingham Symphony Orchestra from 1993 (Mahler's Fourth Symphony and Beethoven's Second Piano Concerto at the 1993 Proms). *Honour:* Honorary degree, Royal Academy of Music, 1984. *Address:* 4 Ripplevale Grove, London N1, England.

ELIAS Brian David, b. 30 Aug 1948, Bombay, India. Composer. *Education:* Royal College of Music, 1966; Private studies with Elisabeth Lutyens; Extra-mural composition workshop, New York, USA. *Career:* Freelance editor, arranger and copyist; Worked as Clerk and Statistician Assistant, 1972-78; Now composes full time with some teaching commitments. *Compositions include:* La Chevelure for soprano and chamber orchestra; Somnia for tenor and orchestra; L'Eylah for orchestra, commissioned by BBC for Promenade Concerts, 1984; Tzigane for solo violin; Peroration for solo soprano; Geranos for chamber ensemble, commissioned by The Fires of London, 1985; 5 songs to Poems by Irina Ratushinskaya for mezzo-soprano and orchestra commissioned by BBC for Winter Season 1989-; The Judas Tree, ballet score commissioned by The Royal Ballet choreographed by Kennth MacMillan, 1992. *Honour:* Joint 2nd Prize for Proverbs of Hell, Radcliffe Music Award, 1977. *Membership:* Association of Professional Composers. *Hobbies:* Reading; Gardening. *Address:* c/o Chester Music, 8/9 Frith Street, London W1V 5TZ, England.

ELIAS Rosalind, b. 13 Mar 1929, Lowell, Massachusetts, USA. Singer; Opera Director. *Education:* Studied at the New England Conservatory, Boston, and at the Accademia di Santa Cecilia, Rome; Further study with Daniel Ferro in New York. *Career:* Sang with New England Opera, 1948-52; Metropolitan Opera from 1954, as Cherubino, Dorabella, Rosina and Hansel and in the premieres of Barber's Vanessa and Antony and Cleopatra; Scottish Opera 1970, as Rossini's Cenerentola; Vienna Staatsoper 1972, as Carmen; Glyndebourne Festival 1975, as Baba the Turk in The Rake's Progress; Other appearances in Hamburg, Monte Carlo, Barcelona, Lisbon and Aix-en-Provence; Other roles include Verdi's Amneris and Azucena, Massenet's Charlotte and Giulietta in Les Contes d'Hoffmann; Sang Herodias in Salome at Houston, 1987; Produced Carmen at Cincinnati, 1988; Il Barbiere di Siviglia for Opera Pacific, Costa Mesa, 1989. *Recordings:* La Gioconda, La Forza del Destno, Il Trovatore, Falstaff, Madama Butterfly, Rigoletto (RCA); Der fliegende Holländer, La Forza del destino (Decca). *Address:* c/o Opera Pacific, 3187 Red Hill Avenue, Suite 230, Costa Mesa, CA 92626, USA.

ELIASON Robert Erwin, b. 28 Mar 1933, Flint, USA. Musician. m. Ellen Irene Easter, 30 Aug 1958, 2 sons, 1 daughter. *Education:* BM, University of Michigan, 1955; MM, Manhattan School of Music, 1959; DMA, University of Missouri, Kansas City, 1968. *Career:* 7th Army Symphony Orchestra, Principal Tuba, 1955-57; Public School Teacher, 1957-58, 1960, 1969-70; Principal Tuba, Kansas City Philharmonic, 1960-69; Research associate, Smithsonian Institution, 1970-71; Curator, Musical Instruments, Henry Ford Museum, Greenfield Village, 1971-85; Technical writer, New England Digital Corporation, 1985-90; Technical writer Geographic Data Technology Inc, 1993-; started Toad Hill Nusic, a computerized music engraving business, 1987. *Recordings:* Detroit Concert Band Recordings of Sousa Marches and Concert Band Repertoire, 1975-83; 19th Century Ballroom Music, 1976; Our Musical Past, 1976. *Publications:* Keyed Bugles in the United States, 1972; Graves & Co. Musical Instrument Makers, 1975; Early American Brass Makers, 1979. *Contributions to:* 30 articles for Harvard Dictionary of

Music, 1986; 19 Articles, Grove Dictionary, 1980, American Grove, 1985; over 25 articles for various journals and magazines. *Hobbies:* Flying; Commercial Pilots Licence with Multi Engine, Instrument, Flight Instructor and Instrument Instructor Ratings. *Address:* RR 3, Box 466, Lyme, NH 03768, USA.

ELIASSON Sven Olaf, b. 4 Apr 1933, Boliden, Sweden. Singer (Tenor). *Education:* Royal Music Academy, Stockholm. *Career:* Sang at Oslo from 1961, Stockholm from 1965; Guest appearances at the Hamburg Staatsoper 1968-74; Further engagements at Zurich, Dusseldorf and Frankfurt; Glyndebourne 1967, as Don Ottavio; Drottningholm Opera 1967, as Belmonte in Die Entführung; Zurich Opera 1968, 1975, as Pfitzner's Palestrina and in the premiere of Klebe's Ein Wahrer Held; Stockholm Opera 1970, in the premiere of Rosenberg's Hus med Dubbel Ingang; Sang Schoenberg's Aron with the Hamburg Staatsoper in Israel, 1974; Other roles include Don José, Riccardo in Un Ballo in Maschera, Peter Grimes and Tom Rakewell in The Rake's Progress. *Recordings include:* Il Ritorno d'Ulisse in Patria by Monteverdi (Telefunken); Video of Swedish Opera production of Die Meistersinger. *Address:* Kungliga Teatern, PO Box 16094, S-10322 Stockholm, Sweden.

ELKINS Margreta, b. 16 Oct 1932, Brisbane, Australia. Singer (Mezzo-Soprano). *Education:* Studied with Ruby Dent in Brisbane, with Pauline Bindley in Melbourne and Vera Rozsa in London; Further study with Campogalliani in Milan. *Debut:* Brisbane Opera Company 1955, Azucena. *Career:* Joined Royal Opera, London, in 1958 and sang Octavian, Adalgisa (Norma), Amneris and Marina (Boris Godunov); Sang Helen in the premiere of Tippett's King Priam, with the Royal Opera at Coventry, 1962; Sadler's Wells Theatre 1963, in Giulio Cesare by Handel; Many appearances with Joan Sutherland; Guest engagements in Genoa, Naples, Barcelona, Naples, Boston, New Orleans and Philadelphia; Amsterdam 1974, in Handel's Rodelinda; Sang with Australian Opera, Sydney, from 1975; Sang Amneris at Brisbane, 1988, Azucena, 1990; Repertoire ranges from Monteverdi to Wagner; Many concert appearances. *Recordings include:* Many opera sets for Decca, with Joan Sutherland: I Puritani, La Sonnambula, Faust, Rosina by Shield, Giulio Cesare, Griselda by Bononcini. *Address:* c/o Lyric Opera of Queensland, PO Box 677, South Brisbane QLD 4101, Australia.

ELKUS Jonathan Britton, b. 8 Aug 1931, San Francisco, California, USA. Musician and Teacher. m. Marilyn McCormick, 30 July 1966, 1 son. *Education:* BA, University of California at Berkeley, 1953; MA, Stanford University, 1954. *Career:* Professor of Music, Lehigh University, 1957-73; Freelance Musical Editor and Consultant, 1973-; Editorial Associate, Charles Ives Society, 1973-; Director of Music, 1979-85, Cape Cod Academy, Osterville; Chairman, Department of Humanities, ibid, 1985-89; Chairman, Department of History, Stuart Hall School, Staunton, 1989-; Proprietor, J B Elkus and Son, Music Publishers, Laureate Music Press, and Overland Music Distributors, Staunton. *Compositions:* Tom Sawyer (Musical play); Treasure Island (Musical play); Five Sketches for Two Clarinets and Bassoon; Three Medieval Pieces, (Organ); The Dorados, (Chorus); Of Players to Come (Chorus); Numerous compositions and transcriptions for concert band; Act Your Age (Musical Play); The Mandarin (Opera, with Richard Franko Goldman); The Outcasts of Poker Flat (Opera). *Publication:* Charles Ives and the American Band Tradition: A Centennial Tribute, 1975. *Contributions to:* The Instrumentalist; Opera Journal; Yale Review; Nineteenth Century Music. *Honour:* Recipient of Ford Foundation Fellowship, 1962. *Membership:* American Society of Composers, Authors and Publishers. *Address:* PO Box 9526, Berkeley, CA 94709, USA.

ELLA István, b. 1947, Veresegyház, Hungary. Organist. *Education:* Béla Bartók Conservatory; Ferenc Liszt Academy of Music; Graduate, Budapest Academy of Music, 1971; Studied organ and improvisation under

Professor Ernst Köhler and Conducting under Professor Olaf Koch, Weimar and Leipzig; Conductor's Diploma, Wittenberg, 1974. *Career:* Artistic Director and Soloist, Corelli Chamber Orchestra. *Honours:* Prize Winner, Prague International Organ Competition, 1971; 2nd Prize, Bach International Organ Concours, Leipzig, 1972; 1st prize, Anton Bruckner International Organ Competition, Linz, 1974; 1st Prize, J S Bach International Organ Concours, Brugge, 1976.

ELLERO D'ARTEGNA Francesco, b. 15 Dec 1948, Ravascletto, Italy. Signer (Bass). *Education:* Studied at the Udine Conservatory and with Ettore Campogalliani. *Debut:* Verona Arena, 1981, as High Priest in Nabucco. *Career:* Appearances at such Italian opera centres as Trieste, Modena, Genoa, Carcalla, (Timur in Turandot, 1986), Parma, Venice and Milan; Further engagements at Monte Carlo (Raimondo, 1987 Barcelona, Hamburg and Madrid (Leporello, 1989); Sang Ramphis in Aida at Verona, 1988-89 and Raimondo in Lucia di Lammermoor at the Lyric Opera Chicago, 1990; Other roles have included Bellini's Oroveso and Rodolfo, Verdi's Silva, Zaccaria, Sparafucile, Fiesco, Parde Guardiano and Fernando; Mephistopheles in Faust and Haly in L'Italiana in Algeri; Sang Banquo at Reggio Emilia and Timur at the Festival of Caracalla, 1992; Sang in the Verdi Requiem at Wembley, London, 1994. *Recordings:* La Bohème and Falstaff; Maria Stuarda; La Sonnambula. *Address:* c/o Arena di Verona, Piazza Bra 28, 37121 Verona, Italy.

ELLINGBOE Bradley Ross, b. 16 Apr 1958, Farmington, Minnesota, USA. University Professor; Singer; Conductor. m. Karen Hersey, 18 July 1981. 2 sons, 1 daughter. *Education:* BA, cum laude, Music Theory & Composition, Saint Olaf College, 1980; Certificate, University of Oslo, 1984. Music Education: MM Vocal Performance 1983, MM Choral Cond 1984, Eastman School of Music. *Debut:* Opera Southwest, 1987. *Career:* Concert and Oratorio soloist with the Orchestras of: Aspen, San Antonio, Santa Fe, Grand Rapids, New Mexico, Jackson, Chamber Orchestra of Albuquerque, Chamber Orchestra of Denver; Tokyo Symphony, Shinsei Nihon Symphony Orchestra, Japan, Las Vagas Symphony; Concert tours in Korea, Japan and Scandinavia; Soloist under Robert Shaw, David Willcocks, Gregg Smith, Eric Ericson, Kenneth Jennings. *Compositions:* Choral music published by Augsburg, Kjos, Hal Leonard, Mark Foster. *Hobbies:* Tennis; Golf; Reading; Films. *Address:* Department of Music, University of New Mexico, Albuquerque, NM 87131, USA.

ELLIOTT Alasdair, b. 1954, Hamilton, Scotland. Singer (Tenor). *Education:* Studied at the Royal Scottish Academy in Glasgow and with Laura Sarti at the Guildhall School of Music; Further study at the Pears-Britten School of Advanced Musical Studies and the National Opera Studio. *Career:* Opera: Has sung with Kent Opera; Curzio (Nozzi di Figaro), Flich (Beggar's Opera); English Touring Opera; Ramiro (La Cenerentola), Belmonte (Il Seraglio), also for Glyndebourne Touring Opera; Opera Northern Ireland; Leicester (Maria Stuarda), Pedrillio (Il Seraglio); Scottish Opera; Squeak (Billy Budd), Basilio (Nozzi di Figaro), Iodas (Les Troyens), Rector (Peter Grimes); English National Opera; Jew (Salome), Priest (Christmas Eve), Andrés (Wozzeck), Servant, (The Baccai, John Buller, World Premiere); ROH; Fisherman (Guillaume Tell), Gelsomina (Il Viaggio a Reims), Vogel Gesang (Die Meistersinger Von Nürnberg), Priest (Die Zauberflöte), Junger Deiner (Electra); CBTO, Calasis (Les Boréades, Rameau) Covent Garden Festival Opera; Tamino (Die Zauberflöte); Edinburgh International Festival; Gerry (Tourist Variations, James Macmillan, World Premiere); Netherlands Opera; Host (Benvenutu Cellini); Drottingholm Court Theatre; Armida (Haydn); Opera Comique; Azeste (Ascanio in Alba); Concerts: Spain, Switzerland, Holland, Canada, Trevor Pinnock and the English Concert, LMP, Jane Glover (including the first performance of the Vessel, Stephen Oliver); Recitals: Queen's Hall, Edinburgh; Jubilee Hall, Aldeburgh; Purcell Room, Wigmore Hall, ROH, London. *Recordings*

include: Arturo in La Straniera by Bellini. *Address:* c/o Athole Still Ltd., Greystoke House, 80-86 Weston Street, London SE19 3AF, England.

ELLIOTT Anthony, b. 3 Sept 1948, Rome, New York, USA. Conductor; Concert Cellist. m. Paula Sokol, 9 June 1975, 4 daughters. *Education:* Rome Free Academy, Rome, New York, USA; Performers Certificate, 1969, School of Music, Indiana University; Bachelor of Music with Distinction, 1970, Indiana University. *Debut:* St Lawrence Centre of Performing Arts, Toronto, Ontario, Canada. *Career:* Soloist with Detroit Symphony, New York Philharmonic, CBC Toronto Orchestra, Minnesota Orchestra, Vancouver Symphony, Colorado Philharmonic; Recitals broadcast on NET, NPR and CBC, including premiere performances of 20th century compositions; formerly Musical Director, University Symphony Orchestra, Western Michigan University; formerly Assistant Music Director, Marrowstone Music Festival; presently Professor of Music, University of Houston; Music Director of the Houston Youth Symphony and Ballet. *Recordings:* Solo cellist: Ravel, Mother Goose (complete ballet) Vox Records (2); Ravel, La Valse and Alborada del Gracioso, Vox Records; Ravel, Une Barque sur L'Ocean Vox; Rimsky-Korsakov, Russian Easter Overture, CBC Records; Holst, The Planets; CBC; Koch International Classics Series, Music by Slavic Composers. *Hobbies:* Reading; Outdoor sports. *Address:* School of Music, University of Houston, Houston, TX 77204, USA.

ELLIOTT David John, b. 15 Mar 1958, London, England. Director of Music. *Education:* B.Mus., Royal Holloway College, University of London, 1979; Music Teacher's Certificate, University of London Institute of Education, 1981; MA, Music Education, 1985. *Career:* Music Teacher, Strode's College, Egham, Surrey, 1980; Music Teacher, The Latymer School, Edmonton, London, 1981-, Director of Music, 1987-; Part-time Lecturer in Music Education, Middlesex University, 1989-92. *Contributions to:* British Journal of Music Education, Volume I, 1984 and Volume IV, 1987. *Memberships:* Incorporated Society of Musicians; National Trust. *Hobbies:* Entertaining; Food & Drink; European Travel, especially Venice. *Address:* 60 Gladbeck Way, Enfield, Middlesex EN2 7EL, England.

ELLIOTT Martin Alastair, b. 28 May 1954, London, England. Concert Singer. *Education:* Westminster Abbey Choir School, 1964-67; King's School Canterbury, 1968-72; MA, Philosophy, Politics, Economics, Choral Scholar, Christ Church, Oxford, 1973-76; Guildhall School of Music & Drama, 1976-77. *Debut:* Barbican, London. *Career:* Director, Wren Singers, 1978-; Solo Singer: Ballet Rambert, 1981-83; Soloist, Title Music, BBC TV Film, Cruel Garden, by Ballet Rambert; Soloist, Crucible Theatre, Sheffield, 1983-84; Actor, BBC TV Serial By The Sword Divided, 1985; German Debut, Kurhaussaall, Wiesbaden, 1985; Debut with London Symphony Orchestra, Barbican Concert Hall, 1985; Founder, Wren Consort, 1986; Founder, Wren Music, 1987; Voice Tutor, Ardingly School, W. Sussex, 1989-; Norwegian Debut: Essette Imar, Giorgios Koumendakis, 1990; Founder and Director of the Wren Baroque Soloists, 1992; Voice Tutor, Brighton College, Sussex, Eastbourne College, Sussex, 1991-. *Recordings:* London Early Music Group, Tudor Music; Singcircle - A Vinao Son Entero; A Caldara, Madrigals and Cantatas, Wren Baroque Soloists, S Montague, Tigida Pipa, Singcircle. *Hobbies:* Bridge; Travel; Swimming; Sailing. *Current Management:* Wren Music UK. *Address:* 8 Park Lane, Selsey, Sussex PO20 0HD, England.

ELLIOTT Paul, b. 19 Mar 1950, Macclesfield, Cheshire, England. Tenor; Teacher. m. Wendy Gillespie, 1982, 2 sons.*Education:* Chorister, St Paul's Cathedral, London, England, 1959-62; The King's School, Canterbury, 1964-69; Choral Scholar, Magdalen College, Oxford 1969-72; BA 1973, MA 1977, University of Oxford; Principal voice teachers: David Johnston and Peter Pears. *Career:* Vicar choral, St Paul's Cathedral, 1972-75; Member, John Alldis Choir, 1972-76;

Cantores in Ecclesia, 1972-76; Schutz Choir of London, 1972-78; Monteverdi Choir, 1973-78; Founder-member, Hilliard Ensemble, 1974-84; London Early Music Group, 1976-79; Vocal consort member, Consort of Musicke, 1972-74; Academy of Ancient Music, 1973-; Early Music Consort of London, 1973-76; Deller Consort, 1973-82; Baccholian Singers of London, 1974-82; Newberry Consort, Chicago, 1984-89; Tours of Europe and USA as solo concert artist; Operatic engagements including: Handel's Acis in St Gall, 1984, Mozart's Belmonte Indiana University, 1988, Mozart's Arbace in Chicago, 1988, Handel's Jonathan (Saul, staged), San Antonio Festival, 1986, Consort member, Music Everywhere, 1986-; Artist-in-residence, Washington University, St Louis, 1984, 1985; Visiting Lecturer, Indiana University School of Music, Bloomington, 1985-87; Associate Professor of Music, Early Music Institute, Indiana University School of Music, 1987-92; Professor of Music, 1992-; Participant in various workshops and seminars. *Recordings:* Numerous discs as member of various vocal ensembles; Many discs as soloist in works by Bach, Handel, Purcell. *Memberships:* National Early Music Association, NEMA; Early Music America, EMA; National Association of Teachers of Singing, NATS America. *Current Management:* Ariëtte Drost, Europe; California Artists Management, USA and Canada. *Address:* 3702 Tamorron Dr, Bloomington, IN 47408, USA.

ELLIOTT Vernon Pelling, b. 27 July 1912, Surrey, England. Bassoonist; Conductor; Composer. m. Nora Janne Mukle, 25 Sept 1937, 2d. *Education:* Royal College of Music, 1934-36. *Debut:* Bournemouth, 1937. *Career includes:* Principal Bassoonist: Bournemouth Orchestra, 1936-38, Sadler's Wells Opera and Ballet, 1938-39; Royal Opera Covent Garden, 1949-53; English Opera Group and Aldeburgh Festival, 1954-60; Assistant and Sub Principal Philharmonia Orchestra, 1945-75; Principal Woodwind Coach, Kent Youth Orchestra, 1963-87; Professor: Royal College of Music, 1941-45, Trinity College of Music, 1945-86 and London College of Music, 1970-72. *Compositions:* Television music for films for children; Double Bass solo, Odd Man Out; Wind quintet, Woodbridge Sketches. *Recordings:* Turn of the Screw, Britten; Instruments of the Orchestra; Brandenburg Concerto No 1 in F major; Mozart Seranader for 13 wind. *Honours:* Edwin F James Prize, RCM, 1935; Hon FTCL, 1963. *Hobbies:* Sailing; Skiing; Riding; Bee-keeping; Winemaking. *Current Management* Rachael Macdonald Concert Direction, 13a Palmerston Road, London N22 4QH. *Address:* 12 Ash Close, Woodbridge, Suffolk IP12 4BP, England.

ELLIS Brent, b. 20 June 1944, Kansas City, Missouri. Singer (Baritone). *Education:* Studied with Daniel Ferro in New York and with Luigi Ricci in Rome. *Debut:* Washington DC 1967, in the premiere of Ginastera's Bomarzo. *Career:* Santa Fe Opera from 1972, notably as Mozart's Figaro, in the 1982 premiere of Rochberg's The Confidence Man and as Kunrad in Strauss's Feuersnot; New York City Opera debut 1974, as Ottone in L'Incoronazione di Poppea; Glyndebourne from 1977, as Ford in Falstaff, Marcello, Don Giovanni and Germont in the Peter Hall production of La Traviata; Metropolitan Opera from 1979, as Silvio in Pagliacci, Rossini's Figaro and Donizetti's Belcore; Opera North, Leeds, as Scarpia and Macbeth; Welsh National Opera as Zurga in Les Pêcheurs de Perles; Cologne Opera from 1984, in La Gazza Ladra, Wozzeck, Rigoletto and Eine Florentinische Tragödie by Zemlinsky; Appearances in the premieres of Pasatieri's Washington Square for Michigan Opera and The Seagull for Seattle Opera; Sang Germont at Glyndebourne, 1987, Santa Fe, 1989, also Kunrad in Feuersnot, 1988; San Francisco, 1989, as Iago, followed by Rigoletto at Covent Garden; Season 1992 as Amonasro at Seattle; Concert appearances in Mahler's 8th Symphony with the Chicago Symphony and with orchestras in San Francisco, Minnesota, Baltimore, Houston and Denver; Great Woods Festival with Michael Tilson Thomas. *Address:* c/o Harrison/Parrott Ltd., 12 Penzance Place, London W11 4PA, England.

ELLIS David, b. 10 Mar 1933, Liverpool, England.

Composer. *Education:* Liverpool Institute 1944-51; Royal Manchester College of Music 1953-57; FRNCM, ARMCM. *Career:* BBC Music Producer 1964-77; BBC Head of Music 1977-86; Artistic Director, Northern Chamber Orchestra 1986-. *Compositions:* Sinfonietta, 1953; String Trio 1954; Dewpoint for soprano, clarinet and strings 1955; Piano Sonata; Diversions on a theme of Purcell for strings 1956; Violin Concerto 1958; Opera Crito 1963; Magnificat and Nunc Dimittis for choir and organ 1964; Elegy for orchestra 1966; Fanfares and Cadenzas for orchestra 1968; Carols for an Island Christmas 1971; Symphony No.1 1973; Solus for strings 1973; L for orchestra 1977; Sonata for solo double bass 1977; String Quartet No. 1 1980; Berceuse for clarinet and piano 1981; Aubade for horn and piano 1981; Suite Française for strings 1987. *Honours:* Royal Philharmonic Prize 1956; Royal College of Music Patrons' Award 1956; Theodore Holland Award 1957; Royal Manchester Institution Silver Medal 1957; Ricordi Prize 1957. *Address:* Vassaras, 14 Patch Lane, Bramhall, Cheshire, England.

ELLIS Gregory Charles, b. 3 Nov 1960, Preston, Lancashire, England. Violinist. m. Leslie Gail Toney, 22 Dec 1985, 2 daughters, 1 son. *Education:* Royal Academy of Music, London; DipRAM, 1983; ARAM, 1989; Student of Carmel Kaine, Frederick Grinke, Shmuel Ashkenasi. *Debut:* Wigmore Hall, London. *Career:* Violinist and Leader, Vanbrugh String Quartet, resident to Radio Telefis Eireann; Frequent tours, UK, Europe, North and South America; Broadcasts on Radio 3, BBC World Service, RTE TV and Radio, Sky Channel (Arts), US and Canadian Radio, French TV, Brasilian and Mexican TV. *Recordings:* C.D., Collins Classics; Hyperion, Meridian, Chandos. *Honour:* Vanbrugh String Quartet 1st British string quartet to win the London International String Quartet Competition, 1988. *Hobbies:* Aikido; Yoga; Gardening. *Current Management:* Neil Chaffey Concert Promotions. *Address:* Vanbrugh House, Castle Treasure, Douglas, Co Cork, Republic of Ireland.

ELLIS James Antony, b. 5 Mar 1954, Ashton-under-Lyne, England. Composer and Conductor. m. Fiona Anne Johnson, 25 Feb 1978, 4 daughters. *Education:* Music Scholar, King's College, Cambridge, 1972-75; MA (Cantab); MMus, King's College, London, 1982. *Career:* Violinist Member of Royal Philharmonic Orchestra, 1977-80; Violinist Member, Philharmonia, 1980-81; Assistant Tutor, King's College, London, 1982-84; Lecturer in Music, University of Keele, 1984-86; Composer-in-Residence, National Centre of Orchestral Studies, Goldsmiths' College, London, 1986-87; Lecturer in music, City University, 1989-; Conductor, Thames Chamber Players, Oxford Haydn Players. Appearances with National Centre of Orchestral Studies, European Community Youth Orchestra, Capricorn. *Compositions:* Works include: Chamber (String Quartet No. 1); Summer Song; Works for Piano: Sonata No. 1; Autumn Tale, piano and orchestra (Serenata), orchestra (Variations, 1979; Festive Fanfare; Prelude, dream sequence and the song of the washerwomen, from Yerma (opera); Appearances; The Name of the Rose (forthcoming); Chamber ensemble; Summer cycle including Summer Night; Summer's Apotheose; String Quartet 1 and 2 (L'Eveil Av Désir); Canti Cantici (Libro 1). *Contributions to:* Music Analysis (Editorial Assistant) and Contributor of reviews. *Address:* 2 Stanley Avenue, Chesham, Buckinghamshire HP5 2JF, England.

ELLIS Osian Gwynn, b. 8 Feb 1928, Ffynnongroew, Flint, Wales. Harpist. m. Rene Ellis Jones, 1951, 2 sons. *Education:* Royal Academy of Music. *Career:* Numerous radio & television broadcasts; Recitals, concerts, all over the world; Shared poetry & music recitals with Dame Peggy Ashcroft, Paul Robeson, Burton, C. Day-Lewis, etc. Member, Melos Ensemble; Solo harpist with London Symphony Orchestra; Professor of Harp, Royal Academy of Music, 1959-89; Works Written for him include: Harp Concertos by Hoddinott 1957, Mathias 1970, Jersild 1972, Gian Carlo Menotti 1977, William Schuman 1978; From 1960 worked with Benjamin Britten who wrote for him Harp Suite in C (opus 83), & (for performance with Sir Peter Pears), Canticle V, Birthday Hansel, folk songs. With Sir Peter Pears on recital tours, Europe & USA, 1974-. *Recordings include:* Concertos; Recitals; Folk Songs; etc. *Publications:* The Story of the Harp in Wales, 1991. *Honours:* Film, The Harp, Paris award; Others include Grand Prix du Disque, French Radio Critics' Award. FRAM, 1960; CBE, 1971; Hon.D.Mus., U.Wales, 1970. *Membership:* Former member, Music & Welsh Advisory Committees, British Council. *Address:* 90 Chandos Avenue, London N20, England.

ELLISON Joan Audrey, b. Workington, Cumbria, England. Food Consultant; Writer. m. Donald Roy Ellison, 24 Aug 1954, divorced 1975, 1 son, 1 daughter. *Education:* BSc., Honours; FIFST; FLS; FIHE; Music Studies, University of Oslo, 1952. *Career:* J Audrey Ellison, International Artists Management, 1989; Former Honorary Secretary, now UK Representative, International Liszt Centre for 19th Century Music; Newsletter Editor, Liszt Society, 1987; Publicity and Information officer, British Kodály Society; Former Honorary secretary, Treasurer, The Rudolf Kempe Society; Former Chairman, The Chopin Society. *Publications:* Norman Tucker, Musician Before & after 2 Decades at Sadler's Wells, 1978; In Memoriam, NWGT 1910-78, 1978. *Contributions to:* Music & Musicians. *Honours:* Liszt Medal of Honour, Hungarian Ministry of Culture & Education, 1986. *Hobbies:* Music; Travel; Study of New Useful Plants. *Address:* 135 Stevenage Road, Fulham, London SW6 6PB, England.

ELMING Poul, b. 1949, Aalborg, Denmark. Singer (Tenor). *Education:* Studied at the Conservatoires in Aalborg and Aarhus, and with Paul Lohmann in Wiesbaden. *Debut:* Sang in recital from 1978. *Career:* Performed baritone roles with Jutland Opera, Aarhus, from 1979; Royal Opera Copenhagen from 1984, as Mozart's Count, Eugene Onegin, Malatesta and Verdi's Germont, Posa and many other roles; Further Private Studies with Susanna Eken of the Royal Danish Music Conservatory and Professor Oren Brown of the Juilliard School of Music, New York, and made his tenor debut as Parsifal at The Royal Opera, Copenhagen in 1989; Has sung Erik in Der fliegende Holländer and Spalanzani in Les contes d'Hoffmann; Bayreuth Festival, Covent Garden, Deutsche Oper Berlin and the Vienna Staatsoper, Hannover and Mannheim, 1990-, as Siegmund in Die Walküre and Parsifal; Many recitals and concerts, including appearances with the Danish Radio Symphony Orchestra in Copenhagen. *Address:* c/o Ingpen and Williams Ltd, 14 Kensington Court, London, W8 5DN, England.

ELMORE Cenieth Catherine, b. 4 July 1930, North Carolina, USA. Professor of Music. *Education:* BMus, University of North Carolina, 1953; MMus Composition, 1962; MA Musicology, 1963, PhD Musicology, 1972, UNC Chapel Hill. *Career:* Private Piano Teacher, 1953-60; Teacher of Piano Music Theory, Musicology and Piano Pedagogy, Campbell University, 1963-; Piano Recitalist, Adjudicator, Lecturer; Part-time Church Organist. *Compositions:* A Secular Cantata, with Text by Thomas Wolf; Five Piano Pieces; American Carolina Suite for Piano. *Publications:* Article, A Secular Cantata with Text by Thomas Wolf, reviewed in The Thomas Wolf Review. *Honours:* Professorship, 1992; Biography in Contemporary American Composers Based at American Colleges and Universities. *Memberships:* American Musicological Society; North Carolina Music Teachers Association; North Carolina Federation of Music Clubs; Raleigh Piano Teachers Association. *Hobbies:* Painting; Flower gardening; Reading; Travel. *Address:* Route 2 Box 377, Franklinton, NC 27525, USA

ELMS Lauris, b. 20 Oct 1931, Melbourne, Australia. Singer (Contralto). *Education:* Studied with Katherine Wielaert in Melbourne and Dominique Modesti in Paris. *Career:* Sang in concerts and oratorios, then made stage debut at Covent Garden, 1957, as Ulrica (Un Ballo in Maschera); Appeared with the Royal Opera on tour, and in London as Mrs Sedley in Peter Grimes; Returned to Australia 1959 and sang with local companies as Azucena, Lucretia, Olga and the Princess in Suor Angelica; Toured with J C Williamson's Company, 1965, as Arsace in Semiramide (with Joan Sutherland). *Recordings:* Peter Grimes and highlights from Graun's Montezuma and the Bononcini's Griselda. Video of Il Trovatore, from Sydney Opera House. *Address:* c/o Australian Opera, Sydney Opera House, New South Wales, Australia

ELMS Roderick James Charles, b. 18 Oct 1951, Ilford, England. Pianist/Organist. *Education:* Licentiate, Guildhall School of Music, 1965; Licentiate, Royal Academy of Music, 1970; Fellow, Royal College of Organists, 1974. *Debut:* Wigmore Hall and Purcell Room, 1976. *Career:* Regular Recitalist on Organ and Piano; Participant in Recordings and Public Concerts given by all major Symphony Orchestras, some broadcast on Radio or Television; Member of GNAFF Ensemble, with which made successful Television debut, December, 1982. *Compositions:* Numerous arrangements and original compositions performed and broadcast by BBC; Several Christmas arrangements recorded on Christmas Gift; Original Music to Love is a Gift recorded on Just For Today. *Recordings:* Numerous works recorded with orchestras and choirs; Organ Music of Percy Whitlock, album on the Libra label; Solo piano album for Weinberger, London. *Honours:* Kate-Steele Prize for piano playing, Royal Academy of Music, 1973; Fellow, Royal Society of Arts, 1979. *Memberships:* Royal Academy of Music Club, Royal College of Organists. *Hobbies:* Sound Recording; Photography. *Address:* 23 Bethell Avenue, Cranbrook, Ilford, Essex, IG1 4UX, England.

ELSTE Rudolf Otto Martin, b. 11 Sept 1952, Bremen, Federal Republic of Germany. Musicologist; Discologist; Music Critic. *Education:* University of Cologne; Rheinische Musikschule, Cologne; King's College, London University, England; Dr Phil, Technische Universität, West Berlin. *Career:* Curator, Staatliches Institut für Musikforschung Preussischer Kulturbesitz, 1982-; Review Editor, IASA Phonographic Bulletin, 1983-92; Chairman, IASA Discography Committee; Consulting Musicologist, Bach-Tage Berlin, 1986-87. *Publications:* Internationale Heinrich Schütz Diskographie, 1928-72, 1972; Verzeichnis deutschsprachiger Musiksoziologie, 1975; Bachs Kunst der Fuge auf Schallplatten, 1981; Musikinstrumenten-Museum Berlin, 1986 (with other contributors), Handwerk im Dienste der Musik, 1987 (with other contributors); 100 Jahre Berliner Musikinstrumenten-Museum, 1988, (with other contributors); Kleines Tonträger-Lexikon, 1989; Kielklaviere, 1991, with other contributors; Musikalische Interpretation, 1992 (with other contributors). *Contributions to:* The New Grove; Fono Forum; Fanfare; Die Musikforschung. *Address:* Regensburger Strasse 5a, D-10777 Berlin, Germany.

ELTON Antony, b. 3 July 1935, Romford, Essex, England. Composer; Pianist. 2 sons, 2 daughters. *Education:* Royal Academy of Music, 1952-53, 1955-56, LRAM (Piano); BMus, Durham University, 1966-68; MMus, Surrey University, 1976-77. *Career:* RAF Music, 1953-55; NZBC, NZ Ballet, 1957-62; Australian Ballet ABC, 1962-65; Head of Music, Durham Technical College, 1968-72; Tutor, Lecturer, Nigeria, Nsukka, 1973-76; Music Director, Durham Theatre Company, 1978-82; Tutor: Beamish Hall, Billingham College, and Open University Summer Schools. *Compositions:* Song cycles: Lyrical Love Songs; The Poet's Soul; Songs of Women; Canine Epitaphs; Piano Suites, Chamber Music, Operas: The Senate meets; The Trojan Women; Ballets: The Exile, Anne Frank, Fate; Cantata for Chorus and Orchestra; Symphony in 1 movement; Sonata for Trumpets and Organ; Sonata for two pianos; Pantomime, Rannulf the Rover; More recently, Russian Impressions, piano; Heart of Albania, violin suite; Italiano; Finnish Suite; Memories of Portugal; Devon 1,2,3,4 for flute; Bulgarian Excursion; Spain Then and Now; 4 Woodwind quartets, 1992. *Publications:* Music and Life, 1985; Memoirs, 1988; Youth Love and Age, 1990; Songs of Life and Death, A Female Heart, Love

Found and Lost, 1992; 500 articles for Durham Advertisesr, 1978-86; Books: The Kovac Letters, Not Always Music. *Address:* Mole Cottage, 17 Prospect Terr, New Brancepeth, Durham DH7 7EJ, England.

ELVIRA Pablo, b. 24 Sept 1938, San Juan, Puerto Rico. Singer (Baritone). *Education:* Studied at the Pablo Casals Conservatory, Puerto Rico. *Debut:* Indiana University, Bloomington, as Rigoletto, 1968. *Career:* Sang at opera houses in Santa Fe, San Diego and New Orleans; New York City Opera from 1974, debut as Germont; Metropolitan Opera from 1978, as Rigoletto, Lescaut, Rossini's Figaro and Don Carlo in Ernani and La Forza del Destino; Chicago Lyric Opera 1985, as Germont; Other roles include Berg's Wozzeck and Strauss's Mandryka; Sang Sharpless in Madam Butterfly at Pittsburgh, 1989; Also performs in concert. *Recordings include:* Amore dei Tre Re (RCA); Cavalleria Rusticana; La Favorita. *Address:* c/o Pittsburgh Opera Inc., 711 Penn Avenue, 8th Floor, Pittsburgh, PA 15222, USA.

ELWES John, b. 1946, England. Singer (Tenor). *Education:* Studied with Gorge Malcolm at Westminster Cathedral; Further study at the Royal College of Music. *Career:* Chorister at Westminster Cathedral; Soloist in Britten's Missa brevis and Abraham and Isaac; Frequent broadcaster for the BBC; Repertoire includes Baroque, Lieder and contemporary music on the concert platform and operas by Gluck, Handel, Mozart and Monteverdi on stage; Sang Orfeo in Monteverdi's opera with Phillipe Herreweghe and La Chapelle Royale at the Montpellier opera house and with Flanders Opera, Antwerp, 1989-90. *Recordings include:* Orfeo in The Death of Orpheus by Stefano Landi, with Tragicomedia directed by Stephen Stubbs. *Address:* c/o Allied Artists Agency, 42 Montpelier Square, London, SW7 1JZ.

EMERSON Stephen Harold, b. 26 Dec 1948, Southgate, California, USA. Cellist. m. Linda Lee Allen, 23 Aug 1969, 4 sons. *Education:* BA, California State University, Long Beach, 1971; MM, Hartt School of Music, 1974; Cello studies with Eileen Strang, Naoum Benditzky, Paul Olefsky and Raya Garbousova. *Career:* Member, Hartford Symphony, 1972-74; Principal Cello, Hartford Chamber Orchestra, 1973-74; Member, Utah Symphony, 1974-; Assistant Principal Cello, Utah Symphony, 1978-; Member, New Hartford String Quartet, 1972-73; Co-Founder, Member, Cantilena String Trio, 1975-78; Member, Salt Lake Chamber Ensemble, 1986-88; Adjunct Assistant Professor of Music, University of Utah, 1988-; Part time faculty, Brigham Young University, 1991-; Member, Desret Piano Quartet, 1991-. *Hobbies:* Chess; Reading; Drawing; Sports. *Address:* 1968 Bryan Avenue, Salt Lake City, UT 84108, USA.

EMMERLICH Gunther, b. 18 Sept 1944, Thuringia, Germany. Singer (bass). *Education:* Studied in Weimar and Dresden and with Pavel Lisitsian. *Debut:* Sang the Peasant in Die Kluge by Orff at the Dresden Staatsoper, 1978. *Career:* Appeared as Kuno in Der Freischutz at the re-opening of the Semper Oper, Dresden, and has sung with the Dresden ensemble at the Vienna Volksoper and in Amsterdam (Don Alfonso, 1988); Other roles have included Osmin (Die Entführung), Geronimo (Matrimonio Segreto), Rocco, Dulcamara and the Hermit in Der Freischütz; Many concert appearances. *Recordings:* Der Freischütz; Eugene Onegin. *Address:* c/o Staatsoper, 8012 Dresden, Germany.

EMMERSON Simon Thomas, b. 15 Sept 1950, Wolverhampton, England. Lecturer; Composer. *Education:* BA, Cambridge, 1972; PhD, City University London, 1982. *Career:* City University London: Visiting Lecturer, 1976-78; Lecturer, Senior Lecturer then Reader in Music, 1978-; Director of Electroacoustic Music Studio. *Compositions:* Ophelia's Dream, voices, electronics; Time Past IV, voice, electronics; Shades of Night and Day, piano, electronics; Pathways, guitar, tablas, flute, cello, electronics; Sentences, soprano electronics; Antiphonies, 2 pianos. *Recordings:*

Ophelia's Dream II; Time Past IV; Piano Piece IV; Shades of Night and Day; Songs from Time Regained. *Publications:* Editor and contributor to The Language of Electroacoustic Music, 1986; also Contemporary Music Review, and Computer Music Association Proceedings. *Honours:* First Prize, Bourges Electroacoustic Awards, 1985. *Memberships:* Sonic Arts Network; SPNM; Royal Society of Musicians; Association of Professional Composers. *Address:* 15 Holligrave Road, Bromley, Kent BR1 3PJ, England.

ENCINAS Ignacio, b. 1958, Spain. Singer (Tenor). *Education:* Studied with Enzo Costantini and in Madrid; Master classes with Gianni Poggi and Gino Bechi. *Career:* Sang in Trovatore and La Favourita at the Santander Festival, Rigoletto at the Zarzuela Theatre Madrid and appeared further in Oviedo, Vallodilid and Malaga; At Dijon has sung in Norma (Pollione), Traviata (Alfredo), Rigoletto and Ballo in maschera (Riccardo); Season 1989-90 as Maurizio (Adriana Lecouvreur) at Liege, returning as Turiddu and Rodolfo (Le Boheme); Sang in Verdi's Attila at the Theatro Romano of Benevento and as Macduff in a concert performance of Macbeth at the 1990 Gstaad Festival; Performances of Nabucco in Nimes and Puritani (as Arturo at Marseille, 1990-91). *Honours:* Winner of numerous international competitions. *Address:* c/o Opera de Marseille, 2 Rue Moliere, F-1321 Mareseille Cedex 1, France.

ENDERLE Matthias, b. 16 June 1956, Switzerland. Violinist. *Education:* Studied at the Winterthur Conservatory, in Indiana, the University International Menuhin Academy in Gstaad. *Career:* Co-founder and leader of the Carmina Quartet 1984; Appearances from 1987 in Europe, Israel, Japan, USA; Regular concerts at the Wigmore Hall from Oct 1987; Concerts at the South Bank Centre, London, Amsterdam Concertgebouw, the Kleine Philharmonie in Berlin, Konzertverein Vienna; Four engagements in Paris 1990-91, seven in London; Tours in Australasia, the USA, Japan; concerts at the Hohenems, Graz, Hong Kong, Montreux, Schleswig-Holstein, Bath, Lucerne, Prague Spring Festivals; Collaborations with Dietrich Fischer-Dieskau, Olaf Bär and Mitsuko Uchida. *Recordings:* Albums for Ex Libris, Bayer, Claves and Denon, 1991. *Honour:* Joint winner (with members of Carmina Quartet) Paolo Borciani String Quartet Competition in Reggio Emilia, Italy, 1987; Gramophone prize for Best Chamber Music Recording, 1992. *Address:* c/o Intermusica Artists' Management, 16 Duncan Terrace, London N1 8BZ, England.

ENDO Akira, b. 16 Nov 1938, Shido, Japan. Conductor. *Education:* Studied violin with Vera Barstow, Eudice Shapiro, Jascha Heifetz; BM, MM 1962, University of Southern California, Los Angeles. *Career:* Violinist, Trojan String Quartet, 1960-62; 2nd violinist, Pacific String Quartet, 1962-69; Conductor, Long Beach (California) Symphony Orchestra, 1966-69; West Side Symphony Orchestra, Los Angeles, 1968-69; Music Director, American Ballet Theatre, NY, 1969-79; Resident Conductor, Houston Symphony Orchestra, 1974-76; Music Director, Austin (Texas) Symphony Orchestra, 1975-82; Louisville Orchestra, 1980-83.

ENGEL Karl, b. 1 June 1923, Basle, Switzerland. Concert Pianist. m. Barbara Wackernagel, 26 Oct 1976, 1 son, 1 daughter. *Education:* Humanistisches Gymnasium Basle; Basle Conservatory with Paul Baumgartner; Ecole Normale Paris with Alfred Cortot. *Career:* International career as concert pianist since 1948; Cycles of all Mozart piano sonatas in Paris, Berlin, Munich, Salzburg, Vienna, Zurich; Cycles of all Beethoven piano sonatas in West Germany and Tel-Aviv; Series of all Mozart piano concertos in Salzburg; Concert tours in Europe, USA, Japan; Guest of all major music festivals in Europe; Chamber music with Pablo Casals (Prades), Menuhin, Tortelier and Fournier; Lieder recitals with Dietrich Fischer-Dieskau, Hermann Prey and Peter Schreier; 1959-86 Professsor of piano at Hochschule für Musik Hanover; Masterclass at Bern Conservatory. *Recordings:* Complete piano works of Schumann, Audvis/France; Complete Mozart piano concertos with the Mozarteum Orchestra conducted by Leopold Hager (Teldec); Complete solo piano music by Mozart (Teldec); Chamber music and Lieder (Deutsche Grammophon, Electrola). *Honour:* Prize, Queen Elisabeth Competition Belgium 1952. *Membership:* Schweizerischer Tonkunstlerverein. *Hobbies:* Chess; Walking. *Current Management:* Konzertgesellschaft Zurich, Steinwiesstrasse 2, CH 8032, Zurich. *Address:* 2 Chemin des Frenes, CH 1805, Jongny (VD), Switzerland.

ENGELER Margaret, b. 1 Aug 1933, Heiden, Switzerland. Musicologist. m. Erwin Engeler, 14 Apr 1956, 1 son, 1 daughter. *Education:* Dr Phil, University of Zurich, 1980. *Publications:* Das Musikleben im Launde Appenzell dargestellt anhand der Schriftlichen Quellen, 1979; Das Bezichungsfeld Zwischen Volkmusik, Volksmusiker und Volkmusikpflege, Verlag Schlapfer, 1984; Briefe an Volkmar Andreae, Ein halbes Jahrhundert Zurcher Musikleben 1902-1959, 1986; Das Zürcher Konzertleben, Rothenhäusler, 1990; Unterhaltungsmusik am Schweizer Radio, 1993. *Contributions to:* Swissair Gazette; Schweiz Musiker Revue; Schweiz Archiv f Volkskkunde. *Honour:* Forderpreis, FDP Frauen der Stadt Zurich, 1986. *Memberships:* Schweiz Tonkunstlerverein; Schweiz Gesellschaft für Volkmusik (GVS); International Council for Traditional Music (ICTM). *Address:* zum Sillerblick 6, CH-8053 Zurich, Switzerland.

ENGELMANN Hans Ulrich, b. 8 Sept 1921, Darmstadt, Germany. Composer; Professor. *Education:* Studied composition with Fortner, Heidelberg, 1945-49, with Leibowitz and Krenek, Darmstadt, 1948-50; Musicology with Gennrich and Osthoff, Philosophy with Adorno, University of Frankfurt am Main, PhD, 1952. *Career:* Music Advisor, Hessisches Landestheater, Darmstadt, 1954-61; Lecturer 1969-73; Professor 1973-, in composition, Hochschule für Musik, Frankfurt am Main. *Compositions:* Operas: Doktor Fausts Hollenfahrt, 1949-50; Verlorener Schatten, 1960; Der Fall Van Damm, 1966-67; Music Theatre pieces; Ballets: Ballet Colore, 1948; Noche de Luna, 1958; Serpentina, 1962-63; Incidental music to plays; Film scores; Orchestral: Kaleidoskop, suite, 1941; Concerto for Cello and Strings, 1948; Musik for Strings, Brass and Percussion, 1948; Impromptu, 1949; Leopoldskron for Chamber Orchestra, 1949; Orchester-Fantasie, 1951, revised as Symphony No 1, 1963; Partita, 1953; Strukturen for Chamber Orchestra, 1954; 5 Orchestra Pieces, 1956; Polifonica for Chamber Orchestra, 1957; Ezra Pound Music, 1959; Trias for Piano, Orchestra and Tape, 1962; Shadows, 1964; Sonata for Jazz orchestra, 1967; Capricciosi, 1968; Symphony No 2, 1968; Sinfonia da Camera for Chamber Orchestra, 1981; Stele für Buchner, canto sinfonico for Soloist, Chorus and Orchestra, 1986; Chamber: Cello Sonata, 1948; String Quartet, 1952; Integrale for Saxophone and Piano, 1954; Permutazioni for Flute, Oboe, Clarinet and Bassoon, 1959; Timbres for Harp, Celesta, Piano, Percussion and Tape, 1963; Mobile II for Clarinet and Piano, 1968; Modelle I oder I Love You Babi for Amplified Instruments, 1970, and II for Trombone and Percussion Ensemble, 1970; Les chansons for Chamber Ensemble, 1982; Epitah for trumpet and piano, 1983; Chamber-Symphonie, 1984; Stele for Chorus, Solists, Symphonie Orchestra, 1987; Duettini for Piano and Percussion, 1984; Piano pieces; Choral music, including cantatas; New Works: Dialogue Piano Percussion, 1991; Clarinota, 1991; Tastenstück, 1991. *Publication:* Bela Bartóks Mikrokosmos, 1953; Monografie Commedia humana. *Address:* Park Rosenhohe, Engelweg 15, 6100 Darmstadt, Germany.

ENGEN Keith, b. 5 Apr 1925, Irazee, Minnesota, USA. Singer (Bass). *Education:* Studied at Berkeley, California, and with Tino Pattiera and Pavel Ludikar in Vienna. *Career:* Appeared as concert singer; Stage debut Graz 1954; Bavarian State Opera Munich from 1955 in repertory operas and in the premieres of Hindemith's Harmonie der Welt (1957) and David Kirchner's Belshazar (1986); Bayreuth 1958, as King Henry in Lohengrin; Guest appearances in Germany,

Amsterdam, Turin, Florence, Buenos Aires and Edinburgh; Stuttgart 1968 in the premiere of Orff's Prometheus; Concert engagements in oratorios by Bach and Handel and in Lieder recitals. *Recordings:* Bach's B Minor Mass and St Matthew Passion, Fidelio, Orff's Oedipus der Tyrann and Schoenberg's Gurrrelieder (Deutsche Grammophon); Verdi's Giovanna d'Arco (HMV); Idomeneo (Telefunken); Prometheus (RCA); Strauss's Feuersnot (Acanta). *Address:* c/o Bavarian State Opera, Postfach 745, D-8000 Munich 1, Germany.

ENGERER Brigitte. b. 27 Oct 1952, Tunis, Algeria. French Pianist. *Education:* Commenced piano lessons with Lucette Descaves, Paris, at five years; 1st Prize, Paris Conservatory, aged 15; Studied with Stanislav Neuhaus, Moscow Conservatory, 1970-75. *Career:* Major career since 1975: Soloist with many of the leading orchestras including: Orchestre de Paris, Berlin Philharmonic Orchestra, London Symphony Orchestra, Vienna Symphony Orchestra, Chicago Symphony Orchestra with Daniel Baremboim, Czech Philharmonic Orchestra, Minnesota Orchestra, Los Angeles Philharmonic Orchestra, and Toronto Symphony; Numerous recitals around the world; Many festival appearances; Many TV appearances; Video with Switzerland Orchestra with Strauss Burlesque. *Recordings:* For Philips, Denon, Harmonia Mundi. *Honours:* 6th Prize, Long-Thibaud Competition, Paris, 1969; 6th prize, Tchaikovsky Competition, Moscow, 1974; 3rd prize, Queen Elisabeth of Belgium Competition, 1978; Grand Prix du Disque with Schumann Carnaval. *Address:* c/o ICM Artists Ltd, 40 West 57th Street, New York, NY 10019, USA.

ENGERT Ruth, b. 9 Oct 1946, Frankfurt-am-Main, Germany. Singer (Mezzo-soprano). *Education:* Studied at the Frankfurt Musikhochschule and with Josef Metternich in Cologne. *Career:* Sang at Koblenz, Freiburg and Hanover, 1969-79; Member of the Deutsche Oper Berlin from 1979, notably as Mozart's Cherubino and Dorabella, Verdi's Eboli and Meg Page, Wagner's Fricka, Brangaene and Waltraute; Octavian, Nicklausse in Les Contes d'Hoffmann and Charlotte in Die Soldaten; Guest appearans at Turin (Clytemnestra, 1987), Venice, (The Composer, Ariadne auf Naxos), Genoa, Madrid, and Lisbon; Bayreuth festival, 1989, as Venus in Tannhäuser; Sang Kundry at the Spoleto Festival in Italy and in Charleston USA, 1986-90; Octavian in Rosenkavalier at Catania, 1992, *Recordings:* Feuersnot by Strauss; Parsifal, Bayreuth, 1985; Die Walküre, Bayreuth, 1987; Eugene Onegin; Funeral Cantata by Cherubini.

ENGLISH Gerald, b. 6 Nov 1925, England. Lyric Tenor; Educator; Administrator. m. (1) Jennifer Ryan, 1954, 2 sons, 2 daughters, (2) Linda Jacoby, 1974, 1 son. *Education:* Royal College of Music. *Career:* After war service began career as lyric tenor, subsequently travelled, USA, Europe; appeared at Sadler's Wells, Covent Garden, Glyndebourne; often heard in operas by Mozart and Monteverdi, concert music by Bach, Stravinsky, Fauré and Dallapiccola; Professor, Royal College of Music, 1960-77; Director, Opera Studio, Victorian College for the Arts, Melbourne, Australia, 1977-. *Recordings:* For major gramophone companies. *Address:* c/o Victorian College for the Arts, 234 St. Kilda Road, Victoria 3003, Australia.

ENGLISH Jon (Arthur), b. 22 March 1942, Kankakee, Illinois. Composer; Trombonist; Percussionist; Double Bass Player. m. Candace Natwig. *Education:* Studied at the University of Illinois with Kenneth Gaburo, BM 1965. *Career:* Member of the Harry Partch Ensemble 1961-62, the Illinois Contemporary Chamber Players, 1963-66 and the Savannah Symphony Orchestra, 1967; Associate Artist of the University of Iowa Center for New Music and New Performing Arts until 1974; Has worked from Cologne since 1976; Performances in Europe as soloist, with Candace Natwig (singer) and in new- music groups. *Compositions include:* 404 1/2 E. Green Street for tape, 1965; Sequent Cycles for 6 players 1968; .... whose circumference is a nowhere 1970; Used Furniture Sale for tape 1971; Summerstalks for performer and tape 1973; Shagbolt for trombone 1978; Electrotrombonics 1979; Foursome 1979; Dog Dreams 1982; Harmonies for Charlie Mingus 1983. *Address:* c/o ASCAP, ASCAP Building, One Lincoln Plaza, New York, NY 10023, USA.

ENGLUND Sven Einer, b. 17 June 1916, Ljugarn, Gotland, Sweden. Composer; Pianist; Professor. m. (2) Maynie Sirén Smolander, 3 Oct 1958, 2 sons, 2 daughters. *Education:* Sibelius Academy, Helsinki, 1933-41; Tanglewood Music Center, USA, 1949. *Career:* Composer of numerous works, Professor; Lecturer in Composition and Music Theory, Sibelius Academy, 1957-81; Music Critic, Helsinki's daily, Hufvudsbladet, 1956-76. *Compositions include:* Symphony Nos. 1, 2, 3, 4, 5, 6, 7, 1976-88; Concerto for Cello and Orchestra, 1954, Piano and Orchestra, 1954, Piano and Orchestra, I, 1956, II, 1974, for Violin and Orchestra, 1981, for Flute and Orchestra, 1985, for 12 Cellos, 1981; Chamber music includes, Sonata for violin and piano, 1979; Sonata for Cello and Piano, 1982, Trio for piano, violin and cello, 1982; Works for solo instruments, Kanteletar-sarja, for women's choir, 1984, Works for the stage; Choral works; String Quartet, 1985; Concerto for Clarinet and Orchestra, 1991, Ep.Helsinki Festival, 1991. *Recordings:* Concerto for Piano and Orchestra No 1, EMI CD; The Complete Pianomusic; Concerto for Violin and Orchestra; Symphony No 1; Symphony No 2; Symphony No 4; Sonato for Cello and Piano; Serenade for Strings, Symphony No 5 (Fennica); Piano Trio; Sonata for violin and piano; Concerto for 12 cellos; Concerto fro flute and orchestra; Wind Quintet; Hymnus Sepulcralis. *Address:* Lallukan Taiteilijakoti, Appollonkatu 13 A 48, SF-00100 Helsinki 10, Finland.

ENGSTRÖM Bengt Olof, b. 25 May 1926, Umeå, Sweden. Orchestra & Concert Hall Executive. m. Anne-Marie Lemner, 19 Apr 1954, 2 sons, 1 daughter. *Education:* Graduated as: Music teacher 1949, Higher kantor 1951, Higher organist 1952, Swedish Royal Academy of Music. *Career:* Organist, music teacher, Iggesund, Sweden, 1952-55; Music teacher, Uppsala, Sweden, 1955-58; Music consultant, Stockholm, 1958-61; Manager, Norrköping Symphony Orchestra, 1961-64; Music consultant, Royal Board of Education, 1964-69; Lektor, Teachers Training College, Umeå, 1969-74; Secretary, Local Authorities Music Association, Stockholm, 1974-76; President, Stockholm Philharmonic Orchestra & Concert Hall, 1976-86. *Publications:* Form och stil i musiken, 1959; Brevkurs i musikhistoria, 1959-61; En bok om musik, 1966-69; Vi Gör musik, co-author, 1970-81; Lek med toner, co-author, 1971; Den Kommunala musikskolan, 1976; 75 år med Stockholms Konsertförening, 1977. *Memberships:* Music Education Committee, 1964-68; Board, Stockholm Conservatory of Music, 1976-87; Central Music Committee, 1984-88; Board, Royal Academy of Music (Deputy Chairman); Board, Konstnarsnamnden, 1985-91; Board, Stockholm Opera College, 1988-91; Board, Swedish Singers Association (Chairman); Board, The Norrbotten Academy, Permanent Secretary; Various clubs. *Address:* Johan Enbergs Väg 54A, S-17161 Solna, Sweden.

ENTREMONT Philippe, b. 7 June 1934, Rheims, France. Conductor; Pianist. *Education:* Studied under Jean Doyen, Paris Conservatoire. *Debut:* Barcelona, age 15. *Career:* US debut, National Gallery, Washington DC and with National Orchestral Association, New York, 1953; Appearances as Recitalist and Guest Artist (conductor, pianist) with major orchestras, worldwide; Music Director, Conductor, Pianist, Vienna Chamber Orchestra; Has conducted Royal Philharmonic Orchestra, Orchestre National de France, Ensemble Orchestral de Paris, St Martin-in-the Fields Academy Orchestra, Mostly Mozart Orchestra, New York, also Orchestras of Philadelphia, St Louis, Dallas, Atlanta, Detroit, Pittsburgh, San Francisco, Montreal, Quebec; Appeared, many major summer festivals, recently including Vienna Chamber Orchestra at Schleswig-Holstein and Carinthian Festivals, Philadelphia Orchestra at Saratoga, Orchestra of St Luke's at

Caramoor; World tour with Vienna Chamber Orchestra for Bicentennial of Mozart's Death, 1991; Former President, Ravel Academy, St Jean-de-Luz; Juror, Santander International Piano Competition, 1990, Van Cliburn Piano Competition, 1992; Permanent Conductor of the Netherland's Chamber Orchestra, 1993. *Recordings:* Chopin, Mozart, also Schubert and Dvořák works for piano and string quartet with Vienna Chamber Orchestra soloists, Debussy's Printemps and Prélude a l'apres-midi d'une faune, Ravel's Bolero, Rapsodie espagnole and Alborada del gracioso with Denver Symphony, Pro Arte; Stravinsky, Bernstein, Milhaud, Jolivet, Satie, Dohnanyi, Richard Strauss, Saint-Saëns, Litolff, CBS Masterworks; Others for Teldec, Sonata, EMI. *Honours:* Numerous including: 1st Laureate/ Grand Prize Winner, Marguerite Long/Jacques Thibaud Competition; Grand Prix de Disque; Edison Award, Netherlands; Knight, Legion of Honour; 1st Class Cross of Honour for Arts and Sciences, Austria. *Current Management:* ICM Artists, USA. *Address:* c/o ICM Artists, 40 West 57th Street, New York, NY 10010, USA.

EOLIAN Isabella, b. 12 Mar 1928, Armenia. Musicologist. 1 daughter. *Education:* Studied at the State Conservatory, 1977-79; Moscow Conservatory, 1950-53. *Debut:* Erevan Conservatory, Armenia, 1954. *Career:* Lecturer, Moscow Conservatory, 1955-64 and Specialist in Oriental Music for the Composers Union; Head of Department of Asian and African Arts, Russian Research Institute of Art Criticism, Moscow, 1956-. *Publications:* Books: Alexander Arutyunian, 1964; Gregor Egiazazian, 1968; Komitas: Founder of Armenian classical music, 1969; Arab Music Essays, 1977; Traditional music of the Arab East, 1990; More than 50 articles published in various Russian and Foreign journals. *Honours:* PhD, 1956; Professo, 1988; Book Prizes, 1970, and 1991. *Memberships:* Russian Composers Union; International Council for Traditional Music. *Hobbies:* Collecting dolls in international dress; Swimming. *Address:* Moskva 129626, Prospekt Mira 116-5, KV 65, USSR.

EÖSZE László, b. 17 Nov 1923, Budapest, Hungary. Art Director. m. (1) 2 children, (2) 24 Sept. 1983. *Education:* PhD, Aesthetics and Literature. *Career:* Music Teacher and Pianist; Concerts in Hungary and Europe, 1946-51. *Publications:* 16 books including, Zoltán Kodály élete és munkássága (Life and Work of ZK), 1956; Zoltán Kodály élete képekben (K's Life in Pictures), 1957; Az opera utja (History of Opera), 1960; Giuseppe Verdi, 1961, 2nd edition, 1966; Enlarged, 1975; Zoltán Kodály, His Life and Work, English, 1962, German, 1965; Zoltán Kodály, 1967; Kodály, His Life in Pictures, 1971, English and German; Richard Wagner, 1969; Richard Wagner, Eine Chronik seines Lebens und Schaffens, 1969; Zoltán Kodály, életének kroñikája, 1977; 119 római Liszt dokumentum, 1980; Essays and articles in various languages. *Contributions to:* The New Grove Dictionary of Music and Musicians; Brockhaus Riemann Musiklexikon; Numerous professional publications. *Honours:* Erkel Prize, 1977; Gramma Award, 1978. *Memberships:* Co-president, F. Liszt Society; Executive Secretary, International Kodály Society. *Current Management:* International Kodály Society, Budapest. *Address:* Attila ut 133, 1012 Budapest, Hungary.

EÖTVÖS Peter, b. 2 Jan 1944, Hungary. Composer; Conductor. *Education:* Budapest Academy of Music, 1958-65; Cologne Musikhochschule, 1966-68. *Career:* Music Director, Ensemble InterContemporain, Paris, 1979-91; Principal Guest Conductor, BBC Symphony Orchestra, 1985-88; First Guest Conductor, Budapest Festival Orchestra; Conducted first performance pieces by Birtwistle, Boulez, Danatoni, Kurtag, Reich, Stockhausen and Xenakis; Operas include premiere of Stockhausen's Donnerstag aus Licht, Milan Scala, Covent Garden; Maderna; Hyperion, Paris; Stravinsky: Rake's Progress, Lille; Mozart: Don Giovanni, Lyon; Engaged by most major festivals in Europe as conductor and artistic advisor; Professor, Hochschule für Musik, Karlsruhe, Bartok Seminar Szombathely; Founder and President, International Eotvos Institute for Young

Conductors. *Compositions include:* for orchestra: Chinese Opera, Psychokosmos, Atlantis; for ensemble: Intervalles-Interieurs, Windsequenzen, Brass the Metalspace, Steine, Triangel; for string quartet: Korrespondenz; for vocalensemble: 3 comedy madrigals; for solo: Psalm 151 for percussion. *Recordings:* Chinese Opera, 1986; Intervalles-Interieurs, 1974-81; Mese, 1968; Cricket-music, 1970; Sequenzes of the Wind, 1975; Moro Lasso, 1963. *Honours:* Officier de l'ordere de l'art et des lettres, France, 1986. *Address:* 1015 Budapest, Szabo Ilonka U 30, Hungary.

EPPERSON Gordon, b. 18 Jan 1921, Williston, Florida, USA. Professor; Cellist; Author. m. 27 Aug 1941, 2 daughters. *Education:* B.Mus., Cincinnati Conservatory of Music, 1941; M.Mus., Eastman School of Music, 1949; MusAD, Boston University, 1960. *Debut:* Town Hall New York City, 1956; Wigmore Hall, London, England, 1969. *Career:* Seasons with major orchestras; Recital Tours in USA, Canada, Europe, Far East, 1952-; Numerous Master Classes; Faculty: University of Puget Sound, 1946-52; Louisiana State University, 1952-61; Ohio State University, 1961-67; Professor, Cello, University of Arizona, 1967-; Professor, Cello, University of Arizona, 1967; Professor Emeritus, 1988. *Recordings:* Zoltán Kodály, Sonata Op. 8; G. Fletcher, Sónata for Cello & Piano; Samuel Barber, Sonata Op. 6; B. Martinu, Sonata 2. *Publications:* The Musical Symbol, 1967, DaCapo Edition 1990; The Art of Cello Teaching, 1980; A Manual of Essential Cello Techniques, 1963; Editor, Violoncello Technique, Mark Yampolsky, 1971. *Contributions to:* Music, Art of, Encyclopaedia Britannica, 15th Edition; many articles in professional journals. *Honours:* Fulbright Artist, New Zealand, 1981. *Memberships:* Violoncello Society; Pi Kappa Lambda; American String Teachers Association; American Society of Aesthetics. *Address:* 3248 N. Olsen Avenue, Tucson, AZ 85719, USA.

EPPSTEIN Hans, b. 25 Feb 1911, Mannheim, Germany. Musicologist. m. Lilli Lipsky, 27 Sept 1936, 1 son. *Education:* Private studies with Max Sinzheimer; Examination in Teaching Piano and Theory of Music, Karlsruhe, 1931; Studied Musicology, Universities of Heidelberg, Freiburg and Bern, Switzerland; Dr.phi (Bern), 1934; fil.dr (Uppsala), 1966. *Career:* Editor-in-Chief, Tonkonsten (Swedish dictionary of music), 1953-57; Leader of music classes, Framnäs folkhögskola, Ojebyn, Sweden, 1957-63; Docent in Musicology, University of Uppsala, 1966-77. *Publications:* Nicolas Gombert als Motettenkomponist, 1935; Brahms, 1948; Studien über J.S. Bachs Sonaten für ein Melodieinstrument und obligates Cembalo, 1966, 2nd ed., 1983; Heinrich Schütz, Swedish version, 1971, German version, 1975. *Contributions to:* Die Musikforschung; Osterreichische Musikzeitschrift; Bach-Jahrbuch; Archiv für Musikwissenschaft; Svensk tidskrift för musikforskning; Schütz-Jahrbuch. *Honour:* Member, Royal Swedish Academy of Music, 1974-. *Memberships:* Swedish Society for Musicology; Neue Bach-Gesellschaft; Gesellschaft für Musikforschung; Internationale Heinrich-Schütz-Gesellschaft; Internationale Joseph Martin Kraus-Gesellschaft; Others. *Address:* Edsviksvägen 1 C, 182 33 Danderyd, Sweden.

EPPSTEIN Ury, b. 3 Feb 1925, Saarbrücken, Germany. Musicologist. m. Kikue Iguchi, 2 Jan. 1965, 2 sons. *Education:* MA, Hebrew University of Jerusalem, 1945-49; Diploma in Music Theory, Jerusalem Academy of Music, 1950-53; Diploma in Japanese Language, Tokyo University of Foreign Studies, 1958-59; Diploma in Japanese Music, Tokyo University of Fine Arts, Japan, 1959-63; PhD, Tel Aviv University, 1984. *Career:* Secretary, Music Research Centre, Hebrew University, Jerusalem, 1966-72; Lecturer, Tel Aviv University, Theatre and Musicology Departments, 1972-77; Hebrew University, Theatre and Musicology Departments, 1972-; Guest Lecturer, Copenhagen University, East Asian Institute, 1981, 1986; Lund University, Sweden, East Asian Institute and Musicology Department, 1986. *Recordings:* The Nuns of Gethsemane sing Russian-Orthodox Chants, 1972;

Hassidic Tunes of Dancing and Rejoicing, 1976; Sephardic Songs of the Balkans, 1980; Jewish Yemenite Songs from the Diwan, 1982; Taqsim - Instrumental Improvisation in Near Eastern Traditions, 1991. *Contributions to:* Transactions of the International Conference of Orientalists in Japan, 1961; Orient/West, 1967; Studies on Japanese Culture, 1973; China - Tradition versus Changes, 1979; Ha-aretz; Monumenta Nipponica; New Grove Dictionary of Music and Musicians; The Israel General Encyclopedia; Maske und Kothurn; Israel Broadcasting Authority (radio programmes); Encyclopedia Judaica Yearbooks, 1988-91; Jerusalem Post, 1990-1993. *Address:* 80 Tchernihovsky Street, Jerusalem, Israel.

EPSTEIN David M, b. 3 Oct 1930, New York City, USA. Composer; Conductor; Theorist; Professor. m. Anne Merrick, 21 June 1953, 2 daughters. *Education:* AB, Antioch College, 1952; MMus, New England Conservatory of Music, 1953; MFA, Brandeis University, 1954; PhD, Princeton University, 1968. *Career includes:* Professor of Music, Massachusetts Institute of Technology, current; Professor, International Sommerakademie Mozarteum, Salzburg, Austria (conducting master classes), 1984, 1985; Guest conductor, well-known orchestras, Germany, Austria, Czechoslovakia, Israel, France, Belgium, USA, etc. Member, Herbert von Karajan Musikgespräche, Salzburg, 1983-88. *Compositions include:* String Trio; Sonority - Variations for Orchestra; Fantasy Variations for Solo Viola or Violin; The Seasons; String Quartet, 1971; The Concord Psalter, 1978; Music for theatre, film & television. *Recordings include:* Bloch, Concerto Grosso for String Orchestra & Piano Obbligato, Czech Radio Orchestra; Scriabin, Piano Concerto, Abbott Ruskin & MIT Symphony Orchestra; Dugger Music for Synthesiser & 6 Instruments. *Publications:* Beyond Orpheus, Studies in Musical Structure, 1979; The Sounding Stream, Studies of Time in Music, in press; Various articles, musical arrangements. *Contributions to:* Various professional journals. *Hobbies Include:* Skiing; Sailing. *Address:* Department of Music, Massachusetts Institute of Technology, Cambridge, MA 02139, USA.

EPSTEIN Matthew A, b. 23 Dec 1947, New York City, New York, USA. Opera Impressario; Consultant. *Education:* BA European History, University of Pennsylvania, 1969. *Career:* Manager Representative with extensive list of operatic artists; Consultant to opera companies and symphony orchestras on production concepts and casting, USA and Europe; Formerly Artistic Director of BAM Opera at the Brooklyn Academy of Music and Artistic Consultant for a Concert Opera series at Carnegie Hall. General Director, Welsh National Opera, 1994; Vice President, Columbia Artists Management Incorporated; Artistic Advisor to Lyric Opera of Chicago and Artistic Consultant to Santa Fe Opera. *Address:* Columbia Artists, 165 W 57th Street, New York, NY 10019, USA.

EQUILUZ Kurt, b. 13 June 1929, Vienna, Austria. Singer (Tenor). *Education:* Studied in Vienna with Adolf Vogel. *Career:* Sang as chorister in Vienna from 1945; Solo career at the Vienna Staatsoper from 1957, notably as Mozart's Pedrillo, Beethoven's Jacquino and in operas by Strauss; Sang at the Salzburg Festival in the premieres of Liebermann's Penelope (1954), Martin's Le Mystère de la Nativité (1960) and Wagner-Regeny's Das Bergwerk zu Falun (1961); Many concert appearances as Lieder singer and in religious music; Professor at the Graz Musikhochschule from 1971; Professor of Lieder and Oratorio at the Academy for Music in Vienna from 1982. *Recordings:* Monteverdi's Orfeo and Il Ritorno di Ulisse; Cantatas by Bach and the St John and St Matthew Passions (Telefunken); Cavalieri's La Rappresentazione di Anima e di Corpo (Deutsche Grammophon). *Address:* Osterreichische Akademie der Wissenschaften, Fleichmarkt 22, 1010 Vienna, Austria.

ERB Donald (James), b. 17 Jan 1927, Youngstown, Ohio, USA. Composer; Music Educator. m. Lucille

Hyman, 10 June 1950, 1 son, 3 daughters. *Education:* BS, Kent State University, 1950; MM, Cleveland Institute of Music, 1953; DMus, Indiana University School of Music, 1964; Studied with Harold Miles, Kenneth Gaburo, Marcel Dick, Bernhard Heiden, USA and Nadia Boulanger, Paris, 1953. *Career:* Teacher 1953-61, Composer-in-residence 1966-81, Professor of Composition 1987-, Cleveland Institute of Music; Composer-in-residence, Dallas Symphony Orchestra, 1968-69; Staff composer, Bennington (Vt) Composers Conference, 1969-74; Visiting Professor 1975-76, Professor of Music 1984-87, Indiana University School of Music; Meadows Professor of Composition, Southern Methodist University, 1981-84; Composer-in-residence, St Louis Symphony Orchestra, 1988-90. *Compositions:* Orchestral: Chamber Concerto for Piano and Strings, 1958; Concertant for Harpsichord and Strings, 1963; Symphony of Overtures, 1964; Reticulation for Symphonic Band and Tape, 1965; Stargazing for Band and Tape, 1966; Concerto for Solo Percussionist and Orchestra, 1966; Christmasmusic, 1967; The Seventh Trumpet, 1969; Klangfarbenfunk I for Orchestra, Rock Band and Electronic Sounds, 1970; Autumnmusic for Orchestra and Electronic Sounds, 1973; Treasures of the Snow, 1973; Music for a Festive Occasion for Orchestra and Electronic Sounds, 1975; Cello Concerto, 1975; Trombone Concerto, 1976; Concerto for Keyboards and Orchestra, 1978; The Hawk for Alto Saxophone, Jazz Ensemble and Percussion, 1979; Cenotaph (for EV) for Symphonic Band, 1979; Trumpet Concerto, 1980; Sonneries, 1981; Prismatic Variations, 1983; Contrabassoon Concerto, 1984; Clarinet Concerto, 1984; The dreamtime, 1985; Concerto for Orchestra, 1985; Concerto for Brass and Orchestra, 1986; Chamber music; Choral works and piano pieces. *Recordings:* Several works recorded. *Contribution to :* Article on orchestration in Encyclopaedia Britannica, 15th edition, 1974. *Address:* 4073 Bluestone Road, Cleveland Heights, OH 44121, USA.

ERBEN Valentin, b. 14 Mar 1945, Austria. Cellist. *Education:* Studied in Vienna, Munich and Paris. *Career:* Co-founder and cellist of the Alban Berg Quartet from 1971; Many concert engagements, all around the world, including complete cycles of the Beethoven Quartets in 15 European cities, 1987-88, 1988-89 seasons; Bartók/Mozart cycle in London, Vienna, Paris, Frankfurt, Munich, Geneva, Turin 1990-91; Annual concert series at the Vienna Konzerthaus and festival engagements worldwide; Associate Artist at the South Bank Centre, London; US appearances in Washington DC, San Francisco and New York (Carnegie Hall). *Recordings* include: Complete quartets of Beethoven, Brahms, Berg, Webern and Bartók; Late quartets of Mozart, Schubert, Haydn and Dvořák; Ravel, Debussy and Schumann quartets; Live recordings from Carnegie Hall (Mozart, Schumann); Konzerthaus in Vienna (Brahms); Opéra-Comique Paris (Brahms). *Honours include:* Grand Prix du Disque; Deutsche Schallplatenpreis; Edison Prize; Japan Grand Prix; Gromophone Magazine award. *Address:* Intermusica Artists' Management, 16 Duncan Terrace, London N1 8BZ, England.

ERBSE Heimo, b. 27 Feb 1924, Rudolstadt, Germany. Composer. *Education:* Studied at the Musikhochschule of Weimar and Berlin, with Boris Blacher. *Debut:* Conducted in Berlin, 1951. *Career:* Freelance composer; Has conducted, and directed opera; Moved to Salzburg 1957: his opera Julietta performed there 1959. *Compositions:* Stage: Julietta, opera 1957; Ruth, ballet 1958; Der Herr in Grau, comic opera 1966; Orchestral: Symphony in 4 Movements 1964; Das Hohelied Salomons 1969; For String and Wind Players 1971; Symphony No 2 1970; Triple Concerto 1972; Chamber music and music for chorus. *Honours include:* Beethoven Prize, Bonn, 1961; Appreciation Award for Music, Austrian Ministry for Education and Art, 1973. *Hobbies:* Mountain Climbing; Skiing. *Address:* c/o GEMA, Rosenheimer Street 11, D-8000 Munchen 80, Germany.

ERDÉLYI Csaba, b. 15 May 1946, Budapest, Hungary. Viola Player; Conductor. m. Ju-Ping Chi, 8 Oct 1989, 2 sons. *Education:* General - Bartók High School 1965; Musical: Artist-Teacher Diploma, Franz Liszt Academy of Music, 1970, influential teachers, Pál Lukács, Yehudi Menuhin, Bruno Giuranna. *Career:* Franz Liszt Chamber Orchestra 1968-72; Eszterházy Baryton Trio, 1973-78; Principal Viola of Philharmonia Orchestra, London 1974-78; Professor of Viola at Guildhall School of Music, London 1980-87; Chilingirian String Quartet, 1981-87; Professor of Viola at Indiana University, Bloomington, 1987-91; Rice University, Houston, Texas, 1991-; Soloist in RFH, Promenade Concerts; Frequent partner with Yehudi Menuhin; Master classes in London RAM, Edinburgh, Aldebugh, Isle of Man, Alaska, New Zealand, Hong Kong, Beijing, Mexico, Budapest and throughout USA, annual summer classes in Gubbio Festival, Italy; Jury Member in BBC Young Musician of the Year; Lionel Tertis Viola Competition on Isle of Man; First US performance of Brahms-Berio Sonata for viola and Orchestra; Opening recital at the International World Viola Congress in Redlands, California, June 1989 and in Vienna, June 1992. *Recordings:* Hoddinott Viola Concerto (Decca); Strauss Songs with Jessye Norman (Philips). *Publications:* Bartók: Viola Concerto strictly based on the composer's manuscript; Bach: Suite pour la Luth (BWV 995) for viola; Hummel: Fantasia; Mozart: Erdélys Sinfonia, Concertante KV 364 for string sextet; De Falla Erdélys Spanish suited for viola and piano; Arrangement for viola and piano of Brahms' Sonata op 78; viola part to Schubert's Arpeggione Sonata. *Contributions to:* Music and the fear of violence in Classical Music; Lecture tours: The Breath of Performance; The History of the Viola and Viola Players. *Honour:* First Prize in Carl Flesch Competition, 1972. *Memberships:* Institute for the Development of Intercultural Relations through the Arts (Geneva). *Hobbies:* Rebirthing; Yoga; Massage; Cooking; Body-mind control; Mountain walking. *Address:* Rice University, School of Music, Houston, TX 77005, USA.

ERDING-SWIRIDOFF Susanne, b, 16 Nov 1955, Schwabisch Hall, Germany. Composer. m. Paul Swiridoff, 11 Mar 1988. *Education:* Stuttgart University, 1975-77; Oxford and Cambridge, England, summers 1976-80; Yale University, USA, 1976; Universite de Montreal, Canada, 1978; Studied music, piano and composirtion with Milko Kelemen, Stuttgart Academy of Music, 1974-79; Composition with Dieter Acker, Munich, 1980; Seminars on composition, Buenos Aires, Argentina, 1981; International Summer School of Music, with Peter Maxwell Davies, Dartington, England, 1985; Composition with Agosto Benjamin Rattenbach, Buenos Aires, 1985. *Career:* Many TV appearances, 1983-88. *Compositions:* Orchestra: Yellan, 1981; Modi Giocosi, 1985, II, 1990; Event, 1985; Kassandra, 1986; Il Visconte Dimezzato, 1994; Hommage a Telemann, 1994; Concertos: Konzert, 1983; La Mia Isola Vera, 1984; Tierra Querida, 1986; Maske und Kristall IX, 1992; Operas: Joy, chamber opera, 1983; Der Schneemann, 1989-90; Die Wundersame Geschichte des Peter Schlemihl, marionette opera, 1991; Ballet: Yellan, 1981; Piano: Klaviersuite, 1982; Cadeau Cosmique, 1982; Maske und Kristall IV, 1992; Hommage a Schubert, 1994; Chamber music: Grotesques Arabesques, 1980; El sueno, 1981; Rotor, 1982; Ausweg, 1984-85; Homage to the City of Dresden, 1985; Eine Brucke zwischen Gestern und Morgen, 1985; Variations Serieuses, Fayence, 1986; Aragonesa, 1987; Labirinto del Sole, 1987; Delirio; 1987; Gioielli Rubati, 1987; Lieder, 1988; Blumen und Blut, 1988; Maske und Kristall I, II, 1991, III, V-VIII, 1992, XI, 1993; Zeitstimmen, 1993; Capriccio, 1994; Vocal: Okteondo, 1979; Spuren im Spiegellicht, 1984; Initialen, 1986; Frohliche Wehmut, 1990; Maske und Kristall X, 1993, XII, 1994. *Hobbies:* Languages; Travel; Cooking; Literature; Art; Painting. *Address:* Am Postgutle 14, Post Box 620, D-74506 Schwabisch Hall, Germany.

ERDMANN Martin, b. 14 Sept 1960, Bottrop; Musicologist; Pianist. *Education:* Studied at Bonn University; Private lessons in violin, viola, organ and piano with Rose Marie Schwabe-Zartner in Bonn. *Career:* Chamber and solo concerts, mostly the music of Cage, Feldman and other US avant-garde composers;

Also tutor and lecturer all over Europe. *Publications:* Untersuchvugen zum Gesamtwerk von John Cage, 1993; Contributions to Musik Kouzepte, Neue Zeitschrift fur Music, Archiv fur Musikwissenschaft and others. *Address:* Viktoriastrasse 11, 53173 Bonn, Germany.

EREDE Alberto, b. 8 Nov 1908, Genoa, Italy. Conductor. *Education:* Studied in Genoa and at the Milan Conservatory; Conducting studies with Weingartner in Basle and Fritz Busch in Dresden. *Debut:* Accademia di Santa Cecilia, Rome, 1930. *Career:* Musical Director of the Salzburg Opera Guild 1935-38; US debut with the NBC Symphony orchestra 1937; Glyndebourne Festival 1939-39, conducting Le Nozze di Figaro and Don Giovanni; Chief Conductor of the Turin Radio Symphony Orchestra 1945-46; Musical Director of the New London Opera Company 1946-48; Metropolitan Opera 1950-55 and 1974-75, notably in La Traviata, Tosca and Turandot; Music Director of the Deutsche Oper am Rhein Dusseldorf 1958-61; Chief Conductor of the Gothenburg Symphony Orchestra 1961-; Conducted the San Carlo Opera, Naples, at the Edinburgh Festival, 1963; Bayreuth Festival 1968, Lohengrin; Artistic director of the Paganini International Competition at Genoa, from 1975. *Recordings include:* 14 Complete Opera Sets, largely of works by Puccini and Verdi and La Favorita, Cavalleria Rusticana, Roméo et Juliette and Il Barbiere di Siviglia. *Address:* c/o SA Gorlinsky Ltd, 33 Dover Street, London W1X 4NJ, England.

ERICKSON Kaaren, b. 9 Feb 1953, Seattle, USA. Singer (Soprano). *Education:* Studied at Western Washington University, Bellingham, WA, 1970-74 and the Music Academy of the West with Martial Singher and Maurice Abravanel. *Career:* Sang Gilda in 1982 and won 1st prize 1982 Munich Competition; Sang at the Deutsche Oper Berlin and the Munich Staatsoper; Piccola Scala 1983, in Les Pelerins de la Mecque; US engagements at Seattle, San Francisco, Houston, Cincinnati and the City Opera New York; Metropolitan Opera from 1985 as Susanna in new production of Le Nozze di Figaro; Appears in the Met videos of Wagner's Ring; Blanche in Dialogues of the Carmelites, as Zerlina in Don Giovanni and a Flowermaiden in a new production of Parsifal (1991); Other roles have included Mozart's Pamina, Susanna, Fiordiligi Micaela, Contessa, Ellen Orford, and Aennchen in Der Freischutz; Sang in the premiere of The Voyage by Philip Glass, Metropolitan, 1992; Many Lieder recitals and concert appearances. *Recordings:* Le Cinesi by Gluck; The White Election by Gordon Getty; Messiah Handel Atlanta Symphony. *Address:* c/o Metropolitan Opera, Lincoln Center, NY 10023, USA.

ERICKSON Robert, b. 7 Mar 1917, Marquette, Michigan, USA. Composer; Professor. *Education:* BA 1943, MA 1947, Hamline University; Studied composition with May Strong, Wesley La Violette, Ernst Krenek, Roger Sessions. *Career:* Teacher, College of St Catherine, St Paul, Minn, 1947-53; San Francisco State College, 1953-54; University of California, Berkeley, 1956-58; San Francisco Conservatory of Music, 1957-66; Director, Pacifica Foundation, Berkeley, 1954-63; Professor of Music, University of California, San Diego, 1967-. *Compositions:* Stage: Monodrama: Cardenitas 68, 1968; Orchestral: Introduction and Allegro, 1948; Divertimento for Flute, Clarinet and Strings, 1953; Fantasy for Cello and Orchestra, 1953; Variations, 1957; Sirens and Other Flyers, 1965; Rainbow Rising, 1974; Garden for Violin and Orchestra, 1977; East of the Beach, 1980; Auroras, 1982; Chamber: Piano Sonata, 1948; 2 string quartets, 1950, 1956; Trio for Violin, Viola and Piano, 1953; Duo for Violin and Piano, 1959; Chamber Concerto, 1960; Toccata: Ramus for Piano, 1962; Concerto for Piano and 7 Instruments, 1963; Scapes for 9 Instruments, 1966; Scapes II, 1966; Ricercar a 5 for Trombone, 1966; Ricercar à 3 for Double Bass, 1967; Drum Studies, 1968; General Speech for Trombone, 1969; High Flyer for Flute, 1969; Cradle for 2 Tube Drums and Chamber Ensemble, 1971; Cradle II for 4 Tube Drums and Ensemble, 1972; Loops for 6 Instruments, 1973; Percussion Loops, 1973; White

Lady for Wind Ensemble, 1975; Kryl for Trumpet, 1977; Night Music for Trumpet and Chamber Ensemble, 1978; Quoq for Flute, 1978; The Pleiades for Violin, 1981; Solstice for String Quartet, 1984-85; Dunbar's Delight for Timpani, 1985; Vocal: Rilke Songs, 1940; The End of the Mime of Mick, Nick and the Maggies for Chorus, 1963; Do it for Speaker, Chorus, Percussion, Bassoon and Double Bass, 1968; The Idea of Order at Key West for Soprano and Chamber Ensemble, 1979; Night Sky for Voices and Chamber Ensemble, 1981; Postcards for Mezzo-soprano and Lute, 1981; Sierra for Tenor or baritone and Chamber Orchestra, 1984; Several tape pieces. *Publications:* The Structure of Music, 1955; Sound Structures in Music, 1975. *Address:* c/o Music Department, University of California at San Diego, La Jolla, CA 92093, USA.

ERICSDOTTER Siw, b. 9 Feb 1919 Norrkoping, Sweden. Singer (Soprano). *Education:* Studied in Stockholm with Nanny Larsen-Todsen. *Career:* Member of the Royal Opera Stockholm 1951-54; Sang with the Hamburg Staatsoper 1954-59; Appeared in Berlin from 1959, notably as Wagner's Elsa, Eva and Sieglinde; Guest appearances in Vienna, Paris and in Italy; Stuttgart Staatsoper 1962-70; Other roles include Leonore, Amneris, Tosca and the title role in Judith by N. Berg. *Recordings include:* Herodias in Salome (Electrola); Der Evangelimann by Kienzl (Deutsche Grammophon).

ERICSON Barbro, b. 2 Apr 1930, Halmstad, Sweden. Singer (Mezzo-Soprano). *Education:* Studied in Stockholm with Arne Sunnegard. *Debut:* Stockholm 1956, as Eboli in Don Carlos. *Career:* Guest appearances in London, Berlin, Hamburg, Edinburgh, and Helsinki, and in France, Holland and Italy; Paris Opera 1964, as Venus in Tannhäuser; Bayreuth Festival from 1964, as Kundry and Venus; Salzburg Easter Festival 1967 in Die Walküre, conducted by Karajan; Metropolitan Opera debut 1968, as Fricka; returned to New York 1976, as Herodias in Salome. *Recordings include:* Die Walküre (Deutsche Grammophon); Requiem and other works by Ligeti.

ERIKSEN Ib, b. 7 Aug 1942, Fredericia, Denmark. Choirmaster; Teacher. *Education:* Singing studied at the Royal Danish School of Educational Studies; Conducting courses in different countries. *Career:* Choirmaster, Midtbyskolens Kor, since 1967; Concerts in many European countries. Since 1977, also teacher at Horsens Music School (Singing and recorder); Writer and reviewer for the music periodical, Dansk Sang. *Recordings:* 15 Songs for Equal Voices. *Honours:* The Lyngsie Prize, 1992. *Memberships:* VP, 1985-91, Secretary, 1991-93, VP, 1993-, The Danish Kodaly Society. *Hobbies:* Topography; Railway History. *Address:* Lokes Alle 17B Thorsted, 8700 Horsens, Denmark.

ERLMANN Veit, b. 13 Feb 1951, Essen, Federal Republic of Germany. Ethnomusicologist. *Education:* University of Cologne, 1969-72; Free University Berlin 1973-74; University of Cologne 1975-78, PhD 1978. *Career:* Lecturer, University of Natal, Durban, South Africa, 1981-85; Senior Research Officer, University of Witwatersrand, 1986-87; Abt, Musikethnologie, Ethnographic Museum, West Berlin, 1987-89; Visiting Professor, University of Chicago, 1990-91. *Publications:* Die Macht des Wortes, 1980; Booku, 1979; Music and the Islamic Reform in the Sokoto Empire, 1986; African Stars, 1991. *Contributions to:* Ethnomusicology, ICTM Yearbook, American Ethnologist. *Honours:* Grammy Nomination, 1987. *Membership:* Society for Ethnomusicology. *Address:* Bennigsenstr 2, 1 Berlin 41, Germany.

ERLO Louis, b. 26 Apr 1929, Lyon, France. Stage Director. *Education:* Studied electrical engineering at Lyon, 1944-48. *Career:* Stage Manager, Lyon Opera, 1950, followed by production of Lohengrin, and directorship, 1953; Head of Production, 1969, Administrator, 1973, Paris Opera-Studio; Directed Rabaud's Marouf at Venice 1956, and worked further at San Francisco, Buenos Aires Paris and many European centres; Director, Aix-en Provence Festival, from 1981, staging Don Giovanni and Pelléas et Mélisande, Les Contes d'Hoffmann, 1982, and Chabrier's L'Etoile; Other productions include Ohana's Autodafe, 1973, The Love for Three Orangea and Martinu's Les Trois Souhaits at Lyon, 1973, 1990 and Don Giovanni at Nice, 1991; Les Contes d'Hoffmann, 1993. *Address:* c/o Opera de Lyon, 1 Place de la Comédie, F-69001 Lyon, France.

ERMLER Mark, b. 5 May 1932, Leningrad, USSR. Conductor. *Education:* Studied at the Leningrad Conservatory with Khaikin and Rabinovich. *Debut:* Conducted the Leningrad Philharmonic 1952. *Career:* Opera debut 1953, Die Entführung in Leningrad; Joined the staff of the Bolshoi Opera, Moscow, 1956: conducted Fidelio, Il Barbiere di Siviglia, Eugene Onegin and Le Nozze di Figaro in his first season; Ballet debut 1964, with The Firebird and Petrushka; British debut with the Bolshoi Ballet at the London Coliseum, 1974; Opera tours with the Bolshoi Company to Montreal 1967, Paris l970, Tokyo 1970, 1989, Prague 1973, Milan 1974, New York and Washington l975, West Berlin l980: Carmen, Faust, Werther, Così fan Tutte, Tosca, Butterfly, Aida, Otello Rigoletto, Traviata, Trovatore and Don Carlos; Vienna Staatsoper with Boris Godunov, Don Carlos, Eugene Onegin, Cavalleria Rusticana and Pagliacci; Bayerische Oper Munchen new production Prince Igor, Vancouver Opera new production Eugene Onegin; New Productions of Eugene Onegin and The Bartered Bride for Welsh National Opera; Royal Ballet debut 1985, Sleeping Beauty; Royal Opera debut, Carmen 1986; Guest conductor with USSR State Symphony Orchestra: tours to Italy, West and East Germany, USA, Canada, Japan, France, Holland, Hungary and Yugoslavia from 1976; Guest in Italy, USA, Bulgaria, Czechoslovakia and Hungary; Concerts with the Royal Liverpool Philharmonic, Royal Philharmonic Orchestra, London Symphony and the Orchestra of the Welsh National Opera; Khovanshchina, Sadko, Legend of Kitezh, Snowmaiden, Tzar's Bride and Mozart and Salieri by Rimsky-Korsakov; Rusalka by Dargomizksky; Ruslan and Ludmila by Glinka at the Bolshoi Theatre; Seattle Opera, 1990, new production of War and Peace; Royal Opera House, Covent Garden: Butterfly, Onegin, Medea, Attila, Fanciulla del West; Guest in Germany, Japan, Sweden, Spain, Yugoslavia; Season 1992 with La Bohème and Samson et Dalila at Covent Garden; Tchaikovsky's The Oprichnik at the 1992 Edinburgh Festival. *Recordings:* Prince Igor, Francesca da Rimini by Rachmaninov, Iolanta, Eugene Onegin, The Queen of Spades, The Stone Guest (Dargomizhsky), Tosca, Butterfly, Norma, Così fan Tutte, Boris Godunov, Khovanshchina and War and Peace by Prokoviev; Recording with Royal Opera House Orchestra, Swan Lake, The Nutcracker and Sleeping Beauty; Ivan Susanin by Glinka; The Story about a Real Man by Prokofiev; Vera Sheloga, Mozart and Salieri by Rimsky-Korsakov; symphonic pieces of Prokofiev, Shostakovich, Liszt, Haydn and others. *Honours include:* Winner, Conducting Competition of Bolshoi Theatre, 1956; Glinka Prize, USSR, 1978. *Address:* c/o Allied Artists, 42 Montpelier Square, London SW7 1JZ, England.

EROD Ivan, b. 2 Jan 1936, Budapest, Hungary. Composer; Professor; Pianist. m. Marie-Luce Guy, 11 Apr 1969, 3 sons, 2 daughters. *Education:* Academy of Music, Budapest, 1951-56; Academy of Music, Vienna, Austria, 1957-61. *Debut:* Budapest. *Career:* Coach, Vienna State Opera, 1962-64; Concert Pianist, 5 continents; Appearances include Salzburg Festival, Vienna Philharmonic with Karl Bohm; Full Professor for Composition and Music Theory: Hochschule fur Musik und darstellende Kunst, Graz, Austria, 1971-89; Hochschule fur Musik, Vienna, 1989-. *Compositions:* 2 operas; Orchestral works; Concertos; Chamber music; Cantatas; Lieder; Chorus works; Main publishers: Doblinger, Boosey & Hawkes, Universal. *Recordings:* As pianist: 10 records with Rudolf Schock, tenor, Pierrot Lunaire (die reihe, Vienna), recordings in about 10 countries; As composer: Amadeo 419071-1; Crest Records INC-81-3, Da capo 7127 a/b, Preiser Records SPR 10043, numerous radio recordings, BBC.

Contributions to: Articles in Osterreichische Musikzeitschrift. *Current Management:* Verlag Doblinger, Vienna, Austria. *Hobbies:* Literature; Theatre; Arts; Walking tours; Swimming; Travel; Games; Family. *Address:* Gumpendorfer Strasse 9/13. A-1060 Vienna, Austria.

ERÖS Peter, b. 22 Sept 1936, Budapest, Hungary. Symphony & Opera Conductor. m. Georgia Weiser, 4 Dec 1956, 2 sons. *Education:* Franz Liszt Music Academy, Budapest; Studies with: Zoltán Kodály, Leó Weiner, Laszlo Somogyi. *Career:* Associate Conductor, Amsterdam Concertgebouw Orkest, 1960-65; Music Director, Malmo Symphony, 1966-68; Permanent Guest Conductor, Melbourne Symphony, 1968-69; Music Director, San Diego Symphony Orchestra, 1971-80; Conductor, Australian Broadcasting Commission, 1975-79; Music Director, Aalborg Symphony Orchestra, 1983-; Guest Conductor, worldwide. *Recordings:* Siegfried Wagner, Orchestral Works; Gabriel von Wayditch, Jesus before Herod; Many recordings for Australian Broadcasting Commission and Swedish Radio. *Contributions to:* Various professional journals and newspapers. *Current Management:* Janina K. Burns. *Hobbies:* Reading; Theatre; Astronomy. *Address:* c/o 136 Kingsland, Nutley, NJ 07110, USA.

ESCHBACH Jesse Ernest, b. 6 Nov 1950, Warsaw, Indiana. USA. Organist; Professor of Music. *Education:* BM, 1973, MM, 1975, Indiana University; DMA, University of Michigan, 1980; Conservatoire de Rueil-Malmaison, France; Teachers: Oswald Ragatz, Robert Glasgow, Marie-Claire Alain, Marie-Madeleine Duruflé. *Career:* Performed, national and regional conventions, American Guild of Organists; Numerous broadcasts for Pipedreams, Public Radio programme; Co-Founder, Summer Institute for French Organ Studies; Professor of Music, College of Music, University of North Texas, Denton. *Recordings:* Music of Cesar Franck and Alexandre Guilmant, Cantaur label, 1988. *Publications:* Fantaisie en UT Majeur of Cesar Franck in Three versions, 1979. *Contributions to:* Garland Press Encylopedia of Keyboard Instruments; Internationalism in the Work of Aristide Cavaille-Coll, In Memoriam Maurice Duruflé, other articles, The American Organist; History of the Grand-Orgue at St Sulpice, Paris, other articles, Diapason. *Honours:* Prix d'Excellence, Prix de Virtuosité, Conservatoire de Rueil-Malmaison. *Memberships:*American Guild of Organists; Association Aristide Cavaille-Coll; Association des Amis de Jeanne Demessieux. *Hobbies:* Organbuilding; Antiques; Travel. *Current Management:* Philip Truckenbrod Concert Artists, Hartford, Connecticut, USA. *Address:* College of Music, University of North Texas, PO Box 13887, Denton, TX 76203, USA.

ESCHENBACH (Ringmann) Christoph, b. 20 Feb 1940, Breslau, Germany. Pianist; Conductor. *Education:* Piano studies with foster mother, age 8; with Eliza Hansen and conducting with Wilhelm Bruckner-Ruggeberg, Hamburg Conservatory. *Career:* London debut, 1966; Gave the premiere of Henze's 2nd Concerto, Bielefeld 1968; USA debut as soloist with Cleveland Orchestra, 1969; Many tours of the world both as soloist with leading orchestras and as recitalist; Many duo piano appearances with Justus Frantz; Debut as Opera Conductor with La traviata, Darmstadt, 1978; Generalmusikdirektor, Rheinland-Pflaz State Philharmonic Orchestra, 1979-81; 1st permanent guest conductor 1981-82, Chief Conductor 1982-85, Tonhalle Orchestra, Zurich; Covent Garden debut 1984, Così fan Tutte; Music Director, Houston Symphony Orchestra, 1988-; conducted Robert Wilson's production of Parsifal, 1992; Guest Conductor with many major orchestras of the world. *Recordings:* For Angel-EMI; Deutsche Grammophon; CD of Schumann's Violin Concerto and Fantasie in C, with Thomas Zehetmar and the Philharmonia. *Honours:* 1st prize, Steinway Piano Competition, 1952; 2nd prize, Munich International Competition, 1962; 1st prize, Clara Haskil Competition, Montreux, 1965; Recording prizes. *Address:* c/o Houston Symphony Orchestra, 615 Louisiana Street, Houston, TX 77002, USA.

ESCHKENAZY Vesko, b. 3 Dec 1970, Sofia, Bulgaria. Violinist. *Education:* Studied with Yfrah Neaman in London, Pierre Amoyal in Lausanne and at the Bulgarian Conservatory where he left with an Honours degree. *Career:* Leader, Pioneer Youth Philharmonic Orchestra in Sofia, 1979, touring France, Italy, Germany and Brazil; Solo performances with the English Chamber Orchestra, Royal Philharmonic Orchestra, Sofia Philharmonic, Bulgarian Festival Symphony, Monte Carlo Symphony, City of London Sinfonia, Philharmonia and London Philharmonic (Beethoven Concerto, 1992); Festival engagements in Sofia, Varna, Cannes, Montpellier and nantes, with tours to the former Soviet Union, throughout Europea, India, Brazil and China. Repertoire includes concertos by Bach, Brahms, Mozart, Prokofiev, Sibelius and Shostakovich; Sonatas by Tartini, Bach, Mozart, Beethoven, Franck and Schumann. *Honours:* Winner of various competitions in Europe and China. *Recordings include:* Bruch and Mendelssohn Concertos, conducted by Emil Tchakarov. *Address:* World Wide Artists Ltd, 6 Petersfield Crescent, Coulsdon, Surrey CR5 2JQ, England.

ESCHRICH Jane, b. 12 Dec 1955, Johnstown, USA. General Manager. m. Phillip Sargeant, 14 Aug 1977. *Education:* BMus, West Virginia University, 1977; MMus., Southern Methodist Universiy, 1981. *Career:* Instructor, Oboe, West Virginia University Preparatory, 1975-77; Teaching Assistant, Music, Southern Methodist University, 1977-79; Manager, Whittle Music Company, Printed Music Orders Dept, 1979-85, Manager, Printed Music Division, 1985-87; General Manager, Adams Music Co, 1987-92. *Publications:* The Fourteenth-Century Italian Motet and Its Place in the Music of the Trecento, 1981; Chansons de Cyrnos, 1988. *Contributions to:* Journal of the International Double Reed Society; International Trumpet Guild Journal. *Hobbies:* Russian Art; 19th Century French Literature; Corsican Folksongs. *Address:* 9515 Claychin Court, Burke, VA 22015, USA.

ESCHRIG Ralph, b. 2 Apr 1959, Dresden, Germany. Singer (Tenor). *Education:* Studied at the Musikhochschule Dresden. *Career:* Sang at the Dresden Staatsoper, 1984-87, notably in the local premiere of The Nose by Shostakovich; Lyric Tenor at the Berlin Staatsoper from 1987, notably as Mozart's Ottavio, Belmonte, Tamino and Ferrando, Fenton by Nicolai and in the Singspiels Erwin und Elmire by Reichardt and Zar und Zimmerman by Lortzing; Concert appearances as the Evangelist in Bach's Passions, Lieder by Schubert and Schumann and The Diary of one who Disappeared by Janacek. Engagemnts with the Dresden Kreuz Choir and Chorus of St Thomas's Leipzig and broadcasting stations in Germany and Finland. *Recordings include:* Mendelssohn Motets and Bastien und Bastienne by Mozart.*Honours:* Prizewinner, 1984 International Bach Competition;, 1987 Mozart Competition at Salzburg. *Address:* c/o Berlin Staatsoper, Unter den Linden 7, 1086 Berlin, Germany.

ESCOBAR Roberto B, b. 11 May 1926, Santiago, Chile. University Professor; Musician. m. Marta Cruchaga, 19 Mar 1950, 2 sons. *Education:* MA, Philosophy, Catholic University, Valparaiso; Escuela Moderna de Musica, Santiago; Manhattan School of Music, New York. *Career:* Composer; Conductor, Chilean Modern Music Ensemble, 1973-78; Musicologist. *Compositions:* Over 60 works publicly performed; Symphonia de Fluminis, 1987, first performance, USA 1992; Sinfonia Andres Bello, 1992, first performance, Chile 1993. *Recording:* Preludios Franceses; Homenaje a Amengual; Talagante; Cuarteto Estructural, Cuarteto Funcional, Macul, La Grenja, Quinteto La Paloma. *Publications:* Catalogue of Chilean Music, 1969; Chilean Musicians & Their Music, 1971. *Contributions to:* various journals. *Honours:* Goethe Prize for Composition, 1982; Claudio Arru Prize (Chile), 1992; Honorary Professor, University of Missouri, 1989. *Memberships:* President, Chilean Composers Association; President, Sociedad Chilena de Filosofia, 1985-88. *Hobby:* Cooking. *Address:* PO Box 16360, Santiago 9, Chile.

ESCOT Pozzi (Olga), b. 1 Oct 1931, Lima, Peru. Composer; Teacher; Writer on Music. m. Robert Cogan. *Education:* Studied with Andres Sas, Sas-Rosary Academy of Music, Lima, 1949-53; Mathematics, San Marcos University, Lima, 1950-52; BS 1956, MA 1957, Juilliard School of Music, New York; Studied with Philipp Jarnach, Hamburg Hochschule für Musik, 1957-61. *Career:* Teacher, New England Conservatory of Music, Boston, 1964-67, 1980-81; Wheaton College, Norton, Mass, 1972-; Lecturer, University of Peking and University of Shanghai, 1984; Editor, Sonus journal, 1980-. *Compositions:* 3 symphonies: 1952-53, 1955, 1957; Sands..for Orchestra, 1965; Concerto for Piano and Chamber Orchestra, 1982; 3 Poems of Rilke for Narrator and String Quartet, 1959; 3 Movements for Violin and Piano, 1959-60; Lamentus; Trilogy No 1 for Soprano and 8 Players, 1962; Cristhos: Trilogy No 2 for 6 Players, 1963; Visione: Trilogy No 3 for Soprano, Speaker and 5 Players, 1964; Neyrac lux for 2 Guitars and Electric Guitar, 1978; Eure pax for Violin, 1980; Trio in Memoriam Solrac for Violin, Cello and Piano, 1984; Piano pieces; Pieces for instrument and tape. *Publications:* Sonic Design: the nature of Sound and Music, with Robert Cogan, 1976; Sonic Design: Practice and Problems, 1981. *Honours:* MacDowell Colony Fellowships, 1962-65; Ford Foundation grant, 1966; Radcliffe Institute Fellowships, 1968-70; Camargo Foundation Residence, Cassis, France, 1982. *Address:* c/o Music Department, Wheaton College, Norton, MA 02766, USA.

ESHAM Faith, b. 6 Aug 1948, Vanceburg, Kentucky, USA. Singer (Soprano). *Education:* Studied at Juilliard with Jennie Tourel and Beverly Johnson. *Debut:* New York City Opera 1977, as Cherubino. *Career:* European debut in Nancy as Nedda (Pagliacci); Sang Cherubino at Glyndebourne in 1981 and at La Scala 1982; Vienna Staatsoper 1984, as Micaela in Carmen; Geneva Opera 1984, as Mélisande; New York City Opera as Pamina in Die Zauberflöte, Leila in Les Pêcheurs de Perles, Marguerite in Faust and Massenet's Cendrillon; Washington DC as Zerlina in Don Giovanni; Pittsburgh Opera as Gilda; Las Palmas as Antonia in Les Contes d'Hoffmann; Metropolitan Opera debut 1986, as Marzelline in Fidelio; Season 1990-91 as Musetta at Cologne, Pamina for Washington Opera and Susanna at Fort Lauderdale; Micaela for Cincinnati Opera, Butterfly at St Louis and Cherubino at the Dallas Opera, 1992; Concert apperances at the mostly Mozart Festival, New York, Requiem and Schubert's A flat Mass, and Fauré's Requiem with the Pittsburgh Symphony under Charles Dutoit. *Recordings include:* Le Nozze di Figaro conducted by Haitink; Video of Carmen, with Domingo. *Honours include:* Young Artists Award from the National Opera Institute, 1978-79; Concours International de Chant de Paris prize 1981. *Address:* c/o Harrison/Parrott Ltd, 12 Penzance Place, London W11 4PA, England.

ESHPAI Andrey Yakoulevitch, b. 15 May 1925, Kozmodemiansk, USSR. Composer; Pianist. m. Alexandra Stempnevski, 2 sons. *Education:* Studied with Khachaturian at the Moscow Conservatory. *Career:* Regular TV and radio appearances. *Compositions:* 4 Symphonies: 1959, 1962, 1964, 1982; Symphonic Dances 1951; Hungarian Melodies for violin and orchestra 1942; 2 Piano Concertos 1954, 1972; Concerto for Orchestra 1967; Festival Overture 1970; 2 Violin Sonatas 1966, 1970; Ballet The Circle 1981; Oboe Concerto 1982; Music for 30 Films; 5th Symphonie, 1985-86; 6th Symphonie, 1988-89; 7th Symphonie, 1991; Violin concerto No.3, 1990; Viola concerto, 1988; Cello concerto, 1989; Cello-sonate, 1990; Music for 50 films; Concerto for saxaphone, soprano and orchestra, 1986. *Memberships:* Secretary, Union of Composers of USSR; First Secretary, Union of Composers of RSFSR. *Address:* G-165, Studentcheskaya 44/28 R12 Moscow, Russia.

ESKEW Harry L, b. 2 July 1936, Spartanburg, South Carolina, USA. Teacher; Music Librarian; Hymnologist. m. Margaret Hodges, 20 Dec 1965, 1 son, 1 daughter. *Education:* BA Music, Church Music major, Furman

University, 1958; MSM, Musicology, New Orleans Baptist Theological Seminary, 1960; PhD, American Musical Studies, Tulane University, 1966. *Career:* Faculty, 1965-, currently Professor of Music History and Hymnology, Music Librarian, New Orleans Baptist Theological Seminary, New Orleans, Louisiana. *Publications:* Sing with Understanding (with Hugh T McElvath), 1980. *Contributions to:* Over 200 articles and reviews, The New Grove Dictionary of Music and Musicians, The New Grove Dictionary of American Music. *Hobbies:* Organic gardening; Hymnal collecting; Travel; Photography. *Address:* New Orleans Baptist Theological Seminary, 3939 Gentilly Boulevard, New Orleans, LA 70126, USA.

ESMILLA Sergio Zalamea, Jr, b. 22 Feb 1927, Manila, Philippines. Music Educator; Orchestra Conductor; Consultant. m. Araceli Prociuncula, 9 Dec 1958, 2 sons, 2 daughters. *Education:* Music diploma, University of Philippines, Quezon City, 1948; BMus, University of St Tomas, Manila, 1953; Postgraduate study, Peabody Conservatory of Music, Baltimore, USA, 1954-55, Juilliard School of Music, New York City, 1955-56. *Career includes:* Concertmaster, Manila Municipal Symphony Orchestra, 1948; Assistant concertmaster 1949-54, concertmaster 1956-58, Manila Little Symphony; Leader, 1st violinist, Manila String Quartet 1956-62, University of Philippines String Quartet 1969-78; Music director/conductor, Philippines Youth Orchestra 1974-, Manila Symphony Orchestra 1979-. *Membership:* Director 1979-, National Music Council of the Philippines. *Address:* c/o Manila Symphony Orchestra, Liwasany Bonifacio, Metro Manila, Philippines.

ESPERIAN Kallen, b. 8 June 1961, Waukegan, Illinois, USA. Singer (Soprano). *Education:* Studied at the University of Illinois. *Career:* Sang in various opera houses and concert halls in the USA then won 1985 Pavarotti Competition and toured with the tenor to China, singing mimi in La Boheme; Further appearances as Mimi at the Berlin Vienna Statsopers 1986, the Lyric Opera of Chicago and the Metropolitan New York, 1989; Returend to the Met as Elena in I Vespri Siciliani; Has sung Verdi's Luisa Miller in Vienna, 1986, Verona and Geneva, 1993; Desdemona at the Opera Bastille in Paris, and Reggio Emilia, 1992, Mozart's Countess at St Louis, the Trovatore Leonora at Chicago and Nedda for Connecticut Grand Opera; San Francisco, 1991, as Donna ELvira in Don Giovanni. *Address:* c/o Grand Theatre de Geneve, 11 Boulevard du Theatre, CH-1211 Geneva 11, Switzerland.

ESPERT Nuria, b. 1935, Barcelona, Spain. Stage Director. m. Armando Moreno 1954. *Career:* Performed as actress with Compania Titular Infantil del Teatro Romea, in Barcelona, 1947-52; Formed theatre company with husband and acted in performances in Spain, France, Germany, Iran and Britain (World Theatre season at the Aldwych); First production The House of Bernarda Alba by Lorca at the Lyric, Hammersmith 1986; Staged Madama Butterfly for Scottish Opera and at Covent Garden; La Traviata for Scottish Opera 1989, seen at the Teatro La'Zarzuela, Madrid 1990; Elektra at Barcelona 1990; Returned to Covent Garden for Rigoletto 1988 and Carmen 1991 (also at the Seville Expo 1992). *Address:* c/o Royal Opera House, Covent Garden, London WC2, England.

ESPOSITO Valeria, b. 10 Apr 1961, Naples, Italy. Singer (Soprano). *Education:* Studied at the Salerno Conservatoire. *Debut:* Teatro del Giglio in Lucca, as Zerlina in Don Giovanni, 1986. *Career:* Appeared in concert productions at La Scala of Riccardo III by Flavio Testi and Berg's Lulu Suite; Amsterdam 1987, as Nausicca in Ulisse by Dallapiccola; Lucca 1987, in Domenici Puccini's Il Ciarlatano; Teatro Lirico Milan, as Sophie in Werther; US debut Houston 1988, in Werther; Teatro San Carlo Naples 1988, as Amor in Orfeo e Euridice; La Scala 1989, in Pergolesi's Lo Frate Innamorato; Radio France 1989, in the title role of Linda di Chamounix, by Donizetti; Welsh National Opera 1989, as Amina in La Sonnambula; Sang Ippodamia in Paer's

Achille at Lugo di Romagna, 1988; Amina in La Sonnambula at the 1992 Macerata Festival; Featured Artist, Opera Now magazine, Nov 1992. *Honours:* Winner, Aslico Competition Milan, Feb 1987; Winner, Cardiff Singer of the World Competition, July 1987. *Address:* c/o Athole Still Management, 113 Church Road, Crystal Palace, London SE19 2PR, England.

ESSER Hermin, b. 1 Apr 1928, Rheydt, Germany. Singer (Tenor). *Education:* Studied at the Schumann Conservatory Dusseldorf with Franziak Martiensen-Lohmann. *Debut:* Krefeld 1954. *Career:* Sang at Gelsenkirchen, the Komische Oper Berlin and Wiesbaden; Member of the Deutsche Oper am Rhein Dusseldorf 1964-; Bayreuth Festival from 1966, as Froh, Erik, Tristan, Tannhäuser, Siegmund and Loge; Sang Tristan at Monte Carlo in 1973 and Parsifal at Rome in 1974; Sadler's Wells Opera 1973, with Scottish Opera, as Tristan; Guest appearances in Paris, Moscow, Warsaw, Brussels, Zurich, Chicago, Geneva and Zurich; Sang Herod in Salome at the Staatsoper Berlin, 1988. *Recordings:* Das Rheingold; Der fliegende Holländer. *Address:* c/o Deutsche Staatsoper, Unter den Linden 7, D-1086 Berlin, Germany.

ESSWOOD Paul, b. 6 June 1942, Nottingham, England. Singer (Counter Tenor); m. (1) Mary L Cantrill, 12 Feb 1966, (2) Aimee D Blattmann, 1990. 2 son, 1 daughter. *Education:* Royal College of Music, 1961-64. *Debut:* Operatic: Berkeley University of California, 1968; concert: BBC Messiah, 1965. *Career:* Lay-Vicar, Westminster Abbey, 1964-71; Professor: RCM, 1977-80, Baroque Vocal Interpretation, RAM, 1985-; European Operatic Debut, Basle, Title role in Il Tigrane, A Scarlatti; World premieres: 1979, Lyric Opera, Chicago, Paradise Lost, Penderecki, 1984, Stuttgart State Opera title role, Akhnaten, Philip Glass; Major performances in Zurich, Cologne, Stuttgart, Milan and Covent Garden. Performed in major centres and festivals including Edinburgh, Leeds Triennial, English Bach, Three Choirs, Vienna, Salzburg, Zurich, Naples, Israel, Holland and Wexford, among others. *Recordings:* All Bach's cantatas; Bach: Matthew Passion, Christmas Oratorio; Handel: Jephtha, Saul, Belshazzar, Messiah, Il pastor Fido Rinaldo, Xerxes, Chamber Duets; Monteverdi: Poppea, Ulisses (also on film); Vespers 1610; Solo recordings: Songs to my Lady (Lute Songs); Music for a While (Purcell songs), Schumann Liederkreis op 39 and Dichterliebe. *Honours:* ARCM, Teachers and Performers, 1964; Hon RAM, 1990; German Handel Prize, 1992. *Memberships:* Incorporated Society of Musicians. *Hobbies:* Organic Gardening; Apiculture. *Current management* Transart (UK) Ltd. *Address:* Jasmine Cottage, 42 Ferring Lane, Ferring, West Sussex BN12 6QT, England.

ESTES Richard, b. 21 Jan 1948, Louisville, Kentucky, USA. Operatic Tenor. m. Nancy Elizabeth Stelling, 19 Aug 1978, 2 daughters. *Education:* BM, Stetson University, 1970; MM, Catholic University of America, 1974; The Juilliard School, American Opera Center, 1980. *Debut:* As Jean Baptiste in Herodiade with Opera Orchestra of New York in Carnegie Hall, New York, 1980. *Career:* Has appeared with the Opera Companies of Houston, Baltimore, Rochester, Minnesota, Kentucky, Atlanta, Piedmont, Augusta, Chattanooga, Sante Fe, San Francisco, Lake George, Wolf Trap, etc. and with Symphony Orchestras of Florida, Rochester, Charlotte, National, Charleston. *Honour:* District Winner of Metropolitan Opera Regional Auditions 1967, 1969. *Memberships:* Actors' Equity Association; American Guild of Musical Artists; The College Music Society. *Current Management:* Robert Lombardo Associates, New York City. *Address:* c/o Robert Lombardo Associates, 61 West 62nd Street, Suite 6F, New York, NY 10023, USA.

ESTES Simon, b. 2 Mar 1938, Centreville, Iowa, USA. Singer (Bass-Baritone). *Education:* Studied with Charles Kellis at the University of Iowa and at the Juilliard School, New York. *Career:* Sang at opera houses in Germany from 1965, debut at the Deutsche Oper Berlin as Ramfis in Aida; Member of the Zurich Opera 1976;

Metropolitan Opera from 1976, as Oroveso in Norma, Herman in The Queen of Spades, Amfortas, Amonasro, Gershwin's Porgy and Orestes in Elektra; La Scala Milan 1977, as Arkel in Pelléas et Mélisande; Hamburg Staatsoper 1978, as King Philip in Don Carlos; Bayreuth Festival from 1978, as the Dutchman and Amfortas; Geneva Opera 1984, as Jochanaan in Salome; Covent Garden debut 1986, as Wagner's Dutchman; Sang Wotan in new productions of Der Ring des Nibelungen at Berlin (1984-85) and the Metropolitan (1986-88); Appearances at San Francisco, the Glyndebourne Festival, Paris Opera, Munich and Vienna; Other roles include the villains in Les Contes d'Hoffmann, Escamillo, King Mark, Gounod's Mephistopheles, the Pharoah in Rossini's Moses and Boris Godunov; Concert engagements include the US premiere of the 14th Symphony by Shostakovich, with the Philadelphia Orchestra; Other concerts with the New York Philharmonic, Chicago Symphony, Boston Symphony and the Berlin Philharmonic; London Promenade Concerts debut 1989, Act III Die Walküre; Sang title role in the musical King, London, 1990; Jochanaan in Salome at the Deutsche Oper Berlin; Season 1992 as the Padre Guardiano in La Forza del Destino at Zurich, Macbeth for Greater Miami Opera, and Wotan at Bonn. *Recordings include:* Simon Boccanegra; Oberto by Verdi; Judas Maccabeus by Handel (RCA); Idomeneo (Telefunken); Mahler's 8th Symphony (CBS); Don Carlos; Koanga by Delius; Messiah, Fauré's Requiem and Beethoven's 9th Symphony, conducted by Colin Davis (Philips). *Address:* c/o Harrison/Parrot Ltd, 12 Penzance Place, London W11 4PA, England.

ESTRIN Morton, b. 29 Dec 1923, Burlington, Vermont, USA. Concert Pianist; Teacher. m. Eleanor Glassman (divorced), 17 June 1944, 1 son, 1 daughter. *Education:* School of Education, New York University, 1942-44; Juilliard Graduate School, 1945; Studied piano privately with Vera Maurina-Press, 1941-49. *Debut:* Town Hall, New York, 1949. *Career:* Private Piano Teacher, 1942-; Professor of Piano and Theory, Hofstra University, 1958-; Numerous concerts and recitals, Town Hall, Carnegie Hall, Alice Tully Hall, Merkin Concert Hall, New York; Tours, USA, London, Amsterdam, Berlin, 1982. *Recordings:* Works of Brahms, Rachmaninov. 1st ever recording of Scriabin's Etudes, Opus 8, Connoisseur Society records and tapes; Serenus Records; Book-of-the-Month Club; Fantasy Records; Raff, Suite in D minor, Opus 91; Scriabin-Etudes Opus 8; Tchaikowsky-Sonata in G; Anton Rubinstein, Six Etudes. *Contributions to:* Article on Rachmaninov's Preludes, Clavier Magazine, 1972. *Hobbies:* Gourmet cookery; Cyclist. *Address:* 9 Clotilde Court, Hicksville, NY 11801, USA.

ETHERDEN Alan B, b. 18 Apr 1956, Coventry, England. Pianist. m. Hazel E Sherwood, 30 June 1990. *Education:* Coventry School of Music, 1972-74; Royal Academy of Music, 1974-80; Studying with Louis Kentner; ARCM, 1976; LRAM, 1973; Dip RAM, 1980; ARAM, 1988. *Debut:* Beethoven concerto, Birmingham Town Hall. *Career:* Recital and concerto appearances; Specialist interest in neglected 19th century piano works; Recordings frequently broadcast on radio, TV in England and abroad. *Recordings:* The Robin's Return and Enchanging Melodies, both drawingroom collections; Also Field, FX Mozart and Beethoven. *Honours:* ARAM, 1988. *Memberships* ISM. *Hoby:* Inland waterways. *Current Management* Hunters Moon Promotions. *Address:* 14A Abbey Hill, Kenilworth, Warwicks CV8 1LU, England.

ETZKORN K Peter, b. 18 Apr 1932, Karlsruhe, Germany. Sociologist/Anthropologist of Music; Ethnomusicologist. m. Hildegard Garve Etzkorn, 2 sons. *Education:* AB, Ohio State University, Columbus, USA; AM, PhD, Princeton University; Studied organ with Walter Schwan, Anton Boellinger, Carl Weinrich; studied Musicology with August Herden & Arthur Mendel; studied Ethnomusicology with George Herzog. *Career:* Assistant Professor, University of California, Santa Barbara, 1959-63; Associate Professor, University of Nev, 1964-67; Professor, University of W

Florida, California State University, Northridge; University of Missouri, St Louis, 1969-; Fulbright Professor Hochschule für Musik, Wien, 1987-89. *Publications:* Sociologists and Music, 1989; Music & Society, 1973; Editor, Journal of Ethnomusicology, 1985-88. *Contributions to:* Ethnomusicology; Kölner Zeitschrift fur Soziologie & Sozialpsychologie; Social Forces; Journal for Research in Music Education; American Sociological Review; Sociology & Social Research; International Folk Music Council Yearbook. *Hobbies:* Tennis; Chamber Music. *Address:* 21 Ladue Ridge Road, St Louis, MO 63124, USA.

EVANGELATOS Daphne, b. 1952, Athens, Greece. Singer (Mezzo-Soprano). *Education:* Studied in Athens, Minuch and Vienna. *Career:* Sang first at the Bayerische Staatsoper, Munich, then in Vienna, Cologne, Frankfurt, Hamburg and Vienna; Théâtre de la Monnaie Brussels 1982, in La Clemenza di Tito; Hamburg Staatsoper 1984, in Cavall's L'Ormindo; Salzburg Festival 1985, in Henze's version of Monteverdi's Il Ritorno d'Ulisse as Melanto; Cologne 1986, as the Prince in Massenet's Cendrillon; Other roles include Octavian in Der Rosenkavalier, Mozart's Cherubino, Sextus and Annius, Preziosilla in La Forza del Destino, the Composer in Ariadne auf Naxos and Wagner's Waltraute; Sang Tisbe in Cenerentola at the 1988 Salzburg Festival; Wolf-Ferrari's Le Donne Curiose at the 1990, Munich Festival; Has also appeared in Campra's Tancrède, Aix, 1986, Ramiro in La Finta Giardiniera, Orpheus, Annius and Sextus in La Clemenza di Tito, Fricka, Waltraute and Varvara in Katya Kabanova. *Address:* c/o Music International, 13 Ardilaun Road, London, N5 2QR.

EVANGELIDES Petros, b. 1949, Limasol, Cyprus. Singer (Tenor). *Education:* Studied in Athens and Vienna. *Career:* Sang at Klagenfurt 1973-74, and Ernesto on tour in Switzerland, Germany and Holland, 1974; Stadttheater Berne, 1976-82, National Theatre Mannheim, 1982-84 Glyndebourne Festival 1983 as Pedrillo in Die Entführung, Deutsche Oper Berlin as Monostatos and Pedrillo; Further appearances in Stuttgart, Amsterdam and Berlin, returned to Glyndebourne, 1984-88, in L'Incoronazione di Poppea, Falstaff, Entführung and Carmen; Vienna Staatsoper from 1984, notably in 1986 tour to Japan in Manon Lescaut and Tristan und Isolde; La Scala debut, 1986 as Monostatos; Sang Johannes in the premiere of Der Rattenfänger by Friedrich Cerha, Graz, 1987; Guest engagemnts at Hamburg, (Brighella in Ariadne), Bonn, Zurich (Singer in Rosenkavalier), Strasbourg and Vichy. *Recordings include:* Video of L'Incoronazione di Poppea. *Address:* Staatsoper, Opernring 2, A-1010 Vienna, Austria.

EVANS Anne, b. 20 Aug 1941, London, England. Soprano. *Education:* Royal College of Music, London; Conservatoire de Musique, Geneva. *Career:* Principal soprano, English National Opera 1968-78: debut as Mimi in La Bohème, then Mozart's Fiordiligi, Verdi's Violetta, Strauss's Marschallin, Wagner's Elsa, Sieglinde and Kundry and Smetana's Mlada; subsequently guest with Welsh National Opera: Strauss's Chrysothemis and Empress, Beethoven's Leonore, Mozart's Donna Anna, Dyer's Wife and Wagner's Brünnhilde and Isolde; has sung extensively in Germany, Italy, France and America, including Brünnhilde in Berlin, Nice, Paris, Turin, Zurich, Vienna and at the 1989-92 Bayreuth Festivals; sang the title role in Ariadne auf Naxos for ENO, 1990; made Metropolitan, New York debut with Elisabeth in Tannhäuses, 1992; recital Edinburgh Festival, 1993; Returned to ENO as the Marschallin, 1994. *Recordings:* Helmwige and Third Norn in ENO Ring conducted by Goodall; Brünnhilde's Immolation scene; Brünnhilde in Der Ring des Nibelungen, from Bayreuth (CD, video and laserdisc). *Current Management:* Ingpen and Williams, London. *Address:* Ingpen and Williams, 14 Kensington Court, London W8 5DN, England.

EVANS D John O, b. 17 Nov 1953, Morriston, South Wales. Music Producer; Musicologist; Broadcaster. *Education:* University College, Cardiff, 1972-78; ATCL

Piano, 1974; BMus, 1975; MA, 1976; PhD, University of Wales, 1984. *Career:* First Research Scholar, Britten-Pears Library and Archive, Red House, Aldeburgh, England. 1980-85; Senior Music Producer, BBC Radio 3, 1985-; Chief Producer, BBC Radio 3, 1992; Head of Radio 3 Music Department, 1993-; Artistic Director, Volte Face Opera Project, 1986-89; Executive Trustee of The Peter Pears Award, 1989-92; Artistic Director, Covent Garden Chamber Orchestra, 1990-; Guest lectures: National Film Theatre; English National Opera, Fairfield Halls, Croydon; Britten-Pears School; Aldeburgh Festival; Royal College of Music; Goldsmiths' College, University of London; Hull University; Camden Festival; Bath Festival; International Brown Symposium on Benjamin Britten, Southwestern University, Georgetown, Texas, USA; Postgraduate Music Tutor, University College, Cardiff, Wales, 1986-87. *Publications:* Benjamin Britten: Pictures from a Life 1913-1976 (with Donald Mitchell), 1978; A Britten Source Book, 1987; Editor, revised 2nd Edition, Benjamin Britten: His Life and Operas (Eric Walter White). *Contributions to:* The Britten Companion, 1984; The Turn of the Screw, Cambridge Opera Handbook, 1985; Death in Venice, Cambridge Opera Handbook, 1987; Magazine articles: Interview with Joan Cross and Sir Peter Pears in ENO/ROH Opera Guide on Peter Grimes and Gloriana; Britten's Venice Workshop, in Soundings Vols 12 and 13, 1986; Death in Venice: the Apollonian Dionysian Conflict, in Opera Quarterly, autumn 1986. *Honours:* Prix Italia and Charles Heidsieck Award as Music Producer of BBC film of Bartók's opera, Bluebeard's Castle. *Hobbies:* Theatre, Musicals; Contemporary dance; Travel; Cooking; Entertaining; Interior decorating. *Address:* 114 Lauderdale Mansions, Lauderdale Road, Maida Vale, London, W9 1NF, England.

EVANS Damon, b. 1960, Baltimore, Maryland, USA. Singer (Tenor). *Education:* Studied at the Interlochen Arts Academy on a Reader's Digest Foundation Scholarship. *Career:* Sang Amon in Akhnaten by Philip Glass at the New York City Opera, 1985; Virginia Opera Association 1985, as Benji in the premiere of Musgrave's Harriet: The Woman Called Moses; Glyndebourne Festival 1986 as Sportin' Life in Porgy and Bess; Has also sung Sportin' Life at Charleston, Boston, London (Philharmonic Orchestra) and Moscow (with the Finnish National Opera, 1988); Concert engagements include Beethoven's Ninth and Pulcinella, conducted by Simon Rattle; Bernstein's West Side Story at the Usher Hall Edinburgh and a Bernstein Celebration at Alice Tully Hall, New York; the British premiere of Blitzstein's Airborne Symphony, with the London Symphony; A Child of our Time at the City of London Festival and Weill's 3 Concert Suites at the Almeida Festival; Carnegie Hall Debut 1989, in the premiere of a suite from Weill's Lost in the Stars; Has also sung Janáček's Diary of One who Disappeared, with Matrix at the Elizabeth Hall; Sang Don José in Carmen Jones (London, 1991); Sang Porgy and Bess at Covent Garden, 1992 and in Weill/Grosz concert at the 1993 London Proms. *Address:* John Coast, 31 Sinclair Road, London W14 0NS, England.

EVANS David Gruffydd, b. 8 May 1925, Treherbert, Wales. Conductor; Repetiteur; Accompanist. m. Maja Moebius, 1 son, 1 daughter. *Education:* AGSM in Conducting, Guildhall School of Music, 1951; Diploma in Conducting, State High School for Music, Hamburg, 1954. *Career:* Freelance Orchestral, choral and operatic Conductor, Coach, Accompanist, Germany, Wales, Republic of Ireland; Staff Conductor Repetiteur; Welsh National Opera, 1962-72; Conductor, Repetiteur and Deputy Chorus Master, Oldenburgisches Staatstheater, 1973-92; Now Freelance Conductor, Number of conducting engagements with British Broadcasting Corporation, Cardiff and RTE Dublin. *Memberships:* ISM; Guild for Promotion of Welsh Music; Genossenschaft Deutscher Bühnenangehöriger. *Hobbies:* Reading; Walking. *Address:* Heinrich-Schütte-Strasse 33, D-26123 Oldenburg, Germany.

EVANS Edgar, b. 9 June 1912, Cardiganshire, England. Opera Singer. m. Nan Walters, 1 son. *Education:* Private study with Dawson Freer, London and Luigi Ricci, Rome Opera. *Debut:* London, 1947. *Career:* Professor of Singing, Royal College of Music; Founder Member and Principal Tenor, Royal Opera House, 1946- as Don José, Alfredo, Mussorgsky's Dimitri, Calaf, Captain Vere, Tchaikovsky's Herman and Janáčeks's Laca; Numerous Radio and Television Programmes. *Recordings:* Tristan und Isolde (HMV); Albert Herring (Decca). *Honours:* Honorary RCM, 1977. *Membership:* Incorporated Society of Musicians. *Hobbies:* Reading; Motoring; Gardening. *Address:* The White House, 110 Preston Hill, Harrow, Middlesex, HA3 9SJ, England.

EVANS Joseph, b. 1950, USA. Singer (Tenor). *Career:* Sang with the New York City Opera 1976-, in Les Pêcheurs de Perles, Maria Stuarda, Don Giovanni, The Love of Three Oranges, Attila and La Traviata; Appearances with the Opera Company of Boston in Don Pasquale, Rigoletto, Benvenuto Cellini, War and Peace, I Capuleti e i Montecchi, Ruslan and Ludmilla, Die Soldaten by Zimmermann, Montezuma by Sessions and Orphée aux Enfers; Has also sung with Houston Grand Opera and with opera companies in San Diego, Palm Beach, Cincinnati, Cleveland, Hawaii, Fort Worth and Colorado; Sang in The Love of Three Oranges in Geneva, The Prodigal Son in Venice; Persephone by Stravinsky at Nancy; Guidon in Rimsky's Tsar Saltan at La Scala; Season 1988-89 with The Devil and Kate and Marschner's Die Templar und die Jüdin at Wexford; Alwa in Lulu for the Opera de Nantes; Max in Der Freischütz for Welsh National Opera; Concert engagements with Bernstein and the New York Philharmonic, Lukas Foss and the Brooklyn Philharmonic and with Julius Rudel and Michael Tilson Thomas; Has also sung with the Pittsburgh, Atlanta and Indianapolis Symphony Orchestras and appeared in concerts with the Orchestre de l'Isle de France. *Address:* Music International, 13 Ardilaun Road, London N5 2QR, England.

EVANS Nancy, b. 19 March 1915, Liverpool, England. Singer (Mezzo-Soprano). m. (1) Walter Legge, (2) Eric Crozier. *Education:* Studied with John Tobin in Liverpool, then Maggie Teyte and others. *Debut:* Liverpool 1933, in recital. *Career:* Stage debut in Sullivan's The Rose of Persia, 1938; Sang minor roles at Covent Garden and in Glyndeourne Chorus in 1930s; Associated with Benjamin Britten, who wrote A Charm of Lullabies for her; Glyndebourne 1946-47, in the premieres of Britten's The Rape of Lucretia and Albert Herring; Sang with the English Opera Group in Britten's version of The Beggar's Opera; Created 8 roles in the premiere of Williamson's The Growing Castle, 1968; Also heard in recital, notably with French and British songs; Glyndebourne 1957-60, in Die Zauberflöte and Der Rosenkavalier. *Recordings include:* Dido and Aeneas (Decca); The Rape of Lucretia (HMV).

EVANS Peter Angus, b. 7 Nov 1929, West Hartlepool, England. Musicologist. *Education:* Studied with Arthur Hutchings and A E Dickinson at Durham University, 1947-51 (BA 1950); FRCO 1952; BMus Durham 1953, MA 1953; DMus 1958. *Career:* Music master, Bishop Wordsworth's School, Salisbury, 1951-52; Lecturer, Durham University, 1953-61; Professor of Music, Southampton University, from 1961. *Publications include:* Articles on Britten and Jonathan Harvey in Tempo and The Musical Times; Chapter The Vocal Works in Michael Tippett: A Symposium 1965; The Music of Benjamin Britten 1979; Articles on Britten and Rawsthorne in The New Grove Dictionary of Music and Musicians 1980.

EVANS Peter Geoffrey, b. 13 Jan 1950, Redhill, Surrey, England. Freelance Pianist; Teacher; Conductor. *Education:* Honours, ARCM piano performance diploma (age 16), 1966; BMus, Honours, University of Edinburgh, 1972; Hochschule für Musik, Vienna, Austria, 1972-74. *Career:* Performances as solo pianist & in various duos & ensembles throughout UK (including Aldeburgh, Edinburgh Festivals, London's South Bank & Wigmore

Halls, St John's Smith Square), also in Austria, Germany, France, Republic of Ireland, USA, USSR and Japan 1974-. Appearances on Scottish, Tyne-Tees, BBC Television, including BBC 2 Beethoven cello/piano sonatas series, recordings for French & Swedish Radio; Radio 3. Soloist with all major orchestras in Scotland; Principal conductor, Edinburgh's Meadows Chamber Orchestra, 1972-; Conducting debut in Spain, Festival of Torroella de Montgri, Catalonia, 1986; Close association with International Musicians Seminar, Cornwall, 1982-; Master classes, Oberlin College, Ohio, USA 1980, Deal Summer Music Festival 1985-; Artistic co-director of Hebrides Ensemble, 1991-; Membership of London-based Première Ensemble, 1990-. *Recordings:* Over 60 for BBC, including large number for Radio 3. For Hyperion Records: Brahms and Martinů sonatas for cello & piano, with Steven Isserlis, cello, for Unicorn Kanchana: cello and piano recital record with Alexander Baillie, cello, 1988; For ASV: Solo piano in Britten's, Young Apollo, with Scottish Chamber Orchestra, Serebrier, 1990; For Linn Records: recital of French music for cello and piano; Works by Webern, Lutoslawski and Rachmaninov for cello and piano with William Conway, 1992. *Address:* 49 Spottiswoode Road, Edinburgh, EH9 1DA, Scotland.

EVANS Rebecca Ann, b. 19 Aug 1963, Neath, Wales. Opera Singer (Soprano). *Education:* Guildhall School of Music and Drama, London. *Debut:* As Gretel in Hansel and Gretel, Welsh National Opera, 1990. *Career:* Has appeared in TV series Encore and Rebecca Evans; Roles include Ilia in Idomeneo, Oscar in Un Ballo in Maschera, Inez in La Favorita, title role in Massenet's Cendrillon, the Countess in Rossini's Count Ory. *Recordings:* Mabel in Pirates of Penzance. *Honours:* Prizewinner, BP Peter Pears, 1990; Young Welsh Singer of the Year, 1991. *Hobbies:* Cooking; Walking; Going to the cinema. *Current Management:* Harlequin Agency Ltd. *Address:* 203 Fidlas Rd, Llanishen, Cardiff CF4 5NA, Wales.

EVEN-OR Mary, b. 8 Sept 1939, Israel. Musician; Composer; Music Educator. m. Dan, 30 June 1960, 1 son, 1 daughter. *Education:* BA, Musicology and Theory, Tel-Aviv University and Academy of Music, 1981; MMus, Composition, Rubin Academy of Music, 1983. *Career:* Appeared several times on Radio and TV in Israel in concerts. *Compositions:* Music for Strings, 1979; Esspresioni-Musicali, The Italian Music Terms for Children's Choir, 1981; Numerous compositions for various ensembles; Pieces for solo instruments and for choirs; Cardioyda; Ad Infinitum; Musikinesis; Holy Curtain. *Contributions to:* Programme notes for Haifa Symphony Orchestra Subscription Concerts, for 2 seasons, 20 programmes, 1979-81. *Honours:* Recipient, 1st Prize, Musikinesis, ACUM Ltd, 1983; Winner, Competition in Germany with Cardioyda, 1982; Ad Infinitum commissioned by Rubin Academy of Music in memory of Oedoen Partos. *Memberships:* League of Composers in Israel; Acum Ltd (societe d'auteurs, compositeurs et editeurs de musique in Israel); International League of Women Composers. *Address:* 16 Yitzhak Avenue, Haifa 34 482, Israel.

EVERDING August, b. 31 Oct 1928, Bottrop, Germany. Head Manager; Producer. m. Gustava von Vogel, 30 July 1963, 4 sons. *Education:* Universities of Bonn and Munich, studies of Germanic studies, philosophy, theology and dramatic science. *Career:* Assistant Producer, Munich Chamber Players (Münchner Kammerspiele) to Kortner, Schweikart; Producer in Munich and Abroad; Stage Manager, Münchner Kammerspiele, 1959; Artistic Director, 1960; Manager, Munchner Kammerspiele, 1963, State Opera, Hamburg, 1973, Bavarian Opera, 1977; Head Manager, Bavarian State Theatre, 1982; Lecturer, Ludwig-Maximillian University, Munich; Professor, College of Music, Munich; Productions have included, Die Zauberflöte at the Savonlinna Festival, Der fliegende Holländer at Bayreuth, 1969, Tristan und Isolde, 1971, Boris Godunov, 1974, Lohengrin, 1976, and Khovanshchina, 1985, and Fliegende Holländer, 1990, at the Metropolitan; Recent work has included Salome at Covent Garden, 1988 and Munich, Fidelio at

Dusseldorf, 1990, and Mitridate, Re di ponto at the 1990 Munich Festival; Engaged for the Ring cycle at the Lyric Opera, Chicago, 1992-. *Recordings include:* Videos of Hansel and Gretel, 1981, and Die Zauberflöte. *Memberships:* President, International Theatre Institute, Germany; Vice-President, German Stage Association; Chairman, Manager's Group, German Stage Association; Broadcasting Council, Federal Republic of Germany; Praesidium, Goethe Institute; Academic Advisor, Research Institute for Musical Theatre at University of Bayreuth; Curatorium of Richard Strauss Foundation. *Address:* Generalintendanz der Bayerische Staattheater, Prinzregenstheater, Prinzregentenplatz, 8000 München 80, Germany.

EVERETT Paul Joseph, b. 6 May 1955, London, England. Lecturer in Music, University College, Cork. m. Margaret Mary Bernadette McLoughlin, 21 July 1979, 1 son. *Education:* BMus (Hons), Sheffield University, 1976; PhD, Liverpool University, 1984. *Career:* Lecturer in Music, Liverpool University, 1980-81; Lecturer in Music, University College, Cork, 1981-. *Publications:* Editor of various modern editions of music by D Purcell, J C Schickhardt, J B Loeillet and several works by Vivaldi for the Istituto Italiano Antonio Vivaldi; Scholarly articles on Italian sources, especially those of Vivaldi's music; The Manchester Concerto Partbooks, 2 Vols, 1989. *Contributions to:* Music and Letters, and the Musical Times. *Membership:* RMA. *Address:* Music Department, University College, Cork, Republic of Ireland.

EVROVA Katia (Ekaterina), b. 5 Oct 1947, Sofia, Bulgaria. Pianist (Chamber Music); Teacher of Piano. div. *Education:* Diploma of Excellence in Piano and Musical Pedagogy classes, Bulgarian Superior Conservatoire of Music, Sofia, 1971; Diploma of Excellence in Professor Justus von Websky's Chamber Music class, A Debussy Conservatoire, Paris, 1982. *Career:* First appearance, with aunt Yova Kallova, teacher of piano, Sofia, 1952; Concerts as member of violin and piano duo and trio with piano, 1976-81; Concerts as violin and piano duo with Vladimir Lazov, 1983-89, performances including cycle of Schubert sonatas, 1987, cycle of 19 sonatas for piano and violin by Mozart, 1989; Concert tours, Europe and Asia; Piano Teacher, Chaumont, France, 1989; Founded the Mezzo-Forte Ensemble (piano, flute classical guitar) with Franck Douvin and Gerard Montaudoin, 1989; Piano Teacher at School of Music, Pays de Langres, 1990; Concerts with the Mezzo-Forte Ensemble at Chaumont and 4th European Congress of Jewish Studies, Troyes, 1990; Debut, cycle of Mozart works for piano and violin as duo with Svetoslav Marinov, 1990; Cycle of Mozart works for piano and violin, Chaumont, Apr, June, Oct and Dec 1991; Tour of Brazil and Mexico, Aug 1991; Concerts-duo piano and violin with Sue Toslav Marinov in France, 1992, 1993; Tour of Brazil, May 1993. *Membership:* Former Dramaturgist of the Sofia weeks of Music Bulgarian International Festival. *Address:* 1 rue Bartholdi, Chaumont 52000, France.

EVSTATIEVA Stefka, b. 7 May 1947, Rousse, Bulgaria. Singer (Soprano). *Education:* Sofia Conservatoire with Elena Kiselova. *Career:* Member of Rousse Opera 1971-79: roles included Verdi's Amelia, Elisabeth de Valois, Aida and Desdemona; Margarita in Mefistofele; Yaroslavna in Prince Igor; Puccini's Mimi and Suor Angelica; Member of Bulgarian National Opera in Sofia from 1978; Guest appearances in Vienna, Frankfurt, Munich, Hamburg, New York, Berlin, Milan, Verona, Madrid and Paris; Roles include Leonora (Il Trovatore), Elvira (Ernani), Madeleine de Coigny (Andrea Chénier) Donna Elvira (Don Giovanni) and Lisa (Queen of Spades); Royal Opera debut in Manchester as Desdemona in Otello: London 1983 as Elisabeth de Valois; Metropolitan Opera debut, 1983, as Elisabeth de Valois; San Francisco, 1984 and 1986, as Aida; Toronto, 1989-90, as Tosca, Mimi, Leonora in La Forza del Destino, and Desdemona; Appeared at Nimes, 1986, as Medora in the French Premiere of Verdi's Il Corsaro; Sang at the Savonlinna Festival, 1990, as Aida; Season 1991-92 as Amelia in Ballo in Maschera at Antwerp,

Tosca at Buenos Aires and the Forza Leonora at Florence; Many engagements as concert singer. *Recordings:* Rimsky-Korsakov's Boyartinya Vera Sheloga and The Maid of Pskov; 2 Recitals of Italian arias. *Address:* c/o San Francisco Opera, War Memorial Opera House, San Francisco, CA 94102, USA.

EWING Alan, b. 1959, Northern Ireland. Singer (Bass). *Education:* Read music, University of East Anglia; Choral Scholar, Norwich Cathedral Choir; Guildhall School of Music, 1980-84 with Rudolf Piernay. *Career:* Roles at the GSM included Sarastro, Colline, Bottom, Collatinus (The Rape of Lucretia) and Falstaff in The Merry Wives of Windsor; Has sung widely with Renaissance and Baroque groups, notably with the Consort of Musicke at major festivals in the USA, Australia, Japan, Israel and Europe; Has sung in oratorios throughout Europe and with the 1989 Young Songmakers' Almanac concert; Appearances in The Rape of Lucretia at the Aldeburgh Festival and as the Voice of Neptune (Idomeneo) with Rattle at the Elizabeth Hall; Trulove in The Rake's Progress conducted by John Lubbock and in Kopernicus by Claude Vivier in a Pierre Audi production at the Almeida Festival; Osmin in Die Entführung at the 1991 Buxton Festival. *Recordings:* Albums for Hyperion, EMI and Virgin Classics with the Consort of Musicke. *Address:* Kaye Artists Management, Barratt House, 7 Chertsey Road, Woking, GU21 5AB, England.

EWING Maria Louise, b. 27 Mar 1950, Detroit, Michigan, USA. Soprano. m. Sir Peter Hall, 14 Feb 1982, 1 daughter, Divorced 1990. *Education:* Piano studies with Mabel Barel and Gizo Santo; Studied singing with Marjorie Gordon, Eleanor Steber, Jennie Tourel and Otto Guth; Music Scholarship, Cleveland Institute of Music. *Debut:* Meadow Brook Festival, 1968. *Career:* Debut as Cherubino, New York Metropolitan Opera, 1976 and at La Scala, (Pelléas and Mélisande); Is particularly known for her interpretations of Dorabella in Così, Susanna and Cherubino in Figaro and the title roles in La Périchole and La Cenerentola; Appearances at Glyndebourne include, Carmen, Così, Poppea, Barber of Seville and Ariadne; Concerts and with Haitink and Concertgebouw Orchestra, and with James Levine, Simon Rattle and Abbado, in London, Paris, Amsterdam, New York, Chicago and at Los Angeles; Autumn tour 1985 included recitals at La Scala and in Geneva, Paris and London; Sang Salome at Los Angeles and Ravel's Shéhérezade with Simon Rattle and Concertgebouw Orchestra in late 1986; In Spring 1988 gave recitals in Paris, Vienna & Florence, followed by highly acclaimed Covent Garden debut in the role of Salome; Highlights of 88/89 season included performances of Così in Los Angeles, Salome in Chicago & Los Angeles, Strauss Four Last Songs with the BBC Symphony Orchestra and John Pritchard, Carmen at Earls Court,London, 1989; Damnation of Faust with Hessischer Rundfunk - recorded by Denon & concerts in Amsterdam and Paris; Tosca, Los Angeles; Shéhérezade, with Rattle and the CBSO; Carmen, Tokyo; Four Last Songs, with Ashkenazy and the Royal Philharmonic Orchestra also recitals in London and Florence, spring 1990; Sang Carmen in a new production of Bizet's opera at Covent Garden, 1991; Carmen arena production, Earls Court 1989 subsequently toured Japan and Australia; Carmen at Covent Garden, cond Mehta, filmed for BBC TV 1991; Salome at Covent Garden filmed for TV, 1992; Performed with BPO/Abbado and Los Angeles PO/ Boulez at the Salzburg and Luzern Festivals, summer 1992; Messiaen Poèmes pour Mi: Philharmonia/Boulez in London and Paris, 1993; Sang closing scene from Salome, at 1993 London Proms; Season 1993/94, premiere of new works by Michael Tilson Thomas, with LSO, Tosca and Madame Butterfly at the Vienna State Opera and The Trojans with Levine at the Metropolitan Opera. *Recordings:* Andrea Chénier (RCA), Don Giovanni (EMI); Mozart's Requiem, (DG) conducted by Bernstein, 1988 and Shostakovich, Lady Macbeth of Mtzensk, title role, (DG) with Bastille Opera, 1993; Sheherazade (EMI) with CBSO/Rattle and Pelléas et Mélisande conducted by Abbado, (DG). *Hobby:* Gardening. *Current*

Management & Address: Harold Holt Limited, 31 Sinclair Road, London W14 0NS, England.

EYSER Eberhard, b. 1 Aug 1932, Marienwerder, Prussia, Germany. Composer; Violist. *Education:* Akademie für Musik und Theater, Hannover; Mozarteum, Salzburg; Accademia Chigiana, Siena, Italy. *Career:* Violist, Royal Swedish Opera Orchester. *Compositions:* About 100 works, including chamber and orchestral music, vocal and electronic music, computer-music; operas and chamber operas, including Molonn, 1970, The Death of a Bird, 1971, A Dream of Man, 1972, Last Voyage, 1973, King of Heart, 1973, Abu Said, 1976, Summer's Day, 1979, The Deep Water, 1980, Bermuda Triangle, 1981, Via Gravis, 1981, The Ravens, 1982, Roses and Ruins, 1982, The Last Day on Earth, 1982, The Red Book Mystery, 1984, Twilight in Granada, 1984, It Was Raining Yesterday, 1985, The Picture of Dorian Gray, 1986; The Aspern Papers, 1989; 5 saxophone-quartets, orchestral works, Itabol, Metastrophy, Macbeth Overture; Chamber Opera: Charly McDeath, 1992. *Recordings:* King of Hearts, Last Voyage, The Deep Water, Overture, Circus Overture. *Honour:* Awarded 1st Carl Maria von Weber Prize for Chamber Operas, Dresden, Germany, 1978 and 1986; 1st prize Florilège Vocal, Tours 1990; 1990-prize of the Fundació pública de les Balears per a la Música. *Memberships:* FST; STIM; International Society for Contemporary Music. *Address:* Karlbergsv 71B, S-11335, Stockholm, Sweden.

F

FABBRI Franca, b. 28 May 1935, Milan, Italy. Singer (Soprano). *Education:* Studied in Milan with Adelina Fiori, Adelaide Saraceni and Giuseppe Pais. *Debut:* Spoleto 1963, as Violetta. *Career:* Has sung widely in Italy, and in Berlin, Hamburg, Cologne, Budapest, Warsaw, San Francisco and Aix-en-Provence; Sang in the premieres of L'Idiota and Riva delle sirti by Chailly, Orfeo vedevo by Savino and Al gran Sole carico d'amore by Nono (1975); Repertoire includes Lucia di Lammermoor, Musetta, Nedda, Fiordiligi, Gilda, Marguerite de Valois in Les Huguenots, the Queen of Night, and Pamira in L'Assedio di Corinto by Rossini; Roles in operas by Britten, Shostakovich, Maderna and Malipiero. *Address:* c/o Opera La Scala, Via Filodrammatici 2, Milan, Italy.

FABBRI Franco, b. 7 Sept 1949, Sao Paulo, Brazil. Musician; Musicologist. m. Monica Silvestris, 31 May 1980, 1 daughter. *Education:* Chemistry, State University of Milan; Composition, Conservatory Giuseppe Verdi of Milan; Musicology, University of Gothenburg, Sweden. *Career:* Member of the Experimental Rock Group Stormy Six/Macchina Maccheronica, 1965-82; Freelance Writer and Lecturer, 1983-85; Consultant to Musical Institutions, Musica nel Nostró Tempo, Milan and Publishers, G. Ricordi & C, Milan. *Recordings:* 9 LPs with Group, La Chitarra Rotta, 1981; Domestic Flights, 1983; La Casa Parlante, 1984; Tempo Rubato, 1983; Various soundtracks and stage musics. *Publications:* La Musica in Mano, 1978; Elettronica e Musica, 1984; La Musica che si Consuma, 1985; What Is Popular Music? 1985 (Editor), Compositore, 1986. *Address:* Strada Anulare, Torre 1, San Felice, 20090 Segrate, Italy.

FABBRICINI Tiziana, b. 1961, Asti, Piemont, Italy. Singer (Soprano). *Education:* Studied in Milan and other centres in Italy. *Career:* Won Various singing Competitions, 1982-85 and sang minor roles in provincial Italian opera houses; made successful La Scala, Milan debut, 1990, as Violetta; Season 1991 in La Traviata at Naples and Elvire in a revival of La Muette di Portici by Auber at Ravenna; Sang Lucia di Lammermoor at La Scala, 1992. *Address:* c/o Teatro alla Scala, Via Filodrammatici 2, 20121 Milan, Italy.

FABIAN Marta, b. 1946, Budapest, Hungary. Dulcimer Player. *Education:* Started playing dulcimer at age 8; Béla Bartók Conservatory, 1960-64; Ferenc Liszt Academy of Music, Budapest, 1967. *Career:* Soloist, Budapest Chamber Ensemble; Has made numerous guest performances in Austria, Belgium, Bulgaria, Czechoslovakia, Finland, France, Federal Republic of Germany; Democratic Republic of Germany, United Kingdom, The Netherlands, Italy, Latin America, Mexico, Poland, USSR, Spain, Sweden, Switzerland, Turkey, USA, West Berlin and Yugoslavia; Bratislava Festival; Darmstadt Festival; The Holland Festival; The Lucerne Festival; IGNM (SIMC) Festivals of Athens and Graz; Warsaw Autumn Festival of Modern Music; The Witten Festival; Zagreb Biennial Festival of Modern Music. *Recordings:* Has made numerous recordings including: Cimbalom Recital. *Honours:* Grand Prize, French National Record Academy, 1977; Liszt Prize.

FAERBER Jorg, b. 18 June 1929, Stuttgart, Germany. Conductor; Composer. *Education:* Studied at the Hochschule für Musik, Stuttgart. *Career:* Theatre conductor and composer in Stuttgart and Heilbronn, 1952-60; Founded Wurttemberg Chamber Orchestra 1960; Tours to Austria, Britain, France, Italy, USA and South Africa; Many performances in the Baroque repertory; Appearances with the European Community Chamber Orchestra, various BBC Orchestras, the Bournemouth Sinfonietta, the Thames Chamber Orchestra, and the Northern Sinfonia; Festival engagements at Swansea and with the English Bach Festival. *Recordings:* Bach Brandenburg Concertos; Boyce Symphonies; Vivaldi Four Seasons and other concertos; Bassoon Concertos by Weber, Graun, J C Bach, K Stamitz, Boismortier and Mozart; Concertos for cello, clarinet, viola and flute by Stamitz; Trumpet concertos by Torelli, Albinoni, Biber, Stölzel and Manfredini; Mozart piano concertos K413 and K450, violin concertos, K218 and K219, flute concertos, sinfonia concertante, K297b and overtures. *Address:* c/o Basil Douglas Artists' Management, 8 St George's Terrace, London NW1 8XJ, England.

FAGGIONI Piero, b. 12 Aug 1936, Carrara, Italy. Opera Producer. *Education:* Worked under Jean Vilar and Luchino Visconti in Italy. *Debut:* La Bohème, Venice, 1964. *Career:* Produced Alceste at La Scala, 1972; La Fanciulla del West in Turin (1974) and at Covent Garden; Norma (Vienna, 1977); Carmen (Edinburgh, 1977); Macbeth (Salzburg, 1984); Metropolitan Opera 1984, Francesca da Rimini; Production of Boris Godunov at Barcelona; Staging of Massenet's Don Quichotte seen at Paris Opéra, 1986, Florence and Monte Carlo, 1992; Produced Il Trovatore at Covent Garden in 1989: first of a projected series to include all the Spanish operas of Verdi; Principal Guest Producer at Covent Garden, until 1990. *Address:* c/o Royal Opera House, Covent Garden, London, WC2.

FAHBERG Antonia, b. 19 May 1928, Vienna, Austria. Singer (Soprano). *Education:* Studied at the Vienna Music Academy. *Career:* Sang at Innsbruck from 1950, Munich from 1952; Opera engagements in Hamburg, Vienna, Brussels and Amsterdam; Radio and TV engagements; Noted concert interpreter of works by Rossini (Stabat Mater), Beethoven (Christ at the Mount of Olives), Bruckner (Te Deum) and Bach. *Recordings include:* St Matthew Passion and Cantatas by Bach (Deutsche Grammophon); Alexander Balus by Handel; Il Ritorno d'Ulisse and L'Incoronazione di Poppea (Vox); Diana in Gluck's Iphigénie en Tauride (Cetra). *Address:* c/o Bayerische Staatsoper, Postfach 745, D-8000 Munich 1, Germany.

FAHNDRICH Walter, b. 1 Apr 1944, Menzingen, Switzerland. Musician. 1d. *Education:* Studied music theory and viola at Lucerne, 1965-71. *Career:* International activities as a viola player, composer and improviser; Solo concerts: Music for Spaces; Improvisation; professorship for improvisation, Basel; Organisation of International Congresses. *Compositions:* Works for viola solo; Music for Spaces (sound installations); Musical landscape-projects; Chamber music; Electroacoustical music. *Recordings:* Viola solo and various radio and television recordings. *Publications:* Publisher of Improvisation, 1992. *Honours:* First Musical Prize of Lucerne, 1989, and of Zug, 1992; various publications on Music and Space. *Memberships:* Schweizerischer Tonkunstler-Verein; Intercommunication Center, Tokyo. *Hobbies:* Mountaineering; Pistol-shooting; *Current Management:* Kunstler-Agentur ERNI. *Address:* Unterdorf 10, CH-4203 Grellingen, Switzerland.

FAIRBAIRN Clive Stuart, b. 21 Apr 1946, London, England. Conductor. m. Nicola Swann, 18 Aug 1979, 1 daughter. *Education:* Royal Academy of Music, London. *Debut:* St Johns, Smith Square, London, 1977. *Career:* Principal Conductor, New Mozart Orchestra, 1977-; Principal Conductor, Lindstrom Philharmonic Orchestra, 1984-; Guest appearances include London Symphony Orchestra, London Philharmonic, Philharmonia, Wren Orchestra; Has broadcast with New Mozart Orchestra, London Symphony Orchestra, Wren Orchestra; Conducted in Germany, Switzerland, Turkey, Portugal. *Membership:* Incorporated Society of Musicians. *Current Management:* N. McCann International Artists Ltd, London, England. *Address:* c/o N. McCann International Artists Ltd, The Coach House, 56 Lawrie Park Gardens, London, SE26 6XJ, England.

FAIRLEY Janet Christine, b. 16 Mar 1949, Birkenhead, Cheshire, England. Ethnomusicologist; Singer. m. Stephen Platt, 23 July 1972, divorced, Feb 1991, 1 son, 2 daughters. *Education:* BA Hons, Comparative Studies, University of Essex; MPhil, Latin American Studies, University of Oxford; PhD,

Ethnomusicology, University of Edinburgh. *Career:* Singing since age 8; Classical, folk and popular songs as solo singer, in madrigals and with choirs; Broadcaster, Radio 3 specialist music programmes and occasional contributor of Kaleidoscope, Radio 4; Fellow, Institute of Latin-American Studies, University of Glasgow: Presenter BBC Radio Scotlands Weekly World Music Programme, Earthbeat, 1991-; Half hour feature documentaries on Arts in Chile, 1991; Basque Country, 1992; Finland, 1992 for R4 and BBC World Service. *Address:* 7A Cluny Gardens, Edinburgh EH10 6BE, Scotland.

FALCON Ruth, b. 2 Nov 1946, Residence, Louisiana, USA. Singer (Soprano).*Education:* After studies in New Orleans she moved to New York and was a semi-finalist in the Metropolitan Auditions of 1972; further study in Italy with Tito Gobbi and Luigi Ricci. *Debut:* New York City Opera 1974, as Micaela in Carmen. *Career:* Title role in Mayr's Medea in Corinto, Bern 1975; Bayerische Staatsoper Munich 1976-80 as Leonora (Trovatore and La Forza del Destino), and Mozart's Countess and Elettra; guest artist in New York, Canada, Germany and France as Puccini's Manon Lescaut and Weber's Agathe; Paris Opera debut 1981, as Mozart's Donna Anna; Covent Garden London and Vienna Staatsoper 1983, as the Trovatore Leonora; Sang Anna Bolena at Nice, 1985; Nancy Opera, 1986, as Norma; Aix-en-Provence Festival as Ariadne; Covent Garden, 1987 and Metropolitan, 1989, as the Empress in Die Frau ohne Schatten; concert repertory includes Mahler's 8th Symphony, Beethoven's Missa Solemnis, Verdi's Requiem and works by Handel, Mozart, Brahms, Dvořák and Strauss. *Recordings include:* Die Walküre and Götterdämmerung for Eurodisc. *Address:* c/o Royal Opera House, Covent Garden, London, WC2.

FALEWICZ Magdalena, b. 11 Feb 1946, Lublin, Poland. Soprano. *Education:* Studied at the Warsaw Conservatory with Olga Olgina and Maria Kuninska-Opacka. *Career:* Member of the Warsaw Chamber Opera 1971-72; Solo debut as Oscar in Un ballo in maschera at the Komische Oper, Berlin, 1973; Sang Madame Butterfly with Welsh National Opera, 1978, and the London Coliseum, 1986; Member of the Staatsoper Berlin from 1984, guest appearances in Frankfurst and Leipzig, and in the USA, Bulgaria, Finland and Holland; Dresden Staatsoper 1985 as the Countess in the premiere of Siegfried Matthus's Weise von Liebe und Tod des Comten Christoph Rilke. *Recordings include:* Schubert's Alfonso und Estrella (Electrola); Amor in Gluck's Orfeo ed Euridice (Accent); Die Kluge by Orff (Philips). *Address:* c/o Deutsche Staatsoper, Uner den Linden, 1086 Berlin, Germany.

FALIK Yuri, b. 30 July 1936, Odessa, Russia. Composer; Conductor; Cellist. *Education:* Studied Cello and Composition at the Leningrad Conservatory with Boris Arapov, graduated, 1964. *Career:* Teacher of cello and composition, St Petersburg Conservatory; Active member of the Composer's Union. *Compositions:* Stage works Till Euelenspiegel, mystery ballet, 1967; Oresteai, choreographic tragedy, 1968; Les Fourberries de Scapin, opera, 1984; Polly and the Dinosaurs, operas, performed in concert in Chicago, 1990; Orchestral: Concertino, oboe and chamber orchestra, 1961; Symphony, string orchestra and percussion, 1963; Concerto for Orchestra, 1967; Music for Strings, 1968; Easy Symphony, 1971; Concerto for Orchestra No 2, Symphonic Etudes, 1977; Chamber: 7 string quartets, 1955-93; Trio for oboe, cello and piano, 1959; Wind quintet, 1964; Concerto for 6 Winds and Percussion (Bufoons), 1966; English Divertimento, flute, clarinet and bassoon; Vocal music including Solemn song, catata, 1968, Winter songs, 1975, Autumn Songs, 1970 for a cappella chorus; Estonian Watercolours, Suite for women's Chorus, 1976; 3 Concertos for Chorus a capella, 1979, 1987, 1988; Russian Orthodox Liturgical Songs for mixed Chrous and Soloists, 1990-92; Solo songs. *Address:* St Petersburg N Rimsky Korsakov Conservatory, Teatralnaya Pl 3, 190001 St Petersburg, Russia.

FALK Nina, b. 5 May 1947, New York City, New York,

USA. Violist; Violinist. *Education:* Juilliard Preparatory Division, 1958- 64; BM, Oberlin Conservatory, 1968; Fromm Foundation Fellow, Tanglewood, 1968; Diploma with honour, Accademia Chigiana, Siena, Italy, 1969; MA, University of Iowa, 1977; Oberlin Baroque Performance Institute, 1985. *Career:* Participant: Tanglewood Festival, 1968; Marlboro Festival, 1970; Aspen Festival, 1975; Chamber Music West, 1980; Violist with: Baltimore Symphony, 1972-74; Cincinnati Symphony, 1978-80; San Francisco Opera, 1980-81; Principal Viola, Washington Opera Terrace Theatre, 1982-85; European debut, Copenhagen, Denmark, Apr. 1988; Frequent performances in National Symphony, Washington DC; Member, Sistrum Ensemble for New Music; Member, Smithsonian Chamber Orchestra; Faculty, Levine School of Music, Washington DC, 1982- . *Recordings:* With Smithsonian Chamber Orchestra and National Symphony. *Honour:* Fulbright Fellowship, 1968. *Memberships:* Member, City Musick, Chicago. *Address:* c/o Levine School of Music, 1690 36th Street NW, Washington, DC 20007, USA.

FALKNER (Donald) Keith (Sir), b. 1 Mar 1900, Sawston, Cambridgeshire, England. Musician. m. Christabel Margaret Fullard, 1930, 2 daughters. *Education:* New College School, Oxford; Perse School, Cambridge; Royal College of Music, London. *Debut:* Singer, 1923. *Career:* Pilot, RNAS, 1917-18; Professional Singer, 1923-46; often appeared in oratorio: Bach's St Matthew Passion and Handel's Alexander's Feast among his recordings; Squadron Leader, RAFVR, 1940-45; Music Officer, British Council in Italy, 1946-50; Visiting Professor, Cornell University, 1950-51; Associate Professor, 1952, Professor, 1956-60; Director, Royal College of Music, 1960-74; Joint Artistic Director, Kings Lynn Festival, 1981-83. *Publication:* Voice (in Menuhin series of guide books for young musicians), 1983. *Honours:* Honorary RAM, FGSM, Fellow, Trinity College of Music, London; Hon D Mus, (Oxford); Humane Society Medal, for Life Saving at Sea; Vice President, Royal College of Music; Vice President, The Bach Choir. *Hobbies:* Golf; Cricket; Squash racquets; Walking; Reading. *Address:* Low Cottages, Ilketshall, Bungay, Suffolk, England.

FALLETTA JoAnn, b. 1960, New York, USA. Conductor. *Education:* Studied at Juilliard, Queens College and Mannes College of Music. *Career:* Soloist with orchestras on classical guitar, lute, mandolin, cello and piano; Has conducted leading orchestras at Denver, Indianapolis, Phoenix, St Paul, Richmond, Toledo, Tucson and Columbus; European engagements in Italy, Franc, Switzerland and Denmark; Music Director of the Long Beach Symphony Orchestra 1989; Music Director of the Virginia Symphony Orchestra, 1991, with guest appearances with the Symphony Orchestras of San Francisco, Savanah, Delaware, Hamilton and Antwerp; German debut with the Mannheim National Theatre Orchestra, in works by Barber, Gershwin and Brahms. *Honours include:* Winner of Stokowski, 1985, Toscanini, 1985, and Brno Walter Awards, 1982-87. *Address:* c/o Athole Still Ltd, Greystoke House, 80-86 Westow Street, London SE19 3AF, England.

FALLOWS David, b. 20 Dec 1945, Buxton, England. Musicologist. m. Paulène Oliver, 1 son, 1 daughter. *Education:* BA, Jesus College, Cambridge; MMus., King's College, London; PhD, University of California, Berkeley, USA. *Career:* Lecturer, Music, University of Wisconsin, Madison, 1973-74; Lecturer, Music, 1976-82, Senior Lecturer, 1982-, University of Manchester; Visiting Associate Professor, University of North Carolina, Chapel Hill, 1982-83. *Publications:* Dufay, 1982; articles in Musicological Journals; Editions of early music. *Contributions to:* Gramophone; Times; Review Editor, Early Music. *Honours:* 1st Ingolf Dahl Prize in Musicology, 1971; Dent Medal, 1982. *Address:* 10 Chatham Road, Manchester M16 0DR, England.

FALVAY Attila, b. 7 Sept 1958, Budapest. Violinist. First Violinist of Kodály String Quartet; Soloist. m. Maria Farnadi, 28 June 1983, 2 daughters. *Education:* Musical: Budapest, Liszt Ferenc Academy of Music,

(Professor Semyon Snitkowsky); Vienna Music Academy, (Professor Josef Sivo). *Debut:* 9 years old, Budapest. *Career:* First Violinist of Kodály Quartet, 1980-; First Concertmaster of Budapest Symphony Orchestra; Miss Dorothy DeLay invited him to Aspen Colorado, USA in 1981. *Recordings:* Hungaroton Record Company, Last Release - 1 and 2 String Quartets; Naxos Record Company: Haydn String Quartets: Op 54, 55, 64, 71, 74, 76, 103; Debussy String Quartet; Ravel String Quartet; The Last Seven Words of Jesus Christus; Debussy, Ravel, String Quartet, Schumann, Brahms Piano Quintet with Jenö Jandó. *Honours:* Il Szigeti Competition Budapest, II Prize and the Jury Special Prize for the best Bartók solo Sonata performing, 1978; Hubay Prize, 1980; Carl Flesch Competition London, 5th prize, 1986; Merited Artist of The Hungarian Republic, 1990. *Memberships:* Magyar Kodály Társaság (Hungarian Kodály Society). *Hobbies:* Collecting 17th and 18th Century Hungarian Maps and Prints. *Current Management:* Gergely Arts Budapest. *Address:* 1121 Budapest, Kázmér UTCA40, H1121 Budapest.

FALVO Robert J, b. 27 Aug 1963, New York City, New York, USA. Percussionist. *Education:* BM, Music Education, Performers Certificate, State University of New York, Fredonia, 1985; MM, Percussion Performance, 1987, DMA, Percussion Performance, Manhattan School of Music; Studied with Fred Hinger, Christopher Lamb, James Presiss, Claire Heldrich, Lynn Harbold, Theodore Frazeur, others. *Career:* Performances with: The New Music Consort, New York City, 1987-; NOA, Carnegie Hall, New York City, 1988-; English Chamber Orchestra, US tour, 1988; Pierre Boulez and the Scotia Festival Orchestra, Nova Scotia, Canada, June 1991; Frick Hawkins Dance Company Orchestra, touring Tokyo, Shanghai, Hong Kong, throughout USA, 1991-; Tokyo Symphony, world tour, 1991; Has also appeared with Erie Chamber Orchestra, Hudson Valley Symphony Orchestra, New Music Orchestral Project; Xylophone Soloist, Fredonia Symphony Orchestra; Many contemporary music recitals throughout New York area, including Carnegie Hall, Merkin Hall, Miller Hall, Hubbard Hall, Town Hall; Has conducted Manhattan School of Music Contemporary and Percussion ensembles; Frequent lectures, contemporary composition techniques for percussion instruments; Assistant Professor of Music, teaching percussion at School of Music, Appalachian State University in North Carolina. *Recordings:* Recordings on DRG, Koch, Newport Classics. *Address:* PO Box 368-DTS, Boone, North Carolina 28607, USA.

FALVY Zoltán, b. 28 Aug 1928, Budapest, Hungary. Musicologist. m. Eva Kardos, 15 Aug 1957, 1 son. *Education:* Philosophy, University of Eötvös Loránd, Budapest; Conservatory of Music, Budapest. *Debut:* 1952.*Career:* Director of the Hungarian Institut for Musicology, Budapest. *Compositions:* Reconstructions: Daniel Speer - Musicalisch Türkischer Eulen-Spiegel, 1688, 1963; Peire Vidal - Troubadour Songs, 1979; Gaucelm Faidit, Troubadour Songs, 1985. *Publications:* A Magyar Zene Története, 1987; Mediterranean Culture and Troubadour Music, 1986; Editor: Studies in Central and Eastern European Music; Studia Musicologica. *Contributions to:* Studia Musicologica, Budapest. *Hobby:* Fishing. *Address:* H-1014 Budapest, Szentha'romsa'g-U 9-11, Hungary.

FAN Paula, b. 2 Feb 1952, Illinois, USA. Pianist. m. John Denman, 6 Oct 1982. *Education:* BMus, University of Arizona; MMus, DMA summa cum laude, University of Southern California. *Debut:* Wigmore Hall, London, 1978. *Career:* Concerts in US, China, Japan, Australia, Mexico, Hong Kong, England and France; Broadcasts on American Public Radio, BBC, China Radio and TV; Currently Professor of Piano and Head of Department, University of Arizona. *Recordings:* England-New England; Masterworks; Art of John Denman; Le Beau Dussek; English Wind Music Vols 2 and 3; Potpourri; Sonatas of Reger, Mendelssohn. *Memberships:* Pi Kappa Lambda; Phi Kappa Phi. *Hobbies:* Cats; Golf. *Address:* 1542 E Lester, Tucson, AZ 85719, USA.

FANDREY Birgit, b. 1963, Germany. Singer (Soprano). *Education:* Studied at the Carl Maria von Weber Musikhochschule, Dresden. *Career:* Associated with the Opera Studio of the Dresden Staatsoper, then appeared with the main company from 1987, notably as Mozart's Susanna, Papagena, Pamina and Zerlina, Euridice, Mimi, Gretel, Sophie Scholl in Udo Zimmermann's Die Weisse Rose and parts in operas by Siegfried Matthus; Sang Handel's Galatea at the Halle Festival, 1987, Amor in Orfeo ed Euridice at the Leipzig Gewandhaus, Mozart's Constanze at Amsterdam and Pamina at St Gallen; Lieder recitals in works by Schubert, Schumann, Brahams, and Strauss; Concert repertoire includes Beethoven's Mass in C (Amsterdam Concertgebouw), Bach's St John Passion, Messiah and Mozart's Exsultate Jubilate. *Address:* c/o Dresden Staatsoper, 8012 Dresden, Germany.

FANNING David John, b. 5 Mar 1955, Reading, Berkshire, England. University Lecturer; Concert Pianist. m. 26 July 1975, 1 son. *Education:* MusB, Manchester University, 1973-77; PhD, 1984; GRNCM Royal Northern College of Music, 1973-77. *Career:* Lecturer, Manchester University. *Publications:* The Breath of the Symphonist: Shostakovich's Tenth. *Contributions to:* Gramophone; Music and Letters; The Independent. *Membership:* Royal Musical Association. *Hobby:* Languages. *Address:* c/o Department of Music, Denmark Road, Manchester, M15 6FY, England.

FANSHAWE David Arthur, b. 19 Apr 1942, Paignton, Devon, England. Composer; Explorer; Sound Recordist; Ethnomusicologist; Multi-media Guest Speaker; Author; Photographer; Record Producer; Music Documentary Presenter. m. (1) Judith Grant, 8 May 1971, div. 1985, 1 son, 1 daughter. (2) Jane Bishop, 14 Dec 1986, 1 daughter. *Education:* St George's Choir School, Stowe; Foundation Scholar, Royal College of Music. *Debut:* Composer and Cantor Soloist, Queen Elizabeth Hall, London, 1970. *Career:* Composer for BBC, ITV including Yorkshire and Anglia TV, British Film Institute, documentaries, feature films, private commissions; International University and College multi-media speaker on indigenous/traditional music and own compositions (One World-One Music), active promoter and participant in concerts of own works worldwide, researcher and founder, The Fanshawe Collections, 1965-92, 3000 tapes of traditional music from Arabia, Africa and the Pacific; Currently publishing, copying, cataloguing The Pacific Collections, establishing The World Music Foundation, completing major work Pacific Odyssey for world premiere at Sydney Opera House. *Compositions include:* African Sanctus; Salaams; Requiem for the Children of Aberfan; Fantasy on Dover Castle; The Clowns Concerto;; Mini-Serenade; The Strange Lady; Coloured Hats; Arabian Fantasy; The Pensive Clown; The Awakening; Ring Out the Bells; Holy Jesus; Sing Christians Sing; Romanza Burlesque; Dona Nobis Pacem. Film music. *Recordings:* African Sanctus, 1973, 1987, 1994; Arabian Fantasy; Salaams; The Awakening, Musical Mariner. Ring Out the Bells; The Lord's Prayer; Dona Nobis Pacem. Ethinic Compilations include: Heartbeat of Africa Series, 1973; Island Music of the South Pacific, Musical Mariner, Spirit of African Sanctus, Spirit of Polynesia, Spirit of Micronesia and Melanesia, 1994. *Address:* Little Orchard House, Preston, Ramsbury, Marlborough, Wiltshire SN8 2HF, England.

FARBAKY GÉZÁNÉ Charlotte, b. 18 Mar 1924, Budapest, Hungary. Music Master; Choir Conductor. m. Dr Farbaky Geza, 17 Jan 1950, 1 son, 1 daughter. *Education:* Diploma, music master, 1950, Conservatoire of Pecs; Diploma, solfeggio teacher and conductor of choir, 1959, Conservatoire of Miskolc. *Debut:* With Children's choir, 1953. *Career:* Egressy Beni School of Music, Miskolc, 1952-83; Leader of practical teaching, Liszt Ferenc Academy of Music, Miskolc; Teacher of Kodály method to American holders of Ford scholarships, Kodály Centre of Yale University; Most noted pupil was Peter Eötvös; Founder, Chorus Master, Children's Choir, Egressy Beni School of Music, Egressy Beni Zeneiskola Gyermekkorusa (produced with this choir the first performances of numerous new Hungarian choral works and numerous tours abroad); Music Master, Music School of Budapest, 1983-. *Recordings:* With Children's Choir for recording and for television in Hungary, Finland, Sweden, Germany, Belgium and Bulgaria. *Honours:* Numerous with children's choir; Music Prize, Remenyi Ede, 1980; Excellent Teacher Prize, 1978. *Memberships:* International Society of Music Education; Founder member, Hungarian Kodály Society; Society of Artists of Music, Hungary. *Hobbies:* Swimming; Outings; Reading. *Address:* Népfürdö U 21, 1138, Budapest, Hungary.

FARBERMAN Harold, b. 2 Nov 1929, New York City, USA. Conductor; Composer. m. Corinne Curry, 22 June 1958. 1 son, 1 daughter. *Education:* Scholarship student, diploma 1951, Juilliard School of Music, NY; BS 1956, MS 1957, New England Conservatory of Music, Boston. *Career:* Percussionist, Boston Symphony Orchestra, 1951-63; Conductor, New Arts Orchestra, Boston, 1955-63; Colorado Springs (Colo) Philharmonic Orchestra, 1967-68; Oakland (Calif) Symphony Orchestra, 1971-79; Principal Guest Conductor, Bournemouth Sinfonietta, 1986-; Founder-first president, Conductors' Guild, 1975; Founder, Conductors' Institute, University of West Virginia, 1980 (relocated to University of South Carolina 1987). *Compositions:* Operas: Medea, 1960-61; The Losers, 1971; Mixed-Media: If Music Be, 1965; Ballets; Film scores; orchestral: Concerto for Bassoon and Strings, 1956; Symphony, 1956-57; Timpani Concerto, 1958; Impressions for Oboe with Strings and Percussion, 1959-60; Concerto for Alto Saxophone and Strings, 1965; Elegy, Fanfare and March, 1965; Violin Concerto, 1976; The You Name it March, 1981; Shapings for English Horn, Strings and Percussion, 1984; A Summer's Day in Central Park, 1987; Chamber: Variations for Percussion and Piano, 1954; Variations on a Familiar Theme for Percussion, 1955; Music Inn Suite for 6 Percussion, 1958; String Quartet, 1960; Quintessence for Woodwind Quintet, 1962; Trio for Violin, Piano and Percussion, 1963; Images for Brass for 5 Brass, 1964; The Preacher for Electric Trumpet and 4 Percussion, 1969; Alea for 6 Percussion, 1976; Duo for English Horn and Percussion, 1981; A few vocal works. *Recordings:* For Boston Records; Cambridge; Capitol; Mercury; Serenus; Vanguard, including symphonies by Mozart, Schumann and Beethoven; Bartók's Divertimento and Sonata for Two Pianos and Percussion; Schoenberg/Handel Concerto; Bassoon Concertos by Weber and Hummel. *Address:* c/o ASCAP, ASCAP Building, One Lincoln PLaza, New York, NY 10023, USA.

FARKAS Andras, b. 14 Apr 1945, Budapest. Conductor. m. Francoise Viquerat, 23 June 1973, 1 son, 1 daughter. *Education:* Bela Bartok Academy, Budapest; Franz Liszt Academy, Budapest; Orchestra conducting with Hans Swarowsky, and Horn, Akademie fru Musik und Darstellende Kunst, Vienna. *Debut:* Budapest, 1973. *Career:* Settled in Switzerland in 1974 and performed in concerts throughout Europe; Invited Conductor, Orchestre Symphonique de la Radio Hongroise, Orchestre Philharmonique de Budapest, Orchestre de la Suisse Romande, Orchestre de Chamber de Lusanne, Orchestre Symphonique de la Radio Slovaque, Bratislava, Orchestre symphonique de la Radio de Pilzen, Orchestre de Seville; Artistic Director and Founder, Nouvel Orchestre de Montreux, 1987. *Recordings:* Several recordings for Hungarian and Swiss radio and television. *Contributions to:* Swiss Musical Review, 1975-77. *Honours:* Vermeil medal, Arts, Sciences et Lettres, Paris, 1990. *Memberships:* Swiss Musicians Association; Centre Europeen de la Culture, Geneva. *Address:* Chemin des Bouvreuils 12, 1009 Pully, Switzerland.

FARKAS Andrew, b. 7 Apr 1936, Budapest, Hungary. Librarian; Educator. Divorced. *Education:* Eötvös Lorand University of Law, Budapest, 1954-56; BA, Occidental College, Los Angeles, 1959; Master of Library Science, University of California-Berkeley, 1962. *Career:* Gift &

Exchange Librarian, Chief Bibliographer and Assistant Head, Acquisitions Department, University of California, Davis, 1962-67; Walter J. Johnson, Inc., New York City, 1967-70; Director of Libraries and Professor of Library Science, University of North Florida, Jacksonville, Florida, 1970-. *Publications:* Music Editor to newspaper Daily Democrat, Woodland, California, 1965-67; Advisory Editor: 42 Volume Series entitled Opera Biographies, 1977; Titta Ruffo: An Anthology, 1984; Opera and Concert Singers: An Annotated International Bibliography, 1985; Editor: Lawrence Tibbett, Singing Actor, 1989; Enrico Caruso: My Father and My Family, joint author with Enrico Caruso, Jr., 1990; Series Editor ''Opera Biographies'' for Amadeus Press, 1989-; Librarians' Calendar & Pocket Reference, annual since 1984; Advisor & Contributor: International Dictionary of Opera, 1993. *Contributions to:* Opera; Opera News; The Opera Quarterly; The Record Collector, Previews; Library Journal; Member, Editorial Board: The Opera Quarterly, 1993-. *Honours:* Distinguished Professor Award, University of North Florida, 1991. *Memberships:* American Library Association; Duval County Library Association. *Hobbies:* Writing; Photography; Book and Record Collecting; Travel. *Address:* Director of Libraries, University of North Florida, PO Box 17605, Jacksonville, FL 32216, USA.

FARKAS Ferenc, b. 15 Dec 1905, Nagykanizsa, Hungary. Composer; Professor of Composition. m. Margit Kummer, 1 son. *Education:* Graduate, Academy of Music, Budapest, 1928; Corso Superiore, Accad. Sta Cecillia, Rome, Study with Respighi, 1929-31. *Debut:* Concert of own works, Budapest, 1930. *Career:* Composer, Conductor, film music, Vienna, 1932, Copenhagen, 1934-36; Professor of Composition, Municipal Music School, Budapest, 1935-41; Conservatory in Kolozsvar, 1941-46; Director, Conservatory in Szekesfehervar, 1946-49; Professor, Academy of Music, Budapest, 1949-75, retired. *Compositions Include:* Operas and Ballets - The Magic Cupboard, The Sly Students, Panegyricus - A Gentleman from Venise; Cantatas and Oratorios - Cantata Lirica, Cantus Pannonicus, Waiting for the Spring, Unfurled Flags; Aspirationes Principis, Vita Poetae (Oratorio); Vivit Dominus, Omaggio a Pessoa; Requiem pro memoria M, 1992; Number of orchestral works and concertos and chamber music; 2 masses, other choral works and songs, many recorded. *Honours:* Franz Joseph Prize, 1934; Klebelsberg Prize, 1942; Kossuth Prize, 1950 & 1991; Erkel Prize, 1960; Merited Artist, 1965; Honoured Artist, 1970; Herder Prize, 1979; Cavaliere dell'ord. della Repubblica Italiana, 1984. *Memberships:* Member, Hungarian Union of Musicians; National Choir Council; Chairman, Budapest Choir Council. *Address:* Nagyajtai utca 12, H-1026 Budapest II, Hungary.

FARKAS Katalin, b. 5 Jan 1954, Budapest, Hungary. Singer (Soprano). *Education:* Studied in Budapest. *Career:* Has sung at the Hungarian State Opera from 1982 as Rosina, Frasquita, Sophie in Werther, Zerbinetta and Mozart's Blondchen (1987); Glynderbourne Festival debut 1985, as Zdenka in Arabella; Season 1986-87 in Liszt's Don Sanche at Naples and Amaryllis in Il Pastor Fido at the Göttingen Festival; Other roles include Beethoven's Marzelline, Lola and Gianetta in L'Elisir d'amore. *Recordings include:* Don Sanche, conducted by Tamás Pal (Hungaroton). *Address:* Hungarian State Opera House, Nepoztarsasag utja 22, 1061 Budapest, Hungary.

FARLEY Carole, b. 29 Nov 1946, Le Mars, Iowa, USA. Soprano. m. José Serebrier, 29 Mar 1969, 1 daughter. *Education:* BMus, Indiana University, 1968; Fulbright Scholar, Hochschule für Musik, Munich, 1968-69. *Debut:* American debut, Town Hall, New York City, 1969; Paris debut, National Orchestra, 1975; London debut, Royal Philharmonic Society, 1975; South American debut, Teatro Colon, Philharmonic Orchestra, Buenos Aires, 1975. *Career:* Soloist with major American and European Symphony Orchestras, 1970-; Soloist, Welsh National Opera 1971, (as Lulu, in the first production by a British Company of Berg's opera) 1972, Cologne Opera 1972-75, Philadelphia Lyric Opera

1974, Brussels Opera 1972, Lyon Opera 1976, 1977, Strasbourg Opera 1975, Linz Opera 1969, New York City Opera 1976, as Offenbach's Hélène, New Orleans Opera 1977, Cincinnati Opera 1977, Metropolitan Opera Company, New York City 1977-, Zurich Opera 1979, Chicago Lyric Opera 1981, Canadian Opera Company 1980, Dusseldorf Opera 1980, 1981, 1984, Palm Beach Opera 1982; Théâtre Municipale, Paris, 1983, Théâtre Regale de la Monnaie Brussels, 1983; Teatro Regio, Turin, Italy, 1983; Nice Opera, France, 1984; Cologne Opera, Salome, conducted by John Pritchard, 1985; Firenze (Florence) Maggio Musicale, Teatro Comunale, 1985, as Lulu; TV film for ABC Australia La Voix Humaine; Sang Marie in Wozzeck at Buenos Aires, 1989. *Recordings:* for Deutsche Grammophon, CBS, BBC records; Final Scenes from Daphne and Capriccio by Strauss, Belgian Radio Orchestra, conductor Jose Serebrier (Chandos) and Songs by Prokofieff (Chandos); Songs by Prokofiev and Weill; Britten's Les Illuminations; CD, Video, Poulenc La Voix Humaine and Menotti The Telephone; Tchaikovsky Opera Arias; Milhaud Songs. *Membership:* American Guild of Musical Artists. *Hobbies:* Skiing; Jogging; Swimming; Dancing; Cooking; Entertaining; Reading.*Current Management:* Robert Lombardo Associates, New York, USA. *Address:* 270 Riverside Drive, New York, NY 10025, USA.

FARNCOMBE Charles Frederick, b. 29 July 1919, London, England. Musical Conductor. m. Sally Mae Felps, 23 May 1963, 1 daughter. *Education:* BSc Engineering, London University, 1940; LRAM, 1952. *Career:* Musical Director, Handel Opera Society, 1955-, conducted first modern British performances of Rinaldo, Alcina and Deidamia; Rodelinda, Radamisto, Riccardo Primo, Scipione, Ottone, Atalanta, Ariodante, Ezio, Giustino, Rodrigo; Chief Conductor, Royal Court Theatre, Drottningholm, Sweden, 1972-79; Chief Guest Conductor, Badisches Staats Theater, Karlsruhe, Germany, 1979-; Musical Director, London Chamber Opera, 1983-; Musical Director, Malcolm Sargent Festival Choir, 1986-; has conducted all the oratorios by Handel and Choral Works of Berlioz, Mahler and Verdi; Conducted Handel's Admeto at the 1990 Karlsruhe Festival; Artistic Director, Llantilio Crossenny Festival: Don Pasquale, 1992. *Recordings:* Castor and Pollux, Rameau; Great Handel Choruses; Drottningholm Music, Roman; Castor & Pollux (President's Prize Grand Prix Du Disque); Rodrigo, Handel; CD of Handel Highlights, 1993. *Honours:* Archibald Dawnay Scholarship in Civil Engineering, 1936, London University; Augustus Mann Prize, Royal Academy of Music, 1952; Royal Gold Medal of Drottningholm, 1972; Commander of the Order of the British Empire, 1976; Order of the Royal Northern Star, Sweden, 1982; Honorary D.Mus. City University, 1988. *Memberships:* Fellow, Royal Academy of Music; Royal Swedish Academy. *Current Management:* Werner Kühnly, Wörthstrasse 31, 7000 Stuttgart, Germany. *Hobby:* Farm Cottage on Offa's Dyke. *Address:* c/o Child & Co, 1 Fleet Street, London, EC4Y 1BD, England.

FARNON Robert Joseph, b. 24 July 1917, Toronto, Ontario, Canada. Musician; Composer. m. Patricia Mary Smith, 13 Aug 1963, 4 sons, 1 daughter. *Education:* Student, Broadus Farmer School of Music 1930-32; Humberside College 1932-34; Toronto Technical College 1934-35. *Career:* Principal Trumpet, CBC Concert Orchestra 1936-38; Musical Director, CBC 1939-42; Conductor, BBC TV and Radio 1946-; Served with Canadian Army 1943-46; Member, BBC Music Advisory Committee; Guest Conductor, international orchestras. *Compositions include:* Symphony No. 1 1939, Symphony No. 2 1941, Rhapsody for Violin and Orchestra 1956, Saxophone Triparte 1974, Prelude and Dance for Harmonica and Orchestra 1969, Canadian Impressions Suite 1952, Composer of Film Music in Great Britain, Canada and US 1946-. *Address:* c/o Warner Chappell Music Limited, 129 Park Street, London, W1Y 3FA.

FARQUHAR David Andross, b. 5 Apr 1928, Cambridge, New Zealand. Composer. m. Raydia d'Elsa,

2 June 1954, 1 son, 1 daughter. *Education:* BMus, University of New Zealand; MA, Cambridge University; Guildhall School of Music. *Career:* Lecturer, 1953-; Professor of Music, Victoria University of Wellington, New Zealand, 1976-93. *Compositions:* And One Makes Ten; Anniversary Duets, (2 sets); Concertino for Piano and Strings; Evocation; Five Scenes for Guitar; On Your Own; Partita; Ring Round the Moon: dance suite; Three Pieces for Double Bass; Three Scots Ballads; Concerto for wind quintet; Three Improvisations, 1988; Three Songs of Cilla McQueen; Eight Blake Songs, Three Echoes, Symphony No2, String Quartet, 1989, Waiata Maori. *Recordings:* Concerto for Wind Quintet; Symphony No 1; Three Improvisations; Three Pieces for Violin and Piano; Concertino for Piano and Strings; Evocation; Partita; Ring Round the Moon; Three Scots Ballads; In Despite of Death, Homage to Stravinsky, Magpies and Other Birds, String Quartet, 1989. *Memberships:* Composers Association of New Zealand, Founding President; Board Member, New Zealand Composers' Foundation. *Address:* 15 Nottingham Street, Wellington 5, New Zealand.

FARRELL Eileen, b. 13 Feb 1920, Williamantic, Connecticut, USA. Opera Singer. m. Robert V. Reagan 1976, 1 son 1 daughter. *Career:* Debut with Columbia Broadcasting Company 1941, own programme for six years; Opera debut with San Francisco Opera (Il Trovatore); Carnegie Hall, 1951, as Marie in a concert performance of Wozzeck; Toured throughout the USA and in other parts of the world; sang Berg's Marie and Cherubini's Medea in New York concert performances; Metropolitan Opera 1960 as Gluck's Alceste, followed by Santuzza, Gioconda, Maddalena and Leonora in La Forza del Destino; sang Wagner's Brünnhilde and Isolde, under Leonard Bernstein. *Honours:* Several honorary degrees; Grammy Award. *Address:* c/o Metropolitan Opera, Lincoln Center, New york, NY 10023, USA.

FARRELL Peter Snow, b. 13 Sept 1924, Greensboro, North Carolina, USA. Professor; Concert Artist, cello and viola da gamba. m. Miriam, 2 sons. *Education:* MMus, Eastman School of Music, University of Rochester; Artists Diploma, Eastman School. *Career:* Solo and Chamber Music performances throughout USA and Great Britain, German Federal Republic, Poland, France and Hawaii; Appearances at major festivals; Specialisation on performances of contemporary music (cello) and Renaissance and Baroque Music (gamba); Former Principal Cellist, Columbus Philharmonic Orchestra and San Diego Symphony Orchestra; Former Faculty Member, Eastman School of Music and National Music Camp, Interlochen; Former Professor of Music, University of Illinois at Urbana; Professor, Music Department, University of California, San Diego; Chair, Music Department University of California, San Diego; Numerous orchestral and chamber music recordings; Professor Emeritus, Music Department, University of California, San Diego. *Hobbies:* Sailing; Hiking. *Address:* University of California, San Diego, La Jolla, CA 92093, USA.

FARREN-PRICE Ronald William, b. 2 July 1930, Brisbane, Australia. Pianist; University Academic. m. Margaret Lillian Cameron, 15 Jan 1982, 3 sons, 2 daughters. *Education:* Brisbane Grammar School; Diploma in Music, University of Melbourne, 1951; Studies with Claudio Arrau on a personal scholarship donated by him, 1952-55, London and New York. *Debut:* Melbourne, S.O. Concerto, 1947; Wigmore Hall, London, 1955. *Career:* Has played in over 30 countries around the world including, 7 concert tours of USSR, and many performances at London's Wigmore Hall, Queen Elizabeth Hall, Purcell Room and St John's, Smith Square; Performances at, Carnegie Recital Hall, New York; National Gallery, Washington; Tchaikovsky Hall, Moscow; Reader in Music, 1975-, Dean, Faculty of Music, 1986-, University of Melbourne; Has performed concertos with many of the leading conductors of the world including, Antal Dorati, Ferdinand Leitner, Eugene Goossens, Charles Groves, Hiroyuki Iwaki, Willem van Otterloo, John Hopkins, Moshe Atzmon and Harry Blech; Has broadcast recitals in many countries and also appeared in television recitals. *Hobbies:* Swimming; Walking; Travelling. *Address:* Faculty of Music, University of Melbourne, Parkville, VIC 3052, Australia.

FARULLI Piero, b. 13 Jan 1920, Florence, Italy. Professor of Viola. *Education:* Conservatorio Statale Luigi Cherubini, Florence (under Gioacchino Maglioni). *Career:* Professor of Viola 1957-77; For thirty years a member of Quartetto Italiano; Has also collaborated with Amadeus and Berg Quartets; appeared with Trio di Trieste 1978; Has lectured at Accademia Chigiana di Siena and at Salzburg Mozarteum; Member of judging panel at several international competitions and has been active in many aspects of musical life and education in Italy, notably in Fiesole. *Honours:* Medaglia della Cultura e dell'Arte; Premio Massimo Mila. *Address:* Via G d'Annunzio 153, Florence, Italy.

FASSBAENDER Brigitte, b. 3 July 1939, Berlin, Germany. Singer (Mezzo-Soprano); Stage Producer. *Education:* Studied in Nuremberg with her father, Willi Domgraf-Fassbaender. *Debut:* Munich 1961, as Nicklausse in Les Contes d'Hoffmann. *Career:* Has sung in Munich, Dusseldorf, Frankfurt and Milan as Eboli, Sextus, Hansel, Carlotta in Die schweigsame Frau, Clarice in La Pietra del Paragone, Marina, and the Countess Geschwitz in Lulu; San Francisco 1970, as Carmen; Covent Garden debut 1971, as Octavian; Paris Opera 1972, Brangaene; Salzburg Festival 1972-78, as Dorabella in Così fan Tutte; Metropolitan Opera debut 1974, as Octavian: returned to New York 1986, as Fricka in Die Walküre; Vienna Staatsoper 1976, in the premiere of Kabale und Liebe by Von Einem; Bayreuth Festival 1983-84; La Scala Milan 1986, in Die Frau ohne Schatten; Metropolitan Opera, 1986, as Fricka in Die Walküre; Salzburg Festival, 1989, as Clytennestra in Elektra; Produced Der Rosenkavalier at Munich, 1989, Cenerentola at Coburg 1990, Der Ferne Klang for Opera North, 1992; Hansel and Gretel in Augsburg, 1992; A Midsummer Night's Dream in Amsterdam, 1993; Die Zauberflöte in Coburg, 1993; Sang Clairon in Capriccio at the 1990 Glynderbourne Festival; Concert artist in works by Bach and Mahler, and song recitalist; Masterclasses at the 1992 Brereton International Symposium. *Recordings include:* More than 100 recordings since 1964 comprising Opera, Recital, Concert and Oratorio works from Scarlatti to Schoenberg and La Clemenza di Tito and Lulu (Decca); Die Zauberflöte and Die Fledermaus (Electrola); St John Passion by Bach; Messiah; Pfitzner's Palestrina, Il Giardino d'Amore by Scarlatti, Mozart's La Finta Giardiniera and Tristan und Isolde (Deutsche Grammophon); Christmas Oratorio by Bach and Mahler's Das Lied von der Erde; Video of Elektra (as Clytennestra) conducted by Abbado, Virgin. *Address:* c/o Sekretariat, Haiming, 83119 Obing, Germany.

FAST George Allan, b. 27 Mar 1954, Leamington, Ontario, Canada. Countertenor Soloist; Voice Professor; Writer on Music. *Education:* BMusA, University of Western Ontario. *Debut:* With Waverly Consort, Kennedy Center, Washington DC, USA, 1979. *Career:* Soloist with Tafelmusik Baroque Orchestra, The Bach Ensemble, National Arts Centre Orchestra (Ottawa), CBC Vancouver Orchestra, Smithsonian Chamber Players, New York Oratorio Society, Oregon Symphony, Opera Atelier (Toronto), Casals Festival, Madeira Bach Festival, Wratislavia Cantans, Pacific Opera Victoria, Les Violons du Roy, Studio de Musique Ancienne de Montreal, L'Orchestre de la Nouvelle France, Edmonton Symphony, Louisville Bach Society and others; Assistant Professor of Early Music Voice, Director of Cappella Antica, McGill University. *Recordings:* The Christmas Story, The Waverly Consort, CBS Masterworks, 1983; Renaissance Favorites, The Waverly Consort, CBS Masterworks, 1985; Bach Cantatas 8, 78 and 99, Bach Ensemble, Joshua Rifkin, Decca, 1989; Complete Alto Cantatas of Buxtehude, McGill Records, 1989. *Hobbies:* Gardening; Painting. *Current Management:* Colwell Arts Management, RR No 1, New Hamburg, Ontario, Canada. *Address:* 263 Bourchemin Ouest, St-Hugues, Quebec, Canada, J0H 1N0.

FATH Karl, b. 1941, Germany. Singer (Bass). *Career:* Sang at Giessen 1963-67, Koblenz, 1968-72, Brunswick, 1972-74 and Saarbrucken 1974- 77; Engaged at Gelsenkirchen from 1977 and has made guest appearances at Stuttgart, Garlsruhe, Frankfurt, 1984-86 and Cologne, 1987-88; Tour of Brazil, 1982, singing in Jakob Lenz by Wolfgang Rihm; appeared as Don Magnifico in La Cenerentola at Bielefeld, 1989, Lunardo in I Quattro Rusteghi by Wolf-Ferrari at Hanover, 1991; Many Lieder recitals and concert appearances. *Recordings:* Petite messe solonnelle by Rossini. *Address:* c/o Niedersachsiche Staatstheater, Opernplatz 1, 3000 Hannover, Germany.

FAUBERT Jacques, b. 1952, Valleyfield, Canada. Composer; Professor. *Education:* Studied at Conservatoire de Montréal at age of 18; Studied ear training with Andrée Germain and Marcel Laurencelle, harmony with Gaston Arel, counterpoint, fugue, orchestration and composition with Jean-Louis Martinet, electro-acousties with Micheline Coulombe Saint-Marcoux, 1970-76; Studied composition and orchestration under Jean-Louis Martinet in Paris, 1976-79, studied fugue under Marcel Bitsch 1978; studied analysis under Jacque Castéréde 1979; Conservatoire National Supérieur de Musique. *Career:* Choirmaster, St. Joseph de Ville Mount-Royal Church 1979; Professor of harmony, counterpoint, fugue and orchestration, Conservatoire de Trois-Rivières; Professor of harmony and fugue, Conservatoire de Montréal; several of his works have been commissioned, created, published and broadcast in Canada and France. *Compositions include:* Requiem sans parole. *Address:* Louise Ostiguy, 1906 H Bourassa Est, Apt 405, Montreal, Quebec H2B 1S1, Canada.

FAULL Ellen, b. 14 Oct 1918, Pittsburgh, Pennsylvania, USA. Singer (Soprano). *Education:* Studied in Pittsburgh, then at the Curtis Institute and in New York. *Career:* Sang at the New York City Opera 1947-70, as Donna Anna, Madama Butterfly, Eva and Mozart's Countess, and in the 1965 premiere of Lizzie Borden by Jack Beeson; Many appearances with regional companies in the USA; Concert appearances with orchestras in San Francisco, Boston, Chicago, Los Angeles, Cincinnati and Pittsburgh; Conductors include Solti, Serafin, Ormandy, Koussevitsky, Stokowski and De Sabata; Member of the voice department at the Juilliard School; Adjudicator for singing competitions, including the Metropolitan Opera Auditions. *Address:* c/o The Juilliard School of Music, Lincoln Center Plaza, New York, NY 10023, USA.

FAUST Isabelle, b. 19 Mar 1972, Esslingen/N, West Germany. Violinist. *Education:* Gymnasium Gerlingen, Baden-Wurttemberg; Musikhochschule des Saarlandes, Saarbrücken. *Career:* Recitals, Schleswig-Holstein Festival 1987, Mozart Festival, Hildesheim 1988; Soloist at concerts with: Hamburg Philharmonic Orchestra (conductor Sir Yehudi Menuhin), Rias Symphony Orchestra, Wurttemberg Chamber & Philharmonic Orchestras, State Philharmonic of Rheinland-Pfalz, Orchestra of Padua (conductor, Bruno Giuranna). *Recordings:* Radio: Bartók's Solo Sonata for Violin; Mozart's Violin Concerto in A major (K 219); Dvořák's Violin Concerto in A minor; J. S. Bach's Violin Concerto in A minor. *Honours:* 1st prize, International Leopold Mozart Competition for Violinists, 1987; Prizes, International Radio Competitions Concertino Praha, 1984, 1987. *Hobbies:* Reading; Table tennis; Writing letters; Foreign languages & literature. *Address:* Lontelstrasse 19, 7016 Gerlingen, Germany.

FEAR Arthur, b. 1902, Blaina, Monmouthshire, Wales. Singer (Baritone). *Education:* Studied at the Royal Academy of Music with Thomas Meux. *Career:* Sang Falstaff and Hans Sachs while at College; Sang Sachs with the British National Opera Company at Leeds, 1927; Covent Garden 1929, in the premiere of Judith by Eugene Goossens; Sang with the Royal Opera as Rigoletto, the villains in Les Contes d'Hoffmann, Gunther in Götterdämmerung, Donner, Sharpless, Telramund, Kaspar in Der Freischütz, Renato in Un Ballo in Maschera, Sachs and Escamillo; Concert tours of USA 1936, 1938 with visits to Boston, Cincinnati and New York; Tours of Britain with the Covent Garden Company and the British National Opera Company; Sang with the Carl Rosa Company after the War. *Recordings include:* Gunther in Götterdämmerung.

FEDER Donn-Alexandre, b. 23 June 1935, Philadelphia, Pennsylvania, USA. Concert Pianist; Teacher. m. Janet Landis, 26 Aug 1960, 1 daughter. *Education:* DMA, 1973, MS, 1959, BS, 1958, Juilliard School of Music; Studies with Rosina Lhevinne, Kabos and Gorodnitzki; Study at Eastman and with Jorge Bolet. *Debut:* New York Town Hall, 1963. *Career:* Extensive concertizing throughout Europe, Mexico, Canada and USA NBC and ABC-TV; BBC England; Appearances with major European and American orchestras; Faculty, Philadelphia College of Performing Arts, 1971-81; Piano Faculty Member, Manhattan School of Music, 1978-; Part of professional two-piano team, Feder and Gilgore; Co-Director, Musicisti Americani Festival and Institute, Rome and Sulmona, Italy; Artist-Teacher, Tawain International Festival, Republic of China, 1988 and 1989. *Recordings:* Recordings with Netherlands Radio Philharmonic under Allers and Van Otterloo; Recording artist for Protone and Chandos; Szymanowski Piano Music; Excursions for Two Pianos, Music of Barber, Copland and Gershwin (with Elisha Gilgore); Bartók Sonata for Two Pianos and Percussion, Stravinsky Concerto for Two Solo Pianos (with Elisha Gilgore). *Current Management:* Nicholas Choveaux Management, England. *Address:* 755 Palm Avenue No.306, Sarasota, Florida 34236, USA.

FEDER Susan (Elisabeth), b. 21 Feb 1955, New York City, New York, USA. Writer; Editor on Music. m. Todd I Gordon, 10 Apr 1983. *Education:* BA, Princeton University, 1976; MA, University of California, Berkeley, 1979. *Career:* Vice President and Director of Promotion, G Schirmer Incorporated, 1986-; Editorial Co-ordinator, New Grove Dictionary of American Music, 1981-86; Programme Editor, San Francisco Symphony, 1979-81; Freelance Writer. *Publications:* Editorial Co-ordinator, New Grove Dictionary of American Music; Music Performance Trust Fund Orchestral Guide, 1982-83. *Contributions to:* Musical Times; Musical America; Stagebill; Programme Annotator for American Composers Orchestra, 1981-91, San Francisco Symphony, Boston Symphony, Dallas Opera; Grove's Dictionary articles. *Honours:* ASCAP Deems Taylor Award, 1986. *Memberships:* MPA (Board of Directors, 1988-); AMS; MCA; ASOL; Sonneck Society. *Address:* 53 Jaffray Court, Irvington, NY 10533, USA.

FEDOSEYEV Vladimir Ivanovich, b. 5 Aug 1932, Leningrad, Russia. Conductor. m. Olga Ivanovna Dobrohotova. *Education:* Moscow Musical Institute; Moscow State Conservatory. *Debut:* With Mravinsky Orchestra, Leningrad Philharmonic Concert Hall. *Career:* Principal Conductor, Academic Orchestra of Russian Folk Instruments, TV-Radio USSR, 1957-74; Principal Conductor, Moscow Radio Symphony Orchestra, 1974-; Appeared regularly with RAI Milano Symphony Orchestra, French National Orchestra; Appeared in last 4 years: Munich Symphony Orchestra, Vienna Philharmonic Orchestra, Hamburg Radio Symphony, La Scala Opera, Milan, Istanbul and Ankara Symphony Orchestras, Antwerp Symphony Orchestra, Tokyo Philharmonic Orchestra, NHK Orchestra, Osaka Symphony Orchestra, Japan; Conducted the Vienna Symphony Orchestra in La Damnation de Faust at the 1992 Bregenz Festival; conducted Carmen, performance in Staatsoper in Vienna, 1993; conducted 3 performances of Requiem Verdi with Luciano Pavarotti and World Festival Choir in Oslo, Stockholm, 1992, Munich, 1993. *Recordings:* About 100 with Grand Moscow Radio Symphony Orchestra. *Honours:* 2nd Prize for Record of the Year, Tchaikovsky 6th Symphony, Tokyo, 1983; Crystal Award, International Music Awards, Osaka, 1988; Silver Award for the best Concert of the season, Osaka, 1989; Golden Orpheus Award of the French National Academy for the recording of the opera, May Night. *Hobby:* Fishing. *Current*

Management: Moscow Radio Symphony Orchestra. *Address:* Moscow Radio Symphony Orchestra, Piatnitskaia Str 25, 113326 Moscow, Russia.

FEINSTEIN Martin, b. 12 Apr 1921, New York, USA. Music Administrator. *Education:* Studied at Wayne State University and the City College of New York. *Career:* Director of Publicity for Sol Hurok Concerts in New York, 1945-50; Vice-president of Sol Hurok Concerts 1950-71; In addition, served as visiting Professor at Yale University, 1971-73; Executive Director of the John F Kennedy Center for the Performing Arts in Washington DC, 1972-80; President and Chief Executive Officer of the National Symphony, 1979-80; General Director, Washington Opera, 1980-. *Address:* The Washington Opera, John F Kennedy Center for the Performing Arts, Washington DC 20566, USA.

FEJER András, b. 1950, Hungary. Cellist. *Education:* Studied with András Mihaly at the Franz Liszt Academy, Budapest, with members of the Amadeua Quartet and Zoltán Szekely. *Career:* Founder member of the Takacs Quartet, 1975; Many concert appearances in all major centres of Europe and the USA; Tours of Australia, New Zealand, Japan, South America, England, Norway, Sweden, Greece, Belgium and Ireland; Bartók Cycle for the Bartók-Solti Festival at South Bank, 1990; Great Performers Series at Lincoln Center and Mostly Mozart Festival at Alice Tully Hall, New York; Visits to Japan 1989 and 1992; Mozart Festivals at South Bank, Wigmore Hall and Barbican Centre 1991; Bartók Cycle at the Théâtre des Champs-Elysées 1991; Beethoven Cycles at the Zurich Tonhalle, in Dublin, at the Wigmore Hall and in Paris, 1991-92; Resident at the University of Colorado, Resident at the London Barbican 1988-91, with master classes at the Guildhall School of Music; Plays Amati instrument made for the French Royal Family and loaned by the Corcoran Gallery, Gallery of Art, Washington DC. *Honours:* Winner, International Quartet Competition, Evian 1977; Winner, Portsmouth International Quartet Competition, 1979. *Recordings:* Schumann Quartets Op 41, Mozart String Quintets (with Denes Koromzay), Bartók 6 Quartets, Schubert Trout Quintet (with Zoltán Kocsis) Hungaroton; Haydn Op 76, Brahms Op 51 nos 1 and 2, Chausson Concerto (with Joshua Bell and Jean-Yves Thibaudet); Works by Schubert, Mozart, Dvořák and Bartók (Decca). *Address:* Artists Management International, 12/13 Richmond Buildings, Dean Street, London W1V 5AF, England.

FELCIANO Richard (James), b. 7 Dec 1930, Santa Rosa, California, USA. Composer; Teacher. *Education:* Pupil of Milhaud, Mills College, Oakland, California, MA 1955; Continued studies with Milhaud and Ple-Caussade, Paris Conservatory, 2 diplomas, 1955; Privately with Dallapiccola, Florence, 1958-59; with Bezanson, University of Iowa, PhD, 1959. *Career:* Composer-in-Residence, National Center for Experiments in Television, San Francisco, 1967-71; City of Boston, 1971-73; Chairman, Music Department, Lone Mountain College, San Francisco, 1959-67; Professor, University of California, Berkeley, 1967-; Founding Director, Center for New Music and Audio Technologies, University of California, Berkeley, 1987. *Compositions:* Chamber Opera: Sir Gawain and the Green Knight, 1964; Experimented television works; Orchestral: Mutations, 1966; Galactic Rounds, 1972; Orchestra, 1980; Concerto for Organ and Orchestra, 1986; Symphony for string orchestra, 1993; Chamber: Evolutions for Clarinet and Piano, 1962; Contractions for Woodwind Quintet, 1965; Glossolalia for Baritone, Organ, Percussion and Tape, 1967; Crasis for flute, clarinet, violin, cello, harp, piano, percussion and tape, 1967; Chod for Violin, Cello, Double Bass, Piano, Percussion and Live Electronics, 1972; Salvadore Allende for String Quartet, Clarinet and Percussion, 1983; Alleluia to the Heart of Stone for Reverberated Recorder, 1984; Lontano for harp and piano, 1986; Shadows for flute, clarinet, violin, cello, piano and percussion, 1987; Palladio for violin, piano and percussion, 1989; Camp Songs for chamber orchestra (15 instruments), 1992; Piano pieces; Various choral works. *Recordings:* Conducted own works on discs.

Honours: Fulbright Fellowship, 1958; Guggenheim Fellowship, 1969; American Academy of Arts and Letters Award, 1974; Various grants and commissions. *Address:* c/o Music Department, University of California, Berkeley, CA 94720, USA.

FELD Jindrich, b. 19 Feb. 1925, Prague, Czechoslovakia. Composer; Music Teacher. m. Helena Feldova, 22 Jul. 1955. 1 daughter. *Education:* Prague Conservatoire, 1945-48; Academy of Music Prague, 1948-52; PhD, Charles University, Prague. *Career:* Composer; Music Teacher; Vic. Composer-in-Residence, University of Adelaide, Australia, 1968-69; Professor, Conservatoire of Prague, 1972-1986; Head, Department of Music, Czechoslovak Radio Prague, 1990-; Guest lectures in Germany, Denmark, Norway, several Universities in the USA and Japan. *Compositions include:* Sonatina for 2 Violins, 1952-53; Concerto for Flute and Orchestra, 1954; Rhapsody for Violin and Orchestra, 1956; Sonata for Flute and Piano, 1957; Concerto for Cello and Orchestra, 1958; 3 Frescoes for Grand Symphony Orchestra, 1963; String Quartet No. 4, 1965; Inventions for Mixed Chamber Choir, 1966; 1 Symphony for Grand Symphony Orchestra, 1966-67; Wind Quintet No 2, 1968, Dramatic Fantasy, The Days of August, for Symphony Orchestra, 1968-69, Brass Quintet, 1970; Concerto for Piano and Orchestra, 1973; Concert Suite for percussion instruments, 1976; String Quartet No. 5, 1979; Violin Concerto, 1977; Saxophone Concerto, 1980; Harp Concerto, 1982; Symphony No. 2, 1983; Laus Cantus, for Soprano Voice and String Quartet, 1985; Concerto da camera, for 2 string quartets, 1987; Cosmae Chronica Boemorum, Oratorio-Cantata for Mixed Chorus, Soli and Symphony Orchestra, 1988; Sonata for Alto Saxophone and Piano, 1990; Numerous other symphonic, concerto, chamber, vocal, stage and pedagogic works published and recorded. *Contributions to:* Hudebni Rozhledy (Musical Review), Prague. *Hobbies:* History, Violin and Viola; Tennis; Skiing. *Address:* Peckova 17, 186 00, Prague 8, Czech Republic.

FELDBUSCH Eric, b. 2 mar 1922, Grivegnee, Belgium. Composer; Cellist. *Education:* Studied at the Liege Conservatory, 1934-39. *Career:* Active as concert cellist and teacher, Mons Conservatory, Professor de Violincello, 1953-63, Directeur, 1963-1973; Brussels Conservatory, Directeur, 1974-87. *Compositions include:* Opera Orestes 1969 and Ballet El Diablo Cojuelo, 1972; Orchestral: Contrastes 1956; Les Moin eaux de Baltimore, suite, 1958; Mosäique for strings 1961; Three Lorca Poems for voice and orchestra 1964; violin Concerto 1967; Fentaisie- Divertissement, 1967; Cantique des cantiques for soprano and orchestra, 1970; Piccola musica for strings 1971; Triade for chamber orchestra, 1977; Concertante for 2 pianos and orchestra, 1986; Cello concerto, 1988; Chamber: Violin Sonata, 1957; 4 String quartets, 1955-71; Duo for flute and piano, 1959; Trio for flute, cello and violin, 1961; Septet for soprano and ensemble, 1969; Cheminement for violin and violin ensemble, 1984; Piano music; Incidental music for plays. *Address:* SABM (Belgium), c/o PRS Ltd Member Registration, 29-33 Berners Street, London WIP 4AA, England.

FELDERER Ingeborg, b. 28 Nov 1933, Innsbruck, Austria. Singer (Soprano). *Education:* Studied in Vienna and Milan. *Career:* Engaged at the Basle Stadttheater 1955-59, notably in the premiere of Titus Feuerfuchs by Sutermeister and the local premiere of The Fiery Angel by Prokofiev, 1957; Wuppertal, 1959-62, Karlsruhe, 1962-65, Basle, 1962-67; Sang minor roles at the Bayreuth Festival 1961-63 and made guest appearances in Copenhagen, Frankfurt, Barcelona, Brussels, Zurich and Paris; Metropolitan Opera New York, 1967-70 as Santuzza and the Trovatore Leonora; Vienna Staatsoper as Senta, Chyrsothemis in Elektra and Woglinde; Barcelona, 1969, as Elisabetta in Maria Stuarda; Other roles were Hecuba in King Priam (German premiere Karlsruhe, 1963), Tosca, Poppea, Katya Kabanova and the Duchess of Parma in Dokotr Faust by Busoni; Frequent concert appearances. *Address:* c/o Bayerische Staatsoper, Postfach 100148, 8000 Munich 1, Germany.

FELDERHOF Jan Reindent Adriaan, b. 25 Sept 1907, Bussum, The Netherlands, Composer, Violinist, Conductor. m. Petronella J Mulder, 2 sons, 1 daughter. *Education:* Violin and Composition Certificate, Amsterdam Conservatory; Certificate, Schoolmusic, Utrecht University Conservatory. *Career:* Headteacher Amsterdam and Utrecht Conservatories; Director, Rotterdam Conservatory; Adjunct Director, Amsterdam Conservatory; Teacher at a Girls' High School and at the Folk Music School; Conductor of many choirs and orchestras; Guest Conductor, Broadcasting Orchestras and the Concertgebouw Orchestra; Has given many radio violin recitals. *Compositions include:* for orchestra: Introduction and Rondo, Chanterelle, Suite nostalgique, Elegie, Sinfonietta, Symphonie, Overture, Funeral Music (with vocalising choir), Flute Concerto, Complimento (string orchestra), Omaggio (orchestra), Cantata, 'To Whom Shall We Go', (with vocal soloists); Groen is de gong (with choir); Facetten (choir and piano with vocal soloists); Compositie (female choir with flute and harp); 5 String Quartets; 1 Brass Quartet; 2 Operas; Chamber Music. *Recordings:* Concerto for Flute and string orchestra. *Honour:* Knight in the Order of Oranje Nassau, 1970. *Membership:* Society of Netherlands Composers. *Hobbies:* Former hobbies: Tennis; Bridge; Mountain-sports. *Address:* Iris-Straat 2, 1402 ER, Bussum, The Netherlands.

FELDHOF Gerd, b. 29 Oct 1931, Radevormwald, Cologne, Germany. Singer (Baritone). *Education:* Studied in Detmold. *Debut:* Essen 1959, as Mozart's Figaro. *Career:* Guest engagement at Buenos Aires 1960; Städtische Oper Berlin and Frankfurt Opera from 1961; Metropolitan Opera from 1961, debut as Kaspar in Der Freischütz; Further appearances in Helsinki, Hamburg, Copenhagen, Amsterdam, Montreal, Mexico City, Japan and Korea; Bayreuth Festival 1968-78, notably as Amfortas; Also sings Barak in Die Frau ohne Schatten. *Recordings include:* Lulu, and Kothner in Die Meistersinger; Beethoven's 9th Symphony; Jonny spielt auf by Krenek; Hindemith's Mathis der Maler. *Address:* Festspielhaus, 85008 Bayreuth, Germany.

FELDMAN Barbara Monk, b. 18 Jan 1953, Quebec, Canada. Composer; Theorist. m. Morton Feldman, 6 June 1987. *Education:* MMus, McGill University, 1983; PhD, Composition, SUNY Buffalo, 1987. *Career:* Faculty member, Internationale Ferienkurse fur Neue Musik, Darmstadt, 1988, 1990. *Compositions:* Trio for Violin, Cello and Piano, 1983; Variations for Six Strings Instruments, 1986; Variations for String Quartet and Chorus, 1987; Duo for Piano and Percussion, 1988; Two Pianos, 1989; The I and Thou, solo paino, 1988; Infinite Other, choir and instruments, 1992; Pure difference, instrumental ensemble, 1991; The Immutable Silence, instrumental ensemble, 1990. *Publications:* Article, All Things Being Unmeasured, New Observations, 1989. *Honours:* Edgard Varese Fellowship, SUNY Buffalo, 1984-87. *Address:* 83 Oriole Road, Toronto, Ontario M4V 2G2, Canada.

FELDMAN Jill, b. 21 Apr 1952, Los Angeles, USA. Signer (Soprano). *Education:* Studied at San Francisco, Basle and the University of California at Santa Barbara (Musicology). *Career:* Has sung in France and elsewhere in Europe in many performances of early music; US opera debut, 1979, as Music in Monteverdi's Orfeo; Europe opera debut, 1980, as Clerio in Cavalli's Erismana, at Spoleto; Concerts with William Christie include Charpentier's Médée at the Salle Pleyel, Paris, 1984; Sang Vita in the first modern revival of Marco Marazolli's La vita Humana, at the Tramway, Glasgow, with the Scottish Early Music Consort, 1990. *Recordings:* Rameau's Anacreon, Cesti's Orontea, Cavalli's Xerse; Charpentier's Médée, Acteon, Les Arts Florissants and the incidental music for Molière's Le Malade Imaginaire, conducted by Marc Minkowski. *Address:* c/o Scottish Early Music Consort, 22 Falkland Street, Glasgow G12 9PR, Scotland.

FELIX Václav, b. 29 Mar 1928, Prague, Czechoslovakia. Composer; Musicologist; Educator. m. Danuse Felixová, 1 son, 2 daughters. *Education:*

Graduate, Musical Faculty, Academy of Musical Arts, Prague, 1953; PhD and Candidate of Science, Charles University, Prague. *Career:* Editor, Hudebni Rozhledy, Prague, 1959-61; Assistant, Musical Faculty, 1951-54, Special Assistant, 1960-73, Docent in Music Theory, 1973-84, Professor, Composition and Music Theory, 1985-92, Dean of Musical Faculty, 1985-90. *Compositions include:* Sonata Capricciosa for flute and piano, 1981; Concerto for trumpet and orchestra, 1984; Symphony No. 1, for female voice and orchestra, 1974; The Advertisement, chamber mini-opera, 1977; Sonata Lirica for oboe and piano, 1978; Double Concerto for violoncello, piano and string orchestra, 1978; Quartetto Amoroso, for string quartet, 1979; Symphony No. 2, for small orchestra, 1981; Mariana, Opera in 4 acts, 1982; Sonata Poetica for piano solo, 1988; Sonata Concertante for viola and piano, 1989; Concerto for violoncello and orchestra, 1990; Symphony No.3, for mixed choir and large orchestra, 1986; Symphony No.4, for large orchestra, 1987; Symphony No.5, for chamber orchestra, 1987; Symphony No.6, for large wind orchestra, 1990; Numerous other published compositions. *Publications:* Janaček's Sonata Style, 1980; The Fundamental Problems of Musical Forms, 1983. *Contributions to:* Hudebni Rozhledy; Ziva hudba. *Memberships:* Member, Association of Musical Artists and Scientists, 1990. *Hobby:* Entomology. *Address:* K Betáni 1099, 148 00 Praha 4-Kunratice, Czech Republic.

FELLEGI Adam, b. 1941, Budapest, Hungary. Concert Pianist. *Education:* Budapest Academy of Music, 1963; Master Class for Young Pianists conducted by P Badura-Skoda, Alfred Brendel and Jörg Demus, 1966. *Career:* Has given recitals, concerts appearing as soloist; Guest performances in Austria, Canada, Czechoslovakia, France, Germany, Great Britain, Italy, the Netherlands, USA and USSR. *Recordings:* Has made numerous recordings. *Honours:* 1st Prize, International Cultural Centre, Vienna, Austria, 1966; Special Prize, Liszt-Bartók International Music Competition, Budapest, 1966; Artur Rubinstein Prize, Rio de Janeiro International Piano Concours, 1974; Liszt Prize, 1981.

FELLER Carlos, b. 30 July 1922, Buenos Aires, Argentina. Singer (Bass). *Education:* Studied at the opera studio of the Teatro Colon. *Debut:* Sang the Doctor in Pelléas et Mélisande, Buenos Aires 1946. *Career:* Sang widely in South America and toured Europe with the Argentinian Chamber Orchestra, 1958; Resident in West Germany from 1958, notably at the Cologne Opera where he has sung Don Pasquale, Dulcamara, Dr Bartolo, Leporello and Don Alfonso; Glyndebourne Festival 1959-60, as Don Alfonso, Figaro, the Speaker in Die Zauberflöte and Dr Bombasto in the British premiere of Busoni's Arlecchino; Appearances at the Salzburg, Edinburgh and Holland Festivals and in most major opera houses in Europe and the Americas; Metropolitan Opera debut 1988, as Don Alfonso, followed by Dr Bartolo, 1990; Buenos Aires and Santiago, 1990-91; Other roles in Il Matrimonio Segreto (Venice and Washington); Wozzeck (Seattle); Zar und Zimmermann, Der Rosenkavalier, La Cambiale di Matrimonio and Il Signor Bruschino (Cologne); Season 1992 as Don Alfonso in performances of Così fan Tutte in Paris and Lisbon conducted by John Eliot Gardiner; Season 1992-93, Nozze di Figaro on tour with Monteverdi C & O (John Eliot Gardiner) to Lisbon, Paris, London; Recorded by DGG for future release and video recording by Cameras Continentals. *Recordings include:* Don Alfonso and Mozart's Bartolo, with the Drottningholm ensemble conducted by Arnold Oestmann (Decca); Videos of Il Barbiere di Siviglia, Il Matrimonio Segreto, La Gazza Ladra and Agrippina. *Address:* c/o Haydn Rawstron Ltd, PO Box 654, London SE26 4DZ, England.

FELLINGER Imogen, b. 9 Sept 1928, Munich, Germany, Musicologist. *Education:* University of Munich and Tübingen; PhD, University of Tübingen, 1956. *Career:* Research Collaborator, International Inventory of Musical Sources, RISM, German Federal Republic, 1957-62; Chairman, Research Department for Music Bibliography, 19th Century, Institute of Musicology,

University of Cologne, 1963-70; Chairman, Music Archive of the 19th century State Institute for Music Research, Prussian Culture Collection, Berlin, 1970-93; Head, Library, 1971-93; Scientific Councillor, 1974, Scientific Super Councillor, 1983. *Publications:* Über die Dynamik in der Musik von Johannes Brahms, 1961; Verzeichnis der Musikzeitschriften des 19 Jahrhunderts, 1968; Periodica Musicalia (1789-1830), 1986; Editor, Klavierstücke op 118 and 119 von J Brahms, 1974. *Contributions to:* MGG Ed, 1-2; Riemann Musik Lexikon; Neue deutsche Biographie; Die Musikforschung; Studien zur Musikgeschichte des 19 Jahrhunderts; Beiträge zur rheinischen Musikgeschichte; The New Grove Dictionary of Music and Musicians; Fontes Artis Musicae; Mozart-Jahrbuch, 1978-79, 1980-83; Acta Musicologica, 1983-84; Bruckner-Symposium, Linz, 1983-85; Hamburger Jahrbuch für Musikwissenschaft, vol 7-8; Brahms-Studien, 1981, 1983, 1985; Brahms 1-2, Cambridge 1983, 1987; Jahrbuch des Staatlichen Instituts für Musikforschung, 1971, 1987-88; The New Grove Dictionary of Opera; The New Grove Dictionary of American Music. *Address:* 10 St Anna-Platz, 80538 Munich, Germany.

FELTSMAN Vladimir, b. 8 Jan 1952, Moscow, USSR. Pianist; Teacher. *Education:* Began piano lessons at age 6 with mother; Studied at Central Music School Moscow and with Yakov Flier, Moscow Conservatory. *Debut:* Soloist with Moscow Philharmonic, 1963. *Career:* Toured Soviet Union and Eastern Europe from 1971; Played in Japan 1977, France 1978; emigrated to USA, 1987; Performed at the White House, 1987; NY Recital debut, Carnegie Hall, 1987; Professor, State University of New York at New Paltz, 1987-. *Recordings:* For CBS Masterworks; Sony Classical and Music Masters. *Honours:* 1st prize, Prague Concertino Competition, 1967; joint 1st prize, Marguerite Long-Jacques Thibaud Competition, Paris, 1971. *Address:* c/o Music Department, State University of New York at New Paltz, New Paltz, NY 12561, USA.

FENBY Eric William, b. 22 Apr 1906, Scarborough, Yorkshire, England. Musician; Author; Conductor. m. Rowena Marshall, 1 son, 1 daughter. *Education:* Privately and largely self-taught in music; Amanuensis to Frederick Delius, 1928-34. *Debut:* As Composer, Promenade Concerts; As Conductor of Appalachia with LSO Choir and Orchestra, Royal Festival Hall, London. *Career:* Past Professor of Composition, Royal Academy of Music; Yorkshire Television Documentary Film, A Song of Farewell; Conductor of Delius's music (World Premiere of Delius's Opera, Margot-La-Rouge, Opera Theatre, St Louis, Missouri, 1983). *Recordings:* Award winning Fenby Legacy (Conductor), 2 discs of all the works taken down from Delius dictation, 1981; Delius Arrangements, Bournemouth Sinfonietta; Delius Violin Sonatas with Yehudi Menuhin; also with Ralph Holmes, violin, Eric Fenby, piano. *Publications:* Delius As I Know Him, 1936, revised, 1966; Delius (Great Composer Series), 1971; Menuhin's House of Music, 1969. *Contributions to:* Music and Musicians; Books and Bookmen. *Honours:* OBE; Award winning script of A Song of Summer (Ken Russell TV Documentary); Hon DMus (Jacksonville); Hon DLitt (Warwick and Bradford), 1978; Honorary Member of Royal Philharmonic Society, 1984; Honorary Fellow of the Royal College of Music, 1985 and Trinity College of Music, London, 1986. *Memberships:* Council Member, Former Chairman, Composers' Guild of Great Britain; President, Delius Society. *Address:* 1 Raincliffe Court, Stepney Road, Scarborough, North Yorkshire YO12 5BT, England.

FENNELL Frederick, b. 2 July 1914, Cleveland, Ohio, USA. Conductor; Teacher. *Education:* BM 1937, MM 1939, Eastman School of Music, Rochester, NY. *Career:* Conductor, National Music Camp, Interlochen, Michigan, summers 1931-33; Faculty Member, Conducted various ensembles, Eastman School of Music, 1939-65; Founder-Conductor, Eastman Wind Ensemble, 1952; Conductor-in-Residence, University of Miami School of Music, Coral Gables, Florida, 1965-80; Conductor, Kosei Wind Orchestra, Tokyo, 1984-;

Guest conductor with many USA ensembles. *Recordings:* Numerous discs for Mercury and Telarc. *Publications:* Time and the Winds, 1954; The Drummers Heritage, 1956. *Contributions:* Articles in The Instrumentalist. *Honours:* Many citations for championing the cause of wind ensembles.

FENNELLY Brian, b. 14 Aug 1937, Kingston, New York, USA. Composer; Theorist; Pianist; Professor of Music. m. Jacqueline Burhans Baczynsky, 1 son (from previous marriage). *Education:* B Mechanical Engineering 1958; BA 1963, Union College; MMusic, School of Music, 1965; PhD, Graduate School, 1968, Yale University. *Career:* USAF, 1958-61; Teacher, Union College and Yale University Faculty 1962-68; Professor, New York University; Editor, Contemporary Music Newsletter, 1969-77; Composers' Forum, 1968; various performances, USA and ISCM International Festival, 1973, 1980, 1981, 1984. *Compositions:* Numerous including Wind Quintet, 1967; Evanescences, 1969; SUNYATA, 1970; String Quartet in Two Movements, 1971-74; Prelude and Elegy, 1973; In Wildness Is The Preservation of the World, 1974-75; Sonata Seria, 1976; Quintuplo, 1977-78; Scintilla Prisca, 1979; Tropes and Echoes, 1981; Canzona and Dance, 1982-83; Tesserae I-IX, 1971-80; Concerto for Saxophone and String Orchestra, 1983-84; Fantasy Variations, 1984-85; Thoreau Fantasy No. 2, 1985; Brass Quintet, 1987; Keats on Love, 1988-89; Corollaries I-III, 1986-89; Lunar Halos, 1990; A Sprig of Andromeda, 1991-92; On Civil Disobedience, 1992-93. *Recordings:* Wind Quintet; Evanescences; String Quartet in Two Movements; In Wildness Is The Preservation of the World; Sonata Seria; Scintilla Prisca; Prelude and Elegy; Empirical Rag; For Solo Flute, Tesserae VII; Concerto for Saxophone and String Orchestra; Tesserae II; Fantasy Variations; Two Poems of Shelley. *Contributions to:* Dictionary of Contemporary Music, 1974; The New Grove Dictionary of Music and Musicians; Perspectives of New Music; Journal of Music Theory. *Address:* 2 Schryver Court, Kingston, NY 12401, USA.

FERENCZI Ilona, b. 15 Feb 1949, Miskolc, Hungary. Musicologist. *Education:* Diploma as Musicologist, Franz Liszt Academy of Music, Budapest, 1975. *Career:* Musicologist, Musicological Institute, Hungarian Academy of Sciences; Co-author, Co-Editor, Hungarian source music series Musicalia Danubiana. *Publications:* Editor: Tabulatura Vietoris saeculi XVII, Musicalia Danubiana 5 (with Marta Hulkova), 1986; Zacharias Zarewutius: Magnificats and Motets, Musicalia Danubia 8, 1987; Graduale Ecclesiae Hungaricae Epperiensis, 1635, Musicalia Danubiana 9, 1988. *Contributions to:* Studies on Hungarian music of the 16th-17th centuries in Studia Musicologia and other reviews. *Memberships:* The Art Foundation of Hungary; International Fellowship for Hymnology. *Hobby:* Leader of the choir Gál Huszár, singing 16th and 17th century material from her research. *Address:* MTA Zenetudomanyi Intezet, H-1014 Tancsics u 7, Hungary.

FERGUSON Barry William Cammack, b. 18 July 1942, London, England. Cathedral Organist; Master of the Choristers. m.(1) Marjorie Kemp, 20 Oct. 1971, (dec 1987), 1 daughter (2) Sandra Wibrew, 30 Sep. 1989. *Education:* MA, Cambridge University; FRCO; Exeter Cathedral Choristers School; Clifton College, Bristol; Organ Scholar, Peterhouse, Cambridge University; Honours degree in Music; Postgraduate, Royal College of Music. *Career:* Assistant Organist, Peterborough Cathedral, 1964-71; Organist, Wimborne Minster, 1971-77; Organist and Master of the Choristers, Rochester Cathedral, 1977-; Conductor, Rochester Choral Society; directed courses for Royal School of Church Music in USA, Australia, New Zealand; Musical Advisor Rochester Diocesan Church Music Committee. *Compositions include:* Six Organ Pieces; Death and Darkness; Aubade, for choir piano and speaker; Two Organ pieces; Dialogue Between BVM and the Christ Child; A Song of Creation; O God I Love Thee; Potsdam Prelude for organ; Christ's Lovesong to Man; Two hymn-tunes; The Annunciation; The Transfiguration; South and West Organ Suite, 1993. *Recordings:* Has had a number of his own compositions recorded; Music from Rochester Cathedral, volumes 1 and 2; The Organ of Rochester Cathedral; Music from Rochester Cathedral Vol.3; Te Deum and Jubilate, 1993. *Memberships:* Royal College of Organists. *Hobbies:* Poetry; Collecting West Country books and postcards; playing Scrabble; Visiting his Devon cottage; Art Galleries; Family. *Address:* 7 Minor Canon Row, Rochester, Kent ME1 1ST, England.

FERGUSON Howard, b. 21 Oct 1908, Belfast, N. Ireland. Pianist; Musicologist; Composer. *Education:* Studied with Harold Samuel and with Morris and Sargent at the Royal College of Music, London. *Career:* Violin Sonata No.1 performed at the Wigmore Hall, 1932; Two Ballads performed at the Three Choirs Festival, 1935; Assisted Myra Hess with wartime concerts at the National Gallery; Piano recitalist and duet partnerships with Denis Matthews (piano) and Yfrah Neaman (violin); Editions of early keyboard music; Professor of Composition at the Royal Academy of Music 1948-63. *Compositions:* Two Ballads for baritone, chorus and orchestra 1928-32; 2 Sonatas for violin and piano 1931, 1946; Octet 1933; Partita for orchestra 1935-36; Four Diversions on Ulster Airs for orchestra 1939-42; Piano Sonata 1938-40; Piano Concerto 1951; Overture for an Occasion 1953; Amore langueo for tenor, chorus and orchestra 1956; The Dream of the Rood for high voice, chorus and orchestra 1959. *Recordings:* Partita, Op.5b, Piano Sonata, Op.8, Octet, Op.4, Bagatelles, Op.9, Violin Sonata No.2, Amore Langueo, Op.18, Piano Concerto, Op.12; 2 Ballards, Op.5a; Overture for an Occasion, Op.16; Dream of the Rood, Op.19. *Publications:* Editions of: Tisdall, Complete keyboard works, 1957; Purcell, Complete harpsichord works, 1964; Blow, Six Suites 1965; Style and Interpretation, 1-VI, 1963-69; Early French, Italian, German, English Keyboard Music, 2 volumes of each, 1966-69; Dagincourt, Pièces de clavecin, 1969; Keyboard Interpretation, 1975; Croft, Complete harpsichord works, 1974; Schubert, Complete Piano Works, 1978; Pichi, Complete Keyboard works, 1979; The Music of Howard Ferguson, 1989. *Honours include:* Hon. MusD, Queen's University, Belfast, 1959. *Hobbies:* Reading; Cooking. *Address:* 51 Barton Road, Cambridge CB3 9LG.

FERGUSON Robert Stanley, b. 6 May 1948, London, England. Pianist. *Education:* Studied Piano with Cyril Smith, Royal College of Music; ARCM; LRAM; LGSM. *Debut:* Royal Festival Hall, 1973. *Career:* Piano due with Christopher Kite, debuting at Wigmore Hall, 1973, also giving regular Purcell Room Recitals, 1974-83, including use of original early pianos; Solo recital of 20th Century Music, Purcell Room, 1975; Appointed Examiner for Associated Board of Royal Schools of Music, 1982; Regular BBC Radio Broadcasts with Christopher Kite, 1979, 1983 and tours of Ireland, 1983. *Honours:* Hopkinson Gold Medal, 1969; Dannreuther Prize, 1970, Royal College of Music. *Memberships:* Incorporated Society of Musicians. *Hobbies:* Genealogy; Tropical Fish. *Address:* 98 Riverside, Cambridge CB5 8HN, England.

FERNANDEZ Nohema, b. 23 May 1944, Havana Cuba. Pianist. 1 daughter. *Education:* Diploma, Conservatorio Internacional, Havana, 1960; BMus, DePaul University, USA, 1965; MMus, Northwestern University, 1966; DMA, Stanford University, 1983; Piano studies with Jorge Bolet, Adolph Baller, and duo-pianists Vronsky and Babin. *Debut:* Havana, Cuba, 1960; New York Debut, Carnegie Recital Hall, 1983. *Career:* Appearances: Festival de Musica Latino-Americana, Mexico City; Cabrillo Festival; Sunriver Festival; Recitals in Glasgow, Edinburgh, Vienna, Amsterdam, New York, Miami and San Francisco; Radio broadcasts in Mexico City, New York, San Francisco; Television appearances in Chicago and San Jose; Recitalist and soloist worldwide. *Recording:* Musical Heritage Society, MusicMasters, Protone Records and Centaur Records also recorded Latin-American music for the Saarländisches Rundfunk. *Contributions to:* Articles in Piano Quarterly and Latin American Music Review. *Current Management:* Joanne Rile Artists

Management. *Address:* c/o School of Music, University of Arizona, Tucson, AZ 85721, USA.

FERNANDEZ Wilhelmina, b. 5 Jan 1949, Philadelphia, USA. Singer (Soprano). *Education:* Studied at Philadelphia 1969-73 and at the Juilliard School. *Debut:* Houston Opera 1977, as Gershwin's Bess. *Career:* Sang in Porgy and Bess on tour in the USA and Europe; Paris Opera 1979, as Musetta in La Bohéme; appearances at the New York City Opera, in Boston and Michigan, and at Toulouse as Aida; Opéra du Rhin Strasbourg and Liège, 1987-88, as Marguerite; Theater des Westens Berlin 1988, as Bess; Bonn Opera 1989, as Aida; Sang the title role in Carmen Jones, London 1991; Winner of the Evening Standard, Best Actress in a Musical, award; National Indoor Arena, Birmingham, 1992; Other roles include Mozart's Countess and Donna Anna, Purcell's Dido and the title role in Luisa Miller; concert engagements include Beethoven's Ninth; recital at Kensington Palace in the presence of HRH Princess of Wales, recitals in 1993 at Aix-en-Provence Festival and Paris; Appeared in the film Diva. *Address:* Marks Management Ltd, 14 New Burlington Street, London W1X 1FF, England.

FERNANDEZ-GUERRA Jorge, b. 17 July 1952, Madrid, Spain. Composer. *Education:* Studied at the Madrid Conservatory. *Career:* From 1970 has worked a smusician, composer and actor in the Independent Theatre Movement; Opera Sin Demonio no hay fortuna, based on the Faust legend, performed at Madrid's Sala Olimpia, 1987. *Compositions include:* Sin Demonio no hay fortuna, opera; Incidental music to plays by Aeschylus, Wilde, Beckett, Brecht and others; Chamber and orchestral music. *Address:* SGAE (Spain), c/o PRS Ltd Member Registration, 29-32 Berners Street, London W1P 4AA, England.

FERNANDEZ-IZNAOLA Ricardo J, b. 21 Feb 1949, Havana, Cuba. Concert Artist; Pedagogue (Classical Guitar); Composer. m. Maria Victoria Santos Brandys, 22 Aug 1974. 2 sons. *Education:* Colegio Americano, Caracas, 1966; Diplomas: Manuel de Falla Courses, Granada, 1971, 1972, 1974; Escuela Lino Gallardo, Caracas, summa cum laude, 1968; Royal Conservatory, Madrid, 1978 (Post graduate studies in composition). *Debut:* Madrid, May 1969. *Career:* Chair, Guitar Department, University of Denver's Lamont School of Music, 1983-; Director, International Guitar Week, Denver, 1984-; Over 1500 concerts, lectures, master classes, in Europe, North and South America and Japan; Appearances include BBC (London), RTVE (Madrid), Bayerische Rundfunk (Munich), since 1970-; Masterclasses, since 1990, for, Mannes College of Music, Manhatten School of Music, Yale University, The Cleveland Institute, The Royal Academy of Music, Trinity College of Music, the Guildhall School of Music; Recent Concerts in New York City, Madrid. *Compositions:* 10 Concert Etudes; Death of Icarus (Etude No 11); Variations on a Theme of A Lauro; Monologue I; Monologue II; Musique de Salon; 5 Miniatures; Berceuse; Prelude and Valse; Chanson. *Recordings:* Numerous. *Contributions:* Guitar and Lute Magazine; Ritmo; Cuadernos de Musica; Guitar International. *Hobbies:* Reading; Haute cuisine; Travelling. *Current Management:* Victoria Brandys Artists Management. *Address:* Lamont School of Music, 7111 Montview Blvd, Denver, Colorado 80220, USA.

FERNEYHOUGH Brian, b. 16 Jan 1943, Coventry, England. Composer. *Education:* Birmingham School of Music, 1961-63; Royal Academy of Music, with Lennox Berkeley, 1966-67; Amsterdam Conservatory, with Ton de Leeuw, 1968-69; Basle Academy, with Klaus Huber, 1969-71. *Career:* Emigrated to Switzerland 1969; 1973-86 Lecturer at Freiburg Musikhochschule; 1986-87 Composition Teacher at Royal Conservatoire The Hague; 1987-, Professor of Music, University of California San Diego; Terrain performed at the 1993 Prom Concerts, London. *Compositions:* Sonatina for 3 clarinets and bassoon, 1963; Four Miniatures for flute and piano, 1965; Coloratura for oboe and piano, 1966; Epigrams for piano, 1966; Sonata for Two Pianos, 1966; Three

Pieces for Piano, 1966-67; Prometheus for wind sextet, 1967; Sonatas for String Quartet, 1967; Epicycle for 20 strings, 1968; Missa Brevis for 12 voices, 1969; Firecycle Beta for orchestra, 1969-71; Cassandra's Dream Song for flute, 1970; Sieben Sterne for organ 1970; Transit for 6 amplified voices and chamber orchestra, 1972-75; Time and Motion Study I for bass clarinet, II for cello and electronics, III for 16 voices, percussion and electronics, 1971-77; Unity Capsule for flute, 1975-76; Funerailles for string septet and harp, 1969-80; La Terre est un Homme for orchestra, 1976-79; String Quartet No.2, 1980; Lemma-Icon-Epigram for piano, 1981; Superscriptio for piccolo, 1981; Carceri d'Invenzione I for chamber orchestra, II for flute and chamber orchestra, III for woodwind, brass and percussion, 1982-86; Adagissimo for string quartet, 1983; Etudes Transcendantales for soprano and quartet, 1982-85; Intermedio alla ciaccona for violin, 1986; Mnemosyne for bass flute and tape, 1986; String Quartet No 3, 1987; La Chute d'Icare for clarinet and ensemble, 1988; Quartet No.4 1990; Kurze Schatten for guitar, 1983-89; Tritticoper G.S. for double bass, 1989; Bone Alphabet for solo percussion, 1991; Terrain, for solo violin and ensemble, 1992. *Recordings include:* Superscriptio, Intermedio alla Ciaconna, Etudes Transcendantales, Mnemosyne and La Chute d'Icare; String Quartets played by the Arditti Quartet. *Address:* c/o Peters Edition Ltd, 10-12 Baches Street, London W1, England.

FERRAND Emma, b. 1 Oct 1948, London, England. Cellist. m. Richard Deakin, 6 Sept 1969, 3 sons. *Education:* International Cello Centre, London, 1965-66; Royal Academy of Music, London; Pupil of Pierre Fournier, Geneva. *Debut:* Wigmore Hall, 1974. *Career:* Solo concerts; BBC recordings; BBC Television, Elgar Concerto, 1975; Chamber music concerts; Member, Deakin Piano Trio; Senior lecturer, Royal Northern College of Music, 1983-; Artist-in-Residence, Stowe Summer School, Lake District Summer Music; Solo concerts; BBC Recordings; BBC TV; Elgar concerto, 1975; Member of Deakin Piano Trio & The Prelude Ensemble. *Recordings:* C Hubert Parry, complete piano trios, piano quartet. *Honour:* Winner, Young Concert Artists Award, National Federation of Music Societies, 1974. *Membership:* Incorporated Society of Musicians.*Current Management:* J Audrey Ellison International. *Address:* 26 Woodgrange Avenue, Ealing, London W5, England.

FERRARINI Alida, b. 9 July 1946, Villafranca, Verona, Italy. Singer (Soprano). *Education:* Studied at the Verona Conservatory and in Venice. *Debut:* Trevisto 1974, as Mimi. *Career:* Appearances at the Verona Arena from 1975 as Mercedes and Micaela in Carmen, Oscar and Gilda; Further performances in Rigoletto at Parma, 1987, Paris Opera 1988, and Bilbao 1990; Micaela and Adina (L'elisir d'amore) at La Scala, Milan; Other roles have included Xenia in Boris Godunov and Liu in Turandot (Verona), Norina, Euridice, Ines in La Favorita (Bregenz), Nanette and Lauretta in Gianni Schicchi; Season 1984 sang Gilda at Covent Garden, and made American debut, as Adina at San Francisco: Appeared as Marie in La Fille du Regiment at the Paris Opera and the Teatro Sao Carlos, Lisbon, 1988-89; Sang Pergolesi's Serpetta at Reggio Emilia, Micaela at Genoa and Liu at the Festival of Caracalla, 1992. *Address:* c/o Teatro alla Scala, Via Filodrammatici 2, 20121 Milan, Italy.

FERRÉ Susan Ingrid, b. 5 Sept 1945, Boston, Massachusetts, USA. Concert Organist; Harpsichordist. m. Kenneth Charles Lang, 18 June 1980, 1 son. *Education:* BA Philosophy and Music Literature, BMus, Texas Christian University, 1968; Diplôme, d'Orgue et Improvisation, Schola Cantorum, Paris, France, 1969; MMus, Eastman School of Music, New York, USA, 1971; DMA, North Texas State University, 1979; Studies with Jean Langlais, Marcel Dupré, France, and David Craighead, USA. *Career:* Currently, Musical Director, Texas Baroque Ensemble, and Adjunct Faculty member, North Texas State University, Denton; Organ and Harpsichord performances in North and South America,

Europe and Scandinavia; Feature Artist, Lahti Organ Festival, Finland, and at the World Council of Churches, Switzerland; Recitals at the Cathedral of Notre-Dame, Paris, France; Numerous radio broadcasts, USA; Musical Director, Texas Baroque Ensemble; Director, Early Music Festival Weekend, Round Top, Texas, 1986-. *Compositions:* Numerous compositions published and recorded by Avant Quart Company, France. *Recordings:* Works of Langlais on the Cavaillé-Col organ at Ste Clotilde, Paris; Messe Solonelle by Louis Vierne (VQR Digital Recordings); Recordings for national radio and television, France, Hungary, Sweden, Finland, USA. *Contributions to:* The Diapason. *Current Management:* Independent Concert Artists, Garland, Texas, USA. *Hobbies:* Sailing; Hiking. *Address:* 2221 Royal Crest Drive, Garland, TX 75043, USA.

FERREIRA Paulo Affonso De Moura, b. 11 Nov 1940, Araraquara, Brazil. Pianist; University Professor. m.(1) 1 son, 1 daughter, m. (2) Claudia Felícia Balduíno Ferreira, 1989. *Education:* Colégio Estadual Bento de Abreu Sampaio Vidal, Araraquara; Pianist, Conservatório Dramático e Musical de S. Paulo, 1959; Music Teacher, Instituto de Educacão Caetano de Campos, 1961; GRF, Piano Teacher, Hochschulinstitut für Musik in Trossingen, 1966. *Career:* Piano Recitals, Solo and Chamber Music, in Brazil, Uruguay, Argentina, Peru, Spain, Austria, Federal German Republic, Senegal, German Democratic Republic, Costa Rica, Colômbia, México; Adjunct Professor 1969-; Head of Music Department 1969-71; University of Brasilia; President, Sociedade Brasileira de Música Contemporânea, 1974-82, 1985-87; Produced programs about contemporary music for Brasilia Super Rádio F.M., since March 1987-89. *Recordings:* For Radio Bremen, Westdeutscher Rundfunk, Bayerischer Rundfunk, Norddeutscher Rundfunk, Radio Hilversum. *Publications:* Catalogues of 43 Brazilian Composers, 1975-80; New Brazilian Piano Music, 1977; Nova Música Brasileira para Piano, 1970. *Address:* Superquadra Sul 105 - Bloco B - Apto 506, 70344 Brasilia (DF), Brazil.

FERRERO Lorenzo, b. 17 Nov 1951, Turin, Italy. Composer. *Education:* Studied with massimo Bruni and Neore Zaffiri, at Bourges (electronic resources) and Turin University. *Career:* Collaboration with the Musik Dia Licht Galarie in Munich from 1974, producing multi-media works; Artistic Consultant at the Puccini Festival at Torre del Lago, 1980-84; Artistic Director of the Arena di Verona from 1991; Works attempt a reconciliation between 19th century Italian opera and pop music. Works include: theatre pieces Rimbaud, Avignon, 1978; Marilyn, Rome, 1980; La Figlia del mago, Montepulciano, 1981; Carlotte Corday, Rome, 1989; Le Bleu- blanc-rouge et le noir, Paris, Centre George Pompidou, 1989. *Address:* c/o Arena di Verona, Piazza Bra 28, 37121 Verona, Italy.

FERREYRA Beatriz Mercedes, b. 21 June 1937, Cordoba, Argentina. Composer. *Education:* Studied Piano with C. Bronstein (Buenos Aires) 1950-56; Harmony with Nadia Boulanger, 1962-63; Composition with György Ligeti and Earle Brown (Darmstadt), 1967; Electronic Techniques with Pierre Schaeffer (G.R.M. Paris), 1963-64. *Debut:* G.R.M. Paris, 1964. *Career:* Professor assistant: GRM, 1965-70; GMEB, 1973; B. Baschet Musical Instrument Development, 1970; Music Therapy, 1973-76; Darthmouth College's Computer System, 1975; Jury in 4th International Music. Competition, (GMEB, Bourges), 1976. Films: Musiques en Feu, 1981; Antartide, 1971; Mutations, 1972. A la lueur de la lampe (Ballet, S. Birge), 1973; Homo Sapiens (TV), 1975; La Baie St. James (TV), 1980. *Compositions:* Demeures Aquatiques, 1967; Médisances, 1968; L'Orvietan, 1970; Etude aux son Flegmatiques 1971; Le Recit, 1971; Siesta Blanca, 1972; Jeux des Rondes, 1980/84; Canto del Loco, 1974; Tierra Quebrada, 1976; Echos, 1978; Cercles des Rondes, 1982; Boucles, rosettes et serpentins, 1982; La Calesita, 1982; Bruissements, 1983; Arabesques autour d'une corde raide, 1984; Passacaille déboitée pour un lutin, 1984; Petit Poucet Magazine, 1985; The UFO Forest, 1986;

L'Autre....ou le chant des marécages, 1987; Souffle d'un petit Dieu Distrait, 1988; Brise sur une fourmillère, 1988. *Recordings:* Solfège de l'Objet Sonore (Pierre Schaeffer), Assistant and Co-author, 1967; Médisances: Collection Prospective XXI Siecle, 1969; Siesta Blanca: Electronic Music Competition, 1975 (Fylkingen). *Address:* Bethleem, Nesle Hodeng, 76270 Neufchâtel-en-bray, France.

FERREYRA Marcelo Cesar, b. 4 Sept 1926, Cordoba, Argentina. Choirmaster. m. Leonor Bregant, 14 Dec 1957, 1 son, 1 daughter. *Education:* La Salle Institute, Buenos Aires; Music self-taught. *Debut:* Argentine Association of British Culture, Cordoba, 19 Sept 1949. *Career:* Research on choral music and performance; Creation and training of 2 major choruses and various popular choruses; European, Latin American and Argentine tours; Performances at Colon Theatre, Buenos Aires. *Recordings:* 7 records containing music by Byrd, Brahms, Mendelssohn and XVIth century Spanish composers: Victoria and others; Palestrina and others. *Publication:* Interpretacion coral, 1993. *Contributions to:* Regularly to national and local newspapers and serials. *Honours:* Honorary Collaborator, University of Barcelona; Lifelong Award, Municipality of Cordoba. *Memberships:* Choral Association of La Plata, Argentina; Argentine Choral Federation. *Hobbies:* Cycling; Trekking; Gourmet cooking. *Address:* Lastra y Gordillo 4543, 5009 Cordoba, Argentina.

FERRO Gabriele, b. 15 Nov 1937, Pescara, Italy. Conductor. *Education:* Studied Piano and Composition at the Accademia di Santa Cecilia in Rome with Franco Ferrara. *Career:* Has appeared at leading opera houses and concert halls in Italy from 1964; Founded the Symphony Orchestra of Bari, 1967; Regular concerts with the orchestras of Sta. Cecilia, Suisse Romande, National de France, BBC London, Wiener Symphoniker, Bayerisches Staatsorchester, WDR Köln and the orchestras of RAI; Music Director of the Sicilian Symphony Orchestra at Palermo and permanent conductor of RAI Symphony Orchestra in Rome; Opera performances at La Scala, Milan; Covent Garden, London; San Francisco Opera; Lyric Opera Chicago; Opera de Bastille, Paris; De Nederlandse Opera, Amsterdam; Bayerische Staatsoper, München; Grand Théâtre de Genève; Maggio Musicale Firenze; General Music Director of the Stuttgart Staatsoper from 1992. *Recordings include:* Recordings with CBS, DDG, Erato, Sony Classical and EMI. *Honours:* Winner, RAI Young Conductor's Competition, 1964. *Address:* c/o Staststheater Stuttgart, Oberer Schlossgarten 6, 70173 Stuttgart, Germany.

FERWERDA John Diedrich, b. 1942, Holland (now Australian citizen). Violin Maker. *Education:* Adelaide Conservatorium, Australia, under James Whitehead; Mittenwald School of Violin Making, Germany, Rudolf van Merrebach. *Career includes:* Cellist, New Zealand Symphony Orchestra, Brabants Orchestra, Holland, Concertgebouw Orchestra & Radio Philharmonic Orchestra (Holland), Rheinische Philharmonic, Germany. Established own business as violin/other stringed instrument maker, Adelaide, Australia, removed to Melbourne, 1978. Orders for Ferwerda handcrafted instruments from Germany, UK, Austria, Holland, Israel, New Zealand, Australia, numerous well-known orchestras/players; instruments usually based on traditional Stradivarius model, although can be made to personal requirements; Over 100 instruments completed including violins, violas, cellos, double bass, gambas, bowed guitar, etc, 1974-; Exhibited, Australia, USA, Europe; Films & slides made demonstrating techniques of handcrafting. Early instruments commissioned, Victorian College of the Arts, grants from Utah Foundation. *Hobbies:* Antiques; Paintings; Books; Classical music. *Address:* 291 Auburn Road, Hawthorn East, Melbourne, Victoria 3123, Australia.

FETTA Frank Paul, b. 11 Feb 1944, Perth Amboy, New Jersey, USA. Conductor; Pianist; Music Director. m. Susan Kathelen Henninger, 25 Sept 1976, 1 son.

Education: BMus., Ithaca (New York) College School of Music. *Career:* Assistant Conductor, San Diego Opera, 1975-76; Music Director, Principal Conductor, Los Angeles Community College Opera Theater, 1973-76; Music Director, Marina/Westchester Symphony, 1976- ; Conductor, Los Angeles Chamber Ensemble, 1985- Artistic Director, Principal Conductor, Opera Theater of the Inland Empire, 1978-; Conductor, Opera-A-La-Carte, 1975-; Music Director, Los Angeles Concert Opera Association, 1987-; Music Director, West Coast Opera, 1986-; Music Director, Conductor, Redlands Bowl Festival Symphony & Opera, 1985-; Guest Conductor, Utah Opera, Stern Grove Festival, Flagstaff Festival, Los Angeles Doctors Symphony, Los Angeles Opera Theater, Los Angeles Pops Orchestra. *Membership:* Phi Mu Alpha Sinfonia. *Address:* 5843 Eucalyptus Lane, Los Angeles, CA 90042, USA.

FIALA George, b. 31 March 1922, Kiev, Ukraine. Composer; Pianist; Conductor. *Education:* Tchaikovsky State Conservatory, 1939-41; Studied with Hansmaria Dombrowski (Composition) and Wilhelm Furtwängler (Conducting), Akademische Hochschule für Musik, Berlin 1942-45; Leon Jongen at Conservatoire Royal de Musique. *Career:* Active member of well-known Seminaire des Arts Brussels, participated in many musical events as composer, pianist and conductor. Arrived in Canada and settled in Montreal 1949, active as Composer, Pianist, Organist and Teacher; currently producer for Radio Canada International. *Compositions:* Soloist with Orchestra: Capriccio 1962; Concerto for Violin and Orchestra 1973; Divertimento Concertante 1965; Introduction and Fugato 1961; Musique Concertante 1968; Serenade Concertante 1968; Sinfonietta Concertata 1971. Voices with Orchestra: Canadian Credo 1966; Five Ukrainian Songs 1973. Orchestral: Autumn Music 1949; Eulogy (in Memory of President John Fitzgerald Kennedy) 1965; The Kurelek Suite 1982; Montreal 1967; Ouverture Burlesque 1972; Overtura Buffa 1981; Sinfonico 1975; Symphony No. 4 1973; Ukrainian Triptych 1975. Chamber Music: Cantilena and Rondo 1963; Chamber Music for Five Wind Instruments 1948; Concertino Canadese 1972; Duettino Concertante 1981; Duo Sonata for Violin and Harp 1971; Musique a Quatre 1972; Musique a Trois 1970; Partita Concertata 1982; Pastorale and Allegretto 1963; Quintet 1982; Sonata Breve 1972; Sonata-Fantasia for Cello and Piano 1971; Sonata for Alto Saxophone and Piano 1970; Sonata for Cello and Piano 1969; Sonata for Violin and Piano 1969; Terzetto Concertante 1981; Three Movements 1957; Ukrainian Suite 1948, revised 1982; Wallaby's Lullaby 1964. Voice: Four Russian Poems 1968; The Heart's Memory 1981; My Journey 1982; Psalm 1974. Piano Solos and Duos. *Recordings:* Chamber Music for Five Wind Instruments; Montreal; Concertino; Suite Concertante; Three Movements; Sonatat Breve; Sonata I for two pianos; Duo Sonata; The Kurelek Suite; Quartet No. 2 for Saxophones; Sinfonietta Concertata. *Address:* PO Box 66, Station B, Montreal, Quebec, Canada, H3B 3J5.

FIALKOWSKA Janina, b. 1951, Canada. Pianist. *Education:* Studied at the Ecole de Musique Vincent d'Indy in Montreal and in Paris with Yvonne Lefebure; Further study at the Juilliard School with Sasha Gorodnitzki. *Career:*Performed the World Premiere of the Newly Re-Discovered 3rd Piano Concerto of Franz Liszt with the Chicago Symphony; Has appeared from 1974 with the Cleveland Orchestra, the Detroit Symphony, Los Angeles Philharmonic, Minnesota Orchestra, New Orleans Philharmonic, Philadelphia Orchestra, Pittsburgh Symphony, and the Seattle Symphony; Further engagements with orchestras in Canada and Mexico; European appearances with the Concertgebouw, the Bonn Philharmonic, London Philharmonic, Hallé, Philharmonia London, Royal Philharmonic, Scottish National, Warsaw and Israel Philharmonics and the French and Belgian National Radio Orchestras; Season 1984-85 included debut with the Chicago Symphony, under Solti; To commemorate the 1986 centenary of Liszt's death gave the Twelve Transcendental Studies in New York, Paris, Chicago, Los Angeles and London; In 1989 gave concert tour

of Britain, including appearances with the Royal Philharmonic, and with the Hallé Orchestra at the Promenade Concerts; Season 1989-90 included Bartók's Third Concerto at the Festival Hall, the Brahms D minor Concerto with the BBC Sumphony and Szymanowski's Symphonie Concertante with the Philharmonia; Concerts with the Cincinnati Symphony conducted by Edo de Waart. *Honours include:* Prizewinner, First International Arthur Rubinstein Master Piano Competition, 1974. *Address:* c/o Ingpen and Williams Ltd., 14 Kensington Court, London W5 5DN, England.

FIASCONARO Gregorio, b. 5 Mar 1915, Palermo, Sicily. Baritone; Stage Director. *Education:* Studied in Genoa and with Riccardo Stracciari in Rome. *Debut:* Genoa 1937, as Germont in La Traviata. *Career:* Settled in Dublin after wartime internment; Director of the Opera School at the University of Cape Town, 1952-80; Produced and sang with the University of Cape Town Opera Company, including the title role in the British stage premiere of Duke Bluebeard's Castle, Rudolf Steiner Theatre, London, 1957; Also sang Puccini's Scarpia and produced operas by Verdi and Puccini at many South African centres. *Publications include:* I'd Do it Again (Cape Town, 1982).

FICKLER Yehuda, b. 1925, Rumania, Symphony Orchestra Director. m. Erica Fickler, 3 Nov 1953, 2 children. *Education:* Student, Liceul Laurian 1948; Conservatoire Ciprian Porumbecou, Bucharest, 1951; Jerusalem Music Academy, 1957; BA, Hebrew University, 1965. *Career:* Choir Conductor, Bucharest; Trumpet Player, Jerusalem's Radio Orchestra; Personnel Manager, Radio Orchestra, Jerusalem; Assistant Manager, Jerusalem Symphony Orchestra; General Manager, New Israeli Opera; Music Adviser, Producer, Concerts, Hebrew University; Producer, Israeli Festival; Founder, Jerusalem Chamber Orchestra; Music Advisor, Old Acre Concert Series. *Address:* 56 Harlap, Jerusalem, Israel.

FIEBIG Kurt, b. 28 Feb 1908, Berlin, Germany. Composer; Organist (also playing Piano and Cembalo); Choir Leader. m. Dorothea Simke, 2 sons. *Education:* Studied Piano with Gertud Wetheim, Rudolph Schmidt; Organ with Arnold Dreyer and Composition with Karol Rathaus and Franz Schreker; State Exam for Organists and Choir Director, Berlin, 1933. *Career:* Organist, Choir Leader, Berlin, 1926-36; Cathedral Organist, Quedinburg, 1936-38; Director, Church Music School, Halle, 1939-50; member, Faculty, 1951-, Lecturer, Composition 1960-, Hamburg Institute of Music. *Compositions:* Markuspassion; Kantate Et Unum Sanctam; Missa secunda; Missa Media vita; Paul-Gerhardt Kantate; Concertino, violin and string orchestra; Easter oratorio; Cantata Wie nach einer Wasserquelle; Concerto Cembalo and String orchestra; works for organ, piano and cembalo; Stons: a Song Cycle Advent Oratorio. *Publications:* Psalmkantaten (Anthems) G.F. Handel, 1947; 73 choral preludes, 1952. *Honours:* Mendelssohn Prize, Composition. *Hobbies:* Literature; Theatre. *Address:* Görlitzer Strasse 20, 2 Hamburg 70, Germany.

FIEDUKIEWICZ Krzysztof Aleksander, b. 2 Oct 1968, Wroclaw, Poland. Bassoon Player. *Education:* Academy of Music in Wroclaw, 1987- 91. *Debut:* Festival Warsaw Autumn as a soloist, 1990. *Career:* Concert in Leningrad Conservatoire as a soloist in 1989; Concert during Warsaw Autumn, 1990; Concert of the Year, Warsaw, 1991. *Recordings:* Many recordings for Polish Radio with contemporary music. *Hobbies:* Tennis; Basketball. *Address:* ul Czarnieckiego 74/4, 53-627 Wroclaw, Poland.

FIELD Helen, b. 14 May 1951, Awyn, N Wales. Singer (Soprano). *Education:* Royal Northern College of Music; Royal College of Music. *Career:* Has sung with Welsh National Opera as Poppea, Musetta, Mimi, Tatyana, Butterfly, Marenka, Jenůfa, Marzellina, Vixen, Desdemona; Appeared with Opera North in first UK production of R Strauss' Daphne, 1987, and Massenet's Manon; Appeared with English National Opera as Nedda, Pamina, Donna Anna, Violetta, Jenifer in Midsummer Marriage, and Gilda (also at Metropolitan, New York); Sang Jo-Ann in premiere of Tippett's New Year at Houston, 1989, and Glyndebourne, 1990, the Governess in Turn of the Screw for Netherlands Festival and Cologne and Montpellier Operas, Butterfly at Deutsche Oper Berlin, Katya for Scottish Opera, and Emma in Kovanshchina for Royal Opera, Covent Garden; Concerts with all major UK orchestras; Butterfly and Liu sung in concert at Gewandhaus with Kurt Masur; R Strauss' Vier Letzte Lieder with Gunther Wand, Norddeutscher Rundfunk and with BBC Symphony Orchestra at Proms. *Recordings:* Gilda; Village Romeo and Juliet; Rossini's Stabat Mater; Rossini's Petit Messe Solenelle; Hiawatha; Janaček's Osud. *Address:* c/o Lies Askonas Ltd, 6 Henrietta St, London, England.

FIELD-HYDE Margaret, b. 4 May 1905. Musician. *Education:* Studied with father and in Germany; Studied performance of vocal music of 12th and 15th centuries. *Debut:* First stage revival of Purcell's King Arthur, 1928. *Career:* Numerous appearances in oratorio, opera and recitals, singing in most cathedrals in Britain and at the Albert Hall, Queen's Hall and Festival Hall, most notably Bach, Purcell and Fauré; Founder and Directgor, The Golden Age Singers (Quintet); Toured in most European countries, North Africa, Canada and USA; Appeared at many festivals including Kings Lynn; Also TV and radio broadcasts; Poetry Readings for the BBC and British Council; Lecturer on Teaching of solo singing. *Memberships:* Royal Musical Association; Incorporated Society of Musicians. *Hobbies:* Gardening; Painting; Sewing. *Address:* Dulas Court, Dulas, Hereford HR2 OHL, England.

FIERENS Guillermo, b. 1940, Argentina. Classical Guitarist. *Education:* Studied with Andres Segovia. *Debut:* Spain, 1963. *Career:* US debut, 1965, thirty conert tour of Mexico, 1967; Regular engagements in Britain with the LSO, Halle Orchestra, English Chamber, royal and London Philharmonics, Philharmonia and Orchestra of the Welsh National Opera; Queen's Hall Edinburgh, 1983; Festival appearances at Norwich, St Andrews, Harrogate, Lichfield, Newbury and Belfast; Further concerts in Holland, Switzerland, Spain, Hong Kong Czechoslovakia, USA, Italy and Canada. *Recordings:* Music by Castlenuovo-Tedesco, Albeniz, Turina, Sor and Villa-Lobos. *Honours include:* Winner, 1967 Caracas International Guitar Competition; Citta d'Alessandria Competition in Italy; Gold Medal, Villa-Lobos Competition, Rio de Janeiro, 1971. *Address:* Anglo Swiss Ltd, 3 Primrose Hill, 1a Sharpleshall Street, London NW1 8YW, England.

FIFIELD Christopher, b. 1945, Croydon, Surrey, England. Conductor; Music Writer. *Education:* Studied at Manchester University, Royal Manchester College of Music, Guildhall School and Cologne Musikhochschule. *Career:* Assistant Director of Music, Capetown Opera, followed by 12 years on music staff at Glyndebourne; Assisted Solti on 1977 recording of Otello; Former Music Director of the London Contemporary Dance Theatre, currently Director of the Lambeth Orchestra, Northampton Symphony Orchestra and Central Festival Opera; Frequent conductor at the GSM and Trinity College of Music; Director of Music, University College London, 1980-90, leading Massenet's Herodiade, Sphoh's Faust, (1852 version), Verdi's Il Corsaro, Giovanna d'Arco and Un Giorno di Regno, Puccini's Le Villi and Edgar; British premieres of Verdi's Oberto, Chabrier's Gwendoline, Bruch's Die Loreley and The Devil's Wall by Smetana; Music Director of the Jubilate Choir and the Reigate and Redhill Choral Society; Guest chorus master, Chelsea Opera Group; Conducted a revival of Max Bruch's Oratorio Odysseus at the Queen Elizabeth Hall, 1988. *Publications:* Contributions to Wagner in Performance, 1992; Viking Opera Guide, International Opera Guide and New Grove Dictionary of Opera, 1992; Reviews for BBC Music Magazine; Writes Sleeve notes for Philips; Author: Max Bruch, his Life and Works, 1988; True Artist and True Friend: A

Biography of Hans Richter, 1993. *Address:* Music International, 13 Ardilaun Road, London N5 2QR, England.

FIGUEROA Rafael, b. 27 Mar 1961, San Juan, Puerto Rico. Cellist. m. Irma I Justicia, 18 Apr 1987. *Education:* BM and Performer's Certificate, Indiana University School of Music; Violoncello studies with Janos Starker and Gary Hoffman. *Debut:* Recital debut at Terrace Theater, Kennedy Center for the Arts, Washington DC. *Career:* Recitals in major concert halls such as Library of Congress, Kennedy Center, National Gallery of Art, Jordan Hall, Shriver Hall, Merkin Hall, Casals Hall in Tokyo, Carnegie Recital Hall; Numerous radio broadcasts on National Public Radio. *Recordings:* F Mendelssohn: Concerto for Violin and Piano, with Orpheus Chamber Orchestra, 1989; Schoenberg: Verklarte Nacht, 1990; R Strauss: Le Bourgeois Gentilhomme and Divertimento Op 86, 1992; Weber: Clarinet Concertos and Rossini Variations, 1992. *Contributions to:* Review, The Strad Magazine; Reviews, Strings Magazine. *Hobbies:* Gourmet cooking; Wines; Reading. *Current Management:* Columbia Artists Management. *Address:* 16 Magaw Place 52C, New York, NY 10033, USA.

FIKEJZ Daniel, b. 21 June 1954, Prague, Czechoslovakia. Composer. m. 21 June 1979, 1s, 1d. *Education:* Technical University, Prague; Private lessons with Marta Oberthorova. *Debut:* Keyboard player and composer of group, Combo FH, 1974. *Career:* Continued with Combo FH, performing jazz and rock from 1974-88; Music for theatre plays, television, film and ballet, 1983-. *Compositions:* Laser pilgrimage-audiovisual performance, 1979; Dried Strawberry's Dream, 1981; Music for Krizik Fountain, 1991; Shake-up, ballet, 1993; New Testament, 1993. *Recordings:* Things, 1981; Situation on the Roof, 1986; Music for Kriziks Fountain, 1991; Don Juan, 1992. *Publication:* Article, Music and technology, 1989. *Honours:* Musical Prize, Czech critics, Cena Molodie, 1978. *Memberships:* OSA; SAI, both Czech. *Hobbies:* Formula 1 races; Literature; Theatre. *Address:* 100 00 Praha 10, Kounicka 65, Czech Republic.

FILIPOVA Elena, b. 2 Dec 1957, Pasardjk, Bulgaria. Opera Singer (Soprano). *Education:* Sofia Music High School; Piano and Oboe, Sofia Music Conservatory. *Debut:* Marie in Bartered Bride, Bad. Staatstheater Karlsruhe, 1981. *Career:* Badisches Staatstheater Karlsruhe, 1981-86; debut as Marenka in The Bartered Bride; Salzburg Festival, 1983; Guest Performances, Hamburg, Frankfurt, Barcelona, Luxemburg, Hanover, (as Violetta, 1989) Bern, Vienna, Nurenberg; Has also sung Donne Anna, Amelia Boccanegra and Tatiana; Sang Aida at Hanover, 1990; Concerts in Germany, Austria, France, Italy, Switzerland; TV, ORF Salzburg Festival, 1983, ZDF, Berlin, 1983, SWF, Baden Baden, 1985, Mozart & Handel Arias. *Honours:* 1st Prize, Karajan Foundation, Salzburg Festival, 1982. *Hobbies:* Cooking; Reading; Piano; Languages. *Address:* Staatstheater, Opernplatz 1, 3000 Hannover, Germany.

FILIPOVIC Igor, b. 18 Apr 1951, Ljubljana, Slovenija. Singer (Tenor). *Education:* Studied in Ljubljana and in Italy. *Debut:* Sang Ernesto in Don Pasquale, 1976. *Career:* Member of the Vienna Kammeroper 1976-77, Lucerne Opera, 1977-78; Guest appearances in Europe, the USA and Canada as Rossini's Amenofi (Mosè in Egitto) and Arnoldo (Wilhelm Tell), Arturo in I Puritani, Edgardo in Lucia di Lammermoor, Enrico in Maria di Rudenz, Tonio in La Fille du Regiment, the Duke of Mantua in Rigoletto, Alfredo in La Traviata, Riccardo in Ballo in maschera, Rodolfo in Luisa Miller, Cavaradossi in Tosca, Don José at Bregenzer Festspiele in summer 1992, sang also at Prague, Venice, Milan, Rome, Turin, Palermo, Vienna (Staats and Volksoper), Stuttgart, Mannheim, Frankfurt, Brussels, Chicago and New York (City Opera); Broadcasting engagements throughout Europe. *Address:* c/o Opernhaus Dortmund, Kuhstraße 12, 44137 Dortmund, Germany.

FILSELL Jeremy Daniell, b. 10 Apr 1964, Brentwood,

Essex, England. Pianist; Organist. m. 20 Oct 1990. *Education:* BA 1985, MA, 1990, (Organ), Keble College, Oxford University; Piano, Royal College of Music, studied with David Parkhouse and Hilary McNamara. *Debut:* St John's South Square, January 1993. *Career:* Concerto and piano solo appearances throughout UK; As concert organist, appearances in virtually all UK major cathdrals, town halls as well as West Germany and North America; Presently accompanist to Alistair Mackie (Trumpet). *Compositions:* Church music for Ely Cathedral Choir and a popular arrangement for rite A use of the Missa de Angelis. *Recordings:* CDs of English orgam music, Marcel Dupré organ music, Vierne 3rd Symphony and Widor/Tournemire, Howells and Stevens Piano music and music by Daniel Lesur with BBC Symphony Chorus and Stephen Jackson. *Honours:* Silver Medal, Worshipful Company of Musicians, 1983; Limpus, Shinn and Durrant Prizes, FRCO, 1983; LRAM (Piano performance). *Hobbies:* Club cricketer; Squash. *Current Management* Chameleon Arts Management. *Address:* Music Office, St Luke's Church, Sydney Street, Chelsea, London SW3 6NH, England.

FINCKEL David, b. 6 Dec 1951, Kutztown, Pennsylvania, USA. Cellist. *Career:* Member of the Emerson String Quartet from 1977; Premiere concert at Alice Tully Hall, New York in 1977, with works by Mozart, Smetana and Bartók; European debut at Spoleto, Italy, in 1981; Quartet-in- residence at the Smithsonian Institute, Washington, from 1980, at the Hartt School from 1981 and at the Spoleto aned Aspen Festivals from 1981; First resident quartet at the Chamber Music Society of Lincoln Center, season 1982- 83; Many performances of works by Bartók, including all six quartets in a single evening, and contemporary works; Premieres include Mario Davidovsky's 4th Quartet and works by Maurice Wright and George Tsontakis. *Recordings include:* Walter Piston's Concerto for string quartet, Winds and percussion (CRI); Works by Andrew Imbrie, Henry Howell, Roy Harris and Gunther Schuller (New World); Bartók's Six Quartets (Deutsche Grammophon).

FINDLAY Jane, b. 1960, England. Singer (Mezzo-soprano). *Education:* Studied at the Royal Northern College of Music and with Peter Harrison and Paul Hamburger. *Career:* Sang with the Glyndebourne Festival Chorus, then Hermia and Dorabella with the Touring Opera; Third Boy in Die Zauberflöte at the Festival; Has sung Dorabella with the Northern Ireland Opera Trust in Belfast and with Opera 80 on tour; Appearances at the Wexford Festival and with Opera Nancy; Sang in Margot-la-Rouge at the Camden Festival, 1984, and in Monteverdi's L'Orfeo at Florence under Roger Norrington; Tour of Germany with the Monteverdi Choir in 1985, including Irene in Handel's Tamerlano at the Göttingen Festival and concert performances in Cologne; Season 1987-88 in Opera 80's Cenerentola and appearances in The Gondoliers and La Belle Hélène for New Sadler's Wells Opera; Welsh National Opera debut 1989, in La Traviata; Covent Garden debut April 1990 as Magdalena in Die Meistersinger; Concert repertoire includes the Dream of Gerontius, Shéhérazade by Ravel, Bach's Christmas Oratorio, and Messiah. *Honours include:* South East Arts Award; Miriam Licette Award 1985. *Address:* c/o Korman International Management, Crunnells Green Cottage, Preston, Herts SG4 7UQ, England.

FINE Vivian, b. 28 Sept 1913, Chicago, Illinois, USA. Composer; Teacher. m. Benjamin Karp, 5 Apr 1935. 2 daughters. *Education:* Studied piano, Chicago Music College; Piano pupil of Djane Lavoie-Herz; Harmony and composition with Ruth Crawford, Adolf Weidig and Henry Cowell; Piano with Abby Whiteside, composition with Roger Sessions; Orchestration with George Szell. *Career:* Teacher, New York University, 1945-48; Juilliard School of Music, 1948; State University of New York at Potsdam, 1951; Connecticut College School of Dance, 1963-64; Bennington (Vt) College, 1964- 87. *Compositions:* Chamber Opera: The Women in the Garden, 1977; Theatre pieces; Orchestral: Elegiac Song for Strings, 1937; Concertante for Piano and Orchestra,

1944; Romantic Ode for Violin, Viola, Cello and Strings, 1976; Drama, 1982; Poetic Fires for Piano and Orchestra, 1984; Dancing Winds, 1987; After the Tradition for Chamber Orchestra, 1988; Chamber: String Trio, 1930; Violin Sonata, 1952; String Quartet, 1957; Dreamscape for 3 Flutes, Cello, Piano and Percussion Ensemble, 1964; Chamber Concerto for 7 Instruments, 1966; Quintet for String Trio, Trumpet and Harp, 1967; Brass Quintet, 1978; Piano Trio, 1980; Quintet for Oboe, Clarinet, Violin, Cello and Piano, 1984; Cello Sonata, 1986; Piano pieces; Choral music; Works for voice and instruments. *Honours:* Many grants; commissions; Guggenheim Fellowship, 1980. *Memberships:* American Society of Composers, Authors and Publishers; American Academy and Institute of Arts and Letters, 1980-. *Address:* RFD 2, Box 630, Hoosick Falls, NY 12090, USA.

FINE Wendy, b. 19 Dec 1943, Durban, South Africa. Singer (Soprano). *Education:* Studied with John van Zyl in Durban and with Christian Mueller, Erik Werba and Maria Hittorf at the Vienna Music Academy. *Debut:* Stadttheater Berne, as Madame Butterfly. *Career:* Appearances at opera houses in London, Hamburg, Munich, Stuttgart, Berlin, Lisbon, Vienna and Geneva; Bayreuth Festival 1971; Roles include Nedda, Micaela, Marguerite, Mimi, Sophie in Der Rosenkavalier, Desdemona, Fiordiligi, Donna Elvira, Pamina, Luise in Der junge Lord, (British Premiere, 1965) Ophelia in Szokolay's Hamlet and Maria in The Miracles of Our Lady, by Martinů; sang at Covent Garden 1971-77 as Musetta, Gutrune, Donna Elvira, Fiordiligi and Jenůfa; La Scala Milan, 1977, as Berg's Marie.

FINGERHUT Margaret, b. 30 Mar 1955, London, England. Pianist. *Education:* Royal College of Music, London; Peabody Conservatory, Baltimore. *Career:* Performed in UK, America, Europe, Scandinavia, USA, Africa, India, Turkey and Israel. Played with London Symphony, Royal Philharmonic, London Philharmonic and Philharmonia Orchestras. Broadcasts for BBC Radio and WFMT, Chicago. Appeared on film and television. *Recordings:* For Chandos Records; Several Recordings with the London Philharmonic and London Symphony Orchestra, including world premiere recording of Arnold Bax's Winter Legends; Has also recorded music by Grieg, Dukas, Falla, Suk, Stanford and Moeran; collections of Russian and French Composers. *Honours:* Hopkinson Gold Medal, 1977; Boise Foundation Scholarship, 1977; Greater London Arts Association, Young Musician of the Year, 1981. *Current Management:* Jane Piper. *Address:* c/o Chandos Records, Chandos House, Commerce Way, Colchester, Essex CO2 8HQ, England.

FINK Manfred, b. 15 Apr 1954, Frankfurt am Main, Germany. *Education:* Studied in Frankfurt.*Career:* Chorus of the Cologne Opera, 1979-81; Soloist with the Mainz Opera from 1981, debut as Tamino; Deutsche Oper am Rhein Dusseldorf from 1982, as Mozart's Ferrando, Belmonte and Don Ottavio; Guest appearances from 1984 at Buenos Aires, Venice, Roma, Nice, Florence (David in Die Meistersinger, 1985), Frankfurt and Vienna; Other roles have included Edgardo in Lucia di Lammermoor, Des Grieux in Manon Lescaut, Rinuccio and Nemorino; Sang the Steuermann in Der fliegende Holländer for Cologne Oper 1991, Pedrillo in Die Entführung at the Schwetzingen Festival, 1991. *Recordings:* Handel Dettingen Te Deum. *Address:* c/o Oper der Stadt Koln, Offenbachplatz, 5000 Cologne, Germany.

FINK Michael Jon, b. 7 Dec 1954, Los Angeles, USA. Composer; Teacher. *Education:* Studied at the California Institute of the Arts with William Kraft, Harold Budd, Barney Childs and Mel Powell (MFA 1980). *Career:* Performances with the Negative Band and Stillife; Composer-in- Residence, North Michigan University, 1985; Teacher at California Institue of the Arts from 1982. *Compositions include:* Two pieces for piano, 1983; Work for chamber orchestra, 1986; Living to be Hunted by the Moon, for clarinet, bass clarinet, electronics,

1987; A Temperament for Angels, electronics and keyboards, 1989; Sound Shroud Garden, with Jim Fox, 1989; Epitaph, bass clarinet, 1990. *Recordings include:* Album vocalise. *Publications include:* Inside the Music Business; Music in Comtemporary Life, 1989. *Address:* c/o ASCAP, ASCAP Building, One Lincoln Plaze, New York, NY 10023, USA.

FINK Myron S, b. 19 Apr 1932, Chicago, USA. Composer. *Education:* Studied at Julliard with Bernard Wagenaar and Castelnuovo- Tesdesco, Burrill Phillips at the University of Illinois; Cornell University with Robert Palmer and in Vienna, 1955-56; Former teacher at Alma College, Hunter College New York, the Curtis Institute and the City University of New York. *Compositions:* Operas The Boor, after Chekov, 1955; Susanna and the Elders, 1955; Jeremiah, 1962; Judit and Holofernes, 1978; Chinchilla, 1986; The Island of Tomorrow, 1986. *Honours include:* Woodrow Wilsom Memorial Fellowship, 1954. *Address:* c/o ASCAP, ASCAP Building, One Lincoln Plaza, NY 10023, USA.

FINK Petr, b. 3 Feb 1943, Brno, Czechoslovakia. Composer; Conductor; m. Jana Horackova, 19 July 1974, 1 son, 1 daughter. *Education:* Conservatory in Plzen. *Debut:* Trumpet, 1968. *Career:* Trumpet player in jazz orchestras in Prague; Director of Music, Department of Radio Prague, 1977-; Since 1978, has recorded for Czech and German television. *Compositions:* 100 pop music and jazz, 150 brass music; All recorded on Czech radio and televison. *Recordings:* 8 LPs and CDs as author and conductor including: Liebesgrusse aus Bohmen, 1989; Czech Polkas Waltzes and Songs, 1988. *Honours:* Czech festival of pop music composers prize, 1974, 1978; Prize winner, Radio Prague Brass Composers Competition, 1985-89. *Memberships:* Czech Union of composers and Musicians; Czech Union for the Protection of Composers. *Hobbies:* Cars. *Address:* Jestrebicka 12, 181 00 Praha 8, Czech Republic.

FINK Richard Paul, b. 23 Mar 1955, USA. Singer (Baritone). *Education:* Kent State University; Oberlin College. *Career:* Worked and performed with the Houston Symphony, Pops, Houston Ballet, Houston Theatre Under the Stars; Other concerts include Youngstown Symphony, A Night at the Opera as well as benefit concerts for churches and the homeless in Houston; Other productions include: Falstaff, Boris Godunov, Eugene Onegin, (Houston Opera); Tosca's Scarpia, (Bremer Stadt Theater of Germany), 1988; Jokanaan in Salome, Enrico in Lucia Di Lammermoor and Tchelio in the Love for Three Oranges (Bremen Opera), 1988-89; Kaspar in Der Freischütz, 1988-89, Escamillo in Carmen and Rigoletto title role, 1990-91, (Welsh National Opera); The Watergnome in Rusalka and Klingsor in Parsifal, 1991-92, (Houston Grand Opera); 1992-93 season opened as Sid in Albert Herring with the Atlanta Opera; Kurwenal in Tristan, Count de Luna in Il Trovatore, Pizzaro in Fidelio and Sebastiano at the Washington Opera Kennedy Center's staging of D'Albert's Tiefland. *Honours include:* Metropolitan Opera Western Regional Winner, 1984; San Diego Opera, Richard Tucker Memorial Award, Marguerite McCammon Fort Worth Opera, 1985; Stuart Awards, Oklahoma, 1986. *Current Management:* William Guerri, Trawick Artists Management, 129 West 72nd Street, NY 10023, USA. *Address:* 1310 Bridle Spur Ln, Houston, TX 77055, USA.

FINKE Martin, b. 1948, Rhede bei Bocholt, Germany. Singer (Tenor). *Education:* Studied with Hilde Wesselman at the Folkwang Hochschule Essen. *Career:* Sang first at opera houses in Augsburg, Cologne and Stuttgart; Bayreuth Festival 1975; Appearances at Munich, Hanover, Nuremberg, Frankfurt and Wiesbaden; Barcelona 1983, as Jacquino in Fidelio; Bregenz Festival 1984; Sang David in Die Meistersinger at the Théâtre de la Monnaie, Brussels, 1985; Salzburg Festival 1986, in the premiere of Penderecki's Die schwarze Maske; Other roles include Mozart's Pedrillo and Monostatos and Mime in Der Ring des Nibelungen, Nice Opera, 1988; Concert singer in the Passions of Bach, Messiah, and the Missa Solemnis. *Recordings:* Pagliacci, Intermezzo and Ariadne auf Naxos, Die Verschworenen by Schubert, Operettas by Lehar. *Address:* c/o Oper der Stadt Köln, Offenbachplatz, D-5000 Cologne, Germany.

FINKO David, b. 15 May 1936, Leningrad, Russia. Composer; Conductor. *Education:* Studied at the Leningrad School of Performing Arts, 1950-58; Leningrad Conservatory, 1960-65. *Career:* Emigrated to the USA, 1979; Visiting lecturer, University of Pennsylvania, 1979-81; Lecturer and Composer-in-residence, University of Texas, El Paso, 1981; *Compositions:* Polinka, after Chekov, 1965; In a Torture Chamber of the Gestapo, 1970; The Enchanted Tailor, 1983; Orchestral: 6 Tone Poems, 1965-78; Symphony No 1, 69; Piano Concerto, 1971; Viola Concerto, 1971; 2nd Symphony, 1972; Double Concerto for violin, viola and orchestra, 1973; Double Concerto for viola, double bass and orchestra, 1975; Harp concerto, 1976; Conceto for 3 violins, and orchestra, 1981; Pilgrimage to Jerusalem, 1983; Chamber: Mass without words for violin and organ 1968; Lamentations of Jeremiah for violin, 1969; Fromm Septet, 1983; Piano Sonata, 1964. *Honours include:* Grants and fellowships, ASCAP, the Fromm Foundation and the Memorial Foundation of Jewish Culture.

FINLEY Gerald, b. 30 Jan 1960, Montreal, Canada. Singer (Baritone). m. Louise Winter. *Education:* Studied at King's College Cambridge, the Royal College of Music and the National Opera Studio. *Career:* Glyndebourne Festival from 1986, as Sid in Albert Herring, Kuligin (Katya Kabanova), Count Dominik (Arabella) and the Touring Opera in Il barbiere di Siviglia, Death in Venice and Die Zauberflöte; Sang Papageno as part of Roger Norrington's Mozart Experience; Covent Garden debut in Don Carlos; Other opera roles include Mozart's Figaro for Mecklenburgh Opera, Guglielmo for the Britten Pears School and Glyndebourne, and Britten's Demetrius at Aix-en-Provence; Salzburg Festival 1991, in Der Schauspieldirektor; Concert appearances with the Northern Sinfonia, the City of London Sinfonia, the Orchestra of the Age of Enlightenment, the Hanover Band, The Sixteen and Monteverdi Choir and Orchestra; North American engagements in Messiah at St Louis, Ottawa and Montreal, Arvo Pärt's Passion in Chicago and at the Lincoln Center, New York; Has sung in works by Haydn, Handel and Mozart in Utrecht, Vienna and elsewhere in Europe; Wigmore Hall, London, debut in September 1989, in a programme of Beethoven Lieder; BBC Radio 3 in the Mass by Amy Beach and Vivaldi's serenata La Senna Festeggiante; BBC TV in Britten's Death in Venice; Sang in Haydn's The Seasons at the 1993 London Proms. *Recordings include:* L'Enfance du Christ by Berlioz (EMI); Albums of sacred music with the King's College Choir. *Address:* c/o Harrison Parrott Ltd., 12 Penzance Place, London W11 4PA, England.

FINNEY Ross Lee, b. 23 Dec 1906, Wells, Minnesota, USA. Composer. m. Gretchen Ludke, 3 Sept 1930, 2 sons. *Education:* BA, Carleton College, 1927; Nadia Boulanger, 1927-28; Alban Berg, 1931; Roger Sessions, 1935. *Career:* Professor of Music, Smith College, 1929-49; Composer in Residence, Professor of Music, Emeritus, 1974, University of Michigan, 1949-74. *Compositions:* Symphonies Nos 1, 2, 3, 4, 1942-47; Earthrise; Piano Concerto; Violin Concerto; John Brown for tenor, male chorus and chamber orchestra; Chamber Music includes 8 String Quartets 1935-60; Piano Trio; 4 Piano Sonatas; 8 Poems for Soprano, tenor and piano. *Recordings:* Piano Quintet; String Quartet No 6; Concerto for Alto Saxophone. *Honours:* Pulitzer Scholarship, 1937; Guggenheim Fellowship, 1937, 1947; Boston Symphony Award, 1955; Brandise Gold Medal, 1967. *Memberships:* Phi Beta Kappa; Academy/ Institute of Arts and Letters; Academy of Arts and Sciences. *Hobby:* Cooking. *Address:* University of Michigan, School of Music, Ann Arbor, MI 48109, USA.

FINNIE Linda, b. 9 May 1952, Paisley, Scotland. Singer (Mezzo-Soprano). *Education:* Royal Scottish Academy of Music with Winifred Busfield. *Debut:*

Scottish Opera, Glasgow, 1976. *Career:* After winning Kathleen Ferrier Prize at the 1977 's-Hertogenbosch Competition in the Netherlands sang widely in Europe: Brussels, Paris Opéra, Madrid, Lyon, Bordeaux and the Ludwigsburg Festival; Welsh National Opera from 1979; Roles with the English National Opera have included Brangaene in Tristan and Isolde, Eboli in Don Carlos, Amneris and Ortrud in Lohengrin; Guest Appearances in the Ring at Covent Garden; 1986 sang in Mahler's 8th Symphony at the Promenade Concerts and under Claudio Abbado in Verdi's Requiem in Chicago; 1987 season included Prokofiev's Alexander Nevsky at the Proms, the Choral Symphony in Edinburgh, Messiah in San Francisco, Mahler's Lieder eines fahrenden Gesellen and Resurrection Symphony, and Elgar's Sea Pictures; Frankfurt and Nice Opera debuts 1987, as Amneris, and as Waltraute in Götterdämmerung; Bayreuth debut 1988, in a new production of the Ring cycle conducted by Daniel Barenboim; sang Fricka, Siegrune and Second Norm at the 1990 Festival; Appearing in the Ring production at Vienna State Opera in 1995; engaged as Ortrud in Lohengrin at Bayreuth, 1993-94; Concert season 1992-93 with the New Japan Philharmonic, Orchestra National de France, Berlin Symphony, Czech Philharmonic and the Santa Cecilia Orchestra, Rome. *Recordings:* Alexander Nevsky and the Choral Symphony for Chandos; Elgar Sea Pictures (LPO/Thomson), Ravel Sheherazade (P.Tortelier), Respighi Il Tramonto (Vasary), La Rondine, (LSO/Maazel-CBS), L'Enfant et les Sortilèges, (LSO/Previn-EMI), Eugene Onegin, (Mackerras-EMI), Prokofiev Ivan the Terrible. (Philharmonia/Järvi-Chandos). *Address:* c/o Christopher Tennant, Unit 2, 39 Tadema Road, London SW10 0PY, England.

FINNILA Birgit, b. 20 Jan 1931, Falkenberg, Sweden. Singer (Contralto). m. Allan Finnila, 2 sons, 3 daughters. *Education:* Studied in Goteborg with Ingalli Linden; Royal Academy of Music with Roy Henderson. *Career:* Concerts in Sweden from 1963; London debut 1966, followed by concerts in Berlin, Hamburg, Hanover, Stuttgart and Dusseldorf; Tours of USA, Australia, USSR and Israel from 1968; Opera debut Goteborg 1967, as Gluck's Orpheus; Guest appearances at La Scala Milan and the Munich Staatsoper; Salzburg Easter Festival 1973/74 as Erda in the Ring, conducted by Karajan; 1976 Brangaene in Tristan und Isolde at the Paris Opéra. *Recordings:* Cimarosa's Requiem, Mozart's Betulia Liberata, Bach's Magnificat (Philips); Bruckner's Te Deum (Electrola); Dvořák's Requiem (RCA); Strauss's Aegyptische Helena (Decca); Bach's B Minor Mass (Erato); Vivaldi's Tito Manlio, Eterna; Awarded Grand Prix du Disque for Juditha Triumphans by Vivaldi. *Address:* c/o Svensk Konsertdirektion AB, Box 5076, 40222 Goteborg, Sweden.

FINNISSY Michael Peter, b. 17 Mar 1946, London, England. Composer. *Education:* Royal College of Music, London. *Career:* Director of Music, London School of Contemporary Dance, 1969-74; Lecturer at Chelsea College, Chelsea School of Art, Dartington Summer School; Guest Artist of The Victorian College of The Arts, Melbourne, 1982-83; Composition teacher at Winchester College, 1987-; Sussex University 1989-90; Chairman British Section, ISCM, 1989-90; President, ISCM, 1991-; Executive Councillor, ISCM, 1990-. *Compositions:* World, 1968-74; Mysteries, 1972-79; Tsuru Kame, 1971-73; Folk-Song Set, 1969-70; Cipriano, 1974; 7 Piano Concertos, 1975-81; Offshore, 1975-76; Mr. Punch, 1976-77, English Country-Tunes, 1977; Alongside, 1979; Sea and Sky, 1979-80; Kelir, 1981; Dilok, 1982; Whitman, 1981-83; Vaudeville, 1983; Ngano, 1983-84; String Quartet, 1984; Cabaret Vert, 1985; The Undivine Comedy, Opera 1988; Red Earth, 1987-88; Gershwin Arrangements and more Gershwin, 1975-90; Obrecht Motetten, 1988-; Unknown Ground, 1989-90; Thérèse Raquin, Opera 1992-93. *Current Management:* Oxford University Press, United Music Publishers, Universal Edition, London. *Address:* c/o Oxford University Press, Walton Street, Oxford OX2 6DP, England.

FINSCHER Ludwig, b. 14 Mar 1930, Kassel,

Germany. Musicologist; Professor. *Education:* Pupil of Rudolf Gerber, PhD, University of Göttingen, 1954; Completed Habilitation, University of Saarbrücken, 1967. *Career:* Research Assistant, Deutsches Volksliedarchiv; Assistant Lecturer, Institute of Musicology, University of Kiel, 1960-65; Assistant Lecturer, University of Saarbrücken, 1965-68; Professor of Musicology, University of Frankfurt am Main, 1968-81; University of Heidelberg, 1981-; Editor 1961-68, co-editor 1968-74, Die Musikforschung. *Publications:* Loyset Compère (c 1450-1518): Life and Works, 1964; edited with F Blume et al, Geschichte der Evangelischen Kirchenmusik, 2nd edition, 1965, English translation, augmented, 1974 as Protestant Church Music: A History; edited with C-H Mahling, Festschrift Walter Wiora zum 30 Dezember 1966, 1967; Studien zur Geschichte des Streichquartetts: I, Die Entstehung des klassischen Streichquartetts: Von den Vorformen zur Grundlegung durch Joseph Haydn, 1974; edited Renaissance-Studien: Helmuth Osthoff zum 80. Geburtstag, 1979; edited Quellenstudien zur Musik der Renaissance: I, Formen und Probleme der Uberlieferung mehrstimmiger Musik im Zeitalter Josquins Desprez, 1981, II, Datierung und Filiation von Musikhandschriften der Josquin-Zeit, 1983; edited Ludwig van Beethoven, 1983; edited Claudio Monteverdi: Festschrift Reinhold Hammerstein zum 70. Geburtstag, 1986; edited, Die Musik des 15 und 16, Jahrhunderts, Neues Handbuh der Musikwissenschaft, vol. 3/1-2, 1989-90 . *Contributions tto:* Edited the complete musical works of Gaffurius, 1955, 1960; the collected works of Compère, 1958-72; with K von Fischer, the collected works of Hindemith, 1976-; edited works for the Neue Mozart-Ausgabe and the complete works of Gluck. *Memberships:* International Musicological Society, vice president 1972-77, president 1977-82; Gesellschaft für Musikforschung, president 1974-77; Honorary foreign member, Royal Musical Association, London, 1978-; Mainz Academy of Sciences; Heidelberg Academy of Sciences. *Address:* Klingenstrasse 5, D-6932 Hirschhorn, Germany.

FIRKUSNY Rudolf, b. 11 Feb 1912, Napajedla, Czechoslovakia. Pianist; Teacher. m. Tatiana Nevole, 9 June 1965, 1 son, 1 daughter. *Education:* Private composition lessons with Janáček, 1919; Studied piano with Ruzena Kurzova, Brno Conservatory, 1920-27; University of Brno; Pupil in Music Theory, Vilem Kurz and Rudolf Karel, Prague Conservatory; Composition with Suk, 1929-30; Completed piano studies with Artur Schnabel, 1932. *Debut:* As Soloist in Mozart piano concerto at age 10 in Prague. *Career:* Toured Central Europe; London debut, 1933; US debut, NY, 1938; Regular tours to all major music centres after World War II, appearing as soloist with orchestras, recitalist and chamber-music player; Has given the premieres of works by Menotti, Barber, Hanson, Martinů and Ginastera; Celebrated 65th anniversary of debut, 1985; Teacher, Juilliard School of Music, NY. *Compositions:* Piano Concerto; String Quartet; Various piano pieces. *Recordings:* Numerous discs; including music by Janáček. *Publication:* Edited with Rafael Druian, violin sonatas of Mozart. *Honours:* Ethnic New Yorker Award, 1989; T G Masaryk Order, 1st Class , Vaclav Havel, 1991; Honorary Doctorate of Philosophy, Charles University, Prague, 1990 & Masaryk University, Brno, 1991; Bard College, USA, 1993, Janáček Academy of Music, Brno, 1993; Honorary Citizenship of Prague and Napajedla, 1990; Citizenship, Brno, 1991; . *Current Management:* Columbia Artists Management, New York, Van Walsum Management, London. *Address:* P O Box 355, Staatsburg, NY 12580, USA.

FIRSOVA Elena, b. 21 Mar 1950, Leningrad, USSR. Composer. m. Dmitri Smirnov. *Education:* Began music studies at college in Moscow, 1966; Moscow Conservatoire 1970-75, with Alexander Pirumov (composition) and Yury Kholopov (analysis); further study with Edison Denisov. *Career:* Her music was first featured outside the Soviet Union in 1979, in Cologne, Paris and Venice; British debut with Petraca's Sonnets, 1980; BBC commissions: Eartly Life, 1986; Augury, 1991; Cassandra, 1993; Professor and Composer in residence at Keele University, 1993. *Compositions:*

Scherzo for woodwind quartet and piano, 1967; Suite for viola solo, 1967; Three Poems by Osip Mandelstam for mixed chorus, 1970; String Quartet No.1, 1970; Sonata for cello and piano, 1971; Five Pieces for orchestra, 1971; A Feast in Time of Plague, chamber opera after Pushkin, 1972; Piano Trio, 1972; Chamber Music for string orchestra, 1973; Cello Concerto No.1, 1973; String Quartet No.2, 1974; Autumn Songs for voice and piano, 1974; Stanzas for orchestra, 1975; Violin Concerto No.1, 1976; Capriccio for flute and saxophone quartet, 1976; Sonata for clarinet solo, 1976; Petrarca's Sonnets for voice and ensemble, 1976; Postlude for harp and orchestra, 1977; Chamber Concerto No.1 for flute and strings, 1978; Elegy for piano, 1979; Tristia, cantata for voice and chamber orchestra, 1979; Three Poems by Osip Mandelstam, 1980; Misterioso, String Quartet No.3, 1980; Shakespeare's Sonnets for voice and organ, 1981; Chamber Concerto No.2 for cello and orchestra, 1982; Spring Sonata for flute and piano, 1982; The Stone, cantata for voice and orchestra, 1983; Violin Concerto No.2, 1983; Mysteria for organ and percussion, 1984; Earthly Life, cantata for soprano and ensemble, 1984; Fantasie for violin solo, 1985; Chamber Concerto No.3 for piano and orchestra, 1985; Music for 12, 1986; Piano Sonata, 1986; Forest Walks for soprano and ensemble, 1987; Chamber Concerto No.4 for horn and ensemble, 1987; Augury for orchestra and chorus, 1988; Autumn Music, 1988; Amoroso, String Quartet No.4, 1989; Monologue for bassoon, 1989; Nostalgia for orchestra, 1989; Stygian Song for soprano and ensemble, 1989; Odyssey for 7 performers, 1990; Verdehr-Terzett for violin, clarinet and piano, 1990; The Nightingale and the Rose, chamber opera after Wilde, 1991; Seven Haiku for voice and lyre, 1991; Far Away for saxophone quartet, 1991; Sea Shell for voice and ensemble, 1991; Whirpool for voice, flute and percussion, 1991; Silentium for voice and string quartet, 1991; Secret Way for orchestra and voice, 1992; Distance, for voice and ensemble, 1992; Meditation in the Japanese Garden for flute, viola and piano, 1992; You and I for cello and piano, 1992; Starry Flute for flute, 1992; Vigilia for violin and piano, 1992; Lagrimoso, String Quartet No.5, 1992; Otzvuki for flute and guitar, 1992; Cassandra for orchestra, 1992; Phantom for four viols, 1993. *Address:* 32 Larchwood, Keele, Newcastle, Staffordshire ST5 5BB, England.

FIRTICH Georgy Ivanovich, b. 20 Oct 1938, Russia. Composer. div. 2 sons. *Education:* Leningrad Music College; Leningrad Conservatoire. *Debut:* Leningrad, 1953 as composer and musician. *Career:* Composer or symphonies, film scores, music for radio and theatre; Currently Chairman of St Peterburg Association of Modern Music. *Compositions include:* Bug and Return, (ballets), 1961, 1964; Baths (opera), 1971; About motherland (symphony), 1963; Concerto-symphony, 1986; Seven sonatas for piano and for viola and piano, 1960-90; Vocal cycle for baritone, 1988; vocal cycle for Soprano and Piano, 1990; Choral works include: Leningrad, cantata for soprano, baritone, chorus and symphony orchestra in 6 movements, 1976. *Recordings include:* Adventures of captain Vrungel, 1986; Edwards. *Honours:* Laureate of Leningrad Competitions; Honoured Worker of Arts, Russia, 1993. *Memberships:* Composers Union of St Petersburg. *Hobbies:* Driving; Fishing; Mushrooms. *Address:* Novoalexandrovskaya St 11-29, St Petersburg 193012, Russia.

FISCHER Adam, b. 9 Sept 1949, Budapest, Hungary. Conductor. *Education:* Kodály School Budapest; Studied conducting in Budapest, Vienna and Rome. *Career:* Since winning Milan Cantelli Competition in 1973 has conducted widely in Germany and Austria; Regular guest at the Hamburg and Munich State Operas; At the Vienna State Opera has conducted new productions of The Bartered Bride 1982, Manon 1983, Cavalleria Rusticana and Pagliacci 1985, Maria Stuarda and La Gioconda 1986; Further Viennese productions include Fidelio, Die Fledermaus, Otello and Così fan Tutte; Paris Opéra debut 1984, Der Rosenkavalier; US debut 1984, with the Boston and Chicago Symphony Orchestras; 1986 guest conductor with the Cincinnati, Denver, Detroit and Toronto orchestras; Season 1986-87 Die

Zauberflöte at La Scala Milan; BBC TV recording of Bartók's Bluebeard's Castle, with the London Philharmonic Orchestra 1989; Currently Music Director of the Austro-Hungarian Haydn Festival in Eisenstadt; Conducted the Premiere of Patmos by Wolfgang Von Schweinitz at Kassel Opera, 1990; Music Directorship of Kassel Opera relnquished at end of 1991/92 season; Royal Opera House debut, Die Fledermaus, 1988/89 season; ENO debut, 1991, Bluebeard's Castle; 1993/94, Smetana, The Two Widows; Conducted the Austro-Hungarian Haydn Orchestra at the 1993 London Proms, Beethoven's Third Concerto and Haydn's 97th Symphony. *Recordings:* Haydn's complete Symphonies, with the Austro-Hungarian Haydn Orchestra, Nimbus; Goldmark: Queen of Sheba (first recording), Grand Prix du Disque, 1982; 1990: contract with Nimbus to record Hungarian repertoire (esp Bartók) with the Hungarian State Symphony. *Honours:* BBC TV Recording of Duke Bluebeard's Castle with the LPO won Italia Prize, 1989. *Address:* c/o Harold Holt Ltd., 31 Sinclair Road, London W14 ONS, England.

FISCHER Annie, b. 5 July 1914, Budapest, Hungary. Pianist. m. Aladar Toth (deceased). *Education:* Budapest Academy of Music; Studied with Arnold Szekely and Ernö von Dohnányi. *Debut:* Beethoven's C Major Concerto, 1922. *Career:* Numerous concerts, tours and recordings 1926-; often heard in Brahms, Mozart, Bartók and Schumann. *Honours:* 1st Prize, International Liszt Competition, Budapest 1933; Kossuth Prizes 1949, 1955 and 1965; Honorary Professor of Academy of Music, Budapest 1965; Decorated Eminent Artist; Red Banner Order of Labour 1974. *Address:* Szent Istvan Park 14, H-1137 Budapest XIII, Hungary.

FISCHER Enrico, b. 25 Aug 1950, Muri, Switzerland. Conductor. 2 sons. *Education:* Zurich University; Voice training with Margrit Conrad; Conducting with Erich Schmid. *Debut:* As Conductor: Purcell, Dido and Aeneas; Vivaldi, the Four Seasons. *Career:* Founder Director, Conductor of the Opera company Cappella dei Grilli producing operas, musicals, oratorios, concerts, touring as an ensemble with 15-25 performances a year; Swiss first performances include: Lully's Alceste, 1981; Loewe Lerner's Brigadoon, 1982; Gesner's You're a Good Man Charlie Brown, 1986; Rodgers and Hammersteins' South Pacific, 1990. *Compositions:* Orchestral work, Uberdie Geburt Jesu, for strings and soli. Quintet for wind and piano, Se non evero, è ben trovato; Miscellaneous chamber music. *Memberships:* Committee, Allgemeine Musikgesellschaft Zurich; Steering committee, Willy Burkhard Association. *Address:* Bergstrasse 2, CH-5736 Burg, Switzerland.

FISCHER György, b. 12 Aug 1935, Budapest, Hungary. Conductor; Pianist and Harpsichordist. *Education:* Franz Liszt Academy, Budapest; Salzburg Mozarteum. *Career:* Assistant to Karajan at the Vienna State Opera, where he conducted Die Zauberflöte and Die Entführung; Currently Principal Conductor at the Cologne Opera, notably in a Mozart cycle produced by Jean Pierre Ponnelle; Bavarian State Opera, Don Giovanni; Idomeneo and Die Zauberflöte in South America; Cimarosa's Le Astuzie Femminili at Wexford; UK debut with the Welsh National Opera, 1973; returned for Così fan Tutte and Le Nozze di Figaro; London debut 1979 with the UK premiere of Mozart's Mitridate at the Camden Festival; English Chamber Orchestra from 1980; Debut with Australian Opera 1987/88, conducted Cosi Fan Tutte, 1990; Don Giovanni for Vancouver Opera 1988; Season 1992 with Le Nozze di Figaro at Sydney; Accompanist to leading singers, including his former wife the late Lucia Popp. *Recordings include:* Mozart arias for soprano voice with Kiri Te Kanawa, Teresa Berganza and Cecilia Bartoli (Decca). *Address:* c/o Lies Askonas Ltd., 186 Drury Lane, London WC2B 5RY, England.

FISCHER Ivan, b. 20 Jan 1951, Budapest, Hungary. Conductor. *Education:* Studied cello and composition in Budapest; Conducting studies with Hans Swarowsky in Vienna and Nikolaus Harnoncourt in Salzburg. *Career:* Many engagements with British orchestras from 1976;

Music Director of the Northern Sinfonia of England, 1979-82; Toured Britain with the London Symphony Orchestra 1980; Founded the Budapest Festival Orchestra 1983; Music Director of Kent Opera 1984-89, conducting Agrippina, L'Incoronazione di Poppea, Die Entführung aus dem Serail, Le Nozze di Figaro, Carmen, La Traviata, Die Zauberflöte, Il re Pastore, Le Comte Ory, Fidelio, Don Giovanni and Peter Grimes; Season 1987-88 directed Die Zauberflöte for English National Opera and La Gazza Ladra at the Paris Opera; Season 1988-89 conducted Don Giovanni at the Vienna Staatsoper, returning for Le nozze di Figaro and Die Entführung; US engagements with orchestras in Pittsburgh, San Francisco, Los Angeles, Chicago and Cincinnati (Principal Guest Conductor of the Symphony Orchestra); Also conducts the St Paul Chamber Orchestra and in Montreal and Toronto; Recent engagements with the Royal Concertgebouw, Amsterdam, the Berlin Philharmonic and the Israel Philharmonic; Toured Switzerland 1989 with the Budapest Festival Orchestra and pianist Zoltan Kocsis, ending with a visit to the Barbican Hall, London; Conducted the Orchestra of the Age of Enlightenment in Zaide at the Elizabeth Hall, 1991; Bluebeard's Castle at the 1992 Promenade Concerts. *Recordings include:* Symphonies by Schubert, Mahler, Mozart and Mendelsshon, the Brahms Violin Concerto (with Boris Belkin and the LSO) and Don Pasquale, Bartók Concertos with the Budapest Festival Orchestra and Zoltan Kocsis (Philips); Other labels include CBS, CBS Sony, Hungaroton and Decca. *Honours include:* First Prize, Firenze International Concours 1976; Rupert Foundation Competition 1976; MUM Prize in USA and ERASMUS Prize in Holland for Bartók recordings. *Address:* c/o Linda Marks, Harrison Parrott Ltd., 12 Penzance Place, London W11 4PA, England.

FISCHER Jan F, b. 15 Sept 1921, Louny, Czechoslovakia. *Education:* Studied at the Prague Conservatory, 1940-45, Master Schl for Composers, 1945-48, with Jaroslav Rídký, Prague University, 1945-48. *Career:* Committee member of the Pritomnost Association for Contemporary Music, 1945-49, and of the Union of Czechoslovak Composers, 1953-70. *Compositions include:* Operas: The Bridegrooms, Brno, 1957; Romeo Juliet and Darkness, 1962; Oh, Mr Fogg (after Around the World in 80 Days), 1971; The Miracle-Theatre, Radio Prague, 1973; Dekameron, 1977; Copernicus, 1983; Orchestral: Pastoral Sinfonietta, 1944; Violin concerto, 1946; Dance Suite, 1957; Fantasia for piano and orchestra, 1958; Symphony, 1959; Clarinet concerto 1963; Harp Concerto, 1973; Commemoration 1973; Night Music for strings 1973; Concerto for Orchestra, 1980; Partita for string Orchestra, 1983; Chamber; Suite for wind sextet, 1944; Ballad for string quarter and clarinet, 1949; Piano Quintet, 1949; Conversations with harp, for string trio, harp and flute, 1979; Brass Quintet, 1983. *Address:* SOZA (Czechoslovakia), c/o PRS Ltd Member Registration, 29-33 Berners Street, London W1P 4AA, England.

FISCHER Klaus Peter, b. 16 Jan 1937, Breslau, Silesia, Germany. Musicologist. *Education:* Diploma in School Music, Franz-Liszt- Hochschule, Weimar, 1958; PhD, Cologne University, 1970. *Career:* Scholarship Holder: German Historical Institute, Rome, 1970-72, German Research Association, 1972-76; Scientific Collaborator, Institute for Hymnological and Ethnological Studies, Cologne-Maria Laach, 1977-78; Lecturer, 1982-87, Associate Professor, 1988-, University of Pavia (Scuola di Paleografia e Filologia Musicale), Italy. *Publications:* Die Psalmkompositionen in Rom um 1600 (ca 1570-1630), 1979. *Contributions to:* Analecta Musicologica; Archiv fur Musikwissenschaft; Studi Musicali; Die Musikforschung; Grove's Dictionary of Music and Musicians, 6th edition; Kirchenmusikalisches Jahrbuch; Die Musik in Geschichte und Gegenwart (MGG), 2nd edition; Congress Reports. *Memberships:* Gesellschaft fur Musikforschung; International Musicological Society; Societa Italiana di Musicologia. *Hobbies:* Chess; Literature. *Address:* Via Villa Glori 5, 1-26100 Cremore, Italy.

FISCHER Miroslav, b. 6 Dec 1932, Slovakia. Master of Stage; Regisseur of Opera. m. (1) Olga Hanakova, 17 Oct 1977, (2) Jitka Saparova, 19 Oct 1977, 1 son, 1 daughter. *Education:* School of Musical Arts, Bratislava, 1955. *Debut:* Traviata, in Slovak National Theatre, Bratislava, 1955. *Career:* More than 130 operas and operettas performed in Bratislava, Banska, Bystrica, Kosice, Brno, Plzen, Ankara, Bilbao, Brussels, most notably: Pelléas et Melisande, 1958; Fidelio, 1960; La Forza del Destino, 1964; Consul, 1956; Midsummer Night's Dream, 1963; Greek Passions, 1969; Salome, 1976; Elektra, 1980; Fliegende Hollander, 1957; Lohengrin, 1976; Falstaff, 1978; Don Carlos, 1981; Un Ballo di Maschera, 1985; Katarina Izmailova, 1984; Wozzeck, 1985. *Hobbies:* Dogs; Cooking; History; Gardening. *Address:* Dankovskeho 14, 811 03 Bratislava, Slovakia.

FISCHER Norman, b. 25 May 1949, Plymouth, Michigan, USA. Cellist. *Education:* Studied at the Interlochen Arts Academy and with Richard Kapuscinski at the Oberlin College Conservatory. *Career:* Member of the Concord String Quartet from 1971; Nationwide performances in a wide repertory, including many works by American composers; George Rochberg has written his Piano Quintet, String Quintet and String Quartets nos. 3-7 for the ensemble; Other composers who have been premiered include Lukas Foss (Third Quartet), Ben Johnston (Crossings) and Jacob Druckman (Third Quartet); Quartet-in- residence at Dartmouth College, New Hampshire, from 1974. *Honours include:* Naumburg Award 1971. *Recordings include:* Fourth, Fifth and Sixth Quartets of George Rochberg. *Address:* c/o Dartmouth College, Hanover, NH 03755, USA.

FISCHER-DIESKAU Dietrich, b. 28 May 1925, Berlin. Baritone. m. (1) Irmgard Poppen 1949 (died 1963) 3 sons; (2) Ruth Leuwerik 1965 (divorced 1967); (3) Kristina Pugell 1968; (4) Julia Varady 1978. *Education:* High School in Berlin; Singing studies with Professor Georg Walter and Professor Hermann Weissenborn. *Career:* Military service 1943-45, POW in Italy until 1947; First Lyric and Character Baritone, Berlin State Opera 1948-, debut as Posa in Don Carlos; Member, Vienna State Opera Company 1957-; Professor, Hochschule der Kunste, Berlin, 1982-; numerous concert tours of Europe, USA and Asia, in Lieder by Strauss, Schubert, Wolf and Schumann; Appeared at a number of festivals: Bayreuth, Salzburg, Lucerne, Montreux, Edinburgh, Vienna, Holland, Munich, Berlin, Coventry etc. Best-known roles in Falstaff, Don Giovanni, The Marriage of Figaro, Wozzeck and Die Frau ohne Schatten; First performances of contemporary composers such as Britten (War Requiem, 1962), Henze (Elegy for Young Lovers, 1961), König Hirsch, 1956 and Tippett (The Vision of St Augustine, 1966); Also premiered Von Einem's An die Nachgeborenen, 1975, Hartmann's Gesangssszene, 1964, Henze's Neapolitan Lieder, 1956, Lutoslawski's Les Espaces du Sommeil, 1978; Holofornes by Matthus, 1981, Reimann's Totentanz, Requiem Zyklus, Lear, 1978, and Three Poems of Michelangelo, 1986; Dies by Wolfgang Rihm, 1986, Stravinsky's Abraham and Isaac, 1964, and 5th Symphony by Isang Yun, 1987; Retired 1992. *Recordings include:* Leading roles in Tosca, Macbeth, La Traviata, Parsifal and Götterdämmerung; Le Nozze di Figaro, Tristan und Isolde, Genoveva, Les Contes d'Hoffmann, Lohengrin and Othello; Capriccio; Falstaff; Orfeo ed Euridice, Don Giovanni, Figaro, Cosi fan Tutte, Die Zauberflöte, Fidelio, Salome, Elektra, Meistersinger, Tannhäuser, La Damnation de Faust, Arabella, Wozzeck, Lulu, Cardillac, Giulio Cesare, Doktor Faust; St Matthew Passion, Bach Cantatas; Complete male voice Lieder of Schubert, Wolf, Mahler, Strauss, Brahms, Schumann, Haydn, Mozart, Beethoven, over 1,000 recordings in all. *Publications:* Texte deutscher Lieder, 1968; Aus den Spuren de Schubert-Lieder, 1971; Wagner und Nietzsche, der Mystagoge und sein Abtrunniger, 1974; Franz Schubert, ein Portrait, 1976; Robert Schumann-Wort und Musik, 1981; Nachlang, Echoes of a Lifetime, 1987; Wenn Musik der Liebe Nahrung ist, Künstlerschicksale im 19 Jahrhundert Deutsche Verlaganstalt, Stuttgart, 1990; Weil nicht alle Blütenrëume reiften, Johann Friedrich Reichardt,

Hofkapallmeister dreier Preusenkönige; Deutsche Verlangsanstalt, Stuttgart, 1992. *Hobby:* Painting. *Address:* c/o Deutsche Verlangsanstalt, Stuttgart, Germany.

FISER Lubos, b. 30 Sept 1935, Prague, Czechoslovakia. Composer. *Education:* Studied with Hlobil at the Prague Conservatory and with Borkovec at the Prague Academy of Music. *Career:* Worked with Vit Nejedly Military Ensemble; First work publicly performed Four Pieces for violin and piano, 1954; Emigrated to the USA 1971 and became composer-in-residence with the American Wind Symphony Orchestra in Pittsburgh. *Compositions include:* Lancelot, chamber opera 1961; The Good Soldier Schweik 1962; Changing Game, ballet, 1971; Orchestra: Suite 1964; 2 Symphonies 1956, 1960; Symphonic Fresco 1963; Chamber Concerto for piano and orchestra 1964; 15 Prints after Dürer's Apocolypse 1965; Pieta 1967; Report for wind instruments 1971; Kreutzer Etude for chamber orchestra 1974; Labyrinth 1977; Serenade for Salzburg 1978; Albert Einstein for organ and orchestra 1979; Piano Concerto 1980; Meridian 1980; Romance for violin and orchestra 1980; Centaurs 1983; Chamber: Four pieces 1954; String Quartet 1955; Sextet for wind quintet and piano 1956; Cello Sonata 1975; Piano Trio 1978; Sonata for 2 cellos and piano 1979; Testris for string quartet 1981; Sonata for solo violin 1981; Vocal: Caprichos for soloists and chorus 1966; Requiem 1968; Lament over the Destruction of the City of Ur 1969; Ave Imperator 1977; Per Vittoria Colona for celo and female chorus 1979; Istannu, melodrama, 1980; The Signe for soloists, chorus and orchestra 1981; Address to Music 1982; 6 Piano Sonatas, 1955-78. *Honours include:* UNESCO Prize (1967) for 15 Prints after Durer's Apocolypse. *Address:* c/o ASCAP, ASCAP Building, One Lincoln Plaza, New York, NY 10023, USA.

FISH Adrian Vernon, b. 20 Jan 1956, Bristol, England. composer; Radio Presenter. m. Margaret Crichton, 19 Aug 1978, 2 sons. *Education:* Dartington College of Arts, 1973-74; Royal College of Music, 1975-78. *Career:* Church Organist, 1974-78; Founding Committee, Presteigne Festival, Wales, 1982-83; Founder and Artistic Director, Hexagon Ensemble, 1984-; Freelance Radio Presenter, 1988-; Jack Kennedy Selection (dance band), 1988-90; Salon Duo (pianist), 1990-93; First concert tour of Greenland by a classical musician, 1991, Second Tour, 1994. *Compositions:* Symphonies I-XII, 1978-93; A Dartmoor Cabaret, 1984; A Greenland Organ Book, 1992; Kalaallit Nunaat, (organ), 1980; Hawker, (chamber opera), 1979-87; Moraine (chamber ensemble), 1986; Septem Verba (organ), 1984. *Publications:* Publishers: Mayhew, RSCM, Delamuse, Brunton; Several editions as well as compositions including The Salon Duo Collection; Festival for flute/Carnival for Clarinet; Preludes and Verses, 1992; Kalaallet Nunaat, 1986. *Memberships:* Composers' Guild of Great Britain; Performing Right Society. *Hobbies:* Study of the Arctic; Photography; *Current Management* Darose Agency, Leicester. *Address:* Brownson House, Grenofen, Tavistock, Devon PL19 9ER, England.

FISHER David John, b. 7 Dec 1952, Northumberland, England. Teacher; Composer; Conductor. m. Pauline Russell, 27 July 1974, 2 stepsons. *Education:* Durham University, 1971-74; Sheffield University, 1986-87; BA, MMus; LTCL. *Career:* Head of Music, King Edward VII College, Leics, 1976-86, 1987-; Musical Director, Derby Choral Union and Kingfisher Chorale and GCSE Chief Examiner, Leics, 1989-90. *Compositions:* Mary Laid Her Child, 1972; Viva Italia, 1991; Aspects of Time, 1983; All is Well, 1989; Congissima, 1989; Le Destine de Sparky, 1992. *Recordings:* Ave Regina Caelorum, Lincoln Cathedral Choir, 1983; Litanie, Jacquelyn Parker soprano, Buttows Choir, 1988. *Publications:* Harpsichord: Listen, Compose and Perform, 1986; Advanced Listening, 1986. *Honours:* Young Composer Award with The Litanie, Northern Sinfonia Chorus, 1977. *Memberships:* Composers Guild of Great Britain. *Hobbies:* Gardening; Travel; Architecture. *Address:* Holly

Tree House, 13 Braunstone Lane East, Leics LE3 2FD, England.

FISHER Gillian, b. 1955, England. Singer (Soprano). m. Brian Kay. *Education:* Studied with John Carol Case, at the Royal College of Music and with Jessica Cash. *Career:* Appearances in the world's leading concert halls, including Albert, Festival and Barbican Halls (London), Amsterdam Concertgebouw, Lincoln Center New York and Suntory Hall Tokyo; Handel Festivals in London and in Maryland, USA; Frequent broadcasts with repertoire ranging from Baroque music to the vocal symphonies of Milhaud; Featured in Central TV series Man and his Music; Sang in Theodora and other works by Handel for tercentenary year, 1985; Sang in Messiah with Ton Koopman and the Amsterdam Baroque Orchestra, Japan 1987; Appearances in Italy, Japan & Australia with vocal group The Sixteen. *Recordings include:* Purcell's King Arthur and Dioclesian with John Eliot Gardiner and the Monteverdi Choir; The Triumph of Time and Truth with Denys Darlow and the London Handel Orchestra; Great Baroque Arias and Pergolesi's Stabat Mater with the King's Consort and Michael Chance; Purcell's, Fairy Queen and Bach Cantatas with The Sixteen and Harry Christophers and Handel duets with The Kings Consort and James Bowman. *Current Management:* Magenta Music. *Address:* c/o Magenta Music, 64 Highgate Street, London, N6 5HX, England.

FISHER Helen Wynfreda McKee, b. 4 Feb 1942, Nelson, New Zealand. Composer. m. Peter Fisher, 14 May 1966, 3 daughters. *Education:* BA, English, Canterbury University, 1964; Diploma of Teaching, 1965; BM, Musicology, 1982, BM (Hons), Composition, 1991, Victoria University, Wellington. *Career:* Teaching Music and English, 1966-; Appointed by Arts Council to New Zealand Composer-in-Schools residency, 1990, 1991; Received New Zealand Japan Foundation Travel Award to attend performance of Pounamu at 1990 Asian Music Festival in Japan; Initiator, Artistic Coordinator for first New Zealand Composing Women's Festival, 1993. *Compositions:* Te Tangi A Te Matui, 1986; Woodwind Trio, 1987; Pounamu, 1989; Nga Taniwha, 1991; Nga Tapuwae o Kupe, 1992; Wahine Toa, 1992; Bone of Contention, 1993. *Honours:* 1st Prize for Woodwind Trio, Composers Competition, Victoria University, 1987. *Memberships:* Composers Association of New Zealand; New Zealand Society of Music Education. *Hobbies:* Reading; Theatre. *Address:* 10 Winston St, Crofton Downs, Wellington 6004, New Zealand.

FISHER John, b. 1950, Scotland. Conductor. *Education:* Studied at the University of Glasgow and the Royal Academy of Music. *Debut:* Former member of the music staff at the Theatre La Monnaie, Brussels; has conducted opera companies, including Netherlands, Opera, Cologne Opera, the Maggio Musicale (Florence) and La Scala Milan; Artistic Director of Teatro La Fenice, Venice, from 1990; has conducted Le nozze di Figaro 1991, Semele, Rinaldo 1989 and Cosi fan Tutte (1990); Technical Consultant for Unitel films, including Jean-Pierre Ponnelle's Rigoletto; former Artistic Director of the Rossini Opera Festival at Pesaro; Covent Garden debut, 1992, Alcina. *Recordings include:* Rinaldo, with Marilyn Horne; Plays harpsichord on video of Mozart's Mitridate, conducted by Harnoncourt. *Address:* c/o Teatro La Fenice, Campo S Fantin 1965, 30124 Venice, Italy.

FISHER Norma, b. 11 May 1940, London, England. Concert Pianist. m. Barrington Saipe, 3 Sept 1967, 2 sons. *Education:* Guildhall School of Music with Sidney Harrison, 1951-57; Privately with Ilona Kabos, 1957-68 and Jacques Fevrier, Paris, 1962. *Debut:* Wigmore Hall, 1956; Proms, Royal Albert Hall, 1963. *Career:* Performances throughout Great Britain, Europe, USA, Canada and Israel, in Recitals, Concertos and Chamber Music; Regular Performer for BBC, London; Represented Great Britain twice at International Jeunesses Musicales Congress. *Honours:* 2nd Prize, Busoni International Piano Competition, Italy, 1961; Piano Prize (Joint holder with Vladimir Ashkenazy), Harriet Cohen

International Awards, 1963. *Hobbies:* Tennis; Theatre; Cooking. *Current Management:* Anglo-Swiss Management, London. *Address:* 5 Lyndhurst Gardens, Finchley, London N3 1TA, England.

FISHER Stephen Carey, b. 18 May 1948, Norfolk, Virginia, USA. Musicologist. *Education:* BA, University of Virginia, 1969; PhD, University of Pennsylvania, 1985. *Career:* Assistant Professor, Widener University, 1985-87; Lecturer, University of Pennsylvania, 1989- . *Publications:* The Symphony 1720-1840, Series B, Volume IX, Witt, Reicha, Eberl, 1983; Joseph Haydn Werke, series I, volumes 9-10, Sinfoniem um 1778-81, 1. und 2. Folge. *Contributions to:* Haydn-Studien; Mitteilungen der Internationalen Stiftung Mozarteum; Current Musicology; Haydn Studies, 1975; The Haydn Yearbook; The Eighteenth Century: A Current Bibliography; Eighteenth-Century Studies, Journal of Musicology; New Grove Dictionary of Opera; Notes; Journal of the American Musicological Society. *Honours:* Fulbright-Hays Grant, 1976-77. *Memberships:* American Musicological Society; International Musicological Society; Music Library Association. *Hobbies:* Writing science fiction. *Address:* Department of Music, University of Pennsylvania, 201 S 34th Street, Philadelphia, PA 19104, USA.

FISHER Sylvia Gwendoline Victoria, b. 18 Apr 1910, Melbourne, Australia. Soprano. m. Ubaldo Gardini, 1954 (div.). *Education:* Melbourne Conservatorium of Music, Australia. *Debuts:* Operatic debut in Lully's Cadmus & Hermione, 1932; Covent Garden (UK) debut in Fidelio (Leonore), 1948. *Career:* International Celebrity Concert, Australia, 1947; Tour of Australia, 1955. Appeared in: Rome (Sieglinde), 1952; Cagliari (Isolde), 1954; Bologna (Gutrune), 1955; Covent Garden (Brünnhilde), 1956; Frankfurt Opera House/Der Rosenkavalier, 1957; Created Mrs Wingrave in Britten's Owen Wingrave 1971; Sang Kabanichka in Katya Kabanova at the London Coliseum, 1973; Former Principal Soprano, Royal Opera House, Covent Garden, London, UK. *Honour:* Winner, Sun Aria Competition, Melbourne, 1936. *Hobbies:* Gardening; Rare books on singing. *Address:* Hochschule für Musik, Cologne, Germany.

FISK Eliot (Hamilton), b. 10 Aug 1954, Philadelphia, Pennsylvania, USA. Guitarist; Professor. *Education:* Pupil of Oscar Ghiglia, Aspen Music School, 1970-76; Ralph Kirkpatrick and Albert Fuller, BA 1972, MMA 1977, Yale University. *Debut:* Solo recital debut, Alice Tully Hall, NY, 1976. *Career:* Toured throughout the world as Soloist with orchestras, as recitalist and chamber-music performer; Teacher, Aspen Music School, 1973-82; Yale University, 1977-82; Mannes College of Music, 1978-82; Professor, Cologne Hochschule für Musik, 1982-; Prepared transcriptions of works by Bach, Scarlatti, Mozart, Paganini for guitar. *Recordings:* Various discs. *Honour:* Winner, International Classical Guitar Competition, Gargano, Italy, 1980. *Address:* c/o ICM Artists Ltd, 40 West 57th Street, New York, NY 10019, USA.

FISTOULARI Anatole, b. 20 Aug 1907, Kiev, USSR. Conductor. m. (1) Anna Mahler 1942 (dissolved) 1 daughter; (2) Mary Elizabeth Lockhart 1957. *Education:* Kiev, Berlin and Paris. *Debut:* First symphony concert, Kiev 1914. *Career:* Conducted all over Russia; Concerts in Western Europe 1920; Conducted Grand Opera Russe, Paris with Chaliapin 1931; Conducted Ballet de Monte Carlo with Massine in England, France, Italy and USA; First symphony concert with London Symphony Orchestra 1942; Principal Conductor, London Philharmonic Orchestra 1943-44; Founder and Principal Conductor of London International Orchestra 1943, now guest conductor; Numerous engagements in Europe, Israel, South Africa and the Americas; Numerous recordings, including Liszt's Les Préludes, Mazeppa and Totentanz; d'Indy's Symphonie; Poulenc's Les Biches and Aubade; Brahms and Beethoven violin Concertos, Saint-Saëns 3rd and Chausson Poème, Milstein; Liszt Piano Concertos, Kempff; Tchaikovsky's ballet music and 1st piano concerto, Earl Wilde. *Address:* 65 Redington Road, London NW3, England.

FITZGERALD Daire, b. 1966, Dublin, Ireland. Concert Cellist. *Education:* Studied with Rostropovitch, at the Menuhin School with William Pleeth and the Menuhin Academy with Radu Aldulescu. *Career:* Concerts throughout Western Europe, China, India, Israel and Czechoslovakia, while a student at the Menuhin School; Engagements with the hamber Music Society of Lincoln Center, New York, and concerts with such orchestras as the Royal Philharmonic, Warsaw Sinfonia, Central Philharmonic of Peking, Hallé and Berlin Radio Symphony; Soloist with the Camerata Lysy Gstaad on tour to Japan and Canada; Berlin debut with the Saint-Saens A minor concerto; New Year's Concert for Finnish TV, tour of USA playing chamber music with Menuhin and participation on Julian Lloyd Webber's Cellothon at South Bank, London. *Address:* c/o Anglo Swiss Ltd, 3 Primrose Mews, 1a Sharpleshall St, London NW1 8YW, England.

FIZDALE Robert, b. 12 Apr 1920, Chicago, Illinois, New York. Pianist; Writer on music. *Education:* Studied at the Juilliard School, New York. *Career:* Formed piano duo with Arthur Gold and debut recital at the New School for Social Research, with the premiere of two works by John Cage; New York Town Hall debut 1946; First performances of works by Ned Rorem, Vittorio Rieti, Samuel Barber and Virgil Thomson; French composers include Milhaud (Carnaval pour La Nouvelle-Orleans, 1947, Suite op.300 and Concertino d'automne), Auric (Partita), Poulenc (Sonata for Two Pianos), Tailleferre, Henri Sauguet; Premiere of Berio's Concerto for Two Pianos and Orchestra, with the New York Philharmonic, 1972; Further repertoire includes Mendelssohn's Concertos in E and A flat, Bartók's Concerto for Two Pianos and Percussion, Rorem's Four Dialogues and Mozart's Concerto K365; World wide tours until 1982. *Publication include:* Misia: the Life of Misoa Sert (with Arthur Gold) 1980.

FLAGELLO Ezio, b. 28 Jan 1931, New York City, USA. Singer (Bass). *Education:* Studied with Friedrich Schorr and John Brownlee at the Manhattan School of Music; Further study with Luigi Ricci in Rome. *Debut:* Concert performance of Boris Godunov at Carnegie Hall, 1952. *Career:* Sang Dulcamara in Rome, 1956; After winning Metropolitan Auditions of the Air (1957) appeared in New York, until 1987, as Leporello, Fiesco in Simon Boccanegra, Pogner, Philip II and Rossini's Basilio; Sang Enobarbus in the inaugural production of the Metropolitan Opera at Lincln Center, Antony and Cleopatra by Barber (1966); Guest appearances in San Francisco, Dallas, Houston, Milan, Vienna, Berlin, Prague and Florence; Screen debut, Francis Ford Coppola's Godfather II; Sang Sarastro for Pennsylvania Opera Theater, 1991. *Recordings include:* Così fan Tutte, Lucrezia Borgia, Lucia di Lammermoor, Un Ballo in Maschera, Ernani, Luisa Miller, Rigoletto, La Forza del Destino (RCA); Alcina, I Puritani (Decca); Don Giovanni (Deutsche Grammophon); Oedipus Rex (CBS). *Address:* 2005 Samontee Road, Jacksonville, Florida 32211, USA.

FLAGELLO Nicolas (Oreste), b. 15 Mar 1928, New York City, USA. Pianist; Conductor; Professor; Composer. *Education:* Began piano lessons at age 3; Violin lessons at age 6 with Francesco di Giacomo; Oboe lessons; Pupil of Harold Bauer, Hugo Kortschak, Hugo Ross and Vittorio Giannini, BM 1949, MM 1950, Manhattan School of Music; Studied conducting with Dimitri Mitropoulos; Composition lessons with Ildebrando Pizzetti, DMus 1956, Accademia di Santa Cecilia, Rome. *Career:* First appeared in public as pianist at age 5; Violinist, All American Youth Orchestra, 1945-46; Professor of Composition and Conducting, Manhattan School of Music, 1950-77; Guest conductor of opera and symphony in USA and overseas; Piano Accompanist to various singers. *Compositions:* Operas: Mirra, 1953; The Wig, 1953; Rip van Winkle, 1957; The Sisters, 1958; The Judgment of St Francis, 1959; The Piper of Hamelin, 1970; Beyond the Horizon, 1983; Orchestral: Beowulf, 1949; 4 piano concertos, 1950, 1956, 1962, 1975; Symphonic Aria, 1951; Overture giocosa, 1952; Flute Concerto, 1956; Missa sinfonica,

1957; Concerto for Strings, 1959; Capriccio for Cello and Orchestra, 1962; Lautrec, 1965; 2 symphonies: 1968, 1970; Serenata, 1968; Credendum for Violin and Orchestra, 1974; Odyssey for Band, 1981; Concerto sinfonico for Saxophone Quartet and Orchestra, 1985; Chamber: Harp Sonata, 1961; Piano Sonata, 1962; Concertino for Piano, Brass and Timpani, 1963; Violin Sonata, 1963; Suite for Harp and String Trio, 1965; Electra for Piano and Percussion, 1966; Ricercare for Brass and Percussions, 1971; Prisma for 7 Horns, 1974; Diptych for 2 Trumpets and Trombone, 1979; Vocal: Passion of Martin Luther King, oratorio for Bass-baritone, Chorus and Orchestra, 1968; Choruses; Songs. *Recordings:* Many discs of his own works under his direction for Serenus Recorded Editions.

FLAKE Uta-Maria, b. 2 Feb 1951, Germany. Singer (Soprano). *Education:* Studied at the Hamburg Musikhochschule, at Bloomington and with Tito Gobbi and Mario del Monaco. *Career:* Sang in Offenbach's Orphee aux Enfers at the Hamburg Staatsoper, while still a student; Professional debut Ulm, 1974, as the Forza Leonora; Dortmund Opera, 1976-80, notably as Eve in the German premiere of Penderecki's Paradise Lost; Stuttgart Staatsoper from 1980, as Leonore (Fidelio), Agathe, Elsa, Eva and Giulietta; Guest engagements at the Munich Staatsoper, Salzburg (in concert), Dusseldorf, Berlin Staatsoper (Lisa in The Queen of Spades) and Deutsche Oper (leonore), Covent Garden (Elsa and Freia), Lisbon (Gutrune and Third Norn), Cologne, Trieste and Basle (Sieglinde). *Recordings include:* Daphne by Strauss. *Address:* c/o Stuttgart Staatsoper, Oberer Schlossgarten 6, 7000 Stuttgart, Germany.

FLAKSMAN Michael, b. 3 May 1946, Akron, Ohio, USA. Cellist. *Education:* BA, Harvard College, 1969; Teachers of Music; Nadia Boulanger, Pablo Casals, Ernst Silberstein, Maurice Eisenberg; also Antonio Janigro, Stuttgart Musikhochschule (Kuenstlerische Abschlusspruefung) 1978. *Debut:* Cleveland Orchestra 1963. *Career:* Marlboro Festival, 1964-65; Appearances Salzburg, 1973, 1974; Prizewinner in International Competitions: Francesco Serato, Bologna, 1974; Pablo Casals, Barcelona, 1975; Rockefeller Fund Award, New York, 1981; Current Positions held: Professor of Violoncello at: Musikkonservatorium Schaffhausen (Switzerland) (Violoncello-Meisterklasse) and California State University, Northridge, California, USA; Stuttgart Musikhochschule. *Recordings:* Pergolesi Sinfonia (VOX); Works of Schumann and Mendelssohn (VERITON).

FLEET Marlene Rose, b. 13 Feb. 1942, Grimsby, South Humberside, England. Concert Pianist. m. Harry Terence Harvey Taylor, 5 June 1972. *Education:* LRAM, ARCM, Grimsby Technical College; Royal Academy of Music, 1960-65. *Debut:* Wigmore Hall, 1964. *Career:* Numerous concerts in Great Britain, Europe and America; Appearances at Wigmore Hall, Purcell Room, Queen Elizabeth Hall, Royal Festival Hall, London; Plays regularly for BBC and has performed on BBC TV; Played with most of the leading British orchestras and with many distinguished conductors. *Recordings:* Numerous recordings for BBC Radio 3. *Honours:* Winner of most of solo pianist prizes, Royal Academy of Music, 1960-65; Countess of Munster Scholarships; Martin Musical Scholarships. *Address:* 22 Fairefield Crescent, Glenfield, Leicester LE3 8EH, England.

FLEISCHER Edytha, b. 5 Apr 1898, Falkenstein, Germany. Singer (Soprano). *Education:* Studied in Berlin with Lilli Lehmann. *Debut:* Deutsche Opernhaus 1918. *Career:* Early success as Mozart's Constanze; Salzburg Festival 1922, as Zerlina and Susanna; Tour of North America with the German Opera Company; Sang coloratura roles at the Metropolitan Opera 1926-36; appeared in the first local performances of Rimsky-Korsakov's Sadko (1930) and Rossini's Il Signor Bruschino (1932); Also heard in La Rondine, Suppé's Boccaccio and Il Serva Padrona; Engagements at the Teatro Colon Buenos Aires 1936-49; Teacher at the Vienna Conservatory from 1949. *Recordings include:* Scenes from Götterdämmerung.

FLEISCHER Randall Craig, b. 14 Mar 1959, Ohio, USA. Conductor. m. Heidi Joyce, 18 Dec 1982. *Education:* BMus Oberlin Conservatory of Music; MMus, Conducting, Indiana University; Private study with Otto-Werner Mueller. *Career:* Associate Conductor: National Symphony; Music Director: Hudson Valley Phil; Adjunct Associate Professor, Catholic University of America; CBS National Broadcast: Kennedy Center Honours. *Recordings:* Dvořák Cello Concerto, Mstislav Rostropovich, Cellist. Live performance with NSO from St Petersburg. *Honours:* Fellowship, Aspen Choral Inst, 1982; Conducting Fellowship, 1989. *Memberships:* American Symphony Orchestra League. *Hobbies:* Weightlifting; Aerobics. *Address:* 225S Whiting Street, No 718, Alexandria, VA 22304, USA.

FLEISCHMANN Aloys Georg, b. 1910, Munich, Germany. Composer; Conductor; Professor of Music. m. Anne Madden, 2 sons, 3 daughters. *Education:* MA, University College, Cork, Ireland; MusD, National University of Ireland; MusD, Dublin University; State Academy of Music, Munich, Germany. *Career:* Conductor, Cork Symphony Orchestra, 1934-; Director, Cork International Choral & Folk Dance Festival, 1954-87; Emeritus Professor of Music, University College, Cork. *Compositions:* Overture, The Four Masters; Introduction & Funeral March, for large orchestra; Song of the Provinces, choir & orchestra with audience participation; Songs of Colmcille, choir & chamber orchestra; Clare's Dragoons, baritone, war pipes, choir & orchestra; Cornucopia, horn & orchestra; 4 Song Cycles, voice & orchestra; Sinfonia Votiva, large orchestra; Mass for Peace; 4 ballets, including The Táin (full length ballet produced at Gaiety Theatre, Dublin, 1981). *Publication:* Music in Ireland: A Symposium, 1953. *Contributions to:* Grove's Dictionary; Various professional journals and encyclopaedias. *Address:* Glen House, Ballyvolane, Cork, Eire.

FLEISCHMANN Ernest Martin, b. 7 Dec 1924, Frankfurt, Germany. Music Administrator. Divorced; 1 son, 2 daughters. *Education:* Bachelor of Commerce, Chartered Accountant, (S.A.), University of the Witwatersrand, Johannesburg, South Africa, 1950; Bachelor of Music, University of Cape Town, 1954; Postgraduate work, South African College of Music, 1954-56. *Debut:* Conductor with Johannesburg Symphony Orchestra, 1942. *Career:* Conductor, various symphony orchestras, operas, 1942-55; Music Organizer, Van Riebeeck Festival, Cape Town, 1952; Director of Music and Drama, Johannesburg Festival, 1956; General Manager, London Symphony Orchestra, 1959-67; Director for Europe, CBS Records, 1967-69; Executive Director, Los Angeles Philharmonic, and General Director, Hollywood Bowl, 1969-88; Vice President and Managing Director, Los Angeles Philharmonic Association, 1988-. *Honours:* John Steinway Award for Distinguished Service to Music, 1979; President's Special Award, Association of California Symphony Orchestras, 1980; Award of Merit, Los Angeles Junior Chamber of Commerce, 1985; Honorary Doctor of Music, Cleveland Institute of Music, 1987. *Memberships:* Vice-Chairman, Board of Directors, American Symphony Orchestra League; Member, Board of Directors, California Confederation of the Arts; Member, Board of Directors, American Music Center, Inc. *Address:* c/o Los Angeles Philharmonic, 135 N. Grand Avenue, Los Angeles, CA 90012, USA.

FLEISHER Leon, b. 23 July 1928, San Francisco, California, USA. Pianist; Conductor. *Education:* Studied piano with Artur Schnabel, 1938-48; Conducting with Pierre Monteux. *Career:* First public recital 1934; Played Liszt's A Major Concerto with the San Francisco Symphony, 1942; Brahms D Minor Concerto in San Francisco and New York, 1943, 1944; International career from 1952; Gave concerts with George Szell and the Cleveland Orchestra; Joined faculty of the Peabody Conservatory of Music, Baltimore, 1959; Premiered Leon Kirchner's Concerto, Seattle 1963; Lost use of right hand 1965, and later played Piano Left Hand repertoire; Co-Director of the Theatre Chamber Players Washington DC 1968; Associate Conductor of the Baltimore Symphony Orchestra 1973-78; Guest engagements as conductor with leading orchestras in the USA; Resumed bimanual solo pianist career 1982; Artistic Director of the Tanglewood Music Center, 1985.

FLEMING Amaryllis, b. 1920, London, England. Cellist. *Education:* Studied at the Royal College of Music, London, and with Pierre Fournier and Pablo Casals. *Career:* Has played at the Wigmore Hall, Albert Hall, and many other venues in Britain and abroad; Until 1987 played in Piano Trio with Manoug Parikian and Bernard Roberts; Professor of Cello at the Royal College of Music. *Recordings include:* Bach Suites for Solo Cello; Works for cello and piano. *Honours include:* Queen's Prize, Munich International Competition. *Membership:* ISM. *Hobby:* Studying Bach. *Address:* 137 Old Church Street, London SW3, England.

FLEMING Renée, b. 1960, Rochester, New York, USA. Singer (Soprano). *Education:* Studied in New York. *Career:* Frist major role as Mozart's Countess at the Metropolitan, New York, returning as Pamina and Tatiana and as Rosina in the premiere of John Corigliano's The Ghosts of Versailles, 1991; Other appearances include Dvorak's Rusalka at Houston and Seattle (1990, Donna Elvira at La Scala Milan, Massenet's Thais in Washington, Fiordiligi in Geneva and at Glyndebourne, 1992 and the title role in Donizetti's Maria Padilla at Omaha, 1990; Further engagements as Mozart's Countess at Houston, San Francisco and Buenos Aires, 1991; Sang Dirce in Cherubini's Médée at Covent Garden, 1989, returning as Comtesse de Folleville in Rossini's Il Viaggio a Reims, 1992; Sang Anna in La Dame Blanche at Carnegie Hall and Mimi for Bath City Opera, 1992. *Honours:* Richard Tucker Award, 1990; Metropolitan Opera Auditions. *Address:* c/o Royal Opera House, Covent Garden, London WC2, England.

FLETCHER Andrew Illston, b. 25 Nov 1950, Birmingham, England. Freelance Musician; Organist; Choir Trainer; Teacher; Composer; Arranger; Accompanist. *Education:* FLCM, 1969; FRCO, 1971; CHM, 1974; MA (Oxon), 1976; Keble College, Oxford University, 1969-72; London University Institute of Education, 1972-73. *Career:* Director of Music, St Mary's, Warwick, 1973-81; Director of Music, St Mark's Swindon, 1982-85; Director of Music, St Peter's, Hall Green, Birmingham, 1985-93; Numerous recital tours, USA. *Compositions:* Church and organ music; various anthems recorded on Abbey label. *Recordings:* Late Romantic Masterworks - St Mary's, Warwick, 1990; The Majesty of Riverside, New York, 1993; Recording contract with Mirabilis Records. *Publications:* Organ Music published by OECUMUSE and MAYHEW; Church Music published by OUP (New York), Mayhew and OECUMUSE. *Contributions to:* Analyses of set works, Music Teacher magazine. *Honours:* Turpin Prize, FRCO, 1971. *Memberships:* Assistant Music Masters Association; Incorporated Society of Musicians. *Hobbies:* Swimming; Crosswords. *Address:* 230 The Avenue, Acocks Green, Birmingham B27 6NU, England.

FLETCHER H Grant, b. 25 Oct 1913, Hartsburg, Illinois, USA. Composer; Conductor. m. Gretchen Anna Walton, 30 June 1967, 3 sons, 2 daughters. *Education:* BM, Illinois Wesleyan University, Bloomington, Illinois, 1935; MM, University of Michigan, Ann Arbor, 1939; PhD, Eastman School, University of Rochester, New York, 1951. *Career:* Head, Theory Department, Winthrop College, 1941-45; Orchestra Conductor, Akron Symphony, Akron, Ohio, 1945-48; Head Conductor, Chicago Music College, 1949-51; Conductor and Composer, Professor, Arizona State University, Tempe, Arizona, 1956; Conductor, film score for Julius Caesar. *Compositions:* 2 operas; 4 sonatas; 5 ballets; Over 300 other works. *Recordings:* Son; Toccata No 1. *Publications:* Syllabus for Advanced Integrated Theory, 1962-76; Rhythm Production and Notation, 1969; Chromatic, Functional Modality, 1979; Editor, New World Encyclopaedia, 1956-. *Contributor to:* Numerous monographs, articles and critiques. *Hobbies:* Swimming; Psychology. *Address:* 1626 E Williams Street, Tempe, AZ 85281, USA.

FLETCHER Reg(inald) Donald, b. 3 Nov 1939, Derbyshire, England. Music Educator; Singer. m. Brenda Warner, 29 July 1964, 2 sons. *Education:* Royal Manchester College of Music; Guidhall School of Music and Drama; University of London Institute of Education. *Career:* Soloist (bass-baritone): Lieder Oratorio, Recitals, Opera: Schoolteacher, Nottingham 1963-65, Hucknall, 1965-67, Bristol, 1967-69; Music Adviser, Hampshire, 1969-88, County General Inspector for Music, 1988-93; Freelance Consultant, 1994-; Writer; Broadcaster; Lecturer. *Publications:* GCSE Music, a Teacher's Guide, 1985; Sounds Inventive, I and II, 1986, 1987. *Contributions to:* magazines. *Memberships:* ISM; MANA; SMA; MENC; NAIEAC; ISME. *Hobbies:* Arts; Design; Driving; Boating; Gardening. *Address:* 8 Olivers Battery Gardens, Olivers Battery, Winchester, Hampshire SO22 4HF, England.

FLETZBERGER Matthias, b. 24 Aug 1965, Vienna, Austria. Pianist. *Education:* Hochschule für Musik, Vienna. *Career:* Musikverein Wien; Mozarteum Salzburg Festival; Festivals in Puerto Rico, Lockenhaus, Athens, Naples, Soloist, Israel Philharmonic, Orchestre de Bordeaux, R. Schumann Philarmonie, Hochschulorchester Vienna, Orquestra Sinfonica da Chile; Recitals in Europe, America, Australia; Musical Assistant to Elisabeth Schwarzkopf, Renata Tebaldi; Musical Director and Principal Conductor of the Superdstilthcater, in Vienna. *Recordings:* Production of Video Clips for ORF; Radio Recordings; TV Recordings; Conductor of the TV Production of The Magic Flute at the Vienna Festival, 1991. *Honours:* Recipient, various prizes & awards. *Hobbies:* Musical Director, Opera Productions & Staging Assistance; Architecture; Mathematics. *Address:* Alban Bergweg 11, A 1130 Vienna, Austria.

FLEURY André, b. 1903, Neuilly-sur-Seine, France. Organist; Composer. *Education:* Conservatoire de Paris; Studied with Marcel Dupré. *Career:* Assistant to organist Eugene Gigout, St Augustin, at age 17; Assistant to Tournemire, Sainte-Clotilde; Appointed Organist, Sainte Augustin, 1930; Jury Member, Conservatoire de Paris; Professor, Ecole Normale de Musique, Paris; Professor, Conservatory of Dijon, 1949-71; Organist, Dijon Cathedral, 1949-71; Co-Organist, St Eustache, Paris; Professor, Schola Cantorum, Paris; Numerous recitals, Paris and provinces, England, Germany, Switzerland, Belgium, Netherlands, Rome; Participated at Besançon, Vichy, Bordeaux, Toulon and York Festivals. *Compositions include:* Organ works: 2 Preludes and Fugues; Allegro Symphonique; 1 Triptych (Prelude, Andante and Toccata); 2 Symphonies; 1 Fantasia; 24 pieces for organ without pedals; Piano pieces; Others. *Honours:* 1st Prize for Organ and Improvisation, Conservatoire de Paris, 1926; Various awards for composition. *Address:* 30 rue Georges Chafiélier Le Chesney 78150, France.

FLIETHER Herbert, b. 29 Oct 1911, Velbert, Germany. Singer (Baritone). *Education:* Studied with Ivo H Gotte in Berlin, 1949-53. *Debut:* Essen 1953, as Orestes in Elektra. *Career:* Member of the Hamburg Staatsoper from 1957: roles include Hans Sachs, Telramund, the Dutchman, Scarpia, Kaspar in Der Freischütz and Wotan in Der Ring des Nibelungen; sang in the 1960 premiere of Henze's Der Prinz von Homburg; Glyndebourne Festival 1961, 1963, as Pizarro in Fidelio; Metropolitan Opera 1962-63; Sang The Wanderer in Siegfried at Covent Garden; Many concert appearances. *Address:* c/o Hamburgische Staatsoper, Grosse-Theaterstrasse 34, D-2000 Hamburg 36, Germany.

FLOR Claus Peter, b. 16 Mar 1953, Leipzig, Germany. Conductor. *Education:* Robert Schumann Conservatory, Zwickau, age 10; Franz Liszt Institute for Music, Weimar, 1966; Mendelssohn Bartholdy High School for Music,

Leipzig, under Rolf Reuter and Felix Mendelssohn; Studied with Rafael Kubelik and Kurt Sanderling. *Career:* Principal Conductor, Suhler Philharmonic, 1981; Guest Conductor, Gewandhaus Orchestra Leipzig, Dresden Staatskapelle, Berlin Symphony Orchestra; Principal Conductor, Artistic Advisor, 1984, General Music Director, 1985, Berlin Symphony Orchestra, with world tour, 1988, at Edinburgh Festival, 1990; US debut, Los Angeles Philharmonic, 1985; Berlin Philharmonic debut, 1988, and concerts, Berlin Festival, 1993; Vienna Symphony Orchestra, 1991; New York Philharmonic debut, Principal Guest Conductor, Philharmonia, London, Principal Guest Conductor, Artistic Advisor, Tonhalle Orchestra, Zurich, 1991; Conducted Philharmonia at 1993 London Proms, Mendelssohn's 5th and Szymanowski's 3rd Symphonies, Bartok's 3rd Piano Concerto; Regularly with Munich Philharmonic, Bayerische Rundfunk Symphony, Radio Symphony Orchestras of Frankfurt, Hamburg, Cologne, Berlin, Orchestre de Paris (debut with Bruckner's 7th Symphony), Royal Concertgebouw Amsterdam, Rotterdam Philharmonic Orchestra; Recent guest engagements include Israel Philharmonic, NHK Symphony, Tokyo; Has worked with Boston, St Louis, Dallas, Montreal, Cincinnati and London Symphonies, Minnesota and Philadelphia Orchestras, Royal Philharmonic; Opera engagements, Deutsche Oper Berlin, Bayerische Staatsoper, Semper Oper Dresden; Regular visitor, Berlin Staatsoper, recently conducting La Traviata, Der Freischutz, Lohengrin; Conducted new Schaaf production of Entfuehrung at Staatsoper Hamburg, 1992-93. *Recordings include:* Mendelssohn: A Midsummer Night's Dream; Martinu symphonies; Cherubini Requiem; New Year's Day concert of popular classics; Franck Symphony in D minor, Dvořák Symphony No 8, Royal Philharmonic; Mozart's Coronation Mass, Philharmonia; Shostakovich: 10th Symphony, Royal Concertgebouw. *Honours include:* Mendelssohn Scholar, 1979; 1st Prizes, competitions, Poland, Denmark. *Address:* c/o Intermusica Artists Management, 16 Duncan Terrace, London N1 8BZ, England.

FLOROS Constantin, b. 4 Jan 1930, Saloniki, Greece. Professor. *Education:* Diplomas in Composition and Conducting, Academy of Music, Vienna, 1953; Dr, University of Vienna, 1955; Habilitation, Hamburg University, 1961. *Career:* Professor of Science of Music, Hamburg University, 1967; Editor, Hamburger Beitrage zur Musikwissenschaft, 1971-; Editor, Hamburger Jahrbuch für Musikwissenschaft, 1975-. *Compositions:* Zwei Tricinien, 1958; various Lieder; Compositions for chorus, piano and organ. *Publications:* Das mittelbyzantinische Kontakienrepertoire, 3 volumes, 1961; Universale Neumenkunde, 3 volumes, 1970; Die geistige Welt Gustav Mahlers, 1977; Mahler und die Symphonik des 19. Jahrhunderts in neuer Deutung, 1977; Beethovens Eroica und Prometheus-Musik, 1978; Mozart-Studien, 1979; Einfuehrung in die Neumenkunde, 1980; Brahms und Bruckner, 1980; Johannes Brahms: Sinfonie Nr. 2, 1984; Gustav Mahler, Die Symphonien, 1985; Musik als Botschaft, 1989; Alban Berg, 1993; President of the Gustav Mahler Vereinigung, Hamburg. *Address:* Schlangenkoppel 18, 2 Hamburg 74, Germany.

FLOWERS Kate, b. 1950, Cheshire, England. Singer (Soprano). *Education:* Studied at the Northern School of Music and the Royal Northern College of Music; Further study in Paris. *Career:* Glyndebourne Festival from 1976, as Despina, Isotta in Die schweigsame Frau, Norina in La Fedeltà Premiata and the title role in The Cunning Little Vixen; Appearances with Opera North as Gretel, Despina, Susanna, Zerlina, Aennchen in Der Freischütz and Thérèse in Les mamelles de Tirésias; Polly Peachum in The Beggar's Opera for Scottish Opera; Micaela, Marenka and Jenůfa for the Welsh National Opera; Concert engagements in Europe, and on London's South Bank with the Philharmonia, the English Chamber Orchestra, Royal Philharmonic, Hallé Orchestra, London Philharmonic and the Academy of St Martin in the Fields; sang Jenny in The Threepenny Opera, for Opera North, 1990. *Honours include:* John Christie Award and Royal Society of Arts Scholarship,

1977. *Address:* c/o The Grand Theatre, 46 New Briggate, Leeds, LS1 6N11, England.

FLOYD Carlisle, b. 11 June 1926, Latta, South Carolina, USA. Composer; Teacher. *Education:* Studied at Converse College, Spartenburg and with Ernest Bacon at Syracuse University (BA 1946, MA 1949); Piano with Rudolf Firkusny and Sidney Foster. *Career:* Teacher at Florida State University 1947-76; M.D. Anderson Professor of Music at the University of Houston, 1976-. *Compositions:* Operas: Slow Dusk 1949; Susannah 1951; Wuthering Heights 1958; The Passion of Jonathan Wade 1962; The Sojourner and Mollie Sinclair 1963; Markheim 1966; Of Mice and Men 1969; Bilby's Doll 1976; Willie Stark 1981; Pilgrimage, song cycle, 1956; Piano Sonata 1957; The Mystery, song cycle, 1960; Flower and Hawk, monodrama for soprano and orchestra 1972; Citizen of Paradise, song cycle, 1983. *Address:* c/o ASCAP, ASCAP Building, One Lincoln Plaza, New York, NY 10023, USA.

FLOYD Samuel A (Jr), b. 1 Feb 1937, Florida, USA. Scholar. m. Barbara Nely, 1956, 1 son, 2 daughter. *Education:* BME, Florida A&M University; MME, PhD, Southern Illinois University. *Publications:* Black Music in the Harlem Renaissance, 1990; Black Music in the United States: A Bibliography of selected reference and research materials, 1983. Author of: Ring Shout Literary Studies; Historial Studies and Black Music Inquiry; The Power of Black Music. *Honours:* Irving Lowens Award for distinguished scholarship in American Music. *Memberships:* American Musicological Society; College Music Society. *Hobbies:* Reading. *Address:* 901 S Plymouth Court, No 206, Chicago, IL 60605, USA.

FLYNN George William, b. 21 Jan 1937, Miles City, Montana, USA. Professor; Musicianship Studies and Composition; Chairman, Musicianship Studies and Composition. *Education:* BS, Music, Columbia University, 1964; MA, Music Composition, 1966, DMA, 1972, Columbia University. *Career:* Faculty Member, Columbia University, 1966-73; City University of New York, 1973-76 and DePaul University, Chicago; Chairman, Board of Directors, Chicago Soundings; Professor, Musicianship Studies, and Composition, School of Music, DePaul University, Chicago. *Compositions:* Recorded - Wound, 1968 for solo piano, Finnadar Records; Four pieces for Violin and Piano, 1965, Kanal, 1988; Finnadar records; Javeh: Amen; Lammy, all 1974, ATCO records; Published - Wound; Four pieces for violin and piano Imprimis Music Co; Fantasy Etudes, solo violin, American String Teachers Association; Kanal, Finnadar Records, 1976. *Recordings:* Winter Music; Theme and Variation; Six Melodies; Pre-First Sonata; Wound; Piano Music for Composer and Performer with Ilhan Mimaroglu, 1967. *Contributions to:* Listening to Berio's Music; Musical Quarterly, 1975; Music and Idealogy, Chicago Symphony Orchestra, Programme Guide, 1980. *Hobby:* Philosophy. *Address:* 824, Webster Avenue, Chicago, IL 60614, USA.

FOCILE Nuccia, b. 1959, Catania, Sicily. Singer (Soprano). *Education:* Protegee of Pavarotti. *Debut:* Sang Mimi at Turin, 1984. *Career:* Season 1986-87, as Oscar in Ballo in Maschera at Turin and Philadelphia, Clarine, Thalia, in Rameau's Platée at Spoleto, Elvira (L'Italiana in Algeri) at Schwetzingen and Mistress Ford in Salieri's Falstaff at Peralade; Further engagements at Buenos Aires as Musetta, Valencienne in the Merry Widow a Venice and Nannetta at Covent Garden, 1988; Rio de Janeiro in 1989 as Rossini's Rosina, and Oscar at Naples, and Ascanio in Pergolesi's Lo frate 'nnamorato at La Scala; Returned to Milan in 1990 as Servilia in La Clemenza di Tito and appeared at Bergamo as Eleanora in Donizetti's L'Assedio di Calais; Pesaro Festival 1990, as Giulia in La Scala di Seta, Teatro Valle Rome as Countess in Paisiello's Don Chisciotte; Returned to Philadelphia 1991, as Norina, sang Mozart's Susanna at Houston and appeared at the Oper Bastille, Paris, as Illia in Idomeneo; Barcelona and Dallas 1992, as Adina in L'Elisir d'amore, Oscar at the Opera Bastille, Paris, Tatiana at the Théâtre du Châtelet and Carolina

(Matrimonio Segreto) at the 1992 Ravenna Festival. *Honours:* Turin International Competition, 1983; Pavarotti Competition, Philadelphia, 1986. *Recordings include:* Lo frate 'nnamorato and L'Assedio di Calais. *Address:* c/o Teatro Alla Scala, Via Filodrammatici 2, 20121 Milan, Italy.

FODI John, b. 22 Mar 1944, Hungary. Composer; Music Librarian. m. 22 Oct 1971, 1 son, 1 daughter. *Education:* Studied composition with Lorne Betts; BMUS and MMus, University of Toronto, 1966-72; MLS, University of Toronto, 1987-90. *Career:* Supervisor, Sniderman Recordings Archive, University of Toronto, 1982-92; Head Cataloguer for recordings and supervisor of Sniderman Recordings Archive, 1992-. *Compositions:* Pi, trombone and piano; Division IV, guitar; Concerto in four parts, accordion; bagatelles; tuba; Sonata: Cor Vigilans, bassoon and cello; Adagio, string orchestra; Kootenay, chamber orchestra; Rhapsody, bass clarinet and piano; Ballades, cello. *Publications:* Musical examples: Brian Cherney's Harry Somers, 1975; Stephen Adams' Murray Schafer, 1982-83; Tim McGee's Early Music Performance, 1984. *Hobbies:* Reading science fiction; Cogitation. *Address:* 14 Times Road, Toronto, Ontario M6E 3B9, Canada.

FODOR Eugene (Nicholas, Jr), b. 5 Mar 1950, Turkey Creek, Colorado, USA. Violinist. *Education:* Studied with Harold Wippler, Denver; Ivan Galamian, Juilliard School of Music, NY, 1966-68; Josef Gingold, Harry Farbiman and William Primrose, Indiana University School of Music, diploma, 1970; Jascha Heifetz, University of Southern California at Los Angeles, 1970-71. *Debut:* Soloist at age 10 with Denver Symphony Orchestra. *Career:* Soloist with major orchestras, 1974-; Recitalist; Performed at the White House, Washington, DC, 1974, 1986. *Recordings:* For RCA. *Honours:* 1st Prize, Merriweather Post Competition, 1967; Paganini Competition, Genoa, 1972; co-2nd Prize, Tchaikovsky Competition, Moscow, 1974. *Address:* c/o Hillyer International Inc, 888 Seventh Avenue Suite 300, New York, NY 10106, USA.

FOGELL Martin Maurice, b. 3 Aug 1929, Glasgow, Scotland. Conductor; Teacher; Accompanist. m. Anne Goldwater, 20 Oct 1953, 1 son, 1 daughter. *Education:* BA; BMUs; FTCL; ARCM; LTCL; studying for PhD on music of Coleridge-Taylor. *Career:* Conductor, Fogell Ensemble, 1955-64; London Students Opera Society, 1956-65; Reading Symphony Orchestra, 1958-64; Southern Sinfonia Orchestra, 1964; Guest with Boyd Neel Orchestra, London Mozart Players, New London Orchestra, Nottingham Symphony Orchestra, Ostrava Symphony Orchestra; Broadcasts in Italy, Holland, Czechoslovakia. *Compositions include:* Part-song, The Gravedigger, Orchestra and Instrumental works; 1-Act Opera, Kirsteen. *Recordings:* 3 Highland Sketches; Toy Symphonies of Haydn & Romberg; Peter & the Wolf. *Publications:* in preparation: Critical Appreciation and Analysis of the music of Coleridge-Taylor. *Honours:* Freeman of Ostrava, 1961; Barlow Cup for composition, 1973, 1975, 1976, 1984-89. *Memberships:* Composers' Guild of Gt Britain; Royal Musical Association. *Hobbies:* Walking; Reading; Research. *Address:* 63 Lache Lane, Chester, CH4 7LP, England.

FOLDES Andor, b. 21 Dec 1913, Budapest, Hungary. Pianist-Conductor. m. Lili Rendy, 1 July 1940. *Education:* Classical Gymnasium, finished 1932; Liszt Music Academy, Masters Degree, 1933. *Debut:* Philharmonic Orchestra, Budapest, 1921. *Career:* Concert Tours in all countries of Europe, Gt Britain, USA, Japan, Australia, New Zealand, India, Far East; Frequent TV appearances in Western Germany and France. *Compositions:* Little Suite for Strings (Bärenreiter Verlag); Prelude for piano (Carl Fischer, New York). *Recordings:* Complete Solo Works of Bartók, Schumann, Mozart and Beethoven with recording companies such as EMI and Deutsche Grammophon; 17 LPs (DGG); 7 LPs (EMI - Elektrola); Schumann Piano Works, CD - EMI; Bartók Piano Works, CD - DGG. *Publications:* Keys To The Keyboard, 1950; also published in German, Italian, Spanish, Portuguese, Norwegian, Finnish, Japanese,

Korean, Hungarian, Turkish, Dutch; Gibt es einen Zeitgenössischen Beethoven Stil? 1963. *Contributions to:* Several articles in Reader's Digest. *Honours:* Grand Cross of Merit of Western Germany, 1964; Medaille d'argent de la ville de Paris, 1969; Grand Prix Du Disques, Paris, 1956; Deutscher Schallplattenpreis, 1982. *Hobbies:* Literature; Art; People. *Address:* CH-8704 Herrliberg/ZH, Switzerland.

FÖLDES Imre, b. 8 Mar 1934, Budapest, Hungary. Musicologist; Profesor of History. m. Dr Zsuzsa Vadász, 1 daughter. *Education:* Graduate in composition, Ferenc Liszt Academy of Music, Budapest. *Career:* Musicologist, Professor of Music History and Theory, Ferenc Liszt Academy of Music, Department of Teachers Training Institute; Educational Lecturer on Music for the general public and radio. *Publications:* Harmincasok, Beszélgetések magyar zeneszerzökkel (Generation of the Thirties - Talks with Hungarian Composers), 1969; Life and Works of J S Bach, 1976; The Melody Dies Irae, 1977. *Contributions to:* Az ének-zene tanitása; Muzsika; Parlando. *Honours:* Art Prize for Socialist Culture, 1974; Art Prize, National Council of Trade Unions, 1975; Szabolcsi Prize, 1977; Ferenc Erkel Prize, 1986. *Memberships:* Hungarian Musicians Association; President, Music Department, Society for Propagating Sciences and Arts; Hungarian Ferenc Liszt Society; Hungarian Kodály Society; Lajos Bárdos Society; International Society for Music Education. *Hobbies:* Collecting gramophone records; Hiking; Photography. *Address:* Kresz Géza utca 26, 1132 Budapest, Hungary.

FOLDI Andrew Harry, b. 20 July 1926, Budapest, Hungary. Opera Director; Singer (Bass). m. Marta Justus, 19 May 1977, 1 son, 1 daughter. *Education:* MA Musicology, 1948, PhB Philosophy, 1945, University of Chicago. *Debut:* La Boheme, 1950. *Career:* Director of Music, Department of Adult Education, University of Chicago, 1949-61; Chairman of the Opera Department, DePaul University, 51-57; Advisor, Netherlands Opera, 1977-80; Chairman and Artistic Director, Opera Dept, Cleveland Institute of Music, 1981-91; Director, Chicago Lyric Opera Center for American Artists, 1991-. Stage direction includes: The Barber of Seville (Atlanta Opera), 1989; The Merry Wives of Windsor, (Chicago Opera Theatre), 1990; La Tragedie de Carmen, (Lyric Opera Center, Chicago), 1992. Television performances of The Barbiere di Siviglia, 1967, The Merry Widow, 1977, Elixir of Love, 1978, and Lulu, 1980. Selected performances include: Alberich in the Ring and Schigolch in Lulu at the Metropolitan Opera, Bartolo in Il Barbiere di Siviglia, Vienna Staatsoper and San Francisco, Cardillac at La Scala. *Recordings include:* Fiddler on the Roof, 1974; A Modern Psalm, 1975. *Publications:* Articles in Opera News, Alban Berg Society Newsletter. *Memberships:* American Musicological Society. *Address:* Lyric Opera Center for American Artist, 20 N Wacker Drive Suite 830, Chicago, IL 60606, USA.

FOLWELL Nicholas, b. 1953, England. Singer (Baritone). *Education:* Studied with Raimund Herincx; Royal Academy of Music, London Opera Centre & Raimund Herincx. *Career:* Sang with Welsh National Opera from 1978 as Mozart's Figaro and Leporello, Pizarro, Melitone, Escamillo, The Poacher in The Cunning Little Vixen, Alberich in The Ring of the Nibelung (also at Covent Garden with WNO, 1986) and Wagner's Melot and Klingsor; As guest with other British companies has sung the villians in The Tales of Hoffmann, Tonio, Beckmesser, Schaunard, Creon and The Messenger in Oedipus Rex, Alberich and Papageno (ENO 1990); Sang in Weill's Seven Deadly Sins with the London Sinfonietta, 1988; Debuts in France, Italy, Austria and West Germany, 1987-90; Created Koroviev in York Höller's Master and Margarita in Paris, 1989; Covent Garden and Glyndebourne 1990 as The Poacher (conducted by Simon Rattle) and Beethoven's Pizarro; Sang in The Weill Event at the 1990 Almeida Festival; Promenade Concerts 1991, in Prokofiev's The Fiery Angel; Alberich in Rheingold (Opera de Nantes), 1992; Mozart's Figaro for Glyndebourne Touring Opera at Sadler's Wells; Cecil, Maria Stuarda, Buxton Festival, 1993; Alberich, Siegfried, Opera de Nantes, 1993.

Recordings: Tristan and Isolde and Parsifal, conducted by Reginald Goodall (EMI); Poacher (Cunning Little Vixen, EMI); Pish-Tush, (The Mikado), Telarc. *Honour:* ARAM, 1990. *Current Management:* Robert Gilder & Co. *Address:* c/o Robert Gilder & Co, Enterprise House, 59/65 Upper Ground, London, SE1 9PQ, England.

FONDA Jean Pierre, b. 12 Dec 1937, Boulogne sur Seine, Paris, France. Concert Pianist. *Educaion:* Virtuosity Prize, Piano Instrumentation, Geneva Conservatory, Switzerland. *Debut:* Germany, 1958. *Career:* Concert tours in Europe, South America, USA, Japan, Middle East, Turkey etc; TV in Paris, Munich; Major European Summer Festivals including: Lucerne, Montreux, Edinburgh, Monte Carlo etc. *Compositions:* Cadenzas for Different Piano Concertos. *Recordings:* Numerous. *Honours:* Recipient, Harriet Cohen Medal, London, 1968; Awarded by French culture minister, Chevalier des Arts et Lettres, 1980. *Hobbies:* Reading; Theatre; Films; Collecting and purchasing autographs. *Current Management:* Ingpen and Williams Limited, 14 Kensington Court, London W8, England. *Address:* 20 Parc Chateau Benquet, 1202 Geneva, Switzerland.

FONDARY Alain, b. 1932, Bagnolet, France. Singer (Baritone). *Education:* Studied in Paris. *Debut:* Tonio in Pagliacci, Cherbourg, 1968. *Career:* Sang in many provincial French opera houses in 1970s; Appearances at the Paris Opera, 1985 and 1991, in Jerusalem by Verdi and as the High Priest in Samson et Delila; Royal Opera House Covent Garden in La Fanciulla del West, La Scala Milan as Amonsasro, Metropolitan Opera in Cavalleria Rusticana; Sang Scarpia at San Francisco, returning in 1990 as Renato in Un ballo in Maschera; Vienna Staatsoper and Barcelona, 1991, as the High Priest and Scarpia; Festival engagements include Orange, 1992, as Count Luna and Bregenz, 1993, as Nabucco; Sang Massenet's Sancho Panza at Toulouse 1992 and Count Luna at Orange; La Scala, 1993, as Scarpia. *Recordings include:* Sancho Panza in Don Quichotte, conducted by Michel Plasson. *Address:* c/o Opera de la Bastille, 120 Rue de Lyon, F-75012, France.

FONSECA Regina, b. 1932, Portugal. Singer (Mezzo-soprano). *Career:* Sang at Dusseldorf, 1958-59, Bremen, Saarbrucken, Mainz, Kiel and Kassel, 1959-69; Engaged at the Mannheim National Theatre 1969-81, Gelsenkirchen, 1981-82, Dortmund, 1983-84; Guest appearances at Cologne and Nuremberg, Naples, Hamburg, (Brangaene in Tristan und Isolde, 1967), Monte Carlo and the Deutsche Oper Berlin, 1975; Sang Kundry at the 1976 Bayreuth Festival and the Composer in Ariadne auf Nexos at the Vienna Staatsoper; Deutsche Oper am Rhein Dusseldort, 1983; Other roles have included Wagner's Venus, Ortrud, Waltraute and Fricka, Strauss's Clytemnestra and Nurse, Countess Geschwitz in Lulu, Verdi's Eboli, Lady Macbeth and Azucena, Zenobia in Handel's Radamisto and the Countess in Zimmerman's Die Soldaten. *Address:* c/o Opernhaus, Kuhstrasse 12, 4600 Dortmund, Germany.

FONTANA Bill, b. 25 Apr 1947, Cleveland, Ohio, USA. Composer; Radio Producer. *Education:* Studied at John Carroll University and at the New School for Social Research, BA 1970; Private study with Louis Lane and Philip Corner. *Career:* Composer-in-residence and music director for the Toronto Free Theater, 1972-73; Compiled archive of natural sounds for the Australian Broadcasting Commission, 1975-78; Natural sound archive for the Oakland Museum in California, 1979; Assembled material for series of 365 programmes broadcast in San Francisco 1983 as Soundscapes; Composer sound sculptor and radio producer on various broadcasting stations. *Compositions include:* Phantom Clarinets 1975; Handbell Sculptures 1977; Wave Spiral 1977; Music for a Resonant Space 1977; Music for Carillon; Standing Wave Sculpture 1978; Piano Sculpture 1978; Ocarina Sculpture; Sound Sculpture for Brass Band; Space between Sounds 1980; Flight Paths out to Sea; Grid Projections; Landscape Sculpture with Foghorns 1981; Oscillating Steel Grids along the Brooklyn Bridge 1983; Sound Recycling Sculpture 1983;

Soundscapes 1983. *Address:* c/o ASCAP, ASCAP Building, One Lincoln Plaza, Lincoln Center, New York, NY 10023, USA.

FONTANA Gabriele, b. 1958, Innsbruck, Austria. Singer (Soprano). *Education:* Studied with Ilse Rapf at the Vienna Musikhochschule. *Career:* Sang Echo in Ariadne and Lauretta in Gianni Schicchi at the Opera Studio of the Vienna Staatsoper; Sang Pamina at Frankfurt; Hamburg Staatsoper from 1982, as Susanna, Servilia in La Clemenza di Tito and Sophie in Der Rosenkavalier; Sang in the premiere of Udo Zimmermann's Die Weisse Rose, revised version; Guest appearances in Bremen and Hanover; Glyndebourne 1984, as the Countess in Le Nozze di Figaro; Bregenz Festival 1985, as Pamina; Vienna Staatsoper and Glyndebourne Festival, 1987, as Fiordiligi; Sang in Die weisse Rose at Innsbruck, 1989; Lieder recitals in London, Berlin, Brussels and Vienna. *Recordings include:* Schubert Lieder and Bach Cantatas; Idomeneo, Arabella; Gluck's Paride ed Elena; Die grossmutige Tomyris by Reinhard Keiser. *Address:* c/o Tiroler Landestheater, Rennweg 2, A-6020 Innsbruck, Austria.

FONTYN Jacqueline, b. 27 Dec 1930, Antwerp, Belgium. Composer; Professor of Composition. m. Camille Schmit (dec) 2 children. *Education:* Studied theory and composition. with Marcel Quinet; Studied in Paris and Vienna; Grand Prix de Rome, for composition - diploma. *Career:* Professor of Counterpoint, Royal Conservatory, Antwerp 1963-70; Professor of Composition, Conservatoire Royal de Bruxelles 1971-1990; participant in many international festivals. *Compositions include:* Galaxie for chamber orchestra 1965; Pour 11 Archets 1971; Evoluonn for orchestra 1972; Concerto for violin and orchestra 1975; Frises for great symphonic band 1975; Halo for harp and 16 instruments or chamber orchestra 1978; Quatre Sites for orchestra; Creneaux for Youth Orchestra 1982; In the Green Shade for orchestra 1988; Vocal music: Madrigale e Canzone, for mixed choir a cappella, 1968; Ephémères for mezzo soprano and orchestra or 11 instruments 1979; Alba for soprano and 4 instruments 1981; Pro & Antiverbs, for Soprano and Cello, 1984; Rosa, Rosae for Soprano, Contralto, Clarinet, Violin, Harp and Piano, 1986; Chamber music: Nonetto for flute, oboe, clarinet, bassoon, French horn, violin, viola, cello and double bass 1969; Spirales for 2 pianos 1971; Six Climats, for cello and piano 1972; Horizons for string quartet 1977; Zones for flute, clarinet and cello, percussion and piano 1979; Rhumbs for 2 trumpets, French horn, trombone and tuba 1980; Fougères (Ferns) for viola and harp; Controversy for bass-clarinet or B Flat clarinet or tenor saxophone and percussion 1983; Either Or for string quintet (2 violas) or string quartet and clarinet 1984; Cheminement for 9 performers 1986; La Deviniére, eleven light pieces for violin with piano accompaniement, 1988; Scurochiatro for flute, clarinet, bassoon, piano, violin, cello and double bass, 1989; Compagnon de la nuit, for oboe and piano, 1989; Orchestral works: Reverie and Turbelence, piano concerto, 1989; A l'orée du Songe, viola concerto, 1990; Colinda, cello concerto, 1991; Vocal works: Rose des Sables, Radiophonic work for Mezzo, speaker, Womens Choir, Orchestra. *Address:* Rue Leon Dekaise 6, B1342 Limelette, Belgium.

FORBES Elizabeth, b. 3 Aug 1924, Camberley, Surrey, England. Critic; Writer on Music; Translator. *Education:* Autodidact. *Career:* Freelance Music Critic; Financial Times 1970-80; Reviews and articles for FT, Independent, Opera, Musical Times, Music & Musicians, Opera News, Opera International, Opera Canada, The Listener, About the House. *Contributions to:* Encyclopedia of Opera, 1976; New Grove Dictionary of Music and Musicians 1980; The Peforming Arts 1980; New Grove Dictionary of American Music 1986; New Grove Dictionary of Opera, 4 volumes, 1992; Viking Opera Guide, 1993. *Publications:* Opera from A to Z 1977; Observer's Book of Opera 1982; Mario and Grisi 1985; Old Scores, detective story; Translations of Spontini's La Vestale, Auber's La Muette de Portici, Meyerbeer's Robert le Diable and Berwald's Queen of

Golconda for Nottingham University; Schubert's Claudine von Villa Bella, Brand's Maschinist Hopkins and Wagner-Regeny's Die Bürger von Calais for Radio 3. *Address:* Flat 3, I Bryanston Square, London W1H 7FE, England.

FORBES Elliot, b. 30 Aug 1917, Massachusets, USA. Retired Professsor. m. Kathleen Brooke Allen, 7 June 1941, 3 daughters. *Education:* MA, Harvard, 1947; Mozarteum, Salzburg, 1937; Westminister Choir College, 1946. *Debut:* Conductor, Harvard Glee Club and Radcliff Choral Society, 1958. *Career:* Teacher: Cate School, California, 1941-43, Belmont HIll School, Massachusetts, 1943-45; Assistant Professor, 1947-54, Associate Professor, 1954-58, Princeton University; Professor Music, Harvard University, 1958-84. *Publications:* Editor: Thayer's Life of Beethoven, 1964; Beethoven's Fifth, 1971; A History of Music at Harvard to 1972, 1988; A Report of Music at Harvard 1972-90, 1993. Articles in American Choral Review and Musical Quarterly. *Honours:* Phi Beta Kappa; Signet Society Medal, 1985; Harvard Medal, 1991. *Memberships:* AAAS; American Musicological Society; College Music Association. *Hobbies:* Nature Walks. *Address:* 975 Memorial Drive, Apt 210, Cambridge, MA 02138, USA.

FORBES Rupert Oliver, b. 27 Jan 1944, London, England. Singer (Tenor). *Education:* Studied at Cambridge University with Pierre Bernac in Paris and Luigi Ricci in Rome. *Career:* Sang at the Zurich Oper 1970-75; Engaged at the Stadttheater Basel from 1975, singing Mozart's Monostatos and Pedrillo, Jacquino in Fidelio, Tybalt in Romeo et Juliette, Lindoro, (Hadyn's La Fedelta Premiata), the comic roles in Les contes d'Hoffmann, Wagner's Steuermann and Lord Barrat in Der Junge Lord; Guest appearances in Mannheim, Wiesbaden, Kassel, Breman and Freiburg; Theater am Gärtnerplatz Munich, 1977-78; Many engagements in concert and oratorio, notably in works by Bach. *Address:* Theater Basel, Theatrerstrasse 7, CH-4010 Basel, Switzerland.

FORBES Sebastian, b. 22 May 1941, Amersham, Buckinghamshire, England. Composer; University Lecturer; Conductor. m. (1) Hilary Spaight Taylor, 2 daughters, (2) Tessa Brady, 24 Sept 1983, 1 son, 1 daughter. *Education:* Royal Academy of Music, 1958-60; Kings College, Cambridge University, 1960-64; MA, Cantab; MusB, Cantab; Mus D, Cantab; LRAM; ARCO; ARCM. *Career:* Treble Soloist, 1953-56; Organist, Trinity College, Cambridge, 1968; Conductor, Aeolian Singers, 1965-69; Seiriol Singers, 1969-72; Horniman Singers, 1981-90; BBC Producer, 1964-67; University Lecturer, Bangor, 1968-72, Surrey, 1972-; Professor of Music, 1981-; Principal Commissions: Essay for Clarinet and Orchestra, Proms, 1970; Symphony, Edinburgh Festival, 1972; String Quartet No. 3, BBC, 1982. *Compositions:* Various Orchestral, Chamber, Vocal, Organ and Choral compositions; Sinfonia 2, Brighton PO, 1978; Sinfonia 3, Guildford Festival, 1991. *Recordings:* Treble: few minor records; Conductor: Bach Motets, Aeolian Singers; Composer: String Quartet No. 1; Capriccio for organ; Triple canon for trumpet and delays. *Publications:* Various publications. *Honours:* McEwen Memorial Prize, 1962; Clements Memorial Prize, 1963; Radcliffe Music Award, 1969; SPNM, prize 1979. *Memberships:* Composers' Guild of Great Britain; Association of Professional Composers. *Hobbies include:* Playing with his children. *Address:* 32 Wykeham Road, Merrow, Guildford, Surrey GU1 2SE, England.

FORBES Watson, b. 16 Nov 1909, St Andrews, Scotland. Viola Player. m. (1)Mary Hunt, 1937; (2) Jean Beckwith, 1967, 2 sons. *Education:* Royal Academy of Music (RAM), London, with Albert Sammons; Studied with Professor Sevcik in Czechoslovakia; RAM, 1930. *Career:* Solo Viola player, 1932-64; Aeolian String Quartet, 1932-64; London String Trio and London Piano Quartet, 1946-64; London Philharmonic, 1932-36; London Symphony Orchestra, 1936-46; Professor of Chamber Music, RAM; Examiner, RAM; Head of Music, BBC Scotland, 1964-72. *Compositions:* Editions and arrangements. *Recordings:* Various. *Publications:* Catalogue of Chamber Music, 1965, National Fed of Music Societies; Articles in the Radio Times; The Strad; Musical Times. *Honours:* FRAM; Hon Dr of Music, Glasgow University, 1970; Cobbett Memorial Prize for Services to Chamber Music, 1972. *Memberships:* Fellow, Royal Scottish Academy of Music in Drama, 1956; Panel, Inc Society of Musicians. *Hobbies:* Philosophy; Gardening. *Address:* The Coach House, Great Wolford, Shipston-on-Stour, Warwicks CV36 5NQ, England.

FORD Andrew, b. 1957, Liverpool, England. Composer; Conductor. *Education:* Graduated with honours, Composition, University of Lancaster, 1978; Composition study with Edward Cowie & John Buller. *Career:* Fellow in Music, University of Bradford, 1978-82; Founder, Music Director, Performer, Big Bird Music Theatre, 1982; Lecturer, School of Creative Arts, University of Wollongong, New South Wales, Australia, 1983-; Numerous world and Australian premieres with the School's contemporary music ensemble, SCAW, 1984-, including Stockhausen's Stimmung, 1986; Conductor, Australia Ensemble, Seymour Group and Magpie Musicians; Composer-in-Residence, Bennelong Programme, Sydney Opera House, 1985; Own works performed, Australia, Europe, America; Various commissions; Writer and broadcaster on music; Featured composer at many Festivals, including: Aspekte, Salzburg, 1984; Ferrara, 1985; Istanbul, Buffalo, Up-Beat to The Tate, Liverpool, Aspen, 1988; Composer in Residence, Australian Chamber Orchestra, 1993; Conductor, Australian Chamber Orchestra. *Compositions:* Music-theatre: Songs for the Lady Pan, 1981-83; From Hand to Mouth, 1984-85; Poe, opera, 1981-83; Whispers, 1990; Children's opera: The Piper's Promise, 1986-87; The World Knot, 1987-88; Orchestral: Concerto for Orchestra, 1980; Prologue, Chorale and Melodrama, 1981; Epilogue to an Opera, 1982; Serenade for 20 Solo Strings and Percussion, 1984; The Big Parade, 1985-86; Choral: Season Song, also a cappella version, 1981-82; Chamber ensemble: Sonata for 4 Instruments, 1978; Chamber Concerto No 1, 1979; Bright Ringing Morning, 1981; Pit, 1981; Boatsong, 1982; Chamber Concerto No 2: Cries in Summer, 1983; Rant, 1984; Pea Soup, 1984; Four Winds, saxophone quartet, 1984; Foolish Fires, 1985; String Quartet, 1985; Deep Blue, 1986; On Canaan's Happier Shore, 1987; Instrumental: Portraits, solo piano, 1981; Like Icarus Ascending, solo violin, 1984; A Kumquat for John Keats, solo piano, 1987; Swansong, solo viola, 1987; Several vocal works; Imaginings for piano and orchestra, 1991; Chamber: The Art of Puffing, 1989, Parabola, 1989, Ringing the Changes, 1990, Pastoral, 1991, Clarion, 1991; Harbour, for tenor and strings; les débris d'un rêve, for piccolo & reverb, 1992; In somnia, for chorus & ensemble, 1992. *Recordings:* Boatsong, Pro Viva ISPV 140; String Quartet, ABC Classics/Polygram 426 992; Ringing the Changes, Attacca-Babel 9161-4. *Publications:* Composer to Composer: Conversations about contemporary music, Allen & Unwin Sydney, 1993. *Address:* c/o Virginia Braden, Arts Management, 56 Keller Street, Potts Point, Sydney, New South Wales, Australia.

FORD Anthony Dudley, b. 19 Sept 1935, Birmingham, England. Senior Lecturer in Music; Pianist; Harpsichordist; Conductor. m. Diane Clare Anwyl, 1 son, 1 daughter. *Education:* BMus, University of Birmingham. *Career:* Senior Lecturer in Music, University of Hull; Conductor, Hull Bach Choir. *Publications:* Editor, Purcell-Fantasias and In Nomines; Editor, G Bononcini-Arias from the Vienna Operas; Editor, G Bononcini-Aeterna Fac; G Bononcini-Funeral Anthem. *Contributions to:* Musical Times; Proceedings of the Royal Musical Association; Encyclopaedia Britannica. *Honour:* Barber Post Graduate Scholarship, 1957. *Membership:* Life Member, Royal Musical Association. *Hobbies:* Transport; Photography. *Address:* Music Department, University of Hull, Cottingham Road, Hull, Humberside, England.

FORD Bruce, b. 15 Aug 1956, Lubbock, Texas, USA.

Singer (Lyric Tenor). *Education:* Studied at the West Texas State University, Texas Tech University and the Houston Opera Studio. *Career:* Sang with Wuppertal Opera from 1983, as Belmonte, Rameau's Dardanus, Nurredin (Der Barbier von Bagdad) and Ramiro; Bordeaux 1985, as Almaviva; Minnesota Opera 1985, as Tamino; Mannheim Opera from 1985, as Fenton, Tamino, Ferrando and Ramiro; Appeared at the 1986 Wexford Festival as Argirio in Rossini's Tancredi; Since 1987 has sung Mozart's Mitridate at the Concertgebouw Amsterdam, the Netherlands Opera, and the Royal Opera House, Covent Garden; Ferrando at the Volksoper in Vienna and the Salzburg Festival; Season 1988-89 sang Lindoro at Strasbourg; Rinaldo in Armida by both Haydn and Rossini for Dutch broadcasting; Berlioz's Lelio for the Dusseldorf Symphonic; Sang Agorante in Ricciardo e Zoraide at Pesaro, 1990; Also heard as Uberto in La Donna del Lago at Dusseldorf and Don Ottavio, for Opera Pacific and Bologna; Covent Garden debut 1991, Almaviva; La Donna del Lago (Uberto) at La Scala with Muti, 1992; Mitridate (title role) at Covent Garden & Amsterdam, 1991, 1993. *Recordings include:* Messiah, Imeneo and Bertoni's Orfeo with the Solisti Veneti conducted by Claudio Scimone, Ghernando in Rossini's Armida; Adriano in Il Crociato in Egitto by Meyerbeer (Opera Rara); Giasone in Medea in Corinto by Mayr for Opera Rara and Horace in Le Domino Noir for Decca. *Address:* c/o Athole Still, Greystoke House, 80-86 Westow Street, London, SE19 3AF, England.

FORD Frederic Hugh, b. 5 Feb 1939, Woonsocket, Rhode Island, USA. Conductor; Educator. m. Kathleen Hoffman, 12 Oct 1968, 1 son, 1 daughter. *Education:* AB, Music, Harvard College, 1960; AMT, Harvard Graduate School of Education, 1962; MA, Music History, State University of New York, Buffalo, 1969. *Career:* Choral Conductor, Faculty Member, University of Virginia, 1966-67, State University of New York, Buffalo, 1967-68, Wabash College, Indiana, 1972-79, Rutgers University, 1979- (University Choir, Glee Club, Queens Chorale and Collegium Musicum). *Recordings:* Orff: Carmina Burana. *Memberships:* American Choral Directors Association, New Jersey Board of Directors, 1984-; Intercollegiate Musical Council, Board of Directors, 1975-78, 1983-85, Secretary 1985-; American Musicological Society; College Music Society; American Choral Foundation; American Association of University Professors. *Address:* Dept of Music, Mason Gross School of the Arts, Rutgers University, New Brunswick, NJ 08903, USA.

FORD Peter John, b. 25 Sept 1946, Staffordshire, England. Repetiteur; Opera Coach; Chorus Master; Conductor. m. (1) Carol Henley, 1967, (2) Penelope Davis, 1971, (3) Seona Denholm, 1980, 1 son, 1 daughter. *Education:* Guildhall School of Music & Drama, 1971-72; London Opera Centre, 1972-73; GBSM; ABSM Teacher(Organ); ARCO. *Debut:* English National Opera, 1975. *Career:* English National Opera 1974-81, Repetiteur, Assistant Chorus Master, Conductor; Visiting Professor, Guildhall School of Music & Drama, 1981; Chef des Choeurs, Conductor, Opera of Nancy, 1982-84; Choral Concerts in France; Private Coaching, Teaching, 1988-; Freelance work for Royal Opera House, Covent Garden. *Membership:* Incorporated Society of Musicians. *Address:* 104 Pirbright Road, Southfields, London SW18 5NA, England.

FORD Trevor. b. 28 Nov 1951, London, England. Flautist; Editor. m. Marianne Barton, 13 Dec 1979, 2 sons. *Education:* Dip, Royal Academy of Music, 1972-76. *Career:* Orchestral Flautist, 1976-; Personnel Manager, English Sinfonia, 1979-; Orchestral Manager, Philomusica of London, 1981-, Midland Philharmonic, 1982-, Ambache Chamber Orchestra, 1984-89; General Manager, English Festival Orchestra, 1984-, Opera in Concert Orchestra, 1993-; Board of Directors, Association of British Orchestras, 1985-88. *Publications:* Editor: The Musician's Handbook, 1986; The Art of Auditioning, 1988; Church Music Quarterly, 1989-. *Honours:* ARAM, 1992. *Memberships:* Musicians Union; Inc Society of Musicians; Royal School of Church Music; Association of British Choral Directors. *Hobbies:* Architecture; Antiques; Antique maps. *Address:* 151 Mount View Road, London N4 4JT, England

FORRAI Miklós, b. 19 Oct 1913, Magyarszék, Hungary. Professor. m. Mária Gyurkovics, 2 daughters. *Education:* Studied under Zoltán Kodály, Artúr Harmath, Lajos Bárdos; Chorus Master, 1934, Singing Master, 1935, Artist of Trumpet, 1937, F Liszt Academy of Music, Budapest.*Debut:* as Chorus Master of the Forrai Chamber Choir, 1936. *Career:* Leader of concert series Kis Filharmónia, Organised for children, 1936-44; Chorus Master of Budapesti Kórus, 1948-78; Music Programmes on Hungarian Radio, 1936-; Music Programmes on Hungarian Television, 1958-; Professor, F Liszt Academy of Music, 1941-83. *Recordings:* Cantata Lyrica, 1960 and Cantus Pannonicus by F Farkas, 1961; Missa Choralis, 1963; Psalms, 1965; Christus, 1971; Prometheus by F Liszt, 1974; Requiem by R Schumann, 1976. *Publications:* A Karvezetó (Book for chorusmasters), 1936, Ötévszázad kórusa (Choral works of 500 years, 1956); Ezer év kórusa (Choral works of 1000 years) 1943; Deep River (Negro Spirituals), 1963; Singing Exercises, 1963. *Contributor to:* Musica Hungarica, 1965; Musica Mundana, 1974. *Address:* Budenz út 18, 1021 Budapest, Hungary.

FORRER Felix, b. 22 May 1930, Rorschach, Switzerland. Musician. m. Maria Rohr, 12 Sept 1981, 2 sons, 1 daughter. *Education:* Studied at the Conservatory of Winterthur with Peter Rybar and at the Conservatoire Royale de Musique Bruxelles with Andre Gretler. *Career:* Teacher of Violin, Conservatory of Zurich; Member of the orchestras of Zurich, Berne, Geneva (Orchestre de la Suisse Romande, E Ansermet) and Winterthur; Since 1973, Professor for violin and viola at Aarau. *Publications:* Violin Tutor for Beginners, vol I-III (ed Hug, Zürich); The Forrer's Positions Puzzle for Violin or Viola, 1991 (ed PAN, Zürich), featuring a new presentation of the musical notation with movable staves. *Honours:* First prize for Violin, Conservatoire Royale de Musique Bruxelles. *Memberships:* European String Teachers Association. *Hobbies:* Collecting old books; Cycling; Swimming. *Address:* Bündtenweg 19, 5000 Aarau, Switzerland.

FORREST Sidney, b. 21 Aug 1918, New York City, USA. Clarinettist; Educator; Arranger. m. Faith Levine Forrest, 16 Nov 1941, 1 daughter. *Education:* Juilliard School of Music; BA, University of Miami, 1939; MA, Columbia University, 1941. *Career:* Clarinet Soloist, US Marine Band & Symphony Orchestra, 1941-45; Clarinettist, Major radio networks, New York City, 1945-47; Principal Clarinet, National Symphony Orchestra, Washington, 1946-47, summers 1948-51; Professor, Peabody Conservatory of Johns Hopkins University, 1946-85; Director, Placement and Counselling, 1969-85; Adjunct Professor, Catholic University of America, 1954-; Professor, clarinet, ensembles, National Music Camp, Interlochen Center for the Arts, 1959-; American University, 1961-; Clincian, chamber music coach; member of National Woodwind and Brass Jury of Fulbright Commission, 1980-84; member clarinet Jury, Quebec, Conservatoire of Music, 1969-85; Students in major symphonies in USA and Europe. *Compositions:* Arrangements for Piano & Clarinet: Nocturne 20, F Chopin; Entrance March of the Boyards; Halvorsen Revisions for Clarinet & Piano; Pastorale, Carl Baermann; Theme and Variations by Carl Baermann; Divertimento, Carl Baermann; Twelve Fantasias for Solo Clarinet by Georg Philip Telemann; Variations on a theme by Corelli, by G Tartini, for piano and clarinet. *Recordings:* Mozart Clarinet Quintet in A Major; Clarinet Trio in E Flat Major; Brahms Trio in A Minor. *Address:* 9611 Kingston Road, Kensington, MD 20895, USA.

FORRESTER Maureen, b. 25 July 1930, Montreal, Canada. Singer (Contralto). *Education:* Studied with Barnard Diamant in Montreal. *Debut:* Sang in concert at Montreal, 1953. *Career:* Alto solo in Mahler's 2nd Symphony at New York Town Hall, conducted by Bruno Waletr, 1956; Many concert appearances with leading

US orchestras in Boston, San Francisco, Philadelphia and elsewhere; Tours to Holland, Germany, France, Belgium, Spain and Scandinavia; Sang Gluck's Orpheus in Toronto 1961 and appeared as Cornelia in Giulio Cesare to open New York City Opera's first season in Lincoln Center (1966); San Francisco debut 1967, as La Cieca in La Gioconda, Metropolitan Opera 1975 as Erda in Das Rheingold; Covent Garden 1971, as Fricka in Der Ring des Nibelungen; Paris 1981, in Massenet's Cendrillon; Has also sung at opera houses in Canada and South America; Other roles have included Mistress Quickly, Monteverdi's Arnalta, Brangaene (Tristan and Isolde), Ulrica, and the Witch in Hansel and Gretel; Sang with the Bach Aria Group 1964-74 and toured the USA with the Montreal Symphony 1982, with Les Nuits d'Ete by Berlioz; Pittsburgh Opera 1989 as Clytemnestra in Elektra; Sang at San Diego and La Scala Milan 1990, as Mme. de Croissy in Dialogues des Carmélites and the Countess in The Queen of Spades. *Recordings:* Giulio Cesare (RCA); Beethoven's 9th and the Alto Rhapsody (Deutsche Grammophon); Handel's Serse and Rodelinda (Westminster); Elektra (Harmonia Mundi). *Memberships:* Chairman of the voice department at the Phildelphia Academy, 1966-71; Chairman of the Canada Council, 1984. *Address:* c/o Pittsburgh Opera Inc, 711 Penn Avenue, 8th Floor, Pittsburgh, PA 15222, USA.

FORSBERG Roland, b. 18 Sept 1939, Stockholm, Sweden. Director of Music; Organist. m. (1) Margaretha Widlund, 1967-91, (2) Lisbeth Carlborg, 1992, 2 sons, 1 daughter. *Education:* Professor of Music, Royal Academy of Music, Stockholm, 1961; Higher Organist Exam, 1963; Higher Cantor Exam, 1964; Diploma, Organist, 1968. *Career:* Director of Music, Norrmalm's Church, Stockholm, 1964-89; Organists in Immanuels Church, Stockholm 1989-; Musical Expert in Swedish State Psalm Committee, 1976-86. *Compositions include:* Liten Svit (organ), 1959; Passacaglia (organ), 1960; Verbum Christi (vocal), 1963; 12 Sacred Songs, 1964; Musica solenne (organ), 1965; Orgeljojk (2 organs), 1975; Sicut Cervus Organ Symphony, 1977; Sonata lapponica (violin, piano), 1980; Sonatina da cappella (violin, organ), 1983; 3 piano sonatas; Concertos for flute and oboe; Sacred concertos for solo voices and organ; Songs; Hymns; Motets; Cantatas; Oratorios; Masses and other Choral works; 8 Organ Suites, Psalm Sonata for mixed chorus, 1984, (English words); Credo Triptych, organ 1988, Memoria viola, organ/piano, 1988. *Recordings:* Karlekens musik; Tre orglar i Vastervik; En gang blir allting stilla; Sjogrens Legender; Autography, Swedish Composers play their own works; Orgelmusik i Sjovik. *Publications:* Red, of Sjung svenska kanon (Sing Swedish Cannons), 1977 Fader war (Gustaf Duben), Ed Reimers, 1980; Seven Sacred Songs (Anders Bond) 1981; Organ Fantasy (Otto Olsson), 1983; Two Organ Pieces (Anders Bond), 1985; 88 preludes Anders Band, 1989; Organ Preluded I-III, 1990-93. *Honours:* Numerous honours including Composers Scholarships, STIM, Stockholm, 1974, 81, 85. *Memberships:* Kammarmusikforeningen Samtida Musik; Foreningen Svenska Tonsattare, Stockholm. *Address:* Dalaro Prastgard, 13054 Dalaro, Sweden.

FORSMAN John Väinö William, b. 11 Aug 1924, Tavastehus, Finland. Composer. m. Maria Luisa Chavez, 26 Apr 1958, 1 son, 3 daughters. *Education:* Royal Conservatory of Denmark, 1945-48; Studies with Paul Hindemith, Salzburg 1948, A. Honegger, Paris 1949, Luigi Dallapiccola, Florence, Italy 1954. *Compositions include:* 3 symphonic ballets; 1st Symphony, A Symphonic Song; 7 Piano Sonatas; Chamber Opera, Ein Lyrisches Märchen; Various piano works; Choral works; Christmas oratorio for children. *Recordings:* Tono, Romance for Violin & Piano, Copenhagen; Nordisk Polyphon, Christmas Oratorio for Children, Copenhagen. *Contributions:* Music critic, Berlingske Aftenavis, Børsen; Articles to Musikrevyn, Verdems Gang, Dagbladet. *Hobbies:* Chess; Ping pong; Reading. *Address:* Ap Postal 4.004, Mexico 4 DF, CP 06400, Mexico.

FORST Judith, b. 7 Nov 1943, British Columbia, Canada. Singer (Mezzo-soprano). *Education:* Studied with Bliss Hebert in New York and with Robert Keyes in London. *Debut:* Vancouver, 1967, as Lola in Cavallieria Rusticana. *Career:* Sang at the Metropolitan Opera from 1968, as Hansel, Siebel and Lola; San Francisco debut, 1974, as Suzuki; Appearances at New Orleans, Santa Fe, Miami (Donna Elvira, 1988), Detroit and Toronto, 1987, as Preziosilla; Seattle 1991, as Dorabella and Jane Seymour in Anna Bolena; Returned to the Met 1991, as Donna Elvira; other roles include Mozart's Cherubino, Olga (Eugene Onegin), Maddalena, Octavian, Carmen and Cererentola; Sang Andromaca in the first British performance (Concert) of Rossini's Ermione, Elizabeth Hall, 1992. *Honours:* winner, Metropolitan Auditions, 1968. *Address:* c/o Metropolitan Opera, Lincoln Center, NY 10023, USA.

FORSTER Andreas, b. 17 Sept 1949, Naumburg, Germany. Singer (Baritone). *Education:* Studied in Berlin and in Essen with Gladys Kuchta. *Debut:* Detmold, 1974, as Schaunard in La Boheme. *Career:* Sang at Kaiserslautern, 1975-76, Saarbrucken, 1976-78, Nuremberg, 1978-88; Staatstheater Hanover from 1988; Guest appearances at the Staatsoper Berlin, Dusseldorf, Cologne, Dortmund, Stuttgart, Munich, Wiesbaden and Orlando, Florida, USA. Other roles have included Verdi's Nabucco, Rigoletto, Macbeth and Simon Boccanegra, Germont, Renato, Iago and Amonasro, Rodrigo, Luna; Donizetti's Enrico, Belcore and Dulcamara, Gerard, Escamillo, Eugene Onegin, Wolfram, Amfortas, Marcello, Olivier in Capriccio and Mozart's Don Giovanni and Count; Concert engagements in works by Bach, Handel, Beethoven, Brahms, Mahler and Penderecki; Lieder recitals and broadcast concerts in Germany, France and Italy. *Address:* Niedersachische Staatstheater, Opernplatz 1, 30159 Hannover, Germany.

FORSTER Heinrich, b. 22 Sept 1938, Munich, Germany. Viola Player. *Education:* Mozarteum, Salzburg, 1958-63; Oberlin College, USA, 1960. *Career:* Camerata Academica, Salzburg; Ramat Gan, Israel Chamber Orchestra; Zurich Chamber Orchestra; Berner Streichquartett; Camerata Bern; Assistant Director, Berne Conservatory, 1977-; Director, Mastercourses, Berne Conservatory. *Address:* Steinbachstrasse 61, CH-3123 Belp, Switzerland.

FORSYTH Malcolm Denis, b. 8 Dec 1936, Pietermaritzburg, South Africa. Composer; Conductor. m. (1) Lesley Eales, 1965, div 1984, (2) Constance Braun, 1992, 1 daughter. *Education:* BMus, 1963, MMus, 1966, DMus, 1972, University of Cape Town; Conductors class, Canford Summer School of Music, 1980-84. *Career:* Conductor: Chamber Choir and Orchestra, University of Cape Town, 1962-64; St Cecilia Orchestra, 1977-86; Edmonton Wind Sinfonia, 1978-79; West Wind Chamber Ensemble, 1980-83; Chamber Choir, University of Witwatersrand, 1983; Guest Conductor: Cape Town, CAPAB and Edmonton Symphony Orchestras, Alberta Ballet Orchestra, National Orchestra, SABC, Johannesburg; As Trombonist: Assistant Principal, Cape Town Symphony Orchestra, 1961-67; Co-Principal, CAPAB Symphony Orchestra, 1971-72; Principal, Edmonton Symphony Orchestra, 1973-80; Junior Lecturer, College of Music, University of Cape Town, 1967; Assistant Professor, 1968-71, Associate Professor, 1971-77, Professor, Music, 1977-, Division Chairman, Assistant to Concert Activity Chairman, 1984-86, Artistic Director, Music Department, 1987-89, McCalla Professor, 1990-91, University of Alberta, Edmonton, Canada; Visiting Professor: Cape Town and Witwatersrand Universities; Composer-in-Residence: Banff Centre, 1975-78; Festival of the Sound, 1991; Juror; Commissions include: Canada Council, CBC, University of Cape Town. *Compositions:* Works for orchestra, band, ensembles, piano and vocal solos. *Address:* 9259 Strathearn Drive, Edmonton, Alberta, Canada, T6C 4E1.

FORTE Allen, b. 23 Dec 1926, Portland, Oregon, USA. Music Theorist. *Education:* Studied at Columbia University, MA 1952. *Career:* Taught at Teachers College of Columbia 1953-59; Member of theory faculty at Mannes College, 1957-59; Yale University from 1959, Professor from 1968; Editor of the Journal of Music Theory 1960-67; President of the Society for Music Theory, 1977. *Publications include:* Schenker's Conception of Musical Structure 1959; Bartok's 'Serial' Composition 1960; The Compositional Matrix 1961; Tonal Harmony in Concept and Practice 1962; A Theory of Set-complexes for Music 1964; A Program for the Analytical Reading of Scores 1966; Computer-implemented Analysis of Musical Structure 1966; Music and Computing: the Present Situation 1967; The Structure of Atonal Music 1970; The Harmonic Organization of The Rite of Spring 1978. *Address:* c/o Yale University, Music Department, New Haven, CT 06520, USA.

FORTUNATO D'Anna, b. 21 Feb 1945, Pittsburgh, Pennsylvania, USA. Singer (Mezzo-soprano). *Education:* Studied with Frederick Jagel and Gladys Miller at the New England Conservatory, 1965-72; Further study with Phyllis Curtin at the Berkshire Music Center. *Career:* Concert appearances in Pittsburgh, Detroit, Louisville, Atlanta and Minnesota; Recitals with the Chamber Music Society of Lincoln Center and with the Boston Musica Viva ensemble; Taught at Longy School of Music, Cambridge, 1974-82; Member of the Liederkreis Ensemble; European debut Paris 1980, as Purcell's Dido with the Boston Camerata; New York recital debut 1981; Sang in the premiere of John Harbison's opera Full Moon in March, New York 1979; New York City Opera debut 1983, as Ruggiero in Handel's Alcina. *Honours include:* Co-winner, Naumburg Chamber Music Prize, 1980. *Address:* New York City Opera, Lincoln Plaza, New York, NY 10023, USA.

FORTUNE George, b. 13 Dec 1935, Boston, Massachuetts, USA. Singer (Baritone). *Education:* Brown University, Providence; Boston University; Vocal studies with Todd Duncan. *Debut:* Ulm 1960, as Fluth in Die Lustigen Weiber von Windsor. *Career:* Guest appearances in Bordeaux, Brussels, Strasbourg, Hamburg and Munich; Glyndebourne 1964, as the Count in Le Nozze di Figaro; Santa Fe 1967, in the US premiere of Henze's Boulevard Solitude; Member of the Deutsche Oper Berlin from 1967: roles include Mozart's Figaro and Guglielmo, Rigoletto, Giulio Cesare, Iago, Amonasro, Posa, Scarpia and Wolfram; Further appearances in Dusseldorf, Frankfurt, Milan and Zurich; sang Scarpia at the Teatro San Carlos, Lison, 1988, the High Preist in Samson and Delilah at the Deutsche Oper Berlin, 1989; Many concert engagements. *Recordings include:* Thérèse by Massenet (Schwann); Christus by Liszt. *Address:* c/o Deutsche Oper Berlin, Richard Wagnerstrasse 10, D-1000 Berlin, Germany.

FORTUNE Nigel (Cameron), b. 5 Dec 1924, Birmingham, England. Musicologist. *Education:* Studied music and Italian at Birmingham University (BA 1950) and researched Italian monody at Cambridge under Thurston Dart (PhD 1954). *Career:* Music Librarian at London University, 1956- 59; Lecturer in music at Birmingham University 1959-69, reader in music from 1969; Secretary of the Royal Musical Association 1957-71, Vice-President 1971; Member of editorial committee, Musica Brittanice, 1975-77; Senior member, editorial committee, New Grove Dictionary of Music and Musicians, 1970-80; Editorial work for the New Oxford History of Music; Writings include: Continuo Instruments in Italian Monodies 1953; Italian Secular Song from 1600 to 1635, 1954; Italian 17th Century Singing 1954; Purcell's Autographs (with F B Zimmerman) 1959; A New Purcell Source 1964; Philip Rosseter and his Songs 1965; Editor, with Dennis Arnold, The Monteverdi Companion (1968) and The Beethoven Companion (1971); Editor, with Anthony Lewis, Opera and Church Music, 1630-1750, 1975; Editions of John Dowland and sacred music by Purcell (with Thurston Dart and Anthony Lewis).

FOSS Lukas, b. 15 Aug 1922, Berlin, Germany. Composer; Conductor; Pianist. m. Cornelia Brendel, 1950, 1 son, 1 daughter. *Education:* Studied at the Curtis Institute of Music (piano, composition, conducting), Yale University (composition), Berkshire Music Center (composing and conducting). *Career includes:* Pianist, Boston Symphony Orchestra, 1944-50; Professor of Conducting and Composition, University of California, 1953-62; Music Direcctor: Ojai Festival, Buffalo Philharmonic Orchestra, 1963-70; Founder-Director, Center for Creative and Performing Arts, SUNY at Buffalo, 1963; Music Director, Brooklyn Philharmonic, 1971-82, Brooklyn Philharmonic, 1982-; Conductor, Jerusalem Symphony Orchestra, 1972-76; Music Director, Milwaukee Symphony Orchestra, 1981-86; Composer in Residence, Tanglewood, summers, 1989, 1990. *Compositions:* Over 120 including operas The Jumping Frog, 1949 and Griffelkin, 1955 and most recently: Solo for piano, 1982; Symphony No 3, 1992; Renaissance concerto for flute and orchestra, 1986; Chamber: 3 string quartets, 1947, 1973, 1975; Brass Quintet, 1978; Percussion Quartet, 1983; Tashi for clarinet, string quartet and piano, 1986; Piano pieces; Choral music. *Recordings:* Over 30 works recorded, some of which were also conducted by Foss. *Publications:* A Bio-bibliography, USA, 1991. *Honours:* NY Music Critics Circle Awards, 1944, 1954; Guggenheim Fellowships, 1945, 1960; Fellow, American Academy, Rome, 1950-51; Fulbright Grant, 1950-52; Brandeis University, Creative Arts Award, 1983; 9 honorary doctorates. *Membership:* American Academy of Arts and Letters. *Address:* 1140 Fifth Avenue, New York, NY 10128, USA.

FOSTER Donald H, b. 30 Apr 1934, Detroit, Michigan, USA. Professor. *Education:* BS, Wayne State University, 1956; MMus, 1960, PhD, 1967, University of Michigan. *Career:* Music Faculty, Olivet College, Michigan, 1960-67; Professor of Musicology, College Conservatory of Music, University of Cincinnati, 1967-. *Publications:* L'histoire de la femme adultere by Louis Nicolas Clerambault, 1974; Louis-Nicolas Clerambault 1676-1749: Two Cantatas for Soprano and Chamber Ensemble, 1979; Symphonies concertantes of Jean-Baptiste Davaux; Overtures of Franz Beck; Jean-Philippe Rameau: A Guide to Research, 1989; Co-author, Sourcebook for Research in Music, 1993; Contributor to: Symphony Orchestras of the United States: Selected profiles, 1986; Opera Quarterly; Recherches sur la musique francaise classique; The Diapason; Acta Musicologica; Current Musicology; The Eighteenth Century. *Honours:* Fulbright Grant, 1962. *Memberships:* American Musicological Society; Societe francaise d'etude du XVIIIe siecle; American Association of University Professors. *Hobbies:* Travel; Hiking. *Address:* 393 Amazon Avenue, Cincinnati, OH 45220, USA.

FOSTER Dudley Edwards Jr, b. 5 Oct 1935, Orange, New Jersey, USA. College Professor; Organist; Conductor; Composer. *Education:* Occidental College, Los Angeles, 1953-56; AB, 1957, MA, 1958, Composition & Theory, Doctoral Study, 1959-63, University of California at Los Angeles; FTCL, Organ, Trinity College of Music, London, 1960. *Debut:* Los Angeles, 1957. *Career:* Teaching Assistant, University of California, Los Angeles, 1959-61; Lecturer in Music, Immaculate Heart College, Los Angeles, 1961-63; Director of Music, Holy Trinity Episcopal Church, Alhambra, California, 1959-62; Lecturer in Music, California State University, Los Angeles, 1968-71; Director of Music, First Lutheran Church, Los Angeles, 1968-73; Professor of Music, Los Angeles Mission College, 1975-, Chairman, Music Department, 1979-. *Compositions:* String Quartet; Passacaglia for Brass Instruments; Introduction, Arioso & Fugue for Cello and Piano; O Sacrum Convivium, for Trumpet and Organ; Numerous choral and organ works. *Recordings:* Baroque Organ Music; Piece in Free Form for Organ (Original work). *Contributor to:* Worship and Arts. *Honours:* Associated Students Faculty Award, LA Mission College, 1988; Graduate representative to Music Department, Chair, University of California at Los Angeles, 1959-60. *Memberships:* Los Angeles College Teachers' Association, District Vice-President, 1981; American Guild of Organists; International Platform Association; Mediaeval Academy of America; National Association of Scholars. *Hobbies:* Reading; Travel. *Address:*

Department of Music, Los Angeles Mission College, 13356 Eldridge Avenue, Sylmar, CA 91342, USA.

FOSTER Lawrence (Thomas), b. 23 Oct 1941, Los Angeles, California, USA. *Education:* Studied conducting with Fritz Zweig, Los Angeles; Attended the Bayreuth Master Classes and the Berkshire Music Center, Tanglewood, Mass. *Debut:* Young Musicians Foundation Debut Orchestra, Los Angeles, 1960. *Career:* Assistant Conductor, Los Angeles Philharmonic Orchestra, 1965-68; Chief Guest Conductor, Royal Philharmonic Orchestra, London, 1969-74; Conductor-in-Chief, Houston Symphony Orchestra, 1971-78; Chief Conductor, Opera de Monte Carlo and Orchestre National (renamed Orchestre Philharmonique) de Monte Carlo, 1979-; General Music Director, Duisburg, 1981-88; Music Director, Lausanne Chamber Orchestra, 1985-; Jerusalem Symphony Orchestra, 1988-; Conducted new production of Hamlet by Ambroise Thomas at Monte Carlo, 1993. *Recordings:* For Angel-EMI; Candide; CBS; Decca-London; Desto; Erato; New World; Philips. *Honour:* Koussevitzky Prize, 1966. *Address:* c/o Orchestre Philharmonique de Monte Carlo, Casino, Monte Carlo, Monaco.

FOSTER Richard, b. 30 Mar 1930, Bangor, Maine, USA. Piano Accompanist; Vocal Coach. *Education:* Studied with Nadia Boulanger, Paris, 1955-56; Song Literature with Felix Wolfes, Povla Frijsh and Pierre Bernac; MusB, 1953, MusM, 1957, New England Conservatory. *Career:* Accompanist and Coach for artists of Metropolitan Opera and New York City Opera on national tours; Tours of USA and Canada; State department tours of Europe with Schola Cantorum, tours of Middle East with Ambassadors of Opera, 1984 and 1985, and the Philippines and People's Republic of China, 1986; Organist and continuo with Symphony of Air, 1963-65; New York performance with Royal Philharmonic of London, 1963; Assistant Conductor of Central City and St Paul Operas, 1973-74; Assistant Conductor, Coach of Zero Mostel, BBC television, London, 1966; Opera Coach, Temple University, 1969; Visiting Lecturer, vocal coaching and accompanist, University of Hartford, 1970-. *Honour:* Recipient of Sally Eisemann Award, Tanglewood Festival, 1958. *Hobby:* Swimming.

FOTEK Jan, b. 28 Nov 1928, Czerwinsk nad Wisla, Poland. Composer. *Education:* Studied with Stanislav Wiechowicz in Krakow and Szeligowski in Warsaw. *Compositions:* Operas: The Sea of Recovered Unity, Polish Radio, 1967; Galileo, 1969; Vir sapiens dominabitur astris, after Dante, Copernicus, St Francis and Michelangelo, Polish Radio, 1983; The Spoons and the Moon, 1973-76; The Woodland Princess, opera-ballet, Warsaw, 1978; Man and Angels, misterium sacrum, 1982; Opus Concertante for organ, piano and percussion, 1959; Gregorian Hymn for chorus and orchestra, 1963; A Cycle of Verses for children's chorus and orchestra, 1963; Epitasis for orchestra, 1967; The Last War for narrator, chorus and orchestra, 1971; Partita for 12 bassonss and 3 double bassoons, 1973; Musica Chromatica for strings, 1982; Sonata for tuba and piano, 1984; Czarnolas Suite for strings, 1986; Ecloga for counter-tenor and ensemble, 1987. *Address:* ZAIKS (Poland), PRS Ltd Member Registration, 29-33 Berners Street, London W1P 4AA, England.

FOU TS'ONG b. 10 Mar 1934, Shanghai, China. Pianist. *Education:* Studied in China with Mario Paci and at the Warsaw Conservatory with Zbigniew Drzewiecki. *Debut:* With the Shanghai Municipal Orchestra, playing Beethoven's Emperor Concerto, 1951. *Career:* Gave 500 concerts in Eastern Europe while studying in Poland; Moved to London 1958; Solo appearances in Europe, Scandinavia, the Far East, Australia and New Zealand, North and South America. *Recordings include:* Concertos by Beethoven, Haydn, Chopin. Solo recitals by Chopin, Debussy, Bach, Handel, Mozart, Beethoven, Schubert. *Honours include:* Third Prize, Bucharest Piano Competition 1953; Third Prize, International Chopin Competition, Warsaw, 1955.

Address: Intermusica Artists' Management, 16 Duncan Terrace, London N1 8BZ, England.

FOUNTAIN Ian, b. 15 Oct 1969, Welwyn Garden City, England. Concert Pianist. *Education:* Chorister at New College Oxford from 1976; Westminster College 1982; Studied with Sulamita Aronovsky at the Royal Northern College of Music. *Career:* Has performed widely in Europe from 1986; Recital debuts in Frankfurt and Munich, season 1989-90; Further concerts in Madrid, Warsaw, Pasadena and Savannah (Georgia) and at the Sintra Festival (Portugal) and Montpellier Festival (France); Toured Germany with the Arthur Rubinstein Philharmonie, Lodz; Debut with the Royal Liverpool Philharmonic Feb. 1990; Autumn 1991 with the Berlin Radio Symphony Orchestra (Rachmaninov 3) and London recital debut in the International Piano Series at South Bank. *Honours include:* Winner, Viotti-Valsesia International Piano Competition (Italy) 1986; Joint winner, Arthur Rubinstein International Piano Competition, 1989. *Address:* c/o Terry Harrison Artists Management, 3 Clarendon Court, Park Street, Charlbury, OX7 3PS, England.

FOUNTAIN Primous III, b. 1 Aug 1949, St Petersburg, Florida, USA. Composer. *Education:* Studied at DePaul University in Chicago, 1968-69. *Career:* Freelance composer from 1968, including association with the Arthur Mitchell Dance Theatre of Harlem. *Compositions include:* Manifestations for orchestra 1969; Grudges for orchestra 1972; Ritual Dance of the Amaks for orchestra 1973; Duet for flute and bassoon 1974; Cello Concerto 1976; Ricia for violin, cello and piano 1980. *Honours include:* BMI composition award 1968; Guggenheim Fellowships 1974, 1977; American Academy and Institute of Arts and Letters award.

FOURNET Jean, b. 14 Apr 1913, Rouen, France. Conductor. *Education:* Studied with Philippe Gaubert at the Paris Conservatoire. *Debut:* Rouen 1936. *Career:* Conducted in Rouen and Marseilles until 1944; Music Director of the Opéra-Comique, Paris, 1944-57; Conducting courses at the Ecole Normale, Paris, 1944-62; Conducted Pelléas et Mélisande in Tokyo, 1958; Conductor of the Netherlands Radio Orchestra 1961-68; Chicago Lyric Opera 1965; Principal Conductor of the Rotterdam Philharmonic from 1968-73; Guest conductor in Europe, South America, USA and Israel; Metropolitan Opera debut 1987, Samson et Dalila; Conducted Les Dialogues des Carmélites at Seattle, 1990. *Recordings include:* Berlioz Grande Messe des Morts, 1943; Louise by Charpentier, Pelléas et Mélisande and Les Pêcheurs de Perles, Mignon; d'Indy Symphonie; Saint-Saëns Piano Concertos; Fauré Requiem; Franck Symphonic Poems; Debussy La Damoiselle élue, (Janine Micheau), Nocturnes, Ibéria and Prélude. *Address:* c/o Seattle Opera Association, PO Box 9248, Seattle WA 98109, USA.

FOUVY Charles Louis, b. 25 Sept 1928, Melbourne, Australia. Consultant in Acoustics, Music & Theology. m. Valda Rose Vaughan, 5 May 1955, 2 sons, 1 daughter. *Education:* BEE, Melbourne University 1954; MS Civil Engineering, University of California, Berkeley 1974; BD Melbourne College of Divinity 1986; Matriculation,Music (theoretical) Melbourne, 1950. *Career:* Engineer, Melbourne and Metropolitan Tramways Board/Metropolitan Transit Authority of Victoria, 1954-88; Australian Hymn Book Committee 1968- (first secretary 1968-72); Director, Australian Hymn Book P/L, 1974-; Kew Philharmonic Society deputy choir conductor, Musicology/Acoustics Consultant. *Publications:* Editor, Music for Christmas, carols for 4-part flute choir, 1983, 1991. *Contributor to:* various engineering, musicological and theological journals and magazines. *Memberships:* Musicological Society of Australia; Australian Acoustical Society; The Hymn Society of Great Britain and Ireland; Hymn Society of America. *Hobbies:* Photography; Walking. *Address:* 241 Cotham Rd, Kew, VIC 3101, Australia.

FOWKE Philip Francis, b. 28 June 1950, Gerrards

Cross, England. Concert Pianist. *Education:* Downside School, Somerset, England, 1964-67; Scholarship to Royal Academy of Music, England, 1967-74; Piano Studies with Majorie Withers and Gordon Green; LRAM (Piano Performance); ARCM (Piano Performance); Recital Diploma. *Debut:* Wigmore Hall, 1974. *Career:* Professor of Pianoforte, Royal Academy of Music, London; Performs regularly with all major British Orchestras including the four principal London Orchestras; frequent Radio and TV Broadcasts; Regular performer at the London Promenade Concerts since 1979; Toured with throughout Europe; Made his USA Debut 1982; tours throughout Europe and Australia; has played in Hong Kong and the Emirate of Oman; Invited to perform at the Serate Musicale de Milano; Appeared at Salzburg Mozartweek, 1984. *Recordings include:* Carnival of the Animals; The Bliss Piano Concerto; Virtuoso Piano Transcriptions; Britten's Scottish Ballad; complete Chopin Waltzes; Chopin Sonatas Nos 2 & 3; Tchaikovsky's First and Third Piano Concertos; Rachmaninoff Concerto No. 2; Paganini Rhapsody; Ravel Piano Concerto in G and Concerto for the left hand; Chopin Waltzes and Brahms Intermezzo; Delius Piano Concerto; Bliss Piano Recital. *Contributor to:* Times Educational Supplement, Review of Rubinstein Biography. *Honours:* Many prizes and awards including Church Fellowship, 1976; Fellow Royal Academy of Music. *Memberships:* Incorporated Society of Musicians; Chelsea Arts Club. *Hobbies:* Architecture; Reading; DIY. *Current Management:* Kaye Artists Management, London, England. *Address:* Kaye Artists Management, Barratt House, 7 Chertsey Road, Woking GU21 5AB, England.

FOWLER Charles Bruner, b. 12 May 1931, Peekskill, New York, USA. Arts Consultant; Writer. *Education:* BSMusEd, State University of New York, Potsdam, 1952; MMMus Ed, Northwestern University, 1957; DMA, Boston University, 1964. *Career:* Education Editor, Musical America Magazine, 1974-; Created education materials for the New York Philharmonic, Metropolitan Opera, John F Kennedy Center; Special Events Consultant, Writer, Grand Openings, John F Kennedy Center, 1971, Walt Disney World, 1971, Knoxville's World Fair, 1982, Epcot Center, 1982; Consultant, Writer, various education projects sponsored by National Endowment for the Arts, etc; Speaker on arts education; Scriptwriter for radio, TV, film and theatre; Director of Publications; Editor; Teacher and guest professor. *Publications:* The Search for Musical Understanding (co-author), 1973; An Arts Education Source Book (editor), 1980; Arts in Education/Education in Arts (editor), 1984; The Crane Symposium: Toward an Understanding of the Teaching and Learning of Musical Performance (editor), 1988; Can We Rescue the Arts for America's Children? (author), 1988; Sing! a secondary school choral textbook (editor), 1988; Music! Its Role and Importance in Our Lives (author), 1993. Many booklets and reports. *Hobbies:* Painting; Theatre. *Address:* 320 Second Street SE, Washington, DC 20003, USA.

FOWLER Jennifer, b. 14 Apr 1939, Bunbury, Western Australia. Composer. *Education:* University of Western Australia, BA Hons, 1961, Dip Ed, 1962, B.Mus, 1967; Further study at the Studio for Electronic Music, Utrecht, 1968-69. *Career:* Resident in London from 1969; Music Teacher in schools, 1962-72; free-lance composer. *Compositions:* Hours of the Day for four mezzos, 2 oboes, 2 clarinets 1968; Ravelation for string quintet 1971; Chimes, Fractured for ensemble 1971; Look on this Oedipus for orchestra 1973; Piece for an Opera House for 2 pianists 1973; Chant with Garlands for orchestra 1974; Voice of the Shades for soprano and ensemble 1977; Ring out the Changes for strings and bells 1978; Tell Out, my Soul: Magnificat for soprano, cello and piano 1980; Music for Piano-Ascending and Descending, Piece for E.L. for solo piano 1981; The Arrows of St Sebastian II for bass clarinet, cello and tape 1981; The Arrows of St Sebastian I, for ensemble, 1982; Invocation to the Veiled Mysteries for ensemble, 1982; Line Spun with Stars for Piano Trio 1983; When David Heard.... for choir and piano 1983; Echoes from an Antique Land for ensemble, 1983; Threaded Stars

for solo harp, 1983; Blow Flute for solo flute, 1983; Letter from Haworth for mezzo, clarinet, cello and piano 1984; Between Silence and the World, for wind quintet, 1987; Lament for baroque oboe and bass viol. 1987; We Call to You, Brother for ensemble, 1988; Restless Dust for cello and piano, 1988; And Ever Shall Be for mezzo and ensemble, 1989; Reeds, Refections...for oboe and string trio, 1990. *Recordings:* Chimes Fractured on Festival Records: Australian Festival of Music, Vol.10; Blow Flute on The Flute Ascendent, Vox Australis CD. *Publications:* Article in New Music Articles, vol 4, Australia, 1985; Article in Contemporary Music Review, 1993. *Honours:* Prize from Berlin Academy of the Arts for Hours of the Day; First prize in chamber music in the International Contest for Women Composers, Mannheim, 1974; Radcliffe Award of Great Britain, 1971. *Memberships:* Member: Fellowship of Australian Composers; Composers Guild of Great Britain; Sonic Arts Network; Women in Music; Int League of Women Composers. *Address:* 21 Deodar Road, London SW15 2NP, England.

FOWLER John, b. 1956, USA. Singer (Tenor). *Career:* Sang in the USA as Edgardo in Lucia di Lammermoor, and in Norma; European engagements form 1983, including Rodolfo at Cologne and Hoffmann at Liège, 1985; Vienna Staatsoper, 1984-85, as Des Grieux, Leicester in Maria Stuarda and Arturo in I Puritani; Hamburg Staatsoper, 1984-85, in Rosenkavalier, Traviata and La Bohème; Welsh National Opera, 1986-87, as Edgardo and as Tonio in La Fille du Regiment; Further appearances in New Orleans, Houston, (as Faust), Miami (Hoffmann, 1989), with Edmonton Opera (Duke of Mantua) and Liège (Gounod's Romeo, 1988); Concert showings in works by Respighi, Verdi (Requiem) and Mendelssohn (Elijah); Sang Percy in Anna Bolena at Barcelona and Donizetti's Edgardo at Dublin, 1991; Sang Hoffmann at Cincinnati, 1992. *Honours:* Winner, Metropolitan Opera Auditions, 1981. *Address:* c/o Herbert Barrett Management, 1776 Broadway, Suite 1610, New York, NY 10019, USA.

FOWLES Glenys, b. 4 Nov 1946, Perth, Western Australia. Singer (SOprano). *Education:* Studied with Margarita Mayer in Sydney, Kurt Adler in New York and Jani Strasser in London. *Debut:* Sang Oscar (Ballo in Maschera), Australian Opera in Sydney, 1969. *Career:* Sang in the USA 1974-81, notably at the City Opera New York as Poppea, Susanna, Melisande, 1976, Mimi, and Micaela; European engagements have included Ilia in Idomeneo at Glyndebourne (1974), Sophie and Titania for Scottish Opera (Midsummer Night's Dream); Other roles include Gounod's Juilette, Mozart's Zerlina and Pamina, Marzelline, Marguerite (Faust), Nannetta, Anne Trulove, Mimi and Lauretta; Sang Liu in Turandot for Australian Opera, 1991; the Marschallin, 1992. *Address:* Australian Opera, Sydney Opera House, New South Wales, Australia.

FOX Delores, b. 30 Nov 1938, Ohio, USA. Conductor; Singer. m. Michael D Park, 22 May 1992, 2 daughters. *Education:* BMus, Boston University. Tutors include Robert Shaw, Mary Curtis Verna, David Dahl, Bela Nagy and Katheryn Habedank. *Career:* Conductor in Seattle, Washington, 1972-; Organist and Choir Director, Seattle and Brookline, 1967-92; Faculty staff of Boston Conservatory, 1979-80 and University of Connecticut, 1980-82; Currently at Shoreline Community College, since 1984; Soprano soloist specialising in contemporary music. Numerous premieres of new works by Bavicchi, Adler, Haflich and Kacinskas. Member of the Robert Shaw Chamber Chorus, France, 1988. *Honours include:* Grant, Boston Universiyt, 1962; Indianapolis Foundation Grant, 1956; Various scholarships from Indiana University, 1956, University of Washington, 1982-83. *Memberships:* National Association of Teachers of Singing; American Guild of Organists; Conductors' Guild; American Choral Directors Association. *Current management* Career Impact. 4206 NE 65th Street, Seattle, WA 98115, USA.

FOX Erika, b. 3 Oct 1936, Vienna, Austria. Composer. m. 3 Sept 1961 (now separated), 1 son, 1 daughter.

Education: ARCM, Royal College of Music, London; Also private study with Jeremy Dale Roberts and Harrison Birtwistle. *Career:* Numerous commissions from leading contemporary music groups; Works performed at London's South Bank, Canada, Greece, Turkey, Czechoslovakia, Festivals and Broadcast; Rehearsed orchestra at Menuhin School; Teaching includes Centre for Young Musicians, Pimlico; Junior Department, Guildhall School of Music and Drama; Composition workshops in various schools and privately. Sometime ballet pianist Arts Educational Schools. *Compositions include:* Lamentations for Four, 1973; The Slaughterer, chamber opera, 1975; Paths Where the Mournerrs Tread, 1980; Litany for Strings, 1981; Movement for String Sextet, 1982; Shir, 1983; Kaleidoscope, 1983; Quasi Una Cadenza, 1983; Nick's Lament, 1984; Osen Shomaat, 1985; Silver Homage, 1986; Rivka's Fiddle, 1986; On Visiting Stravinsky's Grave at San Michele, 1988; Hungarian Rhapsody, 1989; The Bet, puuppet music drama, 1990; The Dancer Hotoke, chamber opera, Garden Venture commission, 1992 (Olivier Award Nomination); Meditation on Sibyls', 1991; The Moon of Moses, 1992; Currently writing piano concerto commissioned by Julian Jacobson, 1993. *Hobbies:* Reading; Theatre. *Current Management:* Elinor Kelly, WestBrook Farm Cottage, Boxford, Nr Newbury, Berkshire, RG16 8DL, England. *Address:* 78 Peterborough Road, London SW6 3EB, England.

FOX Fred(erick Alfred), b. 17 Jan 1931, Detroit, Michigan, USA. Composer. *Education:* Studied at Wayne State University, the University of Michigan, Indiana University, Bloomington, with Bernhard Heiden. *Career:* Teacher, Franklin College, Indiana and Sam Houston University, Huntsville; Worked in Minneapolis; Assistant, Contemporary Music Project, Washington DC; Teacher, California State University, Hayward, 1964-74; Teacher, Indiana University 1974-; Chairman of Composition Department 1980-. *Compositions include:* A Stone, a Leaf, an Unfound Door for soprano and ensemble, 1966; BEC for chamber ensemble, 1968; Quantic for woodwind quintet, 1969; The Descent for chorus and percussion, 1969; Violin Concerto 1971; Matrix for cello, strings and percussion, 1972; Ternion for oboe and orchestra, 1973; Variables no 5 for orchestra 1974; Variables nos 1-4 and 6 for instruments 1976; Time Excursions for soprano, speaker and instruments, 1976; Beyond Winterlock for orchestra 1977; Ambient Shadows for 8 instruments 1978; Night Ceremonies for orchestra 1979; Sonaspheres nos 1-5 for chamber ensemble 1980-83; Nilrem's Odyssey for baritone, speaker and chorus 1980; Tracings for orchestra 1981; Bren for 13 brass 1982; Visitations for 2 saxophones 1983; Januaries for orchestra, 1984; Devil's Tramping Ground, chamber ensemble, 1991; Echo Blues, orchestra, 1992; Auras, chamber ensemble, 1989; Nightscenes, strings & percussion, 1989. *Address:* Music Department, Indiana University, Bloomington, IN 47045, USA.

FOX Leland Stanford, b. 25 Jan 1931, Worcester, Massachusetts, USA. University Music Professor and Administrator. m. Wanda R. Nelson, 1 Mar 1955, 1 son, 1 daughter. *Education:* BM, 1956; MM, 1957, Baylor University; PhD, Florida State University, 1962. *Career:* Hearst Publications, New York City, 1948-51; Graduate Assistant, 1956-57, Instructor of Music, 1957-60, Baylor University; Graduate Assistant, Florida State University, 1960-62; Instructor in Music, Pensacola Junior College, 1962-63; Associate Professor of Music, University of Oklahoma, 1963-66; Associate Professor to Professor, Director of Opera Theater, 1966; Associate Dean of Graduate School, University of Mississippi, 1986-; Principal Tenor, Asolo Festival, 1962; Opera and Oratorio performances in USA. *Publications include:* Index of Italian Opera 1900-1970; Opera Comique: A Vehicle for Classic Style, 1964; From Out of the Ashes: Santa Fe Opera's New Theater, 1968; La Belle Arsène (1773) by Pierre Alexandre Monsigny, 1969; The State of Opera: A Dialogue Between Boris Goldovsky and Carlisle Floyd, 1971; Editor of numerous books. *Contributions to:* New Grove Dictionary of Music and Musicians; The Opera Quarterly; Editor, The Opera Journal, 1968-88. *Hobbies:* Golf; Smoking Pipes. *Address:* University of Mississippi, MS 38677, USA.

FOX Malcolm, b. 13 Oct 1946, Windsor, England. Composer. m. Pauline Elizabeth Scholz, 5 Apr 1980, 1 son. *Education:* Royal College of Music, University of London; ARCM, 1966; BMus(Hons), 1967; MMusRCM, 1968. *Career:* Music Director, Cockpit Theatre, London, 1972-74; Lecturer in Music, 1974-79, Senior Lecturer, 1980-, University of Adelaide, South Australia. *Compositions:* Sid the Serpent, opera, 1976; Six Miniatures, violin and piano, 1977; Violin Concerto, 1980; The Iron Man, opera, 1987; Pathways of Ancient Dreaming, string orchestra, 1990; Ten Thousand Years Goodbye, soprano, piano and clarinet, 1992. *Publications:* Music Education in South Education (1836-1986), chapter in From Colonel Light into the Footlights - The Performing Arts in South Australia from 1936 to the present, 1988. *Contributions:* Siegfried's Death, 1989; The Swan Knight in Wagner's Lohengrin, 1989; Wotan's Spear, 1993. *Memberships:* Australasian Performing Right Association; Australia Music Centre; Fellowship of Australian Composers; Association of Professional Composers (UK). *Address:* 13 Whinham Street, Fitzroy, Adelaide, South Australia 5082, Australia.

FOX Tom, b. 1950, USA. Singer (Baritone). *Education:* Studied at the College Conservatory of Music in Cincinnati Opera Company. *Career:* Appeared with Texas Opera Theater, 1974, then with Houston Grand Opera; Resident member of Cincinnati Opera 1976-80; Frankfurt Opera from 1981 as Orestes (Elektra), Amonasro, Don Pizarro, Escamillo, Klingsor, Ford, Figaro and Nick Shadow in The Rake's Progress, Wiesbaden 1981, as Don Giovanni; Hamburg Staatsoper 1983, as Arcalems in Amadis de Gaule by J C Bach; Has sung with Canadian Opera as Orestes, Jochanaan and Escamillo; Welsh National Opera 1985 as Escamillo; Other roles include Iago (Teatro Colon 1986), Claudius in Hamlet by Thomas (Pittsburgh), Alberich in The Ring for Nice Opera, at the Théâtre des Champs Elysées and in San Francisco; Gessler in Guillaume Tell in Nice; Dutchman, Amonasro, the villains in Hoffmann and Scarpia (Pittsburgh); Giovanni (Francesca di Rimini) in Turin; Barnaba in La Gioconda with Rome Opera; Invited to San Francisco for the US premiere of Henze's Das Verratene Meer; Season 1992/93 with debut in Washington as Iago, the role of Vesco Di Blois in Massenet's Esclamonde in Palermo, Telramund in Montpellier, debut at the Metropolitan Opera, New York as Alberich, Jokanaan in San Francisco, 1993/94, Prus (Makropulos Case) in San Francisco and Bologna, his debut at the Lyric Opera of Chicago as Scarpia, his debut as Wotan at the Santiago Opera in Chile, Klingsor in a new production of Parsifal at the Munich Staatsoper and Kurwenal in a new production of Tristan at La Monnaie in Brussels. *Address:* Kaye Artists Management Ltd, Barratt House, 7 Chertsey Road, Woking, GU21 5AB, England.

FRACKENPOHL Arthur (Roland), b. 23 Apr 1924, Irvington, New Jersey, USA. Composer; Professor. *Education:* Studied with Bernard Rogers, Eastman School of Music, BA 1947, MA 1949; Darius Milhaud, Berkshire Music Center, Tanglewood, summer 1948; Nadia Boulanger, Fontainebleau, 1950; Mus Doc, McGill University, Montreal, 1957. *Career:* Teacher 1949-61, Professor 1961-85, Crane School of Music, State University of New York at Potsdam. *Compositions:* Chamber Opera: Domestic Relations (To Beat or Not to Beat), 1964; Orchestral: A Jubilant Overture, 1957; Allegro scherzando, 1957; Overture, 1957; Symphony for Strings, 1960; Largo and Allegro for Horn and Strings, 1962; Short Overture, 1965; Concertino for Tuba and Strings, 1967; Suite for Trumpet and Strings, 1970; Band music: Chamber: Brass Quartet, 1950; 2 brass quintets, 1963, 1972; Trombone Quartet, 1967; Brass Trio, 1967; String Quartet, 1971; Breviates for Brass Ensemble, 1973; Trio for Oboe, Horn and Bassoon, 1982; Tuba Sonata, 1983; Piano pieces; Choral works; Song cycles; Solo songs. *Publications:* Harmonization at the Piano, 1962, 4th edition, 1981, 6th edition, 1990;

Concerto for Brass Quintet and Strings, 1986; Mass for Chorus and Orchestra, 1990; Suite for Brass Trio and Percussion, 1973. *Address:* c/o 13 Hillcrest Drive, Potsdam, NY 13676, USA.

FRANCAIX Jean, b. 23 May 1912, Le Mans, France. Composer; Pianist. *Education:* Studied at the Le Mans Conservatory and at the Paris Conservatoire, with Isidor Phillip and Nadia Boulanger. *Career:* Many tours of Europe and the USA as a piano virtuoso; Performances of his music at many festivals including ISCM Festivals at Vienna 1932 and Palermo, 1949. *Compositions:* Operas: Le Diable Boiteux, 1937; La Main de Gloire, 1945; Paris a nous deux, 1954; La Princesse de Cleves, 1961-65; Ballets: Les Malheurs de Sophie, 1935; Le Jeu Sentimental, 1936; Le Jugement du fou, 1938; Les Demoiselles de la nuit, 1948; La Dame dans le lune, 1958; Oratorio L'Apocalypse selon St Jean, 1942; Orchestral: Symphony, 1932; Concertino for piano and orchestra, 1932; Serenade for chamber orchestra, 1934; Fantasie for cello and orchestra, 1934; Quadruple Concerto, 1935; Piano Concerto, 1936; La Douce France, 1946; Symphony, 1953; Divertimento for horn and chamber orchestra, 1958; L'Horloge de Flore, suite for oboe and orchestra; 2-Piano Concerto, 1965; Flute Concerto, 1967; 2 Violin Concertos, 1970, 1979; Theme and Variations for orchestra, 1973; Concerto for double bass and orchestra, 1974; Theme and Variations for clarinet and strings, 1978; Concerto for 2 Harps and strings, 1979; Bassoon Concerto, 1980; Chamber Music including Clarinet Quintet, 1978 and 6 Impromptus for flute and bassoon, 1979; Piano Sonata, 1960. *Address:* SACEM, 225 Avenue Charles de Gaulle, 92521 Neuilly sur Seine Cedex, France.

FRANCI Carlo, b. 18 July 1927, Buenos Aires, Argentina. Composer; Conductor. *Education:* Studied at the Rome Conservatory and with Fernando Previtali at the Accademia di Santa Cecilia. *Career:* Conducted symphonic music at first, then Hansel und Gretel at Spoleto, 1959; Appearances at many opera houses in Italy and abroad, including the Vienna Staatsoper; Led the company of Rome Opera in Rossini's Otello at the New York Metropolitan, 1968, returning as guest, 1969-72; Other repertoire includes Spontini's Fernand Cortez and Verdi's Nabucco, Berne, 1990; Conducted the Seven Stars concert at the Baths of Caracalla, 1991. *Compositions include:* L'Impertaore (opera), produced at Bergamo, 1958. *Address:* c/o Teatro dell'Opera di Roma, Piazza B Gigli 8, 00184 Rome, Italy.

FRANCI Francesca, b. 1962, Rome, Italy. Singer (Mezzo-soprano). *Education:* Studied with Rodolfo Celletti and Tito Gobbi. *Debut:* Sang Mahler's Lieder eines fahrenden Gesellen at Verona, 1984. *Career:* Appeared as Maddalena in Rigoletto at Genoa and Naples, Rosina at Bari and Suzuki in Bologna, 1988; Festival della Valle d'Itria 1988 in Donizetti's Maria di Rohan, as Armando; Edvige in Guillaume Tell at La Scala, Milan, returning as Fatima in Oberon; Sang Ernestina in Rossini's L'Occasione fa il Ladro at Pesaro; Further engagements at Rome and Naples (from 1987), Florence, Monteverdi's Otho, 1992, Paris and Wiesbaden; Franca 1992, as Stephano in Gounod's Romeo et Juliette. *Recordings include:* Maria di Rohan. *Address:* c/o Teatro Alla Scala, Via Filodrammatici 2, 20121 Milan, Italy.

FRANCIS Alun, b. 1943, Kidderminster, England. Conductor. *Education:* Royal Manchester College of Music, 1960-63. *Career:* Played the horn in Halle and Bournemouth Symphony Orchestra; From 1966 has conducted more than 60 orchestras in over 20 countries; Guest conductor at the Vienna Festival, Hong Kong Arts Festival with the BBC Scottish Symphony, Arhus Festival in Denmark with the Philharmonia Hungarica, Promenade Concerts London with the Royal Philharmonic and Festival Hall 1983 in Henryk Szeryng Golden Jubilee concert; Chief Conductor and Artistic Director of the Ulster Orchestra, 1966-67, and the Northern Ireland Opera Trust, 1974-84; Director, Northwest Chamber Orchestra in Seattle, 1980-85; Director and Artistic Advisor, Overijssels Philharmonic

in Holland, 1985-87; Currently Chief Conductor of the NordWestDeutsche Philharmonie and Principal Conductor of Berlin Symphony (from 1989); Repertoire includes Bel Canto opera (1978 revival of Donizetti Gabriella di Vergy, premiere of revised version, at Belfast) and 20th century music ranging from Berio to Stockhausen; Has composed music for the concert hall, films and theatre. *Recordings:* Donizetti's Ugo, Conte di Parigi, with the Philharmonia Orchestra; Offenbach's Christopher Columbus, with the London Mozart Players (Opera Rara); Other albums with the London Symphony, Royal Philharmonic, English Chamber and Northwest Chamber Orchestras. *Address:* Anglo-Swiss Management, 4-5 Primrose Mews, Sharpeshall Street, London NW1 8YW, England.

FRANCIS David Edward, b. 27 Feb 1953, London, England. Harpsichordist; Performer; Teacher. m. Susan Elson, 7 Aug 1982, 3 sons. *Education:* Manchester University 1971-75; Royal Manchester College of Music, 1971-75; Royal Northern College of Music, 1975-78; MusB, GRNCM; ARNCM; LRAM; LTCL. *Debut:* Cheltenham International Festival, 1980. *Career:* Harpsichord Tutor at Chetham's School of Music, 1975-; Harpsichord Tutor at Junior School of Royal Northern College of Music, 1976-, and Assistant Administrator, 1980-; Tutor in harpsichord and baroque ensemble at Royal Northern College of Music, 1978-; Solo recitalist and member of Manchester Camerata, the Goldberg Ensemble, Contrasts and Musical Offering; Co-ordinator of Early Music Studies, Royal Northern College of Music, 1991-; Harpsichord Tutor at Chethams School of Music, 1975-; Harpsichord Tutor at Junior School of Royal Northern College of Music, 1976-92 & Assistant Administrator, 1980-92; Tutor in Harpsichord and Baroque Ensemble at Royal Northern College of Music, 1976-, and Co-ordinator of Early Music Studies, 1991-; Administrator of School of Keyboard Studies at Royal Northern College of Music, 1992-. *Recordings:* Haydn violin and Harpsichord Concerto, with Goldberg Ensemble for Meridan. *Hobby:* Photography. *Address:* 36 Grant Close, Old Hall, Warrington, Cheshire WA5 5QY, England.

FRANCIS Sarah Janet, b. 1935, London, England. Oboist. m. Michael D C Johnson, 2 daughters. *Education:* ARCM, Scholar, Royal College of Music, London; Boise Foundation Scholarship to Pierre Pierlot, Paris, France. *Career:* Principal Oboe BBC Welsh Orchestra; BBC Recitalist; Soloist Chamber Music and Orchestral Player; Professor, Royal College of Music, London; Director London Harpsichord Ensemble; Dedicatee of many concerto and chamber music works. *Recordings:* Britten Metamorphoses, Quartet, Crosse Ariadne; Boccherini Quintets, Decca Argo; Crusell, Reicha Quintets; Howells, Rubbra Sonatas; Rutland Boughton Oboe Concerto, RPO; Mozart & Krommer Concertos, LMP; On Hyperion Bax, Holst Quintets; Moeran, Jacob Quartets, Chandos; Complete Albinoni and Telemann Concetos LHE, Unicorn-Kanchana. *Publications:* Oboe Music to Enjoy, Novas Music. *Honour:* Somerville Prize for Wind instrumenys, RCM, 1959. *Memberships:* British Music Society; Royal Society of Musicians; Incorporated Society of Musicians, BDRS. *Hobbies:* Theatre; Travel; Walking. *Address:* 10 Avenue Road, London N6 5DW, England.

FRANCKE Donald Max, b. 26 Oct 1929, London, England. Singer. m. Margaret Rose Lindsay, 1 son, 1 daughter. *Education:* Harrow; St. Catharine's College, Cambridge University, England; The Royal College of Music. *Debut:* with New Opera Company, Sadler's Wells Theatre. *Career:* Regular Broadcasts for BBC Sound Opera and TV; Recital with Gerald Moore at Wigmore Hall; Editor, Royal College of Music Magazine, 1969-74; Recital with John Ireland Society; Intimate Opera Company; Opera Players; Royal Opera, Covent Garden, London; Scottish National Opera; Phoenix Opera; New Opera Company; Park Lane Opera Company; Welsh National Opera; Opera North; Currently singing lead, Old Deuteronomy, in Andrew Lloyd Webber Musical, Cats, in London's West End; Adjudicator, at all major Festivals in Great Britain, 1969-; Adjudicator in Canada,

Trinidad and Tobago, Hong Kong, Bermuda. *Compositions include:* Mass; Lux et Origo; Anthem and Songs. *Recordings:* with Purcell Singers. *Publications include:* Editor, The Ways and Means of Voice Expression - Dr Arnold Smith, 1974. *Current Management:* Evan Dunstan Associates, 1B Montagu Mews North, London, W1, England. *Address:* Orama House, 263 Sheen Lane, London SW14 8RN, England.

FRANDSEN John, b. 13 Mar 1956, Aalborg, Denmark. Composer and Organist. m. Kirsten Grove, 5 Jan 1985, 1 daughter. *Education:* Aalborghus Statsgymnasium; MA in Music, Aarhus University; Composition, Organ, Royal Academy of Music, Aarhus. *Career:* Organist, Ellevang Church, 1982-84; Organist, Holy Ghost Church, Aarhus, 1984-; Teacher, Aarhus University, 1979-83; Teacher, The Royal Academy of Music, Aarhus, 1980-; Conductor of Cantilena Choir, 1983-. *Compositions:* String song for String Quartet, 1980; Wo Immer Wir Spielen, for mixed choir, 1982; Songs of Innocence for Soprano and Guitar, 1984; Amalie Lever, Opera, 1984; Avers/Revers for Wind Quintet, 1985; Deux Poëmes Sur Le Temps for Mixed Choir, 1985; Amalie Suite, for Chamber Orchestra, 1985; Stabat Mater for Tenor and Organ, 1986; Petite Suite Pour La Guitare for Guitar, 1986; De/Cadences for Wind Quintet, 1987. *Recordings:* Songs of Innocence (Ellen Lunde, Soprano/Erling Møldrup, Guitar, SUDM). *Contributions to:* Organistbladet, Dansk Mussiktidsskrift, *Memberships:* Chairman: Young Nordic Music (Danish Section, 1983-87; Aarhus Unge Tonekunstnere, 1983-; Danish Composers' Society. *Address:* Odinsvej 7, DK-8230 Aabyhøj, Denmark.

FRANK Claude, b. 2 Dec 1925, Nurnberg, Germany. Musician (Pianist). m. 29 Aug 1959, 1 daughter. *Education:* Studies, France & USA with Artur Schnabel, K.U. Schnabel. *Debut:* New York Philharmonic 1959. *Career:* Appearances with most major orchestras including: New York Philharmonic, Boston Symphony, Chicago Symphony, Cleveland Orchestra, Philadelphia Orchestra, Berlin Philharmonic, Concertgebouw, London Symphony, Royal Philharmonic; Performed with Conductors including Bernstein, Giuliui, Leinsdorf, Mehta, Szell, etc.; Tours of Australia, Africa, Israel, Taiwan; Appearances at most major music festivals; Master Classes, etc. *Recordings:* 32 Beethoven Piano Sonatas; Mozart Concertos; Beethoven Trios; Numerous other works. *Contributions to:* Piano Quarterly; Keynote Magazine. *Honours:* Emmy Award Nomination, 1966; Beethoven Society Award, 1979. *Hobbies:* Languages; Sports; Bridge. *Current Management:* Columbia Artists Management Inc. *Address:* 825 West End Avenue, New York, NY 10025, USA.

FRANK Susanne, b. 2 Nov 1962, Switzerland. Violinist. *Education:* Studied at the Winterthur Conservatory in Paris, the International Menuhin Academy in Gstaad. *Career:* 2nd violin of the Carmina Quartet since 1987; Appearances from 1987 in Europe, Israel, Japan and the USA; Regular concerts at the Wigmore Hall from Oct 1987; Concerts at the South Bank Centre, London, Amsterdam Concertgebouw, the Kleine Philharmonie in Berlin, Konzertverein Vienna; Four engagements in Paris, 1990-91, seven in London; Tours to Australasia, USA, Japan and concerts at the Hohenems, Graz, Hong Kong, Montreux, Schleswig Holstein, Bath, Lucerne and Prague Spring Festivals; Collaborations with Dietrich Fischer-Dieskau, Olaf Bär and Mitsuko Uchida. *Recordings:* Albums for Ex Libris, Bayer, Claves and Denon (from 1991). *Honour:* Joint winner (with members of Carmina Quartet) Paolo Borciani String Quartet Competition in Reggio Emilia, Italy, 1987; Gramophone prize for best recording of chamber music, 1992. *Address:* c/o Intermusica Artists' Management, 16 Duncan Terrace, London N1 8BZ, England.

FRANKL Peter, b. 2 Oct 1935, Budapest, Hungary. Pianist. m. Annie Feiner, 1958, 1 son, 1 daughter. *Education:* Franz Liszt Academy of Music, Budapest, 1943-56.*Debut:* London, 1962; USA, 1965. *Career:* Regular concert tours with leading orchestras &

conductors throughout the world; Numerous festival appearances, including Edinburgh, Cheltenham, Lucerne, Flanders, Aldeburgh, Adelaide, Windsor; Piano Trio Performances with György Pauk, violin, and Ralph Kirshbaum, cello; with György Pauk and the Wind Soloists of the Chamber Orchestra of Europe played in Mozart Festival, London, 1991; Played with Tama's Vásáry at the 1993 London Proms, Brahms Liebeslieder and Schubert F minor Fantasia. *Recordings include:* Complete works for piano by Schumann & Debussy; Orchestral & chamber pieces. *Honours:* Winner, international competitions in: Paris, 1957; Munich, 1957; Rio de Janeiro, 1959. Franz Liszt Award, Budapest, 1958, Honorary citizen, Rio de Janeiro, 1960. *Hobbies:* Football; Opera; Theatre. *Address:* 5 Gresham Gardens, London NW11 8NX, England.

FRANKLIN Peter Robert, b. 19 Dec 1947, London, England. University Teacher. *Education:* BA, D Phil, University of York, 1966-72. *Career:* Teacher of Music and German at Harlaxton College, Lincolnshire, 1974-79, and at William Jewell College, Liberty, Missouri, USA, 1979; Lecturer, Department of Music, University of Leeds, 1980-. *Publications:* Edited and annotated: Natalie Bauer-Lechner - Recollections of Gustav Mahler, 1980; Author: The Idea of Music, Schoenberg and Others, 1985. *Contributions to:* Many journals including: The Music Review, Music and Letters, Opera (1992), The Musical Quarterly and The Musical Times on Mahler, Schreker. *Address:* Department of Music, University of Leeds, 14 Cromer Terrace, Leeds, West Yorkshire LS2 9JR, England.

FRANOVA Tatiana, b. 3 Aug 1945, Czechoslovakia. Pianist. m. Eduard Ihring, 20 Aug 1966, 1 daughter. *Education:* Bratislava Conservatoire, 1959-64; The Academy of Music and Dramatic Arts, Bratislava, 1964-69; The Music Academy, Vienna, 1969-73; Postgraduate studies in Bratislava, 1980-83. *Career:* Concert Tours: Austria, Brazil, Cuba, Egypt, France, Germany, Hungary, India, Italy, Luxembourg, Poland, Romania, Spain, Gran Canaria, Switzerland, Sweden, USSR; Professor, Academy of Arts, Cairo, Egypt, 1983-87; Professor of Piano, Academy of Music Arts, Bratislava, 1987-. *Recordings:* 1975: J Brahms: Sonata F sharp minor Op 2; S Rachmaninov: Sonata B minor Op 36; 1978: Etudes - Chopin, Liszt, Scriabin, Rachmaninov; 1982: S Rachmaninov: Concerto No 1, F sharp minor, M De Falla: Nights in the Gardens of Spain; 1991: Complete Work of A Glazunov. *Honours:* 1st prize in the Radio Competition, Young People's Studio, 1964; Silver Medal in International Festival, Bordeaux, 1974; Prize of F Kafenda, 1980. *Membership:* Slovak Music Union. *Hobbies:* Painting; Reading; Travelling. *Current Management:* Slovkoncert. *Address:* Gorkeho 7, 81101 Bratislava, Slovakia.

FRANTZ Justus, b. 18 May 1944, Hohensalza, Germany. Pianist. *Education:* Hamburg Hochschule für Musik, with Eliza Hansen; Wilhelm Kempff in Positano. *Career:* European concerts from 1960; Mozart Concerto series with Karajan and the Berlin Philharmonic; US debut 1975 with the New York Philharmonic under Bernstein; later performances in New York and Washington with Kempe, Giulini and Haitink; 1983 tour of US, Japan and Europe with pianist Christoff Eschenbach; Professor, Hamburg Musikhochschule, 1985-; Founded Schleswig-Holstein Music Festival, 1986; performed the Beethoven Concertos, 1988; performed complete cycle of Mozart concerti in several European cities, season, 1987-88. *Recordings:* Concertos by Dvořák and Schumann under Bernstein; Duos by Mozart and Schubert with Eschenbach; Bach Concerti for Deutsche Grammophon, 1985; Mozart concerti for two and three pianos with Eschenbach, Helmut Schmidt and the London Philharmonic. *Address:* c/o Anglo-Swiss Artists Management, 4/5 Primrose Mews, 1a Sharpleshall Street, London NW1 8YW, England.

FRANZEN Olov Alfred, b. 22 Jan 1946, Umeå, Sweden. Composer; Cellist. m. Ingeborg Axner, 12 Nov 1977. *Education:* Stockholm Music Academy, 1966-73;

Music Teacher Examination, 1970; Cello with Gunnar Norrby, 1966-72; Composition with Ingvar Lidholm, 1969-73. *Debut:* As composer: A Wind Quintet in Lund, 1963; as Cellist, 1971, Nyström. *Career:* Cellist in Norrkoping Symphony Orchestra, 1971-72; Harpans Kraft, Stockholm, 1971-77; Since 1977-92 freelance in Härnösand and founder of the ensemble HND; From 1992 freelance in Skokloster; Has played with Harpans Kraft and HND in Sweden, Finland and Austria on radio, Swedish TV-Film Sundcreme with Harpans Kraft, 1976; Compositions played in all Nordic countries, France, West and East Germany, Czechoslovakia, USA and Canada; cellist in the Sundsvall Chamber Orchestra, 1983-90; Teacher of composition at Kapellsberg Music School, Härnösand, 1983-92; In 1986 started Faimo Edition for publishing music scores and recordings. *Compositions include:* Cytoplasma, song, piano, 1968; Saiva, Symphony Orchestra, 1972; Fiesta, percussion ensemble, 1982; The Vacuum State, Symphony Orchestra, 1983; Har, soprano harp, 1983; Intenso, string orchestra, 1984; From the Junction Point, bassoon, live electronics, 1985; Der vater gebirt sinen sun, mezzo soprano, flute, violon-cello, 1986; Suite for three flutes, 1986; Heptyk, for saxophone quartet 1987; Agnim, for symphony orchestra, 1987; Death and Entrances, mixed choir, 1988; It's getting sunny, Brass Band, 1988; Concert Overture, symphony orchestra, 1989; Purity 6.5, clarinet, violin, violoncello, piano, 1990; Gaps, violin, piano, 1990; In Memoriam 1791 sopra Requiem di Mozart, 10 winds, 1991. *Address:* Abbotvägen 18, Skokloster, S-746 95 BÅLSTA, Sweden.

FRASER Malcolm Henry, b. 1 Aug 1939, Kingston upon Thames, England. Opera Director. m. 25 Apr 1964, 4 sons. *Education:* Surbiton County Grammar School. *Career:* Associate Director, Lincoln Repertory, 1966-68; Resident Director, Welsh National Opera Company, 1968-76; Senior Lecturer, Royal Northern College of Music, 1976-87; Founder, Artistic Director, Buxton International Festival, 1979-87; J. Ralph Corbett Distinguished Professor of Opera, University of Cincinnati, 1987-; Guest Director: London Opera Centre, New Sadler's Wells Opera, Portland Opera, Seattle Opera, Calgary Opera, Edmonton Opera, Virginia Opera, Arkansas Opera; permanent Guest Director, Arkansas Opera, 1988-; Associate Artistic Director, Buxton International Festival, 1988-; Florenetine Opera of Milwaukee. *Honours:* Kodály Medal, Hungarian Government, 1982; Prague International TV Festival Prize for Mise-en-Scene, 1975; Churchill Fellow, 1969. *Address:* College Conservatory of Music, University of Cincinnati, Cincinnati, OH 45221, USA.

FRECCIA Massimo, b. 19 Sept 1906, Florence, Italy. (American). Conductor. *Education:* Cherubini Royal Conservatoire, Florence. *Career:* Guest Conductor, New York Philharmonic Orchestra, 1938, 1939, 1940; Musical Director, Conductor, Havana Philharmonic Orchestra, 1939-43, New Orleans Symphony Orchestra, 1944-52, Baltimore Symphony Orchestra, 1952-59; Chief Conductor, Rome (RAI) Orchestra, 1959-65; Frequent appearances as guest conductor of famous orchestras in Europe, and US; Tours in Australia, 1963, Japan, 1967, South Africa, 1969; Appearances at various International Festivals including, Vienna, Prague, Berlin, Lisbon, Montreux. *Honours:* Hon DMus, Tulane University, New Orleans; Order of the Star of Italian Solidarity. *Recordings include:* Symphonies by Haydn, Mozart and Mendelssohn, with the Santa Celicia Orchestra; Shostakovich 5th Symphony and Symphonie Fantastique, Royal Philharmonic.

FREDIN Thorvald, b. 28 Feb 1928, Soderhamn, Sweden. Double Bassist. m. Gunnel Johanson, 28 Sept 1957, 1 daughter. *Education:* Royal Academy of Music, Stockholm; Akademie fur Musik und Dahrstellende Kunst, Vienna. *Career:* Stockholm's Royal Court Orchestra, 1952, principal Double Bass, 1958; Toured Europe, North America and USSR; Principal player, Theatre of Drottningholm, 1952-1974, touring to Versailles and Brighton, 1972-73; Co-Founder, Stockholm Chamber Orchestra, 1952 and Stockholm Sinfonietta, 1980, Royal Court Chamber Orchestra,

1986; Professor, Academy of Music, Stockholm, 1961-; Double Bass Coach, National Youth Orchestra of Canada, 1980-. *Recordings:* Solo pieces for Double Bass and piano; concertos for Double Bass; Double-Bass School, 1969, updated, 1989. *Memberships:* Fellow, Royal Academy of Music. *Hobbies:* Chess; Fishing; Avid berry and mushroom picker. *Address:* Norlindsvagen 9, 161 52 Bromma, Sweden.

FREDMAN Myer, b. 29 Jan 1932, Plymouth, Devon, England. Conductor. m. Jeanne Winfield, 26 Aug 1954, 2 sons. *Education:* Torquay Grammar School; Dartington Hall; The Opera School, London. *Debut:* Cork. *Career:* Glyndebourne Festival (Operas by Mozart, Verdi, Maw and Von Einem); Glyndebourne Touring Opera, 1968-74; State Opera of South Australia; Seymour Group; Guest Conductor throughout Europe, America, Australia; BBC TV; Wexford Festival; Perth Festival; Adelaide Festival; Hong Kong Fest; Poland; Belgium; Romania; Germany; conducted Cavalli's L'Ormindo, Brussels, 1972; Bizet's Carmen, Hamburg 1973 and Il Barbiere di Siviglia, Sydney 1974; Season 1992 with La Bohème for the Canadian Opera Company at Toronto and Le Nozze di Figaro in Sydney; Head of Opera at the New South Wales Conservatorium, 1981-92 (premiere of Lawrence Hargrave by Nigel Butterfly, 1988); Associate Artist, The Australian Opera, 1991-; Concert debut, South America (Montevideo and Buenos Aries), 1992; Conducted Australian premiers of Midsummer Marriage Death in Venice and One Man Show. *Recordings:* Bax Symphonies 1/2 LPO, No. 3 Sydney Symphony; H. Brian Symphonies 16/22 LPO; Delius Paradise Garden LPO; Benjamin Overture To An Italian Comedy; Respighi Sinfonia Drammatica/Piano Concerto, Sydney Symphony; Puccini Le Villi, Adelaide Symphony. *Honours:* Bronze Medal by Italian Government, 1965. *Current Management:* Jenifer Eddy, Australia. *Hobbies:* Walking; Theatre; Scrabble. *Address:* 7/16 Rose Street, Birchgrove, New South Wales 2041, Australia.

FREED Dorothy Whitson, b. 10 Feb 1919, Dunedin, New Zealand. Retired Librarian and Musician. m. 19 Nov 1940, 1 son, 2 daughters. *Education:* Victoria University of Wellington, 1952-57; MusB, 1958; New Zealand Library School, 1959-60; Composition study with Peter Racine Fricker, London, 1964-65, Elizabeth Lutyens, 1965. *Career:* Composer, mainly unpublished music for local stage choirs, small orchestras, chamber groups, singers, 1957; Works performed publicly and broadcast on Radio New Zealand's concert programmes, 1957-; Reference Librarian, Victoria University of Wellington, 1968-85; Work to improve music in New Zealand libraries, including establishment of Music Section, National Library of New Zealand, 1971-; Founded New Zealand branch, International Association of Music Libraries, 1982. *Compositions:* Whence comes this rush of wings afar, carol for women's voices, published 1967, recorded 1964; Published: Nursery Tale for Brass Quintet, 1980; The Chinese Terracotta Soldiers, piano solo, 1985; The Sea Child, Kowhai, solo songs, 1994. *Publications:* Music for amateur choirs and orchestras in New Zealand, 1960; Orchestral scores: a finding list...in some New Zealand musical societies and libraries (with Gerald Seaman), 1978, 1983; Directory of New Zealand music organisation, 1983, 1986; Contributor to Groves Dictionary, 6th edition. *Contributions:* Frequent to: Fonts arts musicae; Crescendo: Canzona. *Honours:* Australian Performing Right Association and Radio New Zealand Prize, New Zealand ballad, 1958; Philip Neill Memorial Prize, woodwind quintet, University of Otago, 1959; Services to Music Award, Australasian Performing Right Association, 1980; Lilburn Trust Award, Services to Music, 1991. *Memberships:* Full Composer Member, Australasian Performing Right Society; Composers Association of New Zealand; New Zealand Library Association; International Association of Music Libraries, New Zealand. *Hobbies:* Swimming; Travel; Writing; Listening to music. *Address:* 48 Standen Street, Karori, Wellington 5, New Zealand.

FREED Richard D(onald), b. 27 Dec 1928, Chicago,

Illinois, USA. Music Critic; Annotator; Broadcaster. *Education:* University of Chicago, graduated 1947. *Career:* Contributor, Saturday Review, 1959- 71; Critic, New York Times, 1965-66; Assistant to the Director, Eastman School of Music, 1966-70; Contributing Editor, Stereo Review, 1973-; Opus, 1984-86; Record Critic, Washington Star, 1972-75; Washington Post, 1976-84; WETA-FM Radio, Washington, DC, 1985-; National Public Radio, 1986-92; New York Times, 1989-92; Programme Annotator, St Louis Symphony Orchestra, 1973-; Philadelphia Orchestra, 1974-84; Houston Symphony Orchestra, 1977-80; National Symphony Orchestra, Washington, DC, 1977-; Baltimore Symphony Orchestra, 1984-92; Executive Director, Music Critics Association, 1974-90; Consultant to the Music Director, National Symphony Orchestra, 1981- . *Honours:* ASCAP-Deems Taylor Awards, 1984, 1986, Life Member Music Critics Association. *Address:* 6201 Tuckerman Lane, Rockville, MD 20852, USA.

FREEDMAN Harry, b. 5 Apr 1922, Lodz, Poland. Composer. m. Mary Louise Freedman, 15 Sept 1951, 3 daughters. *Education:* Senior Matriculation, St John's High School, Winnipeg, Manitoba, 1938; Winnipeg School of Art, 1936-40; Royal Conservatory of Music, Toronto, 1945-50; Tanglewood Music Centre, 1949. *Career:* English Horn, Toronto Symphony Orchestra, 1946-70; Host, Junior Round-Up, Music Segment, CBC-TV, 1958-60; Host, CBC Thursday Music, 1967-69; Many guest appearances in television and radio. *Compositions:* Tableau; Images; 3 Symphonies; 9 Ballets; 2 String Quartets; Numerous Orchestral Works, Chamber Works, Choral works, Song cycles; Scores for films, television, theatrical and radio; 1 act opera, Abracadabra. *Recordings:* Images, Columbia, Toronto, Symphony, Ozawa; Tangents, CBC, Vancouver Symphony, Akiyama; The Flame Within, Decca Festival Singers, Iseler; Poems of Young People, CBC, Maureen Forrester. *Hobbies:* Golf; Painting. *Address:* 35 St Andrew's Gardens, Toronto, Ontario, Canada, M4W 2C9.

FREEGARD Michael John, b. 3 Mar 1933, London, England. Manager. *Education:* Fellow, Institute of Chartered Secretaries and Administrators; Haileybury and Imperial Service College, 1947-50. *Career:* Joined Head Office Staff, The Performing Right Society, London as Assistant Secretary, Nov 1964, Appointed Secretary, July 1966, Deputy General Manager, 1968, General Manager, 1969, Chief Executive, July 1980, retired, 1993; Radio appearances; Lectures, Great Britain, France, Commonwealth, USA. *Contributions to:* Numerous articles on questions relating to copyright in newspapers and magazines and other publications in Britain, Commonwealth and USA. *Honours:* Honorary member, Royal Society of Musicians, 1975; Order of Arts and Sciences, (Egypt) 1976; Honorary member, Royal Northern College of Music, 1991. *Memberships include:* Executive Bureau and Administrative Council of Confédération Internationale des Sociétes d'Auteurs et Compositeurs, 1969-1993, President of its Executive Bureau, 1972-75; Vice-President, Association Littéraire et Artistique Internationale, 1981-91. *Address:* 15 Highgate Close, Highgate, London N6 4SD, England.

FREEMAN Carroll Benton, b. 16 Dec 1951, Memphis, Tennessee, USA. Tenor. m. Elizabeth Kay Pashal, 31 May 1975. *Debut:* First Spirit in The Magic Flute, New York City Opera, 1966. *Career:* Opera: New York City; Houston; Miami; St Louis; Kentucky; Michigan; Minnesota; Portland; Kansas City; Columbus; Toledo; Fort Worth; Dallas; Texas; Philadelphia; Boston; Tulsa; Omaha, Mobile; Long Beach; Mississippi; Arizona; Festivals: Edinburgh; Lake George; Chautauqua; Central City; Castle Hill; Saratoga Springs; Symphony: Dallas; St Louis; Houston; Minnesota; St Paul Chamber; National; New York Philharmonic; Little Orchestra Society; Kansas City; Toronto; Philadelphia; Portland (Maine); Delaware; Victoria (Texas); Spokane; Musica Sacra; Chautauqua; Artistic Director, Mississippi Opera and Artistic Director, Opera in the Ozarks at Inspiration Point. *Recordings:* Don Giovanni, by Plaza Media Munich, Germany & released as video-cassette by London Records; Joruri, Japanese premiere, released as laser-disc & video-cassette by Dream Corporation, Tokyo, Japan and HMS Gilbert & Sullivan, CD of Highlights from HMS Pinafore, The Pirates of Penzance and The Mikado released by ProArte. *Hobbies:* Art; Water sports. *Address:* 5801 Lumberdale Road No.155, Houston, TX 77092, USA.

FREEMAN David, b. 1 May 1952, Sydney, Australia. Stage Director. m. Marie Angel. *Career:* Founded Opera Factory in Sydney 1973 and in Zurich 1976 (20 Swiss productions); Productions for Opera Factory in London (founded 1981) have included The Knot Garden, Punch and Judy, The Beggar's Opera, Cavalli's La Calisto, Birtwistle's Yan Tan Tethera (world premiere 1986); Eight Songs for a Mad King by Peter Maxwell Davies, Ligeti's Aventures/Nouvelles Aventures and Reimann's The Ghost Sonata; Mozart's three Da Ponte operas presented at the Elizabeth Hall as part of the bicentenary celebrations; Has also produced Osborne's Hells Angels; Founded Opera Factory Films in 1991; Directed Prokofiev's The Fiery Angel for Marinsky Theatre, St Petersburg, Covent Garden and The Metropolitan, New York; Operas by Birtwistle, Maxwell Davies, Ligeti and Mozart have been shown on BBC and Channel 4 television; For English National Opera has produced Orfeo, Akhnaten by Glass (British premiere), The Mask of Orpheus (world premiere), and The Return of Ulysses; Productions elsewhere have included La Bohème for Opera North, Manon Lescaut at the Opéra-Comique Paris and work in Germany, Houston and New York. *Honour:* Chevalier dans l'Ordre des Arts er Lettres, 1985. *Current Management:* Allied Artists. *Address:* c/o Opera Factory, 8a The Leather Market, Weston Street, London, SE1 3ER, England.

FREEMAN Paul (Douglas), b. 2 Jan 1936, Richmond, Virginia, USA. Conductor. m. Cornelia Perry. 1 son. *Education:* Received lessons in piano, clarinet and cello; BMus 1956, MMus 1957, PhD 1963, Eastman school of Music; Berlin Hochschule für Musik, 1957-59; Studied conducting with Richard Lert and Pierre Monteux. *Career:* Director, Hochstein Music School, Rochester, NY, 1960-66; Music Director, Opera Theater, Rochester, 1961-66; Director, San Francisco Community Music Center, 1966-68; Conductor, San Francisco Conservatory Orchestra, 1966-67; Music Director, San Francisco Little Symphony Orchestra, 1967-68; Associate Conductor, Dallas Symphony Orchestra, 1968-70; Resident Conductor, Detroit Symphony Orchestra, 1970-79; Principal Guest Conductor, Helsinki Philharmonic Orchestra, 1974-76; Music Director, Victoria (BC) Symphony Orchestra, 1979-; Chicago Sinfonietta, 1987-; Guest Conductor, North America and Europe. *Recordings:* For Columbia, Fanfare, Finlandia, Laurel, Orion, Seraphin, Spectrum and Vox. *Address:* c/o Victoria Symphony Orchestra, 631 Superior Street, Victoria, British Columbia V8V 1V1, Canada.

FREEMAN Robert S., b. 26 Aug 1935, Rochester, NY, USA. Pianist; Musicologist; Music School Director. m. Carol M Henry, 10 Dec 1976, 2 sons, 1 daughter. *Education:* BA, Harvard, 1957; MFA, 1960, PhD, 1967, Princeton University; Longy School of Music, Tanglewood; Kneisel Hall, Marlboro. *Recordings:* David Epstein, The Seasons; Robert Schumann, Andante and Variations, Opus 46; Anthology of early 20th-century conversational duets, Cuddle up a little Closer. *Publications:* Opera without Drama, 1981; Notenband and Kritischer Bericht for Bach Cantata 176 in vol 1/15 of the Neue Bach Ausgabe, 1971. Articles in JAMS, MQ, Notes, MEJ and in Festschrifts honoring Oliver Strunk and Arthur Mendel. *Memberships:* AMS; IMS; CMS; NASM: Neue Bach Gesellschaft. *Hobbies:* Reading; Hiking; Animal welfare. *Address:* Eastman School of Music, 26 Gibbs Street, Rochester NY 14604, USA.

FREIMANIS Walter John, b. 6 May 1937, Goldingen, Latvia. Cellist; Composer; Educator. m. Edith Freimanis, 12 June 1983. *Education:* New School of Music, Philadelphia, 1956-58; Curtis Institute of Music,

Philadelphia, 1958-60; BM, MM, Manhattan School of Music, 1960-65; Studied with bassist Roger Scott and cellist Benar Heifetz, Bernard Greenhouse and William Stokking. *Career:* Professor of Music, Music Department, State University College at Oswego, New York, 1965-; Concert Cellist, solo and recital appearances, USA and Canada; Former Member of Sheldon String Trio; Former Conductor, College Community Orchestra; Member of Vahana Duo with Harvey Jacobson; Soloist with Marlboro Festival; Participant, Casals competition, Budapest, Hungary, 1968; Librettist for Sherwood Shaffer's opera A Winter's Tale; Lecturer on dreams, creativity, soul travel and ECKANKAR New Age Religion. *Address:* 130 East 7th St, Oswego, NY 13126, USA.

FREITAG Erik, b. 1 Feb 1940, Vienna, Austria. Composer; Violin Teacher. *Education:* Diploma, Academy of Music, Vienna. *Career:* With Radio Sweden, 1964-66; Violinist, Philharmonic Orchestra, Stockholm, 1967-70; Teacher, Conservatory of Vienna, 1970-. *Compositions:* Suite for Orchestra; Overture Danoise; 2 pieces for Strings; Music in memory of a great artist; Quintet, Cello sonata, Helle Nacht, for strings, Reflections in Air violin, viola, violoncello, Symphony Nocturnes. *Recordings:* For Radio - 3 pieces for String Quartet; Divertimento for Wind Quintet; Limericks, 5 songs for medium voice and 6 instruments; Elegie und Tanz, Oboe and string quartet; Quasi una Marcia, for 15 players; Nachtstücke for violin and viola; for radio: Passages in the Wind; CD, Helle Nacht for strings; CD, sonata for cello and piano. *Address:* Schippergasse 20, A-1210 Vienna, Austria.

FRÉMAUX Louis Joseph Felix, b. 13 Aug 1921, Aire-sur-Lys, France. Orchestral Conductor. *Education:* Conservatoire National Supérieur de Musique, Paris. *Career:* Musical Director and Permanent Conductor of Orchestre National de l'Opéra de Monte-Carlo, Monaco, 1955-66; Principal Conductor, Rhones-Alpes Philharmonic Orchestra, Lyons, 1968-71; Principal Conductor and Musical Director, City of Birmingham Symphony Orchestra, 1969-78; Particularly known for performances of Berlioz; Chief Conductor, Sydney Symphony Orchestra, 1979-81, Principal Guest Conductor, 1982-85; Guest appearances in Austria, Belgium, Holland, France, Italy, New Zealand, Norway, Switzerland, South America and Germany; Has premiered Panufnik's Sinfonia Sacra, 1964, McCabe's 2nd Symphony, 1971, and Columbia Falls by Nicola Le Fanu, 1975. *Recordings include:* French Baroque music by Gilles, De La Lande, Rameau, Campra, Mouret and Charpentier; Poulenc Stabat Mater and La Bal Masqué; Berlioz Grande Messe des Morts and overtures, Bizet Symphony, Saint-Saëns 3rd Symphony; Poulenc Les Biches, Piano Concerto and Gloria; Symphonie Fantastique; Rimsky's Scheherazade. *Honours:* 8 Grand Prix du Disque Awards; Koussevitsky Award. *Address:* Christopher Tennant Management, Unit 2, 39 Tadema Road, London, SW10 0PY.

FRENI Mirella, b. 27 Feb 1935, Modena, Italy. Opera Singer (Soprano). m. (1) Leone Magiera, 1955, 1 daughter, (2) Nicolai Ghiarouv. *Debut:* 1955, at Modena, as Micaela. *Career:* Glyndebourne Festival, 1961; Royal Opera House, Covent Garden, 1961; Metropolitan Opera House, New York, 1965; Appearances at Vienna State Opera and Salzburg Festival and in leading opera houses throughout the world; Major roles include, Nannetta in Falstaff, Mimi in La Bohème, Zerlina in Don Giovanni, Susanna, Adina in L'elisir d'amore; Violetta in La Traviata, Desdemona in Otello, centenary performance at La Scala, 1987; Grand Opera Houston, 1987, as Aida; marked 35th anniversary of debut in 1990 at Modena, as Manon Lescaut; Gala concert with the Boston Opera/Boston Symphony 1990; Gran Teatre del Liceo Barcelona, 1989, as Tatyana and Adriana Lecouvreur, Manon Lescaut, 1990; La Scala Milan, 1990, as Lisa in The Queen of Spades; Sang Alice Ford at the Metropolitan, 1992; Rome Opera and Barcelona 1992 as Mimi. *Recordings include:* Carmen, Falstaff; La Bohème, Madame Butterfly, Alcina, Tosca, Guillaume Tell; Verdi Requiem, Simon Boccanegra; Don Carlos,

Aida, Faust, Turandot, L'Amico Fritz, Don Giovanni L'Elisir d'Amore; Le Nozze di Figaro and Don Giovanni; Video of Madame Butterfly (Decca). *Address:* c/o John Coast Concerts, 31 Sinclair Road, London WC4 ONS, England.

FRENKLOVA Jana, b. 17 Sept 1947, Prague, Czechoslovakia. Pianist. 1 daughter. *Education:* Prague Conservatoire, 1962-67, Honours Graduate; Leningrad Conservatoire, 1967-68 (studies curtailed after Russian invasion of Czechoslovakia). *Debut:* Prague, 1956. *Career:* Pianist-in-Residence, Lancaster University, 1975-79; Pianist-in-Residence, University College of North Wales, 1979-; Recording Artist for BBC Radio 3, 1977-. *Honours:* Numerous first prizes in Czechoslovakia up to 1968; Finalist, Alfredo Casella Competition, Naples, 1970; Winner, Dudley Competition, 1971. *Hobby:* Enjoying rural peace. *Current Management:* Encore Concerts. *Address:* Maen Hir Bach, Dwyran, Anglesey, Gwynedd LL61 6UU, North Wales.

FRETWELL Elizabeth, b. 13 Aug 1920, Melbourne, Australia. Operatic Soprano, Adjudicator and Vocal Consultant. m. Robert Simmons, 1 son, 1 daughter. *Career:* Joined National Theatre, Melbourne, 1950; Came to Britain, 1955; Joined Sadler's Wells, 1956, Elizabethan Opera Company, Australia, 1963; Tours, West Germany 1963, USA, Canada & Covent Garden 1964, Europe 1965. Guest soprano with Cape Town & Durban Opera Companys, South Africa, 1970; Joined Australian Opera, 1970. *Roles include:* Violetta/La Traviata; Leonore/Fidelio; Ariadne/Ariadne auf Naxos; Senta/Flying Dutchman; Minnie/Girl of the Golden West; Leonora/Il Trovatore; Aida; Ellen Orford/Peter Grimes; Leonora/Forza del Destino; Alice Ford/Falstaff; Amelia/Masked Ball; Giorgetta/Il Tabarro, opening season, Sydney Opera House, 1973. Has sung in BBC Promenade Concerts, and on TV. *Recordings:* Il Trovatore, Verdi; Land of Smiles, Lehar. *Honour:* Order of British Empire, 1977. *Membership:* Music board, Australian Opera Foundation, 1982-. *Address:* 47 Kananook Av Bayview, NSW. 2104 Australia.

FREUDENTHAL Otto, b. 29 July 1934, Gothenburg, Sweden. Composer; Pianist; Violist. 1 son. *Education:* TCL, England; Studied piano with Ilona Kabos. *Debut:* (as pianist) Wigmore Hall, London. *Career:* Recitals and Concerts in Great Britain, Germany, Switzerland, Netherlands, Scandinavia and Japan; Broadcasts; Teacher, Royal College of Music, Manchester; Assistant to Dr Otto Klemperer to 1973. *Compositions:* Chamber music, viola concerto, concert piece for trombone and orchestra; In Highgate Cemetery for strings; Chamber opera; A BankoMat cantata; The Song About Our Town; a cantata to Linkopings 700 year jubilee; Symphony, 1989; String Quartet, 1991; Saxophone Quartet, 1992. *Recording:* Coliseum records, BBC, Swedish Radio; CD Wir Wandelten, with Cheryl Jonsson, soprano, WANDA CD. *Publication:* (essay) Music and Equity (with Irene Lotz); Chamber Music with Wollenweber Edition, Munich. *Honours include:* Harriet Cohen Memorial Medal for interpretation of Beethoven; Swedish State Cultural Stipend, 1977, 1987. *Memberships:* Swedish Society of Composers, STIM. *Address:* Västanâgatan 25, 58235 Linköping, Sweden.

FREY Paul, b. 1942, Heidelberg, Toronto, Canada. Singer (Tenor). *Education:* Studied at the Toronto Conservatory with Louis Quilico. *Career:* Played professional ice hockey until retirement through injury; Sang at first in concert then appeared in Toronto as Werther; Member of the Basle Opera from 1978, notably in operas by Strauss and Wagner; Sang Lohengrin at Karlsruhe 1985, Florestan at Heidelberg 1984-85; Guest appearances at Mannheim and Lyon; Bayreuth Festival 1987-89, as Lohengrin; Munich Festival 1986 and 1988, as Apollo in Daphne and Midas in Die Liebe der Danae; Metropolitan Opera debut 1987, as Bacchus in Ariadne auf Naxos; Karlsruhe and Santiago 1988, as Lohengrin and Walther von Stolzing; La Scala Milan 1989, as Huon in Oberon; Has also sung in Tel-Aviv and Sydney (Walther, 1988); Cologne Opera 1990-91, as Siegmund in Die Walküre; Other roles include Parsifal, Peter Grimes, Flamand in Capriccio, the Emperor in Die Frau ohne Schatten and Mozart's Don Ottavio and Titus; Sang Siegmund at Bonn, 1992. *Recordings include:* Die Frau ohne Schatten (EMI); Ariadne auf Naxos conducted by Kurt Masur. *Address:* Theateragentur Dr. Germinal Hilbert, Maximilianstrasse 22, D-8000 Müchen, Germany.

FREY-RABINE Lia, b. 12 Aug 1950, Crosby, Minnesota, USA. Opera Singer; Dramatic Soprano. m. Eugene Rabine, 27 June 1976, 1 son. *Education:* BMus, MMus, Indiana University, Bloomington; Private Vocal Studies with Eugene Rabine, Founder & Director of the Rabine Institute for Functional Voice Pedagogy, Bönstadt, Germany. *Debut:* Municipal Theatre, Bern, Switzerland, 1973. *Career:* Principal Singer, Bern, Switzerland, 1973-75; Flensburg, 1975-77; Nürnberg, 1977-79; Hagen, 1979-84; Frankfurt, 1984-; Guest Appearances in numerous other German, Austrian and Swiss Theatres and in Barcelona, Ghent, Rome, Naples, Vienna State Opera and other European Cities; Sang the Siegfried Brünnhilde at Dortmund, 1991. *Honours:* Metropolitan Opera Auditions National Finalist, 1971; Outstanding Musician of 1983, The State of Nordrhein-Westfalen. *Hobbies:* Baking; Cooking; Children's activities. *Current Management:* Kühnly Agency, Stuttgart, Germany. *Address:* Kleinstr 6, 61194 Niddatal-2, Germany.

FREYER Achim, b. 30 Mar 1934, Berlin, Germany. Stage Director; Theatre Designer. *Education:* Studied at the Akademie der Kunste, East Berlin. *Debut:* Designed sets and costumes for the Ruth Berghaus production of Il barbiere di Siviglia at the Berlin Staatsoper, 1967. *Career:* Emigrated to the West, 1973, and created designs for Cardillac and Pelleas et Melisande at the Cologne Opera, 1973-75; Directed and designed Iphigénie en Tauride at the Munich Staatsoper 1979 (seen at Amsterdam and Basle, 1990); Philip Glass' Satyagraha and the premiere of Akhnaten at the Stuttgart Staatsoper (1981, 1984); Orfeo ed Euridice at the Deutsche Oper Berlin, 1982, Die Zauberflöte at Hamburg (seen at the Vienna Festival, 1991); Iphigénie en Tauride at the Deutsche Staatsoper, 1994. *Address:* c/o Deutsche Staatsoper, Unter den Linden 7, 1086 Berlin, Germany.

FREYHAN Michael, b. 31 Aug 1940, London, England. Performer; Writer; Lecturer. *Education:* Violin player 1954-59, Leader 1956-59, National Youth Orchestra; King's College, Cambridge University, 1958-62. BA; MA(Cantab); LRAM. *Debut:* Wigmore Hall, 1963. *Career:* Piano: Soloist, with George Malcolm, Royal Festival Hall, 1966; Chamber music tours, British & American musicians, Europe, Australasia, North & South America, 1969-; Numerous broadcasts, radio & television. Harpsichord & Organ: Continuo, with London Bach Society, London Festival Orchestra. Violin, Viola: With London Mozart Players, 1964-73. Guest Lecturer: Universities of Stanford, Harvard, Princeton, New York, London, Cambridge, Leipzig, 1984-. *Compositions:* Toy Symphony; Piano reduction, Recorder Concerto in G Major, by Anton Heberle. *Recordings:* Spohr Trios Nos. 1 & 2, with Frances Mason (violin) & Joy Hall (cello); Schubert Violin Sonatinas, with F. Mason (violin). Both recordings feature Broadwood piano of 1823. *Contributions to:* Journal, American Musicological Society; The Strad; London correspondent 1987-, numerous articles, Strings. *Memberships:* Incorporated Society of Musicians; Musicians Union. *Hobby:* Travel. *Address:* 15 Chelmsford Square, London NW10 3AP, England.

FRIBBINS Peter, b. 4 June 1969, London, England. Composer. *Education:* Royal Academy of Music, 1987-90, studied with Hans Werner Henze; BMus, London, and LRAM, 1990; MMus, University of London, 1992. *Career:* Opera Anna Bella, 1989 Montepulciano Festival, Italy; Tutor, London University. *Compositions include:* 3 Elegies; Horn Concerto; Pavane for Brass; Guitar Concertino; Inferno; Opera Anna Bella; Wind Quintet In Xanadu; String quartet, I have the serpent brought;

Two songs, Nocturne. *Recordings include:* London Cantilena quintet play In Xanadu; Serendipity, 1992. *Publications:* Articles in the Classical Music magazine and Composers Guild Journal. *Honours:* Runner-up, Royal Philharmonic Society Prize, (composition), 1991. *Memberships:* Composers Guild of Great Britain; Performing Rights Society; MCPS. *Hobbies:* Tennis; Walking; Genealogy. *Address:* 64 Courtlands Close, Watford, Herts WD2 5GT, England.

FRICK Gottlob, b. 28 July 1908, Olbronn, Germany. Singer (Bass). *Education:* Studied at the Stuttgart Conservatory and with Neudorfer-Opitz. *debut:* Coburg 1934, as Wagner's Daland. *Career:* Sang at Freiburg and Konigsberg 1934-39; Member of the Dresden Staatsoper 1939-50, taking part in the premieres of Die Zauberinsel by Sutermeister 1942 and Die Hochzeit des Jobs by Haas 1944; also sang Gremin, Rocco, Nicolai's Falstaff and bass roles by Wagner; Stadtische Oper Berlin 1950; Covent Garden 1951-71, notably as Hunding, Hagen, Gurnemanz, Daland and Rocco; Salzburg Festival 1955-60, as Sarastro and the Commendatore, in Pfitzner's Palestrina and in the premiere of Egk's Irische Legende 1955; Bayreuth Festival 1957-64, as Pogner and in Der Ring des Nibelungen; Metropolitan Opera 1961, as Fafner; Regular appearances in Munich and Vienna. *Recordings:* Fidelio, Die Entführung, Lohengrin, Die Meistersinger, Die Zauberflöte, Tannhäuser, Der Freischütz (EMI); Parsifal and Der Ring des Nibelungen. *Address:* c/o Bayerische Staatsoper, Postfach 745, D-8000 Munich 1, Germany.

FRIED Joel Ethan, b. 22 Apr 1954, California, USA. Conductor. m. Mary Anne Massad, 9 Dec 1990, 1 step-daughter. *Education:* BMus, 1973; MMus, Piano Performance, DMA, 1979, University of Southern California. *Debut:* Hidden Valley Opera, 1978; Europe: Heidelberg Castle Festival, 1981. *Career:* Assistant Conductor, NY City Opera, 1980-82; Studienleiter, Saarland State Theater, 1983-86; Chorus Master, Cleveland Opera, 1990-92; Chorus Master and Music Administrator, Pittsburgh Opera, 1992-; Resident Conductor, Heidelberg Castle Festival, 1981-; Conducting appearances with Zurich Opera, Fort Worth Opera, and Cleveland Opera. *Honours:* Second Prize, American Conductors' Competition, 1978; Special Prize for contemporary Music, Hans Swarowsky International Conducting Competition, Vienna, 1984. *Address:* c/o Pittsburgh Opera, 711 Penn Avenue, Pittsburgh, PA 15222, USA.

FRIED Miriam, b. 9 Sept 1946, Satu-Mare, Rumania. Violinist. *Education:* Rubin Academy of Music, Tel Aviv, Israel; Graduate studies, Europe & USA (Juilliard School, Ivan Galamian). *Debut:* Carnegie Hall, New York, USA, 1969; Royal Festival Hall, UK. *Career:* Appearances, orchestras worldwide including: Boston Symphony; Los Angeles Philharmonic; Philadelpia, Cleveland, Chicago Symphonies; New York Philharmonic; Berlin & Munich Philharmonics; Vienna Symphony; Zurich Tonhalle; Orchestre Nationale de France. Recent appearances include: Stuttgart Radio Orchestra (conducted Neville Marriner); Danish Radio (Kurt Sanderling); Jerusalem Symphony at Berlin Festival; Orchestre Nationale, Belgium; Philharmonic Orchestras, Monte Carlo, Stuttgart, Nuremburg; Nouvel Orchestre Philharmonique, Paris; Opened Helsinki Festival (with Helsinki Philharmonic, conducted Gennadi Rozhdestvensky), 1988; Hollywood Bowl (Yuri Temirkanov), 1988; Cleveland Orchestra (Mariss Jansons), 1989; Santa Cecilia (Yuri Temirkanov), 1989; Orchestre de Paris (Kurt Sanderling), 1989; American engagments for 1994-95: Chicago Symphony Orchestra, Cleveland Orchestra, Boston Symphony Orchestra, Philadelphia Orchestra; Frequent engagements, Royal Philharmonic Orchestra; BBC TV, & Promenade Concerts; Edinburgh Festival; Scottish National Orchestra; Bournemouth Symphony; Numerous recitals. *Recordings:* Recital LP, Deutsche Grammophon; Solo violin works, Bach; Sibelius Violin Concerto, Helsinki Philharmonic (Okko Kamu), 1988. *Honours include:* Scholarship, overseas studies,

American Israel Cultural Foundation; 1st prizes, Paganini International Competition, Genoa, Italy 1968, Queen Elisabeth Competition, Belgium 1971. *Current Management:* Agence de Concerts et Spectacles Caecilia. *Address:* c/o Agence de Concerts et Spectacles Caecilia, 5, place de la Fusterie, 1204 Genève, Switzerland.

FRIEDERICH (Albert) Matthias, b. 16 June 1954, Heidelberg, Germany. Oboist; Recorder Player; Composer. m. Margaret Joy Stone, 30 Aug 1980, 1 son. *Education:* Studied at Cologne Music College with G Hoeller, H Hucke and A Meidhof. *Debut:* Recorder Soloist, Vivaldi's Sopranino recorder concerto C major, Heidelberg, 1966. *Career:* Concerts with George Malcolm, Amadeus Quartet, Mozarteum Quartet, Munich String Trio, and Sinfonia Varsovia, Poland; Since 1988, member of Pifferari di Santo Spirito trio, Heidelberg, (with Margaret Friederich and Peter Schumann). Concerts Berlin, Paris, Dallas and Tokyo. *Compositions:* Happy Birthday Variations, 1989; Highstreet Dixie, 1990; Enigma Blues for FGB, 1991; Jubilee Stomp, 1992. *Recordings:* CD, Music for Fun, 1991; CD, Pifferari Safari, 1993. *Contributions to:* Rohrblatt, article, Jazz on the oboe and the cor anglais, 1993. *Memberships:* International Double Reed Society. *Hobbies:* Table Tennis; Swimming; Painting and Drawing. *Current Management* Konzertdirektion Buescher, Postf 101424, 69004 Heidelberg, Germany. *Address:* Floringasse 2, 69117 Heidelberg, Germany.

FRIEDMAN Erick, b. 16 Aug 1939, Newark, New Jersey, USA. Violinist; Professor. *Education:* Pupil of Samuel Applebaum; Studied with Ivan Galamian, Juilliard School of Music; with Nathan Milstein; Private studies with Jascha Heifetz, 1956-58. *Career:* Professional debut as Soloist, Little Orchestra Society, NY, 1953; Carnegie Hall recital debut, NY, 1956; Soloist with leading orchestras, as Recitalist and Chamber-Music player; Mischa Elman Professor, Eastman School of Music, Rochester, NY, 1975-. *Recordings:* for RCA. *Honour:* Winner, Music Education League Competition, 1953. *Address:* c/o Eastman School of Music, University of Rochester, Rochester, NY 14627, USA.

FRIEDMAN Leonard Matthew, b. 11 Dec 1930, London, England. Violinist. m. twice, 2 sons, 3 daughters. *Education:* Guildhall School of Music and Drama. *Debut:* Central Hall, 1938; Conway Hall, 1949. *Career:* Joint Founder, Haydn Orchestra; Joint Founder, Cremona Quartet; Member, Adolph Busch Chamber Orchestra, English Chamber Orchestra, Rostal, Hurwitz, Bath Festival; Founder Leader, Northern Symphony; Deputy Leader and RPO Leader, Bremen Philharmonic; Leader, Westphalia Symphony; Founder, Scottish Ensemble; Guest Leader, Scottish Chamber; London Festival; Member, Melos of London; Duo with Allan Schiller; Duo with son, Richard Friedman; Director, Friedman Ensemble. *Recordings:* Director, Music at Hopetoun; Director, Music at Drumlanrig; Scandinavian Serenade, CRD; String Orchestra Music by Mozart; Baroque Cello Concertos; English Serenade, Abbey; Schubert String Quintet; Bach Concertos; Tribute to Kreisler, Syrinx. *Honours:* Gold Medal, Guildhall, 1953; Royal patronage of Duke of Edinburgh, 1975; Citizenship Prize of Edinburgh, 1980-81; Founder/Director, Camerata of St Andrew, 1988. *Memberships:* Honorary member, Royal Overseas Scottish Arts; New Club. *Hobbies:* Cricket; Comparative religion; Global politics; History of art. *Address:* 17a Dublin Street, Edinburgh, EH1 3PG, Scotland.

FRIEDMAN Victor, b. 23 Sept 1938, Moscow, USSR. Musician; Pianist; Teacher. *Education:* High School, 1947-56; Musical School, Moscow Conservatory, 1957; PhD, 1962-65, Moscow Conservatory. *Career:* Concert Pianist, Moscow Philharmonic Concert Society, 1962-74; Professor of Piano, Moscow State Conservatory, 1965-77; Concert Pianist, Various Managements, USA and Europe, 1974-; Master Classes, Various Conservatories, USA, Europe and Israel, 1974-. *Recordings:* Works by Haydn, Beethoven, Liszt and Prokofiev, Orion Master Recording, USA. *Honour:* Gold

Medal with Honours, for Graduation, Moscow Conservatory, 1962.

FRIEDRICH Götz, b. 4 Aug 1930, Naumburg, Germany. Opera Producer. m. Karan Armstrong. *Education:* Studied at the German Theatre Institute in Weimar. *Career:* Worked at the Komische Oper Berlin 1953-72 (Director of Productions from 1968); Stagings included Jenůfa, Tosca, Così fan Tutte and Porgy and Bess; Principal Producer, Hamburg Staatsoper, 1973-81; Staged Schoenberg's Moses und Aron at Vienna 1973 and La Scala 1975; Principal Producer, Royal Opera House, Covent Garden, 1976-81: Lulu and Der Ring des Nibelungen; Other productions include Tannhäuser 1972, Lohengrin 1978 and Parsifal 1982 at Bayreuth; Die Meistersinger in Stockholm 1977; Fidelio in Munich 1977; Tristan und Isolde in Berlin 1980; World premiere of Un Re in Ascolto by Berio (Salzburg 1984); Der Ring des Nibelungen at the Deutsche Oper Berlin 1984-85; Schoenberg's Erwartung and Duke Bluebeard's Castle by Bartók (Vienna 1985); Oedipus by Wolfgang Rihm in Berlin 1988; US productions include Wozzeck in Houston 1982, Otello and Katya Kabanova in Los Angeles 1986, 1988; Production of The Ring at Covent Garden, 1989-91; Staged Tannhäuser at the Deutsche Oper Berlin, 1992; Director of the Deutsche Oper from 1981; TV films of many productions including Die Meistersinger and Elektra. *Publications include:* Walter Felsenstein-Weg und Werk 1961. *Address:* c/o Deutsche Oper Berlin, Richard Wagner Strasse 10, 1000 Berlin 10, Germany.

FRIEND Caroline, b. 1950, England. Singer (Soprano). *Career:* Concert appearances in Britain, Switzerland, Belgium, France, Germany and the Netherlands; Repertoire includes Handel's Oratorios, Bach's Oratorios and Cantatas; Schubert's A flat Masses; Mozart's Oratorio; Britten's War Requiem under Stephen Cleobury in King's College, Vaughan Williams, Sea Symphony, Howells Hymnus Paradisi; Rossini, Stabat Mater, Dvořák Stabat Mater; Mahler's 4th Symphony and Les Nuits d'Eté with the Netherlands Philharmonic under Franz-Paul Decker; Appearances with the Songmakers' Almanac in England and Ireland, performing Robin Holloway's Women in War; Sang Diane in Rameau's Hippolyte et Aricie for the English Bach Festival under Jean-Claude Malgoire in Athens and Versailles and at Covent Garden; Other roles include Mozart's Donna Anna, Susanna, Pamina, Countess and Fiordiligi (Pavilion Opera); Rosalinde (Die Fledermaus), Norina (Don Pasquale), Hannah, The Merry Widow, Tosca and Mimi, Puccini, Berta, Barber of Seville and performances of Balfe's The Siege of Rochelle; Engagements in all the major London concert halls and with many choral societies; conductors include Adrian Boult, John Eliot Gardiner and Charles Mackerras. *Address:* 33 Wetherby Mansions, Earls Court Square, London, SW5 9BH, England.

FRIEND Lionel, b. 13 Mar 1945, London, England. Conductor. m. Jane Hyland, 2 Aug 1969, 1 son, 2 daughters. *Education:* Royal College of Music, London, 1963-67; London Opera Centre, 1967-68. *Debut:* Welsh National Opera 1969. *Career:* Welsh National Opera, 1968-72; Glyndebourne Festival Opera, 1969-72; Staatstheater, Kassel, Germany, 1972-75; Staff Conductor, English National Opera, 1976-89; Musical Director, Nexus Opera, 1981-; Musical Director New Sussex Opera, 1989-. *Recordings:* Works by Anthony Milner, Havergal Brian (BBC Symphony Orchestra), Nicholas Maw, Anthony Payne, Bliss, Poulenc, Colin Matthews, Debussy, Simon Holt, Schoenberg (Nash Ensemble), Stravinsky (Scottish Chamber Orchestra). *Hobbies:* Theatre; Reading. *Current Management:* Allied Artists, London, SW7 1JZ. *Address:* 136 Rosendale Road, London SE21 8LG, England.

FRIGERIO Ezio, b. 16 July 1930, Como, Italy. Stage Designer. *Education:* Studied architecture at Milan Polytechnic. *Career:* Costume Designer, Giorgio Strehler's Piccolo Teatro d'Arte from 1955; Collaborations with Strehler, Eduardo de Filippo and other directors in Italy and elsewhere; Designed Don Pasquale at the Edinburgh Festival, 1962, Tosca at Cologne, 1976 and Carmen at Hamburg, 1988; Collaborations with Nuria Espert for Madame Butterfly and Traviata at Scottish Opera (1987 and 1989), Rigoletto at Covent Garden, 1988 and Elektra at Barcelona, 1990; La Scala Milan, 1990 with Fidelio and The Queen of Spades; Designs for Il Turco in Italia and Anna Bolena at Madrid, season, 1990-91; Frequent associations with costume designer, Franca Squarciapino. *Address:* c/o Royal Opera House (Contracts), Covent Garden, London WC2, England.

FRISCH Walter M., b. 26 Feb 1951, New York City, USA. Professor of Music. m. Anne-Marie Bouché, 27 Aug 1981, 1 son. *Education:* BA, Yale University, 1973; MA 1977, PhD 1981, University of California, Berkeley. *Career:* Assistant professor, music, Columbia University, 1982-; Research, music of 19th & 20th centuries, especially Austrian tradition - Schubert, Brahms, Schoenberg. *Publications:* Brahms & the Principle of Developing Variation, 1984; Schubert: Critical & Analytical Studies, editor, 1986; Brahms' Alto Rhapsody, editor, facsimile edition, 1983. *Contributions to:* 19th Century Music, co-editor 1984-. *Honours:* Winner, ASCAP-Deems Taylor Award, outstanding book on music, 1984. *Memberships:* American Musicological Society; President, American Brahms Society. *Address:* Department of Music, Columbia University, New York, NY 10027, USA.

FRISCHKNECHT Hans Eugen, b. 8 May 1939, St Gallen, Switzerland. Musician. m. Eliane Kneuss, 5 July 1969. *Education:* Orgeldiplom, Hochschule für Musik, Berlin, 1962; 1er prix d'analyse 1964 (Olivier Messiaen), Conservatoire Paris; Ecole César Franck Paris, Diplome de clavecin, 1964; Theorielehrer-Diplom, Konservatorium Bern, 1969. *Career:* Organist, Johanneskirche, Bern, 1964; Music Teacher, Lehrerinnenseminar Bern, 1965-86; Music Teacher, Conservatory Biel, 1983-; Choirmaster, IGNM-Vokalsolisten Bern, 1970-; Choirmaster, Berner Jugendsinglager, 1979-85; Radio lectures. *Compositions:* Numerous for orchestra, organ, piano, choir, chamber music and brass band. *Contributions:* Articles for reviews. *Address:* Krayigenweg 93, CH-3074 Muri, Switzerland.

FRISELL Sonja, b. 5 Aug 1937, Richmond, Surrey, England. Stage Director. *Education:* Studied piano and acting at the Guildhall School. *Career:* Associated with Carl Ebert at the Stadtische Oper Berlin and at Glyndebourne; Staff Producer, La Scala, solo Producer in North and South America, directed La Favorite at the 1977 Bregenz Festival, Vivaldi's Tito Manlio at La Scala 1979 and Handel's Agrippina at Venice, 1985; Directed Carmen at Buenos Aires 1985, Aida at the Metropolitan, 1988; Lyric Opera of Chicago 1989-90, Don Carlos: Khovanshchina at San Francisco, 1990; Directed Die Zauberflöte for Washington Opera at Kennedy Center, 1991; Forza Del Destino at San Francisco, 1992, Otello at Chicago, 1993. *Address:* c/o Drosslweg 45, 85667 Oberpframmern, Germany.

FRISS Gábor, b. 28 June 1926, Budapest, Hungary. Professor; Conductor; Composer. m. Magda Klein. *Education:* Diploma, Budapest Academy of Music. *Career includes:* Head, Methodology Faculty, Teachers Training Institution, Budapest Academy of Music, 1966; Teacher and Lecturer, various institutions, Benelux, Denmark, Austria, Germany, Mexico and USA; Concerts and Choir and Orchestras throughout Europe. *Compositions:* A Story in the Forest; Choral Works; Songs; Accompaniments. *Recordings:* Contemporary and Danish Broadcast Choir; pre-classical works, with Danish Broadcast Choir. *Publications:* Numerous publications including Musical Education in Hungary, 1966; Methods for the Teaching of Music to Children, 1971; From So-Mi to Folksong, 1971; Pre-instrumental Music, 1976; Editor, Parlando Educational Journal; MI-RE-DO 1-4, Wilhelm Hansen, Copenhagen, 1973-77; Musica Para Todos 1-2 Ricordi, Mexico, 1984-85; Pictures and Symbols Mora, Budapest, 1987, 55

Famous Operas Moara, Budapest, 1993. *Honours:* Recipient of numerous musical and teaching honours. *Memberships:* National Council of Choirs; Association of Hungarian Musicians. *Hobbies:* Collecting Folk Art and Music; Photography. *Address:* Damjanich utca 14, 1071 Budapest, Hungary.

FRITH Benjamin, b. 11 Oct 1957, Sheffield, England. Concert Pianist. m. Donna Sansom, Apr 1989, 3 daughters. *Education:* Dinnington High School, 1969-76; Leeds University, 1976-79; BA (Hons.) Music (1st Class); Private Study with Fanny Waterman, OBE, since childhood; Leeds University. *Debut:* Official London debut Recital, Wigmore Hall, 1981 sponsored by Countess of Munster Trust. *Career:* Performing career of recitals, concertos and participation in chamber music ensembles in London and the Provinces including South Bank, Wigmore Hall, Usher Hall Edinburgh, Aldeburgh, Harrogate and many major festivals; TV and Radio appearances; Concerts in Italy, Spain, Germany, Poland, Israel and America.*Recordings:* with ASV, Diabelli and 32 variations by Beethoven; Chamber music; Naxos label, on one CD: Schumann piano music, Davids bündlertänza (opus 6), Fantasiestücke (opus 12); Serendipity label: Martin Ellerby, piano & chamber works and Collage, clarinet & piano music with Linda Merrick. *Honours:* Gold Medallist and Joint first prize winner, Arthur Rubinstein International Piano Masters Competition, 1989; Joint Top Prize Winner, Busoni International Pianoforte Competition, 1986- *Current Management:* Tim Bullamore Management. *Address:* 6 Carisbrook Road, Carlton in Lindrick, Nr Worksop, Notts, S81 9NJ.

FRITSCH Markus Heinz, b. 29 June 1963, Dinkelsbuehl, Germany. Bassist; Composer. *Education:* Professional Music Diploma, Berklee College of Music, 1987; Tutors include Rich Appleman, Kai Echardt, Jerry Bergonzi. *Career:* As Electric Bass Player, live appearances with Gloria Gaynor, Joan Orleans, Drafi Deutscher, Joy Fleming, Margerie Barnes, Howard Carpendale, Ricky Shane, Wencke Myrhe, Chris Andrews and Tony Christie; Studio appearances and radio shows. *Compositions:* Don't Steal my heart Away; Clea's Blues; Gold and Diamonds; Walk in Rhythm; Dance with me; Island in the Dusk; Southern Comfort; I love you, Don't you love me.*Recordings:* Conny Wagner Band Greatest Hits. *Publications:* Bass Masters of Heavy Metal, 1994; Jazz Bass I, 1990; Songwriting and Harmony, 1994; Arranging and Producing, 1994; Contributor to Sound Check, Artist, and The Bass. *Memberships:* GEMA; GVL; Deutscher Komponistenverband, Vereingung Deutscher Musikbearbeiter. *Hobbies:* Travel; Wine; Gourmet Food. *Address:* Sternbergstrasse 12, D-93047 Regensburg, Germany.

FRITZSCH Johannes, b. 1960, Meissen, Germany. Conductor. *Education:* Studied with his father and at the Dresden Hochschule für Musik, from 1975. *Career:* Second Kapellmeister at the Rostock Opera 1982-87; Conducted Il Barbiere di Siviglia and Il Matrimonio Segreto at the Semper Opera Dresden, 1987; Nearly 200 performances as the Dresden Staatsoper with the Dresdener Staatskapelle; Guest Conductor at the Royal Swedish Opera in Stockholm; Regular orchestra concerts in former East Germany; West German debut Oct 1990 with Beethoven's 5th Piano Concerto and the New World Symphony with the National Theatre Orchestra, Mannheim; Danish debut Oct 1991, with the Orchestra of Danish Radio at Copenhagen; also engaged for: Don Giovanni, Royal Opera Stockholm, 1991; Rialto Theatre, Copenhagen, 1991; Entführung, Nozze di Figaro & Don Giovanni, Royal Opera Stockholm, 1991; La Traviata, Hanover, 1991; Hansel and Gretel, Sydney (Australian Opera), 1992; Die Bassariden at Freiburg, 1993, (Music Director from 1993). *Address:* c/o Haydn Rawstron Management, PO Box 654, London SE26 4DZ, England.

FROBENIUS Wolf, b. 1 June 1940, Speyer/Rhein, Federal Republic of Germany. Musicologist. *Education:* Studies in Musicology, history of art and history,

Freiburg i/Br., Germany and Paris, France; PhD, Freiburg i/Br., 1968; Habilitation, Freiburg i/Br., 1988. *Career:* Staff member, Handwörterbuch der musikalischen Terminologie, Akademie der Wissenschaften und der Literatur, Mainz, 1968-88; Teacher, University of Freiburg i/Br., 1971-88; Professor, University of Saarbrücken. *Publications:* Johannes Boens Musica und seine Konsonanzenlehre, 1971. *Contributions to:* Handwörterbuch der musikalischen Terminologie; Archiv für Musikwissenschaft; The New Grove; Die Musik in Geschichte und Gegenwart. *Address:* Akazienweg 56, D-6601 Saarbrücken, Schafbrücke, Germany.

FROLOV Sergei Vladimirovich, b. 23 Jan 1948, Russia. Musicologist; Music Historian. div. 1 son, 1 daughter. *Education:* Samar Music College, 1967; St Petersburg Conservatoire, 1972; DMus, 1980. *Career:* Researcher, Russian Literature Institute, Academy of Science, SPB, 1971-83; Profesor, Head of Faculty of History of Russian Music, SPB Conservatoire, 1973-; Writer, Consultant, SPB TV and film Studio, 1979-. *Recordings:* Two LPs, Songs of Smolensk Podneprovie (Russian musical folklore); Melodia. *Publications include:* Over 40 articles including Musical Manuscripts in Karelian Collection, 1988, and contributor to Soviet Music magazine. *Memberships:* St Petersburg Composers Union. *Hobbies:* Reading; Travel. *Address:* Plehanova Str, 26/27 apt 24, St Petersburg, Russia 190000.

FROOM David, b. 14 Dec 1951, Petaluma, California, USA. Composer; Assistant Professor of Music. m. Eliza Garth, 29 June 1986. *Education:* BA (Highest Hons.), University of California, Berkeley, 1976; MMus (Most Outstanding), University of Southern California, 1978; Doctor of Musical Arts, Columbia University, 1984; Fellowship, Composition, Tanglewood, 1981; Fulbright Grant for study with Alexander Goehr, Cambridge University, 1983. *Career:* Assistant Music Editor, Garland Publishing, 1981-82; Past teaching: Columbia University, City University of New York, 1980-85; Assistant Professor of Music, University of Utah, 1985-; Associate Professor of Music, University of Utah, 1985-89; St Mary's College of Maryland, 1989-. *Compositions include:* Piano Sonata; Piano Concerto; Quartet for Piano and Strings; Rhapsody for String Orchestra; Down to a Sunless Sea. *Recording:* Ballade for Piano and Fender Rhodes; Piano Sonata, Quartet for Piano and Strings, Down to a Sunless Sea. *Contributions to:* Issue editor: Contemporary Music Review, The Emerging Generation. *Address:* Music Department, St Mary's College of Maryland, St Mary's City, Maryland 20686, USA.

FROUNBERG Ivar, b. 12 Apr 1950, Copenhagen, Denmark. Composer. m. Inge Sønderskov Madsen, 1 son. *Education:* Diploma, Organist and Choirleader, 1976; MA, Composition, State University of New York, USA, 1981; Royal Danish Academy of Music, 1986. *Career:* Giving courses, electro-acoustic music, Royal Danish Academy of Music, 1986-; 1992, Assistant Professor at the Royal Danish Academy of Music, Musical Coordinator of then 1994 ICMC. *Compositions:* Peripeti; Phantasia Dekadenz; Five echoes of a sonata; Thrice-told tunes; Faust Variations II; en vue de Roesnaes; Drei-Klang; Frescobaldi - epitaph; pro pacem pugnandum est; Haliksa'i; Henri Michaux preludes; Embryo; D; Multiple Forms; And the fire and the rose are one; At the stillpoint of the Turning World; Other echoes inhabit the garden; What did the Sirens Sing as Ulyssus sailed by?; A Pattern of Timeless Motion, 1989; Time and the Bell, 1990; Kreppvaar, 1991. *Recordings:* Henri Michaux preludes; Phantasie DeKadenz; Five echoes of a Sonata; Haliksa'i; Drei-Klang; A Pattern of Timeless Motion. *Publications:* Theory and Praxis in the compositional methods of Iannis Xenakis - an exemplification; Komponisten Pierre Boulez, 1985. *Contributions to:* Dansk Musiktidskrift; Nutida Musik. *Address:* Melchiorsvej 1, DK 3450 Alleroad, Denmark.

FRUGONI Orazio, b. 28 Jan 1921, Davos,

Switzerland. Pianist. *Education:* Graduated Milan Conservatory 1939; Attended master classes of Alfredo Casella at the Accademia Chigiana, Siena, and Dinu Lipatti at the Geneva Conservatory. *Career:* Played in concerts in Italy from 1939 and in the USA from 1947; Piano professor at the Eastman School, Rochester, until 1967; Director 1967-72; Teacher of piano at the Conservatory Luigi Cherubini at Florence from 1972. *Recordings include:* Beethoven's E flat concerto of 1784 (premiere recording); Mendelssohn's Piano Concertos; Lalo's Piano Concerto. *Honours Include:* Prix de Virtuosite, Geneva Conservatory, 1945. *Address:* Conservatorio di Musica L Cherubini, Piazzetta delle Belle Arti, Florence, Italy.

FRUSONI Maurizio, b. 22 Sept 1945, Rome, Italy. Singer (Tenor). *Education:* Studied in Rome. *Career:* Sang at Siena from 1971, Florence from 1973 (as Andrei in Khovanshchina); Appeared at the Piccola Scala, 1974, Schwetzingen Festival, 1976, in Paer's Leonora; Florence 1975, as Lensky; US debut at the Spoleto Festival, Charleston, 1978; Sang with the Welsh National Opera, 1980, 1982, Radames at Buenos Aires and Verona, 1983-84; Appearances at Livorno 1990, as Nanni in La Lupa by Marco Tutino, and as Manrico at the Teatro Colon Buenos Aires, 1991; Has also sung at the Paris Opera, Pittsburgh, Toronto, Zurich, Bologna, Strasbourg, Macerata and Parma; Other roles include the Duke of Manuta, Alfredo, Pollione (Norma), Licinio in La Vestale, the Rodolfo of Puccini and Leoncavallo, Pinkerton, Cavaradossi, Gregor in The Makropoulos Case and Tom Rakewell. *Address:* c/o Teatro Colon, Cerrito 618, 1010 Buenos Aires, Argentina.

FRÜHBECK DE BURGOS Rafael, b. 15 Sept 1933, Burgos, Spain. Conductor. m. Maria Carmen Martinez 1959, 1 son 1 daughter. *Education:* Music Academies in Bilbao, Madrid and Munich and University of Madrid. *Career:* Chief Conductor, Municipal Orchestra, Bilbao 1958-62; Music Director and Chief Conductor, Spanish National Orchestra, Madrid, 1962-78; Music Director of Dusseldorf and Chief Conductor, Dusseldorf Symphoniker 1966-70; Musical Director, Montreal Symphony Orchestra 1974-76; Principal Guest Conductor, National Symphony Orchestra, Washington, USA, 1980-1990; Principal Guest Conductor, Yomiuri Nippon Symphony Orchestra, Tokyo, 1980-1990; Honorary Conductor, Yoniuri Nippon Symphony Orchestra, Tokyo, 1991; Conducted opening concert of 1989 Edinburgh Festival, Falla's Atlantida and La Vida Breve; Chefdirigent of the Vienna Symphony Orchestra, 1991; Music Director, Deutsche Oper Berlin, 1992; Conducted Carmen at Genoa, 1992; Don Carlos in Berlin. *Recordings include:* Falla El amor brujo; La vida breve, Nights in the Gardens of Spain and L'Atlantida; Mozart Requiem and Schumann 3rd Symphony; Mendelssohn Elijah and St Paul; Orff Carmina Burana, Le Sacre du Printemps, Prokofiev Violin Concertos, Mendlessohn Violin Concerto; Beethoven's Symphonies and the complete works of Falla, with ballets by Stravinsky and Bartók with the LSO, for Collins Classics. *Honours:* Gran Cruz al Mérito Civil Orden de Alfonso X, Orden de Isabel la Catolica. *Address:* Plaza Reyes Magos 13, Madrid 28007, Spain.

FRY James W.H., b. 14 Aug 1974. *Education:* Clarinet Diploma, Licentiate in Music Australia, 1990; University of Melbourne, 1993-. Tutors include Peter Clinch, Ruth Collins, Stephen Colebrook, (clarinet); Meryl Ross, Beverly Norris, Anne-Marie Kriewalt, (piano). *Career:* Has played as principal clarinet in eight youth orchestras including the Melbourne Youth Orchestra, Melbourne Sinfonia and Melbourne University (Conservatorium) Orchestra. Has performed works by Schubert, Spohr, Shostakovich, Mozart, Beethoven, Saint-Saens; Soloist with five orchestras playing all four concertos of Louis Spohr, the Potpourri, Opus 80 for clarinet and orchestra; and the Mozart Clarinet Concerto. *Recordings:* Mozart Clarinet concerto in A Major, Collingwood Chamber Orchestra, 1991. *Honours:* Scholarships to study with Professor Sidney Forrest, Catholic University of America, 1991- 92, and John Denman, AZ, USA, 1992-93; Preston Orchestra

Youth Concerto Competition, Finalist, 1992; Melbourne Youth Orchestra Musical Award, 1992. *Address:* 16 Howard Street, Kew 3101, Victoria, Australia.

FU Haijing, b. 1960, China. Singer (Baritone). *Education:* Studied in London and New York. *Career:* Concert engagements include Mozart's Requiem with the Montreal Symphony Orchestra, Zemlinsky's Lyric Symphony, Beethoven's Ninth, Carmina Burana with the Pacific Symphony and the Cleveland Orchestra; Verdi's Requiem in Geneva; Mendelssohn's Erste Walpurgisnacht with the Boston Symphony and Mozart's C minor Mass with the Cincinnati Orchestra; Metropolitan Opera debut, 1990, as Germont, followed by Sir Richard Forth in I Puritani; Renato with Atlanta Opera, Enrico and Verdi's Miller at Philadelphia and Filippo in Bellini's Bianca e Fernando at Catania, Italy, 1992; Appearances as Rigoletto with the San Diego and Edmonton Opera companies; Other roles include Marcello in La Bohème, and Posa in Don Carlos; Sang Germont at Philadelphia, 1992. *Honours include:* Second prize, Benson and Hedges Gold Award International Competition, London, 1987; Winner, Metropolitan Opera National Council Competition, 1988. *Address:* IMG Artists, Media House, 3 Burlington, London W4 2TH, England.

FUGELLE Jacquelyn, b. 1950, London, England. Singer (Soprano). m. George Johnston, 1975, 1 daughters. *Education:* Studied at Guildhall School of Music, Vienna Academy and in Rome. *Debut:* Wigmore Hall, London, 1975. *Career:* Extensive repertoire in oratorio, recital and opera; Appearances in England, Canada and Europe; Television and radio appearances in the Netherlands, Sweden and for the BBC; Debut at Royal Opera House, Covent Garden 1991 as Arbate in Mozart's Mitridate; Other roles at ROH include, Falcon in Die Frau Ohne Schatten; Debut with Scottish Opera, 1993; Major oratorio performances include, Elijah with LPO, conducted by Kurt Masur; Broadcasts include Messiah in Norway, Mendelssohn's 2nd Symphony in Paris and the B minor Mass in Iceland. *Recordings:* Operatic Favourites with Joan Sutherland, Luciano Pavarotti; Music by Bottesini with Tomas Martin on double bass and Anthony Halstead on piano. *Honours:* Silver medal, Worshipful Company of Musicians; Countess of Munster and Royal Society of Arts Scholarships; 2nd Prize, Kathleen Ferrier Competition. *Memberships:* ISM; Equity. *Hobbies:* Geology; Gardening. *Address:* 38 Wadham Road, Portsmouth, Hants PO2 9EE, England.

FUJIKAWA Mayumi, b. 27 July 1946, Asahigawa City, Japan. Solo Violinist. *Education:* Toho Conservatoire in Tokyo; Antwerp Conservatory, Belgium; Further study with Leonid Kogan in Nice. *Career:* Concerts with leading orchestras in South America, Australia, Israel, Asia, Japan and Europe; American orchestras in Philadelphia, Boston, Chicago, Pittsburgh and Cleveland; Festival engagements at Aldeburgh with Previn, Edinburgh with the Concertgebouw Orchestra and Kondrashin; Other conductors include Barenboim, Dutoit, Foster, Haitink, Levine, Ormandy, Sanderling and Rattle; TV appearances playing the Mozart Concertos with the Scottish Chamber Orchestra; Promenade Concerts, London, 1991, in Mozart's Sinfonia Concertante. *Recordings:* Mozart Concertos with the Royal Philharmonic conducted by Walter Weller; Beethoven's Kreutzer and Franck's Sonata, with Michael Roll; Tchaikovsky and Bruch Concertos with the Rotterdam Philharmonic; Sonatas by Prokofiev and Fauré. *Honours:* 2nd Prize, Tchaikovsky International Competition, Moscow, 1970; First Prize, Henri Vieuxtemps Competition in Verviers, Belgium, 1970. *Hobbies include:* Chamber Music; Reading; Plays; Movies; Concerts; Being with Friends; Drawing. *Current Management:* Terry Harrison Artists Management, 3 Clarendon Court, Park Street, Charlbury, OX7 3PS, England.

FULKERSON James Orville, b. 2 July 1945, Manville, Illinois, USA. Composer; Trombonist. *Education:* Studied trombone and composition at Illinois Wesleyan University, composition at the University of Illinois, MM 1966. *Career:* Fellow at the Center for Creative Performing Arts at SUNY, Buffalo, 1969-72; Residencies at the Deutscher Akademischer Austauschdienst in Berlin, 1973, and the Victorian College of the Arts, Melbourne, 1977-79; From 1981 resident at Dartington College, South Devon. *Compositions include:* Guitar Concerto 1972; To See a thing Clearly for orchestra 1972; Orchestral Piece 1974; Co-ordinative systems nos. 1-10, 1972-76; Music for Brass Instruments nos. 1-6, 1975-78; Raucasity and the Cisco Kid or, I Skate in the Sun, theatre piece 1978; Concerto for amplified cello and chamber orchestra 1978; Vicarious Thrills for amplified trombone and pornographic film 1979; Symphony 1980; Force Fields and Spaces for trombone, tape and dancers 1981; Cheap Imitations IV for soloist, tape and films 1982; Put Your foot down Charlie for 3 dancers, speaker and ensemble 1982; Rats Tale for 6 dancers, trombone and ensemble 1983; Mixed-media works, television and film music; Various instrumental pieces under the titles Space Music, Patterns, Metamorphosis and Chamber Musics. *Address:* c/o ASCAP, ASCAP Building, One Lincoln Plaza, NY 10023, New York, USA.

FULLER Albert, b. 21 July 1926, Washington DC, USA. Harpsichordist; Conductor. *Education:* Studied organ with Paul Callaway at the National Cathedral in Washington; Peabody Conservatory; Georgetown, Johns Hopkins and Yale Universities (Ralph Kirkpatrick and Paul Hindemith); Studied French Baroque keyboard music in Paris. *Career:* Performer on the harpsichord in New York from 1957, Europe from 1959; Repertoire includes French music and the sonatas of Scarlatti; Professor of Harpsichord at the Juilliard School from 1964; President and Artistic Director of the Aston Magna Foundation (for the study of Baroque music) 1972-83; Summer Academies at Great Barrington, Massachusetts; Conductor of Rameau's Dardanus and Les Sauvages (Les Indes Galantes); Handel's Acis and Galatea and Xerxes 1978, 1985; Teacher at Yale University 1976-79. *Publications include:* Edition of the harpsichord music of Gaspard Le Roux. *Address:* c/o Juilliard School of Music, Lincoln Plaza, New York, NY 10023, USA.

FULLER David Randall, b. 1 May 1927, Newton, Massachusetts, USA. Harpsichordist; Organist; Musicologist. *Education:* Studied at Harvard University MA 1951, PhD 1965; Organ with E. Power Biggs, William Self and André Marchal; Harpsichord with Albert Fuller. *Career:* Has performed widely in the USA, mainly in French Baroque repertory; Professor of Music at the State University of New York, Buffalo, from 1963. *Publications:* Editions of keyboard works by Armand-Louis Couperin and Handel; Numerous articles in The New Grove Dictionary of Music and Musicians 1980; The New Harvard Dictionary of Music, 1986, Early Music and others; A Catalogue of French Harpsichord Music, 1699-1780, 1990. *Recordings include:* Music by Armand-Louis Couperin (with William Christie). *Address:* c/o State University of New York, Buffalo, New York State, USA.

FULLER Louisa, b. 1964, England, Violinist. *Education:* Studied at the Royal Academy of Music with Emanuel Hurwitz; Further study with David Takeno. *Career:* Principal second Violin of the Kreisler String Orchestra (winners, 1984 Jeunesses Musicales Competition, Belgrade); extensive tours of Europe; Co-founder and leader of the Duke String Quartet from 1985; Performances at the Wigmore Hall, Purcell Room, Conway Hall and throughout Britain; Tours to Germany, Italy, Austria and the Baltic States; South Bank series 1991, with Mozart's early quartets; Soundtrack for Ingmar Bergman documentary The Magic Lantern, Channel 4, 1988; BBC Debut feature; Features for French television 1990-91, playing Mozart, Mendelssohn, Britten and Tippett; Brahms Clarinet Quintet for Dutch Radio with Janet Hilton; Live Music Now series with concerts for disadvantaged people; The Duke Quartet invites.... at the Derngate Northampton

1991, with Duncan Prescott and Rohan O'Hara; Resident quartet of the Rydale Festival 1991; Residency at Trinity College, Oxford, tours to Scotland and Northern Ireland and concert at the Elizabeth Hall 1991; Top of the Pops and Radio 1 and no.1 album Jan 93 with Little Angels; BBC Def II feature, 20 mins documentary German TV on the Duke. *Recordings include:* Quartets by Tippett, Shostakovich and Britten 3 for Factory Classics; Collins Classics Duke recording Dvořák American and Barber Quartet. *Honours include:* Awards from the Craxton Memorial Trust and the Ian Fleming Trust; Macklin Bursary and the Poulet award from the RAM. *Current Management:* Lorraine Lyons. *Address:* c/o 21 Loftus Road, London, W12 7EH, England.

FULTON Thomas, b. 18 Sept 1949, Memphis, Tennessee, USA. Conductor. *Education:* Studied with Eugene Ormandy at the Curtis Institute, Philadelphia. *Career:* Has conducted at the Hamburg Staatsoper and the San Francisco Opera; Metropolitan Opera on tour; New York performances from 1981, including Manon Lescaut, Madama Butterfly and works by Verdi; Paris Opéra 1979, Robert le Diable by Meyerbeer; Deutsche Oper Berlin 1986, Macbeth; Conducted La Voix Humaine and Il Tabarro for Miami Greater Opera, 1989; Billy Budd at the Metropolitan and Nabucco at the Orange Festival, France; Don Carlos, 1990. *Address:* c/o Greater Miami Opera Association, 1200 Coral Way, Miami, FL 33145, USA.

FUQUA David, b. 22 June 1967, Massachusetts, USA. Composer. m. Michelle Koenig, 27 June 1992. *Education:* BA, Oberlin College; BMus, Composition. *Compositions:* Eyes Dulled by Frustration and Sadness, for chamber orchestra; Once again, once again I am for you a Star, for solo piano; Bigsounds-Smallsounds, for electric guitar and electronics. *Recordings:* Bigsounds-Smallsounds. *Honours:* Arts International Travel Grant Pilot, 1994; New Hampshire State Council for the Arts, Artist Opportunity Grant. *Memberships:* BMI. *Address:* 104A South Main Street, Hanover, NH 03755, USA.

FURLANETTO Ferruccio, b. 16 May 1949, Sacile, Italy. Singer (Bass). *Education:* Studied with Campogaliahi and Casagrande. *Career:* Sang at Vicenza in 1974 as Sparafucile in Rigoletto; Trieste 1974, as Colline in La Bohème, with José Carreras and Katia Ricciarelli; Appearances at La Scala, Banquo, Turin, Leporello and San Francisco as Alvise in La Gioconda; Metropolitan Opera, 1980; Salzburg Festival from 1986, as Philip II and Leporello, 1990 conducted by Riccardo Muti; San Diego and Covent Garden 1988, as Mephistopheles and Leporello; In 1989 sang Mozart's Figaro at Geneva and Fernando in La Gazza Ladra at the Pesaro Festival; Season 1991-92 included Le nozze di Figaro in Paris, London, Salzburg and New York; Semiramide and Don Giovanni at the Metropolitan; concert performances of Mozart's Da Ponte operas with the Chicago Symphony; Other roles include Philippe II, Don Giovanni, Leporello with Karajan, Figaro (Salzburg) Figaro, Bastille, Procida in Vespri Siciliani, Scala. *Recordings include:* Don Alfonso in Così fan Tutte, conducted by James Levine; Roles in Mozart's Da Ponte operas, conducted by Daniel Barenboim; videos of Don Carlos, Metropolitan and Salzburg, Rigoletto, Metropolitan, Vespri Siciliani, La Scala, and Don Giovanni, Metropolitan and Salzburg; Innumerable CDs by Sony, DGG, Philips, EMI also many films and videos. *Membership:* Ambassador of Honour of the United Nations. *Hobbies:* Le Golf; Les Porsches. *Address:* Musicaglotz, 11 Rue de Verrier, 75006 Paris, France.

FURRER-MÜNCH Franz, b. 2 Mar 1924, Winterthur, Switzerland. Composer. m. Cécile Brosy. *Education:* 1st artistic training, Zürich and Basel; Studied Flute, Piano, Harmony, Counterpoint and Composition, Basel Konservatorium; Scientific studies, ETH, Zürich; Musicology with K. von Fischer and P. Müller, Zürich University; Study visits: Federal Republic of Germany including Studio für elektronische Musik, Freiburg i Br, and USA including State University of New York at Stonybrook and University of Bennington, Vermont.

Compositions: 6 published by Edition Modern Munich; Recorded: Timbral Variations, 1973, Dialogue for oboe and clarinet, 1972, CS-301, Ubres Recording, USA; Images sans cadres, 1982, for voice and clarinet quartet, CD Classic 2000, C' 2/4 Aton, 1990; Souvenir mis en scène, 1988-89, for 2 cellos, Thomas and Patrick Demenga, CD 50-8909 Claves. *Publications:* Walter Gieseler: Zur Semiotik graphischer Notation, NZ 1/1978; W. Gieseler, L. Lombardi, R. D. Weyer: Instrumentation in der Musik des 20 Jahrhunderts, 1985; Das geistige Ameublement in Eugen Gomringers Konstellationen, betrachtet vom Standpunkt eines Musikers, in Deine Träume - mein Gedicht, Greno Verlag 1989, C. Schnauber, Hrsg, 1989. *Contributions to:* Thomas Meyer: Aus dem Notenbuch eines Träumers: der Komponist Franz Furrer-Münch, 1993. *Honours:* Composition commissions: City of Zurich, 1989; Stiftung proArte, 1989; Canton of Zurich, 1990. *Memberships:* Schweizerische   Tonkunstlerverein;   SUISA; Musikforschende Gesellschaft der Schweiz, Zurich. *Hobbies:* Guest recitals. *Address:* Hohfurristrasse 4, CH-8172 Niederglatt, Switzerland.

FÜRST Janos, b. 1935, Budapest, Hungary. Conductor. *Education:* Studied at the Liszt Academy, Budapest, and in Brussels. *Career:* Formed Irish Chamber Orchestra 1963; London debut 1972, with the Royal Philharmonic Orchestra; Appearances with all major London orchestras; Engagements in Finland, Sweden, Denmark, Germany, Spain, Italy and Israel; Tours of Australia and New Zealand; Chief Conductor of Orchestra of Malmo, 1974-78; Music Director of the Aalborg Symphony Orchestra Denmark, 1980-83; Music Director of the Opera and Philharmonic Orchestra in Marseille; Former Conductor of the Irish Radio Orchestra in Dublin; Currently Music Director of the Stadtorchester Winterthur, Switzerland; Has conducted opera in Stuttgart, Gothenburg and Copenhagen and for English National Opera and Scottish Opera; Elektra at Marseille, 1989; Creator and leader of the International Conductors' Course for the Dublin Master Classes, 1982-89; Mahler series with the RTE Orchestra, 1988-89; US debut 1990, with the Indianapolis Symphony Orchestra. *Recordings include:* Salome by Peter Maxwell Davies (EMI); Numerous recordings with Swedish companies; Mahler's Lieder eines fahrenden Gesellen and Kindertotenlieder, with the RTE Orchestra. *Honours include:* Premier Prix at the Brusells Conservatory; Swedish Gramophone Prize, 1980. *Address:* c/o EMI Classics, 30 Gloucester Place, London, W1A ES, England.

FUSCO Laura de, b. 1950, Catellammare di Stabia, Italy. Concert Pianist. *Education:* Studied at the Conservatorium San Pietro a Maiella in Naples. *Career:* Many concert appearances from 1966, notably in Europe, United States, South America and Japan; Orchestras have included the Detroit Symphony, Philadelphia, Orchestre National de Paris, Budapest Philharmonic, Santa Cecilia Rome, Moscow Symphony, Residentie Den Haag and the Yomiuri Nippon Symphony; Conductors have featured Muti, Mehta, Ceccato, Chailly, Inbal, Maag, De Burgos and Fedoseyev; Marlboro Festival concerts at the invitation of the late Rudolf Serkin; Debut with the BBC Philharmonic Feb 1991. *Recordings:* Albums for RCA Italiana, Ricordi and Fonit-Cetra. *Address:* c/o Anglo-Swiss Management, 4-5 Primrose Mews, Sharpeshall Street, London NW1 8YW, England.

FUSSELL Charles C(lement), b. 14 Feb 1938, Winston-Salem, North Caroline, USA. Composer; Conductor; Teacher. *Education:* Studied piano with Clemes Sandresky, Winston-Salem; BM, Composition 1960 with Thomas Canning, Wayne Barlow and Bernard Rogers; Piano with Jose Echaniz; Conducting with Herman Genhart, Eastman School of Music, Rochester, NY; Pupil of Boris Blacher, Berlin Hochschule für Musik, 1962; MM, Eastman School of Music, 1964. *Career:* Teacher of Theory and Composition, University of Massachusetts, 1966; Founder-Director of its Group for New Music 1974, later renamed Pro Musica Moderna; Teacher of Composition, North Carolina School of the

Arts, Winston-Salem, 1976-77; Boston University, 1981; Conductor, Longy School Chamber Orchestra, Cambridge, Mass, 1981-82; Artistic Director, New Music Harvet/Boston, Boston's first city-wide contemporary music festival, 1989. *Compositions:* Opera: Caligula, 1962; Orchestral: 3 symphonies: No 1 1963, No 2, 1964-67, No 3, Landscapes, 1978-81; 3 Processionals, 1972-73; Northern Lights for Chamber Orchestra, 1977-79; 4 Fairy Tales, 1980-81; Three Portraits for Chamber Orchestra, 1986; Chamber: Trio for Violin, Cello and Piano, 1962; Dance Suite for 5 Players, 1963; Ballades for cello and Piano, 1968, revised 1976; Greenwood Sketches: Music for String Quartet, 1976; Free-fall for 7 Players, 1988; Vocal: Saint Stephen and Herod, drama, 1964; Voyages for Soprano, Tenor, Women's Chorus, Piano, Winds and Recorded Speaker, 1970; Julian, drama, 1969-71; Eurydice for Soprano and Chamber Ensemble, 1973-75; Resume, song cycle for Soprano and 3 Instruments, 1975-76; A Prophecy for Chorus and Piano, 1976; Song of Return for Chorus and Piano, 1983; Cymbeline, romance for Soprano, Tenor, Narrator and Chamber Ensemble, 1984; The Gift for Soprano and Chorus, 1986; 5 Goethe Lieder for Soprano or Tenor and Piano, 1987; A Song of Return for Chorus and Orchestra, 1989; Wilde, Symphony for Baritone and Orchestra; Last Trombones, 1990 for 5 Percussionists, 2 pano, 6 trombones; 5 Gaethe Lieder version for Orchestra, 1991, soprano on tenor. *Recordings:* Several works recorded. *Honours:* Various grants and commissions. *Address:* ASCAP, ASCAP House, One Lincoln Plaza, New York, NY 10023, USA.

G

GABEL Gerald R, b. 5 Apr 1950, Dodge City, Kansas, USA. Composer; Theorist; Conductor; Educator. m. Jeraldine Kotani, 9 Oct 1977, 1 daughter. *Education:* BM, University of Northern Iowa, 1974; MA, 1977, PhD, 1984, University of California at San Diego. *Career:* Choral Director, University of California at San Diego, 1977-81; Director, La Jolla Civic/University Chorus, 1980-81; Assistant Professor, Music and Arts Institute, San Francisco, 1982; Instructor, San Diego Mesa College, 1983-84; Visiting Professor, Dartmouth College, 1984-87; Assistant Professor, Texas Christian University, 1987-; Composer-in-Residence, New Hampshire Music Festival, 1985-; Co-editor, ex tempore, 1983-; Director, New Hampshire Music Festival Composers Conference, 1986-; Founder and Director, Upchurch Studio for Electro-Acoustic Music, 1989-. *Compositions:* Three Songs: Nocturnes for Piano; Statics for Bass Clarinet Solo; The Wicked Walk on Every Side; The Labyrinth; Saraph for Three Bassoons; Songs and Epitaphs of the Golden Sun; Flight; Fantasy for Woodwind Quintet, all works published by Seesaw Music Corp, New York; The Garden of Forking Paths I; The Garden at Forking Paths Ib; Cantos de Lorca; Una Bofetada Para La Luna Naciente; A Dream!. *Address:* Department of Music, Texas Christian University, Fort Worth, TX 76129, USA.

GABOS Gábor, b. 4 Jan 1930, Budapest, Hungary. Pianist. m. Ingeborg Sandor, 20 Oct 1951, 1 son, 1 daughter. *Education:* Performers Diploma, Ferenc Liszt Academy of Music, Budapest. *Debut:* Budapest, 1952. *Career:* Festival Hall, London; Musikverein, Vienna; Chatelet, Paris; Palais des Beaux-Arts, Brussels; Further appearances in Italy, USSR, Japan, Federal Republic of Germany, Sweden, Greece, Switzerland, Peru, South America and throughout Europe. *Recordings:* Hungaroton; Pathe-Marconi; Top Award of the Japan Record Academy, 1968. *Honours:* Hungarian Government Award Liszt Ferenc, 1959; Merited Artist of the Hungarian People's Republic, 1976; Musica prizes, International Liszt-Bartók Competition, 1st Prize, 1961; Laureat du Concours International Reine Elisabeth, Brussels, 1960. *Hobby:* Bridge. *Current Management:* Interkoncert, Budapest, Hungary. *Address:* Nyul utca 1o, 1026 Budapest, Hungary.

GABRIELOVA Jarmila, b. 2 July 1948, Bohemia. Musicologist. m. 6 Nov 1981, 2d. *Education:* PhD Musicology, Charles University. *Publications:* The early creative period of Antonin Dvořák, 1991; Contributor to: Hudebni Veda, Hudebni Rozhledy, Opus Musicum, Miscellanea Musicologica. *Honours:* Honorary Citizen of New Orleans, USA, 1991; Antonin Dvořák 150th Anniversary Medal, 1991. *Memberships:* International Musicology Society; Antonin Dvořák Society, Prague. *Address:* 181 00 Praha 8, Mazurska 522/24, Czech Republic.

GABRIELSSON Alf Gunnar Hakan, b. 18 June, 1936, Varnhem, Sweden. Music Psychologist. m. Barbro Gabrielsson, 1 Jan 1963, 1 son 2 daughters. *Education:* Royal College of Music, Stockholm, Sweden 1960-63 qualified as organist and music director. PhD, Psychology, Uppsala University, 1973. *Career:* Academic career in Psychology, specialising in music psychology and auditory perception; Numerous publications on music psychology and perceived sound quality of sound-reproducing systems. *Publication:* Gabrielsson A (Ed) Action and perception in rhythm and music, Stockholm, 1987. *Contributions to:* Professional journals and publications, including: Rhythm in music in J R Evans and M Clynes (Eds) Rhythm in Psychological, Linguistic and Musical Processes, Springfield, Illinois: Charles C Thomas, 1986; Timing in music performance and its relations to music experience, in J Sloboda (Ed) Generative processes in music. The psychology of performance, improvisation and composition. Oxford: Clarendon Press, 1988; Music psychology - A survey of problems and current research activities., In Basic musical functions and musical ability. Publications issued by the Royal Swedish Academy of Music, Stockholm, No 32, 1981; Interplay between analysis and synthesis in studies of music performance and music experience. Music Perception 3, 1985; Once again: The theme from Mozart's Piano Sonata in A major (K.331). A comparison of five performances. In A Gabrielsson (Ed) Action and perception of rhythm and music, Publications issued by the Royal Swedish Academy of Music, Stockholm, No 55, 1987. *Address:* Department of Psychology, Uppsala University, Box 1854, S-75148 Uppsala, Sweden.

GADD Stephen, b. 1964, England. Singer (bass-baritone). *Education:* St John's College, Cambridge and Royal Northern College of Music; Appearances with Scottish Opera as Colline in La Boheme and for Opera North as Le Herault in the British stage premiere of Verdi's Jerusalem, 1991; Royal Opera Covent Garden as Angelotti in Tosca, 1992, followed by Purcell's Faery Queen in Lisbon and Die Zauberflöte in Geneva; Sang Pisander in Dallapiccola's Ulisse for the BBC, 1993; concert repertoire includes the Verdi Requiem under Charles Groves, Messiah in Singapore, Handel's Samson under Ivor Bolton, A Child of our Time, Belshazzar's Feast, the Missa Solemnis in Seville. Forthcoming bookings: as Rangoni (Boris Godunov) in Tel Aviv; Count in The Marriage of Figaro for Scottish Opera. *Recordings include:* Mozart's Coronation Mass and Purcell's Dioclesian for D.G. with Trevor Pinnock and the English Concert. *Honours include:* Kathleen Ferrier Memorial Scholarship. *Address:* c/o IMG Artists, Media House, 3 Burlington Lane, London W4 2TH, England.

GADDARN James, b. 12 Mar 1924, Pembrokshire, Wales. Conductor. *Education:* Trinity College of Music, London. *Debut:* St Peter's, Eaton Square, 1951. *Career:* Conductor, London Orpheus Choir, 1952- Founder and Conductor, London Orpheus Orchestra, 1960-; Conductorl Ealing Choral Society, 1968-; Music Director, Croydon Philharmonic Society, 1973-; Director, Opera Seria, 1962-67; BBC Broadcasts; Royal Albert Hall, Festival Hall, Queen Elizabeth Hall, Wigmore Hall; Professor, Trinity College of Music, 1957-92. *Compositions:* Conductor: Donizetti Requiem Mass with Ealing Choral Society; Elizabeth Maconchy's Heloise and Abelard and Antonin Tucapskys Stabat Mater with Croydon Philharmonic Society; Kennedy Scott's Everyman with the BBC. *Honours:* Hon FTCL, 1963; GTCL; LRAM; ARCM. *Memberships:* Royal Philharmonic Society; Incorporated Society of Musicians; Royal Society of Musicians of Great Britain. *Hobbies:* Reading; Travel; Classic Cars. *Address:* 2 Tenby Mansions, Nottingham Street, London W1M 3RD, England.

GADDES Richard, b. 23 May 1942, Wallsend, Newcastle upon Tyne, England. Opera Administrator. *Education:* Studied at Trinity College of Music, London. *Career:* Founded Wigmore Hall Lunchtime Concerts 1965; Emigrated to USA 1969; Artistic Administrator of Santa Fe Opera 1969-78; Founded Opera Theater of St Louis 1975; Production by Jonathan Miller of Così fan Tutte for BBC TV 1982; Visited Edinburgh Festival with St Louis Company in 1983, bringing the first production of Margot-le-Rouge by Delius. *Honours include:* Award from MU Phi Epsilon for services to music in the USA and abroad. *Memberships:* Boards of Directors, William Matheus Sullivan Foundation and Opera America Inc.

GADE Per, b. 26 May 1944, Aalborg, Denmark. Professor of Music; Trombonist; Concert Artist. m. Masae Iwamoto, 7 May 1977, 1 daughter. *Education:* Graduation Diploma, Pedagogue and Teachers Diploma, Performers Diploma on Trombone, Royal Academy of Music, Copenhagen, Denmark; Extra studies Conducting, Composition and Instrumentation; Soloist Class under Professor Denis Wick, London Symphony Orchestra, Guildhall School of Music and Drama, London, England; Further studies with Jay Friedman, Chicago Symphony Orchestra, USA. *Debut:* Solo Trombone Recital, Royal Danish Academy of Music, 1974. *Career:* Solo Trombone in Jazz ensembles, Big Bands and various orchestras, tours of Denmark,

Sweden and England, 1962-69; From 1970 Classical music only; Assistant and Solo Trombonist with various symphony orchestras; Soloist in concerts, International Music Festivals; Radio and TV broadcasts in several countries; Trombone and Brass Instructor, Clinics and Workshops; Brass Teacher, Government Schools, Copenhagen; Assistant Instructor, Trombone, Royal Danish Academy of Music; Professor of Trombone, Baritone Euphonium and Brass Ensemble, Sakuyo College & Academy of Music, Japan. *Recordings:* Gramophone, tapes, Video. *Publications:* Editor of Brass Instrumental Music for several Music Publishers internationally. *Current Management:* Charles Finch Music Agency, Morden, Surrey, England; Ongaku Geijytsuka-kyo-kai, Japan. *Address:* Apt. 801, 3-11-27 Setagaya, Setagaya-ku, Tokyo 154, Japan.

GAGE Irwin, b. 4 Sept 1939, Cleveland, Ohio, USA. Pianist. *Education:* Studied with Eugene Bossart at the University of Michigan; Yale University; Ward Davenny; Vienna Akademie with Erik Werba, Klaus Vokurka and Hilde Langer-Rühl. *Career:* Accompanist to leading singers, including Hermann Prey, Dietrich Fischer-Dieskau, Christa Ludwig, Gundula Janowitz, Jessye Norman, Elly Ameling, Lucia Popp, Brigitte Fassbaender, Tom Krause, Arleen Auger, Anna Reynolds, Rene Kollo, Peter Schreier and Edita Gruberova plus younger singers François Le Roux, Cheryl Studer, Thomas Hampson, Siegfried Lorenz and Francisco Araiza; Festival appearances at every major festival in the world; Professor at the Zurich Conservatory and master classes throughout the world. *Recordings:* over 50 recordings, some of which have won prizes such as the Gramophone award (3 times), Grand Prix du disque, Deutsche Schallplatten preis (5 times), Edison Prize, Recording prizes from Spain, Belgium, Finland, Japan and the Ovation-Mumm awards in USA.

GAGNE Marc, b. 16 Dec 1939, Saint Joseph de Beauce, Quebec, Canada. Professor; Composer. m. Monique Poulin, 27 Dec 1969, 1 son, 2 daughters. *Education:* Doctor of Letters, University Laval, Quebec, 1970; 3 years at School of Music, University Laval with Jacques Hétu, José Evangélista and Roger Matton. *Career:* His Symphonie de chants paysans created at Moncton Choralies Internationals, 1979; His Symphonie-itineraire was Principal work by Quebec Symphony Orchestra at Festival marking 375th anniversary of the discovery of Canada; L'opéra Menaud a été créé et présenté à la télévision sous sa forme de cantate scénique en mai 1992. *Compositions:* Les Chansons de la tourelle, in the folklore mode, 1975; Jeu a deux faces, Piano Sonata No. 1; Ceremonial d'orgue pour la fete du Tres Saint-Sacrement, 1976; Deux chorals pour le temps de la Passion, organ, 1976; Les Jeunes filles a marier (suite for a capella choir on folklore themes), 1977; Short Mass, Du Peuple de Dieu, 1981; Sonate du roi Renaud, alto saxophone and piano, 1983; Vari-anes et moulin-ations, solo marimba, 1983; Symphonie-itineraire, 1983-84; Menaud, opera en 3 actes et un prologue, 1984-86; Évangéline Et Gabriel, opéra en 2 actes, 1987-1990; Le Père Noël, la sorcière et l'enfant conte de Noël pour orchestre de chambre, choeurs et solistes, 1993. *Hobbies:* Walking; Physical Activities Generally; Reading. *Address:* 677 Avenue du Chateau, Sainte-Foy, Quebec G1X 3N8, Canada.

GAGNON Alain, b. Trois-Pistoles, Québec, 1938. Composer. *Education:* Ecole de Musique, Laval University, Graduate degree in Composition studying under Jeanne Landry, Jocelyne Binet and Roger Matton; Studied with Henry Dutilleux, Ecole Normale de Musique, Paris; Studied with Olivier Alain, Ecole César-Franck, Paris; Studied composition and Orchestration with André-François Marescotti, Geneva Conservatory; Initiated into electro-acoustic music at University of Utrecht. *Career:* His works have been performed in France, Switzerland, Germany, Latin America and Canada and several have been recorded or published. Sat on several juries including Competition for Young Composers 1980, with Murray Schafer, Barbara Pentland and Toru Takemitsu; Teacher, Techniques of Composition, Ecole de Musique, Laval University 1967-

; Director of Composition Programme, Laval University 1977-. *Compositions:* These include works for orchestra, chamber music, string quartets and piano; Trio pour flûte, violon et violoncelle, Septuor, Les oies sauvages; Prélude pour orchestre 1969; Ballet score 1983. *Honours:* Received Prix d'Europe 1961; Association de musique actuelle de Québec (AMAQ) honoured him by performing three of his works including Incandescence 1982.

GAHL Dankwart Arnold, b. 18 Dec 1939, Korbach, Germany. Cellist; Professor. m. Irmgard Schuster, 23 May, 1964, 1 son, 1 daughter. *Education:* Matriculation, with Latin and Greek, Gumanistic Gymnasium, 1959; Private cello and viola da gamba instruction (with Johannes Koch/Kassel); Summer class with Casals 1959; Entry to the Akademie für Musik und darstellende Kunst, Vienna, Austria, Oct 1959; Student of Wilfried Boettcher; Theory with Erwin Ratz; Pedagogics Diploma 1963, Final Concert Diploma with first class honours. *Career:* Foundation member of the Vienna Soloists, 1959, touring with this formation all over the world, participating in many famous festivals, e.g. playing with Casals in Prades festival. Originating from this same ensemble - Alban Berg Quartet and Austrian String Quartet of which he has been a member since 1972; Quartet in residence at Mozarteum, Salzburg 1972-, holder of cello class 1972-; Ordinary Professor at the Hochschule 1984-; Foundation member of the piano trio, Trio Amade, Salzburg, 1979; Concerts in the USA and several tours to Far East; Guest classes in South Korea on many occasions; Has given classes with the Quartet at Salzburg Summer Academy Mozarteum for many years; Invited jurist of international chamber music competitions on many occasions. *Honours:* Scholarship, Studienstiftung des deutschen Volkes. *Memberships:* Vienna Symphony Orchestra. *Hobbies:* Books; Jogging; Mountain biking; Hiking. *Address:* Carl Storch- strasse 10, Salzburg, Austria.

GAHL-SCHUSTER Irmgard Elisabeth, b. 14 Nov 1939, Vienna, Austria. Violinist; Professor.m. Dankwart Gahl, 23 May, 1964, 1 son, 1 daughter. *Education:* Private Studies with Josef Drevo; Entered class of Franz Samohyl, Akademie für Musik und Darstellende Kunst, Vienna, 1954; Gained all possible diplomas. *Career:* Leader, Vienna Academy Quartet; Foundation Member, Vienna Soloists; Member, Austrian String Quartet, 1972-; Violin Classes, 1972, Ordinary Professor, 1982- , Hochschule Mozarteum, Salzburg; Foundation Member, Trio Amadé, Salzburg; Tours; Classes; Far East and International Summer Academy Mozarteum, Salzburg. *Hobbies:* Family; Literature; Cooking; Hiking. *Address:* Carl Storch-Strasse 10, Salzburg, Austria.

GÄHMLICH Wilfried, b. 14 July 1939, Halle, Germany. Singer (Tenor). *Education:* Studied at the Musikhochschule Freiburg and with Alfred Pfeifle in Stuttgart. *Debut:* Giessen 1968, as Pedrillo in Die Entführung. *Career:* Sang at Wuppertal 1973, in the premiere of Blacher's Yvonne, Prinzessin von Burgund; Appearances in Dusseldorf, Zurich, Vienna, Stuttgart, Wiesbaden and London; Salzburg 1983, in Dantons Tod by Von Einem; Other roles include Florestan, the Drum Major in Wozzeck, Tamino, Andrea Chénier, Don José and Max in Der Freischütz; Bregenz Festival 1987-88, in Les Contes d'Hoffmann; sang Pedrillo in Die Entführung at the Theater an der Wien, Vienna, 1989; The Sailor in Krenek's Orpheus und Eurydike for the Austrian Radio; Salzburg Festival 1992 as The Hunchback in Die Frau ohne Schatten. *Recordings:* Dantons Tod; Die Entführung; Video of Elektra conducted by Abbado (as the Young Servant - Decca). *Address:* c/o Staatsoper, Ringstrasse, Vienna, Austria.

GAILLARD Paul André, b. 26 Apr 1922, Veytaux-Montreux, Switzerland. Chorus Master; Composer; Musicologist. *Education:* Studied at Montreux and the Lausanne Conservatory, the Winterthur School of Music and the Geneva Conservatory; Conducting with Franz von Hoesslin and violin at the Zurich Conservatory; Study with Hindemith, Willy Burkhard and Willi Schuh. *Career:* Played viola in various Swiss chamber orchestras; Conducted choirs in Luxembourg, Germany, Britain, Belgium, Spain and Poland; Directed the Wagner Seminar at the Bayreuth Festival 1951-59; Conductor of the Chor des Festspieltreffens 1957, Musical Assistant 1961; Professor of Musical History at the Lausanne Conservatory 1956; President of the Swiss Society of Professional Music Directors, 1962; Founded International Choir Festival at Montreux 1964; Professor of Musicology at Zurich 1973-79; Chorus Master at the Geneva Opera 1969-87. *Compositions include:* Choral, vocal, piano and chamber music. *Recordings include:* Handel's Belshazzar (Collegium Academicum de Geneve).*Publications include:* Die Formen des Troubadours-Melodien, Zurich, 1945; Zeitgenössische Schweizer Musik, Bayreuth, 1950; Adolphe Appia, 1955; Il coro nell opera di Wagner, 1961; Les Compositeurs Suisses et l'opéra, 1974; Articles in Musik in Geschichte und Gegenwart.

GAJEWSKI Jaromir Zbigniew, b. 2 Apr 1961, Pyryce, Poland. Musician; Composer; Conductor. *Education:* MA, Academy of Music, Poznan, Poland. *Debut:* Poznan 1986. *Career:* Teacher of Conducting, Composition and Harmony, 1988-; Founder of Academy orchestra 1991. *Compositions:* Altana - Songs, 1986 for voice and piano; String Quartet, 1986; String Quartet, 1988 - all recorded; Penetration for symphony orchestra, 1989; From Dawn to Dusk for orchestra, 1989; To Cage, Opera 1990. *Recordings:* Altana - Songs, 1986; String Quartet 1986; String Quartet, 1988. *Memberships:* Polish Composers Society; Polish Society for Contemporary Music. *Hobbies:* Physics; Swimming. *Address:* ul Boguslawa 24/3, 79-200 Pyrzyce, Poland.

GAL Zahava, b. 29 Aug 1948, Haifa, Israel. Singer (Mezzo-soprano). *Education:* Piano, Rubin Academy, Jerusalem; Voice, Opera, Juilliard School with Jennie Tourel and Daniel Fero. *Career:* Feodor in Boris Godunov, La Scala, 1979; Salzburg Easter Festival production of Parsifal, 1980; Angelina in La Cenerentola, Netherlands Opera, Amsterdam, 1980; Feodor, Carmen, Paris Opera, 1981; Sang Carmen Carmen in Peter Brook's Carmen, Hamburg, Zurich; Rosina in The Barber of Sevilla, Washington DC (2 seasons), Glyndebourne Festival Operas, at Santiago de Chile, Scottish Opera in Lyon, Avignon, Nantes, Dario Fo's Amsterdam production, 2 seasons with Frankfurt Opera; Isolier in Le Conte d'Ory, Pesaro, Italy, Cherubino in The Marriage of Figaro, Monte Carlo, Vienna Staatsoper, Santa Fe Festival; L'incoronazione di Poppea, Mezier Festival; Ariodante in Nancy, Paris, Lausanne, Dejanira in Hercules, title role in Teseo, Covent Garden, Siena, Athens Summer Festival, Handel Year, 1985; Nicklausse, Rosina, Carmen with New Israeli Opera, 1988-89; Rinaldo, Paris; Elmira in Floridante with Tafel Baroque Orchestra in Toronto, San Francisco; Zerlina in Don Giovanni, Nancy; Concert repertoire includes Shererazade, L'enfant et le Sortliege (Ravel), Songs of Wayfarer, 3rd and 4th Symphonies (Mahler), Romeo and Juliet (Berlioz), Requiem, C-Minor Mass (Mozart), Bruckner's Te Deum, Beethoven's 9th, Pergolesi's Stabat Mater; Has sung with Mehta and Israel Philharmonic, Barenboim and New York Philharmonic, Abbado with La Scala Orchestra and Chicago Symphony, Armin Jordan and Orchestra de la Suisse Romande, Matta with Pittsburg and Dallas Symphonies; Sang on TV, Italy, Switerland, France, Israel. *Recordings include:* Moussorgsky's choral works with Abbado; Amaltea in Moses in Egypt; L'incoronazione di Poppea (disc, videocassette); Selection of duets; Donizetti cantata. Honours: Grand Prix, 1st Prize, Melodie Francaise; Coucours International de Chant de Paris; Top Prize, Lieder, Munich International Competition; 1st Place, Kathleen Ferrier Young Artists Award. *Current Management:* Robert Lombardo, New York, USA. *Address:*c/o Robert Lombardo, 61 West 62nd St 6F, New York, NY 10023, USA.

GAL Zoltan, b. 1960, Hungary, Violist. *Education:* Studied at the Franz Liszt Academy, Budapest and with Sandor Devich, György Kurtag and András Mihaly. *Career:* Member of the Keller String Quartet from 1986,

debut concert at Budapest March 1987; Played Beethoven's Grosse Fuge and Schubert's Death and the Maiden Quartet at Interforum 87; Series of concerts in Budapest with Zoltán Kocsis and Deszo Ranki (piano) and Kalman Berkes (clarinet); Further appearances in Nuremberg, at the Chamber Music Festival La Baule and tours of Bulgaria, Austria, Switzerland, Italy (Ateforum 88 Ferrara), Belgium and Ireland; Concerts for Hungarian Radio nd Television. *Recordings:* Albums for Hungaroton (from 1989). *Honour:* 2nd Prize, Evian International String Quartet Competition, May 1988. *Address:* c/o Artist Management International, 12/13 Richmond Buildings, Dean Street, London W1V 5AF, England.

GALANTE Jane H, b. 14 Feb 1924, San Francisco, California, USA. Pianist; Music Historian. m. Clement Galante, 26 Dec 1956. 2 sons. *Education:* AB, Vassar College, 1944; MA, University of California at Berkeley, 1949. *Career:* Instructor Extension Division, University of California at Berkeley, 1948-52; Instructor, Mills College, Oakland, California, 1950-52; Music Editor, Berkeley, A Journal of Modern Culture, 1944-52; Concert Tours in Europe and USA, 1952-. *Recording:* Carlos Salzedo Sonata for harp and piano. *Publication:* Translation of Darius Milhaud (Paul Collaer) edited and revised catalogue of works by D Milhaud, 1988. *Honour:* Chevalier de l'Ordre des Arts et des Lettres, 1983. *Memberships:* Founder, Director, Composers' Forum of San Francisco, 1946-56; Honorary Trustee, San Francisco Conservatory of Music; Trustee, Morrison Chamber Music Foundation, San Francisco State College. *Address:* 8 Sea Cliff Avenue, San Francisco, CA 94121, USA.

GALAS Diamanda, b. 29 Aug 1955, San Diego, California, USA. Vocalist; Composer. *Education:* BA, MA Music, University of California, San Diego. *Career:* Lead role in Globokar's Un Jour Comme Une Autre, Avignon Festival, 1979; Sang her solo works at Theatre Gerard Phillipe St Denis, Paris. also festivals throughout Europe; US and Central America premieres of works by Iannis Xenakis and Vinko Globokar with L'Ensemble Intercontemporaire, Musique Viuvante and Brooklyn Philharmonic; Solo Performances, New York Philharmonic's Horizons Festival, Pepsico Festival, Brooklyn Philharmonic's Meet the Moderns, 1982, 1983, 1984, San Francisco Symhony's New and Unusual Music, 1984, Creative Time's Arts in the Anchorage, many others; Appeared in film Positive Positive; Solo tour, Australia, Sweden, Yugoslavia, Netherlands, Italy, Spain, Bavaria, 1988; UK premiere of Masque of the Red Death, Queen Elizabeth Hall, London, 1989, then Lincoln Center, New York; Plague Mass performed, 1990, Berlin, Basel, Barcelona Olympic Festival, Helsinki Festival, also with world premiere of newest section at St John the Divine Cathedral, New York, then 1991 Athens Festival; World premiere of Vena Cava, the Kitchen, New York City, 1992; Opened 1993 Serious Fun! Festival, Lincoln Center, with electroacoustic work Insekt; 1993 world tour included USA, Spain, Netherlands, Austria, Slovenia, Switzerland, Belgium, Norway; Director, Intravenal Sound Operations, New York. *Compositions include:* Published: Tragouthia ap to Aima Exoun Iona, 1981; The Litanies of Satan, 1981; Panoptikon, 1982; Wild Women with Steak Knives, 1982; Eyes without Blood, 1984; Free among the Dead, 1985; Deliver Me from Mine Enemies, 1986; Recorded: The Litanies of Satan, 1982; Diamanda Galas, 1984; The Divine Punishment, 1986; Saint of the Pit, 1987; You Must Be Certain Of The Devil, 1988; The Masque of the Red Death, 1985, trilogy, 1989; The Singer, 1992; Vena Cava, 1993; Film music. *Honours:* Research Fellow, Center for Music Experiments, 1981-82; Grants: Meet the Composer; Ford Foundation. *Memberships:* American Society of Composers, Authors and Publishers. *Current Management:* International Production Associates, 584 Broadway, Suite 1008, New York, NY 10012, USA. *Address:* 2425 First Avenue, San Diego, CA 92101, USA.

GALE Elizabeth, b. 8 Nov 1948, Sheffield, Yorkshire,

England. Singer (Soprano). *Education:* Studied at the Guildhall School of Music, London, with Winifred Radford. *Debut:* With the English Opera Group, in Purcell's King Arthur. *Career includes:* Appeared in The Turn of the Screw with the EOG; Scottish Opera (Glasgow) as the Queen of Shemakha in The Golden Cockerel; Welsh National Opera (Cardiff) as Blondchen in Die Entführung; Glyndebourne 1973-86, as Barbarina, Papagena, Susanna, Nannetta, Zerlina, Marzelline in Fidelio, Drusilla in L'Incoronazione di Poppea, Titania (A Midsummer Night's Dream, 1984) and Miss Wordsworth (Albert Herring, 1985); Covent Garden as Zerlina and as Adele in Die Fledermaus; Zurich Opera as Susanna, Ilia (Idomeneo), Ismene (Mitridate), Nannetta and Drusilla; Frankfurt 1980, in Castor et Pollux by Rameau; Guest appearances in Amsterdam, Geneva and Cologne; Sang at San Diego, in La Voix Humaine by Poulenc, 1986, US debut; Appeared with Chelsea Opera Group at the Elizabeth Hall 1989, as Massenet's Thais; in Glyndebourne Festival 1990, as Miss Wordsworth, repeated at Los Angeles, 1992; Many concert engagements, in particular in works by Handel; Guest, Opera Houses, Vienna and Paris. *Recordings include:* Le Nozze di Figaro and Don Giovanni; Amor in Orfeo ed Euridice; Israel in Egypt; Messiah; Handel's Saul; Dido and Aeneas; Semele in Die Liebe der Danae, in a BBC recording of Strauss's Opera. *Address:* Harrison/Parrott Ltd., 12 Penzance Place, London, W11 4PA, England.

GALIMIR Felix, b. 20 May 1910, Vienna, Austria. Violinist. m. Suzanne Hirsch, 18 Feb 1945. *Education:* Pupil of Adolf Bak, Vienna Conservatory, Diploma, 1928; Carl Flesch, Berlin and Baden-Baden, 1929-30. *Career:* Founder, Galimir String Quartet, Vienna, 1929; US debut, Town Hall, New York, 1938; Founder, reconstituted Galimir String Quarter, NY, 1938; 1st Violinist, NBC Symphony Orchestra, NY, 1939-54; Concertmaster, Symphony of the Air, NY, 1954-56; Teacher-Performer, Marlboro, (VT, Festival and Music School, 1954-); Teacher, Juilliard School of Music, NY, 1962; Head, Chamber Music Dept, Curtis Institute of Music, Philadelphia, 1972-; Teacher, Mannes College of Music, NY, 1977-. *Recordings:* Various. *Honours:* Grand Prix du Disque, 1937, 1938; Hon DMus, New School of Music, Philadelphia, 1984 and Mannes College of Music, 1987. *Address:* 225 East 74th Street, NY 10021, USA.

GALL Hughes, b. 1940, Honfleur, France. Opera Intendant. *Education:* Studied at the Sorbonne and Ludwig Maximilian University, Munster. *Career:* Worked in French education and cultural ministries; Secretaire General de la Reunion des Theatres Lyriques Nationaux, 1969; Deputy Director of the Paris Opera, 1973-80; Intendant of the Grand Theatre de Geneve from 1980; Has been responsible for more than 100 opera productions in Geneva. *Address:* Intendant Grand Theatre de Geneve, 11 Boulevard de Theatre CH-1211 Geneva 11, Switzerland.

GALL Jeffrey Charles, b. 19 Sept 1950, Cleveland, Ohio, USA. Counter Tenor. m. Karen Rosenberg, 24 June 1978. *Education:* BA, Princeton University, 1968-72; MPhil, Yale University, 1972-76; Private study with: Blake Stern, Yale School of Music, 1972-75; Arthur Burrows, 1976-80. *Career:* Member, Waverly Consort, 1974-78; Debuts: Brooklyn Academy of Music on Cavalli's Erismena; Spoleto Festival, Italy, 1980; La Scala, 1981; Edinburgh Festival, 1982; San Francisco Opera, 1982; La Fenice, 1984; Teatro di San Carlo, Naples, 1984; Canadian Opera, 1984; Handel festival at Carnegie Hall, 1984; Chicago Lyric Opera, 1986; Santa Fe Opera, 1986; Metropolitan Opera, 1988 as Tolomeo in Giulio Cesare; Sang Ruggiero in Orlando Furioso at San Francisco 1989, Polinesso in Ariodante at Philadelphia 1990, Handel's Flavio at Monte Carlo; Has also sung in operas by Jommelli, Lully, Pergolesi, Cesti, Purcell, Scarlatti and Mozart; television appearances include title role in Handel's Giulio Cesare, in production by Peter Sellars; Season 1992 as Farnace in Mozart's Mitridate at Amsterdam, Britten's Oberon at Los Angeles and in Conti's Don Chisciotte at the Innsbruck Festival of Early Music; Performed Oberon in Britten's Midsummer Night's Dream with the Frankfurt Opera, Ottone in Monteverdi's Poppea for the Köln Opera, the role of David in Handel's Saul, with the Boston Cecelia Society, 1993; Returning to the Metropolitan Opera in Britten's Death in Venice, 1994. *Recordings:* For Columbia; Nonesuch; Titanic; Smithsonian; Harmonia Mundi, including Flavio, conducted by René Jacobs. *Honours:* First Prize, Bodky Award for Performance of Early Music, 1977. *Current Management:* William Knight. *Address:* c/o William Knight, 309 Wood Street, Burlington. New Jersey 08016, USA.

GALLAGHER Jack B, b. 27 June 1947, Forest Hills, New York, USA. Composer; Conductor; Trumpeter; Educator. m. April Lorenz, 19 Aug. 1977. 1 son, 1 daughter. *Education:* BA, cum laude, Hofstra University, 1969; MFA, Composition 1975, DMA, Composition 1982, Cornell University. *Debut:* Carnegie Recital Hall, New York City, 1978. *Career:* Associate Principal Trumpet, National Orchestral Association, New York City, 1968-70; Graduate Teaching Assistant, Cornell University, 1971-75; Professor of Composition, Music Theory and Trumpet, The College of Wooster, Ohio, 1977-; Associate Music Director, Wooster Symphony Orchestra, 1984-85; Music Director, 1985-86; Acting Chair, Department of Music, 1992-93. *Compositions:* Divertimento for Orchestra; Diversions Overture; Berceuse; Two Pieces for String Orchestra; The Persistence of Memory (In Memoriam: Brian Israel); Diversions; Mist-covered Mountain; Heritage Music; Three Wordsworth Poems; To Those Who've Failed; Invocation; Sonatas for Cello, Piano, Trumpet, Tuba; Variations for Woodwind Quintet; Celebration and Reflection; Three Songs of Love, Joy and the Beauty of Night; Symphony in One Movement: Threnody, 1991. *Recordings:* Toccata for Brass Quintet, 1986; Diversions, 1988; Mist-covered Mountain, 1988. *Publications:* Toccata for Brass Quintet, 1981; Sonata for Unaccompanied Trumpet, 1982; Sonata Breve for Unaccompanied Tuba, 1983; Resonances, 1984; Elegy, 1987; Capriccio for Two Trumpets, 1987; Berceuse for Orchestra, 1993; Celebration and Reflection, 1994; Intrada from Diversions, 1994. *Hobbies:* Reading; Films; Sports. *Address:* Scheide Music Center, The College of Wooster, Wooster, OH 44691, USA.

GALLI Dorothea, b. 11 Nov 1951, Zurich, Switzerland. Singer (Soprano). m. Rudolf Bamert. *Education:* Studied with Elsa Cavelti and Elisabeth Schwarzkopf and at the Salzburg Mozarteum. *Career:* Sang at the Zurich Opera, 1976-78, Kaiserslautern 1978-79, Gelsenkirchen 1979-82; Guest appearances at the Deutsche Oper am Rhein Dusseldorf, Karlsruhe, Mannheim, Dortmund, Heidelberg and Amsterdam; Roles have included Mozart's Donna Elvira, Fiordiligi and Ramiro (La Finta Giardiniera); Leonore, Marguerite, Mimi, Tatiana, the Marschallin, Arabella, Emilia Marty and Giorgietta in Gianni Schicchi; Many Lieder recitals and performancces of oratorio. *Address:* c/o Opernhaus Zurich, Falkenstrasse 1, CH-8008 Zurich, Switzerland.

GALLIA Thomas Nicolas, b. 27 Sept 1921, Budapest, Hungary. Engineer. m. Brigitte Deloche, 4 Apr 1970. 1 daughter. *Education:* History of Arts, Asthetics, Unviersity Peter Pazany, Budapest; Telecommunications Engineer, State Polytechnical University of Budapest; Piano Diploma, Liszt Ferenc Academy of Music, Budapest, 1944. *Debut:* Hungarian Radio. *Career:* Hungarian Radio, 1947-51; Chief Engineer, Hungarian State Gramophone Record Company, 1951-56; Pathe Marconi, Paris, France, 1957-60; Disquest Charlin, 1960-65; Studio Director, Angelicum Milano Gramophon Company, 1961-75; Artistic and Technical Director, Sonart Recordings, Milan, Italy, 1975-. *Recordings:* Produced or Directed more than 1300 records of classical music. *Publications:* Schalltechnik; Journal of the Audio Engineering Society; Il Suono Milano; La Revue du Son, Paris. *Honours:* 32 Awards. *Membership:* Aduio Engineering Society. *Hobby:* Research of Folcloric Music. *Address:* 13 Via della Moscova, 20121 Milan, Italy.

GALLIERA Alceo, b. 3 May 1910, Milan, Italy. Conductor; Composer. *Education:* Studied with his father and at the Parma and Milan Conservatories. *Career:* Lecturer in organ and organ composition at the Milan Conservatory, 1932; Debut as conductor 1941, Orchestra di santa Cecilia, Rome; Conducted at the Lucerne Festival 1945; Tours of Israel, North and South America, Europe and Australia; Teatro San Carlo Naples 1957-60, with operas by Verdi, Rossini and Puccini; Artistic Director and resident conductor of the Strasbourg Municipal Orchestra from 1964. *Compositions include:* Scherzo tarantella and Poema dell'Ala for orchestra; Ballet Le Vergini savie e le Vergini folli (The Wise and Foolish Virgins), produced at La Scala. *Recordings:* Music by Franck, Falla, Stravinsky, Debussy and Beethoven with the Philharmonia Orchestra; Rossini and Verdi overtures; Carmen, and Il Barbiere di Siviglia, with Callas; Tchaikovsky overtures and 1st Piano Concerto; Tod und Verklärung and Strauss Oboe Concerto, with Leon Goossens (EMI); Monteverdi's Orfeo; Symphonies, Piano Concertos, Clarinet Concerto and Sinfonie Concertante K364 and 297b by Mozart; Rigoletto, with the Bavarian State Opera Orchestra (Electrola).

GALLO F Alberto, b. 17 Oct 1932, Verona, Italy. Professor, History of Music. *Education:* LLD; PhD. *Publications include:* Antonii Romani Opera, 1965; Mensurabilis Musicae Tractatuli, 1966; Franchini Gafurii Extractus Paruvs Musicae, 1969; Petrus Picardus Ars Motettorium Compilata Breviten, 1971; Johannes Boen Ars Musicae, 1972; La Prima Rappresentazione al Teatro Olimpico, 1973; Italian Sacred Music, 1976; Storia Della Musica: Il Medioevo, 1977; Il Codice Musicale 2216 della Biblioteca Universitaria di Bologna, 1968-70; Il Codice Musicale Panciatichi 26 della Biblioteca Nazionale di Firenze, 1981; Geschichte der Musiktheorie, 1984; Music of the Middle Ages, 1985; Musica e Storia tra Medio Evole Eta moderna, 1986; Italian Sacred and Ceremonial Music, 1987; Musica nel castella, Bologna, 1992; Il codice Squarcialupi, Firenze, 1992. *Contributions to:* Acta Musicologica; Annales Musicologiques; Archiv für Musikwissenschaft; Die Musik in Geschichte und Gegenwart; Grove's Dictionary; Handworterbuch der Musikalischen Terminologie; Musica Disciplina; Quadrivium. *Honour:* Dent Medal, 1966; Premio Iglesias, 1992. *Memberships:* International Italian & American Musicological Societies; Gesellschaft fur Musikforschung. *Address:* L Alberti 34, 40137 Bologna, Italy.

GALLOIS Henri, b. 11 May 1944, Alger, France. Conductor. *Education:* Studied in Nice, Grenoble and Paris. *Career:* Made conducting tour of France 1964; Permanent Conductor. Dijon Opera 1970-72; Theatre du Capitole Toulouse 1972-79; Music Director of the Opera du Nord 1979-; Has conducted revivals of Gounod's Philémon et Baucis and the oratorio Mors et Vita; D'Albert's Tiefland and La Testament de tante Caroline by Roussel; Premieres conducted include Evening Shadows by Nikiprowetszky, 1974 and Aliana by Ancelin, 1981. *Honours include:* Prize winner, Besançon International Competition, 1969.

GALOS Andrew John, b. 18 Feb 1918, Hungary. Violinist; Conductor; Educator. m. Ruth Fishberg, 2 Nov 1945. 1 son. *Education:* City College of New York; Teachers College, Columbia University; MA, Music Education and Conducting, 1952; EdD, 1958; BS 1942; MD 1952; Scholarship in Violin; Juilliard School of Music; Fellowship in conducting. *Debut:* Brahms Violin Concerto A, Abravanel conducting The Utah Symphony, Utah 1956. *Career:* 1st Violinist, NBC Symphony under Toscanini; Assistant Concert Master, Baltimore Symphony, Maryland, 1946-48; Violin Professor, Peabody Conservatory of Music, Baltimore; Concert Master, Assistant Conductor 1969-74, Portland Symphony, Maine; Savannah Symphony, Georgia; Soloist with Boston Pops, 1973, 1974; New Orleans Symphony; Columbus Symphony, Georgia; Violin Professor, Chamber Music Professor and Director of Orchestra, Utah State University, 1956-60; University of New Hampshire, 1956-60; University of Akron, Ohio; University of Tulsa, Oklahoma; Chairman of The Music Department, Columbus College, 1969-80; Violin Professor, University of South Florida, 1982-; Member of Mischakoff and Galimir String Quartets, 1950; Assistant Conductor, Co-Concert Master, Fort Meyers Symphony Florida, 1986-; Wilkes Un 1988; Pacific Un 1990; Un of Tampa. *Recordings:* RCA Victor Labels: Symphonies 1-9 by Beethoven, as 1st Violinist, NBC Symphony, under Toscanini; Same with Brahms Symphonies, 1-4. *Hobbies:* Swimming; Photography. *Address:* 4214 Golf Club Lane, Tampa, FL 33624, USA.

GALTERIO Lou, b. 29 Nov 1942, New York, USA. Opera Director and Administrator. *Education:* Studied at Marquette Univertsity, Milwaukee (BA 1964). *Career:* Worked as an actor and theatre director; Opera productions for the Opera Theater of St Louis include Così fan Tutte, Le Nozze di Figaro, Albert Herring, Ariadne auf Naxos and the US premiere of Prokofiev's Maddalena, 1982; Director of opera production at the Manhattan School from 1977; Santa Fe Opera, Il Barbire di Siviglia and Hindemith's Neues vom Tage 1981; Kennedy Center Washington, Argento's Postcard from Morocco 1979; New York City Opera 1980, La Cenerentola; Chicago Opera Theater 1984, Don Giovanni; Staged Don Giovanni at Santa Fe, 1992. *Address:* Manhattan School of Music, 120 Claremont Avenue, New York, NY 10027, USA.

GALVANY Marisa, b. 19 June 1936, Paterson, New Jersey, USA. Singer (Soprano). *Education:* Studied with Armen Boyajian. *Debut:* Seattle Opera 1968, as Tosca. *Career:* New York City Opera from 1972, as Elizabeth I in Maria Stuarda, Anna Bolena, Medée, Santuzza and Violetta; Mexico City and San Francisco 1972-73, Aida; New Orleans 1974, as Rachel in La Juive; Guest appearances in Philadelphia, Warsaw, Prague, Belgrade and Rouen; Metropolitan Opera from 1979, as Norma, Ortrud, and the Kostelnička in Jenůfa; other roles include Verdi's Hélène, Abigaille and Elvira, Turandot, Mozart's Countess, Massenet's Salomé and Tchaikosky's Iolanta. *Recordings include:* Title role in Medea in Corinto by Giovanni Simone Mayr. *Address:* c/o Metropolitan Opera, Lincoln Center, NY 10023, New York, USA.

GALWAY James, b. 8 Dec 1939, Belfast, Northern Ireland. Flute player. m. (1) 1965, 1 son. (2) 1972, 1 son, 2 daughters. (3) Jeanne Cinnante, 1984. *Education:* RCM; Guildhall School of Music, London; Conservatoire National Superieur de Musique, Paris, France. *Career:* First post, wind band of Royal Shakespeare Theatre, Stratford-on-Avon; worked with Sadler's Wells Orchestra, Royal Opera House Orchestra, BBC Symphony Orchestra. Principal Flute, London Symphony Orchestra, 1966; Royal Philharmonic Orchestra, 1967-69; Principal Solo Flute, Berlin Philharmonic orchestra, 1969-75; International soloist, 1975-. *Recordings:* Works by CPE Bach, JS Bach, Beethoven, Corigliano, Debussy, Franck, Handel, Khachaturian, Mancini, Mozart, Nielsen, Prokofiev, Reicha, Reinecke, Rodrigo, Schubert, Stamitz, Telemann, Vivaldi; albums of flute showpieces, Australian, Irish and Japanese collections. *Publications:* James Galway: An Autobiography, 1978; Flute (Menuhin Music Guide), 1982; James Galway's Music in Time, 1983 (TV series, 1983); Masterclass; performance editions of great flute literature, 1987. *Honours:* OBE, 1977; FRCM, 1983; Grand Prix du Disque, 1976; Hon MA Open University, 1979; Hon DMus Queen's University, 1979; Hon DMus New England Conservatory of Music, 1980; Officier Arts et des Lettres, 1987. *Membership:* FBSM, Fellow of Birmingham Schools of Music. *Hobbies:* Music; Walking; Swimming; Films; Theatre; TV; Chess; Backgammon; Computing; Talking to people. *Current Management:* IMG Artists (Europe). *Address:* c/o Kathryn Enticott IMG Artists, Media House, 3 Burlington Lane, Chiswick, London, W4 2TH, England.

GAMBA Piero, b. 16 Sept 1936, Rome, Italy. Conductor. *Education:* Studied piano and score-reading with his father. *Career:* Conducted Beethoven's 1st Symphony at the Rome Opera House, aged 8; Tours of Europe and North and South America while a child; British debut 1948, conducting Beethoven and Dvořák in London; Moved to Madrid 1952; Guest engagements in London 1959-63, often with the London Symphony Orchestra; Musical Director, Winnipeg Symphony Orchestra, Canada, 1970-81; Principal Conductor, Adelaide Symphony Orchestra, from 1982-88. *Recordings include:* Rossini Overtures with the London Symphony Orchestra; Beethoven's Piano Concertos, with Julius Katchen as soloist. *Address:* c/o Adelaide Symphony Orchestra, ABC, GPO Box 9994, Adelaide 5A 5001.

GAMBERINI Leopoldo, b. 12 Mar 1922, Como, Italy. Composer; Musicologist. m. Graziella Benini, 27 Dec 1961. 2 children. *Education:* Graduate, Conservatory of Genoa, Italy; Student of Markevich (Salzburg, Austria); Academia Chigiana (Siena, Italy). *Career includes:* Founder and conductor, I Madriagalisti, Genoa; Numerous conducting tours, Europe; Lecturer, history of music theory, Professor, music history, Faculty of Arts, University of Genoa; Music critic, Il Nuovo Cittadino, Genoa. *Compositions include:* Sonata for Flute & harpsichord, 1974; Various piano works, symphonic suites & symphonies, chamber music. *Recordings:* Numerous recordings, ancient & Renaissance music. *Contributions to:* Various scholarly journals. *Honours:* Decoration, Belgian Government; Award, International Music Festival, Belgium. *Memberships:* Royaume de la Musique (honorary); Fondatore della Associazione I Madrigalisti de Genova. *Address:* Via Trieste 8/13, Genova, Italy.

GAMBERONI Kathryn, b. 11 June 1955, Pennsylvania, USA. Singer (Soprano). *Education:* Studied at the Curtis Institute. *Debut:* St Louis, 1981, as Gerda in the US premiere of Fennimore and Gerda by Delius. *Career:* Sang with the St Louis Company at the Edinburgh Festival, 1983 (Margot la Rouge by Delius); Seattle Opera from 1985 as Adina, Despina, Adele Juliette Zerbinetta and Marzelline, 1991; Santa Fe, 1985, in the US premiere of The English Cat by Henze, returning in 1989 in Judith Weir's A Night at the Chinese Opera and as Satirino in La Calisto; Guest appearances in Paris, Dallas, Cologne, Chicago, and Melbourne; Other roles include Mozart's Blondchen, Susanna and Papagena, and Fanny in Rossini's La Cambiale di Matrimonio; Sang Rosina in Paisiello's Il Barbiere di Siviglia for Long Beach Opera, 1989, and the title role in The Cunning Little Vixen at the New York City Opera, 1991.

GAMBILL Robert, b. 1955, Indianapolis, Indiana, USA. Singer (Tenor). *Education:* Studied at the Hamburg Musikhochschule with Hans Kagel; Debut at Milan 1981, as Michael in the premiere of Stockhausen's Donnerstag aus Licht. *Career:* Sang at Frankfurt from 1981, notably in Die Gezeichneten by Schreker; Sang at Wiesbaden as Ernsto, Tamino, Don Ottavio and Nicolai's Fenton; Glyndebourne 1982-85, as Almaviva in Il Barbiere di Siviglia and Don Ramiro in La Cenerentola; La Scala Milan 1982; Teatro La Fenice, Venice, as Ferrando in Così fan Tutte, 1983; Sang David in Die Meistersinger, at the renovated Zurich Opera, 1984; Geneva and Aix-en-Provence 1984, as Rossini's Lindoro and Almaviva; Season 1987/88 as Belmonte at Buenos Aires and the Steersman in Fliegende Holländer at La Scala, also at the Metropolitan 1989; Schwetzingen Festival 1987, as Rossini's Almaviva; Theater au der Wien Vienna 1988, in Schubert's Fierrabras; sang Almaviva at Munich 1990, Wagner's David at Covent Garden; other roles include Mozart's Ferrando, Renaud in Armide, Verdi's Fenton and Iopas in Les Troyens; Sang in Rossini double bill at Cologne and Schwetzingen, 1992. *Recordings include:* Rossini, Stabat Mater; Evander in Gluck's Orfeo ed Euridice; Tenor Solo in Messiah. *Address:* c/o Royal Opera House, Covent Garden, London, WC2.

GAMMON Philip Greenway, b. 17 May 1940, Chippenham, Wiltshire, England. Pianist; Conductor. m.

Floretta Volovini 1963, 2 sons. *Education:* Royal Academy of Music 1956-61; Pupil of Harold Craxton; Badische Musikhochschule 1961-64; Pupil of Yvonne Loriod. *Career:* Joined Royal Ballet, Covent Garden, 1964; Ballet for All Principal pianist 1968-71; Teaching appointments at Watford School of Music and Trinity College; Returned to Royal Ballet 1972; Solo pianist for many ballets including Elite Syncopations, A Month in the Country and Return to the Strange Land; Conducting debut with Ballet for All at Richmond Theatre 1970; At Covent Garden 1978, Sleeping Beauty; Radio 3 broadcasts in recitals as soloist and accompanist; Debut Festival Hall and Barbican Hall in 1984 as piano soloist. *Recordings:* Elite Syncopations, with musicians from the Covent Garden Orchestra; A Month in the Country, Chopin/Lanchbery. *Publication:* First orchestral arrangement of La Chatte Metamorphosée en femme, premiered in 1985 at the Royal Opera House. *Honours:* Recital Diploma 1960; MacFarren Gold Medal 1961; Karlsruhe Culture Prize 1962; Badische Musikhochschule Diplom 1963; ARCM (Performers) 1969; ARAM, 1991. *Hobbies:* Walking; Yoga; Reading. *Address:* 19 Downs Avenue, Pinner, Middlesex HA5 5AQ, England.

GANSEMANS Jos, b. 7 Dec 1942, Buizingen, Belgium. Ethnomusicologist. m. Chris Nieuwenhuysen, 20 Jan 1967, 2 sons, 1 daughter. *Education:* Katholieke Universiteit, Leuven; Conservatory of Music, Halle, 1962; Doctor 1973. *Career:* Radio Lectures on Folk Music; Visiting Professor, Musicology, KUL, 1982-83; Head, Ethnomusicological Section, Royal Museum of Central Africa, Tervuren, Belgium. *Recordings:* Various records; 3 cassettes. *Publications:* La musique et son rôle dans la vie sociale et rituelle des Luba, 1978; Les instruments de musique Luba, 1980; Zentralafrika, 1986; Les instruments de musique du Rwanda, 1988. *Memberships:* International Council for Traditional Music; Ethnomusicology Society. *Hobbies:* Sports; Films. *Address:* Oude Baan 121, 3060 Bertem, Belgium.

GANZ Isabelle Myra, b. 9 Dec 1937, New York City, USA. Mezzo-Soprano. m. Abbie Lipschutz, 1966, 2 daughters. *Education:* BA, 1964, MM, 1968, University of Houston; DMA, Eastman School of Music, 1980. *Debut:* As Pianist with New York Philharmonic, 1947. *Career:* Soloist, Brooklyn Philharmonic Orchestra; New York City Symphony; New Jersey Symphony; Midland-Odessa Symphony; Arad Philharmonic, Romania; Houston Grand Opera; Solo appearances: Aspen Music Festival, Vermont Mozart Festival; St Cyprien International Festival of the Arts, France; Concert Tours: British Isles, Spain, Korea, Holland, Israel, Turkey, Lithuania, Colombia, Canada; Director, Alhambra ensemble. *Recordings:* Ryoanji; John Cage, Three Spanish Songs; The Art of Judeo-Spanish Song; Folksongs; Master Musicians' Collective, Three Songs of Pablo Neruda, McKinley. *Hobbies:* Composing; Swimming. *Address:* 2317 Southgate, Houston, TX 77030, USA.

GANZAROLLI Wladimiro, b. 9 Jan 1932, Venice, Italy. Singer (Bass). *Education:* Studied at the Bendetto Marcello Conservatory, Venice. *Debut:* Teatro Nuovo Milan 1958, as Mephistopheles in Faust. *Career:* Sang at La Scala Milan from 1959, notably as Falstaff and as Bottom in the local premiere of Britten's A Midsummer Night's Dream; Spoleto 1959, in a revival of Il Duca d'Alba by Donizetti; Monte Carlo 1960; Vienna Staatsoper from 1964; Teatro Colón Buenos Aires 1966, as Leporello in Don Giovanni; Sang as guest in the USA, notably in San Francisco, Chicago, Dallas and at the Metropolitan Opera 1968. *Recordings:* Le Nozze di Figaro, Così fan Tutte and Don Giovanni, conducted by Colin Davis (Philips); La Vera Costanza by Haydn, conducted by Antal Dorati; Un Giorno di Regno and Stiffelio by Verdi; Les Huguenots by Meyerbeer; Luisa Miller. *Address:* c/o Teatra alla Scala, Via Filodrammatici 2, Milan, Italy.

GARAVANTA Ottavio, b. 26 Jan 1934, Genoa, Italy. Singer (Tenor). *Education:* Studied with Rosetta Noli and Vladimiro Badiali. *Debut:* Milan 1954, as Don Ottavio.

Career: Sang major roles in Italy at La Scala and in Rome, Florence and Verona; Guest engagements in Vienna, Buenos Aires, Berlin, Marseilles, Brussels, Chicago, San Francisco, Lisbon and Belgrade; Glyndebourne Festival 1967, as Rodolfo in La Bohème; Has often appeared in revivals of neglected Italian operas: Théâtre de la Monnaie Brussels 1980, in Donizetti's Il Duca d'Alba, Genoa 1985 as Cadmo in Donizetti's Il Diluvio Universale; Sang Carlo in a concert performance of Verdi's Giovanna d'Arco opposite Margaret Price, Festival Hall, London 1989; Teatro Regio Turin 1990, as Radames. *Recordings:* Scenes from Rossini's Otello, with Virginia Zeani (Philips); Mosè in Egitto by Rossini (Estro Armonico); Admeti in Dejanice by Catalani (Bongiovanni). *Honours:* Winner of the Verdi Competition at Bussetto and competitions at Genoa and Modena. *Address:* c/o Teatro Regio di Torino, Piazza Castello 215, I- 10124 Turin, Italy.

GARAZZI Peyo, b. 31 Mar 1937, St Jean Pied de Port, Basses Pyrenees, France. Singer (Tenor). *Education:* Studied in Bordeaux and Paris. *Career:* Sang first at the Théâtre de la Monnaie Brussels; Royal Opera Ghent 1962, as Nadir in Les Pêcheurs de Perles; Paris 1977, in Gwendoline by Chabrier; Guest appearances in Bordeaux, Munich and Berlin; Covent Garden Opera 1983, as Don Carlos in a French language revival of Verdi's opera; Other roles include Florestan, Aron in Moses and Aron by Schoenberg and parts in operas by Delibes, Donizetti, Offfenbach and Puccini. *Recordings include:* Don Quichotte by Massenet (Decca).

GARBOUSOVA Raya, b. 25 Sept 1906, Tbilsi, Georgia, Russia. Cellist; Professor of Cello. *Education:* Studied at the Tbilsi Conservatory, 1914-23. *Debut:* Moscow 1923. *Career:* Left USSR 1925 and appeared in Berlin, Paris and London, 1926-28; New York debut 1935, settled in USA 1939; Concerts with leading orchestras in the US and Europe; Gave the premieres of works written for her by Samuel Barber (Concerto, with the Boston Symphony conducted by Koussevitsky, 1946), Karol Rathaus and Vittorio Rieti; Edited for publication and premiered works by Paul Creston, Hindemith, Martinů and Prokofiev; Master classes at Aspen, the Cleveland Institute of Music and Indiana University; Professor of Cello at Hartt College, University of Hartford, Connecticut, from 1970.

GARCIA Orlando, b. 13 Feb 1954, Havana, Cuba. Composer; Professor. m. 31 July 1982, 2 sons. *Education:* BA, Frostburg State University; BMus, Florida International University; MMus, DMA, Composition, University of Miami. *Career:* Associate Professor and Director of Music Theory/Composition at Florida International University; Founder and President, South Florida Composers Alliance; Founder and Co-Director: FIU May in Miami Young Composers Festival, FIU Electronic Music Stiduo, FIU New Music Ensemble. *Compositions:* Threnody for the Americas, soprano and orchestra, 1988; Improvisations with Metallic Images, wind synthesizer and tape; Varadero memories (Recuerdos), for orchestra; Spheres; La Luz Penetra el Cristal; Despues del 24 de Agosto, 1992. *Recordings:* Spheres; Four Individual Migrations; The Beauty of Silence; Escher Waterfall, Images of Wood and Wire. *Honours:* Fulbright Scholar, 1991-92; Various grants from FIU, NEA Dade County and State of Florida. *Address:* 13525 SW 115 Place, Miami, FL 33176, USA.

GARCIA NAVARRO Luis, b. 30 Apr 1941, Chiva, (Valencia), Spain. Conductor. *Education:* Studied at Conservatories of Valencia and Madrid and in Italy with Franco Ferrara; Vienna Academy with Hans Swarowsky. *Career:* Founded the Orchestra of the Spanish University Society, 1963; Permanent conductor of the Valencia Symphony 1970-74; Musical Director of San Carlos Theatre at Lisbon, 1980-82; Principal Guest Conductor of the Radio Symphony Orchestra Stuttgart, 1984-87; Generalmusikdirektor of the Stuttgart State Opera 1987-91; Principal Guest Conductor of the Vienna State Opera, 1987-91; Musical and artistic Conductor of the Barcelona Symphony Orchestra, 1991-93. Since 1992 Principal Guest Conductor of the Tokyo Philharmonic Orchestra (Japan), and Permanent Guest Conductor at Deutsche Oper Berlin. Appearances in most of the major Opera Theatres in the World such as Covent Garden: Bohème, 1979 and Tosca, 1983; Paris Opera: Carmen, 1982; San Fe Opera, Aida, 1980, Bohème, 1982, Carmen, 1983; Chicago Lyric Opera: Bohéme, 1983; Metropolitan Cav/Pag, 1986, Tosca, 1987; Scala Milano: Madame Butterfly, 1987, Colon Buenos Aires: Otello, 1988; Vienna State Opera: Falstaff, Bohème, Tosca, Cav/Pag, La Forza del Destino, Andrea Chenier. Also has conducted among others the Vienna Philharmonic, London Symphony and Philharmonia, Leningrad Philharmonic, the Chicago Symphony, Pittsburgh Symphony, Los Angeles Philharmonic. *Recordings:* Several, including those for DG, CBS, EMI, RCA, Cappiccio. *Honours:* First Prize, Madrid Conservatory 1963; Prize winner, International Competition Besançon 1967; Gold Medal, Paris City, 1983. *Memberships:* Royal Academy of San Carlos, Spain. *Address:* Conciertos Vitoria, Amaniel 5-50-2, 28015 Madrid, Spain.

GARCIA-ASENSIO Enrique, b. 22 Aug 1937, Valencia, Spain. Conductor. *Education:* Royal Conservatory of Music, Madrid, gaining Master's degree in Violin, Harmony, Counterpoint, Fugue, Chamber Music and Composition; Orchestra Conducting at Higher School of Music, Munich, with Professors Lessing, Eichhorn and Mennerich; Further study, Accademia Chigiana, Siena, with Sergiu Celibidache. *Career:* Has conducted all leading Spanish orchestras; Music Director, Conductor, Philharmonic of Las Palmas, Canary Islands, 1962-64, Valencia Municipal Orchestra, 1964-65, Spanish Radio and TV Orchestra, Madrid, 1966-84; Assistant Conductor, National Symphony Orchestra, Washington DC, season 1967-68; Currently Principal Guest Conductor, Valencia Orchestra, Music Director and Conductor, Madrid Symphonic Municipal Band; Has led orchestras in Canada, US, Mexico, Dominican Republic, Brazil, Uruguay, Argentina, Portugal, France, Italy, England, Belgium, Russia, Japan, Northern Ireland, Israel, Greece, Netherlands, Denmark, Rumania, Puerto Rico, Czechoslovakia, Austria, Germany, Bulgaria, Switzerland, Iceland; Symphonic and operatic repertory; Assistant to Celibadache at master classes, Bologna, Munich; Professor of Conducting, Royal Conservatory of Music, Madrid, 1970-; Has given international master classes, Netherlands, Dominican Republic; Presentes The World of Music educational TV programme for 4 years. *Recordings:* Numerous including: Zarzuela, Teresa Berganza and English Chamber Orchestra, 1976; Ernesto Halffter, English Chamber Orchestra, 1991. *Honours:* RAI Prize, 1962; Chigiana Academy Prize, 1963; 1st Prize and Gold Medal, Dimitri Mitropoulos International Competition for Conductors, 1967; Prize, Best Conductor in Madrid Opera Season, 1967; Charles Cros Academy Prize for recording, 1976; Ministry of Culture Prize, Best Interpretation of Spanish composition recorded by Spanish company, 1991; National Music Prize, life dedicated to Music, Cultura Viva, 1992. *Memberships:* San Carlos Royal Academy of Fine Arts, Valencia; Cultural Council, Government of Valencia. *Address:* Gavilan 8, 28230 Las Rozas, Madrid, Spain.

GARCISANZ Isabel, b. 29 June 1934, Madrid, Spain. Singer (Soprano). *Education:* Studied with Angeles Ottein in Spain and with Erik Werba in Vienna. *Debut:* Vienna Volksoper 1964, as Adèle in Le Comte Ory. *Career:* Sang in Paris at the Opéra and the Opéra-Comique; Guest appearances in Bordeaux, Marseille, Nancy, Nice, Cologne, Barcelona and Miami; Glyndebourne 1966-68, 1970, as Concepcion in L'Heure Espagnole, Nerillo in L'Ormindo and Zaida (Il Turco in Italia); Toulouse 1972-73, in the premieres of operas by Casanova and Niki Prowetsky; Strasbourg 1974, in the premiere of Delereue's Medis et Alissio; Engagements with French Radio, Paris, in the first performances of works by Mihalovici, she was also the first singer of Hahn's Sybille. *Recordings:* L'Ormindo (Decca); Le maître de Chapelle by Paer (Barclay); Le Roi malgré Lui by Chabrier (RCA); Cantigas, Sybille, Mass by Ohana (Erato); 3 centuries of spanish melodies

(Arion); Spanish songs, by Rodrigo, Falla, Garcia. *Memberships:* Acanthes; Uffam (Union des Femmes Artists Musiciennes). *Current Management:* Agence Thérèse Cedelle, 78 Blvd Makesherres, 75008 Paris, France. *Address:* c/o Opéra du Rhin, 19 Place Broglie, F-67008 Strasbourg-Cédex, France.

GARD Robert, b. 7 Mar 1927, Cornwall, England. Singer (Tenor). *Education:* Studied with Dino Borgoli, with Walter Hyde at the Guildhall School of Music and with Professor Kaiser Breme in Bayreuth. *Debut:* English Opera Group in Lennox Berkeley's, Ruth, 1957. *Career:* Sang for Welsh National Opera then at Aldeburgh and in Australia as Britten's Peter Quint (The Turn of the Screw), Albert Herring, Male Chorus and Aschenbach; Sang Anatol in War and Peace at the opening of the Sydney Opera House, 1973, and appeared on television in this production, Charpentier's Louise and Manon; Sang Aschenbach in a film version of Britten's Death in Venice, 1981, commissioned by the Britten Foundation; Other roles have included Aegist, Herod, Loge, Siegmund, Tamino, Steva in Jenufa, Peter Grimes, Tom Rakewell and Le Mesurier in the premiere of Meale's Voss 1986. *Honours:* Awarded the OBE, 1981. *Address:* c/o Australian Opera, Sydney Opera House, Sydney, NSW, Australia.

GARDELLI Lamberto, b. 8 Nov 1914, Venice, Italy. Conductor. *Education:* Studied at the Liceo Musicale Rossini in Peasro, and in Rome. *Career:* Assistant to Serafin in Rome; Opera debut Teatro Reale Rome 1944, La Traviata; Conducted the Royal Opera Stiockholm 1946-55; Conductor of the Danish Radio Symphony Orchestra 1955-61; Guest appearances in Berlin and Helsinki; Music Director Budapest Opera from 1961; US debut Carnegie Hall New York 1964, Bellini's I Capuleti e i Montecchi; Glyndebourne 1964, l968 (Macbeth and Anna Bolena); Metropolitan Opera from 1966, with Andrea Chénier, Rigoletto and Madama Butterfly; Royal Opera Covent Garden 1969, Otello; Royal Opera Copenhagen from 1973; Conducted La Forza del Destino at Budapest, 1990; Rossini's Moise et Pharaon, 1992. *Recordings include:* Guillaume Tell by Rossini; Verdi's La Forza del Destino, Macbeth, I Lombardi and Nabucco; Respighi's La Fiamma, Belfagor and Maria Egiziaca. *Address:* c/o Hungarian State Opera, Nepoztarsasag Utja 22, 1061 Budapest, Hungary.

GARDINER John Eliot, b. 20 Apr 1943, Dorset, England. conductor. m. Elizabeth Suzanne Wilcock, 1981, 3 daughters. *Education:* King's College Cambridge, Certificate of Advanced Studies in Music; Studied with Nadia Boulanger in Paris, 1967-68. *Debut:* Sadler's Wells Opera, London, The Magic Flute, 1969. *Career:* Founder and Artistic Director of Monteverdi Choir, 1964, Orchestra, 1968, The English Baroque Soloists, 1978 and Orchestre Révolutionnaire et Romantique, 1990; Conductor, CBC Vancouver Orchestra, 1980- 83, Opera de Lyon, 1983-88; Artistic Director: Gottingen Handel Festival, 1988-90, Veneto Music Festival, 1986; Principal Conductor, NDR Symphony Orchestra, 1991-. Festivals at Aix-en-Provence, Aldeburgh, Bath, Berlin, Edinburgh, Flanders, Holland, City of London and Salzburg. *Recordings:* Numerous recordings of works by Handel, Haydn, Monteverdi, Mozart, Purcell and Schumann, among others. *Honours include:* DHon, University of Lyons, 1987; Officier de L'Ordre des Arts et Des Lettres, 1989; CBE, 1989; Honorary Fellow: King's College, London, 1992, RAM, London, 1992; International Classical Music Awards, Best Choir of the Year, with Monteverdi Choir, 1993. *Address:* Media House, 3 Burlington Lane, Chiswick, London W4 2TH, England.

GARDNER Gary David, b. 30 Apr 1949, Chicago, Illinois, USA. Conductor, Principal Hornist and Horn Professor. *Education:* MM, Chicago Musical College of Roosevelt University, 1967-68; 1982; 1986-87; BA, Delta State University, 1981-82; Kalamazoo College, Michigan, 1971-72; Ambassador College, St. Albans, England, 1968-71; Music Studies with Neill Sanders, Eugene Chausow and Rudolph Macciocchi. *Career includes:* Principal Horn, Orquesta Sinfonica del Noroeste de Guadalajara, Mexico, 1972-73; Principal Horn, Savannah, Georgia, Symphony Orchestra, 1973-78; Principal Horn, Jackson, Mississippi, Symphony Orchestra, 1978-81; Principal Horn, Singapore Symphony Orchestra, 1983-86; Principal Horn and Assistant Conductor, Rishon Le-Zion, Israel Symphony Orchestra, 1988-89; Artist/Clinician, The Selmer Company, 1978-82; Artist-Faculty, Sessione Senese per la Musica e l'Arte, Siena, Italy, 1979; Ensemble Coach, 12th International Horn Workshop, Indiana University, 1980; Adjunct Professor, Delta State University, 1981-82; Coach/Conductor, Singapore Youth Orchestra, 1983-86; Profesor, XVIII Festival Inverno de Campos do Jordao, Brazil, 1987; Conductor, Prism Music Festival Brass Choir, University of Chicago, 1988; Horn Instructor, VanderCook College of Music, 1988; Professor/Conductor, Escuela de Musica Victoriano Lopez, San Pedro Sula, Honduras, 1989-90; Special Workshop Instructor, University of Illinois at Chicago, 1990-91. *Compositions include:* Singapore Suite, for Flute and Horn, 1983, published by Israel Brass Woodwind Publications, 1989. *Hobby:* Running. *Address:* 1708 Emery Drive, Dellwood, MO 63136-2214, USA.

GARDNER Jake, b. 14 Nov 1947, Oneonta, NY, USA. Singer (Baritone). *Career:* Spent the first 10 years of career studying and performing with the Tri-Cities Opera, Binghamton, New York; Sang Valentin in Faust at Houston, 1975; Carnegie Hall 1976, in a concert performance of Le Cid by Massenet; Sang James Stewart in the premiere of Thea Musgrave's Mary Queen of Scots at the 1977 Edinburgh Festival, and repeated the role at Norfolk, Virginia (1978) and elsewhere; Appeared with Boston Opera in the 1979 US premiere of Tippett's The Ice Break and has sung at opera houses in Washington, Detroit, San Diego, San Francisco, New Orleans and St Louis; Has sung Mozart's Guglielmo and Figaro with Netherlands Opera, Escamillo in Peter Brook's version of Carmen throughout Europe and at Lincoln Center; Wexford Festival debut 1987 as Valdeburgo in La Straniera; Has also sung the title role in Il Ritorno di Ulisse conducted by Nicholas McGegean for Long Beach Opera and in the premiere of Musgrave's Incident at Owl Creek Bridge, for BBC Radio 3; Principal baritone at Cologne Opera from 1989, as Valentin, Nardo in La Finta Giardiniera, Mozart's Count, Puccini's Lescaut and Marcello, Belcore in L'Elisir d'Amore; Concert performances of Figaro and the Glagolitic Mass, conducted by Simon Rattle; Glyndebourne Festival debut 1991, as Guglielmo; Other roles include Rossini's Figaro (Miami Opera, 1989), Don Carlos in La Forza del Destino, Germont, Enrico in Lucia (San Francisco), Donner (Rheingold) and Zurga in Les Pêcheurs de Perles; Sang Lockit in The Beggar's Opera at Santa Fe, 1992; Weill/Grosz concert at the 1993 London Proms. *Recordings include:* Le Cid (CBS); Mary, Queen of Scots. *Address:* c/o John Coast Ltd, 31 Sinclair Road, London WC4 ONS, England.

GARDNER John Linton, b. 2 Mar 1917, Manchester, England. Composer. m. Jane Margaret Mary Abercrombie, 19 Feb 1955, 1 son, 2 daughters. *Education:* BMus, Exeter College, Oxford. *Career includes:* Music staff, Royal Opera House, 1946-52; Tutor, Morley College, 1952-76 (Director of Music 1965-69); Professor, Royal Academy of Music, 1956-86. *Compositions:* 5 operas, including The Moon & Sixpence; 3 symphonies; 3 string quartets; 3 piano sonatas, concertos for Piano, trumpet, organ and oboe; brass chamber music; brass chamber music; 6 major cantatas for chorus & orchestra, including The Ballad of the White Horse; Music for smaller groups; Much unaccompanied choral music. *Recordings:* A Latter-Day Athenian Speaks; Theme & Variations for Brass; Quartet for Saxes; Tomorrow Shall Be My Dancing Day. *Contributions to:* Schumann, A Symposium; Musical Companion. Journals including: Listener; Musical Times; RAM Magazine; Tempo; Dublin Review. *Honours:* Gold Medal, Bax Society, 1958; C.B.E., 1976. *Memberships:* Deputy Chairman, PRS, 1983-88; Chairman 1963, Composers' Guild. *Hobbies:* Tesseraphily; Egrephily. *Address:* 20 Firswood Avenue, Ewell, Epsom, Surrey. KT19 0PR, England.

GARDNER Kay L, b. 8 Feb 1941, Freeport, New York, USA. Composer; Performer; Teacher of Healing Properties of Music. Divorced, 2 children. *Education:* MMus, State University of New York at Stony Brook; Private study with Samuel Baron and Antonia Brico; Master class with Jean Pierre Rampal; Workshops with Charlotte Selver in Sensory Awareness and with Paul Winter in ethnomusicology and improvisation; Seminars with Elizabeth Green in orchestral conducting. *Career:* Appearances in concert and recital in 40 USA States and three Canadian Provinces; TV interviews on local stations throughout USA; Regular playing of compositions on national radio series: Morning Pro Musica; Music from the Hearts of Space and All Things Considered; Playing of compositions in England, Finland, Japan, Denmark, Austrian radio; Music used in National Public TV science series, Nova, USA; Concert appearances in Scotland, England, Canada and Mexico. *Compositions:* A Rainbow Path, 1984; Golden City, 1983; The Rootwomen, 1982; The Seasons, 1982; Ladies Voices, 1981; The Rising Sun, 1981; Winter Night, Gibbons Moon, 1980; Mooncircles, 1975; Vocalise; A River Sings, 1985; Samba for Sunwomyn; The Elusive White Roebuck; Rainforest, 1986; North Coast Nights for String Quartet 1990; Viriditas 1989; Dancing 1988. *Recordings:* Fishers daughter; Troubadour Songs, 1986; Mooncircles 1975; Emerging 1978; Moods and Rituals 1981; Women's Orchestral Works 1981; A Rainbow Path 1984; Fishersdaughter 1986; Avalon 1989; Garden of Ecstasy 1989; Sounding the Inner Landscape 1990; Ocean Moon 1991.*Publications:* author of book, Sounding the Inner Landscape: Music as Medicine, 1990. *Hobbies:* Swimming; Hiking; Kayaking. *Address:* Box 33, Stonington, ME 04681, USA.

GARDOW Helrun, b. 8 Jan 1944, Eisenach, Germany. Singer (Mezzo- soprano). *Education:* Studied in Berlin and Milan and with Josef Metternich in Cologne. *Career:* Sang at the Bonn Opera 1969-76; Zurich Opera, 1976-87 in various roles including Orpheus and Dorabella; Appeared in the premieres of Kelterborn's Ein Engel Kommt nach Babyon, 1977 and Der Kirschgarten, 1984; Guest appearances at Copenhagen, Dusselsorf, Edinburgh, Berlin, Dresden, Munich, Milan and Vienna; Concert engagements in Frankfurt, Madrid, Amsterdam, Cologne and Naples; Active in Seoul, Korea from 1987 as singer and Director of Art-Com, Computer visual Art and Music. *Recordings:* Minerva in Il Ritorno di Ulisse, L'Incoronazione di Poppea, Dido and Aeneas, Bach Cantatas and Magnificat; Haydn's Theresia Mass and Mozart's Missa Brevis in D. *Address:* c/o Opernhaus Zurich, Falkenstrasse 1, CH-8008 Zurich, Switzerland.

GARETTI Helene, b. 1943, France. Singer (Soprano). *Education:* Studied at the Paris Conservatoire, and with Regine Crespin. *Career:* Sang first at Nice then Paris Opera from 1968, as Marguerite, Iphigenie (en Tauride), Médée, Chrysothemis (1987) and Desdemona (1988); Appearances at the Paris Opera-Comique as Mimi, Butterfly, Katya Kabanova and Donna Elvira (1988); San Sieglinde at Rouen, Marseille and elsewhere in France; Other roles have included Leonore, Ariadne and Marguerite in La Damnation de Faust; Sang Massenet's Grisélidis at Strasbourg, 1986.

GARIBOVA Karine, b. 1960, Moscow, Russia. Violinist. *Education:* Studied at the Central Music School, Moscow. *Career:* Co-founder, Quartet Veronique, 1989; Many concerts in the former Soviet Union and Russia, notably in the Russian Chamber Music Series and the 150th birthday celebrations for Tchaikovsky, 1990; Masterclasses at the Aldeburgh Festival 1991; Concert tour of Britain in season 1992-93; Repertoire includes works by Beethoven, Brahms, Tchaikovsky, Bartok, Shostakovich and Schnittke. *Recordings include:* Schnittke's 3rd Quartet. *Honours include:* Winner, all-Union String Quartet Competition, St Petersburg, 1990-91; Third Place, International Shostakovich Competition at St Petersburg, 1991, both with the Quartet Veronique. *Address:* c/o Sonata (Quartet Veronique), 11 Northgate Street, Glasgow G20 7AA, Scotland.

GARILLI Fabrizio, b. 29 July 1941, Monticelli d'Ongina, Piacenza, Italy. Musician (Pianist); Composer. m. Anna Paola Rossi, 8 Sept 1968, 1 son. *Education:* Diploma in Piano, Composition, Choral Music; Teaching qualification. *Debut:* Piano Soloist with orchestra, Beethoven's 3rd Concerto, Teatro Municipale, Piacenza. *Career:* Concerts as Solo Pianist with orchestra and chamber music; Conservatory Director. *Compositions:* Fantasie for piano; Cantico delle creature for soloists, choir and organ; Contrappunti su temi Gregoriani for organ and orchestra; Metamorfosi for 2 pianos and percussion; Laude for female choir and orchestra and narrator. *Recordings:* Music of 700 Italiano, Ciampi, Geluppi and Scarletti, and J S Bach's Il Clavicembalo ben Temperato (2 records). *Publications:* Studi per pianoforte; La Cartellina; Pezzi per cordo di voci bianche; Pezzi per organo. *Honours:* 1st Prize, F M Neapolitano Competition for Composition, Naples; 2nd Prize, Pedrollo, Milan; 1st Place, Assisi Prize; Various compositions commended in other composition competitions. *Hobby:* Music. *Address:* via A da Sangallo 22, 29100 Piacenza, Italy.

GARINO Gerard, b. 1 June 1949, Lancon, Provence, France. Singer (Tenor). *Education:* Studied at the Bordeaux Conservatoire and in Italy. *Debut:* Bordeaux, 1977, as Rossini's Almaviva. *Career:* Appearances at Bordeaux as Gerald in Lakmé and in La Dame Blanche and Gounod's Mireille; Further engagements as Mozart's Ferrando at Toulouse and Nadir in Les pecheurs de Perles at Aix; Paris Opera and Liege 1981, in Il matrimonio Segreto and Don Pasquale (Ernesto); Returned to Liege 1982 and 1987, as Idomeneo and in Gretry's Zemire; Portrait de Manon, Monte Carlo 1989; Season 1991 as Nadir at the Opera-Comique, Paris, Pylades in Iphigenie en Tauride by Piccinni at Rome and Masaniello in La Muette de Portici at Marseille; Other rules include Tonio (La Fille du Regiment), Macduff, Ismaele (Nabucco) and Nicias (Thais); Traviata et Romeo and Juliette à Lieges, Bohème à Toulouse, Thérèse (Massenet) à Monte Carlo, 1989; Manon (Massenet) à Bordeaux, Anna Bolena à Marseille, 1990; Werther at Festival Massenet and Festival de La Coruna, Spain, 1993. *Recordings:* L'Abandon d'Ariadne by Milhaud; Don Sanche by Liszt; Messiaen's St François d' Assise; Il Pitor Parigino by Cimarosa; Video of Carmen (as Remendado); Phantom of the Opera, film with Tony Richardson, La Mort d'Orphée, Berlioz. Honours include: Winner, 1973 Enrico Caruso Competition. *Address:* Teatro dell'Opera, Piazza B. Gigli, 00184 Rome, Italy.

GARLICK Nancy, b. 1 Feb 1946, New York, USA. Clarinetist; Conductor. m. Stevens Garlick, 30 Aug 1980. *Education:* BS Crane School of Music, NY, 1968; MMus, Manhattan School of Music, 1970; DMA, Catholic University of America, 1993. *Debut:* Carnegie Recital Hall, 1981. *Career:* Solo appearances at Boston Pops, Crane Symphony, Wooster Symphony, Charlottesville University Symphony, Paul Hill Chorale, Pennsylvania Sinfonia; Orchestral and chamber music experience with orchestras throughout America; Member of the Wooster Brio, Rbio Trio and currently, the Albemarle Ensemble; Artistic Director, Artist Faculty Chamber Music Series, UVA; Music Director and Conductor, Wooster Symphony Orchestra and Youth Orchestra of Charlottesville-Albemarle; The Mozart Ensemble; Artist in Residence, University of Virginia. *Recordings include:* Beethoven, Eroica Symphony and Barber, Knoxville 1915, 1982; Persichetti's King Lear, 1992. *Memberships:* Musician's Federation; College Music Society. *Hobbies:* Celtic Studies; Photography; Tennis. *Address:* 1831 Brenda Court, Charlottesville, VA 22901, USA.

GARNER Françoise, b. 17 Oct 1933, Nerac, Lot-et-Garonne, France. Singer (Soprano). *Education:* Studied at the Paris Conservatoire, the Accademia di Santa Cecilia Rome and in Vienna. *Debut:* Paris Opéra-Comique 1963, in the premiere of Menotti's Le Dernier

Sauvage. *Career:* Sang in Paris as Rosina, Leïla, Lakmé and Olympia; Paris Opera as Gilda and Lucia di Lammermoor; Aix-en-Provence Festival 1971, as the Queen of Night in Die Zauberflöte; Sang Marguerite in Faust at La Scala Milan 1977; At the Verona Arena appeared as Butterfly and Gounod's Juliette, 1977-79; Many performances in France and Italy in operas by Bellini. *Address:* c/o Teatro alla Scala, Via Filodrammatici 2, I-20121 Milan, Italy.

GARRARD Don, b. 31 July 1929, Vancouver, Canada. Singer (Bass). *Education:* Studied at the Toronto and Vancouver Conservatories; Music Academy of the West at Santa Barbara with Lotte Lehmann. *Debut:* Vancouver 1952, as the Speaker in Die Zauberflöte. *Career:* Sang Don Giovanni for Canadian TV; Sadler's Wells Opera London from 1961, as Attila, Sarastro, Rocco, Raleigh in Gloriana, Trulove (The Rake's Progress) and in the British premiere of Pizzetti's L'Assassinio nella Cattedrale 1962; Scottish Opera 1963, in the British premiere of Dallapiccola's Volo di Notte; Aldeburgh Festival 1964, in the world premiere of Curlew River by Britten; Glyndebourne Festival 1965-76, as Rochefort in Anna Bolena, Gremin, Pastor in the local premiere of Von Einem's The Visit of the Old Lady, Trulove and Arkel (Pelléas et Mélisande); Hamburg Staatsoper debut 1968; Covent Garden debut 1970, Ferrando in Il Trovatore; English National Opera as The Wanderer, in Siegfried; Guest appearances in Santa Fe, Johannesburg, Toronto, Ottawa, Washington and Edinburgh; sang the Grand Inquisitor in Don Carlos at Toronto 1988, Daland in Der fliegende Holländer for Pacific Opera at Victoria, B.C., 1989; Sang King Mark in Tristan und Isolde for Capab Opera at Cape Town, 1992; Many concert appearances. *Recordings include:* The Rake's Progress (CBS). *Address:* Capab, PO Box 4107, Cape Town 8000, South Africa.

GARRETT Eric, b. 1935, Yorkshire, England. Singer (Bass- Baritone). *Education:* Studied at the Royal College of Music, London, and with Eva Turner and Tito Gobbi. *Debut:* Covent Garden 1962, in La Bohème. *Career:* Many character roles at Covent Garden from 1962; Appearances with Scottish Opera and the Welsh National Opera; Brussels and Ghent 1978-79, as Bartolo in Il Barbiere di Siviglia, Dulcamara (L'Elisir d'Amore) and in Adriana Lecouvreur; Antwerp 1981, Baron Ochs in Der Rosenkavalier; sang Mustafà in L'Italiana in Algeri at Covent Garden 1988; Ceprano in Rigoletto 1989, Skula in a new production of Prince Igor 1990, followed by Don Pasquale and Alcindoro; Other roles at Covent Garden have included Gianni Schicchi, Don Fernando, Sacristan, Swallow, Varlaam and Frank; has also sung Falstaff, Melitone, Scarpia, Ochs, Kecal Schigolch (Lulu) and Rocco; guest appearances include San Francisco, Los Angeles, Marseilles, Montpellier and Munich. *Recordings include:* La Fanciulla del West (Deutsche Grammophon); Billy Budd (Decca). *Address:* Stafford Law Associates, 26 Firlands, Weybridge, Surrey KT13 OHR.

GARRETT Lesley, b. 10 Apr 1955, Thorne, Doncaster. Singer (Soprano). *Education:* Studied at the Royal Academy of Music; further study with Joy Mammen. *Career:* Has sung Dorinda in Handel's Orlando, the title role in Mozart's Zaide at the Wexford Festival and Hysiphile in Cavalli's Giasone at the Buxton Festival; Further appearances with the Glyndebourne Festival and Touring Company (Zerlina and Despina) and with Opera North as Sophie in Werther; European engagements include Servilia in La Clemenza di Tito (Geneva), The Fairy Queen (Maggio Musicale, Florence) and a Schoenberg cabaret song recital at the Pompidou Centre, Paris; English National Opera from 1984, as Bella in The Midsummer Marriage, Valencienne in The Merry Widow, Atalanta in Xerxes (also televised) and Yum-Yum in Jonathan Miller's production of The Mikado (Thames TV); Further appearances as Eurydice in Orpheus in the Underworld, Papagena, Zerlina, Alsi in the European premiere of The Making of the Representative for Planet 8 by Philip Glass (1988), Oscar in a new production of A Masked Ball and Princess Ninetta in The Love for Three Oranges, 1989; Susanna

at ENO 1990, Atalanta on tour to USSR and Brazil, Papagena in a revival of The Magic Flute; sang in concert performance of Nabucco at the Festival Hall, 1991; Season 1991/92 as Adele in Die Fledermaus, Rose in Weill's Street Scene and Zerlina, at the Coliseum. *Recordings include:* Diva and Primadonna. *Honours include:* Winner, Kathleen Ferrier Memorial Competition, 1979. *Address:* c/o Allied Artists, 42 Montpelier Square, London SW7 1JZ, England.

GARRIGUENC Pierre, b. 20 Aug 1921, Narbonne, France. Composer. m. Michelle, 7 Apr 1979. *Education:* Technical College of Narbonne, 1938-40; BM, Ithaca College, 1968; MM, Eastman School of Music, Rochester, New York, USA, 1971. *Career:* Staff Composer, Columbia Broadcasting System, Hollywood, California, USA, 1948-62; Instructor in Theory and Composition, Private teacher of Theory and Composition and Piano Technology, Lecturer, Tuner/Technician for Music Department, State University College, Oswego, NY, 1973-86. Performances of compositions in Europe and throughout the United States and in various Universities; 1st performances of compositions by members of Music Department, State University College, Oswego, New York, 1973-86. *Memberships:* American Society of Composers, Authors and Publishers; American Society of University Composers. *Hobbies:* Painting; Picture framing; Book binding.

GARRISON Jon, b. 11 Dec 1944, Higginsville, Missouri, USA. Singer (Tenor). *Career:* Has sung widely in North America, notably at opera houses in Houston, Montreal, Santa Fe and San Diego; Metropolitan Opera from 1974, in Death in Venice, Manon Lescaut, Così fan Tutte (Ferrando) and Die Zauberflöte (Tamino); New York City Opera from 1982, as Admete in Alceste, Don Ottario, Rodolfo, Nadir, the Duke of Mantua, Tom Rakewell, Tamino and Nicholas in the premiere of Reise's Rasputin, 1988; sang Prince Edmund in the premiere of Stewart Copeland's Holy Blood and Crescent Moon, Cleveland 1989; sang Shuratov in the US stage premiere of From the House of the Dead, New York 1990. *Address:* c/o New York City Opera, Lincoln Center, New York, NY 10023, USA.

GARTON Graham, b. 25 Apr 1929, Hull, England. Director of Music. m. Barbara Howson, 3 Sept 1955, 1 son, 3 daughters. *Education:* Lincoln Cathedral Choir; Royal Academy of Music: GRSM; LRAM; ARCO; ARAM. *Career:* Assistant Dir of Music, Repton, 1953; Dir of Music, Royal Masonic School, 1955-77; Director of Music, St Margaret's School, Bushey, 1977-89; Conductor: Wetford Philharmonic Society, 1967-89, Bermuda Philharmonic Society, 1989-; conductor, Geoffrey Tankard Foundation Choir; Director, Dunbarton School of Music, Bermuda. *Compositions:* Anthems, graces, songs, song cycles and organ music. *Address:* PO Box HM 1420, Hamilton HM FX, Bermuda.

GARWOOD (Miriam) Margaret, b. 22 Mar 1927, New Jersey, USA. Composer; Pianist; Teacher. m. Donald Chittum, 18 July 1981. *Education:* Private Study, Piano, 1938-69; MA, Music Composition, Philadelphia Colleges of the Arts, 1975; Self-taught in Composition. *Debut:* Carnegie Recital Hall, 1965. *Career:* Teacher, Philadelphia Musical Academy and Muhlenberg College, 1953-84; Concert Pianist; Vocal Coach/ Accompanist; Composer; Accompanist, 1965-. *Compositions:* The Trojan Women, opera, 1967; The Nightingale and the Rose, opera, 1973; Roppaccini's Daughter, opera, 1983; The Cliff's Edge, song cycle, 1968; Lovesongs, 1970; Joringel and the Songflower, opera, 1986; Springsongs, 1969; Six Japanese Songs, 1985; A Joyous Lament for a Gilly Flower, 1982; Autumn Soliloquy, 1985; Aesop's Fables, short ballet, 1968; Haiku, 1978; Tombsongs, chorus and orchestra, 1989. *Hobbies:* Reading; Gardening; Tropical fish. *Address:* 6056 N 10th Street, Philadelphia, PA 19141, USA.

GASDIA Cecilia, b. 14 Aug 1960, Verona, Italy. Singer (Soprano). *Education:* Studied classics and piano in Verona. *Debut:* Florence 1982, as Giulietta in I

Capuleti e i Montecchi by Bellini. *Career:* La Scala l982, as Anna Bolena in the opera by Donizetti; Perugia and Naples 1982, in Demophoon by Cherubini and as Amina in La Sonnambula; Paris Opéra debut 1983, as Anais in Moise by Rossini; Pesaro 1984, in a revival of Il Viaggio a Reims by Rossini; US debut Philadelphia 1985, as Gilda in a concert performance of Rigoletto; Chicago Lyric Opera and Metropolitan Opera 1986, as Giulietta and as Gounod's Juliette; Other roles include Violetta, Liu in Turandot, Hélène in Verdi's Jérusalem and Mrs Ford in Salieri's Falstaff; sang Rosa in Fioravanti's Le Cantatrici villane, Naples 1990; Season 1991/92 as Adina at Chicago, Mimi at Bonn, Nedda at Rome, Elena in La Donna, del Lago at La Scala and Rosina at the Festival of Caracalla. *Recordings include:* Catone in Utica, and Motets by Vivaldi (RCA); Il Viaggio a Reims (Deutsche Grammophon); Video of Turandot (Thorn-EMI); Rossini's Armida and Ermione. *Address:* c/o Teatro San Carlo, Via San Carlo 98F, 1-80132 Naples, Italy.

GASTEEN Lisa, b. 1957, Queensland, Australia. Singer (Soprano). *Education:* Studied at the Queensland Conservatorium, with teacher, Margaret Nickson in San Francisco and at the London Opera Studio. *Debut:* Lyric Opera of Queensland, 1985, as the High Priestess in Aida and Diana in Orpheus in the Underworld. *Career:* Appearances with Australian Opera as Miss Jessel (Turn of the Screw), Frasquita, Madame Lidoine (Carmelites), the Forza Leonora, Elsa, Donna Elvira and Leonore in Fidelio; Victorian State Opera as Elisabeth in Tannhauser, Elisabeth de Valois and Desdemona, 1993; Season 1991-92 as the Trovatore and Forza Leonoras for Scottish Opera, Amelia (UnBallo in Maschera) for Welsh National Opera and Washington Opera, Donna Anna in Prague and Leonore in Stuttgart; Concert repertoire includes Rossini's Stabat Mater and Elijah for the Sydney Philharmonia, Beethoven's Ninth in Sydney, Melbourne and Tasmania; Verdi Requiem, Hungarian Radio, Budapest, 1993; Maddelena, Andrea Chenier, for Deutsche Oper, Berlin, 1994; Aida for Australian Opera, 1995. *Honours:* Winner, Metropolitan Opera, N.Y. Competition Australian Regional Finals, 1982; First Australian Recipient of Met. Opera Educational Fund Grant, (used for study with Blanche Thebom); Received Advance Australia Award, 1991; Covent Garden Scholarship, 1984; Winner, Cardiff Singer of the World Competition, 1991. *Address:* c/o IMG Artists, Media House, 3 Burlington Lane, Chiswisk, London W4 2TH, England.

GASZTOWT-ADAMS Helen Catriona, b. 29 Sept 1956, Geelong, Victoria, Australia of Polish-Scottish parents. Opera, Concert and Recital Singer (Soprano). *Education:* Victorian College of the Arts, Melbourne; National Opera Studio, London, 1989; Studied with Audrey Langford and Janice Chapman. *Debut:* Pamina, Die Zauberflöte, State Opera of South Australia, 1983. *Career:* Sang in Don Giovanni, Manon, Countess Maritza, Figaro, State Opera of South Australia, 1985-86; With Australian Opera: Debut, Nannetta, Falstaff, 1986, then in Suor Angelica, Il Tabarro, Médée, Poppea, Carmen; London Debut, Anna Bolena, National Opera Studio Showcase, Queen Elizabeth Hall, 1989; BBC Cardiff Singer of the World finals, 1989; European concert debut, Grusse aus Wien, Robert Stolz Club, recorded Belgian Radio and TV, 1990; Gilda in Rigoletto, Australian Opera, 1990; English National Opera debut, Donna Elvira, Don Giovanni, 1991; Other appearances include: Rossini's Petite Messe Solennelle, Netherlands and Belgium tour; Strauss's Vier Letzte Lieder, Koninklijk Ballet van Vlaanderen, Antwerp, Belgium; Mozart's Requiem, English String Orchestra, Bath Mozart Festival; Pamina in Die Zauberflöte, Victoria State Opera, Melbourne; Extensive radio and TV recital and concert work, ABC, Australia, including Handel's Messiah, Mendelssohn's Elijah, A Midsummer Night's Dream, Carl Orff's Carmina Burana, Strauss's Vier Letzte Lieder; Performed with Melbourne and Sydney Symphony Orchestras, Australian Chamber Orchestra; Opera and Concert performances in Britain, Barbados, Australia, France and Spain. *Address:* London, England.

GATES Crawford, b. 29 Dec 1921, San Francisco, USA. Conductor; Composer. m. Georgia Lauper, 19 Dec 1952, 2 sons, 2 daughters. *Education:* BA San Jose State College; MA Brigham Young University; PhD music, Eastman School of Music, University of Rochester; Conducting studies with Eleazar de Carvalho, Hans Swarowsky. *Debut:* Stanford University, 1938 (composer); Utah Symphony, 1948, (conductor). *Career:* Chairman, Music Dept and Conductor, Symphony Orchestra and Opera, Brigham Young University, 1960-66; Music Director, Beloit Janesville Symphony, 1966-; Quincy Symphony, 1969-70; Artist in Residence, Professor, Chair of Music Dept, Beloit College, 1966-89. *Compositions include:* Five stage works, 5 symphonies, numerous choral arrangements, 4 major choral works, trumpet concertino and horn Sonata; Pentameron, for piano and orchestra, commissioned by Grant Johannesen; Over 100 titles in publication including Suite for String Orchestra. *Recordings:* Symphony No 2, Orchestral Setting of beloved Mormon Hymns on Philadelphia Orchestra Album; The Lord's Prayer and A Jubilant Song; Music to the New Hill Cumorah Pageant, 1988, Promised Valley. *Publications:* Non-Music: Catalogue of published American Choral Works. *Hobbies:* Tennis; Running; Swimming; Reading; Travel. *Address:* 911 Park Avenue, Beloit, WI 53511, USA.

GATI Istvan, b. 1947, Budapest, Hungary. Singer (tenor). *Education:* Studied at the Franz Liszt Academy, Budapest. *Career:* Member of the Hungarian State Opera from 1972, notably in the premieres of Csongor and Tunde by Attila Bozay, 1985 and Ecce Homo by Sandor Szokolay, 1987; Appearances at the Vienna Staatsoper from 1986; Sang Don Giovanni at Liège, 1988, Nick Shadow, at the Deutsche Oper Berlin,1989, and Antonio in Le nozze di Figaro at the 1991 Vienna Festival; Guest appearances in Italy, France, Poland, Spain, Holland and Austria; Concert engagements in works by Bach, Handel, Mozart, Mozart, Beethoven and Liszt. *Recordings include:* Cantatas by Bach, Don Sanche and The Legend of St Elisabeth by Liszt, Salieri's Falstaff, Paisiello's Barbiere di Siviglia, Don Pasquale, Simon Boccanegra, Telemann's Der Geduldige Sokrates, Balthazar and Jonas by Carissimi, Ein Deutsches Requiem, Mahler's Lieder eines fahrenden Gesellen; Oronte in Handel's Floridante. *Honours:* Competition winner at Salzburg, Vienna, Trevisto and Moscow (Tchaikovsky International, 1974). *Address:* c/o Hungarian State Opera, Nepoztarsasag utja 22, 1061 Budapest, Hungary.

GATTI Daniele, b. 1962, Milan, Italy. Conductor. *Education:* Studied at the Giuseppe Verdi Conservatory, Milan. *Career:* Conducted Verdi's Giovanna d'Arco, 1982; Concerts with the Maggio Musicale Fiorentino Orchestra, the Milan Angelicum and the Bologna Municipal Orchestra; Appearances with the regional orchestras of Italian radio; Gianni Schicchi at the Osimo Festival, 1987, the premiere of Rabarbaro by Pedini, and Werther in Milan, Bergamo and Brescia; Season 1988-89 with Il Barbiere di Siviglia in Bari, Linda di Chamounix in Milan and Cremona; La Scala debut 1988 with Rossini's L'Occasione fa il Ladro; Rossini Festival Pesaro 1989, Bianca e Falliero; Led Bellini's I Capuleti e i Montecchi and Rigoletto at Bologna; US debut Chicago 1991, Madama Butterfly; New production of I Puritani at Covent Garden, 1992; also engaged for Toronto Symphony Orchestra, 1991 and Bologna, Rigoletto, 1992; Other repertory includes Rossini's Mosè in Egitto and Verdi's Un Ballo in Maschera and Simon Boccanegra; Carnegie Hall debut 1990; Verdi's Requiem at the Spoleto Festival, 1990; Forthcoming: engaged to conduct the Covent Garden premiere of I Due Foscari by Verdi, 1994-95; concerts with the Bavarian Radio Symphony, London Philharmonic, Cleveland Orchestra, Boston and Chicago Symphonies and the Accademia Santa Cecilia, Rome. *Address:* Stage Door Management, Via Giardini 941/2 - 41040, Saliceta San Ginliano, Modena, Italy.

GATTI Gabriella, b. 5 July 1908, Rome, Italy. Soprano. *Education:* Studied piano at the Accademia di Santa Cecilia in Rome. *Debut:* Rome 1933, as Anna in Verdi's Nabucco. *Career:* Rome 1934, in a concert performance of Monteverdi's Orfeo; Verona 1937-38, as Elena in Mefistofele and Elisabeth in Tannhäuser; Maggio Musicale Florence 1939-40, as Rossini's Semitamide, in the premiere of Frazzi's Re Lear and in the title role of Gluck's Iphigénie en Aulide; La Scala debut 1940, as Reiza in Oberon; Rome 1942, as Marie in the Italian premiere of Berg's Wozzeck, with Tito Gobbi. Concert performances in London; Retired as singer 1952 and taught at the Accademia di Santa Cecilia; Other roles were Abigaille in Nabucco, Mozart's Countess, Desdemona and Mathilde in Rossini's Guillaume Tell. *Recordings include:* Le nozze di Figaro and Nabucco (Cetra).

GAVAZZENI Gianandrea, b. 27 July 1909, Bergamo, Italy. Conductor and Writer. *Education:* Milan Conservatory under Renzo Lorenzoni, Ildebrando Pizzetti and Mario Pilati. *Debut:* As conductor, 1940. *Career:* Conductor, 1940-; Associated with La Scala, Milan, 1948, Artistic Director, 1966-68; Has participated in many festivals with La Scala including the Edinburgh Festival, 1957; World Fair, Brussels, 1957; Expo 1967 Montreal; also at the Bolshoi and Kremlin Theatres, Moscow, 1964; Has directed numerous operatic recordings with La Scala; Conducted Donizetti, Anna Bolena at Glyndebourne, 1965; Conducted Madame Butterfly at La Scala, 1990; Season 1992 with Donizatti's Roberto Devereux at Bologna, Lucia di Lammemoor at La Scala aand Donizetti's Poliuto at the Ravenna Festival; As a music Critic has written studies of Donizetti, Pizzetti, Mascagni, Mussorgsky, Janáček, Bartók, Sibelius, guides to the operas of Mozart, Wagner. *Recordings include:* Madame Chénier, Andrea Chénier, Il Turco in Italia, Rigoletto, L'Elisir d'Amore, L'Amico Fritz; La Gioconda and Simon Boccanegra, for EMI, Decca, RCA, Cetra, Mercury and Deutsche Grammophon. *Address:* c/o Teatro alla Scala, Via Filodrammatici 2, 1-20121 Milan, Italy.

GAVAZZI Ernesto, b. 7 May 1941, Seregno, Monza, Italy. Singer (Tenor). *Education:* Studied at the Milan Conservatoire with Bruno Carmassi and at the Scuola della Scala with Vladimiro Badiali. *Debut:* Treviso 1971, as Nemorino in L'Elisir d'Amore. *Career:* Many appearances in Italy and elsewhere in Europe as Elvino in La Sonnambula, Paolino in Il Matrimonio Segreto and Rossini's Almaviva, Don Ramiro, Giocondo (La Pietra del Paragone), Edward Milfort (Il Cambiale di Matrimonio), Rodolphe (Guillaume Tell) and Don Eusebio (L'Occasione fa il Ladro); Has sung at Pesaro and La Scala in several Rossini revivals, including Zefirio in Il Viaggio a Reims (1984-85); Sang Goro (Madama Butterfly) and Chekalinsky (The Queen of Spades) at La Scala, 1990. *Recordings include:* Il Viaggio a Reims (Deutsche Grammophon); Verdi's Captain (Simon Boccanegra), Borsa (Rigoletto) and Uldino (Attila) for Decca and EMI; Guillaume Tell conducted by Riccardo Muti (Philips). *Address:* c/o Teatro alla Scala, Via Filodrammatici 2, I-20121 Milan, Italy.

GAVENELLI Paolo, b. 1959, Padua, Italy. Singer (Baritone). *Debut:* Sang Leporello at the Teatro Donizetti, Bergamo, 1985. *Career:* Season 1988-89, as Mephistopheles at Barcelona and Marcello in La Boheme in Madrid; Further engagements as Marcello at Venice, Bologna, and the State Operas of Munich and Vienna (1991); Sang Luna in Trovatore at the Metropolitan 1990, returning in Puritani and as Germont, 1992; Gerard in Andrea Chenier at San Francisco and Stuttgart 1998, 1992), Renato (Ballo in Maschera) at Chicago and Verdi's Falstaff the Rome Opera; Festival appearances at Pesaro (Germano in La Scala di Seta, 1990) and the Arena Verona; Has also appeared at La Scala (from 1991) and Genoa (as Renato); Other roles include Rossini's Figaro and Verdi's Iago, Rigoletto and Amonasro. *Recordings:* Marcello in La Bohème. *Address:* c/o Metropolitan Opera House, Lincoln Center, NY 10023, USA.

GAVRILOV Andrei, b. 21 Sept 1955, Moscow, USSR. Pianist. *Career:* Following London Debut, Philharmonia

Orchestra/Muti, 1976, has appeared with all major London orchestras; Recitals, Queen Elizabeth Hall & Barbican, Royal Festival Hall, London; also in Austria, Belgium, France, Germany, Holland, Spain, Switzerland, Italy, Japan, Kanada, New Zealand; Festivals in Salzburg, Roque d'Antheron, Schleswig Holstein, New Zealand, 1986; Regular visits to USA include concerts with Philadelphia Orchestra, with Muti & Frühbeck de Burgos; other conductor's include Abbado, Haitink, Muti, Ozawa, Svetlanov and Tennstedt. *Recordings:* EMI: Scriabin, Chopin; Rachmaninov: Concerto No. 3, Concerto No. 2, Paganini Variations; Tchaikovsky: Concerto No. 1, Philadelphia/Muti, (second version), Concertos No. 1, 3, Berlin Philharmonic/Ashkenazy; Bach Concertos, Academy of St Martin-in-the- Fields/ Marriner; Chopin; New DG recordings include: 4 Ballades, Sonata No 2, Chopin; Sonatas No 3, 7, 8; Prokofiev: Romeo and Juliet; Ravel: Gaspard de la nuit; Bach: Goldberg Variations; One record specially negotiated for Decca, Stravinsky: Concerto, Rite for Spring, etc with Vladimir Ashkenazy; Chamber recordings: Shostakovich: Violin Sonata: Gavrilov/ Kremer (Melodia); Britten: The Golden Vanity, Friday Afternoons, with Vienna Knabenchor, solo pieces (DG). *Honours:* 1st prize, Tchaikovsky Piano Competition, 1974; Contract with EMI 1976-90; Deutsche Grammophon from 1990 (Romeo and Juliet, Goldberg Variation); Recordings of Ravel & Prokofiev, International Awards; winner, Premio Internationale Academia Musicale Chigiana, 1989. *Address:* Am Walberstück 7, 65520 Bad Camberg, Germany.

GAWRILOFF Saschko, b. 20 Oct 1929, Leipzig, Germany. Violinist. *Education:* Early studies with his father; Leipzig Conservatory 1942-44, with Gustav Havemann and Martin Kovacz in Berlin, 1945-47. *Career:* Leader of the Dresden Philharmonic 1947-48, Berlin Philharmonic 1948-49, Berlin Radio Symphony 1949-53, Museum Orchestra of Frankfurt am Main 1953-57, Hamburg Radio Symphony 1961-66; Teacher at the Nuremberg Conservatory 1957-61; Professor at the North-West German Music Academy 1966-69; Professor at the Folkwanghochschule in Essen from 1969; Currently Head of Master Classes for Violin at the Cologne Musikhochschule; Appearances with the leading orchestras in Germany, Britain and elsewhere: concerts in Vienna, Milan, Madrid, Rome, Paris, India and Japan; Conductors include Boulez (Berg Concerto), Solti, Dohnányi, Gielen and Inbal; Has given the premieres of works by Maderna, Dieter Kaufmann and Schnittke; Formed a Trio with Alfons Kontarsky and Klaus Storck 1971; Currently member of the Robert Schumann Trio, with Johannes Goritzki and David Levine; Contemporary music with Siegfried Palm and Bruno Canino. *Recordings:* Labels include CBS and Deutsche Grammophon. *Honours:* Winner, International Competitions at Berlin and Munich, 1953; Genoa Paganini Competition and City of Nuremberg Prize, 1959. *Address:* c/o Ingpen & Williams Ltd., 14 Kensington Court, London W8 5DN.

GAYER Catherine, b. 11 Feb 1937, Los Angeles, California. Singer (Soprano). *Education:* Studied in Los Angeles. *Career:* Sang in the premiere of Nono's Intolleranza 1960, Venice 1961; Covent Garden 1962, as the Queen of Night; Deutsche Oper Berlin from 1963, notably as Hilde Mack in Henze's Elegie für junge Liebende, Berg's Lulu and Marie in Zimmermann's, Die Soldaten, and Nausicca in the 1968 premiere of Dallapiccola's Ulisse; Scottish Opera from 1968, as Susanna, Hilde Mack, the Queen of Shemakha (The Golden Cockerel) and in the 1975 premiere of Orr's Hermiston; Schwetzingen Festival 1971, in the premiere of Reimann's Melusine; Edinburgh Festival 1972, with the company of the Deutsche Oper Berlin in Zimmermann's Die Soldaten; Sang the leading role in the premiere of Joseph Tal's Der Versuchung, Munich 1976; Other roles include: La Scala: Ulisse-Dallapiccola; Zerbinetta, Gilda and Mélisande; sang The Woman in Schoenberg's Erwartung at the Komische Oper Berlin, 1988; songs by Reimann and Szymanowski at the 1990 Aldeburgh Festival; Berlin Kammeroper, 1991 with Berio's Sequenza III, Tal's Die Hand, The Medium by Maxwell Davies and Weisgall's The Stronger; Stuttgart

1992, as the Grand-Mother in Dinescu's Eréndira and in Rag Time (arrangement of Joplin's Treemonisha) at the 1992 Schwetzingen Festival; 2 Productions Schoenberg's Pierrot Lunaire. *Recordings:* Woodbird in Siegfried (Deutsche Grammophon); Elegie für junge Liebende; Die Israeliten in der Wüste by CPE Bach; Il Giardino d'Amore by Scarlatti. *Honours:* Winner, 1960 San Francisco Opera Auditions; Berlin Kammersängerin 1970. *Address:* c/o Deutsche Oper, Berlin, Germany.

GAYFORD Christopher, b. 1963, Wilmslow, England. Conductor. *Education:* Studied at the Royal College of Music with Christopher Adey, John Forster and Norman del Mar. *Career:* Repetiteur at Graz Opera, 1987; Junior Fellow in Conducting at the Royal Northern College of Music, 1988; Conducted Don Carlos and A Midsummer Night's Dream at the RNCM, 1990; Debut with the London Mozart Players at the Barbican Hall, 1990; L'Elisir d'Amore for RNCM; Don Giovanni for Opera North, Assistant Conductor to Royal Liverpool Philharmonic Orchestra, 1992/93; Conducted Così fan Tutte for British Youth Opera at Sadler's Wells, 1992. *Honours:* Winner, 39th Besançon International Competition for Young Conductors, 1989. *Address:* c/o Christopher Tennant Management, Unit 2, 39 Tadema Road, London SW10 0PY, England.

GEBHARDT Horst, b. 17 June 1940, Silberhausen, Germany. Singer (Tenor). *Education:* Studied in Weimar and Berlin. *Debut:* Schwerin 1972, as Chateauneuf in Lortzing's Zar und Zimmermann. *Career:* Sang at Leipzig, the Staatsoper Dresden and Berlin; Member of the Leipzig Opera from 1985 (Erik in Fliegende Hollander, 1989) and has made guest appearances in France, Italy, Spain, England, Yugoslavia, Russia, Poland, Japan and Cuba; Other roles have included Max, Mozart's Belmonte, Ottavio, Titus, Tamino and Ferrando; Lensky, Fenton, Strauss's Narraboth and Flamand, Jacquino in Fidelio, David (Die Meistersinger), Alfredo and Sextus in Giulio Cesare. *Recordings:* Idomeneo, Parsifal, Palestrina and Alfonso und Estrella. *Honours include:* Prize winner, International Bach Competition, Leipsiz and National Opera Competition, E Germany, 1972. *Address:* Stadtische Theatre, 7010 Leipzig, Germany.

GEDDA Nicolai, b. 11 July 1925, Stockholm, Sweden. Operatic tenor. *Education:* Musical Academy, Stockholm. *Debut:* Stockholm, 1952. *Career:* Concert appearances, Rome, 1952; Paris 1953 and 1955; Vienna 1955; Aix-en-Provence and Rome, 1953; Paris, London and Vienna, 1954; Salzburg Festival, 1957-59; Edinburgh Festival, 1958-59; with Metropolitan Opera, New York, 1957-, created role of Anatol in Barber's Vanessa, 1958; World-wide appearances in opera, concerts and recitals; numerous recordings; including Les Contes d'Hoffmann, Boris Godunov, Il Barbiere di Siviglia, Il Turco in Italia, I Capuleti e i Montecchi, La Damnation de Faust, Carmen, Les Pêcheurs de Perles, Faust, A Life for the Tsar, Louise, Fra Diavolo, Lady Macbeth of Mtsensk, Manon, Thais, Così fan Tutte, Die Zauberflöte, Don Giovanni, Padmâvati by Roussel, Bach's St. Matthew Passion and Rossini's Petite Messe Solonnelle (EMI); La Bohème, Carmen (with Callas), Werther, Der Barbier von Bagdad, Der Rosenkavalier, Capricco, Die Fledermaus (Columbia); Rigoletto and Vanessa (RCA), Così fan Tutte and Benvenuto Cellini (Philips); War and Peace (Erato) Pfitzner's Palestrina (Deutsche Grammophon); Schubert's Die Zwillingsbrüder, Weber's Abu Hassan, Der Freischütz, Gluck's Le Cadi Dupé, Die Entführung and Lortzing's Undine (Electrola); First London recital, 1986; sang in concert performances of Bernstein's Candide, Barbican Hall, London, 1989; Sang Christian II in the first modern performance of Naumann's Gustaf Wasa, Stockholm 1991. *Address:* c/o Lies Askonas, 186 Drury Lane, London WC2, England.

GEFORS Hans, b. 8 Dec 1952, Stockholm, Sweden. Composer. *Education:* Studied composition with Per-Gunnar Alldahl and Maurice Karkoff; Pupil of Ingvar Lidholm, Stockholm Academy of Music, 1972; Per Nørgård, Arhus Conservatory, Diploma 1977. *Career:*

Active as composer, music critic and editor; Professor in composition, Malmö College of Music, 1988; Der Park premiere at the 1992 Wiesbaden Festival. *Compositions:* Operas: The Poet and the Glazier, 1979; Christina, 1986; Der Park, 1991; Music Theatre: Me morire en Paris, 1979; The Creation no.2, 1988; Orchestral Music: Slits, 1981; Christina Scenes, 1987; Twine, 1988; Die Erscheinung im Park, 1990; Chamber Music: Aprahishtita, 1970-71; La Boîte Chinoise, 1976; L'invitation au voyage, for voice, guitar and violin, 1981; Krigets Eko for Percussionist, 1982; Tjurens Död, 1982; Flickan Och Den Gamle, 1983; Galjonsfiguren, 1983; One Two, 1983; Vocal Music: singer on förtröstan for voice and guitar, 1970; Whales Weep Not! for 16-part choir, 1987; En Obol, sonnets for voice, clarinet, cornet, cello and piano, 1989. *Address:* STIM, Sandhamnsgatan 79, PO Box 27327, S-102 54 Stockholm, Sweden.

GEIGER Hans, b. 3 Jan 1920, Moson-Magyarovar, Hungary. Violinist. m. Johanna Angela, 28 Feb 1963, 1 son. *Education:* Royal College of Music; Studied with W H Reed, Guido Brandweiner in Vienna and Max Rostal in London. *Career:* Member of the London Harpsichord Ensemble, English Opera Group, Chamber Orchestra (leader), Philharmonia Orchestra, London Symphony Orchestra, (Principal) and London Mozart Players. *Memberships:* Incorporated Society of Musicians. *Hobbies:* Chamber music; Reading; Motorcars. *Address:* 8 Tiviton Road, London, NW10 3HL, England.

GEIGER Ruth, b. 30 Jan 1923, Vienna, Austria. Pianist. *Education:* Studied in Vienna with Hans Gal and Julius Isserlis, Juilliard School, New York, with Josef Lhevinne. *Debut:* Town Hall, New York, 1944. *Career:* Recitals and appearances with orchestras in USA; Radio and TV broadcasts in New York; Annual concert tours of Europe from 1957: orchestras include Suisse Romande, New Philharmonia, English Chamber Orchestra; BBC Series My Favourite Concertos; Appearances on BBC solo recital series at St. Johns Smith Square, London; Live broadcasts, Pebble Mill, Birmingham, Concert Hall, Broadcasting House London, Live concerto broadcasts with Glasgow BBC Orchestra; Complete Schubert Sonatas for Basle Radio; Toured Sweden, Holland, Belgium, Switzerland, Austria, England; Master Classes at University of Sussex, 1971: chamber music with the Allegri Quartet; concert and teaching week's residency at Yale University, USA; Most recent appearances on Live BBC Concert series: Lunchtime Recital at St David's Hall, Cardiff, 1992; Live Broadcast of Lunchtime Recital at St John's Smith Square, London, 1992. *Recordings include:* Schubert Sonatas for Critics Choice Records. *Honours:* Naumburg Award, New York, 1943; Finalist, Leventritt Competition 1944 and Rachmaninov Competition 1948. *Hobbies:* Photography; Literature; Nature. *Current Management:* Helen Jennings Concert Agency, London. *Address:* 160 W 73 Street, New York, NY 10023, USA.

GEIRINGER Bernice, b. 24 Apr 1918, Minnesota, USA. Internationally-known Musicologist. m. Karl Geiringer, 1987, 2s, 1d. *Education:* University of California, Los Angeles; Studied with Arnold Schoenberg; Alfred Mirovitch, Victor Aller, and Dusi Mura. *Debut:* Beau Arts Theatre, Los Angeles, 1940. *Career:* Guest artist with La Mirada Symphony, UCSB Symphony, Santa Babrara Symphony and West Coast Symphony Chamber Orchestra. *Publications:* This I remember, (co-author), 1993. *Honours:* National Federation of Music Clubs. *Memberships:* American Musicological Society. *Hobbies:* Writing. *Address:* 161 Rametto Road, Santa Barbara, CA 93108, USA.

GELIOT Michael, b. 27 Sept 1933, London, England. Opera and Theatre Director. m. Diana Geliot, 2 children. *Education:* BA Cambridge University. *Career:* Staged first UK production of Liebermann's School for Wives while at Cambridge, 1958; Sadler's Wells from 1960: Burt's Volpone for the New Opera Company 1961; Weill's Mahagonny 1963; Resident Producer, then Director of Productions, Welsh National Opera 1965-78; Productions for Scottish Opera, Kassel, Zurich,

Barcelona, Wexford, Amsterdam, Ottawa, Lausanne, Netherlands Opera (Wozzeck 1973) and Munich Opera (Fidelio 1974); Staged the premiere of Maxwell Davies's Taverner at Covent Garden, 1972; Translations of Mozart's Zauberflöte and Nozze di Figaro; Stagings at Kassel Opera include Le nozze di Figaro, 1980; Collaborations with the designer Ralph Koltai. *Honours include:* Critics' Prize, Barcelona, 1974. *Hobbies:* Cricket; Sailing; Walking; Chess.

GELLHORN Peter, b. 24 Oct 1912. Conductor; Pianist; Composer. 2 sons, 2 daughters. *Education:* University of Berlin; Music Academy, Berlin. *Career:* Musical Director, Toynbee Hall, London, 1935-39; Assistant Conductor, Sadler's Wells Opera, 1941-43; Conductor, Royal Carl Rosa Opera, 1945-46; Conductor and Head of Staff, Royal Opera House, Covent Garden, 1947-53; conductor and Chorus Master, Glyndebourne Festival Opera, 1954-61; Director, BBC Chorus, 1961-72; Co-Founder, Director, Opera Barga, Italy, 1967-69; Musical Director, Barnes Choir, The Oper Players Limited; Professor, Guildhall School of Music and Drama, 1981-92; Visiting Coach, Opera Schol of the RCM, 1980-88. *Publications:* Contributions to music journals. *Honours:* FGSM, 1989. *Memberships:* Incorporated Society of Musicians; Musicians Union; RPS; BBC Club; President, Twickenham Choral Society. *Hobbies:* Walking; Swimming; Theatre. *Address:* 33 Leinster Avenue, London, SW14 7JW, England.

GELLMAN Steven D., b. 16 Sept 1947, Toronto, Ontario, Canada. Composer; Pianist; Professor of Music. m. Cheryl, 18 Oct 1970, 1 son, 1 daughter. *Education:* Juilliard School of Music, New York, USA; Conservatoire de Paris. *Career:* Soloist with CBC Symphony Orchestra in own Concerto for Piano and Orchestra, aged 16; Compositions performed, USA, Canada, France, Europe, South America, Japan; Currently Associate Professor, Department of Composition and Theory, Faculty of Music, University of Ottawa; European Tour of Toronto Symphony, 1983; Gellman's Awakening, performed 10 times throughout Europe; Universe Symphony; Inaugurated the International Year of Canadian Music, Toronto, 1986. *Compositions include:* Orchestral: Chori, 1976; Anima, Animus (orchestra), 1976; Odyssey, 1971; Symphony in Two Movements, 1971 (recorded); Symphony No. 2, 1972; Awakening, 1982; The Bride's Reception, 1983; Universe Symphony for large orchestra and 3 polyphonic synthesizers, 1984-85; Chamber Music; Mythos II, for flute and string quartet, 1968 (recorded); Soliloquy, cello solo, 1966, (revised 1982); Wind Music, for Brass Quintet, 1978 (recorded); Deux Tapisseries, 1978; Dialogue for solo horn, 1978; Trikaya, 1981; Transformation, 1980; Piano: Melodic Suite, 1972; Sonata, 1964; Poeme, 1976 (recorded); The Warrior, 1978 (recorded); Waves and Ripples, 1979; Fantasia on a theme of Schumann, (recorded), 1983; Keyboard Triptych for piano/synthesizer, 1986; Orchestra: Love's Garden for Soprano and Orchestra, 1987; Canticles for Choir and Orchestra, 1989; Piano Concerto, 1988-89; Chamber: Chiaroscuro, 1988; Concertino for Guitar and String Quartet, 1988; Burnt Offerings for String Orchestra, 1990; Red Shoes, 1990; Musica Eterna, for String Quartet, 1991; Child-Play, for Chamber Orchestra, 1992. *Honour:* Named Composer of the Year, 1987. *Address:* c/o Music Department, Stewart Street, University of Ottawa, Ottawa, Ontario, K1N 6N5, Canada.

GELMETTI Gianluigi, b. 11 Sept 1945, Rome, Italy. Conductor. *Education:* Studied at the Accademia di Santa Cecilia, Rome, with Franco Ferrara; Further study with Sergiu Celibidache and in Vienna with Hans Swarowsky. *Career:* Musical Director of Pomeriggi Musicale of Milan, and teacher at the Conservatory until 1980; Artistic Director of RAI Symphony Orchestra at Rome 1980-84; Musical Director of Rome Opera 1984-85; Chief Conductor of the South German Radio Symphony Orchestra 1989; Musical Director, Orchestre Philharmonique de Monte Carlo, 1990; Has conducted the first performances of Castiglioni's Sacro Concerto, 1982, Donatoni's In cauda, 1983 and Henze's 7th Symphony, 1984; Conducted Tosca at La Fenice Venice

1989 and a double bill of Rossini's La Cambiale di Matrimonio and Il Signor Bruschino at the 1989 Schwetzingen Festival; Rossini's La Gazza Ladra, with Katia Ricciarelli at Pesaro, 1989; Conducted Salieri's Les Danaides at the 1990 Ravenna Festival; Season 1992 with Tancredi at Bologna, Rossini double bill at Schwetzingen and Il Matrimonio Segreto at the Ravenna Festival. *Recordings include:* Telerecording of Rossini Double Bill. *Address:* Symphonie Orchester des Suddeutscher Rundfunks, Neckarstrasse 230, Postfach 837, D-7000 Stuttgart, Germany.

GELT Andrew Lloyd, b. 2 Feb 1951, New Mexico, USA. Composer; Arranger; Conductor; Performer. *Education:* BM, cum laude with distinction, Music Theory, University of New Mexico 1973; MM, Clarinet Performance, University of Southern California; DMA, Theory and Composition, University of Miami; studied at University of Denver; Clarinet Student of Mitchell Lurie; also studied with Stanley Drucker. *Career:* Popular Music and Jazz Performer appearing on Radio, TV and many recordings; Professor at several Universities and Colleges; specialises in the analysis of microprocessor devices as applied to Music; his main expertise is in the theory and composition of music in the eclectic vein. *Compositions:* Symphony No. 1, Op. 34, The Art of Eclecticism, premiered by Frederick Fennell, second performance by the Orchestra Society of Philadelphia. *Publications:* Index to Alcohol, Drugs and Intoxicants In Music 1982 (also published in French); Eclecticism, Composional Process and Elements...(UMI); A Statement Concerning Eclecticism and the Gesamtstilwerk, (SCI Series). *Contributions to:* The Instrumentalist; Polyphony. *Hobbies:* Shooting and Marksmanship including Olympic Competition and Army National Guard. *Current Management:* Music Associates of Florida Inc., Hallandale, Florida. *Address:* 10919 Fairbanks Road, NE, Albuquerque, NM 87112, USA.

GEMERT Theo van, b. 20 Oct 1940, Kerkrade, Holland. Singer (Baritone). *Education:* Studied at the Maastricht Conservatory. *Career:* Professional Footballer (including Dutch national team) before career as singer; Sang at Aachen, 1970-71, as Germont and Jochanaan; Wuppertal from 1973, as Wotan and Gunther in The Ring Creonte in Médée, Rigoletto, Iago, Nabucco, Count Iuna, Simon Boccanegra, Telramund, Amfortas and Orestes; Guest appearances in Germany, Franc, Holland and Barcelona. *Address:* c/o Stadische Buhnen, Spinnstrasse 4, 5600 Wuppertal, Germany.

GEMROT Jiri, b. 15 Apr 1957, Prague, Czechoslovakia. Composer. m. 16 October 1982. *Education:* Prague Conservatorium, 1972-76; Graduated, Composition, Academy of Musical Arts, Prague, 1981; Master Composers Course with Franco Donatoni, Accademia Chigiana, Siena, Italy, 1981. *Career:* Music Director, Radio Prague, 1982-86, 1990-; Editor, Panton Publishing House, 1986-90. *Compositions:* Published: Sonata for Piano No 1, 1981; Tributes for orchestra, 1983; 5 lyrical songs to poems by Ingeborg Bachmann for soprano and piano, 1984; Inventions for violin and viola, 1984; Sonata for Piano No 2, 1985; Maxims for 15 strings, 1986; Rhapsody for Bassoon and Piano, 1986; Recorded: Tributes; Dances and Reflections; Cello Concerto; Sonata for Harp; Bucolic for string quartet; meditation for viola and organ; Invocation for violin and organ; Sonatina for flute and piano; Maxims for 15 strings; Piano sonatas. *Hobbies:* Gardening; Cycling. *Address:* Na valech 32, Prague 6, Czech Republic.

GENCER Leyla, b. 10 Oct 1921, Ankara, Turkey. Singer (Soprano). *Education:* Studied at the Ankara Conservatory; Further study with Giannina Arangi-Lombardi and Apollo Granforte. *Debut:* Ankara 1950, as Santuzza. *Career:* Teatro San Carlo Naples 1953, as Madama Butterfly; Milan La Scala from 1956, notably in the premieres of Poulenc's Dialogues des Carmélites 1957 and Pizzetti's L'Assassinio nella Cattedrale 1958; San Francisco from 1956; Spoleto Festival 1959, as Renata in The Fiery Angel by Prokofiev; Salzburg Festival

1961, as Amelia in Simon Boccanegra; Covent Garden 1962, Elisabeth de Valois and Donna Anna; Sang Norma at the Verona Arena, 1965; Glyndebourne 1962-63 (Mozart's Countess) and 1965 (Anna Bolena); Rome Opera 1971, as Giulia in La Vestale by Spontini; Naples 1972, in a revival of Caterina Cornaro by Donizetti; Edinburgh Festival 1969, 1972; Further appearances in Vienna, Munich, Moscow, Warsaw, Oslo, Buenos Aires and Rio de Janeiro. *Recordings:* Ascanio in Alba by Mozart; Donizetti's Belisario and Caterina Cornaro; I Due Foscari, Il Trovatore, I Lombardi, Attila and Simon Boccanegra by Verdi; Pacini's Safo; La Vestale; I Puritani. *Address:* c/o Viale Majno 17/A, 92122 Milan, Italy.

GENTILE Ada, b. 26 July 1947, Avezzano, Italy. Composer. m. Franco Mastroviti, 2 July 1972. *Education:* Diploma, Piano, 1972, Diploma, Composition, 1974, S Cecilia Conservatoire, Rome; Advanced course with Goffredo Petrassi, Academia di Santa Cecilia, 1975-76. *Career:* Participant, international composition competitions; Her works performed throughout Europe, Canada, USA, Australia; Invited to festivals of contemporary music festivals including Huddersfield, Aarhus, Zagreb, Warsaw, Alicante, Bacau, Kassel; Commissions from RAI, French Ministry of Culture, Academia di Santa Cecilia; Artistic Director, G Petrassi Chamber Orchestra, 1986-88; Artistic Director, Nuovi Spazi Musicali festival, Rome; Currently teaches, S Cecilia Conservatoire; Presents contemporary music festivals, RAI-Radiotre. *Compositions:* 34 published works; 8 recorded works. *Recordings:* Monographic record with 4 works, FDI-PAN; Record with 2 works, RCA Italiana; Record with 1 work, BEAT Records; CD with 1 work, Canadian Radio. *Hobbies:* Books; Cuisine; Cats. *Address:* Via Divisione Torino 139, 00149 Rome, Italy.

GENTILE Louis, b. 2 Sept 1957, Connecticut, USA. Singer (tenor). *Education:* Studied in New York. *Career:* Guest appearances in opera and broadcasting houses in Europe and the USA; Sang a Darmstadt, 1983- 86; Krefeld, 1986-88 as Alfredo, among other roles; Netherlands Opera at Amsterdam, 1988, in Fidelio, Berlin Staatsoper, 1988, in Judith by Siegfried Matthus; Appeared at the Deutsche Oper Berlin, 1990, as Schwalb in Mathis der Maler; Pedro in Tiefland at the Theater am Gartnerplatz, Munich, 1991; Sang Don Jose at Oslo, 1991; Other roles include Tamino, Rossini's Almaviva, Boris in Katya Kabaova, Cavalli's Ormindo, Rodolfo, and Erik in Der Fliegende Holländer; Sang Bibalo's Macbeth for Norwegian Opera at Oslo, 1992. *Honours:* Winner Young Talent Presents, Competition, 1981. *Address:* c/o Deutsche Oper Berlin, Richard Wagnerstrasse 10, D-1000 Berlin, Germany.

GENTILESCA Franco J., b. 30 May 1943, New York, NY, USA. Stage Director; Producer. *Education:* Sacred Heart, Chicago, 1960; St. Johns University, New York, 1964; Pace University, New York, 1967; Private studies in Piano and Voice. *Debut:* With Andrea Chenier, Richard Tucker at Philadelphia Grand Opera, 1973. *Career:* Assistant to Luchino Visconti, Roman Polanski, Spoleto, 1974; Assistant Artistic Director, Artists International, 1975; Resident Stage Director, Connecticut Grand Opera, 1983-92; Stage Director: New Jersey State Opera, Philadelphia Grand Opera, New York Grand Opera, Florentine Opera, Milwaukee, Connecticut Opera Association, Tulsa Opera, Oklahoma, Opera Metropolitana, Caracas, Venezuela. Teaching: New York School of Opera; IIVA; MCA, Franklyn Institute; AIMS, Graz, Austria; Escuela de Opera, Caracas, Venezuela. *Memberships:* Member, Board of Governors: 5th Vice-President, American Guild of Musical Artists; Member: Actor's Equity. *Address:* 2109 Broadway, Apartment 14-10, New York City, NY 10023, USA.

GENZMER Harold (Professor), b. 9 Feb 1909, Bremen, Germany. Composer. m. 1949. *Education:* Abitur, Marburg; Berlin College of Music. *Career:* Director of Studies and Choral Repetitor, Opera House, Breslau, 1934-37; Berlin, 1938-; Professor, Freiburg, 1946-57; Professor, National College of Music, Munich, 1957-. *Compositions:* 3 Symphonies, Concertos for

piano, flute, trautonium, violins, violas, cello and orchestra; Zauberspiegel Suite for orchestra; Numerous works for chamber orchestra; Chamber music, organ works, choral works and electronic works. *Recordings:* 2 Concertos for trautonium and orchestra; Organ works; Harp music; Irische Harfe - Irish Harp; Concerto for trumpet and orchestra; Concerto for 2 clarinets. *Publications:* Harald Genzmer. *Honours:* Arts Prize, Bavarian Academy of Fine Arts, 1961. *Memberships:* Academy of Fine Arts, Munich; Academy of Fine Arts, Berlin; 1989 Medaille: München Lenchtet. *Hobbies:* Astronomy; Natural Sciences. *Address:* 8 München 80, Eisensteinstr 10, Germany.

GEORGE Alan Norman, b. 23 Dec 1949, Newquay, Cornwall, England. Violist. m. Lesley Schatzberger, 2 daughters. *Education:* MA, King's College, Cambridge University. *Debut:* As member of Fitzwilliam Quartet, Purcell Room, London, 1973. *Career:* Member, Fitzwilliam Quartet, 1969-, Quartet in Residence, University of York, 1971-74 & 1977-86, University of Warwick 1974-77; Lecturer, University of York, 1986-88, Finchcocks Quartet, 1992-; Participant, 1st performance of Quartets, No 2 by Sebastian Forbes, Edward Cowie, David Blake, Cuaderna by Bernard Rands, Clarinet Quintet by David Blake; Michael Blake Clarinet Quintet, 1st British performances, Shostakovich Quartets 13, 14 & 15; Alfred Schnittke, Canon in Memory of I. F. Stravinsky; Fitzwilliam Quartet, affiliate artists at Bucknell University, Pennsylvania, USA, 1978-86; Principal Viola, English Baroque soloists, Orchestra Révolutionnaire et Romantique; Member, Lumina (contemporary music group); 1st performances, ... et Quart by John Paynter, Clarinet Trio by William Sweeney; Concerts and recordings, London Classical Players, Age of Enlightenment, Academy of Ancient Music, English Baroque Soloists, New London Consort, Hanover Band, Yorkshire Baroque Soloists. *Recordings:* Shostakovich Quartets Nos 1-15; Franck, Quartet in D; Borodin, Quartets Nos 1 & 2; Delius Quartet; Sibelius, Voces Intimae; Brahms, Clarinet Quintet; Wolf, Italian Serenade; Schubert, String Quintet; Beethoven, Quartets opuses 130, 132, 127, 133, 135; Shostakovich, Piano Quintet, with V. Ashkenazy; Mozart Clarinet Trio, with A. Hacker & K. Evans; Schumann: piano quintet and piano quartet with R. Burnett; Mozart clarinet quintet with L. Schatzberger. *Publication:* Shostakovich Chamber Music. *Address:* 10 Bootham Terrace, York YO3 7DH, England.

GEORGE Donald, b. 13 Sept 1955, San Francisco, USA. Singer (Tenor). *Education:* Studied at Louisiana State University in Berlin and with Josef Metternich in Munich. *Career:* Sang lyric tenor roles at the Theater am Gartnerplatz, Munich; Brussels and the Vienna Staatsoper, 1986, in the premiere of Das Schloss by Andre Laporte and as Belmonte; Deutsche Oper Berlin, 1988-89, as Bernstein's Candide and as Fento in Die Lustigen Weiber von Windsor; Guest appearances at Madrid in the local premiere of Lulu, Wurzburg (as Belmonte), Komische Oper Berlin (Tamino), Leopold in La Juive, (Bielefeld, 1989); Giessen (Mozart's Titus) and Bregenz (Stuermann in Der fliegende Holländer: Other roles include Faust, Ferrando, Leukippos (Daphne), Jason in Médée and Jenik in The Bartered Bride; Sang Antonio in Prokofiev's The Duenna at the 1989 Wexford Festival, Candide in a concert performance at the Barbican Hall, London; Other repertoire includes works by Bach, Handel, Orff and Vaughan Williams. *Recordings include:* Alzira by Verdi. *Address:* c/o Deutsche Oper Berlin, Richard Wagnerstrasse 10, D-1000 Berlin, Germany.

GEORGE Michael, b. 1950. England. Singer (Baritone). *Education:* Chorister at King's College, Cambridge; Royal College of Music, London. *Career:* Solo engagements and as member of leading early music ensembles in Britain and Europe; Handel's L'Allegro at the 1988 Promenade Concerts; Brahms Requiem with the London Symphony Orchestra and Kurt Sanderling; Haydn's Creation in Madrid; Beethoven's Missa Solemnis and Choral Symphony with the Hanover Band; Purcell's Dioclesian with John Eliot Gardiner;

Performances of Messiah with The Sixteen in London, Italy, Spain, Poland and France; Engagements at the Three Choirs Festival, the Royal Festival Hall, Oslo, Brussels; Tour of Austria, Germany and Yugoslavia with the Orchestra of St Johns; Twentieth Century repertoire includes Stravinsky's Threni for the BBC, A Child of our Time with the Bournemouth Symphony Orchestra, premiere of John Metcalf's The Boundaries of Time for the BBC at the Swansea Festival and Christus in the St John Passion by Arvo Pärt (tour of Britain with the Contemporary Music Network); 3 Promenade concerts, 1990, in Bach's cantata Herz und Mund und Tat und Leben, Bonfire of the Vanities and Janáček's Glagolitic Mass; Sang Abinoam in Handel's Deborah at the 1993 Proms. *Recordings include:* Medieval Carmina Burana; Monteverdi's Vespers of 1610; Messiah, with The Sixteen; At the Boar's Head by Holst; Purcell's St Cecilia Ode; Bach Cantatas; Baroque Arias; Beethoven's Choral Symphony and Missa Solemnis; Haydn's Creation (Decca); complete Purcell Odes with the King's Consort (Hyperion).*Current Management:* IMG Artists, Europe, Media House, 3 Burlington Lane, Chiswick, London W4 2TH, England.

GEORGESCU Dan Corneliu, b. 1 Jan 1938, Craivoa, Rumania, Composer; Ethnomusicologist. m. Teodora Georgescu, 28 Jan 1984. *Education:* C. Porumbescu High School of Music, Bucharest. *Career:* Institute for Dialectological and Ethnological Research, 1962-83; Muzica review 1983-84; Scientific Researcher, Institute for History of Art, 1984-. *Compositions:* 3 symphonies; 5 string quartets; Symphonic cycles Plays (10 pieces); Models (5 pieces); Opera Model Mioritic; Studies atemporales (electronic music). *Publications:* Rumanian Dance Music; Alphorn Signals; Dance Music from Oltenia. *Contributions to:* Studies, articles. *Honours:* Prizes, Union of Rumanian Composers, 1969, 1970, 1974, 1978, 1981, 1984, 1985; G. Enescu Prize, Rumanian Academy, 1974; Prize, Rumanian Radio and Television Broadcasting. *Memberships:* Committee Member, Union of Rumanian Composers; European Seminar in Ethnomusicology; SACEM. *Hobbies:* Computers; Painting. *Address:* Am Schiessrain 7, 7630 Lahr/Schwarzwald, Germany.

GEORGIADIS Nicholas b. 14 Sept 1925, Athens, Greece. Stage Designer. *Education:* Studied architecrure in Athens and New York, painting and theatre design at the Slade School, London, 1953-54. *Career:* Collaborations with the late Kenneth Macmillan at Sadler's Wells, the Royal Ballet, the Stuttgart Ballet and the Deutsche Oper Berlin; Teacher at the Slade Schoool, 1960-86; Designed productions of Aida and Les Troyens at Covent Garden, 1968-69; Cherubini's Médée at Frankfurt, 1971, Anna Bolena (1976) and Don Giovanni in Athens; La Clemenza di Tito at Aix-en-Provence, 1988. *Honours include:* CBE, 1984. *Address:* c/o Teatre d'Opera du Festival, Aix en Provence, France.

GEORGIAN Karine, b. 5 Jan 1944, Moscow. Solo cellist. m. 15 Dec 1990, Anthony Philips, 1 son. *Education:* Gnessin School, Moscow 1950-61; Private studies with Armen Georgian, father, 1949-61; Moscow conservatory with Mstislav Rostropovich, 1961-68. *Career:* Regular appearances, Leading Soviet, European and American Orchestra and Festivals. Debut tour, Carnegie Hall, Chicago Symphony, 1969. Performance of Khatchaturian Cello Rhapsody; Return tour, Carnegie Hall, recital, Prague 1970; Berlin Philharmonic Orchestra, 1970; Leningrad Philharmonic Orchestra, 1973; Royal Philharmonic Orchestra, 1982; Debut: Professor of cello at Staatliche Hochschule für Musik, since 1984; BBC Proms, Henry Wood Promenade Concerts, 1985 and 1990; Philadelphia Orchehstra, 1990. *Recordings:* Melodia, Brahms Trio in B with Dmitri Alexeyev, Liane Isakadze; Denisov Concerto in C Moscow Philharmonic, Dmitri Kitayenko; Khatchaturian Cello Rhapsody, Bolshoi Radio Symphony Aram Khatchaturian; Sonatas by Shostakovich and Locatelli, Aza Amintayeva; Couperin Music for 2 Cellos with Natalia Gutman; Hyperion, Brahms Trio in A minor with Thea King, Clifford Benson. *Honours:* 1st Prize, All Union Music Competition 1966; Tchaikovsky International Competition, Moscow 1966, First prize and gold medal *Address:* c/o Olivia Ma Artists Management, 28 Sheffield Terrace, London W8 7MA, England.

GERAETS Theodora, b. 13 Oct 1961, Bosch en Duin, Holland. Concert Violinist. *Education:* Studied in Amsterdam, with Dorothy Delay in New York and with Kyung Wha-Chung in London. *Career:* American debut 1980, with the St Louis Symphony under Leonard Slatkin; British debut at the Wigmore Hall, 1979; Regular appearances on radio and TV and in concert throughout Europe, and USA, Central and South America; Repertoire includes the Mendelssohn Concerto, Mozart's Sonata K380, Ravel's Sonata and Ysaye's Extase; Teacher at the Hague Conservatory. *Honours include:* Second prize, National Youth Violin Competition, Amsterdam, 1971; Finalist, International Conservatory at Glasgow, 1976; Winner, National Oskar Back Concours in Amsterdam, 1979; Winner, International Bartók Competition, in Aspen, Colarodo, 1980; Netherlandse Muziekprijs, 1989. *Address:* c/o World Wide Artists Ltd, 6 Petersfield Crescent, Coulsden, Surrey CR5 2JQ, England.

GERBER Steven Roy, b. 28 Sept 1948, Washington, USA. Composer; Pianist. m. Theresa Aiello, 10 June 1972, divorced 1988. *Education:* BA Haverford College, 1969; MFA Princeton University, 1971; Studied Composition with Robert Parris, Milton Babbitt, Earl Kim, JK Randall, Harvey Sollberger; Piano with Robert Parris, Agi Jambor, Irwin Gelber. *Career:* At age of 19 years was commissioned by the Kindler Foundation to write a Trio For Violin, Cello and Piano for the Trio of the University of Maryland; Frequent performances with such distinguished soloists as sopranos Christine Schadeberg and Johana Arnold and violinists Kurt Nikkanen and Rolf Schulte; Tour of the former Soviet Union in 1991, as composer and pianist, including world premieres of Symphony no.1 and Serenade for String Orchestra. *Compositions include:* Soprano and Orchestra: Harmonium: Six Poems of Wallace Stevens, 1981; Choral: Ceremony After a Fire Raid (Dylan Thomas), 1973; Illuminations (Rimbaud), 1972; Vocal: Desert Places: Five Poems of Robert Frost, 1982; Drum Taps: Three Patriotic Poems (Frost, Whitman and Emerson), 1984; Words for Music Perhaps (WB Yeats), 1984; Solo Piano: Piano Sonata, 1982; Voices, 1976; Solo Winds or Strings: Epithalamium (flute), 1971; High Wood (oboe). 1978; Chamber Music: Dreamwork (flute, viola, cello, and piano), 1978; String Quartets, Nos. 1 and 2, 1973-81; Trio (violin, cello and piano), 1968; Woodwind Quartet (flute, oboe, clarinet and bassoon), 1967; Symphony No.1, 1989; String Quartet No.3, 1988; Six Songs of William Shakespeare, 1988; Serenade for String Orchestra, 1990; Woodwind Quintet, 1986. *Recordings:* As pianist recorded music by Milton Babbitt, Frank Martin and Robert Evett as well as his own compositions. *Memberships:* Several professional organizations. *Address:* 639 West End Avenue, 10D, New York, NY 10025, USA.

GERGIEV Valery, b. 2 May 1953, Moscow, USSR. Conductor. *Education:* Studied piano and conducting in Ordzhonikidze, later moved to Leningrad Conservatory; while a student won the All Union Conductors Competition Prize in Moscow and the Karajan Competition in Berlin. *Career:* Conductor at Kirov Opera, 1977-, and Chief Conductor of the Armenian State Orchestra; appeared with the USSR State Symphony Orchestra in France, 1987; guest engagements with the Berlin Philharmonic, L'Orchestre de France and Dresden Philharmonic; London debut 1988, with the London Symphony Orchestra at the Barbican; later engagements with the City of Birmingham Symphony Orchestra, Royal Liverpool Philharmonic and Bournemouth Symphony; BBC Philharmonic succeeded Yuri Temirkanov as Music Director of Kirov Opera and Ballet Theatre, May 1988; Conducted Welcome Back St Petersburg, Kirov gala at Covent Garden, 1990 (debut in opera there with Eugene Onegin, 1993); Boris Godunov at the Helsinki Fair Centre, Khovanshchina at Rome, 1992; Kirov Opera at the Metropolitan, 1992, with The Fiery Angel, The Queen of Spades and Boris

Godunov; Prince Igor at Caesarea, Israel; Met 1994, Otello. *Address:* c/o Harold Holt Ltd, 31 Sinclair Road, London W14 ONS, England.

GERINGAS David, b. 29 July 1946, Vilna, USSR. Concert Cellist. m. Tatiana Schatz. *Education:* Studied with Rostropovitch at the Moscow Conservatoire, 1963-71. *Career:* Concert tours of Germany 1970 and Hungary 1973; Resident in Germany from 1976: many recitals with pianist Tatiana Schatz and Professor at Hamburg Conservatoire; Played in Orchestra of the North German Radio, and given solo performances of works by Honegger, Milhaud, Hindemith and Kabalevsky; Premiered the sonata for solo cello by Gottfried von Einem, 1987; Piano Trio performances with Gerhard Oppitz and Dmitri Sitkovetsky; Also plays the baryton and has formed the Trio Geringas with the violinist Vladimir Mendelssohn and the cellist Emil Klein. *Recordings include:* Gubaidulina Offertorium, Boston Symphony/Charles Dutoit (Deutsche Grammophon). *Honours include:* First Prize, Baku Competition, 1969; Winner, Tchaikovsky International Competition, 1970. *Address:* c/o DGG (contracts), 1 Sussex Place, London W6 AX5, England.

GERLE Robert, b. 1 Apr 1924, Abbazia, Italy. Violinist; Conductor; Teacher. *Education:* Franz Liszt Academy of Music, Budapest; National Conservatory, Budapest. *Career:* Soloist with many European Orchestras; Toured as Recitalist in Europe; Head, String Department, University of Olkahoma, 1950-54; Teacher, Peabody Conservatory of Music, 1955- 68; Mannes College of Music, 1959-70; Manhattan School of Music, 1967-70; Ohio State University, 1968-72; Head, Instrumental Program, University of Maryland, 1972-. *Recordings:* Several discs. *Publications:* The Art of Practising the Violin, 1983. *Honour:* Hubay Prize, 1942. *Address:* c/o Siegel Artist Management, 3003 Van Ness Street North West, Suite 205, Washington, DC 20008, USA.

GERSTENENGST Iosif, b. 3 July 1920, Ciacova, Romania. Organist. *Education:* Graduate of Normal High School, Timisoara, 1939; Graduate, Theological Academy, Timisoara, 1944; 8 years piano and musical theory with Professor Elizabeth Andrée; 4 summer Master-courses of Organ with Professor Franz Xaver Dressler, Sibiu. *Debut:* Timisoara, 1945. *Career:* Performed concerts and recitals in all main Cathedrals in Romania such as in Bucharest, Timisoara, Arad, Alba Iulia, Jassy, Oradea, Satu-Mare, Sibiu and abroad in Vienna, Salzburg, West Berlin, Hamburg, East Berlin, Cologne, Munich, Paris, Rome, Brussels, Stockholm, Warsaw, Belgrade, Sofia, Leipzig, Riga, Odessa, Prague and New York. *Recordings:* Disc issued LP with pieces by Frescobaldi and Pachelbel; Organ collaborations in the issue of other disc records. *Hobby:* Reading Classics in Music and Literature. *Current Management:* Romanian Agency of Artists Management, Bucharest. *Address:* Str Nuferilor 19, 70749 Bucharest, Romania.

GERTLER André, b. 26 July 1907, Budapest, Hungary. Violinist; Professor. *Education:* Studied with Professors Hubay, Kodaly; Violin Diploma, Budapest, 1925. *Career:* Founder, Leader, Gertler Quartet, 1931-51; Soloist, Recitalist, Europe, USA, Africa, Asia and Australia; numerous sonata recitals with Bartók; Professor, Cologne Academy of Music, 1954-58; Professor, Hanover Academy of Music, 1964-78; Professor, Royal Conservatory of Music, Brussels; Professor, Chapelle Musicale Reine Elisabeth, Founder of Konzertarbeitswochen Goslar (GFR), JMAS (Internationale Musikakademie für Solisten, Wolfenbuttel (GFR). *Recordings:* Numerous recordings made. *Publications:* Transcriptions of works by Bartók, Geza Frid. *Contributions to:* Revue Musicale; The Score. *Honours:* Knight, Order of Leopold and Order of the Crown, Belgium; Officer, Order of Gustav Vasa Sweden; Order of the Flag, Hungary; Order of Merit, 1st Class, German Federal Republic; Honorary Fellow, Royal Academy of Music, London; Order of Freedom and Friendship, Hungary; Order of Merit, Poland; Bundesverdienstkreuz 1 Klasse, GFR. *Address:* 28 Avenue d'Overhem, 1180 Brussels, Belgium.

GESSENDORF Mechthild, b. 1937, Munich, Germany. Singer (Soprano). m. Ernö Weil. *Education:* Studied at the Munich Musikhochschule and with Joseph Metternich in Cologne. *Career:* Sang with the Vienna Kammeroper, from 1961, then at Bremen and Bonn; Staatsoper Munich from 1981, as Aida, the Empress in Die Frau ohne Schatten, Rosenkavalier, Don Carlos and in The Turn of the Screw; Salzburg Festival 1981, as Amelia Boccanegra; Bregenz Festival 1983, Agathe; US debut 1983, Marschallin (Rosenkavalier) at Tulsa; Philadelphia 1985, as Ariadne; Metropolitan Opera debut 1986, the Marschallin (returned 1989, as the Empress in Die Frau ohne Schatten, Senta 1990); Vienna State Opera, Oper Köln, Düsseldorf, Deutsche Oper Berlin, Staatsoper Hamburg, Grand Opera Paris, Covent Garden London 1987 Tannhäuser, 1988 Lohengrin, Scala Milano as Senta (Holländer) 1988; Savonlinna Festival, Aix en Provence, Edinburgh Festival, Lyric Chicago, Toronto, Montreal, Detroit; Sang Sieglinde in Die Walküre for Greater Miami Opera, 1989, Ariadne at Lyon and Barcelona, the Marschallin in Paris and Agathe in Der Freischütz at Monte Carlo; sang Elsa in Lohengrin at Lisbon 1990, the Marschallin at the Metropolitan, 1991; Sang in Beethoven's Choral Symphony at the 1989 Promenade Concerts, London. *Recordings include:* Die Lustige Witwe (Deutsche Grammophon); Penthesilea by Schoeck. *Address:* c/o Kaye Artists, Barratt House, 7 Chertsey Road, Woking, GU21 5AB, England.

GESZTY Sylvia, b. 28 Feb 1934, Budapest, Hungary. Singer (Soprano). *Education:* Studied at the Budapest Conservatory and the Budapest Music Academy, with Erszebeth Hoor-Tempis. *Career:* Sang at the Budapest Opera from 1959; Berlin Staatsoper from 1961, debut as Amor in Orfeo ed Euridice; Komische Oper Berlin 1963-70; Hamburg Staatsoper 1966-72; Covent Garden and Salzburg Festival debuts 1966, 1967, as the Queen of Night; Stuttgart Opera from 1971; Glyndebourne Festival 1971-72, as Zerbinetta and Constanze; Los Angeles 1973, with the company of the New York City Opera, as Sophie in Der Rosenkavalier; Schwetzingen Festival 1976, as Gismonda in Cimarosa's Il Marito desperato; Sang Rosina in Haydn's La Vera Costanza at Vienna, Schönbrunn, 1984 (also televised); Guest appearances in Buenos Aires, Vienna, Paris, Brussels, Amsterdam and Moscow; many concert appearances. *Recordings include:* Ariadne auf Naxos (EMI); Die Israeliten in der Wüste by CPE Bach, Cantatas by JS Bach and La Rappresentazione di Anima e di Corpo by Cavalieri (Deutsche Grammophon); Die Zauberflöte, Cosi fan Tutte, Barbier von Bagdad by Cornelius (Eurodisc); Mozart's Die Schuldigkeit des ersten Gebotes. *Address:* c/o Staatliche Hochschule für Musik, Urgansplatz 2, D-70000 Stuttgart, Germany.

GETREAU Florence, b. 16 May 1951, Boulogne-Billancourt, Seine, France. Curator. m. Ingofried Muthesius, 12 Oct 1982, 1 son. *Education:* Licence Modern Literature, Licence, History of Modern Art, University of Aix-Marseille, 1973; Maitrise, History of Art, 1976; Doctor in Musicology, 1991, University of Paris, Sorbonne. *Career:* Previously Assistant, then Curator, 1979-, Museum of Musical Instruments, Conservatoire de Paris; Leader of Project for Museum of Music, Paris, 1988-92; Director, until Jan 1992, CNRS research team on musical iconography and organology; Professor for musicaliconography and organology, Conservatoire de Paris, Paris, 1993; Member, ICOM; Member, International Committee of Musical Instrument Collections. *Publications:* Restauration des instruments des musique (as Florence Abondance), 1981; La facture instrumentale européenne: suprematies nationales et enrichissement mutuel (editor), 1985; Instrumentistes et luthiers parisiens (editor), 1988; Des cabinets de musique aux musées d'instruments, Le Musée Instrumental du Conservatoire de Paris. 1793-1993. *Address:* 57 Allée d'Alsace (Gretz), F-77220 Tournan, France.

GHAZARIAN Sona, b. 2 Sept 1945, Beirut, Lebanon. Singer (Soprano). *Education:* Studied at the Armenian College, Beirut, at the Accademia Chigiana, Siena, and at the Accademia di Santa Cecilia, Rome. *Career:* Member of the Vienna Staatsoper from 1972, notably as Oscar (Un Ballo in Maschera) and as Violetta; Bregenz Festival 1983, as Aennchen in Der Freischütz; Guest appearances in Hamburg, Paris, Brussels, Geneva and Salzburg; Verona Arena, 1985, Barcelona, 1988; Metropolitan Opera, 1989, as Musetta in La Bohème; Sang in J.C. Bach's Adriano in Siria for Austrian Radio, conducted by Charles Mackerras. *Recordings:* Il Re Pastore by Mozart (RCA); Marzelline in Fidelio (Decca); Un Ballo in Maschera (Philips). *Address:* c/o Metropolitan Opera, Lincoln Center, New York, NY 10023, USA.

GHENT Emmanuel (Robert), b. 15 May 1925, Montreal, Quebec, Canada. Composer. *Education:* Studied at McGill University, and with Ralf Shapey in the US. *Career:* Freelance composer of electronic music; From 1969 has worked at Bell Telephone Laboratories; Has practised psychiatry in New York and invented the Polynome, for the reproduction of multiple rhythms. *Compositions include:* Movement for wind quintet 1944; 3 Duos for flutes 1944; Lament for string quartet 1958; Quartet for winds 1960; Dance Movement for trumpet and string quartet 1962; Triality I and II for violin, trumpet and bassoon 1964; Dithyrambos for brass quintet 1965; Hex, an Ellipsis for trumpet, ensemble and tape 1966; Helices for violin, piano and tape 1969; Lady Chatterly's Lover, L'Apres-midi d'un Summit Meeting, Our Daily Bread and 12 Electronic Highlights, all for tape, 1969-70; Phosphones 1971; Lustrum 1974; Program Music 1-29, 1977-79; Baobab 1979. *Contributions to:* Perspectives of New Music; Electronic Music Review. *Honours include:* MacDowell Fellowships, 1964-65; Guggenheim Fellowship 1967; NEA Grants 1974, 1975. *Address:* c/o ASCAP, ASCAP Building, One Lincoln Plaza, New York, NY 10023, USA.

GHEZZO Dinu, b. 2 July 1941, Tuzla, Romania. Composer; Conductor. m. Marta, 3 Oct. 1961, 1 daughter. *Education:* State Diploma in Education, 1964, State Diploma in Composition, 1966, Romanian Conservatory; PhD, University of California, Los Angeles, USA, 1973. *Career:* Program Director, Composition, Director, New York University Music in Italy, Professor of Composition, New York University; Director, George Enescu International Composition Competition; Co-Director, New Repertory Ensemble of New York. *Compositions include:* Aphorisms; Structures; Sketches (with Seesaw Music, New York) recorded on Orion Masters and Grenadilla; Breezes of Yesteryear (with Editions Salabert); Sound Shapes I & II; From Here To There; Two Prayers for Soprano and Tape; A Book of Songs; Ostrom; Doina, etc. *Recordings:* Several recordings with Orion Master Recordings, Grenadilla and West Deutscher Rundfunk. *Publications:* Most works published with Editions Salabert, Seesaw Music Corporation and Musica Scritta. *Contributions to:* Tomis; Living Musician. *Hobbies:* Photography; Computers; Travel. *Address:* New York University, Music Department, 35 West 4th Street, New York, NY 10003, USA.

GHIAUROV Nicolai, b. 13 Sept 1929, Velingrad, Bulgaria, Singer (Bass). m. Mirella Freni. *Education:* Sofia Music Academy, Moscow Conservatoire. *Debut:* Played violin and piano, clarinet from a very early age, Sofia Opera House as Don Basilio in Barber of Seville, 1955. *Career:* Bologna, 1958, La Scala, Milan, as Varlaam in Boris Godunov, 1959; Regular appearances at La Scala, Covent Garden, 1962-, Metropolitan Opera New York, 1965-, as Mephistopheles (debut), King Philip, Padre Guardiano and Fiesco in Simon Boccanegra; Vienna State Opera; Major roles include title role in Boris Godunov, Mephistopheles in Faust, Don Giovanni, Philip II in Don Carlos and Massenet's Don Quixote; sang Ramphis at the opening of Houston Grand Opera, 1987, Ivan Khovansky in Khovanshchina at the Vienna Staatsoper, 1989; Gran Teatre del Liceu Barcelona, 1989-90, as Gremin in Eugene Onegin and Boris; Season 1992 as Colline in La Bohème at Rome and Goryanshikov in From the House of the Dead at the Salzburg Festival; returned to Covent Garden 1993

as Gremin. *Address:* Royal Opera House, Covent Garden, London WC2, England.

GHIGLIA Lorenzo, b. 26 Nov 1936, Florence, Italy. Stage Designer. *Education:* studied in Florence. *Career:* Worked at the Bergamo Festival 1958 then designed the premier of Pizzetti's Il Calzare d'argento at La Scala, 1961, for director Margherita Wallmann; Has also collaborated with Franco Enriquez, Mario Missiroli and Filippo Crivelli; Designed La Bohème at Palermo (1961), Attila at Florence (1962) and Petrassi's Il Cordovano at Turin, 1966; US commissions include Pagliacci and Rigoletto for Houston Opera and Samson et Delilah at Dallas; Glyndebourne, 1965-66, Anna Bolen and Dido and Aeneas; Further designs at Florence (le Villi and Busoni's Aralecchino, 1972, and 1975); La Scala, Suor Angelica, 1973) and Catania, (Médée, 1977). *Address:* c/o Teatro alla Scala, Via Filodrammatici 2, 20121 Milan Italy.

GHIGLIA Oscar, b. 13 Aug 1938, Livorno, Italy. Concert Artist; Guitarist. m. Anne-Marie d'Hauteserre, 6 Dec 1966, 1 daughter. *Education:* Honours Graduate, Conservatory Santa Cecilia, Rome, 1962. *Career:* Concert Tours in North America, 1965-; Performed with Juilliard, Tokyo, Emerson String Quartets, Julius Baker, Victoria de los Angeles, Jean Pierre Rampal; Performances all over the world including Europe, Turkey, Israel, Japan, Far East, Australia, New Zealand; Artist in Residence, Hartt School of Music, University of Hartford, USA; Musik Akademie de Stadt, Basel; Instructor, Summers, Aspen, Colorado Music Festival, 1969; Academia Musicale Chigiano, Siena, Italy, 1976; Banff Centre for the Arts, Canada, 1978-. *Recordings:* Paganini Sonata; The Guitar in Spain; The Spanish Guitar of Oscar Ghiglia; Numerous recordings. *Current Management:* 197 S Quaker Lane, W Hartford, CT 06119. *Address:* Helfenberg Strasse 14, Basel, CH-4059, Switzerland.

GHIUSELEV Nicola, b. 14 Aug 1936, Pavlikeni, Bulgaria. Singer (Bass). *Education:* Studied with Khristo Nrambarov at the Sofia National Opera School. *Debut:* Sofia 1961, as Timur in Turandot. *Career:* Metropolitan Opera from 1965, debut as Ramphis in Aida; Holland Festival 1966, as King Philip; Guest appearances in Vienna, Paris, Moscow and Milan; Stockholm 1974, as Rossini's Moses; Covent Garden debut 1976, as Pagano in I Lombardi (sang Boris Godunov, 1984); Further engagements in Bucharest, Budapest, Monte Carlo, Naples, Leipzig and Berlin; Sang title role in Czechoslovak TV film of Don Giovanni; Rossini's Basilio at Chicago, 1989; sang Ramphis in Aida at Caracalla, Rome, 1990; Prince Galitzky in a new production of Prince Igor at Covent Garden, 1990; Silva in Ernani at Parma, Verdi's Attila at the Vienna Staatsoper; Season 1992 as Colline in La Bohème at Bonn and Mustafa in L'Italiana in Algeri at the Deutsche Oper, Berlin. *Recordings include:* Khovanshchina; Aleko by Rachmaninov; La Gioconda and Les Huguenots (Decca); Les Contes d'Hoffmann, La Bohème, Turandot (EMI); La Battaglia di Legnano by Verdi (Philips). *Honours include:* Prizewinner at Competitions in Sofia, Prague and Helsinki. *Address:* c/o Kaye Artists Management, Barratt House, 7 Chertsey Road, Woking, Surrey, GU21 5AB, England.

GIACOMINI Giuseppe, b. 7 Sept 1940, Veggiano, Padua, Italy. Tenor. *Education:* Studied with Elena Fava Ceriati in Padua, Marcello del Monaco in Treviso and Vladimiro Badiali in Milan. *Debut:* 1966, as Pinkerton in Madame Butterfly. *Career:* Sang in Berlin and Vienna from 1972, Hamburg from 1973; La Scala debut 1974; Paris Opera Debut 1975; US debut Cincinnati Opera from 1976, as Alvaro (La forza del destino), Verdi's Macduff, Don Carlos and Manrico, Puccini's Cavaradossi and Canio in Pagliacci; Further appearances in Barcelona, Boston, Budapest, London, Munich, Tokyo; sang Verdi's Otello at San Diego in 1986; Season 1992 as Alvaro at Naples, Canio at Rome and Radames at the Festival of Caracalla; other roles include Puccini's Calaf, Luigi, Rodolfo and Des Grieux, Pollione (Norma), Turiddu (Cavalleria Rusticana), Giordano's Andrea

Chenier, Verdi's Radames (Aida) and Ernani. *Recordings include:* Norma (CBS); Fausta by Donizetti (HRE); Manon Lescaut (RCA); Cavalleria Rusticana (Philips); Tabarro, Tosca (both new editions, recorded in Philadelphia, conductor Riccardo Muti). *Honours include:* Prizewinner in Competitions at Naples, Vercelli and Milan.

GIAIOTTO Bonaldo, b. 25 Dec 1932, Ziracco, Udine, Italy. Singer (Bass). *Education:* Studied in Udine and with Alfredo Starno in Milan. *Debut:* Teatro Nuovo Milan, 1957. *Career:* Sang widely in Italy then appeared as Rossini's Bartolo at Cincinnati. 1959; Metropolitan Opera debut 1960, as Zaccaria in Nabucco, and has sung in New York for 25 years in 300 performances, notably as Ramphis, Raimondo and Timur; Further engagements in Paris, London, Bordeaux, Rome, Geneva, Vienna, Hamburg and Madrid; Concert tour of South America 1970; Season 1985 as Banquo in Zurich, Attila at the Verona Arena and in a revival of Donizetti's Il Diluvio Universale at Geneva (as Noah); La Scala Milan debut 1986, as Rodolfo in La Sonnambula; Season 1988-89 as Ramphis in Aida at Chicago, Fiesco (Simon Boccanegra) at Piacenza and Padre Guardiano in Miami and Verona; Sang Timur in Turandot at Turin, 1990; Season 1992 as Alvise in La Gioconda at Rome and Philipp II and Ramphis at the Verona Arena. *Recordings:* Ferrando in Il Trovatore, Brogni in La Juive (RCA); Luisa Miller (Decca); Aida , La Traviata and Turandot (HMV); La Cieco in Massenet's Iris, conducted by Patanè (CBS). *Address:* c/o Arena di Verona, Piazza Bra 28, I-37121 Verona, Italy.

GIBAULT Claire, b. 1955, Le Mans, France. Conductor. *Education:* Studied at the Le Mans Conservatory and in Paris. *Career:* Staff conductor and assistant to John Eliot Gardiner at the Lyons Opera 1983-89, leading Pelléas et Mélisande, La Finta Giardiniera, Il Barbiere di Siviglia and Iphigénie en Tauride: For Nice Opera has conducted Mitridate, Rossini's Donna del Lago, La Traviate and Die Zauberflöte; Idomeneo at Liège: Assistant to Claudio Abbado at the Vienna Staatsoper, 1986, engaged there 1988; Debut with the Royal Opera at Covent Garden, 1993, Pelléas et Mélisande. *Address:* c/o Royal Opera House (Contracts), Covent Garden, London WC2, England.

GIBBONS Jack, b. 2 Mar 1962, England. Pianist. *Career:* Numerous solo and concerto appearances from the age of ten. London solo debut 1979; Queen Elizabeth Hall, solo debut, 1984; Appearances on BBC Radio television, and Classic FM radio, and with various orchestras. *Compositions:* Solo piano arrangements of Gershwin's Concert Works and Overtures, and transcriptions of Gershwin's original piano improvisations from recordings and piano-rolls. *Recordings:* For Hyperion; Lambert's Rio Grande with English Northern Philharmonia Orchestra, Opera North, conductor David Lloyd-Jones; For ASV: series of solo piano albums: The Authentic George Gershwin, Volume 1, 2 and 3. *Current Management:* Norman McCann International Artists Ltd, London. *Address:* c/o Norman McCann International Artists Ltd, 56 Lawrie Park Gardens, London SE26 6XJ, England.

GIBBS Robert Whysall, b. 1 Jan 1965, Isleworth, Middlesex, England. Violinist. *Education:* Yehudi Menuhin School, 1973-83; ARCM Performers' with honours, 1983; Royal College of Music, 1983-; RCM course completed 1988. *Debut:* Wigmore Hall, London, 19 June 1983. *Career:* Concerto and other solo, quartet and orchestral engagements in UK and abroad including Korea, Hong Kong, People's Republic of China, Germany, India, France, Netherlands, Spain, South America & the Caribbean, Switzerland; 5 appearances, Queen Elizabeth Hall, St John's, Smith Square and Wigmore Hall including Leader of quartet in Priaulx Rainier Birthday Concert; Mendelssohn Octet with Yehudi Menuhin, including at David Niven's funeral; Regularly plays with the London Festival Orchestra. *Recordings:* Recital for French Radio, 1983. *Hobbies:* 20th century history; Cricket; Cars. *Address:* 8 St Margaret's Drive, Twickenham, Middlesex, TW1 1QN, England.

GIBIN Joao, b. 1929, Lima, Peru. Singer (Tenor). *Education:* Studied in Lima and at the Scuola della Scala, Milan, Italy. *Career:* Sang first in Italy then guested with the Netherlands Opera in Amsterdam as Andrea Chénier and Calaf; Vienna Staatsoper from 1958; Covent Garden 1959, as Edgardo opposite Joan Sutherland's Lucia; Leading roles at La Scala from 1960; New York City Opera and Maggio Musicale, Florence 1961, as Radames and Don Carlos. *Recordings:* La Fanciulla del West, with Birgit Nilsson (Columbia); Lucia di Lammermoor, with Sutherland. *Honour:* Winner, MGM South American Caruso Competition, 1954. *Address:* c/o Teatro alla Scala, Via Filodrammatici 2, I-20121 Milan, Italy.

GIBSON Alexander Drummond, (Sir), b. 11 Feb 1926, Motherwell, Scotland. Conductor. m. Ann Veronica Waggett, 3 sons, 1 daughter. *Education:* Dalziel School; Glasgow University; Royal Scottish Academy of Music; Royal College of Music, London; Mozarteum, Salzburg; Academy Chigiana, Siena. *Career:* Royal Corps of Signals, 1944-48; Assistant Conductor, BBC Scottish Orchestra, 1952-54; Repetiteur and Assistant Conductor, Sadler's Wells Opera, 1951-52, Staff Conductor, 1954-57; Musical Director, 1957-59 (Premiere of John Gardner's The Moon and Sixpence); Guest Conductor, Royal Opera House, Covent Garden, 1957-58; Musical Director and Principal Conductor, Scottish National Orchestra, 1959-84; Founder, Artistic Director and Principal Conductor, Scottish Opera, 1962-87 (Les Troyens 1969, first German language Ring Cycle in Scotland, 1971); Guest Conductor all major symphony orchestras of Great Britain and many in Europe and America; Conducted Tosca for Scottish Opera, 1990, Otello for Kentucky Opera; Bruckner Festival Linz 1990, concert performance of Tristan und Isolde. *Recordings include:* Symphonies by Sibelius, Dvořák, Tchaikovsky, Bizet, Mendelssohn, Elgar and Prokofiev; Beethoven Piano Concertos with John Lill; Das Lied von der Erde, with Alfreda Hodgson; Berlioz Overtures; Walton Belshazzar's Feast; Collins Classics Sibelius series with the Royal Philharmonic. *Honours:* Knighted, 1977; Hon Dmus, Newcastle University, 1990; Hon Dmus, York University, 1991. *Address:* 15 Cleveden Gardens, Glasgow, G12 0PU, Scotland.

GIBSON Jon (Charles). b. 11 Mar 1940, Los Angeles, California, USA. Composer; Flautist; Saxophonist. *Education:* Studied at Sacramento and San Francisco State Universities. *Career:* Co-founded the New Music Ensemble 1961; Association with minimalist group of composers includes participation in the premiere of Terry Riley's In C (1964) and membership from 1968 of the Philip Glass Ensemble; Visual arts involved in compositions, some of which written for dancers; Solo appearances as instrumentalist in the USA and Europe. *Recordings include:* Einstein on the Beach, with the Philip Glass Ensemble. *Compositions include:* Opera Voyage of the Beagle 1985; Who are You, Vocal/Tape Delay, Visitations: an Environmental Soundscape and Radioland for tape, 1966-72; Instrumental: Multiples 1972; Song I-IV 1972-79; Melody I-IV 1973-75; Cycles for organ 1973; Recycle I and II 1977; Call 1978; Return, and Variations, both for small ensemble 1979-80; Extensions, dance score 1980; Relative Calm, dance score for small ensemble and tape 1981; Interval for video tape, 1985. *Honours include:* Grants from the Creative Artist Public Service Program 1974, 1981; Rockefeller Foundation grant 1982. *Address:* c/o ASCAP, ASCAP Building, One Lincoln Plaza, New York, NY 10023, USA.

GIBSON Rodney, b. 1960, Winchester, England. Singer (Baritone). *Education:* Studied at the Royal College of Music and with Paolo Silveri and Raimund Herincx. *Career:* Sang first at the Teatro Ghione in Rome; Early roles were the Forester in The Cunning Little Vixen, Falstaff, Pistol (At the Boar's Head by Holst) and Don Alfonso; Season 1985-86 with Mecklenburgh Opera and Abbey Opera, at the Camden Festival in the Tsar has his Photograph Taken by Weill, and with the Modern Music Theatre Troupe; Further appearances as Dapertutto with Beaufort Opera and concerts with Baroque Music; Has sung Ping in Turandot for Regency Opera and at the Royal Albert Hall; Concert repertoire includes Puccini's Gloria and Mozart's Coronation Mass; Moses and Aron by Schoenberg and Carmina Burana by Orff. *Address:* c/o Korman International Management, Crunnells Green Cottage, Preston, Herts SG4 7UQ, England.

GIBSON Stephen Brodie, b. 27 Mar 1957, Barnet, Hertfordshire, England. Composer. *Education:* BMus Honours degree, Composition, Birmingham University, 1978; Studied with John Casken, John Joubert, G W Hopkins. *Career:* Composer, Banff Centre Music Theatre Studio Ensemble, Alberta, Canada, 1982-84; Music performed extensively in Netherlands, Belgium, Canada, Spain, USA, and in Britain at Huddersfield Festival, 1982-83; Commissions from Banff Centre, Birmingham University, also various ensembles and performers including Copas Ensemble, Catherine Pluygers (oboe), David Wilson (oboe). *Compositions include:* Meridian for 4 violins, 2 violas and oboe, for video piece OLAM, 1982; From the Seed There Weeps a Willow..... (published by The Premiere Magazine), 1983-85; Self-published major works: Extensions II-IV for various combinations, 1979-82; Mystery-Bouffe, 1-act music theatre work, 1979-84; Baby on a Leash, opera in 6 scenes, 1982-83; Stomp for piano, 1982 (also recorded); Ghost Town, 2-act music theatre work, 1983; Sub-class Four Million, 1-act music theatre work, 1983-84; There Was Once A Time for baritone and ensemble, 1984; Symphony - Urban Street Songs for large orchestra, 1985-86. *Honours:* Bursaries: Vaughan Williams Trust; Hinrichsen Foundation; The Banff Centre. *Memberships:* Performing Rights Society; The Composers' Guild; Society for the Promotion of New Music. *Address:* 40 Campbell Close, London, SE16 6NG, England.

GIEBEL Agnes, b. 10 Aug 1921, Heerlen, Holland. Singer (Soprano). m. Herbert Kanders, 1 son, 2 daughters. *Education:* Studied at the Folkwang-Schule Essen with Hilde Wesselmann. *Career:* Gave first public concert 1933, with Lieder by Strauss and Reger; Adult career from 1947, giving many concerts and recitals in Europe and North America; Bach Cantata series with Karl Ristenpart for Berlin Radio, 1950-51; Repertoire includes 20th Century works, Mozart arias and much Baroque music. *Recordings include:* Bach, Christmas Oratorio (EMI); St Matthew Passion (Oiseau Lyre); St John Passion (Deutsche Grammmophon); St Matthew Passion, Beethoven's Missa Solemnis, Die Schöpfung, Bach Cantatas (Philips); Ein Deutsches Requiem (Decca); Song recitals for EMI; Hunt Production CD with Hermann Prey and Celibidache. *Address:* EMI Records, Publicity, Classical, 20 Manchester Square, London, W1A 1ES, England.

GIELEN Michael Andreas, b. 20 July 1927, Dresden, Germany. Conductor. m. Helga Augsten, 20 May 1957, 1 son 1 daughter. *Education:* Dresden, 1936; Berlin, 1937; Vienna, 1940; after imigration 1940, studied music in Buenos Aires with Dr Erwin Leuchter. *Career:* Coach, Teatro Colon, Buenos Aires, Argentina, 1947-50; Conductor, Vienna State Opera, 1950-60; Chief conductor, Stockholm Royal Opera, 1960-65; Freelance conductor, Cologne, West Germany, 1965-68; conducted the premiere of Zimmermann's Die Soldaten, 1965; Music Director, Belgian National Orchestra, Brussels, 1969-73; Chief conductor, Netherlands Opera, 1973-75; Music Director-General Manager, Frankfurt Opera House, 1977-87; Music Director, Cincinnati Symphony Orchestra, USA, 1980-86; Chief Conductor, SWF Radio Orchestra, Baden-Baden, Federal Republic of Germany, 1986-; Professor conducting Mozarteum, Salkzburg, 1987-; (SWF-Orchestra), Television Series in 6 parts, Orchester-Farben, 1993. *Compositions:* 4 Gedichte von Stefan George, 1958; Variations for 40 instruments, 1959; Un dia sobresale, 1963; Die glocken sind auf falscher spur, 1969; Mitbestimmungs Modell, 1974; String quartet, 1983; Pflicht und Neigang, for ensemble, 1988; Rückblick, trio for 3 cellos, 1989;

Weitblick, Sonata for cello solo, 1991.*Recordings include:* Schoenberg's Moses und Aron; Schoenberg's Piano and Violin Concertos; Alfred Brendel, Wolfgang Marschner; Zimmermann's Die Soldaten; Ligeti's Requiem and Cello Concerto (Siegfried Palm); Stockhausen's Carré; Werle's Dreaming of Thérèse, with the Royal Stockholm Orchestra; Recordings with Cincinnati CSO, a series of 15 CD's, Jieleen Edition, with SWF Orchestra. *Address:* c/o South West German Radio, D-7570 Baden-Baden, Germany.

GIERSTER Hans, b. 12 Jan 1925, Germany. Musical Director. *Education:* Musikhochschule, Munich; Mozarteum, Salzburg. *Career:* Formerly, Musical Director, Freiburg-im-Breisgau Municipal Theatres; General Musical Director, Nuremburg, 1965; Director, Musiktheater Nuremburg, 1971; Currently, Conductor, Munich Staatsoper; Guest Conductor, State Operas of Hamburg, Munich and Vienna; Guest appearances at festivals in Munich, 1964; Edinburgh (with Bavarian State Opera) Così fan Tutte, 1965; Glyndebourne (presented Magic Flute), 1966, Zurich, 1971, Vienna, 1972; Concerts with Philharmonic Orchestras of Bamberg, Berlin, Munich, Vienna, London, Mexico City. *Address:* Musiktheater Nürnberg, 8500 Nuremberg, Hallerweisse 4, Germany.

GIERZOD Kazimierz, b. 6 Aug 1936, Warsaw, Poland. Pianist. m. Jolanta Zegadlo, 14 Jul 1974. *Education:* Secondary School Leaving Certificate, 1953; Graduated, Warsaw Frederic Chopin Academy of Music, 1962, studied with Professor Margerita Trombini-Kazuro; Diploma of Merit, Accademia Chigiana, Siena, studied under Professor Guido Agosti. *Career:* Regular recitals and concerts in Europe, Japan, USA and South America, 1964-; Pedagogical career: F Chopin Academy of Music in Warsaw, tutor 1969-73, Assistant Professor, 1973-86, Professor 1986-, Dean of the Piano Department, 1975-87, Elected as Rector of F Chopin Academy of Music, 1987, 1990-93 (two terms of office). *Recordings:* Archival recordings for Polish Radio (pre-performances of Polish music), recordings for foreign radio (USA, Cyprus), tv recordings (Poland, Japan). Creative Works: Lectures on musical interpretation, Master Classes (Poland, Japan, USA, Venezuela, Cyprus); radio and tv commentator during International F Chopin Piano Competition in Warsaw, 1985, 1990; radio and tv interviews; interviews for local and foreign press. *Address:* ul Sygietynskiego 36, 05-805 Otrebusy, Poland.

GIFFORD Anthea, b. 17 Feb. 1949, Bristol, England. Classical Guitarist. m. John Trusler, 18 July 1970, 1 son, 1 daughter. *Education:* Accademia Musicale Chigiana, Siena, Italy; Royal College of Music, London. *Debut:* Purcell Room, London. *Career:* Many Solo Recitals on BBC Radio 3; over 30 Programmes on BBC Radio 3 with violinist Jean-Jacques Kantorow; Recitals; Purcell Room, Wigmore Hall, Fairfield Hall; Barbican Centre, Queen Elizabeth & Festival Halls; TV Appearances on Channel 4, BBC2, TSW etc.; frequent chamber music recitals with Delme string quartet; Adjudicator, overseas league; Performances in Italy, France, Spain Germany. *Recordings:* Paganini and his Contemporaries, Kantorow-Gifford duo, BBC realesed 1991; Paganini Ensemble, Denon released 1991; Solo Recital, National Trust record label, 1991; Paganini Ensemble National Trust record label, 1991; Kantorow-Gifford violin and guitar duos, National Trust record label 1993; Dodgson duo concerto with Northern Sinfonia, Biddalph recordings, 1994. *Contributions to:* Guitar International. *Honours:* Recipient, Young Musician of the Year, Greater London Arts Association Award. *Memberships:* Incorporated Society of Musicians; Overseas League. *Address:* 24 Donovan Avenue, London N10 2JX, England.

GIFFORD Gerald Michael, b. 12 Jan 1949, Cambridge, England. Professor; Director of Music; Recitalist. *Education:* Royal College of Music, 1969-72; MA, Cambridge University; BMus, Dunelm; GRSM; FRCM; FRCO; FRSA. *Career:* Assistant Organist, Ely Cathedral, 1973-76; Director of Music, King's School,

Ely, 1974-77; Professor, Royal College of Music, London, 1975-; Academic Tutor, M.Mus (RCM) Degree Course in Performance Studies; Fellow and Director of Music, Wolfson College, Cambridge, 1978-. *Recordings:* Over 40 recordings as organist, harpsichordist or director. *Publications:* John Stanley's Keyboard Concertos, 1986; Loeillet's Harpsichord Suites, 1986. *Contributions to:* Musical Times; Organists' Review; RCM Magazine; The New Grove; Die Musik in Geschichte und Gegenwart. *Memberships:* RMA; RCO; RSCM; ISM. *Address:* Wolfson College, Cambridge CB3 9BB, England.

GIFFORD Helen, b. 5 Sept 1935, Melbourne, Victoria, Australia. Composer. *Education:* MusBach, Melbourne University Conservatorium of Music, 1958; Composer-in-Residence, Melbourne Theatre Company, 1970-; Commissions, Melbourne Chorale, Astra Chamber Music Society, Australian Broadcasting Commission, Australian Percussion Ensemble. *Compositions:* Chamber music: Fantasy, flute, piano, 1958; Septet, harpsichord, flute, oboe, bassoon, violin, viola, cello, 1962; Skiagram, flute, viola, vibraphone, 1963; Lyric, flute, clarinet, cello, 1964; String Quartet, 1965; Fable, harp, 1967; Canzone, chamber orchestra (recorded), 1968; Myriad, from Indian advasi melodies, 1969; Sonnet, flute, guitar, harpshichord, 1969; Of Old Angkor, French horn, marimba, 1970; Overture, chamber orchestra, 1970; The Wanderer, male speaker, flute, cor anglais, viola, percussion with celesta, 1963; Images for Christmas, speaker, electric guitar, small organ, with percussion, celesta and effects for 5 players, 1973; Piano works: Piano Sonata, 1960; Catalysis, 1964; Waltz, The Spell, Cantillation, 1966; Souvenance, 1973; Orchestral: Phantasma (recorded), string orchestra, 1963; Chimaera (recorded), 1967; Imperium, 1969; On Reflection, 2 solo violins, string orchestra, 1972; Vocal/choral: As Dew in Aprille, Christmas carol for boy or female soprano, piano or harp or guitar, 1955; Red Autumn in Valvins, mezzo soprano, piano, 1964; Vigil, a cappella, 1966; The Glass Castle, Soprano solo, a cappella, 1968; Bird Calls From An Old Land, 5 soprano soloists, a cappella female choir, 1971; Foretold At Delphi, soprano, piccolo, oboe, pre-recorded bass crumhorn, Arabian drum, 1978; Brass: Company of Brass, ensemble, 1972; Play, brass and woodwind ensemble with percussion, 1979; Theatre music: Incidental music, songs; Jo Being, 1-act opera, 1974. *Address:* c/o J Albert & Son, 139 King Street, Sydney, New South Wales 2000, Australia.

GILBERT Anthony John, b. 26 July 1934, London, England. Composer; Teacher of Composition. *Education:* D. Mus. MA, Leeds; Fellow, Royal Northern College of Music; Composition with Anthony Milner, Matyas Seiber, Alexander Goehr and Gunther Schuller, Conducting with Lawrence Leonard, Morley College, London. *Career:* Lecturer in Composition, Goldsmiths' College, 1968-73; Composer-in-Residence, University of Lancaster, 1970-71; Lecturer in Composition, Morley College, London, 1972-75; Senior Lecturer in Composition, Sydney Conservatorium, Australia, 1978-79; Composer-in-Residence, City of Bendigo, Victoria, 1981; Currently Principal Lecturer in Composition, Royal Northern College of Music, England. *Compositions include:* Orchestral: Symphony; Sinfonia; Ghost and Dream Dancing; Crow Cry; Towards Asavari; Tree of Singing Names; Operas, 1990: The Scene Machine (with George MacBeth), The Chakravaka-Bird (with Mahadevi and A K Ramanujan); Chamber: 3 String Quartets; Saxophone Quartet; Quartet of Beasts; Nine or Ten Osannas; Vasanta with Dancing; Instrumental: Moonfaring; Dawnfaring; Igorochki; 2 Piano Sonatas; Spell Respell; The Incredible Flute Music; Treatment of Silence; Vocal: Certain Lights Reflecting; Love Poems; Inscapes; Long White Moonlight; Beastly Jingles.*Recordings:*Nine or ten osannas (Music projects, London). *Memberships include:* Composers' Guild; Association of Professional Composers; Performing Right Society. *Hobbies:* Walking; Running; Conservation; Art galleries; Photography. *Address:* c/o Royal Northern College of Music, 124 Oxford Road, Manchester M13 9RD, England.

GILBERT Kenneth, b. 16 Dec 1931, Montreal, Canada. Harpsichordist; Organist. *Education:* MusD (Honorary), McGill University. *Career:* Professor of Harpsichord, Hochschule für Musik, Stuttgart, and the Mozarteum, Salzburg; Summer Courses at Accademia Chigiana, Siena. *Recordings include:* Complete Harpsichord Works of François Couperin (Harmonia Mundi) and Rameau (Archiv); Bach's English and French Suites (Harmonia Mundi) and Well-tempered Clavier (Archiv, 1984); Goldberg Variations, 1987; music by Lully 1988, Bach English Suites 1988, Couperin's Four Books for Harpsichord 1989 (Harmonia Mundi); music by Frescobaldi, Byrd, Froberger, Purcell, Handel, Rameau, Bach, Couperin and Scarlatti, 1988 (Novalis). *Publications:* Complete Harpsichord works of Rameau, François Couperin, D'Anglebert; Bach's Goldberg Variations, Frescobaldi Toccatas; Complete Keyboard Sonatas of Scarlatti in 11 Volumes. *Honours:* International Calouste Gulbenkian Foundation Award, 1970; Canada Council Arts Fellowship, 1968, 1974; Artist of the Year, Canada, 1978; Officer, Order of Canada, 1986; Professor of Harpsichord, Paris Conservatoire, 1988. *Current Management:* Basil Douglas Artists' Management, 8 St. George's Terrace, London NW1 8XJ, England. *Address:* 11 Rue Ernest-Psichari, F-75007, Paris, France.

GILBERT Steven E, b. 20 Apr 1943, New York, USA. Professor of Music; Author. m. Patricia Jean King, 8 May 1977, (div), 2s. *Education:* BA, CUNY, 1964; MMus 1967, Composition, MPhil, PhD, 1969, 1970, Yale University. *Career:* Professor, California State University, Fresno, 1970-; Music reviewer for the Fesno Bee; Cocktail pianist; . *Publications:* The Music of George Gershwin, forthcoming; Introduction to Schenkerian Analysis, with Allen Forte, 1982; Articles in Musical Quarterly, Journal of Music Theory, and other journals. *Honours:* BMI Student Composers Awards, 1963, 1966, 1967. *Memberships:* American Musicological Society; College Music Society; Society for Music Theory; The Sonneck Society. *Hobbies:* Stockmarket spectulating; Car club tours and racing. *Address:* Music Department, California State University, Fresno, CA 93740-0077, USA.

GILBOA Jacob, b. 2 May 1920, Kosice, Czechoslovakia. Composer. m. Shoshana Bregman, 22 Mar 1961, 1 daughter. *Education:* Academy of Music, Jerusalem; Music Teacher's Seminary, Jerusalem. *Compositions:* (Orchestra) The Twelve Chagall Windows; Cedars; From the Dead Sea Scrolls; Kathros Upsanterin; 7 Ornaments to a Theme by Paul Ben Haim; The Beth Alpha Mosaic; Safiah; The Lament of Kalonymos; (Chamber Music): Dew; Steps of Spring; Toccata in Black, White & Grey; Sonata for Cello; C'est q'ua vu le vent d'Est; Reflections on Three Chords by Alban Berg; Crystals; Three lyric pieces in Mediterranean Style; Irith Flowers; Bedu; Melancoly-Triptychon; String Quartet; 7 Little Insects; The Grey Colours of Kaethe Kollwitz, 1990; Blossoms in the Desert, 1991; Three-Coloured Melancholy, 1992. *Recordings:* The Twelve Chagall Windows; The Beth Alpha Mosaic; Three lyric pieces in Mediterranean style. *Honours:* Acum Prize, 1968, 1970, 1973, 1989; Engel Prize, 1972, 1979; Prize, Prime Minister of Israel, 1982. *Memberships:* Israeli Composers' Association. *Hobby:* Painting. *Address:* Israeli Music Publication (IMO), 25 Karen Hayessod-Street, Jerusalem.

GILDER Eric, b. 25 Dec 1911, London, England. Lecturer; Author; Composer. m. 23 Dec 1939, 2 daughters. *Education:* Royal College of Music. *Career:* About 1000 radio and television appearances as Pianist, Conductor, Actor, Playwright, Singer, Story and Script Writer. *Compositions:* Symphonic works; 200 songs; 13 stage musicals. *Publications:* Dictionary of Composers and Their Works, 1978 and 1985; Catterels; Sharing Music with Eric Gilder; Many Parts. *Address:* 21 Fieldend, Twickenham, Middlesex TW1 4TF, England.

GILES Alice, b. 1961, Australia. Concert Harpist. *Education:* Studied in Australia and with Alice Chalifoux in Cleveland. *Career:* Has concertised extensively in

Australia, the USA, Israel and Germany; Festival engagements at Schleswig-Holstein, Bayreuth (International Youth Festival) and Dusseldorf New Music Festivals, Adelaide (Britten's Canticles with Barry Tuckwell and Gerald English), Marlboro, and Bath Mozart Festival; New York Merkin Hall debut 1984, 92nd street 'Y' Concert 1988; Wigmore Hall debut, June 1989 and tour with Luciano Berio; Chamber concerts with violinist Thomas Zehetmair and pianst Arnan Wiesel. *Recordings include:* Two solo CD recitals for the KOCH label; one chamber music for CDI; one flute and harp wth Tall Poppies. *Honours include:* Winner, International Harp Competition, Israel, 1982; Churchill International Fellowship, 1980. *Address:* Robert Gilder & Co, Enterprise House, 59/65 Upper Ground, London SE1 9PQ, England.

GILL Timothy, b. 1960, England. Cellist. *Career:* Co-founded the Chagall Piano Trio at the Banff Centre for the Arts in Canada (currently resident artist); Debut concert at the Blackheath Concert Halls in London 1991; Further appearances at the Barbican's Prokofiev Centenary Festival, the Warwick Festival and the South Place Sunday Concerts at the Conway Hall, London; Purcell Room London recitals 1993 with the London premiere of Piano Trios by Tristan Keuris, Nicholas Maw and Dame Ethel Smyth (composed 1880); Premiere of Piano Trio no 2 by David Matthews at the Norfolk and Norwich Festival, 1993; Engaged for the Malvern Festival, 1994. *Address:* Chagall Trio, South Bank Centre, Press Office (Pamela Chowham Management), London SE1, England.

GILLARD David Owen, b. 8 Feb 1947, Croydon, Surrey, England. Critic; Writer. *Education:* Tavistock; Croydon. *Career:* Scriptwriter, Associated British Pathé, 1967-69; Film and Theatre Critic, Daily Sketch 1969-70; Ballet Critic, Daily Mail, 1971-89; Opera Critic, Daily Mail, 1971-; Founder Editor, ENO and Friends 1982-92; Radio Correspondent, Radio Times, 1983-91. *Publication:* Beryl Grey: A Biography 1977. *Contributions to:* Daily Mail; Radio Times; BBC Music Magazine; Music and Musicians. *Memberships:* The Critics Circle; The Green Room Club. *Hobbies:* Hill Walking; Collecting Children's Books. *Address:* 16 Grasmere Road, Bromley, Kent BR1 4BA, England.

GILLES Marie-Louise, b. 1937, Duren, Germany. Singer (Mezzo-Soprano). *Education:* Studied at the Folkwang-Hochschule Essen with Hilde Wesselmann. *Career:* Wiesbaden Opera from 1962, as Octavian, Dorabella and the Composer in Ariadne auf Naxos; Staatsoper Munich 1964-66; Bremen 1966-68; Sang at Hanover from 1968, notably as Azucena, Brangaene, Eboli, Waltraute, Fricka, Ortrud, Berg's Marie and Countess Geschwitz and Santuzza; Bayreuth Festival 1968-69; Appearances at the Dubrovnik and Salzburg Easter Festivals; Concert engagements in Washington, New York, Vienna, Paris and Lisbon; Professor at the Hanover Musikhochschule from 1982. *Recordings:* Petite Messe Solennelle by Rossini; Bach Cantatas (Telefunken); Hans Heiling by Marschner. *Address:* Hochschuele für Musik und Theater, Emmichplatz 1, 3 Hannover, Germany.

GILLESPIE Rhondda Marie, b. 3 Aug 1941, Sydney, Australia. Concert Pianist. m. Denby Richards 1973. *Education:* New South Wales Conservatory, Sydney, with Alexander Svergensky; UK with Denis Matthews and Louis Kentner. *Career:* Recitals and concerto appearances throughout world, including UK, USA, Australia, Far and Near East, Europe and Scandinavia; BBC TV series on Liszt's Christmas Tree; from 1984 many tours with Robert Weatherburn as Duo, Two's Company. *Recordings:* Duets (with Robert Weatherburn); Sonatas by Bliss and Lambert (Argo); Concertos by Usko Merilainen (Philips and EMI); Sonata, 2 Ballads and Christmas Tree Suite by Liszt (Chandos); Works by Camilleri (Vista). *Contributions to:* Musical Opinion 1989. *Honours:* New South Wales Concerto Prize 1959; Harriet Cohen Commonwealth Medal 1966. *Membership:* Landsdowne Club. *Hobbies:* Exotic Cooking; Golf. *Address:* 2 Princes Road, St Leonards-on-Sea, East Sussex, TN37 6EL, England.

GILLESPIE Wendy, b. 1950, New York. Viol Player. *Career:* Member of Fretwork, first London concert at the Wigmore Hall, London, July 1986; Appearances in the Renaissance and Baroque repertoire in Sweden, France, Belgium, Holland, Germany, Austria, Switzerland and Italy; Radio broadcasts in Sweden, Holland, Germany and Austria; Televised concert on ZDF, Mainz; Tour of Soviet Union Sept 1989 and Japan, June 1991; Festival engagements in Britain; Repertory includes In Nomines and Fantasias by Tallis, Parsons and Byrd; Dance music by Holborne and Dowland (including Lachrimae); Six-part consorts by Gibbons and William Lawes; Songs and instrumental works by Purcell; Collaborations with vocal group Red Byrd in verse anthems by Byrd and Tomkins, London Cries by Gibbons and Dering; Resurrection Story and Seven Last Words by Schütz; Gave George Benjamin's Upon Silence at the Elizabethan Hall, Oct 1990; Wigmore Hall concerts 1990-91 with music by Lawes, Purcell, Locke, Dowland and Byrd. *Recordings:* Heart's Ease (late Tudor and early Stuart); Armada (Courts of Philip II and Elizabeth II); Night's Black Bird (Dowland and Byrd); Cries and Fancies (Fantasies, In Nomines and The Cries of London by Gibbons); Go Nightly Cares (Consort songs, dances and In Nomines by Byrd and Dowland): all on Virgin Classics Veritas label. *Address:* Robert White Management, 182 Moselle Avenue, London N22 6EX, England.

GILLETT Christopher, b. 1958, London. Singer (Tenor). *Education:* Studied at the Royal College of Music with Robert Tear and Edgar Evans; National Opera Studio, London. *Debut:* Sadler's Wells 1981 as Edwin in The Gypsy Princess. *Career:* Sang with New Sadler's Wells Opera in Gilbert and Sullivan; Has appeared with Glyndebourne Touring Opera as Ferrando and Albert Herring; Hermes in King Priam for Kent Opera; Royal Opera House Covent Garden from 1984 as Flute (Midsummer Night's Dream), Roderigo (Otello), Dov (Knot Garden), Pang and Hermes, and in Parsifal, Un Re in Ascolto and Idomeneo; Sang Nooni in The Making of the Representative for Planet 8 at the London Coliseum and in Amsterdam; Season 1990-91 with the Martyrdom of St Magnus by Maxwell Davies in London and Glasgow; Mozart's Ferrando at Garsington Manor and Arbace with the English Bach Festival at Covent Garden and in the Vichy Festival, France; Pysander in Netherlands Opera Ulisses; Sang Musil in the premiere of Broken Strings by ParamVir, Amersterdam, 1992; Tichon in Katya Kabonova for Glyndebourne Touring Opera and Britten's Flute at the 1992 Aix-en-Provence Festival; Concert engagements include Elgar's The Kingdom with the London Philharmonic, Tippett's Mask of Time with the Hallé; Bach's St John Passion in Hong Kong, Cambridge and Greenwich and Elijah with the Bach Choir. *Honours include:* Winner, Grimsby Singing Competition 1980; Countess of Munster Award 1981. *Address:* Magenta Music International, 4 Highgate High Street, London N6 5JL, England.

GILMORE Gail, b. 21 Sept 1950, Washinton DC, USA. Singer (Mezzo-Soprano). *Education:* Studied at Xaver University New Orleans and at Indiana University, Bloomington. *Career:* Sang at Krefeld, Germany, 1975-79; Appearances at Giesen, Enschede (Holland) and the Vienna Staatsoper; Staatsoper Wiesbaden 1979-82; Deutsche Oper am Rhein Dusseldorf 1981-82, 1986 (Penthesilea by Schoeck); New York City Opera 1981-82; Teatro La Fenice Venice 1983-84, Kundry in Parsifal; Sang at the Verona Arena 1983-86, as Carmen and as Ulrica (Un Ballo in Maschera); Further engagements in Frankfurt, Nice, Cologne, Nuremberg, Barcelona and Hanover; Other roles include Cassandre (Les Troyens), Octavian, the Composer, Eboli, Gluck's Orpheus, Fricka, Brangaene, Cenerentola, Begonia (Der junge Lord) and Venus; Teatro Fenice Venice 1987, as Ortrud; Metropolitan Opera debut 1987, as Fricka in Das Rheingold; Zurich Opera 1990, as Azucena; Season 1992 as Amneris at San Juan and the Festival of Caracalla; Concert performances of Schoenberg's

Gurrelieder, Passions by Bach and the Brahms Alto Rhapsody. *Address:* c/o Metropolitan Opera, Lincoln Center, New York, NY 10023, USA.

GIMENEZ Eduardo, b. 2 June 1940, Mataro, Barcelona, Spain. Singer (Tenor). *Education:* Studied with Carmen Bracons de Clomer and Juan Sabater in Barcelona; Vladirimo Badiali in Rome. *Debut:* Reggio Emilia 1967, as Nemorino in L'Elisir d'Amore. *Career:* Has sung widely in Italy and at the Teatro Liceo, Barcelona; Holland Festival 1970, in La Fedeltà Premiata by Haydn; Guest appearances in Brussels, Nice, Monte Carlo, Venice, Budapest, Bordeaux, Tel Aviv, Seattle and Washington; Pesaro and La Scala Milan 1984-85, in a revival of Rossini's Il Viaggio a Reims; Well known in operas by Cimarosa, Bellini, Paisiello, Galuppi, Mozart, Verdi and Puccini; has sung in Paisiello's Il Barbiere di Siviglia at Leningrad; Barcelona 1988, in the premiere of Llibre Vermell by Xavier Benguere (Ferrando in Così fan Tutte, 1990); Season 1992 as Rossini's Don Ramiro at the Semper Oper Dresden and in Barcelona. *Recordings include:* Elvino in La Sonnambula; Don Pasquale; L'Atlantida by Falla (EMI); Rossini's Armida. *Address:* John Coast, 31 Sinclair Road, London W14 0NS, England.

GIMENEZ Raul, b. 14 Sept 1950, Argentina. Singer (Tenor). *Education:* Studied in Buenos Aires. *Debut:* Teatro Colon Buenos Aires 1980, as Ernesto in Don Pasquale. *Career:* Sang in concert and opera throughout South America before European debut, as Filandro in Cimarosa's Le astuzie femminili at the 1984 Wexford Festival; Sang in Paris and Venice as Roderigo in Rossini's Otello and appeared at the Théâtre des Champs-Elysées as Elvino, 1989, in La Sonnambula; Season 1987 sang at the Pesaro Festival in Rossini's L'Occasione fa il ladro, as Ernesto at Amsterdam and Alessandro in Il re Pastore by Mozart at Rome; Aix-en-Provence 1988, as Gernando and Carlo in Rossini's Armida; Toronto and Zurich 1989, as Almaviva; US debut at Dallas as Ernesto; Lisbon 1989, as Tonio in La Fille du Régiment; Covent Garden 1990-91-93, as Almaviva, Ernesto and Ramiro; Season 1990 appearances in Tancredi (as Argirio) at Geneva, Così fan Tutte at Buenos Aires and Salieri's Les Danaides at the Ravenna Festival (as Lyncée); Debut: Tancredi at La Scala, 1993; Cenerentola in Florence, 1993; Debut: Vienna State Opera, 1990, Almaviva in Il Barbiere di Siviglia; Further guest appearances in Naples, Bologna, Verona, Turin, Frankfurt, Los Angeles, Toulouse, Monte Carlo, Lausanne, Schwetzingen Festival and Brussels. *Recordings include:* Rossini arias, Bellini and Donizetti arias; Les Danaides, L'Occasione fa il ladro for Nimbus, EMI and Fonit Cetra, conducted by Michelangelo Veltri; Il Turco in Italia; Rossini Messa di Gloria (Philips), 1992; Il Barbiere di Siviglia (Teldec); Viaggio a Reims, (Sony); Nimbus: Mozart Arias. *Address:* c/o Patricia Greenan, 19b Belsize Park, London NW3 4DU, England.

GIMSE Havard, b. 15 Sept 1966, Kongsvinger, Norway. Pianist. *Education:* Norway State Academy of Music; Bergen Music Conservatory; Mozarteum, Salzburg; Musikhochschule, Berlin. *Debut:* Trondheim Symphony Orchestra, 1981. *Career:* Soloist with Major Scandinavan orchestras, such as Oslo Philharmonic, Bergen Philharmonic, Helsinki Radio, since 1981; Concerts in Europe and North and South America; Played with conductors including Kitajenko, Talmi, Schönwandt, Iona Brown; Several chamber music appearances. *Recordings:* Liszt: Piano Sonata; Chopin: Piano Music; Grieg: Piano and chamber music. *Honours:* Princess Astrid's Music Prize, 1985; Robert Levin Festival Prize, 1986; Jugend Musiziert Frankfurt, 1987. *Current management* Oslo Arts Management. *Address:* Storetveitasen 13, 5032 Minde, Norway.

GINGOLD Josef, b. 28 Oct 1909, Brest-Litovsk, Russia. Violinist; Professor. *Education:* Pupil of Vladimir Graffman, New York; Eugene Ysaÿe, Brussels. *Career:* 1st Violinist, NBC Symphony orchestra, NY, 1937-43; Concertmaster, Detroit Symphony orchestra 1943-46, Cleveland orchestra 1947-60; Teacher, Case Western Reserve University, 1950-60; Professor of Chamber Music, Meadowmount School of Music, 1955-81; Teacher 1960-65, Distinguished Professor of Music 1965-, Indiana University School of Music; Mischa Elman Chair, Manhattan School of Music, 1980-81; Various master classes; 1st Honorary Chairman and President of the Jury, International Violin Competititon of Indianapolis, 1982, 1986. *Recordings: Several discs.* *Address:* c/o School of Music, Indiana University, Bloomington, IN 47405, USA.

GINGOLD Norbert, b. 26 Sept 1902, Czernowitz (former Austria). Composer; Conductor. m. (1) Heddy Grabscheid, 7 Mar 1926, (2) Venetia Gatsos, 26 Aug. 1983. *Education:* PhD, Vienna and Friedrich-Wilhelm University, Berlin, 1931; Music Academy, Vienna (with Joseph Marx); Diplomas, Composition and Conducting, Musikhochschule, Berlin (with Franz Schreker). *Career:* Conductor, Threepenny Opera (Weill), Vienna, 1929; Theatrical works, with books by Heddy Gingold, performed: Cinderella (Vienna, 1930, Otto Preminger, director); Mozart auf der Reise nach Prag (Berlin, 1932); Pour un baiser de vous (Paris, 1947); series of children's operas: Théâtre Charles-Perrault, Marseilles, 1947-51 and New York, 1951-52, Amato Opera House, San Francisco, 1952-, Founder and Director, San Francisco Children's Opera, at Herbst Theatre. *Compositions:* Published: Rumanian Rhapsody (Ries and Erler, Berlin 1931); Lieder and songs (Editions Mondia, Paris; Editions Magali, Marseilles); Chansons Petites-Russiennes (Metropolis, Paris.) *Memberships:* SACEM (France); ASCAP (USA). *Address:* PO Box 18143, San Francisco, CA 94118, USA.

GINKEL Peter van, b. 10 Mar 1933, Eindhoven, Holland. Singer. (Bass-baritone). *Education:* Studied at the Quebec Conservatory and with Kurt Herbert Adler in San Francisco. *Debut:* Woodstock, New York, as Colonel Ibbetson in Peter Ibbetson by Deems Taylor. *Career:* Has appeared at most Canadian opera houses and in Chicago (premiere of Penderecki's Paradise Lost, 1978); German engagement at Cologne, Dortmund, Stutgart, Mannheim, Dusseldorf and Nuremberg; Rules have included Mozart's Figaro and Alfonso, Verdi's Iago and Rigoletto, Caspar, Wagner' Dutchman, Wotan and Alberich, Escamillo, Wozzeck and Jochanaan; Many concert appearances. *Recordings include::* Lieder by Beethoven and Wolf. *Address:* c/o Stadtische Buhnenn Richard Wagner-Platz 2-10, 8500 Nuremberg Germany.

GINZER Frances, b. 19 Sept 1955, Calgary, Alberta, Canada. Singer (Soprano). *Education:* Studied at Calgary, North Texas State and Toronto Universities. *Debut:* Canadian Opera Toronto, as Clothilde in Norma. *Career:* Sang Antonia in Les Contes d'Hoffmann at Toronto, followed by the Verdi Requiem, Messiah, Beethoven's Ninth and Die Schopfung; European opera debut Karlsruhe, 1983, as Antonia; Engaged at Dusseldorf from 1987 and has made guest appearances at Hamburg, Stuttgart, Cologne, Bonn, London (English National Opera), Munich State Opera, Frankfurt, Zurich, Warsaw, Maastricht, Vancouver, Calgary, Edmonton, Winnipeg and USA debut in Dallas, Texas; Welsh National opera,1991, as Violetta; Duisburg, 1991, as Frau Fluth in Die Lustige Weiber von Windsor; Early roles included Micaela, Constanze, Donna Anna and Mozart Countess; Lucia, Cleopatra, Sophie in Der Rosenkavalier, Aminta (Die schweigsame Frau), Jenůfa, Leila (Les Pecheurs de perles), and Mimi; Present Repertoire include Turandot, Ariadne, Senta and Tosca. *Recordings include:* Handel's Rodrigo; Ariana Lecouvreur. *Address:* c/o Welsh National Opera, John Street, Cardiff, Wales CF1 4SP.

GIOMBI Claudio, b. 22 June 1937, Trieste, Italy. Singer. Divorced, 1 son, 1 daughter. *Education:* Diploma, Drama & Singing; La Scala; Metropolitan Opera; Staatsoper, Vienna; Maggio Musicale Florence. *Debut:* Teatro Verdi, Trieste. *Career:* Bohème with Karajan; Bohème with Kleiber; Le Nozze di Figaro, Muti; The Nose, De Filippo; Nozze di Figaro, Strehler; Master Classes: Juilliard, Ohio, Tokyo, Korea, Strasbourg. *Honours:* Recipient, many honours & awards. *Hobbies:*

Agriculture; Philosophy; Photography; Food. *Address:* Via Chopin 13, Milan 20141, Italy.

GIOVANINETTI Christoph. b. 1960, France. Violinist. *Education:* Studied at the Paris Conservatoire with Jean-Claude Pennetier and with members of the Amadeus and Alban Berg Quartets. *Career:* Member of the Ysaÿe String Quartet from 1984; Many concert performances in France, Europe, America and the Far East; Festival engagements at Salzburg, Tivoli (Copenhagen), Bergen, Lockenhaus, Barcelona and Stresa; Many appearances in Italy, notably with the 'Haydn' Quartets of Mozart; Tours of Japan and the USA 1990 and 1992. *Recordings:* Mozart Quartet K421 and Quintet K516 (Harmonia Mundi); Ravel, Debussy and Mendelssohn Quartets (Decca). *Honours:* Grand Prix Evian International String Quartet Competition, May 1988; special prizes for best performances of a Mozart quartet, the Debussy quartet and a contemporary work; 2nd Prize, Portsmouth International String Quartet Competition, 1988. *Address:* c/o Artist Management International, 12/13 Richmond Buildings, Dean Street, London W1V 5AF, England.

GIPPS Ruth Dorothy Louisa, b. 20 Feb 1921, Bexhill, Sussex, England. Musician; Composer; Conductor; Organist. m. Robert Baker, 19 Mar 1942, 1 son. *Education:* Bexhill School of Music; Private Tuition; Oxford School Certificate, 1936; ARCM, Piano Performers, 1936; Royal College of Music, 1937-42 Caird Scholarship, 5 prizes, B Mus (Dunelm) by Examination, 1941; Matthay Piano School, 1942-43 D Mus (Dunelm) by Examination, 1948. *Debut:* Wigmore Hall, 1940. *Career:* Concert Pianist and Orchestral Oboist until 1952; Chorus Master, City of Birmingham Choir, 1948-50; Lecturer in Music, Oxford Extra-Mural Delegacy, 1948-59; Professor, TCL, 1959-66; Professor, RCM, 1967-77; Principal Lecturer in Music, Kingston Polytechnic, 1977-79; Conductor, London Repertoire Orchestra, 1955-86; London Chanticleer Orchestra, 1961-; Organist, High Hurstwood Parish Church, 1986-90; Organist, Ripe with Chalvington, 1990-93; Conductor, Heathfield Choral Society, 1990-92; Chalvington Singers, 1992-. *Compositions:* 5 Symphonies; 6 concertos; Choral Works: The Cat; Goblin Market; Seascape, for 10 wind instruments; Wind Octet; Sinfonetta for 10 wind & tam-tam; Numerous songs; Chamber music. *Recordings:* Numerous recordings made. *Contributions to:* Musical Times; Musical Opinion; Composer. *Honours:* FRCM, Honorary RAM, FRSA; Cobbett Prize; MBE, 1981. *Memberships:* Chairman, Composers Guild, 1967; Member of Council, Composers' Guild, 1991-; President, Hastings Festival, 1957-88; President, John Bate Choir; Vice-President, London Repertoire Orchestra. *Hobby:* Photography. *Address:* Tickerage Castle, Pound Lane, Framfield, Uckfield, East Sussex TN22 5RT, England.

GIRAUDEAU Jean, b. 1 July 1916, Toulon, France. Singer (Tenor). *Education:* Studied in Toulon and Paris. *Debut:* Montpelier 1942, in Mignon by Thomas. *Career:* Strasbourg 1947, in the premiere of Rabaud's Martine; Paris Opéra-Comique 1947, as Nadir in Les Pêcheurs de Perles: later appeared in the premieres of operas by Wisser and Tailleferre, and in a revival of Philidor's Blaise le Savetier; Paris Opéra as Tamino, and in the premiere of Milhaud's Bolivar 1950; Guest appearances in Nice, Monte Carlo, Marseilles and Brussels; BBC, London, 1952 as Aeneas in Les Troyens; Director of the Paris Opéra-Comique 1968-71. *Recordings:* Thaïs by Massenet; L'Heure Espagnole; Les Mamelles de Tiresias by Poulenc; The Nightingale by Stravinsky; The Fiery Angel by Prokofiev; Les Troyens (Westminster).

GIROLANI Renato, b. 1959, Amelia (TR), Italy. Singer (Baritone). *Education:* Studied in Germany with Ernst Haefliger and Dietrich Fischer-Dieskau and in Italy with Sesto Bruscantini. *Career:* Sang Mozart roles, Figaro and Leporello at Passau, Germany, St Gallen, Switzerland and at Salzburg Landestheater, 1987-89; From 1989, ensemble at Vienna Volksoper, singing Figaro, Leporello and Guglielmo in Così fan Tutte; From 1991, member of Vienna Staatsoper where he added

Bartolo in Barber of Seville, also in Stuttgart, 1992-94, Belcore in L'Elisir d'amore, Sharpless in Madame Butterfly and Taddeo in L'Italiana in Algieri; Other roles include Somarone with Neville Marriner in London, 1990, Papageno at Barcelona, 1991, the Count in Nozze di Figaro at Bari, 1991, Schaunard in La Bohème at Naples, 1992 and at Tokyo, 1993, and Enrico in Lucia di Lammermoor at Marseilles, 1994. *Address:* Friedlgasse 57-2, A-1190 Vienna, Austria.

GIRÓN Arsenio, b. 15 Dec 1932, Renteria, Spain. Composer; Professor of Theory and Composition. m. Patricia Day, 14 July 1956, 1 son, 1 daughter. *Education:* BMus, Oberlin Conservatory of Music, USA, 1956; MA, Tulane University, 1962; Washington University. *Career:* Performances by various chamber groups, orchestras, choirs and soloists, in concert halls and on radio. *Compositions:* Symphonias, concerti, numerous chamber works, songs, choral pieces and one opera. *Honours:* Numerous Commissions; Ford Foundation Grant; Ontario Arts Council Grants; Wolf Trap Residency. *Membership:* Canadian League of Composers. *Address:* 114 Edgar Drive, London, Ontario N6G 1K1, Canada.

GISCA Nicolae, b. 30 Sept 1942, Tibirica, Romania. Conductor; Professor of Conducting and Orchestration. m. Elena, 28 Jan 1965, 1 daughter. *Education:* Music Conservatory George Enescu, Iasi, Romania, 1960-65. *Debut:* Conductor with Choir of Conservatory, 1962. *Career:* Conductor of more than 400 choral, chamber and symphony concerts with Conservatory Symphony and Chamber Orchestras and Conservatory Choir and Chamber Choir; Performances and tours of concerts in Romania, Austria, West Germany, Belgium, Luxembourg, Switzerland, Wales, France with Chamber Choir, Cantores Amicitiae, TV and radio appearances; Professor of Conducting and Orchestration, George Enescu Arts Academy. *Compositions:* Arrangements and choral processing of European, American, African and Asian Folksongs for choir; 100 musical pieces. *Recordings:* The Tour of the World in 16 Melodies; Winter Songs from Everywhere; The Festival of Political Song; two CD audio production: Christmas Carols from Romania and from the World, and Romanian Choral Music. *Publications:* Year Book of Music Conservatory George Enescu, 1970; 4 Choir Collections for Mixed Voices, 1978-82; Conduct Art, Didact and Pedagogue House, 1982; Handbook of Instrumentation, Musical House, 1987; Choir Conductor, Hyperion House, 1993. *Hobby:* Travel. *Current Management:* Rector of Arts Academy, George Enescu, from Iasi. *Address:* Str Gr Ureche, No 1, Bl Maracineanu, et 9; ap 33, 6600 Iasi, Romania.

GITECK Janice, b. 27 June 1946, New York, USA. Composer; Pianist. *Education:* Studied at Mills College with Darius Milhaud and Morton Subotnick; Paris Conservatoire with Olivier Messiaen, 1969-70; Aspen School with Milhaud and Charles Jones; Has also studied electronic music, Javanese gamelan and West African percussion. *Career:* Taught at Hayward State University and the University of California at Berkeley, 1974-76; Cornish Institute, Seattle, from 1979; Co-director of the Port Costa Players 1972-79. *Compositions include:* Piano Quintet 1965; 2 String Quartets; How to Invoke a Garden, cantata 1968; Traffic Acts for 4-track taoe 1969; Sun of the Center cantata 1970; Magic Words 1973; Messalina 1973; Helixes for ensemble 1974; A'gita, opera, 1976; Sandbars on the Takano River 1976; Thunder Like a White Bear Dancing 1977; Callin' Home Coyote, burlesque 1978; Far North Beast Ghosts the Clearing 1978; Peter and the Wolves for trombone with actor and tape 1978; Breathing Songs from a Turning Sky 1980; When the Crones Stop Counting for 60 flutes 1980; Tree, chamber symphony 1981; Hopi: Songs of the Fourth World 1983; Loo-wit for viola and orchestra 1983. *Honours include:* Grants from the California Arts Council 1978 and the National Endowment for the Arts, 1979 and 1983; Commissions from soloists and ensembles. *Address:* c/o ASCAP, ASCAP Building, One Lincoln Plaza, New York, NY 10023, USA.

GITLIS Ivry, b. 22 Aug 1922, Haifa, Israel. Concert Violinist. m. Paule Deglon. *Education:* Studied at the Ecole Normale de Musique, Paris, and with Flesch, Enescu and Thibaud. *Career:* First played in public aged 8, in Israel; Worked in British troop entertainment during the War; Debuts with the London Philharmonic, BBC Symphony and other British orchestras during the 1940s; Paris debut 1951, Israel debut 1952; Many recitals, and concert appearances with leading orchestras; US debut 1955; Often heard in works by 20th Century composers. *Recordings include:* Concertos by Berg, Stravinsky, Bartók and Tchaikovsky. *Honour:* Winner, Thibaud Prize, 1951.

GIULEANU Victor, b. 11 Nov 1914, Stroesti, Romania. Professor at Academy of Music; Musicologist; Chorus Conductor. m. Miseta Chivulescu, 17 Apr 1947. *Education:* Graduate Academy of Music, Bucharest, 1941, Graduate Faculty of Law, Bucharest, 1952; Graduate University Pedagogic Seminar, Bucharest, 1945; Doctor of Musicology, 1976. *Debut:* Chorus Conductor, 1949. *Career:* Chorus Conductor of the Health Department Trade Union, 1949-52; Conductor of the Ciocirlia State Ensemble, 1954-59; Professor in Music Theory, Academy of Music, Bucharest, 1953-85; Head, Chair Theory, Conducting and Pedagogy, 1964-85; Dean, Composition, Musicology, Music Teaching Faculty, 1960-62; Rector, Academy of Music, Bucharest, 1962-72. *Publications:* Author: Music Theory Treatise, 2 volumes, 1962; Musical Rhythm 2 volumes, 1968, 69; Fundamental Principles in Music Theory, 1975; Byzantine Melody, 1981; New Music Theory Treatise, 1986. *Contributions to:* Romanian and foreign publications of articles and essays; Scientific Papers at ISME (International Society for Music Education) in Buenos Aires, Tunis, Montreux, Graz, Paris, Geneva, Dijon. *Address:* Str. Tudor Arghezi 54, Bucharest sector 2, Romania.

GIULINI Carlo Maria, b. 9 May 1914, Barletta, Italy. Conductor, Former Music Director, Los Angeles Philharmonic Orchestra. m. 3 sons. *Education:* Accademia Santa Cecilia, Rome. *Debut:* as conductor, Rome 1944. *Career:* Formed Orchestra of Milan Radio, 1950; Principal Conductor, La Scala, Milan 1953-55; associated with Callas and conducted her in La Traviata and Gluck's Alceste; Debut in Great Britain conducting Verdi's Falstaff, Edinburgh Festival, 1955; Closely associated with Philharmonia Orchestra 1955-; Debut at Royal Opera House, Covent Garden, Don Carlos, 1958; Principal Guest Conductor, Chicago Symphony Orchestra 1969-78; Music Director, Vienna Symphony Orchestra 1973-76; Music Director, Los Angeles Philharmonic Orchestra 1978-84; often heard in music by Verdi, Bach, Mozart and Beethoven; Conducted new production of Falstaff in Los Angeles and at Covent Garden, 1982, after 14 years absence from opera (co-production by Los Angeles Philharmonic, Covent Garden and Teatro Comunale). *Recordings include:* CDs on EMI of Brahms's Violin Concerto (Chicago Symphony, Perlman); Le Nozze di Figaro and Don Giovanni (Philharmonia); Mozart arias (Schwarzkopf); Schubert 8th Symphony (Philharmonia), Schumann 3rd (Los Angeles Philharmonic); Don Carlos (Covent Garden Orchestra). *Honours:* Honorary Member, Gesellschaft der Musikfreunde, Vienna 1978; Honorary DHL DePaul University, Chicago, 1979; Gold Medal, Bruckner Society, 1978. *Memberships:* International Mahler Society; Una Vita Nella Musica. *Hobby:* Sailing. *Address:* c/o Robert Leslie, 53 Bedford Road, London, SW4. England.

GIUNTA Joseph, b. 8 May 1951, Atlantic City, New Jersey, USA. Music Director; Conductor. m. Cynthia Reid, 5 June 1982. *Education:* BMus, Theory, Northwestern University School of Music, 1973; MMus, Conducting, 1974 Northwestern University; DFA, Honorary, Simpson College, 1986. *Career:* Music Director, Conductor, Waterloo Cedar Falls Symphony Orchestra and Chamber Orchestra of Iowa, 1974-; Numerous Guest Conducting including: Chicago Symphony, Philharmonia Orchestra, London, Minnesota Orchestra, Indianapolis Symphony, Phoenix Symphony, Florida Symphony, Akron Symphony, Syracuse Symphony, Rhode Island Philharmonic. *Honours:* Helen M Thompson Award, Outstanding Young Conductor in USA, 1984; Honorary DFA, Simpson College, 1986. *Memberships:* Pi Kappa Lambda; Phi Mu Alpha; Iowa Arts Council. *Hobbies:* Tennis; Golf. *Address:* 1630 Aspen Drive, Waterloo, IA 50701, USA.

GIZBERT STUDNICKA Bogumila, b.16 Mar 1949, Cracow, Poland. Musician (Harpsichordist). 1 son. *Education:* MMus with honours, Academy of Music, Cracow, 1973; Study under Jos van Immersel, Conservatoire Royal, Antwerp, Belgium; Diploma with special honours, Conservatoire Royal, 1979; Master classes with Zuzana Ruzickova, Kenneth Gilbert, Ton Koopman. *Career:* Numerous concert appearances including with Polish Orchestra of Wojciech Rajski, Poland and other European countries; Active participant in many chamber music ensembles; Currently Assistant Professor, Department of Harpsichord and Early Instruments and Department of Chamber Music, Academy of Music, Cracow. *Recordings:* Concertos of Antonio Vivaldi, J S Bach's transcriptions, Polskie Nagrania Musa; Recordings for Polish and Belgian radio and TV, and Dutch radio. *Honours include:* Prize, Polish Piano Festival, Slupsk, 1974; Prize (distinction), International Harpsichord Competition, Bruges, Belgium, 1977. *Membership:* Polish Society of Musicians. *Hobbies:* Riding; Skiing. *Address:* ul Meissnera 4 m 66, 31462 Cracow, Poland.

GJERDE Rosalie Carolyn Prince, b. 23 May 1941, Fort Bragg, California, USA. Music Educator; Choral Director. m. Marion Wilbur Gjerde, 27 Aug 1966, 2 sons, 1 daughter. *Education:* BS, Humboldt State University, 1963; California Lifetime Teaching Credentials. *Career:* Teacher, Fort Bragg Schools, 1964-69; Consultant, Mendocino Schools, 1978-79; Teacher, Music Department, College of the Redwoods, 1971-78; Owner, Principal Teacher, Gjerde Music Studio, 1979-; Music Director, Mendocino Presbyterian Church, 1986-. *Publications:* Hosanna, Ride On; Rhapsody for the Young; Various choral responses and service music. *Contributions to:* California Association of Professional Music Teachers Communique. *Memberships:* Nationally Certified, Music Teachers National Association; Accredited, National Guild of Piano Teachers. *Hobby:* Photography. *Address:* 315 Park Street, Fort Bragg, CA 95437, USA.

GJEVANG Anne, b. 1948, Norway. Singer (Contralto Mezzo-Soprano). *Education:* Studied in Oslo, the Accademia di Santa Cecilia, Rome, and with Erik Werba, Music Academy, Vienna. *Debut:* Klagenfurt 1972, as Baba the Turk in The Rake's Progress. *Career:* Sang in Ulm from 1973, Bremerhaven 1977-79; Staatstheater Karlsruhe 1979-80, as Carmen, Ulrica and Orpheus; Bayreuth 1983-86, as Erda in Der Ring des Nibelungen and again for a new production Ring 1988, 1989, 1990 (Erda and First Norn); Zurich Opera 1985-90, as Maddalena in Die Meistersinger, Carmen, L'Italiana in Algeri, Ulrica, Erda; Many concert appearances, notably in Messiah (Chicago 1984) and the Missa Solemnis, Lied von der Erde; Lieder recitals in Germany and Austria; La Scala Missa Solemnis (Giulini) and Salome, 1987; Metropolitan Opera Ring des Nibelungen new production, 1988 and 1990; sang Lady Macbeth in the premiere of Bibalo's Macbeth at Oslo, 1990, repeated 1992; Covent Garden 1991, as Erda in the Ring. *Recordings:* Tiefland (RCA); Norn in Götterdämmerung (Eurodisc); Messiah (Decca); Das Paradies und die Peri (Schumann) Erato and Supraphon; La Gioconda (Ponchielli) RCA; Solo-recital (Wolf, Sibelius, Liszt, Grieg, de Falla) label Victoria; Video of Mitridate by Mozart as Farnace (Decca). *Address:* c/o Den Norske Opera, Storgarten 23, N-0184 Oslo 1, Norway.

GLADD Neil Laurence, b. 4 Sept 1955, Rochester, New York, USA. Classical Mandolinist; Composer. *Education:* BA, Musicology, Virginia Polytechnic Institute & State University, 1978; Self-taught as Mandolinist. *Career:* Appearance as a Concerto Soloist with: Handel Festival Orchestra, Now Music Orchestra, Alexandria Symphony; Recitals in USA and Europe, including premiere of new Mandolin Music by Carman Moore, Brian Israel, Elizabeth Vorcoe & others; Music Editor, Plucket, 1982-; String Editor, Faculty Member, Shenandor College & Conservatory of Music, 1982-. *Compositions:* The Red Bach Book: 3 Rags After Bach; Partita a Dodic Toni; Sonata for Solo Mandolin; Le Tombeau de Scarlatti; Farewell to a Hubbard Harpsichord. *Recordings:* The Sole Mandolin: Baroque to Modern. *Publications:* Music Editor: Anon (18th Century) 3 Divertimenti for 2 Mandolins or Guitar, 1982; Leoni - 2 Airs for Solo Mandolin, 1982; Barbelh - Six Duettes for 2 Mandolins or Violins, 1983; Arrigoni - Sonata in D for Mandolins Continuo, 1984. *Memberships:* American Music Center; Classical Mandolin Society of America; Broadcast Music Inc. *Hobby:* Instrument Building. *Address:* 6538 Marlo Dr, Falls Church, VA 22042, USA.

GLANVILLE Mark, b. 24 May 1959, London, England. Singer (Bass). *Education:* Studied at Oxford University and the Royal Northern College of Music. *Debut:* Sang the 2nd Soldier in Les Troyens and the Doctor in Macbeth for Opera North, 1987. *Career:* Has sung Nourabad (Les Pêcheurs de Perles), the King (Aida), the King of Clubs in The Love for Three Oranges, Hobson in Peter Grimes and Betto di Signa in Gianni Schicchi for Opera North; Scottish Opera debut 1988, as the Commendatore in Don Giovanni; Radio Vara Amsterdam as Lord Rochefort in Anna Bolena; Omaha Opera as Ferrando in Il Trovatore; Concert engagements include Bruckner's Te Deum for the Hallé Orchestra and Messiah with the Royal Liverpool Philharmonic; Opera: King (Oranges) in Lisbon, 1991; New Israeli Opera, 1992; Father (Jewel Box), for Opera North, 1991; Concerts: Beethoven 9 (Ulster Orchestra cond. Tortelier, Netherlands Philharmonic, cond. Menuhin); Mozart Requiem, Bournemouth Sinfonietta cond. Menuhin, City of London Orchestra cond. Judd, Stravinsky's Oedipus (RAI Milano cond. Gatti). *Recordings include:* Donizetti's L'Assedio di Calais (Opera Rara); Schubert's Mass in G. *Honours include:* Scholarships from the Peter Moores Foundation and the Countess of Munster and Ian Fleming Trusts; Ricordi Opera Prize and Elsie Sykes Fellowship, RNCM. *Address:* c/o Athole Still Ltd, 80-86 Greystoke House, Westrow Street, London SE19 3AF, England.

GLASER Werner Wolf, b. 14 Apr 1910, Cologne, Germany. Composer; Pianist; Conductor. m. Renée Glaser, 3 children. *Education:* University; Pupil of Abendroth, Dahmen, Jarnach and Hindemith. *Debut:* Pianist, 1918. *Career:* Conductor, Opera of Chemnitz, 1929-31; Teacher in Denmark; Teacher, Västerås, Sweden, 1945-; Composer; Critic; Soloist; Various programmes at the Swedish Broadcasting Service; Series of recitals, Conferences; Vice-Director, Town Music School, Västerås. *Compositions:* 13 symphonies; 5 operas; 14 string quartets; Col Legno, German Recital; chamber music; 2 ballets; cantatas; work for solo instruments, concertos; Stage work performances at Stockholm, Gothenberg, Västerås. *Recordings:* Phono Suecia (Linnea rezza for solo and orchestra); Opus III, (Duo); Fermat (Duo); Coronet (sax-quartet); Caprice (Trio). *Publications:* Trumma och triangel, 1946; Den sköna leken, 1947; Poems 1-7, 1969-77; Poems, 1981; Poems, 1992. *Address:* Djäknegatan 16, 722 15 Västerås, Sweden.

GLASOW Glenn (Loren), b. 24 July 1924, Pine City, Minnesota, USA. Composer; Educator. *Education:* Studied with Ernst Krenek at Hamline University, MA 1948, and at the University of Illinois; Further study with Wolfgang Fortner at Detmold. *Career:* Member of music faculty at California State University, Hayward, from 1961. Writings include: Variation technique in Schoenberg's String Quartet op 30 (dissertation). *Honours include:* Piano Sonata, 1948; Requiem, 1954; Grass Harp, incidental music, 1957; Two Egrets for chorus, 1957; Piano Trio, 1958; Canto Kechwa for alto and ensemble; Fantasy Variations for orchestra, 1967; Rakka for violin and tape, 1970. *Address:* c/o ASCAP,

ASCAP Building, One Lincoln Plaza, New York, NY 10023, USA.

GLASS Beaumont, b. 25 Oct 1925, New York, USA. Opera Coach; Stage Director; Recital Accompanist; Author; Lecturer; University Professor. m. Evangeline Noël Young, 7 June 1958, 1 daughter. *Education:* BS, US Naval Academy, Annapolis, 1949; Graduate Studies, San Francisco State College, 1955, University of California, Berkeley, 1955; Private Music Study, Piano, Violin, Theory. *Debut:* As A Stage Director, Northwest Grand Opera, Seattle, 1956. *Career:* Northwest Grand Opera, 1956-57; Assistant to Lotte Lehmann, Music Academy of the West, 1957-59, 1961; Coach, New York City Opera, 1959; Coach, Studienleiter, Zurich Opera, 1961-80; Accompanist, Grace Bumbry Recital, Holland Festival, 1965; Accompanist, Grace Bumbry Brahms Lieder Recital, Salzburg Festival, 1965; Coach, Harpsichordist, Recital Accompanist, Festival of Aix-en-Provence, 1974, 1976-78; Director, Opera, University of Iowa, 1980-; Stage Director, Utah Opera Company, Fall 1988; Cedar Rapids Symphony, 1987, 1989, 1991, 1993. *Publications:* Biography of Lotte Lehmann, 1988. Contributing, Consulting Editor, The Opera Quarterly, 1983-89. *Memberships:* National Opera Association. *Hobbies:* Translating Operas; History; Art; Travel; Nature; Shakespeare; Theatre. *Address:* 301 Richards St, Iowa City, IA 52246, USA.

GLASS Philip, b. 31 Jan 1937, Baltimore, Maryland, US. Composer; Musician. m. (1) Jo Anne Akalaitis, 1 son, 1 daughter, (2) Luba Burtyk. *Education:* Studied Flute, Peabody Conservatory of Music, Baltimore; Piano, Mathematics, Philosophy, University of Chicago, 1952-56; Composition with Persichetti, Juilliard School of Music, New York, MS 1962; Counterpoint with Boulanger, Paris, 1964. *Career:* Founder-Director, Philip Glass Ensemble, 1968; Many tours with Ensemble, North America and abroad; Trilogy of Satyagraha, Akhnaten and Einstein on the Beach performed in Stuttgart, 1990; Piano recital, Festival Hall, London, 1992. *Compositions:* Dramatic: Einstein on the Beach, 1976; Madrigal Opera: The Panther, 1980; Satyagraha, 1980; The Photographer, 1983; Akhnaten, 1983; The Civil Wars: A Tree is Best Measured When It is Down, 1983; The Juniper Tree, 1985; A Descent into the Maelstrom, 1986; In the Upper Room, 1986; The Making of the Representative for Planet 8, 1988; The Fall of the House of Usher, 1988; 1000 Airplanes on the Roof, 1988; Hydrogen Jukebox, 1989; The Voyage, 1992; The White Raven, 1993; Incidental music; Film scores; Violin Concerto, 1987; The Light for Orchestra, 1987; Chamber music; Choral works; Songs. *Recordings:* Various discs with Philip Glass Ensemble. *Honours:* BMI Award, 1960; Lado Prize, 1961; Benjamin Award, 1961-62; Ford Foundation Young Composer's Award, 1964-66; Fulbright Scholarship, 1966-67; Musician of the Year, Musical America magazine, 1985. *Memberships:* American Society of Composers, Authors and Publishers; SACEM, France. *Address:* ASCAP, ASCAP Building, One Lincoln Plaza, New York, NY 10023, USA.

GLASSMAN Allan, b. 1950, Brooklyn, New York, USA. Singer (Tenor; Baritone). *Education:* Studied at Hartt College of Music and Juilliard School. *Career:* Sang as a baritone at Michigan Opera from 1975, then at Philadelphia, Washington and the City Opera, New York; Roles have included Dandini in La Cenerentola, Rossini's Figaro, Belcore, Enrico (Lucia di Lammermoor), Ford and Schaunard; Studied further in New York and sang tenor roles at the Metropolitan, 1985-, debut as Edmondo in Manon Lescaut; Further appearances, USA and at Frankfurt as Tybalt in Romeo et Juliette, Cassio, Bacchus, Alfredo, Hoffman, Faust and Eisenstein; Sang Tichon in Katya Kabanova at the Met, 1991; Marcello in Leoncavallo's La Bohème at St Louis; Sang Dimitri in Boris Godunov at Pittsburgh, 1991, Arrigo in I Vespri Siciliani at Nice, 1992. *Address:* c/o Metropolitan Opera, Lincoln Center, New York, NY 10023, USA.

GLAUSER Elisabeth, b. 1 June 1943, Interlaken, Switzerland. Singer (Mezzo-soprano). *Education:* Studied in Berne, Stockholm and Italy. *Career:* Sang in Pforzheim, 1971-73, Freiburg, 1973-75, Dortmund, 1975-82: Staatsoper Stuttgart, 1982-88; Sang Rossweise at Bayreuth Festival, 1976-80, Adelaide in Arabella at Glyndebourne Festival, 1989; Guest appearances, Rome Opera (Herodias in Salome, 1988) and Komische Oper Berlin, in Dusseldorf, Zurich, Bologna, Venice, Cologne, Lisbon, Hanover and Schwetzingen Festival; Other roles have been Marcellina, Maddalena, Kundry, Fricka, Waltraute, Octavian, Clytemnestra and the Countess Geschwitz in Lulu; Concert soloist in works by Bach, Handel, Mozart, Brahms, Beethoven and Liszt; Teacher, Berne Conservatory, 1988-. *Address:* c/o Konservatorium fur Musik und Theater, Kramgasse 36, CH-3011, Switzerland.

GLAZ Herta, b. 16 Sept 1908, Vienna, Austria. Singer (Mezzo-Soprano). m. Josef Rosenstock, (deceased 1985). *Education:* Studied in Vienna. *Debut:* Breslau 1931, as Erda in Der Ring des Nibelungen. *Career:* Left Germany 1933 and gave concerts in Austria and Scandinavia; German Theatre Prague 1935-36; Toured North America 1936 with the Salzburg Opera Guild; Los Angeles 1937, in Das Lied von der Erde and the St Matthew Passion, conducted by Klemperer; Chicago Lyric Opera 1940-42; Metropolitan Opera 1942-56, as Annina in Der Rosenkavalier, Mary in Der fliegende Holländer, Berta in Il Barbiere di Siviglia; Nicklausse, Mozart's Marcellina and Wagner's Magdalena; Taught at the Manhattan School of Music from 1956. *Recordings include:* Tristan Love Duet (as Brangaene) with Helen Traubel and Torsten Ralf. *Address:* c/o Manhattan School of Music, 120 Claremont Avenue, New York, NY 10027, USA.

GLAZER David, b. 7 May 1913, Milwaukee, Wisconsin, USA. Clarinettist; Teacher. m. Mia Helen Deutsch, 16 Feb 1959. *Education:* BE, Milwaukee State Teachers College, 1935; Berkshire Music Center, Tanglewood, Massachusetts, summers 1940-42. *Career:* Bandleader, Plymouth (Wisconsin) High School, 1935-37; Teacher, Longy School of Music, Cambridge, Massachusetts, 1937-42; Member, Cleveland Orchestra 1946-51, New York Woodwind Quintet, 1951-85; Soloist with various orchestras; Numerous recitals; Teacher, Mannes College of Music, New York College of Music, New York University, State University of New York at Stony Brook, Hebrew Arts School; Master classes around the globe; Served on the juries of various competitions. *Recordings:* For Angel-EMI; Vox. *Address:* 25 Central Park West, New York, NY 10023, USA.

GLAZER Gilda, b. 1943, New York City, USA. Pianist. m. Robert Glazer. *Education:* BA, Music, Queens College, City University of New York; MA, Music, Columbia University; Piano student of Nadia Reisenberg. *Debut:* Kaufmann Concert Hall, New York. *Career:* Resident Keyboardist, Chicago Symphony; Resident Keyboardist, St Louis Symphony; Guest Soloist, Chicago, St Louis, North Carolina Symphonies; Resident Soloist, New York String Symphony; Pianist, Glazer Duo, 1970-; Pianist, New York Piano Quartet; Guest Pianist with Mendelssohn Quartet; World Premieres of works by Leo Ornstein, David Ott; Piano Faculties, Hartt College of Music and Chicago Musical College; Extensive solo tours; Appearances in Lincoln Center, Carnegie Hall and Ravinia Festival; Pianist, New Friends of Chamber Music, New York. *Recordings:* Piano solos and chamber music of Leo Ornstein, Joaquin Turina, Easley Blackwood and David Amram. *Publications:* Schubert Arpeggione Sonata, Edited 1993, MMB; Album of works for Piano and Viola Edited 1980, Brodt Music Company. *Contributions to:* American Piano Magazine. *Current Management:* Robert M Gewald Management. *Address:* Prestige Concerts International, 14 Summit, Englewood, NJ 07632, USA.

GLAZER Robert, b. 1945, Anderson, Indiana, USA. Violist; Conductor. m. Gilda. *Education:* BMus, MMus, Chicago Musical College; Studied Viola with William Primrose, Conducting with Franco Ferrara. *Career:* String Faculty, Columbia University; Member, Chicago Symphony; Co-Principal Viola, St Louis Symphony;

Violist, Hartt String Quartet; Music Director, New York String Symphony; Violist of Glazer Duo, 1970-; Guest Soloist, St Louis Symphony, Louisville Orchestra, Hartford Symphony; Guest Violist with Lenox Quartet, Manhattan and Mendelssohn Quartets; Extensive solo tours; World Premieres of works by David Epstein, Leo Ornstein; Conductor, American Chamber Orchestra, Brevard Music Festival. *Recordings:* Soloist, Morton Gould Viola Concerto with Louisville Orchestra, First Edition Records; Violist, Lyric by George Walker, Orion Records; Works by Joaquin Turina and Easley Blackwood. *Publications:* Schubert Arpeggione Sonata, 1993, Edited, MMB; Album for Viola and Piano, 1980, Edited, Brodt Music Company. *Contributions to:* Conductors Guild Journal; Instrumentalist. *Current Management:* Robert M Gewald Management. *Address:* Prestige Concerts International, 14 Summit, Englewood, NJ 07632, USA.

GLENN Bonita, b. 1960, Washington, USA. Singer (Soprano). *Education:* Studied at the Philadelphia Academy of Music. *Career:* Sang with the Vereingten State Orchestra under Eugene Ormandy, the Oakland Symphony, Toronto Symphony and Rochester Orchestra; Recitals at Carnegie Hall, Avery Fisher Hall, Tully Hall, Kennedy Hall and in Canada and Costa Rica; Sang in La Bohème with Philadelphia Grand Opera and in Turandot at the Salzburg Landestheater, conducted by Leopold Hager; Sang Manon in Houston and Pamina with Santa Fe Opera; At Berne and St Gallen, Switzerland, appeared as Musetta, Suppé's Galatea and Corilla in Viva la Mamma; Concert engagements in Europe, Canada and the USA; Germany with the Nuremberg Symphony Orchestra, the Stuttgart Symphony (Four Last Songs, conducted by Neville Marriner) and the Bavarian Radio Symphony Orchestra; Sang Clara in Porgy and Bess with the Royal Liverpool Philharmonic, conducted by Libor Pešek, and with the Scottish Chamber Orchestra under Carl Davis, 1989-90. *Honour:* Winner, Philadelphia Orchestra Vocal Competition. *Address:* c/o Norman McCann Ltd, The Coach House, 56 Lawrie Park Gardens, London SE26 6XJ, England.

GLENNIE Evelyn, b. 19 July 1965, Aberdeen, Scotland. Professional Musician (Timpani and Percussion). m. 1993. *Education:* Studied from age 12; Entered Royal Academy of Music 1982; GRSM (Hons); LRAM; ARAM. *Career:* Played in National Youth Orchestra of Scotland: tours of Britain, the Faroe Islands and Scandinavia; Wigmore Hall debut 1986; Concerts with the London Symphony Orchestra, London Sinfonietta, Scottish Chamber Orchestra, Bournemouth Symphony, the Philharmonia and English Chamber Orchestra; Festival engagements at Edinburgh, Chichester, Salisbury and Harrogate; Performed Bartók's Sonata for Two Pianos and Percussion 1987, in Paris, Zurich, London, Oxford and Aldeburgh; US concerts in New York, St Louis and Los Angeles; Season 1989-90 engagements with the Northern Sinfonia, Scottish Chamber Orchestra and the Ulster Orchestra; London Promenade Concerts 1989, with the world premiere of John McLeod's The Song of Dionysius; Subject of TV Documentaries by BBC and ITV. *Recordings include:* Bartók's Sonata for Two Pianos and Percussion, with Solti (CBS); Rhythm Song; Light in Darkness; Dancin and Rebounds. *Publications:* Good Vibrations, autobiography. *Honours include:* Gold Medal in Shell/London Symphony Orchestra Musical Scholarship, 1984; Queens Commendation Award for all-round excellence, 1985; Munster Trust Scholarship, 1986; Leonardo da Vinci Prize 1987; Young Professional Allmusic Musician of the Year 1988; Grammy Award for Bartók Recording, 1988; OBE, 1993; Personality of the Year, International Classical Music Awards; Hon DMus, Aberdeen University, 1991; Hon DMus, Warwick University, 1993. *Address:* c/o Harrison/Parrott Ltd, 12 Penzance Place, London W11 4PA, England.

GLICK Srul Irving, b. 8 Sept 1934, Toronto, Canada. Composer. m. 18 Sept 1957, 1 son, 2 daughters. *Education:* BMus 1955; MMus, 1958; University of Toronto; Continued studies with Darius Milhaud, Louis

Saguer and Max Deutch. *Career:* Teacher of Theory and Composition, Royal Conservatory of Music and York University; Composer-in-Residence, Beth Tikvah Synagogue, Toronto 1969-. *Compositions include:* Chamber Music, Orchestral, Works for Solo Instruments with Orchestra, Vocal, Choir with Instruments, Piano. *Recordings:* 4 Preludes for Piano; Petite Suite for Solo Flute; Suite Hebraique No 1; Songs from The Sabbath Festivals and High Holy Days; I Never Saw Another Butterfly; Gathering In, a Symphonic Concept for Strings; Suite Hebraique No 2; 2 Landscapes for Tenor and Piano; Music for Passover; Suite Hebraique No 4; Prayer and Dance for Cello and Piano; String Quartet No 1; Violin Concerto; 4 compact disc anthology released by CBC including 17 works including Northern Sketches and fantasy for violin and orchestra (Vision of Ezekiel). *Address:* CAPAC, 1240 Bay Street, Toronto, Ontario M5R 2C2, Canada.

GLIGO Niksa, b. 6 Apr 1946, Split, Croatia. Musicologist. m. Mirjana Zabcic, 24 Jan 1981, 1 son. *Education:* BA, Comparative Literature, English Language and Literature, 1969; BA, Musicology, University of Ljubljana, 1973; Later studies, Cologne, Berlin, Freiburg i B; MA, Musicology, Zagreb, 1981; PhD, Musicology, Ljubljna, 1984. *Career:* Head, Music Department, Zagreb University Student Centre, 1969-86; Artistic Director, Zagreb Music Biennale, 1977-79; Assistant Professor, 1981- 86, Senior Lecturer, 1986-92, Reader in Musicology, 1992-, Zagreb Unversity Music Academy. *Publications:* Vrijeme glazbe (The Time of Music), 1977; Varijacije razvojnog kontinuiteta: skladetelj Natko Devcic (The Variations of Development Continuity: the Composer Natk Devcic), 1985; The Problems of the 20th Century New Music: Theoretical Background and Evaluation Criteria, 1987. *Contributions to:* Numerous, Croatia and abroad. *Hobbies:* Skiing; Sailing; Tennis; Chess. *Address:* Preradoviceva 34, HR 41000 Zagreb, Croatia.

GLOBOKAR Vinko, b. 7 July 1934, Anderny, Meurthe-et-Moselle, France. Composer; Trombonist. m. Tatjana Kristan, 27 June 1963, 2 sons. *Education:* Diploma, Ljubljana Conservatory, 1954; Trombone, Conservatoire National de Musique, Paris, 1954-59; Composition, Conducting, with Rene Leibowitz, 1959-63; Composition with Berio, 1965; University Physics, 2 years. *Career:* Trombone Soloist, Conductor; Played with group for new music, Buffalo University, 1966; Teacher, Trombone, Staatliche Hochschule fur Musik, Cologne, 1968-76; Composition, New Music Courses, Cologne; Founder: Free Music Group, 1969, New Phonic Art quartet; Director of Department for Instrumental and Vocal Research, IRCAM, Paris, 1973-79; Professor, Scuola di Musica, Florence, 1983-; Solo performer, works written for him by Stockhausen, Berio, Kagel, others; UK premiere with Heinz Holliger, of Gemeaux by Toru Takemitsu, Edinburgh, 1989; Played his Kolo at Dartington Summer School, 1992. *Compositions:* Voie, narrator, chorus, orchestra, 1965; Accord, soprano, ensemble, 1966; Traumdeutung, voices, ensemble, 1967; Etude pour folklora I, II, 19 instruments and for orchestra, 1968; Concerto Grosso, 5 instruments, chorus, orchestra, 1970; Ausstrahlungen, 1972; Vendre le vent, 11 instruments; Airs de voyages vers l'interieur, choir, 2 soloists, 1972; Laboratorium, ensemble, 1973; Das Orchester, 1974; Carousel, 4 solo voices, 16 instruments, 1977; Les Emigres, 1982-86; L'Armonia Drammatica, 1986-89; Labour, 1992; Blinde Zeit, ensemble, 1993; Fluide, brass, percussion, 1967; Discours II-IX: II - for 5 trombones, 1968; III - 5 oboes, 1969; IV - 3 clarinets, 1974; V - saxophone quartet, 1981; VI - string quartet, 1982; VII - brass quintet, 1987; VIII - wind quintet, 1989; IX - 2 pianos, 1993; Drama, piano, percussion, 1971; Atemstudie, oboe, 1972; Notes, piano, 1972; Limites, violin or viola, 1973; Voix instrumentalisee, bass clarinet, 1973; Toucher, percussion, 1973; Dedoublement, clarinet, 1975. *Recordings:* Globokar by Globokar; Les Emigres; Vinko Globokar; Globokar by Aulos. *Publications:* Vzdih-Izdih; Komposition und Improvisation by Vinko Globokar. *Contributions to:* About 30 articles in musical magazines. *Honours:* 1 Prix de Paris, Trombone, 1959; 1 Prix Gaudeamus, Composition, 1968; 1st Prize Radio

Yugoslavia, 1973. *Hobbies:* Tennis; Skiing; Jogging. *Address:* 2 Rue Pierre et Marie Curie, 75005 Paris, France.

GLOCK William Frederick, (Sir) b. 3 May 1908, London, England. Musician; Pianist; Music Critic; Administrator. m. (1) Clement Davenport Hale, 1944, 1 daughter; (2) Anne Balfour Geoffroy-Dechaume, 1952. *Education:* Christ's Hospital, 1919-1926; Gonville & Caius College, Cambridge University, 1926-30 Honours Degree; pupil of Artur Schnabel, Berlin, 1930-33. *Career:* Music Critic, Daily Telegraph, 1934; The Observer, 1934-45; New Statesman, 1958-59; Service with RAF World War II, 1941-46; Director, Summer School of Music, Bryanston, 1948-52; Dartington Hall, Devon, 1953-79; Founder & Editor, The Score, 1949-61; Controller of Music, British Broadcasting Corporation, 1959-72; Director, Bath Festival, 1975-84; Chairman, London Orchestra Concert Board, 1975-86; Chairman, British Section, ISCM, 1954-58. *Publication:* Editor, Eulenburg books on Music, 1973-86; Autobiography, 1991. *Honours:* Knight; Commander of the Order of the British Empire; DMus, Nottingham University; Doctor of University of York; Albert Medal, Royal Society of Arts, 1971; Fellowship, Royal Northern College of Music, 1981; DLitt, Bath University, 1984; DMus, Plymouth University, 1993. *Memberships:* Board of Directors, Royal Opera House, Covent Garden, 1968-72; Honorary Royal Philharmonic Society, 1971; Arts Council of Great Britain, 1971-75; Member of the South Bank Board, 1986-91. *Address:* Vine House, Brightwell-cum-Sotwell, Wallingford, Oxon OX10 0RT, England.

GLOSSOP Peter, b. 6 July 1928, Sheffield, England. Opera Singer (Baritone). m. (1) Joyce Blackham, 1955 (div 1976); (2) Michele Yvonne Amos, 1977, 1 daughter. *Education:* High Storrs Grammar School, Sheffield. *Career:* Joined Sadler's Wells Opera, 1952; Covent Garden Opera Company, 1962-66, as Renato, Amonasro, Iago, Rigoletto, Nabucco, Escamillo, Britten's Demetrius, Verdi's Posa and Boccanegra; at Salzburg sang Verdi's Iago; Freelance Singer, 1966-; Metropolitan Opera from 1971, as Scarpia, Don Carlo in La Forza del Destino, Britten's Mr Redburn and Balstrode, Falstaff and Wozzeck; English National Opera 1980, as Mandryka. *Honours:* 1st Prize, Bulgarian First Competition for Young Opera Singers, 1961; Honorary D Music, Sheffield, 1970. *Hobby:* Golf. *Address:* Elmcroft, 91 Cambridge Road, Teddington, Middlesex, England.

GLOVER Jane Alison, b. 13 May 1949, Helmsley, Yorkshire, England. Conductor; Musical Director. *Education:* BA, MA, DPhil, St Hugh's College, Oxford University. *Debut:* Oxford University Opera Group, 1971, Le Nozze di Figaro; As professional conductor, Wexford Festival, 1975, Cavalli's Eritrea. *Career:* Research fellow, St Hugh's College, 1973-75; Lecturer in Music, ibid, 1976-84, St Anne's College, 1976-80, Pembroke College, 1979-84; Elected to Oxford University Faculty of Music, 1979; Musical director, London Choral Society, 1983-; Artistic director, London Mozart Players, 1984-91; Senior research fellow, St Hugh's College, Oxford, 1982-91; Honorary Fellow, St Hugh's College, 1991-; Operas & Concerts for: BBC; Musica nel Chiostro; English Bach Festival; Glyndebourne Festival Opera; (Musical director, Touring Opera, 1982-85); Conducted Don Giovanni at the Festival 1982; Teatro la Fenice, Venice; London Symphony Orchestra; London Philharmonic Orchestra; Royal Philharmonic Orchestra; English Chamber Orchestra; Bournemouth Sinfonietta; City of Birmingham Symphony Orchestra; Netherlands Radio Chamber Orchestra; Covent Garden debut 1988, Die Entführung. Television: Documentaries & presentation for BBC & London Weekend TV, especially Orchestra and Mozart series, South Bank Show; Conducted Mozart's Requiem at St Pauls Cathedral, 1991; Conducted new production of Sullivan's Princess Ida at the London Coliseum 1992; Brahms Liebeslieder at the 1993 London Proms. *Recordings:* series of Haydn and Mozart symphonies for ASV. *Publication:* Cavalli, 1978. *Contributions to:* Music & Letters; Proceedings, Royal Musical Association; Musical Times; The Listener;

Times Literary Supplement; Early Music; etc. *Honours:* Hon DMus, Exeter, 1986; Hon DLH, Longborough, 1988; Hon DUniv, 1988; Hon DMus, CNAA, 1991; ABSA/Daily Telegraph Arts Award, 1990; Hon DLitt, Bradford, 1992; Hon DLitt, London, 1992. *Hobbies:* Times crossword puzzle; Theatre. *Address:* c/o Lies Askonas Limited, 186 Drury Lane, London, WC2, England.

GLUSHCHENKO Fedor, b. 1944, Rostov-on-Don, USSR. Conductor. *Education:* Studied at the Rostov Musical Academy and the Moscow and Leningrad Conservatories. *Career:* Chief Conductor of the Karelian Radio and TV Symphony Orchestra, Finland, 1971; Formerly Chief Conductor of the Ukrainian State Symphony Orchestra; Regular guest conductor with the Moscow Philharmonic, the USSR State Symphony Orchestra, the Moscow Symphony and the Ministry of Culture Orchestra and orchestras in Riga, Vilnius, Sverdlovsky, Tbilisi and Tashkent; Season 1989-90 with appearances at the Soviet Contemporary Music Festival, Cheliabinsk and at the Athens Festival with the Athens Broadcasting Orchestra; Concerts with the Prague Symphony Orchestra and visits to Belgium, Greece and Istanbul; British debut 1989, with the BBC Scottish Symphony; Returned to appear with Royal Liverpool Philharmonic and the Scottish Chamber Orchestra. *Honours:* Diploma of Distinction at the Soviet Concourse of Conductors; People's Artist of the Ukrainian SSR. *Address:* c/o Norman McCann International Artists Ltd, The Coach House, 56 Lawrie Park Gardens, London SE26 6XJ, England.

GNAM Adrian, b. 4 Sept 1940, New York City, New York, US. Conductor; Symphony Music Director; Oboist. m. Catharine Dee Morningstar, 16 Aug 1983, 1 son, 1 daughter. *Education:* BMus, 1961, MMus, 1962, College-Conservatory of Music, Cincinnati; BSc, 1962, DMus, ABD, University of Cincinnati, 1962. *Debut:* Carnegie Recital Hall and Town Hall, New York, 1962. *Career:* Principal Oboe: American Symphony Orchestra under Stokowski, Cleveland Orchestra under Szell; Member: Heritage Chamber Quartet, Carnegie Wind Quintet, Chamber Arts Ensemble; Faculties: University of Cincinnati College-Conservatory of Music, 1967-76, Ohio University, 1969-76; Guest Conductor: Florida, Grand Rapids, Indianpolis, Louisville, Jacksonville, Charleston (South Carolina and West Virginia), Vermont, South Dakota, Santa Cruz, Columbia, Trenton, Puerto Rico, Anchorage, Alabama, Youngstown, Santa Fe, Beaumont, Columbus (Georgia), Abilene, Amarillo Symphonies; Cincinnati Ballet, Dance Theatre of Erie, Eugene Ballet; Eastern, Spoleto, Oklahoma, Interlochen, Shreveport, Sewanee, Colorado, Texas Music Festivals; Orchestras in Rumania, Yugoslavia, Venezuela, Mexico City, Italy; Congress of Strings, Temple University, Peabody Conservatory, University of Michigan, Georgetown University, University of Georgia, Colorado Philharmonic, University of Houston; Assistant Music Director, 1976-82, Music Director, 1982-84, National Endowment for the Arts; Music Director: Midland Symphony, Michigan, 1982-86; Macon Symphony, Georgia, 1983-, and Tuscaloosa symphony, Alabama, 1993-; Eugene Symphony, Oregon, 1985-89; Principal Guest Conductor, Philadelphia Concerto Soloists Chamber Orchestra, 1977-88. *Recordings:* For several labels. *Memberships:* President-Elect, Conductors' Guild; Other professional organizations including AFM, American Symphony Orchestra League. *Hobbies:* Golf; Tennis; Skiing; Photography. *Address:* 85440 Appletree Court, Eugene, OR 97405, USA.

GNEUSS Helmut Walter Georg, b. 29 Oct 1927, Berlin, Germany. University Professor; Hymnologist. *Education:* Free University, West Berlin, 1948-53; Research Student, St John's College, Cambridge, 1953-55. *Career:* Lektor, Durham University, 1955-56; Assistant Lecturer, Lecturer, Free University, Berlin, 1956-62; Lecturer, Heidelberg University, 1962-65; Professor, University of Munich, 1965-; Visiting Professorial Fellow, Emmanuel College, Cambridge, 1970; Visiting Professor, University of North Carolina, Chapel Hill, USA, 1974. *Publications:* Hymnar und Hymnen im englischen Mittelalter, 1968; Latin Hymns

in Medieval England; The State of Scholarship in RH Robbins Festschrift, London, 1973; Liturgical Books in Anglo-Saxon England and their Old English Terminology in Learning and Literature; Studies presented to Peter Clemoes on the occasion of his sixty-fifth birthday, edited by M Lapidge and H Gneuss, 1985. *Address:* Schellingstrasse 3, D-80799 Munich, Germany.

GNIEWEK Raymond, b. 13 Nov 1931, East Meadow, New York, USA. Violinist. m. (1) 2 daughters, (2) Judith Blegen. *Education:* MusB, Eastman School of Music, Rochester, New York, 1953. *Career:* Member 1949-53, Concertmaster 1953-57, Rochester (NY) Philharmonic Orchestra; Concertmaster, Metropolitan Opera Orchestra, New York, 1957-; Sante Fe (NM) Opera Orchestra, 1958; Solo engagements with USA Orchestras; Recitals. *Honour:* Distinguished Alumni Award, Eastman School of Music, 1977. *Address:* c/o Metropolitan Opera, Lincoln Center Plaza, New York, NY 10023, USA.

GOBBATO Angelo Mario Giulio, b. 5 July 1943, Milan, Italy. Opera Producer, Singer (Baritone), Artistic Director Opera. CAPAB (Cape Town). *Education:* Marist Brothers College (High School), Rondebosch; BSc (Hons), University of Cape Town; LTCL (Piano); Studied singing with Albina Bini, Carlo Tagliabue and Fred Dalberg. *Debut:* Cape Town. *Career:* Sang in Opera, Oratorio and Concerts throughout Republic of South Africa as well as broadcasting and TV appearances; Roles include: Figaro (Mozart and Rossini); Papageno, Guglielmo, Sharpless, Ford (Falstaff), Enrico (Lucia); Produced for PACT, CAPAB, NAPAC and PACOFS (Aida, Forza Del Destino, Trovatore, Tosca, Figaro, Così fan Tutte, Magic Flute); Resident Producer, Opera for CAPAB for 5 years, Head of Opera School at University of Cape Town, 1982-1988; Artistic Director CAPAB Opera, Director of the UCT Opera School, 1993-. *Honours:* Awarded Cavaliere al Merito della Republica Italiana 1986; 1st Nederburg prize for Opera (Papageno) 1971 - Cape Province; Nederburg Prize for Opera (Production of Forza del Destino) - Cape 1981. *Memberships:* Owl Club, Cape Town. *Hobby:* Bridge. *Address:* Cape Performing Arts Board, PO Box 4107, Cape Town 8000, Republic of South Africa.

GOCKLEY David, b. 13 July 1943, Philadelphia, Pennsylvania, USA. Administrator. *Education:* Studied at Brown and Columbia Universities and New England Conservatory, Boston. *Career:* Sang at first in opera and became House Manager at Santa Fe Opera, 1968; Assistant Managing Director, Lincoln Center, New York City, 1970; General Director, Houston Opera, 1972, presiding over premieres of Pasatieri's The Seagull, 1974, Floyd's Bilby's Doll, 1976, Willie Stark, 1981, and revised version of The Passion of Jonathan Wade, 1991, Glass's Akhnaten, 1984 and The Making of the Representative for Planet 8, 1988, Nixon in China by John Adams, 1987, Tippett's New Year, 1989, Meredith Monk's Atlas, 1991 and Robert Moran's Desert of Roses, 1992; Has introduced surtitles and educational programmes and initiated the touring Texas Opera Theatre. *Honours include:* Honorary Doctorate of Humane Letters, University of Houston, 1992 and Honorary Doctorate of Fine Arts, Brown University, 1993. *Address:* c/o Houston Grand Opera Association, 510 Preston Avenue, Houston, TX 77002, USA.

GODÁR Vladimir, b. 1956, Czechoslovakia. Composer. *Education:* Bratislava Conservatory; Academy of Music and Drama, 1980. *Career:* Editor, OPUS, publishing house. *Compositions include:* Fugue for String Orchestra, 1975; Three Songs, 1977; Overture for symphony orchestra, 1978; Symphony, 1980; Trio for oboe, violin and piano, 1973; Wind Quintet, 1980; Melodarium, 20 dances, 1980; Melodiarium, 72 duets, 1981; Trio for violin, clarinet and piano, 1980; Ricercar, 1980; Grave Passacaglia for piano, 1983; Lyrical Cantata, 1981; Partita, 1983; Talisman, 1983; Four Serious Songs, 1984; Orbis sensualium pictus, oratorio, 1984; Concerto grosso per archi e cembalo, 1985; Sonata in memorium Viktor Shklovski, 1985. *Honours:*

Jan Levoslav Bella Prize, Slovak Music Fund. *Address:* SOZA, Kollarova nam 20, 813 27 Bratislava, Slovakia.

GODFREY Daniel Strong, b. 20 Nov 1949. Bryn Mawr, Pennsylvania, USA. Composer; Music Professor. m. Diana Carol Bottum, 13 Mar 1976, 1 son. *Education:* BA, magna cum laude, Yale University, 1973; MMus, Composition, Yale School of Music, 1975; PhD, Composition, University of Iowa, 1982. *Career:* Director, Yale Russian Chorus, including tours of the USA and USSR, 1969-72; Visiting Assistant Professor, Music Composition and Theory, University of Pittsburgh, 1981-83; Assistant Professor, 1983-88, Associate Professor, 1988-, Syracuse University School of Music. *Compositions:* String Quartet, 1974; Progression, 1975; Trio, 1976; Five Character Pieces for viola and piano, 1976; Celebration, 1977; Music for Marimba and Vibraphone, 1981; Scrimshaw for flute and violin, 1985; Concentus for small orchestra, 1985; Dickinson Triptych for soprano and piano, 1986; Three Marian Eulogies for high voice, viola and piano, 1987; Mestengo for orchestra, 1988; Numina for six instruments, 1991; Clarion Sky for orchestra, 1992. *Recordings:* Scrimshaw; Trio; Five Character Pieces; Celebration; String Quartet; Progression; Music for Marimba and Vibraphone. *Publications:* Music since 1945, Elliott Schwartz, Co-author, Schirmer Books. *Contributions to:* Elliott Carter's String Quartet No 3: A Unique Vision of Musical Time, Sonus, Volume 8, No 1. *Address:* 222 Kensington Place, Syracuse, NY 13210, USA.

GODFREY Peter David Hensman, b. 3 Apr 1922, Bluntisham, Huntingdon, England. Musician. m. Sheila Margarette McNeile 1945, 4 daughters. *Education:* King's College Cambridge 1941-42, 1945-46; Royal College of Music 1946-47. *Career:* Assistant Music Master, then Director of Music, Marlborough College, 1949-58; Lecturer, Auckland University, New Zealand, 1958-71; Associate Professor, 1971-73; Dean and Head of Department, 1974-82; Director of Music Auckland Cathedral, 1958-74; Conductor, Auckland Dorian Choir, 1961-83; Conductor, Symphonia of Auckland, 1959-68; Professor Emeritus Auckland University, 1983-; Director of Music Wellington Cathedral 1983-89; Founder and President New Zealand Choral Federation, 1985-; Director National Youth Choir of NZ, 1982-86; tour of England and Europe 1988; Director of Music, Trinity College, Melbourne, 1989-91; Conductor of Wellington Orpheus Choir, 1984-91; Advisor to the Board of the International Federation of Choral Music, 1990-; Conductor Kapiti Chamber Choir, 1992; Conductor Cantoris, Wellington, 1993. *Recordings:* Music of the Church's Year; The Way of the Cross, The Dorian Singers, 1969; Five Centuries of Sacred Music, 1975; Visions I, 1977; The Blue Bird; Motets of Peter Philips, 1981; The Dorians Sing 1982; Hail Gladdening Light, 1989; Wellington Cathedral Choir, 1991; Carols, Anthems, Psalms, Trinity College Chapel Choir, Melbourne. *Honours:* MBE, 1978; CBE, 1988. *Hobby:* Gardening. *Address:* 11 Karaka Grove, Waikanae, New Zealand 6454.

GODFREY Victor, b. 10 Sept 1934, Deloraine, Canada. Singer (Bass-Baritone). *Education:* Studied with Gladys Whitehead in Winnipeg and Joan Cross in London; Further study with Hans Hotter in Munich and with Giovanni Inghilleri. *Debut:* Covent Garden, 1960, as the Doctor in Macbeth. *Career:* Appeared with the Covent Garden company at Coventry 1962, in the premiere of King Priam by Tippett; Aldeburgh Festival, 1966, in the premiere of The Burning Fiery Furnace by Britten; Guest appearances at Drottningholm and at opera houses in Glasgow (Scottish Opera), Edinburgh, Florence, Naples, Berlin, Dusseldorf, Montreal, Nice and Amsterdam; Other roles include Scarpia, Amonasro, Zaccaria (Nabucco), Wotan, Wolfram, Orestes and Jochanaan; Also sang in operas by Busoni, Dallapiccola and Hindemith; Many concert engagements.

GODSON Daphne, b. 16 Mar 1932, Edinburgh, Scotland. Violinist. *Education:* LRAM; ARAM; Royal Academy of Music, London; Brussels Conservatoire. *Career:* Principal Soloist, Scottish Baroque Ensemble,

1969-87; Principal, Scottish Chamber Orchestra, 1974-76; member, Bernicia Ensemble, Scottish Early Music Consort; Leader, Edinburgh Bach Players; Soloist with BBC Scottish, Scottish National Orchestra and Bournemouth Symphony Orchestra; Teacher, RSAMD, Broughton High School Special Music Unit. *Recordings:* Various. *Honours:* Premiere Prize, Brussels Conservatoire, 1956; ARAM, 1988. *Memberships:* Incorporated Society of Musician's Soroptimist International. *Address:* 48/11 Lwarmonth Avenue, Edinburgh EH4 1HT, Scotland.

GODWIN Joscelyn, b. 16 Jan 1945, Kelmscott, Oxon, England. University Teacher. m. (1) Sharyn Cook, (2) Janet Matthews, 1 son. *Education:* BA, 1965, MusB, 1966, Magdalene College, Cambridge; PhD, Cornell University, 1969; FRCO, 1965. *Career:* Cleveland State University, 1969-71; Professor, Music, Colgate University, 1971-. *Publications:* Editor: Schirmer Scores, 1975; Editor, A Scarlatti, Marco Attilio Regolo, 1975; Robert Fludd, 1979; Athanasius Kircher, 1979; Editor, Music, Mysticism & Magic, 1986; Editor, M Maier, Atalanta Fugiens, 1987; Harmonies of Heaven & Earth, 1987; Editor, Fabre d'Olivet, Music Explained as Science & Art, 1988; Editor, Cosmic Music, 1989; Mystery of the Seven Vowels, 1991; L'Esotérisme Musical en France, 1991; Editor, Harmony of the Spheres, 1991. *Contributions to:* Musical Times; Musical Quarterly; Notes; Galpin Society Journal; The Consort; Music and Letters. *Membership:* American Musicological Society. *Address:* Music Dept, Colgate University, Hamilton, NY 13346, USA.

GODZISZEWSKI Jerzy, b. 24 Apr 1935, Wilno, Poland. Artist Musician; Pianist. *Education:* Diploma with distinction, 1960, MA, Superior Music School, Warsaw; Summer Master Classes in piano with Benedetti Michelangeli, Arezzo, Italy, 1960, 1961. *Career:* Regular apperances as Soloist and with orchestras, Poland and abroad; Performed: Complete piano works of Maurice Ravel, 1975; Complete piano works of Karol Szymanowski, 1982; Chamber music appearances; Piano classes, Superior Music School, Wroclaw, 1967-77; piano classes, 1978-, Professor, 1988-, Academy of Music, Bydgoszcz; Appearance in International Music Festivals (among others: Warsaw Autumn, Chopin Festivals in Duszniki, Gaming). *Recordings:* Piano works of Chopin, Szymanowski, Debussy, Ravel, Prokofieff and others, for Polish Radio and TV, also Polish record companies Muza and Wifon. *Honours:* Distinction, 6th F Chopin International Piano Competition, Warsaw, 1960. *Address:* ul Zamojskiego 17 m 4, 85-063 Bydgoszcz, Poland.

GOEBEL Reinhard, b. 31 July 1952, Siegen, Westphalia, Germany. Violinist. *Education:* Studied in Cologne and Amsterdam, principal teachers: Maier, Gawriloff and Leonhardt. *Career:* Founder, Musica Antiqua Köln for the performance of early music, 1973; Many tours with it in Europe, North and South America, the Far East and Australia; Concert at the 1989 York Festival, England, with music by Legrenzi, Schmelzer, and Biber. *Recordings:* For Deutsche Grammophon including CDs of Bach's Art of Fugue and Musical Offering, Biber's Mensa Sonora and Solo violin Sonata in A, Orchestral Suites by Telemann. *Address:* Hochstadenstrasse 10, 5 Cologne 1, Germany.

GOEBELS Franzpeter, b. 5 Mar 1920, Mülheim-Rhur, Germany. Pianist; Harpsichordist; Professor. m. Gertraud Kockler, 1 son, 1 daughter. *Education:* Universities of Cologne and Berlin. *Debut:* 1940. *Career:* Solo Pianist, Deutschanlandsender, Berlin; Docent, Robert Schumann Konservatorium, Dusseldorf; Professor, Hochschule für Musik, Detmold. *Compositions:* (pseudonym Angfied Traudger): Dependances for harpsichord and strings, 1970; Byrd-Boogy, 1971; Bach: Goldberg variations for harpsichordist and strings. *Recordings include:* Bach, 6 sonatas; Bach, Concertos for harpsichord. *Publications:* Das Sammelsurium, 1968; Handbuch der Pianistik, 1973. *Contributions to:* Melos; Musica; Musik und Bildung. *Honours:* Honorable professor, University of Barcelona; IAM; Ruhr Preis für Kunst und Wissenschaft, 1969. *Membership:* VDMK. *Hobbies:* MSS; Sculpture; Modern graphics. *Address:* An der Pyramideneiche, (Privatzufahrt: Clara-Schumann Weg), Postfach 4023, D-493 Detmold 14, Germany.

GOEHR Alexander, b. 10 Aug 1932, Berlin, Germany. Composer; Professor of Music; Fellow of Trinity Hall, University of Cambridge since 1976. *Education:* Berkhamsted; Royal Manchester College of Music; Paris Conservatoire. *Career:* Lecturer, Morley College, 1955-57; Music Assistant, BBC, 1960-67; Winston Churchill Trust Fellowship, 1968; Composer-in-Residence, New England Conservatory, Boston, Massachusetts, 1968-69; Associate Professor of Music, Yale University, 1969-70; West Riding Professor of Music, Leeds University, 1971-76; Artistic Director, Leeds Festival, 1975; Visiting Professor, Peking Conservatoire of Music, 1980; Board Directors, Royal Opera House, 1982-87. *Compositions include:* Fantasia Opus 4; Violin Concerto; Little Symphony; Pastorals; Romanza for cello; Symphony in one Movement, Op 29; Piano Concerto, 1970; Concerto for Eleven, 1972; Metamorphosis/Dance, 1973; Lyric Pieces, 1974; Konzertstuck, 1974; Kafka Fragments, 1979; Sinfonia, 1980; Deux Etudes, 1981; Symphony with Chaconne, 1986; Operas include, Arden must die, 1967; Behold the Sun, 1985; Cantatas, Sutter's Gold; The Deluge; Triptych (Naboth's Vineyard; Shadowplay; Sonata about Jerusalem); Babylon the Great is Fallen; Carol for St Steven, 1989; Eve dreams in Paradise for mezzo, tenor and orchestra, 1988; Sing, Ariel for mezzo, two sopranos and five instruments, 1989-90; Still Lands, 3 pieces for small orchestra, 1990; 4 string quartets: 1957 (revised 1988), 1967, 1976, 1990; ...a musical offering (JSB 1985)... for 14 players; Variations on Bach's Sarabande from the English Suite in E minor for wind instruments and timpani, 1990; ...in real time, cycle of pieces for solo piano, in progress from 1989. *Honours:* Honorary Vice-President, SPNM, 1983-; Honorary FRMCM; Honorary FRAM, 1975; Honorary FRNCM, 1980; Honorary FRCM, 1981; Honorary DMus, Southampton, 1973. *Address:* Trinity Hall, Cambridge University Music School, West Road, Cambridge, England.

GOEKE Leo, b. 6 Nov 1936, Kirksville, Missouri, USA. Singer (Tenor). *Education:* Studied at Louisiana State University; State University of Iowa with David Lloyd; New York with Hans Heinz and Margaret Harshaw. *Debut:* Metropolitan Opera 1971, as Gaston in La Traviata: later sang Tamino, Edgardo, Alfredo, the Duke of Mantua, Ferrando and Don Ottavio in New York; Glyndebourne Festival 1973-78, as Flamand in Capriccio, Idamante, Tom Rakewell, Don Ottavio and Tamino; Stuttgart 1981, in the German premiere of Satyagraha by Philip Glass, (repeated 1990) Other roles include Ernesto in Don Pasquale, Almaviva, Rodolfo, Belmonte, Pinkerton and Massenet's Des Grieux; Guest engagements at the New York City Opera and in Seattle, Strasbourg, Baltimore and Amsterdam; Television appearances include Gandhi in the Stattgart production of Satyagraha, 1983. *Address:* Staatstheater Stuttgart, Oberer Schlossgarten 6, D-7000 Stuttgart 1, Germany.

GOENNENWEIN Wolfgang, b. 29 Jan 1933, Schwabisch-Hall, Germany. Conductor; Educationist. *Education:* Studied music in Stuttgart, Philosophy at Heidelberg and Tubingen Universities. *Career:* Director of the South German Madrigal Choir at Stuttgart, 1959; Tours throughout Europe from 1964 and to South America, 1971; Director of the Cologne Bach Choir, 1969-73; Repertoire has included Palestrina, Bach, Schütz, Dallapiccola and Stravinsky; Chair of Choirmastership at the Stuttgart Musikhochschule, 1968; Principal of the Hochschule für Musik und Darstellende Kunst at Stuttgart, 1973; Artistic Director at the Ludwigsburg Castle festivals from 1972, conducting Die Zauberflöte, Fidelio and Der Freischütz, 1972-89; Has also conducted Bach Passions and Christmas Oratorio, Haydn Oratorios, and Masses by Mozart and Bruckner; General Director, Staatstheater Stuttgart (Opera, Ballet, Theatre), 1985; Ludwigsburg Festival, 1990, Die Entführung. *Recordings include:* Bach Cantatas, St Matthew Passion and Magnificat; Mozart Requiem, with the Consortium Musicum; Handel Dettinger Te Deum; Haydn Creation and Seasons, with the Ludwigsburg Festival Orchestra; Mozart Mass in C Minor; Beethoven Missa Solemnis, with the Collegium Aureum; Brahms Ein Deutsches Requiem; Bruckner E minor Mass. *Address:* Staatstheater Stuttgart, Oberer Schlossgarten 6, D-7000 Stuttgart 1, Germany.

GOERGEN Viviane, b. 17 June 1948, Paris, France. Pianist. *Education:* Graduated, Secondary School in Luxembourg, 1967; Studied French and German, Nancy University; Graduated, Conservatoire de la Ville de Luxembourg, 1965; Graduated, Conservatory of Nancy, France, 1967; Licence de Piano, Paris Conservatory and Ecole Nationale de Musique, Paris. *Debut:* Luxembourg. *Career:* First appeared: Paris, 1971; London, 1973; Zurich, 1974; Bonn, 1975; Brussels, 1976; Prague, 1978; Vienna, 1979; Frankfurt, 1982; Madrid, 1983; Berlin, 1991; Since 1978 has taken part in regular foreign tours to Czechoslovakia (Prague Philharmony) and Austria; Numerous radio appearances; Several first performances of works, partly especially composed for her; Currently devotes her attention to the music of Robert Schumann and Claude Debussy. *Recordings:* Schumann: Davidsbündlertänze, Drei Romanzen Op 28; K D Richter: Feininger Impulse; Johannes Brahms: Sonata Op 5 G minor; Johannes Brahms: Sonata op 38; Cesar Franck: Sonata in A Major; Ludwig van Beethoven: Sonata op 5; Dimitri Shostakovitch: Sonata op 40. *Hobby:* Psychology. *Address:* Nelkenstr 1, D-63322 Rödermark 2, Germany.

GOERNER Stephan, b. 23 Oct 1957, Switzerland. Cellist. *Education:* Studied at the Winterthur Conservatory at Juilliard, the International Menuhin Academy in Gstaad. *Career:* Co-founder and cellist of the Carmina Quartet 1984; Appearances from 1987 in Europe, Israel, Japan and USA; Regular concerts at the Wigmore Hall from Oct 1987; Concerts at the South Bank Centre, London, Amsterdam Concertgebouw, the Kleine Philharmonie in Berlin, Konzertverein Wien (Vienna); Four engagements in Paris 1990-91, seven in London; Tours to Australasia, USA, Japan, concerts at the Hohenems, Graz, Hong Kong, Montreux, Schleswig-Holstein, Bath, Lucerne, Prague Spring Festivals; Collaborations with Dietrich Fischer-Dieskau, Olaf Bär and Mitsuko Uchida. *Recordings:* Albums for Ex Libris, Bayer, Claves and Denon, 1991. *Honour:* Joint winner (with members of Carmina Quartet) Paolo Borciani String Quartet Competition in Regio Emilia, Italy, 1987. *Address:* c/o Intermusica Artists' Management, 16 Duncan Terrace, London N1 8BZ, England.

GOERTZ Harald, b. 31 Oct 1924, Vienna, Austria. Conductor; Musicologist; Pianist; Manager. m. Carola Renner, 1 son, 1 daughter. *Education:* PhD, University of Vienna, 1947; advanced studies of piano with Wührer and conducting with Reichwein, Krips and Swarowsky, Academy of Music, Vienna. *Career:* Assistant to von Karajan, Scala di Milano, Lucerne, etc.; Music Director, opera and concerts, Ulm, Germany, 1955-63; Guest Conductor, Stuttgart, Vienna, Berlin and others; Teacher, Academy of Music, Stuttgart and Salzburg Mozarteum; Professor, Leader of Conductors' Class, Opera Section, Hochschule für Musik, Vienna and seminars for interpretation; Chorus director Vienna Opera to 1991; President, Austrian Society of Music, 1963-; Writer and Commentator, Austrian Television. *Publications:* Editor, Osterreichisches Musikhandbuch, Dictionary of Contemporary Austrian Composers, Vienna, 1989, New Edition, 1993; Author, Mozarts Dichter Lorenzo da Ponte, Piper, Munich, 1988; Gerhard Wimberger, Vienna, 1990 (a monography about the Austrian composer). *Honours:* Recipient OBE; Bundesverdienst-Kreuz, Federal Republic of Germany. *Hobbies:* Literature; Archaeology; Architecture. *Address:* Wiedner Hauptstrasse 40, A-1040 Vienna, Austria.

GOETHALS Lucien Gustave Georges, b. 26 June

1931, Ghent, Belgium. Composer. m. Maria De Wandelaer, 12 July 1958, 1 son. *Education:* Royal Conservatory of Ghent; studied composition with Norbert Rosseau and modern technics with Godfried Michael Koenig. *Career:* Organist, 1958-62; Producer, IPEM, 1962; Professor, Analysis, Royal Conservatory, Ghent; Producer, BRT 3, 1964. *Compositions:* Cellotape for cello, piano & electronic music, 1969; Endomorfie for violin, piano and electronic music, 1969; Contrapuntos, electronic music, 1974; Llanto por Salvador Allende for trombone solo; Klankstrukturen organ solo; Triptiek, violin & harpsichord; Sinfonía en Grismayor, 2 orchestras and electronic music; many electronic compositions, chamber music and compositions for orchestra. *Publications:* Lucien Goethals, Le Constructivisne Bifuntionel by Dr H Sabbe; Lucien Goethals, Composer, by H Sabbe. *Contributions to:* Professional journals. *Honours:* Mathieu Prize, 1956; Provincial Composition Prize, 1960; Koopal Prize, 1977; Cultur Prize, City of Ghent, 1981. *Hobby:* Literature. *Address:* Verschansingsstraat 32, B 9030, Ghent, Mariakerke, Belgium.

GOEYVAERTS Karel (August), b. 8 June 1923, Antwerp, Belgium, Composer. *Education:* Studied at Antwerp Conservatory, 1943-47, and with Milhaud, Messiaen and Martenot, Paris, 1947-50. *Career:* Taught Music History, Antwerp Conservatory, 1950-57; Organised Ghent Institute for Psychoacoustics and Electronic Music, 1970-74; Producer of new music concerts on Flemish Radio, 1974-87. *Compositions include:* Aquarius, opera, produced at Rotterdam, 1990; Sonata for 2 pianos, Op 1, 1951; Ops 2-7, various works for electronics, 1951-55; Diaphonie, suite for orchestra, 1957; Improperia, cantata for Good Friday, 1958; Jeux d'ete for 3 orchestral groups, 1961; La Passion for orchestra, 1962; Cataclysme, ballet, 1963; Mass in Memory of Pope John XXIII for chorus and 10 winds, 1968; Al naar gelang for 5 instrumental groups, 1971; Piano Quartet, with tape, 1972; Belise dans un jardin for chorus and 6 instruments, 1972; Nachklange aus dem Theater for tape, 1972; Landscape for harpsichord, 1973; Litanie III, ballet, 1980; Litanie IV for soprano and ensemble, 1981; Zum Wassermann for chamber ensemble, 1984; De Heilige Stad for chamber ensemble, 1986. *Address:* c/o SABAM (Belgium), c/o PRS Ltd, Member Registration, 29-33 Berners Street, London W1P 4AA, England.

GOJOWY Peter Lars Detlef, b. 7 Oct 1934, Freital, Saxony, Germany. Musicologist; Journalist; Writer. m. Christiane Otto, 5 May 1959. *Education:* Humboldt-Universität Berlin; Freie Universität Berlin; Universität Göttingen; Musicology, Hochschule für Musik Berlin-Charlottenburg; Staatsexamen, 1961, Dr Phil, 1966, Universität Göttingen. *Debut:* Die Matthäuspassion und die Köthener Trauermusik, Bach-Jahrbuch, 1965. *Career:* Lectures on music in Yugoslavia, Brazil, Switzerland, USA and Poland. *Publications:* Neue Sowjetische Musik det 20-er Jahre, manuscript 1965, book 1980; Dimitri Shostakovich, 1983. *Contributions to:* Music journals including: Neue Zeitschrift für Musik; Die Musiksforschung; Musica; Ruch Muzyczny; Newspapers including Die Welt. *Current Management:* Radio Redactor, Westdeutscher Rundfunk, Cologne. *Address:* Auf dem Kreuzbüchel 16, D 5463 Unkel, Germany.

GOLAB Maciej, b. 25 Oct 1952, Lebork, Poland. Musicologist. m. Halina Wiercinska, 17 Feb 1979, 1 son, 1 daughter. *Education:* MA, 1976, PhD, 1981, Habilitation, 1990, Warsaw University; all in the field of Musicology. *Career:* Assistant, 1978-81, Lecturer, 1981-91, Deputy Director, 1991-, Institute of Musicology, Warsaw University. *Publications:* Dodekafonia. Studia nad teoria i kompozycja I polowy XX wieku, Bydgoszcz 1987; Chromatyka i tonalnosc w muzyce Chopina, Krakow, 1991; Professor at the University Wrocław, 1991. *Contributions to:* Muzyka, Ruch Muzyczny, International Review of the Aesthetics and Sociology of Music; Musik des Ostens; Polish Music; Rocznik Chopinowski; Chopin Studies; Komponisten der Gegenwart, München, 1992. *Memberships:* Zwiazek

Kompozytorow Polskich 1982; Rada Naukowa Towarzystwa im Fryderyka Chopina w Warszawie, 1987-91; Vice President, International Foundation for the Promotion of Polish Music, 1992. *Hobbies:* Literature; Poetry. *Address:* Institute of Musicology, Warsaw University, ul Zwirki i Wigury 93, PL - 02- 089 Warsaw, Poland.

GOLANI Rivka, b. 1946, Tel Aviv, Israel. Viola Virtuoso Soloist. *Education:* University of Tel Aviv, with Professor Oedon Partos. *Career:* One of the world's most highly acclaimed soloists, giving concerts throughout the world in both traditional and contemporary repertoire; Inspired over 180 works to date of which 22 are concerti; Examples are: Viola concerti by Holloway (UK); Hummel (Germany); Fontajn (Belgium); Colgrass (USA) and others; Solo works by Holliger (Switzerland); Von Holmboe (Denmark); Colgrass (USA); many others. *Recordings include:* the Elgar Cello Concerto in England and many others with Vernon Handley and the Royal Philharmonic; The Bartók Viola Concerto in Hungary with Andras Ligeti and the Budapest Radio Symphony; Martinů's Rhapsody Concerto with Peter Maag and the Berne Symphony; Viola with piano Brahms Sonatas, Joachim (Conifer Records). Contemporary Recordings include Chaconne (CBC) and Viola Nouveau and Prouesse (Centredisc) among many others. *Publications:* A book of drawings entitled Birds of Another Feather, Mosaic Press, Canada,*Honour:* Grand Prix du Disque for Viola Nouveau, 1985. *Current Management:* Carol Ross, 6 Petersfield Crescent, Coulsdon, Surrey CR5 2JQ, England. *Address:* c/o Fox Jones & Associates, 50 Prince Arthur Avenue, Suite 107, Toronto, Ontario, M5R 1B5, Canada.

GOLD Edward (Jay), b. 25 July 1936, Brooklyn, New York, USA. Pianist; Music Educator. *Education:* BA Music, New York City College, (CUNY), 1957; MMus, Yale School of Music, 1960; Private piano instruction: Nadia Reisenberg, 1963-64; Ellsworth Grumman (Yale), 1957-60; Elise Braun- Barnett, 1950-57. *Debut:* Carnegie Recital Hall, 1967. *Career:* Appearances on radio stations, WQXR, WNYC, WFUV; Solo recital tour of Mexico under USA Information Service, 1963; Private teacher, 1960-; Teacher, Henry St Music School, 1961-66; Dalcroze School, 1961-, (School Closed 1993); Staten Island Jewish Community Center, 1978-. *Compositions:* 10 Canticles for Unison Voices and Organ, Music for Liturgy, 1967; Schratlieder 1985-86 (poems of Paul Becker) Bass-baritone and piano. *Recordings:* JL Dussek: Sonata in F minor Op 77; 3 pieces, also author of liner notes, 1974; Gottschalk: Piano Music, also author of liner notes, 1973; As accompanist, Music by Israeli Composers, 1973; Made arrangement of song Y'rushalayim for tenor, cello and piano, 1971, all recorded by Musical Heritage Society. *Publication:* Bicentennial Collection of American Keyboard Music from 1790-1900, Editor, 1975. *Contributions to:* Music for the Holy Eucharist and the Daily Office; Editorial assistant and contributor to one setting of Phos hilaron, 1971. *Honour:* Grace Spofford Scholarship, Henry St Music School, 1956-57. *Memberships:* American Liszt Society, 1967-68; New York Liszt Society, 1968-69. *Address:* 205 West 79th Street 2E, New York, NY 10024-6244, USA.

GOLD Ernest, b. 13 July 1921, Vienna, Austria. Composer; Conductor. m. (1) Marni Nixon, 1 son, 2 daughters; (2) Jeannette Keller, 29 Nov 1975. *Education:* Vienna Conservatory; State Academy of Music, Vienna; Studied conducting, National Orchestral Association; Private study with Otto Cesana, Leon Barzin and George Antheil. *Career:* Musical Director and Conductor, Santa Barbara Symphony, California, USA, 1958-60; Conductor, Santa Barbara Civic Opera Association; Broadway Musicals; Various Community Orchestras; Founder, Senior Citizens' Orchestra, Los Angeles. *Compositions Include:* 2 symphonies; Piano concerto; Chamber and Vocal Music; Choral Compositions; Symphony for 5 instruments; Introduction and Fugue, Gavotte and March; 3 Miniatures for the Piano; A Song

Cycle; Songs of Love and Parting; About 75 film scores including On The Beach, 1959; Exodus, 1960; It's a Mad, Mad, Mad, Mad World, 1963; The Secret of Santa Vittoria, 1969; Broadway Musical, I'm Solomon, 1968; Numerous popular songs, 1939-45. *Recordings:* Numerous recordings of film soundtracks. *Contributions to:* Professional Journals and Daily Press. *Honours:* Academy Award (Oscar) for Exodus. *Hobbies:* Tennis; Painting. *Current Management:* Robert Light Agency, 6404 Wilshire Blvd, Ste. 900, Los Angeles 90048, USA. *Address:* 269 N. Bellino Drive, Pacific Palisades, CA 90272, USA.

GOLDBERG Reiner, b. 17 Oct 1939, Crostau, Germany. Singer (Tenor). *Education:* Carl Maria von Weber Hochschule fur Musik, Dresden, with Arno Schellenberg. *Debut:* As Luigi in Il Tabarro, Dresden, 1966. *Career:* Dresden State Opera, 1973-77; Deutsche Staatsoper East Berlin from 1977; Roles include Florestan, Turiddu, Cavarodossi, Hermann in The Queen of Spades, Aron in Schoenberg's Moses und Aron, and Sergei in Katerina Ismailova; Guest appearances in Leipzig, Leningrad, Vienna, Prague and in Italy; Toured Japan with Dresden company, 1980; Covent Garden debut, 1982, as Walther in Die Meistersinger; Paris, 1982, in a concert performance of Strauss's Die Liebe der Danae; Bayreuth Festival, 1988, in a new production of the Ring produced by Harry Kupfer; New York debut, 1983, in a concert performance of Strauss's Guntram; La Scala Milan, 1984, as Tannhäuser; Teatro Liceo Barcelona, 1985, as Siegfried; Sang Walther at Covent Garden, 1990 (replaced by Ben Heppner), Erik in Der Fliegende Holländer at Bayreuth, 1990; Sang Florestan and Tannhäuser at the Metropolitan, 1992; Bayreuth Festival, 1992, as Erik in Fliegende Holländer. *Recordings:* Drum Major in Wozzeck (Eterna); Parsifal in film version of Wagner's opera by Syberberg, (with role mimed by a woman); Max in Der Freischütz (Denon); Guntram (Hungaroton); Siegmund in Haitink's recording of Die Walküre (EMI). *Address:* c/o Allied Artists Ltd., 42 Montpelier Square, London SW7 1JZ, England.

GOLDBERGER David, b. 25 July 1925, Memphis, Tennessee, USA. Pianist; Teacher; Editor; Writer. m. Helen Rothenberg, 2 Feb 1952 (deceased 1963). *Education:* BA, Regents External Degree Programme, University of State of New York, 1975; MA, 1976, MEd, 1977, EdD, 1978, Columbia University; Private Piano study with Artur Schnabel, Karl Ulrich Schnabel, Leonard Shure, Egon Petri. *Debut:* New York, 1955. *Career:* Recitals, chamber music, orchestral appearances, lecture-recitals in New York, Mexico City, Paris; Television in Philadelphia, Memphis, Mexico City; Lecture and lecture recitals at universities and for teachers groups throughout the USA; Leacturer, Mannes College of Music, 1955-; Lecturer at Long Island University, 1981-, and Hunter College (CUNY), 1986-. *Recordings:* Piano Sonatinas of Beethoven and Clementi; Mozart Piano Works; Piano Works of Beethoven; Piano Music of Schubert. *Publications include:* Easy Original Piano Duets, 1959; CMP Piano Library, (23 volumes) 1961-73; Classical Dances of Mozart and Beethoven, 1963; Russian Music for Young Pianists (6 volumes), 1967-69; Muzio Clementi, Six Sonatas for Piano Four Hands, 1960; Eleven Piano Duets by the Masters, 1964; Johann Anton Andre, Six Sonatinas for Piano Four Hands, 1959; F J Haydn, A Digest of Short Piano Works, 1972; Ignaz Pleyel, Sonata in G Minor for Piano Four Hands, 1961; Kleine Klavierstuecke I (Neue Schubert-Ausgabe) appeared with copyright 1988. *Address:* 375 Riverside Drive, New York, NY 10025, USA.

GOLDENZWEIG Hugo de la Paz, b. 21 Aug 1943, Rosario (SF), Argentina. Concert Pianist; Artist Teacher. m. Virginia Strazziuso, 8 May 1969. *Education:* Undergraduate degree, University of Rosario; Postgraduate Diploma, The Mannes College of Music, New York City; MMus, Manhattan School of Music; PhD, Music (Piano Performance), New York University. *Debut:* Carnegie Recital Hall, New York, 1976; Wigmore Hall, London, 1981. *Career:* Recitals and concerto appearances, Netherlands, Spain, Italy, England, USA,

Argentina, TV and Radio as well as concert stage in major halls; World premieres: Lanza's Concerto for Piano and Chamber Orchestra, National Symphony of Argentina, 1993; Camarero's Finale (dedicated to H Goldenzweig), Palma de Mallorca, 1993. *Recordings:* Live recording of public performances in New York City; Works by William Mathias (New York premiere), Mario Davidovsky, Alcides Lanza (US premiere), Ginastera Melopea-CD (Buenos Aires); 2 videos: 27 Chopin Etudes (complete); Argentine Piano Music of the last fifty years - a lecture and demonstration. *Publication:* Selected Piano Etudes of Frederic Chopin: A Performance Guide, microfilm, 1987. *Honours:* Jóvenes Concertistas Prize, Buenos Aires, 1966; Jóvenes Solistas Prize, Santa Fe, Argentina, 1967. *Membership:* College Music Society, USA; Faculty Member, Piano and Piano Peddgogy, The Mannes College of Music, New York City, since 1989. *Hobbies:* Reading; Cycling; Visiting art galleries and museums. *Current Management:* PAMAR - Pan Americn Musical Art Research Inc. *Address:* 116 East 57th Street, 3rd Floor, New York, NY 10022, USA.

GOLDING Robin Mavesyn, b. 4 June 1928, London, England. Administrator; Freelance Writer; Editor. m. (1) Claire Simpson, 18 Aug. 1956, 1 daughter, (2) Felicity Lott, 22 Dec. 1973. *Education:* Westminster School; MA, Christ Church, Oxford. *Career:* Freelance writer on musical subjects; Experience of local journalism (The Kensington News), the record industry (Vox), music and general publishing (George Rainbird); Librarian, Boyd Neel Orchestra, 1953-56; Administrative Assistant, 1961-65, Registrar, 1966-87, Royal Academy of Music. *Publications:* Editor, Royal Academy of Music Magazine, 1963-87; Innumerable programme notes, 1953-. *Contributions to:* Gramophone; Musical Times; Music and Musicians; Records and Recording; The Strad; Arts Review. *Honours:* Hon ARAM, 1965; Hon RCM, 1971; Hon RAM, 1976. *Memberships:* Savage Club; Garrick Club; Chelsea Arts Club; Royal Musical Association; Royal Society of Musicians; Critics' Circle. *Hobbies:* Interests: People; Buildings; Pictures; Italy; Greece; Hungary. *Address:* 33 Prentice Street, Lavenham, Sudbury, Suffolk CO10 9RD, England.

GOLDOVSKY Boris, b. 7 June 1908, Moscow, Russia. Pianist; Conductor; Opera producer; Lecturer; Broadcaster. m. Margaret Codd, 1933. 1 son, 1 daughter. *Education:* Studied piano with uncle, Pierre Luboschutz; Attended Moscow Conservatory, 1918-21; Studied with Schnabel and Kreutzer, Berlin Academy of Music, 1921-23; Attended Dohnányi's Master class, Budapest Academy of Music, graduated 1930; Studied conducting with Reiner, Curtis Institute of Music, Philadelphia, 1932. *Debut:* Soloist, Berlin Philharmonic Orchestra, 1921. *Career:* Head, Opera Department, New England Conservatory of Music, Boston, 1942-64, Berkshire Music Center, Tanglewood 1946-61, Curtis Institute of Music, 1977-; Founder-director, New England Opera Theater, Boston, 1946 which became Goldovsky Opera Institute, 1963; Toured with own opera company until 1984; Commentator, Metropolitan Opera Radio Broadcasts, 1946-; Lecturer; Translator of opera librettos into English. *Publications:* Accents on Opera, 1953; Bringing Opera to Life, 1968; Bringing Soprano Arias to Life, with A Schoep, 1973; Manual of Operatic Touring, with T Wolf, 1975; My Road to Opera, with C Cate, 1979; Good Afternoon, Ladies and Gentlemen!: Intermission Scripts from the Met Broadcasts, 1984. *Honours:* Honorary MusD, Bates College 1956, Cleveland Institute of Music 1969, Southeastern Massachusetts University 1981; Honorary DFA, Northwestern University, 1972; Fellow, American Academy of Arts and Sciences. *Address:* c/o Herbert Barrett Management Inc, 1776 Broadway, New York, NY 10019, USA.

GOLDRING Malcolm David, b. 12 July 1949, Croydon, England. Lecturer; Conductor; m. Susan Elizabeth Austin, 11 Sept. 1971, 3 sons. *Education:* MEd, Nottingham University, 1982; PGCE, Durham University, 1972; GRSM, ARCM, 1971, Royal College of Music, London. *Career:* Assistant Teacher of Music, Southmoor School, Sunderland, 1972-74; Head of

Music, Shepshed High School, Leicestershire, 1974-81; Head of Music, Charles Keene College of Further Education, Leicester; Lecturer, Leicestershire School of Music, 1981-86; Inspector of Schools (Music), Metropolitan Borough of Solihull, West Midlands, 1986-; Guest Conductor, including Leicester Philharmonic Choir, Cecilian Singers, Cambridge Youth Orchestra, Guernsey Symphony Orchestra, Guernsey Youth Orchestra; Conductor of Choral Workshop, Cavendish Singers, Royal Leamington Spa Bach Choir, Solihull Youth Orchestra, Solihull Youth Chamber Orchestra. *Honours:* Winston Churchill Fellow, 1990; Fellow of Royal Society of Arts, 1991. *Hobbies:* Food; Photography; Gardens. *Address:* 145 Widney Lane, Solihull, West Midlands, England.

GOLDSCHMIDT Berthold, b. 18 Jan. 1903, Hamburg, Germany. Composer; Conductor. *Education:* Studied at the University of Hamburg and the Friedrich Wilhelm University, Berlin; Berlin State Academy of Music with Franz Schreker, 1922-25. *Career:* Assistant conductor at the Berlin Staatsoper 1926; Conductor of the Darmstadt Opera 1927-29; Piano Sonata performed at the 1928 ISCM Festival Geneva; Guest Conductor Leningrad Philharmonic Orchestra 1931; Conducted for the Berlin Radio, and Artistic Adviser to the Berlin Stadtische Oper 1931-33; Der gewaltige Hahnerei performed: Mannheim, 1932; Emigrated to Britain 1935, British citizen 1947; Ballet Chronica performed by the Ballets Joos at Cambridge, 1939; Conducted the Glyndebourne Opera company in Macbeth at the 1947 Edinburgh Festival; Prizewiner in the Arts Council competition for new operas, 1951: Beatrice Cenci given concert premiere at the Elizabeth Hall, 1988; UK premiere of Ciacona Sinfonica by the City of Birmingham Symphony and Simon Rattlle, Oct 1990; performed at the 1993 London Proms; Early champion of Mahler in Britain, and conducted the premiere of Deryck Cooke's full performing version of the 10th Symphony, Albert Hall 1964. *Compositions:* Overture Comedy of Errors 1925; Ist String Quartet 1925; Passacaglia for orchestra 1925; Piano Sonata 1926; Der gewaltige Hahnrei, opera 1931; Violin Concerto 1933, rev. 1955; 2nd String Quartet 1936; Ballet Chronica 1938; Sinfonietta 1945; Radio Scores Dream Play (after Strindberg) 1948 and Investigations of a Dog (after Kafka) 1969; Chaconne for orchestra 1949; Beatrice Cenci, opera 1950; Cello Concerto 1953; Clarinet Concerto 1954; Mediterranaean Songs 1958; String Quartet No. 4, 1992. *Address:* 13 Belsize Crescent, London NW3, England.

GOLDSTEIN Louis R., b. 20 Dec. 1947, Kenosha, Wisconsin, USA. Pianist; Teacher. m. Vicki Freedman, 2 Feb. 1971, 1 son, 2 daughters. *Education:* Interlochen Arts Academy, Interlochen, Michigan 1966; BM, Oberlin College Conservatory of Music 1970; MFA, California Institute of The Arts 1972; DMA, Eastman School of Music 1980; Study with Joseph Hungate, Leonid Hambro, Rudolf Ganz, David Burge. *Career:* Orchestra Hall, Chicago 1965; Hollywood Bowl 1973; Carnegie Recital Hall and Town Hall 1974; Co-Founder and Co-Director, California New Music Ensemble 1972-76; Monday Evening Concerts, Los Angeles; also member, Los Angeles Group For Contemporary Music 1975; and NEWBAND (in NYC) 1977-79; Wake Forest University, Professor of Music 1979; Faculty Coordinator, American Foundations Seminar on American Art, Music, Literature and History (Reynolda House Museum of American Art) 1982; American Dance Festival Workshop On Music and Dance 1980, 1981; Frequent Performer as Soloist, Chamber Musician and Accompanist. *Compositions:* Chukchi for 2 pianos 1979; Foundations Music, for 14 percussionists and solo woodwind 1982. *Recordings:* Keyboard Music of Dan Locklair (Orion Recording). *Address:* Wake Forest University, Department of Music, Box 7345, Winston-Salem, NC 27109, USA.

GOLDSTEIN Malcolm, b. 27 March 1936, Brooklyn, New York, USA. Composer; Violinist. *Education:* Studied at Columbia University with Otto Luening. *Career:* Has taught at Columbia-Princeton Electronic Music Center,

1959-60; Columbia University 1961-65; New England Conservatory 1965-67; Goddard College, Vermont 1972-74; Bowdoin College, Brunswick, Maine 1978-82; Co-director of the concert series Tone Roads 1967-69, giving performances of works by Ives, Varése and Cage; Director of the New Music Ensemble and Collegium at Dartmouth College, 1975-78. Has toured Europe and North America as violinist. *Compositions include:* Emanations for violin and cello 1962; Ludlow Blues for wind and tape 1963; Overture to Fantastic Gardens 1964; Majority-1964 for string trio; Sirens for Edgard Varése 1965; Sheep Meadow, tape collage 1967; Frog Pond at Dusk 1972; Upon the Seashore of Endless Worlds 1974; Yosha's Morning Song Extended 1974; Hues of the Golden Ascending for flute and ensemble 1979; On the First Day of Spring there were 40 Pianos 1981; A Breaking of Vessels, becoming Song, flute concerto, 1981; The Seasons, Vermont, 1980-82; Of Bright Mushrooms Bursting in my Head for ensemble 1984; Cascades of the Brook (Bachwasserfall) for orchestra 1984. *Publications include:* Edition of the 2nd Symphony by Ives; From Wheelock Mountain, scores and writings (Toronto, 1977). *Address:* c/o ASCAP, ASCAP Building, One Lincoln Plaza, New York, NY 10023, USA.

GOLDSTONE Anthony Keith, b. 25 July 1944, Liverpool, England. Concert Pianist. m. Caroline Clemmow, 26 July 1989. *Education:* Royal Manchester College of Music. *Debut:* Wigmore Hall, London, 23 Feb 1969. *Career:* Appearances throughout Great Britain with all major symphony orchestras and in recital; Many festivals; Several London Promenade Concerts including the Last Night in 1976; Very frequent broadcaster; Tours, North and South America, Africa, Asia, Europe, Australasia; Flourishing piano duo with wife Caroline Clemmow and numerous chamber activities including founding Musicians of the Royal Exchange in 1978. *Recordings:* Solo piano: Holst, Lambert, Moussorgsky, Britten, Bridge, others; Chamber: Beethoven, Sibelius, Mendelssohn, Holst, others; Piano Duo: Rimsky-Korsakov, Stravinsky, virtuoso variations, romantic sonatas, others; Concertos: Alkan, Saint-Saens. *Honours:* International Piano Competitions, Munich, Vienna, 1967; BBC Piano Competition, 1968; Gulbenkian Fellowship, 1968-71; Fellow, Royal Manchester College of Music, 1973. *Membership:* Incorporated Society of Musicians. *Hobbies:* Antique maps; Birdwatching. *Address:* 41 West St, Oundle, Peterborough PE8 4EJ, England.

GOLDTHORPE (John) Michael, b. 7 Feb. 1942, York, England. Singer (Tenor). *Education:* MA, Trinity College, Cambridge, 1964; Certificate of Education, King's College, London, 1965. Guildhall School of Music & Drama, London, 1966-67. *Debut:* Purcell Room, London, Jan. 1970. *Career includes:* Paris debut, 1972; Opera Royal, Versailles, 1977; Royal Opera, Covent Garden & BBC Television, 1980; Regular broadcaster, BBC Radio; US debut, Miami Festival, 1986; Appearances in Singapore, Iceland, most countries Western Europe; Concertgebouw, Amsterdam, 1986, Directed Mediaeval Concert in Rome, 1987. Noted Bach Evangelist & exponent of French baroque, lecturer; Lucerne Festival's performance of Frank Martin's Golgotha, 1990; Series of concerts for the Sorbonne, Paris, 1992; Recent London performances Verdi Requiem, Janáček's Glagolotic Mass, Britten's Cantata Misericordium; Beethoven's Missa Solemnis. *Recordings include:* Rameau: Hippolyte et Aricie, La Princesse de Navarre, Pygmalion; Charpentier: Missa Assumpta est Maria, Judith; Mondonville: Motets; Cavalli: Ercole Amante; 100 Years of Italian Opera; Delius: Irmelin; L'Incoronazione di Poppea; Monteverdi Madrigali Libro Sesto; Blanchard cantatas. *Honours:* Lieder Prize, GSM, 1967; Choral exhibition, Cambridge, 1961; GLAA Young Musician Award, ISM Young Musician Award, Park Lane Group's Young Musician Award, early 1970's. *Hobbies:* Languages; Reading; Brewing; Gardening; Computing. *Address:* 23 King Edward's Road, Ruislip, Middlesex HA4 7AQ, England.

GOLIGHTLY David Frederick, b. 17 Nov. 1948,

England. Composer; Lecturer. *Education:* BA Hons 2:1, Huddersfield University, Post Graduate Certificate of Advance Studies Composition, Guildhall school of Music and Drama; Post graduate certificate of Education, Leeds University. *Career:* Composer. *Compositions:* Star Flight, a contest piece for brass band; Crimond, a symphonic arrangement for brass band; Northumbrian Fantasy, a concert piece for brass band; Septet for Brass, Little Suite for Brass Quintet; Three Pieces for Trombone Quartet Vol 1 and 2; Concert Fanfare for brass and percussion; Four Preludes for flute and guitar; Moods for solo clarinet; Serenade for solo tuba; Two pieces for solo brass instrument; Two pieces for solo brass instrument; Two pieces for solo trombone; Three simple dance episodes for flute and piano; A three hour Comic Opera, The Eye New Music for the theatre, The Railway Children, Suddenly Last Summer, Something Outspoken; Grange Arts Centre, The Eye Chamber Opera premiered 1992; Songs of The Cliff Top, for baritone, piano; Rites of Passage for The Rouss-Land Male Voice Choir of St Peterburg, premiered 1993. *Recordings:* Septet; Three Pieces for Trombone Quartet Vol I & II; Four Preludes for Flute and guitar; Music for the Theatre, incidental music composed for the following plays: Snow Queen, Disorderly Women, The Glass Menagerie, Hans, Witch and the Gobin, On the Razzle, Blood Wedding, The Voyage of the Dawn Treader, Under Milkwood; Rites of Passage, The Eye (Video). *Memberships:* Performing Rights Society; Composers Guild of Great Britain. *Address:* c/o Modrana Music Publishers, 17 Paragon Street, Stanhope, Co Durham, DL13 2NN, England.

GÖLLNER Marie Louise, b. 27 June 1932, Fort Collins, Colorado, USA. Professor. m. Theodor Göllner, 30 Sept. 1959, 1 son, 1 daughter. *Education:* BA, Vassar College, 1953; University of Heidelberg, 1954-56; University of Munich, 1956-62; PhD, summa cum laude, 1962; Aspen School of Music, Summers, 1951, 1952; Eastman School of Music, 1953-54. *Career:* Research assistant, Bavarian State Library, Munich, 1965-67, 1969-70; Lecturer, College of Creative Studies, University of California, Santa Barbara, 1968; Assistant Professor, 1970, Associate Professor, 1974, Professor, 1978, Chairman, Music, 1976-80, Chairman, Musicology 1985-89, University of California, Los Angeles. *Publications:* Die Musik des frühen Trecento, 1963; Rules for Cataloguing Music Manuscripts, 1975; Orlando di Lasso: Sämtliche Werke, Neue Reihe, Das Hymnarium 1580-81, 1980; Katalog der Musikhandschriften der Bayerischen Staatsbibliothek München, II 1979, I 1989; Joseph Haydn: Sinfonie Nr. 94, 1979; Eine neue Quelle zur italienischen Orgelmusik des Cinquecento, 1982; The Manuscript Cod. lat. 5539 of the Bavarian State Library (MSD43), AIM, 1993. *Contributions to:* Numerous articles in professional journals including: Fontes; Grove VI. *Address:* Dept. of Music, University of California, 405 Hilgard Ave, Los Angeles, CA 90024, USA.

GÖLLNER Theodor, b. 25 Nov. 1929, Bielefeld, Germany. Musicologist; Administrator. m. Marie Louise Martinez, 1 son, 1 daughter. *Education:* PhD, University of Heidelberg, 1957; Phil habil., University of Munich, 1967. *Career:* Lecturer, 1958-62, Assistant, 1962-67, Associate Professor, 1967, Professor, 1973-; Chair in Musicology and Director, Institute of Musicology, 1973-, Dean, Division of History and Fine Arts, 1975-77, University of Munich; Associate Professor, 1967-71, Professor, 1971-73, University of California, Santa Barbara, USA; Member, Bavarian Academy of Sciences, 1982-. *Publications:* Formen früher Mehrstimmigkeit, 1961; Die mehrstimmigen liturgischen Lesungen, 2 vols, 1969; Die Sieben Worte am Kreuz bei Schütz und Haydn, 1986; Editor, Münchener Veröffentlichungen zur Musikgeschichte, 1977-; Editor, Münchener Editionen zur Musikgeschichte, 1979-. *Contributions to:* Various publications. *Memberships:* International Musicological Society; Gesellschaft für Musikforschung; Gesellschaft für Bayerische Musikgeschichte, President 1981-. *Address:* Musikwiss Institut, University of Munich, Geschw Scholl Platz I, 8 Munich 22, Germany.

GOLOVIN Andre, b. 11 Aug 1950, Moscow, Russia. Composer. *Education:* Moscow Conservatoire, 1971-76; Postgraduate course, 1977- 79. *Career:* Teaching Composition: Musical School, 1975-; Gnesin's Musical Pedagogical Institute, 1989-. *Compositions:* Published: Cadence and Ostinato for 5 Timpani, Bells, Tam-tam and Piano, 1979; Concerto Symphony for Viola, Cello and Symphony Orchestra, 1980; Sonata for Oboe and Cembalo, 1980; Sonata for Piano, 1981; Duet for Violin and Piano, 1981; Duet for Viola and Cello, 1981; Sonata breve for Viola and Piano, 1982, 2nd edition, for Japan, 1992; 2 pieces for Piano, 1982; Sonata for Cello solo, 1983; 2 pieces for Flute and Piano: 1. Portrait, 2. Landscape, 1983; Prelude for Vibraphone, 1984; Legend for Piano, 1984; 3 Easy pieces for Piano, 1985; 1st Quartet for 2 Violins, Viola and Cello, 1986; Music for String Quartet, 1986; Sonatina for Piano, 1986, 2nd edition, for Japan, 1991; Fairy-tale for Horn and Piano, 1987; Concert Symphony for Viola, Piano and Orchestra, 1988; Symphony for Full Symphony Orchestra, 1990; Elegy for Cello solo, 1990; Poeme Nocturne for Viola and Piano, 1991; Plain Songs: Cantata to Verses by N Rubtsov for Mezzo-soprano, Bass, Piano and Chamber Orchestra, 1991; Remote Past for Piano, 1991. *Recordings:* Simple songs: Cantata, Elegy for Cello solo; Sonata breve for Viola and Piano; Elegy for Cello solo; Concert Symphony for Viola, Piano and Orchestra; Quartet for 2 Violins, Viola and Cello; 2 pieces for Flute and Piano. *Membership:* Russian Composers Union. *Address:* Shumkin St 3, k2, ap 45, Moscow 107113, Russia.

GOLOVINSKY Grigory, b. 18 Feb. 1923, Gitomir, USSR. Musicologist. m. Margarita Kapnist, 30 July 1946. 1 daughter. *Education:* Postgraduate of the Mosco Conservatory. *Career:* Teacher, Musical School, 1945-55; Teacher, Musical College, 1954-60; Chief Assistant of the Musicology Commission (of the Union of Soviet Composers), 1957-67; Senior Researcher, Institute of Art Studies, 1967. *Publications:* Borodin's chamber ensembles, 1972; Composer and Folklore, 1981; Sergei Balasanian (with B Schachnasarova), 1972; Book of Music (one of the authors and as an editor), 1975; M P Mussorgsky and Twentieth-Century Music (one of the authors and as an editor), 1990; Mussorgsky and folklore, 1991. *Contributions to:* Articles in History of Music of the Soviet Peoples, 1973 and 1974; Questions of Art Sociology; Social Function of Art and Its Forms; Perception of Music; Come into existance a sound image; Sovjetskaja muzika magazine. *Honour:* Doctor of Science (1985) musicology (Doctor of Art Studies). *Memberships:* Union of Soviet Composers; Institute Mediacult, Vienna. *Address:* Uralska Street No 8 Ap 97, 107207 Moscow, Russia.

GOLTZ Christel, b. 8 July 1912, Dortmund, Germany. Singer (Soprano). m. Theodor Schenk. *Education:* Studied with Ornelli-Leeb in Munich, and with Theodor Schenk. *Career:* Sang first at Plauen, as Eva, Santuzza and Octavian ; Sang at the Dresden Staatsoper from 1936, notably as Reiza in Oberon, in the premiere of Sutermeister's Romeo und Julia 1941 and in the local premiere of Orff's Antigonae 1950; Sang in Berlin from 1947, then in Munich and Vienna as Salome, Electra, the Countess in Capriccio, Tosca and Leonore; Covent Garden 1951-52, as Salome and as Marie in the local stage premiere of Wozzeck; Salzburg Festival from 1954, in the premiere of Liebermann's Penelope and as Electra and Leonore; Metropolitan Opera 1954, Salome; Guest engagements in Paris, Brussels and Milan; Sang at the State Operas of Munich and Vienna until 1970. *Recordings:* Salome and Die Frau ohne Schatten (Decca). *Address:* c/o Vienna State Opera, Ring Strasse, Vienna, Austria.

GOLUB David, b. 22 March 1950, Chicago, USA. Pianist. *Education:* Studied with Alexander Uninsky in Dallas and with Beveridge Webster at the Juilliard School, N.Y.; graduated 1974. *Career:* Debut 1964 with Dallas Symphony Orchestra; after graduation appeared with orchestras in Philadelphia, Cleveland, Dallas, St Louis, Pittsburgh, Cincinnati, Chicago, Minnesota, Washington, and Atlanta; solo appearances with orchestras of Toronto, Ottawa, Edmonton, Montreal, Calgary and Vancouver and has performed at all the major North American music festivals; international appearances with such conductors as Maazel, Mata, Horst Stein, Zinman, Conlon, Chailly, Levine, Dutoit, Bychkov, DeWaart, Foster, Skrowaczewski and Albrecht; European engagements with orchestras in London, Rome, Paris, Milan, Geneva, Florence and Rotterdam; Appeared in film, From Mao to Mozart, which documented tour to China in 1979 with Isaac Stern and formed a Piano Trio with Colin Carr and Mark Kaplan. *Recordings:* Gershwin and Rachmaninov with the London Symphony Orchestra and the complete piano trios of Schubert, Mendelssohn and Brahms. *Address:* c/o Harold Holt Ltd., 31 Sinclair Road, London W14 ONS, England.

GOMEZ Jill, b. 21 Sept. 1942, New Amsterdam, British Guyana. Singer (Soprano). *Education:* Royal Academy of Music; Guildhall School of Music, London, England. *Debut:* (Operatic) Adina in L'Elisir d'Amore, Glyndebourne Touring Opera, 1968; Operatic debut with Glyndebourne Festival Opera, 1969 as Mélisande; has since sung La Calisto, 1971 and Ann Truelove in The Rake's Progress, 1975. *Career includes:* Appearances with: Royal Opera, English Opera, Scottish Opera, roles including Pamina, Ilia, Fiordiligi, Countess (Figaro), Elisabeth (Elegy for Young Lovers), Tytania, Lauretta (Gianni Schicchi), Governess (Turn of the Screw). Created role by Flora, Tippett's Knot Garden, 1970 and The Countess in Thea Musgrave's The Voice od Ariande, Aldeburgh, 1974; Title role, Massenet's Thais, Wexford, 1974; Jenifer (Midsummer Marriage), Welsh National Opera, 1976. Created title role in William Alwyn's Miss Julie, 1977; Created roles: Flora, Tippett's Knot Garden, Covent Garden 1970; Title role, William Alwyn's Miss Julie, radio, 1977; Tatiana (Eugene Onegin), Kent Opera, 1977; Donna Elvira (Don Giovanni), Ludwigsburg Festival, 1978; Created title role, Maddalena; Title role, BBC world premiere, Prokofiev's Maddalena, 1979; Fiordiligi (Cosi fan Tutte), Bordeaux, 1979; Premiere of Eighth Book of Madrigals, Zurich Monteverdi Festival, 1979; Violetta, La Traviata, Kent Opera, Edinburgh Festival, 1979; Cinna, Lucio Silla, Zurich, 1981; Governess, The Turn of the Screw, Geneva, 1981; Cleopatra, Giulio Cesare, Frankfurt, 1981; Teresa, Benvenuto Cellini, Berlioz Festival, Lyon, 1982; Leila, Les Pêcheurs de Perles, Scottish Opera, 1982-83; Governess, The Turn of the Screw, English Nat Opera, 1984; Helena, Britten's A Midsummer Night's Dream, Glyndebourne; Donna Anna, Don Giovanni, Frankfurt Opera, 1985; Amyntas, Il Re Pastore, Kent Opera, 1987; Donna Anna, Don Giovanni, Kent Opera, 1988; Rosario in Goyescas by Granados, 1988; Regular engagements including recitals and concert appearances in: France, Austria, Belgium, Netherlands, Germany, Scandinavia, Switzerland, Italy, Spain and USA. Festival appearances include: Aix-en-Provence, Spoleto, Bergen, Versailles, Flanders, Netherlands, Prague, Edinburgh and BBC Promenade concerts; World premiere performance in 1988 Proms of Cantiga - The Song of Inês de Castro commissioned by her from David Matthews, 1988; Sang songs by Berlioz and Canteloube with the RPO at the Festival Hall, 1992. *Recordings:* Vespro della Beata Vergine 1610 (Monteverdi); Acis and Galatea (Handel); The Knot Garden (Tippett); Three recital discs of French, Spanish and Mozart songs; Quatre Chansons Françaises (Britten); Trois Poèmes de Mallarmé (Ravel); Chants d'Auvergne (Canteloube); Les Illuminations (Britten); Bachianas Brasileiras No 5 (Villa Lobos); Knoxville-Summer of 1915 (S Barber) and Cabaret Classics with John Constable: and South of the Border (down Mexico Way...); Britten's Blues, Cabaret Songs by Britten and Cole Porter, premiere recordings of: Cantiga, The Song of Inês de Castro (Matthews) and Seven Early Songs (Mahler); Songs by Britten and Cole Porter. *Honour:* FRAM, 1986.*Address:* 16 Milton Park, London N6 5QA, England.

GOMEZ-MARTINEZ Miguel-Angel, b. 17 Sept 1949, Granada, Spain. Conductor; Composer. *Education:* Studied at Granada and Madrid Conservatory, in USA and in Vienna with Hans Swarowsky. *Career:* Has conducted opera in Lucerne, Berlin, Frankfurt, Munich and Hamburg, Royal Opera House Covent Garden London, Paris, Geneva, Houston, Chicago, Florence, Venice, Rome, Palermo; Resident Conductor, Berlin Deutsche Oper, 1973-77; Vienna Staatsoper, 1977-82; Festivals in Berlin, Vienna, Munich, Macerata (Italy), Granada, Santander, San Sebastián, Savonlinna (Finland), Helsink; Repertoire includes operas by: Beethoven (Fidelio), Bellini, (Puritani), Bizet (Carmen), Donizetti (Don Pasquale, Maria Stusrda), Leoncavallo (Pagliacci), Mascagni (Cavalleria Rusticana), Massenet, (Werther), Mozart (Cosí fan tutte), Entführung, Figaro, Giovanni, L'Oca del Cairo, Schauspieldirektor, Zauberflöte), Pergolessi (Serva padrona), Ponchielli (Gioconda), Puccini (Bohème, Butterfly, Fanciulla del West, Manon Lescaut, Tabarro, Suor Angelica, Gianni Schichi, Tosca, Turandot), Rossini (Cambiale di Matrimonio, Cenerentola). Conductor, Radiotelevision Española Orchestra, 1984-87; Artistic Director and Chief Conductor, Teatro Lérico Nacional Madrid, 1985-91, General Musikdirektor Nationaltheater Mannheim and Chief Conductor of the Nationaltheater Orchestra, 1990-93, Chief Conductor Hamburg Symphony, 1992-, General Music Director, Finnish National Opera, Helsinki, 1993-. *Compositions include:* Suite Burlesca; Sinfonia del Descubrimiento (first performed 1992), at Mozart Saal, Rosengarten, Mannheim. *Honours:* Several decorations and nominations. *Address:* c/o Finnish National Opera, Helsingin katu 58, SF 00260 Helsinki, Finland.

GONDA-NIGG Anna, b. Jan 1950, Miskole, Hungary. Singer (Mezzo- soprano). *Education:* Studied at Franz Liszt Academy, Budapest, and in Berlin. *Debut:* Sang Gluck's Orpheus in Berlin, 1976. *Career:* Sang at Rostock, 1976-78; Vienna Staatsoper, 1981-, notably on tour to Japan, 1986; Salzburg Festival, 1984, in premiere of Un Re in Ascolto by Berio; Appeared in Zigeunerbaron at Zurich Opera, conducted by Nikolaus Harnoncourt, 1990; Lieder recitals and concerts, Austria, France and Switzerland; Other roles have included Verdi's Azucena, Ulrica, Mistress Quickly, Amneris, Maddalena and Preziosilla, Wagner's Erda and Brangaene, Marina in Boris Godunov, Clytemnestra and Penelope in Il Ritorno di Ulisse. *Recordings include:* Zulma in L'Italiana in Algeri, Margret in Wozzeck. *Address:* c/o Opernhaus Zurich, Falkenstrasse 1, CH-8008 Zurich, Switzerland.

GONDEK Juliana Kathleen, b. 20 May 1953, Pasadena, California, USA. Soprano. m. Carl Della Peruti, 22 June 1985, 1 daughter. *Education:* Violin study; BM, 1975, MM, 1977, University of Southern California School of Music; Britten-Pears School of Advanced Musical Studies, Aldeburgh, England. *Debut:* San Diego Opera. *Career:* Opera highlights: Contessa, Le Nozze di Figaro, Netherlands Opera, 1986; Heroines, The Tales of Hoffmann, 1986, title role, Alcina, 1987, Opera Theatre of St Louis; Bianca, Bianca e Falliero, Greater Miami Opera, 1987; Fiordiligi, Così fan tutte, Hawaii Opera, 1989; Metropolitan Opera, 1990-92; Vitellia, La Clemenza di Tito, Scottish Opera, 1991; Title role, Beatrice di Tenda, 1991; Elvira, Don Giovanni, Seattle Opera, 1991; Gismonda, Ottone, Handel Festival, Göttingen, 1992; Concert highlights: Soloist, Montreal, Toronto, Vancouver, San Francisco, Dallas, St Louis, Indianapolis, Detroit Symphonies, Orchestre de la Suisse Romande, Stuttgart Radio Symphony, Brucknerorchester Linz, Gran Liceo of Barcelona, National Radio/TV Orchestra of Spain, Madrid; Festival Soloist: Edinburgh, Caramoor, Marlboro, Newport, Avignon; Recitals, New York, Los Angeles, Chicago, Geneva, Lucerne, Berlin, Venice; Aspasia, Mitridate, New York, mostly Mozart Festival, 1992; Göttingen Handel Festival, 1993; Gilda, Rigoletto, Opéra de Nice, 1993; New York Philharmonic, as soloist; Bard Festival, New York, mostly Mozart. *Recordings:* Harmonia Mundi: Handel Ottone (Gismonda), 1992; Harmonia Mundi: Handel Radamisto (Zenobia), 1993; The Orion Records: The Yoav Chamber Ensemble, 1983; Video: Live From the Met, Die Zauberflöte, 1st Dame, Metropolitan Opera, 1992; BBC Documentary, The Making of West Side Story. *Current Management:* Colbert Artists Management Inc, USA. *Address:* c/o Colbert Artists

Management Inc, 111 West 57th Street, New York, NY 10019, USA.

GONLEY Stephanie, b. 1960, England. Violinist. *Education:* Studied at Chetham's School of Music, at Guildhall School of Music, with Dorothy DeLay at Juilliard, and in Berlin. *Career:* Played the Weill Concerto with London Symphony Orchestra, 1986, Mozart Concertos with Manchester Camerata, Mendelssohn and Bruch with Royal Philharmonic, Brahms with London Philharmonic Orchestra and Beethoven in Netherlands, conducted by Adrian Leaper; Further engagements with English Chamber Orchestra, 1990, Philharmonia and Halle, at Montpellier Festival and in Hong Kong, Belgium and Canada, played Vivaldi's Four Seasons with English Chamber Orchestra, Festival Hall, 1993; Leader, English Chamber Orchestra; Masterclasses, Banff, Canada, Aspen, USA, and Prussia Cove, Cornwall, England; Co-founded Vellinger String Quartet, 1990; Participated in masterclasses with Borodin Quartet, Pears- Britten School, 1991; Concerts at Ferrara Musica Festival, Italy and debut on South Bank with London premiere of Robert Simpson's 13th Quartet; BBC Radio 3 debut, Dec 1991; Season 1992-93 with concerts in London, Glasgow, Cambridge, at Davos Festival, Switzerland, and Crickdale Festival, Wiltshire; Wigmore Hall with Haydn (Op 54 no 2), Gubaidulina and Beethoven (Op 59 no 2), Purcell Room with Haydn's Last Seven Words. *Recordings include:* Elgar's Quartet and Quintet, with Piers Lane. *Address:* c/o Georgina Ivor Associates (Vellinger Quartet), 66 Alderbrook Road, London SW12 8AB, England.

GONNEVILLE Michel, b. 1950, Montreal, Canada. Lecturer; Composer. *Education:* Studied piano at an early age; Studied at Ecole de musique Vincent-d'Indy, 1968-72; BMus, 1972. *Career:* Composer, studying analysis and composition with Gilles Tremblay, Conservatoire de musique de Montreal, 1973; Obtained First Prizes in Analysis and Composition from Conservatoire de musique de Montreal, 1974 and 1975; attended Stockhausen's seminars in Darmstadt, 1974; attended Stockhausen's Composition Classes in Cologne for three semesters also working in Electronic Studio, Musikhochschule, Cologne; Student and Personal Assistant to Henri Pousseur, Liège; His professors during three-year European sojourn included: Frederic Rzewski and Joh Fritsch; returning to Canada, 1978, lectured on Analysis and Composition at Montreal and Rimouski Conservatories and at Universities of Montreal and Ottawa. *Compositions:* Composed works for Louis-Philippe Pelletier, Michael Laucke, Robert Leroux, Gropus 7, l'Ensemble d'Ondes de Montreal, the SMCQ and a recent work premiered by the Orchestre des jeunes du Quebec; his works have been performed in Montreal, Quebec, Toronto, Metz, Cologne, Bonn, Liège, Paris and several have been recorded and broadcast by CBC and WDR in Cologne. *Membership:* Member of Board of Directors of Societe de musique contemporaine du Quebec.

GONZAGA Otoniel, b. 1944, Phlippines. Singer (Tenor). *Career:* Has appeared at opera houses in Europe and North America, 1967-; Engaged at Trier, 1973-77, Frankfurt-am-Main, 1977-88; Member of Cologne Opera, 1988-; Guest engagements at Stuttgart, Munich (Theater am Gartnerplatz), Vienna (Volksoper), Barcelona, Berne and Genoa; Sang Otello at Aachen, Edgardo in Lucia di Lammermoor at Cincinnati, 1990; Other roles have included Ferrando, Faust, Almavivaa and Luigi in Il Tabarro; Many concert appearances. *Address:* c/o Stadttheater, Theaterstrasse 1-3, 5100 Aachen, Germany.

GONZALEZ Carmen, b. 16 April 1939, Vallodid, Spain. Singer (Mezzo-Soprano). *Career:* Studied at the Madrid Conservatory and with Magda Piccarolo and Rodolfo Celetti in Milan. *Debut:* Madrid Chamber Opera 1968, as Isolier in Le Comte Ory. *Career:* Sang in Rome, Bolgna, Trieste and Venice; Turin 1974, in the local premiere of Die drei Pintos by Weber/Mahler; La Scala Milan 1979, in a revival of Tito Manlio by Vivaldi; Turin 1986, as Ulrica (Un Ballo in Maschera); Further

appearances in Washington, Florence, Rome, Paris, Brussels, Mexico City, Belgrade and New York (City Opera); Sang Mistress Quickly in Falstaff at Rome, 1989; Holland Festival 1990, as Fortune-teller and Mother Superior in The Fiery Angel by Prokofiev. *Recordings:* Orlando Furioso by Vivaldi (RCA); Anacreon by Cherubini. *Address:* c/o Netherlands Opera, Waterlooplein 22, 1011 PG, Amsterdam, Holland.

GONZALES Dalmacio, b. 12 May 1945, Olot, Spain. Singer (Tenor). *Education:* Studied in Barcelona and at the Salzburg Mozarteum with Arleen Auger and Paul Schilharsky; Further study with the late Anton Dermota in Vienna. *Debut:* Teatro Liceo Barcelona 1978, as Ugo in Parisina by Donizetti. *Career:* Metropolitan Opera from 1980, as Ernesto in Don Pasquale: later appeared as Almaviva, Fenton and Nemorino; New York City Opera and San Francisco 1979, as Alfredo and in Rossini's Semiramide and Tancredi; La Scala Milan and Aix-en-Provence 1981, in Ariodante and Tancredi; Pesaro and La Scala 1984-85, in a revival of Rossini's Il Viaggio a Reims; Further appearances in Rome, Los Angeles, Chicago, Berlin, Zurich, Trieste and London; Sang Ford in Salieri's Falstaff at Parma, 1987; Munich Festival 1990, as Catullus in Catulli Carmina by Orff; Ugo in Donizetti's Parisina at the 1990 Maggio Musicale, Florence; Other roles include Rossini's Argiro (Tancredi), Idreno (Semiramide), Lindoro, James V (La Donna del Iago) and Rénaldo in Armida; Season 1992 as Nemorino at Barcelona and Demetrio in Rossini's Demeterio e Polibio at Martina Franca. *Recordings:* Verdi Requiem, Falstaff and Il Viaggio a Reims (Deutsche Grammophon); La Donna del Lago by Rossini (CBS).*Address:* c/o Teatre alla Scala, Via Filodrammatici 2, 1-20121 Milan, Italy.

GONZALEZ Manuel, b. 30 April 1944, Madrid, Sapin. Singer (Baritone). *Education:* Studied at the Madrid Conservatoire. *Debut:* Théâtre de la Monnaie Brussels 1971, as Ping in Turandot. *Career:* Many appearances in the lyric baritone repertoire at opera houses in Brussels, Antwerp, Ghent and Liège; Guest engagements in Dortmund, Essen, Frankfurt, Hamburg, Stuttgart and Mannheim; Barcelona, Lisbon, Paris, Nice, Marseilles and Geneva, and at the Vienna Volksoper; Sang roles in operas by Donizetti, Bizet, Mozart, Puccini, Rossini, Massenet and Verdi; Wagner's Wolfram von Eschenbach and Tarquinius in Britten's The Rape of Lucretia; Wexford Festival 1973, in Donizetti's L'Ajo nell'imbarazzo (The Tutor in a Fix); Many concert appearances. *Address:* c/o Théâtre de la Monaie, 4 Leopoldstrasse, B-1000 Brussels, Belgium.

GOODALL Howard Lindsay, b. 26 May 1958, London, England. Composer; Arranger. *Education:* ARCO, 1975; Chorister, New College, Oxford; Music Scholar, Christ Church, Oxford. *Career:* Composer, TV Scores & songs of: Not the Nine O'Clock News; The Black Adder; Composer & Performer in: Rowan Atkinson in Revue, UK Tours 1977-87, World Tour 1982, West End 1981, 1986, Broadway 1986. *Compositions:* Musicals: The Hired Man, with Melvyn Bragg, 1984; Girlfriends, 1987, Days of Hope, 1991. Operas: Der Glöchner von Notre-Dame, 1983; Silas Marner, 1993; Choral: Psalm 122, 1992; Let Us Be True to One Another, 1990; Christ Church Mass, 1993. Orchestral: Land of the Lakes Suite, 1986; Voces Redentes, 1988; The Borrowers, 1992. *Recordings:* The Hired Man; Rowan Atkinson Live in Belfast; Not Just a Pretty Face; Not the Nine O'Clock News; Hedgehog Sandwich; The Memory Lingers; Days of Hope, 1991; The Hired Man, at the Palace Theatre, 1992 . *Honours:* MA, Oxon; Ivor Novello Award, Best Musical, 1984. *Memberships:* BASCA; Liberal Club; PRS; MU; European Movement; Liberal Club. *Hobbies:* Gardening; Cricket; Reading. *Current Management:* PBJ Management. *Address:* c/o 47 Dean Street, London W1V 5HL, England.

GOODALL Valorie, b. 23 Sept. 1936, Waco, Texas, USA. Soprano; Voice Teacher; Opera Director. m. William P Mooney, 21 Jan. 1962. 2 sons. *Education:* BM cum laude, Baylor University, 1958; MM, University of Colorado, 1959; Advanced study with Paola Novikova, Berton Coffin and Werner Singer. *Debut:* Graz Opera

House, Austria. *Career:* Leading Lyric Soprano, roles of Mimi, Micaela, Mélisande, Zdenka, Composer, Fiordiligi, Cherubino, Graz Opera; Performances at opera houses of Graz, Geneva, Bern, Theatre an der Wien in Vienna, Prague; Star/producer, State museum tour of Venus and Adonis with early instruments, New Jersey, USA, 1981; Founder/director of Opera at Rutgers; Performer in oratorio, song recital and musical theatre; Resident Stage Director: New England Lyric Operetta, Stamford, Conn. *Recordings:* Land des Lächelns by Lehar, opposite Giuseppe di Stefano, London Records. *Address:* Voice Department, Mason Gross School of the Arts, Rutgers University, New Brunswick, NJ 08903, USA.

GOODE Richard Stephen, b. 1 June 1943, New York City, USA. Pianist. m. Marcia Weinfeld, 10 Apr. 1987. *Education:* Diploma, Curtis Institute of Music, 1961-64; BSc, Mannes College of Music, 1967-69; Marlboro School of Music. *Debut:* New York Young Concert Artists, 1962. *Career:* Concerts in USA, England, Europe, South America, Australia, Far East with various orchestras including: New York Philharmonic, Los Angeles Philharmonic, Baltimore, Orpheus, Philadelphia, ECO, Royal Philharmonic; Founding Member, Chamber Music Society of Lincoln Center; European Tours with Orpheus. *Recordings:* Complete cycle of 32 Beethoven Sonatas; Schumann, Fantasy, Humoresque; Schubert, 3 Posthumous Sonatas; Brahms, Late Piano Music; Mozart, Piano Concerti; Various chamber music recordings. *Honours:* Clara Haskil 1st Prize, 1973; Avery Fisher Prize, 1980. *Hobbies:* Book collecting; Museums. *Current Management:* Frank Salomon Association, New York City. *Address:* 12 East 87th Street Apt 5A, New York, NY 10128, USA.

GOODLOE Robert, b. 5 Oct. 1936, St Petersburg, Florida, USA. Singer (Baritone). *Education:* Studied at Simpson College Indianola (Iowa) and with Harvey Brown and Armen Boyajian. *Debut:* Des Moines, Iowa, 1963, as Mozart's Figaro. *Career:* Has sung principally at the Metropolitan Opera, also in Hartford, Baltimore, Philadelphia and San Francisco; Roles include Puccini's Scarpia, Michele and Marcello; Enrico (Lucia di Lammermoor); Mercutio in Roméo et Juliette; Germont in La Traviata and Paolo in Simon Boccanegra. *Address:* c/o Metropolitan Opera, Lincoln Center, New York, NY 10023, USA.

GOODMAN Alfred, b. 1 Mar. 1920, Berlin, Germany. Composer; Musicologist. m. Renate Roessig, 14 July 1967. 1 son. *Education:* BS, Columbia College, New York; MA, Composition, musicology, Columbia University; PhD, Technische Universitaet, Berlin. *Career:* Editor, Westminster Records, New York; Composer, Movietone, New York; Music Editor, Bavarian Broadcasting Commission Lecturer, Academy of Music, Munich Service, 1971-; Lecturer, Academy of Music, College of Music, Munich, 1976-. *Compositions:* Psalm XII; The Audition, opera in one act; Pro Memoria for orchestra; Individuation, symphonic work; Chamber works, songs, choral compositions; Television and film scores; orchestral works; The Lady and the Maid, opera in one scene; Across the Board for Brass ensemble (Locke Brass Consort, London); Brassology for Eleven (Brunn Brass Ensemble CSSR); Works for organ and brass; Timpani; Works for organ saxophone, organ and flute or trumpet; Universe of Freeedom - Orchestrology, 1991; Orchestrette in 7 parts, 1992; Lecture, Arnold Schoenberg Symposion Duisburg, Germany, 1993. *Publications:* Musik im Blut; Lexikon; Music von A-Z; Die Amerikanischen Schuler Franz Liszts; Dictionary of Musical Terms, 1982. *Hobbies:* Walking; Reading. *Address:* Bodenstedt St 31, 8124 Munich, Germany.

GOODMAN Bernard Maurice, b. 12 June 1914, Cleveland, Ohio, USA. Violinist; Conductor; University Professor of Music. m. Margaret Ann Carfray (deceased) 1 Sept. 1937. 2 sons. *Education:* BS, Western Reserve University; Cleveland Institute of Music; Private study with Joseph Fuchs, Carlton Cooley, Arthur Shepherd, George Szell. *Debut:* As member of Walden String Quartet, Cleveland, 1934. *Career:* Member, Cleveland Orchestra, 1936-46; Assistant Professor of Music and Artist-in-Residence, Cornell University, 1946-47; Professor of Music and Artist-in-Residence, University of Illinois, 1947-74; Conductor, University of Illinois Symphony Orchestra, 1950-74; Conductor, Champaigne-Urbana Symphony Orchestra, 1960-74; Conductor, Bloomington Normal Symphony, 1971-74; Member, Walden String Quartet, 1934-74, including tours in USA and West Europe, major music festivals, concerts; Conductor, University of Illinois Symphony Orchestra, tour of Latin America, 1964. *Recordings:* Music by Walter Piston, Robert Palmer, Martinu, Kodály, Szymanowski, Elliott Carter and Charles Ives (with Walden String Quartet). *Address:* Pemaquid Point, HC 61 Box 382, New Harbor, Maine 04554, USA.

GOODMAN Craig Stephen, b. 6 July 1957, Pittsburgh, Pennsylvania, USA. Flautist; Conductor; Educator. *Education:* BA, Yale University, 1978; MM, Yale School of Music, 1979; Private Study with Marcel Moyse and theory with Narcis Bonet. *Debut:* Konzerthaus, Vienna, Austria, 1975. *Career:* Solo Flutist, Opera Company, Philadelphia, 1978-79; Freelance, American Symphony, New York City Ballet, St Luke's Chamber Orchestra, Musica Aeterna, 1979-86; Solo engagements, Australia, Europe, USA; Musical Director, The Players of the New World, New York; Chamber Music performances with L'Ensemble, New York City, Bach Aria Group, New York City and Ensemble i, Vienna, Austria; Solo videos of Bach and Gossec, WYNC Television, New York; Featured artist in Allan Miller Bach documentary; Appearances on Sunday Morning with Charles Kuratt, CBS TV. *Recordings:* Bach Aria Group, Bach Brandenburg Concerto No 4 with James Buswell, Samuel Baron and Festival Strings, Ensemble I recording, Bach Trio Sonata in G for 2 flutes and continuo; Musical Heritage Society recording, Morton Gould's Concerto for wind quartet, piano and violin. *Hobbies:* Wilderness and outdoor activities; Art.

GOODMAN Richard Edwin, b. 25 Dec. 1935, New York City, USA. Baritone; Artistic Director. 3 daughters. *Education:* BA 1955, MS 1958, Cornell University; PhD, University of California, Berkeley, 1964; Studied piano and musicianship with Hedy Spielter, as a child; Piano coaching with Alexander Aronowsky; Voice studies with Janet Parlova, Frederick Sharp, Lenoir Hosack and others; Attended AIMS, Graz, Austria. *Career:* Founder, Artistic Director, Berkeley Opera Company; Over 40 opera roles in Berkeley Opera, West Bay Opera, Lamplighters, Pocket Opera; Recitals and appearances, London and Austria; Main roles include Falstaff (Verdi and Vaughan Williams), Don Pasquale, Figaro (Mozart), Rigoletto, Rocco, George (Of Mice and Men) and Bartolo (Rossini and Paisiello). *Address:* 715 Arlington, Berkeley, CA 94707, USA.

GOODMAN Roy, b. 26 Jan 1951, Guilford, Surrey. Conductor; Director; Violinist. *Education:* Chorister, King's College, Cambridge, 1959-64; Hull Grammar School 1965-68; Royal College of Music 1968-70; Berkshire College of Education, 1970-71. *Career:* From 1971-: Successively Head of Music at two comprehensive schools, Senior String Tutor for Berkshire, Director of Music, University of Kent and Director of Early Music, Royal Academy of Music; Founded the Brandenburg Consort (Reading 1975); Co-Director of the Parley of Instruments, 1979-1986; Principal Conductor of the Hanover Band 1986-; Three tours of the USA 1988-90; Guest Conductor 1991 with the Finnish Radio Symphony Orchestra, German Handel Soloists, I Virtuosi di Praga and the Gran Canaria Philharmonic Choir and Orchestra; Conducted Handel's Tamerlano in Paris, Bastien and Bastienne in Portugal and complete Beethoven Symphonies in Hanover. *Recordings:* (On Nimbus), Beethoven 6 Symphonies; Beethoven and the Philharmonic; Overtures by Weber and Beethoven; 8 Symphonies by Schubert; Mozart Horn Concertos; Clarinet Concerto; Requiem; Piano Concerto K466 and Symphonies K550 and K551; Mendelssohn 4th Symphony and Violin Concerto; The Symphonies of Haydn (Hyperion). *Hobbies:* Squash; Windsurfing;

Skiing. *Address:* 97 Mill Lane, Lower Earley, Reading, Berkshire. RG6 3UH, England.

GOODWIN Andrew John, b. 11 Nov 1947, Hillingdon, Middlesex, England. Cathedral Organist. *Education:* BA (Honours), Music, University of Liverpool, 1970; FRCO, 1970; MA, University College of North Wales, Bangor, 1972. *Career:* Organist, Master of the Choristers, Bangor Cathedral, Wales, 1972-; Visiting Teacher, Organ, University College of North Wales, Bangor, 1972-; Examiner, Associated Boad of Royal Society of Music, 1978-; Organ Recitalist, several cathedrals and other venues; Radio and TV broadcasts as Organist and as Conductor of the Cathedral Choir. *Recordings:* Diolch a Chan, organist, 1984; Music from Bangor Cathedral, conductor and organist, 1985; Celebration, organist, 1986. *Publication:* The Anthems of Maurice Greene, MA thesis, 1972. *Memberships:* Incorporated Society of Musicians; Guild for Promotion of Welsh Music. *Hobbies:* Railways; Wildlife conservation; Cycling. *Address:* The Diocesan Centre, Clos y Gadeirlan, Bangor, Gwynedd LL57 1RL, Wales.

GOODWIN (Trevor) Noël, b. 25 Dec 1927, Fowey, Cornwall, England. Writer and Critic specialising in Music and Dance. m. Anne Mason Myers, 23 Nov. 1963, 1 stepson. *Education:* BA (London). *Career:* Assistant Music Critic, News Chronicle, 1952-54, Manchester Guardian, 1954-55; Music and Dance Critic, Daily Express, 1956-78; Associate Editor, Dance and Dancers, 1958-; Executive Editor, Music and Musicians, 1963-71; London Dance Critic, International Herald Tribune, Paris, 1978-83; London Correspondent, Opera News (NY), 1980-91; Overseas News Editor, Opera, 1985-91; Planned and presented numerous radio programmes of music and records for BBC Home and World Services during past 25 years; Frequent contributor to music and arts programmes on Radios 3 and 4; London Correspondent, Opera News (NY), 1980-91; Overseas News Editor, Opera, 1985-91; Editorial Board Member, Opera, 1991-. *Publications:* London Symphony, portrait of an orchestra, 1954; A Ballet for Scotland, 1979; A Knight at the Opera (with Sir Geraint Evans), 1984; Editor, Royal Opera and Royal Ballet Yearbooks, 1978, 1979, 1980; Area Editor and Writer, New Grove Dictionary of Music and Musicians, 1980; Editor, A Portrait of the Royal Ballet, 1988. *Contributions to:* Encyclopaedia Britannica, 15th edition, 1974; Encyclopaedia of Opera, 1976; Britannica Books of the Year, annually, 1980-93; Cambridge Encyclopaedia of Russia and the Soviet Union, 1982; New Oxford Companion to Music, 1983; Pipers Enzyklopädie des Musiktheaters, 1986-91; Numerous other magazines and journals; New Grove Dictionary of Opera, 1992; Viking Opera Guide, 1993; International Dictionary of Ballet, 1993; Metropolitan Opera Guide to Recorded Opera, 1993. *Memberships include:* Arts Council of Great Britain, 1979-81, Dance Advisory Panel, 1973-81, Music Advisory Panel, 1974-81; Arts Council Representative on Visiting Arts Unit of GB, 1979-81; Drama and Dance Advisory Committee, British Council, 1973-89; HRH The Duke of Kent's UK Committee for European Music Year 1985, 1982-84; Trustee-Director, International Dance Course for Professional Choreographers and Composers since 1975. *Address:* 76 Skeena Hill, London SW18 5PN, England.

GOOSSENS Sidonie, b. 19 Oct. 1899, Liscard, Cheshire, England. Harpist. m. (1) Hyam Greenbaum 1924, (2) Norman K. Millar 19 Dec. 1945. *Education:* Studied at the Royal College of Music. *Debut:* Played with orchestra 1921. *Career:* Played at Savoy Hill 1924, with the British Broadcasting Company and the 2LO Wireless Orchestra; Appeared on television 1936; Founder member of the BBC Symphony Orchestra 1930; Played with BBC SO until 1980, notably in modern scores conducted by Boulez: subsequent guest appearances; Participation in many first performances; Professor of Harp at the Guildhall School of Music from 1960. *Honours:* Order of the British Empire; FGSM; FRCM; Hon. RAM. *Address:* Woodstck Farm, Gadbrook, Betchworth, Surrey RH3 7AH, England.

GORBENKO Pavel, b. 1956, Moscow, Russia. Violinist. *Education:* Studied at Gnessin Music Institute with Dr Kiselyev. *Career:* Co-founded Amistad Quartet, 1973; Many concerts in former USSR and Russia, with repertoire including works by Haydn, Mozart, Beethoven, Schubert, Brahms, Tchaikovsky, Borodin, Prokofiev, Shostakovich, Bartók, Barber, Bucci, Golovin and Tikhomirov; Recent concert tours to Mexico, Italy and Germany. *Recordings include:* Recitals for a US-Russian company. *Honours include:* Prizewinner (with Amistad Quartet) at Bela Bartók Festival, 1976, and Bucchi Competition, Rome, 1990. *Address:* c/o Sonata (Amistad Quartet), 11 Northgate Street, Glasgow G20 7AA, Scotland.

GORCHAKOVA Galina, b. 1960, Novokuznetsk, Russia. Singer (Soprano). *Education:* Studied at Novosibirsk Academy and Conservatory. *Career:* Appearances with Sverdlovsk Opera, 1988-, as Tatyana, Butterfly, Yaroslavna in Prince Igor, Santuzza, Katerina (Lady Macbeth of Mtsensk), Liu, Militrissa (The Legend of Tsar Saltan), Tamara (The Demon by Rubinstein), and Clara in Prokofiev's The Duenna; Guest appearances elsewhere in Russia, notably as the Trovatore Leonora, Yaroslavna and Lisa in The Queen of Spades at Maryinsky Theatre; Sang Renata in The Fiery Angel by Prokofiev at 1991 Promenade Concerts (UK debut), at St Petersburg, and at Covent Garden (UK stage premiere of the opera in the original Russian), 1992; Sang Natalya in concert performance of Tchaikovsky's The Oprichnik, Edinburgh, 1992, Renata at the Metropolitan, New York. *Honours include:* Prizewinner, Mussorgsky and Glinka Competitions. *Address:* c/o Royal Opera House, Covent Garden, London WC2, England.

GORDIEJUK Marian Stanislaw Wlodzimierz, b. 9 Feb 1954, Bydgoszcz, Poland. Composer; Music Theory Lecturer; Music Journalist; Musicologist. m. 2 Jul 1977, 1 son, 2 daughters. *Education:* State College of Music, Lodz, Pedagogic studies with Assistant Professor Antoni Kedra, 1976; Studies in Music Theory under Professor Franciszek Wesolowski, 1977; Studies in conducting vocal-instrumental groups with Professor Zygmunt Gzella, 1978; Studies in Composition, with Professor Jerzy Bauer, 1979. *Compositions include:* Suite, Birds, for two transverse flutes (Lodz) 1976, published: Edition Agencja Autorska Warszawa, 1986, Contemporary Polish Music, Series of Chamber Music Compositions; Games, for flute and harp (Gdansk) 1987, recorded: Polskie Radio, Gdansk, 1987; Children's Quart Miniature for Oboe or Flute and Piano (Lodz) 1987, recorded: Telewizja Polska, Lodz, 1987; String Quartet (with amplifier) Gdansk, 1991. *Contributions to:* Reviews of Concerts at Filharmonia Pomorska im. T. J. Paderewskiego in Bydgoszcz published in Ilustrowany Kurier Polski 1977-78; Discussions of Compositions for Programme Leaflets of Concerts in Filharmonia Pomorska in T J Paderewskiego in Bydgoszcz during 1978-88. *Publication:* Edition Agencja Antorsko, Promocja, Warsaw, 1993. *Hobbies:* Artistic photography; Numismatics; History of Art. *Address:* ul Tczewska 12, 85-382 Bydgoszcz, Poland.

GORDON Alexandra, b. 1945, Dannevirke, New Zealand. Singer (Soprano). *Education:* Studied at London Opera Centre and with Walter Midgley. *Debut:* Sang First Boy in Die Zauberflote and Despina in Cosi fan Tutte for New Zealand Opera, aged 19. *Career:* Sang with Opera for All at Glyndebourne and with Scottish Opera, notably as the Queen of Night and Flotow's Martha, and in The Nightingale by Stravinsky; Many concert appearances and radio broadcasts; Sang Delia in new production of Rossini's Il Viaggio a Reims, Covent Garden, 1992. *Honours include:* Friends of Covent Garden Scholarship, at London Opera Centre. *Address:* c/o Royal Opera House, Covent Garden, London WC2, England.

GORDON David Jamieson, b. 7 Dec 1947, Philadelphia, USA. Concert/Opera Singer (Tenor). m. Barbara Bixby, 14 June 1969. *Education:* College of Wooster; McGill University; Conservatoire de Quebec. *Debut:* Lyric Opera of Chicago, 1973. *Career:* Frequent appearances with North American and European orchestras and opera companies, including Metropolitan Opera, Lyric Opera of Chicago, San Francisco Opera, Hamburg Staatsoper, Boston Symphony, Philadelphia Orchestra, Cleveland Orchestra, Los Angeles Philharmonic; Specialist in music by J S Bach; Also appears regularly as master class teacher and lecturer; Bach Festivals of Bethlehem, Carmel, Oregon and Winter Park (USA) Stuttgart, Tokyo. *Recordings:* Bach Magnificat - R Shaw/Atlantic Symphony; Acis and Galatea, Seattle Symphony; Pulcinella, St Paul Chamber Orchestra; other recordings on Telarc, London Decca, Delos, RCA Red Seal and Nonesuch/Electra. *Hobbies:* Wilderness canoeing; Photography. *Current Management:* Thea Dispeker, Inc, 59 East 54 Street, New York, NY 10022, USA. *Address:* PO Box 577, Sunneytown, PA 18084, USA.

GORDON Marjorie, b. New York City, USA. Lyric-Coloratura Soprano; Opera Producer; Teacher. m. Nathan Gordon, 1 son, 1 daughter. *Education:* BA, cum laude, Hunter College; Studied piano & voice. *Debut:* New York City Opera, 1955. *Career:* Performed in all media in USA Canada, South of the Border, Hawaii & Parts of Europe & Israel; Professor of Voice: Duguesne University, Pittsburgh, PA; University of Michigan at Interlocken, MICH; Michigan State University in East Lansing; Wayne State University, Detroit; Special Education Consultant, Detroit Grand Opera Association; General Director and Founder: Detroit Opera Theatre, 1960-62; Piccolo Opera Company, 1962-. *Recordings:* Shadows of the Heart. *Publications:* Opera Study Guide. *Contributions to:* various articles. *Hobbies:* Reading; Handicrafts; Swimming; Sketching. *Current Management:* Lee Jon Associates. *Address:* 18662 Fairfield Ave., Detroit, MI 48221, USA.

GORDON Peter, b. 20 June 1951, New York, USA. Composer; Saxophonist. *Education:* Studied at the University of California, San Diego, and Mills College; Teachers included Robert Ashley, Kenneth Gaburo, Terry Riley and Pauline Oliveros. *Career:* Co-founded the art-rock group Love of Life Orchestra 1977; Performances and recordings in the USA, Europe and Canada; Collaborations with the Italian group Falso Movimento; Co- founded video and music production company Antarctica 1982. *Honours include:* Obie award for music to Otello, 1985. *Recordings:* Albums of his own music; Albums as saxophonist and clarinettist playing music by various groups. *Compositions include:* The Birth of a Poet, text by Kathy Acker; The Return of the Native, after Hardy; Shoptalk, collage based on talk by eight composers; Frozen Moments of Passion for saxophone, speech fragments and tape; Otello, mixed media work based on Shakespeare; Collaboration with Robert Ashley on Perfect Lives (Private Parts). *Address:* c/o ASCAP, ASCAP Building, One Lincoln Plaza, New York, NY 10023, USA.

GORDON Priscilla Ann, b. 2 Jan. 1938, Martinsville, Virginia, USA. Singer (Soprano). m. Alberto Figols, 12 Sept. 1962. 1 son, 2 daughters. *Education:* Madison College, Harrisonburg, Virginia; BM, New England Conservatory of Music, Boston, Massachusetts, 1960; Scuola Basiola, Milan, Italy; Nadia Boulanger, Paris, France. *Debut:* At age 5. *Career:* Performances at Metropolitan Opera, State Theatre, Gran teatro del Liceo, Barcelona, Opera Houses of Toulouse, France, Geneva, Switzerland; San Jose, Costa Rica; Amsterdam, The Netherlands; Toured internationally with Touring Concert Opera Company; Boston Symphony Orchestra. *Recordings include:* Numerous recordings sung at live performances, including opera; operetta; popular; oratorio; sacred music as well as French, German and English concert songs. Recuerdos de Navidad, Arias and Duets from Spanish Opera and Zarzuela; Beethoven's Ninth Symphony, with Boston Symphony Orchestra. *Contributions to:* Numerous newspapers and magazines. *Hobbies:* Travel; Taking care of 15 acre estate. *Address:* c/o Ramon Alsina, 228 E 80th Street, New York, NY 10021, USA.

GORDON Stewart Lynell, b. 28 Aug. 1930, Olathe,

Kansas, USA. Pianist; Composer; Teacher; Adminsitrator. *Education:* DMA, Eastman School of Music, University of Rochester, 1965. *Career:* Tour of USA, Canada, Europe and the Middle East, 1950s and 1960s; University of Maryland Faculty, 1960-85, Chair, Piano Division, 1965-78, Chair, Department of Music, 1979-85; Founded Maryland Piano Festival, 1971 and acted as its Director 1971- 78 and 1982-85; Vice President for Academic Affairs and Provost, Queens College, City University of New York, 1985-88; Professor of Music, University of Southern California, Los Angeles, 1988-; Adjudicator of Gina Bachauer Competition 1975 and 1979; Young Keyboard Aritsts 1983 and 1985; Continues to teach and in concert activity; Artistic Director of Music Festival, Savannah Onstaga, (a festival in Savvanah, Georgia) 1990-92. *Compositions:* Music and lyrics composed for Shows produced, Runaway, 1978; Aunt Polly, 1981; Sweet Mississippi, 1982; Hello, I Love You, 1982. *Recordings:* Schubert Sonata Op 143, Schumann Sonata Op 11; Schubert-German Dances, all on Washington Records; Piano Favorites (Beethoven Op 10 no 2; Rachmaninoff; Debussy; Falla). Refirmation Records. *Publications:* Co-Author of The Well-Tempered Keyboard Teacher, 1990. *Address:* School of Music, University of Southern California, University Park, Los Angeles, CA 90089, USA.

GORECKI Henryk Mikolaj, b. 6 Dec. 1933, Czernica, near Rybnik, Poland. Composer. m. Jadwiga Gorecki, 1959. 2 children. *Education:* Composition, Katowice State Higher School of Music, under B Szabelski. *Career:* Docent, Faculty of Composition, State Higher School 1975-79, Extraordinary Professor 1977-, State Higher School of Music, Katowice. *Compositions:* Symphony No.1, for strings and percussion, 1959; Scontri for orchestra, 1960; Concerto for 5 Instruments and String Quartet, 1957; Genesis for instrumental ensemble and soprano, 1963; Cantata for organ, 1968; Canticum Graduum for orchestra, 1989; Ad matrem for soprano, chorus and orchestra, 1971; Symphony No.2 Copernican, 1972, No.3 Lamentation Songs, 1976; Beatus Vir for baritone, chorus and orchestra, 1979; Harpsichord Concerto, 1980; Lullabies and Dances for violin and piano, 1982; O Domina Noztra for soprano and organ, 1985/90; Already it is Dusk, String Quartet, 1988; Good Night, for soprano and ensemble, 1990. *Honours:* 1st Prize, Young Composers Competition, Warsaw for Monologhi, 1960; 1st Prize, Parish Youth Biennale, for 1st symphony, 1961; Prize, UNESCO International Tribune for Composers for Refrain, 1967; for Ad Matrem, 1973; 1st prize, Composers Competition, Szczecin for Kantata, 1968; Prize, Union of Polish Composers, 1970; prize, Committee for Polish Radio & TV, 1974; Prize, Minister of Culture & Arts, 1965, 1969, 1973; State Prize 1st Class for Ad Matrem & Nicolaus Copernicus Symphony, 1978. *Membership:* Council of Higher Artistic Education, Ministry of Culture & Arts. *Address:* U1 Feliksa Kona 4 m.1, 40-133 Katowice, Poland.

GOREN Eli, b. 23 Jan. 1923, Vienna, Austria. Violinist; College Professor. m. Doreen Stanfield. *Education:* Studied in Vienna and at the Jerusalem Conservatory; Further study with Max Rostal in London. *Career:* Leader of the Jerusalem Symphony Orchestra 1947-50; London Mozart Players 1953-59; Melos Ensemble 1952-57; Leader of the Allegri String Quartet 1953-68, co-leader of the BBC Symphony Orchestra 1968-77; Has given early performances of music by Tal, Maconchy and Seiber; Professor of Violin and Chamber Music at the Guildhall School of Music and Drama from 1961; Member of jury on international competitions. *Address:* c/o Guildhall School of Music and Drama, Barbican, London EC2, England.

GORNE Matthias, b. 1966, Chemnitz, Germany. Singer (Baritone). *Education:* Studied in Leipzig from 1985, then with Fischer-Dieskau and Elisabeth Schwarzkopf. *Career:* Performed with the children's choir at Chemnitz Opera; Sang in Bach's St Matthew Passion under Kurt Masur, Leipzig, 1990; Appearances with Hanns Martin Schneidt and Munich Bach Choir, and with NDR Symphony Orchestra Hamburg; Further engagements under Horst Stein, with Bamberg

Symphony and in Hindemith's Requiem under Wolfgang Sawallisch; Concerts at Leipzig Gewandhaus under Helmuth Rilling and in Amsterdam and Paris; Lieder recitals with pianist Eric Schneider; Sang title role in Henze's Prinz von Homburg, Cologne, 1992, Marcello in La Bohème at Komische Oper Berlin, 1993; Broadcasts with Hessischer Rundfunk, RIAS Berlin, Sender Freies Berlin. *Address:* c/o IMG Artists, Media House, 3 Burlington Lane, Chiswick, London W4 2TH, England.

GOROKHOVSKAYA Yevgena, b. 1944, Baku, Russia. Singer (Mezzo- soprano). *Education:* Studied at Leningrad Conservatory. *Debut:* Maly Theatre, Leningrad, as Lehl in The Snow Maiden by Rimsky-Korsakov, 1969. *Career:* Member, Maryinsky Opera Leningrad (now St Petersburg), 1976-; Roles have included Lubasha in The Tsar's Bride by Rimsky, Eboli (Don Carlos) and Azucena; Guest appearances, Germany, Rumania, Spain, France, Greece, USA, Switzerland, Czechoslovakia; On tour to UK, 1991, sang Mme Larina in Eugene Onegin at Birmingham and Marfa in Khovanshchina at Edinburgh Festival. *Recordings:* Several albums. *Address:* c/o Maryinsky Opera and Ballet Theatre, St Petersburg, Russia, CIS.

GORR Rita, b. 18 Feb. 1926, Zelzaete, Belgium. Singer (Mezzo-Soprano). *Education:* Studied in Ghent and at the Brussels Conservatory. *Debut:* Antwerp 1949, as Fricka in Die Walküre; Strasbourg Opera 1949-52, as Orpheus, Amneris and Carmen; Paris Opéra-Comique and Opéra debuts 1952, as Charlotte (Werther) and as Magdalene in Die Meistersinger; Bayreuth Festival 1958, as Ortrud and Fricka; La Scala Milan 1960, as Kundry; Covent Garden 1959-71, debut as Amneris; Edinburgh Festival 1961 in Iphigénie en Tauride, with the Covent Garden company; Metropolitan Opera from 1962, as Amneris, Eboli, Santuzza, Azucena and Dalila; London Coliseum 1969, in a concert performance of Roussel's Padmavati (British premiere); Other roles include Margared (Le Roi d'Ys), Massenet's Herodiade, the title role in Medée by Cherubini and Didon in Les Troyens by Berlioz; Sang the Mother in Louise by Charpentier at Brussels, 1990; First Prioress in Dialogues des Carmélites at Lyon, 1990 followed by Herodias in Salome. *Recordings:* Pelléas et Mélisande (Philips); Dialogues des Carmélites, Iphigénie en Tauride (EMI), Aida, Lohengrin (RCA); Louise by Charpentier (Erato). *Honours include:* Winner, Competition at Verviers, 1946; Winner, Lausanne International Singing Competition, 1952. 21. *Address:* c/o Opéra de Lyon, 9 Quai Jen Moulin, F-69001 Lyon, France.

GORRARA Riccardo (Richard), b. 29 May 1964, Metz, France. Classical Guitarist; Lutenist; Conductor. *Education:* Studied science, general art, Italy and England; Graduated, science diploma, London; Studied music, major colleges, London including Guildhall School of Music; Diploma, Royal Academy of Music; Studied, Paris Music College. *Debut:* Genoa Cathedral, Italy. *Career:* Appeared in most European halls and festivals, Milan, Rome, Turin, London, Paris, Madrid. Paris Festival, Edinburgh Festival. *Compositions:* Varied; Music for guitar and lute from 15th Century to present, including Dowland, Frescobaldi, Ferrabasco, Couperin, Weiss, Bach, Sor, etc. *Recordings:* Various major recordings for guitar and lute, particularly works from 15th Century to 20th Century rarely played; 7 Gramophone recordings, also for radio broadcasting; Various national radio stations in Italy, Denmark, Switzerland. *Contributions to:* Various reviews for Guitar and lute method, technique, interpretation, for Italian guitar and music magazines. *Honours:* 2 certificates with merit, guitar, Royal Academy of Music, 1984. *Memberships:* Royal Philharmonic Society; National Early Music Association; Lute Society; Dutch Lute Society; Brussels Philharmonique Society. *Address:* PO Box 195, London WC1H 8NA, England.

GORZYNSKA Barbara, b. 4 Dec. 1953, Cmielow, Poland. Violinist. m. Ryszard Rasinski, 5 June 1982. 1 son. *Education:* MA (honours), Lodz Academy of Music, 1977. *Debut:* Played the Mendelssohn Concerto with the Great Symphony Orchestra of Polish Radio, 1969. *Career:* Solo appearances with London Philharmonic Orchestra, Royal Philharmonic Orchestra, Dresden Staatskapelle, Warsaw Philharmonic Orchestra; London debut at the Festival Hall, 1981, with the London Philharmonic followed by concerts with the Royal Philharmonic and the English Chamber Orchestra;; Tour of Britain with the Warsaw Philharmonic, 1987; Further engagements in France, Mexico, the USSR and Czechoslovakia; Professor of violin at the Lodz Academy of Music. *Recordings:* Studio recordings for Polish Radio & TV, Westdeutscher Rundfunk and the BBC. Gramophone recordings for Le Chant Du Monde and Wifon labels. *Honours:* First prize, Carl Flesch International Violin Competition, London, 1980; First Prize and the Henryk Szeryng Special Prize, Zagreb International Competition, 1977. *Hobbies:* Film; Theatre. *Current Management:* Christopher Tennant Artists' Management, London. *Address:* Sienkiewicza 101-109 m.48, 90-301 Lodz, Poland.

GOSMAN Lazar, b. 27 May 1926, Kiev, USSR. Violinist; Conductor. m. Eugenia Gosman, 16 Apr. 1950. 1 son. *Education:* Central Music School, Moscow, 1934-44; Diploma, Honours, Tchaikovsky Conservatory of Music, Moscow, 1945-49. *Career:* Violinist, Leningrad Philharmonic Orchestra; Music Director, Leningrad Chamber Orchestra, 1962-77; Associate Concertmaster, St Louis Symphony, USA, 1977-82; Music Director, Tchaikovsky Chamber Orchestra, formerly Soviet Emigré Orchestra; Music Director, Kammergild Chamber Orchestra; Professor, Violin, State University of New York, Stonybrook. *Recordings:* Over 40 with Leningrad Chamber Orchestra; Two records with Tchaikovsky Chamber Orchestra. *Current Management:* Herbert Barrett Management, New York. *Address:* 3 East Gate Lane, Setauket, NY 11733, USA.

GOSSETT Philip, b. 27 Sept. 1941. Music Professor. m. 2 children. *Education:* BA, Amherst College 1958-61; 1962-63; Columbia University 1961-62; MFA 1963-65; PhD (1970), 1967-68; Princeton University; Research in France and Italy 1965-67. *Career:* Assistant in Instruction, Princeton University 1964-65; Assistant Professor 1968-73; Associate Professor 1973-77; Professor 1977-84; Robert W. Reneker Distinguished Service Professor 1984-; Chairman, Department of Music 1978-84; The University of Chicago; Visiting Associate Professor, Columbia University, Spring 1975; Meadows Visiting Professor, Southern Methodist University, Fall 1980; Radio Programmes for Metropolitan Opera, NY; WFMT, Chicago; Lectures for Metropolitan Opera, Lyric Opera of Chicago, Chicago Symphony Orchestra, Philadelphia Orchestra, Chicago Chamber Choir, Houston Grand Opera, Teatro La Fenice (Venice), Teatro Comunale (Florence), Rossini Opera Festival (Pesaro), Dailey-Thorpe tours, Colleges and Universities; Consultant, National Endowment for Humanities, Illinois Humanities Council; Social Sciences and Humanities Research Council of Canada, various University Presses; Board of Directors, Chicago Theatre; Dean, Division of the Humanities, University of Chicago, 1989-; Gauss Seminars, Princeton University, 1991; Vocal ornamentation and stylistic advisor for various opera houses, including: Metropolitan Opera; Teatro dell'Opera (Rome); Rossini Opera Festival (Pesaro); St Louis Opera Theatre; Chicago, Lyric Opera; and Miami Opera; Fellow, American Academy of Arts and Sciences, 1989-. *Publications include:* Articles in Renaissance Music, Music Theory, Beethoven, Record Notes; Encyclopaedia articles; Articles for Opera News; English National Opera Guides; Programme notes for various organisations including Carnegie Hall, San Francisco Opera, Lincoln Center, Spoleto Festival (Charleston); General Editor, The Works of Giuseppe Verdi; General Editor of Edizione critica delle opere di Gioachino Rossini; Editorial Board, The Journal of The American Musicological Society 1972-78; Anna Bolena and the Maturity of Gaetano Donizetti; Early Romantic Opera, with Charles Rosen, New York 1978-83; Il Barbiere di Siviglia, Facsimile edition, Rome, 1993; Honorary member, Academia Filarmonica di Bologna, 1992; Doctor of Humane Letters, Amherst College, 1993. *Memberships include:* President, American

Musicological Society, 1994-; International Musicological Society; American Institute of Verdi Studies; Society for Textual Scholarship; President, Society for Textual Scholarship, 1993. *Address:* Department of Music, The University of Chicago, 5845 S. Ellis Avenue, Chicago, IL 60637, USA.

GOTSINDER Mikhail, b. 1950, Moscow, Russia. Violinist. *Education:* Studied at Moscow Conservatoire with David Oistrakh. *Career:* Co-founded Amistad Quartet, 1973; Many concerts in former USSR and Russia, with repertoire including works by Haydn, Mozart, Beethoven, Schubert, Brahms, Tchaikovsky, Borodin, Prokofiev, Shostakovich, Bartok, Barber, Bucci, Golovin and Tikhomirov; Recent concert tours to Mexico, Italy and Germany. *Honours include:* Prizewinner (with Amistad Quartet), Bela Bartok Festival, 1976, and Bucchi Competition, Rome, 1990. *Recordings include:* Recitals for a US-Russian company. *Address:* c/o Sonata (Amistad Quartet), 11 Northgate Street, Glasgow G20 7AA, Scotland.

GOTTLIEB Gordon, b. 23 Oct. 1948, Brooklyn, New York, USA. Percussionist; Conductor; Composer. *Education:* Graduate, High School of Performing Arts, 1966; BM 1970, MS 1971, Juilliard School of Music; Timpani and Percussion, Saul Goodman, 1966-71; Total Musicianship, James Wimer, 1961-71. *Career:* Extensive performing with New York Philharmonic, including solo appearances in 1974 and 1986; Commissioning and performing new works for piano and percussion with brother, Jay; active in contemporary music and has played with Contemporary Chamber Ensemble, Speculum Musicae, The Juilliard Ensemble, the group for Contemporary Music, etc; As Conductor performed the New York premiere of Vesalii Icones by Peter Maxwell Davies and made his Carnegie Hall debut conducting William Walton's Facade with Anna Russell narrating, 1981; In 1986 conducted Histoire du Soldât of Stravinsky with L'Ensemble and Shaker Loops of John Adams at the Santa Fe Chamber Musical Festival; In 1984 became first American to play with an escola de samba in Carnival parade in Rio de Janeiro. *Compositions:* Graines gemellaires (improvisation 1); Traversees (improvisation 2), Saudades do Brasil. *Recordings:* Bartok for 2 pianos and percussion, Histoire Du Soldat, I Stravinsky, Music Masters Records, 1993-. *Hobbies:* Scuba diving; Underwater Photography. *Address:* 29 W 17th Street, 8th Floor, New York, NY 10011, USA.

GOTTLIEB Jack S., b. 12 Oct. 1930, New Rochelle, New York, USA. Composer. *Education:* Studied at Queens College, Brandeis University, the University of Illinois and the Berkshire Music Center; Teachers included Karol Rathaus, Irving Fine, Aaron Copland and Boris Blacher. *Career:* Assistant to Bernstein at the New York Philharmonic, 1958-66; Music Director at Temple Israel, St Louis, 1970-73; Composer-in-residence then assistant professor at Hebrew Union College, New York, 1973; Publications director at Amberson Enterprises from 1977. *Compositions include:* String Quartet 1954; Tea Party, opera 1955; Kids' Calls for chorus and piano 1957; Piano Sonata 1960; In Memory of ..... for chorus and organ 1960; Wind Quintet 1961; Love Songs for Sabbath 1965; Articles of Faith for orchestra and tape 1965; Shout for Joy 1967; The Silent Flickers for piano four hands 1968; New Year's Service for Young People 1970; Sharing the Prophets for solo voices, chorus and ensemble 1975; The Song of Songs, which is Solomon's, opera 1976; Four Affirmatuons for baritone, chorus and brass sextet or organ 1976; Psalmistry 1979; The Movie Opera: a Music Drama for Torch Singer and a Chorus of People in her Life. *Honours include:* Awards from Brown and Ohio Universities; National Federation of Music Clubs and NEA awards. *Address:* c/o ASCAP, ASCAP Building, One Lincoln Plaza, New York, NY 10023, USA.

GOTTLIEB Jay Mitchell, b. 23 Oct. 1952, New York, USA. Pianist; Composer. *Education:* BA, Hunter College, 1970; MA, Harvard University, 1972; Chatham Square Music School, NY; Conservatoire Americain de Fontainebleau, France with Nadia Boulanger; Festivals of Tanglewood and Darmstadt with Messiaen, Loriod, Ligeti, Kontarsky. *Career:* Recitals in New York: Alice Tully Hall, Merkin Hall, Carnegie Recital Hall, Third Street Settlement, Cooper Union, Radios WQXR, WNYC, New York University, Theâtre des Champs-Elysées, Paris, Alte Oper, Frankfurt; Soloist with Boston Symphony, Orchestra Della Radiotelevisione in Italy, Nouvel Orchestre Philharmonique, Paris, L'Orchestre Philharmonique d'Europe, Paris, L'Orchestre du Rhin, Geneva and Radio & TV in New York, Boston, Washington, Paris, Switzerland, Frankfurt, Cologne, Rome; Festivals of Berlin, Rome, Milan, Paris, Almeida, Aldeburgh, Musica in Strassburg, Avignon, Toulouse, Frankfurt, Amsterdam. *Compositions:* Synchronisms for Two Percussionists and Tape; Sonata for Violin and Piano; Improvisations for Piano & Percussion; Essay for Orchestra; Soundtrack for film, La Discrète. *Recordings:* Trios Contes de l'Honorable Fleur; Lys de Madrigaux; Piano & Percussion-Jay and Gordon Gottlieb; Appello of Barbara Kolb; Harawi of Messiaen; Figure of Michèle Reverdy; La Discrète, soundtrack. *Contributions to:* Professional journals; Jury member for advanced piano examinations at Paris Conservatory; Piano Faculty at conservatoire Américain in Fontainebleau; Master Classes at Schola Cantorum, Paris. *Hobbies:* Travel; Theatre; Cinema; Reading. *Address:* 484 West 43rd Street Apt 3M, New York, NY 10036, USA.

GOTTLIEB Peter, b. 18 Sept. 1930, Brno, Czechoslovakia. Singer (Baritone). *Education:* Studied in Rio de Janeiro and in Florence with Raoul Frazzi. *Career:* Sang at first in Italy, Belgium and North America; Paris Opéra in the 1962 premiere of L'Opéra d'Aran by Becaud and as Don Giovanni, Figaro, Papageno, Scarpia, and Wozzeck 1985; Glyndebourne Festival 1966-79, as Albert in Werther, Barber in the schweigsame Frau, Mercurio in the first modern performance of Cavalli's La Calisto 1970, and Zastrow in The Rising of the Moon by Nicholas Maw; Théâtre de la Monnaie Brussels 1983, in the premiere of La Passion de Gilles by Boesmans; Opéra du Rhin, Strasbourg, in the 1984 premiere of H.H. Ulysses by Jean Prodromides; Other roles include Iago, Don Carlos in La Forza del Destino and the Count in Capriccio; Professor at the Paris Conservatoire from 1982. *Recordings include:* La Calisto (Decca); Opera D'Aran (Pathe); La Passion de Gilles (Ricercare); H.H. Ulysses (Harmonia Mundi); La Cocarde de Mimi Pinson (Decca); La Traviata (Sofca). *Address:* Conservatoire National, 361 rue Lecourbe, 75015 Paris, France.

GÖTZ Werner, b. 7 Dec. 1934, Berlin, Germany. Singer (Tenor). *Education:* Studied with Friedrick Wilcke and W. Kelch in Berlin. *Debut:* Oldenburg 1967, as Alvaro in La Forza del Destino. *Career:* Sang in Dusseldorf, Karlsruhe, Munich, Stuttgart and Hamburg; Roles include Wagner's Erik, Lohengrin and Parsifal, Mozart's Tamino, Lionel in Martha by Flotow and parts in operas by Puccini, Janácek and Verdi; Further engagements in London, Zurich, Lodz, Barcelona, Amsterdam and Frankfurt; Munich Opera 1978, in the premiere of Lear by Reimann. *Recordings include:* Lear (Deutsche Grammophon); Melot in Tristan und Isolde; Eine Florentinische Tragödie by Zemlinsky (Fonit-Cetra). *Address:* c/o Bayerische Staatsoper, Postfach 745, D-8000 Munich 1, Germany.

GOUGH John, b. 28 Jan. 1957, Chester, England. Pianist; Teacher. *Education:* RNCM Junior School, 1972-75; RNCM, 1975-80; GMus, RNCM (Hons); Professional Performance Diploma with Distinction, ARCM. *Debut:* BBC, 1981; Wigmore Hall, 1982; Purcell Room, 1984. *Career:* Recitals and concerts throughout England; Concertos with Royal Liverpool Philharmonic, Northern Chamber Orchestra; Several BBC Broadcasts; Appearances at Bowdon and Chester Festivals. *Honour:* Winner, John Ireland Centenary Piano Competition at Wigmore Hall, 1979. *Address:* 1 Makepeace Close, Vicars Cross, Chester, Cheshire CH3 5LU, England.

GOULD Morton, b. 10 Dec. 1913, Richmond Hill, New York, USA. Composer; Conductor. m., 4 children.

Education: Piano lessons with Joseph Kardos and Abby Whiteside; Studied composition with Vincent Jones, New York University. *Career:* Began career as a pianist; Active as a composer-conductor for radio from 1934; Guest Conductor with many US orchestras; Van Cliburn International Piano Competition, 1993; Commission, Ghost Waltzes for solo piano, Pittsbough Symphony Association for the Pittsburgh Youth Orchestra Commission, 1993, The Jogger and the Dinosaur for Rapper and Orchestra. *Compositions:* Stage: Musicals: Billion Dollar Baby, 1945; Arms and the Girl, 1950; Cantata-musical: Something to Do, 1976; Ballets: Interplay, 1945; Fall River Legend, 1947; Fiesta, 1957; Clarinade, 1964; I'm Old Fashioned, 1983; Orchestral: 3 American Symphonettes, 1933, 1935, 1937; Piano Concerto, 1937; Violin Concerto, 1938; Stephen Foster Gallery, 1940; Latin-American Symphonette, 1941; Spirituals, 1941; Lincoln Legend, 1942; American Salute, 1943; Symphony No 1, 1943; Viola Concerto, 1943; Symphony on Marching Tunes, 1944; Concerto for Orchestra, 1945; Harvest, 1945; Minstrel Show, 1946; Symphony No 3, 1947, revised 1948; Serenade of Carols, 1949; Tap Dance Concerto, 1952; Dance Variations for 2 Pianos and Orchestra, 1953; Inventions for 4 Pianos, Brass, and Percussion, 1953; Showpiece, 1954; Jekyll and Hyde Variations, 1957; Dialogues for Piano and Strings, 1958; Festive Music, 1965; Columbia: Broadsides, 1967; Venice for Double Orchestra and Brass Bands, 1967; Vivaldi Gallery, 1968; Soundings, 1969; Troubador Music for 4 Guitars and Orchestra, 1969; American Ballads, 1976; Symphony of Spirituals, 1976; Cheers!, 1979; Burchfield Gallery, 1981; Housewarming, 1982; Apple Waltzes, 1983; Flourishes and Galop, 1983; Flute Concerto, 1984; Classical Variations on Colonial Themes, 1986; Chorales and Rags, 1988; Concerto Grosso, 1988; Film and television scores; Band: Symphony, 1952; Centennial Symphony, 1983; Chamber: Concerto Concertante for Violin, Woodwind Quintet, and Piano, 1983; Piano pieces; Choruses. *Recordings:* Ghost Waltzes for piano solo; The Jogger and the Dinosaur; Many compositions recorded. *Honours:* National Arts Award, 1983; American Symphony Orchestra League Gold Baton Award, 1983. *Memberships:* American Academy and Institute of Arts and Letters, 1986-; ASCAP, President, 1986-. *Address:* c/o ASCAP, 1 Lincoln Plaza, New York, NY 10023, USA.

GOY Pierre, b. 29 Nov. 1961, Lausanne, Switzerland. Pianist. *Education:* Conservatoire Lausanne, 1979-82; Ecole Internationale, Piano Lausanne 1982-85. *Debut:* Montreux, 1983. *Career:* Radio Suisse Romande, 1976; Concerto with Orchestra TV Romanian, 1982; Recital Trento, 1984; Recital Roma, 1985; Chamber Music Karlsruhe, Germany, 1986; Solisten Audition, 1987; Festival Piano Roque-d'Antheron, 1987; Bern Concerto 1988; Professor, Lausanne Conservatoire, 1990-. *Honours:* Swiss Competition for Young Musicians, 1976, 1979; Vercelli International Piano Competition, Gold Medal, 1985; University of Maryland USA, William Kapell International Piano Competition, Boucher Memorial Prize, 1988. *Memberships:* European Piano Teachers Association; Swiss Society of Musical Pedagogy; Frank Martin Society. *Hobbies:* Bonzai; Pianoforte. *Address:* Ricercare Case Postale 56, 1820 Montreux 2, Switzerland.

GRADENWITZ Peter Werner Emanuel, b. 24 Jan. 1910, Berlin, Germany. Musicologist. m. (1) Rosi Wolfsohn, 1933, deceased 1965, 1 son, deceased 1963, 1 daughter. (2) Ursula Mayer-Reinach, 1967. *Education:* Studies at Universities of Berlin, Freiburg/Br, Prague and London Polytechnik; PhD, Musicology, German University of Prague; composition studies with Julius Weismann, Joseph Rufer. *Career:* Honorary Professor, University of Freiburg/Br, 1980; Lecturer at European and American Universities; Lecturer, Musicology, Tel Aviv University, 1968-76, Freiburg/Br, 1980-; Founder, Editor-Director of Israeli Music Publications Ltd, 1949-82; *Compositions:* Editor of newly discovered works by Salomone Rossi, Johann Stamitz, Karl Stamitz, Anton Stamitz, Franz Schubert; Symphony and Chamber Music. *Publications include:* Johann Stamitz Das Leben, 1936; Johann Stamitz, Life and Works, 2 vols 1984;

The Music of Israel, 1949; Music and Musicians in Israel, 1978; Leonard Bernstein, Infinite Variety of a Musician, 1984; Third edition, 1992, published in five languages; Arnold Schoenberg's 4th String Quartet, 1986; Kleine Kulturgeschichte der Klaviermusik, 1986; editor, Yiddish Love Songs, 1988. *Honours:* International Critics' Prize, Salzburg, 1971; Golden Insignia of Salzburg, 1978; Frank Pelleg Memorial prize, Haifa, 1988. *Memberships:* International Musicological Society; Israeli Section of International Music Council. *Hobby:* Mountain tours. *Address:* PO Box 6011, Tel Aviv 61060, Israel.

GRAEBNER Eric Hans, b. 8 Jan. 1943, Berrington, England. Lecturer; Pianist; Composer; Conductor. *Education:* MA, Cambridge University; PhD, York University; ARCO. *Career:* Lecturer in Music, University of Southampton, 1968-; Visiting Fellow, Princeton, New Jersey, USA, 1973, 1981-82, 1983; Assistant Professor, William Paterson College, New Jersey, 1981-82. *Compositions:* Thalia, 1975; Between Words, 1976; String Quartet No 1, 1979; String Quartet, No 2, 1984; 4 Songs and an Aria, 1980; Aspects of 3 Tetrachords, Quintet, 1981; The Winter Palace, 1982; La mer retrouvée, 1985-86; 3rd Quartet, 1985; Dollbreaker, 1987; Trapeze Act, 1988; Berenice, 1990-91. *Publications:* New Berlioz Edition Volume 4; Some Aspects of Rhythm in Berlioz, 1971-72. *Contributions to:* Soundings; Perspectives of New Music; In Theory Only; Music Analysis. *Honours:* Fulbright-Hayes Fellowship, 1973; Dio Award, 1977; Fellow, Salzburg Seminar of American Studies, 1976. *Membership:* EMAS (Sonic Arts Network), PRS. *Current Management:* STR Music Marketing. *Address:* Music Department, University of Southampton, Highfield, Southampton, Hampshire, England.

GRAEME Peter, b. 17 Apr. 1921, Petersfield, England. Oboist. nm. Inge Anderl, 14 June 1952. 1 son, 3 daughters. *Education:* Royal College of Music. *Career:* LPO, 1938-42; Military Service, 1942-46, then Freelance Oboist; 1st Oboe in various orchestras including: Kalmar Orchestra; Haydn Orchestra; Boyd Neel Orchestral; Philomusica; Goldsborough Orchestra; English Chamber Orchestra; Melos Ensemble of London; Oboe Professor, Royal College of Music, 1949-71, 1991; Royal Northern College of Music, 1974-90; Teaching and Adjudicating with occasional free-lance playing, currently. *Recordings:* Various with: Kalmar Orchestra, Melos Ensemble of London, English Chamber Orchestra. *Honours:* Hon ARCM, 1959; FRCM, 1979; FRNCM, 1989. *Memberships:* MU. *Address:* Grenovic, 4 French Mill Lane, Shaftesbury, Dorset SP7 8EU, England.

GRAF Hans, b. 16 Mar 1928, Vienna, Austria. Pianist; Professor. m. Carmen Graf-Adnet, 27 Jan 1953, 2 daughters. *Education:* Architecture studies, Vienna; Vienna Music Academy with Bruno Seidlhofer. *Debut:* Schubert-Saal, Vienna, Dec 1950. *Career:* Concerts in Europe, North, South and Latin America, Near East, Japan, Korea; Appearances with major orchestras and chamber music ensembles; Master courses in USA, Japan, Americas, Europe; Jury Member, almost all major competitions; Founded Music School, Rio de Janeiro; Professor, Hochschule für Musik, Vienna; TV and radio appearances. *Honours:* Ehrenzeichen, Austrian, Polish and Brazilian Governments; Prizes at international piano competitions. *Membership:* Piano Teachers Association. *Hobbies:* Bridge; Puzzles; Fencing. *Address:* Laudongasse 44/8, 1080 Vienna, Austria.

GRAF Hans, b. 15 Feb 1949, Linz, Austria. Conductor. *Education:* Studied at the Bruckner Conservatory of Linz and the Academy of Music at Graz; Further study with Franco Ferrara, Sergiu Celibidache and Arvid Yansons. *Career:* Director of the Iraqi National Symphony Orchestra, 1975; Vienna Staatsoper debut 1977, conducted new production of Petrushka, 1981; Munich and Vienna Festivals, 1980; In 1984 conducted Rigoletto at the Maggio Musicale Florence and appeared at the Prague Spring, Bregenz, Helsinki and Salzburg Festivals; Paris Opera 1984, with Die Entführung and Il Barbiere di Siviglia; Music Director of the Mozarteum Orchestra of Salzburg, 1984; Guest appearances with the Vienna Symphony; Vienna, Leningrad, Dresden, Helsinki and Liverpool Philharmonic Orchestras; Leipzig Gewandhaus, RAI Symphony of Milan and the ORF (Austria) Symphony; Bournemouth Symphony Orchestra; Has led productions of Der Ring des Nibelungen at the Grossesfestspielhaus, Salzburg; Fidelio at La Fenice, Venice; Così fan Tutte at the Deutsche Oper Berlin; Otello at the Salzburger Kulturtage; Conducted Die Zauberflöte at the 1986 Orange Festival at Tokyo with the Vienna Staatsoper 1989 and the 1992 Savonlinna Festival; production of Ariande auf Naxos with John Cox for TV, 1994. *Honours include:* First prize, Karl Böhm Conductors Competition, Salzburg, 1979. *Recordings include:* Songs, with Brigitte Fassbaender; Zemlinsky's Es war Einmal; Complete Symphonies of Mozart, with the Mozarteum Orchestra of Salzburg. *Address:* Unit 2, 39 Tadema Road, London SW10 0PY, England.

GRAF Peter-Lukas, b. 5 Jan 1929, Zurich, Switzerland. Flautist; Conductor. *Education:* Studied at the Paris Conservatoire with Marcel Moyse (flute) and Eugene Bigot (conducting). *Career:* First flautist with the Winterthur Orchestra, 1951-57; Conductor at the Lucerne State Theatre 1961-66; Played in the Lucerne Festival Orchestra 1957- and toured as soloist with Edwin Fischer and Gunther Ramin; Performances with the English Chamber Orchestra, the Academy of St Martin in the Fields and the Lucerne Festival Strings; As soloist and conductor, tours of Europe, South America, Australia, Japan and Israel; Teacher at the Basle Conservatory 1973-. *Recordings include:* Spohr Concertante for violin, harp and orchestra; Bach A minor Triple Concerto and Saint-Saens A minor Concerto (English Chamber Orchestra); Mozart Flute Concertos and Concerto K299 (Lausanne Chamber Orchestra); Swiss music with Orchestra della Radio Svizzera, and the Zurich Tonhalle. *Honours include:* First prizes in flute and conducting, Paris Conservatoire, 1950, 1951; Winner, International ARD Competition, 1953; Bablock Prize, Harriet Cohen International Music Award, London, 1958.

GRAF Uta, b. 5 Jan. 1915, Karlsruhe, Germany. Singer (Soprano). *Education:* Studied with Heinrich Schlusnus and Anna Bahr- Mildenburg. *Career:* From 1940 sang in Dortmund, Dresden, Stuttgart, Aachen and Cologne; US debut San Antonio 1948, as Sophie in Der Rosenkavalier; Sang in opera at San Francisco and Toronto and made concert tour of South America; US concerts with Leopold Stokowski; Covent Garden 1950-51, as Sophie and Pamina, conducted by Kleiber, and Marcellina in Fidelio; Munich Staatsoper 1954; Holland Festival 1955-58, notably in the 1956 premiere of Sampiero Corso by Tomasi; Teacher at the Peabody Conservatory 1958-66, Manhattan School of Music from 1964. *Recordings:* Don Giovanni; Les Contes d'Hoffmann; Bach B Minor Mass; Soprano Solo in Schoenberg's 2nd String Quartet, with the Juilliard Quartet.

GRAF-ADNET Carmen, b. 23 July 1929, Vitoria, Brazil. Pianist; Professor. m. Hans Graf, 27 Jan 1953, 2 daughters. *Education:* University of Rio de Janeiro; Music Academy , Vienna; Studied with Profs Josef Turczynsky and Bruno Seidlhofer; Master courses with Edwin Fisher and Alfred Cortot; Language studies, English, French, German, Spanish, Italian. *Debut:* Vitoria, Brazil, age 11. *Career:* Concerts in Europe, North and South America; Master courses, Salzburg, Austria and Indiana University, USA; Radio appearances; Soloist with major orchestras; Professor, Hochschule fur Musik, Vienna. *Recordings:* With Vienna Symphony Orchestra under Hans Swarowsky. *Honours:* Prizes at piano competitions, Warsaw and Munich; Officer, Cruzeiro do Sul, Brazilian Government; Villa-Lobos Medal. *Membership:* Piano Teachers Association. *Hobbies:* Bridge; Movies; Crossword puzzles; Travel by car. *Address:* Laudongasse 44/6, 1080 Vienna, Austria.

GRAFFMAN Gary, b. 14 Oct. 1928, New York, USA.

Pianist. m. Naomi Helfman, 1952. *Education:* Curtis Institute of Music under Mme Isabelle Vengerova. *Debut:* with Philadelphia Orchestra, 1947. *Career includes:* Concert tours worldwide; Annual appearances with major orchestras, USA; Teacher, Curtis Institute, Manhattan School of Music, 1980-. *Recordings:* For Columbia, Masterworks, RCA Victor, including concertos of Tchaikovsky, Rachmaninoff, Brahms, Beethoven, Chopin, Prokofiev; Also plays piano left hand repertory. *Publication:* I Really Should Be Practising, autobiography, 1981. *Honour:* Leventritt Award, 1949. *Address:* c/o Harry Beall Management, 119 West 57th Street, New York, NY 10019, USA.

GRAHAM Alasdair, b. 19 Apr 1934, Glasgow, Scotland. Pianist; Professor. *Education:* BMus, Edinburgh University; Performers Diploma, Vienna Hochschule fur Musik; Royal Academy of Music with Peter Katin. *Debut:* Bishopsgate Hall, 1958. *Career:* Soloist with Scottish National Orchestra, London Philharmonic Orchestra, BBC Symphony Orchestra (Proms, 1963), Royal Liverpool Philharmonic, Halle Orchestra, Sydney Symphony Orchestra, Melbourne Symphony Orchestra (Australian tour), 1967; Recitals, BBC, TV, Britain, Turkey, India; As Accompanist with Elisabeth Soderstrom, Josef Suk, John Shirley-Quiz R; Professor, Royal College of Music, London. *Recordings:* Schubert: Sonata in B flat, 8 Ecossaises. *Honours:* Harriet Cohen Commonwealth Medal, 1963; Honorary RCM, 1973. *Membership:* Royal Society of Musicians of Great Britain. *Address:* 184 Cann Hall Road, London E11 3NH, England.

GRAHAM Colin, b. 22 Sept. 1931, Hove, Sussex, England. Stage Director; Librettist; Artistic Director. *Education:* Stowe School, 1946-52; New Covenant School of Ministry, St Louis, 1985-87; Honorary Doctor of Arts, Webster University, 1985; Honorary Dr of Arts, University of Missouri, 1992; Diploma, Royal Academy of Dramatic Art; Private study. *Debut:* Playhouse Theatre, Nottingham, England. *Career:* Artistic Director, Aldeburgh Festival, 1969-82; English Music Theatre, 1976-; Opera Theater of St Louis, 1982-; Director of Productions, English National Opera, Sadler's Wells Opera, 1976-82; Over 350 productions in Opera, TV and Theatre. *Publications:* Opera Libretti; King Arthur (Purcell), 1972; The Golden Vanity (Britten), 1970; The Postman Always Rings Twice (Paulus), 1983; Joruri (Miki), 1985; The Woodlanders (Paulus), 1985; Penny for A Song (Bennett), 1970; Staged the premiere of Corigliano's The Ghosts of Versailles at the Metropolitan, 1991; A Midsummer Night's Dream at St Louis, 1992; Production of Britten's Death in Venice at Covent Garden, 1992. *Contributions to:* Opera Magazine; Musical Times; Opera News, 1992. *Honours:* Prize for Opera Production (Orpheus) Germany, 1977; Winston Churchill Fellowship, 1975. *Memberships:* Equity; Canadian Equity; American Guild of Musical Artists; Ordained Minister, 1988; Arts and Educational Council 1993; Award Personal Achievement in the Arts. *Hobbies:* Weightlifting; Motorcycles; The Bible. *Address:* PO Box 191910, St Louis, MO 63119, USA.

GRAHAM Susan, b. 1960, USA. Singer (Mezzo-soprano). *Education:* Studied at Manhattan School of Music; Texas Tech University. *Career:* Sang Masseenet's Cherubin while a student; Engagements with St Louis Opera as Erika in Vanessa, Charlotte and at Seattle as Stephano in Romeo et Juliette; Season 1989-90 included Chicago Lyric Opera debut as Annius in La Clemenza di Tito, Sonia in Argento's Aspern Papers at Washington, Dorabella and the Composer at Santa Fe; Carnegie Hall debut in Des Knaben Wunderhorn and Bernstein concert in New York; Season 1990-91 as Octavian with San Francisco Symphony, Minerva in Monteverdi's Ulisse with San Francisco Opera, Berlioz' Beatrice at Lyon, Cherubino at Santa Fe; Mozart's C minor Mass under Edo de Waart and with Philadelphia Orchestra under Neville Marriner; Season 1991-92 at Metropolitan as Second Lady, Cherubino, and Tebaldo in Don Carlos; L'Opera de Nice as Cherubino and Les Nuits d'ete in Lyon; Beethoven's 9th in Spain conducted by Marriner; Salzburg Mozart Week,

1993, as Cecilio in Lucio Silla, Easter and Summer Festivals as Meg Page in Falstaff; Season 1993-94 as Massenet's Cherubin and Dorabella at Covent Garden, Ascanio in Les Troyens at the Met, Annius in Tito at San Francisco and 1994 Salzburg Festival; Engaged as Octavian for Welsh National Opera, and Vienna State Opera and Marguerite in La Damnation de Faust for L'Opera de Lyon. *Recordings include:* Falstaff conducted by Solti; La Damnation de Faust conducted by Kent Nagano; Beatrice et Benedict conducted by John Nelson; Stravinsky's Pulcinella. *Honours include:* Winner, Metropolitan Opera National Council Auditions. *Address:* c/o IMG Artists, Media House, 3 Burlington Lane, London W4 2TH, England.

GRAHAM-HALL John, b. 1955, Middlesex, England. Singer (Tenor). *Education:* Studied at King's College, Cambridge and Royal College of Music. *Debut:* Opera North, as Ferrando in Cosi fan Tutte, 1983. *Career:* Has sung Albert Herring at Covent Garden and Glyndebourne, Pedrillo for Kent Opera, Cassio for Welsh National Opera and Don Ottavio for Opera Northern Ireland; Glyndebourne Touring Opera as Britten's Aschenbach, Lysander, Basilio and Ferrando; English National Opera debut as Cyril in Princess Ida, 1992; Engagements at Lyon as Lensky and Frère Massee in Messiaen's St Francois d'Assise, Vancouver as Ferrando, Brussels and Lisbon as Cassio and Antwerp as Achilles in King Priam; Conductors have included Haitink, Janowski, Tate, Rattle and Abbado; Concert career with most British orchestras including Pulcinella with BBC Symphony, 1993; Engaged to sing Bob Boles at 1995 Glyndebourne Festival; *Recordings include:* Carmina Burana, L'Incoronazione di Poppea and A Midsummer Night's Dream. *Address:* c/o IMG Artists, Media House, 3 Burlington Lane, London W4 2TH, England.

GRAHN Ulf (Ake Wilhelm), b. 17 Jan. 1942, Solna, Sweden. Composer. m. Barbro Dahlman, 15 Aug. 1969. 1 son. *Education:* Degree in Violin Pedagogy, SMI, Stockholm, 1968; MM, Catholic University, Washington, DC, USA, 1973; Business Administration, Development Studies, Uppsala University, Sweden, 1986. *Career:* Music Instructor, Stockholm and Lidingo schools, 1964-72; Teaching Assistant, Instructor, Catholic University, Washington, USA, 1972-76; Founder, Music Director, Contemporary Music Forum, 1973-85; Lecturer, Northern Virginia Community College, 1975-79; Lecturer, Associate Professor, George Washington University, 1983-; Founder, Artistic Director, The Aurora Players, 1983-; Artistic and Managing Director, Lake at Siljan Festival, Sweden, 1988; Composer-in-Residence, Charles Ives Center, USA, 1988; Publisher, Owner, Edition NGLANI, 1985-. *Compositions:* Major orchestral works including Symphonies Nos 1 and 2; Concertos for piano, guitar, double bass; Chamber music; Choral music; Solo works for guitar, piano, violin. *Recordings:* Cinq Preludes; Snapshots; Sonata for piano with flute and percussion; In the Shade, Caprice; Sonata for piano. *Contributions to:* Articles; Tonfallet; Musik Revy and Ord och Ton; Reviews, Europe. *Honours:* Stockholm International Organ Days, 1973; League International Society for Contemporary Music International Piano Competition, 1976. *Memberships:* STIM Sweden; Society of Swedish Composers. *Hobby:* Photography. *Address:* PO Box 5684, Takoma Park, MD 20913-5684, USA.

GRANAT Juan Wolfgang, b. 29 Nov. 1918, Karlsruhe, Baden, West Germany. Viola Player; Member of The Philadelphia Orchestra. *Education:* High School of Education, Munich; Studied under Rudolf Zwinkel, grandfather; Sevcik-Marteau Master School, Munich with Herma Studeny; with Alexander Petschnikoff, Buenos Aires. *Career:* Member, Jewish Kulturbund Orchestra, Frankfurt/Main, 1937-38; Violist of The Kleinberg Quartet, 1937-38; Solo Violist with Swiss Italian Broadcasting Symphony, Monteceneri, 1939-40; Violist with Monteceneri String Quartet, Lugano, Switzerland, 1939-40; Emigrated to Argentina, 1940; Distinguished Recital career, Soloist in the first Latin American performance of William Walton's Viola

Concerto with The Cordoba Symphony, Teodoro Fuchs conductor, 1945; Solo Violist with The Havana Philharmonic, 1945-53, invited by Erich Kleiber, numerous recitals and first performances, also played with The Cuban Chamber Music Society, Violist; Violist with The Minneapolis Symphony, 1954-56; Violist, The Philadelphia Orchestra, 1956; Solo recital engagements, 1956; Gave the first New York City performance of I Handoshkin's Viola Concerto, 1962; Gave first Washington DC performance of Elizabeth Gould's Viola Sonata, 1970; Debut with The Liberty Bell String Trio, 1984; Inaugurated New Philadelphia orchestra Chamber Music Series, 1985; Instrumental in having abolished compulsary retirement for musicians, 1986/87; Retired, Philadelphia Orchestra since 1991. *Hobbies:* Listening to records and tapes; Reading; Hiking; Swimming; International and exotic foods. *Address:* 4738 Osage Avenue, Philadelphia, PA 19143-1815, USA.

GRANDI Margherita, b. 4 Oct. 1894, Hobart, Tasmania. Singer (Soprano). *Education:* Studied at the Royal College of Music, London, and with Emma Calvé in Paris. *Debut:* Paris Opera-Comique, in Werther. *Career:* Sang the title role in the premiere of Amadis by Massenet (Monte Carlo 1922); Teatro Carcano Milan 1932, as Aida; La Scala Milan 1934 as Elena in Mefistofele; Sang widely in Italy and in Holland during 1930s; Glyndebourne Festival 1939, 1947, 1949, as Lady Macbeth and as Amelia (Un Ballo in Maschera); La Scala 1940, as Maria in the local premiere of Friedenstag by Strauss; Cambridge Theatre London 1947, as Tosca and Donna Anna; Covent Garden in the 1949 premiere of The Olympians by Bliss and as Tosca and the Trovatore Leonora; Retired from stage 1951.

GRANGE Philip Roy, b. 17 Nov. 1956, London, England. Composer. m. Elizabeth Caroline Hemming 1986. *Education:* York University 1976-82; BA 1979, Doctorate in Composition 1984; Dartington Summer School of Music, Composition Class with Peter Maxwell Davies, 1975-81. *Career:* Promenade Concert debut 1983; Fellow in the Creative Arts at Trinity College, Cambridge, 1985-87; Northern Arts Fellow in Composition at Durham University 1988-89; Appointed Lecturer in Composition at Exeter University 1989; Performances of music at most major festivals in Britain, and in Europe and USA. *Compositions:* Cimmerian Nocturne 1979; Sextet 1980; The Kingdom of Bones 1983; La Ville Entière 1984; Variations 1986; Out in the Dark 1986; In Memoriam HK 1986; The Dark Labyrinth 1987; Concerto for Orchestra; Labyrinthine Images 1988; In A Dark Time, 1989; Changing Landscapes, 1990; Focus and Fade, 1992; Lowry Dreamscape, 1992. *Recordings:* La Ville Entière for clarinet and piano (NATO 1180); In Memoriam HK for solo trombone. *Publications:* In Memoriam HK, Comus Publications; All other pieces, Maecenas Music. *Hobbies:* Languages; Linguistics; Literature; Classics. *Current Management:* Maecenas Music, 5 Bushey Close, Old Barn Lane, Kenley, Surrey, CR8 5AU. *Address:* Department of Music, University of Exeter, Knightley, Streatham Drive, Exeter EX4 4PD, England.

GRANT Clifford Scantlebury, b. 11 Sept 1930, Randwick, New South Wales, Australia. Singer (Bass). m. (1) Jeanette Earle, 1 son, 2 daughters, (2) Ruth Anders, 1992. *Education:* Studied at Sydney Conservatorium with Isolde Hill; Melbourne with Annie Portnoj; London with Otakar Kraus. *Debut:* New South Wales Opera Company, as Raimondo in Lucia di Lammermoor, 1952. *Career:* Sang with Sadler's Wells/ English National Opera from 1966, debut as Silva in Ernani; Leading roles in Oedipus Rex, The Mastersingers, Peter Grimes, The Magic Flute, Madame Butterfly, The Barber of Seville, The Ring of the Nibelung, Don Giovanni, The Coronation of Poppea, and Don Carlos; Sang in San Francisco from 1966; Glyndebourne Festival as Nettuno in Il Ritorno d'Ulisse, 1972; Further engagements with Covent Garden Opera, Welsh National Opera and in Europe; Sang in Sydney from 1976, as Nilakantha (Lakme), 1986; Retired, 1990, after singing in Les Huguenots with Australian Opera; Returned to UK, 1992; Returned to stage, May 1993, as Alvise in new production of La Gioconda, Opera North; Many concert appearances. *Recordings:* Don Giovanni; Rigoletto; Esclarmondo; L'Oracolo; Fafner in The Rhinegold and Hunding in The Valkryie, conducted by Reginald Goodall; Bartolo in Le Nozze di Figaro; Il Corsaro; The Apostles by Elgar; Tosca; Les Huguenots. *Hobbies:* Gallery owner; Oil painting; Making scones. *Address:* c/o Australian Opera, Sydney Opera House, Sydney, NSW, Australia.

GRAUBART Michael, b. 26 Nov 1930, Vienna, Austria. Composer; Conductor; Lecturer. m. Ellen Barbour, 1962, 1 son, 2 daughters. *Education:* BSc, Physics, University of Manchester, England, 1952; Studied Composition privately with Matyas Seiber, 1953-57; Flute with Geoffrey Gilbert, 1953-56. *Career:* Conductor, Ars Nova Chamber Orchestra, 1960; Conductor, Hampstead Chamber Orchestra, 1962-66; Music Director, Focus Opera Group, 1967-71; Director of Music, Morley College, 1969-91; Adjunct Professor of Music, Syracuse University London Centre, 1989-91; Senior Lecturer, School of Academic Studies, Royal Northern College of Music, Manchester, 1991-. *Compositions:* Quasi una Sonata for piano; Three Bagatelles for cello and piano; Sure I am only of uncertain things for a cappella chorus; Two songs for mezzo-soprano and piano; Concertino da Camera for viola and four woodwings; Declensions for 10 instruments; Metabola for flute, bass clarinet, viola and tape; Four Observations for mezzo-soprano and piano; Quintet for flute, clarinet, viola, cello and vibraphone; Sonato for cello and piano; Sinfonia a 10 for 10 winds; Aria for Orchestra; Untergang for baritone, chorus, wind, piano and percussion; Diptych (The Seed and the Harvest, Broken Mirror) for 4 winds; Scena and Capriccio for piano; Variants and Cadenzas for orchestra; Nightfall for chorus and piano; Elegy for orchestra; Speculum Noctuinum for 9 winds, cello and bass; Diaphony for flute and cor anglais, 1992; Scena II for euphonium, 2 flutes, viola and cello, 1992; Scena IIa for euphonium and piano, 1992; To a Dead Lover for soprano and 7 instruments, 1993; Various choral arrangements. *Publications:* Editions: Music by Pergolesi, Dufay and Josquin. *Contributions to:* Several articles on Leopold Spinner; Articles, reviews and translations in Tempo and Encounter. *Memberships:* Composers' Guild of Great Britain; NATFHE. *Hobbies:* Hill walking; Philosophy and aesthetics; Modern art and architecture. *Address:* 64 Moor End Road, Mellor, Stockport, Cheshire SK6 5PT, England.

GRAULTY John Patrick, b. 3 Dec 1962, Pittsburgh, Pennsylvania, USA. Conductor; Clarinettist. m. Charlotte Frasier, 7 July 1987. *Education:* BMus, Peabody Conservatory, Baltimore; MMus, New England Conservatory, Boston; EdD, College Music Teaching, Columbia University Teachers College. *Appointments:* Clarinettist, US Military Academy Band, West Point, New York, 1986-90; Deputy Commander, Assistant Conductor, US Air Force Academy Band, Colorado, 1990-93; Deputy Commander, Assistant Conductor, Band of the US Air Forces in Europe, Ramstein, Germany, 1993-; Performed throughout Europe and on National Public Radio. *Recordings:* Public Service recordings for US Army and US Air Force. *Publication:* The Status of the Double-Lip Clarinet Embouchure in Present-Day Pedagogy and Performance, 1989. *Contributions to:* Articles in The Instrumentalist, The Clarinet and International Military Music Society Journals. *Honours:* Evergreen House Foundation Prize, Outstanding Graduate, Peabody Conservatory, 1984-85; Only American Semi-Finalist in 1984 International Clarinet Competition, London, England. *Memberships:* Phi Mu Alpha; Pi Kappa Lambda; College Band Directors National Association; International Military Music Society. *Hobbies:* Ice-skating; Ice hockey; Swimming; Travel. *Address:* 11 AM Wartenwald, D-67753 Rothselberg, Germany.

GRAUNKE Kurt, b. 30 Sept. 1915, Stettin, Germany. Violinist; Conductor; Composer. *Education:* Pupil in violin of Gustav Havemann, Berlin Hochschule für Musik; Received training in composition from Adolf Lessle and Hermann Grabner, in violin from Hanns Weisse and Hans Dunschede, and in conducting from Felix Husadel; Completed violin studies with Wolfgang Schneiderhan. *Career:* Played violin in the Vienna Radio Orchestra; Founder-Conductor, Graunke Symphony Orchestra, Munich, 1945-. *Compositions:* 8 symphonies: 1969, 1972, 1975, 1981, 1982, 1983, 1985; Violin Concerto, 1959; Other orchestral works. *Recordings:* Numerous discs as well as movie and television sound tracks. *Address:* c/o Symphonie Orchester Graunke, Schornstrasse 13, D-8000 Munich 30, Germany.

GRAY Linda Esther, b. 29 May 1948, Greenock, Scotland. Opera Singer (Soprano). m. Peter McCrorie. 1 daughter. *Education:* Royal Scottish Academy of Music and Drama, Cinzano Scholarship, 1969; Goldsmith School, 1970; James Caird school, 1971. *Career:* London Opera Centre, 1969-71; Glyndebourne Festival Opera, as Mimi and Mozart's Electra, 1972-75; Scottish Opera, 1974-79; Welsh Opera, 1980-; English National Opera, as Donna Anna, Wagner's Eva, Strauss's Ariadne and Verdi's Amelia, 1979-; American Debut, 1981; Royal Opera House, Sieglinde, 1982; Fidelio, 1983; Record of Tristan and Isolde, 1981; Principal Roles: Isolde, Sieglinde, Kundry (Wagner); Tosca (Puccini); Fidelio (Beethoven). *Honours:* Kathleen Ferrier Award, 1972; Christie Award, 1972. *Hobbies:* Cooking; Swimming. *Address:* 171 Queens Road, London SW19, England.

GREAGER Richard, b. 5 Nov. 1946, Christchurch, New Zealand. Singer (Tenor). *Education:* Studied in Australia. *Career:* Junior principal at Covent Garden until 1975; Lyric tenor at Scottish Opera from 1975 then sang widely in Germany, notably at Hanover, Dortmund, Wiesbaden, Karlsruhe and Bonn; Roles included Don Ottavio, Ferrando, Tamino, Rodolfo, the Duke of Mantua, Fenton and Ernesto; Australian Opera from 1980, as The Painter in Lulu, Edgardo (opposite Sutherland's Lucia), Peter Grimes, Lensky, Don José and Peter Quint (The Turn of the Screw); Guest appearances at the Grand Théâtre Geneva as Peter Quint, the Painter and the Negro in Lulu (Jeffrey Tate conducting) and Edgardo; Opéra de Lyon as Huon in Oberon; Season 1988-89 as Rodolfo at Melbourne and Covent Garden; Eisenstein in Die Fledermaus for Scottish Opera; Peter Quint in Schwetzingen and Cologne; Covent Garden 1991, as Arthur in the world premiere of Gawain by Harrison Birtwistle; Other roles include Tonio (La Fille du Régiment) and Werther; Season 1991/92 as Arbace in Idomeneo at Helsinki, Herod in Salome at Wellington and Mozart's Basilio with the Royal Opera in Japan. *Honours include:* Winner, Sun Aria Competition, Australia. *Address:* c/o Judith Alexander, Cameron's, 163 Brougham Street, Wooloomooloo, Sydney, NSW 2011, Australia.

GREAVES Terence G, b. 16 Nov 1933, Hodthorpe, Derbyshire, England. Freelance Musician. m. Janet Sheila Nichols, 27 July 1962, 3 daughters. *Education:* Chorister, Welbeck Abbey; LRAM, Piano Performance; ARCM, Piano Teachers; Royal Signals Staff Band (National Service), 1952-57; Keble College, Oxford, 1957-61; BA, MA, BMus, Oxford. *Career:* Lecturer, then Director of Studies, Birmingham School of Music, 1961-73; Extra-Mural Lecturer, Birmingham University; Dean of Studies, Royal Northern College of Music, Manchester, 1973-89; Freelance Composer, Lecturer, Examiner, Pianist in Duos, Choral and Opera Accompanist, 1990-; Academic Consultant to Associated Board of the Royal Schools of Music. *Compositions:* Arachne, play with music; A Garden of Weeds for clarinet, soprano and piano; Ingestre Portraits, suite for orchestra; Numerous published piano, vocal and instrumental pieces. *Recordings:* Numerous BBC broadcasts with clarinettist John Fuest. *Memberships:* Fellow, Birmingham School of Music; Fellow, Royal Northern College of Music. *Hobbies:* Tennis; Sport in general; Walking. *Address:* 85 Broad Walk, Wilmslow, Cheshire SK9 5PN, England.

GREEN Anna, b. 27 Jan. 1933, Southampton, England. Singer (Soprano). m. Howard Vandenburg. *Education:* Studied at the Royal College of Music 1951-54, and with Rodolfo Mele in London. *Debut:* Deutsche Oper am Rhein Dusseldorf 1961, as Amelia (Un Ballo in Maschera). *Career:* Has sung in Hamburg, Nuremberg, London, Cologne, Barcelona, Graz, Ottawa, Toronto, San Diego, Barcelona and Washington; Roles include Brünnhilde, Leonore, Donna Anna, Aida, Amelia Boccanegra, Ariadne, Tosca, Desdemona, Isolde, Marie (Wozzeck), and the Mother in Il Prigioniero by Dallapiccola; Teatro Liceo Barcelona, 1986 as Brünnhilde in Götterdämmerung. *Address:* Ingpen and Williams Ltd, 14 Kensington Court, London W8 5DN, England.

GREEN Barry, b. 10 Apr. 1945, Newark, New Jersey, USA. Symphony Bassist; Professor; Author; Solist. m. Mary Tarbell Green, 7 Oct. 1984. 2 sons, 1 stepson. *Education:* BMus, Indiana University School of Music; Performers Certificate; MMus, University of Cincinnati. *Career:* Principal Bassist, Nashville Symphony, 1965-66; Principal Bassist, Cincinnati Symphony, 1967-; Faculty, University of Cincinnati, 1967-; Cassals Festival Orchestra, 1979-87; International Workshops, 1982-86. *Recordings:* (Solos) Baroque Bass; Romantic Music for Double Bass; New Music for Double Bass; Bass Evolution; Sound of Bass, Volume 1 (Chamber Music Recordings) Heritage Chamber Quartet; Music Now; What of My Music Opus One. *Publications:* Fundamentals of Double Bass Playing; Advanced Techniques of Double Bass Playing, 1976; Inner Game of Music, 1986. *Contributions to:* Founder-Executive Director, International Society of Bassists, Suzuki Journal, 1975-82; Articles in ASTA Music Journal; Suzuki Journal; American Music Teacher; Instrumentalist; Bass World. *Memberships:* International Society of Bassists, Founder Director, Life Member; ASTA. *Hobbies:* Skiing; Tennis; Golf; Running. *Address:* 3449 Lyleburn Place, Cincinnati, OH 45220, USA.

GREEN Christopher John Charles, b. 3 Nov 1942, Ipswich, England. Educator; Lecturer; Music Critic. m. Sylvia Buckenham, Aug 1968, 2 sons. *Education:* BA (Hons), Psychology/Sociology, then Research Fellow, 1964-67, Doctor of Philosophy, Psychology of Music Education, 1968, University of Leeds. *Career:* Lecturer, Hockerill College, 1968-71; Senior Lecturer, Middlesex Polytechnic, 1971-76; Head of Department, Essex Institute, 1984-88; Anglia Polytechnic, Director, Essex Centre, 1988-, Professor of Continuing and Adult Education; Director, Regional Office, Anglia Polytechnic University, 1992-; Music Director, Braintree Choral Society 1992-; Conductor, Anglia University Singers (Chelmsford), 1992-. *Publications:* A social and psychological study of factors influencing music appreciation, 1968. *Contributions to:* Reviews: Arts Alive; Images; East Anglian Daily Times; Essex Chronicle; Music Education; Programme notes for orchestras including Royal Philharmonic Orchestra, London Mozart Players, Philharmonia. *Memberships:* Chair, National Association of Youth Orchestras; Artistic Director, Trianon Music Group of East Anglia; Associate Fellow, British Psychological Society; Critics Circle; Fwllow, Royal Society of Arts. *Hobbies:* Reading; Conducting. *Address:* 25 The Avenue, Braintree, Essex CM7 6HY, England.

GREENAWALD Sheri (Kay), b. 12 Nov. 1947, Iowa City, Iowa, USA. Soprano. *Eucation:* Studied with Charles Matheson at the University of Northern Iowa; and with Hans Heinz, Daniel Ferro and Maria DeVarady in New York; Further studies with Audrey Langford in London. *Debut:* Manhattan Theater Club 1974, in Les mamelles de Tiresias by Poulenc. *Career:* Sang in the premieres of Bilby's Doll by Carlisle Floyd and Washington Square by Thomas Pasatieri (Houston and Detroit, 1976); European debut with Netherlands Opera as Susanna in Le nozze di Figaro, 1980; Regular concert appearances with the St Louis and San Francisco Symphony Orchestras and the Rotterdam Philharmonic; Sang in the premiere of Bernstein's A Quiet Place,

Houston 1983; Other roles include Violetta, Ellen Orford (Peter Grimes), Mozart's Despina and Zerlina, Sophie in Werther and Norina in Don Pasquale; Season 1991/92 at Chicago as Pauline in the US Stage premiere of Prokofiev's The Gambler and Mozart's Donna Anna, Fiordiligi at Seattle and Rosalinde in Fledermaus at the Santa Fe Festival. *Address:* c/o Houston Grand Opera Association, 510 Preston Avenue, Houston, TX 77002, USA.

GREENBERG Sylvia, b. 1955, Rumania. Singer (Soprano). *Education:* Studied at the Tel Aviv Academy of Music and with Marc Belfort in Zurich. *Debut:* Tel Aviv concert, conducted by Zubin Mehta. *Career:* Stage debut Zurich 1977, as the Queen of Night; later sang Zerbinetta, Olympia in Les Contes d'Hoffmann, and in operas by Monteverdi; Guest appearances in Hamburg, Berlin, Vienna, Munich and Cologne; Glyndebourne Festival 1978, Die Zauberflöte; US debut Chicago 1981, in Die Schöpfung, conducted by Solti; Bayreuth Festival 1983, as Waldvogel in Siegfried; Salzburg Festival 1984, premiere of Un Re in Ascolto by Berio; At La Scala in 1985 sang the Queen of Night; Aix-en-Provence as Ilia in Idomeneo, 1986; Sang in Doktor Faustus by Giacomo Manzoni at La Scala, 1989. *Recordings include:* Die Schöpfung (Decca); Te Deum by Bizet; Poulenc's Gloria; Carmina Burana (Decca). *Address:* c/o Teatro all Scala, Via Filodrammatici 2, I-20121 Milan, Italy.

GREENE Gary (Allen), b. 31 Oct 1952, Danville, Illinois, USA. Teacher; Musicologist; Hornist; Writer. *Education:* BS magna cum laude with distinction, Music Education, University of Indianapolis, 1974; MM, Butler University, 1978; PhD, University of Maryland, 1987. *Career:* Music Teacher, Elementary, Secondary, Indiana and Illinois, 1975-80; Instructor, Danville Area Community College, 1978-83; Reference Specialist, Librarian, American Symphony Orchestra League, 1987-88; Assistant Professor of Music, Northeast Louisiana University, 1988-; Section and Principal Horn: Danville Symphony, 1968-70, 1976, 1977-83, Danville Municipal Band, 1968-83; Co-Founder, Danville Woodwind and Brass Quintets; Section Horn, Prince George's Symphony, 1984; Assistant Principal Horn, Prince George's Philharmonic, 1985- 89; Principal Horn, Monroe Symphony Orchestra, 1988-; Horn, Chamber Arts Brass Quintet, 1988-. *Compositions:* Dies Irae for mixed chorus, soprano, organ. *Publications:* Richard Strauss: The Two Concertos for Horn and Orchestra, 1978; The Life and Music of Henry Holden Huss, 1987; In progress: Henry Holden Huss: An American Composer's Life; Twentieth-Century Conductors. *Contributions to:* Response to Johnson, Horn Call, 1982; The Community Music Ensemble, Sinfonian, 1984; Corresponding editor, Current Musicology, 1985-87; Master Pianist: The Artistry of Carl Friedberg, IPAM, 1102/3; De Capite Haydnii, Nebraska Society for Masonic Research Newsletter, 1987; Understanding Past Currency in Modern Terms, Sonneck Society Bulletin, 1987; Editorial Board, Horn Call Annual, 1988-; Nadia Reisenberg Collection, International Piano Archives at Maryland Newsletter, 1988; Response to William Scharnberg: Rhythm, Horn Call, 1993; The Musical Huss Family in America, American Music, 1984; Programme annotator, Laurel, Maryland Oratorio Society, Cleveland Quartet, Orlando Quartet, Rosen-Schub Duo, Bach Aria Group, Trevor Pinnock, Hopkinson Smith, Ruth Laredo, Monroe Symphony Orchestra. *Hobbies:* Photography; Travel. *Address:* 3904 Blanks Street, Monroe, LA 71203, USA.

GREENE Gordon K., b. 27 Dec 1927, Cardston Alberta, Canada. Musicologist. m. Lucy Seneshen, divorced, 2 sons, 4 daughters. *Education:* AMus, 1953; BA, 1954; BEd., 1955, MA 1962, University of Alberta; PhD, Musicology, Indiana University, USA, 1970. *Career:* Extension Dept., University of Alberta, 1955-63; Chairman, Music History, University of Western Ontario, 1966-76; Dean, Music, Wilfrid Laurier University, 1979-89. *Publications:* 5 Volumes, French Secular Music in the series, Polyphonic Music of the Fourteenth Century, 1980-88. *Memberships:* International Musicological Society; Canadian

University Music Society President, 1985-87. *Address:* c/o Faculty of Music, Wilfrid Laurier University, Waterloo, Ontario, Canada N2L 3C5.

GREENE Susan, b. 1 Jan 1955, Passaic, New Jersey, USA. Music Book Editor. *Education:* BA, Musicology, Drew University, 1976; MA, Mus Ed, New York University, 1978. *Career:* Editor, Music Publications, Silver Burdett Company, 1976-; Research Associate, Opera Orchestra of New York, 1979-; Research Assistant, Educational Materials, Metropolitan Opera, 1980-; Vice President, Education, New York City Opera Guild, 1985-. *Publications:* A Guide to Children's Opera, 1982; Teachers' Guides to Tannhäuser and Arabella, 1982; Editor, The Queens College Choral Society: An Historical Narrative, 1984; Comedy and Puccini's Operas, Opera Quarterly, 1984; Wozzeck and Marie: Two Characters in Search of an Honest Morality, in Opera Quarterly, 1985. *Contributions to:* Professional Journals including Opera Quarterly. *Address:* 105 Ridgedale Avenue, Madison, NJ 07940, USA.

GREENFIELD Edward Harry, b. 30 July 1928. Music Critic. *Education:* Trinity Hall, University of Cambridge (MA). *Career:* Joined staff of Manchester Guardian, 1953; Record Critic, 1955; Music Critic, 1964; Succeeded Sir Neville Cardus as Chief Music Critic, 1977 until 1993; Broadcaster on Music and Records for BBC Radio, 1957-; Member, Critics Panel, Gramophone, 1960-; Goldener Verdienstzeichen, Salzburg, 1980. *Publications:* Puccini: Keeper of the Seal, 1958; Monographs on Joan Sutherland, 1972, André Previn, 1973; With Robert Layton, Ivan March and initially Denis Stevens, Stereo Record Guide, 9 volumes, 1960-74; Penguin Stereo Record Guide, 1st Edition, 1975, 4th Edition 1984. *Hobbies:* Work; Living in Spitalfields. *Address:* 16 Folgate Street, London E1, England.

GREENHOUSE Bernard, b. 3 Jan 1916, Newark, New Jersey, USA. Cellist; Teacher. m. Aurora Greenhouse. 2 daughters. *Education:* Diploma, Juilliard Graduate School of Music, New York, 1938; Studied with William Berce, Felix Salmond, Emanuel Feuermann, Diran Alexanian, Pablo Casals. *Career:* Principal Cellist, CBS Symphony Orchestra, New York, 1938-42; Member, Dorian String Quartet, 1939-42; Solo Cellist, US Navy Symphony Orchestra; Member, Navy String Quartet, 1942-45; Annual recitals, Town Hall, New York, 1946-57; Member, Harpsichord Quartet, 1947-51; Bach Aria Group, 1948-76; Founder-member, Beaux Arts Trio, 1955-87; Guest artist, Juilliard, Guarneri and Cleveland String Quartets; Numerous appearances on major concert series and with festivals worldwide; Professor, Manhattan School of Music, New York, 1950-82; Juilliard School of Music, New York, 1951-61; Hart Conservatory, Hartford, Connecticut, 1956-65; Indiana University School of Music, Bloomington, summers 1956-65; State University of New York, Stony Brook, 1960-85; New England Conservatory of Music, Boston, 1986-; Rutgers, the State University of New Jersey, 1987-; Master classes around the globe. *Recordings:* Numerous. *Honours:* Many recording awards including Prix Mondial du Disque; Union de la Presse Musicale Belge; Gramophone Record of the Year; Stereo Review Record of the Year; 3 Grand Prix du Disques; American String Teachers Association Teacher of the Year Award, 1982; US Presidential Medallion, 1985; Honorary Doctorate, State University of New York, Stony Brook, 1988. *Memberships:* Cello Society, president, 1955- 59, 1987- ; Honorary Member, American String Teachers Association. *Address:* 12 East 86th Street, New York, NY 10028, USA.

GREENSMITH John Brian, b. 12 Apr 1029, Bournemouth, England. Cellist; Orchestra Manager and Administrator. m. Magdalen Aurelia Green, 3 sons. *Education:* Birmingham School of Music; Guildhall School of Music; Licentiate, Trinity College of London; Associate, Royal College of Music.*Career:* Bournemouth Municipal Orchestra, 1952-53; Principal, British Broadcasting Corporation, Glasgow, 1956-63;

Instrumental Teacher, West Riding County Council, 1963-74; Visiting Tutor, Bretton Hall, 1965-82; Teacher in charge, Batley Music Centre, 1967-74; Advisory Committee, 1968-73, Governor, 1988-, City of Leeds College of Music; Coordinator for Instrumental Music, Barnsley Metropolitan Borough Council, 1974-90; Visiting Tutor, Wakefield Tertiary College, 1982-90; Freelance with leading orchestras; Orchestral Manager, Yorkshire Concert Orchestra, 1965-72; Yorkshire Sinfonia, 1972-75; General Manager, Yorkshire Philharmonic Orchestras, 1975-; Director, Company Secretary: Wakefield Metropolitan Festival Co Ltd, 1975-, Wakefield Opera House, 1981-; Arts and Financial Marketing Consultant, 1982-; Managing Director, Music for All Occasionsm, 1988-. *Recordings:* Various. *Address:* Torridon House, 104 Bradford Road, Wrenthorpe, Wakefield WF1 2AH, England.

GREENWOOD Andrew, b. 1954, Todmorden, Yorkshire, England. Conductor. *Education:* Studied at Clare College, Cambridge and at the London Opera Centre. *Career:* Opera For All, 1976; Member of the music staff of Covent Garden 1977-84, studying with Edward Downes and conducting the Dutch Radio and Television Orchestra; Principal Guest Chorus Master of the Philharmonia Chorus from 1981: concerts with Previn, Davis, Giulini, Sinopoli and Solti; Conducted Rossini's Petite Messe Solennelle at the Istanbul Festival 1985; Chorus master at Welsh National Opera from 1984, and has conducted performances of operas by Mozart, Bizet, Puccini, Verdi, Berlioz (The Trojans), Beethoven, Strauss and Smetana; Many concerts on BBC Radio 2 and 3, notably with the BBC Welsh Symphony Orchestra; Debut with the Rotterdam Philharmonic 1990, Cologne Opera 1990, The Bartered Bride and Die Fledermaus; English National Opera 1990-92, The Magic Flute and Madame Butterfly; Conducted Manon Lescaut for the Chelsea Opera Group, 1992, Don Giovanni for ENO. *Address:* Kaye Artists Management, Barratt House, 7 Chertsey Road, Woking GU21 5AB, England.

GREER David Clive, b. 8 May 1937, London, England. Professor of Music. m. Patricia Regan, 25 Aug 1961. 2 sons, 1 daughter. *Education:* Reading Blue Coat School, 1947-52; Dulwich College, 1952-55; Oxford University, 1957-60, BA, 1960, MA 1964, MusD, Dublin, 1991. *Career:* Lecturer in Music, Birmingham University, 1963-72; Hamilton Harty Professor of Music, Queen's University, Belfast, 1972-84; Professor of Music, Newcastle University, 1984-86; Professor of Music, Durham University, 1986-. *Publications:* Editor with F W Sternfeld, English Madrigal Verse, 3rd Edition, 1967; English Lute Songs, facsimile series, 1967-71; Hamilton Harty, His Life and Music, 1979; Songs from Manuscript Sources, 1979; Collected English Lutenist Partsongs (Musica Britannica, vols 53-4), 1987-89; Editor, Journal (formerly Proceedings) of the Royal Musical Association, vols 103-115. *Contributions to:* Music and Letters; Proceedings of the Royal Musical Association; Lute Society Journal; Musical Times; Shakespeare Quarterly; English Studies; Notes and Queries; Early Music; Music Review. *Honour:* Fellow, Royal Society of Arts, 1986. *Address:* Department of Music, University of Durham, Palace Green, Durham DH1 3RL, England.

GREEVE Gilbert-Jean de, b. 11 Nov 1944, St Truiden, Belgium. Concert Pianist. *Education:* Studied Piano with Eugene Traey, Royal Conservatory of Antwerp, Belgium, 1958-69; Performing major, with First Prizes in Piano and Chamber Music and a Diplome superieur for Chamber music; Composition major, with First Prizes in Music Theory, Harmony, Analysis, Counterpoint and Fugue; 1970 Peabody Institute of Music, Baltimore, Maryland, USA; Private studies with Rudolph Serkin, Eugene Ormandy and Leonard Pearlmann; 1972, Franz Liszt Academy of Budapest, Hungary. *Career:* Active world-wide as pianist 1970- ; Director of the State Music Academy of Antwerp and Professor of the Royal Conservatory of Antwerp, 1970- ; Working in a permanemt duo with the Belgian soprano Martine De Craene, 1988-, repertoire of more than 14 hours music from Baroque until today, including 3 books of melodies by Gabriel Fauré; Lieder cycles by composers from Hungary and Canada have been dedicated to and world-created by the Duo. Concerts and Master Classes in 5 continents; Major foreign tours: Canada, Australia, New Zealand, Africa, Finland, Netherlands, Antilles, Greece. *Compositions:* Chamber Music, a Lieder cycle of 36 Lieder on poems by James Joyce. *Recordings:* Belgian Radio and Television; CBC Canada; Hungarian Radio Budapest. *Address:* Anselmostraat 38, 2018 Antwerpen, Belgium.

GREEVY Bernadette, b. 3 July 1940, Dublin, Ireland. Singer (Mezzo-Soprano). *Career:* Concert appearances with with many of the world's great orchestras and numerous recitals in all the major capitals of the world; Operatic repertoire includes Eboli, Charlotte, Dalila, Herodiade in the opera by Massenet and Gluck's Orfeo; Tour of the People's Republic of China 1985, giving recitals and holding Master Classes; Recital series at the National Concert Hall in Dublin and on RTE Radio and Television; Has sung Mahler's Rückert Lieder and the Choral Symphony with the Oslo Philharmonic; the Brahms Alto Rhapsody and Elgar's Sea Pictures in Ottawa; Recent concerts in Denmark, Italy, Spain, USA, France, Finland and Norway; Mahler series in London with the Royal Philharmonic under Charles Dutoit, 1989. *Recordings:* Handel Arias, Orlando, Ariodante; Brahms Lieder; Nuits d'Été by Berlioz and songs by Duparc, with the Ulster Orchestra (Chandos); Bach Arias; Sea Pictures; Mahler's Lieder eines fahrenden Gesellen and Kindertotenlieder, with the RTE Orchestra. *Honours:* Harriet Cohen International Music Award; Order of Merit of the order of Malta; Honorary DMus, National University of Ireland; DMus, Trinity College Dublin, 1988; Pro Ecclesia et Pontifice, 1988. *Address:* c/o Trinity College, Dublin, Eire.

GREGOR Bohumil, b. 14 July 1926, Prague, Czechoslovakia. Conductor. *Education:* Studied with Alois Klima at the Prague Conservatory. *Career:* Worked at the Prague 5th May (Smetana) Theatre from 1947; Conducted at the Brno Opera 1949-51; Musical Director Ostrava Opera 1958-62: performances of Janáček's Katya Kabanova and The Excursions of Mr Brouček, and premieres of works by Pauer, Kaslik and Trojan; Conductor at the Prague National Theatre from 1962: led the company in the first British productions of Janáček's From the House of the Dead and The Excursions of Mr Brouček (Edinburgh 1964 and 1970); Royal Opera Stockholm 1966-69, Hamburg Staatsoper 1969-72: premiere of Kelemen's Belagerungzustand (after The Plague by Camus, 1970) and operas by Verdi, Smetana and Janáček; Performances of The Cunning Little Vixen in Vienna, Edinburgh, Brussels and Amsterdam; San Francisco Opera from 1969, Jenůfa, Otello and Salome; Conducted The Cunning Little Vixen at Zurich, 1989 and at the Bayreuth Youth Festival, 1990; New production of Dvořák's The Devil and Kate at Prague, 1990; Season 1993 with Katya Kabanova and a new production of The Bartered Bride. *Recordings:* Several sets of Czech opera for Supraphon: The Makropoulos Case, The Cunning Little Vixen, Jenůfa and From the House of the Dead. *Address:* National Theatre, PO Box 865, 112 30 Prague 1, Czech Republic.

GREGOR Joszef, b. 8 Aug 1940, Rakosliget, Hungary. Singer (Bass). *Education:* Studied in Budapest with Endreh Poessler and sang in choir of Hungarian army. *Career:* Appearances at the Szeged Opera from 1964; Sang Sarastro at the Hungarian State Opera, Budapest, 1966; Played title role in Hungarian premiere of Attila, 1972 and appeared in operas by Goldmark, Rossini, Donizetti, Puccini and Bartok (title role in Duke Bluebeard's Castle); Visited the Wiesbaden Festival 1970 and sang elsewhere in Germany as guest; Houston Grand Opera 1986 as Varlaam in Boris Godunov, Monte Carlo Opera 1988, in Cimarosa's Il Pittore Parigino; Many radio and television performances from 1975; Frequent concert engagements. *Recordings:* Goldmark's Die Königin von Saba; Haydn's L'Infedeltà delusa and La Fedeltà Premiata; Paisiello's Barbiere di Siviglia; Guntram (Strauss), Nerone (Boito) and Mosè in Egitto

(Rossini); Don Pasquale, Gianni Schicchi and La Fiamma by Respighi; Duke Bluebeard's Castle; Liszt's Missa solemnis and Legend of St Elisabeth; Beethoven's Missa solemnis and 9th Symphony; Salieri's Falstaff La Serva Padrona; Il Pittore Parigino; Andrea Chénier and Fedora; Der Geduldige Sokrates by Telemann (Hungaroton). *Address:* Hungarian State Opera House, Nepoztarsasag utja 22, 1061 Budapest, Hungary.

GREGOR-SMITH Bernard, b. 1945, England. Cellist. *Education:* Studied with Douglas Cameron, at the Royal Academy of Music, with Sandor Vegh at the University of Keele and with Vilmos Tatrai in Budapest. *Career:* Founder member of the Lindsay String Quartet 1966; Regular tours of Europe, Britain and the United States; From 1974 quartet in residence at Sheffield University, then Manchester University (1979); Premiered the 4th Quartet of Tippett at the 1979 Bath Festival and commissioned Tippett's 5th Quartet 1992; Chamber Music Festival established at Sheffield, 1984; Regular concerts at the Wigmore Hall, including Haydn series 1987; Plays a Ruggieri cello of 1694. *Recordings include:* Complete cycles of Bartók, Tippett and Beethoven; CDs of Haydn quartets Live from the Wigmore Hall (ASV). *Honours:* Prize winner (with members Lindsay Quartet) at Liege International Competition 1969; Gramophone Chamber Award for late Beethoven quartets 1984. *Address:* c/o Ingpen and Williams Ltd, 14 Kensington Court, London W8 5DN, England.

GREGSON Edward, b. 23 July 1945, Sunderland, County Durham, England. Composer; Lecturer; Conductor. m. Susan Carole Smith, 30 Sept 1967, 2 sons. *Education:* Royal Academy of Music, 1963-67; BMus (London) 1977; LRAM 1966; GRSM 1967; ARAM 1983; FRAM, 1990. *Career:* Lecturer, 1976-, Reader in Music, 1989-, Professor of Music, 1993-, Goldsmiths' College, University of London, 1976-; Active as Conductor, particularly of contemporary music; Has written to commission only since 1970; commissioned by many orchestras, organisations and ensembles in this country and abroad; also English Chamber Orchestra to compose Music for Chamber Orchestra, 1968; Commissioned by York Festival to write the music for the York Cycle of Mystery Plays, 1976; Received commissions from National centre for Orchestral Studies and Wren Orchestra of London, BBC; Has worked widely on various judging panels including BBC Young Musicians of the Yea, Royal Philharmonic Society Awards for composition, Ivor Novello Awards; Chairman, Association of Professional Composers, 1989-91. *Compositions include:* Orchestral: Music for Chamber Orchestra, 1968; Tuba Concerto, 1976; Trombone Concerto, 1979; Metamorphoses, 1979; Contrasts, 1983; Trumpet Concerto, 1983; Celebration, 1991; Blazon, 1992; Clarinet Concerto, 1993. Choral and Vocal: In the Beginning, 1966; 5 Songs of Innocence and Experience, 1979; Missa Brevis Pacem, 1988; Make a Joyful Noise (anthem), 1988; Instrumental and Chamber Music: Divertimento, 1967; 6 Little Piano Pieces, 1982; Piano Sonata in one movement, 1986; Brass Band: Connotations, 1977; Dances and Arias, 1984; Of Men and Mountains, 1990; Educational: Fairground Songs, 1982; 15 Duets, 1982; Refrains, 1982; Music for Television: Title Music for BBC Young Musician of the Year, 1988; Music for Theatre: Commissioned to write music for the Plantagenet Trilogy (Shakespeare) at RSC, Stratford, 1988; Henry IV pts 1 & 2, RSC, Stratford, 1991. Commissions: English Chamber Orchestra, York Festival, Royal Liverpool Philharmonic Orchestra, BBC (for BBC Philharmonic); Blazon, commissioned by the Bournemouth Festival, 1992; The Sword and the Crown, Symphonic suite for symphonic wind band, adapted from music for the RSC. *Recordings:* Tuba Concerto; Horn Concerto; Intrada, Connotations, Gregson: Brass music composed and conducted by the composer, (Doyen Label), 1992; Horn Concerto, Cannotations, Dances and Arias of Men and Mountains; Make a Joyful Noise, (Koch International label); The Sword and the Crown, (Polyphonic), and several other recordings. *Publication:* The Contemporary Repertoire of Brass Bands in the 20th Century, ed V & G Brand, 1979. *Current Management:* c/o Novello and Company, 8/9 Frith Street, London W1V 5TZ,

England. *Address:* 15 Farnaby Road, Shortlands, Bromley, Kent BR1 4BL, England.

GRELLA-MOZEJKO Piotr, b. 15 Mar 1961, Bytom, Poland. Composer; Music Critic. m. Kasia Zoledziowski 30 June 1990. *Education:* MA, University of Silesia, Katowice; Studied Composition with Dr Edward Boguslawski, Katowice, Dr Boguslaw Schaeffer, Cracow, Dr Alfred Fisher, University of Alberta. *Debut:* The Silesian Tribune of Composers, 1982. *Career:* 1st performance of work, 1977; Works performed at major festivals such as Warsaw Autumn Festival, Poznan Music Spring Festival, Gdansk Meetings of Young Composers; Founder, Fascinating Music Festival, Katowice, 1983-86; Co-Founder, J S Bach Festival, Cracow-Katowice, 1985; Took part in many exhibitions of musical scores, Institut Polonais, Paris, Royal Academy of Music, London, Warsaw, Salzburg, Katowice; Numerous interviews, Polish TV and Radio, also CBC; Polish TV documentary on activities and the Fascinating Music Festival, 1986; Founder, The Edmonton New Music Festival, 1992; Completed M.Mus Degree in Composition at the University of Alberta, Edmonton, 1992. *Compositions:* Archival radio recordings, Poland, Canada, USA: ravenna, harpsichord; minimum-optimum-maximum, chamber ensemble; en attendant Bergson, string quartet; The Dreams of Odysseus, tape (performed in Warsaw, Poland, as part of the first exhibition of Polish artists in exile, Jestesmy); Epitaph for Jerzy, for tape included in A BEAMS Compilation; Other works: Xylotet Concerto, saxophone, orchestra; Horror Vacui, strings; Ordines, saxophone, organ, cello; Melodramas I-VI, solo instruments; Festivals: Canada, Pacific Market, Fringe, The Edmonton Music Festival, Warsaw. *Hobbies:* Reading; Cooking; Photography. *Address:* No 8 8807 101st Street, Edmonton, Alberta, Canada T6E 3Z9.

GRICE Garry Bruce, b. 25 Jan 1942, Dayton, Ohio, USA. Opera Singer (Tenor). m. Patricia A Michael, 9 July 1983, 1 son, 2 daughters. *Education:* BA, History, University of Dayton, 1964; Musical studies with Hubert Kockritz, Cincinnati and Adelaide Saraceni, Milan. *Debut:* National Opera, USA, 1970-71. *Career:* 8 seasons in German and Swiss opera houses including: Debut, Stadttheater, St Gallen, Switzerland, 1974, Debut, Bavarian State Opera, 1974; Debut as Don José in Carmen, Florentine Opera, Milwaukee, 1980; Bacchus in Ariadne auf Naxos, Des Moines Metro Opera, 1980; Debut, New York City Opera, 1981; Bermuda Festival, 1981; Debut, Chicago as Don Jose in Carmen, 1983; Debut, Calgary Opera Association, 1985; Debut. Cairo, 1990; Has sung with conductors Kleiber, Prêtre, Guadagno, Keene, Pallo and Rescigno; Has appeared in over 50 roles including Otello, Florestan, Bacchus, Canio, Max and Radames; Has sung throughout USA, also Canada, Bermuda and Europe mainly Germany, Austria, Switzerland; Faculty Voice and Opera, University of Notre Dame, 1991; Artistic Director, Indiana Opera North since 1990; Performance: New Orleans Debut, Verdi Rerqium, 1992. *Recordings:* Title role in Otello, TV Public Broadcasting, 1982; Radames in Aida, TV Public Broadcasting, 1984; Turiddu in Cavalleria Rusticana, Canadian Public Radio, 1985. *Publications:* Translations into English of Otello, Il Trovatore and Tales of Hoffmann. *Current Management:* Warden Associates Inc. *Address:* c/o Warden Associated Inc. 127 W 72nd Street, SSuite 2-R, New York, NY 10023, USA.

GRIER Francis, b. 1955, England. Organist; Pianist; Composer. *Education:* Chorister at St George's Chapel, Windsor Castle; Eton College; Organ scholar at King's College, Cambridge; Piano studies with Joseph Cooper, Fanny Waterman and Bernard Roberts; Organ with Gillian Weir. *Career:* Assistant organist at Christ Church Cathedral, Oxford (to Simon Preston), Organist and Director of Music 1981; Organ recitals throughout Britain; First organ recital at the BBC Promenade Concerts, 1985; Studied in India from 1985 then worked with mentally-handicapped in London and Bangladore; Resident in England from 1989. *Compositions:* Advent Responsories for King's College Chapel 1990; Mass with

motets for Westminster Abbey; Sequence of Readings and Music for Ascension, for the 550th anniversary of Eton College 1990; The Cry of Mary, for BBC2, 1992; St Francis, Opera, for Eton College and National Youth Music Theatre, 1993. *Recordings:* Bach, Mendelssohn, Couperin, Franck and Messiaen (Messe de la Pentecôte and L'Ascension) on the Rieger organ at Christ Church Cathedral. *Address:* 65 Tynemouth Road, London N15 4AU, England.

GRIER Hugh Christopher, b. 4 Dec 1922, Derby, England. Music Critic; Lecturer. m. Mary Elisabeth Martin, 1 son. *Education:* King's College, Cambridge, MA, MusB. *Career:* Music Officer, Scandinavia, British Council, 1947-49; Music Critic, The Scotsman, 1949-63, Music Critic, The Standard, 1970-93; Freelance, 1970-; Professor, Royal College of Music, 1971-84; Professor, Royal Academy of Music, 1976-83. *Honours:* Honorary RCM, 1975; Honorary RAM, 1979. *Memberships:* Incorporated Society of Musicians; Institute of Journalists; Critics Circle; Scottish Arts Club. *Hobbies:* Skiing; Tennis; Reading. *Address:* 10 Hospital of St Cross, St Cross Road, Winchester SO23 9SD, England.

GRIESBACH Karl-Rudi, b. 14 June 1916, Breckerfeld, Westphalia, Germany. Composer. *Education:* Studied Composition with Philipp Jarnach at Cologne Hochschule fur Musik (graduated 1941). *Career:* Worked in Hamburg as Composer and Pianist, then moved to Dresden, 1950; Music Critic, Lecturer, Artistic Adviser to Dresden Staatsoper; Professor of composition at the Carl Maria von Weber Academy of Music. *Compositions include:* Kolumbus, opera, first performed Erfurt and Neustrelitz, 1958; Die Weibermuhle, opera, first performed Weimar, 1960; Marike Weiden, opera, first performed Weimar, Görlitz and Neustrelitz, 1960; Der Schwarze, der Weiße und die Frau, opera, first performed Dresden, 1963; Aulus und sein Papagei, opera, first performed Dresden, 1982; Florian, opera, 1984; Noah, opera, 1987; Belle und Armand, opera, 1988; Ballets: Kleider machen Leute, first performed Berlin, 1954; Schneewittchen, first performed, Berlin, 1956; Reineke Fuchs, first performed Dresden, 1985, Samson, 1982; Works for Orchestra: Afrikanische Sinfonie, first performed Berlin, 1962; Konzertante Musik für Klavier und Kammerorchester, first performed Berlin, 1964; Sinfonie 1967, first performed Dresden, 1967; Ostinati für Orchester, first performed Dresden, 1967; Kontemplationen für großes Orchester, first performed Dresden, 1986; Chamber Music: Blues- Impressions, Klavierstücke im Jazzstil, first performed Dresden, 1962; Streichquartett, first performed Berlin, 1977; Vocal Music: Nacht der Faeben, Lieder Für Streichquintett und Harfe, first performed Berlin, 1967; Und Va kamst Du, sieben Lieberlieder für mittlere Stimme und Klavier, first performed Berlin, 1967. *Address:* c/o GEMA (Germany), PRS Ltd, 29-33 Berners Street, London W1P 4AA, England.

GRIFFEL Kay, b. 26 Dec 1940, Eldora, Iowa, USA. Singer (Soprano). m. Eckhard Sellheim. *Education:* Studied at Northwestern University, Illinois, in Berlin and with Lotte Lehmann at Santa Barbara. *Debut:* Chicago 1960, as Mercédès in Carmen. *Career:* Sang at the Deutsche Oper Berlin and in Bremen, Mainz, Karlsruhe, Hamburg and Dusseldorf; Salzburg 1973, in the premiere of De Temporum fine Comoedia by Orf; Glyndebourne Festival 1976-77, as Alice Ford in Falstaff; Tour of Japan with the Staatsoper Berlin 1977, as the Marschallin, Donna Elvira and Mozart's Countess; Lisbon 1978, Eva in Die Meistersinger; Metropolitan Opera from 1982, as Electra in Idomeneo, Rosalinde, Arabella, Tatiana and the Countess; Further appearances in Brussels, Moscow, Cologne and at the Orange Festival; Sang Eva in Die Meistersinger at Wellington, New Zealand, 1990. *Recordings:* Janáček Diary of one who Disappeared (Deutsche Grammophon); De Temporum fine Comoedia; Italian Arias. *Honour:* Doctorate of Fine Arts, Simpson College, Indianola, Iowa 1983. *Current Management:* Robert Lombardo, New York, USA; Stoll and Hilbert in Germany. *Address:* c/

o Wellington City Opera (contracts), PO Box 6588, New Zealand.

GRIFFIN Judson, b. 7 Sept 1951, Lewes, Delaware, USA. Violist; Violinist. m. Mara Paske, 7 May 1988. *Education:* DMA 1977, MM 1975, Juilliard School of Music; BM, Eastman School of Music, 1973. *Debut:* Carnegie Recital Hall, New York City, January 1981. *Career:* Violist, Rochester Philharmonic Orchestra, 1970-73; Freelance Violist, New York City, 1973-77; Assistant Professor, University of North Carolina at Greensboro, 1977-79; Principal Viola, Aspen Chamber Symphony, 1977-80; Freelance Violinist and Violist, New York City, 1979-; Current activities, Violist of Smithson String Quartet and Smithsonian Chamber Players (Smithsonian Institution, Washington DC); Atlantis Ensemble (Europe); Violinist of Four Nations and Sonata a quattro (New York); Regular appearances with almost all period-instrument organisations in USA. *Recordings:* Chamber music on labels, Nonesuch, Grenadilla, Smithsonian Collection, Arabesque, Harmonia Mundi (France, USA), L'Oiseau-Lyre, Reference, Harmonia Mundi (Germany), Columbia, CRI, CP2, Pro Arte, Newport; Many radio recordings. *Address:* 170 Claremont Avenue No 7, New York, NY 10027, USA.

GRIFFITH-SMITH Bella, b. 1920, USA. President, Coral Gables Civic Opera and Orchestra, Inc; Opera Singer; Coach; Conductor. *Education:* Private tutors; Howard Thain, Franco Iglesias, Dr Paul Csonka. *Debut:* Civic Opera of the Palm Beaches. *Career:* Appeared with Louis Quilico, Metropolitan Artist; Robert Merill, Guiseppe Campora, a Television Concert Version-Spanish Translation, Channel 2, Miami; Madam Butterfly; Radio-La Traviata; Leading Roles in Madam Butterfly, La Bohème, Tosca, Cavalleria Rusticana, Pagliacci, Suor Angelica, Il Tabarro, Faust, Carmen (Micaela), Così Fan Tutte (Fiordiligi), Tales of Hoffmann (Antonia), Don Pasquale-Norina, L'Oca del Cairo (Celidora), La Traviata, Oratorio-Elijah, L'Enfant Prodigue, Messiah, Vivaldi's Gloria, Stabat Mater, Rossini; Concerts-Salome, Otello, Turandot, with Alain Lombard/Greater Miami Philharmonic, Guest Soloist. *Hobbies:* Writing; Painting; Reading-research; History; Literature. *Address:* 700 Santander Avenue, Coral Gables, FL 33134, USA.

GRIFFITHS Graham Charles Thomas, b. 13 May 1954, Tiverton, England. Conductor; Pianist; Lecturer. m. Miriam Regina Zillo, 18 Jan 1985, 1 son. *Education:* Bryanston School 1967-72; B Mus (Hons) Edinburgh University, 1976; PGCE (Cantab) Cambridge University, 1977. *Career:* Founder-member, Edinburgh Experimental Arts Society, 1972-76; Founder- member, Grand Toxic Opera Company, Edinburgh, 1974-76; Member, Cambridge Contemporary Music Ensemble, 1976-78; Marketing/Education Officer, Scottish National Orchestra, 1978-81; Co-Administrator, International Musica Nova Festival, Glasgow, 1978-81; Arts Journalist, Scottish Television, 1981-86; Principal Conductor, Glasgow Chamber Orchestra, 1985-86; Lecturer in Twentieth Century Music, Sao Paulo State University, Brazil, 1987-89; Founder-Director, Jardim Musical Arts Centre, 1987-; Founder-Conductor, Ensemble Grupo Novo Horizonte, 1988-; Director of Education, Mozarteum Brasileiro, 1987-; Conductor, Choir of Cultura Inglesa, Sao Paulo, 1988-90; Choral Director, 1st National Festival of Brazilian Colonial Music (Juiz de Fora) 1990; Guest Conductor, Campos do Jordao Festival, 1990; Guest Conductor, Orquestra Sinfonica e Madrigal da Universidade Federal da Bahia, Salvador, 1990-; Director of Conducting Course, Festival Seminarios Internacionais Salvador, 1991; Lecture-Recital piano tours: 1990 Bridges Across Time, Brazil, Denmark, United Kingdom; 1991 New World Experience, Brazil, Denmark (25 concerts); Co-Founder-Director, Mostra de Musica Contemporanea, Ouro Preto, 1991; Regular broadcasts on Radio e Televisao Cultura, Sao Paulo, 1988-; Visiting lecturer, Federal Universities of Rio de Janeiro 1990, Bahia 1990/91, Uberlandia 1992; Guest Conductor, Camerata Antigua de Curitiba, 1993. *Compositions:* Sacred Choral Works include:

Anglican Hymn Collection, 1988-; The Lords Prayer, 1990; Ta Voix, 1991; Cançao de Quatá for Trombone Quartet, 1993. *Current Management:* Jardim Musical, Sao Paulo. *Address:* Rua Angatuba 97, Pacaembú, 01247-000 Sao Paulo, SP, Brazil.

GRIFFITHS Gwyneth Grace, b. 19 Sept 1943, Welwyn Garden City, Hertfordshire, England. Singer (Mezzo-soprano). m. J M Heraud, 1971, dec. *Education:* Latymer School; Guildhall School of Music and Drama, London; AGSM in Singing (Teaching and Performing) and Piano Teaching; Further study with Roy Henderson and Paul Hamburger. *Career:* Sang regularly at South Bank Halls, Royal Albert Hall, numerous cathedrals, concert halls and music festivals; Appearances, Brazil, Switzerland, Netherlands and Belgium; Retired from singing for health reasons; Currently gives courses in major choral works and German Lieder, Cambridge. *Honours:* Kathleen Ferrier Memorial Scholarship, 1968; Bronze Medal, Royal Overseas League, 1968; Leverhulme Scholarship for study in Germany, 1970; Award of Merit, Hertogenbosch International Vocal Concours, 1974. *Membership:* Incorporated Society of Musicians. *Address:* Nimrod, 8 Cook Close, Milton Road, Cambridge CB4 1PH, England.

GRIFFITHS Howard Laurence, b. 24 Feb 1950, Hastings, England. Conductor. m. Semra, 24 July 1971, 1 son, 1 daughter. *Education:* Studied viola with Cecil Aronowitz, Royal College of Music, London ARCM; Studied Conducting with Leon Barzin in Paris and Erich Schmid in Zurich. *Debut:* QEH with ECO 1989; RFH with RPO 1991. *Career:* Principal viola, Ankara State Opera until 1979; Member of Lucern String Quartet; Conducted many prominent orchestras, including Royal Philharmonic Orchestra, London; the English Chamber Orchestra; the Warsaw Philharmonic Orchestra; The Basel Radio Symphony Orchestra; Istanbul State Symphony Orchestra; the AML Lucern; the Northern Sinfonia of England; Stadtorchester Winterthur, The Kristiansand Symphony Orchestra, Strings of Zurich, the Polish Chamber Orchestra; Tonhalle Orchestra, Zürich, Zürich Chamber Orchestra. *Recordings include:* 18th century Swiss Composers, Stalder and Reindl with English Chamber Orchestra; Instrumental Works of Othmar Schoeck - ECO; Mozart Horn Concertos, Kalinski and Polish Chamber Orchestra; Works of Max Bruch with the Royal Philharmonic Orchestra; For Koch International, 3 CDs of music by Turkish composers (Saygun, Erkin, Rey), with the Northern Sinfonia of England, Baroque Oboe concertos and Mozart Sinfonia, Concertante for Sony. *Contributions to:* Discovered oldest Swiss Violin Concerto by Caspar Fritz, performed in Lucern and Zurich, to be recorded with ECO in 1993. *Memberships:* Artistic Director, Allensbach Chamber Music festival, Germany since 1992. *Hobbies:* Tennis; Reading; Playing chamber music. *Current Management:* Henrietta Brougham, 6 Bedford Court, Grena Road, Richmond, Surrey TW9 1XT, England. *Address:* Bondlerstr 25, 8802 Kilchberg, Switzerland.

GRIFFITHS Paul, b. 24 Nov 1947, Bridgend, Glamorgan, Wales. Critic; Writer on Music. m. Rachel Griffiths. *Education:* BA, MSc, Lincoln College, Oxford. *Career:* Music critic for various journals from 1971; Area Editor, 20th Century Music, New Grove Dictionary of Music (1980) and New Oxford Companion to Music (1983); Chief Music Critic, The Times, 1982-92; New Yorker from 1992; Author of 3 novels; Compiled Mozart pasticcio The Jewel Box for Opera North, 1991. *Publications:* A Concise History of Modern Music 1978; Modern Music: The Avant-Garde since 1945, 1981; The String Quartet 1983; New Sounds, New Personalities: British Composers of the 1980s, 1985; An Encyclopedia of 20th-Century Music 1986; Studies of Boulez, Cage, Stravinsky's The Rake's Progress, Ligeti, Davies, Bartók and Messiaen. *Contributions to:* The Grove Concise Dictionary of Music and Musicians 1988; Numerous professional journals. *Address:* Darville Cottage, Lower Heyford, Oxford, England.

GRIFFITHS Paul Wynne, b. 1958, England. Conductor. *Education:* Studied at Royal Northern College of Music and London Opera Centre. *Career:* Conducted The Judgement of Paris by John Woolrich in Royal Opera House Garden Venture Series, Orchestra of Royal Opera at Windsor Festival and Symphony Hall, Birmingham; Paris debut at Théâtre du Champs Elysées, with Orchestre du Conservatoire National; Further concerts with Royal Philharmonic, English Chamber Orchestra and Tokyo Philharmonic; Season 1992-93 with Il Trovatore for Scottish Opera, L'Elisir d'Amore at Gothenburg, concert in Athens with Grace Bumbry and London with Josephine Barstow and Montserrat Caballe; Artistic Director and Accompanist of Luciano Pavarotti Master Class; Recital Accompanist with Geraint Evans, Jose Carreras, Katia Ricciarelli, James King, Thomas Allen and Yevgeny Nesterenko; Staff Conductor, Royal Opera House, Covent Garden. *Address:* c/o John Coast Ltd, 31 Sinclair Road, London W14 0NS, England.

GRIGORIU Theodor, b. 25 July 1926, Galatzi, Rumania. Composer. m. 28 Mar 1951. *Education:* Studied with Mihail Jora, Conservatory of Bucharest, Rumania, with Aram Khachaturian, P I Tchaikovsky Conservatory, Moscow, USSR; Faculty of Architecture, Bucharest. *Career:* Secretary-General, Union of Rumanian Composers; Freelance Composer; His works performed worldwide. *Compositions:* Orchestral works include: Sinfonia Cantabile, percussion and strings, 1950, revised, 1966; Variations Symphoniques sur une Chanson d'Anton Pann, 1955; Concerto pour Double Orchestre de Chamber et Hautbois, 1957; Vis cosmic, 1959; Omagiu Lui Enescue, violins, 1960; orchestral version of Sept Chansons (works Clement Marot), 1964; Melodie Infinita; string orchestra, 1969; Tristia, in memoriam Ionel Perlea, violins, violas, 1972; Suite Carpatine, string orchestra, 1980; Pastorale si Idile Transilvane, 1984; Choral music; Elegia Pontica, choir, baritone-bass, instrumental ensemble, 1969; Canti per Europa (oratorio), mixed choir and orchestra, 1976; Vocalizele Marii (choral symphony), mixed choir and organ, 1984; Columna Modala (chamber music), piano, 1984; Others include: Codin, 1963; La Foret des Pendus, 1965; Theatre music. *Recordings:* Various works, Electrocord. *Publication:* Muzica si Numbul Poeziei. *Hobbies:* Painting; Design; Graphics. *Address:* Str Pictor Rosenthal 2, Bucharest 71288, Rumania.

GRILLO Joann, b. 14 May 1939, New York, USA. Singer (Mezzo-Soprano). m. Richard Kness, 1 son. *Education:* BS, Hunter College, New York; Private study with Loretta Corelli, Franco Iglesias and Daniel Ferro. *Debut:* New York City Opera 1962, as Gertrude in Louise; Metropolitan Opera from 1963, as Carmen, Meg Page in Falstaff, Preziosilla in La Forza del Destino, Santuzza, Laura in La Gioconda, Neocle in The Siege of Corinth and Suzuki (226 performances); Sang Massenet's Charlotte at Barcelona in 1963; Amneris at Frankfurt (1967); Carmen at the Vienna Staatsoper and in Paris (1978, 1981); Guest appearances in Essen, Hamburg, Zurich, Dallas, Philadelphia, Lisbon and Marseille; Other roles included Marguerite in The Damnation of Faust, Saint-Saëns's Dalila, Olga in Eugene Onegin, Fricka in The Ring and Verdi's Eboli, Ulrica and Azucena; Sang Amneris at Rio de Janeiro, 1988; Concert appearances as Jocasta in Oedipus Rex. *Hobbies:* Egyptology; Cooking; Travel. *Current Management:* Eric Semon Associates, 111 W. 57 Street, New York City, NY 10019, USA. *Address:* 1550-75 Street, Brooklyn, NY 11228, USA.

GRIMM Hans-Gunther, b. 1925, Germany. Singer (Baritone); Professor. *Education:* Studied in East Berlin. *Career:* Sang at Berlin Staatsoper, 1950-52, Bremen, 1952-54, Mannheim, 1954-60; Engaged at Cologne, 1960-64, Theater am Gartnerplatz, Munich, 1964-66, Dortmund, 1966-70; Sang in Cologne, 1961, in German premiere of Nono's Intolleranza 60; Guest appearances as concert and opera singer, Frankfurt, Japan, North America, France and Barcelona; Roles included Mozart's Count, Don Giovanni, Guglielmo and Papageno, Malatesta, Marcello, Wolfram, Escamillo, Don Fernando in Fidelio and Carlos in Forza del Destino; Professor at Maastrich Conservatory, Netherlands, 1973-82.

Recordings include: Undine by Lortzing; Eine Nacht in Venedig; Rossini's Petite Messe solennelle; Beethoven's Ninth.

GRIMS-LAND Ebbe B V, b. 11 June 1915, Malmo, Sweden. Composer; Musician. m. Vera Annerstedt. 2 sons. *Education:* Studied music in Scandinavia and Internationally; Instruments, Viola, Violin, Mandolin. *Debut:* Malmo, 1932. *Career:* Performed with Swedish Radio-Symphony Orchestra, 1943-74; Gitarr-Kammartrion, 1955; Tonkonstnarstrion, 1970; Drottningholms and Nationalmusei Chamber Orchestra, Stockholms Baroque Ensemble, 1973; Floridsdorfer-Kammerspieler, 1974; Gesellschaft der Musikfreunde, Wien, 1983; Soloist on Radio and television. *Compositions:* Several compositions including: Sinfonietta Carl von Linné; Montafoni; Concertino; Concerto rondoso; Instrumentality Ballad; Konnexion; Canzona; Eloge for Bibi Andersson; Songs with Flutem, Mandolin, Viola, Guitar; Compositions for Wind Ensemble and for Orchestra. *Address:* Nissastigen 1, S-12841 Bagarmossen, Sweden.

GRIMSTAD Birgitte, b. 15 Dec 1935, Copenhagen, Denmark. Folksinger; Actor; Voice Teacher. div., 2 sons, 1 daughter. *Education:* BA, Theatre Arts, University of Minnesota, USA, 1959; Self-taught, Singing, Guitar; 1-year Teaching Certificate, Norwegian State Conservatory, 1983. *Debut:* Oslo, 1966. *Career:* TV Producer for children's programmes, 1960-63; Extensive concert touring in Nordic countries and internationally. *Compositions:* Music with voice as only instrument; Performance projects: Last Bird, 1988; Music for Living Windharp, 1989; What the windharp sang, 1-woman theatre production, 1991; Music for A Portrait, 1-woman dance performance by Alison Chase, premiere at Pilobolus Dance Theatre, New York City, 1993; Various folk songs. *Recordings:* 18 LPs, Norway and Denmark; 1 LP, Minnesota; Nordic and international folk songs; Wondering and Calling, MC with meditative music, voice only; After a visit in the greenhouse of dreams, CD, voice only, 1991. *Publication:* Menneskeviser, collection of her repertoire, 1972. *Contributions:* Articles on cultural policy issues. *Honours:* Music Critics Prize, 1971; Spellemanns prisen (Grand Prix du Disque, 1972, 1978. *Memberships:* Norwegian Musicians Union; Norsk Tonekunstner Samfunnet. *Hobbies:* Painting; Textile work. *Address:* Evensgate 2, 0655 Oslo, Norway.

GRINDE Nils, b. 8 Jan 1927, Enebakk, Norway. Musicologist; Organist. m. Kirsti Wilhelmsen. *Education:* Candidate Mag. Musicology, University of Oslo, 1953; Higher Examination in Organ, Oslo Music Conservatory, 1959. *Career:* Docent in Musicology; Currently, professor of Musicology, University of Oslo. *Publications include:* The Halfdan Kjerulf Bibliography, 1956; Halfdan Kjerulf's Piano Music, 1961; Textbook in Counterpoint in the Style of Bach, 1966; History of Norwegian Music, 1971; Norwegian Music: An Anthology, 1974; Contemporary Norwegian Music, 1920-80, 1981; History of Norwegian Music, Russion Ed, 1982; A History of Norwegian Music, English Ed, 1991; Editor, Studia Musicologica Norwegica Volumes 2-4, 1976-78; Editor, Halfdan Kjerulf-Collected Songs, Volume 1-2, 1978; Halfdan Kjerulf-Collected Piano Pieces, 1980; History of Norwegian Music, 3th edition, 1993; Editor, Edvard Grieg Piano Duet, dramatic music (GGA v6), 1982; Edit with Don, Edvard Grieg Songs (GGA v14,15), 1990-91. *Contributions to:* Grove's Dictionary, 6th Edition; Sohlmans Musiklexikon, 2nd edition. *Address:* Slemdalsvn 91 B, 0373 Oslo 3, Norway.

GRINDENKO Tatyana, b. 1946, Kharkov, Ukraine. Concert Violinist. *Education:* Studied at Central Music School, Kharkov, and Moscow Conservatoire. *Debut:* Kharkov, playing works by Bach, Wieniawski and Paganini, with orchestra, 1954 (aged 8). *Career:* Gave concerts throughout Russia and Europe as soloist and with major ensembles and in chamber concerts; Prevented by Soviet authorities from touring, 1979-88, but appeared with New York Philharmonic, London Symphony Orchestra, Leipzig Gewandhaus, Berlin

Radio Symphony, Vienna Symphony and Chamber Orchestra of Europe; Conductors have included Mravinsky, Kondrashin, Kurt Masur and Nikolaus Harnoncourts; With Alexei Lyubimov formed Academy of Ancient Music, Moscow, 1982, the only ensemble in former USSR performing on authentic instruments; Tours, 1988-, USA, Germany, France, Italy, Nwetherlands, India, Austria, Belgium Czechoslovakia, Hungary, Finland; Festival engagements, Namur, Schleswig-Holstein, Passau, Lockenhaus, Brno and Bratislava; London debut playing the Roslavetz Violin Concerto with Royal Philharmonic under Ashkenazy, 1991. *Recordings:* For various well-known labels. *Honours include:* 1st Prize, World Youth Festival, Sofia, Bulgaria, 1968; Prizewinner, Tchaikovsky Competition, Moscow, 1970. *Address:* c/o Sonata, 11 Northpark Street, Glasgow G20 7AA, Scotland.

GRIST Reri, b. 29 Feb 1932, New York, USA. Coloratura Soprano. *Education:* Music and Art High School, New York; Queens College. *Debut:* Consuelo, West Side Story, 1957. *Career:* Santa Fe Opera Company and New York City Opera, 1959; Washington Opera Society, 1960, 1962; Vancouver Opera Association, 1962, 1964; San Francisco Opera, 1963, 1964, 1965, 1966; Chicago Lyric Opera, 1964; Montreal debut as Gilda, Rigoletto, 1966; Metropolitan Opera debut as Rosina, Barber of Seville, 1966; Has sung in numerous opera houses and festivals in Europe including debut as Queen of Night, Magic Flute, Cologne; Despina, Glyndebourne, 1962; Zerbinetta, Ariadne, Naples, 1963; Holland Festival, 1963; Piccola Scala, Milan, 1963; Bordeaux Opera, 1964; Munich State Opera, 1965; Regular appearances Zurich Opera, 1960-; Covent Garden, 1962, 1966 as Olympia, Gilda and Susanna; Vienna State Opera, 1963-; Salzburg Festival, 1964-. *Recordings:* Don Giovanni, Cosi Fan Tutte, Ariadne auf Naxos, Scarlatti's Endimione e Cintia (Deutsche Grammophon); Un Ballo in Maschera, Il Re Pastore and Der Schauspieldirektor (RCA); Le Nozze di Figaro (Electrola); La Rossignol (CBS); Rigoletto (EMI). *Address:* c/o Columbia Artists Management, 165 West 57th Street, New York, NY 10019, USA.

GRITTON Robin William Langford, b. 5 Feb 1939, Reigate, Surrey, England. Conductor. m. Patricia Elspeth Swift, 11 Aug 1962. 1 son, 2 daughters. *Education:* Royal College of Music, London. *Career:* Assistant Director of Music, Epsom College, 1961-64; Conductor, Kent Music School, 1965-69; Freelance Conductor, Pianist, Singer, Cellist, 1970-79; Examiner, Associated Board of Royal Schools of Music; Guest Conductor, Belgian Radio, Westdeutscher Rundfunk, Norddeutscher Rundfunk, Conductor, Dutch Radio Choir, 1980-. *Recordings:* Various Dutch Contemporary (Donemus); as Chorus Master Dutch Radio, Stockhausen Michaels Heimkehr, Mahler 2nd Symphony, Beethoven 9th with Haitink and Concertgebouw Amsterdam. *Honours:* FRCO; LRAM (Singing Performance); ARCM (Organ performing, Piano teaching). *Memberships:* Musicians Union; Incorporated Society of Musicians. *Hobbies:* Graphology; Gardening; Walking; Canals. *Address:* Heath Farm, Reigate, Surrey RH2 8QP, England.

GRONER Brian Timothy, b. 19 June 1956, Frankfort, Michigan, USA. Conductor; Violinist. m. Teresa K Fream, 14 June 1980, 1 daughter. *Education:* BA cum laude, Classical Greek, Music Performance, Social Work, Michigan State University, 1979. *Career:* Violinist, Oklahoma Symphony, 1979-80; Co-Founder, Conductor, West Texas Youth Orchestras, 1981-82; Violinist, 1982-91, Assistant Conductor, 1988-91, Nashville Symphony Orchestra; Conductor: Nashville Junior Symphony, 1984-86; Nashville Youth Symphony, 1984-88; Nashville Little Symphony, 1987-88; Nashville Symphony String Orchestra, 1988-91; Music Director, Nashville Cello Ensemble, 1989-91; Music Director, Conductor, Kokomo Symphony Orchestra, 1991-; Conductor, Birch Creek Music Festival, 1993; Guest Conductor: Lake Shore Symphony, Nashville Ballet, Indianapolis Chamber Orchestra, Nashville Symphony Orchestra, Chicago Sinfonietta; Conducted premieres:

The Emperor's Nightingale (Herbert Donaldson), ballet, 1987; Free from Seasons Passing (Lee Gannon), 1988; Saints and Sinners (Kristin Wilkinson), cello ensemble, 1989; Broadcasts, National Public Radio, 1989, 1990; Teaching: Adjunct Faculty, Blair School of Music, Vanderbilt University, 1984-85; Faculty, Tennessee Governor's School for the Arts, 1987; Artist Faculty, Concordia University, 1992. *Publication:* A Child's Guide to the Symphony: A curriculum for preschools on the orchestra, 1989. *Memberships:* Conductors Guild; American Federation of Musicians; American Symphony Orchestra League. *Hobbies:* Cycling; Automobile restoration. *Address:* 531 Illinois Ave, Glenwood, IL 60425, USA.

GRONER Earl, b. 23 Oct 1935, Stroudsburg, Pennsylvania, USA. Conductor; Teacher. *Education:* Bmus, University of Michigan, Ann Arbor; MMus, New England Conservatory of Music; Scholarship Fellow, Tanglewood Music Center, 1956-57; Scholarship Student, National Orchestral Association, New York City, 1961-62. *Career:* Teacher, Lakeland Schools, Shrub Oak, New York, 1962-72; Teacher, Scarsdale Public Schools, Scarsdale, New York, 1972-; Conductor, Scarsdale High School Orchestra and Chamber Orchestra; Music Director, Conductor, Empire State Symphony Orchestra, Empire State Pops Orchestra, Empire State Chamber Orchestra, Scarsdale, 1987-. *Honours:* Phi Mu Alpha Sinfonia, 1956; Pi Kappa Lambda, 1958. *Memberships:* Former Member: 7th Army Symphony Orchestra, Stuttgart, Germany; Past President, Westchester County (NY) School Music Association; Former Member, Alumni Board of Governors, University of Michigan School of Music; American String Teachers Association; American Symphony Orchestra League; Conductors Guild; Music Educators National Conference; National School Orchestra Association; Chair, Council of Music Education Associations, New York State; Advisory Council, New York State School Music Association. *Hobby:* Making own conducting batons. *Current Management:* Empire State Concert Productions, 130 Garth Road, Suite 123, Scarsdale, NY 10583, USA. *Address:* 142 Garth Road, Scarsdale, NY 10583, USA.

GRONNIER Henry Maurice Pierre, b. 7 May 1960, Saint Quentin, France. Opera Manager. *Education:* Baccalaureat, Mathematics, Physics, Chemistry, Lycee Henry Martin, Saint Quentin, 1978; Gold Medal in Violin, Piano and Chamber Music, Versailles Conservatory, 1980; Artist Diploma in Violin, University International, Paris, 1981; Student of Zino Francescatti and Michele Avclair, 1984-86. *Debut:* With Brahms Concerto, Gaveau Hall, Paris, 7 May 1981. *Career:* Owner, Henry Gronnier Artists Management, New York City, USA, 1990-; Specialises in managing opera singers, notably soprano Margarita Castro Alberty, countertenor Brian Asawa, tenor Gregory Cross and bass Alexander Anisimov. *Hobbies:* Playing chamber music; Opera. *Address:* 107 West 89th Street PH-B, New York, NY 10024, USA.

GRONOWETTER Freda, b. 10 Feb 1918, Toronto, Canada. Concert Cellist; Teacher. m. George J Herman, 15 Dec 1945, dec 1970. *Education:* Royal Conservatory of Music, Toronto; Cello study under Serge Stupin, then with Alfred Wallenstein, Joseph Schuster, Emanuel Feuermann. *Debut:* Town Hall, New York City. *Career:* Cellist, Toronto Symphony Orchestra; 1st Cellist, American Symphony Orchestra, New York City Opera Company Orchestra, Ballet Theatre Orchestra; Soloist with Markova-Dolin Ballet Company; Recital, Carnegie Hall; Guest Soloist, The White House, Washington; Recitals, broadcasts and concerts as Soloist with symphony orchestras, throughout USA, Canada and Mexico; Currently Soloist, Musical Arts Trio; Taught YMHA, New York City, Long Island School of Music, Great Neck School of Music and Arts, Brooklyn Music School, etc; Music Director, Professor of Music, Southampton College, Long Island University, 1965; Master classes; Cello workshops; Judge, Israel Cello Competition, Feuermann International Cello Competition, Austin, Texas, etc; Competition Director,

5 Towns Music and Art Foundation; Director, Celebrity Concert Series, Zinman Hall, Boca Raton, Florida, 1991. *Compositions:* In A Sacred Mood, for violoncello and piano or orchestra. *Publications:* Manual of Basic Cello Instruction; 16 hours of film from Elementary to Artist. *Hobbies:* Interior Decorating; Writing; Gardening. *Address:* 557 West Market Street, Long Beach, NY 11561, USA.

GRONROOS Walton, b. 1939, Aland Islands, Finland. Singer (Baritone); Administrator. *Education:* Graduated as organist, Sibelius Academy, Helsinki 1966. *Career:* Served as cantor and organist at Lapinjarvi, 1964-71; Studied voice in Vienna and gave first concert 1971; Helsinki concert debut 1971, Stockholm 1973; Deutsche Oper Berlin from 1975, as Antonio in Le Nozze di Figaro (debut), Mozart's Count, Papageno and Don Giovanni; Posa in Don Carlos and Malatesta in Don Pasquale; Cardinal Morone in Palestrina and Wolfram in Tannhäuser; Finnish National Opera from 1974, and Posa at the Savonlinna Festival; Maggio Musicale, Florence, 1983-87, all over the world; US debut, 1984, Chicago, Boston, Cleveland, New York; As concert artist has sung in Bach's St Matthew Passion in London and Paris (1979, 1981); Artistic Director, Savonlinna Festival 1987-91; Finnish National Opera from 1992. *Recordings:* Lieder by Schubert, Tannhäuser (EMI); Songs by Brahms, Sibelius and Rangström (BIS); Iphigénie en Tauride (Orfeo); Tchaikovsky Iolanta (Erato). *Address:* c/o Helsingink katu, Helsinki 00250, Finland.

GROOM Lester Herbert, b. 19 Jan 1929, Chicago, Illinois, USA. Organist; Music Educator. m. Myrtle Vera Jacobson, 14 June 1955, 1 son, 2 daughters. *Education:* BMus, Wheaton College, Wheaton, Illinois, 1951; MMus, Northwestern University, Evanston, Illinois, 1952; AAGO, 1954; Private Study in Composition with Stella Roberts, American Conservatory of Music, 1953-54. *Career:* Instructor, Moody Bible Institute, Chicago, 1953-55; Assistant Professor, Blue Mountain College, Mississippi, 1957-62; Baker University, Kansas, 1962-67; Associate Professor, Seattle Pacific University, Seattle, 1969-, Professor Emeritus, 1991; Faculty, Evergreen Conference School of Church Music, Colorado, 1965-77; President, Evergreen Conference, 1973-78; Organist-Choirmaster Positions: Illinois; Georgia; Mississippi; Kansas and Washington. *Compositions:* 24 Psalm-Voluntaries; Six Preludes for Organ; Easter Alleluia; Grant To Us, Lord; and other compositions for organ and choral works. *Address:* 10629 NE 26th Street, Bellevue, WA 98004, USA.

GROOP Monica, b. 1958, Finland. Singer (Mezzo-soprano). *Education:* Studied at the Conservatory and Sibelius Academy in Helsinki; Masterclasses with Kim Borg, Hartmut Holl, Mitsuko Shirai and Erik Werba. *Career:* Has appeared with the Savonlinna Opera Festival from 1986 and the Finnish National Opera in Helsinki from 1987; Sang Dorabella in a production of Così fan Tutte conducted by Salvatore Accardo at Naples, 1989; Concert performance of Così fan Tutte in Rome, 1991; Concert engagements with leading Finnish and other Scandinavian orchestras under Erich Bergel, Jukka-Pekka Saraste, Leif Segerstam and Walter Weller; Tour of West Germany 1989 with the Drottningholm Baroque Orchestra in Bach's St John Passion (Bachwoche Ansbach Festival); Season 1989-90 with the Bach B minor Mass and St John Passion in Stockholm, Berlin and Edmonton, Canada; Mozart's Betulia Liberata with the Bachakademie in Stuttgart under Helmuth Rilling, 1991; Mahler/Schoenberg project with Philippe Herreweghe and the Ensemble Musique Oblique; Season 1991/92 with Cherubino at Aix-en-Provence, Wellgunde and the Walküre Waltraute at Covent Garden (debut), the Missa Solemnis at Aix, 1992; tour of Così fan Tutte with Sigiswald Kuijken to Spain, France and Portugal and appearances with the Drottningholm Theatre at the Barbican; Season 1993 with Cherubino at Toulouse, the Composer at the Paris Opéra Comique and Bach's St John Passion in Spain, Lucerne and Stockholm. *Recordings include:* Bach B minor Mass; Così fan Tutte for television. *Current Management:* IMG Artists Europe (UK); Nordic Artists

Management (GM). *Address:* c/o IMG Artists Europe, Media House, 3 Burlington Lane, London W4 2TH, England.

GROSCHEL Werner, b. 18 Sept 1940, Nuremberg, Germany. Singer (Bass). *Education:* Studied at the Richard Strauss Conservatory Munich with Marcel Cordes and Josef Metternich. *Debut:* Flensburg 1967, as Fiesco in Simon Boccanegra. *Career:* Member of the Zurich Opera from 1972, as Rocco, Mephistopheles, Falstaff (Nicolai) and Dikoy in Katya Kabanova; Mozart's Osmin, Don Giovanni and Sarastro; Verdi's King Philip, Silva (Ernani) and Zaccaria (Nabucco); Wagner's Daland, Landgrave, King Henry and Pogner; Sang in the 1975 premiere of Klebe's Ein Wahrer Held and the premiere of Kalterborn's Ein Engel kommt nach Babylon, 1977; Guest appearances elsewhere in Switzerland and in Germany; Many concert engagements, notably in music by Bach and Monteverdi. *Recordings include:* Plutone in Monteverdi's Orfeo, L'Incoronazione di Poppea and Il Ritorno di Ulisse (Telefunken). *Address:* c/o Opernhaus Zurich, Falkenstrasse 1, CH-8008 Zurich, Switzerland.

GROSGURIN Daniel, b. 13 July 1949, Geneva, Switzerland. Cellist. m. Ferhan Güraydin, 21 June 1990. *Education:* Classical Baccalaureat, Geneva, 1967; Conservatoire Geneva, 1st Prize 1968, Master of Music, Indiana University, 1972. *Debut:* London 1976. *Career:* Lucerne Festival 1975; Salzburg Festival 1990, regular appearances with Orchestre de la Suisse Romande 1978-, tours with Stuttgart Philharmonic 1987, Festival Strings, Lucerne, 1975 and 1978; London Festival Hall with LSCO 1991, Tibor Varga Festival 1991, Eastern Music Festival (USA) 1992; Chamber Music with Martha Argerich. Professor, State Music College, Heidelberg-Mannheim, Germany, 1978-90; Professor, Geneva Conservatory of Music, 1990. *Recordings:* Swiss and German Radio recordings; TV programme with Pierre Fournier. *Hobbies:* Literature; Swimming; Hiking. *Address:* 15 Route de Florissant, 1206 Geneva, Switzerland.

GROSS Ruth, b. 1959, Kleve, Germany. Singer (Soprano). *Education:* Studied Viola at Essen, Voice with Edda Moser, Cologne. *Debut, Regensburg, as Leonore in Fidelio, 1987.* *Career:* Sang at Ulm, 1988-89, notably in Golem by d'Albert and in operetta; Bayreuth Festival, 1989-90, as Ortlinde in Die Walkure; Sang Leonore at Basle, 1989; Has appeared at Staatsoper Stuttgart, 1989-, as Iphigénie (in Aulide), Arabella, and Elsa in production of Lohengrin conducted by Silvio Varviso. *Address:* Staatsoper Stuttgart, Oberer Schlossgarten 6, 7000 Stuttgart, Germany.

GRUBE Michael, b. 12 May 1954, Uberlingen. Violin-Virtuoso; Violin Professor. *Education:* Privately with his violinist father, Professor Max-Ludwig Grube; Further violinistic studies with Professor Henryk Szeryng, Professor Ivan Galamian, Professor Eugene Effenberger; Conservatory Diploma, 1975; Studies of Musicology and Composition (Professor Gunther Becker). *Debut:* West Berlin, 1964. *Career:* Concert Soloist in 110 countries of all continents, performances before His Majesty King Tupou IV of Tonga and Queen of Tonga; Concerts and Festival Performances in Vienna, Copenhagen, Prague, Warsaw, Leningrad, Moscow, New York, Washington DC, Jerusalem, Caracas, Buenos Aires, Canberra, Singapore, Osaka, Bangkok, Bogota, Sao Paulo, Delhi, Panama City, Madrid, Istanbul; Pro Musica International USA. *Compositions:* Souvenir de Senegal for Solo Violin (Radio Dakar); Hommage a Colville Young and Olanchito (Landestonkunstler Festival 1986-87). *Recordings:* Garnet Records, Dusseldorf; Violin Concertos by Bruch, Mendelssohn, Mozart; Violin Music by Dvořák; Smetana, Suk, Handel, Paganini, Reger, Haas, also with Max-Ludwig Grube (Violin) and Helen Grube (Piano). *Hobbies:* Philosophy; Indian classical music; Austrian bakery of the old tradition. *Current Management:* Konzertdirektion Olga Altmann, Austria. *Address:* c/o Konzertdirektion Olga Altmann, Jaquingasse 37/55, A-1030 Wien, Austria.

GRUBER H(einz) K(arl), b. 3 Jan 1943, Vienna, Austria. Composer. *Education:* Studied at the Vienna Hochschule für Musik 1957-63 and with Gottfried von Einem 1963-64. *Career:* Sang in Vienna Boys' Choir 1953-57; Double Bass player in ensemble Die Reihe from 1961; Principal Double Bass Tonkunstler Orchestra 1963-69; Co-Founder of MOB Art and Tone ART ensemble 1968-71; Has worked with Austrian Radio, Vienna, from 1969; conducted the premiere of his opera Gomorrah at the Vienna Volksoper, 1993. *Compositions:* 4 Pieces for solo violin 1963; Manhattan Broadcasts 1962-64; 5 Kinderlider for female voices 1965, revised 1980; The Expulsion from Paradise for speakers and 6 solo instruments 1966, revised 1979; 3 MOB Pieces for 7 instruments and percussion 1968, revised 1977; 6 Episodes from a Discontinued Chronicle for piano 1967; Frankenstein !! for baritone, chansonnier and orchestra 1976-77; Phantom-Bilder for small orchestra 1977; Violin Concerto 1977-78; Demilitarized Zones for brass band 1979; Charivari for orchestra 1981; Castles in the Air for piano 1981; Rough Music, concerto for percussion and orchestra 1982; Anagram for 6 cellos 1987; Nebelsteinmusik (2nd Violin Concerto) 1988; Cello Concerto 1989; Gomorrah (opera), 1992; Gloria von Jaxtberg, music theatre, 1993; Television appearances include Nekrophilius the Pawnbroker in Bring me the Head of Amadeus (for the Mozart Bicentenary, 1991). *Address:* c/o Boosey & Hawkes Ltd., 295 Regent Street, London W1, England.

GRUBEROVA Edita, b. 23 Dec 1946, Bratislava, Czechoslovakia. Singer (Soprano). *Education:* Studied with Maria Medvecka in Prague and with Ruthilde Boesch in Vienna. *Debut:* Bratislava 1968, as Rosina. *Career:* Sang at the Vienna Staatsoper 1970, as the Queen of Night: sang Zerbinetta in Vienna 1976; Glyndebourne Festival 1973; Salzburg Festival from 1974, notably as Elisabeth de Valois in Don Carlos, conducted by Herbert von Karajan; Metropolitan Opera debut 1977, as the Queen of Night; Covent Garden 1984, as Giulietta in a new production of I Capuleti e i Montecchi by Bellini; Guest appearances at the Bregenz Festival and at La Scala, the Munich Staatsoper (Massenet's Manon) and the Hamburg Staatsoper; Other roles include Gilda, Lucia, Constanze and Violetta; Sang Lucia at La Scala, 1984, Chicago 1986 and Barcelona 1987; La Scala 1987, Donna Anna, Zurich Opera 1988, as Marie in La Fille du Régiment; Metropolitan Opera 1989, as Violetta; Sang Rossini's Rosina and Semiramide (concert) at Munich 1990; Barcelona 1990, as Ariadne; Vienna Staatsoper Oct 1990, as Elizabeth I in Donizetti's Roberto Devereux; Season 1992 as Lucia at Munich and Semiramide at Zurich. *Recordings:* Don Carlos (EMI); Die Zauberflöte; I Capuleti e i Montecchi; Lucia d Lammermoor; Leonore by Paer and Ariadne auf Naxos (Decca); Mitridate by Mozart (Deutsche Grammophon); Rigoletto (Philips); Die Schöpfung (Telefunken); Video of Rigoletto, with Luciano Pavarotti. *Address:* John Coast, 31 Sinclair Road, London W14 ONS, England.

GRUBERT Naum, b. 1951, Riga, USSR. Pianist. *Education:* Studied at the Riga Conservatory and with Professor Gutman in Moscow. *Career:* Performed first in Russia, Eastern Europe, Italy and Finland; Emigrated from USSR 1983 and has performed with the London Symphony, the Hague Philharmonic, Netherlands Philharmonic, Orchestre de la Suisse Romande, Helsinki Philharmonic and orchestras in Germany and Spain; Conductors include Paavo Berglund, Sergiu Commisiona, Franz-Paul Decker, Valeri Gergiev, Hartmut Haenchen, Vernon Handley, Thomas Sanderling, Horst Stein and Christopher Seaman; Further engagements with the Rotterdam Philharmonic, the Tonkunstler Orchestra Vienna and the Scottish National Orchestra. *Honours include:* 2nd Prize, International Piano Competition, Montreal, 1977; Prize winner at the 1978 Tchaikovsky Competition, Moscow. *Address:* c/o Ingpen and Williams Ltd., 14 Kensington Court, London W8 5DN, England.

GRUENBERG Erich, b. 12 Oct 1924, Vienna, Austria. Violinist. *Education:* Studied in Vienna and at the Jerusalem Conservatory. *Debut:* Jerusalem 1938. *Career:* Leader of the Palestine Broadcasting Corporation Orchestra 1938-45; Moved to London 1946 and took British nationality 1950; Solo career from 1947; Leader of the Stockholm Philharmonic orchestra 1956-58, the London Symphony 1962-65, Royal Philharmonic 1972-76; Appearances as soloist throughout Europe, the USA and Canada, Australia, Holland, Germany, Switzerland and Scandinavia; Gave the first Russian performance of Britten's Concerto, in Moscow; Engagements with the Hungarian State Symphony Orchestra in Budapest and visits to to the Far East; Associated with contemporary works by Goehr, Gerhard and David Morgan; Formerly leader of the London String Quartet and chamber music player with William Glock, Franz Reizenstein, Edmund Rubbra and William Pleeth; Professor at the Royal Academy of Music; Master Classes and Competitiion Jury appearances around the world. *Recordings:* Beethoven's Concerto conducted by Horenstein and the complete Violin Sonatas with David Wilde; Works by Bach, Stravinsky, Messiaen (Quatuor pour le fin du Temps), Durko, Parry and Vaughan Williams; Labels include EMI, Decca, Argo, Chandos, Hyperion, Hungaroton and Lyrita. *Honours include:* Winner, Carl Flesch Competition, London, 1947. *Address:* c/o Intermusica, 16 Duncan Terrace, London N1 8BZ, England.

GRUENBERG Joanna, b. 1957, Stockholm, Sweden. Concert Pianist. *Education:* Studied with Fanny Waterman, Louis Kentner and Peter Frankl; Guildhall School of Music with James Gibb. *Career:* Appearances at the Aldeburgh and Harrogate Festivals, at the Fairfields Hall, Croydon and for the City Music Society, London; Festival Hall debut 1978, with the Royal Philharmonic Orchestra; Recital tours with her father, Erich Gruenberg; Concerts with the GLC series at Ranger House and visits to Ireland and Spain; Played with the Bournemouth Symphony and Sinfonietta 1983-85; Barbican Centre with Tchaikovsky's 1st Concerto and the Grieg Concerto with the Royal Liverpool Philharmonic, 1984-85; Further engagements with the Hallé Orchestra (Mendelssohn's 1st Concerto, 1988) the Philharmonia at the Barbican. *Recordings include:* Album for Unicorn Records. *Honours include:* RAOS, Silver Medal 1980. *Address:* Intermusica Artists' Management, 16 Duncan Terrace, London N1 8BZ, England.

GRUESSER Eva, b. 1965, Black Forest, Germany. Violinist. *Education:* Studied at Freiburg Hochschule, Rubin Academy in Jerusalem, and Juilliard School, USA. *Career:* Leader of Lark Quartet, USA; Recent concert tours to Australia, Taiwan, Hong Kong, China, Germany and Netherlands; US appearances at Lincoln Center, New York, Kennedy Center, Washington DC and in Boston, Los Angeles, Philadelphia, St Louis and San Francisco; Repertoire includes quartets by Haydn, Mozart, Beethoven, Schubert, Dvořák, Brahms, Borodin, Bartók, Debussy and Shostakovich. *Honours include:* With Lark Quartet: Gold Medals at 1990 Naumberg and 1991 Shostakovitch Competitions; Prizewinner: Premio Paulio Borciani, Reggio Emilia, 1990; Karl Klinger Competition, Munich, 1990; London International String Quartet, 1991; Melbourne Chamber Music, 1991. *Address:* c/o Sonata (Lark Quartet), 11 Northgate Street, Glasgow G20 7AA, Scotland.

GRUHN Nora, b. 6 Mar 1905, London, England. Singer (Soprano). *Education:* Studied with her father, Hermann Grunebaum, and with Hermine Bosetti in Munich. *Debut:* Kaiserslautern 1928. *Career:* Sang at the Cologne Opera 1929-30; Covent Garden 1929-32 and 1936, as Adele in Die Fledermaus and as Gretel; Sang at Sadler's Wells from 1945, notably in the 1946 British premiere of I Quattro Rusteghi, by Wolf-Ferrari. *Recordings include:* Woodbird in Siegfried, with Lauritz Melchior (HMV). *Contributions to:* Opera Magazine (Articles, Not Quite a Prima Donna).

GRUMBACH Raimund, b. 20 Jan 1934, Eibelstadt, Wurzburg, Germany. Singer (Baritone). *Education:* Studied in Wurzburg. *Career:* Sang at the Stadttheater

Wurzburg 1956-59; Nuremberg Opera 1959-62; Bayerische Staatsoper Munich from 1962, as Mozart's Figaro, Masetto, Guglielmo, and Papageno; Puccini's Sharpless and Marcello; Wolfram in Tannhäuser. Guest appearances in Edinburgh (1965, with the Munich company), Paris, Vienna, Madrid and Tokio; Many concert appearances; Teacher at the Munich Hochschule from 1972. *Recordings:* Il Barbiere di Siviglia (Deutsche Grammophon); Der Mond by Orff (Eurodisc); Leoncavallo's La Bohème (Orfeo); Feuersnot by Strauss (Acanta); Sutermeister's Romeo und Julia; Der Freischütz (Decca); Tristan und Isolde (Philips); Intermezzo (EMI). *Address:* c/o Staatliche Hochschule für Musik, Arcisstrasse 12, Munich 2, Germany.

GRUNDHEBER Franz, b. 27 Sept 1937, Trier, Germany. Singer (Baritone). *Education:* After service in the Luftwaffe studied in Trier and Hamburg; Further study at Indiana University and the Music Academy of the West, San Diego. *Career:* Has sung at the Hamburg Staatsoper from 1966; Tours of the USA and many appearances in European opera houses; Vienna Staatsoper 1983, as Mandryka in Arabella; Salzburg Festival 1985, as Olivier in Capriccio; Other roles include Mozart's Masetto and Guglielmo, Faninal in Der Rosenkavalier, and Escamillo; Salzburg and Savonnlina Festivals 1989, as Orestes and Amonasro; Sang Barak in Die Frau ohne Schatten at the Holland Festival, 1990; Season 1992 as Germont at Barcelona; Wozzeck at the Châtelet, Paris, and Macbeth at Cologne. *Recordings include:* Video of Elecktra (as Orestes) conducted by Abbado (Virgin), Don Giovanni (Electrola); Doktor Faust by Busoni (Deutsche Grammophon); Die drei Pintos by Weber/Mahler (RCA). *Address:* Kaye Artists Management, 7 Chertsey Road, Woking GU21 5AB, England.

GRUSKIN Shelley b. 20 July 1936, New York, USA. Flautist; Recorder Player. *Education:* Studied at Eastman School, Rochester, graduated 1956. *Career:* Member, New York Pro Musica, 1961-74, playing recorder and other early wind instruments; Associated with such singers as Charles Bressler, Bethany Beardslee, Jan DeGaetani, Russell Oberlin; Premiere of liturgical drama The Play of Herod at the Cloisters, New York 1963; Tour of Europe 1963, USSR 1964; Final performances with group in Marco de Gagliano's La Dafne, 1974; Formed Philidor Trio 1965, with soprano Elizabeth Humes and harpsichordist Edward Smith; Performances with group until 1980; Teacher of music history and early music performance practice at various institutions; Artist-in-residence, College of St Scholastica, Duluth, Minnesota 1978-; President of the American Recorder Society, 1980-88. *Recordings include:* Albums with New York Pro Musica and Philidor Trio. *Address:* College of St Scholastica, Duluth, Minnesota 55811, USA.

GSTREIN Rainer Johannes, b. 4 Dec 1960, Lienz, Austria. Musicologist. *Education:* Mag.Phil., 1984, Dr.Phil., 1986, University of Innsbruck. *Career:* Student Assistant, 1983-84, Assistant, 1984-, University of Innsbruck; Visiting Professor, University of New Orleans, USA, 1988. *Publications:* Die vokale Romanze in der Zeit von 1750 bis 1850, 1989. *Contributions to:* Muziek oon het hof van Margaretha von Oostenrijk, 1987; Mozart in der Tanzkultur seiner Zeit, 1990; Zarabanda/Sarabande, ir: Handwörterbuch der musikalischen Terminologie 20, 1992. *Memberships:* International Council for Traditional Music; Gesellschaft für Musikforschung; International Musicological Society. *Hobbies:* Skiing; Mountain Hiking. *Address:* Innerkoflerstr. 4, A 6020 Innsbruck, Austria.

GUADAGNO Anton, b. 2 May 1925, Castellammare del Golfo, Trapani, Italy. Conductor. m. Dolores Guidone, 1 son. *Education:* Graduate, Conservatory of Vincenzo Bellini; Degree in Conducting, Degree Composition, Conservatory Santa Cecilia, Rome; Postgraduate Conducting, Academia Mozarteum. *Career:* Conducted Opera in Mexico City then made Carnegie Hall Début 1952; also conducted Philadelphia Lyric Opera and the Vienna Staatsoper; London début 1970 at Drury Lane, Andrea Chénier; Covent Garden début 1971, Un Ballo

in Maschera; Conducted La Fanciulla del West at the Deutsche Oper Berlin 1989, Luisa Miller at the Shubert Theatre Philadelphia and Andrea Chénier at Versailles. *Compositions:* Hymn for Holy Infancy, Vatican, Holy Year, 1950. *Recordings:* On Angel Records, RCA Victor, London Decca and EMI. *Honours:* 1st prize conducting, Academia Mozarteum, 1948; Silver Medal, Lima, Peru, 1953; Gold Medal, Mexico, 1957; Order of Cavalier, Italian Government, 1965; Gold Medal, Chile, 1970, Spain, 1971; Critic's Award, Chile, 1970; Grand Prix du Disque, Paris, 1973. *Current Management:* Columbia Artists Management Inc, New York. *Address:* Deutsche Oper Berlin, Richard Wagnerstr 10, D-1000 Berlin, Germany.

GUARRERA Frank, b. 3 Dec 1923, Philadelphia, Pennsylvania, USA. Singer (Baritone). *Education:* Studied with Richard Bonelli at the Curtis Institute, Philadelphia. *Debut:* New York Cty Opera 1947, as Silvio in Pagliacci. *Career:* Metropolitan Opera from 1948, as Escamillo, Amonasro, Don Alfonso, Eugene Onegin, Gianni Schicchi, Germont and Ford, 34 roles in 427 performances; La Scala Mialn 1958, as Zurga in Les Pêcheurs de Perles; Other appearances in London, San Francisco, Paris, Chicago, and Los Angeles. *Recordings include:* Faust (Philips); Cavalleria Rusticana, Così fan Tutte and Lucia di Lammermoor (CBS); Falstaff conducted by Toscanini (RCA). *Address:*423 Second Avenue, Bellmawr, NJ 08031, USA.

GUBAIDULINA Sofia, b. 24 Oct 1931, Chistopol, USSR. Composer. *Education:* Graduated from Kazan Conservatory, 1954; Moscow Conservatory, 1954-59, with Nikolai Peiko; Postgraduate work under Vissarion Shebalin. *Career:* Has lived in Moscow as freelance composer, 1963-91, since 1991 in Germany; Regarded as a leading representative of New Music in Russia; Offertorium performed at the 1991 Promenade Concerts, London; Opera-oratorio-ballet Prayer for the Age of Aquarius premiered at Genoa, 1991, conducted by Rostropovitch. *Compositions:* Orchestral: Fairytale Poem, 1971; Stufen (Steps), 1972-92; Detto II for cello and ensemble, 1972; Concerto for bassoon and low strings, 1975; Concerto for orchestra and jazz band, 1976; Te Salutant, Capriccio for large light orchestra, 1978; Introitus, concerto for piano and chamber orchestra, 1978; Offertorium, concerto for violin and orchestra, 1980-86; Seven Words for cello, bayan and strings, 1982; Stimmen...verstummen, symphony in 12 movements, 1986; Answer without Question, collage for 3 orchestras, 1988; Pro et Contra for large orchestra, 1989; The Feast is in Full Swing, for cello and orchestra, 1993; Vocal: Fatseliya, vocal-symphonic cycle for soprano and orchestra, 1956; Night in Memphis, cantata for mezzo-soprano, male chorus and orchestra, 1968-92; Rubayat, cantata for baritone and orchestra, 1969; Roses, 5 romances for soprano and piano, 1972; Counting Rhymes, 5 children's songs, 1973; Hour of the Soul for mezzo-soprano and winds, 1974, for percussion, mezzo-soprano and large orchestra, 1976-82; Laudatio Pacis, oratorio on texts by Johannes Comenius, 1975; Perception for soprano, baritone and 7 string instruments, 1983; Hommage à Marina Tsvetaeva, suite in 5 movements for chorus a cappella, 1984; Hommage à T S Eliot for soprano and octet, 1987; Witty Waltzing in the style of Johann Strauss for soprano and octet, 1987, for piano and string quartet, 1989; Jauchzt vor Gott for chorus and organ, 1989; Alleluja for chorus, boy's soprano, organ and large orchestra, 1990; Aus dem Stundenbuch for cello, orchestra, male chorus and female speaker, 1991; Chamber: Now Always Snow for chamber ensemble and chamber choir on poems of Gennady Aigi, 1993; Piano Quintet, 1957; Allegro rustico for flute and piano, 1963; Five Etudes for harp, double bass and percussion, 1965; Vivente-non vivente for synthesizer, 1970; Concordanza for chamber ensemble, 1971; String Quartet No 1, 1971; Music for harpsichord and percussion, 1972; Rumore e Silenzio for percussion and harpsichord, 1974; Ten Preludes for solo cello, 1974; Quattro for 2 trumpets and 2 trombones, 1974; Sonata for double bass and piano, 1975; Light and Darkness for solo organ, 1976; Dots, Lines and Zig-zag for bass clarinet and piano, 1976; Trio for 3 trumpets, 1976; Duo-Sonata for 2 bassoons, 1977; Quartet for 4 flutes, 1977; Misterioso for 7 percussionists, 1977; Detto I, sonata for organ and percussion, 1978; De profundis for solo bayan, 1978; Sounds of the Forest for flute and piano, 1978; In Croce for cello and organ, 1979; Jubilatio for 4 percussionists, 1979; Garten von Freuden und Traurigkeiten for flute, harp and viola (speaker ad lib), 1980; Rejoice, sonata for violin and cello, 1981; Descensio for ensemble, 1981; In the Beginning there was Rhythm for 7 percussionists, 1984; Et exspecto, sonata for solo bayan, 1985; Quasi Hoquetus for viola, bassoon and piano, 1985; String Quartet No 2, 1987, String Quartet No 3, 1987; Two Songs on German Folk Poetry for soprano, flute, harpsichord and cello, 1988; String Trio, 1988; Silenzio, 5 pieces for bayan, violin and cello, 1991; Even and Uneven for 7 percussionists, 1991; Tatar dance for 2 double basses and bayan, 1992; The Ropedancer for violin and piano, 1993; Meditation on the Bach-Choral Vor deinen Thron tret ich hiermit, for harpsichord, 2 violins, alto, cello and double bass, 1993; String quartet No 4, 1993; Piano music. *Address:* Internationale Musikverlage Hans Sikorski, Johnsallee 23, 20139 Hamburg, Germany.

GUBRUD Irene (Ann), b. 4 Jan 1947, Canby, Minnesota, USA. Singer (Soprano). *Education:* Studied at St Olaf College, Northfield, Minnesota, and at Juilliard, New York. *Career:* Concert engagements with leading US orchestras; Tour of East Germany with the Baltimore Symphony; Premiere of Star-Child by George Crumb with the New York Philharmonic conducted by Pierre Boulez, 1977; European engagements with the Stuttgart and Bavarian Radio Orchestras; Opera debut 1981, as Mimi with the Minnesota Opera, St Paul; Recitals at Lincoln and Kennedy Centers 1981; Appearances at the Aspen, Blossom and Meadowbrook Festivals; Teacher at Washington University, St Louis, 1976-81. *Honours include:* First prize, Concert Artists Guild competition 1970; Ford Foundation performance competition 1971; Rockefeller and Minna Kaufmann Ruud competitions, 1972; Winner, Naumburg International Voice Competition, 1980.

GUDBJORNSSON Gunnar, b. 1965, Reykjavik, Iceland. Singer (Tenor). *Education:* Studied at New Music School, Reykjavik, with Hannelore Kuhse in Berlin, and with Nicolai Gedda in London. *Debut:* Icelandic Opera, as Don Ottavio, 1988; Sang Clotarco in Haydn's Armida at Buxton Festival, 1988; Appearances with Opera North and Welsh National Opera; Opera galas at St David's Hall, Cardiff, and with Royal Philharmonic; Sang the Lawyer in Punch and Judy at Aldeburgh Festival and engaged with Wiesbaden Opera as Almaviva, Ottavio and Tamino; Concert repertoire includes St Matthew Passion (Queen's Hall, Edinburgh), Britten's Serende, Die Schöne Müllerin; Recitals at Covent Garden and Wigmore Hall, 1993. *Recordings include:* Die schöne Müllerin; Albums in Mozart complete edition. *Address:* John Coast Ltd, 31 Sinclair Road, London W14 0NS, England.

GUDMUNDSEN-HOLMGREEN Pelle, b. 21 Nov 1932, Copenhagen, Denmark. Composer. m. Gunvor Kaarsberg, 21 Nov 1959, 1 son, 1 daughter. *Education:* Studied Theory and History of Music at The Royal Danish Conservatory of Music, 1953-58. *Career:* Teacher, Royal Danish Academy of Music in Aarhus, 1967-73; Works have been played at Scandinavian Music Days, Royal Danish Ballet and Music Festival, ISCM; on Danish television, on radio throughout the world; Music for plays and films. *Compositions include:* Terrace in 5 stages, (woodwind quintet), 1990; Plateaux por deux (cello and percussion), 1970; Mirror II (orchestra), 1973; Songs Without (mezzo soprano, piano), 1976; Symphony, Antiphony (orchestra), 1977; String Quartet V Step by Step, 1982; VI Parting, 1983; VII Parted, 1984; VIII Ground, 1986 (commissioned by the Kronos Quartet), Concord (Sinfonietta) 1987; Octopus (organ, 2 players), 1989; Concerto Grosso for String Quartet and Symphonic Ensemble, 1990, for piano, 1992. *Recordings:* Solo for Electric Guitar, 1972; Symphony, Antiphony (orchestra), 1977; Prelude to Your Silence (octet), 1978; Your Silence (soprano, septet), 1978;

Mirror Pieces (clarinet trio) 1980, Triptych (percussion Concerto) 1985. *Contributions to:* Dansk Musiktidsskrift; Nutida Musik. *Honour:* Symphony, Antiphony was awarded the 1980 Music Prize of the Nordic Council. *Membership:* The Society for the Publication of Danish Music. *Address:* Eggersvej 29, 2900 Hellerup, Denmark.

GUELFI Giangiacomo, b. 21 Dec 1924, Rome, Italy. Singer (Baritone). *Education:* Studied in Florence and with Titta Ruffo. *Debut:* Spoleto 1950, as Rigoletto. *Career:* Sang at the Teatro Fenice Venice and in Catania; La Scala Milan from 1952; Chicago Lyric Opera from 1954; Appearances in Rome, Paris, Cairo, Naples, Berlin and Dallas; Covent Garden 1975, as Scarpia; Theatre Royal Drury Lane 1958, as Gerard in Andrea Chénier; Verona Arena 1960, 1970, 1972; Rio de Janeiro 1964, as Macbeth and Scarpia; Lisbon 1965, as Guillaume Tell; Metropolitan Opera 1970, as Scarpia, and Jack Rance in La Fanciulla del West; Appeared at the Maggio Musicale Florence in revivals of L'Africaine by Meyerbeer 1971 and Agnese di Hohenstaufen by Spontini; Sang in Giordano's La Cene delle Beffe at La Scala 1977. *Recordings include:* Tosca and Aida (Cetra); Cavalleria Rusticana (Deutsche Grammophon); Verdi's I Due Foscari, I Lombardi, Nabucco and Attila. *Address:* c/o Teatro alla Scala, Via Filodrammatici 2, 1-20121 Milan, Italy.

GUEST Douglas Albert, b. 9 May 1916, Mortomley, Yorkshire, England. English Organist and Conductor; Emeritus Organist of Westminster Abbey. m. Peggie Florentia Falconer, 4 Dec 1941, 2 daughters. *Education:* MA; MusB, (Cantab); MusD, (Cantuar); FRCM; FRCO; Hon. RAM; FRSCM; Reading School, 1929-33; Royal College of Music, London, 1933-35; King's College, Cambridge, 1935-39. Organ Scholar of King's College, Cambridge, 1935-39; Cambridge University - Stewart of Rannoch Scholar, 1935-39. *Career:* War Service, Major, Royal Artillery, (Mentioned in Despatches, Normandy, 1944), 1939-45; Director of Music, Uppingham School, 1945-50; Organist, Salisbury Cathedral, 1950-57; Organist, Worcester Cathedral, 1957-63; Organist, Westminster Abbey, 1963-81; Emeritus Organist and Master of Choristers, Westminster Abbey, 1981-; Professor, Royal College of Music, London, 1963-81. *Compositions:* Miscellaneous small works for special occasions at Westminster Abbey. *Recordings:* Several recordings from Westminster Abbey. *Honours:* Appointed Commander of the Royal Victorian Order, CVO, 1975; Mentioned in Despatches, Normandy, June, 1944. *Memberships:* Many musical societies and associations. *Hobbies:* Fly fishing; Golf. *Address:* The Gables, Minchinhampton, Glos. GL6 9JE, England.

GUEST George Hywel, b. 9 Feb 1924, Bangor, Wales. Choral Director, Organist. m. Nancy Mary Talbot, 31 Oct 1959, 1 son, 1 daughter. *Education:* Friars School, Bangor, 1933-35; Chester Cathedral Choir School, 1935-39; King's School, Chester, 1939-42; MA, MusB (Cantab); Organ Student, St. John's College, Cambridge, 1947-51; FRCO, 1942. *Career:* Served in RAF, 1942-46; John Stewart of Rannoch Scholar in Sacred Music, 1948; Organist and Choirmaster, St. John's College, Cambridge, 1951-91; University Assistant Lecturer in Music, Cambridge, 1953-56, University Lecturer, 1956-82; Professor of Harmony and Counterpoint, RAM, London, 1960-61; Director, Berkshire Boy Choir, USA, 1967, 1970; University Organist, Cambridge University, 1974-91; Special Commissioner, Royal School of Church Music, 1953-; Examiner to Associated Board of Royal Schools of Music, 1959-92, Director, Côr Cenedlaethol leuenctid Cymru, 1984-86; Artistic Director, Llandaf Festival, 1985. Concerts with St. John's College Choir in USA, Canada, Japan, Australia, Brazil, most countries in W. Europe; Concerts and Choral Seminars in the Philippines and in S. Africa. *Compositions:* Arrangements of church music. *Recordings:* Some 100 recordings with St. John's College Choir for various record companies including Haydn Masses; Victoria Litaniae de beata Virgine, Mass and Requiem; Palestrina Masses; Purcell Funeral Music, Verse anthems and Te Deum; Monteverdi Masses and

Laudate Pueri; Michael Haydn Salve Regina; Liszt Missa Choralis; Beethoven Mass in C; Schubert Masses in A flat and E flat; Fauré Requiem and works by Britten. *Contributions to:* Various magazines. *Honour:* CBE, 1987. *Hobby:* Welsh Language. *Address:* Saint John's College, Cambridge, England CB2 1TP.

GUI Henry, b. 1926, Bordeaux, France. Singer (Baritone). *Education:* Studied in Paris. *Career:* Sang in operetta at the Théâtre du Chatelet, Paris; Sang Debussy's Pelléas at the Vienna Staatsoper and at the Glyndebourne Festival, 1962; Wexford Festival 1967-68, as Mercutio in Roméo et Juliette and as Pelléas; Strasbourg 1967, in Der junge Lord by Henze; Brussels 1973, in The Mines of Sulphur by Bennett; Appearances at the Aix-en-Provence Festival, the Paris Opéra-Comique, La Scala Milan and the Teatro Liceo Barcelona.

GUIDARINI Marco, b. 1950, Genoa, Italy. Conductor. *Education:* Studied conducting with Mario Gusella at Pescara, cello in Vienna with Andre Navarra; Master-classes with Franco Ferrara in Verona and Assisi. *Career:* Conducting career began in Italy; Conducted Falstaff with the Opéra de Lyon 1986; Le Comte Ory in Lyon, Annecy and St Etienne; Wexford Festival and Queen Elizabeth Hall, London 1988- 89, with Mercadante's Elisa e Claudio and Mozart's Mitridate; Season 1989-90 with Il Barbiere di Siviglia for Opera North, Madame Butterfly in Dublin, 1990-91 included Tosca with English National Opera, Le Nozze di Figaro for Welsh National Opera, La Bohème for Scottish Opera; Concerts with the RAI in Rome; Season 1991-92, Die Fledermaus and The Magic Flute for WNO, Carmen with Scottish Opera and debut with Australian Opera at Sydney, Tosca; 1993 and 1994: Orphée in Sydney, Traviata in Stockholm, Elisir d'Amore Scottish Opera; Barbiere di Siviglia at Deutsche Staatsoper, Berlin. *Address:* Allied Artists Ltd, 42 Montpelier Square, London SW7 1JZ, England.

GUILLAUME Edith, b. 14 June 1943, Bergerac, France. Opera and Concert Singer; Lyric Mezzo; Resident Member, Royal Danish Opera, Copenhagan. m. Niels Hvass, 2 children. *Education:* Soloist Diploma, Royal Danish College of Music, Copenhagen; Private study, Copenhagen and Paris. *Debut:* (Opera) Therese, Dreaming of Therese, Jutland Opera. *Career includes:* Sang with opera in Copenhagen, Aarhus, Hamburg, Mannheim, Geneva, Montpelier, Nancy, Metz, Lille, Liège, Le Havre; Roles with these companies include Bartók, Judith (Bluebeard's Castle); Bibalo, Julie (Miss Julie); Bizet, Carmen (Carmen); Campra, Clorinde (Tancrède); Davies, Miss Donnithorne's Maggott; Gluck, Orfeo; Gounod, Siebel (Faust); Mascagni, Santuzza (Cavalleria Rusticana); Massenet, Charlotte (Werther); Monteverdi, Ottavia and Poppea (L'Incoronazione di Poppea), Penelope (Ritorno d'Ulisse); Mozart, Cherubino (Le Nozze di Figaro), Dorabella (Così fan Tutte), Idamante (Idomeneo); Offenbach, La perichole (La Perichole); Penderecki, Jeanne (The Devils of Loudun); Poulenc (Voix Humaine); Ravel, Concepcion (L'Heure Espagnole); Rossini, Zaida (Turco in Italia), Angelina (Cenerentola); Strauss, Octavian (Der Rosenkavalier); Verdi, Maddalena (Rigoletto), Meg (Falstaff). *Recordings:* Various Danish Songs. *Honours include:* Critics Prize of Honour, 1970; Tagea Brandt Memorial Fund, 1977. *Address:* Ellebakken 2, 2900 Hellerup, Copenhagen, Denmark.

GUILLOU Jean, b. 18 Apr 1930, Angers, France. Organist; Composer; Pianist. *Education:* Paris Conservatoire from 1945, with Dupre, Durufle and Messiaen. *Career:* Professor, Instituto de Alta Cultura, Lisbon, 1953-57; Recitalist in residence in west Berlin, 1958-62; Organist at St Eustache, Paris, 1963; Professor, International Master Class, Zürich, 1970-. *Compositions:* Organ: Sinfonietta, 18 Variations, Fantaisie, 1958; Pour le Tombeau de Colbert, Toccata, 1966; Sagas, Symphonie Initiatique, La Chapelle des abimes, 1970; Scènes d'Enfants, Sonate en Trio, 1985, 5 Concertos for Organ and Orchestra; Hyperion, 1987; Chamber works: Colloques no 1 to 6 Concertos no 1

and 2 for Piano and Orchestra; Judith-Symphonie for Mezzo-Soprano and orchestra; Peace and Aube, for 12 voices and Organ, 1991. *Publications:* Author of the book about organ, history and design, L'Orgue, Souvenir et Avenir, Ed Bucher Chastel. *Recordings:* Many by Philips and Dorian including: J S Bach, Goldberg Variations, Complete Organ works; C Franck, complete Organ works; Vivaldi: 5 Concertos; J Reubke: piano and organ Sonatas; Mussorgsky: Pictures at an Exhibition and Stravinsky: Petrushka; The Art of Improvisation. *Honours:* Gramophon, Critics Prize, 1980; International Performer of the Year, USA, 1980; Prize of the Liszt Academy, Budapest, 1982; Diapason d'Or and Prix Choc of Le Monde, 1991. *Address:* 25 rue Gay-Lussac, 75005 Paris, France.

GUIOT Andrea, b. 11 Jan 1928, Garon-Saint-Gilles, Nimes, France. Singer (Soprano). *Education:* Studied in Nîmes and with Janine Micheau in Paris. *Debut:* Nancy Opera 1955, in Faust. *Career:* Sang at the Opéra-Comique Paris as Antonia in Les Contes d'Hoffmann, Micaela, Mireille, Mimi and Manon; Paris Opéra debut as Marguerite; Wexford Festival 1961, Chicago Lyric Opera 1963; Carnegie Hall New York 1964 in Dialogues des Carmélites by Poulenc; Retired as Singer 1973; Professor at the Paris Conservatoire from 1977.

GULDA Friedrich, b. 16 May 1930, Vienna, Austria. Pianist; Composer. *Education:* Grossmann Conservatory; High School of Music and Dramatic Art, Vienna, with Bruno Seidhofer and Joseph Marx. *Debut:* 1944. *Career:* Numerous concert tours with leading orchestras; Carnegie Hall debut 1950; Often heard in Bach, Beethoven, Mozart and Schubert; Founded Classical Gulda Orchestra of the Vienna Symphony; Founded small jazz band; Jazz club engagements from 1956; Founded Eurojazz Orchestra; Modern Jazz Competition in Vienna 1966; Has performed flute and baritone saxophone with various partners; Founded International Musikforum at Ossiach, Carinthia, 1968; TV series playing Mozart Sonatas; Played Mozart's Concerto K488 with the Vienna Philharmonic at gala concert conducted by Claudio Abbado. *Compositions include:* 2 Piano Concertos; Cadenzas for repertory works; Galgenlieder for baritone and orchestra 1951; Numerous jazz compositions. *Recordings:* Classical Sonatas and Concertos for Decca. *Publication:* Worte zur Musik 1971. *Contribution to:* Osiach müsste erfunden werden 1971. *Honours include:* First Prize, Geneva International Competition 1946; Beethoven Ring from the Vienna Academy of Music 1970. *Hobbies:* Chess; Record Collecting. *Address:* c/o Wiener Philharmoniker, Bösondorfstrasse 12, A-1030 Vienna, Austria.

GULIN Angeles, b. 18 Feb 1943, Ribadavia, Orense, Spain. Singer (Soprano). m. Antonio Blancas-La Plaza. *Education:* Studied with her father. *Debut:* Montevideo 1963, as the Queen of Night. *Career:* Appearances in Barcelona, London, San Francisco, Dusseldorf, Amsterdam, Naples, Turin, Monte Carlo and Mexico City; Festivals of Edinburgh, Aix-en- Provence, Rome, Florence and Verona; Hamburg Staatsoper 1973-77; Other roles include Abigaille, Aida, Norma, Valentine in Les Huguenots, Donna Anna, Senta, Turandot and La Gioconda; Many concert appearances. *Recordings include:* Oberto, Il Corsaro and Stiffelio by Verdi; Fernand Cortez by Spontini; Andrea Chénier. *Honours:* Winner, Verdi Competition at Busseto 1968; International Competition Madrid 1970. *Address:* c/o Hamburg Staatsoper, Grosse-Theaterstrasse 34, D-2000 Hamburg, Germany.

GULKE Peter, b. 29 Apr 1934, Weimar, Germany. Conductor. *Education:* Studied at the Franz Liszt Hochschule Weimar, the Friedrich Schiller University Jena and the Karl Marx University, Leipzig (PhD 1958). *Career:* Repetiteur at the Rudolstadt Theatre 1959; Music Director at Stendal 1964 and Potsdam 1966; Stralsund 1972-76; Kapellmeister at the Dresden Opera 1976; Musical Director at Weimar 1981; as Musicologist Technical University, Berlin 1984; Musical Director, Wuppertal Opera, 1986; Work as musicologist includes edition of a 10th Symphony by Schubert, from sketches, broadcast at the Schubert Congress in Detroit, 1978; Lecturer at the Hochschule für musik in Dresden; Conducted Poulenc's Dialogues des Carmélites at Wuppertal 1989, to commemorate the bicentenary of the French Revolution and numerous other operas including the Ring et Wuppertal, Graz, Kassel. *Publications:* Bruckner, Brahms, zwei Studien (Kassel, 1989); Schubert und seine Zeit, 1991. *Recordings include:* Beethoven Piano Concerto of 1784 and Udo Zimmermann's Der Schuhu und der fliegende Prinzessin (Eterna), works by Berg, Webern, Baird, Schubert. *Address:* Wuppertaler Buhnen, Spinnstrasse 4, D-5600 Wuppertal, Germany.

GULLI Franco, b. 1 Sept 1926, Trieste, Italy. Concert Violinist. m. Enrica Cavallo. *Education:* Studied with father and at Trieste Conservatory; Accademia Chigiana, Siena. *Debut:* 1932. *Career:* Worldwide appearances with leading orchestras, including Cleveland, Pittsburgh, Ottawa; Chamber music activity with wife and with Trio Italiano d'Archi; Former member, Pomeriggi Musical Orchestra of Milan and of I Virtuosi di Roma; Gave premieres of concertos by Malipiero and Viozzi and of Paganini's 5th Concerto (1959); Master Classes, Accademia Chigiana, Siena, 1964-72; Professor of Music, Lucerne Conservatory 1971-72; Professor of Music, Indiana University from 1972. *Recordings include:* Duos with Bruno Giuranna; String Trios by Beethoven with the Italian Trio; Paganini's Concerto No. 5; Beethoven Sonatas; Mendelssohn Sonata in F. *Memberships include:* Accademia Nazionale Santa Cecilia, Rome. *Honours include:* Premio dell'Accademia Chigiana, Siena. *Address:* 1000 S Ballantine Road, Bloomington, IL 47401, USA.

GULYAS Dénes, b. 31 Mar 1954, Budapest, Hungary. Singer (Tenor); Producer. *Education:* Studied at the Liszt Academy and the Budapest Conservatory. *Debut:* Budapest 1978, as Alfredo. *Career:* Vienna Staatsoper debut 1978; Sang in the Verdi Requiem at Budapest and La Scala Milan 1981; US debut Philadelphia 1981; Royal Opera House Covent Garden 1984-85; Metropolitan Opera from 1985, as the Singer in Der Rosenkavalier, Romeo, Rodolfo, Massenet's Des Grieux and Andrei in Khovanshchina; Appearances in Belgium, France, Germany and Italy; Other roles include Don Ottavio, Ferrando, the Duke of Mantua, Almaviva and Ernani; Performances in La Bohème, Rigoletto, Massenet's, Manon, Khovanshchina, Gounod's Romeo and Juliet; San Francisco, Così fan Tutte, 1986; Florence - Elisir d'amore, Genoa; Staged and sang leading role in Roméo et Juliette at Budapest, 1988-89; Sang Faust with the Florentine Opera at Milwaukee, 1989 (recreated at Montreal); San Diego, 1990 as Tamino; Debut at Barcelona, 1989, as Lensky in Eugene Onegon; Sang Lensky at Tel Aviv, 1992. *Recordings:* Gianni Schicchi, Salieri's Falstaff, Hunyadi Laszlo by Erkel, Paisiello's Il Barbiere di Siviglia, Liszt's Hungarian Coronation Mass (Hungaroton). *Honours:* Winner, Pavarotti Competition, Philadelphia 1981. *Address:* c/ o Hungarian State Opera House, Népoztársaság utja 22, 1061 Budapest, Hungary.

GULYAS György, b. 11 Apr 1916, Korostarca, Hungary. Conductor. m. Eva Manya, 6 Nov 1958, 3 daughters. *Education:* Composition and Conducting, Academy of Music, Budapest, 1942. *Career:* Teacher, Music Teachers' Training College, Debrecen, 1942-46; Founder-Director, Music High School, Bekestarhos, also conductor, Tarhosi Korus, 1946-54; Director, Music High School, Debrecen, 1954-66; Debrecen Academy of Music, Budapest, 1966-76; Founder, Chief Conductor, Kodály Choir, Debrecen, 1955-83; Békéstarhosi Zenei Napok, music director 1976-. *Publications:* Author, Bekestarhos Zenei tanulsagai, 1968; Az enekkari intonacio kerdesei, 1972; Articles in various professional journals; Büneim...Büneim?, biography, 1988. *Address:* 8 Blaháné, Debrecen 4024, Hungary.

GÜMPEL Karl-Werner, b. 6 Jan 1930, Duderstadt, Germany. Professor, Musicology. m. Isolde Ambs, 1 son, 2 daughters. *Education:* University of Göttingen; PhD,

University of Freiburg i Br. 1955. *Career:* Research Assistant, German Research Union, 1955-57; Assistant Professor, Musicology, University of Freiburg i. Br., 1958-69; Research Fellow, Görresgesellschaft, 1962-63, 1981; Associate Professor, Musicology, University of Louisville, Kentucky, USA, 1969-74; Professor, 1974-, Chairman, 1974-75, Musicology, University of Louisville. *Publications:* Die Musiktraktate Conrads von Zabern, 1956; Hugo Spechtshart von Reutlingen: Flores Musicae, 1958; Zur Frühgeschichte der vulgärsprachlichen spanischen und katalanischen Musiktheorie, 1968. *Honours:* Foreign Corresponding Member, Institut d'Estudis Catalans, Barcelona, 1979; Corresponding Academician, Reial Acadèmia Catalana de Belles Arts de Sant Jordi, Barcelona, 1984. *Memberships:* American Musicological Society; Mediaeval Academy of America; International Musicological Society. *Hobbies:* Art History; Photography; Hiking. *Address:* 1803 Devondale Drive, Louisville, KY 40222, USA.

GUNDE Peter, b 1942, Budapest, Hungary. Conductor. *Education:* Studied oboe at the Budapest Conservatory; Composition and conducting at the Franz Liszt Academy, Budapest; Seminars in Weimar and Petersburg with Arvid Jansons, 1965-75. *Career:* Oboist with the National Orchestra Budapest 1961-63; Kapellmeister in Miskolc, Hungary, 1969-71; First Opera Kapellmeister in Pecs, 1972-73; Opera Kappellmeister, Hungarian State Opera 1973-75; Founder and Director of the Corelli Chamber Orchestra Budapest 1975-77; Conductor and Artistic Director of the chorus and orchestra Kapisztran and Palestrina Choir, Budapest 1973-77; Director of the Chamber Orchestra and Lecturer at the International Youth Festival in Bayreuth 1975-77; Assistant to Peter Maag, Christoph von Dohnanyi, and Herbert von Karajan at the Salzburg Festival 1977-78; Lecturer at the University of Bielefeld and University of Osnabrüeck; Guest conductor in Stavanger, Oslo and Hungary 1981-83; Concerts with the Sudwestdeutschen Kammerorchester in Pforzheim and Reutlingen; Concerts in Hungary and USA, 1984; Guest Conductor in Tokyo and Israel, and broadcasts with the Westdeutschen Rundfunk Cologne, 1985-89; Concert Tour with the Hungarian Virtuosi Orchestra, 1990-93-. *Address:* Heeperstrasse 52a, 33607 Bielefeld 1, Germany.

GUNDRY Inglis, b. 8 May 1905, Wimbledon, England. Composer and Lecturer on Music. m. Nina Peggy Maggs, 22 Aug 1957, 2 daughters. *Education:* Mill Hill School 1918-23; MA, Balliol College, Oxford 1923-27; Middle Temple 1927-29; Barrister-at-Law; ARCM, Royal College of Music 1935-38; Founder: The Sacred Music-Drama Society - Music Director, 1960-86. *Compositions include:* Unpublished: Operas: Naaman, The Return of Odysseus, Avon, The Tinners of Cornwall, The Horses of The Dawn, The Logan Rock, The Three Wise Men, The Prisoner Paul, The Prince of Coxcombs (Morley College Prize 1964); A Will of Her Own, The Rubicon, Lindisfarne, Claudia's Dream, 2 Symphonies, Harp Concerto, orchestral suite The Logan Rock; 5 Song-Cycles; Cantata, The Daytime of Christ. Published: Opera: The Partisans (WMA); Orchestral Suite: Heyday Freedom (Hinrichsen); Choral Suite with Orchestra: Five Bells (Hinrichsen); The Shepherds (Ed. Medieval Music-Drama), OUP; Male Voice Choir: Sing From The Chamber To The Grave, OUP; First Will and Testament, OUP; Cornish Carols: Now Carol We, OUP; Harp Variations (Thames); Orchestral Suite: Lindisfarne, 1992; Galileo, opera in 5 Acts and 5 Choral Episodes, 1993. *Recordings:* Discs: Excerpts From The Three Wise Men; Excerpts From The Prisoner Paul; Song Cycles: The Black Mountains, Woman's Heart and Songs of Experience; Harp Variations and Two Songs from A Will of Her Own; Medieval Music Dramas for Christmas and Easter. Tape-Recordings: A Will of Her Own, A Fountain of Gardens; Songs of Friendship. *Publications:* The Nature of Opera as A Composite Art (Royal Music Association) 1947; Canow Kernow - Songs and Dances from Cornwall 1966, 3rd Edition 1984; Composers by the Grace of God, a study of Music and Religion, 1989; Libretto of Galileo, 1993. *Contributions to:* The Composer 1964; Composition In More Than Twelve

Tones. *Honours:* Cobbett Prize at RCM 1936; Won Morley College Opera Competition 1964; The Horses of The Dawn was one of the winning librettos in a Competition for School Operas sponsored by The Council For Social Services 1951. *Memberships:* Composers' Guild Performing Right Society. *Hobbies:* Pastel Painting; Gardening. *Address:* 11 Winterstoke Gardens, Mill Hill, London NW7 2RA, England.

GUNS Jan, b. 22 Nov 1951, Antwerp, Belgium. Bass Clarinet Player; Soloist. 1 son, 2 daughters. *Education:* Royal Flemish Conservatorium, Antwerp; Summer courses, Nice, France. *Debut:* Royal Flemish Opera, Antwerp, 1971. *Career:* Assistant Professor of Clarinet, Royal Conservatorium, Gent, 1979; Played with: Opera of Flanders, 1980; BRT Philharmonic Orchestra, 1983; Associate Professor, 1984, Professor of Bass Clarinet, 1991-, Royal Flemish Conservatorium, Antwerp; Bass Clarinet Player and Percussionist with Gemini Ensemble, 1990-. *Recordings:* Introduction and Concertante for Bass Clarinet and Clarinet Choir, opus 58 (Norman Heim), with Walter Boeykens Clarinet Choir, 1986; Harry's Wonderland for Bass Clarinet and 2 Tapes (Andre Laporte), 1987; Mladi sextet (Leos Janáček), with Walter Boeykens Ensemble, 1992; Spotlights on the Bass Clarinet, Concerto for Bass Clarinet and Concert Band (Jan Hadermann), with Concert Band of the Belgian Guides, conducted by N Nozy, 1993; With Gemini Ensemble, 1993: Sonata (Frits Celis); Van Heinde en Verre (Wilfried Westerlinck); Due Concertante (Ivana Loudova); Giuco per Due (Dietrich Erdmann); Exercices (Jean Segers); Tango (Frederic Devreese). *Address:* Hagelandstraat 48, B-2660 Hoboken (Antwerp), Belgium.

GUNSON Ameral, b. 1960. England. Singer (Mezzo-Soprano). *Career:* Many concerts and broadcasts in Britain and Europe; Frequent appearances at the Promenade Concerts London; Season 1985-86 with Walton's Gloria at the Last Night of the Proms and Hecuba and Anna in a concert performance of Les Troyens by Berlioz at Portsmouth, conducted by Roger Norrington; Sang Lady Toodle in a Frankfurt Opera production of The English Cat by Henze; L'Enfant et les Sortilèges in Rotterdam, conducted by Simon Rattle; Verdi's Aida in Glasgow and Requiem at the Albert Hall, conducted by David Willcocks; Elgar's Sea Pictures and Mozart's Mass in C Minor, conducted by Richard Hickox; Bach's Mass in B Minor and the Choral Symphony with the Bournemouth Symphony orchestra; Haydn Masses televised by Austrian TV, with Roger Norrington; Tour of France with the Bach B Minor Mass; Many recitals with the pianist Paul Hamburger; Premiere recording of Britten's The Rescue for the BBC; Sang in the premiere of Goehr's Eve Dreams of Paradise 1989, (Prom Concerts 1990), Season 1990/91 in Texeira's Mass, with The Sixteen, Berg's Altenberg Lieder with the Rotterdam Philharmonic, Hindemith's Requiem in Geneva and Mozart's Requiem conducted by Jane Glover; Covent Garden 1992 as a Young Nun in Prokofiev's The Fiery Angel. *Recordings include:* Maw's Scenes and Arias (EMI); Copland's In the Beginning, with the choir of King's College, Cambridge. *Address:* Magenta Music International, 64 Highgate High Street, London N6 5HX, England.

GÜNTER Horst (Professor), b. 23 May 1913, Leipzig, Germany. Voice Teacher; Professor of Voice; Singer; Baritone. m. 4 May 1938, 2 sons, 2 daughters. *Education:* Choirboy, St. Thomas, Leipzig; Musicology and Philosophy, Universities of Leipzig and Bologna; Voice, Leipzig Conservatory; Most influential teachers: Karl Straube, Fritz Polster, Emmi Leisner. *Debut:* Matthäus-Passion, St. Thomas, Leipzig 1939; Count in Marriage of Figaro, Schwerin State Opera, 1941. *Career:* Leading Lyric Baritone, Hamburg State Opera 1950-68; Knappertsbusch and Böhm, Munich State Opera 1958-63; Edinburgh Festival, 1952 and 1956; Holland Festival 1961; Guest Singer: Vienna State Opera, Frankfurt, with Solti; Ansbach Bach Festival, 1951-58; TV: 12 Operas and numerous Radio Recordings; First Performance of Moses and Aaron in Hamburg; Teaching Career: Nordwestdeutsche Musikakademie Detmold 1959-65;

Staatliche Musikhochschule, Freiburg 1965-78; University of Southern California, Los Angeles 1978-80; University of California, Los Angeles (UCLA), 1981; Visiting Professor at many universities in USA: Southern Methodist Universities, Dallas; North Texas State University, Denton; Oberlin Conservatory of Music; University of Minneapolis, Minneapolis; University of Alaska and many others; Musashino Academia Musicae, Tokyo 1984, 1986, 1987, 1990, 1991 and 1992; Frequent judge at International Voice Competitions such as: Munich, Budapest, Leipzig, s'Hertogenbosch, Los Angeles, Dallas, Osaka and others. *Recordings:* Lohengrin (HMV); Schüchter, Moses und Aron (Columbia); Zillich, Così fan Tutte, Jochum, Don Giovanni, Klemperer, Zauberflöte, Rother, La Traviata, Wagner, Die Fledermaus (Elektrola), Schüchter, Weihnachts Oratorium (Decca); Karl Richter; Matthäus-Passion (Phillips), Kurt Redel; Zar und Zimmermann (Deutsche Grammophon), Leitner; La Bohème (DGG), Erede; and many others. *Hobbies:* Scientific work about The History of Singing; Collecting Books about the human voice; Gardening. *Address:* Unterer Heimbach 5, D-79280 AU bei Freiburg, Germany. 43. 92.

GÜNTHER Odin, b. 13 Nov 1948, Ludwigshafen, Germany. Director of Music School; Music Teacher. m. JoAnne Linda Walker, 1 Oct 1976, 2 daughters. *Education:* Study for Private Music Teacher, School of Music, University of Heidelberg, 1968-74; Orchestral Music, University of Karlsruhe, 1975-76; Violin studies with Professor Assmann, 1968- 74, Professor Hans Borner, Concertmaster, Karlsruhe, 1975-76. *Career:* Played with Camarate Palatina ensemble for Mozart Society, Schwetzingen; Hebraische Melodien radio recording, 1975, Scottish Folk Music in German Music radio recording, 1977, Studio Heidelberg; Performed at Stadttheater Pforzheim, 1976-79; Director, Music School in Sinsheim, 1980-; Teacher of Violin, Viola, Guitar and Piano, 1980-. *Recordings:* Audite records: Englische Dichtung im Spiegel romantischer Musik, 1976; Antike dichtung im Spiegel der Musik, 1976. *Memberships:* Association of German Music Schools; German Orchestra Union. *Hobbies:* Piano restoration; Carpentry. *Address:* HC 65 Box 233, Oark, AR 72852-9505, USA.

GUNZENHAUSER Stephen (Charles), b. 8 Apr 1942, New York City, USA. Conductor. m. Rochelle E Davis, 14 June 1970. 2 daughters. *Education:* BMus, Oberlin College, 1963; Diploma, Salzburg Mozarteum, 1962; MMus, New England Conservatory of Music, 1965; Artist diploma, Cologne Hochschule für Musik, 1968. *Career:* Assistant conductor, Monte Carlo National Orchestra, 1968-69; American Symphony Orchestra, New York, 1969-70; Music Director, Brooklyn Center Chamber Orchestra, 1970-72; Kennett (Pennsylvania) Symphony Orchestra, 1974-78; Wilmington (Delaware) Chamber Orchestra, 1976-79; Delaware Symphony Orchestra, Wilmington, 1978-; Principal Conductor 1978-81, Music Director 1981-, Lancaster (Pennsylvania) Symphony Orchestra; Artistic director, 1974-82, Artistic Administrator 1982-87, Wilmington Music School; Guest conductor with various North American and European orchestras; Recording Contract, HNH International, 1985; Named as Cultural Ambassador for the State of Delaware, 1990. *Recordings:* Several discs; Over 35 CDs recorded. *Address:* c/o Delaware Symphony Orchestra, P O Box 1870, Wilmington, DE 19899, USA.

GURTNER Heinrich, b. 15 Oct 1924, Wattenwil, Switzerland. Organist. m. Eugenie Tenger, 12 Apr 1950, 2 sons, 2 daughters. *Education:* Training College, Berne; Organ and Piano, Conservatory of Music, Berne; Further studies with Maurice Durufle in Paris and Adriaan Engels in den Haag. *Career:* Organist, Petruskirche, Berne and Teacher, Training College, Berne, 1949-66; Organist, Berne Cathedral, including Artistic Leader of Abendmusiken, 1966-89; Teacher, Conservatory of Music, Berne, 1966-89; International concert work, Europe and USA. *Recordings:* Bach: 6 Trio Sonatas; Mendelssohn: Organ works. *Honours:* Music Prize, City of Berne, 1974. *Memberships:* Honorary Member, Bernischer Organistenverband; Schweizerischer Tonkunstlerverein. *Hobbies:* Travel; Hiking. *Address:* Krayigenweg 41, CH 3074 Muri b Bern, Switzerland.

GUSCHLBAUER Theodor, 14 Apr 1939, Vienna, Austria. Conductor. *Education:* Studied at the Vienna Academy of Music. *Career:* Conducted the Vienna Baroque Ensemble 1961-69; Assistant at the Vienna Volksoper 1964-66; Chief Conductor of the Salzburg Landestheater 1966- 68; Lyon Opera 1969-75; Conducted the Linz-Bruckner Symphony Orchestra and the Landestheater Linz 1975-83; Chief Conductor of the Strasbourg Philharmonic; Guest appearances at many festivals including those at Salzburg, Aix-en-Provence, Prague, Bregenz, Flanders, Oxford, Luzern, Montreux, Ascona, Maggio Musicale Fiorentino, Regular Guest conductor with the Vienna and Hamburg Operas, Geneva, Paris (Bastille), Munich, Cologne and Lisbon. Conducted Così fan Tutte at Strasbourg 1990, Die Fledermaus at Bonn. *Recordings:* Symphonies by Mozart, Haydn, Schubert and Beethoven; Concertos by Strauss, Marcello, Mozart, Haydn, Mendelssohn and Weber (Erato); Mozart's Divertimento K287, Cassation K99, Oboe Concerto K314, Masses K194 and K220, Vesperae Solennes, Sinfonia Concertante K297b, Bassoon Concerto, Flute Concertos (Rampal), and Piano Concertos K271, K453 and K467 (Maria Joao Pires); Music by Cesti (Il Pomo d'Oro), Fux, Dittersdorf, Schmelzer, Wagenseil and Muffat; Strauss Burleske, Horn Concerto No.2 and Oboe Concerto; Beethoven's 6th symphony and Schubert's Ninth, with the New Philharmonia.*Honours:* Received Grand Prix du Disque, for seven of his numerous recordings; The Goeth Foundation in Basel awarded him The Mozart Prize, 1988. *Address:* c/o Orchestre Philharmonique de Strasbourg, 9 Rue Brûlée, F-67000 Strasbourg, France.

GUSTAFSON Nancy, b. 27 June 1956, Evanston, Illinois, USA. Singer (Soprano). m. Brian Dickie. *Education:* Studied in San Francisco on the Adler Fellowship Program. *Career:* San Francisco Opera debut as Freia in Das Rheingold: returned as Musetta in La Bohème and Antonia in Les Contes d'Hoffmann and Elettra in Idomeneo; Opera Colorado as Donna Elvira; Minnesota Opera as Leila in Les Pêcheurs de Perles; Canadian debut as Violetta for Edmonton Opera; Festival performances as Rosalinda in Santa Fe and Britten's Helena for Chatauqua Opera; European debut as Rosalinda in Paris, season 1984-85; Glyndebourne debut as Donna Elvira, while on tour to Hong Kong: Festival appearances as Katya Kabanova, in a new production of Janáček's opera, 1988, returned 1990; Chicago Lyric Opera debut as Marguerite in Faust; Covent Garden debut 1988, as Freia; Scottish Opera 1989, as Violetta; Metropolitan Opera debut 1989, as Musetta; Sang Freia in Rheingold at Munich, 1990; Seattle Opera 1989, as Elettra in Idomeneo, Antonia in Les Contes d'Hoffmann 1990; Sang Eva at La Scala and Amelia in a new production of Simon Boccanegra at Brussels 1990; sang for Lisa in The Queen of Spades at Glyndebourne 1992; Season 1991/92 as Violetta and Alice Ford at Toronto; Sang the Letter Scene from Eugene Onegin at the 1993 London Proms; Eva in a new production of Die Meistersinger at Covent Garden, 1993; Concert engagements in Mahler's 8th Symphony, with the San Francisco Symphony, and at the Carmel Bach Festival, California. *Address:* Harrison/Parrott Ltd., 12 Penzance Place, London W11 4PA, England.

GUSTIN Denis-Pierre, b. 25 Jan 1971, Brussels, Belgium. Flautist. *Education:* General Certificate of education, St Michael College, Brussels, 1988; First Prizes in flute and chamber music at Brussels and Paris High Conservatories, - 1991, teachers A Marion and M Bourgue. *Debut:* Soloist of the Ensemble Jeunes Solistes RTBF, 1988. *Career:* Foreign tours: Czechoslovakia 1989; Germany, Spain 1990; France 1991; Italy 1992; Debut with BRT Philharmonic Orchestra, 1990; TV and Radio appearances: RTBF, BRT, NHK, BBC, TVE, Radio-France. Collaboration with main Belgian orchestras: National Orchestra, New Belgian Chamber Orchestra, RTBF Symphonic Orchestra.

Honours: First Prizes of: Pro Civitate Competition, 1988; National Competition for Musicians, 1989; Tenuto Competition, 1990; Second Prize of the Brussels Mozart International Competition, First Flautist nominated, 1991; Laureate of the Yehudi Menuhin Foundation and of the Vocation Foundation. *Address:* 236 Avenue Albert, 1180 Brussels, Belgium.

GUTCHË Gene, b. 3 July 1907, Berlin, Germany. Composer. m. Marion Frances Buchan, 1 Dec 1935. *Education:* MA, University of Minnesota, 1950; PhD, State University of Iowa, 1953. *Career:* World Premieres include, Piano Concerto Opus 24, Minneapolis Summer Session, 1956, Third String Quartet, Opus 12, No. 3, Arts Quartet, 1958; Holofernes Overture, Opus 27 No. 1, Minneapolis Symphony Orchestra, 1959; Rondo Capriccioso Opus 21, New York Chamber Orchestra, 1960; Concertino for Orchestra Opus 28, Minneapolis Summer session, 1961; Fourth String Quartet Opus 29 No. 1, Fine Arts Quartet, 1962; Symphony VI Opus 30, Albuquerque Symphony, 1962; Timpani Concertante Opus 31, Oakland Symphony, 1962; Symphony V for Strings Opus 34, Chautauqua Festival, 1962; Bongo Divertimento Opus 35, St Paul Chamber Orchestra, 1962; Raquel Opus 38, Tulsa Philharmonic, 1963; Genghis Khan Opus 37, Minneapolis Symphony, 1963; Rites in Tenochtitlan Opus 39, St Paul Chamber Orchestra, 1965; Appearances with various orchestras and symphonies throughout USA and abroad including, Munich Philharmonic, Radio-Tele, Luxembourg, Trieste, Oslo Philharmonic, Stockholm Philharmonic, American Symphony, Australian Broadcasting, Helsinki, Curtis Symphony; Also national broadcast on public and communal radio, 1980, 84; 4th String Quartet, Opus 29 no. 1, Voice of America, 1983; Numerous commissions including, Rochester (New York) Philharmonic, 1975, Cincinnati Symphony, 1976, Florida Philharmonic, 1978. *Memberships include:* American Federation of Musicians; American Composers' Alliance; American Music Center. *Address:* Regus Publishers, 10 Birchwood Lane, White Bear Lake, MN 55110, USA.

GUTHRIE Frederick, b. 31 Mar 1924, Pocatello, Idaho, USA. Singer (Bass). *Eucation:* Studied with Glynn Ross and Hugo Strelitzer in Los Angeles; Later study with Elisabeth Rado, Ludwig Weber and Josef Witt in Vienna. *Career:* Sang in a concert performance of Oedipus Rex conducted by Karajan, Vienna 1953; Vienna Staatsoper 1954-74; Glyndebourne Festival 1956, as Sarastro in Die Zauberflöte; Frankfurt from 1958 and made guest appearances in Trieste, Munich and Rome; Salzburg Festival 1960, in the premiere of Le mystere de la Nativite by Frank Martin. *Recordings include:* Die Schöpfung by Haydn (Vanguard); Das Buch mit sieben Siegeln by Franz Schmidt; Bruckner's F minor Mass (Melodram).

GUTIERREZ Horacio, b. 28 Aug 1948, Havana, Cuba. Pianist. m. Patricia Asher. *Education:* Juilliard School of Music, New York City, 1967-70. *Debut:* At age 11 with Havana Symphony Orchestra. *Career:* Performed most major symphony orchestras as soloist in recitals throughout the world; Appearances on BBC-TV and also in France and USA; Tours in USA, Canada, Europe, South America, Israel, USSR. *Recordings:* Many for Angel (EMI) Records; Telarc and Chandos Recordings. *Honours:* Recipient, 2nd Prize, Tchaikowsky Competition, 1970; Avery Fisher Prize, 1982. *Current Management:* c/o Columbia Artists' Management, *Address:* Columbia Artists' Management, 165 W 57th Street, New York, NY 10019, USA.

GUTMAN Natalia, b. 14 June 1942, Moscow, Soviet Union. Cellist. *Education:* Began cello studies aged five at Gnessin Music School Moscow under R. Saposhnikov; later studied at Moscow Conservatory with Rostropovich. *Career:* After winning awards at competitions in Moscow, Prague, Munich and Vienna she has made many tours of Europe, America and Japan, appearing with the Vienna Philharmonic Orchestra, Orchestre National de France, Berlin Philharmonic Orchestra, the Philharmonia and the Concertgebouw

Orchestra; conductors with whom she has performed include Abbado, Sawallisch, Muti, Rozhdestvensy, Stokowski, Svetlanov and Sinopoli; tours of the USA with the USSR State Symphony Orchestra and of the USSR with the BBC Symphony Orchestra and John Pritchard; she plays chamber music in the Russia and Europe with Eliso Virsaladze and Oleg Kagan; chamber concerts with Sviatoslav Richter; Russian composers she has performed include Gubaidulina, Denisov and Schnittke. *Recordings include:* Both Shostakovich Concertos for RCA. *Address:* c/o Harold Holt Ltd., 31 Sinclair Road, London W14 ONS, England.

GUTSTEIN Ernst, b. 15 May 1924, Vienna, Austria. Singer (Baritone). *Education:* Studied at the Vienna Music Academy. *Debut:* Innsbruck 1948, as Fernando in Fidelio. *Career:* Sang at Innsbruck 1949-52; Heidelberg 1953-54; Kassel 1954-56; Deutsche Oper am Rhein Dusseldorf 1958-59; Frankfurt-am-Main 1956-67; Vienna 1967-89; Further appearances in London, Cologne, Florence, Moscow, Paris, Chicago, Rome and Brussels; Salzburg Festival 1959, in Il Mondo della Luna by Haydn; Zurich Opera 1975, in the premiere of Ein Wahrer Held by Klebe; Many engagements in operas by Verdi and Wagner; Sang in Berg's Lulu at the Festival Hall, London, 1994. *Recordings:* Jochanaan in Salome (Electrola); Rigoletto; La Rappresentazione di Anima e di Corpo by Cavalieri (Deutsche Grammophon); Notre Dame by Schmidt.*Address:* Puchheimerg 23, A-2851 Krumbach, Austria.

GUTTLER Ludwig, b. 13 June 1943, Sosa, Germany. Trumpeter; Conductor; Professor. *Education:* Degree in architecture; Studied trumpet with Armin Mennel, Leipzig Hochschule für Musik, 1961-65. *Debut:* Soloist with orchestra, 1958. *Career:* Solo Trumpeter, Handel Festival Orchestra, Halle, 1965-; Dresden Philharmonic, 1969-81; Founder-Director, Leipziger Bach-Collegium, 1976-; Blechbläserensemble Ludwig Guttler, 1978-; Virtuosi Saxoniae, 1985-; Solo tours throughout the world; Lecturer 1972-80, Professor 1980-, Head of master classes in wind playing 1982-, Dresden Hochschule für Musik; Guest Teacher, Weimar International Music Seminar, 1977-; also in Austria, Japan and the USA. *Recordings:* over 21 discs for Capriccio. *Honours:* National Prize, German Democratic Republic, 1978; German Phonoakademie recording prize, 1983; Music Prize, City of Frankfurt, 1989. *Address:* c/o Gotthart Wilke, Edinger Konzer-und Kunstleragentur, Lindenstrasse 26, D-8011 Zorneding, Germany.

GUTTMAN Albert, b. 12 Oct 1937, Galati, Romania. Pianist. *Education:* Conservatoire of Music, Bucharest; Graduate, Piano, Florica Musicescu; Studied Piano Accompaniment under Dagobert Buchholz; Graduate, Biennial Master Classes, magna cum laude, Santa Cecilia Conservatoire, Rome, Teacher Guido Agosti; *Career:* Professor of Piano, Chamber Music and Piano Accompaniment, Bucharest Conservatoire of Music, 1960-76; Official Assistant for Chamber Music, Santa Cecilia National Academy in Rome, 1972; Invited by Yehudi Menuhin to teach Chamber Music at International Menuhin Academy of Music, Gstaad, Switzerland, 1982-84; Taught summer courses at Taormina and Vicenze, Italy and Gstaad, Switzerland, 1969, 1970, 1977, 1981, 1982, 1983; Professor of Piano, Musikschule Saanenland, Gstaad, Switzerland and Professor of Piano Accompaniment, including permanent Master Class for Graduate Pianists specializing in Piano Accompaniment, Musik Akademie der Stadt Basel, 1983-; Worldwide Tours and participant in numerous festivals; recitals with Radu Aldulescu and Silvia Marcovici, and has often performed with Yehudi Menuhin, Pierre Fournier, Ruggiero Ricci, Enrico Mainardi, Jean Pierre Rampal, Christian Ferras, Lola Bobesco, Pina Carmirelli, Ivry Gitlis, Raphael Sommer. *Recordings:* Radio and Television recordings in Baden-Baden, Belgrade, Berlin, Bucharest, Bulawayo, Frankfurt, Jerusalem, Johannesburg, Karlsruhe, Köln, Madrid, Moscow, Paris, Rome, Stuttgart, Tokyo, Torina, Venezia, Warsaw; Discography: Beethoven; Integral Edition; Five Sonatas for Piano and Cello; Radu

Aldulescu - cello. Schumann; Frauenliebe und Leben; De Falla Siete Canciones Populares Espanolas, Elena Cernei, mezzo; Shostakovitch Sonata Op.40 for cello and piano. Hindemith Sonata Op.11 No. 3 for cello and piano, Radu Aldeluscu; cello. Bach; Sonata No.4 for violin and piano BWV 1017. Beethoven; Sonata Op.30 No.3 for piano and violin, Lola Bobesco; violin. Brahms; Sonata No.2 Op.100 in A major for piano and violin, Sonata No.3 Op.108 in D minor for piano and violin; Angela Gavrila Dieterle, Beethoven, Sieben Variationen in Es-dur Wo046 for piano and cello, Mirel Iancovici; cello. *Honours include:* The Hephzibah Menuhin International Prize for Pianists, 1981. *Address:* Chalet Bel Air, App. 216 3780 Gstaad, Switzerland.

GUY Barry John, b. 22 Apr 1947, Lewisham, London, England. Musician (Double Bass; Violone); Composer. *Education:* AGSM. *Career includes:* Freelance Bassist; Principal, City of London Sinfonia; Solo Recitalist; Artistic Director, London Jazz Composers Orchestra; Plays with improvisation groups, Evan Parker trio; Marilyn Crispell; Gerry Hemingway; Barry Guy trio; Cecil Taylor; Roo; Mats Gustafsson and Iskra 1903. *Compositions:* Statements II, 1972; String Quartet III, 1973; Anna, 1974; Play, 1976; EOS for Double Bass and Orchestra, 1977; Details, 1978; Hold Hands and Sing, 1978; Waiata, 1980; Pfiff, 1981; Flagwalk, 1983; Voyages of the Moon, 1983; RondOH!, 1985; Cirular for solo oboe(s), 1985; The Road to Ruin, 1986; Video/Life (Ballet for London Contemporary Dance Theatre), 1986; Harmos, 1987; The Eye of Silence, 1988; UM 1788, 1989; Look Up!, 1990; Theoria, 1991; After the Rain, 1992; Bird Gong Game, 1992; Mobile Herbarium, 1992; Portraits, 1993; Witch Gong Game, 1993. *Recordings:* Over 40 albums including: Ode, 1972; Statements V-XI, 1976; No Fear, 1977; Improvisations are Forever Now, 1977; Endgame, 1979; Paintings, 1981; Facets, 1979; Incision, 1981; Tracks, 1983; Stringer, 1984; Hook, Drift and Shuffle, 1985; Tai Kyoku, 1985; Assist, 1985; Zurich Concerts, 1988; Harmos, 1989; Double Trouble, 1990; Atlanta, 1990; Arcus, 1991; Elsie Jo Live, 1992; Theoria, 1992; After the Rain, 1993; Fizzles, 1993. *Honour:* Radcliffe Award 1st Prize, 1973; Royal Philharmonic Prize for chamber scale composition, 1991. *Memberships:* Professional organisations including Musicians Union; PRS; MCPS; APC; RPS; ISM. *Hobbies:* Squash; Sailing; Painting. *Address:* Bramley's House, Shudy Camps, Cambridge, CB1 6RA.

GUY Ruth Maureen, b. 10 July 1932, Penclawdd, Glamorgan, South Wales. Mezzo-soprano. *Education:* Guildhall School of Music and Drama. *Debut:* As Dryad in Ariadne auf Naxos, Sadlers Wells. *Career:* Principal Mezzo-soprano, Sadlers Wells, Royal Opera House Covent Garden, Frankfurt Opera; Recitals, oratorio and orchestral concerts worldwide; Tours, New Zealand, Australia, Europe; Performed in opera, New Zealand, Spain, Portugal, France and Budapest, Hungary; Her roles include: Delilah; Eboli; Amneris; Azucena; Fricka; Erda; Orpheus; Mrs Sedley; Adriano in Rienzi; Performed Oedipus Rex in Herodus Atticus (Athens), conducted by Stravinsky; Presently Welsh College of Music and Drama as Vocal Tutor. *Recordings:* Solti, Götterdämmerung, Decca; Leinsdorf, Walküre; Sadlers Wells, Rigoletto (Maddalena). *Honour:* Glamorgan Country Scholarship to Guildhall School. *Hobby:* Interior decoration. *Address:* The Verzons Granary, Munsley, Ledbury, Herefordshire, England.

GUZMAN Rodolfo, b. 8 Mar 1956, Guananacoa, Cuba. Music Specialist. m. Iris Vila, 1 Feb 1980, 1 daughter. *Education:* BMus magna cum laude, Theory, Composition, University of Miami, Coral Gables, Florida, USA, 1979. *Career:* Music Specialist for US Information Agency; Have been active as composer of music for piano, voice, chamber groups and orchestra, and as recorder soloist for Potomac Consort, Washington Camerata and Musica Antiqua of Miami. *Compositions include:* Incidental music for film Our Lady of Charity, 1992; Fantasia Ritmica for piano; String Quartet; Recorder Quartet. *Honours:* 2nd Prize for String Quartet No 1, South Florida Composers Contest, 1981;

Honourable Mention, American Recorder Society Compositon Contest, 1986. *Memberships:* Broadcast Music Inc; American Recorder Society. *Hobbies:* Reading; Listening to music. *Address:* 6091 Belleview Drive Apt 102, Falls Church, VA 22041, USA.

GWIZDALANKA Danuta, b. 22 June 1955, Poznan, Poland. Musicologist. *Education:* MA, 1979, Doctorate, 1989, Mickiewicz University, Poznan. *Publications:* Brzemienie Kwartetow Smyczkowych Beethovena (Sonority in String Quartets of Beethoven), Poznan, 1990; Slowniczek Skrotow i Oznaczen Muzycznych (Little Dictionary of Musical Terminology), Poznan, 1994; Co-author: Tadeusz Szeligowski, Bydgoszcz, 1987; Konstanty Regamey, Warsaw, 1988; Editor: Chopin Studies, I, 1985, II, 1987. *Contributions to:* Various journals in Poland and Sweden, papers issued by Music Academies, musical encyclopaedia, Cracow, 1978-. *Membership:* Union of Polish Composers. *Address:* Kurt Schumacher 10 W 51, 51427 Bergisch Gladbach, Germany.

GYLDENFELDT Graciela von, b. 22 June 1958, Buenos Aires, Argentin. Singer (Soprano). *Education:* Studied in Buenos Aires. *Debut:* Sang Norina in Don Pasquale at Buenos Aires, 1979. *Career:* Sang at Bern Opera from 1980, debut as Gilda, later appearing as Zerlina, Martha, Pamina, Echo in Ariadne auf Naxos and Corilla in Donzietti's Convenzione Teatrali; Sang at Vienna Staatsoper, 1982-86, Salzburg Festival, 1984-88, as Frasquita and Tebaldo in productions of Carmen and Don Carlos conducted by Karajan; Enschede, Netherlands, from 1988, as Suor Angelica, Mimi and Donna Elvira; Currently member of Kiel Opera, as Chrysothemis, Katya Kabanova and Ellen Orford; Sang the Princess in Zemlinsky's Es War Einmal, 1991, Marietta in Die Tote Stadt, 1992; Cincinnati, 1991, as Carmen; Appearances at Teatro Comunale, Florence, as Elena in Mefistofele and concert engagements in Beethovens Ninth and Janáček's Glagolitic Mass; Salud in La vida breve of Manuel de Falla, at the Dallas Opera, 1993. *Address:* c/o Buhnen des Landeshaupstadt, Rathausplatz, 2300 Kiel, Germany.

GYSELYNCK Jean-Baptiste, b. 22 Mar 1946, Ghent, Belgium. Professor at the Royal Music Conservatory of Brussels. m. Bruyneel Arlette, 1 June 1946, 1 son, 1 daughter. *Education:* General; Royal Atheneum of Ghent; Musical; Royal Music Conservatory of Ghent; 1962-66; Conservatory of Brussels, 1966-78. *Career:* BRT Brussels (classical music) 1969; Teacher at the Royal Flemish Music Conservatory of Antwerp (counterpoint) 1970; Professor of Harmony, counterpoint and composition at the Lemmens Institute of Louvain, 1970-79; Professor of Harmony, Art Humanities Department, Royal Music Conservatory of Brussels, 1974-75; Professor of Written Harmony, Royal Music Concervatory of Brussels, 1970-. *Compositions:* Recorded: Simfonia da Camera, radio and TV, 1975; Intermezzi, (wood instruments) Long playing record and radio, 1977; Trio per strumenti a corde archi, (strings) radio, 1979; Adagio en Allegro voor altsaxofoon, radio, 1979; Adagio en allegro voor altsaxofoon; Diptyque, for violin and piano, radio, 1980; Diptyque, for violin and piano, radio, 1982, Published: Intermezzi, (Andel-Ostend); Illuminatio, (ANZ Brussels); Diptyque, (Metropolis Antwerp); Music for 6 poems written by Johan Daisne (Royal Academy of Brussels). *Honours include:* International Music Competition Queen Elisabeth Laureat of composition Diptyque for violin and piano (set piece), 1980; Silver Prize of Her Majesty Queen Fabiola Composition Competition Sabam, Diptyque, for violin and piano, 1980; 6 poems of Johan Daisne given at the Albertine, Brussels, 1985. *Address:* Kortrijksesteenweg 934, 9000 Ghent, Belgium.

H

HAAR James, b. 4 July 1929, St Louis, Missouri, USA. Musicologist. *Education:* Harvard University, BA, 1950, PhD, 1961, University of North Carolina, MA, 1954. *Career:* Faculty member, Harvard University, 1960-67, University of Pennsylvania, 1967-69, New York University, 1979-78, University of North Carolina, 1978-; General Editor, Journal of the American Musicological Society, 1966-69. *Publications:* The Tugendsterne of Harsdorffer and Staden, 1965; Essays on Italian Poetry and Music in the Renaissance, 1350-1600, 1986. *Contributions to:* Articles in many journals. *Memberships:* American Musicological Society, President, 1976-78. *Address:* c/o Department of Music, University of North Carolina, Chapel Hill, NC 27599, USA.

HAAS Kenneth, b. 8 July 1943, Washington DC, USA. Symphony Orchestra Executive. m. (1) Barbara Dooneief, 14 Feb 1964, 2 daughters, divorced, 1 Mar 1990 (2) Signe Johnson, 23 Mar 1990, 1 s. *Education:* BA, Columbia College, 1964. *Appointments:* Assistant to Managing Director, New York Philharmonic, 1966-70; Assistant General Manager, 1970-75, General Manager, 1976-87, Cleveland Orchestra; General Manager, Cincinnati Symphony Orchestra, 1975-76; Managing Director, Boston Symphony Orchestra, 1987-; Chairman, Orchestra Panel, National Endowment for the Arts, 1982-85; Co-Chairman, Music Overview Panel, National Endowment for the Arts, 1983-85; Chairman, Challenge Grant Panel, Ohio Arts Council, 1985-86. *Memberships:* American Symphony Orchestra League, Executive Committee, 1980-82; Managers, Major Orchestras, US, Chairman, 1980-82. *Hobby:* Bicycling. *Address:* Symphony Hall, 301 Massachusetts Avenue, Boston, MA 02115, USA.

HAASEMANN Frauke, b. 25 Nov 1922, Rendsburg, Germany. Professor of Voice and Conducting. Widow. *Education:* Studied Church Music, qualification: Kirchenmusikdirector, Church Music School of Wwestphalia, Herford, West Germany; Studies of Voice, Folkwang Hochschule/Essen-Werden and Musik Hochschule, Hannover. *Career:* Contra-Alto Soloist, Oratorios and Lieder, all over Europe, 1951-77; Soloist of the Westfaelische Kantorei (conductor Wilhelm Ehmann) which toured Europe, Asia, North America; Numerous appearances on tv and radio stations; Co-tutor of Westminster Symphonic choir for concerts with New York and Philadelphia Symphonic for conductors such as: Bernstein, Mehta, Muti, Masur, Abbado, Levine, Giulini. Conductor of many All Sate and Honours Choirs; Leader of hundreds of workshops for Group Vocal Techniques all over the USA. *Recordings:* As the alto soloist of the Westfaelische Kantorei, appearance on about 90 recordings (Cantate, Musicaphon, Musical Heritage, Laudate). *Publications:* Handbuch der Chorischen Stimmbildung, Baerenreiter 1984; Voice building for Choirs, Hinshaw music, 1981; Group Vocal technique, Hinshaw music, 1990; Group vocal technique, the vocalise cards, Hinshaw 1990; Group Vocal Technique, Video, Hinshaw, 1990. *Contributions to:* Lied und Chor, Deutscher Saengerbund; Musik und Kirche, Baerenreiter; Choral Journal, publication of ACDA. *Memberships:* Internationale Heinrich Schütz Gesellschaft; Internationale Bach Gesellschaft; American Choral Directors Association. *Address:* Eichsfelderstrasse 44, 3000 Hannover-Stoecken, Germany.

HAASS Erich Walter, b. 25 Sept 1936, Cologne, Germany. Music Publisher. m. 17 July 1965, 1 son, 1 daughter. *Education:* Piano instruction with Professor Hans Haass, Kläre Bormann and Lia Kipper, 1943; Academy of Music, Cologne, 1956-59; Examination as Teacher of Music and Literature; Doctor of Musicology, Universities of Cologne and Marburg, 1983. *Debut:* Competitor in Youth Makes Music, Dusseldorf, 1948. *Career:* Organ concert, WDR, Cologne, 1958; Piano and choir concerts, Cologne and Leverkusen; Co-Partner, Hans Gerig music publishers, Cologne, 1978; Owner, music publishing house. *Publications:* Cantata for soli, choir and orchestra, 1955; Compositions for choir; Compositions for piano. *Recordings:* Tapes of works by Bach, Handel, Debussy and Haass for flute played by Hans-Jürgen Horn, for piano played by Walter Haass, and piano solo. *Publications:* Studies about the 'L'homme arme' Masses of the 15th and 16th centuries, 1984; Poems, in preparation. *Contributions to:* The song 'L'homme arme' in publication in honour of Prof Dr Heinrich Huschen; Article on Hans Haass, in Contr hist Rh mus. *Honours:* Oberstudienrat, 1974; Doctor phil, 1983. *Memberships:* GEMA, Berlin; Committee, Youth Makes Music, Cologne. *Hobbies:* Hiking; Photography. *Address:* Kermeterstrasse 24, D-50935 Cologne, Germany.

HAASS Hans, b. 15 Sept 1897, Cologne, Germany. Professor. m. Irmgard Gerig, 6 July 1929, 1 son, 1 daughter. *Education:* First piano instruction with brother Willi Haass; With Lonny Epstein and Professor Carl Friedberg, Academy of Music, Cologne, 1911; Composition with Boelsche, Klanwell, Ramroth, Straesser. *Debut:* Prizewinner, piano, 1916. *Career:* Teacher of Piano, Academy of Music, Krefeld, 1918; Teacher of Piano, Academy of Music, Viersen and Rheydt; Pianist and Artistic Director with firm Welte, producer of mechanical pianos, Freiburg/Breisgau, 1925; Performance of mechanical compositions at Donaueschingen Festival; Established Haass Archives, Cologne. *Compositions:* Fantasy of Russian dances for piano and orchestra; Irish folkdance; Fugue for mechanical piano; Sinfonietta; Songs; Arrangements. *Recordings:* Rolls of mechanical music including under pseudonyms Hans Haeuser, John Hare, Jean Maison; Recordings for WDR, SWF and other broadcasting stations, also in Austria, as composer and/or pianist. *Publications:* Little pictures for piano; 9 pieces for piano, op 16; Fantasy of Russian dances. *Contributions to:* About the character of mechanical music. *Honours:* Ibach Prize for Piano, 1916; Professor, Academy of Music, Cologne and Detmold. *Membership:* GEMA, Berlin. *Hobbies:* Photography; Hiking. *Address:* Goldammerweg 183/Haassweg 10, D-50829, Cologne, Germany.

HABBESTAD Kjell Helge, b. 13 Apr 1955, Bomlo, Hordaland, Norway. Teacher; Composer. m. Inger Elisabeth Brammer, 30 Dec 1976, 1 son, 2 daughters. *Education:* Studies of Church Music (organ), 1975-79; Studied Composition, Norwegian State Academy of Music, 1979-81. *Career:* Organist: Snaroya Church, Baerum, 1977-81, Langhus Church, Ski, 1986-87; Teacher of Harmony, Counterpoint, Composition: Bergen Conservatory of Music, 1981-86, Ostlandets Conservatory of Music, Oslo, 1986-. *Compositions:* 3 Cantica (Magnificat, Nunc Dimittis, Benedictus Dominus), 1978-83; Lament, soprano and orchestra, 1981; Mostraspelet, baritone solo, choir, orchestra and mediaeval instruments, 1983; Ave Maria, concerto for organ and string orchestra, 1984; Something New - Below Ground, concerto for tuba and brass band, 1985; Mostrasuite for baritone solo, unison choir and orchestra, 1986; Liturgic dramas/church plays, choral works, chamber music, cantatas, organ chorals, motets. *Publications:* Cantate - Handbook of Norwegian Sacred Choral Works, 1989. *Address:* Wesselsvei 5, N-1412 Sofiemyr, Norway.

HABERMANN Michael Robert, b. 23 Feb 1950, Paris, France. Pianist; Piano Instructor; Composer. *Education:* AAS, Nassau Community College, Garden City, NY 1976; BA 1978; MA 1979; Long Island University, Greenvale, NY; DMA, Peabody Conservatory, Baltimore, Maryland, 1985. *Debut:* Carnegie Recital Hall, NYC 1977. *Career:* American Liszt Festival appearances 1978, 1982, 1993; International Piano Festival, University of Maryland 1979; Grand Piano Programme, National Public Radio Piano Recital 1981; McMaster University, Hamilton, Ontario, Canada 1983; Rocky River Chamber Music Society, Ohio 1984. *Recordings:* Sorabji: A Legend In His Own Time; Sorabji: Le Jardin Parfumé; Sorabji, piano music (vol 3); Piano Music of Alexandre Rey Colaço Educo. *Publications:* Kaikhosru Shapurji Sorabji, The Piano Quarterly,

Summer 1983; The Exotic Piano Masterpieces of Sorabji, Soundpage and Score, Keyboard Magazine, April 1986; A Style Analysis of The Nocturnes for Solo Piano by Kaikhosru Shapurji Sorabji with special emphasis on Le Jardin Parfumé, University Microfilms International No 8506576; Author of Sorabji's Piano Music in Sorabji: A Critical Celebration, 1993; author: Essay for Remembering Horowitz: 125 Pianists recall a legend, ed by David Dupal, 1993. *Hobbies:* Computers; Jogging; Movies; Swimming; Cycling. *Address:* 4208 Harford Terrace, Baltimore, MD 21214, USA.

HACKER Alan Ray, b. 30 Sept 1938. Clarinettist; Conductor; Lecturer. m. (1) Anna Maria Sroka, 1959, 2 daughters; (2) Karen Evans, 1977 (now separated), 1 son. *Education:* Royal Academy of Music; FRAM. *Career:* Joined LPO, 1958; Professor, Royal Academy of Music, 1960-76; Founded, Pierrot Players (with S Pruslin and H Birtwistle), 1965; Matrix, 1971; Music Party for authentic performance of classical music, 1972; Classical Orchestra, 1977; Guest Conductor, Orchestra la Fenice, Venice, 1981; First Modern authentic, performances 1977-, including: Mozart's Symphonies 39, 40; Beethoven's Symphonies, 2, 3, 7, 9 and Egmont; Haydn's Harmonie and Creation Masses; Symphony 104 and Trumpet Concerto; Revived basset clarinet and restored original text, Mozart's concerto and quintet, 1967; revived baroque clarinet (hitherto unplayed), 1975; Premieres of music by Birtwistle, Boulez, Feldman, Goehr, Maxwell Davies, Stockhausen, Blake, Mellers and Sciarrino; Conductor, 5 staged performances of Bach's St John Passion for European Music Year, 1984; Sir Robert Mayer Lecturer, Leeds University, 1972-73; Member, Fires of London, 1970-76; Director, York Early Music Festival; Directed the revival of Den Bergtagna by Hallström, Swedish National Opera, 1986-87 (for Norrlands Operan), directed the first production of the complete La Finta Giardiniera; conducted Keiser's Claudius at the Vadstena Academy, Sweden, 1989; Premiere of Judith Weir's The Vanishing Bridegroom for Scottish Opera, 1990; Così fan Tutte and La Finta Giardiniera for Opera North, 1990-91; Stuttgart Opera 1990-92, Don Giovanni and Monteverdi's Ulisse; Conducted Traviata and La Cenerentola at Barcelona 1992, Giulio Cesare at the Halle Handel Festival; Senior Lecturer, Music, York University, 1976-85. *Recordings:* Many, including Brahms Clarinet Sonatas, Saydisc, 1989. *Publications:* Scores of Mozart Concerto and Quintet, 1972; 1st Edition of reconstructed Mozart Concerto, 1973; Schumann's Soirestücke 1985. *Honours:* OBE, 1988; Patron of Artlink, 1993. *Hobby:* Cookery. *Current Management:* Haydn Rawstron, PO Box 654, London, SE26 4DZ. *Address:* Hindlea, Broughton, Malton, North Yorkshire YO17 0QJ, England.

HADARI Omri, b. 10 Sept 1941, Israel. Conductor. m. Osnat Hadari, 29 June 1965, 1 son, 1 daughter. *Education:* Tel-Aviv Music College; Guildhall School of Music and Drama, London. *Debut:* London, 1974. *Career:* Conductor, London Lyric Orchestra; Principal Guest Conductor, Adelaide Symphony Orchestra; Music Director and Principal Conductor, Cape Town Symphony Orchestra, South Africa, 1989-; Debut with Australian Opera 1988, La Bohème; Guest Conductor: Royal Philharmonic Orchestra, London Symphony Orchestra, City of Birmingham Symphony Orchestra, The Australian Opera, Sydney Symphony Orchestra, Melbourne Symphony Orchestra, South Australia Symphony Orchestra, Queensland Symphony Orchestra, Israel Chamber Orchestra, Jerusalem Symphony Orchestra, Beer-Sheva Sinfonietta, Het Brabant Symphony Orchestra, Dutch National Ballet, The Australian Opera, The Victorian State Opera, Ulster Orchestra, The National Symphony Orchestra of South Africa, Natal Philharmonic, Columbus (Ohio) Symphony Orchestra, San Francisco Chamber Orchestra, Orchestra of Radio City New York, Lahti Symphony Orchestra, Avanti Orchestra, Tasmania Symphony Orchestra; conducted Shostakovich's New Babylon in London, 1982, New York and Helsinki and at the Flanders Festival. *Honours:* Dr Leo Kestenberg Prize (1st), Israel, 1969; Conducting Prize, Guildhall School of Music, 1974; Capsalic Cup for Conducting, 1974;

Fellow, Guildhall School of Music, 1983. *Membership:* Incorporated Society of Musicians. *Current Management:* Christopher Tennant Artists' Management. *Address:* 7 Hurstwood Road, London NW11 0AS, England.

HADDOCK Marcus, b. 19 June 1957, Fort Worth, Texas, USA. Singer (Tenor). *Career:* Appearances at opera houses of Fort Worth and Dallas, Baton Rouge, Boston, Miami, Atlanta and Pennsylvania, 1984-; Roles have included Lindoro (L'Italiana in Algeri), Almaviva, Ramiro (Cenerentola) and Pinkerton; Washington Opera, 1987-88, as Gounod's Romeo, Lindoro and Jacquino; European engagements include Ford in Salieri's Falstaff and Nemorino for Hungarian National Opera at Bordeaux, Ernesto, Tamino, Rodolfo and Edgardo at Aachen, 1988-90; Karlsruhe, 1990-, as Edgardo, Rudolfo, Alfredo and Tamino; Guest appearances at Cologne as Pinkerton and Nemorino, Vienna, Zurich, Hamburg (Wilhelm Meister in Mignon) and Opera Bastille, Paris (Idomeneo, 1991); La Scala Milan debut, 1992, as Matteo in Arabella; Season 1992-93 at Bonn (Hoffmann, Werther), Reggio Emilia (Cassio), Cologne, Munich (Mitridate) and Essen; Sang Rodolfo in La Bohème for Bath City Opera, 1992; Concert appearances with Leonard Slatkin and Simon Rattle in USA in works by Britten, Janáček, Berlioz and Mozart; Further showings with Dusseldorf and Aachen Symphonies, Philharmonica Hungarica and Berlin Concert Choir. *Address:* Atholl Still Ltd, 80-86 Westow Street, London SE19 3AF, England.

HADJINIKOS George, b. 3 May 1923, Volos, Greece. Conductor; Concert Pianist; Lecturer; Teacher. m. Matina Crithary, 1 son. *Education:* Athens University; Diploma, Athens Conservatoire; Soloist and Conducting degrees with distinction, Mozarteum, Salzburg; Postgraduate with Carl Orff, Munich, Ed Erdmann, Hamburg, G Chavchavadze, Paris. *Career:* Concert Soloist, Conductor, Lecturer, Europe, USA, South Africa, India, Brazil; World premieres of works by Nikos Skalkottas; Soloist with Berlin Philharmonic, BBC Orchestra with Antal Dorati, Halle Orchestra with Sir John Barbirolli, NDR with Herman Scherchen, Schmidt-Isserstedt, ORTF, France, Suisse Romande, Stockholm Philharmonic, Vienna, Zurich, Copenhagen Radio; Conductor: London Bach Festival Ensemble, Northern Sinfonia, Athens State and Radio Orchestras, RAI Milan Orchestra (Athens Festival Opening Concert), Stockholm Radio Orchestra, Rio de Janeiro Radio Orchestra, Danish Radio Orchestra (European Broadcast Union Concert), Slovakian State Philharmonic, Sinfonie Orchester Berlin, others, numerous international youth orchestras; Concert tour, US universities; Prepared and conducted 1st Greek performance of Brahms' German Requiem, 1992; Nexus Opera Workshop; Lectured, Wuerzburg European Council Symposium; Developed fresh approach Logic and Foundations of Musical Interpretation, presented in open seminars and articles; Music Director, Coordinator, annual Hortos Seminars and Festivals; Taught, Royal Manchester and Royal Northern Colleges of Music. *Recordings:* Album with works by Bach, Bartok, Skalkottas, Konstantinidis, Poniridis. *Publications:* Monographs on Skalkottas, 1981, Mozart's Recitative, 1991; The Complete Works by Nikos Skalkottas (co-editor). *Current Management:* PIA Agency, Amerikis 15, Athens 10672, Greece. *Address:* PIA Agency, Smerkis 15, Athens 10672, Greece.

HADLEY Jerry, b. 16 June 1952, Peoria, Illinois. Singer (Tenor) m. Cheryll Drake Hadley. *Education:* Studied at University of Illinois and with Thomas LoMonaco. *Debut:* Sarasota, Florida, 1978, as Lionel in Martha. *Career:* New York City Opera debut 1979, as Arturo in Lucia di Lammermoor; returned as Werther, Tom Rakewell, Rodolfo, Nadir and Pinkerton; Vienna Staatsoper debut 1982, as Nemorino in L'Elisir d'Amore; Glyndebourne debut 1984, as Idamante in Trevor Nunn's production of Idomeneo; Covent Garden 1984, as Fenton in Falstaff; Metropolitan Opera debut 1987, as Des Grieux in Manon; Guest engagements in Chicago, Hamburg, Berlin, Munich and Geneva; Other roles include Gounod's Faust, Mozart's Tamino, Ferrando and Alessandro in Il Re Pastore; the Duke of Mantua, Alfredo in La Traviata and the tenor leads in Anna Bolena and Maria Stuarda; Hamburg 1987, as Tamino; sang Edgardo at the Deutsche Oper Berlin and Washington 1988-89; Candide in a concert performance of Bernstein's work, London 1989; Ferrando and Ottavio at the Metropolitan 1990; sang Rodolfo at Covent Garden, 1990; returned 1993 as the Berlioz Faust; sang Hoffmann in London, 1992; Concert engagements with the Pittsburgh Symphony, Boston Symphony, Chicago Symphony, Philadelphia Orchestra, Vienna Philharmonic and Los Angeles Philharmonic; Recitals with Cheryll Drake Hadley, piano. *Recordings:* Schubert Mass in E flat and La Bohème (Deutsche Grammophon); Anna Bolena (Decca); Beethoven's Choral Symphony and the Requiems of Mozart and Verdi, with the Robert Shaw Chorale; Britten's Serenade, Nocturne and Les Illuminations (Nimbus); Il Re Pastore conducted by Neville Marriner (Philips). *Address:* c/o Harrison/Parrott Ltd, 12 Penzance Place, London W11 4PA, England.

HAEBLER Ingrid, b. 20 June 1926, Vienna, Austria. Concert Pianist. *Education:* Studied at the Salzburg Mozarteum, the Vienna Academy and the Geneva Conservatory; Further study in Paris with Marguerite Long. *Debut:* Salzburg 1937. *Career:* Many concert tours of Europe, Australia, USA, Canada, South Africa and Japan; Festival appearances at Salzburg, Edinburgh, Wiesbaden, Bath, Amsterdam and Prague; Concerts with the Concertgebouw Orchestra, London Symphony, Royal Philharmonic, Vienna and Berlin Philharmonics, Boston Symphony, Lamoureux Orchestra, Stockholm and Warsaw Philharmonics, London Mozart Players; Teacher at the Salzburg Mozarteum from 1969. *Recordings include:* Two Cycles of the Complete Piano Concertos of Mozart; Complete Sonatas of Mozart and Schubert; Beethoven's 2nd and 4th Concertos; Schumann Piano Concerto; Symphonic Variations by Franck; Works by J.C. Bach on the Fortepiano. *Honours:* Winner, International Competition Munich, and Schubert Competition Geneva, 1954; Beethoven Medal, Harriet Cohen Foundation, 1957; Grand Prix du Disque, Paris, 1958; Puthon Prize, Salzburg Festival; Mozart Medal, Vienna, 1971. *Address:* 5412 St Jakob am Thurn, Post Buch Bei Hallein, Land Salzburg, Austria.

HAEFLIGER Ernst, b. 6 July 1919, Davos, Switzerland. Singer (Tenor). *Education:* Studied in Zurich, and with Fernando Carpi in Geneva; Further study with Julius Patzak in Vienna. *Debut:* 1942, as the Evangelist in Bach's St John Passion. *Career:* Sang with Zurich Opera 1943-52; Many concert appearances in Switzerland, Germany, Austria, France and Holland, notably in the St Matthew Passion and Lieder cycles by Schubert; Salzburg Festival 1949, as Tiresias in the premiere of Antigonae by Orff; returned to Salzburg for Idomeneo and the Choral Symphony; Glyndebourne Festival 1956-57, as Tamino in Die Zauberflöte and as Belmonte in Die Entführung; Guest appearances in Munich, Hamburg, Florence, Aix-en-Provence, Brussels and Berlin (Deutsche Oper 1952-74); Sang in the first performances of the Oratorios Le Vin Herbé, Golgotha and In Terra Pax, by Frank Martin; Visited Moscow and Leningrad with the Munich Bach Choir, 1968; Professor at the Musikhochschule Munich from 1971. *Recordings:* St Matthew Passion, Missa Solemnis (Philips); Oedipus Rex (Decca); Pelléas and Mélisande (Harmonia Mundi); Die Entführung, Fidelio, Don Giovanni, Die Zauberflöte, Der fliegende Holländer, Brockes Passion by Handel, Die Israeliten in der Wüste by CPE Bach (Deutsche Grammophon). *Publication:* Die Singstimme, 1984. *Address:* c/o Ingpen and Williams Ltd, 14 Kensington Court, London W8 5DN, England.

HAENCHEN Hartmut, b. 21 Mar 1943, Dresden, Germany. Conductor. *Education:* Member of the Dresden Kreuzchor 1953-60, under Rudolf Mauersbergee and student at the Dresden Musikhochschule, 1960- 66. *Career:* Directed the Robert-Franz-Singakademie and the Halle Symphony 1966-72; Music Director at the Zwickau Opera 1972-73; Permanent conductor of the Dresden Philharmonic

1973-76, Philharmonic Chorus of Dresden 1974-76, and permanent guest conductor of the Staatsoper Dresden; Musical Director of the Schwerin Staatstheater and conductor of the Mecklenburg Staatskapelle 1976-79; Professor of Conducting at the Dresden Musikhochschule, 1980-86; Permanent guest conductor at the Komische Oper Berlin, Berlin Staatsoper; Guest appearances in England and elsewhere in Western Europe, USA, Canada, Japan; Guest appearances in the Opera Houses of Bologna, Vienna, Munich, Stuttgart, Warsaw, Geneva, Kirishima Festival in Japan; From 1980 director of the Chamber Orchestra C P E Bach, Berlin; From 1986 musical director of the Netherlands Opera, Amsterdam, and principal conductor of the Netherlands Philharmonic Orchestra, founded in 1985, and the Netherlands Chamber Orchestra; Conducted Bluebeard's Castle, La Damnation de Faust, Elektra, Salome, Rosenkavalier, Le Nozze di Figaro, Entführung, Don Carlos, Tristan, Parsifal, Don Carlos, Boris Godunov, Orphée et Euridice; Conducted Gluck's Orfeo ed Euridice at Covent Garden, 1991, followed by Mozart's Mitridate; Conducted Die Frau ohne Schatten, Mitridate, La Damnation de Faust and Samson et Dalila at Amsterdam, 1992. *Recordings:* Numerous Records, including Gluck's Orfeo ed Euridice which was given the Preis der Deutschen Schallphatten and the Gramophone Award Nomination. *Address:* c/o Royal Opera House, Covent Garden, London WC2, England.

HAENDEL Ida, b. 15 Dec 1923, Chelm, Poland. Concert Violinist. *Education:* Gold Medal at age of 7, Warsaw Conservatorium; Private Teachers, Carl Flesch and Georges Enesco. *Debut:* British: Queen's Hall London: Brahms Concerto under Henry Wood. *Career:* After debut as child prodigy gave concerts for British and US Troops and in factories, World War II; thereafter career developed to take in North and South America, USSR and Far East as well as Europe; has played with conductors such as Beecham, Klemperer, Szell, Barenboim, Mata, Pritchard, Rattle and has accompanied British orchestras on tours to China, Hong Kong, Australia; Performances with major orchestras worldwide include Boston Symphony, New York Philharmonic, Berlin Philharmonic, City of Birmingham Symphony Orchestra, London Philharmonic, Philharmonia and Royal Philharmonic Orchestra. Major festival appearances including regular performances at BBC Promenade Concerts, London. *Recordings:* Numerous records for EMI Label. *Publications:* Autobiography: Woman With Violin, 1970. *Honours:* Huberman Prize, 1935; Sibelius Medal (Sibelius Society of Finland), 1982; New Years Honours List Awarded CBE for Outstanding Services to Music, 1991. *Current Management and Address:* c/o Harold Holt Ltd, 31 Sinclair Road, London W14 0NS, England.

HAENEN Tom, b. 1960, Amsterdam, Netherlands. Singer (Bass). *Education:* Studied at Amsterdam Conservatoire. *Debut:* Sang Don Alfonso in Così fan Tutte for Netherlands Opera. *Career:* Appearances in Netherlands and elsewhere as the General in Prokofiev's The Gambler, Arkel in Pelléas et Mélisande and Ferrando in Il Trovatore; Osmin in Die Entführung for Opera North and Leporello and Geronte (Manon Lescaut) in Dublin; Further engagements as Sparafucile in Rigoletto at Barcelona, Don Cassandro in La Finta Semplice and Tom in Ballo in Maschera for Flanders Opera, 1992; Guest appearances at Spoleto, Israel and Las Palmas Festivals. *Honours include:* Prizewinner at the internationals' Hertogenbosch and Rio de Janeiro Competitions. *Address:* c/o Anglo Swiss Ltd, 3 Primrose Mews, 1a Sharpleshall St, London NW1 8YW, England.

HAGEGARD Erland, b. 27 Feb 1944, Brunskog, Sweden. Singer (Baritone). m. Anne Terelius. *Education:* Studied in Sweden with Arne Sunnegaard, with Erik Werba in Vienna and with Gerald Moore in Vienna. *Debut:* Vienna Volksoper, 1968, in Trois Opéras Minutes by Milhaud. *Career:* Sang with Frankfurt Opera, 1971-74; Member of the Hamburg Staatsoper from 1974; Guest with the Vienna Staatsoper from 1976; Appearances at the Drottningholm Court Opera,

Sweden; Danish TV in Xerxes by Handel; Roles include Escamillo, Valentin, Don Giovanni, Eugene Onegin, Albert in Werther and Germont in La Traviata; Lieder singer in works by Schubert; television appearences include Suppé's Boccaccio. *Address:* c/o Drottningsholm Slottsteater, PO Box 27050, 5-102 51 Stockholm, Sweden.

HAGEGARD Håkan, b. 25 Nov 1945, Karlstad, Sweden. Baritone. m. Barbara Bonney, 2 children. *Education:* Music Academy of Stockholm; Student of Tito Gobbi, Rome, Gerald Moore, London, Erik Werba, Vienna. *Debut:* As Papageno in The Magic Flute, Royal Opera, Sweden, 1968. *Career:* Metropolitan Opera debut, 1978 as Donizetti's Malatesta; Member, Royal Opera Stockholm; appeared with major opera companies throughout Europe; in film, The Magic Flute, 1975; Glyndebourne 1973-, as the Count in Figaro and Capriccio and Mozart's Guglielmo; created role of Crispin in Tintomara, Royal Opera, Stockholm, 1973; Covent Garden debut 1987, as Wolfram in Tannhäuser (also at Chicago, 1988); Metropolitan Opera 1988, Guglielmo; Eisenstein in Die Fledermaus at Chicago, 1989; Created Beaumarchais in The Ghosts of Versailles by Corigliano at the Metropolitan, 1991; Deutsche Oper Berlin, 1992, as Wolfram; Recitalist. *Recordings include:* Die Zauberflöte, conducted by Armin Jordan (Erato); Don Giovanni (title role) from Drottningholm (L'Oiseau Lyre). *Current Management and Address:* c/o Thea Dispeker Artists' Management, 59 E 54th Street, New York, NY 10022, USA.

HAGEN Christina, b. 1956, Hamburg, Germany. Singer (Mezzo-soprano). *Education:* Studied singing with Naan Pold and Hilde Nadolowitsch; Concert Diploma, Exam as Private Music Instructor, Opera Diploma with distinction, Hochschule für Musik und darstellende Kunst, Hamburg; Masterclasses including with Sena Jurinac and at International Studio for Singing, Herbert von Karajan Stiftung, with Christa Ludwig. *Career:* Engaged at Staatstheater Oldenburg, 1983-84, then Deutsche Oper am Rhein, Dusseldorf-Duisburg, 1984-; Guest appearances at Wiesbaden, Hanover, Hamburg, Cologne, Munich, Bolshoi Theatre in Moscow, Antwerp, Amsterdam, Staatsoper Berlin; Participant, Bayreuth Festival, 1989, 1990, 1991; Has sung Rosina in Barber in Seville, Micha in Samson (Handel), Judith in Bluebeard's Castle (Bartók) and Jocasta in Oedipus Rex at Oldenburg, Olga in Eugene Onegin and Second Woman in Die Zauberflöte at Oldenburg and Dusseldorf, Composer in Ariadne auf Naxas, Dorabella in Così fan Tutte, Nicklausse in Tales of Hoffmann, Orlowsky in Die Fledermaus, Maddalena in Rigoletto, Fatima in Oberon (Weber), Sextus in Julius Caesar (Handel), Flosshilde, Erda and Fricka in Rheingold, Fricka in Walküre, Second Norn and Waltraute in Götterdämmerung, Fenena in Nabucco, Lucretia in Rape of Lucretia (Britten), Olga in Das Schloss (A Reimann), Ottavia in L'Incoronazione di Poppea (Monteverdi) and Eboli in Don Carlos at Dusseldorf, Clytemnestra in Iphigenie in Aulis (Gluck) at Dusseldorf and Berlin, Fricka in Walküre at Dusseldorf and Munich, Santuzza in Cavalleria Rusticana at Eutiner Festival; Many Lieder recitals and concert appearances. *Honours:* Nominated Chamber Singer of Deutschem Oper am Rhein at Dusseldorf, 1992. *Address:* c/o Deutsche Oper am Rhein, Heinrich-Heine Allee 16, 40213 Dusseldorf, Germany.

HAGEN-GROLL Walter, b. 15 Apr 1927, Chemnitz, Germany. Choral Conductor. *Education:* Studied at the Stuttgart Musikhochschule 1947-52. *Career:* Assistant conductor at the Stuttgart Opera, 1952; Chorus master at the Heidelberg Opera, 1957, Deutsche Oper Berlin 1961; Directed the chorus of the Berlin Philharmonic from 1961; Assisted Wilhelm Pitz at Bayreuth, 1960-62; Chorus Master at the Salzburg Festival from 1965; Philharmonia Chorus, London, 1971-74; Chorus master at the Vienna Staatsoper 1984, Vienna Singakademie 1987; Choral director at the Salzburg Mozarteum from 1986.

HAGENAH Elizabeth Artman, b. 1930, USA. Concert Pianist; Conductor; Pedagogue. m. Henry H Hagenah, 20 June 1953, 2 sons, 1 daughter. *Education:* BM, MM, Performer's Certificate, Graduate with distinction, Eastman School of Music, Rochester, New York; Advanced Study with Isabella Vengerova, Chairman of Piano Department of Curtis School of Musik, Hochschule fur Musik, Freiburg im Breisgau; Hochschule für Musik, Hamburg; Doctoral candidate, School of Music, Boston University. *Debut:* Manhattan's Town Hall, New York City; Orchestral debut: Eastman Theatre, Rochester, New York. *Career:* Faculty Member, Eastman School of Music, 1953-55; Fulbright Scholar to Germany, 1955-57; 3 Solo Concerts, Town Hall, New York, 1968; Teaching Fellow, Doctoral Candidate and Professor of Piano, Boston University, 1965-84; Performer on New York's radio WNYC, Keyboard Masters Series 1968-69; Founder and Artist Director, Stockbridge Concerts International, Inc, 1975-; Organized Summer Konzerte Mulkenkur, Heidelberg, 1983; Collaborator with Principals and Member of Boston Symphony Orchestra; Frequent recitalist and soloist with orchestral and chamber ensemble in major cities in USA, Canada and Europe; Leader of International Piano Seminar, Mitterfels, Germany, 1991, 1992. *Recordings:* Debussy, Preludes, Book II for Radio Station WNYC, New York; Schumann, Piano Concerto in A Minor, Eastman School of Music; Complete standard works for clarinet and piano (on tape) with Gino Cioffi. *Publications:* Works of Girolamo Frescobaldi, 1969; A Study of the Fitzwilliam Virginal Book and Comparison with the Manuscript, 1971; The Biblical Sonatas of Johann Kuhnau, 1970. *Hobbies:* Walking; Swimming; Playing chamber music with her children. *Current Management:* Stockbridge Concerts International, Inc. *Address:* 68, Kenilworth Street, Pittsfield, MA 01201, USA.

HAGER Leopold, b. 6 Oct 1935, Salzburg, Austria. Conductor. m. Gertrude Entleitner, 2 July 1960, 1 daughter. *Education:* Graduated in organ, piano, conducting, harpsichord, High School for Music (Mozarteum), Salzburg. *Career:* Assistant Conductor, Staedtische Buhnen, Mainz, West Germany, 1957-62; Principal Conductor, Landestheater, Linz, Austria, 1962-64; Opernhaus, Cologne, West Germany, 1964-65; General Music Director, Staedtische Buhnen, Freiburg, West Germany, 1965-69; Principal Conductor, Mozarteum Orchestra, Salzburg, 1969-81; has conducted many performances of early operas by Mozart; led the first modern performance of Mitridate, Salzburg, 1971; Symphony Orchestra, Radio Luxembourg, 1981-; Guest Conductor, Vienna Opera, Munich Opera, Metropolitan Opera, Covent Garden, Teatro Colón, Buenos Aires, Berliner Philharmoniker, Wiener Philharmoniker; Conducted Così fan Tutte at the Metropolitan, 1991. *Recordings:* Mozart Piano Concertos, with Karl Engel (Telefunken); Bastien und Bastienne, Lucio Silla, Il re Pastore, Ascanio in Alba (BASF); Mitridate, Re di Ponto (Deutsche Grammophon); CD of La Finta Semplice released 1990 (Orfeo). *Honour:* Decorated, Ehrenkreuz 1 klasse fur Kunst und Wissenschaft, Austria. *Address:* Morzgerstr. 102, A-5020 Salzburg, Austria.

HÅGGANDER Mari Anne, b. 23 Oct 1951, Trokorna, Sweden. Opera Singer (Soprano). *Education:* Opera School, Gothenburg. *Debut:* Michaela in Carmen, Ponelle production, Royal Opera, Stockholm. *Career:* Has sung Cherubino in Stockholm, Elisabetta in Don Carlo in Savonlinna (Finland), Pamina and the Countess in Figaro in Bonn and at Buxton Festival, Eva in Meistersinger in Bayreuth 1981, Mimi in Stockholm and Hamburg, Eva at the Metropolitan 1985, New York, and Elsa in Lohengrin in San Francisco; Guest in Berlin, Munich, Paris, Brussels, Vienna, New York, Seattle, Toronto, London, elsewhere; Other roles include: Butterfly, Amelia in Ballo in Maschera and Simone Boccanegra, Marschallin, Titania in Onegin, Lisa in Pique Dame, Sieglinde, Arabella, Donna Anna. *Recordings:* Das Rheingold with Levine; Peer Gynt with Blomstedt; Several of Lieder and sacred music. *Honours:* Appointed Court Singer to His Majesty the King of Sweden. *Current Management:* Ulf Tornqvist, Stockhol, Sweden. *Address:* c/o Artistsekretariat Ulf Tornqvist,

Sankt Eriksgatan 100, 2 tr, S-113 31 Stockholm, Sweden.

HAGLEY Alison, b. 9 May 1961, London. Singer (Soprano). *Education:* Studied at the Guildhall School of Music and the National Opera Studio. *Career:* Sang in Handel's Rodelinda at the Aldeburgh Festival; Handel's Flavio with Musica nel Chiostro at the 1985 Batignano Festival, Italy; Camden Festival 1986 in La Finta Giardiniera by Mozart; Sang Clorinda in Opera 80's 1987 production of La Cenerentola; Glyndebourne debut 1988, as the Little Owl in L'Enfant et Les Sortilèges, returning in Jenůfa and as Susanna, Nannetta, Papagena and Zerlina; Glyndebourne Tour as Varvara in Katya Kabanova, Despina and Papagena; Covent Garden as a Flowermaiden in Parsifal and in Peter Grimes; English National Opera 1991, as Lauretta in a new production of Gianni Schicchi and Gretel (Hansel and Gretel); Scottish Opera appearances as Musetta in La Bohème and Adele in Die Fledermaus; sang Mélisande, Feb 92, with Boulez and Peter Stein (WNO); Sang Nannetta for ENO, 1992. *Honours include:* FPC Opera Singer of the Year, National Opera Studio. *Address:* Harrison Parrott Ltd, 12 Penzance Place, London W11 4PA, England.

HAHN Barbara, b. 1965, Stuttgart, Germany. Singer (Mezzo-soprano). *Education:* Studied in Stuttgart and at Salzburg Mozarteum. *Career:* Sang at Bielefeld from 1987 as Dorabella, Cherubino and Orlofsky; Nicklausse in Les contes d'Hoffmann at Bregenz Festival, 1987; Appeared as Dorabella and Nicklausse at Hanover, 1988, and sang Grimgerde in Die Walküre at Bologna and Angelina in La Cenerentola at Passau; Freiburg Opera, 1989-91, as Octavian, Idamantes, Hansel and Sonja in Der Zarewitsch; Concert performance of Schreker's Der ferne Klang in Berlin, 1990; Frankfurt Opera, 1992-, debut as Dorabella. *Recordings:* Der ferne Klang, conducted by Gerd Albrecht. *Address:* c/o Atholle Still Ltd, Greystoke House, 80-86 Westrow Street, London SE19 3AF, England.

HAIGH Andrew Wilfred, b. 26 Apr. 1954, Lagos, Nigeria. Pianist. *Education:* Student 1969-74, Associate 1975, Royal College of Music, London, England; Studied with the late Cyril Smith, Phyllis Sellick, Albert Ferber, 1974; Licenciate, Royal Academy of Music, 1975. *Debut:* London Philharmonic Orchestra, Royal Festival Hall, 1965; Wigmore Hall, 1971. *Career:* Soloist with all major British orchestras including London Symphony, London Philharmonic, Philharmonia, Royal Philharmonic, BBC Philharmonic Orchestras; Soloist, Herbert von Karajan Festival, Berlin, 1970; Presented to H M The Queen, and performed for Princess Alexandra, St James' Palace; Recitals in Europe; Head of Piano at Kent Centre for Young Instrumentalists; Examiner and Adjudicator. *Honours:* Gold Medallist, 1969; Winner, BBC Mozart Competition, 1969; Winner, Royal Overseas Competition; National Piano Competition; Hopkinson Silver Medal, 1973; Dannreuther Concerto Prize, Royal College of Music. *Membership:* Incorporated Society of Musicians. *Hobbies:* Swimming; Hill walking; Classic cars. *Address:* 15 Dornden Drive, Langton Green, Tunbridge Wells, Kent TN3 0AA, England.

HAILSTORK Adolphus (Cunningham), b. 17 Apr 1941, Rochester, New York, USA. Composer. *Education:* Studied at Howard University, Washington DC, with Nadia Boulanger in France and at the Manhattan School, MMus 1966; Further study at Michigan State University, PhD 1971. *Career:* Teacher at Michigan State 1969-71, Youngstown State University 1971-76; Norfolk Virginia State College from 1977. *Honours include:* Ernest Bloch award 1971; Commissions from the Edward Tarr Brass Ensemble and the Virginia Symphony. *Compositions include:* The Race for Space, theatre piece 1963; Phaedra tone poem 1966; Horn Sonata 1966; Statement, Variation and Fugue for orchestra 1966; Sextet for strings 1971; Violin Sonata 1972; Bagatelles for brass quintet 1973; Pulse for percussion ensemble 1974; Bellevue and Celebration, both for orchestra, 1974; Concerto for violin, horn and orchestra 1975; Spiritual for brass octet 1975; American Landscape nos 1, 3 and 4 for orchestra 1977-84; American Landscape for violin and cello 1978; Piano Sonata 1981; Sport of Strings 1981; Unaccompanied choral music, and with brass and percussion accompaniment. *Address:* c/o ASCAP, ASCAP Building, One Lincoln Plaza, New York, NY 10023, USA.

HAIMOVITZ Matt, b. 3 Dec 1970, Tel Aviv, Israel. Solo Concert Cellist. *Education:* Juilliard School of Music, New York, 1982-87; Graduated, The Collegiate School, New York, 1989; Princeton University, 1989-91; Harvard University, 1993-; Studied Cello with Gabor Rejto and Leonard Rose, Music Analysis with Carl Schahter. *Career:* Appeared with Israel Philharmonic Orchestra, conductor Zubin Mehta, Mann Auditorium, Tel Aviv, broadcast Israel National TV, 1985; London debut with English Chamber Orchestra, conductor Daniel Barenboim, Barbican, 1985; Appearances with many conductors and orchestras, and regular recitals throughout USA and Europe, 1985-; Debut with Philharmonia Orchestra and Giuseppe Sinopoli, Royal Festival Hall, London, 1987; Debut with Chicago Symphony Orchestra, conductor James Levine, Ravinia Festival, 1988; 1st tour to Japan, 1988; Live concert appearance, The Performing Arts pay tribute to Public Television, PBS TV, 1988; Documentary on early life, CBS Sunday Morning TV programme, 1989; 1st European recital tour, 1989; 1st American recital tour, 1990; Debut with Berlin Philharmonic, conductor James Levine, Berlin, 1990; Lucerne Festival debut, solo recital programme, 1990; Recital debuts, all solo cello repertoire, Montreux Festival, Washington DC, New York, Paris, 1991; 1st Australian tour, appeared with Sydney Symphony and Melbourne Symphony Orchestra, 1991; Debut with Dalla Symphony, 1992. *Recordings:* Lalo and Saint-Saëns Concerti with Chicago Symphony, conductor James Levine, 1989; Haydn C Major, Boccherini and C P E Bach with English Chamber Orchestra/Andrew Davies, 1990; Solo Cello, Reger, Britten, Crumb, Ligeti, 1991; All Deutsche Grammophon. *Honours:* Avery Fisher Career Grant Award, 1985. *Hobbies:* Hiking; Tennis; Writing; Reading. *Current Management:* Harold Holt Ltd, England. *Address:* c/o Harold Holt Ld, 31 Sinclair Road, London W14 0NS, England.

HAINE Malou, b. 22 Oct 1945, Liège, Belgium. Musicologist. *Education:* Piano with Marcelle Mercenier, Solfege with Mme Deschamp, Royal Conservatoire, Liege, 1957-65; Licence, English-German Translation, Institut Superieur de Traducteurs et Interpretes, Brussels, 1970; Licence, Musicology, 1974, Agregee, Higher Secondary Teaching, 1976, Doctor of Philosophy & Letters, highest distinction, Musicology, 1983, Free University, Brussels; Laureate, Royal Academy, Brussels, 1977; Organology under Prof Francois Lesure, Ecole Pratique des Hautes Etudes, Paris, 1978-83. *Career:* Scientific research, Musée Instrumental, Brussels, 1971-; Lecturer, Musicology, Free University, Brussels, 1983-; Lecturer, Musicology, Organology, University of Liege, 1984-93; Visiting Professor, University of Illinois, Urbana-Champaign, 1986; Editor, MUSIQUE/MUSICOLOGIE collection, Editions Pierre Mardaga, Liège, 1988-; Invited Professor, Ecole Normale Superieure, Paris, 1991 & 1994. *Publications:* Adolphe Sax. Sa vie, son oeuvre et ses instruments de musique, 1980; Catalogue des instruments Sax au Musee Instrumental de Bruxelles suivi de la liste de 400 instruments Sax conserves dans des collections publiques et privees (with Ignace De Keyser), 1980; Saxinstrumenten. Tentoonstellingsgids Oudergem, Kunstcentrum (with Ignace De Keyser), 1980. *Address:* Universite Libre de Bruxelles, Faculte Philosophie et Lettres, 50 Avenue Roosevelt, 1050 Brussels, Belgium.

HAITINK Bernard Johan Herman, b. 4 Mar 1929, Amsterdam, Holland. Conductor. *Education:* Studied Conducting with Felix Hupke, Amsterdam Conservatory. *Debut:* Holland, 1956. *Career:* First conducted Concertgebouw, 1956; USA debut, 1958 with Los Angeles Philharmonic; Appointed (with Jochum) Concertgebouw's Permanent Conductor, 1961, became

Chief Conductor, 1964-88; Principal Conductor, London Philharmonic, 1967-79; Music Director, Glyndebourne Opera, 1978-88; Glyndebourne debut, 1972; Music Director, Royal Opera House, 1988- with Ring Cycle, 1989-91, Prince Igor 1990, Katya Kabanova 1994; President, London Philharmonic, 1990-; Guest Conductor, Berlin Philharmonic, Boston Symphony, Bayerischer Rundfunk, Concertgebouw, Vienna Phlharmonic, Salzburg, Berlin and Tanglewood Festivals; Conducts at re-opening of Glyndebourne Opera, 1994. *Recordings:* Numerous recordings for Philips, EMI and Decca including complete cycles of symphonies by Bruckner, Mahler, Beethoven and numerous opera recordings including Ring Cycle. *Honours:* Order of Oranje Nassau, 1988; Bruckner Medal of Honour, 1970; Gold Medal, International Gustav Mahler Society, 1971; Chevalier de l'Ordre des Arts et des Lettres, 1972; Hon RAM, 1973; Order of the Crown (Belgium), 1977; Hon KBE, 1977; FRCM, 1984; Honorary Doctorates of Music from the Universities of Oxford and Leeds. *Current Management:* Harold Holt Limited. *Address:* c/o Harold Holt Ltd, 31 Sinclair Road, London, W14 0NS, England.

HAJOSSYVOVA Magdalena, b. 25 Jul 1946, Bratislava, Czechoslovakia. Singer (Soprano). *Education:* Studied at the Bratislava Music Academy. *Debut:* Slovak National Theatre Bratislava 1971, as Marenka in The Bartered Bride. *Career:* Sang at the National Theatre Prague and elsewhere in Czechoslovakia; Berlin Staatsoper from 1975, as Mozart's Pamina, Fiordiligi, Contessa, Donna Anna, Handel's Alcina, Wagner's Eva, Elsa, Strauss's Arabella, Marschallin, Capriccio, Dvořák's Rusalka; Has also sung in the operas of Jan Cikker; Guest appearances as opera and concert singer in England, Belgium Spain, Holland, Greece, Italy, France, USA, Japan, Russia, Austria, Persia and German Capitals. *Recordings include:* The Cunning Little Vixen, Don Giovanni and Mahler's 4th Symphony (Supraphon); Erindo by Sigismund Kusser; Beethoven's 9th Symphony (Denon); Mozart's Requiem; Dvořák's Requiem, Stabat Mater; Britten: Illuminations/OPUS; Janáček: Missa Glagolitica/OPUS; Dvořak: Dimitri/Supraphon: Mahler-II Symphony/Eterna; Schumann; Paradies und der Peri/OPUS; Gounod: Margarethe/OPUS; Wagner: Wesendonk-Lieder/Supraphon; Strauss: Brentano-Lieder, 4 letzte Lieder/Panton; OPUS; Bruckner: Te Deum, F-Moll Messe/OPUS Schubert: G-Dur Messe: Stabat Mater/ETERNA H Wolf: Italienisches Liederbuch/OPUS; Mahler G, Alma: Lieder/OPUS J Brahms: Lieder/OPUS. *Current Management:* Deutsche Staatsoper Berlin, Unter den Linden 7, O-Germany. *Address:* Magdaléna Hajossyová, Köpenicker Str 104, O-Berlin 10179, Germany.

HALASZ Laszlo, b. 6 June 1905, Debrecen, Austria-Hungary (Naturalized US citizen, 1943). Conductor; Teacher. m. Suzette F Forgues, 1 son, 1 daughter. *Education:* Studied piano and conducting, Budapest Conservatory, graduated 1929. *Career:* Toured Europe as a pianist and conductor, 1929-36; Music Director, St Louis Grand Opera, 1937-42; General Director, New York City Opera, 1944-51; Conductor, Chicago Opera Company, 1949-52; Music Director, Remington Records Inc, 1953-55; Conductor, German repertory, Gran Teatro del Liceo, Barcelona, 1955-59; Artistic Director, Empire State Music Festival, New York, 1957-65, National Grand Opera, New York, 1983-; Head, Conducting Department, Eastman School of Music, Rochester, New York, 1965-67; Faculty member, State University of New York College at Old Westbury, 1968-71, State University of New York at Stony Brook, 1971-75. *Recordings:* Several discs. *Address:* 3 Leeds Drive, Port Washington, NY 11050, USA.

HALBREICH Harry Leopold, b. 9 Feb 1931, Berlin, Germany. Musicologist. m. Helène Chait, 11 Apr 1961, now separated; 1 son, 2 daughters. Companion to Elizabeth Buzzard since 1980. *Education:* Geneva Conservatory, 1949-52; Studies with Arthur Honegger Ecole Normale de Musique, Paris, 1952-54; Study at Paris Conservatory, 1955-58. *Career:* Teacher of Musical Analysis, Royal Conservatory, Mons, Belgium, 1970-; Artistic Director of Festival of Contemporary Music, Royan, France, 1973-77; Teacher at Summer Courses of Contemporary Music, Darmstadt, Germany 1982-; Federal of Contemporary Music Musica Libera in Brussels, beginning Apr 1988; Numerous appointments for lectures, seminaries, etc. In Italy at Turin, Cagliari, Milan, and other places; Member of several international juries (International Record Critics Award, High Fidelity, New York; Academie Charles-Cros, Paris; Prix Cecilia, Brussels); Member of several Composition Competition Juries (Parma, Turin.); Regular Producer of Radio Programmes (RTB Brussels; RSR Geneva). *Publications:* Bohuslav Martinů (in German) 1968; Edgard Varèse (in French) 1970; Olivier Messiaen (in French) 1980; Claude Debussy (in French) 1980; several more in preparation. *Contributions to:* Regular Contributions to Harmonie (Paris), 1965-84; Le Monde de la Musique (Paris), 1982-; Compact (Paris), 1985-; L'Avant Scène Opera (Paris); Encyclopaedia Universalis (Paris); High Fidelity (New York); Tempo (London) Journal de Genéve (Geneva). *Address:* Avenue des Phalènes 36, 1050 Brussels, Belgium.

HALDAS Beatrice, b. 1952, Switzerland. Singer (Soprano). *Education:* Studied in Berne and Milan. *Debut:* Stadttheater Berne, 1976, as Mozart's Countess. *Career:* Sang at Basle, 1977-79; Opéra du Rhin Strasbourg, 1979, as Gluck's Euridice; Vienna Staatsoper, 1980, as Micaela; Has been based at the Hamburg Staatsoper from 1980; Other roles include Mozart's Fiordiligi and Ilia, Handel's Cleopatra, Liu in Turandot and Antonia in Les Contes d'Hoffmann; Has sung Mimi at Lucerne aand has appeared widely in opera and concert. *Recordings include:* Die Sieben letzten Worte unseres Erlösers am Kreuz by Haydn (Acanta); Zemlinsky's Der Zwerg (Schwann).

HALE Nathan Kelly, b. 13 Oct 1942, Oklahoma, USA. Professor; Musician. m. Natalie Cecile Schuppert, 6 May 1972, 1 son, 1 daughter. *Education:* BME, University of Oklahoma, 1964; MM, DMA, University of Texas, Austin, 1974; Studied piano, voice, organ and conducting. *Career:* Assistant Conductor, Santa Fe Opera, 1963-65; Lincoln Square Opera, Harlem Opera, Christian Arts Inc; Accompanist for Gramercy Quartet and many singers including John Alexander, Jerome Hines, John Stewart, Kathleen Kaun (European debut, Brucknerhaus, Linz, Austria, 1982); Artist-in-Residence, Bay View Music Festival, 1979-; Associate Professor of Opera, College-Conservatory of Music, University of Cincinnati, Cincinnati, Ohio. *Recordings:* Extensive educational recordings for Holt, Reinhart and Winston, Lorenz Press, SBSSB, etc. *Publication:* Performance edition in English of The White Lady (La Dame Blanche) by A Boieldieu, 1974. *Honour:* Martha Baird Rockefeller Grant, 1964. *Memberships:* Central Opera Service; National Opera Association; American Guild of Organists; McDowell Society. *Hobbies:* Gardener and Rosarian. *Address:* 1457 Aster Place, Cincinnati, OH 45224, USA.

HALE Robert, b. 22 Aug 1943, Kerrville, Texas. Singer (Bass-Baritone). m. Inga Nielsen, 3 sons. *Education:* Studied at the New England Conservatory with Gladys Miller; Boston University with Ludwig Bergman; Oklahoma University; With Boris Goldovsky in New York. *Debut:* Denver 1965, as Mozart's Figaro. *Career:* Sang with New York City Opera from 1967, debut in La Bohème; Guest appearances in Philadalphia, Pittsburgh, San Diego, Frankfurt, Paris, Munich, Berlin, London, San Francisco, Tokyo, Buenos Aires, Vienna, Zurich; Cologne Opera 1983, as Escamillo; Metropolitan debut, 1990, Dutchman; Concert appearances with the Orchestras of Chicago, Boston and Montreal; Festival engagements at Wolf Trap, Tanglewood, Lausanne and Bordeaux; Repertoire includes roles in operas by Handel, Mozart, Gounod, Bizet and Wagner; has sung Wagner's Wotan at Wiesbaden and with Deutsche Oper Berlin tour to Japan 1987, and Washington DC, 1989; Berlin 1987, as Scarpia, Covent Garden debut 1988, as Jochanaan in Salome, returned 1990, as Orestes in Elektra; sang the Dutchman at the 1989 Bregenz Festival; San Francisco Opera 1990, as Wotan; Pizarro in Fidelio at the 1990 Salzburg Festival; Sang Wotan in a new production Der Ring des Nibelungen at the Vienna Staatsoper, 1992-93, Salzburg Festival 1992 as Barak in Die Frau ohne Schatten. *Recordings include:* Bellini Requiem; Messiah (Philips); Der Ring des Nibelungen, conducted by Christoph Von Dohnányi; Fliegende Holländer (Decca), Verdi Requiem (BMG); Video of Die Frau ohne Schatten (Decca). *Honours include:* Singer of the Year. *Hobbies:* Photography; Antique Cars. *Address:* c/o Deutsche Oper Berlin, Richard Wagnerstrasse 10, D-1000 Berlin, Germany.

HALE Una, b. 1922, Adelaide, South Australia, Australia. Singer (Soprano). m. Martin Carr, 1960. *Education:* Studied in Adelaide and at Royal College of Music, London. *Career:* Sang with Carl Rosa Opera Company in many roles, notably as Marguerite in Faust; Royal Opera House, Covent Garden from 1953, as Micaela, Mimi, Musetta, Mozart's Countess, Eva, Ellen Orford, Liu (Turandot), Freia, Marschallin and Walton's Cressida; Sang with Sadler's Wells from 1964, Tosca, Ellen Orford, tour of Australia with the Elizabethan Opera Company, 1962, Theatre de la Monnaie, Brussels, 1963; Further appearances at Aldeburgh Festival and Gubenkian Festival in Portugal; Further study with Tiana Lemnitz in Berlin and Hilde Konetzui in Vienna; Sang Ariadne, Donna Anna and Alice Ford on tour in Australia. *Address:* Madron, Ostlings Lane, Bathford, Bath BA1 7RW, Avon, England.

HALEM Victor von, b. 26 March 1940, Berlin, Germany. Singer (Bass). *Education:* Studied at the Musikhochschule Munich, with Else Domberger. *Career:* Has sung at the Deutsche Oper Berlin from 1966; Guest appearances in Hamburg, Munich, Stuttgart, Cologne, Rome, Geneva, Montreal, Athens and London; Roles include Wagner's Daland, Pogner, King Henry, Fafner, Fasolt and Hans Sachs; Padre Guardiano and the Grand Inquisitor, by Verdi; Mozart's Sarastro and Osmin; Puccini's Colline; Season 1987-88 as Mephistopheles at Strasbourg, St. Bris in Les Huguenots at Berlin and at the Spoleto Festival as Gurnemanz and in Antigone by Traetta; sang King Heinrich (Lohengrin) at Nice 1990, the Hermit in Der Freischütz with the Komische Oper Berlin at Wiesbaden and in Parsifal at Spoleto, Charleston; Many concert appearances. *Address:* c/o Deutsche Oper Berlin, Richard Wagnerstrasse 10, D-10585 Berlin, Germany.

HALFFTER Cristobal, b. 24 March 1930, Madrid, Spain. Composer; Conductor. m. Maria Manuela Caro, 2 sons, 1 daughter. *Education:* Madrid Conservatory 1947-51, with Del Campo; Private studies with Alexander Tansman. *Career:* Studied harmony and composition with Conrado del Campo and at the Real Conservatorio de Musica in Madrid, graduated in 1951; 1961-1966 teacher of composition and musical forms at the Real Conservatorio de Musica in Madrid and director of this institute 1964-1966; scholarships for the United States (Ford Foundation) and Berlin (DAAD); 1970-1978 lecturer at the University of Navarra; lecturer at the internationale Ferienkurse für Neue Musik at Darmstadt; 1976-1978 president of the Spainish section of the ISCM; 1979: artistic director of the Studio for electronic music at the Heinrich Strobel-Stiftung in Freiburg; 1980: member of the European Academy of Science, Arts and Humanities, Paris; 1981: was awarded the Gold Medal for the Fine Arts by King Juan Carlos of Spain, 1983; member of the Royal Academy of the Fine Arts San Fernando, Madrid; since 1989 Principal Guest Conductor of the National Orchestra, Madrid; since 1970 conductor of the chief orchestras in Europe and America; lives in Madrid. *Compositions:* Stage: Ballet Saeta 1955; Orchestral: Piano Concerto 1955; 5 Microformas 1960; Rhapsodia espanola de Albeniz for piano and orchestra 1960; Sinfonia for 3 instrumental groups 1963; Sequencias 1964; Lineas y Puntos for 20 winds and tape 1967; Anillos 1968; Fibonaciana for flute and strings 1970; Plaint for the Victims of Violence 1971; Requiem por la libertad imaginada 1971; Pinturas negras 1972; Processional 1974; Tiempo para espacios for harpsichord and strings 1974; Cello Concerto 1975; Elegias a la muerte de tres

poetas espanoles, 1975; Officium defunctorum 1979; Violin Concerto; Tiento 1980; Handel Fantasia 1981; Sinfonia Ricercata 1982; Versus 1983; Parafrasis 1984; 2nd Cello Concerto 1985; Double Concerto for violin, viola and orchestra 1984; Tiento del Primer tono y Batalla Imperial 1986; Concert for Cello and Orchester, N 2 (first performed by Rostropovitch), 1986; Dortmund Variations 1987; Piano Concerto 1988; Preludio and Nemesis 1989; Concerto for saxophone quartet and orchestra 1989; Vocal: Regina Coeli 1951; Misa Ducal 1956; In exspectatione resurrectionis Domini 1962; Brecht-Lieder 1967; Symposium 1968; Yes Speak Out 1968; Noche pasiva del sentido 1971; Gaudium et Spes for 32 voices and tapes 1972; Oracion a Platero 1975; Officium Defunitorum 1978; Noche Pasiva del Sentido 1979; eyendo a Jorge Guillen 1982; Dona Nobis Pacem 1984; Tres Poemes de la Lirica Eśpanola 1984-86; Dos Motetes para Caro a Cappella 1988; muerte, Mudanza y Locura, for tape and voices, 1989 (text by Cervantes); Chamber: 2 String Quartets 1955, 1970; Solo Violin Sonata 1959; Codex for guitar 1963; Antiphonismoi for 7 players 1967; Noche activa del espiritu 1973; Mizar for 2 flutes and electronic ensemble 1980; Piano Music. *Recordings:* For Soprano, Baritone and Orchestra: 2 Cello Concert, Rostropovitch and Orchestra National De France, Erato. *Publications:* Universal Edition. *Memberships:* Real Academia De Bellas Artes, Spain; Akademie Der Künste, Berlin; Kungl Musikaliska Akademien, Sweden, Stockholm. *Current Management:* Jürgen Erlebach, Konzertdirektion, Erlebach. *Address:* Universal Edition, Bösel Dorfer Strasse 12, A1015 Wien, Austria.

HALFVARSON Eric, b. 1953, Texas, USA. Singer (Bass). *Education:* Studied at Houston Opera Studio. *Career:* Sang at Houston from 1977, notably as Sarastro, 1980; Carnegie Hall, New York, in Hamlet by Amboise Thomas, 1981; San Francisco, 1982-, notably as Hagen in The Ring, 1990; Spoleto, 1983, in European premiere of Barber's Antony and Cleopatra; Further appearances at Chicago, Toronto, Miami, St Louis (US premiere of Il Viaggio a Reims, 1986) and Dallas (premiere of The Aspern Papers by Dominick Argento, 1988); Sang Raimondo in Lucia di Lammermoor at Washington, 1989, Wagner's King Henry at Dallas and the Landgrave in Tannhauser at Montpellier, 1991; Engagements at Santa Fe as Baron Ochs, 1989, 1992, and Morosus in Die Schweigsame Frau, 1991; Other roles include Ramphis (Dallas, 1991), Banquo, Rocco, Sparafucile, the Commendatore in Don Giovanni, Alvise, Puccini's Colline, Alvise in La Gioconda and Gremin in Eugene Onegin; Sang the King in Schreker's Der Schatzgräber at the 1992 Holland Festival. *Recordings include:* Enobarbus in Antony and Cleopatra. *Address:* c/o Santa Fe Opera, PO Box 2408, Santa Fe, NM 87504, USA.

HALGRIMSON Amanda, b. 28 Nov 1956, Fargo, North Dakota, USA. Singer (Soprano). *Education:* Studied at Northern Illinois University. *Career:* Appearances at opera houses in 32 American States, notably as Fiordiligi, Norina, Clarice in Il Mondo della Luna and Rosalinde; Sang with Texas Opera on tour, 1987-88, as Lucia di Lammermoor; European debut, 1988, as the Queen of Night, with Netherlands Opera; Further engagements in Vienna (Volksoper and Staatsoper), St Gallen and Dusseldorf; Concert performnces include Mozart's Schauspieldirektor and Salieri's Prima la musica, poi le parole with Houston Symphony; Sang the Queen of Night in a new production of Die Zauberflöte at the Deutsche Oper Berlin, 1991; Member of the ensemble of the Deutsche Oper Berlin, 1992-93; Sang Beethoven's Missa Solemnis with the Boston Symphony Orchestra under Roger Norrington, 1993; Sang Beethoven's 9th Symphony at the re-opening of the Liederhalle in Stuttgart under G Gelmetti, 1993; Schumann's Faust/Gretchen with the Minnesota Orchestra as well as Beethoven's Missa Solemnis with the Boston Symphony Orchestra at the Tanglewood Festival; Sang Donna Anna with the Birmingham Symphony Orchestra under Simon Rattle, 1993; Concerts of Mozart's Requiem in London, Berlin and Paris with the Chamber Orchestra of Europe, 1993; Queen of the Night at the Grand Théatre de Genève, 1994. *Honours include:* Prize winner at Voci Verdiana

(Bussetto) Competition, 1985, and the Metropolitan Auditions, 1987. *Address:* c/o Deutsche Oper Berlin, Richard Wagnerstrasse 10, D-1000 Berlin, Germany.

HALL Janice, b. 28 Sept 1953, San Francisco, USA. Singer (Soprano). *Education:* Studied in Boston with Grace Hunter. *Career:* Sang in Cavalli's Egisto for the Wolf Trap Opera Company, 1977; New York City Opera 1978-81, as Ann in Die Lustigen Weiber von Windsor, and Mozart's Servilia; European debut with the Hamburg Opera 1982; Further appearances in Tel-Aviv, Venice and Drottningholm; Salzburg Festival 1985, as Fortuna in the premiere of Henze's version of Il Ritorno di Ulisse; Cologne 1985, as Poppea in Handel's Agrippina; Has returned to the USA to sing at Houston, Washington DC and Santa Fe (Cavalli's Calisto, 1989); Sang Janáček's Vixen at Cologne, 1987, Fanny in Rossini's Cambiale di Matrimonio at the 1989 Schwetzingen Festival; Other roles include Verdi's Oscar, Gilda and Violetta, Rosina, Pamina and Lauretta.

HALL John, b. 1958, Wales. Singer (Bass). *Education:* Studied at the Birmingham School of Music and at the Royal College of Music with Frederick Sharp. *Career:* Sang Rossini's Basilio and Mozart's Bartolo for Opera 80; Appearances with the English Bach Festival at Covent Garden and the Athens Festival; Glyndebourne Festival from 1981; Glyndebourne Touring Opera as Masetto in Don Giovanni (Hong Kong 1986), Mozart's Figaro and Quince in A Midsummer Night's Dream; Théâtre du Châtelet Paris 1985, in The Golden Cockerel; Opera North 1986, in The Trojans and Madame Butterfly, and returned in Carmen, Tosca, Nielsen's Maskarade and Don Giovanni (as Leporello); Kent Opera 1989, in The Return of Ulysses; Almeida Festival 1989, in the premiere of Golem by John Casken; Glyndebourne Touring Opera 1989-90 as Basilio and Rocco in Fidelio; Covent Garden 1991, in Boris Godunov, as Mitiukha; ENO, 1992, in Return of Ulysses, as Time, Antinous; Concert repertory includes Vaughan Williams's Serenade to Music (Last Night of the Proms, 1987) Messiah and Elijah. *Address:* c/o Korman International Management, Crunnells Green Cottage, Preston, Herts SG4 7UQ, England.

HALL Martin C, b. 27 Oct 1950, Portsmouth, England. Organist. *Education:* Southern Grammar School, Portsmouth, 1962-69; Bristol University, 1969-72; Cambridge University, 1972-73; BA Hons Music, Bristol University, 1972; CPGCE, Cambridge, 1973; ARCO, 1973. *Career:* Assistant Director of Music, St Edmund's School, Canterbury, 1973-84; Director of Music, King Edward VI School, Southampton, 1984-; Director of Music, Southampton City Centre Parish, 1985-; Assistant Conductor, Canterbury Orchestra, 1980-84; Member, Portsmouth Cathedral Choir, 1984-85; Assistant Conductor, BBC Songs of Praise from Portsmouth, Nov 1984; Member of Cathedral Choir for BBC Choral Evensong Broadcasts from Portsmouth Cathedral, 1985; Acting Assistant Organist, Portsmouth Cathedral, Jan-Feb, 1987; Organ Recitals given in Portsmouth, Leicester and Canterbury Cathedrals and in churches in Portsmouth, Leicester, Bristol and Canterbury, Southampton Guildhall and appearances as Organist with Bournemouth Symphony Orchestra in Southampton Guildhall; Played for Services in: York Miniter, Westminister Abbey, St Pauls, Winchester, Canterbury, Hereford, Lincoln, Peterborough, Lichfield Cathedrals and St Mary's Edinburgh, Concert Tours in Sweden, Switzerland and Italy. *Memberships:* Royal College of Organists; Music Masters Association. *Hobbies:* Travelling; Theatre; Concerts; Railways; Architecture. *Address:* King Edward VI School, Kellett Road, Southampton SO9 3FP, England.

HALL Peter John, b. 7 Apr 1940, Surbiton, UK. Tenor. *Education:* BA, 1964, MA, 1968, King's College, Cambridge; Choral scholarship; Private vocal study with Arthur Reckless, John Carol Case. *Career includes:* Lay-Vicar, Chichester Cathedral, 1965-66; Vicar-Choral, St Paul's Cathedral, London, 1972-; Member, various professional choral groups including John Alldis Choir; Schütz Choir of London; London Sinfonietta Voices;

Sang Ugo & Il Prete, La Vera Storia (Berio), Florence 1986, at composer's personal request. *Recordings:* Carmina Burana (Orff), with Hallé Orchestra; Transit (Ferneyhough), with London Sinfonietta; At the Boar's Head (Holst), with Royal Liverpool Philharmonic Orchestra; Christmas Vespers (Monteverdi), with Denis Stevens. *Honour:* Choral scholarship, Cambridge. *Memberships:* Savage Club; Incorporated Society of Musicians. *Hobbies:* Good food & wine; Travel; Motoring; Languages. *Address:* 51 Treachers Close, Chesham, Bucks HP5 2HD, England.

HALL Peter Reginald Frederick (Sir), b. 22 Nov 1930, Bury St Edmunds, Suffolk, England. Theatre Director. m. (1) Leslie Caron (diss 1965), (2) Jacqueline Taylor (diss 1982), (3) Maria Ewing (diss 1989), 2 sons, 3 daughters. *Education:* Perse School and St Catharine's College Cambridge; MA (Hons) Cantab. *Career:* Director, Oxford Playhouse, 1954-55; Founder, International Playwrights' Theatre, 1957; Managing Director, Royal Shakespeare Company, 1960-68; created RSC as permanent ensemble and opened its home at Aldwych Theatre; Succeeded Sir Laurence Olivier as Director of National Theatre of Great Britain (1973), which transferred from Old Vic to London's South Bank, 1976; Artistic Director, Glyndebourne Festival Opera, 1984-90; Opera Productions include: The Moon and Sixpence by John Gardner, Sadler's Wells 1957; Covent Garden: Moses and Aaron 1965, The Magic Flute 1966, The Knot Garden 1970, Eugene Onegin 1971, Tristan und Isolde 1971; Glyndebourne: La Calisto 1970, Il Ritorno d'Ulisse in Patria 1972, Le Nozze di Figaro 1973, Don Giovanni 1977, Così fan Tutte 1978, Fidelio 1979, A Midsummer Night's Dream 1981, Orfeo ed Euridice 1982, L'Incoronazione di Poppea 1984, Albert Herring 1985, Carmen 1985, Simon Boccanegra 1986, La Traviata 1987, Falstaff 1988, Le Nozze di Figaro 1989; Metropolitan Opera New York 1982, Macbeth; Bayreuth Festival 1983, Der Ring des Nibelungen, Salome in Los Angeles, 1986; Production of Albert Herring seen at Covent Garden 1989; New Year 1989, Houston Grand Opera (Glyndebourne 1990). *Publications include:* Peter Hall's Diaries. *Honours include:* Sidney Edwards Award 1982; Honorary Doctorates, York, Reading, Liverpool, Leicester and Cornell Universities; CBE, 1963; KBE, 1977. *Memberships:* Garrick; Athenaeum; RAC. *Hobbies:* Music; Literature. *Address:* The Peter Hall Company, 18 Exeter Street, London, WC2E 7DU, England.

HALL Tom, b. 13 Feb 1955, Teaneck, New Jersey, USA. Conductor. m. Linell Nash Smith, 16 Nov 1986. *Education:* BM magna cum laude, Music, Ithaca College, 1977; MM Music, Boston University, Massachusetts, 1981. *Career:* Faculty, Longy School, 1978-81; Music Director, Concord Chorus, 1979-81; Music Director, Baltimore Choral Arts Society, Baltimore, Maryland, 1982-; Chorusmaster, Baltimore Opera Company, 1983-; Director of Choral Activities, Goucher College, 1983-; Guest Conductor, Handel and Haydn Society, 1985-86. *Honours:* Theodore Presser Award, Ithaca College, 1976; Outstanding Student Award, Ithaca College, 1977; Elected President, Senior Honour Society, Ithaca College, 1977. *Current Management:* Mary Schretlen, Executive Director, Baltimore Choral Arts Society, Baltimore, Maryland, USA. *Address:* Baltimore Choral Arts Society, 1316 Park Avenue, Baltimore, MD 21217, USA.

HALL Vicki, b. 13 Nov 1943, Jefferson, Texas, USA. Singer (Soprano). *Education:* Studied in New York and with Josef Metterson in Cologne. *Career:* Sang at New York City Opera, 1970-; Made guest appearances in Vienna (Volksoper), Munich (Theater am Gartnesplatz), Cologne, Wuppertal and Bregenz; Roles have included Mozart's Susanna and Blondchen, Carolina in Matrimonio Segreto, Frau Fluth in Die Lustige Weiber von Windsor, Olympia, Strauss's Sophie, Adele in Fledermaus, Gretel, and Janáček's Vixen; Many concert appearances.

HALLDÓRSSON Skúli Kristján, b. 28 Apr 1914, Flateyri, Ónundarfjódur, Iceland. Composer. m.

Steinunn Gudný Magnúsdóttir, 14 May 1937, 1 son, 1 daughter. *Education:* Degree from the Commercial School of Iceland, Reykjavík, 1932; Diplomas as a Pianist and Composer, Reykjavík Conservatory, 1947 and 1948. *Career:* Performed with many soloists and choirs as an accompanist and also as a solo pianist. *Compositions:* More than 140 songs (Lieder), 20 piano works and 16 orchestral works, including a symphony, ballet suites, a cantata and overtures; Chamber Music: Flautosolo, Duo, Trios, Quintett, Sextett and Nonett. *Recordings:* LP Record: Sounds From Iceland, Saunamusiikki, Helsinki and many recordings for the Icelandic Radio and Television. *Memberships:* Board Member, The Icelandic Composers Society and STEF (PRS) 1950-87, President of STEF (PRS) 1968-87. *Honours:* Prize from the Icelandic Radio Love Songs by Jónas Hallgrímsson, 1960. *Address:* Bakkastígur 1, 101 Reykjavík, Iceland.

HALLER Hermann, b. 9 June 1914, Burgdorf, Switzerland. Composer; Professor of Piano; Pianist. m. Margret Huber, 2 daughters. *Education:* BA; Diplomas for piano and composition, Zurich Conservatory; Studied composition with Nadia Boulanger, Paris, France and piano with C Marek, Zurich, Switzerland. *Career:* President, Swiss Association for Musical Copyrights (SUISA), 1979-. *Compositions include:* Works for organ; Variations for Orchestra; Exoratio for alto and strings; Ed e subito sera (Quassimodo) with orchestra; 2nd Concerto for piano; Trio for violin, cello and piano; 3 Nocturnes for viola and piano; Herbst (Morgenstern) for alto and piano; 3 String Quartets; Concerto per Archi; Per la Camerata (16 strings); 2 Concertos (piano and orchestra); Symphony; 5 Lieder for deep voice and orchestra; Hiob (oratorio); Elegia variata (piano); Extension-Contraction, for cello and orchestra; Resonances fur 2 oboes, 2 horns, violas and Orchestra; Funf Aspekte fur Orchestra; Episoden, for viola and orchestra. *Publication:* Harmonie-Lehre, 1949. *Honours include:* Musikpreis der Stadt Zurich, 1976; Komponisten-Preis of Swiss Composers Association, 1985. *Memberships include:* Swiss Composers Association, Past President. *Address:* Alte Landstrasse 84a, CH-8700 Kusnacht-Zurich, Switzerland.

HALLGRIMSSON Haflidi, b. 18 Sept 1941, Akureyri, Iceland. Composer; Cellist. m. 31 Aug 1975, 3 sons. *Education:* The Music School, Reykjavík, Iceland; Accademia Sancta Cecilia, Roma; Royal Academy of Music, London; Private studies in composition with Dr Alan Bush and Sir Peter Maxwell Davies. *Career:* Member of Haydn String Trio, 1967-70; English Chamber Orchestra, 1971-76; Principal Cellist, Scottish Chamber Orchestra, 1977-83; Mondrian Trio, 1984-88; Many recitals, appeared as Soloist with Symphony Orchestras and performed on BBC Radio 3. *Compositions:* Poemi; Verse I; Five Pieces for Piano; Seven Folksongs from Iceland; Scenes from Poland. *Recordings:* Strond; Poemi; Verse I; Daydreams in Numbers; Tristia; Jacob's Ladder. *Honours:* Suggia Prize for Cello playing, 1967; Viotti Prize, Italy, 1975; Nordic Council Prize, 1986. *Memberships:* Society of Promotion for New Music; Society of Scottish Composers; Performing Right Society. *Hobbies:* Reading; Drawing; Walking. *Current Management:* Chester Music. *Address:* 5 Merchiston Bank Gardens, Edinburgh EH10 5EB, Scotland.

HALLIGAN Susan Claire, b. 15 Nov 1938, New York City, USA. Pianist; Professor. *Education:* BM, Baldwin-Wallace College, Berea, Ohio; MS, Juilliard School of Music. *Debut:* Town Hall, New York City, Dec 1967. *Career:* Radio & television appearances, Ohio, 1959-60; Chamber music pianist, Berkshire Music Centre, Massachusetts, 1960; Staff accompanist, University of Illinois 1960, Interlochen National Music Camp 1963, Aspen Music Festival 1964, Meadowmount School for Strings 1965; Artist-in-Residence, Bowdoin College Summer Music Programme, 1966, 1967; Staff accompanist, Juilliard School, 1962-67; Solo & chamber music performances, 1964-70; Pianist, Alvin Ailey Dance Company, 1967-70, New York City Ballet, 1967-68; Radio/TV appearances, New York City, 1966-69; Recitals, Carnegie Recital Hall, 1966, 1968; Faculty,

Ithaca College summer 1970, Brooklyn College 1970-74, Orpheus Piano Festival 1975, 1976, 1977; Solo, chamber music, concerto performances, Vermont, 1975-. Member, Craftsbury Chamber Players, 1981-86; Radio/TV, Vermont 1982-85, Boston 1985; Duo-piano concert, Juilliard School, 1984; Faculty, Johnson State College 1976-, Associate Professor 1983-. *Address:* PO Box 425, Johnson, VT 05656, USA.

HALLIN Margareta, b. 22 Feb 1931, Karlskoga, Sweden. Singer (Soprano); Composer. *Education:* Studied at the Royal Stockholm Conservatory with Ragnar Hulten. *Career:* Sang at the Royal Opera, Stockholm 1954-84, in the premieres of Blomdahl's Aniara 1959 and Drommen om Therese 1964 and Tintomara 1973 by Werle; Also heard as Constanze, Blondchen, Lucia di Lammermoor, Gilda and Leonora in Il Trovatore; Sang Anne Trulove in the Swedish premiere of The Rake's Progress 1961; Glyndebourne Festival 1957, 1960 as the Queen of Night; Covent Garden 1960, with the Stockholm Company in Alcina by Handel; Drottningholm Court Opera from 1962, notably in the Abbé Vogler's Gustaf Adolf och Ebba Brahe 1973; Appearances in Florence, Edinburgh, Hamburg, Zurich, Rome and Munich; Later in career sang Elsa, Elisabeth de Valois, Mathilde in Guillaume Tell, the heroines in Les Contes d' Hoffmann, Violetta, Donna Anna, Senta, Butterfly and the Marschallin; Sang Cherubini's Medée, 1984.*Compositions include:* Miss Julie, opera after Strindberg. *Honours:* Swedish Court Singer 1966; Order Litteris et artibus 1976. *Address:* c/o Kurgliga Teatera, PO Box 16094, 5-10322 Stockholm, Sweden.

HALLMAN Ludlow Boyd, b. 1 Aug 1941, Dayton, Ohio, USA. College Professor. m. Laura-Jean Beal, 1 Sept 1985, 3 sons. *Education:* BM, Oberlin College, 1963; MM, Southern Illinois University, 1965; Kapellmeister Diplom, Mozarteum, Salzburg, Austria, 1970. *Career:* Santa Fe Opera Company, USA, 1964-65; Salzburg Festival, Austria, 1968-70; Salzburg Baroque Ensemble, 1968-70; Mozart Opera, Salzburg, 1969; Appearances with St Louis, Mozarteum, Portland (Maine) and Bangor orchestras; Wichita Summer Music Theater, USA; Artistic Director, University of Maine Opera Theater; Chairman, Department of Music, University of Maine, Academic Year. *Hobbies:* Sailing; Running. *Address:* 298 Forest Avenue, Orono, ME 04473, USA.

HALLSTEIN Ingeborg, b. 23 May 1937, Munich, Germany. Singer (Soprano). *Education:* Studied with her mother. *Debut:* Stadttheatre Passau 1956, as Musetta in La Bohème. *Career:* Sang at Basle 158-59, Munich from 1959; Salzburg Festival from 1960, as Rosina in La Finta Semplice and in the premiere of The Bassarids by Henze (1966); Theater an der Wien 1962, as the Queen of Night in Die Zauberflöte, conducted by Karajan; Sang in the first performance of Henze's Cantata Being Beauteous, Berlin 1964; Guest appearances in Hamburg, Stuttgart, Dresden, Karlsruhe, Kassel, Venice, Paris, Montreal, Ottawa, Stockholm and Amsterdam, Royal Opera House Covent Garden, as the Queen of Night; Other roles include Mozart's Constanze, Fiordiligi and Susanna; Sophie in Der Rosenkavalier and Zerbinetta; Norina (Don Pasquale) and Aennchen in Der Freischütz; Professor at the Wurzburg Musikhochschule from 1981. *Recordings:* Die Frau ohne Schatten (Deutsche Grammophon); Marzelline in Fidelio, conducted by Klemperer; Operettas by Lortzing and Benatzky. *Address:* c/o Hochschule für Musik, Holfstallstrasse 6-8, D-8700 Würzburg, Germany.

HALMEN Pet(re), b. 14 Nov 1943, Talmaciu, Rumania. Stage and Costume Designer; Director. *Education:* Studied in Berlin. *Career:* Worked at Kiel and Dusseldorf, then collaborated with director Jean-Pierre Ponnelle at Zurich from 1975 in cycles of operas by Monteverdi and Mozart; Munich, 1978-, with premiere of Reimann's Lear and Troades, 1986, Das Liebesverbot by Wagner and Berg's Lulu, 1985; Designs for Aida at Berlin, Chicago and Covent Garden, 1982-84, Parsifal at San Francisco, 1988, and 2 Ring cycles; Designed and directed Lohengrin at Dusseldorf, 1987, Paer's Achille at Bologna, 1988, La Straniera at Spoleto Festival, Charleston, 1989, and Nabucco for Munich Festival, 1990; Designs for Parsifal seen at Mainz, 1991, Mozart's Lucio Silla at Vienna Staatsoper; Directed The Golden Cockerel at Duisburg, 1991, La Clemenza di Tito at Toulouse, 1992; Directed and Designed, Turandot at Deutsche Oper am Rhein, Düsseldorf, 1993. *Address:* Tengstrasse 26, D-80798 Munich, Germany.

HALMO Joan Marie, b. 8 Dec 1945, Kuroki, Saskatchewan, Canada. Musicologist; Liturgist; Writer on Music and Liturgy. *Education:* University of Saskatchewan, Saskatoon; BA, University of Regina, Regina, 1977; MLM, 1978, PhD, Musicology, 1993, Catholic University of America, Washington DC; Saint Paul University, Ottawa, MA, St John's University, Collegeville, Minnesota, 1982; AMUS; LTCL. *Career:* Consultant and Lecturer in music and liturgy across Canada and in USA, 1978-; University Lecturer, Newman Theological College, Edmonton, and University of Saskatchewan, Saskatoon; Visiting Professor, Saint Paul University, Ottawa; Private Music Teacher. *Compositions:* Various liturgical works. *Publication:* Celebrating the Church Year with Young Children, 1988, 2nd printing, 1992; Antiphons for Paschal Triduum-Easter in Medieval Offices, 1994. *Contributions to:* Worship; The Canadian Catholic Review. *Honours:* University Medal and President's Medal, University of Regina, 1977; Dom Mocquereau Foundation Grant, New York, 1990; Publication grants, 1988-, scholarships, 1989-. *Memberships:* International Musicological Society; The Plainsong and Medieval Music Society; Neue Bachgesellschaft; Institutum Musices Feldkirchense; North American Academy of Liturgy; American Musicological Society; Early Music America. *Address:* 47 Riverside Estates, Saskatoon, Saskatchewan, Canada S7K 3J8.

HALMRAST Tor, b. 26 Apr 1951, Sarpsborg, Norway. Composer. *Education:* MSc, Engineering (Acoustics), 1976; BMus, University of Trondheim, 1984; Private studies in Composition; State Scholarship, Sweelinck Conservatory, Amsterdam, 1988. *Career:* Composer-in-Residence, Music Conservatory, Tromsoe, 1988-90; Festival Composer, Northern Norwegian Festival, 1990; In charge of acoustic design of several buildings for music, concerts and theatre, and studios. *Compositions:* Several for symphony orchestra, chamber music, soloists, installations and for TV, films and records, including: The Music for the Norwegian Pavilion at EXPO 92 in Seville; Piece Fausse for chamber orchestra and soprano; Batseba, church play with recorders and dance. *Recordings:* Hemera 2901; Music for EXPO 92 and other electroacoustic works: Aqueduct, Icille, Oppbrudd, Varang, Motgift. *Publications:* Several papers on room acoustics. *Honours:* European Broadcasting Union, Rostrum for Electro-Acoustic Music, 1990; AMI, for Norwegian Pavilion at EXPO 92. *Membership:* Co-Founder, Norwegian Section, International Conference of Electroacoustic Music. *Address:* Spangberg vn 28a, N-0853 Oslo, Norway.

HALSEY Simon Patrick, b. 8 Mar 1958, Kingston, Surrey, England. Conductor. m. Lucy Lunt, 14 June 1986. *Education:* Winchester College, 1971-75; King's College, Cambridge, 1976-79; MA(Cantab); Conducting Scholar, Royal College of Music, 1979-80. *Career:* Conductor, Scottish Opera-Go-Round, 1980, 1981; Director of Music, University of Warwick, 1980-88; Chorus Master, City of Birmingham Symphony Oorchestra, 1982-; Associate Director, Philharmonia Chorus, 1986-; Music Director, City of Birmingham Touring Opera, 1987- (Wagner's Ring, 1990-91); Director, Academy of Ancient Music Chorus, 1988-92; Director, Salisbury Festival, 1989-93; Chorus Director of the Flanders Opera in Antwerp, 1991-; Guest Conductor, Chicago Symphony Chorus, 1993. *Recordings:* Over 20 with EMI, Conifer, Chandos, Hyperion and Decca, including Rossini's Petite Messe Solennelle and Bruckner's Mass in E minor, 1990. *Publications:* Editor, Choral Music, Faber Music. *Current Management:* Magenta Music International, 4 Highgate Street, Highgate Village, N6 5JL. *Address:* 279 High Street, Henley in Arden, B95 5BG, England.

HALTON Richard, b. 1963, Devon, England. Singer (Baritone). *Education:* Studied at the University of Kent and the Guildhall School of Music, with Johanna Peters. *Career:* Concert appearances in Bach's Magnificat and Christmas Oratorio, Handel's Messiah and Fauré's Requiem; Barbican debut in Britten's Cantata Academica; Recital engagements with the New Songmakers' Almanac and in Die Schöne Magelone by Brahms and Wolf's Italienisches Liederbuch; Glyndebourne Festival Opera 1989, Opera 80, 1990 as Danilo in The Merry Widow; Has toured Britain as Ravenal in Opera North's RSC Showboat; Appeared in Capriccio at Covent Garden 1991; in Billy Budd (ENO) and La Bohème (GTO); Repertoire also includes Mozart's Count in Figaro, Tarquinius in The Rape of Lucretia and the Duke of Rothsay in La Jolie Fille de Perth by Bizet; Street Scene, by Kurt Weill, ENO, 1992; Italian Girl in Algiers by Rossini, Buxton Festival, 1992; Dancairo, Carmen, Dorset Opera, 1992; Janko, Petrified by Juraj Beneš Mecklenburgh Opera, 1992-1993; Papageno, The Magic Flute, Scottish Opera, 1993. *Honours include:* Walter Hyde Memorial Prize; Schubert Prize; Lawrence Classical Singing Bursary. *Address:* Magenta Music International, 64 Highgate High Street, London N6 5HX, England.

HALTON Rosalind, b. 4 Oct 1951, Dunedin, New Zealand. Harpsichordist; Musicologist. m. David Halton, 24 Mar 1979. *Education:* New Zealand Junior Scholarship; Otago University, 1969-72, BA (Honours); Commonwealth Scholarship to: Oxford University, 1973-80, St Hilda's College, DPhil (Oxon). *Career:* Research and Editing of Classical Symphonies (Beck-Holzbauer) and Cantatas of Alessandro Scarlatti; Concerts of 17th and 18th Century Chamber Music using period instruments; Solo performances on Harpsichord and pianos of 18th and early 19th century; Lecturer, Performance, University of New England, Armidale, Australia, 1986-; Senior Lecturer, Performance, UNE, 1991. *Publications:* Various reviews. *Contributions to:* Music and Letters. *Hobbies:* Cricket; Musical Instruments. *Address:* 72 Dangar Street, Armidale, NSW 2350 Australia.

HAMARI Julia, b. 21 Nov 1942, Budapest, Hungary. Singer (Mezzo-Soprano). *Education:* Studied piano at first, then singing with Fatima Martin and at the Music Academy Budapest. *Debut:* Vienna, 1966, in the St Matthew Passion conducted by Karl Richter. *Career:* Rome, 1966, in the Brahms Alto Rhapsody, conducted by Vittorio Gui; Concert appearances with Karajan, Kubelik, Solti, Böhm, Boulez and Celibidache: most often heard in works by Mahler, Monteverdi, Handel, Bach, Beethoven, Mozart and Verdi; Stage debut Salzburg, 1967; Stuttgart, 1968, as Carmen; US debut with Chicago Symphony Orchestra, 1972; Sang Celia in Haydn's La Fedeltà Premiata at Glyndebourne, 1979; Metropolitan Opera from 1984, as Rosina and Despina; Stuttgart and Philadelphia 1984, as Sinaide in Mosè and as Cenerentola in the opera by Rossini; sang Vivald's Griselda at Ludwigshaven, 1989. *Recordings:* St Matthew Passion (Electrola); Oberon, Il Matrimonio Segreto, Giulio Cesare, Beethoven Mass in C, Mozart Requiem (Deutsche Grammophon); Ernani (RCA); Tito Manlio by Vivaldi (Philips); Cavalleria Rusticana, I Puritani (EMI); Bach B minor Mass (CBS); Pergolesi Stabat Mater (Hungaroton); Hansel und Gretel, Die Meistersinger, Eugene Onegin (Decca). *Address:* c/o Staatsheater Stuttgart, Oberer Schlossgarten 6, D-7000 Stuttgart 1, Germany.

HAMBLIN Pamela, b. 14 June 1954, Cookeville, Tennessee, USA. Singer (Soprano). *Education:* Studied at North Texas State University and Salzburg Mozarteum. *Debut:* Karlsruhe, as Euridice in Orphée aux Enfers by Offenbach, 1980. *Career:* Has sung at Karlsruhe in such roles as Handel's Florinda (Rodrigo), Almirena (Rinaldo) and Romilda (Serse); Micaela, Mozart's Susanna, Pamina, Constanze and Sandrina, Verdi's Gilda and Oscar, Constance in Cherubini's Les

Deux Journées, Strauss's Sophie and Aminta (Die schweigsame Frau) and Titania in A Midsummer Night's Dream; Guest appearances at Dresden, Stuttgart, Zurich, Essen, Heidelberg, Strasbourg, Madrid, Barcelona and Athens; Sang Zdenka in Arabella at Karlsruhe, Dec 1989. *Recordings include:* Rodrigo. *Address:* Kriegsstrasse 71, 76133 Karlsruhe, Germany.

HAMBRAEUS Bengt, b. 29 Jan 1928, Stockholm, Sweden. Composer; Organist; Musicologist. *Education:* Studied organ with Alf Linder, 1944-48; Uppsala University, PhD 1956; Summer Courses at Darmstadt 1951-55, with Krenek, Messiaen and Fortner; Worked for Swedish Broadcasting Corporation from 1957: Director of chamber music 1965-68, Production Director 1968-72; Composed at Electronic Studios of Cologne, Munich and Milan; Professor at McGill University, Montreal, from 1972. *Compositions:* Chamber operas Experiment X 1971; Se Människan 1972; Sagan 1979; L'ouï-dire, 1985-86; 3 String Quartets 1948-64; Concerto for organ and harpsichord 1951; Antiphones en rondes for soprano and 24 instruments 1953; Crystal Sequence, for soprano choir and ensemble 1954; Rota for 3 orchestras and tape, 1956-62; Transfiguration for orchestra, 1962-63; Constellations I-V, 1958-83; Segnali for 7 instruments, 1960; Mikrogram for ensemble 1961; Interferences for organ 1962; Klassiskt spel, electronic ballet 1965; Fresque Sonore for soprano and ensemble 1967; Rencontres for orchestra 1971; Pianissimo in due tempi for 20 string instruments 1972; Ricercare for organ 1974; Advent for organ 10 brass instruments and percussion 1975; Ricordanza for orchestra 1976; Continuo for organ and orchestra, 1975; Livre d'orgue 1980-81; Symphonia Sacra for 5 soloists, choir, wind instruments and percussion 1985-86; Apocalypsis cum figuris for Bass solo, choir and organ 1987; Five Psalms for choir 1987; Litanies for orchestra 1988-89; Nocturnals for chamber orchestra 1989; Piano Concerto, 1992; St Michael's Liturgy, 1992; Missa pro Organo, 1992; Organum Sancti Jacobi, 1993; Meteoros, 1993; Songs of the Mountain, The Moon, and Television, 1993; Eco dalla montagna lontana, 1993. *Publications:* Codex Carminum Gallicorum, 1961; Om Notskifter (On Notation) 1970; Numerous articles and essays published since 1948. *Address:* RR1, Apple Hill, Ontario, K0C 1B0, Canada.

HAMBURGER Paul, b. 3 Sept 1920, Vienna, Austria. Pianist; Writer; Educator. m. Clare Walmesley, dec, 1 son, 1 daughter. *Education:* Vienna State Academy; ARCM, London. *Career:* Freelance Accompanist and Chamber Music Player; Member, Coach, English Opera Group, 1953-56; Member, Coach, Glyndebourne Opera, 1956-62; Staff Accompanist, 1962-75, Radio Producer, 1976-81, BBC; Currently Professor, Guildhall School of Music and Royal College of Music, London; Seminars for singers and accompanists in England, Germany, Austria. *Recordings:* With various singers including April Cantelo, Bernadette Greevy, Janet Baker, Heather Harper, Laura Surti, Clare Walmesley; Benvenuto Duo. *Publications:* Mozart Songs, annotated edition, 1991; Translations: Music and Music Making (Bruno Walter), 1961; Leoš Janáček (Hans Hollander), 1963. *Contributions to:* A Britten Symposium, 1954; A Mozart Companion, 1956; A Chopin Symposium, 1966; Music Survey; Music Review; Tempo; Music and Musicians. *Honours:* FGSM, 1982; Honorary RAM, 1992; Austrian Order of Science and Art, 1992. *Memberships:* Incorporated Society of Musicians; Society for the Promotion of New Music. *Address:* The Bakery, East Stoke House, Stoke sub Hamdon, Somerset TA14 6UF, England.

HÄMEENNIEMI Eero Olavi, b. 29 Apr 1951, Valkeakoski, Finland. Composer. m. Leena Peltola, 7 Oct 1977, (div Oct 28, 1989), 1 daughter. *Education:* Diploma, Sibelius Academy, 1977; State Higher School of Music, Cracow, 1979; Eastman School of Music, Rochester, New York, USA, 1980-81. *Career:* Commissions for the Finnish Radio SO, Swedish RSO, Helsinki Festival, Finnish National Ballet; Works performed by (the above) and Scottish National Orchestra, Malmo Symphony Orchestra, Gothenburg

Symphony Orchestra, etc; Senior Lecturer, Sibelius Academy, 1982-. *Compositions:* Symphony, 1982-83, 1984; Dialogue for Piano and Orchestra, 1987; Sonata for Clarinet and Piano; Loviisa, a ballet in two acts, premier 19 Mar. 1987, Finnish National Ballet; Second Symphony, 1988; String Quartet, 1989. *Recordings:* Duo I, for Flute and Cello; Pianosonata, 1979; Sonata for Clarinet and Piano, 1987. *Publication:* ABO - johdatus uuden musiikin teoriaan, Sibelius Academy Publications, 1982 (An Introduction to the Theory of Contemporary Music). *Hobbies:* Cooking; Oriental Literature; Squash. *Address:* Lapilantie 8B7, 04200 Kerava, Finland.

HAMELIN Marc-Andre, b. 1961, Montreal, Canada. Concert Pianist. *Education:* Studied, Vincent d'Indy School of Music and Temple University, Philadelphia. *Career:* Recitals in Montreal, Toronto, New York and Philadelphia; Concerto appearances in Toronto, Quebec, Ottawa, Albany, Detroit, Indianapolis, Minneapolis, New York (Manhattan Philharmonic and Riverside Symphony) and Philadelphia; Toured with the Montreal Symphony to Spain, Portugal and East Germany, 1987; Duo partnership with cellist Sophie Rolland from 1988: Beethoven cycles in New York, Washington, Montreal and London (Wigmore Hall, Mar 1991). *Recordings include:* Works by Leopold Godowsky (CBS Enterprises); William Bolcom Twelve New Etudes, Stefan Wolpe Battle Piece and Ives Concord Sonata (New World Records); Sorabji Sonata No 1, Rzewski The People Will Never be Defeated (Altarus). *Honours:* First Prize, Carnegie Hall International American Music Competition, 1985; Virginia P Moore Prize, Canada, 1989. *Address:* c/o Norman McCann International Artists Ltd, The Coach House, 56 Lawrie Park Gardens, London SE26 6XJ, England.

HAMES Richard David, b. 2 Sept 1945, Chelwood Gate, England. Composer. m. Valerie MacDonald, 3 Apr 1974, 2 sons, 6 daughters. *Education:* Royal College of Music, 1963-66; Paris Conservatoire, 1970-71; University of Southampton, 1971-72; Accademia di Santa Cecilia, Rome, 1972-73. *Career:* Director, Arts Technology, Dartington College of Arts, 1973-76; Head, Graduate Studies, Victorian College of the Arts, Melbourne, Victoria, Australia, 1976-83; Head, Australian Film, TV and Radio School, 1986-88. *Compositions:* Music for ensemble (with and without voices); Works for solo instruments and orchestra. *Honours:* Lord Attlee Fellow, 1969; French Government Scholarship, 1970; Leverhulme European Fellow, 1972; Spivakovsky Scholarship, 1979. *Membership:* Performing Rights Society. *Address:* 69 Balaka Drive, Carlingford, NSW 2118, Australia.

HAMILTON David (Peter), b. 18 Jan 1935, New York, New York, USA. Music Critic; Writer on Music. *Education:* Princeton University, AB, 1956, MFA in Music History, 1960. *Career:* Music and Record Librarian, Princeton University, 1961-65; Assistant Music Editor, 1965-68, Music Editor, 1968-74, W W Norton & Company, New York; Music Critic, The Nation, 1968-; Music Correspondent, Financial Times, London, 1969-74; Associate Editor, Musical Newsletter, 1971-77. *Publications:* The Listener's Guide to Great Instrumentalists, 1981; The Music Game: An Autobiography, 1986; Editor, Metropolitan Opera Encyclopedia: A Guide to the World of Opera, 1987. *Contributions to:* Many articles and reviews in periodicals. *Address:* c/o The Nation, 72 Fifth Avenue, New York, NY 10011, USA.

HAMILTON David, b. 1960, USA. Singer (Tenor). *Career:* Appearances with opera companies at Philadelphia, San Diego, Tulsa, Sarasota, Hawaii, New York (City Opera), Milwaukee and St Louis; Metropolitan Opera debut, season 1986-87; Season 1991-92 as Tamino for Opera de Nice, Lensky with Manitoba Opera, and Pinkerton with Chattanooga Opera; Season 1992-93 as Tamino with Vancouver Opera, Peter Quint in Turn of the Screw for Edmonton Opera and Lensky with Scottish Opera; Concert repertoire includes Messiah, Rinaldo by Brahms, Mozart's Requiem, Dvořák's Stabat

Mater, the Berlioz Romeo et Juliette and Schumann's Scenes from Faust; Soloist with Israel Philharmonic, Baltimore Symphony, Mostly Mozart Festival Orchestra and Indianapolis Symphony under Raymond Leppard; As recitalist gave premiere of Hugo Weisgall's cycle Lyric Interval; Sang Belmonte in Die Entführung with the Metropolitan Opera. *Honours include:* Winner, Paris International Voice Competition, 1984. *Address:* c/o IMG Artists, Media House, 3 Burlington Lane, London W4 2TH, England.

HAMILTON Iain Ellis, b. 6 June 1922, Glasgow, Scotland. Composer. *Education:* MusB, University of London, 1950; MusD (Hons), University of Glasgow, 1970; USA, 1961. *Career:* Engineer, 1939-47; Lecturer, London University, 1952-60; Morley College, London, 1951-60; Mary Duke Biddle Professor of Music, Duke University, USA, 1961-78, Chairman of Department, 1966-67; Composer in Residence, Tanglewood, Massachusetts, 1962; Chairman, Composers' Guild of Great Britain, 1958; Chairman, Secretary, Institute of Contemporary Arts, London, 1958-60. *Compositions:* (Operas) Royal Hunt of the Sun, 1968; Agamemnon, 1961, 68; The Catiline Conspiracy, 1973; Tamburlaine, 1976; Anna Karenina, 1978; Raleigh's Dream, 1984; Lancelot, 1983; The Tragedy of Macbeth, 1990; London's Fair, 1992; also Symphonies, Chamber Works and Vocal Works. *Recordings:* Symposium Records 1121, Le Jardin de monet: Palinodes (solo piano): String Quartet No 3. *Honours:* Recipient Koussevitsky Foundation Award, 1951; Royal Philharmonic Prize, 1951; Arnold Bax Gold Medal, 1957; Vaughan Williams Award, 1974. *Memberships:* Fellow, Royal Academy of Music; International Webern Society, Founding Member; American Society of University Composers, Founding Member. *Address:* 85, Cornwall Gardens, Flat 4, London, SW7 4XY, England.

HAMILTON Robert, b. 1 Apr 1937, South Bend, Indiana, USA. Pianist; Educator. m. Beverley Daube, 23 Aug 1958, 1 son, 3 daughters. *Education:* Indiana University School of Music. *Debut:* Town Hall, New York City, 1963; With Orchestra, Chicago, 1965. *Career:* Major appearances in, New York Town Hall; Orchestra Hall, Chicago; Kennedy Center, Washington; Wigmore Hall, London; Concertgebouw, Amsterdam; Tchaikovsky Hall, Moscow; Mozarteum, Salzburg; Teatro San Carlo, Naples; with Major Orchestras, Chicago, National, Milwaukee; SODRE, Chautauqua Festival; 14 tours of Europe; Official Pianist, US Army, 1959-63; Indiana University, 1967-75; Arizona State University, 1980-89; Appeared on BBC Radio, London; Radio Zurich; ABC Network (USA); National Public Radio (USA); Voice of America; Radio Warsaw, Polish National Television; 20 tours of Europe; Annual tours of the Far East; Artistic Director of London Piano Festival (annual/summer). *Recordings:* BBC; Philips; Orion; Advance. *Address:* School of Music, Arizona State University, Tempe, AZ 85287, USA.

HAMILTON Stuart, b. 28 Sept 1929, Regina, Saskatchewan, Canada. Pianist. *Education:* ARCT, Royal Conservatory, Canada; Studied privately with Alberto Guerrero. *Debut:* New York Town Hall, 1967. *Career:* Solo concerts across Canada, New York, London, Paris; Accompanist for Maureen Forrester, Lois Marshall, José Carreras, Louis Quilico, Jon Vickers; Producer and Musical Director, Opera in Concert, 1974-; Broadcaster for CBC since 82 and at Metropolitan Opera, New York, 1991-; Many radio and TV appearances on CBC. *Recording:* With Lois Marshall, CBC recording. *Contributions to:* Reviews in Opera Magazine, 1962-72. *Address:* 424 Yonge Street Apt 612, Toronto, Ontario, Canada M5B 2H3.

HAMMES Lieselotte, b. 1932, Siegburg, Germany. Singer (Soprano); Professor. *Education:* Studied in Cologne. *Debut:* Cologne, as Amor in Orfeo ed Euridice, 1957. *Career:* Guest appearances at Stuttgart, Hamburg, Berlin (Deutsche Oper), Naples, Rome, Lisbon and Paris (1971); Glyndebourne Festival, 1965, as Sophie in Der Rosenkavalier; Sang at Cologne until 1975 as Mozart's Pamina, Susanna and Papagena,

Marzelline, Mimi, Manon Lescaut, Nedda, Marenka in The Bartered Bride and Anne Trulove in The Rake's Progress; Teacher at Bonn, then Siegburg from 1973; Professor at Cologne Musikhochschule, 1985-. *Address:* Staatliche Hochschule fur Musik, Dagobertstrasse 38, 5000 Cologne 1, Germany.

HAMMOND Joan (Dame), b. 24 May 1912, Christchurch, New Zealand. Singer. *Education:* Presbyterian Ladies College, Pymble, Sydney, Australia; Singing and Violin, Sydney Conservatorium of Music. *Debut:* London Debut, Messiah, 1938; Operatic Debut, Vienna, 1939. *Career:* Guest Artist, Royal Opera House, Convent Garden; Vienna State Opera; Bolshoi Theatre, Moscow; Barcelona, Liceo; Kirov, Leningrad; New York City Center; Nederlands Opera; Sadler's Wells; World Tours include Europe; SA; Canada; Australasia; India; S Africa; USSR; Scandinavia. *Recording:* HMV artist; 62 records, most famous was the first recording made in the world of O My Beloved Father (Gianni Schicchi) having now sold over 1 million copies. *Publications:* Autobiography, A Voice, A Life, 1970. *Honours:* OBE, 1953; Coronation Medal, 1953; CBE, 1963; Sir Charles Santley Award, Worshipful Company of Musicians, 1970; CMG, 1972; DBE, 1974; Hon DMus, Western Australia, 1979; Hon Life Member, Australian Opera, Victoria State Opera, Lifetime Achievement Award: Green Room Awards Assea, 1988; Head of Vocal Studies, Victorian College of the Arts and Vocal Consultant. *Hobbies:* Golf; Reading; Writing; Swimming. *Address:* 46 Lansell Road, Toorak, Victoria 3142, Australia.

HAMMOND-STROUD Derek, b. 10 Jan 1926, London, England. Concert and Operatic Baritone. *Education:* Studies with Elena Gerhardt and Gerhard Hüsch, Trinity College of Music, London. *Career:* Debut: London 1955 in the British Premiere of Haydn's Orfeo ed Euridice; Guest Artist with numerous opera companies; Principal Baritone, English National Opera, 1961-71, as Rossini's Bartolo, Verdi's Melitone and Rigoletto, and Wagner's Alberich and Beckmesser; Glyndebourne 1973-; Royal Opera, Covent Garden 1971-; Broadcasts on BBC and European radio; Opera and recital appearances, Netherlands, Denmark, Iceland, Federal Republic of Germany, Austria, Spain, USA; Opera Appearances, Metropolitan Opera, New York, 1977-89; Teatro Colón, Buenos Aires, 1981; National Theatre, Munich, 1983; Other roles include Publio in La Clemenza di Tito and Don Magnifico, and roles in the British Premieres of La Pietra del Paragone and Der Besuch der Alter Dame; also Faninal in Der Rosenkavalier. *Recordings:* Recording for HMV, RCA, Célèbre; Symposium. *Honours:* OBE, 1987; Honorary Member, Royal Academy of Music; Honorary Fellow, Trinity College of Music, London; Sir Charles Santley Memorial Gift by Worshipful Company of Musicians. *Membership:* Incorporated Society of Musicians. *Hobbies:* Chess; Philosophy. *Address:* 18 Sutton Road, Muswell Hill, London N10 1HE, England.

HAMPE Michael, b. 3 June 1935, Heidelberg, Germany. Actor; Director in International Opera Houses and Theatres. *Education:* Study of Music (Cello), Syracuse University, USA; Study of Literature, Musicology, Philosophy at Munich and Vienna Universities; PhD. *Career:* Vice-Director, Schauspielhaus, Zürich 1965-70; Intendant, National Theatre, Mannheim 1972-75; Member of Salzburg Festival Board of Directors, 1985-89; Intendant, Cologne Opera; Director, Opera: Scala, Milan; Covent Garden, London (Andrea Chenier 1984, Il Barbiere di Siviglia 1985, Cenerentola 1990); Paris Opera; Salzburg and Edinburgh Festivals; Munich, Stockholm, Cologne, Geneva, Zurich Operas; German, Austrian, Swedish TV; Director of Drama: Munich, Bavarian State Theatre; Zurich, Schauspielhaus; Schwetzingen Festival (Double-bills of Rossini seen at Cologne, Schwetzingen and the Paris Opéra-Comique); Director of TV: German and Swiss TV; Actor: TV and Film (Leading Parts in German TV features: Der Kunstfehler 1983; Verworrene Bilanzen 1985, etc.); Teaching: Professor at: State-Music-Academy, Cologne; Cologne University;

Consulting: Consultant For Theatre-Building 1977-82; Vice-President, Deutsche Bühnentechnische Gesellschaft, Jury Opéra Bastille, Paris; Actor, Director in German Theatres; About 160 Productions in Opera, Plays, TV; Languages: English, French, Italian. *Address:* Oper der Stadt Köln, 5000 Köln 1, Germany.

HAMPSON Thomas, b. 28 June 1955, Elkhart, Indiana, USA. Singer (Baritone). *Education:* BA, Government, Eastern Washington University, Cheney; BFA, Voice with Marietta Coyle, Fort Wright College; Studied with Gwendolyn Koldowsky and Martial Singher, Music Academy of the West, summers 1978-79, with Elisabeth Schwarzkopf (Merola), 1980. *Debut:* Hansel and Gretel, 1974. *Career:* Sang first Marcello in La Boheme, 1981; Dusseldorf Ensemble, 1981-84; Guglielmo in Così fan Tutte, St Louis Opera, sang title role, Der Prinz von Homburg, Darmstadt, 1982; Debuts, Cologne, Hamburg, Munich, Santa Fe, 1982-84; Engaged as principal lyric baritone, Opernhaus Zurich, Wigmore Hall recital debut, St John's Passion (Bach's 300th birthday), Alte Oper Frankfurt, 1984; Metropolitan debut as Count in Nozze di Figaro, Town Hall recital debut, Vienna Staatsoper debut as Guglielmo in Così fan Tutte, 1986; Don Giovanni, Zurich, 1987; Alice Tully Hall recital debut, Roland in Schubert's Fierrabras, Vienna, Salzburg Festival debut as Count, 1988; La Scala Milan recital debut, Deutsche Oper Berlin debut as Don Giovanni, 1989; Mahler's Rückert Lieder and Lieder eines fahrenden Gesellen with Leonard Bernstein and Wiener Philharmoniker at Musikverein, Carnegie Hall debut with Bernstein in 2 Mahler cycles, San Francisco Opera debut as Ulisse in Il Ritorno d'Ulisse in Patria, 1990; Opened New York Philharmonic season with Copland's Old American Songs, Lincoln Center and London Philharmonic season with Lieder eines fahrenden Gesellen, sang in Met's 25th Anniversary Gala, 1991; Rossini's 200th Birthday Gala, Avery Fisher Hall, title role in Billy Budd at Met, Count in Nozze, Maggio Musicale, Florence, opened Chicago Symphony season with Brahms Requiem, Schumann's 20 Lieder und Gesange aus dem Lyrischen Intermezzo im Buch der Lieder von Heinrich Heine, Geneva, repeated at Carnegie Hall recital debut (including Walt Whitman songs), 1992; Title role in Hamlet by Thomas, Opera de Monte Carlo, Covent Garden debut in Il Barbiere di Siviglia, Posa in Verdi's Don Carlo, Zurich; recital, concert and master classes at Tanglewood Festival, 1993; Has appeared with Harnoncourt, Abbado, Levine, Masur, Mehta. *Recordings:* La Bohème, Mahler songs, with Bernstein; Des Knaben Wunderhorn solo album; Hamlet; Mahler songs with Geoffrey Parsons, critical edition. *Publication:* Co-editor: Mahler songs critical edition, 1993. *Honours include:* Lotte Lehmann Medal, Music Academy of the West, 1979; 1st Prize, Met Auditions, 1981; Des Knaben Wunderhorn: Netherlands Edison Prize (also Mahler cycles, 1992), Grand Prix du Disque, Deutsche Schallplattenpreis; 5 Grammy nominations; Best Male Singer of the Year, Classical Music Awards, 1994. *Address:* c/o Sekretariat T Hampson, Starkfriedgasse 53, 1180 Vienna, Austria.

HANAK Bohus, b. 8 Jan 1925, Banovce, Czechoslovakia. Singer (Bass-baritone). *Education:* Studied in Bratislava. *Career:* Sang at Bratislava from 1950 and made guest appearances with the company at Prague, Sofia and Wiesbaden; Engaged at Linz, 1958-60, and at Stadttheater Basle, 1968-88; Further performances at the Komische Oper Berlin, Bolshoi Moscow, Leningrad, State Operas of Dresden and Munich, Naples, Geneva, Innsbruck, Berne and Paris (Théâtre des Champs Elysées); Roles have included Mozart's Figaro and Don Giovanni, Pizarro, Rigoletto, Renato, Amonasro, Count Luna, Macbeth, Simon Boccanegra, Wolfram, Telramund, the Dutchman, Alberich, Prince Igor, Eugene Onegin, Scarpia, Cardillac, Nabucco and Mandryka. *Address:* c/o Theater Basel, Theaterstrasse 7, CH-4010 Basel, Switzerland.

HANANI Yehuda, b. 19 Dec 1943, Jerusalem, Israel. Cellist. m. Hannah Glatstein, 21 Mar 1971, 1 son. *Education:* Rubin Academy of Music, Israel; Juilliard School, USA. *Career:* Guest Performer with Chicago Symphony, Philadelphia Orchestra, Baltimore Symphony, St Paul Chamber Orchestra, Berlin Radio Symphony, Israel Philharmonic; BBC Welsh Symphony etc; Aspen Music Festival; Chautauqua; Marlboro. Artistic Director, Chamber Music Series, Miami Center for the Fine Arts; Cello Faculty, The Peabody Conservatory and Cincinnati College - Conservatory. *Recordings:* Miaskovsky Cello Sonatas; Alkan Cello Sonata; Vivaldi Cello Sonatas; Aleksander Obradovic Cello Concerto; Leo Ornstein Sonata, Samuel Barber Sonata; Lukas Foss Capricco. *Honours:* Nomination for Grand Prix du Disque; Recipient of 3 Martha Baird Rockefeller Grants for Music; America Israel Cultural Foundation Award.

HANCOCK Paul, b. 6 May 1952, Plymouth, Devon, England. Composer. m. Joan Baigent, 11 Oct 1986, 3 stepsons, 1 stepdaughter. *Education:* Sherborne School, 1965-71; MA; MusB, Trinity Hall, Cambridge, 1971-76. *Career:* Composing and Private Music Teaching in: Plymouth 1976-79; York 1979-83; Oxford 1983-85; Cambridge 1985-87; First London Recital at BMIC, January 1986. *Compositions:* Main Compositions: 24 Preludes (Piano Solo) 1979-81; String Quartet, 1982; Who? (Songs for Children) 1981; With The Mermaids (Wind Quartet) 1983; The Gift Of A Lamb (Children's Opera) 1985; Maen Tans-Boskednan (Piano Solo) 1984; Silent Love (Song Cycle) 1985; Zennor (Clarinet and Viola) 1986; Little Gidding Variations (Orchestra) 1985-86; Viola Concerto, 1986. (All Published by Trewhella Music); The Mermaid of Zennor (Opera), 1986-88; ...O Very Most The Hidden Love... (Song Cycle), 1986; The Voice of the Hidden Waterfall (Ensemble), 1987; Nocturne for Ragnhild (Soprano & Piano Duet), 1988; Dancing On A Point Of Light (Ensemble), 1988; Round 12 O'Clock Rock (baritone and piano), Sea Change, percussion ensemble, 1989, Vespers of St Mary Magdalene, soprano and organ, 1990, piano sonatas 1, 2, and 3, 1990-91, Ogo Pour, percussion solo, 1991; Matrice, piano duet, 1991; The Ring of Fire, piano solo, 1992; Journey Out of Essex, baritone and ensemble, 1993. *Recordings:* Two Cassettes of Piano Music produced by Trewhella Music. *Membership:* Composers' Guild of Great Britain. *Address:* Brunnion Farmhouse, Lelant Downs, Hayle, Cornwall TR27 6NT, England.

HANCORN John, b. 1954, Inverness, Scotland. Singer (Baritone). *Education:* Studied at Trinity College of Music and the National Opera Studio; Further studies with Hans Hotter in Munich and London. *Debut:* Edinburgh 1981, as Masetto in Don Giovanni. *Career:* Aldeburgh from 1981, in Albert Herring, The Rape of Lucretia and Eugene Onegin; Glyndebourne Touring Opera from 1983, in The Love of Three Oranges, Kent Opera, Don Giovanni (Masetto) and Fidelio; Debut at Covent Garden as Hermann in Les Contes d'Hoffmann; Tour of Italy 1986 with Monteverdi's L'Orfeo, conducted by Roger Norrington; Concert performance of Charpentier's Médée with the Orchestra of the Age of Enlightenment, 1987; Season 1989-90 with Welsh National Opera as Kilian in Der Freischütz; Hector in King Priam with Musica nel Chiostro in Batignano, Italy; Handel's Israel in Egypt with the Royal Choral Society, 1990; Concert repertory also includes the Brahms Requiem; Appearances with the Royal Philharmonic Orchestra, Scottish Chamber Orchestra, Bournemouth Sinfonietta, Northern Sinfonia and at the Festivals of Camden, Greenwich, Brighton, Aldeburgh, Flanders and Frankfurt; Sang in Weber's Oberon at the Edinburgh and Tanglewood Festivals and at the Alte Oper, Frankfurt, conducted by Ozawa. *Honours include:* Countess of Munster Trust Scholarship; South East Arts Musicians Platform, 1980; Richard Tauber award 1982; Prizewinner at s'Hertogenbosch, 1983. *Address:* Korman International Management, Crunnells Green Cottage, Preston, Herts SG4 7UQ, England.

HANDLEY Vernon George, b. 11 Nov 1930, Enfield, England. Conductor. m. (1) Barbara Black, 1954, divorced, 1 son, 1 daughter (1 son deceased); m. (2) Victoria Parry-Jones, (divorced), 1 son, 1 daughter; (3) Catherine Margaret Newby, 1 son. *Education:* Balliol College, Oxford; Guildhall School of Music. *Career:*

Conductor, Oxford University Musical Club and Union, 1953-54; Oxford University Dramatic Society, 1953-54, Tonbridge Philharmonic Society, 1958-61, Hatfield School of Music and Drama, 1959-61; Proteus Choir, 1962-81; Musical Director, Conductor, Guildford Corporation, Conductor, Guildford Philharmonic Orchestra & Choir, 1962-83; (Guest Conductor 1961-83; Professor, Orchestra & Conducting, Royal College of Music, 1966-72, for Choral Class, 1969-72; Guest Conductor, 1961-; Bournemouth Symphony Orchestra, City of Birmingham Symphony Orchestra, Royal Philharmonic Orchestra, BBC Welsh Orchestra, BBC Northern Symphony (now BBC Philharmonic) Orchestra, London Philharmonic Orchestra, New Philharmonia (now Philharmonia) Orchestra; Conducted London Symphony Orchestra in International Series, London, 1971; tours of Germany, 1966, 1980, South Africa, 1974, Holland, 1980, Sweden, 1980, 1981, Germany, Sweden, Holland and France, 1982-83; Conducted the BBC Concert Orchestra at the 1993 London Proms (Delius Cello Concerto, Vaughan Williams On Wenlock Edge and Bliss Colour Symphony); Chief Guest Conductor, Royal Liverpool Philharmonc Orchestra, and Melbourne Symphony Orchestra; Chief Conductor, West Australian Orchestra; Associate Conductor, Royal Philharmonic Orchestra. *Recordings include:* CDs of Elgar Violin Concerto (Kennedy), Wand of Youth and 2nd Symphony (London Philharmonic); Vaughan Williams 5th Symphony and Flos Campi (Liverpool Philharmonic); Bridge The Sea and Britten Sea Interludes (Ulster Orchestra); Bax Enchanted Summer, Walsinghame and Fatherland (Royal Philharmonic); Delius Florida Suite, North Country Sketches, Violin Concerto, Suite and Légende (Ralph Holmes); Dvořák Overtures and Scherzo Capriccioso; Finzi Cello Concerto (Rafael Wallfisch); Moeran Symphony; Simpson 2nd, 4th, 6th, 7th, 9th and 10th Symphonies, all Stanford Symphonies; all Vaughan Williams Symphonies, Elgar Dream of Gerontius. *Address:* Hen Gerrig, Pen-y-Fan, nr Monmouth, Gwent, Wales.

HANDT Herbert, b. 26 May 1926, Philadelphia, Pennsylvania, USA. Tenor; Conductor; Musicologist. *Education:* Juilliard School New York; Vienna Academy. *Debut:* Vienna Staatsoper 1949; Sang in the premieres of Venere Prigioniera by Malipiero (Florence 1957) and Maria Golovin by Menotti (Brussels 1958); Appeared in the Italian and French premieres of works by Henze, Berg, Busoni, and Britten; Debut as conductor Rome 1960; Founded own opera group and gave revivals of works by Boccherini, Rossini and Geminiani; Also heard in Haydn's Orfeo ed Euridice (L'Anima del Filosofo); Settled in Lucca, Italy, and founded the Associazione Musicale Lucchese and the Lucca Chamber Orchestra. *Recordings:* Maria Golovin (RCA); Don Giovanni, Haydn's Orfeo, Idomeneo (Nixa); Giuseppe, Figlio di Giacobbe by Luigi Rossi; Rossini's Otello; Temistocle by JC Bach; Sesto in Giulio Cesare by Handel (Vox). *Publications include:* Performing editions of early Italian vocal music.

HANGEN Bruce (Boyer), b. 2 Feb 1947, Pottstown, Pennsylvania, USA. Conductor. *Education:* MusB, Eastman School of Music, 1970; Postgraduate studies, summers 1972, 1973, Berkshire Music Center. *Career:* Conducting assistant, Buffalo Philharmonic Orchestra, 1972-73; Assistant Conductor, Syracuse (NY) Symphony Orchestra, 1972-73; Assistant Conductor 1973-76, Associate Conductor 1976-79, Denver Symphony Orchestra; Music Director, Portland (Maine) Symphony Orchestra, 1976-86; Omaha Symphony Orchestra, 1984-. *Honours:* Eleanor Crane Prize, Berkshire Music Center, 1972; Honorary DFA, University of New England, Biddeford, Maine, 1982; Bruce Hangen Day observed by City of Portland, Maine, 1986. *Hobby:* Bicycling. *Address:* c/o Omaha Symphony Orchestra, 310 Aquila Court, 1615 Howard Street, Omaha, NE 68102, USA.

HANKINSON Michael, b. 23 Jan 1946, Maghull, Liverpool, England. Conductor; Composer. m. Kay Connett, 1 son. *Education:* TCL; FTCL; LTCL (Music Education). *Career:* Conductor, Durban Philharmonic Orchestra, 1980-87; City Organist, Durban, 1977-87; Arranger and conductor of many highly successful concerts in Durban ranging from his ballet suite With a Little Help From My Friends through Rick Wakeman's Journey to The Centre of the Earth; Resident Ballet Conductor, PACT, State Theatre, Pretoria, 1989-. *Compositions:* Magnificat and Nunc Dimittis - A Hereford Service; Christus Vincit, An Easter Oratorio; In Time of War, poems by Fernando Pessoa for contralto, chorus and orchestra; Concertino for trombone; Five Piano Pieces; A Christmas Festival Overture; A Republic Festival Suite. *Recordings:* Tchaikovsky, Francesca da Rimini, Von Einem, Philadelphia Symphony with Nurnberg Symphony Orchestra; Songs I Love with Mimi Coertse; Festival Suite, 1981- Cape Town Symphony Orchestra. *Membership:* CGGB. *Hobbies:* Amateur Radio; Computers; Interest in scientific developments in chemistry and physics. *Current Management:* Milecourt Limited. *Address:* c/o Milecourt Ltd, 32 Warren Road, Chingford, London E4 6QS, England.

HANLON Kevin (Francis), b. 1 Jan 1953, South Bend, Indiana, USA. Composer. *Education:* Studied at Indiana University, the Eastman School of Music and the University of Texas, DMA 1983; Further study with Mario Davidovsky at the Berkshire Music Center. *Career:* Taught at the University of Kentucky 1982-83; Composition and electronic music faculty at the University of Arizona, Tucson; Director of the Arizona Contemporary Music Ensemble; Appearances as singer and conductor. *Honours include:* Joseph H Bearns Prize 1978; Koussevitzky Prize 1981. *Composition include:* Through to the End of the Tunnel for low voice and tape delay 1976, revised 1980; Second Childhood for soprano and ensemble 1976; Cumulus numbus for orchestra 1977; Variations for alto saxophone and tape delay 1977; Toccata for piano 1980; String Trio 1981; An die ferne Geliebte for low voice and piano 1980; Lullaby of my Sorrows for chamber orchestra 1982; Ostinato Suite for harpsichord 1982; Centered for chamber ensemble and tape 1983; A E Housman Song Cycle for low voice and chamber ensemble 1982; Choral Introits for chorus and ensemble 1982; Trumpet Sonata 1983; Sratae for orchestra 1983; Relentless Time for small orchestra 1984. *Address:* c/o ASCAP, ASCAP Building, One Lincoln Plaza, New York, NY 10023, USA.

HANLY Brian Vaughan, b. 3 Sept 1940, Perth, Australia. Concert Violinist; Music Professor. m. Jeri Ryan Hanly, 25 Aug 1968, 2 sons. *Education:* Performers diploma, 1960, Teachers diploma, 1961, Australian Music Examinations Board. *Career:* Violinist, Arts Trio, in residence at University of Wyoming and University of Houston, Texas, USA; Numerous tours with Western Arts Trio, Europe, USA, Mexico, also concerts throughout South America and Australia; Soloist with orchestras throughout Australia, Mexico, USA, with particular success with Beethoven and Prokofiev concerts. *Recordings:* 1st recording of Claude Debussy's recently discovered piano trio; 7 LPs with Western Arts Trio. *Honour:* Winner, Australian Broadcasting Commission concerto competition. *Hobby:* Swimming. *Address:* Music Department, University of Wyoming, Laramie, WY 82071, USA.

HANNAH Ron, b. 14 Dec 1945, Moose Jaw, Saskatchewan, Canada. Composer; Teacher. *Education:* BSc, Chemistry, 1969, BMus, Theory, Composition, 1973, MMus, Composition, 1975, EdDip, 1980, University of Alberta, Edmonton; Student of Violet Archer, Manus Sasonkin, Malcolm Forsyth. *Career:* Mbr, Da Camera Singers, 1973-; Instructor, Department of Extension, University of Alberta, 1975-76; Instructor, Harmony, Ear Training, Red Deer College, 1977-78; Music Instructor, Edmonton Public Schools, 1980-; Founder, Owner, Composer Publications, Edmonton, 1989; Commissions include 2 from Canadian Broadcasting Corporation. *Compositions include:* From Song of Solomon, SATB, piano, 1972; An Immorality, SATB, piano, 1972; The Dinner Party, song cycle, soprano, clarinet, piano, 1973; String Quartet No 1, 1973; Sonata for Violoncello and Piano, 1973; Three African Songs, tenor, piano, 1974; The Shrine of Kotje, chorus, orchestra, 1975; Variations on a Theme of Violet Archer, piano, 1975; Concert Piece, flute, piano, 1975; Visions of Nothingness, piano sonata in 2 movements, 1975; Sonata for French Horn and Piano, 1976; Prelude and Meditation on Coventry Cathedral, trumpet, organ, 1978; Five Preludes, organ, 1978; Songs of Myself, song cycle, soprano, violin, piano, French horn, 1979; The Lonely Princess, flute, guitar, 1981; Suite for Elan, piano, 1982; Piano Trio No 1, 1982; Four Canons for three Voices, mixed chorus, piano, 1983; Mademoiselle Fifi, chamber opera, 1983; Three Songs on Poems of Robert Graves, voice, electronic tape, 1984; Fantasia on 'Ein' Feste Burg, organ, 1984; Hypatia, a play with songs, 1984; Three Romantic Madrigals, 1985; Concerto for Piano and Tape, 1986; Morning's Minion: 4 songs after G M Hopkins, soprano, piano, 1987; Alleluia, SATB, 1989; Credo, mezzo-soprano, viola, piano, 1990; Divertimento for Strings, 1991. *Address:* 11627-46 Avenue, Edmonton, Alberta, Canada T6H 0A6.

HANNAN Eilene, b. 4 Nov 1946, Melbourne, Australia. Singer (Soprano). *Education:* Studied in Australia and London. *Debut:* Australian Opera 1971 as Barbarina in Le nozze di Figaro. *Career:* Sang Natasha in Prokofiev's War and Peace at the opening of the Sydney Opera House, 1973; Other Australian roles have been Janáček's Vixen, Santuzza, Mozart's Zerlina and Cherubino and Leila in Les pêcheurs de Perles; Glyndebourne and Wexford 1977, as the Vixen and as Salomé in Herodiade by Massenet; English National Opera from 1978 as Janáček's Mila (Osud) and Katya Kabanova, the Duchess of Parma in Busoni's Doctor Faust, Mozart's Pamina and Susanna, Mélisande, Poppea (Monteverdi) and Natasha; Covent Garden debut 1978, in the British premiere of The King goes forth to France, by Sallinen; Sang in Britten's The Turn of the Screw at Brisbane in 1988; Season 1992 as Jenůfa at Sydney, Pat Nixon for the State Opera of South Australia and at Dusseldorf. *Address:* c/o Ingpen and Williams, 14 Kensington Court, London W8 5DN, England.

HANNAN Michael Francis, b. 19 Nov 1949, Newcastle, New South Wales, Australia. Composer; Writer; Educator; Keyboard Performer. *Education:* BA, 1972, PhD, 1979, University of Sydney; Graduate Diploma of Musical Composition, University of Sydney, 1982. *Career:* Teacher: University of New South Wales, 1975-76, University of Sydney, 1977-83; Lecturer in Composition, Queensland Conservatorium of Music, 1985-86; Head of Music, Northern Rivers College of Advanced Education, 1986-; Research: Post-doctoral Scholar, University of California, Los Angeles, 1983-84; Research Affiliate, University of Sydney, 1985-. *Compositions:* Voices in the Sky for piano, 1980; Rajas for solo cello, 1982; Zen Variations for piano, 1982; Island Song for recorders, percussion and organ, 1983; In the Utter Darkness for solo flute, 1983; Callisto for tape, 1984; Alphabeat for tape, 1984; Resonances for piano, 1986. *Recording:* The Piano Music of Peter Sculthorpe, Move Records, 1982. *Publication:* Peter Sculthorpe: His Music and Ideas, 1929-79, 1982. *Contributions to:* Various publications. *Hobbies:* Surfing; Cooking; Wine; Ornithology. *Address:* c/o School of the Arts, Northern Rivers College of Advanced Education, Lismore, New South Wales 2480, Australia.

HANNAY Roger Durham, b. 22 Sept 1930, Plattsburg, New York, USA. Composer; Conductor; Teacher. m. Janet Roberts, 1 daughter. *Education:* BMus, Syracuse University, 1948-52; MMus, Boston University, 1952-53; PhD, Eastman School of Music, 1954-56; Berkshire Music School, 1959; Princeton Seminar for Advanced Studies, 1960; Bennington Composers Conference, 1964-65. *Debut:* Music in Our Time, New York City, 1964. *Career:* Teacher on the faculties of SUNY, Hamilton College, University of Wyoming, Concordia College; Teacher, University of North Carolina, where founded and directed Electronic Studio and the New Music Ensemble, 1967-82; Conducted the North Carolina Symphony Orchestra in his Symphony No 4, American Classic, 1983; Greensboro Symphony Orchestra premiere of his orchestral suite, The Age of Innocence, 1985, Peter Fuchs Conductor; Residencies: Charles Ives Center for American Music. *Compositions include:* Sphinx, trumpet and tape; Pied Piper, clarinet and tape; Clarinet Voltaire, saxophone, percussion and speaker; Rhapsody, flute and piano; The Nightingale and the Rose, 1986; Ye Musick for the Globe Theatre, 1985; Sic Transit Spiritus, 1984; Souvenir and Souvenir II, 1984 and 1986; The Journey of Edith Wharton, opera, in 2 acts for 5 voices and chamber orchestra, 1982; Prologue to Chaucer's Canterbury Tales, commissioned. *Recordings:* Symphony for Band, Crest Records. *Publications:* Transcribed and edited, Sonate for viola and piano by Mrs H H Beach, 1984. *Hobbies:* Literature; Travel. *Address:* 609 Morgan Creek Road, Chapel Hill, NC 27514, USA.

HANNIKAINEN Ann-Elise, b. Hangö, Finland, 14 Jan 1946. Composer; Pianist. *Education:* Schools in Sweden, Finland, New York, 1953-63; Academia Moderna de Musica, Peru, 1964-66; Diploma, Sibelius Academy, Finland, 1967-72; Studies with composer Ernesto Halffter, Spain, 1972-. *Debut:* As composer, orchestral piece, Anerfálicas, Valencia, Spain, 1973. *Career includes:* Tournée as pianist, Andalucia, 1975; Performance, world premiere, Piano Concerto, Helsinki, Finland, 1976; Anerfálicas, Teatro Real, Madrid, Spain, 1977; Finnish Radio broadcasts, Spanish Radio; Piano recitals; Festival Kuhmoinen, Andalucia, Madrid, etc. *Compositions include:* Anerfálicas, orchestral, 1973; Pensamientos, piano, 1974; Toccata Fantasia, piano, 1975. Concierto for Piano & Orchestra, in memoriam Manuel de Falla's 100th anniversary, 1976; Cosmos, orchestral, 1977; Trio, Sextetto, 1979; Chachara, flute & piano, 1980; Solemne, piano solo, 1982; Zafra, violin & piano, 1986. *Recordings:* Tape recordings, Finnish Radio. *Publications:* Pensamientos 1974, Toccato Fantasia, Chachara, Edition Fazer, Finland. Some works included in 'Centre de Documentation de la Musique Contemporaine' Paris, France. *Compositions:* 1st prize, 2nd contest for young composers, JJMM Barcelona, 1980. *Memberships:* Société des Auteurs, Compositeurs et Editeurs de Musique, Paris; Society of Finnish Composers. *Hobby:* Oil painting. *Address:* Mannerheimintie, 21-23b, 00250 Helsinki 25, Finland.

HANNULA Tero, b. 1950, Vehmaa, Finland. Singer (Baritone). *Education:* Studied in Finland with P Salomaa, in Rome with Luigi Ricci and at Musikhochschule Vienna. *Career:* Sang Escamillo and Posa in Don Carlos at Kaiserslautern, 1976; Nationaltheater Mannheim from 1977, as Wolfram, Enrico, Counts Luna and Almaviva, Eugene Onegin, Marcello, Rossini's Figaro and Lortzing's Tsar; Sang Almaviva at Ludwigsburg, 1980-81, Savonlinna Festival, 1981-89, as Papageno and in the 1984 premiere of Sallinen's The King goes forth to France; Stuttgart Staatsoper, 1982-, notably in the 1984 premiere of Akhnaten by Philip Glass; Guest appearances at Hamburg, Hanover, Karlsruhe, Aachen, Vienna, Moscow, Leningrad and Munich; Finnish National Opera, Helsinki, as Rigoletto, Deutsche Oper Berlin as Thoas in Iphigenie en Aulide; Sang Blancsac in La Scala di Seta at Stuttgart Staatsoper, 1991. *Recordings include:* Akhnaten. *Address:* c/o Stuttgart Statsoper, Oberer Schlossgarten 6, 7000 Stuttgart, Germany.

HANSEL Stanislaw b. 19 Nov 1950, Peterborough, England. Composer. m. 1 son, 1 daughter. *Education:* Composition with John Tavener, LTCL, Amus TCL, GTCL diplomas, Trinity College of Music, London, 1969-72. *Career:* Music teaching, various institutions, 1974-77; Founder, Director, Peterborough Festival of Electronic and Modern Music, 1985-86-; Member, Electro Acoustic Ensemble, Hull, 1987; Member, Contemporary Open Studio, English National Opera, 1989; Commissions from Peterborough Arts Council and Ferens Art Gallery, Hull. *Compositions include:* Kharaja for strings, 1984; Forcefields for piano, 1985; Ponderables, dance piece with poetry by Paul Green, 1985; Forcefields for Keyboards, 1985; Forcefields, sound poem, 1985; Children of Atlantic, multi-lingual poem, 1985; Psychic Music II for piano, 1986; Telepathia I for 2 accordians, 1 out of earshot of auditorium, 1987; Telepathia II for flute, 3 synthesisers players, 1 our of earshot of auditorium, 1987; Micromusics for string quartet and synthesiser, 1987; Ripening, settings of poetry by Paul Buck, 1987; Glimmer Twins, full-length opera, words by Paul Buck, 1987-88, both represented by Music International Network, 1991; Currently working on a new opera to a libretto by Paul Buck, Through the Opening. *Contributions to:* Composer and H/Ear magazines, mid-80s; Unknown Public; Psychic Music II issued on CD with issue 03 of Unknown Public. *Hobbies:* Foreign langages; Theories of single origin of all languages. *Address:* 38 West Parade, Peterborough, Cambs, PE3 6BA, England.

HANSELL Kathleen Amy Kuzmick, b. 21 Sept 1941, Bridgeport, Connecticut, USA. Musicologist; Organist; Harpsichordist. 1 son, 1 daughter. *Education:* BA, Wellesley College, Massachusetts, 1963; MMus, University of Illinois at Urbana, 1969; PhD, University of California at Berkeley, 1980; Studied, piano organ and harpsichord with private teachers. *Career:* Instructor in music history, by correspondence, University of Illinois, 1967-68; Organist, Lutheran Church of the Good Shepherd, Sacramento, California, 1969-71, Gloria Dei Lutheran Church, Iowa City, Iowa, 1973-74; Instructor in musicology and harpsichord, Grinnell College, Iowa, 1976; Instructor in music history, Cornell College, Mt Vernon, Iowa, 1979; Archivist, Swedish Music History Archive, Stockholm, Sweden, 1982-. *Publications:* Editor, Mozart: Lucio Silla for Neue Mozart Ausgabe, 1986; Franz Berwald Complete Works, Volume 14, Duos (Barenreiter), 1987, Hindemith, Organ Concerto, 1962 for Hindemith-Ausgabe; Il Balletto e l'Opera Italiana, in Storia dell'opera Italiana (Turin), 1988; Editor, Rossini: Zelmira, for Tutte le opere di Gioachino Rossini. *Contributions to:* Numerous professional magazines and publications including, Grove's Dictionary, 6th edition. *Memberships:* American, International, Italian and Swedish Musicology Societies; International Association of Music Libraries; College Music Society; Chairman, Editorial Board, Monumenta Musicae Svecicae.

HANSEN Flemming Christian, b. 1 Jan 1968, Copenhagen, Denmark. Organist (Composer). *Education:* Recorder, Clarinet, Saxophne, Piano, in childhood; Preliminary Organ studies, to 1988; Organ at Royal Danish Academy of Music, 1992-; Composition studies with Professor Ib Nørholm, Andy Pape and Bent Sørensen. *Career:* As composer: Performances in Denmark, Norway, Finland, Germany, USSR, Hungary, France, Belgium; Attended festivals in Russia, 1989, 1990, 1992, and Moldavia, 1991. *Compositions:* November-Music for clarinet, vibraphone and viola, 1986; Andre Nætter for orchestra, 1988; Kantele for tape, 1988; A la Memoire de Dali for saxophone quartet, 1989; De Profundis for organ, 1990. *Recording:* CD: A la Memoire de Dali with New Danish Saxophone Quartet. *Honours:* Several scholarships, Art Foundation of the Danish State; Participant in Rostrum 91. *Membership:* Danish Composers Society. *Hobby:* Travel. *Address:* H C Andersensgade 9 I, 4800 Nykøbing F, Denmark.

HANSEN Peter, b. 15 Aug 1917, The Hague, Netherlands. Pianist; Musician. m. Atie den Dulk, 4 Sept 1948, 2 sons. *Education:* Studied piano with Cor de Groot, Royal Conservatory, The Hague 1936-41; Degree C1 in 1939, Degree C2 in 1941. Studied with Jaap Spaanderman, Amsterdam 1950-60. *Debut:* The Hague. *Career:* Played piano concertos by Khachaturian and Badings with The Hague Philharmony conducted by Louis Stotijn and Willem van Otterloo, 1953 and 1956; Piano concertos with several orchestras: Utrecht, Groningen, Enschede, Deventer, Arnhem. Accompanist to many soloists including: Herman Krebbers, Theo Olof, Willem Noske, Thomas Magyar and Hermann Schey, Bernard Kruysen, Max van Egmond, Robert Holl. Manager of De Zingende Zolder in The Hague with 500 concerts, 1952-; given 4,000 school concerts all over The Netherlands 1947-; Played 127 times for Radio

Corporations in Holland, Belgium, France, Germany and Switzerland; Piano teacher at Royal Conservatory of Music in The Hague, retired in 1982. *Memberships:* Royal Netherlands Musicians Society; EPTA; Cultural Council of South Holland. *Honours:* Order of Knighthood of Oranje Nassau 1978. *Hobbies:* Visiting Concerts, Theatre, Operas, Ballet; Nature; Photography. *Address:* Jozef Israëlslaan 34, The Hague, The Netherlands.

HANSON Robert Frederic, b. 24 Oct 1948, Birmingham, England. Composer; Musicologist; Teacher. m. (1) Anthea Judith Carter, 11 July 1970, 1 daughter, (2) Rosalind Thurston, 1 Nov 1980, 2 sons. *Education:* ARCO, 1967, BA, 1970, PhD, 1976, Southampton University. *Career:* Founder/Conductor, Southampton University Chamber Orchestra, 1970-72; Analytical Research into the music of Webern, 1970-73; Freelance Teacher and Composer, 1973-74; Lecturer in Music, Dartington College of Arts, 1974-91; Degree Course Leader, 1983-91; Acting Head of Music, 1990-91; Director of Studies, Morley College, 1991-. *Compositions:* Numerous unpublished compositions. *Contributions to:* Tempo: Lutoslawski's Mi-Parti; Music Analysis: Webern's Chromatic Organisation. *Memberships:* Society for the Promotion of New Music; Performing Rights Society. *Hobby:* Architecture. *Address:* Morley College, 61 Westminister Bridge Road, London, England.

HANUŠ Jan, b. 2 May 1915, Prague, Czechoslovakia. Composer. *Education:* Studied Composition with O Jeremias, 1932-40. *Career:* Has worked for music publishers, 1934-, notably Panton, 1963-70 (editions of Dvorak and Fibich). *Compositions include:* Operas: Flames, Plzen, 1956; The Servant of Two Masters, Plzen, 1959; Prometheus's Torch, Prague, 1965; The Story of One Night, 1961-63; A Dispute over the Goddess, Czech Television, 1986; Ballets: Othello, Prague, 1952; Salt Above Gold, Olomouc, 1953; Labyrinth, Prague, 1983; 7 symphonies, 1942-78; Concertante Symphony for organ, harp, timpani and strings, 1954; Double Concerto for oboe, harp and orchestra; Three Essays for orchestra, 1975-76; Chamber: Serenade for nonet, 1953; Viola sonatina, 1958; Frescoes, Piano Trio, 1961; Suite domestica for wind quintet, 1964; Concertino for timpani and tape, 1972; Tower Music for brass quintet, 1976; The Praise of Chamber Music for flute, oboe, string trio and harpsichord, 1979; Ecce Homo, oratorio, 1980; Glagolitic Mass for bass, chorus, organ and bells, 1985. *Address:* 169 00 Prague 6, Tomanova 38, Czech Republic.

HANUSZEWSKA-SCHAEFFER Mieczyslawa, b. 1 Oct 1929, Borszow, near Tarnopol, Poland. Musicologist; Philosopher; Journalist. m. Boguslaw Schaeffer, 23 Nov 1953, 1 son. *Education:* Languages, Philosophy, Musicology, Jagiellonian University, Cracow; Music Theory, State Higher School of Music. *Debut:* 1953. *Publications:* Collaborated in Lexicon of 20th Century Composers, 1965 and New Grove Dictionary; Editor: Almanach kompozytorów polskich (Lexicon of Polish Contemporary Composers), 3rd edition, 1981; Tysiac kompozytorow (Lexicon of 1000 Composers), 4th edition, 1985; Musical Editor, Zycie Literackie. *Contributions to:* Some 400 articles in magazines such as Zycie Literackie, Ruch Muzyczny. *Honour:* Music Prize for Music Journalism, 1989. *Membership:* Grupa Krakowska. *Hobbies:* Philosophy; Reading. *Address:* Osiedle Kolorowe 4, Cracow 31 938, Poland.

HARA Kazuko, b. 10 Feb 1935, Tokyo, Japan. Composer. *Education:* Studied in Japan, with Dutilleux in Paris and with Tcherepnin, 1962; Singing at Venice Conservatory, 1963, Gregorian Chant in Tokyo. *Career:* Her operas have been successfully performed in Tokyo. *Compositions include:* Operas: The Casebook of Sherlock Holmes: the Confession, 1981; On the Merry Night, 1984; A Selection for Chieko, 1985; Sute-Hime: the Woman who Bit off a man's Tongue, 1986; A Love Suicide at Sonezaki, 1987; Beyond Brain Death, 1988; Yosakoi-bushi: Junshin and Omma, 1990; Princess Iwanaga, 1990; Pedro Kibe: recanted not, 1992;

Nasuno-Yoichi, 1992; Tonnerre's miraculous tree, 1993. *Address:* JASRAC (Japan), c/o PRS Ltd, Member Registration, 29-33 Berners Street, London W1P 4AA, England.

HARADA Sadao, b. 4 Jan 1944, Tokyo, Japan. Cellist. *Education:* Studied at the Juilliard School with members of the Juilliard Quartet. *Career:* Cellist of the Tokyo Quartet, 1969-; Regular concerts in the USA and abroad; First cycle of the complete quartets of Beethoven at the Yale at Norfolk Chamber Music Festival, 1986; Repeated cycles at the 92nd Street Y (New York), Ravinia and Israel Festivals and Yale and Princeton Universities; Season 1990-91 at Alice Tully Hall, the Metropolitan Museum of Art, New York and in Boston, Washington DC, Los Angeles, Cleveland, Detroit, Chicago, Miami, Seattle, San Francisco, Toronto; Tour of South America, two tours of Europe including Paris, Amsterdam, Bonn, Milan, Munich, Dublin, London, Berlin; Quartet-in-residence at Yale University, the University of Cincinnati College-Conservatory of Music. *Recordings:* Schubert's major Quartets; Mozart Flute Quartets with James Galway and Clarinet Quintet with Richard Stolzman; Quartets by Bartók, Brahms, Debussy, Haydn, Mozart and Ravel; Beethoven Middle Period Quartets (RCA). *Honours:* Grand Prix du Disque du Montreux; Best Chamber Music Recording of the Year from Stereo review and the Gramophone; Four Grammy nominations. *Address:* Intermusica Artists' Management, 16 Duncan Terrace, London N1 8BZ, England.

HARBISON John (Harris), b. 20 Dec 1938, Orange, New Jersey, USA. Composer; Conductor. *Education:* Pupil of Walter Piston, Harvard College, BA, 1960, Boris Blacher, Berlin Hochschule für Musik, 1961, and Roger Sessions and Earl Kim, Princeton University, MFA, 1983; Studied conducting with Eleazer de Carvalho, Berkshire Music Center, Tanglewood, Massachusetts, and with Dean Dixon, Salzburg. *Career:* Teacher, Massachusetts Institute of Technology, 1969-82; Conductor, Cantata Singers and Ensemble, 1969-73, 1980-82; Composer-in-residence, Reed College, 1968-69, Pittsburgh Symphony Orchestra, 1982-84, Berkshire Music Center, 1984; New Music Adviser, 1985-86, Composer-in-residence, 1986-88, Los Angeles Philharmonic Orchestra. *Compositions:* Operas: The Winter's Tale, 1974; Full Moon in March, 1977; Ballets: Ulysses' Bow, 1984; Ulysses Raft, 1983; Orchestral: Sinfonia for Violin and Double Orchestra, 1963; Confinement for Chamber Ensemble, 1965; Elegiac Songs for Mezzo-soprano and Chamber Orchestra, 1973; Descant-Nocturne, 1976; Diotima, 1976; Piano Concerto, 1978; Snow Country for Oboe and Strings, 1979; Violin Concerto, 1980; Symphony No 1, 1981; Deep Potomac Bells for 250 Tubas, 1983; Remembering Gatsby, 1986; Viola Concerto, 1989; Chamber: Serenade for 6 Instruments, 1968; Piano Trio, 1969; Bermuda Triangle for Amplified Cello, Tenor Saxophone, and Electric Organ, 1970; Die Kurze for 5 Instruments, 1970; Woodwind Quintet, 1979; Organum for Paul Fromm for Chamber Group, 1981; Piano Quintet, 1981; Exequien for Carlo Simmons for 7 Instruments, 1982; Overture: Michael Kohlhass for Brass Ensemble, 1982; Variations for Clarinet, Violin, and Piano, 1982; String Quartet, 1985; Choral pieces; Songs. *Recordings:* Several compositions recorded. *Honours:* Guggenheim Fellowship, 1978; Pulitzer Prize in Music, 1986; Many commissions. *Address:* 4037 Highway 19, De Forest, WI 53532, USA.

HARDENBERGER Håkan, b. 27 Oct 1961, Malmo, Sweden. Trumpeter. *Education:* Trumpet with Bo Nilsson in Malmo aged 8; Royal College of Music Malmo; Paris Conservatoire with Pierre Thibaud. *Career:* Prizewinner at competitions in Paris, Munich, Toulon and Geneva; Extensive tours of Europe and North and South America; UK debut Aug 1984. playing the Howarth Trumpet Concerto at Crystal Palace; Tour of Germany 1984 with the Dresdner Baroque Soloists; 1985 Bournemouth Sinfonietta with Andrew Parrott, playing Hummel and Bach; Harrogate and Warwick Festivals 1985, and South American tour with the Munich Bach Collegium; London Promenade Concert debut 1986, with the premiere of Array by Gordon Crosse conducted by James Loughran; May 1987 premiere of Harrison Birtwistle's Endless Parade with the Collegium Musicum Zurich conducted by Paul Sacher; Aug 1987 premiere of John McCabe's Rainforest II at the Harrogate Festival; Concerts with the Scottish National Orchestra and Neeme Jarvi and the Northern Sinfonia with George Malcolm; Other conductors with whom he has worked include Peter Eötvös, Charles Mackerras, John Pritchard, Seiji Ozawa and Rostropovitch; Edinburgh Festival debut 1988, playing the Haydn Concerto with Esa-Pekka Salonen conducting the Swedish Radio Symphony; Premiered Henze's Concerto 1992 (Japan); Season 1993/94 with South America tour, appearances at Salzburg and the London Proms, tour of Europe with the London Sinfonietta. *Recordings:* Concertos by Haydn, Hummel, Hertel, Stamitz and Telemann with the Academy of St Martin in the Fields under Neville Marriner (Philips); Birtwistle Endless Parade, Concertos by Davies and Watkins; Mysteries of the Macabre, Baroque Trumpet Recital, At the Beach. *Honours:* RPO Charles Heidseele Music Award for best instrumentalist in 1988, 1989. *Current Management:* Svenek Konsertdirektion AB. *Address:* c/o Svensk Konsertdirektion AB, Henrik F Lodding, Box 5076, 402 22 Göteborg, Sweden.

HARDY Janet, b. 1940, Atlanta, Georgia, USA. Singer (Dramatic Soprano). *Education:* Studied at the Mississippi Southern and Louisiana Colleges; BM in Music Education, Louisiana College; Further study with Dorothy Hulse, Dominique Modesti, Gladys Kuchta and Hilde Zadek. *Career:* Has sung in Gelsenkirchen, Kassel and Augsburg as Elektra, Ortrud, Leonore in Fidelio, the Kostelnička in Jenůfa, Kundry, Isolde, Senta and Turandot; Guest appearances in Frankfurt, Salzburg, Copenhagen, the Berlin Staatsoper, Trieste, Leipzig, Berne, Mannheim, Toulon and Dusseldorf; Season 1988-89 with the title role in new productions of Mona Lisa by Schillings in Augsburg and Elektra in Innsbruck; sang Elektra at the Vienna Staatsoper, June 1991; Brünnhilde in Die Walküre at Liège, the Dyer's Wife in Die Frau ohne Schatten at Augsburg, Nov 1991; Sang Elektra with Welsh National Opera, 1992. *Address:* Music International, 13 Ardilaun Road, London N5 2QR, England.

HARDY Rosemary, b. 1949, England. Singer (Soprano), *Education:* Studied at the Royal College of Music and at the Franz Liszt Academy, Budapest. *Career:* Performances with Roger Norrington, Michel Corboz and John Eliot Gardiner in the Baroque repertoire; Solo cantatas with the Drottningholm Baroque Ensemble, Sweden, at the Berlin Staatsoper and the Wigmore Hall; Sang in Jonathan Miller's production of Orfeo by Monteverdi; Modern repertoire includes Webern's music for voice at the Venice Biennale 1983 and the Cheltenham Festival; Webern recital at the Vienna Konzerthaus 1983; Schoenberg's 2nd Quartet (Arditti) for the Maggio Musicale, in Geneva and in London (BBC); Premieres of Jonathan Harvey's Passion and Resurrection and Song Offerings; Tours of France with Ensemble Intercontemporain, performing Boulez, Ravel, Varèse and Kurtag (Scenes from a Novel): has also given Kurtag's Sayings of R V Troussova; Appearances at the Glyndebourne Festival in Knussen's Where the Wild Things Are and Higgelty Piggelty Pop: concert showings with the Hallé, City of Birmingham, San Diego, Danish Radio, BBC Symphony and London Symphony Orchestras; Has sung in Henze's The English Cat for the BBC and in Frankfurt and Italy; Concert with the Schoenberg Ensemble and the Nieuw Ensemble at the Holland Festival: Pierrot Lunaire in Milan, 1991; Tour with Capricorn on the Contemporary Music Network; Has also sung in Schubert Masses with the London Philharmonic, Mozart and Handel concert for the Cambridge Festival and concerts at the Aldeburgh Festival. *Honours include:* Artijus Prize, Hungary, 1983. *Recordings:* Cavalli's Ercole Amante (Erato); Monteverdi's Combattimento, Il Ballo delle Ingrate and Scherzi Musicale. *Address:* Magenta Music International, 4 Highgate High Street, London N6 5JL, England.

HARE Ian Christopher, b. 26 Dec 1949, Kingston upon Hull, England. Organist; Conductor; Composer. m. (1) Carol Russell, 23 Apr 1973, (2) Pauline Crosland, 21 Mar 1985, 2 daughters. *Education:* Organ Scholar, MA, Mus B, King's College, Cambridge, 1968-72; Associate, Royal College of Music, 1973-74; Fellow, Royal College of Organists (CHM); ADCM. *Career:* Lecturer in Music, University of Lancaster, 1974-; Musical Director, Lancaster Singers, 1975-; Organist and Master of the Choristers, Cartmel Priory, 1981-89; Sub-Organist, Carlisle Cathedral, 1989-; University Organist, Lancaster, 1983-. *Compositions:* Thou, O God, Art Praised in Sion, anthem, 1973; Beethoven's Hymn to Joy, organ arrangement, 1974; A Child is Born, anthem, 1987; Triptych, for organ, 1993; Sing Praises unto the Lord, anthem, 1993. *Recordings:* Handel's Messiah, Bach Cantata 147 and motets, Britten's Missa Brevis, St Nicolas, Once in Royal David's City, Hymns for All Seasons, King's College Choir, Cambridge, 1968-72; The Organ of Carmel Priory, 1985; Cassette: English Organ Music, 1987; Haydn & Schubert CD, 1989 (Haydn Society of Great Britain). *Contributions to:* The Organ. *Honour:* John Stewart of Rannoch Scholarship in Sacred Music, 1969-72. *Memberships:* Fellow, Royal College of Organists; Incorporated Association of Organists; Incorporated Society of Musicians. *Hobbies:* Reading; Walking; Gardening. *Address:* Prior Slee Gatehouse, The Abbey, Carlisle, Cumbria, CA3 8TZ, England.

HAREWOOD The Earl of (George Henry Hubert Lascelles), b. 7 Feb. 1923, London, England. Musical Administrator. m. (1) Maria Donata Stein, 1949 (divorced 1967), (2) Patricia Tuckwell, 1967, 4 sons. *Education:* King's College, Cambridge University. *Career includes:* Board of Directors, 1951-53, 1969-72, Administrative Executive, 1953-60, Royal Opera House, Covent Garden, London; Director-General, 1958-74, Chairman, 1988-90, Leeds Musical Festival; Artistic Director, Edinburgh International Festival, 1961-65; Artistic Advisor, New Philharmonia Orchestra, 1966-76; Artistic Advisor, Buxton Festival, 1993-; Chairman, British Council Music Advisory Committee, 1956-66; Arts Council Music Panel, 1966-72; General Advisory Council, BBC, 1969-77; Managing Director, Sadler's Wells Opera, 1972; Managing Director, 1974-85, Chairman, 1986-, English National Opera; Governor, BBC, 1985-87; President, British Board of Film Classification, 1985-; Artistic Director, Adelaide Festival, 1988. *Publications:* Editor, Opera, 1950-53; Editor, Kobbés Complete Opera Book, 1954, 1973, 1987; Autobiography, The Tongs and the Bones, 1982; Kobbe's Illustrated Opera Books, 1989. *Honours:* Honorary LLD, Leeds, Aberdeen and Bradford; Honorary DMus, Hull; Austrian Government Silver Medal of Honour, 1959; Lebanese Order of Cedar, 1970; Janáček Medal, 1978; Honorary Doctorate, York University, 1982; Honorary Member, Royal Academy of Music, 1983; Honorary Fellow King's College, Cambridge, 1985; KBE, 1987. *Current Management:* Ingpen & Williams. *Hobbies:* Opera; Theatre; Association Football. *Address:* Harewood House, Leeds LS17 9LG, England.

HARGAN Alison, b. 1943, Yorkshire, England. Singer (Soprano). *Education:* Studied piano and singing at the Royal Northern College of Music. *Debut:* With Welsh National Opera, as Pamina in Die Zauberflöte. *Career:* Concert performances of music by Strauss and Mahler, Four Last Songs and Resurrection Symphony, and Verdi (Requiem); Appearances include Tippett's A Child of our Time with Neville Marriner, the Fauré Requiem with the Royal Philharmonic Orchestra and Bach's B Minor Mass in Lisbon; Britten's War Requiem with the Boston Symphony Orchestra and Mahler's 8th Symphony at La Fenice, Venice, conducted by I Inbal; Has also worked with Andrew Davis, Eugen Jochum, Erich Leinsdorf, Leppard, Ozawa, Pritchard, Colin Davis, Lorin Maazel, Simon Rattle, Richard Hickox and Rozhdestvensky; Orchestras include the Vienna Philharmonic, Munich Philharmonic and Los Angeles Philharmonic, as well as leading orchestras in Britain. *Address:* c/o IMG Artists Europe, Media House, 3 Burlington Lane, Chiswick, London, W4 2TH, England.

HARGITAI Geza, b. 1940, Hungary. Violinist. *Education:* Studied at the Franz Liszt Academy, Budapest. *Career:* Second Violinist of the Bartók Quartet from 1985; Performances in nearly every European country and tours of Australia, Canada, Japan, New Zealand and the USA; Festival appearances at Adelaide, Ascona, Aix, Venice, Dubrovnik, Edinburgh, Helsinki, Lucerne, Menton, Prague, Vienna, Spoleto and Schwetzingen; Tour of Britain 1986 including concerts at Cheltenham, Dartington, Philharmonic Hall Liverpool, RNCM Manchester and the Wigmore Hall; Tours of Britain 1988 and 1990, featuring visits to the Sheldonian Theatre, Oxford, Wigmore Hall, Harewood House and Birmingham; Repertoire includes standard classics and Hungarian works by Bartók, Durko, Bozay, Kadosa, Soproni, Farkas, Szabo and Lang. *Recordings include:* Complete quartets of Mozart, Beethoven and Brahms; Major works of Haydn and Schubert (Hungarton); Complete quartets of Bartók (Erato). *Address:* c/o Ingpen and Williams Ltd, 14 Kensington Court, London W8 5DN, England.

HARGREAVES Glenville, b. 1950, Bradford, England. Singer (Baritone). *Education:* Studied at St John's College, York, the Royal Northern College of Music and at the London Opera Centre. *Debut:* Title role in Il Barbiere di Siviglia, 1981. *Career:* Covent Garden debut 1982, in Les Contes d'Hoffmann; English National Opera from 1982, notably in The Magic Flute, War and Peace and Salome; Modern repertory includes The Old Man in Purgatory by Gordon Crosse; Walworth in Wat Tyler by Alan Bush; Longinus in The Catiline Conspiracy by Iain Hamilton (creation); Ullmann's Emperor of Atlantis; Mittenhofer in Henze's Elegy for Young Lovers (Queen Elizabeth Hall, London) and Sir Charles Keighley in John Metcalf's Tornrak (creation, 1990); Appearances with Opera North as The Dark Fiddler in A Village Romeo and Juliet, Kothner in Meistersinger and roles in Tosca and The Bartered Bride; Welsh National Opera debut as Marcello in La Bohème; Has sung Rossini's Figaro in the Netherlands and Belgium and Falstaff with the City of Birmingham Touring Opera; Other roles include Zurga (Les Pêcheurs de Perles), Nick Shadow, Germont, Don Giovanni, Mandryka, Paolo (Simon Boccanegra), Tonio, Scarpia, Demetrius (A Midsummer Night's Dream) and Mozart's Count; Season 1992 with Don Magnifico for Pimlico Opera and the Guardian in Elektra for Welsh National Opera; Concert repertory includes Elijah, Judas Maccabeus, The Kingdom, Messiah, Bruch's Odysseus, Puccini's Messa di Gloria, Sea Drift by Delius and Lieder eines fahrenden Gesellen by Mahler; Has sung with the Hallé Choir, the National Orchestra of Spain, Royal Choral Society and the Royal Philharmonic Orchestra; Also sings in Bach's Passions and Carmina Burana. *Address:* c/o Korman International Management, Crunnells Green Cottage, Preston, Herts SG4 7UQ, England.

HARLAN Christoph, b. 30 Mar 1952, Dreilingen, Germany. Classical Guitarist; Educator. m. Iris Mallet, 27 July 1975, 2 sons. *Education:* Abitur, Gymnasium, West Germany, 1970; Teaching Certificate 1972, Performance Diploma with Distinction 1973, Vienna Academy of Music, Austria. *Career:* Numerous radio broadcasts, WCLV Cleveland, CIM Concert Hall, Kent in Concert, USA; Television broadcasts, Continental Cable, 1983; Concert tours, 18 recitals, Essen, Hannover, Osnabruck, other venues, Germany; Concert appearances, New York, Buffalo, Pittsburgh, Cleveland, Cincinnati, Lubbock, Toronto, Quebec (USA & Canada); Has held various masterclasses; Appearances, most major concert series, solo/chamber music, Ohio; Many world & American premieres, various works including own compositions; Appearances, several American Festivals, Guitar Symposia (USA/Canada). *Compositions:* Anthologia Judaica, Vol I, II; Romanesca; Fantasy and Ecstasy; Trilogy; Tsigayner Doyna; Choral Variations; Britten's Ayre. *Recordings:* With members of Cleveland Orchestra, 2 records, works by Vivaldi, Bach, Boccherini, Haydn, Handel. *Publications:* Editions of chamber music, 1982; 3 suites by J J Froberger, transcribed & fingered, 1983. *Address:* c/o Iris Rozanski, 1215 Driftwood Drive, Pittsburgh, PA 5243, USA.

HARLING Stuart, b. 1955, Bournemouth, England. Singer (Baritone). *Education:* Studied at St John's College Cambridge and at the London Opera Centre. *Career:* Has appeared with the Royal Opera, Covent Garden, in Le Rossignol, Don Carlos, The King goes Forth to France, La Fanciulla del West and Lohengrin; English National Opera in The Merry Widow, Romeo and Juliet and Les Mamelles de Tiresias; Mozart's Count and Eugene Onegin for Welsh National Opera; Has sung Papageno, The Dark Fiddler (A Village Romeo and Juliet), Albert (Werther) and Ned Keene (Peter Grimes) with Opera North; Netherlands Opera as Sandini in La Cenerentola and Don Giovanni for Northern Ireland Opera Trust; Sang Nardo in La Finta Giardiniera for English Music Theatre; Took the title role in Ullmann's The Emperor of Atlantis at the Imperial War Museum, 1985; Toured Japan as Morales in Carmen, 1989; Concert engagements with the London Symphony under Claudio Abbado and Gennadi Rozhdestvensky. *Address:* c/o Korman International Management, Crunnells Green Cottage, Preston, Herts SG4 7UQ, England.

HARMAN David Rex, b. 9 Nov 1948, Redding, California, USA. Conductor; Clarinettist. m. 15 May 1981, 2 daughters. *Education:* BA 1970, MA 1971, California State University, Sacramento; Boursier de l'État Français, Paris, 1971-72; Advanced study, Paris Conservatory; DMA, Eastman School of Music, University of Rochester, 1974. *Career:* Conductor, orchestra, opera, University of Louisville, Kentucky; Visiting Professor and Director of Orchestral Avtivities; The University of Rochester (NY) and Conductor of the Rochester Philharmonic Youth Orchestra, assistant conductor, The Louisville Orchestra, 1986-87; Guest conductor; Cincinatti Symphony, Kentucky Opera, Opera Theater of Rochester, Rochester Philharmonic National Opera Orchestra of Slovenia, Tucson Symphony; Clarinet Debut: Carnegie Recital Hall, New York City, 1981; Clarinet recitals: BBC Radio III, Wigmore Hall, Purcell Room, London, UK; National Public Radio, WGBH, WQXR; ORTF, Paris. *Recordings:* Crystal Records; Garparo Records; Musical Heritage Society. *Publications:* Editor, Quartet for Clarinet & String Trio, Jean Lefèvre, Musica Rara. *Honours:* Yamaha performance award, 1973; French Govt Scholar, 1971; Executive Secretary, Grawemeyer Award for Music Composition. *Memberships:* ASOL; Conductors' Guild; ASTA. *Hobbies:* Languages; Hiking; Fishing. *Address:* 1000 Park Avenue, Rochester, NY 14610, USA.

HARNONCOURT Nikolaus, b. 6 Dec 1929, Berlin, Germany. Musician (Conductor and Cellist). m. Alice Hoffelner 1953, 3 sons, 1 daughter. *Education:* Studied in Graz, then with Paul Grummer and Emanuel Brabec at the Vienna Academy. *Career:* Cellist with the Vienna Symphony Orchestra 1952-69; Gave concerts as solo performer on the viola da gamba; Formed Vienna Concentus Musicus 1953, tours from 1957 in early and Baroque repertory; UK debut 1966, Handel's Messiah; Debut in US and Canada 1966; Professor, Mozarteum and Institute of Musicology, University of Salzburg, 1972-; Conductor, Zurich Opera, notably in works by Monteverdi, and the Amsterdam Concertgebouw Orchestra; Conducted Monteverdi's Il Ritorno d'Ulisse (Vienna 1971) and Orfeo (Amsterdam 1972); Tours in Europe, Australia and the USA; Conducted the Chamber Orchestra of Europe at the 1989 Promenade Concerts, London; Conducted La Clemenze di Tito at Zurich, 1989, Cosi fan Tutte for Netherlands Opera, 1990; Beethoven's Ninth at the Barbican Centre, London, 1991. *Recordings:* Many works with the Concentus Musicus, notably Messiah, the Brandenburg Concertos and Cantatas by Bach, operas by Monteverdi and Rameau (Castor et Pollux) and Bach's B Minor Mass; Don Giovanni (Teldec, 1990); Die Schöpfung (Vienna Symphony Orchestra); Idomeneo (Zurich Opera); Telemann Tafelmusik. *Publications:* Musik als Klangrede, Wege zu einem neuen Musikverständnis, 1982; Der Musikalische Dialog, 1984. *Honours:* Shared Erasmus Prize, 1980; HG Nägeli Medal, Zurich, 1983; Awards for recordings include Prix Mondiale du Disque, Grand Prix du Disque, Deutscher Schallplattenpreis; University of Edinburgh Honorary Degree, DMus, 1987. *Hobbies:* Cultural

History; Woodwork. *Address:* 38 Piaristengasse, A-1080 Vienna, Austria.

HARNOY Ofra, b. 31 Jan 1965, Hadera, Israel. Cellist. *Education:* Studied with father, Vladimir Orloff, William Pleeth; Master Classes with Mistislav Rostroprovich, Pierre Fournier, Jacqueline du Pre. *Debut:* Aged 10, as Soloist with Dr Boyd Neel and his Orchestra. *Career:* Soloist with numerous major orchestras, and solo recitals, USA, Canada, Japan, France, Austria, Hong Kong, Italy, Turkey, Germany, England, Israel, Australia, Holland, Belgium, Spain, Luxemburg, Venezuela; Featured in over 500 nationally televised solo-concerts or documentaries in Canada, England, Japan, Australia, Holland, Belgium, Italy, France; Radio broadcasts throughout the world; Regular Soloist, World Premiere of Jacques Offenbach Cello Concerto, North American Premiere, Sir Arthur Bliss Cello Concerto. *Recordings:* 29 solo albums RCA Victor; London; Pro Arte, including Vivaldi Cello Concertos. *Honours:* 1st Prize, Montreal Symphony Competition, 1978; Canadian Music Competition Winner, 1979; Concert Artists Guild Award, New York, 1982; Grand Prix du Disque, 1988; Juno, (as Best Classical Soloist, Canada), Award, 1988, 1989 and 1990. *Address:* 122 Alfred Ave, Willowdale, Ontario M2N 3H9, Canada.

HARPER Edward James, b. 17 Mar 1941, Taunton, Somerset, England. Composer; University Reader. m. Dorothy Shanks, 22 Oct 1984, 1 son, 1 daughter. *Education:* Studied Music, Christ Church, Oxford, 1959-63; Composition with Gordon Jacob, Royal College of Music; Further study with Franco Donatoni, Milan, 1968. *Career:* Lecturer, 1964-, currently Reader, Faculty of Music, Edinburgh University; Director, New Music Group of Scotland, 1973-91. *Compositions include:* Fanny Robin, chamber opera, 1975; Hedda Gabler, full-length opera, 1985; Piano Concerto, 1969; Sonata for chamber orchestra, 1971; Bartók Games for orchestra, 1972; Quintet for piano, flute, clarinet, violin and cello, 1974; Ricecari in Memoriam Luigi Dallapiccola for 11 instruments, 1975; Fantasia I for chamber orchestra, 1976; Fantasia II for 11 strings, 1976; Fantasia III for brass quintet, 1977; Fern Hill for chamber orchestra, 1977; 7 Poems, to texts by E E Cummings for soprano and orchestra, 1977; Chester Mass for chorus and orchestra, 1979; Symphony, 1979; Clarinet Concerto, 1982; Intrada after Monteverdi for chamber orchestra, 1982; Mass; Qui Creavit Coelum, 1986; In Memorian Kenneth Leighton for cello and piano, 1989; Homage to Thomas Hardy for baritone and orchestra, 1990; The Lamb for soprano, chorus and orchestra, 1990. *Recordings:* Bartók Games; Fanny Robin. *Address:* 7 Morningside Park, Edinburgh EH10 5HD, Scotland.

HARPER Heather, b. 8 May 1930, Belfast, N. Ireland. Soprano. m. 2nd Eduardo J Benarroch, 1973. *Education:* Trinity College of Music, London. *Career:* Created Soprano Role in Britten's War Requiem, Coventry Cathedral, 1962; Toured USA with BBC Symphony Orchestra, 1965; USSR 1967; Soloist, Opening Concerts, Maltings, Snape, 1967, Queen Elizabeth Hall, 1967; Annual Concert & Opera tours, USA, 1967; principal Soloist, BBC Symphony Orchestra on 1982 tour of Hong Kong and Australia; Principal Soloist, Royal Opera House, La Scala, Milan, 1976, Japan and Korea, 1979, USA Visit 1984; Professor and Consultant, Royal College of Music, London, 1985-; Director of Singing Studies, Britten-Pears School, Snape, 1986-; First Visiting Lecturer in Residence, Royal Scottish Academy, Glasgow, 1987-; Concerts in Asia, Middle East, Australia, European Music Festivals, South America; Principal Roles at Covent Garden, Bayreuth Festivals, La Scala (Milan), Teatro Colon (Buenos Aires), Edinburgh Festival, Glyndebourne, Sadler's Wells, Metropolitan Opera House (New York), San Francisco, Frankfurt, Deutsche Oper (Berlin), Japan (with Royal Opera House Covent Garden Co), Netherlands Opera House, New York City Opera; renowned performances of Arabella, Ariadne, Chrysothemis, Empress, Marschallin; TV Roles include Ellen Orford; Mrs Coyle (Owen Wingrave); Ilia; Donna Elvira; La Traviata, La Bohème; Principal Soloist, Promenade Concerts, 25 consecutive years; sang in the first performance of Britten's War Requiem 1962 and Tippett's 3rd Symphony 1972; Last solo appearance in the Four Last Songs of Strauss, Belfast March 1989; Nadia in The Ice Break at the 1990 Promenade Concerts. *Recordings include:* Les Illuminations (Britten); Symphony No 8 (Mahler); Don Giovanni (Mozart); Requiem (Verdi) and Missa Solemnis (Beethoven); Seven Early Songs (Berg); Marriage of Figaro; Peter Grimes; Strauss's Four Last Songs (First British Soprano Recording). *Honours:* CBE; Honorary Fellow, Trinity College of Music; Honorary Member, RAM; Hon DMus, Queen's University; Edison Award, 1971; Grammy Award, 1979; Grand Prix Du Disque, 1979; Grammy Award (Best Solo Recording), 1984. *Hobbies:* Gardening; Cooking.

HARPER Josephine Cook, b. 16 Sept 1929, Nashville, Tennessee, USA. Concert Pianist; Teacher of Piano and Theory. m. Jewel B Harper, 12 Feb 1953, 2 daughters. *Education includes:* BMus 1951, MMus 1952, University of Cincinnati Conservatory of Music; Postgraduate, Universities of Louisville, Memphis State, Jacksonville. *Career:* Artist Performer, WCPO-TV, Cincinnati, Ohio, 1952-53; Belmont College Faculty, 1952-55; Accompanist, Nashville Ballet Society, Tennessee, 1956-61; State Competition Adjudicator, Adviser, National Federation of Music Clubs, National Music Teachers Association, 1972-; Faculty, National Guild of Piano Teachers; Director of Music, Durham Academy, 1976-77; Music Specialist, Institute of Arts and Sciences, Music Faculty, New Hampshire Department of Education, 1977-82; Director, Studio of Talent Education, Nashville, Tennessee, 1982-; SAA registered Suzuki piano teacher, 1983-. *Recordings:* Circuit Rider, WRAL, Raleigh, North Carolina, 1968-69; Director, Producer, National Federation of Music Clubs' radio music broadcast, Duke Veterans Administration Medical Center, Durham, NC 1972-76. *Address:* 503 Cunniff Court, Goodlettsville, TN 37072, USA.

HARPER Thomas, b. 1950, Oklahoma, USA. Singer (Tenor). *Education:* Studied in Los Angeles, Kansas City, Paris and Italy. *Career:* Sang in opera at Coburg, 1982-85, Kaiserslautern, 1985-87, in buffo and character roles; Stadttheater Hagen, 1987-, as the Duke of Mantua, Radames, Almaviva, Don Ottavio, Alwa in Lulu and Daniel in Belshazar by David Kirchner; Sang Fritz in Der Ferne Klang by Schreker, 1989; Seattle Opera, 1991, as Mime in Der Ring des Nibelungen; Dortmund Opera, 1991-92, as Mime and in premiere of Sekunden und Jahre des Caspar Hauser, by Reinhard Febel. *Recordings include:* Der Ferne Klang (Marco Polo). *Address:* c/o Seattle Opera Association, PO Box 9248, Seattle, WA 98109, USA.

HARRELL Lynn, b. 30 Jan 1944, New York City, USA. Solo Cellist. m. Linda Blandford, 7 Sept 1976, 1 son, 1 daughter. *Education:* Studies with: Lev Aronson, Dallas; Leonard Rose, Juilliard School; Orlando Cole, Curtis Institute; Master classes, Gregor Piatigorsky, Casals. *Debut:* Dallas Symphony Orchestra, 1957. *Career:* Solo principal cellist, Cleveland Orchestra (conductor, George Szell), 1963-71; Numerous appearances with major orchestras, USA, Europe, Japan, & worldwide recitals, 1971-; Piatigorsky Chair of Cello, University of Southern California, Los Angeles, 1986-92; International Chair of Cello Studies, Royal Academy of Music, London, UK, 1986-92; Artistic Director, Los Angeles Philharmonic Institute, 1988, 1989, 1990, 1991; Music adviser, San Diego Symphony, 1988, 1989; Principal, Royal Academy of Music. *Recordings:* Dvořák Concerto (with Askenazy, Cleveland); Lalo (Chailly, RSO); Shostakovich 1 & Bloch Schelomo (Haitink, Concert); Schumann Concerto (Marriner, Cleveland); Brahms & Beethoven Sonatas (Ashkenazy); Beethoven Trios (Ashkenazy, Perlman); Solo Bach Suites. *Honours:* Merriweather Post Contest, 1960; Piatigorsky Award, 1962; 1st winner (with Murray Perahia), Avery Fisher Prize, 1974. *Hobbies:* Chess; Opera; Fishing. *Current Management:* Media House, 3 Burlington Lane, Chiswick, London W4 2TH, England. *Address:* c/o Royal Academy of Music, Marylebone Road, London NW1 5HT, England.

HARRELL Ray Evans, b. 3 Dec 1941, Ada, Oklahoma, USA. Teacher of Voice and Vocal Performance; Opera Stage Director. m. Dr Valentina Harrell PhD, 1 daughter. *Education:* BM, Voice and Pedagogy, University of Tulsa, 1972; Manhattan School of Music, 1974; Voice-studied with Dame Eva Turner, 1957, Louis Cunningham, 1959-64, Frederick Wilkerson, 1965-70, Daniel Ferro, 1970-85. *Debut:* Alice Tully Hall, New York. *Career:* Soloist in major New York City performance halls; Co-founder of New York Group for Vocal Research, 1975; Director of Singers' Workshop, 1976-79; Director of The Singers' and Composers' Workshop, Manhattan School of Music and Vocal Arts Institute, 1979-86; Teacher of Vocal Anatomy, Manhattan School of Music and The Magic Circle Opera Training Programme, 1984-85; Teacher and Stage Director at the Mannes College of Music, Summer Opera Programme, 1986-. Private teaching at his New York City Vocal Studio, 1975, and also currently developing new works and performance techniques with the Magic Circle Opera Repertory Ensemble, where he is Artistic Director. *Address:* The Magic Circle Opera Repertory Ensemble, 235 West 102nd Street, Suite 7-1, New York, NY 10025, USA.

HARRHY Eiddwen, b. 14 April 1949, Trowbridge, Wiltshire, England. Singer (Soprano). *Education:* Studied at the Royal Manchester College of Music and in London and Paris. *Career:* Sang in concert at Welsh Eisteddfods and with the Royal Liverpool Philharmonic; Queen Elizabeth Hall 1974, in Rinaldo; Alcina with the Handel Opera Society at Sadler's Wells; Covent Garden debut 1974; English National Opera from 1977, debut as Adele in Le Comte Ory; Kent Opera as Pamina and the title role in Iphigénie en Tauride; Glyndebourne Touring Opera as Donna Anna; Glyndebourne debut 1979, as Diana in La Fedeltà Premiata; Sang Madama Butterfly at the London Coliseum 1984 and Berg's Marie with Welsh National Opera 1986; Other roles include Dido in Les Troyens (concert performance conducted by Roger Norrington); Sang Mercian in the premiere of David Blake's The Plumber's Gift, ENO, 1989; Hecuba in a new production of King Priam for Opera North, 1991; Sang Kabanicha in Katya Kabanova for Glyndebourne Tour, 1992; Concert appearances include Promenade Concerts London 1989, in Vivaldi's Gloria and Bach's Magnificat, conducted by Richard Hickox. *Recordings include:* Isabelle in Rossini's L'Assedio di Corinto and A Hundred Years of Italian Opera, 1810-20, (Opera Rara). *Address:* c/o Rawstron Still Management Ltd, 113 Church Road, London SE19 2PR.

HARRHY Paul, b. 6 Sept 1957, Port Talbot, Wales. Singer (Tenor). *Education:* Studied at Guildhall School of Music and Drama. *Debut:* Sang Alfredo with Opera 80, returning as Tom Rakewell. Career: English National Opera, 1986-, as High Priest in Akhnaten, Valzacchi in Der Rosenkavalier, Truffaldino in Love for Three Oranges and Janek in The Makropoulos Case; Appearances with Scottish Opera as Pedrillo, Mime, the Novice in Billy Budd and Remendado in Carmen; Opera North as Tom Rakewell and Truffaldino (also televised); Engagements with Glyndebourne Festival and Touring Opera, The Chelsea Opera Group, Opera Factory and Musica nel Chiostro in Batignano; Almeida Festival, 1988, 1989, 1990, in Wolpe's Anna Blume and Street Music, and in premieres of John Casken's Golem and Gerald Barry's Intelligence Park; Other festivals in Strasbourg, Frankfurt (Les Malheurs d'Orphée by Milhaud), Venice, South Bank, Bath, Cheltenham, Florence and Henry Wood Promenade Concerts, Royal Albert Hall; Wexford Festival, 1989, in Der Templer und die Judin by Marschner and as Marzio in Mozart's Mitridate (also at Queen Elizabeth Hall); Sang Mime and Loge with City of Birmingham Touring Opera, 1990-91; Pedrillo in Die Entführung for Opera 80 at Garsington Manor, 1991, also 1993 Nenus in Haydn's L'Infedelta; Appeared with New Israeli Opera as Truffaldino in Love for Three Oranges, 1992, returning to sing the role in 1995; Appeared as Pong in Turandot with Royal Opera House at Wembley Arena; Appeared in European premiere of Sondheim's Assassins at Donmar Warehouse, as Giuseppe Zangara; Opera Factory appearances have included Pylades in Iphigenias and Lucano in Poppea; Goro in Madame

Butterfly for Opera Forum, Netherlands, 1993. *Recordings:* Casken's Golem; Stravinsky's Renard and Milhaud's Les Malheurs d'Orphée with Matrix Ensemble. *Honours include:* BP Opera and Boise Foundation Scholarships to Guildhall School. *Address:* c/o Atholl Still Ltd, Greystoke House, 80-86 Westow Street, London, SE19 3AF, England.

HARRIES Clive, b. 5 June 1951, Clivedon, England. Conductor; Harpsichordist; Organist; Counter-Tenor. m. Catherine Tyzack, 22 Oct 1982, 4 sons. *Education:* MA, Open Choral Scholar, Kings College, Cambridge University, 1973; Fellow, Royal College of Organists; Church Music/Choir Training Diploma; LRAM; ARCM. *Career:* Conductor, Kings Consort of Voices (Choir and Orchestra), Conductor, Choral Scholars from Kings, 1970-73; Assistant Director, Music, Millfield, 1973-77; Conductor, Clive Harries Singers and Orchestra, 1974-77; Director of Music, Ipswich School, 1977-78; Director of Music, Cranborne Chase, 1978-82; Organist, Master of Choristers, Christchurch Priory, 1980-83; Artistic Director, Finance Director, Christchurch International Summer Festival, 1981-83; Conductor, Christchurch Festival Orchestra, 1981-83; Examiner, Associated Board, Royal Schools of Music, 1981-; Director, Musica Reservata Singers, 1982-; Director of Music, Polam Hall, 1983-85; Conductor, York Early Music Choir and English Renaissance Orchestra, 1986-; Harpsichordist, The Heritage Orchestra, 1987-; Adjudicator-member, British Federation of Music Festivals, 1971-; Musical Director of English Renaissance Orchestra & York Early Music Choir. *Recordings:* 35 with Kings College, Cambridge, for record, radio and TV; with Bach Choir, Vienna Concentus Musicus, Britten, Solo Organ Recording from Christchurch. *Honours:* Freedom of the City of London, 1989. *Membership:* Fellowship of Royal Society of Arts, 1991-. *Hobbies:* Rotary; Squash; Golf; Country Pursuits. *Current Management:* Direct Booking. *Address:* Hill Top House, Birkby, Northallerton, North Yorkshire, DL7 0EF, England.

HARRIES Kathryn, b. 15 Feb 1951, Hampton Court, Middlesex, England. Singer (Soprano). *Education:* Studied at the Royal Academy of Music with Constance Shacklock. *Career:* Presented BBC Television series Music Time; Festival Hall, London, debut 1977: concert repertoire ranges from Monteverdi to the 20th Century; Operatic debut with the Welsh National Opera 1982, as Leonore: returned as Sieglinde and Gutrune (also at Covent Garden, 1986), Adalgisa, and the Composer in Ariadne auf Naxos; English National Opera as Eva, Female Chorus in The Rape of Lucretia, Irene (Rienzi) and Donna Anna in The Stone Guest by Darghomyzhsky; Appearances with Scottish Opera as Leonore, the title role in the premiere of Hedda Gabler by Edward Harper, and Senta; Metropolitan Opera 1986, as Kundry in Parsifal: returned 1989, as Gutrune in a new production of Götterdämmerung; Sang Dido in the first complete peformance of Les Troyens in France, Lyon 1987, Senta for Paris Opéra, Sieglinde in Nice and Paris and Leonore in Buenos Aires; Covent Garden debut 1989, in the British premiere of Un Re in Ascolto by Berio; returned 1991 as Gutrune in a new production of Göttdämmerung; Dido in Les Troyens for Scottish opera, 1990, also at Covent Garden; season 1990-91 with Katya Kabanova at ENO, Bartók's Judith for Scottish Opera, Dukas' Ariane, Netherlands Opera, Massenet's Cléopâtre in St Etienne and Giulietta in Les Contes d'Hoffmann at the Châtelet in Paris; Season 1992 with the Berlioz Dido in Brussels and Carmen at Orange. *Address:* c/o Ingpen & Williams Ltd, 14 Kensington Court, London W8 5DN, England.

HARRIS Alice Eaton, b. 5 Aug 1924, Milwaukee, Wisconsin, USA. Pianist; Harpsichordist; Clavichordist; Forte Pianist; Educator. m. David H Harris, 18 June 1947, 1 daughter. *Education:* Vassar College 1940-41; BA Barnard College (Columbia University) 1944; As student of Mikhail Sheyne received Professional Artist's Diploma from Westchester Conservatory of Music; Graduate Studies at SUNY, Purchase, New York with Anthony Newman; also studied with Malcolm Bilson. *Debut:* Solo Piano Recital, New York Times Hall, 1945.

Career: Solo Piano Recitals, Carnegie Recital Hall and Town Hall, New York City; Solo Harpsichordist with Westchester Chamber Music Society; and Westchester Symphony Orchestra; Founder/Director of Scarsdale Baroque Ensemble; Inaugural Recital Fortepiano, University of California, Riverside; Fortepiano Recitals, White Plains, New York, 1979 and 1983; Many lecture-recitals and workshops on early keyboard instruments in New York State and California; Faculty Member, Westchester Conservatory of Music 1944-. *Address:* 58 Brite Avenue, Scarsdale, NY 10583, USA.

HARRIS Donald, b. 7 Apr 1931, St Paul, Minnesota, USA. Composer; Administrator; Musicologist; Dean. m. Marilyn Hackett, 29 Jan 1983, 2 sons, from previous marriage. *Education:* BMus, 1952, MMus, 1954, University of Michigan; Studied with Paul Wilkinson, St Paul, Minnesota, Ross Lee Finney, University of Michigan, Nadia Boulanger, Max Deutsch and André Jolivet in Paris, France. *Career:* Dean, Hartt School of Music, University of Hartford; Incidental Music, Poet with the Blue Guitar, Connecticut Public Radio, 1979; Incidental Music, Fires, Connecticut Public radio, 1983. *Compositions:* Numerous, including: Piano Sonata; Violin Fantasy; Symphony in Two Movements; On Variations; For the Night to Wear; Balladen; Little Mermaid, opera; String Quartet; Ludus I; Ludus II; Of Hartford in a Purple Light (Wallace Stevens); Les Mains (Marguerite Yourcenar). *Recordings:* CRI, Delos Records, Golden Crest. *Publications:* Co-Editor, Correspondence between Alban Berg and Arnold Schoenberg, New York; Music: Editions Jobert, Paris, France; Theodore Presser, Bryn Mawr, Pennsylvania. *Contributor to:* Journal of the Arnold Schoenberg Institute; Perspective of New Music; Newsletter, International Alban Berg Society; Music Journal; Alban Berg Studien, Universal Edition. *Address:* c/o ASCAP, ASCAP Building, One Lincoln Plaza, New York, NY 10023, USA.

HARRIS Hilda, b. 1930, Warrenton, North Carolina, USA. Singer (Mezzo-soprano). *Education:* Studied at North Carolina State University and in New York. *Career:* Sang in musicals on Broadway; Made opera debut at St Gallen, Switzerland, 1971, as Carmen; Returned to New York, 1973, as Nicklause in Les contes d'Hoffmann at City Opera and in Virgil Thomson's Four Saints in Three Acts (as St Theresa) at the Metropolitan; Further roles at the Met have included the Child in L'Enfant et les Sortileges, Cherubino, Hansel, Stephano in Romeo et Juliette and parts in Lulu; Sang Nicklausse at Seattle, 1990, Cherubino at the 1990 Spoleto Festival; Frequent concert appearances. *Address:* c/o Metropolitan Opera, Lincoln Center, New York, NY 10023, USA.

HARRIS Keith David, b. 26 Jan 1949, Sydney, Australia. Mandolinist. *Education:* BA, Sydney University, 1975; Artistic Diploma/Concert Diploma; State Music Hochschule, Rhineland/Wuppertal, Federal Republic of Germany. *Career:* Solo recitals in London, Tokyo, Australia, USA and throughout Europe. Recent important music festivals with major orchestras: Carinthian Summer, Bratislava Music Festival, Festival of Flanders. *Recordings:* for Hyperion (London), Plucked String (USA), Opus (Czechoslovakia). *Publication:* Translated: Wölki, History of the Mandolin, published 1984. *Honours:* International Fellow of the Music Board of the Australia Council, 1980, 1981, 1982. *Memberships:* Armin Kaufmann Society (Vienna); Music Director of German Federation of Plucked Instruments (BDZ) in Hessen. *Hobbies:* Squash; Jogging; Chess; Reading; Cooking. *Address:* c/o 17 Thomas Street, Hurstville 2220, Australia.

HARRIS Matthew, b. 18 Feb 1956, North Tarrytown, New York, USA. Composer. m. 4 Dec 1988. *Education:* New England Conservatory, with Donald Martino, 1974-75; Fontainebleau School, with Nadia Boulanger, France, 1976; BM, 1978, MM, 1979, DMA, 1982, Juilliard School of Music; Harvard Graduate School, 1985-86. *Career:* Major performances: New York New Music Ensemble, 1983; Houston Symphony, 1986; Minnesota Orchestra, 1987; League/ISCM, New York,

1987; Florida Symphony Orchestra, 1988; Alea III, Boston, 1988; Assistant Professor, Fordham University, 1982-84; Instructor, Kingsborough College, City University of New York, 1985; Music Editor, Carl Fischer Inc, 1987-. *Compositions:* Music After Rimbaud; Songs of the Night, soprano, orchestra; Ancient Greek Melodies, orchestra; As You Choose, monodrama; Starry Night, piano trio; Invitation of the Waltz, string quartet; String Quartet No 7. *Recording:* Music After Rimbaud, Opus One Commissions: Casa Verde Trio, 1984; Haydn-Mozart Orchestra, 1985; Scott Stevens: Leigh Howard Stevens, marimbist, 1986; Minnesota Composers Forum: Omega String Quartet, 1988; The Schubert Club: Anthony Ross, cellist, 1988. *Memberships:* Broadcast Music Inc; Composers Forum; American Music Center; Board Member, League-International Society for Contemporary Music. *Address:* American Composers Edition, 170 W 74th Street, New York, NY 10023, USA.

HARRIS Paul David, b. 7 Jan 1957, London, England. Musician. *Education:* Royal Academy of Music, 1974-78; LRAM; GRSM; ARCM; MTC, London University, 1978. *Career:* Administrative Director, Kaleidoscope Chamber Orchestra, 1978-80; Teacher, Harrow School, 1979-82; Teacher, Perse School for Girls, Cambridge, 1982; Head of Woodwind and Brass, Stowe School, 1983-; Examiner for Associated Board; Adjudicator; Director, Stowe Woodwind Workshop; Performances around Britain; Conductor. *Compositions:* Sonatina for Clarinet; Adagio for Clarinet and Piano; Concerto for 2 Oboes and 2 Clarinets; Sonatina for Piano; Noel, A Christmas Cantata; Visions for Clarinet; The Meal, an opera; Sonatina for cor anglais; Divertimento for Wind Quintet; Six Miniatures for Trumpet and Piano; Five Bagatelles for Horn and Piano; Summer Sketches for Clarinet and Piano; Funfare for Horn and Piano; Suite in five for Clarinet and Piano; Clowns for Flute and Piano; 80 Graded Studies for Flute, Clarinet, Oboe and Saxophone; Chalumeau Sonatina for Clarinet; The Second Book of Clarinet Solos; Rainbow for Piano; 7 Dances for Saxophone and Piano; 6 Clerihew Songs for Voice, Clarinet and Piano. *Publications:* Cambridge Clarinet Tutor, 1982; The Improve Your Sight-Reading Series, 1987; Essential Clarinet Technique, 1988; Making the Grade, 1991; Music Through Time, 1992. *Hobbies:* Antique furniture; Haute cuisine; Shakespeare. *Address:* 5 Fox Way, Buckingham, Buckinghamshire MK18 7EH, England.

HARRIS Richard Leigh, b. 4 Jan 1956, Bristol, England. Harpsichordist; Composer; Lecturer; Critic; Writer. *Education:* Birmingham School of Music, 1975-78; GBSM; University of Reading, 1978-79; PG Cert Ed, 1986-89-; MMus, 1989; Studied harpsichord with Robert Woolley and Virginia Black; Masterclasses with George Malcolm, Kenneth Gilbert, Jill Severs and Davitt Moroney. *Career:* Head of Music, Bicester School, Oxon, 1979-80; Associate Lecturer in Music, Oxford Polytechnic, 1984-88; Visiting Tutor, Birmingham Conservatoire, 1990; Radio includes: Satiés Vexations on Today Programme, 1977; BBC R 4 John Wain's Oxford, Pride of Place, 1984; BBC R Oxford: Contemporary British Harpsichord Music, 1987 & 1990; Visiting Tutor in Composition, Birmingham Conservatoire, 1991-93. *Compositions include:* Skullscape I for soprano and tape; Baroque Flickers, piccolo, oboe and clarinet; Still Life, solo guitar; Cantata: The Return of Spring; O Magnum Mysterium, SSA Chorus; Aria for Orpheus, oboe and tape; Magnificat and Nunc Dimittis, SATB and Organ; Three Celtic Folksongs, ensemble; Epiphany Preludes, 1992, for bass clarinet, marima & cello; String Quartet No 2 (Paraboolya I), 1993. *Recordings:* Richard Leigh Harris plays Bach, Couperin, Scarlatti and Soler (RLH8) (digital cassette). *Address:* 1 Ferry Road, New Marston, Oxford OX3 0ET, England.

HARRIS Robert A, b. 8 May 1928, Rich Hill, Missouri, USA. Musician. *Education:* BMus, 1950; MS in ED, 1953; Pittsburg, Kansas State College; 7 years Advanced Study with Madame Rosina Lhevinne; Aspen Music School, 1958; 1965-70. *Career:* Private Piano Instructor 1949-; College Teacher for over 20 years; Musical

Consultant to KXMS, the classical music voice of MSSC; Missouri Southern State College 1971-; Organist, First United Methodist Church, Carthage 1955-; Adjudicator, National Piano Guild. *Memberships:* National Certification - Piano - Music Teachers' National Association; Certified Director of Music - Missouri West Conference, United Methodist Church. *Address:* 1344 S Main Street, Carthage, Missouri 64836, USA.

HARRIS William Lewarne Capes, b. 23 May 1929, Birkenhead, England. Composer; Pianist; Conductor. m. Josephine Patricia McGovern, 25 Nov 1955, divorced. 2 sons, 1 daughter. *Education:* Royal College of Music, 1950-52, Composition with Patrick Hadley and Herbert Howells; Piano with Norman Greenwood. *Debut:* Broadcast, 1953. *Career:* Broadcast of Suite for Viola and Piano, BBC 3rd Programme, 1953; Recital, Leighton House, 1961; Recital of Music, Wigmore Hall, 1973; Work with ILEA, Pianist and Teacher; Performances of chamber opera, The Woman on the Hill, 1980, at the Golden Lane Theatre, London. *Compositions:* Suite for Viola and Piano; Variations on a Cornish Tune for Brass Trio; Operas: The Countess Cathleen; The Woman on the Hill; Orchestral: The Dance of Life; A Celtic Triptych; Ow Bro (My Country); 2 Song Cycles; Bassoon Sonatina; Chansons de Baudelaire Overture: Rex Quondam, First performed Sept 1989; Two chorals from The Sunken City for Brass Quintet; The Sunken City, Opera in Three Acts, Prologue and Epilogue, 1992. *Recordings:* As conductor and pianist on Music by Inglis Gundry. *Address:* 26 Park Court, Park Hall Road, London SE21 8DZ, England.

HARRISON Jonty, b. 27 Apr 1952, Scunthorpe, England. Composer; Lecturer. m. Alison Warne, 28 May 1985. *Education:* BA, DPhil, University of York, 1970-76; British Youth Symphony Orchestra, National Youth Orchestra of Great Britain; Studied composition with Bernard Rands. *Career:* National Theatre, London; Visiting Composer, University of East Anglia Recording and Electronic Music Studio, 1978; Visiting Lecturer, The City University, London, 1978-80; Lecturer in Music, Director of Electro-Acoustic Music Studio, University of Birmingham, 1980-; Hungarian Radio, 1982; IRCAM, 1985; Groupe De Recherches Musicales, Paris, 1986; Groupe De Musique Experimentale De Bourges, 1987. *Compositions:* Rosaces 2; Rosaces 3; Rosaces 4; EQ; Lunga; Q; Lament (with Douglas Doherty); Pair/Impair; Fair Tune; A Vent; Aurora; SQ, Luftfut, Klang, Manodies, Hammer and Tongs; Sons transmutants/sans transmutant; Aria; Ripieno; Concertino. Recorded: Klang; Sons Transmutants/Sans Transmutant; EQ. *Contributions to:* Electro-Acoustic Music; Music and Letters; The Musical Times; Lien (Musiques Et Recherches - Belgium); Upbeat to the Tate 88 - Liverpool (Programme Book). *Hobbies:* Travel; Reading; Food and drink; Conducting. *Address:* 64 Rotton Park Road, Edgbaston, Birmingham, B16 0LH, England.

HARRISON Lou, b. 14 May 1917, Portland, Oregon, USA. Composer. *Education:* Studied with Henry Cowell, San Francisco, 1934-35, Arnold Schoenberg, Los Angeles, 1941, 1942; Grant, American Academy and Institute of Arts and Letters, 1947. *Career:* Positions as: Florist; Record Clerk; Poet; Dancer; Dance Critic; Music Copyist; Playright; Instrument Builder; Teacher, Portland, Oregon, Black Mountain College; Animal Hospital Worker, 1957-60; Senior Scholar, East-West Centre, University of Hawaii, 1963; Teacher, various Universities Including: Stanford, 1974, San Jose State, 1974-82, Centre for World Music, Berkeley, 1975, Southern California, 1977, Mills College, 1980-82; Milhaud Chair, Mills College, until his retirement, 1985. *Compositions:* Works include: Javanese Gamelan; American Gamelan; Cirebon Gamelan; European Orchestral; Sudanese Gamelan Degung; Ensemble; Solo Instrumental Works; Solo Vocal Works; Orchestrations; Choral; and Stage Works; Film Scores etc; Co-Designer with William Colvig of 2 Javanese Gamelan Orchestras. *Recordings:* Numerous including; Double Concerto; Gending Pak Cokro; Fugue for Percussion; Concerto for Violin and Percussion Orchestra; Concerto for Organ and Percussion

Orchestra; String Trio; Serenade for Guitar. *Publications include:* About Carl Ruggles, 1946; Lou Harrison's Music Primer, 1969; 19 Items, 1970; Articles in professional journals. *Honours include:* Fromm Award, 1955; Rockefeller Grant, Recipient, numerous other honours and awards. *Memberships:* American Institute of Arts & Letters. *Address:* 7121 Viewpoint Road, Aptos, CA 95003, USA.

HARRISON Margaret Maud, b. 20 Apr 1899, Chatham, England. Violinist. *Education:* Private Tutors and Kensington High School; Royal College of Music; Guildhall and Hochschule fur Musik, Berlin and St Petersburg Conservatory. *Debut:* December 1918, Wigmore Hall. *Career:* Surviving member of an exceptionally musical family which included Beatrice Harrison cellist and May Harrison violinist; Played the Bach No 1 Concerto at the Promenade Concerts in 1925; Toured extensively in Europe and America; Taught at Royal College of Music in 1945. *Recordings:* Aus der Heimat; Southland Sketches. *Hobbies:* Dog-breeding - leading breeder of Irish Wolfhounds. *Address:* Hollesley Farm, Smallfield, Nr Horley, Surrey.

HARRISON Sally, b. 1965, England. Singer (Soprano). *Education:* Studied at Oxford and Royal Northern College of Music; Further study with Ava June. *Career:* Sang Manon and Gilda with Royal Northern College of Music, 1987-88; Season 1988-89 as Musetta in Singapore, Handel's Morgana at Royal Northern College of Music and Amour in Rameau's Pygmalion for the English Bach Festival at Elizabeth Hall; Season 1989-90 with Scottish Opera as Polly in The Threepenny Opera, Minette in Henze's English Cat at Guttersloh and Berlin, repeated at Montepulciano Festival and for BBC, and Messiah with Bournemouth Sinfonietta; English National Opera debut, 1991, as Barbarina in Le nozze di Figaro; Sang Handel's Galatea with the English Bach Festival at Elizabeth Hall, 1992; Despina, with Scottish Opera and Poppe in Handel's Agrippina at the 1992 Buxton Festival; Other concert repertoire includes Elgar's The Kingdom, Henze's Being Beauteous (Barbican Hall debut, 1990) and works with the Hague Philharmonic and Ensemble Modern of Frankfurt; Television appearance in The English Cat, for Germany TV. *Honours include:* Peter Moores Foundation Scholarship. *Address:* c/o English National Opera, St Martin's Lane, London WC2, England.

HARSHAW Margaret, b. 12 May 1909, Philadelphia, Pennsylnania, USA. Singer (Soprano); Teacher. *Education:* Studied at the Curtis Institute, then the Juilliard School New York with Anna Schoen-Rene. *Career:* Sang first with various opera companies in Philadelphia; Steel Peer Grand Opera in New York, 1934; Metropolitan Opera from 1942-64 as Second Norn in Götterdämmerung (debut), Azucena, Mistress Quickly, Amneris, Isolde, Kundry, Santuzza, Ortrud, Senta and Brünnhilde; Paris Opéra 1948, as Dalila, Amneris and Brangaene; Covent Garden 1953-56, as Brünnhilde; Glyndebourne Festival 1954, Donna Anna; Teacher at Indiana University School of Music, Bloomington, from 1962: sang Brünnhilde there 1970. *Recordings:* Duets with Zinka Milanov and Eleanor Steber; Private recordings from the Metropolitan Opera. 21.

HART William Sebastian, b. 30 Oct. 1920, Baltimore, Maryland, USA. Symphony Orchestra Conductor. m. Regina Margaret Litsch, 10 Apr. 1950. *Education:* Graduate cum laude, Peabody Conservatory of Music, Baltimore, 1939; BA Political Science, Johns Hopkins University, 1940; PhD Psychology, Golden State University, 1956; Advanced studies in conducting with Franz Bornschein, Stanley Chapple, Felix Robert Mendelssohn. *Career:* Timpanist, Baltimore Symphony Orchestra, 20 years; Teacher, Peabody Conservatory of Music; Radio, then TV Conductor, Commentator, Concert Hall, Maryland and 13 other states, 1939-69; Founder, Conductor, Gettysburg Symphony Orchestra, 1958-; Appeared as Conductor, Royal Philharmonic Orchestra, 1965, 1969, 1977, 1983; Conductor, National Symphony Orchestra, Washington, 1969,

London Philharmonic Orchestra, England, 1983, London Mozart Players, 1983. *Composition:* Timpani duet. *Recordings:* Dominion Records: Gettysburg Symphony Orchestra; Concerto 1 piano, F. Chopin; Concerto for piano 1, Mendelssohn; Rienzi Overture, Wagner/ Cinderella Fantasy, Coates; Masquerade Suite, Khachaturian; Operatic Arias. *Contributor To:* Baltimore newspapers; Musical journals. *Current Management:* John Higham International Artists Ltd, 16 Lauriston Road, London, SW19 4TQ. *Address:* 1800 Cromwell Bridge Road, Baltimore, MD 21234, USA.

HARTH Sidney, b. 5 Oct. 1929, Cleveland, Ohio, USA. Violinist; Conductor; Professor. m. Teresa Testa Harth. *Education:* Cleveland Institute of Music, MB, 1947; Pupil of Joseph Fuchs and Georges Enesco. *Career:* Debut, Carnegie Hall, New York, 1949; Concertmaster and Assistant Conductor, Louisville Orchestra, 1953-58; Faculty member, University of Louisville; Concertmaster, Chicago Symphony Orchestra, 1959-62; Faculty member, De Paul University; Concertmaster, Casals Festival Orchestra, San Juan, 1959-65, 1972; Professor of Music and Chairman of the Music Department, Carnegie-Mellon University, Pittsburgh, 1963-73; Concertmaster and Associate Conductor, Los Angeles Philharmonic Orchestra, 1973-79; Music Director, Puerto Rico Symphony Orchestra, 1977-79; Interim Conductor, New York Philharmonic Orchestra, 1980; Orchestral Director, Mannes College of Music, New York, 1981- ; Professor of Violin, State University of New York, Stony Brook, 1981-. *Recordings:* Various discs. *Address:* c/o Mannes College of Music, 150 West 85th Street, New York, NY 10024, USA.

HARTINGER Albert F, b. 13 July 1946, Seekirchen, Salzburg, Austria. Singer (baritone). m. Heather G Woodall, 3 children. *Education:* Arbitur; Doctor (Education and Psychology); Voice and Opera, Mozarteum, Salzburg; Graduate, authentic interpretation of baroque music, music and education. *Career:* Concerts, Austria, Germany, Italy; TV and Radio recordings, oratorios, cantatas, and Lieder, Austria and Germany; Member, Salzburg Baroque Ensemble; Art Director, Salzburger Bach-Gesellschaft; Professor for Voice, Mozarteum, Salzburg. *Honour:* Winner, Mozart Competition, Mozarteum, 1970. *Hobbies:* Mountaineering; kiing; Model railways. *Address:* Molckhofgasse 3a, A-5020 Salzburg, Austria.

HARTKE Stephen Paul, b. 6 July 1952, New Jersey, USA. Composer. m. Lisa Stidham, 12 Sept. 1981. *Education:* BA, magna cum laude, Yale University, 1973; MA, University of Pennsylvania, 1976; PhD, University of California at Santa Barbara, 1982; Composition study with James Drew, George Rochberg and Edward Applebaum. *Career:* Fulbright Professor of Composition, University of Sao Paulo, Brazil, 1984-85; Associate Professor of Compositions, University of Southern California, 1987-; Composer-in-Residence, Los Angeles Chamber Orchestra, 1988-1992. *Compositions:* Alvorada; Iglesia Abandonada; The King of The Sun; Maltese Cat Blues; Oh Them Rats Is Mean in my Kitchen; Pacific Rim; Sonata Variations; Songs for an Uncertain Age; Caoine; Night Rubrics; Post-Modern Homages; Symphony No.2; Four Madrigals on Old Portuguese Texts; Wir Küssen Ihnen tausendmal die Hände; Violin Concerto. *Recordings:* Caoine and Iglesia Abandonada; Oh Them Rats Is Mean In My Kitchen; Wir Küssen Ihnen tausendmal die Hände. *Contributions to:* Minnesota Composers Forum Newsletter, 1988; Caderno de Musica, 1985. *Hobbies:* Walking; Reading; Day-dreaming. *Address:* School of Music, University of Southern California, Los Angeles, California 90089, USA.

HARTMAN Vernon, b. 12 July 1952, Dallas, Texas, USA. Singer (Baritone). *Education:* Studied at West Texas State University and in Philadelphia. *Debut:* Philadelphia, as Masetto, 1977. *Career:* Sang with New York City Opera from 1977 and made guest appearances at Cincinnati, San Antonio and Seattle; Spoleto Festival, 1977-78, as Guglielmo; Metropolitan Opera, 1983-, as Rossini's Figaro, Count Almaviva, Schaunard and

Guglielmo; Other roles have included Rigoletto, Malatesta, Silvio, Marcello, Frank in Die Tote Stadt and Falke in Fledermaus; Sang Almaviva and Marcello at Milwaukee, 1991; *Address:* c/o Metropolitan Opera, Lincoln Center, New York, NY 10023, USA.

HARTMANN Donald Conrad, b. 28 Mar. 1954, Greensboro, USA. Singer; Voice Instructor; Opera Director. *Education:* BM, University of North Carolina, Greensboro, 1977; MM, 1982; American Institute of Musical Studies, Graz, Austria, 1979; Hochschule für Musik, Dortmund, West Germany, 1980. *Debut:* Stadttheater Regensburg. *Career:* Stadttheater Regensburg, Vereinigte Städtische Buhnen Krefeld-Mönchen-Gladbach; Virginia Opera Association; Greensboro Opera Company; Eastern Music Festival; Peabody Conservatory; Toledo Choral Society; Bowling Green State University Opera Theatre; Roles include: Marcello, Guglielmo, Dr Bartolo, Mephistopheles, Pistol, Second Prisoner; Verdi Requiem; Assistant Professor of Music, Eastern Michigan University. *Contribution to:* Opera Roles: Don Giovanni, Dandini. *Honours:* USAO Regents Award for Superior Teaching, 1986; Finalist: San Antonio Opera Guild Talent Search, 1990. *Memberships:* National Association of Teachers of Singing; National Opera Association; Board of Directors, National Opera Association. *Address:* 2215 S Huron Parkway, Apt. No. 4, Ann Arbor, Michigan 48104, USA.

HARTWIG Hildegard, b. 1951, Munich, Germany. Singer (Mezzo- soprano). m. Diether Jacob. *Education:* Studied in Munich and at Cologne Opera Studio. *Career:* Sang minor roles at Cologne, then engaged at Bonn, 1976-81, Deutsche Oper am Rhein, 1980-86, notably in the 1985 premiere of Goehr's Behold the Sun; Schwetzingen Festival, 1986, as Lotte in premiere of Bose's Die Leiden des Jungen Werthers; Guest engagements at Hamburg, 1982, and Copenhagen, 1989, as Bartok's Judith; Other roles include Dorabella, Magdalena, Octavian, Lola, the Countess Geschwitz in Lulu and Meroe in Schoeck's Penthesilea; Many concert appearances. *Recordings include:* Beethoven's Ninth, conducted by Gunter Wand.

HARVEY Jean, b. 2 Jan 1932, Glasgow, Scotland. Professor of Music; Concert Pianist; Violinist. *Education:* Studied at Royal Academy of Music, London with Frederick Grinke and Harold Craxton; Child Prodigy with Moisewitsch, Myra Hess and Albert Sammons. *Debut:* 7 years old with Scottish National Orchestra. *Career:* Broadcasts regularly as violinist and pianist after giving a Promenade Concert with a Piano and Violin Concerto; Chief Examiner to Associated Board of the Royal Schools of Music, London; Head of String Faculty & Chamber Music, 1991, at RAM. *Honours:* Fellow of Royal Academy of Music; Silver Medal, Worshipful Company of Musicians. *Memberships:* Incorporated Society of Musicians; European String Teachers' Association; IPTEC. *Address:* Kittswood, Three Gates Lane, Haslemere, Surrey, England.

HARVEY Jonathan Dean, b. 3 May 1939, Sutton Coldfield, England. Composer; Professor of Music. m. Rosaleen Marie Barry, 1960. 1 son, 1 daughter. *Education:* St Michael's College, Tenbury; Repton; MA, DMus, St John's College, Cambridge; PhD, Glasgow University. *Career:* Lecturer, Southampton University, 1964-77; Reader 1977-80, Professor of Music 1980-, Sussex University; Harkness Fellow, Princeton University, 1969-70; Works performed at many festivals and international centres. *Compositions:* Persephone Dream for orchestra, 1972; Inner Light (trilogy) for performers and tape, 1973-77; Smiling Immortal, for chamber orchestra, 1977; String Quartet, 1977; Magnificat and Nunc Dimittis, for choir and organ, 1978; Album, for wind quintet, 1978; Hymn, for choir and orchestra, 1979; Be(com)ing for clarinet and piano, 1979; Concelebration, instrumental 1979, rev, 1981; Mortuos Plango, Vivos Voco, for tape, 1980; Passion and Resurrection, church opera, 1981; Resurrection, for double chorus and organ, 1981; Bhakti, for 15 instruments and tape, 1982; Easter Orisons, for chamber orchestra, 1983; The Path of Devotion, for choir

and orchestra, 1983; Nachtlied, for soprano, piano and tape, 1984; Gong-Ring, for ensemble with electronics, 1984; Song Offerings, for soprano and players, 1985; Madonna of Winter and Spring, for orchestra, synthesizers and electronics, 1986; Lightness and Weight, for tuba and orchestra, 1986; Forms of Emptiness, for choir, 1986; Tendril, for ensemble, 1987; Timepieces, for orchestra, 1987; From Silence for soprano, instrumentalist and tape, 1988; Valley of Aosta for 13 players, 1988; String Quartet no 2, 1989; Ritual Melodies for tape, 1989; Cello Concerto, 1990; Serenade for 10 Wind, 1991; Inquest of Love, opera, 1992; Lotuses, for flute quartet; Scena, for violin and ensemble; One Evening for voices, instruments and electronics. *Recordings:* Bhakti NMCD001, Mortuos Plango, Vivos Voco WER2025-2, Song Offerings NI5167, Valley of Aosta RIC073052; Cello Concerto, KTC 1148; From Silence, BCD 9031. *Publication:* The Music of Stockhausen, 1975; numerous articles. *Honour:* Hon. Doctor of Music, Southampton, 1991. *Membership:* Academia Europaea, 1990; The Britten Award for Composition, 1993. *Hobbies:* Tennis; Walking; Meditation. *Address:* 35 Houndean Rise, Lewes, Sussex BN7 1EQ, England.

HARVEY Keith, b. 1950, England. Cellist. *Education:* Studied with Douglas Cameron at Royal Academy of Music and with Gregor Piatigorsky in Los Angeles. *Career:* Formerly youngest ever principal cellist of London Philharmonic Orchestra, then principal of English Chamber Orchestra; Plays cello by Montagnana of 1733, formerly belonging to Bernard Romberg; Founder member of Gabrieli Ensemble, with chamber music performances in UK and abroad; Co-founded the Gabrieli Quartet, 1967, and toured with them to Europe, North America, Far East and Australia; Festival engagements in UK, including Aldeburgh, City of London and Cheltenham; Concerts every season in London, participation in Barbican Centre's Mostly Mozart Festival; Resident Artist at University of Essex, 1991-; Has co-premiered works by William Alwyn, Britten, Alan Bush, Daniel Jones and Gordon Crosse, 2nd Quartets of Nicholas Maw and Panufnik (1983, 1980) and 3rd Quartet of John McCabe (1979); UK premiere of the Piano Quintet by Sibelius, 1990. *Recordings include:* 50 CDs including early pieces by Britten, Dohnanyi's Piano Quintet with Wolfgang Manz, Walton's Quartets and the Sibelius Quartet and Quintet, with Anthony Goldstone. *Honours include:* Emmy Award for solo playing in films. *Address:* c/o Anglo Swiss Ltd, 3 Primrose Mews, 1s Sharpleshall Street, London NW1 8YW, England.

HARVEY Peter, b. 1958, England. Singer (Baritone). *Education:* Choral Scholar at Magdalen College Oxford, Guildhall School of Music. *Career:* Concert appearances with the St James Baroque Players in Telemann's St Matthew Passion at Aldeburgh and London; Visit to Lisbon with The Sixteen; Concerts of Monteverdi and Purcell in Poland and the Flanders Festival with London Baroque; Sang with Joshua Rifkin and the Bach Ensemble at St James Piccadilly, 1990; Engagements with La Chapelle Royale and Collegium Vocale in Belgium, France and Spain; Bach Cantatas for French television and tour of Messiah with Le Concert Spirituel; Other repertoire includes the War Requiem, Elijah and the Five Mystical Songs of Vaughan Williams; St John in The Cry of the Ikon by John Tavener (also televised); Bach's St John Passion (Westminster Abbey) and Christmas Oratorio; Schubert's E flat Mass; Visited Brazil 1989 with The Sixteen for Messiah; Belgium 1991 in Teixeira's Te Deum, conducted by Harry Christophers. *Recordings:* Dido and Aeneas; Sacred music by CPE Bach with La Chapelle Royale (Virgin Classics); Gilles Requiem with Le Concert Spirituel. *Honours include:* Walther Gruner International Lieder Competition, 2nd Prize winner; Nonie Morton Award (leading to Wigmore Hall debut). *Address:* c/o Magenta Music International, 64 Highgate High Street, London N6 5HX, England.

HARVEY Raymond Curtis, b. 9 Dec. 1950, New York, USA. Conductor. *Education:* BMus, 1973, MMus, 1973, Oberlin College; MMA, 1978, DMA, 1984, Yale

University. *Career:* Music Director, Texas Opera Theatre, 1978-80; Exxon/Arts Endowment Conductor, Indianapolis Symphony, 1980-83; Associate Conductor, Buffalo Philharmonic, 1983-86; Music Director, Springfield Symphony (MA), 1986-. *Membership:* National Arts Associate of Sigma Alpha Iota. *Address:* c/o Springfield Symphony, 1391 Main Street, Springfield, MA 01103, USA.

HARVEY Richard Allen, b. 25 Sept. 1953, London, England. Composer/Performer. *Education:* Associate, Royal College of Music, 1971. *Debut:* Conductor, London Symphony Orchestra, Barbican Centre, 1985. *Career:* Recorder/Woodwind Player; Conductor and Composer; Founder, London Vivaldi Orchestra; Guest Conductor, Royal Philharmonic and London Symphony Orchestras; Toured with guitarist John Williams, 1984-; Conductor and Performer with English Chamber Orchestra, Barbican Centre, London, 1987. *Compositions:* La Citadelle and L'Homme Armé, both for 13 brass and percussion instruments; Elegy for viola, strings and harp; Compositions for films and television. *Recordings:* Italian Recorder Concertos; The Genteel Companion; Brass at La Sauve-Majeure; Four Concertos for Violins and Recorder. *Membership:* Founder member, ARC. *Hobbies:* Cricket; Alvis cars; Travel. *Current Management:* Tony Prior, London, England. *Address:* 90 Lots Road, London SW10 0QD, England.

HASELBACH Richard, b. 21 Sept 1914, Uznach, Switzerland. Musician (Teacher, Director). m. Wolf Agnes (Violinist) 20 Jul 1955, 3 daughters. *Education:* Studies in Philosophy, Munich; Diplomas: Schulmusik, 1944, Piano, 1946, Theory, 1947; All Diplomas by Zurich Conservatory; Doctor of Musicology, University of Zurich, 1952. *Career:* Repetitor, Opera Zurich, 1948-50; Teacher, Zurich Conservatory, 1950-60; Director of choirs and orchestras, Zurich, 1950- 60; Founder and Director, Zurcher Kantorei (concert choir) 1948-88; Foreign tours to Germany and Holland; Teacher, Lehrerseminar Rickenbach 1960-79; Director of Music, St Martin, Schwyz, 1968-87. *Compositions:* German mass (Hug); Marien-Motette (Lucerna). *Recordings:* Radio performances: Kodály: Missa brevis; Sutermeister (T Gryphius): Senfl: Missa brevis. Bassani : Op 8 Nr 1 Bassani Op 9 Nr 1-4; J B Hilber: Missa vox clamantis in deserto; Sutermeister: Missa in Es. *Publication:* J B Bassani (Barenreiter). *Contributions to:* Herder: Lexikon fur Theologie und Kirche; Ricordi: Lexikon of music. *Memberships:* International Association of Musicology; Swiss Association of Musicology; Swiss Association of Musicians. *Hobby:* Chess. *Address:* Perfidenstr 5, CH 6432 Rickenbach, Switzerland.

HASHIMOTO Eiji, b. 7 Aug. 1931, Tokyo, Japan. Harpsichordist. m. Ruth Anne Laves, 8 June 1963, 1 son, 2 daughters. *Education:* BM, Organ, 1954, Graduate Diploma, Organ, 1955, Tokyo University of Fine Arts; MA, Composition, University of Chicago, 1959; MM, Harpsichord, Yale University School of Music, 1962. *Career:* Instructor of Harpsichord, Toho Gakuen School of Music, Tokyo, 1966; Assistant Professor of Harpsichord and Artist-in-Residence, 1968-72, Associate Professor of Harpsichord & Artist-in-Residence, 1972-77, Professor of Harpsichord and Artist-in-Residence, 1977-, University of Cincinnati College Conservatory of Music; concerts, recitals and/or solo appearances in Australia, Austria, Belgium, Brazil, Canada, Chile, England, Finland, France, Germany, Holland, Hong Kong, Iran, Italy, Japan, Luxembourg, Mexico, New Zealand the Philippines, Spain, Switzerland, the USA and Venezuela. *Recordings:* Eight solo albums from Camerata Tokyo, Fontec, Inc., (Tokyo); The Musical Heritage Society, Inc., (New York); several albums of chamber music under various labels. *Publications:* Editions: D. Scarlatti, 100 Sonatas, (3 vols), G. Schirmer, 1985, Zen-On 1975; J.B. Loeillet, Pièces pour Clavecin, Heugel & Cie, 1985; C.P.E. Bach, Sonatas (3 vols), G Shirmer, 1988, Zen-On, 1984; Vivaldi-Hashimoto, Concerto for four harpsichords and strings in E minor, Zen-On, 1990. *Current Management:* ICA Management (USA and Europe); Camerata Tokyo, Inc., (Japan). *Address:* 4579 English Creek Dr, Cincinnati, Ohio 45245, USA.

HASS Sabine, b. 8 April 1949, Brunswick, Germany. Singer (Soprano). m. Artur Korn, 1979. *Education:* Studied with Karl-Heinz Lohmann in Berlin; Munich with Esther Muhlbauer; Richard Strauss Conservatory Munich. *Career:* Sang at the Stuttgart Staatsoper from 1970; State Operas of Munich and Vienna 1976, as Senta and Ariadne; Bregenz Festival 1977, as Reiza in Oberon; Guest appearances in Paris, London, Lisbon, Trieste, Venice, Turin, Rome, Barcelona and Buenos Aires; Munich Staatsoper and La Scala Milan 1983, as Isabella in Das Liebesverbot and as Elsa in Lohengrin; Metropolitan Opera 1985-86, as Elsa and Senta; Sang the title role in a new production of Die Liebe der Danae by Strauss at the 1988 Munich Festival; Season 1987/88 as Senta at Philadelphia and Leonore at Frankfurt and with the company of the Cologne Opera at Tel-Aviv; Deutsche Oper Berlin 1988, as Sieglinde; Seattle and Théâtre du Châtelet Paris 1989, as Leonore; Sang Isolde at Basle, Feb 1990; Season 1992 with Wagner's Elisabeth at the Deutsche Oper Berlin and Senta at the Bayreuth Festival; Many concert appearances. *Recordings include:* Der Wein by Berg (Deutsche Grammophon). *Address:* c/o Bayerische Staatsoper, Postfach 745, D-8000 Munich 1, Germany.

HASSAN Tarek Hassan Ali, b. 19 Oct 1937, Cairo, Egypt. Physician; Composer; Dramatist; Anthropologist. m. Jane Blenkinsop, 17 Feb 1968. *Education:* Ain Shams and Cairo Universities; Royal Colleges of Physicians, London, Edinburgh and Glasgow; FRCP (Edinburgh), 1978; Postgraduate Medical School, Hammersmith; Studied Turkish Sufi Tradition and Violin with Ahmad Dada, Violin and Rudiments of Music with Arturo Saino, Shultz and Tigerman Conservatories, Cairo, Orchestra with Hans Hickman; Studied with Andrew Byrne, Royal Academy of Music, London. *Career:* Medical: Graded medical posts in Egyptian and British university hospitals, from House Officer to full Professor; Currently Chairman, Department of Endocrinology; Music and drama: Founding Chairman, Egyptian National Cultural Centre and The New Opera; Performances of dramatic works, London, Edinburgh, Brighton, Birmingham; Several radio and TV com-commercial appearances for dissemination, of culture and music. *Compositions:* Sinfonietta for strings, 1st performance Vienna 1989; Fanfare for the Opera, Ministry of Culture commission, 1st performance Manchester, 1990; Al Mansoura symphonic suite; Variations for strings; Introduction and Allegro for winds, commissioned for Naples Festival of Contemporary Music; Sonatina for flute and piano; Songs for voice and piano, performed Cairo, Vienna, New York. *Publications include:* Crisis of Modern Sciences and the Place for Music, 1985. *Honours:* Gold Medal for Musical Composition, Damascus, 1961; Commendation for Conceptual Contributions in Science and Music, International Cultural Council, Mexico, 1987; Commandeur des Arts et des Lettres, France, 1991. *Memberships include:* Musicians Union. *Hobbies:* Painting; Philosophy; History; Farming. *Address:* 18 Mohammad Saleh Street, Dokki, Cairo, Egypt.

HASSELL Jon, b. 22 Mar 1937, Memphis, Tennessee, USA. Composer; Trumpeter. *Education:* Trained as trumpeter then studied composition with Karlheinz Stockhausen and Henri Pousseur in Cologne; Further study at the Eastman School of Music, Rochester. *Career:* As composer and performer has been concerned with electronic music, minimalism and Indian music. *Compositions include:* Music for Vibraphones 1965; Blackboard Piece with Girls and Loops 1968; Goodbye Music 1969; Maps nos. 1-2 for hand-held magnetic playback heads 1969; Solid State for 2 synthesizers 1969; Superball 1969; Landscape Series 1969-72; Sulla Strada, theatre piece after Kerouac's On the Road, performed Venice 1982. *Recordings include:* Vernal Equinox; Earthquake Island; Volumes in Fourth World series; Aka-Dhari-Java: Magic Realism. *Address:* c/o ASCAP, ASCAP Building, One Lincoln Plaza, New York, NY 10023, USA.

HASSON Maurice, b. 6 July 1934, Berck-Plage, France. Concert Violinist. *Education:* Studied at Paris Conservatoire and with Henryk Szeryng. *Career:* Played the Mendelssohn Concerto in Paris, aged 16; Resident in London, 1973-; Has appeared with orchestras and given recitals in Europe, Israel, USA, South America, Australia, New Zealand and Hong Kong; Conductors have included Masur, Mata, Rattle and Alexander Gibson; US debut with Cleveland Orchestra under Lorin Maazel, 1978; Guest concerts with European broadcasting stations; Colin Davis, Rafael Fruebeck De Burgos; Professor of Royal Academy of Music, 1986; Plays a Benvenuti violin by Stradivarius, 1727. *Recordings include:* Paganini Concerto No 1, Prokofiev No 1 - Brahms - Bruch and Bach Double Concerto, with Szeryng and the Academy of St Martin in the Fields; Brilliant showpieces for the Violin, Virtuoso Violin and Concerto by Gonzalo Castellano-Yumar; Recently recorded French Sonatas (Franck - Debussy - Fauré), with Charles Ivalsi and Favourite for the violin with Ian Brown. *Honours include:* Grand Prix and Prix d'Honneur at Paris Conservatoire; Honorary Member of the Royal Academy. *Address:* Manygate, John Boyden and James Thompson, Directors, 12 Cotswald Mews, 30 Battersea Square, London SW11 3RA, England.

HASTINGS Baird, b. 14 May 1919, New York City, New York, USA. Musician; Writer; Educator. m. Louise (Lily) Laurent, 22 Dec 1945. *Education:* AB, Harvard College, 1939; Diploma, Paris Conservatory, 1946; Diploma, Tanglewood, 1957; Diploma, Mozarteum, Salzburg, 1961; MA, Queens College, 1966; PhD, Sussex College, 1976. *Career:* Conductor, Mozart Chamber Players, 1957-60; Conductor, Mozart Festival Orchestra, 1960-; Music Advisor, Eglevsky Ballet, 1961-78; Lecturer in Music, Conductor of Band and Orchestra, Trinity College, 1965-70; Administrator, Juilliard School of Music, New York City, 1972-85; Music Advisor, School of American Ballet, New York City, 1973-85; Music Director, Westport Point, Massachusetts, Summer Episcopal Church, 1974-92; Guest Conductor, American Symphony, New York State Theatre, Holyoke, Tufts Recorder Society, Queens Philharmonic; Consultant, Royal Academy of Music, London; Panelist, Hofstra Mozart Conference, New York. *Recordings:* Music for Strings; Mozart Concerto for Piano and Orchestra, with Beveridge Webster; Michael Haydn Symphony; Other Mozart works. *Publications:* Berard, 1960; Sonata Form in Classic Orchestra, 1966; Treasury of Librettos, 1969; Don Quixote by Minkus, 1975; Choreographers and Composers, 1983; Mozart Research Guide, 1989. *Contributions to:* American Record Guide; Carnegie Hall programmes; Alice Tully Hall programmes; Prose of Distinction to Ballet Review; Juilliard Journal; Guide to Thamos by Mozart, Conductor's Journal. *Honours:* Fulbright Fellowship, 1949-50; Tanglewood, 1957. *Memberships:* The Bohemians; Musicians Union; American Musicological Society. *Hobbies:* Collecting art; Tennis. *Address:* 33 Greenwich Avenue, New York, NY 10014, USA.

HATRÏK Juraj, b. 1 May 1941, Orkucany, Prešov, Czechoslovakia. Composer. m. 17 Apr 1965, 2 sons. *Education:* Academy of Music and Dramatic Arts, Bratislava. *Debut:* Sinfonietta, 1963. *Career:* Musical Education, Aesthetics and Psychology of Music, Academy of Music. *Compositions include:* Double Portrait for orchestra, 1971; Da Capo al Fine for orchestra, 1976; Diary of Tanja Savitchova for brass quintet and soprano, 1976, TV version, 1983; Happy Prince, opera after Oscar Wilde, 1978; Sans Souci, 1 symphony, 1979; Vox memoriae, cycle for 4 instruments, 1983; Canzona for organ, alto and viola, after John Roberts, R. Tagore, 1984; Submerged Music for soprano and strings, 1985; Moment musical avec J.S.Bach for soprano and chamber group, 1985; Victor, 2 symphony, 1988; Compositions for children, choirs, 4 monologues for accordion; Adam's Children, chamber opera after Slovak national proverbs and bywords, 1991; Diptych for Vlno, Vlello, Pft, 1989; The Lost Children, string quartet with basso solo after Gregory Orr, 1993. *Contributions to:* Slovenská hudba (Slovak Music); Hudobný život (Musical Life). *Hobbies:* Educational projects for children; Moderation of music programmes;

Creative art; Literature; Nature. *Current Management:* Academy of Music and Dramatic Arts, Bratislava, music analysis, composition. *Address:* Dubnická 2, 85102 Bratislava, Slovakia.

HATTEBERG Kent E, b. 22 Oct 1954, Savanna, Illinois, USA. Conductor. m. Hope Burton, 8 Aug 1981, 3 daughters. *Education:* BMus, University of Dubuque, Dubuque, Iowa; MMus, Choral Conducting, University of Iowa; Studied Conducting with Don V Moses and Uwe Gronostay; DMA in progress, University of Iowa. *Debut:* As Guest Conductor with Nederlands Kamerkoor, Amsterdam, Jan 1993. *Career:* Present position: Director of Choral Activities at Sam Houston State University. *Honours:* Fulbright Scholar, Berlin, 1990-91. *Memberships:* American Choral Directors Association; Conductors Guild Inc. *Hobbies:* Sports: Basketball and baseball. *Address:* 121 Willow Bend, Huntsville, TX 77340, USA.

HATTON Gaylen A, b. 4 Oct. 1928, Red Mountain, California, USA. Music Professor; Composer; Performer. m. Marianne Johnson, 6 Aug. 1958, 2 sons, 2 daughters. *Education:* Elementary School, Red Mountain, California, 1941; High School, Barstow, California, 1942-45; BA, 1951, MA, 1954, Brigham Young University; PhD, University of Utah, 1960. *Career:* French horn student of Mario Marianni, Los Angeles, Edmund Stegner, Frankfurt, Joseph Singer, New York City; Utah Symphony, 1956-64; Sun Valley Music Festival, 1960-68; Sacramento Symphony, 1965-77; Bedford Springs Festival, 1982-84; Member of Brassworks (quintet), 1979-86; Member of Orpheus Winds, 1979-86. *Compositions:* Editor, Noche de los Tropicos by Gottschalk, Boosey & Hawkes; Coventry Carol, Organ Prelude, Harold Flammer; Organ Preludes, Deseret Press. *Recordings:* Music for Orchestra, 1958 recorded by Maurice Abravanel and the Utah Symphony Orchestra under the auspices of the Koussevitsky Foundation. *Address:* 560 South 500 East, Orem, UT 84057, USA.

HATTORI Joji, b. 1969, Japan. Concert Violinist. *Education:* Studied in Vienna with Rainer Kuchl; Further lessons with Robert Masters and masterclasses with Nathan Milstein. *Career:* Played the Beethoven Concerto in Vienna, 1985; Concert engagements throughout Europe and USA; UK debut with the Royal Philharmonic Orchestra; Concerts with Yehudi Menuhin at the Festival Hall and with Vienna Kammerorchester at the Vienna Konzerthaus; Appearances with the English Chamber Orchestra, the Radio Symphony of Netherlands and the European Community Chamber Orchestra; Season 1991-92 included Mozart concertos at Vienna Mozart Festival and tour of Japan with Yehudi Menuhin and the New Japan Philharmonic Orchestra; World tour with Waseda University Orchestra; Plays a Stradivari violin (Hamma, 1773). *Honours include:* Winner, Carl Nielsen International Violin Competition and Menuhin International Violin Competition, Folkestone. *Address:* c/o Robert Gilder and Company, Enterprise House, 59-65 Upper Ground, London SE1 1PQ, England.

HAUBENSTOCK-RAMATI Roman, b. 27 Feb. 1919, Cracow, Poland. Composer. *Education:* Studied with Artur Malawski at the Cracow Conservatory 1934-38 and with Josef Koffler at the Lwow Academy of Music 1939-41. *Career:* Director of Music of Cracow radio 1947-50; Secretary of the Polish section of the ISCM 1947-50; Emigrated to Tel-Aviv 1950, and has taught at the Academy of Music there (Director of the State Music Library 1950-56); Worked for Universal Edition, Vienna, 1957-68; Organized exhibition of graphic scores at Darmstadt, 1959; Directed the Gaudeamus Foundation Week at Bilthoven 1967; Guest Lecturer in Buenos Aires 1968 and at the Stockholm Academy of Music 1968. *Compositions:* Ricecari for string trio 1950; Blessings for voice and 9 players 1952; Recitativo ed Aria for harpsichord and orchestra 1954; Papageno's Pocket-Size Concerto for glockenspiel and orchestra 1955; Les Symphonies des Timbres for orchestra 1957; Chants des prismes for orchestra, 1957, 1967;

Sequences for violin and orchestra 1958; Interpolation for solo flute 1958; Liasions for vibraphone and marimbaphone 1958; Petite Musique de Nuit, mobile for small orchestra 1959; Mobile for Shakespeare for voice and 6 players 1960; Decisions, 10 pieces of musical graphics 1960-68; Jeux 6, mobile for 6 percusssionists 1960; Amerika, opera after Kafka 1962-64; Hotel Occidental for speech-chorus, after Kafka 1967; La Comedie, anti-opera after Beckett 1969; Tableau I, II and III for orchestra 1967-70; Symphonie K 1967; Psalm for orchestra 1967; Multiple I-VI 1969; Alone for trombone and mime 1969; Madrigal for 16 part chorus; Konstellations, 25 etchings 1971; Poetics, cycle for various instruments 1972; Concerto a tre, for trombone, piano and percussion 1973; 2 String Quartets 1973, 1978; Endless, mobile for 7 players and conductor 1974; Solo Cello Sonata 1975; Musik for 12 instrumemts 1976; Ulysses, ballet 1977; Concerto per archi 1977; Symphonien 1977; Self for bass clarinet and 3 tapes 1978. 21. *Address:* c/o Zaiks, 00-092 Warszawa, Ul Hipotecznaz, Post Box P-16, Poland.

HAUBOLD Ingrid, b. 1943, Berlin. Singer (Soprano), m. Heikki Toivannen. *Education:* Studied in Detmold and at the Munich Musikhochschule with Annelies Kupper. *Career:* Sang at the Munich Theater am Gärtnerplatz 1965-66; Detmold Landestheater 1970-72, Bielefeld 1972, Lubeck from 1979; Guest engagements at Hanover (from 1981) and Karlsruhe (1981-84); Sang Isolde at Madrid 1986, Turin and Berlin 1988, Lucerne Festival 1989; Has also appeared at the Teatro Massimo Palermo, Teatro Comunale Bologna, the Vienna Staatsoper, Schwetzingen Festival (Ariadne, 1989) and the Metropolitan Opera, 1990-91; Other roles include Senta (Savonlinna Festival, 1990), Pamina, Wagner's Elsa, Elisabeth, Gutrune, Eva, Freia, Sieglinde, Irene (Rienzi) and Ada (Die Feen); Leonore, Strauss's Chrysothemis and Marschallin, Janáček's Jenůfa and Katya Kabanova; Many concert appearances. *Address:* c/o Deutsche Oper Berlin, Richard Wagnerstrasse 10, Berlin, Germany.

HAUGLAND Aage, b. 1 Feb. 1944, Copenhagen, Denmark. Singer (Bass). *Education:* Studied medicine at first, then music with Moegens Wöldike and Kristian Riis in Denmark. *Career:* Sang in Oslo from 1968, then Bremen; Member of the Royal Opera Copenhagen from 1973; Covent Garden debut 1975 as Hunding in the Friedrich production of Die Walküre; Hagen in Götterdämmerung with English National Opera; returned to London for new productions of Boris Godunov and Der Rosenkavalier, 1984; Appearances in Venice as Mussorgsky's Varlaam, Geneva, (Ochs in Der Rosenkavalier), Paris and Viennna; Netherlands Opera as Banquo in Macbeth; US debut 1979, as Boris Godunov in St Louis; Metropolitan Opera in works by Wagner, Mussorgsky and Tchaikovsky; Salzburg debut 1982, as Rocco in Fidelio; Bayreuth Festival from 1983, as Hagen and Fafner in the Ring; Edinburgh Festsival 1990 as Marke in Tristan and Isolde (Concert); Sang at the Metropolitan 1990-91 as Baron Ochs and in Katya Kabanova and Parsifal; Season 1992 with Boris in Lady Macbeth of Mtsensk at La Scala and King Mark at Aarhus; Concert appearances with the London Symphony, London Philharmonic, Philharmonia, Vienna Philharmonic and the Philadelphia, Boston and Chicago Symphony Orchestras. *Recordings:* Roles in Götterdämmerung, Boris Godunov, Katerina Ismailova, Parsifal and Moses und Aron; Video of Wozzeck, as the Doctor, conducted by Abbado (Virgin). *Address:* c/o Lies Askonas Ltd., 186 Drury Lane, London, England, WC2B 5RY.

HAUPTMANN Cornelius, b. 1951, Stuttgart, Germany. Singer (Bass). *Education:* Graduated Stuttgart Musikhochschule 1982; Berne Conservatoire with Jakob Stämpfli; Further study with Dietrich Fischer-Dieskau in Berlin and masterclasses in Salzburg with Eric Tappy and Elisabeth Schwarzkopf. *Career:* Sang at Stuttgart from 1981, notably as Masetto; Heidelberg Opera 1985-87, as King Philip in Don Carlos and Osmin; Stadttheater Karlsruhe from 1987, as Sparafucile (Rigoletto), Plutone (Orfeo), Sarastro and Mozart's

Figaro; Festival appearances at Lucerne, Salzburg, Singapore, Sapporo, Schwetzingen (1983 premiere of Henze's The English Cat) and Ludwigsburg (recital 1991); Further engagements in Munich, Paris, Berlin, Leipzig, Orleans and London (Publio and Sarastro in concert performances of La Clemenza di Tito and Die Zauberflöte, 1990); Sang Sarastro at Ludwigsburg, 1992; Conductors include John Eliot Gardiner, Hogwood, Janowski, Tilson Thomas, Masur, Barenboim, Maazel, Lothar Zagrosek and Roger Norrington; Concert performances include the St Matthew Passion (Gardiner) and Mozart's Requiem (Bernstein) in 1988; Frequent Lieder recitals, and other concerts under Nikolaus Harnoncourt, Trevor Pinnock, Helmut Rilling and Garry Bertini. *Recordings:* Bach St John and St Matthew Passion, Mozart C minor Mass, Idomeneo, La Clemenza di Tito, and Die Entführung, with Gardiner and Mozart Requiem and C minor Mass (Bernstein) for Deutsche Grammophon; Haydn Stabat Mater, with Pinnock (DG) and Die Zauberflöte with Norrington; Enescu Oedipe with Foster (EMI); Akhnaten by Philip Glass (CBS). *Address:* Lies Askonas Ltd, 186 Drury Lane, London WC2B 5RY, England.

HAUSCHILD Wolf-Dieter, b. 6 Sept 1937, Greiz, Germany. Conductor. *Education:* Studied at Franz Liszt Musikhochschule, Weimar, with Ottmar Gerster and Hermann Abendroth; Further study with Hermann Scherchen and Sergiu Celibidache. *Career:* Conductor of the Deutsche National theater Weiners and from 1963 Chief Conductor of the Kleist Theatre at Frankfurt Oder (also of Frankfurt Philharmonic); Chorus Master for RDA Radio, 1971-74, joint Conductor of Berlin Radio Symphony Orchestra, 1974-78; Chief Conductor of the Symphony Orchestra of Radio Leipzig, 1978-85; Professor of Conducting at the Musikhochschule of Berlin and Leipzig from 1981; Guest Conductor of Berlin Symphony Orchestra; Chief Conductor of Stuttgart Philharmonic Orchestra, 1985-91; Professor of Conducting at Karlsruhe Musikhochschule, 1988; Artistic Director and Chief Conductor at Essen Opera, 1991; Guest appearances at Berlin Staatsoper and Komische Oper and the Semper-Oper Dresden; Conducted a new production of Tristan und Isolde at Essen, 1992. *Address:* c/o Theater und Philharmonie, Rolandstrasse 10, 45128 Essen, Germany.

HAUSER Alexis, b. 1947, Vienna, Austria. Music Director. *Education:* Student at the Conservatory and the Academy of Music and Performing Arts in Vienna; Graduated summa cum laude in the masterclass of Professor Hans Swarowsky; Also studied with Franco Ferrara in Italy and Herbert von Karajan, Salzburg, Mozarteum. *Debut:* With Vienna Symphony, 1973. *Career:* Several concerts and broadcasts with Vienna Symphony; Invitations to conduct many other European orchestras including the Berlin RIAS Symphony, Belgrade Philharmonic and the Vienna Chamber Orchestra; Invited by Seiji Ozawa to spend summer of 1974 in Tanglewood; USA Debut with New York City Opera, 1975; Conducted Atlanta Symphony with Itzhak Perlman as soloist, 1975; Subsequently conducted with Symphonies of San Francisco, Minnesota, Seattle, Kansas City (with Maureen Forrester as soloist) and the Rochester Philharmonic; Music Director, Orchestra London Canada, 1981-; Led orchestra on its first European tour to the Festival Internationale dell Aquila in Italy; Directed Conductors' Seminar at the Royal Conservatory of Music in Toronto; Conducted the Toronto, Winnipeg and Kansas City Symphonies; Appeared at Chicago's Grant Park Festival. *Honours:* Winner of several conducting awards in Austria including 1st International Hans Swarowsky Conducting Competition in Vienna; Awarded Koussevitzky Conducting Prize at Tanglewood, 1974; In 1984 Orchestra London Canada received the Award of Merit presented by the Canadian Performing Rights Organization.

HAUSER Michael Leon, b. 28 Apr. 1930, Copenhagen, Denmark. Lecturer. m. Henriette, 21 Jan. 1956. 3 sons. *Education:* University of Copenhagen, cand mag, 1958; Studied Ethnomusicology. *Career:*

Ethnomusicologist, Greenlandic traditional music; Music teacher, Roskilde Katedralskole, 1958-; Det kgl danske Musikkonservatorium, 1965-90; Conductor, Roskilde Katedralskoles Kammerkor, 1958-88; Musik og Ungdoms Kor, 1967-73. *Compositions:* For chorus, edition Egtved, Denmark. *Recordings:* Traditional Songs of Greenland, 1965. *Publications:* Classification of traditional Greenlandic music, 1985 and 1987; Traditional Greenlandic Music, 1992. *Contributions:* Numerous articles to professional journals including: Tidsskriftet Gronland; Publikationen zu wissenschaftlichen Filmen; Humaniora 1974-76; Hainang-Qaanaaq, 1984; Gronland-Kobenhavn, 1985; Arctic Anthropology, 1986; Hymns of the Moravian Church in Greenland, 1987. *Honour:* Jacob Gade Prize, 1970. *Memberships:* International Council for Traditional Music; Dansk Selskab for Musikforskning. *Hobbies:* Nature; Chamber music. *Address:* Haraldsborgvej 35, 4000 Roskilde, Denmark.

HAUTZIG Walter, b. 28 Sept. 1921, Vienna, Austria. Concert Pianist. m. Esther Rudomin, 10 Sept. 1950, 1 son, 1 daughter. *Education:* Public and High School, Vienna; State Academy of Vienna; Jerusalem Conservatory; Curtis Institute, Philadelphia; Principal Teacher, Mieczyslaw Munz; Private Study with Artur Schnabel. *Debut:* Town Hall, New York, 31 Oct. 1943. *Career:* Recitals and Orchestral Appearances in over 50 Countries; Soloist with Berlin Philharmonic, Orchestra National Belgique, Oslo, Stockholm,Copenhagen, Helsinki, Zurich, New York, Baltimore, St Louis, Buffalo, Vancouver, Honolulu, Tokyo, Sydney, Melbourne, Auckland, Wellington, Mexico, Bogota, Jerusalem and Tel Aviv etc; Played for BBC, Australian, New Zealand, Japanese, USA and Canadian Radio; Professor of Piano, Peabody Conservatory of the Johns Hopkins University, Baltimore, USA, 1960-87. *Recordings:* Numerous for labels including, RCA, Monitor, Vox, Turnabout, Musical Heritage Society. *Contributions to:* Musical America; American Record Guide. *Hobbies:* Ping Pong; Photography; Swimming. *Current Management:* Eric Semon Associates, 111 W 57th Street, New York, NY 10019, USA. *Address:* 505 West End Avenue, New York, NY 10024, USA.

HAVAS Kato, b. 5 Nov 1920, Hungary. Violinist; Lecturer; Teacher; Author. 3 daughters. *Education:* Scholarship and Diploma, Ferenc Liszt Academy of Music, Budapest. *Debut:* Carnegie Hall, USA, 1939. *Career:* Concert tours and broadcasts; Developed new method of violin teaching; Founder, International Music Festival at Oxford, Annual Seminar at St Edmund Hall, Oxford University, England; President of Kato Havas Association for the New Approach. *Publications:* A New Approach to Violin Playing, 1961; The Twelve Lesson Course, 1964; The Violin and I, 1968; Stage Fright (Its Causes and Cures), 1993; Video: The Release of Tension and Stage Fright in Performance - 1 hour duration, 1991. *Honours:* Tourt/bow at Student Competition; Recipient, American String Teachers Association International Award. *Membership:* Honorary Member, Ysaye Foundation, Belgium. *Hobbies:* Theatre; Gardening. *Address:* 72 Victoria Road, Oxford OX2 7QE, England.

HAWES Jack Richards, b. 18 May 1916, Ipswich, Suffolk, England. Composer. *Education:* Piano, Organ & Theory with Dr George Gray, starting as boy chorister at St Mary-le-Tower Church, Ipswich; Studied Cello with Alfred Earnshaw, Ipswich Conservatoire. *Compositions:* Piano Solos: Improvisation; Christmas Idyll; Burlesque; Pastorale; Nocturne; Toccata; Three Whimsical Pieces; A Handful of Pieces; Brackenbury Suite. Organ Solos: A Wedding Fanfare; For a Festive Occasion; Five Diversions; Manual Miniatures. Choral (Secular): Choral Suite-The Bells of Youth; Three English Lyrics. Choral (Sacred): Magnificat & Nunc Dimittis in D and B flat; Psalm Trilogy; Holy Communion Service-Rite A; Sanctus & Benedictus (ASB); Anthems: O Sing unto the Lord a New Song; Grant, we beseech thee; A Morning Song; Drop, drop, slow tears; Stir up, we beseech thee. Carols: Christ is born; Children's Carol; Carol for the Nativity; The Gift of Christmas. Instrumental: Festival Pieces

(Brass Quintet); Three Commands (Brass Band); Pieces of Eight (Woodwind Octet); Birthday Bagatelles (Oboe & Piano); A Suite for Harp (Harp solo); Concertino Lirico (Flute & String orchestra); Sinfonietta (String orchestra); Full Orchestra: An English Overture; Piano Concerto; Prelude-In Celebration; Overture-Suffolk Spree; Jack & the Magic Beans (Narrator, orchestra and audience); Romanza, for string orchestra; Venite, for SATB and Organ; Preces and Responses, SATB; Three Child Portraits, Piano; Rhapsodic Duo, Cello and Piano; Three Duos, Harp and Harpsichord; To Music, Three Choral Songs, 1991; Three Novelettes, piano duet, 1992. *Address:* 29 Lynwood Avenue, Felixstowe, Suffolk IP11 9HS, England.

HAWES Patrick Thomas, b. 5 Dec 1958, Grimsby, England. Composer; Teacher. *Education:* St Chad's College, Durham University, 1977-81; BA Hons, Music, 1980; MA, Early Baroque Music, 1981. *Career:* Associate Director of Music, Pangbourne College, Berkshire, 1981-90; Composer-in- Residence, Charterhouse, 1990-. *Compositions:* The Wedding at Cana, dramatic cantata; A King's Ransom, children's opera; The Song of Guthlac for male voice choir, harp, strings and percussion; The Far Seeing Land, Lincolnshire song cycle; Deep Harvests, SATB and 2 pianos; When Israel was a Child, SATB and organ. *Memberships:* Fellow, Royal College of Organists; Performing Rights Society; MCPS. *Hobbies:* Horse racing; Swimming. *Address:* Lessington Brake, Charterhouse, Godalming, Surrey GU7 2DE, England.

HAWKES Tom, b. 21 June 1938, England. Stage Director. *Education:* Trained at the Royal Academy of Music. *Career:* Resident Staff Producer at Sadler's Wells 1965-69; For English National Opera has produced Un Ballo in Maschera, Madama Butterfly, La Vie Parisienne, La Gazza Ladra and Die Fledermaus; English Bach Festivals (seen at Covent Garden and in France, Greece, Italy and Spain) include Rameau's Castor et Pollux and Platée, Handel's Teseo and Gluck's Alceste and Orphée et Eurydice; Dido and Aeneas in London and at the Athens Festival; Artistic Director for Phoenix Opera and Director of Productions for the Handel Opera Society; La Finta Giardiniera for the English Music Theatre; Wat Tyler by Alan Bush, Hansel and Gretel and operettas at the Sadler's Wells Theatre; Season 1990-91 with The Maid of Orleans for Northern Opera, La Bohème in Hong Kong, Mitridate in Monte Carlo and Handel's Riccardo Primo at the Royal Opera House and in Limasol for the English Bach Festival; Has also produced in Dublin, Nottingham, Oxford, Belgium and Guelph and St Louis, USA; Season 1993/94 with Rigoletto and Die Fledermaus at Singapore, L'Orfeo, for E.B.F. at Royal Opera House, Covent Garden and in Spain; Director of Productions for the Singapore Lyric Theatre and for Crystal Clear Productions UK. *Address:* c/o Music International, 13 Ardilaun Road, London N5 2QR, England.

HAWKINS Brian, b. 13 Oct. 1936, York, England. Viola Player/Teacher. m. Mavis Spreadborough, 30 Dec. 1960, 1 son, 1 daughter. *Education:* National Youth Orchestra, 1951-54; Royal College of Music, 1954-60. *Career:* Chamber Music, Edinburgh Quartet; Martin Quartet; Vesuvius Ensemble; Nash Ensemble; London Oboe Quartet; Gagliano String Trio; Member, English Chamber Orchestra, Academy of St Martin-in-The-Fields, London Sinfonietta, London Virtuosi; Professor, Viola & Chamber Music, Royal College of Music, 1967- ; String Faculty Adviser, Royal College of Music, 1989; Head of String Faculty Royal College of Music, 1992. *Recordings:* With the Nash Ensemble, London Virtuosi, London Oboe Quartet & Gagliano Trio. *Honours:* Silver Medal, Worshipful Company of Musicians, 1960; Fellowship of The Royal College of Music, 1991. *Memberships:* Royal Society of Musicians; European String teachers' Association; Incorporated Society of Musicians. *Hobbies:* Food; Wine; Travel; Photography. *Address:* The Old Vicarage, 129 Arthur Road, London SW19 7DR, England.

HAWKINS John, b. 26 July 1944, Montreal, Canada.

Composer; Pianist. *Education:* Studied under Istvan Anhalt and received Master's degree in Composition, McGill University. *Career:* Joined Faculty of Music, University of Toronto, teaches theory and composition 1970-; Remained active as pianist and performed frequently in the concerts of Société de Musique Contemporaine du Québec as well as Toronto's New Music Concerts, of which he is a member of Board of Directors; Conductor, Pierre Boulez' conducting seminar, Switzerland 1969. *Compositions:* Composed over 70 new works which include pieces for harpsichord and organ. *Honours:* Won several major awards including first John Adaskin Memorial Fund Award 1968 and BMI Student Composers' Award 1969. *Address:*CAPAC, 1240 Bay Street, Toronto, Ontario M5R 2C2, Canada.

HAWKINS Malcolm, b. 8 Mar. 1944, Oporto, Portugal. Composer; Teacher. m. 2 Aug 1987 *Education:* Rugby School; Royal Academy of Music; B. Mus. (London), 1966; LRAM; Mozarteum, Salzburg; Diploma in Composition, 1970; M. Mus. (London), 1976. *Career:* Freelance Double Bass Player and Pianist; Assistant Director of Music, Cranleigh School, 1971-76; Professor, Royal Academy of Music, 1979-88; Wells Cathedral School, 1988-90. *Compositions:* A Day in Town (suite for orchestra), UMP; This Endris Night (carol), UMP; On Stage (suite for Piano Duet), Stainer and Bell; (version for orchestra) Basil Ramsey; Animal City (8 songs for school choirs) S and B; Glimpses of a Garden (flute or recorder and keyboard) Bardie edition; The Riders (Carol) Stainer and Bell; Stepping Out for Flute and Jazz Trio (BBC) commission RVW Trust 1987; Cantata, Sancta Sophia, Litchfield Festival, 1991. *Recordings:* On Stage (suite for orchestra) BBC Radio 3; Diversions for Oboe Quartet (Berlin); Dancing Partners for Wind Quartet (Berlin); Four Songs for Baritone, Saxophone and Piano (DRF Salzburg); Festival Fanfare La Marseillaise Round Top, Texas, 1989; Ghost Games for Piano, 1991; Oboe Concerto, 1991. *Honour:* First Prize in International Song Competition, Das Neue Lied, Salzburg, 1975. *Memberships:* Composers' Guild; Savile Club. *Address:* Old Forge, Old Frome Road, East Horrington, Wells, Somerset, BA5 3DP, England.

HAWKINS Osie, b. 16 Aug. 1913, Phenix City, Alabama, USA. Singer (Baritone). *Education:* Studied in Atlanta and with Friedrich Schorr in New York; Sang at the Metropolitan Opera from 1942, as Wagner's Telramund, Kurwenal, Bitterolf, Wotan, Amfortas, Donner and Gunther; Zuniga in Carmen and Monterone in Rigoletto; Also sang with Central City Opera, Colorado, and the Cincinnati Summer Opera; Many concert appearances; Executive Stage Manager at the Metropolitan 1963-78; 926 performances with the Metropolitan Opera, played 54 roles in 39 different operas in German, Italian, French and English. *Honours:* Awarded Metropolitan Opera National Council Verdi Memorial Award of Achievement, 1978; Inducted into Philadelphia Academy of Vocal Arts Hall of Fame, 1987. *Address:* c/o Metropolitan Opera, Lincoln Center, New York, NY 10023, USA.

HAWLEY William Palmer, b. 4 Nov. 1950, Bronxville, New York, USA. Composer. m. Kiyoko Jyoti Hawley, 12 June 1975. *Education:* BFA, 1974, MFA Composition, 1976, California Institute of the Arts; Ithaca College School of Music, 1969-71. *Compositions Include:* Hagoromo, opera in 1 act; Te Deum, soloists, chorus, orchestra; 2 orchestral serenades; Sappho Songs, mezzo-soprano and orchestra; 2 motets; 6 madrigals; 3 songs, soprano, violin, piano; Six Dickinson Settings; 1 string quartet; 1 piano trio; Sonata for Violin and Piano; 2 fantasies for piano, various other chamber works; numerous songs. *Address:* 347 West 57th Street Apt 5F, New York, NY 10019, USA.

HAYASHI Yasuko, b. 19 July 1948, Kanagawa, Japan. Singer (Soprano). m. Giannicola Piglucci. *Education:* Studied in Tokyo with Shibata and Rucci; With Lia Gurani and Campogalliani in Milan. *Debut:* La Scala 1972, as Madama Butterfly. *Career:* Appearances in Florence, Rome, London, Venice, Turin,

Barcelona, Chicago and Aix-en-Provence; Other roles include Donna Anna, Fiordiligi, Carolina in Il Matrimonio Segreto, Luisa Miller, Anne Trulove, and Liu in Turandot; Turin 1976, in Bianca e Fernando by Bellini; Sang Donna Anna at the reopening of the Stuttgart Staatsoper, 1984; Genoa 1985, in a revival of Il Diluvio Universale by Donizetti; Season 1987/88 as Butterfly at Verona and Leonora (La Forza del Destino) in Tokyo; Appearances on TV and in concert. *Recordings:* I Lituani by Ponchielli; Rachel in La Juive; Requiem by Bottesini (Fonit-Cetra); Video of Madama Butterfly from La Scala. *Address:* c/o Marks Management Ltd, 14 New Burlington Street, London W1X 1FF, England.

HAYES Gary J. b. 14 Dec. 1948, Hamilton, Ontario, Canada. Composer. *Education:* Studied violin and percussion; Studied John Beckwith, Contemporary Trends, at University of Toronto's Faculty of Music; Studied with John Weinzweig, Composition; Graduated, University of Toronto 1972. *Career:* Freelance Composer, and Music Director for theatrical productions; Artist-in-classroom, North York Board of Education, Toronto; toured with folksingers Ian and Sylvia Tyson as sound and lighting technician; served as technical co-ordinator and board member for Toronto's Mariposa Folk Festival; Founding member of Array; Producer of radio music for CBC 1975-; produced series Music of The Twentieth Century and prepared several programmes documenting new music in Canada; Has produced four broadcast recordings by Ottawa's National Arts Centre Orchestra; Founding member of Ottawa concert organization Espace Musique. *Compositions:* Orchestral: Dementia 1974; Nuances Du Nord 1975; Two Studies in Strings 1978. Instrumental Ensemble: Dementia II 1974; Dialogues 1975; Experiments in Burnt Offerings 1979; Falling Leaves 1970; Fanfare for International Music Day 1978; First Perceptions 1979; Four Pieces for Three Performers 1973; Idiosyncracies 1972; Mists and the Dream of Mists 1973; Musical Journal 1973; Preludes and Dances Book I 1976; Quatre Jouets 1977; Quintet No. 1 for Brass, Convolutions 1975; Surges 1977. Instrumental Solo: Directions 1972; Soring 1975. Voices: Dog (A Poem by Lawrence Ferlinghetti) 1971; Five Haiku 1972; Pythian I 1973; Two Songs 1970. Piano IV Journeys 1979. Incidental Music: More Than Ever 1977; Music for The Devil's Instrument 1972; Music for Hamlet 1973. *Honours:* Won first prize for best work by an Ontario Composer, Ontario Arts Council in CBC/Canada Council Competition for Young Composers 1973. *Membership:* Canadian League of Composers.

HAYES Malcolm Lionel Fitzroy, b. 22 Aug. 1951, Overton, Marlborough, Wiltshire, England. Music Critic; Writer; Composer. *Education:* St Andrews University; BMus, Honours, Edinburgh University, 1974. *Career:* Music Critic, The Times, 1985-86; Music Critic, The Sunday Telegraph, 1986-89; Music Critic, The Daily Telegraph, 1989-; Frequent broadcasts (talks) for BBC Radio 3, 1985- and Radio 4, 1986-; Music performed at Bath Festival, 1985, ICA, London, 1985, Viitasaari Festival, Finland, 1987 and BBC, London 1986. *Publication:* Co-editor: New Music 88, 1988. *Contributions to:* Numerous articles for The Listener, 1985-; Musical Times, 1985-86; Tempo, 1982-; International Music & Opera Guide, 1987; New Music 87, 1987. *Honour:* Tovey Prize for Composition, Edinburgh University, 1974. *Address:* Daily Telegraph, Peterborough Court at South Quay, 181 Marsh Wall, London E14 9SR, England.

HAYMAN Richard Warren Joseph, b. 27 Mar. 1920, Cambridge, Massachusetts, USA. Composer; Conductor. m. Mary-Ellen, 25 June 1960, 2 daughters. *Education:* Freelance Composer, Arranger, 20th Century Fox, Warner Bros. Metro-Goldwyn-Mayer, Universal Film Studios; Music Arranger, Director, Vaughn Monroe Orchestra records and TV show, New York City, 1945-50; Chief Arranger, Arthur Fiedler, John Williams and Boston Pops Orchestra, 1950-90; Musical and A&R director, Mercury; Record Corporation, New York City, 1950-65; Music Director, Time-Mainstream Records, New York City, 1960-70; Principal Pops Conductor,

Detroit Symphony Orchestra, St Louis, Birmingham (Alabama), Hartford (Connecticut), Calgary (Canada). *Honours:* Best Instrumental Record WERE, Cleveland, 1963. *Hobbies:* Golf; Astronomy; Water-skiing; Photography. *Current Management:* Shaw Concerts, 1900 Broadway, New York, NY 10023, USA. *Address:* Richard Hayman Productions Inc, 1020 Park Avenue, Suite 5A, New York, NY 10028, USA.

HAYMON Cynthia, b. 6 Sept 1958, Jacksonville, Florida, USA. Singer (Soprano). m. Barrington Coleman. *Education:* Graduate, Northwestern University. *Debut:* Santa Fe Opera, as Diana in Orpheus in the Underworld, 1985. *Career:* Sang Xanthe in US premiere of Die Liebe der Danae, Santa Fe, 1985; Has sung Micaela for Seattle Opera and Liu in Boston; Created Harriet, A Woman Called Moses, Virginia, 1985; European debut, 1986, as Gershwin's Bess at Glyndebourne; With Covent Garden has sung Liu on tour to Far East and Mimi in London; State Operas, Hamburg, Munich, as Liu, Theatre de la Monnaie, Brussels, as Gluck's Amor; Israel Philharmonic as Micaela, conducted by Zubin Mehta; Season 1988-89 with Eurydice at Glyndebourne, Mimi for Baltimore Opera, Marguerite with Opera Grand Rapids; Season 1989-90 includes Susanna for Seattle Opera, Canadian Opera debut as Micaela; Coretta King opposite Simon Estes, West End; 1990-91 highlights: Lauretta in Gianni Schicchi at Seattle, Liu in Miami, and Mozart's Pamina at Bastille Opera, Paris; 1991-92 highlights: San Francisco Opera debut as Micaela in Carmen, premiere of Rorem's Swords and Plowshares with Boston Symphony, Pamina at Opera Bastille, Liu at Royal Opera House, Covent Garden, Gershwin in concert at Teatro La Fenice, Venice, recital at Northwestern University, Carmina Burana with Detroit Symphony Orchestra, Mendelssohn's Symphony No 2 for RAI, Rome, Gershwin and Tippett concert with London Symphony Orchestra, Gala concert, Glyndebourne Festival; 1992-93 highlights: Bess in Porgy and Bess, Royal Opera House, Pamina at Opera Bastille, Micaela in Birmingham and Dortmund, Marguerite at Deutsche Oper Berlin, Mimi at Santa Fe Opera; Concert engagements in Brahms Requiem conducted by Kurt Masur, Rossini's Stabat Mater (London debut) with London Symphony Orchestra conducted by Michael Tilson Thomas; Other conductors: Seiji Ozawa, Bernard Haitink, Isaiah Jackson. *Recordings include:* Tippett's A Child of Our Time, London Symphony Orchestra, Richard Hickox, Conductor; Bess in Porgy and Bess, Glyndebourne Festival Opera, Simon Rattle, Conductor. *Honour:* Grammy Award, 1990. *Address:* c/o Columbia Artists Management Inc, 165 West 57th Street, New York, NY 10019, USA.

HAYNES Eugene Jr, b. 1925, East St Louis, Illinois, USA. Pianist. Composer. *Education:* Undergraduate Diploma, Juilliard School of Music, 1947, Postgraduate Diploma, 1949; Studies with Nadia Boulanger, Paris, 1951-54; Isador Philipp, 1954, Isabella Vengeroua, New York City, 1955. *Debut:* European Concert Tour for USIS, 1956, Carnegie Hall, 1958. *Career:* Concerts, Carnegie Hall, 1962 and 1969; European concert tour, 1964, South America, 1959; Composer of incidental music for Riddersalen Teater, Copenhagen, 1954; Soloist, Indianapolis Symphony Orchestra, Oklahoma City Symphony Orchestra, Detroit Symphony Orchestra; Host, Wonderful World of Music with Eugene Haynes, KSD Radio, St Louis, 1965-73; Professor of Music, Lincoln University, Jefferson City, Missouri, 1973-79; Professor of Music, Artist-in-Residence, East Saint Louis campus, Southern Illinois University, 1979-80, Director, Performing Arts Training Center, 1980-; Music Director, Radio Station KSCFM, Florissant, Missouri. *Compositions:* String Quartet, 1951; Song Cycle, 1952; Fantasy for Piano, and Orchestra, 1956; Symphony, 1960; Rhapsody on a Gospel Song, 1978. *Address:* 710 Lafayette Street, Jefferson City, MO 65101, USA.

HAYNES Stanley, b. 21 Mar. 1950, London, England. Musician; Computer Programmer. m. Melanie Davey, 26 Oct. 1976, 2 daughters. *Education:* BA (Hons.), York University, 1971; BMus, Composition, 1974, PhD,

Music, 1981, Southampton University. *Career:* Computer Music Fellow, City University, 1976-78; On Staff of IRCAM (Paris) under Pierre Boulez, 1980-82; Concert Manager for Experimental Arts Productions, 1975-; Computer Programmer, London, 1983-. *Compositions:* Pyramids, Prisms for piano, modulators and computer synthesized tape; O Alter Duft for solo violin, and 4 other compositions. *Recording:* Prisms for piano and computer synthesized tape Adam Wodnicki (piano) on American Folkways Computer Music Record. *Contributions to:* Computer Music Journal; Interface. *Memberships:* Performing Right Society; British Computer Society; EMAS; Society for the Promotion of New Music. *Hobbies:* Cinema; Politics (Labour). *Current Management:* Experimental Arts Productions. *Address:* 37 Woodcock Hill, Kenton, Harrow, Middlesex HA3 0JH, England.

HAYS Sorrel Doris, b. 6 Aug. 1941, Memphis, Tennessee, USA. Composer; Keyboard Musician; Media Artist in Audio and Film/Video. *Education:* Artist Diploma, Hochschule für Musik, Munich, Germany, 1966; MMus, University of Wisconsin, 1968; Studies with Hilda Somer, Paul Badura-Skoda, Harold Cadek, Hedwig Bilgram. *Career:* Recently in 80's added film and video to media art; Commissions from West German Radio Hoerspiel, 1984, 1986; Commissioned film and music for 1984 Pro Musica Nova Festival, Germany; Film, music video production shown at Museum of Modern Art, New York and Stedelijk Museum, Amsterdam; Commissions from Westdentscher Rundfonk, Cologne, 1988; Echo, Whatchasay Wie Bitte, 1989; The Hub, Megopolis Atlanta and Sound Shadows, commissioned as opening work for Whitney Museum Acoustica Festival, April 1990; Bits, NY City premiere, 1993, Merkin Hall; Performances of Opera, The Glass Woman, NYC, Interant Theater, 1993; Premiere, The Clearing Way, Chattanooga Symphony, 1992. *Compositions:* Southern Voices for Orchestra and Soprano, 1982, 21 minutes; Celebration of No, tape, Soprano, Violin, Piano, Cello, 1983; Sunday Nights, Piano, 1979; H.U.S.H., Soprano, 2 Percussion, 1986; The Clearing Way, for full orchestra, contralto, SATB chorus; 3 act opera, 11 soloists and chorus, The Glass Woman, 1993. *Honours:* Opera America, production award for opera, The Glass Woman, 1989 and National Endowment for the Arts, 1992. *Memberships:* ASCAP International League of Women Composers Frau und Musik. *Hobby:* Herb and Flower Gardening. *Address:* 697 West End Avenue, PHB, New York, NY 10025, USA.

HAYWARD Robert, b. 1956, England. Singer (Bass-baritone). *Education:* Studied at the Guildhall School of Music and the National Opera Studio. *Career:* Sang Falstaff and Mozart's Figaro while at college; Glyndebourne Touring Opers 1986, as Don Giovanni; Has sung Figaro, Don Giovanni, Marcello and Sharpless for Welsh National Opers; Theseus and Haushofmeister (Capricco) for Glyndebourne Festival; English National Opera appearances as Tomsky in The Queen of Spades; US debut as Figaro for Houston Grand Opera, 1988; German debut 1990 as Don Giovanni for the Bayerische Staatsoper on tour to Teatro Liceo Barcelona; Invited by Opera North for Guglielmo, Figaro, Count, Escamillo, Don Giovanni, Malatesca, Marcello and Robert (Iolanta); For Royal Opera House, Spirit Messenger (Frau); Concert engagements include Messiah with the Royal Liverpool Philharmonic, Hallé and London Philharmonic Orchestras; The Mask of Time, Elijah, Beethoven's Ninth and the Brahms Requiem with the Hallé; Das klagende Lied and Gurreleider with the English Northern Philharmonia; The Dream of Gerontius with the Scottish National Orchestra; Haydn's Creation with the Bournemouth Sinfonietta and the Philharmonia conducted by Claus Peter Flor; Mozart Requiem with Georg Solti, 1991. *Current Management:* Ingpen & Williams. *Address:* Ingpen & Williams, 14 Kensington Court, London W8 5DN, England.

HAYWOOD Lorna Marie, b. 29 Jan. 1939, Birmingham, England. Singer (Soprano). m. Paul Crook. *Education:* Royal College of Music, with Mary Parsons and Gordon Cinton; Juilliard School with Sergius Kagen and Beverley Johnson. *Debut:* Juilliard 1964, as Katya Kabanova. *Career:* Covent Garden debut 1966, in Die Zauberflöte: sang Jenůfa in 1972; English National Opera from 1970, notably in Janáček's The Makropoulos Case and Katya Kabanova; Appearances with Welsh National Opera and at the Glyndebourne Festival; Guest engagements in Prague, Brussels, New York, Chicago, Dallas, Washington and Seattle: roles include Marenka in The Bartered Bride, Mimi, Micaela in Carmen, Sieglinde, Elizabeth Zimmer in Elegy for Young Lovers, Mozart's Countess, Madam Butterfly, Ariadne, the Marschallin and Lady Billows in Billy Budd. *Address:* Stafford Law Associates, 26 Mayfield Road, Weybridge, Surrey KT13 8XB, England.

HAZELL Andrea, b. 1965, Southampton, England. Singer (Mezzo- soprano). *Education:* Studied at Royal Academy of Music. *Career:* Many appearances throughout UK in oratorio; Sang Second Witch in Dido and Aeneas for Amersham Festival, Offenbach's Perichole in Reading and Dorabella at the 1990 Cheltenham Festival; Sang in Carmen at Earl's Court, 1989, and on tour to Japan; Royal Opera, Covent Garden, 1990-, in Les Huguenots and Die Frau ohne Schatten and as Tefka in Jenůfa, 1993; Other roles include Marcellina in Le nozze di Figaro. *Address:* c/o Royal Opera House, Covent Garden, London WC2, England.

HAZEN Robert Miller, b. 1 Nov. 1948, Rockville Center, New York, USA. Professional Trumpeter; Musicologist; Research Scientist. m. Margaret Hazen, 9 Aug. 1969, 1 son, 1 daughter. *Education:* BS, SM, Massachusetts Institute of Technology, 1971; PhD, Harvard University, 1975; Musical studies with A.Ghitalla, A.Come, N.Paella, A.Sanchez. *Career:* Professional trumpeter, member of National Chamber Orchestra, Smithsonian Chamber Orchestra, National Gallery Orchestra (all in District of Columbia); Soloist: BBC, Boston Esplanade Concerts, Handel Festival Orchestra, National Gallery Orchestra. *Recordings:* With Smithsonian Chamber Orchestra on Argos, DDG, Pro Arte; Other chamber recordings. *Publication:* The Music Men, 1987. *Hobby:* Double volleyball. *Address:* 10430 Masters Terrace, Potomac, MD 20854, USA.

HAZUCHOVÁ Nina, b. 24 May 1926, Slovakia, Opera Singer (Mezzo-soprano). *Education:* Conservatory, Bratislava. *Career:* Appeared with Slovak National Theatre; Roles include: Carmen, Amneris in Aida; Azucena in Il Trovatore; Eboli in Don Carlos; Maddalena in Rigoletto; Suzuki in Madame Butterfly; Rosina, in the Barber of Seville; Marina in Boris Godunov; Cherubino in The Marriage of Figaro; Nancy in Martha; Isabella in The Italian Girl in Algiers; Catherine in The Taming of the Shrew; Appears as a Concert Singer performing with the best Czech orchestras; Has toured many countries including USSR, Germany, Austria, Belgium, Italy, Yugoslavia, Arabia, China, Mongolia; Vocal-Teacher, Academy of Music Arts (Vysokà škola múzických umení) Bratislava. *Recordings:* Has made numerous records. *Honours:* Meritorious Artist, 1968. *Membership:* Slovak Music Foundation, Bratislava. *Address:* Grösslingova 6, 811 08 Bratislava, Slovakia.

HEADINGTON Christopher John Magenis, b. 28 April 1930, London, England. Musician. *Education:* Taunton School, Royal Academy of Music. *Career:* Assistant Music Master, Trinity College, Glenalmond, Perthshire, 1951-54; Deputy Director of Music, Lancing College, Sussex, 1954-64; Senior Assistant Music Presentation, BBC, London, 1964-65; Tutor in Music, Department for External Studies, Oxford University, 1965-72; Part-time Association Tutor, 1972-82; Freelance Composer, Pianist, Broadcaster, Author, 1950-; Piano Concert Appearances in Europe, Middle and Far East, West Indies, etc. *Compositions:* String Quartets Nos. 1, 2 and 3, 1954, 1974, 1982; Three Piano Sonatas, 1956, 1974, 1985; Violin Concerto, 1959; Song Cycles including Reflections of Summer and A Clouded Starre, 1965 and 1975; A Bradfield Mass, 1977; Piano Quartet, 1978; The Healing Fountain (In Memoriam Benjamin Britten), 1979; Piano Concerto,

1982; Sinfonietta, 1985. *Recordings:* Recitals of Solo piano music: Pictures and Pleasures and Russian Trinkets for Kingdom records. *Publications:* The Bodley Head History of Western Music, 1974; The Orchestra and Its Instruments, 1965; Chapters on Various Composers in A Dictionary of Composers, 1977; Illustrated Dictionary of Musical Terms, 1980; Britten 1981; The Performing World of The Musician, 1981; The Listener's Guide To Chamber Music, 1982; The Rape of Lucretia (Chapter in The Britten Companion), 1984, Opera: A History, 1987. *Contributions to:* The Concerto, Illustrated Encyclopedia of Classical Music; Regular criticism for Gramophone Magazine. *Honours:* Leonard Borwick Prize, Royal Academy of Music; Awarded Major Arts Council of Great Britain Bursary for Composers, 1978. *Hobbies:* Aviation; Skiing; Travel; Cooking; Languages. *Address:* 19 Falkland Drive, Kingsteignton, Newton Abbot, Devon, TQ12 3RH. England.

HEADLEY Erin, b. 1948, Texas, USA. Lirone and Viola da Gamba player. *Career:* Member of Tragicomedia, three musicians performing in the Renaissance and Baroque repertory; Concerts in Britain and at leading European early music festivals; Gave Stefano Landi's La Morte d'Orfeo at the 1987 Flanders Festival; Francesca Caccini's La liberazione di Ruggiero dall'isola d'Alcina at the 1989 Swedish Baroque Festival, Malmo. *Recordings* (on Hyperion and Virgin) include: Proensa (troubadour songs), My Mind to me a Kingdom is (Elizabethan ballads, with David Cordier); A Musicall Dreame (duets from Robert Jones's 1609 collection); Biber's Mystery Sonatas; Concert programmes include The Lyre of Timotheus (incidental music by Handel, Bach, Vivaldi and Abel); Orpheus I Am (music based on the Orpheus myth by Landi, Monteverdi, Lawes and Johnson); Il Basso Virtuoso (songs by Landi, Monteverdi, Strozzi, Huygens and Purcell, with Harry van der Kamp); Three Singing Ladies of Rome; Monteverdi Madrigals from Book VIII and L'Orfeo; Early Opera: Peri's Euridice, Landi's La Morte d'Orfeo and Rossi's Orfeo. *Address:* Robert White Management, 182 Moselle Avenue, London N22 6EX, England.

HEADRICK Samuel Philip, b. 14 Sept. 1952, St Louis, Missouri, USA. Composer; Conductor; Professor. m. Kathryn Ann Marshall, 16 Aug. 1974, 3 sons, 1 daughter. *Education:* BM 1975, MM 1977, North Texas State University; PhD Music Composition, Eastman School of Music, 1981; Courses in Computer Music, Massachusetts Institute of Technology, 1983; Composition Study with Samuel Adler, Warren Bensen, Martin Mailman, Joseph Schwanter and James Sellers. *Career:* Teaching Fellowships in Composition and Electronic Music, North Texas State University 1977, Eastman School of Music 1979-80; Visiting Instructor of Music, Crane School of Music, State University of New York, 1980-81; Assistant Professor of Composition and Theory, Boston University, 1981-; Co-Director, Boston University Contemporary Collegium, 1983-84; Guest Conductor, 2nd Annual Festival of Contemporary Chamber Music at the State University of New York, Potsdam, 1984; Director of Electronic Music, Boston University, 1981-; Music Director, Huntington Theater Company, 1984; Guest Conductor, St Louis Symphony Chamber Players, 1987. *Compositions:* Commissions and performances include ALEA III, St Louis Symphony Chamber Players, Dinosaur Annex, Boston Conservatory Wind Ensemble, Boston University Contemporary Collegium, NUMA New Music; The Eyes of My Eyes, for orchestra, 1992; Hostage - an opera, 1993; Numerous chamebr compositions. *Address:* 11 Hagar Lane, Waltham, MA 02154, USA.

HEALD-SMITH Geoffrey, b. 30 Mar. 1930, Mexborough, South Yorkshire, England. Musician. Divorced, 1 son, 1 daughter. *Education:* Mexborough Grammar School; Royal College of Music. *Career:* Music Adviser, Hull; Pianist; Conductor; Artistic Director from age 32 years; Orchestras conducted include: Sadler's Wells, English Northern Philharmonic, Stavanger Symphony, Siegerland Orchestra, Radio and TV Eirean, Sao Paulo Municipal, Chamber Orchestra of Brazil.

Compositions: Film Score: Eve Island; Local radio music. *Recordings:* Edward German, Norwich Symphony; Granville Bantock Hebridean Symphony; Overture Macbeth; Overture Little Minister, Mackenzie, Holbrooke; Piano Concerto, 3 discs Havergal Brian World Premiere recordings. *Publications:* Group of Songs to be published by Da Capo. *Hobbies:* Model Railways; Boating; Gardening; Travel. *Address:* Tir Nan Og 7, Ganavan Road, Ganavan By Oban, Argyll PA34 5TU, Scotland.

HEALEY Derek, b. 2 May 1936, England. Composer. *Education:* Studied organ with Harol Darke and composition with Herbert Howells at Durham University; Further study at the Royal College of Music and with Petrassi and Celibidache in Italy. *Career:* Tutor: University of Victoria, BC, 1969-71, College of Arts, University of Guelph, 1972-78; Professor of Composition and Theory, University of Oregon, 1979, returning to Britain in 1988. *Compositions include:* Opera Seabird Island, 1977, and children's opera, Mr Punch, 1969; Ballets Il Carcerato 1965 and The Three Thieves, 1967; Orchestral: The Willow Pattern Plate, 1957; Concerto for organ, strings and timpani, 1960; Butterflies for mezzo and chamber orchestra, 1970; Artic Images, 1971; Tribulation, 1977; Music for a Small Planet, 1984; Mountain Music, 1985; Chamber: String Quartet, 1961; Cello sonata, 1961; Mobile for flute and ensemble, 1963; Laudes for flute and ensemble, 1966; Maschere for violin and piano, 1967; Wood II for soprano and string quartet, 1978, rev, 1981; Solana Grove for wind quintet, 1982; Piano music including Lieber Robert, 1974; Organ music and songs. *Address:* 29 Stafford Road, Ruislip Gardens, Middlesex HA4 6PB, England.

HEARTZ Daniel Leonard, b. 5 Oct. 1928, Exeter, New Hampshire, USA. Educator. *Education:* AB, University of New Hampshire, 1950; MA, 1951; PhD, 1957, Harvard University. *Career:* Assistant Professor, Music, University of Chicago, 1957-60; Assistant Professor, 1960-64, Associate Professor, 1964-66, Professor, 1966-, Chairman, 1968-72, Music, University of California, Berkeley. *Publications:* Pierre Attaingnant, Royal Printer of Music, 1969; Edition of Mozart's Idomeneo, Neue Mozart Ausgabe, 1972; Mozart's Operas, 1990. *Contributions to:* Professional journals. *Honours:* Dent Medal, RMA, 1970; Kinkeldey Prize, American Musicological Society, 1970; Guggenheim Fellowship (2), 1967-68, 1978-79; Elected Fellow of the American Academy of Arts and Sciences, 1988. *Memberships:* American Musicological Society, Vice President, 1974-76; IMS; RMA; Societe Française de Musicologie; Gesellschaft fur Musikforschung. *Address:* 1098 Keith Ave., Berkeley, CA 94708, USA.

HEATER Claude, b. 1930, Oakland, California, USA. Singer (Tenor). *Education:* Studied in Los Angeles; Further study in Europe with Mario del Monaco and Max Lorenz. *Career:* Sang at first as baritone, on radio and TV and in Broadway Musicals; Bayerische Staatsoper 1964, in König Hirsch by Henze; Sang Wagner roles in Amsterdam, Brussels, Hamburg, Berlin and Milan; Bayreuth Festival 1966, as Siegmund and Melot; Other roles include Turiddu, Otello, Florestan and Samson; Guest appearances in South America; Sang Tristan at Spoleto, 1968 and appeared at Dresden, 1968, Barcelona, Bordeaux and Geneva, 1968-69; Budapest and Venice, 1970. *Recording:* Tristan und Isolde, conducted by Karl Böhm (Deutsche Grammophon).

HEATH Edward Richard George, Rt Hon. b. 9 July 1916, St Peter-in-Thanet, Kent, England. Conductor; Writer on Music. *Education:* Chatham House School, Ramsgate, Kent, 1926-35; Balliol College, Oxford 1935-39, MA (Organ Scholar). *Career:* Has conducted the London Symphony Orchestra, Royal Philharmonic, Philharmonia, Liverpool Philharmonic, Birmingham and Bournemouth Symphony Orchestras, Northern Sinfonia, Zurich Chamber Orchestra, Leningrad Conservatoire Symphony Orchestra, Georgian TV Orchestra Tbilisi (USSR), Prague Opera Chamber Orchestra, Calgary Symphony Orchestra, Berlin

Philharmonic, Barcelona Symphony Orchestra; European Community Youth Orchestra; Chicago, Cleveland and Philadelphia Symphony Orchestras; Shanghai Symphony Orchestra and Central Philharmonic Orchestra of China, Peking. *Recordings:* Elgar Cockaigne overture with the LSO (EMI); Robert Mayer Christmas Concert 1973 with the Academy of the BBC orchestra and the BBC Singers; Carols, The Joy of Christmas with the English Chamber Orchestra and the George Mitchell Singers (EMI) Black Dyke Mills Band (RCA) 1977; Carols, The Joy of Christmas, 1980 (Toshiba-EMI Tokyo); Beethoven Triple Concerto and Boccherini Cello Concerto in G with Trio Zingara, Felix Schmidt and the ECO (Pickwick 1989). *Publications:* Music - A Joy for Life and Carols - the Joy of Christmas (Sidgwick and Jackson). *Memberships:* Trustee, LSO; Vice-President, London Bach Choir; Vice-President, Oxford Bach Choir; Governor of RCM 1961-70; President, European Community Youth Orchestra, 1977-83; Chairman of The London Symphony Orchestra Trust, 1963-70; Governor of The Royal College of Music, 1960-70. *Hobbies:* Sailing; Travel. *Address:* House of Commons, Westminster, London SW1 0AA, England.

HEBERT Bliss, b. 30 Nov. 1930, Faust, New York, USA. Stage Director. *Education:* Studied piano at Syracuse University with Dika Newlin, William Fleming and Kirk Ridge. *Career:* Debut as stage director Santa Fe 1957; General Manager Washington DC Opera Company 1960-63; Productions for New York City Opera 1963-75; Productions for Santa Fe Opera, San Francisco Opera from 1963; Metropolitan Opera debut 1973, Les Contes d'Hoffmann; Stage director for Stravinsky's recordings of Oedipus Rex and The Nightingale; Faust for Opera Northern Ireland, 1989; Staged Turandot for the Opera Company of Philadelphia, 1992. *Address:* c/o Metropolitan Opera, Lincoln Center, New York, NY 10023, USA.

HEBERT Pamela, b. 31 Aug. 1946, Los Angeles, California, USA. Singer (Soprano). *Education:* Studied at the Juilliard School with Maria Callas, Tito Capobianco, Margaret Hoswell and Boris Goldovsky. *Debut:* New York City Opera 1972, as Donn Anna. *Career:* Appearances in New York as Mimi, title role in L'Incoronazione di Poppea, Vespina in Haydn's L'Infedeltà delusa and the Composer in Ariadne auf Naxos; Frequent concert engagements.

HECHT Joshua, b. 1929, New York City, USA. Singer (Baritone). *Education:* Studied with Lili Wexberg and Eva Hecht in New York and with Walter Tassoni in Rome. *Debut:* Baltimore 1953, as Des Grieux in Manon. *Career:* Sang in Boston, Chicago, Miami, Pittsburgh, San Francisco, Seattle and New Orleans; Metropolitan Oppera from 1964; Further apearances at the New York City Opera and in Graz, Johannesburg, Barcelona, Bucharest, Dublin and Vancouver; Roles include the Wanderer in Siegfried, Amfortas, Rigoletto, Iago, Scarpia and the title role in Einstein by Dessau (Gelsenkirchen 1980); Sang Prospero in Martin's Der Sturm, Bremen, 1992. *Address:* c/o New York City Opera, Lincoln Center, NY 10023, New York, USA.

HECKMANN Harald, b. 6 Dec. 1924, Dortmund, Germany. Director, Deutsches Rundfunkarchiv (German Broadcast Archives). m. Elisabeth Dohrn, 25 Aug. 1953, 1 son. *Education:* Gymnasium, Dortmund, 1934-43; Musicology, Freiburg/Breisgau, 1944-52; Assistant to Wilibald Gurlitt, Freiburg/Breisgau, 1952-54. *Career:* Teacher of Church Music History, College of Music, Freiburg/Breisgau, 1950-54; Director, German History of Music Archive, Kassel, 1955-71; Director, German Broadcasting Archive, Frankfurt am Main, 1971-1991. *Publications:* Deutsches Musikgeschichtliches Archiv, Katalog der Filmsammlung, 1955; W A Mozart, Thamos, Koenig in Aegypten, Choere und Zwischenaktmusiken, 1956; W A Mozart, Musik zu Pantomimen und Balletten, 1963; Ch W Gluck, La Rencontre imprévue, Editor and Critic, 1964; Elektronische Datenverarbeitung in der Musikwissenschaft, 1967; various essays on musicology. *Memberships:* International Association of Music Libraries, Hon President; International Inventory of Musical Sources, President; Board Member of the Robert-Schumann Society; International Repertoire of Musical Iconography, Co-President; History of Music Commission, FRG; International Schubert Society, President; Rotary. *Address:* Im Vogelshaag 3, 6233 Ruppertshain/Ts, Germany.

HEDFWIG Douglas Frederick, b. 24 June 1951. Trumpeter; Educator; Scholar. m. Mary Frances Jones, 6 June 1982, 1 son. *Education:* BM, Manhattan School of Music, 1973; MM 1976, DMA 1986, Juilliard School. *Career:* Spoleto festival, Italy, 1972, 1974 and 1975; Mel Torme, 1973; Extra Trumpet 1973-84, Associate member 1984-, Metropolitan Opera Orchestra; Founding member, Metropolitan Brass Quartet, 1976- ; Assistant Principal Cornet, Goldman Band, 1977-; Broadway shows, 1976-78; Mexico City Philharmonic, 1982; Chairman, Brass department, Brooklyn College Conservatory of Music, City University of New York, 1985-; Lecturer in Music History, Juilliard School, 1986- . *Recordings include:* Discoveries, with Metropolitan Brass Quartet; Noel We Sing, with Metropolitan Brass Quartet and New York Choral Society; She is Thy Life by B Adolphe, with Metropolitan Brass Quartet and the Gregg Smith Singers. *Contributions to:* The Symphony 1720-1840; Repertoire Internationale de la Literature Musique; Quatour en Forme de Sonatine.*Memberships include:* College Music Society; International Trumpet Guild; Music Educators National Conference. *Address:* 255 West 95th Street Apt No.3a, New York, NY 10025, USA.

HEDGES Anthony John, b. 5 March 1931, Bicester, England. Reader in Composition; Composer. m. Delia Joy Marsden 1957, 2 sons, 2 daughters. *Education:* Keble College Oxford, MA, BMus, LRAM. *Career:* Teacher and lecturer, Royal Scottish Academy of Music, 1957-63; Lecturer in Music, University of Hull, 1963, Senior Lecturer 1968; Reader in Composition, 1978- ; Founder-conductor, The Humberside Sinfonia, 1978-81. *Compositions include:* Orchestral: Comedy Overture, 1962; Sinfonia Semplice, 1963; Expressions, 1964; Prelude, Romance and Rondo for strings, 1965; Concertante Music, 1965; Variations on a theme of Rameau, 1969; An Ayrshire Serenade, 1969; Celebrations, 1973; Symphony, 1972-73; Sinfonia Concertante,1980; Scenes from the Humber, 1981; Concertino for horn and strings, 1987; Choral: Gloria, unaccompanied, 1965; Epithalamium for chorus and orchestra, to text by Spenser, 1969; To Music, 1972; A Manchester Mass for chorus, orchestra and brass band; A Humberside Cantata, 1976; Songs of David, 1978; I Sing the Birth: canticles for Christmas, 1985; Aspects of Love, 1987; I'll Make Me A World, chorus and orchestra, 1990; Chamber: Flute Trios, 1985, 1989; Bassoon Quintet, 1991; Piano Quartet, 1992; Orchestral: Sinfonia Giovanile, 1992. Chamber: Five Preludes for piano, 1959; Rondo Concertante for violin, clarinet, horn and cello, 1967; Sonata for violin and harpsichord; String Quartet, 1970; Fantasy for violin and piano, 1981; Sonatinas for flute, viola and cello, 1982; Wind Quintet, 1984; Clarinet Quintet, 1987; opera Shadows in the Sun, 1976; many anthems, partsongs, albums of music for children; music for television, film and stage. *Recordings:* Scenes from the Humber, Kingston Sketches and Bridge for the Living on Meridian. *Publications:* Basic Tonal Harmony, 1987, Comprehensive Archive in Hall Central Music Library. *Contributions to:* 1957-63 regular contributor to The Guardian, The Scotsman, The Glasgow Herald and The Musical Times; The Yorkshire Post 1963-73. *Memberships:* Chairman, Composers' Guild of Great Britain, 1972, Joint Chairman 1973; Executive Committee of Composers' Guild 1969-73, 1977-81, 1982-87; Council Member Composers' Guild. *Address:* 76 Walkergate, Beverley, East Yorks, HU17 9ER, England.

HEDWALL Lennart, b. 16 Sept. 1932, Gothenburg, Sweden. Composer; Conductor. m. Ingegerd Henrietta Bergman, 13 Apr. 1957, 4 sons. *Education:* Royal College of Music, Stockholm, 1951-59; Composing and Conducting, Darmstadt, Vienna, Hilversum and Paris.

Debut: As Composer, 1950; As Professional Conductor, Messiah, 1954. *Career:* Conductor: Riksteatern 1958-60; Great Theatre Gothenburg 1962-65, Drottningholmteatern 1966-70, Royal Theatre 1967-68, Orebro Orchestra Society 1968-74; Teacher, Dramatic School in Gothenburg 1963-67, State Opera School 1968-70, 1974-80, 1985-; Director of Swedish National Music Museum 1981-83. *Compositions:* 2 Operas: Herr Sleeman Kommer; America, America; Sagan, symphonic phantasy; Juligen, a Christmas Rhapsody, Several Works for String Orchestra; Concertos for Oboe, Violoncello; Chamber Music (2 String Quartets, 2 String Trios); Organ and Piano Works; Several Song Cycles; Choir Pieces and Cantatas; Stage and Television Works. *Recordings:* As Conductor with Orebro Chamber Orchestra, Värmland Sinfonietta and Musica Vitae; As Accompanist Several Song Recitals; Also others as Organist and Pianist. *Publications:* Hugo Alfvén, a monography, 1973; Operettas and Musicals, 1976; The Swedish Symphony, 1983; Wilhelm Peterson-Berger, a biography in pictures, 1983; The Concert Life in Åbo 1872-76, 1989; Hugo Alfvén, a biography in pictures, 1990; The musical life in the manors of Vermland, 1770-1830, 1992. *Hobbies:* Literature; Theatre. *Address:* Mårdvägen 37, 16137 Bromma, Sweden.

HEELEY Desmond, b. 1 June 1931, West Bromwich, England. Stage Designer. *Education:* Trained at the Shakespeare Memorial Theatre, Stratford, 1974-52. *Debut:* La Traviata for Sadler's Wells 1960. *Career:* Productions for Glyndebourne (I Puritani, 1960) and English National Opera (Maria Stuarda, 1973); Work for the Metropolitan Opera includes Norma 1970, Pelléas et Mélisande 1972, Don Pasquale 1978 and Manon Lescaut 1980. *Address:* c/o Metropolitan Opera, Lincoln Center, New York NY 10023, USA.

HEENAN Ashley David Joseph, b. 11 Sept. 1925, Wellington, New Zealand. Composer; Conductor; Lecturer; Broadcaster. m. (1) Jean Margaret Ross, 30 Mar. 1951, 2 sons, 2 daughters, (2) Maureen Elizabeth Roberts. *Education:* Diploma Music, Mus B, Victoria University of Wellington; Royal College of Music, London, England. *Career:* Musical Director, Schola Musica of New Zealand, Symphony Orchestra, 1961-84; New Zealand Youth Orchestra, 1965-75; Musical Advisor and Orchestra Co-ordinator, QE II Arts Council, 1964-65; Musical Director, New Zealand Ballet Trust, 1966-68; New Zealand Writer Director Apra, 1966-80; Chairman, New Zealand Composers' Foundation, 1981- . *Compositions:* Moana Roa; Rotorua Symphony, (Film scores): Jack Winters Dream, (Radio Drama); War and Peace, (incidental music) Scottish Dances; A College Overture; Maori Suite; Cindy; Sea Songs, Orchestra works; various vocal and instrument works, arrangements and transcriptions of traditional Maori music. *Recordings:* Numerous with Schola Musica and New Zealand Symphony Orchestra. *Publications:* The New Zealand Symphony Orchestra, 1971; Schola Musica, 1974. *Contributions to:* Challenges in Music Education; Indiana Musicator; Journal of the Polynesian Society. *Honours:* New Zealand Music Bursar, 1948-50; UNESCO, Bursar, 1961-62; New Zealand Phonographic Award, 1976; Composers' Association New Zealand Citation, 1981; OBE, 1983; New Zealand Commemoration Medal, 1990. *Memberships:* New Zealand Composers' Foundation; Composers' Association of New Zealand; Australasian Performing Right Association; New Zealand Musicians Union; New Zealand Society of Genealogists. *Hobbies:* Croquet; Private Aviation; New Zealand History. *Address:* 11 Kiwi Street, Alicetown, Wellington, New Zealand.

HEGAARD Lars, b. 13 Mar 1950, Svendborg, Denmark. Music Teacher; Composer. m. Susanne Taub, 10 Oct 1984, 4 sons. *Education:* High School 1966-69; Diploma in Guitar 1973; Examination of Teaching 1977; Diploma in Composition 1980; BA in Music, 1975. *Career:* Have played at all major Festivals in Denmark and Scandinavia including on Radio; Have several commissions through The Danish Arts Foundation and 3-year Stipendium 1983. *Compositions:* Orchestra:

Symphony No. 1 and 2, Letter To My Son; Chamber Orchestra: Decet, Intersections; The Rolling Force (Cello Concerto). Chamber Works: Five Fragments for String Quartet; The Four Winds (Clarinet, Cello, Piano); Music For Chameleons (Wind Quintet); Configerations (Alto Flute), Guitar); Six Studies for Two Guitars, Song-lines (Guitar Trio); 13 Short pieces (Flute, Viola, Harp); Dreamtracks (Flute, Clarinet, Horn, Percussion, Guitar, Cello); Four Square Dances for Saxophone Quartet, Partials' Play (Flute, Guitar, Cello). Solo Works: Variations (Guitar), The Conditions Of a Solitary Bird (Guitar); Canto (Cello); The Great Beam... (Piano); Worldes Bliss (Organ); Labyrinthus (Electric Guitar). Vocal: Hymns (Baryton, Sinfonietta); Haiku (Soprano, Violin, Pinao); Far Calls, Coming Far (Mezzo Soprano, Electric Guitar, Percussion, Text: James Joyce); The Dimension Of Stillness (Soprano, Flute, Guitar, Cello, Text: Ezra Pound); Night Flower, (Mezzo-Soprano, Percussion, Piano, Viola, Double-Bass, Text: Sylviia Plath). Recordings: Five Fragments for String Quartet; Decet (Wind Quintet and String Quintet); The Great Beam of The Milky Way, (Piano). Contributions to: Interviews in Dansk Musiktidskrift. Membership: Danish Composers' Society.Current Management: Publishers: The Society For Publication of Danish Music, Gråbrødrestræde 18,1, 1156 Copenhagen K, Denmark. Address: c/o Danish Composers' Society, Gråbrødre Torv 16, 1154 Copenhagen K, Denmark.

HEGARTY Mary, b. 1960, Cork, Eire. Singer (Soprano). Education: Studied at the Cork School of Music, at Aldeburgh and the National Opera Studio in London; Further study with Josephine Veasey. Career: Has sung for Radio Telefis Eireann in Britten's Quatres chansons Françaises and the Brahms Requiem; Bach's Christmas Oratorio with Harry Christophers; Recitals in Ireland, the USA and at the Aix-en-Provence Festival (Une Heure avec Mary Hegarty); Covent Garden debut as a Flowermaiden in Parsifal, followed by Pousette in Manon; English National Opera as Nannetta and Naiad (Ariadne); Appearances with Opera Factory in La Calisto; With Opera North as Leonora in the British premiere of Nielsen's Maskarade (1989) in Ariane at Barbe-Bleue, the Mozart pasticcio The Jewel Box (1991) and as Frasquita; Buxton Festival 1991, in Mozart's Il Sogno di Scipione; Requiem for RTE; Princess Laula in Chabrier's Etoile, (Opera North); Papagena in Magic Flute, (ENO); Eurydice in Orpheus in The Underworld, (D'Oyly Carte); Adele in Die Fledermaus, (Dublin Grand Opera Society). Recordings: Debut solo album, A Voice is Calling. Honours include: Winner, Golden Voice of Ireland, 1984; Bursary for study at Aldeburgh; Irish Life, Sunday Independent Classical Music Award, 1988; Allied Irish Bank, RTE National Entertainments Award for Classical Section, 1987. Address: c/o John Coast, 31 Sinclair Road, London W14 0NS, England.

HEGEDUS Olga, b. 18 Oct. 1920, London, England. Musician (Cellist). Education: London Violoncello School; Private Study, Pierre Fournier. Debut: Recital, Wigmore Hall, London. Career: Solo recitals; Many BBC & Television appearances with trios, chamber ensembles, etc; Co-principal cello, English Chamber Orchestra. Recordings: Art of Fugue, Bach & Musical Offering, with Tilford Festival Ensemble; The Curlew, Warlock, with Haffner Ensemble; Vivaldi Motets with Teresa Berganza & English Chamber Orchestra; Dvořák Serenade, with English Chamber Orchestra Wind Ensemble; Schubert Quintet in C, with Gabrieli Quartet. Contributions to: A Pictorial Review, English Chamber Orchestra, 1983. Memberships: Incorporated Society of Musicians; Musicians Union. Hobbies: Reading; Visiting art galleries; Swimming. Address: 8 Kensington Place, London W8 7PT, England.

HEGGEN Almar, b. 25 May 1933, Valldal, Norway. Singer (Bass). Education: Studied at the Oslo Conservatory, with Paul Lohmann in Wiesbaden and with Clemens Kaiser-Breme in Essen. Debut: Oslo 1957, as Masetto in Don Giovanni. Career: Sang in Wuppertal, Berlin, Frieburg, Wiesbaden, Nuremburg, Munich; Guest Performances in Sweden and Yugoslavia amongst others; Nuremberg 1969, in the premiere of

The Dream of Liu-Tung, by Isang Yun; Roles include Rocco (also filmed), King Philip, Padre Guardiano, Sarastro, Don Alfonso, Tiresias (Oedipus Rex), Daland, Pogner, Fafner, Hagen, Baron Ochs, Ptolomeo in Giulio Cesare; Wagner: Landgraf, King Henry, Marke, Hunding; Verdi: Zacharias, Ramphis; Mozart: Osmin; Rossini: Don Basilio; Smetana: Kezal; Many Oratorios including Genesis and Seasons of Haydn, Requiem of Verdi, Requiem of Mozart; Teacher of singing. Memberships: Norsk Operasangerforbund (Norsk Musikerforening), Norsk Tonekunstnersamfunn, Kunsterforeningen. Address: Hareveien 40A, N-1413 Tårnasen, Norway.

HEGYI Erzsébet, b. 4 Nov. 1927, Nagykanizsa. Full Professor of Liszt Academy of Music, Budapest. m. Dezsö Legány, 23 Sept. 1961, 1 son. Education: Professor of Music, Liszt Academy of Music, Budapest 1951. Career: Professor, 1951-79; Full Professor 1979-; Liszt Academy of Music, Budapest; Professor of Kodály Seminars, Kodály Institute, Kecskemét, Hungary; Kodály Summer Courses in USA/Wellesley, Binghamton, Oakland, Milwaukee, Tallahassee, Tucson, Philadelphia, Millersville, West Chester; London, England; Sapporo, Japan; Aarhus, Denmark. Publications: Collection of Bach Examples, Volume 1, 1971, 12th edition 1989, Japanese Translation 1977, Volume 2, 1974, 9th edition 1989; Solfege According to the Kodály Concept, Volume 1, 1975, Its Pupil's Book 1985, Volume 2, 1979, Its Pupil's Book 1987; In Hungarian: Singing Teachers Training On The Basis of Kodály's Pedagogical Music Works, 1976; Stylistic Knowledge, Volume 1, Characteristics of Folk Music and Renaissance Style, in Hungarian 1982, in English 1983, Volume 2, Stylistic Marks of Baroque Music and Viennese Classicism, in Hungarian 1984, Volume 3, Musical Characteristics of the Romantic Style, in Hungarian 1987. Address: Apahida u 11, Budapest H-1112, Hungary.

HEIBERG Harold Willard, b. 6 Feb. 1922, Twin Valley, Minnesota, USA. Pianist; Vocal Coach. m. Eva Margrethe Lundberg, 21 Sept. 1957. Education: BMus, St Olaf College, 1943; MA, Columbia Teachers College, 1949; Advanced Piano study with Karl Ulrich Schnabel and Leonard Shure; Advanced Voice Study with Gerhard Hüsch and Cornelius Reid. Debut: Tully Hall, Lincoln Center, New York, 1971. Career: Solo recitals in Germany, Austria, Italy, Switzerland, England, France, Norway, USA and Puerto Rico; Appearances with orchestra in USA and in chamber music and as accompanist in USA, Germany, Austria, Canada and Taiwan; Professor of Music, University of North Texas, Denton, 1971-; Member of Faculty of Summer Vocal Institute of the American Institute of Musical Studies, Graz, Austria, 1969-. Publications: Translator of texts of over 200 Operatic and Choral works including, Il Prigioniero (Dallapiccola), Songs of Nature (Dvořák), Laud to the Nativity (Respighi), Stabat Mater (Poulenc), and with Ernst Oster, Der freie Satz (Schenker). Hobby: Gardening. Address: 2111 North Locust Street, Denton, TX 76201, USA.

HEICHELE Hildegard, b. Sept 1947, Obernburg am Main, Germany. Singer (Soprano). m. Ulrich Schwalb. Education: Studied at the Munich Musichochschule. Debut: Klagenfurt, as Jennie in Aufstieg und fall der Stadt Mahagonny. Career: Munich Staatsoper from 1971, notably as Mozart's Zerlina, Despina, Susanna and Ilia; Appearances in Vienna, Cologne (as Gretel), Karlsruhe (as Adina), Berlin, Zurich and Barcelona; Covent Garden 1977, 1983, as Adele in Die Fledermaus; Frankfurt 1981, in the Symphony of a Thousand, by Mahler; Monte Carlo 1982, Brussels 1984, as Susanna; Bayreuth Festival 1984, as the Woodbird in Siegfried; Sang at Kassel and Hanover 1988, as Elsa and Elisabeth; Concert engagements in Vienna, Graz and Venice (1985). Recordings include: Mahler's 8th Symphony; Egisto by Cavlli (Eurodisc); Bach Magnificat, Handel Dettinger Te Deum (Telefunken); Video of Die Fledermaus (Covent Garden 1983). Address: c/o Lies Askonas Ltd., 186 Drury Lane, London WC2B 5QD, England.

HEIDEN Bernhard, b. 24 Aug 1910, Frankfurt am

Main, Germany. Composer; Pianist; Harpsichordist; Conductor; Professor Emeritus. *Education:* Training in piano, clarinet, violin, theory, and harmony; Student of Paul Hindemith, Berlin Hochschule für Musik, 1929-33, of Donald Grout, Cornell University, AM, 1946. *Career:* Teacher, Detroit Art Center Music School; Conductor, Detroit Chamber Orchestra; Faculty member, Indiana University School of Music, Bloomington, 1946-81. *Compositions:* Opera: The Darkened City, 1962; Incidental music to plays; Orchestral: 2 symphonies, 1938, 1954; Euphorion: Scene, 1949; Concerto for Small Orchestra, 1949; Memorial, 1955; Concerto for Piano, Violin, Cello, and Orchestra, 1956; Philharmonic Fanfare, 1958; Variations, 1960; Envoy, 1963; Cello Concerto, 1967; Concerto for Strings, 1967; Horn Concerto, 1969; Partita, 1970; Tuba Concerto, 1976; Concerto for Trumpet and Winds, 1981; Recitative and Aria for Cello and Orchestra, 1985; Fantasia Concertante for Alto Sax, Winds and Percussion, 1987; Recorder Concerto for Recorders and Chamber Orchestra, 1987; Salute for Orchestra, 1989; Bassoon Concerto for Bassoon and Chamber Orchestra, 1990; Preludes for Flute, Bass and Harp, 1988; Chamber: Sonata for Alto Saxophone and Piano, 1937; Sonata for Horn and Piano, 1939; 2 string quartets, 1947, 1951; Sinfonia for Woodwind Quintet, 1949; Quintet for Horn and String Quartet, 1952; 2 sonatas for Violin and Piano, 1954, 1959; Quintet for Clarinet and Strings, 1955; Trio for Violin, Cello, and Piano, 1956; Sonata for Cello and Piano, 1958; Quintet for Oboe and Strings, 1962; Woodwind Quintet, 1965; Intrada for Woodwind Quintet and Saxophone, 1970; Quintet for Flute, Violin, Viola, Bassoon, and Contrabass, 1975; Terzetto for 2 Flutes and Cello, 1979; Quartet for Horns, 1981; Piano music, including 2 sonatas, 1941, 1952; Choral works; Songs; Voyage for symphonic wind ensemble, 1991; Trio for oboe, bassoon and piano, 1992; Divertimento for tuba and 8 solo instruments, 1992. *Honours:* Guggenheim, 1976; Mendelssohn Prize, 1933. *Address:* c/o School of Music, Indiana University, Bloomington, IN 47405, USA.

HEIFETZ Daniel (Alan), b. 20 Nov. 1948, Kansas City, Missouri, USA. Violinist; Teacher. *Education:* Pupil of Theodore Norman; Studied with Sascha Jacobson, Israel Baker, and Heimann Weinstine, Los Angeles Conservatory, 1962-65, and with Efrem Zimbalist, Ivan Galamian, and Jascha Brodsky, Curtis Institute of Music, Philadelphia, 1966-71. *Career:* Debut as soloist in the Tchaikovsky Violin Concerto with the National Symphony Orchestra of Washington DC, on tour in New York; Thereafter regular tours of North America and the world; Appointed to the faculty of the Peabody Conservatory of Music, Baltimore, 1980. *Recordings:* For Leonarda. *Honours:* 1st prize, Merriweather-Post Competition, Washington DC, 1969; 4th prize, Tchaikovsky Competition, Moscow, 1978. *Address:* c/ o Shaw Concerts Inc, ASCAP Building, 1900 Broadway, New York, NY 10023, USA.

HEIFETZ Robin (Julian), b. 1 Aug. 1951, Los Angeles, California, USA. Composer. *Education:* Studied at UCLA with Paul Chihara and Roy Travis; University of Illinois with Salvatore Martirano and Ben Johnston, DMA 1978. *Career:* Composer-in-residence at Shiftelsen Electronic Studio, Stockholm 1978-79; Worked at various music departments in Canada and the USA; Director of the Centre for Experimental Music at the Hebreew University of Jerusalem, 1980. *Honours:* Awards at the Concours International de Musique Electro-acoustique, Bouges, France, 1979, 1981; International Computer Music Competition at Boston, 1983. *Compositions include:* 2 Pieces for Piano 1972; Leviathan for piano 1975; Chirp for euphonium and piano 1976; Susurrus for computer and tape 1978; Child of the Water for piano 1978; For Anders Lundberg: Mardrom 29 30 10 for tape 1978; Harbinger/18:30 PST for brass and tape 1978; Flykt for piano and computer 1979; Wasteland for tape 1979; A Clear and Present Danger for tape 1980; Spectre for tape 1980; Wanderer for synthesizer 1980; The Unforgiving Minute for 9 instruments 1981; In the Last, Frightened Moment for tape 1980; The Vengeance for synthesizer 1980; The Arc of Crisis for tape 1982; A Bird in Hand is Safer than one Overhead

for 2 or more performers 1983; At Daggers Drawn for tape 1983. *Address:* c/o ASCAP, ASCAP Building, One Lincoln Plaza, New York, NY 10023, USA.

HEILGENDORFF Simone, b. 4 Apr 1961, Opladen, West Germany. Violist; Musicologist. *Education:* Graduated. Zeugnis der allgemeinen Hochschulreife, Leverkusen, Germany, 1979; Final Artistic Examination in Viola Performance, Staatliche Hochschule fuer Musik im Rheinland, Cologne, Germany, 1987; Magister Artium in Musicology, Albert-Ludwigs-University in Freiburg, Germany, 1989; Master of Music in Viola Performance, University of Michigan, 1991. *Career:* Member of symphonic orchestras: Junge Deutsche Philharmonie 1985-87, German training orchestra; Sinfonietta Basel, Philharmonische Werkstatt Switzerland, Serenata Basel (chamber orchestra) and the Freiburger Bachorchester; Conductors: Gerd Albrecht, Rudolf Barschai, David Shallon, Mario Venzago, Laurence Foster. Performances: Contemporary Music: Ensemble Modern (ISCM-Ens), Aventure Freiburg, Contemp. Directions, Ann Arbor, Contemporary Ensemble (Aspen Music Festival 1991); Opera: Opera Factory Zurich - Apr-June 1990 with Figaros Hochzeit; Early Music: Camerata delle Voile Frieburg, Early Music Ensemble Ann Arbor; Tours of Germany, France, Italy, Poland, Spain and the United States; Radio and sic recordings. Conception, management and performance of her own concert programmes. *Publications:* Various musicological publications; glossolalie von Dieter Schnebel - Anmerkungen aur Konstruktion in Schnebel 60 edited by W Gruenzweig, G Schroeder und M Supper, Hofheim 1990. *Address:* Reusratherstr 26, 5090 Leverkusen 3, Germany.

HEILMANN Uwe, b. 7 Sept 1960, Darmstadt, German. Singer (Tenor). m. Tomoko Nakamura. *Education:* Studied in Detmold with Helmut Kretschmar. *Career:* Sang at Detmold from 1981 as Tamino, Don Ottavio and the Italian Singer in Rosenkavalier; Stuttgart Staatsoper from 1985, notably as Tamino, Belmonte, Don Ottavio, Cassio in Otello and Max in Der Freischutz; Munich Staatsoper as Don Ottavio, Vienna as Tamino; Sang Pylades in Iphigénie en Tauride at the Deutsche Oper Berlin; Appearances at the Salzburg and Ludiwgsburg Festivals, 1988-89, including Max; Concert engagements and Lieder recitals, notably in works by Schubert and Wolf; Sang Cassio in Metropolitan Oper Gala, 1991. *Recordings include:* Tamino in Die Zauberflöte, conducted by Solti; Belmonte in Die Entfuhrung conducted by Hogwood. *Address:* Stuttgart Staatsoper, Oberer Schlossgarten 6, 7000 Stuttgart, Germany.

HEIM Norman Michael, b. 30 Sept. 1929, Chicago, Illinois, USA. Professor of Music. m. Catherine Tiemann, 5 June 1951, 2 daughters. *Education:* BMusEd, University of Evansville, 1951; MM, 1952, DMA, 1962, University of Rochester, USA. *Career:* Professor, Central Missouri College, 1952-53; Professor, University of Evansville, 1953-60; Professor, University of Maryland, 1960-; Performs with Maryland Woodwind Quintet; Solo Clarinettist and Director, Maryland Ensemble. *Compositions:* 115 published compositions including major works, Concerto da Camera for two clarinets and horn; Symphonic Sketches for Clarinet and choir; Incantations of Mephistopheles for bass clarinet and piano; Sinfonia for three clarinets. *Recordings:* Preludium and Canzona; Celebrations Suite; Sonata da Chiesa. *Publications:* Author of 17 books including, Style Studies for Clarinet, 1978; The Clarinet Instructor and Technical Studies for Clarinet, 1968. *Contributions to:* Author of over 252 articles in journals such as The Clarinet; The Instrumentalist. *Hobbies:* Travel; Woodworking; Gardening. *Address:* 7402 Wells Blvd, Hyattsville, MD 20783, USA.

HEININEN Paavo, b. 18 Jan 1938, Järvenpää, Finland. Composer. *Education:* Studied Theory and Composition, Sibelius Academy, Helsinki, Finland, College of Music, Cologne, Federal Republic of Germany and at Juilliard School of Music, New York, USA, 1956-

62; Training as pianist, conductor and musicologist. *Career:* Teacher of Theory and Composition, Turku Institute of Music, Turku, Finland; Teacher of Theory and Composition, Sibelius Academy, Helsinki, 1966-. *Compositions include:* Orchestral works: Symphony No 1, 1958, revised 1960; Piano Sonata; Symphony No 3, 1969, revised 1977; Dia, 1979; Works for solo instrument and orchestra: Concerto for piano and orchestra No 3, 1981; Chamber Music: Jeu I and II, 1980; Works for solo instrument: Gymel for bassoon and tape, 1978; Vocal and choral works; The Silken Drum, opera, 1980-83; Floral View With Maidens Singing, folk melody, 1980-83; Dicta computer music, 1980-83. Recorded: Adagio, Royal Philharmonic Orchestra, conductor Walter Süsskind, Philips; Arioso, Heidelberg Chamber Orchestra, conductor Andreas von Lukácsy, Da Camera Magna; Sonatine, Izumi Tateno on piano, Toshiba, 1957; Sonatina Della Primavera, Liisa Pohjola on piano, Konserttikeskus; The Autumns, Finnish Radio Chamber Choir, conductor Harald Andersén, Fennica Nova; Maiandros, tape composition, Fennica Nova; Poesia Squillante ed Incandescente, Paavo Heininen on piano, Tactus; Discantus 1, Ilari Lehtinen on flute on Cipango/Asia Records and Anne Raitio on flute on Sibelius-Akatemia; Touching, Jukka Savijoki on guitar, Bis; Concerto III, Paavo Heininen on piano, Sibelius Symphony Orchestra, conductor Ulf Söderblom, Sibelius-Akatemia. *Address:* TEOSTO, Lauttassarentie I, 00200 Helsinki 20, Finland.

HEINIÖ Mikko, b. 18 May 1948, Tampere, Finland. Composer. Professor of Musicology. m. Riitta Pylvänäinen, 2 Apr 1977, 1s, 1d. *Education:* MA, 1972, PhD, 1984, University of Helsinki; Diploma in Composition, Sibelius Academy, 1977; Hochschule der Kunste, W Berlin, 1975-77. *Career:* Composer, 1972-, Teacher, University of Helsinki, 1977-85; Professor of Musicology, University of Turku, 1985-. *Compositions include:* Orchestral: 5 piano concertos; Concerto for French Horn and orchestra; Concerto for Orchestra; Possible Worlds; Dall'ombra all'ombra; Chamber music: Duo for Violin and Piano; Brass Mass; Piano Trio; In 6 for violoncello and piano; Wintertime for harp and marimba/vibraphone, Piano Quintet; Vocal: Landet som icke är for children's choir and piano; Vuelo de alambre for soprano and orchestra; The Shadow of The Future for Soprano and Brass Instruments; La for piano and 4 voices; Wind Pictures for choir and orchestra. *Recordings include:* Notturno di fiordo for flute and harp; Champignons a l'hermeneutique; Genom kvällen; Vuelo de alambre; Possible Worlds; Wind Pictures. *Publications:* Contemporary Finnish Composers and their background, 1981; Contemporary Finnish Music, 1982; The Idea of Innovation and Tradition, 1984; The Reception of New Classicism in Finnish Music, 1985; The Twelve Tone Age in Finnish Music, 1986; Postmodern features in new Finnish Music, 1988; Contextualisation in the research of art music, 1992. *Memberships:* Board, Society for Finnish composers; Performing rights Society, Teosto; Foundation for Promotion of Finnish Music; Finnish Musicological Society; Chairman: Society of Finnish Symphony Orchestras and Society of Finnish Composers. *Address:* University of Turku, Department of Musicology, 20500 Turku 50, Finland.

HEINRICH Adel Verna, b. 20 Jul 1926, Cleveland, Ohio, USA. Professor of Music Emeritus. *Education:* BA, magna cum laude, Flora Stone Mather College, Case Western Reserve University, Cleveland, Ohio; MSM, Union Theological Seminary, New York City; A Mus D, The University of Wisconsin-Madison; Studied organ with Hugh Porter and John Harvey, and in master classes with E Power Biggs, André Marchal and Jean Langlais; Studied conducting with Robert Shaw and Robert Fountain. *Career:* Held several full-time Church positions before 1964; Assistant Orchestra Conductor of the Colby Community Symphony Orchestra, preparing and conducting several concerts, 1964-74; Served on the faculty each summer of the Colby Church Music Institute, 1964-87; Full-time faculty member, Colby College, Waterville, Maine, 1964-88. Numerous recitals or lecture/recitals. *Compositions:* Over 55 Works include Carol Dramas, Choric-Dances, choral works on American poet texts, solo works for instruments or voice, chamber ensembles, an oratorio, chamber dance-drama, and nature portraits. *Publications:* Bach's Die Kunst der Fuge: A Living Compendium of Fugal Procedures, University Press of America, Washington DC 1982; Organ and Harpsichord Music by Women Composers, Greenwood Press, Westport, Connecticut, 1991. *Contributions to:* Article in Bach Vol XII No 2, April 1981, entitled A Collation of the Expositions in Die Kunst der Fuge of J S Bach; Bach Vol XV, No 3, Jul 1984, entitled Significance of the Original Subject and Its Variants in Bach's Die Kunst der Fuge; Bach Vol XVII No 4, Oct 1986 entitled Heretofore Unpublished Conclusions for the Incomplete Quadruple Fugue (Die Kunst Der Fuge), includes her own original conclusion. *Hobbies:* Oil painting; Writing poetry. *Address:* Hemlock Hills, 14903 Hook Hollow Road, Russell, OH 44072, USA.

HEINRICH Siegfried, b. 10 Jan 1935, Dresden, Germany. Künstlerischer Direktor für Oper und Festspielkonzerte Bad Hersfeld. *Education:* Studied in Dresden and Frankfurt-on-Main, 1954-61. *Debut:* Sänger im Dresden Kreuzchor, 1948. *Career:* Conductor, Frankfurt Chamber Orchestra, 1957; Since 1961-: Artistic Director, Hersfeld Festival Operas and Concerts; Lecturer, Music Academy of Kassel; Conductor, Radio Symphony Orchestras, Prague, Frankfurt-on-Main, Hanover, Luxemburg, ORTF, France, Budapest, Warsaw, Venice, Stuttgart; Concert tours throughout Europe; New Interpretations of Bach's The Art of the Fugue, Beethoven's opera Fidelio with parts of Leonore I, Handel's Messiah, Monteverdi's Marian Vespers, Orfeo, Poppea, Il ritorno d'Ulisse. *Recordings:* Bach, Brahms, Bruckner, Carissimi, Liszt, Monteverdi, Ockeghem, Spohr, Telemann; Prospectusses and press reviews from Jubilate Schallplatten, Oberhöchstädter Weg 48, 60488 Frankfurt-on-Main, Germany; Bärenreiter, Koch International. *Current Management:* Rainer Zagovec, Rathausstr. 42, 65428 Rüsselsheim. *Address:* Sekretariat Nachtigallenstr 9, D-36251 Bad Hersfeld, Germany.

HEINS Ernst Lodewijk, b. 21 May 1937, Amsterdam, Netherlands. Ethnomusicologist. 2 sons, 2 daughters. *Education:* Cand.ex.1960, Doct.ex.1964, Doctor's degree & dissertation, 1977, musicology, University of Amsterdam. *Career:* Senior Fellow, Ethnomusicology Centre Jaap Kunst, University of Amsterdam, 1964-; Leader, Javanese & Balinese gamelan performance groups, Royal Tropical Institute, Amsterdam, 1965-; Church choir conductor, 1958-65. *Publications:* Tempo in Javanese Gamelan Performance, 1969; Goong Renteng; Aspects of Musical Life in a Sudanese Village (dissertation, 1977); 2 documentary films, Javanese dance & wayang puppetry. *Contributions to:* Ethnomusicology; Indonesia; Grove's Dictionary of Music & Musicians. *Honour:* Award (1st prize), International Festival of Scientific Films, Cairo, 1978. *Membership:* Society of Ethnomusicology. *Address:* Valeriusstrasse 100, 1075 GC Amsterdam, Netherlands.

HEISINGER Harold Brent, b. 27 Jan. 1937, Stockton, California, USA. Professor of Music. m. Barbara Anne Dale, 15 June 1958, 3 sons. *Education:* BA, 1958, MA, 1962, Music, San Jose State University; DMA, Stanford University, 1968; Student of Stanley Hollingsworth, Leland Smith, Leonard Ratner and Humphrey Searle. *Career:* Public School Music Teacher, 1958-62; Professor of Music, San Jose State University, 1962-; Composer-in-Residence, Montalvo Centre for the Arts, 1982-84; Planner - Writer, Hawaii Curriculum and Research Group, 1970-72; Pianist/Trombonist, Hawaii New Music Ensemble, 1971-72; Project Director, SJSU Programmes, Contemporary Music Project, 1969-70. *Compositions:* Minim for piano, 1985; Concerto for Piano, Winds and Percussion, 1984; Fanfare and Prayer for band, 1981; Fantasy on a B Flat Blues for piano, 1979; Ekelktikos In Five Pieces, piano, 1973; Statement, band, 1971; A Cycle of Thoughts, soprano and piano, 1971; Hymn for Band, 1970; Soliloquy for Band, 1968; O Praise the Lord, choir and brass, 1967; Fantasia for

Band, 1966; Essay for Band, 1965; March for Timpani and Brass, 1964. *Recordings:* Eklektikos, In Five Pieces, CRS Aiko Onishi piano; Essay for Band, Vorstelijke Melodieen, Basart Records; March for Timpani and Brass, Pembroke Records Inc. *Publications:* Comprehensive Musicianship through Band Performance, Zone 5 Book A, 1972, Zone 4 Book A, 1973, Zone 4 Book B, 1976. *Contributions to:* Living Music, 1987; Music Educators' Journal, 1965. *Address:* 1315 Avalon Drive, San Jose, CA 95125, USA.

HEISS John, b. 23 Oct. 1938, New York, USA. Composer; Flautist. m. Arlene Tubio, 6 June 1964, 1 son, 1 daughter. *Education:* BA, Mathematics, Lehigh University, 1960; Study, composition, with Babbitt, Kim, Luening, Milhaud, Westergaard; Flute with Hosmer, Lora, Tipton; Graduate study in music, teaching assistantships, instructorship, Columbia University, Aspen Music School; MFA Music (Wilson & Ford Fellowships), Princeton University, 1967. *Career:* Principal flute, Boston Musica Viva; Freelance performances with Boston Symphony Orchestra, Boston Ballet Company, other area ensembles; Jordan Hall recitals, annually. Board memberships: Kodály Musical Training Institute; Collage; Artists Foundation; Charles Ives Society; National Flute Association; Commodore, Community Boating. Current faculty, New England Conservatory (composition, director of contemporary ensemble, flute, chamber music, music history, theory); Former faculty, Columbia University, Barnard College, Massachusetts Institute of Technology. *Compositions:* Over 50 including: Pieces for solo flute, flute & piano, flute & cello, songs, music for orchestra. *Recordings:* 4 movements for 3 flutes, 1969; Quartet, flute, clarinet, cello & piano, 1971; Inventions, Contours & Colors, 1973; Songs of Nature, 1975; Capriccio for flute, clarinet & percussion, 1976. *Address:* 61 Hancock Street, Auburndale, MA 02166, USA.

HELESFAY Andrea, b. 18 Nov. 1948, Budapest, Hungary. Violinist. *Education:* Bela Bartók Conservatoire, 1968-73; Franz Liszt University of Music; Study with Vilmos Tatrai, Andras Mihaly. *Debut:* Aged 11, Budapest. *Career:* Member, Hungarian Chamber Orchestra, Budapest Chamber Ensemble, often as Soloist; Zurich Chamber Orchestra, Tonhalle Orchestra, Zurich, 1973-; Many appearances as soloist in Germany, Switzerland; frequent appearances on Radio & TV; Founder, Trio Turicum. *Honours:* Award Winner, International Mozart Violin Competition, Salzburg. *Memberships:* various professional organisations. *Hobbies:* Hiking; Travel; Cooking; Photography; Children. *Address:* Hadlaubstrasse 148, CH 8006 Zurich, Switzerland.

HELFFER Claude, b. 18 June 1922, Paris, France. Pianist. m. Mireille de Nervo, 3 June 1946, 2 sons, 2 daughters. *Education:* Ecole Polytechnique, 1942. *Career:* Numerous recital tours and concert tours with orchestra, Europe, USA, North and South America, Australia, Japan, etc. *Recordings:* Various including music by Boulez, Xenakis, Debussy and Schoenberg. *Honours:* Chevaler de la Legion d'Honneur; Croix de guerre, 1939-45; Officier des arts et lettres; Numerous prizes for records including President of the Republic's Prizes for record of contemporary music, 1986, 1993. *Hobby:* Religious problems. *Address:* 6 rue Mignet, 75016, Paris, France.

HELFRICH Paul M., b. 5 May 1955, Philedelphia, USA. *Education:* BMus, Pennsylvania State University, 1978; MMus, Composition, Temple University, 1980; DMA, Composition, Temple University, 1986, studied with Clifford Taylor and Maurice Wright. *Career includes:* Owner, Nu Trax Recording Studio, Upper Darby, PA, 1981-; Senior Project Manager, 1987-91, Assistant Director, Exhibit Development, 1991-, Franklin Institute Science Museum, PA. *Compositions include:* Sine Nomine for brass chorale, 1974; Metamorphosis 1 for string orchestra, 1976; Theme and Five Variations for string orchestra and percussion, 1977; Five Short pieces for piano, 1977; Sonata Allegro in G for symphonic wind ensemble, 1978; Winds from a longer

Distance, for tape and seven dancers, 1989; Song for healing, tape and solo dancer, 1990; The Robot Game Show, for tape, 1990; Movie soundtracks: Spirits in the Valley II, 1991, The Alchemist's Cookbook, 1991. *Address:* 130 Cunningham Avenue, Upper Darby, PA 19082, USA.

HELIN Jacquelyn, b. 24 Sept. 1951, Chicago, Illinois, USA. Concert Pianist. *Education:* BM, University of Oregon, 1973; Graduate Studies, Yale University School of Music, 1973-74; MA, Stanford University, 1976; DMA, University of Texas, 1982. *Career:* Performances at Wigmore Hall, London, The Chagall Museum, Nice, American Embassy, Paris, Merkin Hall and Town Hall, New York, Dumbarton Oaks, The Corcoran Gallery, Hirshhorn Museum, Washington DC and The Brooklyn College Conservatory of Music. The Dame Myra Hess Series; The Beethoven Discovery Series, The Aspen Music Festival; Featured Artist, PBS TV programme honouring Virgil Thomson's 90th birthday; Premiered Joan Tower's Piano Concerto with Hudson Valley Philharmonic, 1986; Numerous radio appearances: WFMT Chicago, WNCN New York, WGMS Washington and throughout USA on National Public Radio. *Recordings:* For Musical Heritage, Virgil Thomson Ballet and Film Scores for Piano. *Honours:* Winner, Artists International Competition, 1984. *Memberships:* Grove Music Society; Mu Phi Epsilon; Phi Kappa Phi; Pi Kappa Lambda. *Hobbies:* Films; Theatre; Travel; Hiking..

HELLAWELL Piers, b. 14 July 1956, Chinley, Derbyshire, England. Composer; University Lecturer. *Education:* New England College, Oxford, 1975-78; BA (Hons. 1st Class), 1978; MA, 1984; Postgraduate Research, 1978-81. *Career:* Appointed Composer-in-Residence, Queens University of Belfast, 1981-85; Northern Ireland Coordinator, European Music Year, 1985; Appointed Lecturer in Music, Queens University of Belfast, 1986-; Regular Broadcasts BBC Radio Ulster; BBC Radio 3, Who Needs Programme Notes; Lecturer to schools. *Compositions:* Xenophon: commissioned, performed Belfast and elsewhere and Radio 3 broadcast by Ulster Orchestra, 1985; How Should I Your True Love Know: first perfomed by The Fires of London, Elizabeth Hall, conducted by Peter Maxwell Davies, 1986; Seal Songs for Flute: first US performance, New Hampshire Music Festival, 1987; Seal Songs/Squam Songs (clarinet), 1987; Sound Carvings From Rano Raraku: commissioned (ACNI), first performed N Ireland tour and BBC broadcast, Martin Feinstein Quartet, 1988; Das Leonora Notenbuch: commissioned North West Arts and first performed Buxton Festival by William Howard; Oh Whistle and I'll Come to You: commissioned and performed Washington, DC and elsewhere by Collaborations, 1988; Soundtrack: first performed Almeida Theatre, London by Innererkland Music Theatre, 1989; Squam Songs: Dance premiere, Project Arts Theatre, Dublin and elsewhere, by Barefoot Dance Company, 1989; The Erratic Aviator's Dance: commissioned and performed at the Dance Place, Washington, DC and elsewhere by Alvin Mayes Dance and Collaborations Ensemble, 1989; Oh Whistle: UK premiere at Barber Festival, Birmingham, 1990; Das Leonora Notenbuch: 1st broadcast BBC Radio 3, 1990; Truth or Consequences: commissioned (ABSA) and first performed by Sequenza at Award Ceremony, 1991; Improvise! Improvise!: US premiere at The Phillips Collection, Washington DC, by William Feasley, 1991. *Hobbies:* Concert Organising and Conducting; Balinese Camelan; Photography; Walking. *Address:* Department of Music, Queens University of Belfast, Belfast, BT7 1NN, Northern Ireland.

HELLER Alfred, b. 8 Dec. 1931, New York City, USA. Composer; Conductor; Pianist. m. (1) Alice Ewing Jones, 31 Mar. 1965, 1 son, (2) Karen S. Cottrell, 28 Nov. 1981. *Education:* High School of Music and Art, New York City, 1949; BM, Composition, Syracuse University, 1952; MM, Piano, Manhattan School of Music, 1954; Fulbright Scholar, Italy, Opera Conducting, 1954-55; DMus, Instrumental Conducting, Indiana University, 1974. *Debut:* Opera, La Vacanze Musicali, Venice, 1955; Symphony, Adzerbaijan, USSR, 1971; Composer, High

School of M & A, 1949. *Career:* Protege of Heitor Villa-Lobos, 1956-59; Assistant Conductor, Chicago Lyric Opera, New York City Opera, 1958-63; Coach/Accompanist for Frank Guarrera, Jan Peerce, Giuseppe di Stefano, John Brownlee, 1954-80; Guest Conductor: Hungarian State Symphony, Adzerbaijan State Symphony, Georgian State Symphony, Brasov Philharmonic, Tatar State Symphony, Latvian Radio and Television Symphony, Baton Rouge Symphony. *Compositions:* Compositions performed in West Germany, Austria, Mexico, USSR, UK and USA; Songs on Emily Dickinson Poems sung by Arleen Auger.*Recordings include:* Villa-Lobos Violin Sonatas and Piano Suites, KTC 1101; Villa-Lobos Piano Works, KTC 1123; Villa-Lobos Vocal Music, Vol II, 1994. *Address:* 153 East 92nd Street, 4R, New York, NY 10128-2479, USA.

HELLER Jack Joseph, b. 30 Nov. 1932, New Orleans, Louisiana, USA. College Professor; Conductor. m. Judith A. Krawetz, 9 June 1957, 2 sons, 1 daughter. *Education:* Diploma, Violin, Juilliard School of Music 1952; MMus. University of Michigan 1958; PhD, University of Iowa 1962. *Debut:* Violin Soloist, New Orleans Symphony 1947. *Career:* Assistant Concert Master, New Orleans opera 1947-49; Freelance Violinist, NYC (Radio, TV, Chamber Groups) 1950-55; Concertmaster, Toledo Symphony 1955-58; Professor, University of Connecticut 1960-85; Conductor and Music Director, Manchester (CT) Symphony and Chorale 1968-85; Founder and Conductor, Nutmeg Chamber Orchestra 1984-; Conductor and Music Director, Tampa Bay Symphony 1986-; Conductor and Music Director, Spanish Lyric Theatre, 1992-; Professor and Director, Music School, University of South Florida, Tampa 1985-. *Contributions to:* Numerous contributions on Research In The Psychology of Music in Professional Journals 1968-. *Address:* Music School, FAH 110, University of South Florida, Tampa, Florida 33620, USA.

HELLER Richard, (Rainer), b. 19 Apr. 1954, Vienna, Austria. Composer. m. Shihomi Inoue, 26 Aug. 1980. *Education:* Diploma in Composition, 1979; Final Examination composition for Audio-visual media, 1978, Final examination for cultural management, 1979, Hochschule für Musik und Darstellende Kunst, Vienna. *Career:* Numerous performances of own works in Argentina, Austria, CSFR, Denmark, Egypt, France, Germany, Greece, Hungary, Italy, Japan, Yugoslavia, The Netherlands, Russia, Switzerland, Spain, Saudi Arabia, Turkey, Greece, Hungary, South Africa, Uruguay, CSFR, Russia; Teaching Composition and Music Theory, Music Academy, Augsburg, 1979-. *Compositions include:* Concerto for violin; Concerto for 2 pianos and orchestra; Sinfonietta for wind orchestra; Concerto for bass clarinet; Concerto for Marimba; Concertino for orchestra; Concerto per fiati; Toccata for wind orchestra; Novelette (piano trio); 3 moments musicaux (guitar quartet), string quartet; Cellophonie (8 violon cellos); Statement, (string trio); Elegy on texts out of Duineser Elepien by RM Rilke; Ballade (piano 4 hands), various pieces for chamber ensembles; songs; solo pieces for piano, organ, bass clarinet; numerous commissions. *Recordings:* LP (Augsburger Gitarrenquartett), CD (organ-piano), MC (Live documentations); numerous radio recordings. *Address:* Reichenberger Strasse 24, D-86161 Augsburg, Germany.

HELLERMANN William, b. 15 July 1939, Wisconsin, USA. Composer. m. 17 Sept 1985, 1s, 1d. *Education:* MA Composition, 1969, DMA, 1976, Columbia University School of Arts. Private Study with Stefan Wolfe. *Compositions:* Time and Again for orchestra, 1967; anyway ... for orchestra, 1976; But, The Moon..., for guitar and orchestra, 1975; Tremble, for solo guitar; Squebek for desk Chair, 1978; Post/Pone for guitar and 5 instruments, 1990. *Recordings:* Ariel, for electronic tape, 1967; At Sea; Ek-Stasis II; Passages 13 -The Fire. *Publications:* Scores published by Theodore Preeser and ACA; Articles: Boyond Categories, 1981; Experimental Music, 1985. *Honours:* Prix de Rome, American Academy, 1972; NEA Fellowship, 1976-79; Composer

in Residence, Centre for Culture and Performing Arts, SUNY at Buffalo. *Memberships:* BMI; ACA. *Address:* Box 850, Philmont, NY 12565, USA.

HELLMANN Claudia, b. 1931, Berlin, Germany. Singer (Mezzo- soprano). *Education:* Studied in Berlin. *Debut:* Oper, Munster, 1958-60. *Career:* Stuttgart Staatsoper, 1960-66, Nuremberg, 1966-75; Appearances at the Bayeruth Festsival, 1958-61, as Wellgunde and a Flower Maiden; La Scala Milan, 1963, as Flosshilde; Sang in concerta at the Salzburg Festival, 1961-85; Hamburg Staatsoper from 19960, Theatre de la Monnaie Brussels, 1963-67; Other roles have included Marcellina, Magdalena in Die Meistersinger, Mistress Quickly, Fidalma in Matrimonio Segreto and Frau von Hufnagel in Henze's Der Junge Lord; Many concert and oratorio appearances. *Recordings:* Ismene in Orff's Antigonae, Bruckner's F minor Mass; Die Walküre; Bach's Easter Oratorio; Bach Church Cantatas. *Address:* c/o Stuttgart Staatsoper, Ober Schlossgaten 6, 7000 Stuttgart, Germany.

HELLWIG Klaus, b. 3 Aug 1941, Essen, Germany. Pianist; Educator. m. Mi-Joo Lee (pianist). *Education:* Folkwang Hochschule Essen with Detlef Kraus, in Paris with Pierre Sancan; Summer courses with Guido Agoshi and Wilhelm Kempff. *Career:* Concerts throughout Europe, US and Canada, Far and Middle East; all German radio stations, BBC London, NHK Tokyo. Professor at the Hochschule der Künste, Berlin. *Recordings:* FX Mozart Concerti in C and E Flat, Cologne Radio Orchestra, conductor Roland Bader (Schwann); Haydn Concerto in D, Mozart Concerto KV 537, Sinfonietta (Toshiba-EMI); Bach Inventions (RSM), together with other recordings a total of 20 records. *Honours:* Prize at the Concours Internationale M Long, J Thibaud, Paris, 1965; First Prize at the Concorso Internazionale G B Viotti Vercelli, Italy, 1966. *Current Management:* Raymond Weiss Artist Management, New York. *Address:* Regensburgerstr 27, 10777 Berlin 30, Germany.

HELM E(rnest) Eugene, b. 23 Jan. 1928, New Orleans, Louisiana, USA. Musicologist; Professor. *Education:* Southeastern Louisiana College, BME, 1950; Louisiana State University, MME, 1955, North Texas State University, PhD, 1958. *Career:* Faculty member, Louisiana College, 1953-55, Wayne (Neb) State College, 1958-59, University of Iowa, 1960-68; Associate Professor, 1968-69, Professor, 1969-, of Music, Chairman, Musicology Division, 1971-87, University of Maryland; Coordinating Editor, Carl Philipp Emanuel Bach Edition, 1982-. *Publications:* Music at the Court of Frederick the Great, 1960; with A.Luper, Words and Music, 1971, 2nd edition, 1982; A Thematic Catalogue of the Works of Carl Philipp Emanuel Bach, 1987. *Contributions to:* Articles in numerous periodicals and other publications. *Address:* c/o Department of Music, University of Maryland, College Park, MD 20742, USA.

HELM Everett (Burton), b. 17 July 1913, Minneapolis, Minnesota, USA. Composer; Writer on Music. *Education:* Studied at Harvard University, PhD 1939; Studies in Europe with Malipiero and Vaughan Williams. *Career:* Head of music department of Western College, Oxford, Ohio 1944-46; Music Officer with the US Military in Germany 1948-50; Resident in Asolo, near Venice, from 1963; Guest lecturer at the University of Ljubljana 1966-68; Editor of Musical America, New York, 1961-63; Compositions have been performed by the New York Philharmonic, Berlin Philharmonic and BBC Symphony Orchestras. *Publications:* The Beginnings of the Italian Madrigal and the Works of Arcadelt 1939; The Chansons of Arcadelt 1942; Bela Bartók in Selbsteugnissen und Bilddokumenten Hamburg 1965; Composer, Performer, Public, Florence 1970; Bartók London 1971; Franz Liszt, Hamburg 1971; Music and Tomorrow's Public, Wilmeshaven 1981. *Compositions include:* Two Piano Concertos 1951, 1956; Adam and Eve, adaptation of a medieval mystery play 1951; Concerto for 5 instruments, percussion and strings 1953; The Siege of Tottenburg, radio opera 1956; Le Roy fait battre tambour, ballet 1956; 500 Dragon-

Thalers, singspiel 1956; Divertimento for flutes 1957; Sinfonia da Camera 1961; Concerto for double bass and string orchestra 1968; 2 String Quartets; Woodwind Quintet 1967; Songs and piano music. *Address:* c/o ASCAP, ASCAP Building, One Lincoln Plaza, New York, NY 10023, USA.

HELM Hans, b. 12 April 1934, Passau, Germany. Singer (Baritone). *Education:* Studied with Else Zeidler and Franz Reuter-Wolf in Munich, Emmi Muller in Krefeld. *Debut:* Graz 1957, in Boris Godunov. *Career:* Sang in Vienna, Cologne, Frankfurt, Munich, Dusseldorf and Hanover; Salzburg Festival 1973, in the premiere of De Temporum fine Comoedia by Orff; Glyndebourne Festival 1976, as the Count in Le Nozze di Figaro; Vienna Staatsoper, 1987 and 1990, as Agamemnon in Iphigénie en Aulide, and in Die Soldaten; Munich 1989, as Faninal in Der Rosenkavalier; Sang The Forester in The Cunning Little Vixen at the Vienna Volksoper, 1992; Many concert appearances. *Recordings:* Otello (EMI); De Temporum fine Comoedia and Die Frau ohne Schatten (Deutsche Grammophon). *Address:* c/o Staatsoper, Opernring 2, A-1010 Vienna, Austria.

HELM Karl, b. 3 Oct. 1938, Passau, Germany. Singer (Bass). *Education:* Studied with Else Zeidler in Dresden and with Franz Reuter-Wolf in Munich. *Debut:* Berne 1968, as Don Alfonso in Così fan Tutte. *Career:* Member of the Bayerische Staatsoper, Munich; Guest appearances in Geneva, Paris, Dusseldorf, Hamburg and Stuttgart; Other roles include Arkel in Pelléas et Mélisande, Rocco, King Philip, Zaccaria, Varlaam, Fasolt, Falstaff in Die Lustigen Weiber von Windsor, Dulcamara, and Melitone in La Forza del Destino; Berlin Staatsoper 1987, in La Cenerentola; Munich 1990, as First Nazarene in Salome; Sang Swallow in Peter Grimes at Munich, 1991; Many concert appearances. *Recordings include:* Die Feen by Wagner. *Address:* Bayerische Staatsoper, Postfach 745, D-8000 Munich 1, Germany.

HELMAN Zofia, b. 8 Mar. 1937, Radom, Poland. Musicologist. m. A Bednarczyk, 10 Sept. 1968. *Education:* Prof Dr, Musicology, University of Warsaw. *Career:* Assistant Professor, Institute of Musicology, University of Warsaw, 1980-; Professor, 1990-, Director, 1991-, Institute of Musicology. *Publications:* Book: Neoclassicism in the Polish Music of the XX Century, 1985; Art on XIX and Century Music; Editor Works of K Szymanowski. *Contributions to:* Muzyka, Warsaw; Polish Art Studies, Warsaw. *Memberships:* International Society of Musicology; Schumann-Gesellschaft in Dusseldorf; Gesellschaft für Musikforschnng, Kassel. *Address:* Institute of Musicology, Warsaw University, Zwirki i Wigury 93, PL-02-089 Warszawa, Poland.

HELMS Joachim, b. 24 June, 1943, Rostock, Germany. Singer (Tenor). *Education:* Studied at the Franz Liszt Musikhochschule Weimar and in Dresden. *Debut:* Erfurt, 1974, as Ernesto in Don Pasquale. *Career:* Sant at Erfurt, 1974-83, as Mozart's Ferrando and Tamino, the Duke of Mantua, Nemorino, Don Carlos, Max in Der Freischütz and Sergei in Katerina Ismailova; Dresden Staatsoper from 1984, as Rodolfo, Alfredo and Don Ottavio; Guest appearances in the former Soviet Union, Poland, Bulgaria, Austria and Switzerland; Sang Ernesto at Leipzig, 1989; Many concert appearances and broadcasting engagements. *Address:* c/o Staatsoper, 8012 Dresden, Germany

HELPS Robert, b. 23 Sept 1928, New Jersey, USA. Composer; Pianist; Professor. *Education:* Julliard Preparatory Dept and Institute of Music Arts, 1936-43; Private study with Abby Whiteside, piano; and Roger Sessions, composition, 1943-60. *Debut:* Recital, New York, 1990. *Career:* Active piano and chamber music performances including many premieres with leading contemporary music groups in New York, Boston, Chicago, San Francisco, Los Angeles; Tours with Bethany Beardslee, Soprano, Rudolf Kolisch, Ididone Cohen, Jorja Freezanis, Violin. *Compositions:* Symphony, Two Piano Concertos, various chamber music and songs; Many solo piano pieces, voice and orchestra. *Recordings include:* Nocturne, 3 Hommages; Hommage a Fauvre; 3 Hommages, Nocture for string quartet. *Publications include:* Nocturne, 1975; False Mirage, 1978; Eventually the Carousel Begins, 1991; The Running Sun, 1976; Symphony No 1; Piano Concerto No 1. *Address:* 11500 Summit West Blvd 16F, Tampa, FL 33617, USA.

HELTAY Laszlo Istvan, b. 5 Jan. 1930, Budapest, Hungary. Conductor. *Education:* MA, Franz Liszt Academy of Music, Budapest, with Kodály and Bardos; BLitt, Oxford. *Career:* Director of Music, Merton College, Oxford, 1960-64; Associate Conductor, New Zealand Broacasting Corporation Symphony Orchestra 1964-65; Musical Director, New Zealand Opera Company, 1964-66; Conductor, Phoenix Opera Company, London, 1967-69, 1973; Conductor, Collegium Musicum of London, 1970-1989; Director of Music, Gardner Centre, Sussex University from 1968-1978; Founded Brighton Festival Chorus; Chorus of the Academy of St Martin in the Fields, 1975-; Director of Royal Choral Society, 1985-; Has conducted leading orchestras in Britain and Abroad including the Philharmonia, the Royal Philharmonic, the London Philharmonic & the Dallas Symphony Orchestras. *Recordings:* Choral works of Kodály, Resphighi, Rossini & Haydn on Argos & Decca Labels; Paco Pena, Misa Flamenca for Virgin *Honours:* International Kodaly Medal, 1982. *Hobbies:* Chess; Skiing; Tennis. *Current Management:* Influence. *Address:* c/o International House, Wendell Road, W12 9RT, England.

HEMBERG (Bengt Sven) Eskil, b. 19 Jan. 1938, Stockholm, Sweden. General Director. m. Birgit Sofia Ohlsson, 8 July 1962, 2 sons, 1 daughter. *Education:* Music Teachers Degree. *Debut:* Conductor, Uppsala, 1961; Higher Organist's Degree; Higher Cantors Degree; Orchestra Conducting Class. *Career:* Executive Producer, Swedish Radio, 1963-70; Planning Manager, Head, Foreign Relations, National Institute of Concerts, 1970-83; General Director, Stora Teatern Gothenburg, 1983-87; Royal Opera, Stockholm, 1987-. *Compositions:* Operas: Love, Love, Love; Pirates of the Deep Green Sea; Saint Erik's Crown; Herr Apfelstadt wird Künstler, chamber Opera, 1989. *Recordings:* Compositions on EMI & Phono Suecia; Caprice. *Publications:* Eskil Hemberg - Swedish Composer, Choral Conductor & Administrator: A Survey of His Works, 1987. *Address:* Floravagen 3, S-131, 41 Nacka, Sweden.

HEMM Manfred, b. 1961, Modlin, Austria. Singer (Baritone). *Education:* Studied at the Vienna Conservatory with Waldemar Kmentt. *Debut:* Klagenfurt 1984, as Mozart's Figaro. *Career:* Sang at Augsburg 1984-86, Graz, 1986-88, notably as Papageno, Leporello, and Polyphemus in Acis and Galatea; Vienna Staatsoper from 1988 (title role in the premiere of Von Einem's Tuliphant, 1990); Guest appearances as Bayreuth, Basel, Berne, Zurich, Salzburg (Figaro, 1989-91) and Orange; Sang Figaro at the Deutsche Oper Berlin, 1990, Aix-en-Provence Festival, 1991; Metropolitan Opera debut 1991, as Papageno; Salzburg Festival, 1992, as the One Eyed Brother in Die Frau ohne Schatten; Frequent Lieder recitals and concert appearances. *Recordings include:* Video of Die Zauberflöte, from the Met.

HEMMINGS Peter William, b. 10 Apr. 1934, London, England. Opera Company Administrator. m. Jane Frances Kearnes, 19 May 1962, 2 sons, 3 daughters. *Education:* Mill Hill School, London 1947-52; Gonville and Caius College, Cambridge 1954-57; Choral Exhibitioner, Cambridge. *Career:* Harold Holt Ltd., London 1958; Repertory and Planning Manager, Sadler's Wells Opera 1959-65; General Manager, New Opera Co., 1957-65; General Administrator, Scottish Opera 1962-77; General Manager, Australian Opera 1977-79; Managing Director, London Symphony 1980-84; General Director, Los Angeles Music Center Opera 1984-. *Honours:* Fellow of The Royal Scottish Academy of Music; Hon. LLD., University of Strathclyde; Honorary

Fellow of The Royal Academy of Music. *Memberships:* Governor of Royal Academy of Music; Director of Sadler's Wells Association; Board member, opera America; Member, Garrick Club; Vice President of Opera America. *Address:* 775 South Madison Avenue, Pasadena, CA 91106, USA.

HEMSLEY Thomas, b. 12 Apr 1927, Coalville, Leicestershire, England. Opera and Concert Singer; Producer; Teacher; Lecturer. m. Gwenllian James, 9 Nov 1960, 3 sons. *Education:* Brasenose College, Oxford; Private music studies. *Debut:* Opera, Mermaid Theatre, London, 1951. *Career:* St Paul's Cathedral, London, 1950-51; Stadttheater, Aachen, Federal Republic of Germany, 1953-56; Deutsche Oper am Rhein, 1957-63; Opernhaus Zurich, Switzerland, 1963-67; Performed at Glyndebourne, 1953-83, as Hercule (Alceste), Masetto (Don Giovanni), Sprecher (Zauberflöte), Minister (Fidelio), Dr Reischmann (Elegy for Young Lovers), Musiklehrer (Ariadne), Aeneas (Dido), Arbace (Idomeneo); Edinburgh and Bayreuth Festivals, (1968-70, as Beckmesser), Covent Garden, Scottish Opera, Welsh Opera, English National Opera, English Opera Group, Kent Opera (Falstaff, 1980); Created Demetrius in A Midsummer Night's Dream (Aldeburgh 1960), Mangus in The Knot Garden at Covent Garden, 1970, and Caesar in Iain Hamilton's Catiline Conspiracy; Alfonso with Welsh National Opera, 1986; Produced The Return of Ulysses for Kent Opera, 1989; Soloist with many major orchestras; Frequent broadcasts on radio and TV; Repertoire includes more than 150 Operatic Roles; Masterclasses, BBC TV, Danish TV, Music colleges in Britain, Denmark, Sweden, Norway; Visiting Professor, Royal College of Music, London, and Royal Northern College of Music; Guest Professor, Royal Danish Academy of Music. *Recordings:* Operas: Dido and Aeneas; The Fairy Queen; Saul; Xerxes; Alcina; Alceste; Midsummer Night's Dream; Savitri; The Knot Garden; Meistersinger; Cantatas: Bach; Handel; Schütz; Songs: Schubert; Schumann; Wolf; Berkeley; Choral: Delius Requiem. *Honour:* Honorary RAM, 1974; Hon FTCL, 1988. *Memberships:* Equity; ISM; Garrick Club; Member, Royal Philharmonic Society; Fellow Royal Society of Arts. *Hobbies:* Gardening; Mountain walking. *Current Management:* Harold Holt Ltd. *Address:* 10 Denewood Road, London N6 4AJ, England. 1.

HENAHAN Donal, b. 28 Feb. 1921, Cleveland, Ohio, USA. Music Critic. *Education:* Ohio University; Northwestern University, BA, 1948. *Career:* Staff Writer, 1947-57, Music Critic, 1957-67, Chicago Daily News; Staff Writer, 1967-80, Chief Music Critic, 1980-, New York Times. *Honour:* Pulitzer Prize in music criticism, 1986. *Address:* 229 West 43rd Street, New York, NY 10036, USA.

HENDERSON Roy (Galbraith), b. 4 July 1899, Edinburgh, Scotland. Retired Baritone & Teacher of Singing (Private); Professor of Singing. m. Bertha Collin Smyth, 1926 (dec. 1985), 1 son, 2 daughters. *Education:* Royal Academy of Music, London (Worshipful Company of Musicians Medal). *Debut:* As Baritone Singer, Queen's Hall, London, 1925. *Career:* Has sung at all leading Festivals in England, International Festival for Contemporary Music, Amsterdam, 1933; Recitals at first two Edinburgh Festivals, 1947, 1948; principal parts in all Glyndebourne Opera Festivals, 1934-40 as Mozart's Count, Guglielmo, Papageno and Masetto; Associated chiefly with works of Delius, Elgar, and Vaughan Williams, and sang many first performances of contemporary music; Retired from Concert Platform, 1952, to devote his whole time to teaching (among his pupils was late Kathleen Ferrier); Conductor, Huddersfield Glee and Madrigal Society, 1932-39; Founder, Conductor, Nottingham Oriana Choir, 1937-52; Conductor, Bournemouth Municipal Choir, 1942-53; Adjudicator, International Concours, Geneva, 1952, and Triennially, 1956-65; Member, Jury of International Muziekstad's Hertogenbosch, Holland, 1955-62, 1965, and Barcelona, 1965; Master Classes in Singing: Royal Conservatory of Music, Toronto, 1956; Toonkunst Conservatorium, Rotterdam, 1957, 1958; Hertogenbosch, 1967; Professor, Singing, Royal

Academy of Music, London, 1940-74. *Recordings:* Decca's first classical artist. *Publications:* Contributed to: Kathleen Ferrier, ed Neville Cardus 1954; Opera Annual 1958; The Voice, editor Sir Keith Falkner, 1983.*Honours:* FRAM, 1932; CBE, 1970. *Membership:* Incorporated Society of Musicians. *Address:* Ivor Newton House, Edward Road, Bromley, Kent BR1 3NQ, England.

HENDL Walter, b. 12 Jan. 1917, West New York, New Jersey, USA. Conductor; Pianist; Composer. m. Barbara Heisley, 1 daughter by previous marriage. *Education:* Studied piano with Clarence Adler; Piano scholarship student of David Saperton and conducting scholarship student of Fritz Reiner, Curtis Institute of Music, Philadelphia; Conducting student of Serge Koussevtizky, Berkshire Music Center, Tanglewood, Massachusetts, summers 1941-42. *Career:* Assistant Conductor, New York Philharmonic Orchestra, 1945-49; Music Director, Dallas Symphony Orchestra, 1953-72; Associate Conductor, Chicago Symphony Orchestra, 1958-64; Music Director, Ravinia Festival, 1959-63; Director, Eastman School of Music, Rochester, New York, 1964-72; Music Director, Erie (Pa) Philharmonic Orchestra, 1976-. *Recordings:* For Desto and RCA. *Address:* c/o Erie Philharmonic Orchestra, 409 G. Daniel Baldwin Building, Erie, PA 16501, USA.

HENDRICKS Barbara, b. 20 Nov. 1948, Stephens, Arkanas, USA. Singer (Soprano). *Education:* Juilliard School of Music with Jennie Tourel. *Debut:* Mini-Met, New York, 1973 in Four Saints in Three Acts. *Career:* Glyndebourne 1974, in La Calisto; San Francisco 1976, as Monteverdi's Poppea; Berlin Deutsche Oper 1978, as Susanna in Le Nozze di Figaro; Orange Festival 1980, as Gilda; Paris Opera 1982, as Gounod's Juliette; Los Angeles and Covent Garden 1982, as Nannetta in a new production of Falstaff conducted by Giulini; Metropolitan Opera debut 1986, as Sophie in Der Rosenkavalier (returned 1987, as Susanna); Song recitals in the US, Europe and Russia with Dmitri Alexeev, Daniel Barenboim, Michel Béroff and Radu Lupu as accompanists; Concert appearances with Barenboim, Bernstein, Dorati, Giulini, Karajan, Maazel, Mehta and Solti; Tours of Japan with Karajan, Bernstein and the Vienna State Opera; Festival engagements at Aix, Edinburgh, Montreux, Orange, Prague, Salzburg and Vienna; Debut at La Scala 1987, Susanna; Sang at the opening concert of the Opéra Bastille Paris, 1989; Norina in Don Pasquale at Lyons, 1989 (also at Venice 1990); Debut as Manon at Parma, 1991; Sang Micaela at Orange, 1992. *Recordings include:* Mahler 2nd Symphony and Mozart Masses (Deutsche Grammophon); Haydn Nelson Mass (EMI); Handel's Solomon, Les Pêcheurs de Perles (Philips); La Bohème, Don Pasquale and Le Roi d'Ys (Erato); Orphée et Eurydice and Hänsel und Gretel (EMI). *Honours include:* Commandeur des Arts et des Lettres 1986; Goodwill Ambassador of the High Commissioner for Refugees at the United Nations 1987. *Address:* IMG, MCAIA House, 3 Burlington Lane, London W4, England.

HENDRICKS Marijke, b. 18 Apr 1956, Schinveld, Holland. Singer (Mezzo-soprano). *Education:* Studied in Maastricht and Cologne. *Career:* Sang at the Cologne Opera 1981-85, notably as Nancy in Martha, Cherubino, Hansel, Meg Page, and Olga in Eugene Onegin; Sang the Marchesa in Musgrave's The Voice of Ariande at the 1982 Edinburgh Festival; Guest appearances at Geneva 1985, as Cherubino, Salzburg 1986 as Second Lady in Die Zauberflöte and Innsburck, 1986 in the title role of Cesti's Orontea; Bordeaux and Lyon 1987, as Ramiro in La Finta Giardiniera; Amsterdam 1987, in a concert performance of Tancredi, as Isaura; Visits to the Orange Festival and to Israel with the company of Cologne Opera, 1984; Antwerp 1988, as Dulcinée in Massenet's Don Quichotte; Maastricht 1989 in La Belle Helene; Television appearances in Austria and Switzerland. *Address:* Oper der Stadt Koln, Offenbachplatz, 5000 Cologne, Germany.

HENDRIE Gerald Mills,b. 28 Oct. 1935. Professor of Music. m. (1) Dinah Florence Barsham, 1962, deceased, 1985, 2 sons; (2) Lynette Anne Maddern,

1986. *Education:* Royal College of Music; MA MusB, PhD, Selwyn College, Cambridge; FRCO; ARCM. *Career:* Director of Music, Homerton College, Cambridge, 1962-63; Lecturer, History of Music, University of Manchester, 1963-67; Professor, Chairman, Department of Music, University of Victoria BC, Canada, 1967-69; Professor, Open University, 1969-90 (retired); Director of Studies, Music, St. Johns College, Cambridge, 1981-85 (Supervisor, 1977-85); Visiting Fellow in Music, University of Western Unviersity, 1985. *Publications:* Musica Britannica XX, Orlando Gibbons : Keyboard Music, 1962, 2nd revised edition 1967; Anthems für Cannons (3 volumes, 1985, 1987, 1991), Anthems für die Chapel Royal (1992), Utrecht Te Deum and Jubilate (in press), all for Halle Handel Society's Collected edition of Handel's works; Iolanthe, Critical edition in full score for the new Collected Edition of the Gilbert and Sullivan operas published by Broude Brothers, New York (in press); own compositions include Quintet for Brass, 1988; Magnificat and Nunc Dimittis for Boys' Voices for St Paul's Cathedral, 1988; Te Deum and Jubilate for Men's Voices for St Paul's Cathedral 1988; other Services for St John's College Cambridge, New College, Oxford, Canterbury Cathedral; organ music includes Choral: Hommage à César Franck, 1990; Le Tombeau de Marcel Dupré, 1991-93, comprising Toccata and Fugue, Prelude and Fugue on B.A.C.H., Two Sketches on B.A.C.H.; various other published compositions; articles for professional journals. *Address:* The Garth, 17 The Avenue, Dallington, Northampton NN5 7AJ, England.

HENDRIKX Louis, b. 13 Mar. 1927, Antwerp, Belgium. Singer (Bass). *Education:* Studied at the Antwerp Conservatory and with Willem Ravelli. *Debut:* Antwerp 1963, as Samuel in Un Ballo in Maschera. *Career:* Sang in Antwerp and Kassel; Further appearances in Hannover, Cologne; Dortmund; Munich, Hamburg, Nuernberg, Lyon, Bordeaux, Toulose, Venice, Palermo, Milan, Monte Carlo, Stockholm, Glasgow and London (Gurnemanz at Covent Garden); Promenade Concerts 1972; Théâtre de la Monnaie and Rome Opera 1973, as Boris Godunov and as King Mark in Tristan und Isolde; Also Salzburg, Fafner in Rheingold and Pogner in Mastersingers for the Easter Festivals. *Recordings include:* Gessler in Guillaume Tell (EMI); Rheingold with Herbert Karajan. *Address:* c/o Théâtre de la Monnaie, 4 Léopoldstrasse, B-1000 Brussels, Belgium.

HENN Brigitte, b. 21 Oct 1939, Freudenthal, Czecholosvakia. Singer (Soprano). m. Raymond Henn. *Education:* Studied in Frankfurt, in Weisbaden with Helena Braun and in Basle. *Debut:* Sang at the Basle Opera, 1968-75, Deutsche Oper Berlin, 1976-80; Guest appearances at Basle from 1982, and in Dusseldorf, Frankfurt, Zurich and Hanover; Roles have included Mozart's Countess, Donna Anna and Fiordiligi, Agathe, Euridice, Marenka in The Bartered Bride, Wagner's Senta, Elsa and Sieglinde, Elisabeth de Velois, Alice Ford and Amemlia in Un Ballo in Maschera; Operetta engagements in works by Lehar and Zeller; Many concert appearances. *Address:* Theater Basel, Theatrestrasse 7, CH-4010 Basel, Switzerland

HENNING Dave, b. 27 July 1956, Wisconsin, USA. Band Director. m. Rita Evertts, 16 Sept 1972, 1 s. *Education:* BMus, University of Wisconsin at Madison; MMus, Texas Christian University, 1982. *Career:* Ensembles under his direction have performed in films, live radio broadcasts and at major professional conventions including CBDNA, Midwest International Band Clinic. Bank Director and Music Professor at the University of Iowa, 1993-; Band Director and Instructor, Texas Christian University, 1990-93; Band Director and Teacher, Arlington, TX, 1982-90; Active as an arranger and composer and has published works for band. *Honours:* Bravo Award, Arlington Texas, 1990; Outstanding Young Men, 1989; Pi Kappa Lambda, 1982. *Memberships:* CBDNA; TMEA; IAJE; TBA. *Current Management* Matarix Publishing. *Address:* 7007 Greenspring Drive, Arlington, TX 76016, USA.

HENSCHEL Jane, b. 1950, California. Singer (Mezzo Soprano). *Education:* Studied at the University of Southern California, *Career:* Sang Gilbert and Sullivan with Opera a la Carte in Los Angeles; Aspen Music Festival 1977, with Haydn's Berenice, Respighi's Il Tramonto with the Cleveland Quartet and Ottavia in L'Incorohazione di Poppea; Aachen Opera 1977-80; Sang at Wuppertal from 1980, notably as Schoeck's Penthesilea; Dortmund Opera as Eboli, Nancy (Martha), Amneris, Brangaene and the Witch in Rusalka; Concert engagements with the Frankfurt Radio Orchestra in Mahler's 8th Symphony and Beethoven's 9th, conducted by Eliahu Inbal; Baroque repertoire includes Vivaldi's oratorio Juditha Triumphans (Radio France); Sang the Nurse in Die Frau ohne Schatten at Covent Garden 1992, Judy in Birtwistle's Punch and Judy for Netherlands Opera, 1993. *Address:* c/o Music International, 13 Ardilaun Road, London N5 2QR, England.

HENSHALL Dalwyn James, b. 20 Feb. 1957, Liverpool, England. Composer. *Education:* B.Mus., M.Mus., PhD., UCNW, Bangor; Sibelius Academy, Helsinki. *Compositions:* Variations & Fugue, 1982; Oboe Concerto, 1979; Harp Concerto, 1980; The Silent Land, 1982; Cello Concerto, 1982; Et in terra pax, 1983; Sinfonietta No 1, 1980; Sinfonietta No 2, 1982; Sinfonietta No 3, 1987; Dic Penderyn, 1986; Twin Sion Cati, 1988. *Contributions to:* Welsh Music; Western Mail. *Memberships:* Chairman, Young Welsh Composers' Guild; Gorsedd of Bards, Royal National Eisteddfod; Performing Rights Society. *Hobbies:* Conducting; Adjudicating. *Address:* 10 Lon-y-Tresglen, Caerfilli, Wales CF8 2QP.

HENSHILWOOD Donald Keith, b. 16 July 1930, Bradford, Yorkshire, England. Musician. *Education:* Bingley Grammar School, Yorkshire and Private schools in Wales; Mainly self-taught musician; Attended Composition classes at Dartington Summer School 1957-63. *Career:* Founded own Electronic Studio, 1961; Became full-time Composer/Arranger, 1964; Works performed throughout the UK. *Compositions include:* 5 Symphonies; Music for Brass and Wind Ensemble, Brass and Symphonic Band; Incidental music (Theatre, Documentary, Film, etc.); Publishes own music. *Recording:* Toccata (James Shepherd Versatile Brass) on Look Records, also released on Australia. *Contributions to:* Regular contributor to Composer and Winds. *Memberships:* Composers Guild of Great Britain; British Association of Symphonic Bands and Wind Ensembles (BASBWE); PRS; MCPS. *Hobbies:* Films; Cryptozoology; Conservation. *Address:* 130 Frankby Road, Newton, West Kirby, Wirral L48 9UX, England.

HENZE Hans Werner, b. 1 July 1926, Gutersloh, Germany. Composer; Conductor. *Education:* Studied at the Staatsmusikhochschule Brunswick; Kirchenmusikalisches Institut, Heidelberg. *Career:* Musical Director at the Deutsches Theatre Constanze 1948; Artistic Director, Ballet of the Hessian State Theatre, Wiesbaden, 1950; Has lived in Italy as an independent artist from 1953; Professor of Composition, Mozarteum, Salzburg, 1961; Artistic Director, Accademia Filarmonia Romana, 1982; Founder and Artistic Director of the Munich Biennale for Contemporary Music Theatre since, 1988; BBC Henze Festival at the Barbican, 1991; First Composer-in-Residence, Berlin Philharmonic Orchestra, 1990; British premiere of Requiem at the 1993 London Proms. *Compositions:* Operas and Music Theatre: Das Wundertheater 1948; Boulevard Solitude 1951; Ein Landarzt 1951; Das Ende einer Welt 1953; König Hirsch 1955: rev. as Il Re Cervo 1962; Der Prinz von Homburg 1958; Elegy for Young Lovers 1961; Der junge Lord l964; The Bassarids 1965; Moralties, scenic cantatas 1967; Der langwierige Weg in die Wohnung der Natascha Ungeheuer 1971; La Cubana 1973; We Come to the River 1976; Don Chisciotte della Mancia, after Paisiello 1976; Pollicino, for children 1979; Il Ritorno d'Ulisse in Patria, after Monteverdi 1982; The English Cat 1983; Das Verratene Meer, 1990; Ballets: Jack Pudding 1949; Ballet-Variationen 1949; Rosa Silber

1950; Die Schlafende Prinzessin 1951; Labyrinth 1951; Der Idiot 1952; Maratona 1956; Des Kaisers Nachtigall 1959; Undine 1956-71; Tancredi 1964; Orpheus 1978; Orchestral: 8 Symphonies 1947-93; Quattro Poemi 1955; Antifone 1960; Los Caprichos 1963; Telemanniana 1967; Heliogabalus Imperator 1972; Tristan, preludes for piano, orchestra and tape 1973; Ragtimes and Habaneras for brass band 1975; Barcarola 1983; Chamber Orchestra: Sinfonie 1947; Symphonic Variations 1950; Sonata for Strings 1958; 3 Dithyrambs 1958; In Memoriam: Amicizia 1976; Aria de la folia espanola 1977; Apollo Trionfante 1979; Canzona 1982; I Sentimenti di Carl P.E. Bach 1982; Sonata for 6 1984; Concertos: 2 for Violin, 1947, 1971; 2 for Piano, 1950, 1967; Jeux des Tritons 1957; Ode to the West Wind for cello and orchestra 1953; Concerto per il Marigny 1956; Double Concerto, with oboe and harp 1966; Double Bass Concerto 1966; Compases para preguntas ensimisadas 1970; Il Vitalino raddoppiato 1977; Le Miracle de la Rose for clarinet and 13 players 1981; Guitar Concerto 1986; Sieben liebeslieder for cello and orchestra, 1986; Allegro brillante, 1989; Requiem for instruments, 1990-91, Trumpet Concerto, 1992; Vocal: Whispers from Heavenly Death 1948; Der Vorwurf 1948; Apollo and Hyacinth 1949; 5 Neapolitan Songs 1956; Nocturnes and Arias 1957; Chamber Music I958; Novae de Infinito Laudes 1962; Ariosi 1963; Being Beateous 1963; Choral Fantasia 1964; Muses of Sicily 1966; Essay on Pigs 1968; Das Floss der Medusa 1968; El Cimarron 1970; Voices 1973; Jephte, after Carissimi 1976; The King of Harlem 1979; Canzoni for Orpheus 1980; Chamber music includes 5 String Quartets, 1947-76, 2 Wind Quintets, 1952, 1977, Royal Winter Music for guitar, 1976, 1979 and Capriccio for cello 1983; Serenade for solo violin, 1986; Keyboard music.Honours: Siemens Prize, Munich, 1990; Apollo d'Oro, Bilbao, 1990. Address: c/o Schott & Co. Ltd., 48 Great Marlborough Street, London W1, England.

HEPPLEWHITE Lionel Karl, b. 4 Feb 1936, Rawmarsh, Yorkshire, England. Violin, Viola, Cello Maker. m. Margaret Waterhouse, 13 Apr. 1957, 4 sons. Education: HNC, Applied Physics, 1967; Studied Violin from age 13 with William Kendal, O. Sevcik; First Violin made at age 18. Career: National Service, RAF, 1955-57; Scientific Work, Cambridge University, Manchester University, Sheffield University, Royal Radar Establishment, Malvern; Self Employed, Violin, Viola & Cello Maker, 1980- (Previously part-time); Instruments sold to leading players and frequently heard live and on radio & TV; Customers include: New Welsh String Quartet, City of Birmingham Symphony Orchestra, BBC Philharmonic, BBC Midland Radio Orchestra, English National Opera Orchestra, Welsh National Opera Orchestra, English Opera. Contributions to: Strad Magazine. Honours: Diploma, Best Toned Viola, Newark Violin Making Competition, 1978; Member, Crafts Council Index of Selected Makers. Memberships: Leader of The Worcester Concert Orchestra. Hobbies: Photography; Sailing; Hill Walking; Violin Playing. Address: Soundpost, 8 North End Lane, Malvern, Worcs WR14 2ES, England.

HEPPNER Ben, b. 14 Jan 1956, Murrayville, British Columbia, Canada. Singer (Tenor). Career: Many oratorio and concert performances in Canada; Opera debut 1987 with the Victoria State Opera, Australia as Bacchus in Ariadne auf Naxos; Canadian Opera Company as Zinovy in Lady Macbeth of Mtsensk; American debut in Tannhäuser at the Chicago Lyric Opera, 1988; Has sung the Prince in Rusalka with the Philadelphia Opera Company, Seattle Opera (1990) and at the Vienna State Opera (1991); European debut at the Royal Opera Stockholm 1989, as Lohengrin; Sang Walther von Stolzing on his La Scala and Covent Garden debuts (1990) and in Seattle and Toronto; San Francisco Opera debut 1989, as Lohengrin; Season 1991-92 with Janáček's Laca at Brussels, the Emperor in Die Frau ohne Schatten at Amsterdam and the premiere of William Bolcom's McTeague in Chicago; Season 1992 with Dvořáks Dimitrij at Munich, Mozart's Titus at Salzburg; Engaged to sing Lohengrin at Seattle, 1994. Recording: Die Meistersinger, conducted by Wolfgang Sawallisch; Andrey in Tchaikovsky's Mazeppa (DGG).

Address: c/o Columbia Artists Management, 165 West 57th Street, New York, NY 10019, USA.

HERBERT Jocelyn, b. 23 Feb. 1917, London, England. Stage Designer. Career: Designed in London for productions of avant-garde plays at the Royal Court Theatre and the National Theatre; Designed Monteverdi's Orfeo for Sadler's Wells, 1967; La Forza del Destino at the Paris Opéra 1975; For the Metropolitan Opera has designed productions of Lulu (local premiere, 1977), Die Entführung, and Aufstieg und Fall der Stadt Mahagonny (both 1979). Address: c/o Metropoliton Opera, Lincoln Center, New York, NY 10023, USA.

HERBIG Gunther, b. 30 Nov 1931, Usti-nad-Labem, Czech Republic. Conductor. Education: Studied with Hermann Abendroth at the Franz Liszt Academy, Weimar, and with Hermann Scherchen; Further study with Herbert von Karajan. Career: Held posts in Erfurt, Weimar, Potsdam and East Berlin; General Music Director, Dresden Philharmonic Orchestra 1972-77; London debut with the New Philharmonia Orchestra, 1973; Music Director, Berlin Symphony Orchestra 1977-83; Guest Conductor Dallas Symphony Orchestra 1979-81; Principal Guest Conductor, BBC Philharmonic Orchestra, 1982-86; Music Director, Detroit Symphony 1984-90; Debut with London Symphony Orchestra 1986; Orchestre de Paris 1986; Appearances with the New York Philharmonic, Boston Symphony, Philadelphia Orchestra and Los Angeles Philharmonic from 1984; Music Director Toronto Symphony 1989-94; Toured Europe 1989 with the Detroit Symphony Orchestra and Gidon Kremer as soloist. Recordings include: Haydn's London Symphonies; Reger's Piano Concerto; Beethoven's ballet Die Geschöpfe des Prometheus; Brahms 4 Symphonies and Nielsen's 5th. Address: c/o Terry Harrison Artists Management, 3 Clarendon Court, Park Street, Charibury, Oxon OX7 3PS, England.

HERBINE Lois Lorraine, b. 6 Oct 1961, Abington, USA. Flautist; Piccolo Specialist; Instructor. m. David Herbine, 9 June 1984. Education: BMus., New School of Music, 1984. Career: Freelance Performances with: The Concerto Soloists of Philadelphia, Pennsylvania Ballet, The Delaware Symphony Orchestra, Pennsylvania Pro Musica, Opera Company of Philadelphia, Philadelphia Promenade Orchestra, Ocean City Pops Orchestra, 1987 Hollybush Festival, The Performance Organization and the Davidsbund Chamber Players; Flute & Harp Recitals. Honours: Winner, Musical Fund Society Solo Competition, 1982; Catherine Drinker Bowen Scholarship, New School of Music, 1983. Memberships: Piccolo Society Inc., Vice President 1983-86; American Federation of Musicians; National Flute Association. Hobbies: Woodwork; Skiing; Racquetball. Address: 1826 Willard Avenue, Willow Grove, PA 19090, USA.

HERFORD (Richard) Henry, b. 24 Feb 1947, Edinburgh, Scotland. Singer. m. Lindsay John, 14 Feb 1982, 2 sons, 1 daughter. Education: Kings College, Cambridge (Classics, English), 1965-68; MA (Hons.); Royal Northern College of Music, 1971-76; ARNCM (Performers and Teachers) with Distinction; GRNCM. Career: Glyndebourne Chorus, 1976-78; Forester in Cunning Little Vixen (Janáček); Roles with Royal Opera House, Covent Garden; Scottish Opera; Handel Opera; Chelsea Opera Group; Batignano; Nancy; English Bach Festival; Frequent Concerts with leading orchestras in Britain. Europe & North and South America; Nash Ensemble; Fires of London: Koenig Ensemble; Ensemble Modern; BBC Radio and TV; Numerous Recitals. Recordings: Recital of American Songs (Shepherd, Weber, Corigliano, Susa), New World Records; Rameau, Castor et Pollux (High Priest), Erato; Handel, Messiah (excerpts), Scottish Chamber Orchestra and George Malcolm, Contour; Biggin, The Gates of Greenham, Sain; A Dylan Thomas Song Cycle; Handel's Dixit Dominus with King's College Cambridge Choir; Joubert, The Instant Moment, with the English String Orchestra; Vaughan Williams's Five Tudor Portraits: Five Mystical Songs; Britten, A Midsummer Night's Dream, Virgin;

Charles Ives: Songs (2 vols), Unicorn-Kanchana; Songs with instruments, Ensemble Modern, EMI. *Honours:* Curtis Gold Medal, (RNCM), 1977; Benson and Hedges Gold Award, Aldeburgh, 1980; 1st Prize, American Music Competition, Carnegie Hall, 1982; Record of the Year (M.R.A.). *Hobbies:* Family; House Renovation; Reading; Hill Walking. *Current Management:* Ron Gonsalves, London. *Address:* Pencots, Northmoor, Oxon, OX8 1AX, England.

HERINCX Raimund, b. 23 Aug 1927, London, England. Singer (Bass-Baritone). *Education:* Studied with Van Dyck in Belgium and with Valli in Mllan. *Career:* Concerts in Belgium and France, 1950; Stage debut Welsh National Opera 1950, as Mozart's Figaro; Sang Mephistopheles in Faust 1956; Sadler's Wells Opera from 1956, as Count Almaviva, Rigoletto, Germont, Pizarro, Nick Shadow, Creon in Oedipus Rex, and in the premiere of Our Man in Havana by Malcolm Williamson 1963; Sang in the 1964 British premiere of The Makropoulos Case; Philharmonic Hall New York 1966, in A Mass of Life by Delius; Boston Opera 1967; BBC 1967, in L'Erismena by Cavalli; Covent Garden from 1968, as King Fisher in The Midsummer Marriage and in the premieres of The Knot Garden 1970 and Taverner 1972; Other Covent Garden roles include Escamillo, Macbeth and Alfio; Salzburg Easter Festival 1973-74, as Pogner in Die Meistersinger and Fafner in Siegfried, conducted by Karajan; English National Opera 1974-76, in the British stage premiere of The Bassarids by Henze and as Wotan and Hagen in The Ring; Seattle Opera 1977-81; Metropolitan Opera debut 1977, as Matthisen in Le Prophète; San Francisco 1983 in The Midsummer Marriage; Les Contes d'Hoffmann for Opera North 1983; sang in the US premiere of Taverner at Boston, 1986; Has Reviewed opera for Music and Musicians magazine. *Recordings include:* Dido and Aeneas (Decca); Les Contes d'Hoffmann (Electrola); Hansel and Gretel, Koanga, A Village Romeo and Juliet, I Capuleti e i Montecchi, The Pilgrim's Progress, Aronte in Armide by Gluck, Oedipus Rex (EMI); The Midsummer Marriage (Philips); Das Liebesverbot by Wagner. *Address:* c/o English National Opera, St. Martins Lane, London, WC2, England.

HERING Karl-Josef, b. 14 Feb 1929, Westonnen, Germany. Singer (Tenor). *Education:* Studied with Fred Husler, Max Lorenz and Franz Volker. *Debut:* Hanover 1958, as Max in Der Freischütz. *Career:* Engagements at the Deutsche Oper Berlin and in Cologne, Karlsruhe, Stuttgart, Vienna and Hamburg; Royal Opera House Covent Garden, as Siegfried in Der Ring des Nibelungen, 1966; Further appearances in Trieste, Toronto, Barcelona, Marseille and Buenos Aires; Other roles include Florestan, Canio, Aegisthus, Hermann in The Queen of Spades and Erik in Der fliegende Holländer; Many concert performances. *Address:* c/o Deutsche Oper Berlin, Richard Wagnerstrasse 10, D-1000 Berlin, Germany.

HERLEA Nicolae, b. 28 Aug 1927, Bucharest, Rumania. Singer (Baritone). *Education:* Studied at the Bucharest Conservatory with Aurelius Costescu-Duca and at the Accademia di Santa Cecilia, Rome. *Debut:* Bucharest 1951, as Silvio in Pagliacci; Guest appearances at Covent Garden (Rossini's Figaro, 1960), Milan, Prague, Brussels, Moscow, Boston, Cleveland and Vienna; Metropolitan Opera debut 1964; Other roles include Verdi's Germont, Luna and Rigoletto. *Recordings Include:* Il barbiere di Siviglia, La Traviata, Rigoletto and Pagliacci (Electrocord); Opera arias (Deutsche Grammophon).

HERMAN Silvia, b. 1954, Vienna, Austria. Singer (Soprano). *Education:* Studied in Vienna with Anton Dermota: worked at the Opera Studio of the Vienna Staatsoper, 1976-79. *Career:* Appearances in Vienna 1979-82, Hamurg, 1983-85; Guest engagements in Stuttgart, Geneva, Barcelona, Madrid and Cologne, 1989-90; Salzburg Festival, 1978-81; Bayreuth Festival 1978 as a Flowermaiden, 1985-88 as Wellgunde and Waltraute in Die Walkure; Bruckner Festival in Linz, 1982-88, and elsewhere, in Lieder recitals and concert

showings. *Recordings:* Das Rheingold and Die Walkure, conducted by Haitink; Schumann's Das Paradies und der Peri. *Address:* Oper der Stadt Koln, Offenbachplatz, 5000 Cologne, Germany.

HERMAN Vasile, b. 10 June 1929, Satu Mare, Rumania. Composer. m. Titina Herman, 2 children. *Education:* Diploma of Composition, 1957, Doctor of Musicology, 1974, High School; Diploma of Teacher of Music, 1960. *Career:* TV and radio appearances. *Compositions:* Double Concerto; Poliphony; Concert of Strings; Chamber works, Melopee, Variante, Epsodi; 5 Symphonies, Concerto for Strings and Percussion. *Recordings:* Cantilations; Rimes nostalgique; Symphonie No.2, Variante, Poleommusica. *Publication:* Form and Style in the Contemporary Rumanian Music, 1977. *Contributions to:* Muzica, Steaua; Tribuna; Utunk (Rumania). *Honours:* Prize, Composers' Union, Rumania; Prize, Rumanian Academy. *Membership:* Composers' Union of Rumania. *Hobbies:* Numismatics; National history. *Address:* Str Jozsa Bela Nr 33 ap 4, 3400 Cluj-Napoca, Rumania.

HERMAN Witold Walenty, b. 14 Feb 1932, Torun, Poland. Solo Cellist; Professor of Music. m. Catherine Bromboszcz, 1 June 1970, 1 son, 1 daughter. *Education:* Bachalaureat Diploma, Copernic Lyceum, Torun, 1950; Diploma with Distinction, Szymanowski Conservatory, Torun, 1950; MA, Academy of Music, Cracow, 1956; Diploma, Ecole Normale de Musique, Paris, France, 1960; Culture Doctorate in Philosophy of Music, World University, Tucson, Arizona, USA, 1984. *Debut:* State Philharmonie, Cracow, Poland, May 1954. *Career:* Cello concerts with orchestras and cello recitals in Poland and other European countries; Professor, Music Academy, Cracow. Visitor-Professor of the Franz Liszt Musik Akademie in Weimar, 1972; Jury of The International Pablo Casals Cello-Competition in Budapest, 1968. *Recordings:* Recordings for radio and television in Poland and the rest of Europe including Radio Luxembourg; Recordings as a solo cellist with great symphony orchestras. *Publications:* Notes for Cello, edited in Poland, Polish Music Edition. *Honours:* Special Prize 1st Class, Polish Minister of Culture and Arts, 1982; Golden Cross of Merit, Polish Government, 1977; Honour Medal, XL Anniversary of the Polish Republic, 1985; Chevalier-Cross of the Order "Polonia Restituta' 1986. *Hobbies:* Sociology; Theatre; Tennis. *Current Management:* Academy of Music, Kracow, ul Starowiślna 3, Poland. *Address:* ul. Friedleina 49 m 5, 30- 009 Kracow, Poland.

HERMANN Roland, b. 17 Sept 1936, Bochum, Germany. Singer (Baritone). *Education:* Vocal studies with Paul Lohmann, Margarethe von Wintrefeldt and Flaminio Contini. *Debut:* Trier 1967 as Count Almaviva. *Career:* Member of the Zurich Opera from 1968; Guest appearances in Munich, Paris, Berlin and Cologne; Buenos Aires 1974, as Jochanaan in Salome and Wolfram in Tannhäuser; US debut 1983, with the New York Philharmonic; La Scala Milan debut 1986, with Claudio Abbado; Roles include Don Giovanni, Amfortas, Germont, Gunther in Götterdämmerung and the title roles in Karl V by Krenek and Doktor Faust by Busoni; Apollo (L'Orfeo), Cinna (Lucio Silla), Morald (Die Feen), Forester (The Cunning Little Vixen); Mauregato (Alfonso und Estrella); Beckmesser, Achill (Penthesilea), Vendramin (Massimila Doni), Orff's Prometheus; Took part in the European stage premiere of Die Jakobsleiter by Schoenberg (Hamburg 1983) and the world premiere of Kelterborn's Der Kirschgarten (Zurich 1984); Sang in the premiere of Krenek's Oratorio Symeon der Stylites at the 1988 Salzburg Festival, conducted by Lothar Zagrosek; BBC London 1989, in the title role of Der Prinz von Homburg by Henze; sang the Forester in The Cunning Little Vixen at Zurich 1989, The Master in the premiere of York Höller's Der Meister und Margarita (Paris 1989) and Gunther at a concert performance of Götterdämmerung at the Holland Festival; Season 1992 as Nekrotzar in Le Grand Macabre at Zurich, followed by the Count in Capriccio; Many Lieder recitals and concert appearances. *Recordings include:* Penthesilea by Schoeck (BASF); Prometheus and Trionfi by Orff, Die

Meistersinger, CPE Bach's Magnificat (Deutsche Grammophon); Moses und Aron by Schoenberg (CBS); Zemlinsky's Der Kreidekreis; Mathis der Maler by Hindemith; Peer Gynt by Werner Egk; Der Vampyr by Marschner; Schumann's Genoveva. *Address:* c/o Ingpen & Williams Ltd., 14 Kensington Court, London W8 5DN, England.

HERMANSON Åke Oscar Werner, b. 16 June 1923, Mollösund, Sweden. Composer. m. Britt Anderson, 10 Apr 1948, 1 daughter. *Education:* Studies in Composition, Counter Point, Instrumentation with Hilding Rosenberg; Piano with Knut Back; Organ with Alf Linder. *Career:* Chairman and Board Member, Swedish Society of Composers, 1967-71; Royal Swedish Academy of Music, 1973-; Composer for Whole Times. *Compositions:* 4 Symphonies for Orchestras; Utopia, for orchestra; Ultima for orchestra; In Voco, for string orchestra; 2 String Quartets; Vocal Music for Choirs; Solo works for French Horn, Flute and Oboe; Rockall, op 29 for Winds Vision; Hymn to Salto, op 31; All works recorded. *Publications:* Konsertnytt, 1983; Nutida Musik. *Hobby:* Sailing. *Address:* Villa Vindila Sma, S-13054 Dalarö, Sweden.

HERNANDEZ-LARGUIA Cristian, b. 6 Oct 1921, Buenos Aires, Argentina. Choir Conductor. m. Eugenia Barbarich, 29 Dec 1953. *Education:* Studied with T Fuchs, E Leuchter, R Shaw, N Greenberg and G Graetzer. *Debut:* Madrigal Group, Asoc Ros de Cultura Inglesa, 1941. *Career:* Conductor, Coro Estable de Rosario, since 1946; Founder and Conductor, Pro Musica de Rosario, 1962; Appearances in concert tours to North, Central and South America and Europe, 1967-92, Hunter College, NY, Coolidge Aud, Washingdon DC and St Martin in the Fields, London; Professor of Choir Conducting, Musical Morphology and Acoustics, University of Litoral, University Rosario. *Recordings:* 35 titles including LP, Cassettes and CD's. *Publications:* Performances: Mass in B Minor, Bach's first version with Argentine cast, 1985; St Johns version, Bach, 1977; First Argentine audition of complete and original version Messiah, 1973, Brocke's Passion, 1980, Handel. *Honours include:* Numerous personal and joint awards (with Pro Musica and CER) as well as National Culture Glory, 1984, Illustrious citizen, 1985, Concorso Internazionale Guido D'Arezzo, Italy, 1967-81. *Hobbies:* Model Railroads; Electronics; Handcraft; Repairing musical instruments. *Address:* San Luis 860, 4J 2000 Rosario, Argentina.

HERNON Paul, b. 1947, Northumberland, England. Director; Designer. *Career:* Co-founded the London Music Theatre Group 1982 and directed the British stage premieres of Martin's Le Vin Herbé and Vivaldi's Juditha Triumphans at the Camden Festival, London; British premieres of Salieri's Prima la Musica and Ward's The Crucible; Directed a tercentenary production of Handel's Acis and Galatea for the English Bach Festival in Reggio Emilia, Seville and Madrid; In Northern Ireland has directed Don Giovanni, Così fan Tutte, Le Nozze di Figaro, Die Zauberflöte and Der Schauspieldirektor and works by Haydn, Donizetti, Puccini and Purcell; Has designed productions of Hansel and Gretel at Sadler's Wells, La Favorita in Dublin, Offenbach operas in Belfast and Crispino e la Comare at the Camden Festival; Designed the Yuri Lyubimov productions of Jenůfa (first in Zurich, 1986) and Das Rheingold at Covent Garden, 1986, 1988; Eugene Onegin for Bonn 1987 and Tannhäuser for Stuttgart 1988. *Address:* Music International, 13 Ardilaun Road, London N5 2QR, England.

HERREMA Robert Dale, b. 2 Apr 1941, Grand Rapids, Michigan, USA. Conductor; Music Professor. m. Joyce A Peuler, 10 Aug 1962, 2 sons, 1 daughter. *Education:* AB, Calvin College, 1964; MM, Choral Music Education, University of Michigan, 1966; Indiana University School of Music, 1966-68; workshops with Helmuth Rilling and Robert Shaw, seminars. *Career:* Minister of Music, Eastminster Presbyterian, Grand Rapids, 1961-64; Conductor, Calvin College Meistersingers, 1962-64; Director, Music, Alger Park Church, Grand Rapids, 1964-65; Vocal Music Teacher,

South Christian High School, Cutlerville, 1964-65; Lecturer, Choral Director, Stillman College, 1968-70; Co-Founder, Musical Director, Community Singers of Tuscaloosa, 1969-70; Director, Music, Covenant Presbyterian Church, Tuscaloosa, 1969-70; Choral Director, Elmira College, 1970-73; Musical Director, Cantata Singers of Elmira, 1971-75; Associate Professor, Director of Choirs and Orchestra, Marywood College, 1973-; Choirmaster, St Peter's Cathedral, Scranton, 1974-76; Founder, Musical Director, Robert Dale Chorale, 1977-; Chorusmaster, Northeastern Pennsylvania Philharmonic, 1978-87; Faculty, Summer Choral Institute, Saratoga Music Festival, 1980; Minister of Music, First Presbyterian Church, Clarks Summit, 1982-85; Choirmaster St Luke's Episcopal Church, Scranton, 1986-. *Compositions:* A Day is Coming; Ave Maria; Calvin Torch Song; Eloquence (Haydn); Et in Terra Pax; Fog; Gloria; Hammer; Let us Break Bread Together; Lo, How a Rose E'er Blooming; Lord, Thou Hast Been our Dwelling Place; O Filii et Filiae; Shepherd of Eager Youth; Tenting Tonight; Three Early Christmas Songs. *Hobbies:* Boating; Skiing; Travel. *Address:* 111 Columbus Circle, Clarks Summit, PA 18411, USA.

HERREWEGHE Philippe, b. 2 May 1947, Ghent, Belgium. Conductor; Choral Director. *Education:* Studied at Conservatoire of Ghent. *Career:* Founded the Collegium Vocale of Ghent 1969; Collaborations with the harpsichordists Ton Koopman and Gustav Leonhardt in the performance of early music; With Philippe Beaussant founded the Ensemble Vocal La Chapelle Royal, 1977; Performances of Bach's church cantatas and the B minor Mass with Nikolaus Harnoncourt; Participation with the Kuijken brothers and others in the Towards Bach series on South Bank, London, 1989; Conductor of the European Vocal Ensemble from 1989; Led the Ensemble Musique Oblique in a series of Mahler/Schoenberg concerts, 1991; Conducted Dido and Aeneas at Brussels, 1992.

HERRMANN Karl Ernst, b. 1936, Neukirch, Upper Lusatia, Germany. Stage Director and Designer. *Education:* Studied at the Hochschule fur Bildende Kunst at Berlin. *Career:* Designed for the theatre at Ulm from 1961 and associated with Peter Stein at Bremen and Berlin, 1969-78; Designed Das Rheingold and Die Walküre at the Paris Opéra, 1976; Theatre de la Monnaie Brussels from 1978, with a cycle of seven operas by Mozart, La Traviata and Orfeo ed Euridice; Eugene Onegin at Hamburg, 1979; Die Zauberflöte at the Salzburg Landestheater, to inaugurate the Mozart Bicentenary, 1991; Die Entführung at the Vienna Staatsoper, 1991; Brussels productions of La Clemenza di Tito and La Finta Giardiniera seen at Salzburg Festival, 1992; Designed sets for Peter Stein Production of Pelléas et Mélisande at Welsh National Opera, 1992. *Address:* Theatre Royale de La Monnaie, 4 Leopoldstrasse, B-1000 Brussels, Belgium.

HERZ Gerhard, b. 24 Sept 1911, Düsseldorf, Germany. Musicologist. m. Mary Jo Fink, 2 June 1943. *Education:* University of Freiburg/Br, 1930; University of Vienna, 1931; Berlin University, 1931-33; Zurich University, 1933-34; PhD magna cum laude. *Career:* University of Louisville, USA, 1938; Indiana University, 1945-46; Professor, 1946-78, Chairman, Department of Music History, 1956-78, Emeritus Professor, 1978-, University of Louisville, USA; Visiting Professor, Chicago University, 1965. *Publications:* Joh Seb Bach im Zeitalter des Rationalismus und der Frühromantik, 1935, 1936, reprint, 1985; Bach, Cantata No 4, 1967; Bach, Cantata No 140, 1972; Bach-Quellen in Amerika/Bach Sources in America, 1984; Essays on J S Bach, 1985; Essays on the Music of J S Bach and other Divers Subjects; A Tribute to Gerhard Herz, 1981. *Contributions to:* The Musical Quarterly, 1938-77; Bach, Riemenschneider Bach Institute quarterly, 1970-; Bach-Jahrbuch, 1974, 1978, 1986; American Choral Review, 1970s, 1980s; Orbis Musicae, 1986. *Address:* 729 Middle Way, Louisville, KY 40206, USA.

HERZ Joachim, b. 15 June 1924, Dresden, Germany. Professor; Director of Production. m. Charlotte Kitze, 17

July 1954, 1 son. *Education:* Colleges of Music, Leipzig/ Dresden, 1942, 1945-49, State Exams; Musicology, Humboldt University, Berlin, 1949-51. *Debut:* Dresden National Opera: Die Bremer Stadtmusikanten, 1950. *Career:* Producer: Dresden Touring Opera, 1951-53; Berlin Komische Oper, 1956; Cologne, 1957; Director, Leipzig Opera, 1976; Managing Director, Berlin Komische Oper, 1981; Dresden National Opera, 1981-; Chief, Music Theatre Department, College of Music, Dresden; Music Coach, Dresden, 1946-49; Assistant, 1949-51; Teacher, 1951-53; Dresden Drama Studio; Teacher: Berlin, 1953-56; Cologne, 1957; Lecturer, Berlin University, 1956; produced Lohengrin at Vienna, 1975; Professor, Leipzig University, 1976-; Visiting Lecturer: Leipzig Drama College; Universities of Munich, Salzburg, Eichstätt, Paris VIII, London, California, Cincinnati, British Columbia, New York City, Banff Centre; Guest Producer: Buenos Aires, London, Cardiff, Moscow, Stockholm, Belgrade, Bern, Munich, Hamburg, Frankfurt, Vienna, Vancouver, Zurich, Salzburg, Helsinki. Film: The Flying Dutchman (DEFA); TV: Xerxes, Copenhagen; Radio Producer; produced Così fan Tutte at Helsinki 1989, The Love for Three Oranges at the Dresden Music Festival; Director of Productions at the Desden National Opera 1991; Tours with Salzburg Così fan Tutte to Japan and with Leipzig to Xerxes through 13 countries; Guest Lecturer in Europe and the former Soviet Union. *Recordings:* Freischütz, Carlos Kleiber; Zauberflöte, Colin Davis; Eroffnung Leipzig, Meistersinger, Dresden Semperoper: Freischütz and Rosenkavalier. *Publications:* Musiktheater - Felsenstein/Herz; Joachim Herz, Regisseur im Musiktheater - Irmer/Stein; Oper als Idee und Interpretation - Herz; Joachim Herz über Musiktheater; Gesammelte Schriften. *Contributor to:* Magazines, Newspapers, programmes and congresses etc. *Memberships:* Academy of Arts, Berlin; Honorary Board, Music Theatre Committee and Music Theatre Society, Vienna. *Current Management:* Staatsoper Dresden. *Hobbies:* Early Music; Travel; Museums. *Address:* Staatsoper PF75, 8012 Dresden, Germany.

HESS Andrea Megaery, b. 7 May 1954, London, England. Cellist. m. John Leonard, 20 Jan 1985. *Education:* Recital Diploma, Royal Academy of Music, 1974; Nordwestdeutschemusikakademie, Detmold, Federal Republic of Germany. *Debut:* Wigmore Hall, London, 1979. *Career:* Numerous performances as a soloist throughout UK, Europe, Canada and the Far East; Performed as a member of several chamber ensembles notably the Kreisler Trio of Germany and the Raphael Ensemble of London; Appeared on stage as solo cellist in National Theatre production of The Elephant Man, 1980-81; Solo cellist for Royal Shakespeare Company, 1982-87; Appearances in drama productions for BBC and major independent television companies; Several broadcasts for BBC Radio 3. *Recordings:* Volker David Kirchner Trio, with The Kreisler Trio of Germany, Wergo; Cello Works, Chopin Chamber Music, with The Kreisler Trio of Germany, Pantheon; Hyperion recordings of both Brahms sextets, Dvořák Quintet and Sextet, Korngold Sextet and Schoenberg's Verklärte nacht, Martinů & Ervin Schulhoff Sextets, Arensky Quartet for violin, viola & two cellos & Tchaikovsky's Souvenir de Florence Sextet with the Raphael Ensemble. *Hobbies:* Cinema; Theatre; Reading; Travel; Philosophy; Cooking; People. *Address:* 10 Belsize Park, London NW3 4ES, England.

HESS Robert W, b. 17 May 1930, Brooklyn, New York, USA. Vocal Coach; Translator. *Education:* BMus Piano, Carnegie Mellon University 1952; MMus Opera, New England Conservatory, 1954. *Career:* Musical Assistant, New England Opera Theater; Faculty, American Musical and Dramatic Academy 1968-79; Visiting Lecturer, Hartt School of Music, University of Hartford, 1971-1992; Recital Accompanist for Singers; Musical Director, Musicals-New York, Hyannis, Massachusetts & Beverly, Massachusetts; Master Classes in Musical Theatre; 92nd St 'Y', 1993-94. *Publications:* Translations: Puccini La Rondine, 1969; Haydn: Die Reisende Ceres, 1977; Offenbach-Les Bavards, 1982; Rimsky Korsakov-Complete Songs, 7 volumes 1980; Sadko, Snegurochka, 1985. *Honours:* National Endowment for the Arts; Grant for Translation

of Haydn's La Vera Costanza, 1974, performed at Caramoor Festival, 1980. *Memberships:* ASCAP; American Federation of Musicians. *Hobbies:* Travel; Architecture. *Address:* 115 W 73rd Street Apt 9D, New York, NY 10023, USA.

HESSE Axel Ernst, b. 16 July 1935, Berlin, Germany. Musicologist; Educator. m. Flora Perez Diaz, 29 Feb 1964, 1 son, 1 daughter. *Education:* Musicologist: Latin American Music History, German Folk Song, Musical Transculturation Theory, Humboldt University (Berlin), Karl Marx University (Leipzig), Cuban Biblioteca Nacional (Havana), 1963-65; Diploma of Philosophy, 1961; Doctor of Philosophy, 1971. *Career:* Oberassistent musicologist, Humboldt University, 1970; Visiting Professor of Ethnomusicology, Lima, Peru, 1978; Academy of Sciences, German Democratic Republic, 1987-89; Co-Founder, Ciplice Folk Sound Archives, Freyburg, 1989; Lecturer, Humboldt University, 1990; Visiting Professor, Musicology, Catedra Francisco Salinas, University of Salamanca, Spain, 1990-93, founding the multidisciplinary Salinas Coloquium on Rhythm. *Recordings:* Cuban folk music, in field, 1965; Afro-Peruvian music, 1978; German folk song, Hungary & GDR, 1975-1982; Children's holiday camp songs, GDR, 1975-1987. Approx. 10,000 items, Folk Sound Archive, Hesse. *Publications:* Cancronero Violeta Parra (transcriber, editor), 1977; Chapters on Aztec, Mayan & Inca music, Geschichte der Musik, vol 1, 1977; Ungarndeutscher Rosengarten, German Songs from hungary. *Address:* Apartado 29, E-370080 Salamanca, Spain.

HESSE Ruth, b. 18 Sept 1936, Wuppertal, Germany. Singer (Mezzo-Soprano). *Education:* Studied with Peter Offermans in Wuppertal and with Hildegard Scharf in Hamburg. *Career:* Sang in Lubeck from 1958; Hamburg Staatsoper from 1960; Operas by Wagner, Verdi and Strauss at the Deutsche Oper Berlin from 1962; Bayreuth Festival as Mary, Magdalene and Ortrud; Berlin 1965, in the premiere of Der junge Lord by Henze; Vienna Staatoper 1966, Ortrud, Brangaene and Eboli; Paris Opéra 1966, 1972, as Kundry and as The Nurse in Die Frau ohne Schatten; Salzburg Festival 1974-75, as The Nurse; sang Clytemmnestra in Elektra at the Deutsche Oper Berlin, 1988; Concert and oratorio appeaances. *Recordings:* Die Meistersinger (Electrola); Die Frau ohne Schatten and Der junge Lord (Deutsche Grammophon); Fricka in Der Ring des Nibelungen (Westminster); Violanta by Korngold (CBS). *Address:* c/ o Deutsche Oper Berlin, Richard Wagnerstrasse 10, D-1000 Berlin, Germany.

HESTER Mark Bowman, b. 27 June 1956, Roxboro, North Carolina, USA. Tenor. *Education:* BM, University of North Carolina, 1974-78; MM, Performer's Certificate, Eastman School of Music, 1979-81; Certificate, Indiana University, 1981-85; University of Houston, 1986-87; American Institute of Musical Studies, Graz, 1986. *Career:* Houston Grand Opera; New Jersey State Opera; Orlando Opera; Bronx Opera; Brevard Music Festival; Aspen Music Festival; June Opera Festival, Princeton, New Jersey; Connecticut Early Music Festival; San Antonio Festival; Houston Symphony Orchestra; North Carolina Symphony; Canton Symphony Orchestra; Rochester Philharmonic Orchestra; Houston Opera Studio, 1986-87; Theater der Stadt Heidelberg, 1987-. *Hobby:* Philately. *Address:* Rt 2 Box 73, Hurdle Mills, NC 27541, USA.

HETHERINGTON Hugh, b. 1958, England. Singer (Tenor). *Education:* Studied at the Guildhall School of Music, as St John's College Cambridge and with Frederick Cox in Manchester; Further study with Audrey Langford. *Career:* With Glyndebourne Festival and Touring companies has sung Dr Caius (Falstaff) and Truffaldino (Love of Three Oranges) and Where the Wild Things Are, and Idomeneo; Appearances with Scottish Opera as Dema in Cavalli's L'Egisto, Pang in Turandot, The Devil in The Soldier's Tale, Basilio in Le Nozze di Figaro and roles in Iolanthe, Lulu, La Vie Parisienne and Eugene Onegin; With English National Opera as Piet in Ligeti's Le Grand Macabre and in The Return of Ulysses and L'Orfeo (1992); Covent Garden from 1985 in King Priam and Samson et Dalila; Further engagements with University Opera, New Sussex Opera, Opera Factory, Zurich and London Sinfoniettas, the Singers' Company, Channel 4 TV and the Endymion Ensemble double bill of Monteverdi and Michael Nyman (1987); New York debut 1989 in HMS Pinafore with New Sadler's Wells Opera at the City Center Theater; Concerts with the City of Birmingham Symphony and the Matrix Ensemble. *Address:* c/o Opera Factory, 8a The Leather Market, Weston Street, London SE1 3ER, England.

HETTRICK Jane Schatkin, b. 1940, New York City, USA. Musicologist. m. William E Hettrick. *Education:* AB, Queens College, CUNY; MM, DMA, University of Michigan; Study at Hochschule für Musik und darstellende Kunst, Vienna. *Career:* Professor of Music, Rider College, 1974-; Solo concert organist with numerous recitals; Musicologist. *Publications:* Critical Editions: Arnolt Schlick, Spiegel der Orgelmacher und Organisten (1511): Translation, Transcription, and Study, Colorado College Music Press; Antonio Salieri, Concerto per l'organo, Doblinger, 1981; Antonio Salieri, Three Symphonies, Italians in Vienna, Series B, vol 2 of The Symphony, 1720-1840: A Comprehensive Collection of Full Scores in Sixty Volumes. Garland, 1983; Antonio Salieri, Messe in B-Dur (1809), Denkmaeler der Tonkunst in Oesterreich. Graz 1988; Antonio Salieri, Mass in D (1788), Recent Researches in the Music of the Classical Era. A-R Editions, 1994; Antonio Salieri, Missa stylo a capella. Doblinger, 1993. *Contributions to:* The American Organist; The Diapason; Journal of Church Music; Fontes Artis Musicae; Studien zur Musikwissenschaft. *Address:* 48-21 Glenwood Street, Little Neck, NY 11362, USA.

HETTRICK William Eugene, b. 15 Nov 1939, Toledo, Ohio, USA. Musicologist; University Professor. m. Jane Schatkin Hettrick, 5 Jun 1966. *Education:* BMus, 1962, MA, 1964, PhD, 1968, University of Michigan; University of Munich, Germany, 1966-67. *Career:* Professor, Music, Hofstra University. *Publications:* Editor: Gregor Aichinger, Cantiones ecclesiasticae (1607), 1972; Bernhard Klingenstein, Rosetum Marianum (1604), 1977; Gregor Aichinger, The Vocal Concertos, 1986; Translator and Editor: The Musica instrumentalis deudsch of Martin Agricola: A Treatise on Musical Instruments, 1529 and 1545; Editor, Journal of the American Musical Instrument Society, 1979-85, 92, Board Member 1986-. *Contributions to:* Notes; The New Grove; Journal of the American Musical Instrument Society; American Recorder; Journal of the American Musicological Society; Recorder & Music Magazine; Studien zur Musikwissenschaft. *Address:* 48-21 Glenwood Street, Little Neck, NY 11362, USA.

HETU Jacques, b. 8 Aug 1938, Trois-Rivières, Quebec, Canada. *Education:* Classical Studies, Jean-de-Brebeuf College, Montreal, 1949-55; Piano and Harmony studies, School of Music of University of Ottawa for a year; Studied Composition with Clermont Pepin, Conservatoire de Musique de Montreal; Received tutelage from Lukas Foss, Berkshire Music Centre, Tanglewood, Massachusetts, summer 1959; Studied with Henri Dutilleux, obtaining a degree in composition, Ecole Normale Superieure, Paris, 1961-63; Student in Oliver Messiaen's analysis class, Paris Conservatoire, winter season 1962-63. *Career:* Teacher, Analysis, School of Music, Laval University, 1963-77; Teacher, University of Montreal 1972-73 and 1978-79; Appointed professor, University of Quebec, Montreal currently teaches analysis, orchestration and composition, 1979-; Hosted 13 programmes on French Network of CBC-TV; Research in music therapy at Sainte-Anne Hospital, Baie-Saint Paul and participated in public conferences. *Compositions:* Orchestral: Adagio et Rondo pour Orchestre a Cordes, Opus 3, No 1b 1960; Antinomie, Opus 1977, L'Apocalypse, Opus 14 1967; Passacaille, Opus 17, 1970; Prelude, Opus 5, 1961; Soloists with Orchestra; Concerto pour basson, Opus 31, 1979; Concerto pour Piano et Orchestre, Opus 15, 1969; Double Concerto, Opus 12, 1967; Fantaisie pour Piano et Orchestre, Opus 21, 1973; Rondo pour Violoncelle et Orchestre a Cordes, Opus 9, 1965. Voices: Les Clartes de la nuit, Opus 20, 1972; Les Djinns, Opus 22, 1975; Piano: Ballade, Opus 30, 1978; Prelude et danse, Opus 24, 1977; Sonate pour deux pianos, Opus 6, 1962; Toccata; Variations pour piano, Opus 8, 1964. *Recordings:* Concerto pour piano et orchestre; Cycle; Petite Suite; Quatre Pieces pour flute et piano; Quintette pour instruments a vent; Sonate pour deux pianos; symphonie pour cordes; Symphonie No 3; Variations pour piano. *Address:* CAPAC (Canada), c/o PRS Ltd, Berners Street, London W1P 4AA, England.

HEUCKE Stefan, b. 24 May 1959, Gaildorf, Germany. Composer. *Education:* Studied Piano with Professor Renate Werner, Stuttgart, 1978-82; Piano with Professor A von Arnim, Composition with Professor G Schafer, Musikhochschule, Dortmund, 1982-86. *Debut:* Premiere of Vier Orchesterstucke op 5 performed by Saarland State Orchestra, Saarbrucken, 1985. *Career:* Dozent (University Lecturer) in Theory of Music, Musikhochschule, Dortmund, 1989-; Production and editing live for WDR, SDR and Saarlandischer Rundfunk broadcasting stations; Numerous performances in Germany, Russia, Netherlands and Chile. *Compositions:* Self-published: Vier Orchesterstucke, op 5, 1983; Holderlin-Frgmente, op 7, 1985; Symphony No 1, op 12, 1990; Quartet for bayan and strings, op 16, 1991-92; Symphony No 2, op 19, 1993; Variations on a theme of Webern, op 10, for orchestra. *Recording:* CD, Abendgebete, op 14, with Berthold Schmid, tenor, and Sinfonietta Tubingen. *Honours:* Prize, Forum of Young German Composers Competition, 1985; Grant, City of Dortmund, 1990. *Memberships:* GEMA; Interessenverband deutscher Komponisten. *Hobbies:* Reading; Cooking; Hiking. *Address:* Markt 10a, D59174 Kamen, Germany.

HEUERMANN Patricia Calhoun, b. 4 Aug 1936, Atlanta, Georgia, USA. Stage Director; Designation, Set Designer. m. (1) Eric Heuermann Jr, 12 June 1956, (2) Vete Nowik, 29 Mar 1985, 1 son, 3 daughters. *Education:* Westminster School, Atlanta, Georgia; Voice Performance, Curtis Institute of Music, 1956; Private study, Stage Direction: Frank Corsare, Wesley Balk; Voice: Ludwig Fabri, Eufemia Giannini; Gregory Wilfred Pelletier, New York. *Career:* Director, Emory Opera Theatre, Emory University, 1967-73; Director, Opera Theater, Clark College, 1971-73; Founder, Artistic Director, Georgia Opera, 1974-78; Artistic Director, Atlanta Civic Opera, 1978-80; Managing Director, North Carolina Opera, 1980-82; Artistic Director, Theater of New York, 1982-; Director, Performance Workshop for Young Professional Singers, Manhattan School of Music, 1986-; Artistic Director, Reimann Opera Theatre of New York University, 1989-; Guest Director with regional opera companies throughout USA. *Current management:* Association of Artistic Enterprises. *Address:* 481 Ft Washington Avenue No 68, New York, NY 10033, USA.

HEWITT Harry Donald, b. 4 Mar 1921, Detroit, Michigan, USA. Composer. m. Elizabeth Rolfe, 15 May 1943. *Education:* Studies with Homer LaGassey; Edward Murray; Joseph Barone. *Career includes:* Composer, over 60 years; Over 400 pieces publicly performed; Works played throughout USA by orchestras including: New York Little Symphony; Pennsylvaniaa Philharmonic; Egerinsky Sinfonia; Concerto Soloists of Philadelphia; Orchestra Society, Philadelphia; Chamber works performed at many colleges, numerous broadcasts. *Compositions include:* Major works: 29 symphonies, 23 string quartets, operas, concerti; Most recent: 24 preludes for 2 Euphoniums (TUBA Press, 1989). *Contributions to:* Numerous journals & other publications; Editor, Penn Sounds, 1989-. *Memberships:* Founder, President 1976-88, Delaware Valley Composers; Writer member, American Society of Composers, Authors & Publishers; Past Secretary, Guild for Contemporary Music; Past Music Director, Main Line Playhouse; Currently Pres/Ceo of Composer Services, Inc; Director of CSI Publications, 1990-.

Address: 345 South 19th Street, Philadelphia, PA 19103, USA.

HEYER John Hajdu (formerly HAJDU, John H), b. 4 Jan 1945, Altoona Pennsylvania, USA. Musicologist; Conductor. m. Sandra Lee Heyer, 1 Sept 1973, 2 sons. *Education:* BMus, Composition, DePauw University, 1966; MA, PhD, Musicology, University of Colorado, 1971-73; Studied with Nadia Boulanger, 1967-70. *Career:* Teacher, University of Colorado, 1971-73; Teacher, 1973-87, Music Department Chairman, 1980, University of California, Santa Cruz; Lecturer, Programme Annotator, Carmel Bach Festival, 1979-; Dean, College of Fine Arts, Indiana University of Pennsylvania, Indiana, Pennsylvania, 1987-; Member of International Committee preparing the New Collected Works of Jean-Baptiste Lully for publication; President, Rocky Ridge Music Center Foundation, 1989-. *Recordings:* Conducted J Gilles, Messe des Morts, Musical Heritage Society, 1981. *Publications:* Critical Edition: Jean Gilles, Messe des Morts, 1983; Lully and the Music of the French Baroque, 1989. *Contributions to:* Notes; The New Grove. *Address:* College of Fine Arts, Indiana University of Pennsylvania, 110 Sprowls Hall, Indiana University of Pennsylvania, Indiana, PA 15705, USA.

HEYNIS Aafje, b. 2 May 1924, Krommenie, Holland. Singer (Contralto). *Education:* Studied with Aaltje Noordewier-Reddingius, Laurens Bogtman and Bodi Rapp; Further study with Roy Henderson in England. *Career:* Sang at first in oratorio and other sacred music; Amsterdam 1956, in Der Wildschütz by Lortzing; Concertgebouw Amsterdam 1958, in the Alto Rhapsody by Brahms; Many concert engagements in music by Mahler, Bach (St Matthew Passion, B Minor Mass), Monteverdi, Schubert, Handel, Beethoven and Frank Martin. *Recordings:* Orfeo ed Euridice by Gluck; Madrigals by Monteverdi (Telefunkem); Music by Bach. *Honours include:* Harriet Cohen Medal 1961. *Address:* c/o Concertgebouworkest, Jacob Obredhstrasse 51, 1017 Amsterdam, Holland.

HICKOX Richard Sidney, b. 5 Mar 1948, Stokenchurch, Bucks, England. Conductor; Music Director. m. Frances Ina Sheldon-Williams, 1976, 1 son. *Education:* Royal Academy of Music (LRAM); Organ Scholar, Queens College, Cambridge (MA). *Debut:* As Professional Conductor, St Johns Smith Square, 1971. *Career:* Organist, Master of Music, St Margarets, Westminster, 1972-82; Prom Debut, 1973; Artistic Director, Woburn Festival, 1967-; St Endellion Festival, 1974-; Christ Church Spitalfields Festival, 1978-; Truro Festival, 1981-; Summer Music Festival, 1989; Principal Guest Conductor, Dutch Radio Orchestra, 1980-85; Associate Conductor, San Diego Symphony Orchestra, 1983-84; regularly conducts LSO, RPO, Bournemouth Symphony Orchestra and Sinfonietta, Royal Liverpool Philharmonic Orchestra, BBC Symphony, Concert, Scottish and Welsh Orchestras, BBC Singers, Aarhus and Odens Orchestras, Hallé Orchestra; Conducted: ENO, 1979; Opera North, 1982, 1986; Los Angeles Opera, 1986; Scottish Opera, 1985, 1987; Royal Opera, 1985; appearances, many music festivals including Proms, Flanders, Edinburgh, Bath and Cheltenham; Artistic Director, Northern Sinfonia, 1982-; Associate Conductor, London Symphony Orchestra; Conductor, Music Director, City of London Sinfonia, 1971-; Richard Hickox Singers, 1971-; London Symphony Chorus, 1976-; Bradford Festival Choral Society, 1978-; Conducted Rimsky's Mozart and Salieri at the Festival Hall 1990, A Midsummer Nights Dream at Sadler's Wells; Season 1992/93 with Rossini Birthday Gala at the Barbican Hall and Giulio Cesare at Schwetzingen; Conducted the City of London Sinfonia at the 1993 Prom Concerts (Strauss's Oboe Concerto, Saxton's Viola Concerto and Mendelssohn's Fourth Symphony). *Recordings:* Virgin EMI, Decca, including Belshazzar's Feast, with David Wilson-Johnson; Britten's Frank Bridge Variations; Elgar's Cello Concerto and Bloch's Schelomo (Steven Isserlis); Moeran's Sinfonietta and Serenade in G; Finzi Dies Natalis and Clarinet Concerto (Martyn Hill, Michael Collins); Rossini Stabat Mater

(Field, D Jones, A Davies, Earle); L'Incoronazione di Poppea (Auger, Jones); Alcina (Auger); A Midsummer Night's Dream. *Address:* 35 Ellington Street, London N7, England.

HIDAS Frigyes, b. 25 May 1928, Budapest, Hungary. Composer. m. Erzsebet Zombori, 5 July 1966. 1 daughter. *Education:* Degree in composing, Academy of Music, Budapest, 1946-51. *Career:* Music Director, Budapest National Theatre, 1951-66; Music Director, Budapest Operetta Theatre, 1974-79; Freelance Composer. *Compositions include:* Chamber music: Three Sketches, 1982; Hungarian Folksongs, 1985; Divertimento, 1982; Pian-Org, 1985; Musique pour six, 1985; Brass Chamber Music: Trio, 1980; Six Etudes, 1980; Play, 1981; Three Little Scherzos, 1982; Movement, 1982; Septet, 1982; 5 x 5, 1983l; Trumpet Fantasy, 1983; Little Suite, 1983; Academic quintet, 1983; Musik fur Blaser, 1983; Training Patterns, 1982; Four-in-Hand, 1985; Works for Concert Band: Ballet Music, 1980; Merry Music, 1980; Concertino, 1981; Suite, 1981; Fantasy and Fugue, 1984; Folksong Suite No 1, 1985, No 2, 1985; Circus Suite, 1985; Festive Music, 1985. Concertos: Ballad, 1982; Trumpet Concerto No 2, 1983; Baroque Concerto, 1984; Quintetto concertante, 1985; Concertos for Concert Band: Rhapsody, 1982; Flute Concerto No 2, 1983; Quintetto concertante, 1985. *Recordings:* Wind Quintet No 2; Flute Concerto No 2; Toccata, Movement No 3 of Organ Sonata; Violin Concertino; Oboe Concerto; Rhapsody for Brass Trombone; Training Patterns, excerpts; Four in Hand. *Publications:* Cedar, Ballett in two acts, 1975; Alteba Trio, 1986; String Quartet, Nos.1, 2 and 3; Symphonic Works: Széchenyi Concerto, 1984; Three Movements for Orchestra, 1987; The Undanced Ballett, 1989; 1 & 5 Sextet for Bass Trombone and Wind Quintet, 1986; Tuba Quartet, 1990; Saxaphone Quartet, 1990; 17 Concertos for various instruments; Oratories; Music for Films, TV and Theatre. *Honours:* Merited Artist of the Hungarian Republic, 1987; Erkel Prize, 1958 and 1982. *Address:* Attila ut 133, 1012 Budapest, Hungary.

HIEBERT Thomas Nels, b. 3 July 1955, Göttingen, Germany. Assistant Professor of Horn and Theory. m. Lenore Eileen Hiebert, 7 July 1984, 1 daughter. *Education:* Staatliche Hochschule für Musik Rheinland, Cologne, 1976-77; BA, Music, Bethel College, Kansas, USA, 1978; MM, Eastman School of Music, 1980; DMA, University of Wisconsin, Madison, 1989. *Career:* Teaching positions: University of Wisconsin, Oshkosh, 1984-85; University of Nebraska, Lincoln, 1987; California State University, Fresno, 1987-91; Played horn with: Boston Lyric Opera, 1980-82; Oshkosh Symphony, 1984-85; Wisconsin Chamber Orchestra, 1986-87; Lincoln Symphony Orchestra, 1987; Orpheus Contemporary Chamber Ensemble, Fresno, 1987-91. *Publication:* The Horn in Early Eighteenth-Century Dresden: The Players and Their Repertory (dissertation). *Address:* California State University at Fresno, Department of Music, Fresno, CA 93740, USA.

HIELSCHER Ulrich, b. 29 Apr 1943, Schwarzengrund, Germany. Singer (Bass). *Education:* Studied in Dusseldorf and with Paul Lohmann in Wiesbaden. *Career:* Sang at Essen from 1967, member of the Cologne Opera from 1974; Guest appearances at Hamburg, Hanover, Wuppertal, Frankfurt, Dusseldorf, Stuttgart and the Vienna Staatsoper Ghent Opera, 1984-85 and further engagements as concert singer in Holland, Belgium, France, Switzerland and Colombia; Opera roles have included Mozart's Osmin, Figaro, Leoporello, Alfonso, Sarastro and Speaker, Verdi's Falstaff and Padre Guardiano, Kecal in The Bartered Bride, Mephistopheles in Faust Plunket in Martha; Wagner Daland, Hagen and Gurnemanz, Baron Ochs, the Doktor in Wozzeck, and Don Pasquale; Concert showings in works by Bach, Handel, Haydn, Mozart, Beethoven and Bruckner. *Recordings include:* Messa di Gloria by Puccini. *Address:* Oper der Stadt Koln, Offenbachplatz, 50667 Cologne, Germany.

HIESTERMANN Horst, b. 14 Aug 1934, Ballenstadt, Harz, Germany. Singer (Tenor). *Career:* Staddtheater

Brandenburg from 1957, debut as Pedrillo in Die Entführung; Sang in Leipzig, Weimar, Berlin and Dresden; Deutsche Oper am Rhein Dusseldorf 1976-84; Salzburg Festival from 1978, as Monostatos, as the Dancing Master in Ariadne auf Naxos, and as Robespierre in Dantons Tod 1983; Dallas Opera 1982, as Loge in Das Rheingold; Tokyo 1983, as Mime in Siegfried; Other appearances in Geneva, Rouen, Amsterdam, Houston and New York (Metropolitan Opera); Barcelona 1984, as Aegisthus in Elektra; Member of the Zurich Opera from 1984; Deutsche Oper Berlin, 1984, in the premiere of Reimann's Gespenstersonate; Vienna Staatsoper 1987, as Herod in Salome; sang Mime in a new production the Ring at the Metropolitan 1988-90; Shuisky in Boris Godunov at Barcelona, 1990; Herod in Berlin; Sang Aegisthus at Athens, 1992; Other roles include, the Captain in Wozzeck, Shuisky in Boris Godunov and David in Die Meistersinger. Recordings: Wozzeck, The Duenna by Prokofiev, Puntila by Dessau (Eterna); Carmina Burana and Trionfi by Orff Philips); Die Zauberflöte (RCA); Karl V by Krenek; Die Meistersinger conducted by Karajan (EMI). Address: c/o Deutsche Oper Berlin, Richard Wagnerstrasse 10, D-1000 Berlin, Germany.

HIGGINBOTTOM Edward, b. 16 Nov 1946, Kendal, Cumbria, England. University Lecturer; Director of Music, New College, Oxford. m. Caroline M F Barrowcliff, 30 Oct 1971, 2 sons, 4 daughters. Education: FRCO; John Stewart of Rannoch Scholar in Sacred Music; MA; PhD; MusB; Corpus Christi College, Cambridge, 1966-73; Organ Scholar, 1966-69. Career: Research Fellow of Corpus Christi College, Cambridge, 1973-76; Director of Music and Fellow of New College, Oxford, 1976-; Conseiller to the French Ministry of Culture. Recordings: Organ Music and as Director of New College Choir, Oxford (over 40 issues). Publications: Various editions of music and contributions to Grove 6 Contributions to: Musical Times; Organists Review; Music and Letters. Honours: Harding and Read Prizes, Royal College of Organists; Officier de l'Ordre des Arts et des Lettres. Address: New College, Oxford, England.

HILEY David, b. 9 May 1947, Littleborough, England. University Professor. m. Ann Fahrni, 28 Feb 1975, 2 daughters. Education: BA Oxon, 1973; PhD London, 1981. Career: Assistant Music Master, Eton College, 1968-73; Lecturer, Royal Holloway College, 1976-86; Professor Regensburg University, 1986-. Publications: Nex Oxford History of Music II (co-editor), 1990; Western Plainchant: A Handbook, 1993. Memberships: Royal Musical Association; Plainsong and Mediaeval Music Society; Gesellschaft für Musikforschung; American Musicological Society; International Musicological Society; Henry Bradshaw Society. Address: Sonnenstrasse 10, 93152 Nittendorf, Germany.

HILL David Neil, b. 13 May 1957. Master of Music; Organist. m. Hilary Llystn Jones, 1979, 1 son, 1 daughter. Education: Chetham's School of Music, Manchester; St John's College, Cambridge (organ Scholar - toured Australia, 1977, USA and Canada, 1978, Japan, 1979; MA). Career: Conductor, Alexandria Choir, 1979-; Musical Director, Alexandra Choir, London, 1980-87; Sub Organist, Durham Cathedral, 1980-82; Organist, Master of Music, Westminster Cathedral, 1982-88; Organist and Master of Choristers at Winchester Cathedral from 1988 and Artistic Director, Philharmonia Chrous, the first British conductor to hold the post; Concerts in 1993 included performances with the Bournemouth Sinfonietta, Bournemouth Symphony and the Philharmonia Orchestra and Chorus, also conducted the Bournemouth Symphony Orchestra, the Waynflete Singers and the Cathedral Choir in a concert televised for ITV at Christmas; In 1994 is to conduct in South Africa, Singapore, Denmark and Spain; Frequently invited to direct choral workshops and summers schools, particularly in Britain, USA and Australaisia and has written several articles on choir training. Recordings: With Westminster Cathedral Choir. Honours: Gramophone Award, 1985. Hobbies: Wine; Beer; Cricket; Reading; Snooker. Address: 5 The Close, Winchester Cathedral, Winchester, Hants, England.

HILL George R, b. 12 July 1943, Denver, Colorado, USA. Musicologist; Music Bibliographer. m. Janet McMonagle, 26 June 1982. Education: AB Music, with Departmental Honours, Stanford University, 1965; AM Library Science, University of Chicago, 1966; PhD Historical Musicology, New York University, 1975. Career: Librarian, Music Division, New York Public Library, 1966-70; Assistant Music Librarian, New York University, 1971-72; Fine Arts Librarian, University of California, Irvine, 1972-73; Associate Professor of Music, Baruch College, City University of New York, 1973-. Publications: A Thematic Locator for Mozart's Works as Listed in Kochel's Chronologisch-Thematisches Verzeichnis - 6th Edition (principal author), 1970; A Preliminary Checklist of Research on the Classic Symphony and Concerto to the Time of Beethoven (excluding Haydn and Mozart), 1970; A Thematic Catalogue of the Instrumental Music of Florian Leopold Gassmann, 1976; Florian Leopold Gassmann, Seven Symphonies, 1981; Joseph Haydn Werke, Floetenuhrstuecke, 1984; A Handbook of Basic Tonal Practice, 1985. Contributions to: Articles and Reviews to various professional journals, including The New Grove Dictionary of Music and Musicians. Address: 84 Highgate Terrace, Bergenfield, NJ 07621-3922, USA.

HILL Jackson, b. 23 May 1941, Birmingham, Alabama, USA. Composer; University Professor of Music. m. Martha Gibbs, 5 June 1966, 1 son. Education: AB, 1963, MA, 1966, PhD Musicology, 1970, University of North Carolina; Composition with Iain Hamilton, 1964-66 and Roger Hannay, 1967-68. Career: Conductor, Bucknell Symphony Orchestra, 1969-79; Member, Research Unit, Manchester College, Oxford, 1975; Choral Conductor Assistant, Exeter College, Oxford; Assistant/Associate Professor of Music, 1968-80; Head of Department of Music, 1980-90, Associate Dean of Faculty, 1990-, Bucknell University; Hays-Fulbright Fellow, Japan, 1977; Visiting Fellow, Clare Hall, Cambridge, England, 1982-83. Compositions: More than 100 works including: Serenade, 1970; Three Mysteries, 1973; Paganini Set, 1973; Missa Brevis, 1974; English Mass, 1975; Sonata: By the Waters of Babylon, 1976; Whispers of the Dead, 1976; Streams of Love, 1989; Enigma Elegg, 1987; Symphony No 1, 1990. Recordings: Sonata: By the Waters of Babylon; Ecce vidimus eum. Publications: The Music of Kees van Baaren, 1970; The Harold E Cook Collection of Musical Instruments, 1975 and numerous articles on music and mysticism, Japanese Music and Buddhist Liturgical Music. Contributions to: Ethnomusicology; Studio Mystica and Notes. Hobbies: Travel; History; Book Collecting. Address: Bucknell University, Lewisburg, PA 17837, USA.

HILL Jenny, b. 20 June 1944. Opera and Concert Singer (Soprano). div. 2 daughters. Education: National School of Opera, London Opera Centre. Debut: Sandman, Hansel and Gretel, Sadler's Wells Opera Co, (now known as English National Opera). Career: English opera Group with Benjamin Britten performing in London, Russia and Canada; Created role of Pretty Polly in Punch & Judy premiere, Aldeburgh and Edinburgh Festivals, and Mrs Green in Birtwistle's Down by the Greenwood Side, premiere at the London and Brighton Festivals, 1968; Repertory operas performed include, Traviata, Lucia, La Sonnambula, Rigoletto, Marriage of Figaro, Magic Flute, A Midsummer Nights Dream; Concerts appearances include: A Mother Goose Primer, with Pierrot Players, Petrassi's Magnificat, with Giulini both British premieres at the RFH, 1972; City of London Opening Concert Bach's B minor Mass with Giulini at St Paul's Cathedral; Opening Concert, English Bach Festival, Blenheim Palace; Performances on radio and television as well as numerous song recitals of classical and advante garde music. Recordings include: The Rape of Lucretia, as Lucia; Schumann's Faust; Bach's St John's Passion. Honours: Leverhulme Scholarship, 1960-63; Gulbenkian Fellowship for Most Outstanding Young Performer, 1969-72. Memberships: Equity;

Incorporated Society of Musicians; Association of Singing Teachers. *Hobbies:* Swimming; Reading; Travel. *Current Management:* Direct Booking Only. *Address:* 5 Oaklands Grove, London W12 OJD, England.

HILL John Walter, b. 7 Dec 1942, Chicago, Illinois, USA. Professor of Music. m. 4 sons, 2 daughters. *Education:* AB, University of Chicago, 1963; MA, 1966, PhD, 1972, Harvard University, Cambridge, Massachusetts. *Career:* Assistant Professor, University of Pennsylvania, 1971-78; Associate Professor, 1978-84, Professor of Music, 1984-, University of Illinois; Editor-in-Chief, Journal of the American Musicological Society, 1983-86. *Publications:* The Life and Works of F M Veracini, 1979; Studies in Musicology in Honor of Otto E Albrecht, 1980; Vivaldi's Ottone in Villa: A Study in Musical Drama, 1983. *Contributions to:* The Journal of the American Musicological Society; Music and Letters; Acta Musicologica. *Memberships:* American Musicological Society; International Musicological Society; Società Italiana di Musicologia. *Address:* 2136 Music Building, University of Illinois, 1114 West Nevada, Urbana, IL 61801, USA.

HILL Keith Richard, b. 8 May 1948, Tungan, Fukien, China. Musical Instrument Maker. m. Marianne Ploger, 3 Apr 1984. *Education:* BA, Western Michigan University, 1970. *Career:* Began professional career making Harpsichords, 1972; Began Structured investigation into the Art & Science of acoustic enhancement of musical instruments, 1979-86; Began making Harpsichords with highly advanced acoustic properties, 1986-; Instruments made include: 114 Double Manual Harpsichords; 59 Single Manual Harpsichords; 25 Spinets; 9 Fortepianos; 3 Gothic Harps; 1 Three Rank Wooden Pipe Organ; 22 Clavichords; 11 Pedal Harpsichords; 1 Pedal Clavichord; 5 Cellos; 4 Violas; 33 Violins; 3 Double Basses; 36 Violas da Gamba; 2 Violas d'Amore; 1 Psaltry; 3 Rebecs; 1 Fiddle. *Contributions to:* Continuo Magazine; Luthiers Society Journal. *Hobbies:* Landscape Painting; Soundboard Painting; Writing Music; Gardening. *Address:* 110332 Chelsea - Manchester Road, Manchester, MI 48158, USA.

HILL Martyn, b. 14 Sept 1944, England. Singer (Tenor). m. Marleen De Maesschalck 1974, 3 sons, 1 daughter. *Education:* Royal College of Music (ARCM); Vocal studies with Audrey Langford. *Career:* Worldwide appearances in concert and opera; Sang Arbace in the Ponnelle/Harnoncourt production of Idomeneo in Zurich; Glyndebourne Opera 1985, as Idomeneo; Scottish Opera 1986, as Quint in The Turn of the Screw; US debut in New Hampshire as Tom Rakewell in The Rake's Progress; Metz Opera as Flamand in Capriccio and Ferrando in Così fan Tutte ; Glyndebourne Opera 1988, as Belmonte; sang Mozart in Rimsky's Mozart and Salieri at the Festival Hall, 1990, Edrisi in Szymanowski's King Roger at the Festival Hall; Concert engagements include: world premiere of Carter's In Sleep, in Thunder, London 1982; Amsterdam Concertgebouw in Holst's Savitri, Stravinsky's Threni and the St Matthew Passion; Britten's War Requiem in Hanover, Spring Symphony in Los Angeles, and Serenade at Ludwgisburg; Messiah with the Washington National Symphony; London concerts singing Schubert with Sanderling, Stravinsky with Ozawa and Bruckner's Te Deum with Matacic; UK tour with the Contemporary Music Network; Bach's Magnificat at the 1989 Promenade Concerts. *Recordings include:* Britten's Serenade with the City of London Sinfonia; Walsinghame by Bax (Royal Philharmonia); Hoist Choral Hymns from the Rig Veda; Finzi Dies Natals (Virgin Classics); Handel L'Allegro il Penseroso ed il Moderato (Erato) and Acis and Galatea (Archiv). *Address:* c/o Harrison/Parrott Ltd, 12 Penzance Place, London W11 4PA, England.

HILL Peter, b. 14 June 1948, Lyndhurst, England. Pianist; University Lecturer. m. Charlotte Huggins, 21 Apr 1981, 2 daughters. *Education:* MA, Oxford University; Royal College of Music. *Debut:* Wigmore Hall, London, 1974. *Career:* Regular Broadcasts, BBC;

International Festival Appearances include: Harrogate, Bath, English Bach, Dublin, Stuttgart; Founder Member, Ensemble Dreamtiger; Senior Lecturer, University of Sheffield. *Recordings:* Complete Piano Music of Havergal Brian; Dreamtiger: East-West Encounters; Nigel Osborne: Remembering Esenin; Piano works by Nigel Osborne, Douglas Young, Howard Skempton; Messiaen: The Complete Piano Music. *Contributions to:* Tempo. *Honours:* Chappell Gold Medal, Royal College of Music, 1971; Darmstadt Ferienkurst, 1st Prize, 1974. *Current Management:* STR Music Marketing and Management. *Hobbies:* Photography; Golf. *Address:* c/o Dept of Music, University of Sheffield, Sheffield S10 2TN, England.

HILL Robert Stephen, b. 6 Nov 1953, Philippines. Harpsichordist; Fortepianist; Musicologist. *Education:* Solo Diploma, Amsterdam Conservatory, 1974; Licentiate, Trinity College of Music, London, 1974; MA, 1982, PhD, 1987, Harvard University, USA. *Career:* Tours with Musica Antiqua Köln; Radio & TV Broadcasts for West German, British, Dutch, Belgian, French networks, & National Public Radio & CBC, USA. *Recordings:* J S Bach, Sonatas for Violin & Harpsichord with Reinhard Goebel; J S Bach, Art of Fugue, early version; Solo Harpsichord. *Contributions to:* Early Music; Bach Jahrbuch. *Honours:* NEA, Solo Recitalist Award, 1983; Erwin Bodky Award, 1982; American Musicological Society Noah Greenberg Award, 1988. *Interests:* Early 20th Century Recordings. *Management:* Andreas Braun, Cologne, West Germany. *Address:* Staatliche Hochschule fuer Musik Freiburg, Freiburg, Germany.

HILL SMITH Marilyn, b. 9 Feb 1952, Carshalton, Surrey. Singer (Soprano). *Education:* Guildhall School of Music. *Career:* Toured in USA, Canada, Australia and New Zealand; Appearances at Sydney Opera House and Hollywood Bowl; English National Opera from 1978 as Adele in Die Fledermaus, Susanna in Le Nozze di Figaro, Olympia in Les Contes d'Hoffmann, Zerbinetta and Mozart's Despina, Papagena and Blonde; Covent Garden debut 1981 in Peter Grimes; New Sadler's Wells Opera in works by Lehar, Kalman and Sullivan; Principal roles with Canadian Opera, Welsh National, Scottish Opera and Lyric Opera of Singapore; Other engagements include Camden Festival, English Bach Festival, London Promenade Concerts and regular concerts and broadcasts; Foreign appearances in Hong Kong, Coburg, Versailles, Granada, Siena, Cologne, Athens, Rome, Madrid, Seville, Oman & Cannes. *Recordings:* Several works for Chandos, That's Entertainment, Opera Rara (including A Hundred Years of Italian Opera, and award-winning operetta series for Chandos. *Address:* c/o Music International, 13 Ardilaun Road, Highbury, London N5 2QR, England.

HILLEBRAND Nikolaus, b. 1948, Oberschlesien, Germany. Singer (Bass). *Education:* Studied with Rolf Dieter Knoll in Cologne and Hanno Blaschke in Munich. *Debut:* Lubeck, 1972. *Career:* Israel 1972, as Mosè in the opera by Rossini; Salzburg Easter Festival 1974, in Die Meistersinger; Vienna Staatsoper 1974; Bayreuth Festival 1974-75, in Parsifal and Die Meistersinger; Further engagements in Munich (Lohengrin), Karlsruhe, London, Paris, Rome and Brussels; many concert appearances, notably in music by Bach; conductors include Abbado, Böhm, Kleiber, Karajan and Muti. *Recordings include:* Stefano Colonna in Rienzi (EMI); Johannes Passion by Bach (Deutsche Grammophon); Egisto by Cavalli (Eurodisc); Romeo und Julia by Sutermeister; Reger's Requiem, Schwann. *Address:* c/o Ingpen & Williams Ltd, 14 Kensington Court, London W8 5DN, England.

HILLEBRANDT Oskar, b. 15 Mar 1943, Schopfheim, Baden, Germany. Singer (Baritone). *Education:* Studied at Cologne Musikhochschule with Josef Matternich. *Career:* Sang at the Stuttgart Staatsoper from 1969; Appearances at Saarbrucken, Kiel and Brunswick from 1971; Member of the Dortmund Opera from 1985; Guest appearances at Hamburg, Munich, Dusseldorf, Mannheim and Zurich; La Scala Milan as Telramund and the Teatro Zarzuela Madrid as Achillas in Giulio Cesare by Handel; Seattle Opera as Alberich in the Ring; Further engagements in Antwerp, Copenhagen and at the Santander Festival, Marseilles and Turin 1986, as Kaspar and Donner; British debut 1989, as Mandryka at the Glyndebourne Festival; Other roles include Pizarro, Scarpia, Count Luna, Amonasro, Simon Boccanegra and Jochanaan in Salome; Wagner's Dutchman, Amfortas and Klingsor; Concert showings in Paris, London, New York, Barcelona and Rome. *Address:* Opernhaus, Kuhstrasse 12, D-4600 Dortmund, Germany.

HILLEBRECHT Hildegard, b. 26 Nov 1927, Hanover, Germany. Singer (Soprano). *Education:* Studied with Margarethe von Winterfeldt, Franziska Martianssen Lohmann and Paul Lohmann. *Debut:* Freiburg 1951, as Leonora in Il Trovatore. *Career:* Sang at Zurich 1952-54, notably in the premiere of the revised version of Hindemith's Cardillac (1952); Dusseldorf 1954-59, Cologne 1956-61; sang Maria in Strauss's Friedenstag at Munich 1961; Many appearances at the State Operas of Vienna, Hamburg and Munich; Salzburg Festival 1956, 1964 as Ilia, Chrysothemis and Ariadne; Deutsche Oper Berlin 1968, in the premiere of Ulisse by Dallapiccola; Covent Garden 1967, as the Empress in Die Frau ohne Schatten; Metropolitan Opera 1968-69; sang with the Zurich Opera from 1972; Appearances in Rio de Janeiro, Paris, Rome, San Francisco, Edinburgh, Copenhagen, Barcelona, Dresden, Brussels and Prague; Repertoire includes works by Wagner, Puccini (Tosca), Verdi and Strauss; Elena in I vespri siciliani, Elisabeth de Valois, Desdemona, Sieglinde, Jenůfa and Ursula in Mathis der Maler. *Recordings:* Excerpts from Don Giovanni and Tannhäuser; Cavalleria Rusticana; Der Rosenkavalier; Ariadne auf Naxos, Don Giovanni, Duchess of Parma in Doktor Faust by Busoni, Die Zauberflöte (Deutsche Grammophon).

HILLEN Kees, b. 25 Jan 1946, Amsterdam, Holland. Musicologist. m. Bartje Nauta, 13 June 1970, 1 son, 1 daughter. *Education:* Degree, Musicology, University of Utrecht. *Career:* Head of Music Radio, VARA, until 1983; Promotion Manager of Donemus Publishing House and Library of Contemporary Dutch Music, Amsterdam, 1973-90; Artistic Director, Rotterdam Philharmonic Orchestra, 1990-. *Publications:* Contributor to various magazines. *Hobbies:* Gipsy Music; Sport. *Address:* Van Eeghenstraat 167, 1071 GC Amsterdam, The Netherlands.

HILLER Lejaran Arthur, b. 23 Feb 1924, New York City, USA. Composer; Conductor. m. 18 Apr 1945, 1 son, 1 daughter. *Education:* BA 1944, MA 1946, PhD 1947, Princeton University; MMus, University of Illinois, 1958. *Career includes:* Many television & radio interviews, conferences. *Compositions include:* Orchestral & chamber music; Vocal music; Electronic music; Instrumental/tape combinations, etc. *Recordings include:* Appalachian Ballads, voice & guitar, Winifred Balck & David Sussman, 1977; Sonata no 5, piano, Kenwyn Boldt, 1975; 8 Electronic Studies, 1965, 1966; Computer Cantata, Helen Hamm with University of Illinois Contemporary Chamber Players, 1967, 1973; suite, 2 pianos & tapes, Roger Shields & Neely Bruce, 1970, 1979; Quartet no 6 for strings, Concord String Quartet, 1974; An Apotheosis for Archaeopterix for Piccolo & Berimbau, Laurence Trott & Jan Williams, 1981; Quadrilateral, piano & tape, Yvar Mikhashoff, 1984; Expo '85, studies for tape & synthesisers, 1986; String Quartets Nos 3 and 7 (1953 and 1979); Electronic Sonata (1976); Three Compositions for Tape (1983). *Publication:* Co-author, Experimental Music, 1959, 1982. *Hobbies:* Sports including tennis; Carpentry. *Address:* Department of Music, State University of New York at Buffalo, Buffalo, NY 14260, USA.

HILLIER Paul Douglas, b. 9 Feb 1949, Dorchester, England. Singer; Conductor; Writer. m. Lena-Liis Kiesel, 19 Mar 1977, 1 daughter. *Education:* AGSM, 1970; Guildhall School of Music. *Debut:* Purcell Room, London, 1974. *Career:* Vicar-Choral, St Paul's Cathedral, 1973-74; Early Music Masterclasses, York, London,

Vancouver, Canada; Visiting Lecturer, University of California, Santa Cruz, 1980-81; Copland Fellow, Amherst College, Massachusetts, 1984; Director, Hilliard Ensemble, 1974-90; Professor of Music, University of California at Davis, 1990-; Director, Theatre of Voices, 1989-; TV Debut, Music in Time, 1983. *Recordings:* EMI International; ECM Records; EMI Reflexe; Harmonia Mundi, France; Hyperion; Saga; Meridian; Plant life; UEA Records. *Publications:* 300 Years of English Partsongs, Faber Music, 1983; Romantic English Partsongs, 1986; The Catch Book, 1987. *Honour:* Edison Klassik, 1986. *Hobbies:* Books; Looking at Islands; Composing. *Address:* Music Department, University of California, Davis, CA 95616, USA.

HILLIS Margaret (Eleanor), b. 1 Oct 1921, Kokomo, Indiana, USA. Conductor: Professor. *Education:* Indiana University, BA, 1947; Juilliard School of Music, New York, graduate student in choral conducting, 1947-49; Studies with Robert Shaw. *Career:* Music Director, American Concert Choir and Orchestra, New York, from 1950; Assistant Conductor, Collegiate Chorale, New York, 1952-53; Conductor, American Opera Society Chorus, New York, 1952-68; Choral Director, New York City Opera, 1955-56; Music Director, New York Chamber Soloists, 1956-60; Founder-Conductor, Chicago Symphony Orchestra Chorus, 1957-; Choral Director, Santa Fe (NM) Opera, 1958-59; Music Director, Kenosha (Wis) Symphony Orchestra, 1961-68; Resident Conductor, Chicago Civic Orchestra, 1967-; Conductor, Cleveland Orchestra Chorus, 1969-71; Music Director, Elgin (Ill) Symphony Orchestra, 1971-85; Conductor, San Francisco Symphony Orchestra Chorus, 1982-83; Guest Conductor with various US orchestras; Teacher, Juilliard School of Music, 1951-53; Director of choral activities, Northwestern University, 1970-77; Visiting Professor of Conducting, Indiana University School of Music, Bloomington, 1978-; Master classes in choral conducting; Founder-Director, American Choral Foundation, 1954-. *Recordings:* Prepared choruses for many award-winning discs by the Chicago Symphony Orchestra. *Memberships:* American Choral Directors Association; Association of Choral Conductors; Chors America; Kappa Kappa Gamma. *Address:* c/o Chicago Symphony Orchestra, Orchestra Hall, 220 S Michigan Avenue, Chicago, IL 60604, USA.

HILLMAN Jennifer (nee Glass), b. 29 Sept 1944, Stockton-on-Tees, England. Pianist; Composer; Journalist; Teacher. m. Basil Hillman, 13 Aug 1970, 2 sons. *Education:* Tiffin Girls' School, Kingston-upon-Thames 1955-62; Newnham College, University of Cambridge 1962-66; ARCM (Performance) 1962; LTCL (Performance) 1962; BA Hons Cantab 1965. *Career:* Head of Music Department, Francis Holland School, London NW1, 1966-69; Music Correspondent, The Times 1966-69; Lecturer, Homerton College, Cambridge 1969-70; Music Correspondent, Cambridge Evening News 1969-70; Professor of Musicianship, Trinity College of Music 1966-72; Professor of Musicianship and Piano, Guildhall School of Music and Drama 1970-; Freelance Accompanist and Duo Partnership with Pianist, Marion Raper 1984-. *Compositions:* Sonatina for Tuba and Piano, 1963; (Published by Emmerson; Recorded with John Fletcher and Reeves, Japan). *Address:* 24 Hill Top, London NW11 6EE, England.

HILLSMAN Walter Lee, b. 25 Feb 1943, Dallas, Texas, USA. Musician. *Education:* BMus, The Curtis Institute of Music, Philadelphia, 1960-64; MA, DPhil, New College, Oxford University, England, 1964-67, 1978-85; State Music Academy, Munich, Federal Republic of Germany, 1967-69; FRCO, Royal College of Organists, London, England, 1973. *Career:* Organist-Choirmaster, Old Christ Church, Philadelphia, USA, 1962-64; Organ Scholar, New College, Oxford, England, 1964-67; Organist-Choirmaster, Church of the Ascension, Munich, 1968-69; Director of Music, St Margaret's Church, Oxford, England, 1972-79; Organ Professor, Trinity College of Music, London, 1974-78; Sessional organ teacher, Reading University, 1974-78; Freelance Music Tutor, Oxford University, 1976-;

Member of Faculty of Music, Oxford University, 1981-; Organist, Manchester College, Oxford, 1985-; Solo organ recitals for BBC, Radio France, RIAS Berlin, Sender Freies Berlin, State radios of North and South Germany, Bavaria, Austria, Holland, Denmark. *Contributions to:* Articles in The American Organist; The Galpin Society Journal; Jeunesse et Orgue; The Musical Times. *Hobbies:* Swimming; Cycling; Weighttraining. *Address:* 13 Norham Road, Oxford OX2 6SF, England.

HILTON Janet Lesley, b. 1 Jan 1945, Liverpool, England. Clarinettist. m. David Richardson, 6 July 1968, 2 sons, 1 daughter. *Education:* Music, Royal Manchester College of Music, 1961-65; ARMCM; Vienna Konservatorium, 1966. *Career:* Soloist with BBC Philharmonic, Concert tours with Margaret Price; Festival appearances include: Bath, Cheltenham, Aldeburgh, Henry Wood Proms, 1979; Edinburgh; BBC2 Television with Lindsay Quartet; Principal Clarinettist, Welsh National Opera, 1970-73; Scottish Chamber Orchestra, 1973-80; Kent Opera, 1984; Teacher, RSAMD, 1974-80; RNCM, 1982-86; Head of Woodwind, Birmingham Conservatoire, 1992; Principal Clarinet of Manchester Camerata & Director of Camerata Wind Soloists. *Recordings:* For EMI; Chandos including Stanford Clarinet Concerto. *Honours:* Boise Foundation Scholarship; National Federation of Music Societies Prize. *Hobbies:* Cooking; Reading; Walking. *Current Management:* Robert Gilder & Company. *Address:* 27 Cassel Ave, Poole, Dorset BH13 6JD, England.

HIND Rolf, b. 1964, England. Concert Pianist. *Education:* Studied at Royal College of Music with John Constable and Kendall Taylor; Los Angeles with Johanna Harris-Heggie. *Career:* Played piano solo in Des Canyons aux Etoiles and Sept Haikai by Messiaen; Has premiered works by Ligeti, Xenakis, David Sawer and Tristan Murail; Concerts at the main London venues and at the Bath, Canterbury, Cheltenham, Brighton, King's Lynn and Avignon Festivals; Has appeared with London Brass, Spectrum, the London Sinfonietta and the Ulster Orchestra (Szymanowski conducted by Jan Latham Koenig); Played in St Lucia 1990 and was soloist in Eight Ligeti Piano Studies for a Belgian dance company; Seasons 1990-92 in Grenoble, Rotterdam, Metz, Brussels, Antwerp, Paris, Essen, Salzburg, Utrecht and New York. *Recordings include:* Solo works by Ligeti, Carter and Martland (Factory Classics); Xenakis Econta and Ruders Breakdance, with London Brass (Teldec); Messiaen Trois Petites Liturgies de la Presence Divine, with the London Sinfonietta (Virgin Classics). *Address:* c/o Norman McCann International Artists Ltd, The Coach House, 56 Lawrie Park Gardens, London SE26 6XJ, England.

HIND O'MALLEY Pamela, b. 27 Feb 1923, London, England. Composer; Cellist and Pianist. m. Raymond O'Malley, 2 sons, 1 daughter. *Education:* ARCM (performance); Studied cello with Ivor James, Piet Lentz and Pablo Casals; Piano with Dorothea Aspinall and Imogen Holst; Composition with Herbert Howells. *Debut:* Wigmore Hall 1963. *Career:* Cello Soloist and Ensemble Player; As One Pair of Hands, gives recitals for solo cello and solo piano in programmes that always include one contemporary work; Solo recitals playing cello and piano from 1967: Wigmore Hall 1969 and 1970; Teacher of cello and piano, Cambridge; Part time cello teacher, Kings College School; Part time ensemble coach, Cambridge University Music Society. *Compositions:* Keyboard Music, Songs, Duo for Violin and Cello, Trio for Flute, violin and cello; Suite for string orchestra. *Contributions to:* Royal College of Music magazine; Casals as Teacher (RCM Magazine 1950); Casals and Intonation (ESTA News and views 1981, and re-printed in the STRAD, 1983). *Publications:* Cycle of Four Rounds for Four Violins (Stainer & Bell, 1984); Arrangements of two Fauré songs for either viola or cello with piano (S J Music, 1991). *Memberships:* Incorporated Society of Musicians; European String Teachers Association; International Cello Centre; Herbert Howells Society; Cambridge University Music Society. *Hobbies:* Walking; Reading; Gardening. *Address:* 23 Nightingale Avenue, Cambridge, CB1 4SG, England.

HINDERAS Natalie (Henderson), b. 16 June 1927, Oberlin, Ohio, USA. Pianist; Teacher. *Education:* Studied at the Juilliard School and with Eduard Steuermann at the Philadelphia Conservatory. *Debut:* Played the Grieg Concerto with the Cleveland Women's Symphony Orchestra, 1939. *Career:* Gave concerts in Europe after completing studies and made New York debut in 1954; Toured for the US State Department in Africa, Poland, Sweden and Yugoslavia in the 1960s; Toured black colleges of the southern United States 1968, presenting classical music of black composers; Solo appearances with the Chicago Symphony Orchestra, the Cleveland Orchestra and the New York Philharmonic; Teacher at Temple University. *Honours include:* Honorary doctorate, Swathmore College 1976.

HINDS Esther, b. 3 Jan 1943, Barbados, West Indies. Singer (Soprano). *Education:* Studied with Clyde Burrows in New York, and at Hartt College, Hartford, with Helen Hubbard. *Debut:* New York City Opera 1970, as First Lady in Die Zauberflöte. *Career:* Has sung in New York as Donna Elvira, Madama Butterfly and Gershwin's Bess (on Broadway); Engagements at opera houses in Houston, Cincinnati and San Diego; Other roles include Liu (Turandot) and Micaela; Spoleto Festival 1983, as Cleopatra in Antony and Cleopatra by Samuel Barber; Many concert performances. *Address:* c/o New York City Opera, Lincoln Center, New York, NY 10023, USA.

HINDS Geoffrey William John, b. 2 Apr 1950, Auckland, New Zealand. Composer; Piano Teacher. *Education:* BA, Auckland, 1974; MPhil (Mus), Auckland, 1976; BDiv, Melbourne College of Divinity, 1976; LRSM (Piano Teachers), 1983. *Compositions:* Held in New Zealand Music Archive Canterbury University - Sonata for Viola and Pianoforte, 1975; Suite for String Quintet, 1975; String Quartet, 1976; Cantata Upon This Rock, 1982; Held in Music Library, Radio New Zealand, Wellington Motet for the Lord has Purposed, 1980-81; Overture into a Broad Place, 1981; String Quartet, 1981; Symphonic Moments of Our Time, 1982; And His Name Shall be Called, 1981; Through the Grapevine, 1982; Anthems written for St Barnabas Choir; Song Cycle, Water Water Everywhere, 1985; Song Cycle, Pieces of Peace, 1986; Colyton Overture, 1986-87, written for Manawatu Youth Orchestra; String Quartet 1983-84; Song Cycle, Innocence and Experience, 1987; Blowing in the Wind for wind quintet, 1987; Song Cycle, Nine Mystical Songs, 1988-89; Godzone Re-evaluated for Youth Orchestra, 1989; Great Outdoors Suite for Piano, 1989; String Quartet 1989; Symphony, St. Barnabas Ballads (Ten & Pf), Creation Cantata, The Good Life (Musical), 1990; Piano Sonata, Two Edged Sword (Song Cycle for Sop & Pf), Sonata for Trombone, Organ, 1991-; Flights of Fancy, for Clarinet & String Quartet, Gardens (SATB), Suite for Viola, Our Good Keen Men (Song cycle for Tenor & Pf), 1992. *Hobbies:* Political Science; Crossword Puzzles; Cycling. *Address:* 72 Valley Road, Mount Eden, Auckland 1003, New Zealand.

HINES Jerome, b. 8 Nov 1921, Hollywood, California, USA. Singer (Bass); Composer. *Education:* Studied with Gennaro Curci in Los Angeles and with Samuel Margolis in New York. *Debut:* San Francisco 1941, as Monterone in Rigoletto. *Career:* Metropolitan Opera from 1946, as Sparafucile, Mephistopheles, the Grand Inquisitor, Gurnemanz, Sarastro, Boris Godunov and Don Basilio; 454 Performances in 30 Years; Engagements in Rio de Janeiro, Mexico City and Buenos Aires; Concerts with Toscanini; Glyndebourne and Edinburgh 1953 as Nick Shadow in the British premiere of The Rake's Progress; Munich 1954, as Don Giovanni; Further European appearances in Paris, Vienna, Florence and Milan; Bayreuth 1958-61, as Gurnemanz, King Marke and Wotan; Moscow 1962, as Boris; Sang Fiesco in Simon Boccanegra for Long Beach Opera, 1992. *Compositions include:* Opera, I am the Way, on the life of Christ. *Publications include:* This is my Story, this is my Song 1968; Great Singers on Great Singing 1982. *Recordings:* Beethoven Missa Solemnis, conducted by Toscanini; Macbeth, Lohengrin (RCA); La favorite (Decca); Messiah (Columbia); Le Prophète, Duke

Bluebeard's Castle (CBS); Don Carlos (Estro Armonico). *Honours include:* Caruso Award 1946. *Address:* c/o Metropolitan Opera, Lincoln Center, New York, NY 10023, USA.

HINES Robert Stephan, b. 30 Sept 1926, Kingston, New York, USA. University Professor; Dean. m. Germaine Lahiff, 9 Dec 1950. *Education:* BS, Juilliard School, 1952; MM, University of Michigan, 1956. *Career:* Assistant Professor, Southern Illinois University, 1957-61; Professor, Wichita State University, 1961-71; Professor, University of Hawaii, 1972-80, Chairman, 1980-84, Acting Dean, 1984-85, Dean, 1986-. University of Hawaii. *Compositions:* Over 250 choral editions and arrangements. *Publications:* The Composer's Point of View: Essays on Twentieth Century Choral Music By Those Who Wrote It, 1963, reprinted 1980; The Orchestral Composer's Point of View: Essays on Twentieth Century Music By Those Who Wrote It, 1970, essays from both books reprinted in French, German, Italian, Polish, Swedish, English; Singer's Manual of Latin Diction & Phonetics, 1975; Ear Training and Sight-Singing: An Integrated Approach, Co-author, Book, 1979, Book II, 1980; Booklet and articles in professional journals. *Hobby:* Travel. *Address:* 555 University Ave, 3500, Honolulu, HI 96826, USA.

HINSHAW Donald Gray, b. 23 Aug 1934, North Carolina, USA. Music Publisher. *Education:* Public School, Boonville, North Carolina; BMus, Davidson College; Master of Sacred Music, New Orleans Seminary. *Career:* Public School Music Teacher, 1955-56; Minister of Music, 1958-64; Professor of Music, 1959-64; Industry Management, 1964-67; Music Editor, 1968-75; Chief Executive Officer, Hinshaw Music, Hindon Publications and Chapel Hill Music, 1975-. *Compositions:* Editor/Arranger of In Babylon Town/Copley; Thou Wilt Keep Him In Perfect Peace/Wesley; Sing We Gloria/Dufay; Arranger of various choral works for hire under the name of John Hines. *Honours:* Board of Trustees, Westminster Choir College, Princeton New Jersey, 1984-87; Commissioned Kentucky Colonel, Commonwealth of Kentucky, 1971-. *Memberships:* Phi Mu Alpha Sinfonia; American Society of Composers, Authors and Publishers; Broadcast Music Incorporated; SESAC; National Music Publishers Association. *Address:* Hinshaw Music Incorporated, PO Box 470, Chapel Hill, NC 27514-0470, USA.

HINTERMEIER Margareta, b. 11 Sept 1954, St Polten, Austria. Singer (Mezzo-soprano). *Education:* Studied in Vienna with Hilde Konetzi. *Career:* Has sung at the Vienna Staatsoper from 1982 as Dola, Cherubino, Octavian, the Composer in Ariande auf Nxos and Federica (Luisa Miller); Tour of Japan with the Staatsoper Company as Cherubino; Guest appearances at Geneva, Lisbon (as Orlofsky), Liege, (Idamante in Idomeneo) and Dresden; Salzburg Festival, 1978-83, as Idamante; Concert appearances include Beethoven's Ninth at the 1989 Vienna Festival and Wagner's Wesendonck Lieder; Schubert Festival Hohenems, Carinthia Summer and Flanders Festivals; Further concert engagements in Istanbul, Nice and Bologna; Sang in Mahler's 3rd Symphony with the Vienna Symphony Orchestra at the Festival Hall, London, 1993. *Recordings include:* Maidservant in video of Elektra, conducted by Abbado, Die Walküre; Beethoven's Ninth. *Address:* c/o Staatsoper, Opernring 2, A-1010 Vienna, Austria.

HIROKAMI Jun'ichi, b. 5 May 1958, Tokyo, Japan. Conductor. *Education:* Studied at the Tokyo Music University. *Career:* Assistant Conductor, Nagoya Philharmonic Orchestra, 1983; International career from 1984; Conducted the NHK Symphony Orchestra, 1985, Orchestre National de France, 1986; Debut with Israel Philharmonic Orchestra, 1988; London debut Jan 1989, London Symphony Orchestra; Royal Philharmonic Orchestra, May 1990; Further engagements with the Stockholm Philharmonic, the Norrkoeping Symphony Orchestra (Principal Conductor from 1991), the Malmo and Gothenbury Symphony Orchestras and radio orchestras in Holland and Italy; Operatic debut (July

1989), Un Ballo in Maschera followed by Rigoletto and La Forza del Destino all with the Australian Opera; International concert activities spread to other countries eg Spanish National Orchestra, Berlin Radio Symphony, Royal Concertgebouw Amsterdam, Montreal Symphony and with many European Orchestras; Conducted all major Japanese orchestras and appointed Principal Guest Conductor of the Japanese Philharmonic Orchestra. *Recordings:* Debut with the London Symphony Orchestra (BMG) and subsequent recordings with BIS Records (of Sweden) and Fun House Records (Japan) mainly made with his own Norrkoping Symphony Orchestra. *Honours:* Winner, first International Kondrashin Conducting Competition, Amsterdam, 1984. *Address:* c/o Terry Harrison Artists Management, 3 Clarendon Court, Park Street, Charlbury, Oxon OX7 3PS, England.

HIRSBRUNNER Theo, b. 2 Apr 1931, Thun, Switzerland. Writer. *Education:* Pupil of Pierre Boulez. *Career:* Teacher, Berne Conservatory until 1987. *Publications:* Books on: Debussy, 1981, Stravinsky 1982, Messiaen, 1988, Boulez, 1985, Ravel, 1989. *Contributor to:* many articles in periodicals. *Honours:* Janáček Medal, 1978; Year of Czech Music Medal, 1984; Hon Member, Accademia Musicale Ottorino Respighi, 1988. *Address:* Optingenstr 53, CH-3013, Bern, Switzerland.

HIRSCH Leonard, b. 19 Dec 1902, Dublin, Ireland. Music Educator; Conductor; Violinist. m. Anne Richardson, 2 daughters. *Education:* Royal Manchester College of Music with Adolph Brodsky, FRCM; FRCM, London. *Debut:* Dublin. *Career includes:* Halle Orchestra, 1921-37; Leader and occasional conductor, BBC Empire Orchestra, 1937-39; Toured America with RAF Symphony Orchestra during World War II; Leader, Philharmonia Orchestra, 1941; Hirsch String Quartet, re-established, 1944; Played in front of Churchill, Truman and Stalin at the Potsdam Conference, after the War; Associated with National Youth Orchestra, 1948-66; Conductor, Hirsch Chamber Players, 1961-; 1st Musical Director, BBC Training Orchestra, 1966-69; Chief Music Consultant, County of Hertfordshire, 1964-79; Professor, Royal College of Music. *Recordings include:* Bartók Quartet No 1. Bloch No 2 (string quartet); Hugo Wolf Serenade. *Contributor to:* Book, Sir Hamilton Harty, 1978. *Honours:* Fellow, Royal Manchester College of Music; Fellow, Royal College of Music. *Hobbies:* Walking; Gardening; Travel. *Address:* 50 Henleaze Park Drive, Bristol, BS9 4LN, England.

HIRSCH Peter, b. 1956, Cologne, Germany. Conductor. *Education:* Studied at the Hochschule, Cologne. *Career:* Assistant to Michael Gielen at the Frankfurt Opera, 1979; Guest conductor at theatres in Hamburg, Dusseldorf, Karlsruhe and Wiesbaden; Debut at La Scala 1985, with Prometo by Luigi Nono; Has conducted Die Fledermaus and Rigoletto for Vancouver Opera; La Bohème and Der Freischütz for Welsh National Opera and Cosi fan Tutte with Scottish Opera; Season 1990-91 conducted Benvenuto Cellini for Netherlands Opera; Concert engagements with the radio orchestras of Hanover and Berlin, the Residentie Orkest and the Radio Chamber Orchestra of Hilversum, Holland, and orchestras of Bremen, Darmstadt and Nuremberg; Regular engagements with the Bournemouth Sinfonietta and the Bournemouth Symphony; Led the Ensemble InterContemporain, Paris, 1990. *Address:* c/o Ingpen and Williams Ltd, 14 Kensington Court, London W11 4PA, England.

HIRST Grayson, b. 27 Dec 1939, Ojai, California, USA. Singer (Tenor). *Education:* Studied at the Music Academy of the West with Martial Singher, at the Juilliard School with Jennie Tourel. *Debut:* Sang Cavalli's Ormindo with the Opera Society of Washington 1969. *Career:* Sang Tonio in La fille du régiment at Carnegie Hall, 1970; New York City Opera debut 1970, in Britten's The Turn of the Screw; Kennedy Center, Washington, in the premiere of Ginastera's Beatrix Cenci; Other premieres include works by Robert Aitken, Ned Rorem, Robert Starer, Virgil Thomson (Lord Byron) and Jack Beeson; Further appearances in France, Brazil, England and Switzerland; Other roles include Don José, Pelléas, Faust and Mozart's Tamino, Ferrando and Belmonte. *Recordings include:* Schubert's Die schöne Müllerin (Leonarda).

HIRST Linda, b. 1950, Yorkshire. Singer (Mezzo-Soprano). *Education:* Flute and singing at the Guildhall School of Music, London. *Career:* Joined Swingle Singers and often appeared with Cathy Berberian; Concerts with the London Sinfonietta with Berio, Ligeti and Henze conducting their works; Premiere performances of Muldowney's Duration of Exile, Osborne's Alba, Simon Holt's Canciones and Judith Weir's The Consolations of Scholarship; Performances of Schoenberg's Pierrot Lunaire in Paris and Florence and for Channel 4 TV; Glyndebourne Festival debut 1985, Knussens's Where the Wild Things Are; 1986 world premiere of Osborne's The Electrification of the Soviet Union; Appearances at Bath and Almeida Festivals; Frankfurt Opera Henze's Elegy for Young Lovers; Arts Council Network Tour with the London Sinfonietta; Also performs earlier music; Incoronazione di Poppea in Spitalfields for Opera London; sang in the premiere of Vic Hoyland's La Madre (Written for her), London 1990. *Recordings:* Songs Cathy Sang and Ottavia in L'Incoronazione di Poppea for Virgin. *Address:* c/o Norman McCann Internatioanl Artists Ltd, The Coach House, 56 Lawrie Park Gardens, London SE26 6XJ, England.

HIRSTI Marianne, b. 1958, Oslo, Norway. Singer (Soprano). *Education:* Studied in Oslo and Lubeck. *Career:* Sang at Kiel, 1980-81, Staatsoper Hamburg, 1981-85; Cologne, 1985-87, Staatsoper Stuttgart, from 1987; San Meroe in Reinhard Keiser's Die grossmutige Tomyris, at Ludwigsshafen, followed by Constanza in Bononinii's Griselda and Blondchen in Die Entfuhrung; Cologne Opera as Maire in Zar und Zimmermann; Ludwigsburg Festival as Susanna in Le Nozze di Figaro; Theatre de la Monnaie, Brussels, as Berta in Il Barbiere di Siviglia, 1992; Other roles have included Despina, Marzelline, Gretel, Sophie in Werther and Tytania in A Midsummer Night's Dream; Many Lieder recitals and concert appearances, including Wigmore Hall, London 1988. *Recordings include:* Beethoven Missa Solemnis; Die Grossmutige Tomyris; Der Zwerg by Zemlinsky; Blondchen in Die Entführung, conducted by Hogwood. *Address:* c/o Staatsoper Stuttgart, Oberer Schlossgarten 6, 7000 Stuttgart, Germany.

HIRTE Klaus, b. 28 Dec 1937, Berlin, Germany. Singer (Baritone). *Education:* Studied at the Stuttgart Musikhochschule with Hans Hager. *Career:* Sang at the Stuttgart Staatsoper from 1964; Bayreuth Festival 1973-75, as Beckmesser in Die Meistersinger; Salzburg Festival as Antonio in Le Nozze di Figaro; Ludwigsburg Festival 1972, as Papageno; Further appearances in Nuremberg, Munich, Dusseldorf, Mannheim, Venice, Chicago and San Antonio; Other roles include Don Pasquale and Dulcamara by Donizetti; Wagner's Kurwenal and Klingsor and parts in operas by Strauss, Gluck, Mascagni and Weber; Sang Oberon in the premiere of Der Park by Hans Gefors, Wiesbaden, 1992. *Recordings include:* Tannhäuser (Deutsche Grammophon); Die Meistersinger (Philips); Le Cadi Dupé by Gluck (Electrola); Der Schauspieldirektor; Cavalleria Rusticana; Intermezzo; Die schweigsame Frau (EMI). *Address:* c/o Staastheater Stuttgart, Oberer Schlossgarten 6, D-7000 Stuttgart 1, Germany.

HIRZEL Franziska, b. 28 Nov 1952, Zurich, Switzerland. Singer (Soprano). *Education:* Studied in Basel, Fribourg, Frankfurt am Main and Zurich. *Career:* Sang at Darmstadt Opera from 1980, notably in the 1983 premiere of Klebe's Die Fastnachtsbeichte and as Mozart's Blondchen, Donna Elvira, Fiordiligi and Pamina, Micaela, Martha, Euridice, Gilda, Musetta and Gretel; Concert repertoire has included sacred works by Bach, Beethoven, Mozart, Haydn and Schoenberg; Many Lieder recitals and broadcasting engagements; Guest appearances at concert halls and opera houses

throughout Germany. *Address:* Staatstheater, Postfach 111432, 6100 Darmstadt, Germany.

HITCHCOCK Hugh Wiley, b. 28 Sept 1923, Detroit, Michigan, USA. Musicologist; Writer on Music. *Education:* Studied at Dartmouth College (BA 1944) and the University of Michigan (PhD 1954); Additional study with Nadia Boulanger in Paris. *Career:* Taught at Michigan 1947-61; Professor of Music at Hunter College 1961-71; Professor of Music at Brooklyn College from 1971 (Distinguished Professor 1980); Founder-Director of the Institute for Studies in American Music at Brooklyn College, 1971; Getty Scholar at the J Paul Getty Center for Art History and the Humanities, 1985-86; Editor of the Prentice-Hall History of Music Series. 1965-; Member of the executive committee and area editor for the Americas in The New Grove Dictionary of Music and Musicians, 1980; Co-editor of The New Grove Dictionary of American Music, 1984; Research interests include French and Italian Baroque, as well as American, music. *Memberships:* Music Library Association from 1954; American Musicological Society from 1954; President of the Charles Ives Society, from 1973. *Publications:* The Latin Oratorios of MA Charpentier (PhD dissertation, 1954); Editor, Earlier American Music, 1972; Music in the United States: A Historical Introduction, 1969, 1975, 1988; Charles Ives Centennial Festival-Conference 1974; Editor, Recent Researches in American Music, 1976-; Ives, 1977, rev 1983; The Phonograph and our Musical Life 1980; Co-author, The Music of Ainsworth's Psalter 1612, 1981; The Works of MA Charpentier: A Catalogue Raisonné, 1982; Editions of music by Caccini (Le nuove musiche, 1970), Leonardo Leo, Charpentier and Lully. *Honours:* Fulbright Grants, 1954-55, 1968-69; Guggenheim Grants, 1968-69; National Endowment for the Humanities Grants, 1982-83; President-elect, American Musicological Society, 1989-90 (President, 1990-92). *Address:* c/o Music Department, Brooklyn College, City University of New York, USA.

HLAVAC Miroslav (Ing), b. 23 Oct 1923, Protivin, South Bohemia. composer. m. Kvetoslava Zdarkova, 25 Sept 1970, 1 d. *Education:* Music School, Pilsen, studying composition under B Mikoda, J Ridky and K Slavicky. *Debut:* Pilsen, Prague. *Career includes:* Bridge Designer, Civil Engineering College, Prague, 17 years; Professional Composer since 1967; Symphony, Festival of the Czechoslovakia Symphony Orchestras, Prague, 1960; Ballet, The Sorcerer's Apprentice, Pilsen, 1963; Halle, 1977; Ballet, electroacoustic, Nocturne at the Fountain, Pilsen, 1980; Gorlitz, 1981; Opera, Inultus, suite, 1970, Prague. *Compositions:* Over 100 works including electroacoustic with graphic scores; Symphonietta Elegikon; The Sorcerer's Apprentice; Arhythmikon; Episode; Impulsioni; Serenade; Postludium; Stenograms; Inultus. *Publications:* Musica carnevalesca; Leporello; About Johny; Two Pasterales; Childrens Pictures; Pools a Brooks; Slovak Inventions; The Sorcerer's Apprentice, Opera Inultus, two acts, 6 parts. Articles include: Confession: Tradition and Modern; My Ballet Creation; *Honours:* Prizes awarded at the Great Jubilee Artistic Contest, 1955, 1960, 1965 and Contest of the Czech Music Fund, 1972. *Memberships:* Association of Musical Artists and Scientists; Society of the Elecctro-acoustic Music. *Hobbies:* Tourism; Swimming; Reading; Mushroom Picking. *Address:* Zelenecska 26, 194 00 Praha 9, Czech Republic.

HO Allan Benedict, b. 30 Mar 1955, Honolulu, Hawaii, USA. Musicologist. *Education:* BA, Music History, 1978, MA, Musicology, 1980, University of Hawaii; PhD, Musicology, University of Kentucky, 1985. *Career:* Discovered a copy of the "lost" full score of Wilhelm Stenhammar's First Piano Concerto, the manuscript of which was believed destroyed during WW11. This was the most widely performed Swedish composition at the turn of the cenutry. *Publications:* A Biographical Dictionary of Russian/Soviet Composers, 1989; Music for Piano and Orchestra: The Recorded Repertory; Critical editions of the two-piano score and full score of Wilhelm Stenhammar's First

Piano Concerto (Nordiska Musikförlaget, 1993-94). *Contributions to:* Journal of the American Liszt Society, 1984-; Notes; The New Grove Dictionary of American Music. *Memberships:* American Musicological Society; American Liszt Society; Pi Kappa Lambda. *Hobbies:* Record collecting; Sports. *Address:* Box 1771 Music Department, Southern Illinois University, Edwardsville, IL 62026, USA.

HO Edward, b. 27 Sept 1939, Hong Kong. Lecturer; Pianist; Composer; Conductor. *Education:* BA(Hons), Geography and Geology, University of Hong Kong, 1962; LRSM, 1957; Royal School of Church Music, 1962-63; Trinity College of Music, London, England, 1962-64; LMusTCL, 1963; LTCL, 1964; FTCL, 1964; BMus (Durham), MMus (Durham), 1966; DMus (Durham), 1975. *Career:* BBC Programme Assistant; Lecturer, Chairman of Music Department, Chinese University of Hong Kong; Acting Head of Music Department, University of Singapore (established new Music Department); Senior Lecturer, Mabel Fletcher Technical College, Liverpool, England; Currently Professor and Head of School of Music, Kingston University; Examiner, Associated Board of Royal Schools of Music; Conducted orchestras in China and Taiwan, Lectured in the Far East and China. *Compositions:* Unpublished: Symphony (performed 1978/1991), cantatas, choral music, concert overtures, organ music; Commissioned works for Chinese orchestra (performed Hong Kong, China and Taiwan) include: Seasonal Sentiments for Soprano and Orchestra; Orchestral Interludes; Symphony for Chinese Orchestra; Songs for Voice and Chinese Orchestra; Four Tones and Melody for Chamber Ensemble; Void and Concreteness for Orchestra. *Address:* School of Music, Kingston University, Kingston Hill, Kingston-upon-Thames, Surrey, KT2 7LB, England.

HO Sylvia, b. 27 Jan 1952, Hong Kong. Concert Pianist. m. Dr Kam-Yung Lau, 30 June 1979. *Education:* BMus, 1974, MMus, 1976, Temple University, Philadelphia, Pennsylvania; Post-graduate studies, Juilliard School, 1976-78. *Debut:* New York Debut - Carnegie Recital Hall, 1977; Philadelphia Debut - 1979. *Career:* Numerous recitals; TV Broadcasts; Performances at Lincoln Center; Co-Founder of East-West Piano Duo (Coast-to-Coast US Tour 1986); Faculty Member, Settlement Music School, Philadelphia 1974-79; Columbia Basin College, Washington, 1979-80; University of Texas at El Paso, 1982-83. *Honours:* Pi Nu Epsilon Award, 1969; Elmer Yarnall Scholarship, 1974; Winner, Artists International Competition, 1977. *Memberships:* National Guild of Piano Teachers; Music Teachers' Association of California. *Hobbies:* Reading; Gourmet cooking. *Current Management and Address:* Artists International Management, New York City.

HOBBS Allen (Alain), b. 10 May 1937, Denver, Colorado, USA. Organist; Improviser; Musicologist. *Education:* Studies with Simone Plé-Caussade, C-A Estyle, André Marchal, Jean Langlais and Marcel Dupré, Paris, France; Diploma in Virtuosity, Organ and Improvisation, Schola Cantorum, Paris, 1964. *Career:* Organist of the Cathedral, Denver, 1953-70; Organist/ Director of Music, Church of the Holy Ghost, Denver, 1988; Organist/Director of Music, Church of the Blessed Sacrament, Denver, 1993-; Teacher of Improvisation and Score Reading with international reputation, 1991-93; Co-founder with Daniel-Lesur of the International Charles Tournemire Assoociation, 1987; Concert Appearances in USA, France, Italy, Switzerland, Japan and People's Republic of China. *Compositions:* Stabat Mater, 1964; Xristus, 1965; Way of the Cross, 1973; Trilogy of Psalms, 1991; Psalmozum, 1993-. *Publications:* Organ Method, 1980; Manual for Score Reading, 1981; The Essentials of Harmony Explained in Common Language, 1986; Treatise on the Fugue, 1990; Treatise on Strict Counterpont (in collaboration with Yvonne Desportes, 1991); Charles-Marie Widor: Studies for the 50th Anniversary of his Death, 1986; Charles Tournemire (I) 1989, (II) 1992. *Memberships:* Life Member, Société Française de Musicologie, 1968; Les Amis de l'Orgue, Paris. *Hobbies:*

Musicology. *Address:* Brooks Towers, Suite 41 L, 1020 15th Street, Denver, CO 80202, USA.

HOBKIRK Christopher, b. 1965, Henley on Thames, England. Singer (Tenor). *Education:* Studied at the Royal Scottish Academy and at Royal College of Music with Neil Mackie. *Career:* Concert engagements in Finland and Norway with Britten's St Nicolas and Bach's St John Passion; Bach's Magnificat with the Las Palmas Philharmonic, the B minor Mass at Edinburgh and Telemann's Luke Passion at St John's Smith Square; Created Eochd in Edward McGuire's opera, The Loving of Etain, 1990 at Glasgow; Season 1991 with Britten's Serenade at Palma, Bach's St Matthew Passion at Darmstadt and Bergen, Mozart's Requiem with the Manchester Camerata and the B minor Mass conducted by William Boughton; Sang Misael in the Burning Fiery Furnace for St James's Opera, 1991. *Address:* c/o Anglo Swiss Ltd, 3 Primrose Mews, 1a Sharpleshall St, London NW1 8YW, England.

HOBSON Ian, b. 1953, Wolverhampton, England. Pianist; Conductor. m. 4 sons, 1 daughter. *Education:* Began private piano studies aged 5; BA Magdalene College Cambridge; MA, DMus Yale University; Profesor, University of Illinois, 1983-. *Career:* Finalist in 1978 Baltimore Symphony Conducting Competition; Silver Medals at Artur Rubinstein and Vienna-Beethoven Competitions; First Prize Leeds International Piano Competition, 1981; Soloist with Royal Philharmonic, Philharmonia, Scottish National Orchestras; USA with Orchestras of Chicago, Philadelphia, Pittsburgh, St Louis, Baltimore, Indianapolis, Houston; Complete cycles of Beethoven's Sonatas; The Age of Anxiety for Bernstein's 70th birthday, 1988; As conductor has led Mozart's Concertos from the keyboard with English Chamber Orchestra on its Far Eastern Tour; Illinois Opera Theatre in Così fan Tutte and Die Fledermaus; Founded Sinfonia da Camera 1984; 1988-89 season engagements with San Diego Chamber Orchestra and in Israel. *Recordings:* Chopin/Godowsky Etudes and the complete piano sonatas of Hummel (Arabesque); Strauss's Burlesque and the Paregon on the Symphonia Domestica, with the Philharmonia; Concertos by Francaix, Saint-Saëns and Milhaud with the Sinfonia da Camera; 24 Chopin Etudes, Rachmaninov Transcriptions and Mozart's Concertos Nos 23 and 24 (EMI). *Address:* c/o Norman McCann International Artists Ltd, The Coach House, 56 Lawrie Park Gardens, London SE26 6XJ, England.

HOCH Francesco, b. 14 Feb 1943, Lugano, Switzerland. Composer; Professor of Music. m. 1 May 1971, 2 sons. *Education:* G Verdi Conservatory, Milan; Composition, Padua, Darmstadt. *Career:* Professor of Music, Lugano; Assistant, Composition coursee, Chigiana Academy, Siena, Italy, 1974; Invited, International Laboratory, Venice Biennial, 1975; Founded Oggimusica Association of Comtemporary Music, 1977; Regular radio broadcasts of compositions, all Europe, Israel, Canada, Australia; TV (TSI) recordings: Trasparenza per Nuovi Elementi, 1977; Leonardo e/und Gantenbein, 1985; Monographic concerts, 1982, 1987, 1989, 1991; Commissions: Pro Helvetia; Nuova Consonanza, Rome; City of Geneva; Ascona Festival; Luzern Festival; Others. *Compositions:* 34 published works including: Dune, 3 instruments, 2 percussion, 2 voices, 1972; L'Oggetto Disincantato, 13 instruments, 1974; Trittico, clarinet, viola; Leonardo e/und Gantenbein, opera-ballet, 1980-82; Ostinato Variabile, I, bass clarinet, 1981, II, bass clarinet, piano, III, 2 guitars, IV, violin, piano, 1982; Sans, oboe, orchestra, 1985; Un Mattino, 2 flutes, 1986; Der Tod ohne das Maedchen, string quartet, 1990; Memorie da Requiem, choir, orchestra, 1989-91; Postludio degli Spettatori, choir, 1991. *Contributions to:* Schweizer Komponisten Unserer Zeit; Swiss Musica Review; Pro Arte, Bern; Enc Musica Garzanti Prospettive Musicali, Pescara; Encyclopaedia UTET, Turin, 1988; Musikrevy, Stockholm; Swiss Composer. *Honours:* Prove concertanti for orchestra represented Switzerland, International Composers Tribune, Paris, 1973; Premio Angelicum, Milan, 1975; Sans, chosen 20 years of

Union European Radiodiffusion, 1987. *Memberships include:* Association of Swiss Musicians; Swiss Society of Learning. *Address:* Campo dei Fiori 9, 6942 Crocifisso di Savosa, Switzerland.

HOCHMANN Klaus, b. 29 Dec 1932, Ostpreußen, Poland. German Composer. *Education:* Composition and Conducting studied at Stuttgart and Salzburg. *Career:* Piano Teacher in Music, School of Herrenberg. *Compositions:* Der Findling, Opera, 1970; Midsummer Night, 5 choirs, 1963; Requiem für einen Unbekannten, 3 songs for bass and organ, 1965; Bärenreiter-Verlag Kassel; Concertino I for percussion, 1969; Doblinger-Verlag Wien: Concertino III for percussion solo e tutti, 1974. *Recordings:* Requiem für einen Unbekannten, 1968; Tenebrae factae sunt f gem chor, 1982; Jn Memoriam, Song Cycle for baritone and piano, 1980; Und suche Gott, 1991; *Honours:* Composition Prizes, Kassel 1965, Bern 1975, Bonn 1984; Promotion Prizes, 1971, 1977; *Memberships:* Society of Promotion of Radio Symphony Orchestra Stuttgart; Die Künstlergilde e.V. Esslingen; Leoš Janáček Society, Bern. *Hobbies:* Literature; Art; Travel. *Address:* Beethovenstrasse 62, D-71083 Herrenberg, Germany.

HOCHREITHER Karl, b. 27 Oct 1933, Speyer, Germany. Church Musician (Organist and Choirmaster); Conductor; Professor. m. Gertrud Wien, 23 June 1959, 1 son, 2 daughters. *Education:* Studies in German Philology, History and Philosophy, University of Freiburg, 1953-54; Church Music, Organ with M Schneider, Staatliche A-Exam; Continuing studies, Conducting and Chamber Music, Nordwestdeutsche Musikakademie, Detmold, 1954-58; Musicology, Heidelberg University, 1962-63. *Career:* Organist and Choirmaster, Protestant Palatine Church Council, Speyer; Member of Faculty, Berliner Kirchenmusikschule, 1963; Director, Bach-Chor and Bach-Collegium, Kaiser-Wilhelm-Gedächtniskirche, Berlin, 1964; Guest Professor, Wittenberg University, Springfield, Ohio, USA, 1968; Artist-in-Residence, Music Department, University of Western Ontario, London, Ontario, Canada, 1975 and 1977; Artist-in-Residence, Asian Institute for Liturgy and Music, Manila, Philippines, 1984; Artist-in-Residence, Tainan Theological Seminary, Tainan, Taiwan, 1989; Concert tours as organist and conductor, teaching and lecturing, worldwide. *Recordings:* S Scheidt, Motets and Concertos (harpsichord), Bärenreiter, 1964; J S Bach, Cantatas 56 and 82 (conductor), Miller International, 1972; H W Zimmermann, Vesper (harpsichord and organ), Bärenreiter, 1967; Franz Liszt, Organ Works (organ), EMI Electrola, 1974. *Publications:* Ernst Peppings Toccata und Fuge, Mitten wir im Leben sind, 1971; O Messiaen, La Nativité du Seigneur (co-editor), 1974; Zur Aufführungspraxis der Vokal-Instrumentalwerke J S Bachs, 1983. *Address:* Ev Johannesstift, Franckehaus, 1000 Berlin 20, Germany.

HODDINOTT Alun, b. 11 Aug 1929, Bargoed, South Wales. Composer. m. Beti Rhiannon Huws, 1953, 1 son. *Education:* University College, Cardiff. *Career:* Lecturer, Cardiff College of Music and Drama, 1951-59; Lecturer, University College, Cardiff, 1959-65; Reader, 1965-67; Professor, Music, 1967-87, University College; Artistic Director, Cardiff Festival of Twentieth Century Music, 1966-89. *Compositions include:* 9 Symphonies, 1955-93; 11 Sonatas for piano, 1959-93; 5 Violin Sonatas, 1969-92; Sonatas for harp, clarinet, horn; 2 Sonatas for Cello and Piano, 1977; Welsh Dances; Investiture Dances; Black Bart; Dives and Lazarus, 1965; Variants 1966; Fioriture 1968; The Tree of Life 1971; Ritornelli 1974; The Beach at Falesa (opera) 1974; The Magician (Opera); Ancestor Worship, Five Landscapes (Song Cycles); A Contemplation Upon Flowers (songs for soprano & orchestra); What the Old Man Does is Always Right (Opera); Sonatina for Guitar; Sonatina for 2 Pianos; The Rajah's Diamond (opera); The Trumpet Major (opera in 3 acts), 1981; Nocturnes and Cadenzas for solo flute; Doubles for oboe, harpsichord and strings; 5 Studies, for orchestra; 4 Scenes from the Trumpet Major, for orchestra; Quodlibet for orchestra, 1982; Quodlibet for brass quintet, 1983; Masks, oboe, bassoon and piano,

1983; Cantata Lady & Unicorn, Piano Trio No 2, Bagatelles for Oboe & Harp, String Quartet No 2, Scenes & Interludes for Trumpet, Harpsichord & Strings, Cantata Bells fo Paradise, 1984; Scena for String Orchestra, Sonata for 2 Pianos, Song Cycle - The Silver Hound, Fanfare with variants for brass band, Sonata for 4 Clarinets, 1985; Triple Concerto, Divisions for Horn, Harpsichord & Strings, Concerto for Orchestra, 1986; Concerto for Clarinet & Orchestra, 1987; Welsh Dances for Brass Band, 1987; The Legend of St. Julian, 1987; String Quartet no 3, 1988; Lines from Marlowe's Dr Faustus: mixed voices, brass and percussion; Noctus Equi: cello and orchestra, 1989; Songs of Exile: tenor and orchestra; Star Children for orchestra; Symphony for organ and orchestra; Advent Carol SATB/Organ, 1990; Emynan Partycelyn baritone solo, chorus, orchestra, 1990; Novelette, flute, oboe, piano, 1991; Sonata for flute & piano, 1991; Sonata No 5 for violin & piano, 1992; Symphony for Brass & Percussion, 1992; Chorales Variants & Fanfares for Organ & Brass, 1992; A Vision of Eternity: Symphony for Soprano & Orchestra, 1993; Gloria for Chorus and Organ, 1993; Three Motets for Chorus and Organ, 1993; Wind Quintet, 1993. *Recordings:* Symphony No 6, BBC WSO; Thomson, Chandos and Noctis Equi, CSO, Kagaho, Rostropovich, Erato; Star Children, BBC WSO; Passagio, Otaka; Doubles, Hu-Knn; Heaven Tree of Stars, Cowley; Piano Sonatas 1-10, Martin Jones, Nimbus; Three Advent Cards, St John's College Choir, Nimbus. *Honours:* CBE; Hopkins Medal, St Davids Society of New York; Fellow, University College, Cardiff, 1981; Bax Medal, 1957; Walford Davis Prize, 1954; Fellow Welsh College of Music and Drama, 1991; Hon DMus (Sheffield), 1993. *Address:* Maesawelon, Mill Road, Lisvane, Cardiff, Wales.

HODGES Nicolas, b. 4 June, 1970, London, England. Composer; Pianist. *Education:* Studied composition at Dartington and Winchester with Morto Feldman and Michael Finnissy; Piano with Robert Bottone and privately with Susan Bradshaw; Music at Cambridge University. *Career:* As pianist, premieres including music by Finnissy, Weir, Skempton, C Newman, A Pritchart, Toovey, Powerll Morison/Opit, Holloway, Bill Hopkins, Ozzard-Low, Stoneham, some as part of the Bach project, broadcast on Radio 3. *Compositions:* Small Shadows, 1990; Piano Studies, 1988-92, solo piano; toothreefourfive, violin and piano, 1991-92; Do I detect a silver thread between you and this young lady, solo vla, 1993; Concertino, 1993; Scripture, soprano, oboe d'amore, 2 perc, 1994. *Recordings:* Bach Project released on CD. *Publications:* Various articles and reviews to Tempo, Musical Times, including The Music of Bill Hopkins, 1993, The Music of Luigi Nono, 1950-58 - Analytical investigations. *Hobbies:* Reading; Cooking; Wine; Countryside. *Address:* Flat 3, 68 Norwood Road, Herne Hill, London SE24 9BB, England.

HODGSON Julia, b. 1960, England. Viol Player. *Career:* Member of Fretwork, first London concert at the Wigmore Hall, London, July 1986; Appearances in the Renaissance and Baroque repertoire in Sweden, France, Belgium, Holland, Germany, Austria, Switzerland and Italy; Radio broadcasts in Sweden, Holland, Germany and Austria; Televised concert on ZDF, Mainz, Tour of Soviet Union Sept 1989 and Japan June 1991; Festival engagements in Britain; Repertory includes In Nomines and Fantasias by Tallis, Parsons and Byrd; Dance music by Holborne and Dowland (including Lachrimae); Six-part consorts by Gibbons and William Lawes; Songs and instrumental works by Purcell; Collaborations with vocal group Red Byrd in verse anthems by Byrd and Tomkins, London Cries by Gibbons and Dering, Resurrection Story and Seven Last Words by Schütz; Gave George Benjamin's Upon Silence at the Elizabeth Hall, Oct 1990; Wigmore Hall concerts 1990-91 with music by Lawes, Purcell, Locke, Dowland and Byrd. *Recordings:* Heart's Ease (late Tudo and early Stuart); Armada (Courts of Philip II and Elizabeth II); Night's Black Bird (Dowland and Byrd); Cries and Fancies (Fantasias, In Nomines and The Cries of London by Gibbons); Go Nightly Cares (Consort songs, dances and In Nomines by Byrd and Dowland): all on Virgin Classics Veritas label. *Address:* Robert White

Management, 182 Moselle Avenue, London N22 6EX, England.

HODGSON Peter John, b. 6 Apr 1929, Birmingham, England. Music Educator and Administrator. m. Mary Christina Hodgson, April 1958, 1 son. *Education:* LRAM, 1951; LTCL, 1963; ARCM, 1951; ARCO, 1957; PhD, University of Colorado, 1970; MMus, Royal College of Music, 1965; BMus, London University, 1964. *Career:* Faculty, University School, Vancouver, BC, 1952-55; Mount Royal College, Alberta, 1955-65; Banff School of Fine Arts, 1959-64; Ball State University, 1968-78; New England Conservatory of Music, 1978-83; Texas Christian University, 1983-87; Dean of Faculty, Principia College, 1987-. *Publications:* The Music of Herbert Howells, Ann Arbor Microfilms; Toward an Understanding of Renaissance Musical Structure, Ball State University Publications; Toward a Metaphysical Perception of Structure in Music, University of Colorado. *Contributions to:* The Use of Hymn Tunes in Larger Musical Works, Hymn, 1982. *Honours:* Reading University Prize; British Council Award. *Memberships:* College Music Society; American Musicological Society; Hymn Society of America; American Conference of Academic Deans. *Hobbies:* Walking; Gardening; Reading. *Address:* Dean of Faculty, Principia College, Elsah, IL 62028, USA.

HOEKMAN Guus, b. 16 Oct 1913, The Hague, Holland. Singer (Bass). *Education:* Studied with Aaltje Noordewier-Reddingius, N de Haan-Liégeois and Lucie Frateur (singing) and Lothar Wallerstein and Felix Hupka (opera). *Career:* Concert debut 1938; Opera debut 1951, as Osmin with the Flemish Opera at Antwerp; Netherlands Opera from 1953, notably in Don Carlo by Verdi and Don Pasquale by Donizetti; Netherlands Opera from 1956 notably in Die Kluge by Orff and Der Wildschütz by Lortzing; Salzburg Festival 1960, in the stage premiere of Martin's Mystère de la Nativité; Glyndebourne 1962-63, 1969, as Arkel in Pelléas et Mélisande; Deutsche Oper am Rhein Dusseldorf from 1960; Appearances in Boston and at the New York City Opera; Taught in the USA 1972-79; Amsterdam 1981-85, as Lumey (in Thijl by van Gilse), Sarastro, Titurel and Trulove in The Rake's Progress. *Recordings:* Sarastro in Die Zauberflöte; Basilio in Il Barbiere di Siviglia; Bach Mathhäus Passion conducted by Anthon van der Horst; Pélleas et Mélisande conducted by Ansermet (Decca); Bruckner Te Deum (Philips).

HOELSCHER Ludwig, b. 23 Aug 1907, Solingen, Rheinland. Cellist. m. 1940, 1 son, 1 daughter. *Education:* Studied under Lamping, Klengel and Becker. *Career:* Professor, Hochschule für Musik, Berlin, 1936, later at Mozarteum Salzburg; Professor, Staatliche Hochschule fur Musik und Darstellende Kunst, Stuttgart, 1954-; Member of Jury, Moscow and Florence international competitions; Member, Elly-Ney-Trio and Strub Quartet 1931-40; Member, trio with Walter Gieseking and Gerhard Taschner after 1945; has appeared as soloist under many of the world's most famous conductors and given first performances of many cello concertos and sonatas by contemporary composers and new works by Hindemith; has undertaken tours throughout Europe, Asia, Africa and North and South America. *Honours:* Mendelssohn Prize 1930; Honorary Professor of University of Tokyo; Member, Bayerische Akademie der schönen Kunste; Grosses Bundesverdienstkreuz mit Stern; Bayerischer Verdienstorden Bayer, Maximiliansorden für Wissenschaft und Kunst and several other honours and awards. *Address:* 8132 Tutzing bei Munchen, Germany.

HOELSCHER Ulf, b. 17 Jan 1942, Kitzingen, Germany. Violinist. *Education:* Studied first with his father and Bruno Masurat, then with Max Rostal in Cologne; Further study with Josef Gingold at the University of Indiana and with Ivan Galamian at the Curtis Institute in Philadelphia. *Career:* Played with the Philharmonic of the Palatinate while a student, 1956; Concerts in London, Munich, Hamburg, Paris and Berlin; Tours of Europe, Russia, the Far East, Australia, East Germany (with the Dresden Staatskapelle), the USA and

Japan; Beethoven Festival Bonn 1971; Plays the standard concertos and has premiered the Concertos by David Kirchner (1984) and Franz Hummel (1987), both with the Berlin Philharmonic; Premiere of the Concerto for Violin and Cello by Aribert Reimann at the Montreux Festival, 1989; repeated in New York 1990 and with the Berlin Philharmonic 1991; Chamber music collaborations with the pianist Michel Béroff and in trio with Heinrich Schiff and Christian Zacharias; Formerly professor at the Karlsruhe Musikhochschule; Professor at the Hochschule der Kunste in Berlin from 1987; British engagements with BBC Symphony, BBC Welsh and BBC Philharmonic Orchestras, and Royal Scottish Orchestra, under Jane Glover. *Recordings include:* Concertos by Tchaikovsky, Berg, Schumann, Mendelssohn, Korngold, Strauss, Brahms and Beethoven; Shostakovich chamber music with Vishnevskaya and Rostropovitch; Schumann sonatas with Michel Béroff; Chamber works by Bartók, Franck, Szymanowski, Franz Hummel and Schubert. *Address:* c/o Christopher Tennant Management, 11 Lawrence Street, London SW3 5NB, England.

HOEPRICH Thomas Eric, b. 5 Sept 1955, Baltimore, Maryland, USA. Clarinettist. *Education:* AB cum laude, Harvard University, 1976; Solo Diploma, Royal Conservatory of Music, Netherlands, 1982. *Career:* Principal Clarinet, Orchestra of the 18th Century, 1983-; Founding member of Amadeus Winds, Stadler Trio (basset horns), Nachtmusique and Trio d'Amsterdam; Regular appearances with London Classical Players, Tafelmusik and The Orchestra of the Handel and Haydn Society; Professor at Royal Conservatory of Music, Netherlands. *Recordings:* Mozart Clarinet Concerto and Quintet with Orchestra of the 18th Century, Philips; Other recordings as soloist: Taverner Players, EMI; Musica Antiqua Cologne, DGG-Archiv; Other recordings for Decca, Harmonia Mundi, Accent, Erato and SONY Classical. *Contributor to:* Early Music; Tibia; Galpin Society Journal; NOTES. *Honour:* Mozart Clarinet Concerto and Quintet recording named one of the best 15 CDs of 1988, Le Monde de la Musique. *Hobbies:* Squash; Instrument-making. *Address:* Bredeweg 39-2, 1098 BN Amsterdam, Netherlands.

HÖFFGEN Marga, b. 26 Apr 1926, Mulheim an der Ruhr, Germany. Singer (Contralto). m. Theodor Egel. *Education:* Studied with Anna Erler-Schnaudt in Essen, at the Berlin Musikhochschule and with Hermann Weissenborn. *Debut:* Berlin concert 1952. *Career:* Sang in the St Matthew Passion in Vienna 1953, conducted by Karajan; Sang Erda in Siegfried at Covent Garden in 1959, later in Vienna, Buenos Aires and Bayreuth (with the role of First Norn in Götterdämmerung); many concert appearances in music by Bach; Sang at Frankfurt-am-Main Opera 1984. *Recordings:* Beethoven, Missa Solemnis, conducted by Klemperer (EMI); Bach Mass in B Minor conducted by Karajan (Decca); Erda in Siegfried conducted by Solti (Decca); St Matthew Passion (Philips); Church Cantatas by Bach.

HOFFMAN Grace, b. 14 Nov 1926, Cleveland, Ohio, USA. Singer (Mezzo-Soprano). *Education:* Studied with Friedrich Schorr in New York, Mario Basiola in Milan, and with Maria Wetzelsberger in Stuttgart. *Debut:* With the US Touring Company as Lola, 1951. *Career:* Sang at Florence from 1951; Zurich 1952, as Azucena; Wurttemberg Staatsoper Stuttgart from 1955; La Scala Milan 1955, as Fricka in Die Walküre; Bayreuth Festival 1957-70, as Brangaene, Fricka and Waltraute; Metropolitan Opera 1958, Brangaene; Covent Garden debut 1959, as Eboli in Don Carlos; Florence 1961, as Ortrud in Lohengrin; Carnegie Hall New York 1964 as Elisabetta in Donizetti's Maria Stuarda; Appearances in Paris, Vienna, Munich and Dusseldorf; Teacher of singing at the Stuttgart Musikhochschule from 1978; sang Mary in Der fliegende Holländer at Stuttgart, 1989; Other roles include Mother Wesener in Die Soldaten by Zimmermann (Strasbourg, 1988). *Recordings:* Das Lied von der Erde; Salome, Der Barbier von Bagdad; Tristan und Isolde (Cetra). *Address:* c/o Staatsheater Stuttgart, Oberer Schlossgarten 6, D-7000 Stuttgart 1, Germany.

HOFFMAN Irwin, b. 26 Nov 1924, New York City, NY, USA. Symphony Conductor; Violinist. m. Esther Glazer Hoffman, 3 sons, 1 daughter. *Education:* Juilliard School of Music. *Career:* Conductor, Vancouver Symphony, British Columbia, Canada, 1952-64; Associate Conductor and Acting Music Director, Chicago Symphony, Illinois, USA, 1964-70; Music Director, The Florida Orchestra 1968-87; Chef Permanent, Belgian Radio and Television Symphony, 1972, 1976; Guest Conductor, various leading orchestras, Europe, North America, Israel and South America. *Recordings:* DGG. *Current Management:* Everett Wright, 3876 Oak Grove Dr, Sarasota, FL, USA.

HOFFMAN Joel Harvey, b. 27 Sept 1953, Vancouver, British Columbia, Canada. Composer; Pianist; Teacher. m. 30 Dec 1988. *Education:* BM, University of Wales, Cardiff, Wales, 1974; MM, 1976, DMA, 1978, Juilliard School, New York, USA. *Career:* Graduate Teaching Assistant, Juilliard School, New York, 1976-78; Professor of Composition, College-Conservatory of Music, University of Cincinnati, Ohio, 1978-; Commissions: Cincinnati Symphony Orchestra, 1993. *Compositions:* Variations for violin, cello and harp, 1978; September Music for double bass and harp, 1981; Music from Chartres for 10 brass instruments, 1984; Double Concerto, 1984, Sonata for harp, 1985; Chamber Symphony, 1986; 5 pieces for 2 pianos, 1986; Violin Concerto, 1986, Fantasia fiorentina, for violin and piano, 1988, Hands Down, for piano, 1986, Crossing Points, for string orchestra, 1990, Partenze, for solo violin, 1990; 90 for piano solo, 1991; Cubist Blues for violin, cello and piano, 1991; Music in Blue and Green for orchestra, 1991; Metasmo for percussion trio, 1992. *Recordings:* Duo for viola and piano, CRI Recordings, 1991; Partenze, Koch International Recordings, 1992. *Address:* College-Conservatory of Music, University of Cincinnati, Cincinnati, OH 45221, USA.

HOFFMAN Stanley, b. 8 Dec 1929, Baltimore, Maryland, USA. Violinist; Violist. *Education:* Private study with Arthur Grumaux, Belgium; BSc, Juilliard School of Music; Study with Mischa Mischakoff, Raphael Bronstein & Oscar Shumsky. *Debut:* Carnegie Recital Hall, New York City. *Career:* Regular member, New York Philharmonic Orchestra under Leonard Bernstein, 1961-64, Jerusalem Radio Symphony Orchestra, Israel 1981-83. *Recordings:* Vocal Chamber Music, Volume I with Susan Reid-Parsons as soprano, 1971, Volume II with Elinor Amlen & Rose Macdonald, sopranos, 1973; Taping session for Radio Kol Israel, 1984, 1986; Solo violin sonatas, Béla Bartók, Honegger, Hindemith, Ralph Shapey, Paul Ben-Haim, Bach C Major, Roger Sessions. *Memberships:* Bohemians, New York; Local 802, Association Federation of Musicians. *Hobbies:* Jogging; Reading; Travel. *Address:* Poste-Restante, Tel Aviv, Israel.

HOFFMANN Horst, b. 13 June 1935, Oppelen, Germany. Singer (Tenor). *Education:* Studied with Thilde Amelung in Hildesheim and Otto Kohler in Hanover. *Debut:* Hanover 1961, in Zar und Zimmermann. *Career:* Has sung at the Stuttgart and Munich State Operas and the Deutsche Oper am Rhein Dusseldorf; Komische Oper Berlin and the Opéra du Rhin Strasbourg; Bayreuth Festival 1967-68; Further appearances in Cologne, Lisbon, Zurich, Vienna (Volksoper) and Sydney 1984 (Lohengrin and Siegmund, 1987 and 1989); Teatro Regio Turin, 1987 as Don Ottavio; Otello, Sydney and Melbourne, 1988 and in Sydney, 1992; Totenhaus, Köln, Germany, 1992; Tristan and Isolde, Sydney and Melbourne, 1993, and Essen, Germany, 1993; Die Meistersinger, Sydney, 1993; Roles include Tamino, Belmonte, Nemorino, Edgardo, Pinkerton, Alfredo in La Traviata and Alfred in Die Fledermaus; Sang Florestan at Sydney, 1992. *Recordings include:* Bruckner Te Deum (Philips). *Address:* c/o Australan Opera, Sydney Opera House, Sydney, New South Wales, Australia.

HOFFMANN Manfred, b. 10 Oct 1940, Kahl am Main, Germany. Singer (Bass). *Education:* Studied at the Frankfurt Musikhochschule. *Career:* Sang at Saarbrucken, 1970-71, Lucerne, 1972-74, Mainz,

1974-77, St Gallen, 1977-80, Engaged at Berne, 1980-84, Graz from 1984, notably in the 1987 premiere of Der Rattenfänger by Friedrich Cerha; Guest appearances in Germany and Switzerland; Roles have included Rossini's Bartolo, Mozart's Alfonso and Sarastro, Rocco, Raimondo, Geronimo in Matrimonio Segreto, Pietro in Dimon Boccanegra, the Landgrave (Tannhauser), Dulcamara, the Grand Inquisitor (Don Carlos) and Count Waldner in Arabella; Further engagements in operetta. *Address:* c/o Vereinigte Bunnen, Kaiser Josef Platz 10, A-8010 Graz, Austria.

HOFFMANN Richard, b. 20 Apr 1925, Vienna, Austria. Composer; Musicologist. *Education:* Studied at the University of New Zealand and the University of California at Los Angeles; Composition studies with Arnold Schoenberg. *Career:* Secretary and assistant to Schoenberg 1948-51; Teacher at UCLA 1951-52, Oberlin College from 1954; Visiting Professor at the University of California, Berkeley, 1965-66; Co-editor of the complete works of Schoenberg, 1961: edited the score of Von Heute auf Morgen. *Honours include:* Guggenheim Fellowships, 1970, 1977. *Compositions include:* Prelude and Double Fugue for strings, 1944; Piano Sonata, 1946; Violin Concerto, 1948; 4 String Quartets, 1947, 1950, 1974, 1977; 3 Songs, 1948; Duo for violin and cello, 1949; 3 Songs, 1950; Piano Quartet, 1950; Fantasy and Fugue for organ, 1951; Piano Sonatina, 1952; Piano Concerto, 1954; Cello Concerto, 1956-59; String Trio, 1963; Memento Mori for male voices and orchestra, 1966-69; Music for strings, 1971; Decadanse for 10 players, 1972; Changes for 2 chimes, 4 performers, 1974; Souffler for orchestra, 1976; In memorium patris for computer-generated tape, 1976; Intavolatura for strings and percussion, 1980. *Address:* c/o ASCAP, ASCAP Building, One Lincoln Plaza, New York, NY 10023, USA.

HOFFMANN-ERBRECHT Lothar, b. 2 Mar 1925, Strehlen Schlesien, Germany. Professor. m. Margarete Fischer, 2 daughters. *Education:* Graduate, Academy of Music, Weimar, 1949; PhD, University of Jena, 1951; Habilitation, Department of Musicology, University of Frankfurt, 1961. *Career:* Professor of Musicology, University of Frankfurt am Main. *Publications include:* Deutsche und italienische Klaviermusik zur Bachzeit, 1954; Thomas Stoltzer, Leben und Schaffen, 1964; Thomas Stoltzer, Ausgewaehlte Werke II-III; Heinrich Finck, Ausgewaehlte Werke, I-II; Beethoven Klaviersonaten (With Claudio Arrau); Henricus Finck-musicus excellentissimus, 1445-1527, 1982; Musikgeschichte Schlesiens, 1986. *Contributions to:* Various professional journals. *Memberships:* Society for Music Research; International Musicological Society. *Address:* 9 Amselweg, D-63225 Langen, Germany.

HOFMAN Shlomo, b. 24 Apr 1909, Warsaw, Poland. Musicologist; Composer; Conductor; Educator. m. Cyla Pelzmann. 2 daughters. *Education:* Grad, State Music Conserv Warsaw, 1933 & 1934; Conserv Nat de Musique, Paris, France, 1937-38; Gregorian Institute, Paris, 1947-49; Doct, Sorbonne, Paris, 1949. *Career includes:* Lecturer on Methodol of Music Education, Hebrew University, Jerusalem, Israel, 1950-53; Teacher of Music & Methodol of Music Education, State Seminar for Arab Teachers, Jaffa & Haifa, 1954-67; Teacher of History of Music, Israel Acadamy of Music, Tel Aviv University, 1954-. *Compositions:* Several works mainly for voice. *Publications:* L'Oeuvre de Clavecin de François Couperin, 1961; Migra'ey Musica V, 1974; Miqra'ey Musica, Biblical References to Music (Hebrew, English, French Spanish), 1974; Amusia, 1977; The Function of the Brain in Language and Music Processing, 1985; Psalmen Davids, Heinrich Schütz, 1985; The Music of A Z Idelsohn, 1986; Music in the Talmud-Talmudic References to Music (Hebrew, English, French, German), 1989. *Honours:* Recipient several awards and grants. *Memberships:* Member of several musical societies. *Address:* 67 Gordon St, Tel-Aviv 64388, Israel.

HOFMANN Peter, b. 12 Aug 1944, Marienbad, Germany. Singer (Tenor). m. Deborah Sasson 1983, divorced 1990. *Education:* Karlsruhe Hochschule.

Debut: Lubeck 1972, as Tamino in Die Zauberflöte. *Career:* Early engagements at Wuppertal and Stuttgart; Bayreuth Festival from 1976, as Siegmund, Lohengrin and Parsifal; Vienna State Opera 1976 as Loge, then Siegmund and Lohengrin; Covent Garden debut 1976, as Siegmund: returned to London as Max in a new production of Der Freischütz, and as Alfred in Die Fledermaus; Metropolitan Opera debut 1980, as Lohengrin: returned to New York as Parsifal, Siegmund and Walther; Sang Tristan at Bayreuth in 1986, and Siegmund in Harry Kupfer's new production of The Ring 1988; Guest appearances in Moscow, Lisbon, San Francisco, Los Angeles, Munich and Chicago. *Recordings:* Parsifal (Deutsche Grammophon); Die Zauberflöte (HMV); Die Walküre, Tristan und Isolde (Philips); Lohengrin, Orfeo ed Euridice (CBS). *Address:* PO Box 100262 Bayreuther Festspiele, 8580 Bayreuth 1, Germany.

HOFMANN Rosmarie, b. 1 July 1937, Lucerne, Switzerland. Singer (Soprano). *Career:* Concert throughout Europe, overseas; Many regular international festival appearances; Many recent world premieres, including works composed for her; Extensive repertoire includes: J S Bach: Johannes, Matthaus and Markus Passions, Hohe Messe B minor, Messe Nr 2 A major, Weihnachts-Oratorium, Magnificat plus Einlagesatze, 6 solo soprano and some 60 other cantatas; Beethoven: 9th Symphony, Christus am Oelberge, Chorphantasie, Missa solemnis, Messe C major, lieder; Brahms: Ein deutsches Requiem, lieder, duets, quartets; Bruckner: Requiem D minor, Te Deum, Grosse Messe Nr 3 F minor, Grosse Messe D minor; Carissimi: Historia de Jephter; Charpentier: Te Deum, Messe de Minuit; Durufle: Requiem; Dvořák: Te Deum, Stabat Mater, messe in D, Zigeunerlieder; Faure: Requiem; Franck: Messe solenne A-major, Die sieben Worte Christi am Kreuz, Magnificat; Handel: Israel in Aegypten, Dettinger and Utrechter Te Deums, Brockes and Johannes Passions, Messias, Josua, Saul, Jephta, Judas maccabeus, Das Alexanderfest, Belsazar, Psalms 96, 109, 112, 51, German arias, duets, cantatas Cacilien Ode, Ode fur den Geb der Konigin Anna, Salve Regina; J Haydn: L'incontro improvviso (1st Soprano), L'anima del Filosofo (Genio, Euridice), Die Schöpfung, Die Jahreszeiten, Die sieben Worte des Erlosers am Kreuz, Stabat Mater, 6 Grosse Messen, many other Masses, cantata Qual dubbio omai, Offertorium Domine Deus, Cantilena pro Adventu; Honegger: Le Roi David, Jeanne d'Arc au bucher: La Vierge, La danse des morts; Frank Martin; In terra pax, Golgotha; Mendelssohn: Paulus, Elias, 2nd Symphony Lobgesang, Psalms 42, 95, 115, hymn Hor'mein Bitten, Ave Maria Stella, Die Hochzeit des Camacho (main role), lieder, duets; Monteverdi: Vespreae de Maria Vergine, Magnificat, Psalm 111, solo motet, duets; Mozart: Solo motets Exsultate jubilate, Venti, fulgura, procellae, Litanien, Vespreaes, Konzertarien, oratorio La Betulia liberata, operetta Die Schuldigkeit des ersten Gebots, cantatas, funeral music, Requiem, Regina Coeli KV 108, KV 127, many small works, C minor Messe, Davidde penitente, many Masses, lieder; PergolesiL Stabat Mater, Salve Regine, Psalm 112; Poulenc: Gloria; Stabat Mater; Schubert: Magnificat, Salve Regina, Messen C, G and B flat, E flat, A flat, Nr 1 in F, Der Hirt auf dem Felsen, Auf dem Strom; Sainte-Säens: Christmas Oratorio, Messe de Requiem, oratorio Le Deluge; Schutz: Die Weihnachts-Historie, Die Auferstehungs-Historie, sacred Konzerte and duets; Telemann: Matthaus-Passion 1746, Lukas-Passion 1744, Magnificat, Grosse Kantate JNO, many solo cantatas; Vivaldi: Gloria, Magnificat, Psalm Laudate pueri, catatas, solo motets; Wide repertoire of ancient music and lieder; Leading roles in 8 operettas; Has given classes at Musikakademie Basel, Abteilung Schola Cantorum Basiliensis of Lehr-und Forschungs Institut fur Alte Musik, over 10 years. *Recordings:* Phyllis und Thirsis, CPE Bach; Canzonette amorose, Rossi; Stabat Mater, Dvořák; Sacred music, Josef and Michael Hadyn; Bach cantatas; Mozart motets, Orchestra of Schola Cantorum Basiliensis, conductor Peter Sigrist; Quiteria (main role), Die Hochzeit des Camacho, 1993; Many others. *Address:* c/o Sinfonieorchester Luzern, Moostrasse 15, CH-6003 Lucerne, Switzerland.

HOFSTETTER Igo, b. 1 June 1926, Linz, Austria. Composer; Professor of Music. m. Hermine Hofstetter, 1 son. *Education:* Graduate, Bruckner Conservatory, Linz; studies with Professor F H Klein; GMD Ludwig Leschetitzky. *Career:* Radio appearances, Austria, Germany, Belgium, France, Holland, Sweden, Czechoslovakia, Poland, 1945-; Work with ORF (Austrian State Radio), 1965-. *Compositions include:* (Published), Operettas: Roulette der Herzen; Alles spricht von Charpillon; Schach dem Boss; Light Music. *Recordings:* Die Bimmel-Bammel-Bummelbahn; Moldau-Polka; Oberösterreicher-Marsch; Rohrbacher Stadtmarsch; songs from the operettas Alles spricht von Charpillon and Schach dem Boss. *Honours:* Title Professor awarded by the President of the Republic of Austria, 1978; Medal for Art and Culture awarded by the Town Council of Linz, 1983. *Memberships:* Austrian Composers' Group; AKM; AustroMechana; Board, International Society for Operetta, Musical & Light Music. *Hobbies:* Photography; Cinema. *Address:* 20/IX Rilkestrasse, A-4020 Linz/Donau, Austria.

HÖGMAN Christina, b. 1956, Sweden, Singer (Soprano). *Education:* Studied at the Stockholm College of Music and the State Opera School; Further studies in Salzburg. *Debut:* Drottningholm 1985, in Pergolesi's Il Maestro di Musica. *Career:* Member of the Hamburg Staatsoper 1986-88, notably as Cherubino; Guest appearances with the Opera du Rhin, Strasbourg, Opera Montpellier, Monte Carlo Opera, Schwetzingen and Innsbruck; Season, 1991-92, as Annius in La Clemenza di Tito on tour with Christopher Hogwood and the Academy of Ancient Music to Japan; Soprano soloist in Messiah at Santiago, Madrid, Bacelona and Santander, Spain; Sang Elisabetta in Don Carlos with Folkoperan in Stockholm and a tour with Bach's B minor Mass in Spain; Season 1993-94 in concert performances throughout Scandinavia and opera appearances at the Early Music Festival, Innsbruck. *Recordings include:* Vitige in Handel's Flavio, and other Baroque operas conducted by Rene Jacobs. *Address:* Nordic Artists Management, Sveavagen 76, S-11359 Stockholm, Sweden.

HOGWOOD Christopher Jarvis Haley, b. 10 Sept 1941, Nottingham, England. Harpsichordist; Conducter; Musicologist; Author. *Education:* Cambridge University; Charles University, Prague; MA; FRSA. *Career:* Founder Member, Early Music Consort of London, 1967-76; Founder, Director, Academy of Ancient Music, 1973-; Faculty, Cambridge University, 1975-; Artistic Director, Handel & Haydn Society, Boston, USA, 1986-; Hon Professor of Music, Keele University, 1986-89; Director, Music, St Paul Chamber Orchestra, Minnesota, USA, 1987-92; Principal Guest Conductor, St Paul Chamber Orchestra, 1992-; International Professor of Early Music Performance, Royal Academy of Music (London), 1992-; Visiting Professor, Department of Music, King's College London, 1992-. *Recordings:* Many recordings of baroque and classical music including CDs of Bach Double Concertos, Cantatas 211 and 212 (Covey-Crump, Kirkby, Thomas); Handel Italian Cantatas (Kirkby); Athalia (Sutherland); Pergolesi Stabat Mater (Kirkby, Bowman); Stravinsky Dumbarton Oaks and Pulcinella (St Paul Chamber Orchestra); Telemann Orchestral Works; Vivaldi L'Estro Armonico and 12 violin Concertos op 4 La Stravaganza (Huggett); Mozart Symphonies. *Publications:* Music at Court, 1977; The Trio Sonata, 1979; Haydn's Visits to England, 1980; Music in Eighteenth-Century England, co-author, 1983; Handel, 1984; Holmes' Life of Mozart, editor, 1991; many editions of musical scores. *Contributions to:* New Grove Dictionary of Music & Musicians. *Honours:* Walter Wilson Cobbett Medal, 1986; CBE, 1989; Hon. Fellow, Jesus College, Cambridge, 1989; Freeman, Worshipful Company of Musicans, 1989; Hon Fellow, Pembroke College, Cambridge, 1992. *Address:* 10 Brookside, Cambridge CB2 1JE, England.

HOHN Carola, b. 3 Mar 1961, Erfurt, Germany. Singer (Soprano). *Education:* Studied at the Franz Liszt Musikhochschule, Weimar. *Career:* Sang at Eisenach, 1984-87, Altenburg 1987-88; Berlin Staatsoper from

1988, notably as Marie Antoinette in the 1989 premiere of Graf Mirabeau by Siegfried Matthus; Other roles have included Antonia, Mozart's Fiordiligi and Pamina, Gretel, Marie in Zar and Zimmermann and Sophie in Der Rosenkavalier; Concert repertoire includes Carmina Burana by Orff; Guest engagements elsewhere in Germany and broadcasting committments; Pamina in Die Zauberflöte at Bordeaux, 1992. *Address:* Deutsche Staatsoper Berlin, Unter den Linten 7, 1086 Berlin, Germany

HOIBY Lee, b. 17 Feb 1926, Madison, Wisconsin, USA. Composer; Pianist. *Education:* BA, University of Wisconsin, 1947; MA, Mills College, 1952; Diploma, Curtis Institute, 1952; Private Study with Egon Petri and Gunnar Johansen. *Debut:* As Pianist, Alice Tully Hall, New York City, 1978. *Career:* Commissions from Ford Foundation, Curtis Institute, St Paul Opera, Des Moines Metro Opera, USIA, Dorian Wind Quintet, G Schirmer, Library of Congress. *Compositions:* Operas: This is the Rill Speaking, 1993; The Tempest, 1986; Something New for the Zoo, 1980; Summer and Smoke, 1971; A Month in the Country, 1964; The Scarf, 1954; Sonata for Violin and Piano; Serenade for Violin and Orchestra; The Italian Lesson, Musical Monologue; Galilo Galilei, Oratorio; For You O Democracy; A Hymn of the Nativity, Cantatas; The Tides of Sleep, Symphonic Song; Various solo piano works, songs and choral pieces. *Recordings:* After Eden, Ballet; Piano Concerto; Choral Music of Lee Hoiby. *Honours:* Fulbright Fellow, 1952; Arts and Letters Award, 1957; Guggenheim Fellow, 1958; Honorary Member, American Guild of Organists; Honorary DFA, Simpson College, 1983. *Membership:* American Society of Composers, Authors and Publishers. *Address:* 800 Rock Valley, Long Eddy, NY 12760, USA.

HOINIC Bujor, b. 17 Feb 1950, Timisoara, Rumania. Conductor. m. Ayse Bilal, 7 July 1984, 1 son. *Education:* Licentiate in Piano, Timisoara Music School; Licentiate in Composition and Conducting, Bucharest Conservatory. *Debut:* Concerto with Iasi Symphony Orchestra, 1973. *Career:* Conductor, Rumanian Opera, 1973-81; Conductor, Ankara State Opera, 1981-; Concerts and performances in Rumania, Yugoslavia and Turkey; Collaborator for musical broadcasts, Rumanian Radio, 1975-76 and 1982-84; Professor Ankara Conservatory, Turkey, 1986-. *Compositions:* String Quartet, 1970; Pavana for Orchestra, 1972; Concerto for cello and string orchestra, 1973; Prelude, Choral and Fugue for orchestra (recorded Radio Bucharest), 1976; Dacia Felix, ballet (recorded and filmed Rumanian TV), 1980; Angora for orchestra and women's choir (recorded Rumanian Radio), 1982; Balade and Deniz lirikleri, for choir and chamber orchestra (recorded Turkey Radio-Television), 1985. *Recording:* Cornel Trailescu's opera Balcescu, Rumanian Radio and TV, 1979. *Honour:* 1st Prize for performance with ballet Dacia Felix, Cantarea Romaniei National Festival, 1981. *Membership:* Rumanian Composers Union. *Hobby:* Skiing. *Address:* Atac Sok 73/17 Yenisehir, Ankara, Turkey.

HOISETH Kolbjorn, b. 29 Dec 1932, Borsa, Norway. Singer (Tenor). *Education:* Studied with Egil Nordsjo in Oslo and with Ragnar Hulten and Set Svanholm in Stockholm. *Debut:* Stockholm 1959, as Siegmund in Die Walküre. *Career:* Sang Wagner roles in Stockholm: Siegfried, Tristan, Tannhäuser, Walther, Parsifal, Erik and Loge; British debut Covent Garden 1963, as Lohengrin; Guest appearances in Berlin, Dusseldorf, Bordeaux, Lyon and Drottningholm; Edinburgh Festival with the Stockholm Company 1974, as Laca in Jenůfa; Metropolitan Opera 1975, as Froh, Loge and Siegmund, in Der Ring des Nibelungen; Other roles include Florestan, Don Carlos, Gregor in The Makropoulos Case, Radames, Otello, Aegisthus, Herod and Don José. *Honours include:* Set Svanholm Memorial Prize, 1974. Address: c/o Kungliga Teatern, PO Box 16044, 5-10322 Stockholm, Sweden.

HOJSGAARD Erik, b. 3 Oct 1954, Århus, Denmark. Composer. *Education:* Studied Composition with Per Norgard, Royal Academy of Music, Arhus; Diploma, 1978; Student of Composition, Cantiere Internazionale d'Arte, 1976; Royal Academy of Music, Copenhagen, 1982-84. *Career:* Music Copyist, 1977-82; Teacher, Royal Academy of Music, Copenhagen, 1982-; Manager, Århus Young Composers Society, 1974-76; Member of Organising Committee, Young Nordic Music Festival, 1974-81; Music Committee, Århus Regional Council, 1977-78; member of Governing Body, Society for the Publication of Danish Music, 1982-92. *Compositions:* Orchestra: Untitled, symphony, 1974; Cello Concerto, 1975; Refleksion, 1977; Scherzo e notturno, 1982; Four Sketches, 1990; Piano Concerto, 1984-85; Chamber Music: Dialogues, 1972; Solprimser, 1974; The Sunflower, 1978; Intrada, 1981; Watercolours, 1983; Intermezzi, 1983; Fantasy Pieces, 1982-84; Carillon, 1986; Two Mobiles, 1990; Paysage blême, (chamber music), 1991; Solo Instrument: Cendree, 1976; Sonate in C Major, 1980; C'est la mer melee au soleil, 1981; Epreuve, (solo instrument), 1993; Solo Voice with instruments: Landet som icke är, 1974; Tuan's Songs, 1976; Variations: 6 Songs of Autumn, 1976; Vise, ballad, 1977; Täglich kommt die gelbe Sonne 1977; Joyous, 1979; Fragments, 1979; The Lost Forest, 1980; Summer Songs, 1981; The Rose, 1981; Two Songs, 1985; Le città continue, 1986; Choral Music: Two songs for mixed choir, 1985-86; Opera: Don Juan Kommt aus dem Krieg, 1991. *Recordings:* Has made numerous recordings. Has had works performed at various Music Festivals in the Nordic countries and at ISCM-festivals 1980 and 1983. *Address:* Esbern Snaresvej 16, 4180 Sorø, Denmark.

HOKANSON Leonard Ray, b. 13 Aug 1931, Vinalhaven, Maine, USA. Concert Pianist; Professor of Piano. m. Rona Wolk, 17 Apr 1976. *Education:* BA, Clark College, 1952; MA, Bennington College, 1954; Studied piano with: Hedwig Rosenthal, 1947-48; Artur Schnabel, 1948-51; Karl Ulrich Schnabel, 1951-53; Claude Frank, 1952-55. *Debut:* Philadelphia Orchestra, 1949. *Career:* Played at Festivals of Aldeburgh, Berlin, Lucerne, Prague, Salzburg, Vienna; Played with Philadelphia Orchestra, Halle Orchestra, Vienna Symphony, Berlin Philharmonic, Bavarian Radio Symphony Orchestra, Rotterdam Philharmonic; Radio and TV appearances throughout Europe; Extensive touring in North and South America, Europe, USSR and Southeast Asia; Recognised also as a Chamber music player and song accompanist; Professor of Piano, University of Frankfurt School of Music, 1976-86; Professor of Piano, Indiana University School of Music, 1986-. *Recordings:* Solo, chamber music and song recital recordings. *Publications:* Beethoven Piano Sonatas op 49/1 and 2 Fingerings and Notes on Interpretation, 1986. *Current Management:* Wolf Concert Artists. *Hobbies:* Literature; Opera. *Address:* 839 Sheridan Road, Bloomington, IN 47401, USA.

HOLAB William Joshua, b. 6 May 1958, Chicago, Illinois, USA. Composer. *Education:* BA, University of Michigan (Music Composition) 1976-80; The Juilliard School 1980-82. Private study with William Albright, William Bolcom, and David Diamond in Composition; Solfege with Marianne Ploger and Rebecca Scott; Conducting with Vincent La Selva. *Career:* Music Engraver and Editor, Music Publishing Services, 1980-86; Music Editor, C F Peters Corporation, 1983-; Orchestrator, Theater-By-The-Sea, Rhode Island, 1982; Resident Orchestrator, The Candlewood Playhouse, New Fairfield, Connecticut, 1983-; Associate Director, Composers Concordance 1983-. *Compositions include:* Ode To A Nightingale for tenor and orchestra, 1981; Instrumental Chamber Music: Diana In New York for woodwind quintet, 1986; Soliloquy for solo horn, 1983; Twilight, for violin, viola and cello, 1982; In The Twilight for 5 trombones, 1980; Arioso for solo piano, 1980; 3 Airs for solo guitar, 1978; Duo for 2 flutes, 1977; Violin Sonata for violin and piano, 1977. Vocal Chamber Music: To My Dear and Loving Husband for soprano and organ, 1985; The Tracks of Angels for baritone and string quartet, 1985; The Bells for chorus and chamber ensemble, 1982; To Sleep for soprano and harp, 1983; Thoughts While Driving Home for medium voice and piano, 1980; 2 Love Songs for bass-baritone and piano, 1977; Gin and Tonic for vocal quartet, 1977. Music

Theatre/Opera: The Mikado, modern updated arrangement of Gilbert and Sullivan work, 1986; Confidence Game, musical based on The Alchemist by Ben Jonson, 1986. *Hobbies:* Gourmet Cooking. *Address:* 804 West 180th Street, Apartment 43, New York, NY 10033. USA.

HOLBROOK Elizabeth, b. 16 Dec 1937, Altrincham, Cheshire, England. Solo Violist. m. William Redgrave, 4 Jan 1973, deceased, 1986, 1 son, 2 daughters. *Education:* ARMCM, Distinction, Royal Manchester College of Music; Eastman School of Music, USA; University of Southern California, Institute for Special Music Studies with William Primrose. *Debut:* Manchester, 1960; London, Wigmore Hall, 1966. *Career:* Turner String Quartet, 1959-63; Teacher, Royal Manchester College, 1958-72, Royal Northern College of Music, 1973; Solo Programmes in Switzerland, Hungary, Holland; Spain; USA; Viola and Piano Duo with Peter Pettinger; Viola and Organ Recitals with Keith Bond; many first performances given; Solo, Duo and with orchestra. *Recordings:* Reger, Suites for Hilversum. *Publications:* Concert Fantasy - Reizenstein, 1967; The Swan, for viola; Kol Nidrei, 1972. *Hobby:* Languages. *Address:* 23 Hungate Street, Aylsham, Norwich, Norfolk NR11 6AA, England.

HOLC Jan, b. 23 Sept 1942, Warsaw, Poland. Conductor; Choirmaster. m. Ewa Puchala, 4 Apr 1967, 1 daughter. *Education:* MA, Academy of Music, Warsaw, 1969. *Career:* Artistic Director of the Madrigal Ensemble, J Musici Cantanti, 1971-; Founder, Staromiejska Orkiestra Kameralna 1980-; Regular concerts in churches, castles, etc, eg Mont St Michel-France, Helsingfør, Denmark, Malbork-Poland. *Recordings:* Recordings for Polish and Danish Broadcasting Companies. *Contributions to:* Newspapers, Literary periodicals about Music. *Memberships:* Jeunessess Musicales de Pologne, 1967; Warsaw Society of Music, 1970. *Honour:* Prize of Prime Minister of Poland, 1980. *Hobbies:* Photography; Driving; Cycling; Tourism. *Address:* Pereca 13/19 M 1410, 00-849 Warsaw, Poland.

HOLD Trevor James, b. 21 Sept 1939, Northampton, England. University Lecturer. m. Susan Turner, 21 July 1962, 2 daughters. *Education:* Northampton Grammar School, 1950-57; BMus (First Class Honours), 1961; MA, 1963; University of Nottingham, 1957-62. *Career:* Head of Music, Market Harborough Grammar School, 1962-63; Assistant Lecturer in Music, UCW, Aberystwyth, 1963-65; Lecturer in Music, University of Liverpool, 1965-70; Lecturer and Staff Tutor in Music, Department of Adult Education, 1970-89; Senior Lecturer, Department of Adult Education, 1980-; Ph.D, 1989, University of Leicester; since 1989, freelance composer, writer and lecturer. *Compositions:* The Unreturning Spring (song-cycle), 1963; Kemp's Nine Daies Wonder (piano suite), 1970; The Lilford Owl (piano folktune arrangements), 1977; Cello Sonata, 1973; Symphony, 1977; The Second Death, (Opera), 1987; Concerto for String Orchestra, 1991; Piano Concerto, 1992; and many songcycles. *Publications:* The Walled-In Garden, a Study of the Songs of Roger Quilter, 1978; A Northamptonshire Garland, 1989; Three volumes of poetry: Time and the Bell, 1971, Caught in Amber, 1981 and Mermaids and Nightingales, 1991. *Contributions to:* Various contributions and reviews to Music and Letters and Music Review; Musical Times. *Honours:* Clements Memorial Prize, 1965; Royal Amateur Orchestral Society Prize, 1968. *Membership:* CGGB. *Hobbies:* Walking; Ornithology; Gardening; English Literature. *Address:* Dovecote House, Wadenhoe, Northamptonshire, via Peterborough, PE8 5SU, England.

HOLECEK Josef, b. 28 Oct 1939, Prague, Czechoslovakia (Swedish national). Guitarist; Teacher of Classical Guitar; Composer; Editor. m. Marie Sobiskova, 19 June 1964, 1 son. *Education:* Diploma, Conservatory of Music, Prague, 1965; Diploma of Guitar, Akademie für Musik und Darstellende Kunst, Wien, Austria, 1967. *Career:* Soloist and chamber musician with concerts, radio and television appearances and recordings in Europe, USA and Australia; Head, Guitar Department, Gothenburg University, Sweden. *Compositions:* Ministudies, Guitar Moods, Guitar Jokes, Swedish Romance; Nevergreens, Smoke Rings, Two Folksongs in Tremolo, Six Aquarelles. *Recordings Include:* Works by B Britten and M Castelnuovo-Tedesco; Contemporary Swedish Guitar Music. *Publications:* Guitar Method, La Dig Spela Gitarr, 1975; Guitar Method, Gitarrdags, 1979; Guitar Pieces From Five Centuries, anthology, 1986; Guitar music edited: Johanson-Omaggio a Bellman, 1977; Nordgren-Butterflies, 1978; Simai-Impressions, 1977; Sörensson-Sonatina, 1977; Koch-Monologue No 10, 1978; Rautavaara-Serenades of the Unicorn, 1980. *Honours:* Finalist, Concours International de Guitare, ORTF, Paris, France, 1966; Artist Award, Royal Swedish Academy of Music, 1977; Award of Swedish Composers' Association, 1982; Gothenburg University Award for Outstanding Pedagogical Achievements, 1991. *Hobbies:* Photography; Antiques. *Address:* Alfhemsg 5, S-413 10 Göteborg, Sweden.

HOLEK Vlastimil, b. 1950, Czechoslovakia. Violinist. *Education:* Studied at the Prague Conservatory. *Career:* Founder member of the Prazak String Quartet, 1972; Tour of Finland, 1973, followed by appearances at competitions in Prague and Evian; Concerts in Salzburg, Munich, Paris, Rome, Berlin, Cologne and Amsterdam; Tour of Britain, 1985, including Wigmore Hall debut; Tours of Japan, the United States, Australia and New Zealand; Tour of UK, 1988, and concert at the Huddersfield Contemporary Music Festival, 1989; Recitals for the BBC, Radio France, Dutch Radio, the WDR in Cologne and Radio Prague; Appearances with the Smetana and LaSalle Quartets in Mendelssohn's Octet. *Recordings:* Albums for Supraphon, Panton and Orfeo. *Honours:* First Prize, Chamber Music Competition of the Prague Conservatory 1974; Grand Prix International String Quartet Competition, Evian Music Festival, 1978; First Prize, National Competition of String Quartets in Czechoslovakia, 1978; Winner, String Quartet Competition of the Prague Spring Festival, 1978. *Address:* c/o Ingpen and Williams Ltd, 14 Kensington Court, London W8 5DN, England.

HOLICKOVÁ Elena, b. 1950, Czechoslovakia. Soprano. *Education:* Conservatory of Music, Bratislava; Academy of Music and Drama, Bratislava. *Career:* Slovak National Theatre; Musetta in La Bohéme, Lisa in the Queen of Spades, Rusalka in Rusalka, Jenůfa, Julietta, Adriana in Adriana Lecouvreur, Marina in Dimitriy; Verdi's Rigoletto; Fiodor in Mussorgsky's Boris Gudunov; Small Shepherd in Suchon's The Whirlpool; Nuri in The Lowlands; Queen in Dance Over the Crying; Swallow in The Happy Prince; A Servant in Electra; Marenka in The Bartered Bride; Orphan in The Siege of Bystrica; Amelia Grimaldi in Simone Boccanegra 1984-85. *Recordings:* Songs by Mikulus Schneider-Trnavsky; Cycles by Alexander Moyzes; Glimpse into the Unknown; Mutations by Ilja Zeljenka, 1980; Ode to Joy, 1983; Submerged Music. *Honour:* Slovak Music Fund Prize, 1984. *Address:* c/o Slovak National Theatre, Gorkého 2, 815 06 Brastislava, Slovakia.

HOLL Robert, b. 1947, Rotterdam, Holland. Singer (Bass). *Education:* Studied with Jan Veth and David Hollestelle. *Career:* Sang with the Bayerische Staatsoper Munich from 1973; Has concentrated on concert career from 1975: appearances at the Vienna, Holland and Salzburg Festivals, the Schubertiade at Hohenems; Salzburg Mozartwochen, 1981-83, as the Priest in Thamos, König in Agypten, as the Voice of Neptune in Idomeneo and Cassandro in La Finta Giardiniera; Many engagements as a singer of Lieder, in music by Schubert, Brahms and Wolf; Concert appearaces with Bernstein, Giulini, Harnoncourt, Jochum, Karajan, Sawallisch, Stein and De Waart; Promenade Concerts London, 1987, in the Choral Symphony; Judge, Walter Gruener International Lieder Competition, London, 1989; sang in Schubert's Fierrabras at the Theater an der Wien, Vienna, 1988; Season 1992 at Zurich, as Assur in Semiramide and

La Roche in Capriccio. *Recordings include:* Mozart's Requiem (Decca); Mozart and Salieri by Rimsky-Korsakov; Lieder by Pfitzner; Requiems by Bellini and Donizetti; Mozart's Zaide and La Finta Semplice (Orfeo); St Matthew Passion by Bach, Die Schöpfung, Utrecht Te Deum by Handel, Mozart's Mass in C Minor (Telefunken); Bach Mass in C minor (EMI). *Honours include:* Winner, International Vocal Competition at 's Hertogenbosch, 1971; Winner, Munich International Competiton, 1972. *Address:* c/o Ingpen & Williams Ltd, 14 Kensington Court, London W8 5DN, England.

HOLLAND Mark, b. 1960, England. Singer (Baritone). *Education:* Studied with John Cameron at the Royal Northern College of Music and with Roberto Benaglio in Italy. *Career:* Joined Welsh National Opera in 1984 and has appeared as Rossini's Figaro, Mozart's Count, Eugene Onegin, Schaunard in La Bohème, Don Carlo in Ernani and Enrico in Lucia di Lammermoor; Sonora in La Fanciulla del West, 1991; Festival engagements include Piccinni's La Buona Figliola at Buxton; Season 1989-90, as Falke in Fledermaus for Opera Northern Ireland and Masetto for Dublin Grand Opera; Season 1990-91 as Ford in Falstaff at the Théâtre des Champs Elysées, tour to Japan with La Bohème and Carmina Burana with the Royal Philharmonic; Sang Puccini's Marcello and Mozart's Allazim (Zaide) with the City of Birmingham Touring Opera, 1991-92; Bregenz Festival, 1992 as Morales in Carmen. *Address:* c/o Anglo Swiss Ltd, 3 Primrose Mews, 1a Sharpleshall St, London NW1 8YW, England

HOLLANDER Julia, b. 1965, Bristol, England. Stage Director. *Education:* St Catherine's College, Cambridge and also in Paris. *Career:* Opera productions have included Dido and Aeneas' Trial by Jury, the Soldier's Tale, Acis and Galatea and Orfeo ed Euridice for the Cambridge Arts Theatre; Les Mamelles de Tiresias a the Edinburgh Festival; A Midsummer Night's Dream at Avignon, Giovanna d'Arco at the Bloomsbury Theatre London and Samson and Delilah for Northern Opera, Newcastle; Staff producer at ENO, 1988- 91, working on Xerxes, The Return of Ulysses, Lear, Macbeth and Bluebeard's Castle; Solo production debut for ENO with Fennimore and Gerda, 1990, returning for the premiere of John Buller's Bakxai, 1992, and Eugene Onegin in 1994; Further engagements with The Rake's Progress at Aldeburgh, Turn of the Screw at the Royal College of Music, and Xerxes in Sao Paulo and Bologna. *Address:* Ingpen & Williams Ltd, 14 Kensington Court, London W8 5DN, England.

HOLLANDER Lorin (D), b. 19 July 1944, New York, USA. Pianist. *Education:* Studied with Eduard Steuermann at the Juilliard School and with Leon Fleisher and Max Rudolf. *Debut:* Carnegie Hall 1955. *Career:* Has performed with leading orchestras in the USA including the New York Philharmonic, Philadelphia Orchestra, Washington National and Chicago Symphony Orchestra; European engagements with the Warsaw Philharmonic, Orchestre de la Suisse Romande, London Philharmonic and Concertgebouw; Has performed in prisons, hospitals and other institutions; Series of programmes on television; Adviser to the Office of the Gifted and Talented for the US Government; Lecturer on psychological aspects of musical performance.

HÖLLE Matthias, b. 8 July 1951, Rottweil am Nekkar, Germany. Singer (Bass). *Education:* Studied in Stuttgart with Georg Jelden and in Cologne with Josef Metternich. *Career:* Sang first in concerts and oratorios; Sang in opera at Cologne from 1976; Ludwigsburg Festival 1978, as the Commendatore in Don Giovanni; Has appeared at the Bayreuth Festival from 1981 as the Nightwatchman, Titurel, Fasolt and Hunding (1988 in Der Ring des Nibelungen, conducted by Daniel Barenboim); King Marke in Tristan und Isolde at Bologna (1983), Florence (1989) and Cologne (1990); Sang in the premiere of Stockhausen's Donnerstag (1981) and created Lucifer in Stockhausen's Samstag aus Licht at the Palazzo dello Sport with the company of La Scala Milan, 1984; Guest appearances in Hanover, Geneva,

Tel Aviv and New York (Fidelio at the Metropolitan, 1986); Season 1989 as Don Fernando in Fidelio at Brussels, Daland in Stuttgart and the Commendatore at Parma; Sang Hunding at Bonn and the Bayreuth Festival, 1992; Television appearances in Die Schöpfung and Beethoven's Christus am Olberge. *Recordings include:* Don Giovanni (Electrola); Haydn's Seven Last Words on the Cross (Intercord); Handel's Saul (Telefunken); Lieder by Schumann (Capriccio); Fourth Shepherd in Daphne, conducted by Haitink (EMI); Samstag aus Licht (Deutsche Grammophon); Gurnemanz in Parsifal, conducted by Barenboim (Teldec). *Address:* Matthias Hölle, Vischerweg 11, D-7290 Freudenstadt, Germany.

HÖLLER York Georg, b. 11 Jan 1944, Leverkusen, Germany. Composer. *Education:* Studied at the Cologne Musikhochschule 1963-70, with B A Zimmermann and Herbert Eimert; Ferienkurse Darmstadt 1965, with Boulez; Worked at the Electronic Music Studios, Cologne, with Stockhausen. *Career:* Freelance composer from 1965; First orchestral work, Topic, performed at Darmstadt 1970; Invited by Boulez to work at the studios of IRCAM, 1978; Piano Concerto given French premiere by Daniel Barenboim, Paris 1988; Der Meister und Margarita last new production at the Paris Opéra, Salle Garnier, before opening of the Opéra de la Bastille; Professor for anaylis and music theory at the College Musikhochschùle, 1975-89; Director of the Electronic Studio at WDR Cologne, 1990-. *Compositions:* 5 Pieces for piano 1964; Diaphonie for 2 pianos 1965; Topic for orchestra 1967I; Sonate Informelle 1968; Cello Sonata 1969; Epitaph for violin and piano 1969; Piano Concerto 1970; Horizont 1972 and Tangent 1973 for electronics; Chroma for orchestra 1972-74; Klanggitter for electronics 1976; Antiphon for string quartet 1977; Arcus for orchestra 1978; Moments Musicaux for flute and piano 1979; Umbra for orchestra 1979-80; Mythos for orchestra 1979-80; Résouance for orchestra and tape, 1981-82; Schwatze Halbinselu for orchestra and tape, 1982; Traumspiel for soprano, orchestra and tape 1983; Piano Concerto 1983-84; Magische Klanggestalt for orchestra 1984; Improvisation sur le nom de Pierre Boulez 1985; Der Meister und Margarita, opera 1985-89; Piano Sonata No 2 Hommage à Franz Liszt 1987; Fanal, for trumpet and orchestra, 1990; Pensée for piano, orchestra and electronics, 1991; Aùna for large orchestra, 1992; Caligùla Opera, after A Camus, 1992. *Recordings:* Arcùs (Erato), Résonance and Schwarze Halbinselu Oeutsche Harmonia Mundi. *Publications:* Composition of the Gestalt on the making of an organism, London, 1984;; Auf der sùche nach den Klang von morgan, Zurich, 1990; B A Zimmermann Moine et Dionysos, Lausanne, 1985. *Honours:* Cheralier dans L'ordre des arts e des lettres, Paris; Rolf-Liebermann-Preis fùr Opera Komponisten. *Address:* c/o Boosey & Hawkes Ltd, 295 Regent Street, London W1R 8JH, England.

HOLLIDAY Melanie, b. 12 Aug 1951, Houston, Texas, USA. Singer (Soprano). *Education:* Studied at Indiana University School and at the Graz Academy of Music. *Career:* Sang at Hamburg and Klagenfurt from 1973; Basle Opera as Zerbinetta in Ariadne auf Naxos; Vienna Volksoper from 1976, as Olympia in Les Contes d'Hoffmann, Frau Fluth, Constanze, Philine in Mignon, Adele (Die Fledermaus), Valencienne (Die Lustige Witwe) and in Die Schöne Galatea by Suppé; Tours of Japan with the Volksoper 1979, 1982, 1985; Guest appearances in Germany, Italy, Holland, Spain and Switzerland; Vienna Staatsoper; Houston Opera 1983; Operetta tour of West Germany with Rene Kollo, 1984; Theater am Gärtnerplatz Munich 1986, as Musetta in La Bohème. *Recordings include:* Die Fledermaus (Denon); Film of L'Elisir d'Amore. *Address:* c/o Volksoper, Währingerstrasse 78, A-1090 Vienna, Austria.

HOLLIGER Heinz, b. 21 May 1939, Langenthal, Switzerland. Oboist; Composer; Conductor. *Education:* Berne, Paris and Basle under Emile Cassagnaud (oboe) and Pierre Boulez (composition). *Education:* Professor of oboe, Freiburg Music Academy, 1965-; has appeared at all the major European music festivals and in Japan, USA, Australia, Israel; British premiere of Scardanelli Cycle at the Elizabeth Hall, 1988; Has recorded over 200 works, mainly for Philips and Deutsche Grammophon; Berio, Krenek, Henze, Stockhausen and Penderecki have written works for him; Played in the British fp of Gemeux by Takemitsu, Edinburgh, 1989; Has premiered Carter's Oboe Concerto, 1988, Ferneyhough's Coloratura, 1972, Henze's Doppio Concerto, 1966, Ligeti's Double Concerto, 1972, Lutoslawski's Double Concerto, 1980 and Eucalypts I and II by Takemitsu, 1970-71; Conducted the Chamber Orchestra of Europe in Beethoven's 7th Symphony and Schnittke's 3rd Violin Concerto, London, 1992. *Compositions include:* Der magische Tanzer; Trio; Siebengesang; Wind Quintet; Dona nobis pacem; Pneuma; Psalm; Cardiophonie; Kreis; String Quartet; Atembogen; Die Jahreszeiten; Come and Go; Not I; Trema; Turm-Musik, Tonscherben, Scardanelli-Cycle; 2 Liszt Transcriptions; Gesänge der Frühe; What Where. *Honours:* Recipient of several international prizes. *Address:* c/o Ingpen and Williams, 14 Kensington Court, London W8 England.

HOLLIGER Ursula, b. 8 June 1937, Basle, Switzerland. Harpist. m. Heinz Holliger. *Education:* Studied in Basle and at the Brussels Conservatoire. *Career:* World-wide appearances with leading orchestras, including the Philharmonics of Berlin, Vienna and Los Angeles, the Orchestre de Paris, English Chamber Orchestra, Orchestra of South German Radio and the Schweizerisches Festspielorchester Luzern; Conductors have included Pierre Boulez, Michael Gielen, Simon Rattle, André Previn and Neville Marriner; Composers who have written for her and her husband include Edison Denisov, Henze (Doppio Concerto, 1966), André Jolivet, Ernst Krenek, György Ligeti (Double Concerto, 1972), Witold Lutoslawski (Double Concerto, 1977); Several works written for her by her husband; Professor at the Basle Music Academy. *Recordings include:* Spohr Concertos for Harp and Concertos for Violin and Harp. *Address:* c/o Ingpen and Williams Ltd, 14 Kensington Court, London W11 4PA, England.

HOLLISTER David Manship, b. 1 May 1929, New York City, New York, USA. Composer. m. Barbara Witriol, 22 Mar. 1964. *Education:* AB, Harvard University, 1951; MA 1965, MFA 1966, PhD 1968, University of Iowa; Studies at Juilliard School, Manhattan School of Music; Higher School of Music, Warsaw, Poland. *Career:* Composer of concert music and music for film, dance, and musical theatre, 1952-; Commissions by Spoleto Festival, American Chamber Ensemble, Paul Taylor Dance Company, American Dance Machine, Downtown Chamber and Opera Players; Composer; Pianist; Conductor; Arranger; Former Teacher, Hofstra University, York College, and University of New Orleans; Faculty Member, New School for Social Research, 1985-; New York University, 1987-; Adjunct Associate Professor, Long Island University, Brooklyn, NY, 1991-. *Compositions:* Peace-Cry (chamber cantata); String Quartets 1 and 2; Tributaries (clarinet, cello, piano); Sea-Change (flute, viola, piano); Corronach (string orchestra); A Change of Hearts (one-act opera). *Recordings:* String Quartets 1 and 2, Hampshire String Quartet, Opus One Recordings.*Publications:* Editor and Publisher, since Jan. 1989, The Hollister Report, Quarterly. *Memberships:* Dramatists Guild; Romanesque Revival Society (President). *Address:* 10 East 16th Street, Apartment 5, New York, NY 10003, USA.

HOLLOS Mate, b. 18 July 1954, Budapest, Hungary. Composer. *Education:* F Liszt Academy of Music, Budapest. *Career:* Managing Director, Hungarotoon Classic; Artistic Director, Akkord Music Publishers. *Compositions include:* Cantatas: Kajetan Tyl, Voyelles de Rimbaud, Songs of Love; Camera Music: Looking Up on a Star; Duli Duli; Promanade; O Songs Float from my lips; Arparmonia; New song without Words; Toccata Lirica; Hommage a Szeged, for string orchestra; L'EAR-A, sextet; Six and a Half Flute Duets; Rhapsodic Monologue, clarinet solo. *Recordings:* On the Edge of Non-Existence; Impromptu; O Songs Float from my Lips.

Publications: Scores published by Editio Musica Budapest; Works in Kritika, Muzsika, Parlando, Magyar Nemzet. *Honours:* Creative Youth, 1980; Public Prize, Rostrom of the Hungarian RAdio, 1992. *Memberships:* Vice President, Hungarian Composers Union; Hungarian Kodaly Society; Jeunesses Musicales (Board). *Address:* Bimbo ut 5, H-1022 Budapest, Hungary.

HOLLOWAY David, b. 12 Nov 1942, Grandview, Missouri, USA. Singer (Baritone). m. Deborah Seabury. *Education:* Studied at University of Kansas and with Luigi Ricci in Rome. *Debut:* Kansas City Lyric Opera 1968, as Belcore in L'Elisir d'Amore; Sang Britten's Billy Budd in Chicago 1970; New York City Opera 1972, as Guglielmo in Così fan Tutte; Metropolitan Opera debut 1973, in Madama Butterfly: returned as Puccini's Schaunard, Sharpless and Lescaut; Guglielmo 1984; European appearances, in particular at the Deutsche Oper am Rhein, Dusseldorf; Glyndebourne 1985, as Escamillo; Other roles include Mozart's Papageno, Count and Nardo (La Finta Giardiniera), Rossini's Figaro and Dandini, Donizetti's Malatesta, and Nick Shadow in The Rake's Progress. *Recordings include:* The Taming of the Shrew by Goetz. *Honours include:* Hi Fidelity Award, 1971. *Hobbies:* Camping; Fishing; Sailing; Motorcycling; Piano. *Address:* c/o Columbia Artists Management, 165 W 57th Street, New York, NY 10019, USA.

HOLLOWAY Robin Greville, b. 19 Oct 1943, Leamington Spa, England. University Teacher; Critic; Composer. *Education:* St. Paul's Cathedral Choir School; King's College School, Wimbledon; Kings College, Cambridge; New College, Oxford; MA; PhD; DMus. *Compositions:* Numerous compositions in all genres; Opera Clarissa, 1990; principal works for orchestra: Scenes from Schumann, 1970; Domination of Black 1974; Seascape and Harvest 1984; First and Second Concertos for Orchestra, 1969, 1979; principal chamber works: Evening With Angels 1971; The Rivers of Hell 1977; Concertos for horn, harp, oboe, bassoon, violin, clarinet and saxophone; Opera: Clarissa 1976 (premiered 1990); Dramatic Ballads: Brand 1981; Peer Gynt 1985-; Violin Concerto 1990; The Spacious Firmament for chorus and orchestra, 1990; Hymn to the Senses for chorus, 1990; Serenade for strings, 1990; Winter Music for sextet, 1993; Third Concerto for orchestra, 1993. *Recordings:* Sea Surface Full of Clouds, Chamber Cantata, Opus 28; Romanza for violin and small orchestra, Opus 31; Second Concerts for Orchestra Opus 40; The Spacious Firmament, 1990. *Publications:* Debussy and Wagner 1978; Numerous articles and contributions to anthologies. *Address:* Finella, Queen's Road, Cambridge CB3 9AH, England.

HOLLREISER Heinrich, b. 24 June 1913, Munich, Germany. Conductor. *Education:* Akademie der Tonkunst Munich. *Career:* Conducted at opera houses in Wiesbaden, Mannheim, Darmstadt and Duisburg; Munich Opera from 1942, notably with operas by Strauss, then musical director in Dusseldorf; Hamburg Opera 1947, with the local premiere of Peter Grimes by Britten; Vienna Staatsoper from 1952; Principal conductor at the Deutsche Oper Berlin 1961-64: Blacher's Zweihundertausend Thaler 1969; Modern repertory includes operas by Bartók, Hindemith and Berg; Bayreuth Festival 1973-75, Tannhäuser and Die Meistersinger; Wagner's Ring at the Vienna Staatsoper, 1976; Guest Conductor with the Cleveland Orchestra 1978. *Recordings include:* Mozart Piano Concertos, Haebler; Tchaikovsky and Mendlessohn Violin Concertos (Gitlis); Bartók Cantata Profana and Concerto for Orchestra; Symphonies by Schubert, Brahms, Dvořák, Tchaikovsky, Bruckner; Stavinsky's Apollo, Pulcinella and Jeu de Cartes. *Address:* c/o PO Box 100262, Bayreuther Festzpiele, 8580 Bayreuth 1, Germany.

HOLLWEG Werner, b. 13 Sept 1936, Solingen, Germany. Singer (Tenor). m. Constance Daucha, 2 children. *Education:* Studied in Detmold, Munich and Legano. *Debut:* Vienna Kammeroper 1962. *Career:* Bonn 1963-67; Gelsenkirchen 1967-68; Maggio

Musicale Florence 1969, as Belmonte in Die Entführung; Guest appearances in Hamburg, Munich, Berlin, Rome, Paris, New York and Los Angeles; Salzburg Festival as Mozart's Tamino, Ottavio, Ferrando and Belmonte; Osaka, Japan, 1970 in Beethoven's 9th Symphony; Covent Garden debut 1976, as Mozart's Titus; Paris Opera 1986, as Jason in Cherubini's Médée; Promenade Concerts London 1989, in Psalmus Hungaricus by Kodály; Created Matthew Levi in Höller's Der Meister und Margarita, Paris, 1989; sang the High Priest in Idomeneo at Salzburg, 1990. *Recordings:* Haydn, Die Jahreszeiten; Mozart, Le Nozze di Figaro (HMV); Mahler, Das klagende Lied; Mozart, La Finta Giardiniera and Zaide (Philips); Lehar, Die lustige Witwe; Mozart, Mitridate (Deutsche Grammophon); Mozart, Idomeneo; Monteverdi, Il Combattimento; Ballads by Schubert, Schumann and Loewe (Telefunken). *Address:* c/o Ingpen and Williams Ltd., 14 Kensington Court, London W8 5DN, England.

HOLM Mogens Winkel, b. Oct 1936, Copenhagen, Denmark. Composer. *Education:* Studied Oboe and Composition, Royal Danish Academy of Music, Copenhagen. *Career:* Oboe player in various Copenhagen orchestras including the Danish Radio Light Orchestra, 1964-65; Choreographer to his own ballet scores, 1975-. *Compositions Include:* Opera: Aslak, 1961; Sonata for Four Opera Singers, 1967-68; Ballet: Tropisms, 1963; Chronicle, 1968; Galgarien, 1970; Report, 1972; Tarantel, 1975; Eurydice Hesitates, 1977; Whitethroat under an Artificial Firmament, 1979-80; To Bluebeard, 1982; Orchestra: Kammerkoncertante, 1959; Concerto piccolo, 1961; Cumulus, 1965; Ricercare, 1966; The Glass Forest, 1974; Aiolos, symphony in 1 movement, 1972-77; Cries, 1983-84; Chamber Music: Abracadabra, 1960; Tropismer, 1960; Sonata, 1965; Transitions, 1972; Seven Letters to Silence, 1976; Adieu, 1982; Note-book, 1983; Vocal: October Morning, 1964; Transitions, 1971; Nightmare, 1973; For Children 1984. *Recordings:* Has made numerous recordings.*Address:* KODA, Rosenvaengets Hovedvej 14, 2100 Copenhagen, Denmark.

HOLM Peder, b. 30 Sept 1926, Copenhagen, Denmark. Composer; Educator. *Education:* Graduate in Violin and Theory, Royal Danish Conservatorium, 1947; Teacher's Examination in Piano and Violin, 1950. *Career includes:* Director, Western Jutland Conservatorium; Director, West Jutland Symphony Orchestra. *Compositions include:* Orchestral works: Pezzo Concertante, 1964; VYL, 1967; For solo instruments and orchestra: Khebeb for 2 pianos and orchestra, 1968; Concertino for clarinet and chamber orchestra, 1970; For instrumental ensembles: 2 pieces for wind quintet, 1968; Music for brass band, 1969; Works for children's choir: Children's Song, Ole Wivel, 1970; Legend, Erik Knudsen, 1971; Pikkutikka for children and symphony orchestra, 1973; For mixed choir: 5 Choral Songs, Ene Mene, Inscription, Mobile, September Evening, Regards to Børge, 1971; Arrangements: Works by Schumann, Grieg, Couperin and Mozart; Pieces for the Musica Ensemble Series; Works for solo voice, orchestra, symphonic works, concertos and chamber music. *Publications include:* The String Method; Wind Method; Editor, Violin 1 and 2; All part of Wilhelm Hansen's MUSICA-Methods series. *Memberships:* Programme Committee, Danish Radio, 1963-67; Music Committee, State Cultural Foundation, 1965-68. *Address:* Skolegyden 37, Nr Søby, 5792 Årslev, Denmark.

HOLM Renate, b. 10 Aug. 1931, Berlin, Germany. Singer (Soprano). *Education:* Studied with Maria Ivogun in Vienna. *Career:* Sang in films and entertainment programmes from 1953; Vienna Volksoper from 1957, debut as Gretchen in Der Wildschütz by Lortzing; Appearances at the Vienna Staatsoper, Bolshoi Theatre, Moscow, Covent Garden, London, and the Teatro Colon Buenos Aires in the soubrette repertory, including Despina, Norina, Sophie, Zerlina and Marzelline; Saltzburg Festival from 1961, as Blondchen in Die Entführung, Papagena and Musetta. *Recordings:* Die Fledermaus, Der Vogelhändler, Das Land des Lächelns

(Electrola); Die Zauberflöte (Decca); Die Entführung (Melodram). *Address:* c/o Staatsoper, 1010 Wien, Austria.

HOLMAN Peter, b. 1946, London, England. Harpsichordist; Chamber Organist. *Education:* King's College, London with Thurston Dart. *Career:* As student, directed the pioneering early music group Ars Nova; Founded, The Parley of Instruments, with Roy Goodman, 1979, The Purley now recognised as one of the leading exponents of Renaissance and Baroque string consort music; Musical Director, 1985, newly formed Opera Restor'd which specialises in authentic productions of eighteenth century English operas and masques; Past Professor, Royal Academy of Music in London for 10 years and has taught at many conservatoires, universities and summer schools in Britain; Artistic Director of the annual Suffolk Village Festival; Appointed joint Artistic Director, with Paul O'Dette, of the forthcoming Boston Early Music Festival; Presently, Senior Associate Lecturer at Colchester Institute School of Music; Regular Broadcaster on BBC Radio 3; He spends much of his time in writing and research; Special interests in the early history of the violin family, in European instrumental ensemble music of the renaissance and Baroque and in English seventeenth and eighteenth century music. *Publications:* Many editions of early music; Four and Twenty Fiddlers; The Violin at the English Court 1540-1690, 1993; Ed. London: Commonwealth and Restoration in The Early Baroque Era. C A Price in the Man and Music (Music and Society in the USA) series (London), 1993; paper on Monteverdi's string writing in the Nov 1993 issue of Early Music; Presently finishing book on Purcell's music. *Contributions to:* Various articles and reviews to a range of newspapers and journals. *Address:* 119 Maldon Road, Colchester, Essex CO3 3AX, England.

HOLMBOE Vagn, b. 20 Dec 1909, Horsens, Jutland, Denmark. Composer. *Education:* Copenhagen Conservatory with Finn Hofffding and Knud Jeppesen; Studied with Ernest Toch in Berlin. *Career:* Freelance composer from 1934; Taught at Institute of Blind in 1940s; Music Critic of Politiken 1947-55; Professor of Composition at Copenhagen Conservatory 1955-65. *Compositions include:* 12 Symphonies, 1935-88; 13 Chamber Concertos 1939-56; 2 Concertos for flute and orchestra; 20 String Quartets 1948-75; 3 Violin Sonatas; Sonatas for recorder, accordian, guitar; Romanian Suite; Epitaph; Epilogue; Requiem for Nietzsche, 1964; Sextet for flute, clarinet, bassoon and string trio 1973; Piano Music; 2 brass quintets, Concerto for brass band. *Publications include:* Mellemspil 1961; Det uforklarige 1981; Experiencing Music, Paul Rappport, 1991. *Contributions to:* Modern Nordisk Musik 1957. *Address:* Holmboevej 4, Ramlöse, 3200 Helsinge, Tlf 48712045, Denmark.

HOLMES Eugene, b. 7 March 1932, Brownsville, Tennessee, USA. Singer (Baritone), Kammersaenger, Deutsche Oper Am Rhein, Duesseldorf, Germany. m. Katja L Holmes. *Education:* AM and N College, BS Degree, Music Ed, Indiana University, Bloomington, Indiana, Special award: Performers Certificate; Studied with W D Walton in St Louis, Frank St Leger at the Indiana University in Bloomington, and with Dorothy Ziegler in Miami. *Debut:* Goldovsky Opera, New York, 1963, in The Crucible by Ward. *Career:* Sang in San Diego, San Francisco, Seattle and New York (City Opera 1971, in the premiere of The Most Important Man by Menotti; Washington 1970, in the US premiere of Koanga by Delius; Dusseldorf 1983, as Don Carlos in La Forza del Destino, Nabucco, and Enrico in Lucia di Lammermoor; Munich 1983, in a concert performance of Porgy and Bess; Other roles include Amonasro, Macbeth, Iago, Rigoletto, Boccanegra, Jochanaan and parts in operas by Mozart, Wagner and Puccini; Verdi's La Traviata, Germont, Puccini's La Boheme, Marcello, Madame Butterfly, Sharpless, Manon Lescaut, Lescaut, Verdi's Il Trovatore, Count di Luna. Performed with the Deutsche Oper Am Rhein in the USSR, Magic Flute; Concert tours in Japan, Israel. *Recordings include:* Porgy and Bess (EMI); Koanga. *Address:* c/o Deutsche Oper am Rhein, Heinrich Heine Allee 16, D-4000 Dusseldorf, Germany.

HOLMQUIST Ake, b. 2 Aug 1943, Stockholm, Sweden. President; Musical Director. m. Britt Ingrid Kullberg, 3 Nov 1967, 1 son, 2 daughters. *Education:* BA, 1967; MA, 1970; PhD, 1972; Music Theoretical and Pianistic Studies, Stockholm, and Vienna. *Career:* Planning Manager, 1973-74, Regional Director, 1975-80, Programme Director, 1980-86, Institute for National Concerts, Sweden; President, European Music Year, Sweden, 1983-85; Head, Uppsala Music Authorities, 1978-82; Exeecutive and Artistic Director, Stockholm Concert Hall Foundation, Royal Stockholm Philharmonic Orchestra, 1986-; Chairman of the Board, Swedish Festival, 1993-; Director, Stockholm Composer Festival, 1986-; Chairman of the Board, Hugo Alfvén Society, 1993-; Member of the Board, Renewal and Restoration of the City of Stockholm, 1993-; Commissioner, Stockholm Exposition, 1993-; Member of the Board, Swedish-Greek Cultrual Foundation, 1992-. *Publications:* Fran signalgivning till regionmusik, 1974; The Music in Stockholm 1719-1976, 1976; Arnold Schoenberg - a small biography, 1976; To Commission Music for the Regional Music, 1976. *Contributor to:* Musikrevy, 1970-. *Membership:* IMC. *Address:* Stockholm Concert Hall Foundation, Box 7083, S-103 87 Stockholm, Sweden.

HOLOMAN D(allas) Kern, b. 8 Sept 1947, Raleigh, North Carolina, USA. Musicologist; Conductor; Music Educator. m. Elizabeth R Holoman. 1 son, 1 daughter. *Education:* Studied bassoon and conducting, North Caroline School of the Arts; Accademia Musicale Chigiana, Siena, Italy, 1967, 1968; BA, Duke University, 1969; MFA 1971, PhD 1974, Princeton University. *Career:* Founding Director, Early Music Ensemble 1973-77, 1979, Conductor, Symphony Orchestra, 1978-, Chairman Music Department 1980-88, University of California at Davis; Founding Co-editor, 19th Century Music Journal, 1977; General Editor, Recent Researches in the Music of the Nineteenth and Early Twentieth Centuries, 1989; Guest Lecturer, various professional organizations. *Publications:* The Creative Process in the Autograph Musical Documents of Hector Berlioz, c 1818-1840, 1980; edited with C Palisca, Musicology in the 1980s, 1982; Dr Holoman's Handy Guide to Concert-Going, 1983; Catalogue of the Works of Hector Berlioz, 1987; Writing About Music: A Style-Sheet from the Editors of the 19th Century Music, 1988; Berlioz, 1989. *Contributions:* Numerous articles and reviews in journals and other publications; Editor, Berlioz's Roméo et Juliette, New Berlioz Edition. *Memberships:* American Musicological Society; Music Library Association; Association Nationale Hector Berlioz. *Address:* c/o Department of Music, University of California at Davis, Davis, CA 95616, USA.

HOLOUBEK Ladislav, b. 13 Aug 1913, Prague, Czechoslovakia. Composer; Conductor. *Education:* Academy of Music and Dramatic Arts, Bratislava, with Vitezslav Novak, Prague. *Career:* Conductor, National Theatre, Bratislava, 1933-52 and 1958-66; Conductor, State Theatre, Kozice, 1955-58 and 1966-. *Compositions:* Stella, opera in 3 acts, 1937-38; Dawn, opera 3 acts, 1940; Yearning, opera 3 acts, 1943; The Family, opera 3 acts, 1958; Professor Mamlock, opera 2 acts, 1964; Many chamber and orchestra music and song cycles. *Publications:* Translated a number of Russian, Italian and German opera librettos. *Honours:* Recipient of many honours including Excellent Labour, 1960; Order of Labour, 1984. *Membership:* Union of Slovak Composers. *Address:* Rustaveliho 16, 83106 Bratislava, Slovakia.

HOLT Simon, b. 21 Feb 1958, Bolton, Lancashire, England. Composer. *Education:* Bolton College of Art, 1977-78; Composition, Piano, Harpsichord, Royal Northern College of Music, 1978-82. *Career:* Featured composer Bath Festival, 1985; Commissions from London Sinfonietta (Kites, Ballad of the Black Sorrow) and Nash Ensemble (Shadow Realm, Era Madrugada, Canciones, Sparrow Night) and Proms for 1987; Also

featured at Music in London Now Festival in Japan, 1986. *Compositions:* All compositions published by Universal Edition: Lunas Zauberschein; Palace at 4 am; Mirrormaze, Maiastra; Kites; Shadow Realm; Era Madrugada; Burlesca Oscura; Tauromaquia; Canciones; Syrensong; Ballad of the Black Sorrow; Duendecitos; Capriccio Spettrale; String Quartet: Danger of the Disappearance of Things; Sparrow Night; Lilith; Walking With The River's Roar, Tanagra; Figurine; Icarus Lamentations, A Knot of Time; Some Distant Chimes; A Shapeless Flame, Minotaur Games, The Thing That Makes Ashes. *Recordings:* CD, ERA Madrugada, Canciones, Shadow Realm, Sparrow Night, Nash Ensemble, NMC Label. *Address:* c/o Universal Edition, Warwick House, 9 Warwick Street, London, England.

HOLTEN Bo, b. 1948, Denmark. Composer. *Compositions include:* Works for symphony orchestra, with/without chorus; Works for large/small chamber ensembles; Vocal & instrumental music; Choral works, with/without instruments; Opera, The Bond, 1978-79; Tape, film scores. Symphonic works include: Mahler-Impromptu, 1972-73; Caccia, 1979; Symphony, 1981-82; Imperia, 1983; Tertia Die, 1985. Conducts vocal group, Ars Nova, performances of rare works; Music critic & editor, Dansk Musiktidsskrift; Pioneer, many unusual concerts combining classical music/jazz. *Hobby:* Football. *Address:* KODA, Rosenvaengets Hovedvej 14, 2100 Copenhagen, Denmark.

HOLTENAU Rudolf, b. 1937, Salzburg, Austria. Singer (Baritone). *Education:* Stuided in Linz and in Vienna with Alfred Jerger. *Career:* Sang in concert, 1959-61; Opera engagements at Klagenfurt, 1961-62, Regensburg, 1962-65, Bielefeld, 1965-67, Essen, 1967-75; Further appearances at Cologne, 1972-73, Vienna Staatsoper, 1973-75, Graz, 1977-70; Guest throughout the 1970s at Stockholm, Lyon, Brussels, Bacelona, Monte Carlo, Lisbon, Marseille and Bologna; Performances of Der Ring des Nibelungen at Seattle, 1978-79; Sang such roles as Wagner's Dutchman, Sachs, Wotan, Gunther, Kurwenal and Amfortas, Straauss's Mandryka and Verdi's Amonasro at Hamburg, Berlin (Deutsche Oper), Buenos Aires, Venic, San Francisco and Rio de Janiero; Sang at Cape Town, 1982, 1985. *Recordings:* Ballads by Carle Loewe. *Address:* Opera of the Cape Performing Arts Board, PO Box 4017, Cape Town 8000, S Africa.

HOLTHAM Ian, b. 1 Feb 1955, Melbourne, Australia. Concert Pianist; Educationalist. *Education:* BA, Phd, DipEd, Melbourne University; BMus, Durham University; Studied with Peter Fenchtwanger, Geza Anda and Geoffrey Parsons. *Debut:* Purcell Room and Wigmore Hall, both 1977. *Career:* Appearances in UK, Switzerland, France, Austria, Italy, Thailand Hong Kong and Australia; Concerto soloist and recitalist; Frequent appearances for Australian Broadcasting Corporation; Numerous radio and tv appearances. *Recordings:* Chopin: Twenty-four etude, Op 10 and Op 25; Godowsky: Selection of transcriptions of Chopin Etudes. *Publications:* The essentials of Piano Technique, 1992. *Current management* Alan Watkinson Management. *Address:* Heavitree, PO Box 412, Canterbury, Victoria 3126, Australia.

HOLTMANN Heidrun, b. 18 Oct 1961, Münster, Westphalia, Germany. Pianist. *Education:* Study with Eleonore Jäger, Münster, 1966-70; Professor Renate Kretschmar-Fischer, Musikhochschule Detmold/Westphalia, 1970-83; Nikata Magaloff, Geneva, Switzerland, 1978; Vladimir Ashkenazy, Lucerne, Switzerland, 1981. *Career:* Concerts in England, France, Germany, Israel, Italy, Japan, Yugoslavia, North Africa, Austria, Poland, Hungary, Switzerland, USA; Concerts at festivals in Bordeaux (France), Brescia & Bergamo (Italy), Salzburg, Lockenhaus (Austria), Luzern (Switzerland), Berlin (West Germany); Concerts with Detroit Symphony Orchestra (Ivan Fischer), Royal Philharmonic Orchestra, London (Antal Dorati), Mozarteum Orchestra/Salzburg, Tonhalle Orchestra/Zurich (Gerd Albrecht, Ferdinand Leitner, David Zinman), etc. ARD/NDR-ZDF (West Germany), DRS-TV

Zurich (Switzerland), RTV Skopje (Yugoslavia). TV recordings at ARD & ZDF, West Germany; Radio recordings several times with all radio stations in West Germany. *Recordings:* Gidon Kremer Chamber Music Festival, 1983; Anneliese Rothenberger Presents (1984); Bach, Goldberg Variations (1986); Schumann, Carnaval & Kreisleriana (1987). *Hobbies:* Music; Literature; Modern Arts. *Current Management:* Konzertagentur Fahrenholtz, Oberweg 51, D-6000 Frankfurt/Main 1. *Address:* Büsingstrasse 1, D-1000 Berlin 41, Germany.

HOLTON Ruth, b. 1961, England. Singer (Soprano). *Education:* Choral exhibitioner at Clare College, Cambridge; Further study with Elizabeth Lane, Nancy Long and Julie Kennard. *Career:* Appearances from 1985 in Baroque music at Bruges, Turku (Finland), Munich, Amsterdam, Salerno and Innsbruck; Recitals in Cambridge, Oxford, London and at the Three Choirs Festival in Gloucester; Fauré's Requiem at the Théâtre du Châtelet, Paris, and Ilia in Idomeneo (May 1991); Radio Broadcasts: BBC Recital Radio 3, WDR Recital, both in 1992. *Recordings:* Bach's St John Passion and Cantatas, Jephtha by Handel and Carissimi, Dido and Aeneas, Handel's Israel in Egypt and Dixit Dominus, works by Schütz and Buxtehude (conducted by John Eliot Gardiner); Angel in Schütz's Christmas Story with the King's Consort and Mozart's Salzburg Masses with the Quiristers of Winchester College. *Address:* Magenta Music International, 64 Highgate High Street, London N6 5HX, England.

HOLZER Linda Ruth, b. 9 Aug 1963, Chicago, Illinois, USA. Pianist; Teacher. *Education:* BMus, Northwestern University, 1985; MMus, University of N Carolina at Chapel Hill, 1987; DMus, Florida State University, 195; Southeastern Music Centre, 1986; Studies with Donald Isaak, Michael Zenge, Barbara Rowan, Leonard Mastrogiacomo, Nelita True and John Perry. *Debut:* Soloist, Rachmaninoff Concerto No 2, Raleigh Symphony Orchestra, 1987. *Career:* Artist in Residence, North Carolina Visiting Artist Program, 1988-92; Holzer-Chambers-Robertson Trio, 1992-; Doctoral Fellow, Florida State Univ, 1993-; Appearances at the Kennedy Centre, New Orleans Centre for Creative Arts, Guest Artist with the Western Piedmont String Quartet; Soloist, 7th Biennial Festival of New Music, Tallahassee. *Recordings:* A Faun at Late Afternoon, Imprisoned Soul, 1993 (Col Legno/Aurophon). *Honours:* Artist Roster, NC Arts Council, VA Commission for the Arts, 1988-92; Grant, AJ Fletcher Foundation, 1990; First Prize, Wurlitzer Collegiate Artist Competition, 1987. *Memberships:* League of Women Composers; American Music Center; Chamber Music America; Music Teachers National Association; The College Music Society. *Hobbies:* Cycling; Woodwork; Poetry. *Address:* 3907 Paces Place, Tallahassee, FL 32311, USA.

HOLZMAIR Wolfgang, b. 1952, Austria. Singer (Baritone). *Education:* Studied in Vienna. *Career:* Appearances in opera and concert halls throughout Germany, Austria and Switzerland; British Lieder recitals from 1990, including Schubert's Schwanengesang, with Imogen Cooper at the Wigmore Hall, 1993; Engagements with Berne Opera, from 1985, including Rossini's Figaro, Valentin and Papageno, 1985-86, Gluck's Orpheus and Euegene Onegin, 1991; Season 1987-88, in Udo Zimmermann's Die Weisse Rose at the Vienna Kunstlerhaus, as Ireo in Cesti's Semiramide at Innsbruck and as Serezha in The Electrification of the Soviet Union by Nigel Osborne at Wuppertal; Season 1989-90, as Peri's Orfeo at Wuppertal, in Die Weisse Rose at Innsbruck and as Pelléas at Essen; Convent Garden debut 1993, as Papageno. *Recordings:* Lieder albums. *Address:* c/o AMI Ltd, 22 Tower Street, Covent Garden, London WC2H 9NS, England.

HOMO-LECHNER Catherine Anne Francoise, b. 29 May 1958, Maisons-Laffitte, France. Museum Curator. m. Petr Lechner, 20 Dec 1986. *Education:* History of Art and Archaeology, Specialist in Organology and Ethnomusicology; Studied classical guitar and choral singing, Conservatory, 1981; Diploma, Ecole du Louvre, 1984; PhD, 1992, (Les Cordophones dans l'Occident médiéval du VI au XII s. Essai de Paléo organologie), Paris Sorbonne. *Career:* Curator, Museum for Musical Instruments, Paris, 1981-; Contributes to broadcasts on medieval music and Archaeology, France Musique, France-Culture; Organised the 4th International Meeting of the ICTM Study Group on Music Archaeology, St Germain en Laye, 1990; Cambridge Symposium, The Archaeology of Music, 1991; Liege Snus originals, 1992. *Publications:* Editor, Archaeologia Musicalis magazine, 1987-. *Contributions to:* Cahiers de la guitare, 1982; Flute à bec et instruments ancien, 1986; Stockholm Conference, 1986; Imago Musicae, 1987; Revista de musicologia espanola, 1987; Hanover Conference. *Membership:* President, Pro Lyra Society (to establish the French Laboratory for Musical Archaeology); ICTM; ICOM. *Hobbies:* Languages; Trees and arboriculture. *Address:* Cité de la Musique, Museé de la Musique, 2, rue de la Clôture, 75019 Paris, France.

HOMOKI Andreas, b. 16 Feb 1960, Marl, Germany. Director. *Education:* Studied at the Bremen Hochschule and the Academy of Fine Arts in Berlin. *Career:* Assistant at the Deutsche Oper Berlin, the Theater des Westens and the Komische Oper, Berlin; Assistant to Harry Kupfer at the Salzburg Festival, the Stuttgart State Opera and the Cologne Opera, 1986-87; From 1987 has assisted Michael Hampe, Willy Decker and Harry Kupfer at the Cologne Opera; Assistant to Michael Hampe at the Salzburg Festival; Opera productions have included Mozart's Bastien und Bastienne in Oslo, Le Nozze di Figaro for Kammeroper Herdecke (1988); Fidelio and Jakob Lenz by Wolfgang Rihm for the Cologne Music Academy (1989-90); Directed the Michael Hampe/Australian Opera production of Die Meistersinger, 1990, for the New Zealand International Festival of the Arts; Il Trovatore for Wellington City Opera, 1991; Instructor of drama at opera department of the Cologne Music Academy, 1988-1993. Since 1993 Freelance director. Opera productions have included, L'Enfant et les Sortileges in 1992 for the Cologne Music Academy, Die Frau Ohne Schatten, Geneva Grand Opera in 1992, and Cav & Pag in State Theatre, Mainz, 1993; Madame Butterfly, Essen, 1993; Das Schloss, Hannover, 1994; Frau ohne Schatten, Paris, 1994; Wildschütz, Cologne, 1994; Rigoletto, Hamburg, 1994; Tristan und Isolde, Wiesbaden, 1994. *Address:* c/o Haydn Rawstron Ltd, PO Box 654, London SE26 4DZ, England.

HONEGGER Henri Charles, b. 10 June 1904, Geneva, Switzerland. Cellist. m. Claire Pallard, 1 son, 1 daughter. *Education:* Cello studied in Geneva; Leipzig, Germany (with Julius Klengel); Ecole Normale, Paris, France with Diran Alexanian and Pablo Casals. *Career:* Soloist with major European Orchestras, North and South American, Japanese Orchestras; Gave 1st performance of entire set of Bach's Suites in New York, 1950, Leipzig, 1952, China (1st western musician invited to give concerts in Peking, Shanghai, etc); Television appearances, Tokyo, Hong Kong, Singapore, etc; Numerous festival appearances; Numerous recordings. *Current Management:* Basil Douglas Limited, 8 St George's Terrace, London NW1 8XJ, England. *Hobbies:* Mountaineering; Skiing. *Address:* 21 Chemin de Conches, CH 1231 Conches, Switzerland.

HONEYMAN Louise Mary, b. 23 Feb. 1933, Shrewsbury, Shropshire, England. Orchestra management. Divorced, 1 son, 2 daughters. *Education:* Ludlow Girls High School. *Career:* Orchestra Management: London Mozart Players; English Bach Festival; London Bach Society; Steinitz Bach Players; London Bach Orchestra; Fires of London. *Memberships:* Director of the ABO; Elected member of the Council of the National Campaign for the Arts; Currently Executive Director of the London Mozart Players; Board Member, Trinity College of Music; Member of The Arts Club. *Address:* 92 Chatsworth Road, Croydon, CRO 1HB, England.

HÖNGEN Elisabeth, b. 7 Dec. 1906, Gevelsberg, Germany. Singer (Mezzo-Soprano). *Education:* Studied with Hermann Weissenborn in Berlin. *Debut:* Wuppertal 1933, as Lady Macbeth. *Career:* Sang in Dusseldorf 1935-40, Dresden 1940-43; Vienna Staatsoper from 1943; Covent Garden debut 1947, with the Vienna Staatsoper Company, as Dorabella, Herodias and Marcellina; Salzburg Festival 1948-59 as Orpheus, Lucretia in the local premiere of Britten's The Rape of Lucrece, Clairon in Capriccio, Marcellina in Le Nozze di Figaro and Bebett in the 1958 premiere of Julietta by Erbse; Bayreuth Festival 1951, as Fricka and Waltraute; Metropolitan Opera 1952, Clytemnestra, Herodias and Waltraute; Further appearances in Buenos Aires, Florence, Milan, Paris, Munich, Amsterdam and Berlin; Other roles include Baba the Turk, Amneris, Eboli, Carmen, The Nurse in Die Frau ohne Schatten and Venus; Professor at the Vienna Musikakademie from 1957; Retired from stage 1971. *Recordings:* Elektra (Deutsche Grammophon); Macbeth; Die Frau ohne Schatten (Decca); Das Rheingold, Die Walküre and Siegfried.

HOOPER Adrian John, b. 6 May 1953, Sydney, Australia. Conductor; Mandolinist. m. Barbara Michele Jackson, 9 Jan. 1975, 2 sons, 1 daughter. *Education:* Studied at New South Wales Conservatorium of Music. *Career:* Founder and Conductor of Australia's foremost Mandolin Orchestra, The Sydney Mandolins; Regular Player with the Australian Opera and Ballet Orchestra which accompanies the Australian Opera, and performed in such works as Otello and the Merry Widow; Worked with Sydney Symphony Orchestra in such works as Agon by Stravinsky; Regularly takes part in Radio and Concert Performances as a Mandolin Soloist and Conductor for the Australian Broadcasting Commission; Soloist, Australian Chamber Orchestra; Mandolin Teacher, New South Wales State Conservatorium of Music, 1983. *Recordings:* Have released 25 CD's of music by Australian Composers; Three (3) LP records. *Publications:* Published and Edited a number of Ancient Mandolin works; Currently Editing all known Mandolin Concertos. *Address:* 24 Kitchener Street, Oatley 2223, Australia.

HOOPER-ROE Janice, b. Buxton, Derbyshire. Singer (Mezzo-Soprano). *Education:* Studied at the Birmingham School of Music and London Opera Centre. *Career:* Sang with the English Opera Group and English Music Theatre in operas by Mozart, Henze, Oliver, Britten, Tchaikovsky and Weill; Appearances in London, Venice and Brussels and at the Edinburgh, Florence and Schwetzingen Festivals; Sang at the Aldeburgh Festival in the premiere of Death in Venice (1973) and in the British premiere of Paul Bunyan; Covent Garden debut 1979, as Olga in Eugene Onegin, returning in Parsifal, Lohengrin and Alceste; Concert engagements at the Barbican Hall and South Bank; Appearances in musicals and Gilbert and Sullivan in Europe and America. *Address:* c/o Korman International Management, Crunnells Green Cottage, Preston, Herts SG4 7UQ, England.

HOPE Daniel, b. 1974, South Africa. Concert Violinist. *Education:* Studied at the Menuhin School of Music and with Felix Andrievsky at the Royal College of Music Junior Department. *Career:* Played duos with double-bassist Garry Karr, 1983, Bartok Duos with Yehudi Menuhin for German TV, 1984; International debut with the Jyvaskyl Symphony Orchestra of Finland, playing the Mendelssohn Concerto; Brighton Festival in Bach's Fifth Brandenburg concerto, recitals at the Purcell Room London, the Bach Violin Concertos with the Milton Keynes Chamber Orchestra and concert with the Hallé Orchestra under Menuhin; Vivaldi's Four Seasons with the Aachen City Orchestra, Prokofiev's First concerto in Finland and London and the Beethoven Concerto on tour in Europe; Appearances at the Schleswig-Holstein Festival, Germany. *Honours:* Winner, High Bean violin Competition, 1986; Peter Morrison Concerto Competition, 1989. *Address:* c/o Anglo Swiss Ltd, 3 Primrose Mews, 1a Sharpleshall Street, London WN1 8YW, England.

HOPFERWEISER Josef, b. 25 May 1938, Graz,

Austria. Singer (Tenor). *Education:* Musikhochschule Graz. *Career:* Frequent appearances at the Vienna Volksoper, notably in Notre Dame by Schmidt; State Operas of Hamburg, Munich and Stuttgart; Further engagements in Nancy, Frankfurt, Graz, Milan, Rome and San Francisco; Sang in the premiere of Troades by Aribert Reimann, Munich 1986; Sang Froh in Das Rheingold at Munich 1987, Alwa in Lulu at Madrid 1988; Vienna Staatsoper 1990, as Walther in Die Meistersinger. Many concert appearances. *Recordings include:* Alwa in Berg's Lulu, conducted by Christoph von Dohnányi (Decca).

HOPKIN John Arden, b. 11 Feb. 1947, Laramie, Wyoming, USA. Opera Director; Singer; Music Educator. m. D. Lorraine Rudd, 11 Aug. 1969, 5 sons. *Education:* BMus, Brigham Young University, 1971; MMus, North Texas State University, 1974; DMA, Eastman School of Music, 1978. *Debut:* Fort Worth Opera Company. *Career:* Appeared as Baritone in 30 opera/musical theatre roles with: Fort Worth Opera, Boris Goldovsky Opera Company, Chautauqua Opera Company, Syracuse Opera, Beaumont Opera; Recitalist and concert artist, North and Central America; Specialist in Latin American vocal music; Opera Director and Studio Voice Teacher, 1977-, Head of Vocal Studies, 1977-87, Texas Christian University; Opera Director, Bay View Music Festival, 1981-88; Guest Director: Fort Worth Opera, Arkansas Opera, Southwestern Opera Institute. *Recording:* Andrew Barton's The Disappointment (1st American Opera), Vox Turnabout Records. *Publication:* The Influence of the Commedia dell'Arte on Opera Buffa of the Eighteenth Century, 1974. *Memberships:* AGMA; AEA professional unions; National Association of Teachers of Singing; National Opera Association; Pi Kappa Lambda. *Hobbies:* Athletics; Camping; Boy Scouts of America.

HOPKINS Antony, b. 21 March 1921, London, England. Musician; Author. m. Alison Purves 1947, (dec 1991). *Education:* Royal College of Music with Cyril Smith and Gordon Jacob. *Career:* Lecturer, Royal College of Music 15 years; Director, Intimate Opera Company 1952-64; Series of Radio broadcasts Talking about Music, 1954-92. *Compositions include:* Operas: Lady Rohesia; Three's Company; Hands across the Sky; Dr Musikus; Ten o'clock Call; The Man from Tuscany; Ballets: Etude; Cafe des Sports; 3 Piano Sonatas; Numerous scores of incidental music including Oedipus; The Love of Four Colonels; Cast a Dark Shadow; Pickwick Papers, Billy Budd; Decameron Nights. *Publications include:* Understanding Music 1979; The Nine Symphonies of Beethoven 1980; The Concertgoer's Companion, 2 volumes 1984, 1986. *Honours:* Gold Medal at Royal College of Music 1943; Italia Prize for Radio programme, 1951, 1957; Medal, City of Tokyo, for services to music, 1973; Commander of the British Empire 1976. *Address:* Woodyard, Ashridge, Berkhamsted, Herts HP4 1PS, England.

HOPKINS John Raymond, b. 19 July 1927, Preston, England. Conductor; Director. m. (1)Ann Rosemary Blamey, (dec), 5d; (2)Geraldene Catherine Scott, 1 July 1987. *Education:* Cello Student, Associate Fellow, Royal Manchester College of Music. *Career:* Assistant Conductor, BBC Glasgow, 1949-52; Conductor: BBC Northern Orchestra, 1952-57; National Orchestra, New Zealand; Musical Director, New Zealand Opera Comapny, 1957-63; Director of Music, ABC, 1963-73; Dean, School of Music, Victoria College of Arts, Melbourne, 1973-86; Director of New South Wales Conservtorium of Music, 1986-; Artistic Adviser, Sydney Symphony Orchestra, 1986-88; Education Consultant, Sydney Symphony Orchestra; Principal Conductor, Auckland Philharmonic Orchestra, 1983-; Director, NSW State Conservatorium, 1986-93; Principal Conductor, Auckland Philharmonic Orchestra, 1983-91. *Recordings:* Various with Melbourne, New Zealand and Moscow Symphony Orchestras. *Honours:* OBE, 1970; Queen's Silver Jubilee Medal, 1977; Title, Professor, Sidney University, 1991. *Hobbies:* Gardening; Walking. *Address:* 1290 Mountain Lagoon Road, Bilpin, NSW 2758, Australia.

HOPKINS Robert Elliott, b. 2 Oct. 1931, Greensboro, North Carolina, USA. University Professor Emeritus. *Education:* BM, 1953, MM, 1954, DMA, 1959, Eastman School of Music; Postdoctoral study, Akademie für Musik, Vienna, Austria. *Debut:* As Pianist, Vienna, 1960, New York, 1970; As Organist, New York, 1968. *Career:* Instructor, 1954-57, Head of Music Department, 1960-63, Mars Hill College; Professor of Piano, Organ and Harpsichord, Youngstown State University, 1963-1993; Visiting Lecturer in Piano, Westminster College, New Wilmington, Pennsylvania, 1968-81. *Publication:* Alexander Reinagle; The Philadelphia Sonatas (Volume V of Recent Researches in American Music), 1978. *Contributions to:* New Grove Dictionary of Music and Musicians; New Grove Dictionary of American Music; American Music; New Grove Dictionary of Opera. *Address:* 21 Audubon Lane, Poland, OH 44514, USA.

HOPKINS Sarah, b. 1958, Lower Hutt, New Zealand. Composer; Performer. *Education:* New South Wales Conservatorium of Music High School; Victorian College of the Arts Music School. *Career:* Toured extensively throughout Australia, Britain, Europe and the USA; Musician in Residence, GIAE, Gippsland, Victoria, 1978; Musician in Residence, CIT, Caulfield, Victoria, 1979; Composer in Residence, Arts Victoria Music '81, 1981; Musician in Residence 1981, Guest Artist in Residence 1983, Brown's Mart Community Arts Project; Let's Make Music, Northern Territory, 1982; New Music ACTION Residency, Victorian College of the Arts, Melbourne, 1982; Composer-performer in Residence, Darwin Theatre Group, 1984; Artist in Schools, 1985 and 1986; Composer-performer Sky Song project, Brown's Mart, Darwin and major tour 1987 and 1988; Performer in Residence The Exploration San Francisco 1988; Composer in Residence NT Arts Council, Darwin 1989. *Compositions:* Ensemble Works: Cello Timbre 1976; Seasons II, 1978; Cellovoice, 1982; Whirlies, 1983; Sunrise/Sunset, 1983; Interweave 1984; Deep Whirly Duo, 1984; Aura Swirl, 1986; Eclipse 1986; Bougainvillea Bells 1986; Cello Chi 1986; Flight of the Wild Goose, 1987; Ring 1987; Songs of the Wind 1989; Circle Bell Mantra, 1989; Spiral Bells 1989; Soul Song 1989; Transformation 1989; Heart Songs 1989. *Recordings:* Soundworks 1: Collaborative Works; Soundworks 2: Solo and Duo Works; Soundworks 3: Whirliworks Performance; Interweave; Soundworks Performance. *Address:* c/o Australian Music Centre, PO Box 49, Broadway 2007, Australia.

HOPPE Heinz, b. 26 Jan. 1924, Saerbeck, Germany. Singer (Tenor). *Education:* Studied with Fred Husler in Detmold. *Debut:* Munster 1953, as Xerxes in the opera by Handel. *Career:* Bremen 1955-57; First Lyric Tenor at the Hamburg Staatsoper 1957-70; Glyndebourne Festival 1961, as Belmonte in Die Entführung; Concert Tours of North America, Spain, Belgium and France; Successful in operetta and on German television; Teacher at the Musikhochschule Mannheim from 1977. *Recordings include:* Operettas on Telefunken and Deutsche Grammophon; Narraboth in Salome (EMI).

HORÁCEK Jaroslav, b. 29 April 1924, Dehylov, Czechoslovakia. Singer (Bass); Teacher. *Education:* Studied with Rudolf Vasek, Karel Kugler and Peter Burja in Ostrava, Apollo Granforte in Prague. *Debut:* Opava 1945, as Kecal in The Bartered Bride. *Career:* Sang in Ostrava 1951-53, then at the National Theatre Prague: sang in the standard bass repertory, and in operas by Smetana, Janáček and Dvořák; Took part in the 1959 premiere of Mirandolina by Martinů; Guest appearances in Warsaw, Sofia, Amsterdam, Boston, Edinburgh (1964, with the Prague Company), Naples, Barcelona and Boston; Sang Debussy's Arkel at Prague 1986. Don Giovanni at the bicentenary performance of the opera, 1987; Many concert appearances; Producer of Czech operas at La Scala Milan; Teacher at the Prague Conservatory. *Address:* c/o National Theatre, PO Box 865, 112 30 Prague 1, Czech Republic.

HORÁK Josef, b. 24 Mar 1931, Znojmo, Czechoslovakia. Bass Clarinettist; Music Educator. *Education:* State High School of Musical and Dramatic Arts. *Career:* Clarinettist, Czech Radio Symphony Orchestra and State Philharmonic, Brno; Concert Soloist; Professor, State Music High School, Prague; Chamber Music Lecturer, Biberach West Germany; Member, Chamber Music Ensemble Due Boemi di Praga with Emma Kovarnova, Prague 1963-; Concerts in Europe, USA, Asia and Africa; TV programmes in Czechoslovakia, Germany and Romania; Radio programmes, many countries of Europe and USA; Discovered the bass clarinet as a solo instrument, 1955 he played the very first Bass Clar. Recital in the world; Chamber soloist of the Czech Philharmonic Orchestra. *Recordings:* Due Boemi di Praga (Panton); At the New Ways (Supraphon); Bass Clarinet, the New Solo Instrument (Carus); The Paganini of the Bass Clarinet; The Singing Bass Clarinet; CD: Horák-New Age of Bass Clarinet, Horák and his Bass Clarinet-New Sound, The Singing Bass Clarinet (NSS Records), and also about 85 single recordings on various records. *Memberships:* Union of Czech Interpreters; Honorary member, Jeunesses Musicales de Suisse. *Honours:* Gold Medal 1958; Prize, L Janáček Competition, 1959; Hi-Fi Festival, Paris, 1965; Pick of the Year, London, 1974; Clarinet Super Record, Tokyo, 1986 . *Address:* Bubenska 39, 170 21 Prague 7, Czech Republic.

HORIGOME Yuzuko, b. 1960, Tokyo, Japan. Violinist. *Education:* Studied at Toho Gakuen School of Music, Tokyo, with Toshiya Eto; graduated 1980. *Career:* Won Queen Elisabeth of the Belgians International Competition 1980; London debut 1983, concerts with London Symphony Orchestra under Claudio Abbado and André Previn; US debut 1982 at Tanglewood, with Boston Symphony; later appearances in Pittsburgh, Chicago, Los Angeles and Montreal; 1988/9 season includes concerts in Europe and Japan with the Salzburg Camerata, Royal Liverpool Philharmonic and Scottish National Orchestras, and at the Prague Spring Festival; featured in film Testimony on the life of Shostakovich. *Recordings:* Bach Concerti with the English Chamber Orchestra for CBS Sony; Bach's Solo Violin sonatas; Sibelius and Mendelssohn Concertos with the Concertgebouw Orchestra and Ivan Fischer. *Address:* c/o Harrison/Parrott Ltd., 12 Penzance Place, London W11 4PA, England.

HORN Heiner, b. 20 June 1920, Darmstadt, Germany. Singer (Bass-Baritone). *Education:* Studied in Darmstadt and Berlin. *Career:* Sang at first in Darmstadt, then at the Cologne Opera: retired 1985; Sang Jochanaan, Kaspar in Der Freischütz, Wozzeck, Paris Opera, Amsterdam, Brussels, Luxembourg, Zurich, Bern, Venice, Bologna, Trieste, Lisbon, Barcelona; Der fliegende Holländer; Bett in Zar und Zimmermann, Plunkett in Martha and Kothner in Die Meistersinger, other roles: Pizarro, Mephisto (Gounod, Berlioz), Ramphis, Sarastro, Nick Shadow, Dapertutto, King Henry, Gunther, Klingsor, Fasolt, Fafner, Daland, Zar Saltan, Varlaam, Tomsky, Scarpia, Alfio, Escasmillo, Basilio, Father Guardian, Inquisitor, and many others; 15 Years in WDR Operas and about 20 German opera houses; Sang in the 1965 premiere of Die Soldaten by Zimmermann; Concert appearances, and guest engagements at opera houses elsewhere in Germany. *Recordings:* Sparafucile in Rigoletto (Electrola); Die Soldaten. *Address:* c/o Oper der Stadt Köln, Offenbachplate, D-5000 Cologne, Germany.

HORN Volker, b. 1945, Klagenfurt, Germany. Singer (Tenor). *Education:* Studied at the Vienna Musichochschule. *Career:* Sang as boy soprano in the Bayreuth production of Tannhäuser directed by Wieland Wagner, 1954-55; Has sung at the Deutsche Oper Berlin from 1976; Guest appearances in Lyon, Karlsruhe, Munich and Strasbourg as Max in Der Freischütz and Loge in Das Rheingold; Bayreuth and Salzburg Easter Festivals, 1980; Deutsche Oper Berlin 1987, as Galba in Die toten Augen by d'Albert; Sang Hans Kraft in Der Kobold by Siegfried Wagner, Rudolstadt, 1992; Concert and oratorio appearances in Germany, Austria and Switzerland. *Recordings:* Die Zauberflöte and Nabucco (Deutsche Grammophon). *Address:* c/o Deutsche Oper

Berlin, Richard Wagnerstrasse 10, D-1000 Berlin, Germany.

HORNE David, b. 1970, Stirling, Scotland. Concert Pianist; Composer. *Education:* Studied at St Mary's Music School, Edinburgh and the Curtis Institute, Philadelphia and Harvard University. *Career:* Soloist with BBC Philharmonic and Symphony, Welsh and Scottish Orchestras, CBSO the Scottish National and London Sinfonietta; Festival engagements at Edinburgh, Aldeburgh, Almelda, London; BBC Promenade Concert debut, 1990, with Prokofiev's Third Concerto; Other repertoty includes Ravel, G major, Gershwin Concerto, Brahms concerto, D Minor, Beethoven 1st Concerto and Choral Fantasia, Ian Hamilton 2nd concerto (world Premiere), Mozart K271; Frank Symphonic Variations; Tchaikovsky 1st Concerto. *Compositions:* String Quartet, 1988; Splintered Unisons, for clarinet, violin, cello and piano, 1988; Towards Dharma for 6 instruments, 1989; Light Emerging for symphony orchestra, 1989; Out of the Air, 1990; Contraries and Progressions, 1991 for ensemble; Northscape for chamber orchesra, 1992; Piano Concerto, 1992. *Honours:* First Prize, National Mozart Competition, 1987; First, BBC Young Musician of the Year, (piano) 1988; Winner, Huddersfield Contemporary Music Festival Composers Competition, 1988. *Address:* c/o Boosey & Hawkes, 295 Regent Street, London WIR 8JH, England.

HORNE Marilyn, b. 16 Jan. 1934, Bradford, Pennsylvania, USA. American Mezzo-Soprano Singer. Divorced, 1 daughter. *Education:* University of Southern California, studied under William Vennard. *Debut:* Gelsenkirchen, 1957; San Francisco Opera 1960 as Berg's Marie. *Career:* Performed with several German Opera Companies in Europe 1956; Since appeared at Covent Garden, London; The Chicago Lyric Opera; La Scala, Milan; Metropolitan Opera, New York; Repertoire includes: Eboli (Don Carlo), Marie (Wozzeck), Adalgisa (Norma), Jane Seymour (Anna Bolena), Amneris (Aida), Carmen, Rosina (Barbiere di Siviglia), Fides (La Prophète), Mignon, Isabella (L'Italiana in Algeri), Romeo (I Capuleti ed i Montecchi), Tancredi (Tancredi), Orlando (Orlando Furioso), Dalila (Samson et Dalila); Returned to Covent Garden in 1989 as Isabella; Other Rossini roles include Malcolm in La Donna del Lago (Covent Garden, 1985), Falliero and Andromache in Ermione (Pesaro 1986, 1987) and Calbo in Maometto II (San Francisco 1988); Sang Rosina at the Met 1989, Vivaldi's Orlando at San Francisco; Santa Fe 1990 as Gluck's Orpheus; Season 1992 in a Rossini 200th birthday gala at Fisher Hall, New York; Isabella at San Francisco; Last appearance in Rossini as Isabella (Italiana in Algeri), Covent Garden, 1993. *Recordings:* Many recordings including Semiramide, Orfeo ed Euridice, Anna Bolena, Don Giovanni, Il Trovatore (Decca); Le Prophète, Mignon, Tancredi, Il Barbiere di Siviglia, Suor Angelica (CBS); Carmen (DGG); Norma, Falstaff, Orlando Furioso, La Navarraise, L'Italiana in Algeri (RCA); La Damnation de Faust (Decca). *Honours:* 5 Hon. doctorates. *Hobbies:* Needlepoint; Swimming; Reading; Sightseeing. *Address:* c/o Colombia Artists Management, Inc., 165 West 57th Street, New York, NY 10019, USA.

HORNIK Gottfried, b. 5 Aug. 1940, Vienna, Austria. Singer (Baritone). *Education:* Studied in Vienna. *Career:* Sang at Klagenfurt as Papageno and as Silvio in Pagliacci; Graz Opera as Mozart's Figaro, Don Giovanni and Alberich; Deutsche Oper Berlin and San Francisco, as Beckmesser in Die Meistersinger; Salzburg Easter Festival as Kurwenal in Tristan und Isolde, under Karajan; Sang Alberich and other Wagner roles at the Vienna Staatsoper; Leipzig Opera, as the villains in Les Contes d'Hoffmann; Cologne Opera 1983, Klingsor in Parsifal, Covent Garden 1987, as Faninal in Der Rosenkavalier; Deutsche Oper Berlin 1988 as Alberich in the Ring; Sang Wozzeck at the Metropolitan 1990; Orestes in Elektra at Athens, 1992. *Recordings:* Die Zauberflöte, Tosca and Die Meistersinger conducted by Karajan (Deutsche Grammophon); Der Wildschütz by Lortzing.

HORNSBY David McMillan, b. 14 Nov 1928, Texas,

USA. Pianist; Educator. m. Lenda Ruth Jones, 10 Nov 1969, (div). 1s. *Education:* BMus, (piano), Texas Christian University, 1949; MA, (Music and Music Education), Columbia University, 1950; Postgraduate Study, University of Colorado, 1949, 1956-57, 1978; Piano study in Fort Worth with Jeannette Tillett; Performing Member of Master Class under Ernst Von Dohnanyo, 1948; Piano pupil of Dr Edwin Hughes, New York City; Piano study at University of Colorado with Howard Waltz; Piano Pedagogy Classes with Dr Raymond Burrows. *Career includes:* Annual tours of Judging for National Guild of Piano Teachers, 1963-78, 1980-; Piano Studio, San Antonio, Texas, 1980-; Music Director, Colegio Bolivar, Call, Colombia, 1978-79; Piano concerts for nine seasons, at the Chautauqua Piano Studio, Boulder, Colorado, 1956-78; Lecturer, Music Teachers National Association Convention, 1975; Music Director, San Antonio Academy of Texas, 1981-84; Piano Studio, San Antonio, 1980-; Annual tours of judging for the National Guild of Piano Teachers, 1963-78, 1980-; Judging tours have included, Miami and the Guild Auditions, Carnegie Hall in NYC; Numerous solo piano recitals. *Publications include:* Co-author, Bassetti Primer, 1975; also poetry and articles. *Honours:* Piano Guild Hall of Fame, 1971; Margie B Boswell Prize for Best Alumni Poem, Texas Christian University, 1952. *Memberships include:* National Guild of Piano Teachers (Board of Judges); The Bohemians, (New York Musicians Club); The Leschetizky Association; Music Teachers National Association; Texas and San Antonio Music Teachers Associations; Life Member Phi Mu Alpha Sinfonia. *Hobbies:* Creative writing; Travel; Photography. *Address:* 8000 Midcrown, Apt 1507, San Antonio, TX 78218, USA.

HOROVITZ Joseph, b. 26 May 1926, Vienna, Austria. Composer. *Education:* New College Oxford; Royal College of Music, London; Nadia Boulanger, Paris. *Career:* Music Director Bristol Old Vic 1949-51; Conductor Festival Gardens Orchestra, London 1951; Co-conductor Ballets Russes English Season 1952; Associate Director Intimate Opera Company 1952-63; Assistant conductor Glyndebourne Opera 1956; Professor of Composition Royal College of Music 1961- . *Compositions:* 16 ballets including Alice in Wonderland, Les femmes d'Alger, Concerto for Dancers; Two one-act operas: The Dumb Wife and Gentleman's Island; Orchestral: Concertos for violin, trumpet, jazz harpsichord, 2 for clarinet, tuba, oboe, percussion; Horizon Overture; Jubilee Serenade; Sinfonietta; Fantasia on a Theme of Couperin; Toy Symphony for 17 instruments and piano quintet; Choral: Samson, oratorio; Captain Noah and his Floating Zoo; Summer Sunday; Endymion; Brass band music includes a Euphonium concerto, Ballet for Band and Concertino Classico; For wind band: Ad Astra, Windharp, Dance Suite, Bacchus on Blue Ridge; Chamber: 5 String Quartets; Oboe Sonatina; Oboe Quartet; Clarinet sonatina; Two pieces for Hoffnung Concerts: Metamorphoses on a Bed-Time Theme and Horroratorio; Numerous scores for theatre productions, films and TV series. *Memberships:* Council of Composers' Guild 1970; Executive Council of Performing Rights Society 1971-; Fellow, Royal College of Music 1981; President of CIAM of the International Federation of Societies of Authors and Composers 1981-89. *Address:* 7 Dawson Place, London W2 4TD, England.

HORSLEY Colin, b. 23 Apr. 1920, Wanganui, New Zealand. Pianist; Professor. *Education:* Royal College of Music. *Debut:* At Invitation of Sir John Barbirolli at Hallé Concerts, Manchester, 1943. *Career:* Soloist with all leading orchestras of Great Britain, the Royal Philharmonic Society, 1953, 1959, Promenade Concerts; Toured Belgium, Holland, Spain, France, Scandinavia, Malta, Ceylon, Malaya, Australia and New Zealand; Festival appearances include: Aix-en-Provence, International Contemporary Music Festival, Palermo, British Music Festivals in Belgium, Holland and Finland; Broadcasts frequently. *Recordings:* HMV; Meridian; Symposium Records. *Hobby:* Gardening. *Address:* Belmont, Dreemskerry, Maughold, Isle of Man.

HORVAT Milan, b. 28 July 1919, Pakrac, Yugoslavia.

Conductor. *Education:* Studied at the Zagreb Music Academy 1939-46. *Career:* Began as pianist and choral conductor; Conductor of the Zagreb Philharmonic 1946-53 and 1958-59; Chief Conductor of the Radio Telefis Eireann Symphony 1953-58; Principal Conductor of the Zagreb Opera 1958-65: many premieres of Yugoslav music; Guest conductor with major orchestras in Europe and the USA; Musical Director of the Dubrovnik Festival 1965; Principal Conductor of the Austrian Radio Symphony 1969-75; Professor of Conducting at the Graz Academy 1975; Conductor of the Zagreb Symphony Orchestra, 1975-. *Recordings:* Haydn Harpsichord Concertos (with Robert Veryon-Lacroix); Mozart Violin and Piano Concertos (with Jean Fournier and Jörg Demus); Hindemith Mathis der Maler Symphony; Shostakovich Symphonies Nos. 1 and 9, 1st Piano Concerto, with the Zagreb Philharmonic; Beethoven Violin Concerto (with Igor Ozim). *Address:* c/o Zagreb Philharmonic Orchestra, Trjanska 66, 4100 Zagreb, Croatia.

HORVÁTH László, b. 14 July 1945, Koszeg, Hungary. Musician (Clarinettist). div., 1 son, 1 daughter. *Education:* Music Gymnasium, Gyor, 1960-64; Studied with Professor Gyorgy Balassa, 1964-69, MMus with distinction, 1969, Liszt Ference Academy of Music, Budapest; Bursary student, Conservatoire de Musique, Paris, 1969-70; Studied with Professor Ulysse Delecluse. *Debut:* Competition in Budapest, 1965. *Career:* Clarinettist, 1965-68, Soloist, Leading Clarinettist, 1968-, Hungarian State Symphony Orchestra, Budapest; Toured as soloist, Buffet-Crampon Company, Japan, 1981, 1986; Many solo recitals around world, appearances as clarinet- duo with Klara Kormendi, chamber music with Philharmonic Wind Quintett, Europe, USA, Canada, Australia, Japan, 1983-; Recitals, Claude Champagne Hall, Montreal, 1991, 1993; Radio broadcasts, Budapest, Paris, London, Tokyo; TV appearances, Hungary; Professor: Conservatory of Music: Debrecen, 1974-79; Bela Bartók Conservatory of Music, Budapest, 1980-; Masterclasses, Montreal, 1991, 1993; Jury Member, International Competition for Musical Performers, Geneva, 1990. *Recordings:* Works by Leo Weiner, 1970, Attila Bozay, 1976, 1979, Carl and Johann Stamitz, 1979, Johann Molter, 1979, 1991, Mozart, 1981; 20th Century Clarinet Music, 1991; Clarinetto all'ungherese, 1992. *Current Management:* Interkoncert, Vorosmarty ter 1m H-1368 Budapest, Hungary. *Address:* 6 Jászai Mari tér, V/44, H-1137 Budapest, Hungary.

HORWOOD Michael Stephen, b. 24 May 1947, Buffalo, New York, USA. Composer. m. 16 Aug 1974, 2 sons. *Education:* BA, Music, State University of New York, Buffalo, 1969; MA, Composition, State University of New York, Buffalo, 1971. *Debut:* Performance of his works, Baird Hall, State University of New York, Buffalo, 1966. *Career:* Instructor, Music, Humber College of Applied Arts and Technology, Ontario, Canada, 1972-. *Compositions include:* Durations, 1-4 keyboards, 1965; Women of Trachis, Incidental Music, chamber orchestra, 1966; Concerto for Double Bass and String Orchestra, 1967, rev. 1981; Double Quintet, two wind quintets, 1968; Asteroids, brass quartet, 1969; 5,3,4 jazz orchestra and percussion ensemble, 1973; Facets, augmented chamber group, 1974; Bipolarity, accordion & string trio, 1979; Birds, 1979; piccolo & piano, Psalm 121, soprano & piano, 1980; 1, 1982; Exit to Your Left, wind quintet, 1982; String Quartet No. 1, 1982;9 Microduets, 1980-83; Sonata for cello and piano, 1983; Brass-Fast, brass quintet, 1984; Symphony No 1, 1984; Amusement Park Suite, 1986; Nervous Disorder, chamber, 1988; Broken Chords, solo piano, 1990; National Park Suite, orchestra, 1991; Talos IV, solo accordion, 1975; Interphase, chamber sextet, 1975; Suite for Accordion and Percussion, 1985. *Recordings:* Overture for Piano Player and Two Assistants; Piece Percussionique No. 5, 1982; Birds, 1982; Dynamite, 1983; Six Pieces for Piano; Motility, 1986.*Publications:* Brass-Fast, Jamar Music Ltd, 1992. *Address:* 8 Grovetree Place, Bramalea, Ontario L6S 1S8, Canada.

HORYSA Inghild, b. 2 Jan. 1944, Bielitz, Germany.

Singer (Mezzo-Soprano). *Education:* Studied with Helena Braun in Munich. *Debut:* Munich Staatsoper 1966, as Hansel in Hansel and Gretel. *Career:* Munich 1969, in the premiere of The Play of Love and Death by Cikker; Sang at Nuremberg, the Vienna Volksoper, Dusseldorf, Frankfurt, Mannheim, Hamburg and Stuttgart; Other roles include Dorabella, Amneris, Eboli, Venus, Branagene, Marina (Boris Godunov), Orsini (Lucrezia Borgia), Fricka (Walküre), Clytemnestra (Elektra), Baba the Turk (The Rake's Progress) and Octavian; Frequent concert appearances. *Address:* c/o Nuremberg Opera House, Nuremberg, Germany.

HOSE Anthony Paul, b. 24 May 1944, London, England. Musician; Conductor. m. Moira Griffiths, 8 July 1977, 2 daughters.*Education:* Junior Exhibitioner, Royal College of Music, London, 1955-62; Student, Royal College of Music, 1962-66; ARCM. *Career:* Glyndebourne Festival, 1966-68; Bremen Opera, Federal Republic of Germany, 1968-69; Welsh National Opera, 1969-83; Music Director, Buxton Festival, 1979-87; Artistic Director, Welsh Chamber Orchestra, 1986- ; Artistic Director, Beaumaris Festival, 1986-; Realisation of Cavalli's Giasone; Artistic Director, Buxton Festival, 1988-91; Professor, Royal College of Music, 1991-; Professor, Royal Academy of Music, 1992-. *Publications:* English translation: Grétry: Le Huron; Elektra (Strauss); Ariodante (Handel); Don Quixote (Conti). *Hobbies:* Good food and wine; Football. *Address:* Fairfield House, Aberdare, Mid-Glamorgan, CF44 7PL, Wales.

HOSEK Jiri, b. 20 Aug 1955, Prague, Czechoslovakia. Musician; Solo Concert Violoncellist. m. Marie Kaplanova, 2 Apr 1977, 2 daughters. *Education:* Prague Conservatory; Academy of Music, Prague; Conservatory National, Paris; International courses, Nice, Szombately. *Debut:* Tchaikovsky's Rococco variations, 1974. Foreign tours: USSR, Germany, France, Italy, Poland; Many TV and radio appearances including A Kraft concertos. *Recordings:* Elgar Concerto, Panton LP, 1985; A Kraft Concertos, Panton LP; Radio recordings: Vivaldi Concerto, D Popper Konzertstücke; Dvořák's Rondo, Tchaikovsky's Rococco variations; Prokofiev, Symphony Concerto, Elgar Concerto. *Current Management:* Radio Symphony Orchestra, Prague, Czech Republic. *Address:* Sudomerska 29, 13000 Prague 3, Czech Republic.

HOSIER John, b. 18 Nov 1928, England. College Principal. *Education:* MA, St John's College, Cambridge, 1954. *Career:* Lecturer, Ankara, Turkey, 1951-53; Music Producer, BBC Radio for Schools, 1953-59; Seconded to ABC, Sydney to advise on educational music programmes, 1959-60; Music Producer, Subsequently Senior and Executive Producer, BBC TV, pioneering first regular music broadcasts to schools, 1960-73; ILEA Staff Inspector for Music, Director of Centre for Young Musicians, 1973-76; Principal, Guildhall School of Music and Drama, 1978-88; Director, Hong Kong Academy for Performing Arts, 1989-93. *Compositions:* Music for Cambridge Revivals Of Parnassus, 1949, Humourous Lovers, 1951; Somethings Burning, Mermaid, 1974; many Radio and Television productions. *Publications:* The Orchestra, 1961, Revised edition, 1977; various books, songs and arrangements for children; Contributor to professional journals. *Honours:* FGSM, 1978; Honorary RAM, 1980; FRCM, 1989; CBE, 1984; FRNCM, 1985; Hon. D. Mus (The City University) 1986; Hon FTCL 1986. *Memberships:* Founder Member, Vice Chairman, UK Council for Music Education and Training, 1975-81; Gulbenkian Enquiry into Training Musicians, 1978; Trustee, Hirnichsen Foundation, 1981-88; Music Panel, British Council, 1984-88; GLAA, 1984-86; Vice-Chairman, Kent Opera, 1985-88; Council of Management, Royal Philharmonic Society, 1982-89; Governing Body, Chetham's School; Governing Body, NYO FRSA, 1976; Hong Kong Council for the Performing Arts; General Committee, Hong Kong Philharmonic Orchestra. *Address:* 1 Hartham Close, London N7 9JH, England.

HOTTER Hans, b. 19 Jan. 1909, Offenbach, Germany. Singer (Bass-Baritone) m. Helga Fischer

1936, 1 son, 1 daughter. *Education:* Studied with Matthaus Remer in Munich. *Career:* Stage debut Troppau 1930; Sang in Prague 1932-34; Staatsoper Hamburg 1934-37; Munich Staatsoper from (1937), notably in the premieres of Strauss's Friedenstag (1938) and Capriccio (1942); Salzburg from 1942, as Mozart's Count, Sarastro, Don Giovanni, Mandryka (Arabella) and Morosus (Die schweigsame Frau); Sang Jupiter in the premiere of Die Liebe der Danae, 1944; Bayreuth Festival from 1952, notably as Hans Sachs, Wotan, Gurnemanz, Pogner, Kurwenal, Gunther, and as The Dutchman; Sang with the company of the Vienna Staatsoper at Covent Garden in 1947, as Mozart's Count and Don Giovanni; returned as Sachs and Wotan, and as producer of The Ring (1962-64); Metropolitan Opera debut 1950, as The Dutchman; Sang in the premiere of Von Einem's Besuch der Alten Dame, Vienna 1971; Sang Wotan for the last time at the Paris Opéra, 1972, but continued to appear at Munich as Schigolch (Lulu) and as the Speaker in Die Zauberflöte (Milan 1985); Returned to London 1989, as the Speaker in Schoenberg's Gurrelieder, at the Festival Hall; Noted concert singer in the Lieder of Schubert and in the Choral Symphony. *Recordings:* Die Zauberflöte and Die Frau ohne Schatten (Deutsche Grammophon); Die Walküre, Siegfried, Lulu and Parsifal (Decca); Der fliegende Holländer (Vox). *Address:* Emil-Dittler-Str. 26, D-81479 München, Germany.

HOU Runyu, b. 6 Jan. 1945, Kunming, China. Orchestral Conductor. m. Su Jia Hou, 15 Sept. 1971, 1 son, 1 daughter. *Education:* Musical study, Middle School of Shanghai Conservatory; Conducting, Shanghai Conservatory; Study at Musikhochschule, Cologne, Federal Republic of Germany, and Mozarteum, Salzburg, Austria, 1981-85. *Debut:* Kunming, 1954. *Career:* Orchestral Conductor, 1977, Vice Music Director, 1986, Shanghai Symphony Orchestra; Guest Conductor: Rheinische Philharmonic, 1985; China Broadcasting Symphony Orchestra, 1988; China Central Philharmonic, 1988; Hong Kong Philharmonic, 1988; Principal Conductor, 1990 Shanghai Symphony Orchestra, Debut in Carnegie Hall, New York, 1990 (to 100 years celebration of the Carnegie Hall). *Honour:* Honorary Member, Richard Wagner-Verband, Cologne. *Membership:* Chinese Musicians Association. *Hobbies:* Sport; Literature. *Current Management:* Konzertdirektion Drissen, International Artists' Management, Postfach 1666, D-6500 Mainz, Germany. *Address:* 105 Hunan Road, Shanghai, China.

HOUGH Stephen, b. 22 Nov 1961, Heswall, Cheshire, England. Pianist. *Career:* Performances with many leading orchestras including: Chicago, Detroit, Toronto, Baltimore Symphonies, Cleveland, Los Angeles Philharmonic, all major British orchestras including London Symphony, Philharmonia, Royal & London Philharmonics, BBC Symphony, English Chamber; Numerous radio broadcasts, UK & USA; Recitals throughout UK, USA, Germany, France, Italy, Australia and Far East; London Proms debut, 1985; Appeared annually, Ravinia Festival, 1984-88, Mostly Mozart Festival, 1988 and 1989, Hollywood Bowl, annually; Played Bartók's Third Piano Concerto at the 1993 London Proms. *Recordings:* 2 Hummel Piano Concertos (Chandos), Music by Liszt & Schumann, & Piano Albums 1 and 2 (all Virgin Classics); Brahms 2nd Piano COncerto, Britten Piano Music. *Honours:* Dayas Gold Medal, Royal Northern College of Music; Winner, Naumburg International Piano Competition; Best Concerto Record Award, Gramophone magazine, 1987. *Current Management:* Harrison Parrott Ltd. *Address:* c/ o Harrison Parrott Ltd, 12 Penzance Place, London W11 4PA, England.

HOULIHAN Timothy de Quetteville, b. 3 Oct 1954, Jersey, Channel Islands, England. Concert Pianist; Private Tutor. *Education:* Studied piano at RAM, under Green Green, 1972-79, ARCM, 1972; LRAM, 1975; Recital Dipoma, 1977. *Debut:* Jersey Opera House, 1980; Wigmore Hall, London, 1987. *Career:* Recital and concerto engagements in UK and major London venues; St Martin in the fields, Purcell Room, South Bank; Programmes featuring music of Liszt; Recordings for television and radio. *Honours:* Hodgeson Memorial Scholarship, 1975; Martin Musical Scholarship, 1976. *Memberships:* Incorporated Society of Musicians; the Royal Academy of Music CLub; International Liszt Centre. *Hobbies:* Bird watching; Photography; Crossword Puzzles. *Address:* 7 Elizabeth Place, St Helier Jersey, Channel Islands JE2 3PN.

HOVHANESS Alan, b. 8 March 1911, Somerville, Massachusetts, USA. Composer. *Education:* Studied at Tufts University; New England Conservatory with Frederick Converse. *Career:* Freelance composer of over 400 works; Influenced by Armenian and Far Eastern Music; Travelled to India and Japan on Fulbright Fellowship; Composer-in-residence, University of Hawaii, 1962. *Compositions:* Operas: Etchmiadzin 1946; Blue Flame 1959; The Burning House 1960; Spirit of the Avalanche 1962; Pilate 1963; Travellers 1965; Lady of the Light 1969; Pericles 1975; Tale of the Sun Goddess Going into the Stone House 1978; Orchestral: 61 Symphonies 1937-1984, including Mysterious Mountain 1955, Arjuna 1947, St Vartan 1950, All Men are Brothers 1960, Odysseus 1973, Consolation 1975, The Broken Wings 1977, To the Green Mountains 1981, Mount St Helens 1982 and Journey to Vega 1982; Cello Concerto 1936; Artik, Horn Concerto 1948; Zertik Parkim, Concerto for piano and chamber orchestra 1948; Talin, Concerto for viola and strings 1952; Accordian Concerto 1959; Concerto for Harp and Strings 1973; Concerto for soprano saxophone and orchestra 1980; And God Created great Whales, for orchestra with tape of humped back whales; Chamber music includes 5 String Quartets 1936-76; Sonata for 2 bassoons 1973; Fantasy for double-bass and piano 1974; Suite for 4 trumpets and trombone 1976; Sonata for clarinet and harsichord 1978; Saxophone Trio 1979; 2 Sonatas for 3 trumpets and 2 trombones 1979; Psalm for brass quintet 1981; Organ Sonata 1981; Choral Music; Solo Vocal Music; Piano Music. *Membership:* Institute of the American Academy and Institute of Arts and Letters, 1977. *Address:* c/o ASCAP, ASCAP House, One Lincoln Plaza, New York, NY 10023, USA.

HOVHANISIAN Edgar (Sergey), b. 14 Jan 1930, Armenia, Russia. Composer. *Education:* Studied at the Erevan Conservatory and in Moscow with Khachaturian, graduating in 1957. *Career:* Director of the Alexander Spendiaryan Theatre of Opera and Ballet in Erevan, 1962-68; Artistic Director for Armenian radio and television, principal of the Erevan Competition, 1986; *Compositions include:* David of Sasun, opera ballet, 1976; Journey to Erzrum, 1987; Ballets and instrumental music. *Address:* RAIS Russian Federation, c/o PRS Ltd Member Registration, 29-33 Berners Street, London W1P 4AA, England.

HOVLAND Egil, b. 18 Oct 1924, Mysen, Norway. Composer. Organist. *Education:* Studied at Oslo Conservatory, 1946-49, with Holmboe in Copenhagen, Cupland at Tanglewood and Dallapiccola in Florence. *Career:* Music critic and organist in Frederiksrad. *Compositions:* Church opera the Well, 1982; Ballets Dona Nobis Pacem 1982; Den Heliga Dansen, 1982; Veni Creator Spiritus, 1984 Danses de la Mort, 1983; 3 Symphonies, 1953, 1955, 1970; Concertino for 3 trumpets and strings, 1955; Music for 10 instruments, 1957; Suite for flute and strings 1959; Missa Vigilate, 1967; Mass to the Risen Christ, 1968; All Saints' Mass, 1970; The Most Beautiful Rose, after Hans Christian Andersen, 1972; Trombone Concerto, 1972; Missa Verbi, 1973; Violin concerto, 1974; Piano Concerto, 1977; Tombeau de Bach for Orchestra, 1978; Pilgrim's Mass, 1982; Concerto for piccolo and strings, 1986; Chamber music including Piano Trio, 1965, 2 Wind Quintets, 1965, 1980, and String Quartet, 1981; Opera Captive and Free, 1993. *Honours include:* Knight of the Royal Order of St Olva, 1983. *Address:* TONO Norway, c/o PRS Ltd Member Registration, London W1P 4AA, England.

HOW Martin John, b. 3 Apr 1931, Liverpool, England. Choral Trainer; Organist; Composer. *Education:* RSCM,

Clare College Cambridge, 1949-52; MA Cantab; FRCO (CHM); ARCM; LRAM; LTCL: FRSCM. *Career:* National Service Commission, RASC; Choirmaster, Commissioner, Royal School of Church Music; Organist, Choirmaster, Grimsby Parish Church; Founder, Conductor, Croydon Youth Choir and Singers Workshop; Conductor, St James Music Society; Musical Director, Southern Cathedral Singers, Royal School of Church Music; Frequent radio and TV Broadcasts; Tours to USA, Canada, Australia, New Zealand, South Africa, Belgium, Netherlands and Denmark; Piano accompanist to BET Chorister of the Year Award. *Compositions include:* Choral works: Day by Day Sanderstead mass; St Nicholas Mass; Bless O Lord; Songs of the Spirit; Elegy for Organ. *Publications:* Royal School of Church Music Choristers Training Scheme. *Address:* Royal School of Church Music, Addington Palace, Croydon, Surrey CR9 5AD, England.

HOWARD Ann, b. 22 July 1936, Norwood, London, England. Opera Singer (Mezzo-soprano). m. Keith Giles, 1 daughter. *Education:* Studied with Topliss Green and Rodolfa Lhombino; Special grant, Royal Opera House, Covent Garden to study with Modesti, Paris, France. *Debut:* As Czipra, Gypsy Baron, Sadler's Wells Opera, 1964. *Career:* In various shows; chorus, Royal Opera House, Covent Garden; Principal, Sadler's Wells; Freelance appearances with English National Opera, Scottish Opera, Welsh National Opera, Royal Opera House, Santa Fe Festival Opera, Canadian Opera Company, New Opera Company, New York City Opera, Baltimore Opera, New Orleans Opera, Fort Worth Opera taking many leading roles including Carmen, Amneris, Fricka, Brangaene, Dalila, Azucena, Cassandra, Grande Duchess, Hélène, Gingerbread Witch, Herodiade, Clytemnestra, Mescalina (Le Grand Macabre), Princess Eboli, Mrs Danvers (Rebecca), Babushka (The Gambler), Baba The Turk and Stravinsky's Jocasta; Old Lady (Candide), Mrs Worthing (The Plumber's Gift); Katisha (Mikado); Appearances in Mexico, Italy, Chile, Belgium, France, Canada and USA; regular broadcasts, BBC, Radio and TV, Scottish TV; Marzellina, Marriage of Figaro, 1989; Step-mother, Into the Woods, Sondheim, 1990; Auntie, Peter Grimes; Prince Orlofsky, Die Fledermaus; (ENO 1992) Sang the Hostess in Boris Godunov for Opera North, 1992; Strauss concerts at the 1993 London Proms. *Recordings:* Has made many recordings for EMI including the Witch in Hansel and Gretel. *Hobbies:* Gardening; Cooking. *Address:* c/o English National Opera, St Martin's Lane, London WC2, England.

HOWARD Jason, b. 1960, Merthyr Tydfil, Wales. Singer (Baritone). *Education:* Studied at Trinity College of Music and with Norman Bailey at the Royal College of Music (performances of the Ballad Singer in Paul Bunyan, 1988). *Career:* Gained early experience as Alfio, Blow's Adonis, Zurga, Don Giovanni and Sharpless; With Scottish Opera has sung Guglielmo, Don Giovanni, Germont and Figaro; Further engagements as Ned Keene for English National Opera, Billy Budd and Ezio in Attila for Opera North, and Ramiro (L'Heure Espagnole) for Scottish Opera; Concert appearances in Carmina Burana, L'Enfance du Christ, Messiah, Fauré's Requiem, The Kingdom, Elijah and Haydn's Lord Nelson Mass; other engagements include Rossini's Figaro and Eugene Onegin for Seattle Opera (1992-93); Television showings in Scotland and Wales. *Recordings include:* Student Prince, Song of Norway and A Little Night Music (TER). *Honours:* Ricordi Prize, Rowland Jones Award and Singing Faculty Award, from the TCM. *Address:* John Coast, 31 Sinclair Road, London W14 ONS, England.

HOWARD John Stuart, b. 22 Dec 1950, Glasgow, Scotland. Composer; Lecturer; Writer; Conductor. m. Ellen Jane Howard, 15 Apr 1974, 1 daughter, 1 son. *Education:* Ilford County High School; Junior Exhibitioner, Royal College of Music, 1965-69; BA, 1st Class Honours, University of Durham, 1969-72; PhD in Composition awarded, 1979. *Career:* School teaching various posts; Senior Lecturer and Principal Lecturer, Kingston Polytechnic/University, 1979-1992; Associate

Professor and Head of Music, Nanyang Technological University, Singapore, 1993-; Honorary Senior Research Fellow, Kingston University, 1993-1995. *Compositions:* Dunstable Cantus for Piano, 1974; The Two Regions for Brass Band, 1976; Bubbles For Ever? for flute, clarinet, violin and cello, 1981; Games/End Game, for Chinese Orchestra, 1983; Sonata for Brass Quintet, 1983; Fantasia and Dance, for Chinese Orchestra, 1985. *Publications:* Learning to Compose, Cambridge, 1990; Performing & Responding, Cambridge, 1994. *Contributions to:* Various; Schools Council Magazine; Pears Encyclopedia; Music File, four articles, 1991-93; IJME, reviewer; Proceedings of British-Swedish Ethnomusicology Conference, 1991. *Memberships:* PRS: ISME. *Hobbies:* Sport; Reading. *Address:* Division of Music, National Institute of Education, Nanyang Technological University, 469 Bukit Timah Road, Singapore 1025.

HOWARD Leslie John, b. 29 Apr. 1948, Melbourne, Australia. Pianist; Composer. *Education:* AMusA, 1962; LMus., 1966; BA, 1969; MA, Monash University, 1973; Piano studies with June McLean, Donald Britton and Michael Brimer (Australia), Guido Agosti (Italy) and Noretta Conci (London). *Debut:* Melbourne 1967. *Career:* Staff Monash University, 1970-73; Guildhall School of Music and Drama, London, 1987-1992; Concertos with various orchestras in Australia, England, Europe, America, South America, Asia; Regular broadcasts as Pianist, Chamber Musician and Musicologist for BBC, ABC and RAI, and various American networks; Telecasts in Australia, Italy, USA, Hungary, Philippines, Britain. *Compositions:* Fruits of the Earth, ballet; Hreidar the Fool, Opera; Prague Spring, opera; Sonatas for violin, clarinet, percussion, double bass, horn, cello and piano; piano solo; Canzona for brass ensemble; Missa Sancti Petri, 1993; songs motets; Trios, String Quartets. *Recordings:* Complete keyboard works of Grainger; works by Franck, Glazunov, Rubinstein, Granados, Mozart, Beethoven, Tchaikovsky, Stravinsky; 70 CDs of the works and transcriptions of Liszt. *Publications:* Edition of complete works of Liszt for cello and piano, 1992; and for Piano Trio, 1993; A Liszt Catalogue, with Michael Short), 1993. *Contributions to:* Liszt Society Journal, on Liszt; Music and Musicians, on Grainger; Musical Opinion, on Liszt; Viking Opera Guide on Liszt and Rakhmaninov; also Dubal's Horowite Symposium. *Honours:* Diploma d'Onore, Siena, 1972, Naples, 1976; Ferenc Liszt Medal of Honour, 1986; Liszt Grand Prix du Disque, Liszt Academy Budapest, 4 times; Ferenc Liszt Medal of Honour, Hungarian Republic, 1989. *Memberships:* President, Liszt Society; Grainger Society. *Hobbies:* Literature; Languages; Bridge; Snooker; Swimming. *Current Management:* Melanie Turner. *Address:* 128 Norbury Crescent, Norbury, London SW16 4JZ, England.

HOWARD Michael Stockwin, b. 14 Sept. 1922, London, England. Conductor; Organ Recitalist; Composer. *Education:* Ellesmere College; Organ and Composition Scholar, Royal Academy of Music, Studied with G D Cunningham, 1939-43; Studied privately with Marcel Dupré, late 1940's to early 1950's. *Career:* Organist, Tewkesbury Abbey, 1943-44; Director, The Renaissance Singers and Renaissance Society, 1944-64; Organist, Master of Choristers, Ely Cathedral, 1952-59; Conductor, Cantores in Ecclesia, 1964-; Broadcaster and subsequent TV appearances, 1946-; International travel as Broadcaster for Radio and TV; Artistic Director, Rye Spring Music, 1976-79; Various Festival appearances at home and abroad. *Compositions:* Principal works include: Prayer Book Canticles, 1946, 49; Seven Songs for Counter-tenor, 1949; Mass, 1961; Sequentia de Insomnia, 1981; Carillon des Larmes, Organ, 1982; Cantique d'un Oiseau matinal, organ, 1983; Cantiones Iduithae, 1983. *Recordings Include:* Three Mass Settings: Byrd; Lamentations of Jeremiah-Tallis; Missa Aeternae Christi munera- Palestrina; Music for the Fest of Christmas-Dufay to Messiaen; Commemoration of Charles-Marie Widor and Louis Vierne, 1987. *Publication:* A Tribute to Aristide Cavaille-Coll, 1986. *Address:* 40 Chapel Park Road, St. Leonards on Sea, Sussex, England.

HOWARD Patricia, b. 18 Oct. 1937, Birmingham, England. Writer. m. David Louis Howard, 29 July 1960, 2 daughters. *Education:* BA, 1959, MA, 1963, Lady Margaret Hall, Oxford University; PhD, University of Surrey, 1974. *Career:* Lecturer, Tutor, Music, Open University, 1976-; many broadcasts both on network and for Open University. *Publications:* Gluck and the Birth of Modern Opera, 1963; The Operas of Benjamin Britten: an Introduction, 1969; Haydn in London, 1980; Mozart's Marriage of Figaro, 1980; C.W. Gluck: Orfeo, 1981; Haydn's String Quartets, 1984; Beethoven's Eroica Symphony, 1984; Benjamin Britten : The Turn of the Screw, 1985; Christoph Willibald Gluck: A Guide to Research, 1987; Music in Vienna 1790-1800, 1988; Beethoven's Fidelio, 1988; Music and the Enlightenment, 1992. *Contributions to:* Musical Times; Music & Letters; The Consort; The Listener; The Gramophone; Opera; ENO and Friends; Programme books for Covent Garden Opera, Glyndebourne Opera. *Honours:* Susette Taylor Travelling Fellowship, 1971; Leverhulme Research Award, 1976; British Academy Research Award, 1988. *Membership:* Royal Musical Association. *Address:* Stepping Stones, Gomshall, Surrey, GU5 9NZ. England.

HOWARD Yvonne, b.1960, Staffordshire, England. Singer (Mezzo Soprano). *Education:* Studied at the Royal Northern College of Music. *Career:* Operatic appearances as Mozart's Marcellina with Glyndebourne Touring Opera, Cenerentola for English Touring Opera and Suzuki for Birmingham Music Theatre; Sang Fricka and Waltraute in The Ring of the Nibelungen, City of Birmingham Touring Opera; Season, 1990-91: Mercedes at Covent Garden, Meg Page in Falstaff, ENO; Amastris in Xerxes, Meg Page in Falstaff and Maddalena (Rigoletto) for ENO, 1992; Concert engagements include Mozart's Requiem under Menuhin at Gstaad, Messiah with the Tokyo Philharmonic, 1990, Vilvadi's Gloria wih the English Chamber Orchestra; Messiah with the Hallé Orchestra and Liverpool Philharmonic, 1990; De Falla's Three Cornered Hat, Festival Hall and with Ulster Orchestra; Song recitals include Wigmore Hall debut, 1989. *Honours:* Curtis Gold Medal, RNCM. *Address:* Anglo Swiss Ltd 3 Primrose Mews, 1a Sharpleshall St, London NW1 8YW, England.

HOWARTH Elgar, b. 4 Nov. 1935, Cannock, Staffs., England. Freelance Musician (Conductor; Composer; Trumpeter). m. Bridget Neary, 1 son, 2 daughters. *Education:* Manchester University (MusB); Royal Manchester College of Music (ARMCM 1956, FRMCM 1970). *Career:* Played in the orchestra of the Royal Opera House, Covent Garden, 1958-63; Royal Philharmonic Orchestra, 1963-69; Member, London Sinfonietta, 1968-71; Philip Jones Brass Ensemble, 1965-76; Freelance Conductor, 1970-; Conducted the premieres of Ligeti's Le Grand Macabre (Stockholm 1978) and Birtwistle's The Mask of Orpheus (London Coliseum 1986); Musical Advisor, Grimethorpe Colliery Brass Band, 1972-; Principal Guest Conductor, Opera North, 1985-88; Conducted the BBC Symphony Orchestra at the 1989 Promenade Concerts, in a programme of Bartók, Birtwistle and Stravinsky; Conducted Le Grand Macabre at the Festival Hall, 1989; British professional premiere of Nielsen's Maskarade for Opera North, 1990; Premiere of Birtwistle's Gawain at Covent Garden, 1991. *Recordings:* Maxwell Davies's Trumpet Concerto and Birtwistle's Endless Parade, Philips, 1991. *Publications:* Various compositions for brass instruments, and an arrangement of Mussorgsky's Pictures at an Exhibition for Brass Band. *Current Management:* Allied Artists, 42 Montpellier Square, London. *Address:* 27 Cromwell Avenue, London N6, England.

HOWARTH Judith, b. 1960, Ipswich, Suffolk. Singer (Soprano). m. 1 daughetr. *Education:* Studied at the Royal Scottish Academy and at the Opera School; Further studies with Patricia Macmahon. *Debut:* Mozart arias with the English Chamber Orchestra, 1984. *Career:* Student roles included Donna Anna, Countess Almaviva, Pamina, Fiordiligi and Mimi; Covent Garden debut 1985, as First Maid in Zemlinsky's Der Zwerg;

Other roles with the Royal Opera have been Siebel, Frasquita, Barbarina (also televised), Oscar, Elvira (L'Italiana in Algeri), First Niece (Peter Grimes), Iris (Semele), Musetta, Aennchen, Gilda, Adele, Norina and Morgana (Alcina, 1992); For Opera North has sung Susanna and Norina and for Scottish Opera Zerlina in Don Giovanni; Salzburg and Aix-en-Provence debuts 1991, in Der Schauspieldirektor and as Susanna; US debut Seattle 1989 in a concert with Domingo; Further Domingo collaborations in Brussels and Amsterdam (also televised); Concerts with the English Chamber, BBC Symphony and London Philharmonic Orchestras, season 1990-91; Promenade Concerts 1991, in The Spectre's Bride by Dvořák; Further engagements with the City of Birmingham Symphony and Scottish National Orchestras, the Huddersfield Choral Society and the Boston Symphony Orchestra; Appearances in Tony Palmer's films of Handel and Puccini; Concerts with Domingo in Hong Kong, Adelaide & Auckland, 1992; Sang Morgana in a new production of Handel's Alcina, 1992-93, Covent Garden; Beethoven's Ninth at the 1993 London Proms; sang Gilda in Rigoletto at Covent Garden 1989, and Aennchen in Der Freischütz; Norina in Don Pasquale for Opera North, 1990; The Woodbird in Siegfried at Covent Garden, 1991-92, also Marguerite de Valois, Musetta and Norina; *Recordings include:* Menotti's The Boy who Grew too Fast; Madame Butterfly, conducted by Sinopoli (Deutsche Grammophon); Mozart's Requiem with the London Mozart Players; Caractacus for Chandos, 1992; Light of Life, Elgar, Chandos, 1993. *Honours include:* Lieder Prize, Governor's Recital Prize and the Margaret Dick Award at the Royal Scottish Academy; John Noble Prize 1984; Decca-Kathleen Ferrier Prize 1985; Heinz Bursary for Young Singers at Covent Garden, 1985-87. *Address:* c/o Lies Askonas Ltd., 186 Drury Lane, London WC2B 5RY, England.

HOWD Janet, b. 17 Feb. 1940, Birmingham, England. Freelance Concert Singer. m. Barry A Turner, 1 Apr. 1961, 2 daughters. *Education:* Teaching Diploma, City of Birmingham Teacher Training College, 1958-60; Study Scholarships, City of Birmingham School of Music, 1960-63. *Career:* Teaching Drama, Northern Sinfonia, Opera in Miniature, 1962-63; Oratorio Solos with major choral societies, 1956-; Various work in operatic field and music theatre; has sung all major Mozart Soprano roles and works by Benjamin Britten, Weill, Handel, Donizetti and others; Created Role of Countess in the Causley/McNeff ballad opera, Aucassin and Nicolette; Radio Broadcast, BBC Radio 4, 1980; work with major repertory theatres and music clubs as recitalist; Organizer, Originator, International Symposium of Concert Song, UK, June 1985; Opera Singer in Phantom of the Opera, Her Majesty's Theatre, London, 1986; Visiting Lecturer Voice Studies at Australian Universities, 1990. *Composition:* A Buckskin Bag of Gold, (Premiered at Exeter Northcott Theatre, 1982). *Recordings:* A Song Recital, 1976; The Pleasure Gardens of England, with the Cornel Music Group, 1985; Proses Lyriques, Janet Howd sings Berlioz, Dupare, Fauré and Debussy, 1989; Advance Diploma in Voice, 1993. *Hobbies:* Listening to all forms of Music; Translations of Lieder into English; Reading.*Current Management:* Felix de Wolfe Associates, Manfield House, 376-378 The Strand, London WC2R 0LR, England. *Address:* The Voice Practice, 10 St. James' Court, Marlborough Crecent, Chiswick, London, W4 1HE, England.

HOWELL Gwynne Richard, b. 13 June 1938, Gorseinon, Wales. Principal Bass. m. Mary Edwina Morris, 1968, 2 sons. *Education:* BSc., University of Wales, Swansea; DipTP, Manchester University; MRTPI, 1966; studied singing with Redvers Llewellyn while at University; part-time student, Manchester Royal College of Music with Gwilym Jones; studied with Otakar Kraus, 1968-72. *Career:* Sang Pogner in Die Meistersinger; as a result of this role, appointed Principal Bass, at Sadler's Wells, 1968; First season at Sadler's Wells sang 8 roles including Monterone and the Commendatore; appearances with Hallé Orchestra, 1968, 1969; Arkel in Pelléas and Mélisande, Glyndebourne and Covent Garden, 1969; Royal Opera House, Covent Garden:

Debut as First Nazarene, Salome, 1969-70; King in Aida; Timur in Turandot; Mephisto in Damnation of Faust; Prince Gremin in Eugene Onegin; High Priest in Nabucco; Reinmar in Tannhäuser, 1973-74; Hobson in Peter Grimes, 1975; Sparafucile in Rigoletto, 1975-76; Ramfis in Aida, 1977; Tristan and Isolde, 1978, 1982; Luisa Miller, 1978; Samson et Delilah, 1981; Pogner, Die Meistersinger, 1982; Semele, 1982; Die Zauberflöte, 1983; Don Carlos; Metropolitan Opera House, New York: Debut as Lodovico in Otello and Pogner in Die Meistersinger, 1985; sang Gurnemanz in a new production of Parsifal, London Coliseum 1986; The Hermit in Der Freischütz at Covent Garden 1989, Pogner in Die Meistersinger; sang the Parson and the Badger in a new production of The Cunning Little Vixen, 1990; sang the Fliedermonolog at the Reginald Goodall Memorial Concert, London 1991; London Coliseum 1992, as King Philip in a new production of Don Carlos, Daland at Covent Garden and Mozart's Bartolo on tour with the Company to Japan; Sacred Music: Verdi and Mozart Requiems, Missa Solemnis; sings in Europe and USA; records for BBC and major recording companies. *Address:* 197 Fox Lane, London N13 4BB, England.

HOWELLS Anne, b. 12 Jan 1941, Southport, Lancashire, England. Singer (Mezzo-Soprano). m. (1) Ryland Davies, (2) Stafford Dean, 1 son, 1 daughter. *Education:* Royal Manchester College of Music, with Frederick Cox; Later study with Vera Rosza. *Debut:* Manchester 1963, in the British premiere of Gluck's Paride ed Helena. *Career:* Sang Flora in La Traviata with Welsh National Opera, 1966; Covent Garden from 1967, as Annina (Rosenkavalier), Rosina, Cherubino, Hermia, Siebel (Faust), Ascanio (Benvenuto Cellini), Mélisande; Sang Ophelia in the London premiere of Searle's Hamlet and Lena in the world premiere of Bennett's Victory; Glyndebourne Festival from 1967, as Erisbe in L'Ormindo, Dorabella, Minerva (Il Ritorno d'Ulisse), the Composer (Ariadne auf Naxos) and as Cathleen in the 1970 premiere of the The Rising of the Moon, by Maw; US debut 1972, as Dorabella at Chicago; Appearances with Scottish Opera, at the Metropolitan Opera (Dorabella, 1975) and with the Covent Garden company at La Scala Milan (1976); Sang Idamantes in Idomeneo with the Deutsche Oper Berlin (1981) and the Geneva Opera (1984); Geneva Opera 1987, as Régine in the premiere of La Fôret by Liebermann; Paris 1985, as Rameau's Phèdre; Chicago Lyric Opera 1989, as Orlofsky in Die Fldermaus; Sang Magdalene in Die Meistersinger at Covent Garden 1990, Adelaide in Arabella, and Meg Page in Falstaff at the 1990 Glyndebourne Festival; Covent Garden 1992, as Giulietta in Les Contes d'Hoffmann; Season 1992 with Despina at Covent Garden, Weill's Begbick at Geneva. *Recordings include:* L'Ormindo, Der Rosenkavalier and Les Troyens; Labels include Decca, Philips and Argo. *Current Management:* IMG Artists Europe. *Address:* c/o IMG Media House, 3 Burlington Lane, Chiswick, London W4 2TH, England.

HOWELLS David, b. 26 Jan 1954, Bedfordshire, England. Piano Recitalist; Teacher. m. Clare Lange, 22 Oct 1977, 1s, 1d. *Education:* Guildhall School of Music, London Opera Center; Private study with Yonty Solomon. *Debut:* Edinburgh Festival Fringe Recitals, 1985. *Career:* Repetiteur Cologne Opera House Germany, 1978-79; Solo recitals, 1979-; Edinburgh Festival Fringe solo recitals, 1985-91; Purcell Room, 1986; St John's Smith Square, 1989; Extensive recitals for children, 1991-; Piano Professor, Welsh College of Music and Drama, 1991-; Performed Etudes of Henselt at Schwabach, Bavaria at Centenary celebrations; Other works include Complete Transcendental Etudes of Lyapunov, Complete Impromptus Faure, 12 Etudes Saint-Saens, Richard Rodney Bennett 5 studies, Peter and the Wolf, Story of Babar with music and narration; Première of piano version, Little Red Riding Hood, Paul Patterson, 1993, and of The Steadfast Tin Soldier, Keith Amos, 1994. *Memberships:* ISM, Secretary of North London Centre; EPTA; RSM. *Hobbies:* Cycling; Travel; Furniture. *Current Management* Helen Sykes Artists Management. *Address:* 7a Belsize Crescent, Hampstead, London NW3 5QY, England.

HOWLETT Neil Baillie, b. 24 July 1934, Mitcham, Surrey, England. Opera and Concert Singer (Baritone). m. Elizabeth Robson, 2 daughters. *Education:* MA, (Cantab); St Paul's Cathedral Choir School; King's College, Cambridge; Hochschule für Musik, Stuttgart. *Debut:* In the World premiere of Britten's Curlew River at Aldeburgh, 1964. *Career:* Major roles with Sadler's Wells, English Opera Group, Royal Opera House, Covent Garden, Hamburg, Bremen, Nantes, Bordeaux, Toulouse, Nice, Marseille; Principal Baritone, English National Opera, London; Has sung most major baritone roles; Sang title roles in premieres of Toussaint (Blake) and The Story of Vasco (Crosse); Appearances at most major festivals; sang Hector in King Priam with the Royal Opera (Athens 1985) and Amfortas in Buenos Aires 1986; sang Scarpia in Tosca with English National Opera, 1987-1990; Holland Festival 1990, as Ruprecht in The Fiery Angel by Prokofiev; Other roles include Goland (Pelléas), King Fisher in The Midsummer Marriage and Wagner's Dutchman; Recitalist; Teacher; Regular broadcaster; Professor, Guildhall School of Music. *Honours:* Kathleen Ferrier Memorial Prize. *Hobbies:* Sports; Jogging; Cycling; Languages; Reading; Host; Theatre. *Current Management:* Ingpen & Williams Limited. *Address:* c/o English National Opera, London Coliseum, St Martin's Lane, London, WC2, England.

HOYLAND Vic, b. 11 Dec. 1945, Wombwell, Yorkshire, England. Composer. *Education:* Studied Fine Arts, Music and Drama at the University of Hull; DPhil in music at York Univrsity, with Robert Sherlaw Johnson and Bernard Rands. *Career:* Hayward Fellow in Music at the University of Birmingham 1980-83; Visiting Lecturer at York University 1984; Lecturer at the Barber Institute for Fine Arts, University of Birmingham, Birmingham, 1985-; Senior Lecturer, 1993-; Founder member and co-director of the Northern Music Theatre; Compositions have been featured at the Aldeburgh, Bath, Holland and California Contemporary Music Festivals; Survey of works at the 1985 Musica concert series in London; Commissions from the Northern Music Theatre, the Essex Youth Orchestra, New MacNaghten Concerts, Musica, the Barber Institute BBC Promenade series, BCMG, Southbank Summerscope, Huddersfield Festival, Almeida Festival and the York Festival. *Compositions:* Em for 24 voices 1970; Es for ensemble with voices 1971; Jeux-Theme for mezzo and ensemble 1972; Ariel, for voice and ensemble 1975; Esem for double-bass and ensemble 1975; Seranade for 14 players 1979; Xingu, music theatre, 1979; Andacht zum Kleinen for 9 players 1980; Reel for double-reed instruments 1980; Michelagniolo for baritone and ensemble, 1981; Quartet Movement 1982; Fox for chamber ensemble 1983; Head and 2 Tails, 3 pieces for voice(s) and ensemble 1984; Quintet of Brass 1985; Seneca/Medea for voices and ensemble 1985; String Quartet 1985; In Transit for orchestra 1987; Hoquetus David for ensemble 1987; Work-Out for trombone 1987; Crazy Rosa-La Madre for mezzo and ensemble 1988; Work-out for marimba, 1988; Of Fantasy, Of Dreams and Ceremonies for 13 strings 1989; Trio, 1990; Piano Quintet, 1990; The Other Side of the Air for Rolf Hind, piano solo, 1991; In Memoriam P.P.P, 1992; Concerto for Chamber Concerto for pianoforte ensemble, 1993. *Address:* Universal Edition Ltd. 48 Great Marlborough Street, London W1V 2BN, England.

HOYLE Ted, b. 17 Aug. 1942, Huntsville, Alabama, USA. Cellist. *Education:* BMus, Eastman School of Music; MMus, Yale University; DMA, Manhattan School of Music, 1981; Studied with André Navarra, Ecole Normale de Musique, Paris, France. *Career:* Cellist, Kohon Quartet; Professor of Music, Kean College, New Jersey, USA; Cellist, Performing Arts Trio, New Jersey; Co-Director, Hear America First, Manhattan concert series, 1978-81. *Compositions:* Edited works by Bach, Schumann, Scriabin for Belwin Mills. *Recordings:* A number with Kohon Quartet including: String quartets by Walter Piston, Peter Mennin, Charles Ives, William Schuman, Aaron Copland, Julia Smith, Roger Sessions and Penderecki; Quartet of Joseph Fennimore; Quintet of Robert Baksa; Trio Sonatas of J. S. Bach, G. F. Handel, G. Telemann. *Memberships:* Violoncello Society; American String Teachers' Association; Phi Kappa Phi,

Honor Society. *Hobbies:* Swimming; Reading. *Address:* 276 Riverside Drive, New York, NY 10025, USA.

HSIEH Li-Ping (Liu Chere), b. 7 Jan 1941, Nanjing, China. Soprano. m. Hsien-Tung Liu, 5 June 1964, 1 son, 1 daughter. *Education:* Conservatorio di Musica Giuseppe Verdi, Milan; Juilliard School of Music, New York; BM, 1977, MM, 1979, Duquesne University, Pittsburgh; Pupil of Licia Albanese, Eleanor Steber and Martin Rich, New York, Luigi Ricci, Rome, Ettore Campogalliani, Milan; Attended Aspen and Tanglewood. *Career:* Sang with San Francisco Opera, Merola Opera, 1966; Pittsburgh Opera, 1969; Recital tours, USA, 1966-; Tour of Italy and Germany, 1969-, Taiwan, 1985-; Appeared in Vienna, 1986; Tour of Korea, 1989-; Many appearances as soloist with symphony orchestras and choirs including Juilliard, Knoxville, Tennessee, San Francisco Opera, Bach Choir of Pittsburgh; Lecturer of Music: La Roche College, 1978-80, Point Park College, 1983-86. *Recordings:* Mozart Coronation Mass and Mass in C Minor, and Schubert Mass in G Major with St Paul, Pittsburgh; Chinese Art Songs, Bel Canto Arias, Sacred Songs with AirCraft, Pittsburgh, in progress. *Current Management:* Albert Kay Associates Inc, 58 West 58th Street, New York, NY 10019, USA. *Address:* 2205 Bentley Drive, Bloomsburg, PA 17815, USA.

HSU John T., b. 21 Apr. 1931, Swatow, People's Republic of China. Professor of Music; Performer on Cello, Viola da gamba, and Baryton. m. Martha Russell, 31 July 1968. *Education:* B Mus 1953, M Mus 1955, New England Conservatory of Music. *Career:* Teacher 1955-, Fellow, Cornell Society for the Humanities, 1971-72; Instructor, 1955-58; Professorial Staff, 1958-76; Chairman, Department of Music, 1966-71; Old Dominion Professor of Music and Humanities, 1976-, Cornell University, Ithaca, New York; Artist-Faculty, Aston Magna Foundation, 1973-90; Barytonist, Haydn Baryton Trio, 1982-; Artist-in-Residence, University of California, Davis, 1983; Director, Aston Magna Festival, 1984-87; Regents' Lecturer, University of California, Santa Cruz, 1985; Viola da gamba Recitalist, including radio broadcast, in North America and Europe; Director, Aston Magna Performance Practice Institute, 1986-90; Artistic Director, Aston Magna Foundation for Music, 1987-90; Music Director and Conductor, Apollo Ensemble, 1991-; John Hsu in a course in French Baroqua Viol Playing, presented by The Viola da gamba Society of America, 1992. *Recordings:* Pièces de Viole, by Louis de Caix d'Hervelois and Antoine Forqueray, Belgium, 1966; 3 Gamba Sonatas, by J S Bach, Da Camera, Federal Republic of Germany, 1971; Musical Heritage Society, 1972; 1st complete recording of Five Suites for viola da gamba, by Forqueray, MHS, 1972; 5 discs, Pièces de Viole, by Marais, MHS, 1973-77; Pièces de Viole, by Marais, J Morel, Charles Doilé, 1978; 2 discs, Baryton Trios, by J Haydn, MHS, 1981-82, LP; Re-issue of Baryton Trios by J Haydn (CD, LP and cassette), ASV-Gaudeamus, London, 1988-89. *Publications:* Editor, The Instrumental Works, by Marin Marais (1656-1728), volume I 1980, volume II 1987; A Handbook of French Baroque Viol Technique, 1981. *Contributions to:* Early Music, 1978. *Current Management:* Rohr Artists Management (New York and Copenhagen). *Address:* 601 Highland Road, Ithaca, NY 14850, USA.

HSU Madeleine, b. 20 Sept. 1938. Professor of Piano; Pianist; Clinician; Adjudicator; Lecturer. 2 sons. *Education:* Artist Diploma, Ecole Normale de Musique, Paris, France, 1960; Diploma, Warsaw Conservatory, Poland, 1965; BM 1970, MS 1971, Juilliard School of Music, New York, USA; PhD, New York University, 1984. *Debut:* Aged 13, Beethoven Festival, Vichy, France, 1952. *Career:* Performed in recitals and with orchestras in Europe, Africa, South America, USA, 1952-; Television soloist, USA; Author of a multi-media production (video); Professor, Boise State University, Idaho; Hsu & Parkinson Piano Duo, USA. *Contributions to:* Musica; Activités Musicales des Jeunes; Clavier; American Music Teacher; Journal of American Liszt Society, 1993. *Honours:* Award winner, International Piano Contests, Spain 1962, Brazil 1965; Josef

Lhevinne Memorial Award, New York, 1970; Mu Phi Epsilon Doctoral Grant, 1981; Governor's Award for Excellence in The Arts, Idaho, 1990. *Memberships:* Lecturer, Adjudicator, Music Teachers' National Association; Piano Teachers' Guild; National Federation of Music Clubs. *Hobbies:* Swimming; Reading; Art; Pet Care. *Address:* Boise State University, Morrison Center for the Performing Arts, Department of Music, Boise, ID 83725, USA.

HUA Lin, b. 8 Aug 1942, Shanghai, China. Composer; Associate Professor. *Education:* Graduated with honours, Shanghai Conservatory of Music, 1966; Piano and Composition with Sang Tong, Wang Jianzhong, Chen Mingzhi. *Career:* Composer: Shanghai Wind Band, 1967-76, Shanghai Opera and Ballet House, 1976-79; Associate Professor, Counterpoint, Fugue, Shanghai Conservatory of Music, 1979-; Consultant, Shanghai Philharmonic Association, 1982-. *Compositions include:* Bright Mountain Flowers in Full Bloom, ballet, 1976; Fantasy, piano, accordion, 1978; Love of the Great Wall, piano, accordion, 1978; Farewell Refrains at Yang Gate Pass, piano quartet, 1978; Beauty of Peking Opera, string quartet, 1979; Album of Woodcuts, piano quintet, 1979; Amid Flowers Beside a River Under the Spring Moon for four harps, 1979; Flower and Song, concertino for soprano and orchestra, 1980; Suite Tragedy, chamber symphony, 1988; 24 Preludes and fugues on Reading Sikong Tu's Shipin (Personalities of Poetry in Tang Dynasty), 1990; Album of Chinese Folk Songs, piano, 1991; Stage, film, TV music. *Publications:* Guide the Teaching of Polyphony by Using Creative Psychology, 1980; Stravinsky Techniques in Polyphonic Writing, 1987; The Sense of Ugliness and its Application in Western Music, 1988; Abstraction of Art and Abstractionism, 1989. *Address:* 20 Fenyang Road, Shanghai, China.

HUANG An-Lun, b. 15 Mar 1949, Canton, China. Composer. m. Ruili Ouyang, 15 Sept 1974, 1s. *Education:* Conservatory of Music, Beijing; Fellowship in Composition, Trinity College, London, 1983; MMus, Yale University, 1986. *Career:* Composer in Residence, Central Opera House of China, Beijing, 1976-; Freelance Composer, 1980-; President, Canadian Chinese Music Soicety of Ontario, 1987-. Major stage, film, TV and radio appearances. *Compositions:* Two Grand operas, 6 grand opera scores, 1 musical, 3 ballets, 4 movies and more than 20 orchestral works, 2 oratorios as well as chamber, electronic, incidental,choral and vocal music. *Recordings include:* Poem for Dance, piano solo, 1992; Selections from the Ballet Dream of Dunhuang, for orchestra, 1990; Chinese Rhapsody No 2, for piano solo, 1992. *Publications:* Numerous music scores. *Hobbies:* Reading; Travel. *Address:* 123 Sadlee Cove Crescent, Scarborough, Ontario M1V 1Y3, Canada.

HUANG Yijun, b. 4 May 1915, Suzhou, China. Conductor. m. Zhang Han-Zhen, 27 Feb. 1939, 3 sons. *Education:* National Conservatory of Music, Shanghai, China. *Career:* Conductor and composer, Chinese movies and stage productions, Shanghai 1936-56; Trumpet player, Shanghai Municipal Symphony Orchestra 1938-42, French horn player 1946-50; Associate Professor, Trumpet and French Horn, Shanghai Conservatory of Music, 1948-56; Conductor and Director, Shanghai Symphony Orchestra 1950-; Honorary Director, Shanghai Symphony Orchestra 1985-; Guest Conductor: Helsinki Symphony Orchestra 1956; Central Philharmonic Orchestra, Peking, China 1957, 1962; National Symphony Orchestra USSR, 1958; Berlin Philharmonic Orchestra 1981; Singapore Symphony Orchestra 1984; Yomiuri Nippon Symphony Orchestra 1986. *Compositions:* Fair Flowers Under Full Moon, for folk ensemble; Selections from Folk Tunes; The Jiangnan Suite, for orchestra. *Memberships:* Musicians Association, China (member of Standing Committee 1979-, Vice Chairman Shanghai Branch 1962-); National Committee of Chinese People's Political Consultative Conference, 1978-. *Address:* 105 Hunan Lu, Shanghai, China.

HUBARENKO Vitaly, b. 13 June 1934, Kharkov,

Ukraine. Composer. *Education:* Studied at the Kharkov Conservatory. *Career:* Teacher, Theory and Composition, Kharkov Conservatory, 1961-72; Freelance composer of stage music, and other works. *Compositions include:* The Destruction of the Squadron, music drama, 1967; The Story Host (Don Juan), ballet, 1968; Mamay, music drama, 1970; Letters to love, monodrama, 1972; Reborn May, lyric drama, 1974; Through Flames, opera in 3 acts, 1976; Viy, opera-ballet, 1984; The Reluctant Matchmaker, lyric comedy, 1985; Al'piyskaya Ballada, lyric scenes, 1985; In the Steppes of Ukraine, lyric comedy, 1986-87; Remember, my Brotherhood, opera-oratorio, 1990-91; The Lonelness, monodrama, 1993. *Address:* c/o Nikolaeva str, 3B op 151 Kyiv 253225, CIS.

HUBER Klaus, b. 30 Nov. 1924, Berne, Switzerland. Composer. *Education:* Studied at the Zurich Conservatory 1947-49 with Stefi Geyer and Willy Burkhard; Further study with Boris Blacher in Berlin. *Career:* Taught violin at the Zurich Conservatory from 1950; Lucerne Conservatory 1960-63; Basle Music Academy from 1961. *Compositions:* Orchestral: Invention und Choral 1956; Litania instrumentalis 1957; Terzen-Studie 1958; Alveare vernat 1967; James Joyce Chamber Music 1967; Tenebrae 1967; Tempora for violin and orchestra 1970; Turna 1974; Choral: Quem terra 1955; Das Te Deum Laudamus Deutsch 1956; Antiphonische Kantate 1956; Soliloquia 1959-64; Cuius legibus rotantur poli 1960; Musik zu eines Johannes-der-Taufer Gottesdienst 1965; Kleine Deutsche Messe 1969; .... inwendig voller figur.... after the Apocalypse and Durer 1971; Hiob xix 1971; Vocal: Abendkantate 1952; Kleine Tauf Kantate fur Christof 1952; 6 Kleine Vokalisen 1955; Der Abend ist mein Buch 1955; Oratorio Mechtildis 1957; Des Engls Anredung an der Seele 1957; Auf die ruhige Nacht-Zeit 1958; Askese 1966; Psalm of Christ 1967; Grabschrift 1967; Der Mensch 1968; Traumgesicht 1968; ...ausgespant.... 1972; Jot oder Wann kommt der Herr zuruck, opera 1973; Instrumetal: Ciacona for organ 1954; Concerto per la camerata 1955; In Memoriam Willy Burkhard for oragn 1955; Partita 1955; Noctes intelligibis lucis for oboe and harpsichord 1961; Moteti-Cantiones for string quartet 1963; 6 Miniaturen 1963; In te Domine spervai for organ 1964; Sabeth 1967; Ascensus for flute, cello and piano 1969; 3 kleine Meditationen for string trio and harp 1969; Ein Hauch von Unzeit. I-III 1972. *Honours:* First Prize at the 1959 ISCM Competition, Rome (for Die Engels Anredung an die Seele); Arnold Bax Society medal 1962; Beethoven Prize of Bonn 1970 (for Tenebrae). *Address:* Salzgasse 5, D-W-7801 Ehrenkirchen, Germany.

HUBERMAN Lina, b. 1960, Moscow, Russia. Violinist. *Education:* Studied at the Moscow Conservatoire with Yankelevich. *Career:* Member of the Prokofiev Quarter (founded at the Moscow Festival of World Youth and the International Quartet Competition at Budapest); many concerts in the former Soviet Union and on tour to Czechoslovakia, Germany, Australia, the USA, Canada, Spain, Japan and Italy; Repertoire includes works by Haydn, Mozart, Beethoven, Schubert, Debussy, Ravel, Tchaikovsky, Bartók, and Shostakovich. *Address:* c/o Sonata Prokofiev Quartet, 11 Northgate Street, Glasgow G20 7AA, Scotland.

HUBNER Fritz, b. 25 April 1933, Sachsengrun, Czechoslovakia. Singer (Bass). *Education:* Studied at the Dessau Conservatory with J. Stieler. *Debut:* Landestheater Bernburg as Sparafucile in Rigoletto. *Career:* Cothen 1953-55; Dessau 1955-56; Sang in chorus of Leipzig Opera House; Dresden-Radebeul 1960-62; Berlin Komische Opera 1962-74; Staatsoper Berlin from 1974 as Hagen and Fafner in The Ring, Daland in Der fliegende Holländer, Landgrave in Tannhäuser, Osmin in Die Entführung and Sarastro in Die Zauberflöte; Guest appearances in Hamburg and Prague in Wagner roles; Bayreuth Festival 1979-85, as Hagen and Fafner; Las Palmas Festival 1985, as Sarastro; Engagements at Covent Garden, London, in Ring cycles directed by Götz Friedrich; sang Ramfis in Aida with the Deutsche Oper am Rhein 1989, Galitzky

in Prince Igor at the Berlin Staatsoper (Osmin on tour to Japan, 1987). *Recordings include:* Der Ring des Nibelungen, Bayreuth Festival 1980 (Philips). *Address:* c/o Ingpen and Williams Ltd., 14 Kensington Court, London W8 5DN, England.

HUDECEK Vaclav, b. 7 June 1952, Rozmital, Czechoslovakia. Musician (Violinist). m. Eva Trejtnarova, 8 Feb 1977. *Education:* Academy of Music, Prague; Private lessons for 4 years with David Oistrakh, Moscow. *Debut:* With Royal Philharmonic Orchestra in London, 11 Nov 1967. *Career:* Concert tours in Europe, Japan and USA since debut with Royal Philharmonic Orchestra; Tours in Europe, USA, Japan and Australia. *Recordings:* Most of world violin repertoire on Panton, Victor of Japan, and Ex Libris labels; Most of World Violin Repertoire on Panton, Victor of Japan, Ex Libris and Supraphon Labels. *Honours:* Artist of Merit of CSSR, 1980; Soloist, Czech Philharmonic Orchestra, 1983; Record of the Year, 1992 for Vivaldi, Four Season. Best Selling Record of Czechoslovakia, Supraphon Records. *Membership:* Union of CSSR Composers and Concert Artists, Central Committee Member; Association of Czech Musicians. *Hobbies:* Films; Paintings; Sculpture. *Current Management:* Euroconcert Bellebern 10a, 78234 Engen, Germany. *Address:* 120 00 Praha 2, Londýnskà 25, Czech Republic.

HUDEZ Karl, b. 21 Jan. 1904, Salzburg, Austria. Musical Director. m. Gusti Petyrek. *Education:* Mozarteum, Salzburg; State Academy of Music, Vienna. *Career:* Max Reinhardt Productions, 1924-38; Salzburg Festival, 1928-60; Musical Director, State Opera, Vienna, 1945-53; Dramatic Adviser, Musical Director, Vienna Volksoper, 1938-44; Director of Studies, State Opera, Vienna, 1953-68; Director, Conservatory Opera School, Vienna and various Summer Courses including Savonlinna, Finland. *Compositions:* Ballet, Daphnis and Chloe; Lieder; Stage Works. *Recordings:* Salzburg, Everyman; Lied Recital (piano accompanied). *Honours:* 1st Class Cross of the Golden Lion, Finland; Honorary Cross, Litteris and Artibus, Republic of Austria; Golden Sign of Honour, Vienna, Austria, 1976. *Membership:* Honorary President, Austrian-Finnish Society. *Hobbies:* Photography; Books. *Address:* 4 Michael Wengerg, 2380 Perchtoldsdorf, Austria.

HUDSON Barton, b. 20 July 1936, Tenessee, USA. Professor. m. Elizabeth Kesselring, 1 June 1959, 1 d. *Education:* BMus, Midwestern University, 1956; MMus, distinction, 1957, PhD, 1961, Indiana University; Staatliche Hochschule fur Musik, Freiburg, 1960. *Publications:* Contributor to Collected works of Jacob Obrecht, Thomas Crecquillon,1990, Ninot le Petit, 1977, Antoine Brumel, 1969-72; Articles to: Journal of the American Musicological Society; Computer and Music; Musica Disciplina; The Musical Quarterly; Revue Belge de Musicologie; Acta Musicologica; Tijdschrift van de Vereniging voor Nederlandse Muziekgeschiedenis; New Grove Dictionary of Music and Musicians. *Honours:* Pi Kappa Lambda; Fulbright Scholarship, 1959-60, Research Fellowship, 1992; Benedum Distinguished Scholar, West Virginia University, 1987; NEH Grants. *Memberships include:* American and International Musicological Societies; Southeastern and Midwestern Historical Keyboard Societies. *Address:* 473 Devon Road, Morgantown, WV 26505, USA.

HUDSON Benjamin, b. 14 June 1950, Decatur, Illinois, USA. Violinist. *Education:* Studied in New York. *Career:* Co-founded the Schoenberg String Quartet 1977, changing name to Columbia String Quartet 1978; Has performed much modern repertory, including the premieres of Charles Wuorinen's Archangel, 1978, with trombonist David Taylor, and Second String Quartet, 1980, Berg's Lyric Suite in its version with soprano (Bethany Beardslee, New York, 1979), and Roussakis's Ephemeris, 1979; Further premieres include quartets by Morton Feldman 1980, Wayne Peterson 1984 and Larry Bell, 1985. *Honours include:* National Endowment of the Arts grants, 1979-81. *Recordings include:* String Quartet No 3 by Lukas Foss and Ned Rorem's Mourning Song, with William Parker, baritone.

HUEBER Kurt Anton, b. 9 July 1928, Salzburg, Austria. Composer; University Lecturer. *Education:* Diploma, piano and conducting, Musik Hochschule Mozarteum, Salzburg, 1948. *Career:* Section Leader, Konservatorium der Stadt Wien; works performed in concerts and on radio; Teacher, Musical Acoustics, Hochschule für Musik, Vienna, 1980-. *Compositions:* Scenic Music for Stage, Linz, 1958-60; Schwarz auf Weiss, 1st opera composed for Austrian TV, 1968; Symchromie 1, 1970; Symchromie II, 1972; Formant spectrale for string orchestra, 1974; Sonata for viola solo; Sonata for trumpet and piano; Opera, The Canterville Ghost, (O. Wilde), 1990-91. *Recordings:* Glockenspektren, for pipe-bells and piano; Iris, for piano and percussion; Horn und Tuba, Requiem for 4 Wagner-Tubas and Contrabass Tuba, 1977, Osiris Hymnus; Schein und Sein (W. Busch) 22 songs for Baritone and Piano (Koch Digital); CD: Musik for Violoncello and Piano (Koch digital). *Publications:* Mathematisch - physikalische Grundlagen einer ekmelischen Intervallehre. Mikrotone II, 1988; Ekmelische Harmonik, Mikrotone III, 1990. *Contributions to:* Mikrotone 1986; Pseudoharmonische Partialtonreihen, Ihre ekmelischen Intervallstrukturen, Ein Neuer Klangraum der Musiktheorie; Acustica, volumes, 26, 1972; Instrumentenbau Musik International, 1975; various other professional publications. *Hobbies:* Mathematics; Physics; Swimming; Travel. *Address:* A 1190 Wien, Paradisgasse 14, Austria.

HUFFSTODT Karen, b. 31 Dec. 1954, Illinois, USA. Singer (Soprano). *Education:* Studied at the Illinois Wesleyan and Northwestern Universities. *Career:* Sang with the New York City Opera from 1982 as Lehar's Merry Widow, Micaela, Violetta and Donna Anna; Santa Fe Opera 1984, as the Soldier's Wife in the US premiere of Henze's We come to the River; Returned 1989, as L'Ensoleillad in Massenet's Chérubin; Other engagements with Chicago Opera (Magda in La Rondine and Fiordiligi); Illinois Opera (title role in Mary, Queen of Scots by Thea Musgrave); Washington Opera (premiere of Menotti's Goya, 1986); Cologne Opera (Constanze, Agrippina, Donna Anna and Mozart's Countess); Metropolitan Opera (Violetta and Rosalinda, from season 1989-90); Other roles include Musetta (Los Angeles and Hamburg); Thais (Paris Opera, Nancy and Toulouse); Amalia in I Masnadieri by Verdi (Australian Opera); Salome (Lyon); Agathe and Arabella (Catania); Odabella in Attila (Opera North, 1990), and ROH, Covent Garden 1991; Season 1992 as Tosca at Antwerp, Turandot at Lyons, Chrysothemis at the Opera Bastille Paris; Opened season at La Scala 1993 as Spontini's Vestale; Strauss's Ariadne at the Opera Comique, Salome at the Bastille, 1994; Alice Ford at Antwerp, 1994. *Recordings include:* Salome in a French language version of Strauss's opera (Virgin). *Address:* c/o Athole Still Ltd., 113 Church Road, London SE19 2PR, England.

HUGGETT Monica, b. 16 May 1953, London. Violinist. *Education:* Studied at the Royal Academy of Music with Manoug Parikian; Early performance practice with Sigiswald Kuijken, Gustav Leonhardt and Ton Koopman. *Career:* Co-founded the Amsterdam Baroque Orchestra with Koopman 1980 and was its leader until 1987; Many performances on authentic, gut-string violins with such ensembles as the Hanover Band, Academy of Ancient Music, Raglan Baroque Players and Hausmusik; Worldwide tours as soloist, director and chamber musician in a repertoire extending from the late Renaissance to the Romantic with performances and recordings of Mozart, Beethoven, Schubert and Mendelssohn, and the concertos of Vivaldi and Bach: played the Beethoven Concerto with the Orchestra of the Age of Enlightenment under Ivan Fischer at the Elizabeth Hall, April 1991; the Mendelssohn Concerto under Charles Mackerras, 1992. *Recordings include:* Symphonies by Beethoven with the Hanover Band (as director), Nimbus; Vivaldi La Stravaganza and Schubert Octet, with the Academy of Ancient Music (Decca L'Oiseau Lyre); Vivaldi La Cetra and Schubert Trout Quintet, with the Raglan Baroque Players and Hausmusik (EMI); Rameau Pièces de Clavecin en Concerts and Corelli Violin Sonatas Op 5 with Trio Sonnerie, and Vivaldi Four Seasons, Mozart Violin Concertos (Virgin Classics); Bach Violin Concertos, with the Amsterdam Baroque Orchestra (Erato); Beethoven Concerto and Mendelssohn Concerto with the Orchestra of the Age of Enlightenment (EMI Eminence); Professor of Baroque and Classical Violin at the Akademie für Alte Musik, Bremen. *Address:* c/o Francesca McManus, 71 Priory Road, Kew Gardens, Surrey TW9 3DH, England.

HUGHES David Weirick, b. 2 Dec. 1945, Janesville, Wisconsin, USA. Ethnomusicologist. m. Gina Barnes, 16 Aug. 1975. *Education:* BA 1967, MPhil, Linguistics 1972, Yale University; Visiting Researcher, Tokyo University of Fine Arts & Music, 1978-80; MA, Clare Hall, Cambridge, England, 1982-85; PhD, Anthropology/Musicology, University of Michigan, 1985. *Career:* Lecturer in Japanese Linguistics 1972-73; Director, Japanese Music Study Group 1975-76, University of Michigan; Director, Cambridge (England) Gamelan Society, 1984-85; Lecturer in Ethnomusicology, School of Oriental and African Studies, University of London, England, 1987-. *Recording:* Min'yo & Min'yo: Yoshio Tanaka and David Hughes, 1980. *Publications:* The Archaeology of Early Music Cultures, ed with E Hickmann, 1988; The Heart's Home Town: Traditional Folk Song in Modern Japan, 1985. *Address:* Centre of Music Studies, School of Oriental and African Studies, London WC1H 0XG, England.

HUGHES Edward, b. 5 Sept 1920, Wallasey. Retired Headmaster. m. Grace Ollman, 1986. *Education:* Liverpool Matthay School of Music. *Career:* Writing children's songs, song books, musicals and hymns in association with Peter Westmore, lyric writer and librettist. *Recordings:* Come to Bethlehem; Christ in Competition. *Publications:* Come to Bethlehem; Songs from Aesops Fables, song book; Neddy the Donkey, nativity play; Chanticleer and the Fox, musical play; People Who Help Us, song book; Snow White and the Seven Dwarfs, song; Things that Help us, song book; Our Friends the Animals, song book; Brer Rabbit and Brer Fox, song books. *Memberships:* PRS; MCPS. *Hobbies:* Gardening; Walking. *Address:* Pen-y-Bryn, Catch, Halkyn, Holywell, Clwyd CH8 8DU, Wales,

HUGHES Martin Glyn, b. 23 Mar. 1950, Hemel Hempstead, England. Pianist. m. Catherine Elder, 21 Aug. 1979, 1 son, 1 daughter. *Education:* Salisbury Cathedral Choir School, 1960-63; Music scholar, Bryanston School, 1963-66; Paris Conservatoire, France, 1966-67; Private study with Yvonne Lefebuse, 1967-70; Moscow Conservatory, USSR, 1970-71. *Debut:* Wigmore Hall, London, England, 1972. *Career:* Proms, 1972; French radio and television, 1972; Cheltenham Festival, 1973; Making a Name, BBC Television, 1974; Tour of USSR, 1974; RPO and LSO debuts, 1975; Chichester and Llandaff Festivals, 1975; Recital and Concerto debut, Queen Elizabeth Hall, 1977; Tours and radio recitals, Portugal and Germany, 1977; Beethoven Sonata Cycle, 1979; Regular Radio 3 broadcasts, solo appearances including Royal Festival Hall, European tours, 1980-; Founder 1984, Artistic Director Music on the Fens festival and summer school 1984 and 1986, Fengate Music Trust; Director, Annual Summer School, Val de Saire, France, 1988, 1989; Bath Festival, 1983, 1985, 1986; Member, Kreutzer Piano Trio, 1985; Tours: USA, Israel, 1987-88. *Recording:* Beethoven Sonatas op. 110 and 111, 1984. *Publications:* Russian School of Piano Playing, (Translation/editing), 1976. *Honours:* 2nd prize, National Junior Piano Competition, 1964; Martin Musical Fund Scholar, 1967-68; French Government Scholar, 1968-70; Bronze Medal, Marguerite Long Competition, 1969; 2nd Prize, Canals Competition, Barcelona, 1970; British Council Scholar, 1970-71; Kirkman Society Award, 1973-79; Arts Council of Great Britain Award, 1975. *Address:* Fengate, Fen Drayton, Cambridge CB4 5SH, England.

HUGHES Owain Arwel, b. 21 March 1942, Cardiff, Wales. Conductor. m. Jean Bowen Lewis, 23 July, 1966, 1 son, 1 daughter. *Education:* University College Cardiff;

1964-66 Royal College of Music, London, with Adrian Boult and Harvey Philips; Further study with Kempe in London and Haitink in Amsterdam. *Career:* Professional careeer from 1968; Music Director, Royal National Eisteddfod of Wales, 1977; Associate Conductor, BBC Welsh Symphony Orchestra, 1980-; Music Director, Huddersfield Choral Society, 1980-86; Guest conductor with Welsh National Opera and English National Opera; Currently Associate Conductor of the Philharmonia Orchestra: concerts in UK and abroad, including Shostakovich's 10th and Leningrad Symphonies, the Verdi Requiem and Elgar's Violin Concerto with Itzhak Perlman; Guest condcutor in Europe and with the BBC Welsh Symphony and Hallé Orchestras: Mahler's Resurrection Symphony and Tippett's 4th Symphony in Manchester; Founded and became Artistic Director of the Welsh Proms in 1986; Series of programmes for BBC TV 1987 featuring settings of the Requeim Mass; Rossini's Stabat Mater on TV for Holy Week 1988; Conducted Mahler's 8th Symphony on Channel 4 television, 1990. *Honours:* Honorary DMus, University of Wales; Fellowship, University College, Cardiff; Honorary DMus from the Council for National Academic Awards in London; Fellowship from the Polytechnic of Wales; Honorary Bard of the Royal National Eisteddfod of Wales. *Memberships include:* Lord's Taverners. *Recordings:* Music by Paul Patterson withn the London Philharmonic; Works with the Hallé Orchestra and the Huddersfield Choral Society (EMI); Music by Delius and the 2nd Symphony of Vaughan Williams for ASV. *Hobbies:* Rugby; Cricket; Driving; Swimming; Soccer.*Address:* 11 Gerard Road, Harrow, Middlesex HA1 2ND, England.

HUGO Robert, b. 15 June 1962, Praha, Czechoslovakia. Organist; Conductor. *Education:* Charles University, Faculty of Life Sciences; Academy of Music, Prague, 1988-. *Debut:* Dafne M da Gagliano, Summer School of Ancient Music, Czech Republic. *Career:* Organist: Church of Saint Salvator, 1990, Monastery of Saint Franciscus, 1992; Founder, Capella Regia Musicalis (ensemble), 1992; Rappresentatione di Anima et di Corpo E de Cavalieri (as Guest Conductor at Janáček's Opera House, Brno, 1992-93. *Recordings:* Adam Michna CD, Czech Baroque music, 1992. *Hobbies:* Repair of ancient key instruments. *Address:* Jeremenkova 60, 147 00 Praha, Czech Republic.

HULA Pavel, b. 23 Jan 1952, Prague, Czechoslovakia. m. Helena Sirlova, 29 June 1976, 1 d. *Education:* Academy of Music Arts, Prague: Violin, 1970-74, Chamber Music, 1980-82. *Debut:* Festival Prague Spring, 1976. *Career:* First Violin, Kocian Quartet, 1975- with performances at over 1800 concerts in 21 countries, as well as TV and Radio appearnces. *Recordings:* Virtuoso Violin Duetts, 1993; Mozart String Quartets, Dvořák, string quartets, Brahms, sextets and quintets, for Orfeo, Haydn quartets. *Honours:* Kocian Violin Competition 1st Prize, 1963, 1964; Concertino Praga, Radio Competition, 2nd Prize, 1969; Prize, Society of Chamber Music of Czech Philharmonic. *Hobbies:* Photography; Sport. *Address:* Vyzlovska 2251, 100 00 Prague 10, Czech Republic.

HULFORD Denise Lovona, b. 24 Oct. 1944, Christchurch, New Zealand. Composer; Singer; Teacher. m. Commander R.F. Hulford, RNZN, 2 Jan. 1965, 1 son, 1 daughter. *Education:* ATCL, Performance Piano, 1965; BM, Victoria University, Wellington, 1982; MM, Composition, Auckland University, 1985; Studied Piano with Jim Powell, Wollongong; Studied Singing with Joan Howard, 1972; Singing Lessons with Emily Mair, 1979; Post Graduate study at Goldsmiths' College, London University, 1992. *Career:* Board Member and Company Secretary of The New Zealand Music Centre. *Compositions:* Pyramids for String Quartet, Plus Forty Years for Tape; Evolution, for Narrator/Tenor and Orchestra; Fascicle, for Cello, Trumpet and Clarinet; Evanescence, for Bassoon, Flute and Bamboo Flute; Time, for Baritone and String Quartet; Cabaret for Brass Band (Arrangement); Haiku, Song Cycle for Contralto and Piano; Meditations, suite for Orchestra; Bold as Brass, for 2 Trumpets, Horn, Trombone and Tuba.

Publications: Canzona Vol.I 1988 - Editorship; Canzona Volume Eleven, 1989-, Editor. *Address:* 16 Woodcote Drive, Glenfield 10, Auckland, New Zealand.

HUMBLET Ans, b. 17 sept 1957, Maastricht, Netherlands. Singer (Soprano). *Education:* Studied with Elisabeth Ksoll and at Amsterdam. *Career:* Appearances with Netherlands Opera from 1983; Wuppertal Opera 1986-90 in such roles as the Queen of Night, Blundchen, Marie in Zar und Zimmermann, Woglinde, Despina and Musetta; Sang Kunigunde in the German premiere of Bernstein's Canide at Wuppertal, 1990; Enschede Holland 1990, as Ninetta in Mozart's La Finta Giardiniera; Guest appearances at Dussseldort and Aachen as the Queen of Night, at Monchengladbach as Frasquita in Carmen; Concert engagements in Beethoven's Ninth, Mendelssohn's St Paul, Bruckner's Te Deum, Carmina Burana and Masses by Haydn and Mozart; Broadcasts in Holland, Germany and Belgium; Engaged at Maastricht from 1990. *Address:* De Nederlandse Opera, Waterlooplein 22, 1011 PG Amsterdam, Netherlands.

HUMPHREYS Garry Paul, b. 22 Feb 1946, Nottingham, England. Baritone Singer; Lecturer; Writer; m. Janet Zimmermann, 30 July 1977 (div). *Education:* Henry Mellish School, Nottingham, England; Univerity of North London School of Information Studies, ALA, 1970; Studied singing with Norman Platt, Nigel Rogers and (principally) John Carol Case; Conducting with Bryan Fairfax. *Career:* Professional chorister and soloist in concerts, recitals and broadcasts; Song recitals with Patricia Williams; Anthology entertainments with Hardwick Players, Voice & Verse; Lectures and Lecture-recitals for music clubs and recorded music societies; Committee member, English Song Award, 1982-89, Chairman, 1986-89; Secretary of Association of English Singers and Speakers, since 1988; Occasional conductor. *Publications:* Member of editorial committee, A Century of English Song, 1993-; Record sleeve and concert programme notes, periodical articles, book reviews, including, The Year in Reference, 1993-. *Honour:* FRSA. *Memberships:* Association of English Singers and Speakers; Elgar Society; Incorporated Society of Musicians; Library Association. *Hobbies:* Listening to music; Books; Theatre; Walking; Watching Cricket. *Address:* 25 Tamar House, Kennington Lane, London SE11 4XA, England.

HÜNGSBERG Gottfried Heinrich, b. 22 Nov. 1944, Tutzing, Bavaria, Federal Republic of Germany. Composer; Microelectronics Consultant. m. Elfriede Jelinek, 12 June 1974. *Education:* BS Engineering, University of Aachen, 1968. *Career:* Leader, Arbeitsgruppe Elektronische Musik, Munich, 1967-; Owner, microelectronics consultants firm, Vienna and Munich, 1975-; Founder, Electronic Films, 1980. *Compositions:* Screen music for Welt am Draht, directed by Rainer Werner Fassbinder, 1973; Numerous compositions for radio, theatre and films. *Memberships:* German Composers Association; International Software Users Association. *Address:* 42 Sendlingerstrasse, Munich 2, D-8000, Germany.

HUNKA Pavlo, b. 7 Apr 1959, England. Singer (Bass). *Education:* Studied with Joseph Ward at the Royal Northern College of Music. *Career:* Has performed in concerts throughout Britain as soloist and conductor; Royal Albert Hall London 1988 in a concert celebrating 1000 years of Christianity in the Ukraine; Opera debut as Melisso in a 1989 production of Handel's Alcina at the RNCM; Has also sung Theseus in A Midsummer Night's Dream and Philip II in Don Carlos with the RNCM; Professional opera debut as Basilio in Il barbiere di Siviglia, Welsh National Opera 1990; Recent engagements as Rangoni in Boris Godunov for Basle Opera, and Dulcamara (L'Elisir d'Amore); Other roles include Colline in La Bohème and Prince Gremin in Eugene Onegin; Now on contract to Basel Stadttheater, Switzerland. *Honours include:* Diploma with Distinction in Performance, RNCM 1990; Ricordi Opera Prize; Peter Moores Foundation and Wolfson Foundation

Scholarships. *Address:* c/o Harrison Parrott Ltd., 12 Penzance Place, London W11 4PA, England.

HUNT Alexandra, b. 1940, USA. Opera and Concert Singer, Librettist and Libretto Translator. *Education:* BA, Vassar College; BS, Juilliard School of Music; Sorbonne University, Paris, France. *Debut:* As Marie in La Scala's first production of Wozzeck in German, 1971, conducted by Claudio Abbado. *Career:* Title role, Lulu at Metropolitan Opera, Katya Kabanova sung in Czech, Janácek Festival, Brno; Jenůfa, Lincoln Center, New York City; Soprano soloist, Penderecki Passion According to St. Luke, Philadelphia Orchestra; Amelia in Ballo in Maschera, Providence, Rhode Island and Bucharest; Title role, Tosca, Bulgaria, Romania and Czechoslovakia; Marie in Wozzeck, Hamburg Staatsoper; Lady Macbeth in Macbeth, Florentine Opera and Kentucky Opera; Soprano Soloist, Mahler Fourth Symphony, Bogota Filarmonica, in Beethoven's Ninth Symphony, Omaha and Des Moines Symphonies, many other roles. *Recordings:* Songs of John Alden Carpenter, Charles T. Griffes and Edward MacDowell, Orion Recordings ORS 77272. *Publications:* Author, New English Translation of Mozart's Don Giovanni and Così fan Tutte; Book reviewer for Best Sellers Magazine. *Address:* 170 W 74th Street, Apartment 1106, New York, NY 10023, USA.

HUNT Donald, b. 26 July 1930, Gloucester, England. Director of Music. m. Josephine Benbow, 24 July 1954, 2s, 2d. *Education:* Private study with Herbert Sumsion; FRCO; ARCM. *Career:* Assistant Organist, Gloucester Cathedral, 1947-54; Director of Music, King's School, Gloucester, 1951-54; Master of the Music, St John's Torquay, 1954-57; Director of Music, Leeds Parish Church, 1957-74; Organist and Master of the Choristers, Worcester Cathedral, 1974-; Conductor, Halifax Choral Society, 1957-88; Conductor: Worcester Three Choirs Festival and Worcester Festival Choral Society, 1975-. *Compositions:* Suite for Organ; Missa Brevis; Missa Nova; The Worcester Service Song Cycle Strings in the earth and air; Magnificat and Nunc Dimittis; Christmas Night; Te Deum; Several short choral works. *Recordings:* 8 with Leeds Parish Church Choir; 26 with Worcester Cathedral Choir and Festival Choral Society; 6 organ recitals; 1 with Halifax Choral Society. *Publications:* SS Wesley: Cathedral Musician. *Honours:* Hon DMus, Leeds University, 1975; OBE, 1993. *Hobbies:* Sport; Reading; Poetry. *Address:* 13 College Green, Worcester WR1 2DH, England.

HUNT Fionnuala, b. 1960, Belfast, Northern Ireland. Concert Violinist. *Education:* Studied at Ulster College of Music, Royal College of Music and the Vienna Hochschule für Musik with Wolfgang Schneiderhan. *Career:* Leader and soloist with the Vienna Chamber Former member of the Bavarian State Opera Orchestra in Munich and co-leader of the RTE Symphony Orchestra in Dublin; Guest leader of the Ulster Orchestra and the Irish Chamber Orchestra; Duo recitals with pianist sister Una Hunt, performing throughout Ireland and in Austria, Germany, Czechoslovakia, Italy and Britain; Member of the Dublin Piano Trio and the contemporary music group, Sequenzo; Solo appearances with the National Symphony Orchestra of Ireland, the RTE Concert Orchestra and the Ulster Orchestra; Played Lutoslawski's Partita at the Maltings Concert Hall, Snape. *Address:* c/o Owen and White Management, 14 Nightingale Lane London N8 7QU. England.

HUNT Michael Francis, b. 28 Nov. 1945, USA. Composer. m. Patricia Gilbert Hunt, 15 July 1972, 2 sons, 2 daughters. *Education:* BM, St Louis Institute of Music, 1968; PhD, Washington University, 1974. *Career:* Performance of works by Los Angeles Philharmonic, St Louis Symphony, Jackson Symphony, Springfield Symphony, Kirkwood and Webster Symphonies; Chamber works performed internationally; Composer-in-Residence, Fontbonne College, 1977-86; Visiting Fulbright Scholar, Trinity College, Dublin, Ireland, 1985-86; Adjunct Professor of Music Compostion, St Louis University, 1988; Program Development Specialist, Missouri Arts Council, 1990. *Compositions:* Lento for Strings; Asymptopia, Other Realities, Space: Inner/Outer, Music for Multiple Keyboards, Metal Ensemble, Avatar, Tao Shu, Orpheus, St Louis; Music for Brass and Percussion, Theme in Two Moods, Moon Shadows, Emerald Reflections published by Magnamusic-Baton, (MMB); Three Contemporary Interval Studies, The Television Suite, published by Magnamusic-Baton (MMB). *Recordings:* Other Realities recorded on Reflections album, New Music Circle records; Before the Wave and Winds Answer recorded on Multiphase Records. *Publication:* Figuered Brass Primer, 1979. *Memberships:* ASCAP; American Society of Composers, Inc; American Music Center. *Address:* 2019 Sidney, St Louis, MO 63104, USA.

HUNTER Carol, b. 25 May 1949, Washington, USA. Choral Director. m. Douglas R Hunter, 28 June 1969, 1s. *Education:* BMus, Westminster Choir College, 1973; Conservatory of Geneva, 1983; MMus Conducting, University of Maryland, 1990. *Career:* Founder, Artistic and Music Director, VOCE, a semi-professional choral ensemble of 26 voices; Director of Music Ministries at Messiah UMC, Springfield, VA: Soloist in major choral works in Switzerland and France. *Memberships:* Conductor's Guild: ACDA; Chorus America, AGO; Friday Morning Music Club; Early Music America, Hymn Society of America. *Hobbies:* Skiing; Languages; Archaeology; Travel; Sailing. *Address:* VOCE, 1559 Inlet Ct, Reston VA 22090-4423, USA.

HUNTER Rita, b. 15 Aug. 1933, Wallasey, Cheshire, England. Prima Donna; Leading Soprano. m. John Darnley Thomas, 1960, 1 daughter. *Education:* Wallasey; joined Carl Rosa, 1950. *Debut:* Berlin 1970; Covent Garden, 1972; Metropolitan, New York, 1972 as Brünnhilde in Die Walküre; Munich 1973; Australia 1978 (returned 1980, 1981); Seattle Wagner Festival, 1980. *Career:* Sang Brünnhilde in first complete Ring cycle with Sadler's Wells, 1973; Norma at New York Metropolitan, 1975; Leading Roles in Aida, Trovatore, Masked Ball, Cavalleria Rusticana, Lohengrin, Flying Dutchman, Idomeneo, Don Carlos, Turandot, Nabucco, Macbeth, Tristan and Isolde, Elektra; Leading Soprano, Sadler's Wells, 1958-, Australian Opera, 1981-; Lecturer in Voice U.C.L.A., USA; sang in Act III of Die Walküre at the Festival Hall, 1990; Title role in concert performances of Turandot at the Albert Hall, 1990. *Recordings:* Ritorna Vincitor, ABC/Polygram; Many including complete Ring, complete Euryanthe, and several recital discs. *Publications:* Autiobiography, Wait Till The Sunshines Nellie 1986. *Honours:* CBE, 1980; Hon DMus, Liverpool, 1983, RAM, 1978; D.Litt Warwick, 1978. *Hobbies:* Sewing; Oil Painting; Reading; Gardening (Member Royal National Rose Society); Caravanning; Swimming. *Current Management* Mark Bonello, 52 Dean Street, Soho, London, W1V 5HJ, England. *Address:* 305 Bobbin Head Road, North Turramurra, NSW 2074, Australia.

HURD Michael John, b. 19 Dec 1928, Gloucester, England. Composer; Author. *Education:* Pembroke College, Oxford University, 1950-53. *Career:* Professor of Theory, Royal Marines School of Music, 1953-59; Freelance composer & author, 1959-. *Compositions include:* Opera: Widow of Ephesus, 1971; The Aspern Papers, 1993; Choral: Missa Brevis, 1966; Music's Praise, 1968; This Day to Man, 1974; Shepherd's Calendar, 1975; Phoenix & Turtle, 1975; Genesis, 1987; Night Songs of Edward Thomas, 1990. Orchestral: Dance Diversions, 1972; Concerto da Camera, 1987; Overture to Unwritten Comedy, 1987. Chamber music: Flute Sonatina, 1964; Violin Sonata, 1987. Various other works. *Publications include:* Immortal Hour: Life & Times of Rutland Boughton, 1962; Outline History of European Music, 1968; Ordeal of Ivor Gurney, 1978; Vincent Novello & Company, 1981; Rutland Boughton and the Glastonbury Festivals, 1993. *Contributions to:* New Grove Dictionary of Music & Musicians; New Oxford Companion to Music; Athlone History of British Music; Musik in Geschichte und Gegenwart. *Address:*

4 Church Street, West Liss, Hampshire GU33 6JX, England.

HURFORD Peter, b. 22 Nov 1930, Somerset, England. Organist. m. Patricia Matthews, 6 Aug 1955, 2s. 1d. *Education:* Royal College of Music, 1948-49; ARCM; Organ Scholar, Jesus College, Cambridge, 1949-53; MA Music and Law; BMus; FRCO. *Debut:* Royal Festival Hall, London, 1957. *Career:* Master of the Music, St Albans Cathedral, 1958-78; Concert tours of Europe, America, Australasia and Japan, 1958-; Founder, International Organ Festival, 1963; Visiting Professor, Universities of Cincinnati, 1967-68 and Western Ontario, 1976-77; Visiting Artist in Residence, Sydney Opera House, 1980-82; Betts Fellow, University of Oxford, 1992-93; Radio and television appearances. *Recordings:* Over 65 including: Complete Organ Works of J S Bach, F Couperin, Handel, and Hindemith. *Publications:* Making Music on the Organ, 1988; Articles in Musical Times. *Honours:* FRSCM, 1977; Gramophone Award, 1979; DMus, Baldwin-Wallace College, Ohio, 1981, and Bristol University, 1992; Hon Member, RAM, 1982; OBE, 1984; FRCM, 1987. *Memberships:* Council, 1964-, President, 1980-82, Royal College of Organists; Incorporated Society of Musicians; Royal Philharmonic Society. *Hobbies:* Walking; Wine. *Current Management* North America only: Karen McFarlane Artists Inc, 12429 Cedar Road, Suite 5, Cleveland, OH 44106, USA. *Address:* Broom House, St Bernard's Road, St Albans, Herts AL3 5RA, England.

HURLEY Laurel, b. 14 Feb. 1927, Allentown, Pennsylvania, USA. Singer (Soprano). *Education:* Studied with her mother. *Debut:* Sang in the Student Prince, New York 1943. *Career:* New York City Opera debut as Zerlina, 1952; Sang at the Metropolitan Opera from 1955 as Oscar, Musetta, Mimi, Adele, Susanna, Olympia, Papagena, Zerlina and Perichole; Also sang in I Capuleti e i Montecchi by Bellini; Many concert appearances in North America.

HURNEY Kate, b. 14 Sept. 1941, Quincy, Massachusetts, USA. Singer (Lyric Coloratura Soprano. m. Robert J. Braverman, 1 son, 1 daughter. *Education:* BA, Tufts University; Columbia University; New England Conservatory; Juilliard School; Manhattan School; Accademia Chigiana; International Opernstudio, Zurich; Dalcroze School. *Debut:* With American Opera Society, Carnegie Hall. *Career includes:* Appearances with Houston, Miami and Buffalo Symphonies; National Orchestra: Santo Domingo; Sudwest Funk; Extensive chamber music and recital work; American Opera Society; Houston Grand Opera; Opera Company of Boston; Dallas Civic Opera; Opera Rara; London; Théâtre Monnaie, Brussels; Zurich Opera; Freiburg Opera, Germany; New Opera Theatre, Brooklyn Academy; San Juan; Guggenheim Museum (Virgil Thomson); Kennedy Center; Wolf Trap Festival; Co-Founder, Public Opera Theater, 1972; Concerts of Irish-related material including, St Patrick's Cathedral, New York City, 1986 and 1987; Opéra de Nice, Théâtre Champs Elysées, Paris, France; Belfast Festival, Wexford Festival. *Recordings:* Decca, Poseidon and Ardee, Rubini Society, 1992. *Honours:* Recipient of various musical honours. *Memberships:* AGMA; Equity. *Hobbies:* Travel; Gardening; Cooking; Antiques. *Current Management:* Tornay Management, 127 W 72nd Street, New York, NY 10023, USA. *Address:* Apt 10B, 235 W 76th Street, New York, NY 10023, USA.

HURNÍK Ilja, b. 25 Nov 1922, Ostrava, Czechoslovakia. Composer; Pianist; Writer. m. Jana Hurnikova, 26 Mar 1966, 1 son. *Education:* Academy of Musical Arts, Prague. *Debut:* As Composer, Piano Piece, 1933; As Pianist, Concert, Prague, 1942. *Career:* Professor, Prague Conservatorium; As Pianist gave concerts in Europe and USA, including piano duo with wife Jana; Regular guest appearances on radio and TV as composer, pianist and music commentator. *Compositions:* Lady Killers, opera; Diogenes, opera; Ezop, cantata; Sonata da camera; Variations on a theme of Pergolesi. *Recordings:* Compositions: Oboe Concerto; Sulamith; Esercizi for wind quartet; Maryka, cantata;

Musica da camera for strings; Ezop; As pianist: Debussy, Preludes, Images, Estampes, Arabesques. *Publications:* Beletrie: Trumpeter of Jericho, 1965; The Geese of the Capitol, 1969; En Route with the Aviator; 2 radio plays. *Honours:* Grand Prix for Variations on a Theme of Pergolesi, Piano Duo Association of Japan, 1990; 1st Prize for Innocenza, International Competition, Piano Duo Association of Japan, 1992; DSc honoris causa, 1992. *Membership:* Association of Composers, Prague. *Hobby:* Natural science (botany). *Address:* 11000 Prague, Varodni tr 35, Czech Republic.

HURSHELL Edmund, b. 1921, USA. Singer (Bass-baritone). *Education:* Studied in the USA and Germany. *Career:* Engaged at the Stadtische Oper Berlin, 1952-53, Kiel, 1953-55; Vienna Staatsoper, 1955- 60, as Amonasro, Scarpia, Alfio, izarro Hans Sachs, Orestes and Mandryka; Theatre de la Monnaie Brussels, 1961, as the villains in Les Contes d'Hoffmann; Bologna and Amsterdam, 1963, as Wolfram and Wotan; Sang Handel's Giulio Cesare at Barcelona 1964, the Dutchman and the Wanderer at Buenos Aires and Lille, 1965; Further engagements at Nuremberg, Rome, Tel Aviv, Athens and Philadelphia; Metropolitan Opera, 1967, as Kurwenal in Tristan; Appearances at Graz 1967-69; Other roles include Kaspar, the Grand Inquisitor and Falstaff. *Address:* c/o Vereinigte Buhnen, Kaisre Josef Platz 10, A-8010 Graz, Austria.

HURST George, b. 20 May 1926, Edinburgh, Scotland. Conductor. *Education:* Various preparatory and public schools in the UK and Canada; Royal Conservatory, Toronto. *Career:* Assistant Conductor, Opera, Royal Conservatory of Music, Toronto, 1946; Lecturer, Harmony & Counterpoint, Composition, etc., Peabody Conservatory of Music, Baltimore, USA, 1947; Conductor, York Pennsylvania Symphony Orchestra, 1950-55, concurrently of Peabody Conservatory Orchestra, 1952-55; Assistant Conductor, LPO 1955-57 with tour of Russia, 1956; Associate Conductor, BBC Northern Symphony orchestra, 1957; Principal Conductor, BBC Northern Symphony Orchestra (previously BBC Northern Orchestra), 1958-68; Artistic Adviser, Western Orchestral Society 1968-73; Staff Conductor, Western Orchestral Society (Bournemouth Symphony orchestra and Bournemouth Sinfonietta), 1973-; Principal Guest Conductor, BBC Scottish Symphony Orchestra, 1986-1989; Principal Conductor, National Symphony Orchestra of Ireland, 1990-93; Frequent Guest Conductor, Europe, Israel, Canada, 1956-. *Address:* 21 Oslo Court, London NW8, England.

HURTEAU Jean-Pierre, b. 5 Dec 1924, Montreal, Canada. Singer (Bass). *Education:* Studied in Montreal and with Marital Singher, 1950- 52. *Debut:* Sang in concert at Montreal, 1949. *Career:* Opera debut Montreal, 1950, as Frere Laurent in Romeo et Juliette; Studied further in Europe and sang in Toulouse from 1957; Pairs Opera and Opera-Comique, 1958- 70, as Mozart's Commendatore, Alfonso and Figaro, La Roche in Capriccio and Mephistopheles; Guest appearances in Lyon, Marseilles and Monte Carlo; Rome, 1974, Toronto, 1976, festival engagements at Orange; Sang in concert from 1970 after returning to Canada. *Address:* c/o Canadian Opera Company 227 Front Street East, Toronto, Ontario M5A 1EB, Canada .

HURWITZ Emanuel, b. 7 May 1919, London, England. Violinist. *Education:* Royal Academy of Music and with Bronislav Huberman. *Career:* Led the Hurwitz String Quartet 1946-51 and the Goldsborough (later English Chamber) Orchestra 1946-68; Leader of the Melos Ensemble 1956-72 and the New Philharmonia Orchestra 1969-71; Leader of the Aeolian Quartet from 1970. *Recordings include* Brandenburg Concertos; Handel's Concerti Grossi with the English Chamber Orchestra; Schubert's Octet and Trout Quintet, Mozart and Brahms Clarinet Quintets with the Melos Ensemble; Complete Haydn Quartets edited by H.C. Robbins Landon; Ravel, Debussy and Late Beethoven Quartets. *Membership:* ISM. *Honours:* Gold Medal, Worshipful Company of Musicians, 1967; CBE 1978. *Hobbies:* Collecting books and antique bows for string instruments; Photography. *Address:* 25 Dollis Avenue, London N3 1DA, England.

HUS Walter, b. 2 July 1959, Mol, Belgium. Composer; Pianist. *Education:* Diploma supérieur, Brussels Royal Conservatory, 1984. *Career Includes:* Recitals as classical pianist since early childhood, Italy, Germany, Poland; Performances as improviser/interpreter of own compositions, 1982-; Concerts throughout Europe with group Maximalist, own compositions, 1984-. Member, Belgisch Pianokwartet, Simpletones, etc. Various radio & television appearances; Video film with Marie André & Walter Verdin; Currently active as composer, several works for ballet, full-sized opera. *Compositions Include:* 8 etudes on improvisation, piano solo; Music for fashion show, Yamamoto, Brussels; Muurwerk, music for choreography, Roxane Huilmand; Die Nacht, opera, 2 acts, libretto by Wolfgang Kolb (unfinished); Compositie, video film by Marie André about W. Hus; Hus/Verdin, video tape by Walter Verdin; Liefde, composition for 4 pianists at 2 pianos; La Theorie, idem, both written for Belgisch Pianokwartet. *Recordings:* 8 etudes on improvisation, 1984; Maximalist, LP, 1985; Muurwerk, 1986; Die Nacht, radio recording, 1987. *Honours:* 1st prize, piano 1981, harmony 1981, practical harmony 1983, Brussels Royal Conservatory. *Current Management:* Lucifer Productions.

HUSA Karel, b. 7 Aug 1921, Prague, Czechoslovakia. Composer; Conductor; Professor Emeritus. m. Simone Perault, 23 Feb 1926, 4d. *Education:* Conservatory of Music, 1941-45, Academy of Music, 1945-47, Prague; Ecole Normale de Musique de Paris, 1946-48; Conservatoire de Musique de Paris, 1948-49; Private study with Nadia Boulanger (composition), Andre Cluytens, (conducting). *Career includes:* Assistant Professor, 1954, Associate Professor, 1957, Full Professor, 1961, Teaching composition, theory, conducting and orchestration, Cornell University; Conductor, Cornell University Orchestra, 1956-75, Ithaca Chamber ;Orchestra, 1955-61, Cayuga Chamber Orchestra, 1978-84; Guest conductor with national orchestras throughout Europe, USA, Hong Kong and Puerto Rico, Asia and Japan. *Compositions include:* Fanfare for Brass and Timpani, 1980; Patoral for String Orchestra, 1980; Three Dance Sketches, 1980; Intradas and Interludes, 1980; The Trojan Women, 1981; Concertino for Piano, 1983; Symphonic Suite 1986; Concerto for Orchestra, 1984; Concerto fo Organ, 1987; Concerto for Trumpet, 1987; Frammenti for Organ, 1987; Concerto for Violoncello, 1988; String Quartet No 4, 1990; Concerto for Violin, 1993. *Recordings include:* Conducted recordings with Cento Soli Orchestra in Paris (Bartok and Brahms), Stockholm and Prague Symphonies (Husa); Orchestre des Solistes (Husa: Fantasies); CD Discs: Music for Prague, 1968; String Quartets, No 2 and 3 and Evocations of Slovakia; Symphony No 1 Serenade, Mosaiques, Landscapes; Apotheosis of this Earth, Monodrama; Concerto for Percussion. *Publications include:* Variations for piano Quartet, 1984; Concerto for Orchestra, 1986; Concerto for violoncello, 1989 among many others; Karel Husa, a Bio Bibliography, USA. *Address:* 1030 Hanshaw Road, Ithaca, NY 14850, USA

HUSS Hugo Jan, b. 26 Jan 1934, Timisoara, Roumania. Symphony Orchestra Conductor. m. Mirella Regis, 1 July 1970, 1 d. *Education:* Bucharest Conservatory of Music and Roosevelt University of Chicago. *Debut:* Concert, Roumanian Atheneum, Bucharest. Career: TV Appearance Performance of Tosca with Placido Domingo; Radio Broadcast on WLXR of Each Concert of La Crosse Symphony Orchestra, Last Major Appearance Performing Berliozs Damnation of Faust; Broadcasts on Radio Louisville, Kentucky, with Louisville Symphony Orchestra; Alabama Symphony Orchestra; Cape Town Symphony Orchestra, South Africa; Tbilisi, Russia; Krakow, Poland; Brno, Czechoslovakia; Sarejevo, Yugoslavia; Grand Rapids, USA; Guadalajara Symphny, Mexico. *Hobbies:* Philately; Computers; Nature. *Address:* N1972 Hickory Lane, La Crosse, WI 54601, USA.

HUSSON Robert Farrin, b. 28 May 1938, Bromley, Kent. Organist; Teacher; Examiner; Adjudicator. m. Sheila Randell, 1 son, 1 daughter by first marriage. *Career:* Professor, Blackheath Conservatoire of Music, 1972-87; Examiner, Associated Board of RSM 1979-; Organist and Music Director, Engerdal Kommune, Norway 1989-93; Organist Borge (Fredrikstad Kommune), 1993-; Recitals at major cathedrals, churches and town halls in British Isles; Also recitals in Hong Kong, Singapore and Malaysia. *Recordings:* Music of Langlais and Vierne at All Saints, Blackheath; Music of Peeters and Karg-Elert at St George's, Hanover Square; Music of Karg-Elert at All Souls, Langham Place; Music of Guilmant and others at All Souls, Langham Place. *Honours:* Silver Medal (LGSM piano performers) for highest marks in British Isles, 1962; Limpus Prize for ARCO, 1972; Coventry Cathedral Recital Award for FRCO, 1973. *Memberships:* Royal College of Organists; Norsk Kantor og Organistforbund. *Hobbies:* Reading; Cricket. *Address:* Løenveien 7, 1653 Sellebakk, Norway.

HUSSON Suzanne, b. 4 Apr. 1943, Buenos Aires, Argentina. Pianist. *Education:* Began musical studies at age 5 with Mrs. E. Westerkamp; Later attended: Conservatoire M. de Falla, Buenos Aires; Conservatory of Geneva (Prof. Hilbrandt); Staatliche Hochschule für Musik, Köln (Prof B. Seidlhofer); and special courses given by Maestro Arturo Benedetti Michelangeli (Italy and Switzerland). *Debut:* 1st Public Recital at age 8, Buenos Aires. *Career:* Various International Performances in Recitals and as Soloist with Chefs such as: J. Guyonnet, Marc Andrae, W. Sawallisch, C. Dutoit, and Orchestra Philarmonique de Lyon, Orchestra Philarmonique de Stuttgart, Orchestra de la Radio Suisse Italienne and Orchestra of Swiss Romande; TV and Radio Appearances in Germany and Switzerland; Radio Appearances in Argentina, Poland and France. *Recordings:* Stravinsky, Les Noces, Directed by Charles Dutoit, Erato Label, 1973; R. Vuataz, Concert for Piano and Orchestra, Opus 112, Orchestra of Swiss Romande, Directed by Wolfgang Sawallisch, CBS Label, 1981; Scarlatti-Ginastera-Debussy-Ravel, Fono Label, 1987. *Hobbies:* Swimming; TV; Reading. *Current Management:* Wismer-Casetti, Rue Merle-d'Aubigné 26, 1207 Geneva, Switzerland. *Address:* 8 Rue Daubin, 1203 Geneva, Switzerland.

HUSZÁR Lajos, b. 26 Sept. 1948, Szeged, Hungary. Composer. *Education:* Secondary Music School, Szeged, Istvan Vantus, 1963-67; Academy of Music, Budapest, Endre Szervanszky, Zsolt Durko, 1967-73; Academy of St Cecilia, Rome, Italy, Goffredo Petrassi, 1975. *Compositions include:* 5 Monologues to poems by Janos Parancs for mezzosoprano and orchestra; Csomorkany, for 10 players, 1973; Hold-lepte uton, cantata for children's or female choir and orchestra; Musica concertante for 13 players, 1975; 69th Psalm, for tenor and piano, 1976; 5 pieces for piano, 1977; 2 Songs to poems by Endre Ady for bass and piano, 1977-83; Scherzo and Adagio, for chamber orchestra, 1979; Sonata for harpischord, 1979-85; 5 Variations for cello solo; Brass Quintet, 1980; 3 Songs to poems by Else Lasker-Schüler for soprano and viola, 1981-89; Serenata Concertante, flute and string orchestra; Songs of Solitude for soprano and percussion, 1983; Notturno for piano, 1984; Concerto rustico for chamber orchestra, 1985; Chamber concerto for cello and 17 strings, 1987; String quartet, 1991; Choirs: Caligaverunt, Dies Sanctificatus, Ave Maria, Song of Fate - female; Under the Silver rose - male; 2 madrigals to poems by Sándor Weöres, The Flower of Silence - mixed; pedagogic pieces, choirs; Libera me for organ, 1993. *Recordings:* Musica concertante; Ave Maria, Dies Sanctificatus - female choirs; Chamber concerto. *Memberships:* Association of Hungarian Composers; Hungarian Society of Music. *Address:* Posta's u. 12., 6729 Szeged, Hungary.

HUSZTI Joseph Bela, b. 27 Sept. 1936, Lorain, Ohio, USA. Conductor; Professor; Voice Teacher. m. Melinda Murray, 1 daughter. *Education:* BMus, MMus, School of Music, Northwestern University; Oberlin Conservatory; University of Southern California;

Occidental College; Conducting studies with Otto Werner-Mueller, Howard Swan, Helmut Rilling and voice with William Vennard and Todd Duncan. *Career:* Director of Choral Activities, Bakersfield College, California, 1959-66; Director of Choral and Voice, University of Delaware, Newark, 1966-72; Director of Choral Activities, Boston University, Massachusetts, 1972-77; Director, Head, Young Vocalists Programme, Tanglewood, 1972-77; Director of Choral and Voice, University of California, 1977-; Founder-Director, California Chamber Singers, 1978; Adjudicator, Clinician in 30 states, Far East and Europe; Choir tours worldwide including Europe 1965, 1971, 1979 and the Far East 1982, Britain 1984, Europe 1986, England, Hungary, Poland, Austria Concert Tour, 1988; Far East Concert Tour, Korea, Hong Kong, Macau, Japan, 1990. *Recordings:* Music at Tanglewood; International Koren Concert, Holland; IMAX production To the LIMIT, UC Irvine Chamber Singers, 1990. *Publications:* Chorhythmics, 1975; In Search of Answers, 1977; In Quest of Answers, Hinshaw Publisher, 1991. *Hobbies:* Travel; Sports; Chamber music. *Address:* University of California Music Department, School of Fine Arts, Irvine, CA 92717, USA.

HUTCHESON Jere Trent, b. 16 Sept. 1938, Marietta, Georgia, USA. Composer; Professor of Music. m. (1) Virginia Bagby, 1 daughter; (2) Mary Ellen Gayley Cleland, 21 June 1982, 1 son, 1 daughter. *Education:* BMus, Stetson University; MMus, Louisiana State University; PhD, Michigan State University; Berkshire Music Center. *Compositions include:* Passacaglia for band; 3 things for Dr. Seuss; Shadows of Floating Life; Wonder Music, I, II, III, IV, V; Sensations; Transitions; Construction Set; Colossus; 3 Pictures of Satan; Electrons; Fantaisie-Impromptu; Nocturnes of the Inferno; Passing, Passing, Passing; Patterns; Cosmic Suite; Earth Gods Symphony; Chromphonic Images for Symphonic Band; Will-O-The-Wisps for Solo Violin; The Song Book for Tenor and Flute; Duo Sonata for Clarinet and Percussion; Concerto for Piano and Wind Orchestra; Metaphors for Orchestra; Interplay for Alto Saxophone and Mallet Percussion; Ritual and Dance for female chorus; Five French Portraits for Wind Orchestra; Duo Concertante in memoria di Margot Evans for Violin and Piano; Concerto to Violin and Small Orchestra; Chamber Opera: Long Live the Composer. *Hobbies:* Chess; French; Travel; Gardening. *Address:* 6064 Abbott Road, East Lansing, MI 48823, USA.

HUTCHINSON Nigel, b. 1963, England. Concert Pianist. *Education:* University of Glasgow, Guildhall School with Craig Sheppard and Juillard with Earl Wild. *Career:* Wigmore Hall debut, 1988 followed by concerts in France, Germany, Italy, Czechoslovakia and elsewhere in Europe; Concerto debut with the London Mozart Players under Jane Glover; Festival engagements at Horrogate and Glasgow, and recitals at the Salle Pleyel Paris, Barbican Center and Festival Hall London and Symphony Hall Birmingham; broadcasts for BBC and Italian Radio; Purcell Room recital, 1993, with Schubert (D664), Liszt and Debussy. *Recordings:* Rachmaninov music for six hands, with John Ogdon and Brenda Lucas, and Carnival for the Animals, with the London Symphony Orchestra under Barry Wordsworth. *Address:* c/o South Bank Centre, Press Office, Opian Productions, London SE1, England

HUTCHINSON Stuart, b. 3 Mar 1956, London, England. Conductor; Concert Accompanist. *Education:* Royal Academy of Music, London; Cambridge University; BMus (Honours), 1977; LRAM, 1979; Studied with Bernstein and Pritchard. *Career:* Opera, Ballet and Music-Theatre Conductor: Productions for English National Opera, Scottish Opera, New Sadler's Wells Opera Company, Sadler's Wells Theatre/ROH, London International Opera Festival, Royal Academy of Music; Conductor, Scottish Ballet, 1991; Chorus Master, Dublin Grand Opera and Wexford Festival Opera; Music Staff, English National Opera, Opera North; Director of Music, Organist, University of London Chaplaincy, 1976-89; Music Director, Northcott Theatre, Exeter, 1982-84; Music Director, Artistic Director, Morley Opera, London,

1986-90; Music Director, Jonathan Miller's company/ Old Vic Theatre, 1988-89; World premiere, Alice in Wonderland, (Carl Davis), Lyric Theatre, Hammersmith, 1986; British premiere, Postcard From Morocco, (Dominick Argento) LIOF, 1988; World premiere, Tables Meet, (Stephen Oliver), Royal Festival Hall, 1990; Also productions for the Royal Shakespeare Company, (London), On Your Toes, with Makarova, West End, 1984. *Compositions:* Music for Little Women and Good Wives, (BBC Twelve-part series); Incidental theatre music including King Lear (Miller/Old Vic); Frequent arranger and orchestrator. *Recordings:* National Philharmonic Orchestra with James Galway, RCA; Several recordings for BBC Radio 3 and 4; Many for BBC Radio Drama; BBC and Independent Television. *Current Management:* Music International, 13 Ardilaun Road, London N5 2QR, England. *Address:* 149 De Beauvoir Road, London N1 4DL, England.

HUTCHISON D Warner, b. 15 Dec. 1930, Denver, Colorado, USA. Composer; French Hornist; Author; Educator. m. Merilyn Etheridge Hutchison (pianist, cellist), 27 Jan. 1967, 1 son, 1 daughter. *Education:* Bachelor of Sacred Music, S W Baptist Theological Seminary, Fort Worth, Texas, 1954; MMus, 1956, PhD, 1971, University of North Texas School of Music; Studies in Composition with Samuel Adler (University of North Texas), Wayne Barlow and Kent Kennan (Eastman School of Music), Roy Harris (Indiana University). *Debut:* Premieres at Lincoln Center for Performing Arts, Tully Hall, New York City: Hornpiece I - Horn and Tape, 1971 (nominated for Pulitzer Prize); Narnian Suite - Chorus, Percussion, Horn, 1977. *Career:* Member of various Graduate faculties; University Lecturer, Avant Garde Music and New Musical Notation: Professor of Music, Composition and Director of Experimental Music Laboratory, New Mexico State University; Visiting Professor, London, American Institute Foreign Study; Adjunct Professor, Fairfax University (US). *Compositions:* Numerous compositions include: The Sacrilege of Alan Kent for orchestra, baritone and tape; Dirge and Hosanna, Fantasy Variations for Band; Psalm 135 for Chorus and Organ; Narnian Suite (C S Lewis) for Chorus, Percussion and Horn; Homage to Jackson Pollock for percussion, tape, slides, speaker; Ceremonies Ballet for oboe, interior piano, tape; Three Love Songs (Joyce) soprano and orchestra; Apocalypse for Brass quintet, Tam-tam bells, Varied Carols and The Desert Shall Bloom As the Rose for orchestra. *Recordings:* Apocalpse I, for Brass Quintet, CD, Crystal Records; Several recordings on Crest Label, numerous published works. *Publications:* User Manual for Electronic Music, 1973, 1975, 1982 3rd edition; Editor: Proceedings, Journal of American Society of University Composers, 1971-76. *Address:* 3025 Broadmoor Drive, Las Cruces, NM 88001, USA.

HUTTENLOCHER Philippe, b. 29 Nov. 1942, Neuchâtel, Switzerland. Singer (Baritone). *Education:* Studied with Juliette Bise in Fribourg. *Career:* Sang with the Ensemble Vocal de Lausanne and with the Choeurs de la Foundation Gulbenkian, Lisbon; Festival appearances in Montreux, Lausanne, Strasbourg and Ansbach in the Baroque repertory; Tour of Japan 1974; Zurich Opera 1975, as the title role in Monteverdi's Orfeo, produced by the late Jean-Pierre Ponnelle; London Bach Festival 1978; Guest appearances in Vienna, Berlin, Hamburg, Milan and Edinburgh. *Recordings include:* Bach Cantatas and operas by Monteverdi including Il Ritorno di Ulisse, (Telefunken); St Matthew Passion (CBS); Le Devin du Village by Rousseau; Die Jahreszeiten by Haydn, Bach B Minor Mass (RCA); Les Indes Galantes by Rameau, Così fan Tutte, Il Maestro di Capella, Pénélope, St John Pasion, Handel Dettingen Te Deum and works by Carissimi, MA Charpentier and Gabrieli (Erato).

HUXLEY Marcus Richard, b. 11 Dec. 1949, Chelmsford, England. Organist. Master of Choristers, Birmingham Cathedral. m. Sally Anne Bamforth, 28 July 1982, 2 sons. *Education:* MA (Oxon); FRCO; ARCM (Organ Playing) Pembroke College, Oxford, 1968-72; Worcester College, Oxford, 1972-74; Privately with

Marie Claire Alain, 1971-74. *Career:* Your Hundred Best Hymns & Morning Worship for ITV; Epilogues for TT TV; Choral Evensong for BBC Radio 3 & 4; Morning Service for BBC Radio 4; Solo Organ Music for BBC Radio 3; Assistant Organist, Ripon Cathedral, 1974-86; Conductor, Ilkley Choral Society & Otley Choral Society, 1980-84; Director, York Early Music Choir 1980-86. *Compositions:* Of a Rose, Christmas Carol, 1981. *Honours:* Joint 2nd Prize, and Audience Prize, Interpretation Competition, St Albans International Organ Festival, 1977; Organ Scholarship, Worcester College, 1972-74; French Government Scholarship, 1974. *Memberships:* RCO; Cathedral Organists Association. *Address:* 25 Cranfield Grove, Birmingham B26 2LR, England.

HUYBRECHTS François, b. 15 June 1946, Antwerp, Belgium. Conductor. *Education:* Studied cello and clarinet at the Antwerp Conservatory; Conducting studies with Daniel Sternefeld, Bruno Maderna and Hans Swarowsky. *Career:* Debut as cellist 1960; Conducting debut 1963, The Fairy Queen by Purcell at the Royal Flemish Opera; Conducted the Netherlands Chamber Opera 1966-67; Concerts at the Salzburg Mozarteum 1967; Assisted Bernstein at the New York Philharmonic and conducted the Los Angeles Philharmonic and the Berlin Philharmonic; Musical Director of the Wichita Symphony 1972-79, San Antonio Symphony 1979-80. *Recordings* include: Janáček's Taras Bulba and Lachian Dances (London Philharmonic); Nielsen's 3rd Symphony (LSO, Decca). *Honours:* Winner, Dimitri Mitropoulos Competition, New York, 1968; Prizewinner, Herbert von Karajan Foundation Competition 1969. *Address:* c/o Polygram Classics, PO Box 1420, 1 Sussex Place, Hammersmith, London, W6 9XS, England.

HUYS Bernard, b. 7 Sept 1934, Hulste, Belgium. Musicologist; Professor of Music. m. Marie-Louise Garré, 1 child. *Education:* LLD; Licenciate, History of Art and Archaeology (Musicology); Studied Piano and History of Music, Royal Conservatory, Ghent. *Career:* Head of Music Department, Royal Library of Belgium; Professor of Music, Hoger St Lukasinstituut, Brussels. *Publications include:* Catalogue des imprimés musicaux des XVe, XVIe et XVIIe siecles, 2 vols, 1965, 1974; Van Paus Gregorius tot Stockhausen. Twaalf eeuwen muzieknotatie, 1966; Belgische en buitenlandse muziekbibliotheken, 1966; Bibliografie van de werken van Antoine Auda, 1879-1964, 1967; De Afdeling Muziek van de Koninklijke Bibliotheek, 1969; Muziekdocumenten, 1969; Twee huldemotetten ter gelegenheid van Blijde Intreden te Antwerpen door Plantijn gedrukt, 1969; Jacques Champion de Chambonnières, humanist, klavecinist en komponist, 1972; Catalogue des imprimés musicaux du XVIIIe siècle. Fonds général (Catalogus van de muziekdrukken van de 18de eeuw), 1974; Various biographical contributions to Biographie nationale, Nationaal Biografisch Woordenboek, Algemene Muziekencyclopedie, 1976-; Occo Codex, facsimile edition, 1979; Historiek van de Brabançonne; haar editio princeps en andere vroege uitgaven, 1987; Belgian music periodicals: their national and international interest, 1988; Les imprimeurs de musique á Bruxelles au X1Xe siècle, 1988; Edgar Tinel en Pol De Mont: Een artistieke samenwerking, 1991; Jeugdbrieven van Gustave Huberti aan zijn tekstdichter Henri Delmotte, 1991. *Contributions to:* Various journals. *Memberships include:* Executive Committee, AIBM; Editorial Committe, Catalogus musicus; President, Belgian Committee, RILM; Working Member, Koninklijke Academie van Belgie. *Address:* Kasteelstraat 5, 1703 Schepdaal, Belgium.

HVOROSTOVSKY Dmitri, b. 16 Oct 1962, Krasnoyarsk, Siberia, USSR. Singer (Baritone). *Education:* Studied at the Krasnoyarsk High School of Arts with Jekatherina Yofel, 1982-86. *Career:* Soloist with the Krasnoyarsk Opera 1986-; Appeared on BBC television as winner of the Cardiff Singer of the World Competition, 1989; Sang songs by Tchaikovsky and Rachmaninov at the Wigmore Hall, Dec 1989; Recitals at New York Alice Tully and at Washington Kennedy Canter March 1990; Opera engagements include Yeletsky in The Queen of Spades at Nice, 1989 (Western operatic debut), Eugene Onegin in Venice, 1991; I Puritani at Covent Garden, 1992; Sang Onegin at the Paris Châtelet 1992, Germont at the Chicago Lyric Opera, Season 1993/94; Promenade Concert debut 1993, Mussorgsky's Songs and Dances of Death; Concert showings in Boston, Paris, Moscow and Leningrad. *Recordings include:* Arias by Tchaikovsky and Verdi with the Rotterdam Philharmonic conducted by Valery Gergiev; Arias from Cavalleria Rusticana, Eugene Onegin and Don Carlos (Philips Classics). *Honours:* First Prize, USSR National Competition 1987; Toulouse Singing Competition 1988; BBC Cardiff Singer of the World Competition, 1989. *Address:* Philips/Polygram Artists, PO Box 1420, 1 Sussex Place, London W6 9XS, England.

HYDE Derek, b. 1 Nov 1931, Gloucestershire, England. Lecturer. m. 29 July 1957, 2s. *Education:* BA, BMus, Durham University, 1950-53; ARCM (Piano Performer), 1952; St John's College, Cambridge University, 1955-56; M.Phil Reading University, 1973; PhD, Reading University, 1979; Trinity College of Music, 1986-87. *Career:* Director of Music, Woodbridge School, 1956-61; Head of Music and Performaing Arts, Nonington College of Higher Ed, 1961-86; Exchange Professor, Eastern Michigan University, 1965-66; Tutor, Open University, 1973-; Senior Lecturer, Canterbury Christ Church College, 1987-; Examiner, Trinity College of Music, 1988-. *Compositions:* Psalm of Celebration; Carol for Today; Forlana. *Publications:* New Found Voices - Women and Music in 19th Century England, 1984. Articles on Gustav Holst in Music Education, 1971, 1974; Contributor to Europa Biographical Dictionary of British Women, 1983. *Honours:* Elisabeth Schumann Prize for Accompaniment; Alec Rowley memorial Prize, Trinity College of Music, 1987. *Memberships:* Adjudicator, British Federation of Music Festivals. *Hobbies:* Sport; Hockey (Cambridge Blue and England B, 1956); Gardening. *Address:* Cowslip Cottage, Cop Street, Ash Near Canterbury, Kent CT3 2DJ, England.

HYDE Miriam Beatrice, b. 15 Jan 1913, Adelaide, South Australia. Composer/Pianist. m. Marcus B Edwards, 26 Dec 1939, 1 son, 1 daughter. *Education:* Tormore House, and Riverside Schools; AMUA and LAB, 1928; Mus.BAC, Elder Conservatorium, University of Adelaide, 1931; ARCM, Composition and Piano, 1935; LRAM, London, 1935. *Career:* Over 50 years broadcasting for ABC; Soloist with major orchestras in England and Australia with conductors, Sir Malcolm Sargent, Schneevoigt, Constant Lambert, Aylmer Buesst (BBC), Sir Bernard Heinze, Dr. Edgar Bainton, Geoffrey Simon. chiefly in own works; Examiner for Australian Music Examination Board for 37 years; small private teaching practice; lecturer in seminars throughout Australia. *Compositions:* 2 piano concerti, 1934, 1935, 4 overtures, Symphonic, 1933; Adelaide, 1935; Happy Occasion, 1957; Kelso, 1959; Sonatas for piano, 1941-44; Viola, 1937; Clarinet, 1949; Flute, 1962. *Recordings:* CD of own piano works for Southern Cross Label, 1993. *Publication:* Autobiography, Complete Accord, 1991. *Honours:* OBE, 1981; AO, (Officer for the Order of Australia), 1991; Hon D.Litt, Macquarie University. *Hobbies:* Gardening; Writing; Italian. *Address:* 12 Kelso Street, Burwood Heights, New South Wales 2136, Australia.

HYDE-SMITH Christopher, b. 11 March 1935, Cairo, Egypt. Flautist; Teacher. 1 son, 1 daughter. *Education:* Eton College, England; Royal College of Music, London. *Debut:* Royal Festival Hall, 1962. *Career:* Member, Camden Wind Quintet, London Mozart Players; Many flute and piano and/or harpsichord concerts with Jane Dodd; Appearances in Holland, Switzerland, Italy, France, Germany, Spain, Portugal, Scandinavia, Russia, North and South America; Professor, Royal College of Music; Dedicatee of works by Alwyn, Dodgson, Horovitz, Mathias and Rawsthorne; Judge, at Leeds, Mozart and Tunbridge Wells Competitions. *Recordings:* Numerous recordings. *Memberships:* Haydn Mozart Society; Chairman, British Flute Society. *Current Management:* Lotte Nicholls, 16 Upper Wimpole Street, London WC1, England. *Address:* 94 Dorien Road, London SW20 8EJ, England.

HYKES David (Bond), b. 2 Mar 1953, Taos, New Mexico, USA. Composer. *Education:* Studied classical Azerbaijani and Armenian music with Zevulon Avshalomov 1975-77; North Indian raga singing with S Dhar from 1982. *Career:* Founded the Harmonic Choir 1975: Resident at the Cathedral of St John the Divine, New York, from 1979; Tours of the USA and Europe from 1980. *Compositions:* Harmonic Tissues fro electronics 1971; Shadow Frequencies for piano and electronics 1975; Looking for Gold/Life in the Sun for children's voices and ensemble 1975; Well-struck Strings for dulcimer 1975-83; Special Delivery/ Rainbow Voice for low voice 1975-84; Test Studies for Harmonic Orchestra for ensemble 1975-85; Hearing Solar Winds for voices 1977-83; Outside of Being There for voices 1981; Turkestan for synthesizer 1979; Current Circulation for voices 1984; Subject to Change for low voice and drones 1983; Desert Hymns 1984. *Honours:* Grants from the National Endowment for the Arts (1978, 1983), the Rockefeller Foundation (1980-83) and UNESCO (1983). *Address:* c/o ASCAP, ASCAP Building, One Lincoln Plaza, New York, NY 10023, USA.

HYNNINEN Jorma Kalervo, b. 3 Apr 1941, Leppavirta, Finland. Opera Singer (Baritone). m. Reetta Salo, 6 Aug 1961, 1s, 2d. *Education:* Sibelius Academy, Helsinki, 1969. *Debut:* As Silvio in Pagliacci, Finnish National Opera, 1969. *Career:* Staatsoper Vienna, 1977; La Scala, 1977; Paris Opera, 1978; Bavarian State Opera, Munchen, 1979; Metropolitan Opera, 1984; Lyric Opera of Chicago, 1989; San Francisco Opera, 1988; Deutsche Oper Berlin, 1991; Lied Recitals: New York, London, Europe and Beijing; Soloist with Vienna Philharmonic, London Philharmonic, London Symphony, Boston Symphony, and Israel Philharmonic. *Recordings:* Le Nozze di Figaro with Riccardo Muti; Orest in Elektra with Seizi Ozawa; Brahms Requiem and Mahler's Eighth with Klaus Tennstedt; Winterreise, Die Schöne Mullerin, Dichterliebe; Songs of Sibelius, Die Schöne Magelone; Lieder Eines Fahrenden Gesellen; Evergreen Love Songs. *Honours:* Professor of Arts, Finland, 1990. *Hobbies:* Painting; Cross Country Skiing; Jogging. *Current management* Allied Artists, London Opera et Concert Paris. *Address:* Ruskokuja 3B, 01620 Vantaa, Finland.

HYTNER Nicholas, b. 7 May 1956, Manchester, England. Opera Producer.*Education:* Trinity Hall, Cambridge; graduated 1977. *Debut:* Dreigroschenoper at Cambridge. *Career:* The Turn of the Screw for Kent Opera, 1979: Tippett's King Priam in season 1984-85; Wagner's Rienzi for English National Opera 1983; Xerxes 1985; Covent Garden debut 1987, with the British premiere of Sallinen's The King Goes forth to France; The Knot Garden 1988; The Magic Flute for English National Opera and Netherlands Opera; Debut with Geneva Opera 1989, Le Nozze di Figaro; Glyndebourne debut 1991, La Clemenza di Tito; Engaged to produce La Forza del Destino, for ENO, 1992. *Recordings include:* Videos of Xerxes and King Priam. *Address:* c/o Lies Askonas Ltd., 186 Drury Lane, London WC2B 5RY, England.

I

IANNACCONE Anthony, b. 14 Oct 1943, New York, USA. Composer; Conductor; Teacher. m. Judith Trostle, 1 son, 1 daughter. *Education:* BMus, MMus, Manhattan School of Music; PhD, Eastman School of Music. *Career:* Conducted orchestras, choruses, wind ensembles and chamber groups throughout the USA including: Lincoln Centre, New York; Many University appearances as guest conductor and composer; Record debut as conductor of Cornell Wind Ensemble, 1983; Teacher, Manhattan School of Music, 1967-68; Composition Professor, 1971, Director of Collegium Musicum, 1973. *Compositions include:* Approximately 40 published works, 14 commercially recorded for orchestra, chorus, Wind Ensemble and Chamber ensembles. *Recordings include:* Partita for piano, 1967; Hades, for brass quartet, 1968; Bicinia for flute and alto saxophone, 1974; Sonatina for trumpet and tuba, 1975; After a Gentle Rain, for concert band, 1979; Walt Whitman Song for chorus, soloists and winds, 1981; No 2 Terpsichore, 1981; Images of Song and Dance, No 1 Orpheus, 1982; Two Piano Invention, 1985; Divertimento, for orchestra, 1983; Night Rivers, Symphony No.3, 1992. *Address:* 521 Kewanee, Ypsilanti, MI 48197, USA.

IBBOTT Daphne, b. 29 Apr 1918, London, England. Pianist. m. (1) Rev John Frost (deceased), (2) Wilfred Smith, 2 daughters. *Education:* Royal Academy of Music; LRAM; FRAM. *Career:* Specialist in chamber music and accompaniment in particular in association with violinist Nona Liddell; Conducts master classes for accompanists; Adjudicator. *Recordings:* Vaughan Williams music with Jean Stewart, Viola; Songs by Elgar, Warlock, Gurney, Britten and Quilter with various artists; Voice of the Violin with Derek Collier; Somervell's Maud and Butterworth's Shropshire Lad with John Carol Case; Spanish Dances by Sarasate and Wieniawski with Campoli. *Address:* 8 Riverview Gardens, Barnes, London, SW13, England.

IHLE Andrea, b. 17 Apr 1953, Dresden, Germany. Singer (Soprano). *Education:* Studied at Musikhochschule Dresden. *Debut:* Dresden Staatsoper, 1976, as Giannetta in L'Elisir d'Amore. *Career:* Appearances in Dresden have included Aennchen and Marianne, in the productions of Freischutz and Rosenkavalier which opened the rebuild Semperoper, 1985; Other roles in Dresden and elsewhere in Germany, have included Mozart's Papagena and Despina, Euridice, Gretel, Sophie (Der Rosenkavalier), Carolina (Il Matrimonio Segreto) and Marie in La Fille du Regiment; Concert and oratorio engagements. *Recordings:* Fesischütz and Rosenkavalier; Bach's Christmas Oratorio; Missa Brevis by Carl Friedrich Fasch. *Address:* Semper Oper Dresden, 8012 Dresden, Germany.

IHLOFF Jutta-Renate, b. 1 Nov 1944, Winteberg, Germany. Singer (Soprano). *Education:* Studied with Marja Stein in Hamburg and with Giorgio Favaretto in Rome and Siena. *Debut:* Staatsoper Hamburg 1973, as Zerlina in Don Giovanni. *Career:* Has sung in Munich, Berlin, Vienna and Salzburg; Frequent guest apparances elsewhere in Europe; Other roles include Mozart's Despina, Susanna, Blondchen and Pamina; Marzelline in Fidelio; Monteverdi's Poppea; Sophie and Zdenka; Mimi; Marie in Die Soldaten by Zimmermann; Adele (Die Fledermaus); Nannetta (Falstaff). *Recordings include:* Serpetta in La Finta Giardiniera by Mozart (Deutsche Grammophon).

IKEDA Kikuei, b. 31 Aug 1947, Yokosuka, Japan. Violinist. Studied at the Juilliard School with Dorothy DeLay and members of the Juilliard Quartet. *Career:* Second violin, Tokyo Quartet from 1974; Regular concerts in the USA and abroad; First cycle of the complete quartets of Beethoven at the Yale at Norfolk Chamber Music Festival, 1986; Repeated cycles at the 92nd Street Y (New York), Ravinia and Israel Festivals, Yale, Princeton Universities; Season 1990-91 at Alice Tully Hall, the Metropolitan Museum of Art, New York, Boston, Washington DC, Los Angeles, Cleveland, Detroit, Chicago, Miami, Seattle, San Francisco, Toronto; Tour of South America, two tours of Europe including Paris, Amsterdam, Bonn, Milan, Munich, Dublin, London, Berlin; Quartet-in- residence at Yale University and at the University of Cincinnati College- Conservatory of Music. *Recordings:* Schubert's major Quartets; Mozart Flute Quartets with James Galway and Clarinet Quintet with Richard Stolzman; Quartets by Bartók, Brahms, Debussy, Haydn, Mozart and Ravel; Beethoven Middle Period Quartets (RCA), *Honours:* Grand Prix du Disque du Montreux; Best Chamber Music Recording of the Year from Stereo Review and the Gramophone; Four Grammy nominations. *Address:* Intermusica Artists' Management, 16 Duncan Terrace, London N1 8BZ, England.

ILES Edna, b. 1919, Birmingham, West Midlands, England. Concert Pianist. *Education:* Studied with Russian Composer, Nicolas Medtner for several years in UK, he regarded her as the authority on his music. *Career:* Played all 3 Medtner Concertos with London Symphony Orchestra, Royal Albert Hall, 1946, further performances of these works include, No. 1, with Philharmonia Orchestra, London, 1947, No. 2 with Bournemouth Symphony Orchestra, 1950, No. 1, first performance in Manchester with Hallé Orchestra, 1960, first broadcast of No. 1 with City of Birmingham Symphony Orchestra, 1947, also broadcast with BBC Northern Orchestra, 1961; Many performances of Medtner's piano solo works, recent ones include, BBC Radio 3 Recital, 1979, and Medtner's Birth Centenary Concert, Birmingham, 1980; Soloist, Beethoven Concertos 4 and 5 with Philharmonia Orchestra on their first provincial tour, 1949; Bloch Concerto Symphonique in London and Bournemouth with Bournemouth Symphony Orchestra, 1956; 1st performance, 1958, first broadcast, 1959, Alan Bush Variations, Nocturne and Finale on an English Sea Song; Appearances with most major British Orchestras and Conductors including Mengelberg, Beecham, Boult, Goossens, Groves and others; Numerous recitals in UK and Europe. *Recordings:* Medtner's works broadcast, USSR; Various recordings of broadcasts and private recordings in National Sound Archives. *Contributions to:* Biography of Medtner published in Moscow, 1981. *Membership:* Incorporated Society of Musicians. *Address:* 86 Grange Road, Olton, Solihull, West Midlands, B91 1DA, England.

ILIFF James, b. 4 Jan 1923, Wolverhampton, England. *Education:* Royal Academy of Music, 1939-45. *Career:* Professor of Composition, Royal Academy of Music, 1957-88; Senior Harmony Tutor, Morley College, 1955-88. *Compositions:* Piano Sonata, 1957; Duo for cello and double bass, 1980; Contrapunctus 19, (Art of Fuge); completed, 1984; String Quartet, 1988; Gone, Gone Again, (Edward Thomas) for Soprano and Violin, 1992; Ave Maris Stella, for organ, 1993. *Publications:* An index of symmetrical all-interval series (Composer No 12, 1963). *Honours:* BMus, London, 1947. *Memberships:* Composers' Guild of Great Britain; Botanical Society of the British Isles; International Organisation for Succulent Plant Study. *Address:* Eithin Tewion, Cilycwm, Llandovery, Dyfed SA20 OTF, Wales.

ILOSVALVY Robert, b. 18 June 1927, Hodmezovasarhely, Hungary. Singer (Tenor). *Education:* Studied with Andor Lendvai at the Budapest Academy. *Career:* Soloist with the Artistic Ensemble of the People's Army from 1949; Budapest Opera from 1954, debut in the title role of Erkel's Hunyadi Laszlo; Sang widely in eastern Europe; San Francisco Opera 1964-68; New York Metropolitan Opera 1966; Member of Cologne Opera from 1966; Covent Garden 1968, as Des Grieux in Manon Lescaut; Concerts with the Berlin Philharmonic and the Orchestra of the Accademia di Santa Cecilia; Career has centred on the Budapest Opera from 1981; Théâtre de la Monnaie Brussels 1985, as Walther in Die Meistersinger; Sang Walther von Stolzing at the 1986 Maggio Musicale, Florence; Other roles include Rodolfo, Tamino, Dick Johnson, Don José, Alfredo, Manrico and the Duke of Mantua. *Recordings:* Madama Butterfly and Manon Lescaut (Hungaroton);

Roberto Devereux, with Beverly Sills (EMI); Requiem by Dvořák, conducted by Kertesz (Decca). *Address:* c/o Hungarian State Opera House, Népöztársaság utja 22, 1061 Budapest, Hungary.

IMAI Nobuko, b. 18 Mar 1943, Tokyo, Japan. Violist. m. Aart von Bochove, 1981, 1 son, 1 daughter. *Education:* Toho School of Music, Tokyo; Yale University; Juilliard School of Music, New York. *Career:* Member of Vermeer Quartet 1974-79; Soloist with the London Symphon Orchestra, Royal Philharmonic, Chicago Symphony, Concertgebouw Orchestra, Montreal Symphony, Boston Symphony, Vienna Symphony, Stockholm Philharmonic; Festivals include Marlboro, Casals, South Bank Summer Music, Bath, Cheltenham, Aldeburgh, London Promenade Concerts, International Viola Congress, Houston. *Recordings:* Tippett Triple Concerto and Berlioz Harold in Italy with the London Symphony Orchestra conducted by Colin Davis; Mozart/Haydn Duos with Mark Lubotsky (Philips); Brahms Sonatas/Schumann Märchenbilder; Schubert Arpeggione/Beethoven Notturno Op 42 with Roger Vignoles (Chandos); Shostakovich Sonata, Glinka Sonata, Schnittke Viola Concerto and Mozart Quintets with the Orlando Quartet (BIS); Mozart Sinfonia Concertante with Iona Brown; Hindemith Sonatas for solo viola, Denisov Concertos, (BIS), Walton Concerto, Franck and Vieuxtemps Sonatas (Chandos). *Honours:* First Prize Munich International Viola Competition; First Prize Geneva International Viola Competition. *Hobbies:* Golf; Cooking. *Address:* c/o Terry Harrison Artists Management, 3 Clarendon Court, Park Street, Charlbury, OX7 3PS, England.

IMBRIE Andrew W., b. 6 Apr 1921, New York, USA. Composer; Professor. m. Barbara Cushing, 31 Jan 1953, 2 sons (1 deceased). *Education:* Studied piano with Leo Ornstein and Robert Casadesus; Composition with Roger Sessions. *Career:* Professor, University of California at Berkeley, 1949-1991. *Compositions include:* Orchestral: Three symphonies, 1965, 1970; Violin Certo, 1954; Cello Concerto, 1972; 3 piano concertos, 1973 1974, 1992; Flute concerto, 1977; Chamber: 5 string quartets, 1942-87; To a traveller, clarinet violin and piano, 1971; Pilgrimage for flute, clarinet, violin, cello, piano and percussion, 1983; Dream Sesquence for flute, oboe, clarinet, violin, viola, cello, piano and percusson, 1986; Vocal: Opera: Angle of Response (Stegner-Hall), 1975, commissioned by the San Francisco Opera; Requiem for Soprano, chorus and orchestra, 1984. *Recordings:* Pilgrimage; Collage Ensemble, Gunther Schuller; Trio No 2, Francesco Trio; QUartet No.4, Emerson Qt. *Publications:* Extra Measures and Metrical Ambiguity in Beethoven, 1973. *Honours include:* Guggenheim Fellowship, 1953-54, 1959-60; Naumberg Award, 1960; Holder, Jerry and Evelyn Hemmings Chambers Chair in Music, University of California, Berkeley, 1989-91; Various grants and commissions. *Memberships:* American Academy of Arts and Letters; American Academy of Arts and Sciences; Phi Betta Kappa. *Address:* 2625 Rose Street, Berkeley, CA 94708, USA.

IMDAHL Heinz, b. 9 Aug 1924, Dusseldorf, Germany. Singer (Baritone). *Education:* Studied with Berthold Putz in Krefeld and at the Cologne Musikhochschule. *Debut:* Detmold 1948, as Morales in Carmen. *Career:* Sang in Bremen, Berlin and Dusseldorf, then became a member of the Bayerische Staatsoper Munich; Guest appearances in Florence 1953, Rio de Janeiro, Turin 1972 and Oslo 1973; Repertoire included leading roles in operas by Wagner, Verdi, Strauss and Verdi. *Recordings include:* Das Liebesverbot by Wagner.

IMRIE Martyn, b. 4 Mar 1947, Bangor, County Down, Northern Ireland. Music Publisher. m. 1976, div., 1 son, 1 daughter. *Education:* BA (Hons), Queen's University, Belfast, 1969; BA (Hons), Music, Bristol University, 1977. *Career:* Co-Founder (with Bruno Turner) of Mapa Mundi series of Renaissance Performing Scores; Editor, numerous editions published and unpublished of Renaissance Church Music, principally late 15th and early 16th century Spanish, including editions of

Guerrero, Penalosa, La Rue (Requiem), Morales, Wert, etc; Publisher of 20th century music by Bourgeois, Victory, Moody, Beaumont, Butterworth, Painter, Ward, as Founder of Vanderbeek and Imrie Ltd. *Recordings:* Editions recorded by Westminster Cathedral Choir, Pro Cantione Antiqua, Hilliard Ensemble on Hyperion, EMI. *Publications:* Major contributor to Mapa Mundi series of Renaissance Performing Scores, including 20 works by Guerrero, also 17 complete motets for 4 and 5 voices by Penalosa, 1990. *Hobbies:* Sailing; Golf; Cycling; Running; Reading (astronomy, biology, palaeontology). *Address:* 15 Marvig, Lochs, Isle of Lewis, Scotland PA86 9QP.

INBAL Eliahu, b. 16 Feb 1936, Jerusalem. Conductor. m. Helga Fritzsche, 19 July 1968, 2 sons, 1 daughter. *Education:* Diploma in Violin and Music Theory, Academy of Music, Jerusalem, 1956; Study of Conducting, Conservatoire National Superieur, Paris, 1960-62; Courses with Fr. Ferrara, Hilversum. *Career:* Opera debut at the Verona Arena 1969, Don Carlos; Chief Conductor, Frankfurt Radio Symphony Orchestra, 1974-; Guest Conductor of major orchestras in Milan, Rome, Florence, Venice, Berlin, Munich, Hamburg, Vienna, London, Paris, Tel-Aviv, New York, Chicago, Tokyo; Appearances at festivals in Salzburg, Lucerne, Berlin and Holland; Chief Conductor, Teatro La Fenice, 1984-; Maria di Rudenz at Venice 1981; Conducted La Forza del Destino at Zurich, 1992. *Recordings:* Schumann; Complete Works for Orchestra, with NPO, London; Debussy, La Mer, Trois Nocturnes with Concertgebouw, Amsterdam; Chopin, Complete Works for Piano and Orchestra, with Arrau, LPO; Scriabin, Complete Works for Orchestra, with RSO, Frankfurt; Donizetti, Maria di Rudenz with La Fenice Venice; Bruckner, Symphonies Nos. 3, 4, and 8 in their first edition, with RSO Frankfurt; Bartók, Works for Orchestra, with RSO, Frankfurt; Saint-Saëns, Symphonies Nos. 1 and 2, RSO, Frankfurt; Schoenberg, Chamber Symphonies Nos. 1 and 2, RSO, Frankfurt; Puccini, Messa da Gloria with RSO, Frankfurt; Gustav Mahler, all Symphonies which received the German critic prize, 1988, Ravel Orchestral works; Bruckner all symphonies. *Honours:* First Prize, Guido Cantelli International Competition for Conductors, Novara, Italy, 1963; Premio Decennale, Palermo, 1975; Israel Prize for Interpretation, 1980. *Current Management:* Harold Holt Ltd., 31 Sinclair Road, London W14 0NS, England. *Hobbies:* Hi-Fi; Photography. *Address:* c/o Hessischer Rundfunk, Bertram Str. 8, 6000 Frankfurt, Germany.

INCIHARA Taro, b. 2 Jan 1950, Yamagata, Japan. Singer (Tenor). *Education:* Studied in Japan and at the Julliard School, New York. *Debut:* Tokyo, 1980, as Gounod's Faust. *Career:* European debut, 1982, as Calaf at the Teatro San Carlo, Naples; Paris Oper from 1983 as Macduff, Riccardo, Don Carlos, and the Duke of Mantua; Guest appearances at Nice, Turin, Naples, Santiago and Buenos Aires (Verdi's Requiem, 1987); Macerata Festival, 1987, Orange, 1989 (as Isamale in Nabucco); Metropolitan Opera, 1987-89, as the Italian Singer and the Duke of Mantua; Further European engagements at Turin and Genoa; Sang Riccardo in Un Ballo in Maschera for Opera Pacific at Costa Califronia, 1991; Other roles include Gabriele Adorno (La Scala), 1989, Verdi's Rodolfo and Alfredo, Enzo in La Gioconda and Edgardo (Lucia di Lammermoor). *Address:* c/o Opera Pacific, 3187 Red Hill Avenue, Suite 230, Costa Mesa, CA 92626, USA.

INGLE William, b. 17 Dec 1934, Texhoma, Texas, USA. Singer (Tenor). *Education:* Studied at the Academy of Vocal Arts in Philadelphia with Dorothy di Scala; With Sidney Dietsch in New York and Luigi Ricci in Rome. *Debut:* Flensburg 1965, as Tamino. *Career:* Sang at the Linz Opera, Dusseldorf, Kassel, Frankfurt, Graz, Leipzig, Montreal, Hanover, Wellington and Vienna; Other roles include Ernesto, Don Ottavio, Manrico, Lohengrin, Parsifal, Walther, Canio, Erik, Radames, Ferrando, Rodolfo, Almaviva, Flamand in Capriccio, the Duke of Mantua and Alfredo; Sang at Linz, 1976, in the premiere of Der Aufstand by Nikolaus Eder; Masaniello in La Muette de Portici by Auber, 1989; TV appearances as

Herod (Salome) in Canada and Tom Rakewell (The Rake's Progress) in Austria . *Address:* Landestheater, Promenade 39, A-4010 Linz, Austria.

INGÓLFSSON Atli, b. 21 Aug 1962, Keflavik, Iceland. Composer. m. Thuridúr Jónsdóttir, 18 Aug 1990. *Education:* Diploma in Classical Guitar, 1983, BM, Theory and Composition, 1984, Reykjavik School of Music; BA, Philosophy, University of Iceland, 1986; Study with D Anzaghi, Milan Conservatory, 1985-88; Private study with G Grisey and Auditor at CNSMP, Paris, 1988-90. *Career:* Performances at Young Nordic music festivals, other Nordic music festivals and various occasions in Iceland, 1981-; His Due Bagatelle for Clarinet premiered in Milan, 1986 and widely performed; Various performances in Europe, 1990-, including Montreuil, May 1991, Varese, July 1991, Amsterdam, Sept 1991, Milan, Nov and Dec 1991; commissioned by IRCAM, Paris to write for computer piano and ensemble, 1993. *Compositions:* Recorded on CD, ITM 6-03 ITM Reykjavik: Due Bagettelle for Clarinet; CD ENMD 03 Paris: Et Toi Pale Soleil, for 4 voices and instruments; A Verso for piano, and O Versa for piano and 12 instruments, OPNA for bassclarinet and marimba; Le Pas Les Pentes for 8 instruments. *Address:* Borgarvegur 28, 260 Njardvik, Iceland.

INGRAM Jaime Ricardo Jaen, b. 13 Feb 1928, Panama City, Panama. Concert Pianist; Diplomat. m. Nelly Hirsch, 29 Jan 1950, 2 sons, 1 daughter. *Education:* Piano Diploma, Juilliard Institute of Music, New York, USA, 1949, studied with Olga Samarof and Joseph Bloch; Piano Diploma, Conservatoire Nationale de Paris, France, 1950, studied with Yves Nat; Additional studies with Alberto Sciarretti, Panama, and Bruno Seidlhofer, Vienna. *Career:* Professor of Piano, National Conservatory of Music, Panama, 1952-56; Escuela Paulista de Musica, São Paulo, Brazil, 1958-60; Escuela Profesional, Panama, 1962-64; Conservatorio Jaime Ingram, 1964-69, University of Panama, 1972-74; Director of Culture, 1969-73; General Director of Culture, 1974-78, Panamanian Ambassador to Spain, 1978-82; Panamanian Ambassador to the Holy See, 1982-; Concert tours as soloist and piano duo with Nelly Hirsch, South and Central America, Cuba, Spain, Italy, Federal Republic of Germany; Bulgaria; Poland, Zurich and Geneva, Switzerland, London, England, Amsterdam, Netherlands, USSR, Israel. *Publications:* Hector Villa Lobas; Muzio Clementi, the Father of the Pianoforte; Antonio de Cabezón, Tientos y Diferencias; Orientación Musical 1974; Historia, Compositores y Repertorio del Piano 1978. *Hobbies:* Chess; Philately; Books; Painting.

INOUE Michiyoshi, b. 23 Dec 1946, Tokyo, Japan. Conductor. *Education:* Studied at the Toho Gakuen Academy of Music with Saito. *Career:* Associate Conductor of the Tokyo Metropolitan Symphony Orchestra; Conducted at La Scala 1971; Has conducted orchestras in Paris, Vienna, Geneva, Berlin, Brussels, Hamburg, Stuttgart, Madrid, Naples, Turin, Florence, Lisbon, London, Helsinki and Copenhagen; Tours of Israel, Eastern Europe and the USSR; Conducted the East Berlin Orchestra on tour to Japan; Concerts in Australia and New Zealand and with the Washington National Symphony in the USA; Has conducted opera in Vienna and at Cluj, Rumania; Music Director of the Japan Philharmonic Orchestra from 1983; Season 1989-90 with the Orchestre National de France, the Munich Philharmonic and the Royal Philharmonic; Conducted the Royal Liverpool Philharmonic in Bruckner's 8th Symphony, 1990; Music Director of the Kyoto Symphony Orchestra, 1990. *Recordings include:* Mahler's 6th and 4th Symphonies with the Royal Philharmonic; Mahler's 5th Symphony; Albums with the Netherlands Chamber Orchestra (Nippon Columbia). *Honours include:* First prize, Guido Cantelli Competition, Milan, 1971. *Address:* c/o Terry Harrison Artists Management, 3 Claredon Court, Park Street, Charlbury, Oxon, OX7 3PS, England.

INWOOD Mary Ruth Brink, b. 27 July 1928, Boston, Massachusetts. Composer. m. (1) The Rev. Charles P. Berger, 18 June 1946, deceased, 4 sons, 1 daughter (2) The Rev. Jay M. Inwood, May 1957, divorced 1968. *Education:* Yale School of Music, 1946-47; BA, Music, Piano, magna cum laude, Queens College, 1975; MA, Composition, Queens College, 1979; Current studies: Graduate School and University Center, doctoral program in composition; Fellowship and Faculty of the New York University doctoral Program in composition. *Career:* Performances of own music at Brooklyn Academy of Music; Queens College; Brooklyn College; The Graduate School and University Center; Performances at New York University and Merkin Hall, New York; Trio for flute, cello and piano published by Seesaw, New York; Park Slope Music Forum; The Episcopal Cathedral at Panama City, Panama; Various churches in the Brooklyn Heights area; Ensemble Librarian, Brooklyn College, several years; Teacher, The Roosa School of Music, 1980-86; Published Compositions (Seesaw N.Y., NY and L'Art de Musique, Boston, MA); Currently Assistant Director, Composition Program, NYU Sehnap, Department of Music and Music Profession, NY; Faculty member, NYU. *Compositions:* 3 Movements for Brass Sextet; String Quartet No. III; Trio for Oboe, Horn and Piano; Suite for Clarinet Bb and Bassoon; Verses from The Song of Songs, Flute and Soprano; Cheerful and Tender Songs; Brass Quintet II, recently performed at Weill Hall, New York (Carnegie Recital Hall). *Publications:* Edited Sinfonia turchesca in C Major by Franz Xavier Süssmayr in Volume XIV of The Symphony 1720-1840. *Address:* 166 Congress Street, Brooklyn, NY 11201, USA.

IOACHIMESCU Calin, b. 29 Mar 1949, Bucharest, Romania. Composer. m. Anca Vartolomei-Ioachimescu, 1 son, 1 daughter. *Education:* Graduate, Bucharest Music College, 1968; Graduate, 1st place, Bucharest High School, Academy of Music, composition class of Stefan Niculescu, 1975; Computer music courses, IRCAM Paris, 1985; International New Music Holiday Courses, Darmstadt, 1980, 84. *Debut:* In concert, Bucharest Radio Symphonic Orchestra, 1978. *Career:* Symphonic, chamber & electronic works played by orchestras, chamber ensembles, or wellknown contemporary music soloists throughout Romania, also in France, Germany, Italy, England, Canada, Greece, Hungary; Film music; Compositions broadcast by Bucharest Radio, Radio France, Radio Bruxeles; Member composer's Forum invited by Internationales Musikinstitut Darmstadt, 1986; Sound Engineer, Romanian Broadcasting; Head of Computer Music Studio (SMEI), Bucharest. *Compositions include:* Tempo 80, Oratorio II, Two String Quartets, Concerto for trombone, doublebass and orchestra, Concerto for saxophones and orchestra (Ministry of Culture of France command), Magic Spell for Celliphonia for cello & tape, Palindrom/7. *Recordings:* Electrecord, Attacca Records, Holland. *Publications:* Oratio II, Editions Salabert, Paris; Tempo 80, String Quartet no.2 and Celliphonia, Music Publishing, Bucharest. *Address:* str Ardeleni 28, sect 2, 72164-Bucharest, Romania.

IONESCO-VOVU Constantin, b. 27 May 1932, Floresti, Romania. Pianist; Professor. m. Margareta Gabriel, 7 Sept 1961, deceased 1983. *Education:* Bucharest Superior Music Conservatory Hochschule, (Academy of Music), 1955. *Career:* Concerts as Soloist with Symphony Orchestras, Piano Recitals and Chamber Music in Romania, France, German Federal Republic, Poland, USSR, Sweden, Denmark, Netherlands, Hungary, Czechoslovakia, Switzerland, Austria, Warsaw Autumn Festival, Evian Festival; Professor, (concert class, piano) Head of Piano Section, Academy of Music Bucharest; Masterclasses Member of International Juries for Piano Competitions in Romania, Europe, France, Germany, Italy. *Publications:* Editor, Romanian Piano Music, C, Silvestri Piano Works, 1st Volume 1973, II Volume, 1979. *Contributions to:* Music Critics And Studies in several Romanian Reviews. *Memberships:* European Piano Teachers Association (EPTA). *Hobbies:* Books; Mountains; Natre; Travel. *Address:* Str. Vasile Lascar, 35, 70211 Bucharest, Romania.

IRANYI Gabriel, b. 6 June 1946, Cluj, Romania. Composer; Pianist; Lecturer. m. Elena Nistor, 20 Aug 1969, 1 son. *Education:* Special School of Music, Cluj, 1955-65; George Dima High School of Music, Cluj, Composition and Musicology Department, Student of Prof. Dr. Sigismund Todutza. *Career:* Teaching Assistant, George Enesco High School of Music, Jassy, Romania, 1971-76; Lecturer, Rubin Academy of Musc, Tel-Aviv, 1977-80; Lecturer, Cfar Saba Conservatoire, 1982-86; since 1988 Professor of the Leo - Borchara - Musikschule in Berlin. *Compositions:* Segments, De Profundis; Bird of Wonder; Until the Day Breaks; Portraits of JS Bach; for solo piano; Laudae for 2 pianos; Song of Degrees for chamber ensemble; Alternances for percussion; Alef for soprano voice, clarinet, cello and piano; Realm for solo cello and electric amplification; Solstice for violin, cello and clarinet; and electric amplification; Shir Hamaalot for organ; Tempora for string quartet, Meditation and Prayer, for violin and 15 strings; Laudae, for 2 pianos (or with chamber orchestra). *Hobbies:* Chess; Swimming; Excursions. *Address:* Gierkeplatz 10, Berlin 10585, Germany.

IRELAND William Patrick, b. 20 Nov 1923, Helston, Cornwall, England. Viola Player. m. Peggy Gray, 4 children. *Education:* Wellington College; Worcester College, Oxford; ARCM; MMus, Hull University. *Career:* Viola, Allegri String Quartet, 1953-77 and 1988-; has taken part in the premieres of quartets by Martin Dalby, 1972, Nicola LeFanu, Peter Sculthorpe, Elisabeth Maconchy, Robert Sherlaw-Johnson, Sebastian Forbes, 1969; Two Clarinet Quintets by Jennifer Fowler and Nicola Lefanu, 1971; 4 Quartets by Barry Guy, Jonathan Harvey, Alison Bauld, Edward Cowie, 1973; Complete Beethoven Quartets at the 1974 Cheltenham Festival. *Recordings:* With Allegri String Quartet; Bach Brandenburg Concertos with Menuhin and Bath Festival Orchestra. *Honours:* Radcliffe Trust Chamber Music Prize. *Hobbies:* Bird-watching; Antique clocks and musical boxes; Carpentry. *Address:* Hillgrove House, Dunkerton, Bath, Avon BA2 8AS, England.

IROSCH Mirjana, b. 24 Oct 1939, Zagreb, Yugoslavia. Singer (Soprano). *Education:* Studied at the Zagreb Conservatory with Fritz Lunzer. *Debut:* Linz 1962, as Mercedes in Carmen. *Career:* Sang for many years at the Vienna Volksoper; took part in the 1968 premiere of the revised version of Der Zerrissene by Von Einem; Tour of Japan 1982; Guest appearances in Graz, Frankfurt, Basle, Brussels and Munich; Other roles include Micaela, Marenka in The Bartered Bride, Fiordiligi, Donna Elvira, Judith in Duke Bluebeard's Castle, Concepcion (L'Heure Espagnole), Rosina and Rosalinde. *Recordings include:* Die Lustige Witwe (Denon). *Address:* Volksoper, Wahringerstrasse 78, A-1090 Vienna, Austria.

IRVINE Robert, b. 11 May 1963, Glasgow, Scotland. Cellist. *Education:* Royal College of Music, London; Studied with Christopher Bunting, Amaryllis Fleming. *Career:* Member, Brindisi String Quartet, 1984-; Philharmonia Orchestra, 1986-; Appeared on Channel 4 TV, and BBC TV and Radio; Principal Cello, London Soloists Chamber Orchestra, Britten-Pears Orchestra, 1985-86. *Recordings:* Britten 2nd Quartet; Berg Op. 3 Quartet, Merlin Records. *Honours:* Foundation Scholar, Royal College of Music; Ivor James Cello Prize; Stern Award for Diploma Recital; Dip.RCM; ARCM. *Membership:* Musicians Union. *Hobbies:* Fly Fishing; Hang-Gliding; Cooking; Travel; Eating Out; Wine Connoisseur. *Address:* 8 Berwyn Road, London SE24 9BD, England.

IRVING David Gerow, b. 23 May 1935, Kankakee, Illinois, USA. Composer; Conductor; French Horn Player. *Education:* BA, MA, Columbia University; New England Conservatory of Music; Vienna Academy of Music, Austria. *Career:* Director and Founder of Phoenix, a New York City new music organization; Compositions performed in Europe and USA including Concerts at Caecelia Society, Columbia Composers and Composers Concordance; The Witch, an opera in one act premiered by the Concert Society of Putnam and Northern Westchester, New York; Featured Guest at Museum of the American Piano in New York for series Contemporary Trends in Piano Music. *Contributions to:* The Horn Call, Journal of the International Horn Society, Fresno, California, 1978. *Honour:* Magna cum laude, Columbia University. *Membership:* Phi Beta Kappa. *Address:* 100 W 67th Street, Apt. 5NW, New York, NY 10023, USA.

IRVING Howard Lee, b. 21 June 1951, Alexandria, Louisiana, USA. Associate Professor of Music. m. Carolyn Irving, 9 June 1973. *Education:* McNeese State University, Lake Charles, Louisiana, 1969-71; BM, Centenary College, Shreveport, Louisiana, 1973; MM, Piano, 1976, PhD, Music History and Theory, 1980, Louisiana State University. *Career:* Graduate Assistant, Secondary Piano, Louisiana State University, 1977-78; Instructor of Music, Bethel College, McKenzie, Tennessee, 1978-81; Assistant Professor of Music, 1981-87, Acting Chairman, Music Department, autumn 1984, Associate Professor of Music, 1987-, University of Alabama at Birmingham. *Contributions to:* Haydn and Laurence Sterne: Similarities in Eighteenth-Century Literary and Musical Wit, in Current Musicology, 1985; Haydn's Deutscher Tanz Finales, in Studies in Music, 1986; Amateurism, in The American Music Teacher, 1987; Creative Sightseeing (with H.Lee Riggins), in Journal of Music Theory Pedagogy, 1988; Advanced Uses of Mode Mixture in Haydn's Late Instrumental Works (with H.Lee Riggins), in Canadian University Music Review. *Address:* Music Department, University of Alabama at Birmingham, Birmingham, AL 35294, USA.

ISAACS Jeremy, b. 28 Sept 1932, Glasgow, Scotland, England. General Director. m. (1) Tamara Weinreich, 1958, dec 1986, (2) Gillian Widdicombe, 1988. *Education:* Glasgow Academy; MA, Merton College, Oxford. *Career:* Television Producer, Granada TV, 1958; BBC TV, Panorama, 1965; Controller of Features, Thames Television, 1968-74; Director of Programmes 1974-78; Chief Executive, Channel Four TV Company 1981-87; Member, Board of Directors, Royal Opera House Covent Garden, 1985-, General Director 1988-. *Publication:* Storm over Four: a personal account, 1989. *Honours include:* Desmond David Award for outstanding creative contribution to television, 1972; Cyril Bennett Award for outstanding contribution to television programming, RTS, 1982; Lord Willis Award for Distinguished Services to Television, 1985; Lifetime Achievement Award, Banff, 1988; Commandeur de l'Ordre des Arts et des Lettres, France, 1988. *Hobbies:* Reading; Walking. *Address:* Royal Opera House, 45 Floral Street, London WC2E 9DD, England.

ISAACS Maurice, b. 31 Aug 1922, Rangoon, Burma. Violinist. m. Isabel Stewart, 28 Dec 1949, 2 daughters. *Education:* LRAM, ARAM, Rangoon University; Studied at the Royal Academy of Music, Max Rostal and Alfredo Campoli. *Career:* Member, Peter Gibbs String Quartet, 1949-53; Formed Duo with Maisie Balch, 1953-75; Member, The London Harpsichord Ensemble, 1956-58; Leader, Marylebone String Quartet, 1956-62, Leader, Tilford Festival Orchestra, 1958-66; Member, Menuhin Festival Orchestra, 1959-67; Leader, Isaacs String Quartet, 1979-83. *Memberships:* Royal Society of Musicians. *Hobbies:* Swimming; Walking; Painting. *Address:* 84 Sutton Road, London, N10 1HG, England.

ISAKOVIC Smiljka, b. 23 Mar 1953, Belgrade, Yugoslavia. Harpsichordist; Pianist. *Education:* Music secondary school, with honours, Belgrade, 1965-69; American Community Schools, Athens, National Honour Society, 1969-1971; Graduated, Belgrade Music Academy, 1974; Master's degree, Faculty of Music, Belgrade, 1979; Postgraduate piano studies, Tchaikovsky Conservatory, Moscow, USSR, 1978-79; Graduate, harpsichord, Royal Conservatory of Music, Madrid, Spain, 1984. *Debut:* Belgrade, 1972. *Career:* Performances throughout the former Yugoslavia, including festivals at Dubrovnik, Ljubljana, Ohrid, Belgrade, East & West Europe, UK, USSR, USA, Cuba, Colombia; Master classes, harpsichord, International

Centre des Jeunesses Musicales, Groznjan, Yugoslavia; Lectures, harpsichord; Music reviews, Evening News & Student newspapers, & Radio Belgrade. *Recordings:* LP records and CD; Radio and TV appearances (Yugoslavia, Spain, Colombia). *Honour:* First Lady of the Harpsichord. *Membership:* President, Association of Serbian Musicians (UMUS). *Hobby:* Music. *Current Management:* Direccion artisitca Daniel, Los Madrazo, 16, 28014 Madrid, Spain. *Address:* Admirala Geprata 10, 11000 Belgrade, Serbia.

ISBIN Sharon, b. 7 Aug 1956, Minneapolis, Minnesota, USA. Guitarist; Teacher. *Education:* Pupil of Jeffrey Van, Minneapolis; Yale University, BA, 1978, MA, 1979; Lessons with Rosalyn Tureck; Pupil of Oscar Ghiglia, Aspen Music School, summers 1971-75, and of Alirio Diaz, Banff Music Festival, 1972. *Career:* International career as a soloist with orchestras and as a recitalist; Professor of Guitar, Manhattan School of Music, New York, 1979-, Mannes College of Music, New York, 1984-. *Recordings:* For Denon, ProArte, and TR. *Honours:* 1st prize, Toronto International Guitar Competition, 1975, Munich International Guitar Competition, 1976, Queen Sofia Competition, Madrid, 1979. *Address:* c/o Mannes College of Music, 150 West 85th Street, New York, NY 10024, USA.

ISEPP Martin Johannes Sebastian, b. 30 Sept 1930, Vienna, Austria. Pianist; Harpsichordist; Conductor. m. Rose Henrietta Harris, 1966, 2 sons. *Education:* St. Pauls School; Lincoln College, Oxford; Private study with Professor Leonie Gombrich, Oxford; Associate, Royal College of Music, London. *Career:* English Opera Group, 1950's; Music Staff, Glyndebourne Festival Opera, 1957; Chief Coach, 1973, Head of Music Staff, 1978-1993; Head of Opera Training, Juilliard School of Music, New York City, USA, 1973-77; Head of Music Studies, National Opera Studio, London, 1978; Head of Academy of Singing, Banff Centre School of Fine Arts, Banff, Alberta, Canada, 1981; Accompanist to leading singers including: Ilse Wolf, Janet Baker, John Shirley-Quirk, Elisabeth Schwarzkopf, Elisabeth Söderström, Jessye Norman, Anne Howells, Sheila Armstrong and Hugues Cuenod; As Conductor: Le Nozze di Figaro, 1984; Don Giovanni, 1986; Glyndebourne Touring Company; Seraglio, Washington Opera, 1986-87 season; Music Director for The Actor in Opera Courses at William Walton Foundation on Ischia, 1992-. *Recordings:* As accompanist and continuo player for various record labels. *Honour:* Carroll Donner Stuchell Medal for accompanying, Harriet Cohen International Musical Foundation, 1965. *Hobbies:* Swimming; Walking; Photography. *Address:* 37A Steeles Road, London NW3 4RG, England.

ISHII Kan, b. 30 Mar 1921, Tokyo, Japan. Composer. *Education:* Studied at the Mmasashino School of Music, 1939-43 and with Carl Orff in Munich, 1952-54. *Career:* Taught at the Toho Gakuen School of Music, 1954-56, the Aichi Prefectural Arts University at Nagoya, 1966-86, and 1939-43 and with Carl Orff in Munich, 1952-54. *Career:* Taught at the Toho Gakuen School of Music, 1954-56, the Aichi Prefectural Arts University at Nagoya, 1966-86, and Showa Music College at Tokyo, from 1986. *Compositions:* The Mermaid and the Red Candle, 1 act opera, 1961; Princess Kaguya, 1 act opera, 1963; En no Gyoja, 3 act opera, 1965; Kesa and Morito, 3 act opera, 1968; Women are Wonderful, comic opera in 1 act, 1978; Kantomi, 3 act opera, 1981; Blue Lion, operetta, 1989. *Address:* JASRAC (Japan), c/o PRS Ltd Member Registration, 28-33 Berners Street, London W1P 4AA, England.

ISHIKAWA Shizuka, b. 2 Oct 1954, Tokyo, Japan. Violinist. m. Jiri Schultz, 26 May 1978. *Education:* Diploma, Prague Music Academy, 1978; Studied with Professor Shin-ichi Suzuki and Saburo Sumi. *Career:* Performances at The Prague Spring Festival; Belgrade Music Festival; Warsaw Autumn Festival; Hungarian Music Week; Helsinki Music Festival; Czechoslovak Music Festival in Japan; Performances in Tokyo, Copenhagen, Prague, Vienna, Brussels, Bonn; Numerous Radio and television broadcasts; Soloist with many major orchestras. *Recordings:* Concertos by Bartók, Bruch, Mozart, Myslivecek and Paganini. *Honours:* 2nd Prize, Wieniawski International Violin Competition, 1972; Silver Medal, Queen Elisabeth in Brussels, 1976; 3rd Prize, International Violin Competition of F Kreisler, 1979. *Current Management:* Konzertburo Andreas Braun, Koln 41, Lindenthal; Japan Arts Corp., Tokyo, Japan.

ISHIKAWA Yoshiyuki (Yoshi), b. 26 Jan 1953, Tokyo, Japan. Bassoonist; Artistic Director. m. Brenda F Ishikawa. *Education:* BMusEd, MMus, Northwestern University; DMA Bassoon Performance, University of Michigan; Studied bassoon with L Hugh Cooper, Alan Goodman, Wilbur Simpson, Bernard Garfield, Norman Herzburg. *Career:* Active as soloist and clinician; Performance credits include tour of Japan, and solo and chamber music performances throughout the United States; Performances with Chicago Opera Studio Orchestra, Chicago Civic Orchestra, Ann Arbor Symphony Orchestra; Currently: Artistic Director (and Founder), Sierra Wind Quintet; Principal Bassoon, Las Vegas Symphony Orchestra, and Reno Philharmonic; Solo Bassoon and Personnel Manager, Las Vegas Chamber Players; Faculty, University of Nevada, Las Vegas, and Nevada School of Arts. *Honour:* Director and Host, 1987 Conference of the International Double Reed Society. *Address:* 3023 East Chapala, Las Vegas, NV 89120, USA.

ISOKOSKI Soile, b. 1960, Finland. Singer (Soprano). *Education:* Studied at the Sibelius Academy, Kuopio and with Dorothy Irving in Sweden. *Debut:* Formerly church organist, then gave concerto debut as singer at Helsinki, 1986; Guest appearances at concert halls in Europe, and Japan; Sibelius's Kullervo Symphony with the LSO under Colin Davis, 1991 (also televised); Les Illumniations by Britten with the English String Orchestra; Engagements with the Finnish National Opera at Helsinki as Mimi, Liu and Mozard's Countess and Fiordiligi; Guest appearances as Sonna Elvira in Cologne, Gluck's Alceste at Ludwigschafen, Fiordiligi in Stuttgart and Micaela in Holland; Season 1993 with Salzburg Festival debut, as First Lady in Die Zauberflote, and Mozart's Countess at Hamburg. *Honours:* Winner, Lapland Singing Competition, 1987; Second Prize, Cardiff Singer of the World Competition, 1987; Winner, Elly Ameling and Tokyo International Competitions. *Address:* IMG Artists, Media House, 3 Burlington Lane, London W4 2TH, England.

ISOMURA Kazuhide, b. 27 Dec 1945, Tokyohashi, Japan. Violinist. *Education:* Studied at the Juilliard School with members of the Juilliard Quartet. *Career:* Violist of the Tokyo Quartet from 1969; Regular concerts in the USA and abroad; First cycle of the complete quartets of Beethoven at the Yale at Norfolk Chamber Music Festival, 1986; Repeated cycles at the 92nd Street Y (New York), Ravinia and Israel Festivals, Yale, Princeton Universities; Season 1990-91 at Alice Tully Hall, Metropolitan Museum of Art, New York, Boston, Washington DC, Los Angeles, Cleveland, Detroit, Chicago, Miami, Seattle, San Francisco, Toronto; Tour of South America and two tours of Europe including Paris, Amsterdam, Bonn, Milan, Munich, Dublin, London, Berlin; Quartet-in-residence at Yale University, the University of Cincinnati College-Conservatory of Music. *Recordings:* Schubert's major Quartets; Mozart Flute Quartets with James Galway and Clarinet Quintet with Richard Stolzman; Quartets by Bartók, Brahms, Debussy, Haydn, Mozart and Ravel; Beethoven Middle Period Quartets (RCA). *Honours:* Grand Prix du Disque du Montreux; Best Chamber Music Recording of the Year from Stereo Review and the Gramophone; Four Grammy nominations. *Address:* Intermusica Artists' Management, 16 Duncan Terrace, London N1 8BZ, England.

ISRAEL Robert, b. 12 June 1918, Berlin, Germany. Violist; Teacher; Composer. m. Tamar Amrami, 20 Dec 1951, 1 son, 1 daughter. *Education:* Studied violin with Rudolph Bergmann, Viola with Oedeon Partos; Theory, Harmony Counterpoint Composition, with Yitshak Edel,

Rosowsky and Mordecai Seter; Teaching Diploma, 1942; Viola Diploma, Rubin Academy, Jerusalem and Tel Aviv. *Debut:* Elegie for Viola with string orchestra by Mordecal Seter, 1969. *Career:* Violist and Tubist Opera Orchestra Tel Aviv; Violin Teacher at various Kibbazine, 1946-48; Teacher of Violin and Viola and Theory at Conservatory Hadera, 1952-; Member, bass, Rinat Choir 1957-58; Principal Violist, Haifa Symphony Orchestra 1962-83; Performed with many chamber music groups. *Compositions include:* Five verses from Song of Songs for 2-voice choir 1955; 3 pieces for violin and Piano, 1988; Arrangement of Rosamunde, the Trout, Marche militaire (Schubert), 3 violons or 2 violins and viola, 1989; 14 songs, 1990; 27 pieces for violin or any melody instrument and guitar, Marom, 68 Pinsker Street, Tel-Aviv, 1991; Saraband, Bourrée, Polonais (J S Bach), Sonitne (Beethoven), arranged for two Violas, 1993. *Recordings:* Baroque music with recorder and harpsichord 1973. *Honours:* Rinat Choir, awarded Premier Prix, Paris 1957. *Hobbies:* Drawing landscapes, people and animals in motion; Reading; Walking; Swimming. *Address:* Ytsiat-Europa st 11, Beth Eliezer POB 10772, Hadera 38484, Israel.

ISSERLIS Steven, b. 19 Dec 1958, London, England. Cellist. *Education:* City of London School; International Cello Centre, 1969-76; Oberlin College, Ohio, 1976-78. *Debut:* Wigmore Hall, London, 1977. *Career:* Concerto, Recital and Chamber Music Performances Worldwide; Artistic Advisor to Cricklade Music Festival, Wiltshire. *Compositions:* Arrangement for Violin/Cello with piano/Harpsichord of Beethoven's Mandolin Variations (Faber). *Recordings include:* Britten Cello Symphony with City of London Sinfonia; Elgar Concerto, Bloch Schelomo with LSO, Hickox; Tschaikowsky: Rocco variations with Chamber Orchestra of Europe, Gardiner; Boccherini Concertos and Sonatas; John Tavener: The Protecting Veil with LSO, Rozhdestvensky; Strauss: Don Quixote with Minnesota Orchestra, de Waart; Saint-Saens: Concerto No.1, Sonata No.1, The Swan with LSO, Tilson Thomas, Dudley Moore, CD & Video; Tavener, Eternal Memory, Bloch, From Jewish Life with Moscow Virtuosi Spivakov. *Memberships:* Liszt Society, London; Dvořák Society. *Hobbies:* Literature; Films; Videos; Eating; Sleeping; Telephoning. *Address:* c/o Harrison and Parrott Limited, 12 Penzance Place, London W11 4PA.

ISTOMIN Eugene George, b. 26 Nov 1925, New York, USA. Pianist. m. Marta Montanez Casals, 1975. *Education:* Curtis Institute, Philadelphia; Studied under Kyriena Silote, Rudolf Serkin. *Debut:* As Concert Pianist, 1943. *Career:* Toured with Adolf Busch Chamber Players, 1944-45; First European Appearance, 1950; Several World tours; Founded Trio with Isaac Stern and Leonard Rose, 1961. *Recordings:* Numerous recordings of solo, chamber works and orchestral music. *Honour:* Leventritt Award, 1943. *Membership:* Charter Member, Casals Prades and Puerto Rico Festivals, 1950-. *Hobbies:* Archaeology; History; Painting; Baseball. *Address:* c/o ICM Concerts, 40 West 57th Street, New York, NY 10019, USA.

ITTZÉS Mihály, b. 8 Oct. 1938, Sárkeresztur, Hungary. Music Teacher; Choir Conductor. m. Kata Kövendi, 25 Aug. 1966, 3 sons. *Education:* Gyor Conservatory, 1953-58; F. Liszt Academy of Music, Budapest, 1958-63; Graduated as Music Teacher and Choir Conductor. *Career:* Teacher of Music Theory, Leader of Youth Orchestra, Gyor Conservatory, 1963-70; Music Teacher, Choir Conductor, Musical Secondary School, Kecskemét, 1970-73; Associate Professor, 1973, Deputy Director, 1980-90, Professor, 1993, Acting Director, 1990-92, 1990-, Z. Kodály Pedagogical Institute of Music, Kecskemét; Lectured and taught in Kodály courses in Australia, Greece, Ireland, Italy, Japan, Poland, the U.K., Norway and Finland. *Publications:* Several articles on music pedagogy, musicology (mainly Kodály's compositions) in Hungarian, English. *Address:* Zoltán Kodály Pedagogical Institute of Music, Kéttemplom Köz 1, POB 188, H-6001 Kecskemét, Hungary.

IVALDI Jean-Marc, b. 6 May 1953, Toulon, France. Singer (Baritone). *Education:* Studied in Paris at the Conservatoire National and the School of the Grand Opera. *Debut:* Paris Opera, 1983, as Yamadori in Butterfly. *Career:* Sang Rossini's Figaro at Liege, 1983, and appeared at Bordeaux, Toulouse, Nancy, Metz, Dijon and Tours; Bretigny in Manon and Ramiro in L'Heure Espagnole at Paris; Philadelphia 1986 as Morales in Carmen, Heidenheim 1989, as Escamillo; Other roles have included Alfonso in La Favorite, Belcore, Albert in Werther, Ourrias in Mireille, Manuel (La Vida Breve), Germont, Paquiro (Goyescas), Frederic in Lakme and Jarno in Mignon; Sang Valentin in Faust at St Etienne, 1990; Concert engagements include Carmina Burana at St Etienne and Joseph in L'Enfance du Christ at Nancy. *Recordings:* La Favorite (Erato); Sonora in La Fanciulla del West, conducted by Leonard Slatkin. *Address:* Saison Lyrique de Saint Etienne, 8 Place de l'Hotel de Ville, F-42000 St Etienne, France.

IVEY Jean Eichelberger, b. 3 July 1923, Washington, DC, USA. Composer. *Education:* MM in piano Peabody Conservatory 1946; MM in composition Eastman School 1956; DMus University of Toronto, 1972. *Career:* Founded electronic music studio at Peabody Conservatory, 1969: co-ordinator of the composition department, 1982; Tours of Europe, the USA and Mexico as piano soloist. *Compositions include:* Bismarck, opera, 1982; Little Symphony, 1948; Passacaglia for chamber orchestra, 1954; Festive Symphony, 1955; Piano Sonata, 1957; String Quartet, 1960; Woman's Love song cycle, 1962; Terminus for mezzo and tape, 1970; Forms in Motion symphony, 1972; 3 Songs of Night for soprano, instruments and tape, 1972; Aldebaran for viola and tape, 1972; Hera, Hung from the Sky for mezzo and ensemble, 1973; Testament of Eve, monodrama for mezzo, tape and orchestra, 1976; Solstice for soprano and ensemble, 1977; Prospero scena, 1978; Cortege-for Charles Kent, electronics, 1979; Sea-Change for orchestra and tape, 1979; Ariel in Flight for violin and tape, 1983; Notes toward Time, 3 sons for mezzo and ensemble, 1984; Cello Concerto, 1985. *Contributions to:* Musical Quarterly; Music Educators Journal. *Honours:* Grant from National Endowment for the Arts; Awards for Martha Baird Rockefeller Fund. *Memberships:* Board of Directors, League of Composers-ISCM, 1972-75, 1979. *Address:* c/o ASCAP, ASCAP Building, One Lincoln Plaza, New York, NY 10023, USA.

IWAKI Hiroyuki, b. 6 Sept 1932, Tokyo, Japan. Conductor. *Education:* Studied percussion at the Tokyo Music Academy and conducting with Akeo Watanabe. *Career:* Assistant Conductor of the NHK (Japanese Broadcasting) Symphony Orchestra, 1954; Conducted many premieres between 1957 and 1960; Conducted the Philharmonic Choir of Tokyo and was Musical Director of the Fujiwara Opera Company, 1965-67; Guest conductor of orchestras in Hamburg, Vienna and Berlin, 1966-69; Musical Director of the NHK Symphony from 1969, the Melbourne Symphony Orchestra from 1974; Director of the Orchestra-Ensemble Kanazawa, 1988; Conducted the first performances of works by Dallapiccola (Concerto per la notte di natale de l'anno 1956); Takemitsu (Marginilia 1976), Dreatime 1982), A Way To Love, 1982 and Star-Isle 1982); Isang Yun (Symphony No 4 1986). *Recordings include:* Beethoven's 9th Symphony, with the NHK Orchestra; Bartók Concerto for Orchestra (Melbourne Symphony); Hungarian Rhapsodies by Liszt (Vienna State Opera Orchestra); Messiaen Couleurs de la cité céleste, Oiseaux Exotiques, Reveil des Oiseaux and Sept Hai-Kai (Decca); Dutch music with the Hague Philharmonic. *Address:* c/o Melbourne Symphony, PO Box 443, East Caulfield, Vic 3145, Australia.

IWASAKI Ko, b. 16 Aug 1944, Tokyo, Japan. Cellist. m. Yurie Ishio, 21 Dec 1979, 2 sons. *Education:* Toho Conservatoire; Juilliard School of Music, USA, 1964-66; Studied with: Leonard Rose, Harvey Shapiro, 1964-66; Pablo Casals, Puerto Rico, 1966. *Debut:* Recital at Carnegie Recital Hall, New York, 1966; Recital at Wigmore Hall, London, England, 1968; Performed with: London Symphony, 1972; participant, Summer

Festivals, Marlboro, Portland, Oregon, Kuhmo, Finland, Lockenhaus, Austria; Performances in USA, Europe, Russia and the Orient; Director, Moonbeach Music Camp, Okinawa, Japan, 1979-; Director, Cello Master Class, Illinois State University, USA. *Recordings:* Ko Iwasaki Plays Schubert Arpeggione Sonata; Beethoven Sonatas; Shostakovich Sonata; Japanese Contemporary Works for Cello; Ko Iwasaki and Staffan Scheja Play Sonata (Rachmaninoff and Grieg); Iwasaki/Requibros; 19 Short Pieces (compact disc); Beethoven: 2 Trios; Dvořák, Tchaikovsky with Polish National Radio Symphony; Haydn Cello Concerto No.1 & No.2 with Polish Chamber Orchestra. *Honours:* 3rd Prizes: Vienna International Cello Competition, 1967; Munich International Competition, 1967, Budapest International Cello Competition, 1968, Tchaikovsky International Competition; 2nd Prize, Casado International Cello Competition. *Hobby:* Driving a Car. *Address:* 3109 Bristol Dr., Bloomington, IL 61701, USA.

IZZO D'AMICO Fiamma, b. 1964, Rome, Italy. Singer (Soprano). *Education:* Studied at Santa Cecilia Conservatory, Rome, 1981-84. *Debut:* Sang Mimi in La Bohème at the Teatro Regio, Turin, 1984. *Career:* Sang Violetta at Treviso 1985, was discovered by Herbert von Karajan, sang Elisabeth de Valois at the 1986 Salzburg Festival followed by Micaela in Carmen; US debut Philadelphia 1986 in La Bohème, with Luciano Pavarotti (celebrated his 15th anniversary with him at Modena) 1986; Bologna 1986 in La Traviata, conducted by Riccardo Chailly; Season 1987-88 with appearances in Boheme at Vienna, Metropolitan, New York; Manon in Genoa, Tosca and the Verdi Requiem at Salzburg; Further engagements at the Paris Opera, London, Chicago, Monte Carlo, Monaco and Hamburg. *Address:* Metropolitan Opera, Lincoln Center, New York, NY 10023, USA.

J

JABLONSKI Krzysztof, b. 2 Mar 1965, Wroclaw, Poland. Musician (Pianist). *Education:* Karol Szymanowski Academy of Music in Katowice, 1986 with Professor Andrzej Jasinski. *Career:* Numerous concert engagements in Poland and abroad, including Austria, Belgium, Bulgaria, Canada, Czechoslovakia, Denmark, Germany, Finland, Great Britain, Holland, Israel, Italy, Japan, Norway, Soviet Union, Spain and USA. Many recordings for radio and TV in Poland and abroad. *Recordings include:* Chopin: 24 Preludes Op 28; Haydn: Sonata in C Minor No 33/Beethoven: Sonata in C Minor Op 13, Pathetique, Aperto 86 404; Mozart: Piano Concerto in F Major K 459, Orchester der Ludwigsburger Festpiele/W Goennenwein, Bayer Records; Chopin: 24 Preludes Op 28/Polonaise in A flat Major, Op 53, Heroique/Study in G flat Major Op 10/5 Black Keys/Study in C Minor Op 10/12 Revolutionary, Yamaha Piano Player; Chopin: Sonata in B Minor Op 58/Barcarolle in F sharp Major Op 60/Polonaises - in A flat Major Op 53, Heroique in G Minor in B flat Major, in A flat Major/Nocturnes - in B flat Major Op 9/3 in F sharp Major Op 15/2, Crown Records; more recently: Mussorgsky: Piano solo, Pictures at an Exhibition; Schumann: Kinderszenen Op. 15; Debussy: Children's Corner, Kos Records, Kos CD 10 (CD), 1993. *Address:* Ul. Kwiska 43/9, 54-210 Wroclaw, Poland.

JACKSON Francis Alan, b. 2 Oct 1917, Yorkshire, England. Organist; Composer. m. Priscilla Procter, 1 Nov 1950, 2 sons, 1 daughter. *Eduation:* Sir Edward Bairstow; DMus, Durham, 1957. *Career:* Chorister York Minster, 1929-33; Master of Music, York Minister, 1946-82; Conductor York Musical Society, 1947-82 and York Symphony Orchestra, 1947-80; Patron, Percy Whitlock Trust. *Compositions:* Symphony in D minor; Concerto for organ, strings, timpani and celesta; Missa Matris Dei; Services in G minor F sharp. *Recordings:* Complete Bairstow Organ works, Mirabilis; The Composer (Amphion) plays his own works; Stanford at Sledmere, 1994; Own Works (Priory), 1994; Whitlock Sonata, Royal Albert Hall, 1994. *Honours:* OBE; Doctor of York University, 1982; Limpus Prize, FRCO, 1937. *Memberships:* Royal College of Organists; ISM. *Hobbies:* Gardening; Art; Architecture. *Address:* Nether Garth, Acklam, Malton, North Yorks YO17 9RG, England.

JACKSON Isaiah, b. 22 Jan 1945, Virginia, USA. Conductor. m. Helen Tuntland, 6 Aug 1977, 1 son, 2 daughters. *Education:* MS Julliard School of Music, 1969; DMA, 1973. *Career:* Assistant Director, American Symphony 1970-71; Assoc Conductor, Rochester Philharmonic, 1973-87; Music Director, Royal Ballet, Covent Garden, 1987-90; Music Director, Dayton Philharmonic, 1987-; Principal Guest Conductor, Queensland Symphony Orchestra, 1993-; Guest Conductng: New York Philharmonic, Cleveland Orchestra, Boston Pops, San Francisco Symphony, Orchestre de la Suisse Romande, BBC Concert Orchestra, Berlin Symphony. *Recordings:* String orchestra compositions of Herrmann, Waxman, RozsaBerlin Symphony (Koch); Dance music of William Grant Still; Berlin Symphony (Koch), Gospel at the Symphony, Louisville Orchestra (Koch). *Honours:* First Governor's Award for Arts, Virginia, 1979. *Address:* c/o United Arts, 3906 Sunbeam Drive, Los Angeles, CA 90065, USA.

JACKSON Laurence, b. 1967, Lancashire, England. Concert Violinist. *Education:* Studied at Chethams School of Music and at the Royal Academy with Maurice Hasson and Anne-Sophie Mutter. *Career:* Concerto repertoire includes works by Bruch, Mendelssohn, Vaughan Williams and Tchaikovsky; Aldeburgh Festival 1988 in the Concerto Grosso by Schmittke; Soloist at the Casals Festival in France, 1988; Purcell Room debut 1989, Festival Hall 1990, in the Four Seasons; Recitals at the Fairfields Halls, Queens Hall, Edinburgh, Brangwyn Hall and Turner Sims Hall; Member of Britten-Pears Ensemble, tour of USA 1991; As member of Borante Piano Trio has performed from 1982 at the Purcell Room and Wigmore Hall in Dublin and Paris and at the 1989 Festival Wiener Klassik (Beethoven's Triple Concerto); Season 1990 at the Bath and Perth Festivals, tour of Scandinavia, Russia and the Baltic States and master classes with Andras Schiff at Prussia Cove, Cornwall; Duo partnership with pianist Scott Mitchell; Solo concert tour of Chile, Columbia and Venezuela 1991; Concerto and Recital Performances in Spain, 1992. *Recordings:* Solo recording for Trittiko records with the ensemble Laureate, 1991. *Honours include:* David Martin Concerto Prize 1987 and Principal's Prize 1988 at the Royal English Heritage Award 1983, 1985, 1986; First Prize at Vina del Mar, Chile, 1990; Third Prize, First International Violin Competition, Pablo Sarasate, 1991. *Current Management:* Scott Mitchell Management, 26 Childebert Road, London SW17 8EX. *Address:* 23 Fulwell Park Avenue, Twickenham, Middlesex TW2 5HF, England.

JACKSON Nicholas Fane St George (Bart.) Sir, b. 4 Sept 1934, London, England. Organist; Harpsichordist; Composer. m. Nadia Michard 1971, 1 son. *Education:* Radley College; Wadham College, Oxford; Royal Academy of Music, with C.H. Trevor, George Malcolm, Gustav Leonhardt; LRAM, ARCM. *Debut:* Wigmore Hall 1964. *Career:* Organist at St James's Piccadilly 1971-74; St Lawrence Jewry next Guildhall 1974-77; Organist and Master of the Choristers St David's Cathedral 1977-84; Organ Recital at the Royal Festival Hall, 1984; Director of the Concertante of London 1987-; Master Classes at Segovia, Spain, 1989; Director of Festival Bach, Santes Creus Spain; Solo performances at the South Bank, London, and at Nôtre Dame Paris, Teatro Real Madrid, New York. *Compositions:* Mass for a Saint's Day; 4 Images for organ; 20th Century Merbecke; Divertissement for organ; Anthems and Choral Settings; Opera: The Reluctant Highwayman, 1992. *Recordings:* The Organ of St David's Cathedral; Bach's Christmas Organ Music, Trumpet and Organ, 2 Lps with Maurice Murphy; Flute and Organ with Edward Beckett; Complete organ works of Richard Arnell; Bach's 2 and 3 part Inventions; François Couperin; Harpsichord Concertos; Mass for a Saint's Day: Companies include Abbey Records, Spectrum. Vista, Decca and RCA; Spanish Organ Music, Segovia Cathedral, Priory Records. *Current Management:* Nuria Corts de Vila, Reus, Spain. *Address:* 42a Hereford Road, London W2 5AJ, England.

JACKSON Richard, b. 15 Feb 1936, New Orleans, Louisiana, USA. Music Librarian. *Education:* BMus, Loyola University; MA, Tulane University; MSLS, Pratt Insitute. *Career:* Head, Americana Collection, New York Public Library. *Publications include:* United States Music - Sources of Bibliography and Collective Biography, 1973; Piano Music of Louis Moreau Gottschalk, 1973; Popular Songs of 19th Century America, 1976; Numerous articles for encyclopeadias. *Contributions to:* Library Journal; Notes; New World Records (notes). *Memberships:* Music Library Association; Sonneck Society; International Association for the Study of Popular Music. *Hobbies:* Films; Reading. *Address:* 111 Amsterdam Avenue, New York, NY 10023, USA.

JACKSON Richard, b. 1960, Cornwall, England. Singer (Baritone). *Education:* Study with Pierre Bernac and Audrey Langford. *Career:* Widely known as a concert singer, in song and oratorio; Founder member of the Songmakers' Almanac: appearances in the USA, at the Saintes Festival, Three Choirs Festival, and the Wigmore and Elizabeth Halls; Solo recital with songs by Poulenc at the Wigmore Hall, 1989; Concerts with David Willcocks, Neville Marriner, Bertini, Rostropovitch, Mackerras and Gardiner; Has sung Bach and Handel in Spain and Portugal; Monteverdi's Vespers in Venice; The Starlight Express by Elgar; Opera engagements at the Glyndebourne and Aldeburgh Festivals and with Kent Opera, New Sadler's Wells Opera and with the Handel Opera Society; Sang Aeneas to the Dido of Janet Baker; Almeida Festival, London, 1987-88 in the British premiere of Jakob Lenz by Wolfgang Rihm and the world premiere of The Undivine Comedy by Michael Finnissy. *Recordings:* For the BBC and for Erato records. *Address:*

c/o Ron Gonsalves, 10 Dagnan Road, London SW12 9LQ, England.

JACOBS Arthur David, b. 14 June 1922, Manchester, England. Critic and Lecturer. m. Betty Upton Hughes, 4 Nov 1953, 2 sons. *Education:* Manchester Grammar School; MA (Oxon), Merton College, Oxford University. *Career:* Music Critic, Daily Express, 1947-52; Freelance Critic, 1952-; Member, Editorial Board, Opera, 1962-; Record Reviewer, Sunday Times, 1964-89; Professor, Royal Academy of Music, London, 1964-79; Head of Department of Music, Huddersfield Polytechnic, 1979-84; Visiting Professor; University of Illinois, 1967; University of Victoria, British Columbia, Canada, 1968; University of California, 1969, 1973; Temple University, Philadelphia, 1970, 1971; University of Western Ontario, 1974; McMaster University, Hamilton, Ontario, Canada, 1975, 1983; University of Queensland, Australia, 1985; Visiting Scholar, Wolfson College, Oxford, 1979, 1984-85, 1991-92. *Publications:* Music Lover's Anthology, 1948; Gilbert and Sullivan, 1951; A New Dictionary of Music (also Spanish, Portuguese, Danish and Swedish editions) 1958; new edition, as The New Penguin Dictionary of Music, 1978; Choral Music (also Spanish and Japanese editions) 1963; Libretto of Opera, One Man Show by Nicholas Maw, 1964; (with Stanley Sadie) Pan Book of Opera, 1966, expanded edition 1984, (US edition, Great Operas In Synopsis) also Partuguese edition; A Short History of Western Music, 1972 (also Italian edition); Editor, Music Education Handbook, 1976; Arthur Sullivan: A Victorian Musician, 1984, Henry J Wood, The Maker of the Proms, 1994; many opera translations; contributor to Shakespeare and The Victorian Stage, 1986; Pan Book of Orchestral Music, 1987; Penguin Dictionary of Musical Performers, 1990. *Contributions to:* Many articles in Times Literary Supplement; Musical Times; High Fidelity/Musical America; New Grove Dictionary of Music and Musicians, 1980; New Grove Dictionary of Opera, 1992; Viking Opera Guide, 1993. *Honours:* Honorary Member, Royal Academy of Music, 1969. *Hobbies:* Walking; Theatre-going. *Address:* 7 Southdale Road, Oxford OX2 7SE, England.

JACOBS René, b. 30 Oct 1946, Ghent, Belgium. Singer (Countertenor); Editor; Conductor. m. Suzy Depoorter. *Education:* Licentiaat Klassieke Filologie, University of Ghent; Solo singing with Louis Devos (Brussels) and Lucie Frateur (The Hague). *Career:* Recitals in Europe, Canada, USA, Mexico and the Philippines; Performances with madrigal ensembles and with such early music groups as the Leonhardt Consort, Il Complesso Barocco, La Petite Bande and groups led by Alan Curtis and Nikolaus Harnoncourt; Sings Baroque music and directs his own ensemble Collegium Vocale; Best known in operas by Monteverdi, Cesti, Handel, Gluck and Cavalli; Sacred music by Charpentier and Couperin; Teacher of performing practice in Baroque singing, Schola Cantorum, Basle; Appointments at the International Summer School for Early Music, Innsbruck, and the Aston Magna Academy for Baroque Music, USA; Conducted Cavalli's Giasone in his own edition at the 1988 Innsbruck Festival, Flavio 1989; L'Incoronazione di Poppea with the ensemble I Febi Armonici, 1989; Conducted Graun's Cleopatra e Cesare at the 1992 Baroque Festival, Versailles; Conti's Don Chisciotte at the 1992 Innsbruck Festival of Early Music. *Recordings:* Cesti's L'Orontea, from the 1982 Holland Festival, arias by Monteverdi and Benedetto Ferrari, Motets by Charpentier, Bach's St Matthew Passion (Harmonia Mundi); Handel's Admeto and Partenope, Lully's Bourgeois Gentilhomme (HMV); Gluck's Orfeo ed Euridice (Accent); and Echo et Narcisse (Harmonia Mundi); Giasone by Cavalli; Handel's Alessandro and Tamerlano (CBS); Charpentier's David et Jonathas (Erato); Handel's Giulio Cesare (Harmonia Mundi). *Address:* Langenakkerlaan 34, 9130 Lochristi, Belgium.

JACOBSON Bernard Isaac, b. 2 Mar 1936, London, England. Writer on Music. m. (1) Bonnie Brodsky, 11 Aug 1968 (marriage dissolved, 1982), 1 son, 1 daughter, (2) Dr. Laura Dale Belcove, 3 Jan 1983. *Education:* City of London School, 1947-54; Corpus Christi College, Oxford (Open Scholar), 1956-60; Classical Honour Moderations, 1958; Lit Hum - BA 1960; MA 1962. *Career:* Sleeve Note Writer, Philips Phonographic Industries, Baarn, Holland, 1960-62; Classical Promotion Executive, EMI International, London, 1962-64; Music Critic, Chicago Daily News, 1967-73; Visiting Professor of Music, Chicago Musical College, Roosevelt University, Chicago, 1972; Director, Southern Arts Association, Winchester, England, 1973-76; Deputy Director of Publications, 1979-81, Director of Promotion, Boosey and Hawkes Music Publishers Limited, London, 1982-84; Manager, Publications and Educational Programmes, 1984-88, Programme Annotator and Musicologist, 1988-91, The Philadelphia Orchestra; Artistic Director, Residentie Orkest (Hague Philharmonic), 1992-94; Independent Associate, Joy Mebus Artists' Management, 1993-. *Composition:* Libretto (16 poems) for Death of a Young Man, song cycle by Wilfred Josephs; Commissioned and performed by 1971 Harrogate Festival, published by Mornington Music, London; poems for songs and other works by Richard Wernick, published by Theodore Presser Co., USA. *Recording:* Schoenberg Ode to Napoleon (Sprechstimme), recorded by Nonesuch, 1968. *Publications:* The Music of Johannes Brahms - Fairleigh Dickinson University Press, USA and The Tantivy Press, London, 1977; Conductors on Conducting, Columbia Publishing Company, USA and Macdonald and Janes, London, 1979; The Songs in Frédéric Chopin, edited by Alan Walker - Barrie, London, 1966; Taplinger, New York, 1967 and in paperback as The Chopin Companion, Norton, New York, 1973; Sonata in Encyclopaedia Britannica 15th Edition, 1974; Contributor, Dictionary of 20th Century Music, 1974 and The New Grove, 1980; Also many translations including Libretto of Henze La Cubana for Schott and English Music Theatre and Matthus's Holofernes and Judith for VEB Deutscher Verlag für Musik. *Hobbies:* Food and Wine; Travel; Photography; Watching Cricket and Baseball. *Address:* Buys Ballotstraat 89, 2563 ZK Den Haag, The Netherlands.

JACOBSON Daniel C, b. 27 July 1959, California, USA. Musicologist. Music Theorist. m. Grace Eugenia Mannion, 20 Dec 1986, 1 daughter. *Education:* BA, Voice, Westminister College, Utah; MA, Music History, California State University; PhD, Musicology and Music Theory, University of California, 1986. *Career:* Faculty, University of California, Santa Barbara, 1986-89; Co-ordinator, Lehmann Centennial, 1988. *Publications:* A Listeners Introduction to Music, 1991; Co-Editor, The Norton CD-Rom Masterworks Series; Contributor to Mozart-Jahrbuch, 1994; Dvořák in America, 1993; The Opera Quarterly, 1991; NATS Journal, 1991. *Honours:* Stanley Krebs Memorial Prize in Musicology, 1983, 1984, 1986; NEH Fellowship grant, 1991; UND College of Fine Arts Faculty Award, 1993. *Memberships:* American Musicological Society; Society for Music Theory; College Music Society; Music Theory Mid-West; International Franz Schubert Society; Lotte Lehmann League. *Hobbies:* Midi Composition; Computer Programming; Baseball; Travel. *Address:* 2210 Highland Court, Grand Forks, ND 58201, USA

JACOBSON Julian, b. 1947, Scotland. Pianist. *Education:* Studied piano with Lamar Crowson and Louis Kentner, composition with Arthur Benjamin and Humphrey Searle; Graduate, Royal College of Music and Oxford University. *Debut:* London, Purcell Room, 1974. *Career:* Appearances in 28 countries including concerto engagements with London Symphony, BBC Symphony, City of Birmingham and English Chamber Orchestras, London Mozart Players and Bournemouth Sinfonietta Chamber music recitals with Nigel Kennedy, Lydia Mordkovitch, Zara Nelsova, Steven Isserlis, Colin Carr, Emma Johnson, Christian Lindberg and the Brodsky and Arditti Quartets; Artistic Director, Paxos Festival, Greece; Teacher, Performer, Dartington International Summer School; Hd of Keyboard Studies, Welsh College of Music and Drama; Partnership with violinist, Susanne Stanzeleit, including Purcell Room recital, 1993, with works by Strauss, Beethoven, and Schubert. *Compositions:* Songs, piano and chamber music, and six film scores. *Recordings:* Albums on various labels. *Address:* 34 St Margaret's Road, London SE4 1YU

JACOBSON Rut, b. 1927, Jokkmokk, Lapaland, Sweden. Singer (Soprano). m. Per Stokholm. *Education:* She studied at the Stockholm Academy of Music and in Vienna. *Career:* Sang first at Graz and at the Vienna Volksoper (1954-58), then at the Stora Theatre Gothenburg; Sang at the Royal Opera Stockholm 1964-65 and Malmo 1970-71; Also sang in Reykjavik; Roles include Constanze, Pamina, Fiordiligi, Gilda, Violetta and Butterfly; From 1971 Professor at the Gothenburg Academy of Music. *Address:*c/o Malmo Stadttheater, Box 17520, S-200 10, Malmo, Sweden.

JACOBSSON John-Eric, b. 6 Oct 1931, Hogran, Sweden. Singer (Tenor). *Education:* Studied in Stockholm with Toivo Ek, Arne Sunnegaard and Sonny Peterson. *Debut:* Royal Opera Stockholm 1964, as Turiddu in Cavalleria Rusticana. *Career:* Sang at Stockholm in the premiere of Kalifens son by Eiyser (1976) and as Alwa in the local premiere of Berg's Lulu; Other roles include Pedrillo in Die Entführung, Jacquino in Fidelio, Cavaradossi, Albert Herring, Eisenstein in Die Fledermaus and Ismaele in Nabucco; Steva in Jenůfa and title role in Xerxes and more than 100 different roles; Guest appearances in Oslo, Copenhagen, Hamburg, Munich, Edinburgh, Moscow, Hong Kong and at the Drottningholm Festival; Many concert appearances. *Address:* c/o Kungliga Teatern, PO Box 16094, S-10322 Stockholm, Sweden.

JACOBY Robert, b. 8 Apr 1940, Sussex, England. Violinist; Conductor; Teacher. m. Elisabeth Duddridge, 3 Sept 1963, 1 son, 1 daughter. *Education:* Guildhall School of Music; Royal College of Music; University of Wales; MA, PhD, FLCM, LRAM, ARCM. *Debut:* Wigmore Hall, London. *Career:* First concert aged 7; Radio and TV appearances as concerto soloist and in chamber music; Sibelius concerto under Sir Adrian Boult; Solo violinist and First Konzertmeister with Westphalian Symphony Orchestra; Leader resident professional String Quartet, University College of Wales; Founder and Conductor, Oakwood Symphony Orchestra, Philomusica of Aberystwyth; Currently, Musical Director, Dorset Chamber Orchestra. *Publications:* Violin Technique, a Practical Analysis for Performers, 1985; Reviews for The Library, British Journal for 18th C Studies. *Hobbies:* Walking; Antiquarian Studies. *Current Management* Direct Booking Only. *Address:* 2 St George's Avenue, Weymouth, Dorset DT4 7TU, England

JAEGER David, b. 1947. Composer. *Education:* Studied composition with Burt Levey, University of Wisconsin at Madison; graduated BMus. Degree and Woodrow Wilson Fellowship 1970. Continued studies with John Weinzweig and Gustav Ciamaga, twice recipient of scholarships, obtained MMus. Degree, University of Toronto, 1972; Attended Summer Electronic Music Institute, Dartmouth, New Hampshire under guidance of Jon Appleton and Hubert Howe. *Career:* Founder-member of Canadian Electronic Ensemble; one of the writers of Outperform, computer sound synthesis programme in use at University of Toronto Electronic Studio; joined CBC Radio Music Department, active in contemporary music as producer of FM Network series, Music of Today 1973-; Main compositional output has been directed toward live performance with the Ensemble 1972-. *Compositions include:* Space To Move Around In 1971; Fancye 1973, commissioned by Faculty of Music, University of Toronto for inauguration of its new Casavanti organ; Quanza Dueto 1976; works have been performed at Fylkingen Festival in Sweden; CBC Radio and on Cologne Radio.

JAFFE Monte, b. 5 June 1940, USA. Singer (Baritone). *Education:* Studied at the Curtis Institue and with Giorgio Tozzi. *Career:* Appearances with Krefeld Opera as Wotan, Kaspar (Der Freischütz), Dr Schön (Lulu), Reimann's Lear, the Dutchman, and in Cerhaa's Baal and the premiere of Judith by Matthus; further engagements at the Metropolitan in Death in Venice,

Lear with ENO, the Hoffmann villains for Israel Opera and Bluebeard (Bartók) for Scottish Opera; Returned to ENO for the title role in the premiere of Timon of Athens by Stephen Oliver, 1991, and has also sung at Karlsruhe (Graf Mirabeau by Matthus), Berne Nekrotzar in Le Grand Macabre, Tel Aviv, (Mephistopheles in Faust), Bonn, (Gianni Schicchi), 1993, Turin (Walküre Wotan), Antwerp (Klingsor) and Bielefeld (Barak in Die Frau ohne Schatten); Other roles include Scarpia, Konchak (Prince Igor), Zaccaria (Nabucco) and Old Sam in Bernstein's A Quiet Place. *Address:* Ingpen & Williams Ltd, 14 Kensington Court, London W8 5DN, England.

JAFFE Stephen, b. 30 Dec 1954, Washington DC, USA. Composer. m. Mindy Oshrain, 29 May 1988, 1 daughter. *Education:* AM, AB summa cum laude, University of Pennsylvania, with George Crumb, George Rochberg and Richard Wernick, 1973-78; Also at University of Massachusetts and Conservatoire de Musique, Geneva. *Career:* Director, Encounters with the music of our Time, Duke University, 1981-; Performances with San Francisco, New Jersey, New Hampshire Symphonies; Rome Radio Orchestra, New York New Music Ensemble, Spectrum concerts, Berlin, Aurora and Ciompi Quartets. *Compositions:* First Quartet, 1991; Double Sonata, two pianos, 1989; Four Songs with Ensemble, for mezzo soprano and ensemble, 1988; Four Images, 1983/87; The Rhythm of The Running Plough, 1988; Triptych, 1993 for piano and wind quintet; Pedal Point, baritone, low strings, harp and timpani, 1992. *Recordings:* First Quartet; Centering for two violins; Three Figures and a Ground; The Rhythm of the Running Plough; Double Sonata; Four Songs with Ensemble. *Publications:* First Quartet, 1991; Double Sonata, 1992; Three Figures and a Grand, 1993; Four Images for Orchestra, 1988; Article: Conversation between JS ands SJ on the New Tonality, 1992. *Current Management* Theodore Presser Co, Bryn Mawr, PA 19010, USA. *Address:* Box 90665, Durham, NC 27708, USA.

JAFFEE Kay, b. 31 Dec 1937, Michigan, USA. Musician; Musicologist. m. Michael Jaffee, 24 July 1964. *Education:* BA, University of Michigan, 11959; MA, New York University, 1965; Private recorder study with Bernard Krainis; Further classes with Frans Bruggen and Hans-Martin Linde. *Debut:* Carnegie Recital Hall, 1966. *Career:* Founding member and Associate Director, The Waverly Consort, 1964-; Performer on Renaissance wind and keyboard instruments, harps, psalteries, percussion; Annual tours of North America since 1967; Also Great Britain, Latin America; Festival appearances include Casals Festival, 1981, 1983, Madeira Bach Festival, 1981, Hong Kong Festival, 1988, Caramoor Festival, New York, 1973 (and annually thereafter); Television appearances in USA. *Recordings:* 9 with the Waverly Consort. *Publications:* Articles and reveiws to the The Journal of Musicology, the American Recorder, The Brass Quarterly. *Memberships:* American Musicology Society; American Musical Instrument Society; American Recorder Society; Early Music America; Renaissance Society of America. *Current Management* Shaw Concerts Incorporated, 1990 Broadway, NY, USA. *Address:* PO Box 386, Patterson, NY 12563, USA.

JAHN Gertrude, b. 13 Aug 1940, Zagreb, Yugoslavia. Singer (Mezzo-Soprano). *Education:* Studied at the Vienna Music Academy with Elisabeth Rado and Lily Kolar; further study with Erik Werba and Josef Witt. *Debut:* Basle 1963, as Gluck's Orpheus. *Career:* Appearances at the State Operas of Vienna, Hamburg, Munich and Stuttgart; Glyndebourne 1968, as Olga in Eugene Onegin; Salzburg Festivals from 1967, as Feodor in Boris Godunor, Mozart's Ascanio, Margret in Wozzeck and Countess Laura in the premiere of Penderecki's Die schwarze Maske, 1986; Munich and Madrid, 1988, as Adelaide in Arabella and the Countess Geschwitz in Lulu; Further engagements in Dusseldorf, Salzburg, Moscow, Trieste and Montreal; Other roles include Carmen, Giulietta in Les Contes d'Hoffmann, Octavian, Eboli, Preziosilla (La Forza del Destino), Fatima in Oberon and Magdalene in Die Meistersinger; Frequent concert appearances. *Recordings include:* Masses by Haydn and Schubert, Missa Choralis by Liszt (Turnabout); Wozzeck.

JAHREN Helen Mai Aase, b. 2 May 1959, Malmo, Sweden. Solo Concert Oboist. *Education:* MFA, 1977, Postgraduate Diploma, Oboe, 1978, Malmoe College of Music; Hochschulabschlussprufung, Staatliche Hochschule fur Musik, Freiburg, 1980; Solistendiplom, Konservatorium fur Musik, Berne, 1983. *Debut:* 1st solo appearance with orchestra, age 17. *Career:* Tours: France, Italy, Spain, Germany, Switzerland, Poland, Denmark, Norway, Finland, Iceland, Japan, 1980-; Belgian tour with Orchestra National de Belgique, 1982; Vienna debut, Grosses Konzerthaus, 1983; Toured Colombia, Ecuador, Peru, Argentina, Uruguay, Brazil, Venezuela, Costa Rica, Mexico, 1984; Debut, Stockholm Philharmonic Orchestra, 1987; Invited to Louisville Symphony Orchestra's 50th Anniversary, USA 1987; Pan Music Festival, Seoul, 1988; Gala Opening Concert, with Hong Kong Philharmonic Orchestra, World Music Days, Hong Kong, 1988; Debut, Swedish Radio Orchestra, 1988; Many TV/radio appearances worldwide; Artist Portrait by Swedish Television, 1991-93; Stockholm Royal College of Music, 1993-; Teaching: Malmo College of Music, 1984-87, Ingesund College of Music, Sweden, 1991-; Masterclasses; Initiator and Artistic Director of Båstad Chamber Music Festival, Sweden. *Recordings:* Swedish music for oboe and organ with Hans-Ola Ericsson, MAP, 1986; Schnittke Double Concerto, oboe, harp, New Stockholm Chamber Orchestra, BIS, 1987; Musica Vitae: J H Roman, Oboe Concerto, Musica Vitae, 1988, L-E Larsoon, Oboe Concertino, 1990. *Current Management:* Svensk Konsertdirektion AB, Sweden. *Address:* c/o Svensk Konsertdirektion AB, Box 5076, S-40222 Gothenburg, Sweden.

JAKOBSSON Claes, b. 1924, Uddevalla, Sweden. Singer (Baritone). m. Suzanna Brenning 1964. *Education:* Studied at the Stockholm Music High School with Gjurja Leppee. *Career:* Sang at the Stora Theatre Gothenburg 1948-78 as Mozart's Count and Don Giovanni, Rigoletto, Germont, Iago, Ford, Escamillo and Eugene Onegin; Guest appearances at the Vienna Volksoper (as Danilo in Die Lustige Witwe), Oslo and Milwaukee; Concert tours of Scandinavia, Austria and the USA (1974); Teacher at the Gothenburg Opera School from 1973. *Recordings include:* Tintomara by Werle (Philips). *Address:* c/o Stora Teatern, Box 53116, S-400 15 Gothenburg, Sweden.

JAKOBY Richard Matthias, b. 11 Sept 1929, Dreis, Kr Wittlich, Germany. m. Irmgard Mohr, 2 sons, 1 daughter. *Education:* Musicology, Music Education, Romance Languages, Philosophy and Psychology, Mainz, 1949-54; Doctorate, 1955. *Career:* Teaching positions, Academy of Music, College of Adult Education and Mainz Conservatory, Mainz, 1954-64; Professor, Hannover, 1964; Principal, State Academy of Music and Drama, Hannover, 1969-93; Honorary Professor of Hannover University, 1981; Chairman, 1973-76, President, 1976-88, Honorary President 1988-, German Music Council; Board Member, International Music Council, 1985. *Publications:* Author of over 200 publications in musicology, music education, cultural-political affairs and various other topics. *Contributions to:* Various professional journals. *Honours:* Gutenberg Prize, 1952; Principal, Society of Music and Music Culture, 1974-76; Niedersachsen-Preis für Wissenschaft und Kulfur, 1989; Deutscher Musikpreis, 1988; Großes Verdienstkreuz der BRD. *Hobbies:* Sport, Archaeology. *Address:* 71 Ostfeldstr 61, 3 30559 Hannover, Germany.

JAKSIC Djura, b. 30 Apr 1924, Karlovac, Yugoslavia. Conductor; Writer on music. m. Slobondanka Ilic, 21 July 1962, 2 sons. *Education:* School of Music, Belgrade, 1939-45; Music Science, Charles University, Prague, 1945-48; Prague Conservatoire, 1945-48; Diploma Academic Musician-Conductor, Academy of Music, Zagreb, 1948-50. *Debut:* Symphonic Concert, Radio Belgrade Symphony, 1950. *Career:* Conductor, Radio Symphony, Radio Chamber, Radio Studio Orchestra,

1950-53; Associate Conductor, Belgrade Philharmonic Orchestra, 1953-66; Art Director, Principal Conductor, Chamber Orchestra Pro Musica, 1967-; Art Director, National Opera/Ballet, Belgrade, 1977-80; Concerts and tours in Yugoslavia, Austria, Belgium, Bulgaria, Czechoslovakia, Denmark, France, Great Britain, Hungary, Italy, Netherlands; Norway; Romania; Spain, Switzerland; Turkey and USSR; autobiography broadcast on Belgrade radio and television, 1987, 1988. *Recordings:* A Vivaldi, The Seasons, Chamber Orchestra Pro Musica; J Slavenski, Suite of Dances, Chamber Orchestra Pro Musica; Pro Musica plays Vivaldi, 1991; Over 300 radio recordings. *Publications:* On the Symphony Orchestra, Belgrade, 1954; State of Music in Serbia, Belgrade, 1969; Two Symphonies of Amando Ivancić, Zagreb; Revisions, Editions and Orchestrations of Yugoslav Composers from the 15th to 19th century; Essays on A Vivaldi, G Ph Telemann, On Conducting; Performers Rights, B Britten's War Requiem, A Berg's Wozzek, Finnish Music, Bulgarian Music; Amando Ivancic and Slovakia, 1986; G.B. Shaw on Music: Selection of music criticisms - Serbocroat translation, selection and comment, 1989, and over 200 other articles. *Contributions to:* Pro Musica magazine, Editor-In-Chief, 1964-90; Yugoslav Music Cyclopedia, 1958-. *Hobbies:* National History; Collecting icons and old prints on Serbia. *Address:* YU-11031 Belgrade, Pozeska 92, Serbia.

JAMES David, b. 1956, England. Singer (Countertenor). *Education:* Choral scholar at Magdalen College, Oxford. *Career:* From 1978 has sung with the Hilliard Ensemble and other early music groups; Tours of Russia and Mexico, Schutz's Psalms of David and Cesti's Orontea in Innsbruck and at the Holland Festival; Handel's Orlando in Spain and Portugal with the Amsterdam Baroque Orchestra; Messiah in Finland and with The Sixteen (tours include visit to Utrecht, 1990); Concerts with the Collegium Vocale Gent and La Chapelle Royale; Bach's St John Passion in London and Salzburg, the B minor Mass at Bruges and Cantatas in Finland (1991); Promenade Concerts 1990, in the cantata Herz und Mund und Tat und Leben; Contemporary Music Network tour with the Hilliard Ensemble in Part's St. John Passion; Has sung at the Aldeburgh Festival, for Handel Opera in London, English National Opera and at Covent Garden. *Recordings:* Orlando; Messiah (Hyperion); Pärt St. John Passion (ECM); Bach St. John Passion (Chandos). *Honour:* Winner, 1978's-Hertogenbosch Competition, Holland. *Address:* Magenta Music International, 64 Highgate High Street, London N6 5HX, England.

JAMES Eirian, b. 1952, Cardigan, Wales. Singer (Mezzo-Soprano). *Education:* Royal College of Music with Ruth Packer. *Debut:* Kent Opera 1977, as Olga in Eugene Onegin: returned as Cherubino, Poppea, Rosina and Meg Page in Falstaff. *Career:* English National Opera in The Makropoulos Case, War and Peace, Rigoletto and Rusalka; Buxton Festival, in Handel's Ariodante; Lyon Opera as Fatima (Oberon) and Rossini's Isolier; Geneva Opera as Hansel; Houston Opera as Siebel in Faust and Sesto in Handel's Giulio Cesare; Aix-en-Provence as Dorabella (Così fan Tutte); Covent Garden debut 1987, as Annina in Der Rosenkavalier: returned as Smeton in Anna Bolena 1988 and Nancy in Albert Herring 1989; Sang Dorabella at Aix-en-Province, 1989, second Lady in Die Zauberflöte at the 1990 Prom Concerts; Ascanio in Benvenuto Cellini for Netherlands Opera, Cherubino at Houston; Concert Appearances at the BBC Promenades, Aldeburgh Festival, the Barbican and with the BBC Welsh Symphony; repertoire includes the Lieder eines fahrenden Gesellen (Lyon), Beethoven's Mass in C (London), Mozart's C minor Mass (Edinburgh and Paris); Haydn's Harmoniemasse; Mendelssohn's Elijah; Gluck's La Corona (City of London Festival); Hermia, Midsummer Night's Dream, Aix-en-Province, 1991; Orlofsky, Fledermaus, 1991; English National Opera: Rosina (Barber of Seville)), 1992; Scottish Opera, Sextus (Julius Caesar), 1992. *Recordings:* 2nd Lady, Magic Flute, conducted by Roger Norrington (EMI); Teseo, conducted by Marc Minkovski (Erato); Despina (Così), conducted by John Gardiner, (Deutsche Grammophon).

Current Management: IMG Artists Europe. *Address:* Media House, 3 Burlington Lane, Chiswick, London W4 2TH, England.

JAMES Ifor, b. 30 Aug 1931, Carlisle, England. Horn Player; Conductor. m. Helen Hames. *Education:* Royal Academy of Music. *Career:* Radio and TV performances in Britain and abroad; Orchestral concerts; Chamber music recitals. *Recordings:* Brahms Trio op.40; Mozart Quintet K407 and Sinfonia Concertante K297b; Solo recital records; Philip Jones Brass Ensemble records. *Publication:* Practice Method 1976. *Contributions to:* Various journals. *Hobby:* Pen drawing. *Address:* Pinnacles, Cutlers Green, Thaxted, Essex, England.

JAMES Peter Haydn, b. 17 Oct 1940, Melbourne, Australia. Vice-Principal, Royal Academy of Music. m. Angela Heather Lewis, 5 Sept 1967, 1 son, 1 daughter. *Education:* BMus; PhD. *Career:* Lecturer, 1970-74, Director of Studies, 1974-83, Birmingham School of Music; Lay-Clerk, Lichfield Cathedral, 1969-74; Warden, Royal Academy of Music, London, 1983-. *Recordings:* Various editions of music by Byrd, East, Alcock, Tomkins and Weelkes; Editions: Know You Not by Tomkins, 1972; Exalt Thyself, O God, by Byrd, 1982. *Contributions to:* Music and Letters; Johnson Society; Soundings. *Honours:* Hon. RAM, RCM, FBSM, 1984. *Memberships:* Royal Music Association. *Hobbies:* Wine; Sport. *Address:* c/o Royal Academy of Music, Marylebone Road, London NW1 5HT, England.

JANACEK Bedrich, b. 18 May 1920, Prague, Czechoslovakia. Organist. m. Elisabet Wentz, 1 Jan 1951, 1 son. *Education:* Soloist examination in organ 1942, master class in organ 1945-46, Diploma 1946, State Conservatory of Music, Prague; Choir Master Degree, Royal High Music School, Stockholm, Sweden, 1961. *Career:* Organist, various concerts in Europe and USA, including Royal Festival Hall, London, England, 1942-; Soloist with orchestras; Teacher of Organ, State Conservatory of Music, Prague, Czechoslovakia, 1946-48; Parish Musician, Cathedral Parish, Lund, Sweden, 1965-85. *Compositions:* organ compositions; Choral works including 2 cantatas with orchestra; Works for brass and organ; various recordings made. *Honours:* City of Lund Cultural Prize, 1980 and 1988; Commander of Merit, Ordo Militaris et Hospotalaris Sancti Lasari Hierosolymitani, 1992; Litteris et Artibus, Sweden, 1993. *Address:* Kyrkogatan 17, 222 22 Lund, Sweden.

JANDER Owen (Hughes), b. 4 June 1930, Mount Kisco, New York, USA. Musicologist; Music Educator. *Education:* BA, University of Virginia, 1951; MA 1952, PhD 1962, Harvard University. *Career:* Faculty Member, Department of Music 1960-, 3 terms as Chairman, Founder, Collegium Musicum, Originated and oversaw project to build the Fisk Organ, Wellesley College; Editor, The Wellesley Edition and The Wellesley Edition Cantata Index Series, 1962-74. *Publication:* Co-editor, Charles Benton Fisk, Organ Builder, 1986. *Contributions to:* Articles on 17th century Italian music and on Beethoven in various journals; 78 articles, The New Grove Dictionary of Music and Musicians, 1980. *Honours:* Guggenheim Fellowship, 1966-67; National Endowment for the Humanities Fellowship for Senior Scholars, 1985; Catherine Mills Davis Professorship in Music History, Wellesley College. *Membership:* American Musicological Society. *Address:* Department of Music, Jewett Arts Center, Wellesley College, Wellesley, MA 02181, USA.

JÁNDÖ Jenö, b. 1952, Pecs, Hungary. Pianist. *Education:* Piano department, Budapest Ferenc Liszt Academy of Music under Professors Katalin Nemes and Pal Kadosa; Graduated, 1974. *Career:* Assistant to Professor Pal Kadosa, Piano Department, Budapest Academy of Music; Soloist with top Hungarian symphony orchestras, giving concerts in concert halls and studios of Hungarian Radio and Television; Guest Performances in most European countries including Austria; Australia; Britain, Canada, Federal Republic of Germany, Finland, France, The Netherlands, Japan, Italy and Turkey. *Address:* Budapest Academy of Music, Budapest, Hungary.

JANEVA-IVELIC Veneta, b. 1950, Bulgaria. Singer (Soprano). *Education:* Studied at Sofia Conservatory. *Career:* Sang at the Sofia Opera from 1973, National Opera Zagreb, from 1980; Guest appearances in Salzburg (with Zagreb company as Norma, 1985), Berlin Staatsoper, Paris Opera (Abigaille in Nabucco), Luxembourg and Karlsruhe: Other roles have included Maddalena (Andre Chenier), the forza dn Trovatore Leonoras, Violetta, Desdemona, Lady Macbeth, Butterfly and Elvira in I Puritani. *Honours:* Prize Winner, 1980 Rio International Competition. *Address:* Slovensko Narodno Gledaslisce, Zupancicava 1, 61000 Ljubljana, Serbia

JANIS Byron, b. 24 Mar 1924, McKeesport, Pennsylvania, USA. Pianist. m. (1) June Dickson-Wright, 1 son, (2) Maria Veronica Cooper. *Education:* Studied with Josef and Rosina Lhevinne in New York and with Adele Marcus and Horowitz. *Debut:* With Pittsburgh Symphony Orchestra 1944, in Rachmaninov's 2nd Concerto. *Career:* Carnegie Hall debut 1948; European debut with Concertgebouw Orchestra 1952; Toured Russia 1960, 1962, appearing with Moscow Philharmonic Orchestra; Further engagements with Boston Symphony, Philadelphia Orchestra and Indianapolis Symphony; Liszt concerts in Boston and New York 1962; Repertoire also includes Chopin, Prokofiev and Gottschalk; Career interrupted by illness in 1960s but resumed 1972; White House concert 1985; Discovered manuscripts of two Chopin waltzes in France, 1967. *Honours:* Harriet Cohen Award; First American to receive Grand Prix du Disque; Chevalier of the Ordre des arts et lettres 1965; Ambassador for the Arts of the National Arthiritis Foundation 1985. *Recordings include:* Concertos by Liszt and Rachmaninov.

JANK Helena, b. 1955, Salvador, Bahia, Brasil. Concert Harpsichordist. m. Eduardo Ostergren, 11 July 1992, 1 d. *Education:* Studied at Staatliche Hochschule Fur Musik, Germany. *Debut:* 1967 Munchen, Germany. *Career:* Professor at Campinas State University; Harpsichordist with Munchener Bach-Orchester; Performances as Soloist and in Chamber Music Ensembles in Germany, USA and Brasil. *Recordings:* Helena Jank Plays Bach, Scarlatti, Ligeti; The Finest Baroque Sonatas Erich; Mozart Sonatas; J S Bach Goldberg Variations: A Guide For the Complete Person. *Publications:* Goldberg Variations. *Honours:* Academic Recognition for Excellence in Teaching. *Membership:* International Bach Society. *Hobbies:* Sport; Theatre; Travel. *Address:* Rua Alvaro Muller 150 Ap 32, 13023 180 Campinas, SP, Brasil.

JANKOVIC Eleonora, b. 18 Feb 1941, Trieste, Italy. Singer (Mezzo- soprano). *Education:* Studied in Trieste and Milan. *Career:* Member of the Opera at Zagreb, then made Italian debut as Trieste 1972, in Smareglia's Nozze Istriane; Appearances at La Scala from 1974, Bologna, 1975, Florence, 1976, Teatro Lirico Milan, 1975, in the premiere of Al gran sole carico d'Amore, by Luigi Nono; Guest engagements at Turin, Venice, Naples, and Catania; Verona Arena, 1975-78, 1983, 1987; Rio de Janeiro and Buenos Aires, 1982-83; Sang Enrichetta in I Puritani at Rome 1990 and appeared in Luisa Miller at Trieste, 1990; Sang in Wolf-Ferrari's I Quattro Rusteghi, for Geneva Opera, 1992; Has also sung the Countess in the Queen of Spades, Ulrica, Amneris, Leonora in La Favorita, Carmen, Charlotte, Marina in Boris Godunov and Mother Goose in The Rake's Progress; Many concert appearances. *Address:* Teatro dell'Opera di Roma, Piazza B Gigli 8, 00184 Rome, Italy.

JANKU Hana, b. 25 Oct 1940, Brno, Czechoslovakia. Singer (Soprano). *Education:* Studied with Jaroslav Kvapil in Prague. *Debut:* Brno 1959, as the Countess in Lucerna by Vitezlav Novak. *Career:* Sang at Brno as the Trovatore Leonora, Libuse, Rusalka, Milada and

Turandot; La Scala Milan debut 1967, as Turandot; Member of the Deutsche Oper Berlin from 1970; Guest appearances in Buenos Aires, San Francisco and Mexico City; Covent Garden 1973, as Tosca; Verona Arena 1973; Teatro Liceo Barcelona 1974, as Leonora in La Forza del Destino; Other roles include Gioconda, Ariadne and Kundry; Many concert appearances. *Recordings include:* Penthesilea by Schoeck (BASF); Dalibor by Smetana (Supraphon). *Address:* c/o Deutsche Oper Berlin, Richard Wagnerstrasse 10, D-1000 Berlin, Germany.

JANOVICKY Karel, b. 18 Feb 1930, Plzen, Czechoslovakia. Composer; Pianist; Broadcaster. m. Sylva Simsova, 22 May 1950, 1 son, 1 daughter. *Education:* Realne Gymnasium; Surrey College of Music, England; Private studies with Jan Sedivka (chamber music) and Matyas Seiber (composition). *Debut:* Wigmore Hall, London, 1956. *Career:* Many scores in MS; Recent performances at British Music Information Centre; Sonata for Bass Clarinet and Piano, Three Cambridge Songs, etc. *Contributions to:* New Edition of Leos Janacek: A Biography by Jaroslav Vogel, for Orbis Publishing, London, 1981; Introducing Mr. Broucek, English National Opera, 1978; Jaroslav Seifert's Nobel Prize, The Listener, 1984. *Honours:* First Prize, Shakespeare Competition, Bournemouth Symphony Orchestra, 1957 for Variations on a Theme of Robert Johnson, Op. 17; Sonata for 2 Violins and Piano on SPNM Recommended List, London. *Membership:* Composers Guild of Great Britain. *Hobbies:* Outdoor Pursuits; Gardening; Photography. *Address:* 18 Muswell Avenue, London N10 2EG, England.

JANOWITZ Gundula, b. 2 Aug 1937, Berlin, Germany. Opera Singer (Soprano). m. 1 daughter. *Education:* Academy of Music and Performing Arts, Graz; Administrator. *Debut:* with Vienna State Opera. *Career:* Sang with Deutsche Oper, Berlin, 1966, Metropolitan Opera, New York, 1967, as Sieglinde in Die Walküre, conducted by Karajan; Salzburg Festival 1968-81 as Mozart's Donna Anna, Fiordiligi and Countess, Strauss's Marschallin and Ariadne; Teatro Colon, Buenos Aires 1970, Munich State Opera 1971, Grand Opera Paris 1973, Covent Garden Opera 1976, La Scala 1978; Concerts in major cities throughout the world; appearances at Bayreuth, Aix-en-Provence, Glyndebourne (as Ilia in Idomeneo), Spoleto, Salzburg, Munich Festivals; Member, Vienna State Opera, Deutsche Oper, Berlin; among her roles are Mozart's Pamina, Wagner's Eva and Elisabeth, Strauss's Empress, and Arabella and Puccini's Mimi; Returned to Covent Garden 1987, as Ariadne; Opera Director at Graz 1990-91. *Recordings:* Deutsche Grammophon, EMI, Decca. *Hobbies:* Modern Literature. *Address:* Vereinigte Bühnen, Kaiser Josef Platz 10, A-8010 Graz, Austria.

JANOWSKI Marek, b. 18 Feb 1939, Warsaw, Poland. Conductor. *Education:* Studied at Cologne Musikhochschule and in Siena. *Career:* Assistant conductor in Aachen, Cologne and Dusseldorf opera houses; London debut 1969, leading the Cologne Opera in the British premiere of Henze's Der junge Lord; musical director, Freiburg and Dortmund Operas, 1973-79; Guest Conductor at opera houses in Hamburg, Paris, Munich and Berlin; American opera debut San Francisco 1983; Metropolitan Opera 1984, Strauss's Arabella; artistic adviser and conductor, Royal Liverpool Philharmonic Orchestra, 1983-6; curently Chief Conductor of the Nouvel Philharmonique de Radio France and the Gurzenich Orchester, Cologne; Conducted the company of the Cologne Opera in Fidelio at Hong Kong, 1989; Die Meistersinger at the Théâtre du Châtelet, Paris, 1990; Conducted Elektra at Orange, 1991. *Recordings:* Opera sets for Eurodisc and Philips include the first compact disc Ring, with the Dresden Staatskapelle, Weber's Euryanthe, Strauss's Die schweigsame Frau and Penderecki's The Devils of Loudun. *Address:* IMG Artists (Europe), Media House, 3 Burlington Lane, Chiswick, London W4 2TH, England.

JANSEN Jacques, b. 22 Nov 1913, Paris, France. Singer (Baritone). *Education:* Studied with Charles Panzera and Claire Croiza in Paris. *Debut:* Opera-Comique, Paris, 1941, as Debussy's Pelleas. *Career:* Sang Pelleas at the Holland Festival 1948, and at Covent Garden in 1949; Further appearances in Vienna (Theater an der Wien, 1946), the Metropolitano Opera and the Opéra-Comique (Valerian in Hahn's Malvina, 1945, and Pierne's Fragonard, 1946;) Paris Opera 1952, as Ali in Les Indes galantes by Rameau and Aix-en-Provence 1956, as Citheron in Rameau's Platée; Other roles were Rabaud's Marouf, and Danilo in Die lustige Witwe, which he sang 1500 times, principally at the Theatre Mogador in Paris. *Recordings include:* Pelléas et Mélisande (HMV); Platée (Pathe).

JANSEN Johannes Felix Johanna Maria, b. 31 July 1923, Tilburg, Netherlands. Conductor; High School Music Teacher. m. Maria van Lierop, 3 Aug. 1948, 1 son, 2 daughters. *Education:* Diplomas in School Music and Conducting, Small Diplomas in Organ, Conservatory. *Debut:* As conductor, Tilburg. *Career:* Conductor for various choirs and orchestras; as Opera Conductor has given performances of major operas including Aida with a chorus of 500 noted Italian soloists and live animals, 1972; conducted numerous oratorios; Guest Conductor, Poznan, Poland; Aida, Il Trovatore and Rigoletto by Verdi; Lodz, Bydgoszcz and Wroczwaw with the operas, Lucia di Lammermoor, Un Ballo in Maschera, Mefistofele, IXe symphony Beethoven; Special concert with music of Dutch Composers. *Contributions to:* Koor and Kunstleven; Mens en Melodie. *Honours:* Concours of Conductors, Besançon, France, 1953; Van Lanschot Prize, Tilburg, 1972; Knight in the Order of Orange Nassau, 1986. *Membership:* Rotary, Tilburg. *Hobbies:* Gardening; Tennis. *Address:* Ottergraaf 15, 5032 EC Tilburg, The Netherlands.

JANSEN Rudolf, b. 19 Jan. 1940, Arnhem, Holland. Pianist. m. (1) Margaret Honig, 2 children, (2) Christa Pfeiler, 2 children. *Education:* Prix d'Excellence, Amsterdam Conservatory. *Career:* Soloist; Accompanist for numerous leading singers and other artists throughout the world. *Recordings:* More than 60 recordings as Lieder Accompanist or Chamber-Music player. *Current Management:* Nederlands Impresariaat, Amsterdam. *Address:* Schepenenlaan 2, 1181 BB Amstelveen, Netherlands.

JANSONS Andrejs, b. 2 Oct 1938, Riga, Latvia. Oboist; Teacher; Conductor; Composer. m. Astrida Ribenieks, 1 son, 1 daughter. *Education:* BSc, Juilliard School of Music, 1960; MMus, Manhattan School of Music, 1973. *Career:* Music Director, Latvian Folk Ensemble, New York Latvian Concert Choir; Guest Conductor, Indianapolis Festival Orchestra, 1988, Bronx Arts Orchestra, Milwaukee Symphony, New England Chamber Orchestra, Philharmonia Hungarica, Moscow Sinfonietta, 1989, Nürnberg Symphony (Germany), 1987; Lithuanian State Phiharmonic; Latvian State Opera, 1987; Latvian Radio Chorus; 20th Song Festival, Riga, Latvia; Principal guest conductor, Bronx Arts Orchestra; Music Director Fordham University Chorus, 1987; Music Director, State Theater Musical Theater Productions, Los Angeles; Visiting Professor, California State University, Los Angeles; Ballet performances, Toronto and New York; Artist in Residence, Bloomfield College; Visiting Professor, Rutgers University, 1986. *Compositions include:* 6 musicals; Orpheus Songs, for voice and chamber orchestra; Suite of Old Lettish Dances; Arrangements, Old American Works for woodwind quintet; 10 Latvian Folk Dances for voices and small orchestra; Orchestrations for Joffrey Ballet; 50 Folk Song settings; works for chorus a capella; 7 Christmas anthems. *Address:* 73 Glenwood Avenue, Leonia, NJ 07605, USA.

JANSONS Mariss, b. 14 Jan 1943, Latvia. Conductor. *Education:* Studied at Leningard Conservatory and in Vienna and Salzburg with Swarowsky and Karajan; winner, Herbert von Karajan Competition, 1971. *Career:* Associate Conductor of Leningrad Philharmonic Orchestra and from 1979

Principal Conductor of the Oslo Philharmonic; successful tours to Italy, Spain, France, the Edinburgh Festival, America and Japan; as guest conductor with BBC Welsh Symphony presented all Tchaikovsky's symphonies on TV; in season 1987/88 made debuts with Montreal Symphony, Los Angeles Philharmonic and Berlin Philharmonic; Conducted the Oslo Philharmonic at the 1993 London Proms (Tchaikovsky Violin Concerto, Strauss Alpine Symphony, Bartók Viola Concerto, Stravinsky Firebird Suite and Dvořák Eighth Symphony). *Recordings:* Symphonies by Tchaikovsky and Shostakovich for EMI with the Oslo Philharmonic; Svendsen's Symphonies Nos 1 and 2. *Address:* IMG Artists, Europe.

JANSSENS Robert, b. 27 July 1939, Brussels, Belgium. Composer; Director. m. Dominique van der Moere, 29 Aug 1962, 2 daughters. *Education:* Advanced Diplomas, Conservatories of Brussels and Liege. *Career:* Director, Brussels Music Academy; Professor, Royal Conservatory, Brussels; Director, Brussels Festival Orchestra; Freelance Director. *Compositions:* Symphonies; 2 piano concertos; 2 violin concertos; 2 horn concertos; Yerma, ballet; Messe des Artistes; Noels da Capo. *Recordings:* Messe des Artistes, Noels da Capo, 3 CDs. *Honours:* Fuerison Prize, Royal Academy for Arts, Belgium; Chevalier de l'Ordre de la Couronne. *Memberships:* SABAM; Cercle Royal Gaulois; Lions Club; Cinquantenaire. *Address:* Rue Albert I 63 B, 1330 Rixensart, Belgium.

JANSSON Henrik Daniel Johannes, b. 20 Mar 1916, Gothenburg, Sweden. Organist; Choirmaster. m. Mildred, 2 daughters. *Education:* Royal Academy of Music, Stockholm. *Career:* Organist and Choirmaster, Sala, 1945-59; Organist and Choirmaster, St Andrew's Church, Malmo, 1959-67; Organist and Choirmaster, Cathedral, Gothenburg, 1968-79 (retired); Several organ recitals and choir concerts for Radio and TV. *Publications:* ABC of Church Music, 1957; Editor, Special Choral Preludes, 1960; List of Choir and Organ Chorals, 1964; The Organ History of Gothenburg Cathedral, 1984; All music performed in Gothenburg Cathedral 1968-79, 1986; Music and Musicians in Gotheburg Cathedral 1824-1979, 1990. *Contributions to:* Arbetet; Various musical magazines. *Address:* St Sigfridsgatan 41, S-412 66 Gothenburg, Sweden.

JANULAKO Vassilio, b. 14 Sept 1933, Athens, Greece. Singer (Baritone). *Education:* Studied at the Athens Conservatory. *Debut:* Athens 1961, as the High Priest in Alceste. *Career:* Engagements at opera houses in Stuttgart, Berlin, Dusseldorf, Hamburg, Munich, Vienna, Frankfurt, Nuremberg, Zurich, Toulouse and San Francisco; Roles include Pizarro, the Dutchman, Telramund, Amfortas, Don Giovanni, Mozart's Count, Gerard, Scarpia, Escamillo, Mandryka, Milhaud's Christopher Columbus and parts in operas by Verdi; Cologne 1986, as Pandolfe in Cendrillon by Massenet; Spoleto and Philadelphia 1988 in Jenůfa and Russalka; Sang Paolo in Simon Boccanegra at Cologne, 1990. *Address:* c/o Oper der Stadt Köln, Offenbachplatz, D-5000 Cologne, Germany.

JAPE Mijndert, b. 11 July 1932, Geleen, Limburg, Netherlands. Lutenist; Guitarist; Writer; Music Historian. m. Marie-Hélène Habets, 2 Aug. 1960 dec. 20 Sept. 1987. *Education:* Guitar: Muzieklyceum Heerlen, 1956, 1957; Conservatory of Maastricht, 1958; Higher Diploma cum laude, Schola Cantorum, Paris, 1960; Studied with Hans-Lutz Niessen, Ida Presti, Alexandre Lagoya; Lute: Royal Conservatory of the Hague, summer schools, England, France, Netherlands, Belgium, Germany, 1972-77; Studied with Toyohiko Satoh, Eugen Dombois, Thomas Binkley, Anthony Bailes. *Career:* Soloist, Accompanist on lute instruments, baroque operas, vocal groups, Belgium, Netherlands, France; Director, Delitiae Musicae, specialising in 1550-1650 music/poetry concerts, Netherlands, Belgium, France; Musicological and pedagogical study, Guest Lecturer; Musical Director, 1986-92, Teacher of Lute and Guitar, Sittard Music School, 1955-92; Plays 1820 Moitessier guitar and 8

lute instruments. Teaching Lute and Guitar, Music Academy, Maasmechelen and Tongeren, Belgium. *Recordings:* 4 (solo, ensemble), Belgium, Netherlands. *Publications:* Fernando Sor - Opera Omnia for the Classic Guitar, 12 vols (with Marie-Hélène Habets), 1980-; On Lute Tuition, 1987; Classical Guitar Music In Print (bibliography), Philadelphia, USA, 1989; Elementa Pro Arte Testvdinis (lute tutor), in progress; Louys de Moy - le Petit Boucquet 1631, Belgium, 1990. *Address:* POB 81, NL-190 AB Bek (Liburg), Netherlands.

JARDA Tudor, b. 11 Feb 1922, Cluj, Romania. Composer. *Education:* Studied in Cluj and Timisoara, 1941-48. *Career:* Played the trumpet at the Rumanian opera in Cluj, 1945-48; Teacher of harmony, Cluj Conservatory, 1949-88; *Compositions:* Operas The Soimaru Kin, 1956; The forest with Vultures, 1961; The Power of Life, 1984; Angel and Demon, 1989; 3 Symphonies; Symphonic Suite; Concert for flute and orchestra; Ballets: Morning Star of the Day; Rounds of the World; the Carol; Instrumental and chamber music. *Address:* Str. Galati 16, 3400 Cluj-Napoca, Rumania.

JARMAN Douglas, b. 21 Nov. 1942, Dewsbury, Yorkshire, England. Lecturer; Writer. m. Angela Elizabeth Brown, 26 Sept. 1970, 2 daughters. *Education:* BA Honours Music, Hull University, 1964; PhD, Durham University, 1968; Research Fellow, Liverpool University, 1968-70. *Career:* Lecturer in Music, University of Leeds, 1970-71; Lecturer 1974-86, Principal Lecturer 1986-, Academic Studies, Royal Northern College of Music, Manchester. *Recordings:* Talk, Lulu; The Historical Background, recording of the Complete Lulu. *Publications:* The Music of Alban Berg, 1979 and 1983; Kurt Weill, 1982; Wozzeck 1989; The Berg Companion, 1989; Alban Berg: Lulu, 1991; Expressionism Reassessed, 1993. *Contributions to:* Perspectives of New Music; Musical Quarterly; Musical Times; Music Review; Journal of Royal Musical Association; Newsletter of International Alban Berg Society; Alban Berg Studien volume 2. *Honours:* Honorary Fellow, Royal Northern College of Music, 1986. *Memberships:* Director, International Alban Berg Society; Director, Square Chapel Building and Arts Trusts; Advisory Board, Music Analysis. *Address:* 1 Birch Villas, Birchcliffe Road, Hebden Bridge, HX7 8DA, England.

JARRETT Keith, b. 8 May 1945, Allentown, Pennsylvania, USA. Pianist; Composer. *Career:* First Solo Concert aged 7, followed by professional appearances; 2 hour solo concert of own compositions, 1962; led own trio in Boston; Worked with Roland Kirk, Tony Scott and others in New York; joined Art Blakely, 1965; toured Europe with Charles Lloyd, 1966, with Miles Davis 1970-71; Soloist and Leader of own groups, 1969-. *Recordings include:* Bach's Well-Tempered Clavier. *Address:* Vincent Ryan, 135 West 16th Street, New York, NY 10011, USA.

JÄRVI Neeme, b. 7 June 1937, Tallinn, Estonia. Conductor/Symphony and Opera. m. 2 Sept. 1961, 2 sons, 1 daughter. *Education:* Tallinn Music School, Estonia; Percussion, Choral Conducting. Under Professor Nicolai Rabinovich and Yevgeni Mravinski, Leningrad State Conservatory, 1955-60; Post Graduate Studies, 1968. *Career:* Music Director, Estonian State Symphony Orchestra, 1960-80; Music Director, Principal Conductor, Theatre Estonia, Tallinn, 1964-77; Guest Conductor with Leningrad Philharmonic; Moscow Philharmonic; USSR Radio Philharmonic Moscow, USSR State Symphony Orchestra; USSR and abroad; New York Philharmonic; Philadelphia, Boston, Chicago, Los Angeles Philharmonic Orchestras; San Francisco, Washington, Toronto, Cincinnati, Atlanta, Montreal, Ottawa, 1980-; Metropolitan Opera, Eugene Onegin, 1979, 1984; Samson and Delila, 1982; New Production Mussorgsky's Khovanshchina 1985/1986 season; Music Director and Principal Conductor, Gothenburg Symphony, Sweden, 1982-; Musical Director and Principal Conductor, Scottish National Orchestra, 1984-88; Music Director, Detroit Symphony Orchestra, 1989-; Guest Conductor, Paris, Cologne Radio, Amsterdam Concertgebouw, Bavarian Radio, Berlin Philharmonic

Hamburg Radio, Bamberg Symphony; Scandinavian Orchestras. *Recordings:* Complete symphonies by Berwald, Niels Gade, Prokofiev, Tubin, Dvořák, Brahms, Rimsky-Korsakov, Stravinsky, Tchaikovsky, Shostakovich, Glazunov, Scriabin, and Rachmaninov. *Honour:* First Prize, Conductor Competition, Academy Santa Cecilia, Rome; Toblach Prize, 1993 for the best Mahler Symphony, new recording (Mahler 3 with Royal Scottish National). *Current Management:* Columbia Artists Management, New York, USA. *Address:* Göteborgs Konserthus, Stenhammarsgatan 1, 41256 Göteborg, Sweden.

JARVIS Edward Keith, b. 13 Mar. 1939, Swindon, England. Organist; Lecturer in Music. m. Janet Keeton, 1 son. *Education:* MA Balliol College, Oxford University; LRAM; ARCM; FRCO. *Career:* Formerly Music Teacher at schools in Swindon and Teignmouth, Devon; Lecturer in Music, School of Music, Huddersfield, 1966; Senior Lecturer, School of Music, University of Huddersfield, 1976; Principal Lecturer, Department of Music, University of Huddersfield, 1981-; Several BBC Organ broadcasts (Huddersfield Town Hall, University of Huddersfield, Universities of York and Keele); Organ Recitalist; University Organist, University of Huddersfield, 1992-; Principal Lecturer, University of Huddersfield, 1992-; Research, Wind Supply Mechanisms to pipe organs. *Recordings:* Baroque and English Organ Music (Huddersfield Polytechnic). *Honours:* ARCO Sawyer Prize; Polytechnic Organist, Huddersfield, 1985. *Hobbies:* Construction and design of organs; Sound recording and reproduction. *Address:* The Woodlands, Thong Lane, Netherthong, Huddersfield, England.

JARVLEPP Jan Eric, b. 3 Jan. 1953, Ottawa, Ontario, Canada. Composer; Teacher; Freelance Cellist. *Education:* B.Mus., University of Ottawa, 1976; MMus, McGill University, Montreal, Canada, 1978; PhD, University of California at San Diego, USA, 1981. *Career:* CBC Chamber Music Broadcasts; Member, Ottawa Symphony Orchestra, 1981-; Nepean Symphony Orchestra, 1981-91; Electronic Compositions performed on several different Canadian and US University Campuses and Radio Stations; Music Director of Espace Musique New Music Concert Society, 1993-. *Compositions:* Lento, 1975; Ice, 1976; Aurora Borealis, 1976; Buoyancy, 1977; Flotation, 1978; Transparency and Density, 1978; Trumpet Piece, 1979; Cello Concerto, 1980; Time Zones, 1981; Night Music, 1982; Harpsichord Piece, 1984; Evening Music for Carillon, 1984; Cadenza for Solo Cello, 1985; Guitar Piece, 1985; Morning Music for Carillon, Afternoon Music for Carillon both 1986; Sunrise, 1987; Sunset, 1987; Trio, 1987; Liquid Crystals, 1988; Camerata Music, 1989; Dream, 1990; Life in the Fast Lane, 1990; Encounter, 1991; Underwater, 1992; Music from Mars, 1993; Moonscape, 1993; Transformations, 1993. *Recordings:* Chronogrammes; Soundtracks of the Imagination. *Publications:* Compositional Aspects of Berio's Tempi Concertati, Interface, Volume II, No 4, 1982; Pitch and Texture Analysis of Ligeti's Lux Aeterna, ex tempore Volume 2-1, 1982. *Address:* 2-424 Lisgar Street, Ottawa, Ontario, Canada, KIR 5H1.

JASIŃSKA Danuta, b. 14 June 1947, Chrzanow, Poland. Musicologist. *Education:* Institute of Musicology, Warsaw University, 1966-71; Editing of Music, Academy of Music, Cracow, 1971-73; Doctor of Liberal Arts in Musicology, Adam Mickiewicz University, Poznań, 1983. *Career:* Assistant Editor, PWM-Edition, Cracow, 1971-73; University Teacher, Jagellonian University, Cracow, 1973-76; University Teacher, Adam Mickiewicz University, Poznań, 1976-. *Publications:* Technique and Musical style of Michal Spisak, in press; Problem of Style Brillante in Chopin's works, 1993, in press. *Contributions to:* Articles to Muzyka periodical on XXth century Polish music; Encyclopedia of Music, Cracow, 1979-; Dictionnaire de la Musique, Bordas, 1986. *Membership:* Musicological Section, Polish Composers Union. *Hobby:* Mountain trips.*Address:* ul Chociszewskiego 54 a 6, 60-261 Poznań, Poland.

JEDLICKA Dalibor, b. 23 May 1929, Svoyanov, Czechoslovakia. Singer (Bass-Baritone). *Education:* Studied in Ostrava with Rudolf Vasek. *Debut:* Opava 1953, as Mumlala in The Two Widows by Smetana. *Career:* Sang at the National Theatre Prague 1957-77: guest appearances with the company in Brno, Amsterdam, Zurich and Edinburgh (1970 in the British premiere of The Excursions of Mr Brouček by Janáček); Engagements at Belgrade, Zagreb, Warsaw, Venice, and Bologna; Repertoire included buffo roles and German, French and Czech operas; Mozart's Figaro and Papageno, Don Pasquale and Kaspar in Der Freischütz; Opéra Comique, Paris 1988, in From the House of the Dead. *Recordings include:* Janáček's Katya Kabanova, The Cunning Little Vixen and From the House of the Dead, conducted by Charles Mackerras (Decca); The Cunning Little Vixen, Pauer's Suzanna Vojirva and Don Giovanni (Supraphon).

JEDLIČKA Rudolf, b. 22 Jan. 1920, Skalice, Czechoslovakia. Singer (Baritone). *Education:* Studied with Tino Pattieri, Pavel Ludikar and Fernando Carpi in Vienna and Prague. *Debut:* Dresden Staatsoper 1944, as Marcel in La Bohème. *Career:* Sang in Prague from 1945; Produced opera at Usti nad Labem 1946-49; Guest with the Staatsoper Berlin from 1958; Appearances at the Vienna Staatsoper and in Russia, German and Polish opera houses as Mozart's Figaro and Don Giovanni, Posa in Don Carlos and Rossini's Figaro; Sang with the Prague National Opera at the Edinburgh Festival 1964, 1970 in the British premieres of Janáček's From the House of the Dead and The Excursions of Mr Brouček; Professor at the Prague Conservatory 1973-75; Director of the National Theatre, Prague 1989; Sang Grigoris in Martinů's Greek Passion at Wiesbaden, 1990. *Recordings:* Jenůfa (Decca). *Address:* National Theatre, PO Box 865, 112 30 Prague 1, Czech Republic.

JEFFERS Ronald (Harrison), b. 25 Mar 1942, Springfield, Ilinois, USA. Composer; Conductor. *Education:* Studied composition with Ross Lee Finney at University of Michigan; University of Carlifornia at San Diego (1970-72) with Pauline Oliveros, Kenneth Gaburo and Robert Erickson; Choral conducting at Occidental College, Los Angeles, 1968-72. *Career:* Director of choral activities at Stony Brook, New York, and at Oregon State University; tours of Europe 1978 and 1982. *Compositions:* Missa concrete for 3 choruses, 1969 revised 1973; In Memoriam for chamber ensemble 1973; Time Passes for mezzo, tape and ensemble 1974-81; Transitiry for chorus and tape 1980; Arise My Love for 12 voices, chimes and gongs 1981; Crabs for tape 1981. *Address:* c/o ASCAP, ASCAP Building, One Lincoln Plaza, New York, NY 10023, USA.

JEFFERSON Alan Rigby, b. 20 Mar. 1921, Ashtead, Surrey, England. Author. m. Antonia Dora Raeburn, 24 Sept. 1976, 2 sons. 3 sons, 1 daughter from 2 previous marriages. *Education:* Rydal School, Colwyn Bay, 1935-7; Old Vic Theatre School, 1947-48. *Career:* Theatre Stage Manager/Director, Administrator, London Symphony Orchestra, 1968-69; Manager, BBC Concert Orchestra, 1969-73; Visiting Professor in Vocal Interpretation, Guildhall School of Music and Drama, London, 1968-74; Editor, The Monthly Guide to Recorded Music, 1980-82. *Publications:* The Operas of Richard Strauss in Great Britain 1910-1963, 1964; The Lieder of Richard Strauss, 1971; Delius (Master Musicians), 1972; The Life of Richard Strauss, 1973; Inside the Orchestra, 1974; Strauss (Music Masters), 1975; The Glory of Opera, 1976; Norwegian version, 1980, 2nd Edition, 1983; Discography of Richard Strauss's Operas, 1977; Strauss (Short Biographies), 1978; Sir Thomas Beecham, 1979; the Complete Gilbert & Sullivan Opera Guide, 1984; Der Rosenkavalier, 1986; Lotte Lehmann, A Centenary Biography, 1988; German Language edition, 1991. *Contributions to:* Opera Magazine; Dancing Times; Blätter: Internationale Richard Strauss Gesellschaft, Vienna; Classical Express, CD Review. *Memberships:* Savile Club. *Hobbies:* Listening to chamber music; Walking; Paternal enjoyment. *Current Management:* Watson, Little Ltd.,

London. *Address:* c/o Watson, Little Ltd., 12 Egbert Street, London, NW1 8LJ, England.

JEFFERY Peter, b. 19 Oct 1953, New York, USA. Professor of Music. m. Margot Fassler, 1983, 2s. *Education:* MFA, 1977, PhD 1980, Princeton University. *Career:* Hill Monastic manuscript Library, 1980-82; Mellon Faculty Fellow, Harvard University, 1982-83; University of Delaware, 1984-92; Boston College, 1992093; Princeton University, 1993-. *Publications:* A Bibliography for Medieval and Renaissance Musical Manuscript Research, 1980; Articles in Journal of the American Musicological Society; Re-Envisioning Past Musical Cultures, 1992. *Honours:* NEH (National Endowment for the Humanities), Grant, 1986-88; Alfred Einstein Award, 1985; John D MacArthur Fellowshp, 1987-92. *Memberships:* American Musicological Society; Medieval Academy of America; North American Academy of Liturgy; Societas Liturgica. *Address:* Music Department, Princeton University, NJ 08544, USA.

JEFFES Peter, b. 1951, London. Singer (Tenor). *Education:* Royal College of Music, London; Rome with Paolo Silveri. *Career:* Italian debut in Rome, Opera: in Spontini's Agnese di Hohenstaufen; Paris Opéra in Doktor Faust; With English Bach Festival at Covent Garden in Rameau's Castor et Pollux; Nero in L'Incoronazione di Poppea for Swiss TV; European engagements as Lohengrin, Tamino and Lensky; Sang Mozart in Rimsky's Mozart and Salieri at Barcelona in 1987; Festival appearances at Aix-en Provence, Orange, Monte Carlo, Athens and in the USA; Engagement with British companies in Roméo et Juliette, Les Contes d'Hoffmann, Die Zauberflöte, The Rake's Progress and A Midsummer Night's Dream; Opera North in the British premiere of Strauss's Daphne, 1987; Season 1988-89 in The Love for Three Oranges for Opera North, Since 1988, repertoire, Cavalleria Rusticana, Pagliacci, Idomeneo, Faust, Werther, Salome, Fliegende Holländer, Macbeth, Attila and Eisenstein; Now sings extensively in Europe and regularly in Israel: The Prince in The Love for Three Oranges, 1992. *Address:* c/o Music International, 13 Ardilaun Road, Highbury, London N5 2QR, England.

JEFFREYS Celia, b. 20 Jan 1948, Southampton, England. Singer (Soprano). *Education:* Studied music at the Royal College of Music, with Meriel St Clair. *Debut:* Welsh National Opera, 1970, as Adele in Die Fledermaus. *Career:* Sang at various regional opera houses in Britain, then appeared in West Germany at Kassel and Darmstadt; Theater am Gärtnerlplatz Munich from 1976, then the Stadtheater Basel, 1978-81; Freelance, 1981-88; Linz, 1988-92; Freelance, 1992-; Other roles have included Mozart's Ilia, Zerlina and Susanna, Caroline in Il Matrimonio Segreto, the Aennchens of Weber and Nicolai, Musetta, Olympia and Corilla in Le Convenzione Teatrali by Donizetti. *Address:* Florians Mülstr 3a, 80939 München, Germany.

JEFFREYS John Michael, b. 4 Dec 1927, Kent, England. Composer; Author. m. Pauline Ashley, 18 Oct 1956. *Education:* LTCL (TTD), 1952, Trinity College of Music. *Career:* Work first brought to public notice in London under John Fry, 1952, & in appraisal made by André Mangeot, BBC European Service Broadcast, 1956; works for single & double string orchestra; unaccompanied voices; voices with organ; Piano; harpsichord; organ; 2 chamber pieces; songs with bassoon; violin concerto. *Compositions:* Over 100 solo songs with piano in 3 vols; settings of English, Scots, Irish & Welsh poetry from 12th-20th centuries: New Brooms, 16 songs for Counter Tenor. *Contributions to:* Frederic Hodgson's anthology of Counter Tenor songs, 1991. *Publications:* The Eccles Family, 1951; Philip Rosseter, his Life & Works, 1990. *Memberships:* Ernest George White Society; TCM Guild; Hardy Plant Society. *Hobbies:* Plantsman; Horticultural Author; Music Research; Poetry. *Address:* Rose Cottage, Stansfield, Clare, Suffolk CO10 9AR, England.

JELEZNOV Irina, b. 4 Oct 1958, Astrakhan, Russia.

Duo Pianist; Docent Chamber Music Cathedra's Tashkent Conservatoire. m. 29 Aug 1980, 1 son. *Education:* Piano Faculty, 1981, Piano Duo Postgraduate course, 1987, Tchaikovsky Conservatoire, Moscow. *Debut:* Tashkent Conservatoire's Hall, 1984. *Career includes:* Recitals and orchestra performances Tashkent, yearly, 1984-93; Appearances, Moscow: The Maly Hall, Moscow Conservatoire, 1986, 1987; Rachmaninov's Hall, 1991; Shuvalova's Home, Moscow, 1991; Piano Duo Festivals: Sverdlovsk, 1989; Leningrad, 1990; Nizny Novgorod, 1991; Novosibirsk, 1992; International Piano Duo Competitions: Belgrade, Yugoslavia, 1989; Caltanissetta, Italy, 1990; Hartford, Connecticut, USA, 1990; Miami, Florida, USA, 1991; TV and radio appearances. *Memberships:* International Piano Duo Association, Tokyo, Japan. *Address:* Prospekt Kosmonavtov d 12-106, 700015 Tashkent, Uzbeckistan.

JELEZNOV Maxim, b. 19 May 1958, Moscow, USSR. Duo Pianist. m. 29 Aug 1980, 1 son. *Education:* Piano Faculty, 1981, Postgraduate course as Piano Duo, 1987, Tchaikovsky Conservatoire, Moscow. *Debut:* Tashkent Conservatoire's Hall, 1984. *Career includes:* Performances: Tashkent, yearly, 1984-93; Maly Hall, Moscow Conservatoire, 1986, 1987; Sverdlovsk Piano Duo Festival, 1989; Belgrade, Yugoslavia, 1989; International Piano Duo Festival, Leningrad, 1990; Hartford, USA, 1990; Caltanissetta, Italy, 1990; Rackmaninoff's Hall, Moscow, 1991; Shuvalova's Home, Moscow, 1991; Nizny Novgorod Piano Duo Festival, 1991; International Piano Duo Festival, Ekatringburg, 1991-93; Piano Duo Festival, The Masters of Piano Duo, Novosibirsk, 1992; TV and radio appearances. *Hobbies:* Football; Table Tennis. *Address:* Prospekt Kosmonavtov d 12-106, 700015 Tashkent, Uzbeckistan.

JELINEK Ladislav, b. 21 Feb 1944, Brno. Concert Pianist. m. 2s. *Education:* State Conservatory in Brno, 1958-62; Janáček University of Musical Arts, Brno, majoring in solo piano under Professor Frantisek Schäfer. *Debut:* Besedni Dum, Brno, 1966. *Career:* Appearances as soloist of Janáček Philharmonic Orchestra, Solo Pianist and Chamber Musician in CSFR and majority of Eastern European Countries; Radio and television appearances in Eastern Europe., 1968-81; Numerous appearances in Westrn Europe, 1981-; University Teacher at the Frankfurter Hochschule für Musik und Darstellende Kunst, 1984-. *Recordings:* Numerous solo recordings at Bayerischer Rundfunk, Munich, with compositions by Liszt, Prokofiev, Jan Novak, Vit. Novak, Smetana, Haydn, Chopin and Dvořák. *Honours:* Piano Competitions: Academy of Music, CSFR, 1961, Hradec Kralove, 1963. *Memberships:* Artistic Adivsory Board, Janáček University of Musical Arts, Brno. *Hobbies:* Travel; History; Cooking; Reading. *Current Management* Conzertmanager Edith Roschlau. *Address:* Friedrichsdorfer Strasse 7, 61352 Bad Homburg, Germany.

JENKINS Carol, b. 1960, Toronto, Canada. Violinist. *Education:* Studied at University of Toronto with Rodney Friend and Victor Danchenki. *Career:* Associate Leader, Denver Symphony Orchestra and other orchestras; Second Violinist, Da Vinci Quartet from 1988, founded in 1980 under the sponsorship of the Fine Arts Quartet; Many concerts in USA and elsewhere in a repertoire including works by Mozart, Beethoven, Brahms, Dvořák, Chostakovich and Bartók. *Honours:* (With the Da Vinci Quartet), Awards and Grants the NEA , the Western States Arts Foundation and the Colorado Council for the Humanities; Artist in Residence, University of Colorado. *Address:* c/o Sonata (Da Vinci Quartet), 11 Northpark Street, Glasgow G20 7AA, Scotland.

JENKINS Graeme James Ewers, b. 1958, England. Conductor. *Education:* Studied at Dulwich College and Cambridge University; Royal College of Music with Norman Del Mar and David Willcocks. *Debut:* Conducted Albert Herring and the Turn of the Screw at College. *Career:* The Beggar's Opera, Die Entfuhrung and Le Nozze di Figaro for Kent Opera; Andrea Chénier, Brighton Festival; Cesti's La Dori (Spitalfields); Il

Trovatore, Le Nozze di Figaro and Così fan Tutte (Scottish Opera); Così fan Tutte with English National Opera, 1988; European debut 1987, Hansel und Gretel and Ravel Double Bill with Geneva Opera; Simon Boccanegra (Netherlands Opera); As Music Director of Glyndebourne Touring Opera has conducted A Midsummer Night's Dream, Albert Herring, Simon Boccanegra and Così fan Tutte; La Traviata and Death in Venice 1989; Glyndebourne Festival debut 1987, with Carmen and Capriccio: returned for Ravel Double Bill and Falstaff; Arabella 1989; Oedipus Rex and Petrushka with Scottish Opera 1989; Scheduled engagements include Carmen and La Rondine with Canadian Opera in Toronto, La Bohème with Australian Opera 1990; Concert appearances with the Hallé Orchestra, BBC Scottish, BBC Philharmonic, BBC Symphony, Royal Philharmonic, Cracow Radio Symphony and Scottish Chamber Orchestra; Fidelio (Glyndebourne Tour); Iphigénie en Tauride (Netherlands Opera); La Bohème (Australian Opera), 1990; Idomeneo (Glyndebourne Festival), 1991; Conducted the world premiere of Stephen Oliver's Timon of Athens, London Coliseum, 1991; Residente Orkest The Hague, Netherlands Chamber Orchestra, 1991; Death in Venice at the 1992 Glyndebourne Festival. *Address:* c/o Lies Askonas Ltd., 186 Drury Lane, London WC2B 5RY, England.

JENKINS Neil, b. 9 Apr 1945, Sussex, England. Opera and Concert Singer, (Tenor). m. Penelope Anne, 26 Apr 1982, 4s, 1 d. *Education:* Choral Scholar, King's College, Cambridge, 1963-66: MA, Royal College of Music, 1966- 68. *Debut:* Purcell Room, London, Song Recital with Roger Vignoles, 1967. *Career:* Guest Soloist, Israel Chamber Orchestra, 1968-69, London Bach Society, 1971, 1973; Member of Deller Consort, 1967-76; Appearances at festivals in Israel, Paris, London and Spain; Performances with Welsh National Opera, Scottish Opera, Opera North, Glyndebourne, Edinburgh and Frankfurt, Kent Opera; New productions of Le Nozze di Figaro and the Ravel double bill in Geneva; Wexford 1989 in Prokofiev's The Duenna; Sang in Bernstein's Candide, 1989; Also heard in oratorio and concert, in the orchecstral version of Tippett's The Heart's Assurance at Canterbury, 1990; Debut at the ENO in Monteverdi's Orfeo and Il Ritorno d'Ulisse, 1992. *Compositions include:* Christmas Carols for unaccompanied SATB singers in, Here we come a-Wassailing, 1993. *Recordings include:* Bernstein Candide; Britten Peter Grimes; Tippett King Priam; Mozart Le Nozze di Figaro; Henze Kammermusik 1958; Britten, Serenade for tenor, horn and Strings with Oriol Ensemble. *Publications:* Editor: The Carol Singer's Handbook, 1993; Editor, the Handbook series. *Hobbies:* Visiting ancient monuments; 18th Century Music Research. *Address:* 10 Hartington Villas, Hove, Sussex, BN3 6HF, England

JENKINS Newell, b. 8 Feb. 1915, New Haven, Connecticut, USA. Conductor; Musicologist. *Education:* Studied in Dresden and with Erich Doflein in Freiburg; Further study with Carl Orff in Munich. *Debut:* Freiburg 1935, Dido and Aeneas; Founded Yale Opera Group 1940; Conducted the Bologna Chamber Orchestra 1948-53; Founded the Piccola Accademia Musicale in Florence 1952; Music Director of the Clarion Music Society New York 1957: performances of Cavalli, Steffani, Monteverdi and J.M. Kraus; Many appearances in Europe as guest conductor; Teacher at New York University 1964-74; Lecturer at University of California, Irvine, 1971-79. *Publications:* Edition of 9 Symphonies by Brunetti 1979. *Recordings:* Operas by Giovanni Simone Mayr and Rossini; Music by Sammartini, Kraus (Funeral Ode for Gustavus III) and Cherubini (Missa Solemnis in D Minor). *Honours:* Commendatore, Italian Order of Merit; Fulbright Scholarship for research on Sammartini.

JENKINS Speight, b. 31 Jan 1937, Dallas, USA. Administrator. *Education:* Studied at the University of Texas and Columbia University Law School, graduating in 1961. *Career:* Editor, Opera News, 1967-73; music critic for the New York Post, 1973-81; Host for the Live from the Met broadcasts, 1981-83; General Director of Seattle Opera, 1983-; Has presided over such productions as The Ring Cycle, 1986-87, 1991, War and Peace, Die Meistersinger, and Werther in the version for baritone , 1989, the US premiere of Gluck's Orphée et Eurydice and the West Coast premiere of Glass's Satyagraha, 1988; Les Dialogues des Carmelites, 1990, Glass artist Dale Chihuly's scenic debut in Pelláas at Mélisande, 1993, Norma, 1994. *Honours:* Honorary Doctorate, Seattle University, 1992; University at Paget Sound, 1992. *Address:* Seattle Opera Association, PO Box 9248, Seattle, WA 98109, USA

JENKINS Terry, b. 9 Oct. 1941, Hertford, England. Operatic Tenor. m. Pamela Ann Jenkins, 14 Sept. 1965, 1 son, 1 daughter. *Education:* BSc (Eng) University College, London, 1964; Guildhall School of Music, 1964-66; London Opera Centre, 1967-68. *Debut:* Opera for All, 1966-67 Nemorino (L'Elisir d'Amore). *Career:* Basilica Opera, 1969-71; Glyndebourne Touring Opera, 1969-71; Malcolm (Macbeth), M. Triquet (Eugene Onegin), Schmidt (Werther) Scarramuccio (Ariadne auf Naxos); Glyndebourne Festival Opera, 1971, Major Domo (Queen of Spades), Officer (Ariadne auf Naxos); Glyndebourne Festival Opera, 1972, Scarramuccio; Sadler's Wells Opera, 1972-74; English National Opera, 1974-, roles include - Basilio (Marriage of Figaro), Pedrillo (Entführung), Remendado (Carmen), Goro (Madam Butterfly), Gaston (La Traviata), Vanya (Katya Kabanova), Spoletta (Tosca), Schmidt (Werther), Fenney (Mines of Sulphur), Tchekalinsky (Queen of Spades), Loge (Rheingold), Borsa (Rigoletto); Duke (Patience); Orpheus (Orpheus in the Underworld); various roles: Pacific Overtures; Hauk Sendorf, Makropulos Case; Schoolmaster, Cunning Little Vixen; Dr Caius (Falstaff); E.N.O. Tour of USA, 1984; New Opera Company, 1976, 1979 and 1980; Royal Opera, Covent Garden, 1976, 1977, 1981; English Bach Festival, 1983 at Versailles and Sadler's Wells; City of London Festival, 1978; Barbican Hall, 1984, 1985, 1986, 1987, 1988; Seattle Opera, 1983, (Loge-Rheingold) Vienna Festival with E.N.O., 1975; Chelsea Opera Group, 1986; Boston Concert Opera (USA), 1986, (Guillot-Manon); Aix-en-Provence Festival, 1991, 1992, Snout, A Midsummer Night's Dream (Britten). *Recordings:* Justice Shallow in Sir John in Love (Vaughan Williams); Borsa in Rigoletto (Verdi); Pacific Overtures; Street Scene; several video recordings. *Contributions to:* Musicians Handbook. *Hobbies:* D.I.Y.; Crosswords. *Current Management:* Music International, Ardilaun Road, London, N7. *Address:* 9 West End Avenue, Pinner, Middlesex, England.

JENKINS Timothy, b. 21 Nov 1951, Oklahoma City, USA. Singer (tenor). *Education:* Studied at Texas State University. *Debut:* Sang Baron Douphol in La Traviata with Fort Worth Opera, 1974. *Career:* Metropolitan Opera deubt, 1979, as Schmidt, in Aufsteig and Fall der Stadt Mahagonny; Returned to the Met as Parsifal, 1983, Laca, (Jenůfa), High Priest in Idomeneo, Macduff, Wagner's Siegmund and Froh and Stravinsky's Oedipus; Bayreuth Festival, 1985, as Froh in Das Rheingold; Guest appearances in concert and opera in the United States. *Recordings:* Idomeneo. *Address:* c/o Metropolitan Opera, Lincoln Center, NY 10023, USA

JENNER Alexander, b. 4 Apr. 1929, Vienna, Austria. Concert pianist; Professor of piano. m. Marytza Rangel, 31 Oct. 1957, 1 son, 2 daughters. *Education:* Realgymnasium, Matura, 1947; Reifeprüfung with Bösendorfer award, 1948, Akademie für Musik, Vienna. *Debut:* Beethoven 5th Piano Concerto, Badgastein, Austria, 1948. *Career:* Recitals and concertos with orchestra and chamber music concerts in most European countries, North and South America, Far and Middle East including live radio and television performances and studio recordings. *Recordings:* Mostly classical and romantic piano music for various record companies and radio and television stations. *Memberships:* Vice-President, International Chopin Society of Vienna; Vienna Beethoven Society. *Address:* Grosse Sperlgasse 16, A-1020 Wien, Austria.

JENNI Donald Martin, b. 4 Oct. 1937, Milwaukee,

Wisconsin, USA. Composer; Professor of Music; Head, Composition and Theory. *Education:* AM, University of Chicago, USA, 1962; BMus, DePaul University, USA, 1958; DMA, Stanford University, 1966. *Career:* Ford Foundation Composer-in-Residence, Ann Arbor, Michigan, USA, 1960; Director of Music, La Compagnie de Danse Jo Lechay, Montreal, Canada, 1975-82; Professor, Music Theory and Composition, The University of Iowa, USA 1974-. *Compositions:* Axis, 1968; R-Music, Asphodel, 1969; Eulalia's Rounds, 1972; Musica dell'autunno, 1975; Long Hill May, 1976; Crux Christi ave! 1977; Canticum Beatae Virginis, 1979; Pharos, 1980; Ballfall, 1981; The Opalion, 1984; Sam mbira, 1985; Figura Circulorum (strings and metallophones), 1993; premiered Center for New Music Iowa City, 1993. *Recordings:* Musique Printaniere, 1967; Cucumber Music, 1969. *Publication:* Cum novo cantico: A Primer of Biblical and Medieval Latin, 1983. *Hobby:* Linguistics. *Address:* 1026MB, The University of Iowa, Iowa City, IA 52242, USA.

JENSON Dylana (Ruth) (Lockington), b. 14 May 1961, Los Angeles, California, USA. Violinist. *Education:* Began violin training with mother; Pupil of Manuel Compinsky, Jascha Heifetz, and Josef Gingold; Master classes with Nathan Milstein, Zurich, 1973-76. *Career:* First public appearance as soloist in the Bach A Minor Concerto at age 7; Professional debut as soloist in the Mendelssohn Concerto with the New York Philharmonic Orchestra, 1973; European debut as soloist with the Zurich Tonhalle Orchestra, 1974; Thereafter regular tours throughout the world as a soloist with leading orchestras, as a recitalist, and as a chamber-music player. *Recordings:* For RCA. *Honours:* 2nd prize, Tchaikovsky International Competition, Moscow, 1978. *Address:* c/o Konzertdirektion Jurgen Erlebach, Beim Schlump 53, D-2000 Hamburg 13, Germany.

JEPPSSON Kerstin Maria, b. 29 Oct. 1948, Nyköping, Sweden. Composer. *Education:* BA, Musicology, Pedagogy, Social Anthropology, University of Stockholm, 1977. Studies 1968-73, music teacher's diploma 1973, Stockholm Conservatory of Music, composition with Maurice Karkoff, Stockholm 1968-73, with Krzysztof Meyer & Krzysztof Penderecki, Cracow Conservatory of Music, Poland 1974, 1977, with Melvin Powell, California Institute of the Arts 1978-79, MFA, ibid 1979. *Compositions include:* Orchestral & chamber music, solo instrumental music, choral music, songs. Titles include 3 Sentenzi, orchestra, 1970; Crisis, string orchestra & percussion, 1976-77; Tre ryska poem, soprano & clarinet, 1973; Hindemith in memoriam, clarinet & piano, 1974; Vocazione, guitar solo, 1982; Prometheus, percussion, 1983; Tendenze, strings & piano, 1986; Piano works; Choral works include Tre visor (1972), Blomstret i Saron (1972), 5 Japanese Images (1973), etc. Songs include Kvinnosånger (Female Songs), edition Suecia, Sweden. *Recordings:* Various pieces. *Address:* Föreningen Svenska Tonsättare, Sandhamnsgatan 79, Box 27 327, S-102 54 Stockholm, Sweden.

JERIE Marek Jan, b. 15 Dec. 1947, Prague, Czechoslovakia. Musician; Cellist. m. Beatrix Elisabeth Schneider, 31 Oct. 1974, 1 son, 2 daughters. *Education:* Prague & Basle Conservatories; Prague Music Academy; Concert and Solo Diplomas; Master Classes with Casals, Rostropovich, Navarra. *Career:* Soloist, Chamber Musician with K. Ragossnig, I. Klansky, I. Straus, Smetana Quartet, etc., 1975-; Professor, Luzern Conservatory, 1979-; TV performances in Prague; Radio Recordings throughout Europe; Discovery of Czech Cello Concertos of 18th Century/Reicha, Fiala. *Compositions:* by Reicha, Tchaikowsky, Valse, Sentimentaler, Cello, Guitar, Fisher Solo-Sonate, Supraphon dedicated to him. *Recordings:* Panton: Reicha Celloconcerto; Supraphon: Cello Miniatures m. I. Klansky, Attaca: Brahms Cello Sonatas. *Publications:* Reicha Cello Concerto, 1980; Tchaikowsky, Valse Sentimental, 1987. *Hobbies:* Skiing; Swimming. *Address:* Engelgasse 104, CH 4052, Basel, Switzerland.

JERSILD Jörgen, b. 1913, Copenhagen, Denmark.

Composer. *Education:* Studied Composition and Music Theory with Poul Schierbeck and piano with Alexander Stoffregen; Studied under Albert Roussel, Paris, France; Further Studies in USA and Italy; MA, University of Copenhagen, 1940. *Career:* Danish radio Music Department, 1939; Professor of Theory, Royal Academy of Music, Copenhagen, 1943-75. *Compositions:* Orchestral: Pastorale, 1946; Little Suite, 1950; The Birthday Concert, 1945; Ballet, Kings Theatre, 1954, Capricious Luicinda de Chamber Music: Music Making in the Forest, 1947; Fantasia e Canto Affetuoso, 1969; String Quartet, 1980; Für Gefühlvolle Spieler for two harps, 1982; Solo Instrument: Trois pièces en Concert, for piano, 1945; Pezzo Elegiaco, for harp, 1968; Fantasia, for harp, 1977; Fantasia for piano, 1987; 15 piano pieces for Julie, 1985; Jeu polyrythmique for piano, 1990; Fantasia per organo, 1985; Vocal Music: 3 songs, 1944; 3 Danish Madrigals 1958; 3 Danish Love Songs; 3 Romantiske Korsange 1984; 3 Latin Madrigals, 1987; Il cantico delle creature 1992; Music for Children: Quaretti Piccolo, 1950; Duo Concertante, 1956. 30 Polyrythmic Etudes, 1975. *Publications:* Laerebog i Rytmelaesning, 2nd edition, 1961; Laerbog i Melodilaesning, 2nd edition, 1963; Ear training I-II, 1966; Elementary Rhythm Exercises; Advanced Rhythmic Studies, 1975; Romantic Harmony, 1970; Analytical Harmony I-II, 1989. *Honours:* Recipient of several honorary appointments. *Address:* Søllerødvej 38, 2840 Holte, Denmark.

JERUSALEM Siegfried, b. 17 Apr. 1940, Oberhausen, Germany. Singer (Tenor). *Education:* Studied violin, piano and bassooon in Essen; Voice with Hertha Kalcher in Stuttgart. *Career:* Played bassoon in various orchestras and made debut as singer at Stuttgart in 1975; Appeared widely in Germany as Lohengrin; Bayreuth Festival from 1977, as Parsifal, Lohengrin, Walther, Siegmund and Siegfried (1988); Deutsche Oper Berlin 1977-80, as Mozart's Tamino and Idomeneo, Weber's Max, Tchaikovsky's Lensky and Beethoven's Florestan; Metropolitan Opera debut 1980, as Lohengrin; Guest appearances in Munich, Milan, Hamburg, San Francisco and Geneva; In 1986 sang Parsifal at the London Coliseum and Erik in Der fliegende Holländer at Covent Garden; Sang Loge and Siegfried in The Ring at the Metropolitan, 1990 (also televised); Siegfried at the 1990 Bayreuth Festival; Season 1992 with Parsifal at the Met and Siegfried at Bayreuth; Featured Artist (People No. 182) Opera Magazine August 1992, pp 904-909; Sang Tristan in a new production at Bayreuth, 1993. *Recordings:* Martha, Les Contes d'Hoffmann, Violanta, Leonore, Die Zauberflöte, Die Walküre, Tannhäuser; Videos of Parsifal and Die Meistersinger; Der Ring des Nibelungen, conducted by Haitink (EMI). *Address:* c/o Theateragentur Dr. G Hilbert, Maximilianstr. 22, D-80539, München.

JESKALIAN Barbara Jean, b. 12 Apr. 1936, Oakland, California, USA. Music Librarian. m. 3 July 1964, divorced, 1 son. *Education:* AB, Berkeley, University of California; MSLS, University of Southern California, Los Angeles; MA, Philosophical and Systematic Theology, Graduate Theological Union, Berkeley; Studies of Piano with Inga Cohelan, 1942-49, Ida Bodanzky Reik, 1950-54, Margaret Jensen Brown, 1955-58, Violoncello, Robert Sayre, 1987-; Margaret Avery Rowell, 1988-. *Career:* Music Librarian, Clark Library, San Jose State University; Micrologus, PBS Broadcast from Music Department, Case Western Reserve University, interviewed on 12th Century Composer, Hildegard of Bingen; Paper delivered to the American Academy of Religion: Hildegard of Bingen-the Music, the Time, the Self. *Publications:* Historical Anthology of Music by Women, 1987, Chapter on Hildegard of Bingen; Background Effects in Music. *Hobbies:* Jungian Psychology; Gardening; Collecting icons; Hiking; Creative writing. *Address:* 321 Brookwood Avenue, San Jose, CA 95116, USA.

JESKO Milan, b. 22 Aug. 1941, Bratislava, Czechoslovakia. Conductor; Composer; Musical Director. m. Klaudia Junosova, 18 Jan. 1969, 3 sons. *Education:* Academy of Music, Bratislava; Doctoral

Degree, Commenius University, 1981. *Career:* Musical Assistant, Banska Bystrica Tajovsky Theatre; Conductor, Organizer of Musical Life in Bratislava; Editor, Czechoslovak Radio, Folk Music Department, Bratislava, 1986-; Director, Slovak Music Fund; Artistic Leader, Folk Ensemble. *Recordings:* Various for Czechoslovak Radio; music for orchestra; Zlata Priadka; Theatre pieces. *Contributions to:* Professional Journals. *Memberships:* Union of Slovak Composers. *Address:* Dostojevského rad 19, 811 09 Bratislava, Slovakia.

JEURISSEN Herman G.A., b. 27 Dec. 1952, Wijchen, Holland. Horn Player; Arranger. *Education:* Soloist Diploma, Brabants Conservatorium, Tilburg, Holland, 1976. *Career:* Co-1st Horn, Utrecht Symphony Orchestra, 1975-78; Solo Horn, The Hague Philharmonic Orchestra, 1978-; Solo and Concerto, Radio and TV appearances with orchestras in Holland, Austria, Germany, France, USA. *Publications:* Compositions: Reconstruction and Completion of Mozart's unfinished Horn Concertos K 370b and 371, K 494A; Compositions and arrangements for horns. Mozart and the Horn, 1978; Contributor to: Mens en Melodie; Praeludium; Horn Call Brass Bulletin. *Recordings:* Mozarts Unfinished Horn Concertos; Complete Horn Music, by Leopold Mozart; Chamber Music, Franz and Richard Strauss; Compositions for horn and organ; Compositions for brass and carillon. *Honours:* Prix d'excellence, 1978; Silver Laurel of the Concertgebouw Friends, 1979. *Address:* Jacob Mosselstraat 58, 2595 RJ The Hague, The Netherlands.

JEWELL Ian, b. 1950, England. Violinist. *Education:* Studied at the Royal college of Music with Cecil Aronowitz and in Italy with Bruno Giuranna. *Career:* Solo performances of the Walton and Rubbra Concertos, Harold in Italy by Berliioz and the Mozart concertante; Philharmonic at The Royal Academy of Music and Head of Strings, Purcell School. Co-founder, Gabriell Quartet, 1967, and toured with them to Europe, North America, the Far East and Australia; Festival engagements in Britain, including the Aldeburgh, City of London and Cheltenham; Concerts every season in London participation in the Barbican Centre's Mostly Mozart Festival; Resident Artist, University of Essex from 1971; Co-Premiered works by William Alwyn, Britten, Alan Bush, Daniel Jones and Gordon Crosse, 2 Quartets of Nicholas Maw and Panufnik, 1980, 1983, and the 3rd Quartets of John MacCabe, 1979; British premiere of the Piano quintet by Sibelius, 1990. *Recordings include:* 50 CDs, including early pieces by Britten, Dohnanyi's Piano Quintet with Wolfgang Manz, Walton's Quartets and the Sibelius Quartet and Quintet, with Anthony Goldstone. *Address:* Gabrieli Quartet, 3 Primrose Mews, 1a Sharpleshall Street, London NW1 8YW, England.

JEZ Jacob, b. 23 Nov. 1928, Bostanj, Yugoslavia. Composer. m. Olga, 1955. *Education:* Diploma, Academy of Music, Ljubljana, Yugoslavia, 1954. *Career:* Chief Editor, Rev Mus, 1968-; Performances of the Nature's Look, World Music Day's, ISCM, Athens, Greece, 1979. *Compositions:* Do Fraig amors, The Monument of Freising, 1970; Star's Look, 1974; Caccia Barbara, 1979; Chamber and Orchestral Music; Children's Music. *Recordings:* Cantatas, 1983; Choral and Children's Music. *Publications:* Compositions (Musik-verlage, West Germany). *Contributions to:* Grlica. *Honours:* Yugoslavian Radio Prize, 1968; Preseren Fond Prize, 1968; Numerous other awards. *Current Management:* Society Slovenian Composers, Trg franc rev 6, Ljubljana, Yugoslavia. *Hobby:* Nature. *Address:* Gradez 27, 61311 Turjak, Slovenia.

JILEK Frantisek, b. 22 May 1913, Brno, Czechoslovakia. Conductor. *Education:* Studied with Kvapil and Chalabala at Brno, with Vitezslav Novak in Prague. *Career:* Repetiteur with the Brno Opera, 1937-39, Conductor of the Ostrava Opera, 1939-48; Returned to Brno 1948, and was Artistic Director at the Opera, 1952-78; Gave the complete operas of Janáček in 1958, and conducted Martinů's Greek Passion and Prokofiev's Fiery Angel and War and peace; Guest appearances in Czechoslovakia, and abroad, notably in works by

Janáček; Chief conductor, Brno State Philharmonic Orchestra from 1978. *Recordings include:* Janáček's The Beginning of a Romance, Osud, Jenůfa and The Excursions of Mr Broucek, 19876-80, Martinů's Comedy on the Bridge and Alexandre Bis, 1985-86. *Address:* c/o Brno State Philharmonic Orchestra, Moravske Namesti 1a, 602 00 Brno, Czech Republic.

JIRACKOVA Marta, b. 22 Mar 1932, Kladno, Czech Republic. Composer. m. 1964, 2d. *Education:* Conservatoire of Music in Prague, Compositon with Emil Hlobil; Modern Harmony and composition with Alois Haba; Janacek's Academy of Performing Arts, Brno, with Alois Pinos. *Career:* Music for orchestra, chamber music, vocal music, scene music electro-acoustic music, including music for stage, film, radio and TV. *Compositions:* The Children's World, piano cycle of etudes, 1977; Ave Seikilos, string orchestra and percussion, 1985; Eight Wonders of the world, human voices, harp and percussion, 1988; Dodekaria I, sonata for violin and piano, 1993; Dodekaria II for flute and cymbal, Dodekaria Tristis, No III for baset, horn and piano; Three songs without words for soprano and instrumental ensemble, 1982; Nanda Devi, First Symphony, 1984; Silbo, 2nd Symphony, 1987; Electroacoustic music: Five Times a Woman; The Ship of Fools by Hieronymus Bosch; The Outlook from my Balcony. *Honours:* Czech Music Fund Annual Prize, 1992. *Hobbies:* Music, Literature; Spending time with the family. *Address:* 169 00 Prague 6, Brevnov, Ve Stresovickach 45, Czech Republic.

JIRASEK Ivo, b. 16 July 1920, Prague, Czech Republic. Composer. *Education:* Studied at the Prague High School of Music, Conservatoire, 1940-45. *Career:* Conductor of Opera in Opava, 1946-56; Teacher and later Freelance Composer from 1956. *Compositions include:* Operas Mr Johanes, 1956; Dawn over the Waters, 1961; The Bear, 1964; Danse Macabra, 1971; Master Jeronym, 1980; The Miracle, 1981; Ballet Faust, 1985. *Address:* 147 00 Praha 4, Braník, U háje 39a.

JIWKOW Wasil, b. 12 Dec. 1926, Jakimowo, Bulgaria. Maker of Musical Instruments especially Violins. *Education:* College for Interior Design, Küstendil 1941-46. *Career:* Master Violin Maker, Kooperativ Gusla, Sofia 1951-65; Violin Maker, Walther KG, Mittenwald/Bavaria 1965-68; Set up own business and violin workshop, Munich 1968-; Took part in various competitions: Concours International de Quatuor a Cordes, Liège, Belgium 1957; Societa Filarmonica Ascolana, Mostra Internazionale di Luteria, Viola Moderna in Ascoli, Italy, Diploma for Modern Viola 1959; Concourse International de Quatuor a Cordès, Liège, Belgium, Certificates for Quartets, 1960 and 1963; Concours International for Stringed Instruments, Poznan, Poland, 2nd prize for violin 1967; Concourse International de Quatuor a Cordès, Liège, Belgium, (1st Prize for quartet, best work and style 1972) 1969 and 1972; International Exhibition and Competition of the Violin Society of America in La Jolla, California, Certificate for Viola Workmanship 1978. *Hobbies:* Cooking; Numismatics. *Address:* Mueller Str. 26, 8000 Munich 5, Germany.

JO Sumi, b. 22 Nov 1962, Seoul, South Korea. Singer (Soprano). *Education:* Studied in Seoul and at the Accademia di Santa Cecilia, Rome, 1983-86. *Debut:* Teatro Verdi Trieste 1986, as Gilda. *Career:* Sang at Lyon, Nice and Marseille, 1987-88; Discovered by Karajan and sang Barbarina at the 1988 Salzburg Festival: Oscar in Un Ballo in Maschera, 1989- 90, conducted by Solti; Guest appearances at Munich from 1988, Vienna from 1989 and Paris; La Scala Milan in Ravel L'Enfant et les Sortilèges conducted by Lorin Maazel and as Zerlina in Auber's Fra Diavolo, 1992; Metropolitan Opera as Gilda, 1988 and 1990; Royal Opera, Covent Garden as Olympia in Tales of Hoffmann and as Elvira in Puritani in 1991 and 1992; Chicago Lyric Opera as Queen of Night in 1990 and as Queen of the Night with Danish Philharmonic conducted by Zubin Mehta in 1991; Season 1992 as Matilde in Rossini's Elisabetta at Naples, Olympia at Covent

Garden (followed by Adina). *Recordings:* Arias (Capriccio); Adèle in Le Comte Ory (Philips); Un Ballo in Maschera (Deutsche Grammophon); Queen of Night in Die Zauberflöte, conducted by Armin Jordan (Erato); and conducted by Solti (Decca/London); Fiorilla in Rossini's Il Turco in Italia, conducted by Neville Marriner (Philips); Soprano soloist in Mahler Symphony 8, conducted by Sinopoli; Soprano soloist in Rossini's Messa di Gloria, conducted by Neville Marriner. *Address:* Columbia Artists Management, 165 West 57th Street, New York, NY 10019, USA.

JOACHIM Otto, b. 13 Oct 1910, Düsseldorf, Germany. Composer; Violist; Violinist; Gambist. Separated, 1 son. *Education:* Concordia School, Düsseldorf; Buths-Neitzel Conservatory, Düsseldorf; Rheinische Musik Schule, Cologne. *Career:* CBC Soloist, Montreal String Quartet, L'Ensemble des Instruments Anciens de Montreal, Canada; 1st Violist, Montreal Symphony. *Compositions include:* Nonet, 1960; Psalm for Choir, 1960; Concertante Number 2 for string quartet and string orchestra, 1961; Fantasia for organ, 1961; 12 Twelve-Tone Pieces for Children, 1961; Contrastes for orchestra, 1967; Kinderspiel for violin, cello, piano and speaker, 1969; 5,9 for 4 channel tape, 1971; Night Music for flute (alto flute) and guitar, 1978; Night Music for alto flute and guitar, 1978; 4 Intermezzi for flute and guitar, 1978; Requiem for violin or viola or cello, 1969; Prix Calixa Lavallée de La Société St Jean Baptiste, 1990; Ordre National du Québec, 1993. *Hobbies:* Musical electronics; Constructing replicas of ancient instruments; Painting. *Address:* 7910 Wavell Road, Côte St-Luc, Montreal, H4W 1L7, Canada.

JOBIN Andre, b. 20 Jan 1933, Quebec, Canada. Singer (Tenor). *Education:* Studied as an actor in Paris and worked with Jean-Louis Barrault. *Career:* Sang at first as a baritone in Parisian musicals; Operatic roles as tenor from 1962, notably Pelleas at Marseilles, Nice, Paris, Madrid, and San Francisco, 1965; Glyndebouren Festival, 976, New York City Opera from 1970; Other roles have been Romeo, Don José, Massenet's Des Grieux, Rodrigo and John the Baptist, Julien (Louise) and Hoffmann; many appearances at Quebec, Lyon, Brussels, Berlin and Madrid; Liège Opera, 1982-87, as Rodrigo in Le Cid, John the Baptist (Herodiade) and Des Grieux; Cologne Opera, 1987, as Werther; Engaged in musical sand operettas in Chicago, London and Detroit. *Recordings:* Albums under various record labels.

JOCHSBERGER Tzipora H, b. 27 Dec 1920, Germany. Composer; Educator; Director of Music. *Education:* Diploma, Palestine Academy of Music, Jerusalem, 1942; Diploma, Music Teachers Seminary, Jerusalem, 1942; MSM, 1959, Doctor of Sacred Music, 1972, Seminary College of Jewish Music, Jewish Theological Seminary, New York. *Career:* Co-Founder, Co-Director, 1947-50, Board of Governors, 1990-, Rubin Academy for Music & Dance, Jerusalem, 1947-50; Founding Director, Hebrew Arts School/Merkin Concert Hall, New York, 1952-86; Assistant Professor, Cantors Institute & Seminary College of Jewish Music, Jewish Theological Seminary, New York, 1954-73; Founder, American Jewish Choral Festival, New York, 1981; Founder, Director, Israel Music Heritage Project, 1985-; Appeared radio & TV, USA, Israel. *Compositions:* Melodies of Israel, duets/trios, recorders & other melody instruments, 1956; Hallel psalms of praise, cantor, choir, children's voices, 1956; B'Kol Zimra, mixed voices, SATB, Piano music and songs. *Hobbies:* Reading; Swimming; Driving. *Address:* POB 7461, Jerusalem 91073, Israel.

JOCHUM Veronica, b. 1930, Berlin, Germany. Pianist. m. Wilhelm Viggo von Moltke, 15 Nov 1961. *Education:* MA, 1955, Concert Diploma, 1957, Staatliche Musikhochschule, Munich, Federal Republic of Germany; Private study with Edwin Fischer, Josef Benvenuti, 1958-59, and Rudolf Serkin, 1959-61. *Debut:* Germany, 1954. *Career:* Numerous appearances as soloist with orchestras, North and South America, 1961-; Appeared with Boston Symphony, London Symphony Orchestra, London Philharmonic Orchestra, Berlin, Hamburg and Munich Philharmonics, Vienna Symphony, Concertgebouw Orchestra, etc; Radio and TV appearances; Recitals in over 50 countries, Europe, North and South America, Africa, Asia; Featured in German film, Self-Attempt, on a novel by Christa Wolf. *Recordings:* Deutsche Grammophon, Laurel, Philips, Golden Crest, PRO ARTE, GM Recordings. *Address* New England Conservatory of Music, 290 Huntington Avenue, Boston, MA 02115, USA.

JOHANNESEN Grant, b. 30 July 1921, Salt Lake City, Utah, USA. Concert Pianist. m. Zara Nelsova, 1963-73. *Education:* Studied with Robert Casadesus at Princeton University and with Egon Petri at Cornell University. *Debut:* Times Hall, New York, 1944. *Career:* First international tour, 1949; Tour of Europe with New York Philharmonic and Mitropoulos, 1956-57; Tour of USSR and Europe with Cleveland Orchestra and George Szell, 1968; Solo tours of the USSR, 1962, 1970; Appearances at all major music festivals; Aspen Festival for 6 seasons; On faculty of Aspen Music School, 1960-66; Music Director of the Cleveland Institute of Music, 1974-84. *Recordings:* Fauré's complete piano music; Works by Dukas, Roussel and De Sévrac; Sonatas for cello and piano with Zara Nelsova.

JOHANNSEN Kay, b. 1 Oct 1961, Giengen. Organist; Church Musician; m. Andrea Ermer, 29 Apr 1987, 1 daughter. *Education:* Studies at Freiburg in organ, conducting; Organ Studies at NEC, Boston, with William Porter. *Career:* Concerts in major German cities and in foreign countries, broadcasted concerts with almost all German stations, several concerts with orchestras as Nurnberg Symphonic, RSO Prague, RSO Hannover, Staatsphilharmonic Rheinland-Pfalz, Philharmonic Orchestra Gelsenkirchen; Teacher, Karlsruhe Conservatory, 1991-, Guest Teacher, Freiburg Conservatory, 1992-93. *Compositions:* CDs: Harmonia Mundi, 1990: Bach, Reger, Fortig; 1993: Christian Hommel, Bach, Mozart Huber ars musici; 1993: French organ music from the 19th C. 1994: Organist of the Stiftskirche Stuttgart. *Honours:* Various prizes in music competitions; German National Foundation Scholarship. *Hobbies:* Windsurfing; Spending time with the family. *Address:* c/o Evang Bezirkskantorat, Altes Schloss, Schillerplatz 6, 70173 Stuttgart, Germany.

JOHANNSSON Kristjan, b. 1950, Akureyi Du, Iceland. Singer (Tenor). *Education:* Studied at the Nicolini Conservatory, Piacenza, and with Campogalliani and Tagliavini. *Debut:* National Theatre of Iceland, Reykjavik, as Rodolfo in 1961. *Career:* Sang Pinkerton in a production of Madam Butterfly, by Ken Russell, at Spoleto, 1983; Engagements as guest artist at the Chicago Lyric Opera (Faust 1991), Metropolitan New York, Vienna, Sttatsoper and La Scala Milan; Roles have included Radames, Alvaro in La Forza del Destino, Cavaradossi and Dick Johnson; Sang Turinddu in Cavalleria Rusticana at Naples and Florence, season 1990-91; Calaf at the Verona Arean, 1991; Sang Manrico in the opening production at the new Teatro, Carol Felice, Geona, 1991; Andrea Chenier at Florence, Calaf at Chicago, Cavaradossi at Rome and Manrico at Turin, 1992. *Address:* c/o Teatro Comunale di Firenze, Via Solferino 15, 50123 Florence, Italy.

JOHANOS Donald, b. 10 Feb 1928, Cedar Rapids, Iowa, USA. Conductor. m. (1) Thelma Trimble, 27 Aug 1950, 2 sons, 3 daughters. (2) Corinne Rutledge, 28 Sept 1985. *Career:* MusB 1950, MusM 1952, Eastman School of Music, Rochester, New York; Advanced conducting studies with Eugene Ormandy, George Szell, Sir Thomas Beecham, Eduard van Beinum, Herbert von Karajan, Otto Klemperer, 1955-58. *Career:* Teacher, Pennsylvania State University, 1953-55; Music Director, Altoona (Pa) Symphony Orchestra, 1953-56; Johnstown (Pa) Symphony Orchestra, 1955-56; Associate Conductor 1957-61, Resident Conductor 1961-62, Music Director 1962-70, Dallas Symphony Orchestra; Teacher, Southern Methodist University, 1958-62; Hockaday School, 1962-65; Associate Conductor, Pittsburgh Symphony Orchestra, 1970-80; Director, Pittsburgh Chamber Orchestra, 1970-80; Music

Director, Honolulu Symphony Orchestra, 1979-; Artistic Director, Hawaii Opera Theatre, 1979-83; Guest conducting engagements with various orchestras at home and abroad. *Recordings:* For Turnabout; Vox; Marco Polo and Naxos. *Honours:* American Symphony Orchestra League and Rockefeller Foundation advanced study grants, 1955-58; Winner, Netherlands Radio Union conducting competition, 1957. *Membership:* American Federation of Musicians. *Address:* c/o Honolulu Symphony Orchestra, 1441 Kapiolani Boulevard Suite 1515, Honolulu, Hawaii 96814, USA.

JOHANSSON Eva, b. 25 Feb 1958, Copenhagen, Denmark. Singer (Soprano). *Education:* Studied at the Copenhagen Conservatory, 1977-81; Opera School of the Royal Opera Copenhagen, 1981-84; Juilliard School, New York, with Oren Brown. *Career:* Sang at the Royal Opera Copenhagen, 1982-88 as the Countess in Figaro (debut), Tatiana, Pamina, Marie in Wozzeck and Chrysothemis (Elektra); Guest appearances in Oslo as Marie and Donna Anna (1985, 1987); Marie at the Paris Opera, 1986; Sang in productions of Der Ring des Nibelungen at Berlin and Bayreuth, 1988, as Gutrune and as Freia and Gerhilde; Sang Freia in a concert performance of Das Rheingold at Paris, 1988, conducted by Daniel Barenboim; Vienna Staatsoper, 1989, as Fiordiligi; Tel Aviv 1990 as Donna Anna in Don Giovanni, conducted by Claudio Abbado; since 1990 Elsa inLohengrin at Bayreuth, Guest appearances in Barcellona, Munich, Dresden, Stuttgart, Cologne, and Hamburg; Debut as Donna Anna, at Covent Garden, 1992; Freia and Gerhilde at the 1992 Bayreuth Festival. *Recordings:* Das Rheingold conducted by Bernard Haitink (EMI); Es War Einmal, by Zemlinsky (Capriccio). *Address:* Buhnenagentur Mariannne Bottger, Dahlmannstrasse 9, D-1000 Berlin 12, Germany.

JOHNS Donald Charles, b. 9 June 1926, Chicago, Illinois, USA. Professor of Music, Emeritus. m. Jorun Bormann Milch, 22 Mar 1955, 2 sons, 1 daughter. *Education:* BMus, 1951, MMus, 1952, PhD, 1960, Northwestern University; Reifezeugnis, Hochschule fur Musik und Darstellende Kunst, Vienna, Austria, 1956. *Career:* Jazz Musician and Arranger, Chicago, 1948-50; Professor of Music, University of California, Riverside, 1957-. *Compositions:* Numerous works including Organ Mass; Fantasia quasi Sonata; Triptych on Aberystwyth; Introduction and Passacaglia; Meditations, Three Partitas on Early American Hymnns for organ; Prelude, Aria and Finale for trumpet and organ; Magnificat, for chorus and organ; Concerto Piccolo, for strings, flute, clarinet and timpani; several motets SAB and SSAA, among others. *Recording:* Praise Ye the Lord, California Boys' Choir. *Publications:* Johann Nepomuk Davids Choralwerk: A Study in the Evolution of a Contemporary Liturgical Organ Style, 1960; Three Partitas on Early American Hymnns for organ, 1992. *Address:* Department of Music, University of California, Riverside, CA 92521, USA.

JOHNS Marian Evelyn Johnson, b. 8 Nov 1920, North Carolina, USA. m. Church Musician (Classical). m. Malcolm M Johns, 2 Oct 1942, 1s, 1d. *Education:* BMus, Salem College; Private lessons in piano, violin, voice, clarinet, oboe, trumpet, cello. *Debut:* Began conducting church choirs at age of 14; Formed and conducted All Women Orchestra, at age of 18. *Career:* Teacher, Vocal and Instrumental pre WWII; Co-Founder with husband, Grosse Pte, Community Chorus, 1952; Director of GP Memorial Ch Youth Choirs, 1956-74; Asst Conductor, Old Christ Church, 1974-87; Choir Director, Assumption Church, 1987. *Publications include:* Editor: Heinz Werner Zimmermann's Psalmkonzert, 1967; Berliner Te Deum, 1992; Numerous short works; Co-Editor, Hugo Distler's Totentanz, 1967-. *Honours:* Moravian Music Foundation, Board, 1984-92; Honorary Life Member, Detroit Chapter, American Guild of Organists. *Memberships:* RCCO; AGO; American Recorder Society; Faculty Wives of Wayne State University. *Hobbies:* Church tours; Coordinating Weddings; Picture Framing; Music by Computer; German translations. *Address:* 906-

3663 Riverside Drive East, Windsor, Ontario N8Y 4V3, Canada.

JOHNS William, b. 2 Oct 1936, Tulsa, Oklahoma, USA. Singer (Tenor). *Education:* Studied in New York. *Debut:* Lake George 1967, as Rodolfo in La Bohème. *Career:* Sang with the Bremen Opera as the Prince in The Love of Three Oranges and the Duke of Mantua; Welsh National Opera 1970-72, as Radames and Calaf; Further appearances in Cologne, Dusseldorf, Dallas, Hamburg, Bregenz, Houston, Vienna, Aix-en-Provence, Rome and New York (Metropolitan Opera); Covent Garden debut 1987, as Bacchus in Ariadne auf Naxos; Philadelphia Opera 1988, as Florestan in Fidelio; Holland Festival 1989, as Siegfried in a concert performance of Götterdämmering; Other roles include Wagner's Lohengrin, Tannhäuser, Siegmund and Tristan, Huon (Oberon), the Emperor in Die Frau ohne Schatten, Jason in Medea in Corinto by Mayr, Hoffmann and Verdi's Otello; Sang Tristan at San Francisco, 1991. *Address:* c/o San Francisco Opera, War Memorial Opera House, San Francisco, CA 94102, USA.

JOHNSEN Dan, b. 17 June 1951, Copenhagen, Denmark. Musician. 1 son. *Education:* Music Pedagogy Examination, Royal Danish Conservatory, 1978. *Career:* Tribunen Theatre, 1978-86; Folketeatret, 1979-83; Radio programmes: Glæde over Danmark, 1979; Morgensange, 1982; Gammel Kærlighed, 1986; Film: Besøget, 1984; TV programme: Cikaden, 1985; Lyngby-Review, 1992. *Compositions:* I'm In No Hurry, 1971; I'm So Sleepy/Bake Your Own Cake, 1971; Månen i sommerlandet, 1981; Alle et livs gode dage, 1981; Kom ud og leg, 1981; Flyvende farver, 1981; Sangen om Niels Ebbesen, 1981; Incidental music for: Kildekabaret (Christian Kronman); Cobra Cabaret (Christian Kronman); Lirekassen (Torben Jetsmark); Et Drømmespil (August Strindberg); Aladdin (Adam Oehlenschläger); Comedy of Errors (William Shakespeare); Det ka' vi alle li' (Hanne Eir), 1986; Livet må vi passe på (Hanne Eir), 1988; Det blæser (Hanne Eir), 1986; Bager-tarantel (Hanne Eir), 1988; Når jeg bager er jeg glad (Hanne Eir), 1988; Incidental music for: Hvordan Maui får solen til at gå langsomt over himlen (Hanne Eir), 1987; Gøglerens Lærling (Anders Ramberg), 1989; Blomstersang (Hanne Eir), 1990; Jeg sidder på en stjerne (Hanne Eir), 1990; En rejse i tiden (Mogens Johansen), 1991. *Address:* Møllegården, Byskovvej 34, Hjortespring, 2730 Herlev, (Copenhagen), Denmark.

JOHNSON Camellia, b. 1960, Delaware, USA. Singer (Soprano). *Education:* Studied at Daytona Beach, Florida and the Manhattan School of Music, New York. *Debut:* Strawberry Woman, in Porgy and Bess at the Metropolitan, 1985. *Career:* Sang in Porgy and Bess at Glyndebourne 1986 and Helsinki, 1989, 1992; Season 1992-93, in Don Carlos at San Francisco and as Aida at Michigan; Beethoven's Ninth in Indianapolis and Montreal; Verdi's Requiem with the Saint Louis Symphony and the Long Island Philharmonic; Metropolitan Opera as Sarena in Porgy and Bess, High Priestess in Aida and Madelon in Andrea Chenier; Mozart's Solemn Vespers and Requiem with the Cincinnati Symphony; Other repertoire includes the Four Last Songs of Strauss, Les Nuits d'Ete, Schubert's Rosamunde; Rossini's Stabat Mater and Beethoven's Missa Solemnis.*Recordings:* Porgy and Bess. *Address:* c/o IMG Artists, Media House, 3 Burlington Lane, London W4 2TH, England.

JOHNSON Christopher Charles, b. 17 Dec 1962, Congleton, Cheshire. Composer; Arranger; Director. *Education:* BA, Hons., Music, Huddersfield Polytechnic, 1984; Countess of Munster Scholarship, 1984; Postgraduate Diploma in Advanced Composition, Guildhall School of Music & Drama, 1984-85. *Career:* Freelance Composer/Arranger, 1985-; Music Assistant, All Souls Church, Langham Place, London; Music Editor, Collins Liturgical Publications; Composer/Arranger, BBC TV and Radio; Musical Director; Pianist. *Publications:* Editor, Sing Alleluia. *Honours:* One of 8 winners, BBC Songs of Praise Competition for New Hymns, 1988. *Memberships:* Composers Guild of Great

Britain; Performing Rights Society; Society for the Promotion of New Music. *Address:* Flat 4 139 Cleveland Street, London W1P 5PH, England.

JOHNSON David (Carl), b. 30 Jan 1940, Batavia, New York, USA. Composer; Flautist. *Education:* Studied composition with Donald Keats and David Epatein at Antioch College; Leon Kirchner at Harvard University and Nadia Boulanger in Paris, 1964-65; Further study in Cologne. *Career:* Teacher at the Rheinische Musikschule Cologne, 1966-67; Worked with Stockhausen in the creation of Hymnen at the studios of West German Radio; Member of the Stockhausen ensemble at the Osaka World Fair, 1970; Co-founded Feedback Studio at Cologne, 1970; Director of the electronic music studio at the Basle Music Academy, 1975. *Compositions:* Five movements for flute, 1962; Bells for flute, guitar and cello, 1964; Thesis for string quartet, 1964; 3 Pieces for string quartet, 1964; 3 Pieces for string quartet, 1966; Tonantiton for tape, 1968; Process of Music for tape and instruments, 1970; Sound- environment pieces Music Makers, Gyromes mit & fur Elise, Cybernet, Gehlhaar, Organica I'IV and Klangkoffer, 1969-74; Proganica for speaker and 2 electric organs, 1973; Audioliven for flute and electronics, 1976; In Memoriam Uschi for tape and 3 instruments, 1977; Jadermann incidental music to play by Hoffmansthal, 1980; Bach: Encounter of the Third Kind, stage piece, 1981; Calls in Search, for tape, 1981. *Address:* c/o ASCAP, ASCAP Building, One Lincoln Plaza, New York, NY 10023, USA.

JOHNSON David Charles, b. 27 Oct 1942, Edinburgh, Scotland. Composer; Musical Historian; Writer; Music Publisher; Performer, cello. 1 son. *Education:* MA, Aberdeen; BA, PhD, Cambridge. *Career:* Various lecturing, including Tutor in musical history, Edinburgh University, 1988-91; Cellist of The McGibbon Ensemble; Organised recitals for the Edinburgh Festival, 1975, 1985, 1986, 1988; Founded self-publishing company, 1990. *Compositions:* Four operas, church music, piobaireached for solo recorder, God, man, and the animals, soprano and instruments, Guess who I met last night?, two school ensembles and symphony orchestra, Piano trio, Sonatas for violin, trumpet and cello, all with piano, Seven MacDiarmid Songs, soprano, trumpet, piano, other songs, chamber and orchestral music. *Publications:* Music and Society in Lowland Scotland, 1972; various editions of 18th century Scottish instrumental music; ed, Ten Georgian Glees for four voices, 1981; contributions to the New Grove Dictionary, 1981; Scottish Fiddle Music in the 18th Century, 1984; The Scots Cello Book, 1990; Stepping Northward, 1990; Scots on the Fiddle, 1991. *Membership:* Music Publishers' Association, PRS, MCPS. *Address:* 1 Hill Square, Edinburgh EH8 9DR, Scotland.

JOHNSON Douglas, b. 1958, California, USA. Singer (tenor). *Education:* Studied at the University of Los Angeles. *Career:* Appearances in Les Dialogues des Carmelites, La Fille du Regiment and La Clemenza di Tito while a student; Sang at Aachen, 1984-87, notably as Don Ottavio, Handel's Serse, Jacquino, Count Almaviva, Rinuccio in Gianni Schicchi Belmonte and the Steuermann; Hanover, 1988-89, Frankfurt am Main, from 1989, notably as Tamino; Salzburg Festival, 1987, 1991 in Moses und Aron and as Arbace in Idomeneo; Guest appearances at Hamburg (Chateauneuf in Zar und Zimmermann), Deutsche Oper Berlin (Nicolai's Fenton), Vienna Staatsoper (Tamino), Cologne (Nemorino, 1987) and Ludiwgshafen (Gualterio in Vivaldi's Griselda, 1989); Sang Rossini's Almaviva at Seattle, 1992. *Recordings include:* L'Oca del Cairo by Mozart. *Address:* c/o Stadtische Buhnen, Untermainanlage 11, 6000 Frankfurt am Main, Germany.

JOHNSON Emma, b. 20 May 1966, Barnet, Hertfordshire, England. Clarinettist. *Education:* Pembroke college, Cambridge University; Studied with John Brightwell, Sidney Fell. *Debut:* Barbican London, 1985. *Career:* Appearances with ECO, London Symphony orchestra, Ulster Orchestra, Royal Liverpool Philharmonic Orchestra, Hallé Orchestra, City of London Sinfonia and Royal Philharmonic Orchestra; Debut in Vienna at the Musikverein, 1985; French Debut, with Polish Chamber Orchestra, 1986; Performances in Holland, Finland, and Monte Carlo; TV and Radio appearances in United Kingdom; Japanese debut, Tokyo, 1990; New York debut, 1992. *Recordings:* Mozart Clarinet Concerto, 1984; Crusell Clarinet Concerto No. 2, 1985; Bottesini Duo for Clarinet and Double Bass, with Tom Martin, 1986; Weber Clarinet Concerto No 1. 1987; Recital Disc La Clarinette Française with Gordon Back, 1988; The Romantic Clarinet (concertos by Weber, Spohr and Crusell); Finzi and Stanford Concertos with Royal Philharmonic Orchestra, 1992; Recital of Encores, 1992; Michael Berkeley Concerto, 1993. *Honours:* BBC TV Young Musician of the Year, 1984; Bronze Award European Young Musician of the Year Compeition, Geneva, 1984; Voted Young Professional All Music Musician, 1986, Wavendon All Music Awards. *Hobbies:* Literature; Theatre; Cinema. *Current Management:* Artist Management International Ltd, Ghenrietta Street, London WC2E 8LA, England.

JOHNSON Gordon James, b. 25 Oct 1949, St Paul, Minnesota, USA. Music Director; Conductor. *Education:* BS, Bemidji State University, 1971; MS, Northwestern University, 1977; DMA, University of Oregon. *Career:* Associate Professor of Music, College of Great Falls (Montana), 1981-present; Conductor, University of Oregon Sinfoniette, 1981-82; Music Director, Conductor, Great Falls Symphony Association, Montana, 1982-; Music Director, Conductor, Glacier Orchestra, Kalispell, Montana, 1984-; Guest Conductor, Spokane Symphony Orchestra, 1984, Dubuque Symphony Orchestra, 1985, Cheyenne Symphony Orchestra, Charlotte Symphony Orchestra, Spokane Symphony Orchestra and Lethbridge Symphony Orchestra, Alberta, Canada, 1986, West Shore Symphony, Michigan 1988, Kumamoto Symphony, Japan, May 1991; Kankakee Symphony, Illinois, 1993; Toulon Symphony, France, 1994; Music Director of Amy Grant's Coming Home For Christmas, NBC Television special; Artistic Director, Flathead Festival (Montana), 1988-. *Recordings:* Mendelssohn's Elijah; Sound Design. *Address:* 1608 Fourth Avenue North, Great Falls, MT 59401, USA.

JOHNSON Graham Rhodes, b. 10 July 1950, Rhodesia. Concert Accompanist. *Education:* Royal Academy of Music, London; FRAM, 1984; FGSM, Guildhall School, 1988. *Debut:* Wigmore Hall, 1972. *Career:* Accompanist to Brigitte Fasabaender, Elisabeth Schwarzkopf, Jessye Norman, Victoria de los Angeles (USA tour 1977), Janet Baker, Peter Pears, Felicity Lott, Margaret Price (USA Tour, 1985), Peter Schreier, John Shirley Quirk, Tom Krause; work with contemporaries led to formation of The Songmakers' Almanac (Artistic Director); has devised and accompanied more than 150 London recitals for this group since Oct. 1976; Tours of USA with Sarah Walker, Richard Jackson and of Australia and New Zealand with the Songmakers' Almanac, 1981; Writer & Presenter, major BBC Radio 3 series on Poulenc Songs, and BBC TV series on Schubert songs; Lecturer, song courses, Savonlinna, Finland, USA and at Pears-Britten School, Snape; Artistic Advisor and Accompanist, Alte Oper Festival, Frankfurt, 1981-82; Appearances at Salzburg, Hohenems, Munich Festivals. *Recordings:* Recitals for Chandos, Harmonia Mundi, Meridian and Virgin; Recital with Felicity Lott and Ann Murray (EMI); Projected complete cycle of Schubert Lieder for Hyperion; Gramophone solo vocal award, 1989, for recital with Janet Baker; Records with Elly Ameling, Peter Schreier, Arleen Anger, Thomas Hampson, Margaret Price, Lucia Popp. *Publications:* (Contributor) The Britten Companion, Editor Christopher Palmer, 1984; Contributor, Gerald Moore, The Unashamed Accompanist, revised edition 1984; reviews in TLS; The Spanish Song Companion, 1992. *Hobby:* Eating in Good Restaurants with Friends and Fine Wine. *Current Management:* Lies Askonas Ltd. *Address:* 83 Fordwych Road, London NW2 3TL, England.

JOHNSON James David, b. 7 Aug 1948, Greenville, South Carolina. Concert Pianist; Professor of Music; Organist-Choirmaster. m. Karen Elizabeth Jacobson, 1 Feb 1975. *Education:* B.Mus., 1970, M.Mus., 1972, DMA, 1976, University of Arizona; Master, Church Music, Westminster Choir College, 1986. *Debut:* Soloist with the Greenville (SC) Symphony, aged 13, 1962. *Career:* Performances with: Royal Philharmonic, London, England, Boston Pops, Victoria Symphony (BC), Yugoslavian National Radio Orchestra, Anchorage and Fairbanks Symphonies; Chamber Musician with Alaska Trio, the Cambridge String Quartet and North Star Consort. *Recordings:* Chaminade, Concertstück; Dohnányi Five Piano Pieces, Orion Records, 1977 (Chosen for inclusion on Clavier Magazine's Ten Best List); Mendelssohn: Concerto in D Minor, Concerto in G Minor, Musical Heritage Society Records, 1978; Beethoven: Concerto No 1 in C Major, Musical Heritage Society, 1979/80. *Contributions to:* Various professional journals. *Address:* University of Alaska, Fairbanks, AK 99775, USA.

JOHNSON Marc, b. 1945, USA. Cellist. *Education:* Studied at the Eastman School of Music and Indiana University. *Career:* Played with the Rochester Philharmonic while a student; Solo appearances in Rochester and with the Denver Philharmonic; Recital and chamber concerts in Washington DC, St Louis and Baltimore; Founder member of the Vermeer Quartet at the Marlboro Festival, 1970: performances in all major US centres, Europe, Israel and Australia; Festival engagements at Tanglewood, Aspen, Spoleto, Edinburgh, Mostly Mozart (New York), Aldeburgh, South Bank, Santa Fe, Chamber Music West, and the Casals Festival; Resident quartet for Chamber Music Chicago; Annual master classes at the Royal Northern College of Music, Manchester; Member of the Resident Artists Faculty of Northern Illinois University. *Recordings:* Quartets by Beethoven, Dvořák, Verdi and Schubert (Teldec); Brahms Clarinet Quintet with Karl Leister (Orfeo). *Honours:* Denver Symphony and Washington International Competitions; Received title of Kämmersängen during the 1960's. *Address:* Allied Artists, 42 Montpelier Square, London SW7 1JZ, England.

JOHNSON Mary Jane, b. 22 Mar 1950, Pampa, Texas, USA. Singer (Soprano). *Education:* Studied at West Texas University, and elsewhere in USA. *Debut:* New York Lyric Opera as Agathe in Der Freischütz, 1981. *Career:* Philadelphia and Santa Fe, 1982, as Musetta and Rosalinde; Sang at the San Francisco Opera from 1983, as Freia in Das Rheingold, Jenifer in the US premiere of The Midsummer Marriage, 1983, Marguerite, and the Empress in Die Frau ohne Schatten; Washington Opera from 1984, Boston and Cincinnati from 1986; European engagements with Opera North at Leeds, Torre del Lago, (Puccini Festival), Bologna, Geneva and the Baths of Caraccala at Rome, (Minnie in La Fanciulla del West); Sang Salome at Santiago, 1990, Desdemona at Pittsburgh and Minnie at the 1991 Santa Fe Festival; Helen of Troy in Mefistofele at Chicago, 1991; La Scala and Opera Bastille, Paris, 1992 in the title role of Lady Macbeth of Mtsensk; Teatro Municipal Santiago as Senta in Der fliegende Holländer, 1992. Other roles include Mozart's Countess, Leonore, Alice in Falstaff, Tosca, Giulietta the Duchess of Parma in Busoni's Faust, and Mrs Jessel in The Turn of the Screw. *Address:* c/o Santa Fe Opera, PO Box 2408 Santa Fe, NM 87504, USA.

JOHNSON Nancy, b. 1954, California, USA. Singer (Soprano). *Education:* Studied at California State University, Hayward. *Career:* Sang at the Landestheater Detmold, 1980-81, Wiesbaden, 1981-82, Mannheim, 1982-87; Engaged at the Stuttgart Staatsoper from 1987 and has made guest appearances at Dusseldorf, the Vienna Staatsoper, San Francisco (Eva in Die Meistersinger, 1988); Other roles have included Manon Lescaut, and The Empress in Die Frau ohns Schatten (Mannheim, 1984). *Address:* c/o Stuttgart Staatsoper, Oberer Schlossgarten 6, 7000 Stuttgart, Germany.

JOHNSON Patricia, b. 1934, London, England. Singer (Mezzo-Soprano). *Education:* Vocal studies with Maria Linker in London. *Career:* Sang at Sadler's Wells Opera as Carmen, Dalila and Azucena; Basle Opera from 1957, notably in the title role of La Cenerentola; Deutsche Oper Berlin from 1961, as Azucena, Eboli, and Fricka; Sang in the premiere of Der junge Lord by Henze 1965 and in Lulu (Countess Geschwitz) and La Calisto, 1975; Salzburg Festival, 1962-63, as Marcellina in Le Nozze di Figaro; Glyndebourne Festival, 1965-68, as Jane Seymour in Anna Bolena, the Sorceress in Dido and Aeneas and Storge in Jephtha; Sang the Countess de Coigny in Andrea Chénier at Covent Garden, 1985; Deutsche Oper Berlin, 1989, in Katya Kabanova (Kabanichka); Sang Dorabella at Salzburg & Lady Billows at Glyndebourne, with video; BBCs Lady Macbeth; Many appearances in concerts and oratorios. *Recordings:* Lulu, Der junge Lord, Le Nozze di Figaro, Dido and Aeneas (Deutsche Grammophon); Video of Andrea Chénier. *Address:* c/o Deutsche Oper Berlin, Richard Wagnerstrasse 10, D-1000 Berlin, Germany.

JOHNSON Robert, b. 10 Dec 1940, Moline, Illinois, USA. Singer (Tenor). *Education:* Studied at Northwestern University in Evanston and at New York. *Debut:* New York City Opera, 1971, as Count Almaviva. *Career:* Sang in New York, Chicago, Baltimore, Houston, New Orleans and Washington as Mozart's Ferrando, Beomote and Tamino; Ernesto, Beppo in Donizetti's Rita, Alfrdo, Fento in Falstaff, Hoffmann, Rodolfo, Sali in A Village Romeo and Juliet and Tome Rakewell; Frequent concert appearances. *Address:* c/o New York City Opera, Lincoln Center, New York, NY 10023, USA.

JOHNSON Russell, b. 14 Sept 1923, Pennsylvania, USA. Architect; Acoustics Designer. *Education:* B.Arch, Yale University, 1951. *Career:* Consultant on Meyerson Symphony Centre, Dallas, Texas, 1981-87; Concert Hall, Birmingham, England, 1984-87; Royal Concert Hall, Nottingham, England, 1979-83; Derngate Centre, Northampton, England, 1979-83; Jack Singer Concert Hall, Calgary, Alberta, Canada, 1974-84; El Pomar Great Hall, Colorado Springs, Colorado, 1981-85; Tampa Centre for the Performing Arts, Tampa, Florida, 1979-87; Palm Beach Centre for The Arts, Palm Beach, Florida, 1984-87; Opera House, National Arts Centre, Ottawa, Canada, 1967-75; Acoustics Adviser to the Royal Opera House on upgrading the main auditorium, Covent Garden, London, 1980-87; Acoustic Design, Hamilton Place, Hamilton, Ontario, Canada, 1969-75. *Memberships:* Acoustical Society of America; United States Institute of Theater Technology. *Hobby:* Sailing.

JOHNSON Theodore, b. 9 Oct 1929, Indiana, USA. Professor of Music. m. Carol A Jolliff, 22 June 1968, 2 sons. 2 daughters. *Education:* BMus, 1951, MMus, 1952, DMa, 1959, University of Michigan. *Career:* Music Faculty, University of Kansas; Professor of Music, Michigan State University; Concertmaster, Lansing Symphony Orchestra, 1967-69; Concertmaster, Grand Rapids Symphony, 1972-73; Principal Violist, Lansing Symphony, 1982-86; Beaumont String Quartet, 1964-80; Recitalist and Chamber Musician; Chair of Music Theory, Michigan State University, 1984-88. *Compositions:* Here on the Cross he Lies; Trust in the Lord with All you Heart. *Publications:* An analytical survey of the fifteen two-part inventions by J S Bach, 1982; An analytical survey of the fifteen Sinfonies (three part inventions) by J S Bach, 1986. *Honours:* Rackham Fellowship, 1957-58; Fulbright Scholarship, 1956-57; Stanley Medal, University of Michigan, 1951. *Memberships:* PHi Kappa Lambda; Phi Mu Alpha; Phi Kappa Phi; Phi Eta Sigma. *Address:* 651 Hillcrest Avenue, East Lansing, Michigan 48823, USA.

JOHNSON Tom, b. 18 Nov 1939, Greeley, Colorado, USA. Composer. *Education:* BA, 1961, M.Mus., 1967, Yale University; private study with Morton Feldman. *Career:* Music Critic, Village Voice, New York, 1971-82; Freelance Composer, 1982-. *Compositions include:* (Operas) The Four Note Opera, 1972; The Masque of Clouds, 1975; Riemannoper, 1988; (Musical Scores) Spaces, 1969; An Hour for Piano, 1971; Septapede,

1973; Verses for Alto Flute, Horn and Harp, 1974; Verses for Viola, 1976; Trinity, SATB, 1978; Dragons in A, 1979; Movements for Wind Quintet, 1980; Harpiano, 1982; Predictables, 1984; Voicings for Four Pianos, 1984; Tango, 1984; Choral Catalogue, 1985; Pascal's Triangle, 1987. *Publications:* Imaginary Music, 1974; Private Pieces, 1976; Symmetries, 1981; Rational Melodies, 1982.

JOHNSSON Bengt Gustaf, b. 17 July 1921, Copenhagen, Denmark. Professor; Pianist; Organist. m. Esther Paustian, 1 daughter. *Education:* Musicology, MA, 1947, University of Copenhagen; Piano Studies with Georg Vasarhelyi and Walter Gieseking; Degree as Organist and Church Musician, 1945, Royal Academy of Music, Copenhagen. *Debut:* Copenhagen, 1944. *Career:* Concert Tours and Broadcasts, Scandinavia, German Federal Republic, Switzerland, France and Netherlands; Recitals in many European countries, Tour of USA, 1964; Organist, Danish Broadcasting, 1949-70; Teacher, Royal Academy, Copenhagen, 1958-61; Professor, Royal Academy of Music, Aarhus, Jutland; Numerous masterclasses held; Studied at Vatican Library, Rome, Italy, 1977, Benedictine Monastery of Montserrat, Spain, 1978, 1980-83; Invited to study in Libraries in Barcelona and Montserrat by Spanish Cultural Department, 1979, 1983. *Recordings include:* N. W. Gade Piano Music; Rissager, Complete Piano Works; Chamber Music of Beethoven, Brahms, Busoni; Roman Organ and Harpsichord Music from the Seventeenth Century, 1982; Rued Langgaard: Piano music, 1985; Catalan Organ Music, 1988. *Publications include:* History of the Danish School of Music until 1739, 1973; Roman Organ Music for the 17th Century; Roman Harpsichord Music from the 17th Century; Piano Music of Manuel Blasco de Nebra, 1984 (Bronze Medal Winner, The International Book Messe, Leipzig 1986); 23 Piano Sonatas of Josep Galles, 1984. Editor: Hans Mikkelsen Ravn; The Vatican Manuscript, 1981; Heptachordum Danicum 1646 (translation with historical comments and studies in sources) 1977; Selected Sonatas of D. Scarlatti including first edition of four new editions, 1985; Selected Piano Music of N. W. Gade, 1986; Catalan Organ Music of the 18th Century, 1986; Scarlatti Vol.II (Henle, W.Germany), 1988; Niels W. Gade: Klavierwerke, 1989; Piano Music for Franz Liszt, 1989; Scarlatti Vol.III, Henle, w Germany, 1992; In preparation: Selected Piano Works of Rued Langgaard, 1994. *Address:* Porsevænget 18, Kgs Lyngby DK-2800, Copenhagen.

JOHNSTON Albert Richard, b. 7 May 1917, Chicago, Illinois, USA. Composer; Administrator. m. Yvonne Jeanne-Marie Guiguet, 13 Aug 1949, 1 son 2 daughters. *Education:* Music Baccalaureat, Northwestern University, Illinois, 1942; M Mus, 1945, PhD, 1951, University of Rochester, New York. *Career:* Frequent appearances on CBC (Canada) as composer, conductor, commentator, interviewer, critic. Music Archivist, University of Calgary. *Compositions:* The Irish Book (songs); Songs for Today (education) 9 vols; Folk Songs of Canada I & II; Folk Songs North America Sings. *Recordings:* Suite for Bassoon and Piano; Folk Love Canadian Style - voice and piano; Folk Songs of Canada. *Publications:* Zoltan Kodály in Education (3 vols) editor; The Poetry of James Nicoll (Canadian poet). *Address:* RR 4, Calgary, Alberta, Canada T2M 4L4.

JOHNSTON Ben(jamin) Burwell, b. 15 Mar 1926, Macon, Georgia, USA. Composer; Teacher. *Education:* College of William and Mary, AB, 1949, Cincinnati Conservatory of Music, MM, 1950, Mills College, MA, 1953. *Career:* Faculty member, University of Illinois, 1951-83. *Compositions:* Operas: Gertrude, or Would She be Pleased to Receive It?, 1965; Carmilla, 1970; Ballets: St Joan, 1955; Gambit, 1959; Orchestral: Concerto for Brass, 1951; Passacaglia and Epilogue, 1955-60; Quintet for Groups, 1966; Symphony, 1988; Chamber: 9 string quartets; Septet for Wind Quintet, Cello, and Bass, 1956-58; Knocking Piece for 2 Percussionists and Piano, 1962; Trio for Clarinet, Violin, and Cello, 1982; The Demon Lover's Doubles for Trumpet and Microtonal Piano, 1985; Piano pieces;

Choruses; Songs. *Honours:* Guggenheim Fellowship, 1959-60. *Address:* c/o Music Department, University of Illinois, Urbana-Champaign, Urbana, IL 61801, USA.

JOHNSTON Richard, b. 7 May 1917, Chicago, Illinois, USA. Music Educator; Professor and Chairman of Division of Theory and Composition, University of Calgary; Composer. *Education:* Obtained Baccalaureate in Composition from Northwestern University, 1942; Studied with Nadia Boulanger, Madison, Wisconsin, 1942-44; MMus, 1945; PhD, 1951 (both in composition), Eastman School of Music, University of Rochester, NY. *Career:* Teacher, Piano and Theory, Luther College, Nebraska, 1942-44; Together with Nadia Boulanger gave world premiere performance of Stravinsky's Sonata for Two Pianos; Teaching Fellow, Eastman School of Music, University of Rochester, NY, 1944-47; Professor of Music Theory and Composition, University of Toronto, 1947-68; during his years in Toronto frequently served Canadian Broadcasting Corporation as composer, arranger, commentator and conductor; Director, Summer School of Royal Conservatory of Music, 1962-; Dean of Faculty of Fine Arts, 1968-73; Professor and Chairman of Division of Theory and Composition, Department of Music, University of Calgary, 1973-; Co-founder of both Canadian Music Educators' Association and Canadian Folk Music Society. *Compositions include:* Orchestral: Canticle of The Sun, 1962; March MS, 1953; Portraits, 1972; Suite for Bassoon and Orchestra, 1946; Symphony No. 1, 1950. Chamber Music: Duo Concertante for Violin and Piano, 1979. *Recordings:* Folk Songs of Canada (excerpts); Folk Songs of Canada (excerpts - Les Raftsmen, When the Ice Worms Nest Again, Mary Ann; Huron Carol; Suite for Bassoon and Piano. *Address:* Dept of Music, University of Alberta, 3-82 Fine Arts Building, Edmonton, Alta T6G 2C9, Canada.

JOHNSTONE Harry Diack, b. 29 Apr 1935, Vancouver, Canada. University Lecturer. m. Jill Margaret Saunders, 5 Aug 1960, dec 8 Apr 1989. 1 son, 1 daughter. *Education:* Royal College of Music, London, 1954-57; Balliol College, Oxford, 1957-63; MA, DPhil (Oxon), 1968; B.Mus (TCD); FRCO; FTCL; ARCM. *Career:* Assistant Organist, New College, Oxford, 1960-61; Assistant Lecturer, Music, University of Reading, 1963; Lecturer, 1965; Senior Lecturer, 1970, Tutorial Fellow, Music, St Anne's College, Oxford; Lecturer, Music, St John's, 1980; Visiting Professor, Music, Memorial University, St John's, Newfoundland, 1983. *Publications:* Editor and part author of the Blackwell History of Music in Britain IV: The Eighteenth Century, 1990; Editor, Maurice Greene: Cambridge Ode and Anthem, Musica Britannica 58, 1991. Numerous editions of 18th century music, mainly English; also articles and reviews in The Musical Times, Music and Letters, Proceedings of the Royal Musical Association, Organists' Review, The New Grove. *Address:* Faculty of Music, University of Oxford, St Aldate's, Oxford, OX1 1DB, England.

JOLAS Betsy, b. 5 Aug. 1926, Paris, France. Composer; Professor of Composition & Advanced Analysis. m. Gabriel Illouz 27 Aug. 1949, 2 sons, 1 daughter. *Education:* French Baccalaureat; Studied composition with Paul Boepple, piano with Helen Schnabel and organ with Carl Weinrich and graduated from Bennington College, USA 1940-46; Studied with Darius Milhaud, Simone Ple-Caussade and Olivier Messiaen, Conservatoire National de Paris, 1946. *Career:* Replaced Oliver Messiaen at his course at the Paris Conservatory, 1971-74; Appointed to Faculty, 1975; Other teaching positions include: Tanglewood, Yale, Darius Milhaud Chair at Mills College, Berkeley, University of Southern California and San Diego University, USA. *Compositions include:* Episode Sixieme pour Alto, 1983; Trois Duos Pour Tuba et Piano, 1983; O Wall, for wind quintet, 1976; Well Met, ensemble, 1973; Points D'Aube, ensemble & soloist; Preludes Fanfares Interludes Sonneries, wind orchestra and percussion, 1983; Trois Rencontres, string trio and orchestra, 1973; Sonate à 12 for 12 voice soloists a capella, 1970; Motet II; Le Pavillon au bord de la rivière; Quatuor II for colorature and string trio, 1964; Tales of a Summer Sea for Orchestra, 1977; Stances for Piano and orchestra, 1978; Liring Ballade for Baritone and orchestra, 1980; Le Cyclope - opera, 1986; Schliemann opera in 3 Acts, 1990; Points d'or our 1 saxophone et 15 instruments, 1982; Trio Les Heures, 1990.*Recordings:* Stances, J.D.E. Points d'aube - D'un opéra de voyage, CD Ades 14. 087-2. *Honours include:* Prizewinner, International Conducting Competition, Besançon, 1953; Copley Foundation of Chicago, 1954; ORTF, 1961; American Academy of Arts, 1973, Grand Prix De La SACEM, 1982; Member of the American Institute of Arts and Letters, 1983; Grand Prix National de la Musique, 1974; Grand Prix de la Ville de Paris, 1981; Prix International Maurice Ravel, 1992; Personnalité de l'année, 1992.*Memberships:* The American Academy of Arts and Letters, 1983. *Address:* 12 Rue Bonaparte, 75006 Paris, France.

JOLL Philip, b. 14 Mar 1954, Merthyr Tydfil, Wales. Singer (Baritone). *Education:* Studied at the Royal Northern College of Music with Nicholas Powell and Frederick Cox; Further study at the National Opera Studio in London. *Career:* Sang with English National Opera from 1979, as Donner and The Dutchman; Welsh National Opera as Wotan (also with the company at Covent Garden, 1986), Kurwenal, Amfortas, Chorebus in The Trojans, The Forester (Cunning Little Vixen), Onegin, Orestes, Don Fernando in Fidelio, Jochanaan in Salome and Barak in Die Frau ohne Schatten; Covent Garden debut 1982, in Salome: has returned in Der Freischütz, Das Rheingold and Die Frau ohne Schatten; German debut Frankfurt 1983, as Amfortas: has returned for The Dutchman; Guest appearances in Dusseldorf 1985-86, Berlin and Wiesbaden (with the Welsh National Company in The Midsummer Marriage, 1986); Metropolitan Opera debut 1988, as Donner in Das Rheingold; Australian debut as Jochanaan, for the Lyric Opera of Queensland, 1988; Bregenz Festival 1989, in Der fliegende Holländer; Lyric Opera of Queensland 1989-90, as Jochanaan in Salome and Marcello; Sang Orestes in Elektra for Welsh National Opera, 1992. *Recordings include:* The Greek Passion by Martinů (Supraphon); Amfortas in Parsifal (EMI); Kurwenal in Tristan und Isolde, conducted by Reginald Goodall (Decca). *Address:* c/o Ingpen & Williams Ltd., 14 Kensington Court, London W8 5DN, England.

JOLY Simon, b. 14 Oct 1952, Exmouth, Devon. Conductor; Repetiteur. *Education:* Corpus Christi College, Cambridge; BA, MA; ARCO; FRCO. *Career:* Music staff, Welsh National Opera, 1974-78; conducted The Barber of Seville, 1978; Assistant chorus master, English National Opera, 1978-79: associate chorus master, 1979-80; Currently Conductor of the BBC Singers, notably in contemporary music; Concerts with BBC Singers: Proms, 1990; Helsinki Biennale, 1991; Peter Grimes, Dublin, 1990; Nicholas Maw's, The Rising of the Moon, 1990 Wexford Festival; Guest conductor of the BBC Symphony Orchestra in works by Hindemith, Bax, Rubbra, Howells and Bedford, Koechlin, Franck, Walton, Debussy and Ives; BBC Philharmonic on 1986 German tour; BBC Welsh Symphony in Swiss music; Concerts with the English Chamber Orchestra and London and Bournemouth Sinfoniettas; Endymion Ensemble in Les Noces at the 1987 Proms and Birtwistle's ...agm...at the Barbican 1988; Opera performances for the BBC; The Bartered Bride for English National Opera; Gazzaniga'a Don Giovanni and Busoni's Turandot at 1988 Wexford Festival; Broadcast premieres of works by Jonathan Lloyd, James Ellis and Many others. *Hobbies:* Food; Cinema. *Address:* c/o Musikmakers, Little Easthall Farm House, St Paul's Walden, Herts, SG4 8DH, England.

JONAS Hilda Klestadt, b. 21 Jan 1913, Düsseldorf, Germany. Concert Harpsichordist and Pianist; Teacher of Harpsichord and Piano. m. Gerald Jonas, 30 Jan 1938, 2 daughters. *Education:* Hochschule für Musik, Cologne, 1932-33; Honour Diploma, Gumpert Conservatory, 1934; Studies with Professor Michael Wittels, Cologne, Rudolf Serkin, Switzerland, and

Wanda Landowska, Paris, France. *Career:* Concert soloist and recitalist worldwide: colleges, universities, museums and art centers - Harvard, Carnegie - Mellon, Cincinnati Taft Museum, Haifa Music Museum, Milano Centro Culturale San Fedele, Empire Saal of Schloss Esterházy, Eisenstadt Brussel's Musée Instrumental, Castello Buoncossiglio, Trento , Palais Wittgenstein, Düsseldorf, Stanford University, California, Palace of the Legion of Honor, San Francisco State University; Soloist with major symphony orchestras: Cleveland, Cincinnati; regular series and May festivals under Max Rudolf and Josef Krips, Honolulu, Oxford, Jerusalem, Strasbourg; Owner of private piano studio, Honolulu, Hawaii, USA, 1938-42, and Cincinnati, Ohio, 1942-75; Founder 1965, Director 1965-75, Harpsichord Festival Put-in-Bay, Ohio; Authority on Johann Sebastian Bach. *Recordings:* Sanjo-Music: Johann Sebastian Bach, Goldberg Variations Italian Concerto, Chromatic Fantasia and Fugue, Capriccio on the Departure of his Beloved Brother, Johann Kuhnau: "Six - Biblical Sonatas", Record for children of all ages, Listen Rebecca, the Harpsichord Sounds.... *Contributions to:* Various Music Magazines. *Memberships:* Life member, Hadassah; Life member, Brandeis University. *Address:* 50 Chumasero Drive 1-L, San Francisco, CA 94132, USA.

JONAS Peter, b. 14 Oct 1946, London, England. General Director, Bavarian State Opera, Munich. m. Lucy Hull, Nov 1989. *Education:* University of Sussex; Northern College of Music; Royal College of Music, London; Eastman School of Music, University of Rochester, USA; BA; LRAM. *Career:* Assistant to Music Director, 1974-76, Artistic Administrator, 1976-85, Chicago Symphony Orchestra; Director, Artistic Administration, Orchestral Association, Chicago, 1977-85; General Director, English National Opera, 1985-93; General Director (Staatsintendant), Bavarian State Opera, Munich 1993-; Board of Management, National Opera Studio, 1985-1993; Member of Council, Royal College of Music, 1988-; Fellow of the Royal College of Music (FRCM), 1989.*Honour:* CBE, 1993. *Membership:* Athenaeum; Fellow Royal Society of Arts. *Hobbies:* Cinema; 20th Century Architecture; Theatre. *Address:* c/o Bayerische Staatsoper, National Theater, Max Josph Platz 2, D-80539, Munich, Germany.

JONES Della, b. 13 Apr 1946, Neath, Wales. Singer (Mezzo-Soprano). *Education:* Studied at the Royal College of Music, London, and at the Centre Lyrique Opera School in Geneva. *Career:* Sang first at the Grand Théâtre, Geneva; Member of the English National Opera, 1977-82, in La Gazza Ladra, Il Barbiere di Siviglia, La Cenerentola, Le Comte Ory, Le Nozze di Figaro, Giulio Cesare, Orfeo, Carmen, L'Incoronazione di Poppea and La Forza del Destino; Has appeared with the Welsh National Opera in Les Troyens, Salome, Il Barbiere di Siviglia and Tristan und Isolde; Scottish Opera in L'Egisto, Hansel and Gretel and Don Giovanni; Appearances with Opera North as Rosina, and in La Cenerentola, Le Comte Ory, Die Meistersinger, Oedipus Rex and Salome; Other engagements with the English Music Theatre (world premiere of Tom Jones by Stephen Oliver and the Threepenny Opera); Dublin Opera and the Handel Opera Society; Baba the Turk in The Rake's Progress in Geneva and Venice; Ruggiero in Alcina for Los Angeles Opera; Sang Cecilio in Lucio Silla also La Finta Giardiniere for the Mostly Mozart Festival in New York; Other Festival appearances in London (English Bach), Cheltenham, Aldeburgh, Chester, Salisbury, Athens, Orange, throughout France, Switzerland and Edinburgh; Sang Preziosilla in La Forza del Destino for Scottish Opera, 1990, Ruggiero in Alcina at Geneva and the Théâtre du Châtelet, Paris; Mrs Noye in Noyes Fludde at the 1990 Promenade Concerts, Hermia in A Midsummer Night's Dream at Sadler's Wells, many other Prom Appearances including Last Night, 1993; Sang Marchesa Melibea at Covent Garden 1992 (Il Viaggio a Reims); Sang Gluck's Armide at the Baroque Festival Versailles, 1992; Welsh National Opera, 1994, as Ariodante. Concerts and recitals in the USSR, USA, Europe and Japan. *Recordings include:* Haydn's L'Incontro Improvviso and Il Ritorno di Tobia, conducted by Dorati (Philips); Alcina, conducted by Hickox; Marcellina in Le Nozze di Figaro and Elvira in Don

Giovanni, conducted by Arnold Oestmann; L'Incoronazione di Poppea; Donizetti's L'Assedio di Calais (Aurelio); Donizetti's, Rossini Stabat Mater and Arias, Bliss Pastoral, conducted by Richard Hickox, (Chandos); Recital of French Songs with Malcolm Martineau (Chandos); The Bear by Walton (Chandos); Dido in Dido & Aeneas (Teldec); Video of ENO production of Giulio Cesare (Sextus).

JONES Geraint Iwan, b. 16 May 1917, Porth, Glamorgan, Wales. Conductor, Organist and Harpsichordist. m. (1) M.A. Kemp, 1940. (2) Winifred Roberts, 1949, 1 daughter. *Education:* Caterham School; Royal Academy of Music. *Career:* Concert Organist, National Gallery Concerts, 1940-44; Conductor, Purcell's Dido and Aeneas, Mermaid Theatre, 1950-53; Founder, Geraint Jones Singers and Orchestra, 1951; Musical Director, Lake District Festival, 1960-78, Kirckman Concert Society, 1963-; Artistic Director, Salisbury Festival of the Arts, 1972-77, Manchester International Organ Festival, 1977-; Professor, Royal Academy of Music; Frequent Harpsichord Recitals with wife Winifred Roberts; Many frequent tours of Europe and America, 1948-. *Recordings:* Has recorded on most historic organs in Europe; Complete organ works of Bach in London, 1945-46 and 1955.*Publications:* Translations: Theorie-Pratique de la Facture de L'Orgue by Cliciquot, Robert Davy's Les Grandes Orgues de L'Abbatiale St Etienne dew Caen, both 1985. *Honour:* Grand Prix du Disque, 1959 and 1966. *Hobbies:* Photography; Antiques; Architecture; Motoring. *Address:* The Long House, Arkley Lane, Barnet Road, Arkley, Hertfordshire, England.

JONES Gordon, b. 1960, Northampton, England. Singer (Bass-baritone). *Education:* Studied at York University; Choral Scholarship to York Minster. *Career:* Concert engagements include visits to the Lincoln Center New York, the Royal Palace in The Hague, Hallé Orchestra, Martin's Le Vin Herbé at the Siena Festival and The Fairy Queen on tour in Italy; Performances of Berio's Sinfonia conducted by the composer, Simon Rattle and Esa Pekka-Salonen; Bach's St John and St Matthew Passions with the Choir of King's College, Cambridge; Sang in Arvo Pärt's St John Passion at the 1986 Almeida Festival and on tour of Britain 1988; Further engagements in Bristol and Aberdeen and at the Malvern and Aix-en-Provence Festivals; Bach's St John Passion with The Sixteen on to Spain. *Recordings:* Vierne's Les Angelus (Hyperion); Lully's Idylle pour la Paix (BBC); Schütz Schwanengesang and Bach Motets, with the Hilliard Ensemble; Pärt St John Passion (ECM). *Address:* Magenta Music International, 64 Highgate High Street, London N6 5HX, England.

JONES Gwyneth, (Dame) b. 7 Nov 1936, Pontenewynydd, Wales. Soprano. m. Till Haberfeld, 1 daughter. *Education:* Royal College of Music, London; Accademy Chigiana, Siena; Zurich International Opera Centre. *Career:* With Zurich Opera House, 1962-63; Royal Opera House, Covent Garden, 1963-; Vienna State Opera House, 1966-; Bavarian State Opera, 1967-; Guest Performances, numerous opera houses world wide including: La Scala, Milan; Rome Opera; Berlin State Opera; Munich State Opera; Hamburg; Paris; Metropolitan Opera, New York; San Francisco; Los Angeles; Zurich; Geneva; Dallas, Barcelona Chicago; Teatro Colon, Buenos Aires; Tokyo; Bayreuth Festival (debut 1966); Salzburg Festival; Arena di Verona; Edinburgh Festival; Welsh National Opera; Known for many opera roles including: Brünnhilde (Ring des Nibelungen), Marschallin (Rosenkavalier), Leonora, Il Trovatore; Desdemona, Otello; Aida, Turandot (Covent Garden 1990); Leonore, Fidelio (Beethoven); Senta, The Flying Dutchman; Medea; Elisabeth, Don Carlos; Madame Butterfly; Tosca; Donna Anna, Don Giovanni; Salome; Kundry, Parsifal; Helena, Aegyptische Helena; Dyer's Wife, Frau ohne Schatten (San Francisco 1989); Elektra, (Geneva 1990); Elisabeth/Venus, Tannhäuser; Sang Brunnhilde at San Francisco 1990, Covent Garden 1990/91; Sang the Dyer's Wife at Covent Garden, 1992, Los Angeles 1993; Wagner's Liebestod at the 1993 Prom Concerts, London; TV Films: Fidelio; Aida; Flying

Dutchman; Beethoven 9th Symphony; Tannhäuser; Poppea (Monteverdi); Rosenkavalier; Die Walküre, Siegfried, Götterdämmerung (Philips); Die Lustige Witwe; Turandot. *Honours:* CBE 1976; DBE 1986; Dr.hc University of Wales; Bundes Verdienstkreuz 1 Klasse; Honorary Member Vienna State Opera. *Recordings:* Decca; DGG; EMI; CBS. *Address:* PO Box, 8037 Zürich, Switzerland.

JONES Harold, b. 30 Jan 1936, Southport, Lancashire, England. Director of Music. m. Helen Richmond, 20 Dec 1969. *Education:* Trinity College of Music, London; MA, Keble College, Oxford University. *Career:* Director of Music, Monkton Combe School, Bath, 1969-86; Lecturer, Trinity College of Music, 1986-; Musical Director, Bath Opera, 1976-89; Director of Music, Church of St John Baptist, Bathwick, Bath, 1980-; Senior Lecturer, Head of the Junior Department, Trinity College of Music, London, 1987-; Examiner, Royal Military School of Music, Kneller Hall, 1988-. *Publications:* Theory of Music Workbooks, grades 1-8, Trinity College of Music, 1985. *Honour:* Honorary Fellow, Trinity College. *Address:* Trinity College of Music, Mandeville Place, London W1M 6AQ, England.

JONES Ieuan, b. 1955, Wales. Harpist. *Education:* Royal College of Music, with Marisa Robles. *Career includes:* Appearances, UK, Dutch, Italian television; Soloist, London Rodrigo Festival, 1986; Soloist, Mozart Concerto for Flute & Harp, with Bournemouth Sinfonietta, 1986; Invited performance, World Harp Congress, Vienna, Austria, 1987; Recitals, Spain, North America; Featured (premiere, Alan Hoddinott's Tarantella for Harp & Orchestra), St David's Day Concert, Cardiff, 1988; Mozart & Daniel Jones Concertos, flute & harp, Swansea & Aberystwyth, 1988; Replaced Marisa Robles, Mozart Flute & Harp Concerto, Debussy's Danses Sacrée et Profane, Margam Festival, Swansea, 1988; Radio 2 Billy Butler Show, Croydon, 1989; USA Miami Recital, North Wales Tour, 1989; Promotional Video, Welsh Development Board, 1990; Brussels, Mozart Concert Recordings release, 1990; Premiere, Rodrigo Concerto in Wales, 1991; Guest Soloist of Enrique Batiz and the State Orchestra of Mexico, 1992; Soloist, Rodrigo Homage Concert, Seville EXPO celebrations, 1992; Welsh premiere of Sonata for Harp by William Mathias (dedicated to Ieuan Jones), at 1993 Machynlleth Festival. *Recordings:* The Uncommon Harp, selection light classics & ballads, BBC Records, 1987; BMG Records, 2 Sides of Ieuan Jones, 1988; New Catalogue...In The French Style, 1990; Belgian Recordings, Mozart In Paris, 1990; All Through the Night, with Huw Rhys-Evans, (tenor(, 1992. *Honours:* All major prizes including Tagore Gold Medal, & 1st-time award from HM Queen Mother, Royal College of Music; All honours including overall Gold Medal, Royal Overseas League Music Competition; Joint winner, Israel International Harp Contest. *Current Management:* Neil Chaffey Concert promotions, 8 Laxton Gardens, Baldock, Herts, SG7 6DA, England.

JONES Isola, b. 27 Dec 1949, Chicago, Illinois, USA. Musician; Mezzo-Soprano. m. Russell Thomas Cormier, 31 Mar 1984. *Education:* Bachelors Degree in Musical Education, Northwestern University, 1971. *Debut:* Olga in Eugene Onegin, Metropolitan Opera, 15 Oct 1977. *Career:* Live From the Met, television series; Maddalena in Rigoletto, 1977, 1981; Lola in Cavalleria Rusticana, 1978; Girl in Mahagonny, 1979; Madrigal in Manon Lescaut, 1980; Recital with Placido Domingo, 1982; The Met Centennial Gala, 1983; Preziosilla in La Forza del Destino, 1984; Smaragdi in Francesca da Rimini; Spoleto Festival 1989, as Giulietta in Les Contes d'Hoffmann. *Recordings:* Porgy and Bess, London Records, Cleveland Orchestra, Lorin Maazel; Flying Dutchman, London Records, Chicago Symphony, Georg Solti; Les Noces, RCA, Chicago Symphony, James Levine; Cavalleria Rusticana, New Philharmonia Orchestra, James Levine. *Honour:* Merit Award, Northwestern University, 1984. *Hobby:* Tennis (husband teaching tennis professional). *Current Management:* Robert Lombardo Associates.

JONES Karen, b. 8 July 1965, Hampton, Middlesex, England. Concert Flautist. *Education:* Studied at the Guidhall School, in Vienna with Wolfgang Schulz, and in New York. *Career:* Played the Ibert Concerto with the LSO, 1985; Concerto performances with Neville Marriner at the QueenElizabeth Hall, Andrew Litton at the Festival Hall and George Malcolm at the Snape Concert Hall; Further engagements with the Ulster Orchestra, the Philharmonia, the Wren Orchestra and London Musici; Solo recitals at the Purcell Room and the Wigmore Hall; Member of the Pears-Britten Ensemble, with performances in Britain and the USA: Guest principal with the Australian Chamber Orchestra at the 1992 Promanade Concerts. *Recordings include:* Arnold's concerto No 1 and Panufnik's Hommage a Chopin. *Honours include:* Winner, Woodwind section, BBC TV Young Musician of the Year, 1982; Gold Medal of the Shell, LSO Scholarship, 1985. *Address:* c/o Owen White Management, 14 Nightingale Lane, London N8 7QU, England.

JONES Kenneth Victor, b. 14 May 1924, Bletchley, Buckinghamshire, England. Composer; Conductor; Professor. m. Anne Marie Heine, 20 Mar 1945, 1 son, 1 daughter. *Education:* King's School, Canterbury; Queen's College, Oxford; Royal College of Music. *Debut:* Royal Festival Hall. *Career:* Assistant Organist, Choirmaster, St Michael's College, Tenbury, 1941; RAF, 1942-47; Assistant Conductor, London Symphonic Players, 1952; Redhill and Reigate Choral Society, 1956-64, Hill Singers, Wimbledon, 1954-60; Professor, Royal College of Music, 1958-91; Conductor, 1961-70, Founder, President, 1970-, Wimbledon Symphony; Conductor, Sinfonia of London, 1966-70; Founder, Member, Governor, Rokeby Educational Trust, 1966-; Visiting Tutor, University of Sussex, 1971-73. *Compositions include:* Paean for Organ; Sussex Suite for junior orchestra; 2 Sinfoniettas; 4 Sonatas; 2 Wind Quintets; String Quartet; 4 works for orchestra; 6 song cycles; collections; 2 brass works; 3 Concerti; 2 Cantatas; 44 piano works; 24 works for violin, viola, cello and piano; 85 film, play, TV scores; Various church music; Dialysis; Rembrancer of an Inward Eye; The Rites Mysterious, for trumpet and organ. *Recordings include:* Dialysis; Chorale, Ceremony and Toccata; Organ Sontata No. 1; A Gay Psaltery; Serpentine Dances; Sonata for solo violin. *Publications:* Numerous books including A Musical Progress for Piano, 43 pieces; Dialysis: for Violin and Harpsichord, Nova Music. *Honour:* FRCM. *Current Management:* CCA. *Memberships:* Royal Philharmonic Society; Composers' Guild; Royal Air Force Club. *Address:* Cleavers, Bishopstone, Seaford, East Sussex BN25 2UD, England.

JONES Martin, b. 4 Feb 1940, England. Concert Pianist. *Education:* Studied in London. *Debut:* Played at the Elizabeth Hall, London, and Carnegie Hall, 1968. *Career:* Regular appearances with the Royal Philharmonic, Royal Liverpool Philharmonic, BBC Symphony, and Halle Orchestra at the Festival Hall, the Barbican and other venues; Tour of Canada with the BC Welsh Symphony Orchestra and recitals in Florida, Tennessee, and California; Broadcasts in Britain, Ireland and the USA; Pianist-in-Residence at University College, Cardiff, 1971-88; Professor, Guildhall School of Music and Drama; Brahms recital at the Wigmore Hall, 1993; repertoire also includes concertos by Busoni, Benjamin, Barber, Mathias, McCabe, Lambert and Scharwenka; Played Grainger's Briadal Lullaby and Mock Morris on the Soundtrack of the film, Howard's End. *Address:* c/o Owen White Management, 14 Nightingale Lane, London N8 7QU, England,

JONES Maureen, b. 1940, Australia. Pianist. *Education:* Studied at the New South Wales Conservatorium, Sydney. *Career:* Formed Trio with Breton Langbein and Barry Tuckwell and gave the premiere of the Horn Trio by Don Banks at the 1962 Edinburgh Festival; Regular tours of Australia and Europe, including recent appearancces in Dublin, Siena, Innsbruck, Paris, Sydney and Melbourne; Duo recitals with Barry Tuckwell; Concert debut playing Beethoven's 1st Concerto with the Sydney Symphony; Appearances at the Edinburgh Festival include concerts with the Berlin Philharmonic. *Address:* c/o Harold Holt Ltd, 31 Sinclair Road, London W14 ONS, England.

JONES Michael Robert, b. 22 Aug 1953, Birmingham, England. Professional Pianist; Teacher. *Education:* Graduate (GBSM) & Associate (ABSM), Piano Teaching & Performing, Birmingham School of Music. *Debut:* Purcell Room, London, 1983. *Career:* Recitals in France, 1977, 1979, 1981, West Berlin 1979; Numerous recitals in Britain, 1974-; Pianist, Anglo-German Youth Music Weeks, 1974-85. *Contributions to:* Composer Magazine, Spring and Summer Edition, 1983; Royal Academy of Music Magazine, Spring Edition, 1985; British Music, 1990 Edition, (Journal). *Memberships:* Incorporated Society of Musicians; European Piano Teachers' Association; Musicians Union. *Address:* 114 Sladepool Farm Road, King's Heath, Birmingham B14 5EF, England.

JONES Philip Burnell Rees, b. 16 Mar 1951, Stourport-on-Severn, England. Lecturer in Music; Conductor; Writer; Arranger. m. Jane Rosamond Hewitt, 8 Sept 1984. *Education:* Worcester Royal Grammar School, 1962-69; Birmingham School of Music, 1969-70; University of York, 1970-74; Eastman School of Music, New York, USA, 1974-75; University of Birmingham, 1975-76. *Debut:* City of Birmingham Symphony Orchestra, 1977. *Career:* Fellow in Music, University of Bradford, 1976-78; Lecturer in Music, University of Keele, 1978-89; Head of Faculty of Art and Music, Bath College of Higher Education, 1989-92; Principal Conductor, English Philharmonic Orchestra, 1976-79; Guest Conductor, Orchestra da Camera, English String Orchestra, BBC Northern Symphony Orchestra, Royal Liverpool Philharmonic Orchestra; Artistic Director, The Fourth Delius Festival, 1982; The First British Music Week, 1984; Artistic Director, Keele Concerts Society, 1983-89. *Contributions to:* Musical Times; Delius Society Journal; Music Quarterly. *Publications:* The American Sources of Delius's Style, Garland Publishing Inc. New York, 1990. *Honours:* BA, York, 1973; BPhil, York, 1974; PhD, Birmingham, 1981. *Memberships:* Royal Musical Association. *Address:* Department of Music, University of Keele, Staffordshire, ST5 5BG, England.

JONES Philip Mark, b. 12 Mar 1928, Bath, England. Musician; Principal, Trinity College of Music, London. m. Ursula Strebi, 1 Aug 1956. *Education:* Royal College of Music, London. *Career:* Principal Trumpet, all major London Orchestras, 1948-72; Founder and Director, Philip Jones Brass Ensemble, 1951-86; Head, Wind and Percussion, Royal Northern College of Music, Manchester, 1975-77; Editor, Just Brass Music Series, Chester Music, London, 1975-89; Head, Wind and Percussion, Guildhall School of Music and Drama, London, 1983-88; Member, Arts Council of Great Britain, 1984-88; Govenor, Chetham's School, Manchester, 1988-; Vice-Chairman, Executive Committee, Musicians Benevolent Fund, 1993-. *Recordings:* Over 50 records with Philip Jones Brass Ensemble. *Honours:* OBE, 1977; CBE, 1986. *Hobbies:* History; Mountain Walking; Skiing. *Address:* 14 Hamilton Terrace, London NW8 9UG, England.

JONES Richard, b. 7 June 1953, Lambeth, London. Producer. *Education:* Studied at the Universities of Hull and London. *Debut:* A Water Bird Talk by Dominick Argento for Scottish Opera, 1982. *Career:* Has directed for the theatre and for the following opera companies: Musica nel Chiostro, Battingano (Mozart's Apollo et Hyacinthus, 1984; Salieri's La Grotta di Trofonio and Paisiello's Il re Teodoro in Venezia, 1985); Opera Northern Ireland (Don Pasquale, 1985); Wexford Festival (Mignon, 1986); Cambridge University Opera (The Magic Flute, 1986); Opera 80 (The Rake's Progress, 1986; Rigoletto, 1987); Opera North (Manon 1987; Carmen and The Love for Three Oranges 1987); Scottish Opera-Go-Round (Macbeth and Die Entführung 1987); Scottish Opera (Scottish Opera 1988; Das Rheingold 1989); Kent Opera (Le Comte Ory and A Night at the Chinese Opera, 1988); The Love for Three Oranges and David Blake's

The Plumber's Gift (world premiere) for English National Opera, 1989. *Honours include:* Laurence Olivier Award as Best Newcomer in Theatre in 1988; Best Director at the 1990 Evening Standard Drama Awards. *Address:* c/o Judy Daish Associates, 83 Eastborne Mews, London, W2, England.

JONES Roland Leo, b. 16 Dec. 1932, Ann Arbor, Michigan, USA. Performer & Teacher of Violin & Viola. *Education:* BMus, University of Michigan; 5 years study in New York City at Columbia University & privately; 3 years with National Orchestra Association Training Orchestra; Summers at Interlochen Music Camp, Meadowmount Music School & Tanglewood Music School. *Career:* Soloist with Ann Arbor Civic Symphony, 1951, 1953; Violinist, Denver Symphony Orchestra, 1960-75; Jackson Hole, Wyoming Fine Arts Festival, 1964-65; Tours throughout USA & Canada; Founder, 1st Violinist, Highland Chamber Players, 1978-79; 1st Violinist, Highland String Quartet, 1979-; Tour with Denver Chamber Orchestra and San Francisco Opera, Western Opera Theater, 1987.*Compositions:* New Cadenzas for all the Mozart Violin Concertos, 1991. *Recordings:* with orchestra, Milena by Alberto Ginastera & Concerto No. 2 of Chopin; Has composed cadenzas for all five Mozart violin concertos. *Publications:* New Cadenzas for all the Mozart Violin Concertos, Presto Publishing, Distributed Internationally, 1992. *Address:* 3004 S Kearney, Denver, CO 80222, USA.

JONES Samuel, b. 2 June 1935, Inverness, Mississippi, USA. Composer; Conductor; Educator. m. (1) 2 daughters, (2) Kristin Barbara Schutte, 22 Dec 1975. *Education:* BA, Millsaps College, 1957; MA, PhD, Eastman School of Music, University of Rochester, 1958-60. *Career:* Director of Instrumental Music, Alma College, Alma, Michigan, 1960-62; Music Director, Saginaw Symphony, 1962-65; Conductor, Rochester Philharmonic, 1965-73; Founding Dean, Shepherd School of Music, 1973-79; Professor of Conducting and Composition, Rice University, 1973-; Guest Conductor: Buffalo Philharmonic, Symphonies of Detroit, Pittsburgh, Houston, Prague and Iceland. *Compositions:* In Retrospect; Symphony No. 1, (recorded); Elegy for String Orchestra, (recorded); Overture for a City; Let Us Now Praise Famous Men, (recorded); Spaces; Contours of Time; Fanfare and Celebration; A Christmas Memory; A Symphonic Requiem; Variations on a Theme of Howard Hanson; The Trumpet of the Swan; Listen Now, My Children (recorded); Two Movements for Harpsichord; Canticles of Time, Symphony No.2; Symphony No.3 (Palo Duro Canyon), 1992; The Seas of God, 1992.*Recordings:* Symphony No.3, recorded by Amarillo Symphony. *Current Management:* Carl Fischer, Inc.*Address:* Shepherd School of Music, Rice University, PO Box 1892, Houston, TX 77251, USA.

JONES Sylvia, b. 7 Aug 1928, New York, USA. m. 12 Feb 1955, 1 son, 3 daughter. *Education:* BMus, New Jersey College for Women, Rutgers; Eastman School of Music. *Debut:* Age 16 Beethoven's 1st Conc with Orchestra. *Career:* Church Organist, Choir Director, Montevideo, Uruguay and Calgary, 20 years. Teacher, Instituto Crandon, Montevideo, Uruguay, five years; Accomp/Coach, Mt Royal College, Calgary, 25 years; Accompanied numerous stage performances and opera productions for Calgary Theatre Singers, Beth Israel Singers, Calgary Opera, University of Calgary, Cappuccino Singers, United Church Concerts and Conferences. *Honours:* Gerald Moore Awards for Accompanying. *Memberships:* Piano Diploma Association; Canadian Association of University Women; Calgary Society of Organists. *Hobbies:* Reading; Swimming; Travel. *Address:* 1106 Crescent Road NW, Calgary Alberta T2M 4A8, Canada.

JONES Warren, b. 11 Dec 1951, Washington DC, USA. Vocal Coach; Accompanist. *Education:* BM New England Conservatory of Music 1973; MM, The San Francisco Conservatory of Music 1977. *Career:* Accompanist to Luciano Pavarotti, Marilyn Horne, Frederica von Stade, Judith Blegen, Håkan Hagegård, Elisabeth Söderström, Martti Talvela, Carol Vaness,

Lynn Harrell; Thomas Allen; Roberta Peters; Roberta Alexander; Samuel Ramey. Appearances at Tanglewood, Ravinia, Caramoor, Salzburg Festivals; Assistant Conductor, Metropolitan Opera, San Francisco Opera; Classes at Harvard, San Francisco Conservatory of Music, Hartt School of Music, California State University; . *Honours:* Who's Who In American Music 1985; Outstanding Young Men of America 1983. *Memberships:* Lifetime Member, Pi Kappa Lambda Fraternity. *Hobbies:* Running; Cooking; Reading. *Address:* 711 West End Avenue, Apartment 6JN, New York, NY 10025, USA.

JONES Wynford Lyn, b. 11 Oct 1948, Merthyr Tydfil, Wales. Teacher. m. Julie Avril Fellingham, 2 sons. *Education:* BA, Music, Leeds University; Graduate Certificate of Education; Associate, Royal College of Music. *Career:* Began Teaching, Wakefield, Yorkshire; Conductor, small group singers, Radio Leeds, 1973; Conductor, Wakefield Youth Choir; Deputy Conductor, Dowlais Male Voice Choir, 1975, making conducting debut with this choir, Luxembourg Cathedral during tour, May 1975; several concerts and on BBC TV, Wales, 1975; Musical Director, Dowlais Male Voice Choir, 1977-87; has conducted over 200 concerts with Dowlais Male Voice Choir; 3 appearances at the Royal Albert Hall; Concert tours of Bulgaria, 1980, USA, 1982, Holland, 1984; Conductor, Wales first Royal Gala Concert; Musical Director, Pontypridd Choral Society, 1988; appearances French TV; Musical Director, Pontypridd Choral Society, 1988-90; Musical Director, Cwmbach Male Choir, 1991; with CWMBACH M.C. First to conduct choir at a Five Nations Rugby International at Cardiff Arms Park, 1992; Tour, Holland and Germany with CWMBACH M.C., 1993. *Address:* 3 Sycamore Close, Landare Park, Aberdare, Glamorganshire, Wales.

JONSSON Anders, b. 24 Oct 1953, Boden, Sweden. Musician. 1 s, 1 d. *Education:* The Academy of Famnas, Musikhogsholan in Stockholm. *Debut:* Swedish Radio Symphony Orchestra and Sergiu Celibidache, 1970. *Career:* Principal Percussionist in Hovliapellet, Royal Opera Stockholm. *Hobbies:* Writing; Travelling. *Address:* Box 132, S-16126 Bromma, Sweden.

JORDA Enrique, b. 24 Mar 1911, San Sebastian, Spain. Conductor. m. Audrey D Blaes, 31 Jan 1944, 2 daughters. *Education:* Colegio Catolico Santa Maria, San Sebastian; Central University, Madrid; Sorbonne, Paris, France; Composition with Paul Le Flem; Organ with Marcel Dupré; Conducting with Francois Ruhlman. *Career:* Madrid Symphony Orchestra, 1940-45; Cape Town Symphony Orchestra, 1948-54; San Francisco Symphony Orchestra, 1954-63; Antwerp Philharmonic Orchestra, 1970-75; Euskadi Symphony Orchestra, 1982-84; Conductor Emeritus, Euskadi Symphony Orchestra; Guest Conductor, France, Belgium, Germany, England, Italy, Luxemburg, Norway, Ireland, Finland, Portugal, Greece, Israel, South America, Canada, Cuba, Switzerland, Australia. *Compositions:* Ballets and Choral Music. *Recordings include:* Lalo Symphonie Espagnole (Ida Haendl); Brahms D Minor Concerto (Clifford Curzon); Falla Nights in the Gardens of Spain (Rubinstein) and The Three-Cornered Hat (London Symphony Orchestra). *Publications:* El director de Orquesta ante la partitura, 1969; De canciomes, denzas y musicos del Pais Vasco, 1978. *Contributions to:* La Vanguardia. *Honours:* Price Conde de Cartagena, Academy of Fine Arts, Madrid, 1941; Comendador of the Order Alfonso el Sabio, 1958. *Hobby:* Reading. *Current Management:* Camile Kiesgen, 252 Faubourg, Saint Honore, Paris, France. *Address:* 64 Avenue Gustave Latinis, 1030 Brussels, Belgium.

JORDAN Armin Georg, b. 9 Apr 1932, Lucerne, Switzerland. Conductor. m. Kate Herkner, 1 son, 1 daughter. *Education:* University of Fribourg; Conservatoire of Lausanne (degrees in piano teaching and conducting). *Debut:* Bienne Opera, 1957. *Career:* Chief Conductor in Biene, 1961-63; First Conductor Zurich Opera, 1963-71; Music Director Basle Opera from 1971; Music Director, Orchestre de Chambre de Lausanne, 1973-85; Music Director, Orchestre de la

Suisse Romande from 1985; Principal Guest Conductor, Ensemble Orchestral de Paris from 1986; Numerous appearances on TV and radio in various countries; International career from 1963: guest conductor at the Lyon, Vienna, Munich, Hamburg, Geneva, Brussels and Seattle Operas; Paris, Orchestre National de France and Nouvel Orchestre Philharmonique; Season, 1991/92 with Die Fledermaus at Geneva and Don Giovanni at Aix-en-Provence. *Recordings:* Actor and Conductor in Syberberg's film of Parsifal; Orchestral works by Dukas, Mozart, Dvořák, Ravel, Chausson, Schubert, Chopin and Franck; Conducted Massenet's Manon at the Geneva Opera, 1989; Mozart Violin Concertos, with Franco Gulli. *Honours:* Grand Prix Academie Charles Cros 1985; Cecilia Award, Belgium, 1985; Academie du disque Lyrique, Paris, 1987; Prix de la critique internationale, 1987; Prix Academie du disque Français, 1988. *Address:* 234 Bunishoferstrasse, CH-8706 Feldmeilen (ZH), Switzerland.

JORDAN Irene, b. 25 Apr 1919, Birmingham, Alabama, USA. Singer (Soprano). Studied at Judson College, Alabama, and with Clyrie Mundy in New York. *Career:* Sang first as mezzo-soprano (Mallika in Lakmé at the Metropolitan, 1946), and after further study sang Donna Anna and Micaela at the Chicago Lyric Theatre, 1954; Appeared at the New York City Opera and the Metropolitan (the Queen of Night) in 1957; Elsewhere in America she sang Verdi's Aida and Lady Macbeth, Madame Butterfly, Weber's Euryanthe, Mozart's Vitellia (La clemenza di Tito) and Leonore in Fidelio. *Recordings include:* Stravinsky's Pulcinella, conducted by the composer, and songs by Schoenberg.

JORDAN Paul, b. 12 Mar 1939, New York City, NY, USA. Conductor; Composer; Organist; Recorder Player; Educator. *Education:* Studied at Harvard and Columbia Universities; Private Studies with Tui St. George Tucker, Emil Platen, Hanns Eppink, Grete Sultan, Helmut Walcha, Irwin Fischer, Jerome Laszloffy; Degrees: Yale School of Music, Frankfurt Staatliche Hochschule für Musik. *Debut:* Performances in NYC beginning at age 12; Carnegie Recital Hall and Tully Hall debuts, 1969, 1971. *Career:* Teaching, Sarah Lawrence College, Yale University, 1967-69; Positions: Director of Music, United Church on the Green, New Haven, Connecticut, 1964-74; Member, Faculty, State University of New York at Binghamton, 1973-; Guest Conductor, California Institute of The Arts, 1984; Concerts in over 100 cities on 4 continents, 1967-; Recordings for the Radio in Berlin, Frankfurt, Hannover, 1973- (including the complete Art of the Fugue by J.S. Bach, Berlin, 1986). *Recordings:* Bach: Complete Orgelbüchlein (Double Album), Pape 1976, Spectrum, 1980; From Amsterdam to Leipzig, Spectrum 1981; Viva Vivaldi, Nonesuch 1984; Buxtehude, Moondog & Co., Spectrum (CD) 1989; earlier (out-of-print) recordings on Kapp, Decca, Classic Editions labels. *Contributions to:* Bachstunden: Festschrift für Helmut Walcha, 1977. Author of An Organ City In Connecticut, The American Organist, 1973; Organ Playing, Epic Poem by Hermann Hesse (Translation), 1973; Helmut Walcha: Artist Teacher, The American Organist, 1984. *Hobbies:* Travel (Europe and Asia); Reading (Philosophy and Psychiatry). *Address:* 39 Lake Avenue, Binghamton, NY 13905, USA.

JORDAN Robert, b. 2 May 1940, Chattanooga, Tennessee, USA. Concert Pianist; Professor of Piano. *Education:* BMus, The Eastman School of Music, 1962; MMus, Juilliard School, 1965. *Career:* Tours of Europe, North and South America and West Africa; Appeared as Soloist with orchestras of Prague, Munich, Baltimore and Buffalo; Annual appearances at the Fêtes Musicale du Touquet in France, 1984-. *Recordings:* Music of Franz Liszt and Dean C. Taylor, David Borden and Talib Rasul Hakim; Schubert, Six Moments Musicaux and Schumann sonata No.2 G Minor, Opus 22. *Honours:* One of 13 Pianists chosen to commission a work from an American composer and give world premiere at Kennedy Center; Chancellor's Award for Excellence in Teaching; Named Martin Luther King Professor, at University of Michigan, March 1991. *Hobbies:*

Languages; Reading. *Address:* State University College, Department of Music, Fredonia, NY 14063, USA.

JORDAN Robert Andrew, b. 25 June 1944, Reading, England. Bassoonist. *Education:* BA, St Edmund Hall, Oxford University, 1967; Royal Academy of Music, 1957-62; BBC Training Orchestra, 1967-69. *Career:* Founder member, Athena Ensemble, 1969-; Co-principal bassoon, Sadler's Wells Orchestra (now English National Opera Orchestra), 1971-; Freelance musician, various major orchestras, chamber groups; Frequent broadcasts. *Recordings:* Numerous. *Address:* 91 Brands Hill Avenue, High Wycombe, Buckinghamshire HP13 5PX, England.

JORGENSEN Jerilyn, b. 1960, New York, USA. Violinist. *Education:* Studied at the Julliard School with Joseph Fuchs. *Career:* Soloist with several orchestras in the Brahms and Tchaikovsky Concertos; Further study with members of the Juilliard Quartet and Co-founded the Da Vinci Quartet, 1980, under the Sponsorship of the Fine Arts Quartet; Many concerts in the USA and elsewhere in the repertoire including works by Mozart, Beethoven, Brahms, Dvorak, Shostakovich and Bartok. *Honours include:* With the Da Vinci Quartet: Awards and grants from the NEA, the Western States Arts Foundation and the Colorado Council for the Humanities; Artist in Residence at the University of Colorado. *Address:* 11 Northpark Street, Glasgow G20 7AA, Scotland.

JORGENSEN Poul, b. 26 Oct 1934, Copenhagen, Denmark. Conductor. m. Marianne Jorgensen, 2 children. *Education:* University of Copenhagen; Royal Academy of Music, Copenhagen. *Debut:* Copenhagen, 1959. *Career:* Past Assistant Permanent Conductor, Former Director, Royal Opera; Royal Conductor, guest conductor, major European orchestras; Former Chairman, Danish State Music Council. *Contributions to:* Danish reviews. *Honours:* Awards at Besançon 1959, Stockholm 1964; Decorated Knight of the Dannebrog. *Address:* Kongelige Teater, PO Box 2185, DK 1017, Copenhagen K, Denmark.

JOSELSON Tedd, b. 4 Oct 1954, Antwerp, Belgium (of American parentage). Pianist. *Education:* Pupil of Adele Marcus, Juilliard School of Music, New York. *Career:* Appeared as a soloist with the Philadelphia Orchestra, 1974; First coast-to-coast recital tour of the US, 1976-77; Thereafter appeared as a soloist and recitalist in many major music centres in the US and overseas.

JOSEPH Charles M., b. 31 Aug 1946, Uniontown, Pennsylvania, USA. Musician; Musicologist. m. Lucy Manning, 30 Aug 1969, 2 daughters. *Education:* PhD, University of Cincinnati College - Conservatory of Music, 1974. *Career:* Teacher, SMU, Dallas, Texas, Williams College, Massachusetts; currently, Professor and Chairman, Music, Skidmore College, Saratoga. *Publications:* Stravinsky and the Piano, 1973. *Contributions to:* Numerous articles for: Musical Quarterly; Music Theory Spectrum; Journal of Musicology; Notes; Piano Quarterly; Journal of Music Theory; Symposium; Clavier. *Address:* Dept. of Music, Skidmore College, Saratoga Springs, NY 12866, USA.

JOSEPHS Norman Arthur, b. 20 June 1943, Berry Hill, Gloucestershire, England. Lecturer in Music. 1 son. *Education:* Birmingham University, 1961-66; Lincoln College, Oxford University, 1967-69; BMus, 1st Class Honours, 1964; Certificate, Education, 1965; MA, 1966. *Career:* Music master, Birmingham, 1967; Assistant Director of Music, 1969-72, Lecturer in Music 1972-84, University of Keele, Staffordshire; Head of Academic Studies (principal lecturer), School of Music, Colchester Institute, Essex, 1984-. *Publications:* 17th Century English Composers, in Grove's Dictionary of Music & Musicians, 6th edition, 1980; Popular Music, Cambridge University Press, 1982-. *Contributions to:* Popular Music; Musical Opinion; Popular Music & Society.

Honours: Barber Scholarships in Music, University of Birmingham, 1961, 1968; Fellow of the Salzburg Seminar, 1976. *Memberships:* Royal Musical Association; Sonneck Society; International Association for the Study of Popular Music; Vincent's, Oxford. *Hobby:* Golf (former county golfer & Oxford Blue). *Address:* 48 Cambridge Road, Colchester, Essex CO3 3NR, England.

JOSEPHS Wilfred, b. 24 July 1927, Newcastle on Tyne, England. Composer. m. Valerie Wisbey, 1956. 2 daughters. *Education:* University of Durham at Newcastle (now Newcastle Univ) (BDS Dunelm) Qual dentistry, 1951; Guildhall School of Music, 1954; Studied musical comp with Maître Max Deutsch, Paris, 1958-59. *Career:* Composer writing many concert works including ten symphonies; many film and television scores and themes; Vis Prof of Comp and Composer-in-Residence, Univ of Wisconsin-Milwaukee, 1970; Vis Prof of Comp and Composer-in-Residence, Roosevelt University, Chicago, 1972. *Compositions include:* Music for: The Great War; I, Claudius; Disraeli; Cider with Rosie; All Creatures Great and Small; Sister Dora; Swallows and Amazons; The Bronte Series; The Somerset Maugham Series; Horizon; Chéri; A Place in Europe; The Inventing of America; The Norman Conquests; The Ghosts of Motley Hall; The House of Bernardo Alba; The Hunchback of Notre Dame; The Voyage of Charles Darwin; Enemy at the Door; People Like Us; Black Sun; The Uncanny; The Atom Spies; Churchill and the Generals; Pride and Prejudice; Strangled; A Walk in the Dark; Gift of Tongues; Miss Morison's Ghosts; The Human Race; Weekend Theatre; The Moles; The Home Front; The Making of Britain; The Brief; A Married Man; The Gay Lord Quex; Martin's Day; Pope John Paul II; Mata Hari; Drummonds; The Return of the Antelope; Art of the Western World; also a television opera, The Appointment; one-act opera, Pathelin; 2 children's operas, Through the Looking-glass and What Alice Found There; Alice in Wonderland; Children's musical, King of the Coast; Equus, the ballet; Rebecca, 3-act opera; Ballet Cyrano de Bereerac, for Covent Garden Royal Ballet. *Publications:* Requiem, Symphonies 1-10, various concertos, sonatas, quartets etc. *Honours:* Recipient of numerous honours including: Hon DMus Newcastle, 1978. *Memberships:* BAFTA; ISM; Council, Composers' Guild of GB; Assoc of Professional Composers; Council of Performing Right Society. *Hobbies:* Writing Music; Swimming; Reading; Opera; Theatre; Videos; Films. *Address:* 15 Douglas Court, Quex Road, London NW6 4PT, England.

JOSHUA Rosemary, b. 1964, Wales. Singer (Soprano). *Education:* Studied in London, Master Clases with Thomas Allen, Graziella Sciutti and Claudio Desderi. *Career:* Engagements with Opera Northern Ireland as Pamina, and at the 1992 Buxton Festival as Blondchen in Die Entfuhrung; English National Opera as Adele in Die Fledermaus, Yum-Yum in The Mikado, Princess Ida, Norina, Sophie in Der Rosenkavalier and Susanna; Covent Garden Festival 1993 as Pamina, Royal Opera debut, 1994, as Pousette in Manon; Angelica in Orlando at Aix en Provence Fesitval, Poppea in Agrippina and Susanna, Cologne Opera, 1994. *Honours include:* Royal Philharmonic Award in debut category. *Address:* IMG Artists, Media House, 3 Burlington Lane, London W4 2TH, England.

JOSIPOVIC Ivo, b. 28 Aug 1957, Zagreb, Yugoslavia. Composer; Lawyer. *Education:* MA, Law, University of Zagreb; Graduate, Music Academy, Zagreb. *Debut:* 1978 (Two children's songs). *Career:* Compositions performed in Yugoslavia, Austria, Canada, Japan, Czechoslovakia, England, Poland, Israel, Spain, Switzerland, Federal Republic of Germany; Concert of EBU transmitted over 33 stations in the world, 1985 (Epicurus Garden); Performances at several music festivals in Europe. *Compositions:* Variations for Piano; Play of the Golden Pearls; Enypnion, for harp solo; Quartetto rusticano, for string quartet; Per fiati, for wind quintet; Samba da camera, for 13 strings; Passacaglia, for string orchestra; Diptych, for large orchestra; Epicurus Garden, for large symphony orchestra; Man and Death, for soloists, choir and orchestra; Pro musica, for accordion orchestra; The

Most Beautiful Flower, for voice and instrumental ensemble; Drmesh for Mr Penderetzky, for folk orchestra; Thousands of Lotuses, for choir and instrumental ensemble. *Address:* Mose Pijade 91, Zagreb, Croatia.

JOST Mack, b. 15 July 1918, Horsham, Victoria, Australia. Concert Pianist; University Lecturer. *Education:* BMus, Master School Diploma, Melbourne University; LRAM. *Debut:* Wigmore Hall, 1948. *Career:* Teachers: Ignaz Friedman, Herbert Fryer, London; Solo Piano Recitals in ten European, Eight Asian Capitals; Soloist with all major Australian Orchestras; Staff Member, Melbourne University, 1949-. *Publications:* Yet Another Guide to Piano Playing, 1975; Practice, Interpretation, Performance, 1984. *Honour:* AM (Member of the Order of Australia), 1986. *Hobby:* Art Collector (has endowed City of Horsham Regional Art Gallery with the Mack Jost Bequest). *Address:* Faculty of Music, University of Melbourne, Parkville, Victoria, Australia 3052.

JOUBERT John Pierre Herman, b. 20 Mar 1927, Cape Town, South Africa. Composer; University Lecturer. m. Florence Mary Litherland 1951, 1 son, 1 daughter. *Education:* Diocesan College, Cape Town; Royal Academy of Music, London. *Career:* Lecturer in Music, University of Hull, 1950- 62; Lecturer (later Reader) in Music, University of Birmingham, 1962-86. *Compositions:* Operatic: Silas Marner 1961; Under Western Eyes 1969; Orchestral: 2 Symphonies, 1955, 1968; Concertos for violin, 1954, piano, 1957, bassoon, 1973; Déploration, 1978; Temps Perdu, 1984; Chamber: 4 String Quartets, 1950, 1977, 1987, 1988; String Trio, 1960; Octet, 1961; Piano Trio, 1987; Solo Vocal: 6 Poems of Emily Brontë, 1969, The Turning Wheel, 1979; Unaccompanied Choral: Pro Pace Motets, 1959, Rovate Coeli, 1985; Choral and Orchestral: Herefordshire Canticles, 1979, Gong-tormented Sea, 1981; Solo Instrumental: 2 Sonatas for piano, 1957, 1972. *Honours:* Fellow of Royal Academy of Music 1957; Royal Philharmonic Society Prize 1949; Hon. Director Music, to be conferred by University of Durham, 1991. *Memberships:* Composers Guild of Great Britain; Association of Professional Composers. *Hobby:* Reading. *Address:* 63 School Road, Moseley, Birmingham B13 9TF, England. 21.

JUDD James, b. 30 Oct 1949, Hertford, England. Conductor. *Education:* Trinity College of Music, London. *Career:* Assistant Conductor, Cleveland Orchestra, 1973-75; Associate Conductor, European Community Youth Orchestra, 1978-; Founder/Director, Chamber Orchestra of Europe; Music Director, Florida Philharmonic Orchestra; Artistic Director, European Communities Youth Orchestra, 1990; Artistic Director of Greater Miami Opera, 1993-; Guest Conductor with the Vienna and Prague Symphonies, Berlin Philharmonic, Orchestre National de France, Zurich Tonhalle and Suisse Romande Orchestra; Conducted La Ceneventola at Glyndebourne, 1985; Traviata, Il Trovatore, Il Barbiere di Siviglia, Rigoletto and Figaro for ENO; US Opera debut 1988, with Don Giovanni in Miami; Season 1992/93 included tours with the Hallé and English Chamber Orchestras, LSO, Royal Philharmonic and the Chamber Orchestra of Europe and Salzburg Festival. *Recordings:* With Chamber Orchestra of Europe (Pickwick and Philips Records); With English Chamber Orchestra (Philips); With Philharmonia Orchestra (Opera Rara). *Current Management:* Christopher Tennant Artist' Management. *Address* Unit 2, 39 Tadema Road, London SW10 0PY, England.

JUDD Wilfred, b. 1945, Hertford, Hertfordshire, England. Opera Director. *Education:* Studied at Oxford and London Opera Centre. *Career:* Began as freelance director, 1979; Has been producer with Royal Opera, 1984-, for which has staged Die Zauberflöte, Tosca, and La Fanciulla del West; Notable recent production Finnissy's Thérèse Raquin for The Garden Venture; Artistic Director, Royal Opera House Garden Venture, 1988-93; Director of Productions, Opera 80, 1988-91.

Address: c/o Royal Opera House, Covent Garden, London WC2, England.

JUDGE Ian, b. 1950, England. Stage Director. *Career:* Joined the Royal Shakespeare Company 1975 and has produced plays in London, Vienna, Stratford and Newcastle; Opera work includes Die Walkure for the Wagner Society, London, Die Entfuhrung at Liverpool, Attila at the Bloomsbury Theatre, 1979 and The Beggar's Opera for LAMDA, 1982; Handel's Ariodante at the Buxton Festival, The Merry Widow and Cavalleria Rusticana and Pagliacci for English National Opera; Ruddigore for New South Wales Opera, Falstaff in Bremen and for Scottish Opera, Tosca in Los Angeles; Work for Opera North includes Faust, Macbeth, Tosca, Acis and Galatea, Boris Godunov and Turandot; Lohengrin at Wiesbaden. *Address:* c/o Diana Morgan, Lies Askonas Ltd, 186 Drury Lane, London WC2, England.

JUHANI Matti, b. 26 Feb 1937, Helsinki, Finland. Singer (Tenor). *Education:* Studied at the Sibelius Academ, Helsinki. *Career:* Member of the Deutsche Opera am Rhein at Dusseldorf, 1964-74; Conductor and teaching of singing at Helsinki, from 1973; Sang with Netherlands Opera, 1974-81, and with the Frankfurt Opera, 1977-84; Guest appearances at the Vienna Staatsoper, Brussels, Savonlinna Festival, 1975, and Marseilles, 1980; Roles have included Pedrillo and Painter in Lulu and the Fox in The Cunning Little Vixen; Concert engagements include the Finnish premiere of Schoenberg's Gurrelieder, 1983. *Recordings:* Evangelist in Bach's St Matthew Passion (Da Camera). *Address:* c/o Stadtische Buhnen, Untermainanlge 11, 6000 Frankfurt am Main, Germany.

JUNE Ava, b. 23 July 1931, London, England. Singer (Soprano). *Education:* Studied with Kate Opperman, Clive Carey and Joan Cross in London. *Career:* Joined Sadler's Wells Chorus 1953; Sang solo roles from 1957, Leila in The Pearl Fishers 1959; Covent Garden debut 1958, as the Heavenly Voice in Don Carlos; sang Mrs Schomberg in the 1970 premiere of Victory by Richard Rodney Bennett; Appearances with the Welsh National Opera, Phoenix Opera, Scottish Opera and in Sofia, Vienna, Dusseldorf, Paris, Zagreb and Johannesburg; English National Opera, 1973 as Sieglinde in The Ring, conducted by Reginald Goodall; US debut San Francisco, 1974, as Ellen Orford; Sang Countess Vrouskaya in the premiere of Iain Hamilton's Anna Karenina, English National Opera, 1981; Other roles included Countess Almaviva, Pamina, Agathe, Musetta, Butterfly, Violetta, Eva, the Marschallin, Elizabeth in Gloriana and in Maria Stuarda, Donna Anna, Marzelline, Micaela, Norina, Marguerite, Tosca, Aida and Santuzza; Currently teacher of singing. *Recordings include:* Mrs Grosse in The Turn of the Screw (Decca); The Ring of the Nibelung, from the London Coliseum (EMI). *Address:* c/o English National Opera, St Martin's Lane, London WC2, England.

JUNG Doris, b. 5 Jan 1924, Centralia, Illinois, USA. Dramatic Soprano. m. Felix Popper, 3 Nov 1951, 1 son. *Education:* University of Illinois; Mannes College of Music; Vienna Academy of Performing Arts; Student of Julius Cohen, Emma Zador, Luise Helletsgruber and Winifred Cecil. *Debut:* As Vitellia in Clemenza di Tito, Zurich Opera, Switzerland, 1955. *Career:* Appearances with Hamburg State Opera, Munich State Opera, Vienna State Opera, Royal Opera Copenhagen, Royal Opera Stockholm, Marseille and Strasbourg, Naples Opera Company, Catania Opera Company, Italy, New York City Opera, Metropolitan Opera, and in Minneapolis, Portland, Oregon, Washington, and Aspen, Colorado; Soloist, Wagner concert conducted by Leopold Stokowski, 1971; Soloist, Syracuse Symphony, New York, 1981; Voice Teacher, New York City, 1970-. *Address:* 40 W 84 St. New York, NY 10024, USA.

JUNG Manfred, b. 9 July 1940, Oberhausen, Germany. Singer (Tenor). *Education:* Studied in essen with Hilde Wesselmann. *Career:* Bayreuth Youth Festival 1967, as Arindal in Die Feen by Wagner; Sang in the Bayreuth Festival chorus, 1970-73; Sang in Dortmund and Kaiserslautern from 1971; Member of the Deutsche Oper am Rhein Dusseldorf from 1977; Bayreuth Festival from 1977 as Tristan, Parsifal and Siegfried (production of Der Ring des Nibelungen, 1983, by John Bury and Peter Hall); Sang in Wagner operas at the Salzburg Easter Festival, under Karajan (Tristan and Parsifal, 1980); Metropolitan Opera debut, 1981; Guest appearances in Zurich, Chicago, Toronto, Vienna, Hamburg, Munich, Barcelona, Cologne, Frankfurt, Lisbon, Rome and Montreal; Other roles include Walther, Florestan, Loge and Siegmund; Sang Herod in Salome at Munich, 1990, Aegisthus in Elektra at the Spoleto Festival; Season, 1991/92 as Herod at Barcelona and Valzaccli in Rosenkavelier at Catania. *Recordings include:* Siegfried in The Ring from Bayreuth (Philips). *Address:* c/o Hilbert Agentur, Maximilianstr 22, 8000 Munich 22, Germany.

JUNGWIRTH Manfred, b. 4 June 1919, St Polten, Germany. Singer (Bass). *Education:* Studied with Alice Goldberg in St Polten; Further study in Vienna, Bucharest, Berlin and Munich. *Debut:* Bucharest 1942, as Mephistopheles. *Career:* Sang at the Salzburg Festival from, 1946; Sang at Innsbruck and after winning the 1948 Interanational Singing Competition appeared at Zurich, the Komische Oper Berlin, Dusseldorf and Frankfurt; Further appearances at Hamburg, Cologne, Stuttgart, Paris, Athens, Lisbon and London; Glyndebourne debut, 1965, as Baron Ochs in Der Rosenkavalier; Vienna Staatsoper from 1967; Member of the Bayerische Staatsoper Munich; Covent Garden debut, 1981, as Waldner in Arabella; Dallas, 1982, as Baron Ochs; Other roles have included Osmin, Rocco, La Scala, 1978, Pietro in Simon Boccanegra and Severolus in Pfitzner's Palestrina; Salzburg Festival, 1985 and Florence, 1987, as La Roche in Capriccio. *Recordings include:* Mozart Arias, Der Rosenkavalier, Biterolf in Tannhäuser (Decca).

JUON Julia, b. 28 Nov 1943, St Gallen, Switzerland. Singer (mezzo- soprano). *Education:* Studied in the Zurich Conservatory. *Career:* Sang in opera at St Gallen, 1975-80, Karlsruhe, 1980-83, Kassel from 1984-, notably as Ortrud and as Tina in the European premiere of The Aspern Papers by Dominick Argento; Guest appearances as Fricks at Amsterdam and at the Hamburg Staatsoper (The Nurse in Die Frau ohne Schatten, 1989); Other roles include Waltraute, Carmen, Agrippina, Donizetti's Leonora, Verdi's Ulrica, Eboli, Amneris and Azucena, Wagner's Kundry, Venus and Brangane; Modern repertoire includes Bartok's Judith, the Priestess in Schoeck's Penthesilea and Catherine in Jeanne d'Arc au Bucher by Honegger; Sang Kabanicha in Katya Kabanova at Basel, 1991; Kundry at Essen, 1992; Concert engagements in Switzerland and Germany, at the Bregenz Festival and in Vienna. *Address:* Staatstheater, Friedrichplatz 15, 3500 Kassel, Germany

JÜRGENS Jürgen, b. 5 Oct 1925, Frankfurt am Main, Germany. Conductor. *Education:* Studied in Frankfurt under Kurt Thomas and at the Musikhochschule Freiburg with Konrad Lechner. *Career:* Director of the Hamburg Monteverdi Choir 1955: many concerts in Europe and the USA in music by Josquin, Mozart, Gagliano, Ockeghem, Dallapiccola and Henze; Director of the Akademische Musikpflege 1960; Music Director at Hamburg University from 1966. *Recordings:* Music by Schütz (St Luke Passion and Seven Last Words), Purcell, Bach, Telemann, Josquin, Brahms and Monteverdi (Vespers and Orfeo) with Hamburg Monteverdi Choir, Bach Cantatas 106 and 182 (Leonhardt Consort), 198 (Amsterdam Concerto); Dallapiccola, Canti di prigionia; Peragallo De Profundis and Gagliano La Dafne. *Publications:* Editions of works by Monteverdi and Alessandro Scarlatti; Urtext und Auffuhrungspraxis bei Monteverdis Orfeo und Marien-Vesper 1968; Die Madrigale Alessandro Scarlattis und Ihre Quellen 1973. *Address:* c/o Hochschule für Musik, Harvestehuderweg 12, 2000 Hamburg 13, Germany.

JURICA Leon, b. 2 May 1935, Orlova, Czech Republic. Conservatory Teacher of Music. m. Helena Moldrzykova, 9 Nov 1963, 2 sons. *Education:* Unfinished study of Medicine, 1953-57; Studied Musicology, J E Purkyne University, 1966-72, BA, 1969, MA, 1972, PhD, 1991. *Career:* Archivist, Czechoslovak Radio, 1963-75; Musical Director, Czechoslovak TV as an external worker. *Compositions include:* The Musicians, play, songs for soprano and piano, 1980; The Stones, songs for soprano and piano, 1980; The Winged Stone, songs for bass and piano, 1980; Only Useless Memories are Left to Me, songs for bass and piano; Three songs to K H Macha, songs for soprano and violoncello; Three songs of Renaissance, songs for soprano and piano, 1989; Music for choirs: Lullaby of a Fisher (for women's choir); Folk Printer (for children's choir); Instrumental compositions include: Sonata for violin and piano; Sonata for violoncello and piano; Roznov Romance; Romance for trumpet and Brass Orchestra, 1978; Musica familiaris-variations (for violin, piano and drums) 1990; The third brass Quintet, 1993; About King Ječmínek, an opera for children, 1993; The lion, fox and deer, miniopera, 1993; Captivating witf a charm, miniopera, 1993; How the egg wandered around the country, a ballet for children, 1993; Characters: 1. Sanguinic, 2. Melancholic, 3. Flegmatic, 4. Choleric, for the basson and piano. *Recordings:* Wail Over Dead Arthur, 1970; Orlova (cantata) 1925; Three Choirs for Children, 1986; Let's Play the Opera, 1986; The Most Beautiful Path, 1989; The Fairy-tale End (ballet) 1989. *Publication:* Harmony of O Hostinsky (Brno 1972). *Address:* 943 V Zimném Dole Street, 735 41 Petrvald, CSFR, Czech Republic.

JURINAC Sena, b. 24 Oct 1921, Travnik, Yugoslavia. Opera Singer, Soprano. m. Dr Josef Lederle. *Education:* Studied with Milka Kostrencic. *Career:* First appearance as Mimi, Zagreb, 1942; Member, Vienna State Opera Company, 1944-83 (last performance as the Marschallin); now works as voice teacher; Sang at Salzberg Festival from 1947, as Dorabella, Cherubino, Amo in Orpheus, Marzellina in Fidelio, Octavian, the Composer in Ariadne and Mozart's Countess; Glyndebourne Festival 1949-56, as Dorabella, Fiordiligi, Ilia, Cherubino, Donna Elvira, Donna Anna and Leonora in La Forza del Destino; Also sang Strauss's Octavian and Tatiana in Eugene Onegin; Sang in Der Rosenkavalier, 1966, 1971, Tosca, 1968, Iphigénie en Tauride 1973, Covent Garden, Austrian State Kammersängerin 1951; numerous tours and recordings; Ehrenkreuz dienste um die Republik Österreich 1967; Ehrenring der Wiener Staatsoper 1968; Ehrenmitglied der Wiener Staatsoper 1971. *Address:* c/o State Opera House, Vienna 1, Austria.

JURTH Attila Ferenc, b. 15 May 1945, Budapest, Hungary. Composer; Music Teacher. m. Reka Kocsardi, 30 Apr 1975, 2 sons, 2 daughters. *Education:* A.Mus.A. Studied cello with Magdalena Kerekes, 1983-86, Richard Dedecius, 1986-87, Gary Williams, 1988-; piano with Yefim Stesin, 1984-88, Attila Jurth, 1988-90, Gwenyth Sitcheff 1990-; percussion with Paul Freer, 1990-91; Cello masterclasses with Kató Havas, Christopher Bunting, Gwyn Roberts; In 1991, at the age of 11, youngest ever candidate to graduate with the Associate Diploma in Music Australia. *Debut:* Leningrad, 1963. *Career:* Composer, 1956-; Piano Recitalist, Leningrad, USSR, 1963-65; Chief Organist, Hungarian Roman Catholic Diocese, Vienna, Austria, 1967-82; Music Director, Organist, Hungarian Pax Romana Congresses, 1971-79; Teacher in Piano, Solfeggio, Theory, Musicianship, 1972-; Artistic Director, LKGT Quartet, 1989-. *Compositions:* Educational piano and string music; Grand Sonata for Piano; The Tale of a Ninth Chord for harp; Spleen for cello and piano; Consonant Music for strings; Lieder; Hungarian folk song arrangements and fantasies: Run, Goat, Run, The Four Mosquitos, Hurdy Birdy for string quartet; A Long Way Off for piano quintet. *Publication:* Orsegi daloskonyv, collection of Hungarian folksongs in East Austria, 1971. *Address:* 17 Shannon Street, Redbank Plains, Brisbane, Queensland 4301, Australia.

JURTH Levente Attila, b. 1965, Vienna, Austria. Cellist; Composer. *Education:* A.Mus.A, Studied Cello with Magdalena Kerekes, 1983-86, Richard Dedecius, 1986-87, Gary Williams 1988-; Piano with Yefim Stesin, 1984-88, Attila Jurth, 1988-90, Gwenyth Sitcheff, 1990-; Percussion with Paul Freer, 1990-91; Cello masterclasses with Kato Havas, Christopher Bunting, Gwyn Roberts; In 1991 at the age of 11, youngest ever candidate to graduate with the Associate Diploma in Music Australia. *Debut:* Brisbane, 1987. *Career:* Speaker, Cellist, LKGT Quartet, 1987-; Performed: World Expo '88, Fiest '89, 1990; Stage: Kolya in A Month in the Country, Royal Queensland Theatre Company, 1990; Oliver in Oliver, Ipswich Orpheus Chorale, 1990. *Compositions:* Chamber music: Melody No 7 for Flute and Cello, 1985; Melody No 18 for String Quartet, 1985; Pieces for Piano. *Current Management:* LKGT (music); Quadran (theatre, film TV). *Address:* 17 Shannon Street, Redbank Plains, Brisbane 4301, Queensland, Australia.

JYRKIAINEN Reijo Einari, b. 6 Apr. 1934, Suistamo, Finland. Cultural Administrator; Composer. m. Rauni Tellervo Savolainen, 15 July 1956, 5 children, 1 dec. *Education:* Candidate Philosophy 1963, Licenciate of Philosophy 1966, Helsinki University; Diploma in composition, Sibelius Academy, Helsinki, 1963. *Career:* Served to Ensign, Finnish Infantry, 1954-55; Technical Controller, Finnish Radio, Helsinki, 1957-66; Librarian, 1966-67, Managing Director, 1971-90, Helsinki Philharmonic Orchestra; Head of music programme, Finnish Radio/Television, Helsinki, 1967-71; Vice-Chairman, Concert Centre, Helsinki, 1980-87; Project Chief (Music), 1990-. *Compositions:* Chamber and electronic music. *Membership:* Vice-Chairman, Association of Finnish Symphony Orchestras, 1972-74. *Address:* Centre for Cultural Affairs, City of Helsinki, Bulevardi 23-27, Fin-00180, Helsinki, Finland.

K

KABAIVANSKA Raina, b. 15 Dec 1934, Burgas, Bulgaria. Singer (Soprano). *Education:* Studied in Bulgaria and in Italy with Zita Fumagalli. *Debut:* Sofia 1957, as Titania in Eugene Onegin. *Career:* Italian debut 1959, as Nedda; La Scala 1961, in Beatrice di Tenda by Bellini, with Sutherland; Covent Garden 1962-64, as Desdemona and Liu; Metropolitan Opera from 1962, Nedda, Mimi, Elisabeth de Valois, Alice Ford, Lisa in The Queen of Spades, and Butterfly; Guest appearances at the Hamburg Staatsoper from 1971; Genoa and Trieste 1973, as Tosca and Gioconda; Turin 1973-74, Elena in I Vespri Siciliani and Francesca da Rimini; Paris Opéra debut 1975 as Leonora in La Forza del Destino; Further engagements in Dallas, Chicago, New Orleans, San Francisco, Buenos Aires and Vienna; Verona Arena 1978-82, Butterfly and Mimi; Sang Adriana Lecouvreur at Rome, 1989; returned 1990, as Butterfly and Hanna Glawari in The Merry Widow; sang the Trovatore Leonora at Parma, 1990; Season 1991/92 as Leonora at the restored Carlo Felice Theatre, Genoa, and Hanna Galwari at Rome. *Recordings include:* Il Trovatore, Francesca da Rimini, Madama Butterfly, Fausta by Donizetti; Wagner's Rienzi; Video of Tosca.

KACZANOWSKI Andrzej, b. 22 Apr 1955, Bialystok, Poland. Musician. m. 14 Dec 1974, 2 sons, 1 daughter. *Education:* Fr Chopin Academy of Music, Warsaw, diploma with honour 1980 MA, Double-bass player. *Debut:* Dregonetti Concert with Bilalystok Philharmonic Orchestra, 1975. *Career:* Regular appearances as chamber player with famous orchestras; Warsaw Chamber Orchestra, 1978-84; Chamber Filharmonic (Karol Teutsch conducting), 1980-84; Polish Chamber Orchestra (Jerzy Maksymiuk), 1984-85; Camerata Vistula Chamber Soloist, 1986; Salle Pleyel (conductor K Teutsch), 1980; Santa Cecilia (conductor J Kasprzyk), 1981; Carnegie Hall (conductor K Teutsch), 1982; Teatro alla Scala (conductor Delmann); Carnegie Hall (conductor J Maksymiuk, Barbican Centre (conductor J Maksymiuk), Teatro alla Scala (conductor C Abbado), 1985; Akademie der Künste, Berlin, 1992; Warsaw Autumn, Warsaw, 1992; Teacher, Josef Elsner First Music School, Warsaw, 1991-. *Recordings:* Polish Chamber Orchestra, Warsaw; Chamber Philharmonic Orchestra, Bach Keyboard concerts 1980; Lutoslawski, Prokofiev, Gorecki, 1990 Olympia. *Honours:* Festivals: Lille, 1979; Bordeaux, 1980; Bergen, Tivoli, 1981; Cheltenham, 1982; Brighton, 1984; Glasgow, 1988; Warsaw Autumn, 1985, 1986, 1988 and 1989. *Hobbies:* Yachting; Cycling; Walking. *Address:* Pradzynskistr 20A/109. 05-200 Wotomin, Poland.

KAGEL Mauricio, b. 24 Dec 1931, Buenos Aires, Argentina. Composer; Film Maker; Dramatist. *Education:* Studied piano, theory, cello, organ, singing and conducting privately; Self-taught as a composer. *Career:* Condutor of the Colon Chamber Orchestra and teatro Colon Buenos Aires 1955; Settled in Cologne 1957; Professor of new music-theatre at the Cologne Musikhochschule 1974; Sle Professor of Composition at Buffalo 1964-65; Lecturer at the Berlin Film and television Academy 1967; Music Director of the Institute of New Music at the Rheinische Musikschule, Cologne, 1969. *Compositions include:* String Sextet 1953; Journal de theatre 1960; Heterophonie for 42 instruments 1959-61; Metapiece for keyboard 1961; Antithese for electronic and public sounds 1962; Die Frauen for 2 solo female voices and other ladies 1962-64; Diaphonie for chorus, orchesra and 2 slide projectors 1962-64; Phonophonie, 4 melodramas 1963-64; Match for 2 cellos and percussion 1965; Trmens, Szenisches Montage 1963-65; Camera Obscura, Chromatisches Spiel 1965; Die Himmelsmechanik 1965; Musik fur Renaissanceinstrumente 1965-66; String Quartet 1965-67; Variaktionen for voices, actors and tape 1967; Kommentar Extempore 1967; Montage 1967; Phantasie for organ with obbligato tape 1967; Hallelujah, chorus (from film) 1968; Der Schall 1968; Unter Strom for 5 players 1969; Luwig Van (from film) 1969; Staatstheater, Ballet for non-dancers with instrumentation including chamber pot; 1969-70; Acustica for tape 1968-70; Klangwehr for military band 1970; Programm, Gasprache mit Kammermusik 1972; Exotica 1972; Variationen ohne Fuge for orchestra 1973; Zwei-Mann-Orchester 1971-73; 1898 for children's chorus and instruments 1973; Kantrimiusik, Pastoral for voices and instrumenmts 1975; Mare Nostrum 1975; Bestiarium 1975; Die Umkehrung Amerikas, radio play 1976; Variete, concert spectacle 1977; Die Erschöpfung der Welt, opera 1979; Aus Deutschland, Liederopera, 1981; Sankt-Bach-Passion 1985; Piano Trio 1985; Nach einer Lektüre von Orwell, stage work 1984; La trahison orale for orchestra 1984; Two Ballads of Guillaume de Machaut 1984; A Letter, concert scene for mezzo and orchestra 1986; Dance School, ballet 1988; Quodlibet for Women's Voices and orchestra 1988; 3rd string quartet 1988; Osten for salon orchestra 1989; Fragende Ode for chorus, wind and percussion, 1989. *Honours include:* Koussevitzky Prize 1966; Karl Sczuka Prize for play Ein Aufnahmezustand 1969; Scotoni Prize of the City of Zurich for film Hallelujah 1969. *Address:* c/o Universal Edition, Bösendorfestrasse 12, Postfach 3, A-1015 Vienna, Austria.

KAHANE Jeffrey Alan, b. 12 Sept 1956, Los Angeles, California, USA. Pianist. m. Martha Philips, 9 Sept 1979, 1 son. *Education:* BMus, San Francisco Conservatory of Music, 1977. *Debut:* San Francisco, California, 1973. *Career:* Soloist, New York, Los Angeles Philharmonics, Pittsburgh, San Francisco and Atlanta Symphonies; Frequent performances with Tokyo String Quartet; has worked with Conductors such as M Tilson Thomas, Zubin Mehta, Edo de Waart, Semyon Bychkov and John Nelson; Soloist in Bernstein's Age of Anxiety at the 1991 Promenade Concerts, London. *Recordings:* Bach D Major Partita; 15 Sinfonias, on Nonesuch Records. *Honours:* Grand Prize, Arthur Rubinstein International Piano Competition, Tel Aviv, Israel, 1983; 4th Prize, Van Cliburn International Piano Competition, 1981. *Membership:* Piano Faculty, New England Conservatory of Music, Boston. *Current Management:* IMG Artists. *Address:* c/o IMG Artists, 22 E 71st, New York, NY 10021, USA.

KAHLER Lia, b. 1952, USA. Singer (Mezzo-soprano). *Education:* Studied in Los Angeles, New York and Milan. *Career:* Sang at the Holland Festival, 1982, Detmold, 1983-85, notably as Eboli and Brangaene; Sang at Gelsenkirchen 1985-89 as Laura in La Gioconda, Monteverdi's Ottavia, the Witch and Mother in Hansel und Gretel, and in the premiere of Deinen Kopf, Holofernes, by Blumenthaler, 1989; Other roles at Gelsenkirchen and elsewhere in Germany have included, Ortrud, Maddalena, Marina in Boris Godunov, Dalila and Baba the Turk in The Rake's Progres; Many concert appearances. *Address:* Musiktheater im Revier, Kennedyplatz, 4650 Gelsenkirchen, Germany

KAHMANN Sieglinde, b. 28 Nov 1937, Dresden, Germany. Singer (Soprano). m. Sigurdur Bjornsson. *Education:* Studied in Stuttgart. *Debut:* Stuttgart Staatsoper, 1959, as Aennchen in Der Freischutz. *Career:* Engaged at the Theater am Gärtnerplatz Munich and Sang at Hamburg, Vienna, Stuttgart, Leipsiz, Karlsruhe and Kassel; Roles have included Mozart's Pamina, Donna Elvira, Countess and Cherubino, Lortzing's Gretchen and Mair, Martha and Musetta; Guest appearances at Lisbon, Strasbourg, Bucharest, Salzburg and Ediburgh, as Micaela, Lisa (Queen of Spades), Maarenka (Bartered Bride) and Adele in Fledermaus. *Address:* c/o Stuttgart Staatsoper, Oberere Schlossgarten 6, 7000 Stuttgart, Germany.

KAIPAINEN Jouni Ilari, b. 24 Nov 1956, Helsinki, Finland. Composer. m. Sari-Anne Liljendahl, 9 Sept 1977, 1 son. *Education:* Sibelius Academy of Helsinki, 1975-81. *Career:* Freelance Composer, 1981-. *Compositions:* The Miracle of Konstanz, TV Opera, 1985-87; Symphony, Opus 20, 1980-85; String Quartets: I, 1973; II, 1974; III, 1984; Ladders To Fire (A Concerto for 2 Pianos), 1979; Trios: I, 1983; II, 1986; III, 1987; Cinq poèmes de René Char, Opus 12a, for soprano and orchestra, 1978-80; Chamber Music; Vocal Music; Incidental Music. *Publications:* Contribution to the book,

Ammatti: säveltäjä (Profession: Composer), edited by R Nieminen and P Hako, Helsinki, 1981. *Contributions to:* Numerous essays and articles in different Finnish magazines including Finnish Music Quarterly (in English). *Honours:* UNESCO International Rostrum, The Chosen Work of the Year Prize, 1981; Spurs of Criticism (The most eminent debut of the year) by The Union of Finnish Critics, 1982. *Hobbies:* Literature; Cinema; Cooking (especially oriental). *Address:* Martinkyläntie 64 G 35, 01660 Vantaa, Finland.

KAISER Barbara, b. 1 June 1947, Bremen, Germany. Conductor. *Education:* Abitur; Studied in Schulmusik, Violin and Singing, Hochschule fur Musik, Freiburg/Breisgau, 1967-73; Studies in Conducting, Hochschule der Künste, Berlin, 1979-85. *Debut:* Guest Conductor, Philharmonisches Staatsorchester, Bremen, 1986. *Career:* Founding Member, Musikfrauen Berlin, 1978; Manager, several projects with contemporary music of women composers; Manager of series of concerts with contemporary music at Hochschule der Künste Berlin, 1984-; Neue Musik im Foyer; Foundation of Ensemble Forum Neue Musik Berlin in cooperation, 1986; Lecturer at Hochschule der Künste Berlin, 1986-; Guest Conductor, Philharmonisches Staatsorchester Bremen, Filharmonia Pomorska, Poland, and Orchester der Stadt Heidelberg. *Recordings:* Instrumental and Vocal. *Publications include:* Die Neue Musik und wir, 1983; Musik von Komponistinnen, 1985; Komponistinnen in Berlin, 1987. *Contributions to:* Some interviews on radio, magazines and journals. *Membership:* International Arbeitskreis Frau und Musik; Kulturinstitut Komponistinnen gestern-heute, Heidleburg. *Address:* Gneisenaustrasse 94, 1000 Berlin 61, Germany.

KAISERMAN David Norman, b. 15 July 1937, Cleveland, Ohio, USA. Pianist; University Professor. m. Sonia Uvezian, 12 Jan 1962. *Education:* BS, 1959; MS, 1960; Juilliard; DMA, University of Iowa, 1977. *Career:* Private Teaching, New York, NY, 1958-63; Assistant Professor, Iowa State University, 1963-68; Artist-in-Residence, Associate Professor, 1968-75; Professor, 1975-77; University of Puget Sound, Tacoma, Washington; Professor, University of Oklahoma, 1977-80; Professor, 1980-85; Chairman, Piano Department, 1983-85; University of Louisville, Kentucky; Professor, Northwestern University, Evanston, Illinois, 1985-, Chair, Piano Department, 1985-91; Concerts and Recitals as Soloist, Chamber Musician and with orchestra throughout US and Canada; appearances on Radio and TV throughout US; Master Classes, Workshops and Adjudications throughout US. *Address:* School of Music, Northwestern University, Evanston, IL 60208, USA.

KAKUSKA Thomas, b. 25 Aug 1940, Austria. Violist. *Education:* Studied in Vienna. *Career:* Violist of the Alban Berg Quartet from 1981; Many concert engagements, including complete cycles of the Beethoven Quartets in 15 European cities, 1987-88, 1988-89 seasons; Bartók/Mozart cycle in London, Vienna, Paris, Frankfurt, Munich, Geneva, Turin 1990-91; Annual concert series at the Vienna Konzerthaus and festival engagements worldwide; Associate Artist at the South Bank Centre, London; US appearances San Francisco and New York (Carnegie Hall). *Recordings include:* Complete quartets of Beethoven, Brahms, Berg, and Bartók; Late quartets of Mozart and Schubert; Ravel, Debussy and Schumann quintet; Live recordings from Carnegie Hall (Mozart, Schumann); Konzerthaus in Vienna (Brahms); Opéra-Comique Paris (Brahms). *Honours include:* Grand Prix du Disque; Deutsche Scallplatenpreis; Edison Prize; Japan Grand Prix; Gromophone Magazine award. *Address:* Intermusica Artists' Management, 16 Duncan Terrace, London N1 8BZ, England.

KALABIS Victor, b. 27 Feb 1923, Cerveny Kostelec, Czech Republic. Composer. m. Zuzana Rusickova, 8 Dec 1952. *Education:* Composition, Prague Competition and Academy of Arts and Music, 1945-52; Philosophy and Musical Science, Charles University, Prague. *Career:* Editor, Musical Producer, Czech Radio, 1953-72; Full-time Composer, 1972-. *Compositions include:* Orchestral works, Five symphonies, 1957, 1961, 1971, 1972, 1976; Concerto for large orchestra, 1966; 9 instrumental concertos; 3 compositions for chamber orchestra; Chamber works include: 2 Nonets; Spring Whistles, octet for wind, 1979; 2 wind quintets; 7 string quartets; Sonatas for violin and harpsichord, violoncello and paino, clarinet and piano, trombone and piano and violin and piano, 1967-82; Solo works include: 3 piano sonatas; 3 pieces for flute; Reminiscences for Guitar, 1979; Several choral works; Five romantic love songs for higher voice and strings, 1977; Ballet: Two worlds (Alice in Wonderland), 1980; 6 string quartet, 1988; Incantations for 13 wind instruments, 1988; Carosal of live songs for bass and piano, 1989; Four enigmas for Graham, piano and solo, 1989. *Recordings:* Diptych for strings, CD; Chant du Monde serie Praga; Chant du monde, Harmonia mundi. *Honours:* Musical Critics Prize, 1967; State Prize, 1969; Artist of Merit, 1983; President, *Memberships:* Bohuslav Martinu Foundation, 1991; Union of Czech Composers; Czech Musical Society. *Address:* Slezska 107, 10300 Prague, Czech Republic.

KALE Stuart, b. 27 Oct 1944, Neath, Glamorgan, Wales. Singer (Tenor). *Education:* Studied at the Guildhall School of Music and Drama and at the London Opera Centre. *Debut:* With Welsh National Opera in 1971, as the Prince in the first production by a British company of Berg's Lulu. *Career:* Sang with English National Opera notably as Don Ottavio and in Jonathan Miller's production of The Mikado; Sang Wagner's Siegfried at Bucharest in 1983 and appeared in the local premiere of Prokofiev's The Fiery Angel for South Australian Opera in 1988; Covent Garden debut 1988, in Manon, returning in 1989 as Bob Boles in Peter Grimes; Has sung the Captain in Wozzeck at Strasbourg, 1987, Reggio Emilia, 1989 and Toronto, 1990; In 1989 sang Lucano in L'Incoronazione di Poppea at the Théâtre du Châtelet, Paris, the Drum Major in Wozzeck at Turin and Zinovy Ismailov in Lady Macbeth of the Mstensk District at Nancy, France; Sang Don Eusebio in Rossini's L'Occasione fa il ladro at the 1992 Schwetzingen festival. *Recordings:* Video of Idomeneo (title role) from Drottningholm (Virgin Classics). *Address:* c/o Athole Still International Management Ltd, 113 Church Road, London SE19 2PR, England.

KALICHSTEIN Joseph, b. 15 Jan 1946, Tel-Aviv, Israel. Pianist. *Education:* Studied at the Juilliard School with Eduard Steuermann and Ilona Kabos. *Debut:* New York recital 1967. *Career:* Appeared with the New York Philharmonic in a televised performance of Beethoven's 4th Piano Concerto, 1968; European debut with Previn and the London Symphony, 1970; Appearances with the London Philharmonic, Israel Philharmonic, Cleveland Orchestra, Chicago Symphony, Boston Symphony and Berlin Philharmonic; Tours to Australia, Japan and South America; Performances in Piano Trio with Jaime Laredo and Sharon Robinson from 1976; Brahms series with the Guarneri Quartet in New York, 1983. *Honours:* Young Concert Artists Award 1967; Winner, Leventritt Competition, 1969. *Address:* c/o Harrison/Parrott Ltd, 12 Penzance Place, London W11 4PA, England.

KALIMULLIN Rashid Fagimovich, b. 6 May 1957, Zelenodolsk, TSSR. Composer. m. Kalimullina Roza Ahmetzyanovna, 7 July 1979, 1 son, 1 daughter. *Education:* Kazan State Conservatory, 1985. *Debut:* Nabereshnye Chelny, TSSR, 1981. *Career:* Currently: Teacher at Kazan State Conservatory; Regular tv and radio appearances, 1984-. *Compositions include:* Rock Opera, Cuckoo's Cry, performed at Tatar State Opera Theatre, 1989; Rock Opera, Cuckoo's Cry, Moscow Theatre of Musical Comedy, 1990; Music for film, Wanderer to Bulgar, 1989; Music for film, Travelling through the Thousand Years, 1989; Symphony-poem: Bulgar; Concert for clarinet and orchestra; three string quartets; Quartet for woodwind instruments; Sonatas for piano, for violoncello solo; instrumental pieces; vocal poems; Romances and songs; Rivayat (legend) - music for voice, flute, violoncello, piano. *Recordings:* Chamber

Music, 1989; Leningrad Melody. *Memberships:* Union of Composers of the USSR, 1986, Chairman for Tatarstan, 1989. *Honours:* Honoured Art Worker of Tatarstan Republic, 1991; First International Chamber Music Competition Prize in Dresden (GDR) 1987. *Hobbies:* Travelling; Reading. *Address:* Flat 49, House 44/6 Dostoyevsky Str, 420043 Kazan, Tatarstan Republic, CIS.

KALININA Galina, b. 1951, Russia. Singer (Soprano). *Education:* Studied in Moscow. *Career:* Member of the Bolshoi Opera, Moscow, from 1977, Notably as Donna Anna, Verdi's Trovatore Leonora, Elisabetta, Desdemona and Amelia (Ballo in Maschera); Tchaikovsky's Tatiana and Lisa and Madama Butterfly; Guest appearances in the West from 1982, notably as Tosca at Stuttgart, 1988 and with Scottish Opera, Yoroslvna in Prince Tgor at Wiesbaden and Zemfira in a Concert performance of Rachmaninov's Aleko at Rome; Season, 1987-88 as Tatiana at Buenos Aires, Butterlfy in Oslo and Yaroslavna at Verona; Covent Garden, 1991 as Tosca. *Recordings:* Fevronia in The Legend of the Invisible City of Kitezh by Rimsky Korsakov.

KALISH Gilbert, b. 2 July 1935, New York, New York, USA. Pianist; Teacher. *Education:* Columbia College, BA, 1956, Columbia University Graduate School of Arts and Sciences, 1956-58; Pupil of Isabelle Vengerova, Leonard Shure and Julius Herford. *Career:* New York recital debut, 1962; European debut, London, 1962; Subsequent tours of the US, Europe, and Australia; Appearances with the Contemporary Chamber Ensemble and the Boston Symphony Chamber Players; Regular accompanist to Jan DeGaetani until 1989; Artist-in-residence, Rutgers, the State University of New Jersey, 1965-67, Swarthmore College, 1966-72; Head of keyboard activities, Berkshire Music Center, Tanglewood, Massachusetts; Faculty member, State University of New York at Stony Brook, 1970-. *Recordings:* Numerous discs as a soloist, chamber player, and accompanist. *Address:* c/o Music Department, State University of New York at Stony Brook, Stony Brook, NY 11794, USA.

KALLIR Lilian, b. 6 May 1931, Prague, Czechoslovakia. Pianist; Teacher. m. Claude Frank, 1959. *Education:* Pupil of Isabelle Vengerova; Studied with Herman de Grab, Mannes College of Music, New York, 1946-49. *Career:* Debut as soloist with the New York Philharmonic Orchestra at age 17; New York recital debut at Town Hall at age 18; Subsequent tours of the US, South America, Europe, and Israel; Many appearances as a soloist with orchestras and as a recitalist, including concerts in season 1990/91 at the Tanglewood, Marlboro, Norfolk, Grant Park and mostly Mozart (Seattle) Festivals; Also duo appearances with husband; Chamber recitals with the Cleveland, Emerson, Guarneri, Juilliard and Tokyo Quartets; European engagements at the Festival Hall, London, the Vienna Musikverieum, the Berlin Philharmonic and in Salzburg, Stuttgart, Munich, Luxembourg and Brussels; Orchestra have included the Chicago Symphony, London Symphony, Royal Concertgebouw, Berlin Philharmonic, Leipzig Gewandhaus, Salzburg Mozarteum and English Chamber; Faculty member, Mannes College of Music, New York, 1975-. *Honours:* Winner, National Music League Award and of the American Artists Award of the Brooklyn Institute of Arts and Sciences. *Address:* c/o Mannes College of Music, 150 West 85th Street, New York, NY 10024, USA.

KALLISCH Cornelia, b. 1955, Marbach am Neckar, Germany. Singer (Mezz-soprano). *Education:* Studied in Stuttgart and Munich, with Jose Metternich in Cologne and with Elisabeth Schwarzkopf. *Career:* Sang at first as Lieder recitalist, then sang in opera at Gelsenkirchen and elsewhere from 1984; Roles have included Orpheus, Octavian, the Composer in Ariande auf Naxos, Monteverdi's Nero, Sesto in La Clemenza di Tito, (Ludwigsburg 1983-84), and Dorabella; Sang Cornelia in a concert performance of Tito at the Grosses Festspielhaus Salzburg, 1991; Arsace in Semiramide and Clairon in Capriccio at Zurich, 1992; Lieder recitals

and concerts at Berlin, Vienna, Stuttgart and Frankfurt and in France and Italy. *Recordings:* Le Roi David by Honegger; Bach's Christmas Oratorio. *Address:* Zurich Opera, Falkenstrasse 1, CH-8008 Zurich, Switzerland

KALLMANN Helmut, b. 7 Aug 1922, Berlin, Germany. Music Librarian; Historian. m. Ruth Singer, 1 stepdaughter. *Education:* BMus, 1949, LLD 1971, University of Toronto; Royal Conservatory of Music, Toronto (piano). *Career:* Music Librarian, 1950-70, Supervisor, 1962-, Canadian Broadcasting Corporation, Toronto; Chief, Music Division, National Library of Canada, Ottawa, 1970-87. *Publications:* Catalogue of Canadian Composers, 1952; A History of Music in Canada 1534-1914, 1960; Encyclopedia of Music in Canada, English, 1981, French 1983, both co-edited with Gilles Potvin & Kenneth Winters; Music for Orchestra I (The Canadian Musical, Heritage series, Vol 8), edited by H K, Ottawa, 1990; Encyclopaedia of Music in Canada, 2nd ed, 1992, English, French, 1993. *Contributions to:* The Canadian Composer; The Canada Music Book; The Canadian Music Journal; Fontes Artis Musicae; Opera Canada; number of dictionaries & encyclopaedias. *Hobbies:* Music; Travel. *Address:* 38 Foothills Drive, Nepean, Ontario, Canada K2H 6K3.

KALMÁR Magda, b. 4 Mar 1944, Budapest, Hungary. Soprano. *Education:* Department of Singing, Bela Bartók Conservatory, Budapest. *Career:* Budapest State Opera, 1969-; Frequent performer in Hungary's concert halls and on Hungarian radio and television; Guest Performer at numerous operas including Austria, Belgium, Cuba, Czechoslovakia, Teatro la Fenice, Italy, Berlin, Leningrad, Stockholm and Paris; roles include Mozart's Blondchen, Despina and Cherubino, Verdi's Oscar, Adele in Die Fledermaus, Don Pasquale and Norina by Donizetti, Adina in L'Elisir d'Amore, Mozart's Pamina, Rossini's Rosina, Alban Berg's Lulu, R Strauss's Sophie in Der Rosenkavalier and Verdi's Gilda in Rigoletto; sang at Budapest 1987, in the premiere of Szokolay's Ecce Homo. *Recordings:* Has made numerous recordings including: Haydn's Il Ritorno di Tobia; Rossini's Mosè in Egitto and Dittersdorf's oratorio Esther; Motets. *Honours:* Grand Prix du Disque, 1975, 1977; 1st prize, International Rostrum for Young Performing Artists, Bratislava, 1972; Scholarship, Budapest State Opera, 1967. *Address:* c/o Hungarian State Opera House, Népöztársaság utja 22, 1061 Budapest, Hungary.

KALUDOV Káludy, b. 1953, Varna, Bulgaria, Singer (Tenor). *Education:* Studied at Sofia Conservatory with Jablenska, graduating in 1976. *Career:* Member of the Sofia Opera from 1978; Guest engagements in Europe and North America, including Dimitri in Boris Godunov at Houston and Chicago, conducted by Abbado; Sang Faust in Mefistofele at Lisbon 1990, Alvaro in La Forza del Destino at Poznan, 1991; Riccardo (Ballo in Maschera) at Genoa 1991, Puccini's Des Grieux at Trieste and Radames at Tel Aviv, 1992; Manrico in Trovatore at Festivals: Salzburg, 1992, Deutsche Oper Berlin, 1992 and 1993, Wiener Staatsoper, 1994; Puccini's Des Grieux at La Scala, Milan, 1992 and at Palermo, 1993; Foresto in Attila at Wiener Staatsoper, 1984, and at La Scala, 1991 (conducted by Riccardo Muti) and RAI Video; Singer in Rosenkavalier at Wiener Staatsoper, 1990, and at Deutsche Oper Berlin, 1993, Staatsoper Berlin, 1992; Don Carlo in Don Carlo at Bayerische Staatsoper, Munich, 1993, National Opera, Sofia, 1988, Madrid, 1986; Requiem, G Verdi at London, 1983 at Festival Hall, Houston, 1992, Tel Aviv with Israel Philharmonic Orchestra conducted by Zubin Mehta; Radames in Aida at Staatsoper Berlin, 1993, Finland, 1994. *Recordings:* Goltsin in Khovanschchina and Vladimir in Prince Igor, with forces of the Sofia Opera conducted by Emil Tchakarov; Janáček's Glagolithic Mass with Charles Dutoit, Montreal, Decca, 1991; Rachmaninov's The Bells with Charles Dutoit, Philadelphia, Decca, 1992; Puccini's Des Grieux Manon Lescaut with BRT Philharmonic Orchestra, Brussels (conducted by Alexander Rahbari), Naxos, 1992. *Address:* Śreniawitów 7 m 59, 03-188 Warsaw, Poland.

KALUZA Stefania, b. 1950, Katowice, Poland. Singer

(Mezzo-soprano). *Education:* Studies in Wroclaw and Vienna with Hans Hotter and Anton Dermota. *Debut:* Opera, Wraclaw. *Career:* Sang in Warsaw and Poznan; Also at the Landestheater Salzburg from 1984, and made guest appearances at the Vienna Staatsoper, Bregenz Festival and Brussels (in The Cunning Little Vixen); Versailles Festival, 1989, as Bersi in Andrea Chenier, Dusseldorf, 1989 as Amneris. Appearances with the Zurich Opera from 1988, as Marcellina in Figaro, Martha in Mefistofele, Pamela in Fra Diavalo and Larina in Eugene Onegin, 1991; Sang Preziosilla at Zurich 1992; Other roles include Dorabella, Frau Fluth, Ulrica and Rosina; Concert engagements in Poland, Hungary, Italy and Russia. *Recordings include:* Frau Litumlei in Zemlinsky's Kleider Machen Leute. *Honours include:* Winner, Belvedere International Competition, Vienna, 1983. *Address:* c/o Opernhaus Zurich, Falkenstrasse 1, CH-8008 Zurich, Switzerland.

KAMENÍKOVÁ Valentina Jurijevna, b. 20 Dec 1930, Odessa, USSR. Pianist. m. Jaroslav Kamenik, 1954, 2 sons. *Education:* Odessa Music High School; Prague Academy of Arts. *Career:* Prague Spring Festival; Salzburg Festival; Concerts in: West Berlin, London, Madrid, Vienna, Palma de Mallorca; Chopin Festival in Polensa; Concert Tour, Europe; Professor, Prague Academy of Arts. *Recordings:* Tchaikovsky: Great Sonate and Dumka; Rachmaninov: Piano Concerto No 1; Rhapsody on Paganini Theme; Chopin: Ballades; Mazurkas; Beethoven: Piano Sonatas No 4 and No 32; Tchaikovsky: Piano Concerto No 1; Mozart: Sonatas No 11 and 12; Haydn: 4 Piano Concertos; Liszt: Sonata in B Minor; Mephisto Waltz; Brahms: Sontata No 1; Rhapsodies; Liszt: Piano Concertos No 1 and 2; Prokofiev: Sonatas No 1 and 3; etc. *Honours:* Prize Supraphon for Recording of Tchaikovsky Piano Concerto No 1, 1973; Wiener Flotenuhr, Preis der Mozartgeminde, Wien. *Membership:* Jury Member, International Piano Competitions. *Hobby:* Cars. *Address:* Cechovo nám 9, 101 00 Prague 10, Czech Republic.

KAMINKOVSKY Rimma, b. 1940, Russia. Violinist. *Education:* Studied in Odessa and Warsaw, at Tel Aviv from 1969 and in the USA with Shmuel Ashkenazi. *Career:* Teacher at the Rubin Academy of Music in Jerusalem, former co-leader of the Jerusalem Symphony Orchestra; Member of the Israel Philharmonic, with appearances as soloist; Co-Founder, Jerusalem String Trio, 1977, performing in Israel and Europe from 1981; Repertoire includes String Trios by Beethoven, Dohnanyi, Mozart, Reger, Schubert and Tanyev, Piano Quartets by Beethoven, Brahms, Dvořák, Mozart and Schumann; Concerts with Radu Lupu and Daniel Adni. *Recordings:* Albums under several record labels. *Address:* Anglo Swiss Ltd, 3 Primrose Mews, 1a Sharpleshall Street, London NW1 8YW, England.

KAMINSKI Pawel Witold, b. 9 Mar 1958, Warsaw, Poland. Pianist; Teacher; Editor of Music. m. Ewa Kaminska, 27 June 1982. *Education:* MA with distinction, Academy of Music, Warsaw, 1983. *Career:* Assistant Professor, Academy of Music, Warsaw 1984- ; Co-editor in the National Edition of F Chopin's works, Polish Music Publications, 1985-; Chopin recitals in Poland and abroad (Austria, France, Arab Emirates) 1980-; Appearances as soloist with Polish orchestras 1983-; Interview on editing Chopin on Polish Radio, 1990. *Publications:* F Chopin: Studies 1990; Various Pieces 1990; Preludes 1991; Various Works 1991. *Honours:* Ministry of Culture and Arts Prize for outstanding achievements in studies, 1983. *Hobbies:* Swimming; Wind-surfing; Trying to understand scientific magazines. *Address:* ul Chocimska 33 m 6, 00-791 Warsaw, Poland.

KAMNITZER Peter, b. 27 Nov 1922, Berlin, Germany. Violist; College Professor. *Education:* Studied at the Juilliard and Manhattan Schools, New York. *Career:* Co-founded the La Salle String Quartet at the Juilliard School, 1949; Many concerts featuring modern composers and the quartets of Beethoven; European debut 1954; Composers who have written for the ensemble include: Hans Erich Apostel, Earle Brown,

Henri Pousseur, Mauricio Kagel, György Ligeti, Penderecki and Witold Lutoslawski; Quartet-in-residence, Colorado College 1949-53, the Quartet-in-residence and Professor, Cincinnati College-Conservatory of Music; Quartet disbanded 1988. *Recordings include:* Works by Berg, Schoenberg, Webern and Zemlinsky; Beethoven's Late Quartets. *Address:* c/o Cincinnati College-Conservatory of Music, Cincinnati, OH 45221, USA.

KAMP Harry van der, b. 1947, Kampen, Holland. Singer (Bass). *Education:* Studied with Alfred Deller, Pierre Bernac, Max von Egmond and Herman Woltman. *Career:* Appearances in solo recitals and in oratorios: conductors include Nikolaus Harnoncourt, Gustav Leonhardt and Ton Koopman; Leading parts in operas by Monteverdi, Handel, Mozart, Pergolesi and Rossini in Milan, Venice and elsewhere in Europe; Engagements at the Berlin, Carinthian, Flanders, Spoleto and Holland Festivals; Founder and director of the Dutch vocal ensemble Gesualdo Consort Amsterdam; Member and artistic adviser of The Netherlands Chamber Choir; Guest teacher at the Early Music Academy in Bremen and Antwerp; Sang in the Towards Bach concert series on London's South Bank, August 1989; sang in Cesti's L'Orontea at the 1990 Innsbruck Festival of Ancient Music. *Recordings include:* Le Testament de François Villon, by Ezra Pound. *Honours include:* Edison Prize, for Ezra Pound recording. *Address:* c/o De Netherlandse Opera, Waterlooplein 22, 1011 PG Amsterdam, Holland.

KAMPEN Bernhardt Anthony van, b. 4 Mar 1943, Bushey, Hertfordshire, England. Double Bass Player. *Education:* Hornsey College of Art; Guildhall School of Music. *Career:* Art Editor, Aldus Books, 1964-66; Founder Member, New British Broadcasting Corporation Orchestra (later Academy of the British Broadcasting Corporation), 1966; Principal Bass, New British Broadcasting Corporation Orchestra, 1967-68; Freelance in London with London Symphony Orchestra, Royal Philharmonic Orchestra, and others; British Broadcasting Corporation Symphony Orchestra, 1972-78; freelance musician and artist, viols, violone, and Baroque and Classical double-bass with various early music groups; Teacher. *Recordings:* With British Broadcasting Corporation Symphony Orchestra, Academy of Ancient Music, London Classical Players, City of London Sinfonia, Hanover Band, London Sinfonietta. *Hobbies:* Double-bass player and artist; Composing; Astronomy; Travel; Reading; History; Natural History; Conservation. *Address:* Borovere, The Chase, Pinner, Middlesex HA5 5QP, England.

KAMU Okko, b. 7 Mar 1946, Helsinki, Finland. Conductor. *Education:* Violin studies with Vaino Arjava at the Sibelius Academy, Helsinki. *Career:* Leader of the Suhonen Quartet 1964; Leader of the Finnish National Opera Orchestra 1966-69; Conducted Britten's The Turn of the Screw in Helsinki 1968; Guest conductor Swedish Royal Opera 1969; Chief Conductor, Finnish Radio Symphony orchestra 1971-77; Music Director, Oslo Philharmonic 1975-79; Music Director, Helsinki Philharmonic, 1981-; Principal Conductor, Dutch Radio Symphony, 1983-86; Principal Guest Conductor, City of Birmingham Symphony Orchestra, 1985-88; Principal Conductor, Sjaelland Symphony Orchestra, Copenhagen, 1988-; Guest engagements with the Berlin Philharmonic, Suisse Romande Orchestra, Vienna Philharmonic and orchestras in Mexico, South America, Australia and Europe; Conducted the premieres of Sallinen's operas The Red Line and The King Goes Forth to France; Metropolitan Opera 1983, US premiere of The Red Line; Covent Garden 1987, in the British premiere of The King Goes Forth to France; Opera conductor at the Savonlinna Festival, Finland; Gothenburg Opera, Don Giovanni and Il Barbiere di Siviglia. *Recordings:* For Deutsche Grammophon, CBS, EMI, BIS and MFP; Sallinen's Shadows, Cello Concerto and 5th Symphony (Finlandia). *Honour:* Winner, First Herbert von Karajan Conductors' Competition, Berlin 1969. *Address:* Terry Harrison Artists Management, 3 Clarendon Court, Park Street, Charlbury, Oxon OX7 3PS, England.

KANAZAWA Masakata, b. 6 Jan 1934, Tokyo, Japan. Musicologist; University Professor. m. Chizuko Yasukawa, 1s. *Education:* BA International Christian University, Tokyo, 1957; AM, 1961, PhD, 1966, Harvard University. *Career:* Teacher, Fellow, Tutor in Music, Harvard University, 1963-66; Lecturer in Music, 1966-82, Professor in Musicology, 1982-, International Christian University, Tokyo; Fellow in Music, Harvard University Centre for Italian Renaissance Studies, Florence, 1970-71; Visiting Professor, various colleges in the USA. *Publications:* The complete works of Anthony Holborne, 1967, 1973; Antonii Janue opera omnia, 1974; The Musical MS Montecassino 871, 1978 (co-author); Contributor to New Grove Dictionary; Musicology Reference Books and Journals. *Honours:* John K Paine Fellowship, 1962; Deems Taylor Award, American Society of Composers, Authors and Publishers, 1980. *Memberships:* Japanese, American and International Musicological Societies. *Hobbies:* Theatre; Travel. *Address:* 2-2-7 Niishikata, Bunkyo, Tokyo 113, Japan

KANG Dong-Suk, b. 28 Apr 1954, Seoul, Korea. Violinist. m. Martine Schittenhelm, 7 Oct 1983, 1 son, 1 daughter. *Education:* Juilliard School, 1967-71; The Curtis Institute of Music, Diploma, 1975. *Career:* Solo appearances with orchestras: Philadelphia, Cleveland, St Louis, San Francisco, National Symphony, Montreal, Stuttgart Philharmonic, Munich Philharmonic, Orchestre National de France, Royal Philharmonic, Philharmonia, BBC Orchestras, Birmingham, Hallé, Scottish National, Bournemouth, Northern Sinfonia, London Mozart Players etc; Promenade Concerts London 1987 (Glazunov Concerto), 1990 (Sibelius) and 1991 (Tchaikovsky); Season 1992/93 included tour to Japan and concerts throughout Britain. *Recordings:* Sibelius Violin Concerto with Orchestre National de Belgique, G Octors Conducting; J Fontyn Violin Concerto, (DG); Franck and Lekeu Violin Sonatas with Pascal Devoyon Piano, (RGIP); Nielsen Violin Concerto, Göteborg Orchestra, M W Chung Conducting, (BIS), 1987; Elgar Concerto (Polish National Radio Symphony/ Leaper). *Honours:* San Francisco Symphony Foundation Competition, 1971; Merriweather Post Competition, 1971; Carl Flesch Competition, 1974; Montreal Competition, 1975; Queen Elizabeth Competition, 1976. *Address:* IMG Artists, 22 E 71st Street, New York, NY 10021, USA.

KANG Philip, b. 10 Apr 1948, Seoul, South Korea. Singer (Bass). *Education:* Studied in Seoul and Berlin. *Career:* Sang small roles at the Deutsche Oper Berlin from 1976; Engagements at Wuppertal, Kiel and Nuremberg, Nationaltheater Mannheim from 1986; Roles have included Sarastro, Rocco, Kaspar, Verdi's Sparafucile, Ramphis, Philip II, Ferrando and Padre Guardiano, Wagner's Saland, Pogner, Mark, King Henry and Gurnemanz; Sang in Italy from 1982, Rodolf in Sonnambula at Toulouse 1983, Lisbon, 1984 as Attila, Sarastro at the Théâtre des Champs Elysées, 1987; American engagements at New York and Philadelphia, European at Madrid, Rome, Frankfurt (As Rocco) and Cologne, as Rossini's Basilio; Théâtre de la Monnaie Brussels as Imen in Boris Godunov and as Antonios in Stephen Climax by Hans Zender, 1990; Bayreuth Festival 1987-92, as Fafner, Hagen and Hunding. *Honours:* Winner, Mario del Monaco Competition, 1979. *Address:* c/o Theatre Royale de la Monnaie, 4 Leopoldstrasse, B-1000 Brussels, Belgium.

KANGA Homi, b. 5 Apr 1922, Bombay, India. Musician, (Violinist). m. Rutty Kapadia, 25 April 1944, 1 son, 1 daughter. *Education:* Bachelor of Engineering (BE/Civil/), Bombay University; Fellow, Trinity College, London; Highest Diploma, Paris Conservatoire. *Debut:* Bombay. *Career:* Soloist, Bombay Symphony Orchestra; Recitalist on All India Radio; Member, London Philharmonic Orchestra, 1950-60; Royal Philharmonic Orchestra, 1960-65; Guest Leader, Royal Philharmonic Orchestra on several occasions; Soloist and Director of London Bach Orchestra in several concerts; Soloist on BBC; Leader, Jupiter String Quartet. *Honours:* 2nd International Wieniawski Competition, Warsaw

(Prizewinner), 1952. *Hobbies:* Tennis (Member, Queen's Club, London); Chess. *Address:* 14 Orchard Gate, London NW9 6HU, England.

KANKA Michal, b. 23 May 1960, Prague, Czechoslovakia. Musician; Violoncello. m. 11 Sept 1982, 1 daughter. *Education:* Prague Conservatory and Academy of Performing Arts; University of Southern California, 1983-84. *Debut:* Dvorak Concerto with Czech Philharmonic Orchestra, 1983. *Career:* Regular appearances with Czech Orcehstras, 1982-; Foreign tours to Europe, America, Japan, Australasia, 1982-; Member of the Prazak Quartet, 1986-; Berlin debut with RIAS, 1987; Regular concerts in Salzburg, Munich, London, Amsterdam, Milan, Tokyo and Sydney. *Recordings:* Chopin, Sonata, Stravinsky, Italian Suite, 1984; Schubert, Sonata C, Franck, Sonata, 1989; Mozard Concertone with S Accardo, 1990; Concertone, with S Accardo, 1990; Martinů, 3 sonatas, 1991; Beethoven, Mozart, and Janáček works with Prazak Quartet, 1989-91; A Vivaldi, 7 cello concerts, Supraphon, 1993. *Honours:* Laureate, Tchaikovsky Competition, Moscow, 1982; First Prize, Prague Spring, Competition, 1983; Winner, Cello International Competition, ARD Munich, 1986. *Hobbies:* Skiing; Tourism. *Address:* Peckova 17, Karlin, 18600 Prague 8, Czech Republic.

KANN Hans, b. 14 Feb 1927, Vienna, Austria. Concert Pianist; Composer; Professor of Piano. m. Kue Hee Ha, 17 Jan 1953, 1 son, 1 daughter. *Education:* Vienna Music Academy, Piano Professors: Bloch, Göllner, Wührer, Schulhof; Composition: Lechthaler, Polnauer. *Debut:* Brahmssaal, Vienna, 1946. *Career:* Concerts in whole of Europe, USSR, Asia, China (3 Concert Tours), South America and USA, 1946-; Professor at Ueno University of Arts, 1955-58; Big concerts in Japan, 1955-58, 1960, 1972, 1974, 1976, 1980, 1981, 1982, 1984, 1985, 1986; Professor at the Hochschule für Musik, 1977-. *Compositions:* Sonatina (for piano); Abschnitt; 10 Stücke ohne Bass-schlüssel; Fingerübungen; Concertino; Chamber Music; Music for Television; Experimental Music. *Recordings:* 120 records for RCA; Musical Heritage Society; Vox; Toshiba-EMI; Amadeo; Phonogram; Supraphon; Muza; Preiser-Records; Toshiba-EMI, popular piano music. *Publications include:* Sonatina; Abschnitt 37; Tägliche Fingerübungen für Pianisten; Models; 4 Stücke für Blockflöte und Klavier; Piano enso oboegaki, 1987; Pianists Memories. *Contributions to:* Österreich Musikzeitung; Gendai Ongaku (Tokyo). *Honours include:* Silver Medal, Concours, Geneva, 1948; Körner Preis, 1962 and 1964; Nestroyring, 1985; Ehrenzeichen für Wissenschaft und Kunst 1 Klasse. *Memberships:* AKM; Austro-Mechana, IGNM, OGZM; Vorstandsmitglied der Austro Mechana, 1987; Vorsitzender des Fonds der Austro Mechana, 1988. *Hobbies:* Collecting Antiques, Instruments, Early Music Prints. *Address:* Wien 1010, Sonnenfelsgasse 11/7, Vienna 1010, Austria.

KANNEN Gunter von, b. 22 Mar 1940, Rheydt, Germany. Singer (Bass-Baritone). *Education:* Studied with Paul Lohmann in Frankfurt. *Career:* Sang first at the Pfalztheater Kaiserslautern; Engagements in Bonn and Gelsenkirchen; Principal Bass at the Karlsruhe opera from 1977, Zurich Opera from 1980; Guest appearances in Vienna, Cologne and Salzburg; Théâtre de la Monnaie Brussels 1983, in Le Comte Ory; Paris Opera and Santa Fe 1983 as Bartolo in Il barbiere di Siviglia and Don Pasquale; Drottningholm 1985, as Osmin and as Claudio in Agrippina; Further appearances in Hamburg, Munich, Berlin and Geneva; Other roles include Dulcamara, Nicolai's Falstaff, Baron Ochs, Don Alfonso, Varlaam (Boris Godunov) and Mustaphà (L'Italiana in Algeri); sang Alberich in the Ring at Munich 1987, Bayreuth 1988-90; Schwetzingen Festival 1987, in L'Italiana in Algeri; Aix-en-Provence 1987 as Osmin; Baron Ochs at the Deutsche Oper Berlin 1988; Season 1992 as the Doctor in Wozzeck at the Châtelet, Paris, and as Alberich at Bayreuth. *Recordings include:* Lebendig begraben by Schoeck (Atlantis). *Address:* Festspielhaus, D-8580 Bayreuth, Germany.

KAŃSKI József Celestyn, b. 21 Oct 1928, Warsaw, Poland. Pianist; Musicologist; Music Critic. m. Teresa Grabowska, 1 daughter. *Education:* MA, University of Warsaw; Piano Diploma, Academy of Music, Warsaw. *Debut:* Bydgoszcz, Poland, 1961. *Career:* Numerous performances including with National Philharmonic, Warsaw; Co-Editor, Ruch Muzyczny; Head, Opera Department, Polish Radio until 1979; Numerous radio appearances. *Publications:* Ludomir Różycki, 1955, 3rd Edition, 1983; Editor, The Stars of the Polish Opera, historical series of LP recordings, 1960; Przewodnik operowy, 1963, 5th Edition, 1984; Golden Pages of Polish Pianistic Art, historical series of LP recordings, 1968; Mistrzowie sceny operowej, 1974; Ludomir Różycki's Symphonic Poems, 1971; Editor, A Chopin Discography, historical catalogue of recordings, 1986. *Hobbies:* Collecting records; Swimming; Tennis; Skiing; Driving. *Address:* ul Perzyńskiego 8 m 14, 01-872 Warsaw, Poland.

KANTA Ludovit, b. 9 July 1957, Bratislava, Czechoslovakia. Solo Cellist. m. 9 July 1977, 2 sons. *Education:* Bratislava Conservatorium; Academy of Music, Prague. *Debut:* With Slovak Philharmonic, International Music Festival, Bratislava, Oct. 1982, Strauß-don Quijote. *Career:* 1st Solo Cello, Slovak Philharmonic, Bratislava, 1983; Concert tours and international festivals as Soloist, Slovak Philharmonic: Bulgaria, 1984, USSR and Poland, 1985, Japan, 1987, Spain, 1988; Other foreign tours, Germany, 1980, 1983, 1986, Italy, 1981, Bulgaria, 1983, 1985, Yugoslavia, 1985, Rumania, 1985, 1987, Sweden, 1985; Solo Cellist, Orchester Ensemble Kanazawa, Japan, 1990-. *Recordings:* Dvořák - Cello Concerto, Haydn - Concerto in D major, with Large Orchestra of Bratislava Radio, conducted by Kurt Hortnagel and Ondrej Lenárd; Igor Dibak - premier recording of Cello Concerto, with Slovak Philharmonic, conductor Bystrik Rezucha, Opus; Haydn - Boccherini Concertos, Capella Istropolitana, conductor Peter Breiner, Naxos. *Honours:* 1st Prize, Beethoven Competition, OPAVA, 1977; 2nd Prize, Prague Spring International Competition, 1980. *Hobbies:* Photography; Walking in the mountains. *Address:* Tsuchishimizu 1-400, 920 Kanazawa, Japan.

KANTROVITCH Vera Evelyn, b. 1920, London, England. Violinist; Teacher. m. Ronald Duncan, 1 son. *Education:* Guildhall School of Music and Drama. *Contributions to:* The Music Teacher. *Honours:* Instrumentalists Gold Medal, Guildhall School of Music; Hon FTCL; LTCL. *Memberships:* Incorporated Society of Musicians; European String Teachers Association. *Hobby:* Watching Tennis. *Address:* 5 Orchard Avenue, Finchley, London N3 3NL, England.

KAPELLMANN Franz-Josef, b. 23 Sept 1945, Cologne, Germany. *Education:* Studied in Cologne. *Career:* Sang at the Deutsche Oper Berlin, 1973-75, Dortmund from 1975, notably as Verdi's Luna, Posa, Germont, Tago and Amonasro, Scarpia, Gianni Schicchi, Wolfram, Beckmesser and Kurwenal; Alberich in a new production of Das Rheingold, 1990; Guest appearances at Dusseldorf, Wiesbaden, Karlsruhe, Klagenfurt, Lubeck and Paris (Alberich in Gotterdammerung); Other roles have included Riccardo in Puritani, Guglielmo, Papageno, Toby in the Red Line by Sallinen, Escamillo (at Regensburg, Mozart's Figaro (Gelsenkirchen) and Don Fernando in Fidelio (Granad Festival); Gala concert at the Alte Oper Frankfurt, 1989; Sang Alberich in Siegfried at Brussels, 1991, Beckmessar at Triests, 1992. *Recordings:* Handel's L'Allegro, il Pensieroso ed il Moderato. *Address:* c/o Operhaus, Ruhstrasse 12, 4600 Dortmund, Germany

KAPLAN Abraham, b. 5 May 1931, Tel-Aviv, Israel. Conductor. *Education:* Studied at the Israel Academy in Jerusalem and at the Juilliard School, 1954-57; Conducting studies with William Steinberg and Frederick Prausnitz, composition with Darius Milhaud. *Career:* Directed the Kol Israel Chorus, 1953-54 and 1958-59; Conductor of the Haifa Oratorio Society, 1958-59; Founded the Camerata Singers, USA, 1960; Director of choral music at Juilliard, 1961-77 and the Symphonic Choral Society of New York, 1968-77; Founded the Camerata Symphony Orchestra 1968 and appeared as guest conductor with leading orchestras in the US and Israel; Teacher at the Berkshire Music Center and at Union Theological Seminary New York, 1961-73; Director of Choral Studies at Chautauqua, New York, 1976; Professor of Music at University of Washington, Seattle, 1977; Many choral engagements and recordings with the New York Philharmonic. *Address:* University of Washington, Music Department, Seattle, Washington State, USA.

KAPLAN Lewis, b. 10 Nov 1933, Passaic, New Jersey, USA. Concert Violinist. m. Adria Goodkin, 6 Aug 1961. 1 son, 1 daughter. *Education:* Bachelors degree, 1958, Masters degree, 1960, Juilliard School. *Debut:* Town Hall, New York, 1961. *Career:* Solo concerts, USA, Europe and Far East, 1953-; Violinist-founder, Aeolian Chamber Players, 1961-; Violin and Chamber music faculties, The Juilliard School, 1964-; Music Director and Co-founder, Bowdoin Summer Music Festival, 1964-; Violin Faculty, Summer Academy Mozarteum, Salzburg, Austria, 1987-; Violin Faculty, Mannes College of Music, 1987-. *Recordings:* Numerous. *Publication:* Edited, Caprice Variations for Unaccompanied Violin by George Rochberg, 1973. *Honours:* Numerous grants from Rockefeller Foundation; National Endowment for the Arts; New York State Council on the Arts. *Memberships:* Board of Directors, Béla Bartók Society; Aeolian Chamber Players (President) Bowdoin Summer Music Festival. *Hobbies:* Cooking; Travelling. *Current Management:* Joanne Rile Artists Management. *Address:* 173 Riverside Drive, New York, NY 10024, USA.

KAPLAN Mark, b. 30 Dec 1953, Boston, Massachusetts, USA. Violinist. *Education:* Studied with Dorothy DeLay at Juilliard School, New York; Fritz Kreisler Memorial Award. *Career:* US engagements from 1973, after gaining the Award of Special Distinction in the Leventritt Competition; performances with the Cleveland, Philadelphia, Los Angeles, Pittsburgh and Baltimore Orchestras; Summer Festivals of Aspen, Blossom, Ambler, Grant Park and Santa Fe; European career from 1980: concerts with the Berlin Philharmonic and Klaus Tennstedt; engagements in UK and Israel with Rudolf Barshai; and thereafter with all major European Orchestras gave the European premiere of Marc Neikrug's Violin Concerto with the Hallé Orchestra; BBC Promenade Concerts and concerts with the Royal Philharmonic in London and Italy; associations with the conductors Marek Janowski, Michael Gielen and Charles Dutoit; Piano Trio with David Golub and Colin Carr; Solo Bach recitals in Europe and America. *Recordings:* Paganini and Wieniawski concertos repertoire; Mendelsohn & Brahms Schubert Piano Trios; Sarasate Solo Violin Works. *Address:* c/o Harold Holt Ltd, 31 Sinclair Road, London W14 ONS, England.

KAPLAN Robert Barnett, b. 26 July 1924, Brookline, Massachusetts, USA. Professor. *Education:* New England Conservatory, 1935-39; Scholarship, Jules Wolffers, 1945-46; Scholarship, Settlement Music School, 1946; Boston University, 1965-67. *Debut:* Vendome, 1939; Composition - Willson Osborne. *Career:* Concert Pianist, WMEX; Composer, WBUR; many local recitals, concerts as Director of Music and Composition, Salon of Allied Arts; Many Concerts as President, American Composers Society for Propagation, Publication and Performance of 20th Century Masterpieces; Many Concerts, Harvard Musical Association; Professor, Pianoforte and Composition. *Compositions:* Opus 1 - Temp di Ballo, 1939; Opus 2 - Intermezzo for String Quartet, 1940; Opus 30 - Five Luna Seas, for Violoncello/Piano, 1951; Opus 31 - Sonatina, Piano, 1953; Sonata, Piano, 1954; Opus 32, Andante con Variazioni - Opus 33 1972; Trio Concertante Opus 34, 1973; Notturno, Flute, 1974; Opus 35, Duo da Camera, 1975; Opus 36, String Quartet, 1976; Opus 37, Concerto for Violin and Orchestra, 1980; Opus 38, Impromptu, Piano, Opus 39, 1980; Fantasy Variations 1981; Opus 40, Sonata, Violin, 1981; Opus 41, Sonata, Cello, 1982; Opus 42,

Rhapsody, 1983; Opus 43, Concerto, Piano, 1984; Opus 44 Capriccio, Piano, 1985; Opus 45 Sonata, Clarinet, 1986, Opus 46; Concerto for Violoncello and Orchestra (1987-88) Opus 47. *Recordings:* Many including early piano and chamber recordings (in the archives of Ventress Library, Marshfield). *Publications:* A Compendium of Orchestral Matters 1982; Notes in the Life of an Artist 1968. *Hobby:* Astronomy. *Address:* 196 Old Ocean Street, Marshfield, MA 02050, USA.

KARAI Jozsef, b. 8 Nov 1927, Budapest, Hungary. Composer; Pianist; Conductor. m. Katalin Kertész, 28 Apr 1958. *Education:* Study of composition and 3 years conductors training, Academy of Music, Budapest, 1947-54. *Debut:* 1950. *Compositions:* Approximately 300 works for chorus mainly based on 20th century Hungarian poets' poems and poems of Goethe, Shelley, C Sandburg, Christina Rossetti, Petrarca, E Lear, Rilke, Trakl, J R Jimenez, G Storm, Christian Morgenstern, G Carducci. Works for wind instruments, strings, piano, organ and orchestra; 88 works published by Edition Musica, Budapest and 48 by other publishers. *Recordings:* 50 works, mainly by Hungaroton, Budapest. *Publications:* Children and Female Choruses, EMB, 1970; Mixed Choruses, EMB, 1977; Twelve Spirituals, EMB, 1978; Easy Children's Choruses, EMB, 1978; Tenders of the Fire, 14 mixed choruses, NPI, 1968-69; Selected Female Choruses, 1992, Zen-on Music Publishers, Tokyo. *Honours:* Erkel Prize, 1972; SZOT Prize, 1980. *Memberships:* Association of Hungarian Composers Composers; Hungarian Art Foundation; Hungarian Kodály Society. *Hobbies:* Drawing; Collecting car and train models; Sport. *Address:* 1151 Budapest, Gyóztes u 19, Hungary.

KARASIK Gita, b. 14 Dec 1949, San Francisco, California, USA. Concert Pianist. m. Lee Caplin, 25 June 1975. *Education:* Private study with Mme. Rosina Lhevinne, Juilliard; Karl Ulrich Schnabel; Lev Schorr; San Francisco Conservatory of Music. *Debut:* San Francisco/SF Symphony, 1958; NYC/Carnegie Hall, 1969. *Career:* First American Pianist to make official concert tour of Peoples Republic of China; Guest Soloist, National Television Debut: The Bell Telephone Hour, NBC, 1963; Guest Soloist; San Francisco Symphony, 1958, 69, 72, 74; Los Angeles Philharmonic, 1971; St Louis Symphony, 1974-75; Boston Pops Orchestra with Arthur Fiedler, 1975; Indianapolis Symphony, 1972, 76; Atlanta Symphony, 1972; Singapore Symphony, 1980-81; Hong Kong Philharmonic, 1980-82; Tours of Latin America, Far East, Europe, USA; Film Scores: Andy Warhol: Made in China, 1986; The Serpent and the Rainbow, 1988; To Die For, 1989; Son of Darkness, 1992. *Composition:* Concerto for Gita Karasik No. 2 by Andrew Imbrie, as first prize Ford Foundation Artists Award, World Premiere with Indianapolis Symphony for BiCentennial, 1976. *Address:* c/o Lee Caplin Productions Inc, 9595 Wilshire Blvd, Suite 505, Beverly Hills, California 90212, USA.

KARAYANIS Plato, b. 26 Dec 1928, Pittsburgh, USA. Administrator. *Education:* Studied singing at Carnegie Mellon University, and at Curtis Institute. *Career:* Sang as baritone in Europe, then directed the Rehearsal Department of the San Francisco Opera, from 1964; Further study of administration and stage technology at Hamburg, then became Assistant State Director of the Metropolitan Opera National Company, 1965-67; Executive Vice-President of Affiliate Artists Inc, until 1977; General Director of Dallas Opera from 1977, presiding over such productions as the US premiere of operas by Vivaldi (Orlando Furioso, 1980), Der Ring des Nibel and works by Monteverdi, Cimarosa, Rossini, Thomas and Britten. *Address:* c/o Dallas Opera, The Centrum, 3102 Oak Lawn Avenue, Suite 450, LB-130 Dallas, TX 75219, USA.

KARCHIN Louis, b. 9 Aug 1951, Pennsylvania, USA. Composer. m. Julie Sirota, 6 July 1987, 1 daughter. *Education:* BMus, Eastman School of Music, 1973; PhD Harvard University, 1978. *Compositions:* Capriccio for violin and seven instruments, 1979; Viola Variations, 1982; Duo for violin and cello, 1981; Songs of John Keats, 1984; Songs of Distance and Light, 1988; Sonata for Cello and Piano, 1987; String Quartet, 1990; Galactic Folds for chamber ensemble, 1992; Remulus and an opera in one act, 1990. *Recordings:* Duo for violin and cello; Songs of John Keats; Capriccio for violin and seven instruments. *Address:* 24 Mohawk Road, Short Hills, NJ 07078, USA

KARCZYKOWSKI Ryszard, b. 6 Apr 1942, Tczew, Poland. Singer (Tenor). *Education:* Studied in Gdansk with Halina Mickiewiczowna. *Career:* Sang in Gdansk and Stettin, then at the Landestheater Dessau (debut as Beppo in Pagliacci, 1969); other roles included Tamino, Ferrando, Fenton and Rodolfo; Sang in Leipzig from 1974, then in Berlin, Dresden (Tamino and Lensky), Moscow, Zurich, Vienna, New York, Rome, Prague and Aix-en-Provence; Covent Garden debut 1977, as Alfred in Die Fledermaus: returned as the Duke of Mantua, Ferrando, and Alwa in the first local production of Berg's Lulu (1981); Sang in the 1981 stage premiere of Prokofiev's Maddalena (Graz) and the same year sang in Haydn's Orlando Paladino, at the Vienna Festival; Other roles include Ernesto, Nemorino, Rinuccio, Lionel (Martha), Jenik (Bartered Bride), Belmonte, Macduff and Elemer in Arabella; Further appearances in Boston (Duke of Mantua, 1981), Washington, Leningrad, Los Angeles, Zagreb and Lisbon; sang in Rigoletto with the company of the Deutsche Oper Berlin at the Wiesbaden Festival, 1989. *Recordings include:* Szymanowski's 3rd Symphony, The Bells by Rachmaninov, Shostakovich 13th Symphony (Decca); Die Lustige Witwe and Die Fledermaus (Denon). *Address:* c/o Allied Artists Agency, 42 Montpelier Square, London SW7 1JZ, England.

KARETNIKOV Nikolay, b. 28 June 1930, Moscow, Russia. Composer. *Education:* Studied with Shebalin at the Moscow Conservatory, 1948-53. *Career:* Freelance composer from 1953 (Underground, 1963-89); Opera Til Ulenshpigel, unpublished and unperformed in former Soviet Union but recorded in secret over one year, premiered at Bielefeld 1993. *Compositions include:* 4 Symphonies; Operas: Til Ulenshpigel, 1985; The Mystery of Apostle Paul, 1987; Ballet: Vanina Vanini, 1961; Eight spiritual songs in memory of B Pasternak, 1969-89; Six spiritual songs, 1992; Chamber Suites: From Shalom-Aleham, 1986; Fragments from Til Ulenshpigel, 1990; Quartet for strings, 1962; Quintet for strings and piano, 1990; The Sonata for violin and piano, 1961; The Piece for piano, 1970; Two pieces for piano, 1978. *Recordings include:* Til'Ulenshpigel (Till Eulenspiegel), CDs issued by Saison Russe. *Address:* Sadovo-Triumphalnya, 14/12 kv 37, Moscow, Russia.

KARIS Aleck, b. 21 Jan 1945, Washington DC, USA. Pianist. *Education:* BM Manhattan School 1976, with Charles Wuorinen; Juilliard School with Beveridge Webster; Private study with Artur Balsam and William Daghlian. *Career:* Latin American debut 1981 at Sao Paulo; New York debut 1984, playing Chopin, Schumann, Stravinsky and Elliott Carter; Has premiered works by Mario Davidovsky, Milton Babbitt and Morton Subotnick; Member of Speculum Musicae from 1983 and has perfromed with the Comtemporary Chamber Ensemble, New York, St Luke's Chamber Ensemble and the Group for Contemporary Music; Associate in music performance at Columbia University from 1983. *Honours include:* Prize winner, Rockefeller Foundation International Competition, 1978; fromm Foundation grant 1983. *Address:* Music Department, Columbia University, City University of New York, USA.

KARKOFF Maurice Ingvar, b. 17 Mar 1927, Stockholm, Sweden. Composer. 2 sons, 1 daughter. *Education:* Music Theory with Karl Birger Blomdahl; Piano, Royal College of Music, Stockholm, 1945; Teachers Degree, 1951; Counterpoint, conducting and composition with Lars Erik Larsson, 1948-53; Additional composition studies with Erland von Koch, Hans Holewa, Wladimir Vogel, André Jolivet. *Debut:* Duo for clarinet and bassoon, Fylkingen, 1951. *Career:* Assistant Music Critic, Stockholmstidningen, 1962-66; Teacher, Stockholm Municipal Institute of Music, 1965-. *Compositions include:* Lyric suite for chamber orchestra,

Nine Aphoristic Variants, 11 symphonies and 5 small symphonies, 14 solo concertos; Dolorous Symphony for String Orchestra No 9; Symphonic Reflections; Voices from the Past for soprano and strings; Quartet, 2 Tr Horn and Trombone; Ballata, intermezzo e leggenda per pianoforte; Glühende Ratsel Fünf Lieder, middle voice and paino; Early summer, songs for middle voice and pianoforte; Scenes in the desert, low voice and pianoforte; Fantasia for left hand; Kleine Music, English horn. *Recordings include:* Six Chinese Impressions; 7 Pezzi per grande orchestra; Swedish Radio Symphony Orchestra; Epitafium for Nonet; Concerto for cello and orchestra; Symphonic Relfections; Symphony No 4 Trio for violin, viola and guitar; Three songs; Piano Sonata; Solo sonata for violin. *Honours:* Swedish Broadcasting Symphony Orchestra Prize, 1962; Christ Johnson Music Prize, 1964; Atterberg Prize, 1983; City of Stockholm Prize of Honour, 1976. *Memberships:* Royal Swedish Academy of Music; Swedish Society of Composers. *Hobby:* Photography. *Address:* Tackjärnsvägen 18, 161 31 Bromma, Sweden.

KARKOSCHKA Erhard, b. 6 Mar 1923, Mor Ostrava, Czechoslovakia. Composer; Composition Teacher. m. Rothraut Leiter, 27 July 1950, 3 sons, 1 daughter. *Education includes:* DPhil. *Career:* Conductor, University Hohenheim, 1948-68; Professor, Musikhochschule Stuttgart, 1958-; Executive Board, Institut für Neue Musik und Musikerziehung, Darmstadt, 1964-72; Lectures worldwide. *Compositions:* About 100 including music for orchestra, chamber music, chorus scenic works, opera, electronic music, organ music and multimedia projects. Recorded: Ad Hoc 1; Four Exercises for Five Players; Desideratio Dei for Organ, 1963; Quattrologe for string quartet, 1966; Antimony for windquintet, 1968; Dialog for Bassoon and Electronics, 1982; Doch Fülle Zwei und Werde Vier, 1982; Salve Regina for female or boys choir and organ, 1980. *Publications:* Das Schriftbild Der Neuen Musik, 1965; Notation in New Music, 1972, Japanese translation 1977; Analyse Neuer Musik, 1976; Hörerziehung Mit Neuer Musik, Ear Education With New Musik, 1981. *Contributions to:* Melos; Musik und Bildung; Musica; Musik und Kirche; Die Musikforschung. *Current Management:* Musikhochschule Stuttgart, Urbanplatz, 7000 Stuttgart 1. *Memberships:* President 1974-80, Gesellschaft für Neue Musik. *Hobby:* Astronomy. *Address:* Nellingerstrasse 45, 7000 Stuttgart 75, Germany.

KARLINS M(artin) William, b. 25 Feb 1932, New York City, New York, USA. Composer; Educator. m. Mickey Cutler, 6 Apr 1952, 1 son, 1 daughter. *Education:* Manhattan School of Music, New York, 1958-61; BM Composition; MM Composition; PhD Composition, University of Iowa, 1965. *Career:* Assistant Professor of Music, Western Illinois University, 1965-67; Associate Professor, 1967-73, Director, Contemporary Music Ensemble, 1967-81; Professor of Theory and Composition, 1973-, Northwestern University, Evanston, Illinois; His music performed worldwide, 1959-; Guest/Visiting Composer in USA and Great Britain, France and Germany. *Compositions include:* Concert Music No I, orchestra, II, chorus and orchestra, III, woodwinds, brass, piano, percussion, IV, and V, orchestra, Symphony No 1 for orchestra; Chamber music includes: Infinity, oboe d'amore, clarinet, viola, female voice; 2 woodwind quintets; 2 saxophone quartets; Quintet, alto saxophone and string quartet; Catena I for clarinet and little orchestra, II for soprano, saxophone and brass quintet and III concerto for horn and orchestra; Various choral works a cappella; 3 piano sonatas; Solo piece with passacaglia, clarinet; Fantasia on My Mother's Name, flute; Relfux, concerto for amplified double bass, solo wind ensemble, piano, percussion; Concerto for alto saxophone and orchestra; Chameleon, harpsichord; Impromptu, alto saxophone and organ; Suite of Preludes for piano 1988; Saxtuper, saxaphone, tuba and percussion; Introduction and Passacaglia, 2 saxaphones and piano; Looking out of My Window, treble chorus and viola; Quartet For Strings, with soprano in the last movement, 1959-60; Nostalgie for ensemble of 12 saxophones, 1991; Elegy for orchestra, 1992; Nightlight for saxophone quartet,

1992-93; Lamentations - In Memoriam, 3 flutes (pieces), 3 trumpets, 3 trombones, tuba, harp, percussion, organ and narrator; All music published by the following: Alphonse Leduc & Cie, C F Peters, Southern Music Co, Pembroke Music Co (Carl Fischer), Tritone Press (Theo Presser), Media Press, Seesaw Music, Needham Publication and American Composers Editions. *Hobbies:* Collecting records; Literature; Art; Cinema; Theatre. *Current Management:* Rosalie Calabrese Management, 170 West 74th Street, New York, NY 10023, USA. *Address:* School of Music, Northwestern University, Evanston, IL 60208, USA.

KARLSOON Lars Olof, b. 24 Jan 1953, Jomala, Finland. Composer. *Education:* Studies, Sibelius Academy, 1972-82; Diploma in Composition, 1983; Higher Degree in Piano, 1979; Chamber Organist, 1976; Studies at the Hochschule der Künste, W Berlin, 1982-83. *Career:* Lecturer at The Sibelius Academy, 1983-86 in Music Analysis and Composition; Founder, The Culture Festival, Aland, 1983-; TV and Film Music. *Compositions:* Five Aphorisms for Piano; Canto Drammatico for Solo Violin; Edition Fazer. Composition for Organ and Wind Ensemble; Arioso for Piano Trio; Composition for Organ and Passacaglia e Fuga (Bach) for Organ; Composer Portrait; Canto dramm; Arioso, Passacaglia e fuga on Ondine Label. *Recordings:* Five Aphorisms on Proprius Label; Dialogue on Sibelius Academy Label. *Contributor to:* Critic at the Huvundstadabladet in Helsinki, 1982-84. *Honours:* 2nd Prize in Composition Competition related to the International Sibelius Violin Competition, 1980; 3 year working stipend from the Swedish Culture Foundation, 1986. *Memberships:* Society of Finnish Composers. *Address:* Helsingegatan 10A 34, 00500 Helsinki 50, Finland.

KAROLYI Otto Jozsef, b. 26 Mar 1934, Paris, France. University Lecturer; Author. m. Benedikte Uttenthal, 17 Apr 1976, 1 son. *Education:* Bela Bartók Conservatoire, Budapest; Akademie für Musik und darstellende Kunst, Vienna; A MUS TCL, Trinity College of Music, London, England; BMus, University of London. *Career:* WEA Tutor, 1963-76; Music Therapist, mental hospitals, 1965-69; Visiting Lecturer, University of London, Imperial College of Science and Technology, 1966, 1968; Tutor, Head, Musicianship, Watford School of Music, 1965-75; Tutor, Counsellor, Open University, 1976; Senior Lecturer, City of Leeds College of Music, 1976-78; Senior Lecturer, in Charge of Music, University of Stirling, 1978-; Honorary Lecturer, University of St Andrews. *Publications:* Introducing Music 1965; Music Session One 1966-68; Erkel and the Hungarian Traditions 1972; Modern British Music, 1994; Introducing Modern Music, 1994. *Contributions to:* Musical Times; Times Educational Supplement; Radio Times; Journal of International Folk Music Council; Making Music. *Address:* Music Dept, University of Stirling, Scotland, FK9 4LA.

KAROLYI Sandor, b. 24 Sept 1931, Budapest, Hungary. Professor. m. Suzanne Godefroid, 3 July 1954, 2 sons, 1 daughter. *Education:* Franz Liszt Music Academy, Budapest, Virtuosity Diploma, 1948; Music Conservatory of Brussels, Virtuosity diploma with distinction, 1954; Teachers include Ede Zathureczky, Leo Weiner, Antal Molnar, Andre Gertler. *Debut:* Franz Liszt Academy, 1941. *Career:* Violin solo, Opera House in Frankfurt, 1956; Professor: Musikhochschule, Frankfurt Main and at the Academie Tonkunst Darmstadt; Concerts for the BBC, and broadcasting companies in Europe; TV appearances in Germany, Japan, Philippines and Australia. *Recordings:* Paul Hindmith: 4 Volin Sonatas with Werner Hoppstock Piano and Károlyi String Quartet recorded No 2 and 6 quartets, plus the Clarinet-Quartet of Paul Hindemith; Max Reger: Violin Sonatas A and C major with Suzanne Godefroid Piano; Prelude and Fugas for violin solo; Giuseppe Tartini Devil's Trill. *Publications:* Gustav Mahler Orchester studies for the 10 symphonies, 1989. *Honours:* Awards: Diploma Contests in Geneva, 1947; Budapest, 1948, London, 1953; Contemporary Contest, Darmstadt, 1952; Vieuxtemps Prize, Belgium, 1959;

Medaille Eugene Ysaye Brussels, 1967. *Memberships:* Deutsche Bachsolisten. *Hobbies:* Gardening; Computer games. *Address:* Dehnhardtstr 30, 60433 Frankfurt am Main, Germany.

KÁRPÁTI János, b. 11 July 1932, Budapest, Hungary. Musicologist; Professor; Librarian. *Education:* PhD, Eotvos Lorand University, Budapest; Diploma, Faculty of Musicology, Ferenc Liszt Academy, Budapest; Candidate in Musicology (CSc), Hungarian Academy of Sciences. *Career:* Folk music research in Morocco, 1957-58; Recording production, Hungaroton, 1959-61; Librarian and Lecturer, Ferenc Liszt Academy of Music, Budapest, 1961-; Folk music research in Japan, 1988. *Recordings:* Kagura: Japanese Shinto Ritual Music (Hungaroton). *Publications:* D Scarlatti, 1959; A Schoenberg, 1963; Muzsikalo zenetortenet, Volumes II, IV, 1965, 1973; Bartók String Quartets, 1975; Bartók kamarezeneje, 1976; Kelet zeneje, Music of the East, 1981; Bartók's Chamber Music, 1993. *Contributions to:* Muzsika; Magyar Zene; Studia Musicologica; Elet es Irodalom; Fontes Artis Musicae; The World of Music; Orbis Musicae (Tel Aviv). *Honour:* Erkel Prize, 1971. *Memberships:* Chairman, Hungarian National Committee, International Association of Music Librarians; Hungarian Music Council; Association of Hungarian Musicians. *Address:* Mester u 77, 1095 Budapest IX, Hungary.

KARR Gary, b. 20 Nov 1941, Los Angeles, California, USA. Double Bass Player. *Education:* Studied with Herman Reinshagen, Warren Benfield and Stuart Sankey. *Debut:* New York 1962 in concert with Leonard Bernstein, and at NY Town Hall. *Career:* European tour 1964, playing at Wigmore Hall London; 1967 founded the International Institute for the String Bass; Teaching appointments at Juilliard School, Yale School of Music, Indiana University, New England Conservatory and Hartt School of Music, Hartford (1976); Formed duo with keyboard player Harmon Lewis in 1972: tours of Europe, the Far East, USA and Canada; Appearances as soloist with the Chicago Symphony, New York Philharmonic, English Chamber Orchestra, London Symphony and Toronto Symphony; Composers who have written for him include Vittorio Giannini, Henze, Wilfred Josephs, Lalo Schifrin, John Downey and Gunther Schuller; Debut tour of Australia 1987-88; Television appearances include series Gary Karr and Friends on CBC in Canada and Bass is Beautiful for Channel 4 in UK; Further TV engagements in France, Belgium, Japan, Norway, Switzerland and USA; Karr Doublebass Foundation Inc. formed 1983, to provide valuable instruments for talented players. *Recordings:* Transcriptions of Paganini's Moses Fantasy and Dvořák's Cello Concerto; Concerto by Lalo Schifrin. *Address:* Kaye Artists Management, 7 Chertsey Road, Woking, SUrrey, GU21 5AB, England.

KARR-BERTOLI Julius, b. 11 June 1920, Munich, Germany. Conductor. m. Charlotte Langesee, 1957, 1 daughter. *Education:* Graduate, Akademie der Tonkunst, Munich, 1939. *Career:* Conductor, Bavarian State Theatres, aged 18: Played Violin, French Horn and Piano; Conductor, Opera of Dortmund, 1942-45; Permanent Freelance at the Bavarian Radio, Munich. 1945-60; Histoire du Soldat by Stravinsky, Munich 1955; Symphony, Harmonie der Welt, by Hindemith, Berlin, 1956; First German performance of the Symphony No 8 by Shostakovich, Munich 1957; First concerts in Italy with the Orchestra del Teatro la Fenice, Venice 1957; Principal concert for the Pergolesi Festival with the first performance of Recitativo e Epitaffio Alla memoria di G B Pergolesi, by Wladimir Vogel, Zurich 1959; Concerts in the Festival-House, Salzburg 1959; Concert for the Sattimane Musicali di Ascona, with the participation of N Milstein and the Swiss first performance of the Symphony No 9 by Shostakovich, Ascona, Switzerland 1960; First concert with the Berlin Philharmonic Orchestra 1965; Symphony No 7 by Dvořák, Munich 1966; First German conductor of the Philharmonic, George Enescu, Bucharest 1966; Permanent guest conducting in Romania 1966-71; Vienna 1967; Rio de Janerio 1967; First concerts in Paris with the Association des Concerts Colonne, 1969; Opera, Production of The Secret Marriage, by Cimarosa, 1971; Professor at the Richard Strauss Conservatory, Munich 1972-85; Concerts in Argentina 1972; Montevideo, Uruguay and Panama 1973; Taiwan and Indonesia 1975; Permanent guest conductor activities in the USSR and Russia, invited by Shostakovich, with concerts in Baku, Tbilisi and Vilnius 1976-; Leningrad Philharmonic Orchestra 1979; Janáček Philharmonic Orchestra, Ostrava, CSSR 1979; Havanna, Cuba 1983; Principal concert for the Musica Bayreuth, with the participation of P Fournier, Bayreuth, Bavaria 1984; Naples with the Scarlatti Orchestra 1984; Concerts in Valletta (Malta) and Palma de Mallorca (Spain) 1985; Concert in honour to Yehudi Menuhin, to his 70th Birthday, Munich 1986; Concert for the Musica Bayreuth, recorded by the Bavarian Radio and transmissioned also in USA, Bayreuth 1987; Guangzhu (Canton) in, China, 1988; Festival concerts in Austria with the Moravian Chamber Philharmonic Orchestra, from Olomouc, CSSR 1988; 50 years of conducting and experience 1989; Music at Pennswood, first concert in US; First Munich performance of the Symphony No 4 by Dvořák, 1989; First German conductor in Tirana, Albania with many concerts throughout the year; Concerts in Havana, Cuba, 1991; First concerts with the Suk-Chamber Orchestra, Prague and nomination as the First Guest-conductor of this orchestra, 1992; Concerts in Sofia, Bulgaria with a performance of the Symphony No 2 by Wilhelm Furtwangler, new concerts in China (Beijing) with the Central Philharmonic Chamber Orchestra, Munich and Ulm with the Suk-Chamber Orchestra, and in Karlovy Vary, Karlsbad, Croatia, 1993. *Recordings:* Lotos, Prague, 1993, Music by Pergolesi and with the participation of Josef Suk, violin. *Publications:* Treatises about classical stylistic problems. *Hobbies:* Climbing; Skiing; Wandering; Reading; Music. *Address:* Sommerstraße 9, D-81543 München, Germany.

KASE Ruriko, b. 7 Nov 1925, Seoul, Korea. Pianist; Music Educator. m. 25 Dec 1957, 1 son, 1 daughter. *Education:* Musashino Music Academy, Japan, 1947; Pupil of Zoltan Kodály, Budapest, Hungary, 1965- 67. *Debut:* Tokyo. *Career:* Leading Educator for Zoltan Kodály System in Japan; Founder, Kodály System Study Society, Tokyo, 1965; A Tour of Hungarian Music telecast, NHK TV, 1966. *Publications:* Piano School 1, 2, 1969; Piano Plaza a, 1977; Piano Plaze b, 1978; A Basket of Songs for Children, 1977; Fun with Music, 1979; A Basket of Piano for Children, 1984; Piano in Singing, 1, 2, 1990, 1991. *Contributions to:* To Music Nova, etc: The Kodály System and Creativity; Piano Teaching Method for the 21st Century; Organization for the Study of Japanese Ethnic Music. *Current Management:* Japan Promotion Association of Piano Culture. *Address:* 6-2-4 Honmachi, Shibuya-ku, Tokyo 151, Japan.

KASHKASHIAN Kim, b. 31 Aug 1952, Detroit, Michigan, USA. Violist; Teacher. *Education:* Studied with Walter Trampler, 1969-70, and Karen Tuttle, 1970-75, Peabody Conservatory of Music, Baltimore. *Career:* Various engagements as a soloist with leading orchestras in North America and Europe; Recitals; Chamber-music appearances; faculty Member, New School of Music, Philadelphia, 1981-86, Mannes College of Music, New York, 1983-86, Indiana University School of Music, Bloomington, 1985-87; Staatliche Hochschule für Musik, Freiburg 1989-; Has prepared transcriptions and has commissioned various works for viola. *Recordings:* Many discs as a soloist and chamber-music artist. *Address:* Hartliebstr 2, 8000 München 19, Germany.

KASPRZYK Jacek, b. 10 Aug 1952, Biala, Poland. Conductor. *Education:* Studied at Warsaw Conservatory. *Career:* Debut at Warsaw Opera, 1975; Principal Conductor and Music Director of the Polish National Radio Symphony until leaving for England 1982; Guest conductor with Berlin Philharmonic, Orchestre National de France, the Stockholm and Oslo Philharmonic orchestras, the Bavarian Radio Symphony and the Rotterdam Philharmonic; 1982 debuts with the

Philharmonia, the Detroit Opera and the San Diego Symphony; British orchestras include the Hallé, Northern Sinfonia, Scottish National Orchestra and regional BBC orchestras; London Prom concert debut 1984, with the BBC Welsh Symphony; Return visits to Frankfurt, Vienna, Hamburg and Scandinavia and to the Cincinnati and San Diego orchestras; Guest at Lyon Opera for A Midsummer Night's Dream, at Bordeaux for Eugene Onegin and at the Stockholm Royal Opera for Die Zauberflöte; Season 1988-89 Fledermaus for Scottish Opera and Der fliegende Holländer for Opera North; English National Opera debut 1992, The Barber of Seville. *Recordings:* For EMI and Cirrus, as well as Polish and Czech companies. *Address:* c/o Harold Holt Ltd, 31 Sinclair Road, London W14 ONS, England.

KASRASHVILI Makvala, b. 13 Mar 1942, Kutaisi, Georgia, USSR. Singer (Soprano). *Education:* Studied with Mdme. Davidova in Tblisi. *Debut:* Bolshoi Theatre Moscow 1968, as Countess Almaviva. *Career:* Member of the Bolshoi ensemble, with guest appearances in Warsaw, Sofia and Brno; Savonlinna Festival Finland 1983, as Elisabeth de Valois; Covent Garden debut 1984, as Donna Anna; Many appearances in operas by Tchaikovsky, Verdi and Puccini; Verona Arena 1985, as Aida; Wiesbaden Festival 1987, as Tosca; sang Voislava in Rimsky's Mlada at the Bolshoi, 1988 (also at Pittsburgh 1989); sang in Mlada at the Barbican Hall, 1989 (first British Performance). *Honours:* Prizewinner, Sofia International Competition 1968; Winner, Montreal Competition 1973. *Recordings include:* Francesca da Rimini by Rachmaninov (Melodyia). *Address:* c/o Bolshoi Theatre, Pr Marxa 8/2, 103009 Moscow, Russia.

KASS Philip Jacob, b. 7 Aug 1954, New York City, New York, USA. Dealer in Rare Violins; Writer on Old Violin Makers. m. Robin Janis Lubert, 30 June 1985. *Education:* BA, Economics, University of Pennsylvania, Philadelphia, 1976. *Career:* American Symphony Orchestra League, 1976-77; Associate, William Moennig & Son Ltd, violin makers, restorers, dealers, appraisers, Philadelphia, 1977-. *Publications:* Entries in: New Grove Dictionary of Musical Instruments, 1984; The New Grove Dictionary of American Music, 1986. *Contributions to:* Journal of the Violin Society of America: Articles including research on the Gemunder family of New York violin makers, the Dodd and Tubbs families of London bow makers, A major work on the workshop of the Cremonese master Nicolo Amati and numerous book reviews; Smithsonian: Article on American violin makers, (Sept 1977); World of Strings (1978-): Numerous articles on violin makers; Liuteria Musica Cultura: short piece on violins by Cremonese masters of the late 18th century; Speeches made on the current state of the violin trade, on modern researches into early violin making, and on the history and use of microphotography as an embellishment to violin bows. *Address:* 209 Park Road, Havertown, PA 19083, USA.

KASSEL Wolfgang, b. 1930, Germany. Singer (Tenor). *Career:* Sang at the Flensburg Opera, 1954-57; Engagements at Mainz, 1957-58, Wuppertal, 1958-60, Krefeld, 1960-66, Bielefeld, 1967-74; Sang at Nuremberg, 1974-80 and made guest apperances at Munich, 1973-76; Appeared as Tannhauser at Covent Garden, 1973, Siegmund at Rouen, 1975; Other roles have inlcuded Lohengrin, Walther, Siegfeied, Florestan, Max, Herod in Salome and Bacchus (Ariadne auf Naxos); Further engagements at Toulouse, Oslo, Warzburg and elsewhere in Europe. *Address:* c/o Stadtische Buhnen, Richard Wagnerplatz 2-10, 8500 Nuremberg, Germany.

KASTU Matti, b. 3 Feb 1943, Turku, Finland. Singer (Tenor). *Education:* School of Royal Opera, Stockholm. *Career:* Principal tenor at Stockholm Opera from 1973; (debut as Laca in Jenůfa, also at Edinburgh, 1974) roles include Rodolfo (La Bohème), Bacchus (Ariadne auf Naxos), Walter (Die Meistersinger), Parsifal, Florestan (Fidelio); Guest appearances in Vienna, San Francisco, Munich, Dusseldorf, Frankfurt and Berlin; Tour of USA 1979, appearing in Detroit, Washington and New York;

Welsh National Opera 1981, as The Emperor in Die Frau ohne Schatten; Milan 1983, in Mahler's Das klagende Lied; Created the Guide in Sallinen's The King Goes Forth to France (Savonlinna, 1984); Edinburgh Festival, 1990, as Tristan in a concert performance of Wagner's opera with the Jutland Opera; Sang Tristan at Aarhus, 1992. *Recordings include:* Menelaos in Aegyptische Helena (Decca). *Address:* c/o Artistsekretariat Ulf Tornqvust, Norrtullsgatan 26, tr 4, 11345 Stockholm, Sweden.

KASZA Katalin, b. 1940, Budapest, Hungary. Soprano. *Education:* Graduate, Ferenc Liszt Academy, Budapest, Hungary, 1967. *Debut:* Abigail in Nabucco, Budapest State Opera, 1967. *Career:* Judith in film, Duke Bluebeard's Castle; Guest Performer as Judith in the Edinburgh Festival (1973), Istanbul Festival and Brussels, Cologne, Florence, Moscow, Paris, Prague, Rome, Salzburg and Vienna; Brünnhilde, in Wagner's Ring, Covent Garden Opera House, London, England, 1974-76; Guest performer as Brünnhilde in Ring, Geneva and various cities of the Federal Republic of Germany, 1977-78; US Debut, Duke Bluebeard's Castle, Los Angeles, California, 1980; Judith at Antal Dorati's Bartók Festival, Detroit and New York, USA, Brussels, Florence, Holland Festival and Paris, France; sang Eudossia in Respighi's La Fiamma, at the Erkel Theatre Budapest, 1989. *Honours:* The Best Dramatic Performer's Diploma, Sofia International Singing Concours, 1968; Liszt Prize. *Address:* c/o Hungarian State Opera House, Népöztársaság utja 22, 1061 Budapest, Hungary.

KATES Stephen (Edward), b. 7 May 1943, New York, New York, USA. Cellist; Teacher. *Education:* Attended Josef Gingold's chamber music classes, Meadowmount School of Music, 1961-62, and Gregor Piatigorsky's master classes, University of Southern California, Los Angeles, 1964-67; Studied with Leonard Rose, Claus Adam, Robert Mann, and Walter Trampler, Juilliard School of Music, New York, diploma, 1968. *Career:* New York debut, 1963; subsequent appearances as a soloist with major US orchestras; Many recitals and chamber-music engagements; Faculty member, Ohio State University, Columbus, 1969-72; Member, Cello and Chamber Music Departments, Peabody Institute, Baltimore, 1974-; Various master classes; Commissioned and played the premiere of Claus Adam's Cello Concerto; Solo Tour of Soviet Union, Nov 1987 guest appearance with Leningrad Philharmonic in Boshoi Hall with Shostakovich Cello Concerto No. 1; Soloist with Baltimore Symphony. Oct. 1989; Member faculty since 1984 at Music Academy of the West in Santa Barbara. California. *Publications:* Articles in Strad, Strings and Musical America. *Recordings:* For Orion, Sonic, RCA, Denon and CRI. *Honours:* 2nd prize, Tchaikovsky Competition, Moscow, 1966. *Memberships:* Violoncello Society, President, 1983-87; Member Jury VIII International Tchaikovsky Cello Competition Moscow, 1988. *Address:* c/o Peabody Institute, Johns Hopkins University, 1 East Mount Vernon Place, Baltimore, MD 21202, USA.

KATIMS Milton, b. 24 June 1909, New York City, USA. Conductor; Violist. m. Virginia Peterson, Cellist, 7 Nov 1940, 1 son, 1 daughter. *Education:* Erasmus Hall High School; BA, Columbia University; Private violin study from age 8; Conducting, National Orchestra Association with Leon Barzin, 1931-35. *Debut:* NBC Symphony, 1947. *Career:* WOR, Mutual Broadcasting Company, Solo Violist and Assistant Conductor, 1935-43; Faculty, Juilliard, 1947-54; NBC (New York) First desk violist with Toscanini, Staff Conductor, 1943-54; Principal Guest-Conductor NBC Symphony 1947-1954 (52 Broadcasts); Music Director, Seattle Symphony, 1954-76; Guest Conductor of Orchestras on five continents; Solo Viola appearances, Chamber Music with Budapest String Quartet, Pablo Casals, Isaac Stern; Artistic Director, University of Houston School of Music, 1976-84. *Compositions:* Editions (viola) for International Music Company include Six Solo Suites of Bach, Three Gamba Sonatas of Bach, Two Brahms Sonatas, Schubert Arpeggione Sonata and 18 other compositions. *Recordings:* Numerous as Conductor and Violist. *Contributions to:* New York Times Magazine; Musical America; Saturday Review; Music Journal. *Honours:* Columbia University Medal of Excellence, 1954; Alice M Ditson Award, 1964; Seattle Man of Year, 1966; Arturo Toscanini Artistic Achievement, 1986; Honorary Doctorates: Whitworth College, 1959, Seattle University, 1972, Cornish Institute, National Orchestral Association, Solo Viola, Chair named Milton Katims Chair, 1982; Milton Katims Scholarship, UH School of Music, 1984; Named Full Professor, Shanghai Conservatory of Music, 1985; American String Teachers 1988 Distinguished Service Award. *Memberships:* American Viola Society; American String Teachers Association. *Hobbies:* Tennis; Chess. *Address:* Fairway Estates, 8001 Sand Point Way NE, Seattle, WA 98115, USA.

KATIN Peter, b. 14 Nov 1930, London, England. Concert Pianist. m. Eva Zweig, 20 Feb 1954, (div) 2 sons. *Education:* Westminster Abbey Choir; Royal Academy of Music. *Debut:* Wigmore Hall, 1948. *Career:* International concert career involving appearances in major concet halls and collaboration with the best known orchestras and conductors; Teaching achievements include professorships at Royal Academy of Music, University of Western Ontario, Royal College of Music. *Recordings:* Approximately 25 recordings for several major companies; complete sets include Greig's Lyric Pieces, Mozart's Sonatas, Chopin's Nocturnes and Impromptus, Rachmaninov's Preludes. *Publications:* Autobiography currently in preparation; Various contributions notably to classical Music (UK) and Clavier, (USA). *Honours:* Brough Memorial Prize, 1944; ARCM, 1952; FRAM, 1960; Chopin Arts Award, 1977. *Memberships:* Incorporated Society of Musicians. *Hobbies:* Reading; Writing; Theatre; Photography; Record collecting; Recording Techniques. *Current Management* Maureen Lunn. *Address:* c/o Maureen Lunn Management, Top Farm, Parish Lane, Hedgerley, Bucks SL2 3JH, England.

KATZ Arnold, b. 18 Sept 1924, Baku, USSR. Conductor. *Education:* Studied violin at the Central Music School and the Moscow State Conservatoire; Conducting at the Leningrad State Conservatoire. *Career:* Conducting career in the USSR from 1956; Founded the USSR Philharmonic of Novosibirsk and brought the orchestra on tour of Britain, 1988; German tour 1989; Guest appearances with the Stockholm Philharmonic, BBC Welsh Symphony Orchestra, Tivoli Orchestra (Copenhagen), Residentie Orchestra (Netherlands) and RT Luxembourg in season 1990-91. *Recordings include:* Music by Shostakovich and Siberian composers with the USSR Philharmonic of Novosibirsk; Russian music with the Leningrad Philharmonic. *Address:* c/o Residentie Orkest, PO Box 11543, 2502 AM The Hague, Netherlands.

KATZ Martin, b. 27 Nov 1945, Los Angeles, California, USA. Pianist; University Professor. *Education:* Studied at the University of Southern California at Los Angeles, accompaniment with Gwendolyn Koldovsky. *Career:* Pianist for the US Army chorus in Washington, 1966-69; Accompanist to such leading singers as José Carreras, Kiri Te Kanawa, Teresa Berganza, Katia Ricciarelli and Nicolai Gedda; Concert tours of North and South America, Australia, Europe and Asia, notably with Marilyn Horne; Editions of Rossini operas performed by Houston Grand Opera and at the Rossini Festival, New York, 1982-83; Edition of Handel's Rinaldo performed at the Ottawa Festival 1982, Metropolitan Opera 1984; Associate Professor at Westminster Choir College 1976; Professor at the University of Michigan 1983. *Address:* Music Department, University of Michigan, Ann Arbor, MI 48109, USA.

KATZ Paul, b. 1941, USA. Cellist. *Career:* Member of the Cleveland Quartet 1969-; Regular tours of the United States, Canada, Europe, Japan, Russia, South America, Australia, New Zealand and the Middle East; On faculty of the Eastman School, Rochester and in residence at the Aspen Music Festival, co-founding the Center for Advanced Quartet Studies; Tour of the Soviet Union and five European countries 1988; Season 1988-89 with appearances at the Metropolitan Museum and Alice Tully Hall, New York; Concerts in Paris, London, Bonn, Prague, Lisbon and Brussels; Festivals of Salzburg, Edinburgh and Lucerne; Many complete Beethoven cycles and annual appearances at Lincoln Center's Mostly Mozart Festival; In addition to standard repertory, has commissioned works by John Harbison, Sergei Slonimsky, Samuel Adler, George Perle, Christopher Rouse, Toru Takemitsu, Stephen Paulus, Libby Larsen, John Corigliano and Oswaldo Golyov. *Recordings:* Repertoire from Mozart to Ravel on CBS Masterworks, Pro Arte, Philips, RCA and Telarc labels; Collaborations with Alfred Brendel (Schubert Trout Quintet), Pinchas Zukerman and Bernard Greenhouse (Brahms Sextets), Emanuel Ax, Yo Yo Ma and Richard Stoltzman; Complete Beethoven Quartets, RCA, 1982; Complete Beethoven Quartets, Telarc, in progress. *Publications:* Interpretation Problems of The Beethoven Quartets, RCA, 1982. *Contributions to:* Numerous articles in Chamber Music Magazine and Editor of Chamber Music Forum for American String Teacher Magazine. *Memberships:* President, Chamber Music America, 1987-93. *Current Management:* ICMm Artists, NY. *Address:* Eastman School of Music, 26 Gibbs Street, Rochester, NY 14604, USA.

KATZER Georg, b. 10 Jan 1935, Habelschwerdt, Germany. Composer. m. Angelika Szostak, 13 May 1975, 3 sons. *Education:* Abitur, 1953; Hochschule fur Musik, Berlin; AMU, Prague; Akademie der Kunste der DDR. *Career:* Freelance Composer, 1960-; Professor for composition (Academy of Fine Arts, Berlin). *Compositions:* Mainly published: Chamber music; More than 10 Symphonic Works; Solo concertos (with orchestra), for flute, oboe, piano, cello, harp and cello; Electro-acoustic works; Multi-media works; 2 ballets; 3 operas. *Recordings:* For Nova, Berlin: Sound House (after F Bacon's The New Atlantis) for 3 orchestras, organ and tape; Kommen und Gehen, woodwind quintet and piano; Aide-Memoire, tape composition; Harpsichord concerto; Konzert fur Orchester No 1; Baukasten for Orchestra; Empfindsame Musik; Streichermusik 1. *Hobbies:* Skiing; Hikibng; Literature; Theatre; Arts; Cooking. *Address:* Weserstrasse 5, 15738 Zeuthen, Germany.

KAUFMAN Frederick, b. 24 Mar 1936, Brooklyn, New York, USA. Composer. *Education:* Studied composition with Vittorio Giannini at the Manhattan School, MMus 1960; Juilliard School with Vincent Persichetti. *Career:* Played trumpet in the New York City Ballet Orchestra, and for various New York bands; Composer-in-residence at the University of Wisconsin, 1969; Director of music for the city of Haifa, Israel, 1971-72; Music performed by major Israeli orchestras and dance companies; Chairman of the music department at Eastern Montane College, 1977-82; Professor of Composition at the Philadelphia College of the Performing Arts, 1982. *Compositions:* A Children's Opera, 1967; The Nothing Ballet, 1975; 3 Symphonies, 1966, 1971, 1978; Concerto for violin and strings, 1967; Interiors for violin and piano, 1970; Violin Sonata, 1970; And the World goes On for percussion and ensemble, 1971; 3 Cantatas for chorus and organ, 1975; Triple Concerto, 1975; 5 Moods for oboe, 1975; Percussion Trio, 1977; Echoes for chorus, clarinet and percussion, 1978; 5 Fragrances for clarinet, harp and percussion, 1980; When the Twain Meet for orchestra, 1981; Metamorphosis for piano, 1981; Southeast Fantasy for wind ensemble, 1982; Mobile for string quartet, 1982; Stars and Distances, spoken sounds and chorus, 1981; Meditation for a Lonely Flute, 1983; Kiddish Concerto for cello and strings, 1984; A/V Slide Show for trombone, 1984; Masada for chorus, clarinet and percussion, 1985. *Publications include:* The African Roots of Jazz, 1979. *Address:* c/o ASCAP, ASCAP Building, One Lincoln Plaza, New York, NY 10023, USA.

KAUFMANN Julie, b. 25 May 1955, Iowa, USA. Singer (Soprano). *Education:* Studied at Iowa University, at the Zurich Opera Studio and at the Musikhochschule in Hamburg. *Career:* Sang at Hagen, then at Frankfurt as Oscar in Un Ballo in Maschera, Blondchen, and Norina; Appearances in Hamburg, Bonn, Stuttgart, Berlin, Salzburg and Dusseldorf; Bayerische Staatsoper Munich 1983, as Despina, Sophie and Zdenka; Aminta in Schweigsame Frau; Covent Garden debut 1984, as Zerlina in Don Giovanni; Gave the premiere of Udo Zimmermann's Gib Licht meiner Augen, 1986; sang at the Salzburg and Wiesbaden Festivals 1987, as Blondchen and Despina; Aminta in Die schweigsame Frau at the Munich Opera 1988 (tour of Japan 1988), Woglinde in the Ring 1989 (also televised); Ludwigsburg Festival 1989, as Susanna, and Carmina Burana at the 1990 Munich Festival; Sang Zdenka in Arabella at La Scala, 1992. *Recordings:* Despina in Così fan Tutte (Harmonia Mundi); Amor in Orfeo ed Euridice, Walther in La Wally (RCA/Ariola); Woglinde in Das Rheingold, conducted by Haitink (EMI), Echo in Ariadne auf Naxos, Schumann's Mignon Requiem and Mendelssohn's Lobgesang; Solo Recital CD with Schönberg, Debussy, Strauss (Orfeo), 1993, with Irwin Gage; Rezia in Pilger from Mecca (Orfeo); Nannetta in Falstaff (BMG) Colin Davis. *Honour:* Bayrische Kammer Sängerin, 1991. *Address:* c/o Bayerische Staatsoper, Postfach 745, D-80539 Munich, Germany.

KAVAFIAN Ani, b. 10 May 1948, Istanbul, Turkey. Violinist; Teacher. *Education:* Pupil of Ara Zerounian, 1957-62, and Mischa Mischakoff, 1962-66, Detroit; Studied with Ivan Galamian and Felix Galimir, Juilliard School of Music, New York, MA, 1972. *Career:* Debut, Carnegie Recital Hall, New York, 1969; European debut, Salle Gaveau, Paris, 1973; Soloist with many major orchestras; Recitalist; Duo recitals with sister, Ida Kavafian; Artist-Member, Chamber Music Society of Lincoln Center, New York, 1980-; Teacher, Mannes College of Music, New York, 1982-, Manhattan School of Music, New York, 1983, Queens College of the City University of New York, 1983-. *Recordings:* Discs as a recitalist and chamber-music artist. *Honours:* Avery Fisher Prize, 1976. *Address:* c/o Herbert Barrett Management, 1776 Broadway, New York, NY 10019, USA.

KAVAFIAN Ida, b. 29 Oct 1952, Istanbul, Turkey. Violinist. *Education:* Studied with Ara Zerounian and Mischa Mischakoff, Detroit, and with Oscar Shumsky and Ivan Galamian, Juilliard School, New York, MA, 1975. *Career:* Founding member of the chamber group Tashi, 1973; New York recital debut, 1978; European debut, London, 1982; Appearances in duo recitals with sister, Ani Kavafian; Violinist of the Beaux Arts Trio, appointed 1992. *Recordings:* Discs as a chamber-music artist; RCA and Nonesuch. *Honours:* Winner, Vianna da Motta International Violin Competition, Lisbon, 1973; Silver medal, International Violin Competition of Indianapolis, 1982; Avery Fisher Career Grant, 1988; Artistic Director of 2 Festivals: Music from Angel Fire, N M and Bravo! Colorado, Vail; Artist member of Chamber Music Society of Lincoln Center. *Current Management:* Harry Bell. *Address:* c/o Beall Management, PO Box 30, Teneafly, NJ 07670, USA.

KAVAKOS Leonidas, b. 1967, Athens, Greece. Violinist. *Education:* Studied at the Greek Conservatory with Stelios Kafantaris; Further studies with Joseph Gingold at the University of Indiana. *Debut:* Athens Festival 1984. *Career:* Cannes Festival, 1985; US debut with the Santa Barbara Symphony, 1986; Athens Festival, 1988, conducted by Rostropovitch, leading to concerts with the National Symphony Orchestra in Washington DC; Concerts at the Helsinki Festival and with the Swedish Radio Symphony conducted by Esa-Pekka Salonen; European tour with the Helsinki Philharmonic conducted by Okku Kamu, 1989; Further appearances in Italy, Spain, France, Cyprus, Turkey, Hungary and Japan; TV and radio recordings in Greece, France, Germany, Spain and Britain. *Honours include:* Winner, 1985 Sibelius Violin Competition, Indianapolis, 1986 International Competition; Winner 1988, Naumburg Competition, New York; Winner 1988 Paganini Competition, Genoa. *Address:* c/o Ingpen and

Williams Ltd, 14 Kensington Court, London W8 5DN, England.

KAVÁSCH Deborah Helene, b. 1945, Washington DC, USA. Composer; Soprano. m. Stephen Scot-Shepherd, 10 June 1977. *Education:* BA, Bowling Green State University, 1971; Mozarteum, University of Salzburg, Austria, 1969-70; BM 1972, MM 1973, Bowling Green; PhD, University of California, San Diego, 1978. *Career:* Founding member, Extended Vocal Techniques Ensemble, 1973; Sang Armide in Gluck's Armide, with Alan Curtis & Berkeley Symphony, US West Coast premiere, 1983; Lecturer in Theory, Bowling Green State University, 1973; Associate in Music, University of California, San Diego, 1976-79; Associate Professor, Theory & Voice, California State University, Stanislaus, 1979-. *Compositions include:* Requiem, performed by Extended Vocal Techniques Ensemble, 1978; Owl & the Pussycat, vocal ensemble, 1974; Soliloquy, solo voice, 1981; Nocturne, solo clarinet, 1982; Beauty & the Beast, Soprano, bass, cello, 1985; Crow & the Pitcher, solo soprano 1984; Tortoise & the Hare, soprano, bass, clarinet/bass clarinet 1983; The Bells, chorus & percussion 1983; Abelard, soprano & viola 1984; Miserve, soprano, clarinet, 1983; Medea, 2 sopranos, 1984; Aviary Suite, solo clarinet, 1985; The Lion and the Mouse, soprano, trombone, 1986. *Publications:* An Introduction to Extended Vocal Techniques: Some Compositional Aspects & Performance Problems, 1980, 1985. *Address:* 6666 Beadnell Way no. 26, San Diego, CA 92117, USA.

KAVRAKOS Dimitri, b. 26 Feb 1946, Athens, Greece. Singer (Bass). *Education:* Athens Conservatory of Music. *Debut:* Athens Opera 1970, as Zaccaria in Nabucco. *Career:* Athens Opera until 1978; US debut at Carnegie Hall, in Refice's Cecilia; Metropolitan Opera debut 1979, as the Grand Inquisitor in Don Carlos; returned to New York as Silva (Ernani), Walter (Luisa Miller), Ferrando (Il Trovatore), Capulet (Roméo et Juliette) and in I Vespri Siciliani; Chicago Lyric Opera in Aida, Lakmé, Les Contes d'Hoffmann and Fidelio; San Francisco Opera in La Gioconda; Guest engagements at La Scala, Paris Opera, Aix-en-Provence, Spoleto, Lyons and Avignon; British debut Glyndebourne 1982, as the Commendatore in Don Giovanni; London debut at the Barbican Hall, in Cherubini's Medée; Covent Garden debut 1984, as Pimen in Boris Godunov; returned in new productions of La Donna del Lago (Douglas, 1985), Le Nozze di Figaro (Bartolo) and Anna Bolena (Enrico VIII, 1988); Rome Opera, 1989, as Silva in Ernani, Bellini's Giorgio in Florence; sang Fiesco in Simon Boccanegra at Cologne, 1990 and Prince Gremin in Eugene Onegin in Chicago; Maggio Musicale Florence, 1990 as Ernest in Donizetti's Parisina; Season 1992/93 as Timur in Turandot at Chicago, Rossini's Mosè with the Israel Philharmonic, Banquo at Cologne and the Commendatore at Aix-en-Provence. *Recordings include:* Don Giovanni. *Address:* c/o Patricia Greenan, 19B Belsize Park, London NW3 4DU, England.

KAWAHARA Yoko, b. 3 Sept 1939, Tokyo, Japan. Singer (Soprano). *Education:* Studied with Toishiko Toda in Tokyo and with Ellen Bosenius at the Cologne Musikhochschule. *Debut:* Niki Kai Opera Tokyo 1958 as Fiordiligi. *Career:* Sang in Bonn as Pamina (1969); Bayreuth Festival 1972-76, as the Woodbird in Siegfried; Member of the Cologne Opera from 1975; Guest appearances in Frankfurt, Hamburg and Tokyo; Staatsoper Hamburg 1986, in La Clemenza di Tito; Other roles include Euridice, Sophie in Der Rosenkavalier, Desdemona, Freia and Liu; many concert appearances. *Recordings include:* Reger's Requiem (Schwann). *Address:* c/o Oper der Stadt Köln, Offenbachplatz, D-5000 Cologne, Germany.

KAWAHITO Makiko, b. 6 Sept 1956, Tokyo, Japan. Viola Player. m. Hideo Etani, 26 Oct 1986. *Education:* Master, Tokyo University of Arts, 1981; Master, Staatliche Musikhochschule, Freiburg, West Germany, 1983. *Debut:* Tokyo, 1985. *Career:* String Quartet with Florin Paul in West Germany and Les Arc, France, 1982-84; Viola Concerto with Orchestra conducted by Yoko

Matsuo in Besançon, France, 1984; Recital in Tokyo, 1985; String Chamber Ensemble with Tokyo Vivaldi Ensemble, 1980-. Radio Appearances on Japan and German Radio. *Honours:* 4th Prize, William Primrose International Viola Competition, USA, 1979. *Memberships:* Tokyo Vivaldi Ensemble. *Hobby:* Appreciation For Arts. *Address:* c/o KAWAHITO, 4-6-6-Fujimicho, Higashimurayama-shi, Tokyo, Japan.

KAWALLA Szymon Piotr, b. 2 June 1949, Cracow, Poland. Conductor; Composer. m. Hanna Kiepuszewska, 28 Apr 1973, 1 daughter. *Education:* Studies as solo concert violinist 1972, as Conductor 1973, as Composer 1974, Chopin Academy of Music, Warsaw. *Debut:* Philharmonic, Cracow, 1964. *Career:* Conductor, Philharmonic Poherien, 1974-78; Conductor-Director, Torun Chamber Orchester, 1978-80; Conductor-Director, Philharmonic and Opera Zielona Gora, 1980-86; Symphonic Orchestra and Chorus, RTV Cracow, 1985-, Concerts in Austria, Bulgaria, Canada, Cuba, England, Germany, Holland, France, Italy, Poland, Romania, Spain, Czechoslovakia, USSR, Vatican, Radio, TV and Films. Professor, Chopin Academy of Music, Warsaw. *Compositions:* Divertimento, Capriccio for violin solo, Oratorio, Pater Kolbe, Cantata, Wit Stwosz, Stabat Mater, Quartet for Strings. *Hobbies:* Car driving; Walking in the mountains; Cooking. *Address:* Lazurowa 6/100, 01-315 Warsaw, Poland.

KAWASAKI Masaru, b. 19 Apr 1924, Tokyo, Japan. University Professor; Composer. m. Taeko Koide, 11 June 1953, 2 sons. *Education:* Diploma 1947, Postgraduate Diploma 1949, Tokyo Academy of Music. *Career:* 1st performance of Compos at Festliche Musiktage Uster, Switzerland, 1971, 1974, 1977, 1981; Director, International Youth Musicale, Shizuoka, Japan, 1979, 1982 and 1985. *Compositions:* March Ray of Hope, 1963; March Forward for Peace, 1966; Essay on a Day for flute and piano, 1969; March Progress and Harmony, 1969; Warabe-Uta for Symphony Band, 1970; Prayer Music Number 1, Dirge, commissioned by Hiroshima City, 1975; Poem for Symphony Band, 1976; Prayer Music Number 2, Elegy, 1977; Romantic Episode, 1979; Romance for Trumpet and Symphony Band, 1982; March Dedicated to Cupid, 1983; In the Depth of Night for flute and cello, 1993. *Publications:* Instrumentation and Arrangement for Wind Ensemble, 1972; New Band Method, 1979. *Contributions to:* Band Journal, Tokyo. *Honours:* Composition Prize, Ministry of Education and President of NHK, 1956; Creative Artists Fellow, UNESCO, 1966-67. *Memberships:* International Society Contemporary Music; Japanese Society Rights Authors and Composers; National Band Association. *Hobby:* Gardening. *Address:* 4-2-38 Hamatake, Chigasaki-shi, Kanagawa-Ken, 253 Japan.

KAY Norman Forber, b. 5 Jan 1929, Bolton, England. Composer; Music Director. m. 22 Jan 1951, 3 sons, 1 daughter. *Education:* Bolton School, 1940-45; ARMCM, Organ, Composition, 1947; ARCO, 1947; Royal Manchester College of Music; Royal College of Music, London. *Career:* Composer-Critic, London, 1950-76; Music Director, HTV, 1976-85; Music Critic, Daily Telegraph, 1964-81; Music Consultant to numerous independent TV Companies, 1989-91. *Compositions:* Miniature Quartet for Woodwind, 1950; String Quartets 1 and 2; Passacaglia for Orchestra, Cheltenham Festival, 1966; Variations for Strings, Harrogate Festival, 1968; King Herod, Cantata, Soloists, Chorus, Orchestra, Llandaff Festival, 1966; 3 Choirs Festival, 1967; Song Without Words, BBC-TV, Winner Italia Prize, 1967; Rose Affair, Opera, BBC-TV, 1968; Xmas Carol, TV Opera, Winner Salzburg Opera Prize, 1980; Robin Hood, Opera for Young People, Buxton Festival, 1986; Daniel, full-scale cantata, St. Davids Hall, Cardiff, starring Sir Geraint Evans, 1988; Piano Trio, Howard Shelley, etc; BBC Radio 3. *Publication:* Shostakovich, Oxford University Press, 1971. *Contributions to:* Articles and Reviews to Musical Times, Music and Musicians, Tempo, Times Literary and Educational Reviews. *Honours:* Italia Prize, 1967; Salzburg TV Opera Prize, 1980. *Membership:* Savile Club, London. *Current Management:* Polygram Ltd, 1993-. *Address:*

Summerhouse, St Donats, Llantwit Major, South Glamorgan CF61 1ZB, Wales.

KAY Ulysses Simpson, b. 7 Jan 1917, Tucson, Arizona, USA. Composer; Professor. m. Barbara Kay. *Education:* Studied piano; University of Arizona, Tucson, MB, 1938; Composition with Bernard Rogers and Howard Hanson, Eastman School of Music, Rochester, New York, MM, 1940, with Paul Hindemith, Berkshire Music Center, Tanglewood, Massachusetts, summers 1941-42, and with Otto Luening, Columbia University, 1946-49. *Career:* Active as a performer, composer, and arranger; Made a consultant to Broadcast Music Inc, New York, 1953; Visiting Professor of Music, Boston University, 1965, University of California, Los Angeles, 1966-67; Professor of Music, 1968-72, Distinguished Professor of Music, 1972-88, Herbert H. Lehman College of the City University of New York. *Compositions:* Operas: The Boor, 1955; The Juggler of Our Lady, 1956; The Capitoline Venus, 1970; Jubilee, 1976; Frederick Douglass, 1980-85; Ballet: Dance Calinda, 1941; Orchestral: Oboe Concerto, 1940; 5 Mosaics for Chamber Orchestra, 1940; Of New Horizons, overture, 1944; Suite in 5 Movements, 1945; A Short Overture, 1947; Portrait Suite, 1948; Suite for Strings, 1949; Sinfonia, 1951; 6 Dances for Strings, 1954; Concerto for Orchestra, 1954; Serenade, 1954; Fantasy Variations, 1963; Umbrian Scene, 1964; Markings, 1966; Symphony, 1967; Theater Set, 1968; Scherzi musicali for Chamber Orchestra, 1969; Aulos for Flute and Chamber Orchestra, 1971; Quintet Concerto for 5 Brass Soli and Orchestra, 1975; Southern Harmony, 1976; Chariots, 1979; String Triptych for String Orchestra, 1987; Chamber: 3 string quartets, 1953, 1956, 1961; Piano Sonata, 1940; Quintet for Flute and Strings, 1947; Piano Quintet, 1949; 5 Portraits for Violin and Piano, 1972; Guitarra, guitar suite, 1973, revised 1985; Tromba for Trumpet and Piano, 1983; Five Winds for Woodwind Quintet, 1984; Pantomime for Clarinet, 1986; 2 impromptus for Piano, 1986; Everett Suite for Bass Trombone, 1988; Many vocal works; Band pieces. *Honours:* Prix de Rome scholarship, American Academy, Rome, 1949-52; Guggenheim Fellowship, 1964-65; Honorary doctorates from various academic institutions. *Address:* 1271 Alicia Avenue, Teaneck, NJ 07666, USA.

KAZARNOVSKAYA Lyubov, b. 1956, Moscow, USSR. Singer (Soprano). *Education:* Studied at the Moscow Conservatory 1976-81, with Irina Arkhipova and Elena Shumilova. *Debut:* Stanislavsky Theatre Moscow 1981 as Tatiana in Eugene Onegin. *Career:* Has sung at the Bolshoi, Moscow, as Nedda Mimi and Lida in La Battaglia di Legnano; Tour of Italy with the Maily Theatre, Leningrad, 1984; Kirov Theatre, Leningrad from 1986 as Leonora (La Forza del Destino and Trovatore), Marina, Violetta, Marguerite, Donna Anna and Tchaikovsky's Iolanta; Paris Opera and Covent Garden 1987, as Tatiana with the Kirov company; Salzburg Festival 1989, in the Verdi Requiem, conducted by Karajan; Zurich Opera 1989-90, as Amelia Boccanegra and the Trovatore Leonora; Cologne Opera 1989-90, as Manon Lescaut and Amelia; Covent Garden 1990, as Desdemona; Concert and oratorio appearances, song recitals with works by Brahms, Wolf, de Falla, Dvořák and Rachmaninov. *Address:* c/o Royal Opera, Covent Garden, London WC2, England.

KEANE David, b. 1940, USA. Composer; Lecturer. *Education:* BSc, BMus, MMus, Ohio State University. *Career:* First composer to use electronic music studio at Ohio State University, 1963; Since 1970, now a Canadian citizen, produced more than 30 major electronic works including those for dance, film, theatre and broadcast; Lectured on aesthetics in new music widely in Europe and North America and published articles in major publications on both continents; conducted lecture series in electronic music at EMS in Stockholm, Musikhochschule in Vienna, National School of Music in Havana, and Cours International in Bourges as well as many places in North America. *Compositions include:* Numerous commissions for non-electronic works including those supported by Canada Council and Ontario Arts Council; produced work for

National Film Board, National Design Council, National Gallery and Canadian Broadcasting Corporation; published works in Canada, USA, Britain and his works have been performed and broadcast throughout North America and Europe; recent commission include those from Cuban Commission of International Music Council (Sinfonia premiered by Trio Jose White in Havana), Groupe de Musique Experimentale de Bourges (Voyage premiered at 10th Festival International de Musique Experimentale), American National Endowment for Arts (Harmonion premiered in Pittsburgh) and Soundstage Canada (Naissance premiered in Yugoslavia at Zagreb Biennial); His music has been a regular feature of annual new music festivals in Brussels and Bourges as well as Warsaw Autumn Festival in Poland and Electronic Music Plus Festival in USA among others.

KEATING Roderic Maurice, b. 14 Dec 1941, Maidenhead, Berkshire, England. Opera and Concert Singer. m. Martha Kathryn Post, 31 Aug 1968, 1 daughter. *Education:* Classics Exhibition, Gonville & Caius College, Cambridge, 1960; BA, Music Tripos, 1963, MA, 1967, Cambridge University; MMus, Yale University, USA, 1965; Doctor of Musical Arts, University of Texas, USA, 1970. *Debut:* Houston Grand Opera, Tales of Hoffmann, 1970. *Career:* Glyndebourne Touring and Festival Opera, 1971-73; Theater an der Wien (Freddy, My Fair Lady), 1971; Permanent contracts in Lübeck, 1972-74, Saarbrücken, 1974-80, Wuppertal, 1980-86, Bonn, 1986-89, Stuttgart, 1989-; Over 80 roles as lyric and buffo tenor; Guest, Kassel, Nuremberg, Hamburg, Düsseldorf, etc.; Guest appearances, Tbilisi, USSR, 1976; Interlaken Festspiel, 1975; Wiesbaden, 1977; Paris Opera, 1981, 1993; London Coliseum, 1982; Warsaw, 1983; Cologne, 1985; Salzburg Festival, 1986; Covent Garden, 1988, Moscow, 1989, Vienna and Schwetzingen Festivals 1990; sang Tiresias in Henze's The Bassarids at Stuttgart 1989; Der Rosenkavalier, Théâtre Châtelet, Paris, 1993; Teacher of Voice at the Freiburger Musikhochschule, Germany; Concerts and radio recordings for BBC, Bavarian Radio, SWF, WDR, and SDR in Germany; Oratorio and church concerts in Italy, France, Spain, Belgium, Holland and Germany. *Publications:* The Songs of Frank Bridge, 1970. *Contributions to:* Musical Times; Musical Opinion. *Hobbies:* Tennis; Photography; Cross Country Skiing. *Current manager:* Inge Tennigkeit, Ottweilerstr 22, 40476 Düsseldorf, Germany. *Address:* Lehenbühlstr 36, 71272 Renningen, Germany.

KEATS Donald (Howard), b. 27 May 1929, New York City, New York, USA. Composer; Professor. m. Eleanor Steinholz, 13 Dec 1953, 2 sons, 2 daughters. *Education:* Mus B primi honoris, Yale University School of Music, 1949; MA, Columbia University, 1952; PhD, University of Minnesota, 1962; Staatliche Hochschule für Musik, Hamburg, Germany, 1954-56. *Career includes:* Professor of Music, Antioch College, Ohio, USA; Visiting Professor of Music, University of Washington, Seattle; Professor of Music, University of Denver, 1975-; Composer, Pianist, at concerts in USA, England and Israel. *Compositions include:* Symphonies No 1 and No 2 (An Elegiac Symphony); String Quartets No 1 and No 2; Piano Sonata The Hollow Men (T S Eliot), for chorus and instruments; Anyone Lived in a Pretty How Town (Cummings), for a cappella chorus; The Naming of Cats (T S Eliot), for chorus and piano; Song cycle, Tierras del Alma (Poemas de Amor) for soprano, flute and guitar; Theme and Variations for Piano; Concerto for Piano and Orchestra; Diptych for Cello and Piano; Polarities for Violin and Piano; Song cycle, A Love Triptych (W B Yeats); Musica Instrumentalis for 9 instruments; Elegy (for full or chamber orchestra); Branchings for Orchestra; Revisitations for Violin, Cello and Piano, 1992. *Recordings:* String Quartets No 1 and No 2; Piano Sonata: Elegy for Orchestra; The Hollow Men; Anyone Lived in a Pretty How Town. *Address:* School of Music, University of Denver, 7111 Montview, Denver, CO 80220, USA.

KEAY Nigel David, b. 13 June 1955, Palmerston North, New Zealand. Musician; Composer. *Education:* Certificate of Executant Music, Wellington Polytechnic,

1978; BMus, Victoria University of Wellington, 1982. *Career:* Active Performer, Contemporary Music (Viola); Mozart Fellow, University of Otago, 1986, 1987; Composer in residence, Nelson School of Music, New Zealand, 1988 & 1989. *Compositions:* Variations for Violin and Piano; Four Piano Pieces, 1983; String Quartet, 1983; Variations for Orchestra, 1983; Variations for Piano; Quartet for Piano, Violin, Viola & Cello, 1986; Diffractions for piano and orchestra, 1987; Interludes for Piano, 1988; Two Pieces for Trumpet, Horn and Trombone, 1988. *Address:* 2 Pollock Street, Dunedin, New Zealand.

KEBERLE David Scott, b. 6 June 1952, Wausau, Wisconsin, USA. Composer; Clarinettist; College Professor. *Education:* BM, Composition, with distinction, Indiana University, 1975; BM, Education, with distinction, Indiana University, 1975; Master of Music in Composition, 1977 New England Conservatory of Music, Boston; Accademia di S Cecilia, Rome, 1980; studied composition with Bernhard Heiden and Donald Martino, clarinet with Earl Bates, Joe Allard and W O Smith. *Career:* Instructor of Music, University of Wisconsin, Baraboo, 1977-81; Co-Founder of Electravox Ensemble, Rome, 1983; Instructor of Music, Loyola University, Chicago, Rome Centre, 1984-88; As clarinet soloist performed in Brazil, Uruguay, Argentina, France, Italy, Israel, Austria and USA; Performed on National Italian Radio 1987, 1988; Instructor of Music, St Mary's College Rome Program, 1991-. *Compositions:* Incantation for Clarinet and Live Electronics published by EDI-PAN Rome 1986; Galoppando Attraverso il Vuoto for solo clarinet 1986 published by EDI-PAN, Rome; Concerto for Trumpet and Chamber Ensemble, 1980, published by EDI-PAN Rome; Murmurs for solo flute published by EDI-PAN Rome, 1989. *Recordings:* ElectraVox Ensemble Incantation for Clarinet and Live Electronics 1986 EDI-PAN Rome; Musicisti Contemporanei: Clarinet and Piano EDI-PAN, 1989. *Honour:* Fulbright Scholarship in Composition, 1979. *Memberships:* American Music Center, New York. *Address:* Via del Pellegrino 75, Int 18, 00186 Rome, Italy.

KECSKEMÉTI István, b. 21 Dec 1920, Budapest, Hungary. Musicologist. *Education:* Doctor in Economics, Budapest University, 1945; Graduate, Pianist, 1943, Musicologist, 1957, Academy of Music, Budapest. *Career:* Dissertation on Mozart's Salzburg Piano Concerto's, 1957; Librarian, Head of Music Division, National Széchényi Library, Budapest, 1957-81; Analysing the music autographs of Z Kodály, Kodály-Archives, Budapest, 1981-; arranger of exhibitions, Hungary and Austria on Haydn, minor classical masters, Dohnányi and Kodály, 1970-80. *Publications:* Kodály, the Composer, Budapest, 1986; Images of Handwriting in Kodály's early music autographs in: Bulletin of the International Kodály-Society, 1988-89; Discoverer and Editor of Autographs by J J Fux, Süssmayr, Schubert, Liszt and has prepared thematic catalogues of the Süssmayr and Dittersdorf manuscripts of the Hungarian National Library; Stylistic studies on the music of Mozart, Chopin, Liszt, Goldmark and Kodály; Z Kodály's compositions. Pecularities of a Thematic Catalogue, 1992. *Honours:* Erkel Prize, 1976. *Address:* Pf14, H-1400 Budapest, Hungary.

KEE Piet, b. 30 Aug 1927, Zaandam, Netherlands. Organist; Composer. 2 children. *Education:* Studied with father, Cor Kee; Organ with Anthon van de Horst, Final Certificate cum laude, 1948, Conservatory of Amsterdam. *Debut:* Zaandam, 1941. *Career:* Organist of Schnitgerorgan, St Laurens Church, Alkmaar, 1952-87; Municipal Organist, St Bavo Church, Haarlem, 1956-1989; Professor of Organ, Conservatory of the Society Muzieklyceum, Sweelinck Conservatory, Amsterdam, until 1987; Professor, International Summer Academy, Haarlem; Many concert tours worldwide; TV films of compositions Confrontation and Integration. *Compositions:* Variations on a Carol, 1954; Triptych on Psalm 86, 1960; Two Organ Works, 1962; Four Manual pieces, 1966; Music and Space for 2 Organs and 5 Brasswinds, 1969; Intrada for 2 Organs; Choral music;

Chamber music; Valerius Gedencklanck, 1976; Confrontation for 3 street organs and church organ, 1979; Integration for mixed choir, flageolet, mechanical birds, barrel organs and church organ, 1980; Frans Hals Suite for Carillon, 1990; Flight for flute solo, 1992. *Recordings:* Baroque music, romantic and modern music, HMV, CNR; Philips, CBS, Telefunken; Confrontation-Piet Kee, Philips; Piet Kee at St Bavo-Haarlem and the Grote Kerk Alkmaar, Guild Records; Since 1989 a new series of Chandos records, featuring Piet Kee, released: Sweelinck-Buxtehude, Buxtehude - Bach (Alkmaar), Hindemith-Reger (St Bavo, Haarlem), Bruhns - Buxtehude (Do Cathedral, Roskilde); Bach organ works I, II and III (Haarlem St Bavo); Franck organworks (San Sebastian); Piet Kee at Weingarten; Piet Kee at the Concertgebouw. *Publications:* The Secrets of Bach's Passacaglia, Musik und Kirche, 1982; The Diapason, 1983. Astronomy in Buxtehude's Passacaglia, The Diapason, Ars Organi, Het Orgel, 1984; Numbers and Symbolism in the Passacaglia and the Ciacona, Het Orgel, 1986, Musik und Kirche, 1988; Loosemore Papers, 1988. *Hobbies:* Ornithology; History. *Address:* Nieuwe Gracht 41, 2011 ND Haarlem, Netherlands.

KEECH Diana, b. 29 May 1945, Hull, England. Peripatetic Woodwind. *Education:* Royal College of Music, 1963-66; ARCM, 1965; GRSM, 1967; Breton Hall College of Education, 1966-67. *Debut:* Cimarosa Oboe Concerto with Scarborough Symphony Orchestra, 1974. *Career:* Peripatetic Wind Teacher, 1967, 1978-91, Senior Woodwind Tutor Hull E A, 1991-, Humberside Woodwind Tutor E A; Music Teacher, St Mary's High School, 1969-71; YTV South Bank Show on Hull Youth Orchestra. *Compositions:* Scherzo Rondoso for Oboe and Piano, 1982; Conversation and Chaser for Oboe and Piano, 1990. *Recordings:* Granville Bantock, Hebridean Symphony, Hull Youth Orchestra, 1977. *Memberships:* ISM, Chairman of Humberside branch; Musicians Union; British Double Reed Society; Royal Scottish Country Dance Society. *Hobbies:* Dancing; Yoga; Photography; Swimming; French. *Address:* 18 Clumber Street, Princes Avenue, Hull HU5 3RL, N Humberside, England.

KEEFFE Bernard, b. 1 Apr 1925, London, England. Conductor; Broadcaster. m. Denise Walker, 10 Sept 1954, 1 son, 1 daughter. *Education:* BA, Honours, Clare College, Cambridge, 1951; Private studies, cello/Di Marco, voice/Roy Henderson & Lucie Manen, conducting/Berthold Goldschmidt. *Career includes:* Appearances as solo baritone in opera (Glyndebourne), concerts, musical plays (London, Edinburgh Festival); Producer & conductor 1955-60, Head of Radio Opera 1959, BBC Music Department; Controller of Opera Planning, Royal Opera House, London, 1960-62; Conductor, BBC Scottish Orchestra, 1962-64; Many appearances, BBC TV, as commentator/conductor; Concerts & broadcasts with major orchestras; Chief conductor, Bournemouth Municipal Choir, 1972-81; Professor, Trinity College of Music, 1966-89. Many engagements as international jurist, various competitions including Italia Prize for Broadcasting, Anvers, Liège, Sofia, London. *Recordings:* L'Oiseau-Lyre, as conductor with Melos Ensemble & Janet Baker; Music of Ravel & Delage. *Publications:* Authorised translations: Janáček, Diary of One Who Disappeared; Petrassi, Death in the Air; English National Opera Guide to Tosca. *Contributions to:* Many talks for BBC Music Magazine, World Service; Hi-Fi News; Music Teacher; Classical Music Fortnightly. *Honour:* Honorary Fellow, Trinity College, London, 1968. *Memberships:* Former warden, Solo Performers Section, Incorporated Society of Musicians; Executive committee, Anglo-Austrian Music Society. *Hobbies:* Photography; Languages. *Address:* 153 Honor Oak Road, London SE23 3RN, England.

KEENE Christopher, b. 21 Dec 1946, Berkeley, California, USA. Conductor; Arts Administrator. m. Sara Frances Rhodes, 21 Dec 1967, 2 sons. *Education:* University of California, Berkeley, 1963-67. *Debut:* Conducting, Britten's The Rape of Lucretia, Berkeley,

1965. *Career:* Assistant Conductor, San Francisco Opera, 1966; San Diego Opera, 1967; European debut conducting Menotti's The Saint of Bleecker Street, Spoleto Festival, 1968; Music Director, American Ballet Company, New York, 1969-70; Co-Music Director 1971-73, General Manager 1973-75, Music Director 1975-76, Spoleto Festival; Music Director 1974-89, President 1975-89, Artpark Summer Festival, Lewiston, New York; Music Director, Syracuse (NY) Symphony orchestra, 1975-84; Spoleto Festival USA; Charleston, SC, 1977-80; Long Island (NY) Philharmonic Orchestra, 1979-90; Artistic Supervisor 1982-83, Music Director 1983-86, General Director 1989-, New York City Opera; Guest Conductor, Metropolitan Opera, New York; Chicago Lyric Opera; Pittsburgh Opera; Santa Fe Opera; Royal Opera, Covent Garden, London; Hamburg State Opera; New York Philharmonic Orchestra; Chicago Symphony Orchestra; Philadelphia Orchestra; Cleveland Orchestra; Boston Symphony Orchestra; St Louis Symphony Orchestra; Conducted Philip Glass's Akhnaten, Satyagraha and Einstein on the Beach, Stuttgart 1990; US stage premiere of From the House of the Dead, New York City Opera, 1990; US stage Premiere of Busoni's Doktor Faust, 1992; Conducted The Rape of Lucretia at San Diego, 1992, Argento's The Voyage of Edgar Allan Poe at Dallas. *Recordings:* For CBS; ECM/Warner Brothers; New World Records; RCA. *Contributions:* Articles in many publications. *Honour:* Julius Rudel Award, 1969. *Address:* c/o New York City Opera, New York State Theater, Lincoln Center for the Performing Arts, New York, NY 10023, USA.

KEENLYSIDE Raymond, b. 9 May 1928, Southsea, Hampshire, England. Musician-Violinist. m. Cynthia J Page, 2 sons, 1 daughter. *Education:* Trinity College of Music, London. *Career:* Principal of Chamber orchestras including Boyd Neel; Philomusica; English Chamber Orchestra; Academy of St Martin-in-the-Fields; Member of London Harpsichord Ensemble, 1959-62; David Martin String Quartet; Aeolian String Quartet, 1962-81; Professor of Violin, Royal College of Music, Senior Tutor, Royal College of Music Junior Department; Numerous Radio appearances; Series on BBC Television of late Beethoven String Quartets; other Television appearances. *Recordings:* Complete Haydn String Quartets; Works by Schubert, Mozart, Elgar, Vaughan Williams, Ravel, Debussy, all with Aeolian Quartet; Others with other groups. *Contributions to:* Daily Telegraph Magazine. *Honours:* LTCL (TTD); Hon MA Newcastle University, 1970; Hon. FTCL, 1983; Hon. FRCM. *Hobbies:* Fly Fishing; Water colour painting; Reading; Beekeeping; Gardening; Bird-watching. *Address:* 100 Westbourne Park Road, London, W2 5PL, England.

KEHL Sigrid, b. 23 Nov 1932, Berlin, Germany. Singer (Soprano and Mezzo-Soprano). *Education:* Studied in Erfurt, at the Berlin Musikhochschule and with Dagmar Freiwald-Lange. *Debut:* Berlin Staatsoper 1956, in Prince Igor. *Career:* Member of the Leipzig Opera from 1957, notably as Brünnhilde in Der Ring des Nibelungen, 1974; Engagements at the Berlin Staatsoper from 1971, Vienna Staatsoper from 1975; Further appearances at the Komische Oper Berlin and in Prague, Bucharest, Rome, Bologna, Geneva, Warsaw and Basle; Lausanne Festival 1983, as Isolde.

KEKULA Josef, b. 1952, Czechoslovakia. Violinist. *Education:* Studied with Václav Snítil and members of Smetana Quartet, Kostecký and Kohout. *Career:* Co-founder and 2nd violinist of the Stamic Quartet of Prague 1977; Performances at the Prague Young Artists and the Bratislava Music Festivals; Tours to Spain, Austria, France, Switzerland, Germany and Eastern Europe; Tour of the USA 1980, debut concerts in Britain at London and Birmingham 1983; further British tours 1985, 1987, 1988 (Warwick Arts Festival) and 1989 (20 concerts); Season 1991-92 with visit to the Channel Islands (Festival of Czech Music), Holland, Finland, Austria and France, Edinburgh Festival and debut tours of Canada, Japan and Indonesia. *Recordings:* Shostakovich No 13, Schnittke No 4 (Panton); Mozart K589 and K370 (Lyrinx); Dvořák, Martinů and Janáček complete quartets

(Cadenza); Conplete Dvořák String Quartets, Complete Maritinů String Quartets. *Publications:* Complete of Smetana and Janáček String Quartet, Bayer Records.*Honours:* (with members of Stamic Quartet): Prize winner, International Festival of Young Soloists, Bordeaux 1977; Winner, 1986 ORF (Austrian Radio) International String Quartet Competition (followed by live broadcast from the Salzburg Mozarteum); Academie Charles Cros Grand Prix du Disque 1991, for Dvořák quartets. *Current Managment:* Robert Gilder & Co, Enterprise House, 59/65 Upper Ground, London SE1 9PQ, England. *Address:* c/o Robertr Gilder and Co, Enterprise House, 59/65 Upper Ground, London SE1 9PE, England.

KELEMEN Milko, b. 30 Mar 1924, Podrawska Slatina, Yugoslavia. Composer. *Education:* Studied at the Zagreb Academy of Music and with Messiaen and Aubin in Paris; Further study with Wolfgang Fortner in Freiburg and at the Siemens electronic music studio in Munich. *Career:* Taught composition at the Zagreb Conservatory, 1955-58, 1960-65; Co-founder of the Zagreb Biennial Festival, president 1961; Taught at the Schumann Conservatory 1969; Professor of composition at the Hochschule for Musik in Stuttgart 1973. *Composition include:* Piano Sonata 1954; Adagio and Allegro for strings 1956; Bassoon Concerto 1957; Dances, song cycle for baritone and strings 1958; Concerto giacoso for chamber orchestra 1958; Concertino for double bass and strings 1958; Constellations for string orchestra 1960; Five Essays for strings 1961; The Mirror ballet 1961; Transfigurations for piano and orchestra 1962; Equilibri for two orchestras 1962; The Abandoned, ballet 1964; O Primavers for tenor and strings 1965; Words cantata for mezzo, choir and orchestra 1966; Compose for 2 pianos and orchestra 1967; Changeant for cello and orchestra 1968; Motion for string quartet 1969; The Siege, opera after Camus 1970; Floreal for orchestra 1970; Varai Melodia for string quartet 1972; Gasho for 4 choir groups 1974; Seven Agonies for mezzo-soprano 1975; Mageia for orchestra 1978; Apocolypse, ballet opera 1979; Grand jeu Classique for violin and orcehstra 1982; Love Song for strings 1984; Dramatico for cello and orchestra 1985; Fantasmas for viola and orchestra 1986; Archetypon for orchestra 1986; Landscapes for mezzo and string quartet 1986; Memories, string trio 1987; Sonnets string quartet 1987; Duo for violin and piano 1988; Nonet 1988. *Address:* Union des Compositeurs de Yugoslavie, 1100 Beograd, Misarska 12-14, Serbia.

KELLA John J, b. 14 Oct 1948, Hilo, Hawaii, USA. Musician; Music Professor; Company President. m. Cecilia Caceres, 21 June 1991. *Education:* BM, 1974, MM, 1975, Teaching Fellow, 1982-83, Juilliard School of Music; PhD, Psychology and Physiology of Skilled Performance in the Arts, New York University, 1984; Certification, Biomechanics of Human Movement, Massachusetts Institute of Technology, 1989. *Career:* Violist, orchestras and chamber music, 1966-, including American Symphony Orchestra, 1976-78, American Ballet Theatre Orchestra, 1976-80, Parnassus String Quartet European tour, 1979, Metropolitan Opera Orchestra, 1980-; Principal Violist: National Ballet of Canada, 1978, New York tours of D'Oyly Carte Opera, 1978, Berlin-Opera Ballet, Joffrey Ballet, Bolshoi Ballet, 1979; Assistant Professor, Violin, Viola, New York University, 1981-; Professor, Violin, Viola, Manhattan School of Music, 1989-; Coordinator, Occupational Rehabilitation and Re-Training Programme for Industry and the Arts, Miller Health Care Institute for Performing Artists, St Luke's-Roosevelt Hospital Center, New York City, 1987-; President, Performing Arts Health Information Services, Editor-in-Chief, Performing Arts Health News, President, Kella Communications Company Inc, Office and Industry Health Training Programmes, 1991-; Lectures and training seminars on medical and psychological problems of musicians. *Recordings:* With Metropolitan Opera: Der Ring des Nibelungen; Rigoletto; Parsifal; Manon Lescaut. *Publications:* Computerized Thermography and Other Technological Aids in the Diagnosis of Musicians' Neuromuscular Disorders (with M M Lee), 1989.

Address: PO Box 566, Radio City Station, New York, NY 10019, USA.

KELLER András, b. 1960, Hungary, Violinist. *Education:* Studied at the Franz Liszt Academy, Budapest and with Sandor Devich, György Kurtág and Andras Mihaly. *Career:* Member of the Keller String Quartet from 1986, debut concert at Budapest March 1987; Played Beethoven's Grosse Fuge and Schubert's Death and the Maiden Quartet at Interforum 87; Series on concerts in Budapest with Zoltán Kocsis and Deszö Ranki (Piano) and Kalman Berkes (clarinet); Further appearances in Nuremberg, at the Chamber Music Festival La Baule and tours of Bulgaria, Austria, Switzerland, Italy (Ateforum 88 Ferrara), Belgium and Ireland; Concerts for Hungarian Radio and Television. *Recordings:* Albums for Hungaroton (from 1989). *Honour:* 2nd Prize, Evian International String Quartet Competition, May 1988. *Address:* c/o Artist Management International, 12/13 Richmond Buildings, Dean Street, London W1V 5AF, England.

KELLER Heinrich, b. 14 Nov 1940, Winterthur, Switzerland. Flautist; Composer. m. 14 June 1968, 3 sons. *Education:* Conservatory, Zurich, 1961-65. *Debut:* 1965. *Career:* Philharmony, Bremen, 1965-66; Orchestra of St Gallen, 1967-72; Musikkollegium Winterthur, solo Flautist, 1972-. *Compositions:* Aleph, 1966; Blaserquintett, 1972; Puzzle, 1973; Streichquartett, 1973-74; Reduktion, 1974; Refrains, 1975; Ritual, 1979; Rencontre, Flue & Harpsichord, 1985. *Recordings:* Flotenmusik aus Frankreich & Italien; Schubert, ihr Blumlein; Baroque & Rokoko, Flute music. *Honour:* Prize for composing String quartet, Tonhalle, Zurich, 1974. *Membership:* Schweizerischer Tonkunstlerverein. *Hobby:* Private concerts, Musica riservata. *Address:* Gruzenstrasse 14, CH-8400 Winterthur, Switzerland.

KELLER Helen, b. 5 Mar 1945, Horgen, Zurich, Switzerland. Singer (Soprano). *Education:* Studied in Zurich and with Agnes Giebel in Cologne. *Career:* Concert performances in Switzerland and elsewhere from 1971 with a repertoire including Rossini's Stabat Mater, L'Enfance du Christ, Schopfung and Jahreszeiten, Elijah and St Paul, works by Bach and Handel and Honegger's Roi David; Appearances at Amsterdam, Antwerp, Paris, Milan, Annsbach, Karlsruhe and the USA in Britten, Brahms, Schubert, Monteverdi, Pergolesi, Vivaldi, and Schumann. Stage engagements as Salome in San Viovanni Battista by Stradella (Berne) at St Gallen and in Le Convenzie Teatrali by Donizetti at Zurich. *Recordings:* Messiah, Schubert's Mass in G and San Giovanni Battista. *Address:* c/o Peter Keller, Opernhaus Zurich, Falkenstrasse 1, CH-8008 Zurich, Switzerland.

KELLER Kjell, b. 25 May 1942, Wilderswil, Switzerland. Musician; Musicologist; Composer. m. 25 Mar 1977, 2 sons, 1 daughter. *Education:* Dr phil, Musicology, University of Berne, 1974; Konservatorium Berne. *Career:* Assistant, Musikwissenschaftliches Seminar, University of Berne, 1972-76; Producer, New Music & Ethnomusicology, Swiss Broadcasting Corporation (Radio & TV), 1976-; University teacher 1991 (Berne). *Compositions:* Numerous lieder, 1981-; Worte und Klänge zu Bruder Klaus, 1987; Wie den Menschen Flügel wachsen (1989); Unter dem schwarzen Regenbogen (1990/92). *Recordings:* Worte und Klänge zu Bruder Klaus, 1988; Numerous lieder; Horspielmusiken. *Publications:* Aspekte der Musik von Klaus Huber, 1976; Musik Dossier Urs Peter Schneider, 1988. *Contributions to:* Neue Musik und ihre Vermittlung, 1986; Numerous articles, various reviews, Switzerland & Germany. *Honour:* Zurcher Radiopreis, 1981. *Memberships:* Arts Council of Switzerland Pro Helvetia. *Address:* Tulpenweg 9, CH-3004 Berne, Switzerland.

KELLER Michael A, b. 5 Apr 1945, Sterling, Colorado, USA. Librarian; Music Bibliographer; Consultant. m. Carol A Lawrence, 6 Oct 1979. 1 son, 3 daughters.

Education: BA cum Laude, Hamilton College, 1967; MA 1970, MLS 1972, PhD abd 1970-, State University of New York. *Career:* Assistant Librarian, Music Library, State University of New York at Buffalo, 1970-73; Music Librarian, Senior Lercturer 1973-81, Acting Undergraduate Librarian 1976, Cornell University; Head, Music Library, University of California at Berkeley, 1981-86; Instructor, Stanford University, 1984; Associate University Librarian, Collection Department, Yale University, 1986-93; Director, Stanford University Librarian, Stanford, California, 1993-; Consultant to numerous Universities. *Publications include:* Music Reference and Research Materials, an annotated Bibliography, 4th ed (co author with Vincent H Duckles), 1988, 1993 (revised); Music and Dance, chapter in The Reader's Adviser, 1986 and 1994; New bibliographic, literary and musical tools-the Italian Music and Lyric Poetry of the Renaissance project in conference proceedings for Conference on Music Bibliography, 1986; Music, chapter in Selection Sources and Strategies: a guide for librarians in larger libraries, 1984; Thinking about music in Critical Thinking, reading across the curriculum, 1984 and 1987. *Contributions to:* New Grove Dictionary of Music and Musicians. *Hobbies:* Travel; Wine and food. *Address:* 4280 Los Palos Circle, Palo Alto, CA 94306, USA.

KELLER Peter, b. 16 Mar 1945, Thurgau, Switzerland. Singer (Tenor). m. Helen Keller. *Education:* Studied in Zurich, with Ernst Haefliger in Berlin and Agnes Giebel in Cologne. *Career:* Has sung at the Zurich Opera from 1973, notably in the Monteverdi series and as Pedrillo, Monostatos, Jacquino, Wagner's David and Steuermann, Valzacchi in Rosenkavalier and M Triquet in Eugene Onegin (1991); Guest engagements at Munich, Hamburg, Dusseldorf (Edgar in Reimann's Lear), Milan, Edinburgh, Berlin and Vienna; Concert singer in Europe and on tour with Helen Keller in the USA. *Recordings include:* Die Zauberflöte, Il Ritorno di Ulisse, L'Incoronaziione di Poppea and Monteverdi Orfen; Diary of One who Disappeared by Janáček; Handel's Israel in Egypt and Mendelssohn's Christus; Haberleins Sonin; Zemlinsky's Kleider Machen Leute. *Address:* c/o Peter Keller Opernhaus Zurich, Falkenstrasse 1, CH-8008 Zurich, Switzerland

KELLER Verena, b. 8 Sept 1942, Schwerin, Germany. Singer (Mezzo- soprano). *Education:* Studied in Vienna with Hans Hotter and in Berlin; Leider with Erik Werba. *Career:* Engaged at Hanover 1963-66, Bonn, 1979-88, Mainz 1983-86; Guest appearances at Cologne, Geneva, Naples, Herrenhausen and Gottingen; Roles have included Mozart's Ramiro, Carmen, Santuzza, Ortrud, Brangaene, Kundry, Venus, Fricka; Verdi's Amneris, Azucena and Ulrica, Strauss's Clytemnestra and Herodias, Janaček's Kabanicha and the Witch in Hansel and Gretel; Concert engagements in Baroque music throughout Germany and in Paris, Rome, Los Angles and Vancouver. *Recordings include:* Dvořák's Mass in D. *Address:* Staatstheater, Gutenbergplatz 7, 6500 Mainz, Germany.

KELLEY Norman, b. 27 Aug 1917, Eddington, Maine, USA. Singer (Tenor). *Education:* Studied at te New England Conservatory and at the Eastman School with Mario B. Pagano. *Debut:* Philadelphia 1947, as Cavaradossi. *Career:* Sang in Baltimore, Boston, San Francisco, Houston, Miami, Mexico City, Brussels, Lyon, Nice, Toulouse, Lisbon, Montreal and Vancouver; Carnegie Hall 1952, in the local premiere of Der Corregidor by Wolf; New York City Opera in the premieres of The Wings of the Dove by Moore and The Crucible by Ward (1961), and The Passion of Jonathan Wade by Carlisle Floyd; Sang lyrical and character roles, as well as parts in modern operas; Frequent concert appearances.

KELLOGG Cal Stewart, b. 26 July 1947, Long Beach, California, USA. Conductor; Composer. *Education:* Conservatorio di Musica S Cecilia Rome, Diplomas in Bassoon, Composition, Conducting. *Debut:* Symphonic: Monte Carlo, Oct. 5, 1975, Opera: Rome Opera, 3 Feb. 1976. *Career:* As bassoonist, Toured with Renato

Fasano's Piccola Teatro Musicale di Roma 1967-72; Soloist with RAI Orchestra of Rome 1972; Conductor: Symphonic Concerts: Baltimore Symphony, New World Symphony, Monte Carlo, Accademia Nazionale di S. Cecilia, Maggio Fiorentino, La Fenice, San Carlo, RAI Orchestras of Rome, Torino and Naples, Antwerp Philharmonic, Spoleto Festival Orchestra, Orchestra of Illinois, Seattle Symphony, Israel Sinfonietta of Beersheva; Opera: Rome Opera, Teatro Communale di Firenze, San Francisco Opera, San Carlo, Teatro Reggio di Parma, NYC Opera, Santa Fe, Washington Opera, St. Louis, Houston Grand Opera, Canadian Opera Company, Opera Montreal, Seattle Opera, Edinburgh Festival, Israel Festival, Spoleto Festival, Chautauqua Festival PBS TV Live From Lincoln Center, New York City Opera production of Menotti's The Saint of Bleecker Street; 1978 Radio Broadcasts: NYCO Tosca 1978, Houston Grand Opera Ballo In Maschera 1981, Canadian Opera Company, Il Trovatore 1984, and Macbeth 1986.*Compositions:* Sullivan Ballou's Letter to his Wife for Bass Baritone and Orchestra, 1990 (A setting of a Civil War Letter). *Recordings:* Thomas Pasatieri: Three Sisters, Opera in 2 Acts, Z Press 1986. *Current Management:* Trawick Artists Management. *Address:* 129 West 72nd Street, New York, NY 10024, USA.

KELLY Bryan, b. 3 Jan 1934, Oxford, England. Composer; Pianist; Conductor. *Education:* Royal College of Music 1951-55, with Gordon Jacob and Herbert Howells; Paris with Boulanger. *Career:* Has taught at the Royal Scottish Academy of Music; Professor of Composition, Royal College of Music, 1962-84; Resident at Castiglione del Lago, Italy, 1984-. *Compositions:* Orchestral: The Tempest Suite, for strings 1964; Cookham Concertino 1969; Divertimento for brass band 1969; Oboe Concerto 1972; Edinburgh Dances for brass band 1973; Guitar Concerto 1978; Andalucia and Concertante Music or brass 1976, 1979; 2 Symphonies 1983, 1986; Vocal: Tenebrare Nocturnes for tenor, chorus and orchestra 1965; Magnificat and Nunc Dimittis for chorus and organ 1965; The Shield of Achilles for tenor and orchestra 1966; Sleep Little Baby, carol 1968; Stabat Mater 1970; At the Round Earth's Imagin'd Corners for tenor, chorus and strings 1972; Abingdon Carols 1973; Let there be Light for soprano, narrator, chorus and orchestra 1973; Latin Magnificat 1979; Te Deum and Jubilate for chorus and organ 1979; Piano Sonata 1971; Prelude and fugue for organ 1960; Pastorale and Paen for organ 1973; Chamber music; Children's Pieces: Herod do your Worst, nativity opera 1968; On Christmas Eve, suite of carols 1968; The Spider Monkey Uncle King, opera pantomime 1971. *Recordings:* The Choral Music of Bryan Kelly, Abbey Records. *Hobby:* Cooking. *Address:* c/o Novello & Co, 8 Lower James Street, London WC1, England.

KELLY Frances, b. 1955, England. Harpist. *Career:* Regular performances with the New London Consort in medieval and renaissance music; Has toured in Europe and the Far East; Early Music Network tours in Britain 1986 and 1988; Freelance engagements with the Consort of Musicke, and the Gabrieli Consort and Players Recitals with soprano Evelyn Tubb; On modern harp was member of the Ondine Ensemble, giving performances in Britain and the USA; Partnership with the flautist Ingrid Culliford from 1977; BBC Recital with tenor Ian Partridge; Concerto soloist in the premieres of Edward Cowie's Concerto in Newcastle and London and for Tyne Tees Television; Season 1988 included Debussy and Ravel with the Lindsay Quartet, chamber music by Bruch for the BBC and concerts in London, Denmark, Bruges and Utrecht as continuo player with the Consort of Musicke; South Bank Summer Music Festival with the New London Consort. *Recordings include:* Debussy's Trio Sonata with the Athena Ensemble; Britten's A Ceremony of Carols with the Choir of Christ Church Cathedral, Oxford; Mozart's Concerto K299 with the Academy of Ancient Music; Solo, Harp collection, (Amon Ra). *Address:* Magenta Music International, 64 Highgate Street, London N6 5HX, England.

KELLY Janis, b. 1955, Glasgow, Scotland. Singer, Soprano. *Education:* Studied at Royal Scottish Academy of Music, the Royal College of Music and in Paris. *Career:* Represented Britain at the UNESCO Young Musicians Rostrum at Bratislava, 1981; Operatic roles include Mimi, Serpettta in La Finta Giardiniera (Camden Festival and Glyndebourne 1991); Flora in The Knot Garden and Mozart's Despina, Zerlina and Susanna, 1991 for Opera Factory; English National Opera as Amor (L'Incoronazione di Poppea), Flora (The Turn of the Screw), Kitty (Anna Karenina by Iain Hamilton), Barbarina, Bekhetaten in Akhnaten, Woman/Fury in The Mask of Orpheus, Papagena, Yum-Yum, and Rose in Street Scene; Polly in The Beggar's Opera for Scottish Opera and Magnolia in Show Boat for Opera North. Concert appearances in the USA, Canada, Paris and Czechoslovakia; Season 1992 as Ottavia, Coronation of Poppea, and Countess in Marriage of Fiagaro for Opera Factory, Governess in Turn of the Season, Bath City Opera, Tatyana in Eugene Onegin for Kentish Opera. *Recordings:* Magnolia, Showboat; Rose, Streetscene; Mozart, Gluck, Puccini, Massenet Arias on Inspector Morse Soundtrack Albums, Virgin Records. *Honours include:* Anna Instone Award, RCM; Countess of Munster, Caird and Royal Society of Arts scholarships. *Current Management:* Ron Gonsalves, 10 Dagnan Road, London SW12 9LQ, England. *Address:* c/o Music International, 13 Ardilaun Road, London N5 2QR, England.

KELLY Robert, b. 26 Sept. 1916, Clarksburg, West Virginia, USA. Composer. m. Mary, 25 Dec. 1942, 3 sons. *Education:* BM, composition, Curtis Institute of Music, 1942; MM, composition, Eastman School of Music, 1952. *Career:* Professor of Composition, University of Illinois, 1946-76; Professor Emeritus of Composition, University of Illinois since 1976. *Compositions:* Chamber music, songs, symphonies, concerti, for large ensembles, operas, ballet, choral works, all published. *Recordings:* Symphony No. 2, Japan Philharmonic, Akeo Watanabe conductor, Composers Recordings Inc; Cello Music by Robert Kelly featuring Roger Drinkall, cellist; Suite for Solo Cello; 3 Expressions for Violin & Cello/Sonata for Cello & Piano, Orion Master Recordings Inc; Sonata for Oboe & Harp, Joseph Robinson, oboe & Deborah Hoffman, harp, Contemporary Record Society. *Publications:* Theme & Variations, A Study of 12-Tone Composition, University of Illinois Press; Audio & Visual Recognition, ear-training series, ibid, both 1965. *Current Management:* Broadcast Music Inc. *Address:* 807 South Urbana Avenue, Urbana, IL 61801, USA.

KELM Linda, b. 11 Dec 1944, Utah, USA. Singer (Soprano). *Education:* Studied with Jennie Tourel at the Aspen School of Music and in New York. *Debut:* Seattle 1977, as Helmwige and Third Norn in the Ring. *Career:* Sang Turandot with Wilmington, 1979, followed by performers at Seattle, New York City Opera, 1983; Chicago, San Francisco and Amsterdam; Sang Salome at St Louis and Princess in Rusalka at Carnegie Hall; Perugia 1983, as Dirce in Cherubini's Demofoonte; Seattle Opera 1985, as Brünnhilde; Further guest appearances include: Helmwige in the Ring. *Address:* c/o Seattle Opera Association, PO Box 9248, USA.

KELTERBORN Rudolf, b. 3 Sept 1931, Basel, Switzerland. Composer; Conductor; Professor. m. Erika Kelterborn Salathe, 6 July 1957, 1s. *Education:* Diplomas in theory and Conducting, Music Academy, Basel, 1953; Studied composition with Blacher and Fortner, Salzburg and Detmold, and conducting with Markewitch. *Career:* Teacher and Conductor, Basel, 1956-60; Professor of Composition, NW German Music Academy, Detmold, 1980-68; Professor of Composition, HS Zurich, Swiss Music Review, 1968-75; Hd of Music Department, Swiss Radio, 1975-80; Professor of Composition, HS Karlsruhe, 1980-83; Director of Music Academy, Basel, 1983-. *Compositions include:* Four Symphonies and five Operas Kaiser Jovian 1967, Ein Engel Kommt nach Babylon 1977, Der Kirschgarten 1984, Ophelia 1984 and Julia, 1990; A Ballet; Various works for Orchestra; Concertos for various solo instruments; Chamber music including 5 string quartets, 1954-89; Cantatas; Piano and organ works. *Recordings:* Several under various labels. *Honours include:* Conrad Ferdinant Meyer Prize, 1971; Zurcher Radio Prize, 1973; Kunstpreis der Stadt, Basel, 1984; Komponistenpreis des Schwerizerisches Tonkünstlervereins, 1984. *Memberships:* Programme Committee, Basler Musik Forum; Association of Swiss Composers and Interpreters (Honorary). *Hobbies:* Contemporary arts and literature; Mountain touring. *Address:* Pilgerstrasse 31, 4055 Basel, Switzerland.

KEMENY Alexander, b. 22 Apr. 1943, Solna, Sweden. Musician (Violinist). Divorced, 1 daughter. *Education:* Bratislava Conservatory, Czechoslovakia, 1960-66; Music Academy, Prague, with Professor A.Plocek, 1966- 70. *Debut:* 1970. *Career:* Concertmaster, Innsbruck Symphonic Orchestra, 1973-75; Violinist, Prague Symphony Orchestra, also Norrkoping Symphony Orchestra, Sweden; Freelance Concert Violinist, 1978-; Soloist with orchestra (works of Myslivecek, Mozart, Beethoven, Brixi, Mendelssohn, Wieniawski, Eklund) and chamber music player (classical and modern music), concerts in Czechoslovakia, Sweden, Denmark and Poland; Performed in Piano Trio and in Duo with guitarist Vladimir Vectomov; Radio performances, Czechoslovakia, Sweden, Austria; Performed at Bornholm Music Festival, Denmark, 1987. *Recordings:* Paganini, Giuliani, Kowalski, Radio Prague and Bratislava; Smetana, Johansson, Telemann, Radio Sweden; Suk, Smetana, Foerster, Suchon, Radio Austria. *Hobbies:* Sport; Reading books; Foreign languages. *Address:* Kristianstadsgatan 13, 21423 Malmo, Sweden.

KEMMER Mariette, b. 1960, Luxembourg. Singer (Soprano). *Education:* Studied at the Luxembourg Conservatoire and at the Rheinland National College of Music in Düsseldorf. *Career:* Sang at the Théâtre de la Monnaie Brussels as Mélisande, Sophie Pamina, Micaela and Mozart's Countess; Guest appearances at the Vienna Staatsoper, Munich, Berlin, Hamburg, Frankfurt, Dresden, Stuttgart, Zürich, Geneva, Basle, Berne, Lausanne, Verona, Karlsruhe, and Liège; Has appeared at the festivals of Aix-en-Provence, Wexford and Bregenz; Other roles include Mozart's Ilia, Fiordiligi and Donna Elvira, Marguerite, Antonia, Tatiana and the Countess in Capriccio. *Address:* Music International, 13 Ardilaun Road, London N5 2QR, England.

KEMP Brian George, b. 29 June 1940, Aberdeen, Scotland. Opera Singer (Baritone). m. Helen Robertson, 27 July 1964, 2 sons. *Education:* London Opera Centre, 1965-67; Private Study with E. Herbet-Caesari, Tito Gobbi, Lorenzo Malfatti. *Debut:* Théâtre Royal De La Monnaie, Brussels as Count, Nozze Di Figaro, 1967. *Career:* Principal Baritone, Scottish Opera, 1967-72; Freelance, Europe, USA; Debut, Royal Opera House, World Premiere of We Come to the River, by Hans Werner Henze, 1976; Formerly Principal Baritone, Stadttheater, Aachen, 1984-88, roles include: Posa, Don Carlos, Don Carlos (Forza Del Destino), etc; Appearances at Wexford Festival, Ledlanet Festival, Edinburgh Festival; Guest Artist, Netherlands Opera, English National Opera, Royal Opera House, Scottish Opera, Brussels, Trieste. *Honour:* Peter Stuyvesant Foundation Scholarship, 1965. *Membership:* Incorporated Society of Musicians. *Current Management:* Athole Still International Management, London. *Hobbies:* Golf; Squash; Horse Riding; History. *Address:* Brüsseler Ring 32, 5100 Aachen, Germany.

KEMP Walter Herbert, b. 16 Nov. 1938, Montreal, Canada. Musicologist; Conductor; Composer; Pianist; Organist; Administrator. m. Valda A Svenne, 1 son, 2 daughters. *Education:* BMus, University of Toronto, 1959; MMus University of Toronto, 1961; AM, Harvard University, 1963; DPhil, Oxford University, England, 1972; FRCCO; ARCT; studied organ with Eric Rollinson, composition with John Weinzweig and Leon Kirchner, musicology with Nino Pirotta and Frank Harrison. *Career:* Conductor, University of Toronto Chorus, 1959-

62; Hart House Glee Club, 1962-63; Kitchener-Waterloo Philharmonic Choir 1966-72; Founder, Chairman, Music Department, Waterloo Lutheran University (now Wilfrid Laurier University) Waterloo, Ontario 1965-75; Director, University Choir; President, RCCO 1974-76; Professor, Music Department, Dalhousie University, Halifax, Nova Scotia 1977-; Professor, University of King's College, Halifax, 1985-; Director, Dalhousie Chorale 1977-; Music Director, St Paul's Church and St Paul's Singers of Halifax 1978-90; Conductor, NS International Tattoo Choir. *Compositions:* Five Poems of William Blake; Five Latvian Folk Songs; Missa Sancti Thomae De Aquino, St Pauls Service (Rite A); Meditations and Commentaries on Ewing's Jerusalem The Golden. *Publications:* The Anon. Chansons Ms. Esc. VIII.24; Burgundian Court Song in the Time of Binchois. *Address:* Department of Music, Dalhousie University, Halifax, Nova Scotia, Canada.

KENDALL Christopher Wolff, b. 9 Sept. 1949, Zanesville, Ohio, USA. Conductor; Lutenist; Artistic Director. *Education:* BA, Antioch College 1972; MM Conducting, University of Cincinnati Conservatory 1974; Dalcroze School of Music, NY 1969-70. *Career:* Director of 20th Century Consort in residence at the Smithsonian Institution, Washington, 1976-, Associate Conductor of the Seattle Symphony, 1987-; Founder and Lutenist of Folger Consort, Ensemble-In-Residence at Folger Shakespeare Library in Washington DC 1977-; Artistic Director of Millennium, Inc., 1980-; Guest Conductor: Seattle Symphony, Chamber Music Society of Lincoln Center, Eastman Musica Nova, Da Capo Chamber Players, Washington Sinfonia. *Recordings:* 20th Century Consort Volume I and II (4 discs), Smithsonian Collection; Into Eclipse (Stephen Albert) 20th Century Consort, Nonesuch; Shakespeare's Music, Folger Consort, Delos; A Distant Mirror, Carmina Burana, Folger Consort, Delos. *Honours:* Gold Award, Houston Film Festival for Millennium: 10 Centuries of Music 1986; Emmy Award for 20th Century Consort PBS Programme on Aaron Copland 1984.

KENDALL Gary K, b. 16 Dec. 1943, Springfield, Missouri, USA. Singer. m. 27 Nov. 1982. *Education:* BS, Education, 1964, MM, Voice, 1966, University of Missouri; Studied for DMA, Indiana University, 1972; Diploma in Opera, Curtis Institute, 1974. *Career:* Soloist with Orchestras of Cleveland, Pittsburgh, Denver, Seattle, Milwaukee, Suisse Romande, St Louis, Atlanta, Memphis, Oklahoma City, National in Washington DC, Wichita, Opera Companies of Miami, Philadelphia, Vienna, Milwaukee Florintine, Kentucky, San Antonio; Affiliate Artist; Resident, Marlboro Festival; Soloist, Spoleto, Italy, Aix-en-Provence, Casals, Mexico City Festivals; Currently, Professor, Voice, College-Conservatory of Music, University of Cincinnati; British Debut, Queen Elizabeth Hall, 1984. *Honours:* 1st Man to win Geneva International Competition by Unanimous Vote of Jury; Fauré Prize, Paris International Competition; Recipient, numerous other honours and awards. *Hobby:* Raising Horses. *Address:* College-Conservatory of Music, University of Cincinnati, Cincinnati, OH 45221, USA.

KENDALL William, b. 1960, London. Singer (Tenor). *Education:* King's School, Canterbury; Choral Scholar at Cambridge University; Further study with Robert Tear and Peter Pears. *Career:* Concert appearances under such conductors as Hogwood, Harnoncourt, Gardiner, Mackerras and Boulez; Works by Tippett and Tavener conducted by the composers; Sang in the world premiere of Penderecki's Polish Requiem; Tour of Germany 1989 with the Monteverdi Choir and Orchestra in the Missa Solemnis and Beethoven's Mass in C; Further appearances in season 1990-91 as the Evangelist in the St John Passion, in The Dream of Gerontius and Britten's Serenade in Australia; Mozart Requiems in Oxford and Cambridge and Bach's B minor Mass with The Sixteen at St John's Smith Square; London Promenade concert appearances and showings at the Holland Festival, Festival Berlin 750 1987 and the 1989 Salzburg Festival. *Recordings:* Beethoven Missa Solemnis and Mass in C (Deutsche Grammophon); Bach

and Schütz with the Stuttgart Kammerchor; Sacred music by Haydn (Hyperion). *Address:* Magenta Music International, 64 Highgate High Street, London N6 5HX, England.

KENGEN Knud-Erik, b. 17 July 1947, Copenhagen, Denmark. Organist, Pianist and Composer. m. Gerlinde Maria Pagel, 6 Dec. 1969, 1 son, 1 daughter. *Education:* Studies in Musicology, University of Copenhagen, 1972-76; Final Diploma, Royal Danish Academy of Music, 1974; Studied under Professor Aksel Andersen; Consultations in Composition with Leif Kayser. *Career:* Assistant Organist, Dome of Copenhagen, 1974; Organist, Gladsaxe Church, Copenhagen, 1979-; Performances: Concert Organist at numerous concerts, mainly in Denmark but also in Germany, England and Sweden; also played as Soloist at first performance of Musica Autumnalis by Axel Borup Jørgensen in The Danish Broadcasting Corporation; as pianist, rehearser and chorus master; accompanist at Lieder-Recitals. *Compositions:* Organ and Choir-Music in style somewhat indebted to modern French church-music since Langlais, Duruflé and early Messiaen; For Organ a.O: Toccata, Opus 5; Choral Preludes, Opus 14 and 26; Rhapsody, Surrexit Dominus, Opus 22; Organ Fantasy, Victimae Paschali, Opus 24; Missa Fons Bonitatis, Opus 26; Proprium For Hallo-Mass, Opus 28; Choral Fantasy, Veni Creator Spiritus, Opus 40; For Choir: Psalm 12, Opus 21; Cantatas with Instruments, Opus 35. *Publications:* Contributed to the lexical part of The History of Music In Denmark, 1978. *Address:* Tranegårdsvej 69, 1 TV, DK 2900 Hellerup, Denmark.

KENINS Talivaldis, b. 23 Apr. 1919, Liepaja, Latvia. Professor of Composition; Composer. *Education:* B es Lettres, Faculty des Lettres, University of Grenoble, France, 1939; studies in piano & composition with Joseph Wihtol, State Conservatory of Music, Latvia, Riga, 1940-44; Conservatoire National Superieur de Musique, with Tony Aubin, Simone Pie-Caussade, Olivier Messiaen, Paris, France, 1945-50; Diploma, Analysis & Aesthetics, Premier Prix Diploma, Composition. *Career:* Instructor, 1952, Sessional Lecturer, 1953, Music, University of Toronto, Canada; Lecturer, 1956, Assistant Professor, 1962, Associate Professor, 1967, Professor, 1973, Composition, Schola Cantorum, Toronto; Instructor, Special Courses, Royal Conservatory for Music; Music Commentator, Radio Canada; Adjudicator, several Canadian Music Competitions & Festivals; Guest Lecturer, various Universities; Professor Emeritus, University of Toronto, 1984; Honorary Professor, Latvian Academy of Music, 1989. *Compositions:* Resident, Kalamazoo College, Michigan; Composer, 8 Symphonies, orchestral works, works for orchestra with soloist(s), works for chorus with orchestra or instrumental accompaniment, choral works, chamber music, keyboard works, educational piano music; Various works commissioned.. *Address:* 73 Parkview Ave, Willowdale, Ontario, M2N 3Y3, Canada.

KENNAN Kent Wheeler, b. 18 Apr. 1913, Milwaukee, Wisconsin, USA. Teacher; Composer; Author. *Education:* University of Michigan, 1930-32; Eastman School of Music; BM, 1934; MM, 1936; studies with Pizzetti, Academy of Santa Cecilia, Rome, Italy, 1938. *Career:* Teacher, Theory and Composition, University of Texas, Austin, retired 1983, now Emeritus; Kent State University, Ohio; Ohio State University; Eastman School of Music; Works performed by major orchestras. *Compositions:* Night Soliloquy; 5 Preludes for piano; Sonata for trumpet and piano; Three Pieces for Orchestra; Scherzo, Aria and Fugato; Retrospectives, 12 earlier pieces for piano, 1992; Numerous others. *Recordings:* Much of his work on record. *Publications:* Counterpoint, 3rd edition, 1987; The Technique of Orchestration, 4th edition, (co-author, Donald Grantham), 1990. *Honours:* Prix de Rome in Music, 1936. *Memberships:* ASCAP; Pi Kappa Lambda, honorary; National Association of Composers USA; Phi Mu Alpha Sinfonia. *Address:* 1513 Westover Road, Austin, TX 78703, USA.

KENNEDY Michael, b. 19 Feb. 1926, Chorlton-cum-Hardy, Manchester, England. Critic; Journalist; Author. m. Eslyn Durdle, 16 May 1947. *Education:* Berkhamsted School. *Career:* Joined editorial staff of The Daily Telegraph in Manchester 1941, Northern editor 1960-86; Staff music critic from 1950, joint Chief Music Critic since 1988; Music Critic, Sunday Telegraph, 1989-. *Publications:* The Hallé Tradition, 1960; The Works of Ralph Vaughan Williams, 1964; Portrait of Elgar, 1968; Portrait of Manchester, 1970; Barbirolli, 1971; History of Royal Manchester College of Music, 1971; Mahler, 1974; Strauss, 1976; Britten, 1980; Concise Oxford Dictionary of Music, 1980; The Hallé 1858- 1983, 1983; Oxford Dictionary of Music, 1985, 2nd edition 1994; Adrian Boult, 1988; Portrait of Walton, 1989. *Contributions:* Gramophone, Listener, Musical Times, Music and Letters. *Honours:* Fellow, Institute of Journalists, 1967; Fellow, Royal Northern College of Music, 1981; Order of the British Empire, 1981. *Hobbies:* Cricket. *Address:* 3 Moorwood Drive, Sale, Cheshire, M33 4QA, England.

KENNEDY Nigel Paul, b. 28 Dec. 1956, Brighton, England. Solo Concert Violinist. *Education:* Yehudi menuhin School; Juilliard Schoool of Performing Arts, New York; ARCM. *Debut:* Royal Festival Hall with the London Philharmonic Orchetra, 1977. *Career:* Regular appearances with London and Provincial orchestras, 1978-; Berlin debut with Berlin Philharmonic, 1980; Henry Wood Promenade debut, 1981; tour of Hong Kong and Australia with the Hallé Orchestra, 1981; Debut with the BBC Symphony Orchestra, 1987; Foreign tours, 1978-; India, Japan, South Korea, Turkey, USA; many appearances as Jazz Violinist with Stephane Grappelli, including Edinburgh Festival, 1974 and Carnegie Hall, 1976; many TV and Radio appearances including Coming Along Nicely, BBC TV documentary on early life, 1973-78; Played the Berg Concerto at the Festival Hall, 1991, dressed in a Dracula outfit; It's about death innit? says Nige; Informal Music Making from 1993. *Recordings:* Exclusive Recording Contract with EMI; Strad Jazz (Oct. 1984); Elgar Sonata with Peter Pettinger (Jan. 1985); Elgar Concerto, London Philharmonic Orchestra, conducted by V Handley; Tchaikovsky, Chausson Poème, London Philharmonic Orchestra (Oct. 1988); Bartók Sonata, Ellington Black, Brown & Beige Suite; Vivaldi - Four Seasons, Sibelius, Bruch, Mendlessohn, Walton Concertos, Walton's Viola Concerto, Brahms Violin Concerto, 1991. *Honours:* Best Classical Record 1985, British Record Industry Awards, for Elgar Concerto; Guiness Book of Records, for Vivaldi Four Seasons a No.1 in UK Classical Chart over one year, 1990; Winner, Golden Rose of Montreux 1990 (TV Special); Variety Club Showbusiness Personality of the Year, 1991. *Hobbies:* Boxing; Football; Cricket; Golf; Driving. *Address:* c/o John Stanley Media Management, 28 Nottingham Place, London, W1M 3FD, England.

KENNEDY Roderick, b. 7 May 1951, Birmingham, England. Singer (Bass Baritone). *Education:* Studied at the Guildhall School and with Otakar Kraus. *Debut:* Covent Garden, 1974. *Career:* More than 30 roles with the Royal Opera; Created Lt of Police in The Ice Break of Tippett, 1977; Appeared with the Royal Opera on visits to La Scala 1976; Korea, and Japan 1979 and 1986; Sang, The Doctor, in Wozzeck at Edinburgh and San Francisco, 1980-81, with further engagements at opera houses throughout Europe; Glyndebourne debut, 1981, as Don Fernando in Fidelio, followed by Alidoro, Rocco, Seneca (Poppea) and Britten's Theseus; Further festival appearances at Aldeburgh, Aix-en-Provence, Montpellier, Strasbourg and Florence; Regular performances with English National, Welsh National and Scottish Operas; Repertoire includes the coloratura works of Handel and Rossini, Roles such as Don Alfonso, King Philip, Pogner, Bottom, as well as many 20th Century works; Regular Promenade and concert appearances at home and abroad; Has worked with such conductors as Muti, Kleiber, Colin Davis, Ozawa, Harnoncourt, Solti, Haitink, Mehta, Pretre, and Mackerras. *Recordings include:* Messiah, Traviata, Herodiade, La Forza del Destino, Maria Padilla, Die Sieben Todessunden, Offenbach's Robinson Crusoe, The Immortal Hour and Le Comte Ory; TV Films and videos of Lucrezia Borgia, Giulio Cesare, Idomeneo, L'Egisto (Cavalli), Herodiade, L'Incoronazione di Poppea, La Cenerentola and a Midsummer Night's Dream. *Current Management* IMG Artists, Media House, 3 Burlington Lane, London W4 2TH. *Address:* Talbot Haven, Nairn Road, Talbot Woods, Bournemouth BH3 7BD, England

KENNER Kevin, b. 19 May 1963, California, USA. Concert Pianist. *Education:* Peabody Conservatory, Baltimore; Hochschule für Musik in Hannover; Studies with Leon Fleisher. *Career:* Has appeared in Europe, North and Central America, The Orient and former Soviet Union, since 1989 performing with St Paul Chamber Orchesstra, Rochester Philharmonic and ensembles in San Diego, San Francisco, Kansas City and Baltimore; Recitals at the Salle Pleyel in Paris, the Chatelet, Elizabeth Hall London (International Piano Series), and at the Kennedy Center, Washington DC; Broadcasts in Japan, Australia, Poland, Germany and Costa Rica. *Honours include:* Winner, International Chopin Piano Competition, 1990; International Terence Judd Award, Manchester, 1990, International Tchaikovsky Competition Moscow, Van Cliburn Competition, Fort Worth, 1989 and the Gina Bachauer Competition, Utah, 1988. *Address:* c/o Ingpen & Williams Ltd, 14 Kensington Court, London W8 5DN, England

KENNY Courtney Arthur Lloyd, b. 8 Nov. 1933, Dublin, Eire. Pianist; Repetiteur; Accompanist. m. Caroline Anne Florence Arthur, 15 Jan. 1972, 1 son. *Education:* Wellington College, Berkshire, 1947-51; Royal College of Music, London, 1951-54. *Career:* Musical Director, Bristol Old Vic, 1954-57; Solo Pianist, Royal Ballet, 1957; Member, Glyndebourne Festival Opera Music Staff; Founder, Western Opera, Ireland, 1963; Wexford Festival Opera Staff since 1963; Head of Music Staff, 1974; Senior Repetiteur, 1982; New Sadler's Wells Opera Head of Music Staff, 1983-89; Associate Music Director, Ohio Light Opera, 1983; Member of various ensembles including, Bureau Piano Trio, Barbican Ensemble, Peter Lloyd Baroque Trio; Faculty, Blossom Festival School of Cleveland Orchestra and Kent State University, 1972-80; Many Concert appearances as soloist and accompanist in Europe, USA, Middle East; One-Man show of songs at the piano called Let Me See You Smile; Conducting Debut, John Curry Theatre of Skating, then Ohio Light Opera, New Sadler's Wells Opera. *Recordings:* With Glyndebourne Festival Opera; Recitals with Ian Wallace. *Contributions to:* Opera. *Memberships:* Incorporated Society of Musicians. *Hobbies:* Musical Theatre; Gardening. *Address:* 14 Grange Grove, London, N1 2NP, England.

KENNY Yvonne, b. 25 Nov. 1950, Sydney, Australia. Singer (Soprano). *Education:* Sydney Conservatory of Music; Opera School of La Scala Milan, 1973-74. *Debut:* London 1975 as Donizetti's Rosamunda d'Inghilterra (concert performance); Covent Garden 1976, in the world premiere of Henze's We Come to the River; later apppeared as Mozart's Susanna, Ilia (Idomeneo) and Pamina, Verdi's Oscar, Bizet's Micaela and Handel's Semele 1988, Liu in Turandot; English National Opera debut 1977, as Sophie, in Der Rosenkavalier, returned as Romilda in Handel's Xerxes; (Also on USSR Tour) Semele at La Fenice, Venice; Guest appearances at La Scala, Paris, Lyon, Vienna, Cologne, Hamburg, Sydney and Munich; Festivals of Salzburg, Aix, Strasbourg, Edinburgh and Glyndebourne (Ilia 1985); Sang Alcina in a new production of Handel's opera at Covent Garden, 1992-93; Deborah in Handel's oratorio in the 1993 Proms; Strauss, Capriccio, at Berlin Staatsoper in 1993; Concert engagements under Pritchard, Colin Davis, Leppard, Harnoncourt, Solti, Abbado, Mackerras and Tennstedt; Featured artist (People, no 185) Opera Magazine, Dec 1992, pp 1385-1393. *Recordings:* Britten folk songs, Etcetera; Barbarina in Figaro, Solti/Decca; Constanze in Die Entführung and Aspasia in Mitridate with Harnoncourt; Donizetti's Ugo Conte di Parigi and Il Castello di Kenilworth; Bach's Cantata Der zufriedengestellte Aeolus, Telefunken; Elgar's The Kingdom, RCA; Mozart's Requiem, Chandos; Sings

Aspasia in Unitel film of Mitridate directed by Jean-Pierre Ponnelle; Vaughan Williams, Sea Symphony (Chandos); Mendelssohn's Elijah (Philips); Stravinsky, Pulcinella (CBS); Mozart's, Coronation Mass (RCA/BMG). *Honours:* Member of Order of Australia (A.M.) for services to music in 1989. *Current Management:* IMG Artists Europe, Media House, 3 Burlington Lane, Chiswick, London W4 2TH, England.

KENT Christopher, b.12 Aug 1949, London, England. Musicologist; Organist; Teacher. m. Angela Thomas, 21 July 1973. *Education:* BMus, University of Manchester; MMus, PhD, Kings College, London; FRCO; ARMCM. *Career:* Assistant Music Master, City of London School for girls, 1975- 80; Editorial Board, Elgar Complete Edition, 1979-. *Publications:* Co- Editor, 5 volumes of Elgar Complete Edition: Symphony No 1, 1981; The Dream of Gerontius, 1982; The Apsotles, 1983; The Kingdom, 1984; Music for Organ, 1987; The Music of Edward Elgar: A Guide to Research, 1993. *Contributions to:* Musical Times, The Listener, Journal of British Institute of Organ Studies; The Organ Year Book, Music and Letters, Journal of the Royal College of Organists; Proceedings of the Royal Musical Association. *Hobbies:* Flying; Railways; Natural History. *Address:* Department of Music, University of Reading, 35 Upper Readlands Rd, Berks RG1 5JE, England.

KENT Richard L., b. 23 Jan 1916, Missouri, USA. m. 1943. 1s. *Education:* BME, Drake University, 1940; MMus, New England Conservatory of Music, 1947; DMA, Boston University, 1961. *Career:* Professor of Music, Fitchburg State College, MA, 1947-82. *Compositions:* Magnificat, SSA chorus, WW quintet, 1981; Two Simple Prayers, SATB chorus music, 1991; The Tide Rises The Tide Falls, five symphonies, 1993. *Publications:* Windows of Song, children's song book, 1968. Magazine articles and several years as music critic for local paper. *Honours:* Sibelius Medal, 1964; Lowell Mason Awrd, 1978. *Memberships:* American Musicological Society; ACDA; ASCAP. *Address:* 1171 Main Street, Leominister, MA 01453, USA.

KENYON Nicholas Roger, b. 23 Feb. 1951, Altrincham, Cheshire, England. Writer on Music; Critic. m. Marie Ghislaine Latham-Koenig. *Education:* BA (Modern History) Balliol College Oxford. *Career includes:* Music Critic, The New Yorker 1979-82; Music Critic, The Times 1982-85; Music Editor, The Listener 1982-87; Formerly Chief Music Critic, The Observer, and Editor, Early Music; Broadcaster, BBC music programmes; Programme Advisor, Mozart Now Festival at South Bank, London, 1991; Controller, BBC Radio 3, 1992-. *Publications include:* The BBC Symphony Orchestra 1930-80; Simon Rattle, the making of a Conductor; Authenticity and Early Music (ed); Co-editor, Viking Opera Guide, 1993. *Membership:* Critics Circle (Music Section). *Address:* BBC, Broadcasting House, London W1A 1AA, England.

KERÉNYI György, b. 9 Mar. 1902, Csorna, Hungary. Musicologist; Folksong Collector; Publisher of Periodicals and Books. *Education:* Doctors Degree, Eötvös College, Budapest, 1924; Studied Composition with Kodály, Hungarian School of Music, 1925. *Debut:* Conductor and Composer, Györ, Hungary 1927. *Career:* Assistant to Bartók, Hungarian Academy of Sciences, 1934-38; First Assistant to Kodály, Folk music reasearch Group, 1950-67; Editor of two Hungarian Musical Periodicals, Eneklö Ifjuság 1941-49, Enekszó 1933-50; Inspector of Singing Teachers, 1947-48; Folk Music Collector, 1929-68. *Compositions include:* Kétágu Sip; Ludasjáték, Virágok vetélkedése; Hét Himnusz; numerous other compositions, including several choruses for church music. *Publications include:* Several volumes of the Corpus Musicae Popularis; Gyermekjátékok Children's Songs, 1951; Jetes Napok Festival Days, 1953; Pározitók Pairing Songs, 1959; Azenékkari muveltseg kezdetei, 1936; 100 Népi Játékdal, 1938, Mozart 30 Canons with Hungarian Texts, 1980; Népies Dalok (Popular Songs) 1961. *Honour:* Pitré Prize 1963. *Memberships include:* International Kodály Society; A Magyar Néköztársaság

Müvészeti Alapja; Magyar Zenemüveszek Szakszervezete. *Hobby:* Composition.

KERMAN Joseph Wilfred, b. 3 Apr. 1924, London. Music Educator; Author. m. Vivian Shaviro, 1945, 2 sons, 1 daughter. *Education:* AB, New York University; PhD, Princeton University. *Career:* Director, Graduate Studies, Westminster Choir College, Princeton, 1949-51; Music Faculty, x 1951-, Chairman, 1960-63, Professor of Music 1974-, J and E.H. Chambers Professor, 1986-88, University of California, Berkeley; Heather Professor of Music, Oxford University/Fellow of Wadham College, Oxford, 1972-74; Co-editor, 19th Century Music, 1977-89; Editor, California Studies in 19th Century Music, 1980-; Fellow, American Academy of Arts & Sciences; etc; Chairman, 1991. *Publications:* Opera as Drama, 1956, new edition, 1988; The Elizabethan Madrigal, 1962; Beethoven Quartets, 1967; History of Art & Music, with H.W. Janson, 1968; Ludwig van Beethoven: Autograph Miscellany 1786-99 (Kafka Sketchbook), editor, 2 volumes, 1970; Listen, 1972; Masses & Motets of William Byrd, 1981; New Grove Beethoven, with A. Tyson, 1983; Musicology, 1985; Music at Turn of Century, 1990, Editor. *Contributions to:* Hudson Review, New York Review, San Francisco Chronicle, etc. *Honours Include:* Guggenheim, Fulbright, NEH Fellowships; Visiting Fellow, All Souls College, Oxford, UK, 1966, Society for the Humanities, Cornell University 1970, Clare Hall, Cambridge, UK 1971; Honorary degrees; Kinkeldey Award x 2; Deems Taylor Award, 1981; Corresponding Member, British Academy.*Membership:* Honorary Foreign Member, Royal Musical Association. *Address:* Music Department, University of California, Berkeley, CA 94720, USA.

KERN Patricia, b. 14 July 1927, Swansea, Wales. Singer (Mezzo-Soprano). *Education:* Guildhall School, London, with Parry Jones (1949-52). *Career:* Sang with Opera for All 1952-55; Sadler's Wells/English National Opera from 1959, debut in Rusalka; appearances as Rossini's Isloier, Rosina, Cinderella and Isabella; Mozart's Cherubino, Monteverdi's Messenger; Sang in the 1966 premiere of Malcolm Williamson's Violins of St Jacques; Covent Garden debut 1967, as Zerlina in Don Giovanni: returned as Cherubino and as Mrs. Herring (1989); US debut 1969, Washington Opera; Scottish Opera in A Midsummer Night's Dream, L'Incoronazione di Poppea, Cenerentola and The Rape of Lucretia; Premiere of Iain Hamilton's Catiline Conspiracy 1974; Foreign engagements include Cherubino at the New York City Center and Dallas Civic Opera; Rossini's Cenerentola in Stratford Ontario and Isolier in Washington: Isabella in Spoleto; Monteverdi's Ottone at Drottningholm; Concerts in Paris, Turin and Hong Kong; Chicago Lyric Opera, 1987, as Marcellina in Le Nozze di Figaro, Repeated for Vancouver Opera, 1992. *Recordings:* Stravinsky, Cantata; Berlioz, Roméo et Juliette conducted by Colin Davis; Anna Bolena, Manon and Les Contes d'Hoffmann with Beverly Sills; Monteverdi Madrigals conducted by Raymond Leppard; Video of L'Incoronazione di Poppea, Glyndebourne, 1984. *Address:* c/o Music International, 13 Ardilaun Road, Highbury, London N5 2QR, England.

KERSJES Anton Frans Jan b. 17 Aug. 1923, Arnhem, Netherlands. Conductor. m. Margaretha van de Groenekan, 8 Aug. 1946. *Career:* 1st Violinist, Arnhem Symphony Orchestra, 194--41; Choir Conductor, 1945-46 and 1949; Co- founder, Kunstamaand Chamber Orchestra, 1953; Conductor, Netherlands Ballet Sonia Gaskell, 1953-61; 1st Conductor 1953-83, Principal Guest Conductor 1983-, Amsterdam Philharmonic Orchestra; Conductor, Netherlands Opera Company, 1955-60; Conductor, Amsterdam Ballet, 1960-62; Conductor of all Dutch symphony orchestras including Concertgebouw Orchestra, Orchestra Radio Hilversum; Guest Conductor, Netherlands Opera Company; Permanent Guest Conductor, Netherlands Philharmonic Orchestra, Amsterdam; Leader of conductors' class, Amsterdam Muzieklyceum, Sweelinck Conservatory, 1969-79; Leader conductors' and opera class, Deputy Director, Maastricht Conservatory; Tours in Europe, Scandinavia,

UK and USSR; Conductor of over 125 concerts, 5 operas on television. *Recordings:* For EMI and HMV. *Honours:* Decorated Officer, Order of Orange Nassau; Silver Medal, City of Amsterdam; Silver Medal, Concertgebouw. *Address:* 6 Honthorst Straat, 1071 Amsterdam, Netherlands.

KERSTERS Willem, b. 9 Feb 1929, Antwerp, Belgium. Composer. *Education:* Studied at the Brussels Conservatoire with Jean Absil, Marcel Quinet and Marcel Poot. *Career:* Teacehr until 1961, then programme Director of Belgian Radio and TV until 1968; Lecturer, Maastricht Conservatory, from 1968, Teacher of Composition at the Antwerp Conservatory, from 1971. *Compositions include:* Tragicomic opera Gansendonk, Antwerp, 1984; Ballets Parwati, 1956, Triomf van de Geest, 1959 and Ulenspiegel de Geus, 1976; Orchestral: Sinfonietta, 1955; Sinfonia Concertante with wind instruments, 1957; Divertimento for strings 1958; 5 Symphonies 1962-87; Sinfonietta for wind orchestra, 1967; Contrasts for percussion and orchestra, 1968; Capriccio 1972; Laudes for brass and percussion, 1973; Serenade for chamber orchestra, 1976; Piano Concerto, 1977; Ballade for alto saxophone and strings, 1987; Chamber: Wind Quintet, 1954; Partita for violin and piano, 1956; 2 String Quartets, 1962, 1964; Solo violin sonata, 1965; Piano Quartet, 1970; Nonetto 1985; Vocal: A Gospel song for soloists, chorus and orchestra, 19654; A hymn of Praise, oratorio, 1966; Canticum Solis Fratris, cantata, 1986; Kinderwereld for trumpet chorus, 2 pianos and timpani, 1988; Songs. *Address:* Vijverlaan 37, 2610-Wilrijk-Antwerp, Belgium.

KERTESZ Otto, b. 1960, Hungary. Cellist. *Education:* Studied at the Franz Liszt Academy, Budapest and with Sandor Devich, György Kurtag and András Mihaly. *Career:* Member of the Keller String Quartet from 1986, debut concert at Budapest March 1987; Played Beethoven's Grosse Fuge and Schubert's Death and the Maiden Quartet at Interforum 87; Series of concerts in Budapest with Zoltán Kocsis and Deszo Ranki (piano) and Kalman Berkes (clarinet); Further appearances in Nuremberg, at the Chamber Music Festival La Baule and tours of Bulgaria, Austria, Switzerland, Italy (Ateforum 88 Ferrara), Belgium and Ireland; Concerts for Hungarian Radio and Television. *Recordings:* Albums for Hungaroton (from 1989). *Honour:* 2nd Prize Evian International String Quartet Competition, May 1988. *Address:* c/o Artist Managment International, 12/13 Richmond Buildings, Dean Street, London W1V 5AF, England.

KESSLER Minuetta Shumiatcher, b. 5 Sept 1914, Gomel, Russia. composer; Pianist; Teacher. m. Dr Myer M Kessler, 14 Sept 1952, 1 s, 1 d. *Education:* Full Scolarship with Ernst Hutcheson from Juilliard School of Music, earned Graduate Diploma in Piano and Postgraduate Diploma as Artist and Teacher, with distinction; Studied with Ania Dorfman in Piano and Ivan Langstroth in Composition. *Career:* Teacher of Piano at Juilliard School of Music; Concerts Throughout Canada, and US; Solo Pinist and Composer, Including Boston Pops with Arthur Fielder, Montreal CBC Orchestra, Radio and TV Appearances; Performed Own Compositions, Including Alberta Concerto for Piano and Orchestra; Also Appeared in Boston at Jordan Hall, Boston Lyric Opera, Morning Pro Musica on WGBH Radio; Creator of Minuetta Kessler Music Kindergarten Method, from 1965; Director, Founder of Concerts in the Home, 1965-79; Private Teaching Studio from 1952-. *Honours include:* 2 CAPAC Awards for Serios Composition; Brookline Library Composition Award; 1st Prize for Left Hand Piano Composition; Nocturne in Purple Commission; 26 Who's Who Listings. *Memberships include:* ASCAP New England Jewish Music Forum; American Women Composers; Boston Juilliard Alumni Association; National League of American Pen Women. *Hobby:* Hiking. *Address:* 30 Hurley Street, Belmont, MA 02178, USA.

KESSNER Daniel Aaron, b. 3 June 1946, Los Angeles, California, USA. Composer/Conductor/ Educator. m. Dolly Eugenio, 29 June 1968, 2 sons. *Education:* AB cum laude 1967; MA 1968; PhD with Distinction 1971; University of California, Los Angeles. *Career:* Guest Conductor, Los Angeles Philharmonic New Music Group (5 concerts 1984-91); Founder and Director of CSUN New Music Ensemble 1970-; Artistic Director, Music on Main Concert Series, Santa Monica, 1987-; Frequent Guest Lecturer for Los Angeles Philharmonic Orchestra (58 appearances to date). *Compositions include:* 63 compositions including 5 orchestral works, a major piano concerto, 7 choral/stage works, 3 pieces for symphonic band, 24 works for various chamber ensembles, and 23 solos and duos. *Hobbies:* Skiing. *Address:* 10955 Cozycroft Avenue, Chatsworth, CA 91311, USA.

KESTEREN John Van, b. 4 May 1921, The Hague, Holland. Singer (Tenor). *Education:* Studied in The Hague with Lothar Wallerstein and with Nadia Boulanger in Paris; Further study with Vera Schwarz in Salzburg. *Debut:* Scheveningen 1947, as the Italian Singer in Der Rosenkavalier. *Career:* Sang operetta in Holland, on Dutch Radio and in Utrecht; Sang at the Komische Oper Berlin from 1951, Städtische Oper Berlin from 1953; Salzburg Festival from 1957, as Basilio in Le Nozze di Figaro and in concerts; Guest appearances in Vienna (from 1954), Dusseldorf, Munich, Stuttgart, Frankfurt, Ghent, Milan, the Drottningholm Festival (Stockholm), New York City Opera, Boston, Cincinnati, Dallas and Buenos Aires; Many concert appearances. *Recordings:* Belmonte in Die Entführung; Le Postillon de Lonjumeau by Adam; Pfitzner's Palestrina, Ariadne auf Naxos, Die Kluge by Orff (Deutsche Grammophon); Leonore by Paer (Decca); Carmina Burana (Eurodisc).

KETELSEN Hans-Joachim, b. 17 Feb 1945, Thuringen, Germany. Singer (Baritone). *Education:* Studied in Dresden with Arno Schellenberg. *Debut:* Freiberg, as Count Eberbach in Lortzing's Wildschutz, 1973. *Career:* Sang at Freiberg, 1973-76, Chemnitz, 1976-82; Dresden Staatsoper, 1982-90; notably in the reopening of the Semper-Oper, 1985 as Ottokar in Der Freischütz; Deutsche Staatsoper Berlin, 1990-93; Sächsische Staatsoper Dresden, Regular starring performances in Berlin, Chemnitz, Solo and ensemble starring performances in Japn, Spain, Greece, Sweden, Italy, Cuba, Suisse, Hungary, Germany, Las Palmas, 1993-; Participation in broadcast and TV, Concerts; Specialisation: German Opera (Wagner, Strauß); Important roles include: Telramund: Lohengrin, Wagner, Staatsoper Dresden; Wolfram: Tannhäuser, Wagner, Staatsoper Berlin and Staatsoper Dresden; Iago: Otello, Verdi, Staatsoper Dresden; Mandryka: Arabella, Strauß, Staatsoper Dresden; In preparation: Die Kluge, Carmina Burana by Carl Orff. *Recordings include:* Palestrina, Morone, Pfitzner; Götterdämmerung, Der Freischütz, as Ottokar. *Address:* c/o Staatsoper Berlin, Unter den Linden 7, 1086 Berlin, Germany

KETTING Otto, b. 3 Sept 1935, Amsterdam, Netherlands. Composer. *Education:* Studied at the Hague Conservatory 1952-58. *Career:* Trumpeter in The Hague Philharmonic Orchestra 1965-60; Teacher of composition, Rotterdam Conservatory 1967-71 and at the Royal Conservatory in The Hague 1971-74; Artistic Adviser to the Utrecht Symphony Orchestra 1983; Opera Ithaka was premiered at the opening of the Muziektheater Amsterdam, 1989. *Compositions include:* Operas: Dummies 1974 and O, Thou Rhinoceros 1977; Ballets The Last Message 1962; Interieur 1963; Barriers 1963; The Golden Key 1964; Choreo-struction 1963; Theatre Pice 1973; Concerto for solo organ 1953; Sinfonietta 1954; Sonata for brass quartet 1955; Piano Sonatina 195 ; Passcagalia for orchestra 1957; Serenade for cello and piano 1957; Concertino 1958; Symphony 1959; Concertino for jazz quintet and orchestra 1960; Variations for wind, harp and percussion 1960; Series of works entitled Collage; Minimal Music for 28 toy instruments 1970; In Memoriam Igor Stravinsky for orchestra 1971; Time Machine for wind and percussion 1972; For Moonlight Nights for flute and 26 players 1973; Adagio for chamber orchestra 1977; Symphony for saxophones and orchestra 1978; Opera Thaka 1989. *Honours include:* Guadeamus Prize 1958; Warsaw Autumn Festival award 1963. *Address:* c/o BUMA/STERMA huis, Postbus 725, 1180 AS Amstelveen, The Netherlands.

KEURIS Tristan, b. 3 Oct. 1946, Amersfoort, Holland. Composer; Lecturer. *Education:* Amersfoort Music School with van Vlijmen; Utrecht Conservatory 1963-69, with Ton de Leeuw. *Career:* Works have been widely performed from 1975; Commission from Houston Symphony Orchestra for Symphonic Transformations; Head of Composition at Sweelinck Conservatory Amsterdam; Visiting lecturer in America, Norway and Berlin. *Compositions:* Orchestral: Concerto for Alto Saxophone and orchestra 1971; Sinfonia 1975; Serenade for oboe and orchestra 1976; Piano Concerto 1980; Movements 1982; Concerto for Saxophone Quartet and orchestra 1986; Aria for Flute and orchestra 1987; Symphonic Transformations 1987; Chamber: Play for clarinet and piano 1968; Piano Sonata 1970; Saxophone Quartet 1970; Concertante Muziek 1973; Muziek for clarinet, violin and piano 1973; Concertino for bass clarinet and string quartet 1977; 2 String Quartets 1975, 1985; Music for Saxophones 1986; Aria for flute and piano 1987; Five Pieces for Brass Quintet 1988; Vocal: To Brooklyn Bridge for 24 voices and ensemble 1988. *Honours:* Composition Prize at Utrecht Conservatory 1969; Matthijs Vermeulen Prize 1975; Cultural Award of Hilversum 1982. *Address:* c/o Novello & Company, 8 Lower James Street, London W1R 4DN, England.

KEYES John, b. 1964, Illinois, USA. Singer (Tenor). *Education:* Studied in Chicago. *Career:* Based with the Chicago Lyric Opera until 1991; Season 1991-92 with Siegmund in Die Walkure for Scottish Opera, Radames at Mexico City and Parsifal in Robert Wilson's production of Wagner's opera for Houston Grand Opera; Concert performances of Otello (as Rodrigo) in Chicago and New York under Solti, 1991; Season 1992-93 as Siegmund at Hamburg and Nantes, Erik in Fliegende Hollander at Toulouse and Parsifal at Antwerp and Hamburg; Other roles include Walther von der Vogelweide and Eisenstein (Houston), Samson, Don Carlos, Don Jose and Dick Johnson, sang Lohengrin in a new production of Wagner's opera for English National Opera, 1993. *Recordings include:* Otello. *Honours include:* Winner, 1990, San Antonio Competition; Ruth Richards Grant in 1990 San Antonio Competition; Ruth Richards Grant in 1990 Richard Tucker Competition; Concert repertoire includes Beethoven's Ninth. *Address:* c/o Joan Coast Ltd, 31 Sinclair Road, London W14 ONS, England.

KEYS Ivor, b. 8 March 1919, Littlehampton, Sussex, England. Musician. m. Margaret Anne Layzell 1944, 2 sons, 2 daughters. *Education:* Christ's Hospital 1931-38; Christ Church Oxford 1938-40, 1946-47, as music scholar and assistant organist; MA, BA BMus 1940, DMus 1947. *Career:* Lecturer at Queen's University Belfast 1947-54; Reader 1950, Sir Hamilton Harty Professor 1951; Professor, Nottingham University 1954-68; Professor Birmingham University 1968-86; Emeritus Professor 1986; Visiting Professor University of Western Australia (Perth); President, Royal College of Organists 1968-70; Currently Council Member Trinity College of Music, and of National Federation of Music Societies; Examiner and Adviser in Music, Kenyatta University, Kenya, 1987-; Active as player of keyboard instruments, in particular the organ. *Compositions:* Clarinet Concerto 1960; Cello Sonata 1960; Miscellaneous Church Music and Editions. *Publications:* The Texture of Music 1964; Mozart 1980; Brahms Chamber Music 1981; Johannes Brahms, 1989. *Contributions to:* Music and Letters; Musical Times. *Honour:* Commander of the British Empire 1976. *Hobbies:* Bridge; Watching Cricket; Railways. *Address:* 6 Eastern Road, Birmingham, B29 7JP, England.

KEYS Robert, b. 30 Jan. 1914, Scholar Green, Cheshire, England. Assistant Head of Music Staff, Royal Opera House (retired). Widower, 1 son, 1 daughter. *Education:* ARMCM; FRMCM. *Career:* Solo Pianist and Broadcaster, 1930-; Light Orchestra Conductor, 1943-

; Repetiteur, English Opera Group, 1948-53; Repetiteur, 1953-72, Senior Repetiteur, 1972-74, Assistant Head of Music Staff, 1974-88, Royal Opera House, Covent Garden, London. *Compositions:* Piano and orchestra pieces for light orchestra; Opera translations. *Recordings:* Prince of the Pagodas; Elisir d'amore, continuo; Peter Grimes, Celesta. *Publication:* Biography of William Baines (with Roger Carpenter), 1976. *Contributions to:* Various music journals. *Honours include:* Hallé Scholarship, 1934; John McCormack Medal, 1984; Robert Stolz Medal, 1985. *Memberships include:* Havergal Brian Society; Johann Strauss Society; Donizetti Society; Founder/Secretary, Friends of Robert Stolz, in Britain. *Hobbies include:* Railway matters; Records. *Address:* Red Lion Court, Stalbridge, Sturminster Newton, Dorset DT10 2LR, England.

KEYTE Christopher Charles, b. 11 Sept. 1935, Shorne, Kent, England. Bass-Baritone. m. June Margaret. *Education:* Choral Scholar, King's College, Cambridge. *Career:* Oratorio, concert and recital appearances; Founder Member, Purcell Consort of Voices, 1963-75; Opera with The Fires of London; Professor of Singing, Royal Academy of Music, 1982-87; Royal Opera House, Covent Garden, 1989-. *Recordings:* Monteverdi Songs, Sacred Concertos, etc; Purcell Anthems, Indian Queen; Haydn and Schubert Masses; Vaughan Williams Serenade to Music, Pilgrim's Progress; Songs by Quilter, Gurney and Glazunov; Mass of the Sea, by Paul Patterson. *Honours:* Hon RAM, 1983. *Hobbies:* Opera; Athletics; Theatre. *Address:* 20 Brycedale Crescent, Southgate, London N14 7EY, England.

KHADEM-MISSAGH Bijan, b. 26 Oct. 1948, Teheran, Iran. Violinist; Conductor; Composer. *Education:* University of Vienna, Austria; Diploma with distinction, Academy of Music, Vienna, 1971. *Debut:* As soloist with orchestra aged 13. *Career:* Concert tours, including radio and TV appearances and Festivals throughout Europe, Asia and Latin America; Founder, Eurasia Quartet, 1969-75; Founder, Tonkuenstler Chamber Orchestra, Vienna, 1974 (Conductor, Soloist); Founder, the Dawnbreakers, Austrian Baha'i Singing group, 1970; Artistic Director, International Chamber Music Festival, Austria, 1979-, Midsummer Music Festival, Sweden, 1981-1990, Badener Beethoventage, 1983-86; Musical Director, Music Forum Landegg, Switzerland, 1991-. *Compositions:* Instrumental and Vocal Works. *Recordings:* LPs, MCs and CDs: Works by Vitali, Paganini, Debussy, Szymanovski, Bach, Tchaikovsky, Haydn, Handel, Dvořák, Respighi, Bartók, Strauss, Kreisler; Dawnbreakers LP 1976, The Child LP, 1979, LP To a Friend, 1982; LP Vision, 1986. Cassettes: Call of the Beloved, Phoenix, Glad Tidings, Wie Sterne. *Publications:* Lieder - Book of Songs, 1976. *Membership:* AKM Vienna. *Honours:* Grand Prize, 1st Prize, International Chamber Music Competition, Colmar-France, 1971; Culture Award of Baden Austria, 1988; Silver Medal, for services to Lower Austria, 1993. *Address:* Secretariat Dr Margaret Ley, Germerg 16, A 2500 Baden/Wien, Austria.

KHANZADIAN Vahan Avedis, b. 23 Jan. 1939, Syracuse, New York, USA. Operatic Tenor; Teacher. *Education:* B.Ed., University of Buffalo, 1961; Curtis Institute of Music, 1963. *Debut:* San Francisco Spring Opera, Ruggero in Puccini's La Rondine, 1968. *Career:* Many Roles in numerous productions including: Wozzeck; Fra Diavolo; Madam Butterfly; Lucia di Lammermoor; Appearances with major opera companies throughout USA and Canada including: New York City Center, Baltimore, Houston, Memphis, New Orleans, St Paul, Providence, Birmingham, Kentucky, Kansas City, Dayton, Toledo, Portland, Honolulu, Montreal, Edmonton, and Vancouver Opera Companies; Guest Soloist with major orchestras including Boston, Chicago, Philadelphia, Baltimore, Boston Pops; numerous recital tours; Master Classes; TV and Radio Broadcasts; Tenor Soloist in World Premiere of Menotti's, Landscapes and Remembrances, at Milwaukee in 1976; European Debuts: Cavaradossi in Tosca at Aachen, 1992; Title Role in Don Carlo at Basel,

1992; Metropolitan Opera Debut: Gustavus in Ballo in Maschera, 1993; Lyric Opera Chicago Debut: Gustavus in Ballo in Maschera, 1993. *Hobbies:* All Major Sports; Tennis. *Current Management:* Thea Dispeker, Inc, 59 E 54th Street, New York, NY 10022, USA. *Address:* 3604 Broadway, Apt 2N, New York, NY 10031, USA.

KHARITONOV Dimitri, b. 1958, Kuibyshev, Russia. Singer (Baritone). *Education:* Rimsky-Korsakov College of Music, Leningrad from 1976; Vocal studies, piano, with honours, Nezhdanova State Conservatory, Odessa, 1978-84. *Career:* Recital singer, Odessa State Philharmonic Society; Principal baritone, Odessa State Opera, 1984; Bolshoi Opera Moscow, 1985-88, as Eugene Onegin, Germont, Silvio-Pagliacci, Rossini's Figaro, Duke Robert - Iolanta, Prince Yeletsky - Queen of Spades, Tchaikovsky's Mazeppa, Ferdinand in Prokofiev's The Duenna, Conte di Luna - Trovatore; Sang in opera houses and concert halls, Moscow, Leningrad, Kiev, Minsk; Appeared regularly on Russian TV; Settled in England, 1989; UK debut as Jochanaan in Salome, Edinburgh Festival, 1989, returning for Tchaikovsky's Cantata Moskow; Season 1989-90 as Germont in Liége and Dublin, Mahagonny and Boris Godunov at the Maggio Musicale - Fiorentino; US debut, 1990, in La Fanciulla del West Chicago; Jochanaan for English National Opera; Recitals, Covent Garden, Buxton, Hamburg; Season 1991-92 engagements included Escamillo and Prince Andrei (War and Peace) at San Francisco War Memorial Opera House and Prince Yeletsky at Barcelona, Florence, Glyndebourne and Chicago, 1992-; Enrico, Lucia di Lammermoor, Los Angeles, 1993; Gerard, Andre Chenier, Enrico and Renato in Un Ballo in Maschera, Los Angeles, 1993. *Recordings include:* Eugene Onegin; Kovanschina; CD's: Shostakovich's romances on Pushkin's poems with City of Birmingham Symphony Orchestra; Tchaikovsky's Ode to Joy; Video of Queen of Spades, Glyndebourne. *Honours include:* Winner: All-Ukrainian Competition for Concert Interpretation, Kiev, 1983; All Ukrainian Lysenko Competition for Opera Singers, Odessa, 1984; All-USSR M I Glinka Competition with special prize for best interpretation of Rimsky-Korsakov works, 1984; Grand Prix, Verviers International Opera Competition, Belgium, 1987; Gold Medal, Bastianini International Competition, Siena, 1988; Voci Verdiane Competition, Busseto, 1988; Carlo Alberto Cappelli Competition, Arena di Verona, for International Competition winners. *Address:* IMG Artists, Media House, 3 Burlington Lane, Chiswick, London W4 2TH, England.

KHARITONOVA Yelena, b. 1960, Moscow, Russia. Violinist. *Education:* Studied at the Moscow Conservatoire with Andrei Shislov. *Career:* Co-Founder, Glazunov Quartet, 1985; Many concerts in the former Soviet Union and recent appearances in Greece, Poland, Belgium, Germany and Italy; Works by Beethoven and Schumann at the Beethoven Haus in Bonn; Further engagements in Canada and Holland; Teacher at the Moscow State Conservatoire and resident at the Tchaikovsky Conservatoire; Repertoire includes works by Borodin, Shostakovich and Tchaikovsky, in addition to the standard works. *Recordings include:* CDs of the six quartets of Glazunov. *Honours include:* Prizewinner of the Borodin Quartet and Shostakovich Chamber Music Competitions with the Glazunov Quartet. *Address:* c/o Sonata (Glazunov Quartet), 11 Northgate Street, Glasgow G20 7AA, Scotland.

KHOLMINOV Alexander, b. 8 Sept 1925, Moscow, Russia. Composer. *Education:* Studied with Golubev at the Moscow conservatory, graduated 1950. *Career:* Stage works have been widely performed in Moscow and elsewhere in Russia. *Compositions:* Operas An Optimistic Tragedy Frunze, 1965; Anna Snegina, Gorky, 1967; The Overcoat, after Gogol, 1975; The Carriage, after Gogol, Moscow, 1975; Chapayev, Moscow Radio, 1977; The Twelfth Series, Moscow, 1977; The Wedding, after Chekhov, Moscow 1984; Vanka, Monodrama after Chekhov, Moscow, 1984; The Brothers Karamzov, after Dostoyevsky, Moscow, 1985; Hot Snow, 1985. *Honours:* USSR State Prize, 1978; People's Artist of the URSSR, 1984. *Address:* RAIS Russian Federation, c/o PRS Ltd

Member Registration, 29-33 Berners Street, London W1P 4AA, England.

KHRENNIKOV Tikhon Nikolayevich, b. 10 June 1913, Elets, Liptsk Region, Russia. Composer. m. Klara Arnoldovna Vax 1936, 1 daughter. *Education:* Moscow Conservatoire; Gnesing School and College, Moscow, 1929-32; Moscow Conservatoire, 1932-36. *Career:* Director of Music, central Theatre of Soviet Army, 1941-54; General Secretary, Soviet Composers' Union, 1948-57, First Secretary 1957-; Deputy to USSR Supreme Soviet, 1962-; Committee Member, USSR Parliamentary Group; member, Central auditing Committee, CPSU, 1961-. *Principal Compositions:* 3 Piano Concertos, 1933, 1971, 1983; 5 Pieces for Piano, 1933; First Symphony, 1935; 3 Pieces for Piano, 1935; Suite for Orchestra from Music for Much Ado About Nothing, 1936; In the Storm (Opera), 1939; Second Symphony 1940-1943; Incidental Music for Play, Long Ago, 1942; Frol Skobeyev (Opera), 1950; Mother (Opera) 1956; Concerto for Violin and Orchestra, 1959; A Hundred Devils and One girl (Operetta), 1961; Concerto for Cello and Orchestra, 1964; White Nights (Operetta), 1967; Boy Giant (opera for Children), 1969; Our Courtyard (ballet for children), 1970; Much Ado About Hearts (Chamber Opera), 1974; Third Symphony, 1973; Love for Love (Ballet), 1976; Concert No 2 for Violin and Orchestra, 1975; The Hussar's Ballard (Ballet), 1979-80; Dorotea - comic opera, 1983; Golden Calf - comic opera, 1985; String Quartette - 1967. *Publications:* Sovetskij Kompozitor; Several Recorded Works. *Memberships:* Member of Santa Cecilia Academy, 1983; Tibara Academy, 1985; Prize of UNESCO International Music Council (IMC), 1977; Chairman of Tchaikovsky Contest Organising Committee, of International Music Festival in the CIS. *Address:* Composers' Union, 103009, Ulitsa Nezhdanovoi str. 8/10, Moscow, Russia.

KIBERG Tina, b. 30 Dec 1958, Copenhagen, Denmark. Singer (Soprano). *Education:* Studied in Copenhagen. *Debut:* Royal Opera Copenhagen, 1983, as Eonora in Nielsen's Maskerade. *Career:* Sang Elsa in Lohengrin at Copenhagen, 1984, the Marschallin 1988, Mozart's Countess and Purcell's Dido, 1990, Helene in Les Vepres Siciliennes, 1991. Guest appearances at Geneva and Frankfurt, 1988, as Agathe and the Countess, at Aarhus as Mimni, Vienna Staatsoper 1990, as Elsa and Opera Bastille Paris, 1991 as Lisa in The Queen of Spades; Lieder recitals in England, Germany and Italy from 1984; Sang Strauss's Ariande at Copenhagen and Elisabeth in Tannhauser at Bayreuth, 1992. Other roles in opera have included Donna Elvira, Pamina, Desdemona, and Tatiana in Eugene Onegin; Concert repertoire includes Schmidt's Das Buch mit Sieben Siegeln (Copenhagen), Beethoven's Mass in C (Lausanne), Haydn's Lord Nelson Mass (Vienna) and Elijah in Berlin; Tour of Moscow, Dresden, Berlin and London with the Missa Solemnis conducted by Antal Dorati. *Recordings include:* Lulu by Kuhlau. *Address:* c/o Det Kongelie Teater, Box 2185, DK 1017 Copengagen, Denmark.

KIEFER Bruno, b. 9 Apr. 1923, Baden-Baden, Germany. Professor; Flautist. m. (2), Nadia Beatriz Nunes Kiefer, 2 sons, 2 daughters. *Education:* Degree in Physics, Engineering School; Degree in flute, compositions studies, Institute of Arts, Federal University of Rio Grande do Sul, Brazil. *Career:* 2nd Flute, Symphony Orchestra of Porte Alegre for 2 years; Flautist with chamber groups; Lecturer on Musical subjects; Professor of Mathematics, School of Philos, until 1969; Professor, History of Music, Institute of Arts, 1969-. *Compositions Include:* Incidental music for theatre; Sonata No. 1 (piano); Madrigals Gauchos Vol. I (chamber chorus); Cantico; Cantata do Encontro, Cântico, Testimunho (chamber chorus); Campeadores for chorus and orchestra; Noite Consoladora for chorus and orchestra; Several chamber music and music for chamber chorus; Reflexões, piece for organ. *Recordings:* No Cimo das Copas (cantata, mezzo-soprano and woodwind quintet); Trio for Violin, violoncello and piano; Monológo (clarinet); Trio for flute, oboe and piano.

Publications include: Elements da Linguagem Musical, 2nd edition, 1973; Historia da Música Brasileira, Vol.I, 1976; Villa-Lobos e o Modernismo na Música Brasileira, 1981; Francisco Mignone - Vida e Obra, 1983; Author of chapter in Estudos Mauricianos, 1983. *Address:* Av. Ganzo, 525 ap 401, 90060 Porto Alegre RS. Brazil.

KIELISCH Melody, b. 2 Sept 1960, Wisconsin, USA. Singer (Soprano). *Education:* Studied at Milwaukee University and in Heidelberg, Milan and Vienna. *Career:* Sang in opera at Passau, then at Essen from 1984; Further engagements at Oberhausen, Coburg, Kiel, and Wuppertal as Gilda, Blondchen, Olympia, Adele, Musetta, Rita by Donizetti, Susanna and Aennchen in Der Freischütz; Concert engagements in Bach's St John Passion, Messiah, Die Schöpfung and works by Mozart, and Schubert at Zurich, Edinburgh, Helsinki, Milwaukee and Chicago. *Address:* c/o Staatstheater, Rolandstrasse 10, 430 Essen, Germany.

KIEMER Hans, b. 9 Feb 1932, Munich, Germany. Singer (Bass Baritone). *Education:* Studied in Munich. *Career:* Engaged at Innsbruck, 1968-70, Augsburg, 1970-76, Wiesbaden, 1976-79; Apperances at Karlsruhe from 1979, notably as the Dutchman and Wagner's Kurwenal, Wotan and Amfortas, Verdi's Falstaff and Amonasro, in the 1986 premiere of Kunaud's Der Meister und Margarita and as Waldner in Arabell, 1989; Guest engagemenst at Amsterdam, Barcelona, Brussels, (the Wanderer in Siegfried, 1981), Bordeaux (as Jochanaan), Triests (Pizarro), Vienna, Lisbon and Warsaw (Wanderer, 1989); Other roles include Strauss's Mandryka and Barak, Borromeo in Palestrina, Baron Ochs, Don Alfonso and Scarpia; Noted interpreter of the Ballades of Carl Loewe; Sang Mefistofele at Innsbruck, 1990. *Address:* Rebisches Staatstheater, Baumeisterstrasse 11, 7500 Karlsruhe, Germany.

KIERNAN Patrick, b. 1960, England. Violinist. *Debut:* Wigmore Hall, 1984 with Peter Pears. *Career:* Co-Founder, Brindisi String Quartet, Aldeburgh, 1984; Concerts in a wide repertory throughout Britain and in France, Germany, Spain, Italy and Switzerland; Festival engagements at Aldeburgh (residency, 1990), Arundel, Bath, Brighton, Huddersfield, Norwich and Warwick; First London Performance of Colin Matthews' 2nd Quartet, 1990, premiere of Davi Matthews' 6th Quartet 1991; Quartet by Mark-Anthony Turnage, 1992; Many BBC recitals and resident artist with the University of Ulster. *Recordings include:* Quartets by Britten, Bridge and Imogen Holst; Works by Pierné and Lekeu. *Honours include:* Prize winner, Third Banff International String Quartet Competition in Canada, 1989, with Brindisi Quartet. *Address:* c/o Owen/White Management, 14 Nightingale Lane, London N8 7QU, England.

KIEVMAN Carson, b. 27 Dec. 1949, Los Angeles, California, USA. Composer; Stage Director. m. Carrie Manfrino, 5 Sept. 1987. *Education:* BFA, 1975, MFA, 1977, California Institute of the Arts. *Career:* The Public Theater, New York City, New York Shakespeare Festival J. Papp; Tanglewood, 1978, Boston Symphony; The Pennsylvania Ballet, Schubert Theater, 1983; Darmstadt, 1976; Rotenfabrick, Zurich, 1976; Basel State Theatre, 1977; Kyoto, 1980, Tokyo, Hong Kong, Philippines, Australia, New Zealand and Singapore; Major commission from New York Shakespeare Festival for Hamlet Opera. *Compositions:* Intelligent Systems; Piano Concerto; California Mystery Park; Wake Up, It's Time To Go To Bed; Multinationals and the Heavens; The Temporary and Tentative Extended Piano; Aspen Symphony; Hamlet-Opera; Tesla (opera). *Recordings:* Belgium Radio Recording, Brussels; Sudwestfunk Radio Recording, Baden Baden, Germany; Japan Radio Recording, Tokyo; National Public Broadcasting Recording, USA. *Address:* 15 Jones Street 6H, New York, NY 10014, USA.

KIKUCHI Yoshinori, b. 16 Sept 1938, Yawatahama, Japan, Conductor. *Education:* Studied at Tokyo National University of Fine Arts and Music. *Career:* Chief

Assistant at the Nikikai Opera, Tokyo, 1961-64; Studied further with Kasei Yamada in Japan, with Peter Maag at the Accademia Chigiana at Siena and with Franco Ferrara in Rome; Engagements at Palermo (Teatro Lirico and Teatro Massimo) 1973-77; Hessisches Staatstheater Wiesbaden 1978-84; Guest conductor in Japan, Italy, Germany, France and Spain; La Scala, Milan and Verona Arena from 1986; Conducted Madama Butterfly at Verona 1987 and Bonn 1989/90. *Address:* c/o Musicart Raphael, Glauburgstraße 95, D-6000 Frankfurt d, Main 1, Germany.

KILDUFF Barbara Jane, b. 31 May 1959, Huntington, New York, USA. Opera Singer. *Education:* BM, State University College, New York at Fredonia (SUCNY Fredonia) 1981; MM, University of Connecticut, Storrs, 1983; MM, Vale University, 1984. *Debut:* Washington Opera, Blonde. *Career:* Performances include: Sang Blonde with Metropolitan Opera, conductor James Levine, 1990, with Baltimore Symphony, David Zinman, Jul 1990, with Zurich Opera, Apr-May 1990 (Edition), Barenreiter - Carlos Kalmar; Sang Zerbinetta in Munich 1987 and 1988, Maestros Bender, Sawallisch, Köhler, in Vienna, 1987 and 1991, Maestro Theodor Guschlbauer, Metropolitan Opera 1987, James Levine, Hamburg, 1988, Julius Rudel, Basel, 1988, Vancouver, Jan 1989, (Martin André); in Vienna, Apr 1991 with Horst Stein; Olympia, Bregenz, Summer 1987 and 88, Marc Soustrot, in Geneva, June 1990; Sang Adele at Metropolitan Opera, 1987, 89, 90 and 91, E Rosenthal, Julius Rudel, in Bonn Dec 1988, Guschlbauer, in San Francisco, Nov 90; Julius Rudel; Cleopatra, Metropolitan, Oct 88, Trevor Pinnock; Sophie, Munich, Oct 1989, 90, 91, Director: Brigitte Fassbaender, Heinrich Hollreiser; Metropolitan Opera, Mar 1991, Jiri Kout; Queen of the Night, Oviedo, Spain, Sept 1991. Many concert appearances and TV and radio performances; Season 1993 as the Countess in Capriccio at Vienna; Appears as Pagagena in Met video of Die Zauberflöte (DGG). *Address:* c/o CAMI, Crittenden Division, 165 West 57 Street, New York, NY 10019, USA.

KILLEBREW Gwendolyn, b. 26 Aug. 1939, Philadelphia, USA. Singer (Mezzo-Soprano). *Education:* Templeton University; Juilliard School; Metropolitan Opera Studio. *Debut:* Metropolitan Opera 1967, in Die Walküre. *Career:* 1968-69 sang Carmen in Munich and at the New York City Opera; 1970 Copenhagen, Geneva and Prague in Handel's Tamerlano; 1972-73 Salzburg Festival, as Amneris and in the premiere of Orff's De Temporum fine Comedia; 1973 Washington Opera as Baba the Turk (The Rake's Progress) and San Francisco as Marina (Boris Godunov); Deutsche Oper am Rhein, Dusseldorf, from 1976, as Gluck's Orfeo, Verdi's Preziosilla and Azucena and Rossini's Isabella; Bayreuth debut 1978, as Waltraute in Götterdämmerung; Zurich 1981, as Mistress Quickly in Falstaff; sang Frau Leimgruber in Klebe's Der Jüngste Tag, Duisburg 1989; Season 1991/92 as the Nurse in Rimsky's Golden Cockerel and Strauss's Herodias at Duisburg; Also sings in concert. *Recordings:* Tamerlano; Orlando Paladino by Haydn (Philips); Edgar, Schvanda the Bagpiper (CBS); De Temporum fine Comedia (Deutsche Grammophon); Mahler's 3rd Symphony (Harmonia Mundi). *Honours:* Outstanding Musician, Temple University, 1971. *Hobbies include:* Creative Cooking; Walking; Modern Dance. *Address:* c/o Ingpen and Williams Ltd., 14 Kensington Court, London W8 5DN, England.

KIM Earl, b. 6 Jan. 1920, Dinuba, California, USA. Composer; Professor; Pianist; Conductor. m. (1) Nora Philipsborn, 1947, 1 daughter. (2) Miriam Odza, 1958. (3) Martha Potter, 1977, 1 daughter. *Education:* Studied piano with Homer Grun; Composition and Theory with Schoenberg, University of California, Los Angeles, 1939; MM 1952, studied composition with Bloch and Sessions, University of California, Berkeley. *Career:* Professor, Princeton University, 1952-67; James Edward Ditson Professor of Music, Harvard University, 1967-90; Pianist and Conductor; Emeritus, 1990-; Composer-in residence, Princeton Seminar in Advanced Musical Studies; Marlboro, Dartmouth, Tanglewood and

Cape and Islands Festivals; Aspen Center for Compositional Studies. *Compositions:* Opera: Footfalls, 1981; Orchestral: Dialogues for Piano and Orchestra, 1959; Violin Concerto, 1979; Chamber: 2 Bagatelles for Piano, 1952; 12 Caprices for Violin, 1980; Scenes from Childhood for Brass Quintet, 1984; Vocal: Letters Found Near a Suicide, song cycle, 1954; Exercises En Route for Soprano and 8 Instruments, 1961-71; Narratives for High Soprano, Woman's Voice, Actor, 7 Instruments, Television and Lights, 1973-76; Now and Then for Soprano, Flute, Harp and Viola, 1981; Where Grief Slumbers for Soprano, Harp and String Orchestra, 1982; Cornet for Narrator and Orchestra, 1983; The 7th Dream for Soprano, Baritone, Violin, Cello and Piano, 1986; The 11th Dream for Soprano, Baritone, Violin, Cello and Piano, 1988; 3 Poems in French for Soprano and String Quartet, 1989; 4 Lines from Mallarmé for voice, flute, vibes, and 4 perucssion 1989; Some Thoughts on Keats and Coleridge for unaccompanied voices SATB 1990. *Recordings:* Two Bagatelles for Piano (Robert Helps: Victor); Earthlight (Merja Sargon, Martha Potter, Earl Kim: New World); Violin Concerto (Itzhak Perlman, Seiji Ozawa, Boston Symphony: EMI); Where Grief Slumbers, chamber version (Dawn Upshaw: Nonesuch); Dear Linda, Womens Voice, flute/picc, Piano Marimba, Percussion, cello. *Publication:* Lawson-Gould, EB Marks, Mobart. *Address:* 57 Francis Avenue, Cambridge, MA 02138, USA.

KIM Ettore, b. 14 Nov 1965, Korea, Singer. (Baritone). *Education:* Studied in South Korea and Italy. *Debut:* Theatro Delle Erbe, Milan, in Salieri's Arlecchinata, 1990. *Career:* Sang in Henze's We Come to the River at La Scala and in the premiere of Ferroro's La Figlia del Mago at the Teatro San Carlo, 1992; Concert performances of Otello, as Iago, at Bordeaux, 1992; Engaged at Germont at Covent Garden, 1993, Chorebus in concerts of Les Troyens with the London Symphony Orchestra and on stage at La Scala, 1993-94, Belcore at Strasbourg, Antonio in Linda di Chamounix at Stockholm and Riccardo in Puritani for Bavarian Radio; Other roles include Scarpia, and Gerard in Andrea Chenier. *Recordings include:* Linda di Chamounix and I Puritani, both with Edita Gruberova. *Honours include:* Gold Medal, International Giuseppe Verdi Competition at Bussetto, 1989. *Address:* Atholl Still Ltd, 80-86 Westrow Street, London SE19 3AF, England.

KIM Sun-Joo, b. 5 Oct. 1929, Sun Cheh Pyung an Buk-Do, Korea. Conductor; Educator. m. Hye Sook Lee, 5 May 1955, 1 child. *Education:* BMus, Kyung Hee University, 1961. *Career:* Principal Associate Conductor, Korean Broadcasting Symphony, Seoul, 1963-; Instructor, Yung-Hee University, Seoul, 1965; Principal Associate Conductor, Seoul Philharmonic, 1965-69; Principal Conductor, National Symphony Korea, 1969-70; Professor, Kyung Hee University; Currently Conductor, Korean Symphony Orchestra, Seoul. *Membership:* Board of Executives 1975-82, Korean Musicians Union. *Address:* Kyung-Hee University School of Music, Whoe Ki Dong, Seoul, Korea.

KIM Young-Mi, b. 6 Nov 1954, Seoul, Korea. Opera and Concert Singer (Soprano). m. Sung-Ha Kim, 21 July 1984. *Education:* Seoul Art School, 1973; BA, Conservatory of San Cecilia, Rome, 1979; MA, Academy of Santa Cecilia, Rome, 1980. *Debut:* Alice Tully Hall, New York Lincoln Center, 1980. *Career:* Appearances with New York City Opera, Los Angeles Music Center Opera, Houston Grand Opera, Opera Company of Philadelphia, Opera de Paris, Bastille Orchestra, National Symphony, Seattle Symphony, San Diego Symphony, Minnesota Orchestra, Colorado Symphony. *Recordings:* Sung-Eum Gramophone. *Honours:* Verona International Contest, 1977; Giacomo Contest, 1979; Maria Callas International Voice Competition, 1980; Luciano Pavarotti International Voice Competition, 1981. *Current Management:* Thea Dispeker Inc, New York, USA.

KIM Young Uck, b. 1 Sept. 1947, Seoul, Korea. Concert Violinist. *Education:* Studied with Ivan Galamian at the Curtis Institute Philadelphia from 1958.

Debut: Philadelphia Orchestra conducted by Ormandy, 1963. *Career:* Tours of South America and Europe: appearances with the Berlin Philharmonic, Concertgebouw Orchestra, Vienna Philharmonic and London Symphony; Season 1987-88 in USA with the St Paul Chamber Orchestra, St Louis Symphony, Cleveland Orchestra, Pittsburgh Symphony and the New York Philharmonic; concerts in Sweden, Italy and the UK; Season 1988-89 with the Hallé and BBC Welsh Orchestras; tours to Eire, Sweden, Norway and Germany; USA recitals with Peter Serkin playing Beethoven sonatas; Piano Trio recitals with Emanuel Ax and Yo-Yo Ma: 1989 concerts in Switzerland, Germany and Italy; Concerto repertoire includes works by Bach, Berg, Mozart, Prokofiev, Sibelius, Stravinsky and Vivaldi; Concerts and Recitals America and Europe: New York Philharmonic, Los Angeles Philharmonic, London Symphony Orchestra, Hong Kong Philharmonic, Rotterdam Philharmonic; Tours, America and Far East; Season 1992 with World and European Premieres of newly commissioned concerto by Gunther Schuller (New York and Rotterdam). *Recordings include:* 5 Mozart Concertos with the London Philharmonic under Christoph Eschenbach (Canyon Classics); Ax/Kim/Ma Trio recording of Dvořák Trios (Sony Classical-Record of the Year Award, 1988); Mozart Piano Quartets with Previn, Heichiro and Gary Hoffman (RCA). *Address:* c/o Harold Holt Ltd., 31 Sinclair Road, London W14 ONS, England.

KIMBROUGH Steven, b. 17 Dec 1936, Athens, Alabama, USA. Singer (Baritone). *Education:* Studied at Birmingham Southern College, Duke University, Princeton Theological Seminary; Further study in Italy. *Debut:* Mantua 1968, as Marcel in La Bohème; Appearances in Mannheim, Frankfurt, London, San Francisco New York and Philadelphia; Member of the Bonn Opera from 1971; Sang in the premiere of Christophorus by Schreker, Freiburg 1978; Essen, 1989 as Mirabeau by Siegfried Matthus; Concert tours of the USA, Germany, Italy and Austria; Guest appearances at the opera houses of Vancouver, Cincinnati, Rio de Janeiro, Barcelona; Repertoire includes roles in operettas and musicals. *Recordings include:* Lieder by Schreker, Korngold, Zemlinsky, Weill, Kienzl, Schönberg, Weigl (EMI and KOCH). *Address:* Gotenstr. 144, 53175 Bonn, Germany.

KIMM Fiona, b. 24 May 1952, Ipswich, Suffolk, England. Singer (Mezzo-Soprano). *Education:* Studied at the Royal College of Music, London. *Career:* Has sung at the Glyndebourne Festival in Die Zauberflöte, The Love for Three Oranges Titus L'Enfant et les Sortilèges; Appearances with Opera North as Hansel, Mercedes, Rosalind in The Mines of Sulphur, Hermia (A Midsummer Night's Dream) and Baba the Turk; Sang in the premiere of Edward Cowie's Kate Kelly's Road Show, Chester 1983; With English National Opera has sung Orlofsky, Lola and Fyodor (Boris Godunov), and in Orpheus in the Underworld and Rusalka; Covent Garden debut in Boris Godunov; Berlioz Festival Dido at Lyon and Aeneas; Sang in the premiere of Greek by Mark Anthony Turnage (Munich 1988) and again at the Edinburgh Festival; Scottish Opera in Lulu, Die Zauberflöte, Eugene Onegin and Das Rheingold; Bath Festival in El Rey de Harlem by Henze, with Ensemble Modern; Sang Smeraldina in The Love for Three Oranges, ENO 1989, Siebel in Faust 1990; Opera North/RSC at Stratford as Julie in Showboat; Glyndebourne Festival 1990, as Third Lady in Die Zauberflöte; Michael Berkeley, Baa Baa Black Sheep, world premiere, 1993; Concert performances with the London Symphony, English Chamber Orchestra, City of Birmingham Symphony and London Sinfonietta; Conductors include Abbado, Haitink, Elder, Hickox, Andrew Davis and Roger Norrington; Television appearances in The Gondoliers, L'Enfance du Christ and Man and Music series on Channel 4. *Address:* c/o Ron Gonsalves Management, 10 Dagnan Road, London SW12 9LQ, England.

KINCSES Veronica. b. 1949, Hungary. Singer (Soprano). *Education:* Studied at the Budapest Academy and the Accademia di Santa Cecilia Rome. *Career:*

Member of the Hungarian State Opera from 1973: roles include Susanna, Fiordiligi, Sulamith in Die Königin von Saba by Goldmark, Euridice, Mimi and Madama Butterfly; Teatro Liceo Barcelona and Montreal 1986, as Donna Elvira and as Suor Angelica; 3 Concerts in Chicago, 1981; Budapest 1986, as Eva in Die Meistersinger; Frequent concert appearances; Has appeared in several Hungarian TV programmes; Guest performer in Austria, Belgium, Czechoslovakia, Germany, France, Holland, Italy and USSR; Teatro Colon, Buenos Aires, Caracas, 1987; Deutsche Oper West-Berlin, 1985, 1986; Sang Madame Butterfly at Chicago 1989. *Recordings:* Die Königin von Saba, Haydn's Der Apotheker and La Fedeltà Premiata; Songs by Bellini; Liszt's Hungarian Coronation Mass; Madama Butterfly; Orfeo ed Euridice (Hungaroton); La Bohème (Supraphon). *Honours:* Winner, Dvořák International Singing Concours, Prague, 1971; Prix de l'Academie du Dusque, Paris, 4 times; Kossuth Prize, Hungarian People's Republic. *Address:* Hungarian State Opera House, Népöztársaság utja 22, 1061 Budapest, Hungary.

KING Alexander Hyatt, b. 18 July 1911, Beckenham, Kent, England. Musical Scholar. m. Evelyn Mary Davies, 1943, 2 sons. *Education:* MA, King's College, Cambridge. *Career:* Entered Department of Printed Books, British Museum, 1934; Deputy Keeper, 1959-76; Superintendent, Music Room, 1944-73; Music Librarian, Reference Division, British Library, 1973-76; Honorary Secretary, British Union Catalogue of Early Music, 1948-57; Council member, Royal Musical Association, 1949-; President, International Association of Music Libraries, 1955-59; Vice chairman, joint committee International Musicological Society/IAML, for International Inventory of Musical Sources, 1961-76; Trustee, Hinrichsen Foundation, 1976-82; President, Royal Musical Association, 1974-78; etc. *Publications include:* Mozart in Retrospect, 1955, 3rd edition 1976; Mozart in the British Museum, 1956, 1975; Some British Collectors of Music, 1963; 400 Years of Music Printing, 1964, 1968; Handel & His Autographs, 1967; Mozart Chamber Music, 1968, 1986; Mozart Wind and String Concertos, 1978, 1986; Printed Music in the British Museum (account of collections, catalogues & their formation, up to 1920), 1979; A Mozart Legacy: Aspects of British Library Collections, 1984; Musical Pursuits, Selected essays, 1987; Various exhibition catalogues, Editor, co-editor, further scholarly works on music. *Contributions to:* Year's Work in Music, 1947-51; Schubert, a symposium, 1947; Music, Libraries & Instruments, 1961; Deutsch Festschrift, 1963; Essays in honour of Victor Scholderer, 1970; Grasberger Festschrift, 1975; Essays in honour of Sir Jack Westrup, 1976; The New Grove, 1980; Rosenthal Festschrift, 1984; Various articles. *Honours include:* Scholarship, King's College, Cambridge; Honorary member, International Association of Music Libraries, 1968; Honorary degrees, Universities of York & St Andrews; Book, Music & Bibliography: Essays in honour of Alec Hyatt King, ed. Oliver Neighbour, 1980. *Hobbies:* Watching cricket; Opera; Exploring Suffolk. *Address:* 37 Pier Avenue, Southwold, Suffolk, IP18 6BU, England.

KING James, b. 22 May 1925, Dodge City, Kansas, USA. Singer (Tenor). *Education:* Studied at Louisina State University, University of Kansas City and with Martial Singher in New York. *Debut:* San Francisco 1961, as Don José. *Career:* Moved to Europe 1961 and sang Cavaradossi in Florence; Deutsche Oper Berlin from 1962; Salzburg Festival 1962-64, as Achilles in Iphigénie en Aulide and Aegisthus in Elektra; Vienna Staatsoper from 1963, debut as Bacchus in Ariadne auf Naxos; Bayreuth Festival 1965, as Siegmund; Covent Garden 1967, as the Emperor in Die Frau ohne Schatten: returned 1985, as Bacchus; Metropolitan Opera from 1966, Florestan, the Emperor, Siegmund, Walther and Don José; La Scala 1983, in Cherubini's Anacreon; Sang Jove Il Ritorno di Ulisse (arranged Henze) at Salzburg 1985 (also televised); returned to Salzburg 1989, as Aegisthus in Elektra; Sang the Drum Major in Wozzeck at the Metropolitan, 1990, Lohengrin at Nice; Holland Festival 1990, as the Emperor in Die Frau ohne Schatten; Sang Aegisthus at the Met, 1992; Other roles include Parsifal, Otello (San Francisco 1974), Pfitzner's

Palestrina, Manrico and Calaf. *Recordings:* Die Frau ohne Schatten, Daphne, Die Meistersinger, Lohengrin, Parsifal (Deutsche Grammophon); Salome, Die Walküre, Fidelio (Decca); Die Walküre (Philips); Mathis der Maler by Hindemith and Ariadne auf Naxos (EMI); Samson et Dalila (RCA); Video of Elektra conducted by Abbado (Virgin). *Address:* c/o Metropolitan Opera, Lincoln Center, New York, NY 10023, USA.

KING Mary, b. 16 June 1952, Tonbridge Wells, England. Singer (Mezzo-soprano). *Education:* BA, English, Birmingham University; PGCE, St Anne's College, Oxford; Postgraduate Diploma, Guildhall School of Music. *Career:* Sang in opera, Glyndebourne, 1980, US debut, 1985, Covent Garden, 1990; Regular appearances with major British orchestras; Spanish tour with BBC Symphony Orchestra, 1991; Proms, 1991; New music a speciality; Many 1st performances: The Undivine Comedy (Finnissy), Paris and London; Valis (Machover), Paris, Boston, Tokyo; Teaching, Guildhall School of Music, London, 1990-; Formed Green Light Music Theatre, 1990; Has sung Marcellina and Baba the Turk at Glyndebourne, The Cockerel in The Cunning Little Vixen at Covent Garden. *Recordings:* Where the Wild Things Are (Knussen); The Cunning Little Vixen, EMI; Praise We Great Men (Britten), EMI; Valis (Machover). *Memberships:* Equity. *Hobbies:* Gardening; Tapestry; Cats; Books. *Current Management:* Quadrivium. *Address:* 34A Garthorne Road, Honor Oak, London SE23 1EW, England.

KING Robert John Stephen, b. 27 June 1960, Wombourne, England. Conductor; Director; Harpsichordist; Editor. *Education:* Radley College 1974-78; MA, St. John's College, Cambridge. *Career:* Director, The King's Consort 1979-; Musical Director, European Baroque Orchestra 1986; Musical Director, National Youth Music Theatre, 1987-; Conductor (Netherlands Chamber Orchestra, Orquesta Sinfonica Euskadi, Orebro Chamber Orchestra, RTL Orchestra Symphonique, Madrid Symphony Orchestra, Filharmonisch Orkest van Vlaanderen) and Editor. *Recordings:* With The King's Consort for Hyperion, (exclusive recording artist). *Hobbies:* Cricket; Skiing; Graphic Design. *Address:* 2 Salisbury Road, Ealing, London W13 9TX, England.

KING Terry B, b. 20 Aug. 1947, Santa Monica, California, USA. Cellist; Conductor; Teacher. m. Leslie Morgan, 18 Dec. 1976. *Education:* BM, Mt St Mary's College, Los Angeles, 1970; Post graduate, Claremont Graduate School, 1974; University of Northern Iowa, 1989-91; Assistant Professor, University of Northern Iowa, 1990-. *Debut:* Carnegie Recital Hall, New York, 1975. *Career:* Assistant to Piatigorsky, University of Southern California, 1971-72; Instructor, San Francisco Conservatory, 1972; Lecturer, Calif St Univ, Fullerton, 1972-75; Artist-in-Residence, Grinnell College, 1975-; Vienna Chamber Orchestra, 1978; St Paul Sunday Morning, 1984-87; Voice of America, America in Concert, Music from the Frick Museum, NY, Austrian Radio, NPR, PBS, several documentaries: Piatigorsky, McPhee, Harrison. *Compositions:* Arrangements: Trio: music by Anderson, Enesco, de Falla, Fauré, Glinka; Voice & Instruments: Mozart, Bachelet, Godard; Cello ensembles: Sibelius, Prokofiev, Shostakovich. *Recordings:* 17 recordings. Cello music by Cowell, Barber, Cooper, Harris; Concertos by Harrison, Reale, Beethoven, Haydn; Trios with Mirecourt Trio, Beethoven to present day composers. *Address:* School of Music, University of Northern Iowa, Cedar Falls, IA 50614, USA.

KING Thea, b. 26 Dec. 1925, Hitchin, Hertfordshire, England. Clarinettist; Professor of Clarinet. m. Frederick Thurston (deceased). *Education:* ARCM, 1944, 1947, FRCM, 1975, Royal College of Music, London. *Career:* Frequent appearances as Soloist, Broadcaster, Recitalist; Principal Clarinet, English Chamber Orchestra; Member, Melos Ensemble of London; Member, Robles Ensemble. *Recordings include:* Mozart, Brahms, Spohr, Finzi, Bruch, Mendelssohn, Stanford, Crusell, 20th century British music. *Publications:* Editor and Arranger, Clarinet Solos; Chester Woodwind Series.

Arrangements of J.S. Bach, Duets for 2 clarinets, Boosey & Hawkes; Schumann for The Clarinet (Associated Board), 1991; Mendelssohn for The Clarinet, (Associated Board), 1993. *Honours:* OBE, 1985; FGSMD, 1992; Fellowship of Guildhall School of Music & Drama. *Hobbies:* Ski-ing; Painting; Lacemaking; Cows. *Address:* 16 Milverton Road, London, NW6 7AS, England.

KINGDOM Elizabeth, b. 1932, USA. Singer (Soprano). *Career:* Sang in opera at Bielefeld, 1958-63, notably in the 1962 German premiere of Scarlatti's Griselda, Nuremberg, 1963-68, (Hostess in the 1980 premiere of Zelminsky's Der Traumgorge); Guest appearances at Cologne, 1964, Oslo, 1970, Graz, 1982, and London, 1988; Other roles have included Mozart's Donna Anna and Fiordiligi, Verdi's Elisabetta, Forza Leonora and Aida, Elisabeth in Tannhauser, Giulietta, and Myrtocle in Die Toten Augen by d'Albert. *Recordings include:* Don Giovanni. *Address:* Stadtische Buhnen, Richard-Wagnerplatz 2-10, 8500 Nuremberg, Germany.

KINGSLEY Colin, b. 15 Apr. 1925, London, England. Lecturer and Pianist. m. 16 Apr. 1955. 2 sons, 2 daughters. *Education:* King's Scholar, Westminster School, 1938-43; BMus, Gonville & Caius College, Cambridge, 1946; DMus, Edinburgh, 1968; RCM, 1943-44 and 1946-47; Leverhulme Scholar, ARCM 1945. *Debut:* 1947. *Career:* Freelance Keyboard Playing, Broadcasting, 1948-; Solo Pianist, Royal Ballet, 1957-59; Several performances of contemporary music, mainly London and Paris; Member of Macnaghten Committee, 1957-63; Pianist, University College of Wales, Aberystwyth, 1963-64; Associated Board Examiner, 1959-93; Princ Radio: Concertos, 1955-; University of Edinburgh Lecturer, 1964; Senior Lecturer, 1968, (ret'd 1992); Series: Piano Music of P R Fricker, 1974 followed by Premiere of his Anniversary for Piano, Cheltenham International Festival, 1978; Series: The English Musical Renaissance, Piano Music, 1977. *Recordings:* Lyrita Sonatas for Piano by John White; Various BBC recordings for broadcasting purposes. *Hobbies:* Gardening; Languages. *Address:* 236 Milton Road East, Edinburgh EH15 2PF, Scotland.

KINGSLEY Margaret, b. 20 Feb 1939, Pool, Cornwall, England. Singer (Soprano and Mezzo-Soprano). m. W.A. Newcombe. *Education:* Royal College of Music; ARCM; LRAM. *Debut:* With Opera for All. *Career:* Glyndebourne debut 1966, in Die Zauberflöte; Appearances with Covent Garden Opera, English National Opera, Scottish Opera, Opera North, State Operas of Hamburg, Munich, Stuttgart and Vienna; Stockholm Royal Opera; Paris Opera; Naples, Miami, Washington, Roles include Wagner's Gutrune; Beethoven's Leonore; Waltraute, Eboli, Elvira, Verdi's Amelia and Lady Macbeth; Mozart's Fiordiligi, Donna Anna and Electra; Cassandre in Les Troyens; Reiza in Oberon; Gluck's Euridice; E.N.O. as Brünnhilde; Title role in Ariadne auf Naxos; Azucena; English National Opera 1983-84, as Amneris, Marina (Boris Godunov), Akhrosimova (War and Peace) and Mrs Grose (The Turn of the Screw); Concert appearances with leading British orchestras and on TV; Professor of Singing, Royal College of Music. *Hobbies:* Gardening; Cooking; Walking. *Address:* Bryher Cottage, Lynx Hill, East Horsley, Surrey KT24 5AX, England.

KIPNIS Igor, b. 27 Sept 1930, Berlin, Germany; Harpsichordist; Fortepianist. m. Judith Robinson, 1s. *Education:* Diploma, Westport School of Music, Connecticut, 1948; Harvard University, 1952. *Debut:* Harpsichordist, NYC, 1959; Fortepianist, Festival Music Society, Indianapolis, 1981. *Career:* Concerts and recitals throughout USA and Canada, 1962-; Extensive tours abroad, 1967-; Faculties, Berkshire Music Centre, Tanglewood, 1964-67; Chairman, Baroque Dept, Berkshire Music Centre, Tanglewood, 1965-67; Visiting Tutor in Harpsichord and Baroque Music Studies, Royal Northern College of Music, Manchester, 1982-; Associate Professor of Fine Arts, 1971-75, Artist in Residence, 1975, Fairfield University, Connecticut; Harpsichord Workshop, Indianapolis, summers, 1974-84; Host of weekly radio programme, Age of Baroque WQXR, NY, 1966-68; Host of syndicated radio series, WGBH, Boston, The Classical Organ, 1992-93. *Recordings:* 74 albums, of which 54 are solo. *Publications include:* A First Harpsichord Book, 1970; Dussek, the Sufferings of the Queen of France, 1975; Telemann, Overture in E Flat, 1977; Kerbs, 6 Preludes, 1985; Vivaldi: Harpsichord Concerto in A (Rv 780), 1987; Contributions and Record Reviewer, Stereophile, Musical America, Stereo Review, the American Record Guide, Opus, Clavier. *Honours:* 6 Grammy Nominations, 3 Record of the Year Awards from Stereo Review; Deutsche Schallplatten Prize, 1969; Gold Star Award, Musica, 1988; Best Harpsichordist, Keyboard magazine, 1978, 1979, 1980; Best classical Keyboardist, 1982, 1986; Hon Dr of Humane Letters, (LHD), Illinos Wesleyan University, 1993. *Memberships include:* Co-artistic Director and VP, Connecticut Early Musical Festival, 1983-. *Hobbies:* Photography; Record Collecting. *Address:* 20 Drummer Lane, West Redding, CT 06896, USA.

KIRBY Frank Eugene, b. 6 Apr. 1928, New York City, New York, USA. Historical Musicologist. m. 17 Aug. 1928, 3 sons, 1 daughter. *Education:* BA, German, Colorado College, 1950; PhD, History of Music, Yale University, 1957; Columbia University, Salzburg Mozarteum, Universities of Zurich, Texas and Hamburg. *Career:* Assistant Professor, Music Librarian, West Virginia University, 1961-63; Faculty, 1963-1993 (retired), currently Professor of Music and Chair, Department of Music, Lake Forest College, Lake Forest, Illinois; Temporary/part-time faculty posts: University of Virginia; University of Texas, Washington (St Louis), Northwestern, De Paul Universities; Music Cataloguer, Peabody Institute Library; Consultant, National Endowment of the Humanities; Editorial Consultant, Schirmer Books, Indiana University Press, World Book; Record Reviewer, Special Projects Editor, Piano Quarterly; Contributing Editor, Journal of the American Liszt Society. *Publications:* A Short History of Keyboard Music, 1966, Japanese Edition, 1979; An Introduction to Western Music: Bach, Beethoven, Wagner, Stravinsky, 1970; Music in the Classic Period: An Anthology with Commentary, 1979; Music in the Romantic Period: An Anthology with Commentary, 1986; Translation of Hanns Neupert, Das Cembalo, 3rd Edition, as Harpsichord Manual, 1960. *Contributions to:* Articles on musicians in New Grove Dictionary of Music and Musicians, 1980, The Academic American Encyclopedia, 1981. *Address:* Department of Music, Lake Forest College, Lake Forest, IL 60045, USA.

KIRCHNER Leon, b. 24 Jan. 1919, Brooklyn, New York, USA. Composer; Pianist; Conductor. *Education:* Studied with Schoenberg at UCLA (BA 1940) and in New York with Sessions; Further study at Berkeley (MA). *Career:* Lecturer at Berkeley from 1949; Lecturer, then Professor at the University of Southern California, 1950-54; Luther Brusie Marchant Professor at Mills College in Oakland 1954-61; Appointed to Harvard faculty 1961, Walter Bigelow Rosen Professor of Music from 1966; Director of the Harvard Chamber Players 1973; Director of the Harvard Chamber Orchestra and Friends 1975; Pianist and conductor of his own music and the Viennese classics; Composer-in-residence and performer at the Santa Fe Chamber Music Festival 1983; Tanglewood Music Center 1985; Soloist and Conductor, Boston Symphony, New York Philharmonic, Philadelphia Orchestra, S. F. Symphony, St Paul Chamber Orchestra, Sudwest Funk Baden Baden, Tonhalle Zurich, London Sinfonietta, Buffalo Philharmonic. *Compositions:* Opera, Lily 1973-76; Orchestral: Sinfonia 1951; 2 Piano Concertos 1953, 1963; Toccata for strings, wind and percussion; Concerto for violin, cello, 10 wind instrumemts and percussion 1960; Music for Orchestra 1969; Music for Flute and Orchestra; Vocal: Words from Wordsworth for chorus 1968; The Twilight Stood, song cycle after Emily Dickinson 1983; Instrumental: Duo for violin and piano 1947; Piano Sonata 1948; Little Suite for piano 1949; 3 String Quartets 1949, 1958, 1966; Sonata Concertante for violin and piano 1952; Trio for violin, cello and piano 1954; A Moment for Roger for piano; Five Pieces for Piano, 1987; Interlude for Piano, 1989; For Solo Violin II, 1987; For Solo Violin II, 1988; Triptych, Violin, Cello, 1988; Five Pieces for piano; Music for Twelve 1985. *Honours:* George Ladd Paris Prize, University of California; Two awards from New York Music Critics' Circle (First two string quartets); Naumburg Award for 1st Piano Concerto; Pulitzer Prize for 3rd String Quartet; Commissions from the Ford Foundation and the New York Philharmonic. *Memberships:* National Institute of Arts and Letters; American Academy of Arts and Sciences. *Address:* c/o ASCAP, ASCAP Building, One Lincoln Plaza, New York, NY 10023, USA.

KIRCHSTEIN Leonore, b. 29 March 1933, Stettin, Germany. Singer (Soprano). *Education:* Studied at the Robert Schumann Conservatory, Dusseldorf, with Franziska Martiensen-Lohmann. *Career:* Sang first with the Städtische Opera Berlin, from 1958; Kiel 1960-63, Augsburg 1963-65, Cologne 1965-68; Has sung with the Bayerische Staatsoper Munich from 1968; Salzburg Festival 1961 and 1970, Edinburgh Festival 1965 and 1971; Montreux Festival 1965; Guest appearances in Hamburg, Stuttgart, Zurich and Vienna; Concert tours of USA, Argentina, England, Italy and Turkey. *Recordings include:* Die Zauberflöte and Cardillac (Electrola); Bach Cantatas; Beethoven's Missa solemnis (RCA).

KIRK Elise Kuhl, b. 14 Feb. 1932, Chicago, Illinois, USA. Musicologist; Pianist; Lecturer. m. Robert L Kirk, 3 children. *Education:* BMus, 1953, MMus, 1954, University of Michigan; PhD, Catholic University of America, 1977; Studies in musicology with Kurt von Fischer, University of Zurich, 1961-63; Studies (piano), with Claudio Arrau, Aspen Institute of Music, 1953. *Career:* Adjunct Lecturer, Baruch College, City University of New York, 1972-77; Visiting Professor, Catholic University of America, summers, 1976, 1977; Adjunct Professor of Music, University of Dallas, 1978-. *Publications:* Editor, Dallas Civic Opera magazine, 1978-; Co-Editor, Opera and Vivaldi, 1984; Music at the White House: A History of the American Spirit, 1986. *Contributor to:* American Music Teacher; Notes; Musical Quarterly; Current Musicology; Symposium; Grove's Dictionary, 6th edition; Opera News; Dallas Civic Opera Magazine; Bulletin for Research in the Humanities; Miscellanea Musicologica; Library of Congress Performing Arts Annual. *Address:* c/o Lyric Opera of Dallas, 2733 Oak Lawn, Suite 201, Dallas, TX 75219, USA.

KIRKBY Emma, b. 26 Feb. 1949, Camberley, Surrey, England. Singer (Soprano). *Education:* Studied Classics at Oxford; Vocal studies with Jessica Cash. *Debut:* London concert 1974. *Career:* Many concert appearances with the Consort of Musicke directed by Anthony Rooley, Andrew Parrott's Taverner Players and the Academy of Ancient Music with Christopher Hogwood; Later repertoire with London Baroque; Tour of USA 1978; Tours of Middle East with Anthony Rooley, 1980-83; Apearances with Andrew Parrott at the Promenade Concerts in Monteverdi's Vespers and the Bach B Minor Mass: Sang Dorinda in Handel's Orlando 1989; Innsbruck Festival 1989, as Guiditta in the opera by Alessandro Scarlatti; TV appearances in Messiah and the Central TV series Man and his Music; Repertoire ranges from 14th Century Italian songs to arias by Haydn and Mozart; London Prom Concerts 1993, in Charpentier's Messe pour les Trépassés and Monteverdi Madrigals Book VI. *Recordings include:* Monteverdi's Orfeo and arias by Handel(EMI); Handel Utrecht Te Deum and Italian cantatas; Mozart Motets (Decca); Bach Mass in B minor and Magnificat (Philips); Dido and Aeneas (Chandos); Florentine Intermedi with the Taverner Players; Venus and Adonis by Blow and Locke's Cupid and Death with the Consort of Musicke; Arne Cantatas (The Parley of Instruments); Bach Cantatas 211 and 212 (Academy of Ancient Music); Handel Aci, Galatea e Polifemo (London Baroque) and Athalia; Monteverdi Sacred Vocal Music; Pergolesi Stabat Mater; Vivaldi In turbato mare irato and Lungi dal vago volto, Cantatas. *Address:* c/o The Consort of Musicke, 54a Leamington Road Villas, London, W11 1HT, England.

KIRKENDALE Ursula, b. 6 Sept. 1932, Dortmund, Germany. Music Historian. m. Warren Kirkendale, 16 June 1959, 3 daughters. *Education:* Dr.phil., Bonn, 1961. *Career:* Taught at University of Southern California, University of California, Duke University, Columbia University, USA (visiting professor). *Publication:* Antonio Caldara: Sein Leben und Seine Venezianisch- Römischen Oratorien, 1966. *Contributor To:* Acta Musicologica; Journal American Musicological Society; Chigiana; Music & Letters; Dizionario Biografico degli Italiani. *Honours:* Fellow, Deutscher Akademischer Austauschdienst, American Council of Learned Societies; Alfred Einstein Award; Deems Taylor Award; Elected Wirkendes Mitglied der Gesellschaft zur Herausgabe von Denkmälern der Tonkunst in Osterreich. *Address:* c/o Via dei Riari 86, 1-00165, Rome, Italy.

KIRKENDALE Warren, b. 14 Aug 1932, Toronto, Canada. Music Historian. m. Ursula Schottler, 1959, 2d. *Education:* BA University of Toronto, 1955; PhD, University of Vienna, Austria, 1961. *Career:* Assistant Professor, University of Southern California, 1963-67; Associate Professor, Duke University, 1967-75, Professor, 1975-82; Professor Ordinarious, University Regensburg, Germany, 1983-92. *Publications:* Fuge and Fugato in der Kammermusik des Rokoko und der Klassik, 1967, English, 1979; L'Aria di Fiorenza, 1972; Madrigali a diversi Linguaggi, 1975; The Court Musicians in Florence during the Principate of the Medici, 1993. Contributor to Journal of American Musicology Society; Acta Musicologica; Music Quarterly; Mozart-Jahrbuch; Quadrivium; Dizionario Biografico degli Italiani. *Honours:* Fellow, Deutscher Akademischer Austauschdienst, NEH, American Council of Learned Societies. Visiting Scholar, Harvard University Center for Italian Renaissance Studies in Florence; Dr h.c. University of Pavia, 1986; Accademico Filarmonico h.c. Bologna, 1987. *Memberships:* International, Italian, American Musicological Societies. *Hobby:* Mountain climbing. *Address:* Via dei Riari 86, I-00165, Rome, Italy.

KIRKOP Oreste, b. 26 July 1923, Hamrun, Malta. Singer (Tenor). *Education:* Studied with Nicolo Baldacchino and Giuseppina Ravaglia in Malta and with Emilio Ghirardini in Milan. *Debut:* Malta 1945, as Turiddu. *Career:* Sang with visiting Italian companies, and with Tito Gobbi and Maria Caniglia; Joined the Carl Rosa Company, England, 1950; Sadler's Wells from 1952, as Turiddu, Cavaradossi, and Rodolfo in Luisa Miller; Appeared as Canio in Pagliacci on BBC TV; Covent Garden debut 1954, as the Duke of Mantua; Contract with Paramount films led to a leading role in The Vagabond King (1956); Sang at Las Vegas and the Hollywood Bowl and appeared on NBC TV in pioneering presentations of Madama Butterfly, La Traviata and Rigoletto; Covent Garden 1958-59 in La Bohème and Rigoletto; Retired 1960.

KIRSHBAUM Ralph, b. 4 Mar 1946, Denton, Texas, USA. Cellist. *Education:* Studied with his father Joseph Kirshbaum, with Lev Aronson and with Aldo Parisot at Yale University. *Debut:* With the Dallas Symphony, 1959. *Career:* Has performed with most leading orchestras from 1970, notably in Berlin, Munich, Cologne, Zurich, Amsterdam, Copenhagen, Stockholm and Paris; US engagements with the Boston Symphony, the Chicago, Cleveland, Detroit, Pittsburgh, San Francisco, Dallas, Baltimore, Houston and Minnesota Symphony Orchestras; Concerts with the Los Angeles Philharmonic at Hollywood Bowl; Tours of Germany, Hungary, Switzerland, Israel, Scandinavia, New Zealand and Australia (September 1990 and July 1993, followed by a tour of Japan); Debut with the Orchestre de Paris December 1990; Festival appearances include Bath, Edinburgh, Lucerne, London's South Bank, ASPEN and the Mostly Mozart Festival, New York; Promenade Concerts, London, include the Elgar Concerto in the Jubilee season, and the premiere of Tippett's Triple Concerto, 1980; Premiered the Cello Concerto by Peter Maxwell Davies with the Cleveland Orchestra under Christoph von Dohnanyi, October 1989; Other conductors with whom he has appeared include George

Solti, John Pritchard, Colin Davis, Leonard Slatkin, Jeffrey Tate, Yuri Temirkanon Simon Rattle, Antal Dorati and André Previn; Tippett's Triple Concerto wuth the LSO and Colin Davis, voted Gramaphone Record of the Year, 1982; Founder and artistic director of the Manchester International Cello Festival at the Royal Northern College of Music in Manchester (held biennially); Fellow and tutor at the RNCM; Regular concerts with György Pauk (violin) and Peter Frankl (piano); Played the six cello suites of Bach at the Wigmore Hall, London, 1987 and in London, Sydney and New York, 1993; Frequent guest of the violinist and conductor Pinchas Zukerman (Brahms Double Concerto in London, 1988) and Edinburgh, 1992. *Recordings include:* Ravel, Brahms and Shostakovich trios (EMI); Elgar and Walton Concertos (Chandos); Tippett Triple Concerto (Phonogram); Barber Concerto and Sonata (Virgin Classics); Bach Suites, Virgin Classics and Haydn Concertos (ECO and Zukerman) BMG. *Honours include:* Winner, 1969 International Cassado Competition in Florence, 1969; Winner, International Tchaikovsky Competition, Moscow, 1970. *Address:* c/o Ingpen and Williams Ltd., 14 Kensington Court, London W8 4PA, London.

KIRYU Yoshihide, b. 15 Aug 1940, Toyko, Japan. Bassoon Player. m. Masae, 13 Dec 1973, 2 s. *Education:* Studied with Professor Kazutsugu Nakata, Professor Heihachirou Mita, Professor Harold Golshire at Juilliard, Professor Leonard Sharow in Aspen and Professor Sherman Walt. *Debut:* 1959 Recital TWIS Woodwind Quintet. *Career:* Member Yomiuri Nippon Symphony Orchestra; Soloist of Mozart bassoon Concert; Member NHK Symphony Orchestra, Principal Player; Soloist of Mozart & Hydn Concertante and Richard Strauss Double Konzert. *Honours:* Japan Music Competition 1st Prize; 10th Arim Prize. *Memberships:* Toyko Fagottiade; TWIS Woodwind Quintet. *Address:* 6-21-3 Shimo-Shakujii, Toyko 177, Japan.

KISCH (Alistair) Royalton, b. 20 Jan. 1919, London, England. Conductor; Artistic Director. m. Aline Stewart, 1940, 1 son, 2 daughters. *Education:* Clare College, Cambridge. *Career includes:* Conductor: Royal Fesitval Hall concerts with London Philharmonic Orchestra; London Symphony Orchestra; Philharmonia Orchestra; Royal Philharmonic Orchestra. Guest conductor: Hallé Orchestra, City of Birmingham Symphony Orchestra. Concerts in Europe with Paris Conservatoire Orchestra, Palestine Symphony Orchestra, Florence Philharmonic Orchestra, Athens State Symphony Orchestra, Pasdeloup Orchestra of Paris, Royal Opera House, Orchestra of Rome, San Carlo Symphony Orchestra of Naples, Vienna Symphony Orchestra, etc. Broadcasts, BBC, with London Symphony Orchestra, Royal Philharmonic Orchestra, Philharmonia Orchestra. Currently Artistic Director, Cork Street Art Gallery (specialist, English & French paintings, 20th Century); Freelance conductor of symphony concerts. *Recordings:* Decca. *Membership:* Friends of Tate Gallery. *Hobbies:* Good food & wine. *Address:* 2 Edwardes Square, Kensington, London W8, England.

KISER Wieslaw Maria, b. 20 July 1937, Poznan, Poland. Conductor; Critic; Composer. *Education:* High School of Music, Poznan. *Debut:* As composer, Poznan, 1965; as conductor, Poznan, 1963. *Career:* Over 750 concerts in Poland, Bulgaria, Finland, France, Germany, USSR and Czechoslovakia; Artistic Manager, The Boys Choir of Gniezno, Poland, 1989; Music Lecturer and Promotor of Music Life, 1990-; The Thrushes; Television and Radio broadcasts in Poland, Finland, France, USSR and Germany. *Compositions:* From the Years 1989-1990: Scherzo for the violin and string orchestra; Aria to J.S. Bach's chorale for the violin and string orchestra; Trio for the viola, violoncello and contrabass; Impromptu for the viola, violoncello and contrabass; Six Children compositions for the piano Sonata for the piano; Over 70 choral compositions. *Recordings:* Radio and TV Poland, Finland, USSR, Germany and France. *Publications:* Organisation and Education of Children's Choirs, 1971; Aerials of Poznan, 1975; The Selected Problems of Music History, 1969; Watchword, The

Music, in Encyklòeadia Wielkopolska (The Great Poland Encyclopaedie); Watchword, The Music, in Dzieje Poznania (The Aets of Poznán), 1989-90. *Hobby:* Working with Youth. *Address:* u. Szelagowska 12, 61-626 Poznan, Poland.

KISSIN Evgeny, b. 10 Oct 1971, Moscow, USSR. Concert Pianist. *Education:* Studied with Anna Cantor at Gnessin Institute of Music from 1977. *Debut:* Played Beethoven sonatas and a Mozart concerto aged 7. *Career:* Appearances with the USSR State Symphony Orchestra under Svetlanov and with the Moscow Philharmonic; Tour of Japan with the Moscow Virtuosi under Vladimir Spivakov; Played with the Berlin Radio Orchestra, November 1986; British debut at the 1987 Lichfield Festival with the BBC Philharmonic; London Symphony Orchestra concert May 1988, conducted by Valery Gergiev; Concerts with the Royal Philharmonic and Yuri Temirkanov March 1990; Promenade concert debut with the BBC Symphony under David Atherton, playing Tchaikovsky's 1st Concerto, 1990; US debut Sept 1990, with the New York Philharmonic conducted by Zubin Mehta; Carnegie Hall recital playing Schumann, Prokofiev, Liszt and Chopin; Tour of America 1991, performing at Tanglewood, Mann Music Center, Ravinia and the Hollywood Bowl; Season 1992/93 at Grammy Award Ceremonies, Performances with the Chicago Symphony, Philadelphia Orchestra and Boston Symphony; London recital debut and concert with the Philharmonia; Prokofiev Concertos with the Berlin Philharmonic under Abbado. *Recordings include:* Rachmaninov 2nd Concerto and Etudes Tableaux with the London Symphony conducted by Gergiev; Carnegie Hall debut recital (BMG/RCA); Profofiev Concertos (RCA and DGG); Haydn and Shostakovich Concertos with The Moscow Virtuosi; Mozart K414 and K466, Rondo K382; Solo Works by Brahms, Schubert and Liszt (DGG). *Address:* IMG Artists, Media House, 3 Burlington Lane, Chiswick, London W4 2TH, England.

KITCHEN Linda b.1960, Morecambe, Lancashire. Soprano. *Education:* Studied at Royal Northern College of Music with Nicholas Powell; National Opera Studio, 1983; later study with David Keren. *Career:* Sang Blonde in Mozart's Die Entführung 1983 and Monteverdi's Amor at the 1984 Glyndebourne Festival; later sang Flora in The Knot Garden at Covent Garden and Barbarina in The Marriage of Figaro at the London Coliseum; other roles include Mozart's Susanna, Papagena and Zerlina; concert repertory includes Rossini's Stabat Mater, Mozart's Requiem, Poulenc's Gloria and Schoenberg's Pierrot Lunaire; in 1988 sang Iris in Handel's Semele, at Covent Garden; Later Studied with David Ceren and Audrey Langford; sang Oscar in Ballo in Maschera, Flora in The Knot Garden, Sophie in Werther, Jemmy in Guillaume Tell (1992), Papagena in Magic Flute, all at Royal Opera House, Covent Garden; In Geneva, Jemmy, Guillaume Tell; In Dublin, Pamina, Magic Flute; Opera North, Cherubino, Zerlina, Serpetta (Finta Gardiniera) and Magnolia (Showboat); Other Roles include Adele; Sang Eurydice in a new production of Orpheus in the Underworld for Opera North, 1992, followed by Susanna in The Marriage of Figaro. *Recordings:* A Serenade to Music, for Hyperion. *Honour:* Heinz Bursary. *Current Management:* Lies Askonas Ltd, 186 Drury Lane, London, WC2B 5RY, England. *Address:* c/o Lies Askonas Ltd, 186 Drury Lane, London, WC2B 5RY, England.

KITCHINER John, b. 2 Dec. 1933, England. Singer (Tenor). *Education:* Studied at the London Opera Centre with Joan Cross. *Debut:* Glyndebourne 1965, as Count Almaviva. *Career:* Appearances with English National Opera, Scottish Opera and Welsh National Opera; Roles include Guglielmo, Don Alfonso, Don Giovanni, Renato (Un Ballo in Maschera), Count di Luna, Figaro and Bartolo in Il Barbiere di Siviglia, Robert (Le Comte Ory), Marcello, Escamillo, and Count Eberbach in Der Wildschütz by Lortzing; Also sang in the British stage premieres of Prokofiev's War and Peace and The Bassarids by Henze, at the London Coliseum (1972, 1974); Frequent concert engagements. *Address:* c/o

English National Opera, London Coliseum, St Martin's Lane, London WC2, England.

KITE Christopher James, b. 5 Nov. 1947, London, England. Harpsichordist; Specialist in Early Piano; Educator. m. Ursula Ksinsik, 16 May 1981, 1 son. *Education:* MA Oxon; ARCM: *Debut:* Wigmore Hall, 1972. *Career:* Debut of Christopher Kite/Robert Ferguson piano duo, Wigmore Hall, 1973; Duo recital series (featuring use of original early pianos), Purcell Room, London, 1974–; Director, Keyboard Department, International Barockensemble-Kurse, Schloss Ebenthal, Austria, annually 1975-80; Director, Askrigg Summer Academy for Baroque Music, Yorkshire, England, 1977; Solo appearances, harpsichord and early piano, Germany, Austria, Switzerland, Italy, Spain, Portugal, France, Belgium, Yugoslavia, Ireland, Sweden, USA, Canada, Israel; Head of Music Studies and Professor of Harpsichord and Fortepiano, Guildhall School of Music and Drama; TV and radio broadcasts, British Broadcasting Corporation. *Recordings:* Dufay and Isaac Secular Music (organ/clavichord), Decca Florilegium; English Virginal Music, Hyperion; Mozart Sonatas (fortepiano), Meridian; Handel Virtuoso Keyboard Music, Ears and Eyes; Mozart and Beethoven, Chamber Music with Fortepiano, Meridan; Mozart Concerto in D Minor, Nimbus; Mendelssohn Concerto in G Minor, Nimbus; Chopin Concerto in E Minor/Weber Konzertstück (Nimbus). *Publications:* Scarlatti Sonatas, 3 volumes, 1978; Editor, Handel: The Eight Great Suites, 1978; John Field: Complete Piano Sonatas, 1980; Handel: Aylesford pieces, 3 vols, 1983; Purcell: Complete Harpsichord Music, 1983. *Contributions to:* Chapter on keyboard instruments, How Music Works; Professional journals. *Honours:* Raymond Russell Memorial Prize, 1972; Bruges International Harpsichord Competition, 1977; Fellowship, Guildhall School of Music and Drama, 1983. *Memberships:* Incorporated Society of Musicians; Music Education Council (UK); Chairman, Early Music Centre Council. *Hobbies:* Cordon Bleu cuisine; Oriental cats; Skiing. *Current Management:* Prima Management. *Address:* 5 Howden Road, London, SE25 4AS, England.

KITE-POWELL Jeffery T, b. 24 June 1941, Miami, Florida, USA. University Professor; Musicologist. m. Helga A M Bordt, 19 Apr 1973, 3 sons. *Education:* BM, College-Conservatory of Music, Cincinnati, Ohio, 1963; BS Music Education, University of Cincinnati, 1964; MA Musicology, University of New Mexico, Albuquerque, 1969; PhD Musicology, University of Hamburg, Federal Republic of Germany, 1976. *Career:* Currently, Director of Early Music Studies and the Early Music Ensembles, Florida State University, Tallahassee, Florida, USA. *Publications:* The Visby (Petri) Organ Tablature-Investigation, Critical Edition, Vols. 14 & 15 of Quellenkataloge zur Musikgeschichte, 1980; Series Editor of Performer's Guides to Early Music and editor/contributor to the Renaissance volume, 1993; The New Grove Dictionary of Music and Musicians, 6th Edition (Contributor), 1980; Hamburgische Kirchenmusik in Reformationszeitalter (Leichsenring), Vol.20 in Hamburger Beiträge zur Musikwissenschaft (Editor), 1982; Syntagma musicum III (translation and edition of Michael Praetorius's treatise of 1619), in progress. *Address:* School of Music, Florida State University, Tallahassee, FL 32306-2098, USA.

KITTS Christopher Martin, b. 7 Apr. 1943, London, England. Conductor; Violinist; Educator. m. 16 Dec. 1982. *Education:* Trinity College of Music, London, 1968; Conducting Studies with Dr Boyd Neel, Toronto, 1964-67, Dr Hans Lert, Virginia, 1966; Violin Studies, with Bernard Robbins, New York Philharmonic, Clifford Evans, Toronto. *Career:* Conductor, Royal Conservatory Orchestra, Toronto, 1967, 1968, 1969; Conductor, Scarborough College, Choir and Band, 1970; Concertmaster, North York Symphony Orchestra, 1971, 1972; Freelance Violinist, Toronto, 1972-85; Conducted Tours in England, France, W. Germany, Netherlands, with Birchmount Park Collegiate, 1980, 1983, 1987, 1991; Adjudicator, Toronto International Music Festival, 1986, 1987; Music Director and Conductor of the Scarborough Philharmonic Orchestra, 1985-1993.

Address: 3663 Danforth Avenue, Scarborough, Ontario, M1N 2GZ, Canada.

KJEAR Kirsten, b. 26 Feb 1938, Copenhagen, Denmark. Musical Director, 1 s. *Education:* Studied at the Royal Conservatory of Copenhagen. *Debut:* Pianist, Copenhagen 1965; Conductor, 1969. *Career:* Chief Conductor, Koge Symphoniorch and Koge Choir; Member of the Danish State Folkmusic Ensemble; Appearances as Soloist and in Chamber Music as Pianist at Copenhagen Theatres, Balletstages; Headmaster of Municipal Music Schools; Founder of the IMUC Institute. *Publications:* Pianoschool for Beginners; Collection of Arrangements for Piano; 3 Songbooks; 3 Music Teaching Videos. *Contributions to:* A Developing Music Teaching Program. *Memberships:* ISME; OMEP. *Hobbies:* History; Archiecture. *Address:* Mollevej 19, PO Box 45, DK 3630 Jaegerspris, Denmark.

KLAAS Rainer Maria, b. 30 Jan. 1950, Recklinghausen, Germany. Pianist; Editor. *Education:* Piano, Conducting, Pedagogics, Musikhochschulen Essen & Hamburg; Piano teachers: Detlef Kraus, Klaus Hellwig, Yara Bernette; Konzertexamen Hamburg, 1977. *Debut:* Recklinghausen, 1968. *Career:* Debuts: USA, Israel, 1986; Schleswig-Holstein Music Festival, 1987; Berliner Festspiele/Rias Berlin Live, 1989; Several radio productions; Founder of Integral-Konzerte Recklinghausen, 1975; Founder and Editor of Piano-Jahrbuch, 1977–; Pianist of Trio Alkan (with Kolja Lessing and Bernhard Schwarz), 1988–; Teacher of Piano, Musikhochschule Detmold/Dep Dortmund, 1985–. *Recording:* Rachmaninov and Prokofiev, 1979. *Publications:* Editor of: Mittagsmusik/Piano I, 1977; Mittagsmusik/Piano II, 1978; Piano-Jahrbuch I 1979, II 1981, III 1983, IV 1989; Publisher of Ferdinand Schulz/Pianography. *Address:* Koernerplatz 8, D-4350 Recklinghausen, Germany.

KLAES Armin, b. 17 Sept 1958, Koblenz, Germany. Conductor. m. Monika Hachmöller, 16 Mar 1982, 1s, 1d. *Education:* Conducting, Reinhard Peters Folkwang-Musikhochschule Essen; Music pedagogy and composition, Musikhochschule, Koln; Musicology, University of Köln; Chamber Music with Günter Kehr. *Debut:* Bedford Springs Festival for the Performing Arts, Pennsylvania, USA. *Career:* Guest conductor with several orchestras since 1978; Founder and regular leader, Kölner Konzertgemeinschaft, 1978-1985; Music Director, Mannesmann-Sinfonieorchester Duisburg, 1985-92; Founder and conductor of the Amadeus Kammerorchester, 1991; Since 1992, Artist leader of the Musikgemeinschaft Marl, symphonic orchestra and oratorio chorus. *Recordings:* Bach, Concert for organ with H Schauerte, Le Carnaval des Animaux. *Honours:* Folkwang – Förderpries, 1987. *Address:* Corneliusstrasse 167, 47918 Tönisvorst, Germany.

KLÁNSKÝ Ivan, b. 13 May 1948, Prague, Czechoslovakia. Pianist. m. 13 June 1987, formerly divorced, 4 sons. *Education:* Prague Conservatory, 1963-68; Prague Academy of Music, 1968-73; Postgraduate Study, Prague Academy of Music, 1975-78. *Career:* Recitals, Orchestral Performances, most European Countries, USA, Japan, Zambia, Canada and South Korea; Lecturer by Professor, Prague Academy of Music and Conservatory, Luzern, Switzerland; Member of Guarneri Trio Prague; TV and Radio appearances in many countries; Lecturer, Prague Academy of Music; Plays with Chamber Ensembles and soloists. *Recordings:* Chopin Sonata in B flat minor Op 35; Prokofiev Sonatas Nos. 1 and 2; Janáček Piano Works; Schubert Impromptus Op 90 and 142; Beethoven 4 Piano Sonatas; Tchaikovsky The Seasons and other piano works. *Honours:* Bolzano, Busoni, 1967; Naples, Casella, 1968; Leipzig, Bach, 1968; Barcelona, M. Canals, 1970; Warsaw, Chopin, 1970; Santander, 1976; Honorary Citizenship, Fort Worth, Texas, Van Cliburn, 1973. *Membership:* Czech Chopin Society, Vice President. *Address:* Pod Klaudiánkou 1016, Prague 4, 147 00 Czech Republic.

KLAPSIS Spyros, b. 25 July 1956, Athens, Greece. Music Professor; Radio Producer. m. Ioanna Delis, 30 July 1983, 1 son, 1 daughter. *Education:* Diplomas in Piano, 1976, Harmony, 1976, Counterpoint, 1978, Fugue, 1979, National Conservatoire of Music, Athens; Political Science Diploma, 1979, Public Administration Diploma, 1981, Pandios University, Athens; 3rd Cycle DEA, Political Sociology, Universite de Nanterre, Paris, France, 1980; Composition Certificate, Conservatoire de Region de Rueil, Malmaison, France, 1981; Orchestra Direction Certificate, Conservatoire Superieur de Strasbourg, 1992; Byzantine Music Diploma, Tournaissen Conservatoire of Music, Athens, 1991. *Career:* Professor of Harmony, Counterpoint, Fugue, History of Music, Analysis, Choir Direction, National Conservatoire of Music and Tournaissen of Music, Athens, 1982-; Radio broadcasts of musical information, 1983-; Founder, Director, conductor, small proclassical group with music students, giving concert of a cappella works, 1984-; Music Consultant, Athens Mayoralty, 1984-85. *Hobbies:* Study of philosophy; Poetry; Composing music. *Address:* 107 Agathoupoleos Str, Athens 10446, Greece.

KLARWEIN Franz, b. 8 March 1914, Garmisch, Germany. Singer (Tenor). m. Sari Barabas. *Education:* Studied with Fritz Kerzman and at the Frankfurt Musikhochschule; Further study in Berlin. *Career:* Sang lyric roles at the Berlin Staatsoper 1937-42; Bayerische Staatsoper Munich from 1942, notably in the world premieres of Capriccio by Strauss (1942) and Hindemith's Die Harmonie der Welt (1957), and in the German premiere of Raskolnikov by Sutermeister (1949); Salzburg Festival 1942-44, tenor solo in the Choral Symphony and in the unofficial premiere of Strauss's Die Liebe der Danae; Sang with the Munich company at Covent Garden 1953, in the British premiere of Capriccio; Maggio Musicale Florence 1957, as Aegisthus in Elektra. *Recordings include:* Elektra (Cetra); Der fliegende Holländer and Der Rosenkavalier (Vox); Der Waffenschmied by Lortzing (Columbia); CDs of Die Meistersinger, as Eisslinger, 1964 (Eurodisc). *Address:* c/o Bayerische Staatsoper, Postfach 745, D-8000 Munich 1, Germany.

KLAS Eri, b. 7 June 1939, Tallin, Estonia. Conductor. *Education:* Studied with parents then at the Tallinn Conservatoire with Gustav Ernesaks. *Debut:* Conducted West Side Story at the Estonia Opera House, 1964. *Career:* Instrumentalist with the Symphony Orchestra of Estonian Radio from 1964; Studied further- at the Leningrad Conservatoire with Nikolai Rabinovich, then at the Bolshoi School, Moscow, with Boris Khaikin, 1969-72; Conducted at the Bolshoi from 1972; Musical Director of Tallinn Opera 1975; Founded the Estonian Chamber Orchestra 1977; Guest engagements at the Paris Opera and in Japan; Conductor of the Royal Opera Stockholm 1985; Conducted Don Giovanni at Stockholm 1988, Eugene Onegin for the Finnish National Opera at Helsinki and Essen, 1989; Music Director, Royal Opera, Stockholm, 1985-89; Chief Conductor, Aarhus Symphony Orchestra, Denmark since 1990; Since 1990 frequent guest conductor of major Symphony Orchestras in USA: Los Angeles, Cleveland, Detroit, Baltimore, Dallas and others; Guest conductor at Hamburg Opera (premiere of Schnittke ballet Peer Gynt, 1989); Debuts with the Los Angeles Philharmonic and the Baltimore Symphony, 1992; Conducted Porgy and Bess at the 1992 Savonlinna Festival. *Recordings:* Recordings for BISA record label includes works by Alfred Schnittke, with the 3rd Symphony (Stockholm Philharmonic) and the 4 Violin Concertos (Malmo Symphony). *Honours:* Order of WASA (Swedish Royal Medal); Order of Finnish Lion, 1992. *Current Management:* c/o Konsertbolaget AB, Kungsgaten 32, S-111 35 Stockholm, Sweden. *Address:* Nurme 54, EE0016 Tallin, Estonia.

KLAUSNER Tiberius, b. 10 Nov. 1931, Arad, Romania. Violinist. m. Carla Levine, 2 June 1963, 3 daughters. *Education:* Academy of Music, Budapest, Hungary; Conservatoire de Musique, Paris, France; Juilliard School of Music, New York. *Career:* Concertmaster, Kuentz Chamber Orchestra, 1950-52; Concertmaster, Kansas City Philharmonic, 1955-67, Kansas City Symphony, 1982-; Professor, Music, Artist in Residence, University of Missouri, Kansas City, 1967-; First Violinist, Volker String Quartet, 1967-. *Publications:* The Orchestra Musician and the Community, The American Symphony Orchestra, 1967. *Honours:* Remenyi Prize, Budapest, 1948; Premier Prix, Paris, 1952; Heifetz Prize, Tanglewood, 1954. *Hobby:* Bridge. *Address:* University of Missouri, Center for the Performing Arts, 4949 Cherry St, Kansas City, MO 64110, USA.

KLEBE Giselher, b. 28 June 1925, Mannheim. Composer. m. Lore Schiller, 1946, 2 daughters. *Education:* Berlin Conservatoire; Studied, Boris Blacher. *Career:* Composer in Berlin 1957; Professor, Composition & Theory of Music, Nordwestdeutsche Musik-Akademie, Detmold, 1957-; Member, Academy of Fine Arts, Berlin 1964 and Hamburg 1963, Bavarian Academy of Fine Arts, 1978. *Composition:* Principal Works include: Operas: Die Räuber (Schiller) 1957; Die tödlichen Wünsche (Balzac) 1959; Die Ermordung Caesars (Shakespeare) 1959; Alkmene (Kleist) 1961; Figaro lässt sich scheiden (Oedoon von Horvath), 1963; Jakobowsky und der Oberst (Werfel), 1965; Das Märchen von der Schönen Lilie (Goethe) 1969; Ein Wahrer Held (Synge/Boell) 1975; Rendezvous (Sostschenko) 1977; Der Juengste Tag (Oedoen von Horvath), 1980; Die Fastnachtsbeichte (Zuckmayer), 1983; Ballets: Signale, 1955; Menagerie, 1958; Orchestral Works: Die Zwitschermaschine 1950; Deux Nocturnes 1952; 5 Sinfonien, 1952, 1953, 1967, 1971, 1977; Adagio und Fuge (with theme from Wagner's Walküre), 1962; Five Lieder, 1962; Vier Vocalisen für Frauenchor, a Cappella 1963; La Tomba di Igor Strawinsky (oboe and chamber orchestra), 1979; Konzert for organ and orchestra, 1980; Church Music : Missa, 1964; Stabat Mater, 1964; Messe (Gebet einer armen Seele), 1966; Chamber Music: 3 String Quartets, 1949, 1963, 1981; 2 Solo Violin Sonatas, 1952, 1955; 2 Sonatas for Violin & Piano, 1953, 1974; Piano Trio Elegia Appasionata, 1955; Clarinet Concerto, 1984; Notturno for orchestra, 1987; Chamber Music: Soirée für Posaune und Kammerensemble, 1987; many other musical works. *Membership:* President of Academy of Fine Arts, Berlin, 1986. *Address:* Bruchstrasse 16, 4930 Detmold 1, Germany.

KLEE Bernhard, b. 19 April 1936, Schleiz, Germany. Conductor. *Education:* Studied piano, composition and conducting at the Cologne Conservatoire; Assistant to Otto Ackermann and Wolfgang Sawallisch at the Cologne opera house. *Career:* Early appointments in Salzburg, Oberhausen and Hanover; Music Director in Lubeck 1966-73; Chief Conductor of the North German Radio in Hanover 1976-79; General Music Director in Dusseldorf from 1977; Chief Guest Conductor of the BBC Philharmonic Orchestra 1985-89: Conducted the orchestra at the 1989 Promenade Concerts, with Berg's Three Pieces from Wozzeck and Mahler's 6th Symphony; Has conducted all the major German and London orchestras, the English Chamber Orchestra, Stockholm and Rotterdam Philharmonics, Zurich Tonhalle, RAI Rome, Vienna Symphony, and NHK Tokyo; US debut 1974, with the New York Philharmonic: has since conducted in San Francisco, Chicago, Detroit and Washington; Regular guest conductor at opera houses in Hamburg, Munich, Berlin, Covent Garden and Geneva; Festival engagements at Edinburgh, Salzburg, Holland, Hong Kong and Dubrovnik; Promenade Concerts, London, 1991, Mozart's Clarinet Concerto and Bruckner's 9th Symphony (BBC Philharmonic). *Recordings:* Extensive catalogue with Polydor and EMI. *Address:* c/o Ingpen & Williams Ltd., 14 Kensington Court, London W8 5DN, England.

KLEEFOOT Michael, b. 9 July 1952, Schleswig, Germany. Musician (Tuba). *Education:* Conducting, Deutscher Sängebund; Violin, composition and sound engineering, Detmold Conservatory; Tuba, with Professor Willi Walther; Musicology with Professor, Dr. Arno Forchert. *Debut:* Violinist, Bundesjugendorchester of Germany, 1971. *Career:* Sound engineer and music manager, Miller Records, Hamburg, 1978; Tuba Player, Gelsenkirchen Opera, 1981; Teacher, Detmold Conservatory, 1984; Solo tubist, Liceo Opera, Barcelona, 1989; Member of Mönchengladbach Opera, 1991; Teacher at Dortmund Conservatory/University, 1993; Solo Tubist, Beethovenhae-Orchestra, Bonn, 1994. *Hobbies:* Yoga; History; Cooking; Jazz. *Address:* Wiesenweg 23, 53121 Bonn, Germany.

KLEIBER Carlos, b. 3 July 1930, Berlin, Germany. Conductor. *Education:* Studied music in Buenos Aires, Chemistry at Zurich University. *Career:* Worked as repetiteur at the Gärtnerplatz theatre, Munich, 1952-53; Conducted at Potsdam from 1954, then at the Deutsche Oper am Rhein, Dusseldorf/Duisburg, 1956-64; Zurich Opera 1964-66; Stuttgart Opera from 1966 and Munich Opera from 1968; Vienna Staatsoper debut 1973, Bayreuth Festival 1974, Tristan und Isolde; US debut at San Francisco 1977, Otello; At Covent Garden (from 1974) has conducted Der Rosenkavalier and Otello; Other operas he has conducted include La Traviata, La Bohème, Der Freischütz, Die Fledermaus, Wozzeck, Carmen and Elektra; Has conducted at the Vienna Festival and the Prague Spring Festival; Engagements with leading orchestras in Europe and North America. *Recordings include:* Der Freischütz (Dresden Staatskapelle); Beethoven's 4th Symphony (Bavarian State Orchestra) and 5th and 7th Symphonies (Vienna Philharmonic); Schubert Symphonies nos. 3 and 8; Brahms Symphony no. 4 (Vienna Philharmonic); Dvořák Piano Concerto (Sviatoslav Richter and the Bavarian Radio Orchestra); Die Fledermaus; La Traviata; Tristan und Isolde, with the Dresden Staatskapelle.

KLEIBERG Ståle, b. 8 Mar 1958, Stavanger. Associate Professor. m. Asta Øvregaard, 25 June 1982, 1d. *Education:* Degree in Musicology, University of Oslo; Diploma, Composing, State Academy of Music, Oslo. *Career:* 26 Opuses since 1981, including commissions; Compositions include large works for full orchestra and church music as well as chamber works for various ensembles and solo works; In addition to numerous concert performances of each work, nearly all have been performed on Norwegian radio; Associate Professor, University of Trondheim. *Compositions:* The Rose Window, 1992; The Bell Reef, Symphony No 1, 1991; Dopo for violoncello solo and strings, 1993; Stilla, orch and tenor/ soprano, 1986; Two poems by Montale, 1986; String Quartet, 1985. *Recordings:* Sonetto di Tasso, 1993. *Publications:* Form in impressionism, 1985; CPE Bach and the individual expression, 1989; David Monrad Johansen's musical thoughts, 1983; Sturm und Drang as style and period designation in music history, 1991; the Music of Hans Abrahamsen, 1986. *Memberships:* Norwegian Society of Composers. *Address:* Stokkanhaugen 201, 7048 Trondheim, Norway.

KLEIN Kenneth, b. 5th Sept 1939, Los Angeles, California, USA. Music Director; Conductor. *Education:* Graduated Magna cum Laude, University of Southern California; Stanford University. *Debut:* Europe, 1970; Paris, 1974; Moscow, 1974; Vienna, 1975. *Career:* Conductor, Stuttgart Ballet in Stuttgart and then the Metropolitan Opera in all major cities of the USA; Toured USSR, Romania and Sweden, 1971, 1972; Invited by Pablo Casals to conduct 4 concerts in Puerto Rico, 1974; Conducted Suisse Romande Orchestra, Geneva, Switzerland, 1977; National Orchestra of France, Lamoureux Orchestra, Paris, France; Vienna Symphony, Montreux Festival; Debut with American Symphony Orchestra at Carnegie Hall, New York; Bruckner Orchestra, Austria, 1978; Debut at Rome Festival, 1979; Debut with Philharmonia Orchestra, Royal Albert Hall, London, England, 1979; Florida Philharmonic, Miami, Florida, USA, 1980-81; Edmonton Symphony; Louisville Orchestra; North Carolina Symphony; Kansas City Philharmonic; San Francisco Chamber Orchestra; Music Director, conducting over 60 concerts per season, Guadalajara, Mexico; Music Director, New York Virtuosi, South Dakota Symphony and the Waterville Valley

Festival; Has made numerous guest appearances worldwide.

KLEIN Lothar, b. 27 Jan. 1932, Hanover, Germany. Composer; Professor of Composition. *Education:* PhD Degree in Musicology and Composition, University of Minnesota 1961. *Career:* As an undergraduate wrote music for many theatre and film productions; Professor of Composition, University of Toronto; Chairman, Graduate Studies in Music; Guest lectures for 150th anniversary of Hochschule für Musik, Berlin, American Society for Aesthetics and Fulbright Commission. *Compositions include:* Stage Works: Canadiana 1980; Lost Love 1950-56; Orpheus 1976; The Prodigal Son 1966. Orchestral: Appassionata for Orchestra 1958; The Bluebird 1952; Charivari: Music for an Imaginary Comedy 1966; Epitaphs for Orchestra 1963; Fanfares for Orchestra 1978; Musique a Go-Go 1966; Orchestral Suite from The Masque of Orianna 1971; Presto for Orchestra 1958; Rondo Giocoso for Orchestra 1964; Symmetries for Orchestra 1958; Symphonic Etudes (Symphony No. 3) 1972; Symphony No. 1, 1955, No. 2, 1966. Band: Divertimento for Band 1953; Eroica: Variations On A Promethean Theme 1970; Gloria for Band 1961. Small Orchestra: Janizary Music 1970; Sinfonia Concertante 1956. String Orchestra: Passacaglia of The Zodiac 1971; Soloists with Orchestra: Boccerini Collage for Cello and Orchestra 1978; Concerto for Winds, Timpani and Strings 1956; Design for Percussion and Orchestra 1970; Ecologues for Horn and Strings 1954; Invention, Blues and Chase 1975; Musica Antiqua, 1975; Music for Violin and Orchestra 1972; Paganini Collage for Violin and Orchestra 1967; Scenes for Timpani and Strings 1979; Slices of Time 1973; Le Tresor des Dieux 1969; Trio Concertante 1961. Voices with Orchestra: Dorick Musick 1973; Herbstlieder 1962; The Masque of Orianna 1973; Meditations on The Passyoun 1961; The Philosopher in The Kitchen 1974; Voices of Earth 1976. Chorus: 8 Madrigals 1957; An Exaltation 1960; Good Night 1970; A Little Book of Hours 1962; 3 Ancient Folksongs 1959; 3 Chinese Laments 1968; 3 Pastoral Songs 1963; 3 Reflections 1976; Travellers 1981; 2 Christmas Madrigals 1961; numerous works for Solo Voices; Solo Voice with Instrumental Ensemble; Instrumental Ensemble, Instrumental Solos; Piano Works. *Address:* PROCAN, 41 Valleybrook Drive, Don Mills, Ontario M3B 2S6, Canada.

KLEIN Mitchell Sardou, b. 13 Aug. 1947, New York City, USA. Conductor, Cellist, Teacher. m. Patricia Whaley (violist), 20 May 1983. *Education:* BA, Brandeis University, 1968; BA, Music, College of Notre Dame, Belmont, California, 1972; MA, California State University, Hayward, 1976; Studied cello with Irving L Klein, conducting with various masters. *Career:* Conductor with various orchestras; Faculty Member, College of Notre Dame and California Music Center, Los Altos; Associate Conductor, Kansas City Philharmonic, 1980-82; Guest Conductor, Seattle Symphony, Buffalo Philharmonic, Kansas City Philharmonic, Santa Cruz Symphony, Flagstaff Festival Symphony, South Bend Symphony, Richmond Symphony, and Lawrence Symphony; Conductor, California Music Center Orchestra, 1972-; National TV appearances and radio performances; Extensive ballet and opera conducting; critic to various newspapers; Music Director and Conductor, Santa Cruz Symphony, 1986-; Peninsula Symphony, 1985-; Faculty, University of California at Santa Cruz. *Memberships:* American Symphony Orchestra League; Conductors' Guild. *Hobbies:* Photography; Sound equipment; Athletics. *Current Management:* Conductors' International Management, 95 Cedar Road, Ringwood, NJ 97456, USA. *Address:* 266 Lennox Avenue, Oakland, CA 94610, USA.

KLEIN Richard Rudolf, b. 21 May 1921, Landau, Germany. Composer; Musicologist. m. Anneliese Schuhle, 12 May 1951, 1 son, 2 daughters. *Education:* Academy of Music, Stuttgart, 1944-48; Diploma, 1948. *Career:* Lecturer, Composition and Theory: Academy of Music, Stuttgart, 1948-49; Academy of Music, Detmold,

1949-60; Lecturer, 1960-85, Professor, 1965-, Academy of Music, Frankfurt. *Compositions:* Nachtvogel, opera; Schwarze Sonne, oratorio; Sinfoniae sacrae; Psalmen; 3 partitas for orchestra; 6 chamber concertos; Choral works; Chamber music; Piano music; Music for children. *Recordings:* Fidelaton (Boppard); Hessischer Rundfunk; Suddeutscher Rundfunk. *Honours:* Chamber Music Prize, Gera, 1953; Youth Music Prize, Bonn, 1954; Prize, City of Stuttgart, 1956; Prize, Rhineland-Palatinate, 1965. *Address:* 15 Heftricher Strasse, 6246 Glashutten 2, Germany.

KLEINKNECHT Daniel, b. 5 May 1960, Indiana. Conductor. *Education:* BMus, Oberlin College Conservatory of Music, 1982; MMus, Indiana University, 1987; DMA, University of Iowa, 1991. *Career:* Music Director, Fort Dodge Area Symphony Orchestra, 1992-; Assistant Conductor, Peoria Civic Opera, Ilinois, 1986-; Music Director, Amahl and the Night Visitors, Aiken Productions, national tours, 1991-; Conducted American Premiere, Nicolae Braetan's Golem, Iowa City, 1992; Assistant Professor of Music, Mount Mercy College, Cedar Rapids, Iowa; Conductor of world premiere of Theodor Grigoriu's Violin Concerto with soloist Sherban Lupu, Indianapolis, Indiana, May 1994. *Address:* 404 C Sixth Street No 1, Coralville, IA 52241, USA.

KLERK Albert, (De),b. 4 Oct 1917, The Netherlands, Organist; Composer. *Education:* Amsterdamsch Conservatorium. *Career:* Organist, St Joseph's Church, Haarlem, 1933-; City Organist, Haarlem, 1956-83; Director of Catholic Choir, Haarlem, 1946-; Professor of Organ and Improvisation, Amsterdamsch Conservatorium (now Sweelinck Conservatorium), 1965-85. *Compositions:* Several works for organ including 3 concertos for organ and orchestra, chamber music and liturgical music, (7 masses). *Recordings:* Has made numerous recordings. *Honours:* Prix d'Excellence, Amsterdam, 1941; Prix du Disque; Prix Edison, 1962. *Address:* Crayenesterlaan 22, Haarlem, The Netherlands.

KLIMOV Valery Alexandrovich, b. 16 Oct 1931, Kiev, USSR. Violinist. *Education:* Studied with Mordkovich in Odessa, then joined David Oistrakh at the Moscow Conservatory, graduated 1959. *Career:* Prizewinner at competitions in Paris and Prague 1956; Soloist with Moscow Philharmonic 1957; Gold Medal Tchaikovsky Competition Moscow 1958; British debut with BBC Symphony Orchestra at the Royal Festival Hall 1967; Regular visits to America, Canada, Australia, Italy, Germany, Switzerland, Sweden; Appearances with such conductors as Ormandy, Svetlanov, Rozdestvensky, Temirkanov and Arvid Yansons; Other than the standard repertoire, plays music by Prokofiev, Khachaturian, Hindemith and Schnittke; Head of violin studies at the Moscow Conservatory, 1975-. *Recordings include:* CD of the Khachaturian Concerto (Olympia). *Honour:* National Artist of the RSFSR 1972. *Address:* c/o Norman McCann International Artists Ltd, The Coach House, 56 Lawrie Park Gardens, London SE26 6XJ, England.

KLINDA Ferdinand, b. 12 Mar 1929, Kosice, Czechoslovakia. Concert Organist; Professor. m. Luba Klindova, 2 daughters. *Education:* Diploma, Bratislava Conservatory, 1950; Med Dr, University of Bratislava, 1952; Concert Diploma, Bratislava Academy of Music, 1954; Studies, Prague, Weimar. *Career:* Concert tours, master classes in Europe, USA, Japan; Festival performances including Rome, Paris, Vienna, Prague, Helsinki, Budapest, Zurich, Leipzig, Moscow, Leningrad; Orchestral concerts with leading conductors including Ancerl, Adler, Baudo, Bour, Dorati, Rozhdestvensky, Herbig, Masur, Matacic, Neumann; Professor, Bratislava Academy of Music, 1962-; Juries, international organ competitions, Leipzig, Chartres, St Albans, Nuremberg, Prague, Budapest. *Publications:* Slovak Organ Music, Volume 1 1957, II 1964; Organ Interpretation, I & II, 1980; Orgelregistrierung, 1987. *Current Management:* Slovkoncert, Bratislava. *Address:* Langsfeldova 23, 81104 Bratislava, Slovakia.

KLIPPSTATTER Kurt, b. 17 Dec 1934, Graz, Austria. Conductor; Director; m. Mignon Dunn, 24 July 1972. *Education:* Conservatory Graz, private studies. *Debut:* Operahouse Graz, 1954. *Career:* Coach and conductor at different opera companies in Austria, Germany; Music Director, Raimundtheater Vienna, 1968-70; Artistic Director, Memphis Opera, 1972-76; Music Director, Arkansas Orchestra, 1973-80; Music Director, Greater Trenton Symphony, 1984-91; Faculty and Dirctor of Orchestral Activities, Hartt College, 1977-90; Director of Opera, Illinois Opera Theatre, 1990-; Guest Conductor, National Opera Bellas Artes, Mexico, Opera Warsaw, City Opera New York, Chautauqua, Michigan, Opera, Saarbrucken, Kassel Opera. *Current Management:* Robert Lombardo. *Address:* Krannert Center for the Performing Arts, 500 S Goodwin, Avenue, Urbana, IL 61801, USA.

KLOBUCAR Berislav, b. 28 Aug 1924, Zagreb, Yugoslavia. Conductor. *Education:* Studied in Salzburg with Lovro von Matacic and Clemens Krauss. *Career:* Assistant at Zagreb Opera 1943-51; Conducted at the Vienna Staatsoper from 1953; General Director Graz Opera, 1960-71; Bayreuth Festival, 1968-69, Die Meistersinger and Lohengrin; Metropolitan Opera, 1968, Der fliegende Holländer, Die Walküre and Lohengrin; Music Director, Royal Opera Stockholm, 1972-81; Principal Conductor, Nice Opera, 1983-; Conducted L'amore dei tre re at Palermo, 1989; Many appearances as guest conductor with leading orchestras. *Address:* Orchestre Philharmonique de Nice, Opéra de Nice, A Rue Saint-François de Paule, F-06300 Nice, France.

KLOPPERS Jacobus Joubert Krige, b. 27 Nov 1937, South Africa. Musicologist; Organist; Composer. m. Wilhelmina Maria McLachlan, 26 Aug 1961, 1 son, 1 daughter. *Education:* BA, 1957, BMus, 1959, University of Potchefstroom; BMus (Hons), 1961; DrPhil, Musicology, Frankfurt/Main, 1966; UPLM, UTLM, Organ, 1959. *Career:* Faculty, University of OFS, 1966-76; Head, Music, King's College, Edmonton, Canada, 1979-; Lecture-Recitals, Canada, USA, West Germany, Austria, South Africa, 1980; Regular organ recitals for SABC, CBC. *Compositions:* Pastorale on 23rd Psalm, 1982; Five chorale Preludes, 1983; Three Plainsong Settings, 1984; 3 Christmas Hymns, 1988; 2 Chorale Preludes, in Six Pieces for Organ by Western Composers, 1988; Hymn Concertato, 1988; Hymn Concertato (CRC Publishers), 1989; Partita on The Old Hundreth (Organ), Brookside Publishers, 1991. *Address:* Dept. of Music, The King's College, 9125 50 St, Edmonton, Alberta, Canada, T6B 2H3.

KLOS Wolfgang, b. 15 July 1953, Vienna, Austria. Viola Professor; Chamber Musician; Soloist. m. Olga Sommer, 20 Feb 1982. *Education:* Law student, University of Vienna; Violin studies 1969, viola 1971-, Final Diploma with Distinction 1977, Musikhochschule, Vienna; Master courses, M. Rostal, U. Koch, B. Giuranna. *Career:* Leader, Viola Sections, Tonhalle Orchestra, Zurich, Switzerland 1977-81, Vienna Symphony Orchestra 1981-89; Teacher, viola, chamber music & orchestra, Vorarlberg State Conservatory of Music, Feldkirch, Austria, 1977-89; Professor, viola & chamber music, & master classes, Vienna Musikhochschule, 1988-; Master classes, various locations, Europe & overseas; Soloist throughout Europe, 1981-; Member (numerous concerts, radio, TV, recordings worldwide), Vienna String Trio. *Recordings include:* Continuous recording, whole String Trio repertory (5 records to date); Numerous recordings with various orchestras & chamber music groups. *Hobbies:* Literature; Swimming; Downhill skiing; Cross-country horse riding; Cultural travel.

KLUSÁK Jan-Filip, b. 18 Apr 1934, Prague, Czechoslovakia. Composer. m. Milena Kaizrova, 29 Mar 1979, 1 son. *Education:* Academy of Music, Dramatic Arts, Prague; Studied composition with Jaroslav Ridky and Pavel Borkovec, 1953-57. *Compositions include:* Published: Four Small Vocal Exercises, 1-4-3-2-5-6-7-

10-9-8-11 for flute, 1965; Rondo for Piano, 1967; Published and recorded: Pictures for 12 wind instruments, 1960; 1st Invention for Chamber Orchestra, 1961; 2nd String Quartet, 1961-62; Variation on a theme by Gustav Mahler for Orchestra, 1960-62; Sonata for Violin and Wind Instruments, 1965-66; Invenzionetta per flauto solo, 1971; 6th Invention for Nonet, 1969; Monody in Memoriam Igor Stravinsky, 1972; 3rd String Quartet, 1975; Variations for two Harps, 1982; Proverbs for Deep Voice and Wind Instruments, 1959; 7th Invention for Orchestra, 1973; Fantasia on Adam Michna of Otradovice for Brass Quintet and Harp, 1983; Six Small Preludes for Orchestra/Vordeinen Thron tret ich hiermit, 1984; Viola, Opera in 2 Acts, 1984-85; The King with the Golden Mask, ballet, 1986; Hero and Leandros, ballet, 1988; Dämmerklarheit, Songs on Friedrich Rückert, 1988; 4th String Quartet; Mozart-Sickness, Fancy for Chamber Orchestra, 1991; Concerto for oboe and small orchestra, 1991; Tetragrammaton sine Nomine Eius for orchestra, 1992; Die Kunst des guten Zusammennspiels for Wind, 1992. *Address:* Blanicka 26, 120 00 Prague 2, Czech Republic.

KLUSON Jospef, b. 1953, Czechoslovakia. Violist. *Education:* Studied at the Prague Conservatory and Academy of Fine Arts. *Career:* Founder member of the Prazak-Quartet, 1972; Tours throughout Europe, America, Japan, Australia and New Zealand; Tours in UK 1982, 1985, 1988, 1989, 1993 (Wigmore Hall, Queen Elizabeth Hall, Huddersfield Contemporary Music Festival); Recitals for BBC, Dutch Radio, Czech Radio, Radio France; Teaching: master classes at Orlando Festival, Mozart European Foundation, Antwerp, Bremen. *Recordings:* Albums for Supraphon, Orfeo, Ottavo, Harmonia Mundi France. *Honours:* First Prize in the Czech National String Quartet Competition, 1978; Grand Prix in Evian, 1978; Grand Prix at Prague Spring Competition, 1979. *Address:* c/o Ingpen and Williams Ltd, 14 Kensington Court, London W8 5DN, England.

KMENTT Waldemar, b. 2 Feb 1929, Vienna, Austria. Singer (Tenor). *Education:* Studied at the Vienna Musikhochschule with Adolf Vogel, Elisabeth Rado and Hans Duhan. *Debut:* Vienna 1950, in the Choral Symphony, conducted by Karl Böhm. *Career:* Toured Europe with Viennese student group, appearing in Die Fledermaus and Le Nozze di Figaro; Vienna Volksoper from 1951, debut as the Prince in The Love for Three Oranges: later roles in Vienna have included Belmonte, Don Ottavio, Ferrando, Idomeneo, Walther, Bacchus and the Emperor in Die Frau ohne Schatten; Sang Jacquino in Fidelio at the opening of the rebuilt Vienna Staatsoper, 1955; Salzburg Festival from 1955, in the premiere of Irische Legende by Egk and as Idamante, Idomeneo, Gabriel in Le Mystère de la Nativité by Martin, Ferrando and Tamino; Bayreuth Festival 1968-70, as Walther von Stolzing; Further engagements in Milan, Dusseldorf, Paris, Amsterdam, Munich and Stuttgart, and at the Drottningholm and Edinburgh Festivals; Many concert appearances, notably in Das Lied von der Erde by Mahler. *Recordings:* Salome, Tiefland, Lulu, Bastien et Bastienne, Così fan Tutte (Philips); Beethoven's Missa solemnis (Electrola); Die Fledermaus, Das Rheingold, Arabella, Tristan und Isolde (Decca); Video of Turandot from the Vienna Staatsoper, 1983. *Address:* c/o Staatsoper, Opernring 2, A-1010 Vienna, Austria.

KNAIFEL Alexander, b. 28 Nov 1943, Tashkent. Composer. m. Tatiana Melentieva, 31 Dec 1965, 1 daughter. *Education:* The Secondary Music School at the Leningrad Conservatoire, 1950-61; Moscow Conservatoire, 1961-63; Leningrad Conservatoire, 1963-67. *Career:* Freelance composer. *Compositions:* Ainana, 1978; Joan, 1970-78; A Chance Occurrence, 1982; Nika, 1983-84; God, 1985; Agnus Dei, 1985; Litania 1988; Through the Rainbow of Involuntary Tears, 1987-88; Voznoshenije (The Holy Oblation), 1991; Svetje Tikhij (O, Gladsome Radiance), 1991; Postludia, 1992; Once Again to the Hypothesis, 1992; Scalae Iacobis, 1992; Chapter Eight, 1993; Maranafá, 1993; Butterfly, 1993; Music for 30 films. *Recordings:* The Canterville Ghost (BBC, 1980; Le Chant du Monde,

1991); Lamento (Le Chant du Monde, 1991); Monodia (Le Chant du Monde, 1990); A Silly Horse (Melodia, 1988). *Publications:* Two Pieces for ensemble, 1975; Classical Suite, 1976; Five Poems by Mikhail Lermontov, 1978; Musique militaire, 1974; The Canterville Ghost, 1977; Lamento, 1979, 1992; The Petrograd Sparrows, 1981; Medea, 1989; Vera (Faith), 1990; Da (Yes), 1991; A Silly Horse, 1985. *Address:* Skobelevski prospekt 5, kv 130, Sankt-Petersburg 194214, Russia.

KNAPP Alexander Victor, b. 13 May 1945, London, England. Musician; Musicologist. m. Caroline Mary Robinson, 2 Apr 1974, 1 son, 1 daughter. *Education:* MA (Hons), MusB (Cantab); Selwyn College, Cambridge, 1963-70; Hon ARAM; LRAM; ARCM. *Debut:* Wigmore Hall, 1975. *Career:* Teacher 1970-72, Royal College of Music Junior Department and Cambridgeshire College of Arts and Technology; Assistant Director of Studies, Royal College of Music, 1977-83; Visiting Scholar, Wolfson College, Cambridge, 1983-86; Joe Loss Research Fellow in Jewish Music, 1992-; Broadcasts on BBC Radio; Numerous lectures and lecture-recitals, consultancy. *Compositions:* Four Sephardi Songs for Voice and Piano, published by Transcontinental Music Publications, New York, 1993. *Recordings:* Accompanist/Arranger for 6 recordings: Cantors Naftali Herstik, Johnny Gluck, Ian Camissar (x 2), The Time of Singing (x2); Highlights from Voice of Jewish Russia (Royal Festival Hall). *Contributions to:* Fontana Dictionary of Modern Thought; The New Grove. *Hobbies:* Philosophy; Table Tennis. *Address:* Music Department, City University, Northampton Square, London EC1V 0HB, England.

KNAPP Peter, b. 4 Aug 1947, St Albans. Opera Singer (Baritone); Director. m. Mary Anne Tennyson, 2 June 1984, 1 son. *Education:* St Albans School; St John's College Cambridge. *Debut:* Glyndebourne Touring Company. *Career:* Kent Opera: Monteverdi's Orfeo (televised on BBC); Eugene Onegin; Don Giovanni; La Traviata; English National Opera: Don Giovanni; The Marriage of Figaro; Abroad: Sofia, Zurich, Frankfurt, Venice, Florence; Tour of Australia; Regular Broadcasts; 1978 began directing own opera company - La Perichole filmed for BBC TV; 1988/89 2 week seasons at Sadler's Wells Theatre, London; Orpheus in the Underworld at the Elizabeth Hall, 1989; sang Mozart's Figaro 1989; Zelta in The Merry Widows for Scottish Opera; sang Wolfram in Tannhäuser for New Sussex Opera, 1990; Made version of Carmen for Travelling Opera, 1992. *Recordings:* Monteverdi Vespers; De Falla Master Peter's Puppet Show. *Publications:* Translations of Così fan Tutte, The Marriage of Figaro, La Perichole, Orpheus in the Underworld, La Bohème, The Barber of Seville. *Honours:* First Benson and Hedges Gold Award, 1977. *Address:* Kaye Artists Management, Barratt House, 7 Chertsey Road, Woking, GV21 5AB, England.

KNEHANS Douglas, b. 3 Apr 1957, St Louis, Missouri, USA. Composer. m. Josephine McLachlan, 4 Dec 1989, 1 daughter. *Education:* BA, Canberra School of Music, Australia, under Don Banks, Larry Sitsky and Donald Hollier; MA, Queens College, CUNY, under Thea Musgrave, Arnold Schwarz Foundation Scholar, Luigi Dallapiccola Composition Award (Inaugural), Queens College, CUNY; DMA candidate, Yale University School of Music, under Jacob Druckman, Sept 1991-. *Career:* Full-time composer 1985-, over a dozen commissions supported by the Australia Council Music Board 1985-89; Victorian Council for the Arts Composition Fellowship, 1987; Australian Bicentennial Authority commission for work for orchestra for the Canberra Symphony Orchestra, 1988; His works have been performed by the Melbourne and Canberra Symphony Orchestras, the Canberra Youth Orchestra, the Australian Boys Choir, ELISION, Ariel New Music, the Adelaide Percussions, Gaudeamus Choir (Canberra), Electric Cellist Jeffrey Krieger, The Australian Opera and the Eastman School of Music, New York. *Compositions include:* Choral Music: Song of the Raven Night, 1984; St Luke Magnificat, 1986; Ensemble music includes: Five Songs to Poems by Sylvia Plath (arranged 1986); Image Shift, 1988; Dawn Panels, 1988; Film

Music: A Song of Air (solo piano) 1987; Instrumental Music includes: Elegies for Merilee (solo contrabass and stereo tape) 1988; ...de la fumee, des voix (solo amplified harpsichord and pre-recorded 4 track tape) 1990; Night Chains, for Electric Cello and FX; Opera: The Ascension of Robert Flau; Orchestral Music: In Light 1987; Passacaglia for Orchestra, 1983. *Address:* c/o Australian Music Centre, PO Box 49, Broadway, NSW 2007, Australia.

KNESS Richard Maynard, b. 23 July 1937, Rockford, Illinois, USA. Tenor. m. Joann Danielle Grillo, 23 July 1967, 1 son; previous marriage: 1 son, 1 daughter. *Education:* BA, San Diego State University, 1958; Hochswang Schule, Essen Werden, Germany, Professor Clemens Kaiser Breme, 1972, Washington National Cathedral, Paul Calloway; Private study with Franco Corelli, 5 years; Voice Teacher, Franco Iglesias. *Career:* Appeared with more than 60 opera companies in Europe & USA including Nantes, France; Hamburg, Düsseldorf, Frankfurt, Essen, Dortmond, Munich, Germany, Brussels, Belgium; Belgrade, Yugoslavia; Teheran, Iran; Tel Aviv, Israel; and Mexico City, 1967-78; Leading dramatic tenor Metropolitan Opera Association, New York City Opera, San Francisco Opera, across the USA, 1967-; Appeared with numerous symphony orchestras across USA including: The New York Philharmonic, The Philadelphia Orchestra, The Pittsburgh Symphony and Cincinnati, 1977-; President, Danielle Maynard Association Inc; Served with US Army Chorus as soloist, 1958-63; Co-founder of The Ambassadors of Opera and Concert Worldwide Ltd, an independent touring company of Metropolitan Opera Artists, 1978-; Performed in more than 45 countries including: the Middle East, Far East, Mainland China, 1983-. *Recordings:* 9th Symphony Steinberg - Pittsburgh Symphony; Catulli Carmina, Ormandy, Philadelphia Orchestra. *Honours:* Grammy award for best classical recording, 1967; Distinguished alumnus San Diego State University, 1992. *Memberships:* Professional organisations: Sigma Alpha Epsilon fraternity, American Legion, Republican Club, Lion's Club. *Hobbies:* Cooking; Precious stones; Fishing; Antiques. *Current Management:* Robert Lombardo, One Harkness Plaza, 61 West 62nd Street, New York City, NY 10023, USA. *Address:* 1550 Bayridge Parkway, Brooklyn, NY 11228, USA.

KNEZKOVA Ludmila, b. 22 Apr 1956, Mukacevo, Ukraine. Concert Pianist. m. Bernard Husey, 17 Nov 1990. *Education:* Tchaikovsly Conservatory, Moscow; Prague Academy of Music; Master classes in Germany and Canada. *Career:* TV and Radio appearances, in Moscow, Prague, Vienna, Austria, Weimar, Germany, New Brunswick, Canada, Italy and the Ukraine. *Honours:* Prize winner, Smetana International Piano Competition, 1980; Best Performer, Weimar Germany, 1987, 1988; Scholarships Czech Musical Foundation, 1987-89, Canada, 1992. *Memberships:* Czech Musician's Association; New Brunswick Musicians Association, Canada; American Federation of Musicians; New Brunswick Music Teacher's Association. *Hobbies:* Travel; Studying; Reading; Swimming. *Current Management* Cyrann Ltd, Canada. *Address:* 840 Grandview St, Bathurst, New Brunswick E2A 3R7, Canada.

KNIE Roberta, b. 13 May 1938, Cordell, Oklahoma, USA. Singer (Soprano). *Education:* Studied at Oklahoma University with Elisabeth Parham, Judy Bounds-Coleman and Eva Turner. *Debut:* Hagen (Germany) 1964, as Elisabeth in Tannhäuser. *Career:* Sang at Freiburg, 1966-69; Graz Opera, 1969, as Salome, Tosca and Leonore; Zurich and Nice, 1972-73, as Brünnhilde in The Ring; Bayreuth Festval 1974, as Brünnhilde; Metropolitan Opera from 1975; Guest appearances in Kassel, Mannheim, Montreal, Buenos Aires, Brussels, Barcelona, Hamburg, Berlin, Munich and Stuttgart; Other roles include Isolde, Senta, Elsa, Sieglinde, Donna Anna, Elektra, the Marschallin, Lisa in The Queen of Spades, Electra in Idomeneo and both Leonoras of Verdi. *Recordings include:* Isolde in Tristan und Isolde.

KNIGHT Gillian, b. 1 Nov 1939, Redditch, Worcs, England. Singer (Mezzo-Soprano). *Education:* LRAM, Royal Academy of Music, London; BA, Open University. *Career:* D'Oyly Carte Opera, 1959-64, sang in contralto rôles as Katisha (Mikado), Ruth (Pirates of Penzance), and Lady Jane (Patience); Sadler's Wells/English National Opera as Suzuki in Butterfly, Ragone (Comte Ory), Juno (Semele) and Carmen; Covent Garden from 1970, in the premiere of Maxwell Davies's Taverner, 1972, Der Ring des Nibelungen, Rigoletto, Eugene Onegin and Semele, 1988; Paris Opera debut, 1978, in Die Zauberflöte; US debut, 1979, as Olga in Eugene Onegin at Tanglewood: tours of USA singing Gilbert and Sullivan; Season 1986/87 Gertrude in Hamlet for Pittsburgh Opera; Nurse in Die Frau ohne Schatten for Welsh National Opera, 1989; sang the Forester's Wife in The Cunnning Little Vixen at Covent Garden; France: Rouen, Lille, Nantes, Avignon, Tours, Paris, Toulouse (Carmen, Don Quixote, Werther); Germany: Frankfurt, Ulrica in Ballo in Maschera; Spain: Carmen with Domingo in Valencia and Saragossa; Switzerland: Rigoletto, Geneva; sang Marguerite in La Dame Blanche at the 1990 Wexford Festival; Sang the title role in the British premiere of Gerhard's The Duenna, Opera North, 1992; Third Maid in Elektra at the First Night of the 1993 London Proms; Concert engagements with conductors such as Bertini, Boulez, Colin Davis, Groves and Solti. *Recordings:* Six Gilbert and Sullivan roles for Decca; Messiah, Damnation of Faust and Mozart Masses with Colin Davis (Philips); Schoenberg's Moses und Aron with Boulez (CBS); Suor Angelica, Il Tabarro and Madama Butterfly with Maazel (CBS); La Forza del Destino with Levine (RCA). *Address:* c/o Kaye Artists Management, Barratt House, 7 Chertsey Road, Woking, GV21 5AB, England.

KNIGHT Katherine, b. 1960, USA. Cellist. *Education:* Johns Hopkins University; New England Conservatory. *Career:* Co-Founder, Da Vinci Quartet, 1980, under the sponsorship of the Fine Arts Quartet; Many concerts in the USA and elsewhere in a repertoire including works by Mozart, Beethoven, Brahms, Dvořák, Shostakovich and Bartók. *Honours:* With the Da Vinci Quartet: Grants from the NEA, Western States Arts Foundation and Colorado Council for the Humanities; Artist in Residence, University of Colorado. *Address:* c/o Sonata (Da Vinci Quartet), 11 Northpark Street, Glasgow G20 7AA, Scotland.

KNIPLOVÁ Nadezda, b. 18 Apr 1932, Ostrava, Czechoslovakia. Singer (Soprano). *Education:* Studied at the Prague Conservatory with Jarmila Vavrdova and at the Academy of Musical Arts with K Ungrova and Zdenek Otava. *Career:* Sang at Usti nad Labem 1956-59 and the Janáček Opera Brno (1959-64), notably as Renata in The Fiery Angel, Katerina in The Greek Passion and Katerina Ismailova; Principal of the Prague National Theatre from 1965: roles include the Kostelnička in Jenůfa, Brünnhilde, Leonore, Milada (Dalibor), Libuse, Emilia Marty, Isolde, Tosca, Aida and Senta; Guest appearances in Salzburg (Brünnhilde, 1967), Barcelona (as Isolde), Turin (in Götterdämmerung) Berlin, Hamburg, New York and San Francsico (Die Walküre); sang with the Berlin Staatsoper on tour in Japan. *Recordings:* Jenůfa, Libuše, Dalibor, Orfeo ed Euridice (Supraphon); Katya Kabanova (Decca); Der Ring des Nibelungen (Westminster). *Honours:* Prizewinner at compettions in Geneva (1958), Vienna (1959) and Toulouse (1959); Czech Artist of Merit 1970. *Address:* National Theatre, PO Box 865, 11230 Prague 1, Czech Republic.

KNODT Erich, b. 1945, Germany. Singer (Bass). *Education:* Studied in Koblenz. *Career:* Sang at the Stadttheater Koblenz, 1970-72; Wuppertal, 1972-76, Mannheim, 1976-87; Guest appearances at Dusseldorf, Hamburg, Stuttgart, Brussels, 1989, Paris, Barcelona, Strasbourg and Madrid; Bregenz and Aix-en-Provence Festivals, 1985, 1989, as Sarastro; Wagner repertoire includes King Mark, Liston 1985, King Henry in Lohengrin 1986, Hunding, Lisbon 1989, Pogner and Hagen; Hal also sang Mozart's Commendatore, Rocco, King Philip, Boris Godunov, Banquo and Ramphis

(Bordeaux 1989); Sang Peneois in a concert performance of Daphne at Rome, 1991; Sarastro at Bordeaux, Pogner at Triests and Roldano in Franchetti's Christoforo Colombo at the Montpellier Festival, 1992. Many further concert engagements. *Address:* Nationaltheater, Am Goetheplatz, 6800 Mannheim, Germany.

KNOUSE Nola Reed, b. 30 June 1956, North Carolina, USA. Research Director. m. Paul Franklin Knouse Jr, 20 Apr 1985. *Education:* BA, Wake Forest University, 1978; MA 1980, PhD 1983, major in Music Theory, minors in Musicology, Math. *Career:* Director of Research and Programmes, Moravian Music Foundation, 1992-; Music Faculty, Salem College, 1983-. *Publications:* Editor, Moravian Music Journal, 1992-; Contributor to Music Theory Spectrum; Current Musicology. *Memberships:* AMS; CMS; SMI; American Music Center. *Hobbies:* Woodworking; Gardening. *Address:* 4281 Bower Lane, Winston-Salem, NC 27104, USA.

KNOX Charles, b. 19 Apr 1929, Atlanta, Georgia, USA. Composer; Professor of Music. m. Ruth Elizabeth McSwain, 31 Aug 1954. *Education:* BFA, University of Georgia, 1951; MMus, 1955, PhD, 1962, Indiana University. *Career:* Principal Trombone, Atlanta Symphony Orchestra, 1949-51; Trombone, Third U.S. Army Band, 1951-54; Faculty, Mississippi College, Clinton, Mississippi, 1955-65; Faculty, Georgia State University, 1965-. *Compositions:* Choral: Festival Procession; A Gloria; Psalm of Praise; Sing We to Our God Above; Hurricane: Concerto for Chorus and Percussion; Brass Choir and Ensemble: Symphony for Brass and Percussion; Voluntary on Hyfrydol; Voluntary on Lauda Anima; Solo for Trumpet with Brass Trio; Solo for Tuba with Brass Trio; Scherzando for Tubular Octet; Triskelion: Music for Brass Quintet and Piano; Orchestra: Paseos; Brazen; Percussion ensemble: Visible Canon; Music for Viola and Percussion; Variations and improvisations on a Bell Theme; Chamber Prelude and Fugue for Cello and Piano; Quintet for Woodwinds. *Recordings:* Symphony for Brass and Percussion; Solo for Trumpet with Brass Trio; Scherzando for Tubular Octet. *Address:* Georgia State University, University Plaza, Atlanta, GA 30303-3083, USA.

KNOX Garth Alexander, b. 8 Oct 1956, Dublin, Republic of Ireland. Violist. *Education:* ARCM, Royal College of Music, London, 1974-77; Studies with Frederick Riddle; Masterclasses with Paul Doktor and Peter Schidloff. *Career:* Member of English Chamber Orchestra, 1979-81, and of London Sinfonietta; Dedicatee and 1st performance of Henze's Viola Sonata, Witten, 1981; 1st performance of James Dillon's Timelag Zero, Brighton, 1981; Guest Principal Viola, Opera la Fenice, Venice, 1981-83; Performances of Harold in Italy and Jonathan Lloyd's Viola Concerto with Danish Radio Symphony Orchestra, Copenhagen, 1982; Member of Pierre Boulez's Ensemble Intercontemporain, Paris, 1983-90; Concertos - Luciano Berio and Marc-Andre Dalbavie conducted by Pierre Boulez in Bordeaux, Lisbon, Paris and New York; Concerto by Karl-Amadeus Hartmann, Théâtre du Rond-Point, Paris, 1987; Tour of USSR with Jan Latham Koenig playing Shostakovich Viola Sonata, 1987; 1st performance of Donatoni's La Souris sans Sourire with Quatuor Ensemble Intercontemporain, Paris, 1989; Joined the Arditti String Quartet, 1990, premiering quartets by Ferneyhough (No 4), Goehr (No 4), Xenakis' Tetora and Feldman's Quintet; 1st Performance of Ligeti's Loop, for solo viola, 1991. *Recordings:* Henze's Viola Sonata, Ricordi, 1981; Schoenberg's Verklärte Nacht, supervised by Boulez, CBS. *Address:* c/o Garth Knox, 6 Willow Road, London, NW3 1TH, England.

KNUSSEN (Stuart), Oliver, b. 12 June 1952, Glasgow, Scotland. Composer; Conductor. m. Susan Freedman, 1972, 1 daughter. *Education:* Purcell School of Music; Private study, composition, with John Lambert, 1963-68. *Debut:* Conducting Symphony No 1, London Symphony Orchestra, 1968. *Career includes:* Study with Gunther Schuller, USA, 1970-73; Koussevitzky Centennial Commission, 1974; Composer-in-residence, Aspen Festival 1976, Arnolfini Gallery 1978; Instructor in composition, Royal College of Music Junior Department, 1977-82; BBC commission, Proms (Symphony No 3), 1979; Guest teacher, Berkshire Music Center, Tanglewood, USA, 1981; Coordinator of Contemporary music activites, Tanglewood, 1986-90; Associate Guest Conductor, BBC Symphony Orchestra, 1989-; Frequent guest conductor, London Sinfonietta, Philharmonia Orchestra, numerous other ensembles, UK & abroad, 1981-; Co-artistic director, Aldeburgh Festival, 1983-; conducted Birtwistle's Punch and Judy for Netherlands Opera, 1993. *Compositions:* Symphony No 1, 1966-67, No 2, 1970-71, No 3, 1973-79; Where the Wild Things Are, opera (Maurice Sendak), 1979-83, staged Glyndebourne 1984); Higglety Pigglety Pop!, opera (Sendak), 1983-85, staged Glyndebourne, 1984, 1985; Numerous orchestral, chamber, vocal works, including Concerto for Orchestra 1968-70, 1974; Cantata for oboe and string trio 1977; Ocean de la Tenre for soprano and chamber ensemble 1972-73, 1976; Autumnal for violin and piano 1976-77; Four Late Poems and an Epigram of Rainer Maria Rilke for soprano 1988; Piano Variations 1989; Secret Song for solo violin 1990. *Contributor to:* Tempo, The Listener, etc. *Honours:* Countess of Munster Awards, 1964, 1965, 1967; Peter Stuyvesant Foundation Award, 1965; Watney-Sargent Award, young conductors, 1969; Fellowships to Berkshire Music Center, Tanglewood, USA, 1970, 1971, 1973; Caird Travel Scholarship, 1971; Margaret Grant Composition Prize, Tanglewood , 1971; Arts Council bursaries, 1979, 1981; Winner, 1st Park Lane Group composer award, 1982; BBC commission, Glyndebourne opera, 1983. *Memberships:* Executive committee, Society for Promotion of New Music, 1978-85; Leopold Stowkowski Society; International Alban Berg Society, New York. *Hobbies:* Cinema; Foreign literature; Record collecting & producing. *Address:* c/o Louise Mitchell, 35 Greenbridge Road, London E9 7DP, England.

KNUTSON David, b. 19 Mar 1946, Wisconsin, USA. Singer (Tenor). *Education:* Studied in Wisconsin. *Career:* Has sung in West Germany from 1971; Sang lyric roles at the Deutsche Oper Berlin from 1972; Guest appearances in Hamburg; Munich 1978, in the premiere of Lear by Reimann; Berlin 1975 and 1980, in the local premieres of La Calisto by Cavalli and Hippolyte et Aricie by Rameau; Spoleto Festival 1986, as the Witch in Hansel and Gretel. *Recordings include:* Lear (Deutsche Grammophon). *Address:* c/o Deutsche Oper Berlin, Richard Wagner Strasse 10, D-1000 Berlin, Germany.

KOBAYASHI Junko, b. September, 1960, Kobe, Japan. Concert Pianist. *Education:* Osaka College of Music; Essen Musik Hochschule; Studied with Maria Curcio and Louis Kentner. *Debut:* Royal Festival Hall, 1988. *Career:* The Purcell Rooom Recitals, 1987-93; Appearances in England, Germany, France, Denmark, Bulgaria, USA, Venezuela, Zambia and Japan. Played with orchestras such as the London Philharmonic Orchestra, the Osaka Philharmonic Orchestra, the New Philharmonic Orchestra, The Academy of St Nicholas; Broadcasts on BBC Radio 3, WKAR Television, USA, ZDF Television, Germany. *Memberships:* Essays for Kansei Music newspaper. *Address:* 11 Rosslyn Hill, London NW3 5UL, England.

KOBAYASHI Marie, b. 31 Aug 1955, Kamakura, Japan. Singer (Mezzo-Soprano). *Education:* Arts and Music National University, Tokyo; National Conservatory of Music, Paris. *Debut:* With 2E2M, International Comtemporary Music Festival, Strasbourg, 1983. *Career:* Appearances: C R Alsina's Prima Sinfonia, Radio France concert with National Orchestra of France, 1985; Satie's La Mort de Socrate, Radio France concert with Nouvel Orchestre Philharmonique, 1989; Smeton in Donizetti's Anna Bolena, Nîmes, 1989; H Birtwistle's Meridian with Pierre Boulez, Châtelet Theatre, 1990; J Fontyn's Roses des Sables, Radio Bruxelles (RTBF), 1991; Has sung in many concerts of oratorios by Bach, Handel, Rossini, Mozart, others. *Recordings:* Les

Madrigaux of G Arrgo, 1990; Motets of Vivaldi, 1990; Mozart's Requiem, 1991. *Hobbies:* Theatre; Films. *Address:* 49 rue Riquet, Apt 2, 75019 Paris, France.

KOBEKIN Vladimir A, b. 22 July 1947, Sverdlovsk, Russia. Composer. *Education:* Studied with Seigei Slonimsky at the Leningrad Conservatory, graduating in 1971. *Career:* Teacher, Urals Conservatory, 1971-80. *Compositions include:* Swan Song, chamber oper after Chekhov, Moscow, 1980; Dairy of a Madman, mono-opera, Moscow 1980; The Boots, chamber opera, 1981; Pugachyov, musical tragedy, Leningrad, 1983; The Prophet, a Pushkin Triptych, Sveerdlovsk 1984; Play about Maximillian, Eleanor and Ivan, Moscow, 1989; The Jester and the King, chamber opera, 1991; The Happy Prince, chamber opera after Wilde, 1991; Instrumental, choral and chamber music. *Honours:* USSR State Prize, 1987; Honoured Artist of the RSFSR. *Address:* R A I S (Russian Federation), c/o PRS Ltd, Member Registration, 29-33 Berners Street, London W1P 4AA5, England.

KOBILZA Siegfried, b. 24 Aug 1954, Villach, Carinthia, Austria. Guitarist. m. Vera Kobilza-Schweder, 7 Feb 1983. *Education:* Finals in Higher Education, Musisch-Padagogisches Realgymnasium, Hermagor, 1973; Diploma in Performance (with distinction), Academy of Music, Vienna, 1981; Pupil of Professor Karl Scheit. *Career:* 1st concert tour, Austrian cities including Vienna, 1979; Recitals in main Austrian venues including Wiener Musikverein, Wiener Konzerthaus, Grosses Festspielhaus Salzburg, Mozarteum Salzburg, Brucknerhaus Linz; Soloist with orchestras including Vienna Symphony, Mozarteumorchester Salzburg, Vienna Chamber Orchestra; TV and radio recordings; Teaching master classes, various European countries and People's Republic of China; Debuts in London, Paris, New York, 1982; Concert tours, Federal Republic of Germany, Switzerland, UK, France, Netherlands, Iceland, Yugoslavia, Hungary, USA, USSR, Czechoslovakia, Turkey, Tunisia, People's Republic of China. *Current Management:* Sekretariat Siegfried Kobilza. *Address:* Servitengasse 7/16, A-1090 Vienna, Austria.

KOBLER Linda, b. 1952, New York City, USA. Harpsichordist. m. Albert Glinsky, 10 June 1979. *Education:* BM, Peabody Conservatory of Music; MM, Juilliard School, 1977. *Debut:* Carnegie Recital Hall, 1984. *Career:* Concerto Soloist with: Zurich Chamber Orchestra, New York Chamber Orchestra, Broadway Bach Ensemble, American Baroque Ensemble, Bach Gesellschaft, Seabrook Chamber Players, Cathedral Orchestra, Chamber Symphony, Toronto Symphony; Former Member, Ensemble Tafelmusik Quartet; performances in New York, Ohio, New Jersey, California, Washington DC, South Carolina, Louisiana, including Philips Collection, Cleveland Institute, University of California, Carnegie Recital Hall, Merkin Concert Hall, Spoleto Festival, Town Hall, New York City; Performances in Switzerland and Germany; Radio appearances in USA. *Recordings:* Musical Heritage Society; Works of Christophe Moyreau and Pancrace Royer; Classic Masters; works of Fresobaldi, Strozzi, Storace et al. *Honours:* Winner, Concert Artists Guild International Competition, 1983; Grant Awards, Harpsichord Music Society, 1984, 1986; Satellite Program Development Fund Grant; Noah Greenberg Award, 1990. *Membership:* Southeastern Historical Keyboard Society. *Address:* 4201 Sassafras St, Erie, PA 16508, USA.

KOCKEN Marcel Elisa Joseph, b. 23 Nov 1935, Mechelen, Belgium. Director, Festival Van Vlaanderen-Mechelen. m. Maria-Luise Fischer, 2 May 1962, 1 daughter. *Education:* Mechelen Royal Atheneum Pitzemburg, Brussels Free University, Licentiate in Modern History. *Career:* Head of the Cultural Service of the City of Mechelen, 1974-, Director, Festival Van Vlaanderen-Mechelen, 1977; Co-founder, Festival Van Vlaanderen-Koepel, 1979. *Memberships:* Kon Kring Oudheidkunde, Letteren & Kunst van Mechelen 1959-. *Honour:* Companion of the Order of Leopold II, 1988.

Hobbies: Music; Fine Arts; Study of History; Track and Field Athletics. *Address:* Frederik de Merodestraat 67, B-2800 Mechelen, Belgium.

KOCMIEROSKI Matthew, b. 18 Aug 1953, Roslyn, New York, USA. Percussionist; Conductor; Historian; Educator. m. Elaine S Schmidt, 28 Dec 1974. *Education:* Studies, Nassau Community College, 1971-74; Mannes College of Music, 1974-77. *Career:* Marimba Concertos performed: Atlantic Wind Symphony (New York), Broadway Chamber Symphony, Thalia Chamber Symphony (Seattle), Philharmonia Northwest, Midsummer Musical Retreat Festival Orchestra; The Bainbridge Orchestra; Recitals, music of American, Japanese and European composers, New York and the Pacific Northwest; Chamber Music performances include New Music, Seattle Chamber Music Festival, 1982 Bergen International Festival, Gooodwill Arts Festival, Seattle Spring Festival of Contemporary Music, 1989, 1990, 1991; Freelance performances, Martha Graham Dance Company, Aeolian Chamber Players, Seattle Symphony, Seattle Opera, Bolshoi Ballet, Northwest Chamber Orchestra; Instructor of Percussion and Music History, Classical New Music Programme, Cornish College of the Arts, Seattle; Member, New Performance Group, 1981-; Artist Director, New Performance Group (Seattle) beginning with the 1984-85 season; currently Principal Percussionist, Pacific Northwest Ballet Orchestra. *Recordings:* Music of Paul Dresher, New Performance Group, New Albion Records 1984; Atlas Eclipticalis, John Cage conducting, Mode Records, 1986. *Address:* 12724 19th Avenue N E, Seattle, WA 98125, USA.

KOCSÁR Miklós, b. 21 Dec 1933, Debrecen, Hungary. Composer. *Education:* Studied with Farkas at the Budapest Academy of Music, 1954-59. *Career:* Teacher, Béla Bartók Conservatory, Budapest, 1972-; Deputy Head of Music, Hungarian Radio, 1983-. *Compositions:* Horn concerto, 1957; Capriccio for orchestra, 1961; Solitary song for soprano and chamber ensemble, 1969; Variations for orchestra, 1977; Capricorn concerto for flute and chamber orchestra, 1978; Metamorphoses for orchestra, 1979; Sequenze for strings, 1980; Elegia for bassoon and chamber ensemble, 1985; Formazioni for orchestra, 1986; Visions of the Night, oratorio for mezzo-soprano solo, mixed choir and orchestra, 1987; Concerto for violoncello and orchestra, 1994; Choral music including I will invoke you, Demon, 1985; Missa in A for equal voices, 1991; Chamber: Wind Quintet, 1959; Brass Trio, 1959; Variaziioni for woodwind quintet, 1968; Sestetto d'ottoni, 1972; 7 Variations for viola, 1983; Wind Quintet, No 3, 1984; Quintetto d'ottoni, 1986; Rhapsody for Trombone, piano and percussion, 1989; Trio for strings, 1990; Music for 4 Trombons e percussion, 1991; Songs and piano pieces. *Honours include:* Erkel Prize, 1973, 1980; Merited Artist of the Hungarian People's Republic, 1987; Bartók-Pasztory Award, 1992. *Address:* Artisjus (Hungary), c/o PRS Member Registration, 29/33 Berners Street, London W1P 4AA, England.

KOCSIS Zoltán, b. 30 May 1952, Budapest, Hungary. Pianist; Composer. m. Adrienne Hauser, 7 Apr 1986. *Education:* Béla Bartók Conservatory, Budapest, 1967-73; Musical Education: Béla Bartók Conservatory, Budapest, 1964-68; Ferenc Liszt Academy of Music, Budapest, 1968-73. *Debut:* 1970; US debut 1971, London and Salzburg, 1972; often heard in Bach and Bartók; in 1988 he played Bartók's 2nd Piano Concerto at the Royal Festival Hall, London. *Compositions:* Premìre, String Ensemble; 33 December, Chamber Ensemble; The Last But One Encounter, for piano or harpsichord. Transcriptions and arrangements for piano and two pianos. *Recordings:* For Hungaroton, Denon and Philips labels. *Contributions to:* Mozgó Világ (Budapest) Music Section, 1982-83; Mozgó Világ (Budapest) Music Section, 1982-83, Holmi (Budapest), 1989-. *Honours:* Liszt Prize, 1973; Kossuth Prize, 1978; Merited Artist, 1984. *Current Management:* Vigadó-Redoute, Budapest, Hungary. *Hobbies:* Collecting Records and Tapes. *Address:* Nárcisz u. 29, Budapest, H-1126 Hungary.

KOEHNE Graeme John, b. 1956, Adelaide, South Australia, Australia. Composer; University Lecturer. *Education:* BMus 1st class honours, MMus, University of Adelaide; Studied composition with Richard Meale, Tristram Cary and Bernard Rands; Composition under Virgil Thomson and Louis Andriessen, School of Music, Yale University, USA. *Career:* Appointed Tutor in Piano and Composition, University of New England, Armidale, New South Wales, 1978; Collaborated with choreographer Graeme Murphy and Sydney Dance Orchestra; Commissions, Australian Bicentenary, West Australian Ballet Company, Queensland Ballet Company, Australian Chamber Orchestra, Seymour Group (Sydney), Australian Ballet; Currently Lecturer in Composition, University of Adelaide. *Compositions:* Orchestral: The Iridian Plateau, 1977; First Blue Hours, 1979; Toccata, 1981; Fanfare, 1981; Rain Forest, 1981; riverrun..., 1982; Ballet Suite from The Selfish Giant, 1985; Capriccio for Piano and Strings, 1987; Ensemble: Sextet, 1975; Cantilene, 1978; Crystal Islands, 1982; Divertissement Trois Pièces Bourgeoises, string quartet, 1983; Ricecare and Burletta, string trio, 1984; Miniature, 1985; Voice and ensemble: Cancion, text F Garcia Lorca, 1975; Fourth Sonnet, text S Mallarmé, 1976; Ballets: The Selfish Giant, 1982; Palm Court Suite, 1984; Nearly Beloved, 1986; Nocturnes, 1987; Keyboard Music: Piano Sonata, 1976; Harmonies in Silver and Blue, piano, 1977; Twilight Rain, piano, 1979; Gothic Toccata, 1984 (aka Toccata Aurora). *Address:* c/o Boosey & Hawkes (Australia) Pty Ltd, Unit 12/6 (PO Box 188), Artarmon, New South Wales 2064, Australia.

KOETSIER Jan, b. 14 Aug 1911, Amsterdam, Netherlands. Composer; Conductor. m. Margarete Trampe. *Education:* Academy of Music, Berlin. *Debut:* As composer and conductor, Concertgebouw, Amsterdam, 1937. *Career:* Second Conductor, Concertgebouw Orchestra, 1942-48; Conductor, Residentieorkest, The Hague, 1949-50; Conductor, Bavarian Radio Symphony Orchestra, Munich, 1950-66; Professor, Musikhochschule, Munich, 1966-76. *Compositions include:* 3 Symphonies; Orchestral works; The Man Lot, Cantata for soli, men's choir and orchestra; Opera, Frans Hals; Chamber Music; Various Solo concertos with orchestra; Piano Music; Lieder. *Recordings:* Petite Suite; Brass Quintet; Partita for English Horn and Organ; Concerto for Trumpet; Trombone and Orchestra; Brass Symphony. *Current Management:* Donemus, Paulus Potterstraat 14, Amsterdam, The Netherlands. *Address:* Florianhaus, Unterkagn, 8251 Heldenstein, Germany.

KOGAN Semjon, b. 24 Apr 1928, Bobruisk, Ukraine. Conductor. *Education:* Studied violin and conducting at the St Petersburg Conservatoire. *Career:* Founded the State Symphony Orchestra at Omsk; Artistic Director, Rostov State Symphony Orchestra, 1976, participating in the 1990 Tchaikovsky International Competition, Moscow; Guest appearances with the USSR State Symphony, Moscow Philharmonic, Moscow Radio and St Peterburg Philharmonic Orchestras and invitations to conduct in Poland, Czechoslovakia and Germany; Repertoire includes Stravinsky and Shostakovich in addition to the standard rpertoire; has given the premieres of works by Denisov, Schedrin and Khrennikov; Professor a the Rostov on Don Conservatoire. *Recordings:* With the Rostov Symphony Orchestra. *Address:* c/o Sonata, 11 Northpark Street, Glasgow G20 7AA, Scotland.

KOHLER Irene, b. 1914, London, England. Pianist. m. Dr Harry Waters, 1950 medical practitioner. *Education:* BMus Royal College of Music, under Arthur Benjamin; Study, Vienna, with Edward Steurmann, Egon Wellesz. *Debut:* 1st professional engagement, Bournemouth, 1933, resulting in BBC engagement, played at 1st night, 40th Promenade Season, 1934. First foreign tour, recitals & broadcasts, Holland, 1938. *Career:* During World War II, concerts for Forces at home & overseas, 1939-45, with ENSA; Subsequently played in many countries of Europe, made tours. Selected by Eugene Goosens, 1st European performance of his

Phantasy Concerto; Broadcast 1st performance, Sonata, by Gunilla Lowenstein, Stockholm. 3 concerts, Festival Hall, Festival of Britain, 1951; Canadian-American tour, 1953; World tour, 1955-56; African tour, 1958; 1959; Bulgarian tour, 1959; 2nd world tour, 1962; Czechoslovakian tour, 1963; Scandinavian tour, 1970; Far/Middle East tour, 1972; Recitals & master classes, Japan 1979, 1981; Polish tour, 1980. *Film appearances include:* Train of Events; Odette; Secret People; Lease of Life; Ministry of Information documentary. *Honours:* Challen Medal, Danreuther Prize, etc, Royal College of Music; Travelling scholarship, Vienna; Honorary FTCL, CRSM, LRAM, ARCM. *Address:* 28 Castelnau, London SW13 9RU, England.

KOHN Karl (George), b. 1 Aug 1926, Vienna, Austria. Pianist; Conductor; Music Educator; Composer. m. Margaret Case Sherman, 23 June 1950, 2 daughters. *Education:* Certificate, New York College of Music, 1944; BA 1950, MA 1955, Harvard University; Studied Piano with Werschinger; Conducting with Prüwer; Composition with Piston, Ballantine, Fine and Thompson. *Career:* Instructor in Music 1950-54, Assistant Professor 1954-59, Associate Professor 1959-65, Professor 1965-85, William M Keck Distinguished Service Professor 1985-, Pomona College, Claremont, California; Teaching Fellow, Harvard University, 1954-55; Teacher, Berkshire Music Center, Tanglewood, summers 1954, 1955, 1957; Appearances as Pianist and Conductor. *Compositions:* Orchestral: Sinfonia concertante for Piano and Orchestra, 1951; Overture for String Orchestra, 1956; Castles and Kings, suite, 1958; 3 Scenes, 1958-60; Concerto mutabile for Piano and Orchestra, 1962; Interlude, 1964; Episodes for Piano and Orchestra, 1966; Interlude I for Flute and String Orchestra, 1969; Interlude II for Piano and String Orchestra, 1969; Esdras for Flute, Piano, Chorus and Orchestra, 1969-70; Centone per orchestra, 1973; Innocent Psaltery, 1976; The Prophet Bird I, 1976; The Prophet Bird II for Chamber Orchestra, 1982; Time Irretrievable, 1983; An Amiable Piece for two pianos, winds and percussion, 1987; Lions on a Banner, Seven Sufi Texts for Soprano solo, chorus and orchestra, 1988; Return-Symphonic Essay for brass, percussion and string orchestra, 1990; Ode for string orchestra; Chamber music includes: Encounters I-VI for various instrumental combinations; Choral works; Songs; Piano pieces; Organ music. *Address:* 674 West 10th Street, Claremont, CA 91711, USA.

KOHN Karl-Christian, b. 21 May 1928, Losheim, Saarbrucken, Germany. Singer (Bass). *Education:* Studied with Irene Eden at the Musikhochschule Saarbrucken. *Career:* Sang at the Deutsche Oper am Rhein Dusseldorf, 1954-57; Städtische Oper Berlin, 1956-58; Sang the title role in Le Nozze di Figaro, at the reopening of the Cuvillies-Theater Munich, 1958; Member of the Bayerische Staastoper Munich from 1958, notably in the 1963 premiere of Die Verlobung in San Domingo by Egk; Schwetzingen Festival, 1961, in the premiere of Elegie fur junge Liebende by Henze; Guest appearances in Hamburg, Vienna, Berlin and elsewhere in Europe; Other roles included Mozart's Osmin, Sarastro and Commendatore. *Recordings:* Der Freischütz, Don Giovanni, Oedipus der Tyrann by Orf (EMI); Arabella, Doktor Faust, Don Giovanni, Wozzeck, Cardillac by Hindemith (Deutsche Grammophon); Bach's Christmas Oratorio. *Address:* c/o Bayerische Staatsoper, Postfach 745, D-8000 Munich 1, Germany.

KOHNEN Robert Stefan, b. 2 June 1932, St Vith, Belgium. Harpsichordist; Organist. m. Francoise Simons, 4 Apr 1970, 3 sons, 1 daughter. *Education:* Lemmens Institut, Mechelen, 1948-49; Royal Conservatory, Brussels for organ, 1950-56; Self-taught harpsichordist. *Career:* One of the founders of the Alarius Ensemble in 1954 playing an important part in the evolution of this group and subsequently with the ensemble formed with the Kuijken brothers, an approach which has brought them world-wide renown. Recitals and radio broadcasts throughout Europe, US, Canada and Japan; Currently Professor at the Royal Conservatory, Brussels, Belgium. *Recordings:* Accent/

Belgium; Harmonia Mundi, Germany; Musical Heritage/USA; Teldec/Germany. *Honours:* Grand Prix for 17th Century Italian Music played by Alarius Ensemble, Paris 1966. *Hobbies:* Cooking; Collecting wine; Gardening. *Address:* Marie-Henriettelaan 37, B 1700 Dilbeek, Brussels, Belgium.

KOHOUTEK Ctirad, b. 18 Mar 1929, Zabreh na Morave, Czechoslovakia. Composer and Theorist. m. Jarmila Chlebnickova, 8 July 1953, 1s, 2d. *Education:* Composition, Conservatory of Brno, 1948-49; Janáček Academy of Music Arts, 1949-53; PhD, Palacky University of Olomouc, 1973; CSc, Masaryk University, Brno, 1980. *Debut:* Munich for ochestra, 1953. *Career:* Junior of Composition, 1953-59, Fellow of Composition, 1959-65, Senior Lecturer of Composition and Theory of Composition, Janáček Academy of Music Arts, Brno, 1965-80; Professor of Composition, Academy of Music Arts, Prague, 1980-90; Artistic Director of Czech Philharmonic, Prague, 1980-87. *Compositions include:* String Quartet, 1959; Concertino for violoncello and chamber orchestra, 1964; Rapsodia eroica for organ, 1965; Inventions for piano, 1965; Miniatures for 4 French horns, 1965; Memento, concert for percussion and wind instruments, 1966; Teatro del mondo for large orchestra, 1969; Panteon, for orchestra, 1970; Festive Prologue for large symphony orchestra, 1971; Celebration of Light, large orchestra, 1975; Symphonical Actualities, for orchestra, 1976-78; Tissues of Time, bass-clarinet and piano, 1977; Minutes of Spring, for wind quintet, 1980; Numerous pieces for choirs; Omaggio a vita, for orchestra, 1989; About Cockerel and Little Hen, opera for children, 1989; Motifs of Summer, for violin, violoncello and piano, 1990; Funs and Smiles, for oboe, clarinet, bassoon, 1991; Winter Silences, for brass and percussion instruments, 1993. *Publications include:* Modern Compositional Theories in Music, 1965; Project Musical Composition, 1969; Musical Styles form the Composer's Viewpoint, 1976; Music Composition, 1989. *Address:* 613 00 Brno-Cerna Pole, Helfertova 40, Czech Republic.

KOHS Ellis Bonoff, b. 12 May 1916, Chicago, USA. Composer; Educator. *Education:* MA, University of Chicago, USA, 1938; Juilliard School of Music, USA, 1938-39; Harvard University, 1939-41. *Career:* Assistant Professor of Music, Wesleyan University, Connecticut, USA, 1946-48; Associate Professor, Music, College of the Pacific, California, USA, 1948-50; Associate Professor, 1950, Professor, 1952, Chairman, Theory Department, 1966, School of Music, University of Southern California, USA, Retired 1985. *Compositions include:* 2 Symphonies, 3 String Quartets; Concerto for Orchestra; Etude in Memory of Bartók; Four Orchestral Songs, Studies in Variation; Calumny; Concerto for Percussion Quartet; Concerto for Violin and Orchestra, commissioned by University of Southern California for its Centennial, 1981; Fantasies, Interludes and Canonic Etudes on the name Eudice Shapiro; Orchestral Suite from the Opera, Amerika; numerous other compositions. *Recordings:* Chamber Concerto for Viola and Strings; Symphony No 1, String Quartet No 2, XXIII Psalm; Chorale Variation No 2 on Hebrew Hymns, Musical Heritage Society. *Publications:* Music Theory, 1961; Musical Form, 1976; Musical Composition, 1980. *Current Management:* Theodore Presser Music, Bryn Mawr, PA 19010, USA. *Address:* 8025 Highland Trail, Los Angeles, CA 90046, USA.

KOITO Kei, b. 4 Jan 1950, Kyoto, Japan. Concert Organist; Composer; Professor. *Education:* Studied Organ, philosophy, musical aesthetics, and psychology, Tokyo University of fine Arts; Studied organ with Pierre Segond at the Geneva Conservatory; analysis, orchestration, composition with Eric Gaudibert; Associated with electro-acoustics studios; Private study of organ with L F Tagliavani (Fribourg), Xavier Darasse (Toulouse), and Reinhard Goebel (Köln). *Debut:* Solo recitalist, Victoria Hall, Geneva, Maurice Ravel Auditorium, Lyons. *Career:* Soloist with symphonic and chamber orchestras, regularly performing at festivals and on radio and television; Since 1978, has performed over 80 new works for organ, premiering a large

number, written specifically for her. Professor of organ at the Conservatoire in Lausanne; Adjudicator, guest lecturer and masterclasses in USA, Europe and Asia. *Compositions include:* Les Tours du silence, narrator and chamber ensemble; Labyrinthe dynamique, brass ensemble; Orestes-Stasimon, choir; Esquisse Alpha, 2 pianos; Wenn aus der Ferne, organ; Splendid Rotation, 2 amplified harpsichords; In Step, string quartet; Poème pulvérisé, voice and percussion; Meta-matic No 22, tape. *Recordings:* 6 Trio Sonatas, 5 Concertos, Canonic Variations of JS Bach; Sonatas of CPE Bach and Contemporary organ music. *Current Management* Europe General: Camille Kiesgen, Bureau International de Concerts et de Conférences, Faubourg Saint-Honoré 252, 75008 Paris, France; USA and Canada: Philip Truckenbrod Concert Artists, 300 Asylum Avenue Suite 290, Hartford, CT 06105-4604, USA.

KOIZUMI Kazuhiro, b. 16 Oct 1949, Japan. Conductor; Music Director. m. Masami. *Education:* University of The Arts, Tokyo; Hochschule für Musik, Berlin; worked with Seiji Ozawa for 2 years. *Career:* Assistant Conductor, Japan Philharmonic, 1970-72; Music Director, New Japan Philharmonic, 1975-80, Winnipeg Symphony Orchestra, 1983-; Chief Conductor, Tokyo Metropolitan Orchestra, 1984-; Guest Conductor, Berlin Philharmonic, Chicago Symphony, National Orchestra of France, Royal Philharmonic, Vienna Philharmonic, Toronto Symphony, Tokyo Metropolitan, Kyoto Symphony, Nagoyo Symphony, Montreal Symphony, RAI in Naples and Munich Philharmonic. *Recordings:* Lalo Concerto Russe/ Concerto in F with Radio France, Decca label; Tchaikovsky, Kodály, Dvořák with WSO. *Honours:* First Prize, 2nd International Conductors Competition (MIN-ONO, 1970); First Prize, von Karajan Competition, 1972; Grand Prix du Disque. *Memberships:* Advisor, Manitoba Conservatory of Music and Arts. *Hobbies:* Golf; Pottery; Baseball; Hiking. *Current Management:* Columbia Artists Management Inc. *Address:* c/o Columbia Artists Management Inc, New York, USA.

KOJIAN Varujan (Haig), b. 12 Mar 1935, Beirut, Lebanon (of American parentage; Naturalized US citizen, 1967). Conductor. *Education:* Studied violin, Paris Conservatory, premier prix, 1956, with Ivan Galamian, Curtis Institute of Music, Philadelphia, and with Jascha Heifetz, Los Angeles, 1960; conducting with Sasha Popov; pupil in conducting of Hans Swarowsky, Vienna, 1971. *Career:* Assistant concermaster, 1965-70, assistant to Zubin Mehta, 1970-71, Los Angeles Philharmonic Orchestra; assistant conductor, Seattle Symphony Orchestra, 1973-76; principal guest conductor, Royal Opera, Stockholm, 1973-80; music director, Utah Symphony Orchestra, Salt Lake City, 1980-83, Chautauqua (NY) Symphony Orchestra, 1981-86, Ballet West, Salt Lake City, 1984-. *Recordings:* For Andante, Louisiville, and Varèse-Sarabande. *Honours:* 1st Prize, Sorrento conducting competition, 1972.

KOK Nicholas, b. 1962, England. Conductor. *Education:* Organ scholar at New College, Oxford; Royal College of Music as Repetiteur. *Career:* Music Director of Janet Smith and Dancers 1985-87; Repetiteur at English National Opera from 1989: Return of Ulysses, 1992; Music Adviser to ENO's Contemporary Opera Studio; Conducted Opera Factory in Reimann's The Ghost Sonata at the Elizabeth Hall, London; For the Almeida Festival has conducted The Intelligence Park by Gerald Barry (premiered 1990); Engagements include Nabucco with Chelmsford Opera Group and The Barber of Seville for Dublin Grand Opera, 1991; Concerts with London Sinfonietta, the Almeida Ensemble, London Pro Arte Orchestra, Chandos Sinfonia and the Cambridge University Chamber Orchestra; Music Director of the Epsom Choral Society, 1989; BBC concerts include The Soldier's Tale and Reginald Smith Brindle's Journey Towards Infinity; Musical commissioned by Framlingham College; Season 1992 with the Return of Ulysses at the London Coliseum, Oliver's Mario and the Magician at the Almeida Festival and Don Giovanni for English Touring Opera. *Honours include:* Countess of Munster Award and Lofthouse Memorial Prize (RCM).

Address: Allied Artists, 42 Montpelier Square, London SW7 1JZ, England.

KOKKONEN Joonas, b. 13 Nov 1921, Iisalmi, Finland. Pianist; Composer. *Education:* MA, Helsinki University, 1948; Diploma in Piano, Sibelius Academy, Helsinki, 1949. *Debut:* 1950. *Career:* Concert Pianist and chamber music performer in Finland; 1st Concert devoted to his compositions, 1953; Music Instructor, Sibelius Academy, 1950-59; Professor of Composition, Sibelius Academy, 1959-63; Music Critic; Writer on musical subjects. *Compositions include:* Orchestral: Music for String Orchestra, 1956-57; Symphony No 1, 1958-60; Sinfonia da camera, 1962; Opus sonorum, 1964; Symphony No 3, 1967; Symphonic Sketches, 1968; Inauguratio, 1971; Concerto for Cello and Orchestra, 1969; Chamber Music: Trio for Piano Violin and Cello, 1948; Duo for violin and piano, 1955; String Quartet No 1, 1958-59; Sonata for cello and piano, 1976; String Quartet No 3, 1976; Vocal Works: Missa a cappella, 1963; Laudatio Domini, 1966; The Evenings, 1955; Sub rosa, 1973; Opera The Last Temptations, 1975. *Recordings:* Has made numerous recordings of his works. *Honour:* Wihuri International Sibelius Prize, 1973. *Memberships:* Chairman, 1965-70, Society of Finnish Composers; Chairman, 1966-, Sibelius Academy Board of Commissioners; Chairman, 1968-, Composers' Copyright Bureau (TEOSTO); Active in several other administrative positions of importance in Finland. *Address:* TEOSTO, Laattasaarentie 1, 00200 Helsinki 20, Finland.

KOKKOS Yannis, b. 1944, Athens, Greece. Stage Director and Designer. *Education:* Studied at the National Theatre of Strasbourg. *Career:* Has created designs for sets and costumes for productions of Macbeth, Lohengrin and Reimann's Lear at Paris Opera Garnier, Pelléas et Mélisande at La Scala and the Vienna Staatsoper, Don Carlos at Bologna and Elektra at Geneva and San Francisco; Directed the Oresteia by Xenakis in Siciliy, directed and designed Boris Godunov in Bologna and Paris (Opera Bastille), Ariane et Barbe Bleue in Geneva, La Damnation de Faust at the Théâtre du Châtelet, Paris; Nancy Opera with Death in Venice, Festival d'Orange with Carmen, and Welsh National Opera with Tristan und Isolde, 1993; Pelléas et Mélisande and Tristan seen at Covent Garden, 1993. *Address:* 7 Rue Bourdaloue 7500, Paris, France.

KOLAFA Jiri, b. 26 Feb 1930, Jicîn, Czechoslovakia. Composer; Performer (Piano, Harpsichord). m. Vera Cihulová, 1 son. *Education:* Graduate, State Conservatoire, Prague; Graduate, Academy of Music, Prague. *Debut:* Song Cycle, 1950. *Career:* Chamber music performances, Czechoslovakia and abroad including Germany and Denmark; Reader in Music, Academy of Dramatic Art, Prague. *Compositions:* About 200 compositions for theatre and film including: Pinocchio, ballet and pantomime; Labyrinth, ditto; Chamber music and orchestral compositions; 2 quintets for wind instruments; Several song cycles; Passacaglia; Manu propria, string quartet in one movement; La Follia e Danza; Racconto, for viola and piano; Orbis terrarum, for cello and tape; Violin sonata; Panychida; La Folla; Nenies, for cello and piano; Struttura di solitudine, for chamber ensemble; Sonata per due Boemi; Oratorios: Stabat mater, Canticum, Victimae paschali laudes; A Lyrical Requiem; Generation (trumpet and organ); Piano sonata; Organ compositions; Madrigalli Boemi for a saxophone quartet; Bagatelles for cello and piano. *Recordings:* As member of chamber ensemble. *Current Management:* OSA, Union protecting Authors Rights, Prague; Dilia, Theatre Agency, Prague. *Address:* Cistovická 20, 163 00 Prague 6, Czech Republic.

KOLB Barbara, b. 10 Feb 1939, Hartford, Connecticut, USA. Composer. *Education:* Studied at the Hartt College of Music, MM 1964 and with Lukas Foss and Gunther Schuller at the Berkshire Music Center. *Career:* Played clarinet in the Hartford Symphony Orchestra 1960-66; Composer-in-residence at the Marlboro Music Festival, 1973, and at the American Academy in Rome, 1975; Taught theory and composition at Brooklyn College and Temple University; Artistic Director of Music New to New York at the Third Street Music School Settlement, 1979. *Compositions:* Rebuttal for 2 clarinets 1964; Chanson bas for voice, harp and percussion 1965; Three Place Settings for narrator and ensemble, 1968; Trobar clus for 13 instruments 1970; Soundings for 11 instruments and tape 1972 (version for orchestra 1975 and 1977); Frailities for tenor, tape and orchestra 1971; Spring, River, Flowers, Moon, Night for 2 pianos and tape 1975; Appello for piano 1976; Musique pour un vernissage for ensemble 1977 (concert version 1979); Songs before an Adieu for flute, guitar and voice 1979; Chromatic Fantasy for narrator and ensemble 1979; 3 Lullabies for guitar 1980; Related Characters for viola and piano 1980; The Point that Divides the Wind for organ and 4 percussionists 1981; Cantico, film score 1982; Millefoglie for ensemble and computer-generated sound 1985; Time....and Again for oboe, string quartet and tape 1985; Umbrian Colours for violin and guitar 1986; Yet that things go Round for Chamber Orchestra, 1986-88; Molto Allegra for guitar 1988; The Enchanted Loom for orchestra 1988-89; Extremes for flute and cello, 1989; Voyants for piano and chamber orchestra, 1991; Clouds for organ and piano, recorded tape, 1992. *Honours:* Rome Prize 1969-71; Fulbright Scholarship 1966-67; MacDowell Colony and Guggenheim Fellowships; Grants from the Ford Foundation and the National Endowment for the Arts (1972-79). *Address:* Boosey & Hawkes Ltd (promotion), 295 Regent Street, London W1R 8JH, England.

KOLLO René, b. 20 Nov 1937, Berlin. Opera Singer (Tenor). m. (1) Dorthe Larsen, 1967, (2) Beatrice Bouquet, 1982, 1 daughter. *Career:* Began with Staatstheater, Brunswick, 1965; First Tenor, Deutsche Oper am Rhein, 1967-71; Guest Appearances with numerous leading opera companies, and at annual Bayreuth Wagner Festival, from 1969; Performances include; The Flying Dutchman, 1969, 1970, Lohengrin 1971, Die Meistersinger von Nurnberg 1973, 1974, Parsifal 1975, Siegfried 1976, 1977; Tristan (Zurich) 1980, (Bayreuth 1981); Covent Garden debut 1976, as Siegmund in Die Walküre; Metropolitan Opera debut, 1976, Lohengrin; Sang Otello at Frankfurt, 1988; Returned to Covent Garden 1989, as Siegmund in a new production of Die Walküre conducted by Bernard Haitink; Young Siegfried 1990; sang Tannhäuser at Hamburg 1990, Siegfried in the Ring at San Francisco; Munich Festival 1990, as Walther in Die Meistersinger; Season 1991/92 as Peter Grimes at Munich, Tannhaüser at the Deutsche Oper Berlin and in Barcelona. *Publication:* Imre Fabian im Gespräch mit René Kollo, 1982. *Hobbies:* Sailing; Tennis; Flying. *Address:* c/o Personal Artists Management, Wilhelm Str 4, 8000 Munchen 40, Germany.

KOLLY Karl-Andreas, b. 26 May 1965, Switzerland. Pianist. *Education:* Music Academy, Zurich, 1988; Studied with Karl Engel and Mieczyslaw Horszowski. *Debut:* Grieg Piano concerto at Zurich, 1982. *Career:* Concerto as soloist and chamber musician all over Europe and at several festivals, including Lucerne, Zurich, Passau and Davos; Piano concertos with Tonhalle Orchester Zurich, and Symphony Orchestra of Berne; Several radio and TV programmes in Switzerland, Germany, Spain, and Czech Republic, 1991; Professor, Winderthur Conservatory, 1991-. *Recordings:* CDs of Schumann, Piano works including Symphonic Etudes; Brahms: The piano Trios, with Trio Novanta. *Honours:* First Prize, Jecklin Competition, 1975, the University Competition of Zurich, 1988; Young Musicians Competition, Union of Swiss Banks, 1990; Tschumi Price for the best soloist diploma of the year, 1991; Prix Maurice Sandoz, 1990. *Hobbies:* Travelling; Architecture; Films. *Address:* Burghaldenstrasse 18, CH-5400 Baden, Switzerland.

KOLOMYJEC Joanne, b. 1960, Canada. Singer (Soprano). *Career:* Appearances in concert and opera throughout Canada, the USA and England from 1985; Opera roles include Mozart's Donna Elvira, Fiordiligi and Countess (all for the Portland and Manitoba companies), and Marguerite; Concert engagements with Toronto

Symphony and Calgary Philharmonic Orchestra; Repertoire includes the Mozart and Verdi Requiems, Messiah, Rossini's Stabat Mater, Bruckner's Te Deum, Beethoven's Ninth and Shostakovich's 14th Symphony; Sang David Del Tredici's Alice for the National Ballet of Canada at the London Coliseum, 1987, followed by Zemlinsky's Lyric Symphony; Sang Donna Elvira in a new production of Don Giovanni, at Toronto (1992) and at the Santa Fe Festival. *Address:* c/o Canadian Opera Company, 227 Front Street East, Toronto, Ontario M5A 1E8, Canada.

KOLTAI Ralph, b. 31 July 1924, Berlin, Germany. Stage Designer. *Education:* Studied in Berlin and at the London School of Arts and Crafts (now Central St Martin's College of Art and Design). *Career:* Angelique, London Opera Club, 1950; Tannhäuser, Royal Opera House, 1955; Il Prigoniero, 1959, Erwartung, 1960, and Volpone, New Opera Company S W, 1961; Murder in the Cathedral, Sadler's Wells, 1962; Boulevard Solitude, New Opera Company S W, 1962; Otello, and Volo Di Notte, Scottish Opera, 1963; Attila, Sadler's Wells, 1963; Don Giovanni, Scottish Opera, 1964; Don Giovanni, Los Angeles, 1965; Boris Gunonov, Scottish Opera, 1965; From The House Of The Dead, Sadler's Wells, 1965; The Rake's Progress, Scottish Opera, 1967 and 1971; The Valkyrie, Coliseum ENO, 1970; Elegy for Young Lovers, Scottish Opera, 1970; Götterdämmerung, ENO Coliseum, 1971; Lulu, National Welsh Opera, 1971; Rhinegold, and Duke Bluebeard's Castle, ENO Coliseum, 1972; Taverner, Royal Opera House, 1972; Siegfried, ENO Coliseum, 1973; Tristan and Isolde, Scottish Opera, 1973; Lulu, Kassel, 1973; Tannhäuser, Sydney Opera House, 1973; Wozzek, Nederlandsche Opera, 1973; Ring Cycle (touring version), ENO, 1974; The Ice Break, Royal Opera House, 1977; Threepenny Opera, Aalborg, Denmark, 1979; Anna Karenina, ENO Coliseum, 1981; Die Soldaten, Opera Lyons, 1983; Italian Girl in Algiers, 1984, and Tannhäuser, 1986, Grand Theatre de Geneva, 1986; The Flying Dutchman (also directed), 1987, and La Traviata (also directed), 1990, Hong Kong Arts Festival; The Makropulos Affair, De Norske Opera, Oslo, 1992; La Traviata, Kungliga Operan, Stockholm, 1993; Otello, Opera Essen, 1994. *Honours:* CBE, 1983. *Address:* c/o London Management, 2-4 Noel Street, London W1V 3RD, England.

KÖLZ Ernst, b. 26 Jan 1929, Vienna, Austria. Composer; Musician (Recorder); Professor. m. Else Krempl, 1 son. *Education:* Conservatory of City of Vienna; Studied with H U Staeps. *Debut:* Austrian Radio, 1947. *Career:* Incidental radio, stage & film music, Austrian radio, television; Stadttheater, Klagenfurt; Theater an der Wien; Volkstheater, Burgtheater, Vienna; Theater am Neumarkt; Thomas-Koerfer film producer, Zürich; Numerous concerts. *Recordings:* Amadeo; Preiserrecords; Musical Heritage Society. *Publications:* L Doblinger, Vienna, A Robitschek, Vienna. *Honours:* Vienna Art Foundation Prize, 1962; Theodor Körner Prize, 1964; Förderungspreis, City of Vienna, 1965. *Memberships:* AKM; Austro-Mechana; IGNM; ÖGZM. *Address:* Garbergasse 14/12, A-1060 Vienna, Austria.

KOMLÓS Katalin, b. 1 Feb 1945, Hidegség, Hungary. Musicologist. *Education:* Diploma Liszt Academy of Budapest, 1969; Master's Degree, Cornell University, USA, 1982; PhD, Cornell University, 1986. *Career:* Kodaly Musical Training Institute, Boston, USA, 1970-73; Faculty of Liszt Academy of Music, Budapest, 1973-; Doctoral Studies, Cornell University, Ithaca, USA, 1980-83. *Publications:* 150 American Folk Songs, 1974; Charles Rosen: The Classical Style, Hungarian translation, 1977. *Contributions to:* Muzsika; Studia Musicologica; New Hungarian Quarterly; Music & Letters; The Musical Times; Historical Performance; Harpsichord & Fortepiano Magazine; The Music review; Mozart-Jahrbuch. *Honour:* Prize of Critics, 1979. *Address:* Szatmár u. 53, 1142 Budapest, Hungary.

KOMLÓS Péter, b. 25 Oct 1935, Budapest, Hungary. Violinist. m. (1) Edit Fehér, 2 sons, (2) Zsuzsa Arki. *Education:* Budapest Music Academy. *Career:* Founded Komlos String Quartet, 1957; 1st Violinist, Budapest Opera Orchestra, 1960; Leader, Bartók String Quartet, 1963; extensive concert tours to USSR, Scandinavia, Italy, Austria, German Democratic Republic, Czechoslovakia, 1958-64, USA, Canada, New Zealand, Australia, 1970, including Day of Human Rights Concert, UN HQ New York, Japan, Spain and Portugal, 1971, Far East, USA and Europe, 1973; performed at Music Festivals of Ascona, Edinburgh, Adelaide, Spoleto, Menton, Schwetzingen, Lucerne, Aix-en-Provence. *Recordings:* Beethoven's String Quartets for Hungaroton, Budapest, and Bartók's String Quartets for Erato, Paris. *Honours:* 1st Prize, International String Quartet Competition, Liège, 1964; Liszt Prize, 1965; Gramophone Record Prize of Germany, 1969; Kossuth Prize, 1970; Eminent Artist title, 1980; UNESCO Music Council Plaque, 1981. *Hobbies:* Ship Model Building; Watching Sports. *Address:* Törökvész ut 94, Budapest 1025, Hungary.

KOMLOSI Ildiko, b. 1959, Békésszentandra's, Hungary. Singer (Mezzo-soprano). *Education:* Studied at Szeged Music Academy with Valeria Berdal and at Franz Liszt Academy, Budapest with András Miko; Guildhall School with Vera Rosza and the Studio of La Scala with Giulietta Simionato. *Career:* Concert appearances have included the Verdi Requiem in Philadelphia, conducted by Lorin Maezel; Concerts with the BBC Symphony, the Royal Philharmonic with Antal Dorati and the Hungarian Radio and State Television Company; Engagements with the Hungarian State Opera Company, Budapest and the State Operas of Berlin, Vienna, La Scala and in America, San Francisco, Portland, Houston, Coloumbus, Ohio; Roles include Carmen, Sextus, Favorita, Laura, Octavian, Giovanna Seymour (Anna Bolena) and Purcell's Dido; Sang Judit in a concert performance of Duke Bluebeard's Castle with the BBC Philharmonic conducted by András Ligeti, Feb 1991, and at the 1992 Prom Concerts London; Jane Seymour in Anna Bolena at Santiago. *Address:* Norman McCann International Artists Ltd, The Coach House, 56 Lawrie Park Gardens, London SE26 6XJ, England.

KOMLOSSY Erzsebet, b. 9 July 1933, Salgotarjan, Hungary. Singer (Contralto). *Education:* Studied at the Bartók Conservatory in Budapest. *Career:* Member of the Hungarian State Opera Budapest; Guest appearances in Moscow, London, Cologne, Edinburgh and elsewhere in Europe; Roles include Azucena (Covent Garden, 1970), Amneris, Ulrica, Preziosilla, Eboli, Carmen, Dalila and parts in operas by Kodály, Szokolay and Erkel. *Recordings:* Aida, Madama Butterfly, Bank Ban by Erkel, The Spinning Room by Kodály and Blood Wedding by Szokolay (Hungaroton); Hungarian Coronation Mass by Liszt (Deutsche Grammophon); Háry János by Kodály (Decca). *Address:* c/o Hungarian State Opera House, Népöztársasáy utja 22, 1061 Budapest, Hungary.

KOMOROUS Rudolf, b. 8 Dec 1931, Prague, Czechoslovakia. Composer and Bassoonist. *Education:* Graduated from Conservatory of Music; Studied composition with Pavel Borkovec at Academy of Musical Arts, Prague. *Appointments:* Teacher, Central Conservatory of Peking, China, 1959-61; Co-founder, Musica Viva Pragensis, Czechoslovakia; Emigrated to Canada 1969; Associate Professor of Composition and Theory, University of Victoria 1971-. *Compositions:* Published by Universal Edition, Vienna and some of them have been issued on Supraphon Records; Mignon for string quartet, 1965; Gone for tape, 1969; Bare and Dainty for Orchestra, 1970; Lady Whiterose Chamber opera, 1971; Anatomy of melancholy for tape, 1974. *Honour:* Won 1st Prize, Concours International d'Exécution Musicale, Geneva, 1957.

KONGSTED Ole Dan, b. 22 Sept 1943, Copenhagen, Denmark. Musicologist; Composer. m. Ida Wieth-Knudsen, 25 Nov 1967, 1 son, 2 daughters. *Education:* Musicology, University of Copenhagen 1976. *Career:* Jazz Musician, 1962-66; High School Teacher, 1969-76; Holder of Scholarship (Danish State), 1976-80; Freelance Collaborator (Danish Radio), 1976-;

Conductor of the choir of Jeunesses Musicales, 1978-86; Choir Master, Church of the Sacred Heart, Copenhagen, 1983-; Assistant Director, Musikhistorisk Museum og Carl Claudius' Samling, Copenhagen, 1980; Composer; Founder and Leader of Capella Hafniensis, 1990. *Compositions:* (Recorded): Opus 2, Puer natus est nobis, for choir, soloists and organ; Opus 3a, Kyrie fons bonitatis, for choir a cappella; till now nineteen opus numbers. *Recordings:* With Choir of the Jeunesses Musicales and with Ben Webster and the Arnved Meyer Band and Capella Hafniensis. *Publications:* Festskrift Johannes Simons, (Editor) in this: e turri tibiis canere - Traek af taarnblaesningens historie (Copenhagen) 1974; Census as Source Material for the History of Music (Copenhagen) 1976; Nils Schiørring: Musikkens Historie i Danmark, Editor (Copenhagen) 1977-78; Heinrich Schütz und die Musik in Dänemark zur Zeit Christians IV, Copenhagen, 1989, Co-Editor; Kronborg-Motetterne Tilegnet Frederik II og Dronning Sophie 1582, Copenhagen 1990. *Address:* Krebsegaarden, Studiestraede 17, 1455 Copenhagen K, Denmark.

KÖNIG Klaus, b. 26 May 1934, Beuthen, Germany. Singer (Tenor). *Education:* Studied with Johannes Kemter in Dresden. *Career:* Sang in Cottbus from 1970; Dessau from 1973, as Max, Don Carlos, and Erik in Der fliegende Holländer; Sang at Leipzig 1978-82, Staatsoper Dresden from 1982; Guest appearances in Karlsruhe 1983-85 (Tristan and Tannhäuser), at La Scala and Covent Garden in 1984 (as Tannhäuser) and the Théâtre de la Monnaie Brussels 1985, as Tristan; Sang Max in Der Freischütz, at the opening of the restored Semper Opera House, Dresden (1985); Guest appearances in Paris, Parma, Strasbourg, Madrid, Venice and Barcelona; Other roles include Lensky, Florestan, Radames, Don José, Alvaro in La Forza del Destino, Lohengrin, Walther, Parsifal and Bacchus; Lisbon 1986, as Florestan; sang Tannhäuser at Cologne and London 1987; Munich Opera 1988, as Menelaos in Die Aegyptische Helena by Strauss; Buenos Aires and Vienna Staatsoper 1988, as Florestan and Bachus; Many engagements in concerts and oratorios. *Recordings:* Tannhäuser (EMI); Der Rosenkavalier (Denon); Choral Symphony (Philips). *Address:* c/o Allied Artists Agency, 42 Montpelier Square, London, SW7 1JZ, England.

KONSULOV Ivan, b. 29 May 1946, Varna, Bulgaria. Singer (Baritone). *Education:* Studied with Jossifov in Sofia and with Aldo Protti in Italy. *Debut:* Opera National Russe (Bulgaria) 1972. *Career:* Sang in Berne from 1977, as Simon Boccanegra, Marcel (La Bohème), Scarpia, Don Giovanni, Mandryka, Tonio, Pizarro, Don Carlos (La Forza del Destino), Alfio and Iago; Bologna 1980, Zurga in Les pecheurs de Perles; Philadelphia Opera 1982, Marcel; Bratislava 1984, as Eugene Onegin; Stuttgart and Berlin 1985, Don Giovanni; At the Monte Carlo opera in 1986 sang Gryaznoy in The Tsar's Bride by Rimsky-Korsakov; Engagements at Graz, Barcelona, Madrid and Karlsruhe; sang Amfortas in Parsifal at Berne, 1989; Season 1992 as the Majordomo in Zemlinsky's Der Zwerg at Trieste. *Recordings include:* La Bohème-Marcello Opus-Bratislava Stereo with P Dvorsky and TV Film 1980; Pique Dame-Tomski, Musik Mundial-Sofia with International Stars, 1988; Don Carlo-Posa, Balkanton, Sofia 1988; Opera Recital Arias Balkanton, 1988. *Address:* c/o Stadttheater Bern, Nägeligasse 1, CH-3011 Bern, Switzerland.

KONT Paul, b. 19 Aug 1920, Vienna, Austria. Composer, 1 son. *Education:* Conductor Diploma 1947, Composer Diploma 1948, Vienna Academy of Music. *Career:* Professor of Composition, Vienna Academy of Music, 1969-86, Emeritus. *Compositions:* Operas: Lysistrate (commissioned by Komische Oper Berlin), 1957; Peter und Susanne (commissioned by Austrian Television), 1959; For the Time Being (commissioned by Austrian Television), 1965; Celestina (commissioned by Städt-Buhnen, Cologne, Federal Republic of Germany), 1966; Plutos (commissioned by Austrian Government), 1976; Musical: Traumleben, 1958; Ballets: Italia Passata; Die Traurigen Jäger; Amores; Il Ballo del Mondo; Ballet film: Monoballette; Oratorio:

Vom Manne und vom Weibe; Symphonies; Concertos; Chamber music; Lieder; Piano Sonatas. *Publications:* Antianorganikum. *Address:* 47 Geusaugasse, Vienna 1030, Austria.

KONTARSKY Alfons, b. 9 Oct 1932, Iserlohn, Germany. Pianist. *Education:* Studied in Cologne with Else Schmidt-Gohr and Maurits Frank; Further study in Hamburg with Eduard Erdmann, 1955-57. *Career:* Many appearances with his brother in modern music programmes from 1955, including works by Earle Brown, Kagel, Stockhausen, Pousseur, Berio and Bussotti; Seminar at Darmstadt, 1962-69; Teacher at the Musikhochschule from 1969; Formed Piano Trio with Saschko Gawriloff and Klaus Storck, 1971. *Publication:* Pro Musica Nova: Studien zum Spielen neuer Musik für Klavier, 1973. *Honours include:* First prize for Piano Duo at the 1955 Munich Radio International Festival. *Recordings include:* Bartók's Sonata for two Pianos and Percussion. *Address:* Stacthiche Hochschule für Musik Rheinland, Degobertstrasse 38, 5000 Köln 1, Germany.

KONTARSKY Alois, b. 14 May 1931, Iserlohn, Germany. Pianist. *Education:* Studied in Cologne with Else Schmitz-Gohr and Maurits Frank; Further study in Hamburg with Eduard Erdmann. *Career:* International performances with his brother from 1955 in modern repertoire: Michael Gielen, de Grandis, Henri Pousseur, Berio and Zimmermann; Gave premiere of Stockhausen's Klavierstücke I-XI, Darmstadt 1966; Concerts with the Stockhausen ensemble and duo with the cellist Siegfried Palm; Master class at the Cologne Muiskhochschule from 1969. *Recordings include:* Bartók's Sonata for Two Pianos and Percussion; Klavierstücke I-XI by Stockhausen. *Honours include:* First prize for Piano Duo at the Munich Radio International Festival, 1955. *Address:* Staatliche Hochschule für Musik Rheinland, Degobertstrasse 38, 5000 Köln 1, Germany.

KONYA Sandor, b. 23 Sept 1923, Sarkad, Hungary. Singer (Tenor). *Education:* Studied at the Budapest Conservatory with Ferenc Szekelyhidy; Further study with Fred Husler in Detmold, and in Milan. *Debut:* Bielefeld, 1951, as Turiddu. *Career:* Sang in Bielefeld until 1954, then in Darmstadt; Städtische Oper Berlin 1956, in the premiere of König Hirsch by Henze; Edinburgh Festival, 1956, in Der Barbier von Bagdad by Cornelius; Bayreuth Festival, 1958-71, as Lohengrin and Parsifal; Sang in San Francisco, 1960-65; Metropolitan Opera, 1961-74, as Lohengrin, Radames, Calaf, Pinkerton, Walther von Stolzing, Edgardo, Max in Der Freischütz and Cavaradossi (212 performances in 21 roles); Covent Garden from 1963; Guest appearances in Paris, Milan, Verona, Rome, Munich and Hamburg; Teacher at the Musikhochschule Stuttgart. *Recordings:* La Bohème, Madama Butterfly, Tosca (Deutsche Grammophon); Die Fledermaus, Lohengrin (RCA); Aida (Hungaroton). *Address:* c/o Staatliche Hochschule für Musik, Urbanplatz 2, D-7000 Stuttgart, Germany.

KOOIMAN Petronella (Elly), b. 24 June 1945, Amsterdam, The Netherlands. Organist. m. Hilbrand Albert Edskes, 17 May 1980, 1 son. *Education:* Gymnasium B, 1963; Concert Diploma, Conservatorium Muzieklyceum, Amsterdam 1969; High School of Music, Vienna, 1972; Studied with: Piet Kee, Amsterdam, Marie-Claire Alain, Paris and Anton Heiller, Vienna; Musicology, University of Utrecht, Doctoral Examination, 1990. *Career:* Concerts in Holland, Denmark, Finland, Germany, Switzerland, Italy, Austria, France, Spain, USA; Radio and TV: Holland, Switzerland, Germany, Finland; Professor of Organ, High School of Arts, Dutch Institute of Church Music, Utrecht, 1978-1990. *Publications:* The Letters of Rodolphus Agricola to Jacobus Barbirianus in: Rodolphus Agricola Phrisius 1444-1485, Leiden 1988. *Contributions to:* Professional Journals including The biography of Jacob Barbireau (1455-1491), reviewed in: TVNM, Vol 38, 1988. *Honours:* 2nd Prize, International Organ Contesst, Kiel, 1972; Prix d'Excellence, Amsterdam, 1972; 1st Prize,

International Organ Contest, Bologna, 1973. *Membership:* NNM.*Address:* Jozef Israëlsstraat 82, 9718 GR Groningen, Netherlands.

KOOPMAN Ton, b. 2 Oct 1944, Zwolle, Netherlands; Conductor; Organist; Harpsichordist. m. Tini Mathot. *Education:* BMus, University of Amsterdam; Solo Degree Organ, 1969; Solo degree harpsichord, 1970. *Career:* Founder, Music ensemble Musica da Camera, 1966 and Music Antiqua Amsterdam, 1970; Numerous concerts and recordings; Founder, Amsterdam Baroque Orchestra, 1979, appearances on radio and TV the world over; Solo tours to USA and Japan, and yearly with Amsterdam Baroque Orchestra, to Europe, USA and Japan; Frequently invited as guest conductor, and forms duo with wife; Professor of Harpsichord, Royal Conservatory, The Hague. *Recordings:* Over 150 records as a soloist, of which 40 with the Amsterdam Baroque Orchestra. *Honours:* Toonkunst Award, 1974; Johan Wagenaar Award, 1978; Edison Awards for Recordings; 3M Award for contribution to Ancient Music, 1989; Crystal Award, Osaka Symphony Hall Japan, 1992. *Hobbies:* Antique books and music; Engravings; Paintings; History of 17th and 18th Century; Laurel and Hardy Movies. *Address:* Amsterdam Baroque Orchestra, Meerweg 23, 1405 BC Bussum, Netherlands.

KOOPMANN Robert John, b. 13 Aug 1946, Waterloo, Iowa, USA. Benedictine Priest; Concert Pianist; Professor of Music; Liturgical Musician; College Administrator. *Education:* BA, 1968, MDiv, 1981, St John's University; MMus, University of Wisconsin, 1970; DMA, University of Iowa, 1976. *Career:* Performances as piano soloist, accompanist, with chamber ensemble, with orchestra, USA and Europe; Featured on commercial and educational television and Minnesota Public Radio; Orchestral appearances include St Paul Chamber Orchestra, Bach Chamber Orchestra, Milwaukee Symphony, St Cloud Civic Orchestra; Solo recitals in Washington, Minneapolis, St Paul, Olympia, Bahama Islands; Chamber musician and accompanist throughout USA and Europe; Professed as Benedictine monk, St John's Abbey, Minnesota, 1971; Professor of Music, 1975-, Chairman, Department of Music, College of St Benedict, 1977-83, 1985-86, St John's University; Organist, 1971-, Director of Music, 1976-86, St John's Abbey Church; Ordained priest, Roman Catholic Church, 1981; Director, International Studies Program, Salzburg, Austria, 1983-83. *Recording:* Christmas Improvisation, 1988. *Publication:* Benedictine Book of Song (edited), 1980. *Hobbies:* Hiking; Swimming. *Address:* St John's Abbey, Collegeville, MN 56321, USA.

KOPPEL Herman D, b. 1 Oct 1908, Copenhagen, Denmark. Composer. *Education:* Conservatory, Copenhagen; Private Study with Anders Rachlev; Further Tuition in Germany, England and France. *Debut:* As Pianist, 1930. *Career:* Concert performances as pianist throughout Scandinavia and in France, Germany and the former Soviet Union; Opera Macbeth performed at the Royal Opera Copenhagen, 1970. *Compositions include:* Orchestral: Festival Overture, 1939; Symphony No 3, 1945; Symphony No 5, 1955; Concertino No 2, 1957; Symphony No 7, 1961; Solo Instrument and Orchestra: Piano Concerto No 1, 1932; Clarinet Concerto, 1941; Concerto for Violin, Viola and Orchestra, 1947; Piano Concerto Nr 3, 1948; Cello Concerto, 1952; Piano Concerto No 4, 1963; Oboe Concerto, 1970; Concertino, 1984; Opera: Macbeth, 1968; Choir: Psalms of David, 1949; Moses Oratorio, 1964; Hymns of Thanksgiving, 1974; 2 Hymns, 1981; Solo Voice: 4 Love Songs, 1949; 3 Songs, 1950; 2 Biblical Songs, 1955; Chamber Music: String Quartet No 2, 1939; String Quartet No 3, 1944; Sonata, 1956; Capriccio, for flute and piano, 1961; String Quartet No 5, 1975; String Quartet No 6, 1979; Solo Instrument: 10 Pieces for Piano, 1933; Suite, 1934; 50 Short Pieces for Piano, 1977; 15 miniatures for piano, 1977; 30 Short Pieces for Piano, 1984. *Recordings:* Has had much of his work recorded. *Address:* Höjbjerg Vang 47, 2840 Holte, Denmark.

KOPTAGEL Yuksel, b. 27 Oct 1931, Istanbul, Turkey. Pianist; Composer. m. Danyal Kerven, 30 Dec 1964. *Education:* English High School, 1948; Private studies with composer Djemal Rechid; Graduated, Real Conservatorio de Music, Madrid, 1955; Diplome Superieur, Schola Cantorum, Ecole Superieur de Musique, Paris, 1958; Certificates on Composition and Spanish Music Interpretation, Santiago, 1959. *Debut:* First public concert, Istanbul, aged 5. *Career:* Concerts in Europe (Spain, France, Italy, Switzerland, Czechoslovakia, Germany), USA, India, Pakistan, USSR; Compositions published by Max Eschig, Paris and Bote Bock, Berlin; International concert career with European Orchestras, 1953-; Member of Jury, Schola Cantorum, Paris; Participant, numerous music festivals. *Compositions:* Tamzara; Toccata; Sonata Menorca; Trois Danses; Pastoral; Etude pour Piano; Deux Chanson du Pecheur Japonais-Hiroshima Lieder; Terezin Lieder (chansons des enfants morts); Zwei Spanische Lieder; Fossil Suite for guitar and piano; Brian's Diary; Epitafio; When We Two Parted, song; Romance de Castille; Prager Lieder. *Recordings:* Deux Chansons du Pecheur Japonais and Zwei Spanische Lieder, sung by Gunther Leib; Tamzara; Toccata. *Contributions to:* Filarmoni and Orkestra magazines. *Honours:* Several mentions and Premiere Prix, Schola Cantorum, Paris, 1958-59; 1st Prize for Toccata, Year's Best Piano Competition, Paris, 1959. *Memberships:* Filarmonic Society, Istanbul; Societe des Auteurs Compositeurs de Musique, France. *Hobbies:* Photography; Filming; Spanish literature; Hispano-American art. *Address:* Caddebostan Plajyolu 21/32, 81060-Istanbul, Turkey.

KOPYTMAN Mark, b. 6 Dec 1929, Kamenetz-Podolski, USSR. Composer; Pianist. m. Miriam Kopytman, 5 July 1955, 2 daughters. *Education:* MD, Tchernovitz, USSR, 1952; MMus, Lvow Academy of Music, USSR, 1955; PhD, Moscow Conservatory, USSR, 1958. *Career:* Senior Teacher, Theory and Composition, USSR State Academies of Music, 1955-72; Chairman of Theory and Composition Department, 1974-76, 1979-82, 1985-, Professor, 1976-, Rubin Academy of Music, Jerusalem, Israel; Deputy Head of Rubin Academy of Music and Dance, Jerusalem, Israel, 1985-; Guest Professor, Hebrew University Musicological Department, Jerusalem, 1979-; Guest Professor of Composition, University of Pennsylvania, USA, 1985 and 1989; Composer in Residence, Canberra School of Music, Australia, 1985. *Compositions:* Casa Mare (Opera), 1966; Songs of Kodr (oratorio), 1966; String Quartet III, 1969; Voices, 1974-75; October Sun, 1974; Monodrama (Ballet), 1975; Concerto for Orchestra, 1976; About an Old Tune, 1977; Rotations, 1979; Cantus II, 1980; Memory, 1981; Kaddish, 1982; Susskind von Trimberg (Opera), 1982-83; Cantus III, 1984; Life of the World to Come, 1985; Variable Structures, 1985-86; Letters of Creation, 1986; Dedication, 1986; Letters of Creation for voice and strings, 1987; Circles for voice, clarinet, cello and piano, 1987; Ornaments for harpsichord and orchestra, 1987; Scattered Rhymes for choir and orchestra, 1988; Eight Pages from the Book of Questions for voice solo, 1988; A Poem for the Numbers for the Dead for baritone and chamber ensemble, 1988; Love Remembered for choir and orchestra, 1989; To Go Away for mezzo-soprano and five instruments, 1989. *Recordings:* Six Moldavian Dances for Orchestra; String Quartet No 2; About an Old Tune; October Sun; For Harp; Memory; Rotations; Cantus II; Lamentation. *Publication:* Choral Composition, 1971. *Hobby:* Graphic Design. *Address:* 4 Tchernichovsky Str, Jerusalem 92581, Israel.

KORD Kazimierz, b. 18 Nov 1930, Pogorze, Poland. Conductor. *Education:* Studied piano at the Leningrad Conservatory, composition and conducting at the Cracow Academy. *Career:* Conducted at the Warsaw Opera, 1960-62; Artistic Director Cracow Opera, 1962-68 (staged own productions of opera); Music Director, Polish National Orchestra, 1968-73; Metropolitan Opera, 1972, The Queen of Spades: returned for Così fan Tutte, Boris Godunov and Aida; San Francisco, 1973, Boris Godunov and Rigoletto; Other opera engagements in London (Eugene Onegin 1976), Amsterdam and Copenhagen; Took the Toronto Symphony Orchestra on its first European tour, 1974: has also conducted the Detroit, Chicago and Cleveland Symphony Orchestras; Artistic Director Warsaw Philharmonic from 1977; Chief Conductor of the South West German Radio in Baden-Baden, 1980; Principal Conductor of the Cincinnati Symphony, 1980-82; Has conducted orchestras in Moscow, Leningrad, New York, London, Stockholm, Rotterdam, Pittsburgh, Vienna and Tokyo; Conducted Othello at San Francisco, 1989. *Address:* c/o Ingpen & Williams Ltd, 14 Kensington Court, London W8 5DN, England.

KORF Anthony, b. 14 Dec 1951, New York City, USA. Composer; Conductor. *Education:* BA, MA, Manhattan School of Music. *Career:* Artistic Director, Conductor, Parnassus, 1975-; Guest Conductor, Group for Contemporary Music, League ISCM; Co-Founder, Associate Director, The Riverside Symphony; Commissioned by San Francisco Symphony, American Composers Orchestra; etc. *Compositions:* Symphony No 2; Symphony in the Twilight; Oriole; A Farewell; Double Take; Brass Quintet; Symphonia; Requiem, 3 Movements for clarinet solo. *Recordings:* A Farewell; As Conductor: Babbitt, Davidovsky, Korf, Lundborg, Olan; Symphony No 2 (New World No 383 Records). *Publications:* Stefan Wolpe Chamber Piece No 2, Editor. *Address:* 258 Riverside Dr, 7C, New York City, NY 10025, USA.

KORMAN Beryl Marie, b. 4 June 1950, Enfield, Middlesex, England. Singer; Agent. *Education:* BA (hons), History, University of Warwick, 1971; Dip RAM, Royal Academy of Music, London, 1975. *Debut:* Purcell Room, London, 1975. *Career:* Sang with Glyndebourne Touring Opera, Scottish Opera, Royal Opera, Northern Ireland Opera, Gilbert and Sullivan for All and London Concert Artists. *Recordings:* Gilbert and Sullivan with Welsh Guards Band; 100 Years of Italian Opera; Yeomen of the Guard, video; Ruddigore; Agent, Lies Askonas Ltd. *Memberships:* Equity; Incorporated Society of Musicians. *Hobbies:* Film; Theatre. *Current Management:* Korman International Management. *Address:* 3 Ladygrove Cottages, Preston, Hitchin, Herts SG4 7SA, England.

KORN Artur, b. 4 Dec 1937, Wuppertal, Germany. Singer (Bass). m. Sabine Hass. *Education:* Studied in Cologne, Munich and Vienna with Clemens Glettenberg and Schuch-Tovini. *Debut:* Cologne Opera Studio 1963, in Un Ballo in Maschera. *Career:* Sang in Graz 1965-68, Vienna Volksoper and Staatsoper from 1968; Glyndebourne Festival 1980-84, as Baron Ochs, Bartolo in Le Nozze di Figaro and Waldner in Arabella; Metropolitan Opera from 1984, as Osmin, Bartolo and Ochs; Engagements in Chicago (debut 1984), San Francisco, Detroit, London and Toronto and in Germany, Italy, South Africa and Switzerland; Salzburg Festival 1987, in Schoenberg's Moses and Aron; Sarastro in Magic Flute, Buenos Aires; Ochs in Rosenkavalier, Santiago de Chile; Met Tour, Japan, 1988; State Opera Munich Tour, Japan, 1988; Vienna Festival State Opera Vienna with Hermanns/Harnoncourt (Osmin-Abduction), 1988; Sang Baron Ochs in Der Rosenkavalier at Toronto, 1990; Season 1991/92 as Hagen at Brussels and Mozart's Bartolo at the Salzburg Festival; Often heard in oratorios and Lieder. *Recordings include:* Alfonso und Estrella by Schubert (PAN); Le Nozze di Figaro with Haitink (EMI); Vespro della Beata Vergine with Harnoncourt (Teldec); Video Recordings: Ariadne (Strauss) Met/Levine; Arabella (Strauss) Glyndebourne/Haitink; Le Nozze de Figaro Met Levine; Die Entführung, Vienna State Opera/Harnoncourt. *Address:* c/o Staatsoper, Opernring 2, A-1010 Vienna, Austria.

KORN Peter Jona, b. 30 Mar 1922, Berlin, Germany. Composer; Conductor. *Education:* Studied at the Berlin Hochschule, with Edmund Ribbra in England and with Stefan Wolpe at the Jerusalem Conservatory, 1936-38; Further study with Schoenberg at UCLA, 1941-42, and with Hanns Eisler, Ernest Toch, Miklos Rozsa and Ingolf Dahl. *Career:* Founder and conductor of the New Orchestra of Los Angeles, 1948-56; Teacher of composition at the Munich Trapp Conservatory, 1960-61; Visiting lecturer at UCLA, 1964-65; Director of the Strauss Conservatory Munich from 1967. *Compositions:* Opera Heidi in Frankfurt, 1963 (performed Saarbrucken 1978); Orchestral: 3 Symphonies, 1941-46, 1956, 1977; Rhapsody for oboe and strings, 1951; Concertino for horn and strings, 1952; Adagietto, 1954; Variations on a theme from the Beggar's Opera, 1955; Saxophone Concerto, 1956; Verolina Suite, 1959; Variations on a German Folksong for cello and orchestra, 1960; Cello Concerto, 1965; Exorcism of a Liszt Fragment, 1968; 4 Pieces for strings, 1970; Morgenmusik for trumpet and strings, 1973; Beckmesser Variations, 1977; Trumpet Concerto, 1979; Salute to the Lone Wolves for winds, 1980; Chamber: Cello sonata, 1949; 2 string quartets, 1950, 1963; Horn sonata, 1952; Aloysia-Serenade, 1953; Wind Quintet, 1966; Serenade for 12 strings, 1968; Piano Trio, 1975; Octet, 1976; Siesta for 12 cellos, 1976; Duo for viola and piano, 1978; Choruses, and cantata Munich, 1979. *Address:* c/o ASCAP, ASCAP Building, One Lincoln Plaza, New York, NY 10023, USA.

KORSAKOVA Natasha, b. 29 Jan 1973, Moscow, Russia. Concert Violinist. *Education:* Studied at Central Music School, Moscow. *Debut:* Concerts with Moscow Chamber Orchestra at the Conservatoire. *Career:* Has given concerts in Bulgaria, Germany, Greece, Yugoslavia, China, Italy, Belgium and Japan, 1989-; Played at the Panatei Festival, Italy, 1991, and the Bruch Second Concerto with the Russian State Symphony Orchestra, Oct 1991; Repertoire also includes works by Vivaldi, Bach, Mendelssohn, Mozart, Tchaikovsky and Lalo; Chamber recitals in Japan, 1991, with her mother Iolanthe Miroshnikova as accompanist in works by Brahms, Saint-Saëns, Beethoven and Prokofiev. *Honours:* Awards at Wieniawski and Lipinski Competitions, Poland, 1988; Young Violinists International Competition, Kloster Schontal, Germany, 1989. *Address:* c/o Sonata, 11 Northpark Street, Glasgow G20 7AA, Scotland.

KORTE Karl (Richard), b. 25 Aug 1928, Ossining, New York, USA. Composer. *Education:* Studied at the Juilliard School with Otto Luening, Peter Mennin, Vincent Persichetti, Goffredo Petrassi and Aaron Copland. *Career:* Teacher at Arizona State University, 1963-64 and at Binghamton, New York, 1964-70; Professor of Music, University of Texas at Austin, 1971. *Compositions:* Orchestral: Concertino on a Choral Theme, 1955; For a Young Audience, 1959; 2 Symphonies, 1961, 1968; Southwest, dance overture, 1963; Concerto for piano and winds, 1976; Chamber: 2 string quartets, 1948, 1965; Quintet for oboe and strings, 1960; Matrix, 1968; Facets, 1969; Remembrances for flute and tape, 1971; Symmetrics, 1973; Piano Trio, 1977; Concertino for base trombone, wind and percussion; The Whistling Wind for mezzo and tape, 1982; Double Concerto for flute, double bass and tape, 1983; Band music and works for chorus including Mass for Youth, 1963, Aspects of Love, 1968; Pale is this Good Prince, oratorio, 1973, Of Time and Seasons, 1975.

KORTEKANGAS Olli, b. 16 May 1955, Turku, Finland. Composer. *Education:* Studied Composition and Music Theory, Sibelius Academy, 1974-81, West Berlin, 1981-82. *Career:* Composer; Journalist; Choral Conductor, Pedagogue (Sibelius Academy, National Theatre Academy). *Compositions include:* TV opera Grand Hotel, 1984-85; Orchestral: Ökologie 1-Vorspiel, 1983; Ökologie, 2: Konzert, 1986-87; Alba, 1988; Amores, 1989; Instrumental Threnody, 1977, Sonata per organo, 1979, Emotion, 1988; Imaggio a M C Escher, 1990, Iscrizione, 1990, Choral MAA, 1984-85, Verbum, 1987, A, 1987-88, Electronic Memoria, 1988-89. *Recordings:* Has made several recordings of his work (on Finlandia and Ondine labels). *Honours:* Salzburg Opera Prize, 1989; Gianfranco Zaffrani Prize, 1989. *Memberships:* Founding Member, Korvat auki Society (society for promotion or new music), Board Member: Society of Finnish Composers, Finnish Composers'

Copyright Bureau TEOSTO. *Address:* Ruoholahdenkatu 20, 00180 Helsinki, Finland.

KOS Bozidar, b. 3 May 1934, Novo Mesto, Slovenia. Composer. m. Milana Karlovac, 29 Apr 1963, 1 daughter. *Education:* BMus, 1974, BMus 1st Class Hons, Composition, 1975, MMus, 1980, University of Adelaide. *Career:* Teacher, Cello, Music Theory, State Music School, Novo Mesto, 1953-54; Lecturer in Music, Torrens College of Advanced Education, Adelaide, South Australia, 1975; Tutor in Composition, Electronic Music, 1976-77, Fellow in Composition, 1978-83, University of Adelaide; Lecturer in Composition, 1984-91, Senior Lecturer in Composition, 1992-, Sydney Conservatorium of Music; Commissions. *Compositions:* Orchestral: Axis 5-1-5, 1973; Meditations, 1974; Metamorphosis, 1978; Sinfonietta, 1983; Violin Concerto, 1986; Guitar Cncerto, 1992; Crosswinds for Jazz trumpet, alto saxophone and orchestra, 1993; Ensemble Works: Integration, 1972; Chamber Piece, 1973; Little Fantasy, 1978; Quartet, 1980; String Quartet, 1982; Three Movements, 1982; Catena 1, 1985; Quasar, 1987; Catena 2, 1989; Ludus ex Nominum, 1989; Bravissssimo, 1991; Solo piano: Reflections, 1976; Piano sonata, 1981; Kolo, 1984; Instrumental works with synthesiser, computer or tape: Modulations, 1974; Spectrum, 1988l, Dialogue 1, tape, 1976. *Recordings:* Quasar for percussion quartet, CD Synergy Percussion, VOX Australia VAST 001-2; Piano Sonata, CD The Hands The Dream, Tall Poppies TPO20. *Address:* Sydney Conservatorium of Music, Macquarie Street, Sydney, New South Wales 2000, Australia.

KOSHELEV Viacheslav, b. 20 June 1947, Petrozavodsk, Russia. Composer. m. Natalia Khilko, Feb 1989, 1 daughter. *Education:* Studied Leningrad Conservatoire, 1972. *Debut:* Second Sonatina for Clarinet, Bassoon and Piano. *Career:* Professor of Petrozavodsk Conservatoire. *Compositions include:* Concert Musik, 4 Dances in Polka Rhythm for Orchetra; Sonata for Violin Solo; Chastushki Suite of Musical Pictures for 2 Flutes, 2 Clarinetes and Saxophone; In Modo for brass Quintet. *Membership:* Composer Union of Russia. *Hobbies:* Skiing; Running. *Address:* Anochina Str 37 Apt 28, Petrozavodsk, Russia 185002.

KOSLER Miroslav, b. 25 July 1931, Prague, Czechoslovakia. Conductor; Choirmaster. m. PhDr Alexandra Rohlena, 3 children. *Education:* Graduate, State Academy of Music, Prague, 1962. *Debut:* Prague. *Career:* Conductor, Czech choirs, tours of France, UK, USSR, Poland, Hungary, Bulgaria, Italy, Germany, Austria, Spain, Japan, Holland; Director, Prague Male Choir, Symphony Orchestra FOK; Jurist, Czechoslovakia, Italy, Bulgaria, Germany. *Honours:* Magister, Conductor, prize-winning choirs, Paris, 1956, Moscow, 1957, Bucharest, 1953, Arezzo, 1965, Prague, 1965, Spittal, 1967, Gorizia, 1969, Pohlheim, 1983, Tolosa, 1984, Cork, 1986. *Hobby:* Hunting. *Address:* Jelínkova 1619, Prague 8, Czech Republic.

KOSLER Zdenek, b. 25 Mar. 1928, Prague, Czechoslovakia. Conductor. m. Jana Svobodova, 1954. *Education:* Academy of Music and Dramatic Arts, Prague. *Career:* In Concentration Camp, 2nd world War; Guest Conductor, Prague National Theatre, 1951-, debut with Il Barbiere di Siviglia, 1951; Artistic Director, Olomouc Opera, 1958-62; Chief, Ostrava Opera, 1962-66; Assistant Conductor, New York Philharmonic Orchestra, 1963-64; FOK Orchestra, Prague, 1965-67; Chief Conductor, Berlin Komische Oper, 1966-68; Chief Conductor Opera of the Slovak National Theatre, Bratislava, 1971-76; Artistic Director and Chief Conductor, Prague National Theatre Opera, 1980-85; Conductor, Czech Philharmonic Orchestra, Prague, 1971-80; Concert Tours of Japan, 1968-; Conducted Salome at the Vienna Staatsoper, 1965; Great Britain, 1975, 1977, Austria, France, Italy, Switzerland, 1976, Canada; Concert tours and opera performances all Europe, USA, Canada, Japan with Czech Philharmonic Orchestra, Wiener Symphoniker, Staatskapelle Berlin and Dresden, Wiener Staatsoper, Leningrad Philharmonic, NHK Orchestra 1958; Conducted

Martinů's Greek Passion at Wiesbaden and in Paris, 1990; The Bartered Bride at Berne, 1992. *Honours:* Award, Outstanding Work, 1958; 1st prize, Young Conductors' Competition, Besancon, 1956; 1st Prize, Gold Medal, D Mitropoulos International Competition, New York, 1963; Artist of Merit, 1974; National Artist, 1984. *Address:* NAD Sarkou 35, 16000 Prague 6, Czech Republic.

KOSOWICZ Francis John, b. 20 July 1946, Lowell, Massachusetts, USA. Concert Organist; Clavichordist. m. Augusta Benning Blundon, 15 Sept 1985. *Education:* Includes Iona College, Manhattanville College, Pius X School of Liturgical Music; Catedra de Francisco Salinas; Universidad de Salamanca, Spain, 1983; University of Massachusetts; Amherst College; Harvard University; Studies with E Power Biggs, Guy Bovet, Montserrat Torrent, William Harris, Walter Ehret, Edgar Hilliar, Richard Casper and others; MMus, Lancashire School of Music, Blackpool, England, 1988. *Debut:* St Catherine's Church, Graniteville, Massachusetts. *Career:* Organist, St Catherine's Church, Graniteville; Chapel of Peace, Kings Point, Bermuda; Holy Trinity Chapel, Gia Lé, Vietnam; numerous solo recitals, Mexico, USA, Switzerland, France, Spain, Bermuda, Bahamas; Soloist with La Sonora Tecolutla, Veracruz, Mexico; Mont La Salle Invitational Concert Series, Napa, California; USA Ambassador to the Commonwealth of the Bahamas Concert at Christ Church Cathedral, Nassau, New Providence Island, Bahamas; All-Bach Concert on Bach's 303rd Birthday, 1988; Programs: Freepost, Bahamas; Charleston, West Virginia; Boston, Massachusetts; Hong Kong Cultural Centre, Tsui Sha Tsui, Kowloon, Hong Kong, 1993. *Compositions:* Wedding; Imperial Suite; Carillon Snow Piece. *Publication:* Book of Worship for United States Forces, 1974. *Address:* 13-C Harmony Route, Spencer, WV 25276-9306, USA.

KOSZEWSKI Andrzej, b. 26 July 1922, Poznan, Poland. Composer; Musicologist. m. Krystyna Jankowska, 1 daughter. *Education:* Studies in Musicology, Poznan University with Adolf Chybinski, Diploma, 1950; Studies in Composition and Theory of Music, State Higher Schools in Poznan with Stefan B Poradowski, Diplomas, 1948 and 1953; With Tadeusz Szeligowski, Warsaw, Diploma, 1958. *Career:* Teacher of Composition and Theory of Music as Professor at Academy of Music, Poznan; Choral works are performed at numerous international festivals and competitions mainly in Europe, America and Asia. *Compositions include:* Concerto Grosso, 1947; Suita Kaszubska (Kashubian Suite), 1952; Allegro Symfoniczne, 1953; Sinfonietta, 1956; Sonata Breve, 1954; Muzyka Fa-Re-Mi-Do-Si, 1960; Tryptyk Wielkopoiski (Great Poland Triptych), 1963; La espero (The Hope), 1963; Nicolao Copernico dedicatum, 1966; Gry (Games), 1968; Przystroje (Ornamentations), 1970; Ba-No-Sche-Ro, 1971-72; Da fischiare, 1973; Canzone e danza, 1974; Trzy koledy (Three Christmas Carols), 1975; Prologus, 1975; 3 Sonatinas, 1978; Ad musicam, 1979; Campana (The Bell), 1980; Angelus Domini, 1981; Three Euphonic Chorales, 1982; Suita Lubuska (Lubusz Suite), 1983; Zaklecia (Incantations), 1983; Strofy trubadura, 1985; Tre pezzi, 1986; Trois chaconnes, 1986; Enigma, 1986, Krople teczy (Drops of a Rainbow), 1988, Serioso-Giocoso, 1989, Miserere, 1989; Canti sacri, 1990; Tristis est anima mea, 1992; Ave Maria, 1992; Trittico di Messa, 1992. *Recordings:* Various recordings. *Publications:* Author of many publications dealing with Chopinology and Musical Education. *Address:* ul Poznanska 37 M 9, 60-850 Poznan, Poland.

KOSZUT Urszula, b. 13 Dec 1940, Psycszyna, Poland. Singer (Soprano). m. Gerhard Geist. *Education:* Studied with Maria Eichler-Cholewa in Katowice and with Bogdan Ruskiewicz in Warsaw. *Debut:* Stuttgart, 1967, as Lucia di Lammermoor. *Career:* Guest appearances in Germany, Warsaw, Geneva, Zurich, Lisbon, Chicago and Toronto; Roles include Regina in Mathis der Maler, Norma, Gounod's Juliette, Mozart's Donna Anna and Fiordiligi and parts in operas by Strauss, Verdi and Puccini; Concert engagements in works by Beethoven,

Bach, Brahms, Handel, Haydn, Mozart and Mahler; Glyndebourne, 1970, as the Queen of Night; Member of the Vienna Staatsoper from 1971; Hamburg Staatsoper in the premieres of Ein Stern geht auf aus Jakob by Burkhard, Staatstheater by Kagel and Under Milkwood by Steffens; Further engagements at Cologne and Stuttgart. *Recordings:* Beethoven's 9th Symphony, conducted by Kempe (HMV); Roles in Don Giovanni, Mathis der Maler, Sutermeister's Romeo and Juliet and Paer's Leonora; Countess de la Roche in Zimmermann's Die Soldeten (Teldec). *Address:* Lilienstrasse 26, 6670 St Ingbert, Germany.

KOSZYKOWSKI Kazimierz, b. 15 Dec 1952, Sopot, Poland. Musician; Composer; Arranger. m. Malgorzata Mackowiak, 24 Sept 1977. *Education:* Degree, Faculty of Education, 1979, Degree, Instrumental Faculty, 1980, Academy of Music, Gdansk. *Debut:* Composition, A Music Tale for Children, performed in Gdynia, 1979. *Career:* Has composed songs for children's dancing and singing groups, 1979-; Radio recordings of compositions for children, popularising activity-music workshops; Arrangement and recording of music for theatre plays; Teledisk recordings of children's songs; Music cooperation with The Polish Saturday School of Liverpool, England; Established The Private Club for Musical Children, 1990; Music compositions for Fund for Artistic Gifted Children, Gdansk, 1992; Some works recorded (studio-musician) for radio and TV, Gdansk, Bydgoszcz, Warsaw. *Compositions:* 200 songs for children and children's chorus; A Woken Windmill, triptych; Published in song-books: Magic World, 1983; Under a Sunshade Umbrella, 1984; Note by Note, 1985; Joy is a Sunny Map, 1986; When You Start to Play and Sing, 1991. *Recordings:* Cassettes with songs for children, composition and arrangement: Children's Hits, 1985; A Tale Disk at the Dreams' Street, 1992; Sun in the Cockle-shell, 1992; A New Song in the Old City of Cracow, 1992. *Contributions:* Methodical Impressions about Composing for Children, Ziemia Gdanska bulletin, 1984-86. *Honours:* Prizes for compositions for children, music festivals, Poland: Siedlce, 1985, Kielce, 1985, Cracow, 1992. *Membership:* Authors Association ZAIKS, Warsaw. *Hobbies:* Tobacco pipes; Tennis; Cycling. *Current Management:* The Bachelors Education Centre in Gdansk, 10 Hallera Street, 80-401 Gdansk, Poland. *Address:* ul Warszawska 18 m 5-6, 81-317 Gdynia, Poland.

KOTCHERGA Anatoly, b. 1947, Ukraine, USSR. Singer (Bass). *Education:* Studied conducting at the Vinitza Conservatory, then singing at the Tchaikovsky Conservatory, Kiev; Further study with Marguerita Corosio and Giulio Cassaletta, 1975-76. *Career:* Leading soloist at the Kiev Opera from 1972, notably as Basilio, Mephistopheles, Pimen and Arkel; Guest appearances at La Scala Milan, and in Canada, Spain, France, Bulgaria, Czechoslovakia, East Germany and Australia; Has sung Boris Godunov with the company of Warsaw Opera (also televised, 1986); Vienna Staatsoper 1988-91, as Shaklovity in Khovanshchina and in Don Carlos; Theater an der Wien, Vienna, as the Commendatore in Don Giovanni (1990); Season 1992 as Boris and The Sergeant in Lady Macbeth of the Mtsensk District at the Opéra Bastille, Paris and La Scala Milan; Concert appearances include Rimsky's Mozart and Salieri in the Vienna Konzerthaus and a recital of Russian songs in Lyons. *Recording:* Khovanshchina by Mussorgsky, conducted by Abbado. *Honours:* Winner, Glinka Competition 1971 (Prize from the Ukrainian Ministry of Culture); Prize winner at international competitions in Berlin 1973 and Moscow (Tchaikovsky Competition) 1974. *Address:* c/o Schaddeck Gasse 5/H, Anately 1060 Wien, Austria.

KOTIK Petr, b. 27 Jan 1942, Prague, Czechoslovakia. Flautist; Composer. m. 30 Sept 1966, 2 sons. *Education:* Flute, State Conservatory, Prague, 1956-62; Composition, Flute, Music Academy, Wien, 1963-66; Flute, Music Academy, Prague, 1962-63, 1966-69. *Career:* In 1964 his group performed with John Cage and Merce Cunningham Dance Company as part of world tour; Founder of SEM Ensemble, group dedicated

to the performance of post-Cagean music including Kotik's compositions, 1970; Since 1972m SEM Ensemble performs yearly concerts in the US and Europe with occasional performances in Canada and South America; In 1992 founded The Orchestra of the SEM Ensemble with which he recorded a CD of works by Cage for Wergo; Conducted The SEM Orchestra, to a critical acclaim, in major concerts at Carnegie Hall, 1992, Schausspielhaus Berlin, and Alice Tully Hall at Lincoln Center. *Compositions include:* Music for Three, 1964; Kontrabandt (Commissioned by WDR Cologne - live electronic music), 1967; There is Singularly Nothing (text Gertrude Stein), 1971-73; John Mary (text Gertrude Stein), 1973; Many Many Women (text Gertrude Stein), 1975-78; Explorations in the Geometry of Thinking (text R Buckminster Fuller), 1978-80; Solos and Instrumental Harmonies, 1981-83; Wilsie Bridge (WDR Cologne commission), 1986-87; Letters to Olga (text Václav Havel), 1989-91. *Recordings include:* First record: There is Singularly Nothing No 1 & 11 Cramps LP, Milan, 1975; Entire Music by Marcel Duchamp: Multhipla LP, Milan, 1976, (with John Cage) on Renee Block Edition, Berlin, 1991; Petr Kotik: SEM Ensemble, Ear-Rational, Berlin, 1989. *Current Management and Address:* SEM Ensemble, 25 Columbia Place, Brooklyn, NY 11201, USA.

KOTONSKI Wlodzimierz, b. 23 Aug 1925, Warsaw, Poland. Composer. m. Jadwiga Chlebowska, 1951, 1 son. *Education:* MMus, Warsaw State Higher School of Music. *Career:* With Experimental Music Studio, Polish Radio and Electronic Music Studio of Westdeutscher Rundfunk, Cologne, Federal Republic of Germany, 1966-67; Professor of Composition, Head of Electronic Music Studio, Academy of Music, Warsaw, Poland, 1967-; Chief Music director, Polish Radio and Television, 1974-76; Lecturer on Composition, USA, 1978; 1983-89, President of the ISCM Polish Section. *Compositions include:* Orchestral and chamber music, electronic and tape music and instrumental theatre. *Publications:* Goralski and Zbojnicki, 1958; Percussion Instruments in the Modern Orchestra, 1967; Muzyka elektroniczna, 1989. *Address:* Academy of Music, Okolnik 2, Warsaw 00-368, Poland.

KOUBA Maria, b. 1924, Altenmarkt, Austria. Singer (Soprano). *Education:* Studied at the Graz Conservatory. *Debut:* Graz, 1957, as Salome. *Career:* Sang at Graz, 1957-61, Frankfurt from 1961: roles include Madama Butterfly, Salome, both Leonoras of Verdi, Alice Ford, Jenufa, Senta, Eva, Tosca and Octavian; Guest appearances in Paris 1962, London 1963; Metropolitan Opera 1964-65; Brussels, Vancouver, Santa Fe, Naples, Vienna, Hamburg and Berlin; Other roles include Donna Anna, Liu, and Marenka in The Bartered Bride.

KOUKL George, b. 23 Mar 1953, Origlio, Switzerland. Pianist; Composer. *Education:* Milan Conservatory; Zurich University, Diploma; Master Classes. *Debut:* 1972. *Career:* Radio Recordings for BBC London, NRK Oslo, Radio Vienna, SR6 Zurich, SSR Lausanne; TV Appearances for Swiss TV; Concerts in Europe, USA, Japan, South America; Festivals, Master Classes. *Compositions:* Pandora's; Te Deum; Quartet, wind instruments; Sonata, clarinet & piano; Ideograms, 1991, Radio Lugano. *Recordings:* Da Camera Verlag-Mannheim; Subiton, Prague. *Publication:* Fylcjur, 1983. *Contributions to:* various journals & magazines. *Honour:* Alienor Award, Washington 1986. *Memberships:* Schweizerisccher Tonkunstlerverein; Mensa Music, USA. *Current Management:* Music Play Management, 6947 Vaglio, Switzerland. *Address:* Casa La Campagnola, 6945 Origlio, Switzerland.

KOUKOS Periklis, b. 3 Jan 1960, Athens, Greece. Composer. *Education:* Studied Composition with Yannis Papaionnou and Dimitris Dragatakis in Athens, with Hans Werner Henze and Paul Patterson in London. *Career:* Teacher of Composition at Athens Conservatory, 1990-. *Compositions include:* Merlin the Magician, children's opera, 1987-89; Conroy's Other Selves, opera in 1 act, Athens, 1990; The Manuscript of Manuel Salinas, opera in 3 acts; A Midsummer Night's Dream, opera-ballet, 1982. *Address:* c/o Skalkottas Conservatory, Agias Lavras 78, Ano Patisia, 11141 Athens, Greece.

KOUNADIS Arghyris, b. 14 Feb 1924, Constantinople, Turkey. Composer. *Education:* Studied Piano at Athens Conservatory and with Yanni Papaionnou at the Hellenic Conservatory; Further studies with Wolfgang Fortner in Freiburg. *Career:* Director of Music Viva concerts at Freiburg from 1963, Professor at Hochschule fur Musik, 1972. *Compositions include:* Operas: The Return (performed Athens, 1991); Der Gumminsarg, Bonn, 1968; Die verhexten Notenstander, Freiburg, 1971; Teirasias, Heidelberg, 1975; Der Ausbruch, Bayreuth, 1975; Die Bassgeige, Freiburg, 1979; Lysistrate, Lubeck, 1983; Der Sandmann, Hamburg, 1987. *Address:* c/o Staatliche Hochschule fur Musik, Freiburg im Breisgau, Schwarzwaldstrasse 141, 7800 Freiburg im Breisgau, Germany.

KOUT Jiri, b. 26 Dec 1937, Novedvory, Czechoslovakia. Conductor. *Eucation:* Studied conducting and organ at the Prague Conservatory; Further studies at the National Academy of Music in Prague. *Career:* Resident conductor at the Pilsener Opera and Symphony Orchestra; Principal conductor of the National Opera in Prague, also appearing with the Prague Symphony Orchestra and the National Radio Orchestra; Principal conductor with the Deutsche Oper am Rhein, Dusseldorf 1978-84; Conducted Der Rosenkavalier at Munich 1985, leading to engagements in Stuttgart, Berlin and Vienna; Debut with the Berlin Philharmonic 1987; Regular appearances in Saarbrucken (The Ring) also Venice, Naples, Florence, Cincinnati and Birmingham; Conducted Katya Kabanova in Paris and Los Angeles, 1988; Lady Macbeth at the Deutsche Oper Berlin (Principal Resident Conductor from 1990), followed by Tristan und Isolde and Mathis der Maler; Bluebeard's Castle at the Vienna Staatsoper; Returned to Los Angeles with Boris Godunov and Parsifal; Metropolitan Opera debut 1991 (Der Rosenkavalier); Season 1992 with Tannhäuser at the Deutsche Oper Berlin and The Makropoulos Case at Los Angeles. *Honours include:* Winner of conducting competitions at Besançon and Brussels, 1965, 1969. *Address:* c/o Athole Still Ltd, 113 Church Road, London SE19 2PR, England.

KOVACEVICH Stephen, b. 17 Oct 1940, San Francisco, California, USA, Pianist; Conductor. *Education:* Studied under Lev Shor and Dame Myra Hess. *Debut:* London Debut, 1961. *Career:* Appeared at International Music Festivals in Edinburgh, Bath, Harrogate, Berlin, San Sebastian and Salzburg; Soloist, Henry Wood Promenade Concerts for 14 seasons; Tours frequently in Europe and America; played Beethoven's Sonatas op 30 nos 1 & 2, op 96 with Kyung Wha Chung, Barbican Centre, 1991; He has conducted in the UK: the City of Birmingham Symphony, BBC Philharmonic, Bournemouth Symphony, and the Royal Liverpool Philharmonic orchestras, Chamber Orchestra of Europe, and National Youth Chamber Orchestra (at the 1993 Promenade Concerts), and abroad: in Copenhagen and Lisbon, the Los Angeles Philharmonic at the Hollywood Bowl Festival, 1990. He also works at the Aspen Music Festival each summer as pianist and conductor of both the Festival Orchestra and the Student Orchestra. *Recordings:* Has made numerous recordings, including CDs of the Grieg and Schumann Concertos (BBC Symphony under C Davis), Mozart Concerto K467 and K503 (London Symphony), Brahms Rhapsodies, Waltzes and Six Piano Pieces, op 118, Schubert Sonata D 960 (Philips and Hyperion), Beethoven Sonatas Op 90, 101, 111 and Brahms Piano Concerto No 1 (London Philharmonic/W Sawallish). *Publications:* Schubert Anthology. *Honours:* Winner, Kimber Award, California, 1959; Mozart Prize, London, 1962; Edison Award for Recording of Bartók's 2nd Piano Concerto; Gramophone Award for recording of Brahms Piano Concerto No 1, 1993. *Hobbies:* Table tennis; Tennis; Chess; Cinema; Indian food. *Current Management:* Van Walsum

Managers. *Address:* c/o Van Walsum Managers, 26 Wadham Road, London SW15 2LR, England.

KOVÁCIC Ernst, b. 12 Apr 1943, Kapfenberg, Styria, Austria. Musician; Violinist. m. Anna Maria Schuster, 29 June 1968, 4 sons. *Education:* Studied, Violin, Composition and Organ, Academy of Music, Vienna. *Career:* Concerts throughout Europe, USA, Australia, Near, Middle, Far East, including performances with LSO, Orchestra RPO, Philharmonia, London Philharmonic, all BBC orchestras, all German radio orchestras, Detroit, Vienna, Prague Symphony, Rotterdam Phileto; Plays British Works by Nigel Osborne and Robin Holloway and gave the Concerto by Thomas Wilson at the 1993 London Proms. *Recordings:* Mozart: All pieces for violin and orchestra, Scottish Chamber Orchestra (Pickwick) Michael Tippett, Triple Concerto (Nimbus), 20th century works, including compositions of Krenek, Schwertsik, Eder, Erod, Pirchner, Gruber, Lampersberg, for ECM, Amadeo, Orfeo, Meridian. Chamber music for two violins and piano (Hyperion). *Honours:* International Competition Prizes: Geneva 1970, Barcelona 1971, Munich ARD, 1972. *Hobbies:* Drawing; Football; Composition; Family life; Reading. *Current Management:* Ingpen and Williams, 14 Kensington Court W8, London. *Address:* Im Muehlfeld 3, A-2102 Bisamberg, Austria.

KOVÁCS Dénes, b. 18 Apr 1930, Vac, Hungary. Violinist. m. 1 son, 1 daughter. *Education:* Budapest Academy of Music under Ede Zathureczky. *Career:* 1st Violinist, Budapest State Opera, 1951-60; leading Violin Professor, Budapest Music Academy, 1957-; Director, Budapest Music Academy, 1967-; Rector, Ferenc Liszt Academy of Music, 1971-80; Dean of String Department, 1980-; Concert tours all over Europe, USA, USSR, Iran, India, China and Japan; Member of Jury in International Competitions: Tchaikovsky, Moscow; Long-Thibaud, Paris; Jean Sibelius, Helsinki; Joseph Joachim, Vienna; Wieniawski, Warsaw; Tokyo. *Honours:* Kossuth prize, 1963; Awarded Eminent Artist Title, 1970; Golden Medal of labour, 1974. *Address:* Music Academy, Liszt Ferenc ter 8, 1061 Budapest VI, Hungary.

KOVÁCS Endre, b. 5 June 1936, Budapest, Hungary. Organist. Church Music Director. m. Zsuzsa Kiss, 24 Oct 1982, 1 daughter. *Education:* Ferenc Liszt Academy of Music, Budapest; Courses in Belgium with Anton Heiller & Marie-Claire Alain. *Career:* Approximately 40-50 concerts a year, Hungary & abroad, including Switzerland, Netherlands, Germany, Austria, Finland, all socialist countries. *Recordings:* Ferenc Liszt, Complete Organ Works, with S Margittay & G Lehotka, Hungaraton. *Honours:* Grand Priz for Liszt recordings, F Liszt Society of Hungary. *Hobbies:* Examining structure & mechanism of old organs; Research, organology. *Address:* Zsókavár u. 55.11.9, H-1157 Budapest, Hungary.

KOVACS Janos, b. 1951, Budapest, Hungary. Conductor. *Education:* Study under Professor Andras Korodi, Ferenc Liszt Academy of Music, Budapest, 1971. *Career:* Coach, Conductor, Budapest State Opera; Musical Assistant, Bayreuth Festival, 1978, 1979; Frequent Conductor of top Hungarian Symphony Orchestras; Has conducted several guest performances given by the Budapest State Opera at the Dresden Festival and in the Berlin State Opera House; Two guest performances with Hungarian State Symphony Orchestra and festive concert series marking opening of Berlin's reconstructed Neues Konzerthaus, 1984; Conductor of several performances at Vienna Chamber Opera, 1984; Suisse Romande Orchestra, Geneva, Switzerland, 1985. *Honour:* Liszt Prize, 1985.

KOVARICEK Frantisek, b. 17 May 1924, Litetiny, Bohemia, Czechoslovakia. Composer. m. Vera Fruhaufova 14 Feb 1957, dec June 1985. *Education:* Faculty of Arts, Charles University, 1945-48; Prague Conservatory, 1945-48; Prague Academy of Music, 1948-52. *Debut:* Overture for Large Orchestra, at Rodolfinum, Prague, 1952. *Career:* All mentioned compositions publicly performed and broadcast many times by Radio Prague; Professor, 1967-85, Director, 1990-91, Prague Conservatory. *Compositions:* Overture for orchestra, 1951; Songs for low voice and piano; Morning Music for large orchestra; The Golden Wave of June, song cycle; The Stolen Moon, lyric comic opera; Mocking Songs for mixed chorus and piano; Capriccio for Chamber Orchestra; Music for Chamber Orchestra, 1982; Concerto for Clarinet and Orchestra; Serenade for Nonet. *Recordings:* Overture, 1952; Mocking Songs; Posmívanky, 1968; Clarinet Concerto; Capriccio for Orchestra. *Hobbies:* Literature; History; Geography; Touring. *Address:* Na Hroude 71, 10000 Prague 10, Czech Republic.

KOVÁTS Kolos, b. 1948, Hungary. Bass. *Education:* Ferenc Liszt Academy of Music, Budapest. *Career:* Budapest State Opera; Has made numerous appearances including operas, The Magic Flute, Eugene Onegin, Boris Godunov, Don Carlos, La forza del destino, Ernani, Simon Boccanegra, Norma and title role in Moses in concert halls and opera houses around the world; Title role in Bartók's Duke Bluebeard's Castle; Sang Zaccaria in Nabucco at Brussels, 1987; Bluebeard at Turin, 1989; Sang in Catalani's La Wally at the 1990 Bregenz Festival; Other roles include Verdi's Philip, Banquo, Sparalucile, Fiesco, Padre Guardiano, Pagno (Lombardi), Fernando, Silva and Ramphis; Mozart's Sarastro and Commendatore, Mephistopheles, Creon, Oroveso, Pimen, Gremin and Henry VIII in Anna Bolena; Has appeared in television and films; Oratorios. *Recordings include:* Has made numerous records; Medea, Ernani, Don Carlos, Lombardi, Macbeth, Liszt's St Elizabeth, Masses by Mozart and Schubert (Hungaraton); Guillaume Tele (EMI); Video of Bluebeard's Castle, conducted by Solti (Decca). *Honours:* 1st Prize, Erkel International Voice Contest; 1st prize, Rio de Janeiro International Vocal Competition, 1973; 2nd Prize, Moscow Tchaikovsky International Vocal Concours, 1974; recipient, Liszt Prize; Korsuth Prize, 1992. *Address:* c/o Hungarian State Opera House, Andrássy U. 22, 1061 Budapest, Hungary.

KOWALKE Kim H, b. 25 June 1948, Monticello, Minnesota, USA. Professor of Music; Musicologist; Foundation President. m. Elizabeth Keagy, 19 Aug 1978, 1 son. *Education:* BA cum laude with special departmental honours in Music, Macalester College, 1970; MA, 1972, MPhil, 1974, PhD, 1977, Yale University. *Career:* Assistant Professor, Music, 1977-82, Associate Professor, 1982-86, Occidental College, Los Angeles, California; Professor of Music/Musicology, Eastman School of Music, University of Rochester, New York, 1986-; President, Kurt Weill Foundation for Music Inc; Member, Editorial Board, Kurt Weill Edition, 1992-. *Publication:* Kurt Weill in Europe, 1979; Accounting for Success: Misunderstanding Die Dreigroschenoper, 1990; Editor: A New Orpheus: Essays on Kurt Weill, 1986; A Stranger Here Myself: Kurt Weil Studien, 1993. *Contributions:* Chapters in Cambridge Opera Handbook, The Brecht Companion, other books; Articles in Musical Quarterly, American Music, Notes, Opera. *Hobbies:* Tennis; Bridge; Running. *Address:* 888 Quaker Rd, Scottsville, NY 14546-9757, USA.

KOWALSKI David Leon, b. 29 Mar 1956, New Haven, Connecticut, USA. Composer; Computer Programmer. m. Michelle Disco, 2 Sept 1983. *Education:* BA, University of Pennsylvania, 1978; MM, Composition, New England Conservatory of Music, 1981; PhD, Composition, Princeton University, 1985; Private Studies with Donald Martino, Arthur Berger, Milton Babbitt. *Career:* Freelance Composer, 1978-. *Compositions include:* Quintus Obscurus for Bass flute, viola, celeste, 2 perc, 1977; Metamorphosis for Jazz Trio & Orchestra, 1978; Dichotomies for solo viola, 1979; Come Sopra, Oboe & cello, 1979; Les Voyageurs for Horn & 3 celli, 1979; Quintetino, String Quartet, Piano, 1980; Concertino, Flute/Piccolo, Clarinet, Horn, Violin, Cello, Bass, Harp, Piano, 2 Percussion, 1980; Double Helix, orchestra, 1980 (rev 1991); Alle Tode, soprano, piano, 1981; String Quartet No 2, 1982; Chamber Concerto, 1982; Toccata, organ, 1982;

Circonspection, soprano & clarinet, 1983; Four Frames, percussion quartet, 1983; Clarinet Quartet, clarinet, violin, cello and piano, 1983; Variations wind quartet, 1983; Premonitions, Piano Solo, 1983; Skid Row, Computer Generated Tape, 1983; Masques, Oboe, 1984; Echoes soprano & computer generated tape, 1984; Windhover soprano & piano, 1985; Masques II, solo Flute, 1986; Masques III, solo clarinet, 1987; The Sea and the Skylark, Computer Synthesized & computer-processed speech; Two Sonnets for Soprano & Piano, 1988; A Memory of Evening for Mezzo and Piano, 1989. *Address:* 32 Academy St, PO Box 501, Kingston, NJ 08528, USA.

KOWALSKI Jochen, b. 30 Jan 1954, Wachow, Brandeburg, Germany. Singer (Counter-tenor). *Education:* Studied at the Berlin Musikhochschule with Heinz Reeh; Further study with Marianne Fischer-Kupfer. *Career:* Sang at the Handel Festival Halle 1982, in the pasticcio Mucio Scevola; Has appeared with the Komische Oper Berlin from 1983, debut as Feodor in Boris Godunov; Guest appearances at the State Operas of Munich and Hamburg; Paris Opera 1987 as Ptolomeo in Giulio Cesare; Vienna Staatsoper 1987 as Orlofsky in Die Fledermaus; Vienna Volksoper in Giustinio by Handel; Has also sung in Dusseldorf, 1989, Amsterdam and Minneapolis; Sang Gluck's Orpheus with the Komische Oper at Covent Garden 1989, returned as Orlofsky 1990, in performances which also featured Joan Sutherland's retirement; Other roles include Daniel in Handel's Belshazzar, and Annio in La Clemenza di Tito; Sang Farnace in Mozart's Mitridate, Covent Garden 1991, Amsterdam 1992; Ottone in L'Incoronazione di Poppea at the 1993 Salzburg Festival. *Recordings include:* Baroque Arias by Prussian composers; Handel and Mozart Arias; Gluck's Orfeo and Euridice; Symphoniae Sacrae by Schütz (Capriccio). *Address:* Komische Oper, Behrenstrasse 55/57, D-1080 Berlin, Germany.

KOX Hans, b. 19 May 1930, Arnhem, Netherlands. Composer. *Education:* Studied at Utrecht Conservatory and with Henk Badings, 1951-55. *Career:* Director of Doetinchem Music School, 1957-71; Teacher at Utrecht Conservatory, 1971-. *Compositions include:* Operas: Dorian Gray, 1974, and Lord Rochester, 1978; Little Symphony, 1956; Concertante Music, 1956; Flute Concerto, 1957; Concerto for Orchestra, 1959; 3 Symphonies, 1959, 1966, 1985; Piano Concerto, 1961; 2 Violin Concertos, 1963, 1981; 12 Cyclophonies, 1964-79; L'Allegria for soprano and orchestra, 1967; Cello Concerto, 1969; Phobos for orchestra, 1970; Gedachtnis lieder for voice and orchestra, 1972; Gothic Concerto for harp and chamber orchestra, 1975; Sinfonia Concertante for violin, cello and orchestra, 1976; Concertino for chamber ensemble, 1982; Le Songe du Vergier for cello and orchestra, 1986; Chamber: 4 Violin Sonatas, 1952, 1955, 1961, 1966; 2 Trios for 2 violins and viola, 1952, 1954; 4 Sextets, 1957-61; String Trio, 1955; String Quintet, 1957; 2 Piano Quartets, 1959, 1968; Serenade for 3 violins, 1968; Preludes for violin, 1971; Piano Trio, 1976; Suite for cello, 1976; Piano and organ music, including 31-tone Passacaglia and Chorale for organ, 1960. *Address:* c/o Utrechts Conservatorium, Mariaplaats 28, 3511 Utrecht, Netherlands.

KOZAR John, b. 12 June 1946, Indiana, USA. Concert Pianist; Conductor. *Education:* Academy of Music, Zagreb, Yugoslavia; BMus, MMus, Indiana University, USA. *Debut:* New York, 1978; British Concerto Debut, 1981. *Career:* Teacher: University of Kansas, Indiana University, New England College, State University of New York, Ball State University; Recitals: New York City, London, Chicago, Munich, Vienna, Zagreb, Hong Kong, Johannesburg, Paris, Vancouver, Sydney; Concertos: Australia, London Philharmonic, Brooklyn Philharmonic, Pretoria (SA) Symphony; Television: Public Broadcasting Systems, Hong Kong Television, Scottish Television, SABC, CBC, Vancouver; Radio: Numerous radio performances, Nationally & Internationally; Conducting: Music Director, Kentish Opera Group, England; Music Director, Opera Program,

State University of New York, Potsdam, 1987-90; Currently Program Director, The Beethoven Foundation, Indianapolis, Indiana; Freelance, Conductor, Opera, Ballet; Founded Piano Productions, 1989; Named a Baldwin Artist by The Baldwin Piano and Organ Company. *Recordings:* Preamble Records; Orion Records. *Publication:* Annotated Bibliography of American Composer Emerson Whithorne, in progress. *Contributions to:* Articles in professional journals. *Current Management:* Talent Centre, PO Box 23220, Cincinnati, OH 45223, USA.

KOZMA Lajos, b. 1938, Lepesny, Hungary. Singer (Tenor). *Education:* Franz Liszt Academy Budapest; Further study at the Accademia di Santa Cecilia Rome with Giorgio Favaretto and Franco Capuana. *Career:* First success as Debussy's Pelléas, Budapest 1962; Appearances from 1964 in Florence, Venice, Rome, Milan, London, Philadelphia, New York and Copenhagen; Amsterdam 1982, as Monteverdi's Orfeo; Teatro San Carlo Naples in Rossellini's La Reine Morte; Further engagements in Paris, Brussels, Aix-en-Provence and Strasbourg; Many concerts in oratorio and Lieder. *Recordings include:* Lucia di Lammermoor (Eurodisc); Monteverdi Orfeo; Orlando Furioso by Vivaldi (Erato). *Address:* c/o Hungarian State Opera House, Népóztársaság utja 22, 1061 Budapest, Hungary.

KOZUBEK Lidia, b. 19 Jan 1927, Poznan, Poland. Pianist; Musicologist; Pedagogue. *Education:* Music Academy, Katowice; MPhil, Cracow Jagellonian University; Music Academy, Warsaw, Studied with A B Michelangeli, Arezzo, Italy. *Debut:* Katowice, 1949. *Career:* Recitalist and Soloist with orchestras in Poland, Austria, Belgium, Bulgaria, Denmark, Finland, France, German, Italy, Norway, Romania, Switzerland, Czechoslovakia, USSR, USA, Cuba, Japan, India, Nigeria, Hong Kong, Philippines and Taiwan; Appearances on Television and Radio and at Festivals; Professor, Music Academy, Frederick Chopin, Warsaw; Guest Professor, Musashino Academia Musicae, Japan; Held piano courses in Norway, Poland and Japan; teacher and Player in New Zealand and Australia, 1983. *Recordings:* Polish piano music. *Publications:* Michelangeli as Man, Artist and Pedagogue (in preparation); Opera Manru of I J Paderewski, ed, 1993. *Hobbies:* Art; Archaeology; Travel; Photography; Films. *Address:* ul J Dabrowskiego 77 m. 9, 02-503 Warsaw, Poland.

KRADER Barbara Lattimer, b. 15 Jan 1922, Columbus, Ohio, USA. Ethnomusicologist. m. Lawrence Krader. *Education:* AB, Music, Vassar College, 1942; Studies with Ernst Krenek and George Dickinson; AM, Russian Language and Literature, Columbia University, 1948; PhD, Slavic Languages and Literatures, Radcliffe College, 1955. *Career:* Sub-Editor for Europe, Grove's Dictionary, 6th edition; Teacher, Harvard University, Ohio State University, Columbia University, Conrad Grebel College, Canada, Free University, Berlin. *Contributions to:* Ethnomusicology: Historical and Regional Studies, ed by H Myers, London, 1993; Ethnomusicology; Journal and Yearbook of the International Folk Music Council/International Council for Traditional Music; Grove's Dictionary, 6th edition. *Honour:* Seeger Lecture of Society for Ethnomusicology, 1985. *Memberships:* Phi Beta Kappa; Executive Secretary, International Folk Music Council, 1965-66; President, Society for Ethnomusicology, 1971-73. *Address:* Babelsberger Str 5, 10715 Berlin, Germany.

KRAEMER Nicholas, b. 7 Mar 1945, Edinburgh. Conductor; Harpsichordist. m. Elizabeth Anderson, 3 sons (1 deceased), 2 daughters. *Career:* Harpsichordist with the Academy of St Martin-in-the-Fields and the English Baroque Soloists; Founded the Raglan Baroque Players 1978: performances on original instruments, often heard on BBC Radio 3; Artistic Director of the London Bach Orchestra and the New Irish Chamber Orchestra 1985; Concerts with the Polish Chamber Orchestra in Poland; Performances of Handel opera in Amsterdam and Geneva; Further concerts with the Israel Chamber Orchestra and the Frysk Orkest in

Holland; Handel in Dublin concerts with the Irish Chamber Orchestra in season 1988-89; Bach's Magnificat with the Royal Philharmonic Orchestra and the City of Birmingham Symphony; Mozart's Requiem with the Manchester Camerata; Concerts with the Australian Chamber Orchestra 1989; Season 1991 with the Orchestra of the Age of Enlightenment in Mozart in London (EBU), Handel's Rinaldo with Teresa Berganza in Lisbon, London Bach Society Concert in Memory of Paul Steinitz; Visit to Switzerland with the Prague Chamber Orchestra and Messiah from Scratch with the (BS) in the new Birmingham Symphony Hall; Principal Conductor Manchester Camerata, 1992-; Artistic Director, London Bach Orchestra, 1985; 1993-1994 season, Series, Distant Echoes with Manchester Camerata Concerts with Scottish Chamber and Northern Sinfonia Orchestra; Messiahs with Ulster Orchestra, Belfast Philharmonic Choir; Made debuts ENO with Magic Flute, 1992, Marseille Opera with Poppea, 1993. *Recordings:* Vivaldi Violin Concertos Op 9 (La Cetra) with Monica Huggett (EMI); Vivaldi Violin Concertos Op 8, including The Four Seasons, with the Raglan Baroque Players (Virgin Classics); Complete harpsichord concertos of Bach (Archiv). *Current Management:* c/o Ron Gonsalve, 10 Dagnan Road, London SW12 9LQ, England. *Address:* 35 Glasslyn Road, London, N8 8RJ, England.

KRAFT Jean, b. 9 Jan 1940, Menasha, Wisconsin, USA. Singer (Mezzo-Soprano). *Education:* Studied with Giannini Gregory at the Curtis Institute, Theodore Harrison in Chicago, William Ernst Vedal in Munich and Povla Frijsch in New York. *Debut:* New York City Opera 1960, in Six Characters in Search of an Author by Weisgall. *Career:* Sang in Houston, Boston, New Orleans, Philadelphia, Santa Fe, Chicago and Dallas; Metropolitan Opera from 1970, as Flora in La Traviata, Emilia (Otello) 1987, Herodias, Ulrica and Suzuki; Maggio Musicale Florence 1988, as Mrs Sedley in Peter Grimes. *Recordings include:* Andrea Chénier and Cavalleria Rusticana (RCA). *Address:* Metropolitan Opera, Lincoln Center, New York, NY 10023, USA.

KRAFT Leo (Abraham), b. 24 July 1922, New York, New York, USA. Composer; Teacher. m. Amy Lager, 16 May 1945, 2 sons. *Education:* Pupil in composition of Karol Rathaus, Queens College of the City University of New York; BA, 1945, Randall Thompson, Princeton University, MFA, 1947, and Nadia Boulanger, Paris, 1954-55. *Career:* Faculty member, Queens College, 1947-. *Compositions:* Orchestral: Concerto for Flute, Clarinet, Trumpet, and Strings, 1951; Variations, 1958; 3 Pieces, 1963; Concerto for Cello, Wind Quintet, and Percussion, 1968; Concerto for 12 Instruments, 1966-72; Music, 1975; Concerto for Piano and 14 Instruments, 1978; Chamber Symphony, 1980; Symphony in One Movement, 1985; Ricercare for Strings, 1985; Concerto for Oboe and Strings, 1986; Chamber: 2 string quartets, 1951, 1959; Sextet, 1952; Partita for Wind Quintet, 1964; Trios and Interludes for Flute, Viola, and Piano, 1965; Dialogues for Flute and Tape, 1968; Line Drawings for Flute and Percussion, 1972; Diaphonies for Oboe and Piano, 1975; Dialectica for Flute, Clarinet, Violin, Cello, and Tape, 1976; Conductus Novus for 4 Trombones, 1979; Episodes for Clarinet and Percussion, 1979; Interplay for Trumpet and Percussion, 1983; Strata for 8 Instruments, 1979-84; Piano pieces; Vocal works. *Publications:* With S Berkowitz and G Fontrier, A New Approach to Sight Singing, 1960, 3rd edition, 1986; A New Appraoch to Ear Training, 1967; Gradus: An Integrated Approach to Harmony, Counterpoint, and Analysis, 1976, 2nd edition, 1987. *Address:* 9 Dunster Road, Great Neck, NY 11021, USA.

KRAFT William, b. 6 Sept 1923, Chicago, Illinois, USA. Composer. m. 2 sons, 1 daughter. *Education:* Bachelor's Degree, cum laude, 1951; Master's Degree, 1954; Columbia University. Studied under Jack Beeson, Seth Bingham, Henry Brant, Henry Cowell, Erich Hertzmann, Paul Henry Lang, Otto Luening, Vladimir Ussachevsky. *Career:* Organised and directed Los Angeles Percussion Ensemble; as percussion soloist performed American premiere of Stockhausen's Zyklus and Boulez's Le Marteau sans Maître; also recorded Histoire du Soldât under Stravinsky's direction; Conductor of contemporary and other music; Assistant Conductor of Los Angeles Philharmonic, 3 years; served as Musical Director and Chief Advisor, Young Musicians Foundation Debut Orchestra, Los Angeles; appeared frequently at Monday Evening Concerts; Visiting Professor in Composition, USC; Guest Lecturer in Composition, California Institute of Arts, Faculty of Banff Center for Performing Arts; similar residences at University of Western Ontario, Royal Northern College of Music, Manchester, England among others; frequent lecturer at festivals and concert series including Percussive Arts Society International Conference, California State University, Sacramento Festival of New American Music, Res Musica Baltimore concert series; given numerous seminars and master classes at universities and music festivals; Composer-in-Residence, Cheltenham International Music Festival, Cheltenham, England, 1986; Visiting Professor in Composition, UCLA, 1988-89. *Compositions include:* Dialogues and Entertainments for soprano solo and wind ensemble, 1980; Double Play for violin, piano and chamber orchestra, 1982; Gallery 83, 1983; Timpani Concerto, 1983; Contextures II: The Final Beast, 1984; Interplay, 1984; Weavings for string quartet, 1984; Gallery 4-5, 1985; Quintessence, 1985; Mélange, 1986; Of Ceremonies, Pageants and Celebrations, 1986; Quartet for the love of Time, 1987; Interplay, 1984; Episodes, 1987; Horn Concerto, 1988; Kennedy Portrait, 1988. *Recordings:* Many of his compositions recorded for various record companies. *Address:* 1437 Crest Drive, Altadena, CA 91001, USA.

KRAINEV Vladimir Vsevolodovich, b. 1 Apr 1944, Krasnoyarsk, USSR. Concert Pianist. *Education:* Studied with Anaida Sumbatian at the Moscow Central Music School and with Heinrich and Stanislav Neuhaus at the Moscow Conservatory (graduated 1967). *Career:* Many recitals, and concert engagements with leading orchestras in the USA and Europe: tours have included England, Germany, France, Portugal, Poland and Hungary; Often heard in Bartók, Prokofiev, Brahms and Beethoven. *Honours:* 2nd Prize at the First Leeds International Piano Competition, 1963; Winner, Vianna da Motta Competition, Lisbon, 1964; Winner, Tchaikovsky Competition Moscow 1970. *Address:* c/o Entertainment Corporation, A Great Newport Street, London, WC2H 7JA, England.

KRAINIK Ardis Joan, b. 8 Mar 1929, Manitowoc, Wisconsin, USA. Director General; Artistic Administrator. *Education:* Studied at Northwestern University. *Career:* Sang sub-principal roles with Lyric Opera of Chicago, 1960, Artistic Administrator, 1975, General Director, 1981; Recent productions have included Alceste with Jessye Norman, Eugene Onegin with Anna Tomowa-Sintow, La Fanciulla del West with Placido Domingo and a Ring cycle conducted by Zubin Mehta; 'Toward the 21st Century' has included revivals of Argento's The Voyage of Edgar Allan Poe, 1990, and Barber's Antony and Cleopatra, 1991, and world premiere of William Bolcom's McTeague, 1992 in USA; First United States staging of Prokofiev's The Gambler, 1991. *Honours include:* Sixteen Honorary Doctorates, 1984-1993; Commendatore della Repubblica Italiana, 1983; Order of Lincoln, State of Illinois, 1985 . *Address:* c/o Lyric Opera of Chicago, 20 North Wacker Drive, Chicago, IL 60606, USA.

KRAINIS Bernard, b. 28 Dec 1924, New Brunswick, New Jersey, USA. Recorder Player; College Professor. *Education:* Studied at Denver University, 1946-48 and with Gustav Reese at New York University, 1948-50. *Career:* With Noah Greenberg founded the New York Pro Musica, 1952: performances until 1959; Toured widely in the USA until 1970 with the Krainis Baroque Trio, Krainis Baroque Ensemble and the Krainis Consort; Teacher at Kirkland College, 1969-71; Eastman School Rochester, 1976, Smith College, 1977-81; Faculty of Mannes College New York from 1980. *Recordings:* Early and Baroque nusic with the New York Pro Musica and

his own ensembles. *Address:* Mannes College of Music, 157 East 74th Street, New York, NY 10021, USA.

KRAJNÝ Boris, b. 28 Nov 1945, Kromeriz, Czechoslovakia. Pianist. *Education:* Conservatory Kromeriz, 1959-63; Academy Prague, 1963-69. *Career:* Soloist, Prague Chamber Orchestra, 1972-80; Soloist, Czech Philharmonic, 1982-. *Compositions:* (Recorded) Bach-Busoni: Organ Preludes, Complete. *Recordings:* Works by Bach, Busoni, Beethoven, Chopin, Ravel, Debussy, Prokofiev, Bartók, Honegger, Roussel, Poulenc, Martinů. *Honours:* Grand Prix du Disque Charles Gros Paris, 1982; 1st Prize, Piano Competition Senigallia, 1976. *Hobby:* Collecting Old Instruments. *Address:* Czech Philharmony, Dum umelcu, 11000 Prague, Czech Republic.

KRAM David Ian, b. 17 Mar 1948, Surrey, England. Orchestral Conductor. m. (1) Toni Anne de Courcy Bennett, 12 Dec 1970, div 1991, 1 son, 1 daughter, (2) Belinda Saltmarsh, 10 Apr 1993. *Education:* Trinity School of John Whitgift, 1959-65; Royal College of Music, London; ARCM; Studied with Maestro Luigi Ricci, Rome; Italian Government Scholarship. *Debut:* Spoleto Festival, Italy, 1969. *Career:* Music Staff, Centre Lyrique, Geneva, Switzerland, 1969-70; Conductor, Stadttheater, Basel, 1970-75; First Conductor, Nationaltheater, Mannheim, Federal Republic of Germany, 1975-77; Resident Conductor, The Australian Opera, 1978-86; Music Director, State Opera of South Australia, 1988-; Artistic Director, Artistic Advisor, Adelaide Chamber Orchestra, 1988; Guest Conductor, Komische Oper (Berlin), Hessisches Staatstheater (Wiesbaden), 1991-92; Musical Director, Ost-West-Jugend-Sinfonie-Orchester, 1992. *Current management:* Wolfgang Stoll, (München). Glado von May (Franfurt). *Hobbies:* Bushwalking; Reading; Travel. *Address:* c/o Agentur Stoll, Martiusstrasse 3, D 8000 München 40, Germany.

KRAMER Gunter, b. 2 Dec 1940, Neustadt an der Weinstrasse, Germany. Stage Director. *Education:* Studied at Heidelberg and Freiburg Universities. *Debut:* First opera production, Krenek's Karl V at Darmstadt, 1979. *Career:* Head of Drama at Bremen and produced Nono's Intelleranza 60 at Hamburg Staatsoper, 1985; Deutsche Oper am Rhein, Dusseldorf, 1986-87, with Die Tote Stadt and Schreker's Die Gezeichneten; Productions at Deutsche Oper Berlin have included The Makropoulos Case (seen also at Los Angeles, 1992); Die Entfuhrung and Die Zauberflote, 1991; Intendant of the Theatre Company of Cologne, 1990, producing Weill's Die Dreigroschenoper with it at the Spoleto Festival, 1991. *Address:* c/o Deutsche Oper, Richard Wagnerstrasse 10, Berlin 1, Germany.

KRAMER Jonathan D., b. 7 Dec 1942, Hartford, Connecticut, USA. Composer; Theorist; Educator; Writer; New Music Advisor; Programme Annotator; Composer in Residence; Broadcaster. m. Norma Berson, 28 Aug 1966, 1 son, 1 daughter. *Education:* BA, magna cum laude, Harvard, 1965; MA, 1967; PhD, 1969; University of California, Berkeley; Post-Doctoral Fellow, School for Criticism and Theory, 1976; University of California, Irvine; Computer Music, Stanford, 1967-68; Music Teachers: K. Stockhausen, R. Sessions, L. Kirchner, A. Imbrie, S. Shifrin, D. Lewin, J. Chowning, J. Kerman. *Career:* Assistant Professor and Director of Undergraduate Composition, Yale University, 1971-78; Professor and Director of Electronic Music, University of Cincinnati, 1978-90; Honorary Research Associate, King's College, University of London, 1986; Professor, Columbia University, 1988-; Programme Annotator and New Music Advisor and Composer in Residence, Cincinnati Symphony, 1980-; Broadcaster, WGUC, 1984-88. *Compositions:* Moments In and Out of Time, orchestra; Music for Piano, No. 5 (recorded); Renascence for Clarinet and Electronics (recorded); No Beginning, No End, for orchestra and chorus; About Face, for orchestra; Five Studies on Six Notes, for percussion trio (recorded); The Canons of Blackearth, for percussion quartet and tape (recorded); Atlanta Licks for Chamber Ensemble. *Hobbies:* Gourmet Cooking; Abstract

Photography. *Address:* 25 Claremont Avenue, New York, NY 10027, USA.

KRÄMER Toni, b. 14 Sept 1935, Malsch, Germany. Singer (Tenor). *Education:* Studied at the Karlsruhe Musikhochschule. *Debut:* Stuttgart 1965, in Les Contes d'Hoffmann. *Career:* Sang in Stuttgart as Pinkerton and Alvaro, and other roles in operas by Puccini and Verdi; Sang Florestan and Erik in Klagenfurt, Parsifal and Lohengrin in Saarbrucken; Stuttgart Staatsoper as Walther in Die Meistersinger, Siegfried, and König Hirsch in the opera by Henze; Munich Staatsoper as Dimitri in Boris Godunov; Bayreuth Festival 1985-86, as Siegfried in Der Ring des Nibelungen; Deutsche Oper Berlin 1987,as Siegfried and Froh in the Ring; Metropolitan 1988, as Siegfried in Götterdämmerung; sang Aegisthus in Elektra at Stuttgart, 1989; Stuttgart Staatsoper 1992, as Bacchus in Ariadne auf Naxos. *Recordings include:* Lohengrin (CBS); Video of Der Freischütz (Thorn-EMI). *Address:* c/o Staatsheater Stuttgart, Oberer Schlossgarten 6, D-7000 Stuttgart 1, Germany.

KRAPF Gerhard W., b. 12 Dec 1924, Meissenheim, Germany. Professor of Organ and Church Music; Composer. m. Gertrud A. Lichti, 30 Dec 1954, 1 son, 3 daughters. *Education:* Staatsexamen Diploma, Musikhochschule, Karlsruhe, 1950; MMus, University of Redlands, California, USA, 1951; AAGO. *Career:* Church Music Supervisor, Synod of Baden, 1951-53; College teaching, Missouri, Wyoming and Iowa, USA; Professor Emeritus of Organ and Church Music, University of Alberta, Canada. *Compositions Include:* Little Organ Psalter, 1971; Fantasia on O Jesus Christ, to Thee May Hymns be Rising; Sing and Rejoice, 6 volumes of organ chorale preludes, 1978-86; Three Triptychs; Cantata, From Heaven Above, voices and instruments, Psalm 148, SATB, soprano solo, brass quartet, organ, 1984. *Recordings:* The Tracker Organ at Iowa, 1973; All organ works taped by CBC; A Sound Story (videotape), University of Alberta Department of Radio and TV, 1979. *Publications Include:* Organ Improvisation: A Practical Approach to Chorale Elaborations for the Service, 1967; Bach; Improvised Ornamentation and Keyboard Cadenzas; An Approach to Creative Performance, 1983; Translations: The Organ Handbook (H. Klotz), 1969; Werckmeister's Orgelprobe of 1698, 1976.

KRAPP Edgar, b. 3 June 1947, Bamberg, Germany. Organist; Harpsichordist; University Professor. m. Dr Maria-Christine Behrens, 22 July 1978, 2 sons. *Education:* Regensburg Cathedral Church Choir, 1956-64; Studied Organ, College of Music, Munich, 1966-71; Pupil of Marie Claire Alain, Paris, 1971-72. *Career:* Concerts in Europe, North and South America, Japan; Radio and TV programmes in Germany and Japan; Succeeded Helmut Walcha as Professor of Organ at the Hochschule fur Musik, Frankfurt, 1974; Visiting Professor at the Salzburg Mozarteum, 1982-91; Professor ofr Organ, Hochschule fur Musik, München, 1993-; Concerts with conductors such as Rafael Kubelik, Colin Devis, Horst Stein, Christoph Eschenbach. *Recordings:* Handel: all organ and harpsichord works; Organ recordings in Haarlem (St Bavo Church), Berlin (St Hedwig's Cathedral), Passau Cathedral, historical instruments in East Germany (Brandenburg Cathedral) and South Germany (Benediktbeuern, Ottobeuren Basilica). *Honours:* 1st Prize, ARD Competition, Munich, 1971; Mendelssohn Prize, Berlin, 1971; German Recording Prizes for Organ, 1981, Harpsichord, 1983; Grand Prix du Disque, 1983; Frankfurt Music Prize, 1983. *Memberships:* Member of Jury for International Organ Competitions at Berlin, Munich, Nurnberg, Linz, Tokyo, Chartres; Member, Bayerische Akademie der Schonen Kunste; Member, Board of Directors, Neue Bachgesellschaft, Leipzig; Artistic Director, Organ Series at New Concert Hall Bamberg. *Hobbies:* Walking; Family. *Address:* Hauptstrasse 15, D-82054 Sauerlach-Altkirchen, Germany.

KRASNER Louis, b. 21 June 1903, Cherkassy, Russia. Musician. *Education:* Teacher's and Soloist Diploma, New England Conservatory of Music, Boston under Eugene Gruenberg, US; Further Studies in Europe with Carl Fleisch, Lucien Capet and Sevcik. *Career:* Solo recitals and soloist with orchestras in Europe including: Vienna Philharmonic, Berlin Philharmonic, BBC London, Paris, Rome, Stockholm, Brussels, Florence, Warsaw, Rotterdam, Munich, Cologne; recitals and Soloist in US with Boston Symphony, New York Philharmonic; Cleveland, Chicago and others; Gave premieres of the Concertos by Berg, Barcelona, 1936 and Schoenberg, Philadelphia, 1940; Concertmaster of Minneapolis Orchestra under Dimitri Mitropoulos, 1944-49; Professor of Violin and Chamber Music, Syracuse University, 1949-71, then Professor Emeritus; Conductor, Syracuse University Orchestra, 1960-; Syracuse Symphony Orchestra, 1960-68. *Recordings include:* Berg and Schoenberg concertos; Schoenberg Serenade; Piston sonata with composer at the piano. *Publications:* Editor, String Problems, Players and Paucity, 1965; In Consideration of the Creative Arts, Aesthetics without Art, 1966; Cross-Fertilization of Conservatory and College on the American Campus, A point of view, 1967; Crisis in the Arts, The Arts Need Government Support, 1969; A Performance History of Schoenberg's Violin Concerto, 1978; Author: The Origins of the Alban Berg Violin Concerto, Vienna, Universal Editor, 1981. *Honours:* Honorary DMus, Syracuse University, 1986; Yale University School of Music, Samuel Simons Sanford Medal, 1983; American String Teachers Association Distinguished Service Award, 1983; Appointed Vice-President, International Alban Berg Society, 1983; Honorary DMus, New England Conservatory, 1981; Elected member, Council, College Music Society, 1969. *Memberships include:* Honorary Member, Academia Filarmonica, Bologna, Italy; Board of Judges, Leventritt and Naumburg Competitions, New York City, 1967; Music Panel, National Endowment for the Arts, 1967-69; Faculty, New England Conservatory of Music; Tanglewood Music Center; Founder, Syracuse Friends of Chamber Music. *Address:* 1501 Beacon Street, Brookline, MA 01246, USA.

KRAUKLIS Georgij, b. 12 May 1922, Moscow, Russia. Musicologist. m. Irina Shklaeva, 4 Aug 1946, 1 daughter. *Education:* Musical College, Conservatory of Moscow, 1946-48; Theoretical studies, Composition Faculty, 1948-53; Postgraduate course in Musical History, 1953-56, Conservatory of Moscow. *Career:* Consultant to Moscow Philharmonic, 1952-60; Teacher, Choral College, Moscow, 1955-62; Teacher, 1956-67, Docent, 1967-80, Dean, 1978-89, Professor, 1980-, Conservatory of Moscow; Director of Stage, France's Violinists, Sarla, France, summer 1982. *Publications:* Piano sonatas of Schubert, 1963; Operatic overtures of R Wagner, 1964; Symphonic poems of R Strauss, 1970; Symphonic poems of F Liszt, 1974. *Contributions include:* Bayreuth Music Festival after 116 years, in Musical Academy, 1993. *Honours:* Prize for article, Ministry of Culture, 1979. *Membership:* Associate Editor, JALS, USA. *Hobbies:* Ornithology; Chess. *Address:* Kostiakova street 9, ap 79, 125422 Moscow, Russia.

KRAUS Adalbert, b. 27 Apr 1937, Aschaffenburg, Germany. Singer (Tenor). *Education:* Studied at the Wurzburg Conservatory with H. Klink-Schneider. *Career:* Sang first in concert hall, with repertoire ranging from Baroque to contemporary works; Sang Belmonte in Die Entführung at Giessen, 1968; Lyric roles at the Hanover opera from 1970; Luwigsburg Festival 1972, as Tamino; Other roles were Mozart's Ferrando, Nemorino, Rossini's Comte Ory, Nureddin in Barbier von Bagdad, Des Grieux in Manon and Florindo in Wolf-Ferrari's Le Donne Curiose; Tour of North and South America 1972, in music by Bach directed by Karl Richter; Concert appearances in London, Rome, Paris and elsewhere in Europe. *Recordings:* Christmas Oratorio by Schütz; Bach Cantatas; Die Schöpfung by Haydn (Vox); Der Barbier von Bagdad; Zar und Zimmermann (BASF); Die Lustigen Weibern von Windsor (Decca). *Address:* c/o Hochschule für Musik, Hofstallstrasse 6-8, D-8700 Würzburg, Germany.

KRAUS Alfredo, b. 24 Nov 1927, Las Palmas, Nationality Spanish. Tenor. *Debut:* in Rigoletto and Tosca, Cairo, 1956. *Career:* Appearances in Venice, Turin, Barcelona and London, at Stoll Theatre, 1958, in Lisbon in La Traviata with Maria Callas, La Scala, Milan, debut 1958, Covent Garden debut, 1959, as Edgardo in Lucia di Lammermoor; Has sung in all major opera houses in Italy, France, and Germany, Vienna, Madrid, Barcelona, Tokyo and Buenos Aires; appeared in Chicago, 1962, Metropolitan New York, in Rigoletto, 1965; Later appeared in New York as Nemorino, Don Ottavio, Ernesto, Alfredo, Faust, Werther, Tonio (La Fille du Régiment), Gounod's Roméo and Hoffman; Debut at Paris Opera as Werther and returned for Romeo & Juliet and La Fille Du Regiment; Recital at the Teatro Colón Buenos Aires, 1989; sang Werther at Lisbon and Rome, 1990; Covent Garden June 1991, in Les Contes d'Hoffmann; returned, 1992, as Nemorino; Sang Fernand in La Favorite at Madrid, 1992. *Recordings:* Numerous recordings include Lucia di Lammermoor and a number of video recordings; Werther, Roméo et Juliette, Manon, La Fille du Regiment, I Puritani, La Traviata, Rigoletto, Don Pasquale, La Jolie Fille de Perth, La Muette de Portici. *Address:* c/o Patricia Greenan, 19B Belsize Park, London, NW3 4DU, England.

KRAUS Philip A., b. 17 Nov 1950, New York City, USA. Baritone, Stage Director, Professor of Opera. *Education:* BME, MM, DM, Northwestern University. *Career:* Artistic director, Light Opera Works, Evanston, Illinois, 1979-; Professor of Opera, De Paul University, Chicago, 1982-87; Baritone, Soloist with, The Chicago Symphony, Milwaukee Symphony, Rochester Philharmonic, Grant Park Symphony, Chicago Lyric Opera, Light Opera Works, Chamber Opera Chicago, Omaha Symphony, Ravinia Festival, Opera Theater of San Antonio, Stage Director, Pamiro Opera of Green Bay, Winsconsin and Gold Coast Opera; Private voice Teacher of Chicago, 1972-; Stage Director, Pamiro Opera of Green Bay, 1988-; Soloist with the Champaign Urbana Symphony, Sioux City Symphony, Civic Orchestra of Chicago, Missouri Symphony, Evansville Philharmonic. *Recordings:* Beethoven, Fidelio, 2nd Prisoner, Solti Conducting on Decca. *Publications:* Translator: The Chocolate Soldier (Oscar Straus), The Waltz Dream (Oscar Straus), Gianni Schiccni (Puccini), Orpheus in the Underworld (Offenbach), The Maid Mistress (Pergolesi). *Hobbies:* Composing; Travel; Restauranteur. *Current Management:* Seidel Management, 4711 N. Leavitt, Chicago, IL 60625, USA. *Address:* 2501 W. Lunt Avenue, Chicago, IL 60645, USA.

KRAUSE Tom, b. 5 July 1934, Helsinki, Finland. Singer (Baritone). *Education:* Studied in Hamburg and Vienna and in Berlin with Margot Skoda, Serjo Nazor and Rudolf Bautz. *Debut:* As Lieder singer in Helsinki, 1957. *Career:* Stage debut at the Städtische Oper Berlin as Escamillo, 1959; Appearances in Milan, Vienna, Paris, Brussels, Bordeaux, Buenos Aires, Cologne, Munich and Toulouse; Bayreuth 1962, as the Herald in Lohengrin; Glyndebourne and London 1963, as the Count in Capriccio and in Britten's War Requiem; Hamburg Staatsoper from 1962, notably in the premieres of Der goldene Bock by Krenek (1964) and Searle's Hamlet (1967); Metropolitan Opera from 1967, Count Almaviva, Malatesta, Escamillo and Guglielmo; Grand Théâtre Geneva 1983, as Golaud in Pelléas et Mélisande; In Chicago with Lyric Opera, San Francisco Opera and Houston Operas, Other roles include Don Giovanni, Renato, Kurwenal, Amonasro, Germont, Pizarro, Amfortas and Mefistopheles; sang at the 1985 Savonlinna Festival as King Philip in Don Carlo; Active career as Lieder recital singer and Oratorio Singer; Kammersänger in Hamburg; Salzburg Festival 1992, as Frère Bernard in St Francois d'Assise by Messiaen. *Recordings:* Tristan und Isolde, Le Nozze di Figaro, Così fan Tutte, Fidelio, Andrea Chénier, La Bohème, Don Pasquale, Turandot, Elektra, Salome, Un Ballo in Maschera and Otello (Decca); Carmen (Deutsche Grammophon); Lohengrin (Philips); Oedipus Rex (CBS); Euryanthe (EMI). *Honours:* Deutsche Schallplatten Prize, Edison Prize, English Gramophone Prize for Sibelius Songs (Decca), 1986. *Address:* c/o Finnish National Opera, Bulevardi 23-27, SF-00180 Helsinki 18, Finland.

KRAUSE-BODOKY Annamaria, b. 8 Aug 1941, Budapest, Hungary. Pianist; Professor. m. Tamas Bodoky, 30 Mar 1970, 2 sons. *Education:* Diploma, F. Liszt Academy of Music, Budapest, 1965; Diploma, Academy of Music, Munich, Germany, 1969; Masterclasses with P. Badura-Skoda & A. Brendel, Vienna, Austria. *Career:* Concerts, Europe & Japan; Head of Department, Piano Teachers Training Institute, F. Liszt Academy of Music, Budapest. *Recordings:* Solo & chamber music, Bavarian Radio, Hungarian Radio. *Publications:* Contributions to: Parlando, Hungarian Music Teachers' Journal; EPTA Documentations; Schriftenreihe der Hochschule für Music Carl Maria von Weber, Dresden. *Current Management:* Interkoncert, H-1051 Budapest, V. ker. Vorosmarthy ter 1. *Address:* Moricz Zsigmond ut 90, H-2016 Leanyfalu, Hungary.

KRAUZE Zygmunt, b. 19 Sept 1938, Warsaw, Poland. Composer; Pianist. *Education:* Studied with Kazimierz Sikorski and Maria Wilkomirska at the Warsaw Conservatory, MA, 1964; Further study with Nadia Boulanger in Paris, 1966-67. *Career:* Soloist in recitals of new music in Europe and the USA; Founded the Warsaw Music Workshop, 1967: group consisting of clarinet, trombone, cello and piano, for which 100 composers have written works; Taught piano at Cleveland State University, 1970-71; Lectures at the International Course for New Music at Darmstadt, in Stockholm, Basle and at US universities; President of the Polish Section of ISCM from, 1980; Resident in Paris from 1982; has worked for IRCAM (Electronic Music Centre) with Boulez; President of the International Society for Contemporary Music, 1987. *Compositions:* Malay Pantuns for 3 flutes and female voice, 1964; Triptych for piano, 1964; Esquisse for piano, 1967; Polychromy, for clarinet, trombone, piano and cello, 1968; Quatuor pour la Naissance, for clarinet, violin, cello and piano, 1985; Voices for 15 instruments, 1968-72; Piece for Orchestra No.1 and 2, 1969-70; 3 String Quartets, 1960, 1969, 1982; Fallingwater for piano, 1971; Folk Music for orchestra, 1972; Aus aller Welt Stammende for 10 strings, 1973; Automatophone for 14 plucked instruments and 7 mechanical instruments, 1974; Fete galante et pastorale, 1975; Piano Concerto, 1974-76; Suite de danses et de chansons for harpsichord and orchestra, 1977; The Star, chamber opera, 1980; Violin Concerto, 1980; Tableva vivant for chamber orchestra 1982; Piece for Orchestra No.3 1982; Arabesque for piano and chamber orchestra 1983; Double Concerto for violin, piano and orchestra 1985; Symphonie Parisienne 1986; Nightmare Tango for piano 1987; From Keyboard to Score for piano 1987; Sigfried und Zygmunt for piano and cello 1988. *Honours include:* Chevalier dans l'ordre des Arts et des Lettres 1984. *Address:* c/o ZAIKS, 2 rue Hippoteczna, 00 092 Warsaw, Poland.

KRAVETZ Nelly, b. 27 Apr 1955, Moscow, Russia. Musicologist. m. Vadim Kravetz, 9 Apr 1977, 1 son, 1 daughter. *Education:* Department of Piano and Musicology, Gnesin's Special Musical School, Moscow, 1968-74; MA, Musicology, Tchaikovsky State Conservatory, Moscow, 1980; Postgraduate studies, All-Union Institute of Art History, Moscow, 1982-89; PhD, 1989. *Career:* Currently Musicologist, Bar-Ilan University, Ramat Gan, Israel. *Publications:* Interaction of Harmony and Texture in the latest Sonatas of Skriabin, MA thesis; Prokofiev's concertos as a new stage in the development of the genre, 1987; Instrumental concertos of S Prokofiev, doctoral dissertation; The play-element as an integral part of Prokofiev's music, 1990. *Hobby:* Jazz. *Address:* Rehov Haviva Reik 3/10, Holan, Israel.

KRAVITZ Ellen King, b. 25 May 1929, Fords, New Jersey, USA. Musicologist; Professor. m. Hilard L Kravitz, 9 Jan 1972, 1 daughter, 3 stepsons. *Education:* BA, Georgian Court College, Lakewood, New Jersey, 1964; MM, 1966, PhD, 1970, University of Southern California. *Career:* Full Professor of Music History, California State University, Los Angeles, 1967;

Researcher in Musicology and related arts; Director, Exhibition of Schoenberg's art, music etc. during Schoenberg Centennial Celebration, USC, 1974; Founder, Friends of Music, California State University, Los Angeles, 1976; Radio Interview as Chairman of Friends of Music Gala in honour of Mona Paulee, 1982; Participant in Faculty Vocal Extravaganza, California State University, Los Angeles, 1981, 1983, 1985, 1987, 1989, 1991, 1993. *Publications:* A Correlation of Concepts Found in German Expressionist Art, Music and Literature 1970; Editor, Journal of the Arnold Schoenberg Institute, Volume 1 No 3, Volume II No 3; Catalogue of Schoenberg's Paintings, Drawings and Sketches; Finding Your Way Through Music in World Culture, 1986. *Hobbies:* Theatre; Travel; Interior decorating. *Address:* 526 N. Foothill Road, Berverly Hills, CA 90210, USA.

KREBBERS Herman (Albertus), b. 18 June 1923, Hengelo, Holland. Violinist. m. A. Torlau, 1 son, 1 daughter. *Education:* Studied at the Amsterdam Musiklyceum with Oscar Back. *Debut:* Gave first concert in 1932. *Career:* Soloist with the Concertgebouw Orchestra 1935; Leader of the Gelderland Orchestra, then the Hague Residentie Orchestra 1950-62; Leader of the Concertgebouw Orchestra from 1962; Many tours of Europe and the USA as soloist; Founded the Guarneri Trio 1963, and played in Violin Duo with Theo Olof; Teacher at the Amsterdam Musiklyceum. *Recordings:* Bach and Badings Concertos for Two Violins, with Theo Olof and the Hague Philharmonic; Beethoven Concerto with the Hague Philharmonic; Brahms and Bruch Concertos with the Brabant Orchestra; Paganini 1st Concerto with the Vienna Symphony; Haydn Concertos with the Amsterdam Chamber orchestra. *Honours include:* Prix d' Excellence, Amsterdam Musiklyceum, 1940; Knight, Oranje Nassau Order; Many Prizes from International Competitions.

KREBS Helmut, b. 8 Oct 1913, Dortmund, Germany. Singer (Tenor). *Education:* Berlin Musikhochschule, 1934-37. *Career:* Began as concert singer; Stage debut, 1937 at the Volksoper, Berlin; Returned to Berlin, 1947; Salzburg Festival, 1949, in the premiere of Orff's Antigonae: Ernesto in Don Pasquale, 1952; Guest appearances in Milan, London, Vienna, Munich, Holland and Belgium; Glyndebourne, 1953 as Mozart's Belmonte and Idamantes; Hamburg Radio, 1954, as Aron in the first performance of Schoenberg's Moses und Aron; Berlin, 1956 and 1965, in the premieres of Henze's König Hirsch and Der junge Lord; Also heard as the Evangelist in the Passions of Bach; Professor at the Frankfurt Musikhochschule from 1966; sang at the Deutsche Oper Berlin, 1988, in From The House of the Dead. *Compositions:* Orchestral, operatic, chamber, choral and vocal works published by Bote & Bock and Astoria Verlag. *Recordings:* Monteverdi Orfeo; Henze Der junge Lord; Bach Christmas Oratorio; Verdi Requiem; Stravinsky Oedipus Rex; Strauss Ariadne auf Naxos; Schoenberg Moses and Aron; Wagner Der fliegende Holländer: Labels include Decca, Deutsche Grammophon, Philips, Vox, Columbia and Melodram. *Honours:* Berliner Künstpreis, 1952; Berliner Kammersänger, 1963. *Address:* 11 Im Dol Berlin 33 (Dahlem), Germany.

KREK UROS, b. 21 May 1922, Ljubljana, Yugoslavia. Composer. m. Lilijana Pauer, 18 June 1960. *Education:* Classical College, Ljubljana; Music High School, Ljubljana. *Debut:* 1st Performance of Compositions, Ljubljana, 1945. *Career:* Performances of compositions on concert stages, radio and television, film, theatre, records and editions. *Compositions:* Concerto for violin and orchestra; Sinfonietta, Concerto for French horn and orchestra; Concertino for piccolo and orchestra; Rhapsodic Dance for orchestra; Sonata for 2 violins; Five Songs for voice and piano; Movements Concertants, Inventions ferales for violin and strings; Symphony for Strings; Duo for violin and violoncello; La Journee d'un Bouffon for brass quintet; Trio for violin, viola and violoncello; String Quartet; Sur un Melodie for piano; 1 Sonatinas for clarinet; Songs for Eva; Concert Diptych for violoncello and orchestra; Sonata for violoncello and

piano; 3 Impromptus for violin solo; Sextett for 2 violins, 2 violas and 2 violoncellos; Espressivo for flute and piano; Songs on Folk Tradition for voice and piano; Chamber music, choir music, film and stage music. *Recordings:* Authors Portrait; Inventiones Ferales; Sonata for 2 violins; Numerous recordings of his compositions. *Hobbies:* Model railways; Mountaineering. *Address:* 64248 Lesce, Na Vrtaci 5, Solvenia.

KREMER Gidon, b. 27 Feb 1947, Riga, Latvia. Violinist. *Education:* Studied at the Moscow Conservatory with David Oistrakh. *Career:* many performances as concert soloist in Europe, the USA and elsewhere in the standard repertoire and in modern works: often heard in Schnittke, and in May 1986 performed Bernstein's Serenade, London; Duo recitals with the pianist Martha Argerich: sonatas by Franck, Schumann and Bartók, London, 1988; Television apperances include Berg Concerto, with the Bavarian Radio Symphony under Colin Davis; Promenade Concerts, London, 1991, with Gubaidulina's Offertorium, conducted by Simon Rattle. *Recordings Include:* Concertos by Mendelssohn, with Martha Argerich, 1989; Gubaidulina's Offertorium, with the Boston Symphony under Charles Dutoit; Mozart Trios K498 and Duos K423 and K424; Schumann Sonatas, with Argerich (Deutsche Grammophon). *Honours:* First Prize of the Latvian Republic, 1963; Winner, Tchaikovsky International Competition, Moscow, 1970. *Address:* c/o Terry Harrison Management, 9 Penzance Place, London W11 4PA, England.

KRENZ Jan, b. 14 July 1926, Wloclawek, Poland. Conductor; Composer. m. Alina Krenz, 1958, 1 son. *Education:* Warsaw and Lodz. *Career:* Conductor, Lodz Philharmonic Orchestra, 1945; Conductor, Poznan Philharmonic Orchestra, 1948-49; Director and First Conductor, Polish Radio Symphony Orchestra, Katowice, 1953-67; British debut 1961; Conducted Polish Music at the 1967 Cheltenham Festival; Artistic Director, First Conductor, Grand Opera House, Warsaw, 1967-73; General Director, Music, Bonn Orchestra, 1978-; tours in Hungary, Romania, Czechoslovakia, France, USSR, Germany, Italy, UK, USA, Japan, Australia. *Compositions include:* Symphony; 2 String Quartets; Nocturnes for orchestra; Rozmowa dwoch miast; Rhapsody for Strings, Xylophone, Tam-Tam, Timpani and Celesta, 1952; Concertino for Piano and Small Symphony Orchestra, 1952; Orchestral transcriptions of Microcosm (B. Bartok, 1958,); Mythes (Szymanowski), 1964. *Recordings:* Paderewski's Piano Concerto; Lutoslawski's 1st Symphony and Wieniawski Violin Concertos; Brahms, Mendelssohn and Tchaikovsky Violin Conertos (Grumiaux); Chopin Piano Concertos. *Hobbies:* Painting. *Address:* Al. 1 Armii Wojaska Polskiego 16/38, 00-582 Warsaw, Poland.

KREPPEL Walter, b. 3 June 1923, Nuremberg, Germany. Singer (Bass). *Education:* Studied at the Nuremberg Conservatory. *Debut:* Nuremberg 1945, as Tommaso in Tiefland. *Career:* Sang in Nuremberg, 1945-48, Wurzburg, 1948-50; Sang in Heidelberg and Gelsenkirchen, 1953-56, Frankfurt, 1956-59; Member of the Bayerische Staatsoper Munich from 1959, Vienna Staatsoper from 1960 (Rocco in Fidelio, 1962); Bayreuth Festival 1962, as Fasolt; Salzburg, 1963-64, as Sarastro; Guest appearances in Zurich, London and Amsterdam. *Recordings:* Kaspar in Der Freischütz, the Commendatore in Don Giovanni (Deutsche Grammophon); Fasolt in Das Rheingold, conducted by Solti (Decca).

KRETH Wolfgang, b. 29 May 1946, Cologne, W. Germany. Lutenist. *Education:* Studied Music, 1967-75 at: Musikhochschule, Köln; Musikhochschule, Düsseldorf; Musikhochschule, Frankfurt; Musikhochschule, Aachen; Musiklehrer-Examen; Staatl. Diplom for Lute, summa cum laude. *Career:* Several Concerts in Europe (Schwetzinger Festspiele, Musica Bayreuth, Dubrovnik-Festival, Wiener Festwochen, Brühler Barock-Fest; Radio Appearances, Interviews. *Recordings:* Lute Music of Anthony Holborne and Nicolas Vallet; Lute Concerto of Antonio Vivaldi. *Contributions to:* Several articles in Gitarre und Laute, Köln. *Memberships:* Lute Society of England; Lute Society of America; Society Nova Giulianiad, Freiburg; Member of EGTA. *Address:* Theophanoplatz Nr. 8, 5 Köln 51, Germany.

KRETSCHMAR Helmut, b. 3 Feb 1928, Kleve, Germany. Singer (Tenor). m. Renate Fischer. *Education:* Studied in Frankfurt with Kurt Thomas and Hans Emge. *Career:* Sang first in concerts and oratorios, from 1953; At Hamburg in 1954 sang in the first performance (concert) of Schoenberg's Moses und Aron; Sacred music by Bach at the Berliner Festwochen and the Bach Festivals at Luneburg and Heidelberg, 1960-62; Further appearances at the Handel Festival at Göttingen and in Dusseldorf, Japan, Korea, Paris, Madrid, Bombay, London and Ceylon; Lieder recitals with Renate Fischer, piano; Repertoire includes sacred music by Handel, Haydn and Mendelssohn, Songs by Wolf, Debussy, Schubert and Schumann; Professor at the Detmold Musikhohschule from 1963. *Recordings include:* Fidelio; Moses und Aron, conducted by Hans Rosbaud (Philips); St Matthew Passion, Christmas Oratorio and B Minor Mass by Bach; Beethoven's Missa solemnis; Schubert's Mass in A flat; Die Jahreszeiten by Haydn. *Honours:* First Prize, German Music High Schools, 1953; Kunstpreis of Nordrhein-Westfalen, 1958.

KRIKORIAN Mari, b. 25 May 1946, Varna, Bulgaria. Opera Singer (Soprano). *Education:* Secondary School of Music, Varna, 1964; Graduated, 1971, Master's Class, 1972, Bulgarian State Conservatorie, Sofia; Specialisation course with James King, Vienna, 1977. *Debut:* As Adalgisa in Norma, Varna National Opera, 1976. *Career:* 1st Soprano, Varna National Opera, in La Bohème, Simon Boccanegra, Fliegende Holländer, Otello, Don Carlo and Tosca; 1st Soprano, Sofia National Opera, 1983-; Permanent Repertoire includes Norma, Attila, Aida, Il Trovatore, La Forze de Destino, Don Carlos, Otello, La Boheme, Madame Butterfly, Tosca, Liu, Senta, Adriana Lecouvreur, Tatiana in Eugene Onegin, Lisa in Queen of Spades, Yaroslavna in Prince Igor, Verdi's Requiem, Donizetti's Requiem, Bruckner's Requiem, Brahms' Deutsches Requiem, Liszt's Christus Oratorio, Rossini's Stabat Mater, Pergolesi's Stabat Mater; Foreign tours, Prague, Budapest, Russia, Armenia, Germany, Italy, Germany, France, Spain, Austria, Greece, Egypt, Cyprus, India, Mexico; Film portrait for Bulgarian Television, 1989; Un Ballo in Maschera, 1993; Foreign Tours: Los Angeles (USA) concerts, 1993. Recordings: Opera recital, airs from Bellini, Verdi and Puccini, with Sofia Opera Orchestra, conductor Ivan Marinov, State Recording Company Balkanton, 1984; Attila, digital, compact discs, with Sofia Philharmonic Orchestra, conductor Valdimir Ghiaurov, Attila N Guzelev; Chants Liturgiques Armeniens CD Edition JADE, Paris, France, 1992; Live and studio recordings for Bulgarian Radio and TV. *Honours:* 1st Prize, Opera Belcanto Competition, Ostende, Belgium, 1980; Honoured Artist of Bulgaria, 1984. *Current Management:* SOFIACONCERT, Bulgaria. *Address:* Druzba 2 bl 213 A ap 11, Sofia 1582, Bulgaria.

KRILOVICI Marina, b. 11 June 1942, Bucharest, Rumania. Singer (Soprano). *Education:* Studied with Mdme. Vrabiescu-Vatianu in Bucharest and with Matia Caniglia and Luigi Ricci in Rome. *Debut:* National Opera Bucharest, 1966, as Donna Anna. *Career:* Sang major roles in the Italian repertory with the Bucharest Opera; Covent Garden debut, 1971, as Aida; Chicago Lyric Opera, 1972, as Mimi; Further appearances in Vienna, Berlin, Munich, Montreal, Lisbon, San Francisco and Strasbourg; Hamburg Staatsoper, 1968-76. *Recordings include:* Cavelleria rusticana (Electrecord); Donizetti's Il Duca d'Alba (Replica).

KRINGELBORN Solveig, b. 1963, Norway. Singer (Soprano). *Education:* Studied at Stockholm Royal Academy. *Career:* Appearances at the Royal Swedish Opera as Susanna and Papagena; Oslo Opera, 1990-91 as Mimi, Jenůfa and Micaela, with further engagements at the Bolshoi, Moscow, Vienna Staatsoper, Strasbourg, Los Angeles (Mozart's Countess, 1993), Brussels (premiere of Reigen by Boesmans), Salzburg (Fiordiligi, 1993), Bastille (Antonia, 1993) and Geneva (Ilia, 1994); Other roles include Musetta, Marguerite, Pamina, Nedda, Serpine in La Serva Padrona, and Drusilla in Poppea; BBC Promenade Concerts, 1991, with premiere of Lutoslawski's Chantefleurs et Chantefables, conducted by the composer (also televised); Other concert repertoire includes Haydn's Jahreszeiten in Paris, Nielsen's 3rd Symphony in London under Simon Rattle, Mahler's 2nd Symphony with Israel Philharmonic and Cleveland Orchestra, and in Los Angeles, 1993; Wigmore Hall recital debut, Dec 1992. *Recordings include:* Grieg Songs conducted by Rozhdestvensky and Tavener choral music conducted by David Hill. *Address:* c/o IMG Artists, Media House, 3 Burlington Lane, London W2 2TH, England.

KRIVINE Emmanuel, b. 7 May 1947, Grenoble, France. Conductor; Violinist. *Education:* Studied violin at Grenoble until 1960; Paris Conservatoire from 1960, violin studies with Henryk Szeryng and Yehudi Menuhin. *Career:* Laureate of Violin competitions during 1960s; Conducted in Belgium from 1964; Chief guest conductor of the New Philharmonic Orchestra of Radio France, 1976; Musical Director of the Lorraine Philharmonic Orchestra at Metz, 1981-83; Teacher of the Lyon Conservatoire, 1979-81; Chief guest conductor, 1983-85, Musical Director from 1987, Orchestre National de Lyon; Conducted the premiere of Michel Legrand's Concertoratorio 89, for the bicentenary of the French Revolution. *Honours:* Prize winner at Violin competitions in Brussels (1965 and 1968), London, Naples and Bratislava. *Address:* Orchestra National de Lyon, 82 Rue de Bonnel, F-69431, Lyon Cedex 03, France.

KROEGER Karl, b. 13 Apr 1932, Louisville, Kentucky, USA. Composer; Musicologist; Music Librarian; Professor. *Education:* Studied composition with Claude Almand and George Perle, University of Louisville, BM. 1954, MM. 1959; Composition with Gordon Binkerd and musicology with Dragan Plamenac, University of Illinois, MS, 1961; Musicology with Janet Knapp, Brown University, PhD, 1976. *Career:* Curator, Americana Collection, Music Division, New York Public Library, 1962-64; Composer-in-residence, Eugene (Oregon) public schools, 1964-67; Teacher, Ohio University, 1967-68, Moorhead (Minn) State College, 1971-72; Director, Moravian Music Foundation, 1972-80, Winston-Salem, North Carolina; Teacher, Wake Forest University, 1974-76, 1982, Winston-Salem, North Carolina, University of Keele, England, 1980-81; Professor and Music Librarian, University of Colorado, Boulder, 1982-; Active as a music editor; Edited with H.Nathan, The Complete Works of William Billings, 4 volumes, 1977-89; Professor and Music Librarian, University of Colorado. *Compositions:* 2 sinfoniettas, 1958, 1965; Chamber Concerto for Oboe and Strings, 1961; Dramatic Overture, 1964; 2 orchestral suites, 1966, 1969; Pax Vobis (Festival Cantata), 1976; Concerto for Alto Saxophone and Winds, 1982; Band pieces; 2 string quartets, 1960, 1966; 4 Canzonas for Brass Sextet, 1961, 1966, 1967, 1988; Partita for Brass Quintet, 1963; Toccata for Clarinet, Trombone, and Percussion, 1968; Fantasy for Brass Quartet, 1969; Sonata for Trombone Quartet, 1978; Suite for Oboe and Harp, 1979; Parataxis for Flute and Percussion, 1989; Piano pieces; Organ music; Choral works; Songs; Anthems; Banchetto Musicale for Saxophone Ensemble, 1993. *Publications:* Catalog of The Musical Works of William Billings, 1991. *Address:* 9260 Newton Street, Westminster, CO 80030, USA.

KROGH Grethe, b. 7 Nov 1928, Viborg, Denmark. Concert Organist, Professor of Organ. m. Richard Dahl Eriksen, 1969. *Education:* Diplomas in Organ, Piano, Harpsichord, Royal Academy of Music, 1951; Studied with André Marchal. *Debut:* Copenhagen, 1953. *Career:* Numerous concerts throughout Europe, Russia and USA; Organist, Holmens Church, Copenhagen, 1964-69; Professor of Organ, Chairman Organ Department, Royal Danish Academy, Copenhagen, 1969-1990.

Recordings: These include several with Danish Music and the organ works of Carl Nielsen. *Honours:* Prize, Copenhagen Music Critics, 1968; Tagea Brandt Prize of Honour, 1972. *Hobbies:* Literature; Swimming; Ballet. *Address:* Allégade 15 A, 2. tv., 2000 Frederiksberg, Denmark.

KROLL Mark, b. 13 Sept 1946, Brooklyn, New York, USA. Harpsichordist; Professor of Music. m. Carol Lieberman, 9 July 1975, 1 son. *Education:* BA, 1968, Graduate School, Musicology, 1968-69, Brooklyn College, City University of New York; MMus Harpsichord, Yale University School of Music, 1971. *Debut:* Carnegie Hall, New York City, New York, 1975 *Career:* Performance in solo recitals, chamber music ensembles and as concerto soloist throughout Europe, South America, USA and Canada including Gulbenkian Foundation, Lisbon, Portugal; Smithsonian Institute, Washington; Centro Venezolano Americano, Caracas, Venezuela; Barcelona, Spain; Associacion Musicale Romana, Rome, Italy; Universities of California and Yale; Museum of Fine Arts; Boston Symphony Orchestra; Tanglewood Festival; Marlboro Festival; Various others; Radio and television appearances include: Westdeutscher Rundfunk, Cologne Federal Republic of Germany; Canadian Broadcasting Corporation; Radio Smithsonian; National Public Radio, Washington; Numerous TV shows for Public Broadcasting System and BBC; Currently Professor of Music, Boston University; Conductor, Orchestral works of Rameau, C.P.E. Bach, Vivaldi; Artist in residence, Lafayette College; Conductor & Artistic Director, Opera New England. *Recordings:* J. S. Bach, complete sonatas for violin and harpsichord; Handel and Scarlatti, harpsichord works; G.F. Handel, complete works for recorder and harpsichord; Balbastre and F. Couperin, harpsichord works; Vivaldi's The Seasons, with Boston Symphony Orchestra; C.P.E. Bach, sonatas for violin and harpsichord; S. LeDuc, sonatas for violin and harpsichord; Monteverdi, madrigals; Solo Harpsichord works of JS Bach; Harpsichord works of JNP Royer; F Schubert, 3 Sonatinas for violin and fortepiano; M de Falla, El Retablo de Maese Pedro, with Montreal Symphony. *Address:* Boston University School of Music, 855 Commonwealth Avenue, Boston, MA 02215, USA.

KROLOPP Wojciech Aleksander, b. 12 Apr 1945, Poznan, Poland. Musician; Manager; Journalist. *Education:* Academy of Music, Poznan, 1973-77; Pedagogy, 1968-70. *Debut:* Soloist soprano, 1957; Soloist baritone, 1964. *Career:* Soloist 1957- (Soprano, bass from 1964), Managing director, 1969-, Poznan Boys' Choir; Director of International Boys' Choirs Festival, Poznan, Poland, 1980-; 3000 concerts with The Poznan Boys' Choir, 400 conducted concerts in 24 countries; Solo parts in big vocal- instrumental works, songs; Camerata (chamber orchestra) 1980-83; Teacher, Conductor, Polish Choir School, Poznan, 1968-; premiere W.A. Mozart opera, Bastien und Bastienne, in Great Theatre in Poznań also in Tawain and Hong Kong; by the end of 1990 nominated as manager and artistic director of the Polish Nightingales. *Recordings:* W.A. Mozart, The Coronation Mass, and K. Szymanowski, Stabat Mater, 1991. *Publications:* Stowiki a la carte, Pomorze, 1989; The Poznan Choir School, Monography, 1989; Poznan, The Poznan Boys' Choir, Monography, 1976. *Current Management:* Polish Artists' Agency, Warsaw and Penta Promotions, Holland. *Address:* Torenstraat 13, B-9160 Lokeren, Belgium.

KROÓ György, b. 26 Aug 1926, Budapest, Hungary. Music Historian and Music Critic. m. Ilona Balogh, 1 son, 1 daughter. *Education:* Music Academy of Budapest. *Career:* Editor, Hungarian Radio Music Department, 1957, Columnist, 1958-; Lecturer in Music History, Music Academy, Budapest, 1961-; Professor of Musicology, 1975-; Ford Scholarship to study Bartók Archives-New York, 1967-68; Represents Hungarian Radio at Rostrum of Composers, UNESCO, Paris. Active as critic for New Music Review, Hungarian Radio, Elet es Irodalom (weekly); Specialist in 19th Century Opera, Bartók and contemporary Hungarian music.

Publications: Robert Schumann, 1958; Hector Berlioz, 1960, 1980; Bartók Bela szinpadi muvei (The Stage Works of BB), 1962; A szabadito opera, 1966; Richard Wagner, 1968; Bartók kalauz (A Guide to B), A magyar zeneszerzes 25 eve (Thirty Years of Hungarian Composition), 1975; Aladar Rácz, 1979; Heilawâc (four Wagner Studies), 1983; Az Elsö Zaràngokèv (The First Year of Pilgrimage, Liszt), 1986. *Honours:* Erkel Prize, 1963; TUC Award, 1970; Labour Order of Merit. *Address:* Liszt Ferenc Zenemuveszeti Foiskola, 1061 Budapest, Liszt Ferenc ter 8, Hungary.

KROSNICK Aaron Burton, b. 28 June 1937, New Haven, Connecticut, USA. Professor of Violin; Artist-in-Residence. m. Mary Lou Wesley, 25 Aug. 1961, 1 son. *Education:* BA, magna cum laude, Yale College, 1959; MS, Juilliard School of Music, 1961; Fulbright Scholar, Royal Conservatory of Music, Brussels, Belgium, 1961-62; Major teachers: Howard Boatwright, Joseph Fuchs, Ivan Galamian, Arthur Grumiaux. *Career:* Concertmaster (and soloist with orchestras): Springfield, Ohio, Symphony Orchestra, 1962-67; Jacksonville Symphony Orchestra, 1969-80; Sewanee Festival Orchestra 1969-82; Florida Bicentennial Chamber Orchestra, 1976; Faculty positions: Wittenberg University, 1962-67; Jacksonville University, 1967-; Summers: Syracuse University, Kneisel Hall Summer School of Ensemble Playing, Sewanee Summer Music Centre, Soloist with extensive concerto repertoire; Appearances with Rome Festival Orchestra, Florida Symphony Chamber Orchestra, Jacksonville University Orchestra and many others; Summers of 1985, 86, Concertmaster and featured artist, Rome Festival in Italy. *Recordings:* Music of Frederick Delius, Musical Heritage Society. *Address:* 5394 Oak Bay Drive N, Jacksonville, FL 32211, USA.

KROSNICK Joel, b. 3 Apr 1941, New Haven, Connecticut, USA. Cellist. *Education:* Studied with William d'Amato, Luigi Silva and Claus Adam; Further study at Columbia University. *Career:* Co-founded and directed the Group for Contemporary Music at Columbia University, 1962; Professor at University of Iowa, 1963-66; Cellist in University String Quartet; Professor at University of Massachusetts, 1966-70; Performed with New York Chamber Soloists and made solo tours to Belgrade, Hamburg, Berlin, London and Amsterdam; New York solo debut, 1970; Has given first performances of works by Babbitt, Subotnick and Ligeti; Taught at California Institute of Arts, 1970-74; Cellist with the Juilliard Quartet from 1974: world wide tours in the standard repertoire and contemporary works; Performances in London, 1990 (works by Mozart). *Recordings* include: Albums with the Juilliard Quartet; Carter's Cello Sonata. *Address:* Juilliard Quartet, c/o Library of Congress, Washington DC, USA.

KROSS Siegfried, b. 24 Aug 1930, Wuppertal, Germany. Professor of Musicology. m. Dorothee Brand, 23 Mar 1962, 2 sons. *Education:* Studied Musicology, German Literature, Psychology, Experimental Physics, Universities of Bonn and Freiburg/Br (Gurlitt); Dr.phil, 1956; Habilitation, 1966. *Career:* Scholar, Deutsche Forschungsgemeinschaft, Vienna, 1959; Assistant, Beethoven Archives, Bonn; Assistant Professor, 1970, Full Professor (tenured), Dean, Faculty of Humanities, 1988, University of Bonn; Vice-Presdident, Landes-Musikrat. *Publications:* Die Chorwerke von J.Brahms, 1957, 2nd Edition, 1963; Das Instrumentalkonzert bei G.Ph.Telemann, 1969; Dokumentation zur Geschichte des deutschen Liedes seit 1973; Geschichte des deutschen Liedes, 1989; Briefe Robert und Clara Schumanns, 1978, 2nd Edition, 1982; Brahms-Bibliographie, 1983. *Contributions to:* Die Musikforschung; 19th Century Music, 1982; American Choral Review 25, 1983; Brahms (ed. Pascall), Brahms (ed. Musgrave), Cambridge University Press, 1983-87; Festschrift: Beiträge zur Geschichle des Konzerts, 1990. *Memberships:* American Musicological Society; Gesellschaft für Musikforschung. *Address:* Musikwissenschaftliches Seminar der Universitat Bonn, Am Hof 34, D-53 217 Bonn, Germany.

KRPAN Vladimir, b. 11 Jan 1938, Zelina, Croatia. Concert Pianist; Professor of Piano. *Education:* Baccalaureate, Zagreb; Diploma of Piano Professor, Zagreb 1960; Masters Degree, Accademia di Santa Cecilia, Rome, Italy 1967; Degree, Accademia Musicale Chigiana, Sienna, Italy 1966. *Debut:* Sienna, Italy 1960. *Career:* Professor of Piano, Zagreb Music Academy, Skopje Music Academy, TRU Zagreb; Appearances as concert pianist at festivals in Europe and abroad; Teacher, Summer courses, Internationale Camp of Jeunesse Musicale, Grožnjan, Istria; Recitals with orchestras; concerts in most European countries and USA, India, Iran, Pakistan, Syria, Lebanon, Korea and USSR; Concerts: Soloist in Recitals and with Orchestras over 3,000 appearances, last years one intensive activity as a member of a piano trio, Orlando, Zagreb, also Cadenzas for a different piano concertos, K D von, Dittersdorf, D V M Puccini, W.A. Mozart; Numerous radio and television appearances. *Recordings:* New CD recordings for Yugoton, Zagreb Antology of Old and Modern Croatian Piano Music, CD, Mozarts Piano Trios and Quartets; Numerous recordings of classical and modern music.*Publications:* Different Studies on Piano Technique and Interpretation Published in Graz/Austria/for EPTA Dokumentation. *Honours:* Prize of SR of Croatia, Vladimir Nazor 1974; Winner of prizes in numerous National Competitions. *Hobbies:* Conducting orchestras; Composition.*Current Management:* Koncertina Direkciya Zagreb, Kneza Mislava 18, Croatia. *Address:* Basaricekova 3, 41000 Zagreb, Croatia.

KRUGER Anna, b. 1965, USA. Violist. *Education:* Studies at Manhattan School of Music and at Indiana Univerity with James Buswell. *Career:* Former principal of New Jersey Symphony; Co-founder of Lark String Quartet, New York; Recent concert tours to Australia, Taiwan, Hong Kong, China, Germany and Netherlands; US appearances at the Lincoln Center, New York, Kennedy Center, Washington DC, and in Boston, Los Angeles, Philadelphia, St Louis and San Francisco; Repertoire includes quartets by Haydn, Mozart, Beethoven, Schubert, Dvorak, Brahms, Borodin, Bartok, Debussy and Shostakovich. *Honours include:* With Lark Quartet: Gold Medals at 1990 Naumberg and 1991 Shostakovich Competitions; Prizewinner at 1991 London International String Quartet, 1991 Melbourne Chamber Music, 1990 Premio Paulio Borciani, Reggio Emilia, and 1990 Karl Klinger Competition, Munich. *Address:* c/o Sonata (Lark Quartet), 11 Northpark Street, Glasgow G20 7AA, Scotland.

KRUGER Harry, b. 20 July 1929, Atlanta, Georgia, USA. Conductor; Music Professor. m. 21 Aug 1957, 1 son, 2 daughters. *Education:* Studied, Emory University, Atlanta, 1947-49; BM, 1953, Further studies, 1954-55, MME, 1959, New England Conservatory of Music, Boston, Massachusetts. *Career:* Conductor, Arlington Symphony, Massachusetts, 1952-53; Conductor, Atlanta Ballet, 1955-61; Assistant Conductor, Atlanta Symphony, 1955-61; Founding Conductor, Atlanta Community Orchestra, 1957-61; Conductor, Macon Civic Youth Orchestra, 1958-61; Assistant Conductor, Toledo Symphony, 1961-65; Conductor, Bowling Green State University Orchestra, 1961-65; Associate Professor of Music, Columbus College, Columbus, GA, 1965-; Conductor, Columbus (Georgia) Symphony, 1965-87; Conductor, Middle Georgia Symphony, 1977-83; Conductor Emeritus, Columbus Symphony Orchestra, 1987-; Music Director/Conductor, La Grange Symphony Orchestra, La Grange, GA, 1990-; Played flute; Boston Pops Tour Orchestra; Portland (Maine) Symphony; Springfield (Massachusetts) Symphony; Atlanta Symphony. *Recordings:* Various recordings with Bowling Green State University Orchestra and Columbus (Georgia) Symphony. *Publications:* Music Column for Columbus (GA) Ledger, Enquirer Newspaper, 1989-; Host and narrator of a music program on Peach State Public Radio Network, 1988-1990. *Contributions to:* Article in Instrumentalist. *Hobbies:* Swimming; Camping; Reading; Travel. *Address:* 6035 Seaton Drive, Columbus, GA 31909, USA.

KRUGER Rudolf, b. 1917, Berlin, Germany. Conductor. m. Ruth Elizabeth Scallan, 25 Aug 1951, 1 son, 1 daughter. *Education:* Conductor's Diploma with highest honours 1938, State Academy of Music, Vienna, Austria, 1936-38; Studied violin with Stefan Frenkel and Boris Schwartz; Piano with Bruno Eisner; Theory and composition with Berthold Goldschmidt and Eric Zeisl; Conducting with Felix Weingartner, Josef Krips and Julius Pruewer. *Career:* Assistant Conductor, Southern Symphony Orchestra and Columbia Choral Society, Columbia, South Carolina, USA, 1939-42; Assistant Conductor, New Orleans Symphony Orchestra and New Orleans Opera House Association, New Orleans, Louisiana, 1942-45; USA Army, 1945-46; Conductor, Mid-western tour, Chicago Light Opera Company, 1946; Musical Director, Jackson Opera Guild, Mississippi, 1948-51; Musical Director, Mobile Opera Guild, Alabama, 1949-55; Musical Director, City of New Orleans Light Opera Company, 1950; Conductor, newly formed Crescent City Concerts Association, New Orleans, 1954; Director of the Opera Workshop, Texas Christian University, Fort Worth, Texas, 1955; Musical Director and Conductor 1955-58, Musical Director and General Manager 1958-, Fort Worth Opera Association; Musical Director, Fort Worth Symphony Orchestra, 1963-65; Appearances as Guest Conductor including: San Juan Opera Casals Festival, Puerto Rico, 1972; State Opera, Hanover, Germany, 1974; Tehran Opera, Iran, 1976; Philippine Philharmonic Orchestra, Manila, Philippines, 1985. *Address:* 5732 Wessex Avenue, Fort Worth, TX 76133, USA.

KRUMM Philip Edwin, b. 7 Apr 1941, Baltimore, Maryland, USA. Composer. *Education:* Studied Orchestration and Composition with Raymond Moses (student of Casals), 1957-59; Studied with Frank Sturchio (student of Puccini), St Mary's University; Student of Ross Lee Finney, University of Michigan, 1962-64; Student of Karlheinz Stockhausen, University of California, Davis, 1966. *Career:* Produced early concert series of major modern works, McNay Art Institute, San Antonio, 1960-61; Performer/Composer, Once Festivals, Ann Arbor, Michigan, 1962-64; Music Hour, TV with Jerry Hunt, 1964; Sampler, TV Program with Robert Wilson, 1964 and others. *Compositions:* Paragenesis for 2 violins and piano, 1959; Axis; Mumma Mix; Soundtrack score for short film, Angel of God; Music for Clocks, 1962, Once Festival Chamber Orchestra; Concerto for Saxophone, Phil Rehfeldt, 1964; Bass Clarinet and Concerto Performance Martin Walker, 1972; by Scott Vance and Redlands Ensemble, 1978 and 1986; Farewell to L.A. (electronic theatre piece), 1975; Sound Machine ('66) rec. Irida Records, 1979; Secret Pleasures, Dance Suite 1988-89; No Time at All, Electronic-Instrumental Set, 1989; Short Pieces for Electronics & Instruments: Into the Pines, The Gabrieli Thing. *Recordings:* Still in print: Sound Machine, performed by Dallas Chamber Ensemble, Jerry Hunt for Irida Records, 1966. *Publication:* Music Without Notes, 1962. *Hobbies:* Host of Weekly New Music Radio Program. *Address:* 103 Erskine Place, San Antonio, TX 78201, USA.

KRUMMACHER Friedhelm (Gustav-Adolf), b. 22 Jan 1936, Berlin, Germany. Professor. m. Aina Maria Landfeldt, 12 June 1964, 1 son, 1 daughter. *Education:* Abitur, 1954; Musicology, Philosophy, Germanistics studies, Berlin, Marburg, and Uppsala, Sweden; Music Teachers Certificate, 1957; DrPhil, Free University of Berlin, 1964; Habilitation, University of Erlangen-Nurnberg, 1972. *Career:* Assistant, 1965, Private Docent, 1973, Erlangen-Nurnberg University; Professor, Musikhochschule Detmold, 1975; Professor, Christian Albrechts University, Kiel, 1976-; Professor, Director, Musicological Institute, University of Kiel, in charge of Brahms section. *Publications:* Die Uberlieferung..., 1965; Mendelssohn - der Komponist, 1978; Die Choralbearbeitung..., 1978; Mahlers III Symphonie, 1991; Editor: Kieler Schriften zur Musikwissenschaft, Vol 22-40, 1978-91. *Contributions to:* About 95 in Archiv fur Musikwissenschaft, Die Musikforschung, Kongressberichte, Festschriften. *Memberships:* Vetenskapssocietet Lund, Sweden, 1975; Jungius-

Gesellschaft der Wissenschaften, Hamburg, 1990. *Address:* Wippen 1, D-2300 Kiel 1, Germany.

KRUMMEL D(onald) W(illiam), b. 12 July 1929, Sioux City, Iowa, USA. Music Librarian; Bibliographer. *Education:* Studied at the University of Michigan, PhD in library science 1958. *Career:* Taught at University of Michigan, 1952-56; Reference librarian in the music division of the Library of Congress, 1956-61; Head of reference department, then associate librarian at New berry Library, Chicago, 1962-70; Professor of library science and music, University of Illinois, 1970; Director of MLA project leading to Resources of American Music History, 1981; President of the American Library Association, 1981-83. *Publications include:* Bibliotheca Bolduaniana: a Renaissance Music Bibliography 1972; Guide for Dating Early Published Music 1974; Early Music Printing, 1533-1700, 1975; Newberry Library, Chicago: Bibliographical Inventory to the Early Music 1976 (editor). *Address:* Music Library, Music Building, University of Illinois at Urbana-Champaign, Urbana, IL 61801, USA.

KRUPOWICZ Stanislaw, b. 25 Nov 1952, Grodno, Poland. Composer. Single. *Education:* Master of Mathematics, University of Warsaw, 1976; Master of Arts, Warsaw Academy of Music, 1981; Doctor of Musical Arts, Stanford University, USA, 1988. *Debut:* Warsaw Autumn 1979. *Career:* Lecturer, Warsaw Academy of Music, 1981; Co-Founder, Independent Electro-Acoustic Music Studio, Warsaw, 1982; Visiting Researcher 1988-90, Teaching Assistant, Instructor, 1990, Stanford University, USA; Co-Founder, Tonus Finalis Ensemble, 1990; Post-doctoral Fellowship, University of Glasgow, 1991. *Compositions:* Music for S, 1984; Thus Spake Bosch, 1985; Farewell, Variations on a Theme by Mozart, 1987; Concerto for Sax and Computers, 1988; Only Beatrice, 1989; Tempo 72, 1981; Smoking Room Blues, 1991. *Recordings:* For Polskie Nagrania, Stanford University Press, Wergo, Polish Radio. *Contributions to:* Articles on computer music for Ruch Muzyczny Bi-weekly, Stanford University Research Report. Alexander Borodin Foundation Award, Warsaw, 1989 and 1990. *Hobbies:* Skiing; Literature; History. *Address:* Music Department, University of Glasgow, 14 University Gardens, Glasgow, G12 8QH, Scotland.

KRUTIKOV Mikhail, b. 23 Aug 1958, Moscow, Russia. Singer (Bass). *Education:* Studies at Moscow State Conservatory and the Opera Studio of Bolshoi Opera, 1982-85; Further studies with Evgeni Nesterenko. *Career:* Appearances with Bolshoi Opera, 1985-, as Boris Godunov, Pimen, Mephistopheles, Basilio, Mendosa in Prokofiev's The Duenna and Dunua in The Maid of Orleans by Tchaikovsky; Sang in La Straniera and La cena delle Beffe at Wexford Festival, and with the Bolshoi Company on tour to UK, 1990; Season 1991-92 as the Inquisitor in Prokofiev's The Fiery Angel at the Prom Concerts, London, The Love for Three Oranges at Florence, the Commendatore in Dargomizhky's Stone Guest at Salzburg and as King Philip in Don Carlos in Deutsche Oper Berlin; Concert engagements at Elizabeth Hall, London, Shostakovich's 14th Symphony in Vancouver and Lausanne, the Verdi Requiem and Tchaikovsky's Moscow Cantata at the Salle Pleyel, Prokofiev's Ivan the Terrible in Rome and Elijah at Dusseldorf. *Recordings include:* Holofernes in Serov's Judith, Saison Russe. *Address:* Atholl Still Ltd, Greystoke House, 80-86 Westrow Street, London SE19 3AF, England.

KRUYSEN (Rene) Bernard, b. 28 Mar 1933, Montreux, Switzerland. Singer (Baritone). *Education:* Studied at the Hague Conservatory from 1953 and with Pierre Bernac. *Career:* Many tours of Europe and the USA in German Lieder and French chansons; Repertoire includes music by Bach, Monteverdi, Schumann, Mussorgsky, Debussy, Poulenc, Faure and Ravel; Recital partnerships with Noel Lee, Hans Henkemans, Paul Niessing and Poulenc; Operatic appearances in Pagliacci and Halka. *Recordings include:* Fauré's Requiem (Philips); Bach Cantatas (Telefunken); Song albums for Westminster, Eurodisc, Epic and Valois. *Honours include:* Prize winner, Gabriel Faure Competition; International Competition of Bois-le-Duc 1958; Grand Prix du Disque 1962, for Debussy songs. *Address:* c/o Royal Conservatory of Music and Dance, Juliana van Stolberglaan 1, 2595 CA Den Haag.

KUBELIK Rafael Jeronym, b. 29 June 1914, Bychory, Nr Prague, Czechoslovakia. Conductor; Composer. m. (1) Ludmila Bertlova, 1942, deceased, 1 son, (2) Elsie Morison, 1963. *Education:* Absolutorium, Prague Conservatory for Music. *Career:* Conductor, 1936, Musical Director, 1941-48, Czech Philharmonic Orchestra; Musical Director, National Opera, Brno, 1939; Musical Director, Chicago Symphony Orchestra, USA, 1950-53; Musical Director, Covent Garden Opera, London, England, 1955-58, giving the British premieres of Janáček's Jenůfa, 1956, and Berlioz' Les Troyens, 1957; Musical Director, Symphony Orchestra, Bavarian Radio, Munich, Germany, 1961-79; Musical Director, Metropolitan Opera, New York, USA, 1973-74; Returned to Czechoslovakia 1990, to conduct performances of Smetana's Má Vlast. *Compositions:* 5 operas; 2 symponies; Symphony in 1 movement; Orphikon, symphony for orchestra; Sequences for orchestra; Peripeteia for organ and orchestra; Invocation Cantata; Cantata without words for chorus and orchestra; 6 string quartets; Trio Concertante; Violin concerto; Cello concerto; Quattro formi per archi; Songs; Piano and violin music. *Recordings:* Beethoven's Symphonies (Deutsche Grammophon); Schoenberg's Gurrelieder; Mahler's Symphonies, with the Bavarian Radio Orchestra; Janáček's Glagolitic Mass, Taras Bulba, Sinfonietta and Diary of One who Disappeared; Pfitzner's Palestrina; Lohengrin and the Siegfried Idyll, Schoenberg's Piano Concerto (Brendel) and Violin Concerto (Szeryng); Mozart's Haffner Serenade, Late Symphonies and Masses K220 and K317; Dvořák Symphonic Poems and Serenade in E; Má Vlast. *Honours:* Grosses Bundesverdienstkreuz, Federal Republic of Germany; Bavarian Order of Merit. *Address:* Im Sand, CH 6047 Kastanienbaum, Switzerland.

KUBERA Joseph, b. 25 May 1949, Buffalo, New York, USA. Pianist. *Education:* Studied at the Community Music School in Buffalo and with Waletr Hautzig at the Peabody Conservatory, MA, 1970. *Career:* Has given performances of works by Howard Riley, John Cage, Tcherepnin and Carson Kievman; Member of the SEM Ensemble, 1972; New Music Ensemble of the San Francisco Conservatory, 1972-74; Steve Reich and Musicians, 1979; Tours of America with the Merce Cunningham Dance Company, 1977-80; Performances of music by Josef Matthias Hauer, originator of a twelve-note theory of composition. *Recordings include:* Hauer's Atonale Musik Op 20 (Arch Records). *Honours include:* Fellowship from the Center for the Creative and Performing Arts, 1974-76; NEA grant to prepare for performance Music of Changes by John cage, 1981.

KUBIAK Teresa, b. 26 Dec 1937, Lodz, Poland. Singer (Soprano). *Education:* Studied at the Lodz Music Academy with Olga Olgina. *Debut:* Lodz 1965, as Halka in the opera by Moniusko. *Career:* Sang Micaela in Carmen 1967; Appeared in the 1969 premiere of The Story of St John and Herod by Twardowski; US debut Carnegie Hall 1970, as Shulamith in Goldmark's Die Königin von Saba; Glyndebourne Festival 1971, as Lisa in The Queen of Spades and Juno in La Calisto by Cavalli-Leppard; Covent Garden 1972, as Madama Butterfly; Metropolitan Opera from 1973, as Lisa, Jenůfa, Giorgietta in Il Tabarro, Tosca and Elisabeth in Tannhäuser; Appearances in San Francisco, Chicago, Houston, Miami, Leipzig, Prague, Venice, Barcelona and Lisbon; Other roles include Aida, Euryanthe, Senta, Tatiana, Tosca and Ellen Orford. *Recordings include:* La Calisto, Eugene Onegin (Decca); Euryanthe (MRF). *Address:* Stafford Law Associates, 26 Mayfield Road, Weybridge, Surrey KT13 8XB, England.

KUBICA Vaclav, b. 20 May 1926, Prague, Czechoslovakia, dec. 15 May 1992. Musician (Clarinettist); Music Scientist (Musicologist). m. Bozena

Kotlandova, 10 Sept 1949. *Education:* Academy of Economics; Studied Clarinet, Prague Conservatoire; Philosophical studies, 1948-53, PhD, 1953, Charles University, Prague. *Career:* Member of Prague National Theatre Orchestra, 1949-60; Scientific Worker, Náprstek Museum, 1970 to 1986; Cultural activities, Morocco, 1957-59; Professor, Institute of Fine Arts, Iraq, 1960-68; Institut National de Musique, Algeria, 1973-75; Organised exhibitions at Naprstek Museum, Prague: The musical instruments of Northern Africa and the Arabic Orient, 1970; The Great Feast, 1973; The Rhythm of Africa, 1979. *Recordings:* Musique populaire traditionnelle d'Iraq, collection of music recordings 1964-68; The Music of Arabic Orient and Northern Africa, 4 LP records, album of authentic recordings, 1976. *Publications:* Arabic Folk Music in Iraq, 1966; Klassische Tradition und Volkstradition der Arabischen Musik im Irak, 1975; The Gipsy Music of Iraq, 1975; La Quasba Algerienne et sa musique, 1980; Contribution to Encyclopedie des instruments de musique, 1980; Les flutes de Pan en Amerique du Sud, 1981; Safari (to) African Culture, 1983. *Membership:* Union of Czech Composers and Concert Artists, Music Science (Musicology) Section.

KUBICKA Vitazoslav, b. 11 Oct 1953, Bratislava, Czechoslovakia. Composer; Broadcasting editor music; Dramaturgist. m. Gabriela Jurolekova, 2 July 1988. 1 son, 1 daughter. *Education:* Composition, University of Music, Bratislava. *Debut:* Rostrum of Composers, UNESCO, Paris, 1982. *Career:* Scenic Music for Radio, 130; Television, 20; Films, 12. *Compositions include:* Orchestral: Dramatic Overture for Large Orchestra, 1980; Concerto for Piano and Orchestra, 1984; Maturing, Overture for Orchestra, 1984; Fantasy for Violoncello and Large Orchestra, 1985; Chamber Opuses: Fantasy for Flute and Piano, 1979; Quintet for Clarinet, Violin, Viola, Violoncello and Piano, 1982; Winter, Sonata for Piano, 1986; Choral: Fugue for Children's Choir, 1982; Electroacoustic: Dedicated to Mussorgski, 1981; Satyr and Nymph, 1985; For Children and Youth: Five Stories for Piano, 1982, 1985, *Honours:* Jan Levoslav Bella Prize, Slovak Music Fund Bratislava, 1988; Priz critique Radiomagazin Bratislava, 1989. *Membership:* Union of Slovak Composer. *Hobbies:* Nature; Tourism. *Address:* Drotarska 9, 811 02 Bratislava, Slovakia.

KUBIK Gerhard, b. 10 Dec 1934, Vienna, Austria. Ethnologist. *Education:* Studied Court Music of Buganda, Kampala, with court musician Evaristo Muyinda, 1959-63; PhD, 1971, Habilitation, 1980, University of Vienna. *Career:* Extensive fieldwork, Uganda, Tanzania, Zambia, Malawi, Angola, Central African Republic, Togo, Cameroun, 1959-, Brazil, 1974-; Major interest in expressive culture of Africa and the Diaspora, including music/dance; Teacher, University of Vienna (Institutes of Ethnology, Musicology, Africanistics); Guest lectures, 33 countries; Regular university visits, Africa, South America and USA. *Recordings:* The Kachamba Brothers' Band, 1972; Donald Kachamba's Kwela Band 1978, 1978; Donald Kachamba's Band. Simanje and Kwela from Malawi, 1979; Donald Kachamba's Kwela Music; Malawi Twist, film, 1978; Donald Kachamba's Kwela Music: Simanje-manje, Chachacha, 1978. *Publications include:* Angolan traits in Black music, games and dances of Brazil, 1979; Musikgeschichte in Bildern: Ostafrika, 1982; Musikgeschichte in Bildern: Westafrika, 1989; Das Khoisan-Erbe im Süden von Angola. Bewegungsformen, Bogenharmonik und tonale Ordnung in der Musik der Kung' und benachbarter Bantu-Population, in Musikkulturen in Afrika, 1987; Makisi-Nyau-Mapiko Maskentraditionen im Bantu-sprachigen Afrika, München: Trickster, 1992. *Contributions to:* Encyclopaedia Britannica, 1974, 1989; Cultural Atlas of Africa, 1981; New Grove Dictionary of Music and Musicians, 1981; Numerous articles on African and Brazilian music culture in professional journals. *Address:* Burghardtgasse 6/9. A-1200 Vienna, Austria.

KUBIK Ladislav, b. 26 Aug 1946, Prague,

Czechoslovakia. Composer. m. Natalie Bartosevicová, 7 Nov 1974, 1 son, 1 daughter. *Education:* Composition, 1970, Theory of Music, 1972, PhD, 1981, Prague Academy of Music. *Career:* Music Director, Czechoslovak Radio Prague, 1979-83; General Secretary, Union of Czech Composers and Concert Artists, 1983-. *Compositions:* Symphonic Works: Symphony, 1970; Drammatic Toccata, 1972; Concerto for piano and orchestra, 1974; Hommage a Majakowski, 1976; Concerto for violin and orchestra, 1980; Choral Works: Songs of Hope, 1982; Chamber-Cantat: Lament of a Warrior's Wife, 1974; Radio Opera: Solaris, 1975; Ballet: Song of Man, 1984; Vocal Symphony Works: February, 1973; Wolkeriana, 1982; To the Earth of Future, 1985; Songs with orchestra: Words; Chamber Music: 2 string quartets, 1981, 1986; Trio Concertante, 1983; Duo Concertante. *Recordings:* 15 works recorded on record and numerous in Czechoslovak and foreign radio broadcasts. *Current Management:* Charles University, Prague. *Address:* Na Brezince 6, 150 00 Praha 5, Czech Republic.

KUBIK Reinhold, b. 22 Mar 1942, Vienna, Austria. Musicologist. 1 son, 1 daughter. *Education:* Abitur, Humanistic College, Vienna II, 1960; PhD, University Erlangen-Nuremberg, Federal Republic of Germany, 1980; Studied Piano, Composition, Conducting with Hans Swarowsky, Hochschule für Musik, Vienna. *Career:* Conductor, Deutsche Oper am Rhein, Dusseldorf (Duisburg) and many European cities including Lille, Barcelona, Ljubljana, 1966-74; Pianist; Composer; Choirmaster; Lecturer, 1980; Proprietor, Hanssler Musik Verlag, Kirchheim, Federal Republic of Germany, 1989-; Visiting Professor, Yale University, USA, 1987-1991; Production Manager at Universal Editon, Vienna, since 1992; Chief editor of Gustav Mahler Gesamtausgabe, and of Wiener Urtext Edition. *Publications:* Handels Rinaldo, 1980; About 120 editions including 80 cantatas by J.S.Bach (Hanssler), EdM 96, 106 and 110, Schubert, Lazarus (Neue Schubert Ausgabe II/10). *Contributions to:* Festschrift Arnold Feil, 1985; KB Stuttgart, 1985; Festschrift Martin Ruhnke, 1986; Veroffentlichungen der International. Handel-Akademie Karlsruhe, Vols 2, 3 and 4, 1988; Handel-Symposium Halle, 1989. *Address:* A-1090 Wien, Liechtenstein Strasse 39/6, Germany.

KUBIZEK Augustin, b. 15 Oct 1918, Vienna, Austria. Professor of Music; Composer. m. Alina Gunia, 5 Feb 1992. 2 sons, 2 daughters. *Education:* Teachers' Training College, 5 years; State Diploma in Singing, 1949; Choral and Orchestral Conducting and Composition, 1955-56. *Career:* Professor, Academy of Music, Vienna, 1956; University Professor, 1979; Professor Emeritus, 1985. *Compositions:* Over 200 works including sacred choral works: Neue Messe, 1970; St Michael-Messe, 1970; Missa a Cappella, 1983; Jakobs Stern, 1985; Motetten: Memento Homo; Psalmen-Motetten, Div Zyklen; Secular works: Symphonic works; Instrumental concerti for clarinet, violoncello, viola and others; Opera: Nathan der Weise, 1994; Oratorios: Stationen; Hadmar der Kuenringer; Works for voice and instruments; Chamber music. *Recordings:* Numerous works recorded on disc and radio.. *Address:* Schoenburgstrasse 13/27, A-1040 Vienna, Austria.

KUBO Yoko, b. 5 Dec 1956, Nishinomiya, Japan. Composer; Pianist; College Lecturer. *Education:* BA, 1979, MA, 1981, Osaka College of Music; Diplome d'Etudes Approfondies, University of Paris, France, 1985. *Debut:* 1979. *Career:* Many concerts of her compositions, Japan and Europe, 1979-; Lecturer, Osaka College of Music, 1981-; Associate, Institut Recherche Coordination Acoustique/Musique, Paris, France, 1984-. *Compositions:* La Sensation de Vingtième Siecle, 12 percussionists, 1977; Collage, orchestra, 1978; Objet, 2 pianos and percussions, 1979; Play, violin, violoncello, piano, 1979; Crossword, piano, 1980; Mon parc, string orchestra, 1980; Quatuor à Cordes No 2, 1980; Concerto pour Violon No 1, 1981; Puzzle, 3 marimbas, 1981; On the tree, soprano, 8 voices, piano, 1981; Chikyu ni hajimete yuki ga futta hi no koto, soprano, 8 voices, piano, 1981; Quatuor à Cordes No 3, 1981; Concerto pour Orgue, 4 Cuivres et Percussions, 1981; Livre Illustré des chats, string orchestra, 1982; . . .SONG. . . , 5 voices and pinao, 1982; Quatuor á Cordes, No 4, 1982; Paysage, flute, percussion, piano, 1983; Quatuor pour Flûte, Hautbois, Violon et Violoncelle, 1983; Quintette pour Piano No 1, 1983; Marche du roi (extract from Le roi nu), string orchestra, 1984; Espace, 11 players, 1985; Vision, piano, 1987; Concerto pour 7 Interprètes, 1987. *Address:* No 9-25 2-chome, Nigawa-cho Nishinomiya-shi, Hyogo-ken, Japan.

KUCEROVA Marie, b. 7 Mar 1959, Brno, Czech Republic. Musicologist; Organiser; Television Producer. m. Radim Kucera, 6 Dec 1980, 1 son, 1 daughter. *Education:* Studied History, History of Music, Musicology, Masaryk University, Brno. *Career includes:* Currently Head of Editing of Musical Programmes, Czech Television, Brno. *Contributions:* La tablature d'epinette de S Mareschall, in Revue Musicale de Suisse Romande; Barbara Celerent...Jakoba Handla, in Opus Musicum. *Memberships:* Janáček Gesellschaft; Ancient Music Society. *Hobby:* Con Stile Agency (baroque music) Festival. *Address:* Popelakova 14, 62800 Brno, Czech Republic.

KUCHTA Gladys, b. 16 June 1923, Chikopee, Massachusetts, USA. Singer (Soprano). *Education:* Studied at Mannes College and the Juilliard School, New York; Further study in Italy. *Debut:* Florence 1951, as Donna Elvira in Don Giovanni. *Career:* Sang at Flensburg from 1953, debut as Leonore in Fidelio; Stuttgart Staatsoper as Tosca; Vienna Staatsoper as Elektra; Sang in Berlin from 1958, notably at the Deutsche Oper; Hamburg Staatsoper as Isolde and in other operas by Wagner; Metropolitan Opera 1961, as Chrysothemis in Elektra; Bayreuth Festival 1968, Sieglinde in Die Walküre; Guest at the Paris Opéra 1972, as the Empress in Die Frau ohne Schatten; Guest appearances in London, Buenos Aires, San Francisco, Tokyo, Dusseldorf and Edinburgh; Retired from stage 1975 and taught in Dusseldorf. *Address:* c/o Staatliche Hochschule für Musik Rheinland, Robert Schumann Institut, Fisherstrasse 110, D-4000 Dusseldorf, Germany.

KUDRIAVCHENKO Katerina, b. 2 Mar 1958, Karpinsk, Sverdlovskaya, Russia. Singer (Soprano). m. Paolo Kudriavchenko. *Education:* Graduated Tchaikovsky Conservatoire, Moscow, 1985. *Career:* Member of Bolshoi Opera, 1986-, as Iolanta, Tatiana, Agnes Sorell in The Maid of Orleans, Marfa in The Tsar's Bride, Gilda, Antonida in A Life for the Tsar, Louisa, Prokofiev's The Duenna, Rachmaninov's Francesca, Violetta, Mimi, Liu and Oxsana in Rimsky's Christmas Eve; Western debut as Iolanta at La Scala, 1989; Season 1990-91 with Bolshoi Opera on tour to Spain, Italy, USA (Metropolitan), Japan and Glasgow, Scotland; Freelance artist debut as Tatiana for New Israel Opera Company at Tel Aviv, 1992; Season 1992-93 as Mimi with Scottish Opera, Liu and Titania at the Bolshoi. *Honours include:* Gold Medallist, Madame Butterfly Competition, Miami, 1990. *Address:* c/o Athole Still Ltd, 80-86 Westow Street, London SE19 3AF, England.

KUDRIAVCHENKO Paolo, b. 12 Aug 1952, Odessa, Crimea, Russia. Singer (Tenor). m. Katerina Kudriavchenko. *Education:* Studied at Tchaikovsky Conservatory, Odessa. *Career:* Sang first with Odessa Opera, then Kiev Opera; Bolshoi Opera, Moscow, 1984-, in Rimsky's Invisible City of Kitezh and as Canio, Turiddu, Dimitri in Boris Godunov, Don José and Jeromir in Mlada; Sang Sobinin in A Life for the Tsar with the Bolshoi Company at La Scala and made US debut, 1989, as Manrico for Greter Miami Opera (repeated for Omaha Opera, 1991); Royal Opera House, Covent Garden, 1990-91, as Turiddu and Dimitri; Season 1991-92 as Turiddu at Munich Staatsoper and as Ernani for Welsh National Opera, followed by Manrico for Scottish Opera, Ishmaele in Nabucco at Bregenz Festival, 1993, and Canio at Rouen; Engaged for season 1993-94 as Calaf and Radames at the Bolshoi; Many concert appearances.

Address: c/o Athole Still Ltd, 80-86 Westow Street, London SE19 3AF, England.

KUEBLER David, b. 23 July 1947, Detroit, Michigan, USA. Singer (Tenor). *Education:* Studied with Thomas Peck in Chicago and Audrey Field in London. *Career:* Sang in the chorus of the Chicago Opera; Solo career with the Santa Fe Opera from 1972; European debut Berne Opera 1974, as Tamino; Sang Mozart and bel canto roles with Cologne Opera; Glyndebourne Festival, 1976, as Ferrando in Così fan Tutte; Metropolitan Opera from 1979; Bayreuth Festival, 1980-82, as the Steersman in Der fliegende Holländer; Santa Fe Opera, 1984, in We Come to the River by Henze; Other roles include Don Ottavio, Rodolfo, Pinkerton, Lionel (Martha), Jacquino in Fidelio, Paolino in Il Matrimonio Segreto and Giannetto in La Gazza Ladra; Donizetti's Ernesto and Nemorino; Glyndebourne, 1987-1990, Strauss's Flamand and Matteo; Schwetzingen Festival, 1988, as Rossini's Almaviva (1989 in La Cambiale di Matrimonio); sang Don Ottavio in Rome and Madrid, 1989; Schwetzingen 1990 as Doric in Rossini's La Scala di Seta; sang in the Spectre's Bride by Dvořák at the 1991 Promenade Concerts, London; Sang the Berlioz Faust at Wellington and Bregenz, 1992. *Recordings include:* Mitridate re di Ponto by Mozart (Deutsche Grammophon); Fidelio (Decca); Videos of La Scala de Seta (Warner Classics) and Idomeneo, as Idamante (Virgin). *Address:* 165 West 57th Street, New York, NY 10019, USA.

KUEN Paul, b. 8 Apr 1910, Sulzberg, Kempten, Germany. Singer (Tenor). *Education:* Studied with Heinrich Knote and Adalbert Ebner in Munich. *Debut:* Konstanz 1933. *Career:* Sang first at opera houses in Bamberg, Freiburg and Nuremberg, 1944-47; Munich Staatsoper from 1947, in character roles; Bayreuth Festival 1951-57, as Mime in Der Ring des Nibelungen; also sang Mime in Holland, Belgium, Frnce, Italy, Spain and South America; Royal Opera House, Covent Garden, 1953; Metropolitan Opera, 1961-62. *Recordings:* Der Freischütz, Le Nozze di Figaro, Oedipus Rex (Deutsche Grammophon); Die Kluge and Der Mond by Orff (Columbia); Mime in Siegfried, conducted by Clemens Krauss, Bayreuth, 1953 (Foyer). *Address:* c/o Bayerische Staatsoper, Postfach 745, D-8000 Munich 1, Germany.

KUENTZ Paul, b. 4 May 1930, Mulhouse, France. Conductor. m. Monique Frasca-Colombier 1956. *Education:* Studied at the Paris Conservatoire, 1947-50, with Noel Gallon, Georges Hugon and Eugene Bigot. *Career:* Founded the Paul Kuentz Chamber Orchestra, 1951; many tours of Europe and the USA, including the orchestrak works of Bach at Saint-Severin and concert at Carnegie Hall, 1968; Frequent performances of French music, including premieres of works by P M Dubois, J Casterede and J Charpentier; Founded Paul Kuentz Chorus, 1972. *Recordings include:* Bach's Orchestral Suites, Mass in B Minor and Musikalisches Opfer; Vivaldi's Four Seasons, and other concertos; Flute concertos by Haydn, Blavet, Mozart, Leclair and Pergolesi; Music by Delalande, Mouret, Gabrieli and Gluck; Mozart's Concerto K299, Requiem, Bastien und Bastienne and Church Sonatas; Harp concertos by Handel, Albrechtsberger, Boieldieu, Wagenseil and Dittersdorf; Haydn Symphonies nos 85 and 101 (EMI); Other labels include Decca and Deutsche Grammophon.

KUERTI Anton Emil, b. Vienna, 1938. Pianist; Composer. m. Kristine Bogyo, 13 Sept 1973, 2 sons. *Education:* BM, Cleveland Institute of Music; Diploma, Curtis Institute, 1959; PhD (Hon.) York University, 1985, Laurentian University, 1985. *Career:* Soloist, New York Philharmonic, Cleveland Orchestra, Detroit Symphony, Philadelphia Orchestra, Buffalo Philarmonic, San Francisco Symphony, Denver Symphony; Over 25 appearances with Toronto Symphony and National Arts Centre Orchestra (Ottawa), Dresden Staatskapelle, Leipzig Gewandhaus,London Symphony; Tours world-wide including Soviet Union, Far East, Australia, Latin America; Numerous TV appearances, radio broadcasts; Founder, Festival of Sound, Parry Sound, Ontario.

Compositions: Linden Suite for Piano, 1970; String Quartet, 1972; Violin Sonata and Symphony Epomeo, 1975; Piano Man Suite and Piano Concerto, 1985; Clarinet Trio, 1989; Complete Schubert Sonatas. *Recordings:* Recordings include complete cycle of Beethoven Sonatas and Concerti; Mendelssohn Piano Concerti.*Honour:* Leventritt Award, 1957. *Memberships:* War Resisters League; Amnesty International; Canadian Scientists and Scholars.*Current Management:* Concertmasters Incorporated, 22 Linden Street, Toronto, M4Y 1V6. *Address:* 20 Linden Street, Toronto, Ontario, Canada M4Y 1V6.

KUHLMANN Kathleen, b. 7 Dec 1950, San Francisco, California, USA. Singer (Mezzo-Soprano). *Education:* Studied at the Opera School of the Lyric Opera Chicago. *Career:* Sang in Chicago from 1979, debut as Maddalena in Rigoletto; Performance of Carmen in open air auditorium; La Scala Milan 1980, as Meg Page in Falstaff; Cologne Opera 1982, as Charlotte and Rosina; British debut Covent Garden 1982, as Ino and Juno in a new production of Semele; Glyndebourne Festival 1983-85, as Cenerentola; Other Rossini roles include Arsace in Semiramide (Parma, Bilbao, Bonn, Naples, Vienna), Tancredi at the 1986 Wexford Festival, Andromace in Ermione (Naples), Fallerio in Bianca e Falliero (Miami) and Isabella in L'Italiana in Algeri (Pisa); Has sung Carmen with Australian Opera and in Montreal and Tel Aviv; Metropolitan Opera debut 1989, as Charlotte in Werther; Salzburg Festival 1985, as Penelope in the Henze realization of Il Ritorno d'Ulisse by Monteverdi; Has returned to Covent Garden as Rosina (1986) and in Semele; sang at Parma 1987, as Orpheus and in La Donna del Lago, Stuttgart 1989 as Cenerentola; San Francisco 1989, as Alcina in Vivaldi's Orlando Furioso, Geneva 1990 as Bradamante in Alcina; Munich Festival 1990, as Arsace in Semiramide (concert); Beethoven's Ninth, Proms 1991; Sang Carmen and Bradamante at Covent Garden, 1991-92; Season 1992 as Cenerentola at the Semper Oper Dresden; Malcolm in La Donna del Lago at the Concertgebouw; Sang in Rossini's Ermione as Andromaca, San Francisco; BBC Proms, Rossini arias; Concert, Seville; Recital, Purcell Room London; Moscow, Concert of Nations in Red Square; Rossini Gala from Lincoln Centre, New York; Carmen, Cologne; Vienna Philharmonic, Brahms Alto Rhapsody; Season 1993: Alcina Covent Garden; Carmen, Barcelona; L'Incoronazione di Poppea, Schwetzingen & Cologne; Dusseldorf Symphony, Stabat Mater; L'Italiana in Algeri, Cologne; ZDF Berlin, Wesendoncklieder; Beethoven 9, Hamburg. *Recordings include:* Video of La Cenerentola, from Glyndebourne. *Address:* c/o Haydn Rawstron, International Management, PO Box 654, London, SE26 4DZ, England.

KUHN Gustav, b. 28 Aug 1947, Turrach, nr Salzburg. Conductor. *Education:* Studied at the Salburg Mozarteum and in Vienna with Karajan, Bruno Maderna and Hans Swarowsky. *Career:* Conducted at the Turkish State Opera at Istanbul 1970-73, debut with Fidelio, Artistic Director Netherlands Opera 1974-75, first conductor at the Dortmund Opera 1975-77; Conducted at the Vienna Staatsoper from 1977, debut with Elektra; Conducted Mozart's Die Entführung aus dem Serail at Glyndebourne 1980, Don Giovanni at Covent Garden 1981; Music Director at Berne Opera 1979-83, Bonn Opera 1982-85; Conducted Tannhäuser at La Scala 1984 and has worked at the Paris Opera, the Lyric Opera of Chicago and the San Carlo, Naples; Artistic Director of Rome Opera from 1986; Conducted the revival of Rossini's Ermione at Pesaro, 1987, and the premiere of Salvatore Gioliano by Lorenzo Ferrero, 1986; Has staged productions of Der fliegende Holländer in Trieste and Parsifal in Naples; Conducted Il Trovatore and Cosí fan Tutte at Macerata, 1990; Produced and conducted La Bohème at Naples, 1992; La Clemenza di Tito at the Salzburg Festival, La Traviata at Macerata and Don Carlos at the Verona Arena, 1992; Festival engagements at Munich and Salzburg. *Recordings:* Otello, with the Tokyo Philharmonic (Koch Schwann). *Address:* c/o Kaye Artists Management, Barratt House, 7 Chertsey Road, Woking GV21 5AB, England.

KUHN Pamela, b. 1960, Oregon, USA. Singer (Soprano). *Education:* Bachelor of Music University of Oregon, Master of Music University of Southern California with Gwendolyn Koldofsky and Margaret Schaper. Debut: London, Wigmore Hall with Graham Johnson, 1984. *Career:* Recitals at the Purcell Room with Stephen Wilder, Stephen Coombs and Geoffrey Parsons; Isle of Man Festival with Roger Steptoe; Oratorio includes Rossini Petite Messe Solennelle at Queen Elizabeth Hall, Verdi Requiem at Fairfield Halls, Dartington (Diego Masson), Oregon Bach Festival (Helmut Rilling), Penderecki Polish Requiem at Oregon Bach Festival (Penderecki), Brahms Requiem at the Royal Festival Hall and in the USA, Beethoven Missa Solemnis in Lugano, Switzerland, Janáček Glagolitic Mass at Salisbury Cathedral; Opera: Ariadne at Dartington, Aida with Florentine Opera in Milwaukee, Rezia with Scottish Opera at La Fenice, Venice, soloist in Oberon conducted by Seiji Ozawa at Tanglewood, Edinburgh Festival and Frankfurt Alte Oper, High Priestess with Scottish Opera; Other roles include Micaela, Tosca, Amelia and Sieglinde; Further concert repertory includes operatic evenings with City of Birmingham Symphony Orchestra, Southampton Symphony and Ernest Read Symphony at the Barbican, Shostakovich Symphony 14 with Mark Wigglesworth at St John's Smith Square and Four Last Songs in Nottingham. *Address:* Lombardo Associates, 61 West 62nd, Suite 6F, New York, NY 10023, USA.

KUHSE Hanne-Lore, b. 28 March 1925, Schwann, Mecklenburg, Germany. Singer (Soprano). *Education:* Studied with Charlotte Menzel in Rostock, at the Stern Conservatory, Berlin, and with Paul Lohmann in Potsdam. *Debut:* Gera 1951, as Leonore in Fidelio. *Career:* Sang at the Staatstheater Schwerin, 1952-59, Leipzig from 1959; Member of the Staatsoper Berlin from 1963; Guest appearances in Dresden, Budapest, Paris, Moscow, Prague, Cologne, Hamburg and Bayreuth; US debut 1967, as Isolde at Philadelphia; London debut Albert Hall 1967; Philharmonic Hall New York 1967, in the US premiere of Turandot by Busoni; London 1973, as Mita in the British premiere of Der Friedensengel by Siegfried Wagner; Other roles include the Queen of Night, Donna Anna, Lady Macbeth, Tosca, Senta, Venus, Brünnhilde, the Marschallin, Marie in Wozzeck, Kundry, Aida, Abigaille and Ariadne; Guest Professor at the Musikhochschule Weimar 1973; Professor at the Musikhochschue Berlin from 1974. *Recordings:* Radamisto by Handel; La Forza del Destino; Der fliegende Holländer; Tiefland; Die Zauberflöte. *Address:* c/o Deutsche Hochschule für Musik, Otto Grotewohlstrasse 19, D-108 Berlin, Germany.

KUIJKEN Barthold, b. 8 March 1949, Dilbeek, Brussels, Belgium. Flautist; Recorder Player; Conductor. *Education:* Studied at the conservatories of Bruges, Brussels and the Hague, with Frans Vester and Frans Brueggen; Self taught on the Baroque flute. *Career:* Concerts in Europe, Australia, Japan and the USA with his brothers, Lucy van Dael, René Jacobs, Frans Brueggen, Gustav Leonhardt, the Parnassus Ensemble, La Petite Bande and the Collegium Aureum; Teacher of Baroque flute at the the Hague Conservatory and the Brussels Conservatory; repertoire includes music by Telemann, Handel, Haydn, Bach and Mozart; Took part in the Towards Bach concert series on the South Bank, London, August 1989. *Recordings include:* Leclair Flute Sonatas, Telemann 12 Fantasies for transverse Flute and German Chamber Music (Accent). *Address:* c/o Allied Artists Agency, 42 Montpelier Square, London, SW7 1J2, England.

KUIJKEN Sigiswald, b. 16 Feb 1944, Dilbeek, near Brussels, Belgium. Violinist; Violin Player; Conductor. *Education:* Studied at Bruges Conservatory from 1952; Conservatoire Royale Brussels from 1960 under M. Raskin; Self-taught on Baroque violin. *Career:* Began to re-establish old technique of violin playing in 1969; Played in the avant-garde group Musique Nouvelle until 1974, and in the Alarius Ensemble 1964-72; Teacher of Baroque violin at the Hague Conservatory from 1971; Founder of the Baroque orchestra La Petite Bande 1972;

Tours of Europe, the USA, Australia and Japan in chamber music and solo programmes; Debut concert with the orchestra of the Age of Enlightenment 1986, Elizabeth Hall London; Collaborations for chamber music mainly with his brothers Barthold and Wieland and Robert Kohnen, as well as Gustav Leonhardt; Founded the Kuijken String Quartet 1986, specializing in Haydn and Mozart; Co-Artistic Director of the Towards Bach concert series on South Bank, London, August 1989; Conducted La Petite Bande in Haydn's L'Infedeltà Delusa at Antwerp, 1990. *Recordings include:* Music by Lully, Rameau (Zoroastre), Muffat, Corelli, Vivaldi, Handel (Partenope and Alessandro), Haydn (Creation, Symphonies), Mozart (Requiem, Davidde Penitente) and Gluck with La Petite Bande; Bach Sonatas for violin and harpsichord with Gustav Leonhardt; Deutsche Schallplattenpreis (several times); Grand Prix due Disque, France (several); Solo-sonatas and partitas for violin, Brandenburg Concertos (with Frans Brueggen and G. Leonhardt), Magnificat and Cantata Ich hatte viel Bekümmernis Virgin Classic), Haydn Symphonies Nos. 26, 52, 82, 83, 84, 85 and 86, L'Infedeltà Delusa (Harmonia Mundi); Mozart Concert Arias; German Chamber Music (Accent). *Honours include:* German award for Bach Sonatas recording. *Address:* c/o Allied Artists Agency, 42 Montpelier Square, London, SW7 1JJ, England.

KUIJKEN Wieland, b. 31 Aug 1938, Dilbeek, Brussels, Belgium. Viola da gamba player; Cellist; Conductor. *Education:* Studied at the Bruges Conservatory and at the Brussels Conservatoire Royale, 1957-62; Self taught on the viola da gamba. *Career:* Played with the Alarius Ensemble, 1959-72; Played in the avant-garde group Musiques Nouvelles from 1962; Kuijken Early Music Group from 1972; Teacher at the Conservatoiries of Antwerp, Brussels and the Hague; Master classes in Britain, Innsbruck and the USA; Festival appearances at Flanders, Saintes and the English Bach Festival; Tour of New Zealand and Australia with Gustav Leonhardt, 1979; Cellist with the Kuijken String Quartet from 1986: London debut 1990; Collaborations with his brothers, Frans Brueggen, Alfred Deller and René Jacobs; Repertoire includes music by French, English, Italian and German composers; Performed in the Towards Bach concert series on the South Bank, London, August 1989. *Recordings include:* Leclair Flute Sonatas, Marais Pièces de Viole du Cinquieme Livre and German Chamber Music (Accent). *Address:* c/o Allied Artists Agency, 42 Montpelier Square, London, SW7 1JZ, England.

KULESHA Gary Alan, b. 22 Aug 1954, Toronto, Canada. Composer; Conductor; Pianist. m. Larysa Kuzmenko, 30 Dec 1983. *Education:* Associate in piano 1973, Associate in composition 1978, Royal Conservatory of Music, Toronto; Private studies with John McCabe, London, England and John Corigliano, New York, USA; L Mus 1976, Fellow 1978, Trinity College, London, England. *Career:* Composer in Residence, Kitchener-Waterloo Symphony, 1989-1992; Composer in Residence, Candia Opera Company. 1993-1995; Guest conducting throughout Canada; Principal Conductor, Festival Theatre, Stratford Festival, Canada; artistic Director and Principal Conductor, Canadian Contemporary Music Workshops and the Composers Orchestra; Works performed throughout North America, Europe, Iceland, Australia and Latin America. *Compositions:* Essay for orchestra; Second Essay for orchestra; Chamber Concertos 1 - 5; Duo for Bass Clarinet and Piano; Second Sonata for piano; Lifesongs for alto and string orchestra, text by composer; Nocturne for chamber orchestra; Angels for marimba and tape, recorded 1986; Scores for several Shakespearean plays including All's Well That Ends Well, Nimrod, Sydney, Australia 1986 and Henry VIII, Stratford 1986; Shama Songs, 1991; Concerto for Recorder, 1992; 3 Essays for Orchestra, 2nd & 3rd Pico Sonata; Concerto for viola, 1992. *Current Management:* Nova Ter Artist Inc, Suite 303, 156 Front Street West, Toronto, Ontario, Canada M5J 2L6. *Address:* 54 Springbrook Gardens, Toronto, Ontario M8Z 3C1, Canada.

KULÍNSKÝ Bohumil, b. 5 May 1959, Prague, Czechoslovakia. Conductor. *Education:* Prague Conservatory, 1978-81; Prague Music Academy, 1981-84; Music Academy of Janácek-Brno, 1984-86. *Career:* Conductor, Czechoslovak Children's Choir Bambini di Praga, 1976-; Concert tours: France; Italy; Democratic Republic of Germany, Federal Republic of Germany, Mongolia, Finland; UK; Japan; Appeared on radio and TV; Conductor, Prague Symphony Orchestra, appearing at concerts and festivals, 1984-; Conductor, Czech Chamber Philharmonic Orchestra; Concert Tours: Spain and Germany. *Recordings:* CBS, Sony, Polydor, King Record Japan, Supraphon, Panton; Recordings with Prague Symphony orchestra. *Hobbies:* Films (camera and direction); Photography. *Address:* Anenská 2, 110 00 Prague 1, Czech Republic.

KULJERIC Igor, b. 1 Feb 1938, Sibenik, Croatia. Composer. *Education:* Studied at Zagreb Academy of Music (graduated 1965) and the electronic music studios in Milan. *Career:* Has conducted various orchestras in Zagreb and elsewhere in Croatia; Employs electronic and other advanced techniques in his music. *Compositions include:* The Ballads of Petric Kerempuh, 1973; Ballets and incidental music; Operas: The Power of Virtue, Zagreb, 1977, and Rikard, 2 acts, after Shakespeare, 1987. *Address:* c/o Zagreb Philharmonic Orchestra, Trnjanska bb, 41000 Zagreb, Croatia.

KULJERICH Davor, b. 23 Apr 1940, Sibenik, Croatia. Musician (Violinist). m. Purificacion Morales, 21 July 1991, 2 daughters. *University of Music (Academy), Zagreb; Master's studies with Professor Bruno Maderna, Mozarteum, Salzburg. Career:* Member: Zagreb Opera House; Philharmonic Orchestra Zagreb; I Solisti di Zagreb. *Recordings:* 40 LPs and CD, as member of I Solisti di Zagreb. *Membership:* European Association of Concert Agents. *Hobby:* Fisherman. *Address:* Pintor Zuloaga 22, 18005 Granada, Spain.

KULKA Janos, b. 11 Dec. 1929, Budapest, Hungary. Conductor. *Education:* Studied at the Franz Liszt Academy, Budapest, with Janos Ferencsik and Laszlo Somogyi. *Career:* Repetiteur and chorus master at the Budapest Opera from 1950; Conducted opera in Budapest from 1953 until the 1956 Revolution; Conducted at the Bavarian State Opera 1957-59, Wurttenberg State Opera, Stuttgart, 1959-61; Principal Conductor of the Hamburg State Opera 1961-64; Music Director at the Wuppertal Opera 1964-75; Chief Conductor at Stuttgart from 1976, Nordwestdeutsche Philharmonie 1976-87; Has worked with leading opera houses in Cologne, Geneva, Vienna, Barcelona, Copenhagen, Boston (1969) and Buenos Aires 1970-73; Conducted the premieres of Blacher's Yvonne, Prinzessin von Burgund (1973), Klebe's Jacobovsky und der Oberst (1982) and Boehmer's Doktor Faustus (1985); Has also led operas by Gluck, Mozart, Verdi, Wagner, Schoenberg, Janáček, Dallapiccola and Penderecki. *Recordings include:* Chopin's 2nd Piano Concerto, with Tamas Vasary and the Berlin Philharmonic; Opera recital albums with Grace Bumbry, Thomas Tipton, Walter Berry, Sandor Konya, Brigitte Fassbaender and Teresa Stratas; Il Trovatore. *Address:* c/o Staatstheater Stuttgart, Oberer Schlossgarten 6, D-7000 Stuttgart, Germany.

KULKA Konstanty Andrzej, b. 5 Mar 1947, Gdansk, Poland. Violinist. m. 2 children. *Education:* Higher State School of Music, Gdansk. *Career:* Participant in 2 music competitions: Paganini Competition, Genoa 1964, Diploma and Special Prize, Music Competition, Munich, 1966, (1st Prize); since 1967 has given concerts all over the world and particpates in many International Festivals including. Lucerne, Prague, Bordeaux, Berlin, Granada, Barcelona; Many recordings both gramophone, and radio/TV. *Honours:* Minister of Culture and Art Prize, 1969, 1973; Minister of Foreign Affairs Prize, 1977; President of Radio and TV Committee Prize, 1978; Prize Winner, 33 Grand Priz du Disque International Sound Festival, Paris, 1980; Gold Cross of Merit. *Hobbies:* Collecting gramophone records; Bridge; Collecting interesting kitchen recipes. *Address:* ul Zwiazku Walki Mlodych 1 m 44, 00-001 Warsaw, Poland.

KUN Hu, b. 1963, China. Concert Violinist. *Education:* Studied at Szechuan and Peking Central Conservatories and at Menuhin International School. *Debut:* Played with Helsinki Radio Symphony and Helsinki Philharmonic Orchestras, 1979. *Career:* London debut, 1985, followed by concerts with London Symphony Orchestra and the Philharmonic at the Barbican; Further concerts at Wigmore Hall and on tour to Canada, Japan, Singapore, Hong Kong, Brazil, Australia and Europe; Engagements at Concertgebouw Amsterdam and Zurich Tonhalle; Vienna and Berlin debuts, 1987, with the Beethoven and Sibelius Concertos. *Recordings include:* Prokofiev First Concerto with the English String Orchestra and the Sibelius and Khachaturian Concertos, both conducted by Yehudi Menuhin. *Honours include:* Winner, City of Paris Menuhin Competition, 1984, Francescatti Competition, 1987, and Lipizer Competition, Italy, 1988. *Address:* c/o Anglo Swiss Ltd, 3 Primrose Mews, 1a Sharpleshall St, London NW1 8YW, England.

KUNAD Rainer, b. 24 Oct 1936, Chemnitz, Germany. Composer. *Education:* Studied at Dresden Conservatory and at Leipzig, 1956-59. *Career:* Lecturer at Zwickau Conservatory from 1960, then Director of incidental music for Dresden theatres; Member of Dresden and Berlin State Operas from 1971; Professor of Composition at Dresden Musikhochschule, 1978; Professor at Salzburg Mozarteum, 1982-84; Emigrated from East Germany, 1984, and settled in Tubingen. *Compositions include:* Operas and music theatre pieces: Bill Brook, Dresden, 1965; Old Fritz, Dresden, 1965; Maitre Pathelin, Dresden, 1969; Sabellicus, after the Faust legends, Berlin, 1974; Der Eiertanz, 1975, staged Tubingen, 1986; Litauische Claviere, Dresden, 1976; Vincent, based on Van Gogh, Dresden, 1979; Amphitryon, Berlin, 1984; Der Meister und Margarita, Karlsruhe, 1986; Scenic mystery play Die Menschen von Babel, 1986; Orchestral: Aphorismen, 1956; Symphonic Variations, 1959; Symphony, 1984; Sinfonietta, 1969; Concerto for Strings, 1967; Piano Concerto, 1969; Choral and chamber music; Piano pieces and songs. *Address:* GEMA (Germany), c/o PRS Ltd, Member Registration, 29-33 Berners Street, London W1P 4A, England.

KUNDE Gregory, b. 1954, Kankakee, Illinois, USA. Singer (Tenor). *Education:* Studied at Illinois State University and the Opera School of Chicago Lyric Opera. *Career:* Sang at Chicago from 1979, Washington Opera, 1983, Dallas, 1986, Seattle, 1987; Metropolitan Opera debut, 1987, as Des Grieux in Manon; European engagements at Nice, Théâtre des Champs Elysées, Paris, 1989, and Geneva, in Guillaume Tell; Montpellier, 1990, as Raoul in Les Huguenots; Detroit, 1989, as Gounod's Romeo; Other roles have included Mozart's Belmonte and Tamino, Ernesto, Alfredo, Riccardo in Ballo in Maschera, Tonio in Fille du Regiment, and Nadir in Les Pecheurs de Perles; Montpellier and Chicago, 1989, as Des Grieux, and Laertes in Hamlet by Thomas; Sang Lindoro in L'Italiana in Algeri at Berlin, 1992, Idreno in Semiramide at the 1992 Pesaro Festival. *Address:* c/o Chicago Lyric Opera, 20 North Wacker Drive, Chicago, IL 60606, USA.

KUNDLAK Josef, b. 1956, Bratislava, Czechoslovakia. Singer (Tenor). *Education:* Studied in Bratislava and at the European Opera Center in Belgium. *Career:* Sang with Bratislava State Opera, 1983-, in works by Janáček and Smetana, in addition to standard repertory; Sang Nemorino in L'elisir d'amore at Teatro Comunale, Bologna, 1987; Ferrando in Cosí fan Tutte at La Scala Milan, 1989, returning in Die Meistersinger, 1990; Donizetti Festival, Bergamo, 1991, in Elisabetta al Castello di Kenilworth; Further engagements at Teatro San Carlo, Naples, and Bayerische Staatsoper, Munich; Appeared as Belmonte in new production of Die Entführung at Deutsche Oper Berlin, 1991; Sang Rossini's Almaviva at Genoa, 1992. *Honours include:* Winner, Luciano Pavarotti Competition, Philadelphia,

1985. *Address:* c/o Deutsche Oper Berlin, Richard Wagnerstrasse 10, 1000 Berlin 10, Germany.

KUNTZSCH Matthias, b. 22 Sept 1935, Karlsruhe, Germany. Conductor (Symphony and Opera). m. Sylvi Anderson, 18 May 1966, 1 son, 1 daughter. *Education:* Studied Piano, Horn, Conducting, Hochschule fur Musik und Theater, Hannover; Master courses, Mozarteum, Salzburg, under Lovro von, Matacic, Hermann Scherchen, Herbert von Karajan, and Zermatt under Pablo Casals, Karl Engel. *Debut:* Conducting Don Pasquale, State Theater, Braunschweig, 1960. *Career:* Conductor, Jeunesse Musicale Orchestra, Braunschweig, 1957; Musical Assistant, Hannover Opera, 1958; Kapellmeister, Opera Braunschweig, 1959; Assistant to Wolfgang and Wieland Wagner, Bayreuth Festival, 1959-64; Principal Conductor: Bonn Opera, 1962-64, Mannheim Opera, 1964-66, Hamburg State Opera, 1966-69; Staatskapellmeister, Munich State Opera, 1969-73; Generalmusikdirektor, Luebeck Opera and Symphony, 1973-77; Generalmusikdirektor and Operndirektor, Saarbruecken State Opera and Symphony, 1977-85; Conductor, International Youth Festival Orchestra, Bayreuth, 1981-86; Principal Guest Conductor and Artistic Advisor, Basque National Symphony, San Sebastian, Spain, 1986-89; Conducted world premieres of operas: Humphrey Searle's Hamlet, Hamburg, 1968, Gian Carlo Menotti's Help help the Globolinks, Hamburg, 1968, Guenter Bialas's Aucassin et Nicolette, Munich, 1969, Detlev Mueller-Siemens's Genovea, Germany TV ZDF. *Recordings:* With soloists Ruggiero Ricci, Eugene List and others. *Honours:* Winner, Lower Saxony Prize for Promotion of Young Musicians and granted concert conducting, Hannover Radio Orchestra, 1963; Special Recognition for performing Cosí fan tutte and Arabella, Orpheus Magazine, 1981. *Memberships:* Rotary International; Conductors Guild of America; Conductors Guild of California. *Hobbies:* Reading; Walking; Swimming. *Current Management:* Kollo Berlin, Kuehnly Stuttgart, Germany; Dorothy Cone, New York City, USA. *Address:* 123 Nantucket Cove, San Rafael, CA 94901, USA.

KUNZ Erich, b. 20 May 1909, Vienna, Austria. Singer (Baritone). *Education:* Studied with Theo Lierhammer and Hans Duhan at the Vienna Music Academy. *Debut:* Troppau, 1933, as Osmin in Die Entführung. *Career:* Sang at Plauen then at Breslau, 1937-41; Member of the Vienna Staatsoper from 1941: visited Covent Garden with the company 1947, as Leporello and Figaro; Salzburg Festival, debut 1941, as Masetto, then 1942-60, as Leporello, Figaro, Guglielmo and Papageno; Glyndebourne Festival, 1948, 1950, as Guglielmo; Bayreuth Festival, 1943, 1951, Beckmesser; Metropolitan Opera from 1952, as Beckmesser, Leporello, Faninal and Figaro; Vienna Staatsoper, 1976, in the premiere of Kabale und Liebe by Einem; Took part in 1978 recording of Salome for EMI. *Recordings include:* Le Nozze di Figaro; Cosí fan Tutte; Die Zauberflöte; Die Fledermaus; Die Lustige Witwe; Salome. *Address:* c/o Staatsoper, Opernring 2, A-1010 Vienna, Austria.

KUNZEL Erich, b. 21 Mar 1935, New York, USA. Conductor. *Education:* Studied at Dartmouth College, A.B. 1957 and at Harvard and Brown Universities, A.M., 1960. *Career:* Assistant to Pierre Monteux 1963-64; Teacher and director of choral music at Brown University, 1958-65; Conducted the Rhode Island Philharmonic, 1960-65; Assistant to Max Rudolf at the Cincinnati Symphony, 1965, Associate conductor, 1967, Resident conductor, 1969-74; Led Pergolesi's La Serva Padrona at Santa Fe, 1957 and the US premiere of The Nose by Shostakovich, 1965; Conducted the Cincinnati Opera 1966; New Haven Symphony Orchestra, 1974-; Founded the Cincinnati Pops Orchestra 1977 and toured with it to the Far East 1990; has also conducted orchestras in Chicago, Boston, Los Angeles, San Francisco, Montreal, Ottawa and Detroit; Music Director of the Indianapolis Symphony Orchestra; Jazz collaborations with Dave Brubeck, Ella Fitzgerald, Duke Ellington, Benny Goodman, George Shearing and Gerry Mulligan. *Recordings include:* Albums with the

Dave Brubeck Trio and the Cincinnati Symphony; Carnaval Roman overture by Berlioz and Pictures at an Exhibition (Decca). *Address:* c/o Cincinnati Symphony Orchestra, 1241 Elm Street, Cincinnati, OH 45210, USA.

KUPFER Harry, b. 12 Aug 1935, Berlin, Germany. Opera Producer. *Career:* Worked at theatres in Halle, Stralsund and Karl-Marx Stadt; Director, National Theatre, Weimar, 1967-72; Chief Producer, Dresden Opera, 1972-81; Chief Producer, Komische Oper, East Berlin from 1981; Premiere production of Penderecki's Die schwarze Maske, Salzburg Festival, 1986; Production of Idomeneo for Stuttgart Opera; Has produced Der fliegende Holländer at Bayreuth: Der Ring des Nibelungen, 1988; Opera productions for Welsh National Opera; Tannhäuser for the Hamburg Staatsoper, 1990; Zimmermann's Soldaten, and Elektra seen at Vienna, Salzburg and Stuttgart; Orfeo ed Euridice at Covent Garden, 1991 (production for the Komische Oper Berlin seen in London, 1989); Season 1992 with Die Frau ohne Schatten at Amsterdam. *Address:* c/o Allied Artists Agency, 42 Montpelier Sqaure, London SW7 1JZ, England.

KUPFERMAN Meyer, b. 3 July 1926, New York City, USA. Composer; College Professor; Clarinettist. m. Pei-Fen Chin, 26 July 1973, 3 sons, 1 daughter. *Education:* High School of Music & Art, New York City; Queens College, New York; Self-taught, musical composition. *Debut:* Steinway Hall, New York City, 1946. *Career:* Composer for symphony, opera, concerto, ballet, cantata, films (12 scores), much chamber music; Director, Sarah Lawrence Improvisation Ensemble, Music By My Friends Ensemble, Spring Trio Ensemble; Teacher, compositions & film music, Sarah Lawrence College, Bronxville, New York. *Compositions:* 11 symphonies; 6 operas; 7 string quartets; 3 piano concerti; 2 cello concerti; Guitar concerto; 5 ballet scores; Torchwine, full length cantata, soprano, basset horn & piano. *Recordings:* Little Symphony; 4th Symphony; Chamber Symphony; Concerto for Cello, Tape & Orchestra; Libretto for Orchestra; Lyric Symphony. *Publications:* Sonata on Jazz Elements; Little Sonata; Infinities No 22; Partita; In A Garden; Draagenfurt Girl; Sound Phantoms No 7; Fantasy Sonata; 5 Little Zeppelins; Halleluja the Hills. *Contributor of:* Major articles on Stravinsky, Acrobat of Apollo, in memorial issue, New Perspectives, 1972. *Honours:* Guggenheim Memorial Grant, 1975; National Endowment for the Arts, 1976-77; Academy & Institute of Arts & Letters, 1981. *Memberships:* American Society of Composers, Authors & Publishers; American Federation of Musicians. *Hobby:* Oil painting. *Address:* 86 Livingston Street, Rhinebeck, NY 12572, USA.

KURTAG György, b. 19 Feb 1926, Lugos, Romania. Composer. *Education:* Budapest Music Academy and in Paris. *Career:* Retired Professor of Chamber Music, Music Academy of Budapest. *Compositions:* Concerto for Viola, 1954; String Quartet, 1959; Quintet for Wind Instruments, 1959; Eight Pieces for piano, 1960; Signs (for solo viola), 1961; Eight duets for violin and Cimbalom, 1961; The Sayings of Peter Bornemissza (for soprano and piano), 1968; In Memory of a Winter Sunset, Four fragments for soprano, Cimbalom and violin, 1969; Four capriccios for soprano and chamber ensemble, 1970; Splinters solo for cimbalom, 1974; Four Pilinszky Songs, S.K. Rememberance Noise, Hommage a Mihaly Andras, Twelve Microludes for String Quartet, Herdecker Eurythmie, Guitar pieces, Omaggio a Luigi Nono, Messages of the late Miss R.V. Troussova, Five Russian Choruses, Rimma Dalos Lieder, Attila Jozsef Fragments, Seven Lieder, Eight Tandori Choruses; Kafka Fragments for Soprano and Violin, 1985; Quasi una fantasia for piano and chamber ensemble; Three Old Inscriptions for soprano and piano 1986; Requiem po drugu for soprano and piano 1987; Introduction, Kyrie A, Hommage à Stockhausen, trumpet, double-bass, piano, 1992; In memoriam Thomas Blum, piano, celesta, double-bass, 1992; Hommage à John Cage, trumpet, double-bass, 1992; Hommage à Tristan, trumpet, double-bass, piano,

celesta, 1992; Les Adieux in Jacačeks Manier, piano solo, 1992; Antiphone in f sharp, trombone, double-bass, piano, celesta, 1992; Kyrie, b, double-bass, piano, 1992; Curriculum vitae, Életút, Op 32, 2 pianos, 2 basset horns, 1992. *Honours:* Erkel Prize, 3 times; Kossuth Prize, 2nd Degree, 1973; Merited Artist, Eminent Artist's Title. *Address:* 2621 Veroce, Lihegoutca 3, Hungary.

KURTZ Efrem, b. 7 Nov 1900, St. Petersburg, Russia. Conductor. m. Elaine Schaffer 1955 (deceased. 1973). *Education:* St. Petersburg Conservatory; Stern Conservatory, Berlin. *Debut:* As conductor, Berlin Philharmonic Orchestra, 1921. *Career:* Conductor, Berlin Philharmonic Orchestra, 1921-24; Musical Director, Stuttgart Philharmonic 1924-33; Guest Conductor, New York Philharmonic NBC Symphony, San Francisco, Cleveland and Chicago Symphony Orchestras, 1933-54; Musical Director, Kansas City Symphony Orchestra, 1941-46, Houston Symphony Orchestra, 1948-54; More recently has been guest conductor of major orchestras of Europe, Japan, Australia, Canada, Israel, USA, USSR, South Africa and at numerous festivals. *Recordings include:* Excerpts from Swan Lake, The Nutcracker and Sleeping Beauty; Prokofiev Symphonies Nos. 1 and 7, Romeo and Juliet Suite; Shostakovich Symphonies Nos. 1 and 10, Age of Gold; Stravinsky The Firebird and Petruska; Mendelssohn Violin Concerto with Menuhin (EMI). *Honours:* Commander, Order of Merit of Italy; Medal of Honor, Bruckner Society of America; Awarded Golden Disc by Columbia Records Inc, after 3 millionth sale of his recordings with New York Philharmonic. *Hobbies:* Drawing; Collecting, paintings, stamps, historical letters; Mountaineering. *Address:* c/o 19 Air Street, Regent Street, London, W1R 6QL, England.

KURTZ Eugene Allen, b. 27 Dec 1923, Atlanta, Georgia, USA. Composer. *Education:* BA, Music, University of Rochester, 1947; MA, Music, Eastman School of Music, 1949; Study with Arthur Honegger and Darius Milhaud, Ecole Normale de Musique, Paris, 1949-51; Study with Max Deutsch, Paris, 1953-57. *Career:* Guest Professor of Composition, University of Michigan, 1967-68, 1970-71, 1973-74, 1980-81, 1988, Eastman School of Music, 1975, University of Illinois, 1976, University of Texas, 1977-78, 1985-86; Hartt School of Music, 1989; Consultant, Editions Jobert, Paris, 1972-. *Compositions:* The Solitary Walker, 1964; Conversations for 12 Players, 1966; Ca...... Diagramme Pour Orchestre, 1972; The Last Contrabass in Las Vegas, 1974; Mécanique, 1975; Logo, 1979; Five-Sixteen, piano, 1982; World Enough and Time, 1982- in progress; String Trio, Time and Again, 1984-85; From Time to Time, violin and piano, 1986-87; also film scores and incidental music for radio, theatre and TV. *Recordings:* Mecanique, with the French National Orchestra, conducted by Alexandre Myrat; Motivations, Books I and II, Piano, Michel Sendrez; The Last Contrabass in Las Vegas, Bertram and Nancy Turetzky; Five-Sixteen, Piano, Geneviève Ibanez; Logo 1, Richard Nunemaker, Clarinet, David Nale, Piano, The Continuum Percussion Quartet, conducted by David Colson; From Time to Time, Adèle Auriol, Violin, Bernard Fauchet, Piano. *Publication:* In preparation, Scott Joplin et le Ragtime Classique, Paris. *Address:* 6 Rue Boulitte, 75014 Paris, France.

KURZ Ivan, b. 29 Nov 1947, Prague, Czechoslovakia. Composer. m. Zdenka Sklenárová, 31 May 1973, 2 sons, 1 daughter. *Education:* Studied music theory privately with Karel Risinger, 1964-66; Emil Hlobil's composition class, 1966-71, postgraduate studies with Vaclav Dobias, 1973-76, Academy of Arts and Music, Prague. *Career:* Dramaturgist, Prague TV, 1972-74; Teacher of Music Theory, Academy of Music, 1976-. *Compositions:* Orchestral works include: Concertino for Piano, Flute, Percussion Instruments and Strings, 1974; Summer Music, chamber string ensemble, 1975; Slanting Plane (symphonic picture), 1979; Absorption (Symphonic picture), 1981; Allegory, 1982; Symphony No 3, 1986; Chamber works: Sonata for Piano, 1976; Vitamins, for flute and piano or string trio, 1977; Circle of Notes, string quartet, 1979; Psalm, sextet, 1981; The Touch, piano trio, 1982; Two Egos, for 2 violins, 1984; Litanie, for organ and percussion instruments, 1984; Sonata for Violin and Piano, 1985; Expectation, for French horn and piano, 1985; Vocal works: For Your Little Mozart, suite for contralto and piano, 1975; Flying Carpet, children's choirs with accompaniment, 1978; Got Mint?, vocal and acting etudes for children's choir, 1982; Moravian Reflection, choirs with accopaniment, 1985; Instructive works: Fiddlers Are Coming, for children's recitation and singing, 1980; Feathers, 5 easy miniatures for 2 violins, 2 guitars, piano, 1982; Reverie (electronic music), 1982; Foolish Message (Symphonic picture), 1987; Toward You I come (Symphonic picture), 1989; Fatima Still Actuell (Oratotium for soli, choir and orchestra), 1992; Evening Meeting (Opera), 1989-90; Advent (Phantasy for organs, harpsihord, chamber strings orchestra, reciter and children choir), 1991; The Confession (Concerto) for bassoon and symphonic orchestra), 1991; Temptation (Quintet for flute, clarinet, piano, cb, percussion instruments), 1988; Sonatina for piano, 1988; Reminiscence (for bassoon solo), 1988. *Hobby:* Theology. *Address:* Drtinova 26, 150 00 Prague 5, Czech Republic.

KUSCHE Benno, b. 30 Jan 1916, Freiburg, Germany. Singer (Bass- Baritone). *Education:* Studied in Karlsruhe and with Fritz Harlan in Freiburg. *Debut:* Koblenz 1938, as Renato. *Career:* Sang in Augsburg, 1939-42; Member of the Bayerische Staatsoper Munich from 1946, Deutsche Oper am Rhein Dusseldorf from 1958; Salzburg Festival 1949, in the premiere of Antigonae by Orff; Covent Garden 1952, as Beckmesser, and 1953, as La Roche in the first British performance of Capriccio; Glyndebourne Festival 1954, 1963-64, as Leporello, La Roche, and Don Fernando in Fidelio; Komische Oper Berlin 1958, as Papageno in Die Zauberflöte; Metropolitan Opera 1971-72, as Beckmesser; Guest appearances in Philadelphia, Amsterdam, Buenos Aires, Zurich, Florence and Bregenz. *Recordings:* Die Meistersinger; Die Kluge and Der Mond by Orff (Columbia); La Bohème; Lulu (Electrola). *Address:* c/o Bayerische Staatsoper, Postfach 745, D-8000 Munich 1, Germany.

KUSHNER David Zakeri, b. 22 Dec 1935, Ellenville, New York, USA. Musicologist; Educator; Lecturer. 4 sons (1 dec). *Education:* BMus, Boston University, 1957; MMus, University of Cincinnati; PhD, University of Michigan, 1966. *Career:* Assistant Professor, Music, Mississippi University for Women, 1964-66; Associate to full Professor, Radford University, 1966-69; Professor, Music, Doctoral Research Faculty, Coordinator, Graduate and Musicological Studies, University of Florida, 1969-; Visiting Professor, Florence Study Center, Florida State University, 1975; Lecturer, colleges, universities, Canada, Australia, Israel, Kenya, Scotland, England, Czech Republic, Slovakia, Poland, Hungary, Austria, Germany, throughout USA; Papers: College Music Society, American Liszt Society, International Musicological Society. *Publications:* Ernest Bloch: Guide to Research, 1988. *Contributions to:* Ernest Bloch, New Grove Dictionary of Music and Musicians, 1980; Jaromir Weinberger: From Bohemia to America, American Music, 1988; Marc Blitzstein: Social Conscience in Music, The Opera Journal, 1993; Ernest Bloch's America, Currents in Musical Thought, 1993. *Address:* Department of Music, University of Florida, Gainesville, FL 32611, USA.

KUSIEWICZ Piotr, b. 30 June, 1953, Gdansk, Poland. Pianist; Singer; Main field of Interest: Baroque Music. *Education:* Pianist Diploma with Professor Zbigniew Sliwinski, 1977; Singer Diploma with Distinction, with Professor Jerzy Szymanski, 1980; Academy of Music, Gdansk. *Career:* Singer: Cooperation with Cracow State Opera, 1981; Teatr STU, 1983-; Warsaw Opera House, 1984-; Wrocaw State Opera, 1986-; Guest Performances in Operas in West Germany, Switzerland, Austria, Holland, Luxemburg, Italy; Cooperation with Philharmonic Societies, Chamber Ensembles, Member of Vocal Ensemble of Ancient Music Bornus Consort. Pianist: Performances with leading Polish Singers as accompanist in Poland and Abroad; Accompanist in

Geneva International Singer Competition, 1978; Both As Singer and Pianist: Festival of Contemporary Music, Warsaw Autumn, 1981, 1983, 1984; 1987 Krzysztof Penderecki's Festival in Lusawice, Poland, (Invited by Composer), 1983; Recordings for the Polish Radio; Vocal: Teacher in Academy of Music in Gdansk, 1986. *Recordings:* G.F. Handel, Sosarme, Opera Seria in 3 Acts Polskie Nagrania, 2 LPs. *Publications:* Gdansk Composers, Co-Author, 1980. *Address:* U1. Michala Glinki 4/9, 80-271 Gdansk, Poland.

KÜTHEN Hans-Werner, b. 26 Aug 1938, Cologne, Germany. Musicologist; Editor, Beethoven Archives, 1968-. Bonn. m. Annette Magdalena Leinen, 1 son. *Education:* Studied Musicology, Bonn University; Civico Museo Bibliografico Musicale, Bologna; MA 1980; PhD 1985; Bonn University. *Publications:* On Beethoven: Kammermusik mit Bläsern, 1969; Article Beethoven, Herder, Das Grosse Lexikon der Musik, 1978; Complete edition, Ouverturen und Wellingtons Sieg, 1974; Critical Report, separately 1991; Klavierkonzerte I, 1984, with Critical Report separately; Klavierkonzerte II (nos. 4 and 5), (in preparation); Klavierkonzerte Nr. 1-3 (Bärenreiter Studienpartituren), 1987; same in practical edition for 2 pianos: no. 3, 1988, no. 1, 1990, no. 2, 1991. *Contributor to:* Professional publications including Beethoven Yearbooks; Gedenkschrift G. Henle, 1980; Festschrift H. J. Abs, 1981; Festgabe U. v. Rauchhaupt, 1982; Beethoven Congress Report Bonn 1984, München, 1987; Beethoven zwischen Revolution und Restauration, 1989; International Musicological Colloquium Bonn 1989, Congress Report, Tutzing, 1990: Schöpferische Rezeption im Finale der 9. Symphonie von Beethoven (Mozarts Offertorium Misericordias Domini KV 222 als Modell für Beethovens Freudenmelodie); International Mozart Conference Prag 1991: Mozart, Schiller, Beethoven, Die Fusion der Embleme im Finale der Neunten Symphonie Prag Hudební Věa; Pragmatic instead of Enigmatic: The Fifty-First Sonata of Beethoven (in Engl), The Beethoven Newsletter, San José, California, 1992; International Congress of the Gesellschaft für Musikforschung Freiburg/Br, 1993: Gradus ad partituram. Erscheinungsbild und Funktionen der Solostimme in Beethovens Klavierkonzerten, Kassel, Basel, 1994; Disk cover texts (Polydor International). On Viadana: Herder, Das Grosse Lexikon der Musik, 1982. *Memberships:* Gesellschaft für Musikforschung; Verein Beethoven, Haus Bonn; VG Musik edition, Kassel. *Hobbies:* Drawing and Painting; Pianoforte Playing; Family. *Address:* Königstr. 8, D-5300 Bonn 1, Germany.

KUULBERG Mati, b. 9 July 1947. Tallinn, Estonia. Composer; Teacher; Violinist. m. Tiiu Aroella, 27 June 1981, 1 daughter. *Education* Tallinn State Conservatoire, 1966-71. *Debut:* 1966. *Career:* Estonian State Symphony Orchestra, 1966-75; Tallinn Secondary Music School, 1978-; Head, Information Centre, Estonian Composers Union, 1987-; Jury Member, new recordings for Estonian Radio collection. *Compositions:* 3 ballets; 5 symphonies; 4 sonatas for solo violin; Sonatas for 2 flutes, 2 pianos, solo clarinet, piano, solo cello; Concerto per Ottoni; Concerto per Fiati; In the Name of Life, oratorio; Wind Quintet; Piano Sextet. *Recordings:* Melodija Recording Company: Wind Quintet, 1973; Sonata No 2 for solo violin, 1975; piano trio, sonata for solo clarinet, concert-sonata for solo cello, 4 Novelettes for alto flute and string quartet, 1977; piano sonata, 1978; Capriccio for 2 pianos and percussion, 1984; saxophone quartet, 1987; 3 and 4 Impressions and Giusto for piano, 1989; sonatas No 1 and 4 for solo violin, 1988; piano trio No 2, Reminder for cello and piano, Attacca for solo trombone, for Tiiu poem for violin and piano, 1991. *Address:* Weizenbergi 19-5, EE0010 Tallinn 10, Estonian Republic.

KVAPIL Jan, b. 1943, Czechoslovakia, Violinist. *Education:* Studied at Prague Academy of Arts, *Career:* Member of the Talich String Quartet from 1962; Tours to most European countries and to Egypt, Iraq, North America, Japan and Indonesia; Chamber Ensemble of the Czech Philharmonic from 1975; Annual visits to France from 1976; Tours of Britain 1990-91, with concerts at the Wigmore Hall, appearances at the Bath and Bournemouth Festivals, Elizabeth Hall and on BBC2's Late Show, with Janáček's 2nd Quartet; Played Beethoven's Quartet Op 74, the Brahms A minor, Smetana D minor and works by Mozart in England, 1991; Festival appearances in Vienna, Besançon, Lucerne, Helsinki, Amsterdam, Prague, Salzburg; Repertoire also includes works by Debussy, Bartók (complete quartets recorded with Supraphon), Shostakovich, Ravel and Dvořák. *Recordings include:* For the French companies Sarastro and Calliope, with the complete quartets of Beethoven; Albums for Collins Classics. *Honours include:* Grand Prix Charles Cros. *Address:* c/o Clarion/Seven Muses, 64 Whitehall Park, London N19 3TN, England.

KVAPIL Radoslav, b. 15 Mar 1934, Brno, Czechoslovakia. Pianist. m. Eva Kvapilová-Mašlanová, 11 June 1960, 1 son. *Education:* Gymnasium Brno, 1952; Janáček Academy of Music, Brno, 1957; Aspirantur, Janáček Academy with Prof L Kundera, 1962. *Debut:* Recital, Brno, 1954. *Career:* Numerous concerts in more than 20 countries including Europe, USA, Canada and Japan, 1956-; Appearances on numerous radio stations including BBC and Radio France; Professor, Conservatory Prague, 1963-73. *Recordings:* Supraphon: All piano works A Dvořák's, 1967-69, All works J H Voříšek, 1975, Concerto A Rejcha, A Dvořák; Panton: All piano works of L Janáček, 1969; Da camera: all polkas of B Smetana, 1969; BIS B Martinů Studies and Polkas, Sonata, 1982; Aurora: Piano works of P M Moussorgsky, Calliope: Works of B. Smetana, and L Janáček; Nimbus: Hindemith, Janáček, with Wallace Collection; ADDA: all piano, violin and violoncello works of L Janáček; 2CD with works of B Martinů/first and last periode/UNICORN-Kanchana: Anthology of czech piano music: Till end of 93 released 5 volumes containing works of Dvořak, Smetana, Martinů/Paris periode/Voříšek, Fibich, Project will continue; Dvořák: Cypresses, Biblical songs with P Langridge Radio recording BBC includes Dvořák piano concerto, Martinů Concertos No.3, 4, Divertimento, Debussy Phantasie for piano and orchestra. *Contributions:* Musical Review Prague. *Honours:* International Competition, Radio ČSSR, 1st prize, 1968; Janáček medaile of Ministry culture ČSSR, 1978; Honorary Vice President, Dvořák Society of GB. *Memberships:* Chairman, EPTA Czech Republic; Chairman, The South Bohemis Festival Society; Chairman, AMAT Czech Republic; Chairman Menuhin Live Music Now Czech Republic, 1992. *Hobby:* Chess. *Address:* Hradecká 5, 13000 Praha 3, Czech Republic.

KVECH Otomar, b. 25 May 1950, Prague, Czechoslovakia. Composer. m. Miluska Wagnerova, 30 Mar 1972, 2 daughters. *Education:* Composition, Organ, Music Conservatory, Prague, 1965-69; Composition with Professor Pauer, Academy of Music Arts, Prague, 1969-74. *Debut:* Symphony for organ and orchestra, Dvorak's Hall, Prague. *Career:* Pianist, National Theatre, Prague, 1974-77; Music Producer, 1977-80, Dramaturgist, Editor, 1988-, Radio Praha; Secretary, Organisation of Czech Composers and Concert Artists, 1980- 90; Professor, Music Conservatory, Prague, 1990-. *Compositions:* 4 symphonies: Organ, 1974, E Flat Major, 1982, D Major, 1984, E Minor with String Quartet, 1987; 5 String Quartets, 1972, 1973, 1974, 1979, 1985; 3 Violin Sonatas, 1974, 1978, 1982; The Honour to Bach, 1971; Wind Quintet, 1975; Transformation, Sinfonietta, Violin, Strings, 1976; Trio, Violin, Cello, Piano, 1976; Sonata for Piano, 1977; The Waz across the room, cantata, 1978; The World Carnival, 1983; Cello Sonata, 1985; Sonata for Organ, 1986; RUR, 1986; Capriccio, concerto, piano trio, orchestra, 1986; The Album for Piano, 1989; Numerous song cycles. *Recordings:* Piano Trio; The Waz across the room; Symphonies 1, 2; RUR; String Quartet No 5; For Radio Praha: Symphony in E Minor, World Carnival, The Honour to Bach, Capriccio, String Quartets 2, 3, 4; Sonatas for Violin 1, 2, 3, Viola Sonata, Cello Sonata, Wind Quintet; Many works recorded in UK, Germany, France. *Publications:* When the Path Disappeared, song cycle; Three Moments for Accordion; Piano Trio; Prague Panorama; Six Preludes for Flute Solo; String Quartet

No 5; Symphony, E Flat Major. *Contributions to:* Hudebni rozhledy, Prague; Opus Musicum, Brno. *Honours:* Prize, Best Chamber Competition, Young Composers Competition, 1973; 2nd Prize, Young Composers Competition, 1975; Prize, Czech Composers and Concert Artists, 1978, 1986; 1st Prize, Young Composers Competition, 1978, 1983; Prize, Minister of Culture, Czechoslovakia, 1982; 1st Prize for Children's Songs, Llangollen, Wales, 1984. *Hobby:* Electric engines. *Address:* Korunni 67, 130 00 Prague 3, Czech Republic.

KVECHOVA Miluska, b. 26 Apr 1947, Prague, Czechoslovakia. Organist. m. Otomar Kvech, 30 Mar 1972, 2 daughters. *Education:* Organ, Music Conservatory, Prague, 1963-68; Organ with Professor Reinberger, Academy of Music Arts, Prague, 1968-73. *Debut:* Dvorak's Hall, Prague, 1973. *Career:* Teacher of Music: Music School, 1973-78; Conservatory of Music, 1978-; Many concerts, recitals and chamber music, Czechoslovakia, USSR, Italy, Germany, Belgium. *Recordings:* Chamber music, Radio Prague; Bach, Reubke, Radio Prague; CD, Baroque music of Bach and others. *Contributor to:* Hudebni roshledy, Prague. *Honours:* Organ Playing Competition, Prague Spring Festival, 1971. *Address:* Korunni 67, 130 00 Prague 3, Czech Republic.

KWELLA Patrizia, b. 26 Apr 1953, Mansfield, England. Singer (Soprano). *Education:* Royal College of Music, London. *Career:* Promenade Concert debut 1979, with John Eliot Gardiner; Concerts and festivals include Ansbach, Bergen, Innsbruck, Aldeburgh, Bologna, Warsaw, Bath, City of London, Edinburgh and Salzburg; Conductors include Richard Hickox, Peter Maag, Christopher Hogwood and Trevor Pinnock; US debut 1983, with the San Diego Symphony; Further concerts with the San Francisco, Houston and Washington Symphony Orchestras; Sang in many of the Bach, Handel and Scarlatti tercentenary concerts of 1985; Premiere of Night's Mask by Colin Matthews at the 1985 Aldeburgh Festival; Handel's Alcina at the 1985 Spitalfields and Cheltenham Festivals; Repertoire includes Haydn, Mozart, Brahms, Mahler, Stravinsky and Britten. *Recordings:* Handel's L'Allegro, Alcina, Alceste, Resurrezione and Esther; Monteverdi's Orfeo and Il Combattimento; Bach's B Minor Mass, Magnificat and St John Passion; Mozart's Coronation Mass, Missa Solemnis, Regina Coeli; Companies include Decca, EMI, Deutsche Grammophon and Hyperion. TV includes many Man and Music appearances for Channel 4. *Address:* c/o Music & Musicians Artist's Management, 54 Regent's Park Road, London NW1 7SX, England.

KWON Hellen, b. 11 Jan 1961, Seoul, South Korea. Singer (Soprano). *Education:* Studied in Cologne. *Debut:* Wiesbaden, as the Queen of Night, 1984. *Career:* Has sung at Mannheim 1985-, Paris Opera, 1986 (Zauberflöte), Hamburg, 1987; Created the role of Alexis de Lechebot in Liebermann's La Forêt at Geneva, 1987; Bayreuth Festival, 1988, as a Flower Maiden; Glyndebourne Festival, 1990, as The Queen of Night, followed by performances at Bonn and Vienna, 1991; Sang Susanna at Hamburg, 1990, Wellgunde in a concert performance of Götterdämmerung at Rome, 1991, and Blondchen in Die Entfuhrung at Salzburg Festival, 1991; Other roles include Strauss's Sophie and Zerbinetta, Rosina, Norina and Musetta; Sang Susanna at the 1992 Israel Festival; Concert tours of USA, France, Italy, Belgium and Netherlands, notably in the B minor Mass and St Matthew Passion of Bach. *Address:* c/o Hamburgische Staatsoper, Grosse-Theaterstrasse 34, 2000 Hamburg 36, Germany.

KYHLE Magnus, b. 1959, Sweden. Singer (Tenor). *Education:* Studied at Stockholm College of Music and the State Opera School in Stockholm. *Debut:* Vadstena Academy, 1983. *Career:* Engaged at the Royal Opera, Stockholm, 1986-89, Stadttheater Darmstadt, 1989-90, and Landestheater Salzburg, 1990-92; Roles have included Mozart's Don Ottavio, Tamino, Monostatos and Ferrando, Pelleas, and Paris in La Belle Hélène; Guest appearances at Tenerife and Tokyo; Season 1990-92 as Tamino and Don Ottavio with the Royal Opera, Stockholm, Tamino at Salzburg Landestheater and Ferrando at Semperoper Dresden; Season 1992-93 as Beppe in new production of Pagliacci at Stockholm, and in a new production of Traviata; Stockholm production of The Phantom of the Opera, 1994-. *Address:* IM Audio & Music HB, Åsögatan 67VI, S-11829 Stockholm, Sweden.

KYLLONEN Timo-Juhani, b. 1 Dec 1955, Saloinen, Finland. Composer; Accordion soloist; Conductor. *Education:* Postgraduate composition studies, solo accordion, conducting and teaching diplomas, Tchaikovsky Conservatoire and Gnesin Music Institute, Moscow. *Debut:* Concert of his works at the Tchaikovsky Conservatory, Moscow, April 1986. *Career:* Biographical programmes, Finnish Television 1982 and 1988; Several concerts and radio and television programmes in Finland, Sweden, USSR, Peru, Ecuador and Norway; Composer-portrait on Netherlands Radio 1990, also on Argentinian and Peruvian radio. *Compositions include:* Elegia: Quasi una sonata for violin and piano, Op 16, 1987; Trio No 1 for Accordion, Violin and Cello, Op 9, 1986; Trilogy for Two Pianos, Op 4, Reflections, 1984; String Quartet No 1, Op 3, In Memory of a Friend, 1984. *Recordings include:* Compositions by Timo-Juhani Kyllonen, Finlandia Records; Elegia quasi una sonata, op 15, 1987; Trio No 1, op 9 1986; Triology for 2 pianos op 4, 1984, String Quartet No 1, op 3, 1984, Ondine records. *Hobbies:* Drawing; Painting; Theatre; Reading. *Current Management:* Finnish Music Information Centre, Helsinki, Finland. *Address:* Joupinmaki 3C49, 02760 Espoo, Finland.

KYNASTON Nicolas, b. 10 Dec 1941, Morebath, Devon, England. Concert Organist. *Education:* Accademia Musicale Chigiana, Siena, 1957; Conservatorio Santa Cecilia, Rome, 1958; Royal College of Music, 1960. *Debut:* Royal Festival Hall, 1966. *Career:* Organist, Westminster Cathedral, 1961-71; Appointed Consultant Tutor, Birmingham School of Music, 1986-; Travels widely giving regular recitals throughout UK, most European countries and to many exotic places including Barbados, Nassau, Ankara, Istanbul, Tokyo, Hong-Kong, Bangkok, Seoul-Korea and the famous bamboo organ of Las Pinas, Philippines and tours of North America. Varied and extensive solo repertoire. Broadcasts regularly on British Broadcasting Corporation radio and television and foreign networks (particularly West Germany). Teaches Cambridge University; Master Classes in USA, Hong-Kong, Norway, Singapore and Germany; Chairman, National Organ Teacher's Encouragement Scheme, 1993-. *Recordings:* Numerous commercial recordings for British, French and German companies; 5 nominated Critics Choice; 2 popular records Great Organ Works at Royal Albert Hall earning EMI Sales Award; Bach from Clifton Cathedral nominated Best Solo Instrumental Record of the Year; received coveted Deutscher Schallplatten preis for Vierne's 6th Symphony (German recording). *Contributions to:* The American Organist; Music and Musicians; Kirche und Musick; RSCM Yearbook; Organ Club Journal and others. *Honours:* Hon. FRCO, 1976; Deutscher Schallplatten preis, 1978; MTA Record award, 1976. *Memberships:* President, Incorporated Association of Organists, 1983-85; Honorary Member of the Organ Club. *Hobbies:* Churches; Pubs. *Address:* 28 High Park Road, Kew Gardens, Richmond-upon-Thames, Surrey, TW9 4BH, England.

KYR Robert Harry, b. 20 Apr 1952, Cleveland, Ohio, USA. Composer; Teacher. *Education:* BA, Yale University, 1974; Royal College of Music, London, England, 1974-76; MA, University of Pennsylvania, 1978; PhD, Harvard University, 1989. *Career:* Composer-in-residence, New England Philharmonic, 1985-89; Resident Composer of Extension Works, Composers and Performers Consortium, Boston, Massachusetts, 1985-; Teacher of Composition and Theory: Harvard University (Teaching Fellow), 1985-89; Longy School of Music (Director of Compositional Studies), 1986-; Hartt School of Music (Visiting Lecturer), Fall 1988; Justus-Liebig University, Giessen,

Federal Republic of Germany (Guest Professor), 1983-84; Yale University, 1982-83; Aspen Summer Music School, 1979-82. *Compositions include:* Commissions: Maelstrom (The Fires of London), 1981; The Greater Changing, Symphony No 2 (Mystic Valley Orchestra, Boston), 1986; A Signal in the Land (Johnson City Symphony Orchestra, Johnson City, Tennessee), 1987; The Fifth Season, Symphony No 3 (Friends of Music at Yale/Yale Symphony Orchestra), 1988; Book of the Hours, Symphony No 1 (New England Philharmonic), 1988; Toward Eternity (Radcliffe Choral Society, Harvard University), 1988; Symphony No 4 (New England Philharmonic), 1989; Symphony No 5 (Pro Arte Orchestra, Boston), 1990; Recently published works: There is a River for soprano, women's chorus and orchestra, 1985; Images from Stillness for string trio, 1986; Images of Reminiscence for piano, 1987; The Fifth Season (Symphony No 3) for large orchestra, 1988; Book of the Hours (Symphony No 1) for soprano, countertenor and orchestra, 1988; Toward Eternity for women's chorus, 1988; One for solo clarinet; Complete Works published by E.C.Schirmer, 138 Ipswich Street, Boston, MA 02215. *Address:* 16 Forest Street, No 41, Cambridge, MA 02140, USA.

L

LA BARBARA Joan Lotz, b. 8 June 1947, Philadelphia, Pennsylvania, USA. Composer; Performer; Writer. m. Morton Subotnick, 18 Dec. 1979, 1 son. *Education:* Syracuse University School of Music, 1965-68; BS, NY University, 1968-70; Tanglewood/Berkshire Music Center, 1967-68. *Debut:* With Steve Reich and Musicians, Town Hall, NY, 1971. *Career:* Worked with Steve Reich, 1971-74; Philip Glass, 1973-76; John Cage (premiered Solo for Voice 45 from Songbooks with Atlas Eclipticlis and Winter Music with Orchestra of the Hague, La Rochelle, France, 1976); performed in Avignon Premiere of Einstein On The Beach (Glass/Wilson); premiered The Double Life of Amphibians, LA Olympics Arts Festival, (Subotnick), 1984; performed own work with Houston Symphony, 1982; San Francisco Symphony, 1982; Los Angeles Philharmonic, 1983; NY Philharmonic, 1984; Composed film score for Elizabeth Harris' Anima, 1991. *Compositions:* The Solar Wind, 1983, NEA Composer Fellowship Commission, (voice and 11 instruments), premiered by Los Angeles Philharmonic, 1983; Klee Alee, 1979 and Shadow Song, 1979 commissioned by RIAS (Berlin); Erin, 1980, commissioned by VPRO (Holland); Helga's Lied, 1986, commissioned by Esbjerg Ensemble, Denmark; Time(d) Trials and Unscheduled Events, 1984, commissioned for LA Olympics Arts Festival; Urban Tropics, 1988, commissioned by New Music America - Miami Festival for Premiere; Meet the Composer, commission for new choral work: To hear the wind roar, 1989-91; WDR commission for self-portrait/sound painting, 1989; 1 of 4 works chosen for Acustica International Competition 1989-90 (WDR); Film work: Composed and performed Angel Voice for Date With An Angel; L'albero dalle foglie azzurre, 1989 commissioned by St Louis Symphony; In The Dreamtime, 1990; Awakening, 1991 commissioned by University of Iowa; Klangbild Köln, 1991. *Recordings:* Voice Is The Original Instrument/Joan La Barbara; Reluctant Gypsy; Tapesongs; As Lightning Comes In Flashes; The Art of Joan La Barbara; Joan La Barbara/Sound Paintings; Joan La Barbara Singing through John Cage; Three Voices for Joan La Barbara by Morton Feldman; Jacob's Room by Morton Subotnick, composed for Joan La Barbara. *Publications:* Articles written for Grove's Dictionary. *Current Management:* Kristina Melcher, Daniel Kosharek, Santa Fe World Music Agency. *Address:* 121 Coronado Lane, Santa Fe, NM 87501, USA.

LA GRANGE Henry Louis de, b. 26 May 1924, Paris, France. Writer on Music. *Education:* Studied at Aix-en-Provence and the Sorbonne, Paris; Yale University School of Music 1941-46; Harmony, Counterpoint, Analysis, Yvonne Lefébure (piano) and Nadia Boulanger, 1945-53. *Career:* Music Critic for French and American publications; Guest Lecturer at Columbia University, Stanford and Indiana Universities, 1974-81; Geneva, 1982, Leipzig, Juilliard, ULCA, 1985, Budapest, 1987, Hamburg, 1988, Oslo, 1993, Paris Conservatory, Kyoto, Hong-Kong,Wellington, Sydney, Camberra, Melbourne etc. Taught a DEA Seminar at the Ecole Normale Supérieure, Paris. Founded the Bibliothèque Musicale Gustav Mahler, Paris, 1986. *Publication includes:* Gustav Mahler: Choronique d'une vie, 3 volumes, 1979-84; Vienna, Une Histoire musicale, 2 volumes, 1990-91; Mahler, to be published in 4 columes by Oxford University Press in England and the USA, from 1994. *Honours include:*Légion d'honneur; Officier Ordre du Merite; Title of Professor granted by Austrian government.*Address:*c/o Bibliothèque Musicale Gustav Mahler, 11 bis, rue de Vézelay, F-75008, France.

LA MONTAINE John, b. 17 Mar 1920, Chicago, Illinois, USA. Composer. *Education:* Studied with Bernard Rogers and Howard Hanson at the Eastman School, with Magenaar at Juilliard and with Nadia Boulanger at the American Conservatory, Fontainebleau. *Career:* Pianist with the NBC Symphony conducted by Toscanini 1950-54; Composer-in-residence at ther American Academy, Rome 1962; Visiting professor at the Eastman School 1964-65; Nixon Chair at Whittier College, California 1977. *Compositions:* Piano Concerto 1958; Jubilant Overture; Colloquy for strings; Spreading the News, opera 1957; Novellis, novellis, Christmas pageant opera 1960; String Quartet 1957; From Sea to Shining Sea for orchestra 1960; Fragments from the Song of Songs for soprano and orchestra 1960; Birds of Paradise for piano and orchestra 1964; Te Deum 1964; Mass of Nature 1966; Wilderness Journal for baritone, organ and orchestra 1972; Be Glad then America, opera 1974; The Nine Lessons of Christmas 1975; Flute Concerto 1981; Concerto for string orchestra 1981; Symphonic Variations for piano and orchestra 1982; The Lessons of Advent 1983; The Marshes of Glyn for baritone, chorus and orchestra 1984. *Honours include:* Guggenheim Fellowships; Pulitzer Prize 1959 for piano concerto; American Academy of Arts and Letters award 1962. *Address:* c/o ASCAP, ASCAP Building, One Lincoln Plaza, New York, NY 10023, USA.

LA RUE, (Adrian) Jan Pieters, b. 31 July 1918, Kisaran, Sumatra. *Education:* SB, Magna cum laude, Phi Beta Kappa, Paine Fellow, Harvard, 1940; MFA, with distinction, Princeton, 1942; PhD, Dissertation: The Okinawan Classical Songs, Harvard, 1952, University Microfilms, 1989. *Career:* Instructor to Associate Professor and Chairman of Music Department, Wellesley College, 1942-43, 1946-57; 1st Lieutenant, Transportation Corps (Okinawa Campaign, 16 months in Pacific Theatre), 1943-46; Professor of Music, Graduate School of Arts and Science, New York University, 1957-88; Visiting Professor, Bar Ilan, Israel, 1980; Executive Dean, 1963-64; Chairman, 1970-71, 1972-73; New York University; Visiting Professor (Summers), UCLA, 1947; University of Michigan, 1963; Fulbright Research Professor Austria, 1954-56; Music Curriculum Project, 1966-67; Councillor, Smithsonian Institution, 1967-73; Musicologist-in-Residence, Kennedy Center, Washington, 1975; Professor Emeritus, 1988. *Compositions:* Concertino, Clarinet and orchestra, 1941; Trio, strings, 1942. *Publications:* Guidelines for Style Analysis, 1970 (Sp.ed. 1988), 2nd Ed, Harmonie Perk Press, 1992; Methods and Models for Musical Style Analysis, with Ohmiya, Makoto, 1988; A Catalogue of 18th-Century Symphonies, 1988. *Contributions to:* Die Musik in Geschichte und Gegenwart, 1968; Grove's Dictionary, 6th Ed. 1980; articles in numerous journals and Festschriften, including Festschriften Davison, 1957; Albrecht, 1962; Voetterie, 1968; Geiringer, 1970; Larsen, 1972; Johnson, 1990; Southern, 1992; Ratner, 1992. Ed. Festschriften Reese, 1966, Deutsch, 1968. *Honours:* Ford Foundation Fellow, 1954; Guggenheim Fellow, 1964-65; ACLS Fellow, 1964-65; N.E.H. Research Grant, 1980-84; Festschrift: Studies in Musicall Sources and Style (ed. Wolf and Roesner), 1990. *Address:* Woods End Road, New Canaan, CT 06840, USA.

LA SCOLA Vincenzo, b. 1958, Palermo, Italy. Singer (Tenor). *Education:* Studied with Carlo Bergonzi. *Debut:* Parma, as Ernesto in Don Pasquale, 1983. *Career:* Sang in Genoa and Liege, 1984, Nemorino in Brussels and Rinuccio (Gianni Schicchi) and Tonio (La fille de regiment) in Paris, 1987-88; La Scala debut, 1988, as Nemorino, returning 1991-92, as Alfredo and Edgardo (Lucia di Lammermoor); Other roles include Elvino in La Sonnambula, Venice, 1989, Orombello in Beatrice di Tenda, Mascagni's Amico Fritz, the Duke of Mantua, and Florindo in Mascagni's Le Maschere; Sang Donizetti's Roberto Devereux at Bologna and Edgardo at La Scala, 1992; Rodolfo in La Bohème at the Verona Arena, 1992. *Recordings include:* Rossini's Petite messe solennelle; Beatrice di Tenda; Rigoletto, conducted by Muti; Le Maschere. *Address:* c/o Teatro alla Scala, Via Filodrammatici 2, 20121 Milan, Italy.

LAADE Wolfgang, b. 13 Jan. 1925, Zeitz, Germany. Ethnomusicologist. m. Dagmar Diedrich, 15 Aug. 1962. *Education:* Musikhochschule Leipzig, 1943; Staatliche Musikhochschule Berlin, 1949-54; PhD, Freie Universitat, Berlin, 1954-60. *Career:* Research Fellow, Australian Institute of Aboriginal Studies, 1963-67; Research Fellow, Deutsche Forschungsgemeinschaft, 1968-70; Lecturer in Ethnomusicology, University of Heidelberg, 1969-71; Professor of Ethnomusicology,

University of Zurich, Switzerland, 1971-90; Guest lectures at German, Austrian, American and Canadian universities; Guest professorships: Helsinki, Stockholm, Innsbruck, Moscow; Field research in Lapland, Corsica, Tunisia, Australia, Torres Straits, New Guinea, New Britain, Sri Lanka, Taiwan, Zimbabwe. *Recordings:* 10 LP records and 7 compact discs. *Publications:* Books: Die Struktur der korsischen Lamento-Melodik, 1962; Die Situation von Musikleben und Musikforschung in den Laendern Afrikas und Asiens und die neuen Aufgaben der Musikethnologie, 1969; Neue Musik in Afrika, Asien und Ozeanien; Diskographie und historisch-stilistischer Ueberblick, 1971; Gegenwartsfragen der Musik in Afrika und Asien: eine grundlegende Bibliographie, 1971; Oral traditions and written documents on the history and ethnography of the Northern Torres Strait Islands, Vol 1, 1971; Klangdokumente historischer Tasteninstrumente, Orgeln, Kiel-und Hammerklaviere, Eine Diskographie, 1972; Das Geisterkanu: Suedseemaerchen aus der Torres-Strasse, 1974; Musik der Goetter, Geister und Menschen; die Musik in der mythischen, fabulierenden und historischen Ueberlieferung der Voelker Afrikas, Nordasiens, Amerikas und Ozeaniens, 1975; Musikwissenschaft zwischen gestern und morgen; Bemerkungen eines Musikethnologen zur einer Diskussion ueber Musikethnologie und Musikgeschichte, 1976; Das korsische Volkslied; ethnographische und historische Fragen, Gattungen und Stil, 3 vols, 1981-87; Musik und Musiker in Maerchen, Sagen und Anekdoten der Voelker Europas, Vol 1: Mitteleuropa, 1988; Music and Culture in South-East New Britain, Auckland, New Zealand; Compact Discs accompanied by books: Jecklin Disco- JD 652-2, The Confucius Temple Ceremony, Taiwan, 1991; JD 653-2, Taiwan: Music of The Aboriginal Tribes, 1991; JD 654-2, Zimbabwe: The Ndebele People, 1991; JD 655-2, Papua New Guinea: The Coast of the Western Province, 1993. *Address:* Holzmoosruetistrasse 11, CH-8820 Waedenswil, Switzerland.

LABELLE Dominique, b. 1960, Montreal, Canada. Singer (Soprano). *Education:* Studied at Boston University and with Phyllis Curtin. *Career:* Concert appearances with Symphony Orchestras of Dallas, Montreal and Boston; Messiah with Pittsburgh Symphony, Mahler's 2nd Symphony in St Louis and Vaughan Williams' Antarctica Symphony at Indianapolis; Other repertory includes the Verdi Quattro Pezzi Sacri, the Requiems of Mozart and Frank Martin, Mahler's Fourth, Les Nuits d'Ete and Mozart's Exsultate Jubilate; Opera engagements as Donna Anna in the Peter Sellars production of Don Giovanni, Elizabeth Zimmer in Elegy for Young Lovers, Mimi for Glimmerglass Opera, New York, the Countess and Susanna in Le Nozze di Figaro at Vancouver (1992); Giuletta in I Capuleti e i Montecchi with Toledo Opera. *Recordings include:* Elektra, with Boston Symphony; Don Giovanni, on video; Masha and Chloe in The Queen of Spades, conducted by Ozawa. *Honours include:* Winner, Metropolitan Opera National Council Auditions, 1989. *Address:* c/o IMG Artists, Media House, 3 Burlington Lane, London W4 2TH, England.

LABÈQUE Katia, b. 3 March 1950, Hendaye, France. Pianist. *Education:* Studied with mother, then at Paris Conservatoire. *Career:* Many appearances with sister in piano duet repertoire, notably in music by Bach, Mozart, Brahms, Gershwin, Messiaen, Boulez and Scott Joplin; Recitals in London, Paris, New York, Chicago and Boston; Appearances with the Cleveland orchestra, Concertgebouw Orchestra, New York Philharmonic, Vienna Philharmonic and London Symphony Orchestra; Festival peformances at Hollywood Bowl, Salzburg, Tanglewood, Edinburgh and Berlin; Conductors include James Conlon, Riccardo Chailly, Simon Rattle and Pinchas Zukerman; Jazz collaborations with John McLaughlin, guitar; Featured in BBC-TV documentary, 1992. *Recordings:* Gershwin Rhapsody in Blue and Concerto in F (Philips); Recitals of Brahms, Liszt, Debussy, Ravel and Stravinsky; Rossini's Petite Messe Solenelle with the choir of King's College Cambridge; Bartók's Concerto for 2 Pianos and Orchestra; Symphonic Dances from West Side Story (CBS).

Honours include: Gold Disc for Gershwin recording with Philips; Dvořák Slavonic Dances, Concertos to two pianos by Bruch and Mendelssohn (Philips); Encore!, (Sony). *Address:* c/o Terry Harrison Artists Management, 9a Penzance Place, London W11 4PE, England.

LABÈQUE Marielle, b. 6 March 1952, Hendaye, France. Pianist. *Education:* Studied with mother and at the Paris Conservatoire. *Career:* Many appearances with sister in piano duet repertoire in music by Mozart, Debussy, Ravel, Schubert, Stravinsky, Berio and Lutoslawski; Recitals in London, Paris, New York, Chicago, Berlin and Boston; Appearances with the Israel Philharmonic, Orchestre de Paris, Philadelphia Orchestra, Boston Symphony and Vienna Philharmonic; Conductors include Semyon Bychkov, Myung-Whun Chung, Jesus Lopez-Cobos, Michael Tilson Thomas and David Zinman; Featured in BBC-TV documentary, 1992. *Recordings include:* Mozart's Concertos K242 and K365, with the Berlin Philharmonic; Carnival of the Animals with the Israel Philharmonic; Poulenc's Concerto for Two Pianos (Philips); Recitals of Liszt, Debussy, Brahms and Stravinsky; Dvořák Slavonic Dances, Concertos to two pianos by Bruch and Mendelssohn (Philips); Encore!, (Sony). *Address:* c/o Terry Harrison Artists Management, 9a Penzance Place, London W11 4PE, England.

LABI Emmanuel Gyimah, b. 27 Sept 1950, Adabraka, Accra, Ghana. Music Lecturer. m. Mary Margaret Blicharz, 31 Aug 1985, 1 daughter. *Education:* BA (Hons), Music with Philosophy, University of Ghana, Legon, 1976; MM, Composition, University of Illinois, Urbana-Champaign, USA, 1979; DMA, Composition, College Conservatory of Music, University of Cincinnati, Ohio, 1983. *Debut:* Break for Music programme, Ghana Broadcasting Corporation Television, 1971. *Career:* Lecturer, Department of Music, University of Nigeria, 1984-85; Adjunct Professor, Mercy College, New York City, USA, 1987-88; Lecturer, Department of Music, University of Ghana, 1988; Assistant Conductor, National Symphony Orchestra, 1988; Periodic Guest Conductor, Ghana National Symphony Orchestra. *Compositions:* 5 Dialects for Piano, op 19, 21, 22, 23, 25; Gentle Winds for violin and piano, 1973; Farewell for violin and piano, 1975; From the Durbar for violin and piano, 1976; 4 orchestral works; Trio for Flute, Bass Clarinet and Piano; 1 string quartet; Commissions: 2 Ancient Perspectives for unaccompanied tuba, op 24, 1972; Ancient Perspectives 3, for E flat tenor saxophone and percussion. *Publication:* Dialects-2 for Pianoforte, Op 21, 1987. *Honours:* Grant, Meet the Composers Inc, New York City, 1986; Winner, Entertainment Critics and Reviewers Association of Ghana Award for Music Composition, 1991. *Hobbies:* Gardening; Swimming; Lawn tennis; Fishing; Working on foundations in African and Western music theory. *Address:* c/o May Acheampong, Box 6646, Accra-North, Accra, Ghana, West Africa.

LACHENMANN Helmut, b. 27 Nov 1935, Stuttgart, Germany. Composer. *Education:* Studied at Stuttgart, with Jurgen Uhde (piano) and Johann Nepomuk David (composition); Venice with Luigi Nono. *Career:* Electronic Music Studio at University of Ghent, Belgium; Taught music theory at Stuttgart Hochschule fur Musik, 1966-70; Ludwigsburg Hochschule, 1970-76; Hanover Hochschule fur Musik, 1976-81; Musikhochschule Stuttgart, 1981-; Master class in composition at Basle Music Academy; Instructor at the Ferienkurse in Darmstadt, 1978, 1982; Instructor at the Cursos Latinamericanos de musica contemporanea in Brazil, 1978, Dominican Republic, 1980; Composition seminars in Toronto, 1982, Buenos Aires, Santiago de Chile, Tokyo, 1984, Villafranca, Spain, 1986, Oslo, Paris, 1989; Member of Akademie der Kunste in Berlin, Akademie Der Schonen Kunste in Munich and Freie Akademie der Kunste in Mannheim, Hamburg, Leipzig. *Compositions:* Souvenir for 41 instrumentalists, 1959; Introversion I and II for 6 instruments, 1964-66; String Trio, 1966; Consolation I and II for solo voices and instruments, 1967-68; Les Consolations for solo voices and orchestra, 1967-68, 1977-78; Notturno for cello and small orchestra, 1968; tema for flute, voice and cello, 1968; Pression for cello, 1969; Air for percussion and orchestra, 1968-69; Kontrakdenz for orchestra, 1970; Dal niente for clarinet, 1970; Gran Torso for string quartet, 1971-76, 1988; Klangschatten for 48 strings and 3 pianos, 1972; Fassade for orchestra, 1973; Accanto for clarinet and orchestra, 1975; Salut fur Caudwell for 2 guitars, 1977; Tanzsuite mit Deutschlandlied for string quartet and orchestra, 1979-80; Ein Kinderspiel for piano, 1980; Harmonica for tuba and orchestra, 1981-83; Mouvement (-vor der Erstarrung) for ensemble, 1982-84; Ausklang for piano and orchestra, 1984-85; Staub for orchestra, 1985-87; Allegro Sostenuto for clarinet, cello and piano, 1986-88; Tableau for orchestra, 1988-89; II Streichquartett 'Reigen seliger Geister' 1989; Zwei Gefuhle. Musik mit Leonardo for ensemble, 1992. *Honours:* Cultural Prize of Music, City of Munich, 1965; Composition Prize, City of Stuttgart, 1968; Bach Prize, City of Hamburg, 1972. *Address:* c/o Breitkopf & Hartel, Walkmuhlstr 52, D-65195 Wiesbaden, Germany.

LACHMANN Elisabeth, b. 20 Apr 1940, Vienna, Austria. Singer (Soprano). *Education:* Studied in Vienna. *Debut:* Berne, 1961, as Despina, and Cagliari in Wiener Slut. *Career:* Sang at Karlsruhe, 1962- 64, as Micaela, Marenka, Cherubino and Regina in Mathis der Maler; Graz, 1964- 68, as Pamina, Susanna, Frau Fluth and Zdenka (Arabella); Engaged at Dortmund from 1968, as Mimi, Sophie, Sieglinde, Desdemona, Donna Anna, the Trovatore Leonora, Wagner's Elisabeth, Venus and Brunnhilde, Tosca, Amelia in Ballo in Maschera, Aida, Senta, Ariadne and Abigaille; These and other roles in guest appearances at Vienna State Opera, Hamburg, Stuttgart, Frankfurt, Cologne, Zurich and Antwerp; Concert and opera tours to Netherlands, France, Far East, Africa, South America and Switzerland; Professor at Detmold Musikhochschule, 1984-. *Address:* Heiligenpesch 18A, D-41069 Mönchengladbach, Germany.

LACHOUT Karel, b. 30 Apr. 1929, Prague, Czechoslovakia. Ethnomusicologist; Composer. *Education:* MusD, University of Prague, Czechoslovakia, 1953; Composition, Academy of Musical Arts in Prague, 1949-54; Private studies. *Career:* Redacteur of Music Department, Prague, 1953-79; Freelance composer and Ethnomusicologist (specialising in Latin American Music and Folklore), 1980-. *Compositions include:* Music for Orchestra, Piano Pieces, suite Such is Cuba, 1962; two String Quartets; Pieces for Dance; Light Music. *Recordings:* Origins of Folkmusic in Latin America, a Selection of music examples in 2 LP records with own textbook produced in cooperation Lyrichord and Supraphon, Prague, 1987; Recordings: Folkmusic of Spain, a selection of 2 LP records with own textbook, 1989. *Publications:* The World Sings, 1957; Music of Chile, 1976; Music of Cuba, 1979; Lexicon of Latin American Music, 1980; Panorama of Spanish Music, 1981; Lullabies from all the World, Collection, 1989. *Hobbies:* Languages (Latin, English, Spanish); Travelling abroad to explore origins of music in foreign countries. *Address:* Viklefova 11, Prague 3, Czech Republic.

LACZO Zoltan, b. 29 Jan 1938, Bekescsaba, Hungary. Music Psychologist. m. 1966, Divorced 1977. *Education:* Bachelor of Psychology, Budapest University, 1968; Bachelor of Music Education, Franz Liszt Academy of Music, 1963. *Career:* Lecturer and Director of Music Teacher Training College, Miskolc, 1963-71; Senior Lecturer, Education and Psychology of Music, Franz Liszt Academy of Music, Budapest, 1971-; Secretary, Hungarian Music Teachers Association, 1972-; Member of Editorial Board, Hungarian Music Education Journal, Parlando, 1972-; Research and lecturing in Europe, Canada 1980-; Artist in Residence at E Cowan University, Perth, Australia, 1991. *Publications:* Music Listening Guidance book for teachers at grade 1-4, 1985 (second edition 1988, third edition 1991); Music Listening Guidance for teachers at grade 7-8, 1987, Budapest. *Contributions to:* Hungarian, English, German, Italian and Polish journals of music education,

especially Journal for Research in Music Education and Canadian Music Educator. *Hobbies:* Swimming; Skiing. *Address:* Bogdanfy u 8/C, 1117 Budapest, Hungary.

LADE John, b. 8 Apr. 1916, Tunbridge Wells, Kent, England. Broadcaster; Writer. m. Susan Ridehalgh-Fisher, 5 Dec. 1942, 1 daughter. *Education:* Licentiate, Trinity College, London, 1946-48. *Career:* Broadcaster, (Music Talks), 1947-; Lecturer, Extra-mural Department, London University; Producer, 1953, then Chief Assistant (Music), Head of Gramophone Programmes, 1972-77, Producer and Initiator, BBC Record Review 1957 for 1,000 programmes, Organ Gallery; Journeys with Music etc. *Publications:* Edited Building a Library and Building a Library 2, based on BBC Record Review, 1979 and 1980; Edited Series The Composer as Contemporary; Record Critic of The Tablet; Has written many record sleeves. *Contributions to:* Musical Times; Listener; Daily Telegraph; Gramophone. *Hobbies:* Good food and drink; Reading; Book collecting. *Address:* Flat 12, 105 Cheyne Walk, London SW10 0DF, England.

LADERMAN Ezra, b. 29 June 1924, Brooklyn, New York, USA. Composer. *Education:* Studied with Stefan Wolpe, 1946-49, and at Brooklyn College with Miriam Gideon, BA 1949; Columbia University with Douglas Moore and Otto Luening. *Career:* Teacher at Sarah Lawrence College 1960-61 and 1965-66; State University if New York at Binghampton 1971-82; Director of the Music Program of the National Endowment for the Arts 1978. *Compositions:* Dramatic: Jacob and the Indians, opera 1954; Goodbye to the Clowns, opera 1956; The Hunting of the Snark, opera-cantata 1958; Sarah, TV opera 1959; Ballets Dance Quartet, Esther, Song of Songs, Solos and Chorale; Air Raid, opera 1965; Shadows among Us, opera 1967; Galileo Galilei, opera 1978; Film and TV scores; Orchestral: Piano Concerto 1939; Leipzig Symphony 1945; Piano Concerto 1957; 9 Symphonies 1964-84; Flute Concerto 1968; Viola Concerto 1975; Violin Concerto 1978; Piano Concerto No.1 1978; Concerto for String Quartet and orchestra 1981; Cello Concerto 1984; Vocal: Oratorios The Eagle Stirred 1961, The Trials of Galileo 1967, A Mass for Cain 1983; Columbus, cantata 1975; Chamber: Wind Octet 1957; Clarinet Sonata 1958; 8 String Quartets 1959-85; Double Helix for flute, oboe and string quartet 1968; Partita for violin 1982; Double String Quartet 1983. *Honours include:* Guggenheim Fellowships, 1955, 1958, 1964; Rome Prize 1963; Oscar for film music to The Eleanor Roosevelt Story 1965. *Address:* c/o ASCAP, ASCAP Building, One Lincoln Plaza, New York, NY 10023, USA.

LADYSZ Bernard, b. 24 July 1922, Vilnius, Poland. Singer (Bass). *Education:* Studied at the Warsaw Conservatory. *Career:* Sang at the Teatr Wielki Warsaw from 1950; From 1956 appeared in Chicago, San Francisco, Moscow, Palermo, Naples and Parma; Hamburg Staatsoper 1969, as Father Barre in The Devils of Loudun by Penderecki; Other roles were Don Giovanni, Boris Godunov, Philip II and the Grand Inquisitor in Don Carlos, Mephistopheles and Szymanowski's King Roger. *Recordings include:* Raimondo in Lucia di Lammermoor, with Maria Callas (Columbia); The Devils of Loudun and Penderecki's St Luke Passion (Philips); Utrenja by Penderecki (RCA).

LAFONT Jean, b. 17 Aug. 1918, Marseille, France. Singer (Baritone). *Education:* Marseille Conservatory with Antonin Trantoul. *Debut:* Marseille Opera 1945. *Career:* Sang in Africa 1946-47, Nancy 1947-48; Théâtre de la Monnaie, Brussels, 1949-59, notably in the first local performances of operas by Stravinsky, Menotti, Rimsky-Korsakov and Moniusko; Guest performances in Wiesbaden, Ostend, Ghent, Amsterdam, Bordeaux, Nantes and Switzerland; Walloon Opera 1967, as Borodin's Prince Igor; Opera producer in Brussels from 1948.

LAFONT Jean-Philippe, b. 4 Feb. 1951, Toulouse, France. Singer (Bass-Baritone). *Education:* Studied in Toulouse with Denise Dupleix and in Paris with Gabriel

Bacquier. *Debut:* Toulouse 1974, as Papageno. *Career:* Paris Opera Studio 1977, as Nick Shadow in The Rake's Progress; Albi from 1977, as Mozart's Guglielmo and in Grétry's Les femmes Vengées and Tom Jones; Paris from 1978, in operas by Gounod, Offenbach, Gluck and Cherubini; Sang in Berlin in the European premiere of Debussy's La Chute de la Maison Usher; Lyon 1980, as Choroebus in the French premiere of Les Troyens; Aix-en-Provence 1982, as Boreas in the stage premiere of Rameau's Les Boréades; Guest appearances in Strasbourg, Geneva, Lille, Hamburg, Hanover and Nimes; New York debut 1983, as Fieramosca in Benvenuto Cellini at Carnegie Hall; Perugia 1983, in Salieri's Les Daniades; Paris Opera 1983, as Rossini's Moïse; Brussels and Barcelona 1984, as Mozart's Count; Rome 1985, in Cherubini's Demophoon; Aix 1986, as Leporello in Don Giovanni; Sang Amonasro at Bonn 1989, Debussy's Golaud at Marseilles, 1990; Alcide in Lully's Alceste at the Théâtre des Champs Elysées, 1991-92. *Recordings include:* Les Boréades (Erato); Gounod's Messe Solonelle (HMV); La Belle Hélène; Le Postillon de Lonjumeau by Adam. *Address:* c/o Opéra de Marseilles, 2 Rue Molière, F-13231 Marseille Cedex 01, France.

LAGRANGE Michele, b. 29 May 1947, Conches, Saone-et-Loire, France. Singer (Soprano). *Education:* Studied in Paris. *Career:* Engaged at Lyon Opera from 1978; Paris Opéra, 1984-85, in Jerusalem by Verdi and as Alice in Robert le Diable by Meyerbeer; Opéra-Comique, 1987, as Donna Anna; Teatro Colon, Buenos Aires, 1982, as Teresa in Benvenuto Cellini; Aix-en-Provence Festival, 1989, as Fata Morgana in The Love for Three Oranges; Sang Marguerite in Faust at Avignon and St Etienne, season 1990-91; Montpellier Festival, 1991, in Bizet's Ivan IV (concert performance); Sang Fiorella in Offenbach's Les Brigands at Amsterdam and Isabella in Franchetti's Christoforo Colombo at Montpellier, 1992; Other roles include Musette and Elisabeth de Valois. *Recordings include:* Poulenc Salve Regina and Stabat Mater; Guercoeur by Magnard; The Love for Three Oranges. *Address:* c/o Saison Lyrique de St Etienne, 8 place de l'Hotel de Ville, F-4200 St Etienne, France.

LAGZDINA Vineta, b. 11 Nov. 1945, Oldenberg, Germany. Composer/Performer. 1 daughter. *Education:* BMus, University of Adelaide, 1976; Instrumental Teachers' Certificate, 1979; Computer Music Studies, Adelaide University Conservatorium, 1980-81. *Career:* Sound works included in exhibitions in Australia, New Zealand and Japan; Film music: electronic, computer generated, instrumental 1978-; Video art music; Grants for experimental music/movement performances 1981-82; Composer's grant for radio 1983; Curated Audio-Eyes, exhibition 1983; Lecturer, Sydney College of the Arts, Music across the Arts, 1984-; ABC Radio, 1987; The White Bird Music Theatre, 1987; Shock of the New, video sound track, 1987; Speaking Out, Film Sound Track, 1987. *Compositions:* Noh-work, a quadrophonic percussion tape, 1982; Obstruction, computer sound tape for dance, 1981; The Black Snake, tape piece for voice and electronics, 1983; Double-Dream, Triple Fate, video sound tracks, 1984-85; Media Massage, spoken song, 1986. *Publications:* 22 Contemporary Australian Composers. *Contributions to:* Article published in Art Network, 1983; Article published in New Music Australia 4 in 1985. *Address:* Flat 11, 26 Pearson Street, Balmain East 2041, Australia.

LAING Alan, b. 16 Sept 1944, Glasgow, Scotland. Lecturer; Composer; Conductor. m. Jennifer Linnell, 25 Mar. 1978, 3 sons. *Education:* B Mus 1966, B Mus honours in Composition 1967, PhD 1973, University of Edinburgh; Licentiate, Royal Academy of Music. *Career:* Repetiteur, London, England, 1968-78; Director of Music, University of Kent, 1968-78; Lecturer, University of Hull, 1978-; Conducting work, in UK and South America, has particularly included opera with professional casts, 1975-3. *Compositions:* Violin Sonata; String Quartet; Witchcraft by a Picture (piano solo); Sul rovescio d'un foglio (full orchestra); Sei Versi (harp solo); Viola Sonata; Music for String Orchestra; Dolce far

niente (orchestra); Octet; 3 Miniatures for the Clarsach; Silver Apples of the Moon (soprano and orchestra); 3 John Donne Sonnets; Transmorphisms (Piano solo); Evocation (Orchestra); Elgiva (Orchestra); Of Music's Wondrous Might (Soprano and 8 cellos); Three for Four (four Saxaphones); Various other songs, choral works, chamber works, incidental stage music. *Address:* 29 Woodlands, Beverley, East Yorkshire HU17 8BT, England.

LAJMING Ziemowit Mikolaj, b. 14 Sept 1964, Gdansk, Poland. Conductor; Cellist. m. Monika Bakowska, 13 July 1990. *Education:* Student, 1971-83, Diploma with honours, 1983, Lyceum of Music, Gdansk; Student, Academy of Music, Gdansk, 1983-84; Student, 1984-90, Diploma with honours, 1990, Academy of Music, Poznan; Hochschule fur Kunste, Bremen, Germany, 1988. *Debut:* Manon Lescaut, Baltic Opera, Gdansk, 1991. *Career:* As Cellist: Numerous concerts with chamber and ancient music ensembles; Tournees: Hamburg, Brussels, London; Founder, Baroque Quartett Quattro a tre, 1988; As Conductor: Works in Baltic Opera, Gdansk; Concerts with Baltic Philharmonic Orchestra and chamber orchestras, 1989-. *Publications:* Conductor as an Accompanist - General Problems and Methods, diploma thesis, 1990. *Honours:* 2nd Prize, Young Cellists Competition, Koszalin. *Memberships:* MENSA-Polska; Karol Szymanowski Musical Society; Art Friends Association, Gdansk. *Hobbies:* Car excursions; Art and architecture. *Address:* 1/4 Weglarska St 20, 80- 834, Gdansk, Poland.

LAKES Gary, b. 26 Sept. 1950, Dallas, Texas. Singer (Tenor). *Education:* Vocal studies with William Eddy at Seattle Opera. *Debut:* Seattle 1981, as Froh in Das Rheingold. *Career:* Mexico City 1983, as Florestan in Fidelio; Charlotte Opera 1984, as Samson in Samson et Dalila; Metropolitan Opera debut 1986, as the High Priest in Idomeneo: returned as Tannhäuser and as Siegmund in a new production of Die Walküre; Sang the Emperor in Die Frau ohne Schatten at the Met 1989, Radames at New Orleans; Erik in Der fliegende Holländer at the Met 1990, followed by Siegmund in New York (also televised) and San Francisco; Sang in Das Lied von der Erde at the 1991 Promenade Concerts, London; Seasom 1991/92 as Lohengrin at Buenos Aires and Erik at the Met. *Recordings include:* Die Walküre, conducted by James Levine. *Address:* c/o Metropolitan Opera, Lincoln Center, New York, NY 10023, USA.

LAKI Krisztina, b. 14 Sept 1944, Budapest, Hungary. Singer (Soprano). *Education:* Studied at Budapest Conservatory. *Debut:* Berne 1976, as Gilda in Rigoletto. *Career:* Sang with the Deutsche Oper am Rhein, Dusseldorf, and in Cologne; Bregenz and Edinburgh Festivals; Glyndebourne 1979-80, as Aminta in Die schweigsame Frau and Sophie in Der Rosenkavalier; Salzburg 1980, as Lucille in Von Einem's Dantons Tod; Tour of East Germany 1984, notably in cantatas by Bach; Paris Opera 1984, as Sophie; Other roles include Zdenka in Arabella; Mozart's Queen of Night, Zerlina and Susanna; Carolina in Il Matrimonio Segreto and Nannetta in Falstaff; Sang Marzelline in Fidelio at Hamburg, 1988; Barcelona 1989, as Zdenka in Arabella, Marzelline with the company of the Cologne Opera at Hong Kong; Also widely heard in oratorio. *Recordings:* St Matthew Passion by Bach (HMV); Handel's Partenope; Masses by Haydn (Electrola); Dantons Tod (Orfeo); Concert Arias by Mozart (Decca); Bach's Christmas Oratorio; Mozart's C Minor Mass (Telefunken); Paisiello's Il Barbiere di Siviglia (Hungaroton); Mozart's Schauspieldirektor and Mysliveček's Il Bellerofonte. *Address:* Oper der Stadt Köln, Offenbachplatz, D-5000 Cologne, Germany.

LAKI Peter, b. 1 Feb 1954, Budapest, Hungary. Musicologist. m. Judit Frigyesi, 12 Apr 1978, div 1991, 1 son. *Education:* Diploma in Musicology, Franz Liszt Conservatory, Budapest, 1979; PhD, Music, University of Pennsylvania, 1989. *Career:* Research Fellow, Franz Liszt Academy of Music, 1979-80; Member, Ethnomusicology Division, Laboratoire des Langues et Civilisations a Tradition Orale, Ivry-sur-Seine, France,

1981-82; Programme Annotator, The Cleveland Orchestra, Cleveland, Ohio, USA, 1990-. *Contributions to:* Free-form Recitative and Strophic Structure in the Hallel Psalms, in Orbis Musicae, 1979-80; Kodaly's First Surviving Composition, in Notes, 1992; G B Marino and Music, in International Journal of Musicology, 1992-93. *Memberships:* American Musicological Society; Society for Ethnomusicology, Past Secretary of Mid-Atlantic Chapter. *Hobbies:* Hiking; Swimming; Reading. *Address:* The Cleveland Orchestra, Severance Hall, 1101 Euclid Avenue, Cleveland, OH 44106, USA.

LAKNER Yehoshua, b. 24 Apr 1924, Bratislava, Czechoslovakia. Composer. *Education:* Studied with Partos and Boscovich in Israel; USA, 1952, with Copland at Tanglewood; West Germany, 1959-60, with Kagel, Koenig, Stockhausen at the electronic music studio of West German Radio; Further study with Bernd-Alois Zimmermann. *Career:* Teacher at Rubin-Academy of Music, in Tel-Aviv from 1950, at Konservatorium und Musikhochschule Zürich from 1974. *Compositions include:* Flute Sonata, 1948; Sextet for Piano and Wind, 1951; Toccata for Orchestra, 1953; Improvisations for viola, 1958; Hexachords for orchestra, 1960; Figures, ballet, 1962; 5 Birthdays for piano, 1965; Dream of Mohamed for chorus and tape, 1968; Kaninchen for speaker, percussion and tape, 1973; Umlaufe for ensemble, 1976; Fermatas for Piano, 1977; Circles and Signals for 2 Pianos, 1985; Aleph-Beth-Gimmel for Piano, 1992; Composed 'concrete music' for various dramatic works at Theater an der Winkelwiese, the Schauspielhaus Zurich (world premiere of Brecht's Turandot, 1969), Theater am Neumarkt; Music for a number of art and commercial films; Composition of AVTS, audio-visual time-structures for computer and screen, 1987-; Musikado, 1987-91; 1987: Mimusini; Meditatives Melisma; Snem 14; November; 1988: Milchstrasse; 12-Ton-Computude; Fest-Farben- Klang; Ostinato/Westinato; Scherzodrama; 1989: Tont so die Rache des Achilles; Gazalut; Alaska 89; Rondudeldo; Scherzo Aldesago; Ornament devours itself; 1990: Wrath of the Bees; Mini-mal-plus; 8 out of 59; Diaguna; 1991: Die-das-den-die; Black, Bluegreen and other Sounds; Summary 15; Colored Interruptions; Trilogy-91; 1992: Nowis; Intermezzo- 92; GRFRGR; Eribo; WHL; 1993: Ba-ne'elam; Rondo 93. *Address:* Ahornstr 1, CH-5442 Fislisbach, Switzerland.

LALANDI Lina Madeleine, b. Athens, Greece. Festival Director. m. Ralph Emery. *Education:* Graduated with Hons, Athens Conservatory; Private Study in England; Harpsichord and Singing. *Debut:* Royal Festival Hall, 1954. *Career:* International Career as Harpsichordist, London, Paris, Geneva, Athens; Radio and TV; Founder and Director, English Bach Festival Trust, 1962, specializing now in baroque opera (Riccardo Primo by Handel, 1991); Iphigénie en Tauride, 1993. *Honours:* OBE, 1975; Officier dans l'Ordre des Arts et des Lettres, France for servicess to culture, 1979. *Hobbies:* Reading, Astrophysics. *Address:* 15 South Eaton Place, London, SW1W 9ER, England.

LALE Peter, b. 1960, England. Violist. *Career:* Founder member of the Britten Quartet, debut concert at the Wigmore Hall 1987; Quartet in Residence at the Dartington Summer School 1987, with quartets by Schnittke; season 1988-89 in the Genius of Prokofiev series at Blackheath and BBC Lunchtime Series at St John's Smith Square; South Bank appearances with the Schoenberg/Handel Quartet Concerto conducted by Neville Marriner, concerts with the Hermann Prey Schubertiade and collaborations with the Alban Berg Quartet in the Beethoven Plus series; Tour of South America, 1988, followed by Scandinavian debut; Season 1989-90 with debut tours of Holland, Germany, Spain, Austria, Finland; Tours from 1990 to the Far East, Malta, Sweden, Norway: Schoenberg/Handel Concerto with the Gothenburg Symphony; festival appearances in Brighton, the City of London, Greenwich, Canterbury, Harrogate, Chester, Spitalfields and Aldeburgh; Collaborations with John Ogdon, Imogen Cooper, Thea King and Lynn Harrell; Formerly resident quartet at Liverpool University; Teaching role at Lake District

Summer Music, 1989; Universities of Bristol and Hong Kong 1990. *Recordings:* Beethoven Op 130 and Schnittke Quartet no 3 (LDR); Vaughan Williams On Wenlock Edge and Ravel Quartet (EMI); Britten, Prokofiev, Tippett, Elgar and Walton Quartets (Collins Classics); Exclusive contract with EMI from 1991. *Address:* c/o Ingpen and William Ltd, 14 Kensington Court, London W8 5DN, England.

LAMA Lina, b. 20 Apr. 1932, Faenza, Italy. Concert Violist; Professor of Viola. *Education:* Diplomas in Violin and Viola; Diplomas in Piano and Composition. *Debut:* Teatro S. Carlo - Naples. *Career:* Professor Conservatorio di Musica S. Cecilia, Roma 1959; Appearances on BBC and Italian TV and Radio; Concerts in Germany, Belgium, Italy, Israel, Hungary, Greece, Finland, France, North and South America, Africa, Asia and Japan; Concerts throughout Europe under Italian and foreign Maestri; Sonata per la Gran Viola by Paganini performed at Teatro San Carlo, Naples; Teacher of Viola at Conservatoire of S. Cecilia, Roma Festival; International Specialisation courses at: Festival of Jywaskyla (Finland); Città di Castello, Lanciano, and Mezzolombardo (Italy); Member of Juries for following international competitions: Viola, Budapest, 1979; N. Paganini, Genova, 1988; Member of jury for national viola competition at Vittaorio Veneto, 1986. *Honours:* Concert Prizes in Italy; Accademico of Accademia di S. Cecilia Roma; Cavaliere al merito della Repubblica Italiana. *Hobby:* Painting. *Address:* Via Ugo de Carolis 31, 00136, Rome, Italy.

LAMARCHINA Robert, b. 3 Sept. 1928, New York City, USA. Cellist; Conductor. *Education:* Paris Conservatoire; Curtis Institute with Piatigorsky and Feuermann. *Debut:* With St Louis Symphony under Vladimir Golschmann 936. *Career:* Played in NBC Symphony Orchestra under Toscanini, 1944; Conductor and Musical Director, Young Musicians Foundation, Los Angeles, 1952-53; Solo cellist with Chicago Symphony under Fritz Reiner, 1960; Conducted at Metropolitan Opera; La Traviata at Spoleto and Menotti's The Medium at the New York City Opera; Artistic and Musical Director, Honolulu Symphony Society and Hawaii Opera Theatre 1967-79; Conductor of numerous symphony orchestras and opera companies, including New York Philharmonic, St Louis Symphony, Chicago Symphony, Radio Italiana, Zurich Symphony, Vancouver Opera Association; Fujiwara Opera Institute.

LAMB Anthony Stuart, b. 4 Jan. 1947, Woodford, England. Clarinettist. m. Philippa Carpenter-Jacobs, 1 son, 2 daughters. *Education:* Royal College of Music; ARCM. *Debut:* With Chamber Ensemble Capricorn, Wigmore Hall, London, 1974. *Career:* Principal Clarinet, Royal Ballet Orchestra, 1969-71; Founder Member, Capricorn (violin, clarinet, cello, piano), 1973, many broadcasts and concerts; Co-Principal with English National Opera Orchestra, 1976-; Several BBC Broadcasts; Freelance Clarinettist with most major British orchestras. *Recordings:* As member of Capricorn: Rimsky-Korsakov, Quintet in B flat for piano and wind; Glinka, Grand Sextet in E flat for piano and strings, 1985. *Membership:* Musicians Union. *Hobby:* Tennis. *Address:* 22 Munster Road, Teddington, Middlesex TW11 9LL, England.

LAMBERTI Giorgio, b. 9 July 1938, Adria, Rovigo, Italy. Singer (Tenor). *Education:* Studied in Mantua. *Debut:* Rome 1964, as Arrigo in I Vespri Siciliani. *Career:* US debut Chicago 1965, as Radames; Rome 1965, in the premiere of Wallenstein by Zafred; Metropolitan Opera from 1974, as Enzo, Cavaradossi, Radames and Turiddu; Engagements in Paris, Brussels, Budapest, Baltimore, Amsterdam, Helsinki, Florence and Venice; Covent Garden debut, Don Carlos, 1979; Other roles include Pollione, Don José, Jason in Medée; Verdi's Ernani, Alvaro, Manrico and Riccardo; Wagner's Tannhäuser and Lohengrin; Edgardo in Lucia di Lammermoor; Sang Radames at Berlin and Luxor, 1987 and Caracalla Festival, Rome, 1989; Andrea Chénier Stuttgart, 1988; appeared as Stiffelio in the first Covent Garden production of Verdi's opera, 1993. *Recordings include:* Ernani and I Lombardi (Hungaroton); Il Corsaro;

Gemma di Vergy by Donizetti; Bellini's Zaira. *Address:* Royal Opera House, Covent Garden London W2, England.

LAMBRO Phillip, b. 2 Sept. 1935, Wellesley Hills, Massachusetts, USA. Composer; Conductor; Pianist. *Education:* Studied music in Boston, later in Miami, Florida; Received Scholarship to The Music Academy of The West in California 1955; Teachers include: Donald Pond and György Sandor. *Debut:* Pianist's Fair, Symphony Hall, Boston 1952. *Career:* Composed and conducted music for several motion pictures including documentaries, Major performances now in Israel, Europe and the Orient. *Compositions include:* Miraflores for string orchestra; Dance Barbaro for percussion; Two Pictures for Solo Percussionist and Orchestra; Four Songs for Soprano and Orchestra; Toccata for Piano; Toccata for Guitar; Parallelograms for Flute Quartet and Jazz Ensemble; Music for Wind, Brass and Percussion; Obelisk for Oboist and Percussionist; Structures for String Orchestra; Fanfare and Tower Music for Brass Quintet; Night Pieces for Piano; Biospheres for 6 Percussionists; Trumpet Voluntary; Eight Little Trigrams for Piano. Compositions performed by Leopold Stokowski, Philippe Entremont, Santiago Rodriguez, The Philadelphia Orchestra, The Rochester Philharmonic, Baltimore, Indianapolis, Miami, Denver, Oklahoma, New Orleans Symphonies. *Address:* 1888 Century Park East, Suite 1900, Century City, CA 90067-1702, USA.

LAMBROS Simon David, b. 17 Jan 1960, Mansfield, Nottinghamshire, England. Composer. *Education:* BSc (Hons), University College, London, 1978; PGCE, Manchester (Victoria) University, 1984; Postgraduate Diploma, Composition, London College of Music; Studied with Tom Williams at Keel University, Simon Parkin, Royal Northern College of Music, Alan Wilson, Goldmsiths and Francis Shaw, National Film and TV School. *Career:* Thames TV appearance to explain film music techniques to Prince Edward, Nov 1992; Important performances of his works. *Compositions include:* Magnificat and Nunc Dimittis, 1st performance Worcester Cathedral, 1981; Preludio for orchestra, Thaxted Festival, 1982; Etude for Strings, Bowdon Festival, 1987; Cello Concerto, Stockport Town Hall with S Callow and BBC Philharmonic, 1989; Psalm 134 for choir and orchestra, Oldham Queen Elizabeth Hall, 1990; In Memoriam for choir and orchestra, Stoke-on-Trent, 1991; Clarinet Concerto, University College London with G Denny, 1992; Mass of St Francis, Granada TV, 1988; Music, award-winning films: Pirates; A Place in Danger; Blindscape; Music, other films including: Reign; 10 Minutes More; Moonlight; Mitologia (Spanish cinema); Fix und Fertig (German cinema); Flying Colours (BBC); Test Flight (BBC). *Address:* 1 Meadow Close, Wycombe Marsh, High Wycombe, Bucks HP11 1RG, England.

LAMIGEON Louise, b. 21 June 1915, Edgware, Middlesex, England. Teacher. *Education:* Royal College of Music; GRSM, ARCM, (Violin Teaching). *Career:* Chief Music Mistress, Various Schools; Staff Hertfordshire Rural Music School; Professor in Charge of School Music; Royal Manchester College of Music; Extra Mural Lecturer, University of Manchester; Adjudicator, Music Festivals; Examiner Associated Board; External Examiner, Music Diplomas, Colchester. *Address:* Via Benozzo Gozzoli 24, E U R, 00142 Rome, Italy.

LAMMEL Inge, b. 8 May 1924, Berlin, Germany. Musicologist. 2 children. *Education:* PhD in Musicology. *Career:* Head, Workers Song Archives, Academy of Arts, German Democratic Republic for 30 years until 1985; Publisher; Lecturer; Issued Records; Exhibitions including, Germany; Austria; Bulgaria; Soviet Union; Czechoslovakia; Finland; Sweden; Japan; France. *Recordings:* Several records on German Workers Song. *Publications include:* Das Arbeiterlied, 1970, 1975, 1980; Bibliographie der deutschen Arbeiterliedblatter, 1973; Bibliographie der deutschen Arbeitliedblatter, 1975; Diskographie der deutschen proletarischen Schallplatten, 1980; Kampfgefahrte unser Lied, 1978; Arbeitermusikkultur

in Deutschland 1844-1945, 1984; Editor of various publications including, song books (10) Das Lied im Kampf geboren, 1956-67; Hundert proletarische Balladen, 1975, 1985; Und weil der Mensch ein Mensch ist, 200 Arbeiterlieder, 1986. *Contributions to:* Books, journals and dictionaries in Germany, Soviet Union, Poland, Sweden, Finland, Japan and Czechoslovakia. *Honours:* Hanns-Eisler prize, 1971. *Hobbies:* Books; Records. *Address:* Wisbyer Straße 59, 10439 Berlin, Germany.

LAMMERS Gerda, b. 13 Feb. 1915, Zeitz, Germany. Singer (Soprano). *Education:* Studied in Berlin with Lula Mysz-Gmeiner and Margret Schwedler-Lohmann. *Debut:* 1940, as concert singer. *Career:* Stage debut 1955, as Ortlinde at Bayreuth; Sang at Kassel 1956-69, notably as Elektra, Marie in Wozzeck, Wagner's Senta, Isolde and Brünnhilde and Cherubini's Medée; Covent Garden 1957, 1959 as Elektra and Kundry; Metropolitan Opera 1962, as Elektra; Hamburg Staatsoper 1959, 1967. *Recordings include:* Hindemith's Das Marienleben; Monteverdi's Orfeo (Vox).

LAMOTHE Donat Romeo, b. 14 Oct 1935, Keene, New Hampshire, USA. Teacher; Musicologist; Performer on Historical Instruments; Roman Catholic Priest. *Education:* Precentors Certificate, Gregorian Plainsong, 1955, AB, 1957, Assumption College; MA, Religious Studies, St John's University, Minnesota, 1969; MMus, Musicology, Boston University School of Fine and Applied Arts, 1973; PhD, Music History, Institute of Musicology, University of Strasbourg, 1980; Diplome du 2e degre, Institut Saint-Gregoire-le-Grand, Plainsong, Lyons, France, 1960. Ordained Member of Religious Order, Augustinians of the Assumption, 1962. *Career:* Founder-Director, Salisbury Consort performance group of Mediaeval and Renaissance music on historical instruments, 1965-; Faculty Member (Music Professor), Assumption College, Worcester, Massachusetts, 1963-. *Publications:* Music in Early Spanish Drama, 1973; Claude Le Jeune (1530-1600) and the Huguenot Psalter, 980; Matins at Cluny for the Feast of St Peter's Chains, 1987; Editor: Two Psalms of Claude Le Jeune, 1987; Georges Migot: 26 Monodies Permodales, 1990. *Contributions to:* Revue Internationale de Musique Francaise; Acta Musicologica. *Hobbies:* Collector of ethnic and antique musical instruments; Stained glass designer and craftsman, *Address:* Assumption College, Worcester, MA 01615-0005, USA.

LAMPART Zbigniew Andrzej, b. 27 Mar 1953, Krakow, Poland. Composer; Music Critic. *Education:* Graduated with Distinction, Academy of Music, Krakow, 1977; Graduated, Arts Critic Studio, Jagiellonian University, Krakow, 1978; Hochschule fur Musik und Darstellende Kunst, Vienna, 1983. *Debut:* Concert of own compositions, Krakow, 1975. *Career:* Lecturer, Academy of Music, Krakow, 1977-82; Editor, TV-Studio, Krakow, 1979-80; Editor, Gazeta Krakowska (Daily); Editor, Depesza (Daily); Musical Manager, Drama Theatre, Tarnow 1988-90. *Compositions:* Synthi, 1973; Wiosna Czasu Zaprzeszlego, 1974; Fragment-H 1977; Maniera Nuova, 1975; Zwierciadlo Chwili, 1976; I Symfonia 1978; Nachtdivertimento, 1982. *Recordings:* Over 50 short films and numerous theatrical musical pieces. *Contributions to:* Numerous musical reviews, articles and overviews. *Memberships:* Polish Composers Society; Authors Society ZAIKS. *Honours:* Nine honours and prizes in composition competitions 1974-91. *Hobbies:* History of civilization and culture; Films. *Address:* Imbramowska 7 m 28, 31-212 Krakow, Poland.

LAMPINEN Elina Eij, b. 25 AQpr 1954, Helsinki, Finland. Lecturer in Music. 1 son, 1 daughter. *Education:* Diploma of Dance Education, Laban School, London, 1978; Music Teacher, University of Helsinki, 1980; Master of Physical Education, University of Jyvaskyla, 1986. *Debut:* As Choreographer, Prayer dance piece, Finnish National Theatre, Helsinki, 1977. *Career:* Choreographer: Modern dance pieces, 1977-; Body percussion pieces with group Syrjahyppy, 1990-;

Shadow theatre pieces, 1993-; Teacher: Kisakallio Sports Institute, 1981-88; University of Jyvaskyla, 1989-. *Compositions:* Various pieces played with percussions, keyboards, drums, for dance or gymnastic choreographies performed on stage, TV or in competitions, 1987-. *Publication:* Music in Dance and in Gymnastics, 1987. *Memberships:* President, Ad lib Finland (Finnish Musicians in Dance); European Guild of Musicians in Dance. *Hobbies:* Sewing; Cross country skiing; Fishing. *Address:* Sippulantie 37 C 5, 40520 Jyvaskyla, Finland.

LANCE Albert, b. 12 July 1925, Menindie, Australia. Singer (Tenor). *Education:* Studied in Australia and sang minor roles and in operetta. *Career:* Sang Cavaradossi in Sydney, 1952; Offenbach's Hoffmann 1954; Paris from 1956: Opéra and Opéra-Comique in operas by Puccini, Gounod and Cherubini; Covent Garden, debut 1958, as the Duke of Mantua, opposite Joan Sutherland; Bolshoy Theatre Moscow 1965-66; Guest appearances in Bordeaux, Lyon, Los Angeles, San Francisco, Vienna, Leningrad, Kiev and Buenos Aires; London Coliseum 1969, in the first British performance of Roussel's Padmâvatî; Teacher at Nice Conservatory from 1974. *Recordings include:* Werther; Madama Butterfly; Tosca.

LANCELOT James Bennett, b. 2 Dec. 1952, Kent. Cathedral Organist. m. Sylvia Jane Hoare, 31 July 1982, 2 daughters. *Education:* St Paul's Cathedral Choir School 1961-66; Ardingly College 1966-70 (ARCO 1968, FRCO 1969); Royal College of Music 1970-71 (ARCM 1971); King's College Cambridge 1971-75 (BA 1974, MusB 1975). *Career:* Organ Scholar, King's College, Cambridge 1971-74; Assistant Organist, St Clement Danes & Hampstead Parish Church, 1974-75; Sub-Organist, Winchester Cathedral, 1975-85; Master of the Choristers and Organist, Durham Cathedral, 1985-; Conductor, Durham University Choral Society 1987-. *Recordings:* Numerous with choirs of King's College Cambridge, Winchester Cathedral and Durham Cathedral; Solo - Great European Organs No. 5. *Publications:* Durham Cathedral Organs with Richard Hird, 1991. *Honours:* Turpin Prize, FRCO, 1969; Stuart Prize, RCM, 1970; Double Distinction, BMus, 1975. *Membership:* Council Member of Royal College of Organists, 1988-. *Hobbies:* Railways; Writings of John Buchan. *Address:* 6, The College, Durham, England.

LANCHBERY John, b. 15 May 1923, London, England. Conductor; Arranger; Composer; Musical Director. m. Elaine Fifield, 17 Dec. 1951, 1 daughter. *Education:* Alleyn's School, Dulwich, 1934-42; Henry Smart Composition Scholarship To Royal Academy of Music, 1942-43; 1945-48; ARAM; FRAM. *Career:* Metropolitan Ballet, 1948-50; Sadler's Wells Theatre Ballet, 1951-59; Royal Ballet at Covent Garden, 1960-72; Australian Ballet, 1972-77; American Ballet, 1978-80; Guest Conductor at: Scala, Milan; Opera, Paris; Staatsoper, Vienna; National Theatre, Munich; Operan, Stockholm; Boston Pops; Houston Symphony Orchestra; Los Angeles Philharmonic; Teatro Municipal, Santiago; Bellas Artes, Mexico; Teatro Municipao, Rio de Janeiro; Toronto Symphony Orchestra; Bolshoi Theatre Medal, 1961; Films: Tales of Beatrix Potter; The Turning Point; Nijinsky; Evil Under The Sun. *Compositions:* Compositions and Arrangements: La Fille Mal Gardée; The Dream; Don Quixote; A Month In The Country; Monotones; Mayerling; The Sentimental Bloke; The Merry Widow Ballet; Rosalinda; Papillon; La Bayadère; The Devil To Pay; Le Chat Botté; Robinson Crusoe; Opportunity Makes the Thief, Figaro (Ballet). *Recordings:* La Fille Mal Gardée (Twice); A Month In The Country; Don Quixote; Merry Widow Ballet (Gold Record); Complete Tchaikovsky Ballets; Corroboree; Jazz Calendar; La Bayadère, etc. *Honours:* Bolshoi Theatre Medal, 1961; OBE, 1990; Carina Ari Medal, 1989; Queen Elizabeth II Coronation Award, 1989. *Memberships:* Garrick Club, London. *Hobbies:* Walking; Reading; Travel. *Current Management:* ICM, NY (For North America); Roger Stone Management, West Grove, Hammers Lane, London NW7 4DY, England. *Address:* Prince's Cottage, 17 Hardwicke Road, London W4 5EA, England.

LANCIE John de, b. 26 July 1921, Berkeley, California, USA. Oboist; Administrator. *Education:* Curtis Institute, Phildelphia, 1936- 40, with Marcel Tabuteau. *Career:* Played oboe in Pittsburgh Symphony Orchestra 1940-42; Met Richard Strauss during war service in Europe and encouraged him to write Oboe Concerto; Philadelphia Orchestra from 1946: principal oboist 1954-74; Teacher at Curtis Institute 1954-74, Director from 1977 to 1985; Commissioned and gave the premieres of Jean Francaix's Horloge de Flore (Philadelphia 1961) and the Concerto by Benjamin Lees (1963); Director, New World School of Music, 1987.

LANDAU Siegfried, b. 4 Sept. 1921, Berlin, Germany. Conductor; Composer. m. Irene Gabriel, 2 sons. *Education:* Stern and Klindworth-Scharwenka Conservatories, Berlin; Trinity College, Cambridge; Conducting Diploma, Mannes College, New York. *Career:* Founded and conductd the Brooklyn Philharmonia 1955-71; Conducted Chatanooga Opera 1960-73; Westphalian Symphony Orchestra 1973-75. *Compositions:* Chassidic Suite for viola and piano 1941; Longing for Jerusalem for soprano and orchestra 1941; Ballet The Golem 1946; Opera The Sons of Aron 1959; Friday Eve Service; Choruses. *Recordings:* Numerous, for Vox-Candide and Turnabout labels. *Honours include:* Fellow, Jewish Academy of Arts and Sciences 1971. *Memberships:* ASCAP; American Musicological Society; National Jewish Music Council. *Hobbies:* Reading; Travel. *Address:* c/o ASCAP, Ascap House, One Lincoln Plaza, New York, NY 10023, USA.

LANDER Thomas, b. 1961, Sweden. Singer (Baritone). *Education:* Studied at Stockholm College of Music and the State Opera School. *Career:* Sang with Norrlandsoperan, 1982-83; Engaged at Hamburg Staatsoper, 1986-87, Vienna Volksoper, 1987-89, as Mozart's Count and Guglielmo; Guest appearances at Aix-en-Provence, Opera de Lyon and in Italy, Iceland and Israel; Engaged at Hanover, 1990-; Other roles have included Mozart's Don Giovanni and Papageno, Malatesta and Harlequin in Ariadne auf Naxos; Sang Christus in Bach's St John Passion at Lucerne Easter Festival, 1993. *Address:* Nordic Artists Management, Sveavagen 76, S-11359 Stockholm, Sweden.

LANDMAN Leonid, b. 17 June 1957, Dushanbe, USSR. Musicologist; Senior Lecturer of Music Theory. m. Lena Negmatullaeva Landman, 2 Dec 1978, 1 daughter. *Education:* Musicology Department, The Dushanbe Musical College, 1972-76; Music Theory Faculty, 1976-81, Postgraduate course, 1983-87, Moscow State Conservatory. *Career:* Lecturer, Ancient and Modern Music, 1987-88, Senior Lecturer, Theory of Music, 1988-90, Department of Music, Institute of Art, Dushanbe; Participant, all-Union and local conferences on Gorky, 1986, ancient and modern music, 1987, 1988, 1989; Emigrated to Israel, 1990. *Publications:* Edition of Musical Culture of Non-European Peoples (V Yunusova), 1989. *Address:* Gordo Vera 7, Tel-Aviv, Israel.

LANDON Howard Chandler Robbins, b. 6 March 1926, Boston, Massachusetts, USA. Musicologist. m. Else Radant. *Education:* BMus, Boston University, 1947. *Career:* Resident in Europe from 1947; Talks on BBC Radio and TV from 1954; Guest teacher, British and American Universities, 1969-; Honorary Professorial Fellow, University College Cardiff, 1972; John Bird Professor of Music at Cardiff; Producer of numerous recordings for the Haydn Society, Vox Library of recorded Masterpieces. *Publications:* The Symphonies of Joseph Haydn, 1955; Collected Correspondence and London Notebooks of Haydn, 1959; Essays on Viennese Classical Style, 1970; Beethoven, 1970; Haydn: Chronicle and Works, 5 volumes, 1976-80; Mozart as a Mason 1983; Edition of Handel's Roman Vespers 1983; Joseph Haydn, single volume reduction of Chronicle and Works, 1988; 1791: Mozart's Last Year; Mozart: The Golden Years 1781-1791, 1989; (with John Julius Norwich) Five Centuries of Music in Venice, 1991; Vivaldi, 1993; Editor of all Haydn's Symphonies, numerous String Quartets and Operas. *Honours:* DMus,

Boston University, 1969; DMus, Queen's College, Belfast, 1974. *Memberships include:* President, International Joseph Haydn Stiftung, Eisenstadt. *Hobbies:* Cooking; Walking; Swimming. *Address:* Château de Foncoussières, 81800 Rabastens (Tarn), France.

LANDOWSKI Marcel François Paul, b. 18 Feb. 1915, Pont-l'Abbe (Finistere) France. Composer. m. Jacqueline Potier, 1941, 2 sons, 1 daughter. *Education:* Lycee Janson-de-Sailly; Conservatoire nationale de musique de Paris. *Career:* Director, Conservatoire Boulogne-sur-Seine, 1960-65; Director of Music, Comedie Francaise, Paris, 1962-66; Inspector-General, Musical Studies, 1964, Director of Music Service, Ministry of Cultural Affairs, 1966-70, Music, Lyric and Dance, 1970-74; Founder, Orchestre de Paris, 1967, Honorary President, 1975-; Inspector-General, de l'instruction publique, 1974-. *Compositions:* Numerous orchestral and choral compositions; Film music, music for Cyrano de Bergerac at Comedie Française. *Honours:* Officer, Legion d'honneur; Commander, des Arts et des Lettres; Croix de guerre. *Membership:* Institute of France, Academy des beaux-arts, 1975. *Address:* 10 rue Max-Blondat, 92100 Boulogne-sur-Seine, France.

LANE Gloria, b. 6 June 1930, Trenton, New Jersey, USA. Singer (Soprano/Mezzo-Soprano). m. Samuel Krachmalnick. *Education:* Studied with Elisabeth Westmoreland in Philadelphia. *Debut:* Philadelphia 1950, in the premiere of Menotti's The Consul. *Career:* Broadway 1954, in the premiere of Menotti's The Saint of Bleecker Street; British debut 1958, as Baba the Turk in The Rake's Progress: returned until 1972 as Dorabella in Così fan Tutte, Strauss's Ariadne and Lady Macbeth; Covent Garden debut 1960, as Carmen; Florence 1966, as Federica in Verdi's Luisa Miller; Guest appearances in Vienna, Paris, Venice, Rome, Palermo, Boston, Chicago and San Francisco; New York City Opera 1971, as Santuzza in Cavalleria Rusticana. *Recordings:* The Consul; Rossini's Mosè in Egitto; The Saint of Bleecker Street (RCA). *Address:* c/o New York City Opera, Lincoln Center, New York, NY 10023, USA.

LANE Jennifer Ruth, b. 25 Nov 1954, Berwyn, Illinois, USA. Opera Singer - Mezzo Soprano. m. James H Carr, 21 Nov 1987. *Education:* B Mus, Chicago Musical College, Roosevelt University, 1977; MA in Performance, City University iof New York, 1980. *Debut:* Elsbeth in Strauss's Feuersnot, Santa Fe Opera, 1988. *Career:* Performances with Santa Fe Opera, New York City Opera, Opera Monte Carlo, L'Opera Français de New York, Opera Omaha, American stage premiere of Handel's Partenope, Milwaukee's Skylight Opera, Opera Ensemble of New York; Prior to operatic career, toured North and South America with The Waverly Consort; Also tours of the Far East with the Gregg Smith Singers; Many concert performances including appearances with the Atlanta Symphony (Robert Shaw), The San Francisco Symphony, The National Symphony, The St Louis Symphony, The Harrisburg Symphony (Mahler's 2nd and 3rd Symphonies; Many radio broadcasts including Mahler's 3rd Symphony, personal interviews and Radio Canada recital with countertenor Allan Fast. *Recordings include:* J S Bach: St John Passion, Smithsonian Collection of Recordings; Handel: Theodora, Harmonia Mundi, Nicholas McGegan conducting; J S Bach: Solo Cantata for alto BWV 169 - Wild Boar; John Adams, Grand Pianola Music. Nonesuch, composer conducting. *Current Management:* Byers, Schwalbe and Associates, Inc, 584 Broadway, Suite 1105, New York, NY 10012, USA. *Address:* 514 West 110th Street, Apt 92, New York, NY 10025, USA.

LANE Louis, b. 25 Dec. 1923, Eagle Pass, Texas, USA. Conductor. *Education:* Studied at the University of Texas; Eastman School of Music, Rochester; Berkshire Music Center, Tanglewood. *Career:* Won 1947 competiton to become apprentice conductor to George Szell; Assistant Conductor Cleveland Orchestra 1956; Principal Conductor Akron Symphony Orchestra 1959; Guest Conductor with Chicago Symphony and Detroit Symphony; Took Cleveland Orchestra on tour

of Europe 1965 and was resident conductor 1970-73; Associate Conductor, Blossom Festival 1968-73; Co-principal conductor, Dallas Symphony Orchestra 1974-77; Principal Conductor, National Symphony Orchestra of the South African Broadcasting Corporation 1983.

LANE Piers, b. 1958, London, England. Concert Pianist. *Education:* Studied with Nancy Weir at the Queensland Conservatorium, Bela Siki in Seattle and Kendall Taylor and Yonty Solomon at the Royal College of Music. *Debut:* Broadcast recital for ABC aged 12. *Career:* Solo and concert appearances in the USA, France, Germany, Spain, Hungary, Italy, India UK, Australia Greece, Middle East and New Zealand; Tour of four Latin American countries 1989; Season 1990-91 with visits to Cyprus and Morocco, concerts in the UK, two visits to Australia and engagements in France and South America; Bliss Piano Concerto at the 1991 Promenade Concerts; Has played with such orchestras as the Philharmonia, Royal Philharmonic, BBC Philharmonic, the Hallé, City of London Sinfonia and the London Festival Orchestra; Frequent recitals on the BBC and chamber concerts with Kathron Sturrock, the New Budapest Quartet, Alexander Baillie and Julian Lloyd Webber; Many recitals at Wigmore Hall; Contemporary repertoire includes Dave Heath's Piano Concerto; Professor of Piano at the Royal Academy of Music. *Recordings:* Music by Shostakovich, Prokofiev, Schnittke, and Rachmaninoff with Alexander Baillie; Moskowski and Paderewski Concertos, The Complete Etudes by Scriabin, Brahms Piano Quintet (Hyperion); Recitals with violinist Tasmin Little; Mussorgsky (Pictures at an Exhibition), Stravinsky (Petroushka) and Balakirev (Islamey), EMI. *Honours include:* Royal Overseas League Outstanding Musician of the Year, 1982. *Memberships:*EPTA (European Piano Teachers Association); The Liszt Society; The Beethoven Pianoforte Society of Europe. *Current Management:* Patrick Garvey Management. *Address:* 51 Portland Road, Hove, East Sussex BN3 5DQ, England.

LANG David, b. 1957, Los Angeles, California, USA. Composer. *Education:* Studied at Stanford University and the University of Iowa; Doctorate from Yale School of Music 1989; teachers have included Jacob Druckman, Hans Werner Henze, Martin Bresnick and Henri Lazarof. *Career:* Freelance composer from 1983; Founded the Bang on a Can Festival New York City. *Compositions:* Orchestral: Eating Living Monkeys 1985, revised 1987; International Business Machine 1990; Bonehead 1990; Stage: Judith and Holofernes puppet opera 1989 (premiered at the 1990 Munich Biennale); Chamber and ensemble: Frag 1985; Spud 1986; Burn Notice 1988; Dance/Drop 1988-89; Are You Experienced? 1987-88; Hammer Amour 1979, rev 1989; Solo and Duo: Illumination Rounds, violin and piano 1982; While Nailing at Random, piano 1983; Orpheus Over and Under, 2 pianos 1989; Vent, flute and piano 1990; The Anvil Chorus, percussion solo 1990; Bitter Herb, cello and piano 1990; My Evil Twin, 1992; Face So Pale, 1992; Cheating, Lying, Stealing, 1993; Music for Gracious Living, 1993; Slow Movement, 1993; Choral: By Fire 1984 (commissioned by the BBC Singers). Other commissions from the City of Munich, Boston Symphony Orchestra, American Composers Orchestra, the Cleveland Orchestra, Santa Fé Opera and the Saint Paul Chamber Orchestra. *Address:* Novello and Co Ltd, 8-9 Frith Street, London W1V 5TZ, England.

LANG Edith, b. 28 April 1927, Chicago, USA. Singer (Soprano). *Education:* Studied in Chicago and Italy. *Career:* Sang in Italy from 1954, debut as Madama Butterfly; Hamburg from 1955, as Verdi's Aida, Amelia, Elisabeth de Valois, Leonora and Abigaille, Beethoven's Leonore and Mozart's Donna Anna; Guest appearances in London, Vienna, Milan and Paris; San Francisco 1959, as the Empress in the US premiere of Die Frau ohne Schattten; Also heard as concert singer; Taught at Lubeck Musikhochschule from 1973. *Address:* Schleswig-Holsteinische Musikakademie, Jerusalemberg 4, Lubeck, Germany.

LANG Istvan, b. 1 Mar. 1933, Budapest, Hungary.

Composer. m. Csilla Fülöp, 27 Dec. 1966, 1 son. *Education:* Academy of Music, Budapest. *Career:* Freelance Composer, 1958-66; Musical Advisor, State Puppet Theatre, 1966-84; Professor, Chamber Music, Academy of Music, 1973-; Secretary General, Association of Hungarian Musicians, 1978-90; Member, Ex.Com. of ISCM, 1984-87; Member, Ex.Com. of International Music Council, 1989-93. *Compositions:* Dream About the Theatre, Rounded up TV Operas; In memoriam N.N.1.; Symphony, 2, 3, 4 & 5; Violin Concerto; Double Concerto (Clarinet & Harp); Concerto Bucolico; Pezzo Lirico; Rhymes; Constellations; Affetti, Intersia Around a Bartók-Theme; Music 2-4-3; Solo pieces for various instruments; String Quartet, 2, 3; Wind Quintet, 1,2,3; Sonatas for violin and piano, 1990; Cimbiosis, 1991. *Recordings:* Several on Hungaroton. *Honours:* Erkel Prize, 1968, 1975; Merit Artist, 1985. *Memberships:* Hungarian Composers' Union. *Address:* Margit Krt, 20, Budapest H1027, Hungary.

LANG Rosemarie, b. 1955, Grunstädtel, Schwarzenberg, Germany. Singer (Mezzo-soprano). *Education:* Studied in Leipzig. *Career:* Sang in opera at Altenburg, then Leipzig; Guest engagements at Dresden as Venus by Wagner, 1988; Berlin Staatsoper as Gluck's Clytemnestra and Wagner's Brangäne, there in Berlin première of Graf Mirabeau by Siegfried Matthus, 1989 (also televised), and as Azucena by Verdi, 1989; Other roles have included Mozart's Dorabella, Cherubino and Sextus, Bellini's Romeo, Rossini's Cenerentola and Rosina, Strauss's Octavian and Komponist in Ariadne; Many concert appearances. *Recordings include:* Mendelssohn's St Paul; Larina in Eugene Onegin; Schönberg's Gurre-Lieder; Mozart's Masses; Songs by Schumann and Brahms; Pfitzner's Palestrina as Silia. *Address:* c/o Staatsoper Berlin, Unter den Linden 7, 10117 Berlin, Germany.

LANG Siegfried, b. 3 Aug. 1919, Millstatt, Austria. Composer; Writer. m. Brunhilde, 1 daughter. *Education:* Conservatoire; Studied composition with Professor Uhl, Vienna Music Academy. *Career:* Has long been active, first as Bandmaster then as Solo Entertainer, in Austria and abroad, toured as Entertainer, with a small band; Has worked in radio as both solo performer and Producer; Writer on musical subjects. *Compositions include:* Edelsteine-Walzer; Wiener Tradition; Ulrichsberg-Polka; Vision im Zwielicht; Alles Schöne; Leute von Heute; Just Dreaming; Secret Love Letter; Never Mind; Exclusiv; Regenmelodie; Eva Claudia's Song; New Edition of Osterreichische Unterhaltungs-Musik Komponisten im 20 Jahrhundert, 1987. *Address:* Poetzleinsdorferstrasse 194/8/3, A-1180 Vienna, Austria.

LANGAN Kevin J, b. 1 Apr. 1955, New York, New York, USA. Singer (Bass). m. Sally Wolf, 16 July 1983. *Education:* New England Conservatory of Music, 1973-75; Indiana University, 1975-80; BM, MM, in Voice, Vocal Instruction with Margaret Harshaw. *Debut:* New Jersey State Opera, in Don Carlos, 1979. *Career:* Principal Bass, San Francisco Opera, 1980-; Appeared with New York City Opera; Houston Grand; Philadelphia; Canadian Opera; Miami; Detroit; Dallas; Geneva; Lyon; Winnipeg; St Louis Opera, Colorado; Santa Fe; Edmonton; Vancouver; Seattle; Tulsa; Pittsburgh; San Diego; Washington DC Opera; Appeared with Chicago Lyric, and Metropolitan Opera; Sang Astofolo in Vivaldi's Orlando Furioso at San Francisco 1989; Colline at San Diego, 1990; Season 1992 as Donizetti's Raimondo at Seattle, followed by Rossini's Basilio; Leporello at the 1992 Santa Fe Festival. *Honours:* Finalist, National Metropolitan Opera, 1980; 2nd Place, San Francisco Opera Auditions, 1980; Richard Tucker Foundation Award for Advanced Studies, 1984. *Hobbies:* Fishing; Racquetball enthusiast. *Current Management:* Elizabeth Crittenden, Columbia Artists, New York. *Address:* Columbia Artists Management Inc, c/o Crittenden Division, 165 W 57th Street, New York, NY 10019, USA.

LANGBEIN Brenton, b. 1935, Australia. Violinist; Conductor. *Career:* Formed Trio with Maureen Jones and Barry Tuckwell and gave premiere of Trio by Don Banks at the 1962 Edinburgh Festival; Regular tours throughout Europe and Australia, including recent engagements in Paris, Dublin, Siena, Innsbruck, Sydney and Melbourne; Founded the ensemble Die Kammermusiker Zurich; Is leader of the Collegium Musicum Zurich and Music Director of Opera Factory Zurich; Regular tours of Australia as conductor and soloist and is Music Director of the Baroness Festival in South Australia. *Address:* c/o Harold Holt Ltd, 31 Sinclair Road, London W14 0NS, England.

LANGDON John David, b. 29 May 1943, Minehead, England. Musician (Organist). *Education:* King's College, Cambridge, 1961-65; New College, Oxford, 1965-67; MA; MusB; FRCO. *Career:* Lecturer, Co-ordinator of Early Music Studies, Royal Scottish Academy of Music & Drama, Glasgow; Frequent appearances as organist on Radio and TV. *Recordings:* Numerous as organist with Choir of King's College, Cambridge; St Clement Dane's Chorale; Paisley Abbey Choir; Scottish Philharmonic Singers. *Publications:* Editions of Works by Christopher Tye. *Contributions to:* Musical Times. *Honours:* John Stewart of Rannoch Scholar in Sacred Music, 1964. *Memberships:* Incorporated Society of Musicians; Royal College of Organists. *Hobby:* Swimming. *Address:* 1058 Cathcart Road, Glasgow G42 9XW, Scotland.

LANGER Milan, b. 10 July 1955, Praha, Czecholvakia. Concert Pianist. m. Marie Sestáková, 30 June 1979, 2 daughters. *Education:* Conservatoire, Prague, 1974; Academy of Music, Prague, 1980; 3 years postgraduate study, Academy of Music, Prague, 1986. *Career:* Free Artist- Pianist, Soloist, Chamber Partner for Ex Ivan Zenaty, Violinist; Member, Ars Cameralis Ensemble of Historic Instruments; Collaboration with Czechoslovak Symphony Orchestras; many Radio & TV appearances; Concerts in Czechoslovakia, Germany, UK, France, Belgium, Austria, Switzerland, Greece, Yugoslavia, Spain, Cuba. *Recordings:* Piano Concerto, Podest; Pezzi Brevi, Filas; Sonata, Amorasa; Kalabis: Sonata for Violin and Piano, Op 58, 1987; Compositions by Stravinsky, Barber, Prokofiev, Bartók; Radio Recordings as Soloist, Liszt, Schumann, Chopin, Bartók, Prokofiev, Gothic Music. *Current Management:* Pragokoncert, Praha, Czechoslovakia. *Address:* Kropackova 559, 149 00 Praha 4-Haje, Czech Republic.

LANGFORD Roger, b. 1865, England. Singer (Baritone). *Education:* Studied at Royal College of Music and Royal Academy of Music. *Career:* Soloist with Yorkshire Bach Choir in the St John Passion, Christmas Oratorio, Bach B minor Mass and Monteverdi Vespers; Concerts in France and Germany, including Purcell's Aeneas for Cologne Radio; Music theatre includes Eight Songs for a Mad King by Maxwell Davies, Master Peter's Puppet Show and Monteverdi's Combattimento; Visits to Europe with Nigel Rogers's group Chiaroscuro, performing English and Italian baroque music; Elijah at Lincoln Cathedral and The Apostles by Elgar at St Albans Abbey; Season 1989-90 as Papageno for British Youth Opera and in Trouble in Tahiti at Edinburgh Festival. *Address:* c/o Anglo Swiss Ltd, 3 Primrose Mews, 1a Sharpeshall St, London NW1 8YW, England.

LANGMAN Krzysztof Maria, b. 22 July 1948, Cracow, Poland. Flautist. *Education:* Academy of Music, Cracow, 1970-74; Study under S.Gazzeloni, S.Cecilia Academy of Music, Rome, 1976-77. *Career:* Principal Flautist, State Opera House and Philharmonic Society, Wroclaw; Principal Solo Flute, Baltic Philharmonic Orchestra, Gdansk, 1974-; Currently Assistant Professor of Flute, Academy of Music, Gdansk; Numerous recordings for Polish Radio and TV; Cooperates with Ensemble MW2 vanguard group; Concerts in various countries including Austria, Federal Republic of Germany, Greece, Norway, Sweden, Denmark, Netherlands, Belgium, UK, Italy, Mexico, Spain, Luxemburg, Switzerland, France. *Current Management:* Polish Artists Agency, Warsaw, Poland. *Address:* ul Pawla Gdanca 4a/42, 80-336 Gdansk, Poland.

LANGRIDGE Philip Gordon, b. 16 Dec. 1939, Hawkhurst, Kent, England. Concert & Opera Singer (Tenor). m. Ann Murray, 1981, 1 son (1 son, 2 daughters, former marriage). *Education:* ARAM, Royal Academy of Music, 1977. *Debut:* Glyndebourne Festival, 1964. *Career:* BBC Promenade Concerts, 1970-; Edinburgh Festival, 1970-; Netherlands Opera, Scottish Opera, Handel Opera, major opera houses Britain & abroad. Concerts with major, international orchestras & conductors including Boston (Previn); Chicago (Solti, Abbado); Los Angeles (Christopher Hogwood); Sydney, (Mackerras); Vienna Philharmonic (Previn); Orchestre de Paris (Barenboim, Mehta), & with all major British orchestras. Many first performances, some dedicated to/written for him. *Compositions include:* Covent Garden/L'Enfant et les Sortilèges, Rossignol; Boris, Jenůfa; English National Opera/Turn of the Screw, Osud; Mask of Orpheus; Glyndebourne/Don Giovanni, Idomeneo, Fidelio; La Scala/Rake's Progress, Wozzeck, Godunov, Idomeneo, Orfeo; Frankfurt Opera/Castor & Pollux, Rigoletto, Die Entführung; Zürich Opera/Poppea, Lucio Silla; Don Giovanni; La Fenice/Janáček's Diary; Palermo/Otello (Rossini); Pesaro/La Donna del Lago; Aix en Provence/Alcina, Les Boréades; Metropolitan Opera, New York/Così fan Tutte; Vienna State Opera/Wozzeck; Salzburg Festival/Moses und Aron; Sang in television production of Tippett's The Midsummer Marriage, 1989; Idomeneo in a new production of Mozart's opera at Covent Garden (1989), Berlioz's Benedict for ENO 1990; Sang Idomeneo at the 1990 Salzburg Festival, Pelegrin in Tippett's New Year at Glyndebourne, Mozart's Titus at Glyndebourne and the Promenade Concerts, 1991; Season 1992/93 as Aschenbach in a new production of Death in Venice at Covent Garden, Macbeth in The Beggar's Opera at Aldeburgh, Skuratov in From The House of the Dead and Nero in Poppea at the Salzburg Festival; Sang in Stravinsky's Pulcinella at the 1993 London Proms. *Recordings:* Over 50 records, early, baroque, classical, romantic & modern music. *Membership:* Music panel, Arts Council of Great Britain. *Hobbies:* Collecting watercolour paintings, Victorian postcards. *Address:* c/o Allied Artists Agency, 42 Montpellier Square, London SW7 1JZ, England.

LANIGAN John, b. 7 Jan 1921, Seddon, Victoria, Australia. Singer (Tenor). *Education:* Studied at the Melbourne Conservatory and in Milan; London with Dino Borgioli. *Career:* Stoll Theatre, London, 1949 as Fenton in Falstaff and Rodolfo in La Bohème; Covent Garden from 1951, debut as the Duke of Mantua; Sang Jack in the 1955 premiere of Tippett's The Midsummer Marriage and the 1956 British premiere of Janáček's Jenůfa; Created Hermes in Tippett's King Priam at Coventry, 1962; From 1963 sang Mime in The Ring; Often heard in character parts such as Shuisky in Boris Godunov; Pandarus in Troilus and Cressida and Sir Philip in Owen Wingrave; Sang at Covent Garden in the premieres of Bennett's Victory (1970), Maxwell Davies's Taverner (1972) and Henze's We Come to the River (1976); Guest appearances in Australia, France and Italy; Often heard in concert and oratorios. *Recordings include:* The Rector in Peter Grimes (Decca); Shuisky in Boris Godunov (EMI). *Address:* c/o Royal Opera House, Covent Garden, London WC2, England.

LANKESTER Michael, b. 12 Nov. 1944, London, England. Conductor; Musical Director; Professor of Conducting. *Education:* Royal College of Music; ARCM; GRSM. *Career:* Musical Director, National Theatre, 1969-75, composing and conducting numerous items to accompany productions; Conductor, Surrey Philharmonic Orchestra, 1972-, English Chamber Orchestra; Founder, Contrapuncti; Radio and TV broadcasts for BBC; Collaborator with Young Vic Theatre in various productions; Conductor, Cheltenham Festival, Sadler's Wells Theatre and at opening of Royal Northern College of Music, 1973; Made orchestral suite of Britten's The Prince of the Pagodas, and conducted it at the 1979 Promenade Concerts. *Recordings include:* Gordon Crosse, Purgatory, Ariadne. *Honours include:* Watney/Sargent Conducting Scholarship, 1967. *Membership:* Noise Abatement Society. *Hobbies:* Reading; Walking; Cricket.

LANSING Robert C, b. 10 Apr. 1915, Chicago, Illinois, USA. Choral Conductor; Bass-baritone; Voice Teacher. m. Gladys Zeiher, 18 June 1943, 1 son, 2 daughters. *Education:* University of Illinois, 1932-33; Chicago Conservatory of Music, 1940-42; American Theater Wing, Manhattan School of Music, 1946-49; Studied voice with Paul Althouse, Friedrich Schorr and Zerline Metzger; Conducting with Hugh Ross. *Debut:* Town Hall, 1949. *Career:* Dulcamara opposite Bidu Sayao, Denver Grand Opera, 1950; Member Metropolitan Opera Chorus, 1945-49 and 1955-60; Sang Escamillo with Boston Opera, 1944; Vocal Teacher, 1950-; Conducted Capitol Opera in Aida, Il Trovatore, Magic Flute, Marriage of Figaro etc, 1950-64; Director, Mountain Bell Singers, 1963-; Directed Rocky Mountain Singers in 7 international concert tours, 1974-88; Bass soloist: Messiah 1984, Elijah, Verdi Requiem 1985, Stainer Crucifixion. *Memberships:* Board of Directors 1956, AGMA; American Guild of Organists; Musicians Union; AFM. *Hobby:* Swimming. *Address:* 940 South Harrison St. Denver, CO 80209, USA.

LANSKY Paul, b. 18 June 1944, New York, USA. Composer. *Education:* Studied with George Perle and Hugo Weisgall at Queens College, New York, BA 1966; Princeton University with Milton Babbitt and Earl Kim, PhD 1969. *Career:* Teacher, Princeton University from 1969; Associate editor of Perspectives of New Music, 1972. *Compositions:* Modal Fantasy for piano 1969; String Quartet 1972-77; Mild und leise for tape 1974; Crossworks for piano and ensemble 1975; Artifice (on Ferdinand's Reflections) for tape 1976; Folk Images for tape 1981; As if, for string trio and electronics 1982; Folk Images, and As it Grew Dark, for tape 1980-83. *Publications include:* Affine Music (dissertation) 1969. *Honours:* League of Composers-ISCM electronic music award 1975; Koussevitsky Foundation award 1981. *Address:* c/o ASCAP, ASCAP Building, One Lincoln Plaza, New York, NY 10023, USA.

LANTOS Istvan, b. 1949, Budapest, Hungary. Pianist. *Education:* Studied Piano under Mme Erzsebet Tusa, Budapest Bela Bartók Conservatory; Ferenc Liszt Academy of Music; Graduate with Distinction, Liszt Academy of Music. *Career:* Played Solo Part, Messiaen's Turangalêla Symphonie, Bayreuth International Youth Festival, 1970; Hitzacker Festival, Federal Republic of Germany; Bratislava International Rostrum of Young Artists; Numerous appearances in Hungarian concert halls and worldwide; Guest performed at most European Socialist countries and Cuba, Austria, Britain, Canada, Germany, The Netherlands, Ireland, Italy and Switzerland; Has twice toured and held master classes in Japan; Soloist, Hungarian State Symphony Orchestra during USA tour; Has toured every 2nd year the major cities of the former Federal Republic of Germany with Hungarian State Symphony Orchestra, 1972-; Also outstanding Organist; Assistant Professor, Budapest Liszt Academy of Music, 1974-.

LANZA Alcides Emigdio, b. 2 June 1929, Rosario, Argentina. Nationalized Canadian Citizen. Composer; Pianist; Conductor; University Professor. 2 sons, 2 daughters. *Education:* Centro de Altos Estudios Musicales, Buenos Aires; Post Graduate Courses, Electronic Music, Columbia University, New York, USA; Studied Composition with Julián Bautista and Alberto Ginastera, Piano with Ruwin Erlich, Conducting with Roberto Kinsky; Further Instruction Courses with various noted artists. *Career includes:* Concert Tours of Europe, North and South America; Artistic Staff, Teatro Colon, Buenos Aires, 1959-65; Pianist, Lecturer and Conductor, Composers/Performers Group, touring Europe; Composer and Teacher, Columbia-Princeton Electronic Music Centre; Director of Electronic Music Studies and Professor of Composition, McGill University, Montreal, Quebec, Canada, 1971-; Artistic Director, Group G.E.M.S. (Group of the Electronic Music Studio). *Compositions include:* Módulos II, 1982; Módulos III, 1983; Sensors I, for organ and two percussionists, 1982; Eidesis VI, for string orchestra with piano, 1983; Interferences III, for chamber ensemble and electronic sounds, 1983; Acúfenos V, for trumpet, piano and electronic-computer tape, 1980; Ekphonesis VI, actress-singer tape, 1988; ...there is a way to sing it...(solo tape), 1988; un mundo imaginario, choir and computer tape, 1989; vôo, for voice, electroacoustic music and digital signal processing, 1992. *Hobbies:* Tennis; Swimming; Bicycling; Walking. *Current Management:* Shelan Concerts. *Address:* 6351 Trans Island Avenue, Montreal, Quebec, H3W 3B7, Canada.

LAPINSKAS Darius, b. 9 Mar. 1934, Kaunas, Lithuania. Composer; Conductor. m. Laima Rastenis, 28 Nov. 1970, 1 son. *Education:* South Boston High School; BA Composition, Conducting, New England Conservatory, Boston, 1953-57; Akademie fuer Musik und darstellende Kunst, Vienna, 1957-58; Musik Hochschule, Stuttgart, 1958-60. *Career:* Musikdirektor, Tuebingen Landestheatre, 1960-65; Kapelmeister, Staatsoper, Stuttgart, 1961-65; Schiedsgericht, Composer-Conductor, Mainz TV; Guest Conductor: Stuttgart Symphony Orchestra; Stuttgart Philharmonic; South German Radio Orchestra; Mannheim Opera Orchestra; National Symphony Orchestra of Bogotà; Symphony Orchestra of Antioquia; Artistic Director of New Opera Company of Chicago. *Compositions:* Operas: Lokys; Maras; Amadar; Dux Magnus; Rex Amos; Ballet: Laima; Concerto for Piano, Strings and Percussion; Concerto for Violin and Orchestra; Haiku (song cycle); Balyvera (song cycle for mezzo soprano and orchestra); Les Sept Solitudes (aria for mezzo soprano and orchestra); Ainiu Dainos (song cycle for voice and chamber orchestra). *Recordings:* Les Sept Solitudes; Ainiu Dainos; Mergaites Dalia recorded on Fine Music Records Labels, Cleveland, Ohio. *Honours:* BML Prize for Composition, Boston, 1955; Wuerttemberg Prize for Composition, 1961; Illinois Arts Council Grant for Composition, 1985, 1986. *Hobbies:* Tennis; Skiing. *Address:* 9368 S. Longwood Drive, Chicago, IL 60620, USA.

LAPLANTE Bruno, b. 1 Aug. 1938, Beauharnois, Quebec, Canada. Singer. 2 sons. *Education:* 1st prize in Vocal Art, Conservatoire de Musique du Québec, Montreal. *Debut:* The Secret Marriage (Cimarosa) in Germany (Weikersheim). *Career:* Under scholarships from Canada Arts Council, The Government of Quebec, private foundations and from Munich (Goethe Institute, worked first in Germany, in Paris under the direction of Pierre Bernac and in Montreal with Lina Narducci); Numerous radio and television appearances including Le Secret de Suzanne; Gounod's Romeo and Juliette; Lehar's La Veuve Joyeuse; Engagements with major Canadian Symphony Orchestras; Les Noces and Carmina Burana with Grands Ballets Canadiens; 30 concerts in Canada for Les Jeunesses Musicales du Canada; A film dealing with his career in the series Les Nouveaux Interprètes; Stage appearances include Carmen, Il Trittico, Manon, Don Giovanni and many others; Regular tours throughout Europe for concerts and festivals including Festival du Marais, Paris, 1979 and 2 recitals at Festival International de Musique et d'art Lyrique of Aix En Provence. *Recordings include:* Integrale des 15 mélodies de Duparc; Mélodies de Lalo et de Bizet; Mélodies de Berlioz; Works by J Offenbach, Jules Massenet, Reynaldo Hahn, Charles Gounod, César Franck and many others. *Honours:* Concours International de Genève 1966 de Barcelone 1966, de Montreal 1967; Grand Prix du Disque 1977. *Membership:* Union des Artistes de Montreal.

LAPORTE André, b. 12 July 1931, Oplinter, Belgium. Composer. *Education:* Studied at Catholic University of Louvain; Organ with Flor Peeters and counterpoint with Marinus de Jong, 1956-58. *Career:* Producer for Belgian Radio 1963; Brussels Conservatory from 1968. *Compositions:* Piano Sonata 1954; Psalm for 6 voices and brass 1956; Jubilus for 12 brass instruments and 3 percussionists 1966; Story for string trio and harpsichord, 1967; Ascension for piano 1967; De Profundis for mixed choir 1968; Le Morte Chitarre for tenor, flute and 14 strings 1969; Night Music for orchestra 1970; La Vita non e Sogno for vocalists, chorus and orchestra 1972; Peripetie for brass sextet; Chamber

Music for soprano and ensemble 1975; Transit for 48 strings, 1978; Das Schloß, opera in three acts after Fr. Kafka, 1986; Fantasia-Rondino for violin and orchestra, 1988; The Magpie on the Gallows, 1989. *Honours:* Lemmens-Tinel Award 1958; Koopal Award from the Belgian Ministry of Culture 1971 & 1976; Prix Italia, 1976. *Address:* c/o SABAM, Rue d'Arlon 75-77, 1040 Brussels, Belgium.

LAPPALAINEN Kimmo, b. 1944, Helsinki, Finland. Singer (Tenor). *Education:* Sibelius Academy 1966-68; Vocal studies with Fred Husler in Lugano; Luigi Rici in Rome, 1969-70. *Career:* Finnish National Opera, Helsinki, 1968-72; Stuttgart Opera from 1972; Glyndebourne Festival 1972-74, as Pedrillo in Die Entführung and Idamantes in Idomeneo; Many performances at the Savonlinna Festival, Finland; Stuttgart 1983, as Britten's Albert Herring; Also heard in concert. *Address:* c/o Finnish National Opera, Bailevardi 23-27, SF 00180 Helsinki 18, Finland.

LARA Christian, b. 15 Aug 1946, Merignac, France. Singer (Tenor). *Education:* Studied in Bordeaux. *Career:* Sang at Lille Opera, 1976-79 and studied further with Michel Senechal in Paris; Sang Juan in Don Quichotte at Venice, 1982, Rodolfo at Nantes, Cavaradossi at Avignon, Faust at Ghent and Antwerp; Theater des Westens, Berlin, 1987, as Sou-Chong in Das Land des Lächelns; Sang Faust at Cologne, 1989, and appeared in La Rondine at Tours, 1991; Concert repertoire includes Mendelssohn's 2nd Symphony; Sang Faust at Vienna, 1991; Also in 1991: Sang Ismaele (Nabucco) at Karlsruhe, Samson, title role, at Besançon, Ruggero (La rondine) at Tours, Mario (Tosca) at Angers, Don José (Carmen) at Bregenz and Liège, Florestan (Fidelio) at Tours; In 1992: he sang Oedipe Roi by Paul Bastide at Strasbourg, Andrei Khovantchi (Khovantchina) at Strasbourg, Ismaele (Nabucco) at Karlsruhe, Florestan (Fidelio) at Angers, Don José (Carmen) at the Festival of Breganz, Jean (Hérodiade) at Liège, Vestale at Nantes; In 1993: he sang Luigi (Il Tabarro) at Tours, Jean (Hérodiade) at Toulon; In 1994: Sang in Manon (Des Grieux), and Carmen at Bordeaux. *Address:* 11 Rue Jean Jaurès, 33127 Martignas-sur-Jalle, France.

LAREDO Jaime, b. 7 June 1941, Cochabamba, Bolivia. Violinist. m. (1) Ruth Laredo 1960 (divorced 1974), (2) Sharon Robinson. *Education:* Studied violin with Antonio de Grassi and Frank Hauser in San Francisco; Josef Gingold and George Szell in Cleveland, and Ivan Galamian at the Curtis Institute in Philadelphia. *Career:* Orchestral debut San Francisco 1952; Won Queen Elisabeth of the Belgians Competition 1959 and subsequently appeared with most major orchestras in Europe and America; New York debut Carnegie Hall 1960; London debut Albert Hall 1961; frequent visitor to summer festivals at Spoleto, Tanglewood, Hollywood Bowl, Ravinia, Marlboro and Edinburgh; repertoire ranges from Baroque to contemporary works: gave the premiere of Ned Rorem's Concerto; as director/soloist he works with St Pauls and Scottish Chamber Orchestras; Director, "Chamber Music at the 92nd Street NY" series in New York; Piano Trio concerts from 1980 with Joseph Kalichstein and Sharon Robinson. *Recordings:* Trios by Mendelssohn, Brahms and Beethoven for Vox Cum Laude and Pickwick International; Brahms Piano Quartets with Emanuel Ax, Isaac Stern, Yo-Yo Ma for Sony Classical. *Honours:* New York City Handel Medallion 1960; Stadium in La Paz named after him; Bolivian stamps with his portrait issued in his honour, enscribed with the notes A, D and C (La-re-do). *Address:* c/o Harold Holt Ltd., 31 Sinclair Road, London W14 ONS, England.

LAREDO Ruth, b. 20 Nov. 1937, Detroit, Michigan, USA. Concert Pianist. m. 1 June 1960, (divorced) 1974, 1 daughter. *Education:* Diploma, Curtis Institute of Music, Philadelphia, BMus. degree 1960. Studied under Rudolf Serkin at Curtis Institute. *Debut:* Carnegie Hall, with New York Orchestra under Leopold Stowkowski. *Career:* Appeared at Carnegie Hall, The Kennedy Center, Library of Congress and The White House with orchestras as The New York Philharmonic, Philadelphia and Cleveland Orchestras, Boston Symphony, St. Louis Symphony, Detroit Symphony, National Symphony, the orchestras of Baltimore, Indianapolis, Houston, Buffalo and American Symphony. Participated in The Music from Marlboro Concerts from their inception 1965-; also performed at The Spoleto Festival USA 1983 and 1985; Frequent Guest Artist with ensembles as The Tokyo and Cleveland Quartets; Tours with flautist Paula Robison. *Recordings:* Complete Works of Rachmaninoff. *Contributions to:* Columnist, Keyboard Classics Magazine; Editor, C.F. Peters Publishing Company. *Hobbies:* Running; Attending Movies and Ballet; Reading. *Address and Current Management:* Herbert Barrett, 1776 Broadway, NYC 10019, USA.

LAREDO Teresa, b. 11 Feb. 1939, Cochabamba, Bolivia. Composer; Pianist; Harpsichordist. *Education:* Academia Santa Cecilia Rome; Mozarteum Salzburg; Accademia Chigiana Siena, with Alfred Cortot; Geneva Music Conservatory. *Career:* 1968-72 Founder and piano soloist of the Panamerican Camerata Ensemble; 1968-72; Founder and harpsichord soloist, Bolivian Baroque Ensemble; 1969-70 Piano soloist with the Bolivian National Orchestra; 1979 Tour with the Orchestre de Chambre de Lausanne; Radio and TV concerts in South America, Australia and Europe; Teacher and lecturer at the La Paz Conservatory, Bolivia, Conservatoire Populaire de Geneve and Conservatoire de Strasbourg; Researcher in Latin-American folklore and Indian music. *Compositions:* Homage to Simone Rapin, Cantata for keyboard; Huayra, Indian air for harpsichord; Colibri, musical poem 1989. *Recordings:* Lyra, Concertino for piano and orchestra by Villapando; Aires tradicionales from South America; Classical Music from the Andes; Latin- American Music for Harpsichord; Music by Ginastera and Bolivian composers; Teresa Laredo at the harpsichord. *Memberships:* Society of Writers and Artists, Geneva; Wagnerian Society, Geneva; Member of the International Committee of the Musique Esperance Association. *Address:* 20 Parc Chateau- Banquet, 1202 Geneva, Switzerland.

LARGE Brian, b. 1937, London, England. Musicologist; Pianist; Writer; TV Producer. *Education:* Studied Royal Academy of Music and London University. *Career:* Producer of opera on BBC TV. *Publications:* Books on Smetana, Martinů and Czech Opera; Wrote entry on Martinů in the New Grove Dictionary of Music and Musicians 1980.

LARMORE Jennifer, b. 1960, Atlanta, Georgia, USA. Singer (Mezzo- soprano). *Debut:* Sang Sesto in La Clemenza di Tito in France. *Career:* Many performances in Europe and USA with a repertoire including operas by Mozart, Rossini, Debussy, Handel and Ravel; From 1990 has sung Rossini's Rosina in Paris, Amsterdam, London and Rome; L'Enfant et les Sortileges at La Scala, Giulio Cesare in Paris, Donna Elvira in Bonn, Rossini's Isabella and Adele (Comte Ory) in Turin and Milan; Season 1992-93 as Rosina in Bilbao and Berlin, Monteverdi's Ottavia in Bologna and Antwerp, Bellini's Romeo at Geneva and Carnegie Hall, Cenerentola in Florence and Dorabella at Salzburg Festival; Wigmore Hall recital, Mar 1933, with arias by Handel and Massenet and French and Spanish songs. *Recordings include:* L'Incoronazione di Poppea; Mozart's C minor Mass; Giulio Cesare; Il Barbiere di Siviglia; Hansel und Gretel; La Cenerentola; Alice in Lucia di Lammermoor; Marianna in Il Signor Bruschino; Arsace in Semiramide; Rossini Songs, Duets and Quartets. *Address:* c/o IMG Artists, Media House, 3 Burlington Lane, Chiswick, London W4 2TH, England.

LARNER Gerald, b. 9 March 1936, Leeds, England. Music Critic. m. Celia Ruth Mary White, 2 daughters. *Education:* BA New College, Oxford. *Career:* Assistant Lecturer, Manchester University, 1960-62; Member of Guardian staff from 1962: chief Northern music critic from 1965; Translated Wolf's Der Corregidor into English; Wrote libretto for John McCabe's The Lion, the Witch and the Wardrobe 1971; Artistic Director, Bowden Festival, 1980-84. *Contributions to:* Musical Times; The Listener. *Membership:* Critics Circle. *Hobbies:* Wine

Drinking; Art; Glass Collecting. *Address:* 11 Higher Downs, Altrincham, Cheshire WA14 2QL.

LARROCHA Alicia de, b. 23 May 1923, Barcelona, Spain. Pianist. m. Juan Torra, 1 son, 1 daughter. *Education:* Studied with Frank Marshall in Barcelona. *Career:* Performed in public from age 4; Concerto debut 1934, with the Madrid Philharmonic; British debut 1953, Wigmore Hall; US debut 1955, with the Los Angeles Philharmonic; Formed Duo with cellist Gaspar Cassado 1956; Solo recitals and concerts with major orchestras in Eurooe, USA, Canada, Central and South America, South Africa, New Zealand, Australia and Japan; Director, Marshall Academy Barcelona, from 1959. Recent British appearances with the City of Birmingham Symphony, Philharmonia Orchestra and the London Symphony Orchestra; Falla's Nights in the Gardens of Spain at the 1986 Promenade Concerts (televised); Barbican Hall recital 1989. *Recordings:* Works by Granados, Falla, Albeniz, Mozart and Romantic composers: Labels include Hispavox, CBS, EMI, Decca. *Honours include:* Paderewski Memorial Medal, London, 1961; Edison Award 1968, 1978; Decorated Spanish Orders of Civil Merit 1962 and Isabel La Catolica 1972; Musician of the Year (USA) 1978; Grammy Award for recording of Iberia by Albeniz, 1989. *Current Management: Address:* c/o Herbert H Breslin Inc. 119 W. 57th Street No. 1505, New York, NY 10019, USA.

LARSEN Bjarne, b. 28 Mar. 1922, Oslo, Norway. Violinist. m. Ruth Steger Larsen, 1 son. *Education:* Studied violin since age 6. *Debut:* Aulaen, Oslo, 1937. *Career:* Solo Appearances in Norway and Scandinavia and on Norwegian radio and television; Leader, Orchestra of Oslo National Theatre, 1947-57; Leader, Oslo Philharmonic Association, 1958-87. *Recordings:* Grieg Sonatas. *Honours:* Critics Prize for performance of Nielsen's violin concerto, 1967; Oslo Town Culture Prize, 1967; His Majesty King Olav V Medal of Merit (Gold), 1983. *Hobby:* Cars. *Address:* Waldemar Thranesgt 62 C 111, Oslo 1, Norway.

LARSON Sophia, b. 1954, Linz, Austria. Singer (Soprano). m. Hans Sisa. *Education:* Salzburg Mozarteum with Seywald-Baumgartner; Further study with Ettore Campogalliani. *Career:* Sang at St Gallen from 1976, as Verdi's Amelia Boccanegra, Mozart's Ilia and Silvia in Mascagni's Zanetto; Ulm 1979-80, as Fiordiligi, the Marschallin, Beethoven's Leonore and Katya Kabanova; Bremen 1980-83; Guest in Hamburg, Stuttgart, Trieste and Rome; Bologna 1985, as the Duchess of Parma in Busoni's Doktor Faust; Turin 1986, as Puccini's Turandot and in Ghedini's Maria d'Alessandria; Further appearances in South America, Berlin, Berne, Wiesbaden and Bratislava; Bayreuth Festival 1984-85, as Gutrune in The Ring; Festival of Verona 1986, as Minnie in La Fanciulla del West; Studio recordings for French and Italian Radio; Venus Tannhäuser, Bayreuth Festival, 1987; Gutrune Ring, Staatsoper Munich, 1987; Tosca, Sieglinde, Turin, 1987; Isolde, Toronto, 1987; War Requiem, Carnegie Hall, New York, 1988; Fedra by Pizzetti, Palermo, 1988; Renata, Fiery Angel by Prokofiev, Grand Theâtre Genève, 1988; Turandot, Zurich, 1988; Senta, Nice, 1988; Senta, San Francisco, 1988; Sieglinde Walküre, Bayreuth Festival, 1989; Renata, Amsterdam, 1989; Lyrische Symphonie Zemlinsky, Amsterdam, 1989; Brucknerhaus: Brünnhilde:- Siegfried, Linz Brucknerfestival, 1989; Fidelio, Catania, 1989; Turin and Zurich 1990, as Turandot and Tosca. *Address:* c/o Opernhaus Zurich, Falkenstrasse 1, CH-8008 Zurich, Switzerland.

LARSSON Charlotte, b. 1966, Sweden. Singer (Soprano). *Education:* Studied at the State Opera School in Stockholm from 1989. *Debut:* Norrlandsoperan as Signe in Stenhammar's Gillet pa Solhaug, 1990. *Career:* Concert appearances including opening of Aarhus Festival, 1991; Sang at Karlstad Opera Festival, 1992, and Liu in Turandot for Stockholm Folkoperan, 1993; Other roles include Mozart's Pamina and Sandrina, Rosalinda and Dvořák's Rusalka; Engaged at Stockholm Royal Opera, 1994. *Address:* Nordic Artists

Management, Sveavagen 76, S-11359 Stockholm, Sweden.

LASKE Otto, b. 23 Apr 1936, Olesnica (Oels), Silesia, Poland. Composer; Poet; Musicologist. *Education:* BMus, Akademie fur Tonkunst, Darmstadt; MMus, Composition, New England Conservatory of Music, Boston, USA; PhD, Philosophy, Goethe University, Frankfurt-am-Main, Germany; EdD, Harvard University, USA; Postdoctoral studies, Institute of Sonology, Utrecht, Netherlands. *Debut:* Composers Forum, New York City, 1969. *Career:* Independent Composer; Professor of Music, Artistic Director, Newcomp Inc, 1981-91. *Compositions:* 65 works for instrumental, vocal and electroacoustic music including: Kyrie Eleison, a cappella, 1969; Distances and Proximities for tape, 1973; Perturbations for chamber orchestra, 1979; Terpsichore for tape, 1980; Soliloquy for double bass, 1984; Furies and Voices, 1989; Treelink for tape, 1992. *Publications:* Music, Memory, and Thought, 1977; Understanding Music with AI (editor with K Ebcioglu and M Balaban), 1992. *Address:* 83 Appleton Street, Arlington, MA 02174, USA.

LÁSZLÓ Eösze, b. 17 Nov 1923, Budapest, Hungary. Musicologist. m. 1. Katalin Kerényi, 16 Oct 1948; 2. Margit Szilléry, 24 Sept 1983, 1 son, 1 daughter. *Education:* PhD, University of Pázmány, Budapest, 1945. Piano Teacher Certificate, F Liszt Academy of Music, Budapest, 1947. *Career:* Artistic Director of Publishing House Editio Musica, Budapest, 1961-87. *Publications:* 15 books including: The Life and Work of Zoltán Kodály in Hungarian, in English 1962, German 1964; Zoltán Kodály: His Life in Pictures, Hungarian, English and German 1971, 1982; History of Opera, 1960, 1962, 1972; Franz Liszt, 119 Roman Documents, 1980; G Verdi 1961; R Wagner, 1969. *Contributions to:* Grove's Dictionary of Music and Musicians; Riemann's Musiklexikon, Hungarian Music Lexikon; Studia Musicologica Hungarica; Magyar Zene (Hungarian Music), Bulletin of the International Kodály Society. *Current Management:* International Kodály Society, P O Box 8, Budapest 1502, Hungary. *Address:* Attila út 133, H-1012 Budapest, Hungary.

LÁSZLÓ Ferenc, b. 8 May 1937, Cluj, Romania. Flautist; Musicologist; Critic; Lecturer of Chamber Music. m. Ilse Herbert, 6 Feb. 1963, 2 sons, 1 daughter. *Education:* Qualified as Flautist, Secondary Music School Cluj, 1954; Qualified as Flautist, Academy of Music Cluj, 1959. *Debut:* As Flautist: 1958; As Musicologist: 1961. *Career:* Flautist with the Sibiu Philharmonic, 1959-66; Teacher of Chamber Music at the Secondary Music School Cluj, 1966-70; Associate Professor of Chamber Music, Academy of Music, Bucharest, 1970-; Collaborator of Romanian Broadcasting, 1963-85; Collaborator of Romanian TV, 1970-81. *Publications include:* Journalist Writings 1971-1974, Hungarian, Bucharest, 1976; Bartók Béla, Tanulmanyok es tanusagok(Béla Bartók, Studies and Testimonies) Hungarian Bucharest, 1980; Utunk Kodályhoz, (Our Way to Kodály) in Hungarian, Bucharest, 1984, editor and co-author; A százegyedik év. Bartókról, Enescuról, Kodályról, (The 101st Year. About Bartók, Enescu and Kodály) in Hungarian, Bucharest, 1984; Bartók Béla. Studii, comunicari, eseuri, (Béla Bartók. Studies, Articles, Essays) in Romanian, Bucharest, 1984; Mosçtenires lui Béla Bartók în România, (Béla Bartók's Inheritance in Romania) in Romanian, Bucharest, in course of publication. *Contributions to:* Over 2,000 contributions to magazines, journals. *Address:* Casutça posçtala 218, RO-3400 Cluj- Napoca, Romania.

LASZLO Magda, b. 1919, Marosvásaŕhely, Hungary. Singer (Soprano). *Education:* Studied Franz Liszt Academy, Budapest, with Irene Stoasser and Ferenc Szekelyhedi. *Debut:* Budapest 1943, as Elisabeth in Tannhäuser and Amelia in Simon Boccanegra. *Career:* Resident in Rome from 1946; Sang in the radio and stage premieres of Dallapiccola's Il Prigioniero, 1949, 1950; Sang further in modern works by Ghedini, Casella, Lualdi and Malipiero; Guest appearances in Austria, Germany, France, Holland and Switzerland; Covent Garden 1954, as Cressida in the premiere of Walton's Troilus and Cressida; Glyndebourne 1953-54, 1962-63, as Mozart's Cherubino, Gluck's Alceste and as Monteverdi's Poppea; Other roles were Marie in Wozzeck, Wagner's Isolde and Senta, Strauss's Daphne, Busoni's Turandot, Alfano's Sakuntala, Prokofiev's Renata, Handel's Agrippina, Roxana in King Roger, Gluck's Elena, and Bellini's Norma. *Recordings:* Bach Cantatas and St Matthew Passion (Nixa); L'Incoronazione di Poppea (HMV).

LATANZA Antonio, b. 13 July 1946, Taranto, Italy. Museum Curator. div., 1 daughter. *Education:* Major in Law, Rome University; Piano studies with Carlo Zecchi; Musicological studies. *Career:* Curator, National Museum of Musical Instruments, Rome; Radio broadcast and television interviews and series. *Publications:* Various, 1987-92. *Contributions to:* Magazines and journals, 1989, 1991, 1992. *Hobbies:* Archive recordings; Archaeology; Collector of mechanical instruments. *Address:* Museo Nazionale degli Strumentali Musicali, Piazza S Croce in Gerusalemme 9A, 00185 Rome, Italy.

LATARCHE Vanessa Jayne, b. 3 Apr. 1959, Isleworth, Middlesex, England. Concert Pianist; Accompanist; Private Teacher; Director, Latarche Trio. *Education:* Foundation Scholarship to Royal College of Music; studied with Kendall Taylor, 1977-82; FTCL; LRAM; ARCM. *Career:* Broadcasts for Radio 3, BBC TV and Cable TV in USA; Piano Teacher, Purcell School and Royal College of Music, Junior Department, Performed at Harrogate International Festival, Battle Festival, various music clubs and concert halls throughout the country including Fairfield Halls, Croydon, Purcell Room and Queen Elizabeth Hall and Wigmore Hall, London; Recital and Concerto appearances. *Honours:* English Speaking Union/Mayer Scholarship to Aspen Summer Festival, USA, 1982; Martin Musical Scholarship Fund Award to study with Vlado Perlemuter in Paris, and Alexander Kelly in London, 1983; Lisa Fuchsova Prize for Chamber Music Pianist; Eric Rice Memorial Prize for an Accompanist, Royal Overseas League Competition, 1984. *Memberships:* Incorporated Society of Musicians; Musicians Union; Ealing and District Music Teachers' Society. *Hobbies:* Driving; Knitting; Dancing. *Address:* 10 Ravenswood Gardens, Isleworth, Middlesex. TW7 4JG, England.

LATCHEM Malcolm, b. 28 Jan 1931, Salisbury, England. Violinist. m. 24 June 1964, 1 son, 3 daughters. *Education:* Royal College of Music, 1947-49, 1951-53; ARCM Performers. *Career:* Philharmonia Orchestra, 1960-65; Sub-Leader, London Philharmonic Orchestra, 1965-69; Dartington String Quartet, 1969-80; Founder Member, 1959, now Principal and Director, Academy of St Martin-in-the-Fields. *Recordings:* Chamber music with Academy of St Martin-in-the-Fields Chamber Ensemble; Handel Trio Sonatas; Mozart's Divertimenti; Spohr's Double Quartets; Other chamber music. *Honours:* Honorary MMus, Bristol University, 1980. *Hobby:* Gardening. *Current management:* ASM (Orchestra) Ltd. *Address:* Station House, Staverton, Totnes, Devon TQ9 6AG, England.

LATEINER Jacob, b. 31 May 1928, Havana, Cuba. Pianist. *Education:* Studied in Havana 1934-40 with Jascha Fischermann; Curtis Institute from 1940, with Isabelle Vengerova; Studied chamber music with Piatigorsky and Primrose. *Debut:* With the Philadelphia Orchestra under Ormandy, 1945. *Career:* Tanglewood Festival with Koussevitsky 1947; New York recital debut 1948; Tours of Europe, the USA and Australia from 1954; Premiered the Concerto by Elliott Carter 1967, and the Third Sonata of Roger Sessions, 1968; Taught at Mannes College 1963-70; Juilliard School, New York, from 1966. *Recordings:* Works by Beethoven and other 19th Century repertory; Contemporary American works. *Address:* Juilliard School of Music, Piano Faculty, Lincoln Plaza, New York, NY 10023, USA.

LATHAM-KOENIG Jan, b. 1953, London, England. Conductor; Pianist. *Education:* Studied at the Royal College of Music with Norman Del Mar, Kendall Taylor and Lamar Crowson. *Career:* Regular appearances as conductor with the Royal Philharmonic, Philharmonia, London Philharmonic, BBC Symphony, BBC Philharmonic and BBC Welsh Symphony Orchestras; Guest conductor of the Los Angeles Philharmonic and St Paul Chamber Orchestras, the Danish and Swedish Radio Orchestras, the Stockholm Philharmonic, the orchestras of the Maggio Musicale in Florence, the RAI (Rome, Turin and Naples), the Zurich Tonhalle and the Gulbenkian Orchestra in Lisbon; Tour with the Stuttgart Philharmonic, in Italy, 1991; Founded the Koenig Ensemble 1976; Concert pianist until 1981; Member of the Cantiere Internazionale d'Arte at Montepulciano 1981-86, and conducted Manon Lescaut, Don Giovanni, Edgar and a cycle of Mahler symphonies; Other opera engagements include: Giulio Cesare with the Royal Swedish Opera 1985; La Vestale and Donizetti's Il Diluvio Universale at Genoa 1984, 1985; From the House of the Dead and The Rake's Progress at Venice 1985-86; Tosca for English National Opera 1987; Attila at Lisbon (1986); L'Italiana in Algeri for Toulouse Opera 1987; The Cunning Little Vixen and Nabucco, Vienna Volksopo, 1992; Festival appearances at Wexford La Straniera, 1987, Macerata (Manon and Macbeth, 1987-88), Maggio Musicale Florence (world premiere of L'Ispirazione by Bussotti, 1988), the Mozart Festival at Vicenza (La Finta Giardiniera, 1986), the Donizetti Festival at Bergamao (concert performances of Fausta, 1987), and Lucca (Catalani's Dejanice); Has conducted Szymanowski's King Roger for Danish Radio and a cycle of Weill operas and cantatas for West German Radio; Rome Opera 1988, with the premiere of Bussotti's Fedra; returned with Donizetti's Poliuto to open the 1988-89 season; Debut at the Vienna Staatsoper 1988, Macbeth: Aida in May 1989; Monte Carlo Opera with Massenet's Thérèse and Le Portrait de Manon; Bregenz Festival, Samson et Dalila; Conducted Leoncavallo's La Bohème at Venice, 1990; Teatro Sao Carlos Lisbon 1990, Un ballo in Maschera and Lohengrin; Montpellier Festival, 1990, Graun's Montezuma and Magnard's Berenice; Conducted Weill's Mahagonny at the 1990 Maggio Musciale, Florence; Permanent Guest Conductor at Vienna State Opera from 1991. *Recordings include:* Weill's Mahagonny with Anja Silja (Capriccio) and Der Zar lässt sich photographieren, Der Lindberghflug, Magna Carta, Street Scene and Der Silbersee; Catalani's Dejanice (Bongiovanni); Walton: Concertos with London Philharmonic Orchestra (for Chandos). *Address:* Unit 2, 39 Tadema Road, London SW10 0PY England.

LAUBACH Mark Edward, b. 18 Jan. 1961, Easton, Pennsylvania, USA. Organist and Choirmaster; Concert Artist; Teacher. *Education:* High School Diploma, Palmerton Area High School, Palmerton, Pennsylvania 1978; Bachelor of Church Music, Westminster Choir College, Princeton, NJ 1982; MMus. Organ Performance and Literature, Eastman School of Music, Rochester, NY 1984; Fellow in Church Music, Washington Cathedral 1985. *Career:* Many solo recitals throughout USA including those at conventions of American Guild of Organists; Solo Recital and Interview featured on Pipedreams, nationally-broadcast programme of organ music via National Public Radio; other local radio broadcasts/interviews throughout USA; Frequent Performances on Music from St. Stephen's, local radio programme from own church. Organist and Choirmaster, St. Stephen's Church, Wilkes-Barre, Pennsylvania. *Honours:* 1st Prize, National Young Artists Competition in Organ Performance, American Guild of Organists, San Francisco 1984; Assistant Conductor and Accompanist, Wyoming Valley Oratorio Society. *Memberships:* American Guild of Organists; Organ Historical Society; Hymn Society of America; Association of Anglican Musicians. *Hobbies:* Golf; Tennis; Walking/Hiking. *Address:* St. Stephen's Church, 35 South Franklin Street, Wilkes-Barre, PA 18701, USA.

LAUBENTHAL Horst, b. 8 March 1939, Duderstadt, Germany. Singer (Tenor). m. Marga Schiml. *Education:* Studied in Munich with Rudolf Laubenthal. *Debut:* Wurzburg 1967, as Mozart's Don Ottavio. *Career:* Staatsoper Stuttgart from 1968, in operas by Wagner, Mozart and Beethoven; Guest appearances in Vienna, Hamburg, and Barcelona; Bayreuth Festival 1970 as the Steersman in Der fliegende Holländer; Deutsche Oper Berlin, as Lensky in Eugene Onegin and Pfitzner's Palestrina; Glyndebourne 1972, as Belmonte in Die Entführung; Paris Opéra 1977; Turin 1985, as Tamino in Die Zauberflöte (returned 1987, as Don Ottavio); Often heard as the Evangelist in the Passions of Bach. *Recordings:* Tannhäuser, Fidelio, Die Meistersinger (Deutsche Grammophon); Wozzeck and Lulu (Decca); Bach Cantatas and Christmas Oratorio (Philips); Trionfi by Orff (BASF); Korngold's Violanta (CBS); Schubert's Lazarus (Orfeo). *Address:* c/o Deutsche Oper Berlin, Richard Wagnerstrasse 10, D-1000 Berlin, Germany.

LAUFER Beatrice, b. 27 Apr 1923, New York City, New York, USA. Composer. *Education:* Studied at Juilliard School from 1944, with Roger Sessions, Marion Bauer and Vittorio Giannini. *Career:* Performances of her music in Germany, Stockholm, China and USA. *Compositions include:* Opera Ile, after O'Neill's Logy Voyage Home, premiered at Stockholm, 1958, revived New at Yale School of Music under Phylis Curtin, 1977, and at Shanghai, 1988; My Brother's Keeper, Biblical opera, 1968; Ballet The Great God Brown, 1966; Adam's Rib for soloists, chorus and orchestra; 2 Symphonies, 1944, 1961; Violin Concerto; Concerto for flute, oboe, trumpet and strings, 1962; Concertante for violin, viola and orchestra, 1986; Lyric for string trio, 1966; Choral music. *Address:* c/o ASCAP, ASCAP Building, One Lincoln Plaza, New York, NY 10023, USA.

LAUGHLIN Roy, b. 1954, Belfast, Northern Ireland. Conductor; Pianist. *Education:* Studied at Edinburgh University and at Durham University. *Career:* Conducted Haydn's L'Infedeltà Delusa at Durham; Head of Music with Opera North, for whom he has conducted The Magic Flute, Orpheus in the Underworld, La Cenerentola and Der Freischütz; twice Chorus Master at Wexford Festival and conducted Die Schöpfung 1989; Assistant Conductor of Halifax Choral Society; recent engagements with Opera North include Fidelio, The Pearl Fishers, Peter Grimes and the British premiere production of Verdi's Jerusalem (1990); also La Traviata, Attila and Faust; Season 1992-93 with Falstaff for English Touring Opera and Cimarosa's Secret Marriage for the Cheltenham and Buxton Festivals. *Address:* Robert Gilder and Co., Enterprise House, 59-65 Upper Ground, London SE1 9PQ, England.

LAUGHTON John Charles, b. 9 Oct. 1946, Sioux City, Iowa, USA. Clarinettist; Professor of Music, St Mary's College of Maryland. (div), 2 sons. *Education:* BM, University of Iowa, 1968; MM, The Catholic University of America, 1972; DMA, The University of Iowa, 1980. *Career:* Solo recitals, concerto performances, and masterclasses given thoughout the USA, Brazil, China, Costa Rica and the Soviet Union. Founding Executive Director of Chesapeake Summer Arts and former director of the Tidewater Music Festival. *Publications:* Featured intervies in Liberal Education 3, and the television specials Evening Magazine, and Capital Edition, The Brazilian Milhaud, published by the Fulbright Foundation of Brazil, and An Overview of the Wind Music of Darius Milhaud, Chamber Music Quarterly. *Contributions to:* Cultural Democracy, Issues of Multiculturalism and the Arts, in the Journal of Art Management, Law and Society. *Address:* Box 83, St Mary's City, MD 20686, USA.

LAUKVIK Jon, b. 16 Dec 1952, Oslo, Norway. Organist; Harpsichordist. *Education:* Studied Organ, Church Music and Piano, Conservatory of Oslo, 1972-74; Organ with Professor M Schneider, Harpsichord with Professor H Ruf, Musikhochschule Cologne, 1974-80; Organ studies with M C Alain, Paris, 1975-77. *Debut:* Oslo, 1973. *Career:* Recitals in Western and Eastern Europe, Israel, Japan and USA; Recordings for several European Radio stations; Master classes; Jury member, international competitions. *Compositions:* Via

Crucis; Triptychon; Suite for organ; Anrufung for 2 organs, tape and brass; EUphonie I for organ and 5 percussionists; EUphonie III for cello and organ; Contredanse for orchestra. *Recordings:* Neresheim monastery (works by J S and C P E Bach, Raison, Kittel). *Publications:* Orgelschule zur historischen Auffuhrungspraxis, 1990; G F Handel: Organ Concertos op 7 and No 13-16 (with W Jacob), 1990. *Honours:* 1st Prize and Bach Prize, International Organ Week, Nuremberg, 1977. *Hobbies:* Cooking; Fine wines; Norway. *Address:* Senefelderstrasse 13, D-70178 Stuttgart, Germany.

LAURENCE Elizabeth, b. 22 Nov 1949, Harrogate, Yorkshire, England. Singer (Mezzo-Soprano). *Education:* Studied clarinet at the Trinity College of Music, London. *Career:* Sang with the Groupe Vocal de France 1981-82; Vienna 1983, in Le Marteau sans Maitre, conducted by Boulez; Further concerts with Barenboim, Casadesus, Downes and Zender; Made video for French TV, L'Heure Espagnole - Ravel, 1985-86; Madrid Opera 1986, as Jocasta in Oedipus Rex; Paris Opéra as Erda in Siegfried and as Cherubino in Le Nozze di Figaro; returned for the 1989 world premiere of Der Meister und Margarita by Höller; Sang in the 1987 world premiere of The Electrification of the Soviet Union, by Nigel Osborne (Glyndebourne Festival); Promenade Concerts 1987, as the Wood-Dove in Schoenberg's Gurrelieder, conducted by Boulez; Tour of Italy and Germany 1987 with the Ensemble InterContemporain, in Pierrot Lunaire; Sang in the 1988 premiere of Le Visage Nuptial by Boulez, revised version; Fricka, Das Rheingold, Paris, 1988; Schoenberg's Op.22 Songs and Mahler's 3rd Symphony in Turin, conducted by Lothar Zagrosek and Rudolf Barshai; Covent Garden debut 1989, in the British premiere of Un Re in Ascolto by Berio; Appeared as Judith in a BBC television production of Bluebeard's Castle by Bartók, 1989; Kindertotenlieder, Milan; Contemporary recital, Berio, Bartók, Britten, Reger & Schoenberg, 'Festival of Montreux'; Gurrelieder, Leeds Town Hall, 1989; Sang Erda in Das Rheingold at Bonn, 1990; Lady de Hautdesert in the premiere of Birtwistle's Gawain, Covent Garden, 1991; Season 1991/92 as Ravel's Conception at Turin and the Duchess of Alba in the premiere of Osborne's Terrible Mouth at the Almeida Theatre. *Recordings:* 'Live' recording, Le Marteau sans maître; Le Visage Nuptial. *Address:* c/o Ingpen & Williams Ltd, 14 Kensington Court, London W8 5DN, England.

LAURENS Guillemette, b. 1950, Fontainebleau, France. Singer (Mezzo-Soprano). *Education:* Studied at the Toulouse Conservatoire and the Paris Opera Studio. *Debut:* Paris Salle Favart, as Anne Trulove on The Rake's Progress. *Career:* Has performed throughout Europe, the USA and South America; Sang Cybele in Lully's Atys at the Paris Opera with Les Arts Florissants; Repertoire includes German Lieder, French and Italian Baroque chamber music; Pierrot Lunaire by Schoenberg; La Clemenza di Tito, Giulio Cesare, I Puritani (Paris Opéra); Appeared with Capriccio Stravagante in the USA, May 1989; Engagements with the Ensemble Sequentia in 12th Century Liturgical Drama; Sang at the Festival of Aix-en-Provence in Iphigénie en Aulide, with John Eliot Gardiner; Towards Bach concert series on London's South Bank, 1989. *Recordings:* Monteverdi's Vespers with Phillipe Herreweghe; Atys and Il Ballo dell'Ingrate, conducted by William Christie; Bach's B Minor Mass with Gustav Leonhardt; Charpentier's Le Malade imaginaire conducted by Marc Minkowski; Diana in Iphigénie en Aulide, under John Eliot Gardiner; Labels include Harmonia Mundi, Erato and Deutsche Grammophon. *Address:* Erato Musifrance, c/o WEA Records, PO Box 59, Alperton Lane, Alperton, Middlesex HA0 1FJ.

LAURIE Alison Margaret, b. 5 Jan. 1935, Glossop, Derbyshire, England. Music Librarian. *Education:* Glasgow University, 1952-57, MA, BMus; Cambridge University, 1957-60, PhD; ARCM. *Career:* Senior Assistant Librarian, Glasgow University, 1961-63; Music Librarian, Reading University Library, 1963-. *Publications:* Editions of Purcell, Dioclesian, 1960 and

Dioclesian (vocal score), 1983; Dido and Aeneas, 1961 and 1979; King Arthur, 1971 and King Arthur (vocal score), 1972; Solo Songs, 1985. *Contributions to:* Neighbour, editor; Music and bibliography, 1980; Bent and Tilmouth, editors, Source materials and the interpretation of music, 1981; Spink, editor, Music in Britain: The Seventeenth Century, 1992; Musical Times; Other journals. *Memberships:* Purcell Society; Royal Musical Association; International Association of Music Libraries Archives and Documentation centres; Library Association. *Hobbies:* Hill walking; Gardening. *Address:* 123 Nightingale Road, Woodley, Reading, Berkshire RG5 3LZ, England.

LAURIE Cynthia, b. 12 Apr. 1924, London, England. Retired, Concert Singer - Soprano; Teacher. m. Trevor Hill, 1 daughter. *Education:* FTCL, Singing; ATCL, Teaching; Studied with Elena Gerhardt, 1950. *Career:* Recitals and broadcasts in England and Scotland, 1949-64; 1st Recital of Mahler and Berg songs on Norwegian radio, 1957; Tutor, University of Ghana and broadcasts on Ghana Radio, 1964-65; Series of recital seminars on German and French romantic song, Simon Fraser University, Canada, 1969; Tutor in Singing, Craigie College of Education, Ayr, Scotland, 1974-76; Lecturer, Institute of Music and Drama, University of Khartoum, Sudan, 1976-80. *Memberships:* Incorporated Society of Musicians; Former Member, Edinburgh Society of Musicians Women's Sect Convener 1959-61. *Hobbies:* Pastel drawing; Reading. *Address:* Sarnia, Shallochpark, Girvan, Ayrshire, KA26 0HW, Scotland.

LAVENDER Justin, b. 4 June 1951, Bedford, England. Singer (Tenor). *Debut:* Sang Nadir in Les Pecheurs de perles at Sydney Opera House, 1982. *Career:* Has sung Medoro in Haydn's Orlando Paladino at St Gallen, Tamino at Vienna Staatsoper, Pilade (Rossini's Hermione) at Madrid, Le Comte Ory at La Scala, Don Ottavio for Rome Opera and Arnold (Guillaume Tell) and Almaviva at Covent Garden; Appearances in premieres of Il Ritorno di Casanova by Arrigo at the Grand Théâtre Geneva and La Noche Triste by Prodomes at Théâtre des Champs Elysées, Paris; Further engagements as Fernande in La Favorite at Vichy, Almaviva at Pittsburgh (US debut), Belmonte in Vienna and Berlin, Ferrando (Cosi fan Tutte) at Essen, Lindoro at Buxton Festival and Neocles in Le Siege de Corinthe by Rossini at Madrid and the Festival Hall, London; Season 1993 in Il Pirata at Lausanne, Marzio in Mitridate and Arone in Mose in Egitto at Covent Garden; Concert repertoire includes Bartok's Cantata Profana with Georg Solti, Schubert's Mass in E flat with Giulini and Berlin Philharmonic, Schnittke's Faust Cantata under Claudio Abbado and Oedipus Rex conducted by Bernard Haitink; Other conductors have included John Lubbock (Dream of Gerontius), John Pritchard, Menuhin, Alberto Zedda and Leonard Slatkin; Regular Contributor to The Singer (Rhinegold Publications). *Address:* c/o Athole Still Ltd, 80-86 Westrow Street, London SE19 3AF, England.

LAVIRGEN Pedro, b. 31 July 1930, Bujalance, Andalusia, Spain. Singer (Tenor). *Education:* Studied with Miguel Barrosa in Madrid. *Debut:* Mexico City 1964, as Radames. *Career:* European debut at the Teatro del Liceo, Barcelona, as Don José; Metropolitan Opera 1969, as Cavaradoss in Tosca; Verona Arena 1974 and 1976, as Radames; Covent Garden 1975 and 1978, as Don José and Pollione (Norma); La Scala Milan 1975, as Don José, which he repeated at the 1978 Edinburgh Festival; Other appearance in Hamburg, Munich, Prague, Budapest and Madrid. *Recordings include:* Il Retablo de maese Pedro by de Falla (HMV).

LAVISTA Mario, b. 3 Apr. 1943, Mexico City. Composer. *Education:* Studied Composition with Carlos Chávez, Musical Analysis with Rodolfo Halffter, National Conservatory of Mexico, 1963-67; Studied in Paris with Jean Etienne- Marie and Nadia Boulanger, in Cologne with K. Stockhausen and Henry Pousseaur, 1967-70. *Career:* Professor, Theory & Composition, National Conservatory of Mexico, 1969-; Founder, Group, Quanta, 1970-73; Editor, Pauta, 1982-. *Compositions:*

(Recent Works 1979-89): Canto Del Alba, For Flute in C; Nocturno, Flute in G; Lamento, Bass Flute; Dusk, Contrabass; Cante, 2 Guitars; Marsias, Oboe & Crystal Cups; Ficciones, Orchestra; Simurg, Piano; Three Songs, Mezzosoprano and Piano (Chinese Poetry of the Tang Dynasty); Reflections of the Night, String Quartet; Hacia el Comienzo; ezzosoprano & orchestra (poems by Octavio Paz); Cuicani, Flute & Clarinet, B Flat; Madrigal, Clarinet, B Flat; Three Nocturnes, Mezzosoprano & orchestra, (poems by Alvaro Mutis); Aura, on act opera (based on Aura, a short story by Carlos Fuentes). *Memberships:* International Society of Contemporary Music; Society of Authors and Composers of Mexico; Mexican Academy of Arts. *Hobbies:* Billiards. *Address:* Yautepec 24, Colonia Condesa, Mexico 06140, D.F.

LAWERGREN Bo, b. 4 Jan. 1937, Hejde, Sweden. Professor. 2 daughters. *Education:* Uppsala University, 1959; PhD, Australian National University, 1963; Studied Composition with: Friedrich Mehler, Chou Wen Chung. *Career:* Professor, Physics, Acoustics, Musical Archaeology, Hunter College, New York City; Associate Director, East & West Artists, New York. *Compositions:* Captain Cook, Chamber Opera; Farfar, Piano Solo; Piano Concerto with Chamber Orchestra; Marche Funebre, Trombone, Piano, Metronome; Semi-Zoo, Chamber Orchestra. *Contributions to:* Numerous articles on ancient instruments in professional journals including: Galpin Society Journal; Acustica; Journal of Egyptian Archaeology; Imago Musicae; Iraq; Journal of the Acoustical Society of America; Beiträge zur allegemeinen und vergleichenden Archäologie, Archéologia; Book and Record Reviews. *Address:* Hunter College, 695 Park Avenue, New York, NY 10021, USA.

LAWLOR Thomas, b. 1938, Dublin, Ireland. Singer (Bass-baritone). *Education:* BA, National University of Ireland; Dublin College of Music; Guildhall School of Music. *Career:* Sang with D'Oyly Carte Company 1963-71 (tours of North America); Glyndebourne 1971- in Eugene Onegin, Ariadne, Cosi fan Tutte, Die Entführung, La Bohème, Le Nozze di Figero, Capriccio, Intermezzo, The Cunning Little Vixen; Engagements with Opera North in A Village Romeo and Juliet, Tosca, Der Rosenkavalier, Der Freischütz, A Midsummer Night's Dream, Manon Lescaut, the premiere of Rebecca by Wilfred Josephs (1983), Werther, La Cenerentola, Beatrice and Benedict, Jonny Spielt Auf, Die Mesitersinger, The Golden Cockerel and Intermezzo; Further appearances with Kent Opera, English Music Theatre, New Sadler's Wells Opera and Opera Northern Ireland; (Royal Opera, Dublin Grand Opera); Rising of the Moon, Wexford Festival 1990; Prokofiev's The Duenna; Regular broadcaster on Radio Telefis Eireann and on BBC radio and television. *Membership:* Faculty Member of Summer Conservatory of Music, Bay View, Michigan, USA. *Address:* Music International, 13 Ardilaun Road, London N5 2QR, England.

LAWRENCE Arthur Peter, b. 15 July 1937, Durham, North Carolina, USA. Organist; Teacher; Editor. *Education:* AB, Music, Davidson College, 1959; MMus, Theory, Florida State University, 1961; Certificate, The Adjutant General's School, 1961; DMusArts, Performance Practice, Stanford University, 1968; AMLS, Music, University of Michigan, 1974; Certificate of Organ Interpretation, University of Salamanca, Spain, 1986. *Career:* Faculty, St Mary's College, Notre Dame, Indiana, 1969-80; Editor, Publisher, The Diapason, Chicago, Illinois, 1976-82; Associate Editor, The American Organist, 1982-92; Organist-Choirmaster, Church of the Good Shepherd, New York City, 1982-; Faculty Member, Manhattan School of Music, 1983-. *Contributions to:* Over 150 feature articles or reviews for American Guild of Organists Quarterly, The American Organist. *Address:* 520 East 20th St., 5-D New York, NY 10009, USA.

LAWRENCE Helen Ruth, b. 22 July 1942, London, England. Opera Singer. m. Abraham Marcus, 1969. *Education:* North London Collegiate School; Royal Academy of Music, London, LRAM; ARAM. *Career:* Guest artist, Covent Garden, English National Opera,

Handel Opera, Chelsea Opera, Phoenix Opera, Ludwigsburg Festival, Germany; Toured Far East with Royal Opera, 1979; Concerts and recitals: Wigmore Hall, South Bank, Barbican and major throughout UK, also Germany, Italy, The Netherlands and Israel; with Songmakers' Almanac, SPNM, Lotano, Halle Orchestra, UK Music Clubs and Choral Societies. Broadcasts and recordings include: BBC Radio: title roles: Ggiordano's, Fedora; Berthold Goldschmidt's, Beatrice Cenci (world premiere QEH, 1988); Decca records: Dama in Macbeth, Mémé in Goldschmidt's Der Gewaltige Hahnrei, Berlin 1992. Other roles include Donna Anna, Constanze, Fiordiligi, Médée (Cherubini), Lucrezia Borgia, Lady Macbeth, Violetta, Leonora, Amelia, Abigaille, Tosca, Santuzza, Carmen, Mezzo-soprano since 1989. Artistic Director and Administrator, New Shakespeare Company's Opera season, Regent's Park Open Air Theatre, 1983; and London Masterclasses, 1989-92. *Publication:* Life of Mozart (translation from Italian), Great Men Series for Children. *Memberships:* Equity; Incorporated Society of Musicians. *Hobbies:* Gardening; Reading; Sewing. *Address:* 5 Greenaway Gardens, London NW3 7DJ, England.

LAWRENCE-KING Andrew, b. 1959, Guernsey, UK. Baroque Harpist. *Career:* Founder-Member of Tragicomedia Baroique Ensemble, now Freelance Soloist and continuo-player appearances with Hilliard Ensemble, Gothic Voices, Hesperion XX, The Kings Singers; Concerts in Britain and at leading European and US early music festivals; Monteverdi's L'Orfeo at the 1986 BBC Proms (director Roger Norrington), in Barcelona Liceo 1993 (dir. Jordi Savall) and 1993 Boston festival (dir. Andrew Parrott); directed Monteverdi Ulisse at 1992 Swedish Baroque Festival, Malmo; Solo recital to open 1992 Utrecht Festival; Professor of Harp and Continuo, Akademie fuer Alte Musik, Bremen, Germany. *Recordings:* On Hyperion, EMI and other include: The Harp of Luduvico; Harp Music of the Italian Renaissance (solo harp music); Biber's Mystery Sonatas (1992 Gramophone award); Handel Harp Concerto; Proensa (troubadour songs); The Lament of Orfeo (songs by d'India). Concert programmes include with Baroque orchestra: Handel Harp Concerto; Early Operas: Monteverdi Orfeo, Poppea, Ulisse (continuo/direction); with Belinda Sykes (voice); Improvisatori (16th century songs and improvisations); Ay! Santa Maria (Spanish Medieval songs); Solo: The lyre of Timotheus, (instrumental music by Handel, Bach, Buxtehude); Harp and Double-harp (Italian and English 17th century); The Harp of Luduvico (Spanish Baroque). *Publications:* Der Harpferschläger, (Historical Harp Technique); Luz y Norte (Spanish 17th century harp music); Article in Companion to Early Music, Dent 1992. *Honours:* First winner of the International Award from Cambridge Early Music Society, 1992; Winner Gramophone Award, 1992. *Current Management:* Robert White. *Address:* Robert White Management, 182 Moselle Avenue, London N22 6EX, England.

LAWSON Colin James, b. 24 July 1949, Saltburn-by-the-Sea, England. Clarinettist; Musicologist. m. Hilary Birch, 16 Apr. 1982, 1 son. *Education:* ARCM, 1967; Keble College, Oxford; BA(Oxon), 1971; MA(Oxon), 1975; MA, Birmingham University, 1972; PhD, Aberdeen University, 1976. *Career:* Lecturer in Music, University of Aberdeen, 1973-77; Lecturer in Music, Sheffield University, 1978-91, Senior Lecturer, 1991-; Professor of Classical Studies and Early Clarinet, Guildhall of Music, London, 1988-91; Visiting Lecturer, RNCM, RAM, 1992; Current specialisation in historical performance; Principal Clarinet, Hanover Band, 1987-, London Classical Players, 1989-; Principal Clarinet, English Concert, 1991-; Guest Principal Clarinet, Orchestra of the Age of Enlightenment, 1987-; Member of contemporary ensemble Lysis; Solo, chamber and orchestral appearances throughout UK, Europe and USA; Performed Mozart Concerto, 1989, on specially designed boxwood basset clarinet at Cheltenham Festival, London and Oxford venues, tourrs throughout Europe and recording for Nimbus. *Recordings:* With Academy of Ancient Music, Albion Ensemble, Classical Winds CM90, Cristofori, English Concert, The Parley of Instruments, La Petite Bande, L'Ecole d'Orphée; The

King's Consort. *Publication:* The Chalumeau in Eighteenth-Century Music, 1981. *Hobbies:* Travel; Acquisition of early clarinets. *Address:* 46 Clitheroe Avenue, Harrow, Middlesex HA2 9UX, England.

LAWSON Peter, b. 11 Apr. 1950, Manchester, England. Musician; Pianist. m. Ariane Dandoy, 3 Apr. 1976, 1 son, 1 daughter. *Education:* Royal Manchester College of Music, 1968-73; Postgraduate Studies, Royal Northern College of Music; GRSM; ARMCM. *Career:* Piano Soloist, Concertos with BBC Philharmonic, BBC Welsh, RLPO, London Sinfonietta, London Mozart Players, etc.; Recitals and Radio in France, Belgium, Holland, Italy, Denmark & throughout UK; 20th Century Specialist; Tutor, Chetham's School of Music, Manchester; Examiner, Associated Board of the Royal Schools of Music. *Recordings:* Satie Piano Music, 1980; New British Piano Music, 1982; American Piano Sonatas, (Virgin Classics), 3 CDs, in preparation. *Hobbies:* Travel; Food. *Address:* 38 Church Street South, Old Glossop, Derbyshire SK13 9RU, England.

LAWTON Jeffrey, b. 1941, Oldham, Lancashire, England. Singer (Tenor). *Education:* Studied wuth Patrick McGuigan. *Career:* With Welsh National Opera has sung Tikhon in Katya Kabanova (also televised), various roles in The Greek Passion by Martinů, Florestan, Huon (Oberon), in Janáček's From the House of the Dead and Jenůfa (Laca), Otello, Aeneas (The Trojans) and Don José; Sang Siegfried in a new production of The Ring (also seen at Covent Garden, 1986) and the Emperor in Die Frau ohne Schatten; Other operatic appearances for Opera North (Erik and Florestan), in Paris, Brussels and Nancy (Otello), and Cologne (Siegmund); Concert engagements include the Choral Symphony with the Royal Liverpool Philharmonic, Das Lied von der Erde with the BBC Symphony at the Brighton Festival and in Paris, Mahler's 8th Symphony in Turin; Season 1989- included Siegfried in Götterdämmerung in Cologne; Edmund in Lear for English National Opera; Edinburgh Festival 1990 in Greek Passion by Martinů; Laca in Jenůfa for Welsh National Opera and Tristan, 1992/93; Shuisky in Boris, Opera North, 1993-94; Laca-Jenůfa, New Israeli Opera and Tristan for Scottish National Opera; Sang Herod in final scene from Salome, Prom Concerts, 1993. *Recordings include:* The Greek Passion. *Current Management:* Music International. *Address:* 13 Ardilaun Road, Highbury, London, England.

LAWTON Sidney Maurice, b. 28 Oct. 1924, Stechford, England. Composer; Arranger; Orchestrator. *Education:* MusB, Manchester University; ARCO; ARMCM. *Career:* Director of Music, Queen's College, Taunton, Somerset, 1947-80; Currently freelance composer, arranger and orchestrator. *Compositions:* The Young Clarinettist, 3 vols; A Book of Clarinet Duets; The Young Flautist, 3 vols; The Clarinettists Book of Carols; The Young Trumpet Player, 3 vols; The Brass Quartet, 2 vols; The Young Oboist, 3 vols; Handel, Overture in C (edited 3 clarinets); A Book of Clarinet Trios; The Young Trombonist, 3 vols; The Young Horn Player, 3 vols; Telemann, Heroic Music (edited trumpet/keyboard, also flute/keyboard); The Windband Book; Old English Trumpet Tunes, Vols 1 and 2; Windscore Series Nos 1-11; Fugue on a Nursery Theme; A Tchaikovsky Clarinet Album; A Wagner Clarinet Album; A Satie Clarinet Album; A Debussy Clarinet Album; The English Baroque Trumpet; An Elgar Clarinet Album; The Young Bassoonist, 3 vols; The Young Recorder Player, 3 vols; Two Fauré Pieces (edited clarinet/piano); Bach, Jesu, Joy (edited clarinet/piano); Jesu, Joy (edited oboe/piano); Bach, Sheep May Safely Graze (edited 2 flutes/keyboard); Carols For Flute; 18th Century Solos For Flute; A Fauré Clarinet Album. *Hobbies:* Dowsing; Healing techniques. *Address:* 10 Margaret's Buildings, Brock Street, Bath, Avon, BA1 2LP, England.

LAYCOCK Mark, b. 30 Aug. 1957, USA. Conductor. m. Emily Muller, 10 July 1982. 1 son. *Education:* New School of Music, Philadelphia, 1975-79; Aspen Music School; Fellow, St Louis Conservatory, 1977; Solfege,

ear training, 1975. *Debut:* Philadelphia Orchestra, 1979. *Career:* Music Director, Chamber Symphony of Princeton; Guest Conductor: Moscow Autumn Festival, 1988; St Paul Chamber Orchestra, 1986 and 1989; Inaugurated New Cairo Opera House, 1988; Middle East Tour, 1988; Philharmonia Orchestra, Royal Festival Hall and Barbican Centre, London, England, 1986; Indianapolis Symphony Orchestra, USA, 1987; Philadelphia Orchestra, 1979. Frequent Guest Lecturer, New Jersey Governor's School for the Arts, Trenton State College; Lecturer, Bishop Grosseteste College, Lincoln, England, 1986. *Compositions:* Published and recorded arranger. *Honours:* Finalist, American Symphony Orchestra Stokowski Conducting Competition, 1988; Outstanding Young Man of America Award, 1986; Winner, Leopold Stokowski Memorial Competition in association with the Philadelphia Orchestra, 1979; Rupert Foundation International Conducting Awards in London, 1980 and 1982; Fellow, Aspen Music Festival, 1977. *Membership:* ASCAP. *Current Management:* Affiliate Artists, Inc. *Address:* Box 271, Villanova, Pennsylvania 19085, USA.

LAYNE Bobby, b. 28 June 1933, Lincoln, Nebraska, USA. Musician. m. 7 June 1958, 5 sons, 1 daughter. *Education:* Private lessons in music; High School Band; 43rd Army Band. *Career:* Played 1st chair trumpet in high school band; Started own 7-piece band in senior year; Began playing alto saxophone and clarinet in 1960s, and became lead saxophone in own band; Extended band to 11 pieces as Bobby Lane Orchestra, 1970s; Repertoire ranges from Dixieland to Big Band sound of Glen Miller; Played at 4 Governor's Inaugural Balls, Nebraska, 1960-88, and Lincoln Center, New York City, 1993; Featured performances: Bob Hope Show, Grand Island, Nebraska, 1981, Nebraska State Fair, Lincoln, 1986, 1987, Four Aces Show, Omaha, Nebraska, 1987, Bob Newhart Show, Topeka, Kansas, 1987, Myron Floren Show, Des Moines, Iowa, 1987, Dave Boyer Show, 1988, NBEA Melody, Caribbean Cruise on Sovereign of the Seas, 1989, Stars of the Lawrence Welk Show, Sioux Falls, South Dakota, 1990, 1991, Corn Palace, Mitchell, South Dakota, 1992; Featured radio shows, South Carolina, Nebraska, Illinois, South Dakota, Kansas, Iowa; Hosted Echos of the Big Bands for Nebraska ETV Network. *Recordings:* Songs from the Heart; Wishing; Swingin' Down the Layne; 40th Year Celebration. *Publication:* 40th Year Celebration, 1993. *Contributions to:* Features in Dancing USA and USA Today. *Honours:* Best Band Award through Voters Poll-KFOR Radio and Lincoln Sound, 1985, 1986, 1987, 1988. *Memberships:* National Orchestra Leaders; National Ballroom Operators. *Hobbies:* Sports; Camping. *Address:* 6600 West O, Lincoln, NE 68528, USA.

LAYTON Billy Jim, b. 14 Nov 1924, Corsicana, Texas, USA. Composer. *Education:* Studied with Francis Judd Cooke and Carl McKinley at the New England Conservatory; Yale University with Quincy Porter, MMus 1950; Harvard University with Walter Piston and Nino Pirrota, PhD 1960. *Career:* Assistant Professor at Harvard 1960-66; Professor of Music and first Chairman of Music Department, State University of New York at Buffalo, 1966-72. *Compositions include:* Five Studies for violin and piano 1952; An American Portrait, overture 1953; Dylan Thomas Poems for chorus and brass sextet 1954-56; String Quartet 1956; Three Studies for piano 1957; Divertimento for clarinet and ensemble 1958-60; Dance Fantasy for orchestra 1964. *Address:* c/o ASCAP, ASCAP Building, One Lincoln Plaza, New York, NY 10023, USA.

LAYTON Richard, b. 1940, Redditch, Worcestershire, England. Violinist. m. 4 children. *Education:* Studied in London. *Career:* Freelance musician, then Co-leader of the Bournemouth Symphony Orchestra from 1964; Leader of the Bournemouth Sinfonietta 1969; Soloist in concertos by Bach, Haydn, Mozart, Prokofiev and in the Brandenburg Concertos; Leader of the Silvestri String Quartet, with concerts at Dartington and at the Bath Festival; Sub-leader of the London Philharmonic Orchestra 1973, including appearances with the Glyndebourne Festival; Guest leader with the BBC Welsh Symphony, English National Opera Orchestra, the Park Lane Players and the Philharmonia; appointed Associate Leader of the Royal Philharmonic Orchestra 1983. *Hobby:* Photography. *Address:* c/o Royal Philharmonic Orchestra, 16 Clerkenwell Green, London EC1R ODP, England.

LAYTON Robert, b. 2 May 1930, London, England. Critic; Producer; Writer on Music. m. Ingrid Nina Thompson. *Education:* Worcester College, Oxford, 1949-53; Universities of Uppsala and Stockholm 1953-55; Studied composition with Edmund Rubbra and history of music with Egon Wellesz; Further studies with Professor Carl-Allan Mobert. *Career:* Swedish Film Industry 1954-55; Teacher in London 1956-59; BBC Music Division 1959- (music presentation, 1959, music talks 1960); General Editor, BBC Music Guides, 1973- ; Producer, BBC Lunchtime Concerts at St John's Smith Quare, 1984-88. *Publications:* Franz Berwald 1959; Jean Sibelius 1965; Sibelius and his World 1970; Dvořák Symphonies and Concertos 1977; Sibelius 1981; Companion to the Concerto 1988; responsible for Scandinavian music in the New Grove Dictionary of Music and Musicians 1980; Translated Erik Tawaststjerna's Sibelius (Vol. 1, 1976, Vol. II, 1985, Vol. III in prep.) Ed. Companion to the symphony (in prep). *Contributions to:* The Symphony (Ed. Robert Simpson) 1966; The Gramophone; The Listener; The Times; Professional journals in Britain and Sweden. *Honours:* Finnish State Literary Prize, 1985; Sibelius Medal, 1987; Knight of the Order of the White Rose of Finland, 1988. *Address:* BBC Radio 3, Broadcasting House, London WA 1AA, England.

LAZAREV Alexander, b. 5 July 1945, USSR. Conductor. *Education:* Studied at the Central Music School and the Moscow and Leningrad Conservatories. *Career:* Has conducted at the Bolshoi Theatre Moscow from 1973, Chief Conductor and Artist Director from 1987; Founded the Ensemble of Soloists of the Bolshoi Theatre 1978, for the promotion of contemporary music; Regular guest conductor of the former Leningrad Philharmonic and the USSR State Symphony; Guest appearances with the Berlin Philharmonic, Dresden, Munich, Rotterdam and Netherlands Radio Philharmonics; the Orchestre National de France and the Orchestra of the Accademia di Santa Cecilia, Rome; UK debut 1987, with the Liverpool Philharmonic; later engagements with the City of Birmingham Symphony, the Scottish National and the BBC Symphony Orchestras; Edinburgh Festival 1987, with the Orchestra of the Bolshoi Theatre; Led the Bolshoi Company in Glasgow with Rimsky-Korsakov's Mlada and Tchaikovsky's Maid of Orleans, 1990; Edinburgh Festival 1990, Prokofiev's The Duenna; Conducted the BBC Symphony Orchestra in Henze's Tristan and 7th Symphony at the Barbican Hall, 1991; Promenade Concerts debut 1991; Principal Guest Conductor of BBC Symphony Orchestra, 1992-; Led the Bolshoi Company on tour to the Metropolitan, New York, 1991; Conducted Salome at Duisburg, 1992; London Proms 1993 with Petrushka and Tchaikovsky's Third Suite. *Recordings:* Albums with the former Leningrad Philharmonic and the USSR State Symphony (Melodiya). *Honours:* First Prize, Young Conductors Competition, Moscow, 1971; Winner Herbert von Karajan Competition, Berlin, 1972. *Address:* c/o Christopher Tennant Management, Unit 2, 39 Tadema Road, London SW10 OPY, England.

LAZARIDIS Stefanos, b. 28 July 1944, Dire-Daw, Ethiopia. Stage Designer. *Education:* Studied in Geneva, 1960-62, and at Central School of Speech and Drama, London. *Career:* Designed Le nozze di Figaro at Covent Garden, 1972, followed by Idomeneo and Werther, 1978-79; Collaborated with John Copley at English National Opera with Die Entfuhrung, 1971, and Il Trovatore, 1972; Further designs for English National Opera have included Katya Kbanova, Dalibor, Euryanthe, Aida, Der fliegende Holländer, Rusalka, Madama Butterfly, Hansel and Gretel and the Mikado; UK stage premieres of Janáček's Osud, 1984, and Busoni's Doktor

Faust, 1986; Tosca at Florence and English National Opera (with Jonathan Miller), 1986, Nabucco for Opera North and Oedipus Rex and Bluebeard's Castle for Scottish Opera (1990); Collaborations with Yuri Lyubimov for Tristan and Isolde at Bologna, 1983, Rigoletto at Florence, 1984, and Fidelio at Stuttgart, 1985; Der fliegende Holländer with David Pountney at Bregenz Festival, 1989; Carmen at Earl's Court, London, 1989, and on tour to Japan and Australia; La Fanciulla del West at La Scala, 1991; Associate Artist at English National Opera. *Address:* English National Opera, St Martin's Lane, London WC2, England.

LAZARO Francisco, b. 13 Mar 1932, Barcelona, Spain. Singer (Tenor). *Education:* Liceo Conservatory, Barcelona. *Debut:* Barcelona 1962, as Gaspare in Donizetti's La Favorita; Sang in Macbeth and Der Rosenkvalier at the 1964 Salzburg Festival, under Karajan; Guest appearances in Berlin, Dusseldorf and Frankfurt; San Francisco 1965; Barcelona 1967, as Calaf in Turandot; Frequent performances at the Munich Staatsoper from 1970; Hamburg 1984, as Otello: Other roles include Verdi's Manrico and Radames; Des Grieux in Manon Lescaut, Rodolfo and Don José.

LAZAROF Henri, b. 12 Apr 1932, Sofia, Bulgaria. Composer. *Education:* Studied with Paul Ben-Haim in Jerusalem; Santa Cecilia Academy Rome with Petrassi, 1955-57; Brandeis University with Harold Shapero, 1957-59. *Career:* Teacher at University of California, Los Angeles, from 1962; Artist-in-Residence at University of West Berlin, 1970-71. *Compositions:* Piano Concerto 1957; Viola Concerto 1962; Concerto for piano and 20 instruments 1963; Odes for orchestra 1963; Double Concerto for violin, viola and chamber orchestra 1964; Structures Sonores for orchestra 1966; Mutazione for orchestra 1967; Cello Concerto 1968; Events, ballet 1973; Concertazioni for orchestra 1973; Spectrum for trumpet, orchestra and tape 1975; Chamber Symphony 1977, Mirrors, Mirrors, ballet 1980; Sinfonietta 1981; 3 String Quartets 1956, 1962, 1980; String Trio 1957; Wind Trio 1981, and other instrumental pieces. *Address:* c/o ASCAP, ASCAP Building, One Lincoln Plaza, New York, NY 10023, USA.

LAZAROV Stefan Stefanov, b. 31 Aug 1935, Sofia, Bulgaria. Musicologist. m. Emilia Tsherkozova, 8 Nov 1977, 1 son. *Education:* Musicology, History of Music, State Conservatoire, Sofia, 1953-58; Diploma, 1958-59; Phil Dr, 1974; Dr Arts, 1989. *Career:* Lecturer, Musicology, Philharmonies of Sofia, 1956-61, Plovdiv, 1959-64, Rousse, 1965-66, Opera of Rousse, 1964-65; Professor, 1960, Associate Professor, 1982, University Professor, 1991, History and Theory of Music, National Academy for Theatre and Film Arts; Professor, History of Opera, Musical Paleography, State Conservatoire, 1963-65; Many public and broadcast lectures; Author, TV plays. *Publications:* General history of Music, 11 books: Brahms, Weber, Mendelsson, Mahler, R Strauss, The Music, Beginning and development of Music, Britten, Honegger, Shostakovitsh, The Old Masters, 1958-88; Bulgarian music: Marin Goleminov, 1971; Pancho Vladigerov and the Theatre, 1974; Musical paleography, medieval: History of Musical Notation, 1965; The Synodikon of Tsar Boril as Musical-historic Monument, 1961; Die altbulgarische Musik und die Kyrillo-Methodianische Tradition, 1966; The Synodikon of Tsar Boril and the Problem of Byzantino-Bulgarian Musical Relations, 1971; The Glagolitic Tradition in Old-Bulgarian Music, 1972; A few Pages from the History of Bulgarian Music, 1973; An Interpretation of the Bulgarian Mediaeval Liturgical Texts, 1974; Die Bogomilen und die Musik, 1975; Pictogrammes et ideogrammes dans l'ecriture musicale byzantine, 1976; A Mediaeval Slavonic Treatise on Music, 1980; Comparative culturology: The Bogomils, the Music and the Theatre, 1985; Trubadures and the Cathares, 1989; The Bogomils and an Old Musical Tradition in Western Europe, 1990; The Role of the Bogomils and the Cathares in development of European Culture, 1990; Literature for Music. Texts in original and translation, 1991. *Address:* Eline-Peline Str 30, 1421 Sofia, Bulgaria.

LAZARTE Julio Ricardo, b . 12 July 1956, Tucuman, Argentina. Pianist; Conductor. *Education:* Medico degree, Faculty of Medicine, National University of Tucuman; Tecnico Instrumentista (Piano), Tecnico en Sonorizaciones, Professor (Piano), School of Musical Arts, National University of Tucuman; Dalcroze Certification, Carnegie Mellon University, Pittsburgh, USA. *Debut:* Pianist, Integral Version of Sonatas and Interludes by John Cage, US Embassy, Argentina, 1985; Conductor, Complete Version of Church Sonatas by Mozart, Santisimo Rosario Basilica, Tucuman, 1990. *Career:* As pianist has performed complete cycles of works for keyboard or chamber music with piano by Pechelbell, Zipoli, Marcello, Haendel, Haydn, Clementi, Mozart, Brahms, von Weber, the Second Viennese School, Debussy, Ravel, Satie, Cage, Ginastera and pioneers of Argentinian and Latin American keyboard music; Tours, USA, Spain, Netherlands, Argentina; Performances abroad have included versions of XXth century piano concertos by Stravinsky, Cage, Balada and Mayuzumi; As conductor he founded and is Artistic/ Music Director, Camerata Lazarte chamber orchestra, which performs intensively including Viena in Tucuman Festival for Mozart Bicentennial, 1991; Has taught in many academic and cultural institutions including National University of Tucuman, Carnegie Mellow University, in Amsterdam and in Madrid; Author of Lazarte Methodology for accelerating learning process in music. *Contributions to:* Analysis of the Complete Work for Piano solo of Alberto Ginastera, in Magazine of the Institute of Aesthetic Research, National University of Tucuman. *Honours:* 1st Prize, Ministry of Social Affairs, Tucuman, 1981; Gold Medal, School of Musical Arts, National University of Tucuman, 1983. *Memberships:* President, Center of Interdisciplinary Semiotic Studies; Principal Researcher, Institute of Aesthetic Research, National University of Tucuman. *Hobby:* Painting. *Current Management:* CESI, Tucuman, Argentina. *Address:* c/o CESI, Marcos Paz 250, Tucuman 250, Argentina.

LAZARUS Bruce, b. 3 Apr 1956, Brooklyn, New York, USA. Composer; Pianist. *Education:* BM, MM, Juilliard School of Music; PhD, Rutgers University. *Career:* Concerts of works at New Jersey Center for Performing Arts, 1985; Carnegie Recital Hall, 1986. *Compositions:* 4 piano sonatas; opera on Little Children Lost; Ballet works; Medieval Scenes; Vision Quest; Garland Epitaphium; Symphony; 2 Flute sonatas; Sonata for Tenor Saxophone and Piano; Pastorale for String Quartet. *Honours:* Rodgers and Hammerstein Scholarship, 1976; New Jersey Council on the Arts Fellowship, 1987. *Address:* 3579 Route 46 No 11a, Parsippany, NJ 07054, USA.

LE BRIS Michele, b. 1938, France. Singer (Soprano). *Education:* Studied at Conservatoire National, Paris. *Debut:* Paris Opera as Marguerite, 1961. *Career:* Many appearances at such French opera centres as Marseilles, Nantes, Vichy, Strasbourg, Toulouse and Rouen; Strasbourg, 1965, in local premiere of Mozart's La finta Giardiniera, Amelia in Ballo in Maschera, Tokyo, 1972; Sang Halevy's Rachel in London, 1973, and at Barcelona, 1974; Barcelona, 1976, as Thais; Other roles have included Rossini's Mathilde, Verdi's Desdemona and Trovatore Leonora, Manon Lescaut, Tosca, Mimi, Minnie and Musetta, Massenet's Salome and Sapho, Regina in Mathis der Maler, Mozart's Countess and Donna, Lisa in The Queen of Spades and Janáček's Jenůfa. *Recordings include:* Highlights from Un Ballo in Maschera and Il Trovatore. *Address:* c/o Theatre National de l'Opera de Paris, 8 Rue Scribe, F-75008 Paris, France.

LE DIZES Maryvonne, b. 25 June 1940, Quimper, France. Violin Soloist; Professor. m. 23 May 1964, 3 sons, 1 daughter. *Education:* 1st Prize, Violin, National Conservatory of Music, Paris, 1957; 1st Prize, Chamber Music, National Conservatory of Music, Paris, 1958. *Debut:* Violin Concert. *Career:* Soloist, Ensemble Intercontemporain, 1978-; Professor, Conservatory of Music, Boulogne Billancourt, France, 1977-. *Recordings:* Pieces of Berio, Messiaen, Chapey, Melby,

Xenakis, Machover, Carter, Brahms. *Honours:* Prize, International Thibaud Competition, Paris, 1961; 1st Prize: N Paganini Competition, Genoa, 1962, International American Music Competition, New York, 1983; SACEM Paris, 1987. *Address:* CIUP, Maison IAA, 5 Bd. Jourdan, 75690 Paris Cedex 14, France.

LE PREVOST Stephen Raymond, b. 23 Jan 1955, Guernsey, Channel Islands. Director of Music; Organist. *Education:* University of East Anglia, 1973-76; Jesus College, Cambridge, 1976-77; BA, FTCL, LRAM; ARCM. *Career:* Assistant Organist and Choirmaster, Ely Cathedral, 1977-89; Director of Music, The King's School, Ely, 1979-89; Conductor, Guernsey Glee Singers, 1990-91; Assistant Organist, Westminster Abbey, Music Master, Westminster Abbey Choir School, 1991-. *Recordings:* Accompanist on Service High and Anthems Clear; Anthems by Purcell and Blow; Music of Six Centuries; Christmas Eve at Ely; The Music of Arthur Wills; Soloist on Music for a Royal Year; Organist Royal Maundy Service, 1987. *Honour:* ARCM, Organ Performance with Honours, 1975. *Memberships:* RCO; MMA. *Hobbies:* Swimming; Theatre; History of Guernsey; Architecture. *Address:* Westminster Abbey Choir School, Dean's Yard, London SW1P 3NY, England.

LE ROUX Francois, b. 30 Oct 1955, Rennes, France. Singer (Baritone). *Education:* Studied with Francois Loup and at the Paris Opéra Studio with Vera Rosza and Elisabeth Grummer. *Career:* Sang at the Opera de Lyon 1980-85 as Mozart's Don Giovanni, Papageno, Guglielmo and Count; From 1985 appeared as Debussy's Pelléas at the Paris Opéra, La Scala, Milan (1986), Vienna Staatsoper (1988), Barcelona, Helsinki (1989), Köln (1992); Covent Garden, 1993; Glyndebourne Festival debut 1987, as Ramiro in L'Heure Espagnole; Hamburg 1987, as Marcello in La Bohème; Sang Lescaut in a new production of Manon at Covent Garden 1988, returning as Papageno 1989; Appeared as Hidraot in Armide at Amsterdam 1988 and Orestes in Iphigénie at Frankfurt, Ulysse in Il Ritorno at Lausanne (1989); Also sings Valentin in Faust and has sung Don Giovanni at the Paris Opéra and in Zurich conducted by Nikolaus Harnoncourt; Created the title role in the world premiere of Birtwistle's Gawain at Covent Garden, May 1991; Season 1992 as Maletesta in Don Pasquale at Covent Garden and the title role in Henze's Der Prinz von Homburg at Munich. *Recordings include:* Pelléas et Mélisande, conducted by Claudio Abbado (DGG). *Honours:* Prizewinner at the International Maria Canals Competition, Barcelona, and the International Competition at Rio de Janeiro. *Address:* c/o Concerts Opera Management, 12 rue des Lions St Paul, 75004 Paris, France.

LE ROUX Maurice, b. 6 Feb 1923, Paris, France. Conductor; Composer. *Education:* Studied at the Paris Conservatoire 1944-52, with Messiaen and Fourestier; Further study with René Leibowitz (composition) and Dimitri Mitropoulos (conducting). *Career:* Worked on musique concrete project with French Radio, 1951; Music Director of the Orchestre National, 1960-68; Artistic Adviser at the Paris Opera, 1969-73; Inspector General of Music for the Ministry of Culture, 1973-88; Conductor of leading orchestras in guest engagements, France and abroad; Repertoire has included the Monteverdi Vespers and music by Berg, Schoenberg and Xenakis; Music programme Arcana for French television, from 1968; Film scores for Truffaut, Godard and others. *Recordings include:* Messiaen Turangalîla-Symphonie. *Publications:* Introduction a la musique contemporaine, 1947; Claudio Monteverdi, 1951; La Musique, 1979; Musorgsky, Boris Godunov, 1980.

LE SAGE Sally, b. 1937, Farnborough, Kent, England. Singer (Soprano); Professor of Singing. *Education:* Studied at the Royal College of Music and with Pierre Bernac on a scholarship in Paris. *Career:* Sang with Deller Consort 1964-67; Concert appearances throughout Britain, Europe and the USA; included the Vienna, Aix, Ghent and Three Choirs Festivals; Many BBC concerts and recitals; Other concert repertoire included L'Enfant et les Sortilèges in Leeds with Simon

Rattle; Haydn Nelson Mass at the Carnegie Hall, New York, USA; Beethoven's 9th for Dutch Television in Amsterdaam; Mozart's C minor Mass, Royal Festival Hall, with Charles Groves; A Child of Our Time in Stockholm conducted by Michael Tippett; Messiah with the Hallé in Manchester; Mahler's 8th Symphony at the Albert Hall in London. Opera appearances with Scottish Opera: The Woodbird in Siegfried, Covent Garden and Glyndebourne; Teofane in Handel's Ottone at Sadler's Wells Theatre; Ann Trulove in The Rake's Progress, Cambridge Arts Theatre. *Recordings include:* Albums for Vanguard, Nonsuch, Harmonia Mundi, Oryx and RCA Victor (with Montserrat Caballé). *Honours:* 1st Prize vocal concours, s'Hertogenbosch, Holland 1967. *Hobbies:* Painting; Crafts; Swimming; Gardening. *Address:* 13 Observatory Road, East Sheen, London SW14 7QB, England.

LEA Yvonne, b. 1960, Cheshire, England. Singer (Contralto). *Education:* Studied at Royal Northern College of Music with Frederick Cox and at the National Opera Studio, London. *Career:* Appearances with Glyndebourne Festival in Die Zauberflote, Hippolyta in A Midsummer Night's Dream, Rosina in Il Barbiere di Siviglia and Linette in The Love for Three Oranges; Royal Opera House, Covent Garden in Der Rosenkavalier and Third Lady in Die Zauberflote; Sang Suzuki with Welsh National Opera and appeared at Batignano and Spitalfields Festivals in Cesti's La Dori; Recent engagements in Graham Vick's version of The Ring for the City of Birmingham Touring Opera, as Hippolyte at the 1991-92 Aix Festivals and Grimgerde in Die Walküre for Scottish Opera; Tour of France with A Midsummer Night's Dream, 1994; Concert repertoire includes Messiah, Elgar's Sea Pictures, Elijah and Beethoven's Mass in C. *Recordings include:* Williamson's Six English Lyrics. *Address:* c/o IMG Artists, Media House, 3 Burlington Lane, London W4 2TH, England.

LEA-COX Graham Russell, b. 15 Feb 1957, Bulawayo, Rhodesia. Conductor. *Education:* Christ Church Cathedral School, Oxford, England, 1965-75; London University; Royal College of Music, London; Magdalen College, Oxford; MA(Oxon); ARCM, ARCO(CHM), MTC, 1975-81. *Debut:* Carnegie Hall, New York, 1983. *Career:* Artistic Director, Texas Boys Choir, USA, 1983-85; Freelance Conductor, Performer, 1985- ; Tours of USA, Canada, Japan, Hong Kong (Columbia Artists, New York, Kambara, Tokyo); Conducting/solo and chamber recitals: Europe, Scandinavia, Africa; Artistic Director, English Performing Arts Ensemble, 1988-; Conductor and Artistic Director, Elizabethan Singers of London, Swedish Tour, 1989, Conductor; British Council Artist to Sweden, 1988; Opera Conductor, Swedish debut, 1988; USA and European Tours, 1990, 1991 and 1992; European, USA tours, 1990, 1992, 1993; Artistic Director and Conductor, Festivals (UK) incl. South Bank (RFH), London. *Compositions:* Recorded: Film and TV music, USA; Sverige Radio, 1989. *Recordings:* Film and TV music; Chamber Music and song from The Court of Queen Victoria, (International release, 1993); Warchild Festival, Highlights, (Festival Hall London). *Publication:* Research for Publication: Gluck: The Swedish Opera Mss, Kungliga Teatran 1770-1815. *Hobbies:* Photography; Travel; Wine. *Current Management:* English Performing Arts (Non Executive). *Address:* English Performing Arts (Non Executive), 11 George's Road, St Margaret's, Twickenham TW1 1QS, England.

LEACH John, b. 29 July 1931, London, England. Musician; Composer; Ethno-musicologist. *Education:* Trinity College London (Stainer); Privately with Solomon, Jackson, Vienna Academy (Reznicek, Schiske). *Career:* Principal Flute, BBC Northern Orchestra, 1954-55; Professor, Beirut Conservatoire, 1957-60; Orchestral Manager, Philharmonia Orchestra, 1963-65; Music Department, BBC TV, 1966-70; Freelance cimbalom player and composer. *Compositions:* Variations for Cimbalom; Suite for double bass. *Recordings:* Kodály, Háry János Suite, Vienna Philharmonic, Kempe; Stravinsky Renard, Suisse Romande, Ansermet; Debussy La Plus Que Lent, Martinon. *Contributions to:*

The Consort; Music & Letters; Composer. *Honour:* Arts Council Award, 1955. *Memberships:* FRAS; FRGS; MIMIT; BBC Club. *Hobbies:* Walking; Good Wine. *Address:* 68 Lysia Street, London SW6 6NG, England.

LEACH Mary Jane, b. 12 June 1949, St Johnsbury, Vermont, USA. Composer; Performer. *Education:* BA, Theatre and Music, University of Vermont; Postgraduate study in composition with Mark Zuckerman, Columbia University, New York. *Career:* Appearances: Experimental Intermedia Foundation, New York City, 1982, 1984, 1987; Relache, Philadelphia, 1984, 1987; Music Gallery, Toronto, Canada, 1985; Metronome, Barcelona, Spain, 1985; Newband, New York City, USA, 1985; Roulette, New York City, 1985; Charles Ives Center, Connecticut, 1986; Logos, Gent, Belgium, 1986, 1987; BACA Downtown, Brooklyn, New York, USA, 1987; New Music America, Philadelphia, 1987; Palais des Beaux Arts, Brussels, 1987; Sankt Peter, Cologne, 1987; Apollohuis, Eindhoven, Holland, 1987; Clocktower, New York City, 1988; Real Art Ways, Hartford, CT, 1989; Franenzcichen Festival, Köln, 1989; Kunsthalle Bremen, 1990, Romanische Summer Festival, Köln, 1990; Ton Gegen Ton, Vienna, 1989; Music To-day, Tokyo, 1990, New Music, America, New York, 1989; Interpretations Series, NYC, 1993; Bangona Can Festival, NYC 1992, 1993; Corn Palace, Minneapolis, 1992; Walker Art Center, 1993; Experimentelle Musik, Munich, 1991; Sound Symposium, NewFoundland, 1992; Ijsbreker, Amsterdam, 1992; Radio performances: John Schaeffer's New Sounds, YMBC, Australia, Radio Bremen, WDR-Köln, Earworks. Television appearances: WDR, Köln. *Compositions:* Note Passing Note, 1981; Solar Spots, 1983; Held Held, 1984; 8x4, 1985; Bare Bones, 1989; Bruckstück, 1989; Pipe Dreams, 1989; Sephardic Fragments, 1989; The Upper Room, 1990; Kirchtraum, 1991; Ariadne's Lament, 1993; He Got Dictators, 1993; Feu de Joie, 1992. *Recordings:* 4BC, 1984; Green Mountain Madrigal, 1985; Trio for Duo, 1985; Lake Eden, 1986; Ariel's Song, 1987; Mountain Echoes, 1987; Guy de Polka, 1987; Her 1001 Nights, 1988. *Current Management:* G Davidge, 990 Glenhill Road, Shoreview, MN 55126, USA. *Address:* PO Box 1635, Canal Street Station, New York, NY 10013, USA.

LEADBETTER Martin John. b. 6 Apr 1945, London, England. Composer. m. Ivy G, 7 June 1969, 2 sons. *Education:* Studied at Associate & Licentiate Trinity College of Music, London; Studied with Dr Alan Bush, 1982-88. *Career:* TV Film, Anglia TV, BBC 3 Music Weekly and BBC 4 Womans Hour. *Compositions include:* 2 Symphonies, 3 String Quartets, An English Requiem; Songs, Instrumental and Choral Works; Laudate Dominium (1992) performed Fontainebleau, France, April 1993; Some 150 Works to date. *Publications include:* Soliloquy; Little Prelude and Fugue. *Honours:* Commissioned By Radio Victory to Compose String Trio. *Memberships:* Performing Right Society; Composers Guild. *Address:* Ivy Lodge, 2 Priory Lane, Little Wymondley, Hertfordshire SG4 7HE, England.

LEAH Philip John, b. 23 Oct 1948, Dulwich, London, England. Music Educator, 2 sons. *Education:* Studied at the Northern School of Music and Padgate College of Education. *Career:* Peripatetic Music Teacher, Glamorgan, 1972-73, City of Birmingham, 1973-90; Founder and Musical Director, West Birmingham Schools Wind Band, 1985, Halesowen Symphony Orchestra, 1986; Lecturer, North Worcs College of Education, 1977-, University of Wolverhampton, 1982- ; Examiner, Guildhall School of Music, 1988-. *Compositions include:* Conversations for Flute & Piano; Fanfare for a Golden Jubilee; Concertino for Bass Tuba and Orchestra; Prelude and Scherzo for String Quartet; Suite for Chamber Orchestra; Various Arrangements for Woodwind Instruments. *Honours:* 1st Prize, Horatio Albert Lumb Composition Competition. *Memberships:* Royal Society of Musicians of Great Britain; Incorporated Society of Musicians; Musicians Union. *Hobbies:* Watching Football and Cricket; Drinking Real Ale. *Address:* 23 New England, Halesowen, West Midlands, B62 9EG, England.

LEAR Evelyn, b. 8 Jan 1926, Brooklyn, New York, USA. Soprano. m. (2) Thomas Stewart (q.v.), 1955; 2 daughters by previous marriage. *Education:* New York University; Hunter College; Juilliard Opera Workshop; Fulbright Scholarship for Study in Germany 1955. *Stage Debut:* As the Composer in Ariadne auf Naxos Berlin 1959; Covent Garden debut 1965 as Donna Elvira; Lulu in Berg's opera at Sadler's Wells Theatre 1966; Debut in UK in Four Last Songs with London Symphony Orchestra 1957; Debut at La Scala, Milan, in Wozzeck 1971; Debut at Metropolitan Opera in the premiere of Levy's Mourning Becomes Electra 1967. *Career:* Deutsche Oper Berlin, 1961, creating the title role in Klebe's Alkmene; Jeanne in the premiere of Egk's Die Verlobung in San Domingo, Munich 1963; Regular performances with leading opera companies and orchestras in Europe and USA; Guest appearances with Berlin Opera and Vienna State Opera; Soloist with leading American Orchestras including: New York Philharmonic, Chicago Symphony, Philadelphia Orchestra, Boston Symphony, San Francisco Symphony and Los Angeles Philharmonic; Has given many recitals and orchestral concerts and operatic performances with Thomas Stewart; Major Roles include: Marie in Wozzeck; Marschallin in Der Rosenkavalier; Countess in The Marriage of Figaro; Fiordiligi in Cosi fan Tutte; Desdemona, Mimi, Dido in The Trojans; Donna Elvira in Don Giovanni; Marina in Boris Godunov; Tatiana in Eugene Onegin; Lavinia in Mourning Becomes Electra; Title Role in Lulu; Appeared in film Buffalo Bill 1976; Sang in the premieres of The Seagull by Pasatieri, 1974, Robert Ward's Minutes to Midnight, 1980 and Kelterborn's Der Kirschgarten, Zurich 1984; Metropolitan Opera, 1985, as the Marschallin; Sang Countess Geschwitz in Lulu at Florence 1985, Chicago 1987 and San Francisco, 1989; Sang Miss Dilly in Bernstein's On the Town at the Barbican Hall, London 1992. *Recordings:* These include: Wozzeck; Lulu; The Flying Dutchman; Excerpts from The Magic Flute; Boris Godunov; Eugene Onegin; Bach's St John Passion; Pergolesi's Stabat Mater; Der Rosenkavalier. *Honour:* Concert Artists Guild Award 1955. *Address:* Columbia Artists Management Inc, 165 West 57th Street, New York, NY 10019, USA.

LEATHERBY Carol Ann, b. 1948, Barking, London, England. Freelance Mezzo-Contralto; Director of Victoriana (Victorian Musical Entertainment). *Education:* Morley College, with Ilse Wolf, 1968-69; Guildhall School of Music and Drama, 1969-71; Vienna, with Eugenie Ludwig, 1981-82; Private study in London with Lyndon Van Der Pump, 1972-. *Debut:* Purcell Room, London, 1973. *Career:* Welsh National Opera, 1973-75; Covent Garden Opera, 1975-78; Glyndebourne Festival Opera, 1979-80; New Opera, 1981; Music in Camera, Southern Television, UK, 1980; Delius Talk, Radio London, 1980; Broadcasts for BBC, London and Cardiff; Recitals at Purcell Room; Wigmore Hall; Concerts at Festival Hall, Queen Elizabeth Hall; Memorial concert for Princess Grace of Monaco, Queen Elizabeth Hall, 1983; Specialist in the songs of Frederick Delius; Athens Festival, 1985; Alte Oper, Frankfurt, 1985 and 1986; Purcell Room Concerts as Member of Quintessence (founded 1984, a group that presents Victorian and Edwardian entertainment in costume and performances of music by Gershwin and Cole Porter), 1984, 1985, 1986; The Vampyr, soap opera for TV-BBC2 TV, music by Heinrich Marschner, 1992. *Recordings:* Czech Songs by Foerster, Smetana and Dvořák, 1983; Songs of Praise, BBC; Sita-Mother Earth-Holst recorded at St John's, Smith Square in conjuction with the Holst Society. *Hobbies:* Cooking; Violin Restoring; Walking; Crossword Puzzles. *Current Management:* Crescendo Concert Agency, 25 Summer House, Bonfield Road, London SE13 6BY, England. *Address:* 278 Monega Road, Manor Park, London E12 6TS, England.

LEAVINS Arthur, b. 14 July 1917, Leicester, England. Violinist. m. Mary Baddeley, 2 sons. *Education:* Royal Academy of Music; LRAM; ARAM. *Debut:* New Zealand, 1925. *Career:* Played with Catterall Quartet; Leader, Royal Philharmonic Orchestra; Sub-leader BBC Symphony Orchestra; Leader, BBC Concert Orchestra; Retired. *Recordings:* Stravinsky's L'Histoire du Soldât.

Honour: Jonathan North Medal. *Membership:* Royal Society of Musicians. *Hobbies:* Reading; Gardening; Golf. *Address:* 17 Highfield Drive, Bromley, Kent, England.

LEAVITT J, b. 1920, Massachusetts, USA. Musician; Producer; Administrator. m. Sally Elissa, 30 Aug 1942, 1 son, 1 daughter. *Education:* Graduate of New England Conservatory of Music, 1940; American University, 1954; Further studies at Boston University, Manhattan School of Music and Harvard Business School Seminars. *Career:* Principal player in 3 major orchestras, recording on RCA, Victor and Columbia labels; Extensive film sound-tracks and TV performances; Principal Player, National Symphony Orchestra, Assistant Manager, 1949-69; General Manager, New Jersey Symphony Orchestra, 1969-71; Executive Director, Executive Producer, Wolf Trap Foundation for Performing Arts, 1970-73; Executive Director, Baltimore Symphony Orchestra, 1973-84; Executive Vice-President, Fort Lauderdale Symphony Orchestra, merged into Philharmonic Orchestra of Florida, 1984-; Panelist, Florida Arts Council, 1985-; Palm Beach Council of the Arts, 1986-. *Recordings:* Adventures in Music, RCA-Victor; Shostakovich, The Symphonies, Age of Gold, on RCA Victor; Appalachian Spring on Westminster; Other works on Decca and Columbia record labels. *Publications:* The Rhythms of Contemporary Music, 1963; Reading by Recognition, 1960. *Contributions to:* Music Journal; Downbeat; Hi-Notes and others. *Address:* 5675 Boca Chica Lane, Boca Raton, FL 33433, USA.

LEBARON Anne, b. 30 May 1953, Baton Rouge, Louisiana, USA. Composer. m. Edward J Eadon, 6 July 1982, 1 daughter. *Education:* Private study with Alice Chalifoux, Salzedo Harp Colony, 1974, 1976; BA, Music, University of Alabama, 1974; MA, Music, State University of New York, Stony Brook, 1978; Darmstadt, 1980; Koln Musikhochschule, 1980-81; National Classical Music Institute, Korea, 1983; DMA, Columbia University, 1989. *Career:* Independent Composer and Harpist; Extensive European tours; Instructor, Music Theory, University of Alabama, 1978; Artist-in-Residence, Decatur, Alabama, 1979-80; Taught Theory, Composition, State University of New York, Stony Brook, 1981-82; Classical and Jazz Music Survey courses, Columbia University, 1984-85; Produced contemporary music series, Washington DC, 1986- 87; Featured, National Public Radio, 1989, 1990; Artist-in-Residence, PASS Studio, 1991. *Compositions:* Orchestral: Strange Attractors; Chamber opera: The E & O Line; Chamber music: Telluris Theoria Sacra; The Sea and the Honeycomb; Noh Reflections; Metamorphosis; Rite of the Black Sea; Planxty Bowerbird; I Am An American...My Government Will Reward You; Lamentation-Invocation; Concerto for Active Frogs; Dish; Waltz for Quintet; Three Motion Atmospheres; Southern Ephemera; Devil in the Belfry; Light Breaks Where No Sun Shines; Story of My Angel. *Recordings include:* Rana, Ritual and Revelations: The Music of Anne LeBaron, 1992; Phantom Orchestra: The Anne LeBaron Quintet, 1992. *Address:* 3338 17th St NW, Washington, DC 20010, USA.

LEBHERZ Louis, b. 14 Apr 1948, Bethesda, Maryland, USA. Singer (Bass). *Education:* Studied at Indiana University. *Debut:* Memphis Opera, as Padre Guardiano in La Forza del Destino, 1974. *Career:* Many appearances at opera houses in North and South America (Caracas, 1981); European engagements at Frankfurt, 1981, Karlsruhe, 1984-85, Berne, 1985-86, Geneva, 1988; Sang Melothal in Guillaume Tell at Covent Garden and the Grand Inquisitor in Don Carlos at Los Angeles, 1990; Appeared in Massenet's La Navarraise with Long Beach Opera, 1990, as Basilio, the Commendatore in Don Giovanni at Los Angeles Music Center, 1991; Sang Rocco at New Orleans, 1992; Other roles include Sarastro, King Mark, Fasolt, Baldassare in La Favorita, Verdi's Zaccaria and Nabucco and Fiesco, Colline, and Dondiego in L'Africaine. *Recordings include:* Verdi's Aroldo; Jone by Petrella.

LEBIČ Lojze, b. 23 Aug 1934, Prevalje, Slovenija. Composer; Conductor; Professor of Music Theory. m. Jelena Ukmar, 2 Aug 1961, 1 daughter. *Education:* Dipl Archaeology, University of Ljubljana, 1957; Academy of Music, Ljubljana, 1972; Studies in Darmstadt. *Career:* Conductor, RTV Ljubljana, 1962-72; App with Festival Musica Antigua Europae Orientalis Bidgoscz, Poland, 1968; Festival van Vlaanderen, 1968; Festival Ohrid, 1968; Festival Jihlava, Czech, 1969; Biennale Zagreb, 1969; Festival Dubrovnik, 1969; University Ljubljana, 1985-. *Compositions include:* Simph music; Voices, November songs, Korant, Sentence, Tangram, Queensland Music Symphony with Organ etc; Burnt Grass (Cantata); Fauvel 86 (vocal-instr-scene); Chamber music: Quartet for Percussion; String Quartet; Ateliers I-III, Vocal Music, Solo Instrument, Electronic, Choral Music. *Recordings:* Various as conductor and composer. *Publications:* Book: The Basis of Music Art, 1982; Sound and Silence, Compositional Synthese of the Eighties, Music Biennale Zagreb, 1985. *Honours:* Winner Class Trophy (Contemporary Music) Let The People Sing, BBC, 1972; Prešeren Fond Prizes (1966-70-87). *Memberships:* Secretary, Yugoslavia ISCM Section, 1981-91; Society of Slovene Composer. *Hobbies:* Archaeology; Travel. *Address:* Bratov Učakar 134, 61000 Ljubljana, Slovenija.

LEBRECHT Norman, b. 11 July 1948, London, England. Writer on Music. m. Elbie Spivack, 1977, 3 daughters. *Education:* Bar Ilan University, Israel. *Career:* Radio and TV producer, 1969-78; Writer and Lecturer 1978-. *Publications:* Discord, 1982; Hush! Handel's in a Passion, 1985; The Book of Musical Anecdotes, 1985; Mahler Remembered, 1987; The Book of Musical Days, 1987; The Maestro Myth, 1991; Music in London, 1992; The Companion to Twentieth Century Music, 1992. *Contributions to:* Sunday Times, The Times, Daily Telegraph, Classical Music, Opera News, Melbourne Age. *Membership:* Society of Authors. *Address:* 3 Bolton Road, London NW8 ORJ, England.

LEDBETTER Steven John, b. 13 Dec 1942, Minneapolis, Minnesota, USA. Musicologist. m. Mary Lee Stewart, 10 Sept 1966, 1 son, 1 daughter. *Education:* BA, Music, Pomona College, 1964; MA, Musicology, 1968, PhD, Musicology, 1971, New York University; Voice (Baritone) with Margery Smith Briggs, Pomona College, 1961-64; Conducting with W F Russell, Pomona College; Voice with Edith Bers, New York, 1969-72. *Career:* Instructor, 1969-71, Assistant Professor of Music, 1971-72, New York University; Assistant Professor of Music, Dartmouth College (music history, choral conductor), 1972-79; Director of Publications, Boston Symphony Orchestra, 1979-; Title changed to Musicologist and Program Annotator in 1984; Freelance Writer; Record Producer. *Recordings:* As Producer: John K Paine, Chamber Music, 1986; chamber works of George W Chadwick, 1988; Liner notes for 90 recordings. *Publications include:* Ornithoparchus, Dowland, A Compendium of Musical Practice, 1973 Ed: George W Chadwick; Songs to Poems by Arlo Bates, 1979, Ed; Luca Marenzio: The Secular Works, vol 7, 1978, Vol 17, 1991; 100 Years of the Boston Pops, 1985; Sennets & Tuckets: A Bernstein Celebration, 1988; Ed: George F Bristow: Rip Van Winkle, 1991; Ed: Gilbert and Sullivan: Trial by Jury, 1993. *Address:* Symphony Hall, Boston, MA 02115, USA.

LEDEC Jan, b. 8 Mar 1922, Prague, Czechoslovakia. Musicologist; Editor; Music Writer. m. Dagmar Capková, 9 Mar 1950. *Education:* Faculty of Philosophy, Charles University, Prague, 1945-49; PhD, 1952; Prague Conservatory, 1945-47; Diploma, Choir Conducting, Academy of Music and Dramatic Arts, 1947. *Career:* Music teacher, Choirmaster, Music Producer, Liberec, 1945-53; Music Administrator, Editor, Head of Music Department, Institute of Cultural Activities, Prague, 1953-65; Music Administrator, Prague Symphony Orchestra, 1965-67; Freelance Writer on Music, specialising in contemporary music and music for choir, 1967-72; Executive Manager, Music Information Centre of Czech Music Fund, Prague, 1972-87; Freelance Musicologist, Music Adviser, 1987-; Secretary, Association for Contemporary Music Prítomnost, Present time, 1991-93; Freelance Musicologist, Music Advisor, 1993-. *Publications:* Editor, Sborový repertoár, 20 volumes, 1960-68; Nástin Vývoje ceské soudobé hudby po roce 1945, 1972; Editor in chief, Music News from Prague, 1978-87; Various cycles for Radio Prague, 1968-75; Editor, Sborový repertoár, 20 Vols. 1960-68; Editor in chief, Music News from Prague, 1978-87; Contributor to Music News from Prague, 1987-. *Address:* Seifertova 25, 130 00 Prague 3-Zizkov, Czech Republic.

LEDEEN Lydia Hailparn, b. 6 Apr 1938, New York City, New York, USA. Professor of Music; Pianist. m. (2) Robert Ledeen, 2 July 1982, 2 daughters. *Education:* BS, 1953, MS, 1954, Juilliard School of Music; Diplome, License de Concert, Conservatoire de Musique, France, 1955; MA, 1957, PhD, 1958, EdD, 1960, Columbia University. *Debut:* All Bach Recital, New York, 1946. *Career:* Member, 2-piano team Hailparn and Sternklar, 20 years; Soloist, performances in USA (East Coast/ West Coast), Europe, Israel, Japan, St Petersburg (Russia) and Vancouver, British Columbia (Canada); Now chamber music performer as Artistic Director and Founder, Drew Chamber Players; Introduced music of Leopoldine Blahetka and Maria Grandval to USA; Professor of Music, Chair of Music Department, Drew University, Madison, New Jersey, 1968-. *Compositions:* Songs My Children Love for soprano and piano; Sonata for Cello and Piano; 5 Diversions for 3 Woodwinds; First Piano Trio, 1988, premiered Drew University, 1990, received critical acclaim. *Recordings:* Lydia Ledeen Plays the Romantic Keyboard, 1986; The Romantic Keyboard, reel-to-reel cassette, 1989. *Publications:* Contemporary Keyboard Literature of Holland, 1960; Editor: Piano Music of Leopoldine Blahetka, 1992; Editor: Maria Grandval, Second Grand Trio, 1994. *Address:* 8 Donald Court, Wayne, NJ 07470, USA.

LEDGER Philip Stevens, b. 12 Dec 1937, Bexhill-on-Sea, England. Conductor; Organist; Academy Principal. m. Mary Erryl Wells, 15 Apr 1963, 1 son, 1 daughter. *Education:* King's College, Cambridge, 1956-61; MA and MusB (Cantab); FRCO. *Career:* Master of the Music, Chelmsford Cathedral, 1962-65; Director of Music, 1965-73, Dean, School of Fine Arts and Music, 1968-71, University of East Anglia, Norwich; Director of Music, King's College, Cambridge, 1974-82; Principal, Royal Scottish Academy of Music and Drama, Glasgow, 1982-. *Recordings:* Many as Director of Music with Choir of King's College, Cambridge, also with the English Chamber Orchestra, Benjamin Britten, Dame Janet Baker, Robert Tear, Pinchas Zukerman and others, including CDs of Elgar's Coronation Ode, Orlando Gibbons Church Music and Organ Music from King's. *Publications:* Tallis to Wesley, Vol 8 William Byrd, 1968; Editor: Anthems for Choirs 2 and 3, 1973; The Oxford Book of English Madrigals, 1978. *Honours:* FRCM, 1983; Honorary RAM, 1984; CBE, 1985; Honorary LLD, University of Strathclyde, 1987; FRNCM, 1989; Hon GSM, 1989; FRSE, 1990; Honorary Professor, University of Glasgow, 1993. *Memberships:* President, Royal College of Organists; President-Elect, Incorporated Society of Musicians; Sette of Odd Volumes. *Hobbies:* Swimming; Theatre-going. *Address:* Royal Scottish Academy of Music and Drama, 100 Renfrew Street, Glasgow G2 3DB, Scotland.

LEDUC Jacques, b. 1 Mar 1932, Brussels, Belgium. Composer; Music Educator. m. Cecile Marion, 10 Apr 1965, 1 son, 1 daughter. *Education:* Classics, Royal Athenaeum, Brussels; Royal Conservatory, Brussels. *Debut:* 1960. *Career:* Director, Academy of Music, Vccle, 1962-83; Professor of Fugue, Royal Conservatory, Brussels; Rector, Chapelle Musicale Reine Elisabeth. *Compositions:* Symphony; Concerto for piano; Concertino for oboe and strings; Divertissement for flute and strings; 5 Croquis for orchestra; Le Printemps, for orchestra; Ouverture d'été, for orchestra; Suite de danses, orchestra; Sonata for violin and piano; Sonata for flute and piano; Trio; Quartet for strings; Suite en quatuor for saxophones; Pieces for piano, guitar, trumpet, bassoon. *Recordings:* Concerto for piano and orchestra; Le Printemps; Instantanés for string ensemble; Ouverture d'été; Concertino for oboe and strings; Divertissement for flute and strings; Others. *Publication:* Brochure sur le Conservatoire Royal de Bruxelles. *Address:* Avenue de l'Hélianthe 24, 1180 Brussels, Belgium.

LEE Andrew Chia-Mu, b. 2 Oct 1961, Taipei, Taiwan. Conductor. *Education:* University studies in Music, History, and Art History; Violin, Piano, Theory, Composition, Musicology and Conducting, privately and at institutions including Accademia Musicale Chigiana, Siena, summers 1988 and 1989, and most recently at Hochschule fur Musik und darstellende Kunst, Vienna. *Debut:* Ottawa, Canada and Vienna, Austria. *Career:* Chief Conductor, Lemberger Philharmoniker. *Recordings:* In preparation. *Honours:* Italy, 1988-90; Ottawa, Vienna-Masterclasses, 1990, 1991. *Memberships:* Conductors Guild; American Symphony Orchestra League; Association of Canadian Orchestras. *Current Management:* Markus Bachmann, AOP Music Agency (Vienna), Wurzbachgasse 22/16, A-1150 Vienna, Austria. *Address:* c/o Decleva, Franz Grassler gasse 8-10/5, 1238 Vienna, Austria.

LEE Dennis Ean Hooi, b. 2 Dec 1946, Penang, Malaysia. Pianist. m. Chee-Hung Toh, 16 Aug 1990. *Education:* BMus, London University; MMus, with Angus Morrison, Royal College of Music, London, 1964-68; Studied with Josef Dichler, Vienna Hochschule, 1968-69; Studied with Ilonka Deckers in Milan. *Debut:* Purcell Room, London and Kennedy Center, Washington DC. *Career:* Concerts (recitals, chamber music and orchestral appearances), TV and radio recordings: UK, Europe, USA, Canada, South America, Hongkong, Japan, South-East Asia, Australia, New Zealand; Radio and TV broadcasts include live transmissions for BBC Radio 3; Festivals include Adelaide, Montreux, Spoleto, Cheltenham, Brighton, Lincoln, Newbury, Warwick, Mananan, Arundel; Orchestral appearances include BBC Regional, Halle, Wiener Symphoniker, London Mozart Players, RAI Milan, Polish and Slovak Chamber Orchestras. *Recordings:* Szymanowski Piano Pieces; Ravel Duets with Philippe Entremont. *Honours:* Prizes: BBC Competition, 1971, Casagrande, Italy, 1975, 1977, Sydney, 1977, Busoni, Italy, 1978. *Address:* Flat 5, 12 St Quintin Avenue, London W10 6NU, England.

LEE Douglas Allen, b. 3 Nov 1932, Carmel, California, USA. Professor of Musicology. m. Beverly Haskell, 2 Sept 1961. *Education:* BMus, DePauw University, 1954; MMus, 1958, Rackham Fellow, 1961-63, PhD, 1968, University of Michigan; National Endowment for the Humanities Seminar in Editing Early Music, 1985; Piano studies with Theodore Lettvin and Gyorgy Sandor. *Career:* Instructor, Mount Union College, Alliance, Ohio, 1959- 61; Professor, Music, Wichita State University, Kansas, 1964-86; Professor, Musicology, Vanderbilt University, Nashville, Tennessee, 1986-; Faculty: Mount Union College, University of Michigan, International Music Camp-Interlochen, Wichita State University, Vanderbilt University; Editor: American Music Teacher, 1968-70; The C P E Bach Edition, 1985-; Sonneck Society Newsletter, 1988-90. *Publications:* The Works of Christoph Nichelmann, 1971; Christoph Nichelmann-Two Concertos, 1977; Six Sonatas of Franz Benda, with Embellishments, 1981; Franz Benda-A Thematic Catalogue, 1984; Chapters in Great Lives in Music-Renaissance to 1800, 1989; 2 chapters in Great Events in History: Arts and Culture, 1993; C P E Bach: Six Keyboard Concertos (Collected Works). *Contributions to:* 23 articles, New Grove Dictionary of Music and Musicians. *Hobbies:* Photography; Sports car mechanics. *Address:* Blair School of Music, Vanderbilt University, 2400 Blakemore Ave, Nashville, TN 37212, USA.

LEE Hope K W, b. 14 Jan 1953, Taiwan, Republic of China. Canadian Citizen. Composer. m. David M Eagle, 23 Aug 1980. *Education:* BSc, University of Toronto, Canada, 1973; BMus, 1978, MMus, 1981, McGill University; Darmstadt Ferienkurs Neue Musik, 1978;

Staatliche Hochschule fur Musik, Freiburg, 1981-83. *Career:* Works heard regularly on CBC and Radio Canada; Work performed in Music Today '85 Festival, Tokyo; ISCM World Music Days, 1987, West Germany; Invited to 1st International Woman Composers' Conference, Berlin, 1982; Invited Guest Composer, Boswil Kunstlerhaus, Switzerland, 1985. *Compositions include:* Instrumental Ensemble: Nabripamo, 1982; M-Nabri, 1983; Nohr, 1983; Luminare, 1984-85; Konductus, 1985; Jygge-Somebody's, 1987; Jygge-Somebody's and Nobody's, 1987; ---I, Laika---, 1988-89; In The Beginning Was the End, 1989; Hsieh Lu Hsing, 1991; Tangram, harpsichord, bass clarinet and tape, 1992; March 3rd, 1911, bass clarinet, piano with/without tape, 1993; Instrumental Ensemble with Voices: Ballad of Endless Woe, 1978-79; In A Mirror of Light, 1988; Solo Works: Dindle for Piano, 1979; Melboac for harpsichord, 1983; Flake Upon Flake Upon...1989, for piano; entends, entends la passé gui marche, piano and tape, 1992; von einem fremden stern for organ, 1993; Orchestral Works: Onomatopoeia, 1979-81; Electronic Works: Study Chant IV, V, 1979; Collaboration Chant VI, 1979; *Performances:* Aspekte Salzburg Festival, 1990; Scotia Festival of Music, 1991. *Address:* 27 Stradwick Rise, SW Calgary, Alberta, Canada.

LEE Michelle, b. 31 May 1952, London, England. Flautist. 1 daughter. *Education:* Bartok Conservatory, Budapest, Hungary, 1970-71; Royal College of Music, London, 1971-75; Robert Schumann Institute, Dusseldorf, Germany, 1975-76, 1977-78; Franz Liszt Academy, Budapest, Hungary, 1978-80; ARCM, Flute & Recorder and Piano; Examiner of Music for Trinity College, London. *Career:* Regular Recitals in Great Britain and Europe; Recorded for Hungarian Radio; Soloist for BBC Radio 3 and given many first performances including the World Premiere of György Kurtág's Seven Bagatelles, Op 14B, 1982 at her Wigmore Recital on 14 June 1982; First Broadcast performance of Fauré's Morceau de Concours for flute and piano on BBC Radio 3, May 1985; First UK broadcast of György Kurtág's Seven Bagatelles, Op 14B on BBC Radio 3, October 1987. *Composition:* Scarlet Runner, for flute, percussion, prerecorded tape and 5 synthesizers. *Recording:* Soloist, German Record of Contemporary Music with Live electronics, VMS 1021; Morton Feldman Flute Concerto with Moscow Philharmonic Orchestra, (CD), 1992. *Memberships:* Incorporated Society of Musicians; Royal College of Music Society; British Flute Society. *Address:* 223 Mellis Road, Thornham Parva, Eye, Suffolk, IP23 8ET, England.

LEE Ming Cho, b. 3 Oct 1930, Shanghai, China. Stage Designer. *Education:* Studied at Occidental College and University of California at Los Angeles, 1950-54. *Career:* Theatre and ballet designs in New York, 1955-59; Peabody Arts Theatre, Baltimore, 1959-63, with designs for Il Turco in Italia, Mahagonny, Werther, Hamlet and Les Pecheurs de perles; Designed Tristan und Isolde for Baltimore Civic Opera and Butterfly for the Opera Company of Boston, 1962; Resident Designer at San Francisco Opera from 1961, Juilliard School, New York, 1964-70; Metropolitan Opera, 1965-, with Figaro, Boris Godunov, Lohengrin and Khovanshchina (1985); Premiere of Ginastera's Bomarzo for the Opera Society of Washington, 1967, Giulio Cesare and Lucia di Lammermoor for Hamburg Staatsoper, 1969, 1971; Teacher of set design at Yale Drama School from 1968. *Address:* c/o Metropolitan Opera, Lincoln Center, New York, NY 10023, USA.

LEE Noël, b. 25 Dec 1924, Nanking, China. Composer; Concert Pianist. *Education:* BA cum laude, Harvard University, Cambridge, Massachusetts, USA, 1948; Artist's Diploma, New England Conservatory of Music, Boston, 1948. *Career:* Numerous concert tours and appearances in North and South America, Europe, Australia; Engagements on every European State Radio; Vast solo, concerto and chamber repertoire. *Compositions include:* Caprices on the name Schönberg, piano and orchestra; 8 études, piano; Dialogues, violin and piano; Convergences, flute and harpsichord; Chroniques, piano; Errances, band; 5 songs on Lorca, soprano, flute, guitar; Songs of Calamus, voice, clarinet, cello, percussion; Triptyque, violin, piano and orchestra; Dance Fantasy, orchestra; 5 Preludes prolonged, piano; Partita, quintet piano & winds; Le tombeau d'Aaron Copland, sextet; Azurs voice & piano 4 hands, plus 7 other song cycles; Variations antiques, flute & piano; 3 Fantasy pieces, flute & guitar. *Recordings include:* 180 LPs and CDs of solo, piano 4-hand, chamber, and vocal works of Schubert, 19th-century French composers, Debussy, Ravel, Stravinsky, Bartók, Copland, Carter and other American composers. *Publication:* Critical edition of Debussy's Two Piano works, 1989. *Honours:* Prix de Composition Lili Boulanger, 1953; National Academy of Arts and Letters Award, 1959; Louisville Orchestra Young Composers' Award, 1954; Grand Prix du Disque, 1959, 1974, 1985, 1989, 1993; Grand Prix des Disquaires Français, 1978; Prizewinner, Arthur Honegger Composition Contest, 1986; Charles Oulmont Foundation Award, 1991. *Membership:* American Music Centre. *Current Management:* Bureau International de Concerts, Kiesgen, France; Roelof Jonker Music Management, Netherlands; Joyce Rohr Management, USA and Scandinavia. *Address:* 4 Villa Laugier, 75017 Paris, France.

LEE Sung-Sook, b. 1948, Korea. Singer (Soprano). *Education:* BA (Music) Sook Myuung Women's University; Juilliard School. *Career:* World premiere of Menotti's Tamu Tamu, Chicago 1973; Leading operatic roles at Spoleto Festival, 1974; San Francisco Opera, 1974; La Scala Milan and Covent Garden, 1975; Frankfurt Opera, 1976-77; Seattle Opera and Miami Opera from 1978; Concert appearances with the Buffalo Philharmonic, Seattle Symphony, Dallas Symphony and Pittsburgh Symphony; New York City Opera, 1975-76. *Recordings include:* Rossini's Stabat Mater (Vox). *Honours include:* Silver Medal, International Madama Buttefly Competition, Japan 1973. *Membership:* American Guild of Musical Artists. *Hobbies:* Sports; Photography.

LEE Yi, b. 3 Mar 1957, Shanghai, China. Classical Musician (Violinist). m. Anita C Gao, 25 May 1986. *Education:* Shanghai Conservatory of Music, Shanghai; Midwest Institute, Crete, Nebraska, USA; University of Illinois, Champaign-Urbana; New England Conservatory of Music, Boston. *Career:* Zong Zheng Symphony, Beijing, 1974-81; Lincoln Symphony and Lincoln Chamber Orchestra, Nebraska, USA, 1982; Symphony Nova Scotia, Halifax, Canada, 1985-; Coach of Nova Scotia Youth Orchestra, Halifax, 1990-; Appearance on CBC Radio Morningside, 1991 and MITV Halifax, 1991-; Leader of Halifax Library Players, 1992-; Violin Professor, Acadia University, Wolfville, 1993-. *Membership:* American Federation of Musicians. *Hobbies:* Sports; Golf; Travel. *Address:* 38 Birchwood Terrace, Dartmouth, Nova Scotia, Canada B3A 3W3.

LEECH Richard, b. 1956, Binghamton, California, USA. Singer (Tenor). *Career:* Sang first as baritone then sang Offenbach's Hoffmann while a student; Many concert and opera appearances from 1980, notably at Cincinnati, Pittsburgh, Baltimore, Houston and Chicago; European debut at the Deutsche Oper Berlin, 1987, as Raoul in Les Huguenots; Chicago Lyric Opera, 1987, and La Scala, 1991, as Rodolfo; Has sung Gounod's Faust at San Diego, 1988 and at the Orange Festival and Metropolitan Opera, 1990; Pinkerton in Washington DC and Florence and La Scala, (debut 1990) 1987 and 1989; Donizetti's Edgardo and Nemorino at the Deutsche Oper Berlin, 1988-89, and the Duke of Mantua at the New York City Opera (1988) and Metropolitan Opera, 1990; Season 1991/92 as Raoul in a new production of Les Huguenots at Covent Garden (debut), Pinkerton at Chicago and the Duke of Mantua at the Met; Rodolfo at the Met, 1994; Concert engagements include Beethoven's Ninth and Verdi Requiem. *Recordings include:* Les Huguenots (Erato); Fledermaus and Salome, (Philips), Faust and Rosenkavalier, EMI. *Address:* c/o Metropolitan Opera, Lincoln Center, New York, NY 10023, USA.

LEEDY Douglas, b. 3 Mar 1938, Portland, Oregon, USA. Composer; Conductor; Educator. *Education:* BA, Pomona College, 1959; MA, University of California, Berkeley, 1962; Karnatic vocal music with K V Narayanaswamy. *Career:* French horn, Oakland Symphony Orchestra, San Francisco Opera, Ballet Orchestras, Cabrillo Festival Orchestra, 1960-65; Music faculty, University of California, Los Angeles, 1967-70; Reed College, 1973-78; Professor of Electronic Music, Centro Simon Bolivar, Caracas, Venezuela, 1972; Musical Director, Portland Baroque Orchestra, 1984-85; Complete performances, Handel's Jephtha and Theodora, Portland Handel Festival, 1985. *Compositions:* Usable Music I for Very Small Instruments with Holes, Source 3, 1968; The Twenty-Fourth Psalm, chorus & orchestra, 1971; Fantasy on Wie Schön Leuchtet der Morgenstern, organ & voice, E C Schirmer; Canti/Music for contrabass & chamber ensemble, Harpsichord Book III (just tuning), Fallen Leaf Press; Music for Meantone Organ, Harmonie Universelle Press; Hymns from the Rig Veda for Chorus & Javanese or American Gamelan; Pastorale (Horace) for Chorus and just-tuned piano, 4-hands, 1987; Three Symphonies for Unison Orchestra, 1993. *Recordings:* Entropical Paradise: 6 Sonic Environments, Seraphim. *Publications:* Chansons from Petrucci in Original Notation, Musica Sacra & Profana, 1983. *Contributions to:* Interval; The Courant; MLA Notes; The New Grove Dictionary of American Music. *Memberships:* Music Library Association; International Heinrich Schütz Society. *Hobbies:* Gardening; Classical philology. *Address:* PO Box 140, Oceanside, OR 97134, USA.

LEEF Yinam Arie, b. 21 Dec 1953, Jerusalem, Israel. Composer. m. Tanya Fonarev, 23 Nov 1978, 1 son, 1 daughter. *Education:* BMus, Artist Diploma, Rubin Academy of Music, Jerusalem; PhD, MA, University of Pennsylvania, USA; Composition Fellow, Tanglewood, 1982. *Career:* Visiting Lecturer, Swarthmore College, 1982-84; Philadelphia College of the Performing Arts, 1984; Teaching Post, University of Pennsylvania, USA, 1984-85; Lecturer, Jerusalem Rubin Academy of Music and Dance, 1985-. *Compositions:* Gilgulim - Woodwind Trio, 1976; Three Pieces for Piano; Fireflies for soprano, flute and harpsichord, 1977; String Quartet, 1978; KO for solo oboe, 1978; Ha'Bor, 1978; Laments for chamber orchestra, 1979; Flowers, Insects and a Very Thin Line, for flute, oboe and piano trio, 1979; Gilgulim for string trio, 1980; Canaanit Fantasy for piano, 1981; The Invisible Carmel for soprano and 5 players, 1982; Violin Concerto, 1983; Octet, 1984; A Place of Fire, for mezzo-soprano and eleven players, 1985; Fanfares and Whispers for trumpet and string orchestra, 1986; Sounds, Shadows for Choir, 1987; How Far East, How Further West? for piano, 1988; Trio for Oboe, Violin and Horn, 1988; Scherzos and Serenades for orchestra, 1989. Elegy for Harpsichord, 1990; Tribute for orchestra, 1991; Elegy for string quartet, 1991; Symphony No 1, 1992; Sea Songs for equal-voice choir, 1993; Cantilena for guitar, 1993; String Quartet, No 2, 1993; Fantasies on a Nocturnal Light for orchestra, 1994. *Recordings:* Numerous pieces for the Israel Broadcasting Authority Commissions include: Fromm Music Foundation at Harvard; Swarthmore Music & Dance Festival; The Concerto Soloists Chamber Orchestra of Philadelphia; Penn Contemporary Players; Israel Sinfonietta Be'er Sheva, Jerusalem Dance Workshop; Rinat Choir. *Publications:* Music published by: 1)Theodore Presser Company, Bryn-Mawr, PA, USA; 2)Israel Music Institute, Tel-Aviv; 3)Israel Music Publications, Jerusalem; 4)Israel Music Center, Tel-Aviv. *Memberships:* ACUM; League of Composers in Israel. *Address:* 1 Ramban Street 10, Jerusalem 92422, Israel.

LEEKE David, b. 10 May 1957, Shropshire, England. Organist; Conductor; Writer; Examiner; Adjudicator. m. Tina M Daler. *Education:* Taught Privately with the Late A S W Baker and Royal College of Music. *Career:* Assistant Organist, Croydon Parish Church, 1977-79; Organist and Master of the Music, Folkestone Parish Church, 1979-90; Music Staff, St Augustine's College, Westgate-On-Sea, 1980-87; Director of Music, St Mary's College, Folkestone, 1987-90; Director of Music, Maidstone Grammar School, 1990-; Organist and

Choirmaster, St Mary's Kemsing, 1990-94; Organist and Choirmaster, St Nicholas', Otham, 1994-; Conductor and Musical Director, East Malling Singers, 1991-. *Compositions:* Hymn Tunes; Anglian Chants; Anthems. *Publications:* Lets Make Music, Music For All. *Recordings:* An Organ Celebration, Folkestone Parish Church, 1980; A Festival of Lessons and Carols, Folkestone Parish Church Choir, 1983. *Memberships:* Royal College of Organists; Royal College of Music Society; Association of British Choral Directors; Music Masters and Mistresses Association. *Hobbies:* Old English Pubs; English History; Driving; Swimming. *Address:* The Old Butchers Shop, Sutton Valence, Maidstone, Kent ME17 3AJ, England.

LEES Benjamin, b. 8 Jan 1924, Harbin, China. Composer. *Education:* Studied at the University of Southern California with Halsey Stevens and Ingolf Dahl; Further study with George Antheil and in Europe; Teacher at the Peabody Conservatory 1962-64, 1966-68; Queens College New York 1964-66, Manhattan School 1972-74, Juilliard School 1976-77; Commissions from the Tokyo String Quartet and the Dallas Symphony Orchestra. *Compositions:* 4 Piano Sonatas 1949, 1950, 1951, 1963; Sonata for 2 pianos 1951; Profile for orchestra 1952; 3 String Quartets 1952, 1955, 1981; Declamations for strings and piano 1953; 4 Symphonies 1953, 1958, 1968, 1985; 2 violin sonatas 1953, 1973; The Oracle music drama 1955; 2 Piano Concertos 1955, 1966; Divertimento burlesca for orchestra, 1957; Violin Concerto, 1958; Concertante breve, 1959; Concerto for Orchestra, 1959; Visions of Poets, cantata after Whitman, 1962; Oboe Concerto, 1963; Spectrum for orchestra, 1964; The Gilded Cage, opera, 1964; Concerto for string quartet and orchestra, 1965; Concerto for chamber orchestra, 1966; Silhouettes for wind and percussion, 1967; Medea of Corinth for vocalists, wind quintet and timpani, 1970; Odyssey for piano trio, 1971; The Trumpet of the Swan for narrator and orchestra, 1972; Collage for string quartet, woodwind quintet and percussion, 1973; Etudes for piano and orchestra, 1974; Variations for piano and orchestra, 1976; Passacaglia for orchestra, 1976; Concerto for woodwind quintet and orchestra, 1976; Scarlatti Portfolio, ballet, 1979; Mobiles for orchestra, 1979; Double Concerto, with piano and cello, 1982; Concerto for brass and orchestra, 1983; Fantasy Variations for piano, 1984; Portrait of Rodin for orchestra, 1984. *Honours:* Fromm Foundation Award, 1953; Guggenheim Fellowship, 1954; National Endowment for the Arts award, 1981. *Address:* c/o ASCAP, ASCAP Building, One Lincoln Plaza, New York, NY 10023, USA.

LEEUW Ton de, b. 16 Nov 1926, Rotterdam, Netherlands. Composer. m. Arlette Reboul 1952, 1 son, 3 daughters. *Education:* Studied piano and composition with Louis Toebosch and Henk Badings, 1947-49; Further study with Olivier Messiaen and Thomas de Hartmann in Paris, 1949-50; Ethnomusicology with Jaap Kunst in Amsterdam, 1950-54. *Career:* Director of sound for the Netherlands Radio Union in Hilversum, 1954-59; Teacher of music at Utrecht and Amsterdam. *Compositions:* Television opera Alceste, 1963; Opera The Dream, 1965; Radio oratorio Job, 1956; Television play Litany of our Time, 1969; Ballets: The Bees, 1965 and Krishna and Radha, 1964; Concerto Grosso, 1946; Sumphony for strings and percussion, 1950; Symphony for strings, 1951; Plutos suite for chamber orchestra, 1952; 2 violin concertos, 1953, 1961; Brabant, symphonic song for middle voice and orchestra, 1959; Ombres for orchestra, 1961; Symphonies for winds, 1963; Spatial Music I-IV, 1965-68; Syntaxis for orchestra, 1966; Lamento pacis for chorus and 16 instruments, 1969; Music for 12 strings, 1970; Music for organ and 12 players, 1972; Gending for gamelan orchestra, 1974; Chamber: String Trio, 1948; Violin Sonata, 1951; 2 string quartets, 1958, 1964; Antiphony for wind quintet and 4 electronic tracks, 1960; Night Music, 1966; Music for solo oboe, 1969, solo trombone, 1974; Rime for flute and harp, 1974; Sweelinck Variations for organ, 1973; Car nos vignes sont en fleur for 12 mixed voices, 1981; And they Shall Reign Forever for mezzo and ensemble, 1981; Chair-Obscur for

electronic sounds, 1982. *Publications include:* Music of the Twentieth Century, Utrecht, 1964. *Honours include:* Dutch government grant, 1961, for study in India and Iran. *Address:* c/o BUMA/STERMA huis, Postbus 725, 1180 AS Amstelveen, The Netherlands.

LEFANU Nicola Frances, b. 28 Apr 1947, Wickham Bishops, Essex, England. Composer. *Education:* MA (Oxon). *Career:* Broadcasts and performances, UK, USA, Europe and Australia. *Compositions:* Over 40 vocal, choral, solo, chamber, orchestral, theatre, ballet works including, Variations for Oboe quartet; The Same Day Dawns, for soprano and chamber ensemble; Columbia Falls, for orchestra; But Stars Remaining, for soprano; Dawnpath, chamber opera, 1977; The Story of Mary O'Neill, radio opera for 17 voices, 1989; Operas: The Green Children, 1990; Blood Wedding, 1992. *Honours:* Cobbett Chamber Music Prize, 1968; 1st Prize, British Broadcasting Corporation Composition Competition, 1971; Mendelssohn Scholarship, 1972; Gulbenkian Dance Award, 1972; Harkness Fellowship, 1973. *Memberships:* Council, Society for Promotion of New Music. *Address:* 9 Kempe Road, London, NW6, England.

LEFEBVRE Claude, b. 11 Nov 1931, Ardres, Calais, France. Composer. m. Ingeborg Giese, 1 May 1965, 2 daughters. *Education:* Prizes in harmony, counterpoint and fugue 1955-57, composition with Darius Milhaud 1959-60, Paris Conservatory; Composition with Pierre Boulez, Musikakademie Basel, Switzerland, 1961-62. *Career:* Teacher of analysis and composition, Metz Conservatory, France, 1966-; Founder and Artistic Director, Centre Européen pour la Recherche Musicale and the International Meeting of Contemporary Music, Metz; Artistic Director of his electro-acoustic studio, Lorraine, 1976-; Lectures in Contemporary Music, Metz University, 1978-. *Compositions include:* Cheminements, 1969; Naissances Pour Quatre Joueurs, 1971; Musiques en Liberté, 1971; Sous le Regard du Silence, 1973; Durchdringen der Nacht, 1976; Verzweigungen-Ramifications, 1976; Ivresse-Absence, 1977; Dérives Nocturnes, 1978; Tourbillonnements, 1979; Mémoires Souterraines, 1980; Océan de Terre, 1981; Lorraine, 1983; Oregon, 1984; Mosella, 1984; La Chute, 1985; Sur le lac...la main, saison, 1991-92; Sur le seuil...Inenfant, 1991; Quand les verres éclatent...; X...1994; 1992-93; Seule la peau..., saison, 1991-92. Recorded: D'Un Arbre de Nuit, 1971; Etwas Weiter, 1972; (Le chant du Monde); Océan de Terre; Vallée; Orégon; Verzweigungen; Savoure; Mosella (Harmonia Mundi HM 83). *Address:* 2 rue du Paradis, F 57000 Metz, France.

LEFKOWITZ Mischa, b. 17 Mar 1954, Riga, Latvia. Concert Violinist. m. Irina Lefkowitz, 15 June 1980. *Education:* Special School of Music, Riga; Moscow Conservatory of Music; Wayne State University, Detroit, USA; Mozarteum Academy, Salzburg. *Debut:* New York, 1984; Paris 1985. *Career:* Radio Show, KPFK; Radio Appearances, KPFC, Los Angeles, KCRW, Los Angeles; TV appearances on CBS; Orchestral appearances with major orchestras and recitals. *Compositions:* (Recorded) Mozart Concerto A Major; Giardini Concerto A Major; Bloch Concerto; Works by Sarasate, Prokofiev. *Recordings:* Laurel and Sequence Records; Recorded with London Philharmonic and English Chamber Orchestras. *Contributions to:* New York Times; Boston Globe; LA Times. *Honours:* City of Paris Prize, 1985; Carnegie Hall American Music Prize, 1983. *Memberships:* Chamber Music America; College Music Society. *Hobbies:* Writing; Basketball; Swimming. *Current Management:* ICA Management. *Address:* 3435 Bonnie Hill Dr, Los Angeles, CA 90068, USA.

LEFORT Bernard, b. 29 July 1922, Paris, France. Singer (Baritone); Administrator. *Education:* Studied at the Paris Conservatoire and with Aureliano Pertile in Milan, Hermann Weissenborn in Berlin and Elisabeth Rado in Vienna. *Career:* Sang at Salle Gaveau during the 1940s and was often heard in music by Auric, Honegger, Milhaud and Poulenc; Sang in the premiere of Tailleferre's Concerto pour Baryton and appeared from 1953 at the Theatre du Chatelet, Paris, in operettas;

Performed at the Lucerne Opera, notably as Don Giovanni and retired from the stage 1960, becoming artistic director of the Lausanne Festival; Director of the Marseille Opera, 1965-68 reviving such operas as La Gioconda, Lucrezia Borgia, Henze's Prince of Homburg and Britten's The Turn of the Screw; Artistic Director of the Théâtre de Ville Paris, 1969-78; Festival of Aix-en-Provence, 1973-80; General Administrator of the Paris Opera, 1980-82; Teacher at Mannes College New York and at the Academy of Vocal Art at Philadelphia; Produced Gounod's Mireille at the Juilliard Opera School, New York, 1986. *Address:* c/o Juilliard School of Music (Opera Dept), Lincoln Plaza, New York, NY 10023, USA.

LEFTERESCU Petre, b. 1 May 1936, Bistrita, Romania. Violinist; Professor. m. Ogneanca Tomici, 27 Sept 1958. *Education:* Bucharest Music Academy, 1953-58; Postgraduate courses, Moscow Conservatory, USSR, at D Oistrakh violin chair, 1967. *Career:* Solo concerts & chamber music tours as violinist, Romania, 1958-; Violin professor, Cluj Music Academy, 1958-69; Professor of Chamber Music, Bucharest Academy of Music, 1969-; 1st violin, Forum String Quartet, 1985; Appearances, Romanian television. *Recordings:* Romanian & universal music, for Romanian Broadcasting Company. *Contributions to:* Muzica, Contemporanul. *Current Management:* ARIA, Romanian Artists Management Company. *Address:* Calea Victoriei Nr 83, B1 81, et IX, ap 37, Bucharest 70176, Romania.

LEGA Luigi, b. 7 Apr 1940, Bordighera, Italy. Singer (Tenor). *Education:* Studied in Rome, Basle and Mannheim, *Debut:* Oberhausen, as Pinkerton, 1961. *Career:* Many appearances at such German opera centres as Munich, Hamburg, Stuttgart, Mannheim, Berlin (Deutsche Oper) and Wuppertal; Further engagements at Amsterdam, Palermo, Barcelona, Rio de Janeiro, Trieste and Vienna as Verdi's Radames, Duke of Mantua, Alvaro, Alfredo, Don Carlos, Manrico and Riccardo; Also a noted interpreter of Don José, Edgardo, Florestan, Andrea Chenier, Turiddu, Rodolfo, Cavaradossi and Des Grieux in Manon Lescaut; Teacher of singing in Wuppertal. *Address:* c/o Buhnen, Spinnstrasse 4, 5600 Wuppertal, Germany.

LEGÁNY Dezsö, b. 19 Jan 1916, Szombathely, Hungary. Musicologist. m. Erzsébet Hegyi, 23 Sept 1961, 2 sons. *Education:* LLD, University of Pécs; Composition, Liszt Academy of Music, Budapest; DMusSc, Hungarian Academy of Sciences, Budapest. *Career:* Professor, Liszt Academy of Music, Budapest, 1951-58; Professor, Bartók Conservatory of Music, Budapest, 1958-73; Head of Hungarian Music Department, Institute for Musicology of Hungarian Academy of Sciences, 1973-83. *Publications:* Liszt and His Country, 1869-1873, 1983; Liszt and His Country, 1874-1886, 1992; F Liszt Unbekannte Presse und Briefe aus Wien 1822-1886, 1984; Henry Purcell, 1959, 2nd Edition, 1981; A Chronicle of Hungarian Music: A Thousand Years of Music History in Documents, 1962; Works of F Erkel, 1975; Liszt in Hungary 1869-1873, 1976; Letters of Z Kodály, 1982; Liszt in Hungary 1874-1886, Budapest, 1986. *Contributions to:* New Grove Dictionary; New Grove Dictionary of Opera; Sohlmans Musiklexikon; The Concise Oxford Dictionary of Opera; Zenei Lexikon; Studia Musicologica; Magyar Zene; The New Hungarian Quarterly; Bulletin of the International Kodály Society; Grazer Musikwissenschaftliche Arbeiten; Journal of the American Liszt Society; Periodica Musica; Vigilia; Nuova Rivista Musicale Italiana; The Liszt Society Journal, London; Liszt Saeculum, Sweden; Dictionary of Opera, London, 1992. *Address:* Apahida u. 11 Budapest, H-1112 Hungary.

LEGGATE Robin, b. 18 Apr 1946, West Kirby, Cheshire. Singer (Tenor). *Education:* Studied at Queen's College Oxford (1964-67) and the Royal Northern College of Music. *Career:* Royal Opera House Covent Garden from 1977, as Cassio in Otello (conducted by Zubin Mehta, Christoph von Dohnányi and Colin Davis), Elemer (Arabella), Narraboth (Salome), the Painter in Lulu and Tamino in a new production of Die Zauberflöte,

1979; Has also sung in Prince Igor and Il Trovatore at Covent Garden; Appearances with the Netherlands Opera and at the Hamburg Staatsoper from 1978; South Australian Opera, 1982, as Ferrando in Così fan Tutte; Théâtre du Châtelet, Paris, as Tamino, 1982; Other Mozart roles include Belmonte and Don Ottavio, which he has sung with most of the regional British companies; Recent engagements in Le nozze di Figaro in Madrid, Weber's Oberon with Scottish Opera, Eisenstein in a new production of Die Fledermaus for Scottish Opera, and the premiere of Andre Laporte's Das Schloss, in Brussels; Has sung at the Festival Hall from 1976 (debut with the London Symphony in Pulcinella); In 1981 sang in Mendelssohn's Elijah at Florence and appeared in Mozart's C minor Mass with the London Philharmonic, conducted by Solti; Sang in the stage premiere of Gerhard's Duenna, Madrid 1992; Sang in world premiere of Life with an Idiot by Schnittke at Netherlands Opera, 1992; Opera Bastille (St Francis D'Assise) and at Salzburg Festival (Salome), 1993; Sang in first production of Stiffelio (Verdi) at Royal Opera House, 1993. *Recordings include:* La Fanciulla del West from Covent Garden; Haydn's Armida; The Light of Life by Elgar. *Current Management:* IMG Artists (Europe). *Address:* Media House, 3 Burlington Lane, Chiswick, London W4 2TH, England.

LEHANE Maureen, b. 19 Sept 1932, London, England. Concert and Opera Singer. m. Peter Wishart, 1966 (d 1984). *Education:* Queen Elizabeth's Girls' Grammar School, Barnet; Guildhall School of Music and Drama; Studied under Hermann Weissenborn, Berlin; and John and Aida Dickens; gained Arts Council Award to study in Berlin. *Career:* Has sung numerous leading roles, (Operas including Arianna and Faramondo) with Handel Opera Societies of England and America, in London and in Carnegie Hall, New York, also in Poland, Sweden and Germany, gave a number of Master Classes on the interpretation of Handel's vocal music (notably at s'Hertogenbosch Festival, Holland, 1972, 1973); debut at Glyndebourne, 1967, as Melide in Cavalli's L'Ormindo; Festival appearances include Stravinsky Festival, Cologne; City of London; Aldeburgh; Cheltenham; Three Choirs; Bath; Oxford Bach; Göttingen Handel Festival; has toured North America; also 3-month tour of Australia and 2-month tour of Far East and Middle East, 1971; sang in Holland and for Belgium TV; visits also to Berlin, Lisbon, Poland and Rome, 1979-80; Warsaw, 1981; Title role of Handel's Ariodante, Sadler's Wells, 1974; Wishart's Clytemnestra, London, 1974; Purcell's Dido and Aeneas, Netherlands Opera, 1976; castrato lead in J C Bach's Adriano In Siria, 1982; female lead in Hugo Cole's The Falcon, Somerset, 1983; Peter Wishart's The Lady of the Inn, Reading University, 1984; Cyrus in first complete recordings of Handel's Belshazzar; appeared regularly on BBC, also in Promenade concerts; Started an annual music festival dedicated to the memory of Peter Wishart, 1986-; Great Elm Music Festival (Jackdaws, Great Elm, devoted to music education). *Recordings:* Made numerous recordings, Bach, Haydn, Mozart, Handel. *Publication:* Songs of Purcell edited with Peter Wishart. *Memberships:* Member, Jury International Singing Competition, s'Hertogenbosch Festival, Holland, 1982- and Llangollen International Eisteddfod from 1991. *Hobbies:* Cooking; Gardening; Reading. *Address:* Bridge House, Great Elm, Frome, Somerset, BA11 3NY, England.

LEHMANN Hans Ulrich, b. 4 May 1937, Biel, Switzerland. Composer; Professor. m. Ursula Lehmann. *Education:* BA, 1956; Universities of Berne, Zurich and Basle, 1956-67; Diplomas: Violoncello, 1960, Music Theory, 1962; Masterclasses in Composition with Boulez and Stockhausen, 1960-63. *Career includes:* Lecturer, Zurich University, 1969-90; Professor, Theory, Composition, 1972-, Director, 1976-, Musikhochschule, Zurich; President, SUISA (Swiss Authors Association), 1991-. *Compositions include:* Quanti, 1962; Mosaik, 1964; Noten, 1964-66; Spiele, 1965; Rondo, 1967; Instants, 1968; Konzert, 1969; Regions III, 1970; discantus I and II, 1970; Sonata di chiesa, 1971; Tractus, 1971; zu streichen, 1974; zu blasen, 1975; Tantris, 1976-77; Motetus Paraburi, 1977-78; Kammermusik I,

1978-79; Kammermusik II, 1979; Duette, 1980; Lege mich wie ein Segel auf dein Herz, 1980-83; Striking, 1980; Canticum I and II, 1981; Stroking, 1982; Mirlitonnades, 1983; battuto a tre - tratto, 1983; Mon amour, 1983; Triplum, 1984; -ludes, 1985; Alleluja, 1985; In Memoriam Nicolai de Flue, 1986-87; Fragmente, 1986-87; Streichquartett, 1987-88; Osculetur me, 1988-89; de profundis, 1988-89; Esercizi, 1989; Wandloser Raum, 1989; ad missam Prolationum, 1989-90; etwas Klang von meiner Oberfläche, 1989-90; Nocturnes, 1990-91; ut signaculum, 1991-92. *Contributor to:* Professional journals; Music Prize, City of Zurich, 1993. *Memberships:* Numerous professional organisations. *Address:* Haldenstrasse 35, CH-8615 Wermatswil, Switzerland.

LEHMSTEDT Sigrid, b. 23 Apr 1929, Weissenfels, Germany. Professor of Piano & Pedagogy. 1 son. *Education:* Abitur, Extended Secondary School; Diploma, Pianist-Pedagogue, F Mendelssohn-Bartholdy Hochschule für Musik, Leipzig, 1953. *Career:* Chamber music concerts, accompanist, recitals; Docent to Professor of Piano: H Eisler Hochschule für Musik, East Berlin 1953-82, F Mendelssohn-Bartholdy Hochschule, Leipzig 1982-; Franz-Liszt Hochschule Weimar, 1982-; Founder, Head, Piano Faculty, special music schools for talented young pianists (65 prize-winners, (national & international competitions); Guest Professor, courses, master classes for young pianists, East & West Germany, Finland, Netherlands, Czechoslovakia, Hungary and USA; Lectures, conferences, courses & seminars for teachers; Juror, piano competitions. *Publications:* Pre-ABC of Piano, 1985; Curriculum, Piano Faculty, Special Schools for Music (Part I 6-11 years, Part II 12-18 years), 1982. *Address:* Schloss Belvedere, 0-5300 Weimar, Germany.

LEHNHOFF Dieter Hasso, b. 27 May 1955, Guatemala City, Guatemala. Musicologist; Conductor. m. Cristina Altamire, 1 Sept 1976, 1 son, 1 daughter. *Education:* Bachiller en Ciencias y Letras, Colegio Aleman, Universidad Francisco Marroquin; Mozarteum, Salzburg; The Benjamin T Rome School of Music, Catholic University of America, Washington DC; MA; PhD, Musicology. *Career:* Founder, Conductor: Capella Antiqua, 1980-, Orquesta Universitaria, 1990-; Founder, Director: Institute of Musicology, Universidad Rafael Landivar, 1989-, Department of Music, Universidad del Valle de Guatemala, 1990-; Conductor, Guatemalam National Choir, 1991-. *Compositions:* Requiem, tape, 1975; Sones de Antano, oboe and choir orchestra (used as soundtrack for film Antigua) 1985; Canto IV, clarinet quartet, 1985; Tientos, violin, clarinet, violoncello, 1988; Praeambulum, brass quintet, 1990. *Recordings:* Pastoras Alegres, 1st recordings of Christmas Music by 17th and 18th century Guatemalan composers. *Address:* 26 Avenida B 16-61 zona 16, San Isidro, Guatemala 01016.

LEHNHOFF Nikolaus, b. 20 May 1939, Hanover, Germany. Opera Producer and Designer. *Education:* Trained as assistant stage director at the Deutsche Oper, Berlin, and at Bayreuth and the Metropolitan Opera, 1963-71; Staged Die Frau ohne Schatten at the Paris Opéra 1971; Director of several opera productuions in Germany and Switzerland; San Francisco 1985, Der Ring des Nibelungen; Produced Katya Kabanova at Glyndebourne and Der fliegende Holländer at Santa Fe, both in 1988; Returned to Glyndebourne 1989, Jenůfa; Idomeneo at the Salzburg Festival, 1990; Munich Opera, 1990, Der fliegende Holländer; Elektra at Leipzig, 1991; Season 1991/92 with Lohengrin at Frankfurt and Henze's Der Prinz von Homburg at the Munich Festival; Engaged for The Makropoulos Case by Janáček at Glyndebourne, 1995. *Address:* c/o Glyndebourne Festival Opera, Lewes, Sussex BN8 5UU, England.

LEHOTKA Gábor, b. 1938, Vac, Hungary. Organist. *Education:* Organ Tuition with Professor Tibor Pikethy; Bartók Conservatory, Budapest, 1953; Budapest Liszt Academy of Music, 1958; Graduate with Distinction, Budapest Academy of Music, 1963; Vacance Musicali Master Class, 1964. *Career:* Professor, Organ Department, Bartók Conservatory, Budapest, 1969-; Professor, Organ Department, Liszt Academy of Music, Budapest, 1975-; Has given numerous concerts throughout Europe, USSR; Expert builder of several organs in Hungary; Jury Member, Ferenc Liszt International Organ Concours, Budapest, 1978, J S Bach International Organ Concours, Leipzig, 1980, Anton Bruckner International Organ Concours, Linz, 1982, and the Budapest Ferenc Liszt International Concours, Budapest, 1983.

LEHRBAUMER Robert, b. 20 July 1960, Vienna, Austria. Pianist. *Education:* Studied Piano, Organ, Conducting, Composition, Vienna School of Music & Dramatic Art; Diplomas with highest distinction, Organ, Piano, 1987, 1988. *Career:* Played with Vienna Philharmonic Orchestra; Vienna Symphonic Orchestra; Austrian Broadcasting Corporation Orchestra; other major orchestras; Conductors: Claudio Abbado, Yehudi Menuhin, Andre Previn, Sandor Vegh; Appeared with: Wolfgang Schneiderhan, Anton Dermota, Walter Berry, Philippe Entremont, Christian Altenburger, Ernst Kovacic; Concerts: most European countries, Korea, Japan, Thailand, Indonesia, Malaysia, Mexico, Argentina, USA (including Schubert Festival, Washington & Carnegie Recital Hall, New York); International Festivals: Vienna, Lucerne, Nurnberg, Prague Spring Festival, Bruckner Festival, Linz Festival Cervantino, Mexico; Many radio & TV performances; Teaching, summer academies, Austria & abroad; World premieres of new works; Specialist, Schubert piano works, Haydn, Mozart, Beethoven piano concertos, A Berg, F Schmidt, E Schulhoff, K Szymanowksy; Recent recitalist in Mastersoloists - Masterensembles & participant in Mozart & Schubert Marathons, Wiener Konzerthaus; Soloist, piano, organ, Mozarteum-Orchestra concert, Salzburg; Soloist, 4 concerts, Vienna Symphonic Orchestra. *Recordings:* LPs: Baroque, Romantic, contemporary piano organ music (Liszt, Weissensteiner, Schollum, Albinoni, Pachelbel, Muffat, Kerll). *Current Management:* Freunde der Claviermusik. *Address:* Freunde der Claviermusik, Penknerg 21, A-3150 Wilhelmsburg, Austria.

LEHRER Phyllis Claire Alpert, b. 13 Mar 1940, New York, USA. Concert Pianist; Professor of Piano; Head of Piano Department. m. Paul M Lehrer, 13 June 1965, 1 son, 1 daughter. *Education:* AB, Music, University of Rochester; MS, Piano, Juilliard School of Music; additional studies at Yale Summer Program, Harvard University; DMA Studies, Stanford University; Dalcroze School of Music, Juilliard School, Eastman School; Chamber Music, Knesal Hall, Blue Hill, Maine. *Debut:* Merkin Hall, New York City, 1982, 1987; London Debut, Wigmore Hall, 1982. *Career:* Rutgers University, Westminster Choir College, Seton Hall University, Keyboard Concerts, Fresno, California; William Paterson State College; McGill University, Montreal; Southeastern Massachusetts University, Solo recital; WQRX Radio, New York City; WCRB Radio, Boston; WWFM Radio, New Jersey; Concerts in Ireland, Scotland, Northern Ireland and England; Chamber concerts, duo piano concerts in various locations including Rutgers University, Meadows Foundation, Princeton University, Kosciusko Foundation, New York City; Glassboro State College; Lecturer and Clinician on Piano Pedagogy and Performance Antlety. *Recordings:* Educo 3130, Schumann Phantasie; Bach Toccata in D, BWV 912. *Hobbies:* Reading; Hiking; Swimming; Cooking. *Address:* Head, Piano Department, Westminster Choir College, Hamilton Avenue and Walnut Lane, Princeton, NJ 08540, USA.

LEHRMAN Leonard Jordan, b. 20 Aug 1949, Kansas, USA. Conductor; Composer; Pianist; Accompanist; Translator; Director. m. Karen S Campbell, 31 July 1978, divorced 1986. *Education:* BA, Harvard College, 1971; MFA, 1975, DMA, composition, 1977, Cornell University; Private study with Elie Siegmeister, 1960-69; Opera conducting, Indiana University, 1975-76; Fontainebleau Conservatoire, 1969; Ecole Normale de Musique, Paris, 1971-72; Salzburg Mozarteum, 1972; MLIS, L I University, 1994. *Debut:* As Pianist,

Carnegie Recital Hall, 1979; As Conductor, Bremerhaven and Berlin, 1981, 1983. *Career:* Assistant Chorus Master and Assistant Conductor, Metropolitan Opera, 1977-78; Assistant Conductor, Heidelberg Festival, 1979, Augsburg Städtische Bühne, 1980, Basler Theater, 1980-81, Conductor; Schauspielhaus Wien, 1981; Kapellmeister, Stadttheater Bremerhaven, 1981-83; Chief Coach, Conductor, Theater des Westens, 1983-85; Laureate Conductor, Jewish Music Theater of Berlin; Has appeared on ZDF, WTIU and WCIC TV and various other TV and radio stations; Faculty, Jewish Academy of Fine Arts. *Compositions:* Tales of Malamud, 2 One-act operas: Idiots First, completion of work begun by Marc Blitzstein, and Karla; Sima; Hannah; The Family Man; Flute Concerto; Violin Concerto; Growing Up Woman; Let's Change the World; EG: A Musical Portrait of Emma Goldman; The Birthday of the Bank, commissioned by Opera America for Lake George Opera Festival; Sisters; Superspy!: The Secret Musical; New World: An Opera About What Columbus Did to the Indians; We Are Innocent (A Rosenberg Cantata). *Current Management:* Jeffrey W James, Artistic Administrator, Prof Edgar H Lehrman Memorial Foundation. *Address:* 10 Nob Hill Gate, Roslyn, NY 11576, USA.

LEHRMAN Paul D, b. 29 Oct 1952, New York, NY, USA. Computer-Music Programmer and Consultant; Composer; Music Journalist. *Education:* BFA, School for The Arts, State University of New York, Purchase 1975; Columbia University, New York 1970-73; Studied with Vladimir Ussachevsky, Mario Davidovsky, Charles Dodge, William Polisi and Donald MacCourt. *Debut:* As Conductor of original work, Purchase Chamber Players/ Percussion Ensemble 1976. *Career:* Stage Musical Director, The Life That We Lead, Boston 1980, Threepenny Opera, Boston 1978, The Great American Backstage Musical, Boston 1979, Marat/Sade, New York 1977; Radio Lecture Performances on Computer Music, WGBH Boston, WCRB Boston, Television Appearances WNEV-TV Boston, WCVB-TV Boston, WBZ-TV Boston, 1979-86; Vice-President, Southworth Music Systems 1985-86; President, LehrWare 1983-; Associate Director, Center for Recording Arts, Technology & Industry, University of Massachusetts-Lowell, College of Music, 1988-. *Compositions:* I Dig A Pygmy, 1990; IRT (In Real Time), 1988; Song Suite (for voice, recorder and two computers), 1987. *Recordings:* The Celtic Macintosh, Themes/KPM, 1986; On Stream, Themes/KPM, 1988; Quick Tunes Library, Passport Designs, 1992. *Publications:* Total Music (Manual) 1985; AKG ADR 68K (Manual), 1986-88; The Personal Computer Programming Encyclopaedia (chapter on music), 1988; The Andy M Stewart Songbook, 1988; Roland S 770 (Manual), 1990-91; Midi For the Professional, 1993; Making Music With Your Computer, (contributor), 1993; Time Code Handbook, (contributor), 1990. *Address:* College of Fine Arts, UMass Lowell, 1 University Avenue, Lowell, MA 01854, USA.

LEIB Gunther, b. 12 Apr 1927, Gotha, Thuringen, Germany. Singer (Baritone); Professor. *Education:* After violin studies entered vocal class at the Weimar Conservatory. *Career:* First violin in Landeskapelle at Gotha from 1949; Stage debut at Kothen 1952, as Bartolo in Il Barbiere di Siviglia. *Career:* Sang at Kothen, Meinigen and Nordhausen; Stadttheater Halle 1956-57; Staatsoper Dresden from 1957, Berlin from 1961; Sang Christus in Bach's St John Passion in Italy 1957, conducted by Franz Konwitschny; Annual appearances at the Handel Festivals, Halle; Salzburg Easter Festival 1974-75, as Beckmesser in Die Meistersinger, conducted by Karajan (also at the Met, 1976); Guest engagements at the Paris Opéra, Moscow Bolshoi, Hamburg Staatsoper, National Operas of Warsaw, Prague and Budapest, Sofia, Stockholm and Helsinki; Other roles were Guglielmo, Raimondo, Papageno, Don Pasquale and Germont; Professor at the Carl Maria von Weber Hochschule, Dresden, 1964-76; Currently Professor at the Musikhochschule Berlin. *Recordings:* Così fan Tutte, Die Zauberflöte, Ein Deutsches Requiem, Lucia di Lammermoor, Don Pasquale and La Traviata (Eterna); St Matthew Passion (Eurodisc); Der

Dorfjahrmarkt by Benda and La Bohème (Deutsche Grammophon); Einstein by Dessau (Nova). *Address:* Hochschule für Musik Hanns Eisler, Otto-Grotewohlstrasse 19, 108 Berlin, Germany.

LEIDEL Wolf-G, b. 14 Dec 1949, Konigsee, Thruingia, East Germany. Professor of Music Theory. m. Sabine Sonsalla, 29 June 1972. *Education:* Studied Conducting and Composition, 1968-73. *Debut:* World premiere of his Symphony No 1 with Jena Philharmonic, 1974. *Career:* Kapellmeister, Theater Weimar, 1974-83; Meisterschuler Berlin, Akademie der Kunste, East Berlin, 1983-85; Assistant, Music Theory, 1985-93, Professor, Music Theory, 1993, Hochschule fur Musik, Weimar; Many world and other premieres of numerous compositions especially music for organ. *Compositions include:* Recorded: Zi Bims Barenreiter for organ played by Kerin Bowyer (A feast of organ exuberance); Meinem Rosengarten for organ and violin, played by Bittotmann (violin) and W Gleidel (organ). *Contributions to:* Orgelmusik, Orgelgutachten, other publications. *Honours include:* 1st Prize in National Improvisation Competition, 1976. *Memberships include:* GdO; Olivier-Messiaen-Association; VDK; Museum fur Orgelbau, Thuringia. *Hobbies include:* Organ; Compositions; Astrophysics; Cosmology; Theology. *Address:* Bauhausstr 12, D-O-5300 Weimar, Germany.

LEIFERKUS Sergei, b. 4 Apr 1946, Leningrad, USSR. Singer (Baritone). *Education:* Studied at the Leningrad Conservatoire, with Barsov and Shaposhnikov. *Career:* Joined the Leningrad Maly Theatre 1972: sang in Eugene Onegen, Iolanta, Il Barbiere di Siviglia and Don Giovanni; Joined Kirov Theatre Leningrad 1977, and sang Prince Andrei in War and Peace by Prokofiev; Sang with Berlin Philharmonic under Kurt Masur 1983; Wexford Festival 1982-86, in Griséledis and Le Jongleur de Notre Dame by Massenet, Hans Heiling by Marschner and Königskinder by Humperdinck; Scottish Opera from 1985, as Don Giovanni, Germont and Eugene Onegin (1988); Covent Garden 1987, as Eugene Onegin and Tomsky in The Queen of Spades, with the Kirov Company; English National Opera 1987, as Zurga in Les pêcheurs de Perles; US debut 1987, in Symphony No 13 by Shostakovich, with the Boston Symphony; In 1989 gave Wigmore hall debut recital, sang Luna in a new production of Il Trovatore at Covent Garden and appeared in a concert performance of Giovanna d'Arco at the Festival Hall; Glyndebourne Opera debut 1989, as Mandryka in Arabella; Concert performance of Mlada by Rimsky-Korsakov, at the Barbican Hall; Season 1989-90 included US opera debut at San Francisco, as Telramund in Lohengrin, and the title role in a new production of Prince Igor at Covent Garden; Sang Rangoni in Boris Godunov at the Kirov Theatre, Leningrad 1990 (also televised); Ruprecht in Prokofiev's The Fiery Angel at the 1991 Promenade Concerts, London and at Covent Garden, 1992; Sang Rangoni at Helsinki, 1992; Tomsky at Barcelona, Rangoni at San Francisco and Iago at Covent Garden; Engaged as Iago in Otello Metropolitan Opera, 1994. *Contributions to:* Opera Magazine (Profile), Feb 1990. *Address:* c/o Allied Artists, 42 Montpelier Square, London SW7 1JZ, England.

LEIGH Adèle, b. 15 June 1928, London, England. Singer (Soprano). *Education:* Studied in New York with Julius Gutmann. *Career:* Sang first in USA; Covent Garden from 1949, as Xenia in Boris Godunov, Mozart's Cherubino and Pamina, Strauss's Sophie and Massenet's Manon; Sang in the premeres of Vaughan Williams's Pilgrim's Progress and Tippett's The Midsummer Marriage; Boston 1959, as Musetta in La Bohème; New York City Centre Opera 1960, as Sophie in Werther; Zurich Opera 1961-; Operetta performances at the Vienna Volksoper from 1965; Brighton Festival 1984, in Offenbach's La Vie Parisienne; Sang in Sondheim's Follies (London 1987); Senior Tutor in Opera Stagecraft at the Royal Northern College of Music, 1990. *Address:* Royal Northern College of Music (opera faculty), 124 Oxford Road, Manchester M15 6FY, England.

LEIGH David Anthony, b. 3 Apr 1953, London,

England. Harpsichordist; Fortepianist. *Education:* Reading University, BA 1975; Guildhall School of Music. *Debut:* Wigmore Hall 1981. *Career:* Recitals all over the UK, Canada, USA, Holland, Belgium, Austria; Lectures in USA and Austria; Masterclasses in USA and UK; Radio broadcasts in UK, Canada and USA; Known for knowledge of early keyboard instruments and their restoration. *Recordings:* Credits with Musicaphon (Germany) and LME (England). *Publications:* Book on early pianos in preparation; Encyclopedia articles on harpsichord and clavichord. *Contribution to:* Antique Collector, on square pianos. *Hobbies:* Collecting old piano and harpsichord records; Theatre; Film; Arts; Antiques; Food and wine. *Address:* Greystones, The Slade, Charlbury, Oxford, OX7 3SJ, England.

LEISNER David, b. 22 Dec 1953, Los Angeles, California, USA. Guitarist; Composer; Teacher. *Education:* Studied privately with John Duarte, David Starobin, Richard Winslow, Virgil Thomson and David Del Tredici Wesleyan University, BA 1976. *Career:* Teacher of Guitar at Amherst College 1976-78, New England Conservatory from 1980; Manhattan School of Music from 1993; New York debut at Merkin Hall 1979, Solo and Chamber music recitals in USA, Canada and Europe; Concerto soloist with L'Orchestre de la Suisse Romande, Australian Chamber Orchestra, New York Chamber Ensemble and others. Compositions performed by The Springfield Symphony Orchestra Fairfield Orchestra, Sanford Sylvan, Paul Sperry, Benjamin Verdery, The Saturday Brass Quintet and the Los Angeles Guitar Quartet. *Compositions include:* Embrace of Peace, Orch. 1991; Dances in the Madhouse, violin/flute and Guitar, 1982; Orchestrated, 1989; Ad Majorem Dei Gloriam, (brass quintet), 1992; Confiding (voice and piano, voice and guitar), 1985-86; Candles in Mecca, (piano trio), 1988. *Recordings:* The Viennese Guitar, Titanic. *Current Management:* Aaron Concert Management. *Address:* Aaron Concert Management, 729 Boylston Street, Suite 600, Boston, MA 02116, USA.

LEITNER Ferdinand, b. 4 Mar 1912, Berlin, Germany. Conductor. m. Gisela Büsing, 14 July 1944, 1 child. *Education:* Graduated Staatliche Akademische Hochschule Musik, Berlin. *Career:* Conductor, Staatsoper, Hamburg, 1945-46; Conductor, Staatsoper Munich, 1946-47; Opera Director, General Music Director, Staatsoper Stuttgart, also symphony orchestra leader, 1947-; Chief Conductor, Zurich Opera, Switzerland, 1969-; Chief Conductor, Philharmonic Orchestra, The Hague, Netherlands, 1975-; While at Stuttgart conducted the premieres of Orff Oedipus der Tyrann 1959 and Prometheus 1968; Guest performances, Tokyo, Japan, and Lyric Opera, Chicago, USA, 1988, Tannhäuser; Guest contracts, Munich and Vienna State Operas; Conducted orchestras, operas, festivals throughout world; Conducted Ariadne and Naxos for RAI, Turin, 1989; Recording artist, including the only recording of Busoni's Doktor Faust; Mozart's Serenades K250 and K320, Piano Concertos (with Wilhelm Kempff and Monique Haas), Beethoven's Piano Concertos (Kempff) and Egmont incidental music; Schumann's 3rd Symphony and Dvořák's 7th; Stage works by Orff (Deutsche Grammophon). *Address:* c/o Orchestro Sinfonico di Torino della RAI, Via Rossini 15, 1-10124, Turin, Italy.

LEIXNER Vladimir, b. 1953, Czechoslovakia, Cellist. *Education:* Studied in Prague with members of the Smetana Quartet. *Career:* Cellist in various Czech ensembles from 1970; Co-founder and cellist of the Stamic Quartet of Prague 1977; Performances at the Prague Young Artists and the Bratislava Music Festivals; Tours to Spain, Austria, France, Switzerland, Germany and Eastern Europe; Tour of the USA 1980, debut concerts in Britain at London and Birmingham 1983; Further British tours 1985, 1988 (Warwick Arts Festival) and 1989 (20 concerts); Gave premiere of Helmut Eder's 3rd Quartet, 1986; Season 1991-92 with visit to the Channel Islands (Festival of Czech Music), Holland, Finland, Austria and France, Edinburgh Festival and debut tours of Canada, Japan and Indonesia.

Recordings: Shostakovich No 13, Schnittke No 4 (Panton); Mozart K589 and K370 (Lyrinx); Dvořák, Martinů and Janáček complete quartets (Cadenza). *Honours:* (with members of Stamic Quartet): Prize winner, International Festival of Young Soloists, Bordeaux 1977; Winner, 1986 ORF (Austrian Radio) International String Quartet Competition (followed by live broadcast from the Salzburg Mozarteum); Academie Charles Cros Grand Prix du Disque 1991, for Dvořák quartets. *Address:* c/o Anglo-Swiss Management, 4-5 Primrose Mews, Sharpeshall Street, London NW1 8YW, England.

LEJET Edith, b. 19 July 1941, Paris, France. Composer; Professor. *Education:* Conservatoire National Superieur de Musique de Paris. *Compositions:* Monodrame, pour violon et orchestre, 1969; Journal D'Anne Frank, oratorio, 1970; Quatuor De Saxophones, 1974; Espaces Nocturnes, 1976; Gemeaux, 1978 & Balance, 1982 for guitar; Harmonie Du Soir, 1977; Triptyque, for organ, 1979; Volubilis for Violoncello, 1981; Aube Marine, 1982; L'Homme Qui Avait Perdu Sa Voix, 1984, Théâtre Musical; Ressac, 1986; Les Rois Mages, oratorio, 1989; 7 Chants Sacrés for female chorus and organ, 1990; Améthyste for 12 strings, 1990. *Publications:* Pedagogic Books: La Precision Rythmique Dans la Musique 3 volumes. *Honours:* Numerous 1st Prizes at Paris Conservatory, Vocation Fondation, 1967; Grand Prix de Rome, 1968; Prix Florence Gould, 1970; Prix Herve Dugardin, 1974; Grand Prix de la Musique de Chambre de la SACEM, 1979. *Address:* 11/13 Rue Cino Del Duca, 75017 Paris, France.

LELIE Martinus Christoffel (Christo), b. 28 Dec 1956, Dordrecht, Netherlands. Writer on Music; Solo Concert Organist; Pianist. *Education:* Piano, 1982, Organ, 1984, Rotterdam Conservatory. *Career:* Organist, Musical Director, Reformed Churches, The Hague, Delft; Critic, Trouw newspaper; Pianist, Rotterdamse Dansacademie; Editor, EPTA Piano Bulletin; Editor, Franz Liszt Kring; Freelance Writer on Music; Numerous organ recitals; Played Liszt organ works in Liszt Cycles, Rotterdam, 1990; Accompanist (Piano, Organ, Harpsichord) in vocal, instrumental concerts and dance performances, Netherlands, Germany; Staff Member, Liszt Festivals: Utrecht, 1988, Amsterdam, 1990; Staff Member, Gina Bachauer Audition, Amsterdam, 1991; Lectures on Liszt, Scarlatti, Italian Organs; BRT Radio Commentary on Harpsichord and Fortepiano, Bruges, Belgium, 1986. *Compositions:* Choral Preludes for organ; Roman Variations; Study 87 for piano; Several religious works for choir; Renaissance Dances transcribed for organ; Fantasy in E minor for organ; Passacaglia for organ. *Publications:* 1685 Europa en de Muziek, Scarlatti, 1985; Liszt in Amsterdam, festival book, 1991; Van Piano tot Forte, 1994. *Contributions:* Numerous reviews, interviews, articles in Trouw: Articles on Liszt, Alkan, Scarlatti, Boely, history of the piano, the pedalier, piano pedagogy, music and the brain in: Mens en Melodie; Muziek en Dans; Piano Bulletin; Piano Wereld; Franz Liszt Kring; Disk; Glenn Gould Society; Others. *Memberships:* Vice-President, Council Member, Franz Liszt Kring; Council, EPTA, Netherlands; President, Historical Dance Ensemble Volta; Council, Ch Tournemire Stichting; Nederlandse Toonkunstenaars Raad; Koninklijke Nederlandse Organisten Vereniging; American Liszt Society; Liszt Society. *Hobbies:* Antiquarian books; Bird watching. *Address:* Havenstraat 12, 2613 VK Delft, Netherlands.

LEMANN Jean (Juan), b. 7 Aug 1928, Vendôme, France. Composer; Pianist; Professor of Composition. m. Maria Luisa Herreros, 28 Sept 1957, 2 daughters. *Education:* BA, Mathematics, 1948; Architecture, Catholic University of Chile, 1948-50; Piano: Student, 1942-54, Postgraduate, 1955-59, University of Chile, National Conservatory of Music; Composition: University of Chile, Catholic University of Chile, privately; Visiting Fulbright Scholar, Juilliard School of Music, New York, 1970-71. *Career:* Professor, Piano, Music Theory, Choral Conductor, Experimental School of Arts, 1957-61; Professor, Piano, Composition, 1961-91, Vice-Dean, 1981-82, Faculty of Arts, University of Chile; Adviser, cultural and artistic institutions; Pianist, Lecturer, Adjudicator; Composer, Professor of Composition at Faculty of Arts, University of Chile. *Compositions:* Orchestral, chamber, choral, mime, theatre, ballet, film music, including: Leyenda del Mar; Tres variables para piano; Sonata Para Arpa; Obertura de Concierto; El Cuerpo y la Sangre; Cuarteto para tres flautas y clavecin; Variaciones para piano; Maestranzas de Noche; Puentes (words, P Neruda); Fantasia Concertante para piano y Orquesta; Eolica para cello solo; Mirado Retrospectiva, 1992, for mixed choir and piano; Akustika, 1992 for recorder, viola da gamba and piano; Barrio sin Luz, 1992 for soprano voice and piano. *Recordings include:* El Cuerpo y la Sangre; Mass, Veni Domine; Ironias Musicales; Variaciones para piano; Tres variables para piano; Leyenda del Mar; Homenaje a Leng; Corranda de la gacela; Aleluya; Ojitos de pena. *Hobby:* Photography. *Address:* Laura de Noves 460, Santiago, Chile.

LEMELIN Stéphane,b. 2 Apr 1960, Rimouski, Quebec, Canada. Pianist. *Education:* BM, 1982, MM, 1983, Peabody Conservatory, USA; Doctor of Musical Arts, Yale University, 1990. *Career:* Performed with Montreal Symphony Orchestra, Quebec Symphony Orchestra, Edmonton Symphony, Luxembourg Radio-Television Orchestra; Frequent CBC broadcasts; Recitals across Canada, in USA and in France; Piano Faculty, Yale University, USA, 1986-90; Piano Faculty, University of Alberta, Canada, 1990-. *Recordings:* Schubert Sonata in A, D 959, Schumann Waldszenen, Opus 82, Fantasiestücke, Opus 111, 1991. *Honours:* Prizewinner, Casadesus International Competition, 1983. *Current Management:* Marie Rakos Concert Management, Canada. *Address:* c/o Marie Rakos Concert Management, 14 Palsen Street, Nepean, Ontario, Canada K2G 2V8.

LENDVAY Kamillo, b. 28 Dec 1928, Budapest, Hungary. Composer; Professor and Head of Music Theory Department. m. 6 June 1972. 1 daughter. *Education:* Academy of Music Ferenc Liszt Budapest, 1959. *Career:* Musical leader, State Puppet Theatre, 1960-66; Musical director, Artistic Ensemble, Hungarian People's Army, 1966-68; Conductor and Artistic director, Operetta Theatre, Budapest; Musical Lector, Hungarian Radio, 1962-; Composer; Professor and Head of the Music Theory Department, Academy of Music Ferenc Liszt, Budapest, 1973-; President, Artisjus the Bureau for Protecting the Author's Rights. *Compositions include:* Oratorio: Orogenesis, 1969-70; Cantatas: Cart-Drive into the Night, 1970; Scenes from Thomas Mann's Joseph and His Brothers, 1978-81; Orchestral Works: Mauthausen-symphonic poem, 1958; Four Invocations, 1966; The Harmony of Silence, 1980; Chaconne for Orchestra, 1988; Concertos: Concertino, 1959; Violin concerto No 1, 1961-62; Pezzo concertato, 1975; Violin Concerto No 2, 1986; Concertino semplice, 1986; Work for Chamber Orchestra: Expressions for 11 strings, 1974. Chamber Music; Solo pieces; several works for wind orchestra and choir, music for films and stage; Stabat Mater. *Recordings:* Numerous. *Honours:* Erkel Musical Prize, 1962, 1964 and 1978; Title of Merited Artist, 1981; Bartók-Pasztory Prize, 1989; Grand Prix International du Disque Lyrique to the Opera: The Respectable Street-Walker, 1983; Trieste Comp, 1975. *Membership:* President of the Association of the Hungarian Composers. *Address:* 1137 Szt Istvan Park 23, Budapest, Hungary.

LENTZ Daniel Kirkland, b. 10 Mar 1942, Latrobe, Pennsylvania, USA. Composer. m. Marlene Helen Wasco, 24 Aug 1964, 1 daughter. *Education:* BS Music, St Vincent College, 1962; MFA, Ohio University, 1965; Brandeis University, 1965-67; Tanglewood, summer 1966; Musicology, Stockholm University, Sweden, 1967-68. *Career:* Founder/Director of ensembles: California Time Machine 1969-73, The San Andreas Fault 1974 and 1976, The Dan'l Lentz Ensemble 1978-80, Lentz 1983-85, Daniel Lentz and Group 1986-; 10 European tours; Major/premiere performances: Gaudeamus Foundation, 1972; New Music America

Festivals, 1983 and 1986; LA Olympic Arts Festival, 1984; Wild Turkeys, Carnegie Hall, 1986; The Crack in the Bell, LAPhil New Music Group, 1986. *Compositions include:* Canon and Fugle, 1971; Loverise, 1971; King Speech Song, 1972; Song(s) of the Sirens, 1973; Missa Umbrarum, 1973; O-Ke-Wa, 1974; Sun Tropes, 1975; Requiem Songs, 1976; Three Pretty Madrigals, 1976; Composition in Contrary and Parallel Motion, 1977; Elysian Nymph, 1978; Wolf is Dead, 1979, 1982); Uitoto, 1980; Music by Candlelight, 1980; Dancing on the Sun, 1980; Point Conception, 1981; Adieu, 1983; On the Leopard Altar, 1983; Lascaux, 1984; Is it Love, 1984; Bacchus, 1985; Topanga Tango, 1985; Time's Trick, 1985; Wild Turkeys, 1985; The Crack in the Bell, 1986. Several recorded. *Address:* Box 311, US Route 30, Latrobe, PA 15650, USA.

LEONARD Lawrence, b. 22 Aug 1928, London, England. Conductor. m. (1) Josephine Duffey, 1 son, 1 daughter, (2) Katharina Wolpe. (3) Rosemary Walker. *Education:* Royal Academy of Music, London. LRAM; L'Ecole Normale de Musique; Studied privately with Ansermet and Kleiber. *Career:* Assistant Conductor, BBC Northern Orchestra, 1 year; Assistant Conductor, Hallé Orchestra, 5 years; Music Director, Edmonton Symphony Orchestra, Canada, 5 years; World Wide Freelance Concerts. *Compositions:* 4 pieces for Orchestra; Group Questions for Orchestra; Symphonic Poem for Orchestra: Mezoon, (for the Sultan of Oman); Pictures From An Exhibition, (Moussorgsky-/Leonard); Various arrangements. *Recordings:* Francesca Da Rimini; Sleeping Beauty Suite; Complete Harpsichord Concerti (Bach); Telemann Flute Suite. *Publication:* Horn of Mortal Danger. *Honours:* FRAM; FGSM. *Memberships:* Composers' Guild (Chairman 1977). *Hobbies:* Chess. *Address:* Boxhurst, Old Reigate Road, Nr Dorking, Surrey RH4 1NT, England. 2, 3.

LEONARD Sarah Jane, b. 10 Apr 1953, Winchester, England. Singer; Soprano. m. Michael Parkinson, 5 Apr 1975, divorced, 1 son, 1 daughter. *Education:* Music Department, Winchester School of Art, 1969-71; GGSM Diploma, Guildhall School of Music and Drama, 1971-76. *Career:* Member, BBC Singers, 1976-81; Member, London Sinfonietta Voices; High Soprano; Broadcasts with BBC Singers, Endymion Ensemble and London Sinfonietta; Television appearances, Video Alice, Channel 4 TV and The Middle of the Road Hour, Channel 4 TV; Sang the Mad Boy in Goehr's Sonata about Jerusalem, Aldeburgh Festival, 1990; Sings with Michael Nyman Band; Guest appearances with Hilliard Ensemble; Sang at La Scala Milan, 1989 and 1992; International Soloist in 20th Century repertoire. *Recordings include:* Drusilla in L'Incoronazione di Poppea (Virgin Classics); Miserere by Arvo Pärt with Hilliard Ensemble; My Heart is Like a Singing Bird, English Song Co. *Honours:* Susan Longfield Award, Guildhall School of Music and Drama, 1976; Winner, Young Artists and 20th Century Music, Park Lane Group, 1984. *Membership:* Incorporated Society of Musicians. *Hobbies:* Theatre; Swimming; Knitting; Sewing. *Current Management:* Allied Artists. *Address:* 42 Montpelier Square, London SW7 1JZ, England.

LEONHARDT Gustav, b. 30 May 1928, Graveland, Holland. Harpsichordist; Organist; Conductor. *Education:* Schola Cantorum Basle 1947-50, with Eduard Muller. *Debut:* Vienna 1950, with Bach's The Art of Fugue on the harpsichord. *Career:* Professor of harpsichord at Vienna Academy of Music 1952-55; Teacher at Amsterdam Conservatory from 1954; Organist at Waalse Kerk, Amsterdam until 1981, since then organist at Nieuwe Kerk, Amsterdam; Founded Leonhardt Consort 1955; Played the organ and harpsichord and acted the part of JS Bach in 1967 film The Chronicle of Anna Magdalena Bach; Visiting Professor at Harvard University 1969-70; Work as conductor includes Monteverdi's L'Incoronazione di Poppea, Amsterdam 1972; Extensive tours of USA and Europe as harpsichordist, notably in the works of Bach, Frescobaldi, Sweelinck, Froberger and Louis Couperin. *Recordings:* ca.150 records for Telefunken, EMI, Philips, BMG, Virgin, including Bach's Goldberg Variations, as harpsichordist. *Publications:* Editions of The Art of Fugue 1952 and keyboard music by Sweelinck for the Dutch critical edition. *Honours:* Erasmus Prize 1980; Honorary Doctorates 1982, 1983, 1991.

LEPPARD Raymond John, b. 11 Aug 1927, London, England. Conductor; Harpsichordist; Composer. *Education:* Trinity College, Cambridge. *Career:* Fellow, Trinity College, University Lecturer in Music, 1958-68; Honorary Keeper of the Music, Fitzwilliam Museum, Cambridge, 1963. Conductor, Covent Garden, (debut 1959, Handel's Solomon), Sadler's Wells, Glyndebourne, (debut 1962, L'Incoronazione di Poppea); various overseas orchestras; Principal conductor, BBC Northern Symphony Orchestra, 1972-80; Principal guest conductor, St Louis Symphony Orchestra, USA, 1984-; Music Director Indianapolis Symphony Orchestra, 1987; London Proms 1993, with Tchaikovsky's Second Symphony and Ravel's Shéhérazade. *Publications:* Realisations of Monteverdi: Il Ballo delle Ingrate, 1958; L'Incoronazione di Poppea, 1962; L'Orfeo, 1965; Il Ritorno d'Ulisse, 1972. Realisations of Francesco Cavalli: Messa Concertata, 1966; L'Ormindo, 1967; La Calisto, 1969; Magnificat, 1970; L'Egisto, 1974; L'Orione, 1983. Realisation of Rameau's Dardanus, 1980. British Academy Italian Lecture, 1969 (Proceedings, Royal Musical Association); Raymond Leppard on Music, 1993. *Honours:* Commendatore al Merito della Republica Italiana, 1974; Commander, Order of British Empire (CBE), 1983. *Hobbies:* Music; Theatre; Books; Friends. *Address:* c/o Colbert Artists Management, 111 West 57th Street, New York, NY 10019, USA.

LERDAHL Fred, b. 10 Mar 1943, Madison, Wisconsin, USA. Composer and Music Theorist. m. 29 Nov 1980, 3 daughters. *Education:* BMus, Lawrence University, 1965; MFA, Princeton University, 1967. *Career:* Professor of Music: University of California at Berkeley, 1969-71, Harvard University, 1971-79, Columbia University, 1979-85, University of Michigan, 1985-; Residency at IRCAM, 1981; Residency at the American Academy in Rome, 1987; Works commissioned by the Fromm Music Foundation, the Koussevitzky Music Foundation, the Juilliard Quartet, the Pro Arte Quartet, the Spoleto Festival. *Compositions:* String Trio, 1966; Wake for soprano and chamber ensemble, 1968; Eros for mezzo-soprano and chamber ensemble, 1975; First String Quartet, 1978; Waltzes for chamber ensemble, 1981; Second String Quartet, 1982; Chords for orchestra, 1974-83; Beyond the Realm of Bird, for soprano and chamber orchestra, 1984; Fantasy Etudes, for chamber ensemble, 1985; Cross-Currents for orchestra, 1987; Waves for chamber orchestra, 1988. *Recordings:* Fantasy Etudes, CRI; First String Quartet, CRI; Second String Quartet, Laurel; Eros, CRI; String Trio, CRI. *Publication:* A Generative Theory of Tonal Music (co-author: Ray Jackendoff), 1983. *Current Management:* Musical Associates of America. *Address:* 1210 W. Liberty Street, Ann Arbor, MI 48103, USA.

LERESCU Emil, b. 26 Jan 1921, Pitesti, Rumania. Composer. *Education:* Studied at Bucharest Conservatory, 1941-48. *Career:* Teacher in Pitesti, 1948-52, Craiova, 1952-54, and Bucharest, 1954-81. *Compositions include:* Ecaterina Teodoroiu, heroic opera, Bucharest, 1971; Penes Curcanul, operatic ballad, Iasi, 1981; Carnival Stories, comic opera, Bucharest TV, 1982; Star without a Name, lyric opera, Bucharest TV, 1983; Symphonic music, chamber music and songs. *Address:* Union of Rumanian Composers, Bucharest, Rumania.

LERNER Mimi, b. 1854, Poland. Singer (Mezzo-soprano). *Education:* Studied at Queens College, New York and Carnegie-Mellon University. *Debut:* New York City Opera, as Sextus in La Clemenza di Tito, 1979. *Career:* Sang at various American opera houses, and at Glyndebourne, 1984, as Marcellina in Le Nozze di Figaro; La Scala, 1985, in Alcina, Théâtre Châtelet, Paris, 1986, as Isabella in L'Italiana in Algeri, Amsterdam, 1987, as Eboli in Don Carlos; Sang with New Orleans Opera Association, 1989-90, as Amneris and Adalgisa; Ruggiero in Alcina at Vancouver, 1990, Rosina at Pittsburgh and Despina at Toronto, 1991; Santa Fe Festival, 1991, as Carlotta in Die schweigsame Frau; Sang Marcellina in Figaro at Orchestra Hall, Chicago, 1992; Other roles include Smeton in Anna Bolena, Suzuki, Siebel and Cenerentola. *Recordings include:* Second Lady in video of Die Zauberflöte, from the Met. *Address:* c/o New Orleans Opera Association, 333 St Charles Avenue, Suite 907, New Orleans, LA 70130, USA.

LESSARD John Ayres, b. 3 July 1920, San Francisco, California, USA. Composer; Professor Emeritus. m. Sarah Fuller, 12 June 1973, 6 daughters. *Education:* Piano with Elise Belenky, Composition wth Henry Cowell, Ernst Levy, Nadia Boulanger; Diploma, Harmonie, Contrepoint, Fugue, Ecole Normale de Musique, Paris, 1938-39; Diploma, Composition, Longy School of Music, Cambridge, Massachusetts, 1940. *Compositions include:* Ariel, 1939; Sonata for Piano, 1940; Box Hill Overture (orchestra), 1946; Full Fathom Five, 1948; When as in Silk My Julia Goes, 1951; Octet for Wind Instruments, 1952; Sonata for Cello and Piano, 1956; Rose Cheek Laura, 1960; Sinfonietta Concertante (orchestra), 1961; Epithalamion, 1962; Concerto for Harp and Orchestra, 1963; 12 songs from Mother Goose, 1964; Trio in Sei Parti, 1967; Fragments from the Cantos of Ezra Pound for Baritone and 9 Instruments, 1969; Brass Quintet, 1971; Pastimes and an Alleluia (orchestra), 1974; Movements for Trumpet and Various Instruments I-VIII, 1976-84; Threads of Sound Recalled, 1980; Concert Duo for Viola and Guitar, 1981; Divertimento for Solo Guitar, 1981; Music for Guitar and Percussion, 1982; Stars, Hill, Valley, song, 1983; Duet for Piano and Percussion, 1984; Pond In A Bowl (soprano, percussion, piano), 1984; Four Pieces for Viola and Percussion, 1985; Album for Guitar, 1986; Bagatelles for Piano I, II, III, IV, 1986-91; Drift, Follow, Persist (solo horn, piano, percussion), 1988; An Assembled Sequence for a Solo Percussionist, 1989; The Seasons (soprano, 2 percussionists), piano, 1992. *Current Management:* American Composers Alliance. *Address:* 15 Scotts Cove Lane, East Setauket, NY 11733, USA.

LESSER Laurence, b. 28 Oct 1938, Los Angeles, California, USA. Cellist. m. Masuko Ushioda, 23 Dec 1971, 1 son, 1 daughter. *Education:* BA, Harvard University, 1961; Fulbright Scholar, Cologne, West Germany, studies with Gaspar Cassadò; Studied with Gregor Piatigorsky, Los Angeles. *Career:* Concert performances in USA, Europe, Japan and South America; Appearances with Boston Symphony, Los Angeles Philharmonic, London Philharmonic and other major orchestras; Assistant to Piatigorsky, University of Southern California, Los Angeles; Teacher, Peabody Institute, Baltimore, Maryland; Visiting Professor, Toho School of Music, Tokyo; Teacher, appointed President, 1983, New England Conservatory, Boston, Massachusetts. *Recordings:* Schoenberg/Monn Concerto; Lazarof Concerto; Chamber Music in Heifetz-Piatigorsky Series. *Honours:* Cassadò Prize, Siena, Italy, 1962; 4th Prize, Tchaikovsky Competition, Moscow, USSR, 1966. *Memberships:* Overseer, Boston Symphony Orchestra; Trustee, WGBH Educational Foundation, Boston; Advisory Council, Chamber Music America; Phi Beta Kappa. *Address:* New England Conservatory, 290 Huntington Avenue, Boston, MA 02115, USA.

LESSING Kolja, b. 15 Oct 1961, Karlsruhe, Germany. Violinist; Pianist; Composer. *Education:* Violin lessons 1964-, piano 1966-, with mother; Violin studies, Hansheinz Schneeberger master classes (Diploma with distinction, 1982), Basel, Switzerland, 1978-; Piano studies, Peter Efler (Diploma, 1983), Basel, 1979-83. *Debut:* Violin recital, Ettlingen Castle, 1981; Piano, Lausanne, 1982. *Career:* Concerts throughout Europe; Solo violin recitals; Chamber music concerts; Orchestral concerts with: Dresdner Philharmonic, Nationaltheaterorchester Mannheim, Radio-Sinfonieorchester Basel and others; Several premieres;

Numerous recitals, violin solo & piano solo with thematic programmes. Founder member (with Rainer Klaas & Bernhard Schwarz), Trio Alkan, 1988-; Professor, Musikhochschule Wurzburg, 1989-. *Compositions:* Mostly recorded, German & Swiss radio stations, Various works for solo violin, solo clarinet, 2 clarinets & violin, 1978-. *Recordings include:* Works by Franz Berwald, Walther Geiser, Karl Michael Komma, Isang Yun; Numerous radio recordings (some 1st), extensive repertoire, Germany, Switzerland, Sweden; Playback recording, Fauré's 2nd sonata, violin & piano, NDR Hannover, 1989.

LESTER Richard, b. 1959, England. Cellist. *Education:* Studies at the Royal College of Music with Ameryllis Fleming. *Career:* Member of Domus from 1979; performances in a portable white geodesic dome on informal locations in Europe and Australia; public workshops, discussion groups and open rehearsals in a wide repertoire; Frequent performances in London at the Wigmore Hall and on the South Bank, thoughout the UK and on Radio 3; Festival engagements at Bath, Cheltenham, Salisbury, Sheffield and the City of London; Tours of South America, Canada, Spain, Italy, Germany, Ireland and Norway; 1991 tours of The Netherlands and New Zealand; Solo concerts and recitals throughout Britain and tours of Europe, Japan and the Middle East; Concerto performances with the Chamber Orchestra of Europe at Carnegie Hall and in Berlin and Vienna; Salzburg Camerata Academica in Austria, Germany and Italy under Sandor Vegh. *Recordings include:* Piano Quartets by Fauré, Dvořák, Brahms, Mozart and Mendelssohn; Schubert's Trout Quintet and Adagio and Rondo Concertante (with pianist Chi- chi Nwanoku); Works by Martinů, Suk, Kodály and Dohnányi (Hyperion and Virgin Classics), Complete cello repertoire of Mendelssohn. *Honours includes:* Deutsche Schallplattenpreis 1986 and Gramophone Magazine award for Best Chamber Music Record of 1986, for Fauré Piano Quartets; Prizewinner at International Scheveninges Cello Competition, 1987. *Address:* Unit 2, Tadema Road, London SW10 0PY, England.

LESURE François, b. 23 May 1923, Paris, France. Musicologist. m. Anik Devriès, 26 Jan 1987. *Education:* Archiviste-paléographe, Ecole des Chartes; Licencié-es-lettres, Sorbonne; Conservatoire de Paris. *Career:* Directeur du Départment de la musique a la Bibliothèque nationale, 1950-88; Directeur d'études a l'Ecole des Hautes Etudes (depuis 1970); Professeur a l'Université de Bruxelles, 1965-77; Chargé du Musée de la musique de La Villette, 1989-91. *Publications:* Music and art in society, 1968; Musique et musiciens francais du XVIe siècle, 1977; Catalogue de l'oeuvre de C Debussy, 1977; Editeur des Chansons polyphoniques de C Janequin (6 vol) et Rédacteur en chef des Oeuvres complètes de C Debussy (5 vol published since 1986); C Debussy avant Pelléas, 1992. *Contributions:* Number of articles in Revue de musicologie; Cahiers Debussy; Fontes artis musicae; Annales musicologiques. *Honour:* Légion d'honneur, Arts et Lettres, Mérite. *Memberships:* American Academy of Arts and Sciences; Académie royale de Belgique; Président de la Société francaise de musicologie, 1988-91. *Address:* 66 rue d'Assas, 75006 Paris, France.

LETELIER-LLONA Alfonso, b. 4 Oct 1912, Santiago, Chile. Composer; Agricultural Engineer; Professor Emeritus. m. Margarita Valdes Subercaseaux, 16 Oct 1937, 3 sons, 1 daughter. *Education:* Agricultural Engineer, Catholic University of Santiago, 1935; Studied Composition, National Conservatory, University of Chile. *Debut:* Petite Suite for Chamber Orchestra, Union Club, 1925. *Career:* Faculty of Arts, Universidad de Chile, 1937-83; Founder Member, Escuela Moderna de Musica, 1940; Dean, Faculty of Arts, 1952-63, Professor Emeritus, 1973, Secretary, Faculty of Music, 1975-77, Universidad de Chile; Director, Revista Musical Chilena, 1957; Dean of Music Department, Ministry of Education, 1973; Dean, Faculty of Arts, Universidad Metropolitana, 1986. *Compositions:* Over 50 choral, chamber, symphonic and solo (piano) works including prizewinning music: Soneto de la Muerte No 3 Malas

Manos, dramatic poem for female voice and orchestra; Variaciones en Fa for piano; Sonata for viola and piano or clarinet and piano. *Recordings:* El honore ante la Ciencia, symphony, 1988; Los vitraces de la Anunciacion for orchestra and chorus, 1988; Canciones Antiguas for voice and piano, 1988; Cassette of SVR Production, Santiago, 1988. *Contributor to:* Revista Musical Chilena; Finisterre; Estudio; Academia; El Mercurio daily. *Honours:* Concourse IV, Santiago-Chile Foundation Centenary, 1942; 1st Prize and 2nd Prize, 1st Music Festival of Chile, 1948; National Prize of Arts in Music, 1968. *Memberships:* Past President, National Association of Composers of Chile; President, Chilean-German Institute of Culture; Academy of Arts, Chilean Institute; Honorary Member; Council of Directors, Universidad de Chile. *Hobby:* Entomomology. *Address:* Benjamin 2929, Las Condes, Santiago, Chile.

LETHIEC Michel, b. 11 Dec 1946, Poitiers, France. Clarinettist. *Education:* Studied in Bordeaux and at the Paris Conservatory. *Career:* Concerto engagements with the Monte Carlo Philharmonic, Radio France Philharmonic, Ensemble Orchestral de Paris and the Lausanne Chamber Orchestra; British appearances with the English Chamber Orchestra, Academy of St Martin in the Fields and the Scottish Ensemble; Recitals and chamber concerts with Leonard Rose, Aurèle Nicolet, Karl Engel, Joseph Suk, Elly Ameling, Philippe Entremont, and the Talich, Vermeer, Takacs and Sibelius Quartets; Has premiered works by Ballif, Boucourechliev, Marco, Corigliano and Scolari; Festival engagements include Edinburgh and the Eastern Music Festival, USA; Concert repertoire includes music by Copland, Crusell, Hindemith, Krommer, Mercadante, Mozart, Pleyel, Spohr, Stamitz and Weber; Boulez Domaines and Busoni Concertino; Double Concertos by Bruch (with viola), Strauss (bassoon), Danzi (flute) and Devienne (clarinet); With string quartets, plays works by Mozart, Brahms, Weber, Reger, Reicha, Hindemith, Birtwistle, Yun and Bloch; Artistic Director of the Pau Casals Festival in Prades. *Honours include:* Interpretation Prize at the International Competition in Belgrade; Grand Prix du Disque 1978 for Asceses by Jolivet. *Address:* Les Templiers, 06790 Aspremont, France.

LETTVIN Theodore, b. 29 Oct 1926, Chicago Illinois, USA. Concert Pianist. m. Joan Rorimer, 2 sons, 1 daughter. *Education:* MusB, Curtis Institute of Music. *Debut:* Ravinia Festival, 1951. *Career:* 1st appearance as concert pianist, 1931; Appeared with Chicago Symphony Orchestra, 1938; Solo, orchestral engagements: Gallery Art, Washington, Philadelphia, Pops Orchestra, Saratoga Springs, Tanglewood, Grant Park Symphony, Florida orchestras, others, 1938-64; Radio appearance, Bell Telephone Hour, 1948; Apprentice to conductor William Steinberg, Buffalo Symphony Orcherstra, 1951; Concert Artist, national Music League, Europe and North Africa, other concerts, France, Corsica, Tunisia, Algeria, Switzerland, Belgium, Germany, 1952; Assistant Artist, Marlboro Music Festival, 1963; New York Philharmonic Promenade concerts, 1970, 1972; American pianist Olympics, 1972; Performed, Salzburg Festival, 1974, also Chautauqua and Ravinia Festivals; Appeared with New York, Cleveland, Minneapolis, Boston, Atlanta, Pittsburgh, Cincinnati orchestras; Town Hall Concerts, New York City; Artist-in-residence, University of Colorado, 1956; Head, Piano Department, Cleveland Music School Settlement, 1958-68; Professor of Music, New England Conservatory of Music, Boston, 1968; Professor of Piano, University of Michigan, Ann Arbor, 1977-87; Director of Doctoral Programe in Performance, The Music Department, Rutgers, The State University of New Jersey. *Address:* 12 Bernard Road, E. Brunswick NJ 08816 USA.

LEUBA (Julian) Christopher, b. 28 Sept 1929, Pittsburgh, Pennsylvania, USA. Professor of Music; Conductor; French Horn Player. *Education:* BMus, Roosevelt University, Chicago, 1951; Carnegie Institute of Technology; Private Study, Conducting, Pierre Monteux, Dr Richard Lert. *Career:* Principal Horn,

Chicago Symphony, Minneapolis Symphony, Philharmonia Hungarica; Chamber Music Performances; Appearances as Conductor; Consultant, Mirafone Corporation and Productiv Genossenschaft Waldkraiburg; Adjunct Professor, Principal Hornist, Portland (Oregon) Opera, 1984-; Oregon Music Theatre, 1990-. *Recordings include:* Horn Omnibus; Mozart, Beethoven. *Publications:* Editor, Musical Publications. *Contributions to:* Professional journals. *Memberships:* Historical Brass Society; AAUP. *Hobbies:* Hiking; Cycling; Linguistics. *Address:* 4800 NE 70th Street, Seattle, WA 98115, USA.

LEUCHTMANN Horst, b. 26 Apr 1927, Brunswick, Germany. Musicologist. m. Brita-Angela von Wentzel, 28 Nov 1952, 1 son, 2 daughters. *Education:* PhD, State Music School, Brunswick, University of Munich, 1957; Honorary Professor, Musikhochschule Munich, 1986. *Career:* Editor, Musikhistorische Kommission, Bayerische Akademie der Wissenschaften; Lecturer, University of Munich and Musikhochschule Munich; ordentliches Mitglied der Bayerischen Akademie der Schönen Künste, 1989. *Publications:* Editor, Complete Works of Orlando di Lasso; Editor, Musik in Bayern; Books, Editions, Dictionaries, Translations. *Honours:* Award, Bayerische Club, Munich, 1979. *Membership:* Der Bayerische Club. *Address:* Markgrafenstrasse 50, D-81827 München 82, Germany.

LEUZINGER Rudolf, b. 2 Mar 1911, Zurich, Switzerland. Musician. m. Helen Schlatter, 16 Nov 1936, 1 son, 2 daughters. *Education:* Private studies as bassoon-player. *Debut:* Solo Bassoon-Player, Orchestra Radio Svizzera Italiana, 1934. *Career:* Principal Bassoon-Player in symphony orchestras in Lugano, Rio de Janerio and Zurich, 1934-1976; General Secretary International Federation of Musicians, 1948-1982; Founder Lucerne Festival Orchestra; Artistic Management of International Music Festival Lucerne, 1943-53; Member, Jury of International Music Competitions in Geneva, Prague and Markneukirchen (GDR); Activities as bassoon soloist and member of Zurich Woodwind Quintet. *Recordings:* For broadcasting programmes in Switzerland, France, Great Britain, Germany, Netherlands, Nordic Countries. *Contributions to:* Magazines, concert programmes, trade-union journals. *Address:* Etzelstrasse 6, 8634 Hombrechtikon, Switzerland.

LEVARIE Siegmund, b. 24 July 1914, Austria. Musician; Educator; Author; Conductor. m. Norma Levarie, 26 Mar 1945, 1 daughter. *Education:* Conductor's Diploma, New Vienna Conservatory, 1935; PhD, University of Vienna, 1938. *Career:* Faculty, Founder of Collegium Musicum, Conductor, Director of Concerts, University of Chicago, USA, 1938-52; Dean, Chicago Music College, 1952-54; Executive Director, Fromm Music Foundation, 1952-56; Chairman, Music Department, 1954-62, Professor of Music, 1954-84, Brooklyn College; Professor of Music, Graduate School, City University of New York, 1963-; Visiting Professor: University of Pisa, Italy, 1984, 1991; Scuola Normale Superiore, Pisa, 1990, 1991. *Publications:* Mozart's Le nozze di Figaro, 1952, reprint, 1977; Fundamentals of Harmony, 1954, reprint, 1962, 1984; Guillaume de Machaut, 1954, reprint, 1970; Musical Italy Revisited, 1963, reprint, 1973; Tone, 1968, 2nd edition, 1980, reprint, 1981; Musical Morphology (with Ernst Levy), 1983; Editor: Lucy Van-Jung Page, 1977; A Theory of Harmony, Ernst Levy, 1985. *Contributions to:* About 80 articles and reviews, also translations. *Membership:* American Musicological Society, National Council for 6 years. *Address:* 624 Third Street, Brooklyn, NY 11215, USA.

LEVI Yoel, b. 16 Aug 1950, Sotmar, Rumania (Israeli)(Naturalized USA citizen 1987). Conductor. m. Jacqueline Levi. 3 sons. *Education:* MA, violin and percussion, University of Tel Aviv, 1975; Graduate degree, Jerusalem Academy of Music, 1976; Diploma, Guildhall School of Music and Drama, London, 1978; Studied with Mendi Rodan, Franco Ferrara, Siena and Kirill Kondrashin, Hilversum; Accademia di Santa Cecilia, Rome. *Career:* Percussionist, Israel Philharmonic Orchestra, 1975; Conducting Assistant, 1978-80, Resident Conductor, 1980-84, Cleveland Orchestra; Music Director and Conductor, Atlanta Symphony Orchestra, 1988-; Guest Conductor with major North American and European orchestras. *Recordings:* For Angel-EMI; Schwann; Telearc. *Honour:* First prize, Conductors' International Competition, Besançon, 1978. *Address:* c/o Atlanta Symphony Orchestra, 1280 Peachtree Street NE, Atlanta, GA 30309, USA.

LEVI MINZI Carlo, b. 10 Dec 1954, Milan, Italy. Pianist. *Education:* Giuseppe Verdi Conservatory, Milan; Piano Diploma, 1974; Tchaikovsky Conservatory, Moscow, Piano Certificate, 1975; Piano Certificate, Curtis Institute of Music, Philadelphia, USA, 1978. *Career:* Recitals and Appearances with Orchestras, Europe and USA, 1972-; TV and Radio Appearances, National Channels in Italy, Switzerland, France, Spain, Austria, West Germany, Poland, Bulgaria, USA, Mexico. *Compositions:* Completion of Schubert's F Sharp Minor Sonata, 1983, with Quirino Principe; First Performance, Town Hall, New York, 1984, First Radio Recording, WDR, Koln, 1985. *Recordings:* On Rusty Records, City Records, RDS. *Contributions to:* Various journals. *Membership:* Classical Frontiers, New York, USA, Vice President. *Address:* Via Copernico 1, 20094 Corsico (MI), Italy.

LEVIN Robert D, b. 13 Oct 1947, Brooklyn, New York, USA. Pianist; Musicologist; Theorist. m. Christine Noël Whittlesey, 18 May 1974, div 1991. *Education:* AB, magna cum laude with highest honours, Music, Harvard University, 1968; Private studies with Nadia Boulanger, 1960-64; Conducting with Hans Swarowsky, 1966. *Career:* Solo and Chamber appearances throughout Europe, USA and Japan, 1970-; Pianist, New York Philomusica, 1971-. *Compositions:* Mozart Completions: Requiem in d, Concerto for piano, violin, orchestra in D (also published); Quintet for Clarinet and strings in B-flat; Symphonie concertante for flute, oboe, horn, bassoon and orchestra in E Flat; Larghetto and Allegro in E Flat for 2 pianos Oboe concerto in F (the 4 latter works recorded); Horn Concertos in Eb & in D; Sonata Movement in G. *Recordings:* Mozart: Sonatas for piano, 4 hands with Malcolm Bilson, Music for 2 pianos, with Malcolm Bilson; Hindemith, Complete viola/piano sonatas with Kim Kashkashian; Mozart, concertos for 2 & 3 Fortepianos (with Malcolm Bilson & Melvyn Tan) and many others; Haydn Trios with Anner Bylsma. *Publications:* Who Wrote the Mozart Four Wind Concertante?, 1988; Sightsinging & Ear Training Through Literature, co-authored with Louis Martin, 1988; Other texts in harmony and counterpoint published privately. *Contributions to:* Mozart-Jahrbuch; High Fidelity; Musical Newsletter, various musicological congress reports; Performance Practice, The New Grove; The Mozart Compendium. *Honours:* Copley Foundation Grant in Composition, 1961; Lili Boulanger Fund Prize, 1966, 71. *Memberships:* Internationale Stiftung Mozarteum; Neue Bachgesellschaft; GEMA. *Hobbies:* Trams and Electric Traction; Hiking. *Current Management:* ARTRA, Chicago, USA. *Address:* Music Dept, Harvard Univ Cambridge, MA 02138, USA.

LEVIN Walter, b. 6 Dec 1924, Berlin, Germany. Violinist; College Professor. *Education:* Studied at the Juilliard School with Ivan Galamian. *Career:* Co-founded the La Salle String Quartet at the Juilliard School, 1949; Many concerts featuring modern composers and the quartets of Beethoven; European debut, 1954; Composers who have written for the ensemble include Hans Erich Apostel, Earle Brown, Henri Pousseur, Mauricio Kagel, György Ligeti, Penderecki and Witold Lutoslawski; Quartet-in-residence at Collorado College, 1949-53, then at the Cincinnati College - Conservatory of Music (also Professor there); Quartet disbanded, 1988. *Recordings Include:* Works by Berg, Schoenberg, Webern and Zemlinsky; Beethoven's Late Quartets.

LEVINE Gilbert, b. 22 Jan 1948, New York City, USA. Conductor. *Education:* Reed College, 1965-67; Juilliard

School of Music, 1967-68; Studied music history with Arthur Mendel and Louis Lockwood; Conducting with Jacques-Louis Monod; Music theory with Milton Babbitt and J K Randall; AB, Princeton University, 1971; MA, music theory, Yale University, 1972; Conducting with Franco Ferrara, Siena. *Debut:* Nouvel Orchestre Philharmonique de Radio France, Paris, 1973. *Career:* Guest conductor with various major North American and European Orchestras including: North German Radio Symphony Orchestra, Hamburg, 1977; Royal Philharmonic Orchestra, London, 1978; (West) Berlin Radio Symnphony Orchlestra, 1980; Minnesota Orchestra, 1984; Toronto Symphony; New York Philharmonic Orchestra; Dresden State Orchestra; San Francisco Symphony; Philadelphia Orchestra, 1986; Music Director, Karkow Philharmonic Orchestra, 1987-. *Address:* 925 West End Avenue, New York, NY 10025, USA.

LEVINE James, b. 23 June 1943, Cincinnati, Ohio, USA. Conductor; Pianist. *Education:* Piano with Rosina Lhevinne and Rudolf Serkin; conducting with Jean Morel, Fausto Cleva, Max Rudolf; style and interpretation with Walter Levin; vocal repertoire with Jennie Tourel, Pierre Bernac, Hans Hotter, Martial Singher, Mack Harrell; student Juilliard School of Music 1961- 64. *Career:* Piano debut 1953 with Cincinnati Symphony; Conducting debut 1961 at Aspen Festival; Cleveland Orchestra: Assistant Conductor to George Szell 1964-70; Metropolitan Opera: Principal Conductor 1974-, Music Director 1976-, Artistic Director 1986-; Ravinia Festival (summer home of Chicago Symphony Orchestra): Music Director 1973-1993; Cincinnati May Festival: Music Director 1973-77; frequent guest both as conductor and pianist throughout US and Europe including: Vienna Philharmonic, Berlin Philharmonic; conducted Metropolitan Opera premieres of Verdi's I Vespri Siciliani, Weill's The Rise and Fall of the City of Mahagonny, Stravinsky's Oedipus Rex, Berg's Lulu, Mozart's Idomeneo and La Clemenza di Tito, Gershwin's Porgy and Bess, Schoenberg's Erwartung; inaugurated the, "Live from the Met", TV series for PBS; conducted the first complete cycles of Wagner's Ring at the Met in 50 years (Spring 1989); Salzburg Festival premiere of Schoenberg's Moses und Aron (1987); Centennial production of Parsifal at the Bayreuth Festival (1982-88); World Premiere of The Ghosts of Versailles (Corigliano), 1991. *Recordings:* Giovanna d'Arco, Otello, Aida, Don Carlo, Luisa Miller, Il Trovatore (Verdi), I Vespri Siciliani (Verdi); Il Barbiere di Siviglia; Parsifal and Ring der Nibelungen (Wagner); La Bohème, Tosca and Manon Lescaut; Die Zauberflöte, Così Fan Tutte, Le Nozze de Figaro (Mozart); Ariadne auf Naxos (Strauss), Eugene Onegin (Tchaikovsky), Erwartung (Schoenberg); Complete Beethoven Piano Concerti (Brendel); Symphonies by Mozart and Mahler with leading orchestras; Recital albums with Christa Ludwig, Kathleen Battle, Jessye Norman, Lynn Harrell; Film soundtracks: La Traviata (Zeffirelli), La Clemenza di Tito (Ponnelle); Domingo in Siviglia (Ponnelle); Mozart and Beethoven Quintets (Ponnelle). *Honours:* Hon. Dr., University of Cincinnati; First recipient of the Cultural Award of the City of New York; Musical America's Musician of the Year Award; Nine-Time Grammy Award winner; Hon Dr. New England Conservatory, 1992, Northwestern University, 1992. *Address:* c/o Ronald Wilford, Columbia Artists Management, Inc., 165 West 57th Street, New York, NY 10019 USA.

LEVINE Joseph Samuel, b. 14 Aug 1912, Philadelphia, Pennsylvania, USA. Symphony Conductor; Concert Pianist. m. Mary Elizabeth Thomas, 16 Feb 1945, 2 sons. *Education:* BMus, Conducting, Piano, The Curtis Institute of Music, Philadelphia; Faculty, The Curtis Institute of Music, 1933-40; Duchesne College, Omaha, 1958-59; Cornish Institute, Seattle, 1969-73, 1976-79. *Debut:* As Piano Soloist with Philadelphia Orchestra, Robin Hood Dell, playing Tchaikovsky Concerto, 1932; As Conductor with New Center of Music Orchestra, Town Hall, Philadelphia, 1940. *Career includes:* Pianist, Philadelphia Orchestra, 1940-43, 1946-50; Founder and Conductor, New Center of Music Orchestra, Philadelphia, 1940-43; Conductor, Philadelphia Chamber Opera, 1946-50; Music Director,

American Ballet Theater, New York City, 1950-58; Foreign tours for US State Department's Exchange Programme, 1950-58; Music Director, Omaha Symphony, Nebraska, 1958-59; American Conductor, England's Royal Ballet, 1963, 1965; Associate Conductor: Seattle Symphony, 1969-73; Honolulu Symphony, 1973-76; Music Director, Bremerton Symphony, Washington, 1978-91; Founder and Music Director, Bainbridge Island Chamber Music Festival, 1984. *Recordings:* 2 as Pianist; 10 as Conductor with Ballet Theater Orchestra. *Contributions to:* Saturday Evening Post; Musical America; High Fidelity. *Honours:* Citations, 1960, 1961, 1962; Key to City of Omaha, 1961; Mercian Medal, College of St Mary, Omaha, 1967. *Memberships:* Numerous professional societies. *Hobby:* Gardening. *Address:* 2917 West Eaton Street, Seattle, WA 98199, USA.

LEVINE Rhoda J, b. 1930, New York City, USA. Opera Director; Choreographer; Teacher; Writer. *Education:* BA, Bard College; Credit towards MA degree, Sarah Lawrence College. *Career:* Director: Netherlands Opera; New York City Opera; Belgian National Opera; San Francisco Opera; Houston Opera; Scottish Opera; Dallas Opera; Festivals: Spoleto, Edinburgh, Cabrillo, Wolftrap, Jerusalem; TV; CBS-TV; NET-TV; NBC-TV; Broadway and Off-Broadway; Teaching Posts: Juilliard School, Curtis Institute of Music; Aaron Copland School at Queens College, Yale School of Drama, Netherlands Opera Studio, Brussels Opera Studio, Music School of the West. *Publications:* Librettos, Opus Number ZOO, Luciano Berio. *Honour:* Fulbright Award: National Institute of Music Theater Award for Contribution to American Music Theater, 1987. *Current Management:* Robert Lantz. *Memberships:* Society Stage Directors and Choreographers; American Guild of Musical Artists; Actors Equity; American Federation of Television Artists. *Address:* c/o Robert Lantz, 888 7th Avenue, New York, NY 10106, USA.

LEVY Edward (Irving), b. 2 May 1929, Brooklyn, New York, USA. Composer. *Education:* BA City College New York, 1957; Princeton University with Milton Babbitt; Columbia University Teachers College, EdD 1967; Further study with Ralf Shapey and Stefan Wolpe. *Career:* Teacher at C W Post College, Long Island University, 1961-67; Professor of Music, Yeshiva University, 1967. *Compositions include:* Duo for violin and cello, 1950; 2 Songs for mezzo and piano, 1951; Clarinet Sonata, 1956; String Trio, 1959; Trio for clarinet, violin and piano, 1961; Images for soprano and piano, 1961; Quintet for flute and ensemble, 1967; Variations on a theme by Brahms for flute, clarinet and horn, 1979; Concatentions for 2 flutes, clarinet and cello, 1980; Movement for brass quintet, 1980; Works for chorus and for chamber orchestra. *Address:* c/o ASCAP, ASCAP Building, One Lincoln Plaza, New York, NY 10023, USA.

LEVY Gerardo, b. 1919, Berlin, Germany. Flautist; Conductor; Teacher. *Education:* Graduate, Collegium Musicum, Buenos Aires, Argentina; BMus magna cum laude, Boston University, Massachusetts, USA. *Debut:* Buenos Aires, Argentina, 1942. *Career:* Soloist, various chamber ensembles, USA, Europe, South America; Principal Flautist, Orquesta Filarmonica, Radio Nacional Orquesta Sinfonica, Amigos de la Musica; Director of Woodwind Studies, New York University; Principal Flautist, White Plains Symphony Orchestra and Clarion Orchestra; Co-Principal Flautist, New York City Opera; Faculty, Sessione Senese per La Musica e l'Arte in Siena, Italy; Florence, Italy; Director and Conductor, Caecilian Chamber Ensemble of New York; Soloist, various chamber ensembles, USA, Europe, South America. *Recordings:* Cri Vox; Vanguard. *Memberships:* Board of Directors, New York Flute Club; National Flute Association. *Hobby:* Philately. *Address:* 123 West 93 Street, Apt. 8F, NY 10025, USA.

LEVY Marvin David, b. 2 Aug 1932, Passaic, New Jersey, USA. Composer. *Education:* BA, New York University, 1954; MA, Columbia University, 1956. *Career includes:* Archivist, American Opera Society,

1952-58; Music Critic, number of leading publications including: Opera News, Musical America, American Record Guide, New York Herald Tribune; Composer. *Compositions include:* (Opera) Mourning Becomes Electra, 1967; Sobata Komachi, 1957; The Tower, 1956; Escorial, 1958; (Vocal): Echoes, 1956; For the Time Being, 1959, One Person, 1962; Sacred Service for the Sabbath Eve: Shir Shel Moshe, 1964; Masada, 1973; In Memoriam W.H. Auden, 1984; (Orchestra): Pascua Florida, 1988; Caramoor Festival Overture, 1958; Symphony, 1960; Kyros, 1961; Piano Concerto, 1970; Trialogus, 1972; Canto De Los Maranos, 1977; (Instrumental) String Quartet, 1955; Rhapsody, 1956; Chassidic Suite, 1956; Arrows of Time, 1988. *Honours:* 2 Prix de Rome Scholarships, 1962, 1965; 2 Guggenheim Fellowships, 1960, 1964; Grants include: Ford Foundation, 1965, Damrosch, 1961, National Endowment for the Arts, 1974, 1978; Recipient, Scroll, City of New York. *Memberships:* ASCAP. *Current Management:* Sheldon Soffer Management. *Address:* c/o Sheldon Soffer Management, 130 W 56, New York City, NY 10019, USA.

LEWANDOWSKI Lynne, b. 14 May 1953, Pennsylvania, USA. Maker of early harps, psalteries & lyres (Luthier). *Education:* BA, Sarah Lawrence College, 1975; Coursework, Mannes College of Music, New York, & School of Visual Arts, 1976-79; Baroque Performance Institute, Oberlin Conservatory of Music, 1976, 1977; Studied with Nora Post, baroque oboe. *Career:* Owner, Lewandowski Workshop, researchers & designers, harps & psalteries from 12th to 18th centuries, specialists in re-creation of Gothic harps painted by Bosch & Memling, 15th century, 1975-; Independent record producer, director, Lady Reason Records, 1984-. *Honours:* Exhibition, The Harmonious Craft, American Musical Instruments, sponsored by Renwick Gallery/Smithsonian Institute, 1978; Grant, National Endowment for the Arts/Windham City Arts Council, 1980. *Memberships:* Board of directors, Womens Crisis Centre, Brattleboro; National Organisation of Women; American Craft Council. *Address:* 67 Main Street, Brattleboro, VT 05301, USA.

LEWIN David (Benjamin), b. 2 July 1933, New York, USA. Composer; Theorist. Studied with Edouard Steuerman 1945-50; Princeton University, MFA 1958, with Milton Babbitt, Roger Sessions and Earl Kim. *Career:* Junior fellowship at Harvard, 1958-61; Computer music at the Bell laboratories, Murray Hill, New Jersey; Teacher at the University of California at Berkeley, 1961-67, Stony Brook, New York, 1967-80, Yale University, 1979-85; Professor at Harvard University, 1985. *Contributions to:* Journal of Music Theory; Perspectives of New Music. *Publications include:* Studies of Parsifal, Moses und Aron and Rameau's Traité de l'harmonie. *Compositions:* Viola Sonata 1958; Essay on a subject by Webern for chamber orchestra 1958; Classical Variations on a theme by Schoenberg for cello and piano, 1960; Fantasia for organ, 1962; Fantasy-adagio for violin and orchestra, 1963-66; Quarter Piece for string quartet, 1969; Woodwind Trio, 1969; Computer Music, 1971; Fanfare, 1980; For Piano, 1982; Generalized Musical Intervals and Transformations (New Haven and London, Yale University Press, 1987). *Address:* Harvard University, Music Building, Harvard, Cambridge, MA 02138, USA.

LEWIN Michael, b. 1 Dec 1948, Epsom, Surrey, England. Professor of Guitar. m. Marylyn Troth, 31 July 1982, 1 son, 2 daughters. *Education:* Royal Academy of Music, London, 1967-71; LRAM (Performer); DipRAM. *Career:* Head of Guitar, Royal Academy of Music; Performances on guitar/lute for Royal Shakespeare Company, Ballet Rambert, English Music Theatre, English National Opera, Scottish Opera, Royal Opera House (Covent Garden), also with Praetorius Consort of London, Monteverdi Orchestra, English Baroque Soloists, English Chamber Orchestra and Orchestra of La Piccola Scala, Milan; Broadcasts for BBC, Thames TV, Yugoslav, Belgian, French and West Germany radio and European Broadcasting Union. *Recordings:* On Pye Virtuoso, Erato and D.G. Archiv

labels. *Publication:* Editor, Trinity College Guitar Grade Syllabus and Albums 1986-9, published 1985 and 1990-93, published 1989. *Address:* c/o Royal Academy of Music, Marylebone Road, London, NW1 5HT, England.

LEWIN-RICHTER Andres, b. 22 Mar 1937, Miranda, Spain. Composer. m. Cristina Vidal-Quadras, 1 son, 1 daughter. *Education:* Dr of Industrial Engineering, Barcelona University; MSEE, Columbia University, New York City, USA. *Career:* Executive Director, Conjunt Catala de Musica Contemporania Barcelona and Phonos Electronic Music Laboratory, Barcelona. *Compositions include:* Study No 1; Study No 2; Densities; Sequenza No 1 for percussion and tape; Sequenza per Anna for voice and tape; Film and stage music; Tinell, 5 percussion and tape. *Contributions to:* Spanish musical and musicological publications. *Memberships:* Acoustical Society of America; Vice-President, Catalan Composers Association. *Address:* Reina Cristina 1, 08003 Barcelona, Spain.

LEWIS Brenda, b. 2 Mar 1921, Harrisburg, Pennsylvania, USA. Singer (Soprano). *Education:* Studied in Philadelphia. *Career:* Sang in The Bartered Bride with the Philadelphia Opera Company; New York City Opera 1943-67, debut as Santuzza in Cavalleria Rusticana; San Francisco 1950, as Salome; Metropolitan Opera from 1952, as Musetta in La Bohéme, Marina in Boris Godunov, Barber's Vanessa and Rosalinde in Die Fledermaus; Chicago 1965, as Marie in Wozzeck; Guest appearances in South America. *Address:* c/o New York City Opera, Lincoln Center, New York, NY 10023, USA.

LEWIS Cary, b. 23 Nov 1942, Uvalde, Texas, USA. Pianist; Associate Professor of Music. m. Dorothy, 28 Dec 1967, 1 son. *Education:* BM, 1964, MM, 1965, University of North Texas; DMA, 1972, Performer's Certificate, Eastman School of Music; The Academy of Music in Vienna. *Career:* Nebraska Wesleyan University, 1971-76; Georgia State University, 1976-; Interlochen Center for the Arts, 1973-; Appearances at, Carnegie Hall, Kennedy Center, Library of Congress; The White House, Wigmore Hall, Warsaw Philharmonic, Vienna Musikvereinsaal; Member of Lanier Trio. *Recordings:* Vanguard; Vox Turnabout; Crystal; Coronet; Orion; Educo; The Musical Heritage Society; Gasparo. *Honours:* Fulbright Scholar, 1969-71. *Address:* School of Music, Georgia State University, Atlanta, GA 30303, USA.

LEWIS Daniel, b. 10 May 1925, Flagstaff, Arizona, USA. Conductor. *Education:* Studied composition with Nino Marcelli in San Diego, 1939-41; BM San Diego State College 1949; Further study with Eugen Jochum in Munich, 1960. *Career:* Leader of the Honolulu Symphony during war service; Assistant Conductor, San Diego Symphony 1954-56; Leader and associate conductor 1956-59; Music Director of the Pasadena Symphony 1972-83, notably in neglected 18th Century and American music; Guest Conductor with the Los Angeles Philharmonic, Oakland Symphony, Atlanta Symphony, Minnesota Orchestra, Utah Symphony, Seattle Symphony, Los Angeles Chamber Orchestra and the Louisville Orchestra; Chairman of the conducting studies department at the University of Southern California.

LEWIS David Sheldon, b. 10 Dec 1929, Baltimore, Maryland, USA. Professor. m. 10 Aug 1985, 2 sons, 4 daughters, previous marriage. *Education:* BS, Music Education, Concord College, West Virginia, 1952; MM, Theory, University of Michigan, 1957; PhD, Theory, West Virginia University, 1968. Additional study, Indiana University, Summers, 1958-61. Clarinet teachers, Angelo Fiorani, William Stubbins, Henry Gulick, Frank Cohen. *Career includes:* Assistant professor, woodwind & theory, Concord College, 1957-63; Teaching fellow, theory, West Virginia University, 1963-64; Assistant professor, woodwind & theory, Frostburg State College, 1964-66; Professor, clarinet & theory, Ohio University, 1966-; Acting Director, School of Music, ibid, 1987-

88; Principal clarinet, Roanoke Symphony Orchestra, 1958-63, Singapore Symphony Orchestra, 1979-80 and 1984; Concerto performances at the Piccolo Spoleto Festival in Charleston, SC, 1989; Performance at, and participation in The International Master Classes and Festival, Porto Carras, Greece, 1989. *Recording:* Ippolitov-Ivanov Symphony no 1, with Singapore Symphony Orchestra. *Publications:* Co-author, Harmonic Dictation: A Programmed Course, 1975. *Hobbies:* Jogging; Sports; Films; Theatre. *Address:* Ohio University, School of Music, Athens, OH 45701, USA.

LEWIS Henry, b. 16 Oct 1932, Los Angeles, California, USA. Conductor. m. Marilyn Horne, 1960 (divorced). *Education:* Studied piano and double bass as a boy; double bass player in the Los Angeles Philharmonic aged 16. *Career:* Played in and conducted the 7th Army Symphony Orchestra overseas, 1955-59; Founded Los Angeles Chamber Orchestra and toured with it to Europe 1963; Conductor and musical director of the New Jersey Symphony, Newark, 1968-76; La Scala Milan debut 1965, Metropolitan Opera 1972, becoming the first black conductor to appear there: productions include La Bohème, Carmen, Un Ballo in Maschera, Le Prophète and Roméo et Juliette; Scottish Opera debut 1978, with Coq d'Or; Hamburg State Opera 1983-, in Les Troyens, Semiramide, Carmen and Turandot; Salome for Los Angeles Opera 1988; has conducted most major orchestras in North America; UK engagements with the London Symphony, London Philharmonic and Royal Liverpol Philharmonic; also with orchestras in Italy, Luxembourg, France, Holland, Germany, Poland and Scandinavia; Chief Conductor, Radio Symphony Orchestra, Holland, 1989-, Live from Lincoln Center televised Gala Concert, April 1990; Conducted Adriana Lecouvreur at the Concertgebouw, 1991. *Address:* c/o Harrison/Parrott Ltd., 12 Penzance Place, London W11 4PA, England.

LEWIS J Reilly, b. 15 Sept 1944, CA, USA. Conductor; Keyboard Artist. m. Kaaren Lynn Ray, 30 Apr 1977, Divorced, 1 daughter. *Education:* Oberlin College Conservatory of Music and Juilliard School of Music. *Career:* Organist, Choirmaster, Church of the Holy Family, The United Nations, NY, 1967-69; Organist, Choirmaster, Clarendon United Methodist Church, 1971-; Resident, Keyboard Artist, National Symphony Orchestra, 1972- 76; Founder, Music Director, Washington Bach Consort, 1977-; Associate Conductor, Keyboard Artist, Handel Festival Orchestra of Kennedy Ctr, 1981-90; Music Director, Cathedral Choral Society, 1985-; Master Schola Conducting Seminar, Attendee, 1992-; Perre Boulez Carnegie Hall Conducting Seminar Attendee, 1993. *Recordings:* Complete Motels of J S Bach; A Thousand Years of Russian Choral Music; Recordings with Handel Festival Orchestra and Musical Heritage Society. *Honours:* Arion Award for Outstanding Musical Achievement; 1st Prize National Organ Playing Competition; Fulbright Scholar; Washington Are Music Awards; Best Conductor, Music Director. *Memberships:* American Bach Society; American Guild of Organists; Association of Professional Vocal Ensembles; American Choral Directors Association; American Musicological Association. *Hobbies:* Scuba Diving; Cycling. *Address:* c/o Cathedral Choral Society, Washington National Cathedral, Mount Saint Alban, Washington DC 20016, USA.

LEWIS Jeffrey, b. 28 Nov 1942, Neath, South Wales. Composer. m. Sheelagh Elizabeth Hywel, 13 May 1983, 1 son, 1 daughter. *Education:* BMus 1st class honours, 1965, MMus, 1967, University College, Cardiff; PhD, University of Wales, 1977; ARCM Organ Performers; Studied composition with Boguslaw Schäffer, Krakow, Poland, with Don Banks, London, with Stockhausen and Ligeti, Darmstadt, Federal Republic of Germany, 1967-68. *Career:* Pianist, Paris Chamber Ensemble, 1967-68; Lecturer in 20th Century Composition Techniques and Experimental Music, City of Leeds College of Music, England, 1969-72; Lecturer, Department of Music, University College of North Wales, Bangor, 1973-; Lecturer, 1973-87, Senior Lecturer, 1987-1993, Department of Music, University College of North Wales,

Bangor. *Compositions:* Orchestral: Mutations I; Antiphony; Fanfares with Variations; Aurora; Memoria; Limina Lucis; Instrumental: Mutations II; Esultante; Momentum for organ; Tableau; Fantasy for piano; Chamber: Epitaph for Abelard and Heloise; Stratos; Ritornel; Mobile II; Time-Passage; Wind Quintet; Sonante; Piano Trio; Choral: Carmen Paschale; Pro Pace; Hymnus Ante Somnum. *Address:* Crafnant, Park Crescent, Llanfairfechan, Gwynedd, LL33 0AU, Wales.

LEWIS John Samuel, b. 12 Nov 1929, Amarillo, Texas, USA. Educator (retired). m. Marjorie Dunlavy, 3 June 1961. *Education:* BS, Kansas State University; PhD, University of Kansas; Studied Violin privately with Janus Hall, Mary Dunn and Max Martin; Also studied with Waldemar Geltch. *Career:* Gave weekly radio musical programme Saturday Night Recorded, KTCU. *Recordings:* As producer, Earle Spencer. *Contributions:* Ragging the Classics, regularly 1976-; Discography in various journals. *Memberships:* Modern Language Association; Renaissance Society. *Hobby:* Record collecting. *Address:* 3120 Spanish Oak Drive, Fort Worth, TX 76109, USA.

LEWIS Keith, b. 6 Oct 1950, Methven, New Zealand. Singer (Tenor). *Education:* Studied in New Zealand; London from 1976; Won Kathleen Ferrier Memorial Prize. *Career:* Sang Alfredo at the 1979 Edinburgh Festival; Premiere of John Tavener's Thérèse at Covent Garden; returned as Rossini's Almaviva and as Bellini's Tebaldo and Tamino in Magic Flute; Appearances in Don Giovanni, (San Francisco), Armide by Rossini (Bonn), Iphigénie en Tauride, La Clemenza di Tito, Eugene Onegin (Frankfurt) and Die Zauberflöte (Zurich); Glyndebourne from 1982, as Mozart's Ferrando, Belmonte and Don Ottavio, Monteverdi's Giove and Strauss's Matteo, 1984; Mozart's Tamino and Rossini's Almaviva with English National Opera; Hamburg and Berlin 1988 and 1989, as Faust by Berlioz and Gounod; Concert engagements in the Damnation of Faust with Solti, Haydn's Creation in Berlin and Frankfurt, Schumann's Paradies und der Peri in Madrid, Milan and Prague, The Dream of Gerontius in Bern, Toronto and London and the Bach B Minor Mass with the Orchestre de Paris conducted by Giulini and Beethoven 9 with Vienna Philharmonic conducted by Abbado; Further appearances include Mendelssohn's Elijah with Colin Davis, Verdi's Requiem, Mozart Requiem, Beethoven 9, Das Lied von der Erde and Bach Mass in B minor with Giulini; Damnation of Faust with Solti (Paris and Salzburg Festival) and Colin Davis (Barbican/ London), Messiah & Beethoven 9 (Solti) and Missa Solemnis with Marriner and Colin Davis; Sang in The Dream of Gerontius at the opening concert of the 1991 Promenade Concerts, London; Oedipus Rex, Stravinsky, Dutoit, Philadelphia, New York; Così fan Tutte, Chicago, 1993; Idomeneo, Glyndebourne, 1991; Opéra de Paris, 1991; Magic Flute, Opéra de Paris, 1991; Britten Tenor Horn Serenade, Giulini, London; Damnation of Faust, Solti, Chicago, London, Salzburg; Haydn Creation, Sinopoli, Dresden. *Recordings include:* Rossini's Tancredi, Otello and Moses; Gluck's Alceste; Don Giovanni conducted by Haitink; Messiah (Solti); Masses by Haydn (Marriner); Paradies und der Peri (Albrecht); Berlioz Lelio and Te Deum & Requiem (Inbal), Berlioz Requiem, G Bertini; Mozart Requiem, F. Welser-Moest and Giulini; Beethoven 9, Gunther Wand and Giulini; Mahler 8, (Sinopoli/DGG); Salome, (Mehta/Sony). *Current Management:* IMG Artists Europe, Media House, 3 Burlington Lane, Chiswick, London W4 2TH, England.

LEWIS Michael, b. 1948, Adelaide, South Australia. Singer (Baritone). *Education:* Studied in Adelaide and at the London Opera Centre. *Career:* Sang first at Wexford Festival, then with Glyndebourne Festival and Touring Operas, Welsh National and Socttish Operas, Frankfurt Opera and companies in Australia; Resident principal with Opera North and Australian Opera; Season 1992-93 as Verdi's Luna, Amonasro, Rigoletto and Renato in Australia, Rigoletto at La Fenice Venice, Rossini's Figaro for English National Opera; Performances of L'Africaine and Tiefland in Berlin, I

Masnadieri and Macbeth in Australia and Bizet's Zurga in San Diego; Other roles include Mozart's Guglielmo, Alfonso, the Count and Papageno, Malatesta, Lescaut in Manon, Riccardo (Puritani), Marcello and Don Carlo in La Forza del Destino; Concert repertoire includes Carmina Burana, Belshazzar's Feast and Elijah. *Address:* c/o IMG Artists, Media House, 3 Burlington Lane, London W4 2TH, England.

LEWIS Richard, b. Trowbridge, Wiltshire, England. Singer; Educationalist; Counsellor. *Education:* Studied at University of North London; Trinity College of Music with John Carol Case and Guildhall School of Music and Drama; MA, B.Ed (Hons), FTCL. *Debut:* Wigmore Hall, as Tenor Soloist with Praetorius Consort. *Career:* Sung with BBC Singers and other leading choirs; much work as oratorio singer; Gentleman of H.M. Chapel Royal Choir, St James's Palace; soloist with Opera for All and also in world premieres in St. Paul's Cathederal and at the South Bank. *Recordings:* Many Recordings as Choirister; Music for the Christening of Prince William; Journey of the Magi. *Honours:* Oriana Madrigal Society Prize; Joseph Maas Prize for Tenors; Vaughan Williams Scholarship; Mitchell City of London Scholarship; Catherine Howard Scholarship; Corporation of London Scholarship. *Memberships:* Equity; NAHT. *Hobbies:* Listening; Friends; Reading; Travel. *Address:* 61 Sydner Road, London N16 7UF, England.

LEWIS Robert Hall, b. 22 Apr 1926, Portland, Oregon, USA. Composer; Conductor; Professor. m. Barbara Bowersock, 8 Aug 1959, 1 daughter. *Education:* BM, Distinction, 1949, MM 1951, PhD, 1964, University of Rochester (Eastman School); Diploma, conducting, Paris Conservatory, 1953; Diploma, Composition, Vienna Academy of Music, 1957; Monteux School of Conducting, Summer, 1954. *Career:* Principal Trumpet, Oklahoma Symphony Orchestra, 1951-52; Assistant Principal Trumpet, Rochester Philharmonic Orchestra, 1953-55; Guest Conductor: Baltimore Symphony Orchestra, Indiana University Orchestra, National Gallery Orchestra; Conducted Recordings of own music with London Symphony, Royal Philharmonic, London Sinfonietta, Philharmonia orchestras; Professor of Music, Goucher College, Baltimore; Professor, Composition, Peabody Institute, Johns Hopkins University. *Compositions:* String Quartets, I, II, III; Music for Twelve Players; Music for Brass Quintet; Osservazioni for Flutes, Piano & Percussion; Monophony I-IX for Solo Winds; Concerto for Chamber Orchestra, Symphony No 2; Nuances II for Orchestra; Osservazioni II for Winds; Keyboard, Harp and Percussion; Moto; Atto for String Orchestra. *Recordings:* Divertimento for 6 Instruments; Toccata for Violin and Percussion; Symphony No 2; Nuances II for Orchestra; Three Prayers of Jane Austen; Concerto for Chamber Orchestra; Serenades for Piano Solo; Moto for Orchestra; Atto for String Orchestra; Combinazioni, I, II, III, IV. *Contributions to:* Professional journals. *Hobbies:* Study of Foreign Languages. *Address:* 328 Broadmoor Road, Baltimore, MD, USA.

LEWIS William, b. 23 Nov 1935, Tulsa, Oklahoma, USA. Singer (Tenor). *Education:* Studied in Fort Worth and New York. *Debut:* Fort Worth 1953, in Gianni Schicchi. *Career:* Early appearances in Cincinnati, San Francisco and Dallas; New York City Opera, 1957, in Die Fledermaus; Metropolitan Opera from 1958, in Salome, Elektra, Boris Godunov, Jenůfa, The Queen of Spades, La Bohème and Francesca da Rimini; Sang Aeneas in the 1983 New York production of Les Troyens; Spoleto, 1959, in the premiere of Barber's A Hand of Bridge; San Francisco, 1984-85, as Loge in The Ring; Wexford Festival and La Scala, 1986-87, in Humperdinck's Königskinder and the title role in the premiere of Testi's Riccardo III; Spoleto Festival, 1989, as Aegisthus in Elektra; Sang Arbace in Idomeneo at San Francisco, 1989 and in the premiere of Blimunda by Azio Corghi at the Teatro Lirico Milan, 1990; Other roles include Pollione in Norma, the Emperor in Die Frau ohne Schatten, Don José, Offenbach's Hoffmann, Radames, Gabriele Adorno in Simon Boccanegra and Strauss's Guntram. *Recordings include:* Adolar in

Euryanthe.*Address:* c/o San Francisco Opera, War Memorial Opera House, San Francisco, CA 94102, USA.

LEWKOVITCH Bernhard, b. 28 May 1927, Denmark. Composer; Organist. *Education:* Graduate, music theory 1948, organ 1949, Royal Danish Conservatory of Music; Composition teachers, Poul Schierbeck, Jørgen Jersild. Studies in France. *Career includes:* Organist, 1947-63, cantor, 1953-63, Sankt Ansgar Catholic Church, Copenhagen; Organist & cantor, Church of Holy Sacrament, Copenhagen, 1973-; Founder & leader, Schola Gregoriana men's choir, Schola Cantorum mixed choir (both now under name Schola Cantorum). *Compositions include:* Vocal music, instrumental music for orchestra, ensemble, piano, organ. Titles include: Mass for 2 corui and mixed choir; Songs of Solomon for tenor and clarinet, coruo and bass trombone; Deprecations for tenor, horn and bass trombone; Preacher and singer for tenor and piano; Six partitas for 5 brass instruments vol. I-II; Improperia per voce (Good Friday); 3 Tasso Madrigali for mixed choir; Responsoria for mixed choir (Good Friday); Helligandskoraler (Holy Ghost Chorales), 4 brass players, 1980; Numerous organ chorales; II Cantico delle Creature, 1962; Memoria Apostolorum, 12 short movements, 1978; Liturgical works. *Address:* Bredgade 69, 1260 K Copenhagen, Denmark.

LEYTENS Luc M E L, b. 14 Nov 1936, Antwerp, Belgium. Administrator. m. Mimi Boereboom, 28 May 1963, 3 daughters. *Education:* LLD, Can Mus, Catholic University of Louvain. *Career:* Barrister, Antwerp, 1960-63; Founder, 1963-, Secretary, Antwerp Cathedral Concerts; Assistant Secretary-General, 1963-69, Secretary-General, 1969-, Youth and Music, Belgium; Lecturer, Musical Aesthetics, Royal Conservatory, Antwerp, 1966-; Permanent Juridical Commission, International Federation Jeunesses Musicales, 1964-74, 1978-82, 1984-; Committee of the FIJM International Music Competition, Belgrade, Yugoslavia, 1977-; Secretary, Treasurer, Flemish Music Council, 1981-; Treasurer, ISME, Belgium, 1983-; Administrator, P Benoit Foundation, 1981-. *Publications:* Jef van Hoof, with Paul de Raedt, 1974; Peter Benoit, with Marc Somers, 1984; Beknopte Kroniek van Jef van Hoof, 1986. *Address:* Cogels Osylei 72, B-2600 Berchem-Antwerp, Belgium.

LI Delun, b. 6 June 1917, Peking, China. Artistic Director; Conductor. m. Li Jue, 1 July 1947, 1 son, 2 daughters. *Education:* Studied Cello, Shanghai Conservatory of Music, 1940; Pursued graduated studies in Conducting under Professor N Anosow at Moscow Conservatory, USSR, 1953-57. *Career:* Conductor, Theatre Orchestras, Shanghai, 1943-46; Conductor, Yannan Orchestra, 1946-49; Conductor, Central Opera, Peking, 1949-53; Trainee, Conductor, State Symphony, USSR, 1957; Artistic Director, China Central Philharmonic Symphony Orchestra, 1958; Guest Conductor, over 20 orchestras in former Soviet Union and has been guest conductor in Finland, Cuba, Czech, Germany, USA, Canada and Portugal, and led the Symphony Orchestra tour to Japan, Spain and Korea. *Recordings:* several. *Honours:* Liszt Memorial Medal, Hungarian Government. *Memberships:* Music Adviser, Peking Symphony; Hon. Advisor, Guanzhou Symphony Orchestra, Chengdu Symphony Orchestra; Vice-President, China Musicians Association. *Hobby:* Photography. *Address:* 11-1 Heping Street, Central Philharmonic Society, 100013 Beijing, China.

LI Hong-Shen, b. 1960, Peking, China. Singer. *Education:* Studied at the Peking Conservatory and the Juilliard School with Ellen Faull. *Career:* Joined the San Francisco Operas Merola Program, 1987, Performing Rinuccio in Gianni Schicchi and Lindoro in L'Italiana in Algeri; Further Appearances as the Duke of Mantua, Aufidio in Mozart's Lucio Silla, The Italian Singer, Alfredo, Tebaldo, Pirro in Ermione and Leukippos in Daphne; Other Roles Include Count Almaviva, Steuermann in Fliegende Holländer, Nadir, Macduff, Nemorino and Idreno in Semiramide; Concert Repertoire icludes the Verdi Requiem and Mozart's Requiem with the Sacramento Symphony. *Honours include:* Highest Fellowship Scholarship at Peking Conservatory. *Address:* c/o IMG Artists, Media Houe, 3 Burlington Lane, London W4 2TH, England.

LI Tian-sheng, b. 14 Aug 1948, Tianshui, Gansu, China. Cellist; Viola de Gamba Player. m. Jian-hua Chen, pianist 20 Mar 1976, 2 daughters. *Education:* Diploma, School of Music attached to Central Conservatory, Peking, China, 1959-67; MMus, Cello Performance, School of Music, Indiana University, Bloomington, 1984; DMA, Cello Performance, Memphis State University, anticipated completion, 1988. *Debut:* Central Ballet Theatre, Peking, China, 1978. *Career:* Cellist, Symphony Orchestra of Central Ballet Theatre, 1968-80; Student of Distinguished Professor of Cello, Janos Starker, 1981-84; Cello and Re-bu (chinese instrument) Solo, Indianapolis TV Arts Network, 1983; Cellist, Memphis Symphony, USA, 1984-; Cello Instructor, Memphis State University Suzuki String Program, 1985-. *Recordings:* Two cello solo recording cassette tapes: Violoncello Recital, Chinese cello music; Violoncello Recital, World Famous Cello Music, published by Hong Kong Audio Production Ltd., 1981. *Address:* c/o The Department of Music, Memphis State University, Memphis, TN 38152, USA.

LIANG Ning, b. 1957, Peking, China. Singer. *Education:* Studied in Gwangdong and Peking. *Debut:* Central Conservatory Peking, 1983 as Cherubino. *Career:* Wigmore Hall Recital, London, 1983; Sang at Peking and Shanghai as Carmen and Rosina, Cenerentola at the 1987 Aspen Festival; Philadelphia and Helsinki, 1988, as Dorabella and Carmen; Studied Further at the Juilliard School, 1986-89; Sang Cherubino in London and Hamburg, 1989-91; La Scala Milan, 1990, as Suzuki in Butterfly; Sang Rosina at Toronto and at the Vienna Festival, 1992; Concert engagements include Beethoven's Ninth in Lisbon and Bellini's Il Pirata in New York. *Recordings Include:* Carmen and Le Nozze Di Figaro. *Address:* c/o Hamburgisches Staatsoper, Grosses-Theaterstasse 34, 2000 Hamburg 36, Germany.

LIAO Naixiong, b. 27 June 1933, Shanghai, China. Director The Institute for Music Research. m. Dec 1954, 1 daughter. *Education:* Studied composition and music theory, 1951-54. Studied piano, 1954-58, Shanghai Conservatory. *Career:* Assistant for piano, 1958-74, Researcher at The Institute for Music Research, 1974-78, Lecturer, 1978-80, Associate Professor, 1980-86, Full Professor, 1986-, Vice-Director, 1982-84, Director, 1984-, Shanghai Conservatory; Research Fellow, Alexander Von Humboldt Foundation, Federal Republic of Germany, 1982-84; Currently working on History of The European Opera, and Carl Orff. *Publications:* The Ocean of Words (Contributor); The Great Chinese Encyclopedia (Contributor); The German Liederalbum 1959; Chopin, 1981; Grieg, 1982; Musik durch die man zu den Quellen steigt, 1985; Quo Vadis The Opera in China?, 1987. *Contributions to:* People's Music; Articles on Music; China im Aufbau; Art of Music; China - Report; Art of Opera; Radio Programmes in Shanghai, Peking, Berlin (West), Munich, Cologne. *Address:* Shanghai Conservatory, Feng Yang Road 20, Shanghai, China.

LIBIN Laurence Elliot, b. 19 Sept 1944, Chicago, Illinois, USA. Museum Curator. *Education:* BMus, Northwestern University, 1966; MMus, Kings College, University of London, England, 1968; Swift Fellow, University of Chicago, USA, 1969-71. *Debut:* Carnegie Recital Hall, New York, 1973. *Career:* Harpsichordist, Teacher and Musicologist; Curator, Department of Musical Instruments, Metropolitan Museum of Art, New York, 1973-; Adjunct Professor, Columbia University, New York University, 1974-. *Recordings:* Producer, 15 recordings at Metropolitan Museum and 30 classical music radio programmes on historic instruments. *Publications:* American Musical Instruments in The Metropolitan Museum of Art, 1985. *Contributions to:* Encyclopaedia Britannica; Grove's 6th edition; JAMS; Early Music etc. *Address:* Department of Musical Instruments, The Metropolitan Museum of Art, Fifth Avenue and 82nd Street, New York, NY 10028, USA.

LICHTMANN Theodor David, b. 25 Dec 1938, Bern, Switzerland. Pianist (Soloist and Chamber Music); University Professor. *Education:* Teacher's Diploma, University of Zurich; Akademie für Musik, Vienna, Austria; Hochschule für Musik, Munich, Federal Republic of Germany; MMus, University of Texas, USA; Piano studies with Irma Schaichet, Zurich, Leonard Shure, New York City. *Debut:* Bern, 1954. *Career:* Recitals in Zurich, Berlin, Vienna, Hamburg, London and smaller cities in Switzerland; Co-founder and pianist of Mendelssohn Trio; Broadcasts on Swiss Radio and TV; Recitals in Philadelphia, Denver, Austin, Roswell, USA; Broadcasts on radio and TV, Denver, Colorado; Full Professor, School of Music, Chairman, Piano Department, University of Denver. *Recordings:* Various records for Decca, London, England: Turicaphon, Fair Play; Summit Brass, Solo Pro; Complete works by Hindemith for Brass and Piano (on SUMMIT RECORDS). *Contributions to:* ARBA; Libraries Unlimited. *Memberships:* College Music Society; Colorado Mountain Club. *Hobbies:* Literature; Photography; Mountaineering. *Address:* 3005 E. Cedar Lane, Denver, CO 80209, USA.

LIDDELL Nona Patricia, b. 9 June 1927, London, England. Musician. m. Ivor McMahon, 15 July 1950, deceased, 1 d. *Education:* Royal Academy of Music. *Career:* Leader, English String Quartet, 1957-73; Leader Richards Piano Quintet, 1964-79; Leader, London Sinfonietta, 1970-; Leader, London Bach Orchestras; Professor, Royal Academy of Music. *Recordings:* Violin Concerto, Kurt Weill; Phantasie by Schoenberg with John Constable; Gemini, Roberto Gerhard with John Constable; Chamber Music by Martinů, Chausson, Herbert Howells; Brahms Horn Trio with Schiller Trio; Stravinsky Soldier's Tale; Chamber Music by Schoenberg. *Honour:* MBE, Fellow of the Royal Academy of Music. *Membership:* Incorporated Society of Musicians. *Hobbies:* Reading; Cooking. *Address:* 28B Ravenscroft Park, Barnet, Herts EN5 4NH, England.

LIDL Vaclav, b. 5 Nov 1922, Brno, Czechoslovakia. Composer. m. Eva Hromadkova, 1 son. *Education:* Graduate Business Academy; Brno Conservatoire. *Career:* Writer of many musical scores for films and television. *Compositions include:* Divertimento for flute, clarinet and bassoon; 3rd string quartet; Dandelions, for flute, soprano and harp; 1st Symphony for Grand Orchestra; Cantus Variabilis for violin, clarinet and piano; Hic Homo Sum, Cantata for mixed choir, tenor, piano and percussion; Our Little Drummer, Cantata for child's voice and Grand Orchestra; 2nd Symphony for Chamber Orchestra; 3rd Symphony for Grand Orchestra; Many compositions for various types of choirs; Ballade on a June Morning (Lidice 1942), for Grand Orchestra; Concerto for trumpet and orchestra. *Honour:* Antonin Zapotocky Prize, for the Ballade on a June Morning, 1984. *Membership:* Association of Musicians and Musicologists. *Hobby:* Skiing. *Current Management:* Music Information Centre, Besedni 3, 118 00 Praha 1, Czech Republic. *Address:* Soukenicka 14, 110 00 Praha 1, Czech Republic.

LIEBER Edvard, b. 11 Apr 1948, Rockville Centre, New York, USA. Composer. Pianist; Composer. *Education:* School of Visual Arts, New York, BFA Film, 1972-76; Manhattan School of Music, 1966-68; Coached Piano with Artur Rubinstein, 1971; Musical Composition with I Xenakis, 1973 and P Boulez, 1977. *Career:* Carnegie Recital Hall, New York, 1976; Alice Tully Hall, Lincoln Center, New York, 1978; Lincoln Center, 1979; WQXR-FM Radio, Live one-hour Concert and Interview, 1978; National Public Radio, Music and Interview, 1981; WQED-TV Pittsburgh, 30 minute special on Lieber, 1980. *Compositions:* Berlinerstück, 1976; Prelude to Jackson Pollock's Autumn Rhythm, 1977; 24 Dekooning Preludes, 1978; 15 Interludes to the Mechanism of Meaning, 1980; Variations on a theme of John Cage, 1982; Discourse and Glimpse, 1986. *Recordings:* Music to Paintings by Edvard Lieber, 1983. *Current Management:* Stephen

White, Representative, 532 La Guardia Place, Suite 114, New York, NY 10012, USA. *Address:* 24 Hay Road, Shirley, NY 11967, USA.

LIEBERMAN Carol, b. 18 Aug 1943, New York City, USA. Musician; Violinist; Baroque Violinist. m. Mark Kroll, 9 July 1975, 1 son. *Education:* BA, City College of New York, 1965; MMus, 1967, DMA, 1974, Yale University School of Music; Violin studies with Raphael Bronstein and Broadus Erle. *Debut:* Carnegie Recital Hall, New York, 1975. *Career:* Faculty, Boston University School of Music, 1979-; Concertmaster, Masterworks Chorale Orchestra, 1980-; Concerts throughout USA and in Rome, Italy, Antwerp, Caracas, Lisbon and Canada; Broadcasts for WGBH radio-TV and WBUR radio, Boston, including 6 part simulcast series for Maine Public Television; Radio and television programmes for Canadian Broadcasting Corporation; Former Member, Israel Philharmonic Orchestra and Toronto Symphony; Assistant Professor, College of Holy Cross, 1985-88, Associate Professor, 1989-; Co-Director, Holy Cross Chamber Players, 1985-; Broadcasts for Radio National de Espana, Madrid, 1985; Soloist with Connecticut Early Music Festival, 1985-; Associate Professor, College of the Holy Cross, 1988-. *Recordings:* Titanic Records; AFKA Records; CD's: Schubert Sonatinas for violin and fortepiano (Newport Classic); Dohnanyi Sonata for violin, piano and second piano quintet, (AFKA); Numerous recordings. *Memberships:* Co-director, Holy Cross Chamber Players; Violinist with Early Music Ensemble of Boston; Violinist of Lieberman/Kroll duo. *Address:* Department of Music, College of the Holy Cross, PO Box 151A, Worcester, MA 01610, USA.

LIEBERMANN Lowell, b. 22 Feb 1961, New York City, New York, USA. Composer; Conductor; Pianist. *Education:* BM 1982, MM 1984, DMA 1987, The Juilliard School, New York; Composition with David Diamond and Vincent Persichetti; Conducting with Laszlo Halasz; Piano with Jacob Lateiner. *Debut:* Carnegie Recital Hall, New York City, 1978. *Compositions:* Published by Theodore Presser, Pennsylvania; Symphony Opus 9; Piano Concerto Opus 11; 2 Piano Sonatas (Opus 1 and 10); Sechs Gesänge Nach Gedichten von Nelly Sachs for Soprano and Orchestra Opus 18; Sonata for Viola and Piano Opus 13; Missa Brevis for Chorus and Organ; Song Cycles; Chamber Music; Sonata for Flute and Piano, Op.24; Quintet for Piano, Clarinet and String Trio, Op. 26; Domain of Arnhiem Op. 33; Quintet for piano and strings Op. 34; Nocturnes Op. 20, 31, 35; Gargoyles Op. 29; Piano Concerto No. 2 Op.36, 1992; Concerto for flute and orchestra, Op.39, 1992; Songs and piano pieces. *Recordings:* Piano Music of Lowell Liebermann, Musical Heritage Society; Recordings on Musical heritage Society; New World Records, Virgin Classics, Centaur Records and Cambria Racords. *Address:* 155 West 68th Street, Apt. 315, New York, NY 10023, USA.

LIEBERMANN Rolf, b. 14 Sept 1910, Zurich, Switzerland. Swiss Musician and Administrator; Composer. *Education:* Zurich Conservatoire, and University of Zurich. *Career:* Member, Musical Department, Swiss Radio Corporation 1945-50; Head of Orchestra Department, Swiss Radio Station, Beromünster 1950-57; Musical Director, N. German Broadcasting System, Hamburg 1957-59; General Manager, State Opera, Hamburg 1959-72; General Manager, Théâtre National de l'Opéra, Paris 1973-80; Guest Professor, Mozarteum, Salzburg, 1982; General Manager, Hamburg State Opera, 1985-. *Compositions:* Operatic: Leonore 1952, Penelope 1954, School for Wives 1955; La Fôret, 1987; Orchestral: Polyphonic Studies 1943, Une das Fins du Monde 1943, Volkslieder Suite, Furioso 1947, Symphony No. 1 1949, The Song of Life and Death 1950, Concerto for Jazzband and Symphony Orchestra 1954, Concerto pour machines à écrire et machines à calculer 1964, Symphonie des Echanges (for business machines) 1964. Liason, for Cello, Piano and Orchestra; Piano Quintet, 1987; Monologue de Medea, for soprano, Choir and orchestra, 1989; Non Lieu Pour Medea, Opera, 1992; Concerto

for Violin and orchestra, 1993. *Honours:* Dr h.c. of the University of Spokane and Berne (USA); Commander Legion d'honneur 1974; Commander de l'Ordre des Arts et des Lettres; Commander de l'Ordre de la Légion d'Honneur. *Memberships:* L'Académie des Beaux Arts de Berlin and of Hamburg; Honorable Mmeber of the Hochschule Mozarteum of Salzburg and of the Royal Academy of Fine Arts of London. *Address:* Hamburg Staatsoper, Hamburg, Germany.

LIEBERSON Peter, b. 25 Oct 1946, NY. USA. Composer. m. Ellen Kearney, 3 d. *Education:* Studied at New York University, Columbia University and Brandeis University; Composition Teachers, Milton Babbitt, Charles Wvorinen, Donald Martino, Martin Boykan. *Compositions include:* Worlds Turning; Drala; Lalita; Ziji; Raising The Gaze; Variations for Violin and Piano; Piano Fantasy; Flute Variations; Concerto for 4 Groups of Instruments. *Recordings:* Piano Concerto; Bagatelles; Lalita; Raising the Gaze; Piano Fantasy; Concerto for 4 groups of Instruments. *Honours:* Charles Ives Fellowship; National Endowment for the Arts; American Academy of Arts and Letters; Brandeis University Creative Arts Award. Membership: BMI. *Hobby:* Golf. *Address:* 47 Anchor Drive, Halifax, Nova Scotia, B3N 3E4, Canada.

LIEBL Karl, b. 16 June 1915, Schiltberg, Germany. Singer (Tenor). *Education:* Studied with Paul Bender in Munich and with Albert Meyer in Augsburg. *Debut:* Regensburg 1950. *Career:* Sang in Wiesbaden from 1951; Cologne Opera 1955-59, notably as Huon in Oberon; Vinna Staatsoper, 1956-59: sang the Cardinal in Mathis der Maler under the direction of Hindemith; Metropolitan Opera, 1959-68, as Wagner's Lohengrin, Tristan, Loge, Walther, Siegfried, Siegmund and Parsifal; Guest appearances in Munich, Hamburg, Chicago, Baltimore, Brussels, Zurich, Venice and Madrid; Teacher at University of Mainz from 1967. *Recordings:* Der fliegende Holländer (RCA); Die Zauberflöte (HMV); Lohengrin; Die Meistersinger; Oberon. *Address:* c/o Staatliche Hochschule für Musik, Bingerstrasse 26, 6500 Mainz, Germany.

LIEBOLD Angela, b. 15 Aug 1958, Dresden, Germany. Singer. *Education:* Studied at Dresden Musikhochschule. *Career:* Appearances at the Dresden Opera from 1985, Title Role in the Premiere of Weise Von Liebe und Tod Des Cornets Christopher Rlike by Siegfried Matthus; Lieder Recitals in Russia, Hungary, France and Germany; Engagements in opera elsewhere in Germany; Teacher of Singing at the Dresden Musikhochschule from 1983. *Honours include:* Prize Winner at the Walter Gruner Lieder Competition; Bach International; Maria Callas Competition Athens; Robert Schumann Competition. *Address:* c/o Semper-Oper, 8012 Dresden, Germany.

LIFCHITZ Max, b. 11 Nov 1948, Mexico City, Mexico. Composer; Conductor; Pianist. *Education:* Studies at the Juilliard School of Muisc, NY and Harvard University, Cambridge, also Berkshire Music Centre. *Debut:* Mexico City, 1955. *Career:* Pianist, Juilliard Ensemble; Lecturer, National Music Camp, Michigan; Faculty Manhattan School of Music; Assistant Professor in Music, Columbia University; Executive Director, Conductor, North South Consonance Inc; Associate Professor in Music, State University of NY. *Compositions Include:* Intervencion, Violin, Orchestra, Duo, Cello; Kaddish, Choir, Chamber, Ensemble, Tiempos; Tientos, Accordion; Recorded Opus one: Affinities, Piano Solo; Transformation, Cello; Yellow Ribbons No 2; Canto de Paz; Yellow Ribbons No. 21; Recorded CRI; Consorte; Winter Counterpoint, Flute, Oboe, Bassoon, Viola; Exceptional String Quartet. *Publications:* String Quartets, Carlos Charez for G Schirmer. *Hobbies:* Sports; Photography. *Address:* PO Box 5081, Albany, NY 12205-0081, USA.

LIELMANE Rasma, b. 1958, Latvia, USSR. Concert Violinist. *Education:* Studied with David Oistrakh at the Moscow Conservatoire. *Career:* Appearances with the leading orchestras of Europe and North America;

Collaborations with the Munich Philharmonic, the Berlin Symphony and the Dresden Philharmonic; Appearances in London, Hamburg, Toronto, Montreal, Nice and Milan. *Honours:* First Prize, International Violin Competition, Sofia; Prizewinner in the Vianna de Motta Competition in Portugal; Nicola Paganini in Italy; Maria Canals Competition in Montreal; Tibor Varga Prize in Switzerland. *Address:* Norman McCann International Artists Ltd, The Coach House, 56 Lawrie Park Gardens, London SE26 6XJ, England.

LIFSON Ludmilla V, b. 27 June 1945, Russia. Pianist; Piano Teacher. m. Dr Jacob S Lifson, 1 Nov 1966, 1 son. *Education:* Special school for musically gifted children, Leningrad, USSR, 1950-59; Special Music High School, Leningrad, 1959-63; Leningrad State Conservatory of Music, 1963-68; MM with Honours Magna Cum Laude for Piano Soloist, ensemble musician, Music Teacher; Artist Diploma. *Career:* Performing; extensive concert appearances throughout USSR and USA in chamber music, member of the Solati Trio. *Recordings:* Compact disk with the Bratislava Radio Orchestra on MMC label; Teaching: Piano, chamber music, Leningrad State Conservatory of Music, 1968-78; Member of Piano Faculty, Longy School of Music, Cambridge Massachusetts, USA, 1979-; Member of Piano faculty, Providence College, Providence, Rhode Island, 1982-. *Address:* 10 Charles Road, Swampscott, MA 01907, USA.

LIGABUE Ilva, b. 23 May 1932, Reggio Emilia, Italy. Singer (Soprano). m. Paolo Pedani. *Education:* Giuseppe Verdi Conservatory Milan and the Scala Opera School. *Debut:* Milan, 1933-53, as Marina in I Quattro Rusteghi. *Career:* Glyndebourne, 1958-65, as Mozart's Donna Elvira and Fiordiligi, Verdi's Alice Ford and Donizetti's Anna Bolena; Chicago, 1961, as Margherita in Mefistofele; La Scala, 1961, as Bellini's Beatrice di Tenda; Guest appearances in Buenos Aires, Dallas, Hamburg, Brussels and Aix-en-Provence; American Opera Society, 1963; Verona Arena, 1971-72; Covent Garden 1963 and 1974, as Alice Ford, Donna Elvira and Elisabeth de Valois. *Recordings:* L'Italiana in Londra by Cimarosa (Philips); Falstaff (RCA); Ascanio in Alba by Mozart (Harmonia Mundi); Cherubini's Lodoiska and L'Osteria Portoghese. *Address:* c/o Teatro alla Scala, Via Filodrammatici 2, 1-20121 Milan, Italy.

LIGENDZA Catarina, b. 18 Oct 1937, Stockholm, Sweden. Singer (Soprano). m. Peter Ligendza. *Education:* Studied in Vienna and Wuerzburg with Henriette Klink; Stuttgart with Trudi Eipperle and Saarbrücken with Josef Greindl. *Debut:* Linz 1963, as Mozart's Countess. *Career:* Sang in Brunswick and Saarbrücken 1966-69, as Verdi's Elisabeth de Valois and Desdemona and Strauss's Arabella; Hamburg Staatsoper from 1967; Deutsche Oper Berlin and Staatsoper Stuttgart from 1970; Staatsoper Wien from 1971 with Wagner's Ring, Isolde with Carlos Kleiber, Lisa in The Queen of Spades, Elsa in Lohengrin with Placido Domingo; Staatsoper München, Fliegende Holländer, Lohengrin from 1978 and Götterdämmerung; Sang Arabella at La Scala in 1970; Salzburg Easter Festival, conducted by Karajan; Metropolitan Opera debut 1971, as Beethoven's Leonore; Bayreuth Festival 1971-77, as Brünnhilde and Isolde, 1986-87 as Elsa in Lohengrin and Isolde; Covent Garden debut 1972, as Senta in Der fliegende Holländer; Wagner's Ring with Deutsche Oper Berlin 1987 in Japan. Retired from stage, 1988. TV-Productions and Operafilms: Der fliegende Holländer (Kaslik/Sawallisch); Lohengrin, Elsa (Everding/Sawallisch); Freischütz, Agathe (Freyer/Russel-Davies); Elektra, Chrysothemis (Friedrich/Karl Böhm). *Recordings:* Third Norn in Götterdämmerung (Deutsche Grammophon); Arias by Handel; (DGG) Eva in Meistersinger von Nuernberg; Lars Erik Larsson Förklädd gud, Three songs Rangström, Sweden. *Address:* c/o Royal Opera, Stockholm, Sweden.

LIGENDZA Peter, b. 4 Mar 1943, Jauer, Schlesien. Solo-Oboist. *Education:* Studied in Staatskonservatorium Würzburg with Prof. Kurt Hausmann, Hochschule für Musik Hannover with Prof.

Kurt Kessler. *Career:* From 1965 Opera Orchestra of Saarbrücken, Chamber Orchestra Karl Ristenpart; From 1972 Member of the Soloists of The Ansbacher Bachwoche, Bach orchestra Karl Richter Munich, Radio orchestra Stockholm with Neville Marriner and Okku Kamu; Teacher at the International Orchestra and Chamber Music Courses in Ljusdal, Sweden; Solo concerts in Germany, France and Sweden; Record, Radio and TV Productions with Deutsche Grammophon, Bayerische Rundfunk, Radio Sweden and Sender Freies Berlin (SFB).

LIGETI András, b. 1953, Hungary. Conductor. *Education:* Franz Liszt Academy, Budapest, violin diploma, 1976; Conducting with Andras Korodi. *Career:* Orchestra Leader, Hungarian State Opera House, 1976-80; Regular concerts as solo violinist in Europe and Canada; Associate Conductor (with György Lehel) of the Budapest Symphony Orchestra 1985, tours of Britain, Europe and America; Regular conductor at the Budapest Opera; British debut 1989, with the BBC Symphony Orchestra; Returned to conduct the BBC Scottish Symphony Orchestra, BBC Philharmonic 1991, with Duke Bluebeard's Castle by Bartók, Weber's 2nd piano concerto and Mahler's 5th Symphony. *Address:* c/o Norman McCann International Artists Ltd, The Coach House, 56 Lawrie Park Gardens, London SE26 6XJ, England.

LIGETI György Sandor, b. 28 May 1923, Dicsöszentmarton, Romania. Composer. m. Dr. Vera Spitz 1957, 1 son. *Education:* Budapest Academy of Music; Studied with Ferenc Farkas and Sándor Veress, Budapest Academy of Music. *Career:* Taught, Budapest Academy of Music, 1950-56; Left Hungary, 1956; Guest Professor, Stockholm Academy of Music, 1961-71; Composer-in-Residence, Stanford University of California, 1972; Worked in Electronic Studios, Cologne, Federal Republic of Germany; Active in Music Composition, Cologne, Vienna, Stockholm and Darmstadt; Professor of Composition, Hamburg Music Academy, 1973-89; Festival of Music, including Le Grand Macabre on London's South Bank, 1989. *Compositions include:* Artikulation (Tape Piece), 1958, Apparitions (Orchestral), 1958-59, Atmosphères (Orchestral), 1960, Volumina (Organ), 1961-62, Poème Symphonique for 100 Metronomes, 1962, Aventures for Three Singers and Seven Instrumentalists, 1962, Requiem for Soprano, Mezzo-Soprano, Two Choirs and Orchestra, 1963-65, Lux Aeterna for 16-part chorus, 1966, Concerto for 'cello and Orchestra, 1966, Lontano (Orchestral), 1967, Ten Pieces for Wind Quintet, 1968, Ramifications for String Orchestra or 12 Solo Strings, 1968-69, String Quartet No. 2, 1968, Chamber Concerto for 13 Players, 1969-70; Melodien (Orchestral), 1971, Double Concerto for Flute, Oboe and Orchestra, 1972; Clocks amd Clouds for 12 female voices and orchestra, 1973; San Francisco Poyphony for Orchestra, 1974; Monument, Selbstportrait, Movement for Two Pianos 1976, Le Grand Macabre (Opera) 1977, Trio (Violin, Horn, Piano) 1982; 3 Phantasies after Hölderlin, 1982; 3 Hungarian Études, 1983 for 16-part mixed chorus; 6 Études for Piano, 1985; Piano Concerto 1985-88; Nonsense Madrigals for 6 voices, 1988. *Honours:* Orden Pour le mérite, Bonn 1975; Prix Ravel, 1984; Prix Honegger 1985; Grawemeyer Award, 1986; Doctor h.c., Hamburg University, 1988; Commandeur dans l'Ordre National des Arts et Lettres, France, 1988; Prix Prince Pierre de Monaco, 1988. *Memberships:* Swedish Royal Academy of Music, 1964; Academy of Arts Berlin, 1968; Free Academy of Arts, Hamburg, 1972; Bavarian Academy of Fine Arts, Munich, 1978; American Academy and Institute of Arts and Letters, 1984. *Address:* Mövenstrasse 3, D-2000 Hamburg 60, Germany.

LILBURN Douglas Gordon, b. 2 Nov 1915, Wanganui, New Zealand. Composer; Professor of Music. *Education:* Canterbury University College, Christchurch, New Zealand; Studied with Vaughan Williams, Royal College of Music, London, England. *Career:* Freelance composer; Composer-in-Residence, Cambridge Summer Music Schools, 1946-49 and 1951; Part-time

Tutor in Music, 1947-49, Lecturer, 1949-55, Senior Lecturer, 1955-63, Associate Professor, 1963-70, Professor with a personal Chair, 1970; Director of Electronic Music Studios, Victoria University, Wellington, New Zealand. *Compositions include:* Overture: Aotearoa, 1940; A Song of Islands, 1947; 3 Symphonies, 1949, 1951, 1961; String Quartet and String Trio; 3 Violin Sonatas; a range of works for piano and chamber music ensembles; Electronic music. *Honours include:* Cobbett Prize, RCM, 1939; 3 New Zealand Centennial Awards, 1940; Philip Neill Memorial Prize, 1944; Hon DMus, University of Otago, 1969; Composers Association of New Zealand Citation for Services to New Zealand Music, 1978; Several awards from APRA and Queen Elizabeth II Arts Council; Order of New Zealand, 1988. *Address:* 22 Ascot Terrace, Wellington I, New Zealand.

LILL John Richard, b. 17 Mar 1944, London, England. Concert Pianist. *Education:* Leyton County High School; FRCM: Hon. FTCL: FLCM: Hon. RAM, Royal College of Music. *Debut:* First Concert at Age 9; Debut in 1963, Royal Festival Hall. *Career:* Gives recitals throughout the world and has appeared as soloist with many leading orchestras; Recitals and Concertos with leading orchestras throughout Great Britain, Europe, United States, Japan & Far East; Australia, New Zealand, Canada & Scandinavia; played complete cycle of Beethoven Sonatas at the Queen Elizabeth Hall, 1982, Barbican Centre, 1986, Tokyo 1987 and in California; Season 1989/90 included concerts with the Royal, Tokyo and Helsinki Philharmonic Orchestras; Season 1990-91, Beethoven Concerto cycle in Hong Kong, tours of Japan and Australia, concerts with the Scottish National and Hallé Orchestra, and Prokofiev Sonatas at the Queen Elizabeth Hall; Beethoven Concertos with the City of Birmingham Symphony under Walter Weller; Royal P.O.; Royal Scottish N.O.; both Brahms concertos with the Hong Kong Philharmonic; a concert in Madrid with the St Petersburg S.O. and recitals at the Royal Festival Hall, Vienna Konzerthaus and Prokofiev series at the Châtelet, Paris; Bath Festival, Colmar and BBC Proms, 1992/93; NHK Symphony/Tokyo, Royal Scottish Orchestra, Weller; Celebrity Recital at Symphony Hall, Birmingham; recital/concert in St Petersburg with the St Petersburg S.O. and Leipzig Gewandhaus Orchestra (Played the Brahms B Flat concerto at the 1993 Proms). *Recordings:* These include complete recordings of Beethoven Piano Sonatas and Concertos and Bagatelles, Chandos (CBSO/Weller), 1992; Both Brahms Piano Concertos; Tchaikovsky Piano Concerto No. 1 with London Symphony Orchestra; complete Prokofiev Sonatas ASV, 1991. *Honours:* Fellow, Trinity College of Music, London College of Music; Numerous Prizes include 1st Prize, Royal Overseas League Competition. 1963; First Prize, International Tchaikovsky Competition, Moscow 1970; Dinu Lipatti, Medal; Chappell Gold Medal; Hon. D.Sc Aston, 1978; Hon. D.Mus, Exeter, 1979; FRCM; OBE, 1978. *Hobbies:* Chess; Amateur Radio; Walking.*Current Management:* Harold Holt Ltd., *Address:* c/o Harold Holt Ltd., 31 Sinclair Road, London W14 ONS, England.

LILOVA Margarita, b. 26 July 1935, Tscherwen Briag, Bulgaria. Singer (Mezzo-soprano), *Education:* Studied in Sofia with Maria Zibulka and Michail Jankov. *Debut:* Varna Opera 1959, as Maddalena in Rigoletto. *Career:* Sang in Varna as the Countess in The Queen of Spades and Azucena; Covent Garden and Vienna Staatsoper debuts 1962 and 1963, as Amneris; Guest appearances at the Paris Opéra, the Komische Oper Berlin and the Teatro Colón Buenos Aires; Cologne, Dusseldorf, Los Angeles, Berlin, Montreal and Moscow; Member of the Vienna Staatsoper from 1963, including tour of Japan, 1986, as Marcellina (Le Nozze di Figaro) and Annina (Der Rosenkavalier); Salzburg Festival, 1965-67, as the Hostess in Boris Godunov, conducted by von Karajan; La Scala Milan 1973, as Ulrica in Un Ballo in Maschera, returned 1988, as Mary in Der fliegende Holländer; Many concert appearances and song recitals. *Recordings:* Les Contes d'Hoffmann, Boris Godunov, Der Rosenkavalier, Bruckner Te Deum and Mass no 2 (Decca), Verdi-Messa da Requiem; Maidservant in Elektra (video, conducted by Abbado-

Virgin). *Honours:* Title: Kammersängerin, 1984, Staatsoper Wien. *Membership:* Professor, Hochschule für Musik und dorstellende Kunst/Wien, 1993. *Address:* c/o Staatsoper, Opernring 2, A-1010 Vienna, Austria.

LILTVED Oystein, b. 20 Jan 1934, Arendal, Norway. Singer (Bass). m. Virginia Oosthuizen. *Education:* Studied with Maria Hittorf in Vienna, Luciano Donaggio in Trieste and Frederick Dalberg in Kapstad, South Africa. *Debut:* Basle 1959, as Konschak in Prince Igor. *Career:* Many appearances at the opera houses of Oslo, Stockholm, Dusseldorf, Kassel and Barcelona; Sang in South Africa at Kapstad and Johannesburg; Seattle Opera as Hagen in Götterdämmerung; Other roles have been Wagner's Daland, Landgave and Fafner; Verdi's King Philip and Fiesco; Mozart's Osmin and Sarastro; Mephistopheles, Varlaam (Boris Godunov), Oroveso, Rocco, Raimondo (Lucia di Lammermoor) and Swallow in Peter Grimes; Many appearances in concerts and oratorios.

LIM Soon Lee, b. 3 Aug 1957, Singapore. Violist, Conductor. m. 23 June 1983. *Education:* Licentiate Royal Schools of Music, Violin and viola), BM with Distinction, University of Rochester, Eastman School of Music. *Debut:* Paganini, Grand Viola Sonata, Kilburn Hall, Eastman School of Music. *Career:* Sub-principal: Singapore Symphony Orchestra; Assistant Conductor: Singapore Youth Orchestra. *Compositions:* Conducted Singapore Symphony Orchestra for the opening and closing ceremony of the 17th South East Asia Games, 1993. *Honours:* 1st Prize, Singapore National Music Competition (Viola/cello open), 1981. *Memberships:* Conductor's Guild, American Viola Society, American String Teachers Association. *Hobby:* Running. *Address:* 69 Bodmin Drive, Singapore 1955.

LIMA Luis, b. 12 Sept 1948, Cordoba, Argentina. Singer (Tenor). *Education:* Studied voice with Carlos Guicchandut in Buenos Aires and with Gina Cigna in Italy. *Debut:* Lisbon 1974, as Turiddu in Cavalleria Rusticana; Guest appearances in Mainz, Munich, Stuttgart and Hamburg; La Scala Milan 1977, as Edgardo in Lucia di Lammermoor; Further appearances in Strasbourg and Spain as Rodolfo, Cavaradossi and Faust in Mefistofele; US debut 1976, in a concert performance of Donizetti's Gemma di Vergy at Carnegie Hall; Metropolitan Opera debut 1978, as Alfredo in La Traviata; New York City Opera 1979, in La Bohème and Rigoletto; Salzburg Festival 1984, as Verdi's Macduff; Maggio Musicale Florence 1985-86, as Don Carlos and as Riccardo in Un Ballo in Maschera; Covent Garden 1985, as Nemorino and Don Carlos: returned to London 1988, as Edgardo; Salzburg Easter Festival, 1988 as Cavaradossi; Sang Faust at the opening of the season of the Teatro Colón Buenos Aires, 1990; Don José in a new production of Carmen at Covent Garden, 1991; Sang Verdi's Don Carlos at San Francisco, Nov 1992; Madrid 1992, as Don José; New York Met 1994, as Cilea's Maurizio. *Recordings include:* Gemma di Vergy (CBS); Le Roi de Lahore (Decca); Thorn-EMI video of Don Carlos from Covent Garden, Video of Covent Garden Carmen. *Address:* c/o Stafford Law Associates, 26 Mayfield Road, Weybridge, Surrey KT13 8XB, England.

LIMA Paulo Costa, b. 26 Sept 1954, Salvador/Bahia. Composer; Professor of Music. m. Ana Margarida Cerqueira Lima e Lima, 2 sons. *Education:* Music School, UFBa, 1969 to 1976; BM, Composition, 1978, MS, 1978, University of Illinois, Urbana, USA. *Career:* Professor of Music Department t Universidade Federal da Bahia, 1979; Head of Music Department, UFBa, 1986-88; Director of Music School, UFBa, 1988-92; Participation as composer in many national and international events. Festivals: Campos de Jordao, Sao Paulo, UFRJ; Director of Music School, Universidade Federal da Bahia, 1988-92; International events: Dresden, Urbana. *Compositions:* Bundle for flute solo, 1977, FCEBa 1981; Ubaba, O Que Diria Bach, 1983, Funarte for chamber orchestra; Atôtô-Balzare, 1985, UFBA for Percussion and Piano; Cuncti-Serenata, 1983, Funarte UFBA for piano solo; Fantasia, 1984, Funarte-UFBA for piano solo. *Recordings:* Compositores Da Bahia 5, 7 and 8.

Publications: Editor of Art - Music Periodical 1981-91. *Address:* Escola de Musica, Universidade Federal da Bahia, Parque Universitario do Canela s/N Salvador 40 000 BA-Brazil.

LIN Cho-Liang, b. 21 Jan 1960, Taiwan. Violinist. *Education:* Studied violin from age 5; Sydney Conservatoire 1972-5; Juilliard School 1975-8, with Dorothy DeLay. *Debut:* Played with the Philadelphia Orchestra under Ormandy and with the London Symphony Orchestra under Previn, 1976. *Career:* Many performances with leading orchestras in Europe and America; Season 1993/94 Concerts in UK, North America, Finland, Germany, Belgium, France and Far East; Plays 1707 Stradivarius once owned by Samuel Dushkin. *Recordings:* Mendelssohn Concerto with the Philharmonia Orchestra conducted by Michael Tilson Thomas; Mozart's 5 Concerti with the English Chamber Orchestra under Raymond Leppard; Concertos by Sibelius and Nielsen conducted by Esa-Pekka Salonen (CBS). *Address:* c/o ICM Artists (London) Ltd, Oxford House, 76 Oxford Street, London, W1N 0AX, England.

LIN Hua, b. 8 Aug 1942, Shanghai, China. Composer; Theorist; Educator. *Education:* Affiliated School of Shanghai Conservatory of Music; Composition Department, Shanghai Conservatory of Music. *Debut:* 1st work, Children's Life piano suite, performed Shanghai, 1960. *Career:* Regular Composer, Shanghai Brass Ensemble, 1968; Regular Composer, Shanghai Opera House, 1976; Associate Professor, Director of Polyphony Music Teaching, Director of Research Section of Composition Department, Shanghai Conservatory of Music. *Compositions:* Bright Mountain Flowers in Full Bloom, for ballet, 1977; Album of Wood Cats, piano quintet, 1980, published 1986; Farewell Refrains at Yang Gate Pass, piano trio, 1980, published 1985; Beauty of Beijing Opera, string quartet, 1983; Fantasy, for accordion and piano, published 1984; Love of the Great Wall, for accordion and piano, published, 1985; Tragedy Suite for Orchestra, 1988; 24 Preludes and Fugues, for piano, 1989; 30 pieces for piano, published, 1991. *Contributions to:* Stravinsky's Technique in Polyphonic Writing, 1984. *Address:* 20 Fen Yang Road, Shanghai, China.

LIND Eva, b. 14 June 1965, Innsbruck, Austria. Singer (Soprano). *Education:* Studied in Vienna. *Debut:* Landestheater Innsbruck 1983, as a Flowermaiden in Parsifal. *Career:* Sang Lucia di Lammermoor at Basle, 1985 and the Queen of Night at Vienna and Paris, 1987; Salzburg Festival 1986 and 1987, as the Italian Singer in Capriccio; Vienna Staatsoper from 1986, as Lucia (Lucia di Lammermoor) and Sophie in Werther; Stuttgart Staatsoper as Adele in Die Fledermaus; British debut as Nannetta in Falstaff, Glyndebourne 1988; Gounod's Juliette at Zurich 1990, followed by Sophie in Der Rosenkavalier at Vienna, Brussels and Berne Opera; Concerts with Francisco Araiza at the Teatro Colon, Buenos Aires, 1990. *Recordings:* Die Fledermaus, conducted by Placido Domingo; Naiad in Ariadne auf Naxos, with the Leipzig Gewandhaus Orchestra conducted by Kurt Masur; Coloratura arias, including Elisabeth ou La Fille proscrit by Donizetti (Philips); Papagena in Die Zauberflöte, conducted by Marriner; Olympia in Tales of Hoffmann, with Jeffrey Tate (EMI); Opera duets with Francisco Araiza; Aennchen in Der Freischüz, conductor, Colin Davis. *Address:* c/o Staatsoper, Opernring 2, A-1010 Vienna, Austria.

LINDBERG Christian, b. 1958, Stockholm, Sweden. Professional Trombone Soloist. m. 4 children. *Education:* Studied trumpet as teenager, then trombone; Further studies in Stockholm, London, Los Angeles, 1978-83. *Career:* Member, Royal Stockholm Opera Orchestra, 1977-78; Currently gives over 100 concerts yearly as trombone soloist with world's major symphony orchestras; Solo programmes including music theatre; Appearances with Per Lundberg, piano, and with Hakan Hardenberger, trumpet; Repertoire includes contemporary music, baroque music played on original instruments, classical and romantic music; Works composed for him include concertos by Schnittke,

Xenakis, Takemitsu and Arvo Part; Played at several UK festivals and Pitea Festival, North Sweden, summer 1993; Season 1993-94 with concerts in Germany, Switzerland, Iceland, Denmark, Sweden, Israel; Tours, USA and with Scottish Chamber Orchestra, Scotland; Schnittke's Dialogue with Nash Ensemble, London; Performances with Prague Symphony Orchestra, Czech Republic, and Gothenburg Symphony Orchestra, Sweden; Carnegie Hall debut with Zwillich Trombone Concerto and world premiere of Trombone Concerto by Toru Takemitsu with St Paul Chamber Orchestra, USA; Several German festivals and Japan tour, summer 1994; 1994-95 season to include performances of Trombone Concerto by Iannis Xenakis, new works by Kalevi Aho and Arvo Part, also tours, Australia, France, Japan; Masterclasses; Designs instruments and mouthpieces for CONN Instrument Company. *Recordings include:* British trombone concerti; American concerti; Italian repertoire for trombone, voice and chamber organ; Gemeaux by Takemitsu; Frank Martin's Ballade with Concertgebouw Orchestra and Riccardo Chailly. *Address:* c/o Clarion/Seven Muses, 47 Whitehall Park, London N19 3TW, England.

LINDBERG Magnus, b. 27 June 1958, Helsinki, Finland. Composer; Pianist. *Education:* Studied at the Sibelius Academy Helsinki; Futher Studies with Globokar in Paris, Donatoni in Siene and Ferneyhough at Darmstadt. *Compositions include:* Three Pieces for Horn & String Trio; Arabesques for Wind Quintet; Quintet for Piano and Wind; De Tartuffe je Croi for String Quartet and Piano; Drama for Orchestra; Sculpture II for Orchestra; Linea d'Ombra for Flute and Ensemble; Action Situation Signification for Horn or Clarinets and Ensemble; Ritratto for Orchestra; Zona for Ensemble; Metal Work for Accordion And Percussion; Kraft for Orchestra; UR for 5 Players and Live Electronics; Twine for Piano; Trios Sculptures for Orchestra; Tape: Etwas Zarter; Ohne Audruck; Faust. *Honours include:* Prix Italia for Faust; Nordic Music Prize for Kraft.

LINDBERG Nils Per Olof, b. 11 June 1933, Uppsala, Sweden. Composer; Organist; Arranger; Pianist. m. Annemarie, 3 sons. *Education:* University of Uppsala; Royal Academy of Music, Stockholm. *Career:* Performances on Swedish Radio & TV; Accompanist to Judy Garland during her Northern Tour; Appearances on Norddeutscher Rundfunk, Hanover, Hamburg and Madrid TV; Tours of Brazil and USA; Tours in Northern Europe as pianist and arranger with Duke Ellington and his orchestra, 1973. *Compositions include:* 7 Dalcarlian Paintings; Trisection; Blues for Bill; Reflections; Petra; Zodiac; Brand New; Ars Gratia Artis; Trumpet Song; In Memoriam Rolf Billberg; Polska with a Trumpet; Lapponian Suite; Noah's Ark; Cubits; Storm Warning; Concerto Grosso; Suite for soprano, choirs, organs and orchestra specially written for the Pope's Mass, June 1989 in the Cathedral of Uppsala; Requiem, 1993. *Recordings:* Music with a Jazz Flavour (Alice Babs); Jan Allan with Music by Nils Lindberg; Own Compositions; 2 recordings with Putte Wickman; O Mistress Mine, suite for soloist and orchestra, 1990; Dalecarlian Legends, suite for soloists and orchestra, 1992. *Address:* Adelborasvägen 10, 78041 Gagnef, Sweden.

LINDE Hans-Martin, b. 24 May 1930, Werne, Germany. Recorder Player; Flautist; Composer. m. Gudrun Olshausen, 1 son, 2 daughters. *Education:* Staatliche Hochschule fur Musik, Freiburg 1947-51, with Konrad Lechner (conducting) and Gustav Scheck (flute). *Career:* Solo flautist of the Cappella Coloniensis of West German Radio, Cologne; Concert tours in Europe, USA, South America, Middle and Far East from 1955; Teacher of Baroque flute, recorder and conducting from 1957; Conductor of vocal ensemble (1965-) and chamber orchestra, 1970- of the Schola Cantorum Basiliensis, Basle; Co-Editor, Zeitschrift für Spielmusik, 1966-; Concert associations with August Wenzinger and Frans Brueggen; Conducted the Basler-Linde Concert in Vivaldi's La Griselda at Ludwigshafen, 1989. *Recordings include:* Flute concertos by Leclair, Stamitz, Dittersdorf and Mozart; Recorder concertos by Sammartini and Vivaldi; English Consort Music and

Chamber Music by Bach, Handel, Haydn with the Linde-Consort; Conductor of the Linde-Consort and the Cappella Coloniensis; Guest conductor of several orchestras und choirs in different European countries and in the USA. Recordings as a conductor include: Bach; Masses, Brandenburg Concertos, Orchestral Suites, Schütz: Exequien, Handel: Water-Music, Music for the Royal Fireworks, Concerti grossi op. 6, Keiser's Der grossmutige Tomyris, (EMI). *Publications:* Kleine Anleitung zum Verrzieren alter Musik 1958; Handbuch des Blockflötenspiels 1962.

LINDENSTRAND Sylvia, b. 24 June 1942, Stockholm, Sweden. Singer (mezzo-soprano). *Education:* Studied at the Opera School of the Royal Oepra, Stockholm. *Debut:* Stockholm 1962, as Olga in Eugene Onegin. *Career:* Has sung at the Royal Opera, Stockholm, as Dorabella, Cherubino, Marina in Boris Godunov, Octavian, Brangäne, Fricka in the Ring and Cenerentola; Sang Tchaikovsky's Maid of Orleans 1986 and sang in Singoalla by Gunnar de Frumerie 1988; Guest appearances at Bayreuth (1964), Copenhagen and the Moscow Bolshoi; Glyndebourne 1975 and 1979, as Dorabella and Amaranta in La Fedeltà Premiata; Aix-en-Provence 1976, Zerlina in Don Giovanni; Sang Idamante in Idomeneo at Drottningholm; Royal Opera Stockholm, 1991 as Dionysus in the premiere of Backanterna by Daniel Börtz (production by Ingmar Bergman); Many concert engagements. *Recordings include:* Songs by Liszt. *Honours include:* Swedish Court Singer, 1982. *Address:* c/o Kungliga Teatern, PO Box 16094, S-102 51 Stockholm, Sweden.

LINDERMEIER Elisabeth, b. 1923, Munich Germany. Singer (Soprano). m. Rudolf Kempe (died 1976). *Education:* Studied at Munich Musikhochschule. *Debut:* Bavarian State Opera, Munich 1946, as the Sandman in Hansel and Gretel. *Career:* Many appearances in Munich in the lyric soprano repertory: appeared with the company at Covent Garden in the British premiere of Strauss's Die Liebe der Danae, 1953; Berlin and Dresden 1956, as Leonora in Il Trovatore; Glyndebourne Festival 1956, Donna Elvira; Sang Freia and Gutrune in Ring cycles at Covent Garden and appeared also in a stage version of Handel's Samson 1958; Further engagements in Vienna, Frankfurt and Amsterdam; Strauss performances at the Munich Festival. *Recordings:* Die Zaubergeige by Werner Egk, Hansel and Gretel (Deutsche Grammophon); Daphne by Strauss, Munich 1950 (Melodram); Finale of Götterdämmerung (Fonit-Cetra). *Address:* c/o Bayerische Staatsoper, Postfach 745, D-80336 Munich 1, Germany.

LINDHOLM Berit Maria, b. 18 Oct 1934, Stockholm, Sweden. Opera Singer (Soprano). m. Hans Lindholm, 2 d. *Education:* Studied at Stockholm Opera School. *Debut:* Countess in Le Nozze de Figaro, Stockholm, 1963. *Career:* Performances all Over The World Including, New York, Carnegie Hall, San Francisco, Chicago, London, Paris, Hamburg, Berlin, Munich, Moscow, Naples, Madrid, Geneva, Düsseldorf, Vienna, Barcelona, Bayreuth; Repertoire Includes, Isolde, Brünnhilde, Kundry, Tosca, Salome, Electra, Turandot, Fidelio, Dyer's Wife in Die Frau ohne Schatten. *Recordings include:* Les Troyens; Songs by Swedish Composers. *Membership:* Swedish Royal Academy of Music. *Honours:* Opera Singer by Appointment of the King of Sweden. *Address:* Artistsekretariat Ulf Tornquist, Sankt Eriksqatan 100, S-11331 Stockholm, Sweden.

LINDLEY Simon Geoffrey, b. 10 Oct 1948, Barnhurst, Kent, England. Cathedral and Concert Organist; Chorus Master. m. Carel Louise McMiram, 20 July 1974, 3 sons, 1 daughter. *Education:* Royal College of Music, London, with John Birch; FRCO(CHM); GRSM; FTCL; ARCM; LRAM. *Debut:* Westminster Cathedral, London, Aug. 1969. *Career:* Deputy Organist, Westminster Cathedral, 1969-73; Assistant Master of Music, St Albans Cathedral, Director of Music, St Albans School, 1970-75; Master of Music, Leeds Parish Church, 1975-; Chorus Master, Halifax Choral Society, 1975-87; Leeds Philharmonic, 1975-83; Leeds City Organist

and Senior Lecturer, Leeds Polytechnic, 1976-; Religious Music Advisor, Yorkshire Television, 1981-. *Compositions include:* Come Sing and Dance (carol); Litany to Mary; Matthew, Mark, Luke and John; Choral Carillon for boys' voices; Arrangements: Jesu joyaunce of my heart (Bach); How dazzling fair (Bourgeois). *Recordings:* Vista: Romantic Organ Music from Leeds Parish Church; Organ Music from Leeds; Rheinberger Trio for Violin, Cello and Organ; Whitetower: Telemann and Music from the Age of Elegance (with London Festival Players); Abbey (with LPC Choir): Elgar and Liszt; 20th Century Church Music; Music for Passiontide; Sacred Songs and Solos. *Publications:* Anthems for Unison and 2-part Singing, Vol 2, 1979. *Address:* Highthorne House, Shadwell Lane, Leeds, West Yorkshire, LS17 8AQ, England.

LINDNER Brigitte, b. 1959, Munich, Germany. Singer (Soprano). *Education:* Studied in Munich. *Debut:* Gärtnerplatz-Theater Munich as a Boy in Die Zauberflöte. *Career:* Sang Gretel in Humperdinck's opera (also televised) and in Mozart's Bastien and Bastienne; adult debut at the Ludwigsburg Festival 1980, as Barbarina in Le Nozze di Figaro; Bayreuth Festival 1985, as the Shepherd boy in Tannhäuser; Sang Despina in Cosi fan Tutte for Kiel Opera, 1990; Other roles include Papagena and parts in operettas by Lehar and Johann Strauss; Concert appearances in oratorios by Bach, Haydn and Mozart. *Recordings:* Hansel and Gretel, Die Zauberflöte (HMV-Electrola).

LINDROOS Peter, b. 26 Feb 1944, Pojo, Finland. m. Anja Hilleri Kervinen, 1963, 4 children. *Education:* Studied in Helsinki, with Jolanda di Maria Tetris, 1966-68, & with Luigi Ricci in Rome and Mario del Monaco in Treviso. *Debut:* Cantor, Organist from Sibelius Academy, 1964; Helsinki 1968, as Rodolfo in La Bohème; Gothenburg 1969, notably as Verdi's Otello; Member of the Royal Opera Copenhagen from 1971, Staastoper Stuttgart from 1974; Covent Garden, 1975-76 as the Duke of Mantua and Bacchus; Guest appearances in Berlin, Munich, San Francisco, London and Vienna; Cologne Opera 1983, as Parsifal; Other roles include Verdi's Manrico and Gabriele Adorno, Don José, Janáček's Laca, David in Nielsen's Saul and David, and Apollo in Strauss's Daphne, Don Carlo, Otello, Alfredo, Rodolpho, Cavaradossi; Helsinki 1985, in the premiere of Rautavaari's Thomas; Sang at the Edinburgh Festival, 1987 in Juha by Merikanto; Lausanne and Graz, 1987 as Bacchus and in the premiere of Cerha's Der Rattenfänger; Sang Apollo in Daphne at Munich, 1988; Radames at the Savonlinna Festival, 1989. *Compositions:* The Singing Tree by Erik Bergman; The Hurt of King Charles by Fredrk Pacius; Guest as Don José at Buenos Aires, 1993, Dimitri (B Godunov) Paris Grand Opera, Bacchus-Opéra-comique, Arimide-Gluck in Madrid and Barcelona, Des Grieux-Edinburgh Festival and Montreal, Apollo in Daphne at La Scala, Lohengrin in Copenhagen and Edmonton; Sang Bacchus at Copenhagen, 1992. *Recordings include:* Liszt's Christus (RCA). *Honours:* The White Rose of Finland, The Knight of the Ivass, 1983; Order of Dannebrog, Denmark, 1982.

LINDSAY L Christeene, b. 2 Mar 1951, San Diego, California, USA. Opera Singer (Soprano). divorced. 2 sons, 4 daughters. *Education:* Studied voice with Robert Austin, 1974-86; with Larra Browning Henderson, 2 years. *Debut:* with Pacific Chamber Opera as Laetitia in Old Maid, 1981,. *Career:* Despina (Così fan Tutte); Sister Marguerite (Sound of Music); Gretel (Hansel & Gretel), 1982; Fanny (Cambiale); Lucieta (Il Quattro Rusteghi), 1984; Maturina (Don Giovanni-Gazzaniga); Martha (Flotow's Martha); Little Match Girl, 1985; Adele (Fledermaus), 1986; Saffi (Gypsy Baron), 1987; Marietta (Naughty Marietta), 1988; Managing Director, Pacific Chamber Opera, 1986-88. *Address:* 7807 Artesian Road, San Diego, CA 92127, USA.

LINDSEY John Russell, b. 26 Aug 1947, Chicago, Illinois, USA. Violinist; Music Educator. Divorced. 2 sons, 1 daughter. *Education:* B.Mus., 1970, M.Mus., 1972, University of Illinois. *Debut:* New York City, 1981. *Career:* Concertmaster, Dallas Chamber Players, 1972-73,

Lexington Philharmonic Orchestra, 1976-81, Warren Chamber Orchestra, 1978-81; Associate Concertmaster, Vermont Symphony Orchestra, 1981-; Concertmaster, The Champlain Valley Symphony Orchestra, 1989-; Concertmaster, The Chamber Orchestra of Northern New York, 1988-; Concertmaster, The Hanover Chamber Orchestra, 1990-; Numerous Solo Recitals in New York, Boston, Montreal, Chicago, Dallas; Member, Lexington String Quartet, 1977-81, Quartetto da Camera, 1976-78, Concord Trio, 1976-81; Violinist, The Miranda Chamber Players, 1990-92; Co-ordinator of Strings, Governor's School of North Carolina (summers), 1971-82, Baylor School of Music, 1973-76; String Chairman, University of Kentucky, 1976-81; String Chairman, Professor, Violin, Crane School of Music, State University of New York, Potsdam, 1981-; Allegro Resident for the City of Dayton, Ohio, 1989; Invited Artist, Stage de Musique, Marcillat-en-Combraille, France, Summer, 1988; Violinist The Ruggieri Chamber Soloists, 1992-. *Recordings:* Violin Concerto, Bartók; 2nd Rhapsody, Bartók; Tzigane, Ravel. *Honour:* Mozart Club Award, Wilkes-Barre. *Memberships:* Pi Kappa Lambda; Triple Nine Society; Phi Mu Alpha.*Hobbies:* Travel, History, Philately. *Address:* Crane School of Music, Potsdam College, Potsdam, NY 13676, USA.

LINETTE Boguslaw, b. 19 Mar 1926, Poznan, Poland. Ethnomusicologist. m. Maria Sluzewska, 20 Dec 1954, 1 son. *Education:* Diploma in Musicology, University of Poznan, 1951; Doctor of Humanities, A Mickiewicz University, Poznan, 1968; Professor A Mickiewicz University, 1980; Diploma in Piano Playing, Academy of Music, Poznan, 1954. *Career:* Transcriber of Folk Music, Institute of Arts, 1953; Assistant Academy of Music, Poznan, 1954; Teacher of Music, Governmental School of Ballet, 1955-63; Professor A (Former Adjunct) Mickiewicz University, Poznan, 1963-; Editor-in-Chief, Oskar Kolberg's Complete Works edition. *Publications:* The Ritual Wedding Songs of the Rzeszow Region, 1981; Contribution to Oscar Kolberg's Opera Omnia vols 43, 48-50, 54-57, 59/1, 1965-85; The Music Life, in Dzieje Wielkopolski (The History of the Province Poznan), vol II 1973; Polish Folk Music and Its Place in Contemporary Culture, in, Lidove umeni a dnesek, Brno 1977. *Address:* Instytut Etnologii, A Mickiewicz University, Poznan, Poland.

LING Jan Nils, b. Apr 1934, Orebro, Sweden. Musicologist; Professor. m. (1) Britt Nyberg, June 1958, 1 son, 1 daughter, (2) Monica Lauritzen, Dec 1981. *Education:* Piano studies, Swedish Royal Academy of Music, 1955-59; Ph. cand. 1959, MA 1961, PhD 1967. *Career:* Professor of Musicology, University of Goteborg. *Publications:* Svensk Folkmusik, 1964; Nyckelharpen (Keyed Fiddle), 1967; Levin Christian Wiedes Vissamling: i 1800-talets Folkligpa Vissång (Study of Folksong in 19th Century Sweden), 1965; Folkmusikboken, 1980; Europas Musikhistoria-1730, 1983; Europas Musikhistoria. Folkmusiken, 1989. Also: Articles on music history, sociology of music, folk music, various journals, different languages. *Honour:* Musical prize, Expressen Spelmannen (The Player), 1983. *Memberships:* Royal Swedish Academy of Music; Kungl Vitterhetssamfundet i Goteborg. *Hobby:* Music. *Address:* Anggardsgatan 31, 413 19 Goteborg, Sweden.

LINGE Ruth, b. 13 Oct 1927, Porsgrunn, Norway. Opera Singer; Lyrical Soprano. m. Tormod Linge. *Education:* Private, Oslo, Stockholm, Vienna. *Debut:* As Norina in Don Pasquale, Oslo, 1951. *Career:* Norsk Operaselskap, 1951-58; Member, Den Norske Opera, 1958-; main roles include Zerlina, Donna Elvira, Donna Anna, Cherubino, Papagena, Adina, Gilda, Rosina, Musetta, Olympia; appearances in TV opera productions, radio concerts. *Memberships:* Secretary, Board Society of Norwegian Opera Singers; Society of Norwegian Musica Artists.

LINGWOOD Tom, b. 15 Sept 1927, Guilford, Surrey, England. Stage Director and Designer. *Education:* Studied at Guildford School of Art and the St Martin's School of Art, London. *Career:* Designs for Martin y

Soler's Una Cosa Rara, Jeannetta Cochrane Theatre, 1965 and Manon Lescaut at Covent Garden, 1968; For Australian opera has designed La Bohème and La Forza del Destino, 1970, Nabucco, 1971; War and Peace for the opening of the Sydney Opera House, 1973 followed by Salome and Don Pasquale, 1976, 1978); Teacher at the New South Wales Conservatorium of Music and the National Institute of Dramatic Art. *Honours:* Emmy Award, 1989, for La Boheme. *Address:* c/o Australian Opera, Sydney Opera House, Sydney, NSW, Australia.

LINJAMA Jouko, b. 1934, Finland. Composer. *Education:* Sibelius Academy; Musicology and Literature, Helsinki University; Further studies in Composition, Cologne, 1962-64; Staatliche Hochschule für Musik; Composers Seminar, Kölner Kurse für Neue Musik. *Career:* Organist, St Henrik's Catholic Church, 1958-60; Cantor-organist, Parish of Tuusula, 1964-. *Compositions include:* Orchestra: 2 Symphonies from oratorio Homage to Aleksis Kivi, 1972; La migration d'oiseaux sauvages, 1977; Choral Works: How it is, Oratorio, 1968; Homage to Aleksis Kivi, Symphonic Oratorio, 1970, 1974, 1976; Missa De angelis, 1969; La sapienza, Oratorio da camera, 1980; Mailman Algusta ia Loomisesta, Oratorio, 1983; Chamber Music: String Concerto No 1, 1978, String Quartet No 2, 1979; Concerto for organ marimba vibraphone and 2 wind quartets, 1981; Works for Organ: Sonatina supra b-a-c-h, 1968; Magnificat per organo, 1970; Partitasonata Veni Creator Spiritus, 1969; Missa Cum jubilo per organo, 1977; Organum supra b-a-c-h, 1982; Toccata in d, 1985; Reflections, duet for organ, 1991; Cappella Choral Works: Two Cantio Motets, 1973; 4 madrigals for male voice choir, 1977, 1982; Partita per coro, 1979; On the Road to Splendour, 1980; Has composed numerous solo songs and music for Shakespeare's play, As You Like It, 1972; Numerous recordings have been made of his work. *Address:* TEOSTO, Lauttasaarentie 1, 00200 Helsinki 20, Finland.

LINKA Arne, b. 6 Feb 1938, Zborovice, Moravia. Associate Professor of Music. *Education:* Studied at the Conservatory of Brno and Janacek Academy of Music; PhD, 1972; Sc, 1989. *Debut:* Conservatory of Music, Brno, 1959. *Career:* Professor of Music, Conservatory of Brno, 1969-73; Assistant Professor of Music, JAMU, 1973-; Professor of Music, Conservatory of Prague, 1983-90; Associate Professor of Music, JAMU, 1990-. *Compositions include:* Sonatina for Piano No 1, 1960-61, NO 2 and No 3, 1990. *Recordings include:* Concerts on Radio Brno, TV Prague and, as well as cassettes and video. *Publications:* The Systhematik and Methodik of Twelve-Ton Compositions, 1966-69; Composer Theodor Schaefer, 1978, 1987-88; Music Therapy, 1993. *Honours:* Prize winner at many piano Concerts on Improvisation, 1950-. *Memberships:* Association of Music Artists, Prague; Czech Music Society; Janacek Society. *Hobbies:* Literature; Art; Cars and Engines. *Address:*Lyskova 13, 635 00 Brno, Czech Republic.

LINKE Fritz, b. 15 May 1923, Claussnitz, Germany. Singer (Bass). *Career:* Sang in Chemnitz from 1950; Dresden Staatsoper, 1951-56; Staatsoper Stuttgart, 1956-86; Guest appearances in Hamburg, Munich, Paris, Barcelona, Venice, Rome, Bologna, Mannheim, Cologne, Zurich and Karlsruhe; Bayreuth Festival, 1963-70; Roles include Mozart's Osmin and Sarastro, Verdi's Padre Guardiano and King Philip, Wagner's Daland, Fafner, Hunding and Landgrave, Beethoven's Rocco and Baron Ochs in Der Rosenkavalier. *Address:* c/o Staatstheater Stuttgart, Oberer Schlossgarten 6, D-7000 Stuttgart 1, Germany.

LINN Robert, b. 11 Aug 1925, San Francisco, California, USA. Composer. *Education:* Studied with Darius Milhaud at Mills College; MM 1950 at UCLA, with Roger Sessions, Bernard Stevens and Ingolf Dahl. *Career:* Faculty member at UCLA 1958; Chairman of the department of music theory and composition, 1973-. *Compositions:* Clarinet sonata, 1949; String Quartet, 1951; Four Pieces for concert band, 1954; 2 Piano Sonatas, 1955, 1964; Symphony, 1956; Concerto Grosso, 1961; Brass Quintet, 1963; Woodwind quintet,

1963; Hexameron for piano and orchestra, 1963; Elevations for wind, 1964; Concertino for violin and wind octet, 1968; Pied Piper of Hamelin, oratorio, 1968; Sinfonia for strings, 1967, revised, 1972; Fantasia for cello and strings, 1976; Twelve, 1977; Concerto for flute and winds, 1980; Partita for winds, 1980; Concertino for woodwind quintet and strings, 1982; Concerto for piano and wind, 1984; Vocal music, including Songs of William Blake for chorus, 1981. *Honours:* Commissions and grants from the American Guild of Organists, the Louisville Orchestra and the Huntingson Hartford Foundation. *Address:* c/o ASCAP, ASCAP Building, One Lincoln Plaza, New York, NY 10023, USA.

LINOS Glenys, b. 29 Sept 1941, Cairo, Egypt. Singer (Mezzo-Soprano). *Education:* Athens Conservatory; London Opera Centre. *Career:* Sang in Mainz, Ulm and Wiesbaden from 1970; Guest appearances in most major German opera houses; Bayreuth and Salzburg Festivals; Toulouse 1983, as Carmen; Festival Hall, London, 1983 in the Verdi Requiem; Ghent 1984, as Santuzza in Cavalleria Rusticana; Zurich 1984-85, as Pensithelia in the opera by Schoeck; Paris Opéra-Comique 1985, in The Stone Guest by Dargomizhsky; Lausanne and La Scala Milan 1986, as The Sorceress in Dido and Aeneas and Geneviève in Pelléas et Mélisande; Rome Opera, 1986 as Ermengarda in Agnese di Hohenstaufen by Spontini; Sang Clairon in Capriccio at Bologna, 1987; Auntie in Peter Grimes at the Zurich Opera, 1989; Clytemnestra in Elektra at the Teatro Nuovo Spoleto, 1990; Television appearances include Adriano in Rienzi, Wiesbaden Opera. *Recordings include:* Monteverdi's Orfeo (Telefunken).*Address:* c/o Opernhaus Zurich, Falkenstrasse 1, CH-8008 Zurich, Switzerland.

LIPKIN Malcolm Leyland, b. 2 May 1932, Liverpool, England. Composer and Lecturer. m. Judith Frankel, 5 Aug 1968, 1 son. *Education:* Liverpool College, 1944-48; Royal College of Music, London, 1949-53; Privately with Mátyás Seiber, 1954-57; D.Mus. (London) 1972; ARCM; LRAM 1953. *Debut:* Gaudeamus Foundation, Netherlands, 1951. *Career:* Numerous Broadcast and Public Performances of own compositions of Orchestral, Choral, Vocal, Chamber and Instrumental Music in many countries 1951-. *Compositions:* Sinfonia di Roma, (Symphony No. 1); The Pursuit (Symphony No. 2), Sun (Symphony No. 3); Two Violin Concertos, Piano Concerto, Flute Concerto; Oboe concerto; Psalm 96 for Chorus and Orchestra; Four Departures for Soprano and Violin; Five Shelley Songs; Clifford's Tower for Instrumental Ensemble; String Trio; Harp Trio; Five Piano Sonatas; Violin Sonata; Wind Quintet; Metamorphosis for Harpsichord; Naboth's Vineyard for Recorders, Cello and Harpsichord; Interplay; Pastorales for Horn and Strings; Piano Trio; Prelude and Dance for Cello and Piano; Nocturne for Piano; Bartók Variations for String Quartet; Dance Fantasy for Solo Violin. *Recordings:* Clifford's Tower; Pastorale, String Trio recorded by Nash Ensemble on Hyperion Label, 1986; Piano trio recorded by English Piano Trio on Kingdom label, 1992. *Publications:* Most compositions listed above are published in England, some by Chester Music, London, but most by The Composer as a Self-Publishing Venture; First work published: Violin Sonata (Chester, London), 1961; Malcolm Lipkin and his recent music by Christopher Headington, Tempo, June 1989. *Contributions to:* The Music of M L, by Hamish Good (Musical Times), 1969; M L Pursuit by Andrew Burn (Musical Times), 1983; Malcolm Lipkin by Malcolm Miller (Musical Opinion), 1992; M L by Lucien Jenkins (Classical Music), 1993. *Hobbies:* Long Country Walks. *Address:* Penlan, Crowborough Hill, Crowborough, Sussex, TN6 2EA, England.

LIPKIN Seymour, b. 14 May 1927, Detroit, Michigan, USA. Pianist; Conductor. *Education:* Studied at the Curtis Institute, 1938-47, with David Sapert, Rudolf Serkin and Horsowski; Conducting studies with Koussevitsky at the Berkshire Music Centre and as apprentice to George Szell at the Cleveland Orchestra, 1947-48. *Debut:* Conducted the Cleveland Little Symphony, 1948. *Career:* Soloist with the New York

Philharmonic, 1949; Concerts with leading American orchestras; Teacher of conducting at the Berkshire Music Center, 1951-64; Conducted the New York City Opera, 1958, New York Philharmonic, 1959, Long Island Symphony, 1963-79; Joffrey Ballet, 1966-79; Teacher of piano at the Curtis Institute from 1969, Manhattan School from 1972; Resumed solo piano career in New York 1981. *Honours include:* Winner, Rachmaninov Piano Competition, 1948. *Address:* c/o Manhattan School for Music, 120 Claremont Avenue, New York, NY 10027, USA.

LIPMAN Michael, b. 15 Mar 1954, Meriden, Connecticut, USA. Cellist; Educator. *Education:* Paul Olefsky, Hartt College of Music; Ronald Leonard and Paul Katz, Eastman School of Music; Leonard Rose, Blossom Music Festival; BMus, Eastman School of Music, 1976; MMus in Performance and Literature, Eastman, 1978. *Debut:* Pittsburgh, 1985. *Career:* Principal Cello, Aspen Chamber Symphony, 1978-80; Associate Principal Cello, New Haven Symphony, 1978-79; Cello, Rochester Philharmonic, 1977-78; Cello, Pittsburgh Symphony, 1979-; Soloist, Pittsburgh Symphony, 1985 and 1993; Soloist, Aspen Philharmonia Orchestra, 1977; Recitals and Chamber Music Concerts throughout USA; Cleveland Chamber Seminar, 1977-78; New York String Seminar, 1976-77; Aspen Music Festival, 1976-80; Grand Teton Music Festival, 1982; Artist Lecturer in Cello, Carnegie-Mellon University, 1986-; Cellist and Founding Member, The California University of Pennsylvania String Quartet, 1986-; Full length radio broadcast of Pittsburgh debut recital, WQED, 1986; Solo and Chamber music performances in Beijing China and in Moscow, Soviet Union, 1987 and 1989 . *Honours:* 1st Prize, Aspen Concerto Competition, 1977; Pittsburgh, Pennsylvania Y Music Society Passamaneck Award, 1985. *Hobbies:* Racquetball; Golf; Running; Reading. *Address:* 4011 Boulevard Drive, Pittsburg, PA 15217, USA.

LIPOVETSKY Leonidas, b. 2 May 1937, Montevideo, Uruguay. Concert Pianist; Lecturer; Educator. m. Astrid Eir Jonsson, 14 April 1973, 1 son, 2 daughters. *Education:* Juilliard School of Music, NYC, USA; Studied Piano with Wilhelm Kolischer at The Kolischer Conservatory, Montevideo, Uruguay and with Rosina Lhevinne and Martin Canin. *Debut:* National Symphony, Montevideo, Uruguay, 1959; NYC, 1967; Recital, NYC, 1964. *Career:* S. American premiere of Britten's Piano Concerto in D, Montevideo, 1959; Concert tours in UK, Europe, Scandinavia, USA, Canada, Central and South America; Soloist on tour with Czech Philharmonic, Leos Janáček in Spain and Czechoslovakia and with English Chamber Orchestra in USA. National Symphony Orchestra, Mexico; National Orchestra Association, NYC, USA; Juilliard Orchestra, NYC, USA; Winnipeg Symphony, Canada; Royal Liverpool Philharmonic, UK; Seville Philharmonic, Spain; National Symphony of Iceland, Reykjavik; Chicago Chamber Orchestra, Chicago; Cedar Rapids Symphony, Iowa; Broadcasts include BBC, London, UK; Rikisutvarpid, Iceland; WNYC, USA; WFMT-FM, Chicago, USA; TV appearances and Special Guest Artist, UN General Assembly; Lectures at Trinity College of Music and Dartington College, UK and at The Juilliard School of Music, NYC, USA; The High Museum of Art,. Atlanta, GA; The Appleton Museum, Ocala, FL as well as in universities, Colleges and Systems of Education in the USA, Alaska, Canada, Puerto Rico, Central and South America; Creator of Project, Music and The Arts; Associate Professor of Piano, School of Music, The Florida State University, USA. *Current Management:* The ALKAHEST Agency, Inc., PO Box 12403, Northside Station, Atlanta, GA 30355, USA. *Address:* 1802 Atapha Nene, Tallahassee, FL 32301, USA.

LIPOVŠEK Marjana, b. 3 Dec 1946, Ljubljana, Yugoslavia. Singer (Mezzo- soprano). *Education:* Studied in Ljubljana and at the Music Academy in Graz; Has sung at the Bavarian State Opera, Munich from 1983, notably as Konchakovna in Prince Igor and Fricka in Der Ring des Nibelungen; Bregenz Festival from 1988 as Dalila and Carmen (1991); Has sung at the Vienna

Staatsoper and in Berlin, Stuttgart, Frankfurt, Hamburg, Madrid and Milan. Covent Garden debut 1990 as Clytemnestra in Elektra conducted by Georg Solti; Other roles include Ulrica, Orfeo, Octavian, Dorabella, Mistress Quickly, Azucena, Amneris, Brangaena, Marfa in Khovanshchina and Marie in Wozzeck; Concert engagements with Abbado, Horst Stein, Harnoncourt, Helmuth Rilling, Colin Davis, Sinopoli, Maazel, Sawallisch and Haitink; Beethoven's Missa Solemnis under Michael Gielen (also televised); London debut 1988 in Das Lied von der Erde with the London Symphony; Salzburg Festival recitals from 1985; Other recitals at the Schleswig-Holstein and Hohenems Festivals, in Brussels, Amsterdam, Vienna and Germany and at the Wigmore Hall, London (1990); Season 1990-91 US concert debut with the New York Philharmonic conducted by Ozawa and the Boston Symphony Orchestra; Sang the Nurse in Die Frau ohne Schatten at the 1992 Salzburg Festival. *Recordings include:* Bach's Passions; Orfeo by Gluck and Messiah; Beethoven's 9th Symphony; Fricka in Das Rheingold and Die Walküre; Orlofsky in Die Fledermaus; the Witch in Hansel and Gretel under Jeffrey Tate; Clytemnestra in Elektra under Sawallisch. *Honours include:* Grand Prix du Disque for recording of Martin's Cornet. *Address:* c/o Lies Askonas Ltd., 186 Drury Lane, London WC2B 5RY, England.

LIPP Wilma, b. 26 Apr 1925, Vienna, Austria. Singer (Soprano). *Education:* Studied in Vienna and with Toti dal Monte in Milan. *Debut:* Vienna 1943, as Rosina in Il Barbiere di Siviglia. *Career:* Member of the Vienna Staatsoper from 1945, notably as Mozart's Queen of Night; Salzburg Festival from 1948, as Mozart's Servilia, Blondchen, Donna Elvira and Queen of Night; Covent Garden 1951, as Gilda in Rigoletto; La Scala Milan 1950 and Glyndebourne 1957, as Constanze in Die Entführung; US debut at San Francisco 1962, as Nannetta in Falstaff; Guest apearances in London, Hamburg, Munich, Berlin and Paris; Returned to Salzburg 1983-84, as the Duenna in Der Rosenkavalier, (also at Turin, 1986). *Recordings:* Brahms Ein Deutsches Requiem (Philips); Die Zauberflöte; Die Entführung; Fra Diavolo; Die Fledermaus; Fidelio; Der Rosenkavalier (Deutsche Grammophon). *Address:* c/o Staatsoper, Opernring 2, A-1010 Vienna, Austria.

LIPPERT Manja, b. 16 Feb 1957, Stuttgart, Germany. Pianist; Professor of Piano. *Education:* Studied with Louis Kentner, Einar Steen-Nokleberg, Arne Torger; Courses with Hans Leygraf; Chamber music with Norbert Brainin, M. Horszowski, others. *Debut:* Steinway Piano Competition, Berlin, 1966. *Career:* Professor of Piano, Hochschule für Musik, Detmold, 1988-; Concert appearances, Germany and abroad. *Recordings:* Various for radio and television. *Honours:* 1st Prize, Steinway Piano Competition, 1966; Several 1st prizes, piano and chamber music competitions. *Address:* Woeste 44, 48291 Telgte, Germany.

LIPPERT Marion, b. 24 Sept 1939, Munich, Germany. Singer (Soprano). *Education:* Studied with the late Annelies Kupper in Munich; Further study in Padua. *Debut:* Hagen 1956, as Aida. *Career:* Augsburg, Cologne and Stuttgart 1959-62; Member of the Bavarian State Opera, Munich; Guest appearances in Germany, Austria, Italy, France and South America; Metropolitan Opera 1969, as Puccini's Turandot; Other roles include Verdi's Lady Macbeth, Abigaille, Leonora and Amelia, Wagner's Brünnhilde, Venus and Senta, Mozart's Donna Anna, the Marschallin in Der Rosenkavalier, Beethoven's Leonore and the Empress in Die Frau ohne Schatten. *Address:* c/o Bayerische Staatsoper, Postfach 745, D-8000 Munich, Germany.

LIPPMANN Friedrich, b. 25 July 1932, Dessau, Germany. Musicologist. m. Gudrun Schuppa, 1 child. *Education:* PhD, 1962. *Career:* Member, Joseph Haydn Institute, Cologne, 1962-64; Director, Music History Department, German Historical Institute, Rome, Italy, 1964-. *Publications:* Editor, J Haydn Harmoniemesse, 1966; Vincenzo Bellini und die Italienische Opera seria seiner Zeit, 1969 (Italian version, 1981); Versificazione

italiana e ritmo musicale, 1985. *Contributions to:* Various professional journals and Editor, Analecta Musicologica and Concentus musicus. *Memberships:* International Musicological Society; Germany Society for Music Research; Italian Musicological Society. *Hobbies:* Literature; Art. *Address:* 391 via Aurelia Antica, 1taly-00165 Rome, Italy.

LIPTAK David, b. 18 Dec 1949, Pittsburgh, Pennsylvania, USA. Composer; Pianist; Teacher. m. Catherine Tait, 1 daughter. *Education:* Duquesne University, 1967-71; BM, Eastman School of Music, 1973-76; MM, DMA, Composition. *Career:* Composition and Theory Faculties, Michigan State University, 1976-80; University of Illinois, 1980-87; Eastman School of Music, 1986-, Chairman of Compositions Department, 1993-. *Compositions:* Loner, 1989; Arcs, 1986; Seven Songs, 1984; Rhapsodies, 1992; Ancient Songs, 1992; Shadower, 1991; Trio, 1990; Duo, 1979/92. *Recordings:* Seven Songs, 1984; Illusions, 1989; Gasparo Records, GSCD-286. *Publications:* All compositions published by Norruth Music, Inc, Saint Louis, Missouri, USA. *Address:* Composition Department, Eastman School of Music, 26 Gibbs Street, Rochester, NY 14064, USA.

LIPTON Daniel B, b. 1950, Paris, France. Conductor; Artistic Director. m. Olga Lucia Gaviria, 7 Mar 1983. *Education:* High School of Music and Art; Manhattan School of Music; Juilliard School; Mannes College; Ecole Normale Superieure; Accademia Chigiana. *Career:* Conductor: Settimane Senese; American Ballet Theater; Denver Symphony; Holland Festival (Concertgebouw); Teatro Comunale, Bologna; Maggio Musicale Fiorentino, Florence; Zurich Opera; Liceo Barcelona; Madrid Opera; Teatra La Fenice, Venice; Chatelet, Paris; Sadler's Wells, London; Houston Grand Opera; Utah Opera; San Antonio Festival; Hamburg Staatsoper; throughout North & South America; Paris Opera Orchestra; Bayerische Staatsoper, Munich; Artistic Director: Bogotà, Colombia, Colombia Symphony Orchestra and Opera de Colombia, 1975-83; Opera Hamilton (Ontario, Canada), 1986-; San Antonio Festival, San Antonio, Texas, 1987-; Conducted World Premiere of Gian Carlo Menotti's The Wedding. *Recordings:* Tosca, Puccini; Recital of Montserrat Caballé and José Carreras at The Gran Teatro del Liceo in Barcelona. Video Tapes: Donizetti: Don Pasquale; Giordano: Andrea Chénier; Leoncavallo: Pagliacci; Mascagni: Cavalleria Rusticana; Mozart: Nozze di Figaro; Ponchielli: Gioconda; Puccini: Bohème, Tosca, Turandot; Verdi: Aida, Ballo, Forza, Rigoletto, Trovatore. *Current Management:* European: Carlos Caballe, Ioan Holender; Canadian: Rosario Farro (Improsario); US: Robert Lombardo; James Harwood Management (NY). *Address:* P.O. Box 2080, Stn. A, Hamilton, Ontario Canada L8N 3Y7.

LIPTON Martha, b. 6 Apr 1916, New York, USA. Singer (Mezzo-Soprano). *Education:* Studied at the Juilliard School, New York. *Debut:* New Opera Company, New York, 1941, as Pauline in The Queen of Spades. *Career:* New York City Opera 1944, in Martha; Metropolitan Opera from 1944, as Siebel in Faust, Verdi's Emilia, Amneris and Maddalena, Bizet's Mercedes and Humperdinck's Hansel; (298 performances in 36 parts), Rio de Janeiro 1950; Carnegie Hall 1952, in a concert performance of Wolf's Der Corregidor; Chicago 1956, as Herodias in Salome; Other roles include Verdi's Meg Page and Ulrica, Mozart's Cherubino, and Strauss's Octavian; Also heard as Lieder singer and in oratorio. *Recordings:* Mother Goose in The Rake's Progress; Orlofsky in Die Fledermaus; Handel's Messiah. *Address:* c/o Metropolitan Opera, Lincoln Center, New York, NY 10023, USA.

LISICHENKO Yuri, b. 1 Feb 1954, Lvov, USSR. Solo Concert Pianist; Professor. m. Irina Plotnikova, 20 Sept 1974, 1 son, 1 daughter. *Education:* Lvov Special Music School; Moscow Conservatory. *Debut:* With Philharmonic Orchestra, Hall of Lvov Philharmonia. *Career:* Professor, Moscow Conservatory; Performed: The Great Hall, 1973, 1975, The Small Hall, 1988, 1989,

Moscow Conservatory; Milan, Turin, Verona, Italy, 1991; Basel, Switzerland, with violinist Tatiana Grindenko, 1991; Many TV and Radio appearances including TV film Avantgarde in Music (Company of Musical Programmes), 1989. *Recordings:* Chopin Sonata, A Rubinstein Sonata, Schumann; Melody, compact disc; Baroque music with chamber orchestra under Tatiana Grindenko, 1990; Ondine, Finland. *Honours:* 3rd Prize, Marguerite Long and Jacques Thibaud Competition, Paris, 1975; Honorary Diploma, Tschaikovsky Competition, 1978. *Memberships:* Union of Musicians, Moscow. *Hobby:* Mountain skiing. *Current Management:* Gosconcert, USSR.; Matteo Tradardi, Itaca, Italy. *Address:* Teply Satn styr 25 K.1, Apt. 244, Moscow 117133, Russia.

LISITSYAN Pavel, b. 6 Nov 1911, Vladikavkas, Russia. Singer (Baritone); Teacher. *Education:* Studied in Leningrad 1932-35. *Career:* Sang first in Leningrad, then at Erivan, Armenia; Appeared as leading baritone at the Bolshoy, Moscow, from 1940; Roles included Tchaikovsky's Yeletsky (Queen of Spades) and Eugene Onegin, Escamillo and Kutuzov in War and Peace; Concert tour of USA in 1960, appearing at the Metropolitan Opera as Amonasro; Tour of Western Europe 1963; Sang in vocal quartet with his three children at Leningrad, 1970; Teacher at Erivan Conservatory 1967-73, Professor from 1970. *Recordings include:* Aida, Carmen, Pagliacci, War and Peace, Rimsky-Korsakov's Sadko. *Address:* c/o Bolshoy Theatre, Pr Marxa 8/2, 103009 Moscow, Russia.

LISNEY James. b. 1960, England. Pianist. *Debut:* Wigmore Hall, 1986. *Career:* Regular Appearances at the Royal Festival and Barbican Halls; Perforamnces with Major Orchestras Such as the Royal Philharmonic, The London Mozart Players, The European Community Chamber Orchestra and the Bournemouth Sinfonietta; Many Prestigious Recital Series and Festivals, and Invitations to Perform in the USA, France, Italy, Germany, Romania and Poland. *Recordings:* Tchaikovsky for IMP Classics. *Honours:* Only Artist to be Selected by the Young Concert Artist Trust, Young Instrumentalists of Outstanding Potential. *Address:* 90 Fulwell Road, Teddington, Middlesex TW11 ORQ, England.

LIST Garrett, b. 10 Sept 1943, Phoenix, Arizona, USA. Composer; Trombonist. *Education:* Studied at California State University, Long Beach, and the Juilliard School. *Career:* Organized concerts of contemporary music and as soloist gave performances of works by Berio, Maderna and Cage; Jazz and immprovised music concerts; Founder member of The Ensemble, with appearances at Lincoln Center, New York: collaborations with Dennis Russel Favies in season 1973-74; Performances with Musica Elettronica Viva from 1971; Co-founded A-I Band 1977; Teacher, Liège Conservatoire from 1980. *Compositions:* 2 Wind Studies 1971; American Images, cantata, 1972; Your Own Self, 1972; Elegy: to the People of Chile, 1973; Orchestral Etudes 1972-79; 9 Sets of 7 for chamber orchestra 1975; Songs for chamber orchestra, 1975; I am Electric for jazz band, 1976; The Girls for narrator and small orchestra, 1977; Escape Story for soloists and orchestra 1979; Requiem for Helen Lopez for piano and ensemble 1981; Flesh and Steel 1982; Baudeliare 1983; Fear and Understanding for jazz band; Hotel des Etrangers 1983; Time and Desire for tape and trombone, 1985. *Address:* c/o Conservatoire Royal de Musique de Liège, Rue Forgeur 14, 4000 Liège, Belgium.

LISTOVA Irene, b. 1960, Moscow, Russia. Violinist. *Education:* Studied at the Moscow Conservatoire with Leonid Kogan. *Career:* Member of the Prokofiev Quartet (founded at the Moscow Festival of World Youth and the International Quartet Competition at Budapest); many concerts in the former Soviet Union and on tour to Czechoslovakia, Germany, Austria, the USA, Canada, Spain, Japan and Italy; repertoire includes works by Hadyn, Mozart, Beethoven, Schubert, Debussy, Ravel, Tchaikovsky, Bartók and Shostakovich. *Address:* c/o Sonata (Prokofiev Quartet), 11 Northgate Street, Glasgow G20 7AA, Scotland.

LITTLE Tasmin, b. 1965, London. Violinist. m. Michael Hatch, 31 July 1993. *Education:* Studied at the Yehudi Menuhin School, the Guildhall School of Music and with Lorand Fenyves in Canada. *Career:* Many solo engagements with leading orchestras, including appearances with the Leipzig Gewandhaus, the Berlin Symphony Orchestra, the Royal Philharmonic, Philharmonia BBC Symphony, Royal Danish and Royal Liverpool Philharmonic; Conductors include Kurt Masur, Vladimir Ashkenazy, Leonard Slatkin, Charles Groves, Vernon Handley, James Loughran, Edward Downes, Sian Edwards, Yehudi Menuhin, Jan Pascal Tortelier, Richard Hickox and Andrew Davis; Performances in East Germany from 1986, including the Delius Concerto and the Concerto by Dvořák; British engagements at the South Bank Centre, Barbican and Harewood House and the Henley, Chester, Chichester, Cambridge and Salisbury Festivals; Three Choirs Festival 1989, Returned 1993 with the Elgar Concerto; Concerto and recital performances in France, Germany, Denmark, Canada, China, Oman, Zimbabwe, Hong Kong and India; BBC Symphony debut 1990, returning to premiere the concerto by Robert Saxton at the Leeds Festival; French debut 1990 with the Haydn C major and Bach A minor concertos; Promenade Concerts 1990 in the London premiere of the concerto by Janáček conducted by Charles Mackerras; Season 1990-91 included debut with the London Symphony and Bournemouth Symphony Orchestras and a return to the Promenade Concerts, with the Dvořák Concerto; Walton Concerto at the 1993 Proms.*Recordings include:* Bruch and Dvořák Concertos with the Liverpool Philharmonic (EMI); Sonatas by George Lloyd, with Martin Roscoe (Albany); Delius Violin and Double Concertos with Rafael Wallfisch and Charles Mackerras (EMI and Decca); Brahms and Sibelius Concertos (EMI); Vaughan Williams' The Lark Ascending conducted by Andrew Davis (WEA). *Honours include:* Finalist, 1982 BBC Young Musician of the Year; Gold Medal, Guildhall School of Music, 1986; Cosmopolitan Magazine's Woman of Tomorrow in the Arts. *Hobbies:* Theatre; Languages; Swimming; Cooking. *Address:* c/o Ingpen and Williams Ltd., 14 Kensington Court, London W8 5DN, England.

LITTLE Vera, b. 10 Dec. 1928, Memphis, Tennesee, USA. Singer (Contralto). m. Professor S. Augustithis. *Education:* Studied in Paris, Rome, Copenhagen and Germany. *Debut:* New York City Opera 1950, as Preziosilla in La Forza del Destino. *Career:* Guest appearances in Israel, Germany and Italy; Deutsche Oper Berlin 1958-85, notably as Carmen and as Melanto in Dallapiccola's Ulisse and in the 1965 premiere of Henze's Der junge Lord; Vatican Concert 1959, in a Bach cantata for the Pope; Salzburg Festival 1966 as Beroe, in the premiere of The Bassarids by Henze. *Recordings:* Gaea in Daphne by Strauss and Begonia in Der junge Lord (Deutsche Grammophon).

LITTON Andrew, b. 16 May 1959, New York City, USA. Conductor. *Education:* Juilliard School of Music. *Career:* Assistant conductor, La Scala, Milan, Italy after graduation; Conducted: Oslo Philharmonic, Swedish Radio Orchestra, Stockholm Philharmonic, Goteborg Symphony Orchestra, Berlin Radio Symphony Orchestra, WDR Koln. In USA has conducted Chicago Symphony, Pittsburgh Symphony, Los Angeles Philharmonic, Philadelphia Orchestra, Utah, Washington National Symphony Orchestras; Appointed principal guest conductor, Bournemouth Symphony Orchestra, 1986; Metropolitan Opera debut 1989, Eugene Onegin; Conducted Bournemouth Symphony in Bernstein's Age of Anxiety and Sibelius's Second Symphony at the 1991 Promenade Concerts, London; Covent Garden debut 1992 with the house premiere of Porgy and Bess; London Proms, 1993 with Walton's Violin Concerto and Tchaikovsky's Fourth Symphony; Music Director & Conductor, Dallas Symphony, 1994- .*Recordings include:* Over 30 including: Elgar Enigma Variations, Mahler Symphony No 1 and Das Lied von der Erde (Virgin Classics); Tchaikovsky's Symphonies

Nos. 1-5, Shostokovich Symphony No. 10, Rachmaninov Symphonies Nos. 1,2,3. *Honours:* Winner, BBC Rupert Foundation International Conductors' Competition, 1982; Winner, Bruno Walter Conducting Scholarship, Juilliard School; Principal Conductor and Artistic Advisor, Bournemouth Symphony Orchestra from 1988. *Current Management:* IMG Artists (Europe), Media House, 3 Burlington Lane, Chiswick, London W4 2TH, England.

LITZ Gisela, b. 14 Dec 1922, Hamburg, Germany. Singer (Soprano). *Education:* Studied in Hamburg. *Career:* After singing in Wiesbaden joined the Hamburg State Opera: visited Edinburgh with the company, 1952; Sang in the 1954 stage premiere of Martinů's The Marriage; Bayreuth Festival, 1953-4; Often heard in operetta and in Bach's cantatas; Guest engagements in Buenos Aires, Rome, Lisbon, Munich and Brussels; Professor at Hamburg Musikhochschule from 1969. *Recordings:* Lortzing's Der Waffenschmied and Die Opernprobe; Nicolai's Die Lustige Weiber von Windsor; Le Nozze di Figaro; Hansel und Gretel; Scenes from operettas. *Address:* Hochschule für Musik and Darstellende Kunst, Harvestehuderweg 12, 2000 Hamburg 13, Germany.

LIVELY David, b. 27 June 1953, Ironton, Ohio, USA. Pianist. *Education:* Ecole Normale de Musique de Paris Licence de Concert, 1970; Studied Privately with Wilhelm Kempff, Claudio Arrau. *Debut:* St Louis Symphony Orchestra, 1968. *Career:* Soloist with: Cleveland Symphony Orchestra; Baltimore Symphony Orchestra; Kennedy Center, Washington, DC; English Chamber Orchestra; RPO; Vienna Symphony Orchestra; Bavarian Radio Orchestra; Berlin Symphony Orchestra; Nouvel Orchestre Philharmonique; Orchestre National de Monte Carlo; La Scala; Orchestre de la Suisse Romande; Director, St Lizier Festival, France. *Recordings:* Deutsche Grammophon; RCA; Decca; Erato; Melodiya; Etcetera, BNL Productions. *Honours:* Prizewinner, Queen Elisabeth Competition, Brussels, 1972, Tchaikovsky, Moscow, 1974, Geneva, 1971, Marguerite Long, 1971, Dino Ciani Award, La Scala, 1977. *Current Management:* Liliane Weinstadt, Brussels, Belgium. *Address:* c/o Liliane Weinstadt, Rue Langeveld 69, 1180 Brussels, Belgium.

LIVINGSTONE Kathleen Mary, b. 26 Dec 1951, Helensburgh, Scotland. Singer (Soprano). m. Neil Mackie (Tenor), 14 July 1973, 2 daughters. *Education:* Royal Scottish Academy of Music and Drama, 1969-73; Royal College of Music, 1973-75; Diploma, Mus.Ed, RSAM&D, (Honours); Diploma, RSAM&D. Wigmore Hall, London, 1976. *Career:* World Wide Concert appearances; Radio and TV Broadcasts in France, Spain, Italy. *Honours:* Countess of Munster Award, 1974, 1975; Caird Scholarship, 1973; Royal College of Music Scholar, 1973; Earl of Dalhousie Award, 1975; Silver Medal, Company of Musicians, 1975; Major Prizewinner, Royal Scottish Academy of Music & Drama and Royal College of Music, 1969, 1975; Professor of Singing, RCM, 1993. *Memberships:* Incorporated Society of Musicians; Equity. *Hobbies:* Gardening; Cooking; Dressmaking. *Address:* 70 Broadwood Avenue, Ruslip, Middlesex, HA4 7XR, England.

LIVINGSTONE Laureen,b. 3 Feb 1946, Dumbarton, Scotland. Singer (Soprano). Teacher. 1 son, 1 daughter. *Education:* Royal Scottish Academy of Music, 1963-66; London Opera Centre, 1967-69; DipMusEd; RSAM. *Career:* Wide variety of operatic, concert and TV appearances, UK and abroad; BBC Proms; Recitals including Wigmore Hall and 1st BBC lunchtime recital in 1976; Guest appearances with London Symphony Orchestra, Halle, English Sinfonia, Northern Sinfonia, Scottish National and Scottish Chamber Orchestras; Operatic roles include: Zerlina, Pamina, Gretal, Lucia (Rape of Lucretia) with Scottish Opera; Susanna, Sophie and Vrenchen (A Village Romeo and Juliet) with English National Opera North; Gilda in Rigoletto and Sophie in Der Rosenkavalier for English National Opera, 1988; Major roles with New Sadler's Wells Opera, Handel Opera, others; Engagements abroad include Woglinde

at Teatro di San Carlo, Naples, 1980, and Gilda for Royal Flemish Opera in Antwerp, 1985; Professor of Singing, Trinity College of Music, London. *Recordings:* Several recital programmes for BBC; Countess Maritza; Gianetta in The Gondoliers, 1st colour production, BBC TV; Ninetta in L'Amour des Trois Oranges, BBC TV, 1980; Elsie in The Yeoman of the Guard, Channel 5 video; Amore in Il Ritorno d'Ulisse in Patria, Glyndebourne, video, 1973. *Honours:* Caird Scholarship, 1968; Winner, Peter Stuyvesant Scholarship, 1969. *Address:* 12 Pymmes Brook Drive, New Barnet, Herts, EN4 9RU, England.

LLEWELLYN Grant, b. 29 Dec 1960, Tenby, Wales. Conductor. m. Charlotte Imogen Rose, 7 Apr 1984. *Education:* Cheetham's School of Music, Manchester, 1972-79; Gonville and Caius College, Cambridge, 1980-83; Royal College of Music, London; Tanglewood Music Center, 1986. *Career:* Has conducted City of Birmingham Symphony Orchestra, English Chamber Orchestra, Scottish National Orchestra, Royal Liverpool Philharmonic Orchestra, Northern Sinfonia, Scottish Chamber Orchestra, City of London Sinfonia and BBC Symphony, Philharmonic and Welsh Orchestras; Took Stockholm Sinfonietta on UK tour, 1986 and conducted at Spoleto, Charleston and Jeunesse Musicale World Orchestra at Berlin Festival; London Proms debut 1993, with the BBC Welsh Symphony in Mendelssohn's Violin Concerto and Beethoven's Seventh Symphony. *Honours:* Royal College of Music Tagore Gold Medal, 1984; Tanglewood Conducting Fellowship and English-Speaking Union Scholar, 1985; Leeds Conductors' Competition, 1986 (first prize). *Hobbies:* Association football (awarded Blue for Cambridge University, 1982); Travel, when not at work. *Current Management:* Van Walsum Management, 40 St Peter's Road, London, W6 9BH, England. *Address:* Bassett Cottage, 43 Main Road, Long Hanborough, Oxfordshire, England.

LLEWELLYN William Benjamin James, b. 6 May 1925, Farnworth, Widnes, England. Director of Music. m. Mildred Stott, 2 sons, 1 daughter. *Education:* Emmanuel College, Cambridge; Royal Academy of Music; B.Mus., London; Fellow, Royal Academy of Music; Associate, Royal College of Organists; Licentiate, Royal Academy of Music. *Career:* Assistant Music Master, Charterhouse, 1950-65; Founder, Conductor, Linden Singers, 1950-59; Director of Music, Charterhouse, 1965-87; Conductor, The Llewellyn Singers, Leith Hill Musical Festival, 1980-; Conductor, Petersfield Musical Festival, 1990-. *Compositions:* Hymns in Anglican Hymn Book; 100 Hymns and Songs; Hymns for Celebration; New Church Praise; Praise and Thanksgiving; Hymns and Psalms; Edited, The Novello Book of Carols, 1986; Jingle, Bells (Novello), 1991; Three Northumbrian Songs, Novello; in progress, Sing with all my soul (RSCM), 1992. *Recordings:* With Linden Singers. *Honours:* MBE, 1987; Fellow, Royal Academy of Music, 1961; Fellow, Royal School of Church Music, 1993; Hon RCM, 1987. *Memberships:* Rotary Club; President, Incorporated Society of Musicians, 1977. *Hobbies:* Photography; Railways; Sound Reproduction. *Address:* Forecourt, Queen's Square, Colyton, Devon, EX13 6JX, England.

LLOVERAS Juan, b. 6 Apr 1934, Barcelona, Spain. Singer (Tenor). *Education:* Studied at the Conservatorio del Liceo, Barcelona. *Debut:* Tel Aviv, 1966, as Rodolfo. *Career:* Sang in Israel until 1969, Krefeld, 1970-71, Essen, 1971-74, Cologne from 1977; Staatsoper Hamburg from 1973 in 200 performances in the Italian repertory; US debut as Manrico at the San Francisco Opera, 1975; Metropolitan Opera debut 1979, as Turiddu, followed by the Duke of Mantua and Manrico; Deutsche Oper Berlin, 1977-83; Further engagements at Dusseldorf, Stuttgart, Lille, Lyon, Paris, Houseon, 1982, Amsterdam and Covent Garden London, 1981; Other roles have included Edgardo, Enzo, Riccardo, Don Carlos, Macduff, Andrea Chenier, Faust, Werther, Laca in Jenůfa and Henry in Die schweigsame Frau. *Address:* c/o Deutsche Oper Berlin, Richard Wagnerstrasse 10, D-1000 Berlin, Germany.

LLOYD David Bellamy, b. 22 Nov 1937, Stockport, Cheshire, England. Piano Accompanist. *Education:* ARMCM (Performance and Teaching). *Debut:* Recital with Heddle Nash, Wigmore Hall, 1956. *Career:* Accompanist to Jan Peerce, Festival Hall, London and tour of France, Germany, Switzerland, Austria and Netherlands; Television appearance with Jack Brymer, Adele Leigh; Regular accompanist to Jack Brymer, Leon Goossens and Elizabeth Harwood in recitals and broadcasts, Singapore, Hong Kong, India, New Zealand and Spain; Senior Lecturer, Royal Northern College of Music, Professional Accompanist, 1967-. *Composition:* (published) Schubert Arpeggione Sonata, arranged by David Lloyd. *Recordings:* Brahms Clarinet Sonata Op 120/1, Weber Duo Concertante; Art of Leon Goossens. *Honour:* Hilary Haworth Prize, RMCM, 1958. *Membership:* Incorporated Society of Musicians. *Hobbies:* Opera; Travel; Railways; Photography; Motor cars. *Address:* 5 Thornhill Road, Heaton Mersey, Stockport, Cheshire, SK4 3HJ, England.

LLOYD David, b. 29 Feb 1920, Minneapolis, Minnesota, USA. Singer (Tenor). *Education:* Minneapolis College of Music; Curtis Institute, Philadelphia; Berkshire Music Center. *Career:* After 1947 debut sang with New York City Opera, then with New England Opera Company; Athens Festival, 1955; Glyndebourne, 1957, as Tamino in Die Zauberflöte and Bacchus in Ariadne auf Naxos; Other roles were Mozart's Belmonte and Idomeneo, Flamand in Capriccio, Rodolfo, Jacquino and Gonslave in L'Heure Espagnole; Also heard in concert and oratorio; Artistic Director, Hunter College, New York; Director of the Lake George Opera Festival, USA, 1974.

LLOYD George, b. 28 June 1913, Cornwall, England. Composer; Conductor; m. Nancy Juvet, 22 Jan 1937. *Education:* Studied violin with Albert Sammons and composition with Harry Farjeon. *Debut:* As conductor with Bournemouth Municipal Orchestra, 1933. *Career:* Has performed at the Lyceum Theatre, London, 1935; BBC Symphony Orchestra, 1935; The Serf, performed by Royal Opera Covent Garden, 1938; John Soeman, Festival of Britain, 1951; BBC Broadcast 8th Symphony, 1977; Principal Guest Conductor, Albany Symphony Orchestra, 1989-91. *Compositions:* 3 operas, 12 symphonies, 4 piano concertos, 2 cantatas: The Vigil of Venus and A Symphonic Mass; 2 violin and piano sonatas; piano solos. *Recordings include:* 12 symphonies; 4 piano conc; The Vigil of Venus; A Symphonic Mass; Violin and piano sonatas; Piano solos; Works for brass band. *Honours:* Hon DMus, Salford University, 1992. *Memberships:* Association of Professional Composers. *Current Management* Albany Records, UK. *Address:* c/o Albany Records (UK), PO Box 12, Carnforth, Lancs LA5 9PD, England.

LLOYD Jonathan, b. 30 Sept 1948, London, England. Composer. *Education:* Studied at the Royal College of Music, London, with Edwin Roxburgh and John Lambert; worked with Tristram Cary at electronic music studio. *Career:* Worked with Twentieth Century Ensemble, 1968; awarded Mendelssohn Scholarship and lived in Paris,1969-70; Occasional work as performer, busker, street musician, 1974-77; Composer-in-Residence at Dartington College Theatre Department, 1978-79. *Compositions:* Orchestral: Cantique, 1968; Symphony No.1, 1983, premiered 19 Jan. 1989 by the City of Birmingham Symphony Orchestra; Symphony No.2, 1983-4; Symphony No.3, 1987; Symphony No.4, premiered 26 July 1988 at a London Promenade Concert; Symphony No. 5 premiered Birmingham, 1990; Rhapsody for cello and orchestra, 1982; Viola Concerto, 1979-80; Everything Returns for soprano and orchestra, 1977-78; Mass or 6 solo voices, 1983; Missa Brevis, 15; Toward the Whitening Dawn for chorus and chamber orchestra, 1980; Revelation for eight voices 1990; Marching to a Different Song for soprano and chamber orchestra, 1991; Almeida Dances, 1986; The New Ear, sonata for winds, 1985; Songs from the other Shore, 4 pieces for ensemble, 1984-86; Waiting for Gozo for ensemble, 1981; Won't it ever be Morning, 1980; He will make it, for solo cello 1988;

Dancing in the Ruins for ensemble, 1990; John's Journal for saxophone and piano, 1980; Oboe sonata, 1985, 2 String Quintets, 1982; Ballad for the Evening of a Man, for mixed quartet, 1992; Dramatic: The Adjudicator, community opera, 1985; Musices Genus, masque for ensemble and piano, 1974; Scattered Ruins, music theatre, 1973; Music for Alfred Hitcock's Blackmail (1929), 1993. *Recordings:* Mass/Second Symphony (Largo Polofonica 5118), 1992.*Address:* c/o Boosey & Hawkes Ltd., 295 Regent Street, London W1R 8JH, England.

LLOYD Robert Andrew, b. 2 Mar 1940, Southend-On-Sea, Essex, England. Opera Singer (Bass). m. 22 Feb 1964, 1 son, 3 daughters. *Education:* BA Hons, Modern History, Keble College, Oxford; Graduate, Modern History, Oxford University, 1962; Private Study with Otakar Kraus, London Opera Centre, 1968-69. *Debut:* Fernando in Beethoven's Leonore, Collegiate Theatre, London, 1969. *Career:* English National Opera, 1969-72; Covent Garden, 1972-83; Freelance in all major opera houses, 1983-; Met debut, 1988; Principal roles, Boris Godunov; Philip II; Sarastro, Gurnemanz, Fiesco; Mephistopheles, Osmin, altogether 120 roles; Appearances with most leading orchestras; Film: Parsifal, Director, Hans Jurgen Syberberg; Video: Notably Don Carlos, Coronation of Poppea, and Tales of Hoffmann, Boris Godunov & Fidelio; First British Bass to sing Boris Godunov at Kirov Opera, 1990 (also televised); Vienna Staatsoper 1990, as King Henry in Lohengrin; At Covent Garden sang Georgio Walton, Arkel and Commendatore, 1993; Sang in Britten's version of The Beggar's Opera at the 1993 Aldeburgh Festival. *Recordings:* Over 50 recordings with all the major companies, Parsifal, Entführung, Barbiere di Siviglia, Nozze de Figaro, Messiah, Mozart Requiem, Il Trovatore, Macbeth, Rigoletto; Romeo and Juliette and Damnation de Faust in Denon's Berlioz Cycle, Elgar's Apostles. *Contributions to:* Frequent contributions to magazines and BBC radio & TV.*Honours:* Grammy (Mozart Requiem); Grammy Nomination (Figaro). Prix Italia, R P Society Award for BBC's Bluebeard's Castle 1989; CBE, 1991; Elected Honorary Fellow, Keble College, Oxford. *Membership:* Garrick Club, London. *Hobbies:* Sailing, Hill Walking. *Current Management:* Lies Askonas Ltd. *Address:* Royal Opera House, Covent Garden, London WC2, England.

LLOYD DAVIES John, b. 1958, England. Stage Director and Designer. *Education:* Studied at Bristol University. *Career:* Directed Le nozze do Figaro for Pavillion Opera, then supervised 1983 tour of Britain; Staff producer, English National Opera from 1984; Freelance productions include: The Cunning Little Vixen, Gianni Schicchi and L'elisir d'Amore; Season 1988-89 with Wozzeck at the Almeida Theatre, Don Giovanni at the Kammeroper Vienna and Assistant to Tim Albery with Les Troyens at Nice and the Scottish Opera; Co-directed Falstaff at ENO and Rusalka for the Frankfurt Opera, with David Pountney; Der fliegende Holländer at the 1989 Bregenz Festival, Die Zauberflöte and Rigoletto for the Kammeroper 1990-91; Madama Butterfly at Ludwigshafen and Dublin, Christmas Eve at the Guildhall School, 1990; Scottish Opera, 1991, with The Cunning Little Vixen; Produced Der Wiederspenstigen Zähmung by Götz at the 1991 Wexford Festival, Figaro at Dublin, Zauberflöte at Klagenfurt and Zar und Zimmermann at Aachen, 1992-93; Produced and designed The Rake's Progress for the New Sussex Opera, 1992. *Address:* c/o Atholl Still Ltd, Greystoke House, 80-86 Westrow Street, London SE19 3AF, England.

LLOYD-HOWELLS David, b. 11 Jan 1942, Cardiff, Wales. Composer. *Education:* South Gwent College, 1974; Pontypridd Technical College, 1972-73; Ealing Music Centre, London, 1960-64; Trinity College of Music, 1967; BMus, Honours, Wales, 1977-80; MMus, Distinction, University of London, 1981-83; FTCL, FLCM Diplomas, 1979-80; York University, 1984-85. *Career:* Tutor in Music, Gwent, 1971-77; Adult Education, 1980-83; Community Musician, 1984; Freelance Composer, Conductor, Artistic Director, Adjudicator; Works mainly with electronic-live mediums; Music Theatre, Modern Dance Groups, Cedar Dance Theatre Company, London, 1983; D.L.H. Productions, music for film, video and self-therapy 1990. *Compositions:* Sound Spaces 1, 2, 3; Solo Piano, Fine Line; 3 sound-scapes, Piano Solo; World Premier String Quartet, 1978 op. 52 Germany, 1991; Choirs and Dialogues for Fifteen Strings and Electronics, 1987 Perf. LRO 1989; Pinocchio, Music Theatre for adults and children in school, Commissioned LEA, 1990; Symphony No. 3 1978-80; Saxophone Quartet, 1993; The Promenade (Music Theatre 1983), Wind Quartet, 1986; String Quintett, 1988; Music for Bass Trio, Commissioned by Welsh Brass Trio, funds from the Welsh Arts Council; Passions for a Moving Image, tape, 1992; Nightcity Pulses, 1992; The Insects Convention for Madrid Radio, 1992 and Tangerine Radio Moscow, 1993; Funk Street Burn at the Celtic Health Farm, 1991; Concerto (Millenium tape), 1992; Clarinet Symphonies, tape, 1990; Sonata for Organ, 1989; Music for solo violin, 1798; Five variations, Sextet, 1978; Five pieces for Five Players, 1985; Kontrasts, Deckette, 1987; Timecycles St Qt., Electronics, 1988. *Recordings:* Piano Sonata 2, 1978, dedicated to John Lill Argos, Welsh Arts Council. *Publications:* Various commissions including folk opera, The Earthdream; Welsh-American Festival of Youth, 1985; World Premiere performances of Cyclomonos in France, USA and Canada. *Address:* 31 Park Street, Abergavenny, Gwent NP7 8YB, Wales.

LLOYD-JONES David Mathias, b. 19 Nov 1934, London, England. Musician. m. Anne Carolyn Whitehead, 1964, 2 sons, 1 daughter. *Education:* Westminster School; Magdalen College, Oxford. *Career:* Chorus Master, New Opera Co, 1961-64; Conducted at Bath Festival, 1966, City of London Festival, 1966, Wexford Festival, 1967-70, Scottish Opera, 1968, Welsh National Opera, 1968, Royal Opera, Covent Garden, 1971, Sadler's Wells, Opera Co (now English National Opera), 1969-; Artistic Director, Opera North, 1977-88; Conductor for TV Operas (Eugene Onegin, The Flying Dutchman, Hansel and Gretel) for operas in Amsterdam and Paris; Conducted The Queen of Spades at Nice, 1989; Don Pasquale for Opera North, 1990; Guildhall School of Music, March 1990, La Vida Breve and Angélique; The Love for Three Oranges at New Israeli Opera, Boris Godunov at Santiago and Tchaikovsky's Yolanta for Opera North at the Edinburgh Festival, 1992; Appearances with most British Symphony Orchestras. *Publications:* Boris Godunov, translation; Vocal Score, Eugene Onegin; Translation, Vocal Score, Boris Godunov - Critical Edition of Original Full Score; numerous contributions to publications including Grove's Dictionary of Music and Musicians, Musik in Geschichte und Gegenwart, Music and Letters, The Listener. *Hobbies:* Theatre; French cuisine; Rose growing. *Address:* 94 Whitelands House, Cheltenham Terrace, London, SW3 4RA, England.

LLOYD WEBBER Andrew, (Sir), b. 22 Mar 1948, London. Composer. m. (1) Sarah Jane Hugill 1971 (divorced 1983), 1 son, 1 daughter, (2) Sarah Brightman 1984 (divorced 1990), (3) Madeleine Gurdon, 1991, 2 sons. *Education:* Westminster School; Oxford University; Royal College of Music, FRCM, 1988. *Compositions:* Joseph and the Amazing Technicolor Dreamcoat (lyrics by Tim Rice, 1968, rev.1973 and 1991); Jesus Christ Superstar (lyrics by Tim Rice, 1970); Jeeves (lyrics by Alan Ayckbourn, 1975); Evita (lyrics by Tim Rice, 1976; stage version 1978); Tell me on a Sunday (lyrics by Don Black, 1980); Cats (based on poems by TS Eliot, 1981); Starlight Express (lyrics by Richard Stilgoe, 1984); The Phantom of the Opera, (lyrics by Richard Stilgoe and Charles Hart, 1986); Aspects of Love, (Don Black and Charles Hart, 1989); Sunset Boulevard, (book and lyrics by Don Black and Christopher Hampton, 1993); Requiem 1985; Variations on a theme of Paganini for orchestra 1986; Deviser of children's board game Calamity! The International High-Risk Insurance Game. *Publications:* Evita (with Timothy Rice, 1978); Joseph and the Amazing Technicolour Dreamcoat (with Rice, 1982). *Honours:* Numerous including: Laurence Olivier, Tony, Drama Desk and Grammy Awards; Knighted 1992. *Hobby:* Architecture. *Address:* 22 Tower Street, London WC2H 9NS, England.

LLOYD WEBBER Julian, b. 14 Apr 1951, London, England. Musician (Cellist). m. (1) Celia Mary Ballantyne, 29 June 1974, (Divorced 1989), (2) Zohra Mahmud Ghazi, 1 July 1989. *Education:* University College School 1964-67; Royal College of Music 1968-72; Study with Pierre Fournier 1973. *Debut:* Queen Elizabeth Hall, London, 1972. *Career:* Appears regularly with world's leading orchestras, including Berlin Philharmonic, Czech Philharmonic, English Chamber, London Symphony, Royal Philharmonic with such conductors as Solti, Maazel, Menuhin and Neumann; Many TV and radio performances including Elgar and Dvořák Concertos, Face the Music and South Bank Show, 1989. *Recordings:* More than 25 world premiere recordings of works by Arnold, Britten, Holst, A. Lloyd Webber, Rodrigo, Sullivan and Vaughan Williams; Complete cello music of Delius; Concertos by Dvorák, Elgar, Lalo, Saint-Saëns, Honneger, Haydn; Sonatas by Britten, Debussy, Ireland, Rachmaninov, Shostakovich. *Publications:* Classical Cello 1980; Romantic Cello 1981; French Cello 1981; Pieces of Frank Bridge 1982; Young Cellist's Repertoire Books 1, 2 and 3 1984; Holst's Invocation 1984; Travels with my Cello 1984; Song of the Birds 1985; Recital Repertoire for Cellists Vols. 1, 2, 3, 4, 1986. *Contributions to:* The Times; Sunday Times; The Composer; Music and Musicians. *Honours:* Suggia Gift 1968; Seymour Whinyates Award 1971; Percy Buck Award 1972; Gold Disc for Variations Recording 1978; Spanish Ministry of Culture Award for world premiere recording of Rodrigo Cello Concerto 1982; Best British classical recording of 1986 for Elgar Cello Concerto - BPI Awards; Professional Societies committee member, solo performers' section, Incorporated Society of Musicians 1982. *Hobbies:* Topography (especially British); Turtle Keeping; Leyton Orient Football Club. *Address:* c/o Kaye Artists Management, 7 Chertsey Road, Woking GU21 5AB, England.

LOBANOV Vassily, b. 1947, Moscow, USSR. Composer; Pianist. *Education:* Studied at the Tchaikovsky Conservatoire, Moscow, 1963-69, with Leo Naumov, Sergei Balasanyan and Alfred Schnittke. *Career:* Has accompanied Natalia Gutman and Oleg Kagan individually and as member of trio; Interpreter of modern works at festivals in Moscow, Witten, Vienna and Kuhmo, Finland; Premiered his Second Piano Sonata at the Moscow Autumn Festival, 1980; Has partnered Sviatoslav Richter in duets; December Nights concert in the Pushkin Museum Moscow, 1981; Soloist with the Moscow Philharmonic from 1982. *Compositions include:* Oratorio Lieutenant Schmidt 1979; Opera Antigone, 1985-88; Orchestra: Symphony for chamber orchestra 1977; Piano Concerto 1981; Cello Concerto 1985; Sinfonietta 1986; Concerto for viola and strings 1989; Chamber: 5 String Quartets, 1966, 1968, 1978, 1987, 1988; Twelve Preludes for Piano 1965; Partita for piano 1967; 2 Cello Sonatas 1971, 1989; 2 Piano Sonatas 1973, 1980; 3 Suites for Piano; Seven Pieces for Cello and Piano 1978; Variations for Two Trumpets 1979; Seven Slow Pieces for Piano 1978-80; Flute Sonata 1983; Clarinet Sonata 1985; Fantasia for solo Cello 1987; Violin Sonata 1989; Vocal: Three Haikus for low voice and piano, 1963; Three Romances (bass) 1965; Five Romances 1971; Four Poems to texts by Alexei Parin (bass) 1984; Eight Poems (soprano) 1984; Stravinsky's Italian Suite adapted for cello and chamber orchestra 1985. *Address:* c/o Boosey & Hawkes Ltd, 195 Regent Street, London W1R 8JH, England.

LOBANOV-ROSTOVSKY Oleg, b. 12 July 1934, San Francisco, California, USA. Arts Executive. m. Susan Waters, 8 Sept 1979, 2 sons, 1 daughter. *Education:* BA, University of Michigan, 1956. *Career:* Community Concert representative, Columbia Artists Management Incorporated, 1958-59; Manager, Columbus Symphony Orchestra, Ohio, 1959-62; Hartford, Connecticut, Symphony Orchestra, 1962-65; Baltimore Symphony, 1965-69; Executive Director, Denver Symphony Orchestra, 1975-76; Managing Director, National Symphony Orchestra, Washington, 1977-80; Consultant, Federal Council on Arts, 1980-81; Executive Vice-President, Managing Director, Detroit Symphony Orchestra, 1982-83; President,

Detroit Symphony Orchestra 1983-. *Membership:* Past member, Board of Directors, American Symphony Orchestra League.

LOCKE Peter, b. 1 Feb 1937, Wolverhampton, England. Accompanist; Pianist; Voice Coach. *Education:* LRAM 1956; MA, King's College, Cambridge 1960; Diploma di Perfezionamento, Accademia di Santa Cecilia, Rome, Italy 1962. *Debut:* Civic Hall, Wolverhampton 1954. *Career:* Actor: Pitlochry, Leicester, Nottingham, Arts Theatre, London 1963-70; Maestro Collaboratore, Teatro La Fenice, Venice 1971-81; Voice Coach for Tito Gobbi's Opera Workshop, Villa Schifanoia, Fiesole, Italy 1979-81; Music Director, Intermezzi Ensemble, London 1981-84; Repetiteur; The Opera House, Belfast, 1982-84; Principal Repetiteur, Lyric Opera, Brisbane, Australia 1984; Chorus Master, Icelandic Opera, Reykjavik 1986-89; Principal Repetiteur and voice coach, Victoria State Opera, Melbourne, Australia, 1986-1989. Formal piano duo with Brian Stacey, Australia, 1989; Pianist and conductor for Chamber Made Opera, Australia in Fall of the House of Usher (Glass), Greek (Turnage), Sweet Death (Greenwell), 1990-92; Chorus-master, Icelandic Opera, Reykjavik; Requiem (Verdi), 1993. *Recordings:* Mona Vanna, Rachmaninov, (Chandos, chorus-master: Icelandic Opera), 1990. *Membership:* ISM. *Current Management:* Performance Management, 120 Johnson Street, Fitzroy 3065, Australia. *Address:* 9 Emperor's Gate, London SW7 4HH, England.

LOCKE Ralph P, b. 9 Mar. 1949, Boston, Massachusetts, USA. Teacher; Author; Musicologist. m. Lona M. Farhi, 26 May 1979, 2 daughters. *Education:* BA, cum laude, in Music, Harvard University, 1970; MA, History and Theory of Music, 1974, PhD, History and Theory of Music, 1980, University of Chicago; Longy School of Music. *Career:* Faculty Member, Musicology, Eastman School of Music, 1975-. *Composition:* Music to Brecht's Mother Courage. *Publication:* Music, Musicians and the Saint Simonians, 1986. *Contributions to:* New Harvard Dictionary of Music; Grove's Dictionary, 6th Edition; New Grove Dictionary of American Music, 1986; Mendelssohn and Schumann, Edited by Todd and Finson; Nineteenth Century Music; JAMS; IMS Proceedings (Strasbourg), 1986 and 1994; Revue de musicologie; Fontes artis musicae; MLA Notes; various Boston newspapers; New Grove Dictionary of Opera; New Grove Dictionary of Women Composers; Cambridge Opera Journal; Music in Paris in the 1830's edited by Bloom; Les Saint-Simoniens et l'Orient, edited by Morsy; Early Romantic Era, edited by Ringer; Opera News; Musical Quarterly; senioe editor of Eastman Studies in Music; editor-in-chief of Journal of Musicological Research. *Address:* 26 Gibbs Street, Rochester, NY 14604-2599, USA.

LOCKEMANN June Elaine Loughridge, b. 27 June 1969, Garnett, Kansas, USA. Concert Singer (Soprano). m. Wolfgang Adolf Richard Lockemann, 28 June 1969, 1 son, 1 daughter. *Education:* BMus, Coe College, Cedar Rapids, Iowa, 1962; MMus, University of Oklahoma, 1966; Certified Concert Singer, Conservatory of Stuttgart, Federal Republic of Germany, 1969. *Debut:* Conservatory of Stuttgart, 13 June 1969. *Career:* Concerts with husband Wolfgang Lockemann, Rice University, Houston, Texas, 1969-72, Hamline University, St Paul, Minnesota, 1975, Ottawa University, 1976, Ottawa, Kansas, 1980, Tulsa (Oklahoma) German American Society, 1984; Appearance at Aaron Copland Festival, Ottawa University, Ottawa, Kansas, 1976. Radio appearances with husband, 1984, presenting Eichendorf, Goethe, Möricke, Rilke, Heine Lieder as composed by Wolf, Schubert, Schumann, Hindemith, Mozart and Brahms. *Address:* 1300 North McKinley, Sand Springs, OK 74063, USA.

LOCKHART James, b. 16 Oct 1930, Edinburgh, Scotland. Conductor; Accompanist. m. Sheila Grogan, 25 Sept 1954, 2 sons, 1 daughter. *Education:* Royal College of Music, London. *Debut:* Yorkshire Symphony Orchestra, 1955. *Career:* Repetiteur, Städtische Bühnen Münster, 1955-56, Bayerische Staatsoper Münches,

1956-57; Director, Opera Workshop, University of Texas, 1957-59; Repetiteur, Glyndebourne Opera, 1957-79, ROH Covent Garden, 1959-60; Assistant Conductor, BBC Scottish Symphony, 1960-61; Conductor, Sadlers Wells Opera, 1961-62; Rep and Cond, ROH Covent Garden, 1962-68; Prof, Royal College of Music, 1962-72; General Music Director, Staatsheater Kassel, 1972-80, Rheinische Philharmonie and Koblenz Stadttheater, 1981-91; Director of Opera, RCM London, 1986-; (Director of Opera, RCM London 1986)-1992; Director of Opera, London Royal Schools Vocal Faculty, 1992-. *Recordings include:* Dittersdorf: Doktor and Apotheker; Brahms, Schumann, French and Spanish Lieder with Margaret Price; Le Flem, and Schmitt, Rheinische Philharmonie; Cras: Piano Conc-Rhein, Phil. *Honours:* ISM, BMus hons, 1950; ARCM, 1951; FRCO (CHM), 1951; FRCM, 1987; Hon, RAM, 1993. *Hobbies:* Mountain hiking; Swimming; Travel; Languages. *Current Management* Thomas Arndt Int, Management. *Address:* 105 Woodcock Hill, Harrow, Middlesex HA3 0JJ, England.

LOCKHART Keith Steven Alan, b. 7 Nov 1959, Poughkeepsie, New York, USA. Conductor; Educator. m. Ann Louise Heatherington, 22 Aug 1981, (divorced), 1983. *Education:* BA, German, BMus, Piano, Furman University, 1981; MFA, Conducting, Carnegie Mellon University, 1983. *Career:* Assistant Conductor, Cincinnati Symphony Orchestra, 1990-; Assistant Conductor, Akron Symphony Orchestra; Music Director, Akron Youth Symphony, 1988-90; Music Director, Pittsburgh Civic Orchestra, 1986-90; Director of Orchestras, Carnegie Mellon University, 1986-89; Guest appearances: Vermont Symphony, Indianapolis Symphony, Akron Symphony, Orquesta Sinfonica de Tucumán (Argentina). *Recordings:* Carnegie Institute Centennial Commemorative Recording - Adolf Forster, Carnegie March, with Carnegie Mellon Philharmonic. *Publications:* new performance edition of Gay: The Beggar's Opera, 1985. *Contributions to:* International Clarinet Society Journal; Journal of the Clarinet & Saxophone Society of Great Britain. *Hobbies:* Skiiing; Reading; Backpacking; Racquet Sports.

LOCKLAIR Dan Steven, b. 7 Aug. 1949, Charlotte, NC, USA. Composer; Organist; at Wake Forest University. m. Paula Welshimer Locklair, 23 July 1983. *Education:* BM, cum laude, Mars Hill College, NC, USA, 1971; SMM, School of Sacred Music of Union Theological Seminary, NYC, 1973; DMA, Eastman School of Music, USA, 1981; Studied Composition with Joseph Goodman, Ezra Laderman, Samuel Adler and Joseph Schwantner. *Career:* Broadcasts of Locklair Compositions over National Public Radio (including performances on St Paul Sunday Morning, Performance Today and Pipe Dreams); over the Canadian Broadcasting Corporation (Arts National); over Voice of America; Composer-in-Residence, Associate Professor of Music, Wake Forest University. *Compositions:* The Breakers Pound (for harpsichord); When Morning Stars Begin To Fall (for orchestra); Constellations (organ and percussion); Inventions (organ); Prism of Life (orchestra); In The Autumn Days (for chamber orchestra); On Cats (for choir); A Christmas Carol (for choir); Ecstasy in Jericho (for guitar); Visions In The Haze (for piano); ...the moon commands... (for chamber ensemble); In The Almost Evening (for chamber ensemble); Break Away! (for choir); Scintillations (ballet); Good Tidings From The Holy Beast (One-Act Opera); Lairs of Soundings (for soprano and double string orchestra); Flutes (for solo flutes, one player); numerous others: changing perceptions, and Epitaph (Choral cycle); Creation's Seeing Order (A Prelude for Orchestra); Clusters's Last Stand, on the ground, for harpsichord; Dancing in the Shadows, for five recorders; The Columbus Madrigals, for treble voices and piano; Stirs the Stars to Sing, A Sinfonia for band; Alleluia Dialogues, for double choir; Rubrics, for organ, 1988, pub 1992; Voyage, for organ, 1991, pub 1992; Primary publisher: E.C. Kerby Ltd, Ricordi. *Address:* 827 Roslyn Road, Winston-Salem, NC 27104, USA.

LOCKWOOD Annea Ferguson, b. 29 July 1939,

Christchurch, New Zealand. Composer; Performer; University Lecturer. *Education:* BMus, University of Canterbury, New Zealand, 1961; Royal College of Music, London, 1961-63, LRAM, ARCM Piano Performance; Musikhochschule Cologne, 1963-64; Institute for Sound and Vibration Research, psychoacoustical research, postgraduate, Southampton University, UK, 1971-73. *Career:* Major performances of own compositions: Cheltenham Festival, UK, 1965, 1969; Commonwealth Festival, UK, 1965; Paris Biennale 1965; Fylkingen Festival, Stockholm, 1970; Queen Elizabeth Hall, London, 1971. Lincoln Center Plaza, New York, 1974; New Music America festivals, 1979,1882, 1986; Autunno Musicale a Como. Italy, 1979; Sydney Biennale, 1982; Westdeutscher Rundfunk 'Meet the USA Festival' 1982; Asia Pacific Festival, 1984; Westdeutscher Rundfunk 'Ives and Co', 1988; New York-Cologne Festival, 1989; *Compositions include:* Recorded: Glass Concert; World Rhythms; Tiger Balm. Published: Malaman; Spirit Catchers; Humming; Delta Run; Sound Map of the Hudson River; Glass Concert, World Rhythms, Tiger Balm, Malolo, A Sound Map of the Hudson River. *Publications:* Malaman, Spirit Catchers, Humming, Delta Run, Amazonia Dreaming, Tiger Balm, Glass Concert. *Honours:* National Endowment for the Arts Composition Fellow, USA, 1979; CAPS Composition Fellowship, USA, 1979; Arts Council of Great Britain, 1972; Gulbenkian Foundation Grants, 1972. *Memberships:* Composers' Forum, New York (Board Member); American Composers' Alliance; BMI inc. *Address:* Baron de Hirsch Road, Crompond, NY 10517, USA.

LOCKWOOD Lewis, b. 16 Dec 1930, New York, USA. Musicologist. *Education:* Queens College, New York, BA 1952; PhD Princeton University 1960. *Career:* Instructor at Princeton from 1958, Professor 1968-80; Professor, Harvard University, 1980-; Editor, Journal of American Musicological Society 1963-66; Consultant editor for New Grove Dictionary of Music and Musicians, 1980; President of the American Musicological Society 1987-88. *Publications include:* Music in Renaissance Ferrara 1984; Beethoven: Studies in The Creative Process, 1992. *Honours:* Recipient of Einstein and Kinkeldey Awards of American Musicological Society; Elected Honorary Member of American Musicological Society, 1993.*Address:* Harvard University, Music Building, Harvard, Cambridge, MA 02138, USA.

LOCKWOOD Normand, b. 19 Mar 1906, New York, USA. Composer. *Education:* Studies under Respighi & Nadia Boulanger. *Career:* Teacher, faculties of Oberlin College, Columbia University, Union Theological Seminary, New York; Universities of Hawaii & Oregon; University of Denver (composer-in-residence, Professor Emeritus). *Compositions:* Published by: American Composers' Alliance; Augsburg; Associated; Broude; Jensen Publications; Kjos Music Company; Mercury Music; C.F. Peters; Theodor Presser; Shawnee Press; Wilshorn Music; World Library; The Kenwood Press. *Recordings:* Concerto for Organ & Brasses, Remington Records; Valley Suite, violin & piano; To Margarita Debayle, soprano & piano, Composers' Recordings Inc.*Publications:* Normand Lockwood: his life and music, by Kay Norton, (The Scarecrow Press, Inc.), 1993 *Honours:* Rome Prize, American Academy in Rome; Guggenheim Fellowship (twice); G. Schirmer Worlds Fair Prize; Award, Music, National Academy & Institute of Arts & Letters; Marjorie Peabody Waite Award, American Academy of Arts & Letters. *Memberships:* American Composers' Alliance; Life member, National Association of American Composers & Conductors; Composer-affiliate Broadcast Music, Inc. *Address:* PO Box 100053, University Park Station, Denver, CO 80250, USA.

LOCKWOOD Ralph Gregory, b. 21 Feb 1942, Cleveland, Ohio, USA. Horn Player; Pianist; Harpsichord Player; Organist; Conductor. m. Marjorie Yates-Lockwood, 1 daughter. *Education:* MMus, New England Conservatory of Music, Boston; Doctoral Study at University of Cincinnati College - Conservatory. *Career:* Music in Maine Chamber Orchestra; 21 years principal

horn and chamber music performer, Eastern Music Festival, Greensboro, North Carolina; Numerous Television Appearances as Recitalist and Chamber Musician; Teacher, University of North Carolina; Currently Professor of Music, Arizona State University School of Music; Former member of Cleveland Orchestra 1975-76, Phoenix Symphony. Member, The Southwest Brass Quintet, Gammage Wind Quintet, Del Sol Brass Quintet, and founding member of Bach West - chamber music ensemble; A number of American and World premieres of works featuring the Horn: Conductor of Arizona State University Brass Choir; World Premiere of Carl Roskott's Concerto for Horn and Orchestra, commissioned by Ralph Lockwood; Visiting Professor of Horn, Oberlin Conservatory of Music, 1991; Professor of Music, the Arizona State University School of Music, 1992; Performances on horn and Wagner tuba in the Arizona Opera's performances of Die Walkure, Solo spot in Richard Strauss' first horn concerto with the Sun Cities Symphony, 1993; Freelance playing with Phoenix Symphony, Mainly Mozart players. *Address:* c/o The School of Music, Arizona State University, Tempe, AZ 85287, USA.

LOEBEL David, b. 7 Mar 1950, Cleveland, Ohio, USA. Conductor. m. Jane Cawthorn, 7 July 1977. *Education:* BS 1972, MMus 1974, Northwestern University. *Career:* Assistant Conductor, Syracuse Symphony Orchestra, 1974-76; Music director, Binghamton Symphony Orchestra, 1977-82; Music adviser, Anchorage Symphony Orchestra, 1983-86; Assistant 1982-86, associate conductor 1986-90, Cincinnati Symphony Orchestra, Associate Conductor, St Louis Symphony Orchestra, 1990-. *Honours:* 3rd Prize 1976, co-winner 1978, Baltimore Symphony Orchestra Young Conductors' Competition; ASCAP award, adventuresome programming, 1981; Seaver/NEA Conductors Award, 1992. *Address:* c/o St Louis Symphony Orchestra, 718 N Grand Blvd, St Louis, MO 63103, USA.

LØEVAAS-GERBER Kari, b. 13 May 1939, Oslo, Norway. Singer (Soprano). m. Manfred Gerber, 1968, 1 daughter. *Education:* Conservatory Oslo; Musikakademie Wien; Studies with KMSGR Erna Westenberger (Frankfurt). *Debut:* Nuri, Oslo, 1959. *Career:* Opera Houses in Dortmund and Mainz; Festivals at Salzburg, Vienna, Lucerne, Bergen, Ludwigsburg, Schwetzigen, Athens, Flandern; Television includes Fischer und seine Fru/Schoeck, 1981 and Peer Gynt, W. Egk, 1983; All major radio stations in Germany, Austria, Norway, Switzerland, France, and Italy. *Recordings include:* Debut record: Lieder (Grieg, Mussorgski, Sibelius) with Erik Werba; Petite Messe Solenelle, Rossini (Sawallisch); Die Feen, Wagner (Sawallisch); War Requiem, Britten (Kegel); more than 30 records. *Honours:* Deutsche Grammophon Sonderpreis, Vienna, 1960. *Hobby:* Painting. *Current Management* Sudwestdeutsche Konzertdirektion Russ, Stuttgart. *Address:* Gugerhalde 10, CH 8207 Schaffhausen, Switzerland.

LOGIE Nicholas, b. 12 May 1950, Hemel Hempstead, Hertfordshire, England. Musician (Viola); Orchestra Manager. m. Marina Orlov, 4 Sept 1972, 2 sons. *Education:* Yehudi Menuhin School, 1963-67; Royal College of Music, London; Northwest Deutsche Musikakademie, Detmold, Federal Republic of Germany; Santa Cecilia, Rome, Italy. *Debut:* Wigmore Hall, London, 1984. *Career:* Member of Vienna Symphony Orchestra, 1973-78; Chilingirian String Quartet, 1978-81; Orchestra Manager, Glyndebourne Touring Opera, 1990; Baroque Viola, London Baroque, 1985-; Viola Tutor, Royal Northern College of Music. *Recordings:* Schubert Cello Quintet, 6 Mozart Quartets, with Chilingirian Quartet. *Contributions to:* 5 Sketches for solo viola by Elizabeth Maconchy; Newsletter No 24, The Viola Society, Mar. 1985. *Address:* Lott's End, Highgate, Forest Row, Sussex, RH18 5BE, England.

LOGOTHETIS Anestis, b. 27 Oct 1921, Burgas, Bulgaria (Greek origin), Austrian Citizen. Composer. m. Maria, 1 daughter. *Education:* Diploma, Academy of

Music, Vienna, Austria. *Career:* Radio plays; Instrumental music; Opera. *Compositions:* Published, Universal Editions, Vienna; Editions Modern, Munich; Ricordi Verlag, Munich; Breitkopf & Hartel, Wiesbaden. *Recordings:* Wergo, Columbia, Thorophon; Amadeo; Jeunesse musicale, Vienna. *Publications:* Zeichen als Aggregatzustand der Musik, Verlag Jugend & Volk, Vienna/Munich; Impulse, Universal Edition, Vienna. *Contributions to:* Melos; Neues Forum; Wort & Wahrheit; Oesterreichische Musikzeitschrift; Erhard Karkoschka, das Schriftbild der Neuen Musik; John Cage, Notations; Otto Breicha, Aufforderung zum Misstrauen. *Honours:* Fellowship to Rome, Italy; 1st prize, Athens competition for modern music, Athens, 1962; Theodor Koerner Prize, Vienna, 1960. *Memberships:* International Society of Modern Music; Grazer Autorenversammlung. *Address:* Hegergasse 4/9, A-1030 Vienna, Austria.

LOHMANN Ludger, b. 9 Mar 1954, Herne. Organist; Professor. m. Gisela Seyfarth, 20 May 1978, 2 sons, 2 daughter. *Education:* Musikhochschule Koln: Organ and Harpsichord; Soloist Diplomas; PhD Musicology, University of Koln, 1981. *Career:* Recitals in Europe, Japan and North and South America. *Recordings include:* Liszt Organ works. *Publications:* Artikulation auf den Tasteninstrumenten, 1982. *Honours:* ARD Competition Munich, 1979; Grand Prix de Chartres, 1982. *Address:* Laquaiweg 11, D-70597 Stuttgart, Germany.

LOIRI Vesa-Matti, b. 4 Jan 1945, Helsinki. Artist; Actor; Singer; Flautist. m. Marita Hakala, (div) 2 sons, 1 daughter. *Education:* Finnish Academy of Actors. *Career:* Performed with Finnish National Opera, 1971-72, Blind singer in Opera Kullervo, Sallinen, Premiere in Los Angeles, 1992; Many musical parts in theatres; own show and many concerts on television from 1967; Annual tour with own band. *Recordings include:* 30 LP records. *Honours:* Finnish prizes for music and acting. *Hobbies:* Billiards; Golf; Painting; Fishing; Horse sport. *Address:* Kalevanvainio 1 C 16, 02100 Espoo, Finland.

LOMBARD Alain, b. 4 Oct 1940, Paris, France. Conductor. *Education:* Studied at the Paris Conservatoire with Line Talleul (violin) and Gaston Poulet (conducting). *Debut:* Salle Gaveau, Pais, aged 11 with the Pasdeloup Orchestra. *Career:* Assistant, the Principal Conductor with Lyon Opera, 1961-65; American Opera Society 1963, with Massenet's Hérodiade; Conducted New York Philharmonic and at Salzburg Festival 1966; Musical Director, Miami Opera, Florida, 1966-74; Metropolitan Opera 1967, Gounod's Faust; Director of the Strasbourg Philharmonic 1972-83; Opéra du Rhin 1974-80; Guest conductor with Schveningen Festival, Holland, Hamburg Opera, L'Orchestre de Paris and other leading orchestras; Conducted Die Zauberflote at Bordeaux, 1992. *Recordings include:* Mozart's Così fan Tutte, with Strasbourg ensemble; Berlioz Symphonie Fantastique, Harold in Italy and Roméo et Juliette; Verdi Requiem; Prokokiev Violin Concertos (Amoyal) and Ballet Suites; Bartók Concerto for Orchestra and Miraculous Mandarin; Ravel Piano Concerto, Queffelec, and Daphnis et Chloë No.2; Gounod Roméo et Juliette. *Honour:* Gold Medal, Dimitri Mitropoulos Competition, 1966. *Address:* c/o S.A. Gorlinsly Ltd., 33 Dover Street, London W1X 4NJ, England.

LOMON Ruth, b. 7 Nov 1930, Montreal, Canada. Composer. m. Earle Lomon, 4 Aug 1951, 1 son, 2 daughters. *Education:* McGill University; New England Conservatory. *Debut:* Piano, Montreal, Canada. *Career:* 2 piano team with Iris Graffman Wenglin, appearances on radio and TV, performing and lecturing on works by women composers, as well as contemporary and classical repertoire, 1973-83; Commissioned works for ALEA III, Boston University Festival; Opus II and III, Michigan University, Canadian Contemporary Music Festival, Music Teachers National Association, National Women's Studies Association, Ohio University; VP, American Women Composers. *Compositions include:* Published: Seven Portals of Vision, organ; Ceremonial

Masks, piano; 5 songs on poems by William Blake, contralto and violin; Dust Devils, harp; Soundings, piano duet; Spells, piano and chamber orchestra; Janus, string quartet; Diptych, woodwind quintet; Metamorphoses, cello, piano; Songs for a Requiem, soprano, piano or woodwinds; Equinox, brass quartet; Celebrations, 2 harps; Bassoon concerto; Dialogue, harpsichord, vibraphone; Requiem Mass for full chorus and brass accompaniement. *Recordings include:* Five Ceremonial Masks for piano; Dust Devils for harp; Soundings for piano four hands; Triptych for two pianos; Esquisses piano solos, 1992 (published); Terra Incognita, for orchestra, 1993. *Honours:* New Mexico Arts Division and NEA 1990; New England Foundation for the Arts, Massachusetts Council on the Art and Humanities Helene Wurlitzer Foundation Grant. *Address:* 2A Forest Street, Cambridge, MA 02140, USA.

LONDON Edwin, b. 16 Mar 1929, Philadelphia, Pennsylvania, USA. Composer. *Education:* Studied at Oberlin College Conservatory and the University of Iowa, PhD 1961; With Gunter Schuller at Manhattan School of Music and with Milhaud and Dallapiccola; Conducting studies with Izler Solomon. *Career:* Teacher at Smith College, Northampton, 1960-68; University of Illinois 1973-83; Chairman of the music department at Cleveland State University 1978-; Founder and leader of the Cleveland Chamber Orchestra. *Compositions:* Santa Claus, mime opera 1960; 3 Settings of Psalm 23 for choruses 1961; Woodwind quintet 1958; Sonatina for viola and piano 1962; Brass Quintet 1965; Portraits of Three Ladies, theatre piece 1967; Four Proverbs 1968; The Iron Hand, otarorio 1975; The Death of Lincoln, opera 1976; Psalms of these Days 1976-80; Metaphysical Vegas, musical 1981. *Honours:* Guggenheim Foundation grant; NEA grants; Hamburg Opera Contemporary Festival grant. *Address:* c/o ASCAP, ASCAP Building, One Lincoln Plaza, New York, NY 10023, USA.

LONGTIN Michel, b. 20 May 1946, Montreal, Canada. Composer; Teacher. *Education:* Acting I, Mime Certificate, 1964; BA, College des Eudistes, 1967; Computer Science Diploma, 1969; Musical studies with Dolin, Hambraeus, Hetu, Lanza, Pedersen, Prevost Garant (Montreal and Toronto), 1968-73; BMus, 1973, MMus, 1975, DMus, Composition, 1982, Universite de Montreal. *Career includes:* Adjunct Professor of Composition and Contemporary Musical Analysis, University of Montreal, 1987-. *Compositions:* Recorded: Deux rubans noirs III for ensemble, RCI, 1979; La Trilogie de la Montagne, electronic music, SNE, 1980; Kata: San Shi Ryu for ensemble, RCI, 1982; Pohjatuuli, hommage a Sibelius for ensemble, Contredisques, 1983; Autour d'Ainola for orchestra, Contredisques, 1986. *Honours:* Broadcast Music Inc Award to Student Composers, New York, 1972; Canadian Choral Alliance Prize for Composition, 1974; Canadian Composers League Prize for Composition, 1975; Prix Jules-Leger for Pohjatuuli, 1986. *Memberships:* Centre de musique canadienne; LCC; Founding Member, ACREQ. *Hobbies:* Cycling; Science; Reading. *Address:* Faculty of Music, Universite de Montreal, CP 6128, Succ A, Montreal, Quebec, Canada H3C 3J7.

LOOSLI Arthur, b. 23 Feb 1926, La Chaux d'Abel, Berner, Jura, Switzerland. Concert Singer. m. Theresia Rothlisberger, 2 sons. *Education:* Conservatoire of Berne with Felix Loeffel; Studies with Mariano Stabile, Venice and Arne Sunnergard, Stockholm, Sweden. *Debut:* Berne, 1958. *Career:* Performances in Switzerland, Belgium, Sweden, Netherlands, Germany and Italy; Guest Artist at Stadttheater, Berne. *Recordings:* Elegie, Lieder (Othmar Schoeck); Winterreise (Schubert); Schwanengesang (Schubert); Johannes- Passion (Bach). *Publications:* Illustrations of Franz Hohler's Tschipo and Der Granitblock im Kino. *Honours:* Recipient, 1st Prize, International Singers Competition, bass baritone, 'sHertogenbosch, Netherlands, 1959; Further professional activities. *Memberships:* Othmar Schoeck Association; Swiss Music Teachers Association. *Hobbies:* Painting and graphics; Drawing

Master at Gymnasium, Thun, Switzerland. *Address:* Gurtenweg 31A, 3074 Muri, Switzerland.

LOOTENS Lena (Helena-Alice), b. 14 Apr 1959, Genk, Belgium. Soprano. m. Matthias Muller, 3 Dec 1988. 1 daughter. *Education:* Royal Atheneum of Maasmechelen; Conservatories of Brussels and Gent; Private studies with Vera Rozsa, London; Margreet Honig, Amersterdam; Kristina Deutekom, Amsterdam. *Career:* Appearances with numerous orchestras; Concert tours to Belgium, Netherlands, Germany, England, Switzerland and Poland; Appearances on radio and television includes: BRT, BBC, WDR, NDR, SDR; Opera engagements in Innsbruck, Monte Carlo, Antwerp, Montpellier, Liège and Versailles. *Recordings:* L'Infedeltà Delusa; Concert arias; Flavio of Händel Deutsche Schallplattenpieis; L'Incoronazion di Poppea of Monteverdi; Die Israeliten in der Wüste, C P E Bach; Requiem/Mozart; La Guiditta/Almeida. *Honours:* 1st prize singing, National Competition for the Youth of Belgium; Alex Devries Scholarship, Roeping Foundation. *Address:* Florastr 57/CH-8620 Wetzikon, Switzerland.

LOPARDO Frank, b. 1958, New York, USA. Singer (Tenor). *Education:* Studied in New York. *Debut:* St Louis, 1984, as Tamino. *Career:* Season 1985-86 at Dallas and Naples, Don Ottavio at Aix and La Scala Milan; Sang Fenton in Falstaff at Amsterdam 1986, Ferrando at Glyndebourne, 1987; Vienna Staatsoper from 1987, notably as Belfiore in Il Viaggo a Reims, conducted by Abbado; Sang Elvino in La Sonnambula and Rossini's Almviva at Chicago, 1989; Sang Lindoro in L'Italiana in Algeri, Covent Garden, 1989; Season 1991 as Elvino and Ferrando at Florence, Don Ottavio at San Francisco; Sang Rossini's Lindoro at San Francisco, 1992. *Recordings include:* Mozart's Requiem and Don Giovanni; L'Italiana in Algeri; Falstaff. *Address:* c/o Royal Opera House (contracts), Covent Garden, London WC2, England.

LOPES-GRAÇA Fernando, b. 17 Dec 1906, Tomar, Portugal. Composer; Writer. *Education:* Philosophy and Literature, Lisbon and Coimbra Universities, 1928, 1932; Musicology, Sorbonne, Paris, 1938-39; Piano, Composition and Musical Sciences, Conservatorio Nacional, Lisbon, 1923-31. *Debut:* Pianist at Cine of Thomar, 1920. *Career:* Composer, 1928-; Teacher, Instituto de Música de Coimbra, 1932-36, Academia de Amadores de Música de Lisbon, 1941-; Conductor, Coro da Academia de Amadores de Musica, 1950-, Artistic Director, 1944-. *Compositions:* Three Portuguese Dances for Orchestra, editor Schott; Sinfonia per Orchestra, editor Suvini Zerboni, Concerto da Camera col Violoncello obligatto, editor Jobert; Pour un enfant qui va naitre, strings, editor Jobert; Album for the Young Pianist, Novello; Preludio e Baileto, for guitar (Suvini Zerboni); Partita for guitar (Suvini Zerboni); Melodias rusticas portuguesas; Sonatina no 2 for piano (Musica, Moscow). *Recordings:* About 45 Orchestral, choral, chamber, piano, songs discs published by HMV, Decca, Columbia, Portugalsm. *Publications:* Obras Literarias, 13 vols 1973-92; Many others to be incorporated in Obras Literarias, 2nd edition. *Address:* Mi Paraiso 2°, Avenue da Republica, 2775 Parede, Portugal.

LOPEZ Peter Dickson, b. 8 July 1950, Berkeley, California, USA. Composer; Software Engineer. m. Irene G. Gee, 18 Aug 1974. *Education:* BA, California State University, Hayward 1972; MA, 1974, PhD, 1978, Composition, University of California, Berkeley. *Career:* Lecturer, Harmony, 1979-80, Lecturer, Electronic Music, Composition, 1982-86, University of California, Davis; Founder, President, Eleusinian Software, 1986-. *Compositions:* Adagio, piano, 1973; Five pieces for piano, 1974; Intrections, 3 Pianos & Electronic Sound, 1974-75; Ship of Death, Male Voice & Chamber Orchestra, 1976-77; Scintilla, piano, 1978; Seven Pieces, violin and piano, 1978-79; IFASIA, octet, 1979; CHominge, Violin and Live Electronics, 1980; Lorinn, Piano Trio and Contralto, 1981; La Casa De Bernarda Alba, Ballet, 1986; Moment Pieces, 4 pianos or piano and tape, 1986; Procedye, extended piano, 1986;

Entropy I, 2 Pianos, 1986; The Embriodery of Imagination, Concerto for Percussion and Orchestra, 1989-90. *Recordings:* The Ship of Death, 1983. *Publications:* Software: Composers' Assistant for Design, Integration and Management, 1987-90; ELUS, Forth Development Environment, 1989-90; ELUS: TD, Remote Tape Deck Controller, 1989; Interactive Screen Designer, Forth Utility, 1989; Automatic Short Glossary Documentor, Forth Utility, 1989. *Address:* Eleusinian Enterprises, 7997 Phaeton Drive, Oakland, CA 94605, USA.

LOPEZ-COBOS Jesus, b. 25 Feb. 1940, Toro, Spain. Conductor. m. Alicia Lopez-Cobos, May 1987, 3 sons. *Education:* PhD, Philosophy, 1964; Diploma in Composition, Madrid Conservatory, 1966; Diploma in Conducting, Vienna Academy, Austria, 1969. *Debut:* Concert, Prague, 1969; Opera, La Fenice, Venice. *Career:* Generalmusikdirektor, Deutsche Oper, Berlin, 1981-90; (Die Zauberflöte, 1969); Debut at the Deutsche Oper 1970 (La Bohème); US debut San Francisco, 1972 (Luciadi Lammermoor); Carmen at Covent Garden, 1975; Adriana Lecouvreur at the Met, 1978; Conducted the company of the Deutsche Oper Berlin in Der Ring des Nibelungen on tour to Japan, 1987; Principal Guest Conductor, London Philharmonic, 1982-86; Principal Conductor, Artistic Director, Spanish National Orchestra, 1984-89; Music Director, Cincinnati Orchestra, 1986-; Music Director Lausanne Chamber Orchestra, 1990-; Concerts with: London Symphony; Royal Philharmonic; Philharmonia Orchestra at Edinburgh Festival; New York Philharmonic; Los Angeles Philharmonic; Chicago Symphony; Cleveland Orchestra; Philadelphia Orchestra; Berlin Philharmonic; Berlin Radio Orchestra; Amsterdam Concertgebouw; Vienna Philharmonic; Suisse Romande; Munich Philharmonic; Hamburg NDR; Oslo Philharmonic; Zurich Tonhalle; Israel Philharmonic; Opera productions: Royal Opera House; Covent Garden; La Scala, Milan; Metropolitan Opera, New York; Paris Opéra. *Recordings:* Franck Symphony in D minor, Ravel Bolero, Bizet Symphony 1 and Carmen Suite, Bruckner Symphonies 4,6 and 7 with Cincinnati Orchestra (Telarc); Donizetti Lucia di Lammermoor, Rossini, Otello, Recital and operatic discs, José Carreras, Liszt Dante Symphony, Falla, Three-Cornered Hat, Rimsky-Korsakov Capricio Espagnole, Chabrier Espana. *Honours:* 1st Prize, Besançon International Conductors Competition, 1969; Prince of Asturias Award, Spanish Government, 1981; Dec 1989 awarded the Cross of Merit, First Class, of Germany. *Hobby:* Tennis. *Current Management:* Terry Harrison Artists Management. *Address:* c/o Terry Harrison Artists Management, 3 Clarendon Court, Park Street, Charlbury, Oxon, OX7 3PS, England.

LORAND Colette, b. 7 Jan 1923, Zurich, Switzerland. Singer (Soprano). *Education:* Musikhochschule Hanover; Zurich with Frau Hirzel. *Debut:* Basle 1946, as Marguerite in Faust. *Career:* Frankfurt Opera 1951-56, notably as the Queen of Night; Hamburg Opera from 1955, often in operas by Henze, Penderecki and Orff; Edinburgh Festival 1955; Lisbon 1961, as Constanze in Die Entführung; Deutsche Oper Berlin 1972, in the premiere of Fortner's Elisabeth Tudor; Created roles in Orff's De Temporum fine Comoedia, Salzburg Festival 1973, and Reimann's Lear, Munich 1978, (as Regan, repeated at the Paris Opéra, 1982). *Recordings:* Lear and De Temporum fine Comoedia (Deutsche Grammophon); Orff's Prometheus (RCA). *Address:*c/o Bayerische Staatsoper, Postfach 745, D-8000 Munich, Germany.

LORD Bernadette, b. 1965, Derby, England. Singer (Soprano). *Education:* Studied at the Guildhall School and with Suzanne Danco in Florence; Further study at the European Arts Centre, 1988. *Career:* Joined Opera Wallonie, Liege, and sang Helena in Schubert's Der hausliche Krieg in Belgium, Holland and Paris; Glyndebourne and Covent Garden debuts as Cis in Albert Herring; Other roles include Despina for British Youth Opera at the Cheltenham Festival, Miss Wordsworth in Albert Herring, Lucia in The Rape of Lucretia, Gretal for Opera East, Susanna and Barbarina in Le nozze di Figaro; Sang Jano in Jenufa at Covent Garden, 1993. *Address:* c/o Royal Opera House (contracts), Covent Garden, London WC2, England.

LORENGAR Pilar, b. 16 Jan 1928, Saragosa, Spain. Singer (Soprano). *Education:* Barcelona Conservatory; With Angeles Otrein in Madrid and with Carl Ebert and Hertha Klust. *Debut:* Madrid 1949, in Zarzuelas. *Career:* Aix-en-Provence 1955, as Cherubino; New York debut 1955, in a concert performance of Goyescas; Covent Garden debut 1955, as Violetta: returned to London as Donna Anna in Don Giovanni and as Gluck's Euridice; Glyndebourne 1956-60,as Mozart's Pamina and Countess, and Echo in Ariadne auf Naxos; Deutsche Oper Berlin from 1958, notably as Regina in Mathis der Maler, Isabella in Falla's L'Atlantida, Janáček's Jenůfa and Debussy's Mélisande; Salzburg Festival 1961-64, in Die Zauberflöte and Idomeneo; Metropolitan Opera from 1966, as Donna Elvira, Wagner's Elsa and Eva, Weber's Agathe and Madama Butterfly; San Francisco Opera from 1964; Deutsche Oper Berlin, 1987 as Valentine in Les Huguenots; Strasbourg and Lyon 1989, as Maddalena in Andrea Chénier. *Recordings:* The Bartered Bride (HMV); Die Zauberflöte, Medée, La Traviata, Orfeo ed Euridice, Don Giovanni, Così fan Tutte (Decca); La Bohème (Deutsche Grammophon). *Honours include:* Ehrenmitglied, Deutsche Oper Berlin, 1984. *Address:* c/o Deutsche Oper Berlin, Richard Wagnerstrasse 10, D-1000 Berlin, Germany.

LORENTZEN Bent, b. 11 Feb 1935, Oerum, Denmark. Composer. m. Edith Kaerulf Moeller, 2 Aug 1958, 1 son, 3 daughter. *Education:* Royal Academy of Music, Copenhagen, 1960. *Career includes:* Performances throughout Europe of works including Euridice, Eine Wundersame Liebesgeschichte, Stalten Mette, Roto, Samba, Pianoconcerto Nordic Music Days, Saxophone Concerto, two choral songs to Enzensberger, 1991, Bill adn Julia (opera), The Magic Brillant, (The Danish National Opera), 1993. *Compositions include:* Purgatorio, choral; Granite; Quartz; Syncretism; Colori; Concerto for oboe; Samba; Paradiesvogel; Graffiti; Genesis; New Choral Dramatics; Ammen Dammen Des; Round; 5 easy Piano Pieces, Olof Palme for mixed choir; Comics, Latin Suite No 2, Tordenskiold. *Recordings include:* The Bottomless Pit; Visions; Cloud-Drift; Mambo, Intersection, Puncti, Triplex, Groppo, Nimbus, Cruor, Umbra, Paesaggio, Dunkelblau, Round, Cyclus II, Mars; Piano and oboe concertos; Regenbogen; Comics. *Publications:* Ej Sikkelej, 1967; Recorder System, 1962-64; Musikens AHC, 1969; Mer om Musiken, 1972; Introduction to Electronic Music, 1969. *Honours:* Prix Italia, 1970; First prize, Nyon Film Festival, 1973, as well as awards in Poland, Austria, and Messiaen-prize, Bergamo, 1988. *Memberships:* Danish Composers Society. *Hobbies:* Gardening. *Current Management* Edition Wilhelm Hansen, Bornholmsgade 1, 1266 Kobenhavn K, Denmark. *Address:* Sotoften 37, 2820 Gentofte, Denmark.

LORENZ Andrew Bela, b. 17 Oct. 1951, Melbourne, Australia. Violinist. m. Wendy Joy Lorenz, 1 son. *Education:* DSCM Performers Diploma and Teachers Diploma, Sydney Conservatory of Music, 1970. *Career:* Recitals; Concerto, Radio and Television performances; Deputy Leader, Melbourne Elizabethan Trust Orchestra, 1972; Led for D'Oyly Carte Opera Company, Sadler's Wells, England, 1973-74; Leader, New England Ensemble (Resident piano quartet) and Lecturer, Music Department, University of New England, Armidale, New South Wales, Australia, 1975-82; Founding Member and Leader, New England Sinfonia; World tours with New England Ensemble; Associate Concertmaster, Adelaide Symphony Orchestra, 1983-86; Leader, Australian Piano Trio, 1983-87; Senior Lecturer in Strings, University College of Southern Queensland, Toowoomba, Queensland, currently; Leader, Darling Downs Trio; Director of McGregor Chamber Music School, currently. *Recordings:* Works by Beethoven, Turina, Margaret Sutherland, Mozart, Fauré, John McCabe, Mendelssohn, Goossens, 6 LPs/CDs including: Sundry Chamber works and Concerto soloist with many of Australia's leading orchestras and Slovak

Radio Symphony; given Australian premieres of Benjamin, McCabe and Mysliveček Concertos. *Honours include:* Victorian ABC Concerto Competition Winner, 1972. *Hobbies:* Sport; Reading. *Address:* 6 Merlin Court, M/S 852, Toowoomba Mail Service, Queensland 4352, Australia.

LORENZ Wendy Joy, b. 25 Oct 1950, Sydney, Australia. Pianist; Teacher. m. Andrew Bela Lorenz, 1 son. *Education:* DSCM Honours in Performing and Teaching, Sydney Conservatory, 1970; L.Mus.A. 1968; studied with Maria Curcio, London, 1973-4. *Career includes:* Recital, Broadcast, Television and concerto soloist appearances in Australia, Europe, Asia and America; Pianist, Young Sydney Piano Trio, 1968-71; Piano Teacher, NSW Conservatory, 1971; Pianist, New England Ensemble and Lecturer in Piano, University of New England, Armidale, NSW, Australia, 1975-82; Pianist, Australian Piano Trio, 1983-87; Pianist, Darling Downs Trio and Lecturer in Piano, University of Southern Queensland, Toowoomba, Queensland, currently. *Recordings:* Seven LP's, CD's including soloist with Adelaide Symphony Orchestra and Slovak Radio Symphony. *Address:* 6 Merlin Court, M/S 852, Toowoomba Mail Service, Q. 4352, Australia.

LORIMER Heather, b. 1961, Wallasey, Cheshire. Singer (Soprano). *Education:* Studied at the Royal Northern College of Music, Manchester with Frederick Cox and now with Iris Dell'Acqua. *Career:* Scottish Opera Go Round, Mimi La Bohème, 1987; Glyndebourne Festival and Touring Opera, Constanze, Die Entfuhrung Aus Dem Serail, 1988; Countess, Le Nozze di Figaro, 1989; Opera 80, Tatiana, Eugene Onegin in 1989 and Hanna Glawari, The Merry Widow, 1990; Travelling Opera, Mimi; Countess;, Donna Elvira; Don Giovani; Flordiligi in Così fan tutte; Opera Interludes Violetta, La Traviata and Micaela, Carmen; English Touring Opera, Mimi, 1994; Education tours for Glyndebourne, Opera 80 and English National Opera's Lillian Bayliss Programmme. Other roles performed include: Giorgetta, Il Tabarro; Liu, Turandot; Norina, Don Pasquale; Rosina, Il Barbiere di Siviglia; Rosalinde, Die Fledermaus; Rosario, Goyescas; Dirce, Medea; Leila, The Pearl Fishers and in 1993 she created the title role in Michael Finnissy's Therese Raquin, for the Royal Opera's Garden Venture; Concert repertoire includes, Verdi Requiem; Rossini Stabat Mater; Dvořák Requiem; Elijah; Carmina Burana; Brahms Requiem; Faure Requiem; Sea Symphony and The Kingdom. *Honours include:* International Opera and Bel Canto Duet Competition, Antwerp, with her husband, the baritone, Gerard Quinn; Scottish Opera John Noble Competition. *Address:* 92 Sturla Road, Chatham, Kent ME4 5QH, England.

LORIMER Michael George, b. 13 Jan 1946, Chicago, Illinois, USA. Guitarist; Baroque Guitarist. m. Judith Ann Weydt, 21 June 1980. *Education:* University of California, Berkeley; Guitar studies with Andrés Segovia. *Debut:* Los Angeles, California 1960. *Career:* Toured USA, USSR 1975, 1977; Appeared in Israel, throughout Europe, on most major North American recital series, Orchestras played with include: Atlanta, Baltimore, Indianapolis, Louisville, New Orleans and San Francisco; Given master classes at universities and conservatories throughout America; Distinguished Visiting Professor of Music, University of North Carolina, Wilmington; subject of special television programme The Artistry of Michael Lorimer. *Recordings include:* Remembranza. *Publications include:* Numerous Guitar Arrrangements (distributed by Mel Bay Publications, Pacific, MO 63069, USA). *Hobbies:* Keeping fit; Reading; Cooking. *Address:* 175 West 73rd Street (Apt. 10-G), New York, NY 10023, USA.

LORIOD Yvonne, b. 20 Jan 1924, Houilles, Seine-et-Oise, France. Pianist. *Education:* National Conservatory of Music, Paris. m. Olivier Messiaen. *Career:* Solo Recitals in most European countries, North and South America, and Japan with leading orchestras; 1st Performances in Paris of 21 concerti by Mozart and Concerti by Bartók and Schoenberg and many works by Jolivet and all Messiaen works with piano including

Visions de l'Amen 1943, Turangalîla Symphonie 1948, Catalogue d'Oiseaux 1958, Des Canyons aux Etoiles 1974; Professor of Piano, Paris Conservatoire of Music; Master Classes at summer schools, Darmstadt and Bayreuth, France and USA. *Recordings:* Numerous works issued. *Honours:* Officer, Legion of Honour; Grand Prix du Disque.

LORRAIN Denis, b. 29 July 1948, Ithaca, New York, USA. Composer. m. Jacqueline Quiniou, 1 Aug. 1970, 1 daughter. *Education:* Baccalaureate, Serie philosophie, 1967; BMus, Composition, University of Montreal, 1971; MMA, Composition, McGill University, 1973; Doctorat, Musique et esthetique, University of Paris, Sorbonne, 1983. *Career:* Assistant, IRCAM, Paris, 1978; Associate Professor, Faculty of Music, University of Montreal, 1980; Maitre assistant, IRCAM, Paris, 1982; Professor, Conservatoire National Superieur de Musique, Lyon, 1988. *Compositions:* Huit pieces pour piano; Arc, string orchestra; P-A, voices; P-A, version Luminy; L'angelus, clarinet and tape; Suite pour deux guitares; Sequence, organ; Polyphrase, orchestra; Generiques, tape; Contra Mortem, clarinet; Droite, homage to Le Corbusier, tape; Le talon d'Achille, flute; Extrema, organ and percussion; Les portes du sombre Dis, tape; 'Di mi se mai...', brass quintet, percussion and tape; The Other Shape, percussion and tape; ...black it stood as night, tape; La nuova ricordanza, two harpsichords. *Address:* SONVS-CNSM de Lyon, C.P. 120, 3 Quai Chauveau, 69266 Lyon Cedex 09, France.

LOTT Felicity Ann, b. 8 May 1947, Cheltenham, Gloucestershire, England. Singer, (Soprano). m. (1) Robin Golding, 22 Dec 1973, (2) Gabriel Woolf, 19 Jan. 1984, 1 daughter. *Education:* BA (Hons.), French, Royal Holloway College, London University, 1965-69; Royal Academy of Music, 1969-73. *Debut:* English National Opera, 1975 as Pamina in Die Zauberflöte. *Career:* Principal roles with Glyndebourne, Covent Garden, ENO, WNO, SNO, Paris Opéra, Brussels Opera, Hamburg, Munich, Chicago, New York, Vienna, Dresden, Metropolitian; Founder Member of Songmakers' Almanac; Wide concert and oratorio and recital repertoire; Glyndebourne; TV appearances in Rake's Progress; Zauberflöte; Midsummer Night's Dream; Intermezzo; roles include Strauss, Arabella, Christine, Octavian, Marschallin and Countess in Capriccio; Mozart, Pamina, Fiordiligi, Donna Elvira, Countess, Xiphares (Mitridate); Amadeus Soundtrack; Royal Wedding, 1986; Sang Eva in Die Meistersinger at Covent Garden 1990, the Countess in Capriccio, Arabella and Marschallin at the 1990 Glyndebourne Festival, Christine Storch in Intermezzo at Munich; Berg's Seven Early Songs at the 1991 Proms; Season 1991/92 with the Countess at Salzburg and Covent Garden, Arabella at La Scala and Strauss's Christine and Marschallin at Munich; Countess in Capriccio at Vienna, season 1993/94. *Recordings:* St Matthew Passion; Messiah; Louise; Mahler 4 and 8; Recitals for Hyperion, Harmonia Mundi, Pickwick, Chandos; Strauss orchestral songs for Chandos, EMI Figaro - Glyndebourne, Amadeus; Peter Grimes, EMI; Duets with Ann Murray, EMI. *Honours:* Fellow, Royal Academy of Music, 1987; Honorary Doctor of University of Sussex, 1989; CBE, New Year's Honours, 1990; Chevalier Dans L'Ordre Des Arts Et Des Lettres, 1993. *Memberships:* Equity; Incorporated Society of Musicians. *Hobbies:* Reading; Gardening; Sleeping. *Current Management:* Lies Askonas Limited. *Address:* c/o Lies Askonas Limited, 186 Drury Lane, London, WC2B 5RY.

LOUDOVÁ Ivana, b. 8 Mar 1941, Chlumec, Czechoslovakia. Composer. m. Milos Haase, 16 Aug 1973. 1 son. *Compositions:* Over 95 works including: two symphonies, Chorale Hymnos, Spleen-Hommage a Charles Baudelaire, Concerto for Percussion, Organ and Wind orchestra; Dramatic concerto for Solo Percussion and Wind Orchestral; Luminous voice, Concerto for English horn and Wind Orchestra; Rhapsody in Black, ballet music; Double Concerto for violin, percussion and strings; Chamber compositions: Suite for solo flute, Per tromba, Gnomai-Trio for soprano, flute and harp; Solo for King David/harp solo/String

quartet No 1, 2; Air, Aulos, Agamemnon, Soli e Tutti, Nocturne for viola and strings, Partita in D, Hukvaldy suite, Meditations, Musica festiva/brass sextet/ Piano Trio in B, Trio italiano for clar, bassoon and piano; Duo concertante; Donn Giovanni's Dream, wind octet; Vocal compositions: Meeting with Love; Kuroshio; Stabat Mater; Ego sapientia; Looking back; Love..!; Fortune; Little prince, cantata; Little Christmas cantata; Children choruses include: Ten minutes silence; Mummy; Riddles; Canonal songs; Songs about roses; Sonetto. *Address:* Aubrechtove 3100, 106 00 Praha 10, Czech Republic.

LOUGHRAN James, b. 30 June 1931, Glasgow, Scotland. Musician. m. (1) Nancy Coggon, 20 Sept 1961; (2) Ludmila Navratil, 15 Apr 1985. 2s. *Debut:* Royal Festival Hall, London, 1961. *Career:* Associate Comductor, Bournemouth S.O. 1962-65; Principal Conductor, BBC Scottish S.O. 1965-71; Principal conductor and Musical Adviser, Hallé Orchestra, 1971-83; Principal Conductor, Bamberg S.O. 1979-83; Guest conductor of principal orchestras of Europe, America, Australasia and Japan; Tours with Munich Philharmonic, BBC Symphony, Stockholm, Lonodn and Japan Philharmonic and Scottish Chamber Orchestra; Permanent Guest Conductor, Japan Philharmonic Symphony Orchestra, 1993. *Recordings include:* Symphonies by Beethoven, Brahms and Elgar, as well as works by Mozart, Berlioz, Schubert, Dvorak, Rachmaninov, Hayergal Brian, Walton, Holst and McCabe. *Honours:* Philharmonic Orchestra Conducting First Prize; FRNCM, 1976; FRSAMD, 1983; Freeman, City of London, 1991; Liveryman, Musicians' Company, 1992; Hon DMus, Sheffield, 1983; Gold Disc, EMI, 1983. *Hobbies:* Golf; Travel. *Current management* Interartists Holland BV. *Address:* The Rookery, Bollington Cross, Macclesfield, Cheshire SK10 5EL, England.

LOUP François, b. 4 Mar 1940, Estavayer-le-lac, Switzerland. Singer (Bass). *Education:* Studied piano, organ, composition and singing at Fribourg. *Career:* Sang at the Geneva Opera 1964-66, notably in the premiere of Monsieur de Pourceaugnac by Martin; Directed various vocal ensembles for which he harmonised motets, madrigals and Swiss folk songs; Soloist with the Ensemble Instrumental de Lausanne, under Michel Corboz; Many performances of Baroque music, notably with the Societa Cameristica di Lugano and with the Opéra de Lyon (in Orfeo by Monteverdi); Oratorio performances in many European countries; Sang in Bizet's Docteur Miracle at the 1975 Spoleto Festival; Sang Bartolo in Le Nozze di Figaro at Houston 1988, repeated at Glyndebourne 1989 (later at the Albert Hall, London); San Diego and the Opera de Lyon 1989, as Don Pasquale and as Balducci in Benvenuto Cellini; Season 1992 with Mozart's Bartolo at San Diego, Don Pasquale at Vancouver and the Sacristan in Tosca at San Francisco; Sang in La Bohème at the Met, 1994; Other roles include Leporello, Figaro, Dulcamara, Masetto, Arkel, Pimen, Frère Laurent in Roméo et Juliette and Sarastro; Dedicatee of several contemporary compositions, and teacher of singing: pupils include François Le Roux. *Address:* c/o Glyndebourne Festival Opera, Lewes, Sussex, England.

LOVE Shirley, b. 6 Jan 1940, Detroit, Michigan, USA. *Education:* Detroit with Avery Crew and New York with Margaret Harshaw. *Debut:* Metropolitan Opera 1963, in Die Zauberflote. *Career:* Remained in New York for 20 seasons, as Carmen, Dalila, Verdi's Maddalena, Amneris and Emilia, Rossini's Angelina and Rosina, Siebel in Faust, Pauline in The Queen of Spades and in operas by Ravel, Menotti and Bernstein; Guest appearances in Cincinnati, Chicago, Miami and Phildadelphia; Baltimore 1962, in the premiere of Kagen's Hamlet; Concert appearances in Amsterdam, Bologna and Florence. *Address:* c/o Metropolitan Opera, Lincoln Center, New York, NY 10023, USA.

LOVEDAY Alan (Raymond), b. 29 Feb 1928, England. Violinist. m. Ruth Stanfield, 1952, 1 son, 1 daughter. *Education:* Private study; Royal College of Music (prizewinner). *Debut:* Childhood debut, age 4;

Debut in England, 1946. *Career:* Numerous concerts, broadcasts, television appearances, Britain & overseas; Played with all leading conductors & composers. *Repertoire:* Ranges from Bach (on un-modernised violin) to contemporary music. *Appointments:* Professor, Royal College of Music, 1955-72; Member & soloist, Academy of St Martin-in-the-Fields. *Hobbies:* Chess; Bridge. *Address:* c/o Academy of St Martin-in-the-Fields, Royal Festival Hall, South Bank, London SE1, England.

LOVELAND Kenneth, b. 12 Oct 1915, Sheerness, Kent, England. Music Critic. m. Anne Edwards. *Career:* Music Critic; Various professional publications; Own music magazine; Radio Wales; Music programmes for Radio Telefis Eireann, Dublin, Republic of Ireland; BBC Kaleidoscope. *Contributions to:* The Times; Opera; Musical Times; Country Life; Music and Musicians. *Honours:* Golden Statue of Vienna, 1970; Cavaliere, Italian Government, 1970; Guild for the Promotion of Welsh Music Award, 1985; Honorary MMus, University College of Wales, 1986. *Memberships:* Critics Circle; Guild of British Newspapers Editors (President 1962); National Training Council (President 1968). *Hobbies:* Watching cricket and soccer; Travel; Food and wine. *Address:* 20 Monmouth House, Cwmbran, Gwent, NP44 1QT, Wales.

LOVETT Terence George, b. 2 July 1922, London, England. Conductor. m. Selina Dorothy Clark, 3 sons. *Education:* Royal Academy of Music; FRAM; LRAM. *Debut:* London, 1941. *Career:* Organist and choirmaster for numerous choirs; Conductor and Artistic Director Hull Philharmonic Society; Plays piano, viola, horn, trumpet and organ; Guest conductor in Sweden, with BBC Symphony and in Europe, Middle and Far East. *Memberships:* Royal Philharmonic Society; ISM; RCM Club; Le Petit Club Français. *Honour:* Royal Academy of Music Prize, 1942. *Hobbies:* Fencing; Reading; Cooking. *Address:* 15 Beauchamp Road, E. Moseley, Surrey KT8 OPA, England.

LOWE Michael Graeme, b. 26 June 1947, Oldham, England. Lute Maker. *Education:* The Manchester Grammar School 1958-65; BA (Honours) in Classics, Grey College, University of Durham 1965-68; Diploma in Classical Archaeology (1970), Merton College, University of Oxford 1968-73. *Career:* Lute-Making 1973-. *Publications:* The New Oxford Companion To Music (Article On The Lute), 1983. *Contributions to:* The Galpin Society Journal; Le Luth et Sa Musique II; Proceedings of The Utrecht Lute Symposium 1986. *Memberships:* British School of Archaeology at Athens; The Lute Society; The Lute Society of America; The Galpin Society. *Hobbies:* Church Organist; Singing; Playing Lute and Viol. *Address:* The Hermitage, Wootton-by-Woodstock, Oxon, England.

LOWE Timothy, b. 20 Jan 1953, Tonbridge, Kent, England. Pianist; Music Teacher. *Education:* Yehudi Menuhin School, 1964-70; Trinity College of Music, 1962-64; Royal College of Music, 1970-73; Paris (Perlemuter), 1973-74. *Debut:* Wigmore Hall, London. *Career:* Appearances throughout Britain, including recitals at Wigmore Hall, Purcell Room, Fairfield Hall (Croydon), Festival Hall, Aldeburgh Festival, Plymouth Mayflower Celebrations; German television. *Recording:* Ernö Dohnányi, Piano Works. *Honours:* Foundation scholarship, 1969; Boise Foundation award, 1973; Chopin Prize, Royal College of Music, 1972; 1st year prize, ibid, 1970; ARCM Diploma with Honours, 1971. *Memberships:* Incorporated Society of Musicians. *Hobbies:* Arts including theatre, cinema. *Address:* 12A Upper Street, Rusthall, Tunbridge Wells, Kent, England.

LOWENBERG Kenneth Dale, b. 15 Nov 1939, Chicago, Illinois, USA. Organist; Conductor; Music Director. *Education:* BMusEd, Northwestern University, Evanston, Illinois, 1961; MMus Composition, University of Southern California, 1966. *Career:* Minister of Music, Chevy Chase Presbyterian Church, Washington DC, 1968-; Founding Director, Chevy Chase Concerts including annual Washington Bach Marathon; Pianist,

Organist: National Symphony Orchestra, District of Columbia Community Orchestra, American Camerata for New Music; Teacher, Columbia Union College, Takoma Park, Maryland; Organ Recitalist: Washington Cathedral, Shrine of the Immaculate Conception, Naval Academy (Annapolis, Maryland), many others; Lectures, workshops, American Guild of Organists; Conductor, choral and orchestral works, Chevy Chase Concert Series; Led Bach Pilgrimage of organists to East Germany, 1985. *Address:* c/o Chevy Chase Presbyterian Church, 1 Chevy Chase Circle, NW, Washington, DC 20015, USA.

LOWENTHAL Jerome, b. 11 Feb 1932, Philadelphia, Pennsylvania, USA. Concert Pianist. m. Ronit Amir, 7 July 1959, 2 daughters. *Education:* BA, University of Pennsylvania, 1953; MS, Juilliard School of Music, 1956; Premier License de Concert, Ecole Normale de Musique/Piano studies, Olga Samaroff, William Kapell, Eduard Steuermann, Alfred Cortot. *Debut:* Philadelphia Orchestra, 1945. *Career includes:* Appearances with orchestras of: New York, Philadelphia, Boston, Cleveland, Israel Philharmonic, Stockholm, Chicago, Los Angeles, Detroit, Pittsburgh; Conductors: Monteux, Stokowski, Bernstein, Ormandy, Giulini, Tennstedt, Mehta, Ozawa, Barenboim, Comissiona; Tours of Southeast Asia, New Zealand, Latin America, Western Europe, USSR, Poland, Romania. *Recordings:* Rorem Concerto no. 3, Louisville/Mester; Tchaikowsky Concerti 1, 2 & 3, London Symphony Orchestra/Comissiona; Liszt Opera Paraphrases; Gershwin Concerto in F, Rhapsody in Blue, Utah Symphony Orchestra; Sinding, Sonata & short pieces for solo piano; Liszt Concerto No.1, No.3, Totentanz, Malédiction; Vancouver Symphony, Commissiona. *Honours:* Laureat, Darmstadt Competition 1957, Busoni Competition 1957, Reine Elizabeth 1960. *Current Management:* Herbert Barrett. *Address:* 865 West End Avenue, Apt 11A, New York, NY 10025, USA.

LU Siqing, b. 26 Nov 1969, Qingdao, China. Violinist. *Education:* Juilliard School of Music, New York; Central Conservatory of Music, Beijing; Yehudi Menuhin School, London. *Debut:* With Royal Philharmonic Orchestra, Fairfield Hall, 1983. *Career:* Regular concert appearances in Asia, Europe, South America, North America; Soloist with: Royal Philharmonic Orchestra; Symphony Orchestra of Genoa Opera House; Vancouver Symphony Orchestra; Bern Symphony Orchestra; National Orchestra of Columbia, 1988; Toured with China Broadcasting Symphony Orchestra in 7 countries, Europe; Numerous appearances, TV and Radio, including Swiss Radio. *Recordings:* Exclusive recording for Chinese company; CD release by Philips for Asian distribution; 2 CDs, China, 1982; Numerous concert and recital works on tape and CDs. *Honours:* Silver Medal, Royal Amateur Philharmonic Society; 1st Prize, 34th International Paganini Violin Competition, Italy, 1987; Many other international prizes. *Hobbies:* Football; Tennis; Reading; Food; Stereo; Cars. *Address:* 251 West 73rd Street, Apartment 3B, New York, NY 10023, USA.

LUBBOCK John, b. 18 Mar 1945, Hertfordshire, England. Conductor. *Education:* Chorister at George's Chapel, Windsor, then Royal Academy of Music; Conducting studies with Sergiu Celibidache. *Career:* Founder, Camden Chamber Orchestra, 1967, becoming in 1972 the Orchestra of St John's Smith Square; Frequent concerts at St John's Church in Westminster and on tour in Great Britain, Europe, USA and Canada; Guest conductor with the City of Birmigham Symphony, London Philharmonic, BBC Scottish Symphony, Bournemouth Symphony and Sinfonietta, London Mozart Players, Irish Chamber Orchestra, Stuttgart Symphony Orchestra and Netherlands Chamber Orchestra; Works regularly with the Ulster Orchestra and Principal Conductor, Belfast Philharmonic Society at the Oxford University Orchestra; Conducted Berio's Sinfonia at the Barbican Hall 1985, and the premiere of Meirion Bowen's Orchestration of Tippett's The Heart's Assurance. *Recordings include:* Arnold Guitar Concerto and Rodrigo Concierto de Aranjuez; Haydn Symphony 44 and 49; Mendelssohn Symphony 3 and

4; Schubert Symphony No 5; Stravinsky Apollo and Orpheus; Tchaikovsky Serenade; Vivaldi concerti Op 10, all with the Orchestra of St John's Smith Square. *Address:* c/o Owen White Management, 14 Nightingale Lane, London N8 7QU, England.

LUBET Alex Jeffery, b. 9 June 1954, Harvey, Illinois, USA. Composer; Theorist; Educator. m. Iris Misae Shiraishi, 9 Aug 1981, 1 daughter. *Education:* BMus. Composition, Chicago Musical College of Roosevelt University 1975; MA 1977; PhD 1979, Composition, University of Iowa. *Career:* Assistant Professor of Music Theory and Composition 1979-86; Associate Professor of Music Theory and Composition 1986-; University of Minnesota; Major performances include: St Paul Chamber Orchestra, Ars Nova Festival (Donaueschingen), Institüt für Neue Musik (Freiburg), Festival Musical du Chateau de Pourtales (Strasbourg); Broadcasts on Sudwestfunk and National Public Radio, USA. *Compositions:* Two Octave Etudes; Lament; Ma Tovu; Psalm 139; M'ein Sheva; La Armonia del Mundo; Rhythm Changes; God's Love Dancing Between The Shadows; Three Short Pieces After Webern; 123454; Jaltgrang; The Song of The Jain Temples; Shabbat Shalom; Masada. *Recordings:* Two Octave Etudes; Ma Tovu. *Address:* School of Music, 100 Ferguson Hall, University of Minnesota, Minneapolis, MN 55455, USA.

LUBIN Steven, b. 22 Feb 1942, New York, USA. Pianist; Musicologist. m. Wendy Lubin, 2 June 1974, 2 sons. *Education:* AB, Harvard College; MS, Juilliard School of Music; PhD, New York University; Piano Studies with Lisa Grad, Nadia Reisenberg, Seymour Lipkin, Rosina Lhevinne and Beveridge Webster; *Debut:* Carnegie Recital Hall, New York, 1977. *Career:* Soloist, Mostly Mozart Festival, Summerfare and other Festivals; Concert tours in North America and Europe, 1977-; Soloist and Conductor, continuing series, The Metropolitan Museum, NYC; Filmed as Soloist in Mozart and Beethoven works for British Documentary TV, London and Vienna, 1986; Repeated appearances Mostly Mozart Festival, Lincoln Center, NYC, Metropolitan Museum Series, Alice Tully Hall, Y Series, Kennedy Center, Ravinia Festival. Director of The Mozartean Players, chamber group performing on 18th century period instruments; Faculty Appointments have included Juilliard, Vassar, Cornell; Concerto performances with Los Angeles and St Paul Chamber Orchestras, as well as the Academy of Ancient Music. *Recordings:* Ongoing cycle of Mozart piano concertos, soloist and conductor, for Arabesque records; cycle of Beethoven piano concertos for London/Decca, soloist with Christopher Hogwood and The Academy of Ancient Music, 1987; for Harmonia Mundi USA, works of Mozart, Beethoven, Schubert and Brahms; Mozart, albums of solo and duo sonatas; Haydn, six trios with The Mozartean Players. *Current Management:* New World Classics, 385 East Mosholu Parkway, 4th Floor, Bronx, NY 10467, USA. *Address:* Music Division, School of the Arts, SUNY, Purchase, NY 10577, USA.

LUBLIN Eliane, b. 10 Apr 1938, Paris, France. Singer (Soprano). *Education:* Studied in Paris, then at the Verdi Conservtory, Paris. *Debut:* Aix-en-Provence, as Debussy's Mélisande. *Career:* Paris Opéra-Comique; Monte Carlo Opera in Menotti's The Medium; Paris Opéra from 1969, in Les Dialogues des Carmélites, as Massenet's Manon, Marguerite in Faust, Ellen Orford in Peter Grimes and in the 1981 French premiere of Ligeti's Le Grand Macabre. *Recordings include:* Sapho by Gounod. *Address:* c/o Théâtre National de l'Opéra de Paris, 8 Ruue Scribe, F-75009 Paris, France.

LUBOTSKY Mark, b. 18 May 1931, Leningrad, USSR. Violinist. *Education:* Moscow Conservatory from 1953, with A. Yampolsky and D. Oistrakh. *Debut:* Bolshoi Hall of Moscow Conservatory 1950, Tchaikovsky's Concerto. *Career:* Solo recitals and concerts with major orchestras in Britain, Scandinavia, Germany, Holland, Italy, USA, Australia, Japan and Israel; Many TV and Radio performances; Teacher at Gnessin Institute, Moscow, from 1967 to 1976; Professor at Sweelinck Conservatory, Amsterdam, from 1976; Professor at

Hochschule für Musik, Hamburg, from 1986; British debut 1970, Britten's Concerto at the Promenade Concerts. *Recordings:* Concertos from the Baroque, by Mozart, Britten, Schnittke, Tubin. Solo sonatas by Bach; Sonatas by Brahms, Mozart, Shostakovich, Schnittke. *Honours:* Mozart International Competition, Salzburg, 1956; Tchaikovsky International Competition, Moscow, 1958. *Address:* c/o Encore Concerts Ltd, Caversham Grange, The Warren, Mapledurham, Berkshire, RG4 7TQ, England.

LUCA Sergiu, b. 4 Apr 1943, Bucharest, Rumania. Violinist; Teacher. *Education:* Studied at the Bucharest Conservatory 1948-50, with Max Rostal in London and at the Berne Conservatory; Curtis Institute with Galamian. *Debut:* With the Philadelphia Orchestra conducted by Eugene Ormany, playing the Sibelius Concerto, 1965. *Career:* Founder and Director, Chamber Music Northwest Festival in Portland, 1971-80; Professor of violin at the University of Illinois 1980-83; Starling Professor of Classical violin and violinist-in-residence at the Shepherd School of Music, Houston, 1983-; Music Director of the Texas Chamber Orchestra, 1983-88; Founder and General Director of Da Camera, in Houston, Texas, an Arts Organisation producing approximately 50 concerts a year of small ensemble repertoir, from Renaissance to Jazz, 1988-; Solo performances in the USA, Europe and Japan; Recitals of the unaccompanied works of Bach with authentic instrument and bow; Mozart sonatas with Malcolm Bilson. *Recordings include:* Bach sonatas and partitas for unaccompanied violin; Bartók works for violin and piano. *Honours:* Finalist, 1965 Leventritt Competition; Winner, 1965 Philadelphia Orchestra Youth Auditions. *Address:* Shepherd School of Music, Rice University, Houston, Texas, USA.

LUCHETTI Veriano, b. 12 Mar 1939, Viterbo, Italy. Singer (Tenor). m. Mietta Sighele. *Education:* Studied with Enrico Piazza and in Milan and Rome. *Debut:* Wexford festival 1965, as Alfredo in La Traviata. *Career:* Spoleto 1967, as Loris in Fedora and in Donizetti's Il Furioso all'isola di San Domingo; Guest appearances in Palermo, Parma, Venice, Vienna, Munich, Paris, Mexico City, Dallas and Houston; Maggio Musicale Florence 1971, 1974, in L'Africaine and Agnes von Hohenstaufen by Spontini; La Scala 1975, in Verdi's Attila; Covent Garden 1973-76, as Rodolfo, Pinkerton and Gabriele Adorno in Simon Boccanegra; Aix-en-Provence 1976, as Jason in Cherubini's Medée; Verona 1984, in Verdi's I Lombardi; Vienna Staatsoper 1988, as Foresto in Attila; sang Radames at Turin (1990), Don José at the Verona Arena; Also heard in concert (Verdi's Requiem at Covent Garden, 1976). *Recordings:* Medée (Hungaroton); Nabucco and Verdi Requiem (HMV); Piccinni's La Cecchina; Griselda by Scarlatti; 2 further recordings of the Verdi Requiem. *Address:* c/o S.A. Gorlinsky Ltd., 33 Dover Street, London W1X 4NJ.

LUCHSINGER Ronald, b. 7 Nov 1940, Dubuque, Iowa. Stage Director/Producer, principally in Opera/Music Theatre. *Education:* BA, University of Dubuque, 1964; Graduate Studies: Wayne State University, Detroit, Michigan, 1964-65; MM, Hartt School of Music, 1972. *Career:* Faculty, Oakland University, Michigan, 1964-65; Faculty, Detroit Music Settlement School, 1965-66; Assistant Stage Director, Hartt Opera Theatre, Hartford, Connecticut, 1969-70; Assistant Stage Director, Aspen Music Festival, 1970; Principal Stage Director, Opera Arts Association, Florida, 1973-76; Stage Director, California Music Center, 1973-83; Faculty, Hartt School of Music, 1975-85; Faculty, Mannes College of Music, 1978-79; Artistic Director, Troupers Light Opera, Connecticut, 1978-92; Resident Stage Director, Connecticut Opera, 1983-88; Artistic Director, Simsbury Light Opera, 1985-; Stage Director, New Britain Opera, 1981-88; Stage Director, Dallas Lyric Opera, 1985-91; General Director, Opera North (VT/NH), 1992-. *Membership:* State Governor (Connecticut, Massachusetts and Rhode Island) National Opera Association. *Hobby:* Student of History. *Address:* 13 Dartmouth College Hwy, Lymer, NH 03768, USA.

LUCIER Alvin, b. 14 May 1931, Nashua, New Hampshire, USA. Composer. m. Wendy Wallbank Stokes, 27 Aug 1979, 1 daughter. *Education:* Nashua, New Hampshire, Parochial and Public Schools; The Portsmouth Abbey School; BA, Yale University, 1954; MFA, Brandeis University, 1960; Fulbright Scholarship, Rome, 1960-62. *Career:* Choral Director, Brandeis University, 1962-70; Professor of Music, Wesleyan University, 1970-, Chair of Department, 1979-84; Co-Founder, Sonic Arts Union, 1966-77; Music Director, Viola Farber Dance Company, 1972-77. *Compositions:* Action Music for Piano, 1962 (BMI Canada); Music for Solo Performer, 1965 for enormously amplified brain waves and percussion; Vespers, 1967; Chambers, 1968; I Am Sitting in a Room, 1970; Still and Moving Lines of Silence in Families of Hyperbolas, 1972-; Bird and Person Dyning, 1975; Music in a Long Thin Wire 1977; Crossings, 1982-84; Seesaw, 1984; Sound on Paper, 1985. Numerous recordings including: Bird and Person Dyning; The Duke of York, Cramps Records, Italy. *Publication:* Chambers in collaboration with Douglas Simon, 1980. *Contributions to:* Professional publications. *Hobbies:* Fly Fishing in the American West; Salmon Fishing in Iceland. *Address:* Music Department, Wesleyan University, Middletown, CT 06457, USA.

LUCIUK Juliusz Mieczyslaw, b. 1 Jan 1927, Brzeznica, Poland. Composer. m. Domicela Dabrowska, 10 Nov 1956, 2 daughters. *Education:* Academy of Music, Cracow; Studied with Nadia Boulanger and Max Deutsch, Paris, France, 1958-59. *Debut:* 3 songs performed, 1954. *Compositions:* Numerous works, various recorded by Polish Radio, BBC, Sender Freies Berlin, ORTF France, Italian radio Palermo, Netherlands Radio, including: Songs, 3 Passion Songs for soprano and organ; Concertino, piano and small symphony orchestra; Concerto, double bass and symphony orchestra; Image, Preludes and Tripticum Paschale for organ; Sonata for bassoon and piano; Variations for cello and piano; Monologues and Dialogues for soprano recorders; Ballets, Niobe, Death of Euridice, Medea; Opera-ballet, L'Amour d'Orphée; Chamber opera, Demiurgos; Works for solo voice and chamber ensemble, Floral Dream, Le Souffle du Vent, Portraits Lyriques; works for solo voice and orchestra; Oratorio, St Francis of Assisi, Polish Litany; The Polish Mass for mezzo-soprano, mixed choir and winds orchestra; Choral works including 4 Antiphonae and Vespera in Assumptione Beate Mariae Virginis for men's choir, The Mass for men's choir and organ, The Mass, Hymnus de Caritate and Magnificat for mixed choir and Apocalypsis for 4 soloists and mixed choir; Osiers, 5 pieces for string chamber orchestra; orchestral works, Four Symphonic Sketches, Symphonic Allegro, Composition for Four Orchestral Ensembles, Speranza Sinfonica, Lamentazioni in memoriam Grazyma Bacewicz, Warsaw Legend (Quasi Cradle - Song). *Address:* Os Kolorowe 6 m 10, 31-938 Krakow, Poland.

LUCK Ray Egan, b. 18 Nov 1942, Guyana, South America. Pianist. *Education:* Royal College of Music, London; Conservatoire National Supérieur de Musique, Paris; DMus., Indiana University 1978. *Debut:* Queen Elizabeth Hall, London 1969. *Career:* Performances in Alice Tully Hall, Merkin Concert Hall, New York; Queen Elizabeth Hall, Wigmore Hall, St. John's Smith Square, London; Théâtre des Champs-Elysées, Paris; Jury Member, Trans-Canada Tour for Canadian Music Competitions 1986; Associate Professor, Music Department, Randolph-Macon Woman's College, Lynchburg, Virginia, USA; Co-Director, Blue Ridge Music Festival, Lynchburg, VA. *Recordings:* Broadcasts on BBC, France-Musique. *Honours:* Premiers Prix (Piano, Chamber Music), Paris Conservatoire 1964, 1965; Prizewinner, Geneva International Piano Competition 1967; American liszt Society. *Current Management:* Leon Yow, 31 Adamson Road, London NW3, England.

LUCKÝ Štěpán, b. 20 Jan 1919, Zilina, Slovakia. Composer. *Education:* Prague Conservatory 1936-39; Studied with Ridky 1945-47; Musicology at Prague University 1945-48. *Career:* Member of Czech resistance, imprisoned in Buchenwald and Auschwitz; Committee member of Pritomnost association for contemporary music 1946-48; Music critic for Prague papers; Head of music for Czech TV 1954-58; Taught at Prague Academy 1956- 61; PhDr. Charles University Prague, 1990. *Compositions:* Opera Midnight Surprise 1959; Divertimento for 3 trombones and strings 1946; Cello Concerto 1946; Piano Concerto 1947; Violin Concerto 1965; Octet for strings 1970; Double Concerto for violin, piano and orchestra 1971; Nenia for violin, cello and orchestra 1974; Concerto for orchestra 1976; Fantasia concertante for bass clarinet, piano and orchestra 1983; Much film music 1950-68; Chamber and instrumental music. *Honours include:* State Order for Outstanding Accomplishment 1969; Artist of Merit 1972. *Hobbies:* Touring; Swimming; Chess. *Address:* Lomena 24, 162 00 Prague 6, Czech Republic.

LUDGIN Chester, b. 20 May 1925, New York, USA. Singer (Baritone). *Education:* Studied in New York with William S. Brady. *Debut:* Experimental Opera Theatre New York as Scarpia in Tosca. *Career:* New York City Opera from 1961, notably in the premieres of The Crucible by Ward and The Golem by Ellstein; Guest appearances in Baltimore, Boston, Chicago, Miami, Toronto, Montreal, Mexico City, San Diego and Milwaukee; San Francisco 1966, in the US premiere of Janáček's The Makropoulos Case; Other roles include Escamillo in Carmen, Mephistopheles in Faust, and Rossini's Figaro; sang at Houston in the 1988 premiere of Bernstein's A Quiet Place; Boston 1988, in the US premiere of Dead Souls; Horace Tabor in The Ballad of Baby Doe at Detroit, 1988. *Address:* c/o Opera Company of Boston, PO Box 50, Boston MA 02112, USA.

LUDVIK Emil, b. 16 Aug 1917, Prague, Czechoslovakia. Composer. m. Gerta, 23 Sept 1946, 1 son, 1 daughter. *Education:* Graduate, Realne Gymnasium, Prague; PhD, Charles University, Prague, 1946. *Career:* Committee member of the Prague Spring Festival, 1946-47; Edited compositions of Dvorak for collection tempo, 1953-54, worked for Artia, 1957, constantly writing music for cinema, screen-play, television music and contemporary dance music; Cinema compositions include, Racquet Masters, 1949, Invitation to a Tradefair, 1949; Small Rasons, 1955; Touriste Toute, 1956; The Exemplary Movie Machine of Jaroslav Hasek, 1956; Prague 1910, 1956; Holiday in the Clouds, The Man Whose Prize Went Up, The Goalkeeper Lives on our Street, Little Babes in Town, K Svolinsky, 1957; Academician Burian, 1957; TV films for children, and cartoons; Also piano compositions, wind instrument quintet, symphonies, saxophone concerto. *Publications include:* Songs: A May in January, The Day Ends, Night Story, To Know a few Magic Tricks, Rememberance of You; contributions to A Hostomska's book Opera, a fairy tail for children. *Honours:* Gold Medal, Brussels; Padova Festival prize, 1955. *Address:* Tychonova 3, 160 00 Prague 6, Czech Republic.

LUDWIG Christa, (Deiber), b. 16 Mar 1924, Berlin, Germany. Singer (Mezzo-Soprano). m. (1) Walter Berry, (2) Paul-Emile Deiber, 3 Mar. 1972, 1 son. *Education:* German Abitur, 1944; Studies with mother, Eugenie Besalla (singing). *Debut:* Frankfurt, Germany, 1946. *Career:* After Frankfurt, Darmstadt, Hanover; Wien Staatsoper, 1955-; All important Opera Houses, London Covent Garden (Amneris and Carmen); Metropolitan, New York; Scala, Milan; Tokyo; Chicago; San Francisco; Berlin; Munich; some opera and concerts, TV, Films, concerts all over the world; Salzburg Festival from 1954, debut as Cherubino (sang Mistress Quickly in Falstaff 1981); Metropolitan Opera 1959-90, as the Dyer's Wife in Die Frau ohne Schatten, Cherbino, Dido in Les Troyens, Fricka and Waltraute in the Ring, Ortrund, Kundry, Charlotte, Clytemnestra and the Marschallin; sang in concert performance of Bernstein's Candide at the Barbican (1989), Clytemnestra in Elektra at Innsbruck 1990; Other roles have included Eboli, Leonore, Dalila, Lady Macbeth, Marie in Wozzeck and Ottavia in L'Incoronazione di Poppea; gave Lieder recital at the Wigmore Hall, London, 1991 (Von Einem, Wolf, Strauss and Schubert); Farewell recitals in London and the USA, 1993. *Recordings:* With Böhm: Così Fan Tutte, Marriage of Figaro, Missa Solemnis; with Karajan: Götterdämmerung, Tristan and Isolde, Verdi's Requiem, Das Lied von der Erde; (Rosenkavalier - Octavian); with Bernstein: Rosenkavalier - Marschallin, Das Lied von der Erde, Brahms - Recital; with Giulini: Verdi's Requiem; with Klemperer: Wesendonck - Lieder, Das Lied von der Erde; Farewell to Salzburg, recital 1993 (RCA). *Publications:* Paul Lorenz; Christa Ludwig - Walter Berry; Eine Künstler Biographie. *Honours:* 1st Prize Radio Frankfurt, 1948; Kammersängerin Staatsoper Wien, 1970; Osterreich Grosses Verdienstkreuz I Classe für Kunst and Wissenschaft, 1980; Ehrenmitglied Staatsoper Wien and Goldenen Ehrenring Ehrenmitglied Konzerthaus Wien/Silberne Rose der Wiener Philharmoniker, 1980; Wolf, Mozart, Mahler Medals; Grammy Awards and many other different prizes; Chevalier Legion D'Honneur, France, 1989; Commandeur De L'Ordre Des Arts Et Des Lettres, France, 1989. *Hobbies:* Reading; Cooking. *Address:* 14 Rigistr. Meggen, Switzerland.

LUEDERS Kurt Demaree, b. 20 Feb 1950, Albuquerque, New Mexico, USA. Organist; Musicologist; Editor. *Education:* BA cum laude, Yale College, 1972; Diplôme de Chef de Choeur, Institute of Liturgical Music, Paris, France, 1978; Diplôme de Virtuosité (Organ), Schola Cantorum, Paris, 1983. *Career:* Concerts, Lectures and demonstrations specialising in 19th-century organ, harmonium and choral aesthetics and repertory, USA and several European countries. *Recording:* L'Orgue Cavaillé-Coll, Motette M10760; Romantic Rarities, Afka SK 514. *Publications:* La Flûte Harmonique (editor); Editor of several anthologies of 19th-century organ music, Federal Republic of Germany. *Contributions to:* Numerous articles and reviews in The American Organist, Ars Organi, La Tribune de L'Orgue, La Flûte Harmonique. *Memberships:* Secretary, International Society of Organbuilders; Vice- President, Association Aristide Cavaillé-Coll, Paris. *Address:* 3840 San Rafael Avenue, Salt Lake City, UT 84109, USA.

LUENING Otto, b. 15 June 1900. Conductor; Flautist; Educator. m. (1) Ethel Codd, 19 Apr 1927 (div), (2) Catherine Brunson, 5 Sept 1959. *Education:* State Academy of Music, Munich, 1915-17; Municipal Conservatory of Music, Zurich, 1917-20; University Zurich, 1919-20; DMus, Wesleyan University, 1963; Wis Conservatory of Music, 1979; DMus Hon, University Wisconsin, Milwaukee, 1985. *Career:* Teaching career includes: Faculty of Eastman School, 1925-28; Assistant Professor, University of Arizona, 1932-34; Faculty of Bennington College, 1934-44; Assoc Professor, Chm, Music Dept, Barnard College, 1944-48; Professor of Music, 1948-68, Professor Emeritus of Music, 1988-, Columbia and Barnard College; Composition Faculty, Juilliard School, NYC, 1971-73; Co-founder, American Music Center, NYC, Chm, 1940-60; Founding member, American Composers Alliance, President, 1945-51; Pioneer of electronic tape music; First US Concert of tape music with Vladimir Ussachevsky at Museum of Modern Art, New York, 1952; Co-founder of Columbia-Princeton Electronic Music Center, 1959; Conductor and guest conductor with American Opera Co, NYC, 1928, Rochester American Opera Co, NY Philharmonic Symphony Chamber Orchestra, 1936, VT Orchestra, 1978, 1985, International Festival of the Americas, 1984; Also appeared as composer and flute soloist at Bennington College summer workshops, 1977-79, performing throughout US, Canada and Europe; Recent performances in Moscow, Zurich Tonhalle, Green Lake Festival, Wisconsin, Dutch Radio Orchestra and San Francisco; CD's on Cri, Newport Classic, Phoenix and Louisville First Edition; Published scores available through C F Peters, E C Schirmer, Boston Music Company. *Publications include:* The Odyssey of an American Composer: Autobiography, 1980; The Development and Practice of Eletonic Music, 1975. *Address:* 460 Riverside Drive No 71, New York City, NY 10027, USA.

LUFF Enid, b. 21 Feb 1935, Glamorgan, Wales. Composer. m. Alan Luff, 30 June 1956, 3 sons, 1 daughter. *Education:* LRAM (Piano Teacher's Diploma), 1965; BMus Hons, 1971, MMus, 1974, University of Wales; Advanced composition with Elisabeth Lutyens and Franco Donatoni. *Career:* Composer, 1971-; Runs Primavera self-publishing company with Julia Usher, 1980-. *Compositions:* Four piano pieces, Tapestries for chamber group, both BBC recordings; Symphony 1; Mathematical Dream, solo harp; Wind Quintet: The Coastal Road; Sheila NaGig for soprano and pianoforte; Dream Time for Bells for chamber group (BBC recording); Sky Whispering for solo piano, (Danish Radio recording); Sonata: Storm Tide for piano (BBC recordings; Come the Morning, for chamber ensemble; RAGS, music for mime, electronic tape, 1990; Peregrinns, Triology for organ, 1991; Listening for the Roar of the Sun, for Oboe, Speaker, Dance and slide projection, 1992; Symphony 2, 1994. *Memberships:* Composers Guild of Great Britain; PRS: MCPS; Women in Music. *Hobbies:* Learning languages; Swimming. *Address:* 119 Selly Park Road, Birmingham B29 7HY, England.

LUITZ Josef, b. 2 Aug 1934, Vienna, Austria. Solo Cellist. m. Sonja Edelgard Mayerhofer, 4 Aug 1962, 1 son, 1 daughter. *Education:* School for Musical Instrument Makers, Vienna; Cello Studies with Professor W. Kleinecke, Konservatorium, Vienna; Master-Course with Professor N. Hubner, Santiago de Compostella. *Debut:* Musikverein, Vienna, 1957. *Career:* 1st Cellist, Tonkuenstler Orchestra, 1957-61; Solo Cellist, 1962-; Member, Haydn Quartett, 1965-72, Ensemble Kontrapunkte, 1968-75, Philharmonia Quintett, 1971-77; Professor, Cello, Konservatorium, Vienna, 1972-; Chairman, Tonkuenstler Chamber Orchestra, 1978-, Concordia Trio, 1979-; Chairman, International Chamber Music Festival, Austria, 1978-. *Recordings:* Chamber music Series for Musical Heritage Society Inc., New York; Spohr Octet with Vienna Octet; With Tonkuenstler Chamber Orchestra; many Radio Productions as Soloist. *Honours:* Professor, Austrian Government, 1985. *Hobbies:* Hiking; Reading. *Address:* Concertmanagement Gerhild Baron, Schulz-Stransnitzkigasse 15, A-1090, Vienna, Austria.

LUKACS Ervin, b. 1928, Budapest, Hungary. Conductor. *Education:* Bela Bartok Conservatory, 1950-51; Conductor's Diploma, Ferenc Liszt Academy of Music, 1956. *Career:* Conductor, Hungarian People's Army Artistic Ensemble, 1954-56; Principal Conductor, Miskolc Opera House and Miskolc Symphony Orchestra, 1956-57; Professor, Department of Conducting, Liszt Academy of Music, Budapest, 1956-59; Conductor, Budapest State Opera, 1957-; Master Class held by Franco Ferrara in Venice and Accademia di Santa Cecilia, Rome, Italy, 1961, 1962; As conductor has made several extensive tours with Hungarian State Symphony Orchestra. *Honours:* 1st Prize, Santa Cecilia International Concours for Conductors, 1962; Liszt Prize; Merited Artist of the Hungarian People's Republic. *Address:* c/o Hungarian State Opera, Budapest, Hungary.

LUKAS Viktor, b. 4 Aug 1931, Rothenburg ob der Tauber, Germany. Organist; Conductor. *Education:* Munich Musikhochschule 1951-53 with Karl Richter and Fritz Lehmann; Paris Conservatoire 1955-56, with Marcel Dupre. *Career:* Organist at Kempten 1956-60; Organist and church music director at the Stadtkirche Bayreuth 1960; Concert tours of Europe, USA and USSR with his consort, directed from the harpsichord; Master class at the Cologne Musikhochschule 1975. *Recordings include:* Complete organ works of Brahms and Mendelssohn.

LUKÁŠ Zdeněk, b. 21 Aug 1928, Prague, Czechoslovakia. Composer. *Education:* Studied in Prague with Modr and Ridky. *Career:* Worked for Czech Radio 1953-65; Choral conductor in Pilsen 1955-65; Freelance composer from 1965. *Compositions:* Radio Opera Long Live the Dead Man 1968; Home Carnival, 1-act opera 1968; Orchestral: Piano Concerto 1955; Violin Concerto 1956; Cello Concerto 1957; 4

Symphonies 1960-66; Concerto Grosso for string quartet and orchestra 1964; Symphonietta solemnis 1965; Sonata concertata for piano, winds and percussion 1966; Concerto for violin, viola and orchestra 1969; Variations for piano and orchestra 1970; Postludium for strings 1970; Choral music includes Adam a Eva, oratorio 1969; Chamber: 3 String Quartets 1960, 1965, 1973; Partita semplice for 4 violins and piano 1964; Wind Quintet 1969; Saxophone Quartet 1970; Electronic work You do not Kill 1971. *Address:* c/o SOZA, Kollarovo nam 20, 813 27 Bratislava, Slovakia.

LUKE Ray, b. 30 May 1926, Fort Worth, Texas, USA. Composer; Conductor. *Education:* Studied at Texas Christian University and at the Eastman School of Music, Rochester with Bernard Rogers. *Career:* Taught at the East Texas State College 1951-62; Oklahoma City University from 1962; Associate Conductor, Oklahoma City Symphony 1969-73; Principal Guest Conductor 1974-78. *Compositions:* Opera Medea 1979; Ballet Tapestry 1975; 4 Symphonies 1959-70; Bassoon Concerto 1965; 2 Suites for Orchestra 1958, 1967; Symphonic Dialogues for violin, oboe and orchestra 1965; String Quartet 1966; Piano Concerto 1970; Septet 1979. *Honours include:* Grand Prix Gold Medal Queen Elisabeth of the Belgians Competition, for Piano Concerto, 1970. *Address:* c/o ASCAP, ASCAP Building, One Lincoln Plaza, New York, NY 10023, USA.

LUKOMSKA Halina, b. 29 May 1929, Suchedniow, Poland. Singer (Soprano). *Education:* State Opera High School, Poznan, 1951-54; Warsaw State Music High School; Further study with Toti dal Monte in Venice. *Career:* Wide appearances as concert singer from 1960, notably in works by Webern, Serocki, Boulez (Pli selon Pli), Maderna, Schoenberg, Nono and Lutoslawski; Festival engagements at Edinburgh, Perugia, Vienna, Toulouse, and Warsaw; Holland Festival 1967, in Monteverdi's Orfeo; North American tour with Cleveland Orchestra 1973. *Recordings:* Works by Berg (Altenberglieder) and Webern (Columbia); Pli Selon Pli; Confitebor Domine by JC Bach (Philips); Boris Godunov (HMV). *Honours include:* Winner, 's-Hertogenbosch Competition, 1956.

LUMSDAINE David, b. 31 Oct 1931, Sydney, New South Wales, Australia. Composer. m. Nicola LeFanu, 1 son, 2 daughters. *Education:* New South Wales Conservatorium of Music; Sydney University; With Matyas Seiber, Royal Academy of Music, London; DMus, 1981. *Career:* Teacher of Composition, Music Editor, London, England; Lecturer in Music, Durham University, 1970-; Founder, Electronic Music Studio, Durham; Lecturer, King's College, London. *Compositions:* Orchestral: Episodes, 1969; Mandela II, 1969; Looking Glass Music, 1970; Salvation Creek with Eagle, 1974; Sunflower for chamber orchestra, 1975; Mandela III for solo piano and ensemble, 1978; Shoalhaven, 1982; Mandela V for Symphony orchestra, 1988; vocal: The Ballad of Perse O'Reilly for tenor, male chorus and 2 pianos, 1953-81; What Shall I Sing for soprano and 2 clarinets, 1982; Annotations of Auschwitz for soprano and ensemble, 1964, 1970; Easter Fresco for soprano and ensemble, 1966, 1971; Aria for Edward Eyre for soprano and doubel bass soloists, chamber ensemble, narrators, tape and electronics, 1972; Tides for narrator, 12 voices, percussion; The Ballad of Perce O'Reilly for tenor Chamber works; Mandela I for wind quartet, 1967; Caliban Impromptu for piano trio, tape and electronica, 1972; Mandala TV for string quartet, 1983; Empty Sky, Mootwingee for ensemble, 1986; A Dance and a Hymn for Alexander Maconochie for ensemble, 1988; Round Dance for sitar, table, flute, cello and keyboard, 1989; piano works include Canberra, piano solo, 1980; Wild Ride to Heaven (with Nicola Le Fanu) for electronics, 1980. *Current management:* Sounds Australian, PO Box N690, Grosvenor Place, Sydney, New South Wales 2000, Australia. *Address:* 9 Kempe Road, London, NW6 6SP, England.

LUMSDEN Andrew, b. 10 Nov 1962, Oxford, England. Organist; Choirmaster. *Education:* Winchester College, 1976-80; RSAMD, 1980-81; St John's College, Cambridge, 1981-84. *Career:* Assistant Organist, Southwark Cathedral, 1985-88; Sub Organist, Westminster Abbey, 1988-91; Organist and Master of the Choristers, Lichfield Cathedral, 1992-; Appeared with ECO, LPO at Barbican, Festival Hall; Live recitals for Radio 3; Appeared with ENO, 1990. *Recordings include:* Recordings under various record labels, organ concerto, solo disc and appearances with Finzi Singers. *Honours:* National Young Organist of the Year, 1985; Winner, Manchester Organ Competition, 1986. *Hobbies:* Travel; Wine. *Current Management* Phillip Truckenbrod Concert Artists. *Address:* 11 The Close, Lichfield, Staffs WS13 7LD, England.

LUMSDEN David James (Sir). b. 19 Mar 1928, Newcastle-upon-Tyne, England. m. Sheila Gladys Daniels, 28 July 1951, 2 sons, 2 daughters. *Education:* Dame Allan's School; Selwyn college, Cambridge. *Career:* Fellow, Organist, New College Oxford; Rector, chori, Southwell Minster, Founder, Conductor, Nottingham Bach Society; Dirctor of Music, Keele University; Visiting Prof, Yale University; Principal: Royal Scottish Academy of Music and Dramma and Royal Academy of Music; Hugh Porter Lecturer, Union Theologial Seminary, NY, 1967. *Publications:* An Anthology of English Lute Music, 1954; Thomas Robinson's Schoole Musike, 1603, 1971; contributions to The Listener, The Score, Music and Letters, Galpin Society Journal, La Luth et sa Musique, La musique de la Renaissance. *Honours:* Kt, 1985; MA, 1955; DPhil, 1957; Hon DLitt, 1990. *Memberships:* Incorporated Society of Musicians; Royal College of Organists; Incorporated Association of Organists, 1966-68; Chairman, National Youth Orchestra of GB, 1985-; Hon Ed, Church Music Society, 1970-73; Chairman, Early Music Society, 1985-89; Member of the Board, Scottish Opera, 1977-83; Member of Board, ENO, 1983-88. *Hobbies:* Photography; Hill Walking; Reading; Theatre; Travel. *Address:* Melton House, Soham, Cambs CB7 5DB, England.

LUMSDEN Ronald, b. 28 May 1938, Dundee, England. Pianist. m. (1) Annon Lee Silver, deceased, 1 son, (2) Alison Paice Hill, 1975, 1 son, 1 daughter. *Education:* Harris Academy, Dundee; Royal College of Music, London; ARCM; LRAM. *Career:* Pianist in Residence, University of Southampton, 1965-68; Henry Wood Promenade Concerts, 1973, 1974; Soloist in Arts Council Contemporary Music Network, 1974-76; Visiting Piano teacher, 1976-; Honorary Director of School of Music, 1984-, Reading University; Frequent broadcasts and recitals in United Kingdom. *Recordings:* Messiaen's Cantéyodjayâ for Gaudeamus Foundation; Open University's Modern Music. *Contributions to:* Bartók, in Makers of Modern Culture, 1981. *Honour:* 1st Prize Winner, International Competition for Interpreters of Contemporary Music, Utrecht, 1968. *Memberships:* Executive Committee, Society for Promotion of New Music, 1975-78; Incorporated Society of Music; European Piano Teachers Association. *Address:* 50 Grosvenor Road, Caversham, Reading, Berkshire RG4 0EN, England.

LUMSDEN Stephen, b. 10 Feb 1956, Nottingham, England. Artists Agent; Concert Promoter. m. Joanna Gruenberg, 17 Nov 1979, 3 daughters. *Education:* Studied at the Guildhall School of Music, London. *Career:* Freelance Bassoonist until 1977; Director, Baril Douglas Ltd, 1978-80; Founding Director, 1980-82, Managing Director, 1992-, Intermusica Artists Management, 1980-92; Founder/Director, International Chamber Music Series, Queen Elizabeth Hall, London, 1991-; Personal manager of international artists, project management, orchestral tours, concert promotions. *Honours:* GGSM, 1977. *Memberships:* British Association of Concert Agents, Deputy Ch, 1987-90; European Association of Concert Agents, Bd, 1985-88. *Hobbies include:* Golf; Skiing; Tennis; Cycling; Art; Theatre. *Address:* 16 Duncan Terrace, London N10 2BU, England.

LUND Tamara, b. 1941, Finland. Singer (Soprano).

Career: Sang with Finnish National Opera from 1967, notably in the 1968 local premiere of Berg's Lulu (title role); Member of the Teater am Gartnerplatz Munich from 1973, with tours to Berlin (Komische Oper and Theater des Westerns) and the Theater an der Wien, Vienna; Engaged at the Zurich Opera, 1979-83; Helsinki 1973, as Daphne in the premiere of Apollo and Marsyas by Rautavaara; Other roles have included Carmen, Musetta, Janáček's Vixen, and Jenny in Aufsteig und Fall der Stadt Mahagonny; Sang Juno in the incidental music to The Tempest by Sibelius, Savonlinna 1986; Many appearances in operetta.

LUNDBERG Gunnar, b. 1958, Sweden. Singer (Baritone). *Education:* Studied at the State Opera School Stockholm and in Salzburg. *Debut:* Vadstena Academy, 1984. *Career:* Member of the Royal Opera Stockholm from 1988, notably as the Heerrufer in Lohengrin, Escamillo, Valentin, Mozart's Count and Figaro, Don Giovanni and Rossini's Figaro; Season 1991 as Barelli in the European premiere of The Aspern Papers by Argento; Engaged for seasons 1992-94 as Silvio in Pagliacci and Marcello in La Bohème; Concert repertoire includes Ein Deutsches Requiem, the Bach Passions and B Minor Mass; St John Passion at the 1993 Lucerne Easter Festival. *Address:* Nordic Artists Management, Sveavagen 76, S-11359 Stockholm, Sweden.

LUNDBERG Robert, b. 25 June 1948, California, USA. Luthier (Lutemaker). m. Linda Toenniessen, 2 sons. *Career:* Apprenticeship in violin making with Paul Schuback, a Mirecourt trained master maker. Journyman work in 1973 with Jacob van de Geest in Vevey, Switzerland. Established workshop in Portland, Oregon in 1974, Master maker; Travelled to major European museums measuring, photographing and analyzing ancient lutes. To date has built over 400 instruments of which 300 are lutes, and restored instruments in many private and public collections. Lecturer; Conservator for musical instruments, Smithsonian Institute, Washington DC, 1980-85; Written over 50 essays, articles and reviews on the history and construction of the lute and related topics including, Sixteenth and Seventeenth Century Lute Making, The Historical Lute Construction. Essay, In tune with the Universe: The physics and metaphysics of Galileo's Lute, 1992. *Memberships:* Lute Society of America (Ed Board); The Lute Society; American Musical Instrument Society; Galpin Society; FOMRHI; AIC; IIC. *Hobbies:* Collecting antiques and textiles; Bookbinding. *Address:* 3344 NE Orgeon Street, Portland, OR 97232, USA.

LUNDBORG (Charles) Erik, b. 31 Jan 1948, Helena, Montana, USA. Composer. m. Zinta Bibelnieks, 14 Nov 1981. *Education:* BM, New England Conservatory of Music, Boston; MA, 1974, DMA, 1985, Columbia University. *Career:* Performances & Commissions by Houston Symphony Orchestra, American Composers Orchestra, Ursula Oppens, Piano, Speculum Musicae, Group for Contemporary Music, Parnassus, New Music Consort, Pittsburgh, New Music Ensemble, Light Fantastic Players, Composers Ensemble, New Jersey Percussion Ensemble, many others. *Compositions:* Passacaglia, Two Symphonies, from Music Forever, No. 2 Piano Concerto; Soundsoup; Solotremolos. *Recordings:* Passacaglia from Music Forever, No. 2; Soundsoup. *Contributions to:* Milton Babbitt, String Quartet No 3, Contemporary Music Newsletter, 1974. *Honours:* Guggenheim, 1976-77; NEA Fellowships, 1975, 1981, 1983. *Memberships:* BMI; American Composers Alliance, Board Member, 1980-82; Board, ISCM, League of Composers, 1975-78. *Address:* 2465 Palisade Ave., 8F, Riverdale, NY 10463, USA.

LUNDE Joan, b. 30 Mar 1939, Long Beach, California, USA. Cellist; Composer. *Education:* Concert Exam Diploma, Vienna Academy of Music, Austria, 1962. *Career:* Member: Academy String Trio, Vienna, Hoffmann Quartet, New York, RKO Quartet; Solo Cellist, Rheinisch Chamber Orchestra, Cologne; Member, Trio Viva, New York; Founder, Director, International Collegium for Musical Communication, Arolsen, Federal

Republic of Germany; Extensive recitals in Europe, USA and Canada; Highly commended as teacher of cello and chamber music producing several international prizewinners. *Recordings:* Golden Crest Records, CRA 4129, New York; With pianist H.J.Spelmanns, WDR Cologne and Bayerische Rundfunk. *Publications:* Piano Studies for Young Fingers, 1989; Vignettes for Violin and Cello, 1989; Vignettes for Piano Trio, 1989. *Current Management:* Soley Management, Post Office Box 2582, Clearwater, FL 34617-2582, USA. *Address:* 303 N Jackson St - 103, Glendale, CA 91206, USA.

LUNDGREN Stefan, b. 5 May 1949, Hogsby, Sweden. Lutenist; Composer; Editor, Luemusic. m. Henrike Brose, 21 Mar 1985. *Education:* Studied Music; Music School, Oskarshann, Sweden, 1972-74; Lund University, 1974-77; Schola Cantonum Basiliensis, Basel, 1977-79. *Career:* Teacher, Performer, Composer, Publisher, Lute Music, 1979-; Director, Annual Lute Course, Ried im Zillertal, 1986-; Teacher, Summer Courses, Svenska Gitarr och Lutasallskapets, 1985. *Compositions:* Sonatas 1-3 for solo lute, 1981-84; Sonata No 4, for solo lute, 1986. *Publications:* New School for the Renaissance Lute, 1985; Publishers of: 50 English Duets in 4 volumes; Charles Mouton: Suite in G Minor; J.A. Losy, Two Suites; Little Book for Lute 1 for Renaissance Lute; Little Book for Lute 2, Baroque Lute; J.S. Bach, Complete Works for lute. *Address:* Barerstrasse 70, D 8000 Munchen 40, Germany.

LUNDQUIST Christie Renis, b. 24 Nov 1946, Chicago, USA. Clarinettist. *Education:* BM, University of Southern California, 1968; MM, Cleveland Institute of Music, 1971. *Debut:* Soloist, 13 years of age with Meremblum Junior Symphony, Los Angeles, California. *Career:* Principal Clarinettist, National Symphony of Mexico, 1972-77; Principal Clarinettist - Casals Festival, 1975; Principal Clarinettist, Utah Symphony, 1977-; Guest Artist and Teacher, The University of Southern California, 1987-88; Soloist, several occasions with: The Utah Symphony, Musgrave Concerto, Mozart Concerto, Debussy - Premiere Rhapsody, C.M. Weber Concertino, Copland Concerto; Numerous Recitals, Master Classes & Lectures. *Compositions:* Works Written for and Dedicated to Christie Lundquist: Twelve Melodic Studies for Clarinet; Sonata for Clarinet and Piano; Duets for Clarinets Ingolf Dahl (Dedication 2nd Movement). *Recordings:* With Utah Symphony, 1978-. *Publications:* (Poems) Constancy, Soul's Sonata, Mozart Alone. *Honours:* Tanglewood- Berkshire Festival Outstanding Musician Award and Koussevitsky Scholarship, 1971. *Hobbies:* Poetry; Skiing; Tennis; Composing. *Address:* 710 East 200 South No. 7-E, Salt Lake City, UT 84102, USA.

LUNDSTEN Ralph, b. 6 Oct 1936, Ersnäs, Sweden's Composer; Filmmaker; Artist; Owner of Swedens most famous picture and electronic music studio, Andromeda, including the Love Machine and other invented synthesizers. *Career:* 500 opus, 60 records, 12 short films, art exhibitions, a book with CD; Work for the Opera House in Stockholm and Oslo, the Modern Museum and the National Museum in Stockholm, the Louvre and the Biennale in Paris, the Triennale in Miland and the Museum of Contemporary Crafts in New York; Subject of a number of Radio and TV portraits, 1971-1993 and a special portrait-exhibition at the Music Museum in Stockholm 1991-1992. *Compositions include:* Nordic Nature Symphony No.1, The Water Sprite; No 2, Johannes and the Lady of Woods; No 3, A Midwintersaga; No 4, a Summer Saga; No 5, Bewitched; No 6, Landscape of Dreams; Erik XIV and Gustav III (2 ballets about Swedish Kings); Cosmic Love; Ourfather; Nightmare; Horrorscope; Shangri-La; Universe; Discophrenia; Alpha Ralpha Boulevard; Paradise Symphony; The New Age; Pop Age; Music for Relaxation and Meditation; Cosmic Phantazy; The Dream Master; The Gate of Time; The Ages of Man; Sea Symphony; Mindscape Music. *Honours:* Grand Prix Biennale, Paris, France, 1967; the Swedish Film Institute prize 1964-1967 and about 40 other awards for music and film making. *Address:* Frankenburgs väg 1, S-132 42 Saltsjö-Boo, Sweden.

LUNETTA Stanley, b. 5 June 1937, Sacramento, California, USA. Composer. *Education:* BA Sacramento State College; MA University of California at Davis, with Jerome Rosen and Larry Austin; Further study with John Cage, David Tudor and Karlheinz Stockhausen. *Career:* Founded New Music Ensemble 1963; Editor of Source: Music of the Avant Garde 1971-77; Percussionist and teacher in Sacramento. *Compositions include:* Many Things for orchestra 1966; Piano Music 1966; A Piece for Bandoneon and Strings 1966; Free Music 1967; Ta-Ta for chorus and mailing tubes 1967; The Wringer (mixed media) 1967; Funkart 1967; Twowomanshow, theatre piece 1968; Spider Song with Lartry Austin, 1968; Mr Machine for flute and tape 1969; A Day in the Life of the Mooscak Machines 1972; The Unseen Force theatre piece with dancers 1978; From 1970 much music from a series of self-playing electronic sound sculptures, e.g. Mooscak Machine, Sound Hat and Cosmic Cube. *Address:* c/o ASCAP, ASCAP Building, One Lincoln Plaza, New York, NY 10023, USA.

LUNKLEY Bruce Glenn,b. 16 Feb. 1929, Minneapolis, Minnesota, USA. Voice Teacher; Choral Conductor. m. 4 June 1960, 1 son, 1 daughter. *Education:* BS (hons) Music, 1951; MMusEd (hons), 1959; Postgraduate study, Meadowbrook School, 1965; Voice study with Roy Schuessler, Aksel Schiøtz, Horst Günter, choral conducting with James Aliferis and Hugh Ross, voice pedagogy with William Vennard. *Career:* Music Assistant, University of Minnesota, 1952, 1954-59; Part-time Theory Instructor, Augsburg College, Minneapolis, 1956-59; Director, Twin City Symphonic Choir, Minneapolis, 1956-59; Professor of Music, Austin College, Sherman, Texas, 1959-, Professor Emeritus, 1991; Founder, Sherman Civic Chorus, Sherman Musical Arts Inc; Visiting Professor of Voice, Southern Methodist University, Dallas, Texas, 1992-95; Co-Founder, Sherman Symphony; Founder, Community Series Inc, Sherman; Masterclasses in Voice in 30 states, USA, Guildhall School of Music and Drama, London, England; London College of Music, Colchester Institute, Trinity College of Music, London; College choir performances throughout USA, Great Britain, Western Europe. *Recordings:* Numerous recordings with Austin College A Cappella Choir including broadcast tapes for National Radio Pulpit and The Protestant Hour. *Address:* 618 West Oxford, Sherman, TX 75092, USA.

LUPERI Mario, b. 1954, Sardinia, Italy. Singer (Bass). *Education:* Studied in Calgliari, Verona and Siena. *Debut:* Perugia 1979, in Olympie by Spontini and in Cherubini's Requiem. *Career:* Palermo and Florence 1981, as Publio in La Clemenza di Tito and as Thomas in Iphigénie en Tauride; La Scala from 1982, as the Emperor in The Nightingale, Somon in Gianni Schicchi and Pluto in the Monteverdi Orfeo; Macerata Festival 1984-86, as Colline and Timur, Salzburg Easter Festival 1986, as the Grand Inquisitor; Sang Ramphis in Aida at the Munich Staatsoper 1986, Luxor 1987; Season 1986-87 as Verdi's Pistol at Brussels, Oroe in Semiramide and Oroveso in Norma at Naples; North American debut 1988, as Timur at Pittsburgh; Sang Colline at Genoa, 1990, Giorgio in I Puritani in Marseilles, 1991; Mozart's Bartolo in Venice 1991 and in Fra Diavolo at La Scala, 1992; Many concert appearances. *Address:* c/o Teatro Alla Scala Via Filiodrammatici 2, 20121 Milan, Italy.

LUPO Benedetto, b. 3 July 1963, Bari, Italy. Pianist; Piano Teacher in the N Piccinni Conservatoire, Bari, Italy. *Education:* Studied at N Piccinni Conservatoire with Michele Marvulli, Pierluigi Camicia. Teachers: Maria Teresa Somma, Aldo Ciccolini. *Debut:* Beethoven 1st Concerto with Bari Symphony Orchestra, December, 1976. *Career:* Antwerp: A. De Vries, Foundation; Naples: Academy San Pietro a Majella, RAI A Scarlatti, Orchestra; Milan: Angelicum, Symphony Orchestra; Marseille: Lundis Du Conservatoire; Nantes: Orchestre Philharmonique des Pays de Loire (conductor Pierre-Michel Durand); Lourmarin: Castle Festival; St-Jean-de-Luz, Orchestre du Capitole de Toulouse (conductor Michel Plasson); Madrid: National Radio Recitals Season; Cordoba, Sevilla, Granada, Burgos, Cleveland:

Severance Hall and IMC Orchestra; Salt Lake City; Utah Symphony (conductor Joseph Silverstein), Temple Square Series; Rio de Janeiro: Brazilian Symphony; Salvador: Castro Alves Theatre; Stresa: International Festival. *Honours:* 1st Prize in the following International Competitions: Senigallia: International Meetings 1977; Milan: Alfred Cortot, Competition, 1980, 26th City of Jáen International Competition, Spain, 1982; 2nd Prize in, R Casadesus, International Competition, Cleveland, 1985. *Address:* Via Caravaggio, I-70021 Acquaviva Delle Fonti-Ba, Italy.

LUPU Radu, b. 30 Nov 1945, Galati, Rumania. Classical Pianist. *Education:* 1st piano lessons, 1951; Scholarship, 1961, Graduated, 1969, Moscow Conservatoire. *Career:* Leading Interpreter for German classical composers; Frequently appears with all major British orchestras; Toured Eastern Europe with London Symphony Orchestra; American debut, 1972; Gave world premiere of André Tchaikovsky's Piano Concerto, London, 1975. *Recordings:* For Decca, including complete Beethoven cycle with Israel Philharmonic and Zubin Mehta, 1979; Mozart sonatas for violin and piano (with Szymon Goldberg); Brahms piano concerto No 1 (with Edo de Waart and The London Philharmonic Orchestra); Mozart piano concerto K467 (with Uri Segal-The Eng Chamber Orchestra); various Beethoven and Schubert sonatas, Mozart and Beethoven Wind Quintets in E Flat, Mozart concerto for 2 pianos, concerto for 3 pianos transcribed for 2 pianos (with Murray Perahia aand The Eng Chamber Orchestra); Schubert Fantasia in F Minor and Mozart in D for 2 pianos (with Murray Perahia). *Honours:* 1st Prize, Van Cliburn Competition, 1966; Enescu International Competition, Bucharest, 1967; Leeds International Competition, 1969. *Hobbies:* Chess; Bridge; History. *Current Management:* Terry Harrison Artists Management. *Address:* c/o Terry Harrison Artists Management, 3 Clarendon Court, Park Street, Charlbury, Oxon OX7 3PS, England.

LUSKIN Evan Ross, b. 20 Mar 1946, Philadelphia, Pennsylvania, USA. Managing Director, Lyric Opera of Kansas City. *Education:* BA, magna cum laude, History, University of Pennsylvania 1967; MA, African History, University of Wisconsin 1969; MBA, State University of New York, Binghamton 1977. *Career:* Assistant Manager, Tulsa Opera 1977-79; Managing Director, Chattanooga Opera 1979-82; Vice-President for Finance and Planning, Michigan Opera Theatre, 1982-86; Managing Director, Lyric Opera of Kansas City 1986-. *Honour:* Phi Beta Kappa. *Address:* Lyric Opera of Kansas City, 1029 Central, Kansas City, MO 64105, USA.

LUTHER Mark, b. 14 Nov 1961, Bristol, England. Singer (Tenor). *Education:* Studied at the National Opera Studio, and at the Guildhall School with Noelle Barker. *Debut:* St John's Smith Square, 1989, in Elijah. *Career:* Concert appearances include Opera Gala Evening at Covent Garden, Vivaldi's Gloria with the Northern Symphonia and showings at the Purcell Room and the Elizabeth Hall; Opera engagements include touring performances with British Youth Opera as Rodolfo; other roles include: Idomeneo, Don Ottavio and Remendado (Carmen); Macduff and Arturo in Lucia di Lammermoor for Welsh National Opera, Don José at Rotterdam and the Verdi Requiem in Holland; Don Ottavio in Schönbrunn Vienna. *Address:* Atholl Still Ltd, 80-86 Westrow Street, London SE19 3AF, England.

LUTOSLAWSKI Witold, b. 25 Jan 1913, Warsaw, Poland. Composer; Conductor. *Education:* Studied Violin with Lidia Kmitowa 1926-32; Studied Theory and Composition with Witold Maliszewski 1927-32; Studied Mathematics, Warsaw University 1931-33; Studied at Warsaw Conservatory under Witold Maliszewski, Composition and Jerzy Lefeld, Piano; Piano Degree 1936; Composition Degree 1937. *Debut:* Orchestral Piece, Warsaw Philharmonic 1933; Sonata for Piano 1935. *Career:* First public performance of Symphonic Variations, Cracow Festival 1939; Took part in clandestine concerts in private houses during war 1939-45; Short period of work with Polish Radio 1945; First performance of orchestral piece in Paris 1946; First performance of Symphony No. 1 Katowice Polish Radio National Symphony conducted by G. Fitelberg 1948; Took part in various social activities as member of Programme Commission of Warsaw Autumn Festival, Chairman of Programme Council of Polish Music Publications, Member, Presidential Committee of International Society for Contemporary Music, Member, International Music Council; Composition Teacher, Berkshire Music Center, Tanglewood, USA 1962; Teaching Composition at Dartington Summer School of Music, 1963 and 1964; Teaching Composition, Conservatory, Aarhus, Denmark 1968; Lecturer in various music centres and universities 1968; Conductor of own works in many European and American countries as well as records 1963-; Conducted Cello Concerto and premiere of Chantefables et Chantefleurs at the 1991 Promenade Concerts, London; Conducted the British premiere of his Fourth Symphony at the 1993 Proms. *Compositions include:* Symphonic Variations 1938; Variations on a theme of Paganini for 2 pianos 1941; First Symphony 1947; Overture for Strings, 1949; Concerto for Orchestra 1954; 5 Songs for female voice and piano 1957; Musique funèbre for string orchestra; Venetian Games for chamber orchestra 1961; 3 Poems of Henri Michaux for choir and orchestra 1963; String Quartet 1964; Paroles Tissées for tenor and chamber orchestra 1965; Second Symphony 1967; Livre pour Orchestre 1968; Concerto for cello and orchestra 1970; Preludes and Fugue for 13 solo strings 1972; Les espaces du sommeil for baritone and orchestra 1975; Mi-Parti for orchestra 1976; Novelette for orchestra 1979; Epitaph for oboe and piano, 1979; Double Concerto for oboe, harp and orchestra 1980; Grave for cello and piano, 1981; Grave version for cello and string orchestra, 1982; Mini Overture for brass quintet, 1982; 3rd Symphony 1983; Chain 1 for chamber orchestra 1984; Partita for violin and piano 1984; Chain 2, Dialogue for violin and orchestra 1985; Sacher variation for cello, 1985; Chain 3 for symphony orchestra 1986; Concerto for Piano and Orchestra, 1988; Partita, version for Violin and Orchestra, 1988; Slides for 11 Soloists, 1988; Lullaby for Anne Sophie 1989; Interludium for Chamber Orchestra 1989; Tarantella for Baritone and piano 1990; Chantefleurs et Chantefables, songs for soprano and chamber orchestra, 1990; Subito for violin and piano 1992; 4th Symphony, 1992. *Honours include:* Numerous honorary degrees, Polish prizes and international prizes in recognition of his compositional works. *Address:* SMIALA 39, 01523 Warsaw, Poland.

LUTZ Verena, b. 6 Feb 1941, Zurich, Switzerland. Concert Organist; Harpsichordist. *Education:* Studied Piano from the age of 8 and Organ from the age of 15; Music Academy, Zurich, Piano Teachers Diploma, 1962, Concert Diploma, Organ, 1963. *Career:* Elementary Studies at the Music Academy in Zurich; Leading Organist, Bruder Klaus Church, Zurich, 1960-; Numerous Concert appearances; toured throughout Europe, Japan and USA; Further Studies with Anton Heiller, Eduard Müller, Michel Chapius, Luigi Ferdinando Tagliavini and other acclaimed artists; Regular TV & Radio broadcasts. *Honours:* 1st Prize at the International Organ Competition in Ravenna, Italy.*Hobbies:* Historical Musical Instruments. *Address:* Langensteinenstr. 3, CH-8057, Zurich, Switzerland.

LUTZE Gert, b. 30 Sept 1917, Leipzig, Germany. Singer (Tenor). *Education:* Sang in the choir of St Thomas' Leipzig from 1928. *Career:* Bach's St Matthew Passion conducted by Gunter Ramin; Many appearances as concert and oratorio singer; Opera roles included Puccini's Pinkerton and Rodolfo, Mozart's Ferrando and Rimsky-Korsakov's Sadko; Engagements as Bach singer in Schaffhausen, Zurich, Basle, Berne, Helsinki, Paris, Brussels and Luxembourg; Sang in Prague and China 1955; St Matthew Passion in Bologna and Florence 1957; Further concerts with Karl Richter as conductor.

LUXON Benjamin, b. 24 Mar 1937, Cornwall, England. Singer (Baritone). m. Sheila Amit, 1969, 2 sons, 1 daughter. *Education:* Westminister Training College, Guildhall School of Music and Drama. *Debut:*

English Opera Group, 1963. *Career:* Sang with the English Opera Group, 1963-70; Royal Opera House, Covent Garden, and Glyndebourne Festival Opera, 1971-; Netherlands Opera, 1976-; Frankfurt Opera House, 1977-. Roles include Monteverdi's Ulisse, Janaček's Forester, Mozart's Don Giovanni and Papageno, Tchaikovsky's Onegin, Verdi's Posa and Falstaff and Wagner's Wolfram, Alban Berg's Wozzeck, Los Angeles, 1988; Recitals and Folk singing; Paris Opera, 1980; La Scala, Milan, 1986. Television appearances include title role in Giulio Cesare by Handel, Theater an der Wien, Vienna, 1985, conducted by Nikolaus Harnoncourt; Sang Falstaff at Los Angeles, 1990; Other roles include Count Almaviva and Sherasmin in Oberon, Edinburgh, 1986 and Falstaff for ENO. *Recordings include:* Mahler's 8th Symphony and Schubert's Song Cycles. *Honours include:* FGSM, 1970; Hon RAM, 1980; Hon DMus, Exeter, 1980; CBE, 1986. *Address:* Lower Cox Street Farm, Detling, Maidstone Kent ME14 3HE, England.

LVOV Boris, b. 1928, Moscow, Russia. Concert Pianist. *Education:* Studied at the Central School of Music and at the Moscow Conservatoire. *Debut:* First public concert aged nine years. *Career:* Performed at the Moscow Conservatoire in 1946 and won the Beethoven Competition for his performance of the Hammerklavier Sonata; many concerts in the former Soviet Union, Eastern Europe and China from 1948; appearances wiht David Oistrakh, Rostropovitch, Kondrashin and Emil Gilels; former Professor of Piano, Moscow Conservatoire, then emigrated to Israel and is currently Professor at the Rubin Academy of Music in Jerusalem; recent concert tours to Europe, Japan, Scandinavia and United States, both in recital and concert; repertoire includes music by Haydn, Mozart, Schumann, Liszt, Prokofiev, Bartók and Stravinsky. *Address:* 11 Northpark Street, Glasgow G20 7AA, Scotland.

LYALL Robert, b. 29 Oct 1948, Shawnee, Oklahoma, USA. Conductor. *Education:* Master of Music, Composition 1972, PhD, Musicology 1974, University of North Texas; Conducting study with Kyril Kondrashin, Amsterdam, 1979, with Richard Lert, Virginia, 1980. *Debut:* Victoria Symphony Orchestra, 1974. *Career:* General Director, The Knoxville Opera Company, 1981-; Music Director, The Oak Ridge Symphony Orchestra, 1979-; Music Director, The Victoria Symphony Orchestra, Texas, 1974-; Guest appearances: 1984 World's Fair; Mexico, New York, North Carolina, Virginia, Texas, Kansas, Colorado, Washington DC, Georgia, Tennessee All-State Orchestra, Seattle Opera; Opera Theatre of St Louis; Baton Rouge Opera; Ballet companies of: Dallas, Fort Worth, San Antonio, Corpus Christi, Chattanooga, Knoxville, Oak Ridge; University of TN Opera Theatre; Radio Concerts: America in Concert with Victoria Symphony Orchestra; General Director, Opera Grand Rapids (Michigan), 1990-. *Publication:* A French Music Aesthetic (writings of MPG Chabanon), 1975. *Address:* 1009 Tokalon Drive, Knoxville, Tennessee 37932, USA.

LYMPANY Moura (Dame), b. 18 Aug 1916, Saltash, Cornwall, England. Concert Pianist. *Debut:* Performance at Harrogate, 1929, Mendelssohn's First Concerto. *Career:* Has played in USA, Canada, South America, Australia, New Zealand, India and most European countries including USSR; Has often been heard in music by Khachaturian, Rachmaninov, Ireland, Delius, Rawsthorne, Cyril Scott and Chopin; Played Mendelssohn at the 1991 Promenade Concerts, London. *Honours:* Commander Order of the Crown, Belgium, 1980; Commander of the British Empire; Fellow, Royal Academy of Musicians; DBE, 1992. *Address:* Château Périgord 2, Appt 81, Monte Carlo, Monaco.

LYNE Richard Clement, b. 15 Nov 1948, London, England. Organist, Conductor, Lecturer. m. Christine Lambie, 9 July 1977, 2 daughters. *Education:* MA, Nottingham, 1978; BMus, London, 1973; GRSM, 1970; ARCO, 1970, ARCM, 1968. *Career:* Organist, St. Anne and St. Agnes, Gresham Street, London, 1972-78;

Conductor, Apollo Singers, 1972-81; Organist, St. John's, Hyde Park Crescent, London, 1980-83; currently, Professor, Royal College of Music, Director, Organist, All Saints', Weston, Surrey, 1989-93; Director Howells Singers; Hon. General Editor, Church Music Society; Presently: Lecturer, Welsh College of Music and Drama; Assistant Organist, Chapel Royal, Hampton Court Palace. *Recordings:* Neapolitan Madrigals and Motets, with Gesualdo Consort. *Publications:* Motets by Dering (Cantica Sacra 1662) RSCM, 1981, Second Set, 1984; Three Motets by Dering, Church Music Society; Anthems by Blow, Boyce and Greene. *Contributions to:* Church Music Quarterly; World of Church Music. *Hobbies:* Cookery; Driving; Gardening. *Address:* 26 Elsworthy, Thames Ditton, Surrey, KT7 0YP, England.

LYON David Norman, b. 29 Dec 1938, Walsall, England. Composer; Pianist; Teacher. m. (1) Kathleen Devney, 31 Mar 1964, 1 son, (2) Elizabeth Buchanan, 27 Oct 1984, 1 daughter, 1 son. *Education:* Royal Academy of Music, 1960-64; BA, Bristol University. *Compositions include:* Divertimento for small orchestra; Piano Concerto; Concerto for horn and strings; Ballet for orchestra; An English Mass; God's Grandeur for tenor and piano; Rhapsodic Prelude for brass band; Violin Sonata; The Reckoning (children's opera); Fleetfoot the Fox for narrator, chorus and orchestra. *Hobbies:* Exploring the countryside; Architecture; Travel; Theatre; Cinema. *Address:* 1 St Rumbolds Road, Shaftesbury, Dorset SP7 8NE, England.

LYSIGHT Michel Thierry, b. 14 Oct 1958, Brussels, Belgium. Composer; Conductor; Professor. *Education:* Candidate in Musicology, Free University of Brussels, 1978; Academy of Schaerbeek; Conservatoire Royal de Musique, Mons; Conservatoire Royal de Musique, Brussels; Advanced Diplomas: Solfege, 1980, Chamber Music, 1988, Composition, 1989. *Career:* Professor, Conservatoire Royal, Brussels, 1980-; Professor: Academies of Schaerbeek, 1979-89, Woluwe Saint-Pierre, 1981-90, Professor, 1989-90, Deputy Director, 1990-, Academy of Brussels; Founder, Michel Lysight Ensemble for contemporary music, 1991; Director, Pedagogical Collection, Alain Van Kerckhoven Publisher. *Compositions include:* Chamber music, orchestral music, piano, percussion including: Reflexion, clarinet or bassoon and piano; Soleil Bleu, 1 wind instrument and piano; Trois Croquis, violin or flute or clarinet and piano or string orchestra, 1990-93; Quatrain, flute, oboe, clarinet, bassoon, 1990; Chronographie II for string orchestra, 1992-93; Vedanta for clarinet, bassoon and piano, 1993; Chronographie III for flute, clarinet, bassoon, violin, viola, cello, double bass and piano, 1993. *Address:* Servranckxplein 3, 1932 Sint Stevens - Woluwe, Belgium.

LYSY Alberto, b. 11 Feb 1935, Buenos Aires, Argentina. Violinist; Teacher. Divorced, 4 children. *Education:* Studied with Ljerko Spiller in Argentina; Further study in Paris and London. *Career:* Solo recitals and performances with orchestras in Italy, France, Israel, Japan, India, USA, USSR, South America; Founder of chamber orchestra in Buenos Aires, 1965; Director of Camerata Lysy, Gstaad; Director, International Menuhin School, Gstaad. *Honours include:* Prizewinner, Queen Elisabeth of Belgium International Competition 1955. *Hobbies:* Cross Country Skiing; Chess; Football. *Address:* Chalet Angela, Gstaad, Switzerland.

LYSY Antonio, b. 1963, Rome, Italy. *Education:* Studied with his father, the violinist Alberto Lysy; Menuhin School with Maurice Gendron and William Pleeth; Menuhin Academy with Raoual Dulescu; Royal Northern College of Music with Ralph Kirshbaum. *Career:* Concert engagements in Austria, Argentina, France, Germany, Israel, Italy and Spain; British venues include the Royal Festival Hall, Wigmore Hall, Queen Elizabeth Hall and St John's Smith Square; chamber concerts with Radu Aldulescu, Gidon Kremer, Lamar Crowson and Yehudi Menuhin; Principal Cellist with the Chamber Orchestra of Europe and appearances with the Manchester-based Goldberg Ensemble; Camerata of Salzburg 1988, with Sandor

Vegh as conductor; solo performances of Tchaikovsky's Rococo Variations in Buenos Aires and Italy; further engagements with the Philharmonia Orchestra and at the Brighton Festival; Artistic Director of Chamber music festival in Tuscany, Incontri Musicali in Terra di Siena, from summer 1989. *Recordings:* Bloch's Prayer and Tchaikovsky's Souvenir de Florence with the Camerata Lysy, for Claves Records. *Address:* c/o Anglo-Swiss Artists Management Ltd., 4/5 Primrose Mews, 1a Sharpleshall Street, London NW1 8YW, England.

LYUBIMOV Yuri (Petrovich), b. 30 Sept 1917, Yaoslal, Russia. Stage Director. *Career:* Actor at the Moscow Arts Theatre and Vakhtangov Theatre; Artistic Director of the Taganka Theatre, Moscow, 1964-84; Opera productions have included The Queen of Spades at the Paris Opera, Don Giovanni in Budapest, Khovanshchina at La Scala, Rigoletto in Florence and Tristan und Isolde at Bologna; Produced Mussorgsky's Salammbo in Paris and Naples, 1986; Royal Opera House Covent Garden 1986 and 1988, with Jenůfa and Das Rheingold; Produced the Queen of Spades at Karlsruhe 1990, The Love for Three Oranges at the Bayerische Staatsoper, Munich, 1991.*Address:* c/o Bayerische Staatsoper, Postfach 100148, 8000 Munich 1, Germany.

M

MA Yo Yo, b. 7 Oct 1955, Paris, France. Cellist. m. Jill Horner, 1978, 1 son, 1 daughter. *Debut:* Aged 5. *Career:* Performed with all major orchestras including Berlin Philharmonic, Boston Symphony, Chicago Symphony, Israel Symphony, London Symphony; Regularly appears at Tanglewood, Salzburg, Edinburgh and other major festivals; Plays regularly in Chamber Music ensemble with Issac Stern and in a duo partnership with Emanuel Ax; Premiered the Concerto by H. K. Gruber, Tanglewood 1989; Beethoven Cello Sonatas from the Edinburgh Festival televised BBC, 1991. *Recordings:* Numerous including: Six Bach Suites for unaccompanied cello, CBS, 1984; CDs of Haydn's Cello Concerto in D (English Chamber Orchestra); Schubert's String Quintet, with the Cleveland Quartet (CBS); Shostakovich Concerto No.1 (Philadelphia Orchestra); Barber Concerto and Britten Cello Symphony (Baltimore Symphony); Brahms Double Concerto (Isaac Stern and the Chicago Symphony); Schumann Works for Cello (Emanuel Ax, Bavarian Radio Symphony). *Honours:* Avery Fisher prize, 1978; Grammy Award, 1984. *Current Management:* ICM Artists Limited. *Address:* c/o ICM Artists Limited, 40 West 57th Street, New York, NY 10019, USA.

MAAG Peter, b. 10 May 1919, St. Gall, Switzerland. Conductor. m. 1 son. *Education:* Theology and Philosophy Studies at Zürich and Basel Universities; Studied piano with Alfred Cortot. *Career:* Began conducting in small theatre; Assistant to Wilhelm Furtwängler; Assistant to Ernest Ansermet, Orchestre de la Suisse Romande; Düsseldorf Opera 1952-55; Chief Conductor Bonn Opera 1956-59; Volksoper, Vienna 1962; Teatro Regio, Turin 1974; Berne Symphony Orchestra 1984-; Former Principal Guest Conductor, Radiotelevisione Italiana (RAI) now Orquesta Nacional, Madrid; Regular Guest Conductor at La Scala, Milan; Metropolitan Opera, (Don Giovanni, 1972, New York); Teatro Colón, Buenos Aires, Venice; Royal Opera House, Covent Garden; also at various festivals including Aix-en-Provence, Zürich, Netherlands, Vienna, Salzburg; Conducted Cosí fan Tutte (and played harpsichord continuo) at the Gran Teatre del Liceu, Barcelona, 1990. *Recordings include:* Mozart Symphonies, Piano Concertos (with Katchen, Gulda and Klien); Posthorn Serenade and Masonic Music; Complete Schubert Symhonies; Britten and Dvořák Violin Concertos; Mendelssohn's 3rd Symphony and Midsummer Night's Dream Music; Mysliveček's oratorio Abraham and Isaac, with the Czech Philharmonic; CDs of Saint-Saëns's 3rd Symphony, d'Indy's Symphonie Cévenole and Martinů's Rhapsody Concerto for viola and orchestra with the Berne Symphony (Conifer). *Honours:* Toscanini Medal, Parma 1969; Verdi Medal 1973. *Hobbies:* Theology. *Address:* Casa Maag, 7504 Pontresina, Switzerland.

MAAZEL Lorin, b. 6 Mar 1930, Neuilly, France. American conductor and musician. m. Dietlinde Turban, 3 sons, 4 daughters. *Education:* Music studies with Vladimir Bakaleinkoff; philosophy major University of Pittsburgh. *Career:* Conductor, American Symphony Orchestras 1938-; European debut 1953; Violin recitalist; Conductor of operas including new productions Metropolitan Opera, New York, Teatro alla Scala Milan, Royal Opera House London, Paris Opera. Festivals include: Bayreuth, (The Ring), Salzburg, Edinburgh, Lucerne; Tours: South America, Australia, former USSR, Japan, China; Artistic Director, Deutsche Oper Berlin, 1965-71; Muscial Director, Radio Symphony Orchestra, Berlin, 1965-75; Associate Principal Conductor, New Philharmonia Orchestra, London, 1970-72; Director, Cleveland Orchestra, 1972-82; Director, Vienna State Opera, 1982-84; Music Director, Pittsburgh Symphony Orchestra, 1988-; Music Director, Bavarian Radio Symphony Orchestra of Munich, 1993-. *Recordings:* Over 350 recordings, including full cycles of Beethoven, Mahler, Rachmaninov, Sibelius, Tchaikovsky symphonic works. Currently completing Puccini opera cycle. Music visualization: Holst, Planets, Vivaldi, Four Seasons, Mozart, Don Giovanni, Bizet, Carmen; Since 1987 participation in over 20 benefit concerts, many to benefit international relief organisations such as UNHCR, UNICEF, WWF. *Hobbies:* Swimming; Tennis; Reading. *Address:* c/o Z. des Aubris, Tal 15-5th Fl, D-80331 Munich, Germany.

MABRY Wilson Drake, b. 20 Jan 1950, Iowa City, Iowa, USA. Composer; Oboist; Lecturer. *Education:* BM (Oboe), Manhattan School of Music, 1971; MM (Composition) Rice University, 1978; PhD (Composition) University of California, San Diego, 1983; Studied oboe with Harold Gomberg, 1967-71; Composition with Wilbur Ogdon, Bernard Rands, Robert Erickson, Paul Cooper, Krzysztof Penderecki, Roger Reynolds. *Career:* Teacher: University of California, San Diego, 1980-83, Dartmouth College, 1983-84, Rice University, 1977-78; Conservatoire Américan, 1989; Principal Oboe: Paris Horn and Synthesizer Ensemble, 1988-; Canadian Opera Orchestra, 1972-73, San Antonio Symphony, 1973-75; Soloist: IRCAM, Paris, 1984, Aspen Music Festival, 1977, Siena, Italy Festival, 1970; Co-founder NAME (New American Music in Europe, Paris), 1984; Concert Producer, Boston Museum of Science, Boston, Massachusetts, 1986. *Compositions:* 7.20.88 for saxophone quartet; 5.4.88 for amplified flute; 6.6.87 for marimba; 9.28.85 for trombone; 5.8.85 for piccolo, trombone, viola, cello and percussion; 12.5.83 for alto recorder, on Neuma compact disc, 1989; 5.1.83 for large orchestra; 3.8.83 for 2 piccolos, oboe, clarinet, trumpet, horn, trombone, piano, string quartet, and double bass; C.S. for jazz ensemble and computer; 9.3.89 for piano and marimba; 9.10.89 for rock ensemble. *Recordings:* The Songs of Robert Burns, Volume II, Volume III, Volume IV, on Philo Records Label.

MACAK Ivan, b. 26 Aug 1935, Gbelce, Czechoslovakia. *Education:* Faculty of Arts, Comenius University, Bratislava. *Career:* Editorial Staff, L'udova Tvorivost and Nasa praca; Music department, Historical Institute of the Slovak national Museum, Bratislava, 1965; College of Music, Academy of Music and Drama; Musico-Folklorist Department, Slovak Academy of Sciences; Researcher, Musical Instrumentary of Indians and Eskimos, Canada, 1972; Competition of Makers of Folk Musical Instruments, Detva, 1977; Musico-Instrumental Programmes, Under-Polana Folk Festival, Detva, 1977-85. *Publications:* Annual Bibliography of European Ethnomusicology, 11 volumes, 1966-80; Musicologia, 2 volumes; Contributions to the Study of Traditional Musical Instruments in Museums.

MÁCAL Zdeněk, b. 8 Jan 1936, Brno, Czechoslovakia. Conductor. *Education:* Brno Conservatory 1951-56; Janacek Academy 1956-60. *Career:* Conductor of the Moravian Symphony Orchestra at Olomouc, 1963-67; Debut with Czech Philharmonic Orchestra 1966, at the Prague Spring Festival: tours to Hungary, Bulgaria, West Germany, Austria and Switzerland; British debut 1969, with the Bournemouth Symphony; Music Director of the Cologne Radio Symphony Orchestra 1970-74; US debut with the Chicago Symphony 1972; Chief Conductor of the orchestra of Hanover Radio from 1980; Music Director, Milwaukee Symphony from 1986, Sydney Symphony, 1986-93; Conducted Prince Igor at the Grant Park Concerts, Chicago, 1990. *Recordings include:* Dvořák's Cello and Piano Concertos; Brahms Alto Rhapsody (Soukupova); Mozart Piano Concertos K488 and K595; Schoeck's Penthesilea; CD of Dvořák's 9th Symphony and Symphonic Variations (Classic for Pleasure). *Honours include:* Winner, International Conductors Competition at Bescancon, 1965; Mitropoulos Competition, New York, 1966. *Address:* c/o Harold Holt Ltd., 31 Sinclair Road, London W14 ONS, England.

MACANN Rodney, b. 1950, New Zealand. Singer (Baritone). *Career:* Sang with New Zealand Opera before studying singing and theology in London; European debut as The Speaker in The Magic Flute, with Welsh National Opera; Appearances with Opera North as Don Alfonso, Sharpless and Jochanaan, and in La Cenerentola and Samson et Dalila; English National Opera as Tchaikovsky's Mazeppa, Ariodates in Xerxes by Handel, Don Alfonso, Klingsor (Parsifal), Scarpia and

Escamillo; With the Royal Opera Covent Garden has sung in Andrea Chénier, King Priam, Les Contes d'Hoffmann and Tosca; Engagements in France, Norway and Italy, as Arthur in The Lighthouse by Peter Maxwell Davies; Adelaide Festival, South Australia as Ruprecht in The Fiery Angel; Sang Cuno in Der Freischütz at Covent Garden 1989, the Music Master in Ariadne for ENO, 1990; Concerts with all the leading British orchestras and frequent performances of Christus in the Bach Passions; Further concerts in Bergen, Florence, New York, and Toulouse. *Recordings include:* Video of Andrea Chénier (Covent Garden 1984). *Address:* c/o Stafford Law Associates, 26 Mayfield Road, Weybridge, Surrey KT13 8XB, England.

MACDONALD David George, b. 9 July 1952, Canada. Musician; Organist; Conductor; Teacher. m. Dr Kathy Schwartzentruber, 23 Aug 1986, 1 son. *Education:* B Mus Ed, Dalhousie University, Halifax, 1974; MMA, McGill University, Montreal, 1977; Diploma, Conservatoire Rueil-Malmaison, France, 1980. *Career:* Professor, Dalhousie University, Halifax, 1985-; Atlantic School of Theology, Halifax, 1985-; Director of Music, First Baptist Church, 1986-; Over 100 broadcasts for Radio Canada; Conductor of concerts throughout Canada: Toronto, Calgary, Montreal, and at Oxford, Stockholm, Paris, Chartres etc. Guest conductor, Symphony of Nova Scotia, 1989, 1990, 1991, 1992; Soloist: Symphony Nova Scotia 1990, Manitoba Chamber Orchetsra, 1992; Soloist: Scotia Festival of Music. *Recordings:* Musica Viva 1030, Radio Canada, Organ Works of J S Bach, 1988, Radio Canada, Hosanna!, 1990, Sing Lullaby, 1992, choral music, Choir of First Baptist Church, Halifax. *Publications:* Soloist Symphony, Nova Scotia, 1990-93. *Hobbies:* Squash; Golf; Hockey. *Current Management:* Hart-Murdock Artists' Management, Toronto, Canada. *Address:* 602 Francklyn Street, Halifax, Nova Scotia, Canada B3H 3B4.

MACDONALD Hugh, b. 31 Jan 1940, Newbury, Berks, England. Professor. m. (1) Naomi Butterworth, 1963, 1 son, 3 daughters; (2) Elizabeth Babb, 1979, 1 son. *Education:* MA, 1966; PhD, 1969, Pembroke College, Cambridge. *Career:* General Editor, Complete works of Berlioz, 1965; Lecturer, Cambridge, University, 1966-71; Oxford University, 1971-80; Visiting Professor, Indiana University, 1979; Gardiner Professor of Music, Glasgow University, 1980-87; Avis Blewett Professor of Music, Washington University, St Louis, 1987-. *Publications:* Editor, New Berlioz Edition, 1967-; Skryabin, 1978; Berlioz, 1982. Contributor to The New Grove Dictionary of Music and Musicians, The New Grove Dictionary of Opera. *Honours:* Szymanowski Medal; FRCM. *Address:* Department of Music, Washington University, Campus Box 1032, St Louis, MO 63130, USA.

MACDONALD Kenneth, b. 1938, Iona, Hebrides. Singer (Tenor). *Education:* Studied at the Guildhall School of Music London with Dino Borgioli. *Career:* Sang in the chorus at Covent Garden from 1946; Solo appearances from 1952, notably as Don Ottavio, and in the 1961 British premiere of Strauss's Die schweigsame Frau and in many character roles; Guest engagements with the Light Opera Company, Sadler's Wells Opera, Welsh National Opera and the English Opera Group; Concert repertoire has included Irish and Scottish Folk Songs, the Steersman in Der fliegende Holländer, conducted by Klemperer. *Recordings include:* Fidelio quartet and Stravinsky's Mavra; Salome.

MACDONALD Malcolm Calum, b. 26 Feb 1948, Nairn, Scotland. Writer on Music; Journalist. *Education:* Downing College, Cambridge. *Career:* Freelance Writer for Musical Journals; Music Copyist; Editor; Managing Editor, Tempo Magazine; Compiler, Gramophone Classical Catalogue. *Compositions:* Surface Measure and Before Urbino, 2 songs with orchestra; At the Firth of Lorne and other songs with piano; Piano Pieces; Arrangements of various contemporary works. *Publications include:* Havergal Brian: Perspective on the Music 1972; John Foulds: His Life in Music 1975; Schoenberg, 1976. *Contributions to:* The Listener,

Musical Times, Tempo, Musical Events; Records and Recordings.*Address:* 95 King Henry's Road, Swiss Cottage, London NW3, England.

MACDOUGALL James, b. 25 Jan 1966, Glasgow, Scotland. Singer (Tenor). *Education:* Studied at the Royal Scottish Academy of Music and the Guildhall School of Music; Italy with Carlo Bergonzi. *Career:* Appeared with Songmakers' Almanac 1988 at the Nottingham Festival, at the Buxton Festival and in London in Handel's Israel in Egypt and Mozart's C minor Mass; Season 1990-91 with Haydn's Creation in Aberdeen and at the Usher Hall, Edinburgh; Bach's Magnificat and Purcell's King Arthur at the Elizabeth Hall; Mozart's C minor Mass conducted by Frans Brueggen; Handel's Belshazzar; Orlando Paladino by Haydn at Garsington Manor; Bach's Magnificat and B Minor Mass in Belgium; Recital in the Szymanowski series at the Purcell Room; Operatic engagements include the Prologue and Quint in The Turn of the Screw and Gluck's Alceste with the English Bach Festival in Monte Carlo and at Covent Garden. *Recordings:* King Arthur conducted by Trevor Pinnock (Deutsche Grammophon). *Honours include:* Jean Highgate Scholarship and Lieder Prize at RSAM; Finalist in the Kathleen Ferrier Singing Competition, 1986. *Address:* Ron Gonsalves Management, 10 Dagnan Road, London SW12 9LQ, England.

MACGREGOR Joanna, b. 1960, England. Concert Pianist. *Education:* Studied at Cambridge, Royal Academy of Music and the Van Cliburn Piano Institute, Texas. *Career:* Concert appearances with the London Symphony Orchestra, Royal Philharmonic, London Mozart Players, CBSO, BBC Symphony, Royal Scottish, ECO, Royal Liverpool; Festival engagements at Shrewsbury, Harrogate, Bath, Edinburgh and Salisbury; Tours of Africa and the Philippines under the British Council; Tivoli Festival Copenhagen recital, 1988; Season 1988-89 with the BBC Scottish Symphony, the City of Birmingham Symphony and the English Chamber Orchestra; Promenade Concerts London, 1990, 1991; International piano series recitals at the South Bank, London, 1990-91; Celebrity Recital Barbican Centre, 1992; Other contemporary repertoire includes works by Berio, Xenakis, Ligeti, Tristan Murail, Takemitsu and James Dillon; Composer of music for various theatre companies, television and radio; Play for radio based on Satie's writings, Memoirs of an Amnesiac; Played in Messiden's Turangalila Symphony at the 1993 London Proms; Founded Contemporary Music Festival, Platform at ICA, 1991-93; World Premiere, Hugh Wood's Piano Concerto Proms, 1991; World Premiere, Birtwistle's Antiphonies with Boulez & Philharmonia, 1993. *Recordings include:* American Piano Classics; Britten Concerto, Satie recital, the Gershwin Songbook and music by Bach, Scarlatti, Bartok, Debussy, Ravel and Messiaen. *Address:* c/o Ingpen and Williams Ltd, 14 Kensington Court, London W8 5DN, England.

MÁCHA Otmar, b. 2 Oct 1922, Ostrava, Czechoslovakia. Composer. m. Marta Hrochová 20 Sept 1947, 1 son, 1 daughter. *Education:* Graduated, Music High School, Prague, 1948. *Career:* Music Dramaturgist, Radio Prague, 1945-61; Full-time composer, 1962. *Compositions include:* String Quartets, 1943, 1982; Violin Sonatas, 1948, 1987; Variations on a Theme by Jan Rychlík, 1964; The Lac Ukereve (opera), 1963; Sinfonietta No 1, 1971, No 2, 1982; Metamorphoses Promethei (opera), 1981; Infidelity Trapped (opera); Night and Hope, Symphonic Poem; Comenius Teestament (oratorio). *Honours:* State Prize, 1967; Merited Artist, 1982. *Membership:* International Music Festival, Prague. *Address:* Hradecká 22, 13000 Prague 3-Vinohrady, Czech Republic.

MACHL Tadeusz, b. 22 Oct 1922, Lwow, Poland. Composer; Organist; Professor. m. Irena Paszkiewicz-Machl, 2 children. *Education:* State College of Music, Krakow, 1949-52, under guidance Professor Malawski and Professor Rutkowski. *Career:* Works recorded in Poland, played through Poland and abroad; Lecturer, State College of Music, Krakow: Director of Chair of Composition, 1966-72; President of Disciplinary

Committee of Pedagogical Staff, 1972-. *Compositions:* 5 Symphonies: 1947, 1948, 1949, 1954, 1963; 7 Organ Concertos (1950-86); Cantata for Youth, 1954; Concerto for Voice, 1958; Violin Concerto, 1960; Harpsichord Concerto, 1962; Piano Concerto, 1964; Arpa Concerto, 1965; Come for Piano and Harpsichord, 1966; Violoncello (or Viola) Concerto, 1967; Trumpet Concerto, 1968; Concerto for 3 organs, 1969; Concerto for 2 pianos, organ and orchestra, 1971; 2 Concertante Concertos: Tcar's Flight, 1968, Blue Cross, 1974; 4 String Quartets 1952, 1957, 1962, 1980; Septet 1980; Choruses; Organ music; Songs. *Honours:* 1st Degree Ministry of Culture and Art, 1971 and 1990. *Membership:* Union of Polish Composers and Zaiks, Warsaw. *Hobbies:* Aviation; Motoring. *Address:* ul. Bal. Chrobrego 29/27, 34-428 Kraków Poland.

MACHLIS Joseph, b. 11 Aug 1906, Latvia. Author and Music Educator. *Education:* BA, College of the City of New York, 1927; MA, Columbia University; Artists Course in Piano, Institute of Musical Art of the Juilliard School, 1928. *Career:* Professor of Music, Queens College of the City University of New York, 1938-74; Graduate Faculty, The Juilliard School of Music, 1976-; Visiting Professor of Music, Northwestern University, 1974. *Recordings:* Record series: The Enjoyment of Music, Lives of the Great Composers. *Publications:* The Enjoyment of Music, 1955, 6th edition, 1990; Introduction to Contemporary Music, 1961, 2nd edition, 1979; Adventures in Listening, 1966; American Composers of Our Time, 1963; 17 operas in English including Dialogues of the Carmelites, La Bohème and War and Peace. *Honours:* Platignum Album, 1980 for the Enjoyment of Music Series; Laurel Leaf Award from American Music Centre, 1980. *Membership:* Century Club, New York City. *Address:* 310 East 55th Street, New York, NY 10022, USA.

MACHOVER Tod, b. 24 Nov 1953, New York, USA. Composer; Cellist. m. Anne Marie Stein, 31 Dec 1984. *Education:* BM, 1975, MM, 1977, Doctoral Studies, Juilliard School of Music; University of California at Santa Cruz, 1971-73; Columbia University, 1973-75. *Career:* Appearances as cellist, including Principal Cello, National Opera of Canada, 1975-76; Has conducted internationally; Director of Musical Research, Institute de recherche et Coordination Acoustique Musique, Paris, France, 1978-84; Currently preparing commission for cellist Yo Yo Ma, and new opera in collaboration with Peter Sellars; Associate Professor of Music and Media, Director of Experimental Media Facility, Media Laboratory, Massachusetts Institute of Technology, Cambridge, Massachusetts, USA. *Compositions include:* Valis, an opera based on a book by Philip K Dick, 1988; Bug-Mudra; Towards the Center; Sun; Inferno; Ye Gentle Birds; Fresh Spring; Concerto for Amplified Guitar and Chamber Ensemble; String Quartet No 1; Chansons D'Amour; Electric Etudes; With Dadaji in Paradise; Deplacements; Desires; Spectres; Parisiens; Hidden Sparks; Nature's Breath; Famine; Epithalamion for vocal soloists, ensenble and electronis, 1990. *Recordings:* Soft Morning; City; Fusione Fugace; Light; Winter Variations; Two Songs; Natures Breath; Spectres Parisien; Valis; Flora; Towards the Center; Famine. *Publications:* Le Compositeur et l'Ordinateur, 1981; Le Conceptyde Recherche en Musique, 1984; Some Thoughts on Computer Music, 1984; A Stubborn Search for Artistic Unity, 1986; The Extended Orchestra, 1985; Computer Music with and without Instruments, 1984; Musical Thought at IRCAM, 1984. *Current Management:* Bridge Management, Great Neck, NY, USA. *Address:* Media Laboratory, E15-487, MIT, Cambridge, MA 02139, USA.

MACILWHAM George, b. 15 May 1926, Cathcart, Glasgow, Scotland. Musician; Composer; Flautist; Piccolo; Alto Flute; Scottish Highland Bagpipe. m. Muriel Watson, 2 Mar. 1955. 2 sons. *Education:* Studied, Royal Scottish Academy of Music, Glasgow; Royal Academy of Music, London; Studied piping with several eminant pipers. *Debut:* Athenaeum Theatre, Glasgow, 1942. *Career:* Freelance experience with British Orchestras; Joined the Scottish Orchestra (Now SNO), 1947; Princ

Piccolo and Flute, BBC Scottish Sym Orch, 1954; Bagpipe Soloist, Edinburgh Festival, Royal Festival Hall, Barbian, Europe and Far East; Flute Soloist; Broadcaster for BBC Radio Scotland. *Compositions:* Orchestral comps include: Cir Mhor (Symphonic Poem); My Native Land (Sym Suite); Dalriada Overture; The Faery Flag (Ballet Suite); Fantasy for Fute and Orchestra Ballygeich; Rhapsody, Flute & Strings; Serenace for Strings and Calder Glen Suite; Fanfare Salute Alba for solo piper, pipe band and orchestra; Songs/Chamber Music; Choral version of Tam O'Shanter (solo bass & piper); Highland Suite Flute & piano; Compositions for Highland Bagpipe. *Address:* 25 Ravelston Road, Bearsden, Glasgow G61 1AW, Scotland.

MACK Kevin L, b. 19 Mar 1956, California, USA. conductor. m. Mary Ellen Baumgardner, 25 Oct 1987. *Education:* BMus, University of the Pacific; MMus, Conducting, Juilliard School. *Debut:* Conductor, Lincoln Center, NY, 1985. *Career:* Conductor of Hartford Philharmonia Society, 1985-; Torrington Symphony, 1990-; University of Bridgeport Chorus, 1991-; Connecticut Community College Chorus, 1988-; Branford Congregational Church, 1989-; Temple Beth-El Keser Israel, 1987-. *Composition:* A Short Gloria. *Publications:* Contributing editor, Connecticut Journal of the American Choral Directors Association. *Honours:* Arline Smith Merit Scholarship, 1984; Merit Awards, Music Broadcasters Association. *Memberships:* College Music Society; Association of Professional Vocal Ensembles; American Choral Director's Association; American Guild of Organists. *Hobbies:* Collecting early choral and orchestral editions, and rare recordings. *Address:* 565 Skiff Street, New Haven, CT 06473, USA.

MACKAY Ann, b. 21 Mar 1956, London, England. Singer (Soprano). m. Donald MacKay, 20 Feb 1976, 1 daughter. *Education:* Associate, Guildhall School of Music and Drama, 1979. *Career:* Singer with major London Orchestras in major concert halls in UK, Carnegie Hall, New York, USA; Appearances with English Bach Festival, Handel Opera and Sadler's Wells Opera; Has given recitals at Wigmore Hall, London, England, Carnegie Hall, New York, USA. *Recording:* My Minstrel Love. *Honours:* Scholarship, Countess of Munster Musical Trust, 1978-80, Royal Society of Arts Travel Scholarship working with Elisabeth Schwarzkopf, 1979; Susan Longfield Award, Lord Mayor of London's Prize and Lieder Prize, Guildhall School of Music; Outstanding Young Musician of the Year, Greater London Arts Association, 1979; Guest Singer of the Year with the European Community Chamber Orchestra, 1990. *Address:* 43 Greenham Road, Muswell Hill, London N10 1LN, England.

MACKAY Penelope Judith, b. 6 Apr 1943, Bradford, Yorkshire, England. Singer (Soprano). *Education:* Secretarial College, Lycée Français, London; Guildhall School of Music and Drama. *Debut:* Glyndebourne, 1970. *Career:* Sang at Glyndebourne, 1970-72, with English Opera Group, 1973-75, English Music Theatre, 1976-78, English National Opera, 1980-83; Freelance work in Britain, Europe and USA; Over 20 leading roles; Sang in premieres of Lutyens' Time Off, 1971, Britten's Death in Venice, 1973, British premieres of Hans Werner Henze's La Cubana (title role), 1978, Krenek's Jonny Spielt Auf (Anita), 1984, Ligeti, Le Grand Macabre (Miranda) 1982; Austrian premiere in modern times of Fux's Angelica, Vincitrice di Alcina (Angelica), 1985, and British premiere in modern times of Handel's Rodrigo (Rodrigo), 1985. *Membership:* Incorporated Society of Musicians; British Voice Association. *Hobbies:* Human potential, e.g. rebirthing; Reading; Good food and good company. *Current Management:* Jeffrey & White. *Address:* c/o Jeffrey & White, 5 Richmond Mews, London W1V 5AG, England.

MACKENZIE Jane Leslie, b. 1956, British Columbia, Canada. Singer (Soprano). *Education:* Studied at the University of Victoria and with Frances Adaskin. *Career:* Concerts throughout Britain and North America, notably with the Stockholm Bach Choir at the Elizabeth Hall, London, with Trevor Pinnock at Aldeburgh, at the

Wigmore Hall with Roger Vignoles and the last night of the 1984 Promenade Conerts; Opera debut as Donna Elvira with Kent Opera; English National Opera as Mozart's Countess and Marzelline in Fidelio; Scottish Opera from 1986 as Micaela, Pamina and the Countess; Appearances with Opera North as Pamina, Anne Trulove, Euridice and Fiordiligi; Welsh National Opera debut 1987, as Mimi; Has returned to Vancouver 1986 and 1988 as Pamina and the Governess in The Turn of the Screw. *Honours include:* Prize winner at competitions in Guelph (Canada), the Belvedere in Vienna and Benson and Hedges at Snape. *Address:* c/o Korman International Management, Crunnells Green Cottage, Preston, Herts SG4 7UQ, England.

MACKENZIE-FORBES Kenneth, b. 18 May 1944, Sydney, Australia. Arts Administrator. *Education:* BA, University of Queensland. *Career:* Senior Music Officer, The Australia Council, 1970-74; Administrator, Elizabethan Trust Orchestras, 1974-76; Consultant, Victorian Ministry for The Arts, 1976-; General Manager, Victoria State Opera, Melbourne, Australia, 1976-. *Contributions to:* Numerous magazines. *Honours:* Mobil Fellowship for Arts Administration, 1981; Member, Order of Australia, (AM, 1987). *Hobbies:* Swimming; Horse Riding; Reading; Skiing. *Current Management:* Victoria State Opera Company Ltd. *Address:* c/o The Victoria State Opera, 77 Southbank Boulevard, South Melbourne, Victoria 3205, Australia.

MACKERRAS (Alan) Charles (Sir), b. 17 Nov 1925, USA. Musician; Conductor. m. Helena Judith Wilkins, 2 daughters. *Education:* Sydney Conservatorium of Music; Prague Academy of Music. *Debut:* Sydney Symphony Orchestra, 1945. *Career:* Principal Oboist, Sydney Symphony Orchestra, 1943-46; Staff Conductor, Sadler's Wells Opera, 1949-53; Freelance Conductor, 1955-66; First Conductor, Hamburg State Opera, 1966-69; Musical Director, ENO, 1970-77; Chief Guest Conductor, BBC Symphony Orchestra, 1976-79;; Chief Conductor, Sydney Symphony Orchestra, 1982-85; Musical Director, Welsh National Opera, 1987-92; Principal Guest Conductor, San Francisco Opera, 1993, Scottish Chamber Orchestra, 1992, Royal Philharmonic Orchestra, 1993. *Compositions include:* Published Ballet arrangements of Pineapple Poll; Lady and Fool; Reconstruction of Sullivan's Lost Cello Concerto. *Recordings include:* Glagolitic Mass and operas by JanaOček; Complete Mozart Symphonies, Prague Chamber Orchestra, Mozart's Die Zauberflöte, Britten's Gloriana, Tchaikovsky's Eugene Onegin. *Publications:* Appendices in A Musician's Musician, and contributions to music magazines. *Honours:* CBE, 1974; Knighted, 1979; Grammy Award, 1981; Hon RAM, 1969; FRCM, 1987; Hon DMus, Hull University, 1990, Nottingham University, 1991. *Hobbies:* Languages; Sailing. *Current Management* Marks Management Ltd. *Address:* 10 Hamilton Terrace, London NW8 9UG, England.

MACKEY Steven, b. 1956, Frankfurt, Germany. Composer. *Education:* PhD, Composition, Brandeis University. *Career:* Commissions from the Koussevitzky and From Foundations, the Kronos and Concord Quartets and soprano Dawn Upshaw; Associate Professor of Music, Princeton University. *Compositions include:* Among the vanishing, soprano and string quartet, Chicago, 1989; On All Fours, string quartet, Chicago, 1990 (Vermeer Quartet); On the Verge/Troubadour Songs, for electric guitar and string quartet, Lubeck, 1992; TILT for orchestra, Carnegie Hall, 1992; Physical Property, electric guitar and string quartet, Lubeck, 1992.*Honours include:* Guggenheim, Lieberson and Tanglewood Fellowships. *Address:* c/o Boosey and Hawkes Ltd, 295 Regent Street, London W1R 8JH, England.

MACKIE David, b. 25 Nov 1943, Greenock, Scotland. Repetiteur; Accompanist; Conductor. *Education:* Royal Scottish Academy of Music, 1961-64; Glasgow University, 1969-72; Birmingham University, 1972-75; MA, BMus, Dip Mus Ed; RSAM; ARCM. *Career:* Repetiteur, D'Oyly Carte Opera, 1975-76; Chorus-Master, Associate Conductor, 1976-82; Music

Associate, BBC Complete Gilbert and Sullivan Operas, 1989; Wrote and presented 14 interval talks; Accompanist, Conductor; Tours of US and Canada in concerts of Gilbert and Sullivan. *Compositions include:* Arthur Sullivan, Cello Concerto Reconstruction, with Sir Charles Mackerras. *Recordings include:* Sullivan, Cello Concerto. *Publications:* Sullivan Cello Concerto, 1986; Piano Reduction, 1987. *Memberships:* ISM; RSM. *Hobbies:* Cartology. *Address:* 187A Worple Road, Raynes Park, London SW20 8RE, England.

MACKIE Neil, b. 1946, Aberdeen, Scotland. Singer (Tenor). *Career:* London debut with the English Chamber Orchestra under Raymond Leppard; European engagements at the Flanders and Savonlinna Festivals, Concertgebouw Orchestra, in Rome for RAI and in Scandinavia; Tours of Holland and Belgium with La Petite Bande conducted by Sigiswald Kuijken; Association with Peter Maxwell Davies includes premieres of The Martyrdom of St Magnus, 1977, The Lighthouse 1980 and Into the Labyrinth 1983; Premiered Henze's Auden Poems at Aldeburgh, 1984; Visitor to Cheltenham and Aldeburgh Festivals; UK engagements with the Hallé, Bournemouth Sinfonietta, BBC Symphony and Scottish Chamber Orchestras, and with the London Sinfonietta under Simon Rattle; June 1988, Into the Labyrinth at the Ojai Festival in America; 1988-89 tour of USA with the Scottish Chamber Orchestra and appearances with the Orchestre National de Paris; Professor of Singing, Royal College of Music, London, 1985-; Head of Vocal Studies, Royal College of Music, 1993. *Recordings:* Mozart's Requiem and Haydn's Die Schöpfung with La Petite Bande; Mozart Masses with the King's College Choir (Decca); Britten's Serenade (with premiere of Now Sleeps the Crimson Petal) and unpublished songs (EMI). *Honours:* FRSAMD, 1992; Hon D Mus, (Aberdeen), 1993. *Membership:* Officer of the Venerable Order of Saint John (OSEJ). *Hobbies:* Reading; Charity work; Occasional gardening. *Address:* c/o Lies Askonas Ltd., 6 Henrietta Street, London WC2E 8LA, England.

MACKINTOSH Catherine, b. 1948, England. Violinist. *Career:* Member of the Purcell Quartet, debut concert at St John's Smith Square, London, 1984; Extensive tours and broadcasts in France, Belgium, Holland, Germany, Austria, Switzerland, Italy and Spain; Tours of the United States and Japan, 1991-92; British appearances include four Purcell concerts at the Wigmore Hall, 1987, later broadcast on Radion 3; Repertoire includes music on the La Folia theme by Vivaldi, Corelli, CPE Bach, Marais, A Scarlatti, Vitali and Geminiani; instrumental works and songs by Purcell, music by Matthew Locke, John Blow and Fantasias and Airs by William Lawes; 17th Cenutry virtuoso Italian music by Marini, Buonamente, Gabrieli, Fontana, Stradella and Lonati; J S Bach and his forerunners - Biber, Scheidt, Schenk, Reincken and Buxtehude. *Recordings include:* Six record set on the La Folia theme (Hyperion); Purcell sonatas for two violins, viola da gamba and continuo; Sonatas by Vivaldi and Corelli (Chandos); Frequent engagements with other ensembles.

MACMILLAN James, b. 1959, Kilwinning, Ayrshire, Scotland. Composer; Lecturer in Music. *Education:* Studied at the Universities of Edinburgh and Durham. *Career:* Formerly lecturer in the music departments of Edinburgh and Manchester Universities; Lecturer at the Royal Scottish Academy of Music and Drama; Performances of his music by the New Music Group of Scotland, Circle, Nomos, Lontano and the Scottish Chamber Orchestra; Commissions from the Edinburgh Contemporary Arts Trust, the Traverse Theatre, Scottish Chamber Orchestra, the Paragon Ensemble, Cappela Nova and the Scottish Chamber Choir; Prom Commission (The Confession of Isobel Gawdie), BBC Scottish Symphony Orchestra, 1990; Featured Composer, 1990 Musica Nova festival, Glasgow; Seven Last Words from the Cross premiered on BBC TV, Easter, 1994. *Compositions:* Study on Two Planes for cello and piano 1981; Three Dawn Rituals for ensemble 1983; Beatus Vir for chorus and organ 1983; The Road to

Ardtalla for ensemble 1983; Songs of a Just War for soprano and ensemble 1984; Piano Sonata 1986; Two Visions of Hoy for oboe and ensemble 1986; The Keening for orchestra 1986; Festival Fanfares for brass band 1986; Litanies of Iron and Stone for ensemble with tape 1987; Untold for ensemble 1987; Visions of a November Spring for string quartet 1988; Busqueda for 8 actors, 3 sopranos, speaker and ensemble 1988; Into the Ferment for orchestra 1988; Cantos Sagrados for chorus and organ 1989; The Exorcism of Rio Sumpul for Chamber Ensemble 1989; As Mothers See Us, for ensemble 1990; The Berserking, Piano Concerto, 1990; The Confession of Isobel Gowdie for orchestra 1990; Soweton Spring for wind band 1990; Catherine's Lullabies for chorus and ensemble 1990; Scots Song for Soprano and Ensemble 1991; Tuireadh for clarinet and string quartet 1991; Sinfonietta 1991; Tourist Variations, 1 act chamber opera 1992; Opera Inés de Castro, 1993; Visitatio Sepulchri for 7 singers and chamber orchestra, 1993; Trumpet Concerto, 1993; Vs for orchestra, 1993; Seven Last Words from the Cross for choir and strings, 1994. Address: c/o Boosey & Hawkes, 295 Regent Street, London, W1R 8JH, England.

MACNEIL Cornell, b. 24 Sept 1922, Minneapolis, Minnesota, USA. Singer (Baritone). Education: Studied at Hartt School, Hartford, with Friedrich Schorr; New York with Virgilio Lazzari and Dick Marzollo; Rome with Luigi Ricci. Debut: Philadelphia 1950, in the premiere of Menotti's The Consul. Career: New York City Opera debut 1953, as Germont; San Francisco 1955, as Escamillo; Chicago 1957, in Manon Lescaut; Metropolitan Opera from 1959-87, as Verdi's Rigoletto, Amonasro, Nabucco, Iago and Luna, Puccini's Scarpia and Michele, and Barnaba in La Gioconda (460 performances in 26 parts); La Scala Milan 1959, as Carlo in Ernani; Covent Garden debut 1964, as Verdi's Macbeth; Verona Arena 1971; Guest appearances in Caracas, Mexico City, Vienna, Buenos Aires, Barcelona, Rome and Naples. Recordings: Un Ballo in Maschera, Rigoletto, Aida, Cavalleria Rusticana, Luisa Miller, La Fanciulla del West, La Gioconda, La Traviata, Falstaff: Labels include Decca, RCA Angel and Melodram. Address: c/o Metropolitan Opera, Lincoln Center, New York, NY 10023, USA.

MACONCHY Elizabeth, (Dame) b. 19 Mar 1907, Broxbourne, Herts, England. Composer. m. William Richard Le Fanu, 1930, 2 daughters. Education: Royal College of Music, London; Pupil of Vaughan-Williams; Travelled overseas, 1929-30. 1st Debut: Piano concerto, Prague Philharmonic Orchestra, 1930; Sir Henry Wood introduced The Land, Promenade Concerts, 1930. Career includes: Works performed at 3 festivals, International Society for Contemporary Music, 1935-47. Largest output, chamber music; String quartets played as series, BBC 3rd Programme, 1955, 1975; Chairman, Composers Guild of Great Britain, 1960; President, Society for Promotion of New Music, 1977-. Recordings: String Quartets 1-13 recorded for CD and Cassette by Unicorn-Kamchama, London 1989-90; Clarinet Quintet, by Hyperion, 1992. Publications: Numerous, 1930-, including chamber music, orchestral, choral works. Most recent: Narration for solo cello, 1984; Still Falls the Rain, double choir, 1984. 4 one-act operas; Concertino for clarinet, 1985; Life Story for strings, 1985; Still Falls the Rain, double chorus, 1985; Narration for cello, 1985; Butterflies for mezzo and harpsichord, 1986. Honours include: Scholarships, prizes, Royal College of Music; Edwin Evans Prize; Radcliffe Award, 1969; Daily Telegraph Prize (oboe quintet); Gedok International Prize, 1961; Commander, Order of British Empire (CBE), 1977; Fellow, Royal College of Music; Honorary Fellow, St. Hilda's College, Oxford, 1978; Dame of the British Empire (DBE), 1987. Current Management: Chester Music, London. Address: Shottesbrook, Boreham, Chelmsford, Essex, England.

MACURDY John, b. 18 Mar 1929, Detroit, Michigan, USA. Singer (Bass). m. Justine May Votypka, 1 son, 1 daughter. Education: Wayne State University, Detroit; Vocal Study with Avery Crew, Detroit. Debut: New

Orleans 1952, in Samson et Dalila; Appearances in Baltimore, Houston, Philadelphia, San Francisco and Santa Fe; New York City Opera debut 1959, in Weill's Street Scene; Metropolitan Opera from 1962, as the Commendatore, Crespel in Les Contes d'Hoffmann and Rocco in Fidelio; Sang in the premieres of Antony and Cleopatra (1966) and Mourning Becomes Elektra (1967) and in the first local performance of Les Troyens (1973); Paris Opera 1973, as Arkel in Pelléas et Mélisande; La Scala Milan 1974, as Rocco in Fidelio; Salzburg Festival 1977-78, as the Commendatore in Don Giovanni; Milan 1984 as the Landgrave in Tannhäuser; Seattle Opera 1986, as Hagen and Hunding in the Ring; Metropolitan 1987, as Fasolt in Das Rheingold; Hunding at San Francisco 1990; Appearances at Aix and Orange Festivals, Hollywood Bowl, Miami Opera and Scottish Opera; Season 1992 in Billy Budd at the Met, as Trulove in The Rake's Progress at Aix-en-Provence, as Fiesco in Simon Boccanegra Montpellier, The Flying Duitchman in Buenos Aires as Daland and L'Africaine in Marseille; 995 performances as Leading Bass; Over 1500 operatic performances. Recordings: Don Giovanni (Deutsche Grammophon); Béatrice et Bénédict; Otello; The Rev. Hale in Ward's The Crucible (Troy). Honours: City of Detroit Medal, 1969; Rockefeller Foundation Grant, 1959; Presently only American to be listed in the Wagnerian Annals for singing all the Bass Roles in the Ring Cycle; Inducted into the Academy of Vocal Arts Hall of Fame. Membership: Bohemian Club. Hobbies: Antiques; Gardening; Tennis; Golf. Address: Tall Oaks Court, Stamford, CT 06903, USA.

MADDALENA James, b. 1954, Lynn, Massachusetts. USA. Singer (Baritone). Education: Studied at the New England Conservatory of Music. Debut: Rogers and Hammerstein medley with the Boston Pops Orchestra, 1974. Career: From 1974 has appeared in a complete cycle of Bach's cantatas at Emmanuel Church Boston, conducted by Craig Smith; Founder member of the Liederkreis Ensemble (Naumburg Award 1980); Association with director Peter Sellars from 1981 includes the title role in Don Giovanni and leading roles in Handel's Orlando (American Repertory Theatre, 1982), Così fan Tutte (Castle Hill Festival, 1984), Haydn's Armida (New Hampshire Symphony, 1983), Giulio Cesare and the Brecht/Weill Kleine Mahagonny (Pepsico Summerfare, 1985); Soloist in Messiah at Carnegie Hall 1984, with Banchetto Musicale; Sang the title role in the world premiere of Nixon in China by John Adams (Houston 1987, repeated at Edinburgh 1988) and The Captain in the premiere of Adams's The Death of Klinghoffer (Brussels 1991, and at Lyon, Vienna and New York); Has appeared as Mozart's Count in the Sellars version of Le Nozze di Figaro, seen at Purchase, New York and Papageno at Glyndebourne, 1990; Created Merlin in Tippett's New Year at Houston 1989 and in the British premiere at Glyndebourne; Season 1992 in Nixon in China at Adelaide and Frankfurt, Don Alfonso at Glyndebourne. Recordings include: Brahms Liebeslieder Waltzes, with Liederkreis; Nixon in China and The Death of Klinghoffer. Address: c/o Houston Grand Opera Association, 510 Preston Avenue, Houston, TX 77002, USA.

MADDISON Dorothy, b. 12 Jan 1956, Fergus Falls, Minnesota, USA. Lyric Coloratura Soprano. m. 29 Dec 1979, Ian Maddison. Education: BMus, St. Olaf College, Minnesota, 1977; Guildhall School of Music & Drama, London, England, 1977-79; Britten-Pears School, Aldeburgh; Private study wtih Audrey Langford and Andrew Field, Cantica Voice Studio, London. Debut: Purcell Room, London, April 1986 with Graham Johnson, piano. Career: Freelance concert & operatic singer; Operatic roles include The Queen of Night/The Magic Flute; Zaide, Madames Herz and Silberklang/The Impresario, Mozart; Norina/Don Pasquale; Adina/Elixir of Love; Rita/Rita, Donizetti; Tytania/Midsummer Night's Dream, Britten; Mable/Pirates of Penzance; Zerbinetta/ Ariadne auf Naxos, Strauss; The Nightingale, Stravinsky; Oratorio repertoire: includes works by Bach, Handel, Haydn, Mozart, Mendelssohn, Orff. Recital Repertoire: standard works by European composers, also Songs from the American Midwest, a programme featuring works by Minnesota composers Argento, Dougherty, Franklin, Larsen, Paulus, first given in April 1988, Purcell Room, London with Robin Bowman, piano; Recent Appearances with: English Bach Festival, New Sadler's Wells Opera Company, Opera Factory, London Opera Players. *Honours:* Honours and Distinction, St Olaf College, Walter Hyde Memorial Prize, Guildhall School. *Membership:* Equity. *Address:* 95 Tanfield Avenue, London NW2 7SB, England.

MADDOCKS James b. 1 Jan 1919, Birkenhead, Cheshire, England. Violinist/Viola; Conductor; Lecturer; Teacher; Chamber Music Player. m. June Mills (Oboist), 15 Oct 1946. *Education:* Royal Manchester College of Music with Henry Holst; Studied with Max Rostal. *Career:* Soloist with City of Birmingham Symphony Orchestra, soloist with major orchestras; Tourned many parts of the world with wife, giving recitals, lectures, concertos; Founded with wife, Winchester International Summer Music Course and Celebrity Concerts, 1960-; Founded and conducts London String Orchestra, 1970, and Philharmonic Chamber Orchestra, 1987. *Recordings:* London String Orchestra. *Contributions to:* Classical Music Magazine and others. *Hobby:* Collecting Antique China. *Address:* 37 St Davids Road, Clifton Campville, Nr Tamworth, Staffordshire B79 0BA, England.

MADER-TODOROVA Marina, b. 20 Aug 1948, Silistra, Bulgaria. Singer (Soprano). *Education:* Studied in Varna, Sofia and Vienna. *Career:* Sang at first in opera at Varna then Mainz and Bremen, 1976-77, as Desdemona and Micaela; Gelsenkirchen 1977-80, as Elisabeth de Valois, Ariadne and Tosca; Further appearances at Dortmund, 1980-83, Hamburg, Stuttgart, Frankfurt, and Basle; Engaged at the Deutsche Opera am Rhein, 1984- 86, Graz, 1984-89, notably as Eva, Amelia (Ballo in Maschera), the Trovatore Leonara, Agathe and Ariadne; Further appearances at the Deutsche Oper Berlin, Budapest, Mannheim, Palermo, Zurich, Copenhagen and Liege; Other roles have included Butterfly, Elisabeth in Tannhäuser, Elsa, Mozart's Fiordiligi and Countess, Mimi and Arabella; Many concert appearances. *Address:* Vereinigte Buhnen, Kaiser Josef Platz 10, A-8010 Graz, Austria.

MAEGAARD Jan Carl Christian, b. Copenhagen, Denmark. m. Kirsten Offer Andersen, 14 Aug 1973, div, 2 daughters. *Education:* Studied at the Royal Danish Conservatory of Music and the University of Copenhagen. PhD, 1972. *Career:* Freelance musician, 1949-56; Music critic, 1952-60; Teacher, Ryal Danish Conservatory of Music, 1953-58; Teaching Assistant, University of Copenhagen, 1959-61; Assoc Professor, 1961-71, Prof, 1971-; Guest Professor, SUNY, 1974; Professor of Music, University of California, Los Angeles, 1978-81. *Compositions include:* Musica riservatna nr 1 op, 52, string quartet; Two choruses, op 57 nr 2 and 3; Musica riservata nr 2, op 61, for oboe, clarinet, bass, and sax; Pastorale, op 63, 2 clarinet; Labirinto 1, op 77, Vla. sola. Orchestration of P Heise, Dyvekes Sange I-VII, op 78, Sopr. Orch; Labirinto II, op 79, guitar; Partita, op 89, for organ; Cello Concerto, op.98. *Recordings include:* Chamber Concerto nr 2, op 38; Octomeri op. 40. Viol. piano; Musica riservata nr 1 op, 52; Trio Serenade, O alter Duft aus Marchenzeit, op 36, Viol, cello, piano. *Publications:* Books: Musikalsk Modernisme, 1964; Studien zur Entwicklung des dodekaphonen Satzes bei Arnold Schonberg I-III, 1972; Numerous articles to magazines and journals including: The Nomenclature of Pitch-Class Sets, 1985; Die Komponisten der Wiener Schule und ihre Textdicher sowie das Komponisten-Dichter-Verhaltnis heute, 1988; Zur harmonischen Analyse der Musik des 19 Jahrhunderts. Eine theoretische Erwägung, 1990. *Memberships include:* Royal Danish Academy, 1986; Norwegian Academy of Science and Letters, 1988 International Musicological Society, 1982. *Address:* Duevej 14 6, 2000 Frederiksberg, Denmark.

MAFFEO Gianni, b. 30 Mar 1939, Vigevano, Milan, Italy. Singer (Baritone). *Education:* Studied at the Liceo

Musiale di Vercelli. *Debut:* Sang Tonionin Pagliacci with the Associazione Lirico Compagnia, 1961. *Career:* Many appearances at such opera centres as La Scala Milan, Genoa, Palermo, Turin and Verona, 1973; Guest engagements at Vienna, Prague, Rouen, Monte Carlo, Brno, Lisbon, Munich and the New York City Opera; Further appearances at Toulouse, Nice, Bordeaux and Frankfurt as Marcello, Sharpless, Germont, Count Luna and Rigoletto. *Recordings include include:* Madama Butterfly; La Bohème. *Address:* Teatro Alla Scala, Via Filodrammatici 2, 20121 Milan, Italy.

MAGA Othmar, b. 30 June 1929, Brno, Czechoslovakia. Conductor. *Education:* Studied at the Stuttgart Hochschule fur Musik 1948-52; Tubingen University 1952-58; Accademia Chigiana at Siena with Paul van Kempen 1954-55; Further studies with Sergiu Celibidache, 1960-62. *Career:* Conducted the Gottingen Symphony Orchestra 1963-67, Nuremberg Symphony 1968-70; Generalmusikdirektor at Bochum 1971-82; Artistic Director of the Odense Symphony Orchestra, Denmark, and permanent conductor of the Orchestra of the Pomeriggi Musicali di Milano, 1987; Also conductor of the Folkswangschule at Essen; Guest conductor with leading orchestras in Europe and tour of Japan with the NHK Symphony Orchestra; from 1992 Chief Conductor of the KBS-Symphony Orchestra in Seoul, Korea. *Recordings:* About 50. *Address:* Merlos 19, 6325 Grebenau, Germany.

MAGAZINER Elliot A., b. 25 Dec 1921, Springfield, Massachusetts, USA. Violinist; Conductor; Educator. m. Sari Magaziner, 2 daughters. *Education:* Princeton University, 1943; National Orchestra Association, 1937-40; Juilliard School of Music, New York, 1946-50. *Debut:* Town Hall, New York, 1952. *Career:* Staff Artist, Concertmaster, CBS TV and Radio Networks, with Conductors Reiner, Ansermet, Beecham, Stokowski; Conductor, Senior Violin Instructor, Westchester Conservatory of Music; Professor of Music, Conductor, Manhattanville College Community Orchestra; Head of Chamber Music and Strings; Affiliated Artist Teacher, State University of New York; Visiting Conductor, Dubuque Symphony; Soloist, New York Philharmonic Symphony, Symphony of the Air, Kol Visrael, Chicago, Fort Myers, Dubuque, York, and St Petersburg symphony orchestras; Recitals in New York, Washington, Detroit, Amsterdam, Paris, Jerusalem; Starred in The Violin, CBS TV. *Recordings:* Charles Ives Sonata No. 2; Charles Ives Trio (with Frank Glazer and David Weber); Vivaldi's Concerto in C and Concerto in B Flat (with Orchestre Symphonique de Paris). *Address:* 250 Garth Road, Scarsdale, NY 10583, USA.

MAGNES Frances, b. 27 Apr 1919, Cleveland, Ohio, USA. Violinist. *Education:* Studied with Herman Rosen. *Debut:* With Cleveland Orchestra under Rodzinski, 1933. *Career:* Studied further with Louis Persinger and Adolf Bushc in New York then toured the USA with the Busch Chamber Players, 1945-46; Recital debut at the Carnegie Hall, 1946, followed by concerts in England, France and Israel; Concet tours of South America, Canada and the USA under such conductors as Boult, Bernstein, Mitropoulos and Monteux; Premiered Wolpe's Violin Sonata , 1949 and Tibor Serly's Sonata for solo violin (1950); Dohnanyi's 2nd concerto 1952, and again at the Carnegie Hall, 1981; Leader of the Westchester Symphony Orchestra under Newell Jenkins, 1963-64, and the Baroque Chamber Orchestra of Scarsdale, 1966-80. *Recordings include:* Bach Concerto for two violins, with Adolf Busch; Wolpe's Violin Sonata and Serly's Sonata for solo violin.

MAGNUSSON Lars, b. 10 Mar 1955, Gothenburg, Sweden. Opera Singer (Tenor). *Education:* Studied at University of Gothenburg and the Opera School in Stockholm. *Career:* Principal tenor at the Royal Opera, Stockholm, from 1982; Roles have included, the Italian Tenor in Der Rosenkavalier, Lensky, the Duke of Mantua, Alfredo, David in Die Meistersinger and Rodolfo in La Bohème; Sang Pedrillo in a new production of Die Entführung at Covent Garden in 1987; further performances in Monte Carlo, Nice, Strasbourg, Vienna

(Staatsoper), and San Francisco (1990); Metropolitan Opera debut 1990 as Pedrillo, returning as David (1992); Royal Opera Stockholm, Gabriele in Verdi's Simon Boccanegra, 1991; Further engagements as David in Paris, Vienna and Marseilles, and the Steersman in Der fliegende Holländer in Geneva; Sang David in a new production of Die Meistersinger at the Metropolitan, 1993 (also San Francisco). *Address:* c/o Athole Still Ltd., 113 Church Road, London SE19 2PR, England.

MAGRO John L., b. 15 Sept 1907, Rochester, New York, USA. Management. m. Nancy Langhorne Post, 30 Jan 1943, 2 sons, 3 daughters. *Education:* BA, Harvard College 1932; Diplomatic & Consular Institute, 1937; Studied Cello under Gerald Mass, Eastman School, Rochester, 1919. *Career:* As General Director managed 60 or more Grand Operas of Cincinnati Summer Opera Association, 1957-64; Co-Founder The American Opera Auditions, Cincinnati, 1957, currently Cincinnati Opera and Project Director. *Recordings:* Zanetto (Mascagni); La Gazzetta (Rossini); La Vestale (Spontini); L'Italiana in Londra (Cimarosa); Comedy on the Bridge, (Martinů); Prima la Musica e poi le parole (Salieri); The Wandering Scholar (Holst); Le'Osteria Portoghese (Cherubini); El Retablo de Maese Pedro (de Falla); Judith (Smith/Smolen); Lucia di Lammermoor (Donizetti). *Publications:* Madrigal Singing Takes Root in Ameria; Musical America, 1940. *Honours:* Award, Cincinnati Opera, 1964; Honoured by President of Italy, 1961, and Associazione Lirica e Concertistica Italiana, Milan, 1969. *Memberships:* Harvard Club of Cincinnati, President, 1953. *Hobbies:* Reading; Sailing; Gardening. *Address:* 8300 Perin Road, Cincinnati, OH 45242, USA.

MAGUIRE Hugh, b. 2 Aug 1927, Dublin, Ireland. Violinist. *Education:* College of Music, Dublin; Royal Academy of Music, London; Studies with George Enescu in Paris, 1949-50. *Debut:* Dublin 1938. *Career:* London debut 1947, Wigmore Hall; Leader of the Bournemouth Municipal (Symphony) Orchestra, 1952-56, London Symphony Orchestra, 1956-62, BBC Symphony, 1962-67; 1968-76 Leader of the Allegri Quartet: performances of contemporary British composers including Nicola LeFanu, Sebastian Forbes and Elizabeth Maconchy; Leader of the Melos Ensemble, 1977; Currently leader of the orchestra of the Royal Opera House, Covent Garden; Tours of British universities giving concerts and lectures under the auspices of the Radcliffe Trust; Professor at the Royal Academy of Music, London; Director of the Orchestra and Director of String Studies at the Britten-Pears School. *Recordings:* Works by Britten, Sherlaw Johnson, Maconchy, Forbes, Elgar, Alexander Goehr and Frank Bridge with the Allegri Quartet. *Address:* c/o Royal Opera House, Covent Garden, London WC2, England.

MAGYAR Gabriel, b. 5 Dec 1914, Budapest, Hungary. Cellist; Teacher. m. Julie Dora, 17 July 1952. *Education:* B, Madacs Imre Gymnazium, Budapest, 1932; Student, National School of Music, Budapest, 1932; M Royal Hungarian Franz Liszt Conservatory, Budapest, 1936. *Debut:* Darius Milhaud, Budapest, 1938. *Career:* Concert Cellist, Europe, 1932-41; S America, 1947-49; Concert Cellist, USA, 1949-; Teacher Solo Cellist, 1949-56, Professor Cello and Chamber Music, University of Oklahoma, 1951-56; Professor Cello and Chamber Music 1973-80, Emeritus 1980-, University of Illinois, Urbana; Prof Chamber Music, Colby College, summers 1962-72; Banff Art Centre, summers 1972-83; Vice Pres Conservatory Cen Illinois, 1986-87; Cellist Hungarian String Quartet, 1956-72. *Recordings:* For Deutsche Grammophon; Pathe; Marconi; Vox records. *Honours:* Recipient Bartók Béla-Pasztory Ditta Award, Bartók-Kuratorium, 1987; Grand Prix du Disque-Paris. *Hobbies:* Drawing; Painting; Photography. *Address:* 101 W. Windsor No.3103, Urbana, IL 61801, USA.

MAHAFFEY Robert Lee, b. 11 June 1930, NY, USA. Organist; Teacher; Conductor. *Education:* BMus, 1951, MMus, 1952, Yale University; MA, 1962, Postgraduate Study, Union Theological Seminary School of Sacred Music, Columbia Unviersity; FAGO; ChM; LTCL; LMus

TCL; FTCL. *Career:* Organist, Director of Music, St John's Church, Brooklyn, NY, 1952-55; Christ Church, Mahasset, NY, 1955-77; Saint John's Churchm Pompano Beach, Florida, 1977-92; Saint Paul the Apostle Church, Lighthouse, Point, Florida, 1992-; Director of Music, The Cathedral School of St Mary, Garden City, NY, 1970-72, The Vincent Smith School, Port Washington, NY, 1966-70, 1972-75, The Kew Forests School, Forest Hills, NY, 1975-77. *Contributions to:* The American Organist. *Memberships:* National Council, American Guild of Organists, 1962-65, National Exaination Committee of AGO, 1971-86; Treasurer, St Wilfred Club of New York; RCO; RSCM; Association of Anglican Musicians; Yale Club of Palm Beaches. *Honours:* Woods Chandler Scholarship, Yale University, 1950, Julia R Sherman Prize, 1951, Yale University, 1950. *Address:* 501 Lake Drive, Delray Beach, Florida 33444-3041, USA.

MAIER Franz-Josef, b. 27 Apr 1925, Memmingen, Germany. Violinist; Conductor. *Education:* Studied at the Augsburg Conservatory, at the Munich Academy of Music and the Music Gymnasium Frankfurt. *Debut:* Violin recital at Munich, 1942. *Career:* Soloist with the Reichs Symphony Orchestra on tour of Germany 1942; Studied further at Saarbrücken and after war service at the Hochschule für Musik, Cologne with Philip Jarnach; Played in Schaffer Quartet and the Schubert Trio; Lecturer at the Robert Schumann Conservatory Dusseldorf 1949-59; Professor and leader of the violin master classes at the Cologne Musikhochschule 1959; Performances of contemporary, Baroque and early classical music; Co-founded the Collegium Aureum 1964, becoming conductor and leader of the ensemble on violin: concerts played on original instruments or copies; Leader of the Collegium Aureum Quartet 1970. *Recordings include:* Suites from Campra's Les Fêtes Venetiennes and Lully's Amadis; Bach Suites, Brandenburg Concertos and Secular Cantatas; CPE Bach Hamburg Symphonies, and Concertos; Haydn Symphonies and Concertos; Pergolesi La Serva Padrona; Mozart Serenades, Divertimenti, Piano Concertos and Symphonies, Coronation Mass, Requiem and Solemn Vespers; Beethoven 3rd Symphony, 4th Piano Concerto and Triple Concerto; Handel Concerti Grossi Op 3, Alexander's Feast, Water Music, Music for the Royal Fireworks and Organ Concertos (Harmonia Mundi and BASF).

MAILMAN Martin, b. 30 June 1932, New York, USA. Composer; Teacher. m. Mary Nan Hudgins, 22 Aug 1959, 1 son, 1 daughter. *Education:* BM, 1954, MM, 1955, PhD, 1960, Eastman School of Music, University of Rochester. *Career:* Composer in Residence, Ford Foundation Young Composers Project, 1959-61; Composer in Residence, East Carolina University, 1961-66; Regents Professor of Music and Composer in Residence, North Texas State University, 1966-. *Compositions:* The Hunted, opera, 1959; Liturgical Music, 1964; Requiem, Requiem, 1970; Decorations, 1974; Symphony No 2, 1979; Concerto for Violin and Orchestra, 1982; Exaltations, 1981; Symphony No 3, 1983; Trio, 1985; Cantata, 1984; Love Letters From Margaret for soprano and orchestra, 1991. *Recording:* Autumn Landscape. *Honours:* Queen Marie Jose Prize for Violin Concerto, 1983; ABA/Ostwald Prize for Exaltations, 1983; Edward Benjamin Award for Autumn Landscape, 1955; Annual ASCAP Awards; Prizes: Queen Marie-Jose Prize for violin Concerto, 1983; Ostwald/ABA Award for Exaltations in 1983, Symphony No. 3, Fantasies, 1983; Trio for Violin, Cello, and Piano, 1985; and for Precious Friends hid in Death's Dateless Night, 1988. *Memberships:* ASCAP; PKL; TMEA; American Bandmasters Association. *Address:* College of Music, University of North Texas, Denton, TX 76203, USA.

MAISKY Mischa (Michael), b. 10 Jan 1948, Riga, Latvia. Concert Cellist. m. M. Kay Lipman, 1 Jan 1983, 1 son, 1 daughter. *Education:* Moscow Conservatory; Studied with Mstislav Rostropovich; Masterclasses with Gregor Piatigorsky. *Debut:* Leningrad Philharmonic Orchestra, 1965. *Career includes:* Appearances at

Carnegie Hall, Royal Festival Hall, Berlin Philharmonic Hall; Recitals with Martha Argerich, Radu Lupu, Boris Belkin, Malcolm Frager; Television & radio, Japan, UK, Germany, Netherlands, France, Spain, Mexico, USA, Israel, USSR; Various films; played the Walton concerto at the Festival Hall, London, 1993; Shostakovich 1st Concerto at the 1993 Proms. *Recordings include:* Bach Sonatas, with Martha Argerich; Bach, 6 Cello Solo Suites; Schumann Cello Concerto with Vienna Philharmonic/Leonard Bernstein (all award winners); Dvořák Cello Concerto with the Israel Philharmonic Orchestra/Leonard Bernstein; Brahms Double Concerto with Gidon Kremer, Vienna Philharmonic/Leonard Bernstein; Haydn Concertos with the Chamber Orchestra of Europe. *Honours:* All Russian Cellists Competition, 1965; Tchaikovsky International Competition, Moscow, 1966; Gaspar Cassado International Competition, Florence, 1973; Grand Prix du Disque, Paris, Record Academy Prize, Tokyo, 1985 and 1989. *Hobby:* Music. *Current Management:* Intermusica Artists Management, London, England. *Address:* 138 Meerlaan, 1900 Overijse, Belgium.

MAIXNEROVA Martina, b. 20 Sept 1947, Prague, Czechoslovakia (now Singapore Citizen); Soloist, Chamber Pianist, Professor of Piano. m. Pavel Prantl (violinist) 24 June 1972, 2 Sons. *Education:* Graduated with Distinction, Conservatory of Music, Prague, 1966; Master's Degree with Distinction, Academy of Musical Arts, Prague, 1972. *Career:* Professor of Piano in Singapore, 1980; Member of the ARS Cameralis Ensemble, 1976-80; Member of the Prague Baroque Ensemble, 1973-80; Assistant Professor of Piano at the Academy of Musical Arts in Prague, 1975-80; Professor of Piano at the Music School for Especially Gifted Children in Prague, 1970-73; Adjudicator at the First Rolex Piano Competition in Singapore, 1987. Festival appearances in England, Germany, Czechoslovakia, Austria, Poland, USA and Korea; Solo appearances with orchestras including: Guest soloist with the Prague Chamber Orchestra without a Conductor, 1980; Guest soloist with the Singapore Symphony Orchestra, 1981, 84, 86, 88; Tours in Germany, Poland, USSR, USA, England, Sweden, Czechoslovakia and Japan. *Address:* 110 Wishart Road, 03-07 Pender Court, Singapore 0409.

MAJOR Malvina Lorraine, (Dame), b. 28 Jan 1943, Hamilton, New Zealand. Opera Singer (Soprano). m. Winston William Richard Fleming, 16 Jan 1965, dec 1990, 1 son, 2 daughters. *Education:* Grade VIII, Piano, Singing, Theory, Convent at Ngaruawahia, Waikato; Singing continued under Dame Sister Mary Leo, St Mary's Music School, Auckland, 1960-65, & Ruth Packer, Royal College of Music, London, London Opera Centre, UK, 1965-67. *Debut:* Camden Town Festival, 1968. *Career includes:* Performances as: Belle, Belle of New York, New Zealand, 1963; Pamina, Magic Flute, London Opera Centre, 1967; 1st non Mormon Soloist to sing with Mormon Tabernacle Choir, 1987; Matilda, Elizabetta Regina d'Inghilterra, Camden Town, 1968; Rosina, Barber of Seville, Salzburg (conductor, Claudio Abbado), 1968-69; Gala Concert, King & Queen of Belgium, Centenary Antwerp Zoological Society, 1969; Marguerite, Gounod's Faust, Neath & London, 1969; Bruckner's Te Deum, conductor Daniel Barenboim, 1968; Cio Cio San, Madam Butterfly; Widow, The Merry Widow; Gilda, Rigoletto; Tosca, Tosca; Constanze, Die Entführung; Arminda, La Finta Giardiniera, Brussels, 1986; Donna Elvira, Don Giovanni, Brighton Festival, 1987; Donna Anna, Don Giovanni, Sydney, Australia, 1987; Operas include recent productions of Rosalinda, Die Fledermaus, & Lucia di Lammermoor, Mimi in La Bohème, Constanze, NY and Australia; sang Arminda in La Finta Giardiniera at Lausanne, 1989, Constanze in Die Entführung with the Lyric Opera of Queensland; Season 1992/93 with Lucia at Adelaide, Arminda at Salzburg, Violetta and Gilda at Wellington. *Recordings:* To The Glory of God, 1964; L'amico Fritz, opera (Caterina), 1969; Songs for All Seasons, Mahler Symphony No 4, 1970; Scottish Soldiers Abroad, 1975; Alleluia, 1974; Operatic Arias, conductor John Matheson, 1987; La Finta Giardiniera, Brussels. *Contributions to:* London Sunday Times (article by

Desmond Shawe- Taylor). *Honours:* NZ Mobil Song Quest, 1963; Melbourne Sun Aria, Australia, 1964; Kathleen Ferrier Scholarship, London, 1966; OBE, 1985; DBE, 1991; Hon D Litt, 1993; Hon D Waik, 1993. *Hobbies:* Golf; Family.*Address:* PO Box 4184, New Plymouth, New Zealand.

MAJOR Margaret, b. 1932, Coventry, England. Violist. *Education:* Royal College of Music. *Debut:* Wigmore Hall, London, 1955 with Gerald Moore. *Career:* Principal viola, Netherlands Chambner Orchestra 1955-59; Oromonte Trio, 1958-65; Principal viola, Philomusica of London, 1960-65; Viola, Aeolian String Quartet, 1965-81; Professor of viola, Royal College of Music, London, 1969-. *Recordings:* Complete String Quartets of Haydn; Late Beethoven Quartets; Ravel and Debussy Quartets; Complete Mozart Viola Quintets. *Honours:* Lionel Tertis Prize 1951; International Music Association Concert Award 1955; MA University of Newcastle-on-Tyne, 1970; FRCM, 1992. *Hobby:* Good food. *Address:* 13 Upper Park Road, Kingston Hill, Kingston-upon-Thames, Surrey, England.

MAKINO Yutaka, b. 5 July 1930, Tokyo, Japan. Composer. *Education:* Studied with Koscak Yamada. *Career:* Freelance composer of operas and instrumental works. *Compositions include:* Operas Ayame, radio opera, CBS, 1960; Mushrooms, comic opera, Tokyo, 1961; Benkei in the Boat, Tokyo, 1962; Hanjo, Tokyo, 1963; Snow-Woman, Yokohama, 1964; The Origin of the Deer Dance, tokyo, 1967; The Millionaire Ayaginu, comic opera, Tokyo 1968; Kurozuka, Tokyo, 1974; Anju and Zushi-ou, Tokyo 1979; The Tale of Ogetsu, 1990. *Honours include:* Argentine Music Festival Prize, 1955; National Arts Festival Grant Priz, 1960; Spanish Radio Prize, 1962. *Address:* JASRAC (Japan), c/o PRS Ltd Member Registration, 29/33 Berners Street, London W1P 4AA, England.

MAKLAKIEWICZ Tadeusz Wojciech, b. 20 Oct 1922, Mszczonow, Poland. Composer. m. Maria Pawluskiewicz, 4 June 1952, 3 daughters. *Education:* Department of Law, Jagiellonian University, Krakow, 1949; State High School of Music, 1958. *Debut:* Festival of Polish Music, Warsaw, 1951. *Career:* Dean of Music Education Faculty, 1968-69, Deputy Rector, 1969-71, State High School of Music, Warsaw; Head of Music Education Department, 1973; Rector, 1975-78. *Compositions:* The Kurpie Suite, for soprano and mixed choir a cappella, 1957; Cantata: Peace; Friendship; Work; 1959 Epitaphium for Symphony Orchestra; Rondo for clarinet and piano or orchestra; 1964 Vienna, vocalisation for soprano and orchestra; Polonais of the Tank Corps; The Clocks are Ringing; Songs for Children for voice and piano; Mazovian Dance for piano, 1977; Hands Friendly With Hands, for mixed choir and organ, 1977; Quintet for flute, 2 clarinets, bassoon and harp, 1977; Above Clouds, for mixed choir, 1978; March for brass band, 1979; Salvum fac, for mixed choir, 1981; The Bible Triptych, for 2 clarinets and bassoon, 1982; Suite for Cello, 1983; The Gorals Mass, for mixed choir and organ, 1983; Chryzea phorminx ode for 4 trombones, 1984; Arch of Triumph, for woodwind quintet, 1984; Wistful Songs for baritone and piano, 1985; Love Letters, variations for string orchestra, 1985; Ave Maria, for 3 violins, 1986; At Zelazowa Wola, 3 stanzas for baritone, flute, alto, horn and harp, 1986; Violin Concerto for Children, 1987; A Memory, for 3 cellos, 1987; A Flag for female choir, 1988. *Memberships:* President, Authors Agency Ltd., Warsaw, 1985; Union of Polish Composers. *Hobby:* History and Culture of Ancient Greece and Rome. *Address:* Smolna 8/90, 00-375 Warsaw, Poland.

MAKRIS Andreas, b. 7 Mar. 1930, Salonica, Greece. Composer. m. Margaret Lubbe, 12 June 1959, 2 sons. *Education:* Phillips University, Enid, Oklahoma, USA, 1950; Postgraduate studies, Kansas City Conservatory, Missouri, and Mannes College of Music, 1956; Aspen Music Festival; Fontainebleau School, France; Studied with Nadia Boulanger. *Career:* Compositions premiered and performed, USA, Canada, Europe, South America, Japan, USSR; Appeared twice with premieres, national

TV networks, USA, 1978, 1984; Composer-in-residence, National Symphony Orchestra, 1979-90; Advisor to Mstislav Rostropovich for new music, 1979-90; His complete short works performed on Voice of America Radio, 1980, 1982. *Compositions:* Principal works include: Scherzo for Violins, 1966; Concerto for Strings, 1966; Aegean Festival, 1967; Concertino for Trombone, 1970; Anamnesis, 1970; Viola Concerto, 1970; Efthymia, 1972; Five Miniatures, 1972; Mediterranean Holiday, 1974; Fantasy and Dance, saxophone, 1974; Sirens, 1976; Chromatokinesis, 1978; In Memory, 1979; Variations and Song, orchestra, 1979; Fanfare Alexander, 1980; 4th of July March, 1982; Life-Nature Symphonic Poem, 1983; Concerto Fantasia for Violin and Orchestra, 1983; Caprice Tonatonal 1986; Intrigues for solo clarinet and wind Ensemble 1987; Concertante for Violin, Cello, French Horn, Clarinet, Percussion and Orchestra, 1988; Sonata for Cello and Piano 1989; Symphony to Youth, 1989; Trilogy for Orchestra, 1990, Alleluia for mixed chorus and brass quintet 1990; Concertino for organ, flute and string quartet, 1992; A Symphony for soprano and strings, 1992; Woodwind Quintet, 1993; Various works for violin, string quartets, voice quintets, duets, arrangements of Paganini and Bach; Compositions for special anniversaries and festival openings. *Address:* 11204 Oak Leaf Drive, Silver Spring, MD 20901, USA.

MAKRIS Cynthia, b. 1956, Sterling, Colorado, USA. Singer (Soprano). *Education:* Studied at the University of Colorado and Adams State College. *Career:* Sang Alice Ford, Donna Elvira and Tosca while a student; European debut at Graz, as Violetta; Stadttheater Freiburg 1980-82, as Constanze, Pamina, Violetta and Saffi in Zigeunerbaron; Sang at Bielefeld from 1982 as Donna Anna, Agathe, Marenka, Lucia di Lammermoor and Manon Lescaut, and in revivals of Schreker's Irrelohe and Max Brand's Maschinist Hopkins; Member of the Dortmund Opera from 1986, as Desdemona, Leonora (Trovatore), Amelia (Un Ballo in Maschera) and Arabella; Other roles include Marietta in Die Tote Stadt (at Dusseldorf), Marie in Wozzeck (Karlsruhe), Mozart's Countess, Wagner's Eva and Freia and the Empress in Die Frau ohne Schatten; Has sung the title role in Salome at Dortmund, Berlin (Staatsoper and Deutsche Oper), Tokyo and Glasgow (Scottish Opera, 1990). *Address:* c/o Opernhaus, Kuhstrasse 12, D-4600 Dortmund, Germany.

MAKSYMIUK Jerzy, b. 9 Apr 1936, Grodno, Poland. Conductor. *Education:* Studied violin, piano, conducting, composition, Warsaw Conservatory, Poland. *Career:* Conducted, Warsaw Grand Theatre, where later founded Polish Chamber Orchestra; Principal conductor, Polish National Radio Orchestra, 1975-77, touring Eastern Europe & USA. UK debut with Polish Chamber Orchestra, 1977, since appearing in Western Europe, Scandinavia, Japan, Australia, New Zealand, also Salzburg & Edinburgh Festivals, festivals at Aix, Flanders, Granada, Lucerne, Vienna, BBC Promenade Concerts (London). Guest conductor, Northern Sinfonia, Scottish Chamber Orchestra, BBC Philharmonic Orchestra, 1980-; Chief Conductor, BBC Scottish Symphony Orchestra, 1983-93, Guest Conductor, London Symphony Orchestra, London Philharmonic Orchestra, Tokyo Metropolitan Orchestra, Indianapolis Symphony, Sydney Symphony; Conducted Don Giovanni for English National Opera, 1991 (debut), Die Fledermaus, 1993; Led the premieres of Macmillan's The Confession of Isobel Gowdie (Proms 1990), and Robin Holloway's Violin Concerto (1992); Season 1992-94 with the Royal Liverpool Philharmonic, the Residentié and Limburg Orchestra and the Hong Kong Philharmonic. *Recordings:* Haydn, Bach, Vivaldi, Tchaikovsky, Mendelssohn (EMI); Music for Pleasure: Schumann with London Philharmonic Orchestra and Devoyon; Shostakovich Piano Concerto, with Dimitri Alexeev and the English Chamber Orchestra (Classics for Pleasure). *Honours:* Doctor of Letters of Strathclyde University, Glasgow, 1990; Gramaphone Award for Contemporary Music, 1993; Honorary title of Conductor Laureate of BBC Scottish Symphony. *Current Management:* IMG Artists. *Address:* c/o IMG Artists,

Media House, 3 Burlington Lane, Chiswick, London, W4 2TH, England.

MALAGNINI Mario, b. 1959, Salo, Italy. Singer (Tenor). *Education:* Studied at the Brescia Conservatory and the Giuseppe Verdi Conservatory, Milan with Piermirando Ferraro; Further study with Tito Gobbi and Giuseppe di Stefano. *Career:* Sang in Frankfurt and Milan (La Scala) 1985, as Radames, and in Il Corsaro; Returned to La Scala 1986-87, as Alfredo and Ismaele in Nabucco; Verona Arena from 1987, as Foresto in Attila, Pinkerton, Riccardo and Radames; Appeared as Don José at Glyndebourne 1987, and in a concert performance of La Battaglia di Legnano at Carnegie Hall (as Arrigo); Further engagements at Florence (as Pinkerton and Gabriele Adorno), Nîmes and Monte Carlo (Pollione in Norma), Vienna, Berlin, Houston, Budapest and Seoul (1988); Teatro La Fenice Venice 1990, as Rodolfo in Leoncavallo's Bohème. *Recordings:* Emilia di Liverpool, with the Philharmonia Orchestra (Opera Rara); Norma conducted by Emil Tchakarov. *Honours:* Winner, Tito Gobbi Competition, 1983; Concorso Enrico Caruso and Belvedere Competition, Vienna, 1984. *Address:* c/o Arena di Verona, Piazza Bra 28, I-37121 Verona, Italy.

MALANIUK Ira, b. 29 Jan 1923, Stanislava, Poland. Singer (Mezzo-Soprano). *Education:* Studid with Adam Didur in Lwow and with Anna Bahr-Mildenburg in Vienna; Salzburg Mozarteum. *Debut:* Graz 1945. *Career:* Sang in Zurich from 1947, notably in The Rake's Progress, 1951; Bayreuth Festival 1951-53, as Brangaene, Magdalena, Fricka and Waltraute; Member of Munich Opera from 1952, as Orpheus, Lady Macbeth and Bartók's Judith; Vienna Opera from 1956; Covent Garden 1953, as Adelaide in Arabella, with the Munich Company; Paris Opera 1956, in Das Rheingold; Salzburg Festival from 1956, notably in the 1958 local premiere of Barber's Vanessa; Concert performances from 1966; Professor at the Graz Conservatory from 1971. *Recordings:* Die Meistersinger, Arabella, Aida, Così fan Tutte, Le Nozze di Figaro; Waltraute in Götterdämmerung, conducted by Clemens Krauss (Bayreuth 1953).

MALAS Spiro, b. 28 Jan 1933, Baltimore, Maryland, USA. Bass-baritone. m. Marlene Kleinman. *Education:* Studied with E Nagy, Peabody Conservatory of Music, Baltimore; E Baklor and D Ferro, New York; Coached by I Chicagov. *Deubt:* Marco, Gianni Schicchi, Baltimore Civic Opera, 1959. *Career:* New York City Opera debut, Spinellocchio, Gianni Schicchi, 1961; Toured Australia with Sutherland-Williamson International Grand Opera Co, 1965; Covent Garden debut, London as Sulpice, La fille du régiment, 1966; Chicago Lyric Opera debut as Assur, Semiramide, 1971; Metropolitan Opera debut New York as Sulpice, 1983; other roles have been the Sacristan in Tosca, Zuniga, Mozart's Bartolo and Frank in Die Fledermaus; Sang Frank Maurrant in the British premiere of Weill's Street Scene, Glasgow 1989, Don Isaac in Prokofiev's Duenna at the 1989 Wexford Festival; Vancouver 1990, as Baron Zeta in The Merry Widow; Many concert engagements; Teacher, Peabody Conservatory of Music. *Recordings:* For Decca-London. *Honour:* Winner, Metropolitan Opera Auditions, 1961. *Address:* c/o Columbia Artists Management Inc, 165 West 57th Street, New York, NY 10019, USA.

MALAS-GODLEWSKA Ewa, b. 1955, Warsaw, Poland. Singer (Coloratura Soprano). *Education:* Studied in Warsaw. *Career:* Sang at the Warsaw Opera from 1978 as Zerbinetta, the Queen of Night, Rosina, Norina, and Constanze in Die Entführung; Leading roles at the Vienna Volksoper, Paris Opera-Comique, Nantes (Olympia), Basle, Berne, Wiesbaden and Dresden; Sang Celia in Mozart's Lucio Silla, produced by Patrice Chereau, at Nanterre and Brussels, 1986; Sang Madeleine in Le Postillon de Longjumeau at the Grand Theatre Geneva, 1990; Queen of Night in new productions of Die Zauberflöte at Houston and Paris (Opera Bastille) 1991; Théâtre du Châtelet Paris in L'Enfant et les Sortileges; Concert performances in Britain, Switzerland, Poland, Germany, Holland,

Belgium, and France. Gstaad Festival, 1987 in Beethoven's Ninth, conducted by Yehudi Menuhin. *Honours:* Winner, Toulouse International Competition, 1978. *Address:* c/o Opera de la Bastille, 120 Rue de Lyon, F-75012 Paris, France.

MALASPINE Massimiliano, b. 17 May 1925, Fara Novarese, Italy. Singer (Bass). *Education:* Studied with Lina Pagliughi. *Career:* Appearances from 1959 at such Italian opera centres as La Scala Milan, Teatro San Carlo Naples, Teatro Fenice Venice and the Teatro Regio Parma; Further engagements at Genoa, Turin, Brussels, Munich Staaatsoper, Montreal, Toulouse, Frankfurt, Rio de Janeiro, Paris, Barcelona and Miami; Roles have included Colline in La Bohème, Oroveso (Norma), Ptolomey (Giulio Cesare), Sarastro and Verdi's Padre Guardino, Banquo and Ramphis; Teacher of singing in Milan after retiring from stage. *Address:* c/o Teatro alla Scala, Via Filodrammatici 2, 20121 Milan, Italy.

MALCOLM Carlos Edmond, b. 24 Nov 1945, Havana City, Cuba. Composer; Pianist. 1 son, 1 daughter. *Education:* Pre-university studies, Vedado Institute, Havana, 1963. Started musical education, 1957; Piano graduate, Amadeo Roldán Conservatory; Degree in Musical Composition, The Superior Institute of Arts, Havana, 1983. *Debut:* National Theatre, Cuba, 1964. *Career:* Composer and Pianist: National Modern Dance Ensemble, 1964-68; Cuban Institute of Radio, (occasionally Cuban Institute of Film), 1968-70; Belongs to The Staff of Composers of The Ministry of Culture of Cuba, 1970-; Toured throughout Mexico, Jamaica and Equador playing own works, teaching and lecturing; works have been played in New Music Concerts, Warsaw Autumn, Berlin's Biennalle, Japan, Argentina, Hungary. *Compositions:* Quetzalcoatl (Song of the Feathered Serpent), for flute and piano; Beny Moré redivivo, for string quartet; Adagio for piano (4 hands); El Remediano; Eclosión; Articulations for piano; 13 studies for piano; Songs set to texts by Caribbean Poets; Rumours, for violin, cello and piano; Meditation for piano, all composed between 1963-1990; New Music Concerts: ACCORDES quartet played, Benny Moré redivivo; played with flautist Robert Aitken, Quetzalcoatl...for flute and piano, other compositions for piano solo, at Toronto's Premier Grand Theater, Royal Conservatory of Music; Bayreuth's Festival of Music: AMBER Trio, Israel, played piano trio, Rumourrs and first performance of Meditation for piano solo, Germany 1990; University of Ann Arbor's Afro American Music Collection, University La Salle of Philadelphia. *Address:* ul. Piekna 16, m.2, 00-539 Warsaw, Poland.

MALCOLM George (John), b. 28 Feb 1917, London, England. Harpsichordist; Pianist; Conductor. *Education:* Wimbledon College; Balliol College, Oxford; MA, BMus, Royal College of Music; originally trained as concert pianist. *Career:* Master of Music, Westminster Cathedral 1947-59, trained Boys' Choir for which Benjamin Britten wrote Missa Brevis Op 63; Harpsichordist, pianist and conductor making frequent tours especially in Europe; Artistic Director, Philomusica of London, 1962-66; Associate Conductor BBC Scottish Orchestra, 1965-67. *Recordings:* Britten Missa Brevis (Decca); Victoria Tenebrae Responsories (Argo); Bach Die Kunst der Fuge and Brandenburg Concertos; Anerio Missa pro Defunctis; Monteverdi Magnificat; Handel Concerti Grossi Op.3; Britten Cantata Academica, Hymn to St. Cecilia and Choral Dances from Gloriana (L'Oiseau Lyre); Poulenc Organ and Harpsichord Concertos (Decca). *Honours:* Honorary Fellow of Balliol College, Oxford, 1966; FRCM; Honorary Member RAM; Papal Knight, Order of St Gregory the Great, 1970; CBE 1965; Honorary Fellow of Royal College of Organists, 1987. *Address:* 99 Wimbledon Hill Road, London SW19 7QT, England.

MALFITANO Catherine, b. 18 Apr 1948, New York, USA. Singer (Soprano). *Education:* Manhattan School of Music and with father, violinist Joseph Malfitano. *Debut:* Central City Opera 1972 as Nannetta in Falstaff. *Career:* Sang with the Minnesota Opera, 1973, then with New York City Opera, 1973-1979; debut as Mimi;

Netherlands Opera 1974 as Susanna in Figaro; Salzburg Festival 1976 as Servilia in Tito, 1981 as Three female roles in Hoffmann, 1992 as Salome; Metropolitan Opera debut in 1979 as Gretel, and returned as Konstanze, Nedda, Violetta, Juliette, Manon, Micaela, Mimi, Three roles in Hoffmann and Lulu; Vienna Staatsoper as Violetta, 1982, Manon 1984, and Grete in Schreker's Der Fernne Klang, 1991; Maggio Musicale Florence 1983 as Suor Angelica and 1990 as Jenny in Weill's Mahagonny; Munich Opera 1985 as Berg's Lulu; Covent Garden as Susanna and Zerlina 1976, Butterfly 1988, and in Stiffelio 1993. Other roles include Puccini's Butterfly, Mimi, Tosca and Liu; Monteverdi's Poppea and Verdi's Amelia in Boccanegra; Geneva Opera as Manon and Poppea 1989; sang Daphne 1988 and Butterfly 1990 at La Scala; Salome at the Deutsche Oper Berlin 1990; at the Lyric Opera of Chicago sung Susanna 1975, Violetta 1985, Lulu 1987, Barber's Cleopatra 1991, Butterfly 1991-92 and Liu 1992; Created roles in the world premieres of Conrad Susa's Transformations 1973, Bilby's Doll by Carlisle Floyd 1976, Thomas Pasatieri's Washington Square 1976 and William Bolcom's McTeague 1992. *Recordings include:* Rossini's Stabat Mater conducted by Muti; Gounod's Roméo et Juliette (HMV) and Monteverdi's Poppea (CBS); Music for Voice and Violin with Joseph Malfitano, (Musical Heritage); Salome conducted by Sinopoli (Teldec); Tosca with Domingo conducted by Mehta (Teldec); Stiffelio with Carreras conducted by Edward Downes (Covent Garden Pioneer).*Current Management:* c/o Rita Schütz, Artists Management, Zurich, Rütistrasse 52, 8044 Zürich-Gockhausen, Switzerland. *Address:* c/o Tom Graham, IMG Artists Europe, Media House, 3 Burlington Lane, London W4 2TH, England.

MALGOIRE Jean-Claude, b. 25 Nov 1940, Avignon, France. Conductor; Oboist. *Education:* Studied in Avignon and at the Paris Conservatory (prizes for oboe and chamber music, 1960). *Career:* 1966 founded La Grande Ecurie et la Chambre du Roy, for the performance of Baroque music; Founded Florilegium Musicum de Paris: concerts of medieval and Renaissance music; Handel's Rinaldo at the Festival Hall, London; Rameau's Hippolyte and Aricie for the English Bach Festival at Covent Garden; Campra's Tancrède for the Copenhagen Royal Opera and at the Aix-en-Provence Festival 1986; L'Incoronazione di Poppea at the Stockholm Opera; Rameau's Les Indes Galantes at the Versailles Opera Royal; Conducted Céphale et Procris by Elisabeth Jacquet de la Guerre at St. Etienne, 1989, Kreutzer's Paul et Virginie at Tourcoing; Season 1992 with Lully's Alceste at the Théâtre des Champs-Elysées, Paris, a Vivaldi pastiche Montezuma at Monte Carlo and Gnecco's Prova di un'opera seria at Montpellier. *Recordings:* Rinaldo; Handel's Xerxes; Hippolyte et Aricie and Les Indes Galantes, Tancrède (Erato); Cavalli's Ercole Amante (CBS); Handel Concerti Grossi Op.3 and 6, Water and Fireworks Music; Lully Alceste, Psyché and Le Bourgeois gentilhomme; Vivaldi Beatus Vir, Gloria and flute concertos; Charpentier Messe de Minuit; Renaissance music with the Florilegium Musicum de Paris. *Honours include:* Prix Internationale de Genève, Oboe, 1968.

MALINOWSKI Wladyslaw, b. 28 June 1931, Sosnowiec, Poland. Musicologist; Music Critic. *Education:* Diploma of Musicology, Warsaw University, under Jozef Chominski, 1957; Piano and Music Study, Warsaw High State School of Music; Doctorate, Polish Academy of Sciences, under Jozef Chominski, 1975. *Career:* Music Critic, many Polish newspapers and magazines including Zycie Warszawy, Wspojczesnosc, Ruch Muzyczny, Chopin Studies; Scientific Collaborator, Institute of Arts, Polish Academy of Sciences; Supernumerary Professor: Music Academy, Poznan, 1985-1986; Music Academy, Lodz, 1986-. *Publications:* Mikojaj Zielenski, Opera omnia (editor), 5 vols, 1966, 1974, 1978, 1989, 1991; Polifonia Mikojaja Zielenskiego, 1981. *Contributions to:* Many musicological papers to: Muzyka; Res Facta; Polish Art Studies; Rivista Italiana di Musicologia; Die Musiktheorie; Others. *Memberships:* Karol Szymanowski Musical Society, Poland, Vice-President 1983-86, President 1986-89; Polish Composers Union,

Musicological Section; Club Polonais de Haute Montagne. *Hobbies:* Mountain climbing; Skiing. *Address:* Lipska 40 m 1, 03-908 Warsaw, Poland.

MALIPIERO Riccardo, b. 24 July 1914, Milan, Italy. Composer. *Education:* Studied at the Milan Conservatory, 1930-37 and with his uncle Gian Francesco Malipiero, at the Venice Conservatory 1937-39. *Career:* Began career as a pianist, interrupted by WWII; After WWII began as Composer and Music Critic; Organized the first International Congress of Dodecaphonic Music, Milan 1949; Lectured in USA 1954 and 1959; Master Classes at the Di Tella Institute Buenos Aires 1963 and the University of Maryland 1969; Director of the Varese Liceo Musicale 1969, 1984. *Compositions:* Operas Minnie la candida 1942; La Donna è Mobile 1954; TV opera Battono alla Porta 1962; Orchestral: Piano Concerto 1937; 2 Cello Concertos 1938, 1959; Balletto 1939; Piccolo Concerto for piano and orchestra 1945; Antico sole for soprano and orchestra 1947; Cantata sacra for soprano, chorus and orchestra 1947; 3 Symphonies 1949, 1956, 1959; Violin Concerto 1952; Studi 1953; Ouverture-Divertimento del Ritorno 1953; Concerto for piano and ensemble, 1955; Concerto Breve for ballerina and chamber orchestra 1956; Cantata di Natale for soprano, chorus and orchestra 1959; Concerto per Dimitri for piano and orchestra 1961; Nykteghersia 1962; Cadencias 1964; Muttermusik 1966; Mirages 1966; Carnet de Notes 1967; Rapsodia for violin and orchestra 1967; Serenata per Alice Tully 1969; Monologo for male voice and strings 1969; Concerto for Piano Trio and orchestra 1976; 2 Piano Concertos 1974; Requiem 1975; Ombre 1986; Go Placidly for baritone and chamber orchestra 1975; Loneliness for soprano and orchestra 1987; Due Arie for soprano 2nd orchestra, 1990; Lieder études for soprano and piano, 1991; Chamber: Musik I for cello and 9 instruments 1938; 3 String Quartets 1941, 1954, 1960; Violin Sonata 1956; Piano Quintet 1957; Musica da camera for wind quintet 1959; Oboe Sonata 1959; 6 Poesie di Dylan Thomas 1959 for soprano and 10 instruments; Mosaico for wind and string quintets 1961; Preludio, Adagio e Finale for soprano, 5 percussionists and piano 1963; In Time of Daffodils (Cummings) for soprano, baritone and 7 instruments 1964; Nuclei for 2 pianos and percussion 1966; Cassazione for string sextet 1967; Piano Trio 1968; Ciaccona di Davide for viola and piano 1970; Giber Folia for clarinet and piano 1973; Memoria for flute and harpsichord 1973; Winter-quintet for clarinet quintet 1976; Aprèsmiró for 11 instruments 1982; Voicequintet for soprano and string quartet 1988; Piano Music. *Address:* Via A Stradella 1, 20129 Milano, Italy.

MALIPONTE Adriana, b. 26 Dec 1938, Brescia, Italy. Singer (Soprano). *Education:* Studied at the Paris Conservatoire and in Milan with Carmen Melis. *Debut:* Teatro Nuovo Milan 1958. *Career:* Sang in Rome, Barcelona, Lisbon, and Brussels; Paris Opéra-Comique 1962, in the premiere of Menotti's The Last Savage; Glyndebourne 1967, as Adina in L'Elisir d'Amore; La Scala Milan 1970, as Massenet's Manon; Metropolitan Opera 1971, as Mimi: returned to New York as Micaela, Luisa Miller, Amelia Boccanegra and Alice Ford in Falstaff (1985); Covent Garden 1976, as Nedda in Pagliacci; Bergamo Festival 1987, as Donizetti's Gemma di Vergy; Verdi's Luisa Miller at Trieste, 1990. *Recordings include:* Micaela in Carmen (Deutsche Grammophon); Le Villi (RCA); Pieces by A. Scarlatti (HMV); Les Pêcheurs de Perles; Poliuto. *Honours:* Winner, Geneva International Competition, 1960; Prizewinner of La Scala and Italian Radio Competitions. *Address:* c/o Teatro Giuseppe Verdi, Riva 3 Novembre 1, 1-34121 Tieste, Italy.

MALKOVICH Mark Paul, b. 10 July 1930, Eveleth, Minnesota, USA. Music Festival Director. m. Joan Shewring, 7 Feb 1959, 3 sons, 1 daughter. *Education:* BS, Columbia University, New York, 1953; Piano with: Dorothy Crost Bourgin, Chicago Musical College; William Beller, Columbia University; Adele Marcus, Juilliard School. *Career:* Artistic and General Director, Newport Music Festival, 1975-; Executive Director, Palm Beach Festival, Florida, 1985-86; Frequent radio and television guest in New York (WQXR), and Boston (WGBH); As one of America's leading impresarios introduced pianists Andrei Gavrilov, Bella Davidovich, Jean-Philippe Collard, and Dimitris Sgouros in their North American debuts as well as nearly 50 other artists; Noted Adjudicator, many American competitions including Beethoven Fellowship, Indiana, and Chopin Foundation, Miami, Florida. *Publications:* Author, Editor, prestigious Festival booklets, 1974-; 100 page publication specialising in Music of the Romantic Era; Articles in Musical America. *Memberships:* Harvard Musical Association; President 1986, Chopin Foundation of the United States, Miami. *Address:* Newport Music Festival, PO Box 3300, Newport, RI 02840 USA.

MALM William Paul, b. 6 Mar 1928, LeGrange, Illinois, USA. Musicologist; Ethnomusicologist; Lecturer. m. Joyce Rutherford Malm. 3 daughters. *Education:* BMus 1949, MMus 1950, Northwestern University; PhD, UCLA 1959. *Career:* Pianist, Composer, Modern Dance, NY American Dance Festival, Jacob's Pillow, Perry-Mansfield School of Theater; Teacher, University of Illinois, US Naval School of Music; Professor, University of Michigan; Director, Stearns Collection. *Publications include:* Music Cultures of the Pacific, The Near East and Asia, 1967, 2nd edition 1977; Japanese Music and Musical Instruments, 1959; Six Hidden Views of Japanese Music, 1986; Theater as Music, 1991. *Contributions to:* Professional journals. *Honours include:* Henry Russel Award, outstanding technologist, 1966; Ernest Bloch Professor, Berkeley, University of California; Koizumi Award in Ethnomusicology, Japan, 1993. *Memberships include:* President, Society of Ethnomusicologist; American Musicological Society. *Address:* School of Music, University of Michigan, Ann Arbor, MI 48109, USA.

MALMBERG Urban, b. 29 Mar 1962, Stockholm, Sweden. Singer (Baritone). *Education:* Sang in the Boys' Choir of the Stockholm Opera and appeared as First Boy in the 1974 Bergman movie version of Die Zauberflöte; Studied in Stockholm with Helge Brilioth and Erik Saeden. *Career:* Sang at Stockholm in works by Peter Maxwell Davies and Janake Hillerud; Hamburg Staatsoper from 1983, as Malatesta (Don Pasquale), Masetto, Papageno, Schaunard (La Boheme), Herlequin (Ariadne) and in Nono's Intolleranza and Die Gespenstersonate by Reimann; Guest appearances in Dusseldorf, Las Palmas, London, Moscow, San Francisco and Tokyo; Other roles have included Guglielmo and Donner (Brussels and Bonn, 1990), Belcore, Marcello and Lescaut; Season 1992 with Malatesta at Vancouver and Frère Léon in Messiaen's St François d'Assise at the Salzburg Festival; Concert repertoire includes the St Matthew Passion, Beethoven's Ninth, Ein Deutsches Requiem and Peer Gynt. *Recordings:* Ariadne auf Naxos and Les Contes d'Hoffmann (Deutsche Grammophon); The Count in Schreker's Der Schatzgräber, with Hamburg forces (Capriccio). *Address:* Hamburgische Staatsoper, Grosse-Theaterstrasse 34, D-2000 Hamburg 36, Germany.

MALMBORG Gunila, b. 26 Feb 1933, Lulea, Sweden. Singer (Soprano). m. Lars af Malmborg. *Education:* Royal Stockholm Academy of Music. *Debut:* Stockhlom 1960, as Marzelline in Fidelio. *Career:* Member of Stockholm Opera from 1960; Guest appearances in Copenhagen, Oslo, Monte Carlo, Cologne and Kiel; Munich 1968, as Salome and Aida; Glyndebourne 1965, as Lady Macbeth; Well known in Wagner roles and as Verdi's Abigaille and Amelia, Mozart's Donna Anna, Puccini's Tosca and Turandot and Offenbach's Giulietta. *Address:* c/o Kungliga Teatern, PO Box 16094, S-10322 Stockholm, Sweden.

MALONE Carol, b. 16 July 1943, Grayson, Kentucky, USA. Singer (Soprano). *Education:* Studied at the University of Indian at Bloomington, at the Hamburg Musikhochschule and with Joseph Metternich in Cologne. *Debut:* Cologen 1966, as Aennchen in Der Freischutz. *Career:* Many appearances at such German opera centres as the State Operas of Hamburg, Munich and Stuttgart, Deutsche Oper am Rhein Dusseldorff, Nationaltheater Mannheim and Frankfurt; Further engagements at Brussels, Vienna Volksoper, Salzburg, San Francisco, Amsterdam, Venice and the Edinburgh Festival; Sang with the Deutsche Oper Berlin in the premiere of Love's Labour Lost by Nabokov (Brussels) 1973 and as Zerlina in Don Giovanni (Berlin, 1988); Other roles have included Marzelline, Nannetta, Despina, Susanna, Blondchen, Sophie, Adele in Die Fledermaus and Adelaide in Blacher's Preussiches Märchen; Many concert appearances. Recordings include: Trionfo d'Afrodite by Orff. *Address:* c/o Deutsche Oper Berlin, Richard Wagnerstrasse 10, D-1000 Berlin, Germany.

MALSBURY Angela Mary, b. 5 May 1945, Preston, Lancashire, England. Freelance Professional Clarinettist. m. David Pettit, 24 July 1965, 1 son. *Education:* Beauchamp School, Kibworth, Leicester, 1960-62; Associated Board Scholar, Royal College of Music, London, 1962-66; ARCM, Clarinet Teacher and Piano Teacher; LRAM, Clarinet Performer. *Debut:* Concert debut, Royal Festival Hall, with London Mozart Players, 1976. *Career:* Concerto Soloist with major orchestras world wide; Clarinet Quintets including classical and contemporary repertoire; Member of De Saram Trio and Cameristi of London, Musicians of the Royal Exchange and Albion Ensembles, Principal Clarinet of London Mozart Players; Clarinet Professor, Royal Academy of Music. *Recordings:* Richard Baker's Musical Menagerie, Cameristi of London; Amadeus, Mozart Serenade for 13 Wind Instruments (Academy of St Martins, Albion and LMP); Mozart: Clarinet Quintet with the String Quartet (LDR); Mozart: Clarinet Concerto, London Mozart Players and Jane Glover (ASV). *Honours:* Philip Cardew Memorial Prize, 1963; Marjorie Whyte Prize, 1964; Mozart Memorial Prize, 1974; Hon. R.A.M., 1991. *Memberships:* Musicians Union. *Hobbies:* Cooking; Swimming. *Current Management:* John Wright. *Address:* 40 Greenford Avenue, Hanwell, London W7, England.

MALTA Alexander, b. 28 Sept 1942, Visp, Wallis Canton, Switzerland. Singer (Bass). *Education:* Studied with Desider Kovacz in Zurich, Barra-Carracciolo in Milan and Enzo Mascherini in Florence. *Debut:* Stuttgart 1962, as the Monk in Don Carlos. *Career:* Sang in Brunswick, Munich, Berlin, Vienna, Frankfurt Geneva, Paris and Venice from 1966; US debut 1976, with the San Francisco Opera; Chicago Lyric Opera in Ariadne auf Naxos; Seattle Opera as Osmin in Die Entführung; Brussels Opera from 1979, notably in Wozzeck, Lulu and Schubert's Fierrabras; Rome Opera as Orestes in Elektra; Maggio Musicale Florence as Wagner's Fasolt and Landgrave; La Scala Milan in Handel's Ariodante; Hamburg Opera as Golaud (Pelléas et Mélisande), Colline (La Bohème), 4 roles (Hoffmann) and Osmin; Paris Opéra (La Bohème, Die Fledermaus), Munich State Opera (Hoffmann, Mosé, Adriana Lecouvreur), Deutsche Oper Berlin as Nicolai's Falstaff, Gounod's Mefistofele and Rocco in Fidelio; Salzburg Festival in Carmen and Don Giovanni, conducted by Karajan; Covent Garden 1985, in Tippett's King Priam (title role); Sang the Voice of Neptune in Idomeneo at the 1990 Salzburg Festival. *Recordings include:* Lady Macbeth of the Mtsenk District (HMV); Carmen, Don Giovanni and the Bruckner Te Deum (Deutsche Grammophon); Rigoletto (Ariola); Zar und Zimmermann (BASF); Wozzeck (Decca). *Address:* c/o Harrison/Parrot Ltd., 12 Penzance Place, London W11 4PA, England.

MAMLOK Ursula, b. 1 Feb 1928, Berlin, Germany. Composer. *Education:* Studied in Berlin and Ecuador, New York with Szell at Mannes Collge and Manhattan School of Music with Vittorio Viannini; Further study with Wolpe, Steuermann, Shapey and Sessions. *Career:* Teacher, NYU, 1967-76, Kingsborough Community College, 1972-75, Manhattan School, 1976- ; Represented USA at the 1984 International Rostrum of Composers. *Compositions include:* Concerto for strings, 1950; Grasshoppers: 6 Humoresques, 1957; Oboe Concerto, 1974; Concertino for wind quintet, 2 percussion and string orchestra, 1987; Woodwind Quintet, 1956; String Quartet, 1962; Capriccios for oboe and piano, 1968; Variations and Interlude for perscussion quartet 1971; Sextet 1978; String Quintet, 1981; From my Garden for violin or viola, 1983; Akarina for flute and ensemble, 1985; Bagatelles for clarinet, violin and cello, 1988; Rhapsody for clarinet, viol and piano, 1989; Stray Birds for soprano, flute and cello, 1963; Hiku settings for soprano and flute, 1967; Der Andreas Garten for mezzo, flutes and harp, 1987; Piano music and pieces for tape. *Recordings include:* Walter Hinrischsen Award, American Academy and Institute of Arts and Letters, 1989. *Address:* c/o ASCAP, ASCAP Building, One Lincoln Plaza, NY 10023, USA.

MANAGER Richetta, b. 1953, USA. Singer (Soprano). *Education:* Studied at Washburn and Kansas Universities, Northwestern University, Evanston, Illinois and at the University of Colorado. *Career:* Sang in concert from 1974, with the Graz Opera 1979-82; Appeared in Chicago 1981 and 1982; With the Gelsenkirchen Opera, and as guest elsewhere in Germany (Cologne, Dusseldorf, Hagen, Munster and Nuremberg) has sung Mozart's Countess and Donna Anna, Agathe, Euridice, Handel's Cleopatra and Alcina, Verdi's Violetta, Amelia and Elena; Drusilla in L'Incoronazione di Poppea, Giulietta, Mimi, Tosca, Elsa (Lohengrin), Countess (Capriccio), the Duchess of Parma in Doktor Faust and Denise in the German premiere of Tippett's Knot Garden (Gelsenkirchen, 1987); Sang Regan in the world premiere of Tippett's New Year (Houston, 1989) and at Glyndebourne 1990; Concert repertoire ranges from Baroque music to contemporary works. *Address:* c/o Houston Grand Opera Association, 510 Preston Avenue, Houston, TX 76107, USA.

MANASSEN Alex Jacques, b. 6 Sept. 1950, Tiel, Netherlands. Composer. *Education:* Studied composition at Sweelinck Conservatory, Amsterdam, with Ton de Leeuw, 1972-79. *Career:* Performances live, on radio and television in the Netherlands; Performances in Italy, France, England, Germany, Israel, Sweden, USA, Poland; Commissions for all important Dutch funds; Teacher of Contemporary and Electronic Music, Sweelinck Conservatory, Amsterdam, 1991; Co-founder, Composer, Manager, Delta Ensemble; Teacher of Music and Informatica, Utrecht Conservatory, 1990; Dean (Director), Teacher of Composition, Zwolle Conservatory, 1991-; Manager DELTA, Ensemble. *Compositions include:* Katarsis-Arsis for organ, 1973; Mei, for flute and string quartet, 1974; Citius, Altius, Fortius, Variable instrumentation, 1979; Pandarus Sings, for mezzo soprano, flute, clarinet and piano, 1980; Pandarus Sings (Higher), for soprano, flute, clarinet and piano, 1980; De Waal, for 1 or more instruments, especially for beginners, 1980; Interlude 1, Sextet, for oboe, bassoon, french horn and string trio, 1980; Bass Clarinet Concerto, for bass clarinet and orchestra, 1981; Quintett, for flute, clarinet and string trio, 1982; Helix for marimba, 1983; Denkmal an der Grenze des Fruchtlandes, for soprano and chamber ensemble, 1983; Air for Orchestra, 1985; Air for electronic music, 1986; Air/Facilmente, clarinet, violin, cello and piano, 1986; Songs and Interludes, for soprano and chamber ensemble, 1979-88; A Call to La Source Possible, for soprano and chamber ensemble, 1988; Air Conditioned, computer controlled player piano, 1988; Lamento for a landscape, electronic music, 1988; Moordunkel, for soprano, accordian, bass clarinet and percussion, 1990; Two Ears to Hear Two Eyes to See, contralto, tenor and piano, 1990; Hallo, Hallo, computer controlled sound generating object on request of the Art Foundation Neerijnen; commissioned by the Amsterdam Fund for the Arts and the Province of Gelderland, 1991; Requiem for a Landscape, based on The Tree Bible by William van Toorn, Gerrit Noordzij and others; commissioned by the Fund for the Creation of Music. *Address:* Ankummerdijk 6, NL 7722, XJ Dalfsen, Netherlands.

MANCINELLI Aldo, b. 29 July 1928, Steubenville, Ohio, USA. Concert Pianist; Professor of Music. m. (1) 1 son, 1 daughter, (2) Judith Elaine Young, 1 June 1971,

1 son, 1 daughter. *Education:* Graduated, 1952, Graduate study, 1953, Oberlin Conservatory of Music; Graduated, Accademia Nazionale di Santa Cecilia, Rome, Italy, 1955; Studied with Claudio Arrau, Rudolf Firkusny and Carlo Zecchi. *Debut:* Beethoven 1st Piano Concerto, with Wheeling (West Virginia) Symphony, 1941. *Career:* Recitals throughout Europe, North Africa, Middle East, North America; Appeared as soloist with major symphony orchestras throughout Europe and USA including Cleveland Symphony, San Antonio Symphony, La Scala (Milan), Royal Liverpool Philharmonic, Santa Cecilia Orchestra (Rome), NDR Orchestra (Hamburg). *Recordings:* Piano music of Charles Griffes, Musical Heritage Society; Beethoven's Concerto No 5 (Emperor), Regal Records; Many recordings for Radiotelevisione Italiana; French North Africa Radio, Tunis; Rumanian Radio, Bucharest. *Contributions to:* Charles Griffes: An American Enigma, in Clavier, 1985. *Address:* c/o School of Music, Millikin University, Decatur, IL 62522, USA.

MANCINI Caterina, b. 1920, Italy. Singer (Soprano). *Education:* Studied in Milan and elsewhere in Italy. *Career:* Many appearances from 1948 at such Italian opera centres as Bologna, Venice, Rome (Leonora in Il Trovatore) and the Baths at Caracalla; La Scala Milan from 1951, debut as Donizetti's Lucrezia Borgia; Sang Agathe at Rome, 1952, and appeared at the Maggio Musicale Florence and the Verona Arena, 1956; Guest engagements in concert and opera elsewhere in Europe. *Recordings include:* La Battaglia di Legnano, Ernani and Il Trovatore; Santuzza in Cavalleria Rusticana and Anaide in Rossini's Mosè in Egitto; Guillaume Tell; Attilia; Il Duca d'Alba by Donizetti. *Address:* c/o Teatro alla Scala, Via Filodrammatici 2, 20121 Milan, Italy.

MANDAC Evelyn, b. 16 Aug. 1945, Malaybalay, Mindanao, Philippines. Singer (Soprano). *Education:* Oberlin College Conservatory; Juilliard School New York. *Debut:* Mobile, Alabama, 1968 in Orff's Carmina Burana. *Career:* Santa Fe 1968, in the US premiere of Henze's Tha Bassarids; Washington DC 1969, as Mimi in La Bohème; Toured with Juilliard Quartet 1969, in Schoenberg's 2nd Quartet; Seattle Opera 1972, in the premiere of Pasatieri's The Black Widow; Sang in the US premiere of Berio's Passaggio; San Francisco 1972, as Inez in L'Africaine; Glyndebourne 1974-75, as Susanna and Despina; Houston Opera 1975, in Handel's Rinaldo; Metropolitan Opera debut 1975, as Lauretta in Gianni Schicchi; Baltimore Opera 1976, in the premiere of Pasatieri's Inez de Castro; Lisa in The Queen of Spades for US TV, 1977; Guest appearances in Toulouse, Turin, Rome, Salzburg Festival and Geneva. *Recordings include:* Carmina Burana, conducted by Ozawa (RCA).

MANDANICI Marcella, b. 15 Apr. 1958, Genoa, Italy. Composer. m. Giuseppe Venturini, 22 Dec. 1978. *Education:* Piano diploma, Brescia, 1979; Harpsichord Diploma 1984, Composition Diploma 1986, Milan; Composition Diploma, Santa Cecilia Academy, Rome 1988. *Career:* Autumn Musicale, Como, 1984; Aspekte, Salzburg, 1986; Nuove Musica Italiana, Rome, 1987-88; Settimana di Musica Contemporanea Desenzano, 1987-88; Musica Rave, Milano, 1985; Spazio Musica, Cagliari, 1988. *Compositions:* Author of many compositions for solo instruments, chamber ensemble and orchestra including: Invenzione a Cinque, for flute, clarinet, viola, cello and piano, 1982; Edipan Steps for piano, 1983; Rugginenti; Senza Testo, for voice, 1987. *Recordings:* Invenzione a Cinque; Senza Testo. *Honours:* Steirischer Herbst Selection, Graz, 1986; IGNM Selection, Koln, 1987 (both with Steps); Antologia Radiotre Selection, Rome, 1988 (with Double Path). *Membership:* Founded, Nuovi Spazi Sonori, Italian Association for Contemporary Music, Artistic Director, 1987-. *Address:* Via Vittorio Emanuele II-60, 25122 Brescia, Italy.

MANDEL Alan Roger, b. 17 July 1935, New York City, USA. Concert Pianist; Professor of Music at The American University; Artistic Director, The Washington Music Ensemble. m. Nancy Siegmeister, 1 June 1963,

divorced 1989. *Education:* BS, 1956, MS, 1957, Juilliard School of Music, New York; Diploma in Piano and Composition, Akademie Mozarteum, Salzburg, Austria, 1962; Diploma, Academia Monteverdi, Bolzano, Italy, 1963. *Debut:* Town Hall, New York City, 1948. *Career:* Over 305 International concert tours in 50 countries; Noted for his repertoire of esoteric and seldom-played masterpieces; Professor of Music The American University, Washington, District of Columbia; Artistic Director, Washington Music Ensemble; Chairman of the Music Division, The American University, Washington DC, 1992. *Compositions:* Composed a Symphony, piano concerto, many piano compositions and songs. *Recordings Include:* The Complete Piano Works of Charles Ives (4 record album); Louis Moreau Gottschalk; Forty Works for the Piano (4 record album); Anthology of American Piano Music, 1790-1970 (3 record album); Three Sides of George Rochberg; Carnival Music; Elie Siegmeister; Sonata No. 4 for Violin and Piano; American Piano (CD); Rags and Riches, CD, Premiere Recordings Inc, New York, 1992. *Publications:* Charles Ives: Study No. 5 for Piano, edited by Alan Mandel, with Preface Performance notes, Editorial notes and Analytical notes, 1988. *Current Management:* Guy Friedman, 37 Robins Crescent, New Rochelle, NY 10801. *Address:* 3113 Northampton St. NW, Washington, DC 20015, USA.

MANDELBAUM (Mayer) Joel, b. 12 Oct 1932, New York, USA. Composer. *Education:* Studied with Walter Piston, Irving Fina and Harold Shapero; BA, Harvard, 1953; PhD Indiana University, 1961. *Career:* Teacher, Queen's College, New York, 1961; Director of the Aaron Copeland School of Music; Fellow, MacDowell Colony 1968. *Compositions include:* Operas: The Man in the Man-Made Moon 1955, The Four Chaplains, 1956 and The Dybbuk, 1971; Light Opera: As you Dislike It, 1973; Orchestra: Concovation overture 1951; Piano Concerto 1953; Sursum Corda 1960; Sinfonia Concertante for oboe, horn, violin, cello and small orchestra, 1962; Memorial for string orchestra, 1965; Trumpet Concerto, 1970; Chamber: Wind Quintet, 1957; 2 string quartets, 1959, 1979; Oboe sonata, 1981; Clarinet sonata, 1983; Piano Sonata, 1958; 4 miniatures in 31-tone temperamane, 1979; Mass for men's voices and organ, 1954; Choruses, songs, musicals and incidental music. *Address:* c/o ASCAP, ASCAP Building, One Lincoln Plaza, NY 10023, USA.

MANDUELL John, (Sir), b. 2 Mar. 1928, Johannesburg. Composer; Educator. m. Renna Kellaway, 1955, 3 sons, 1 daughter. *Education:* Jesus College, Cambridge; Royal Academy of Music. FRAM 1964, FRNCM 1974, FRCM 1980, FRSAMD 1982, Hon. FTCL 1973. *Career includes:* BBC. 1956-68, including chief planner, Music Programme, 1964-68; University of Lancaster, Director of Music 1968-71, Member, Court & Council 1972-77, 1979-; Arts Council, 1973-84; Programme, Cheltenham Festival, 1969-. Also positions with British Council, North West Arts, European Music Year, National Youth Orchestra, etc. Principal, Royal Northern College of Music, 1971-. Engagements & tours as composer, conductor, lecturer in Canada, Europe, Hong Kong, South Africa, USA. *Compositions:* Overture, Sunderland Point, 1969; Diversions for Orchestra, 1970; String Quartet, 1976; Prayers from the Ark, 1981; Double Concerto, 1985. *Contributions to:* Book, The Symphony, ed. Simpson, 1966. *Honours:* CBE, 1982; KBE, 1989. *Memberships include:* Executive Committee, Composers Guild of Great Britain, 1984-; Gulbenkian Foundation Enquiry into Training Musicians; Governor, Chetham's School, 1971-; President, Lakeland Sinfonia, 1972-. Jubilate Choir, 1979-; Director, London Opera Centre, 1971-79, Associated Board, Royal Schools of Music 1971-, Northern Ballet Theatre 1973-, Manchester Palace Theatre Trust 1978-, London Orchestral Concert Board 1980-, Lake District Summer Music 1984-. Honorary member, Royal Society of Musicians, Chopin Society of Warsaw. *Hobbies:* Cricket; Travel; French life, language & literature. *Address:* Royal Northern College of Music, Oxford Road, Manchester M13 9RD, England.

MANGIN Noel, b. 31 Dec. 1932, Wellington, New Zealand. Singer (Bass). *Education:* Marlborough College, Blenheim, New Zealand. *Career:* Sang first as lyric tenor, in such roles as Rodolfo and Cavaradossi; Further study with Domenico Modesti in Paris and Joseph Hislop in London; Debut as bass New Zealand Opera Company 1958; Sadler's Wells London from 1963, notably as Pogner in The Mastersingers, 1968; Hamburg Staatsoper from 1967, as Don Pasquale, Sarastro, Geronimo in Il Matrimonio Segreto, Falstaff, Claggart and Truffaldino in Ariadne auf Naxos; Glyndebourne Festival 1972, as Osmin in Die Entführung; Guest appearances in Buenos Aires, Edinburgh, Paris, Venice and in all other major European and North American opera houses; Has sung for German TV, BBC and Independent TV; Has made films of 14 operas; Teatro Colón Buenos Aires 1987, as Osmin; sang Rocco in Fidelio for the State Opera of South Australia, 1989, the Landgrave in Tannhäuser for the Victoria State Opera (Melbourne). *Recordings:* Excerpts from Die Entführung (Classics for Pleasure); Manon Lescaut; A Village Romeo and Juliet; La Bohème (RCA); Die Winterreise. *Hobbies:* Cooking; Walking; Swimming. *Address:* c/o State Opera of South Australia, GPO Box 1515 Adelaide, SA 5001, Australia.

MANIATES Maria Rika, b. 30 Mar. 1937, Toronto, Canada. Musicologist. *Education:* Associate, Royal Conservatory of Toronto (solo piano), 1958; BA, Music, University of Toronto, 1960; MA, Musicology, 1962, PhD, 1965, University of Columbia. *Career:* Professor of Musicology, Chairman, Department of History and Literature of Music, 1973-78, Faculty of Music, Fellow of Victoria College, University of Toronto; Specialist, Renaissance period and philosophy of music, Director and Performer, Renaissance Music Group, CBC TV Show, Ars Nova Musica, 1969; Visiting Professor of Music, Columbia University, 1976; Associate Dean, Humanities, School of Graduate Studies, University of Toronto, 1990-92; Vice-Dean, School of Graduate Studies, 1992-94. *Publications:* Combinative Techniques in Franco-Flemish Polyphony, 1965; Mannerism in Italian Music and Culture, 1530-1630, 1979; Music and Civilization: Essays in Honor of Paul Henry Long, 1984; The Combinative Chanson: An Anthology, 1989. *Address:* Faculty of Music, University of Toronto, Ontario, Canada M5S 1A1.

MANICKE Hans Detrich, b. 29 Oct 1923, Wurzen, Germany. Composer; Professor. m. Annelies Westen, 7 Nov 1953, 1s, 1d. *Education:* Studied at the Musikakademie, Dresden, 1942-47; PhD, Berlin, 1955. *Career:* Lecturer: Musikakademie, Dresden, 1947-50; Musikhochschule Berlin, 1950- 53; Berliner Kirchenmusikschule, 1957-60; Program Manager, Amerika Haus Berlin, 1956-60; Professor of Composition, Musikhochschule, Detmold, 1960-86. *Compositions:* Orchestral works include: Pass. u. Fuge, Sinfonia brevis, Overture in C, concertos for violin, viola and flute; Chamber music; Organ works; Motets, psalms, Magnificat for choir cappella. *Recordings include:* Trio for piano, Violin and violoncello; Partita Von Gott will ich nicht lassen, for organ. *Publications:* Contributor to: Sas Erbe Deutscher Musik, Der Polyphone Satz. *Honours include:* Carl Maria von Weber Prize, Dresden, 1946; Johann Wenzel Stamitz Prize, Stuttgart, 1983. *Memberships:* Deutscher Komponistenverband; Verband deutscher Musikerzieher und konz. Künstler; Intern H Schütz-Gesellschaft. *Current Management* N Simrock, Hamburg, Merseburger, Berlin, Strube, München. *Address:* Friedrich Pieper-Str 18, D-32760 Detmold, Germany.

MANION Michael Lawrence, b. 6 Aug. 1952, Grand Rapids, Michigan, USA. Composer. *Education:* B.Mus, Oberlin Conservatory, 1977; M.Mus, University of Illinois, 1983; D.Phil (in progress), University of Sussex, 1988; Jenkintown Conservatory, 1966-68; Private Student, Ramon Zupko, 1973; Musikhochschule, Cologne, 1981. *Career:* Percussionist: American Youth Symphony, 1969-70, Grand Rapids Symphony, 1970-74; Freelance, Chicago, San Francisco, Cologne, 1979-82; Freelance Composer, 1980-; Development of Computer Music Software, 1980-86; Performances in West Germany, Holland and USA. *Compositions:* Echoes, Densities, 1974; Orbis Musica, 1975; Combinations, 1976; Wheels, 1976; Meta, 1977; Delta, 1976; Screen, 1979; Islands, 1982; Music for Flute, Bass Clarinet and Tape, 1986. *Publication:* Stockhausen in Den Haag, Editor, 1984. *Honour:* Guest Composer, Institute for Sonology, Utrecht, 1984. *Membership:* American Federation of Musicians. *Address:* 29A St. George Road, Brighton BN2 1ED, East Sussex, England.

MANN Alfred, b. 28 Apr. 1917, Hamburg, Germany. Musicologist; Choral Conductor. m. Carolyn Owens, 23 Aug. 1948. 3 sons. *Education:* Studied with Kurt Thomas, Hans Mahlke, Max Seiffert; Certificate, Berlin Hochschule für Musik, 1937; Milan Conservatory, 1938; Diploma, Curtis Institute of Music, Philadelphia, 1942; Studied with Paul Henry Lang, William J. Mitchell and Erich Hertzmann; MA 1950, PhD 1955, Columbia University. *Career:* Teacher, Berlin Hochschule für Kirchen-und Schulmusik, 1937-38; Scuola Musicale di Milano, 1938-39; Curtis Institute of Music, 1939-42; Rutgers University, 1947-80; Eastman School of Music, Rochester, New York, 1980-; Conductor, Cantata Singers, New York, 1952-59; Bach Choir, Bethlehem, Pennsylvania, 1970-80; Editor, Rutgers Documents of Music, 1951-; American Choral Review, 1962-. *Recordings:* As a choral conductor. *Publications:* Edited J Fux's Gradus ad Parnassum (Die Lehre von Kontrapunkt 1938, 2nd edition 1951, partial English translation as Steps to Parnassus 1943, 2nd edition as The Study of Counterpoint, 1965); The Study of Fugue, 1958, 5th edition 1987; Bethlehem Bach Studies, 1987; Theory and Practice: the Great Composer as Student and Teacher, 1987; edited Modern Music Librarianship, 1989. *Contributions to:* Edited volumes for the Neue-Mozart Ausgabe, 1965, 1988; J J Fux: Sämtliche Werke, 1967, Hallische Händel-Ausgabe, 1979, Neue Schubert-Ausgabe, 1987; Numerous articles in scholarly journals. *Address:* c/o Eastman School of Music, University of Rochester, Rochester, NY 14604, USA.

MANN Robert, b. 19 July 1920, Portland, Oregon, USA. Violinist; Composer; Conductor; Teacher. m. Lucy Rowan. *Education:* Juilliard School of Music with Edouard Dethier, Adolfo Beti, Felix Salmond, Edgar Schenkman, Bernard Wagenar and Stefan Wolpe. *Debut:* Violin recital New York 1941. *Career:* Joined faculty of Juilliard School after wartime service; Founded Juilliard String Quartet 1948: many concert engagements in Europe and USA; Established 1962 as quartet-in-residence under the Whittall Foundation at the Library of Congress, Washington DC; Quartet-in-residence at Michigan State University from 1977; First performances of Quartets by Carter, Kirchner, Schuman, Sessions, Piston, Babbitt, Copland and Foss; First US Quartet to visit USSR, 1961; Repertory of 600 works; Conductor of contemporary music; Has performed and lectured at the Aspen Music Festival; President of the Naumburg Foundation 1971; Chairman of Chamber Muisc panel 1980; Coach to Concord, Tokyo, LaSalle and Emerson String Quartets; Formed Duo with son Nicholas Mann 1980; Visited London with the Juilliard Quartet, 1991. *Recordings include:* Complete Beethoven Quartets and Mozart's Quartets dedicated to Haydn (Columbia); Complete Schoenberg Quartets; Contemporary works. *Address:* c/o Violin Faculty, Juilliard School of Music, Lincoln Plaza, New York, NY 10023, USA.

MANNING Jane, b. 20 Sept 1938, Norwich, England. Singer (Soprano); Lecturer. m. Anthony Payne, 24 Sept 1966. *Education:* LRAM, 1958; GRSM, 1960; ARCM, 1962. *Career:* 20th century music specialist, more than 300 world premieres; Sang in leading concert halls, and festivals worldwide; BBC Broadcasts since 1965, and promanade concerts; Wexford Festival Opera, 1976; New Opera Company, 1978; Scottish Opera, 1979; Brussels Opera, 1981; Garden Venture, 1991, 1993; Founder, Jane's Minstrels, 1988 (ensemble), appearing at the South Bank, Almeida Theatre, Dartington and Aldeburgh Festivals and in Spain and Italy; 1991-92 season with concerts in Oslo, Brussels, Barcelona, London, the USA and Warsaw; Visiting Professor, Mills College, California, 1982-86; Visiting Lecturer, University of York, 1987. *Recordings include:* Complete song cycles of Messiaen; Schoenberg's Pierrot Lunaire, Moses und Aron; Ligeti Aventures-Nouvelles Aventures. *Publications:* Book chapters in How the Voice Works, 1982; New Vocal Repertory-An Introduction, 1986; A Messiaen Companion, 1994; articles in Composer; Music and Musicians; The Independent. *Honours include:* FRAM, 1978; Special Award, Composers Guild of Great Britain, 1973; DUniv, University of York, 1988; OBE, 1990. *Memberships:* VP, Society for Promotion of New Music; Exec Com, Musicians Benevolent Fund; Chairman, Nettlefold Festival Trust; Music Advisory Panel, Arts Council. *Hobbies:* Cinema; Ornithology; Philosophy. *Address:* 2 Wilton Square, London N1 3DL, England.

MANNING Peter, b. 17 July 1956, Manchester, England. Violinist. *Education:* Chathams School 1969-73; Royal Northern College of Music; Indiana University, USA 1973-81. *Career:* Solo appearances with Philharmonia Orchestra, Halle Orchestre, City of Birmingham Symphony; Co- leader, London Philharmonic Orchestra; Professor, Royal Northern College of Music; Founder member of Britten Quartet, debut concert at the Wigmore Hall, 1987; Quartet in Residence at the Dartington Summer School 1987, with quartets by Schnittke; Season 1988-89 in the Genius of Prokofiev series at Blackheath and BBC Lunchtime Series at St John's Smith Square; South Bank appearances with the Schoenberg/Handel Quartet Concerto conducted by Neville Marriner concerts with the Hermann Prey Schubertiade and collaborations with the Alban Berg Quartet in the Beethoven Plus series; Tour of South America 1988, followed by Scandinavian debut; Season 1989-90 with debut tours of Holland, Germany, Spain, Austria and Finland; Tours from 1990 to the Far East, Malta, Sweden and Norway: Schoenberg/Handel Concerto with the Gothenburg Symphony; Festival appearances at Brighton, the City of London, Greenwich, Canterbury, Harrogate, Chester, Spitalfields and Aldeburgh; Collaborations with John Ogdon, Imogen Cooper, Thea King and Lynn Harrell; Formerly resident quartet at Liverpool University; Teaching role at Lake District Summer Music 1989; Universities of Bristol, Hong Kong 1990. *Recordings:* Beethoven Op 130 and Schnittke Quartet no 3 (LDR); Vaughan Williams On Wenlock Edge and Ravel Quartet (EMI); Britten, Prokofiev, Tippett, Elgar and Walton Quartets (Collins Classics); Exclusive contract with EMI from 1991. *Address:* c/o Ingpen and Williams Ltd, 14 Kensington Court, London W8 5DN. England.

MANNING Robert, b. 19 Jan. 1953, Exeter, England. Lecturer in Music; Musicologist; Keyboard Player. *Education:* B.Mus., Honours, Nottingham University; PhD Birmingham University, (Purcell's Anthems: an Analytical Study of the Music and its context), 1979; Revision of Purcell Society Volumes 28 and 29 (Anthems) - unpublished; Dartington College of Arts, South Devon, 1969-71; Nottingham University, 1971-74; Birmingham University, 1974-77. *Career:* Music Assistant, BBC Radio 3, 1977-88; Freelance Lecturer, Music, Royal College of Music, City University; Birkbeck College, University of London Centre for Extra-Mural Studies, Open University, ILEA, WEA, 1980-; Freelance Organist/Continuo Work; (ARCO 1973); Director of Music, Highgate URC, 1989-; Professor of Musicianship and Music History, Royal College of Music, 1992-. *Contributions to:* Adult Education; Music & Letters; Opera; Soundings; Teaching Adults. *Honours:* Nottingham University Exhibition, 1973; Hon. RCM. 1991. *Membership:* Life Member, Royal Musical Association. *Hobbies:* Cricket; Railways. *Address:* 6 Tetherdown, Muswell Hill, London N10 1NB, England.

MANNINO Franco, b. 25 Apr. 1924, Palermo, Italy. Conductor; Composer; Pianist. *Education:* Piano with R.Silvestri, Composition with V.Mortari, Academy of Santa Cecilia, Rome; Graduated in Piano, 1940, Composition, 1947. *Debut:* As Composer, 1932; As Pianist, 1940; As Conductor, 1955. *Career includes:* 1st American tour as Pianist, 1946, as Conductor with Maggio Musicale Fiorentino, 1957; Artistic Director, 1969, 1970, Artistic Advisor, 1974, Teatro San Carlo, Naples; Numerous Guest Conductor appearances including with Leningrad Orchestra, Orchestras of Peking and Shanghai, major US orchestras, etc; Many years as Principal Guest Conductor, Opera of Monte Carlo; Principal Conductor, Artistic Advisor, 1982-86, Principal Conductor, 1986-89; National Arts Centre Orchestra, Ottawa; Numerous US tours; Toured Hong Kong and Japan with National Arts Centre Orchestra, 1985; His works performed by many leading orchestras. *Compositions:* Over 320 works including opera, ballet, oratorios, symphonies, chamber music, music for theatre; Music for over 100 films of directors such as Huston, Visconti, Moguy. *Recordings:* Conductor of own works and works of Bach, Mendelssohn, Mozart, Liszt, Wagner, Schubert, Schumann, Puccini, Franck, Chopin, Verdi, Scarlatti, for Conevox, Melodya (USSR), Curci, CBC, RCA, Fontana, Philips and other labels; Artistic Director, Visconti Record Album, CBS-Sony. *Honours:* Recipient of numerous awards and other honours. *Address:* Via Citta di Castello 14, 00191 Rome, Italy.

MANNION Rosa, b. 1960, Liverpool, England. Singer (Soprano). *Education:* Studied at the Royal Scottish Academy. *Career:* Has sung with Scottish Opera as Gilda, Adina, Pamina, Dorinda (Handel's Orlando), Sophie in Werther and Susanna (1989); English National Opera from 1987 as Sophie in Der Rosenkavalier, Anna in the world premiere of Holloway's Clarissa, Cordelia in King Lear, Oscar, Atalanta (Xerxes) and Nannetta; Has sung Magnolia in Show Boat with Opera North and Donizetti's Lucia for Opera Northern Ireland; Concert appearances with the Manchester Camerata, the Scottish Chamber and National Orchestraas, the City of London Sinfonia and the London Mozart Players; Conductors include Raymond Leppard, Richard Hickox and Jane Glover; Neeme Järvi at the Edinburgh Festival; Glyndebourne Festival debut 1987, as Constanze; Season 1992 as Atalanta at ENO, Dorabella under John Eliot Gardiner at Amsterdam and Lisbon, Gilda for Opera North. *Recordings include:* Mozart's Ascanio in Alba, with Musique en Sorbonne; Così fan Tutte (DGG). *Honours include:* Winner, Scottish Opera International Singing Competition and the John Scott Award, Scottish Opera. *Address:* c/o Lies Askonas Ltd., 186 Drury Lane, London WC2B 5RY, England.

MANNOV Johannes, b. 1965, Copenhagen, Denmark. Singer (Baritone). *Education:* Studied at the Conservatoires of Freiburg and Karlsruhe. *Career:* Sang with the boys' choir Kobenhauns-Drengekor before adult study; Has sung with the Kassel Opera from 1987 as Mozart's Papageno, Masetto and Figaro; Concert performances under such conductors as Helmuth Rilling, Luigi Nono, George Malcolm, Frans Bruggen, Segerstram and Hans Martin Schneidt; Has performed Mozart's Requiem in Bremen, the Christmas Oratorio in Cologne and Frankfurt and an Italian tour with Bach's St John Passion, 1991-92; Britten's War Requiem in Frankfurt; Sang Mozart's Figaro for Opera Northern Ireland, 1991. *Honours include:* Pizewinner, s'Hertogenbosch Competition, 1986, Helsinki Competition, 1989. *Address:* Anglo Swiss Ltd, 3 Primrose Mews, 1a Sharpeshall Street, London NW1 8YW, England.

MANSHARDT Thomas, b. 23 Mar. 1927, Wai, India. Concert Pianist. *Education:* Conservatory of Lausanne, Switzerland; Ecole Normale, Paris, France; Academia Chigiana, Siena; Studied with Alfred Cortot. *Debut:* Vienna, 1954; Bonn, 1954; London, 1956; Los Angeles, USA, 1964; New York City, 1965. *Career:* Concert Tours in Germany, India, Pakistan, USA; Numerous appearances as Soloist with orchestras; Numerous Radio and Television appearances; Professor of Music, University of Regina, Canada, 1966-.*Publications:* Aspects of Alfred Cortot, 1994; CD: A Cortot's Last Pupil. *Address:* Apt. 1301, 1830 College Avenue, Regina, Saskatchewan, Canada S4P 1C2.

MANSON Anne, b. 1960, USA. Conductor. *Education:* Studied at Harvard University, Kings's College London and at the Royal College of Music with Norman del Mar and James Lockhart. *Career:* As Music Director of Mecklenburgh Opera has conducted The Emperor or Atlantis by Viktor Ullmann, Die Weisse Rose (Udo Zimmermann), and Manekiny (Zbigniew Rudzinski); The Soldier's Tale at the Almeida Theatre London and engagements for the British premiere of The Trojan Woman and tours to Austria and Czechoslovakia; Conducted the Endymion Ensemble in the premiere of Nicola LeFanu's Blood Wedding for the Women's Playhouse Trust London, 1992 and the British premiere of Patrified by Juraj Benes; La Monnaie Brussels 1993 in a triple bill of works by Monteverdi and Judith Weir; Conducted John Hawkin's Echoes, at the Riverside Studios for the Covent Garden Project, 1991, and Opera 80 in Don Pasquale and Don Giovanni; Other repertoire includes Le nozze di Figaro, Die Zauberflöte, Albert Herring, Alcina and Suor Angelica; Assistant to Claudio Abbado at the 1992 Salzburg Festival (From the House of the Dead) and in Lohengrin (Vienna Staatsoper); Concerts with the Wiener Kammerorchester; Fellow in Conducting at the Royal Northern College of Music. *Honours include:* Marshall Scholarship; Prizes at the RCM and RNCM. *Address:* c/o Ingpen & Williams Ltd, 14 Kensington Court, London W8 5DN, England.

MANSOURI Lofti, b. 15 June 1929, Teheran, Iran. Administrator; Stage Director. *Education:* Graduate, UCLA, 1953; Opera training from Lotte Lehmann and Herbert Graf. *Debut:* Produced Tosca at Los Angeles, 1959. *Career:* Staff stage director at Zurich, 1960-64; Geneva, 1965- 74 (work included productions of Der Rosenkavalier and Die Entführung); General Director, Canadian Opera Company at Toronto 1976-88: productions during his tenure included Hamlet by Thomas, Anna Bolena, Lady Macbeth of the Mtsensk District, Wozzeck, Otello, Simon Boccanegra, Falstaff, Jenůfa and Tristan und Isolde; Production of Massenet's Esclarmonde seen at the Metropolitan 1976, Covent Garden 1983; Other work includes Les Huguenots for Australian Opera, The Merry Widow at Chicago, 1981 Die Fledermaus at San Francisco (1990) and Elektra at Toronto (1991); General Director of San Francisco Opera from 1988. *Address:* General Director, San Francisco Opera, War Memorial Opera House, CA 94102 USA.

MANTAS Santiago, b. 14 May 1949, London, England. Concert Pianist; Composer. *Education:* Henry Compton School; Trinity College of Music, 1967-71; GTCL; FTCL (Piano); Staatliche Hochschule für Musik, Cologne, 1971-72; Vienna Academy, 1973-75. *Debut:* Vienna, 1976; Wigmore Hall, London, 1983. *Career:* Recital and concerto appearances, BBC Radio 3, 1982- . *Compositions:* The Piano Album, recorded on Studio G Music Library Services. *Honours:* Maud Warrender Prize, 1969; Maud Seton Prize, 1970; (Hon) FTCL 1991. *Hobbies:* Yoga; Swimming; Table tennis. *Current Management:* Manygate Management, 13 Cotswold Mews, 12/16 Battersea High Street, London SW11 3JE, England. *Address:* 18 Furness Road, London SW6 2LH, England.

MANTEL Gerhard Friedrich, b. 31 Dec. 1930, Karlsruhe, Germany. Concert Cellist. m. Renate Mantel, 1 son. *Education:* Music Academies in Mannheim and Paris; Musikhochschule Saarbrücken; Studied with August Eichhorn and Pierre Fournier. *Career:* Solo cellist, Bergen Symphony, Norway; WDR Orchestra, Cologne; Worldwide recital tours, mainly with pianist Erika Friesar; Professor, Frankfurt Musikhochschule, 1973-; Assistant Director 1975-. *Recordings:* With Erika Friesar, Sonatas by Mendelssohn, Strauss, Grieg. *Publications:* Cello Technik 1973. *Memberships:* European String Teachers Association. *Honour:* Kulturpreis der Stadt Karlsruhe, 1955. *Hobbies:* Reading; Family. *Address:* 6236 Eschborn 2, Feldbergstrasse 44, Germany.

MANTLE Neil Christopher, b. 16 Mar. 1951, Essex, England. Conductor. m. Inga Wellesley, 17 Oct. 1980,

1 son, 1 daughter. *Education:* Royal Academy of Music, London, 1969-70; Royal Scottish Academy of Music, 1970-73. *Career:* Conducting with Scottish Sinfonia, 1970-, Edinburgh Opera Company, 1975-81, Sinfonia Opera, 1983-84; Guest Conductor, Scottish National Orchestra, 1984-; Guest Conductor, BBC Scottish Symphony Orchestra, 1986-. *Honours:* Hugh S. Robertson Conducting Prize, Royal Scottish Academy of Music, 1973; 2nd prize, Leeds Conductors Competition, 1986. *Membership:* Elgar Society. *Hobbies:* Old (preferably black-and-white) films; Collecting old records. *Current Management:* Anglo-Swiss Artists Management, London, England. *Address:* c/o Anglo-Swiss Management, PO Box 719, London N6 5UX, England.

MANUGUERRA Matteo, b. 5 Oct. 1924, Tunis, Tunisia. Singer (Baritone). *Education:* Studied in Buenos Aires, Argentina, with Umberto Landi. *Debut:* As tenor in Mozart's Requiem. *Career:* Sang in Europe from 1962, debut at Lyon as Valentin in Faust; Paris Opéra from 1965, as Rigoletto, Escamillo, Germont and Enrico in Lucia di Lammermoor; US debut Seattle 1968, as Gerard in Andrea Chénier; Metropolitan Opera debut 1971, as Enrico: returned to New York 1983 as Barnaba in La Gioconda, and Carlo in La Forza del Destino and Amonasro; Verona Arena 1980-85; Frankfurt 1986, in a concert performance of La Gioconda; Guest appearances Vienna, Hamburg, London, Geneva, Athens and Santiago; sang Carlos in La Forza del Destino at Hanover, 1987; Naples 1989, as Renato in Un ballo in Maschera; Sang Rigoletto at Covent Garden, 1991 and the Metropolitan and Santiago, 1992. *Recordings:* Tosca; Le Villi; Nabucco; La Bohème; Il Barbiere di Siviglia; Werther; I Puritani; La Battaglia di Legnano; Stiffelio; Il Trovatore; Francesca da Rimini. Labels include HMV, Deutsche Grammophon, RCA and Philips. *Address:* c/o Patricia Greenan, 19B Belsize Park, London NW3 4DU, England.

MANVILLE Stewart Roebling, b. 15 Jan. 1927, White Plains, New York, USA. Archivist; Curator. m. Ella Viola Grainger, 19 Jan. 1972. *Education:* BS, Columbia University, 1962; Private Study, Piano, Violin, Voice; Hunter College Opera Workshop; Akademie für Musik, Vienna; Reinhardt Seminar. *Career:* Assistant Stage Director, Opera Companies, Graz, Vienna, and Nürnberg and in Festivals at Passau, Salzburg, 1950's; Curator, Percy Grainger's home. *Compositions:* Archivist, Grainger Works, 1962-. *Contributions to:* Grainger Journal; Opera News; Opera Annual; Opera. *Memberships:* International Percy Grainger Society, Archivist, Corresponding Secretary. *Hobbies:* Genealogy; Hiking. *Address:* Percy Grainger Library, 7 Cromwell Place, White Plains, NY 10601-5005, USA.

MANZ André, b. 15 Dec. 1942, Chur, Switzerland. Musician (Organ, Piano, Harpsichord); Teacher. m. Irene Pomey. *Education:* Music Acad Zurich; Conserv Winterthur; Hochschule für Musik, Cologne, German Federal Republic; Masters degree, Organ & Piano; Concert Dip, Organ. *Debut:* 1964. *Career:* Organ Recitals, Switzerland, Germany, Italy, Denmark, Japan, Poland, USA, Canada, Spain, Austria; Various radio series; Piano-duet with Irene Manz-Pomey. *Composition:* Play b-a-c-h (6 organists & assistants) 1971. *Recordings include:* Swiss Baroque Soloists; Several organ solo recordings including the complete organ music by Franz Liszt. *Contributions to:* Musical journals. *Honours:* Recipient of musical prizes and scholarships. *Memberships:* Schweizer Tonkunstlerverein (STV); Schweizer Musikpadagogischer Verband (SMPV); President of Thurgau Organists Assoc; Rotary. *Hobbies:* Collecting records of great pianists; Long-distance running. *Address:* Brunnenfeldstrasse 11, CH-8580 Amriswil, Switzerland.

MANZ Wolfgang, b. 6 Aug. 1960, Düsseldorf, Germany. Pianist. m. Julia Goldstein, 2 Aug. 1985, 1 son, 1 daughter. *Education:* Studied with Prof. Drahomir Toman, Prague and Prof. Karlheinz Kaemmerling at High School of Music, Hannover. *Career:* Performed at

Promenade Concerts in London, England with BBC Symphony Orchestra, 1984; Gilels Memorial Concert in Dusseldorf, 1986; Recital at Karajan Foundation in Paris, 1987 and Concert Tours, Recitals, Broadcasts and Concerto performances all over Europe; Concert tours since 1988 in Japan. *Recordings:* Beethoven Triple Concerto with English Chamber Orchestra and Saraste, Dohnányi Piano Quintet op 1 with Gabrieli String Quartet (Chandos Records); Solo recital (Europa Records); Chopin Studies (Pavanne Records). *Honours:* First Prize, Mendelssohn Competition, Berlin, 1981; Second Prize, Queen Elisabeth Competition, Brussels, 1983; Second Prize, Leeds Piano Competition, 1981; Van Cliburn International Piano Competition, Texas, USA, Jury Discretionary Award, 1989 . *Memberships:* Chopin Society, Hannover; Mozart Society Dortmund, since 1989. *Current Management:* c/o J Hannemann, Husumer Str. 16, D-2000 Hamburg, Germany. *Address:* Pasteurallee 55, D-3000 Hannover 51, Germany.

MANZINO Leonardo, b. 24 Feb 1962, Montevideo, Uruguay. Pianist; Musicologist. *Education:* Piano Diploma, Kolischer Conservatory, Montevideo, 1978; Licentiate in Musicology, University of Uruguay, 1986; Master of Music in Piano Performance, 1988, PhD, Musicology-Latin American Music, The Catholic University of America, 1993. *Debut:* Sala Martins Pena, Brasilia, 1983. *Career:* International Summer Music Festivals of Brasilia, 1983-84; Uruguayan Music Students Association, 1983; Jeunesses Musicales of Uruguay Series, 1984-85; Argentine Music Foundation Series, 1986; Professor, School of Music, University of Uruguay, 1993. *Publication:* Composers of the Americas, vol 20, editor, 1991; Uruguayan Music in the 1892 Celebrations for the IV Centenary of the Encounter of Two Worlds, Latin American Music Review, 1993. *Memberships:* Jeunesses Musicales - Executive Committee Member for Uruguay; American Musicological Society. *Honours:* Winner, Uruguayan Music Students' Piano Competition, 1983; Winner, Jeunesses Musicales of Uruguay Piano Competition, 1984. *Hobbies:* Swimming; Gardening; Reading. *Address:* Brito del Pino 1423, Montevideo 11600, Uruguay.

MANZONE Jacques-Francis, b. 4 June 1944, Cannes, France. Violinist; Professor of Music. *Education:* Studied at the Nice Conservatoire with Henri Mazioux; Paris Conservatoire with Roland Charmy and Jacques Fevrier; Further study with Eugène Bigot and Henryk Szeryng. *Career:* Soloist with the French Radio Orchestra and at the Société des Concerts du Conservatoire; Co-founded Ensemble Instrumental de France (Paris) 1966; Soloist with the Orchestra of Paris, founded by Charles Munch 1967; Professor at the Nice Conservatoire 1977 and soloist with the Nice Philharmonic Orchestra; Professor of Chamber Music at the Nice International Summer Academy; Musical Director of the Chamber Orchestra of Nice 1984; Plays a Maggini violin. *Address:* Conservatoire Regional de Musique, 7 Avenue des Fleurs, 06000 Nice, France.

MANZONI Giacomo, b. 26 Sept. 1932, Milan, Italy. Composer; Teacher. m. Eugenia Tretti, 1960, 1 son. *Education:* Liceo Mus. Laudamo, Messina and Cons. Verdi, Milan (Composition); Foreign Languages, Università Bocconi, Milan; Piano Diploma, Milan. *Career:* Teacher of Composition: Conserv. Martini, Bologna, 1965-68, 1969-74; Conserv. Verdi, Milan, 1962-64, 1968-69, 1974-91, Scuola di musica, Fiesole, 1988-. Composer, International Festivals (Amsterdam, Berlin, Osaka, Prague, Warsaw, Venice). *Compositions:* Operas: La Sentenza (Bergamo) 1960; Atomtod (Milan, Piccola Scala) 1965; Per Massimiliano Robespierre (Bologna) 1975; Doktor Faustus, by Thomas Mann (Scala, Milan) 1989; Orchestral Works: Insiemi, 1967; Masse: omaggio a E. Varèse, for piano and orchestra, 1977; Modulor, 1979; Ode 1982; Scene Sinfoniche per il Dr. Faustus 1984; Dedica, for flute, bass, orchestra and choir ad lib. 1988. Chorus and Orchestra: 5 Vicariote 1958; Ombre (dedicated to the memory of Che Guevara) 1968; Parole da Beckett 1971; Hölderlin (frammento) 1972 Il deserto cresce (Nietzsche), 1992. Chamber

Music: Musica notturna, for 7 instruments, 1966; Quadruplum for 4 brass instruments, 1968; Spiel for 11 strings, 1969; String Quartet 1971; Percorso GG, for clarinet and tape, 1979; D'improvviso, for percussion, 1981; Klavieralbum 1956; Incontro, for violin and String Quartet, 1983; Opus 50 (Daunium), for 11 instruments, 1984. *Recordings:* Masse: omaggio a E. Varèse; Parole da Beckett; Ode; Dedica; Quadruplum. *Publications:* Guida all'ascolto della musica sinfonica, 1967; A. Schönberg - L'uomo, l'opera, i testi musicati, 1975; Per M. Robespierre - Testo e materiali per le scene musicali (with L. Pestalozza and V. Puecher) 1975; Scritti, 1991. *Contributions to:* Music Critic for l'Unità, 1958-66; Contributions to many Italian and foreign periodicals; Translation of many works by T. W. Adorno and A. Schönberg (from German and English into Italian). *Address:* Viale Papiniano 31, 20123 Milan, Italy.

MARAN George, b. 25 July 1926, Massachusetts, USA. Singer (Tenor). *Education:* Studied at Harvard University and New York. *Career:* Sang in sacred music at the Salzburg Festival, 1951-66; European tour 1956 with the Salzburg Festival Company in Mozart's La Finta Semplice, directed by Bernhard Paumgartner; Sang at the Darmstadt Opera 1956-94, notably in Titus by Mozart-Tod in Venedig by Brittain 1983; Appearances at the Aldeburgh Festival, 1959-60, in The Rape of Lucretia and in the premiere of A Midsummer Night's Dream; Concert and oratorio engagements in Germany, England and Austria, all European Countries. *Recordings include:* La Finta Semplice; Messiah, conducted by Adrian Boult and Elijah under Josef Krips. *Memberships:* Honorary Member, The Staatstheater, Darmstadt *Address:* c/o Staatstheater, Postfach 111432, 64283 Darmstadt, Germany.

MARANGONI Bruno, b. 13 Apr 1935, Rovigo, Italy. Singer (Bass). *Education:* Studied with Campogalliani and in Venice. *Debut:* Venice 1960, as Anselmo in La Molinarelli by Puccinni. *Career:* Many appearances at the Teatro Fenice Venice, Teatro San Carlo Naples, Teatro Massimo Palermo and in Turin, Triste and the Caracalla Baths, Rome; Verona Reana, 1973, 1978, 1983-84; Guest engagements at Aix-en-Provence, Lisbon, Barcelona and Chicago; Other roles have included Geronimo in Il Matrimonio Segreto, Mozart's Leporello, Osmin and Sarastro, Marcel in Les Huguenots, Bartolo in Paisiello's Il Barbiere di Siviglia, Uberto in Pergolesi's La Serva Padrona, Alvise La Gioconda and Wagner's Daland, Pogner and Hunding; Television appearances in La Pietra del Paragone (as Asdrubal), L'Elisir d'Amore, Don Carlos, Il Trovatore, Guillaume Tell and Aida. *Address:* c/o Arena di Verona, Piazza Bra 28, 37121 Verona, Italy.

MARBE Myriam-Lucia, b. 9 Apr 1931, Bucharest, Rumania. Composer. m. Aristide Poulopol, 14 Feb. 1963, 1 daughter. *Education:* Piano studies with Angela Marbe; Graduate, Music Conservatory of Bucharest; Master's degree in progress. *Career:* Musical Editor, Bucharest Film Studio, 1953-54; Tutor, 1954-60, Assistant, 1960-66, Lecturer, 1966-72, Associate Professor, 1972-; Composer, 1988-, Ciprian Porumbescu Academy of Music, Bucharest. Appearances at concerts and conferences; Radio and TV broadcasts. *Compositions include:* Recorded: Incantatio, clarinet solo; Ritual for the Thirst of the Earth for choir and percussion; Jocus secundus; Serenata for chamber orchestra; Saxophone concerto; Trommelbass, string trio; Harpsichord concerto; Le temps retrouvé; La parabole du grenier I for piano, harpsichord and celesta; Cyclus I for flute, guitar and percussion; Chiuituri for children's choir, flute and percussion; Tapes: Sonata for 2 violas; ...En souvenir for choir and orchestra; Quatuor for strings I and II; Concerto for viola; Sonata per due for flute and viola, 1985; Des-Cântec, for wind quintet, 1985; An die Sonne, for voice, 1986; Lui Nau, Streichquartett Nr.3, radio tape, 1988; Ur-Ariadne-Sinfonie Nr. 1, for mezzosopran, saxaphone and orchestra, 1988; Dialogi-Nicht nur ein Bilderbuch für Christian Morgenstern, for Bass clarinet, piano, speaker ad libitum with schlaginstrumenten, 1989; Diapente, for five violins, 1990; Fra Angelico-Chagall-Voronet-

Reguiem, 1990; La Parabole du grenier I for piano, harpsichord and celesta, 1975-79, Quatuor for strings I, 1981; E-Y-Thé, for clarinet and violin, 1990; Preuitorul, Der Schätzer, 1990; Stabat mater, for 12 voices and ensemble, 1991. *Address:* Str Gri-Alexandrescu nr 32, 71128 Bucharest, Romania.

MARCHAND Jacques, b. 1 Dec 1948, Quebec, Canada. *Education:* BAC in Composition, McGill University, Montreal; BAC in Piano, Vincent D'Indy Music School, Montreal. *Career:* Nearer the Stars, Ballet for Violin Solo (Colorado Ballet Comapny), 1981; Founder, Orchestre Symphonique Regional d'Abitibi-Temiscamingue, 1986. *Compositions:* Nearer the Stars, 1981; Suite Pour Orchestre, 1987; Fantaisie Pour Orchestre, 1989; Impromptu Pour Piano et Orchestre, 1993; Un Dimanche À Poznan (Poème Symphonique), 1993. *Recordings include:* Cassett: Jacques Marchand Compositeur, 1988. *Honours:* Citoyen d'Honneur de la Societe Nationale des Quebecois, 1992; Hommage de la Chambre de Commerce de Rouyn-Noranda, 1993. *Memberships:* SOCAN; SODRAC; AOC. *Address:* 22, 8 Rue Rouyn-Noranda, Quebec J9X 2A4, Canada.

MARCIL Monique, b. 28 Apr. 1934, Montreal, Canada. Pianist. *Education:* Studied piano, Conservatoire de Montréal; Private lessons, Professor Bruno Seidlhofer, Vienna Academy of Music, 1954; Worked under direction of Beveridge Webster, professor at Juilliard School, New York, USA, 1956-60; Summer, Aspen School of Music, Colorado, USA, 1956. *Career:* Concerts, recitals; Broadcasts, television performances, Canada; Teacher, Conservatoire de Montréal, 1963-69; Founding member 1963, General Director 1965-, Montreal International Music Competition. *Honour:* 1st prize, Consevatoire de Montreal, aged 16; Special Prize of the Concert Society of the Jewish People's Schools and Peretz Schools, for outstanding Contribution to the Performing Arts; Member of the Order of Canada, 1988. *Address:* 106 Dulwich Avenue, St-Lambert, P.Q., Canada J4P 2Y7.

MARCO Guy Anthony, b. 4 Oct. 1927, New York City, USA. Musicologist; Librarian; University Professor. m. Karen Csontos, 1 son. *Education:* B.Mus., American Conservatory of Music, Chicago, 1951; MA, musicology, 1952, MA, Library Science, 1955, PhD Musicology, 1956, University of Chicago. *Career:* Teacher, Music History & Theory, Chicago Musical College and Chicago City College; Dean, Teacher of Music Bibliography, School of Library Science, Kent State University, Ohio; Chief, General Reference and Bibliography, US Library of Congress; Director, Division of Library Science, San Jose State University, San Jose; Chief of Library Activities, US Army, Fort Dix, New Jersey; Adjunct Professor, Rosary College, River Forest, Illinois. *Publications include:* The Earliest Music Printers of Continental Europe, 1962; The Art of Counterpoint (with Claude Palisca), 1968; Opera: A Research and Information Guide, 1984; Information on Music, 1, 1975, 2 1977, 3, 1984; Editor, Garland Composer Resource Manuals, 1981- (30 volumes through 1989). *Contributions to:* Numerous professional journals. *Memberships:* Numerous American and International Professional Associations. *Hobby:* Travel. *Address:* 3450 Lake Shore Drive 2501, Chicago, IL 60657, USA.

MARCUS Ada Belle Gross, b. 8 July 1929, Chicago, Illinois, USA. Composer; Pianist. m. Isadore Marcus, 2 daughters. *Education:* DePaul University Music School, Chicago, 1939-44; studied Composition, American Conservatory of Music, 1954, Roosevelt University, 1959 and with various masters. *Career:* Concerts, midwest, 1947-; Soloist with major symphonies; Performances of own compositions throughout USA and on TV, 1954-88; Former Faculty, Chicago Conservatory College; Several of her compositions were chosen for exhibition at the 1974 International Society for Contemporary Music World Days, Rotterdam, Holland. *Compositions include:* Snow, chamber opera; Shakespearean Duo; Song for Flute, 1970; Symphony of the Spheres; Zen; Outward Bound; Textures for piano, flute and strings; Song Cycles; numerous piano pieces

and songs; Highlights Suite, composed 1986; World Premiere, Brevities, with Chicago Chamber Orchestra, 1989; Sonata for violin and piano, presented New Music Chicago Festival, 1992; Composed: Commission from Chicagoo Chamber Orchestra, Overture to Unity, Sonata for strings for string orchestra, 1990. *Publications:* International Encyclopedia of Women Composers, current issue; Contemporary Concert Music by Women, A Directory of the Composers and their Works, current issue. *Honour:* ASCAP (American Society of Composers Award Publishers, three special awards, 1991, 1992, 1993. *Current Management:* Independent Concert Management. *Address:* 9374 Landings Lane, Des Plaines, IL 60016, USA.

MARCUSSEN Kjell, b. 19 May 1952, Arendal, Norway. Composer. *Education:* Studied at the Agder Music Conservatorium; Diploma in Guitar and Composition, Guildhall Schol of Music, London, studied with Robert Saxton. *Debut:* Cardiff Festival of Music, 1982. *Compositions:* Cantatas; Orchestral works; Guitar Concerto; Solo and Chamber works. *Recordings include:* NRK Broadcasting. *Publications:* Partita Jubilante (brass), 1993; Guitar Sonata No 1, 1988; Woodcut, for flute, violin and cello, 1988. *Memberships:* Norwegian Composers' Society. *Address:* Skoleveien 6, 1380 Heggedal, Norway.

MARDER Samuel, b. 11 Dec 1930, Czernowitz, Romania. Violinist. m. 1959. *Education:* BMus 1955, MMus, EdM, Manhattan School of Music, NY; Studied with Hubert Aumere, Ralphael Bronstein, Louis Persinger, Nathan Milstein. *Debut:* Lincoln Centre, New York, 1983. *Career:* First performance of Ben Haim Sonata in London and Vienna; First Perforamnce of Earnest Lubin Sonata on radio in WNYC and in New York; Radio performances in Madrid, Helsinki, La Paz, and other cities; Televised concerts in Seoul, Korea, 1988; Concert tours throughout USA, Canada, Israel, South America, Spain, Finland, Bulgaria and South Korea. *Honours include:* Hon Award from Mayor, City of Arequipa, Peru, 1980; First Place, Violin Competition, Czernowitz, Soviet, 1940. *Memberships:* President, Intern Artists Alliance; Director, Riverdale Music Society. *Hobbies:* Writing; Philosophy. *Address:* c/o International Artists Alliance Inc, PO Box 3242, Rockefeller Station, NY 10185, USA.

MAREZ OYENS Tera de, b. 5 Aug. 1932, Velsen, Netherlands. Composer. m. M. S. Arnoni, 8 Mar. 1975, (deceased), 2 sons, 2 daughters. *Education:* Diploma, Conservatorium Amsterdam, 1953; Studied composition with Hans Henkemans, conducting with Frits Kox, electronic music University of Utrecht. *Career:* Composer of about 200 works (orchestral, chamber music, choral, electronic music), most performed in Netherlands, England, Federal Republic of Germany, Israel, USA; Conductor, choirs and orchestras; Performances as pianist; Own music programmes and serial broadcast on radio; Docent in Composition and Contemporary Music, Conservatorium Zwolle, till 1988; Chamber music: Structures and dance for violin and orchestra, Litany of the Victims of War, 1985; for orchestra symmetrical memories, 1988; for cello and orchestra Confrontations for piano and orchestra, 1990, Linzer concert, 1991, for accordion and orchestra Nam San for Marimbasolo, 1993. *Published Compositions include:* Introduzione, orchestra; String quartet; Concertine for piano and orchestra, In Exile; Shoshadre, for string orchestra; The Odyssee of Mr Goodevil for choir, soloists and orchestra, Confrontations, Concerto for piano and orchestra. *Publications:* Werken met Moderne Klanken, 1978; Edited songbooks for children. *Contributions to:* Articles about electronic music, music education, notation, women and music, Dutch magazines, International Society of Music Education publications. *Honours:* 1st prize for Vignettes, Dublin 1990. *Hobbies:* Music; Travel; Reading. *Address:* Celebeslaan 13, 1217 GT Hilversum, Netherlands.

MARGGRAF Wolfgang, b. 2 Dec. 1933, Leipzig, Germany. Musicologist. m. Anne-Marie Lorz, 4 Jan. 1975, 2 sons. *Education:* Studied at Universities of

Leipzig and Jena, 1952-57; PhD, Leipzig, 1964.*Career:* Professor 1987; Rector Musikhochschule Weimar, 1990-93. *Publications:* Franz Schubert, 1967, 2nd edition, 1978; Giacomo Puccini, 1977; Giuseppe Verdi, 1982; Franz Liszt, Schriften zur Tonkunst, 1980; Franz Liszt in Weimar, 1985; Bach in Leipzig, 1985. *Memberships:* The Liszt Society, Weimar, 1984-; Gesellschaft für Musikforschung 1991-. *Address:* Barfüßerstr. 12, Eisenach, Germany.

MARGISON Richard Charles, b. 16 July 1953, Victoria, BC, Canada. Operatic Tenor. m. Valerie Mary Kuinka, 12 Aug 1989. *Education:* University of Victoria, Victoria Conservatory of Music: AVCM; Banff School of Fine Arts; Voice Teacher: Selena James; Coaches Leopold Simoneau, Frances Adaskin. *Debut:* The Bartered Bride with the Pacific Opera Company, Victoria BC. *Career:* Has performed with many orchestras, including: Vancouver 1989, Tornoto 1989, Montreal 1990, London Philharmonic 1991, Chicago 1991, Victoria 1991. Regular appeared with Opera Companies including: English National Opera, 1989 and 1991 as Verdi's Riccardo and as Vakula in Rimsky's Christmas Eve, Montreal Opera 1991, Canadian Opera Company, 1991, Santiago Opera (Teatro Municipal) 1991, Den Norske Opera (Norway) 1991, Calgary Opera 1991 as Nadir in Les Pecheurs de Perles; Other roles include Mozart's Ferrando (Ottawa) and Tito, Pinkerton (Edmonton), Fenton in Falstaff, Faust (at Houston), Don Carlos (San Francisco, 1992), Nemorino, Edgardo, Alfredo, Rodolfo and Lensky; Season 1992/93 as Riccardo at Antwerp, Don José at Brussels, Don Carlos at Melbourne and Cavaradossi at Covent Garden; Many appearances on radio and television in opera, oratorio and concert. *Recordings:* Beethoven 9th with London Philharmonic Orchestra, Yehudi Menuhin conducting, RPO Records 1991; Les Grand Duos D'Amours from French Operas: Quebec Symphony, Simon Streatfield conducting, 1988. *Hobbies:* Fishing; Tennis; Sailing. *Current Management:* Columbia Artists: Zemsky Green Division, New York, USA. *Address:* 42 Aberdeen Avenue, Toronto, Ontario, Canada M4X 1A2.

MARGITA Stefan, b. 3 Aug. 1956, Kosice, Czechoslovakia. Opera Singer (Tenor). *Education:* Conservatoire and Absolutorium, Kosice. *Debut:* Kosice Theatre. *Career:* Stage appearances, National Theatre, Prague, 1986-91; performed in Geneva, Stuttgart, Basel, Berlin, Vienna, Moscow, Turin, Brescia, Milan, Paris, Budapest, Wexford Festival, Oct. 1991 (Lucentio in Der Widerspenstigen Zähmung by Goetz); Tour, Tokyo and Nagasaki, Nov. 1991; Chicago, Feb. 1992. *Recordings:* Mysliveček, Bellerofonte, Supraphon; Martinů, Gilgamesh; Mahler, Das klagende Lied; Contract with Multisonic for 5 compact discs, 1991, 1992. *Honours:* 1st Place, International Festival, Trencianske Teplice, 1984; 1st Place, Prague Spring International Festival, 1986. *Hobbies:* Travel; Music. *Address:* Davidkova 91, Prague, Czech Republic.

MARGOLILNA Yelena, b. 1964, Lvov, Ukraine. Concert Pianist. *Education:* Studied in Lvov and at the St Petersburg State Conservatoire. *Debut:* Beethoven's Second Concerto, Lvov, 1974. *Career:* Notable performances at Moscow, Kiev, Khabarovsk, Lvov and Dnepropetrovsk; Western debut playing Prokofiev's Third Concerto at the Berlin Schauspielhaus, 1985; Concerts at the Prokofiev Centenary Festival in Scotland, 1991; Performs in chamber concerts and as solo recitalist in a repertoire including works by Haydn, Mozart, Liszt, Beethoven, Debussy and Shostakovich; Concerto repertoire includes Beethoven 1-4, Schumann, Chopin, Tchaikovsky, Ravel and Prokofiev; currently resident in Germany. *Honours include:* Scottish International Piano Competition winner, 1990; Casals Monferrato in Italy, 1990. *Address:* c/o Sonata, 11 Northpark Street, Glasgow G20 7AA, Scotland.

MARIANI Lorenzo, b. 1950, NY, USA. Stage Director. *Education:* Studied at Harvard and the University of Florence, Italy. *Debut:* Maggio Musicale Florence, 1982, Bluebeard's Castle. *Career:* Directed L'Heure Espagnole at Florence, La Traviata, Luisa Miller and Offenbach's Barbe-Bleue, 1994 at Bologna; Montepulciano Festival with the Henze-Paisiello Don Chisciotte, Greek by Mark Antony Turnage and Puccini's Edgar; Recent productions include La Forza del Destino at Florence, Massenet's Esclarmonde in Turin, I Quatro Rusteghi in Geneva, La Bohème in Chicago and Don Giovanni in Tel Aviv; Revived Antoine Vitez's production of Pelléas et Mélisande for Covent Garden, 1993.

MARIN Ion, b. 1960, Rumania. Conductor. *Education:* Studied at the George Enescu Music School Bucharest, the Mozarteum Salzburg, Accademia Chigiana in Siena and the International Academy, Nice. *Career:* Music Director, Transylvania Philharmonic, 1981, appearing in Rumania, East Germany, Czechoslovakia, Greece, Italy and France; Resident Conductor, Vienna Staatsoper, 1987-91, with repertoire from Mozart to Berg; Season 1991-92, in Japan for concerts with Margaret Prize and Ruggiero Raimondi, Gala Concert in Prague and Le Nozze di Figaro at the Teatro la Fenice, Venice; London debut with the LSO, 1991, English Chamber Orchestra with Yo-Yo Ma as soloist, 1992; US debut conducting L'Elisir at Dallas 1991, San Francisco, 1992, with Il Barbiere di Siviglia; Led Roman Polanski's production of Les contes d'Hoffmann at the Opera Bastille, Paris, 1992; Metropolitan Opera, 1992-93, Semiramide and Ariadne auf Naxos; Further engagements in L'Italiana in Algeri at Venice, 1992, and with Houston Grand Opera. Concerts with the City of Birmingham Symphony, Philadelphia Orchestra, Soula Cecilia, Rome, BBC Symphony, Rotterdam Philharmonic, Montreal Symphony, 1993. *Recordings include:* Lucia di Lammermoor, with Studer and Domingo, series of Rossini one-acters starting with Il Signor Bruschino, Semiramide and Rossini's Stabat Mater for DGG. *Honours:* Awards Deutsche Schallplatteu; Critics award, Rossini Arias; Nomination for Grammy award. *Address:* 31 Sinclair Road, London W14 0NS, England.

MARINELLI Carlo, b. 13 Dec 1926, Rome, Italy. Musicologist; Discographer. 1 son, 1 daughter. *Education:* Degree in Letters, University of Rome, 1948. *Career:* Founder and editor of the magazine Microsolco, 1952-59; Professor, Storia della Musica, University of L'Aquila, Italy, 1970-, Associate, 1985-; id, Storia della musica moderna e contemporanea, 1992-. *Publications:* La Musica strumentale da camera di Goffredo Petrassi 1967; Lettura di Messiaen 1972; Cronache di Musica Contemporanea 1974; Le Cantate Profane di J S Bach, 1966; L'Opera Cèca, L'Opera russa, L'opera in Polonia e Ungheria, 1977; Opere in disco (da Monteverdi a Berg), 1982; Goffredo Petraassi, an anthology, 1983; Faust e Mefistofele Nelle Opere Sinfonico-Vocali, Discografia, 1986; Le opere di Mozart su libretti di Da Ponte, Discografia, 1988; Mozart, Singspiele, Discografia, 1993; Editor: Quaderni IRTEM; Discografia Mozart, Rossini, Monteverdi; Repertori Fonti sonore audiovisive Italiane Mozart Rossini; Notizie Videoarchivio opera Balletto; Notizie Archivio sonoro musica contemporanea. *Memberships:* President, IRTEM; AIASA; Board Member IMZ; Member: International, American, Australian, French, Spanish and Italian Musicological Societies; IASA; ARSC; ASRA; AFAS; AISNA. *Address:* via Francesco Tamagno 67, 00168 Rome, Italy.

MARINOV Swetoslav, b. 21 Sept 1945, Lom, Bulgaria. Leader: Solo Concert Violinist. m. Elena Maeva, 10 Aug 1967, 2s. *Education:* Music school of Sofia, Bulgaria; Bulgarian State Conservatoire, Sofia; Studied with V Tatrai in Budapest, with Mischa Geler in Moscow Conservatoire, with Yfrah Neaman at the Guildhall School of Music and Drama. *Debut:* Violinist, Orpheus String Quartet, 1969. *Career:* Performed with the Tilev String Quartet from 1973, and the Bulgarian RT String Quartet, 1975; Leader of Sofia Soloist Chamber Orchestra, 1981 and Leader of Bremerhaven's Opera, Germany, 1988; Other concert activity includes violinist and violist of Bulgarian RT String Quartet and Sofia Chamber Orchestra; Concert tours in Europe, Asia, Australia, South America; In duo violin piono, concerts with Katia Evrova in France, (Cycle Mozart 16 sonatas,

1990, 1991 and Beethoven, Schubert, C Franck sonatas, 1992) and Brazil, 1993; In solo viola concert tour with G Tilev (violin) in Symphonie Concertante from Mozart with Niederheinischen Sinfoniker, Mönchengladbach. *Recordings:* In Radio Sofia, Warsaw, Moscow and Paris. *Honour:* Proze winner of competition for string quartet in Kolmae, 1978 and Evian, (France), 1980. *Address:* Rosenweg 5, 27607 Langen, Germany.

MARK Peter, b. 31 Oct 1940, New York City, USA. Conductor. m. Thea Musgrave. *Education:* BA, Musicology, Columbia University, 1961; Juilliard School of Music, with Jean Morel, Joseph Fuchs, Walter Trampler, MS, 1963. *Career:* Boy soprano soloist, Children's Chorus, New York City Opera & Metropolitan Opera, 1953-55; Principal freelance & string quartet violist, Juilliard Orchestra, Princeton Symphony, Trenton Symphony, Tiemann String Quartet, Beaux Arts & Los Angeles String Quartet, Santa Barbara Symphony, Lyric Opera Chicago, 1960-68; Assistant principal violist, Los Angeles Philharmonic Orchestra, 1968-69; Solo Violist, Europe, South America & US tours, 1965-77; General director/conductor, Virginia Opera Association, 1975-; Present Conductor, Chamber Players, Santa Barbara Chamber Orchestra, 1976-77; Guest conductor, Wolf Trap Orchestra 1979, New York Opera 1981, Los Angeles Opera Repertory Theater 1981, Royal Opera House, London 1982, Hong Kong Philharmonic Orchestra 1984; Jerusalem Symphony Orchestra, 1988; Tulsa Opera, 1988; Opera Nacional de Mexico 1989; Conductor, local premiere of Porgy and Bess, Buenos Aires and Sao Paulo, 1992; Guest Conductor, Opera Nacional de Mexico, 1989, 1992; Orlando Opera Company, 1993; Richmond Symphony, 1993; New York Pops, Carnegie Hall, 1991. *Recordings:* As conductor: Mary, Queen of Scots, 1979; A Christmas Carol, 1980; Moss Music Group 301, Moss Music Group 302. Also numerous recordings as violist. *Honours:* Recipient Elias Lifchey viola award Juillard School of Music, 1963. *Memberships:* Musicians Union, New York, London, Los Angeles, Norfolk, Virginia. *Address:* c/o Virginia Opera, PO Box 2580, Norfolk, VA 23501, USA.

MARKERT Annette, b. 1957, Kaltensundheim, Germany. Singer (Mezzo-soprano). *Education:* Studied in Leipzig with Helga Forner and with Hannelore Kuhse and Eleanore Elstermann. *Career:* Has sung with the Landestheater Halle as Handel's Floridante, Rinaldo and Tamerlano, Gluck's Orpheus and Carmen; Bach oratorios on German radio and oratorio performances and Lieder recitals throughout Germany; British debut Dec 1989 in the Alto Rhapsody with the BBC Philharmonic under Kurt Sanderling. *Honours:* Second Prize, Maria Canals Competition, Barcelona, 1985; Handel Prize 1989. *Address:* c/o Landestheater Halle, Universitatsring 24-25, D-4020 Halle, Germany.

MARKEVITCH Dimitry, b. 16 Mar 1923, La Tour de Peilz, Switzerland. Cellist. *Education:* License d'Enseignement Ecole Normale de Paris; Studied with Maurice Eisenberg, Gregor Piatigorsky, Nadia Boulanger. *Recordings include:* 5 Beethoven cello sonatas; 6 Bach suites; Kodaly Sonata, Op 8. *Publications:* Cello Story, 1984; The Solo Cello, 1989; Bach, 6 suites, 1964, 1985; Beethoven Op 64, 1980; Beethoven Kreutzer Sonata Op 47, 1993, for Cello. *Memberships:* American Musicological Society; Societe Francaise de Musicologie. *Current Management* Audrey Ellison, London, England. *Address:* 4 Route de St Maurice, CH-1814 La Tour-de- Peilz, Switzerland.

MARKHAM Elizabeth Jane, b. 7 Oct 1952, Timaru, New Zealand. Musicologist. m. Rembrandt Wolpert, 1981. *Education:* BA, Honours, University of Otago, 1975; PhD, University of Cambridge, England, 1979. *Career:* Alexander-Von-Humboldt Fellow, Far Eastern Musicology, University of Würzburg, Germany, 1981-83; Research Fellow, Music, St Catharine's College, Cambridge, 1983-86; Leverhulme Fellow, Far Eastern Historical Musicology, Queen's University, Belfast, 1986-. *Publications:* Saibara - Japanese Court Songs of the Heian Period, 2 volumes, 1983; Music from the Tang Court, 5 volumes to date, 1981-. *Contributions to:* Monumenta Serica; Musica Asiatica; Bulletin of the School of Oriental and African Studies; Music & Letters. *Memberships:* International Musicological Society; Galpin Society; International Council for Traditional Music. *Hobbies:* Walking; Reading. *Address:* Costerstraat 39, Alkmaar, Holland.

MARKHAM Ralph, b. 1949, Canada. Pianist. *Education: Career:* Studied at the Royal Toronto Conservatory of Music, and at the Cleveland Institute of Music with Vronsky and Babin. Formed Piano Duo partnership with Kenneth Broadway and has given many recitals and concerts in North America and Europe; BBC debut recital 1979 and further broadcasts on CBC TV, Radio France Musique, the Bavarian Radio Hilversum in Holland; Stravinsky's Three Dances from Petrushka at the Théâtre des Champs Elysées, Paris, 1984; Season 1987-88 included 40 North American recitals, concert with the Vancouver Symphony and New York debut on WQXR Radio; Season 1988-89 included the concertos for Two Pianos by Mozart and Bruch in Canada and a recital tour of England and Germany; Recent performances of the Bartok Sonata for Two Pianos and percussion, with Evelyn Glennie and a 1990-91 tour of North America, Europe and the Far East; Festival appearances include Newport USA 1988. *Recordings include:* Duos by Anton Rubinstein; Vaughan Williams Concerto for Two Pianos; Saint-Saëns Carnival of the Animals. *Honours include:* Young Artist of the Year, Musical America Magazine, 1980, with Kenneth Broadway. *Address:* c/o Robert Gilder and Co, Enterprise House, 59/65 Upper Ground, London Se1 9PQ, England.

MARKHAM Richard, b. 23 June 1952, Grimsby, England. Pianist. *Education:* Privately with Shirley Kemp and Max Pirani, RAM; ARAM; LRAM; ARCM; RAM Recital Diploma. *Debut:* Queen Elizabeth Hall, 1974. *Career:* Recitals and concerto performances throughout the United Kingdom and abroad; Several London appearances at Royal Festival Hall, Royal Albert Hall, Queen Elizabeth Hall, Wigmore Hall, Barbican Hall and Purcell Room; The Henry Wood Promenade Concerts; Appearances at Festivals in Aldeburgh, Bath, Berlin, Cheltenham, Harrogate, City of London, Schleswig-Holstein and York; Regular broadcasts of recitals and concerts for BBC and numerous TV and Radio Stations abroad; Has performed with The Philharmonia Orchestra, LSO, RPO, LPO, ECO, SNO, London Mozart Players, Bournemouth Sinfonietta, Hallé, Ulster and BBC Philharmonic and Scottish Symphony Orchestras; Frequent appearances and tours with piano duo partner, David Nettle in Europe, N America, Far East and Middle East. *Recordings:* Kabalevsky, Stravinsky and Rachmaninov with Raphael Wallfisch (cello), Bernstein (Arr. Nettle and Markham), Bennett and Grainger (2 Pianos); Holst, The Planets (2 pianos) and Stravinsky, Petrushka and Le Sacre du Printemps (piano duet) with David Nettle; Elgar, Holst, Grainger and Rossini with CBSO Chorus; Saint-Saëns Carnival of the Animals with Aquarius (Collins Classics); South of the Border, a Latin American Collection with Jill Gomez (Hyperion); Nettle and Markham in England (Pickwick). *Memberships:* Incorporated Society of Musicians; Royal Academy of Music Club. *Hobbies:* Travelling; Cooking; Theatre; Cinema; Playing Cards; Naturism. *Address:* The Old Power House, Atherton Street, London SW11 2JE, England.

MÄRKL Josef, b. 16 Jan 1928, Vilshofen, Germany. Professor, Violin and Chamber Music (Emeritus as of 1 May 1991). m. Brigitte Markl-Jaenisch, 3 children. *Education:* Staatl Hochschule fur Musik, Munich. *Debut:* Munich 1947. *Career:* Violinist, Radio Symphony Orchestras, Munich, Stuttgart, SWF Baden Baden; Concertmaster, Dusseldorf Symphony; Professor, Violin & Chamber Music, Rheinische Musikschule, Cologne; Member, Andrea Wendling Quartet and Stross Quartet; Primarius Markl Quartet. *Recordings:* String Quartet records; Film on Violin Technique. *Honour:* 1st Wetthewerb für junge Kunstler, Radio Stuttgart, 1947. *Membership:* European String Teachers Association.

Hobby: Teaching Chamber Music to Amateurs. *Address:* Bahnhofstrasse 18b, D-82418 Seehausen, Germany.

MARKOV Albert, b. 8 May 1933, Kharkov, USSR. Violinist; Composer. m. Marina Yablonskaya, 7 Feb 1958, 1 son. *Education:* Kharkov Music School; Moscow Gnessin Conservatory; Graduate Master Diploma, 1957; Doctor, 1960. *Career:* Concert Tours in USSR, Eastern and Western Europe, America, Solo with Leningrad Philharmonic, Moscow Philharmonic, major orchestras in Belgium, America, Holland, Sweden, Denmark, Portugal, Poland, Germany, Yugoslavia and other countries, 1978-; Professor, Manhattan School of Music, USA. *Compositions:* 3 Violin Sonatas; 3 Violin Rhapsodies; Concerto 2 Violin Caprices; Duo Sonata for two Violins; Formosa, suite for violin and orchestra. *Recordings:* Paganini Concerto No 2; Other recordings with orchestras and solo compositions by Bach, Veracini, Schubert, Paganini, Prokofiev, Shostakovich (about 30). *Publications:* Sonata for Violin Solo, Violin Technique, 1984; Duo-Sonata Edition of The Tchaikovsky Violin Concerto. *Contributions to:* Sovetskaya Musica, USSR; Novoye Russkoe Slovo, Russian Daily, USA. *Honours:* Gold Medal, Violin National Competition, Moscow, 1957, in Brussels, 1959; Ysaÿe Medal, Belgium. *Membership:* Rondo Music Society, President. *Hobbies:* Inventor; Patent Holder. *Address:* 3 Farm Creek Road, Rowayton, CT 06853, USA.

MARKOVA Juliana, b. 8 July 1945, Sofia, Bulgaria. Pianist. m. Michael Roll, 1 son. *Education:* Sofia Conservatory; Verdi Conservatory Milan with Ilonka Deckers. *Career:* After success in Enescu and Marguerite Long Competitions she performed on both sides of the Atlantic: Berlin Festival, Boston Symphony Orchestra and Andrew Davis and the Los Angeles Philharmonic under Zubin Mehta; Concerto engagements with all major orchestras in the USA and recitals at Lincoln Center New York and in Los Angeles; recent performances in Atlanta, Cleveland, Chicago, Philadelphia, Detroit, Dallas, Montreal, Toronto and Milwaukee; European tours have included Berlin, Florence and Milan; London concerts with the London Symphony Orchestra, Royal Philharmonic and the Philharmonia, with Claudio Abbado and Simon Rattle; regional engagements with the City of Birmingham Symphony and Royal Scottish Orchestra; British tour with the Sofia Philharmonic; season 1991/92 with tour of Japan and debut with the San Francisco Symphony; Repertoire includes concertos by Beethoven, Haydn, Mozart, Prokofiev and Saint-Saëns. *Address:* c/o Harold Holt Ltd, 31 Sinclair Road, London W14 ONS, England.

MARKS Alan, b. 14 May 1949, Chicago, Illinois, USA. Concert Pianist. *Education:* Studied piano with Shirley Parnas Adamas, Juilliard School of Music with Irwin Freundlich; BMus, 1971 and Peabody Conservatory Baltimore wiht Leon Fleisher, 1971-72. *Career:* New York debut Jan 1971 followed by tour of US schools, prisons and hospitals with violinist Daniel Heifetz; Tours as soloist throughout the USA and in Europe and Jaoan; British debut, 1979; Chamber music performances at the Marlboro and Santa Fe Festivals; Premiered Seven Pieces and Caprichos by Carlos Chavez, 1975, 1976; Teacher at the 92nd Street 'Y' in New York, 1972-80, Lincoln Center Institute, 1979-81. *Honours include:* Winner, concert Artists Guild piano Competition, 1970. *Address:* c/o Lincoln Center Institute, Lincoln Center, NY 10023, USA.

MARKUS Urs. b. 29 Sept 1941, Villmergen, Aargau, Switzerland. Singer (Baritone). *Education:* Studied in Zurich, Milan and Fribourg. *Career:* Sang as a bass at the Biel-Solothurn Opera, 1979-81, baritone roles at Trier, 1983-86; Engaged at Brunswick, 1986-88, Nationaltheater Mannheim from 1988; Guest engagements at Geneva, Nancy and Metz; Roles have included Pizarro and Gluck's Agamemnon, Mozart's Count and Alfonso, Verdi's Amonasro and Iago, Telramund, the Dutchman and Hans Sachs, Escamillo and Gerster's Enoch Arden; Concert appearances throughout Switzerland in Berlin, Venice and

Copenhagen. *Address:* c/o Nationaltheater, Am Goetheplatz, 6800 Mannheim, Germany.

MARLEYN Paul, b. 1965, England. Concert Cellist. *Education:* Studied with David Strange at the Royal Academy of Music (from 1981), with Lawrence Lesser in Boston and Aldo Parisot at Yale University. *Career:* Recital and solo appearances from 1988 throughout Europe, Canada and the United States (Jordan Hall Boston, Merkin Hall New York, Chamber Music East and Cape and Island's Music Festivals), Wigmore Hall London; Tour of Europe 1985 as solo-cellist with the European Community Youth Orchestra under Claudio Abbado; Radio and television engagements in Britain, the USA and Switzerland; Tours of Japan, South Korea and Switzerland, 1991. *Honours include:* Suggia Scholarship, Dove Prize and Thomas Igloi Trust Prize at the RAM; First Prize, Hudson Valley National String Competition, New York, 1988. *Address:* c/o Anglo-Swiss Management, 4-5 Primrose Mews, Sharpeshall Street, London NW1 8YW, England.

MARONEY Denman Fowler, b. 25 July 1949, Summit, New Jersey, USA. Composer; Pianist; Editor; Writer. m. Erin Martin, 25 July, 1985, 2 sons. *Education:* BA, Political Science, Williams College, Williamstown, Massachusetts, 1971; MFA, Composition, Piano, California Institute of The Arts, 1974. *Career:* Performances: NYC Experimental Intermedia Foundation, 1986; Logos Studio, Ghent, 1986; Creative Movement Studio, Budapest, 1986; Roulette, NYC, 1982, 1984, 1986; PS 122, NYC, 1985, 1986; Edinburgh Festival Fringe, 1983; The Kitchen, NYC, 1976, 1978; Theater Vanguard, Los Angeles, 1974. *Recordings:* Stockhausen Performed by The Negative Band: Short Wave and Set Sail For The Sun, Finnadar Records, 1976; Tellus Magazine (Cassette) No 15, 1986: Stephanie and Irving Stone Festival of Improvisers, at Roulette, NYC. Composer-in-Residence, Yale Summer School of Music and Art (YSSMA), Norfolk, Connecticut, USA, 1974. *Memberships:* Composers Forum, American Music Center. *Hobbies:* Hatha Yoga; Hiking; Reading. *Address:* 144 Route 306, Monsey, NY 10952, USA.

MAROS Miklos, b. 14 Nov 1943, Pecs, Hungary. Composer; Teacher; Chamber Orchestra Leader. m. Ilona Maros, singer (Soprano). *Education:* Composition and Theory, Academy of Music, Budapest; Composition, State College of Music, Stockholm. *Career:* Leader, Maros Ensemble; Compositions frequently performed in Europe and USA. *Compositions include:* Turba (choir); Denique (soprano and orchestra); Symphonies Nos 1-3; Oolit (chamber orchestra); Divertimento (chamber orchestra); Concerto for Harpsichord and chamber orchestra; Concerto for Trombone and Orchestra; Sinfonietta; Concerto for Alto Saxophone and Orchestra, Concerto for Clarinet and Orchestra; Chamber music; Electronic music etc. *Recordings:* Descort (soprano flute and double bass); Manipulation No 1 (bassoon and live electronic); Divertimento (chamber orchestra); Oolit; Circulation (strings); Dimensions (Percussion); Quartet for Saxophones; Symphony No 1; Stora grusharpan (The Big Gravel-Sifter) (Radio-Opera); 4 songs from Gitanjali (Soprano and chamber ensemble); Concerto for Trombone and Orchestra; Capriccio (Guitar); Undulations (Alto Sax, Piano); Passacaglia (Soprano and Organ), Turba (Choir), Schattierungen (Violoncello), Praefatio (Organ); Concerto for alto saxophone and orchestra; Sinfonia concertante, (Symphony No 3); Trifoglio (harp). *Honour:* Composer in Residence Berlin-West (DAAD/Berliner Künstler program). *Memberships:* Society of Swedish Composers; Society for Contemporary Music (ISCM Swedish Section); Society for Experimental Music and Arts. *Address:* Krukmakargatan 18, S-118 51 Stockholm, Sweden.

MARÓTHY János, b. 23 Dec 1925, Budapest, Hungary. Musicologist. m. Márta Batári, 23 July 1982, 3 sons, 3 daughters. *Education:* PhD, Budapest University, 1948; Composer, Budapest Academy of Music, 1951; Academic Doctor of Musicology, 1967. *Career:* Editor of music journals: Eneklo Nép, 1949-50, Magyar Zene, 1950-51; Research worker, Academy of

Music, Budapest, 1951-61; Head of Music Sociology Department, Institute for Musicology, Hungarian Academy of Sciences, 1961-; Assistant Professor - Professor of Music Aesthetics, Philosophical Faculty, Department for Aesthetics, Budapest University, 1973-. *Publications:* Az Európai Népdal Születése, 1960; Music and the Bourgeois, Music and the Proletarian, Hungarian, 1966, English, 1974; Zene, Forradalom, Szocializmus, 1975; Zene, és Ember, 1980; Apeiron Musikon, (with Márta Batári), 1986; Musica e uomo, 1987. *Contributions to:* Popular Music; Corresponding Editor, Musicà Realtà; Editorial Board, Studia Musicologia; Beitrage Zur Musikwissenschaft; Editorial Board, Magyar Zene; Muzsika. *Honours:* Erkel Prize, 1961; Knight of Labour, 1965; Arts Prize of Hungarian Trade Unions, 1969. *Memberships:* President, Musicological Committee of the Hungarian Academy of Sciences. *Address:* Gellérthegy u. 31, Budapest H 1016, Hungary.

MARQUEZ Marta, b. 1955, San Juan, Puerto Rico. Singer (Soprano, since 1994 Mezzo-Soprano). *Education:* Studied at the Julliard New York and with Tito Gobbi in Florence. *Debut:* New York City Opera, as Oscar in Un ballo in Maschera. *Career:* Sang at Saarbrucken from 1979, notably as Constanze, Frau Fluth, Mimi, Violetta, Susanna and Zdenka in Arabella; Spoleto Festival 1982, as Sylvie in Gounod's La Colombe; Deutsche Oper am Rhein Dusseldorf from 1984 with notable roles including Poppea, Hänsel, Cherubino, Idamantes, Cenerentola, and Rosina (Barbiere), and further engagements throughout Germany; Puerto Rico at the Pablo Casals Festival and appearances in Moscow with the Dusseldorf company; Other roles include Nedda and Musetta; Frequent concert appearances; Guest appearances at Royal Opera House, Covent Garden (Zerlina, Musetta) and Bavarian State Opera, Munich (Susanna, Aennchen). *Address:* c/o Deutsche Oper am Rhein, Heinrich-Heine Allee 16, 4000 Dusseldorf, Germany.

MARRINER Neville, (Sir), b. 15 Apr 1924, Lincoln, England. Musician; Conductor. m. Elizabeth M Sims, 1958, 1 son, 1 daughter. *Education:* Lincoln School; Royal College of Music. *Career:* Director, Academy of St Martin in the Fields, 1959-; Musical Director, Los Angeles Chamber Orchestra, 1969-78; Director, South Bank Festival of Music, 1975-78; Director, Meadowbrook Festival, Detroit, 1979-84; Music Director, Minnesota Orchestra, 1979-86; Music Director Stuttgart Radio Symphony Orchestra, 1986-89; Conducted Béatrice et Bénédict at the Festival Hall, 1989. *Recordings include:* CDs of Dvořák Serenades; Haydn Violin Concerto in C; Mozart Serenade K361; Il Barbiere di Siviglia; Schubert 4th and 5th Symphonies; Baroque Favourites, with Yehudi Menuhin; The English Connection (Vaughan Williams The Lark Ascending, Elgar Serenade and Tippett Corelli Fantasia); Trumpet Concertos, with Håkan Hardenberger; Mendelssohn Piano Works with Murray Perahia, Mozart Haffner Serenade; 200 other recordings include Bach Concertos, Suites and Die Kunst der Fuge; Vivaldi, The Four Seasons and other concertos; Concerti Grossi by Corelli, Geminiani, Torelli, Locatelli and Manfredini, Mozart Symphonies, Concertos, Serenades and Divertimenti, Handel Messiah, Opera overtures and Water and Fireworks music; Die Zauberflöte (Philips, 1980); Handel Arias with Kathleen Battle (EMI); Il Turco in Italia and Don Giovanni (Philips). *Honours:* CBE; FRCM; KBE 1985; Tagore Gold Medal; Six Edison Awards (Netherlands); Two Mozart Gemeinde Awards (Austria); Grand Prix du Disque (France) three times; 2 Grammy Awards(USA); FRAM, Shakespeare Prize; KT of Polar Star. *Address:* 67 Cornwall Gardens, London SW7, England.

MARROCCO William Thomas, b. 5 Dec 1909, West New York, New Jersey, USA. Professor. m. 15 Sept 1937, 1 son, 1 daughter. *Education:* BM, 1934, MA, 1940, Eastman School of Music, University of Rochester; PhD, University of California, Los Angeles, 1952; Licentiate and Magistrate Diplomas, R. Conservatory of Music, Naples, Italy. *Career:* Instructor, Violin, University of Iowa, 1945; Associate Professor,

University of Kansas, Lawrence, 1946-49; Professor, University of California, 1949-77; Associate Director of the Education Abroad Program in Hong Kong during 1976-77. *Recordings:* With the Roth String Quartet: String Quartet in C, by Vernon Duke, 1959; Quartet, Op 74, Ernst Toch, 1961; Quintets in G and C, by Michael Haydn, 1959. *Publications:* Music in America, with Harold Gleason, 1964; Polyphonic Music of the Fourteenth Century, 6 volumes, 1967-78; Medieval Music, with Nicholas Sandon, 1977; Memoirs of a Stradivarius, 1988; Major Article, Anthonius Arena, Master of Law and Dance of the Renaissance, Studi Musicali XVIII, 1989; 9 other publications. *Address:* 2101 Buck Street, Eugene, OR 97405, USA.

MARS Jacques, b. 25 March 1926, Paris, France. Singer (Bass). *Career:* Sang at the Paris Opera from 1955, debut as the Duke in Romeo et Juliette; Other roles include the Commendatore in Don Giovanni, King Philip in Don Carlos, Boris Godunov and Mephistopheles in La Damantion de Faust; Paris Opéra-Comique, 1965, as the villains in Les Contes d'Hoffmann; Glyndebourne Opera, 1969-70, as Golaud in Pelléas et Mélisande; Sang in the premiere of Daniel-Leseur's Andrea del Sarto, Marseilles, 1969; Monte Carlo, 1979, as Massenet's Don Quichotte; Appearances at La Scala Milan and the Maggio Musicale Florence. *Recordings include:* Persée et Andromède by Ibert; Les Abencérages by Cherubini; Pelléas et Mélisande; Les Pêcheurs de Perles. *Address:* c/o Opéra de Monte Carlo, Place du Casino, Monte Carlo, Monaco.

MARSALIS Wynton, b. 18 Oct 1961, New Orleans, Louisiana, USA. Trumpeter. *Education:* Trained in classical music and played with the New Orleans Philharmonic aged 14; Juilliard School, New York. *Career:* Joined Art Blakey and the Jazz Messengers 1980; Toured with Herbie Hancock 1981; Formed own group 1982 with brother Branford Marsalis on tenor saxophone; Grammy Awards 1984 for Jazz album and for Concertos by Haydn, Hummel and Leopold Mozart; Appearances with New York Philharmonic, Cleveland Orchestra, Los Angeles Philharmonic, London Symphony and other major European orchestras; conductors include Lorin Maazel, Zubin Mehta, Leonard Slatkin and Esa-Pekka Salonen. *Recordings:* Exclusive contracts with CBS Masterworks and CBS Records; Awards include Grammy (USA) and Grand Prix du Disque (France). *Address:* c/o Van Walsum Management, 40 St Peter's Road, London W6 9BH, England.

MARSCHNER Wolfgang, b. 23 May 1926, Dresden, Germany. Violinist. *Education:* Studied violin, piano, composition and conducting, Conservatory Dresden and Mozarteum Salzburg. *Debut:* At age 9 with Tartini's Devil's Trill sonata. *Career:* Professor, Folkwang-School, Essen, 1956; Professor, Music Conservatory, Cologne, 1958; Professor, Music Conservatory, Freiburg, 1963-; Regular Mastercourses in Warsaw and Weimar; Director of Pfluger-Foundation for young violinists, Freiburg; International soloist career, concerts in Edinburgh Festival and with Berlin Philharmonic and Royal Philharmonic, London; Premiere, Schoenberg's Violin Concerto in many cities including London, Vienna and Zurich; Founder of: International Ludwig Spohr Violin Competition; Jacobus Stainer Violin Maker's Competition; International Youth Violin Competition; German Spohr Academy; Festival Wolfgang Marschner, Hinterzarten. *Compositions:* Various works for orchestra; 2 concerti for violin and orchestra; Sonata for solo violin; Canto notturno for violin and organ; Rhapsody for viola solo. *Honours:* Kranichsteiner prize for contemporary music, 1954; English record prize for interpretation of Schoenberg's Violin Concerto, Bundesverdienstkreuz, 1986. *Address:* Burgunder Strasse 4, D-7800 Freiburg, Germany.

MARSH Jane, b. 25 June 1944, San Francisco, USA. Singer (Soprano). *Education:* Studied with Ellen Repp at Oberlin College and with Lili Wexberg and Otto Guth in New York. *Debut:* Spoleto Festival 1965, as Desdemona. *Career:* Sang in Essen, Hamburg, Moscow,

Prague, Naples, Trieste and Johannesburg; Member of the Deutsche Oper am Rhein Dusseldorf from 1968; Further appearances in Pittsburgh, San Antonio and San Francisco; Salzburg 1973, in the premiere of Orff's De Temporum fine Comoedia; Often heard as Mozart's Donna Anna, Queen of Night and Constanze. *Recordings:* De Temporum fine Comoedia (Deutsche Grammophon); The Invisible City of Kitezh; Alfonso und Estrella; Penthesilea by Schoeck; Der Vampyr by Marschner (Voce).

MARSH Robert Charles, b. 5 Aug 1924, Columbus, Ohio, USA. Music Critic. m. Kathleen Moscrop, 4 July 1956, divorced 1985, m. Ann Noren, 25 Feb 1987, 1 son. *Education:* BS, Northwestern University, 1945; EdD, Harvard University, 1951; Research at: Cornell University, University of Chicago, Oxford, Cambridge; Private Music Tuition (Voice) and studies at Cornell, Northwestern, Harvard & Cambridge Universities. *Debut:* First published criticism, 1954. *Career:* College and University Teaching, 1946-58; Joined Chicago Sun Times as Music Critic, 1956-. *Compositions:* Toscanini and the Art of Orchestra Performance, 1956, Revised Edition 1962; The Cleveland Orchestra, 1967; Ravina 1985. *Recordings:* Notes for Recordings by Chicago Symphony and many other artists. *Contributions to:* High Fidelity; Gramophone etc. *Honours:* Shared Peabody Award for Educational Broadcasting, 1976; Citation, State of Illinois & City of Chicago for 30 seasons of services to the arts, 1986. *Hobby:* Photography. *Current Management:* Chicago Newspaper Guild. *Address:* 1825 N Lincoln Plaza, Apartment 509, Chicago, IL 60614, USA.

MARSH Roger, b. 10 Dec 1949, Bournemouth, England. Composer; Lecturer. m. (1) Christina Rhys, 24 July 1976, 2 sons, 1 daughter, (2)Anna Myatt, 19 Sept 1992. *Education:* BA, 1971, DPhil, 1975, University of York; Studied with Bernard Rands. *Career:* Harknes Fellow, 1976-78, University of California, San Diego; Lecturer, Keele University, 1978-88; Lecturer, Senior Lecturer, University of York; Member of the Midland Music Theatre. *Compositions:* Not a Soul but Ourselves, for 4 amplified voices, 1977; The Big Bang, (music theatre), 1989; Stepping Out, for piano and orchestra, 1990; Kagura, 1991. *Recordings include:* Not a Soul but Ourselves; Numerous radio broadcasts. *Publications:* Various. *Honours include:* Arts Council Composition Bursary, 1993. *Memberships:* SPNM Reading Panel, 1991-92; BBC Reading Panel, 1987-. *Current management:* Novello. *Address:* Ball Hall Farm, Storwood, York YO4 4TD, England.

MARSH-EDWARDS Michael Richard, b. 7 Apr 1928, Westgate-on-Sea, Kent, England. Composer; Conductor. m. (1) Stella K Parrott, 9 Apr 1952, 1 daughter, (2) Ann Wardleworth, 11 Nov 1971, (3)Srinuan Suwan, 9 Jan 1981, 1 son, 1 daughter. *Education:* Trinity College, London University, Associate and Licentiate Diplomas, Hon PhD, DMus. *Career:* Conductor, Luton Bach Orchestra, 1949-63; Conductor, 1952-63, currently Vice-President, Luton Symphony Orchestra; Director of Music, Luton Industrial Mission and Luton Community Centre, 1957-62; Conductor, Halton Orpheus Choir, 1973-75; Freelance Conductor and Lecturer. *Publications:* Toccata for Percussion and Orchestra; Variations, 8 percussionists; 3 Studies, 12 percussionists; Dance Overture; Birthday Overture; Revolutionary Overture, 1956; Chester Overture; Celebration Overture; Music 1, 60 strings; Music 2, strings and percussion; Music 3, strings and brass; Music 4; Oppositions, 2 orchestras; Structures; Fantasy on the Waltz of Diabelli; Thai Dances; Balinese Dances; Petite Suite pour le Tombeau d'Erik Satie; Treurzang; Suite Guernesiaise; Concerto for 11 Instruments; Horn Concerto; Numerous other instrumental, vocal and electronic pieces; Music for children. *Publications:* Author of concert notes; Author and Presenter of radio scripts. *Honours:* Medal, American Biographical Institute, 1986; Alfred Nobel Medal, 1991. *Memberships:* Life Member, Former Vice-Chairman, British Music Society and Havergal Brian Society; Composers Guild of Great Britain; Performing Right

Society; National Board of Advisors, American Biographical Institute; Vice-President, Former Chairman, Luton Music Club. *Hobbies:* Travel; Photography; Music of South-East Asia. *Address:* 5/ 2440 Muban Prachachuen, Pakkred, Nontaburi 11120, Thailand.

MARSHALL Howard Lowen, b. 21 July 1931, Nokesville, Virginia, USA. University Professor. m. Doris M Rosencranz, 14 Jul 1962. *Education:* Brentsville District High School, Nokesville, Virginia, 1948; BME, Shenandoah Conservatory of Music, Winchester, Virginia, 1952; MM, Conservatory of Music of University of Cincinnati, Ohio, 1958; PhD, Musicology, Eastman School of Music of the University of Rochester, New York, 1968. *Career:* Served in US Navy, 1952-57; Sycamore High School, Cincinnati, 1958-60; Cheltenham High School, Elkins Park, Pennsylvania, 1960-63; Instructor of Music, 1966-68, Assistant Professor of Music, 1968-73, Lake Forest College, Lake Forest, Illinois; Associate Professor of Music, Chair, Music Department, 1974-82, Professor of Music, 1982-84; Roberts Professor of Music, 1984-87, Thompson Professor of Music, 1987-, Mercer University, Macon, Georgia. *Publications:* Book: The Four-Voice Motets of Thomas Crecquillion, published by the Institute of Mediaeval Music, Ltd, Brooklyn, New York, 1971; Critical Edition: The Four-Voice Motets of Thomas Crecquillion, published in three volumes by the Institute of Mediaeval Music, Ltd, Brooklyn, New York, 1971. *Contributions to:* Magazines including: Article: Symbolism in Schubert's Winterreise, published in the journal Studies in Romanticism, 1973. *Address:* 1324 Maplewood Drive, Macon, GA 31210, USA.

MARSHALL Ingram D(ouglas), b. 10 May 1942, New York, USA. Composer. *Education:* BA University of Lake Forest College, 1964; Columbia University with Ussachevsky (electronic music), 1964-66, with Morton Subotnick in New York and California, and traditional Indonesian music at the California Institute of the Arts. *Career:* Taught at the California Institute of the Arts until 9174; Performances in Java, Bali and Scandinavia. *Compositions include:* Transmogrification for tape, 1966; Three Buchla Studies for synthesizer 1969; Cortez, text-sound piece 1973; Vibrosuperball for 4 amplified percussion 1975; Non Confundar for string sextet, alto flute, clarinet and electronics, 1977; Spiritus for 6 strings, 4 flutes, harpsichord and vibraphone, 1981; Frog Tropes for brass sextet and tape, 1982; Voces resonae for string quartet, 1984. *Address:* ASCAP, ASCAP Building, One Lincoln Plaza, NY 10023, USA.

MARSHALL J Richard, b. 28 July 1929, Schenectady, New York, USA. Opera Conductor and Director. *Education:* BA, University of Rochester, 1951; MMus, 1953, DMus, 1963, Indiana University; Arts Management Diploma, Harvard University, 1967. *Career:* Head, Opera and Choral Music, University of Buffalo, New York, 1959-62; Head, Opera, Boston Conservatory, 1965-68; Founder, Director, New England Regional Opera, 1967-76; General Director, Charlotte Opera, Charlotte, North Carolina, 1976-82; Founder, President, Southern Opera Conference; Founder, Director, Center for Contemporary Opera, New York City, 1982-. *Honour:* Award for Service to Opera in New England, Performing Arts Association, Boston, 1975. *Memberships:* President, Southern Opera Conference; Central Opera Service; National Opera Association. *Hobbies:* Photography; Travel. *Address:* 475 Riverside Drive, Room 936, New York, NY 10115, USA.

MARSHALL Lois, b. 29 Jan 1924, Toronto, Canada. Singer (Soprano and Mezzo-Soprano). *Education:* Studied with Weldon Kilburn and Emy Heim. *Debut:* Toronto, 1948, in the St Matthew Passion. *Career:* Sang with Toscanini and Beecham in recordings of music by Beethoven, Handel and Mozart; New York Town Hall recital 1952; Sang in England from 1956, debut under Beecham; Edinburgh and Dublin 1957, in Messiah; Concert tour of Russia 1958; Stage apearances as the Queen of Night in Toronto, as Donna Anna, as Mimi and Tosca in Boston and Ellen Orford in a CBS TV production of Peter Grimes; Duet partnership with Maureen Forrester from 1971; Mezzo-Soprano repertoire from 1975. *Recordings:* Beethoven's Missa Solemnis conducted by Toscanini, 1953; Handel's Solomon and Die Entführung, conducted by Beecham (Columbia).

MARSHALL Margaret Anne, b. 4 Jan 1949, Sterling, Scotland. Concert & Opera Singer (Soprano). m. Graeme Griffiths King Davidson, 2 daughters. *Education:* DRSAMD, Royal Scottish Academy of Music & Drama. *Career:* Performances in Festival Hall, Barbican, Covent Garden; Concerts & Opera in major European events; Has sung Gluck's Euridice and Mozart's Countess at Florence; Covent Garden debut 1980; Sang Fiordiligi at La Scala and Salzburg, 1982; Vienna Staatsoper debut 1988, Mozart's Countess; sang Fiordilng, La Scala 1982 and Salzburg 1982-85 and 1990-91; Season 1990-91 with Countess in Hong Kong and Donna Elvira for ENO; North America Opera debut in Toronto as Vitelia; Season 1991/92 included Violetta at Frankfurt, Mozart Bicentenary Gala at Covent Garden, followed by Fiordiligi and Vitellia in La Clemenza di Tito at the Salzburg Festival; Numerous recordings including Mozart's C Minor Mass and Haydn's Masses, conducted by Marriner; Vivaldi's Tito Manlio and Cantatas (Negri); Handel's Jephtha and Saul; Gluck Orfeo (Muti); Haydn Die Schöpfung and Bach St Matthew Passion (Erato); Pergolesi Stabat Mater (Abbado); Mozart Davidde Penitente and Die Schuldigkeit des Ersten Gebotes; Vaughan Williams Sea Symphony (Virgin Classics); Elgar The Kingdom (Chandos); Hypermnestra in Les Danaïdes by Salieri. *Honour:* 1st prize, Munich International Competition, 1974. *Hobbies:* Squash; Golf. *Address:* 'Woodside' Main Street, Gargunnock, Stirling FK7 0PL, Scotland.

MARSHALL Nicholas, b. 2 June 1942, Plymouth, Devon, England. Composer; Teacher. m. Angela Marshall, 21 July 1982, 1 son, 1 daughter. *Education:* Dartington Hall School; MA, University of Cambridge 1964; Royal College of Music 1964-65. *Career:* Pianist, Conductor; Teacher, Chairman and Artistic Director, Ashburton Festival 1980-84. *Compositions include:* Section: Partita for Guitar; Arion and The Dolphins (Junior operetta); Inscriptions for A Peal of Eight Bells (for SATB); Suite for Guitar, Flute, Clarinet, Violin and Cello; Four Haiku, for Solo Recorder; Trio for Recorders; Sonatina for Solo Flute; Jump, for Flute and Piano; Five West Country Folk Songs; Two West Country Folk Songs; A Playford Garland; The Young King (Childrens Opera); Five Country Dances, Cool Winds for cello and guitar on CD: original music for cello and guitar (EMEC); Three Japanese Fragments for guitar; The Virgin's Song, Carol for Christmas Eve. *Recording:* Music From Dartington. *Membership:* Composers' Guild of Great Britain. *Address:* Aish House, Aish, South Brent, Devon TQ10 9JH, England.

MARSHALL Robert (Lewis), b. 12 Oct 1939, New York City, USA. Musicologist. m. Traute Maass, 9 Sept 1966, 1 son, 1 daughter. *Education:* AB, Columbia University, 1960; MA, 1962, PhD, 1968, Princeton University; French Horn with Gunther Schuller. *Career:* Faculty Member, 1966-83, Chair, 1972-78, Music, University of Chicago; Visiting Professor: Princeton University, 1971-72; Columbia University, 1977; Faculty, 1983-; Incumbent endowed chair: Louis, Frances and Jeffrey Sachar Prof., Chair 1985-, Music, Brandeis University. *Publications:* The Compositional Process of J. S. Bach, 1972; Critical Editor, Cantatas for 9th and 10th Sundays after Trinity, 1985; Studies in Renaissance and Baroque Music in Honour of Arthur Mendel, 1974; J.S. Bach Cantata Autographs in American Collections, 1985; The Music of J. S. Bach; The Sources, the Style, the Significance, 1989; Mozart Speaks: Views on Music, Musicians and The World, 1991. *Contributions to:* Musical Quarterly; Journal of American Music Society. *Address:* Department of Music, Brandeis University, Waltham, MA 02254, USA.

MARSHALL Wayne, b. 31 Jan 1961, Oldham, Lancashire, England. Concert Organist; Conductor.

Education: ARCM Chetham's School Manchester; FRCO Royal College of Music, 1978-83; Austrian Government Scholarship 1983, to study at the Vienna Hochschule. *Career:* Organ scholar at Manchester Cathedral and St George's Chapel Windsor; Recitals at St Paul's Cathedral, Westminster Abbey, Festival Hall, Leeds and Birmingham Town Halls, and King's College Cambridge; Tours of the USA and Yugoslavia; Windsor and Hong Kong Festivals; 1986 worked as repetiteur for Glyndebourne production of Porgy and Bess; appeared as Jasbo Brown the jazz pianist; Assistant Chorus Master at Glyndebourne 1987; 1988-89 seasons included Promenade Concert debut with the Poulenc Concerto and appearances with the City of Birmingham Symphony under Simon Rattle and the BBC Symphony under Paul Daniel; Conducted the premiere of Wilfred Josephs's Alice in Wonderland at the Harrogate Festival, 1990; Carmen Jones in the West End, London, 1991; Recital repertoire includes works by Bach, Dupré, Franck, Liszt, Messiaen, Reger, Schmidt and Vierne. *Address:* c/o Harold Holt Ltd, 31 Sinclair Road, London W14 0NS, England.

MARTA Istvan, b. 14 June 1952, Budapest, Hungary. Composer. 2 daughters. *Education:* Course in Composition in Yugoslavia led by W Lutoslawski, 1979; Diploma in Composition and Teaching from Ferenc Liszt Academy of Music, Budapest, 1981. *Career:* Folk Music Collecting Tour in Moldavia, Romania, 1973; Over 30 pieces of stage and film music composed; Member of Group of 180, 1980-83; Member of Mandel Quartet, playing old and new music on harpsichord, synthesizer and percussion, 1982-; Teacher of History of Classical Music and Analysis of 20th Century Music, Jazz Department, Bela Bartók School of Music, Budapest, 1981-83; Organiser of Planum and Rendezvous, festivals of international contemporary music, 1982 and 1984. *Compositions:* Text and Music, - stage performance based on Samuel Beckett's radioplay, 1978; King of the Dead, cantata 1979; Christmas Day - 24th Lesson, music for chamber ensemble, 1980; Our Hearts, movements for chamber choir and chamber orchestra, 1983; Visions, ballet performed by the ballet corps of the Hungarian State Opera 1984; Dolls House Story, composition for percussion instruments, 1985; Workers' Operetta, musical 1985; ... per quattro tromboni ..., 1986. *Recordings:* Our Hearts, Hungaroton, 1985; Alte und Neue Musik, Thorofon - Hannover 1984; The Wind Arises, Krem, Hungaroton, 1987. *Honours:* Hungarian Television Excellence Prize, 1975; Hungarian Radio Audience Prize, 1982 and 1987; Prize of the Tribune Internationale des Compositeurs, Paris, 1982 and 1987; Erkel Prize, Hungary, 1987. *Membership:* Hungarian Music Union. *Hobbies:* Old houses; Video. *Current Management:* Interkoncert, Budapest. *Address:* Karolyi M.u. 4-8, H-1053 Budapest, Hungary.

MARTELLI Carlo, b. 12 Dec 1935, London, England. Musician. *Education:* Royal College of Music. *Compositions include:* String Quartet No 2, 1955; Symphony No 2, 1956; Terzetto for 2 violins and viola, 1957; Avbade for Orchestra, 1985; Promenade for orchestra, 1985; Prelude and Fugue for orchestra of violas, 1993; Operas: The Monkey's Paw, 1989, The Curse of Christopher Columbus, 1992; Persiflage for String Orchestra, 1983; Church Stretton suite for Strings, Oboes and Horns, 1991; About 200 arrangements for string quartet which are in wide circulation throughout the world, as well as film music. *Address:* 215 Burrage Road, London SE19 7JZ, England.

MARTIN Adrian, b. 1958, England. Singer (Tenor). *Education:* Studied at the London Opera Centre and the National Opera Studio. *Debut:* With Opera for All as Ramiro and Tonio. *Career:* Sang small roles at Covent Garden in Parsifal, Salome and Die Zauberflöte, then the Dancing Master in Ariadne, and Pong in Turandot; Glyndebourne Festival as Tamino and Idamante; Appearances with English National Opera as Cassio, Alfred, the Steersman, Anatol (War and Peace), Don Ottavio, Vincent (Mireille), Tamino, Ferrando and Rodolfo, Nadir, Jenik in The Makropoulos Case and Erik in Fennimore and Gerda; Welsh National Opera as

Lensky in Serban's production of Eugene Onegin; Scottish Opera in La Scala di Seta and La Cambiale di Matrimonio by Rossini; Has sung with Opera North as Rodolfo, Alfredo, Camille, Ismaele (Nabucco), Sali in A Village Romeo and Juliet, Tamino, Jacquino, Nadir and Ernesto; Overseas engagements at St Gallen (Hoffmann and Don Ottavio); Hamburg and Zurich (Hoffmann); Paris (Tybalt in Roméo et Juliette at the Opéra) and Queensland (Nadir and Rodolfo at the Lyric Opera). *Address:* c/o Athole Still Ltd, Greystoke House, 80-86 Westow Street, London SE19 3AF, England.

MARTIN Andrea, b. 9 Mar 1949, Klagenfurt, Germany. Singer (Baritone). *Education:* Studied in Vienna and at the Santa Cecilia Academy in Rome; teachers included Anton Dermota, Hans Hotter, Ettore Campogallian, Mario del Monaco and Giuseppe Taddei. *Career:* Sang with the Wiener Kammeroper and in Klagenfurt, Salzburg, Graz and Munich; Italian debut at Treviso 1979, as Malatesta in Don Pasquale; Further Italian engagements at Rome, Palermo, Bologna, Venice, Naples and Verona; Ravenna Festival as Michonnet in Adriana Lecouvreur; Has sung in Maria di Rudenz by Donizetti at Venice and Wiesbaden, as Luna in Trovatore at the Dresden Staatsoper; Guest appearances at the Théâtre des Champs-Elysées, Paris, Liège, Barcelona, Lisbon and Vienna; Concert tours of Japan, Korea, the USA and Brazil. *Recordings:* Imelda de Lambertazzi and Alcina, Regina di Golconda by Donizetti; Salieri's Axur, and Così fan Tutte (Nuova Era). *Address:* c/o Teatro La Fenice, Campo S Fantin 2519, I-30124 Venice, Italy.

MARTIN David Lloyd, b. 30 Apr 1934, Sydney, Australia. General Manager. m. (1) 5 Oct 1955, divorced 1975, 2 sons, 1 daughter; (2) Alexandra Grace Ross, 4 Feb 1977, 1 daughter. *Education:* BEc, University of Sydney, 1972; ASA, 1972. *Career:* Chairman and Joint Managing Director, Tivoli Circuit Pty Ltd, 1961-66; Chairman and Managing Director, NLT Productions, 1966-70; Deputy General Manager, Sydney Opera House, 1973-79; General Manager, Sydney Opera House, 1979-; Director, National Institute of Dramatic Art, 1979-92; President, Entertainment Industry Employers Association, 1982-91; Chairman, Confederation of Australian Arts Centres, 1989-. *Honour:* Order of Australia (AM), 1987. *Memberships:* Royal Sydney Golf Club; American National Club, Sydney. *Hobbies:* Skiing; Swimming; Walking; Cycling; Tennis. *Address:* Sydney Opera House, GPO Box 4274, Sydney, New South Wales 2001, Australia.

MARTIN George Whitney, b. 25 Jan 1926, New York, USA. Writer. *Education:* BA Harvard College, 1948; Trinity College, Cambridge, 1950; LLB University of Virginia Law School, 1953. *Career:* Practised Law, 1955-59; Full-time Writer, 1959-. *Publications:* The Opera Companion, 4th ed, 1988; Verdi, His Music, Life and Times, 4th ed, 1992, Chinese (pirated ed), 1982, Spanish ed, 1984; The Companion to Twentieth-Century Opera, 3rd Ed, 1989; The Damrosch Dynasty, America's First Family of Music, 1983; Aspects of Verdi, 2nd ed, 1993; Verdi at the Golden Gate, Opera and San Francisco in the Gold Rush Years, 1993. *Address:* 21 Ingleton Circle, Kennett Square, PA 19348, USA.

MARTIN Janis, b. 16 Aug 1939, Sacramento, California, USA. Singer (Soprano). m. Gerhard Hellwig. *Education:* Studied with Julia Monroe in Sacramento and Lili Wexberg and Otto Guth in New York. *Debut:* San Francisco 1960, as Annina in La Traviata. *Career:* Returned to San Francisco as Marina, Venus and Meg Page; New York City Opera debut 1962, as Mrs Grose in The Turn of the Screw; New York Metropolitan Opera from 1962-66, at first in mezzo roles then from 1973 as Sieglinde, Marie in Wozzeck and Kundry; Bayreuth Festival 1968-73, as Magdalene, Eva, Sieglinde and Kundry; Chicago 1971, as Tosca; Deutsche Oper Berlin 1971-88; Covent Garden 1973, as Marie; La Scala 1980, as The Woman in Erwartung; La Scala, Marie; Geneva Opera 1985, as Isolde; Other roles include Wagner's Senta, Brünnhilde, Isolde, Venus and Kundry, Tosca, Fidelio, Santuzza, and Strauss's Ariadne and Dyer's

Wife, Salome, Elektra and Marschallin; Cologne Opera 1988, as the Dyer's Wife; Turin and Bayreuth 1989, as Brünnhilde; Sang Beethoven's Leonore at Dusseldorf, 1990; Season 1991/92 as the Götterdämmerung Brünnhilde at Brussels and Senta at Naples. *Recordings include:* Adriano in Rienzi (EMI); Der fliegende Holländer (Decca); Erwartung (CBS); Sancta Susanna by Hindemith. *Address:* c/o Deutsche Oper am Rhein, Heinrich-Heine Allee 16, D-4000 Dusseldorf, Germany.

MARTIN Kathleen, b. 28 Feb 1948, Texas, USA. Singer (Soprano). *Education:* Studied at UCLA and at California State University Long Beach. *Debut:* San Francisco Opera as Madama Butterfly. *Career:* Engaged at the Lubeck Opera, 1974-80, as Fiordiligi, Donna Elvira, Neddaa, Mimi, Desdemona, the Trovatore Leonora, Elsa, Tatiana and Katya Kabanova; Sang at the Frankfurt Opera, 1980-83, guest engagements at the Theater am Gärtnerplatz, Munich; Sang at Toulouse as Jordane in the 1985 premiere of Landowski's Montsegur and appeared at the Paris Opera 1987. *Address:* c/o Teatre du Capitole, Place du Capitole, F-31000 Toulouse, France.

MARTIN Peter, b. 15 Oct 1933, Hamberg. Flutist. m. Wanda W Sokolowskaja, 7 July 1983, 1 son, 1 daughter. *Education:* Studied Flute Under Nicolet in Berlin, Jaunet in Zurich. *Debut:* Radiokonzert Hannover, 1964. *Career:* Engaged for Kassel Opera; Member of the Bonn Symphony Orchestra; Since 1965 First Solo Flutist with States Orchestra Hannover; Professorship at the Music High School, Hannover. *Recordings:* More Than 10 Records and CD's as Soloist with Orchestras or with Chamber Music. *Publications:* Romberg, Concerto; Concerto d minor, Molique; Concerto G & D Mozart. *Contributions to:* Zum Konzert. *Honours:* Kammer Musiker; Darmstadt Kranichstein; Donemus Found. *Hobbies:* Painting; Literature. *Address:* Föhrenwinkel 8, D 30657 Hannover, Germany.

MARTIN Philip James, b. 27 Oct 1947, Dublin, Republic of Ireland. Pianist; Composer. m. Penelope Price Jones, 22 Aug 1970, 1 son, 1 daughter. *Education:* Read Pianoforte School, Dublin; Associate, FRAM, 1988, Royal Academy of Music, London, England; Private music studies with Louis Kentner, London. *Debut:* Wigmore Hall, 1970. *Career:* Regular soloist with major British orchestras including London Symphony Orchestra, London Sinfonietta, All BBC orchestras; Recital work, solo piano and joint recitals worldwide with wife soprano Penelope Price Jones. *Compositions:* Six Clarinet Dances; Three Childrens Songs, recorded; Over 100 songs, chamber music, piano music and orchestral works including Piano Concerto, 1986; Various unpublished as yet; Several major commissions for 1986-87; Beato Angelico for large orchestra, 1990; Piano concerto No 2: A Day in the City, Thalassa, 1991. *Recordings:* RCA Red Seal, reissued digitally by Chandos Records; Percy Grainger's Music with Bournemouth Sinfonietta; The Piano Music of Louis Moreau Gottechalk, Vol 1, Hyperion; The Music of Percy Grainger, Nimbus; The Piano Music of Franz Reizenstein, Continum. *Address:* Chapel House, Theobalds Green, Calstone, Near Calne, Wiltshire SN11 8QE, England.

MARTIN Ruth Kelley, b. 14 Apr 1914, Jersey City, USA. Writer; Musician; Translator; Librettist. m. Thomas Philipp Martin, 17 June 1939, 1 son, 3 daughters. *Education:* AB, Smith College, 1937; Language Study, Columbia University, University of Munich, Summers, 1934, 35; Private Study of Violin, 1921-31; Voice Study, Lausanne, 1931-32, Smith College, 1932-36; Violin Study at Smith College, 1932-37. *Career:* Premieres of Translations & Adaptations: The Magic Flute, 1941, Abduction from the Seraglio, 1946, Così fan Tutte, 1950, Metropolitan Opera; Marriage of Figaro, 1948, The Trial (von Einem), 1953, Golden Slippers, 1955, Die Fledermaus, 1953, Don Giovanni, 1963, Danton's Death, 1966, Daughter of the Regiment, 1975, Grand Duchess of Gerolstein, 1982, New York City Opera. *Compositions:* 100 songs for Silver Burdett Children's Schools Series; 50 English Translations of Operas &

Operettas; Adaptations and Original with Thomas Martin including Carmen, Gypsy Baron, A Night in Venice, Barber of Seville, La Bohème, Girl of the Golden West, Die Tote Stadt, Tales of Hoffmann. *Recordings:* The Magic Flute; Così fan Tutte; Highlights from Die Fledermaus; A Night in Venice; Mozart Operatic arias. *Publications:* Legend of a Musical City by Max Graf, Translator; Philosophical Library, 1945; The Great Operas of Mozart, 1962; A Treasury of Opera Librettos, 1962. *Hobbies:* Mountain Climbing; Print and Autograph (Musicians) Collecting. *Address:* 219 West 13th Street, Apt 1, New York, NY 10011, USA.

MARTIN Vivian, b. 1945, Detroit, Michigan, USA. Soprano. *Education:* BS, Wayne State University; Student, Detroit Conservatory of Music. *Career:* Soloist, Munich Philharmonic and Nuremburg Symphony and Philharmonic Choir, Federal Republic of Germany, 1970; debut as Leonora in La Forza del Destino, 1971; Rezia in Weber's Oberon, Wexford, Republic of Ireland, Opera Festival, 1972; Royal Opera Ghent, Stadt Opera Essen; Badische Opera, Karlsruhe; Stadt Opera, Bonn; Mainz Opera; Royal Opera Lisbon, Portugal; Stadtheater Bremen; Television broadcasts for BBC, BRT Belgium, Bratislava, Czechoslovakia; Philharmonic Orchestra and Opera; Soloist Gavelborg Symphony, Gayle, Sweden, 1978; Symphony Radio Concert Paris, 1978; Warsaw Symphony Orchestra; Tour of India, Iran, Afghanistan, USA State Department, 1976; Toured with Gavelborg Symphony Orchestra, Sweden, 1981-84; Appeared in opera concert on radio and tv Bucharest, 1979; Sang Leonora in Il Trovatore in opera festival; Constanze, Romania, 1979; Concerts in Belgrade, Tivoli Gardens, Copenhagen, Denmark, Zagreb, Yugoslavia, 1979; Opera concert tour of Sweden with Gayle Symphony Orchestra, 1979; Appeared in Aida and Bess (Porgy and Bess), Bratislava, 1979; As Cio-Cio San in Madam Butterfly and Leonora in Il Trovatore, Constanze, 1980. *Recordings:* Has made numerous recordings. *Honours:* Recipient, numerous scholarships and awards. *Memberships:* Actors Equity; AFTRA, American Guild Musical Artists.

MARTINCEK Dusan, b. 19 June 1936, Presov, Czechslovakia. Composer. m. Magdalene Martincek, 16 Dec 1961, 1 son. *Education:* Piano with A Kafendova, Bratislava Conservatory, 1951-56; Piano under R Macudzinski, Composition under J Cikker, Academy of Music and Drama, Bratislava, 1956-60. *Career:* Composer; Pianist; Senior Lecturer, Theory and Piano, J A Komensky Pedagogic Faculty, Trnava, 1960-72; Associate Professor of Theory and Piano, Department of Music Theory, Academy of Music and Drama, Bratislava, 1973-87; Independent Artist, 1988-; Interpretations of works in Czechoslovakia, Germany, Luxembourg, USSR, Rumania, France; Ordentlisher Professor an der Musikhodischule - vom Fahre, 1993. *Compositions:* Orchestral works: Simple Overture, 1961; Passacaglia for String Orchestra, 1967; 2nd Symphony in memoriam J Haydn, 1981; Animation for 35 String Instruments, 1983-85; Continuity for Orchestra, 1987-88; Interrupted Silence, 1989; Works for piano and orchestra: Rhapsody, 1956; Dialogues in the Form of Variations, 1961; Chamber works: Music (Passionato) for Viola (Clarinet) and Piano, 1959; Concertino for Flute and Piano, 1960; Elegy for Viola Solo, 1975; Bonjour, Monsieur Picasso, flute and guitar, 1983; Elegy for Flute and Guitar, 1983; String Quartet, 1983-85; Reflexions, string quartet, 1988; Solo guitar works; Piano solos: 7 Concertante Etudes, 1954-60; Rumanian Rhapsody - Negrea, 1962; Hommage a Corelli, variations, 1970; 3 Sonatinas, 1966; 12 Preludes, 1979; 3 Piano Pieces, 1982; 7 Piano Sonatas, 1956-84; Preludes and fugues; Communications for violin und klavier, 1988; 10 movements for klevier, 1992; Neues Nocturne for kleviere, 1993; Metamorphoseu for violin, cello, Strings, harp and percussion, 1992-93.*Recordings:* Various compositions on Supraphon and OPUS. *Address:* Lipského 11, 84101 Bratislava, Slovakia.

MARTINEAU Malcolm, b. 1960, Edinburgh, Scotland. Pianist. *Education:* Studied at St Catharine's College, Cambridge, and at the Royal Academy of Music with Kendall Taylor and Geoffrey Parsons; Further study with Joyce Rathbone. *Career:* Has accompanied such leading singers as Janet Baker, Della Jones, Marie McLaughlin, Julia Migenes, Stephen Varcoe and Thomas Allen; Concerts in Fredensborg Palace in Denmark with Laurence Dale, at the Concertgebouw with Sarah Walker and at the Châtelet in Paris with Lorna Anderson; Engagements with clarinettist Emma Johnson; Has played in master classes at the Pears-Britten School for Suzanne Danco, Elisabeth Schwarzkopf, Ileana Cotrubas and Kurt Equiluz; Festival appearances and series of concerts at St John's Smith Square featuring songs by Debussy and Poulenc; Recitals at the Wigmore Hall and on South Bank; Paris, Belgium, Italy and throughout the UK. *Recordings include:* Complete Fauré songs with Sarah Walker; Recital with Della Jones. *Honours include:* Walter Gruener International Lieder Competition, 1984. *Address:* Lies Askonas Ltd, 186 Drury Lane, London WC2B 5RY, England.

MARTINEZ Odaline de la, b. 31 Oct 1949, Matanzas, Cuba. Composer; Conductor; Pianist. *Education:* BFA Tulane University, 1968-72; Royal Academy of Music, 1972-76; GRSM (Composition and Piano); MMus (Composition) University of Surrey, 1975-77; Postgraduate Research (Computer Music), 1977-80. *Career:* Compositions broadcast by BBC, Radio Istanbul, Radio Cork, Radio Belgrade, KPFA San Francisco; Music Director, Cardiff Festival, 1994, conductor of Dame Ethel Smyth's Opera The Wreckers, Proms BBC in 1994 (revival after over 50 years). *Compositions include:* After Sylvia (Song cycle); Phasing for chamber orchestra; A Moment's Madness for flute and piano; Sister Aimee, Opera; 2 American Madrigals for mixed chorus. Conductor of Lontano and London Chamber Symphony: many performances of contemporary music; Conducted the premiere of Berthold Goldschmidt's Beatrix Cenci, 1988; Directed series of Latin American concerts on South Bank 1989. *Recordings:* British Women Composers, Vol I and II, Villa Lobas Chamber and Choral Music, Boulez sans Boulez all on Lorelt label. *Publication:* Mendelssohn's Sister, (forthcoming). *Memberships:* SPNM, Women in Music. *Honours:* 1st woman to conduct BBC Prom concerts at the Royal Albert Hall; Danforth Fellowship; Marshall Scholar; Watson Fellow; National Endowments for the Arts (USA); Joyce Dixie Prize; Villa-Lobos Medal, 1987; Manson Scholarship; Outstanding Alumna Tulane University, FRAM. *Current Management:* Denise Kantor Management. *Hobbies:* Travel; Eating Out; Films. *Address:* c/o Lontano, 47 Queens Drive, London N4 2SZ, England.

MARTINIS Carla, b. 1921, Danculovice, Yugoslavia. Singer (Soprano). *Education:* Zagreb Conservatory, with Professor Martinis. *Career:* Sang first in Zagreb and Prague; New York City Opera 1950-53, debut as Turandot; Vienna Staatsoper from 1951, debut as Aida conducted by Karajan; Salzburg Festival 1951, as Desdemona conducted by Furtwängler; Paris Opéra 1951, as Amelia in Un Ballo in Maschera; La Scala Milan, Aix-en-Provence, Naples and Florence, 1952; San Francisco Opera, 1954; Sang La Gioconda at Trieste, 1956. *Recordings:* Otello from Salzburg (Cetra); Donna Anna in Don Giovanni; La Forza del Destino; Tosca.

MARTINO Donald James, b. 16 May 1931, Plainfield, New Jersey, USA. Composer; Educator; Publisher. *Education:* BM, Syracuse University, 1952; MFA, Princeton University, 1954; MA, Harvard University (honorary), 1983; Fulbright Grant for study with Luigi Dallapiciola, Florence, Italy, 1954-55, 1955-56. *Career:* Associate Professor of Music, Yale University, 1958-69; Chairman of Composition, New England Conservatory, 1969-79; Irving Fine Professor, Brandeis University, 1979-82; Walter Bigelow Rosen Professor, Harvard University, 1983-93, Professor Emeritus, 1993-. *Compositions include:* Contemplations for Orchestra, 1956; Concerto for Wind Quintet, 1964; Concerto for Piano and Orchestra, 1965; Notturno, flute, clarinet, violin, violoncello, percussion, piano, 1973; Paradiso Choruses, chorus, soloists, orchestra, tape, 1974; Ritorno for Orchestra, 1975; Triple Concerto for Clarinet, Bass Clarinet and Contrabass Clarinet with Chamber Ensemble, 1977; Fantasies and Inpromptus, piano solo, 1981; Divertisements for Youth Orchestra, 1981; String Quartet, 1983; The White Island, chorus, chamber orchestra, 1985; Concerto for Alto Saxophone and Chamber Orchestra, 1987; From the Other Side, flute, violoncello, percussion, piano, 1988; Twelve Preludes for Piano, 1991; Three Sad Songs, viola and piano, 1993. *Publications:* Editor: 178 Chorale Harmonizations of J S Bach: A Comparative Edition for Study, 1984. *Contributions to:* The Source Set and its Aggregate Formations, Journal of Music Theory, 1961; Notation in General Articulation in Particular, 1966, An Interview by James Boros, 1991, Perspectives of New Music. *Honours:* Pulitzer Prize, 1974; Kennedy Center-Friedheim Award, 1985; Mark M Horblit Award, Boston Symphony, 1987. *Memberships:* American Academy of Arts and Letters; American Academy of Arts & Sciences; Founder, American Society of Composers; Broadcast Music Inc. *Hobby:* Tennis. *Current Management:* Dantalian Inc, USA. *Address:* c/o Dantalian Inc, 11 Pembroke Street, Newton, MA 02158, USA.

MARTINOTY Jean-Louis, b. 20 Jan 1946, Etampes, France. Stage Director. *Career:* Radio producer for ORTF, then critic for L'Humanite; Assistant to Jean-Pierre Ponnelle, notably in works by Mozart and Monteverdi at Zurich; Baroque repertoire includes productions for the Karlsruhe Handel Festival; Production of Ariande auf Naxos seen at the Paris Opera 1983, Covent Garden 1985; General Administrator of the Paris Opera at the Palais Garnier 1986-89; Productions in season, 1990-91 included Ziegeunerbaron at the Zurich Opera, La Clemenza di Tito at the Deutsche Oper Berlin; Produced Tamerlano at the 1993 Handel Festival, Karlsruhe.

MARTINPELTO Hillevi, b. 9 Jan 1958, Älvalden, Sweden. Singer (Soprano). *Education:* Studied at the Stockholm Opera School. *Career:* Sang Pamina in Die Zauberflöte with the Folksopera in Stockholm and at the Edinburgh Festival; Norrlands Opera from 1987 in Ivar Hallstrom's Den Bergtagna (also on Swedish TV and at the York Festival), Tatiana in Eugene Onegin and Marguerite; Royal Opera Stockholm debut 1987, as Madama Butterfly; Sang the title roles in Gluck's Iphigènie operas at the Drottningholm Festival, 1989-90; Théâtre de la Monnaie Brussels from 1990 as Fiordiligi and the Countess in Le Nozze di Figaro; Season 1991-92 with Fiordiligi at the Hamburg Staatsoper, Wagner's Eva at Nice, Donna Anna at Aix-en-Provence; Season 92-93 included: Don Giovanni, Aix-en-Provence Festival, France; Così fan Tutte, Hamburg State Opera, Germany; Das Rheingold, Lyric Opera of Chicago, USA; Le Nozze di Figaro, Toulouse Opera, France; Châtelet, Monteverdi and Wagner's Eva in Tokyo with Deutsche Oper Berlin; Further engagements include Verdi Desdemona in Helsinki; Concert engagements with Dvořák's Requiem (Scottish National Orchestra, 1987); Residentie Orchestra of The Hague in Mozart; Belgian Radio Orchestra; Philharmonia of London in The Creation, conducted by Claus Peter Flor; engaged as Donna Anna, Don Giovanni, at Glyndebourne, 1994-. *Recordings include:* Elettra in Idomeneo, conducted by John Eliot Gardiner (Deutsche Grammophon); Contessa in Nozze with Gardiner on DGG. *Address:* Artists Sekretariat Ulf Törnqvist, Sankt Eriksgatan 100, 2 tr. S-113 31 Stockholm.

MARTINS Maria de Lourdes, b. 26 May 1926, Lisbon, Portugal. Composition Professor, Conservatorio Nacional, Lisbon. *Education:* Graduate, National Conservatory of Music, Lisbon (Piano and Composition); Advanced studies in Composition with H Genzmer, Music High School, Munich, Germany, 1959-60; Diploma Orff Institute of the Mozarteum, Salzburg, 1964-65. *Career:* Piano Concerts on National and German Radio; TV performances in Portugal; 1st Opera, S Carlos National Theatre, Lisbon, July 1986. *Compositions include:* Encoberto de F Pessoa, 1965; O Litorial de A Negreioas, 1971-76; Rondo for Wind

Orchestra, 1978; Portuguese Christmas Songs for Wind Orchestra, 1978; Portuguese Dances, 1978; Sonatinas 1 and 2 for Piano; Catch, 1981; Ritmite, 1983; Musica de Piano Para Crianças Ed Valentim de Carvalho; Opera: Três Máscaras, 1983; Simetria for Clarinet Solo, 1984; 4 Poemas de F Pessoa, 1984; Moments of Peace by J Gracen Brown, 1989; II String Quartet, 1989; Concerto de piano, 1990; Divertiment on Mozart Themes, 1991. *Recordings:* Educo Edition: Wind Quintet; 12 Choral Port Songs; Piano Works; Decca, Historia de Natal. *Hobby:* Travel. *Address:* R Trindade Coelho 108, 2775 Parede, Portugal.

MARTINUCCI Nicola, b. 28 Mar 1941, Tarent, Italy. Singer (Tenor). *Education:* Studied with Sara Sforni in Milan. *Debut:* Teatro Nuovo Milan 1966, as Manrico. *Career:* Sang at La Scala and at the Teatro La Fenice, Venice; Deutsche Oper am Rhein Dusseldorf from 1973; Florence 1974, as Filippo in a revival of Spontini's Agnese di Hohenstaufen; Verona Arena 1982-86, as Radames, Calaf and Andrea Chénier; Covent Garden debut 1985, as Dick Johnson in La Fanciulla del West; Appearances in Dublin, Teheran, Budapest and Salzburg; Rome Opera, 1989 as Poliuto; Sang Calaf in London, 1990; Pollione at Catania, Manrico at Parma; Season 1992 as Enzo in La Gioconda at Rome and Calaf at the Festival of Caracalla. *Recordings include:* Video of Turandot, from Verona (Thorn-EMI); Donizetti's Poliuto (Nuovo Era). *Address:* Gorlinsky Ltd, 33 Dover Street, London W1X 4NJ, England.

MARTIRANO Salvatore, b. 12 Jan 1927, Yonkers, New York, USA. Composer. *Education:* Studied piano and composition at the Oberlin Conservatory, Eastman School of Music with Bernard Rogers (MM 1952) and with Dallapiccola at the Cherubini Conservatory Florence, 1952-54. *Career:* Played clarinet and cornet with the Paris Island Marine band Fellowship with the American Academy in Rome, 1956-59; Teacher at the University of Illinois at Urbana from 1963. Developed electronic musical instruments and sound systems Malmstadt-Enke Blues, Mar-Vil Construction and Sal-Mar Construction. *Compositions:* Recent works include: Selections for alto flute, bass clarinet, viola and cello, 1970; Sal-Mar Construction I-VII for tape, 1971-75; Fast Forward for tape, 1979; Fifty One for tape, 1978; In Memoriam Luigi Dallapiccola for tape, 1978; Thrown sextet for wind and perecussion, 1984; Look at the Back of my Head for a While, video piece, 1984; Sampler: Everything Goes when the Whistle Blows, for violin and synthetic orchestra, 1985, 1988; Dance Players I and II, video pieces, 1986; 3 not 2, variable-forms piece, 1987; Phleu for amplified flute and synthetic orchestra, 1988; LON/dons for chamber orchestra. *Address:* ASCAP, ASCAP Building, One Lincoln Plaza, NY 10023, USA.

MARTLAND Steve, b. 1958, Liverpool, England. Composer. *Education:* Graduated from Liverpool University, 1981; Royal Conservatory, The Hague, Holland, with Louis Andriessen; Tanglewood USA with Gunther Schuller. *Career:* Works with students and musicians outside the classical tradition; Pieces for informal Dutch ensembles, the Jazz Orchestra Loose Tubes and the band Test Department multi-media project for BBC TV, Joint premiere of Babi-Yar with the Royal Liverpool Philharmonic and the St Louis Symphony Orchestra; American Invention performed in the USA and Japan. *Compositions:* Remembering Lennon for 7 players 1981/85; Lotta Continua for orchestra 1981/84; Duo for trumpet and piano 1982; Canto a la Esperanza for soprano, electric guitar and chamber orchestra 1982; Kgakala for piano 1982; Babi Yar for orchestra 1983; Orc for horn and small orchestra 1984; American Invention for 13 players 1985; Shoulder to Shoulder for 13 players 1986; Dividing the Lines for brass/wind band 1986; Remix for jazz ensemble 1986; Big Mac I/II for 4/8 players 1987; Divisions for electronic tape 1986/87; Drill for 2 pianos 1987; Glad Day for voice and ensemble 1988; Albion for tape and film 1987-88; Terra Firma for 5 voices, with amplification and video 1989; Crossing the Border for Strings, 1991; The Perfect Act for ensemble and voice,

1991. *Honours:* 1981 Mendelssohn Scholarship; 1985 Government Composition Prize, Holland.

MARTON Eva Heinrich, b. 18 June 1943, Budapest, Hungary. Soprano. m. Zoltan Marton, 1 son, 1 daughter. *Education:* Graduate, Franz Lizst Academy. *Debut:* Budapest Opera, 1968. *Career:* Soprano with various opera Companies, including Frankfurt Opera, Vienna State Opera, Hamburg State Opera, Metropolitan Opera, La Scala, Chicago Lyric Opera, San Francisco Opera, Teatro Colon, Buenos Aires, Bayreuth and others. *Roles include:* Empress in Frau ohne Schatten; Salome; all three Brünnhildes in Ring Cycle; Elisabeth and Venus in Tannhäuser; Elsa and Ortrud in Lohengrin; Senta in Fliegende Holländer; title roles of Turandot, Tosca, Manon Lescaut, Fedora, Gioconda, Aida; Amelia in Ballo in Maschera; Leonora in Trovatore; Lady Macbeth in Macbeth; Elisabetta in Don Carlo; Leonore in Fidelio; Maddalena in Andrea Chénier; Leonora in La Forza del Destino; Covent Garden debut 1987, Turandot (returned 1990 as Elektra); Sang Tosca in Budapest, 1989, Elektra at Barcelona 1990; Vienna Staatsoper 1991, as Salome; Season 1992 with Turandot for the Royal Opera at the Wembley Arena and at Chicago, the Walküre Brünnhilde at Bonn, Salome at Barcelona and the Dyer's Wife in Die Frau ohne Schatten at Salzburg. TV films: Two Turandots, Vienna & Met; Toscas, Verona & Florence; Tannhäuser, Lohengrin, Trovatore, All at the Met; Andrea Chénier, La Scala. *Recordings:* Violanta, Turandot, Fedora, Andrea Chénier, Bluebeard's Castle, Gioconda; album of Wagner scenes; album of Puccini arias; album of Richard Strauss songs; Final scene from Salome; Brünnhilde in The Ring conducted by Haitink (EMI); Videos Elektra conducted by Abbado (Virgin) and Il Trovatore from the Met. *Contributions to:* Interview with Alan Blyth (People) Opera magazine, Feb 1990. *Address:* c/o Royal Opera House, Covent Garden, London WC2, England.

MARTTINEN Tauno, b. 27 Sept 1912, Helsinki, Finland. Composer. *Education:* Studied Music, Viipuri, 1920s; Studied Music, Helsinki, 1930s. *Career:* Director, Hameenlinna Music Institute, 1950-75. *Compositions include:* The Cloak, 1962-63; The Engagement, 1964; Burnt Orange, 1968; Maitre Patelin, 1969-72; Shaman's Drum, 1974-76; The Earl's Sister, 1977; The Pharoah's Letter, 1978-80; Song of the Great River, 1982-84; Seven Brothers by Aleksis KIVI, Op 263, 1976-1986; Ballets: A Portrait of Dorian Gray, 1969; Snow Queen, 1970; The Sun Out of the Moon, 1975-77; The Ugly Duckling, 1976, 1982-83; Orchestra: Symphony No 1, 1958; Symphony No 2, 1959; Symphony No 3, 1960-62; Symphony No 4, 1964; Symphony No 7, 1977; panu, God of Fire, 1966; Symphony No 8, 1983; Symphony No 9, 1986; The Maid of Pohjola, 1982; Solo Instrument Concerto for piano and orchestra, 1964; Concerto for flute and orchestra, 1972; Concerto for Clarinet and Orchestra, 1974; Concerto for two pianos and orchestra, 1981; Concerto for piano and orchestra No 4 Op 241, 1984; Chamber Music: Delta, 1962; Alfa op 16, 1963; Visit to the Giant Sage Vipunen, 1969; String Quartet No 2, 1971; Divertimento, 1977; Intermezzo, 1977-78; Le Commencement, 1979; Trio, 1982; Solo Instrument: Titisee for piano, 1965; Adagio for organ, 1967; Sonatina for piano; Nore dame, 1970; The Cupola, for organ, 1971; Sonata for piano, 1975; Impression for cello, 1978; Prophet for organ, 1984. *Honour:* Honorary Professor conferred by the State, 1972. *Address:* TEOSTO, Lauttasaarentie 1, 00200 Helsinki 20, Finland.

MARTURET Eduardo, b. 19 Sept 1953, Caracas. Conductor; Composer. *Education:* Music Degree, Anglia University; Further studies in Cambridge, Siena and Rome. *Debut:* Caracas, 1978. *Career:* Artistic Director, Sinronietta Caracas, 1986; Music Director: Orq Sinfonica Venezuela, 1987-, and Teatro Teresa Carento, 1984-87; Has conducted major orchestras in Germany, Holland, Scandinavia and Hungary. *Compositions include:* Canto Llano, music for six and sax; Tres Tiemtos; Casa Bonita; Oriana. *Recordings:* Brahms complete symphonies, overtures and concertos; Berliner Symphonicer, Mozart, symphonies and complete violin concertos; Concertegbow Chamber Orchestra. *Publications:* Casa Bonita: Catalogue of the Exhibition, 1988; Article, Perspectives of Mozart's Symphonic Music, 1991. *Honours include:* Orden Diego De Losada, 1992; Best Conductor, 1992; Best Classical Record, 1992; Orden Andres Bello, 1992. *Memberships:* SPNM, London; American Symphony Orchestra Legue; Conductors Guild, USA. *Hobbies:* Fishing; Wines; Yachting. *Current Management* John Gingrich, New York. *Address:* PO Box 2912, Caracas, Venezuela.

MARUZIN Yuri, b. 8 Dec 1947, Perm, Russia. Singer (Tenor). *Education:* Studied in Leningrad. *Debut:* Maly Theatre, Laningrad, 1972. *Career:* Appearances with the Kirov Opera Leningrad, St Petersburg from 1978 notably as Hermann in The Queen of Spades and Dimitri in Boris Godunov and touring to Covent Garden, 1987 as Lensky: Sang the Tsarevich in Rimsky's The Tale of Tsar Saltan at La Scala and Reggio Emilia, 1988, Galitsin in Khovanshchina at the Vienna Staatsoper, 1989; San Francisco Opera as Anatol in War and Pieace, Andrei Khovansky in Khovanshchina at Edinburgh, 1991; Other guest engagements at Turin, Nice, Madrid and Toronto; Other roles include Faust, Pinkerton, Rodolfo, Don Carlos, Don Alvaro, Alfredo and the Duke of Mantua; Sang Hermann at Glyndebourne, 1992. *Address:* Kirov Opera and Ballet Theatre, St Petersburg Russia.

MARVIA Einari, b. 21 Nov 1915, Tuusniemi, Finland. Composer; Musicologist. m. Liisa Aroheimo, 28 June 1984, 2 sons, 1 daughter. *Education:* Sibelius Academy, Helsinki; Music studies, Vienna, 1951; MA, 1955; PhLic, 1973. *Debut:* Composition Concert, Helsinki, 1945. *Career:* Director of Publications, Edition Fazer, Helsinki, 1946-80. *Compositions:* Taru, symphonic poem; Piano Sonata in D flat major; Many songs and choral works including: Unhon maa, song cycle; 6 songs to words of Katri Vala. *Publications:* Fazerin Musiikkikauppa, 1897-1947, 1947; Suomen Säveltäjien 25 vuotta, 1970; Sibeliuksen rituaalimusiikki, 1984; Suomen Säveltäjiä I-II, (editor), 1965-66; Documenta Musicae Fennicae I-XVI (editor). *Contributions to:* Many articles on Finnish music history notably academic music and orchestra history. *Honours:* Award Winner, Viotti Song Competition, Vercelli, 1951; Award of Honour, Foundation for the Support of Finnish Music, 1985; Pro Finlandia Medal; Finland's Cross of Freedom; Verdienstkreuz vom Deutschen Adler. *Membership:* Society of Finnish Composers. *Hobby:* Old Finnish books.

MARVIN Frederick, b. 11 June 1923, California, USA. Pianist; Musicologist; Professor. *Education:* Curtis Institute of Music, Philadelphia; Southern California Conservatory, Los Angeles. *Debut:* Carnegie Hall, 1949. *Career:* Toured USA, 1949-54; Concerts in every major capital of Europe from 1954, solo recitals, and concert lectures; Master Classes; Professor of Piano, 1968-, Professor Emeritus and Artist in Residence, 1990, Syracuse University. *Recordings include:* George Antheil Piano Sonata No 4; Liszt Album, Sonatas by Moscheles and L Berger, 3 LPs of sonatas by Dussek; Schubert Album; CD on Dorian Records, Three Sonatas by J L Dussek; Sonatas by Soler, 3 albums. *Publications:* 63 Sontas by Soler; Four Villancicos and Salve, Lamentation, Soler; Edited 8 volumes Sonatas, and Choral Works, Padre Soler; 2 sonatas, J L Dussek; contributions to music magazines. *Address:* c/o Ernst Schuh, 246 Houston Avenue, Syracuse, NY 13224, USA.

MÄRZENDORFER Ernst, b. 26 May 1921, Salzburg, Austria. Conductor. *Education:* Studied with Clemens Krauss at the Salzburg Mozarteum. *Career:* Conducted opera in Salzburg from 1940; Graz Opera, 1945-51; Professor, Salzburg Mozarteum, 1951; Conducted at the Teatro Colon Buenos Aires, 1952-53; Conductor of the Mozarteum orchestra, 1953-58, including tour of the USA, 1956; Conducted at the Deutsche Oper, Berlin from 1958 and at the Vienna Staatsoper from 1961 (premiere of Henze's ballet Tancredi 1966); Recorded the 106 symphonies of Haydn with the Vienna Chamber Orchestra, 1967-71; Premiered his completion of Bruckner's 9th Symphony at Graz, 1969; Conducted first performances of Einem's Turandot, 1954 and Medusa, 1965. *Recordings include:* Early Mozart symphonies, Concerto K299 and Divertimento K334; Mendelssohn Concerto for violin and piano; Donizetti L'Elisir d'Amore, with the Berlin Symphony Orchestra; Eine Nacht in Venedig (Hungaroton); Haydn Complete Symphonies (Musical Heritage Society).

MASCIADRI Milton Walter, b. 15 Nov 1959, Montevideo, Uruguay. Double Bass Player. m. Rosanna Urbani, 19 Dec 1986. *Education:* Studies with Milton Romay Masciadri, Uruguay and Brazil; Master's degree, University of Hartford, with Gary Karr; Doctorate, State University of New York, with Julius Levine, Lawrance Wolfe. *Career:* Formerly: Assistant Principal Bass, Porto Alegre Symphony Orchestra, Brazil; Assistant Professor, Federal University of Rio Grande do Norte (UFRN); Solo Bass, UFRN Chamber Orchestra; Professor, Federal University of Santa Maria; Presently: Assistant Professor of Double Bass, University of Georgia, Athens, USA; Assistant Principal Bass, Charleston Symphony Orchestra; Principal Bass, Macon Symphony Orchestra; Member, Atlanta Virtuosi; Frequent appearances as Solo Bassist with Orchestra and recitals, USA, Uruguay, Argentina, Brazil, Mexico, Central America, Italy, Greece, Germany; Broadcasts, Public Radio, USA, Public Radio and TV, Brazil and Uruguay, American Italian RAI TV; Professor of Double Bass, several music festivals; Teaches at International Music Festival, Brasilia, International Festival, Vale Veneto and Victoria, Brazil, Georgia Music Festival, USA; Lectures extensively on Double Bass, American and Latin American Universities; Has premiered compositions of American and Latin American composers. *Address:* University of Georgia, School of Music, Athens, GA 30602, USA.

MASIN Ronald, b. 9 Aug 1937, Rotterdam, Netherlands. Violinist. m. Maria Keleman, 1 son, 1 daughter. *Education:* Diploma, Royal Brussels Conservatory. *Debut:* With orchestra, aged 14, Johannesburg, South Africa. *Career:* Solo and chamber performances, Netherlands, Belgium, France, Switzerland, Hungary, USSR, Italy, Denmark and South Africa; Numerous solo appearances with Concertgebouw of Amsterdam; leader, Amsterdam Philharmonic Orchestra and Amsterdam Kern Ensemble. *Recordings:* EMI. *Publication:* The Violin Technique-the natural way, 1982. *Honour:* Recipient of professorship, University of Cape Town, South Africa. *Hobbies:* Phogoraphy; Cycling. *Address:* Maartenplein 7, 3633 EJ Vreeland, The Netherlands.

MASLANKA David (Henry), b. 30 Aug 1943, Maryland, USA. Composer. *Education:* Studied at the New England Conservatory 1959-61, Oberlin College, BMus, 1965, and Michigan State University, PhD, 1965-70; Studied conducting with Gerhardt Wimberger, at the Salzburg Mozarteum. *Career:* Taught at Geneso College, New York, 1970-74, Sarah Lawrence College, 1974-80, New York University, 1980-81, Lehmann College from 1981. *Compositions include:* Death and the Maiden, chamber opera, 1974; Orchestra: Symphony, 1970; Fragments, 1971; Concerto for piano, wind and percussion, 1976; Intermezzo for chamber orchestra, 1979; A Child's Garden of Dreams, I and II, 1981-82; Chamber: String Quartet, 1968; 2 Trios for viola, clarinet and piano, 1971-72; Cello Songs for cello and piano, 1978; Arcadia for 4 cellos, 1982; Arcadia II concerto for marimba and percussion ensemble 1982; Vocal: Anne Sexton Songs for soprano and piano, 1975; Hills of May for soprano and string quartet, 1978; medieval and Renaissance music for women's voices, inaccompanied and with instruments. *Honours include:* MacDowell Colony Fellowships; NEA and Martha Baird Rockefeller Fund for Music grants. *Address:* ASCAP, ASCAP Building, One Lincoln Plaza, NY 10023, USA.

MASON Anne, b. 1954, Lincolnshire, England. Singer (Mezzo-soprano). *Education:* Studied at the Royal Academy of Music with Marjorie Thomas and at the National Opera Studie. *Career:* Welsh National Opera Chorus, 1977-79; Opera North from 1982 as Fenena in Nabucco, in Peace by Carl Davis and in Madame Butterfly; English National Opera 1983, as a Valkyrie in a new production of Die Walküre; Innsbruch Early Music Festival 1983, in Cesti's Il Tito, conducted by Alan Curtis; Kent Opera and Scottish Opera 1984, in new productions of King Priam by Tippett and Edward Harper's Hedda Gabler; Covent Garden appearances in Carmen (as Mércèdes), Otello (Emilia), Das Rheingold, Madame Butterfly, Die Walküre, La Clemenza di Tito, Cenerentola, Rosenkavalier, Traviata, and Götterdämmerung; Glyndebourne Tour 1987, as Dorabella in Così fan Tutte; Recent engagements as Annius in La Clemenza di Tito at Aix, Così fan Tutte with Welsh National Opera and as Marcellina in Le nozze di Figaro in Madrid; Season 1992 as Donna Clara in the stage premiere of Gerhard's The Duenna, at Madrid, as Henrietta Maria in I Puritani at Covent Garden and Cornelia in Julius Caeser for Scottish Opera; Second Maid in Elektra at the First Night at the 1993 London Proms; Concerts in Britain, Germany, France, Austria and Belgium, notably in The Dream of Gerontius and Verdi's Requiem. *Recordings include:* Video of HMS Pinafore; Helen in King Priam; Second Bridesmaid in Le nozze di Figaro, conducted by Solti; Marcellina, Figaro with Haitink, EMI; Emilia di Liverpool, Opera Rara. *Honours include:* Gerhardt Lieder Prize, the Recital Diploma and the Countess of Munster Award, at the Royal Academy of Music; Finalist in the 1983 Benson and Hedges Gold Award; ARAM of Royal Academy of Music. *Address:* c/o Harrison Parrott Ltd, 12 Penzance Place, London W11 4PA, England.

MASON Barry, b. 6 Sept 1947, Cottingham, Yorkshire, England. Lutenist; Guitarist; Musical Director. m. Glenda Simpson, 1 Oct 1983. *Education:* Hull College of Technology; Royal Academy of Music with Anthony Rooley and David Munrow, 1969-74; Royal College of Music with Diana Poulton, 1974-75. *Debut:* Purcell Room, 1973. *Career:* Director, Camerata of London, 1974; Director, 1st Early Music Centre Festival, London, 1977; Director, Progress Instruments Tours, Japan, Europe and USA, 1978; The Wicked Lady film, BBC Shakespeare Films; Director, The Guitarist's Companion, 1986. *Recordings:* Popular Music From The Time of Elizabeth I, Saga; The Muses Garden of Delights, Saga; Music For Kings and Courtiers' Saga; The Queens Men, CRD; Thomas Campion, Meridian; Elizabethan Ayres and Duets, Hyperian. *Contributions to:* Guitar International; Early Music News; Early Music Magazine; Music in Education. *Honour:* Peter Latham Award for Musicology, Royal Academy of Music, 1971. *Current Management:* Francesca McManus. *Memberships:* Council member, Early Music Centre. *Address:* Francesca McManus, 71 Priory Road, Kew Gardens, Richmond, Surrey, TW9 3PH, England.

MASON Marilyn, b. 29 June 1925, Oklahoma, USA. Organist. *Education:* Studied in Oklahoma State University, at the University of Michigan, Union Theological Seminary New York, and with Nadia Boulanger, Maurice Durufle and Schoenberg. *Career:* Teacher at the University of Michigan 1946, Chairman of organ department, 1962, Professor, 1965; Recital tours of North America, Europe, Australia, Africa and South America; Concerts with the Detroit and Philadelphia Orchestras; Commissions for such composers as Krenek, Cowell, ALbright, Ulysses Kay, Sowerby and Ross Lee Finney. *Recordings include:* Albums of music by Sessions, Satie, Schoenberg and Virgil Thomson. *Address:* Michigan State University, School of Music, East Lansing, MI 48824, USA.

MASSARD Robert, b. 15 Aug 1925, Pau, France. Singer (Baritone). *Education:* Conservatories of Pau and Bayonne. *Career:* Sang the High Priest in Samson et Dalila at the Paris Opera, 1952; Thoas in Iphigénie en Tauride at Aix, 1952; Sang Ashton in Lucia di Lammermoor at the Paris Opéra 1957; Glyndebourne 1958, in Alceste; Orestes in Iphigénie en Tauride with the Covent Garden company at Edinburgh, 1961: sang Fieramosca in Benvenuto Cellini with the Royal Opera in London; Bolshoy Theatre Moscow 1962, as Rigoletto; La Scala Milan 1967, as Valentin in Faust; Paris 1974, as Sancho Panza in Massenet's Don Quixote; Other roles include Nero in L'Incoronazione di Poppea, the Count in Capriccio, Milhaud's Orpheus, Escamillo and Ravel's Ramiro. *Recordings:* Iphigénie en Tauride (Pathé); Mireille; Thais (Decca); Rigoletto; Benvenuto Cellini (Philips); Raimbaud in Le Comte Ory (Chant du Monde). *Address:* c/o Philips, Polygram Classics, PO Box 1420, 1 Sussex Place, Hammersmith, London W6 9XS, England.

MASSÉUS Jan, b. 28 Jan 1913, Rotterdam, Holland. Composer. *Education:* Studied piano at the Rotterdam Conservatory with Willem Pijper; Studied composition with Henk Badings. *Career:* Music Critic in Rotterdam, 1956-60; Electronic music studios of the Delft Technical High School, 1958-59 Director of the Leeuwarden Music School, 1961-72. *Compositions:* Sinfonietta, 1952; Violin Concerto, 1953; Gezelle liederen for soprano, alto, piano 4 hands and percussion, 1955; Concerto for 2 Flutes and orchestra, 1956; Piano Concerto, 1966; Skirmishes for chorus and orchestra, 1975; 2 Violin Sonatas, 1946, 1950; Quintet for piano and strings, 1952; Partita for violin and piano, 1956; Flute Sonata, 1957; Iowa-Serenade for youth-symph orchestra, 1981; Concerto for euphonium and brassband, 1983; Aquarius foor brassband (dedicated to Marilyn Ferguson); Nada Brahma for piano 4-hands and windband, 1988; Pandora for solo-percussionist and windband, 1990; Wayang-Liedereb (poems) for declamator and percussion, 91; Claviator 94 for brassband, 1993. *Honour:* Visser-Neerlandia Prize, 1956. *Address:* Serviceflat "Het Oosten", Rubenslaan 1 - Flat 71, 3723 BM Bilthoven.

MASSEY Andrew John, b. 1 May 1946, Nottingham, England. Orchestral Conductor. m. Sabra A Todd, 29 May 1982, 1 son, 1 daughter. *Education:* BA, Merton College, Oxford University, 1968; MA, analysis contemporary & conducting techniques, 1969; Dartington Summer School with Hans Keller, Witold Lutoslawski, Luciano Berio. *Debut:* Cleveland, 1978. *Career:* Assistant conductor, Cleveland Orchestra, USA, 1978-80; Associate conductor, New Orleans Symphony Orchestra, 1980-86, San Francisco Symphony Orchestra, 1986-; Music director, Rhode Island Philharmonic, 1986-; Art adviser, prime guest conductor, Fresno Philharmonic, 1986-; Music Director, 1987-. *Membership:* American Federation of Musicians. *Hobbies:* Trees; Computers. *Current Management:* John Gingrich Management, PO Box 1515, NYC, NY 10023, USA. *Address:* c/o San Francisco Symphony, Davies Symphony Hall, San Francisco, CA 94102, USA.

MASSEY Roy Cyril, b. 9 May 1934, England. Organist. m. Ruth Carol Craddock Grove, 1975. *Education:* BMus, University of Birmingham; Private study with David Willcocks. FRCO(chm), ADCM, ARCM. *Career:* Organist: St Alban's, Conybere Street, Birmingham, 1953-60; St Augustine's, Edgbaston, 1960-65; Croydon Parish Church, 1965-68; Warden, Royal School of Church Music, 1965-68; Conductor, Croydon Bach Society, 1966-68; Special commissioner, Royal School of Church Music, 1964-; Organist to City of Birmingham Choir, 1954-; Organist/Master of Choristers, Birmingham Cathedral, 1968-74; Director of Music, King Edward's School, Birmingham, 1968-74; Conductor, Hereford Choral Society, 1974-; Organist/Master of Choristers, Hereford Cathedral, 1974-; Conductor-in-Chief, alternate years associate conductor, Three Choirs Festival, 1975-; Adviser on organs to dioceses of Birmingham & Hereford, 1974- . *Address:* 1 College Cloisters, Hereford HR1 2NG, England.

MASSIMO Alberto, b. 23 June 1962, Cape Town, South Africa. Conductor; Organist. *Education:* BMus, University of Cape Town, 1984; Further studies in Rome and Edinburgh. *Career:* Maestro di Cappella of the Basilica di Santa Cecilia, Rome, 1987 and conducted orchestra del Teatro dell Opera di Roma in Church of Sant Ignazio and the Cancelleria, Rome, 1987- 88; Musical Director, Edinburgh Chamber Orchestra, 1991, and Organist and Choirmaster of St Andrew and St Georges Church, Edinburgh, 1992. *Honours:* Alto

Perfezionamento in Musica Award, Italian Government, 1987; Harry Crossley and Jules Kramer Awards, Cape Town University, 1989; Professional of the Year in Music 1991, ABI, 1991. *Memberships:* Incorporated Society of Musicians; Royal School of Church Music. *Hobbies:* Philately; Steam Locomotives. *Address:* 7/1 Windmill Place, Edinburgh EH8 7XQ, Scotland.

MÁSSON Askell, b. 21 Nov 1953, Reykjavik, Iceland. Composer; Musician. *Education:* Reykjavik Children's School of Music, 1961-63; Reykjavik College of Music, 1968-69; Private Studies, London, England, with: Composition, Patrick Savill, 1975-77, Percussion, James Blades, 1975-76. *Debut:* Icelandic TV Playing Own Music, 1969. *Career:* Commenced composing, 1967; Composer, Instrumentalist, National Theatre of Iceland, 1973-75; Producer, Icelandic State Radio, 1978-83; General Secretary, Icelandic League of Composers, 1983-85; Chairman STEF, Iceland Performing Rights Society, 1989-; Currently working solely on composition. *Publications include:* Silja, 3 Percussionists, 1972; Lagsafn, 1974; Syn, 1975; Tokkata, 1976; Vatnsdropinn, 1977; Blaa Ljosid, 1978; Hrim, solo cello, 1978; Helfro, 1978; Itys, solo flute, 1978; Blik, Solo Clarinet 1979; Galdra Loftur, orchestra, Clarinet concerto, 1980; Sonata; Teikn, solo violin 1982; Viola concerto, 1983; Trio, Clarinet, Violin, Viola, 1983; Myndhvorf, 12 Brass Players, 1983; Prim, solo snare drum, 1984; Duo (Nocturne), 1984; Piano Concerto, 1985; Impromptu, orchestra, 1986; Sonata, organ, 1986; Marimba Concerto, 1987; Trombone Concerto, 1987; Sonata, Solo Percussion, 1987; Fjörg (The Gods) solo percussion and mixed choir, 1989; Sparks, percussion quartet, 1989; Snow, piano trio and percussion, 1992; Meditation, organ, 1992; Sinfonia Trilogia, orchestra, 1992; Sonata, violin and piano, 1993. *Address:* Flokagata 65, 105 Reykjavik, Iceland.

MASSON Diego, b. 21 June 1935, Tossa, Spain. Conductor. *Education:* Paris Conservatoire, 1953-59; Study with Leibowitz, Maderna and Boulez. *Career:* Worked as percussionist in Paris with the ensemble Domaine Musicale; Founded Musique Vivante, 1966; Conducted premieres of Stockhausen's Stop, Setz die Segel zur Sonne; Early performances of works by Boulez (Domaines and.....explosiant fixe.....) and Berio; Musical Director of Marseilles Opera and Ballet-Theatre Contemporain, Angers: conducted the company at Sadler's Wells, London, 1971 and 1973; Guest engagements as orchestral conductor in France and elsewhere in Europe; Conducted La Bohème for Opera North, 1989, premiere of Caritas by Robert Saxton, 1991. *Recordings include:* Boulez, Domaine; Globokar, Fluide and Ausstrahlungen; Berio, Laborintus II; Boulez Le Marteau sans maître, with Yvonne Minton; Stockhausen Aus den sieben tagen, and Liaison; Keuris Alto saxophone concerto. *Address:* Ingpen and Williams Ltd, 14 Kensington Court, London W8 5DN, England.

MASSON Gerard, b. 12 Aug 1936, Paris, France. Composer. *Education:* Largely self-taught; Some study with Henri Pousseur and with Earle Browne and Stockhausen in Cologne, 1965-66. *Compositions:* Piece for 14 instruments and percussion 1964; Dans le deuil des vagues I and II, for 14 instruments and for orchestra 1966; Ouest I and II for 10 instruments and for voice and orchestra 1968, 1970; Bleu Loin for 12 strings 1970; Ici c'est la Tyrannie for orchestra 1973; String Quartet 1973; Hypnopsie for orchestra 1974; Phonies and Phoenemes for chorus and orchestra 1975. *Address:* SACEM, 225 avenue Charles de Gaulle, 92521 Neuilly sur Seine Cedex, France.

MASTERS Rachel, b. 9 Sept 1958, Purley, Surrey, England. Harpist. *Education:* Junior Student, Guildhall School of Music and Drama, 1971-75; National Youth Orchestra, 1972-76; Scholar, Royal College of Music, 1976-80; ARCM, Honours. *Debut:* Wigmore Hall, 22 June 1982. *Career:* Joint Winner, SE Arts Young Musicians Platform, 1979; Finalist, NFMS Young Concert Artists Award, 1979; Joint 2nd Prize, Mobil Oil Harp Competition, 1980; Incorporated Society of Musicians Young Concert Artist, 1981; Principal harp in London Philharmonic Orchestra since 1989; Professor at Royal College of Music. *Recordings:* Mozart Flute and Harp Concerto, with Phillipa Davies, City of London Sinfonia and Richard Hickox; Chandos: Harp concertos by Debussy, Ravel, Glière and Ginastera and Alwyn; Britten: Ceremony of Carols with Kings' College, Cambridge. *Honours:* Jack Morrison, Elisabeth Coates, Harp Prizes, Royal College of Music. *Hobbies:* Tennis, Walking, Cinema. *Address:* 31 Westfield Road, Surbiton, Surrey KT6 4EL, England.

MASTERS Robert, b. 16 Mar 1917, Ilford, Essex, England. Violinist. *Education:* Royal Academy of Music, London. *Career:* Leader, Robert Masters Piano Quartet, 1940-63; Professor of Violin, Royal Academy of Music, London, 1947-64; Leader, Bath Festival Orchestra and Menuhin Festival Orchestra, 1960-75; Leader, London Mozart Players, 1961-78; Director of Music, Yehudi Menuhin School, England, 1968-80; Co-director Menuhin Music Academy, Gstaad, Switzerland, 1980-84; Guest Professor, Taiwan Universities, 1980-; Beijing and Shanghai Conservatories of Music, Banff Arts Centre; Artistic Director, Menuhin International Violin Competition, Folkestone, 1983-; Artistic Director, New Zealand International Violin Competition; Director of Music, Hattori Foundation for Music and Art, 1992. *Recordings:* Robert Masters Piano Quartet, Fauré Piano Quartets (Argo); Walton Piano Quartet (Argo); Skalkottas Piano Trio, with Marcel Gazelle and Derek Simpson. *Honour:* FRAM. *Address:* 72d Leopold Road, London SW19 7JQ, England.

MASTERSON Valerie, b. 3 June 1937, Birkenhead, England. Opera Singer. m. Andrew March, 1 son, 1 daughter. *Education:* Royal College of Music, London; Milan, Won Countess of Munster Scholarship; Gulbenkian Scholarship. *Career:* Performances in Falstaff, Il Turco in Italia and Der Schauspieldirektor, Landestheater, Salzburg; D'Oyly Carte Opera Company including film version of Mikado; Member, English National Opera, 1972-; Roles include, Manon, Traviata, Mimi, Juliet, Louise, Pamina, Gilda, Countess and Suzanna in Figaro; Seraglio, Constanza; Cleopatra in Julius Caesar; Mireille; debut in Covent Garden, 1974, in the Rhinegold; Traviata, Fidelio, We Come To The River by Henze; Semele, Faust (Marguerite), Carmelites, Micaela in Carmen; The King Goes Forth to France (Sallinen); Guest Appearances in Concerts and Opera in many major cities of the world including Paris, Aix, Milan, Munich, New York, Chicago, San Francisco, Barcelona, Geneva, South America; Sang Marguerite in Faust and Mozart's Countess at the London Coliseum, 1990; Fiordiligi for Welsh National Opera and Ilia in Idomeneo for the English Bach Festival at Covent Garden; Season 1992/93 with the Countess at Dublin and the Marschallin at Liège; Vice-President of British Youth Opera. *Honours:* SWET Award, 1983; CBE, 1988; FRCM awarded in 1992. *Address:* c/o English National Opera, St Martin's Lane, London WC2, England.

MASTILOVIC Daniza, b. 7 Nov 1933, Negotin, Serbia. Singer (Soprano). *Education:* Belgrade Conservatory with Nikola Cvejic. *Career:* Sang operetta in Belgrade, 1955-57; Minor roles at Bayreuth from 1956; Joined Georg Solti at Frankfurt Opera, 1959, debut as Tosca; Guest appearances in Hamburg, Dusseldorf, Zagreb, Vienna and Munich; Teatro Colón Buenos Aires 1972, as Abigaille in Nabucco; Zurich 1973, as Ortrud in Lohengrin; Covent Garden 1973-75, as Elektra; Metropolitan Opera 1975, as Elektra; Commemorated the 50th anniversary of Puccini's death with a performance of Turandot at Torre del Lago, 1974; Landestheater Salzburg 1987, as Clytemnestra in Elektra. *Address:* c/o Landestheater, Schwarstrasse 22, A-5020 Salzburg, Austria.

MASTROIANNI Thomas O, b. 1 Sept 1934, Pittsburgh, Pennsylvania, USA. Pianist; Professor. m. Mary Ann Prosser, 25 Jan 1964, 1 son, 2 daughters. *Education:* BS, Piano Performance, 1957, MS, 1958, Juilliard School of Music; DMus, Piano Performance, Indiana University, 1969. *Debut:* Wigmore Hall, London; Concertgebouw, Amsterdam; Carnegie Recital Hall,

New York. *Career:* Tours in Europe, Mexico, Caribbean, USA, Korea & Republic of China, including solo piano concerts, chamber music, piano concerti; Lectures-recitals; Articles & lectures, piano technique. Faculty positions: Professor/Chair, Piano, Texas Technical University, 1961-72; Dean of Music, 1972-81, Chair of Piano, 1972-, Catholic University of America. *Recordings:* 2, Educo Music of Portugal series; Sonatas, Freitas Branco & Freitas (4116); Nocturne, Freitas. *Contributions to:* Technique; Piano Quarterly, summer 1986; Italian Aspect of Liszt, Journal of American Liszt Society, 1985. *Memberships:* Executive secretary, American Liszt Society; Graduate board 1975-81, NASM. *Hobbies:* Tennis; Swimming. *Address:* 1420 Chilton Drive, Silver Spring, MD 20904, USA.

MASTROMEI Giampietro, b. 1 Nov 1932, Camoire, Tuscany, Italy. Singer (Baritone). *Education:* Studied in Buenos Aires with Apollo Granforte, Mario Melani and Hilda Spani. *Career:* Sang at the Teatro Colon, Buenos Aires for 13 seasons from 1952; European debut, 1962, appearing in France and Italy and at the Vienna Staatsoper; Marseilles, 1966; La Scala and Covent Garden, 1973, as Renato (Un Ballo in Maschera) and Amonasro; Verona Arena, 1971-86, as Amonasro and Scarpia; Further appearances at Caracas, Bilbao, Tokyo, Barcelona, Hamburg, Madrid, San Francisco, Dallas and Philadelphia; Also sings Verdi's Iago and Rigoletto and roles in operas by Pergolesi, Scarlatti and Dallapiccola. *Recordings include:* Simon Boccanegra (RCA); Il Corsaro (Philips); Aida (MRF).

MASUR Kurt, b. 18 July 1927, Brig, Silesia. Conductor. *Education:* National Music School, Breslau, 1942-44; Leipzig Conservatory, 1946-48. *Career:* Repetiteur and conductor at the Halle National Theatre, 1948; Conductor at Erfurt City Theatre, 1951-53 and Leipzig City Theatre, 1953-55; Conductor of Dresden Philharmonic, 1955; General Music Director, Mecklenburg Staatstheater, 1958; Musical Director Dresden Philharmonic, 1967-72; Conductor, Leipzig Gewandhaus Orchestra, 1970; Tours of Europe, South America, Japan, USA, Canada and Middle East; British debut, 1973 with the New Philharmonic Orchestra; US debut 1974 with the Cleveland Orchestra; Conducted the London Philharmonic Orchestra in the Choral Symphony at the 1989 Promenade Concerts in London; Britten's War Reqium, 1990; London Proms 1993, with the Gewandhaus Orchestra in Schubert 8 and Bruckner 4, Brahms B flat concerto and A Midsummer Night's Dream by Mendelssohn. *Recordings:* Symphonies by Mendelssohn, Bruckner, Beethoven, Schumann and Tchaikovsky; Prokofiev's Piano Concertos; Beethoven's Missa Solemnis. *Address:* Norman McCann Ltd, The Coach House, 56 Lawrie Park Gardens, London SE26 6XJ, England.

MASUROK Yuri, b. 18 July 1931, Krasnik, Poland. Ukrainian Singer (Baritone). *Education:* Studied at Lvov Institute and Moscow Conservatoire. *Career:* Sang at the Bolshoy, Moscow, from 1963, debut as Eugene Onegin; Vienna Staatsoper as Scarpia, Luna and Escamillo; Aix-en-Provence, 1976, as Germont in La Traviata; Covent Garden debut 1975, as Renato in Un Ballo in Maschera: returned to London as Posa in Don Carlos, Eugene Onegin and Count di Luna; US debut at Metropolitan Opera 1975, with Bolshoy company; San Francisco 1977, as Renato; Metropolitan debut as Germont, 1978; Covent Garden 1983 and 1986, as Luna and Germont; Sang at Wiesbaden 1987 as Scarpia, Budapest as Robert in Iolanta, with the company of the Bolshoi Theatre; Gran Teatre del Liceu Barcelona 1989, as Eugene Onegin; Concerts in Great Britain have included Wigmore Hall recitals and Festival Hall concert conducted by Svetlanov: song repertory includes music by Ravel, Debussy, Schumann and Henze; Other operatic roles include Andrei Bolkonsky in War and Peace, Mazeppa, Rossini's Figaro and Yeletsky in The Queen of Spades; Sang Onegin at Milwaukee, 1992; Scarpia at Metropolitan, New York, 1993. *Recordings:* Eugene Onegin, Tosca, The Queen of Spades and Iolanta on Russian labels; Tosca, Il Trovatore and Boris Godunov

(Philips). *Address:* c/o Bolshoi Theatre, Ochotnyj Rjad 812, 103009 Moscow, Russia.

MATA Eduardo, b. 5 Sept 1942, Mexico City, Mexico. Conductor; Composer. *Eucation:* Studied composition with Rodolfo Halffter 1954-60, Composition and conducting with Julian Orbon 1960-63; Carlos Chávez 1960-65, National Conservatory of Music, Mexico City; Studied conducting with Max Rudolf, Erich Leinsdorf and Gunther Schuller, Berkshire Music Center, Tanglewood, Massachusetts. *Career:* Conductor, Mexican Ballet Company, 1963-64; Guadalajara Symphony Orchestra, 1964-66; Philharmonic Orchestra of the National University of Mexico, 1966-76; Principal Conductor, Phoenix (Ariz) Symphony Orchestra, 1970-78; Music Director, Dallas Symphony Orchestra, 1977-93; Guest Conductor with various orchestras in North America and Europe; Guest conductor, London Symphony Orchestra; Member, Mexico's El Colegio Nacional, 1985-. *Compositions:* 3 symphonies, 1962, 1963, 1966-67; Chamber music. *Recordings include:* Music by Mexican composers; Complete works of Revueltas, with the New Philharmonic (RCA); Falla El amor brujo and The Three-cornered hat (London Symphony); CD of works by Dukas, Enescu, Mussorgsky and Tchaikovsky.

MÁTÉ János, b. 6 June 1934, Tap, Hungary. Professor of Music. m. Julianna Lórincz, 27 June 1964, 1 son, 2 daughters. *Education:* Graduated: Teacher of Piano, Conservatory of Music, Budapest, 1955; Choir Conductor, Music Teacher, 1959, Concert Organist, 1960, Liszt Ferenc Music Academy. *Career:* Music Teacher, Budapest, 1959-71; Organist, Leader of Calvin Choir, Calvin Church, Budapest, 1968-; Piano Teacher, Kodály School, Budapest, 1971-79; Leader of Raday Choir, 1971-; Professor of Church Music, Reformed Theological Academy, Budapest, 1970-. *Compositions:* Choir and organ works. *Publications:* Guide of Church Music, 1969; Collection of Choir Works, 1971; Guide to the Harmonium Play (co-author), 1978; Hungarian Organ Music (co-author), 1978; Hungarian Psalms (co-author), 1979; Guide to the Organ Play (co-author), 1980; Ecumenical Hymn Book (co-author), 1983; Church Music, 1986. *Honour:* Prize for Culture, 1987. *Hobbies:* Gardening; Philately; Riddles. *Address:* Klapka György utca 92, H -1154 Budapest, Hungary.

MATHER Bruce, b. 9 May 1939, Toronto, Canada. Composer; Pianist. m. Pierrette LePage. *Education:* Studied composition at the Royal Conservatory of Music in Toronto, in Paris with Roy Harris, Boulez, Milhaud and Messiaen, and the Universities of Stanford and Toronto (PhD, 1967). *Career:* Teacher at McGill University Montreal from 1966; Solo piano recitals and piano duet performances with Pierrette LePage. *Compositions include:* Five Madrigals for soprano and ensemble, 1967-73; Music for Vancouver, 1969; Musique pour Rouen for string orchestra 1971; Music for Organ, Horn and Gongs, 1973; Eine Kleine Blassermusik, 1975; Au Chateau de Pompairain for mezzo and orchestra 1977; Musique pour Champigny for vocal soloists and ensemble 1976; Ausone for 11 instruments 1979; Musigny for orchestra, 1980; Barbaresco for viola, ccello and double bass, 1984; Scherzo for orchestra 1987; Dialogue pour trio basso et orchestre, 1988; Songs. *Address:* SOCAN (Canada), c/o PRS Ltd Member Registration, 29-33 Berners Street, London W1P 4AA, England.

MATHES Rachel Clarke, b. 14 Mar 1941, Atlanta, Georgia, USA. Opera Singer; College Professor. *Education:* BA, Music, Birmingham-Southern College, 1962; MM, Vocal Performance, 1988, DMA, Vocal Performance, 1991, University of South Carolina; Study at Akademie für Musik und Darstellende Kunst, Vienna, Austria, 1962-63. *Debut:* Aida at Basel, Switzerland, 1965. *Career:* Deutsche Oper am Rhein, Dusseldorf, Germany, 1965-71; Freelance throughout Europe, 1971-74; Debut, Metropolitan Opera, New York City, 1974-77 (debut as Donna Anna); New York City Opera 1975, (debut as Turandot); Wolf Trap Festival (Verdi's Requiem), 1975; Glasgow Opera (as Donna Anna),

1975. *Recordings:* Highlights from Mozart's Don Giovanni with the Glasgow Opera, 1975. *Address:* c/o Augustana College Music Department, Rock Island, IL 61201, USA.

MATHESON-BRUCE Graeme, b. 19 July 1949, Dundee, Scotland. Singer (Tenor). *Education:* Royal Scottish Academy of Music; Royal Manchester College of Music; London Opera Centre; Studies with Hans Hotter in Munich. *Debut:* Wigmore Hall 1973. *Career:* English National Opera and Covent Garden, 1980, in La Traviata and Lohengrin; Guest appearances with Glyndebourne Opera, Opera North and Kent Opera; Roles include Wagner, Siegmund and Parsifal and Walther; Verdi, Otello; Strauss, Bacchus; Puccini, Edgar; Pfitzner, Palestrina; Dvořák, Dmitrij; Beethoven, Florestan; Glass, High Priest in Akhnaten; a member of Darmstadt Opera, notably as Werther, Don José, Peter Grimes, Radames, Hermann (Queen of Spades) and Gabriele Adorno (Simon Boccanegra), 1987-88; US debut Houston Opera as Herod in Salome, 1987: Florestan in San Diego; Concert appearances as Waldemar in Schoenberg's Gurrelieder and in the Berlioz Te Deum, with the Young Musicians Symphony Orchestra, in Mahler's Das klagende Lied and in the Choral Symphony; Sang Lovelace in the premiere of Robin Holloway's Clarissa, ENO, 1990; Erik in Oer fliegende Holländer with the Pittsburgh Opera 1990; Calaf at Haddo House; Sang Tannhäuser for New Sussex Opera at Brighton, 1990; Season 1992 as Pentheus in the premiere of The Bacchae by John Buller at the Coliseum and Tchekalinsky in The Queen of Spades at Glyndebourne. *Address:* c/o Kaye Artists Management, Barratt House, 7 Chertsey Road, Woking, GU21 5AB, England.

MATHIESEN Thomas James, b. 30 Apr 1947, Roslyn Heights, New York, USA. Musicologist. m. Penelope Jay Price, 11 Sept 1971. *Education:* BMus, Willamette University, 1968; MMus, 1970, DMA with honours, 1971, University of Southern California. *Career:* Professor of Music, Indiana University, 1988-; Associate Dean, Honours and General Education, 1986-88, Professor of Music and Head Musicology Area, 1972-86, Brigham Young University, Provo, Utah; Lecturer in Musicology, University of Southern California, Los Angeles, 1971-72. *Publications:* Thesaurus Musicarum Latinarum, Project Director; Ancient Greek Music Theory: A Catalogue Raisonné of Manuscripts, 1988; Aristides Quintilianus on Music in Three Books: Translation, with Introduction, Commentary and Annotations, 1983; A Bibliography of Sources for the Study of Ancient Greek Music, 1974; General editor, Greek and Latin Music Theory, 1982-, 9 volumes to date. *Contributions to:* Acta Musicologica; Fontes Artis Musicae; Journal of Musicology; Journal of Music Theory; Festival Essays for Pauline Alderman; Mousikologia; International Musicological Society Report for the 12th Congress; Musical Humanism and Its Legacy: Essays in Honor of Claude V Palisca. *Address:* School of Music, Indiana University, Bloomington, IN 47405, USA.

MATHIS Edith, b. 11 Feb. 1938, Lucerne, Switzerland. Singer (Soprano). m. Bernhard Klee. *Education:* Studied at the Lucerne Conservatory and in Zurich with Elisabeth Bosshart. *Debut:* Lucerne 1956, im Die Zauberflöte. *Career:* Sang in Cologne from 1959, Berlin from 1963; Salzburg debut 1960, in concert; Glyndebourne, 1962-65, as Cherubino and as Sophie in Der Rosenkavalier; Member of the Hamburg Staatsoper, 1960-72; Metropolitan Opera debut 1970, as Pamina: returned to New York as Annchen in Der Freischütz, Sophie, and Zerlina in Don Giovanni; Covent Garden, 1970-72, as Mozart's Susanna and Despina; Other roles include Ninetta in La Finte Semplice (Salzburg), Beethoven's Marzelline, Debussy's Mélisande, Verdi's Nannetta and Mozart's Aminta; Mozart's Countess; Weber's Agathe, Der Freischütz; Strauss Arabella; Marschallin, Rosenkavalier; Sang in the premieres of Henze's Der junge Lord (Berlin 1965) and Sutermeister's Le Roi Berénger (Munich 1985); Barcelona 1986, as Agathe; debut as the Marschallin at the Berne City Opera, 1990; Concert appearances in Baroque music and as Lieder singer. *Recordings:* Le Nozze di Figaro; Die Zauberflöte; Fidelio; Die Freunde von Salamanka (Schubert), Der Wildschütz (Lortzing); Frau Fluth, Nicolai's Lustige Weiber von Windsor; Mozart's Ascanio in Alba, Il Re Pastore, Il Sogno di Scipione and Apollo et Hyacinthus; Bach Cantatas; Haydn's Il Mondo della Luna and L'Infedeltà Delusa; Handel's Ariodante. *Address:* Ingpen and Williams Ltd, 14 Kensington Court, London W8 5DN, England.

MATOUSEK Bohuslav, b. 1949, Czechoslovakia. Violinist. *Education:* Jaroslav Pekelsky Václav Snitil; Further study with Arthur Grumiaux, Nathan Milstein and Wolfgang Schneiderhan. *Career:* Soloist with the Tokyo Symphony Orchestra 1977-78; Co-founder and leader of the Stamic Quartet of Prague 1980; Performances at the Prague Young Artists and the Bratislava Music Festivals; Tours to Spain, Austria, France, Switzerland, Germany and Eastern Europe; Tour of the USA 1980, debut concerts in Britain at London and Birmingham 1983; Further British tours 1985, 1987, 1988 (Warwick Arts Festival) and 1989 (20 concerts); Gave the premiere of Helmut Eder's 3rd Quartet, 1986; Season 1991-92 with visit to the Channel Islands (Festival of Czech Music), Holland, Finland, Austria and France, Edinburgh Festival and debut tours of Canada, Japan and Indonesia. *Recordings:* Shostakovich No 13, Schnittke No 4 (Panton); Dvořák, Martinů and Janáček complete quartets (Bayer Records); Haydn Violin Concertos 1-6 supraphon, Schubert Sonatinas and grand duo Denon Columbia, Brahms, Bruch Concertos Bayer R; Dvořák Concerto, Mazurek, Romance, Bayer R; Brahms's Sonatas, Bayer R. E; Dvořák Complete violin and piano; Martinů Duo Concertante. *Honours:* (with members of Stamic Quartet): Prize winner, Winner 1986 ORF (Austrian Radio) International String Quartet Competition (followed by live broadcast from the Salzburg Mozarteum); Academie Charles Cros Grand Prix du Disque 1991, for Dvořák quartets; I Prix International Violin Competition Prague (as soloist), 1972. *Current Management:* UK, R Gilder. *Address:* Lhota 68, 25241 Dolni Břežany, Czech Republic.

MATOUSEK Lukás, b. 29 May 1943, Prague, Czechoslovakia. Composer; Clarinettist; Performer of Medieval Instruments. m. Zuzana Matousková, 28 June 1966, 2 daughters. *Education:* Prague Conservatory of Music; Private Study with Mil. Kabelác (Composition), Janáček Academy of Music, Brno. *Career:* Artistic Director, Ars Carmeralis Ensemble; Many concerts and recordings for broadcasting and TV throughout Europe; Recordings as performer, and of own works. *Compositions:* (For orchestra): Radices Temporis, Stories, Concerto for percussion and winds, Metamorphoses of Silent for strings; (Chamber music): Sonata for violin and piano; Sonata for double-bass and chamber ensemble; Wind-Quintet, Aztecs for percussion, Intimate Music for viola or cello, Recollection of Mr. Sudek for brass-sextet, Sonatina for clarinet and piano; (Vocal): Two Cantatas, Colours and Thoughts, The Flower from the Eden, several children's Choir Pieces. *Recordings include:* (As Performer): Hommage à Machaut, with Ars Cameralis, several recordings with Prague Madrigalists; (As Composer). *Address:* Vápencová 10, 14700 Prague 4, Czech Republic.

MATRACKA-KOSCIELNY Alicja, b. 13 Aug 1950, Zawiercie, Poland. Musicologist. m. Jan Koscielny, 22 Sept 1973, 2 daughters. *Education:* Department of Musicology, Warsaw University, Masters degree 1974, Doctoral thesis entitled The Relationship Between Words and Music in Polish Songs, completed in 1983. *Career:* Archivist in Frederik Chopin Society, Editor of the yearly Chopin Studies, Warsaw; One of the organisers of the International Chopin Competitions 1975-80; Custodian in Iwaszkiewicz Museum in Podkowa Lesna, 1984-. *Publications:* Poetry and Music in the Songs of Moniuszko, 1980; Warsaw Composers and their Songs in Second Half 19th Century, 1980; The Relationship Between Words and Music in Chopin

Songs, 1987; Musical Transformation of J Iwaszkiewicz's Poetry, 1988. *Contributions to:* Articles in Ruch Muzyczny, Tworczosc, Muzyka magazines (in Polish). *Membership:* Society of Polish Composers. *Address:* ul Stowackiego 5, 05-807 Podkowa Lesna, Poland.

MATSUBARA Chifuru, b. 15 Oct 1951, Nagano, Japan. Choir Conductor. m. Anja Kaarina Salo, 12 Nov 1982. *Education:* Kunitachi Music College, Tokyo; Sibelius Academy, Helsinki; Choir Conducting Master Class in Zoltan Kodaly Institute - 1984 and several courses of Professor Eric Ericson and Professor Dan-Olof Stenlund; Gregorian Chants in Solesmes, France since 1987. *Career:* Artistic Dorector of Suomen Laulu, 1988-; Singing and Conducting Member of the Finnish Radio Chamber Choir, 1987-; Vice-Conductor, The Helsinki University Male Choir, 1978- and Suoman Laulu, 1979-88; Conducting Cetus Noster (a group performing Finnish Gregorian Chants) 1989-; Conducting several male choirs 1980-88; Assisting the Tapiola Children's Choir (ie on Japan tours); Ellerheim Children's Choir of Estonia, 1991-; Main visiting conductor of the Estonian Philharmonic Choir 1989-; Radio: Several appearances with the Radio Chamber Choir and Cetus Noster, the University Male Choir and Suomen Laulu. *Hobbies:* Literature; Travelling. *Address:* Ilolantie 7 A 1, 01390 Vantaa, Finland.

MATSUDA Nobuya, b. 12 Aug 1931, Kobe, Japan. Composer; Conductor; Pianist; Organist; Music Educator. m. Michiko Tokiwa, 3 May 1956, 2 sons, 1 daughter. *Education:* BA, Tokyo Art University, 1955; MA, Southern Illinois University, 1957; DMA, American Conservatory of Music, 1965; Studied Conducting with Hideo Saito, Tokyo, 1947-52, Thor Johnson, Chicago, 1958- 61, Pierre Monteux, summer school; Composition with Tomojiro Ikenouchi, Tokyo, Roy Harris, Carbondale, Illinois, 1957, Paul Hindemith, Yale University, Leo Sowerby, American Conservatory of Music, Chicago, Elliott Carter and Roger Sessions, Tanglewood Festival. *Career:* Guest Conductor: former Tokyo Symphony Orchestra, Tokyo Glee Club, Fish Creek Music Festival Orchestra; Fellow Conductor, Tanglewood Music Festival; Conductor, Founder, Sioux County Orchestra, Sioux Center, Iowa; Conductor, Westmont College Orchestra; Performed own compositions at concerts; Piano and organ recitalist; Guest Conductor, Southern Illinois University Orchestra with Roy Harris; Faculty: American Conservatory of Music, Chicago, 1965-80; Faculty, Dordt College, 1984-86; Faculty, Westmont College, Santa Barbara, California, 1986-. *Publications:* Harmony (Theory and Practice); Strict Counterpoint. *Address:* c/o Westmont College, Department of Music, 955 La Paz Road, Santa Barbara, CA 93108, USA.

MATSUZAWA Yuki, b. 1960, Tokyo. Concert Pianist. *Education:* Studied with Akiko Iguchi and Hiroshi Tamura and at the Tokyo University of Fine Arts; Further study with Vladimir Ashkenazy in Europe. *Career:* Concert engagements in Europe, Asia and the USA; Radio and television engagements in Britain, Ireland, Holland, Greece, the USA and Japan; Irish debut May 1990 with the Berlin Radio symphony Orchestra, London debut, 1990 at the Wigmore Hall; London appearances at the Wigmore Hall, Barbican Hall and St John's Smith Square; Concerto appearances with the Royal Philhamonic Orchestra, the BBC Symphony Orchestra, Montreal Symphony Orchestra, Athens Radio Symphony Orchestra, Berlin Radio Symphony Orchestra, NHK Symphony Orchestra and the New London Orchestra; Chamber music appearances with the Suk Quartet in Britain and Czechoslovakia and the Martinů Quartet in Britain; Records for the Pianissimo label; Tours of Britian and Europe. *Honours:* Prizewinner at such competitions as Queen Elisabeth, Brussels; Maria Canals, Barcelona; Montreal International, Canada. *Address:* Norman McCann International Artists Ltd, 56 Lawrie Park Gardens, London, SE26 6XJ, England.

MATTEUZZI William, b. 1957, Bologna, Italy. Singer (Tenor). *Education:* Studied with Paride Venturi. *Debut:*

Sang Massenet's Des Grieux in Milan. *Career:* Season 1987 sang Rossini's Ramiro at Bologna, Nemorino at Bergamo and Evander in Alceste at La Scala; Rossini's Comte Ory at Venice, 1988, La Scala, 1991; Pesaro Festival, 1988, in La Scala de Seta, as Rodrigo in Rossini's Otello, 1991; Count Almaviva on Metropolitan Opera debut 1988 and at Barcelona, 1991; Sang Lindoro (L'Italiana in Algeri) at Monte Carlo, 1989, Medoro in Orlando Furioso by Vivaldi at San Francisco; Other roles include Flamand in Capriccio and Ernesto in Don Pasquale. *Recordings:* Le Convenzione Teatrali by Donizetti; Zandonai's Francesca da Rimini: Borsa in Rigoletto; Edmondo in Manon Lescaut and in Barbiere di Siviglia; Rossini's Zelmira; Tonio in La Fille du Regiment; Carlo and Goffredo in Rossini's Armida. *Honours include:* Winner, Caruso International Competition, Milan. *Address:* c/o Teatro alla Scala, Via Filodrammatici 2, 201212 Milan, Italy.

MATTHEWS Andrea, b. 6 Nov 1956, Needham, Massachusetts, USA. Soprano. *Education:* AB, Princeton University, 1978. *Debut:* Marriage of Figaro as Susanna at Virginia Opera, 1984. *Career:* Gretel in Hansel and Gretel, Virginia Opera; Gilda in Rigoletto, Piedmont Opera; Zerlina in Don Giovanni, Greensboro Opera; Euridice in Orfeo ed Euridice, Violetta in La Traviata and Ilia in Idomeneo all at the Stadttheater Aachen, Germany; Other roles: Musetta, Mimi in La Bohème; Pamina in Magic Flute; Lauretta in Gianni Schicchi; Marzelline in Fidelio; Lucy in The Telephone; Marguerite in Faust; Sandrina in La Finta Giardiniera, Mozart; Nannetta in Falstaff; Soloist with Philadelphia Orchestra, Baltimore Symphony, Atlanta Symphony, Puerto Rico Symphony, Honolulu Symphony, Phoenix Symphony, Houston Symphony, La Crosse Symphony, Los Angeles Master Chorale, New York Choral Society, Collegiate Chorale, Dessoff Choirs, Oratorio Society of New York, Mostly Mozart Festival, New Mexico Symphony, Kalamazoo Symphony, Minnesota Orchestra, Northeastern Pennsylvania Philharmonic, American Symphony, Musica Sacra, Florida Orchestra, New Jersey Symphony, Raleigh Symphony, Cincinnati Symphony. Art-song Recitals in: California, Louisiana, New York City, Connecticut, New York State, Oklahoma, Minnesota, Indiana, Texas, New Mexico, Florida and New Jersey; Marie in Bartered Bride. *Recordings:* Vaughan Williams, Serenade to Music, Vox Cum Laude; Handel: Siroe, Muzio, Newport Classics. *Current Management:* Thea Dispeker Artists Representative. *Address:* c/o Thea Dispeker, 59 E 54th Street, New York, NY 10022, USA.

MATTHEWS Colin, b. 13 Feb 1946, London, England. Composer. *Education:* Nottingham University; Composition with Arnold Whittall and Nicholas Maw. *Career:* Collaborated with Deryck Cooke on performing version of Mahler's 10th Symphony; Taught at Sussex University 1972-73, 1976-77; Assistant to Britten in last years; Cortège premiered under Bernard Haitink at Covent Garden 1989, Machines and Dreams by the LSO 1991. *Compositions:* Ceres for nonet, 1972; Sonata No. 4 for orchestra, 1975; Partita for violin, 1975; Five Sonnets to Orpheus for tenor and harp, 1976; Specula for quartet, 1976; Night Music for small orchestra, 1977; Piano Suite, 1979; Rainbow Studies for quintet, 1978; Shadows in the Water for tenor and piano, 1979; String Quartet No.1, 1979; Sonata No.5, Landscape, for orchestra, 1977-81; Oboe Quartet, 1981; Secondhand Flames for five voices, 1982; Divertimento for double string quartet, string orchestra, 1982; The Great Journey for baritone and ensemble, 1981-88; Toccata Meccanica for orchestra, 1984; Triptych for piano quintet, 1984; Night's Mask for soprano and septet, 1984; Cello Concerto, 1984; Three Enigmas for cello and piano, 1985; String Quartet No.2, 1985; Suns Dance for 10 players, 1985; Monody for Orchestra, 1987; Two Part Invention for chamber orchestra, 1987/88; Pursuit for 16 players, 1987; Fuga for 8 players, 1988; Cortège for orchestra, 1989; Second Oboe Quartet, 1989; Hidden variables for 15 players, 1989; Quatrain for wind, brass and percussion, 1989; Chiarisuro for orchestra, 1990; Machines and Dreams for full or small orchestra and children, 1990; Broken Symmetry for Orchestra, 1992; Contraflow for 14 players, 1992; Memorial for

Orchestra, 1993 *Honours include:* BBC chamber music prize, 1970; Ian Whyte Award, 1975; Park Lane Group Composer Award, 1983. *Address:* c/o Faber Ltd., 3 Queen Square, London WC1N 3AU, England.

MATTHEWS David John, b. 9 Mar. 1943, London, England. Composer; Writer. *Education:* BA, Classics, Nottingham University; Private Study in Composition with Anthony Milner.*Career:* Worked with Deryck Cooke on completion of Mahler's 10th Symphony; Assistant to Britten, 1966-69; Musical Director, Deal Festival. *Compositions:* 4 Symphonies, The Music of Dawn for Orchestra, Scherzo Capriccioso for Orchestra, Romanza for Cello and Small Orchestra, Capriccio for Two Horns and Strings, In The Dark Time for Orchestra, Chaconne for Orchestra, A Vision and a Journey for orchestra, From Sea to Sky for Small Orchestra, September Music for Small Orchestra, Serenade for Small Orchestra, Oboe Concerto, Violin Concerto, Variations for Strings, Introit for Two Trumpets and Strings, Cantiga for Soprano and Orchestra, Marina for Baritone, Basset Horn, Viola and Piano, The Sleeping Lord for soprano and Ensemble, 4 Hymns for Chorus, The Company of Lovers for Small Chorus, The Ship of Death for Chorus, 6 String Quartets, String Trio, Concertino for Oboe Quintet, Clarinet Quartet, 2 Piano Trio's, Duet Variations for Flute and Piano, Piano Sonata, Winter Journey for Solo Violin, Three Studies for Solo Violin, From Coastal Stations for Voice and Piano. *Recording:* The Company of Lovers; Romanza; Cantiga; September Music; Introit. *Publications:* Michael Tippett, 1980; Landscape into Sound, 1992; Editor, Mahler, Symphony No. 10, 1976; Editor, Beethoven arr Mahler, String Quartet op 95; Deryck Cooke: Gustav Mahler, 1980; Donald Mitchell: Gustav Mahler, The Early Years, 1980; Schubert arr. Mahler, Death and The Maiden Quartet, 1986. *Contributions to:* Tempo, TLS. *Membership:* Association of Professional Composers. *Hobbies:* Walking; Drawing. *Address:* 12 Woodlands, Clapham Common North Side, London SW4 0RJ, England.

MATTHEWS Gillian Rachel, b. 8 Dec 1962, Huntly, Scotland. Cellist. *Education:* St Mary's Music School, Edinburgh, LTCL, FTCL, LRAM diplomas in Cello, 1981-82; Studied with Maurice Gendron for 3 years and Postgraduate, Guildhall School of Music, London. *Debut:* Purcell Room, London, 1985. *Career:* Recitals in Britain, Eire and France; Gave first performance of Howells Cello Fantasia, 1981; Solo engagements with the Scottish National Orchestra. *Honours:* Finalist, International Feuermann 'Cello Solo Competition, 1985; Prize-winner, Shell-LSO Competition 1978 for strings. *Hobby:* Hill walking. *Address:* Den of Largue Cottage, Forgue, Huntly, Aberdeenshire AB5 6HS, Scotland.

MATTHEWS Michael Gough, b. 12 July 1931, England. *Education:* Royal College of Music, (open scholarship 1947); ARCM, FRCM 1972; ARCO. *Career:* Pianist; recitals; broadcasts and concerts in UK, Europe and Far East; Adjudicator international comppetitions, masterclasses, lecture recitals, piano teacher; Supervisor, Junior Studies, RSAMD, 1964-71; Royal College of Music: Director, Junior Department, and Professor of Piano, 1972-75; Registrar, 1975; Vice-Director, 1978-84; Director, 1985-93; Director Associated Board of the Royal Schools of Music, 1985-93; Trustee, The Countess of Munster Musical Trust, 1985-93; Director, Royal Music Foundation Inc. USA from 1985; Consultant to H M the Sultan of Oman, Jaguar Cars Sponsored Concerts. *Honours:* Hopkinson Gold Medal, for piano, 1953; Diploma di Corso di Perfezionamento Accademia St Cecilia, Rome; Diploma of Honour and Prize, Chopin International Piano Competition, 1955; Italian Government Scholarship, 1956; Chopin Fellowship, Warsaw, (Hon), 1959. *Memberships:* National Youth Orchestra of Great Britain; Royal Philharmonic Society; Board of Management, Music Study Group, European Economic Community (UK representative); Comit d'Honneur, Presence de l'Art, Paris; Council, Purcell Tercentenary Trust; Board of Advisers Bombay Chamber Orchestra from 1992; Vice President, Royal College of Organists. *Publications:* various musical entertainments; arranger of educational music. *Hobby:* Gardening. *Address:* Laurel Cottages, South Street, Mayfield, East Sussex TN20 6DD, England.

MATTHUS Siegfried, b. 13 April 1934, Mallenuppen, Germany. Composer. m. Helga Matthus-Spitzer. *Education:* Deutsche Hochschule für Musik 1952-58, with Wagner-Régeny; Study with Hanns Eisler at the German Academy of Arts. *Career:* Freelance Composer since 1958; Permanent musician for TV, Radio, Film from 1958; Composer-in-residence at the Komische Oper Berlin from 1964; Works performed in all European countries, Japan, North and South America, Australia. *Compositions:* Operas: Lazarillo von Tormes 1964; Der letzte Schuss 1967; Noch ein Loffel Gift, Liebling 1972; Omphale 1976; Judith, 1982-84; Die Weise von Liebe und Tod des Cornets Christoph Rilke, 1983-84; Graf Mirabeau, 1987-88; Desdemona and her Sisters, 1991-92; Orchestral: Kleines Orchesterkonzert 1963; Inventionen 1964; Violin Concerto 1968; Dresdner Sinfonie 1969; Piano Concerto 1970; Serenade 1974; Cello Concerto 1975; 2nd Symphony 1976; Responso, Concerto for Orchestra 1977; Visions for strings 1978; Flute Concerto 1978; Concerto for Trumpet, Kettledrums and Orchestra, 1982; The Wood, Concerto for Kettledrums and Orchestra, 1984; Divertimento for Orchestra, 1985; Oboe Concerto, 1985; The Bride of the Wind, Concerto for Orchestra, 1985; Nächtliche Szene im Park for Orchestra, 1987; Orchestral: Tief ist der Brunnen der Vergangenheit, four pieces for symphonic orchestra, 1991-92; Sinfonie (Gewandhaussinfonie), 1992-93; Piano concerto (based on opus 25 by Johannes Brahms) 1992; Manhattan Concerto, 1993; Weisen von Liebe, Leben und Tod, (Text R M Rilke), Lieder für Countertenor (Alt) und Orchester, 1993; Concerto for percussion instruments and orchestra, 1993; Vocal: 5 Orchester lieder 1962; Wir Zwei 1970; 5 Liebeslieder des Catull 1972; Brennende Stadte 1974; Vocal: Hyperion-Fragmente, 1978-79; Holofernes-Portrait for baritone and orchestra 1981; Die Liebesqualen des Catull, 1985/86; Nachtlieder für Bariton, String Quartet and Harp, 1987; Wem ich zu gefallen suche-Lieder und Duette für Tenor, Bariton und Klavier, 1987; Chamber: Octet 1970; String Quartet 1972; Trio for flute, viola and harp 1972; Octet, 1989. *Honours:* 1969 Hanns Eisler Prize; 1970 Arts Prize DDR; 1972 & 1984 National Prize DDR. *Memberships:* Academy of Arts, Berlin-East; Academy of Arts, Berlin-West; Bayerischen Akademie der Schönen Künste in Munich. *Hobby:* Travel. *Address:* Elisabethweg 10, 13187 Berlin, Germany.

MATTILA Karita, b. 5 Sept 1960, Somero, Finland. Singer (Soprano). *Education:* Studied in Helsinki with Liisa Linko-Malmio; Pupil of Vera Rozsa from 1984. *Career:* Won 1983 Singer of the World Competition in Cardiff; Concert appearances with Abbado, Albrecht, Colin Davis, Dohnányi, Giulini, Salonen and Sinopoli: orchestras include Vienna Philharmonic, Vienna Symphony, Cleveland, London Symphony and the Staatskapelle Dresden; Operatic roles include Fiordiligi at the 1985 and 1987 Munich Festivals; Covent Garden debut 1986, as Fiordiligi; returned for Pamina in Die Zauberflöte; Mozart's Elvira with Washington Opera (US debut), Scottish Opera, Hamburg Opera and Chicago Lyric Opera; Wagner's Eva in Brussels; Sang Emma in Schubert's Fierrabras in Vienna, with Abbado; Other engagements include Elvira and Eva at the Metropolitan Opera, 1990; Sang Ilia in Idomeneo at San Francisco, 1989, Agathe in Der Freischütz at Covent Garden; Sang Donna Elvira at the Vienna Festival, Amelia Grimaldi (Simon Boccanegra) at the Geneva Opera, 1991; Sang Sibelius's Höstkväll and Luonnotar at the 1991 Prom Concerts, London; appeared as Eva in a new production of Die Meistersinger at the Metropolitan, 1993; Sang songs by Grieg at the 1993 Prom Concerts; appearances at the Salzburg Festival and with the Berlin Philharmonic Orchestra, 1993. *Recordings:* Portrait Record with Pritchard; Bruckner's Te Deum with Haitink; Così fan Tutte and Don Giovanni with Marriner (Philips); Recordings for Deutsche Grammophon with Abbado and for Supraphon with Gerd Albrecht; Le nozze di Figaro with Mehta (Sony) and Beethoven's Ninth conducted

by Marriner (Philips). *Address:* c/o Lies Askonas Ltd., 186 Drury Lane, London WC2B 5RY, England.

MATTINSON David, b. 1964, England. Singer (Bass-baritone). *Education:* Choral scholar, Trinity College, Cambridge; Guildhall School of Music with Thomas Hemsley; Further study with Rudolf Pierney. *Career:* Concert repertoire includes the B minor Mass, Messiah, the Creation, Requiems of Brahms, Verdi and Fauré, The Dream of Gerontius and A Child of Our Time; Appearances with the City of London Sinfonia, the Bournemouth Symphony and the London Philharmonic Orchestras; Further concerts include Elijah at the Albert Hall; Christus in the St Matthew Passion at the Festival Hall; Mozart's Requiem, and Beethoven's Ninth in Koblenz; Song recitals with the accompanist Clare Toomer in Winterreise, Dichterliebe, La Bonne Chanson and the Songs of Travel by Vaughan Williams; Appearances with the New Songmakers and the Mistry String Quartet and at the Buxton, Malvern and Warwick Festivals; Operatic roles include Gualtiero in Musgrave's The Voice of Ariadne, Mozart's Figaro, Germont, and Glover in La Jollie Fille de Perth; Scottish Opera debut 1991, as Zuniga in Carmen; Debut as Mozart's Figaro, Opera North, 1992; Season 1992 as Villotto in Haydn's La Vera Costanza for Garsington Opera and in Billy Budd for Scottish Opera. *Recordings include:* Bach St John Passion. *Honours:* Gold Medal Rosebowl and the Worshipful Company of Musicians' Silver Medal, GSM; Gold Medal in the 1988 Royal Overseas League Music Competition; Prizewinner, Walter Gruner International Lider Competition and the Elly Ameling International Lied Concours; First Prize, 1990 BP Peter Pears Award. *Address:* Kaye Artists Management Ltd, Barratt House, 7 Chertsey Road, Woking, Surrey GU21 5AG, England.

MATTON Roger, b. 18 May 1929, Granby, Québec, Canada. Composer. *Education:* Studied in Arthur Letondal's class, Conservatoire de musique du Québec, Montreal; Studied composition under Claude Champagne; Studied under Andrée Vaurabourg-Honegger and Nadia Boulanger, Ecole normale supérieure de musique; attended Olivier Messiaen's analysis classes, Conservatoire de Paris; studied ethnomusicology under Marius Barbeau, National Museum of Canada, Ottawa. *Career:* Joined Archives de folklore, Laval, Quebec; Teacher, History Department, Laval, Québec City; composer of music having received commissions from Canadian Broadcasting Corporation; l'orchestre symphonique de Québec, Montreal Symphony Orchestra, Le Grand Théâtre de Québec. *Compositions include:* Orchestral: Danse Brésilienne 1946; Danse Lente 1947; L'Horoscope 1958; Mouvement Symphonique I, 1960, II, 1962, III, 1974, IV, 1978; Pax 1950. Soloists with Orchestra: Concerto pour deux pianos et orchestre 1964; Concerto pour saxophone et orchestre à cordes 1948. Voices with Orchestra: L'escaouette 1957; Te Deum 1967. Chamber Music: Esquisse pour quatuor à cordes 1949; Etude pour clarinette et piano 1946. Piano: Berceuse 1945; Trois Préludes pour piano 1949. Two Pianos: Concerto pour deux pianos et percussion 1955; Danse brésilienne 1946. Organ: Suite de Pâques 1952. *Recordings:* Berceuse; Concerto pour deux pianos et orchestre; Concerto pour deux pianos et percussion; Danse brésilienne; l'horoscope; Mouvement Symphonique I, II; Suite de Pâques; Te Deum; Trois Préludes pour piano. *Honours:* Awarded distinction at Seventh Gala du Québec, Montreal for choral suite l'Escaouette 1965; Received Prix du Disque Pierre Mercure for Concerto pour deux pianos et orchestre 1966; Presented with Prix Calixa Lavallée by St. Jean Baptiste Society for contribution to French-Canada 1969. *Membership:* Canadian League of Composers. *Address:* c/o CAPAC (Canada) Member Registration, PRS Ltd, Berners Street, London W 1, England.

MATTSSON Jack Christer Randolph, b. 12 Dec 1954, Aland Islands, Finland. Arranger; Composer. *Education:* Sibelius Academy, Helsinki. *Debut:* Finlandia hall, Helsinki, 1974. *Career:* Has appeared regularly on theatre and Finnish TV, radio as a conductor and arranger and composer since 1980; Composer of film scores and stage performances; Performs chamber music in Sandinavia Europe. *Compositions include:* 4 Bagatells, for flute violin and viola; Cavatina et Virace, for flute and piano; Serenado for basson and strings; Alandskt Requiem, orchestra, chorus and soloists; Joy and Thoughts, for organ. *Recordings:* With various Finnish artists in classical folk and rock music. *Honours:* Finnish Swedish Culture Society Prize, 1991/92; Alands Culture Prize, 1992. *Memberships:* Client of Finnish Teosto and Gramex. *Hobbies:* The Beales; Fishing; Bicycling. *Address:* Stationsvagen 1 A 19, SF 01300 Vanda, Finland.

MATUSZCZAK Bernadeta, b. 10 Mar 1937, Torum, Poland. Composer. *Education:* Studied with Szeligowski and Sikorski at the Poznan and Warsaw Conservatories: Paris with Nadia Boulanger. *Compositions include:* Julia i Romeo, chamber opera, Warsaw 1970; Humanae Voces, radio oratorio, 1972; Mysterium Heloizy, opera, 1973-74; The Diary of a Madman, monodrama after Gogol, Warsaw 1978; Apocalypsis, radio oratorio, 1979; Prometheus, chamber opera after Aeschylus, 1981-82. *Address:* c/o PRS Ltd Member Registration, 29-33 Berners Street, London W1P 4AA, England.

MATUZ Istvan, b. 21 Jan 1947, Nagykoros, Hungary. Flautist. m. Katalin Vas, 13 Mar 1976, 2 sons. *Education:* Budapest Music High School, Hungary; Conservatoire Superieur de Musique, Brussels, Belgium. *Career:* Assistant, Conservatoire, Brussels, 1971-72; Solo flautist, Opera de Wallonie, Liège, Belgium; Professor of Flute, Music High School, Liszt Ferenc, Debrecen, 1975-; Soloist, Hungarian Philharmonic Society, 1978-; Soloist, Ensemble Intercontemporain, Paris, 1980-81. *Recordings:* 20th century works for flute; New flute recording with new flute technique, Hungaroton; Matuziada, flute & electronic guitar, Dubrovay; Approximately 12 Hungarian records, Hungarian works. *Hobby:* Languages. *Address:* 1124 Budapest, Tamasi Aron u.23, Hungary.

MATYS Jirí, b. 27 Oct 1927, Bakov, Náchod area, Czechoslovakia. Composer. *Education:* Graduated Brno Conservatory, 1947, studied with Kvapil at the Janacek Academy of Music in Brno. *Career:* Teacher, Janacek Academy, 1953-57, then head of the School of Music at Kralove Pole in Brno, 1957-60. *Compositions include:* Viola Sonata, 1954; 5 String Quartets, 1957-90; Variations on Death for narrator, horn and string quartet of a poem by Milan Kundera, 1959; Morning Music, 1962; Solo viola sonata, 1963; Music for string quartet and orchestra, 1971; Suite for viola and bass clarinet, 1973; Symphonic Overture, 1974; Dialogue for cello and piano, 1976; Suite for flute and guitar, 1981; Music for strings, 1982; Chamber Music includes: Divertimento for Four Horns, 1981; Suite for Wind Quintet, 1984; Compositions for Solo instruments: Sonata for Violin Solo, 1977; Music for Piano, 1985; Poetic Movements V, four compositions for four guitars, 1988; String Quartet No.5, 1989-90; Sonata for Violin Solo, 1991; Night Thoughts, A cykle of piano compositions in five parts, 1992; Plays for 2-3 Horns, 1992-93; Music for Three, 1993; Sonata for Violin Solo, 1993. *Address:* c/o PRS Ltd Member Registration, 29-33 Berners Street, London W1P 4AA, England.

MAUCERI John F., b. 12 Sept 1945, New York, USA. Conductor; Music Director. m. Betty Weiss, 15 June 1968, 1 son. *Education:* M.Phil, 1971, BA, 1967, Yale University; Tanglewood, 1972. *Career:* Music Director: Yale Symphony, 1968-74, American Symphony Orchestra, 1984-87, Washington Opera, 1979-82, Kennedy Center, 1973-, Scottish Opera, 1987-93; Consultant, Music Theater, Kennedy Center, 1982-; Co-Producer, On Your Toes, Musical Play, Broadway & London's West End, 1982; Lyric Opera of Chicago debut, La Bohème, 1987; Music Director, WNET Gala of Stars, A Musical Toast, 1987; Conducted, the New York Philharmonic Metropolitan Opera Orchestra and Empire Brass, Carnegie Hall, 1987; British premiere of Weill's Street Scene, 1989; Conducted new production of La Forza del Destino for Scottish Opera, 1990 followed by revival of Salome and Madame Butterfly; Les Troyens in Glasgow and London; Conducted own edition of Blitzstein's Regina at Glasgow (British premiere, 1991). *Recordings:* Original Cast: Candide, 1973, On Your Toes, 1983; New York City Opera, Candide, 1985; Original Cast, Song and Dance, 1985; My Fair Lady, with Kiri Te Kanawa and Jerry Hadley. *Contributions to:* Opera Magazine, 1985. *Honours:* Antoinette Perry, Outer Critics Circle, Drama Desk Awards, all for On Your Toes, 1982; Yale University Distinguished Alumni Award in Arts, 1985; Grammy Award, Best Opera Recording, Candide, 1987. *Current Management:* Columbia Artists. *Address:* c/o Columbia Artists Management, 165 West 57th Street, New York City, NY 10019, USA.

MAUNDER Charles Richard Francis, b. 23 Nov 1937, Portsmouth, England. m. 3 sons. Lecturer; Musicologist; Early Music Practitioner. *Education:* Jesus College, Cambridge 1955-61; MA, PhD, Cambridge 1962. *Career:* Fellow of Christ's College, Cambridge, 1964-; Lecturer at Universities in Britain (Cambridge, London, Reading, Leeds) and the USA (Philadelphia, Chicago, Northwestern, Northern Illinois) and at musicological conferences (International Mozart Congress, Salzburg, 1991); Performer on the bass viol (Cambridge Consort of Viols), baroque/classical viola (Cambridge Early Music) and violone (concerts in Cambridge and elsewhere include Messiah, St John Passion, Brandenburg Concertos, Bach Christmas Oratorio and Monteverdi Vespers); has restored early keyboard instruments, including square piano by Johannes Zumpe, London 1766, for Emmanuel College, Cambridge; instruments built includes copies of two-manual harpsichord by Thomas Hitchcock and Mozart's fortepiano; Founder of the Cambridge Classical Orchestra, 1990. *Publications:* Mozart's Requiem: On Preparing a New Edition (Clarendon Press, Oxford, 1988); numerous editions of 17th and 18th century music, including 13 of the 48 volumes of J C Bach's Collected Works (Garland, New York); Mozart's Requiem K626 (OUP), C minor Mass K427 (OUP) and Vesperae solennes de confessore K339 (Faber Music). *Contributions to:* Galpin Society Journal, Musical Times, Early Music, Journal of the Royal Musical Association, Music and Letters, Notes, Mozart-Jahrbuch. *Address:* 54 High Street, Sawston, Cambridge CB2 4BG, England.

MAURO Ermanno, b. 20 Jan 1939, Trieste, Italy. Singer (Tenor). *Education:* Studied at the Toronto Conservatory with Herman Geiger-Torel. *Debut:* Canadian Opera Company 1962, as Tamino in Die Zauberflöte. *Career:* Sang Manrico in Toronto 1965; Covent Garden from 1967, debut in Manon Lescaut; Guest appearances with Welsh National Opera, Scottish Opera and at Glyndebourne; New York City Opera 1975, as Calaf in Turandot; BBC TV as Paco in La Vida Breve; Metropolitan Opera from 1978, as Canio, Manrico, Ernani, Pinkerton, Paolo in Zandonai's Francesca da Rimini and Des Grieux; La Scala and Rome 1978; San Francisco 1982; Vienna 1983; Brussels 1984, as Manrico; Dallas Opera 1985, as Otello; Other roles include Male Chorus in The Rape of Lucretia; Donizetti's Edgardo, Gounod's Faust, Verdi's Radames, Riccardo, Alfredo and Gabriele Adorno; Don José, Cavaradossi, Dick Johnson and Enzo in La Gioconda; Sang Cavaradossi at the Met 1986, Turiddu 1989; Calaf at the Deutsche Oper Berlin 1987; San Francisco and Barcelona 1989, as Otello and Enzo; Sang Manrico with Zurich Opera 1990, Maurizio in Adriana Lecouvreur at Montreal; Season 1992 as Radames at Dallas, Puccini's Des Grieux at Miami, Calaf at Philadelphia and Turiddu at the Teatro Colón, Buenos Aires. *Address:* c/o Metropolitan Opera, Lincoln Center, New York, NY 10023, USA.

MAUS Peter, b. 1948, Germany. Singer (Tenor). *Debut:* Bayreuth Youth Festival, 1972, in Wagner's Das Liebesverbot. *Career:* Member of the Deutsche Oper Berlin from 1974, in such character roles as Wenzel in The Bartered Bride, Sparlich (Lustigen Weiber), Peter Ivanov, Zar und Zimmermann, Pong, the count in Zimmermann's Die Soldaten Fatty in Mahagonny and Aljeya in From the House of the Dead; Sang in the 1981 premiere of Kagel's Aus Deutschland; Bayreuth

Festival from 1982, with minor roles in Parsifal and Die Meistersinger; Shepherd in Tristan, 1993; Teacher of Singing at the Hochschule für Kunste in Berlin, from 1987. *Recordings:* Sad Liebesverbot; Die Meistersinger; Masses by Schubert; Donizetti Mass and Wolf's Der Corregidor; Esquire in Parsifal, conducted by Barenboim. *Address:* c/o Deutsche Oper Berlin, Richard Wagnerstrasse 10, D-1000 Berlin 10, Germany.

MAVRODIN Alice, b. 4 Nov 1941, Bucharest, Romania. Musicologist. m. Liuiu Comes, 22 June 1992. *Education:* Bucharest Music Academy, 1960-65; further studies of musical analysis with Igor Markevitch, St Cezaire, France. *Career:* Musical Editor, Romanian Radio, Bucharest, 1965-; served intermittently as musicological assistant to Igor Markevitch in the preparation of his encyclopaedic edition of the Beethoven Symphonies, 1969-80. *Publications:* Monographs on G. Verdi, 1970, and J. Ph. Rameau, 1984. *Contributions to:* 2 articles on Igor Markevitch, Variations, Fugue and Envoi on a Theme of Handel, What the Conductor Owes to the Composer, in Tempo, 1980; over 250 broadcasts on leading Romanian composers, music history, art of conducting. *Memberships:* Romanian Union of Composers and Musicologists. *Hobbies:* Philately. *Address:* Str Vasile Lascan 23, 70211 Bucharest-Romania.

MAW (John) Nicholas, b. 5 Nov 1935, Grantham, England. Composer. m. Karen Graham, 1960, 1 son, 1 daughter. *Education:* Royal Academy of Music; Study with Nadia Boulanger & Max Deutsch, Paris, 1958-59; Fellow Commoner in Creative Arts, Trinity College, Cambridge, 1966-70; Incomplete premiere of Odyssey at the 1987 Promanade Concerts; Complete with the City of Birmingham Symphony under Simon Rattle, 1990, American Games premiered at the 1991 Proms. *Compositions include:* Operas: One-Man Show, 1964; The Rising of the Moon, 1970. Orchestral works: Sinfonia, 1966; Sonata for Strings & Two Horns, 1967; Serenade for Small Orchestra, 1973, 1977; Life Studies, for 15 solo strings, 1973; Odyssey, 1974-85; Summer Dances, 1981; Spring Music, 1983; The World in the Evening, 1986; American Games for wind ensemble, 1990; Shahnama, 1992; Instrumental solos with orchestra: Sonata Notturna, cello & string orchestra, 1985; Little Concert, Oboe and Chamber Orchestra, 1988. Voice & orchestra: Nocturne, 1958; Scenes & Arias, 1962. Chamber Music: String Quartet, 1965; Chamber Music for wind & piano quintet, 1962; Flute Quartet, 1981; String Quartet No 2, 1983; Ghost Dances for Chamber Ensemble, 1988. Instrumental Music: Sonatina for flute & piano, 1957; Essay for Organ, 1961; Personae for piano, Nos I-III, 1973, Nos IV-VI, 1985; Music of Memory for Solo Guitar, 1989. Vocal music: 5 Epigrams, chorus, 1960; Round, chorus & piano, 1963; The Voice of Love, mezzo soprano & piano, 1966; 6 Interiors, high voice & guitar, 1966; 5 Irish Songs, mixed chorus, 1972; Reverie, 5 songs for male voices, 1975; Nonsense Rhymes, songs & rounds for children, 1975-76; La Vita Nuova, soprano & chamber ensemble, 1979; The Ruin, 1980; Three Hymns, SATB and organ, 1989; Roman Canticle, mezzo soprano and chamber ensemble, 1989; Sweté Jesu, 1990. *Honour:* Midsummer Prize, Corporation of London, 1980. *Address:* c/o Faber Music Ltd., 3 Queen Square, London WC1N 3AU, England.

MAWBY Colin, b. 9 May 1936, Portsmouth, England. Choral Conductor; Composer. *Education:* Westminster Cathedral Choir School, 1946-51; Royal College of Music, 1951-54. *Career:* Choirmaster Plymouth Cathedral, 1955-56; Assistant Master of Music, Westminster Cathedral, 1959-61; Master of Music, Westminster Cathedral, 1961-76; Choral Director, Radio Telefis Eireann, Ireland, 1981-. *Compositions:* 9 Masses, Motets, Anthems and Hymns. *Recordings:* With L'Oiseau Lyre, Polydor, Enigma. *Contributions to:* Times; Listener; Tablet; Catholic Herald; Universe. *Honours:* Officer of Merit, Knights of Malta. *Hobbies:* Growing Plants. *Address:* Gerrardstown, Garlow Cross, Navan, Co. Meath, Republic of Ireland.

MAX Robert, b. 7 Feb 1968, London, England. Solo

Cellist; Cellist with Barbican Piano Trio. *Education:* Royal Academy of Music, 1984-87; GRSM Hons (1st class); LRAM, Dip RAM, Royal Northern College of Music, 1987-89; Julliard School, New York, 1990-92. *Career:* Concerts all over UK, Europe, North and South America and the Far East; String Finalist, BBC Young Musician of the Year, 1984; Edward Boyle Memorial Scholarship to Banff Centre for the Arts; Music Director, Nonesuch Orchestra. *Recording:* Barbican Piano Trio: Mendelssohn D Minor, Alan Bush, John Ireland, 1989; Complete Piano Trios of E Lalo. *Honours:* 1st Prize, European Music for Youth Cello Prize, Brussels, 1984; Julius Isserlis Scholarship for Study Abroad; Winner, Strings Section of International Young Concert Artists Competition, 1989. *Hobbies:* Cooking curries; Skiing; Opera. *Address:* 5 Asmuns Hill, London NW11 6ES, England.

MAXWELL Donald, b. 12 Dec 1948, Perth, Scotland. Singer (Baritone). *Education:* Studied Geography in Edinburgh University. *Debut:* With Scottish Opera in Musgrave's Mary Queen of Scots, 1977. *Career:* Has sung Rossini's Figaro and Zurga (Les pêcheurs de Perles) with Scottish Opera, also taking part in Cavalli's Egisto and Janáček's The Cunning Little Vixen and From the House of the Dead; Has sung Verdi's Iago, Renato, Rigoletto and Don Carlo (Ernani) with the Welsh National Opera; Covent Garden debut 1987, in the British premiere of Sallinen's The King goes forth to France; Appeared with the WNO as Falstaff in New York, Milan and Tokyo, 1989; English National Opera in Prokofiev's The Love of Three Oranges and as Baron Prus in The Makropoulos Case, 1989; Appearances with Opera North 1989 as the Dutchman and Scarpia; Vancouver 1989, as Rigoletto; La Monnaie Brussels, Vancouver Opera. Major Roles: Falstaff in Paris, Tokyo, Milan, Vienna, New York and On TV; Iago for TV & Paris Opera; Wozzeck for TV; Rigoletto, Flying Dutchman, Scarpia, Gunther, Figaro, Renato, Pizarro, Don Carlo, Don Alfonso, Zurga, Eisenstein; Sang Wozzeck for ENO 1990, Gunther in Götterdämmerung at Covent Garden; Sang Debussy's Golaud for Welsh National Opera, 1992-, also Paris and TV; Many appearances in light music particularly as member of the Music Box. *Address:* c/o Music International, 13 Ardilaun Road, London N5 2QR, England.

MAY Ernest Dewey, b. 8 May 1942, Jersey City, New Jersey, USA. Department Chairman, Professor of Organ and Musicology. m. (1) Eileen Mayhew, 26 Jan 1963, 2 sons, 5 daughters, (2) Mary Milkey, 29 June 1985. *Education:* AB, Harvard University, 1964; MFA 1968, PhD 1975, Princeton University; Studies in Theory with Nadia Boulanger, 1964-66; Organ studies with Andre Marchal, 1964-66; Musicology studies with Arthur Mendel. *Career:* Assistant Professor of Music 1969-76, Director, Early Music Consort of Amherst 1972-75, Amherst College; Associate Professor, Professor of Organ and Musicology, University of Massachusetts, Amherst, 1976-; Organist and Choirmaster, St James' Church, Greenfield, Massachusetts, 1978-83; Director of Music, South Congregational Church, Springfield, Massachusetts, 1983-; Recitals in USA and Europe. *Recording:* Music for Trumpet and Organ. *Publications:* Breitkopf's Role in the Transmission of J S Bach's Organ Chorales, 1975; J S Bach as Organist (editor with George Stauffer), 1986; Neue Bach-Ausgabe, volume 1/20 (editor with Klaus Hofmann), 1986. *Contributions to:* New Harvard Dictionary of Music, and others. *Address:* 44 Amherst Road, Pelham, MA 01002, USA.

MAY Marius, b. 1950, England. Cellist. *Education:* Studied with André Navarra in Paris and with Pierre Fournier in Geneva. *Career:* Has played in public from age 10, giving a recital at the Royal College of Music, London, and playing the Saint-Saens A minor Concerto in Edinburgh; Wigmore Hall debut 1973 followed by recital and concerto appearances throughout Britain; Festival Hall debut 1976, with the Schumann Concerto and the Philharmonia Orchestra; Edinburgh and Bath Festivals, 1976; Soloist with leading orchestras in Europe; Several tours of Germany have included Berlin

Philharmonic concert 1980; Concerts with Yehudi Menuhin at the Gstaad Festival, Switzerland; Has recently played the Elgar Concerto with the London Philharmonic and the Finzi Concerto at the Three Choirs Festival with the Royal Philharmonic; Has taught at the University of California in Los Angeles; BBC TV concerts include the Tchaikovsky Rococo Variations and a Gala from the Edinburgh Festival. *Address:* c/o Ingpen and Williams Ltd, 14 Kensington Court, London W11 4PA, England.

MAYER Frederic David, b. 21 Apr 1931, Lincoln, Nebraska, USA. Opera singer; Music educator. m. Rosemarie Hege, 2 Aug 1974, 3 sons. *Education:* BA, Midland College; MA, DEd, Columbia University, New York; vocal study with Maestro Luigi Contoni, La Scala, Milan, Italy, Edgar Schofield, New York, USA, Rocco Pandiscio, New York and Munich, Germany and Hans Hopf, Munich. *Debut:* As Ferrando in Così Fan Tutte, Ulm, Germany, 1963. *Career:* With Städtische bühne, Ulm, Germany, 1963-64; Chicago Lyric Opera, Chicago, Illinois, USA, 1965-66; American Opera Society, New York, 1966-68; Staatstheater Am Gärtnerplatz, Munich, Germany, 1968-; Guest appearances, Berlin, Stuttgart, Vienna, Frankfurt, Salzburg Festival, Bregenzer Festival; television appearances on Ed Sullivan Show, Arthur Godfrey, Omnibus, 7 Lively Arts, USA over 25 local and national television shows, Germany; Over 200 concert appearances, USA and Germany and over 350 oratorio appearances, USA and Germany. *Recording:* Im Weissen Roessel. *Publication:* The Changing Voice, 1965; Auf Stieg und Fall der Stadt Mahagonny, Weil Brecht, Capriccio Records; Der Silbersee, Weil Brecht, Capriccio Records. *Honour:* Bayerischer Kammersänger, 1973. *Current Management:* Wolfgang Stoll, Munich, Germany. *Address:* Tirschenreutherstr. 19, 8 Munich 90, Germany.

MAYER George Louis, b. 17 Sept 1929, New Jersey, USA. Music Librarian; Consultant to Libraries and Publishers. *Education:* BA, New York University; MSLS, Columbia University; Graduate study under Fulbright Grant; University of Cologne, Germany, 1960-61. *Career:* Music Librarian, New York Public Library, 1955-65; Supervising Music Librarian, Library & Music of Performing Arts, Lincoln Centre, 1965-73; Principal Music Librarian & Co-ordinator, ibid, 1978-87; Adelphi University, 1988, 1990-; Brooklyn College Music Library, 1988-. *Publications:* Annals of The New York City Opera, 1944-79; published in Sokol, Martin L The New York City Opera: An American Adventure, New York, Macmillan c. 1981, London Collier Macmillan Publishers. *Address:* 150 West End Ave., New York City, NY 10023, USA.

MAYER Thomas, b. 1907, Germany. Conductor. *Education:* Studied conducting and composition, State Academy of Music, Berlin. *Career:* Opera Theatres of Beuthen, Leipzig, Teplitz and Aussig; Assistant to Erich Kleiber, Fritz Busch and Arturo Toscanini, Teatro Colon, Buenos Aires; Director, German Opera season, Santiago, Chile; Director, State Symphony Orchestra, Montevideo; USA debut, Metropolitan Opera, New York, 1947; Conducted Salome with Astrid Varnay, Cincinnati, 1948; Tristan und Isolde with Flagstad, Caracas; First foreign director, Venezuelan Symphony Orchestra; Conductor, Halifax Orchestra, Canada; Ottawa Orchestra became National Orchestra of Canada; Guest conductor, London Symphony, Royal Philharmonic, Chicago, Buffalo, Toronto, Montreal, Cincinnati, Munich Philharmonic, Essen and all the major Australian orchestras, as well as opera in Hamburg, Stuttgart and Australia; Conductor, Sinfonie Orchestra Berlin, 1974-; Frequest guest, Berlin Symphony (East). *Address:* c/o Norman McCann Ltd, c/o Norman McCann Ltd, The Coach House, 56 Lawrie Park Gardens, London SE2 6XJ, England.

MAYER William (Robert), b. 18 Nov 1925, New York. USA. Composer. *Education:* BA, Yale University, 1949; Studied with Roger Sessions at Julliard, 1949 and at the Mannes College of Music, 1949-52. *Career:* Secretary, National Music Council, 1980. Compositions

include: Stage: The Greatest Sound Around, children's opera, 1954; Hello World children's opera, 1956; One Christmas Long Ago, opera in act, 1964; Brief Candle, micro-opera 1964; A Death in the Family, opera, 1983; The Snow Queen, ballet, 1963; Orchestra: Andante for strings, 1955; Hebraic Portrait, 1957; Overture for an American, 1958; Two Pastels, 1960; Octagon for piano and orchestra, 1971; Inner and Outer Strings for string quartet and string orchestra, 1982; Of Rivers and Trains, 1988; String Quartet and other chamber music; Piano Sonata Choruses and songs. *Honours include:* Guggenheim Fellowship, 1966; National Institute for Musical Theater Award, 1983. *Address:* ASCAP, ASCAP Building, One Lincoln Plaza, NY 10023, USA.

MAYER-REINACH Ursula, b. 10 Oct 1920, Russee, Kiel, Germany. Concert and Opera Singer. m. Peter Gradenwitz, 23 Aug 1967. *Career:* Oratorio soloist in German concert halls and churches, 1955-60, Flower Maiden, soloist in Wagner Festival performances, Parsifal, in Bayreuth, 1961; Mrs. Herring in Britten's Albert Herring, on European tour. 1960 - added contemporary music to widen repertoire. Lived in Israel since 1967; Concert appearances, radio and TV in most West European countries, USA, Israel; Soloist in festival performances in Salzburg, Gstaad (Menuhin Festival), Lucerne, Athens, Reykjavik and in Israel; Recordings of classical and contemporary music; Active as pedagogue; Participant in University seminars. *Recordings include:* The Cornet, by Frank Martin, conducted by the composer; Great Artists record Music from Israel, (with Menuhin, Nicolet, Siegfried Palm, Aloys Kontarsky); recital: Songs around the Mediterranean, Homage à Marc Chagall. *Contributions to:* Die Kritik am Singen, in Musica, III 1972; Die Gesangskunst Enrico Carusos, in Musica, IV, 1973; Über Gesang und Sänger, in Musica, V 1984. *Hobbies:* Languages; Mountain tours; Gardening; Animals. *Address:* 6109 Rosehill, Shawnee, KS 66216, USA.

MAYES Samuel (Houston), b. 11 Aug 1917, Missouri, USA. Cellist. *Education:* Studied with Felix Salmond at the Curtis Institute, 1929-37. *Career:* Philadelphia Orchestra 1936, principal from 1939; Principal cellist of the Boston Symphony Orchestra 1948-64, Philadelphia Orchestra 1964-73; Played with the Los Angeles Philharmonic, 1974-75; Many appearances as soloist, notably the US premiere of Kabalevsky's First concerto with the Hartford Symphony and the Boston Symphony, 1953; Former teacher at the New England Conservatory and Boston University, University of Michigan from 1975. *Recordings include:* Prokofiev's Symphony-Concerto with the Boston SO and Don Quixote with the Philadelphia Orchestra. *Address:* Michigan State University, School of Music, East Lansing, MI 48824, USA.

MAYFORTH Robin, b. 1965, USA. Violinist. *Education:* Studied at the Julliard School, New York. *Career:* Appearances with I Solistsi Veneti, under Claudio Scimone; Co-founded the Lark Quartet, USA; Recent concert tours to Australia, Taiwan, Hong Kong, China, Germany and Holland; US appearances at the Lincoln Center New York Kennedy Center Washington DC and in Boston, Los Angeles, Philadelphia, St Louis and San Francisco; Repertoire includes quartets by Haydn, Mozart, Beethoven, Schubert, Dvořak, Brahms, Borodin, Bartók, Debussy and Shostakovich. *Honours:* (with Lark Quartet) Gold medals at the 1990 Naumberg and 1991 Shostakovich Competitions; Prizewinner, 1991 London International String Quartet, 1991 Melbourne Chamber Music, 1990 Premio Paulio Borciani (Reggio Emilia) and 1990 Karl Klinger (Munich) Competitions. *Address:* c/o Sonata (The Lark Quartet), 11 Northpark Street, Glasgow G20 7AA, Scotland.

MAYNOR Kevin Elliott, b. 24 July 1954, Mt Vernon, New York, USA. Classical Singer. *Education:* Diploma, Manhattan School of Music, 1970-72; BME, Bradley University, 1972-76; MM, Northwestern University, 1976-77; MV, Moscow Conservatory, 1979-80; Indiana University, 1980-83; DM, 1988. *Career:* Carnegie Hall debut, Die Leibe der Danal, 1983; Avery Fisher Hall debut, Fidelio, 1985; New York City Opera debut, Akhnaten, 1985; Chicago Lyric Opera; Santa Fe Opera; Virginia Opera; Nashville Opera; Long Beach Opera; Chicago Opera Theater; Mobile Opera; Apprenticeship, 1st from the West, Bolshoi Opera, 1979-80. *Honours:* Richard D Tucker Grant; Fulbright Award, 1979; George London Career Grant, 1986; William Sullivan Award, 1983; NATS Winner, 1984; 1st International Singing Competition, South Africa, 1984; National Arts Club Award, 1984. *Membership:* NAACP. *Current Management:* Herbert Barrett Management. *Address:* 201 Egmont Avenue, Mt Vernon, NY 10552, USA.

MAYR Rupert Erich, b. 1 Apr 1926, Linz, Donau, Austria. Professor of Music and Musicology. m. Erna B. Brandl, 13 June 1955, 3 sons. *Education:* Humanistisches Gymnasium, Linz, Austria; Dr. Phil. Degree, majoring in Musicology and History of Art 1953, University of Innsbruck 1947-53; Piano Lessons with Professor Gisela Pasztory-Göllerich 1934-44; Studies in Violin and Clarinet and Music Theory at school; Organ study at Linz Conservatoire; Conducting at Mozarteum Academy, Salzburg. *Career:* Commenced broadcasting at Studio as Pianist, Linz, Austria, 1946; Organist, City Parish, Linz; Conducted several church choirs; Regular appearances as soloist, accompanist and conductor or vocal and instrumental groups in Austria, and in South Africa 1955-; Conductor, Rhodes University Chamber Choir 1973-; Conductor, Eastern Cape Chamber Orchestra 1978-; Also appearances on South African TV; Various transcription recordings for SA Broadcasting Corporation including two discs in collaboration with flautist, Jean-Pierre Rampal; many tape recordings for SABC. *Publications:* Co-editor to series, Contributions To The Development of The Piano Sonata, published by A.A. Balkema (Amsterdam, Cape Town); The Piano Sonata of The 18th Century in Italy 1967; The Piano Sonata of The 18th Century in Germany 1969. *Hobbies:* Photography; Tennis. *Address:* 22 Southey Street, Grahamstown 6140, South Africa.

MAZURA Franz, b. 22 Apr 1924, Salzburg, Austria. Singer (Bass-Baritone). *Education:* Studied with Fred Husler in Detmold. *Debut:* Kassel 1955. *Career:* Sang at Mainz and Brunswick until 1964; Mannheim 1964-89; Salzburg 1960, in La Finta Semplice; Pizarro Fidelio, 1970; Member of Deutsche Oper Berlin 1963; Paris Opéra from 1973, as Wagner's Wotan, Alberich and Gurnemanz: sang Dr Schön in the 1979 premiere of the 3-act version of Berg's Lulu; Bayreuth Festival from 1971, as Biterolf, Alberich, Gunther, Gurnemanz, Klingsor and the Wanderer in the 1988 Ring cycle directed by Harry Kupfer; Hamburg Opera from 1973; Israel Festival, Caeserea, as Moses in Schoenberg's Moses und Aron; Guest apperances in Vienna, Buenos Aires, San Francisco, Nice and Strasbourg; Metropolitan Opera debut 1980, as Dr Schön: returned to New York as Klingsor, Alberich, Gurnemanz, Creon in Oedipus Rex, Pizarro, Doctor in Wozzeck, Frank in Die Fledermaus, Rangoni in Boris Godunov and the Messenger in Die Frau ohne Schatten, 1989; Bayreuth Festival, 1988-89, as Klingsor and the Wanderer; Season 1991/92 as Voland (the Devil), in Höller's Meister und Margarita at Cologne and Klingsor at the Met and the Bayreuth Festival. *Recordings include:* Dr Schön , Jack the Ripper in Lulu (Grammy Award 1980) (Deutsche Grammophon); Gunther in Götterdämerung (Philips); Schoenberg's Moses (Philips). *Address:* c/o Ingpen & Williams Ltd., 14 Kensington Court, London W8 5DN, England.

MAZURKEVICH Yuri Nicholas, b. 6 May 1941, Lvov, USSR. Professor of Violin; Concert Violinist. m. Dana Mazurkevich, 4 July 1963. 1 daughter. *Education:* School of Gifted Children, Lvov, 1948-60; Moscow State Conservatoire, with D Oistrakh, 1960-65, Postgraduate course, Artist Diploma; Masters degree in Performance, 1965-67. *Career:* Concert Violinist appeared all over the world; Recorded for Radio Moscow, France, BBC, ABC (Australia), CBC (Canada), Sender Freies (West Berlin), WGBH (Boston) and many others; Assistant Professor, Violin, Kiev State Conservatory, 1967-73; Associate Professor, Violin, University of Western Ontario, 1975-

85; Professor of Violin, Chairman of String Department, 1985-, Boston University; Member of Quartet Canada, 1980-. *Recordings:* Works by Beethoven, Paganini, Tartini, Handel, Spohr, Leclair, Prokofiev, Sarasate, Honegger, Telemann and others in Moscow, Toronto and Montreal, Canada. *Honours:* Prize winner of 3 International Violin Competitions, Helsinki 1962, Munich 1966 and Montreal 1969. *Membership:* Music Council of Canada. *Hobbies:* Sport; All kinds of outings. *Current Management:* Robert Gewald, New York City. *Address:* 56 Mason Terrace, Brookline, Massachusetts 02146, USA.

MAZZOLA Denia, b. 1956, Bergamo, Italy. Singer (Soprano). *Education:* Studied with Corinna Malatrasi. *Career:* Sang Amina in La Sonnambula at Brescia, then Lucia di Lammermoor, and Adina at Florence and Milan; Landestheatre Salzburg 1984, as Gilda, St Gallen 1985 as Violetta; Sang at the Zurich Opera 1985-87, notably as Elvira in I Puritani; Appearances as Lucia at Naples, 1988-89, New York City Opera; La Scala Milan, 1987, Sole in Fetonte by Jommelli; Further engagements at Houston, Alice Ford, San Francisco, in Maria Stuarda, Bergamo, Amelia in Elisabetta al Castello di Kenilworth by Donizetti, 1989, Reggio Emilia, Violetta, Barcelona, Elvira, 1990 and the 1990 Montpellier Festival, Palmide in a concert performance of Meyerbeer's Il Crociato in Egitto. *Recordings include:* Lucia di Lammermoor, with forces of the San Carlo, Naples (Nuova Era). *Address:* Teatro San Carlo, Via San Carlo 98F, I-80132 Naples, Italy.

MAZZOLA Patrizio, b. 4 Sept 1956, Chiavari, Italy. Pianist. *Education:* Studied at Lucerne Conservatory under H Harry, 1970; Diploma in Music Education, 1975; Soloist Diploma with distinction, 1978. *Career:* Numerous radio and television performances; Concerts in Switzerland and abroad with Festival Strings/Paul Sacher, International Music Festivals Lucerne; Teacher, Berne Conservatory, 1986-. *Recordings:* First record as soloist, 1980; second record, 1983; third record (Scarlatti Sonatas, 1989). *Honours:* Edwin Fischer Award, 1978; Migros Scholarships, 1975-78; Award of Acknowledgement of the City of Lucerne, 1985. *Membership:* Brahms and Wagner Societies.

MAZZOLA Rudolf, b. 1941, Basle, Switzerland. Singer (Bass). *Education:* Studied in Basle an Zurich. *Debut:* Commendatore in Don Giovanni at St Gallen. *Career:* Sang at St Gallen until 1971, Basle, 1971-75; Engaged at the Vienna Volksoper from 1975, debut in Wolpert's version of Moliere's Le Malade Imaginaire; Sang Osmin in Die Entfuhrung at the Vienna Staatsoper, 1977, returning as Sarastro, Gremin, Pimen, Padre Guardiano and the Grant Inquisitor; Bregenz Festival 1980 and 1984, as Osmin and the Sacristan in Tosca; Salzburg Festival, 1981, in the premiere of Cerha's Baal, Paris Opera 1983 as Truffaldino in Ariadne auf Naxos; Sang the Doctor in Wozzeck at Barcelona 1984, Rossini's Basilio at Liege 1988; Toronto, Don Alfonso, Cosí fan Tutte, 1992; Nice, La Roche, Capricco, 1993; Created roles in Einem's Tulifant and Krenek's Kehraus um St Stephan, Ronach Theater Vienna 1990, and sang Mozart's Bartolo at the Theater an der Wien, 1991; Guest appearances at Frankfurt, Hamburg, Munich, Budapest, Turin, and Zurich; Frequent concert and oratorio appearances. *Address:* c/o Staatsoper, Opernring 2, A-1010 Vienna, Austria.

MCALPINE William, b. 3 Dec 1922, Stenhousemuir, Scotland. Singer (Tenor). *Debut:* First Jew in Salome, at Covent Garden, 1951. *Career:* Sang at Covent Garden as Jacquino, Andres in the first British staging of Wozzeck, Don Basilio and in the premieres of Britten's Billy Budd and Gloriana, 1951, 1953; Glyndebourne Festival, 1956-69, as Idamantes, the Italian Singer and Bacchus; Sadler's Wells English National Opera 1956-74, as Don Ottavio, Rinuccio, Tamino, Alfredo, Belmonte, Boris in Katya Kabanova, Pinkerton, Cavaradossi, Erik and Hoffmann; Appearances with Scottish Opera 1965-74, as Cassio, Faust and Bob Boles in Peter Grimes; Overseas engagements at Vancouver, Paris, Florence, Hamburg, Berlin and Aix; Sang at Covent

Garden, 1960-75 as Grigory (Boris), Alfredo and Hoffmann. *Recordings include:* Handel's Messiah. *Address:* c/o English National Opera, St Martin's Lane, London WC2, England.

MCCABE John, b. 21 Apr 1939, Huyton, Lancashire, England. Classical Musician. *Education:* Manchester University; Royal Manchester College of Music; Hochschule für Musik, Munich, Germany. BMus, FRMCM, FLCM, FRCM, Hon. RAM, FRNCM, FTCL. *Career includes:* Piano recitals, wide repertoire but specialising contemporary music, & Haydn; UK premiere, Corigliano's Piano Concerto; Danish premiere, Delius Piano Concerto. Director, London College of Music, 1983-90. *Compositions:* Operas, symphonies, concertos, choral & keyboard works, TV & film music. Works include: Chagall Windows (orchestra); Notturni ed Alba (soprano & orchestra); Cloudcatcher Fells (brass band); Concerto for Orchestra, US premiere, 1984; Rainforest 1, 1984. Fire at Durilgai (orchestral), premiered BBC Philharmonic Orchestra, Manchester, later performances Prague, London Promenade Concerts, 1989; Flute Concerto, 1990; Red Leaves for orchestra, 1991; Postcards for wind quintet, 1992; Tenebrae for piano, 1993. *Recordings:* Wide range from Scarlatti, Clementi, Bax, Walton & Grieg, to contemporary British, American, Australian composers, including own piano music, & complete Haydn piano music (Decca, 16 discs). *Honours include:* Commander, Order of British Empire, 1985. *Memberships:* Royal Society of Arts; Association of Professional Composers. *Hobbies:* Books; Films, especially Westerns; Cricket; Snooker; Bonfires. *Address:* c/o Novello & Company, 8/9 Frith Str, London, W1V 5TZ, England.

MCCALDIN Denis James, b. 28 May 1933, Nottingham, England. Musician. m. Margaret Anne Smith, 1 son, 1 daughter. *Education:* BSc, PhD, Nottingham University; BMus, Birmingham University. *Career:* Professor and Director of Music, Lancaster University Concerts; Guest appearances as Conductor, Royal Liverpool Philharmonic Orchestra, London Mozart Players, Royal Philharmonic Orchestra, Halle Orchestra, Haydn Orchestra and others, 1970-; BBC Radio programmes including series on virtuoso chamber orchestra. *Recordings:* Haydn and Schubert Masses; Haydn Society Chorus and Orchestra. *Publications:* Stravinsky, 1972; Mahler, 1981; Haydn Mass in F major, 1993; Contributions to Beethoven Companion; Ed, Berlioz Te Deum; Edi, Haydn Little Organ Mass; Haydn Te Deum 1800; Music Review; Music Times; Music and Letters; Music in Education; Times Higher Education Supplement; Soundings and various others. *Hobbies:* Good food; Music. *Address:* Department of Music, University of Lancaster, Bailrigg, Lancaster LA1 4YW, England.

MCCALLUM David Kyle, b. 17 Feb 1948, Giffnock, Glasgow, Scotland. Piano Instructor, Grampian Regional Council; Piano Tutor, Northern College of Education, Aberdeen. m. Rosemary Dale, 14 July 1971, 3 daughters. *Education:* BMus, University of Edinburgh, 1969; Certificate of Education, Aberdeen College of Education, 1970. *Career includes:* Accompanist, Aberdeen Orpheus Choir; Conductor, Aberdeen Orpheus Junior Choir; Musical director, Stonehaven Choral & Orchestral Society, Kelso Operatic Society; Organist, Holburn West Church, Aberdeen, & Dunkeld Cathedral; Resident pianist, Pitlochry Festival Theatre; Director Of Music, Rannoch School; Presently Conductor; Aberdeen Orpheus Choir and organist and choirmaster, Banchory-Ternan East Parish Church; Founding Musical Director, Deeside Singing Festival; Guest Musical Director, Aberdeen Opera Company; President, Aberdeen and District Organists' Association. *Compositions:* Recent works include: Anthem, Easter Sunday; Folk-song Preludes for Organ; Scottish pipe tunes. *Recordings:* Schubert Mass in G, Vivaldi's Gloria, Mendelssohn's Lauda Sion, from chapel of Rannoch School. *Address:* Montgarrie, Raemoir Road, Banchory, Kincardineshire, Scotland.

MCCANN Norman, b. 24 Apr 1920, London,

England. Concert Agent. *Education:* Royal Academy of Music, London. *Career:* Appeared in opera, concerts, musical shows, Shakespeare and on radio and television; Administrative and Artistic Director, British Opera Company; Director of Productions, Hintlesham Festival of the Arts; Artistic Adviser, Battle Festival; Executive Director, Children's Opera Group; Concerts Organiser, International Eisteddfod; Concert Manager, London Bach Society and Goldsmiths Choral Union; Chairman, Minerva Ballet Trust; Concerts Manager and Artistic Adviser, South and North Wales Association of Choirs; President, British Association of Concert Agents; Manager and business adviser to distinguished artists including: Kurt Masur, Kurt Sanderling, Gunther Herbig, Peter Schreier; Executive Member, Visiting Orchestras Consultative Association; Mounted West Side Story, Festival of Szeged, Hungary; Curator of International Music Museum; Artistic Adviser, Dyfel Management. *Honours:* Kyril and Methodus, Bulgarian Government; ARAM, Royal Academy of Music; Fellow, Royal Society of Arts; Fellow, Institute of Directors. *Memberships:* British Institute of Management; President of the English Singers & Speakers Association; President & Chairman of the Lewisham Chamber of Commerce. *Address:* c/o International Artists Limited, The Coach House, 56 Lawrie Park Gardens, London SE26 6XJ, England.

MCCARTHY John, b. 1930, England, Choral Director; Director of Music. *Career:* Musical Director of the Ambrosian Singers and Ambrosian Opera Chorus and many other famous Choral Groups; Director of Music, Carmelite Priory; Former Chorus Master, Royal Opera House, Covent Garden; Professor, Royal College of Music; Choral Director to nearly all the greatest Conductors in the world; Director of many hundreds of very successful recordings and broadcasts and on TV has been Choral Director for many Operas and Music Programmes; In London Theatre has been involved in a number of Musicals and Revivals and several Royal Command Performances; Shows include: Mame; The Great Waltz; Gone With the Wind (Drury Lane); Showboat; The King and I; Choral Director for hundreds of films including the Oscar winning Oliver, Tom Jones, Goodbye Mr. Chips; Scrooge; Cromwell; Fiddler on the Roof; The Great Waltz; Man of la Mancia; Omen 1 & 2 & Final Conflict; Superman; Supergirl; Dracula; Close Encounters; Chariots of Fire; Return of the Jedi; Monsignor; Krull; Yentl; Amadeus. *Recordings:* Over 130 recordings of Operas in French, German, Italian, Russian and English; Conductor of 3 award winning LP's for European Grand Prix du Disques. Operas include: Orfeo; Armida; Semele; Tannhäuser; Don Giovanni; Lucia; Fledermaus. *Publications:* Editor of a new series of Tudor and Renaissance Music; Publisher of compositions and numbers of Orchestral and Choral arrangements. *Honours:* OBE, 1990; Five nominations for USA Grammy Award for Choral Direction and many other honours and awards. *Address:* c/o Ambrosian Singers, 4 Reynolds Road, Beaconsfield, Bucks, HP9 2NJ, England.

MCCARTNEY (James) Paul, b. 28 June 1942, Liverpool, England. Songwriter; Performer. m. Linda Eastman, 1969, 1 son, 3 daughters. *Education:* Self Taught in Playing Guitar, Piano, Organ, Trumpet. *Career:* Wrote First Song, 1956 and Numerous Songs with John Lennon, Joined Pop Group The Quarrymen, 1956; Appeared Under Various Titles Until Formation of the Beatles, 1960; Appeared with The Beatles in the Following Activites, Performances in Hamburg, The Cavern, Liverpool; Worldwide Tours, 1963-66; Attended Transcendental Meditation Course, Maharishis Academy, India, 1968; Founded Apple Limited, After the Collapse of the Apple Corp Limited, Left the Beatles, 1970 and Formed MPL Group of Companies; First Solo Album, 1970; Formed Own Group, Wings, 1971-, Touring Britain and Europe, UK, Australia and the USA; Released Film, Album, Give My Regards to Broad Street, 1984; Tour of Scandinavia, 1989. *Recordings include:* with The Beatles: Please Please Me, 1963; A Hard Days Night, 1964; Beatles for Sale, 1965; Help!, 1965; Rubber Soul, 1966; Revolver, 1966; Sgt Peppers Lonely Hearts Club Band, 1967; Magical Mystery Tour, 1967; The

Beatles, 1968; Yellow Submarine, 1969; Abbey Road, 1969; Let Me Be, 1970. Wings: McCartney, 1970; Ram, 1971; Wild Life, 1971; Red Rose Speedway, 1973; Band On The Run, 1973; Venus and Mars, 1975; Wings at the Speed of Sound, 1976; Wings Over America, 1976; London Town, 1978; Wings Greatest, 1978. Solo: Back To The Egg, 1979; McCartney II, 1980; Tug of War, 1982; Pipes of Peace, 1983; Give My Regards to Broad Street, 1984; Press To Play, 1986; All the Best!, 1987; CHOBA B CCCP, 1988; Flowers in the Dirt, 1989; Tripping the Live Fantastic, 1990; Unplugged: The Official Bootleg, 1991; Paul McCartney's Liverpool Oratorio, 1991, written by Carl Davis. *Honours include:* MBE, 1965; Numerous Grammy Awards; Ivor Novello Awards include: for International Achievement, 1980, for International Hit of the Year (Ebony and Ivory), 1982, for Outstanding Contribution to Music, 1989; Guiness Book of Records; Triple Superlative Award; Freeman of the City of Liverpool, 1984; DUniv Sussex, 1988. *Address:* c/o MPL Communications Ltd, 1 Soho Square, W1V 6BQ, England.

MCCARTY Patricia, b. 16 July 1954, Wichita, Kansas, USA. Viola soloist; Recitalist; Chamber Musician. m. Ronald Wilkison, 29 Aug 1982. *Education:* BMus, University of Michigan, 1974; MMus, University of Michigan, 1976. *Debut:* New York, 1978; Wigmore Hall, London, England, 1986; Beethovenhalle, Bonn, 1991; Japan tour, 1993. *Career:* Viola soloist, recitalist and chamber musician in performances throughout the United States, Europe and Japan; Appearances include Detroit, Houston, Brooklyn, Boston Pops, Beethovenhalle, Suisse Romande, Kyoto and Shinsei Nihon Tokyo orchestras; recitals in New York, San Francisco, Detroit, Boston and London; Chamber music performances at Marlboro, Aspen, Tanglewood, Hokkaido and Sarasota festivals; Faculty the Boston Conservatory. *Recordings:* Viola Works of Rebecca Clarke; Songs of Charles Martin Loeffler; Brahms Viola Quintets; Dvořák String Sextet; Keith Jarrett Concerto. *Current Management:* Ashmont Music, c/o Anne Thomas, 25 Carruth Street, Boston, MA 02124, USA.

MCCAULEY Barry, b. 2 June 1950, Altoon, Pennsylvania, USA. Singer (Tenor). *Education:* Studied at Eastern Kentucky University and Arizona State University. *Debut:* San Francisco Spring Opera 1977, as Don José. *Career:* San Francisco Opera 1977, as Faust; Further appearances in Houston and San Diego; European debut Frankfurt 1979, as Edgardo in Lucia di Lammermoor; New York City Opera from 1980; Aix-en-Provence Festival, 1980, as Don Ottavio; Paris Opera from 1982, Teatro Comunale Florence, 1983 (debut as Wilhelm Meister in Mignon); Théâtre de la Monnaie Brussels, 1984 and 1986, as Idamante and Belfiore in La Finta Giardiniera; Glyndebourne Festival, 1985-88, as Don José and Boris in Katya Kabanova; Metropolitan Opera debut 1985, as Jacquino; Vienna Staatsoper, 1984, Don Ottavio; Has sung Offenbach's Hoffmann at the Spoleto Festival, 1989 and Seattle and Geneva, 1990; Other roles include Alfredo, Seattle, 1988, Maurizio in Adriana Lecouvreur, Trieste, 1989, Belmonte, Gluck's Admète, Nemorino, Robert Dudley in Maria Stuarda, the Duke of Mantua, Fenton, Pinkerton, Gerald in Lakmé, Nadir, Lensky and Froh, Das Rheingold; Debut as Parsifal at Amsterdam, 1991. *Address:* Seattle Opera Association, P O Box 9248, Seattle, WA 98109, USA.

MCCAULEY John J., b. 16 Nov 1937, Des Moines, Iowa, USA. Pianist, Conductor, Teacher. *Education:* MS MusEd Honours, 1960, 1961, University of Illinois at Urbana; Conducting studies, Tanglewood and Aspen, 1960-64; MS, Piano, Juilliard School of Music, 1964; Diplomas in Piano, Chamber Music, Conducting Mozarteum Summer Academy, Salzburg, Austria, 1968-74. *Debut:* Carnegie Recital Hall, New York City, 1975. *Career:* Numerous concerts also chamber music US Coast East and Midwest also in Europe; Frequent radio and television appearances; Recitals, of piano solos and chamber music include, Lincoln Center, 1967-89, Juilliard School of Music Recital Hall, Wave Hill Concert Series; Bronx Symphony Orchestra as concerto soloist,

Lincoln Center Mozart Festival, Research Assistant, 1988; Radio Station WQXR, The Listening Room with Robert Sherman. *Compositions:* Columbia Artists Management Recital Accompanist, Community Concerts throughout USA 1983-1984, 1984-1985. Bronx Symphony Orchestra, Lehman Center for the Performing Arts, Guest Conductor, 1985; Des Moines Metro Opera, Des Moines, IA, Assistant Conductor, Musical Coach, 1984-89, Arizona Opera, Tuscon and Phoenix, AZ, Assistant Conductor Brooklyn Philharmonic, Brooklyn Academy of Music, New York, NY, Associate Conductor, 1985; Eastern Opera Theater, New York, NY, Conductor of East Coast Tours, 1982-84; Bel Canto Opera, New York, NY, Conductor, 1979-1982. *Address:* 212 W. 91 1439, New York, NY 10024, USA.

MCCHESNEY James, b. 2 Apr 1941, Scotland, USA. Musician. *Education:* RSMAD, 1959-63; DRSAM; LRAM; ARCM. *Debut:* Troon, 1966. *Career:* Soloist in recitals and concertos, also conducting from keyboard; Chamber music player; Concerts in UK, USA, Austria, New Zealand; Also radio and television appearances. *Recordings include:* Solo Piano: Schubert Sonata; Eberl Sonata in C minor Op 1 Piano Concerto Op 32 in C; Violin and Piano: Franck Sonata, Constaninidis Suite; Piano Duet: Mozart Beethoven, Schubert recital with Coleen Rae Gerrard. *Memberships:* Incorporated Society of Musicians; Austrian Union for the Arts and Freelance Professionals. *Hobbies:* Fishing; Hill Walking; Aviation. *Address:* Thaliastrasse 96/21, A-1160 Vienna, Austria.

MCCOLL William Duncan, b. 18 May 1933, Port Huron, Michigan, USA. Clarinettist and Bassett Hornist. m. Sue McColl, 1 son. *Education:* 2 years at Oberlin; 1 year at Manhattan School of Music; Graduate with Reifezeugnis, State Academy of Music and Representational Arts, Vienna. *Career:* Solo clarinettist, US Seventh Army Symphony Orchestra, 1957-58; and Philharmonia Hungarica, Vienna, 1959; Clarinettist, Festival Casals; Solo Clarinettist, Puerto Rico Symphony Orchestra, and Clarinet Instructor, Puerto Rico Conservatoire, 1960-68; Clarinettist, Soni Ventorum Wind Quintet, 1963-; Professor, University of Washington, 1968-; Bass Clarinettist, Orquestra Filarmonica de las Americas (Mexico City), summers, 1976-78. *Recordings:* Villa-Lobos, Trio for bassoon, clarinet and oboe, quarter ditto with flute; Reicha Quintet in G major; Haydn Clock Organ pieces (arranged for wind quintet); Beethoven, Clock Organ Pieces (arranged for wind quintet): Reicha, Quintet in E Minor; Danzi-Quintet in F major; Poulenc, Duo for clarinet and bassoon; Villa-Lobos, Trio for clarinet, bassoon and piano, numerous other compositions and arrangements. *Address:* c/o School of Music, University of Washington, Seattle, WA 98195, USA.

MCCORMACK Elizabeth, b. 1964, Fife, Scotland. Singer (Mezzo-soprano). *Education:* BA, Glasgow University, Royal Scottish Academy with Duncan Robertson and at London Opera Studio. *Career:* Edinburgh Festival debut 1986 with Alan Ramsay's The Gentle Shepherd; Concert performances include Handel's Messiah, Samson and Coronation Anthem; Mozart Requiem, Beethoven Missa Solemnis and CPE Bach Magnificat; Stravinsky's Pulcinella with the English Chamber Orchestra at the Barbican; Sang De Nebra's Requiem and Handel's Dixit Dominus with La Chappelle Royale and Philippe Herreweghe 1989; Haydn's Theresian Mass with the Orchestra of the Age of Enlightenment at the Elizabeth Hall; Has also sung in Elgar's The Musicmakers, Vivaldi's Gloria and the Duruflé Requiem; English National Opera debut, 1989 in The Mikado; Scottish Opera 1990 in the premiere of Judith Weir's The Vanishing Bridegroom. *Honours:* Scottish Opera John Noble Bursary, 1987; Decca-Kathleen Ferrier Prize, 1987; Isobel Baillie Perfromance Award, 1987. *Address:* Ron Gonsalves Management, 10 Dagnan Road, London SW12 9LQ, England.

MCCORVEY Everett, b. 3 Dec 1957, Alabama, USA. Opera Singer. m. Alicia Helm, 24 May 1986, 1 daughter. *Education:* BMus, MMus, University of Alabama; DMA,

University of Alabama, 1989. *Debut:* Birmingham Civic Opera, 1979. *Career:* Appearances include: Metropolitan Opera, 1985-86; Radio City Music Hall, 1982; Aspen Music Festival, 1980-82, 1984-85; Whitewater Opera, 1980; Birmingham Civic Opera and Opera Theater, 1979, 1987; Runkamura Theater, Tokyo, Japan, 1990. Solo and duo recitals with Soprano Alicia Helm throughout US and Europe. *Recordings include:* African American Symphonic And Art Songs; Movies: The Long Walk Home; The Cotton Club; Izzi and Moe; TV: Live from Lincoln Center; The Stone Pillow. *Honours:* Advisory Panel, NEA, 1990-92; Society for the Fine Arts, 1991; Oustanding Opera Performance Award, 1981; Winner, National Federation of Music Clubs Competition, 1981. *Memberships:* National Association of Teacher of Singing; AGMA; SAG; AEA; AFTRA; MTNA. *Hobbies:* Tennis; Fishing. *Current Management* Alkahest Agency, Atlanta, Georgia. *Address:* 214 Bell Court East, Lexington, KY 40508, USA.

MCCOY Seth, b. 17 Dec 1928, Sanford, North Carolina, USA. Tenor; Teacher. m. Jane Gunter. *Education:* Graduate, North Carolina Agricultural and Technical College, 1950; Vocal studies with Pauline Thesmacher, Cleveland Music School Settlement, Antonia Lavanne, New York. *Career:* Soloist, Robert Shaw Chorale, 1963-65; Member, Bach Aria Group, 1973-80; Soloist with many major USA orchestras including: New York Philharmonic Orchestra; Boston Symphony Orchestra; Philadelphia Orchestra; Cleveland Orchestra; Chicago Symphony Orchestra; Pittsburgh Symphony Orchestra; San Francisco Symphony Orchestra; Los Angeles Philharmonic Orchestra; Numerous festival appearances in USA; European debut, Aldeburgh Festival, 1978; Metropolitan Opera debut, New York, Tamino, 1979; London debut as soloist, Bach's Christmas Oratorio, 1986; Professor of Voice, Eastman School of Music, Rochester, New York, 1982-. *Recordings:* For American Bicentennial Collection; Composers Recordings Inc; RCA; Vanguard. *Honour:* Recipient of the Albert Schweitzer Award for Artistry.*Address:* c/o Herbert Barrett Management Inc, 1776 Broadway, New York, NY 10019, USA.

MCCRAY James, b. 21 Feb 1939, Warren, Ohio, USA. Singer (Tenor). *Education:* Studied with Raymond Buckingham. *Debut:* Stratford Festival, Canada, in Weill's Aufstieg und Fall der Stadt Mahagonny. *Career:* Appearances in Seattle, Kansas City, Miami, San Francisco and the New York City Opera; Guest with Tel-Aviv Opera, Israel; Roles include Verdi's Ismaele, Radames and Manrico, Wagner's Siegmund and Siegfried, Don José, Samson, Ponchielli's Enzo and Puccini's Calaf, Dick Johnson and Cavaradossi; Sang Florestan at Montreal, 1988; Young Siegfried in the first Polish production of the Ring, Warsaw 1989; Wuppertal 1989, as Tristan. *Address:*c/o Wuppertaler Bühnen, Spinnstrasse 4, D-5600 Wuppertal, Germany.

MCCREADY Ivan, b. 1963, England. Cellist. *Education:* Studied at the Royal Academy of Music with Derek Simpson. *Career:* Member of the Borante Piano Trio from 1982; Concerts at the Wigmore Hall and in Dublin and Paris; Beethoven's Triple Concerto at the Festival Wien Klassik, 1989; Season 1990 at the Perth and Bath Festivals, and tour of Scandinavia, Russia and the Baltic States; Cellist of the Duke String Quartet from 1985; Performances in the Wigmore Hall, Purcell Room, Conway Hall and throughout Britain; Tours of Germany, Italy, Austria and the Baltic States; South Bank series 1991, with Mozart's early quartets; Soundtracks for Ingmar Bergman documentary The Magic Lantern, Channel 4 1988; Features for French television 1990-91, playing Mozart, Mendelssohn, Britten and Tippett; Brahms Clarinet Quintet for Dutch Radio with Janet Hilton; Live Music Now series with concerts for disadvantaged people; The Duke Quartet invites.... at the Derngate, Northampton 1991, with Duncan Prescott and Rohan O'Hara; Resident quartet of the Rydale Festival 1991; Residency at Trinity College, Oxford, tours to Scotland and Northern Ireland and concert at the Elizabeth Hall 1991. *Recordings include:* Quartets by Tippett, Shostakovich and Britten (Third) for Factory

Classics. *Honours include:* Awards include the Harold Craxton at the RAM and the Leche Scholarship. *Address:* Anglo-Swiss Management, 4-5 Primrose Mews, Sharpeshall Street, London NW1 8YW, England.

MCCREESH Paul D., b. 24 May 1960, London, England. Conductor; Baroque Cellist. m. Susan Jones, 23 July 1983. *Education:* University of Manchester. *Career:* Director, Gabrieli Consort and Players (founded 1982); Frequent performances of baroque and renaissance music in UK and abroad. *Recordings:* A & G Gabrieli Music for a Venetian Coronation (Virgin Classics); Venetian Vespers, 1993; exclusive DG/Archiv contract from 1993. *Honour:* Gramophone Award, 1990; ABC record of the year, 1991, Dutch Edison Award, 1991; Gramophone Award, 1993. *Hobbies:* Walking; Travel. *Address:* Beech Cottage, Wartnaby, Leics LE14 3HY, England.

MCCULLOCH Jenifer Susan, b. 3 Aug 1957, London, England. Opera Singer (Lyrico-spinto soprano); Voice Teacher. *Education:* Royal College of Music, 1975-82; ARCM hons, 1979; National Opera Studio, 1985-86. *Debut:* As Countess Almaviva in Mozart's Marriage of Figaro with English National Opera, 1986. *Career:* Concert at the major London venues and at festivals in Edinburgh, Cambridge, Henley and Manchester; Appeared in oratorio all over UK and Europe; Has sung Brahms' Requiem with David Willcocks and Mendelssohn's Infelice with Solti; Recorded Mozart's Exsultate Jubilate and Strauss' Four Last Songs for BBC; American debut in the Four Last Songs, with San Jose Symphony Orchestra; Sings principal roles with ENO, Scottish Opera, Glyndebourne Festival and Touring Opera also Hong Kong, Holland, France, Portugal, Germany and Belgium; appearances include Verdi's Jerusalem for Opera North, Mozart's Countess for ENO, Tosca in Dublin and Mozart's Marcellina in Hong Kong and Holland. *Recordings:* Marriage of Figaro for Deutsche Grammophon. *Hobbies:* Calligraphy; Cooking; Entertaining; Reading; Film-going. *Current Management:* Robert Gilder & Co. *Address:* Flat One, 80 Sunnyhill Road, Streatham, London SW16 2UL, England.

MCCULLY James Kimball, b. 19 Oct 1958, Hot Springs National Park, Arkansas, USA. Administrator, Opera Director and Opera Coach. *Education:* Private operatic study with Wagnerian soprano Marjorie Lawrence, Arno Tourel from the Accademia di Santa Cecilia, and John Moriarty of the Boston Conservatory of Music. B Mus, BA Communications, 1980. *Career:* Executive Director, National Center for the Arts, Washington, D.C. 1986-; Opera Adjudicator, Metropolitan Opera National Council Auditions, New York, New York, 1985; Art Management Fellow, National Endowment for the Arts, Opera-Musical Theater Program, Washington, D.C. 1985; Production Coordinator, Central City Opera House Association, Denver, CO., 1984. *Publications:* A Guide To Operatic Excellence, 1986; A Historical and Critical Study of Opera in the Media, 1987; The Media Arts Center: An Operating Manual, 1988. *Memberships:* National Opera Association; International Society of Professional Arts Administrators; ACUCAA; Phi Mu Alpha Sinfonia. *Address:* 818 Alpine Street, Hot Springs National Park, AR 71913-5142, USA.

MCDANIEL Barry, b. 18 Oct 1930, Lyndon, Kansas, USA. Singer (Baritone). *Education:* Juilliard Schol, New York; Stuttgart Musikhochschule with Alfred Paulus and Hermann Reutter. *Debut:* Sang in recital at Stuttgart in 1953. *Career:* Mainz Opera, 1954-55; Stuttgart Opera, 1957-59; Karlsruhe, 1960-62; Deutsche Oper Berlin from 1962, notably in Baroque and contemporary works, also Mozart and Wagner; Sang in the premieres of Henze's Der junge Lord, 1965 and Reimann's Melusine, 1971; Salzburg Festival, 1968; Metropolitan Opera, 1972, as Debussy's Pelléas; Other roles include the Barber in Die schweigsame Frau and Olivier in Capriccio; Guest engagements in Vienna and Munich; Frequent appearances in Schubert Lieder and as Christus in the St Matthew Passion. *Recordings:* Bach,

Christmas Oratorio; Ariadne auf Naxos, Dido and Aeneas, La Finta Giardiniera and Der junge Lord, Deutsche Grammophon; Orff's Trionfi, BASF. *Address:* c/o Deutsche Oper Berlin, Richard Wagnerstrasse 10, D-1000 Berlin, Germany.

MCDERMOTT Vincent,b. 5 Sept 1933, Atlantic City, New Jersey, USA. Composer; Professor. *Education:* Composition studies with C. Vauclain, D. Milhaud, G. Rochberg and K. Stockhausen; BFA, 1959, PhD, 1966, University of Pennsylvania; MA, University of California, Berkeley, 1961. *Career:* Performances of major works in Zagreb, London, Stockholm, Jakarta, Vancouver, Chicago, Cincinnati, Cleveland, Washington, Seattle, San Antonio, Portland, Milwaukee and New York. *Compositions:* Major works are: He Who Ascends by Ecstasy, (Piano-tape) 1972; Pictures at an Exhibition (tape-slides), 1974; Siftings upon Siftings (orchestra), 1976; A Perpetual Dream (mono-opera), 1978; Slayer of Time (chorus-instruments), 1977; Solonese Concerto (piano-chamber ensemble), 1979; Laudamus (chorus), 1980; The Dark Laments of Ariadne and of Attis (theater piece), 1983; Sweet-Breathed Minstrel, 1983; The Bells of Tajilor (gamelan), 1984; Fiddles, Queens and Laddies, 1987; The King of Bali (opera), 1990; Fugitive Moons (String Quartet), 1991; Mata Har, (Opera), 1993. *Recordings.* The Bells of Tajilor; The Dark Laments of Ariadne and of Attis; Fiddles, Queens and Laddies; Sweet-Breathed Minstral; The Venerable Showers of Beauty. *Address:* School of Music, Lewis and Clark College, Portland, OR 97219, USA.

MCDONALD Gail Faber, b. 24 Oct 1917, Jersey City, New Jersey, USA. Musician (Pianist). m. Angus McDonald, 10 Nov 1946, dec. *Education:* BA, University of Maryland; MM, Catholic University, 1968; DMA, University of Maryland, 1977. *Debut:* National Gallery of Art. *Recordings:* Complete Songs Without Words - Mendelssohn; Complete Sinfonias of J S Bach, Educo, California; Complete Works of Daniel Gregory Mason. *Publications:* Muzio Clementi: Gradus ad Parnassum, 1967; Daniel Gregory Mason - His Life and Piano Works, 1977. *Memberships:* Maryland State Music Teachers Association, President 1977-81; Friday Morning Music Club; District of Columbia Federation of Music Clubs; Washington Music Teachers Association. *Address:* 6807 Farmer Drive, Fort Washington, MD 20744, USA.

MCDONALL Lois, b. 7 Feb 1939, Larkspur, Alberta, Canada. Singer (Soprano). *Education:* Studied in Edmonton, Vancouver and Toronto and with Otakar Kraus in London. *Debut:* Toronto 1969, in Wolf-Ferrari's Il Segreto di Susanna. *Career:* Sang in Ottawa and Toronto, then Flensburg, Germany; Sadler's Wells/English National Opera from 1970, notably as Handel's Semele and in the title role of Hamilton's Anna Karenina (1981); Other roles include Mozart's Countess, Constanze and Fiordiligi, Massenet's Manon and the Marschallin; Sang the Contesse de Coigny in Andrea Chénier at Toronto, 1988; President of Canada, currently teaching at University of Toronto; Feelance singing. roles include: Fedora, Opera in concert, Anna in Anna Karenina and a guest of ENO. *Recordings include:* Freia in The Ring (HMV) and Donizetti's Maria Padilla. *Memberships:* National British Equity, ACTRA Canadian Society. *Address:* c/o Canadian Opera Co, 227 Front Street East, Toronto, Ontario, Canada M5A 1EB.

MCDONNELL Thomas Anthony, b. 27 Apr 1940, Melbourne, Australia. Singer (Baritone).m. Mary Jennifer Smith. *Education:* Melba Conservatorium, Melbourne, with Lennox Brewer. *Debut:* Belcore in L'Elisir d'Amore at Brisbane, 1965. *Career:* Sadler's Wells/English National Opera from 1967, as Mozart's Figaro, Verdi's Germont, Escamillo and in the first British stage performances of Prokofiev's War and Peace (1972) and Henze's The Bassarids (1974); Sang in War and Peace at the opening of the Sydney Opera House (1973); Created roles in Crosse's The Story of Vasco (1974), Henze's We Come to the River and Tippett's The Ice Break (both at Covent Garden), Iain Hamilton's The Royal Hunt of the Sun and Nicola LeFanu's Dawnpath (both 1977); London Collegiate Theatre 1977 in the British

premiere of Nielsen's Saul and David; Well known as Mozart's Papageno and Tchaikovsky's Onegin; Sang Mozart's Commendatore with Opera Factory, Elizabeth Hall, 1990 and Silva in Ernani for Chelsea Opera Group; Sang Lictor in The Coronation of Poppea for Opera Factory, 1992. *Recordings include:* Israel in Egypt; La Fanciulla del West; Tancredi; Donizetti rarities. *Honours include:* Showcase Australia 1965; Leverhulme Youth and Music Scholarship to Rome. *Hobbies:* Shakespeare; Chamber Music; Poetry; Architecture; Jogging; Tennis. *Address:* c/o Opera Factory, 8a The Leather Market, Weston Street, London, SE! 3ER, England.

MCFADDEN Claron, b. 1961, Rochester, New York, USA. Singer (Soprano). *Education:* Studied at the Eastman School, Rochester. *Career:* Has sung in concert, opera and oratorio from 1984; Opera debut 1985 in Hasse's L'Eroe Chinese conducted by Ton Koopman; Regular appearances with William Christie in Europe and North and South America, notably as Amour in Rameau's Anacréon at the Opéra Lyrique du Rhin; Netherlands Opera debut 1989, as Zerbinetta in Ariadne auf Naxos; Season 1991 included Mozart's Impresario at the Salzburg Festival and on South Bank, Acis and Galatea with the King's Consort and Rameau's Les Indes Galantes with Les Arts Florissants in Montpellier; Has also worked in concert with the Schoenberg Ensemble and composers Gunther Schuller, Louis Andriessen and Steve Reich; Carmina Burana conducted by Leopold Hager and L'Enfant et les Sortilèges under Sergiu Comissiona; Sang in Purcell's Fairy Queen with Les Arts Florissants at the Barbican Hall, 1992. *Recordings:* Acis and Galatea, with the King's Consort; Haydn's Orfeo with La Stagione Frankfurt; Vocal works by Glenn Gould (Sony Classical); Les Indes Galantes. *Honours include:* Prize winner at the 1988 International Competition, 's-Hertogenbosch. *Address:* Magenta Music International, 64 Highgate High Street, London N6 5HX, England.

MCFARLAND-JOHNSON Jeffrey Curtis, b. 30 June 1955, Modesto, California, USA. Cellist; Bassist; Composer. m. Cynthia E Hieb, 15 July 1984. *Education:* BM, Conservatory of Music, University of the Pacific, 1977; Sibelius Academy, Helsinki, Finland, 1978; MA, University of California, San Diego, 1986. *Career:* Performances with computers and synthesizers on a solid-bodied cello prototype; Performances with Henri Pousseur, Vinko Globokar, James Newton, Anthony Braxton; Jazz and avant-garde music projects on cello; Principal: University of California, San Diego Chamber Symphony, Merced Symphony Orchestra, Modesto Masterworks Orchestra, Berkeley Chamber Orchestra, Sibelius Academy Chamber Orchestra, University of the Pacific Symphony; Section Member: Napa Valley Symphony Orchestra, Modesto Symphony Orchestra, Stockton Symphony Orchestra, Sibelius Academy Symphony Orchestra, Pacifica Symphony Orchestra; Chamber Music Ensembles. *Address:* 1732 Le Bec Court, Lodi, CA 95240, USA.

MCFARLANE Clare, b. 24 July 1963, Lancashire, England. Violinist; Teacher. m. Leland Chen, 12 Aug 1987, 2 sons. *Education:* The Yehudi Menuhin School, 1973-82; Guildhall School of Music & Drama, 1982-87; Teachers: Margaret Norris, John Glickman, Peter Norris, Hans Keller; ARCM, with Honours. *Career:* BBC Young Musician of the Year, String Section Winner, 1980; Performed in all major concert halls in London; Soloist with RPO, Hallé, Northern Sinfonia, London Mozart Players, Orchestra of St John's, Smith Square; Performed in USA, Canada, India, China & Europe; Duo with Leland Chen for 2 Violin and Violin/Viola works. Performed a cycle of all Beethoven Sonatas in Purcell Room, 1989; Professor of Violin, London College of Music, 1985-89; Violin Teacher, Chetham's School of Music; Chosen for Representation by YCAT; Has given master classes and teaches privately. *Address:* 11 Mayfield Road, Kersal, Salford, Lancs M7 3WZ, England.

MCGEGAN Nicholas, b. 14 Jan 1950, Sawbridgeworth, Herts, England. Conductor; Flautist; Keyboard Player. *Education:* Studied at Oxford and

Cambridge Universities. *Career:* Conducted Handel's Teseo at Pepsico Summer Fare and Boston Early Music Festival, 1985; Music Director of Philharmonia Baroque, San Francisco, 1985-; Conducted John Copley's production of Ariodante at Santa Fe Opera 1986; Has led the Symphonies of San Francisco, Boston, Detroit, St Louis and Washington DC; St Paul and Los Angeles Chamber Orchestras; Baroque Artistic Consultant for Santa Fe Chamber Music Festival, 1990-; Music Director of the Göttingen Handel Festival in Germany; Has conducted Poppea and The Rake's Progress for Washington Opera; Hoffmann, Die Entführung, Paisiello's Barber and The Return of Ulysses at Long Beach Opera; Nakamichi Festival Los Angeles, 1988, with the US premiere of Landi's Il Sant'Alessio; Handel's Guistino at the San Francisco Opera Center, 1989; Season, 1990-91 with Handel's L'Allegro at Brooklyn Academy, La Clemenza di Tito with Scottish Opera and Agrippina at Göttingen; Conducted the Classical Band at the 1990 Schleswig-Holstein Festival; Debut concerts with the Houston and Minnesota Orchestras 1991; Invited to Washington Opera for Agrippina 1992 and to English National Opera 1993 for Ariodante; conducted Ottone at Göttingen and The Beggar's Opera at Santa Fe, 1992. *Recordings:* Handel's Water Music, Mozart's Horn Concertos, Arias for Senesino, with Drew Minter, Arias for Montagnana, with David Thomas, Arias for Cuzzoni, with Lisa Saffer, Handel's Susanna, premiere recording, Clori, Tirsi e Filene, Agrippina, Ottone and Messiah, Corelli's Concerti Grossi Op 6 (Harmonia Mundi) and Vivaldi Recorder Concerti (with Marian Verbrüggen); Three Rameau operas (Erato); Operas by Handel and Telemann, Oratorios by Handel including Floridante, Vivaldi, Telemann and Alessandro Scarlatti (Hungaroton). *Address:* c/o Philharmonia Baroque Orchestra, 57 Post Street, Suite 705, San Francisco, CA 94104, USA.

MCGIBBON Roisin, b. 1960, Northern Ireland. Singer (Soprano). *Education:* Studied with Margaret Lensky at the Guildhall School of Music and at the National Opera Studio. *Career:* Represented Northern Ireland in the Cardiff Singer of the World Competition, 1985; Appearances for Radio Telfis Eireann include Lieder by Schumann and Liszt; Wexford Festival 1986, in Humperdinck's Königskinder and Rossini's Tancredi; Has also sung the Composer in Ariadne auf Naxos; Concert engagements in Messiah at Armagh, Britten's War Requiem in Belfast, Savitri by Holst at Aix and Elgar's Apostles in Nottingham. *Address:* c/o Magenta Music International, 64 Highgate High Street, London N6 5HX, England.

MCGLAUGHLIN William, b. 3 Oct 1943, Philadelphia, Pennsylvania, USA. Conductor; Radio Broadcaster; Trombonist. *Education:* BM, 1967, MM, 1969, Temple University; Studied conducting with Wm R. Smith, Robert Page, Max Rudolph. *Career:* Assistant 1st Trombonist, Philadelphia Orchestra, 1967-68; Co-Principal Trombonist, Pittsburgh Symphony, 1969-75; Exxon-Arts Endowment Conductor, 1975-78, Associate Conductor, 1978-82, St Paul Chamber Orchestra; Music Director, Eugene, Oregon, Symphony, 1981-85, Tucson Symphony, 1982-87, Kansas City Symphony, 1986-, San Francisco Chamber Orchestra, 1986-; Host, Music Director of St Paul Sunday Morning, American Public Radio, 1980-87; Guest Conductor, St Louis, Denver, Houston and Pittsburgh Symphonies, Minnesota Orchestra, Los Angeles and Denver Chamber Orchestras. *Honour:* Exxon-Arts Endowment Conducting Grant with St Paul Chamber Orchestra, 1975-78. *Current Management:* American International Artists Inc, New York, New York, USA.

MCGUINNESS Rosamond, b. 4 Dec 1929, Connecticut, USA. University Professor. div. 1 son, 4 daughter. *Education:* BA, Music, Vassar College, 1951; MA, Music History, Smith College, 1952; DPhil, Music History, Oxford University, 1964. *Career includes:* Lecturer: Royal Academy of Music, 1969-70, London University, 1969-82, Imperial College of Science and Technology, 1976-81; Senior Lecturer, 1980-1990, Royal Holloway College, London University, 1982-,

Professor of Music, Royal Holloway and Bedford New College, 1990. *Publications:* Book, English Court Odes 1660-1820, 1971, as well as book chapters and articles in PRMAM &L: Journal of Newspaper and Periodical History; Quartetly Journal of Social Affairs. *Address:* Dept of Music, Royal Holloway and Bedford New College, Egham Hill, Egham, Surrey TW20 OEX, England.

MCGUIRE Colin John, b. 17 June 1947, London, England. Clarinettist. *Education:* Royal Academy of Music, London. *Debut:* Purcell Room, London, 1973. *Career:* Kent Opera Orchestra, 1973-90; Freelance Clarinet player in London orchestras; Head of Wind and Percussion, Latymer School, Edmonton; Examiner, Music Performance, University of London. *Honours:* R Vaughan Williams Trust Award, Royal Academy of Music. *Memberships:* Incorporated Society of Musicians; RAM Club; Royal Society of Musicians of Great Britain. *Hobbies:* The Times Crossword Puzzle; Food and wine. *Address:* 10 Shirley Road, Enfield, Middlesex EN2 6SB, England.

MCGUIRE Edward, b. 15 Feb 1948, Glasgow, Scotland. Composer. *Education:* Composition study with James Iliff, Royal Academy of Music, 1966-70; Studied with Ingvar Lidholm, The State Academy of Music, Stockholm, Sweden, 1971; ARCM; ARAM. *Career:* Radio broadcasts on BBC Radio 3 include: symphonic poem, Calgacus, 1976; Symphonic Poem, Source, 1979; Euphoria, performed by The Fires of London, 1980, Edinburgh International Festival; Debut at London Proms, 1982; BBC Radio 3 Series features trilogy, Rebirth, Interregnum, Liberation, 1984; Wilde Festival Commission (String trio) for performance by The Nash Ensemble, 1986; Premiere of Guitar Concerto, June 1988; Peter Pan for Scottish Ballet, 1989. *Compositions:* A Glasgow Symphony, 1990; Trombone Concerto, 1991; The Loving of Etain, 1990 for Paragon Opera; Ballet, The Spirit of Flight, 1991; Opera, Cullercoats Tommy, 1993. *Recordings:* Music has featured on CD. eg, Paragon Premieres, Continuum Records, 1993 and Scotland's Music (Linn CD, 1993). *Honours:* Hecht Prize, RAM, 1968; National Young Composers Competition, Liverpool University, 1969; Competition for Test Piece for Carl Flesch International Violin Competition, 1978; Competition for a string quartet for performance at SPNM 40th Anniversary Gala Concert, Barbican, 1983. *Memberships:* Whistlebinkies Folk Music Group, 1973- ; Scottish Arts Council Music Committee, 1980-83. *Address:* c/o Scottish Music Information Centre, 1 Bowmont Gardens, Glasgow G12 9LR, Scotland.

MCINTIRE Dennis (Keith), b. 25 June 1944, Indianapolis, Indiana, USA. Music historian; Lexicographer. *Education:* Indiana University. *Career:* Research editor for general reference works, 1965-79; Editorial associate, Nicolas Slonimsky, 1979-; Advisor, The Oxford Dictionary of Music, 1985-; Advisor and major contributor, The New Grove Dictionary of American Music, 1986; Advisor, The New Everyman Dictionary of Music, 1988-; Advisor, Encyclopaedia Britannica, 1991-; Contributor, The New Grove Dictionary of Opera, 1992. *Publications:* Consultant editor, The International Who's Who in Music and Musicians' Directory, 12th edition, 1990, Compiler, appendices, 13th Edition, 1992, 14th Edition, 1994; Associate editor, Baker's Biographical Dictionary of Musicians, 8th edition, 1992. *Contributions to:* Book reviews; concert reviews; record reviews. *Memberships:* American Musicological Society; Sir Thomas Beecham Society, USA; Christian Church; Freemason, 32nd degree. *Hobbies:* Concerts; Collecting compact discs; Collecting critical editions of major writers of Western civilization; travel. *Address:* 9170 Melrose Court, Indianapolis, IN 46239-1474, USA.

MCINTOSH Thomas Lee, b. 3 Dec 1938, Washington, District of Columbia, USA. Conductor; Concert Pianist. m. M.H.V. Reckett, 30 Sept 1982. *Education:* BS, MS, Juilliard School of Music, New York City; Attended George Washington University, Columbia University, New York University. *Debut:* With National Symphony Orchestra, 1950. *Career:* Conducting and

Piano Concerts in 75 countries of the world. *Recordings:* More than twenty recordings for Unicorn Records, Nippon Columbia, Minstral Records, Kiwi Records and Vox Rcords. *Publication:* Editor, English Symphony Series, Garland Publishing. *Honours:* Winner, International Kranichstein Contest, Darmstadt, Germany; Winner Bolzano Busoni Competition; Elected Fellow, Royal Society of Arts, 1988, President, Brentwood Gramaphone Society, 1990. *Hobby:* Gardening. *Address:* The Old School, Bridge Street, Hadleigh, Suffolk IP7 6BY, England.

MCINTYRE Donald Conroy, (Sir), b. 22 Oct 1934, Auckland, New Zealand. International Opera Singer (Baritone). m. Jill Redington, 29 July 1961, 2 daughters. *Education:* Mt. Albert Grammar School, Auckland; Auckland Teachers' Training College; Guildhall School of Music, London. *Debut:* Welsh National Opera, as Zachariah in Nabucco, 1959. *Career:* Principal Bass, Sadler's Wells Opera, 1960-67; Principal Bass, Royal Opera House, Covent Garden, 1967-; Annual Appearances at Bayreuth Festival, 1967-81; frequent international guest appearances; roles include: Wotan and Wanderer (Der Ring), Dutchman (Der fliegende Holländer); Telramund (Lohengrin); Barak (Die Frau ohne Schatten); Pizarro (Fidelio); Golaud (Pelléas et Mélisande); Kurwenal (Tristan and Isolde); Gurnemanz, Klingsor and Amfortas (Parsifal); Heyst (Victory); Jochanaan (Salome); Macbeth; Scarpia (Tosca); the Count (Marriage of Figaro); Nick Shadow (The Rake's Progress); Hans Sachs (Die Meistersinger); Doctor Schön (Wozzeck); Cardillac (Cardillac, Hindemith); Sang Amfortas at Bayreuth 1987-88; Monterone in a new production of Rigoletto at Covent Garden, 1988, followed by Prospero in the British premiere of Berio's Un Re in Ascolto, 1989; Sang Wotan in Die Walküre for Australian Opera, 1989, Dutchman 1990; debut as Balstrode in Peter Grimes at Covent Garden 1989; Hans Sachs in the New Zealand premiere of Die Meistersinger, Wellington 1990; Teatro San Carlos, Lisbon, 1990, as Telramund; Sang Wagner's Hans Sachs at Covent Garden, 1993; Sang in Lady Macbeth of Mtsensk at Munich, 1993. *Recordings:* Pelléas et Mélisande, Oedipus Rex, Il Trovatore; Video of Der Ring des Nibelungen, from Bayreuth. *Honours:* KBE, 1992, OBE, 1975; CBE, 1985; Fidelio Medal from the International Association of Opera Directors/ Intendants, for outstanding service to the Royal Opera House, 1967-89. *Hobbies:* Sport (particularly Golf, Tennis, Swimming); Gardening; Languages; Farming; Carpentry. *Address:* Foxhill Farm, Jackass Lane, Keston, Bromley, Kent, England.

MCINTYRE Ray, b. 27 Dec 1926, San Jose, California, USA. Harpsichodist; Pianist; Musicologist; Teacher. m. (1) Janet Sutter, 28 Aug 1957, 1 son, 2 daughters, (2) Helga Rausch, 17 Sept 1971, (3) Clare Spring, 17 Dec 1988. *Education:* BA 1948, MA and BLS 1950, University of California, Berkeley; Harvard University, 1957-58; Brandeis University, 1958-60. *Debut:* Carnegie Recital Hall, New York, 1968. *Career:* Music Librarian, Detroit Public Library, 1950-54; Art Archivist, Detroit Institute of Arts, 1955-57; Director of Music and Director of the Music and Art Center, Goddard College, Plainfield, Vermont, 1960-70; Lecturer in Music History, Institute of European Studies, Vienna, 1970-72; Professor of Piano, Vienna Conservatory and Konservatorium für Musik und Dramatische Kunst, Vienna, Austria, 1972-83; Music Director and Performer on old keyboard instruments of 2 art films: A Portrait of Holland in the 17th Century and Venice in the 18th Century produced by Detroit Institute of Arts, 1953; Founder, Renaissance Music Guild, Detroit. *Address:* 1625 Parkside Avenue, San Jose, CA 95125, USA.

MCKAY Elizabeth Norman, b. 21 Nov 1931, London, England. Musicologist, Pianist. m. Gilbert Watt McKay, 7 Dec 1960, 1 son, 2 daughters. *Education:* BSc, Bristol University, 1949-52; LRAM, Pianoforte Performer, 1952; Somerville College Scholar, DPhil, 1961, Oxford University, 1958-61. *Career:* Musicologist, Pianist, chamber music, accompanist, coach, theatre work; Teacher; Lecturer in Musical History. *Publications:*

Proceedings of the Royal Musical Association, 1966-67; Schubert as a Composer of Operas, Schubert Studies, Cambridge, 1982; The Impact of the New Pianoforte: Mozart, Beethoven and Schubert, Lynwood, 1987; Franz Schubert's Music for the Theatre, Hans Schneider, Tutzing 1991; Schuberts Klaviersonaten von 1815 bis 1825', in Franz Schubert Reliquie-Sonate, Hans Schneider, Tutzing, 1992. *Contributions to:* The Music Review; Musical Times; Osterreichisch Musikzeitschrift; Music and Letters. *Honour:* Honorary Member of the Board of the International Franz Schubert Institute. *Address:* Gamrie, Swan Lane, Long Hanborough, Witney, Oxon OX8 8BT, England.

MCKAY James Rae, b. 4 Oct 1944, Toronto, Canada. Professor of Music; Conductor; Bassoonist. *Education:* BA Hons, Music, Trinity College, University of Toronto, 1967; MA Musicology, University of Chicago, USA, 1971. *Career:* Chairman, Performance Department, University of Western Ontario, London, Ontario; Past Chairman, Department of Music, York University, North York, Ontario; Conductor, Music Director, Toronto Community Orchestra; Guest Conductor, Mount Orford, Quebec, Symphony Canada, Orchestra London Canada; Bassoon Soloist with McGill Chamber Orchestra, Chamber Players of Toronto, Contemporary Chamber Players of Chicago, Canadian Broadcasting Corporation; Director, Decoustics/ACS Centre for Acoustical Research at York University. *Recordings:* Three for All, Golden Crest CRS-4217; Solo Bassoon and Piano, Golden Crest; Stravinsky's L'Histoire du soldât, Ultra; Sessions, Concertino, Desto. *Contributions to:* The Breval Manuscript; New Interpretations in Cahiers Debussy Nouvelle Series No. 1, 1977, 1978; Le Trio, op. 120 de Fauré: Une esquisse inconnue du troisième mouvement, Etudes Fauréennes, Paris, 1982. *Address:* Faculty of Music, University of Western Ontario, London, Ontario, Canada N6A 3K7.

MCKAY Marjory Grieve, b. 23 June 1951, Edinburgh, Scotland. Opera Singer (Soprano). m. Frederick Charles McKay, 17 July 1981. *Education:* Trinity Academy, Edinburgh, 1956-69; Royal Manchester College of Music, 1969-74; Royal Northern College of Music, 1974-75. *Debut:* As Esmeralda, Scottish Opera, 1980. *Career:* Scottish opera roles, concerts and recitals; Esmeralda in Bartered Bride, Belleza in L'Egisto and Feklusa in Katya Kabanova; Scottish Opera Go Round, Violetta; Welsh National Opera Workshop, Violetta in La Traviata; Many concerts and recitals in Scotland and the north of England; Now living in Sydney, Australia, Debut in Australian Opera as Gerhilde in Die Walküre, 1985 and Xenia in Boris Godunov, 1986; Debut with Western Australian Opera as Cio Cio San in Madame Butterfly, 1987; Created the title role in Alan Holley's new opera Dorothea; Les Huguenots Video (Joan Sutherland's Farewell), 1990. *Hobbies:* Dressmaking; Knitting; Picture framing; Bakers clay modelling; Various handcrafts; Gardening; swimming; Creating rag dolls. *Current Management:* Australian Opera. *Address:* 25 Gazelle Street, Glenfield, Sydney, NSW 2167, Australia.

MCKAY Neil, b. 16 June 1924, Ashcroft, British Columbia, Canada. Composer; Educator. m. Marion Dyer, 18 Sept 1948, 1 son, 1 daughter. *Education:* BA, University of Western Ontario, 1953; MA, 1955, PhD, 1956, Eastman School of Music. *Career:* Staff Arranger, CFPL, London, 1946-53; Oboist, Duluth Symphony, 1957-64; Professor, Music, University of Wisconsin, Superior, 1957-64, University of Hawaii, 1965-. *Compositions:* Symphony Orchestra: Symphony No 1; Dance Overture; Fantasy on a Quiet Theme; Variations on Twinkle, Twinkle Little Star; Concert Band: Dance Overture; Evocations; Gamelan Gong; Fanfare and Ceremonial; Skye Boat Song; Chamber Ensemble: Kubla Khan; Kaleidoscope; Chorus: A Dream Within A Dream; String Quartet; Piano: Four Miniatures; Soundprints, Clarinet, koto or harp; World(s) Koto or harp; Suite of Miniatures, for clarinet and percussion; From the Mind's Eye, orchestra; There Once Was, medium voice and piano; Patterns, mezzo soprano and piano. *Publications:* Co-Author, Fundamentals of Western Music 1986.

Hobbies: Golf; Fishing. *Address:* Marnie Associates, PO Box 61664, Honolulu, HI 96822, USA.

MCKELLAR FERGUSON Kathleen, b. 1959, Stirling, Scotland. Singer (Mezzo-Soprano). *Education:* Studied at the Royal Scottish Academy and the Royal College of Music; Further study with Margaret Hyde. *Career:* South Bank debut, 1987, with the London Bach Orchestra; Beethoven's Ninth at the Gstaad Festival, 1990 and with the Ulster Orchestra; Other repertoire includes Mozart's Requiem, the Brahms Alto Rhapsody, Mahler's 8th, Songs of the Auvergne and A Child of our Time; Season, 1990-91 with Haydn's Nelson Mass and the English Chamber Orchestra, Messiah with the Liverpool Philharmonic; Also sings Elgar's Sea Pictures and Music Makers, St Matthew Passion (Fairfields Hall) and Elijah; Concerts with Yehudi Menuhin at Festival Halls; Opera repertoire includes Florence Pike in Albert Herring (Aldeburgh 1986), Maketaten in Akhnaten by Philip Glass for ENO, 1987, Mozart's Marcellina and Third Lady for Pavilion Opera, Cherubino, and Handel's Bradamante (Alcina) for Flanders Opera, 1991, Second Lady (Magic Flute) at Theatre Royale de la Monnaie, Brussels, Suzuki (Madam Butterfly) for opera forum in Nederlands and Bradamante (Alcina) with Nicholaus Harnoncourt at Zurich opera. *Address:* IMG Artists Europe, Media House, 3 Burlington Lane, Chiswick, London W4 2TH, England.

MCKENZIE Wallace Chessley, b. 16 June 1928, Alexandria, Louisiana, USA. Professor of Music History. m. Elaine Lamb, 13 July 1951, 1 son, 1 daughter. *Education:* BA Music Theory, Louisiana College, 1949; MA Composition, State University of Iowa, 1950; PhD Musicology, North Texas State University, 1960; Studied composition and musicology with George Morey, Musicology with Helen Hewitt, composition with Philip Greeley Clapp and Kenneth B. Klaus. *Career:* Taught at Louisiana College, summer 1950; Music Theory and Composition, New Orleans Baptist Theological Seminary, 1955-64; Director of Music, St Charles Baptist Church, New Orleans, 1961-64, 1969-70, 1979-80; Head, Department of Music, Wayland Baptist University, 1964-68; Music History, Louisiana State University, 1968-, currently Professor of Music; Co-Founder, New Times Concert; Founder, Director, Louisiana State University Collegium Musicum, 1971-81. *Compositions:* The Church's One Foundation, 1957; We Would See Jesus, 1958; A Charge to Keep (under pseudonym Charles Wilkinson), 1966; Exhortatio for mixed chorus and electronic tape (recorded). *Contributions to:* Webern's Technique of Choral Composition in Anton Von Webern: Perspectives, 1966; Webern's Posthumous Music in Belträge, Oesterreichische Gesellschaft, 1973. *Address:* School of Music, Louisiana State University, Baton Rouge, LA 70803, USA.

MCKERRACHER Colin, b. 1960, Falkirk, Scotland. Singer (Tenor). *Education:* Studied with Joseph Ward at the Royal Northern College of Music and with Nicolai Gedda. *Career:* Has sung with Glyndebourne Touring Opera and the Festival in Simon Boccanegra and Capriccio, 1986-87; Appearances with Scottish Opera-Go-Round as Steva in Jenůfa, Beppe and Turiddu (Cav and Pag) and Don Carlos; Lensky in Eugene Onegin for Opera 80 followed by Monostatos in The Magic Flute and Ernesto in Don Pasquale; English National Opera and Covent Garden debuts season, 1990-91, as Ferrando and in Così fan Tutte. *Honours:* Prizewinner, 1989, Rio de Janiero International Singing Competition. *Address:* Anglo Swiss Ltd, 3 Primrose Mews, 1a Sharpleshall St, London SW1 8YW, England.

MCKINNEY Thomas, b. 5 May 1946, Lufkin, Texas. Singer (Baritone). *Education:* Studied in Houston, Hollywood and New York. *Debut:* Houston, 1971 as Tchelkalov in Boris Godunov. *Career:* Sang in opera in Cincinnati, Houston, San Diego and San Francisco; European engagements at the Wexford Festival (Thais), the Vienna Volksoper and the Theatre Royale de la Monnaie, Brussels; Other roles have included Pelléas, Guglielmo, Don Giovanni, Mozart's Count, Papageno,

Rossini's Figaro, Eugene Onegin, Hamlet, Belcore, Massenet's Herode and Athanael (Thais), Verdi's Posa and Ford and Peachum in The Beggar's Opera; San Diego, 1972, in the premiere of Medea by Alva Henderson; Frequent concert appearances. *Address:* c/o Volksoper, Wahringerstrasse 78, A-1090 Vienna, Austria.

MCLACHLAN Murray, b. 6 Jan 1965, Dundee, Scotland. Concert Pianist. m. Mary Russell, 6 Mar 1993. *Education:* Studied at Chetham's School and at Cambridge with Peter Katin and Norma Fisher. *Debut:* Free Trade Hall, Manchester, 1983. *Career:* Performed extensively throughout Britain as recitalist and concerto soloist with RPO, SCO, BBC Scottish, Manchester Camerata; Toured Belorussia 1991. Has performed complete cycle of 32 Beethoven sonatas from memory in Glasgow, Dundee and Aberdeen. *Recordings include:* Complete Sonatas of Prokofiev, Myaskovsky, Kabalevsky and solo works of Khatchaturian; Piano concerto of Ronald Stevenson. *Honours:* Piano Prize, Chetham's Cambridge Instrumental Exhibition; Penguin Rosette Award, for CD of music from Scotland. *Memberships:* Adjudicator, British Federation of Festivals. *Hobbies:* Hill walking; Films; Cookery; Reading. *Current Management* Anglo-Swiss Artists Management. *Address:* Banrye Cottage, 5 Holburn Place, Aberdeen AB1 6HG, Scotland.

MCLAUGHLIN Marie, b. 2 Nov 1954, Hamilton, Lanarkshire, Scotland. Singer (Soprano). *Education:* Studied at the London Opera Centre and the National Opera Studio. *Career:* Sang Susanna and Lauretta while a student; English National Opera from 1978, in The Consul, Dido and Aeneas, A Night in Venice and Rigoletto; Royal Opera Covent Garden from 1980 as Barbarina and Susanna in Le Nozze di Figaro, Zerlina, Iris in Semele, Marzelline in Fidelio, Nannetta in Falstaff, Zdenka in Arabella and Tytania in A Midsummer Night's Dream; Glyndebourne Festival as Micaela (Carmen) and Violetta, 1985, 1987; Salzburg Festival as Susanna, conducted by James Levine; Scottish Opera in Orfeo ed Euridice and Le Nozze di Figaro; Deutsche Oper Berlin as Susanna and Marzelline; Hamburg: Susanna, Marzelline; Chicago Lyric: Zerlina, Despina; Washington: Susanna; Met. New York: Marzelline; La Scala, Milan: Adina; Paris Opéra in Roméo et Juliette; Sang Zdenka in Arabella at Covent Garden 1990; Marzelline in Fidelio at the 1990 Salzburg Festival, Zerlina at the Vienna Festival; Geneva Opera 1992 as Despina, and Jenny in Mahagonny. Concert appearances in London, Edinburgh, New York, Chicago, Berlin, Spain, France, Belgium and Germany; Conductors worked with include: Maazel, Bernstein, Haitink, Barenboim, Davis, Leppard, Celibidache, Harnoncourt, Mehta and Levine; Season 1992/93 as Blanche in the Carmelites at Geneva, Susanna on tour with the Royal Opera to Japan, Ilia in Idomeneo at Barcelona and Ivy in On the Town at the Barbican Hall. *Recordings include:* Video of Covent Garden Fidelio (Virgin), Handel's L'Allegro, il Pensieroso ed il Moderato; Die Zauberflöte and Dido and Aeneas, Così fan Tutte (Levine), Mozart: Requiem (Bernstein), (Phonogram); Videos of Rigoletto, Carmen, Traviata, Mozart's C Minor Mass and Haydn's Mass in Time of War. *Address:* c/o Harrison/Parrott Ltd., 12 Penzance Place, London W11 4PA, England.

MCLEAN Barton Keith, b. 8 Apr 1938, New York, USA. Composer. m. Priscilla McLean, 28 Aug 1967. *Education:* MusD, Composition, Indiana University, 1972; MM, Music Theory, Eastman School of Music, 1965; BS, Music Education, State University College-Potsdam, New York, 1960. *Career:* Teacher, State University College, Potsdam, 1960-66, Indiana University at South Bend, 1969-76, University of Texas at Austin, 1976-83; Rensselaer Polytechnic Institute I-Ear Studies Director, 1987-88; Rensselaen Polytechnic Institute: EAR studies, teacher 1987-88, 1990-92. *Compositions:* Numerous works include, Metamorphosis for Orchestra, 1975; Dimensions I for violin and tape, 1973, II for piano and tape, 1974, III, for saxophone and tape, 1978, IV, for saxophone and tape, 1979, VIII for piano and tape, 1982; Heavy Music for Four Crobars, electronic, 1979; Ixtlan, for two pianos, 1982; The Last Ten Minutes, computer generated, 1982; The Electric Sinfonia, 1982; from the Good Earth, String quartet, 1985; In The Place of Tears, Chamber Ensemble & Voice, 1985; In Wilderness is the Preservation of the World, environmental- electronic, 1986; Voices of the Wild - Primal Spirits, orchestra, 1987; Visions of a Summer Night, Computer Tape, 1989; Rainforest, 1989; Rainforest Images (comuter tape), 1992; Rainforest Reflections (electronic processed soloists and orchestra), 1993. *Address:* RD Number 2 - Box 33, Petersburg, NY 12138, USA.

MCLEAN Mervyn Evan, b. 17 June 1930, Invercargill, New Zealand. Ethnomusicologist. m. Patricia Anne Taylor, 15 Feb 1964. 1 son 1 daughter. *Education:* BA, University of New Zealand, 1957; MA 1959, PhD 1965, University of Otago. *Career:* Retired, Senior Lecturer, Senior Research Fellow, Research Fellow 1968-74, Associate Professor of Ethnomusicology 1975-92, University of Auckland; Founder and Head, Archive of Maori and Pacific Music, University of Auckland, 1970-92; Visiting Assistant Professor, University of Hawaii, 1968; Visiting Assistant Professor, Indiana University, 1967. *Publications:* Traditional Songs of the Maori (with Margaret Orbell), 1975; An Annotated Bibliography of Oceanic Music and Dance, 1977, Supplement, 1981. *Contributions to:* Over 100 publications on Maori and Pacific music; Contributor of Oceanic entries in New Grove Dictionary of Musical Instruments. *Memberships:* International Council for Traditional Music; Life member Polynesian Society; Life member Society for Ethnomusicology. *Hobbies:* Music; Reading; Computing. *Address:* 17 Vienna Place, Birkenhead, Auckland 1310, New Zealand.

MCLEAN Priscilla Taylor, b. 27 May 1942, Fitchburg, Massachusetts, USA. Composer; Performer. m. Barton Keith McLean, 26 Aug 1967. *Education:* BEd, State College, Fitchburg, 1963; BMusEd, University of Lowell, Massachusetts, 1965; MM Composition, Indiana University, 1969. *Career:* Concerts, The McLean Mix (husband-wife duo performing own electronic-acoustic music), Holland, Belgium, Zagreb Muzicki Biennale, 1981, Amsterdam, Holland Radio, Oslo, Finland, Sweden, 1983, Australia, New Zealand, Hawaii, 1990; tours, USA, 1974-76, 1979, 1981-93, yearly, Canada, 1986; Guest Composer, Kennedy Center for the Performing Arts, 1977, Gaudeamus Musiekweek, Holland, 1979; Guest Professor and Composer/ Performer, University of Hawaii, 1985; Guest Soprano soloist, Cleveland Chamber Orchestra (Wilderness), 1989. *Compositions include:* Variations and Mozaics on a Theme of Stravinsky; Dance of Dawn; Invisible Chariots; The Inner Universe; Fantasies for Adults and Other Children; Beneath the Horizon I, III; Night Images; Messages; Fire and Ice; Elan!; 3 pieces for In Wilderness is the Preservation of the World; In Celebration; Wilderness; A Magic Dwells, (orchestra and tape), 1986; Voices of the Wild, orchestra and soloist (electronic music), 1988; The Dance of Shiva, (electronic tape and multiple slides), 1990; Rainforest (coll with B.McLean), 1990; Everything Awakening Alert and Joyful, (full orchestra and narrator), 1991. *Recordings include:* Dance of Dawn, 1975; Interplanes, 1978; Variations and Mozaics on a Theme of Stravinsky, 1979; Invisible Chariots, 1979; Electronic Music from the Outside In, 1980; Beneath the Horizon III and Salt Canyons, 1983; In Wilderness is the Preservation....1987; Rainforest Images, 1993. *Current Management:* MLC Publications. *Address:* RD2 Box 33, Hill Hollow Farm, Petersburg, New York, NY 12138, USA.

MCLELLAND-YOUNG Thomas, b. 9 Sept 1937, London, England. Conductor; Composer. m. 21 Apr 1979, 1 son, 1 daughter. *Education:* Trinity College of Music with Arnold Cooke, Denys Darlow, John Webster and Edward Krish. *Career:* Director of Musical Studies, The Royal Ballet School Teacher's Course; Master of Music, St Leonards Parish Church, Streatham; Conductor of the St Leonard's Singers, The Academy of St Leonard, Sutton Symphony Orchestra.

Compositions include: Stanzas from Tintern Abbey for tenor and piaon; Blow thou Cleansing Wind from Heaven, for mixed choir and organ; Four plainsong preludes for ogan; Exultet, for children's choir, mixed choir, trumpets, organ and percussion; Prayer for a World in Need, soprano solo, chorus and orchestra; Prosdokia, for horn, harp, piano and strings. *Hobbies:* Cooking; Snooker; Architecture; Long walks in the country. *Address:* 27 Wiseton Road, Wandsworth Common, London SW17 7EE, England.

MCLEOD John, b. 8 Mar 1934, Aberdeen, Scotland. Composer; Conductor; Lecturer. m. Margaret Murray (pianist) 12 Aug 1961, 1 son, 1 daughter. *Education:* Aberdeen Grammar School, 1946-50; Royal Academy of Music, 1957-61, Composition pupil of Lennox Berkeley. *Career:* Woodwind Tutor: Jamaica School of Music, 1961-65, Glenalmond College, 1965-70; Freelance Composer, Conductor, Teacher, 1970-74; Director of Music, Merchiston Castle School, Edinburgh, 1974-85; Visiting Lecturer, Royal Scottish Academy of Music and Drama, 1985-89; Ida Carroll Research Fellow, Royal Northern College of Music, 1988-89; Visiting Lecturer in Composition and Contemporary Music, Napier University of Edinburgh, 1989-; Visiting Composer, Lothian Specialist Music Scheme, 1986-; Conductor, Perth Choral and Orchestral Societies, 1965-73; Conductor, Glasgow Orchestral Society, 1971-75; Conductor, Edinburgh Royal Choral Union, 1977-81; Guest conductor Royal Scottish Orchestra, Scottish Chamber Orchestra, BBC Scottish Symphony Orchestra, Scottish Ballet, Scottish Opera, National Youth Orchestra of Scotland; Course Director, Director, Post Graduate course in Composing for Film and Television, London College of Music, 1991-. *Compositions:* Main works include: The Gokstad Ship for orchestra; Stabat Mater for soloists, choir and orchestra; The Whispered Name for soprano, harp and strings - Jane Manning soloist; Percussion Concerto - Evelyn Glennie soloist; The Song on Dionysius for percussion and piano - Evelyn Glennie and Philip Smith (premiered at the 1989 London Proms); Piano Concerto, soloist Peter Donohoe, 1988; Songs from the Small Zone - poems by Irina Ratushinskaya for soprano, chorus and piano; A Dramatic Landscape for solo clarinet and wind band; Film Scores for many TV and cinema films; Works now performed by leading artists, orchestras and at major Festivals throughout the world. *Hobbies:* Travelling; Books; Art; Films; Theatre; Walking; Conversation; Gardening; Cooking Wine and Malt Whisky. *Address:* 9 Redford Crescent, Colinton, Edinburgh EH13 0BS, Scotland.

MCMASTER Brian John, b. 9 May 1943, Hitchin, England. Opera Administrator. *Education:* Wellington College, 1955-60; LLB, Bristol University, 1963. *Career:* International Artists Department, EMI, 1968-73; Controller, Opera Planning, English National Opera, 1973-76; General Administrator, Welsh National Opera, Cardiff, Wales, 1976-92; Artistic Director, Vancouver Opera, British Columbia, Canada, 1983-89; Director, The Edinburgh Festival, 1992. *Address:* 21 Market Street, Edinburgh, EH1 1BW, Scotland.

MCNAIR Sylvia, b. 23 June 1956, Mansfield, Ohio, USA. Singer (Soprano). *Education:* Studied at Indiana University. *Career:* Sang in Messiah at Indianapolis, 1980; European debut in the premiere of Kelterborn's Ophelia, Schwetzingen, 1984; Concert appearances in Cleveland, Baltimore, San Francisco, Detroit, Montreal, Indianapolis, Atlanta, St. Louis, Washington and Los Angeles; New York at the Carnegie, Avery Fisher and Alice Tully Halls; Season 1991-92 with the Chicago Symphony under Solti, Berlin Philharmonic under Haitink, City of Birmingham Symphony under Rattle, Concentus Musicus under Harnoncourt and London Philharmonic under Masur; Mozart's Ilia and Servilia with the Monteverdi Choir and Orchestra conducted by John Eliot Gardiner; US opera appearances as Pamina at Santa Fe, Ilia; Hero (Béatrice et Bénédict) and Morgana in Alcina at St. Louis; Sang Ilia in Lyon and Strasbourg and Susana with Netherlands Opera; Pamina at the Deutsche Oper Berlin and the Vienna

Staatsoper; Glyndebourne Festival 1989 as Anne Trulove; Covent Garden and Salzburg debuts as Ilia in Idomeneo; Season 1991-92 with Bastille Opera (Paris) and Metropolitan Opera (as Marzelline in Fidelio) debuts; Covent Garden 1992, in Rossini's Il Viaggio a Reims. *Recordings:* Albums with Neville Marriner, Roger Norrington, John Eliot Gardiner, Colin Davis, Kurt Masur, James Levine and Bernard Haitink; Idomeneo with John Eliot Gardiner (Deutsche Grammophon). *Address:* Lies Askonas Ltd., 186 Drury Lane, London WC2B 5RY, England.

MCNEIL-MORALES Albert John, b. 14 Feb 1925, California, USA. Professor; Conductor. m. Helen Rambo, 29 Dec 1953, 1 son. *Education:* BA, University of California; MA, DMA, University of Southern California. *Debut:* Europe, 1968. *Career:* Founder, Albert McNeil Jubilee Singers, 1964; Has travelled to 64 countries and performed over 3,000 concerts, with major performances in Berlin Philharmonie, Salle Gaveau, Paris; Mozarteum, Salzburg; Conservatory de St Cecilia, Rome; Mann Auditorium, Tel Aviv; Alice Tully Hall, New York; Dorothy Chandler Pavillion, Los Angeles. *Publications:* Co-author: Silver Burdett Music (series), 1979-86; Albert McNeil Choral Series. Articles in the Choral Journal and Voice (Chorus America). *Honours:* Alumnus of the Year, UCLA, 1991; Sterling Patron, My Phi Epsilon, 1990. *Memberships:* Phi Mu Alpha; Association of Professional Vocal Ensembles; American Choral Directors Association. *Current Management:* Walter Gould, Century Artists Bureau Inc. *Address:* 447 Herondo St 210, Hermosa Beach, CA 90254, USA.

MCNICOL Richard John, b. 8 Mar 1944, Scarborough, England. Music Educator. m. Barbara Katherine Lawrence, 7 Jan 1967, 3 sons. *Education:* Hadow Music Scholar, Worcester College, Oxford. *Career:* Freelance flautist and member, London Philharmonic Orchestra, 1976-81; Music Animateur London Symphony Orchestra, 1993-; Founder, Apollo Trust, 1977; Pioneered creative music projects involving schools and professional orchestras throughout Great Britain; Introduced first creative music workshops in German schools in 1987 and in Vienna, Spain, Iceland, Norway, Jordan and Canada. *Recordings include:* Athena Ensemble, Debusy, Nielsen, Milhaud and Elgar chamber music. *Publications:* Books and Videos: Create and Discover, OUP, 1988; Sound Interventions Video, OUP, 1993. *Address:* 145 Park Road, Buxton, Derbyshire SK17 6SW, England.

MCPHEE George McBeth, b. 10 Nov 1937, Glasgow, Scotland. Organist; Conductor. m. Margaret Ann Scotland, 3 July 1961, 1 son, 2 daughter. *Education:* Royal Scottish Academy of Music, Edinburgh University; BMus, 1963; FRCO, 1961; DipMusEd, RSAMD, 1959. *Career:* Lecturer, Royal Scottish Academy of Music and Drama, 1963-; Organist and Master of the Choristers, Paisley Abbey, 1963-; Visiting Professor of Organ, St Andrew's University, 1992. *Compositions include:* Magnifact and Nunc Dimittis; Responses; In Bethlehem City; Make we Joy; My Beloved Spake; Missa Brevis, 1989. *Recordings include:* The Organ of Paisley Abbey; Organ Magnificat; Great Organ Music; The Choir of Paisley Abbey; Cantate Domino; Sacred Songs with Kenneth McKeller; Carlos for Culzean; Hymns for Celebrations, 1989; Welcome Sweet and Sacred Feast, 1993; French Organ Music, 1993. *Publications:* Missa Brevis, 1989. *Honours:* FRSCM, 1991. *Hobbies:* Golf; Travel. *Address:* 17 Main Road, Castlehead, Paisley, Renfrewshire PA2 6AJ, Scotland.

MCQUAID John Stephen, b. 14 Mar 1909, Lochgelly, Scotland. Musician; Psychologist. m. Mary Darkin, 1 Nov 1945, dec 10 Nov 1990, 1 son, 1 daughter. *Education:* MA(Hons), Languages, 1932, MEd, 1952, Glasgow University; PhD, Edinburgh University, 1949; Private musical study with Professor Erik Chisholm, 1938-40. *Career:* Taught languages etc, 1935-41; War Service in Intelligence Corps, West Africa, India, Southeast Asia, 1941-46; Teaching, 1946-54; Psychologist, 1954-77; Broadcast, India, 1944; Numerous broadcasts and performances of all kinds of

music, 1948-. *Compositions:* Elegy, Impromptu, piano, 1940; Liturgical music and many hymns, Chapman, St Andrew Hymnal; Three Waltzes for piano, Five Line Publications, 1986; Little Waltzes and Preludes (piano) in six books of twelve each, 1983-90; Three broadcasts of excerpts 1989, 90, 91; Jesus in Picture and Song; Music with nine of his paintings performed in Glasgow, 1993. *Hobby:* Physics experiments. *Address:* 8 Ardrossan Road, Saltcoats KA21 5BW, Scotland.

MCTIER Duncan Paul, b. 21 Nov 1954, Stourbridge, Worcestershire, England. Double Bass Soloist and Teacher. m. Yuko Inoue, 11 Jan 1984. *Education:* King Edward VI Grammar School Stourbridge; Bristol University, 1972-75; BSc(Hons), Mathematical Sciences; ARCM(Hons), 1974. *Career:* Member, BBC Symphony Orchestra, 1975-77; Principal Bass, Netherlands Chamber Orchestra, 1977-84; Senior Double Bass Tutor, Royal Northern College of Music, 1984-; Professor of Double Bass, Royal College of Music, 1987-1991; Double Bass Consultant, Royal Scottish Academy of Music & Drama, 1991-; Solo appearances with Netherlands Chamber Orchestra, Concertgebouw Chamber Orchestra, Bournemouth Sinfonietta, Netherlands Philharmonic Orchestra, Orchestre Regional d'Auvergne, Barcelona Municipal Orchestra, Northern Sinfonia, Orchestre de Chambre Detmold, Nippon Telemann Ensemble of Osaka, Lausanne Chamber Orchestra, BBC Concert Orchestra, Scottish Chamber Orchestra, Bournemouth Symphony Orchestra; World Premieres of Concertos written by Sir Peter Maxwell Davies, John Casken & Derek Bourgeois; Recitals and master classes throughout Europe and Japan. *Recordings:* Solo recordings: Bottesini Grand Duo for Philips; Various pieces with Paganini Ensemble for Denon; Dutch TV recordings of Bottesini Grand Duo and 2nd Concerto; Dvořák String Quintet & Waltzes with Chilingirian Quartet (Chandos); Extensive radio recordings. *Honour:* 1st Prize Winner, Isle of Man International Double Bass Competition, 1982. *Hobbies:* Golf; Carpentry. *Current Management:* Music Productions, London. *Address:* c/o Manager, Music Productions, 'J' House, 6 Studland Street, London W6 0JS, England.

MCVEAGH Diana Mary, b. 6 Sept 1926, Ipoh, Malaya. Writer on Music. m. Dr C.W. Morley, 7 Oct 1950. *Education:* Malvern Girls' College, 1936-44; Royal College of Music, 1944-47, ARCM, GRSM. *Career:* Assistant Editor, Musical Times, 1965-67; Executive Committee of the New Grove, 1970-76; Contributor to The Times, 1947-69, also to Musical Times, The Listener, Records and Recordings; Executive Committee of the GKN English Song Award, 1982-89. *Publications:* Elgar (Dent) 1955; Contributor to New Grove Dictionary of Music (article on Elgar), Twentieth-Century English Masters (MacMillan) 1986. *Memberships:* Royal Musical Association Council 1961-76, Vice-President Royal Music Association 1976-90; Vice-President, Elgar Society. *Address:* Ladygrove, The Lee, Great Missenden, Bucks. HP16 9NA.

MCVICAR George, b. 17 Mar 1919, Dunbarton, Scotland. Adviser in Education. *Education:* Royal Scottish Academy of Music and Drama. *Career:* Teacher, Dunbartonshire schools; Lectuter, Moray House College of Education; Adviser to Music, Stirlingshire and then Central Region, Scotland; Examiner, Trinity College of Music, 1979-91. *Publications:* Saltire Scottish song Book (formerly Oxford Scottish Song Book 1969); New Scottish Song Book, 1987; Saltire Two Part Scottish Song Book, 1989. *Honours:* Diploma in Music Education, RSAM; Hon FTSC. *Memberships:* Federation of Festivals; Scottish Amateur Music Association; Chairman; New Director Lennox Singers. *Address:* 22 Queen Street, Stirling FK8 1HN, Scotland.

MCVICKER William Richard, b. 3 Feb 1961, Radcliffe, England. Organist; Conductor. m. Sally Jane Sherren, 19 Dec 1987. *Education:* BA 1983, PhD, 1987, University of Durham; LRAM, 1984; ARCO, 1985. *Debut:* Royal Albert Hall, 1990. *Career:* Caedmon Fellow, University of Durham, 1987; Director of Music, St

Barnabas Dulwich, 1988; Director of Music, University of Portsmouth, 1990-. *Recordings include:* Hear my Prayer; with Rosebery Chamber Orchestra and Chorus. *Contributions to:* Musical Times; Church Music Quarterly; Organist's Review; Journal of American Choral Directors; Hi-Fi News. *Memberships:* Royal college of Organists; British Institute of Organ Studies; Incorporated Society of Musicians (ISM). *Hobbies:* Food and Wine. *Address:* 79 Landells Road, London SE22, 9PH, England.

MEAD Elizabeth Vaila, b. 19 Aug 1948, Brisbane, Queensland, Australia. Pianist. *Education:* BM 1975, MM 1976, Juilliard School of Music, New York, USA; DSCM (Performers) Diploma, State Conservatorium of Music, Sydney, Australia, 1970; LMusA 1968; AMusA 1965. *Debut:* London, Wigmore Hall, 1977; New York, Alice Tully Hall Lincoln Center, 1979. *Career:* First public performance, Australian Broadcasting Commission aged 11; Radio broadcasts, telecasts; numerous concerts & recitals including appearances as concerto soloist, 1962-70; Recitals 1977-83 including: Special Concert, Palace House, Beaulieu, 1981; National Gallery of Victoria, Melbourne, 1982; University of Hawaii, Honolulu, Recital and Master Class, 1982; Hephzibah Menuhin Memorial Scholarship Recital, Sydney, 1983; Adjudicator, City of Sydney Eisteddfod, 1983; Teaching: Conservatorium of Music (Newcastle branch), 1983-84; Sydney University, 1984-85; Central Coast Music Centre, Gosford, NSW, 1984-87. *Address:* 1311 Addison Road, Manly, NSW 2095, Australia.

MEAD Philip John, b. 8 Sept 1947, Chadwell St Mary, Essex, England. Pianist. m. 2 Aug 1969, 3 daughters. *Education:* ARCM, performing, 1966, FTCL 1982, LRAM 1968, GRSM 1969, Royal Academy of Music. *Debut:* Purcell Room, 1973. *Career includes:* Performances, major festivals, England & overseas; Specialist, 20th century piano music; Commissioned works include a piece for piano and electronics by Dennis Smalley, Norwich Festival, 1990; featured soloist at London South Bank's 1987 Electric Weekend; founded the first British Contemporary Piano Competition, Cambridge 1988; repetoire includes Messiaen, Tippett, Stockhausen and George Crumb. *Recordings:* Numerous, for BBC & European stations, including Stephen Montague, Slow Dance on a Burial Ground. *Contributions to:* Electro Acoustic Music. *Honours:* 5 prizes, Royal Academy of Music; Research awards; Prizewinner, Gaudeamus International Competition for Interpreters of Contemporary Music, 1978. *Membership:* Musicians Union. *Hobbies:* Jogging; Reading. *Current Management and Address:* Magenta Music International Ltd, 64 Highgate High St., Highgate Village, London N6 5HX, England.

MEALE Richard, b. 24 Aug. 1932, Sydney, Australia. Composer. *Education:* New South Wales Conservatorium of Music; University of California at Los Angeles. *Career:* Programme Planning Officer for the Australian Broadcasting Commission 1962-68; Senior Lecturer in the Department of Music at the University of Adelaide from 1969; Active as pianist from 1955, notably in the music of Messiaen. *Compositions:* Stage: The Hypnotist ballet 1956; Incidental music to King Lear; Juliet's Memoirs, opera 1975; Operas Voss, 1986 and Mer de Glace, 1991; Orchestral: Flute Concerto 1959; Sinfonia for piano and strings 1959; Homage to Garcia Lorca for double string orchestra 1964; Images 1966; Very High Kings 1968; Clouds Now and Then 1969; Soon it will Die 1969; Evocations 1973; Viridian 1979; Instrumental: Divertiemnto for Piano Trio 1959; Flute Sonata 1960; Les Alboradas for flute, horn, violin and piano 1963; Wind Quintet 1970; Incredible Floridas for flute, clarinet, violin, cello, piano and percusssion 1971; 2 String Quartets 1974, 1980; Fanfare for brass ensemble 1978; Keyboard: Sonatina Patetica 1957; Orenda 1959; Coruscations 1971. *Honours:* 1971 Member of the British Empire; 1972-75 Composers Fellowship awarded by the South Australian Government *Memberships:* Adelaide Festival Cntre Trust 1972; President of the Australliam Branch of ISCM 1977; Chairman of the Composition Panel of the Music

Board of the Australia Council. *Address:* c/o Universal Edition, 2/3 Fareham Street, London W1V 4DU, England.

MECKNA Robert Michael, b. 13 Feb 1945, California, USA. Musicologist. m. Eva Elizabeth Kartinen, 18 Feb 1976. *Education:* BA, California State University, 1967; PhD, University of California. *Publications:* 20th-Century Brass Soloists, 1993; Collected Works of ALfred B Sedgwick, 1994; Virgil Thomson: A Bio-Bibliography, 1986; The Rise of the American Composer-Critic, 1984; Austrian Cloister Symphonists (co-author), 1982. *Contributions to:* Composers of Latin America, 1993; International Dictionary of Opera, 1993; New Grove Dictionary of Opera; New Grove Dictionary of American Music; American Music, Musical Quarterly, The Musical Times, Music Journal, Oesterreichische Musikzeitschrift, Neue Zeitschrift für Musik. *Hobbies:* Gardening; Ballroom Dancing. *Address:* Music Department, Texas Christian University, Fort Worth, Texas 76129, USA.

MEDEK Tilo, b. 22 Jan 1940, Jena, Germany. Composer. *Education:* Studied in Berlin with E Meyer and Wagner Regeny. *Career:* Moved to West Germany in 1977. *Compositions include:* Operas Einzug, 1969; Icke und die Hexe Yu, 1971; Appetit auf Frukirschen, 1972; Katharina Blum, 1991; Gritzko und der Pan, 1987; Balled David and Goliath, 1972; Orchestral: Triade 1964; Das Zogernde Lied, 1970; Flute concerto, 1973; Piccolo Concerto, 1975; Konig JOhann, concert overture, 1976; Marimba concerto, 1976; 2 Cello Concertos, 1978, 1984; Organ concerto, 1979; violin concerto, 1980; Eisenblatter for organ and orchestra, 1983; Rheinische sinfonie 1986; Chamber: Flute sonata, 1963; 3 wind quintets, 1965-79; String Trio, 1965; Divertissement for wind quintet and harpsichord, 1967; Schwanengesang for clarinet, trombone, cello and piano, 1973; Nonet, 1974; Tagtraum for 7 instruments, 1976; Giebichestein for 8 instruments, 1976; Reliquienschrein for organ and percussion 1980; Vocal: Altägyptische Liebeslieder for 2 voices and orchestra, 1963; Sintflutbestanden for tenor, horn and piano, 1967; Gethsamane, cantata, 1980; Piano and organ music. *Address:* c/o GEMA (Germany), PRS Ltd Membership Registration, London W1P 4AA, England.

MEDINA Jesus, b. 13 Oct 1959, Monterrey, Mexico. Orchestra Conductor. m. Marid Ferndnda, 17 Dec 1983, 2 sons. *Education:* Studied at the College Fednco Mexicano and the Pierre Monteux School. *Debut:* The Mexico City Pholharmonic Orchestra, Conductor, 1982. *Career:* Many Interviews for Mexican TV and Radio. *Compositions:* A New Age Album and Documental Music. *Recordings:* Baroque Music. *Honours:* Prize of the Mexican Union of Music and Art Critics. *Membership:* Pro Musica de Monterrey. *Hobbies:* Movies; Soccer; Network Marketing Direct Distributor. *Address:* Sanchez De La Barquera 97-401, Col Marced Gomez CP 03930, Mexico D F, Mexico.

MEDJIMOREC Heinz, b. 1940, Vienna, Austria. Pianist. *Education:* Studied in Vienna. *Career:* Performances of Haydn and other composers in Vienna and elsewhere from 1968; Co-Founder, Haydn Trio of Vienna, 1968 and has performed in Brussels, Munich, Berlin, Zurich, London, Paris and Rome; New York debut in 1979 and has made frequent North American appearances, with concerts in 25 states; Debut tour of Japan 1984, with further travels to the Near East, Russia, Africa, Central and South America; Series at the Vienna Konzerthaus society from 1976, with performances of more than 100 works; Summer Festivals at Vienna, Salzburg, Aix en Provence, Flanders and Montreaux; Master classes at the Royal College and Royal Academy in London, Stockholm, Bloomington, Tokyo, and the Salzburg Mozarteum. *Recordings include:* Complete piano trios of Beethoven and Schubert, Mendelssohn Di minor, Brahms B major, Tchaikovsky A minor, Schubert Trout Quintet; Albums of works by Haydn, Schumann, Dvořák and Smetana. *Address:* Haydn Trio, Sue Lubbock Concert

Management, 25 Courthorpe Road, London NW3 2LE, England.

MEDLAM Charles, b. 1949, England. Conductor; Cellist. *Education:* Studied the cello in London, Paris (with Maurice Gendron at the Conservatoire), Vienna and Salzburg (performance practice with Nikolaus Harnoncourt). *Career:* Lectured and played in the resident string quartet at the Chinese University of Hong Kong; Founded London Baroque with Ingrid Seifert 1978; Directs the group as chamber orchestra and conducts when larger forces are required; Conducted the first performance of Scarlatti's Une villa di Tuscolo and a revival of Gli Equivoci Sembiante, for the BBC; Season 1990-91 included Dido and Aeneas at the Paris Opéra, Blow and Lully at the Opéra-Comique; Aci, Galatea e Polifemo in Spain, Holland and England, and cantatas by Handel and Rameau in Austria, Sweden and Germany with Emma Kirkby; Other recent repertoire includes Charpentier's Messe de Minuit; 4 violin music by Telemann, Vivaldi and Wassenaar; Bach Brandenburg Concertos; Monteverdi Tancredi and Clorinda; Salzburg Festival debut 1991, with music by Mozart; Further festival engagements at Bath, Beaune, Versailles, Ansbach, Innsbruck and Utrecht; Conducted London Baroque in Handel's Op.6 no.6 and Purcell's Come, Ye Sons of Art Away at the 1993 Proms. *Recordings:* Marais La Gamme, Theile Matthew Passion, Bach Trio Sonatas, Charpentier Theatre Music, Handel Aci, Galatea e Polifemo, Venus and Adonis, Purcell Chamber Music (Harmonia Mundi); Purcell Fantasias, Bach Violin Sonatas, Monteverdi Orfeo, Handel German Arias (EMI); A Vauxhall Gardens Entertainment; English Music of the 18th Century; François Couperin Chamber Music; The complete trio sonatas of Corelli, Handel, Purcell, Lawes; Gamba sonatas by CPE Bach, harpsichord concertos by JC Bach/WA Mozart. *Hobby:* Writing short stories. *Address:* Brick Kiln Cottage, Hollington, nr Newbury, Berkshire RG15 9XX, England.

MEDVECZKY Adam, b. 1941, Budapest, Hungary. Conductor. *Education:* Timpanist Graduate, Bela Bartók Conservatory; Department of Conducting, Liszt Academy of Music, Budapest, 1968; Master Class, Maestro Franco Ferrara, Italy. *Career:* Timpanist, Hungarian State Symphony Orchestra for 9 years; Conductor, Budapest State Opera, 1974; Numerous guest appearances in Bulgaria, Germany, Greece, The Netherlands, Poland, Italy, Romania, Russia and USA; Professor, Ferenc Liszt Academy, Budapest, 1981-. *Recordings:* Has made numerous recordings. *Honours:* Liszt Prize, 1976; 2nd Prize, Hungarian television International Concours for Young Conductors, 1974; 2nd Prize, Hungarian Television International Concours for Young Conductors; Prize of the Public, 1974.

MEEK James, b. 29 July 1957, Winchester, England, Singer (Baritone). *Education:* Studied at the Guildhall School of Music. *Career:* Sang for three seasons at the Buxton Festival and appeared as Owen Wingrave at Aldeburgh; Other roles include Escamillo, Rossini's Figaro, Mozart's Count and Guglielmo, Valentin in Faust and the Doctor in Debussy's posthumous Fall of the House of Usher (Elizabeth Hall 1989); Sang in Haydn's La Vera Costanza in Germany; Concert repertoire includes Elijah, the Petite Messe Solennelle, Handel's Judas Maccabeus (Flanders Festival) Israel in Egypt and Dixit Dominus; Bach's Christmas Oratorio at the Snape Maltings, St John and St Matthew Passions; Britten's War Requiem in Germany and Yugoslavia and the Requiems of Mozart, Fauré and Brahms; Sang Messiah at the National Concert Hall Dublin, Pulcinella at the Barbican and the Missa Solemnis at Guilford Cathedral; Songs by Henri Dutilleux at Aldeburgh and concerts with the Songmakers' Almanac at the Bath, Nottingham, Buxton and Derby festivals; Recitals on South Bank in the Schoenberg Reluctant Revolutionary Series, 1989 and Schubert directed by Hermann Prey, accompanied by Iain Burnside; Sang Starveling in A Midsummer Night's Dream at Aix-en-Provence, 1992. *Address:* c/o Ron Gonsalves Management, 10 Dagnan Road, London SW12 9LQ, England.

MEER Rud van der, b. 23 June 1936, The Hague, Holland. Singer (Baritone). *Education:* Studied oboe and conducting at Royal Conservatory, The Hague; Vocal teachers include Pierre Bernac. *Career:* Played oboe in Hague Philharmonic Orchestra; Teacher at various grammar schools; Conductor of Choir in Holland; Debut as singer 1967; Recitalist and oratorio soloist in major centres, including London, New York, Berlin, Paris, Vienna and Warsaw; Recitals for the BBC and at the Holland, Helsinki and English Bach Festivals; Bregenz Festival and the Belgian Festival of Flanders; Conductors include Gerd Albrecht, Berio, Michel Corboz, Jean Fournet, Harnoncourt, Leitner, Pritchard and Hans Vonk; Performances with Elly Ameling in New York and London of Wolf's Italienisches Liederbuch and Spanisches Liederbuch; Moscow debut 1988, in the Sviatoslav Richter Festival at the Pushkin Museum; Tour of USSR May 1989; Permanent member of the jury of the International Singing Competition of s-Hertogenbosch. *Recordings:* 30 discs of Lieder and oratorio; 40 Bach Cantatas; Bach's St John Passion; Labels include Erato, CBS, Philips, Telefunken, Polydor and Ottavo. *Honours:* Laureate of international vocal competitions of 's-Hertogenbosch, Toulouse and Barcelona; Grand Prix du Disque 1970 for St John Passion. *Hobby:* Ice Hockey. *Address:* c/o Music International, 13 Ardilaun Road, Highbury, London N5 2QR, England.

MEFFEN John, b. 4 Sept 1928, Bedlington, Northumberland. Lecturer. m. Kathleen Parker, 31 Dec 1956. *Education:* BA Hons Music, MA, Durham University; PhD, Leeds University; ARCM; FTCL. *Career:* Principal Lecturer in Music, Darlington College of Education; Director of Music, Queen Elizabeth VIth Form College, Darlington; Specialist in historically accurate harpsichord tuning. *Publications:* A Guide to Tuning Musical Instruments, 1982; A Question of Temperament - Purcell and Croft, in Musical Times, 1978. *Hobbies:* Reading; Writng; Motoring; Gardening. *Address:* 58 Trinity Road, Darlington, Co Durham DL3 7AZ, England.

MEHTA Mehli, b. 25 Sept 1908, Bombay, India. Music Director; Conductor. m. Tehmina Daruvala, 6 Mar 1935, 2 sons. *Education:* BCom, University of Bombay, 1928; FTCM, London, 1929. *Debut:* Wigmore Hall, 1956. *Career:* Concert Master, Halle Orchestra, Sir John Barbirolli, 1955-59; Founder and Conductor, Bombay Symphony Orchestra, 1935; Founder and Leader, Bombay String Quartet, 1940; Five years with the Curtis String Quartet of Philadelphia, 1959-64; Director, UCLA Orchestra, 1964-78; Founder and Director, Conductor, American Youth Symphony, Los Angeles, 1965-; Debut concert, Carnegie Hall, NY, with National Orchestra Association Symphony, 1983; conducted Philadelpia Orchestra, 1978-80, 1982-84, and Israel Philharmonic Orchestra, 1985. *Recordings include:* Preo-Tone, 1983; Tristan and Isolde Synthesis; Rosenkavalier Suite. *Current Management* ICM Artists Ltd, NY. *Address:* American Youth Symphony (Mus Dir Cond), 321 Tilden Avenue, Los Angeles, CA 90049, USA.

MEHTA Ramanlal C., b. 31 Oct 1918, Surat, India. Musician; Professor of Music. m. Shribala, 1 son, 2 daughters. *Education:* BA; DMus (Hon Cau). *Career:* Programme Executive, Music, All India Radio, Bombay-Ahmedabad-Baroda 1945-53; Principal, College of Indian Music, Dance and Dramatics and Professor of Music, MS University, Baroda 1954-76. *Publications:* Psychology of Music (Ed.), 1980; Essays In Musicology, (Ed.), 1983; Studies in Musicology, (Ed.), 1983; Music and Mythology, (Ed.), 1989; On Music, (Ed.), 1989; Thumri-Tradition and Trends, (Ed.), 1990. *Contributions to:* Journal of The Indian Musicological Society and others. *Honours:* Honorary Doctorate in Music, conferred by Akhil Gandharva Mahavidyalaya, Bombay 1968; Emeritus Fellow, (Music), Government of India 1984-86; Gujarat State Award for Music, 1978; Sarangdev Fellowship, Bombay, 1988; Award of Shreshtha Sangeet Acharya, Raipur, 1993. *Membership:* Founder and Secretary, Indian Musicological Society; Vice-Chairman, Gujarat Sangeet

Natak Akademi, Gujarat, 1993-. *Current Management:* Secretary, Indian Musicological Society, Jambu Bet, Dandia Bazar, Baroda-390001, India. *Address:* Jambu Bet, Dandia Bazar, Baroda-390001, India.

MEHTA Zubin, b. 29 Apr 1936, Bombay, India. Conductor; Musician. m. (2) Nancy Diane Kovack, 19 July 1969, 1 son, 1 daughter, from first marriage. *Education:* St Xavier's College, Bombay, India, 1951-53; State Academy of Music, Vienna, 1954-60. *Career:* Music Director, Montreal Symphony, Canada, 1961-67; Music Director, Los Angeles Philharmonic, 1962-78; Music Director for Life, Israel Philharmonic, 1969-; Music Director, New York Philharmonic, 1978-; Frequent Guest Conductor with: Philadelphia Orchestra, Berlin Philharmonic, Vienna Philharmonic, L'Orchestre de Paris, Maggio Musicale Fiorentino; Conducted Il Trovatore and Don Giovanni at Florence 1990; Baths of Caracalla 1990, with three well known tenors; Engaged to conducted Wagner's Ring at Chicago, 1993; Season 1992 with a live Tosca for world-wide television, Aida with the Israel Philharmonic, Tosca at Covent Garden, La Forza del Destino and Le Nozze di Figaro at the Maggio Musicale (engaged for Moses und Aron), 1994. *Recordings:* Salome (Sony); Video of Tosca; CDs of Mozart's Sinfonia Concertante K364 and Concertone K190 (Israel Philharmonic), Tchaikovsky's 1st Piano Concerto and Violin Concerto (Gilels/Zukerman/NYPO), Khachaturian Violin Concerto (Perlman); Saint-Saëns 3rd symphony (Los Angeles Philharmonic); Puccini La Fanciulla del West (Royal Opera House) and Turandot (Sutherland and Pavarotti); Bellini's I Puritani (Gruberova and Merritt). *Honours:* 1st Prize, Liverpool, England - International Conductors' Competition, 1958; Decorated Padma Bhushan of India, 1967; Commendatore of Italy; Medaille d'Or Vermeil of the City of Paris; Honorary Citizen of Tel Aviv, 1986. *Address:* c/o Cynthia Meister, 27 Oakmont Drive, Los Angles, CA 90049, USA.

MEIER Jaroslav, b. 7 Dec 1923, Hronov, Czechoslovakia. Composer. m. Marta Kurbelova, 1950. 2 sons. *Education:* Organ, Academy of Music, Prague, 1939-44; Organ and Composition, Academy of Music, Bratislava, 1947-49. *Career:* Head of Music Department, Radio Bratislava, 1949-56; Head of Music Department, Czechoslovakia TV, Bratislava, 1956-; Music designer (a lot of TV and radio plays and films). *Compositions:* Opera Erindo (rewriting opera by baroque composer J S Kusser); TV opera The Night before Immortality (libretto after A Arbuzov); opera, The Wooden Shoes (libretto after Guy de Maupassant); Orchestral works: Dances from my Country; Songs from my Country; What a Smell (song cycle based on Stefan Zary's poems); Concerto da Camera for organ and orchestra, 1982. *Recordings:* Chamber Music: Trois Impromtus; Prelude and Double Fugue; Divine love; The cycle Nocturnal Songs; Toccata et fuga, Fantasia concertante. *Publications:* Obrazovka plna hudby, (The Screen full of Music), 1970; Johann Sigismund Kusser, 1986. *Contributions to:* Slovenska hudba (Slovak Music); Hudebni zivot (Music Life); Ceskoslovenska televize (TV weekly paper). *Honours:* Prize of Critics at the Int TV Festival The Golden Prague 1976 for TV opera The Night before Immortality. *Memberships:* Union of Czechoslovak Composers; IMZ. *Address:* Andreja Mraza 13, Bratislava 2, Slovakia.

MEIER Johanna, b. 13 Feb 1938, Chicago, USA. Singer (Soprano). m. Guido Della Vecchia. *Education:* Studied at the University of Miami with Arturo di Filippi and at the Manhattan Schoool with John Brownlee. *Debut:* New York City Opera 1969, as the Countess in Capriccio. *Career:* Sang with the City Opera as Donna Anna, Senta, Louise and Tosca; Metropolitan Opera from 1976, as Marguerite, Ariadne, the Marschallin, Ellen Orford, Chrysothemis, Elisabeth, Brünnhilde in Die Walküre and Kaiserin; Guest engagements in Seattle, Washington, Philadelphia, San Diego, Ottawa and Chicago; Other roles include Sieglinde, Musetta, Mozart's Countess, Amelia (Un ballo in Maschera), Agathe and Eva; Bayreuth Festival debut 1981, as Isolde; Vienna Staatsoper from 1983, Fidelio and Senta; Tour

of Japan 1986, as Isolde and the Marschallin; Barcelona and Buenos Aires 1987, as Elisabeth in Tannhäuser and Chrysothemis; Sang Turandot at Dallas and New Orleans, 1987-88; Ariadne at Trieste, 1988; Pittsburgh Opera, 1989 as Chrysothemis; the Dyer's Wife in Die Frau ohne Schatten at the 1990 Holland Festival. *Address:* c/o Metropolitan Opera, Lincoln Center, New York, NY 10023, USA.

MEIER Jost, b. 15 Mar 1939, Solothurn, Switzerland. Composer. Conductor. *Education:* Studied at the Berne Conservatory and with Frank Martin in Holland. *Career:* Conducted at the Biel Opera, 1969-79, Basle, 1980-83. *Compositions include:*Sennentuntschi, dramatic legend, Freiburg, 1983; Der Drache, opera in 2 acts, Basle, 1985; Der Zoobar, opera in 4 scenes, Zurich 1987; Augustin, opera in 4 scenes, Basle 1988; Dreyfus, opera, Berlin (Deutsche Oper), 1994. *Address:* c/o Deutsche Oper Berlin, Richard Wagnerstrasse 10, D-1000 Berlin, Germany.

MEIER Waltraud, b. 9 Jan 1956, Wurzburg, Germany. Singer (Mezzo-Soprano). *Education:* Studied with Dietger Jacob in Cologne. *Career:* Sang in Wurzburg from 1976 as Cherubino, Dorabella, Nicklaus in Les Contes d'Hoffmann and Concepcion in L'Heure Espagnole; Mannheim 1978-80, as Carmen, Fricka, Waltraute and Octavian; Dortmund 1980-83 as Kundry in Parsifal, Eboli in Don Carlos and as Santuzza in Cavalleria Rusticana; Guest appearances in Cologne, Hamburg, Buenos Aires, Opéra de Paris, Staatsoper Wien, Scala di Milano, San Francisco Opera, München; Bayreuth from 1983: sang Kundry in Götz Friedrich's production of Parsifal, Brangäne in Tristan und Isolde, and Waltraute in Harry Kupfer's 1988 production of The Ring; Covent Garden debut 1985, as Eboli: returned to London 1988, as Kundry; made her Metropolitan Opera debut in 1987 as Fricka in Rheingold and Walküre; Other roles include Azucena (Il Trovatore), Venus (Tannhäuser), the Composer (Ariadne auf Naxos); Sang Venus at Hamburg 1990; debut at the Teatro San Carlos, Lisbon, 1990 as Ortrud in Lohengrin; Théâtre du Châtelet, Paris, 1990, as Marguerite in Le Damnation de Faust; Sang Waltraute at the 1990 Bayreuth Festival, Tchaikovsky's Maid of Orleans at Munich. Season 1992/93 as Kundry at La Scala and the Metropolitan, Berg's Marie at the Theâtre du Chatelet, Paris, and Waltraute, Kundry and Isolde at Bayreuth; Also heard as a concert singer, in Brahms, Mahler, and Verdi. *Recordings include:* Dittersdorf's Doktor und Apotheker; Venus and Kundry (EMI & Philips); Brahms Alto Rhapsody; Fricka in James Levine's Die Walküre (Deutsche Grammophon), Wesendonk and Kindertotenlieder (Erato), Missa Solemnis (EMI), Mozart Requiem (EMI). *Address:* PO Box 100262 Bayreuther Festspiele, 8580 Bayreuth 1, Germany.

MEIGS Melinda Moore, b. 28 Nov 1953, Michigan, USA. Singer; Harpsichordist; Teacher; Performer. *Education:* BA, Smith College, Massachusetts, 1975; BMus, 1975; Studies with Ilse Wolf, Ronald Murdoch, Lory Wallfisch; Masterclass with Gustav Leonhardt. *Debut:* Lieder Recital, Boston, Massachusetts, 1975; Harpsichord Concert, Northampton, Massachusetts, 1975. *Career:* Tours throughout Europe, USA and Canada as Soloist, accompanist and soprano soloist in Vivaldi Gloria and Bach Magnificat with choir; Appearance on Athens TV; Broadcast on Paris Radio. *Compositions:* Glissando, for tape recorder, 1981; Spirit Healer, for voices and voice and cello, 1986. *Recordings:* Spanish Villancicos on Diverse Winds, cantatas of Boismortier, Caldara and Telemann. *Honour:* Phi Beta Kappa, 1975. *Membership:* Incorporated Society of Musicians. *Hobbies:* Travel; Reading; Walking. *Address:* 261 Grove Street, London SE8 3PZ, England.

MEIJ Johan de, b. 23 Nov 1953, Voorburg, Netherlands. Professional Musician; Composer; Arranger; Band Conductor. *Education:* Teachers Training College, 1975; Specialised in Trombone and Symphonic Band Conducting, Royal Conservatory of Music, The Hague, graduating, 1983. *Career:* Trombone, Baritone Player, Amsterdam Police Band, 1977-88, The

Dutch Brass Sextet, including numerous radio, television and gramophone recordings and concerts countrywide, 1977-; Band Arranger and Conductor; Trombone with Orkest de Volharding (contemporary music), Amsterdam Trombone Quartet, Amsterdam Wind Orchestra, 1987-; Band Arranger and Conductor; Frequent Guest Conductor performing own works. *Compositions:* Patchwork for brass sextet, 1979; Symphony no 1, The Lord of the Rings, for concert band, 1988; Loch Ness - A Scottish Fantasy, symphonic poem, 1988; Pentagram, for fanfare band, 1989; Aquarium opus 5, for concert band, 1991; Symphony No 2. The Big Apple (A New York Symphony) (opus 6), for concert band, 1991-93; Classical arrangements for band; Arrangements of light music, musical selections and film music; Accompaniments for instrumental and vocal soloists. *Current Management:* Amstel Music, Netherlands. *Address:* c/o Amstel Music, Chr Huygensplein 1st Floor, 1098 PZ Amsterdam, Netherlands.

MEKLER Mani, b. 1951, Haifa, Israel. Singer (Soprano). *Education:* Studied in Italy. *Career:* Sang Leonora in Il Travatore at Stockholm and with Welsh National Opera, 1976, 1977; Glyndebourne debut 1978, as First Lady in Die Zauberflöte; Wexford Festival 1979, as Giulia in Spontini's La Vestale; Deutsche Oper am Rhein, Dusseldorf, from 1979, as Janáček's Jenůfa and Mila (Osud) and Chrysothemis; Further appearances at Drottningholm, Zurich and Milan, La Scala (premiere of Testi's Riccardo III, 1987); Other roles include Puccini's Manon Lescaut, Tosca and Butterfly, Strauss's Salome and Ariadne, and Goneril in Reimann's Lear.

MELBY John B., b. 3 Oct 1941, Wisconsin, USA. Composer. m. Jane H. Thompson, 15 June 1978, 2 sons, 1 daughter. *Education:* Diploma, 1964, BMus, 1966, Curtis Institute of Music; MA, University of Pennsylvania, 1967; MFA, 1971, PhD, 1972, Princeton University. *Career:* Currently, Professor of Music, University of Illinois. *Compositions include:* 2 Concertos for Violin and Computer-Synthesized Tape; Wind, Sand and Stars; Of Quiet Desperation; Concerto for Computer-Synthesized Tape and Orchestra; Symphony, 1993. *Recordings:* 91 Plus 5; Two Stevens Songs; Chor der Steine. Concerto for Violin, English Horn and Computer-Synthesized Tape; Concerto No. 1 for Violin and Computer-Synthesized Tape; Forandre; Chor der Waisen; Concerto No.1 for flute and Computer-Synthesized Tape. *Address:* School of Music, 2136 Music Building, 1114 West Nevada, University of Ilinois, Urbana, IL 61801, USA.

MELBYE Mikael, b. 15 Mar 1955, Frederiksberg, Denmark. Baritone. *Education:* Royal College of Music, Copenhagen. *Debut:* As Guglielmo in Così fan tutte, Royal Opera, Copenhagen 1976. *Career:* Repertoire of 28 lyric baritone roles including Mozart, Rossini and Donizetti; debut abroad at Spoleto Festival 1981; with Hamburg State Opera 1982-; appearances in many other houses in Europe including Théâtre du Châtelet, Aix-en-Provence (Figaro), La Scala, Milan (Guglielmo), Dallas, Santa Fe; Debut at Covent Garden in title role in Il Barbiere di Siviglia 1986, returned 1987, in the British premiere of Sallinen's The King Goes Forth to France; Vienna Staatsoper debut 1988, as Papageno; Copenhagen 1988, as Don Giovanni; Sang Danilo in The Merry Widow at Rome, 1990 (returned 1992); Season 1992 as Escamillo at Copenhagen and Eisenstein at Santa Fe. *Recordings include:* Carmen (Karajan) and Die Zauberflöte (C. Davis). *Honour:* Won Golden Pegasus Award. *Address:* c/o Lies Askonas, 186 Drury Lane, London WC2B 5RY, England.

MELCHER Wilhelm, b. 5 Apr 1940, Hamburg, Germany. Violinist. *Education:* Studied in Hamburg and rome. *Career:* Leader of the Hamburg SO, 1963; Former member of Karl Munchinger's Stuttgart Chamber Orchestra, Heilbroon; Co-Founder, Melos Quartet of Stuttgart, 1965; Represented West Germany at the Jeunesse Musicales in Paris, 1966; International concert tours from 1967; Bicentenary concerts in the Beethoven Haus at Bonn, 1970; British concerts and festival apperances from 1974; Cycle of Beethoven quartets at Edinburgh Festival, 1987; Wigmore Hall, St John's Smith Square and bath Festival, 1990; Associations with Rostropovitch in the Schubert Quintet and the Cleveland Quartet in works by Sphor and Mendelssohn; Teacher, Stuttgart Musikhochschule. *Recordings include:* Complete quartets of Beethoven, Schubert, Mozart and Brahms; Quintets by Boccherini with Narciso Ypes and by Mozart with Frank Beyer. *Honours:* Grand Prix du Disque and Prix Caecilia, Academie du Disque, Brussels (with Melos Quartet). *Address:* Melos Quartet, c/o Ingpen & Williams Ltd, 14 Kensington Court, London W8 5DN, England.

MELCHERT Helmut, b. 24 Sept 1910, Kiel, Germany. Singer (Tenor). *Education:* Studied at the Hamburg Musikhochschule. *Debut:* Began as a concert singer, 1936. *Career:* Sang at Wuppertal Opera from 1939; Member of Hamburg Opera 1943-77, notably in Wagner roles and in the 1960 premiere of Henze's Der Prinz von Homburg; Guest appearances in Berlin, London, Dusseldorf, Munich and Amsterdam; Edinburgh 1956, as Stravinsky's Oedipus; Zurich 1957, as Aron in the stage premiere of Schoenberg's Moses und Aron; Salzburg Festival 1966, in the premiere of Henze's The Bassarids; Taught singing at the Hamburg Musikhochschule. *Recordings:* Salome (HMV); Wozzeck (Deutsche Grammophon); Die Veruteilung des Lukullus by Dessau; Moses und Aron; Karl V by Krenek. *Address:* c/o Hamburgische Staatsoper, Grosse Theaterstrasse 34, D-2000 Hamburg 36, Germany.

MELIS György, b. 2 July 1923, Szarvas, Hungary. Singer (Baritone). *Education:* Studied at the Budapest Academy of Music, with Olga Relevhegyi. *Debut:* Budapest Opera 1949, as Morales in Carmen. *Career:* Many appearances in the major baritone roles of Mozart and Verdi: sang Don Giovanni at Glyndebourne in 1961, and in Brussels, Berlin and Moscow; Further engagements in Edinburgh, (Bartók's Bluebeard, 1973), Vienna and South America; Sang Don Giovanni at Wiesbaden 1987, as guest with the Hungarian State Opera (Bluebeard at Covent Garden 1989); Also heard in concert and oratorio: song recitals include music by Bartók and Kodály. *Recordings:* Kodály's Hary Janos and Budavari Te Deum; Don Giovanni; Rigoletto; Szokolay's Samson; Title role in Bluebeard's Castle by Bartók, conducted by Fricsay. *Honour:* Kossuth Prize 1962. 21. *Address:* Hungarian State Opera, Népoztársaság utja 22, 1061 Budapest, Hungary.

MELKUS Eduard, b. 1 Sept 1928, Baden, Austria. Violinist. m. Marlis Melkus-Selzer, 4 children. *Education:* Studied violin with Ernst Moravec (1942-53), Firmin Touche and Peter Rybar; Musicology at Vienna University with Erich Schenk. *Debut:* Vienna 1944. *Career:* Founded Eduard Melkus Ensemble, playing mainly on original instruments of the 18th Century; Professor of violin and viola at the Vienna Hochschule für Musik from 1958; Founded Vienna Capella Academica 1965; Concerts in all Europe, USA, Australia, Japan, South America; Visiting Professor, University of Georgia, USA, 1973-74, University of Illinois and others. Lectures and master classes in many Universities over all the world. *Recordings:* Concertos by Bach, Tartini, Vivaldi, Haydn; Sonatas by Biber, Corelli, Bach, Mozart and Handel; Solo violin music by Bach; Haydn's La Vera Costanza at the Schönbrunn Palace, Vienna, 1984 (TV). *Publications:* Die Violine, Schott, many articles on interpretation. *Honours include:* Kornerpreis 1967; Edison Prize, Prix Academia Charles C Gross. *Memberships:* Ex-President, Austria ESTA. *Hobbies:* Sightseeing; Music; Collecting old Violins and Fine Art. *Address:* 1020 Wien 2, Obere Donaustrasse 57/14, Austria.

MELL Gertrud Maria, b. 15 Aug 1947, Ed, Sweden. Composer; Organist; Music Teacher; Sea Officer; Sea Captain. *Education:* Organ Diploma, Conservatory of Music, Lund, 1967; Teacher of Music Diploma, Stockholm, 1968; Sea Officer (mate), 1979, Mechanician of Ships, 1979, Sea Captain (Master Mariner), 1981, Engineer of Ships, 1985. *Debut:* Playing own piano composition, Swedish television, 1972. *Career:* Own radio and television programmes, 1973- . *Compositions:* Piano and Organ compositions; Stråkkvartett (string quartet) No. 1, 1969; Fantasie (piano), 1961; Improvisation (piano), 1971; 4 Symphonies; Melodie aus dem Meer (Symfonisk dikt), 1980; Pater Noster (for choir and soloists and instruments), 1983; PT (for piano solo) (Television 1972 and 1982); Celeste Cordialis (for string orchestra), 1985; Piano compositions, also for organ, violin, flute; Symphonic Poem, Andante (for symphony orchestra), 1988; Pacem (for string orchestra), 1990. *Recordings:* LP Mell including string quartet No. 1 played by Royal Court, Orchestra, Sweden, 1971; Single record, Mermaid, 1977. *Honour:* Älvsborgs Läns Landstings Kulturstipendium 10,000. *Memberships:* KMR (Church Musicians Society); STIM (Swedish Composers International Office of Music). *Hobbies:* Pistol Shooting; Driving; Swimming; Animals; Nature. *Address:* Krokegatan 9, 413 18 Göteborg, Sweden.

MELLERS Wilfrid Howard, b. 26 Apr 1914, Leamington, Warwickshire, England. Composer; Author; University Professor (retired). m. (1) Vera Muriel Hobbs, (2) Pauline Peggy Lewis, 3 daughters, (3) Robin Stephanie Hildyard, (4). *Education:* BA (Cantab), 1936; MA (Cantab), 1939; DMus, University of Birmingham, 1960; DPhil., 1980; FGSM, 1982; Studied with Egon Wellesz and Edmund Rubbra. *Career:* College Supervisor in English, Lecturer in Music, Downing College, Cambridge, 1945-48; Staff Tutor in Music, Extra-Mural Department, University of Birmingham, 1948-59; Andrew Mellon Professor of Music, University of Pittsburgh, Pennsylvania, USA, 1960-63; Professor of Music, University of York, England, 1964-81; Visiting Professor, City University, 1984-; Organiser, Attingham Park Summer School of Music, 13 years; Lecturer in Australia, USA, Canada; Work for radio and TV. *Compositions:* About 50 including: Life Cycle, 3 choirs, 2 orchestras; A May Magnificat; Sun-flower; Rosae Hermeticae; Spells, soprano, chamber ensemble; The Ancient Wound, monodrama; Venery for Six Plus; Chants and Litanies of Carl Sandberg; Yeibichai, coloratura soprano, scat singer, jazz trio, orchestra, tape (Proms commission). *Recordings Include:* Voices and Creatures; The Wellspring of Loves; Rose of May; Life-Cycle. *Publications:* 20 books including: Studies in Contemporary Music, 1948; François Couperin, 1950, revised and expanded Edition, 1984; Man and His Music, 2 vols, numerous editions and translations; Music in a New Found Land, 1964; Caliban Reborn, 1966; Twilight of the Gods, 1973; Harmonious Meeting, 1975; Bach and the Dance of God, 1981; Beethoven and the Voice of God, 1983; Vaughan Williams and the Vision of Albion, 1989; The Masks of Orpheus, 1987; The Music of Percy Grainger, 1992; Francis Poulenc, 1993. *Contributions to:* Currently writes regularly for the Times Literary Supplement. *Honours:* Honorary DPhil, City University, 1981; OBE, 1982; Professor Emeritus, University of York, 1984. *Address:* Oliver Sheldon House, 17 Aldwark, York, YO1 2BX, England.

MELLES Carl, b. 15 July 1926, Budapest, Hungary. Conductor. m. Gertrud Dertnig, 1 son, 1 daughter. *Career:* Studied in Budapest. *Career:* Conductor of the Hungarian State orchestra 1951; Conductor of the Symphony Orchestra of Hungarian Radio and Television; Professor at the Budapest Academy of Music 1954-56; Left Hungary during the Revoluton of 1956; Conductor of the Radio Orchestra of Luxembourg 1958-60; Conductor of major orchestras including New Philharmonia and the Vienna and Berlin Philharmonics; Salzburg and Bayreuth Festivals; Concert tours of Japan, South Africa and Europe; Regular conductor of the Vienna Symphony Orchestra and on Austrian Radio. *Recordings:* Mozart Piano Concertos K459 and K466 (Ingrid Haebler, Vienna Symphony Orchestra). *Honours include:* Franz Liszt Prize, Budapest, 1956. *Address:* Grundbergstrasse 4, 1130 Vienna, Austria.

MELLNAS Arne, b. 30 Aug 1933, Stockholm, Sweden. Composer. *Education:* Stockholm Music High School; Further study with Blancher, Max Deutsch and Ligeti, 1962. *Career:* Active at the San Francisco Tape Music Center, 1964; Teacher, Stockholm Citizens School, 1961-63, Music High School, 1963-; Chairman, Swedish Section, ISCM, 1983. *Compositions include:* Concerto for clarinet and strings, 1957; Music for Orchestra, 1959; Chiasmos for orchestra 1961; Collage for orchestra, 1962; Electronic pieces including intensity 6.5 dedicated to Edgar Arese, 1956; Succism for chorus, 1964; Minibuff opera for 2 singers and tape, 1966; Quasi niente for 1 to 4 string trios, 1968; Spots and spaces after E E Cummings, for male chorus; Il strings and winds, 1968; Transparence for orchestra, 1972; Sub Luna for soprano, flute, violin and harp, 1973; Mara, Mara, Minne for chorus and tape, 1973; Blow for wind orchestra, 1974; Church opera Erik the Holy, 1976; Moments Musicaux, for orchestra, 1977; Capriccio for orchestra, 1978; Nocturnes for mezzo and chamber ensemble, 1980; Chamber opera, Bed of Roses, 1984; Symphony No 1 Ikaros, 1986; Gardens for flute, clarinet, percussion, violin, cello and piano, 1986. *Memberships:* Royal Swedish Academy of Stockholm, 1984. *Address:* STIM (Sweden), c/o PRS Ltd Member Registration, 29-33 Berners Street, London W1P 4AA, England.

MELLON Agnes, b. 17 Jan 1958, Epinay-sur-Seine, France. Singer (Soprano). m. Dominique Visse. *Education:* Studied in Paris and San Francisco. *Career:* Sang with the Paris Opera and the Opera-Comique; Later appearances in the Baroque repertoire, notably as Tibrino in Cesti's Orontea at the 1986 Innsbruck Early Music Festival, Eryxene in Hasse's Cleofide, 1987 and Telaire in Rameau's Castor et Pollux at the 1991 Aix-en- Provence Festival; Sang the title role in Rossi's Orfeo at the Queen Elizabeth Hall, London, with Les Arts Florissants, 1990. *Recordings include:* Rossi's Orfeo, Cavalli's Xerxes, Lully's Atys, Charpentier's Médée and David et Jonathas, Hasse's Cleofide, Rameau's Anacreon and Zoroastre: lables include Erato and Harmonia Mundi. *Address:* c/o William Christie, Paris Conservatoire, 14 Rue de Madrid, 75008 Paris, France.

MELNYK Lubomyr Eugene, b. 22 Dec 1948, Munich, Germany. Composer; Pianist. m. Karin Haerdin, 8 May 1978, 2 daughters. *Education:* MA, Queen's University, Kingston, 1971; BA, University of Manitoba, 1969; ARCT, Conservatory of Music, Toronto. *Career:* Pioneered the Continuous technique for piano (technique of separate patterns on each hand); Recorded over 15 works for radio in Canada and Europe; Has written full-length score for 6 modern ballets, premiered in Lyon, New York, Stockholm and Paris; Over 200 concerts given to date. *Compositions:* Major ballet works include, Voice of Trees, The Eastern Horn, Islands, Page Music; 4 symphonies; over 90 pieces for piano or piano ensemble; 2 string quartets in the Continuous mode. *Recordings:* KMH; Poslaniye, Lund-St Petri Symphony; The Song of Galadriel; Concert Requiem; a 6th, A Portrait of Petlurs On The Day He Was Killed. *Publications:* Open Time: The Art of Continuous Music, 1981; Circular Pieces: 22 Etudes for piano, 1982. *Address:* c/o Haerdin, Kadettu 3-F, 19040 Rosersberg, Sweden.

MENARD Pierre, b. 1945, Quebec, Canada. Violinist. *Education:* Studied at Quebec Conservatory and at Juilliard with Dorothy DeLay, Ivan Galamian and the Juilliard Quartet. *Career:* Solo appearances in Canada and the United States; Former concertmaster of the Aspen Festival Orchestra and the Nashville Symphony; Co-founder and second violinist of the Vermeer Quartet from 1970; Performances in most North American centres, Europe, Israel and Australia; Festival engagements at Tanglewood, Aspen, Spoleto, Berlin, Edinburgh, Mostly Mozart (New York), Aldeburgh, South Bank, Santa Fe Chamber Music West, and the Casals Festival; Resident Quartet for Chamber Music Chicago; Master classes at the Royal Northern College of Music, Manchester; Member of the Resident Artists Faculty of Northern Illinois University. *Recordings:* Quartet by Beethoven, Dvořák, Verdi and Schubert (Teldec); Brahms Clarinet Quintet with Karl Leister (Orfeo). *Honours:* First prize in chamber music, Quebec Conservatory; Winner, National Festival of Music Competition; Prix d'Europe from the Quebec government. *Address:* Allied Artists, 42 Montpelier Square, London SW7 1JZ, England.

MENDOZA DE ARCE Daniel Leonel, b. 24 Dec 1940, Montevideo, Uruguay. University Professor. m. Verena Zentner, 14 June 1986. *Education:* Doctor of Law and Social Sciences 1967, PhD equivalent, Sociology 1970, Universidad de la Republica del Uruguay; Magister Diploma in Solfege and Theory of Music, Conservatorio Falleri-Balzo, Montevideo, Uruguay, 1968; Private lessons in singing and harmony. *Publications:* Sociologia del folklore musical uruguayo, 1972; La musica folklorica de Venezuelain Revista Vispera, 1969; On Some Theoretical and Practical Implications of the Structuralist Approach to Ethnomusicology in Sociogram, 1973; Contemporary Sociological Theories and the Sociology of Music in The International Review of the Aesthetics and Sociology of Music, Vol V, 1974. *Address:* College of Arts and Sciences, Governors State University, University Park, IL 60466, USA.

MENESES Antonio, b. 23 Aug 1957, Refice, Brazil. Concert Cellist. *Education:* Studied with the late Antonio Janigro in Dusseldorf and Stuttgart. *Career:* Has appeared widely in Europe and America from 1977; Appearances with the Berlin Philharmonic conducted by Karajan, with the London Symphony Orchestra in London and the USA, and with the Israel Philharmonic, Vienna Philharmonic and Concertgebouw Orchestras; Other conductors include Abbado, Previn, Maazel and Muti; Tours of Australia 1984, 1987; Engagements at the Lucerne and the Salzburg Easter Festivals, with the Berlin Philharmonic. *Recordings include:* Brahms Double Concerto, with Anne-Sophie Mutter; Strauss Don Quixote, conducted by Karajan (Deutsche Grammophon). *Honours include:* Second Prize at International Competitions in Barcelona and Rio de Janeiro; First Pize at ARD Competition, Munich, 1977; Gold Medal, Tchaikovsky International Competition, Moscow, 1982.

MENKOVA Irina, b. 1960, Moscow, Russia. Violinist. *Career:* Co-Founder, Glazunov Quartet, 1985; Concerts in the former Soviet Union and recent appearances in Greece, Poland, Belgium, Germany and Italy; works by Beethoven and Schumann at the Beethoven Haus in Bonn; Further engagements in Canada and Holland; Teacher at the Moscow State Conservatoire and Resident at the Tchaikovsky Conservatoire; repertoire includes works by Barodin, Shostakovich and Tchaikovsky, in addition to the standard works. *Honours:* Prizewinner, Borodin Quartet and Shostakovich Chamber Music Competitions, (with the Glazunov Quartet). *Address:* c/o Sonata (Glazunov Quartet), 11 Northgate Street, Glasgow G20 7AA, Scotland.

MENNINI Louis Alfred, b. 18 Nov 1920, Erie, Pennsylvania, USA. President, School of the Arts. m. 16 June 1956, 2 sons. *Education:* Oberlin Conservatory, 1939-42; BMus, MMus, 1949, Eastman School of Music; PhD, University of Rochester, 1961. *Career:* Professor, University of Texas, 1948-49; Professor of Composition, Eastman School of Music, 1949-65; Dean, School of Music, North Carolina School of the Arts, 1965-71; Director, School of Music, Mercyhurst College, 1973-82; President, Virginia School of the Arts, 1982-. *Compositions:* 2 Chamber operas, The Well, 1951, The Rope, 1955; Allegro Energico, 1948; Andante, Allegro, 1946; Andante, Allegro Energio, 1947; Ariso for Strings, 1948; Canzona for Chorus Orchestra, 1949; Cantilena, 1950; Overture Breve, 1952; Sonata for Violin, 1947; Tenebrae for Chorus, Orchestra, 1948; Sonata for Cello, 1952; Proper of the Mass, 1953; Symphony No. 1 da Chiesa, 1960; Tenebrae for Orchestra, 1963; Symphony No. 2 da Festa, 1963. *Recordings:* Arioso for Strings; Sonatina for Cello, Piano. *Address:* 3700 Crayton Road, Naples, FL 33940, USA.

MENOTTI Gian Carlo, b. 7 July 1911, Cadegliano, Italy. Composer; Stage Director. *Education:* Curtis Institute of Music, Philadelphia, Pennsylvania. *Career:* Went to USA 1928; Member of Teaching Staff, Curtis Institue of Music 1941-45; Founder and President, Festival of Two Worlds, Spoleto, Italy and Charleston, South Carolina. *Compositions include:* Operas: Amelia Goes To The Ball; The Old Maid And The Thief; The Island God; The Telephone; The Medium; The Consul; Amahl and The Night Visitors; The Labyrinth (own libretti); The Saint of Bleecker Street 1954; The Last Savage 1963; Martin's Lie 1964; Help, Help, The Globolinks (Space Opera for Children) 1968; The Most Important Man in The World 1971; Tamu Tamu 1973; Hero, 1976; La Loca 1979; Song of Hope (Cantata) 1980; St. Teresa 1982; The Boy Who Grew Too Fast, 1982; Goya - premiere at Washington Opera, 1986; The Wedding, premiere at Seoul, South Korea, 1988. Ballet: Sebastian; Film: The Medium (Producer); Vanessa (libretto) 1958; The Unicorn, The Gorgon and The Manticore - a Madrigal Fable, Maria Golovin 1959; The Death of The Bishop of Brindisi (Cantata) 1963; Chamber Music, Songs; For The Death of Orpheus, for tenor, chorus and orchestra, 1990. *Honours:* Hon. BM (Curtis Institute of Music); Guggenheim Award 1946, 1947; Pulitzer Prize 1950, 1955; Kennedy Centre Award 1984; New York City Mayor's Liberty Award, 1986; Hon. Association National Institute of Arts and Letters 1953; Richard Tucker Award, 1988. *Address:* ASCAP Building, One Lincoln Plaza, New York, NY 10023, USA.

MENTZER Susanne, b. 21 Jan 1957, Philadelphia, USA. Singer (Mezzo-Soprano). *Education:* Juilliard School, New York, and with Norma Newton. *Debut:* Houston Opera 1981, as Albina in La Donna del Lago. *Career:* Appeared with Dallas Opera 1982, in Gianni Scicchi and Das Rheingold; Washington Opera as Cherubino; Chicago Lyric Opera, Phildalephia Opera and New York City Opera as Rosina in Il Barbiere di Siviglia; Houston Opera as Rossini's Isolier, and at Rossini Festival Pesaro, Italy, the Composer in Ariadne auf Naxos and Giovanna Seymour in Anna Bolena; European debut with Cologne Opera 1983, as Cherubino, later Massenet's Cendrillon; La Scala Milan as Zerlina in Don Giovanni; Vienna Staatsoper as Cherubino; Covent Garden debut 1985, as Rosina: returned as Giovanna Seymour, 1988, and Dorabella in Così fan Tutte, 1989; Metropolitan Opera debut 1989, as Cherubino; Monte Carlo 1988, as Adalgisa in Norma; Sang Octavian at the Théâtre des Champs-Elysées, Paris 1989; Annius in La Clemenza di Tito at La Scala, 1990; Sesto in the Chicago premiere of Mozart's opera Oct 1990; Vienna State Opera, Così Fan Tutte, Der Rosenkavalier, 1991; Salzburg Festival, Cherubino & Zerlina Metropolitan Opera, Idamante, 1991; Les Contes d'Hoffmann, Nicklausse, Octavian in Der Rosenkavalier, Composer, Ariadne auf Naxos, Metropolitan Opera, 1992-93. *Recordings include:* Anna Bolena with Sutherland and Bonynge and Bruckner Te Deum on Phillips label, Mozart Masses with King's College Choir; Barber of Seville, EMI, (Rosina); Idomeneo, Philips, (Idamante); Don Giovanni, EMI, (Zerlina). *Current Management and Address:* c/o IMG Artists Europe, Media House, 3 Burlington Lane, Chiswick, London W4 2TH, England.

MENUHIN Jeremy, b. 2 Nov. 1951, San Francisco, USA. Pianist. *Education:* Paris with Nadia Boulanger; Israel with Mindru Katz (piano) and Vienna with Hans Swarowsky (conducting). *Career:* Public performances from 1965; New York recital debut 1984; Berlin Philharmonic 1984; Dame Myra Hess series in Chicago 1985; Tours of USA with the Czech Philharmonic and the Prague Chamber Orchestra (1989); Guest appearances with the San Francisco and Houston Symphonies; European orchestras include BBC Philharmonic, Royal Philharmonic, Salzburg Mozarteum, Amsterdam Philharmonic and Orchestre National de France; 1987-88 season included Windsor Festival concert with the English Chamber Orchestra; Beethoven's 1st Concerto with the Leningrad Philharmonic conducted by Yehudi Menuhin; 1989 European concert tour with the Toulouse Chamber Orchestra; Chamber music with the cellists Colin Carr, Steven Isserlis and Marius May; Recitals with sopranos Edith Mahis and Arleen Auger (Aldeburgh 1987). *Recordings:* Association with the Polish Chamber

Orchestra (video of Mozart concertos); Recitals of Debussy, Mozart and Schubert; Beethoven's 3rd Concerto with the Royal Philharmonic; Bartók and Beethoven Violin Sonatas with Yehudi Menuhin; Dvořák Quartet & Quintet with Chilingirian Quartet; Schubert Sonatas, piano works, 1993. *Honour:* Grand Prix du Disque, 1981. *Current Management:* Hazard Chase, 25 City Road, Cambrige CB1 1DP, England. *Address:* c/o Clarion Concert Agency, 64 Whitehall Park, London N19 3TN, England.

MENUHIN Yalta, b. 7 Oct 1921, San Francisco, California, USA. Concert Pianist. m. Joel Ryce, 2 sons. *Education:* Studied piano with Marcel Ciampi in Paris and with Carl Friedberg at the Juilliard School, New York. *Career:* Has appeared worldwide as soloist and with leading instrumentalists; Duo pianist with husband Joel Ryce; Appearances at leading European festivals; TV appearances in Paris, London, New York and Geneva. *Recordings:* Several solo and duo piano works for Everest, EMI, World Record Club and Deutsche Grammophon. *Honours:* First Prize with Joel Ryce, Harriet Cohen International Music Award, 1962.

MENUHIN Yehudi (Lord), b. 22 Apr 1916, New York, USA. Violinist; Conductor. m. (1) Nola Ruby Nicholas 1938, 1 son, 1 daughter; (2) Diana Rosamond Gould 1947, 2 sons. *Education:* Privately in America and Europe; Studied with Sigmund Anker, Louis Persinger, Georges Enesco (in Romania) and with Adolph Busch in Basel; *Debut:* New York debut 1925, Paris 1927 and Berlin 1929 (with Bruno Walter and The Berlin Philharmonic). *Career:* First world tour 1935, subsequently appeared as soloist in orchestras under Toscanini, Fricsay, Furtwängler, Stokowski, Koussevitsky, Beecham, Paul Paray, Walter, Mitropoulos; Has undertaken much research and restoration of neglected compositions; Gave numerous benefit concerts during and after World War II; Gave premiere of Bartók's Solo Violin Sonata, 1944; Since 1945 has toured extensively all over the world and has made documentary musical films in Europe and America; Founded The Yehudi Menuhin School, Surrey 1963; Yearly Festival at Gstaad 1957-, Bath 1959-68, Windsor 1969-72; Founder Chairman, Live Music Now 1977; President Royal Philharmonic Orchestra 1982-; Appeared in film, Raga (with George Harrison and Ravi Shankar) 1974. *Recordings include:* CDs of Baroque Favourites (Vivaldi and Corelli; Classics for Pleasure); Elgar Music for Strings (Arabesque) Menuhin Birthday Edition (5 CD's) released April 1991, for 75th birthday: Concertos by Sibelius, Nielsen, Bloch, Berg, Bartók (No.1 and Viola), Beethoven and Mendelssohn; Ravel, Piano Trio, Brahms Horn Trio and chamber music by Debussy, Schubert and Mendelssohn (HMV/EMI). *Publications:* The Violin - Six Lessons with Yehudi Menuhin 1971; Theme and Variations 1972; The Violin 1976; Violin and Viola (with William Primrose) 1976; Sir Edward Elgar: My Musical Grandfather (Essay) 1976; Unfinished Journey (Autobiography) 1977; Conversations with Menuhin, The Music of Man 1980 (Co-author); The King, The Cat and The Fiddle 1983; Life Class, 1986; Visionary Virtuoso (interview) Sunday Times, 21 Apr 1991. *Honours:* Order of Merit; KBE, (UK); Elevated to Peerage, 1993; President, Hallé Orchestra, 1992. *Memberships:* President, Trinity College of Music, 1971 and RPO; Elgar Society 1984-; Goodwill Ambassador of UNESCO, 1992. *Current Management:* SYM Music Co Ltd, London. *Address:* SYM Music Co Ltd, 110 Gloucester Avenue, London NW1 8JA, England.

MERCER Alexandra, b. 12 May 1944, Gravesend, Kent, England. Singer (Mezzo-Soprano). m. Philip Mercer, 2 Oct 1965, 2 daughters (twins). *Education:* Studied with Maestro Antonio and Lina Riccaboni Narducci, Milan, 1963-65, 1967-69; Royal Scottish Academy of Music, 1965-67. *Debut:* Barga Festival, 1970. *Career:* Has appeared in opera throughout UK and Europe, with companies such as English Bach Festival Trust, Kent Opera, Royal Opera House Covent Garden, Opera Rara, Barber Institute; Roles include Poppea, Despina, Dorabella, Rosina, Hansel, Ascanius, Smeton, Isabella, Mrs Sedley, The Sorceress, Samson;

Festival appearances: Barga, 1970, Edinburgh, 1978, 1979, Bath, 1981, Wexford, 1984; Regular appearances in concert, oratorio and recital; BBC Soloist, Radio 3 and 4; BBC recital debut, 1984. *Recordings:* Opera Rara, 100 years of Italian Opera 1800-1910. *Honours:* 2 Vaughan Williams Trust Awards, 1972, 1973. *Memberships:* Equity. *Hobbies:* Politics; Fashion; Travel; Languages; Her family. *Current Management:* Norman McCann International Artists Ltd, London, England. *Address:* Norman McCann International Artists Ltd, The Coach House, 26 Lawrie Park Gardens, London SE26 6XJ, England.

MEREDITH Morley, b. 8 Feb 1922, Winnipeg, Manitoba, Canada. Singer (Baritone). *Education:* Studied with W.H. Anderson in Canada and with Boris Goldowsky at Tanglewood; Further study with Alfredo Martini in New York. *Debut:* New York City Opera 1957, as Escamillo. *Career:* Metropolitan Opera from 1962, in Les Contes d'Hoffmann and as Zuniga (Carmen), Klingsor, Faninal (Der Rosenkavalier), the Emperor in The Nightingale, Doctor in Wozzeck and the Speaker in Die Zauberflöte; Carnegie Hall 1971, in the US premiere of Handel's Ariodante; Guest appearances with Scottish Opera and in Geneva, Chicago, San Francisco and Philadelphia; Sang in Billy Budd at the Metropolitan, 1992. *Address:* c/o Metropolitan Opera, Lincoln Center, New York, NY 10023, USA.

MERIGHI Giorgio, b. 20 Feb 1939, Ferrara, Italy. Singer (Tenor). *Education:* Studied at the Rossini Conservatory, Pesaro. *Debut:* Spoleto Festival 1962, as Riccadro in Un Ballo in Maschera. *Career:* Many appearances on Italian stages, including the Verona Arena and at the Florence Festival (Meyerbeer's Robert le Diable 1968); Covent Garden 1971 and 1974; Metropolitan Opera debut 1978, as Manrico in Il Trovatore; Guest engagements in Berlin, Monte Carlo, Barcelona, Marseilles and Brussels; Geneva 1984, as Pollione in Norma; Wiesbaden Festival 1985, as the Duke of Mantua; Italian TV as Pinkerton in Madame Butterfly; Munich and Palermo 1987-88 as Maurizio in Adriana Lecouvreur; Sang Luigi in Il Tabarro and the Met 1989, Maurizio at Bonn; Season 1992 with Don José at Genoa, Andrea Chénier at Turin and concert in memory of Mario del Monaco at the Torre del Lago Festival. *Address:* c/o S.A. Gorlinsky Ltd., 33 Dover Street, London W1X 4NJ, England.

MERILÄINEN Usko, b. 27 Jan 1930, Tampere, Finland. Composer. *Compositions include:* Ballet & stage music; Orchestral works; Works for solo instrument & orchestra; Chamber music; Works for solo instrument; Electro-acoustic music. Titles include: Partita, brass instruments; 1st Piano Concerto; Concerto for Orchestra, 1956; 2nd Symphony; 1st Piano Sonata, 1960; Arius, ballet; Epyllion, post-serial music, 1963; Symphony No 4, The Anvil, electronic music; Summer Music, flute & tape, 1980; Kinetic Poem for piano and orchestra 1981; The Stonecrushers for orchestra 1982; Visions and Whispers for flute and orchestra 1985; Mouvements circulaires for flute aaquartet, 1985. *Recordings:* Philips; Finlandia; BIS; Toshiba; EMI-HMV. *Honours:* Wihuri Foundation International Sibelius, prize 1965. *Address:* c/o Finnish Music Information Centre, Runeberginkatu 15, A-00100 Helsinki 10, Finland.

MERLIN Jose Luis, b. 24 Dec 1952, Buenos Aires, Argentina. Guiutarist; Composer; Professor. m. Debora Lewin, 22 Apr 1983, 3s. *Education:* BSEE, Buenos Aires National University; Studied Guitar with Abel Carlevaro and vincente Degese; Harmony, counterpoint and morphology with Leonidas Arnedo. *Debut:* Aged 9, Buenos Aires Television. *Compositions:* Suite del recuerdo and Progresiones para Pauline, for guitar, voice, chamber orchestra. *Recordings include:* Travesia; Catedral del los Bajaros; Guitar Recital No 1 and No 2; Teh Amores y recuerdos; Ascencioin. *Publications:* Guitar Body-Functional technique, 1989; Functional and Descriptive Harmony, 1992; 2000 scales for guitar, 1993. *Honours:* Argentina Representative, 1i Tribune, Czechoslovakial; Sponsored by The Argentine Foreign Relations Ministry. *Memberships:* Founder and Past

President, Argentine Guitar Integration Society; Associate, Symphonic and Chamber Music Composer of the Authors and Composers Argentinian Society. *Hobbies:* Photography. *Current Management:* Debora Lewin. *Address:* Pernambuco 2152, 1416 Buenos Aires, Argentina, S America.

MERRILL Nathaniel, b. 8 Feb 1927, Massahcusetts, USA. Stage Director. *Education:* Trained with Boris Goldovsky at New England Conservatory of Music and with Gunther Rennert, Herbert Graf and Carl Ebert in Europe. *Debut:* Boston 1952, with the US premiere of Lully's Amadis. *Career:* Metropolitan Opera New York from 1955, resident stage director from 1960, with productions of Turandot, Meistersinger, Les Troyens, Aida, Rosenkavalier, Adriana Lecouvreur, Luisa Miller, Parsifal, Porgy and Bess, 1985, Il trovatore, Samson et Dalila and L'Elisir d'amore (collaborations with designer Robert O'Hearn); other stagings at Strasbourg, Vancouver, Verona, San Francisco, New York City Opera and the Vienna Staatsoper. *Address:* c/o Metropolitan Opera, Lincoln Center, New York, NY 10023, USA.

MERRILL Robert, b. 4 June 1919, Brooklyn, New York, USA. Singer (Baritone). m. (1) Roberta Peters (2) Marion Machno 1954, 1 son, 1 daughter. *Education:* Studied with mother and with Samuel Margolis in New York. *Career:* Sang with various radio stations; Trenton, New Jersey as Amonasro 1944; Metropolitan Opera from 1945, as Germont: sang more than 800 performances with the company, as Verdi's Renato, Don Carlo, Iago, Di Luna, Rigoletto and Posa, Puccini's Marcello and Scarpia, Gounod's Valentin, and Rossini's Figaro; Sang for both houses of Congress on the occasion of President Roosevelt's funeral, 1945; Performed for every subsequent US President, including Reagan; Guest appearances in Chicago, San Francisco, Milan and Venice; Covent Garden 1967, as Germont; Toured Japan with Metropolitan Opera 1975; Concerts in London, Bournemouth, Geneva and Israel, 1975; Official singer with New York Yankees from 1969-; Numerous TV appearances with: Milton Berle, Ed Sullivan, Jackie Gleason, Red Skeleton, Frank Sinatra and Tonight Show; Performed as Tevye in Fiddler on the Roof over 800 performances 1970-74. *Recordings:* Cavalleria Rusticana; La Bohème; La Traviata; Carmen; Il Barbiere di Sivigilia; La Gioconda; Aida; Falstaff; La Forza del Destino; Il Trovatore; Labels include RCA, HMV and Decca; Fiddler on the Roof, Kismet, Americana, Various other Popular Albums. *Publications:* Between Acts, 1976; The Divas, 1978; Once More from the Beginning, 1965. *Honours include:* Harriet Cohen International Music Award 1961; Handel Medal, City of New York, 1970; The National Medal of The Arts, (USA), 1993. *Memberships:* AGMA, AGVA, AFTRA, SAG, Actors' Equity 1945-; Friar's Club, Monk 1968-. *Hobbies:* Golf; Baseball; Fine Art. *Current Management:* Gurtman and Murtha Associates, 162 West 56th Street, New York, NY 10019, USA. *Address:* Robert Merrill Associates Inc., 79 Oxford Road, New Rochelle, NY 10804, USA.

MERRIMAN Nan, b. 28 Apr 1920, Pittsburgh, USA. Singer (Mezzo-Soprano). m. Tom Brand. *Education:* Studied with Alexia Bassian in Los Angeles and with Lotte Lehmann. *Career:* Debut in concert, 1940; Opera debut as La Cieca in La Gioconda, Cincinnati 1942; Sang in Toscanini's NBC broadcasts as Maddalena in Rigoletto, Gluck's Orpheus and Meg Page in Falstaff; Glyndebourne 1953, 1956, as Baba the Turk in The Rake's Progress and Dorabella in Così fan Tutte; Sang at Aix-en-Provence as Dorabella, at the Holland Festival and La Scala Milan (1955); Piccola Scala 1958, in the local premiere of Dargomizhsky's The Stone Guest; Guest engagements in Paris, Geneva, Amsterdam, Chicago and San Francisco; Many appearances in concert. *Recordings include:* Così fan Tutte conducted by Karajan (Columbia). *Honours include:* 1st Prize, National Federation of Music Clubs 1943.

MERRITT Chris, b. 27 Sept 1952, Oklahoma, USA. Singer (Tenor). *Education:* Studied at Oklahoma City University; Apprentice artist at the Santa Fe Opera.

Career: Sang in Augsburg as Idomeneo, Rossini's Otello, Rodolfo and Julien in Louise; New York City Opera debut 1981, as Arturo in I Puritani; Apppeared in Rossini's Tancredi at Carnegie Hall, Il Viaggio a Reims at the Vienna Staatsoper, Ermione in Naples and Maometto II at San Francisco Opera; Paris Opéra debut 1983, in Rossini's Moïse; Sang Uberto in La Donna del Lago at Covent Garden; Season 1985-86 in Il Viaggio a Reims at La Scala, as Rodrigo (La Donna del Lago) in Paris, Idreno in a concert performance of Semiramide at Covent Garden; Leukippos in Daphne at Carnegie Hall; Maggio Musicale Florence 1986, as Benvenuto Cellini; Aeneas in Les Troyens in Amsterdam; Nemorino in L'Elisir d'Amore at Orlando, Florida; Opened the 1988-89 season at La Scala in Guillaume Tell by Rossini; Title role in Robert le Diable at Carnegie Hall; Sang Arrigo in I Vespri Siciliani at La Scala, 1989; Arturo in I Puritani at the Rome Opera, 1990; Arnold in a new production of Guillaume Tell at Covent Garden, 1990; Sang Admète in Alceste at the opening of the 1990/91 season at Chicago; Benvenuto Cellini at Geneva, 1992; Season 1992/93 as Leicester in Rossini's Elisabetta at Naples, Arnold at Covent Garden and San Francisco, Rodrigo in La Donna del Lago at La Scala and Conte di Libenskof in Il Viaggio a Reims at Pesaro; Featured Artists (People, no.183) Opera Magazine Festival issue, 1992. Concert engagements in Verdi's Requiem; Haydn's Creation and the Choral Symphony in Israel; Rossini's Petite Messe Solennelle in Amsterdam. *Recordings:* Rossini's Stabat Mater, Ermione and Il Viaggio a Reims; Donizetti's Emilia di Liverpool; I Puritani; Faust, conducted by Michel Plasson. *Address:* c/o Harrison/Parrott Ltd., 12 Penzance Place, London W11 4PA, England.

MESHIBOVSKY Alexander, b. 15 Apr 1949, Kharkov, Russia. Concert Violinist; Associate Professor. *Education:* Special School of Music for Gifted Children, Kharkov, 1955-65; Kharkov Conservatory, 1965-70; Masterclasses with Boris Goldstein, Moscow, 1971-74. *Career:* Concertmaster, Soloist, Moscow Chamber Orchestra, Russian Concert Agency, 1971-72; Soloist, Moscow Cocert Agency, 1972-74; Dozent, Innsbruck Conservatory, 1975-76; Concerts in many European Countries, USA; Associate Professor, East Tennessee State University, 1984-; Associate Professor, West Virginia University, 1988. *Compositions:* Paganini Variations; Transcriptions of works by Debussy, Gershwin, Rachmaninoff, and many others. *Hobbies:* Fine Arts; Sport. *Current Management:* Alpha Attractions Incorporated, N.Y. *Address:* 82-46 Lefferts Blvd., Apt 2D, Kew Gardens, NY 11415, USA.

MESPLÉ Mady, b. 7 Mar 1931, Toulouse, France. Singer (Soprano). *Education:* Studied in Toulouse and with Janine Micheau in Paris. *Debut:* Liege 1953, as Lakmé; Paris Opera-Comique from 1956, Opera from 1958, notably as the Queen of Night, Gounod's Juliette, Ophelia in Hamlet, Philine in Mignon, Donizetti's Norina and Lucia and Sophie in Der Rosenkavalier; Aix-en-Provence 1966, as Ariadne; Metropolitan Opera debut 1973, as Gilda; Guest appearances in Buenos Aires, Moscow, Rome and Naples; Concert performances include Schoenberg's Die Jakobsleiter, in London, conducted by Boulez. *Recordings:* Lakmé; Socrate by Satie; Werther; Zémire et Azore by Grétry; Rossini's Barbiere di Siviglia and Guillaume Tell; Operettas by Lecoq, Messager, Planquette, Hahn and Offenbach. *Address:* c/o Conservatoire National de Musique de Lyon, 3 Quai Chauveau, 69009 Lyon, France.

MESSENGER Thomas, b. 15 Oct 1938, Edinburgh, Scotland. University Head of Department and Senior Lecturer. m. Joan Helen Kelly, 22 Mar 1965, 2 sons. *Education:* ARCM, Piano Teacher, George Heriot's School, Edinburgh, Scotland, 1957; BMus, Hons, Organ Scholar, University of Glasgow, Scotland, 1961; ARCO, 1960; Fulbright Scholar, Washington University, USA, 1961-62; PhD, University of Wales, 1979. *Career:* Graduate Assistant, Washington University, USA, 1961-62; Lecturer, Royal Scottish Academy of Music, 1962-68; Conductor, New Consort of Voices, 1966-68; Monteverdi Singers, 1970-79; Examiner, Associated

Board of the Royal Schools of Music, 1969-; Lecturer, Music Department, University College of North Wales, 1968-79; Lecturer, 1979-83, Senior Lecturer and Administrative Head of Department of Music, 1990, Head of Department of Music, University of Surrey, England, 1992-; Various broadcasts as Conductor; Broadcast talk on John Lloyd's Missa O Quam Suavis, 1982; Broadcast performance of his edition of Lloyd's Mass, Taverner Choir, Conductor Andrew Parrott. *Publications:* Two Part Counterpoint from the Great Masters, 1970; *Editions:* Three Chansons for Three Recorders, 1971; Five Imitations for Three Recorders, 1971; Two Books of Canzonets for Four Recorders, 1971 and 1979. *Hobbies:* Hill walking; Opera; Swimming. *Address:* 5 St Mildred's Road, Guildford, Surrey, GU1 1TX, England.

MESSIEREUR Petr, b. 1937, Czechoslovakia. Violinist. *Education:* Studied at Prague Academy of Art. *Career:* Leader of the Talich String Quartet from 1972; Tours to most European countries, Egypt, Iraq, North America, Japan, Indonesia; Chamber Ensemble of the Czech Philharmonnic from 1975; Annual visits to France from 1976; Tours of Britain 1990-91, with concerts at the Wigmore Hall, appearances at the Bath and Bournemouth Festivals, Elizabeth Hall and on BBC2's Late Show, with Janáček's 2nd Quartet; Also played Beethoven's Quartet Op 74, the Brahms A minor, Smetana's D minor and works by Mozart in England; Festival appearances in Vienna, Besançon, Dijon, Helsinki, Amsterdam, Prague and Salzburg; Repertoire also includes works by Debussy, Bartók (complete works recorded by Supraphon), Shostakovich, Ravel and Dvořák. *Recordings include:* For the French companies Sarastro and Calliope, with the complete quartets of Beethoven; Albums for Collins Classics. *Honours include:* Grand Prix Charles Cros. *Address:* c/o Clarion/Seven Muses, 64 Whitehall Park, London N19 3TN, England.

MESSITER Malcolm, b. 1 Apr, Kingston, Surrey, England. Oboist. m. Christine Messiter. *Education:* Paris Conservatoire 1967; Royal College of Music, London; ARCM. *Debut:* Purcell Room, London, 1971. *Career:* Principal Oboe, BBC Concert Orchestra 1972-77; Solo concert engagements; Many appearances as chamber music player. *Honours include:* Royal College of Music Oboe Prize 1970. *Hobbies:* Model Aircraft; Winemaking. *Address:* 67 Crescent W., Hadley Wood, Herts EN4 OEQ, England.

MESTER Jorge, b. 10 Apr 1935, Mexico City, Mexico. *Education:* MA, Juilliard School of Music, New York, 1958; Studied with Leonard Bernstein, Berkshire Music Center, Tanglewood, summer 1955; Albert Wolff, the Netherlands. *Career:* Teacher of conducting, Juilliard School of Music, 1956-67; Music Director, Louisville Orchestra 1967-79; Music Director, Aspen (Colorado) Music Festival, 1970-; Musical Adviser and Principal Conductor, Kansas City (Missouri) Philharmonic Orchestra, 1971-74; Music Director, Casals Festival, Puerto Rico, 1979-; Teacher of conducting, Conductor of school ensembles 1980-; Chairman, conducting department 1984-87, Juilliard School; Music Director, Pasadena (California) Symphony Orchestra, 1984-; Guest conductor in North America and overseas; Chief Conductor of the West Australia Symphony and Principal Guest Conductor of the Adelaide Symphony Orchestra; Conducted Der Rosenkavalier at Sydney, 1992. *Recordings:* For Cambridge; Columbia; Composers Recordings Inc; Desto; Louisville; Mercury; Vanguard including Dallapiccola Piccola musica notturna, Hindemith Concert Music for viola and Kammermusik No. 2; Bruch's 2nd symphony; Ponderecki De Natura Sonoris; Shostakovich Hamlet music; Strauss's Six Songs Op. 68; Milhaud symphony No. 6; Martin Cello Cencerto. *Honour:* Naumburg Award, 1968; Alice M Distwon Award for conductors, 1985. *Address:* c/o The Juilliard School, Lincoln Center, New York, NY 10023, USA.

MÉSZÖLY Katalin,b. 1950, Hungary. Contralto. *Education:* Studied singing under Professor Jenö Sipos,

Budapest; Professor Paula Lindberg, Salzburg, Austria. *Career:* Budapest State Opera, 1976-; from debut, leading contralto of Budapest Opera. Performed title role of Carmen 129 times at Budapest and overseas; Azucena, Il trovatore; Amneris, Aida; Ulrica, Un Ballo in Maschera; Preiosilla, La forza del destino, Marfa in Khovanshchina; Juidith, Bluebeard's Castle, at La Scala 1981; Sang Britten's Mrs Herring at Budapest, 1988, Herodias in Salome, 1989; Ulrica (Un Ballo in Maschera) for Opéra de Montreal, 1990; Has appeared in oratorios including Verdi's Requiem, Mozart's Requiem. Gives song recitals. Guest performer in numerous countries and Operas including Milan Scala, Austria, West Germany, Spain, France, Mexico, Egypt and others. *Honour:* Liszt Prize. *Address:* Hungarian State Opera House, Népötarsaság utja 22, 0161 Budapest, Hungary.

METCALF John Philip, b. 13 Aug 1946, Swansea, Wales. Composer. m. Gillian Alexander, 14 Sept 1972, 2 sons, 1 daughter. *Education:* B Mus 1st class honours, University of Cardiff, 1967. *Career:* Commissions from Festivals of Cardiff, Swansea, and North Wales, Bath, and Cheltenham, England, and Frankfurt, Federal Republic of Germany, also from British Broadcasting Corporation, Gulbenkian Foundation, London Sinfonietta and Welsh National Opera; Currently Associate Artistic Director and Composer-in-Residence, Banff Centre, School of Fine Arts, Alberta, Canada. *Compositions:* Horn Concerto, 1972; PTOC, 1973; Auden Songs, 1973-77; 5 Rags for Charlotte, 1975; Ave Maria (choral), 1977; The Journey (opera), 1981; Music of Changes (orchestra), 1981; Two Carols, 1981; Clarinet Concerto, 1982; The Crossing (music theatre), 1984; The Boundaries of Time (cantata), 1985; Also music for dance, film and television; Piano Trio, 1988; Opera, Tornrak, 1989; Orchestra Variations, 1990. *Honours:* Gulbenkian Dance Fellow, 1973; UK/USA Bicentennial Arts Fellow, 1977-78; University of Wales Creative Arts Fellow, 1984. *Address:* Tŷ YforY, LlanFair Road, Lampeter, Dyfed, SA48 8JZ, Wales.

METCALFE John, b. 1964, England, Violist. *Education:* Studied at the Royal Northern College of Music with Simon Rowland-Jones, at the Guildhall School of Music and with Bruno Giuranna at the Berlin Hochschule. *Career:* Concerts in Europe, the USA and Japan and on Channel 4 and Canadian television; Principal viola with the Kreisler String Orchestra; Violist with the Duke String Quartet from 1985; Performances in the Wigmore Hall, Purcell Room, Conway Hall and throughout Britain; Tours to Germany, Italy, Austria and the Baltic States; South Bank series 1991, with Mozart's early quartets; Soundtrack for Ingmar Bergman documentary The Magic Lantern, Channel 4 1988; BBC Debut feature; Features for French television 1990-91, playing Mozart, Mendelssohn, Britten and Tippett; Brahms Clarinet Quintet for Dutch Radio with Janet Hilton; Live Music Now series with concerts for disadvantaged people; The Duke Quartet invites..... at the Derngate, Northampton 1991, with Duncan Prescott and Rohan O'Hara; Resident quartet of the Rydale Festival 1991; Residency at Trinity College, Oxford, tours to Scotland and Northern Ireland and concert at the Elizabeth Hall, 1991; Founded Factory Classical Label, 1988; Season 1993/94 with Duke Quartet at Casa Manilva Festival in Spain and Tour of Britain. *Recordings include:* Quartets by Tippett, Shostakovich and Britten (Third) for Factory Classics; Further albums with Collins Classics including music by Dvořák, Barber and Glass. *Honours include:* Awards include the Martin Musical Trust and South East Arts scholarships. *Current Management:* Lorraine Lyons. *Address:* 11 Wilmot Place, London, NW1 9JP, England.

METHVEN Jean, b. 1940, St Andrews, Fife, Scotland. Coloratura Soprano. m. Ian C Moore, 7 June 1980. *Education:* ARCM; LRAM; Studied with Ena Mitchell, Roy Henderson and Denis Dowling. *Debut:* Scottish Opera, 1965; Sadlers Wells Opera, 1969; English National Opera, 1974. *Career:* Appearances with Scottish Opera, Sadlers Wells Opera, ENO, including roles of the Queen of The Night in Mozart's The Magic Flute and Olympia in Offenbach's The Tales of

Hoffmann; concerts, oratorios and recitals. *Honours:* Sir James Caird Scholarships 1967-69. *Memberships:* Incorporated Society of Musicians; British Actors Equity. *Hobbies:* Gardening; Photography; Dress making. *Address:* Morven, The Ridgeway, High Wycombe, Bucks HP13 5BE, England.

METSÄLÄ Juha Einari, b. 23 May 1925, Räisälä, Finland. Conductor. m. Vappu Linnea Kuusiluoto. *Education:* BA, Helsinki University, 1953; Politices Magister, 1957; Sibelius Academy, Helsinki. *Career:* Conductor, orchestras in Kemi and Veitsiluoto, 1951-52, Jyväskylä, 1955-56, Kerava, 1959-, Järvenpää, 1965-; Visiting Conductor, Finland, Sweden. *Compositions include:* Works for voice and piano, solo instruments, chamber ensembles, choir; Editor, Pelimannisävelmiä III, 1973. *Honours:* Recipient of various composition prizes in academic competitions, 1951, 1953. *Membership:* Finnish Orchestra Conductors. *Hobbies:* Chess; Travel. *Address:* 17 Sepontie, 04200 Kerava, Finland.

METTERNICH Josef, b. 2 June 1915, Hermuhlheim, nr. Cologne, Germany. Singer (Baritone). *Education:* Studied in Berlin and Cologne. *Career:* Sang with the opera chorus at Cologne and Bonn; Solo debut 1945, as Tonio in Pagliacci at the Berlin Stadtische Oper; Covent Garden debut 1951, as the Dutchman; Metropolitan Opera 1953-56, as Carlo (La forza del destino), Amfortas, Wolfram, Kurwenal, Tonio, Luna, Renato and Amonasro; Further appearances in Paris, Vienna, Hamburg and Edinburgh; Bayerische Staatsoper Munich from 1954, notably as Johannes Kepler in the premiere of Hindemith's Die Harmonie der Welt (1957) and as Kothner in Die Meistersinger at the reopening of the Nationaltheater, 1963; Professor at the Cologne Musikhochschule from 1965, retired as singer 1971. *Recordings include:* Pagliacci (HMV); Hansel and Gretel (Columbia); Salome (Philips); Lohengrin, Fidelio and Der fliegende Holländer (Deutsche Grammophon).

METTERS Colin Raynor, b. 22 Jan. 1948, Plymouth, Devon, England. Conductor. m. Susan Furlong, 28 June 1980, 2 daughters. *Education:* ARCM, Violin and Conducting, Royal College of Music, 1966-71; Studied Conducting under Harvey Phillips, Vernon Handley and George Hurst, 1966-71; Liverpool Seminar under Sir Charles Groves, 1969; Master Classes with Nadia Boulanger, 1968. *Career:* Musical Director, Ballet Rambert, 1972-74; Conductor, Sadler's Wells Royal Ballet, 1974-82; Teacher of Conducting, Canford Summer School of Music, 1973-83; Musical Director, East Sussex Youth Orchestra, 1979-; Guest Conductor with London Schools Symphony Orchestra; British Youth Symphony Orchestra; National Centre for Orchestral Studies; Freelance Conductor, 1982-; Director of Conducting, Royal Academy of Music, 1983-; Conducted major UK, Provincial and BBC Orchestras; Conducted extensively abroad. *Recordings:* BBC Radio and Television and various. *Current Management:* Jean Meikle Management. *Address:* Arnside, 1 Carlton Road, Seaford, Sussex BN25 2LE, England.

METZ Catherine, b. 1965, USA. Violinist. *Education:* studied in New York. *Career:* Recitalist, Lincoln Center's Alice Tully Hall, 92nd Street 'Y' and appearances with major orchestras; Chamber Musician at the Santa Fe Festival, Spoleto Festival and Lockenhaus Kammermusikfest and the International Musicians Seminar in Prussia Cove; Co- founder, Orion Quartet and has given concerts at Washington DC's Kennedy Center, at Boston Gardner Museum and throughout the USA: Carnegie Hall recital, 1991 and as part of the Centenial Celebration tribute; Concerts at Turku Festival in Finland. *Address:* Orion Quartet, Ingpen & Williams Ltd, 14 Kensington Court, London W8 5DN, England.

MEUCCI Renato, b. 8 Nov 1958, Rome, Italy. Organologist; Musicologist. *Education:* Conservatorio S Cecilia, Rome; Conservatorio G Verdi, Milan. *Career:* Collaborator for didactic activities Museo Naz Degli Strumenti Musicali, Rome, 1983-87; Musical

Consultant, Radio Televisione Italiana (RAI), 1988; Currently Teacher, Conservatorio A Pedrollo, Vicenza, 1989- & Conservatorio G Verdi, Milano. *Publications:* Reviews: Rivista di Cultura Classica e Medioevale, 1983; Nuova Rivista Musicale Italiana, 1985; Nuova Rivista Musicale Italiana, 1986; Bonner Jahrbucher, 1987; Studi Verdiani, 1988-89; Galpin Society Journal, 1989; Basler Jahrbuch Für historische Musikpraxis. *Membership:* Societa Italiana di Musicologia (member of the Committee for Musical Iconography, 1989-1992). *Address:* via Neera 14, 20141 Milano, Italy.

MEVEN Peter, b. 1 Oct 1929, Cologne, Germany. Singer (Bass). *Education:* Studied at the Cologne Musikhochschule with Robert Blasius. *Debut:* Hagen, Westfalen, 1957, as Ferrando in Il Trovatore. *Career:* Sang in Mainz, Wiesbaden and Oldenburg from 1959; Deutsche Oper Berlin from 1964; Many guest apperances in Germany and engagements in Amsterdam, Basle, Lisbon, Stockholm, Moscow and San Francisco; Covent Garden London, Gurnemanz in Parsifal; Bayreuth 1971, as Fafner; Salzburg 1974, as Sarastro in Die Zauberflöte; Paris Opera as Daland in Der fliegende Holländer, 1981; Brussels 1983-85, as Kaspar in Der Freischütz and Pogner in Die Meistersinger, (also at the Metropolitan, 1976-77); Sang Lodovico in Schreker's Die Gezeichneten, for Austrian Radio; Sang Hagen and Hunding in the Ring at Geneva, 1988; King Heinrich in Lohengrin at Santiago, 1988; Hagen at the 1988 Holland Festival; Sang Rocco in Fidelio at Dusseldorf, 1990. *Recordings:* Sacred music by Bruckner; Der Freischütz (Deutsche Grammophon); Mathis der Maler by Hindemith (HMV); Fidelio (Eurodisc). *Address:* Deutsche Oper am Rhein, Heinrich Heine Allee 16, D-4000 Dusseldorf, Germany.

MEWES Karsten, b. 18 Mar 1959, Pirna, Saxony, Germany. Singer (Baritone). *Education:* Studied at the Hanns Eisler Musikhochschule Berlin. *Career:* Sang at the Potsdam Opera and the Komische Oper Berlin, 1985-88; Berlin Staatsoper from 1985, notably in the 1989 premiere of Graf Mirabeau by Siegfried Matthus; Guest appearances in Dresden and elsewhere as Mozart's Count, Masetto, Guglielmo and Papageno, Lotzing's Zar, Silvio, Escamillo and Hans Scholl in Udo Zimmermann's Die weisse Rose; concert repertoire includes works by Bach, Handel, Brahms and Fauré; Lieder recitals in Germany, Finland, Norway, Czechoslovakia, Poland and France. *Honours:* Competition prize winner at Zwickau, Verona, Hamburg, Rio de Janeiro, 1985-87. *Address:* c/o Berlin Staatsoper, Unter den Linden 7, 1086 Berlin, Germany.

MEYER Henry, b. 29 June 1923, Dresden, Germany. Violinist; College Professor. *Education:* Studied at Prague Music Academy, in Paris with George Enescu and at the Juilliard School with Ivan Galamian. *Career:* Co-founded the La Salle String Quartet at the Juillliard School, 1949; Many concerts featuring modern composers and the quartets of Beethoven; European debut 1954; Composers who have written for the ensemble include Hans Erich Apostel, Earle Brown, Henri Pousseur, Mauricio Kagel, György Ligeti, Penderecki and Witold Lutoslawski; Quartet-in-residence at Colorado College 1949-53, then Quartet-in-residence and Professor, Cincinnati College-Conservatory of Music; Quartet disbanded 1988. *Recordings include:* Works by Berg, Schoenberg, Webern and Zemlinsky; Beethoven's Late Quartets. *Address:* c/o Cincinnati College-Conservatory of Music, Cincinnati, OH 45221, USA.

MEYER Jurgen, b. 16 Mar 1933, Braunschweig, Germany. Professor of Acoustics. m. Ingeborg Voigt, 23 Nov 1962, 3 sons, 1 daughter. *Education:* Studied violin with Rudolf Sinramm; Dr of Electro Engineering and Acoustics at Technical University Braunschweig. *Debut:* Technical University Orchestra, Barunschweig, 1955. *Career:* Concertmaster, Braunschweigische Musikgesellschaft, 1966; Conductor, Chamber Orchestra Braunschweig, 1989; First performance of the divertimento for string orchestra by Giselher Klebe, 1991; American debut as conductor with the Weber

State University Symphony Orchestra, 1992. *Publications:* Akustik und musikalische Auffuhrungspraxis, 1972; Acoustics and the Performance of Music, 1978; Physikalische Aspekte des Geigenspiels, 1978; Also more than 100 publications on musical acoustics, roomacoustics and psychacoustics in scientific journals and congress reports. *Memberships:* Deutsche Gesellschaft fur Akustik; Acoustical Society of America; Catgut Acoustical Society. *Address:* Bergiusstrasse 2a, D-38116 Braunschweig, Germany.

MEYER Kerstin, b. 3 Apr 1928, Stockholm, Sweden. Opera Singer, Mezzo-Soprano, Principal. m. Björn G. Bexelius, 23 Dec 1974. *Education:* Royal Swedish Conservatory, Stockholm, 1948-50; Swedish College of Opera, 1950-52; Accademia Chigiana, Italy; Mozarteum, Austria. *Debut:* Royal Opera, Stockholm, 1952, as Azucena in Il Trovatore. *Career:* Orchestra Appearances with The Hallé Orchestra, London Philharmonic, Berlin and Vienna Philharmonics, La Suisse Romande, Santa Cecilia, Chicago, ABC, BBC, TV; Leading Roles in most of the important Houses and Festivals in Europe, N. and S. America, Far East, such as Royal Opera House, Covent Garden, Welsh and Scottish Operas, Glyndebourne and Edinburgh Festivals; La Scala, La Fenice and Santa Cecilia, Italy, Vienna and Salzburg, Austria, Munich, Berlin and Hamburg, Germany; Paris, Marseilles, Moscow, Tashkent, Tallin, Riga, USSR, Metropolitan Opera House, San Francisco, Santa Fe, USA; Teatro Colon, Argentina; Mexico City, Tokyo, Hong Kong; Sang in the first British performances of operas by Henze and Einem (Glyndebourne) and in the world premieres of operas by Goehr and Searle (Hamburg), Henze's The Bassarids (Salzburg 1966) and Ligeti's Le Grand Macabre (Stockholm 1978). *Recordings:* Operas, Recitals, etc. with von Karajan, Barbirolli, Solti, Hans Schmidt-Isserstedt, Sixten Ehrling. Appointed Principal of the Swedish State College of Opera (Operahögskolan), Stockholm, Sweden, 1984; Master Classes in Aldeburgh, Mozarteum. *Honours:* Royal Swedish Court Singer, 1963; Commander of the Order of the British Empire, 1985; Bundesverdienstkreutz 1 Klasse (Germany); Officer, Italian Order of Merit; Swedish Vasa Order; Swedish Litteris et Artibus. *Memberships:* Fellow, Royal Swedish Academy of Music, and Member of Board; President, The Royal Opera Houses Soloist Foundation; President, Jussi Bjoerling, Set Svanholm and Joel Berglund Funds; Board Member, Drottingholm Court Theatre; Board Member, Fondation Européene de la Culture, Stockholm. *Address:* Operahögskolan, Strandvägen 82, S-11527 Stockholm, Sweden.

MEYER Krzysztof, b. 11 Aug 1943, Cracow, Poland. Composer; Music Theorist; Pianist. 1 son, 1 daughter. *Education:* High School of Music, Cracow; American Conservatory, Fontainebleau. *Debut:* Warsaw, Autumn 1965. *Career:* Professor: High School of Music, Cracow, 1966-87; High School of Music, Cologne, 1987-; President, Union of Polish Composers, 1985- 88. *Compositions:* Stage works: Cyberiada, opera, premiere 1986; The Countess, ballet, premiere 1981; The Gamblers, completion of Shostakovich's opera, premiere 1984; The Maple Brothers, children's opera, premiere 1990; For orchestra: 4 symphonies, Fireballs, Hommage a Johannes Brahms, Musica incrostata, Carillon; 2 flute concerti; Concertos for piano, violin, violoncello, oboe, trumpet, saxophone; Double concerto for harp and cello; Symphony in Mozartean style, Canti Amadei for cello and orchestra; Caro Luigi for 4 cellos and orchestra; For choir and orchestra: Epitaphium Stanislaw Wiechowicz in memoriam, Symphony No 2; Symphonie d'Orphee, Symphony No 3; Liryc Triptych for tenor and chamber orchestra; Mass for choir and organ; Wjelitchalnaja for choir; Chamber works: Clarinet Quintet; Piano Quintet; 10 string quartets; Piano Trio; String Trio; For various ensembles: Concerto retro; Hommage a Nadia Boulanger; Quattro colori; Capriccio; Canzona and Sonata for cello and piano; For piano: 5 sonatas; 24 Preludes; Solo sonatas for: cello, cembalo, violin, flute; Fantasy for organ. *Recordings include:* String quartets 1-9; Hommage a Brahms; Symphonies 1-6; Canti Amadei; Canzona; Concerto retro: Piano Trio; Clarinet Quintet and others. *Publication:* Dimitri

Shostakovich, 1973. *Contributions to:* Various journals. *Honours:* Award, Minister of Culture and Art, Poland, 1973, 1976; Grand Prix, Prince Pierre de Monaco, 1970; Medal, Government of Brazil, 1975; Gottfried von Herder Preis, Wien, 1984; Award, Polish Composers Union, 1992; Jurzykowski Foundation New York, 1993. *Address:* Kurt Schumacher Str 10W-51, 51427 Bergisch Gladbach, Germany.

MEYER Rudolf, b. Muttenz, Swizerland. Organist. div. 3d. *Education:* Academy of Music, Zurich, 1967; Further studies with Marie-Claire Alain. *Debut:* Switzerland, 1963. *Career:* Organist, choirmaster, Burgendorf, Bern, 1966-71, 1971-76; Organist and Schoolteacher, Rapperswil; Organist, City Church Winterthur and Head Professor Organ, Conservatorium, 1976-; Recitalist, componist, organ-adviser, Jurymember. *Recordings include:* Bach, 1975; W Burkhard, 1980; Romantics, 1984; Baroques, 1984; Romantics, 1993; Founder, Capella Musica Loquens Zurich, 1980; Artistic Dirctor, Internationale Orgeltagungen Wintherthur festival, 1985, 1988, 1990, 1993. *Honours:* Carl Heinrich Ernst Kunstpreis, 1987. *Hobbies:* Mountain walks; Railway-trips; Steamships. *Address:* Mockentobel 14, CH-8400 Winterthur, Switzerland.

MEYER-WOLF Frido, b. 22 Apr 1934, Potsdam, Germany. (Bass- baritone). *Education:* Studied in Berlin, Paris and Hamburg. *Debut:* Straslund 1955 as Mozart's Figaro. *Career:* Appearances at Trier, Hamburg, Kassel, Kiel and the Deutsche Oper Berlin; Opera Comique Paris, 1963, in the premiere of Menotti's The Last Savage; Aix and Spoleto Festivals, 1964, as Ochs in Der Rosenkavalier, Marseilles from 1961, Brussells, 1965, Monte Carol, 1967-94, Nice, 1962-89, Lausanne, 1987; Decorated: Chevalier des Arts et Lettres by the French Government, 1985; direction of open-air theatre Jean Cocteau Cap d'All near Monaco, created and conducted a new chamber orchestra from 1989; Other roles include parts in operas by Verdi, Wagner, Puccini, Strauss, Rossini, Smetana and Moussorgsky; Sang in Wozzeck, Samson et Dallia, Schloß: Reimann, first performance, 1992 at Deutsche Oper, Berlin; Frequent concert appearances. *Current Management:* M Kollo, Lietzensee Lifer 8, 14057 Berlin. Concert Agency: J Jochimsen, Luzerner Str. 14b, 12205 Berlin. *Address:* c/o Deutsche Oper Berlin, Bielerstrasse 9, 13407 Berlin, Germany.

MEYEROWITZ Jan, b. 23 Apr 1913, Beslau, Germany. Composer. *Education:* Studied in Berlin with Zemlinsky and in Rome with Respighi and Casella. *Career:* Resident in Belgium, 1938-46; Naturalized US citizen, 1951; Taught at the Berkshire Music Center, Tanglewood, 1948-51 and at Brooklyn, 1954-61 and City, 1962-80 Colleges of the City University of New York. *Compositions include:* Operas, The Barrier, 1950: Eastward in Eden 1951; Simoon, 1950; Bad Boys in School, 1953; Esther 1957; Port Town, 1960; Godfather Death, 1961; Die Doppelgangerin 1967; Orchestral: Silesian Symphony 1957; Symphony Midrash Esther 1957; Flemish Overture, 1959; Flute Concerto, 1962; Oboe concerto, 1963; Sinfonia brevissima, 1965; 6 pieces of Orchestra, 1967; 7 pieces for orchestra, 1972; 6 songs for soprano and orchestra, 1979; Cantatas and other choral music; Chamber: Woodwind Quintet, 1954; String Quartet, 1955; Violin Sonata, 1960; Flute Sonata, 1961; Piano Sonata, 1958; Songs. *Publications:* Monograph on Schoenberg, 1967 and Der echte Judische Witz Berlin, 1971. *Address:* ASCAP, ASCAP Building, One Lincoln Plaza, NY 10023, USA.

MEYERS Anne Akiko, b. 1970, San Diego, California. Violinist. *Education:* Indiana University with Josef Gingold; University of Southern California Community School with Alice and Eleanore Schoenfeld; Dorothy DeLay and Masao Kawasaki at the Juilliard School, New York. *Career:* Debut as concerto soloist aged 7; later appearances with the Los Angeles Philharmonic, the New York Philharmonic conducted by Mehta and the New York String Orchestra, at Carnegie Hall; participation in Aspen Music Festival, Colorado, and

Orford Festival in Montreal; Far East engagements with the Japan Philharmonic and the NHK Symphony Orchestra; Subject of TV documentaries Beyond the Gift of Music and Teenage Virtuoso; played in Tanglewood, Aspen, Britt, Orford and Bowdoin festivals; toured with Leonard Slatkin and St Louis Symphony; appeared on TV, With John Williams and Boston Pops; played with Montreal, Boston, St. Louis, Philadelphia, Toronto, Swedish Radio, Moscow and Belgium Radio; Orchestra de Paris and Jerusalem Symphonies and Orchestras; Also toured with Moscow Philharmonic, as well as recitals in Chicago, New York, Cincinnati and Japan. *Recordings:* Concertos by Barber and Bruch with the Royal Philharmonic Orchestra and Christopher Seaman and French sonata disc; exclusive RCA Red Seal artist; Lalo Symphonie Espagnole & Bruch Scottish Fantasy RPO/Lopez-Cobos and Cesar Franck & Richard Strauss Sonatas. *Honours:* Epstein Scholarship of the Boys Clubs of America; Philharmonic Society Competition; Youngest to sign with Young Concert Artists; Sole recipient of Avery Fisher Career Grant, 1993. *Current Management:* Jasper Parrott, London; ICM, New York; Japan Arts, Tokyo. *Address:* c/o Harrison/Parrott Ltd., 12 Penzance Place, London W11 4PA, England.

MEYERSON Janice, b. 1950 Omaha, Nebraska, USA. Mezzo-soprano. m. Raymond Scheindlin, 5 Apr 1986. *Education:* BA, Washington University, St. Louis, Missouri, 1972; MM, New England Conservatory, 1975; Fellowship, Berkshire Music Center (Tanglewood), 1976-77. *Career:* Carmen (title role), New York City Opera and Théâtre Royal de la Monnaie, Brussels; Amneris in Aida, Teatro Colón, Buenos Aires and Frankfurt Opera; Santuzza in Cavalleria Rusticana, New York City Opera; Judith in Bluebeard's Castle, New York Philharmonic and Palacio de Bellas Artes, Mexico City; Brangaene in Tristan and Isolde, Leonard Bernstein conducting Philadelphia Orchestra; Soloist, Mahler's 3rd Symphony, American Symphony, Carnegie Hall; Soloist, Boston Symphony, Milwaukee Symphony, Minnesota Orchestra, New Orleans Symphony, National Symphony, Dallas Symphony, Washington Opera, Houston Grand Opera, Montreal Opera, Opera Company of Philadelphia, Aspen Festival, Spoleto USA, Marlboro, Tanglewood, Wolf Trap; Soloist with Schleswig-Holstein Music Festival, Deutsche Oper Berlin, Moscow State Symphony Orchestra. *Address:* 420 Riverside Drive, Apt. GC, New York, NY 10025, USA.

MEYFARTH Jutta, b. 1933, Germany. Singer (Soprano). *Career:* Sang at Basle in 1955; Aachen Opera 1956-59; Member of Frankfurt Opera from 1959; La Scala Milan debut 1960; Maggio Musicale Florence 1961, as Elsa in Lohengrin; Bayreuth Festival 1962-64, as Freia, Gutrune and Sieglinde; Munich Opera 1965, as Donna Anna; Guest appearances in Buenos Aires, Brussels, Rome, London, Lisbon, Athens, Lyon and Antwerp; Other roles include Wagner's Isolde, The Empress in Die Frau ohne Schatten, Aida and Martha in Tiefland.

MEYLAN Jean, b. 22 Dec. 1915, Geneva, Switzerland. Conductor. m. Elisabeth Buscarlet (deceased 1985), 1 son, 1 daughter. *Education:* Licentiate in Law, University of Geneva; Conservatories, Geneva & Lausanne; Private study of music, Switzerland & France, with Felix Weingartner, Carl Schuricht, Paul Kletski, Eugène Bigot. *Debut:* With Collegium Musicum, Geneva, 1941. *Career:* First guest appearances: Paris (Lamoureux), France; Florence, Italy; Cologne, Germany with Gürzenich Orchestra. Chief conductor, Radio Orchestra of Cologne (Nordwestfunk Köln), Geneva Chamber Orchestra, Radio Orchestra of Beromunster, 1954-56; Choirmaster/Conductor, Geneva Opera House, 1958; Musical leader, Opera House, 1962-; Permanent guest conductor, Grand-Théâtre de Genève; Guest conductor with numerous orchestras in Europe, Asia and Latin America; Appeared with Suisse Romande Orchestra, Geneva. *Recordings:* Beethoven, Schubert, Falla, Prokofiev. *Contributions to:* Various anthologies & journals including: Book Ecrits sur la Musique, I, 1993. *Honours:* Arnold Bax Memorial Medal, 1958; Dvořák Medal, 1974; Medal Philharmony, Poznan, Poland,

1980; *Memberships:* Chairman, Geneva Competition for Young Performers, 1969-, Vice-Chairman since 1976; Member of Honour, 1993; AMS; Rotary Club. *Hobbies:* Walking; Reading; Mountaineering. *Address:* 12 route de Drize, CH-1227 Geneva, Switzerland.

MEZO Laszlo, b. 1940, Hungary. Cellist. *Education:* Studied at the Franz Liszt Academy, Budapest. *Career:* Cellist of the Bartók Quartet from 1977; Performances in nearly every European country and tours of Australia, Canada, Japan, New Zealand and the USA; Festival appearances at Adelaide, Ascona, Aix, Venice, Dubrovnik, Edinburgh, Helsinki, Lucerne, Menton, Prague, Vienna, Spoleto and Schwetzingen; Tour of Britain 1986 including concerts at Cheltenham, Dartington, Philharmonic Hall, Liverpool, RNCM, Manchester and the Wigmore Hall; Tours of Britain 1988 and 1990, featuring visits to the Sheldonian Theatre, Oxford, Wigmore Hall, Harewood House and Birmingham; Repertoire includes standard classics and Hungarian works by Bartók, Durkó, Bozay, Kadosa, Soproni, Farkas, Szabo and Lang. *Recordings include:* Complete quartets of Mozart, Beethoven and Brahms; Major works of Haydn and Schubert (Hungaraton); Complete quartets of Bartók (Erato). *Honours:* with members of Bartók Quartet: Kossuth Prize; Outstanding Artists of the Hungarian People's Republic 1981; UNESCO/IMC Prize 1981. *Address:* c/o Ingpen and Williams Ltd, 14 Kensington Court, London W8 5DN, England.

MICHAEL Audrey, b. 11 Nov 1949, Geneva, Switzerland. Singer (Soprano). *Education:* Studied with father, Jean-Marie Auberson, and in Milan and Hamburg. *Career:* Sang with the Hamburg Staatsoper, 1976-81, Deutsche Oper am Rhein Dusseldorf, 1981-86; Guest appearances throughout Europe; Roles have included Gluck's Amor in Orpheus, Ilia (Idomeneo), Mozart's Pamina, Susanna, Countess and Papagena, Elvira (L'Italiana in Algeri), Adina, Lauretta, Zdenka, Melisande and Elisabeth Zimmer in Elegy for Young Lovers by Henze; Sang at Hamburg in the premieres of Kommen und gehen by Heinz Holliger, 1978, William Ratcliff by Ostendorf, 1982 and Jakob Lenz by Wolfgang Rihm, 1979; Theatre Municipal Lausanne, 1991, as Sextus in Gluck's La Clemenza di Tito; Concert engagements in the Baroque and modern repertory throughout Switzerland and in Berlin, Stuttgart, Paris, Lisbon and Buenos Aires. *Recordings include:* Monteverdi Orfeo, L'Enfant et les Sortilèges, Masses by Schubert and Beethoven; Rigoletto, Luisa Miller and Parsifal; Monteverdi Ballo delle Ingrate and Vespers of 1610. *Address:* c/o Opera de Lausanne, PO Box 3972, CH-1002 Lausanne, Switzerland.

MICHAELS-MOORE Anthony, b. 1957, Essex, England. Singer (Baritone). *Education:* Studied at Newcastle University with Denis Matthews and at the Royal Scottish Academy; Further study with Eduardo Asquez. *Career:* Principal Baritone at Covent Garden from 1987, in Jenůfa, Boris Godunov, Turandot, Rigoletto, Pagliacci, Der Freischütz and La Bohème; English National Opera from 1987, as Zurga, Marcello, and the Count in a new production of Figaro (1991); For Opera North has sung Escamillo, Creon (Oedipus Rex) and Figaro; Concert appearances in Bizet's Ivan IV and Massenet's Thais for Chelsea Opera Group; Buxton Festival in Don Quixote by Conti; US debut with Philadelphia Opera 1989 as Guglielmo, followed by the Missa Solemnis in Los Angeles (1990); Other appearances as Germont for Opera North, Falke and the Speaker - Sonora at Covent Garden and Rossini's Figaro at Barcelona; Canadian Opera Company at Toronto as Guglielmo 1991; sang Posa in a new production of Don Carlos for Opera North, 1993; Concert engagements include Oedipus Rex at the Edinburgh Festival and Mehul's Uthal conducted by Neeme Järvi; London concert debut in the Duruflé Requiem at the Elizabeth Hall; L'Enfance du Christ at the Cheltenham Festival and Mahler 8 with the Philharmonia Orchestra; Also sings The Kingdom, Belshazzar's Feast, Carmina Burana, Rossini's Stabat Mater, Elijah and The Creation; Sang as Don Fernando in the world premiere production of Gerhard's The Duenna at Madrid, 1992; Season 1992/93 as Marcello at Covent Garden and in a Rossini Concert at Turin; opened the 1993-94 season at La Scala as Licinius in La Vestale by Spontini. *Honour:* Joint winner, Luciano Pavarotti Opera Company of Phildelphia Competition. *Address:* John Coast Ltd, 31 Sinclair Road, London W14 ONS, England.

MICHALKO Jan Vladimir, b. 6 May 1951, Myslenice, Slovakia. Musician; Concert Organist; Teacher. m. Marta Kacianova, 7 June 1985. 1 son, 1 daughter. *Education:* University of Munich, 1972; Conservatoire, Bratislava, 1975; Graduate School for the Performing Arts, Mus.M., 1979 (with distinction). *Career:* Internal Postgraduate 1980-83, Senior Assistant Lecturer 1983-90, Associate Professor, 1991-, School of Performing Arts; Teacher, Conservatoire, Bratislava, 1983-; Instructor in Organ Improvisation, Conservatoire Bratislava; Senior Organist at the Lutheran Great Church in Bratislava; Concerts in Finland, Austria, Hungary, Rumania, Poland, USA, Switzerland and France; Member, Baroque quartet, Bratislava; Chamber Cembalo-player; Appearances on Czechoslovak Television, Gala concert, 1987, 1988; International Music Festival, MELOS-ETHOS, Bratislava, 1991; International Music Festival, Atelier 90, Praha, 1993; Recitals; Soloist with Slovak Philharmonic, 1985, 1987; State Philharmonic Kosice, 1989; Slovak Chamber Orchestra, 1988. *Composition:* Scenic music for theatre plays, Theatre Nitra, Bratislava. *Recordings:* 6 LP records and 6 CD for Opus. *Publication:* Textbook Hudobna vychova (Musical education), 1987. *Current Management:* Slovkoncert. *Address:* Konventna 11, 811 03 Bratislava, Slovakia.

MICHALOWSKI Kornel, b. 23 Feb. 1923, Poznań, Poland. Music Bibliographer; Music Librarian; Musicologist. m. Helena Mindak, 30 June 1948, 2 sons, 1 daughter. *Education:* Studies in Musicology with Adolf Chybinski, Poznań University, 1947-51; Doctor in Musicology, Jagellonian University, Cracow, 1977. *Career:* Librarian 1945-86, Head of Music Department, 1950-81, Deputy Director 1981-84, Poznań University Library. *Publications Include:* Opery Polskie, 1954; Bibliografia Polskiego Piśmiennictwa Muzycznego, 1955 and supplements 1964, 1978; Karol Szymanowski: Katalog Tematyczny Dziel i Bibliografia, 1967; Bibliografia Chopinowska 1849-1969, 1970; Muzyka w Czasopismach polskich, 1919-1939, 1979; Katalogi Tematyczne: historia i teoria, 1980; Karol Szymanowski: Bibliography and Discography, 1993. *Contributions to:* Numerous music journals. *Honours:* Golden Cross of Merit, 1972; Cultural Award, City of Poznań, 1971; Knight's Cross of Polish Rebirth Order, 1985; Musical Award, Polish Composers Union, 1987. *Memberships:* Musicological Section, Polish Composers Union; Music Libraries Section, National Group of IAML, Polish Librarians Association; Research Council, Chopin Society, Warsaw. *Address:* Orzeszkowej 9/11, 60-778 Poznań, Poland.

MICHALOWSKA Krystyna, b. 13 July 1946, Vilnius, Poland. Singer (Mezzo-soprano). *Education:* Studied in Gdansk. *Debut:* Bydgoszcz 1970, as Azucena. *Career:* Engagements at Szczecin, Poznan and Gdansk; Guest appearances in Germany, Bulgaria, Rumania, Russia and Czechkoslovakia; Appearances at Bielfeld and elsewhere in Germany from 1980, as Leonora in La Favorita, Carmen, Eboli, Lady Macbeth, Ulrica, Fides, Rosina, Konchakovna, Olga and Larina in Eugene Onegin, Dalila, Laura in La Gioconda, Sara in Roberto Devereux and the Nurse in Die Frau ohne Schatten; Bielefeld 1991, in Yerma by Villa-Lobos, as Ortrud and in the premier of Katharin Blum by Tilo Medek; Frequent concert appearances. *Address:* c/o Stadtisches Buhnen, Brunnenstrasse 3, 4800 Bielefeld 1, Germany.

MICHAUD Neil J., b. 14 Oct. 1927, Edmunston, New Brunswick, Canada. Professor of Music. m. Anna E. Malenfant, 25 June 1978. *Education:* BA, Université Saint-Joseph, 1949; MA, Music Education Columbia Teacher's College, NY, USA, 1964. *Career:* NB and NS Tour Orchestra, Les Chanteurs Du Mascaret, 1966, 1967; Many radio and TV appearances on Trans-Canada Network, a capella series on French CBC Network. *Recordings:* Folklore Canadien, 1959; Tournée Trans-Canada, 1960; The University of Moncton Male Choir, 1968; The Voyageur and Their Song, 1967; En Montant la Riviére, 1974; La Chorale de l'Université de Moncton, 1979. *Publication:* The Acadians of the Maritimes: Thematic Studies, 1982. *Address:* Université De Moncton, New Brunswick, Canada E1A 3E9.

MICHEL Winfried, b. 21 Apr 1948, Fulda, Germany. Flautist; Composer. *Education:* Studied at the Royal Conservatoire as a student of Frans Bruggen. *Debut:* Kassel Palais bellevue, 1974. *Career:* Solo performances at Flandern Festival, Concertgebouw Amsterdam, Tage fur Alte Musik Kassel, and Radio BRT Bruxelles, BBC London and Radio Hilversum. *Compositions include:* Klaviertrio, 1990; TU-I for recorder and harpsichord; Horen and Sehen for violoncello; 20 volumes of chamber music. *Recordings include:* Corelli and Vivaldi Concerts; Simonetti, trio sonatas; Kasseler Avantgarde with own compositions; Telemann, 4 sonatas. *Publications:* JJ Quantz, Solfeggi, 1980; V Eych, 1982; J Haydn, first publication of 6 sonatas, 1993. *Honours:* Coupe du Conseil d'lle de France, 1992. *Memberships:* European Recorder Teachers Association; Professor, Akademie Kassel and the Conservatoire in Munster. *Hobbies:* Mountain tours. *Address:* Wiener Str 65a, D-48145 Munster, Germany.

MICHELANGELI Arturo Benedetti, b. 5 Jan. 1920, Brescia, Italy. Concert Pianist. *Education:* Milan Conservatory 1930-33, with Giuseppe Anfossi. *Career:* Professor of Piano at the Martini Conservatory Bologna 1939-41; British debut 1946; US debut 1948; Concert tours of South America, Italy, Japan and South Africa; Master classes in Arezzo, Siena and Lugano; 1964 founded International Pianists' Academy Brescia; Tour of USSR 1964; Repertoire includes music by Ravel, Debussy and Liszt; Teacher at summer school in the Villa Schifanoia, Florence, from 1973; Beethoven and Chopin recitals at the Barbican Centre, London, 1990. *Honours include:* Winner, Grand Prix of Geneva 1939; Gold Medal of Italian Republic. *Memberships include:* Academician, Academy of Santa Cecilia, Rome; Cherubini Academy, Florence.

MICHELOW Sybil, b. 12 Aug 1925, Johannesburg, South Africa. Contralto. m. Derek Goldfoot, 18 Apr 1950. *Education:* Music Diploma, Witwaterstrand University, S.A; Private studies with Franz Reizensten and Mary Jarred. *Debut:* London, 1958. *Career:* Concert performances in UK and abroad, especially of Handel's Messiah; Frequent radio and television appearances, notably in Rule Britannia at the Last Night of the Proms; Singing instructor, Royal Academy of Dramatic Art, 1956-. *Compositions include:* Incidental music for RADA production of Brecht plays Chalk Circle and Mother Courage, Children's stories with music, South African Broadcasting Corp. *Recordings include:* Music of Court Homes, vol 4 and Bach Cantatas 78 and 106; Bliss Pastoral; Dallapicola Sicut Umbra. *Memberships:* Royal Society of Musicians of Great Britain, Governor, 1982-1985, and 1988-93; Incorporated Society of Musicians. *Hobbies:* Piano in chamber music groups; Calligraphy. *Address:* 50 Chatsworth Road, London NW2 4DD, Engalnd.

MICHIELS Jan Prosper, b. 10 Oct. 1966, Izegam, Belgium. Solo Concert Pianist. m. Inge Spinette, 16 Aug 1991. *Education:* Izegem College; Royal Conservatory, Brussels, 1984-88; With Hans Leygraf, Hochschule der Kunste, Berlin. *Career* Many recordings for Radio 3, Belgium; Currently Professor of Piano, Royal Conservatory, Brussels. *Recordings:* Recital, Brahms, Debussy, Goeyvaerts, Ligeti, Bartók, Co-Production Gemeentekrediet-Philharmonische Vereniging, 1992; Beethoven and Poulenc with Wind Quintet Quintessens, 1992. *Honours:* Prizewinner, serveral competitions including Queen Elizabeth Competition, Brussels, 1991. *Hobby:* Contemporary art. *Address:* Klaarhaagstraat 27, B-9310 Meldert (Aalst), Belgium.

MICHNIEWSKI Wojciech, b. 4 Apr 1947, Lódź, Poland. Conductor; Composer. *Education:* Conducting, Theory of Music, Composition, Warsaw Academy of Music, 1966-72; Honours degree with distinction, 1972. *Career:* Assistant Conductor, 1973-76, Conductor, 1976-79, Warsaw National Philharmonic Orchestra; Artistic Director, The Grand Opera Theatre, Lodz, 1979-81; Musical Director, Modern Stage, Warsaw Chamber Opera, 1979-83; Principal Guest Conductor, Polish Chamber Orchestra and Sinfonia Varsovia, 1984-; Conductor, concerts in most European countries, South America, Asia; Appeared West Berlin Philharmonic Hall, La Scala, Milan, Teatro Colon in Buenos Aires, etc; Participant in numerous international festivals including: Steyrischer Herbst, Graz, Austria; International May Festival, Barcelona, Spain; Recontres Musicales, Metz, France; International May Festival, Wiesbaden, Germany; Bemus Festival, Belgrade, Yugoslavia; Dimitria Festival, Thessaloniki, Greece; Warsaw Autumn Festival; Wratisalvia Cantans Music Festival; International Biennale, East Berlin; Polish Chamber Orchestra and Sinfonia Varsovia, 1984-86; General and Artistic Director, The Poznan Philharmonic Orchestra, 1987-; Others. *Recordings:* Gramophone records; CBS Japan; EMI; Pavane Olympia; Polskie Nagrania Muza; Polton; Tonpress; Radio and TV recordings. *Hobbies:* Climbing; Skiing; Sailing; Painting. *Current Management:* Polish Artists Agency PAGART. *Address:* ul Braci Zauskich 3/77, 01 773 Warsaw, Poland.

MIDORI,b. 25 Oct 1971, Osaka, Japan. Violinist. *Education:* Studied with her mother, Setsu Goto, and at Juilliard with Dorothy DeLay, Jens Ellerman and Yang-Ho Kim. *Debut:* Gala concert with the New York Philharmonic, 1982. *Career:* Appearances at the White House, Kennedy Center, Carnegie Hall, the Musikverein, the Philharmonie in Berlin and other major centres; Orchestras include the Berlin Philharmonic, the Boston and Chicago Symphony Orchestras, London Symphony, the Orchestre de Paris, Israel Philharmonic and the Philadelphia Orchestra; Conductors have included Abbado, Ashkenazy, Barenboim, Bernstein (Serenade), Mehta and Rostropovitch; has also appeared at the Concertgebeow, Amsterdam; Founded the Midori Foundation to promote the learning and education of classical music to children of all ages all over the world; Played the Tchaikovsky Concerto on debut at the London Proms, 1993. *Recordings include:* Dvořák Concerto with the New York Philharmonic; Complete Paganini Caprices; Bartók's Concertos with the Berlin Philharmonic and a live recording of Carnegie Hall Recital Debut, (Sony Classical); CD, Encore, released by Sony Classical. *Address:* c/o ICM Artists, 40 West 57th Street, New York, NY 10019, USA.

MIGENES Julia, b. 13 Mar. 1949, New York, USA. Singer (Soprano). *Education:* New York High School for Performing Arts and the Juilliard School; Cologne with Gisela Ultman. *Career:* Appeared on Broadway and at the New York City Opera from 1965 (debut in The Saint of Bleecker Street); Vienna Volksoper 1973-78: roles included Mozart's Despina, Blonchen and Susanna, Schmidt's Esmeralda, Strauss's Sophie and Olympia in Les Contes d'Hoffmann; Metropolitan Opera from 1979, in Mahagonny, Lulu, Pagliacci and La Bohème; Geneva Opera 1983 as Salome; Vienna Staatsoper as Lulu; TV appearances in Germany and on Channel 4, England; Appeared in Francesco Rossi's 1984 film of Carmen; Covent Garden debut 1987, as Manon; sang Tosca at Earl's Court, London, 1991; Concert with Domingo at Buenos Aires, 1992. *Recordings:* Notre Dame; Videos of Carmen and La Voix Humaine. *Honours include:* Golden Bambi awards from German TV, 1980, 1981. *Address:* c/o Stafford Law Associates, 26 Firlands, Weybridge, Surrey KT13 OHR, England.

MIHÁLY András, b. 6 Nov. 1917, Budapest, Hungary. Composer and Professor of Chamber Music. m. (2) Klára Pfeifer 1951, (3) Csilla Varga, 2 sons, 2 daughters. *Education:* Berzsenyi Gymnasium and F. Liszt Conservatory of Music, Budapest. *Career:* First Violoncello Solo in orchestra of Budapest Opera House 1946-47; General Secretary of Budapest Opera 1948-49; Professor of Chamber Music, F. Liszt Music Academy, Budapest 1950-; Reader of Contemporary Music, Musical Department, Hungarian Broadcasting Corporation 1959-; Leader New Hungarian Chamber Ensemble; Director, Hungarian State Opera 1978-; Leader of Chamber Music Class and Pupils Orchestra, Liszt Academy, 1987. *Compositions include:* Concerto for Violoncello and Orchestra 1953; Concerto for Pianoforte and Orchestra 1954; Fantasy for Wind Quintet and String Orchestra 1955; Songs on the Poems of James Joyce 1958; Concerto for Violin and Orchestra 1959; String Quartet 1960; Symphony 1962; Together and Alone (Opera in 2 Acts) 1965; Musica per 15 1974; String quartett No. 3 1975; Musica per Viola 1975. *Honours:* Kossuth Prize 1955; Erkel Prize 1950, 1965; Liszt Prize 1972, Labour Order of Merit (Golden Degree) 1970, Eminent Artist of Hungary, For Socialist Hungary, Order of Merit 1977. *Address:* Vérhalom tér 9b, 1025 Budapest II, Hungary.

MIHELCIC Pavel, b. 8 Nov. 1937, Novo mesto, Yugoslavia. Composer. m. Majda Lovse, 10 Apr. 1965, 2 daughters. *Education:* Diploma 1963, Special Class 1967, Academy of Music, Ljubljana. *Career:* Professor, Conservatory of Music, 1982-; Manager, Department of Smyphonic Music, Ljubljana Broadcasting Corporation, 1982-. *Compositions Include:* Orchestral works: Bridge for strings; Asphalt ballet; Concerto for horn and orchestra; Sinfonietta; Musique Funèbre for violin and orchestra; Chamber works: Limite; Blow Up; Take-off for piano; Sonatine; Sonata 80; Chorus, 1, 2, 3, 4, 5, 10, 13; Games and Reflections; Double Break; Published by Edition DSS, Ljubljana and Edition Peters, Leipzig; Recorded; Quinta Essentia for brass quintet; Timber-line for chamber orchestra; Exposition and Reflections for 9 horns; Stop-time for horn and chamber orchestra; Team for woodwind quintet; Introduction and Sequences for orchestra; Scenes From Bela Krajina; Fading Pictures; Snow of First Youth for orchestra. *Contributions to:* Standing music critic, Delo, Ljubljana; Zvuk, Sarajevo. *Honours:* Preseren Prize, 1979; Zupancic Prize, 1984. *Memberships:* President, Slovenian Composers Society, 1984-. *Address:* Melikova ul 10, 61108 Ljubljana, Slovenia.

MIKI Minoru, b. 16 Mar 1930, Tokushima, Shikoku, Japan. Composer. *Education:* Studied composition with Ifukube at the Tokyo National University of Fine Arts and Music, 1951-55. *Career:* Founder, Ensemble Nipponia, later Pro Musica Nippomia, 1964 (ensemble of traditional Japanese instruments; Foreign tours with the Ensemble from 1972; Founded the music- theatre ensemble Utaza, 1986; Founded the multi-culture ensemble YUI Ensemble, 1990. *Compositions include:*Eurasian Trilogy including symphony for Two Worlds, 1969-81; Shunkin - Sho, opera in 3 acts, Tokyo 1975; Ada (An Actor's Revenge), opear in 2 acts, English Music Theatre at the Old Vic, London, 1979; The Monkey Poet, folk opera, 1983; Joruri, opera in 3 acts, St Louis, 1985; Yomigaeru, musical - opera, Tokyo, 1989; Wakahime, opera in 3 acts, Okayama 1991; Shizuka and Yoshitsune, opera in 3 acts, Kamakura, 1993. *Address:* 1-11-6 Higashi Nogama, Komae-shi, Tokyo 201, Japan.

MIKULAS Peter, b. 1955, Czechoslovakia. Singer (Bass). *Education:* Studied at the College of Music and Drama in Bratislava with Viktoria Stracenska. *Career:* Soloist with the Slovak National Theatre in Bratislava 1978-; Roles have included Kecal in The Bartered Bride, Dulcamara, Gremin, Raimondo, Fiesco (Simon Boccanegra), Don Alfonso and Sarastro; Guest appearances with the National Theatre Prague, the Berlin Staatsoper and other leading European theatres; Concert engagements with the Czech and Slovak Philharmonic Orchestras and at the Bratislava, Prague Spring and Carinthian Summer Festivals; Has sung in Vienna, Salzburg, Leipzig, Berlin, Tokyo, Lisbon, Madrid, Liverpool and most Italian centres. *Honours:* Prizewinner at the 1977 Antonin Dvořák International Singers Competition, Carlsbad; Tchaikovsky Competition, Moscow, 1982; Mirjam Helin Competition,

Helsinki, 1984; Prize of the Union of Slovak Performing Artists for appearance in Suchon's Svatopluk. *Address:* Music International, 13 Ardilaun Road, London N5 2QR, England.

MILAN Susan, b. 1947, England. Flautist. m. 2 sons. *Education:* Junior Exhibitioner, Royal College of Music; Studied with John Francis and Geoffrey Gilbert at the Royal College of Music, and attended the Marcel Moyse Masterclasses in Switzerland; Graduated from the Royal College of Music with Honours. *Career:* Principal Flute of the Bournemouth Sinfonietta, 1968, 1972; Principal Flute of the Royal Philharmonic Orchestra, 1974-1982; Developed solo career; Many commissions, the latest, 1992 Concerto by Robert Simpson; Tours world wide as soloist and recitalist; Records for the Chandos label; Runs two masterclass courses. Ensembles: London Sonata Group; Instrumental Quintet of London; Recital duo with Ian Brown. *Current Management:* Represented by Upbeat Management. *Address:* 18, St Albans Avenue, Weybridge, Surrey KT13 8EN, England.

MILANOVA Stoika, b. 5 Aug. 1945, Plovdiv, Bulgaria. Concert Violinist. *Education:* Studied with father Trendafil Milanov and with David Oistrakh at the Moscow Conservatory. *Career:* Appearances with principal UK orchestras from 1970; Engagements in most European countries; Yamiurti Nippon Symphony Orchestra, Japan, 1976; Concerts with the Hallé Orchestra and at the Hong Kong Festival; Tour for Australian Broadcasting Commission 1976; US and Canadian debuts 1978; tours of Eastern Europe 1975/ 86; Duo recitals with Radu Lupu and the late Malcolm Frager. *Recordings:* Balkanton (Bulgaria), some released by Harmonia Mundi, including the complete Brandenburg Concerts with Karl Munchinger and Prokofiev's Violin Concertos; Sonatas with Malcolm Frager (BASF). *Honours include:* 2nd Prize Queen Elisabeth Competition, Belgium, 1967; First Prize, City of London International Competition (Carl Flesch) 1970; Grand Prix du Disque 1972. *Address:* Terry Harrison Artists Management, 3 Clarendon Court, Park Street, Charlbury, Oxon OX7 3PS, England.

MILASHKINA Tamara (Andreyevna), b. 13 Sept. 1934, Astrakhan, USSR. Singer (Soprano). *Education:* Studied with Elena Katul'skaya at the Moscow Conservatory. *Debut:* Bolshoy theatre 1957, as Titania in Eugene Onegin. *Career:* Has sung Lisa in The Queen of Spades, Zarina in The Legend of Tsar Saltan, Yaroslavna in Prince Igor and Natasha (War and Peace) with the Bolshoy company; Guest appearances at La Scala (Lida in La battaglia di legnano, 1962,), Helsinki, Paris, Wuppertal and in North America; Vienna Staatsoper 1971, as Lisa; Deutsche Oper Berlin 1974, as Tosca; Other roles include Fevronia (The Invisible City of Kitezh), Maria (Tchaikovsky's Mazeppa) and Lyuba (Prokofiev's Semyon Kotko) and Verdi's Elisabeth de Valois and Leonora (Il Trovatore). *Recordings Include:* Mazeppa, Tosca, The Queen of Spades and The Stone Guest. *Address:* c/o Bolshoy Theatre, Pr Marxa 8/2, 103009 Moscow, Russia.

MILBURN Ellsworth, b. 6 Feb 1938, Greensburg, Pennsylvania, USA. Composer. *Education:* Studied with Scot Huston at the University of Cincinnati College-Conservatory of Music, 1956-58, with Roy Travis and Henri Lazarof at the University of California at Los Angeles, 1959-62 and with Milhaud at Mills College in Oakland, 1966-68. *Career:* Teacher, University of Cincinnati College-Conservatory of Music, 1970-75, Rice University, Houston, from 1975. *Compositions include:* Opera Gesualdo 1973; 5 Inventions for 2 flutes, 1965; Massacre of the Innocents, chorus, 1965; Concerto, piano and chamber orchstra, 1967; String Trio, 1968; Soli, 5 players on 10 instruments, 1968; String Quintet, 1969; Soli II for 2 players on flutes and double bass, 1970; Voussoirs for orchestra, 1970; Soli III for clarinet, cello and piano, 1971; Soli IV, flute, oboe, double bass and harpsichord, 1972; Violin Sonata, 1972; Lament, harp, 1972; Spiritus mundi for high voice and 5 instruments, 1974. *Address:* Rice University,

Shepherd School of Music, PO Box 1892, Houston TX 77251, USA.

MILCHEVA-NONOVA Alexandrina, b. 27 Nov. 1936, Shoumen, Bulgaria. Singer (Mezzo-soprano). *Eucation:* Studied with G Cherkin at the Sofia Conservatory. *Debut:* Warna 1961, as Dorabella in Cosi fan Tutte. *Career:* Sang at the Bulgarian National Opera in Sofia from 1968; Guest appearances in Vienna, Brussels, Paris, Amsterdam, Berlin (Komische Oper), London and Zurich; Munich 1979 and 1984; Verona Arena 1980 and 1984; Maggio Musicale Florence 1983, in Suor Angelica; Teatro Liceo Barcelona 1983, as Preziosilla in La forza del Destino; La Scala Milan as Marfa in Khovanshchina, repeated at the Paris Opera 1984; Geneva 1984, as Adalgisa in Norma; Other roles include Azucena, the Princess in Adriana Lecouvreur, Dalila, Carmen and Cenerentola. *Recordings Include:* Carmen, Boris Godunov and Khovanshchina (Balkanton); Aida and songs by Mussorgsky (Harmonia Mundi); Leoncavallo's La Bohème (Orfeo).

MILES Alastair, b. 1961, England. Singer (Bass). *Education:* Studied flute and voice at the Guildhall School, then at National Opera Studio. *Debut:* Sang Trulove in The Rake's Progress for Opera 80, 1985. *Career:* Appearances from 1986 with Glyndebourne Festival and Touring Opera in Capriccio, Katya Kabanova, The Rake's Progress and Die Zauberflöte; Welsh National Opera as Basilio, Sparafucile, Raimondo and Silva in Ernani: Royal Opera Covent Garden in Parsifal, Viaggio a Reims, I Capuleti, Fidelio and Rigoletto; Other engagements in Vancouver, Amsterdam, San Francisco, Lyon and the Deutsche Oper Berlin; Concert appearances under Gardiner in Beethoven's Missa Solemnis, Mozart's Requiem, Handel's Saul and Agrippina and the Verdi Requiem; Handel's Samson and Bach Cantatas under Harnoncourt; With Kurt Masur in Elijah and the St Matthew Passion; Berlioz, La Damnation de Faust and Romeo et Juliette under Colin Davis, Bartolo in Figaro with Simon Rattle and the CBSO and Messiah under Helmut Rilling; Season 1993 in the Choral Symphony under Giulini and title role in Le Nozze di Figaro under Harnoncourt for Netherlands Opera, and Nick Shadow in The Rake's Progress at Cologne and Vienna. *Recordings include:* Lucia di Lammermoor; Saul and Agrippina; Elijah; Le Traviata and Rigoletto; Verdi Requiem; Die Zauberflöte; Don Giovanni; Berlioz Romeo et Juliette. *Address:* IMG Artists, Media House, 3 Burlington Lane, London W4 2TH, England.

MILKINA Nina, b. 27 Jan. 1919, Moscow, USSR. Concert Pianist. m. Alastair Robert Masson Sedgwick, 1943, 1 son, 1 daughter. *Education:* Musical studies with the late Leon Conus, Moscow Conservatoire; Paris Conservatoire; Private study with Professors Harold Craxton, Tobias Matthay, London, England. *Debut:* 1st public appearance, age 11, with Lamoureux Orchestra, Paris. *Career Includes:* Broadcasting, television, touring in Great Britain & abroad. Commissioned by BBC, broadcast series of all Mozart's piano sonatas; Invited to give Mozart recital, bicentenary celebration of Mozart's birth, Edinburgh Festival; Widely noted for interpretation of Mozart's piano works. *Recordings:* For Westminster Company, New York; Pye Record Company and ASV Ltd, London; Mozart, Haydn, Scarlatti, Brahms Piano Trios, Scriabin, Rachmaninov, Prokovlev, Complete Chopin Mazurkas. *Publications:* Works for piano; Early Compositions (Age 11). *Honour:* Honorary member, Royal Academy of Music. *Hobbies:* Chess; Fly fishing. *Current Management:* Marketing and the Arts. *Address:* 17 Montagu Square, London, W1H 1RD, England.

MILL Arnold van, b. 26 March 1921, Schiedam, Holland. Singer (Bass). *Education:* Studied at Rotterdam Conservatory. *Debut:* Brussels, Theatre de la Monnaie, 1946. *Career:* Sang in Holland and Belgium; Antwerp Opera 1950; Wiesbaden 1951-53; Staditsche Oper Berlin 1952, as Zaccaria in Nabucco; Maggio Musicale Florence 1953, in Agnese di Hohenstaufen; Hamburg Opera from 1953, notably in the 1969 premiere of

Penderecki's The Devils of Loudun; Bayreuth Festival 1955-60, as Daland, Titurel, Fasolt and Fafner; Edinburgh Festival 1956, in The Barber of Baghdad and Oedipus Rex; Guest appearances in Vienna, Paris, Lisbon and Rio de Janeiro. *Recordings:* Tristan und Isolde, Die Walküre, Parsifal, Aida, Don Giovanni (Decca); Die Entführung and The Devils of Loudun (Philips).

MILLER Bruce I, b. 12 June 1947, New York City, USA. Conductor; Music Critic; College Teacher. *Education:* BMus, 1969, MMus, 1971, State University of New York, Fredonia; ChM, American Guild of Organists, 1967. *Career:* As a Conductor, Assistant Conductor, Gregg Smith Singers, 1974; Director, College Choir and Chamber Singers, College of the Holy Cross, Worcester, Massachusetts, 1975-; Guest Conductor for various high school festivals; As a Music Critic, awarded Fellowship to the Aspen Music Festival by Music Critics Association Inc, summer, 1973. *Recordings:* Mozart, Requiem, K626, Mozart Mass in C Minor, K427, Lo, He Comes!, (Christmas and Advent Music) conducting the Holy Cross College Choir. *Contributions to:* Music Critic, Baltimore Morning Sun. *Address:* College of the Holy Cross, 1 College Street, PO Box 195A, Worcester, MA 01610, USA.

MILLER Clement A, b. 29 Jan. 1915, Cleveland, Ohio, USA. Musicologist. m. (1) Jean (deceased), 2 sons, 1 daughter. (2), Nancy Voigt, 25 Sep. 1983. *Education:* BM, Piano, 1936, MM, Music Theory, 1937, Cleveland Institute of Music; MA, Western Reserve University, 1942; PhD, Musicology, University of Michigan, 1951. *Career:* Instructor, Head of Music Department (History), Dean of Faculty, Acting Director, 1937-65, Cleveland Institute of Music; Professor of Music, Fine Arts Department, John Carroll University, 1967-79. *Publications:* Heinrich Glarean: Dodecachordon, 1965; Franchinus Gaffurius: Musica Practica, 1968; Johannes Cochlaeus: Tetrachordum Musices, 1970; Sebald Heyden: De Arte Canendi, 1972; Hieronymus Cardanus: Writings on Music, 1973; Le Gendre, Maille, Morpain: Collected Chansons, 1981; Nicolaus Burtius: Musices Opusculum, 1983; Co-editor, A Correspondence of Renaissance Musicians, Oxford University Press, 1990; Commentary and Translation: Musica Practica by Bartolomeo Ramis De Pareia, American Institute of Musicology, 1993. *Contributor To:* The Musical Quarterly; Journal of the American Musicological Society; Die Musik in Geschichte und Gegenwart; New Grove Dictionary of Music and Musicians. *Honours:* Guggenheim Fellowship, 1974-75; Outstanding Educator of America, 1975. *Memberships:* American Musicological Society; Renaissance Society of America; Music Library Association; Musica Disciplina. *Address:* 7922 Bremen Avenue, Parma, OH 44129, USA.

MILLER Gregory, b. 5 Feb 1964, Minneapolis, Minnesota, USA. Harpsichordist; Musicologist; Harpsichord Maker. *Education:* English Literature study, London University, England, 1985; AB with highest honours, Music, Economics, Bowdoin College, 1986; Studied Composition with Peter Lieberson, Harvard University, 1987-88; Last student of Isolde Ahlgrimm, Vienna, 1989-90; MM, Musicology, New England Conservatory, 1991. *Career:* Musicological papers presented in Performance Practices of Harpsichord Music; Trained in Boston; Founded Cambridge Harpsichords, 1991; Instruments built for professional organisations including Boston Symphony Orchestra and Harvard University. *Honours:* Surdna Research Fellowship, 1986; Numerous awards and prizes. *Memberships:* American Musicological Society; Early Music America. *Hobbies:* Collector of music books and recordings; World traveller, 4 continents. *Address:* 19 Watson Street, Cambridge, MA 02139, USA.

MILLER Jonathan, b. 21 July 1934, London, England. Stage Director. *Education:* Studied Natural Sciences, St John's College, Cambridge; MD, 1959. *Career Includes:* Director, Theatre Productions, including: Merchant of Venice; Three Sisters; The Seagull; Eugene O'Neill's Long Day's Journey into Night; The Emperor; The Taming of the Shrew, Royal Shakespeare Company, 1987; Artistic Director, Old Vic, 1988; Director, Opera, British Premiere of Arden Must Die; Orfeo; Janáček's Cunning Little Vixen; The Marriage of Figaro, English National Opera, 1978; Associate Producer, English National Opera, 1980; Productions with the Company include: Arabella, Otello, Rigoletto, Don Giovanni, Magic Flute, Tosca; The Mikado, The Barber of Seville; Director, Tosca, Maggio Musicale, Florence, 1986; Numerous TV appearances, including series on the history of medicine, The Body in Question; Director 12 plays, BBC's Shakespeare Series, 1980-81; Producer, Mozart's Così Fan Tutte, 1985-86; Produced Don Giovanni at Florence, 1990, Le Nozze di Figaro at the Vienna Festival, 1991; Season 1992 with Donizetti's Roberto Devereux at Monte Carlo, Manon Lescaut at La Scala (also at Trieste) and Le Nozze di Figaro at Florence; Der Rosenkavalier for ENO, 1993; Lecturer. *Publications:* The Body in Question; States of Mind; The Human Body; The Facts of Life; Subsequent Performances, 1986; Beyond the Fringe. *Contributions to:* A Profile of Jonathan Miller by Michael Romain, 1992. *Address:* c/o English National Opera, London Coliseum, St Martin's Lane, London WC2, England.

MILLER Kevin, b. 1929, Adelaide, Australia. Singer (Tenor). *Education:* Studied at Elder Conservatory, Adelaide. *Career:* Sang with the Australian National Theatre Company, Melbourne in operas by Mozart, Rossini and Vaughan Williams; Studied further in London and in Rome with Dino Borgioli and toured with the Australian Opera, 1955; Glyndebourne Festival, 1955-57, as Pedrillo, Monostatos and Scaramuccio in Ariadne auf Naxos; Welsh National Opera from 1958, notably as Rossini's Ramiro, Vanja in Katya Kabaova, Sellem in The Rake's Progress and Offenbach's Orpheus; Toured West Germany and Australia, 1962 with Orpheus in the Underworld and The Rake's Progress. *Recordings include:* The Rake's Progress, conducted by the composer.

MILLER Lajos, b. 23 Jan. 1940, Szombathely. Singer; Dramatic Baritone. m. Susanna Dobranszky, 31 Apr. 1964, 1 son. *Education:* Diploma, Hungarian State Academy of Music, 1968. *Debut:* Hungarian State Opera House, 1968, in Szokolay's Hamlet. *Career:* Singer, major companies in: Budapest, Wien, Milan, Rome, Firenze, Paris, Toulouse, Aix-en-Provence, Munich, Hamburg, Bonn, West Berlin, Brussels, Liège, Wexford-Festival, Glasgow, Liverpool, Houston, Buenos Aires, New York (Carnegie), Philadelphia, Caracas; Roles include: Verdi: Simon Boccanegra, Renato (Ballo), Luna (Il Trovatore), Germont (La Traviata), Rigoletto, Carlo (Ernani), Carlo (Forza), Miller, Giacomo (Giovanna d'Arco); Posa (Don Carlo); Macbeth, Rolando (Battaglia); Puccini: Scarpia (Tosca), Marcello (Tabarro), Sharpless (Butterfly); Sang Ivo in Berio's La Vera Storia at the Paris Opéra, 1985; Teatro Colón Buenos Aires 1987, as Grigor, in The Tsar's Bride by Rimsky-Korsakov; Metropolitan 1989-90, as Luna in Il Trovatore; Opéra de Montreal 1990, as Verdi's Renato; Sang Yeletsky in The Queen of Spades at La Scala Milan, 1990; Films & TV Films include: Rigoletto, Leoncavallo: Pagliacci; Silvio, Puccini: Il Tabarro; *Recorded roles:* Vivaldi Olympiade; Verdi; Ernani; Don Carlos; Simon Boccanegra; Attila; Ezio; Puccini; Butterfly; Sharpless; Boito, Nerone (Fanuel); Mercadante Il Giuramento, Manfredo; one record of Verdi baritone arias. *Honours:* Budapest, 3 P. Erkel, 2P. Kodaly, 1972; Toulouse, Grand Prize, 4 extra Prizes, Paris, 1974; Budapest, Kossuth Prize, 1980. *Address:* 28/A Balogh Adam Utca, 1026 Budapest II, Hungary.

MILLER Leta Ellen, b. 30 Sept. 1947, Burbank, California, USA. Musicologist; Flautist; Associate Professor. m. Alan K Miller, 29 June 1969. 1 son, 1 daughter. *Education:* BA 1969, PhD 1978, Stanford University; MM, Hartt College of Music, 1971. *Career:* Associate Professor, University of California, Santa Cruz; Recitalist, baroque and modern flute. *Recordings:* Modern flute: The Prismatic Flute: Dramatic Chamber Works by Lou Harrison, David Cope and Gordon Mumma, with Ensemble Nova, 1988; Lou Harrison:

Solstice, Canticle No 3, Ariadne, A Summerfield Set, 1990; Claude Debussy and the French School: Music for flute and harp, in press; Music of Germaine Tailleferre, in press; Lou Harrison: Chamber Works, in press; Baroque flute: C.P.E. Bach: 6 Sonatas for Flute and Continuo and Flute Unaccompanied (The Later Sonatas), 1988; 6 Sonatas for Flute and Continuo (The Earlier Sonatas), 1990; 4 Sonatas for Flute and Keyboard, 1994; Josef Bodin de Boismortier: Music for -4 Flutes, in press; Renaissance flute: Plaisirs d'armour: Love Songs from the French Renaissance. *Publications:* Music in the Paris Academy of Sciences 1666-1793, with A Cohen, 1979; Editor: Chansons from the French Provinces (1530-1550) Vol 1, 1980, Vol 2 1983; Thirty-Six Chansons by French Provincial Composers (1529-1550), 1981; Gioseppe Caimo: Madrigali and Canzoni for Four and Five Voices, 1990. *Address:* Porter College, University of California, Santa Cruz, CA 95064, USA.

MILLER Margaret, b. 1960, Indiana, USA. Violist. *Education:* Studied at Indiana and Wisconsin Universities. *Career:* Principal violist with the Colorado Springs Orchestra and Co-founded the Da Vinci Quartet, 1980, under the sponsorship of the Fine Arts Quartet; many concerts in the USA and elsewhere in a Repertoire including works by Mozart, Beethoven, Brahms, Dvořák, Shostakovich and Bartók. *Honours:* (with the Da Vinci Quartet) Awards and grants from the National Endowment for the Arts, the Western States Arts Foundation and the Colorado Council for the Humanities; Artist in Residence at the University of Colorado. *Address:* c/o Sonata (Da Vinci Quartet), 11 Northgate Street, Glasgow G20 7AA, Scotland.

MILLER Mildred, b. 16 Dec. 1924, Cleveland, Ohio, USA. Recital Soloist; Impresario. m. Wesley W. Posvar, 30 Apr. 1950, 1 son, 2 daughters. *Education:* BMus, Cleveland Institute of Music, 1946; Artist's Diploma, New England Conservatory, 1948. *Debut:* Metropolitan Opera, 1951. *Career:* Metropolitan Opera, 1951-74 as Siebel (Faust), Nicklausse in Les Contes d'Hoffmann, Susuki, Meg Page and Magdelena in Die Meistersinger (253 performances in 21 parts); TV debut, Voice of Firestone, 1952; Appearances at San Francisco, Chicago Lyric, Cincinnati, San Antonio, Pasadena, Pittsburgh, Kansas City, Fort Worth, Omaha, Vienna, Berlin, Munich, Frankfurt Operas, 1959-73; Film: Merry Wives of Windsor; Musical Comedy, Pittsburgh Civic Light Opera. *Recordings:* Columbia, Musical Heritage, Westminster, Strand and Metropolitan Opera Records. *Publications:* Co-Author, 6 Libretti Translations. *Contributions to:* Opera News; Bravo Magazine. *Memberships:* Director, Gateway to Music; Pittsburgh Opera; Honorary President, Women's Association, University of Pittsburgh; Founder, Artistic Director, Pittsburgh Opera Theater, 1978-. *Current Management:* Robert M. Gewald, New York. *Address:* Pittsburgh Opera Theatre, PO Box 110108 Pittsburgh, PA 15232, USA.

MILLGRAMM Wolfgang, b. 16 Apr 1954, Ostsee bad Kuhlungsborn, Germany. Singer (Tenor). *Education:* Studied with Gunter Leib in Berlin. *Debut:* Semperoper in Dresden, 1992 as Graf Elemer in Arabella; Sang same role in season 1992/93. *Career:* After studying at the Musikhochschule, Berlin, engaged at Deutsche Staatsoper, Berlin Singing the Steeersman in Fliegende Holländer and Walther in Tannhäuser and Alfred in Die Fledermaus; Also visited Japan, Hungary and Switzerland with Deutsche Staatsoper. Solo appearances in Yugoslavia, Rumania and the then Soviet Union; Chamber singer in 1988; Sang the Steersman at Bregenz Festival, 1988 and 1989; Same role at a concert for Radio France, 1990; Season 1992-93 was engaged at the City of Nuremberg theatre, where he made guest appearance in 1991 as Adolar in Euryanthe. Other roles were Erik in Holländer, Hüon in Oberon, José in Carmen; During that period also sang the Drum Major in Wozzeck and Max in Freischütz; Guest at Deutsche Staatsoper as Alfred in Fledermaus, Steersman in Holländer and Walther in Tannhäuser; Further appearances: Frankfurt-am-Main as Alfred in Fledermaus, Mannheim as Max in Freischütz and Gärtnerplatztheater Munich as Duke in Rigoletto.

Recordings include: Ariadne auf Naxos and First Prisoner in Fidelio, conducted by Haitink. *Address:* Bühnen-und Konzertagentur, Sigrid Roslock, Eugen-Schönhaar-Straße 1, 10407 Berlin Germany.

MILLINGTON Andrew, b. 2 May 1952, Willenhall, England. Organist; Choirmaster; Conductor. m. Madeleine, 30 Dec 1978, 1 son, 2 daughters. *Education:* Pupil, Christopher Robinson, Harry Bramma, Worcester Cathedral; Studied piano with Phyllis Palmer, Cambridge; Studied organ with Ralph Downes, London. Fellow, Royal College of Organists, 1972; BA 1974, MA 1978, Downing College, Cambridge. *Career:* Accompanist, City of Birmingham Choir, 1969-71; Conductor, Aldwyn Consort of Voices, Midlands, 1972-82; Assistant music master, Malvern College, 1974; Assistant organist, Gloucester Cathedral, 1975-82; Organist/Master of Choristers, Guildford Cathedral, 1983-; Conductor, St Cecilia Singers 1975-82, Kidderminster Choral Society 1978-87, Birmingham Bach Society 1980-82; Bracknell Choral Society, 1987-. *Recordings:* Music from Gloucester and Guildford Cathedrals. *Honours:* Contemporary Class, 1980, Mixed Voices 1981, Let the People Sing (BBC). *Address:* 5 Cathedral Close, Guildford, Surrey GU2 5TL, England.

MILLIOT Sylvette, b. 6 June 1927, Paris, France. Violoncellist; Musicologist. *Education:* Doctor of Musicology; Studied violoncello, National Conservatory of Music, Paris. *Career:* Research Assistant, National Conservatory of Music, Paris; Soloist, Radio France; Various concert tours; Head of Research, CNRS, French National Centre for Scientific Research in Musicology and Musical Iconography. *Publications:* Documents inédits sur les Luthiers parisiens du 18 siècle, Paris, 1970; La Sonate, Paris, 1978; Le Violoncelle en France au XVIIIe Siècle, Paris, 1981; Le Quatuor, Paris, 1986; Marin Marais, Fayard, Paris, 1991; Entretiens-Avec-Navarra, Societe de musicologie de Languedoc, Beziers, 1991. *Contributions to:* Revue Française de Musicologie; Recherches sur la Musique française classique; The STRAD, articles on La Lutherie Française, 1992 and 1993. *Honours:* 1st Prize for Violoncello, National Conservatory of Music; Hélène Victor Lyon Prize; Solo Artist's Guild Prize. *Memberships:* French Musicology Society; French Society of 18th Century Studies. *Hobbies:* History of art; Psychology. *Address:* 6 Villa de la Réunion, 75016 Paris, France.

MILLO Aprile, b. 14 April 1958, New York, USA. Singer (Soprano). *Education:* Studied with her parents and with Rita Patanè. *Debut:* Salt Lake City 1980, as Aida. *Career:* Gave concert performances in Los Angeles and made La Scala Milan and Welsh National Opera debuts as Elvira in Ernani; Metropolitan Opera debut 1984, as Amelia Boccanegra: returned to New York as Elvira, Elisabeth de Valois and Aida; Guest appearances in Hamburg and Vienna; Other roles include Leonora in Il Trovatore and La Forza del Destino; Sang Aida and Liu at the Metropolitan 1987, followed by Elvira in Ernani, Elisabeth de Valois and Imogene in Il Pirata; Carnegie Hall 1987, Il Battaglia di Legnano (as Lida); Verona Arena and Caracalla festival 1988-90; Sang Aida at Washington 1990, Luisa Miller at Rome; Season 1991/92 as Marguerite at Chicago (debut), Elisabeth de Valois at the Met and Verona and Aida at the Festival of Caracella. *Recordings:* Luisa Miller and Don Carlos conducted by James Levine (Sony); Met productions of Aida on video (DGG) and in Ballo in Maschera. *Address:* c/o S.A. Gorlinsky Ltd., 33 Dover Street, London W1X 4NJ, England.

MILLS Betty, b. 1940, China. Solo and Orchestral Flautist; Solo Pianist. m. Antony Gray. *Education:* Royal Academy of Music, London; Studied piano with Harold Craxton, organ with C H Trevor and flute with Gerald Jackson; ARAM; GRSM. *Career:* Professor of flute, Royal Academy of Music; Principal flute, Sadler's Wells Opera and Royal Ballet at Covent Garden; Solo flautist in Oriel and Oriana Trios; Recitals as flautist and solo pianist for BBC, music clubs and Universities and Schools throughout England; In Spain for Radio Nacional Espana; Has performed concertos for flute and for piano in

London and in provincial concerts; Freelance orchestral work, with BBC Symphony and BBC Regional orchestras and various London orchestras; Also with Hallé and visiting foreign Opera and Ballet Orchestras; Associated Board Examiner in United Kingdom and Far East; Visiting Teacher, Winchester College, Sherborne, Haileybury, King's College, Taunton; Adjudicator; Examiner for Guildhall School of Music and International Baccalaureate. *Hobbies:* Travel; History; Tennis; Swimming; Photography. *Address:* Ferndene, Bracken Close, Storrington, West Sussex, RH20 3HT, England.

MILLS Bronwen, b. 1960, England. Singer (Soprano). *Education:* Studied at London University, the Guildhall School of Music and with Joy Mammon. *Career:* Opera engagements include Dido and Aeneas with Opera Restor'd at the 1986 Edinburgh Festival; Elizabeth Hall 1989 in The Death of Dido by Pepusch and Dibdin's Ephesian Matron; Season 1989/90 with Traviata for New Israeli Opera and Dublin Grand Opera; Elizabeth Zimmer in Henze's Elegy for Young Lovers in London; Norina in Don Pasquale and Madeline in Fall of the House of Usher by Glass in Wales; Donna Anna in Don Giovanni for Opera North, 1992; Man Who Mistook his Wife for a Hat, Michael Nyman, for Music Theatre Wales, 1992-93; Other roles include Mozart's Countess and Fiordiligi (Opera 80), the Governess and Miss Jessel in the Turn of the Screw, and Micaela; Opera North as the Queen of Shemakah in The Golden Cockerel, Strauss's Daphne and Blondchen in Die Entführung; Concert engagements with the Scottish Chamber Orchestra in Handel's Dixit Dominus and Bach's B minor Mass; St Matthew Passion in Stratford and Haydn's Stabat Mater at St John's Smith Square; Mozart's C minor Mass with the Northern Sinfonia, Beethoven's Missa Solemnis at Canterbury Cathedral and the Christmas Oratorio in Belgium; Wexford Festival 1990, in Handel's L'Allegro, il Penseroso ed il Moderato; Tour of English Cathedrals with London Festival Orchestra in 1991, Messiahs in Germany, Norway in 1992 also Messiahs in Lithuania & Moscow (Kremlin) with Yehudi Menuhin; Further appearances at the Malvern, Music at Oxford, Cambridge and Sully-sur-Loire Festivals. *Recordings include:* Solomon by John Blow (Hyperion); Beggar's Opera, Polly Peachum, Hyperion; Dibdin Operas, Hyperion; 100 years of Italian Opera, Opera Rara; Emilia di Liverpool, Opera Rara. *Address:* Magenta Music International, 64 Highgate High Street, London N6 5HX, England.

MILLS Erie, b. 22 June 1953, Granite City, Illinois, USA. Soprano. *Education:* National Music Camp, Interlochen, Michigan; BMus, MA, University of Illinois; Studied with Karl Trump, Grace Wilson and Elena Nikolai. *Debut:* St. Louis 1978, in the US premiere of Martin y Soler's L'Arbore di Diana; Ninette in Love for Three Oranges, Chicago Lyric Opera, 1979. *Career:* Sang New York City Opera debut as Cunegonde, Candide, 1982; Metropolitan Opera debut, New York as Blondchen, Die Entführung aus dem Serail, 1987; New York recital debut, 1989; Guest appearances with Cincinnati Opera; Cleveland Opera; San Francisco Opera; Minnesota Opera; Opera Society of Washington DC; Santa Fe Opera; Houston Grand Opera; Hamburg State Opera; Teatro alla Scala, Milan; Vienna State Opera; Sang Marie in La Fille du Régiment at New Orleans (1989), Blondchen in Die Entführung for Opéra de Montreal 1990; Soloist with many leading orchestras; Numerous recitals; Television appearances; Roles include Rossini's Rosina; Offenbach's Olympia; Donizetti's Lucia; J Strauss's Adele; R Strauss's Zerbinetta. *Recordings:* For New World Records; RCA. *Address:* c/o Metropolitan Opera, Lincoln Center, New York, NY 10023, USA.

MILLS John, b. 13 Sep. 1947, Kingston-upon-Thames, England. Classical Guitarist. m. Jacoba Cornelia Smit, 25 July 1984. *Education:* Hinchley Wood Secondary School, 1958-63; Royal College of Music, 1966-69. *Debut:* Wigmore Hall, 1971. *Career:* Widespread recital work throughout Britain and Europe; Many tours in USA, Canada, Scandinavia, Far East, Australasia; Professor of Guitar, Royal Academy of

Lusic, 1987-; Professor of Guitar Royal Academy of Music & Co-ordinator of Guitar Studies, Welsh College of Music & Drama; Also work in Chamber Music; Frequent Radio Recitals for BBC; TV appearances on Secombe With Music, Yorkshire TV. *Compositions:* For Guitar: Fantasia - Hommage to Frederick Delius; Minner Fra Bergen. *Recordings:* Music from Student Repertoire Vol. I, 1974, Vol. II, 1975; Five Centuries of the Guitar, 1972; 20th Century Guitar Music, 1977; John Mills Guitar Trio, 1981; Guitar Duos, 1983; Music to the John Mills Tutor, 1980. *Publication:* John Mills Classical Guitar Tutor, 1980. *Current Management:* Helen Jennings Concert Agency, 2 Hereford House, Links Road, London, W3 0HX, England. *Address:* 1, Fairways, Dilton Marsh, Westbury, Wiltshire BA13 3RU, England.

MILLS Richard John, b. 14 Nov. 1949, Toowoomba, Queensland, Australia. Composer; Conductor. *Education:* University of Queensland; Queensland Conservatorium; Guildhall School of Music, London, England. *Career:* Regular guest conductor of all major Australian Orchestras; Artist-in-Residence: Australian Ballet, 1987-88; Artist-in-Residence, Australian Broadcasting Corporation, 1989-90; Artistic Director, Adelaide Chamber Orchestra, 1991-1994; Artistic Adviser, Queensland Symphony Orchestra, 1991-94. *Compositions:* Principal works: Music for Strings; Concerti for trumpet and percussion; Bamaga Diptych; Fantastic Pantomimes; Flute Concerto (written for James Galway); Concerto for Violoncello and Orchestra; Violin concerto (for Carl Pini, 1992): Summer of the Seventeenth Doll, 1994. *Current Management:* Arts Management, 180 Goulburn Street, Darlinghurst, NSW 2010, Australia. *Address:* 22 Gray Road, Hill End, Queensland 4101, Australia.

MILNE Hamish, b. 27 Apr. 1939, Salisbury, England. Pianist. m. Margot Gray, 1 son, 2 daughters. *Education:* Royal Academy of Music, London; Guido Agosti, Rome/Siena. *Debut:* 1963. *Career:* Concerto, Recital, Chamber Music in UK, Europe and USSR; Over 100 BBC Broadcasts; Proms Debut, 1978; Professor, Piano, Royal Academy of Music, London. *Recordings:* Piano works by Chopin, Liszt, Haydn, Medtner, Mozart, Reubke, Schumann, Weber. *Publications:* Bartók, 1981; Heritage of Music, Contributor, 1982. *Contributor To:* Medtner-Centenary Appraisal, 1981. *Honours:* Collard Fellowship, 1977; FRAM, 1978. *Address:* 111 Dora Road, London SW19 7JT, England.

MILNER Anthony Francis Dominic, b. 13 May 1925, Bristol, England. Composer. *Education:* Composition with Matyas Seiber, 1944-48; Royal College of Music, 1945-47; DMus, London; FRCM. *Appointments:* Tutor, Music Theory and History, Morley College, London, 1946-64; Extension Lecturer, 1958-65, University of London, 1954-65; Staff Member, 1961-, including Principal Lecturer, 1980-89, Royal College of Music, London; Lecturer, King's College, University of London, 1965-71; Senior Lecturer, 1971-74, Principal Lecturer, 1974-80, Goldsmith's College, University of London; Visiting Lecturer, USA, 1964-88; Composer-in-Residence, Summer School of Liturgical Music, Loyola University, New Orleans, 1965, 1966; Director, Harpsichordist, London Cantata Ensemble baroque music group, 1954-65. *Compositions include:* Variations for Orchestra, 1958; April Prologue, overture, 1961; Divertimento, string orchestra, 1961; Sinfonia Pasquale, string orchestra, optional wind/brass, 1963; Chamber Symphony, 1968; Symphonies Nos 1, 2, 3, 1972, 1978, 1986; Concerto for Symphonic Wind Band, 1979; Concerto, string orchestra, 1982; Chorus/orchestra: 5 Cantatas, 1948, 1955, 1956, 1969, 1974; The Water and the Fire, oratorio, 1960-61; Festival Te Deum, 1967; Motet for Peace, 1973; The Gates of Summer, 1990; Chorus/organ: Anthems, 1958, 1968, 1971, 1976; Processional, 1980; Responsorial Psalm, 1982; Chorus a cappella: Mass, 1951; 2 motets, 1955, 1959; Cantata, 1956; 2 partsongs, 1957, 1974; Turbae for the Passion, according to St John, 1968, according to St Matthew, 1962; Instrumental: Quartet, oboe, strings, 1953; Rondo Saltato, organ, 1955; Fugue for Advent for Organ, 1958; Quintet for Wind Instruments, 1964; String Quartet No

1, 1975; Voice with instrumental accompaniment: The Song of Akhenaten, 1954; Midway, 1974; Our Lady's Hours, song cycle, 1957; Music for children; Music for radio, etc: Congregational music. *Recordings include:* Cantatas Salutatio Angelica and Roman Spring, Decca, 1975; Symphony No 1; Variations for Orchestra. *Publications include:* Harmony for class teaching, 2 vols, 1950; Piano Sonata 1989; Cantata, The Gates of Summer, 1990; Antony Milner, A Bio-Bibliography by James Siddons; Several book-chapters. *Contributor to:* Musical Quarterly; Proceedings of the Royal Musical Association; The Musical Times. *Honours include:* Appointed Knight of St Gregory, Pope John Paul II, 1985. *Address:* 147 Heythorp Street, Southfields, London SW18 5BT, England.

MILNER Howard, b. 1953, England. Singer (Tenor). *Education:* Studied at Cambridge University and the Guildhall School of Music. *Career:* Glyndebourne Opera from 1985, including tour to Hong Kong 1986 and appearances in Albert Herring and Capriccio; Kent Opera title role in Le Comte Ory, Jacquino in Fidelio and Eumeus in The Return of Ulysses; Sang Arnalta (L'Incoronazione di Poppea), and Monostatos for Early Opera Project; Pedrillo (Die Entführung) and Camille (The Merry Widow) for Scottish Opera; Covent Garden 1990-91 in Die Meistersinger and Capriccio; English National Opera, Squeak in Billy Budd; Haydn's Lo Speziale with the Aix-en-Provence Chamber Opera; Don Curzio in Marriage of Figaro with Opera Factory; Frequent concerts in Britain and Europe, Promenade Concerts debut 1988; Arnalta in Coronation of Poppea for Opera Factory, 1992. *Recordings include:* Bach's B minor Mass and Monteverdi's Orfeo with John Eliot Gardiner (Deutsche Grammophon); Beethoven's Choral Fantasia conducted by Roger Norrington (EMI); Video of ENO Billy Budd. *Current Management:* C&M Craig Services Ltd, 3 Kersley Street, London SW11 4PR, England. *Address:* c/o Korman International Management, Crunnells Green Cottage, Preston, Herts. SG4 7UQ, England.

MILNES Rodney, b. 26 July 1936, Stafford, England. Music Critic; Magazine Editor. *Career:* Music Critic, Queen Magazine, later Harpers and Queen, 1968-87; Opera Critic, The Spectator, 1979-90; Opera Critic, London Evening Standard 1990-92; Chief Opera Critic, The Times from 1992; Reviews for Opera Magazine from 1971, Associate Editor, 1976; Editor from 1986. *Publications:* Numerous opera translations; Under original name, Rodney Blumer, has translated such operas as Osud, Giovanna d'Arco, Zemire et Azor, Undine, Tannhäuser, Rusalka and The Jacobin; Consultant editor, Viking Opera Guide, 1993. *Address:* Opera Magazine, 1a Mountgrove Road, London N5 2LU, England.

MILNES Sherrill, b. 10 Jan. 1935, Hinsdale, Illinois, USA. Opera Singer (Baritone). m. (2) Nancy Stokes 1969, 1 son (1 son, 1 daughter by first marriage). *Education:* MMUS, ED, Drake University, Northwestern University; Studied with Boris Goldovsky, Rosa Ponselle, Andrew White, Hermanes Baer with Goldovsky Opera Company 1960-65, NY City Opera Company 1964-67. *Debut:* with Metropolitan Opera, NY 1965 as Valentin in Gounod's Faust. *Career:* Leading Baritone 1965-, as Verdi's Miller, Renato, Amonasro, Don Carlo, Germont, Simon Boccanegra, Iago, Macbeth, Montfort, Paolo, Posa and Rigoletto; has also appeared in New York as Wagner's Herald (Lohengrin) and Donner, Rossini's Figaro, Don Giovanni, Barnaba, Jack Rance, Scarpia, Riccardo in I Puritani and Alphonse in La Favorite; Has performed with all American City Opera Companies and major American Orchestras 1962-73; Performed in Don Giovanni, Vespri Siciliani and all standard Italian repertory baritone roles, and at San Francisco Opera, Hamburg Opera, Frankfurt Opera, La Scala, Milan, Covent Garden, London, Teatro Colón, Buenos Aires; Vienna State Opera, Paris Opera and Chicago Lyric Opera, including Puccini's Scarpia and Verdi's Posa, Boccanegra, Iago and Don Carlo; New York City Opera 1982, as Hamlet in the Opera by Thomas (returned 1990); Season 1991/92 with debut as Falstaff, Jack

Rance at the Met and Scarpia at Buenos Aires; Sang Cilea's Michonnet at the Met, 1994. *Recordings:* For RCA Victor, London Decca, EMI Angel, Philips, Deutsche Grammophon, 60 Albums 1967-; Most recorded American Opera Singer 1978; Videos of Il Trovatore from the Met (DGG) and Tosca in the original locations. *Honours:* 3 Hon. degrees, Order of Merit (Italy) 1984. *Membership:* Chairman of Board, Affiliate Artists Inc.

MILOJKOVIC-DJURIC Jelena, b. 2 Dec 1931, Belgrade. Musicologist. m. Dusan Djuric, 24 Sept 1955, 2d. *Education:* MA 1963, PhD 1982, University of Belgrade. *Career:* Lecturer, University of Belgrade, 1963-65; Research Associate, Musicological Institute, Belgrade, 1963-65; Lecturer, Slavic Languages, University of Colorado, 1968; Lecturer, Russian and German, Texas A&M University, 1972-74; Research Associate, Soviet and Eastern Studies, University of Texas, 1987-. *Publications:* Books: The Music of Eastern Europe, 1978; Tradition and Avant-Garde: The Arts in Serbian Culture between the two World Wars, 1984; Tradition and Avant-Garde: Literature and Arts in Serbian Culture 1900-1918, 1988; Aspects of Soviet Culture: Voices of Glasnost 1960-1900, 1991; also book chapters and articles. *Honours include:* Association of Composers and Writers of Yugoslavia Award, 1969. *Memberships:* American Musicological Society; American Association for the Advancement of Slavic Sudies. *Hobbies:* Collecting art. *Address:* 1018 Holt Street, College Station, TX 77840, USA.

MILOSI Rodrigue, b. 7 Sept. 1935, Clichy, France. Violinist; Music Professor. *Education:* Higher studies, Conservatoire National Superieur de Musique, Paris; Certificate qualifying as teacher in National Conservatories. *Career:* Tours in France, Belgium, Italy, Rumania, Bulgaria, Argentina, Brazil, Chile, Bolivia, Ecuador, Paraguay, Panama; Various contemporary works for violin dedicated to him; Jury Member, Conservatoire Superieur de Musique, Paris; Pedagogical courses. Touquet, Flaine, and Université d'Orsay, Paris; Artistic Director, Festival of Provence; Professor, National Conservatory of the Caen Region; Violin Soloist, Caen Chamber Orchestra. *Recordings:* Complete Grieg Sonatas, with pianist Noël Lee, ADDA, France. *Honours:* Emile Français Prize, 1952; Pablo de Sarasate Prize, 1952; 1st Prize and Prize of Honour, Violin, Conservatoire National Superieur de Musique, Paris. *Hobbies:* Collecting objets d'arts, paintings and drawings of all periods. *Address:* 4 Square La Fontaine, 75016 Paris, France.

MILVEDEN J. Ingmar G., b. 15 Feb. 1920, Göteborg, Sweden. Composer; Assistant Professor. m. Ulla Milveden, 1 son, 1 daughter. *Education:* Licentiate of Philosophy, 1951, PhD, 1972; Musical Theory, counterpoint, composition with Dr S E Svensson, Uppsala; Musicology with Professor C A Moberg; Schola Cantorum Basiliensis, Basel. *Debut:* Serenade for Strings, The Philharmonic Orchestra of Göteborg, Conductor, Issay Dobrowen, 1942. *Career:* Assistant Professor of Musicology, University of Uppsala. *Compositions:* Pezzo Concertante for Orchestra and Soloists, 1971; Clarinet Concerto, 1972; Now, a cantata to Linnean texts for choir and orchestra; Gaudeat Upsalia, a cantata for 500th anniversary of University of Uppsala 1977; Great Mass for Uppsala Cathedral, 1969; Musica in honorem Sanctae Eugeniae, 1982. *Publications:* Zu den liturgischen Hystorie in Schweden; Liturgie-und choralgeschichtliche Untersuchungen, 1972. *Honours:* Uppsala Landstings kulturpris, 1969; Scholarship, Royal Swedish Academy of Music 1972, 1973. *Memberships:* Royal Swedish Academy of Music; Royal Academy of Arts and Sciences of Uppsala; Rotarian; Chairman, Musikaliska Konstföreningen. *Hobby:* Swedish church life. *Address:* Torkelsgatan 16B, S-753 29 Uppsala, Sweden.

MILYAEVA Olga, b. 1960, Moscow, Russia. Violist. *Education:* Studied at the Central Music School, Moscow. *Career:* Co-founder, Quartet Veronique, 1989; many concerts in the former Soviet Union and Russia, notably in the Russian Chamber Music Series and the

150th birthday celebrations for Tchaikovsky, 1990; Mastercalsses at the Aldeburgh Festival, 1991; Concert tour of Britain in season, 1992-93; repertoire includes works by Beethoven, Brahms, Tchaikovsky, Bartok, Shostakovich and Schnittke. *Honours include:* Winner, all-Union String Quartet Competition in St Petersburg, 1990-91; Third place, International Shostakovich Competition at St Petersburg, 1991, (both with the Quartet Veronique). *Address:* c/o Sonata (Quartet Veronique), 11 Northgate Street, Glasgow G2C 7AA, Scotland.

MINDE Stefan P., b. 12 Apr. 1936, Leipzig, Germany. Conductor. m. Edith Halla, 8 July 1961, 2 sons. *Education:* Member of Thomanerchor, Leipzig, 1947-54; MA, Mozarteum, Salzburg, Austria, 1958. *Debut:* State Theatre, Wiesbaden, Germany, Krenek: Life of Orestes. *Career:* Civic Opera Frankfurt/Main under Sir Georg Solti; Hessisches Staatstheater Wiesbaden under Sawallisch; Principal Conductor at Civic Theatre Trier/Mosel; Berkshire Music Festival at Tanglewood, Massachusetts with Eric Leinsdorf; Chorusmaster and Conductor, San Francisco Opera; General Director and Conductor at Portland Opera Association (Oregon), 1970-84; Founder, Music Director and Conductor of Sinfonia Concertante, Chamber Orchestra, Portland, Oregon; Artistic Director and Conductor of Portland Musical Company, Portland, Oregon; Guest appearances with New York City Opera, Philadelphia, Pittsburgh, Cincinnati, San Diego, Phoenix, Los Angeles, Seattle, Vancouver BC, Toronto, Edmonton, Calgary, Lisbon (Portugal), Saarbruecken, Cologne, Nuremberg, Hawaii Opera, Eugene Opera, Utah Opera, Sapporo Japan and others; Guest Professor at Portland State University, Pacific Lutheran University Tacoma/Washington and Florida State University. *Current Management:* Manning Music Management, 935 N.W. 19th Avenue, Portland, OR 97209, USA. *Address:* 1640 S E Holly Street, Portland, OR 97214, USA.

MINDEL Meir, b. 25 Dec 1946, Lvov, Russia. Composer. m. Tzippi Bozian, 25 Dec 1968, 4 daughters. *Education:* Harmony, Counterpoint, Electronic Music with Prof. Itzhak Saday, 1970-71; Rubin Music Academy, Tel Aviv, 1971-75; Composition with Prof. A. Ehrlich, 1975-77. *Debut:* Concert in Rubin Academy Agony for Flute, 1974. *Career:* Radio appearances: Together with..... Meir Mindel, A hour of M.M. Compositions (IX 1988), I.B.A., Israeli Young composer, The Blue & the White, 1982, Circle, A Maya Prophesy, 1987, Israel Broadcasting Authority; Genesis with Morli Consort, Israel Defence Forces Army Broadcasting, 1984; General Director and Secretary of Kibbutz Composers' Organization; Secretary of Management and Board of Israel Composers' League. *Compositions:* The Tie, for strings, 1980; Grotesque, for piano, 1983; Genesis, for recorders, 1983; A Maya Prophecy, for mixed choir, 1985; Grotesque, for recorders, 1985; Agony, for flute, 1986; The Courting Muse, for trombone, 1986; Tamar, for flute, horn and piano. 1988; Poem, for horn, 1988; The Family Tree, for singers ansamble, 1989; Iri, for two choirs, 1989; Koli, songs by Meir Mindel, 1989; Kshatot Letzavta, 18 arrangements for strings, including two compositions, 1989; The Shadow, for children choir, 1989; Murmurs, for trumpet and flugelhorn, 1989. *Recordings:* Negßa 40; Bereshit (Genesis); Song of Songs 85-Duo Beersheba; A Maya Prophecy-Tel-Aviv Philharmonic Choir; Murmurs and A Courting Muse in Composers in search of their roots; Tamar, the first compact disc of compositions by a single Israeli Composer, Completed 1990, by Mindel; Founder of Open Museum Project in Kibbutz Negßa. *Hobbies:* Original combinations for poetry and music; Composing and conducting, court music, within Kibbutz framework; Psychology. *Address:* Kibbutz Negba, 79408 Israel.

MINEVA Stefka, b. 1949, Stara Zagora, Bulgaria. Singer (Mezzo- Soprano). *Education:* Studied in Sofia. *Debut:* Staga Zora 1972, as Berta in Il Barbiere di Siviglia. *Career:* Sang Suzuki, Olga and Amneris at Stara Zagora; Sofia Opera from 1977, notably as Marfa in Khovanshchina. Guest appearances throughout Europe; Metropolitan Opera, 1986- 88, as Marfa; Sang

Konchakovna in Prince Igor at Perugia, 1987, Liubasha in The Tsar's Bride at Rome and Kabanicha in Katya Kabanova at Florence, 1989; Other roles include Marina in Boris Godunov, Eboli, Adalgisa and Leonora in La Favorita; Sang Fenena in Nabucco at the 1991 Verona Arena. *Recordings include:* Rimsky-Korsakov's Vera Sheloga and Prokofiev's War and Peace; Madama Butterfly. *Honours include:* Prize Winner, 1976 Sofia and 1977 Osten International Competitions. *Address:* c/o Arena di Verona, Piazza Bra 28, 37121 Verona, Italy.

MINICH Peter, b. 1928, St Polten, Switzerland. Singer (Tenor). *Education:* Studied at the Horak Conservatory, Vienna. *Debut:* St Polten 1951, in Millocker's Bettelstudent. *Career:* Engaged at St Gallen 1951-55, Graz, 1955-60; Vienna Volksoper from 1960, notably as Eisenstein in Fledermaus on tour to Japan, 1985; Salzburg Festival 1962-63, as Selim in Die Entführung: Other roles have included the Baron in La Vie Parisienne, Paquilo in La Perichole, René in Graf vom Luxembourg by Lehar and Jim Mahoney in Mahagonny; Frequent concert and television appearances. *Address:* c/o Volksoper, Wahringerstrasse 78, A-1090 Vienna, Austria.

MINKOFSKI-GARRIGUES Horst, b. 23 July 1925, Dresden, Germany. Concert Pianist; Composer; Professor. m. Edeltraud Peschke. 1 son, 2 daughters. *Education:* Music Academy & Conservatory, Dresden; Studies with Professor Herbert Wuesthoff, Romana Lowenstein, Karl Knochenhauer, Hermann Werner Finke, Schneider-Marfels. *Debut:* with State Orchestra, Dresden. *Career:* Numerous appearances, concerts and radio broadcasts throughout the world. *Compositions include:* For Orchestra: Klaviermusik, op 15, Piano Concerto, Variations over a theme by Tchaikovsky, op 8, Expo '67 to 2 pianos and orchestra; For piano solo: Impromptus, Preludes, Sonatinas, Sonata op 23 and Scherzo, op 37; For piano, four hands: Eight Miniatures, op 27, Introduction, Theme and Variations for 2 Pianos and Cello, op 14, Andante for 2 pianos, Expo '67 for 2 Pianos op 28, Pictures of a Child for 2 Pianos op 30; Chamber Music includes: Song Cycle, Love and Deception, op 41, works for flute and piano, organ, op 38. *Recordings include:* World Premiere Recording of the Complete works for Piano, Four Hands by Franz Schubert (11 albums) in collaboration with former student, Lothar Kilian; also compositions for 4 hands by Beethoven, Brahms, Tchaikovsky, Saint-Saëns, Dvořák and Smetana; with orchestra: Concerto for 2 pianos by Bach; Concerto in D-Major by Haydn, Klaviermusik, op 15 by Minkofski-Garrigues; Numerous solo and chamber music recordings including Schubert's Sonatas for Violin and Piano with Wolfgang Marschner. *Hobbies:* Antiques; Gardening; Swimming; Jogging. *Address:* 205 Edison Ave, St Lambert, Montreal, Quebec, Canada J4R 2P6.

MINKOWSKI Marc, b. 1962, Paris. France. Conductor. *Education:* Studied at the Hague Conservatory and at the Pierre Monteux Memorial School, USA. *Career:* Founder of and has performed with, Les Musiciens du Louvre, 1984; Has conducted works by Handel including Riccardo Primo, 1991 for the English Bach Festival and Gluck's Iphigénie en Tauride at Covent Garden; French repertoire includes Charpentier's Malade Imaginaire, Alcyone by Marin Marais, Mouret's Les Amours de Ragonde and Titon et l'Aurore by Mondonville; Further engagements with the Ricercar Consort in Gretry's La Caravane du Caire; Mehul, Haydn and Beethoven at the 1991 Flanders Festival; Beethoven concerts with the Australian Chamber Orchestra, Purcell's Dido and Handel's Teseo in Paris, Monteverdi's Orfeo in Valencia, Le Nozze di Figaro in Toronto and Lully's Phaeton, Lyon Opera. *Recordings include:* Les Amours de Ragonde by Mouret; Mondonville's Titon et l'Aurore; Stradella's San Giovanni Battista; Gretry's La Caravane du Caire. *Honours include:* First Prize, First International Concert of Ancient Music, Bruges, 1984. *Address:* c/o Ron Gonsalves, 10 Dagnan Road, London SW12 9LQ, England.

MINNIEAR John, b. 20 July 1938, Louisiana, USA. Professor. m. Evelyn Jean Youker, 10 June 1967, 3s. *Education:* BA, MA, Baylor University; PhD, North Texas University; Studied with Clyde Miller, Helen Hewitt, Lloyd Hibberd, Dika Newlin and Cecil Adkins. *Career:* Principal French Horn player with the Waco TX Symphony and Oskhash Symphony; Also performed with the Shreveport LA Symphony; Tutor at Baylor and North Texas Universities; Chair, Music Department, 1976-80, Associate Dean of Fine and Performing Arts, University of Wisconsin, Oshkosh, 1992-. *Publications:* Contributor to the Grove Dictionary of Music and Musicians and Grove Dictionary of Opera. *Memberships:* American Musicological Society. *Address:* 1306 Washington Avenue, Oshkosh, WI 54901, USA.

MINOR Andrew C., b. 17 Aug. 1918, Atlanta, Georgia, USA. Musicologist. m. Catherine Hogan, 2 daughters. *Education:* BA, Emory University, 1940; MMus 1947, PhD 1950, University of Michigan. *Recordings:* As conductor of Collegium Musicum, University of Missouri-Columbia, 2 masses by J. Michael Haydn, Handel's Joshua, Gossec's Messe des Morts. *Publications:* General editor, American Institute of Musicology's Jean Mouton's Opera Omnia, 4 volumes, 1967-74; Associate editor, Accademia Musicale, 17th century vocal & instrumental music, 10 volumes, 1970. *Contributor To:* Grove's Dictionary, 6th edition. *Memberships:* American Musicologial Society; Music Teachers National Association; Missouri Music Teachers Association; American Choral Revie (associate editor). *Address:* 919 Timberhill Road, Columbia, MO 65201, USA.

MINTER Drew, b. 11 Jan. 1955, Washington DC, USA. Singer (Countertenor). *Education:* Studied at Indiana University and with Rita Streich, Erik Werba and Marcy Lindheimer. *Career:* Performed in concert with various early music ensembles, including the Waverly Consort of New York; Stage debut as Handel's Orlando at the St Paul's Baroque Festival, 1983; Further appearances in early opera at Boston, Brussels and Los Angeles; Omaha and Milwaukee 1988, as Arsace in Handel's Partenope and Otho in L'Incoronazione di Poppea; Santa Fe 1989, in the US premiere of Judith Weir's A Night at the Chinese Opera and as Endimione in La Calisto by Cavalli; television appearances include Ptolemeo in Handel's Giulio Cesare, directed by Peter Sellars; Sang the title role in Handel's Ottone, Göttingen, 1992. *Recordings include:* Ottone in Handel's Agrippina and the title role in Floridante, conducted by Nicholas McGegan. *Address:* c/o Santa Fe Opera, PO Box 2408, Santa Fe, NM 87504, USA

MINTON Yvonne Fay, b. 4 Dec. 1938, Sydney, Australia. Singer (Mezzo Soprano). m. William Barclay, 21 Aug. 1965, 1 son, 1 daughter. *Education:* Sydney Conservatorium. *Career:* Soloist with major Australian orchestras; In 1964 appeared in premiere of Nicholas Maw's One Man Show; subsequently soloist with Royal Opera, Covent Garden, notably as Mussorgsky's Marina, Mozart's Dorabella, Wagner's Waltraute and Thea in the premiere of Tippett's Knot Garden, 1970; has appeared with most major symphony orchestras in the world and at all major opera houses; Sang Octavian at the Metropolitan 1973; Bayreuth Festival 1974, as Brangaene; Fricka and Waltraute in the Centenary Ring 1976; Paris Opéra 1976, as Octavian; Countess Geschwitz in the premiere of the 3-act version of Lulu; Covent Garden 1979, as Kundry in a new production of Parsifal; Turin Opera 1988, as Waltraute in Götterdammerung; Sang Fricka in Die Walküre at Lisbon, 1989; Leokadja Begbick in Mahagonny at the 1990 Maggio Musicale, Florence; Season 1993/94 as Marguerite in La Damnation de Faust at Wellington and Mme Larina in Eugene Onegin at Glyndebourne. *Recordings:* Concert recordings with Chicago Symphony Orchestra; BBC Symphony Orchestra and others; Opera recordings include Rosenkavalier; La Clemenza di Tito; Wagner's Ring; Tristan and Isolde and others. *Honours:* Hon. RAM, 1977; CBE, 1981. *Hobbies:* Gardening; Reading. *Current Management:* Ingpen and Williams,

14 Kensington Court, London W8, England. *Address:* 6 Manor House Court, Heath Road, Reading RG6 1NA, Berkshire, England.

MINTZ Shlomo, b. 30 Oct. 1957, Moscow, USSR. Violinist. m. Corina Ciacci Mintz, 2 sons. *Education:* Diploma, Juilliard School of Music. *Career:* Music Advisor to Israel Chamber Orchestra, 1989-; Conducts and performs with this orchestra in Israel and abroad; Recitals and Chamber Music Concerts throughout the World; Performed with: Israel Philharmonic, Berlin Philharmonic, Vienna Philharmonic, London Symphony, New York Philharmonic, Chicago Symphony, Philadelphia Orchestra, Boston Symphony, Los Angeles Philharmonic, etc. *Recordings:* Works by Bach, Bartók, Bruch, Debussy, Dvořák, Franck, Kreisler, Mendelssohn, Mozart, Paganini, Prokofiev, Ravel, Sibelius, Vivaldi, Beethoven, Brahms, Fauré, Lalo, Vieuxtemps. *Honours:* Grand Prix du Disque, 1981, 1984, 1988; Premio Accademia Musicale Chigiana Siena, 1984. *Management:* ICM Artists Ltd. *Address:* ICM Artists Ltd., 40 West 57 Street, New York, NY 10019, USA.

MIRICIOIU Nelly, b. 31 Mar 1952, Romania. Singer (Soprano). *Education:* Studied in Bucharest and Milan. *Debut:* Sang the Queen of Night in Die Zauberflöte at Iasi, Romania, 1974. *Career:* Appeared with the Brasov Opera 1975-78; Scottish Opera 1981, as Tosca and Violetta; Covent Garden debut 1982, as Nedda in Pagliacci, returning as Musetta (La Bohème), Marguerite and Antonia (Les Contes d'Hoffmann); Further engagements in Toronto, San Diego, San Francisco, Paris, Rome, Hamburg, Milan (La Scala) and Verona; Amsterdam 1988 as Rossini's Armida; In 1989 sang Violetta in Monte Carlo and Ravenna and Yaroslavna (Prince Igor) at Munich; Season 1992 as Violetta at Philadelphia; Maria Stuarda at the Amsterdam Concertgebouw and Amenaide in Tancredi at the Salzburg Festival; Other roles include Puccini's Butterfly, Mimi and Manon Lescaut, Offenbach's Olympia, and Lucia di Lammermoor. *Address:* c/o Royal Opera House (Contracts), Covent Garden, London WC2, England.

MIROGLIO Thierry Jean-Michel, b. 1 Sept. 1963, Paris, France. Percussionist. *Education:* Baccalaureat; Studied Musical Acoustics with Iannis Xenakis, Paris University, Sorbonne; Percussion with J.P Drouet and Sylvie Gualda, National Conservatory, Versailles; Harmony and Counterpoint, Chamber Music, National Conservatory of Boulogne, Billancourt. *Career:* Researcher and Soloist with ensembles: Musique Vivante; Atelier Ville d'Avray; Orchestre Opera de Paris; Orchestre Radio France; Musica Insieme etc...; Soloist, concerts in Festivals of Radio France, Angers, Besançon, Orleans, Nice, Salzburg, Athens, Paris, Ste Baume, Wurzburg, Venice, Bamberg, Rouen, Munich, Trento, Cremona also in South America; Artistic Director, Percussion Season of the French Society of Contemporary Music; Radio broadcasts; Masterclasses, lectures, seminars on the evolution of Percussion style from the origin until our time, numerous countries; Masterclasses, South America, 1990; World or Grand Premieres of works of Cage, Ohana, Boucourechliev, Ballif, Pousseur, Denisov, Stahmer, Donatoni, Kelemen, Henze, several dedicated to him. *Recordings:* For French, German, Austrian, Italian, Canadian and Greek radio. *Honours:* 1st Prize, Percussion, National Conservatory, Versailles; Prize for Chamber Music, National Conservatory of Boulogne. *Address:* 6 rue Leclerc, F-75014 Paris, France.

MIROLYBOV Peter, b. 8 Feb. 1918, Terijoki, Finland. Choir and Orchestra Conductor; Composer. m. Irina Gretschaninoff, 1 son, 1 daughter. *Education:* Graduate, Russian College, Terijoki; College of Music, Viborg. *Career:* Conductor, Church Choir of Terijoki (orthodox) 1935, Helsinki, 1949, Uppenski-Cathedral Choirs, Helsinki, The Balalaika Orchestra of Helsinki (as Pekka Mirola), 1956; several radio and TV performances. *Compositions:* Composer of orthodox music, vesper, liturgy and several hymns to the St Virgin, orchestral music, balalaika music, choir music and vocal music.

Recordings: Of orthodox music as Conductor; 3 recordings of Russian folk music as arranger and conductor. *Honour:* Dir. Cantus, 1973. *Membership:* Society of Finnish Musicians. *Hobby:* Literature. *Address:* Tuulimyllyntie 2 A8, 00920 Helsinki 92, Finland.

MIRSHAKAR Zarina, b. 19 Mar 1947, Dushanbe. Composer; Teacher. *Education:* Studied at the Moscow State Conservatory. *Compositions include:* String Quartet; 24 music pieces for piano; Three frescos of Pamir, violin and piano; Sonata for clarinet solo; Sonata for oboe solo; Respiro for violin, chamber orchestra and timpani; Music for documentary film, Our Baki; Symphonic poem, Colours of Sunny Pamir; Three Pamir Fescos, violin and piano; Sonata for clarinet solo; Symphonietta for string orchestra. *Recordings include:* 24 music pieces for piano; Sonata for clarinet solo; Sonata for oboe solo; Cycle of songs for children on M Mirshaker's poems. *Publications:* Colours of Sunny Pamir, 1989; Three pamir fescos for violin and piano, 1979; Sonata for clarinet-solo, 1982; Six pieces for piano, 1987. *Honours include:* Lenin Komsomol Prize Laureate, 1985. *Memberships:* Union of Composers of Tajikistan. *Hobbies:* Philately; Collecting records and scores. *Address:* Tajikistan, 734003 Dushanbe Pionersky St. proezd I, 12, Russia.

MIRTOVA Elena, b. 1962, South West Siberia, USSR. Singer (Soprano). *Education:* Studied at the Leningrad Conservatory, graduated 1988. *Debut:* Sang at the Musical Academy and Philharmonic Hall in Prague while a student. *Career:* Sang Maria in Rimsky-Korsakov's The Tsar's Bride in Moscow and Leningrad; Series of concerts in Moscow and Leningrad, 1984; Principal soloist at the Kirov Theatre in Leningrad/St Petersburg from 1988: Rimsky's Olga and Maria, Tchaikovsky's Tatiana and Iolanta, and Violetta; Sang in the 14th Symphony of Shostakovich with the Chamber Orchestra of the Lithuanian Philharmonia at the Berliner Philharmonie, 1989; Sang Iolanta at Frankfurt 1990 and Leonora in Il Trovatore with Omaha Opera 1991. *Honours Include:* Winner, Glinka Competition, 1984; First prize, Dvořák Voice Competition, Karlovi Vari, 1987; Winner, Fidenza/Parma Verdi Competition, 1990. *Address:* c/o Athole Still Ltd., 113 Church Road, London SE19 2PR, England.

MIRZOYAN Edward, b. 12 May 1921, Gori, Georgia, USSR. Composer. m. Elena Stepanyan, 1 June 1951, 1 son, 1 daughter. *Education:* Musical College, Yerevan, 1928-36; Yerevan Conservatoire, 1936-41; Postgraduate, Moscow Concervatoire, 1946-48. *Debut:* Yerevan, 1938. *Career includes:* Lecturer 1949, Professor 1965-, Head, Chair of Composition, 1972-87, Yerevan Conservatoire; Secretary 1950-52, Chairman 1956-, Armenian Composers' Union; Chairman 1952-56, Armenian Musical Foundation. *Compositions:* Sako from Lhore, symphonic poem, 1941; Symphonic Dances, suite, 1946; String quartet, 1947; Overture, 1947; Introduction & Perpetuum Mobile, violin & orchestra, 1957; Symphony, 1962; Cantatas, 1948, 1949, 1950; Cello sonata, 1967; Piano pieces, 1983; Epitaph, symphonic poem, 1988. *Recordings:* Introduction & Perpetuum Mobile; Symphony; Symphonic Dances; String Quartet; Cello Sonata; Romances; Piano Poem. *Memberships:* Armenian & CIS Composers' Societies. *Current Management:* Armenian Composers' Union. *Address:* c/o Armenian Composers' Union, Demirchyan str. 25, Yerevan 375002, Armenia, CIS.

MISKELL Austin, b. 14 Oct. 1925, Shawnee, Oklahoma, USA. Professor; Singer. Divorced, 2 sons. *Education:* Oklahoma City University, 1946-47; Hochschule für Musik, Zurich, 1955-65; Mozarteum of Salzburg Austria, 1955-65; LRAM, Royal Academy of Music, London, England. *Career:* Featured Soloist with Elizabethan Consort of Viols, London, Anglian Chamber Soloists London, Ricecare, Ensemble for Ancient Music, Zurich, Arte Antica Zurich; Sang in 25 countries, 1950-86; Performances with Tonhalle Orchestra, Zurich, Orchestra de la Academia Santa Cecilia Rome, London

Symphony Orchestra, Pro Arte, London, Stuttgarter Synfoniker, etc.; Participant, Music Festivals including: Sagra Musicale, Perugia, Italy; Settimane Musicali, Ascona; Salzburg Bach Festival; Britten, Purcell Festival, Buenos Aires; Mozart Festival, Munich, Bergen Festival, Norway, etc., 1970-80; Assistant Professor, Voice, National University of Colombia, Bogotà, 1976-82; Head, Voice, Conservatory of Tolima, Ibague, Colombia, 1978-82; Teacher, Voice, Italian Opera, Teato Colon, National Opera Co., Bogotà, 1978-81; Lecturer, Voice, University of New Mexico, 1982-83; Professor, Voice, College of Santa Fe, 1982-85. *Recordings:* Numerous including: I Sing America, 1969; Radha Krishna, 1971; Pergolesi Requiem, 1972; Ballades Rondeaux and Virelais, 1973. *Publications:* Poetry - The Salt Cathedral, 1981. *Address:* PO Box 204, Manhasset, Long Island, NY 11030, USA.

MISSENHARDT Gunter, b. 29 Mar 1938, Augsburg, Germany. Singer (Bass). m. Agnes Baltsa, 1974. *Education:* Studied at the Augsburg Conservatory and with Helge Roswaenge. *Career:* Sang at the Bayerische Staatsoper Munich, 1965-68, Frankfurt, 1968-72, Berne, 1973-78; Appearances from 1978 at Aachen, Bremen and Darmstadt-Brussels, 1986 Dusseldorf 1988 and Theatre des Champs Elysees Paris, 1989, as Ochs in Der Rosenkavalier; Season 1987-88 as the Doctor in Wozzeck at Strasbourg and Schigolch in Lulu at Brussels; Other roles have included Kecal, Osmin, Bett in Zar und Zimmerman, Masetto, Mozart's Figaro and Varlaam in Boris Godunov. *Address:* c/o Deutsche Oper am Rhein, Heinrich Heine Allee 16, 4000 Dusseldorf, Germany.

MITCHELL Antoine Philip, b. 17 Feb 1954, London, England. Conductor; Pianist; Composer, Harpsichord. *Education:* Trinity College of Music, London; Royal Academy of Music, London; Accademia Musicale Chigiana, Siena. *Career:* Director, London Telemann Ensemble; American Youth Symphony and Chorus, 1972; Sofia Conservatoire Orchestra; Russe Philharmonic Orchestra; Essex Symphony Orchestra; Southend Symphony Orchestra; CSSR State Philharmonic; Estonia Symphony Orchestra; Sao Carlos Opera, Lisbon; Members, Royal Philharmonic Orchestra, Royal Festival Hall, 1987; Artistic Director, Lublin State Philharmonic Orchestra; Director Ferrara Ensemble; Lubliner Bach Ensemble; Estonia Symphony Orchestra; Youth Orchestra, Second Essex Youth Orchestra; Cain Symphony Orchestra; Essex Musical Association; Professor of Piano and Conducting, Anglia University. *Compositions:* Chansons de Charles Baudelaire; Pieces for Solo Viola (Violin); Songs (various); Elegia for Strings; Toccata for Piano; Chansons Pour Petits Enfants, 1988; Canto for a Capella Choir, 1991: Preludes for Piano, 1991; 6 songs for baritone, 1993; Pieces d'Orgues, 1993; Various arrangements. *Current Management:* Anness and Partners, 5 Station Road, Felstead, Essex, England. *Address:* 23 The Avenue, Braintree, Essex CM7 6HY, England.

MITCHELL Clare, b. 1960, England. Costume and Stage Designer. *Education:* Studied at the Bristol Old Vic Theatre School. *Career:* Assist Constume Designer, Royal Shakespeare Company, Stratford; Costumes for premiere of Rebecca by Wilfrid Josephs at Leeds, 1983; English National Oper for Madama Butterfly, Scottish Opera Don Giovanni, and Jenufa in production by Yuri Lyubimov at Zurich and Covent Garden, 1986-93; costumes and sets for Ulisse by Monteverdi and Handel's Flavio at the Batignano Festival, Rigoletto for Opera 80 and Donizetti's Tudor trilogy for Monte Carlo Opera.

MITCHELL Donald Charles Peter, b. 6 Feb. 1925, London, England. Writer on Music; Critic. m. Kathleen Burbidge. *Education:* Dulwich College 1939-42; Durham University 1949-50, with Arthur Hutchings and A.E.F. Dickinson. *Career:* Founded Music Survey 1947: Co-editor until 1952; Music Critic The Musical Times 1953-57; Editor of Tempo 1958-62; Head of Music Department at Faber and Faber 1958; Managing Director of Faber Music 1965-71, Chairman 1977-86; Music Staff of Daily Telegraph 1959-64; Professor of Music at Sussex

University 1971-76, Visiting Professor from 1976; Chairman of Performing Right Society, 1989; Director of Study Courses at the Britten-Pears School, Snape. *Publications include:* Joint Editor Benjamin Britten 1952; The Mozart Companion 1956; Author, 3 volumes of a projected 4 on the life and music of Mahler, 1958-86; The Language of Modern Music 1963; Benjamin Britten, 1913-76: Pictures from a Life, with J. Evans, 1978; Britten and Auden in the Thirties 1981; Benjamin Britten: Death in Venice, 1987; Letters from a Life: Selected Letters and Diaries of Benjamin Britten, Vols. 1 and 2 1923-1945, with Philip Reed. *Contributions to:* Music Survey, The Chesterian, Tempo, Musical Times, Music and Letters and Opera: articles on Reger, Schoenberg, Weill, Berg, Malcolm Arnold, Hindemith, Britten, Prokofiev and Stravinsky. *Honours:* PhD (Southampton), Hon MA (Sussex), Doctor of University of York, Mahler Medal (1987). *Address:* 83 Ridgmount Gardens, London WC1E 7AY, England.

MITCHELL Geoffrey Roger, b. 6 June 1936, Upminster, Essex, England. Counter-Tenor; Conductor; Choral Manager. *Education:* Studied with Alfred Deller & Lucy Menen. *Career:* Counter-tenor/lay-clerk, Ely Cathedral 1957-60, Westminster Cathedral 1960-61; Vicar-choral, St Paul's Cathedral, 1961-66; Founder & conductor, Surrey University Choir, 1966; Manager, John Alldis Choir 1966-, Cantores in Ecclesia 1967-77; BBC Choral Manager, 1977-1992; Conductor, New London Singers 1970-86, Geoffrey Mitchell Choir 1976-; Professor, Royal Academy of Music, 1974-; Singing teacher, King's College & St John's College, Cambridge, 1975-85; Guest Conductor, Camerata Antigua of Curitiba, Brazil. *Recordings:* Various, with John Alldis Choir, Cantores in Ecclesia, Pro Cantione Antiqua, and Opera Rara. *Honours:* Honorary associate, Royal Academy of Music, 1981; Vice chairman, Federation of Cathedral Old Chorister Associations, 1987-1992; Chairman, 1992-; Hon. Fellow, Trinity College London. *Membership:* British Broadcasting Corporation Club. *Hobbies:* Collecting antique prints; Swimming; Food. *Address:* 49 Chelmsford Road, Woodford, London E18 2PW, England.

MITCHELL Ian, b. 14 Feb 1948, South Yorkshire, England. Clarinettist. m. Vanessa Noel-Tod, 5 Sept 1970, 1 son, 1 daughter. *Education:* Royal Academy of Music, 1966-70; GRSM; London University, Goldsmiths' College, 1976-79; BMus, London. *Debut:* Purcell Room, London, 1971. *Career:* Solo appearances throughout Britain, Europe, Middle East, USA (4 tours) Australia, N. Korea; Chamber Concerts widely in Europe; Solo Broadcasts BBC, Swedish, New York, Belgian, Austrian, German Radio Stations; Soloist on British TV and in film of composer Cornelius Cardew; Numerous first performances, many works written for him; Director of Gemini Leading 20th Century Ensemble which is a pioneer in music education; Member of Dreamtiger, Eisler Ensemble of London, Entertainers Clarinet Quartet, AMM. *Recordings:* Works of Nicola LeFanu (with Gemini); Works of Oliver Knussen; Draughtman's Contract, The Masterwork and others with Michael Nyman Band; Eisler with Dagmar Krauze; Works by David Lumsdaine, John White. *Hobbies:* Family; Reading; Badger Watching. *Address:* 137 Upland Road, East Dulwich, London SE22 0DF, England.

MITCHELL Kenneth Stephen, b. 11 Sept 1953, St Louis, Missouri, USA. Musicologist; Harpsichordist-Organist; Conductor. *Education:* BM, Organ Performance, 1978, MM, Conducting, 1980, Webster University; PhD Candidate, Musicology, Washington University, *Career:* Assistant Conductor, St Louis Bach Chorus, 1972-75; Music Director and Conductor, Chamber Academy Orchestra, 1978-81; Specialist in Historical Performance Practice, 17th and 18th century Keyboard Music; Current research in 17th century music theory, philosophy and aesthetics. *Honours:* Conducting Fellow, Aspen Music Festival, 1979; Research Fellow, Washington University, 1986-88; Nussbaum Graduate Research Fellowship, Washington University, 1988-89. *Memberships:* American Musicological Society; Westfield Center for Early Keyboard Studies. *Hobbies:*

Intercultural philosophy and religion; Construction of historical instruments; Observational astronomy; Philosophy of science. *Address:* Washington University, Department of Music, Campus Box 1032, One Brookings Drive, St Louis, MO 63130, USA.

MITCHELL Lee, b. 27 Apr 1951, Wilmington, Delaware, USA. Composer; Pianist; Educator. *Education:* B.Mus., Peabody Institute, Johns Hopkins University, 1970; Studies, University of California, Santa Barbara; PhD, University of Berne, Switzerland, 1976. *Debut:* Wilmington, Delaware. *Career:* Professor, Music Theory & History, Academy of Music, Biel, Switzerland, 1973-76; Professor, Music Theory & History, Peabody Institute, Johns Hopkins University, Baltimore, 1976-86; Chairman, Theory, (Hopkins), 1984-86; Adjunct Professor, Music, Goucher College, Towson, Maryland, 1980-83; Lecturer, University of Esztergom, Hungary, 1980, 1981, 1983; Professor of Music, Johns Hopkins University, School of Continuing Studies, 1986-; TV Appearances, Baltimore, 1969; Radio Appearances, Budapest, 1981, Switzerland, 1993; Piano Concerts, USA, Switzerland, Germany, England, Holland, Greece, Hungary; Compositions performed in USA, Peru, Europe. *Compositions include:* Sonatina, Flute & Piano, 1967; Sonata, Trumpet & Piano, 1968; Pater Noster, 1967; O Surely, Reaving Peace, 1968; Three Songs for Voice and Piano; Chamber Ballet for Broken Consort of Instruments, 1965; Kaleidoscope for Orchestra, 1965; Mass; Two Etudes for Piano; 5 Songs for Voice & Piano; Cycle of Five Sacred Songs of David, 1976; Concerto for Piano & String Orchestra, 1983; A Credo and Agnus Dei, 1984; The Holy Child is Born (A Christmas Oratorio), 1987; Paradisli, 1990-91; Magnificat and Nunc Dimittis 1991; Notebook; Trio Americano for Violin, Piano and Percussion, 1992; Eine Kleine Hochzeitsmusik, 1992; Ave verum corpus; Ave Maria; The Lord is Risen (An Easter Anthem); Seven Gibran Vignettes for Solo Flute, 1993. *Address:* Comanche Circle/Warwick Park, Millsboro, DE 19966, USA.

MITCHELL Leona, b. 13 Oct 1949, Enid, Oklahoma, USA. Singer (Soprano). *Education:* Studied at University of Oklahoma and in Santa Fe and San Francisco; With Ernest St. John Metz in Los Angeles. *Debut:* San Francisco 1972, as Micaela in Carmen; Metropolitan Opera from 1975, as Micaela, Pamina, Puccini's Manon, Liu and Mimi, Elvira in Ernani and Leonora in La Forza del Destino; Barcelona 1975, as Mathilde in Guillaume Tell; Guest appearances in Houston, Washington, Stuttgart and Geneva; Covent Garden debut 1980, as Liu in Turandot; Sydney Opera 1985, as Leonora in Il Trovatore; Nice Opera, 1987, as Salomé in Massenet's Hérodiade; Paris Opéra-Comique in Puccini's Trittico (all 3 soprano leads); Verona 1988, Aida; Sang Elvira in Ernani at Parma, 1990, the Trovatore Leonora at the Teatro Colón Buenos Aires; Season 1992 as Aida for New Israeli Opera. *Recordings include:* Gershwin's Bess (Decca). *Address:* c/o Teatro Regio, Via Garibaldi 16, 1-43100 Parma, Italy.

MITCHELL Madeleine Louise, b. 2 Mar 1957, Essex, England. Concert Violinist. *Education:* Junior Exhibitioner, Royal College of Music, 1969-75; Fondation Scholar, 1975-79; GRSM (1st class hons), 1978; ARCM (Teachers honours and performers honours), 1979; Eastman and Juilliard Schools, New York, MMus (Violin performance), 1981. *Debut:* London, recital South Bank, 1984. *Career:* BBC 1, TV Music Time, 1979; London South Bank recitals include Awards by Park Lane Group, Worshipful Company Musicians, Kirckman Society; Numerous solo tours in concertos & recitals in Britain, Germany, Spain, Czechoslovakia, Italy, USA, Canada; World Tour (British Council), 1989 and 1990; Broadcasts, Australia - ABC & Channel 7 TV, Germany, Britain, Singapore, Italian TV, Canada; Violinist Fires of London, 1985-87; Several solo works written for her; Numerous international Festival appearances including: Huddersfield, Dartington, Malvern, Aspen, Bath, Belfast, Dvořák (CCSR); Schwetzingen, Toronto; Soloist on tour with Wurttemberg, Munich Chamber Orchestras; Ulster, Czech Radio symphony (Plzen), Malaga Symphony of

Spain, Academy of London; London Festival Orchestra; Karlsbad SO (CSSR); Wigmore Hall debut recital, 1989; Solo tour South America, 1991; Concertos with City of London Orchestra, QEH, London 1992, RPO London 1993; Ulster Orchestra; Tours also include Poland, Ukraine, 2 South Bank Recitals, 1993. *Compositions:* Works M Mitchell specially written for her by Brian Elias, Stuart Jones, Piers Hellawell, Anthony Powers, Gorecki, Michael Nyman. *Recordings:* Broadcasts in Hong Kong; Colombia; Czechoslovakia; Messiaen Quartet for the End of Time for Collins Classics with Joanna MacGregor, 1993; Broadcasts also include BBC radio & TV. *Hobbies:* Fine art; Dancing; Swimming; Cycling. *Current Management:* Neil Chaffey Concert Promotions, 8 Laxton Gardens, Baldock, Herts, England. *Address:* 41 Queens Gardens, Lancaster Gate, London W2 3AA, England.

MITCHELL Scott, b. 1964, Perth, Scotland. Pianist. *Education:* Studied at the Royal Academy of Music with Alexander Kelly and John Streets; Further study with members of the Amadeus Quartet. *Career:* Member of the Borante Piano Trio from 1982: London performances at the Purcell Room and Wigmore Hall in the trios of Beethoven; Tours to Dublin, Paris and Vienna Beethoven's Triple Concerto at the 1989 Festival Wiener Klassik; Concerts in Tel Aviv and Jerusalem and association with the Israel Piano trio at the 1988 Dartington Summer School; Season 1990 at the Perth and Bath Festivals, tour of Scandinavia, Russia and the Baltic States; Television appearances on Channel 4 and BSB; Duo partnerships with Laurence Jackson (violin) and Duncan Prescott (clarinet), with concerts at the Wigmore Hall and Purcell Room; Accompanist to Yvonne Howard (mezzo-soprano) and Barry Banks (tenor), including tour of France, Spain and Portugal 1989. *Recordings:* Albums for Chandos with Duncan Prescott and Collins Classics with Jennifer Stinton (flute). *Honours include:* Leverhulme Scholarship; English Speaking Union Scholarship; Lisa Fuchsova Prize, Royal Overseas League Competition 1990. *Current Management:* Scott Mitchell Management. *Address:* 26 Childebert Road, Balham, London SW17 8EX, England.

MITCHINSON John Leslie, b. 31 Mar 1932, Blackrod, Lancashire, England. Opera and Concert Singer (Tenor). m. Maureen Guy (Mezzo-Soprano), 8 Mar 1958, 2 sons. *Education:* Royal Manchester College of Music; ARMCM; FRMCM; Studied singing with Frederick Cox, Heddle Nash and Boriska Gereb. *Debut:* TV Series with Eric Robinson (Music For You); Stage debut as Jupiter in Handel's Semele at Sadler's Wells Theatre, 1959. *Career:* Senior Lecturer, Royal Northern College of Music, 1987-92; Head of Vocal Studies, Welsh College of Music & Drama, 1992-; Many Radio, TV, Concert and Opera appearances worldwide, ENO, WNO, Scottish Opera, Basle Opera, Prague Opera; Most of the world's Music Festivals; Roles include: Idomeneo, Aegisthus, Luca (House of The Dead), Manolios (Greek Passion); Dalibor, Florestan, Siegmund; Sang Svatopluk Cech in the first British production of Janáček's The Excursions of Mr Brouček, ENO 1978; Wagner's Tristan, Beethoven's Florestan and Peter Grimes for Welsh National Opera; Opera North and Buxton Festival, 1983 as Max in Der Freischütz and Gualtiero in Vivaldi's Griselda. *Recordings:* Mahler 8th Symphony, Bernstein; Mahler 8th Symphony, Wyn Morris; Lied von der Erde, Sir Alexander Gibson; Béatrice et Bénedict (Berlioz) Colin Davis; Lelio, (Berlioz) Pierre Boulez; Tristan und Isolde (Wagner) Reginald Goodall; Glagolitic Mass (Janáček) Simon Rattle; The Greek Passion (Martinů) Charles Mackerras; Dream of Gerontius (Elgar), Simon Rattle; Glagolitic Mass, Kurt Masur, Gewandhaus Orch, 1990. *Honours:* Queens Prize and Royal Philharmonic Kathleen Ferrier Prize 1956-57; Curtis Gold Medal (RMCM) 1953; Ricordi Opera Prize 1952. *Hobbies:* Cooking; Boats. *Address:* The Verzons Granary, Munsley, Ledbury, Herefordshire, England.

MITIC Nikola, b. 27 Nov 1938, Nis, Serbia. Singer (Bass- baritone). *Education:* Studied in Belgrade and with V Badiali in Milan. *Career:* Many appearances at the Belgrade National Opera from 1965; Guest engagements with the company at Copenhagen, 1968, Barcelona, 1972. Further appearances at the Vienna Staatsoper, Philadelphia, 1970, Dusseldorf, Perugia Festival, 1973, Rome, 1975 and Dublin; Roles have included Rigoletto, Mozart's Figaro, Eugene Onegin, Mazeppa, Riccardo and I Puritani, Posa in Don Carlos and Enrico in Lucia di Lammermoor. *Address:* c/o Teatro dell'Opera di Roma, Piazza B. Gigli 8, 00184 Rome, Italy.

MITO Motoko, b. 13 June 1957, Kyoto, Japan. Violinist. m. Yoske Otawa, 17 Mar 1989. *Education:* Toho School of Music, Tokyo; Hochschule Mozarteum, Salzburg, Austria. *Debut:* Salzburg. *Career:* Concertmaster, International Music Art Society Orchestra, Tokyo, 1980-81; Soloist, International Mozart Week, Salzburg, 1984; Many recitals and appearances with Professor Erika Frieser, piano, throughout Europe and Japan, 1984-; Member of Salzburger Streichquartett, 1987-. *Recordings:* Preiser Record, 1 Salzburger Streichquartett; Preiser Record, 2 Salzburger Streichquartett. *Current Management:* Sound Gazely, Tokyo, Japan. *Address:* Kamiyasumatsu 11, Tokorozawa, Japan.

MITTELMANN Norman, b. 25 May 1932, Winnipeg, Manitoba, Canada. Opera Singer, Baritone. m. 24 Feb. 1979, 2 daughters. *Education:* Curtis Institute of Music, with Martial Singher, Ernzo Mascherini, diploma, 1959. *Debut:* Toronto Opera Company. *Career includes:* Opera houses, Germany, Italy, Austria; Puerto Rico; Canada; USA; Poland; Switzerland. Roles include: Amonasro/ Aida, Zurich, 1967; William Tell, May Festival, Florence, 1969; Rigoletto/Rigoletto, Chicago Opera Theatre, 1977; Scarpia/Tosca, Venice, 1979; John Falstaff/ Falstaff, Hamburg & Berlin, 1979; Nélusko/L'Africaine, San Francisco Opera; Mandryka/Arabella, La Scala; Sang at Zurich until 1982. *Recordings include:* Video of La Gioconda, from San Francisco, 1979 (Ottocento). *Honours:* Fellow, Rockefeller Foundation, 1956-59; Award, Fischer Foundation, 1959. *Hobby:* Gardening. *Current Management:* Robert Lombardo Associates, 61 West 62nd Street, Suite F, New York, NY 10023, USA. *Address:* c/o Robert Lombardo, NYC.

MIXTER Keith Eugene, b. 22 May 1922, Lansing, Michigan, USA. Musicologist. m. Beatrice Mary Ruf, 30 June 1950, 3 sons, 1 daughter. *Education:* University of Basel 1947-49; BM, Michigan State University 1947; AM, University of Chicago 1952; PhD, University of North Carolina 1962. *Career:* Music Librarian, University of North Carolina 1953-61; Assistant Professor 1961-65; Associate Professor 1965-74; Professor 1974-91; The Ohio State University; Summer Teaching at The University of North Carolina 1961, University of Colorado 1966, and University of Wisconsin 1969; Professor Emeritus, 1991-. *Publications:* Johannes Brassart, Sechs Motetten 1960; General Bibliography For Music Research 1962, 2nd Edition 1975; An Introduction To Library Resources For Music Research 1963; Johannes Brassart, Opera Omnia, 2 Volumes 1965-71. *Contributions to:* Music Journal, Die Musik In Geschichte und Gegenwart, Enciclopedia della Musica; New Grove Dictionary of Music and Musicians; Musica Disciplina and others. *Honours:* University of Chicago Fellow 1950-51; Joint-Recipient, Harriet Cohen Prize for Musicology 1962. *Hobbies:* Chess; Sailing. *Address:* 4455 Shields Place, Columbus, OH 43214, USA.

MIYAZAKI Shigeru, b. 9 Dec 1950, Tokyo, Japan. Composer; Critic. m. Yoko Toriumi, 23 Sept 1976. *Education:* BA, German, Dokkyo University; Private studies with Tomojiro Ikenouchi, 1966-67; Teruyuki Noda, 1967-76. *Debut:* 44 Music Contest of Japan (Nippon Ongaku Concours). *Career:* 44 Music Contest of Japan (NHK Radio), 1975; Orchestral Concert by New Compositions, 1977; The World of Shigeru Miyazaki, 1987 and many composition concerts with other young composers. *Compositions:* Variations (for piano and string quartet), 1969; Hommage (flute, violoncello and harp), 1975; Quintette à Cordes, 1979; 3 Intermazzi for piano, 1983; 2 Kavatinen for Orchestra, 1984; Romanza for viola and Piano, 1985; Scena for Organ, 1986;

Notturno for Strings, 1987; Serenata for Bass clarinet and Piano, 1987. *Memberships:* Japanese Society for Contemporary Music; Japan Federation of Composers; Shin-shin-Kai. *Hobby:* Japanese Chess. *Address:* 4-37-7-604 Honkomagome Bunkyo-ku, Tokyo 113, Japan.

MIYAZAWA Junichi, b. 23 Nov 1963, Gunma, Japan. Music Critic; Writer; Translator; Researcher of Russian Literature. *Education:* Bachelor of Polit Sci, Aoyama Gakuin University, Tokyo, 1986; BA, 1988, MA, 1990, Waseda University, Tokyo. *Career:* Research Assistant, Waseda University, 1993-; Music Critic, GQ Japan, 1993-. *Publications:* Glenn Gould (ed), 1988; Glenn Gould, pluriel (co-translator), 1991; Glenn Gould Studies (co-author), 1991; Glenn Gould: A Life and Variations, (translator), 1992; A Book on Andrei Tarkovsky's The Morror, (co-translator), 1993; Numerous articles, liner notes and translations. *Hobbies:* Jogging; Zen Meditation. *Address:* Apt. 305, 6-3-5 Funabashi, Setagaya-ku, Tokyo 156, Japan.

MIZELLE (Dary) John, b. 14 June 1940, Stillwater, Oklahoma, USA. Composer. *Education:* Studied at the California State University and University of California at Davis, (PhD, 1977). *Career:* Tutor, University of Florida, 1973-75, Oberlin College, 1975-79, State University at Purchase, New York, 1990. *Compositions include:* Polyphonies, I-III, 1975-78; Polytempus I for trumpet and tape, 1976; Primavera-Heterphony for 24 cellos, 1977; Samadhi for quadrophonic tape, 1978; Quanta II and Hymn of the World for 2 choruses and ensemble, 1979; Lake Mountain Thunder for cor anglais and percussion ensemble, 1981; Thunderclap of time, music for a planetarium, 1982; Requiem Mass for chorus and orchestra, 1982; Sonic Adventures, 1982; Quintet for Woodwinds 1983; Contrabass Quartet, 1983; Indian Summer for string quartet and oboe, 1983; Sounds for orchestra, 1984; Concerto for contrabass and orchestra, 1974-85; Genesis for orchestra, 1985; Blue for orchestra 1986; Percussion Concerto 1987; Parameters for percussion solo and chamber orchestra, 1974-87; Earth Mountain Fire, 1987-; Fossy: A Passion Play music theater, 1987; Chance Gives me What I Want, dance, 1988. *Address:* ASCAP, ASCAP Building, One Lincoln Plaza, NY 10023, USA.

MIZZI Alfred (Freddie) Paul, b. 12 Oct 1934, Valletta, Malta. Musician (Clarinettist). m. 24 June 1953. 2 daughters. *Education:* ALCM, 1966. *Debut:* As soloist with the Malta National Orchestra, 1961. *Career includes:* Belfast Arts Festival, 1967; Member, World Symphony Orchestra performances in New York, Washington and Florida, 1971; Soloist in concerts in Bucharest, Mannheim, Mozart Castle, Darmstadt, Wigmore Hall and Barbican Centre, London, 1973-83; Concerts in France and Greece as part of the Mediterranean Arts Festival, 1985; Concerts at the Czechoslovakia Arts Festival, 1986; Soloist with: Stamitz Symphony Orchestra, West Germany; Watford Chamber Orchestra, England; Zapadocesky Symphony Orchester, Czechoslovakia and others. Soloist with string quartets: The Brevis String Quartet, Malta; Salzburg String Quartet, Austria; Sinnhoffer String Quartet, West Germany; Quartetto Academica, Rumania; The Rasumovsky String Quartet, Great Britain and others. Television appearances and radio broadcasts in Malta, Rumania, BBC Germany, USA, France, Greece, Italy. *Honours:* Phoenicia International Culture Award, 1985; Malta Society of Arts Award, 1986. *Membership:* Performing Rights Society, London. *Hobbies:* Paintings; Football. *Current Management:* Corinthia Group of Companies. *Address:* Il Klarinett, Ursuline Sisters Street, G'Mangia, Malta.

MOBBS Kenneth William, b. 4 Aug 1925, Northants, England. Keyboard specialist; Tutor. m. (1) Barbara McNeill, 2 Sept 1950; (2) Mary J Randall, 18 May 1979. 3 daughters. *Education:* Clare College, Cambridge; Royal College of Music. Private studies with Greville Cooke and M P Conway. *Debut:* Organ Recital, Kings College, Cambridge, 1949. *Career:* Lecturer, then Senior Lecturer, Music, University of Bristol, 1950-83; Freelance keyboard performer, including harpsichord

concerto and solo piano, fortepiano recitals and numerous accompaniments on BBC Radio; Director, Mobbs Keyboard Collection. *Compositions include:* Engaged!, comic opera, 1963. *Recordings include:* Mobbs Keyboard Collection, vol I; Golden Age of the Clarinet. *Publications:* Contributor to Encyclopaedia of Keyboard Instruments, 1993; Early Music; Galpin Society Journal; English Harpsichord Magazine. *Hobbies:* Photography; Bird watching. *Address:* 16 All Saints Road, Bristol, BS8 2JJ, England.

MÖDL Martha, b. 22 Mar 1912, Nuremberg, Germany. Singer (Soprano and Mezzo-Soprano). *Education:* Studied in Nuremberg and with Otto Mueller in Milan. *Debut:* Sang Humperdinck's Hansel at Remscheid in 1943. *Career:* Dusseldorf Opera 1945-49 in mezzo roles; Sang at Hamburg from 1949 as a soprano; Covent Garden debut 1950, as Carmen: returned 1966 as Strauss's Clytemnestra and 1972 in Die schweigsame Frau; Bayreuth 1951-67 as Kundry, Brünnhilde, Sieglinde, Waltraute, Gutrune and Isolde; 1955 sang Beethoven's Leonore at the reopening of the Vienna State Opera; Metropolitan Opera debut 1957, as Brünnhilde; 1963 sang the Nurse in the production of Strauss's Die Frau ohne Schatten at the reopening of the Munich Opera; Sang in the premieres of Reimann's Melusine 1971 and Ghost Sonata 1984, Fortner's Elisabeth Tudor 1972, Von Einem's Kabale und Liebe 1978 and Cerha's Baal 1981; sang The Countess in The Queen of Spades at Nice, 1989 and at Essen 1990. *Recordings:* Der Ring des Nibelungen and Fidelio, conducted by Furtwängler; Elektra (Cetra); Oedipus Rex (Philips); Parsifal (Decca); Die Frau ohne Schatten (Deutsche Grammophon). *Address:* c/o Theater Essen, Rolandstrasse 10, D-4300 Essen, Germany.

MOE Bjørn Kåre, b. 10 Aug 1946, Hegra, Norway. Concert organist. m. Kristine Kaasa, 21 June 1975. *Education:* Trondheim School of Music 1963-67; Musik-Akademie der Stadt Basel Abteilung Konservatorium and Schola Cantorum Basiliensis 1968-73 (Eduard Müller and Wolfgang Neininger a.o); Paris (Gaston Litaize) and Praha (Jiri Reinberger). *Career:* Professor at Tröndelag Musik-konservatorium, Trondheim 1973-84; Full-time Concert Organist 1985-; Concerts with the complete works of Olivier Messiaen, the main works of Max Reger and other organ music from all periods; World premiere of several new works from Switzerland, Iceland and Norway (45 minutes work of Ketil Hvoslef Revelations of John in The Bergen International Festival 1986); Co-operates with other arts as theatre, dance and poetry (Exultate, concert with dance recitation and organ, performed 20 times in the main cities in the Nordic countries); Organ Expert/Counsellor. *Address:* Postboks 16, N-7084 Melhus, Norway.

MOENNE-LOCCOZ Philippe, b. 21 Mar 1953, Annecy, France. Musician; Composer. m. 30 Aug 1986, 1 son. *Education:* CAP études secon daires techniques (di éffectué également des études de dessin industriel, nireau BTS (bac technique); Studies electro-acoustic composition, 20th century analysis, string bass, contemporary, classical and popular music. *Debut:* At age 10. *Career:* Teaches aspects of music through animation at special children's Centre; Teacher of Guitar and Electro-acoustic Music; Teacher of electro-acoustique music, Conservatoire de Genève, Switzerland; Director, Collectif et Compagnie (studio for research, creative work and music education), Annecy. *Compositions:* Electro-acoustic works: Boucles; Rèves opaques; Oscillation; Petite musique du Soir; Mixed works (electro-acoustic and traditional instruments): Le cri des idées sur l'eau; Rencontre; Mixage 4; Oscillation No 1, 2, 6; Chaos for tape only; Aspérités (CDO2), 1992; Fermez la porte, 1992; Inventions, 1991. *Recordings:* Rèves opaques, Cassette C1; Le cri des idées sur l'eau, Radio Suisse Romande; CD's, Trola, Chutts etc..., 1989. *Membership:* Association for Electro-acoustic Music, Geneva. *Address:* 16 Impasse des Tablettes, 74940 Annecy Le Vieux, France.

MOEVS Robert Walter, b. 2 Dec 1920, La Crosse,

Wisconsin, USA. Composer; Professor. m. Maria Teresa Marabini, 1 Oct 1953, 1 son, 1 daughter. *Education:* BA, Harvard College, 1942; Conservatoire National, Paris, France, 1947-51; MA, Harvard University, USA, 1952. *Career:* Fellow, American Academy in Rome; Professor, Harvard University, USA, 1955-63; Professor, Rutgers, 1964-91; Professor Emeritus, 1991. *Compositions:* Numerous works for solo instruments, chorus, orchestra, chamber music. *Recordings:* Numerous works recorded. *Publications:* Numerous works published in Paris, Italy and USA. *Contributions to:* Musical Quarterly; Perspectives of New Music; Journal of Music Theory. *Honours:* Award, National Institute of Arts and Letters, 1956; Recipient, Guggenheim Fellowship, 1963-64; Several ASCAP Awards for a number of years. *Memberships:* Founding Member, American Society of University Composers; Executive Committee, International Society for Contemporary Music; National Associate, Sigma Alpha Iota. *Address:* Blackwell's Mills, Belle Mead, NJ 08502, USA.

MOFFAT Alan Lyndon, b. 10 Nov 1949, Sydney, New South Wales, Australia. Cathedral Organist. *Education:* Saint Andrew's Cathedral School, Sydney, 1961-67; FTCL, 1973; LMus (AMEB), 1972; RSCM, 1975; Pupil of Jean Langlais, 1980; Australian Catholic University, 1988-. *Career:* Deputy Organist, 1968-81, Assistant Organist, 1981-84, Saint Andrew's Cathedral, Sydney; Federal Music Librarian, Australian Broadcasting Corporation, 1975-84; Precentor and Organist, Grafton Cathedral, 1984-88; Organist and Master of the Choristers, Holy Trinity Cathedral, Wangaratta, 1988-. *Recordings:* Australian Broadcasting Corporation. *Contributions to:* Sydney Organ Journal. *Memberships:* Royal College of Organists; Royal School of Church Music; Organ Society of Sydney. *Hobbies:* Reading; Cooking; Liturgiology. *Address:* 3 The Close, Wangaratta, Victoria 3677, Australia.

MOFFO Anna, b. 27 June 1932, Wayne, Pennsylvania, USA. Singer (Soprano). *Education:* Studied at the Curtis Institute with E. Giannini-Gregory; Rome with Luigi Ricci and Mercedes Llopart. *Debut:* Sang Norina in Don Pasquale at Spoleto in 1955. *Career:* Madama Butterfly on Italian TV 1954; Sang Mozart's Zerlina at Aix in 1956 and Verdi's Nannetta at Salzburg 1957; Metropolitan Opera from 1959, as Verdi's Violetta and Gilda, Donizetti's Lucia and Adina, Puccini's Liu, Mozart's Pamina, Massenet's Manon, Gounod's Marguerite and Juliette, the soprano roles in Les Contes d'Hoffmann and Debussy's Mélisande; Covent Garden debut 1964, as Gilda; Guest appearances in Berlin, Vienna and Buenos Aires; Sang Thaïs at Seattle, 1976 and Adriana Lecouvreur at Parma, 1978. *Recordings:* La Bohème, Le Nozze di Figaro, Capriccio, Carmen and Falstaff (Columbia); Lucia di Lammermoor, Hänsel und Gretel, Iphigénie en Aulide (Eurodisc); Madama Butterfly, Il Filosofo di Campagna, La Serva Padrona, Luisa Miller (RCA); Film version of La Traviata *Address:* c/o Metropolitan Opera, Lincoln Center, New York, NY 10023, USA.

MOHLER Hubert, b. 1922, Augsburg, Germany. Singer (Tenor). *Education:* Studied in Augsburg. *Career:* Sang in the choir of the Augsburg Stadttheater, 1946-52; Appeared in solo roles at Gelsenkirchen, 1952-57, Oberhausen, 1957-61, Augsburg, 1961-64; Many appearances at the Cologne Opera, 1964-89, as Mozart's Pedrillo, Monostatos and Basilio, Mime in the Ring, David in Die Meistersinger, Valzacchi (Rosenkavalier), the Captain in Wozzeck, the character roles in Les Contes d'Hoffmann and Adam in The Devils of Loudun; Many appearances in Germany and abroad as concert singer. *Recordings include:* Mozart Masses; Les Brigands by Offenbach. *Address:* c/o Oper der Stadt Koln, Offenbachplatz, 5000 Cologne, Germany.

MOHR Thomas, b. 17 Oct 1961, Neumunster, Holstein, Germany. Singer (Baritone). *Education:* Studied in Lubeck, graduating in 1985, and in Hamburg. *Debut:* Lubeck 1984, as Sivio in Pagliacci. *Career:* Sang at Lubeck and Detmold, 1984-85, Bremen, 1985-87,

Nationaltheater Mannheim, from 1987; Guest appearances at the Schleswig-Holstein Festival, 1987, and at Cologne, Hamburg and Ludwigsburg; Other roles include Mozart's Count and Papageno, Rossini's Figaro, Lortzing'z Zar and Count, Der Wildschütz), Wolfram and Billy Budd; Many concerts and Lieder recitals. *Honours include:* Winner, 1984 s'Hertogenbosch Competition, 1985 German Lied Competition, London. *Address:* Nationaltheater, Am Goetheplatz, 6800 Mannheim, Germany.

MÖHRINGER Karel Johannes Frederick, b. 26 July 1930, Zwolle, Netherlands. Cellist; Musician. *Education:* High School, Conservatory, University and Music Academy. *Debut:* Antwerp, 1951. *Career:* Solo Cellist, Rheinisches Kammer-orchester, Cologne; Now Solo Cellist and Gamba Player, Rotterdam Philharmonic Orchestra; Performances all over the world and on film, television and radio. *Recordings:* Numerous. *Contributions to:* Numerous magazines. *Honours:* Kammermusikert der Stadt Köln; 2nd Prize, String quartet competition, Liège. *Memberships:* Alpine Club; Rotary Club. *Hobbies include:* Painting; Since 1984 also very succesful draughtsman of portraits of conductors and soloists. Several exhibitions; Films; Photography. *Address:* Johan Braakensiekstraat 119, 3119 NN Schiedam, Netherlands.

MOLDOVEANU Eugenia, b. 19 Mar 1944, Busteni, Rumania. Singer (Soprano). *Education:* Studied at the Ciprian Porumbescu Conservatory and in Bucharest with Arta Florescu. *Debut:* Bucharest 1968 as Donna Anna in Don Giovanni. *Career:* Guest appearances in Belgrade, Sofia, Athens, Amsterdam, Trieste, Stuttgart, Dresden and Berlin; Repertoire includes roles in operas by Mozart, Verdi and Puccini; Sang Mozart's Countess while on tour to Japan with Vienna Staatsoper, 1986; Season 1987 sang Mozart's Countess at La Scala Milan, Butterfly at Verona and Donna Anna at Turin, (Countess 1989). *Address:* Teatro Regio di Torino, Piazza Castello 215, 1-10124 Turin, Italy.

MOLDOVEANU Vasile, b. 6 Oct 1935, Konstanza, Rumania. Singer (Tenor). *Education:* Studied in Bucharest with Constantin Badescu. *Debut:* Bucharest 1966, as Rinuccio in Gianni Schicchi. *Career:* Stuttgart debut 1972, as Donizetti's Edgardo; Munich Opera from 1976, as Rodolfo and the Duke of Mantua; Deutsche Oper Berlin and Chicago Lyric Opera 1977; Hamburg Opera 1978, as Don Carlos; Metropolitan Opera from 1979, as Pinkerton, Turiddu, Gabriele Adorno, Luigi in Il Tabarro and Henri in Les Vêpres Siciliennes; Covent Garden 1979, as Don Carlos; Zurich Opera 1980, in Verdi's Attila; Monte Carlo 1982, in Lucia di Lammermoor; Guest appearances in Helsinki, Brussels, Barcelona, Dresden, Cologne, Frankfurt and Athens; Other roles include Mozart's Don Ottavio, Pedrillo and Tamino; Stuttgart Staatsoper and Nice 1988, as Cavaradossi and as Puccini's Dick Johnson; Sang Pinkerton at Rome, 1990. *Address:* c/o Lies Askonas Ltd., 186 Drury Lane, London WC2B 5QD, England.

MOLINARI-PRADELLI Francesco, b. 4 July 1911, Bologna, Italy. Conductor; Pianist. *Education:* Studied in Bologna with Ivaldi and Nordio at Bologne; Accademia di Santa Cecilia Rome, with Bernardino Molinari. *Debut:* Concert conductor from 1938. *Career:* Conducted L'Elisir d'Amore at Bologna 1939; La Scala Milan from 1946; Covent Garden 1955, 1960, Tosca and Macbeth; San Francisco Opera from 1957, Vienna Staatsoper from 1959; Metropolitan Opera 1966-73, in Un Ballo in Maschera, Roméo et Juliette and operas by Puccini. *Recordings:* Turandot; La Traviata; Manon Lescaut; La Forza del Destino; La Rondine; Gianni Schicchi, Rigoletto, Don Pasquale, Simon Boccanegra and L'Elisir d'Amore; Rossini songs with Suzanne Danco.

MOLINO Pippo, b. 10 June 1947, Milan, Italy. Composer. m. Giovanna Stucchi, 22 July 1972, 1 son, 2 daughters. *Education:* Degree, Composition and Choral Music. *Debut:* Venezia Opera Prima Festival Competition, 1981. *Compositions include:* Replay I, II, piano, 1978; Tres, violin and viola, 1978; Litanie, orchestra, 1979; II Canto Ritrovato, orchestra, 1980; II Cavalier Selvatico, oratorio, 1981; Cantabile, flute piano, 1983; Jeu, oboe, 1984; Da Lontano, harp, 1985; Per la Festa Della Dedicazione, organ, 1986; Nel Harmonien, wind quintet, 1989; Radici, clarinet, 1991; Ricordando, twelve instruments, 1992; Quintetto, calrinet, string quartet, 1993. *Recordings include:* Tres; Replay II; Frammento A&B; Ritornando; Il Pensiero Dominante; Nel Teempo. *Publications:* Articles in La Musica, Musica e Realta, Reggio Emilia, Il Giornale della musica. *Honours include:* Rimini Aterforum, 1979; Venezia Opera Prima, 1981; Roodeport International Eisteddfod of South Africa, 1983. *Memberships:* Federazione Italiana Compositori di Musica Contemporanea; Nuove Sincronie. *Hobby:* Tennis. *Address:* Via Pistrucci 23, 20137 Milano, Italy.

MOLL Clare, b. 1960, Northumberland, England. Singer (Mezzo- soprano). *Education:* Studied at the Royal Academy of Music. *Career:* Sang in Henze's La Cubana with English Music Theatre and Dorabella with Scottish Opera-go-Round; Opera 80 as Rosina and Mozart's Marcellina; Has sung with Scottish Opera in Die Meistersinger (Magdalena), L'Egisto by Cavalli and L'Enfant et les Sortilèges; With Opera North appeared as Mrs Peachum in The Threepenny Opera and toured for Welsh National Opera in a show featuring Ivor Novello; English National Opera in The Magic Flute, Parsifal and Orpheus in the Underworld; Covent Garden debut 1985, as a Dryad in Ariadne auf Naxos; Concert repertoire ranges from Bach and Handel to Gilbert and Sullivan and musicals. *Address:* c/o Korman International Management, Crunnells Green Cottage, Preston, Herts SG4 7UQ, England.

MOLL Kurt, b. 11 Apr 1938, Buir, Germany. Singer (Bass). *Education:* Studied at Cologne Hochschule and with Emmy Mueller. *Debut:* Lodovico in Otello, Aachen 1961; Sang at Mainz and Wuppertal in 1960s; Bayreuth Festival 1968- as Fafner, Pogner, Gurnemanz and Marke; Member of Hamburg Opera from 1970: sang bass roles in operas by Wagner and took part in the premiere of Bialas's Der gestiefelte Kater at the 1975 Schwetzingen Festival; 1972 Osmin in Die Entführung at La Scala; US debut San Francisco 1974, as Gurnemanz; Covent Garden debut 1977, as Kaspar in a new production of Der Freischütz; Metropolitan Opera debut 1978, as the Landgrave in Tannhäuser: later sang Beethoven's Rocco, Osmin and Ochs in Der Rosenkavalier; Visited Japan with the Hamburg Opera in 1984; Returned to Covent Garden 1987, as Osmin;; San Francisco 1988, Gurnemanz in Parsifal; Metopolitan 1990, as the Commendatore in Don Giovanni, (returned 1992, as Gurnemanz). *Recordings:* Die Entführung, Der Schauspieldirektor, Parsifal, Der Freischütz, Missa Solemnis, Salome, Tristan und Isolde, Die Lustigen Weiber von Windsor, Der Rosenkavalier (Deutsche Grammophon); St John Passion, Die Zauberflöte, Intermezzo, Abu Hassan, Die Zwillingsbrüder, Bastien und Bastienne (Deutsche Grammophon); Don Giovanni, Les Contes d'Hoffmann, Lulu, Le Nozze di Figaro, Die Meistersinger, Otello, Der Freischütz (Electrola); Der fliegende Holländer, Tannhäuser (HMV); Winterreise (Orfeo); Die Zauberflöte from the Met. *Address:* c/o Lies Askonas Ltd., 186 Drury Lane, London WC2 5QD, England.

MOLL Maria, b. 1949, Northumberland, England. Singer (Soprano). *Education:* Studied at the Royal Academy of Music with Marjorie Thomas and at the London Opera Centre. *Career:* Sang Mozart's Countess and the Female Chorus in The Rape of Lucretia at Sadler's Wells Theatre; Glyndebourne Festival Opera from 1975 as Second Lady in Die Zauberflöte, Beethoven's Leonore and Musetta; Appearances as Leonora in La Forza del Destino for Welsh National Opera; Tosca for Scottish Opera and Musetta and Abigaille for Opera North (Fata Morgana in The Love for Three Oranges, 1990); Covent Garden debut 1983, in the Stravinsky/Ravel double bill; Engagements in Don Carlos at Brussels and Macbeth at the Hong Kong Festival; English National Opera from 1987, in Lady

Macbeth of Mtsenk and Reimann's Lear; Has also sung in musical theatre; Season 1992 in Die Königskinder for ENO. *Honours include:* Isobel Jay Prize for Operatic Sopranos and the Robert Radford Prize at the RAM. *Address:* c/o Korman International Management, Crunnells Green Cottage, Preston, Herts SG4 7UQ, England.

MOLLER Anthea Mary, b. 27 Jan 1939, Dunedin, New Zealand. Musician; Voice Teacher. m. (divorced), 1 son, 1 daughter. *Education:* Piano with Mr D J Palmer, Timaru; Voice Teachers: Grace Wilkinson, Joan Davies, Mary Adams Taylor. *Debut:* St Matthew Passion, Christchurch. *Career:* Il Trovatore (Verdi); Television: Old Maid and the Thief (Menotti); Gianni Schicchi (Puccini); Dr Miracle; National Artist for Radio New Zealand; Artist for Australian Broadcasting Commission; Bluebeard's Castle, Sydney Opera House; Hansel and Gretel, Victorian State Opera; Many other operas and oratorio, contemporary music and lieder; Many recordings for Radio New Zealand; Concerts with the New Zealand Symphony Orchestra including, Verdi Requiem, Mahler 8th and Mahler 2nd, Kullervo (Sibelius). *Recordings:* Kiwi: Music by Ronald Tremain; The Flame Tree; Music by Douglas Lilburn. *Hobbies:* Swimming; Walking. *Address:* 44 Rambler Crescent, Beachoven, Auckland, New Zealand.

MÖLLER Mats, b. 13 July 1954, Stockholm, Sweden. Flautist. *Education:* History of Music, University of Stockholm; Diploma, Swedish Academy of Music, 1980; Later studies with André Jaunet, Zürich, Switzerland. *Career:* Freelance appearances in big Swedish orchestras including Radio Symphony Orchestra, also at Royal Opera; Chamber music performances, especially contemporary music; Various TV and radio appearances, Sweden; Appeared, Italy, Switzerland, and France. *Recordings:* Radio DRS, Zürich, Switzerland, and France. *Honours:* Royal Academy of Music Grant, 1981; Recipient of Culture Prize, City of Stockholm, 1986; Member of Samtida Musik.

MOLLER Niels, b. 4 Sept 1922, Gorlev, Denmark. Singer (Tenor). Administrator. *Education:* Studied in Copenhagen, latterly at the Opera School of the Royal Opera. *Debut:* Sang Rossini's Figaro in Copenhagen, 1953. *Career:* Changed to tenor roles 1959 and sang in Copenhagen until 1975 as Florestan, Tannhäuser, Don José, Aegisthus, Shuisky, the Drum Major in Wozzeck and Zeus in Monteverdi's Ulisse; Bayreuth Festival, 1962-65, as Melot and Erik; Guest appearances at Brussels, Vienna, Oslo, Geneva, Venice, Barcelona, 1968, Lisbon, 1972 and Bordeaux; Baritone roles included Renato (Ballo in Maschera), Dandini, and Tarquinius in The Rape of Lucretia; Sang the title role in the premiere of Macbeth by H Koppel and retired as singer, 1975 after appearing as Aegisthus; Director of the Royal Opera Copenhagen 1978-83; Frequent concert engagements. *Recordings include:* Schoenberg Gurrelieder; Parsifal, Bayreuth, 1962; Saul and David by Nielsen. *Address:* c/o Det Kongelige Teatet, Box 2185, DK-1017 Copenhagen, Denmark.

MOLLER Peter, b. 4 Mar 1947, Copenhagen, Denmark. Organist and Composer. m. (1) Anna Sten Andersen, 14 July 1973; (2) Birgit Svendsen, 28 Apr 1983, 4 sons. *Education:* The Royal Danish Music Academy (Academy of Music); Teachers: Professor Aksel Andersen and Charley Olsen, Organ; Leif Kayser, Composition. Master Classes by Professor Anton Heiller 1970 and 1972. *Debut:* Organ, Soloist Class of The Music Academy 1973. *Career:* Organist, Løgumkloster 1973-78; Organist, The Church of Our Saviour, Esbjerg 1978-; Organ Teacher at The Academy of Music, Esbjerg 1975-; Organ Teacher, The School of Church Music, Vestervig 1980-; Many organ recitals on Radio and in Denmark, Germany, England and Finland. *Compositions:* Metamorphoses for Organ 1980; The Miracle of Whitsun for Organ 1983; 47 Easy Choral Preludes for Organ 1974; 12 Danish Songs 1979; 12 Danish Hymns 1986. *Publications:* Textbook in Preparation of Polyphonic Hymn - Introductions (For Hymns From The Period of c.1500-c.1670) 1982.

Contributions to: Articles about Orgelbüchlein by J.S. Bach (In The Magazine For The Members of The Danish Society of Organists) 1985. *Address:* Engparken 32, 6740 Bramming, Denmark.

MOLLET Pierre, b. 23 Mar 1920, Neuchâtel, Switzerland. Singer (Baritone). *Education:* Studied in Neuchâtel, Lausanne and Basle. *Career:* Performed as concert singer in France and Switzerland from 1948; Opera-Comique, Paris from 1952, notably as Debussy's Pelléas; Aix-en-Provence 1952, in Iphigènie en Tauride by Gluck; Paris Opéra 1954, in Gounod's Roméo et Juliette; Geneva 1963, in the premiere of Martin's Monsieur de Pourceaugnac, repeated at the Holland Festival; As a concert singer often appeared in the cantatas of Bach and in music by Honegger, which he studied with the composer. *Recordings include:* Pelléas et Mélisande, Roméo et Juliette and L'Enfant et les Sortilèges (Decca); La Damnation de Faust (Deutsche Grammophon); Iphigénie en Tauride (Pathé).

MOLLOVA Milena, b. 19 Feb 1940, Razgrad, Bulgaria. Concert Pianist; Professor of Piano, 1 son, 2 daughters. *Education:* Studied piano with Pavla Jekova; Studied with composer and pianist Dimitar Nenov, 1947; Studied with Professor Panka Pelisheck from 1949; Studied at the Bulgarian Music Academy with Professor Pelisheck from age 14; Studied in the class of Professor Emil Gilels at the Moscow State Conservatory, 1960-61. *Debut:* First piano concert at age 6. *Career:* Soloist in Sofia State Orchestra with the Beethoven third piano concerto, directed by Professor Sasha Popov; During her education gave numerous concerts in Bulgaria and successful participation in international competitions in Moscow, Paris and Munich; Concert tours in USSR (1958, 1959, 1960), in Czechoslovakia, Poland, Belgium and Yugoslavia; Appointed Assistant to Professor Pelisheck at The Bulgarian Music Academy, Sofia 1963 and as a concert pianist to The Bulgarian Concert Agency; Conducted own class of young piano students 1969-; Tour of Japan and Cuba, 1973; Appointed Reader 1976 and Professor 1989 in the Bulgarian Music Academy; To celebrate 40 years on stage, played in Sofia and Varna the whole 32 Beethoven sonatas in 9 concerts, recorded on compact disks. During last few years has conducted Master Classes in Essen, Germany and Manfredony, Foggia, Italy. *Recordings:* Numerous recordings of piano works from Bach to modern composers.

MOLNÁR András, b. 1948, Hungary, Tenor. *Education:* Hungarian Radio Children's Choir; Studied Singing, 1976. *Career:* Member, Choir of the Hungarian radio and Television, 1977-78; Soloist, Budapest State Opera, 1979-; Appeared in title roles in Erkel's Opera, László Hunyadi, Mozart's Magic Flute, Verdi's Ernani and in La Forza del destino; Don José in Carmen, 1981-82; Title role, Lohengrin, 1981-82; Invited to sing title role in Theo Adam's new production of Wagner's Lohengrin, Berlin State Opera, 1983; Regular appearances with Budapest State Opera, including the premiere of Ecce Homo by Szokolay, 1987; Teatro Colón Buenos Aires 1987, as Donzello in La Fiamma by Respighi; Budapest 1989/90, in Erkel's Hunyadi László and as Tannhäuser. Frequently participates in oratorio performances. *Honours:* 1st Prize, Treviaso Toti dal Monte International Vocal Competition, 1980. *Address:* c/o Hungarian State Opera, Népöztársaság utja 22, 1061 Budapest, Hungary.

MOLNAR-TALAJIC Liljana, b. 30 Dec 1938, Bronsanski, Brod, Yugoslavia. Singer (Soprano). *Education:* Studied in Sarajevo. *Debut:* Sarajevo, 1959, as Mozart's Countess. *Career:* Sang at Sarajevo and Zagreb, 1959-75; Guest appearances at the Vienna Staatsoper, Florence and San Francisco, 1969; Philadelphia from 1970, Naples, 1971; Verona Arena, 1972-73, as Aida and the Forza Leonora; Sang at Covent Garden, 1975, 1977, Metropolitan Opera, 1976 (Aida); Further appearances at Barcelona, Nice and the Deutsche Oper Berlin, 1977-78, Milan, Rome and Marseilles; Other roles have included the Trovatore Leonora, Amelia (ballo in Maschera), Desdemona and

Norma. *Recordings include:* Verdi Requiem. *Address:* c/o Arena di Verona, Piazza Bra 28, 37121 Verona, Italy.

MONELLE Raymond John, b. 19 Aug 1937, Bristol, England. Critic; University Lecturer. m. Hannelore E. M. Schultz 1964 (divorced 1983), 2 daughters. *Education:* Pembroke College, Oxford; Royal College of Music 1964-66 (BMus, London, 1st class honours); PhD (Edinburgh) 1979. *Career:* Senior Lecturer, Bedford College of Physical Education, 1966-69; Lecturer in Music, University of Edinburgh, 1969-; Music Critic, The Scotsman, 1972-88; Music Critic, The Independent, 1986-; Critic, Opera Magazine, 1984-. *Compositions:* Much educational choral music published; Several commissioned works, e.g. Missa Brevis 1979; Cantata, Ballattis of Luve, 1983. *Contributions to:* Music Review; Music and Letters; British Journal of Aesthetics; Music Analysis, Comparative Literature, International Review of the Aesthetics and Sociology of Music. Book: Linguistics and Sematics in Music, published in 1992. *Hobby:* Square-rigged sailing ships. *Address:* 3 Livingstone Place, Edinburgh, EH9 1PB, Scotland.

MONEY David, b. 4 Jan 1912, London, England. Piano Accompanist; Teacher; Music Critic. m. Diana Stone, 4 children. *Education:* Royal College of Music; studied with Louis Kentner, Kathleen Long and George Reeves. *Debut:* Wigmore Hall, London, 1935. *Career:* Numerous appointments as accompanist throughout UK, Europe and Middle East; Broadcasts on BBC Radio and TV, ITV and STV as accompanist and reviewer of records; Assistant Music Critic Daily Telegraph from 1946. *Recordings:* For Parlophone, Waverley, Scots Discs. *Contributions to:* Concise Encyclopedia of Music and Musicians. *Memberships:* Critics Circle; ISM; Musicians Union. *Hobby:* Gardening. *Address:* 16 Devon Rise, London N2 OAA, England.

MONK Allan, b. 19 Aug 1942, Mission City, British Columbia, Canada. Singer (Bass-Baritone). *Education:* Studied in Calgary with Elgar Higgin and in New York with Boris Goldovsky. *Debut:* Western Opera, San Francisco 1967, in Menotti's The Old Maid and the Thief. *Career:* Has sung in Portland, St Louis, Chicago, Hawaii and Vancouver; Canadian National Opera, Tornoto, 1973, in the premiere of Wilson's Abelard and Heloise; Metropolitan Opera from 1976, as Schaunard in La Bohème, The Speaker in Die Zauberflöte, Berg's Wozzeck, Wagner's Wolfram and Verdi's Posa and Ford; Sang Macbeth at Toronto 1986, followed by Carlo in La Forza del Destino; Opéra de Montreal, 1988 as Don Giovanni; Nick Shadow in The Rake's Progress for Vancouver Opera, 1989; Wozzeck and Iago at Toronto, 1990; Sang Simon Boccanegra for Long Beach Opera, 1992. *Recordings include:* Andrea Chénier (RCA); La Traviata. *Address:* c/o Canadian Opera Company, 227 Front Street East, Toronto, Ontario, Canada, M5A 1E8.

MONK Meredith Jane, b. 20 Nov 1942, New York City, New York, USA. Composer; Singer; Director. *Education:* BA, Sarah Lawrence College; Voice Tuition, Vicki Starr, John Devers, Jeanette Lovetri; Composition Study, Ruth Lloyd, Richard Averre, Glenn Mack; Piano, Gershon Konikow. *Debut:* Washington Square Galleries, New York City, 1964. *Career:* Performed worldwide with own vocal ensemble; Appearances include: Carnegie Hall; Town Hall; Guggenheim Museum; Public Theater, New York City; Festivals in London, Paris, Tokyo, Jerusalem, Rome, Stockholm, Munich, Frankfurt, Cologne. *Compositions:* Key; Our Lady of Late; Songs from the Hill; Tablet; Dolmen Music; Vessel: an opera epic; Quarry: an opera; Book of Days; Turtle Dreams; Education of the Girlchild: an opera; Specimen Days; The Games; Acts from Under and Above; Paris; Chacon; Facing North, premiere, 1990; Atlas: an opera in three parts, premiere, Houston Grand Opera, 1991. *Recordings:* Has made numerous recordings including Facing North, ECM New Series, 1992; Atlas: an opera in three parts, 1993. *Hobbies:* Horse riding; Gardening. *Current Management:* The House Foundation for the Arts. *Address:* 228 West Broadway, New York, NY 10013, USA.

MONK Peter Anthony, b. 17 June 1946, Hetton-le-Hole, Durham, England. Composer; Teacher. m. Diana Worthington, 18 Dec 1976, 1 son, 1 daughter. *Education:* Teaching Certificate, Bede College of Education, Durham, 1968; Premier Prix, Conservatoire Royal De Musique, Liège, Belgium, 1975; MMus, King's College, London, 1984. *Career:* Studied composition with Henri Pousseur, Centre de Recherches Musicales de Wallonie, Liège, Belgium; Works performed extensively in Western Europe; Most works have been broadcast on Belgian Radio, several on BBC Radio 3; Funds from Arts Council to write Emperor's New Notes for Brass quintet, Eastern Arts to write Railway Parade for Clarinet and Piano; Greater London Arts Association for Signor Glissando for harpsichord. *Compositions:* Numerous works including, The Emperor's New Notes; The Golden Spike; Troisième Vue sur les Jardins Interdits, Appeelkins; Lasagne da Caccia; Percy, Signor Glissando; Salute to the Third Age, Streamliner; The I Met Pousseur in Rue Forgeur Blues; Danse Sacrée et Danse au Contraire. *Hobbies:* Poetry; O Gauge model railways. *Address:* Fir Tree House, 169b St James's Road, Croydon, Surrey, CR0 2BY, England.

MONNARD Jean-Francois, b. 4 Nov 1941, Lausanne, Switzerland. Conductor. m. Lia Rottier. *Education:* LLM, University of Lausanne; Music Academy, Lausanne; Folkwang Hochschule, Essen, German Federal Republic; Orchestral Conducting Diploma, 1968; International Conductors Course with Jean Fournet, Hilversum, Holland. *Career:* Conductor of Operas, Kaiserslautern; Graz, Austria; Trier, Aachen and Wuppertal GFR; Currently Music Director in Osnabrück; Guest Conductor: Tonhalle Orchestra, Zurich; Residentie Orchestra, The Hague; Philharmonic Orchestra, Stockholm; ORF Symphony Orchestra, Vienna; Orchestre de la Suisse Romande, Geneva; Stockholm Opera; Zurich Opera; Bordeaux Opera. *Contributions to:* Revue des Musiciens Suisses. *Membership:* Association Musiciens Suisses. *Address:* Chemin de l'Eglise, 1066 Epalinges, Switzerland.

MONOD Jacques-Louis, b. 25 Feb 1927, Asnières-Paris, France. Composer; Conductor; Former Pianist. m. (1) Bethany Beardslee (2) Margit Auhagen. *Education:* Paris Conservatoire from 1935: seminars with Messiaen; René Leibowitz 1944-50; Juilliard School with Wagenaar; Further study with Blacher and Rufer in Berlin; DMA, Columbia University, New York. *Debut:* As pianist, Paris, 1949, in Schoenberg concert directed by Leibowitz. *Career:* Directed the first all-Webern concert, Juilliard 1951; Pianist until 1956; Voice and Piano Duo with Bethany Beardslee, USA, 1950-55: first US performances of works by Schoenberg, Berg, Krenek and Webern; Chamber Ensemble Concert Series, Austrian and Italian Institutes, London, 1962-66: several European premieres of American works; Conductor, major orchestras and chamber ensembles; BBC concerts from 1960; Orchestral concerts and broadcasts in Europe, Scandinavia, North and Central America from 1956; Chief Editor, Boelke-Boemart Inc., Hillsdale, New York 1952-82; Teacher at New England Conservatory, Princeton, Harvard and Columbia Universities; Hunter and Queens Colleges, City University of New York. *Compositions:* Setting of Valéry, Renard, Char; 2 Chamber Cantatas; Cantus contra Cantum I, II and III. *Recordings:* Carter's ballet Pocahontas; works by Berg and Webern; Numerous works as pianist and conductor. Memberships include: President, Association René Leibowitz, Paris; Composers' Guild for Performance, New York. *Address:* 395 Riverside Drive, Apartment 10-B, New York, NY 10025, USA.

MONOSOFF Sonya, b. 11 June 1927, Ohio, USA. Violinist; Professor of Music, Cornell University. m. Carl Eugene Pancaldo, 8 Dec 1950. 4 daughters. *Education:* Artists Diploma, Juilliard Graduate School, 1948. *Debut:* New York City, USA. *Career:* Concerts and master classes: USA, Canada, Europe, Israel, Australia and New Zealand. *Recordings:* Heinrich Biber, Mystery Sonatas and 1681 Sonatas; JS Bach, Sonatas for Violin & Harpsichord; Mozart, Sonatas. *Contributions to:* Notes; Early Music; The New Grove; The Musical Times.

Honours: Stereo Review, Best Record of the Year (Bach), 1970; Fulbright Lectureship, New Zealand, 1988; Bunting Institute, 1967-68; Smithsonian Institute, 1971. *Memberships:* Early Music America, Steering Committee; American Musical Instrument Society, Editorial Board. *Hobby:* Chamber music. *Current Management:* Curzon & Kedersha, New York. *Address:* Cornell University, Music Department, Lincoln Hall, Ithaca, New York 14853, USA.

MONOSZON Boris, b. 1955, Kiev, USSR. Violinist; Conductor. *Education:* Graduate, Moscow Conservatoire, 1979; *Career:* Made several concert tours of European and Latin American countries as concert master, Prague Symphony; Interpreted Concerto for Violin and Orchestra by Sibelius, Royal Festival Hall, London, England; Soloist, Teplice State Philharmonic Orchestra, 1982-. *Honours:* Laureate, Tibor Varga International Competition, Switzerland, 1981.

MONOT Pierre-Alain, b. 7 Mar 1961, Fleurier, Switzerland. Trumpeter; Composer. m. Esther Herrmann, 23 Sept 1988. *Education:* Diplome professionnel de trompette; Diplome de virtuosite, Teacher, Andre Besancon. *Career:* 1st Trumpet, Winterthur Symphony Orchestra; 1st Trumpet, Lucern Swiss Festival Orchestra; Member of NOVUS Brass Quartet Concert in Europe (Zurich, Rome, Paris, Lausanne) and Far East (Japan and China). *Compositions:* Quatuor 1980 for Brass Quartet; Trois douces Rêveries Medievales; SR 186 for Vibraphone and Brass Quartet; La Neighe orange for brass quartett; Dans le Chateau de la Fée fluide brass quartet; Trois Ayres de Cour for brass quartet and orchestra. *Recordings:* Novus, 1986; La Neige Orange, 1988. *Honours:* 1st prize, Competition of Union Bank of Switzerland, 1987; 1st Prize, Concours de la Pierre d'Hauterive, 1983. *Membership:* Association des musiciens suisses (AMS). *Hobby:* Photography. *Current Management:* Mrs Indira Tasan.

MONOYIOS Ann, b. 28 Oct 1949, Middletown, Connecticut, USA. Singer (Soprano).*Education:* Studied at Princeton University and with Oren Brown. *Career:* Concert performances in Baroque music with the Folger Consort, Washington DC; Stage debut with the Concert Royal of New York in Rameau's Les Fêtes d'Hébé European debut at the 1986 Gottingen Festival, in Handel's Terpsichore with the English Baroque Soloists conducted by John Eliot Gardiner; Opéra-Comique Paris and Aix-en-Provence Festival 1987, as Lully's Sangaride (Atys) and Psyché; Sang Elisa in Mozart's Il Re Pastore at the Nakamichi Festival, Los Angeles, 1990; Further engagements at Salzburg, Spoleto and Frankfurt. *Recordings:* Iphigénie en Aulide, with the Opéra de Lyon. *Address:* c/o Städtische Buhnen, Untermainalage 11, D-8000 Frankfurt am Main, Germany.

MONTAGUE Diana, b. 8 Apr 1953, Winchester, England. Singer (Mezzo-Soprano). *Education:* Studied at the Royal Manchester School of Music with Ronald Stear, Frederic Cox and Rupert Bruce-Lockhard. *Debut:* With Glyndebourne Touring Opera 1977, as Zerlina. *Career:* Member of the Royal Opera Covent Garden, 1978-83 as Laura in Luisa Miller, Kate Pinkerton, Annius (La Clemenza di Tito), Nicklause, Cherubino and Parseis in Esclarmonde, tour of the Far East; Bayreuth debut 1983, as Wellgunde and Siegrune in Der Ring des Nibelungen; Chicago 1984, in the Missa Solemnis conducted by Solti; Edinburgh Festival 1985, as Mélisande; Salzburg Festival 1986, as Cherubino; Metropolitan Opera debut 1987, Sextus in La Clemenza di Tito: returned to New York as Dorabella and as Nicklausse in Les Contes d'Hoffmann; German operatic debut 1987, Dorabella in a new production of Così fan Tutte at the Frankfurt Opera; Appearances with Scottish Opera as Cherubino and Orlofsky and with English National Opera as Cherubino and Proserpina in Monteverdi's Orfeo; Promenade Concerts London 1988, in Pelléas et Mélisande; Glyndebourne Opera 1989, Gluck's Orfeo; Sang The Fox in The Cunning Little Vixen at Covent Garden 1990; Idamante in Idomeneo at the 1990 Salzburg Festival; Cherubino at the Vienna

Staatsoper 1990, Lucio Silla 1991; Glyndebourne 1991 as Sextus in La Clemenza di Tito (also at the Promenade Concerts, London); Season 1992 sang Gluck's Iphigénie en Tauride for Welsh National Opera, and Dorabella for ENO; Concert engagements in the Mozart Requiem, Bach B Minor Mass, Rossini's Stabat Mater and The Damnation of Faust by Berlioz. *Recordings include:* Title role in Iphigénie en Tauride, Mozart's C Minor Mass (Philips); Handel arias with Simon Preston and Monteverdi's Orfeo (Deutsche Grammophon); Clothilde in Norma (Decca); Cunning Little Vixen (EMI), Romeo in I Capuleti e Montecchi (Nuova Era), Armando in Meyerbeer's Il Crociato in Egitto (Opera Rara). *Address:* c/o Harrison/Parrott Ltd., 12 Penzance Place, London W11 4PA, England.

MONTAGUE Stephen Rowley, b. 10 Mar 1943, Syracuse, New York, USA. Composer; Pianist. m. Patricia Mattin, 10 May 1986, 1 son. 1 daughter. *Education:* BM, (honours), 1965, MM, Theory, 1967, Florida State University; DMA, Composition, Ohio State University, 1972; Post-graduate work, Conducting, Mozarteum, Salzburg, 1966; Fulbright, Warsaw, Poland, 1972-74; Computer Music, IRCAM, Paris, 1982; Stanford University, 1986. *Debut:* Wigmore Hall, London, 1975. *Career:* Warsaw Autumn Festivals, 1974-80; Paris Autumn Festival, 1974; Metz Festival, 1976; Kassel Documenta, 1976; Edinburgh Festival, 1981; Gaudeamus Week, 1977; ISCM, Stockholm, 1978; John Cage Festival, London, 1982; Roulette Series, New York, 1982; Britain Salutes NY, 1983; ASUC Festival, Ohio State University, 1984; New Music America, 1984-87; Sadler's Wells Royal Ballet, 1985; Almeida Festival, 1984-85; Contemporary Dance Theatre, Tours, 1986-87; Almeida Festival commission, London, Sing Circle tour, Ireland, Composer-in-residence, Dublin, New Music America (Miami), Commission, 1988; Südwestfunk Symphony tour of Germany, Ulster Orchestra, Sonorities Festival, National Electronic Studio Commission (UK), Warsaw Autumn Festival, 1989; North American New Music Festival, US tour; Montague/Mead Duo, Festival d'Eté (Quebec), Swedish Electronic Music Festival, Scream, 1990; US tour Montague/Mead Duo, Composer-in-residence, University of Utah, SingCircle tour of Germany, Normandy, Poland, Montague/Mead Duo tour, Eastern Europe, Warsaw, Autumn Festival, 1991; Guest Professor, University of Texas, Austin, 1992; Featured Composer, Speculum Festival (Norway), 1992; Montague/Mead Piano Plus performed 3 concerts at London's ICA on The American Discoveries, series, 1992; 50th Birthday Concert of Montague's music, South Bank Centre, London, 1993; ISCM Festival-Mexicot, 1993, NYYD Festival Estonia, 1993. *Compositions include:* Eyes of Ambush; Quiet Washes; Paramell, I, II, III, IV, V, Va, VI; Strummin' Sound Round; Criseyde; Inundations I, II; Tigida Pipa; At The White Edge of Phrygia; Mouth of Anger, Tongues of Fire; Slow Dance on a Burial Ground (recorded); Scythia; Haiku; Median; Trio; Quintet; Into the Sun; Sotto Voce; Largo Con Moto; Frozen Mirrors, Passim; Piano concerto, 1988; String Quartet: In Memoriam, 1989; Solo Organ, Behold a Pale Horse, 1990; After Ives, 1991; Vlug, 1992; Bright Interiors, 1992; Boombox Virelai, 1992; Aeolian Furies, 1992; Wild Nights, 1993; String Quartet No.2, 1993. *Current Management:* Magenta Music International, 4 Highgate High Street, London, N6 5SL. *Address:* 2 Ryland Road, London, NW5 3EA, England.

MONTAL Andre, b. 18 Nov 1940, Baltimore, USA. Singer (Tenor). *Education:* Studied at the Eastman School, the Music Academy of the West at Santa Barbara and the Curtis Institute. *Debut:* American Opera Societ New York, 1964, as Tebaldo in I Capuleti e i Montecchi. *Career:* Has sung at opera houses in Boston, Chicago, Philadelphia, San Francisco and Vancouver; Metropolitan Oper from 1974; Further engagements with Australian Opera at Sydney; Other roles have included Donizetti's Ernesto, Nemorino, Tonio and Edgardo, Oronte in Alcina, Gounod's Romeo, Rossini's Almaviva, Lindoro, and Idreno (Semiramide), Mozart's Ferrando, Belmonte and Don Ottavio; Memphistopheles in Prokofiev's Fiery Angel, Verdi's Duke, Pinkerton, and the Italian Singer in Rosenkavalier.

MONTARSOLO Paolo, b. 16 Mar 1925, Portici, Naples, Italy. Singer (Bass), Producer. *Education:* Studied with Enrico Conti in Naples and at the La Scala Opera School. *Debut:* La Scala 1954. *Career:* Guest appearances in Italy in operas by Rossini, Donizetti, Wolf-Ferrari and Mozart; Bergamo 1955, in a revival of Donizetti's Rita; Verona 1956; Glyndebourne Festival from 1957, as Mustafà in L'Italiana in Algeri, Selim in Il Turco in Italia, and Mozart's Osmin, Leporello and Don Alfonso; Florence 1966, in Luisa Miller; Deutsche Oper am Rhein Dusseldorf 1973; Paris Opéra 1977, as Don Magnifico in La Cenerentola; Geneva Opera 1984, in L'Italiana in Algeri; Engagements in Moscow, Lisbon, New York, Naples and Rio de Janiero; Sang Don Magnifico at the Berlin Staatsoper, 1987; Mustafà at Covent Garden, debut 1988; Salzburg Festival 1988-89, as Mozart's Bartolo and Don Mangnifico; Staged and sang Don Pasquale at the Dallas Opera, 1989 (Covent Garden, 1990); Sang Donizetti's Dulcamara at the Royal Opera, 1992. *Recordings:* La Cenerentola; Il Barbiere di Siviglia; Rita and Viva la Mamma; La Serva Padrona; Madama Butterfly: Labels include Deutsche Grammophon, HMV and RCA. *Address:* c/o Royal Opera House, Covent Garden, London WC2, England.

MONTEFUSCO Licinio, b. 30 Oct 1936, Milann, Italy. Singer (Baritone). *Education:* Studied in Milan. *Debut:* Teatro Nuovo Milan 1961, as Zurga in Les pecheurs de Perles. *Career:* Sang Renato in Un Ballo in Maschera at Florence, 1963, followed by appearances throughout Italy, notably at the Teatro Reggio Turin; Guest appearances at the Vienna Staatsoper from 1964, Deutsche Oper Berlin from 1966; US debut Philadelphia 1965; La Scala Milan, 1970, as Montfort in I Vespri Siciliani; Sang at Monte Carlo 1967-68, Brussels and Strasbourg, 1972-74, Verona 1972 as Amonasro, Marseilles, 1979; Sang Francesco Foscari in I Due Foscari at Turin, 1984 and Posa in Don Carlos, 1985; Other roles have included Verdi's Germont, Luna, Rigoletto, Macbeth, Carlos and Ford, Enrico in Lucia di Lammermoor, Alfonso in La Favorita, Marcello, Gerard and Valentin. *Address:* c/o Dublin Grand Opera Society, John Player Theatre, 276-288 Circular Road, Dublin 8, Ireland.

MONTENEGRO Roberto, b. 18 Sept 1956, Montevido, Uruguay. Conductor. *Education:* Hamburg Musikhochschule; Studied with Guido Santorsola, Gerhard Markson, Aldo Ceccato and Sergiu Celibidache. *Debut:* Santa Barbara's Festival Symphony Orchestra, California, 1985. *Career:* Artistic director and conductor, Sodre Uruguayan National Symphony Orchestra since 1990; Guest Conductor, France, Spain, Argentina, Venezuela and USA. Conducted the world premiere of the Francisco Rodrico's Guitar Concerto with Venezuela National Orchestra, 1992 and the world premier of the Cesar Cano's Piano Concerto with the Spanish National Orchestra, 1993; Teacher of masterclasses in Uruguay and Argentina; Teacher of Masterclasses in Uruguay, Argentina, Italy (European Community Music High School), and Spain (Santiago de Compostela's International Conductine Masterclasses); Assistant to Aldo Ceccato in Hamburg and Hannover; Jurist, Young Concert Artist, New York, USA. *Hobbies:* Travel; Going to the beach. *Address:* Av. Del Libertador 1684, Apt. 1202, Montevideo, PO Box 1552, Uruguay.

MONTEUX Claude, b. 15 Oct 1920, Brookline, Massachusetts, USA. Conductor; Flautist. *Education:* Studied flute with Georges Laurent. *Career:* Solo debut 1940; Played with Kansas City Philharmonic 1946-; Conductor of the Ballets Russes 1949-; Guest conductor with the London Symphony and with continental orchetras; Member of the Harpsichord Quartet 1947-54; Conductor of Columbus Ohio Orchestra 1953-56; Music Director of the Hudson Valley Philharmonic, New York, 1959-75; Director of the conducting department at the Peabody Conservatory, Baltimore. *Address:* Music Department, Peabody Institute of The John Hopkin's University, 1 East Mt Vernon Place, Baltimore, MD 21202, USA.

MONTGOMERY Kathryn, b. 23 Sept 1952, Canton,

Ohio, USA. Singer (Soprano). *Education:* Studied at the University of Bloomington, Indiana. *Debut:* Bloomington 1972, as Elvira in Ernani. *Career:* Sang at Norfolk from 1978 as Frasquita, and in the premiere of Musgrave's Christmas; European debut at Cologne 1980, as Leonore in Fidelio; sang at Cologne and Zurich 1980-82, Mannheim 1981-85; Guest engagements at Venice, Edinburgh, Barcelona and Brussels; Metropolitan Opera debut 1985, as Chrysothemis; Pretoria, South Africa, 1984 as Salome; other roles include Wagner's Elsa, Senta and Sieglinde, Tosca, Donna Anna, Berg's Marie, Donna Elvira and the Empress in Die Frau ohne Schatten; sang Aksinya in Lady Macbeth of Mtsensk at the Deutsche Oper Berlin, 1988; frequent concert appearances. *Address:* c/o Deutsche Oper Berlin, Richard Wagnerstrasse 10, D-1000 Berlin 1, Germany.

MONTGOMERY Kenneth, b. 28 Oct 1943, Belfast, Ireland. Conductor. *Education:* Royal Belfast Academical Institution; Royal College of Music, London. *Debut:* Glyndebourne Festival 1967; Staff Conductor, Sadler's Wells/English National Opera 1967-70; Assistant Conductor, Bournemouth Symphony Orchestra and Sinfonietta from 1970; Conducted Weber's Oberon at Wexford, 1972; Strauss's Ariadne and Capriccio for Netherlands Opera, 1972, 1975; Director, Bournemouth Sinfonietta, 1974-76; Covent Garden debut 1975, Le Nozze di Figaro; Principal Conductor, Dutch Radio Orchestra from 1976; Musical Director, Glyndebourne Touring Opera 1975-76; Guest appearances with Welsh National Opera, Canadian Opera; Concert performance of Donizeti's Anna Bolena at Amsterdam, 1989; Hansel and Gretel for Netherlands Opera, 1990; Conducted Tosca and The Magic Flute for Opera Northern Ireland at Belfast, 1990; Season 1991 with Alcina for Vancouver Opera, Figaro in Belfast and The Passion of Jonathan Wade for the Monte Carlo Royal Opera. *Honours:* Silver Medal, Worshipful Company of Musicians, 1963; Tagore Gold Medal, Royal College of Music, 1964. *Hobby:* Cooking.

MONTGOMERY Robert William, b. 18 Sept 1933, London, England. Managing Director. m. Margaret Exell, 21 Feb 1959, 2 sons. *Education:* MA, Music and History, Gonville and Caius College, Cambridge University, 1954-57. *Career:* Director, Rank Leisure Services Division, Rank Organisation Ltd, 1968-72; Managing Director, Chappell & Co. Ltd, 1972-76; Mechanical Copyright Protection Society Ltd., 1976-; General Administrator, Mechanical Rights Society Ltd, 1976-. *Memberships:* Deputy Chairman, National Music Council of Great Britain, 1980-; Chairman, Chelsea Opera Group; Trustee, British Music Information Centre. *Hobbies:* Music (Oboe playing); Squash. *Address:* Shores Corner, Shores Road, Woking, Surrey, GU21 4BZ, England.

MONTRESOR Beni, b. 31 Mar 1926, Bussoloegno, Italy. Opera Designer and Producer. *Career:* Designs for Barber's Vanessa seen at Spoleto 1961; Pelléas et Mélisande Glyndebourne 1962; Die Zauberflöte New York City Opera 1966; Metropolitan Opera Menotti's The Last Savage and La Gioconda; Lohengrin for San Francisco Opera; Designs for Massenet's Esclarmonde (San Francisco 1976) were seen also at the Metropolitan and Covent Garden; Falstaff for the opening of the season at the Rome Opera, 1989, Samson et Dalila at Houston, 1990; other productions have included L'elisir d'amore and Benvenuto Cellini at Covent Garden, 1966 and 1976, Madama Butterfly at Verona, 1978, and Zelmira by Rossini at Rome, 1989. *Address:* c/o Houston Grand Opera, 510 Preston Avenue, Houston, TX 77002, USA.

MOODY Ivan William George, b. 11 June 1964, London, England. Composer. m. Susana Simoes Diniz, 2 Sept 1989. *Education:* Royal Holloway College, London University; BMus, 1985; Studies with John Tavener, 1984-86. *Career:* Works performed and broadcast, UK, Austria, Denmark, Portugal, Italy, Germany, Finland, Estonia, Netherlands, Brazil, USA; Lecturing for music festivals, UK, Netherlands, Finland, and courses, UK, Portugal; Conducting of various choirs in Europe in

Orthodox and Renaissance sacred repertoire; Works performed all over Europe, East and West, Brazil and USA; Lecturing for Music Festivals, UK, Netherlands, Finland and courses UK, Portugal, Brazil; Conducting of various choirs in Europe in Orthodox and Renaissance Sacred repertoire. *Compositions include:* Lithuanian Songs, 1986; Cantigas de Amigo; Canticle at the Parting of the Soul; Burial Prayer; Miserere, 1988; Hymn of the Transfiguration; Lament for Christ, 1989; Liturgy of St John Chrysostom, 1991; Cantigas do Mar, 1991; Anamnisis; Hymn of Joseph of Arimathea; Hymn to Christ the Saviour, 1991; Vigil of the Angels, 1991; Passion & Resurrection, 1992. *Recordings:* As Conductor: Ippolitov - Ivanov: Divine Liturgy, Ikon; Moody, Tavener: Various Works, Ikon. *Publications:* Editions of Renaissance polyphony for Mapa Mundi, 1989, 1991, Chester Music, 1990-, Fundacao Calouste Gulbenkian, 1991. *Address:* c/o Vanderbeek & Imrie Ltd, 15 Marvig, Lochs, Isle of Lewis, Scotland PA86 9QP.

MOOG Robert (Arthur), b. 23 May 1934, Flushing, New York, USA. Designer of electronic instruments. *Education:* Studied at Queens College, New York and Columbia University; PhD Engineering Physics, Cornell University, 1965. *Career:* Founded R A Moog company, 1954, for the manufactuer of electronic musical instruments; first synthesizer modules, 1964; portable monophonic instrument and Minimoog 1970; Moog Music established 1971 at Buffalo New York, 1973; Founded Big Briar Company, 1978, producing devices for the control of synthesizers; Has lectured widely on synthesizers and similar products in the US and Europe; Consultant for Kurzweil Music Systems of Boston, 1984, becoming Chief Scientist; Collaborations with Wendy Carlos and various rock musicians. *Address:* c/o Kurzweil Music Systems, Main Street, Boston, Massachusetts, USA.

MOORE Barbara Patricia Hill, b. 28 Dec 1942, St Louis, Missouri, USA. Soprano; Professor and Chair, Department of Voice, SMU. m. Leandrew Moore, 27 Aug 1966, 1 daughter. *Education:* MS, University of Illinois. *Career:* Professor of Voice and Chair, Department of Voice, Southern Methodist University, Dallas, Texas, 1974-; Guest Appearances: Greensboro, N Carolina Symphony; Nuremberg Symphony; Irving, Texas Symphony; Pennsylvania Opera; Beaumont Symphony; Dallas Youth Orchestra; Dallas Chamber Opera; Dallas Symphony; Dallas Civic Symphony; Berlin-Theater Des Westens; Milwaukee, Wisconsin-Florentine Opera, 1989-90; Muenster University Concert, 1990-91; Stuttgart-Theater Des Westens, 1990; Weilheim, Germany, 1990-1991; Saarbrucken, Germany, 1991; Saarlouis, Germany, 1990-1991; Guttenberg, Germany, 1989, 1990, 1991; Eutin Summer Concert Series, 1983-92; Hanover, Germany; Aboard M.S. Europa, concerts in Japan, Hawaii, Central America, Panama, Brazil, and Norway, 1989, 1991 & 1991; Recitals include: Malenta, West Germany, 1985; Cologne, West Germany, 1985; Eutin Civic Summer Concert Series, West Germany, 1983-86; Salzburg College and Salzburg Seminar, Austria, 1984, 1985. *Current Management:* K A Fischer v d Made, Harmsmiihlenstrasse 63, 31832 Springe, Germany. *Address:* 1821 Carmel Cove, Plano, TX 75075, USA.

MOORE Carman Leroy, b. 8 Oct 1936, Lorain, Ohio, USA. Composer; Conductor. Divorced, 2 sons. *Education:* BS Music, Ohio State University, 1958; MS Music (Composition), Juilliard School of Music, 1966; Studied composition with Hall Overton, Luciano Berio, Vincent Persichetti. *Career:* Commissioned performances by New York Philharmonic, San Francisco Symphony, Rochester Philharmonic; Performances by Cleveland Orchestra, Nexus Ensemble, Aeolian Chamber Players; Founder, Composer, Conductor, Skymusic Ensemble, 1978; Taught at Yale School of Music, Queens and Brooklyn Colleges, Manhattanville; Music Critic, Columnist, The Village Voice, 1966-76. *Compositions:* Wildfires and Field Songs; Gospel Fuse; Hit: A Concerto for Percussion and Orchestra; Mass for the 21st Century; Concertos (The Theme Is Freedom) for Skymusic Ensemble; Wild Gardens of the Loup Garou, and The Last Chance Planet opera; Paradise Lost, musical; Four Movements for A Five-Toed Dragon for Orchestra and Chinese Instruments; Berenice Variations, for clarinet, piano, violin and violoncello. *Recordings:* Youth in a Merciful House (sextet), Folkways; Berenice: Variations on A Theme of G.F. Handel, CRI; Four Movements for A Fashionable 5-Toed Dragon, Hong Kong Trade Development Council; Lyrics to all songs on Felix Cavaliere, Bearsville. *Publications:* Somebody's Angel Child: The Story of Bessie Smith, 1970; Rockit. *Contributions to:* Frequently to New York Times, Vogue, others. *Hobbies:* Tennis; Reading. *Address:* 148 Columbus Avenue, 4R, New York, NY 10023, USA.

MOORE Dorothy Rudd, b. 4 June 1940, Deleware, USA. Composer. m. Kermit Moore. *Education:* Studied in Howard University Washington DC, Bmus, 1963, with Nadia Boulanger in France and with Chou Wen-Chung in New York, 1965. *Career:* Teacher of theory and piano at the Harlem School of the Arts, 1965-66; Music history and appreciation at New York University and the Bronx Community College, 1969-71; Co-founder, Society of Black Composers, 1968. *Compositions include:* Opera Frederick Douglas, 1979- 85; Orchestra: Reflections for wind instruments 1962; Symphony 1963; Chamber: Baroque Suite for cello 1965; Adagio for viola and cello, 1965; Three Pieces for violin and piano, 1967; Piano Trio 1970; Night Fantasy for clarinet and piano 1978; A Little Whimsy for piano, 1982; Cycle of 12 songs for soprano and oboe from The Rubaiyat, 1962; Sonnets on Love, Rosebuds and Death for soprano, violin and piano, 1976 and other vocal settings. *Address:* c/o Rud/Mor Corporation, 33 Riverside Drive, NY 10023, USA.

MOORE F. Richard, b. 4 Sept 1944, Uniontown, Pennsylvania, USA. Professor of Music. m. Cynthia Mettge, 24 Mar 1954, 2 daughters. *Education:* BFA, Music Composition, 1966, BFA, Music Performance (piano, percussion), 1966, Carnegie Mellon University; Music Composition and Theory, University of Illinois, 1966-67; MS 1975, PhD, 1977, Computer Engineering, Stanford University. *Career:* Acoustics Research, AT & T Bell Laboratories, 1966-79; Developed MUSIC V and GROOVE computer music systems with Max V Mathews. Currently Professor of Music; and Director, Computer Audio Research Laboratory (CARL), University of California, San Diego (UCSD). Author of cmusic synthesis program. *Compositions:* Computer generated art films (with Lillian Schwartz and Ken Knowlton): Pixillation (1970), Apotheosis (1971), Affinities (1971), Mathoms (1971), Enigma (1972), Galaxies (1975). Computer music: Requiem for computer generated tape. *Publications:* Realtime Interactive Computer Music (PhD dissertation, 1977); Programming in C with a Bit of UNIX (Prentice-Hall, 1985); Elements of Computer Music (Prentice-Hall, 1990). *Contributions to:* CARL Startup Kit; Carnegie Technical; Communications of the Association for Computing Machinery (ACM); Computer Music Journal. *Address:* Center for Research in Computing and The Arts, (CRCA) - 0037, University of California, San Diego (UCSD), La Jolla, CA 92093, USA.

MOORE Jonathan, b. 1960, England. Actor, Writer, Stage Director. *Career:* Has worked in the theatre and for televison; Co-librettist and director of Greek by Mark-Anthony Turnage, premiered at the 1988 Munich Biennale and seen later at the Edinburgh Festival, at the London Coliseum, 1990 and directed the version on BBC television; Directed Henze's Elegy for Young Lovers, at La Fenice, Venice; Wrote the Libretto for Horse Opera, a TV Film opera for Channel Four, Music by Stewart Copeland; Staged the premiere of Hans Jurgen von Bose's 63 Dream Palace at Munich 1990 and engaged for the premiere of Michael Berkeley's Baa Baa Black Sheep, Opera North, 1993; Has been engaged to direct the British Premiere of Schnitke's, Life With an Idiot, ENO London Coliseum. *Honours include:* BMW Prize; Royal Philharmonic Society Award for Best TV Film (Greek), and Midem Award, Cannes; Munich, 1988, 1990. *Address:* c/o Ingpen & Williams Ltd., 14 Kensington Court, London W8 5DN, England.

MOORE Kermit, b. 11 Mar 1929, Akron, Ohio, USA. Cellist; Conductor; Composer. m. Dorothy Rudd, 20 Dec 1964. *Education:* BMus, Cleveland Institute of Music, 1951; MA, New York University, 1952; Paris Conservatory, 1953-56. *Debut:* New York Town Hall, 1949. *Career:* Cello recitals in Paris, Brussels, Vienna, Cologne, Hamburg, Munich, Geneva, Basel, Amsterdam, Tokyo, Seoul, New York, Boston, Chicago and San Francisco; Guest Conductor of, Detroit Symphony, Brooklyn Philharmonic, Symphony of New World; Festival Orchestra at the United Nations; Berkeley (California) Symphony; Dance Theater of Harlem; Opera Ebony. *Compositions:* Music for cello & piano; Music for Viola, Percussion & Piano; Many Thousand Gone, strings, chorus and percussion; Music for Timpani & Orchestra; Music for Flute & Piano; Five Songs for DRM. *Recordings:* Brahms: Sonata in E Minor, Dorothy Rudd Moore; Dirge & Deliverance, Performance Records; Mendelssohn: Sonata in D Major, Kermit Moore: Music for Cello & Piano, Performance Records; Karl Weigl Sonata, Love Song & Wild Dance, Orion Records. *Publication:* Chapter in The Music Makers, 1979. *Hobby:* Hiking. *Current Management:* Rud/Mor Corporation. *Address:* c/o RUD/MOR Corporation, 33 Riverside Drive, NY 10023, USA.

MOORE Philip John, b. 30 Sept 1943, London, England. Organist. *Education:* ARCM; GRSM; FRCO; BMus, Durham University. *Career:* Assistant Music Master, Eton College, 1966-68; Assistant Organist, Canterbury Cathedral, 1968-74; Organist and Master of the Choristers, Guildford Cathedral, 1974-82; Organist and Master of the Music, York Minster, 1983. *Compositions include:* Works for chorus and orchestra, choral and organ works, instrumental works. *Honours include:* Limpus, Turpin and Read Prizes, RCO; Walford Davies Prize, RCM. *Memberships:* RCO; RCM; ISM. *Hobbies:* Collecting fountain pens; Kite Flying. *Address:* 1 Minster Court, York, YO1 2JJ, England.

MOORE Timothy, b. 19 Feb 1922, Cambridge, England. Composer. *Education:* Trinity College, Cambridge, 1939-41 and 1945-46; MA; MusB; Royal College of Music, London, 1946-48. *Career:* Director of Music, Dartington Hall School, 1950-82. *Compositions:* 3 2-part Inventions for Piano, Andante for Cor anglais & Piano; Suite in G for 3 Recorders; Night Song for SA & Piano; Sing Lullaby for SSATB; Westcountry Variations for 2 Cellos & Piano; Trumpet Concerto, 1948; Suite in F for Orchestra, 1949; Clarinet Concerto, 1956; Horn Sonata, 1970; Partita for 2 pianos, 1985; Orchestral Variations on a theme by Fauré, 1987; Piano Duet Concerto, 1989; Variations for Piano and Orchestra on a theme by Mozart, 1992. *Recording:* Suite in G. *Publications:* Brass Quintet; Lullaby for SSATB, 1947; Three 2-part Inventions for Piano, 1948; Andante for Cor Anglais & Piano, 1949; Suite in G for 3 Recorders, 1950; Night Song for SA & Piano, 1967; West Country Variations for 2 Cellos & Piano, 1979; Brass Quintet, 1991. *Address:* 86 Chesterton Road, Cambridge, CB4 1ER, England.

MOORMAN (Madeleine) Charlotte, b. 18 Nov 1933, Little Rock, Arkansas, USA. Cellist. *Education:* BMus, Centenary College, Shreveport, 1955; Juilliard School with Leonard Rose, 1957-58. *Career:* Member of Jacob Glick's Boccherini Players, 1958-63 and the American Symphony Orchestra, until 1967; Founded the Annual New York Avant Garde Festival, 1963; Collaborations with composer and video artist Nam June Paik from 1964, including Cello Sonata No 1 for Adults Only, 1965, Opera Sextronique, 1967, TV Bra for Living Sculpture, 1969, TV Cello, 1971 and Global Groove, 1973; The People of the State of New York against Charlotte Moorman performed 1977; Performances of the cello wrapped in cellophane, in a gondola and in an oildrum, and underwater; Has performed works by John Cage. *Address:* c/o Nam June Paik, ASCAP, ASCAP Building, One Lincoln Plaza, NY 10023, USA.

MORA Barry, b. 1944, New Zealand. Singer (Baritone). *Education:* Studied in London with Otakar Kraus and John Matheson. *Career:* Sang at

Gelsenkirchen 1977-79 as Verdi's Posa and Luna, Mozart's Speaker and Figaro, Monteverdi's Ulisse and Dandini in Cenerentola; Sang at Frankfurt from 1979 as Tamare in Schreker's Die Gezeichneten, Renato (Un Ballo in Maschera), Mary in Die Soldaten, Malatesta, Marcello, Choerebus in Les Troyens and Ford in Falstaff; Festival Hall debut 1979, as Schumann's Faust; Covent Garden debut 1980, as Donner in Das Rheingold; Scottish Opera 1983 as Traveller in Death in Venice and Filitero in Orione by Cavalli; Welsh National Opera from 1986, as Donner, Gunther, the Forester in The Cunning Little Vixen, Germont, Faninal, Don Alfonso, Ford and Frank in Die Fledermaus, 1991; Netherlands Opera 1991, and Fieramosca (Benvenuto Cellini); Engagements at the Deutsche Oper Berlin, the Zurich Opera, Aachen, Dusseldorf, Barcelona and Wellington and Canterbury (New Zealand); Also sang in 1992, Rosenkavalier, Sydney; La Traviata, Barcelona; Parsifal, Frankfurt; Così Fan Tutte, Wellington; Un Ballo in Maschera, Brussels; Concert repertory includes Puccini's Messa di Gloria; Bach's B minor Mass and St John Passion; Carmina Burana; Stravinsky's Canticum Sacrum; Lieder eines fahrenden Gesellen by Mahler; La Traviata, Canterbury Opera, NZ, La Traviata, Wellington Opera, NZ, Lulu, Buenos Aires, Così fan Tutte, Barcelona Opera, Ballo in Maschera, Canterbury Opera, 1993; Lulu, The Australian Opera, La Cenerentola, The Australian Opera, 1994. Address: c/o Haydn Rawstron Limited, PO Box 654, London SE26 4DZ, England.

MORAITIS Nicoclis George, b. 25 July 1924, Andros, Greece. Producer of Classical Operas and Plays. Education: Piano, voice and music theory and analysis to prepare for producer role. Career: Co-Producer for 20th Century Fox, It Happened in Athens, starring Jayne Mansfield; Founder of Apollo Opera & Drama Co, Inc, 1975. Recordings: Private recordings of La Muette de Portici and Dinorah from own live productions by Apollo Opera Inc.; Performance and recordings: Excerpts from Saint-Saens Opera, 3 Halevy Operas, 1988-89; Performance and Recording, Victor Herbert, Magic Knight, Lohengrin, 1990. Publications: Translation: Dumas, Les Deux Diane; Victor Hugo Translation; Greece & travel articles for newspapers; Apollo World Opera Index, listing over 20,000 operas, composers, dates, premieres, 1991. Honour: Athens, Top Scholarship Award of all the schools, 1942. Membership: Montreal Fencing Club. Hobbies: Chess; Oil Paintings; Animal conservation. Address: 2130 Bway, Suite No 1211, New York, NY 10023, USA.

MORALES Abram, b. 30 Nov 1939, Corpus Christi, Texas, USA. Education: BME, MM, Southern Methodist University; Study for DMA, North Texas State University. Career: Dallas Opera; San Francisco Opera; Town Hall, New York City; Seattle Opera; Alice Tully Hall, New York City; Minneapolis Opera; On tour with: Metropolitan Opera Co. in role of Lindoro in Rossini's, L'Italiana in Algieri, May 1986; Buxton Festival, Buxton, England singing Count Alberto in Rossini's L'Occasione fa Il Ladro, August 1987; Concert Opera Orchestra of Manhattan at Town Hall, New York City, as Belfiore in Viaggio a Reims, Oct. 1987. Hobby: Film Festivals. Current Management: Columbia Artists, 165 West 57th Street, New York, NY 10019, USA. Address: 3002 Glenview Road, Wilmette, IL 60091, USA.

MORAN Mike, b. 4 Mar 1948, Yorkshire, England. Composer; Pianist. m. Lynda Elizabeth, 5 Sept 1992, 2 daughters. Education: ARCM, 1966-71; GRSM. Career: Studio musician, Europe and USA, 1971-77; Established player writer and producer with a wide variety of experience in Jazz, 1971-77; Feature films include Time Bandits, The Missionary, Water, as well as The Greek Tycoon, Top secret, Betrayal and an extensive number of television films such as Harry's Game, Taggart, The Contract, El Cid, Love Story Docmentary. Extensive catalogue as writer and producer with artistes such as George Harrison, Paul McCartney, Freddie Mercury, Elvin Jones, Placido Domingo, and Montserrat Caballe; Recently released album of music from TV series, Taggart. Memberships: National Association of Recording Arts and Sciences; PRS; Association of Professional Composers, Royal Aero Club, Crockfords. Hobbies: Flying; Martial Arts. Current Management Olav Wyper Ltd. Address: The Glen, 6 Aldenham Avenue, Radlett, Herts WD7 8HJ, England.

MORAN Robert, b. 8 Jan 1937, Denver, Colorado, USA. Composer. Education: Studied with Hans Erich Apostel and Roman Haubenstock Ramati in Vienna, Luciano Berio and Darius Milhaud at Mills College. Career: Founded and co-directed the New Music Ensemble, San Francisco Conservatory; Performances throughout USA and Europe as pianist; Lecturer on contemporary music. Compositions include: Silver and the Circle of Messages, for chamber orchestra, 1970; Emblems of Passage for 2 orchestras, 1974; Angels of Silence for viola and chamber orchestra, 1975; The Last Station of the Albatross, for 1-8 instruments, 1978; Survivor from Darmstadt, 1984; Mixed media works and stage works including Let's Build a Nut House, chamber Opera, 1969; Erlösung dem Erloser, music drama, 1982; Leipziger Kerzenspiel, 1985; The Juniper Tree, 1985; Desert of Roses, 1992; From the Towers of the Moon, 1992. Address: c/o ASCAP, ASCAP House, One Lincoln Plaza, NY 10023, USA.

MORAVEC (Vincent) Paul, b. 2 Nov 1957, Buffalo, New York, USA. Composer; Professor of Music; Electronic Music Synthesist; Conductor. Education: BA magna cum laude, Music, Harvard University, Cambridge, Massachusetts, 1980; MA Music Composition, 1982, DMA Music Composition, 1987, Columbia University, New York. Career: Currently Assistant Professor of Music, Dartmouth College, Hanover, New Hampshire. Compositions: Missa Miserere, 1981; Ave Verum Corpus, 1981; Pater Noster, 1981; Sacred Songs, 1982; Three Anthems, 1983; Songs for Violin and Piano, 1983; Music for Chamber Ensemble, 1983; Wings, 1983; Spiritdance, 1984; Innocent Dreamers, 1985; Music Remembers, 1985; The Open Secret, 1985; Four Transcendent Love Songs, 1986; Prayers and Praise, 1986; Whispers, 1986; The Kingdom Within, 1987. Current Management: JL Music Productions, 250 West 100th Street Suite 104, New York, NY 10025, USA. Address: c/o Music Department, Dartmouth College, Hanover, NH 03755, USA.

MORAWETZ Oskar, b. 17 Jan 1917, Czechoslovakia. Composer, Professor. m. 1958, 1 son, 1 daughter. Career: Professor of Music, University of Toronto; Ochestral compositions performed frequently by Canadian Orchestras, Canadian Broadcasting Corporation and in USA, Europe and Australia. Among major orchestras abroad, his compositions have been performed by the Philadelphia, Chicago, Detroit, Minneapolis, Indianapolis, Washington and Aspen Festival Orchestras in USA and major orchestras in France, Sweden, Norway, Belgium, Holland, Italy, Czechoslovakia and Greece; Conductors who have programmed his words include William Steinberg, Zubin Mehta, Karel Ancerl, Kubelik, Walter Susskind, Seiji Ozawa, Adrian Boult, Izler Solomon, Sixten Ehrling and Ernest MacMilllan; artists such as Glenn Gould, Rudolf Firkusny and Anton Kuerti have premiered his piano compositions and Maureen Forrester, Jon Vickers, Louis Marshall, Dorothy Maynor, Louis Quilico and Lillian Sukis have included compositions in programmes in Canada, USA, Europe and Australia. Compositions include: Memorial To Martin Luther King for cello and orchestra; Sinfonietta For Winds and Percussion; From The Diary of Anne Frank; Fantasy in D; Piano Concerto. Recordings: Many of his compositions have been recorded by various record companies.

MORAWSKI Jerzy, b. 9 Sept 1932, Warsaw, Poland. Musicologist. m. Katarzyna. Education: Theory, 1957, Piano, 1961, Warsaw Conservatory; MA, Institute of Musicology, Warsaw University, 1958; PhD, Institute of Arts, Polish Academy of Sciences, 1970. Career: Assistant, Department of Theory and History of Music, 1956-70, Doctor, Head, History Music Section, 1970-79, Vice-Director, Institute of Arts and Polish Academy of Sciences, 1979-81; Lecturer, Warsaw University,

1968-70; Academy of Catholic Theology, Warsaw, 1970-73; Jagiellonian University, Cracow, 1971-82. *Publications include:* The Problems of the Tropes Techniques; Research on Liturgical Recitative in Poland; Editor-in-Chief of serial publications: Monumenta Musicae in Polonia and Musica Medii Aevi; Books: Musical Lyric Poetry in Medieval Poland, 1973; Theory of Music in the Middle Ages, 1979; Musica Antiqua Polonica; Anthology, The Middle Ages, 1972; The Rhymed History of St Jadwiga, 1977; The Rhymed History of St Adalbert, 1979; The Polish Cistercian Sequences, 1984; Jan Stefani's Six Partitas for Wind Instruments, 1993. *Contributions to:* Professional publications. *Memberships include:* Past Vice-Secretary and President, Polish Composers' Union, Musicological Section; International Musicological Society. *Address:* ul. Dluga 24 m. 43, 00-238 Warsaw, Poland.

MORDKOVITCH Lydia, b. 1950, Saratov, USSR. Concert Violinist. *Education:* Studied at the Odessa Conservatory and with David Distrakh in Moscow. *Career:* Emigrated to Israel 1974, later resident in London; British debut 1979, with the Halle Orchestra under Waletr Susskind; Appearances with the Philharmonia, London Symphony, London, Royal and Liverpool Philharmonics, Scottish National, City of Birmingham Symphony and all the BBC Symphony Orchestras; US debut with the Chicago Symphony under Solti, returning to play the Brahms Concerto with the Philadelphia Orchestra under Muti; Promenade Concerts debut 1985, returning 1988 with Szymanowski's 2nd Concerto; Further engagements in Finland, Norway, Italy and the Canary Islands; Conductors include Kurt Sanderling, Stanislaw Skrowaczewski, Charles Groves and Marek Janowski. *Recordings:* Shostakovich Concertos with the Scottish National under Neeme Järvi; Complete works for solo violin by Bach; Concertos by Bruch, Prokofiev and Brahms; Moeran Concerto with the Ulster Orchestra under Vernon Handley (Chandos); CD: Solo Sonatas by Ysaÿe. *Honours:* Prize winner, National Young Musicians Competition, Kiev; Long-Thibaud International Competition, Paris; Gramophone Award for Best Concerto Recording, 1990; Diaspason d'or, France, for Prokofiev Concertos. *Address:* c/o Norman McCann International Artists Ltd, The Coach House, 56 Lawrie Park Gardens, London SE26 6XJ, England.

MOREHEN John Manley, b. 3 Sept 1941, Gloucester, England. Lecturer; Musicologist; Organist and Conductor. m. Marie Catherine Jacobus, 26 July 1969, 1 son, 1 daughter. *Education:* Clifton College; Royal School of Church Music; New College, Oxford; College of Church Musicians, Washington DC; King's College, Cambridge. MA (Oxon and Cantab); PhD (Cantab); FRCO (Chm); FRCCO. *Career:* Assistant Director of Music at St. Clement Danes and Hampstead Parish Church; Organist to Hampstead Choral Society, Martindale Sidwell Choir and London Bach Orchestra, 1964-67; Faculty Lecturer, College of Church Musicians, Washington Cathedral and Lecturer in Applied Music at The American University, Washington DC 1967-68; Sub-Organist, St. George's Chapel, Windsor Castle 1968-72; Lecturer in Music, University of Nottingham 1973-82; Senior Lecturer 1982-; Professor of Music, 1989-; Conductor, Nottingham Bach Society 1983-90; BBC Recitalist 1964-; Tours of Europe and North America; Freeman of the City of London, 1991; Liveryman, Worshipful Company of Musicians, 1991; Justice of the Peace, Nottinghamshire, 1991. *Recordings:* With choirs of New College, Oxford and Hampstead Parish Church on EMI, Waverley, Saga and Abbey Labels. *Publications:* Many editions of 16th and 17th Century English Music; Articles in The New Grove Dictionary (6th Edition) and Musical Periodicals; Major editions of the music of Richard Nicolson 1975, Christopher Tye 1979, William Byrd 1987, Thomas Morley 1991. *Address:* Wynstay, Clipstone Lane, Normanton-On-The-Wolds, Plumtree, Nottingham, NG12 5NW, England.

MOREL Francois, b. 14 Mar 1926, Montreal, Canada. Composer. *Education:* Studied piano with private teacher; studied composition with Claude Champagne, Conservatoire de Muique, Montréal. *Career:* Working for Radio-Canada writing background music for theatre, radio and television 1956-81; Professor of composition, orchestration and analysis, l'Ecole de musique, Universitié Laval, Quebec City; President of publishing firm, Les Editions Québec-Musique, Montreal; received commissions for compositions from Canadian Broadcasting Corporation, First International Festival of Contemporary Music For Wind Symphony Orchestra, Edmonton Symphony Orchestra; McGill Chamber Orchestra, Société de Musique Contemporaine du Québec, Guitar Society of Toronto 1976; Olympic Games committee; Montreal International Competition among others. *Compositions:* Orchestral: Antiphonie 1953; Boreal 1959; Departs 1968-69. Diptyque 1948, revised 1955-56; Esquisse 1946-47; L'Etoile noire 1961-62; Iikkii 1971; Jeux 1976; Litanies 1955-56, revised 1970; Melisma 1980; Le mythe de la roche percée 1960-61; Neumes despace et reliefs 1967; Prismes-anamorphoses 1967; Radiance 1970-72; Requiem for Winds 1962-63; Rituel de l'espace 1958-59; Sinfonia 1963; Spirale 1956; Trajectoire 1967. Instrumental Ensemble: Cassation 1954; Etude en forme de toccate 1965; Quatuor No. 1, 1952, No. 2, 1962-63; Quintette pour cuivres 1962; Rhythmologue 1970; Symphonie pour cuivres 1956. Instrumental Solo and Vocal Solos. *Address:* c/o CAPAC (Canada), PRS Ltd, Berners Street, London W1, England.

MORELLE Maureen, b. 1937, Hampshire. Singer (Mezzo-soprano). *Education:* Studied at the Royal College of Music. *Career:* Sang in the original London cast of West Side Story; Opera debut as Smeton in Anna Bolena at the 1960 Glyndebourne Festival; Later appearances as Geneviève in Pelléas et Mélisande, Marcellina (Le Nozze di Figaro) and Madame Larina (Eugene Onegin); Sadlers Wells Opera: Rosina, Barber of Seville; Hansel, H & G; Dorabelle, Cosi; Pippa, Thieving Magpie; Cherubino, Figaro; English National Opera as Ottavia (Coronation of Poppea), Wagner's Fricka, First Norn and Flosshilde, in The Ring conducted by Reginald Goodall; Rosina, Dorabella and Lady Essex (Gloriana); Sang in A Midsummer Night's Dream and Birtwistle's Punch and Judy (world premiere, 1968) for English Opera Group and toured to San Francisco, Brussels, Paris and Montreal; Engagements with Welsh National Opera and Opera North include Cherubino, Fenena (Nabucco), Mrs Sedley (Peter Grimes) and the Hostess in Boris Godunov (1989); Season 1987-88 as The Mayor's Wife in Jenůfa at Covent Garden and Verdi's Azucena for ENO and Scottish Opera; Regular appearances on BBC's Friday Night is Music Night and Melodies for You; ROH Season 1992/93, Mayor's Wife, Jenůfa; Opera North, Lavina, Onegin. *Honours include:* Queen's Prize at the RCM. *Address:* c/o Korman International Management, Crunnells Green Cottage, Preston, Herts SG4 7UQ, England.

MORELLI Adriana, b. 1954, Italy. Singer (Soprano). *Education:* Studied at Reggio Calabria. *Debut:* Spoleto 1978, as Musetta. *Career:* Sang Sophie in Werther at Bergamo 1979, Lauretta in Gianni Schicchi at Lucca, 1981; Further engagements as Butterfly and Mimi at Spoleto and Lille, Elisabeth de Valois at Dijon and Amsterdam, Amelia (Un Ballo in Maschera) at Trieste; Sang Margherita in Mefistofele and Tosca at Genoa, 1987-88, Giorgetta in Il Tabarro at Florence 1988 and Maria Stuarda at Piacenza, 1990; La Scala debut, 1990, as Nedda in I pagliacci; Stage and concert appearances in South America. *Address:* c/o Teatro alla Scala, Via Filodrammatici 2, Milan, Italy.

MORGAN Arwel Huw, b. 1950, Ystalyfera, Swansea, Wales. Singer (Bass). *Career:* Joined the chorus of Welsh National Opera in 1978; Solo roles in Wales have included Don Fernando (Fidelio), Ladas (The Greek Passion), Angelotti (Tosca), Hobson (Peter Grimes) and the Parson (The Cunning Little Vixen); Created the role of Maskull for New Celtic Opera's Voyage to Arcturus; English National Opera from 1987 in Lady Macbeth of Mtsensk and The Cunning Little Vixen; Toured Britain 1988 as Osmin in Opera 80's

Die Entführung aus dem Serail; Season 1992 as Leporello, as Carl Olsen, in Weill's Street Scene for ENO and Fabrizio in The Thieving Magpie for Opera North. *Recordings include:* Polonius in Hamlet by Ambroise Thomas, conducted by Richard Bonynge (Decca). *Address:* c/o Ingpen and Williams Ltd., 14 Kensington Court, London W11 4PA, England.

MORGAN Beverly, b. 17 Mar 1952, Hanover, New Hampshire, USA. Soprano. *Education:* Mt Holyoke College, 1969-71; BMus, Honours, New England Conservatory of Music, 1971-73; MMus, Honours, 1973-75; New York. *Debut:* Recital debut as winner of Concert Artists Guild Award, 1978. *Career:* Operatic Appearances with Wiener Staatsoper, San Francisco Opera, Netherlands Opera, Opera Company of Boston, Pittsburgh, Omaha and Philadelphia Operas, Kennedy Center in Washington and Scottish National Opera; Sang in the premiere of Glass's Satyagraha at Amsterdam, 1980, and in the US Premiere of Zimmermann's Die Soldaten, Boston, 1982; other appearances in Bernstein's A Quiet Place at La Scala and in Vienna at Santa Fe in the US Premieres of Henze's English Cat and Penderecki's Die Schwarze Maske, 1985, 1988, and for Scottish Opera as Berg's Lulu, 1987; other roles include Tatiana and Violetta at Seattle and Fusako in Henze's Das Verratene Meer, Berlin and Milan; Concert Appearances with Boston Symphony, San Francisco Symphony, Chamber Society of Lincoln Center, American String Quartet, Marlboro Music Festival, American Composers Orchestra; Performances under Leonard Bernstein, Seiji Ozawa and Herbert Blomstedt. *Recordings:* DGG; Columbia. *Hobbies:* Backpacking; Vegetarian Cooking. *Current Management:* Columbia Artists Management Incorporated, New York, USA. *Address:* c/o Crittenden Division, Columbia Artists Management Incorporated, 165 West 57th Street, NY 10019, USA.

MORGAN David, b. 18 May 1932, Ewell, Surrey, England. Composer; Arranger; Conductor. 1 son, 2 daughters. *Education:* State Conservatorium of Music, Sydney, Australia, 1947-52; Studied composition with Matyas Seiber and conducting with Walter Goehr and Norman Del Mar; Associate, Royal College of Music, 1957; BMus, Durham, 1970. *Career:* Cor Anglais in Sydney Symphony Orchestra, 1958-59; Tutor of Theoretical Music Subjects, Elder Consevatorium, University of Adelaide, 1959-61; Music Librarian, British Council, London, England, 1964-68; Music Teacher, London, 1971-75; Composer/Arranger, South Australian Education Department, Adelaide, Australia, 1975-93. *Compositions:* 5 symphonies; Concertos for horn, violin and viola; Orchestral, chamber, instrumental, choral, concert band and brass band works. *Publications:* Lullay My Liking and also Weep You No More, Sad Fountains, 1967 and 1969; Miscellany 1 and 2 for Junior Brass Ensemble, 1981 and 1985. *Honours:* S.G. Vicars Composition Scholarship, 1950-52; Martin Fellowship, 1966. *Address:* 13 Berrima Street, Glenelg North, South Australia, 5045, Australia.

MORGAN Michael DeVard, b. 17 Sept 1957, Washington, DC, USA. Conductor. *Education:* Oberlin College Conservatory of Music; Berkshire Music Centre, Tanglewood, 1977. *Debut:* Operatic, Vienna State Opera, 1982. *Career:* Apprentice Conductor, Buffalo Philharmonic, 1979-80; Assistant Conductor, St Louis Symphony, 1980-81; Assistant Conductor, Chicago Symphony, 1986-; Guest Conductor: New York and Warsaw Philharmonics, Vienna, Baltimore, Houston, New Orleans Symphony Orchestras; National Symphony (Washington); Deutsche Staatsoper, Berlin; Summer Opera Theater, Washington, DC; Orchestras in Italy, Denmark and Holland. *Honours:* First Prize, Hans Swarowsky International Conductors Competition Vienna, 1980; Prizes in Conducting Competitions at Baltimore, 1974; San Remo, 1975; Copenhagen, 1980. *Current Management:* Sheldon Soffer Management Inc. New York; Alex Saron, Blaricum, Holland (Europe). *Address:* Sheldon Soffer Management Inc., 130 W. 56th Street, New York, NY 10019, USA.

MORGAN Morris, b. 26 Sept 1940, Berlin, Germany. Singer (Baritone). *Education:* Studied in Dusseldorf, Cologne and Wiesbaden, 1955-71. *Career:* Sang at Cologne in the 1965 premiere of Die Soldaten by Zimmermann; Kiel Opera, 1965-68, notably in the 1965 premiere of Reimann's Traumspiel; Wiesbaden 1968-71, Berne, 1971-79, Freiburg, 1978-81; Further engagements at Dusseldorf, Mannheim, Stuttgart, Bremen, Saarbrucken, Lubeck and Klagenfurt; Returned to Berne 1985, as Marcello in La Boheme; Concert appearances in baroque music and as Lieder singer. *Recordings include:* Die Soldaten; Zemlinsky's Kleider Machen Leute; Israel in Egypt and Carmina Burana. *Address:* Stadttheater Bern, Nageligasse 1, CH-3011 Bern, Switzerland.

MORGAN Robert P, b. 28 July 1934, Nashville, Tennessee, USA. Professor of Music (Music Theory). m. 12 June 1965. *Education:* BA 1956, PhD 1969 Princeton University; MA, University of California, Berkeley, 1958; Hochschule für Musik, Munich, Germany, 1960-62. *Career:* Professor of Music (Music Theory), Yale University. *Compositions:* Numerous works for orchestra, Chamber Ensembles and voice. *Recording:* Trio for Flute, Cello and Harpsichord. *Publication:* Twentieth Century Music; Music: A View from Delft, Selected Essays of Edward T Cone (editor). *Contributions to:* Numerous articles to Musical Quarterly; Journal of Music Theory; 19th Century Music; Perspectives of New Music. *Honours:* Woodrow Wilson Fellowship, 1956-57; German Government Grant, 1960-62; National Endowment of Humanities Senior Fellow, 1983-84. *Memberships:* Society for Music Theory (executive Board 1985-88); American Musicological Society (Council member 1982-85); College Music Society. *Hobbies:* Tennis; Skiing. *Address:* Department of Music, Yale University, New Haven, CT 06520, USA.

MORI Junko, b. 13 Feb 1948, Niigata-ken, Japan. Composer. m. 10 May 1972. *Education:* Tokyo University of Arts, 1966-71; Graduate Course, 1971-75, 1976-78; BA, Composition, 1971; MMus, Composition, 1975; Master of Musicology, Solfeggio, 1978. *Career:* Public Performance, London City, Canada, 1979; NHK-FM Broadcast (choral music), 1979; Chamber Opera, NHK-TV and p.p., 1980; String Quartet III, CCSQWC Concert, USA, 1981; Spring Dawn, Modern Japanese Asian Compositions, USA and KPFA Radio, 1985; Works of Junko Mori Concert for voices, Tokyo, 1986; Two Operette, 1990 & 1992. *Compositions:* String Quartet III; Niji to Atchan, Kudamono no Uta for children (female chorus); Autumn Mist for flute and guitar; Usagi (disk). *Recordings:* Autumn Mist (cassette-tape), USA. *Publications:* String Quartet III, 1985; Niji to Atchan/Kudamono no Uta, 1986; Young Aki's Piano Lesson, 1985; Twelve Children (12 pieces for pf solo) 1989; Nanohana to Watashi, songs for soprano, 1992. *Contributions to:* Guidance and Exercise of Keyboard Harmony, 1981; Guidance of Score-reading, 1980. *Hobby:* Writing Fantastic Stories. *Address:* 2-15-17 Mitsuidai, Hachioji City, Tokyo 192, Japan.

MORIARTY John, b. 30 Sept 1930, Fall River, Massachusetts, USA. Administrator; Educator. *Education:* BM, New England Conservatory, 1952; Mills College with Egon Petri, summers, 1949, 1950 and 1952; Brandeis University, 1954-55. *Career:* Most recent performances include, Tamerlano by Handel, 1970; 6 records as conductor of Chamber Orchestra, Copenhagen and 3 records as piano accompanist, Cambridge; Artistic Administrator, Opera Society of Washington, 1960-62, Santa Fe Opera, New Mexico, 1962-65; Director, Wolf Trap Co, Vienna, Virginia, 1972-77; Principal Conductor, Central City Opera, Denver, 1978-; Artistic Director, 1982-; Panelist, Connecticut Arts Council, 1982 and 1984; Adjudicator, various contests including Metropolitan Opera Auditions, 1965-; Chairman, Opera Department of New England Conservatory. *Publication:* Author, Diction, 1975. *Honours:* D.M. Hon, New England Conservatory, 1992. *Address:* New England Conservatory, 290 Huntington Avenue, Boston, MA 02115, USA.

MORINI Erica, b. 5 Jan 1910, Vienna, Austria. Concert Violinist. m. Felice Siracusano, 1938. *Education:* At age of 4 years under father, Professor Oscar Morini; Age 8, under Professor Ottocar Sevcik, masterclass, Viennese Conservatory. *Debut:* Age 9, under Arthur Nikisch, Leipzig Gewandhaus (Beethoven Festival). *Career includes:* Concert tours to Australia, Asia, Africa, Europe, USA (1920). *Honours:* Honorary member, Sigma Alpha Beta; Honorary MusD, Smith College, Massachusetts, USA, 1955, New England Conservatory of Music, Massachusetts, 1963; City of New York's Mayor Beame presented Certificate of Appreciated and Gold Medal, 1976. *Hobbies:* Mountain climbing; Chamber music. *Address:* 1200 Fifth Avenue, New York, NY 10029, USA.

MORISON Elsie, b. 15 Aug 1924, Victoria, Australia. Singer (Soprano). m. (1) Kenneth Stevenson, 1950; (2) Rafael Kubelik, 1963. *Education:* Melba Conservatorium, Australia; Royal College of Music, London. *Debut:* Melbourne, 1994, in the Messiah. *Career:* Acis and Galatea, Albert Hall, 1948; Sadler's Wells Opera, 1948-54, notably as Fiordiligi, Lauretta, Nannetta; Covent Garden, 1954-62: Pamina, Susanna, Mimi, Marenka in Bartered Bride, and 1958, Blanche in British premiere of Dialogues des Carmelites, by Poulenc. Glyndebourne, 1953-59 in The Rake's Progess and Fidelio. Many appearances at international festivals as a concert singer. *Recordings include:* Haydn The Seasons and Handel, Oratorio Solomon; Handel's Messiah; Mahler's 4th Symphony. *Honours include:* Melba Scholarship. *Address:* Im Sand, CH 6047 Kastanienbaum, Switzerland.

MORK Truls, b. 25 Apr 1961, Bergen, Norway. Concert Cellist. *Education:* Studied with his father and with Frans Helmerson at the Swedish Radio Music School. *Career:* Extensive tours of Europe, USSR, the USA and the Far East from 1984; Performances with the Oslo Philharmonic, Royal Philharmonic, Orchestre National de France, City of Birmingham Symphony, Moscow Philharmonic, Moscow Radio Symphony, Israel Philharmonic, Gothenburg Symphony and Hamburg Philharmonic; Conductors he has worked with include Mariss Jansons, Walter Weller, Vladimir Ashkenazy, Claus Peter Flor, John Nelson, Esa-Pekka Salonen, Neeme Järvi and Witold Lutoslawski; He has also made highly successful recital debuts in London's Wigmore Hall, February 1988 and New York's Town Hall, April 1986; Tours of Australasia with the Adelaide, Sydney and Melbourne Symphony Orchestras and numerous recitals in New Zealand; other engagements include tours of the USA with the Oslo Philharmonic and Mariss Jansons, concerts with the Gulbenkian and Berlin Symphony Orchestras, the Bergen Philharmonic, Atlanta and Detroit Symphony Orchestras, plus tours of Japan and Spain; Participating in Nordic tours, solo recitals and piano quartet recitals); Chamber Festivals include: Prades (Casals Festival), Kuhmo, Korsholm and Naantali; Founder and artistic director of the International Chamber Music Festival in Stavanger; also at Flanders Festival, the Rouen Festival and the Bergen International Festival. *Recordings include:* Haydn Cello Concertos with the Norwegian Chamber Orchestra directed by Iona Brown; and the Schumann, Elgar and Saint-Säens Concertos; Dvořák Cello Concerto, exclusively for Virgin Classics; and Tchaikovsky Rococo Variations, with the Oslo Philharmonic conducted by Mariss Jansons have recently been released to great critical acclaim; Future recording plans include two recital discs with the pianist Jean-Yves Thibaudet, the Shostakovich Cello Concerti, Strauss Don Quixote and the Miaskowsky Cello Concerto. *Honours:* Numerous awards in national and International competitions including: Prizewinner, Tchaikovsky Competition, Moscow, 1982; First Prize, W Naumberg Competition, New York, 1986; First Prize, Cassado Cello Competition, Florence, 1983; UNESCO Prize at the European Radio-Union competition in Bratislava. *Address:* c/o IMG Artists Media House, 3 Burlington Lane, London W4 2TH, England.

MOROZOV Alexander, b. 1950, USSR. Singer (Bass). *Education:* Studied at the Leningrad Conservatory. *Career:* Joined the Kirov Opera, Leningrad, 1983 and has sung Don Basilio, Mephistopheles, Pimen (Boris Godunov) and Surin in The Queen of Spades; Sang at Covent Garden 1987 with the Kirov, as Surin, Pimen and Boris; Tours to Zurich and France (Tours); Sang Zemfira's father in a concert performance pf Rachmaninov's Aleko at the Santa Cecilia, Rome, 1989; Amsterdam 1989, as Pimen; Dolokhov in War and Peace for Seattle Opera, 1990; Scottish Opera 1990 as Padre Guardiano in La Forza del Destino; Covent Garden company as Basilio, and Fiesco in a new production of Simon Boccanegra conducted by Georg Solti, 1991. *Honours:* First Prize at competitions in Rio de Janeiro and Moscow (Tchaikovsky International). *Address:* Allied Artists, 42 Montpelier Square, London SW7 1JZ, England.

MOROZOV Igor, b. 1948, Moscow, USSR. Singer (Baritone). *Education:* Studied at the Moscow Conservatory. *Career:* First engagement at the Kirov Theatre Leningrad, then sang at the Bolshoi, Moscow, from 1976 as Eugene Onegin, Count Luna, Germont, Yeletzky (The Queen of Spades) and Robert in Tchaikovsky's Iolanta; Sang in Shchedrin's Dead Souls at Boston, 1988; Guest engagements in Finland and Hungary as concert and opera artist; British debut at Covent Garden 1988. *Address:* Allied Artists, 42 Montpelier Square, London SW7 1JZ, England.

MOROZOV Vladimir Mikhailovich, b. 1933. Opera Singer (Bass). *Education:* Leningrad Conservatory. *Career:* Soloist with Kirov Opera 1959-, roles include: Varlaam (Boris Godunov), Ivan the Terrible (The Maid of Pskov), Grigory (Quiet Flows the Don), Peter the Great (Peter I). *Honours:* Glinka Prize, 1974; RSFSR People's Artist, 1976; USSR People's Artist 1981. *Membership:* CPSU, 1965-. *Address:* c/o Kirov Opera Company, St Petersburg, Russia.

MORREAU Annette Scawen, b. 4 Feb 1943, Altrincham, England. Writer; Broadcaster. *Education:* BA, Durham University; University of Indiana at Bloomington, USA. *Career:* Founder, The Contemporary Music Network, UK; Music Officer, Arts Council of Great Britain, until 1987; Assistant Editor Arts at Channel 4 TV; Independent TV Producer of music programmes; Devised Not Mozart series on BBC2 TV, 1991. *Contributions to:* Tempo; Contact; Classical Music; BBC Music Magazine; Guardian; Independent; BBC World Service Radio. *Honour:* First woman to win Durham/Bloomington scholarship exchange. *Memberships:* IPPA, IMZ, PACT. *Hobbies:* Cooking; Collecting Oil Lamps; Sailing; Cello. *Address:* 15 Callcott Road, London, NW6, England.

MORRIS Andrew Bryson, b. 14 May 1946, Glasgow, Scotland. Violinist/Administrator. m. Margaret Martin, 28 Mar. 1970, 2 daughters. *Education:* Knightswood Secondary School, Glasgow; DRSAM, Royal Scottish Academy of Music and Drama. *Career:* BBC Northern Ireland Orchestra, Ulster Orchestra, 1970-71; Scottish National Orchestra, 1970-89; Cantilena, Founder Member, 1971-91. *Recordings:* Boccherini Seven Symphonies/Corelli Concerti Grossi Nos 4 and 12; Muffat - Concerto in A Major/Hebden Concerto for Violin No 2 in C Major. *Memberships:* Chairman, Regional Orchestral Committee of Musicians' Union, 1984-86; Rotary Club of Glasgow, 1990-; Events Manager, Glasgow Royal Concert Hall, 1989-92; Managing Director, Pops at The Philharmonic/General Administrator, City of Glasgow Philharmonic Orchestra, 1985-92; Freelance Events and Concert Consultant, projects include Glasgow International Gala Season; Showcase Strathclyde; Tchaikovsky Centenary Festival and Celtic Connections. *Hobbies:* Golf; Badminton; Indian Cookery. *Address:* 3 Coltpark Avenue, Bishopbriggs, Glasgow G64 2AT, Scotland.

MORRIS Andrew William, b. 18 Dec 1948, Kent, England. Director of Music; Conductor; Organist.

Education: Westminster Abbey Choir School; Bembridge School, Isle of Wight; Royal Academy of Music; University of London Goldsmiths' College; The Institute of Education; MA, BMus (London); GRSM; FTCL; ARCO (CHM); LRAM; ARCM. *Career:* Conductor, University of London Choir, 1970-72; Director of Music, Christ's College, Finchley, 1972-79; Organist and Director of Music, The Priory Church of St Bartholomew-the-Great, Smithfield, EC1, 1971-79; Founder and Artistic Director, St Bartholomew's Festivals, 1973, 1977, 1978 and 1979; Musical Director, The New English Singers, 1974-1979; Director of Music, Bedford School, 1979-; Member of the Executive Committee of The New Macnaghten Concerts, 1978-88, Hon. Treasurer, 1980-84, Chairman, 1984-87; Examiner to The Associated Board of the Royal Schools of Music, 1980-; Founder and Director, New Bedford Singers, 1983-93. *Recordings:* In Quires and Places No 13, with St Bartholomew-the-Great Choir; Mozart's Church Music, with St Bartholomew-the-Great Choir, both on ABBEY Label. *Contributions to:* Musical Times 1973 and 1981. *Honour:* ARAM, 1989. *Memberships:* RAM Club; RCO; MMA; Freeman of the City of London, 1978-. *Hobbies:* Cricket (Member of MCC); History and Architecture; Sailing. *Address:* The Music School, Bedford School, Bedford, MK40 2TU, England.

MORRIS Christopher John, b. 13 May 1922, Clevedon, Avon, England. Music Editor; Organist. m. Ruth Early, 31 Dec 1949, 1 son, 1 daughter. *Education:* Hereford Cathedral School; Royal Academy of Music, London; Associate, Royal College of Organists (ARCO), 1942. *Career:* Organist, St George's Church, Hanover Square, London, 1947-72; Music Editor, 1954-75, Head of Music, 1975-86, Oxford University Press. *Compositions:* Various carols and organ pieces (published). *Publications:* Editor: A Sixteenth-Century Anthem Book, 1960; Anthems for Choirs 4, 1976; The Oxford Book of Tudor Anthems, 1978. *Honours:* Fellow, Royal Academy of Music, 1985; Honorary MA (Oxon). 1986. *Address:* 3 Vicarage Gate, London W8 4HH, England.

MORRIS Colin, b. 17 Nov 1952, Sheerness, Kent, England. Baritone Singer. *Education:* BA, 1974, PhD, 1978, Geography, Exeter University; ARCM Performers, 1977; Private study with Derek Hammond-Stroud, OBE. *Debut:* Edinburgh Festival with Kent Opera, 1979. *Career:* Many concert and recital appearances in UK and Netherlands; Lieder repertoire of over 300 songs; Toured UK/USA with Pavilion Opera; London Opera Players, Regency Opera, D'Oyly Carte; Opera debut overseas, Singapore, 1992; Main roles Don Alfonso, Leporello, Magnifico, Bartolo, Pasquale, Dulcamara Falstaff, Rigoletto, Sharpless, Scarpia, Tonio, Operetta. *Recordings:* Several song recitals on British Broadcasting Corporation, Radio Kent; Commercial recordings of Noel Coward, Jerome Kern. *Memberships:* Equity; Incorporated Society of Musicians, Solo Performers Section. *Hobbies:* Gilbert and Sullivan; Works of Noel Coward; Siamese cats. *Current Management:* Music International, 13 Ardilaun Road, Highbury, London N5 2QR, England. *Address:* 49 Winstanley Road, Sheerness, Kent ME12 2PW, England.

MORRIS Gareth Charles Walter, b. 13 May 1920, Clevedon, Somerset, England. Flautist. m. Patricia Mary Murray, 18 Dec 1975, 1 son, 2 daughters and 1 daughter by first marriage. *Education:* Bristol Cathedral School and privately; Royal Academy of Music, London. *Career:* Soloist; Professor, Royal Academy of Music, 1945-85; Principal Flautist, Philharmonia Orchestra, London, 1948-72. *Recordings:* Many. *Publications:* Flute Technique: Oxford University Press, 1991; Numerous Articles in Journals. *Honours:* ARAM, 1945; FRAM, 1949; FRSA, 1967. *Memberships:* Royal Society of Arts, Member of Council, Chairman, Music Committee; Royal Society of Musicians, Governor. *Hobbies:* Antiquarian Horology; Reading and Collecting Books. *Address:* 4 West Mall, Clifton, Bristol, BS8 4BH, England.

MORRIS James, b. 10 Jan 1947, Baltimore,

Maryland, USA. Singer (Bass-Baritone). m. Susan Quittmeyer. *Education:* Studied with Rosa Ponselle in Baltimore, with Frank Valentino and Nicola Moscona in New York. *Debut:* Baltimore Civic Opera 1967, as Crespel in Les Contes d'Hoffmann; Metropolitan Opera from 1971, as Mozart's Commendatore and Don Giovanni, 1975, Verdi's Procida, Padre Guardiano, Grand Inquisitor and Philip II, and the villains in Les Contes d'Hoffmann; Glyndebourne debut 1972, as Verdi's Banquo; At the Salzburg Festival he has sung Guglielmo in Così fan Tutte and Mozart's Figaro, 1986; Received coaching from Hans Hotter and sang Wagner's Wotan in San Francisco and Vienna 1985; Other roles include Gounod's Mephistopheles, Britten's Claggart and Donizetti's Henry VIII; Sang the Dutchman at the Metropolitan 1989, Mephistopheles and Wotan (also televised) 1990; sang Mephistopheles at Cincinnati 1990, with his wife as Siebel; Covent Garden 1990, as the Wanderer in a new production of Siegfried; Season 1992 as the Dutchman in New York and at Covent Garden, Claggart in Billy Budd at the Met and Boris Godunov at San Francisco. *Recordings include:* Wotan in Ring cycles conducted by James Levine and Bernard Haitink, 1988-90. *Address:* c/o Lies Askonas Ltd, 186 Drury Lane, London, WC2B 5QD, England.

MORRIS Joan Clair, b. 10 Feb 1943, Portland, Oregon, USA. Singer; Teacher. m. William Bolcom, 28 Nov 1975. *Education:* Gonzaga University, 1963-65; Diploma, American Academy of Dramatic Arts, 1968. *Debut:* Wigmore Hall, 1993. *Career:* Performed at the Boston Pops, 1976; Alice Tully Hall, Lincoln Center, 1976-83; Polly Peachum in The Beggar's Opera, Guthrie Theatre, Minneapolis, 1979; Soloist, World Premiere of William Bolcom's Songs of Innocence and of Experience, Stuttgart Opera, 1984, and at NY premiere, 1987; Weill Recital Hall, Carnegie Hall, 1987; Soloist, world premiere of William Bolcom's 4th Symphony with the St Louis Symphony 1987; Played the nurse, in world premiere of Casino Paradise, 1990. *Compositions include:* Songs: Carol, 1981; Tears at the Happy Hour, 1983, both with William Bolcom. *Recordings:* After the Ball, A Treasury of Turn of the Century Popular Songs; Who shall rule this American Nation, songs of Henry Clay Work; Vaudeville Songs of the Great Ladies of the Musical Stage; Songs by Ira and George Gershwin; Night and Day, album; Let's Do It, Bolcom and Morris live at Aspen. *Publications:* Contributor to the New Grove Dictionary of American Music. *Hobby:* Photography. *Current management* Shaw Concerts, 1900 Broadway, New York, NY 10023, USA. *Address:* 3080 Whitmore Lake Road, Ann Arbor, MI 48105, USA.

MORRIS Robert Daniel, b. 19 Oct 1943, Cheltenham, England. Composer; Music Theorist; Professor. m. Ellen Koskoff, 10 June 1979, 1 son, 2 daughters. *Education:* BM (with distinction) Eastman School of Music; MM 1966; DMA 1969; University of Michigan. *Career:* Instructor, University of Hawaii, 1968-69; Assistant Professor, 1969-75, Director, Yale Electronic Music Studio, 1973-78, Associate Professor, 1975-78, Chairman, Composition Department, 1974-78, Yale University; Associate Professor, 1977-80, Director, Electronic and Computer Music Studio, 1977-80, University of Pittsburgh; Associate Professor, 1980-85, Professor, 1986-, Eastman School of Music. *Compositions:* Continua for Orchestra, 1969; Thunders of Spring Over Distant Mountains, Electronic Music, 1973; In Different Voices for 5 Wind Ensembles, 1975-76; Plexus for Woodwinds, 1977; Passim, 1982; Exchanges, piano and computer generated tape, 1983; Cuts, wind ensemble, 1984. *Recordings:* Phases for two-pianos and electronics; Motet On Doo-dah; Hamiltonian Cycle; Inter Alia; Karuna. *Publications:* Composition With Pitch-Classes: A Theory of Compositional Design, 1986. *Contributions to:* Reviews and Articles in Journal of Music Theory, Perspectives of New Music; Musical Quarterly; JAMS; In Theory Only. *Hobbies:* Study in Mathematics; Buddhist Scripture; South Indian Classical Music; Philosophy; Camping.

MORRIS Stephen, b. 1970, Bridlington, Yorkshire, England. Violinist. *Education:* Studied with Yfrah

Neaman in London and with Manoug Parikian and Maurice Hasson at the Royal Acadamey of Music. *Career:* Leader of the RAM symphony orchestra 1988; Further study with Howard Davis; Leader of the Pegasus and Thames Chamber Orchestra; As soloist plays Bruch, Bach, Mendelssohn and Lalo; 2nd violin of the Duke String Quartet from 1985; Performances in the Wigmore Hall, Purcell Room, Conway Hall and throughout Britain; Tours to Germany, Italy, Austria and the Baltic States; South Bank series 1991, with Mozart's early quartets; Soundtrack from Ingmar Bergman documentary and The Magic Lantern, Channel 4 1988; BBC Debut feature; Features for French television 1990-91, playing Mozart, Mendelssohn, Britten and Tippett; Brahms Clarinet Quintet for Dutch Radio with Janet Hilton; Live Music Now series with concerts for disadvantaged people; The Duke Quartet invites.... at the Derngate, Northampton, 1991, with Duncan Prescott and Rohan O'Hara; Resident quartet of the Rydale Festival 1991; Residency at Trinity College, Oxford, tours of Scotland and Northern Ireland and concert at the Elizabeth Hall 1991. *Recordings include:* Quartets by Tippett, Shostakovich and Britten (Third) for Factory Classics. *Honours include:* Awards at the RAM include the John Waterhouse Prize, London Orchestral Society Prize, Poulet Award and Inter-collegiate Quartet Prize. *Address:* c/o Anglo-Swiss Management, 4-5 Primose Mews, Sharpeshall Street, London NW1 8YW, England.

MORRIS Wyn, b. 14 Feb 1929, Wales. Conductor; Musical Director. m. Ruth Marie McDowell, 1962, 1 son, 1 daughter. *Education:* Royal Academy of Music; Mozarteum, Salzburg, Austria. *Career:* Apprentice conductor, Yorkshire Symphony Orchestra, 1950-51; Musical director, 17th Training Regiment, Royal Artillery Band, 1951-53; Founder & conductor, Welsh Symphony Orchestra, 1954-57; Koussevitsky Memorial Prize, Boston Symphony Orchestra, 1957; Observer, on invitation George Szell, Cleveland Symphony Orchestra, 1957-60; Conductor, Ohio Bell Chorus, Cleveland Orpheus Choir, Cleveland Chamber Orchestra, 1958-60, choir of Royal National Eisteddfod, Wales, 1960-62; London début, Royal Festival Hall with Royal Philharmonic Orchestra, 1963; Conductor to Royal Choral Society, 1968-70, Huddersfield Choral Society, 1969-74, Ceremony of Investiture for Prince Charles as Prince of Wales, 1969, Royal Choral Society tour of USA, 1969. Chief Conductor/Musical Director, Symphonica of London, current; Specialist, conducting works of Mahler. *Recordings include:* Des Knaben Wunderhorn, with Janet Baker & Geraint Evans; Das klagende Lied; Symphonies 1, 2, 5, 8; No 10, in Deryck Cooke's final performing version. *Honours:* August Mann's Prize, 1950; Fellow, Royal Academy of Music, 1964; Mahler Memorial Medal, Bruckner & Mahler Society of America, 1968. *Hobbies:* Chess, Rugby football; Climbing; Cynghanedd; Telling Welsh stories. *Address:* c/o Manygate Management, 1 Summerhouse Lane, Harmondsworth, Middlesex UB7 0AW, England.

MORRISON Bryce, b. 27 Nov 1938, Leeds, Yorkshire, England. Teacher; Pianist; Critic; Lecturer. *Education:* MA(Oxon); MA(Dalhousie); MMus (SMU); Music Scholar, The Kings School, Canterbury 1952; Studied with Ronald Smith, Kings School; Iso Elinson, Guildhall School of Music and Drama; Alexander Uninsky, Southern Methodist University, Texas, and also with Bomar Cramer, Texas. *Career:* Has published extensively in The Times; The Times Literary Supplement; Observer; Gramophone etc; also in America and Australia; interviews with virtually every pianist of world class including Horowitz, Rubinstein, Clifford Curzon etc; was a major contributor to The Phaidon Book of The Piano; two BBC Talks published in John Lade's Building A Library; has completed a short biography of Liszt and commenced a study of the Cuban pianist, Jorge Bolet; has written over 100 annotations for Decca, EMI, CBS. in England and America, including personal tributes to Solomon (EMI) and Terence Judd (Chandos); musical advisor to EMI for two disc album The Art of Eileen Joyce. Jury Member on several National and International Piano Competitions including the Naumberg in New York, (winners have included Jorge Bolet, Abbey Simon, William Kapell and, most

recently, Stephen Hough); Chairman, First Terence Judd International Award 1982; his students have been international prize winners; he has lectured and given master classes in Australia, Poland, America, Great Britain, China and Japan. Television appearances in Great Britain and Australia and Broadcasts extensively for the BBC, ABC, CBC; also in Poland, USA and New Zealand; Held the Corina Frada Pick Chair of Advanced Piano Studies, Ravinia Festival, Chicago, 1988. *Address:* 19 Hinde House, 11 Hinde Street, London W1M 5AQ, England.

MORTIER Gerard, b. 25 Nov 1943, Ghent, Belgium. Opera Director. *Education:* Student of Law, 1961-66, Journalism and Communications, 1966-67, University of Ghent. *Career:* Administrative Assistant, Festival de Flandre, 1968-72; Assistant Administrator, Oper de Stadt Frankfurt am Main, 1973-77; Director, Artistic Production, Hamburg Staatsoper, 1977-79; Technical Programme Consultant, Théâtre National de l'Opéra de Paris, 1979-81; Director General, Opera National, Brussels, 1981-1991; Director of the Salzburg Festival from 1992; Has commissioned operas from leading composers: Philippe Boesmans (La Passion de Gilles), André Laporte (Das Schloss), and Hans Zender (Stephen Climax); associated with Director Peter Sellars at Brussels (premiere of The Death of Klinghoffer by John Adams, 1991) and Salzburg (Messiaen's St François d'Assise, 1992). *Address:* c/o Festspielhaus, Salzburg, Austria.

MORYL Richard, b. 23 Feb 1929, Newark, New Jersey, USA. Composer; Conductor. *Education:* Studied at Montclair State College, New Jersey and Columbia University, MA, 1959; Further study with Boris Blacher and Arthur Berger. *Career:* Teacher, 1960-72; Founder, New England Contemporary Music Ensemble, 1970; Director, Charles Ives Center for American Music, 1979. *Compositions include:* Ballons for percussion, orchestra, radios and audience, 1971; Volumes for piano, organ and orchestra, 1971; Chroma, 1972; Loops for large orchestra and tape; Particle, 1974; Strobe for large orchestra with any instruments, 1974; The untuning of the Skies, 1981; The Pond, flute and chamber orchestra, 1984; Instrumental music including Rainbows, I and II, 1982-83 and The Golden Phoenix for string quartet and percussion, 1984; Vocal: Flourescents for 2 choruses, 2 percussion and organ, 1970; Illuminations for soprano, 43 choruses and chamber orchestra, 1970; De morte cantoris for soprano, mezzo and ensemble, 1973; Das Lied for soprano and ensemble, 1975; Stabat Mater, 1982; Come, Sweet Death, chorus and piano, 1983; Mixed media works including Passio avium, 1974; Atlantis, 1976; Visiones mortis, 1977; Music of the Spheres, 1977; An Island on the Moon, 1978; A Sunflower for Maggie, 1979; Music for tape (electronics). *Address:* ASCAP, ASCAP Building, One Lincoln Plaza, NY 10023, USA.

MOSCA Silvia, b. 1958, Italy. Singer (Soprano). *Education:* Studied in Naples. *Debut:* Mantua Teatro Sociale as the Trovatore Leonara. *Career:* Has sung at opera houses throughout Italy and appeared as Luisa Miller at the Metropolitan 1988; Leonora at Lieve and Miami 1988-89; Sang Aida at Buenos Aires and the Savonlinna Festival, 1989; Elvira in Ernani at Rome and Venice, 1989-90. *Address:* c/o Teatro La Fenice, Campo S Fantin 1965, 30124 Venice, Italy.

MOSCATO Jacques, b. 1945, France. Conductor; Clarinettist. *Debut:* Municipal Orchestra as Clarinettist, 1955. *Career:* Director, Public concert, Switzerland, 1962; In Charge, Music Department, International University, City of Paris, from 1968; Director, Charleville Mezieres Conservatorium, from 1969; Conductor, Concerts in West Germany, Belgium and France, 1971; Guest Conductor, Australian Broadcasting Commission, 1976; Conductor, Monte Carlo Symphony, The Salle Garnier of Monte Carlo, 1979-; Guest Conductor, Istanbul Symphonic Orchestra, Symphony Orchestra, Pays Loire, France, 1984 and 1989. *Composition:* Music for film, Symphonic Interdite, 1983; A Music Ballet

"Resonances", 1989. *Recordings:* Albums, Symphony no 2, plus eleven Viennese Dances (Beethoven), 1977, Les Musiciens Monegasquesm 1981. *Honours:* Recipient, 1st Prize of Versailles, 1967; Named a director Academie de Musique, Prince Rainier III, Monaco, 1979. *Memberships:* International Jury, Enna piano competition, Sicily, 1985, Stresa, Italy, 1986; Scriptwriter, L'Effet Vicaldi, (translated by Anthony Burgess), 1985; L'Ode a La vie (Beethoven's Life), 1992, written with C Sygala. *Address:* Academie de Musique, Prince Ranier III de Monaco, 1 Boulevard Albert 1er, Monaco.

MOSELEY Carlos (Du Pre), b. 21 Sept 1914, Laurens, South Carolina, USA. Administrator; Pianist. *Education:* Graduated Duke University, 1935; Further studies at the University of Michigan and the Philadelphia Conservatory; Piano studies with Harold Morris and Olga Samaroff. *Career:* Early appearances as piano soloist in recitals and concerts; Director of the School of Music and Professor of Piano at the University of Oklahoma, 1950-55; Director of press and public relations, 1955-59, associate managing director, 1959-61 and managing director, 1961-70, New York Philharmonic Orchestra; President, New York Philharmonic Symphony Society, 1970-78; Developed the New York PO Promenade Concerts, from 1963 concerts in New York Parks, 1965 and the Rug Concerts directed by Pierre Boulez, 1974-78; Chairman of the Board of New York Philharmonic, 1984. *Address:* c/o New York Phillharmonic Orchestra, Avery Fisher Hall, Lincoln Center for the Performing Arts, Broadway at 65th St, NY 10023, USA.

MOSER Edda, b. 27 Oct 1938, Berlin, Germany. Singer (Soprano). *Education:* Studied at the Berlin Conservatory with Hermann Weissenborn and Gerty Konig. *Debut:* Berlin Stadtische Oper 1962, in Madama Butterfly. *Career:* Sang at Hagen and Bielefeld from 1964; Began musical association with Hans Werner Henze at Brunswick in 1967 and sang in the premiere of Das Floss der Medusa, Vienna 1971; 1968 sang Wellgunde in Das Rheingold at the Salzburg Festival and at the Metropolitan: later New York appearances as Mozart's Donna Anna, Queen of Night and Constanze, Puccini's Musetta and Liu and Handel's Armida (Rinaldo, 1984); Guest appearances in Russia, Berlin, Vienna, Salzburg (Aspasia in Mozart's Mitridate), Hamburg (Lucia 1974) and South America; Modern repertory includes music by Nono, Fortner, Zimmermann and Stravinsky (The Nightingale); sang Strauss's Ariadne at Rio de Janerio, 1988; Marie in Wozzeck at the Teatro Valli, Reggio Emilia, 1989. *Recordings:* Der Ring des Nibelungen, Orfeo ed Euridice, Rappresentazione di Anima e di Corpo, Das Floss der Medusa (Deutsche Grammophon); Don Giovanni (CBS: also filmed); Idomeneo, Die Zauberflöte, Das Paradies und die Peri, Leonore (Beethoven); Abu Hassan, Der häusliche Krieg (Schubert), Genoveva (Schumann) and Die Abreise (Electrola). *Address:* Ingpen and Williams Ltd, 14 Kensington Court, London W8 5DN, England.

MOSER Thomas, b. 27 May 1945, Richmond, Virginia, USA. Singer (Tenor). *Education:* Richmond Professional Institute; Curtis Institute Philadelphia; California with Martial Singher, Gerard Souzay and Lotte Lehmann. *Career:* After success at the 1974 Metropolitan Auditions sang in Graz from 1975; Munich Opera, 1976, as Mozart's Belmonte; Vienna State Opera from 1977, as Mozart's Tamino, Ottavio, Titus and Idomeneo, Strauss's Flamand and Henry, and Achilles in Iphigénie en Aulide, conducted by Charles Mackerras; New York City Opera 1979, as Titus; Salzburg Festival 1983, in La Finta Semplice; La Scala Milan, 1985, as Tamino; Rome Opera, 1986, as Achilles; Paris Opéra Comique, 1987, as Mozart's Idomeneo and Tito; Sang the Tenor in the premiere of Berio's Un Re in Ascolto, Salzburg, 1984; Vienna Staatsoper, 1987, as Achilles in Iphigénie en Aulide, Schubert's Fierabras at the Theater an der Wien, 1988; sang Florestan in Fidelio at La Scala and Salzburg, 1990; new production of Lucio Silla at Vienna, 1991, the Emperor in Die Frau ohne Schatten at Geneva, 1992; Season 1992/93 with

Florestan at Zurich & the Emperor at Salzburg; As concert singer in Beethoven's Choral Symphony and Missa Solemnis, Britten's War Requiem, The Bach Passions, Schmidt's Das Buch mit Sieben Siegeln and Mozart's Requiem; Conductors include Giulini, Colin Davis, Mehta, Leinsdorf, Leopold Hager and Horst Stein. *Recordings include:* Roles in Stiffelio (Verdi); Mozart and Salieri (Rimsky-Korsakov); Zaide, La Finta Giardiniera and Don Giovanni (Mozart); Die Freunde von Salamanka (Schubert); Genoveva (Schumann); Oedipus Rex (Stravinsky); Handel's Utrecht Te Deum and Dvořák's Requiem. *Address:* c/o Lies Askonas Ltd, 186 Drury Lane, London WC2B 5RY, England.

MOSES Don V, b. 21 Dec 1936, Kansas, USA. Conductor. m. Ann Swedish, 28 Jan 1973, 1 son, 1 daughter. *Education:* BME, Fort Hays Kansas State College, 1959; MM, 1961, DMA, 1968, Indiana University. *Career:* Assoc Professor Music, Indiana University, 1964-73; Professor, Music, University of Iowa, 1973-86; Professor Music, 1986-88, Director, School of Music, 1988-, University of Illinois; Music Director of Classical Music Seminar, Eisenstadt, Austria, 1976-. *Recordings:* Liebeslieder Waltzes, Brahms; Harmoniemesse, Haydn; Mass in B flat, Hummel. *Publication:* Face to Face With an Orchestra, 1984. *Contributions to:* American Choral Directors Journal. *Honours:* Guest, International Choral Festival, New York City, 1972; Conductor of 30 all-state Festivals; Guest conductor, Györ Philharmonic Orchestra, Hungary, 1983. *Memberships:* American Choral Directors Association; American Choral Foundation; National Association of Music Executives of State Universities. *Hobby:* Golf. *Address:* 1914 Byrnebruk Road, Champaign, IL 61820, USA.

MOSES Geoffrey, b. 24 Sept 1952, Abercynon, Wales. Singer (Bass). *Education:* Emmanuel College, Cambridge; Guildhall School of Music and with Otakar Kraus and Peter Harrison. *Debut:* Welsh National Opera, 1977, as Basilio in Il Barbiere di Siviglia: other roles include Seneca (L'Incoronazione di Poppea), Sarastro and Padre Guardiano (La Forza del Destino); Covent Garden debut 1981, in Les Contes d'Hoffmann: returned in a new production of Otello; Glyndebourne Festival debut 1984; Sang Fiesco in Simon Boccanegra, 1986; Brussels Opera in Hoffmann and Boccanegra; Welsh National Opera in Peter Stein's production of Falstaff; Season 1990-91, with WNO in Figaro, Carmen and Falstaff (also on tour to Japan); Concert engagements include La Damnation de Faust in Frankfurt and the Choral Symphony with the Scottish National Opera; Sang in Strauss's Die Liebe der Danae for BBC Radio 3, conducted by Charles Mackerras. *Recordings include:* Martinů's Greek Passion (Supraphon); Ceprano in Rigoletto (Phonogram). *Address:* c/o Harrison/Parrott Ltd, 12 Penzance Place, London W11 4PA, England.

MOSES Leonard, b. 6 Jan 1932, New York City, NY, USA. Composer. m. Alice Irma Prather, 11 April 1954, 1 son, 1 daughter. *Education:* Studied with: 3rd Generation Master-Student of Brahms; 2nd Generation Master-Student of Glazunov; Howard Hanson and Louis Menini, Eastman School of Music; Thad Jones, Catholic University of America; Musical: BMus. BMusEd., 1955; MMus, 1962; Doctoral Candidate, 1964. *Debut:* Composer, Philadelphia, 1943. *Career:* Washington DC, Good Music Station, a RKO Radio Station, 1987. *Compositions:* Ode to Judith Ivie; In Flanders Fields, 1987; Major Commissions: Under the Auspices of Maryland (State Council of Arts: When I Was One and Twenty (and 11 other Vocal Works), 1984; American Sonatina for Piano and Heenay Mahtov Variations for Violin and Piano, 1985; Symphonic Brass Quintet, 1986; Goodbye My Fancy, A Dance Work with Chamber Orchestra, 1987; Other Major Commissions: Sonata For Flute and Harp; Trio in D for Oboe, Flute and Piano, 1986; The Oratorio (Sermon On The Mount) for Soloists, Chorus and Orchestra, 1987; String Quartet No. 1 - The Folk, 1988; Three Songs for Soprano, Oboe and Piano, 1988; Ballet: Flatland, 1989.*Publications:* Ode to Judith Ivie, 1988; In Flanders Fields, 1988. *Address:* 16 Southgate Avenue, Annapolis, MD 21401, USA.

MOSHINSKY Elijah, b. 8 Jan 1946, Shanghai, China. Opera Producer. m. Ruth Dyttman, 1970, 2 sons. *Education:* BA, Melbourne University, Australia; St Anthony's College, Oxford University, UK. *Career includes:* Original Productions at Covent Garden of: Peter Grimes, 1975; Lohengrin, 1978; The Rake's Progress, 1979; Macbeth, 1981; Samson & Dalilah, 1981. Other opera productions include: Wozzeck, 1976; A Midsummer Night's Dream, 1978; Boris Godonuv, 1980; Un Ballo in Maschera, Metropolitan Opera, New York, 1980; Il Trovatore, Australian Opera, 1983. For English National Opera: Le Grand Macabre, 1982; Mastersingers of Nuremberg, 1984; Bartered Bride, 1985. La Bohème, 1988, Scottish Opera. For Royal Opera: Tannhäuser, 1984; Samson, 1985; Otello, 1986, Die Entführung aus dem Serail 1987. Productions at National Theatre: Troilus & Cressida, 1976; Productions on the West End: Three Sisters, 1986, Ivanov, 1989, Much Ado about Nothing, 1989. Productions for BBC: All's Well That Ends Well, 1980; Midsummer Night's Dream, 1981; Cymbeline, 1982; Coriolanus, 1984; Love's Labour Lost, 1985; Ghosts, 1986; The Rivals, 1987; Television film of Michael Tippett's 'The Midsummer Marriage', 1988; Produced La Forza del Destino for Scottish Opera, 1990, Attila at Covent Garden. *Contributions to:* Opera Magazine, Oct 1992 (Verdi: a Pox on Post-Modernism). *Hobbies:* Painting; Conversation. *Address:* 28 Kidbrooke Grove, London SE3 0LG, England.

MOSLEY George, b. 1960, England. Singer (Baritone). *Education:* Studied with Laura Sarti at the Guildhall School, at the Academic Chigiana in Siena, the Munich Hochschule fur Musik and the National Opera Studio, London. *Career:* Performed in many operas including: Dandini in La Cenerentola, 1987, and Onegin in Tchaikovsky's Eugene Onegin, 1989 both for Opera 80; Orlofsky in Strauss's Die Fledermaus, Scottish Opera, 1990; Marco in Puccini's Gianni Schicchi, 1990, The Sportsman in Delius's Fennimore & Gerda, 1990, and Duke of Albany in Reimann's Lear, 1991, all for the English National Opera; Patroclus in King Priam, Opera North, 1991; Malatesta in Don Pasquale and Guglielmo in Così fan Tutte in 1991, and Dandini in La Cenerentola in 1992 all for Teatro Verdi, Pisa, Italy; Schaunard in La Bohème for Scottish Opera, 1993; Ottone in Incoronazione di Poppea, and Count in Le Nozze di Figaro both for Teatro Verdi, Pisa, Italy in 1993; Father in Baa Baa Black Sheep for Opera North and BBC TV in 1993; Count in Le Nozze di Figaro for Concert Hall, Athens in 1993; Papageno in the Magic Flute for Scottish Opera in 1994. *Recordings include:* Schumann's Dichterliebe and Liederkreis Op, 39; Aeneas in Dido and Aeneas conducted by John Eliot Gardiner. *Honours include:* Schubert Prize and French Song Prize, and first prize, International Mozart Competition at Salzburg, 1988. *Address:* c/o Robert Gilder & Co, Enterprise House, 59/65 Upper Ground, London SE1 9PQ, England.

MOSTAD Jon, b. 21 Apr 1942, Oslo, Norway. Composer. m. Ase S Folleras Mostad, 1 son, 2 daughters. *Education:* MDivinity; Intermediate Grade of Music, University of Oslo, 1969; Diploma, Composition, Music Academy of Oslo, 1974. *Compositions include:* I Forarssol; Den Sommeren; Children's Chorus; Mitt Hjerte alltid Vanker, Mixed Chorus; Sanger I den siste Tid, mixed chorus and organ; Towards Balance, Symphony Orchestra, 1977-78; House, Symphony Orchestra, 1982-85; Amsterdam Trio, 3 Movements for 3 Guitars, 1983; Dawning in The Old Cathedral, Organ and Tape, 1984; Concerto for Violoncello and Orchestra, 1988-90; Choral Works; Orchestral; Instrumental; Piano; Organ; Electro-Acoustical and Chamber Music; works broadcast by Norwegian, Swedish, Yugoslavian and British Radio; Norwegian TV; Performances by the Symphony Orchestras of Oslo, Bergen and Trondheim. *Recordings:* Song, for Symphony Orchestra, Towards Balance; Forthcoming: The Light Shines in the Darkness, Orchestra House, Symphony Orchestra, Voloncello Concerto. *Contributions to:* Und Chopin ist Auch Dabei, Ballade, 1982. *Honours:* Norwegian Broadcasting Competition Prize for Compositions for Childrens and Youth Choirs, 1972; 3rd Prize, Competition for Male

Chorus Composers, 1981. *Memberships:* Norwegian Composers Association; Chairman, Fredrikstad Section and Member National Committee, Ny Musikk, 1976-80, Norwegian Branch of ISCM. *Hobbies:* Forest and Mountain Walking; Skiing; Gardening. *Address:* Skovbølev 3, N-1600 Fredrikstad, Norway.

MOULSON John, b. 25 July 1928, Kansas City, Missouri, USA. Singer (Tenor). *Education:* Studied in Atlanta. *Debut:* Berlin Komische Oper 1961, as Cavaradossi. *Career:* Sang at the Komische Oper until 1982 as Alfredo (Traviata), Hoffmann, the Steersman in Fliegende Holländer, 1969-72, as Lensky, Gabriele Adorno and Oedipus Rex; Sang at Boston 1988, in the US premiere of Dead Souls by Shchedrin; Further guest engagements in Germany, England, Italy, Poland, Russia and the USA.

MOUND Vernon, b. 1954, England. Opera Director. *Education:* Studied at London University. *Career:* Has worked with the Royal Opera, the Scottish Ballet, the Swan Theatre, Opera North and the Black Theatre of Prague as stage manager, administrator, company manager and assistant director; Staff producer at Opera North 1983-88, assisting on new productions and directing revivals; Workshops for children and adults, including community piece Quest of the Hidden Moon; Directed small-scale touring version of Carmen; The Gondoliers for New Sadler's Wells Opera, 1988; Directed the Opera Informal and the Sondheim Workshop at the Royal College of Music, 1989-91; Directed Handel's Ariodante for the Birmingham Conservatoire, 1990 and The Marriage Contract and Le Pauvre Matelot for Morley Opera; Productions of Amahl and the Night Visitors at the Barbican Centre and Alice - the Musical-at St Martin-in-the-Fields; La Finta Giardiniera for the Opera Hogskolan in Stockholm, Mar 1991, and Pedrotti's Tutti in Maschera at the Britten Theatre (La Fille du Régiment, 1992); Associate Director Carmen Jones at The Old Vic. *Address:* c/o Norman McCann International Artists Ltd, The Coach House, 56 Lawrie Park Gardens, London SE26 6XJ, England.

MOUNTAIN Peter, b. 3 Oct 1923, Shipley, Yorkshire, England. Musician (Violinist). m. Angela Dale, 1 son, 2 daughters. *Education:* Royal Academy of Music; Studied violin privately with Sascha Lasserson. *Debut:* Wigmore Hall, London, 1950. *Career:* Regular broadcasts with Angela Dale; Formed Peter Mountain String Quartet; Member Boyd Neel Orchestra; Member Philharmonia Orchestra (played in 2 Brahms concerts conducted by Toscanini on his last visit to England); Leader, Royal Liverpool Philharmonic Orchestra 1955-66; Concertmaster, BBC Training Orchestra 1968-75; Coach, numerous Youth Orchestras, including National Youth Orchestra and Scottish National Youth Orchestra 1979; Currently, Head, String Department Royal Scottish Academy of Music and Drama, Glasgow. *Recordings:* Many works with orchestras and ensembles. *Honour:* FRAM 1963. *Hobbies:* Photography; Camping; Gliding; Reading. *Address:* 23 Kingsborough Gardens, Glasgow G12 9NH, Scotland.

MOURADOGLOU Sarah Lydia, b. 14 Sept 1965, Ixelles, Belgium. Percussionist. *Education:* Royal Music Academy of Brussels, First prizes: solfege 1983, percussion with distinction, 1989, chamber music, 1991. *Career:* Percussion Professor at the Music Schools of Schaerbeek and Woluwé Saint-Lambert; Concerts with the Musique Nouvelle Ensemble; Percussionist of the Michel Lysight Ensemble; Founder member of Flutimba (duo flute-marimba) and of Percusounds (percussion duo); Specialist of mallet instruments (marimba); Frequently working with the National Orchestra of Belgium. *Membership:* Art Exists! (association for the diffusion of the New Consonant Music). *Hobbies:* Theatre; Cinema; Do-It-Yourself; Lecturing; Cookery. *Address:* 88, Rue de la Conciliation, 1070 Brussels, Belgium.

MOUTSOPLOULOS Evanghelos A, b. 25 Jan 1930, Athens, Greece. University Professor; Member of

Academy of Athens. m. Michèle Montaigne. *Education:* MA, University of Athens; State PhD, University of Paris, France; Composition, Athens and Paris. *Compositions:* Suites for Orchestra; Chamber Music; Lieder. *Publications:* Over 50 books and over 450 articles including: La Musique dans l'Oeuvre de Platon, 1959; Aesthetic Categories: An Introduction to the Axiology of the Aesthetic Object, 1970; Rhythms and Dances of Greeks and Bulgarians, 1959; Platon, Dictionnaire de la Musique, Volume II, 1970; La Philosophie de la Musique dans la Dramaturgie Antique: Formation et Structure, 1975; The Aesthetics of J Brahms: An Introduction to the Philosophy of Music, 1986. *Contributions to:* Revue Philosophique; Diotima; Les Etudes Philosophiques; Others. *Memberships:* Société Française de Musicologie; Union of Greek Composers. *Address:* 40 Hypsilantou Street, Athens 11521, Greece.

MOYER Birgitte Plesner, b. 13 Aug 1938, Hellerup, Denmark. m. Carl Moyer, 24 Sept 1960, 1s, 1d. *Education:* University of Copenhagen, 1957-59; BMus 1960, MMus, 1961, PhD Musicology, 1969, Stanford University; MM equivalent, University of Copenhagen, 1965. *Career:* Teaching Assistant, 1962, 1965-66, Research Assistant, 1962, Instructor, 1966-68, Stanford University; Chairman, Music, College of Notre Dame, 1976-; Violinist; Singer; Musicologist; Music Administrator; Member, Accreditation Commission of National Association of Schools of Music, 1988-. *Publications:* A Bibliography of Theoretical Works in Music Published 1700-1750, 1962; A Bibliography of Theoretical Works in Mucic Publisher 1750-1800, 1962; Ombra and Fantasia in Late 18th Century Theory and Practice in Festschrift for Leonard Ratner, 1992. *Contributions to:* Dansk Musik Tidsskrift; New Grove Dictionary of Music and Musicians. *Address:* 160 Erica Way, Menlo Park, CA 94028, USA.

MOYLAN William David, b. 23 Apr 1956, Virginia, Minnesota, USA. Professor; Composer; Recording Producer. m. Vicki Lee Peterlin, 18 Dec 1976. *Education:* BMus Composition, Peabody Conservatory, Johns Hopkins University, 1979; MMus Composition, University of Toronto, Canada, 1980; Doctor of Arts in Theory and Composition, Ball State University, USA, 1983. *Career:* Professor, Sound Recording Technology, College of Fine Arts, University of Massachusetts, Lowell. *Compositions:* Published works include: On Time - On Age (soprano, flute, trumpet, piano and 4-channel tape), 1978; Concerto for Bass Trombone and Orchestra, 1979; Brass Quintet (brass quintet and tape), 1979; Two Movements for String Orchestra, 1980; Duo for Flute and Tape, 1980; Seven Soliloquies (trumpet), 1981; Metamorphic Variations (clarinet), 1983; The Now (high voice, horn and piano), 1983; Trio for Trombones (alto, tenor and bass), 1984; Three Interplays for Trumpet Duo, 1984; Wind Quintet No 2, 1985; Stilled Moments for solo violin, 1988; Evocations for Guitar, 1988; La Liberte (soprano and piano), 1989; Eroica (a Piano Sonata), 1989; Two Suspended Images (wind controller), 1990; Ask Your Mama, 1990; The Dream Deferred (two-channel tape), 1990. *Publications:* The Art of Recording: The Creative Resources of Music Production and Audi; Van Nostrand Reinhold, NYC, 1992. *Address:* College of Fine Arts, University of Massachusetts at Lowell, Lowell, MA 01854, USA.

MOYLE Richard Michael, b. 23 Aug 1944, Paeroa, New Zealand. Ethnomusicologist. m. Linden Averil Evelyn Duncan, 1 son, 2 daughters. *Education:* Licentiate, Trinity College, London 1965; MA 1967; PhD 1971; University of Auckland. *Career:* Visiting Lecturer in Anthropology, Indiana University, USA, 1971-72; Assistant Professor, Music, University of Hawaii, 1972-73; Research Fellow, Ethnomusicology, 1974-77, Research Grantee, 1977-82, Australian Institute of Aboriginal Studies; Senior Research Fellow, Faculty of Arts, University of Auckland, New Zealand, 1983-86; Lecturer in Ethnomusicology, University of Auckland 1986-. *Recordings:* The Music of Samoa; Traditional Music of Tonga; Tonga Today (Compiler). *Publications:* Songs of The Pintupi 1981; Fagogo; Fables From Samoa 1979; Alyawarra Music 1985; Tongan Music 1987;

Traditional Samoan Music, 1988; Sounds of Oceania, 1989; Polynesian Song and Dance, 1991. *Contributions to:* Numerous professional journals. *Address:* Department of Anthropology, University of Auckland, Private Bag, Auckland, New Zealand.

MOYSE Louis Joseph, b. 14 Aug 1912, Scheveningen, Netherlands. Musician; Professor. m. (1) 2 sons, 2 daughters, (2) Janet White, 27 July 1974. *Education:* Flute with Philippe Gaubert and Marcel Moyse, Piano with Joseph Benvenuti and Isidore Philipp, Paris Conservatory of Music. *Career:* Professor of Flute, Paris Conservatory; Member, Moyse Trio, many years; Flautist, French Radiodiffusion and Concerts Lamoureux; Emigrated to USA, 1949; Co-Founder, Marlboro School of Music Festival, USA; Co-Founder, Brattleboro Music Center, Vermont; Professor of Flute, Piano and Chamber Music, Marlboro College, Vermont and University of Toronto, Canada; Guest Professor, University of Boston; Master classes, seminars, concerts, USA, Canada and overseas. *Compositions:* Major works include: Ballad of Vermont for narrator, soloists, chorus and orchestra; Divertimento for 14 instruments; Woodwind Quintet; Quintet for 5 flutes; Sonata for flute and piano; 3 concerti grossi for various instruments and orchestras; Suite in old style for flute ensemble; 4 Pieces for 3 flutes and piano; Suite for 2 flutes, alto and bass flute and piano; Pieces for flute alone; Duets, trios; Many transcriptions for young flautists. *Recordings:* International Prize with Moyse Trio, Paris, 1936. *Publications:* Collaborating with Mrs Joan Bauman on book about his father Marcel Moyse. *Contributions to:* Various articles in Flute Magazines. *Honours:* 1st Prize, Paris Conservatory of Music, 1932. *Hobby:* Drawing. *Address:* RR 2, Box 2446, Westport, NY 12993, USA.

MOYSEOWICZ Gabriela Maria, b. 4 May 1944, Lwów, Poland. Composer; Pianist; Choir Director. *Education:* Lyceum of Music, Cracow, Poland, 1962; Academies of Music, Cracow and Katowice, Poland; MA, 1967. *Debut:* Playing own piano concerto, Cracow, 1957. *Career:* Piano recitals; Public performances of own compositions by known artistes and assemblies; Radio appearances, discussions and interviews. *Compositions:* Media vita, for 2 violins, cello, soprano and bass recitativ; 9 Moments Musicaux, for piano and strings; Rhapsody No 1 for piano; Marche Funebre, for cello and piano; Deux Caprices, for violin solo; Ave Maria, for 2 mixed choirs a capella; Sonata No 1, for cello and piano; Two Canzonas, for viola da gamba solo; Piano Sonata No's 3 to 8 including the 6th Noumenon and 8th Concatenatio; Sonata Polska, for violin and piano; Alleluja for choir. *Address:* Schlossstrasse 50, D-1000 Berlin 19, Germany.

MOZES Robert, b. 1950, Romania. Violist. *Education:* Studied at the Cluj Academy of Music and the Tel Aviv Rubin Music Academy. *Career:* Nember of and solo appearances with the Israel Philharmonic; Chamber music concerts in Israel, the USA, Canada and Japan; Co-Founder, Jerusalem String Trio, 1977, performing in Israel and in Europe from 1981; Repertoire includes string trios by Beethoven, Dohnanyi, Mozart, Reger, Schubert and Tanyev, Piano Quartets by Beethoven, Brahms, Dvořák, Mozart and Schumann; Concerts with Radu Lupu and Daniel Adni. *Recordings include:* Albums for Meridian, Channel Classics Studio, Holland and CDI, Israel. *Address:* c/o Anglo Swiss Ltd, 3 Primrose Mews, la Sharpleshall St, London NW1 8YW, England.

MOZETICH Marjan, b. 7 Jan 1948, Gorizia, Italy. Composer. *Education:* Began piano training at age 9; studied piano and theory with Reginald Bedford; studied with John Weinzweig and Lothar Klein; ARCT Piano Performance Diploma, 1971; BMus, University of Toronto, 1972; Further studies with Luciano Berio in Rome and Franco Donatoni in Siena. *Career:* Teacher of composition, Queen's University, Kingston, Ontario, 1991-. *Compositions include:* Sonata for flute and harp; Songs of Nymphs for harp; Procession, El Dorado, Dance of the Blind and Fantasia, (all recorded). *Honours:* String quartet Changes recognised as outstanding work at

Student Composers Symposium, Montreal, 1971; Wind quintet awarded 2nd Prize at International Gaudeamus Composers Competition, Amsterdam, 1976; String orchestra piece, Nocturne, received 1st Prize in CAPAC-Sir Ernest Macmillan Award, 1977; Viola solo work Disturbances chosen by CBC Radio to represent Canada at 25th Anniversary of International Rostrum of Composers, Paris 1978. *Hobbies:* Avid reader and gardener. *Address:* RR 4 Howe Island, Gananoque, Ontario K7G 2V6, Canada.

MRACEK Jaroslav John Stephen, b. 5 June 1928, Montreal, Canada. Professor of Music (Musicology) Emeritus, 1991 of San Diego State University. m. 5 Aug. 1963. 2 sons. *Education:* Assoc Dip, Royal Conservatory of Music, Toronto, 1948; BMus, University of Toronto, 1951; MA 1962, PhD 1965, Indiana University, studied with Willi Apel, John R White, Paul Nettl, Walter Kaufmann. Bernard Heiden, Marie Zorn (harpsichord); Studied piano with Alberto Guerrero, Toronto. *Career:* Taught instrumental/vocal music English and History at Lisgar Collegiate Institute, Ottawa, Canada, 1953-59; Lecturer: University of Illinois, Urbana 1964-65; Assistant, Associate, Full Professor, San Diego State University, 1965-91; General Director, The Smetana Centennial, International Conference & Festival of Czechoslovak Music, San Diego State University, 1984; General Director, Canadian Music Festival & Conference, San Diego State University, 1987; Conducted at Canadian Music Festival, San Diego State University, 1987. *Publications:* Seventeenth-Century Instrumental Dance Music, 1976; 5 articles, New Grove Dictionary of Music & Musicians, 1980; Papers published in proceedings: Int Musicological Congress-Bach, Handel, Schütz-Stuttgart, 1985; Musica Antiqua Congress, Bydgoszcz, 1985; Rudolf Firkusny at 75, Musical America, 1987; Smetana Centennial, Musical America, 1985. *Honours:* Rudolf Firkušný n Medal, 1992.*Address:* 5307 W Falls View Dr, San Diego, CA 92115, USA.

MUCZYNSKI Robert, b. 19 Mar 1929, Chicago, Illinois, USA. Composer; Professor of Music. *Education:* BM, 1950, MM, 1952, DePaul University, Chicago; Academy of Music, Nice, France, 1961. *Career:* Visiting Lecturer, DePaul University, Chicago, summers 1954-56; Head of Piano Department, Loras College, Dubuque, Iowa, 1956-58; Visiting Lecturer, Roosevelt University, Chicago, 1964-65; Professor, Head of Composition, University of Arizona, Tucson, 1965-87; Professor Emeritus, 1988-. *Compositions:* Over 40 published works including: Concerto for Piano and Orchestra; First Symphony; Suite for Orchestra; Concerto for Alto Saxophone and Chamber Orchestra; 3 Piano Sonatas; 2 piano trios; String Trio; Sonatas for Cello, for Alto Saxophone, for Flute and Piano; Time Pieces, for clarinet/piano; Scores for 9 documentary films; Commission: Dream Cycle, for solo piano, 1983; Quintet for Winds, 1985; Third Piano Trio, 1986-87; For release: Compact Disc recordings of Concerto No. 1 for Piano & Orchestra; A Serenade for Summer; The Three Piano Trios; Trio for Violin, Viola, Cello. *Hobbies:* Films; Reading; Writing; Dogs. *Address:* 2760 N Wentworth, Tucson, AZ 85749, USA.

MUFF Alfred, b. 31 May 1949, Lucerne, Switzerland. Singer (Bass-Baritone). *Education:* Studied with Werner Ernst in Lucerne, Elisabeth Grümmer and Irmgard Hartmann-Dressler in Berlin. *Debut:* Don Ferrando in Fidelio, Lucerne 1974. *Career:* Member of the opera companies in Lucerne, Linz, Mannheim and since 1986/87, Zürich; Opera roles include King Philip in Don Carlos, Falstaff, Hans Sachs, Wotan, Wagner's Dutchman, Gremin in Eugene Onegin and Boris Godunov; Season 87/88 sang Der Fliegende Holländer, La Scala, Milan, Wotan in Die Walküre, Zürich and Gurnemanz in Parsifal, Mannheim; Wanderer in Siegfried at Zürich and Landgraf in Tannhäuser at Bonn in 88/89; sang Wotan at Zurich 1988, Boito's Mefistofele, 1989; Munich and San Francisco, 1988-89, as Barak; Teatro Liceo Barcelona, 1989, as the Dutchman; Jochanaan in Salome, Zürich in 89/90; Scarpia in Tosca and Orest in Elektra, Zürich, Jochanaan

in Salome, Vienna and Kezal in Die Verkaufte Braut, Bonn in 90/91; König Marke in Tristan, San Francisco, König Heinrich in Lohengrin, Zürich, Der Fliegende Holländer, Munich and Hans Sachs in Die Meistersinger, Hannover in 91/92; Sang Pizarro at Zurich, 1992; Wanderer in Siegfried at Hamburg and Wotan in Die Walkure at Munich in 92/93; Gurnemanz in Parsifal, Linz in 93/94. *Recordings include:* The Speaker in Die Zauberflöte, conducted by Armin Jordan (Erato); Barak in Frau ohne Schatten for EMI; Der Fliegende Holländer for Naxos; Hunding in Die Walküre for Decca; Adorno/Capitano for Decca. *Address:* c/o Opernhaus Zurich, Falkenstrasse 1, CH-8008 Zurich, Switzerland.

MULDOWNEY Dominic, b. 19 July 1952, Southampton, England. Composer. m. Diane Trevis, 3 Oct 1986, 1 daughter. *Education:* BA, BPhil, York University. *Career:* Composer in Residence, Southern Arts Association, 1974-76; Composer of Chamber, Choral, Orchestral works including work for theatre and TV; Music Director, National Theatre, 1976-. *Compositions include:* An Heavyweight Dirge, 1971; Driftwood to the Flow for 18 String, 1972; 2 String Quartets, 1973, 1980; Double Helix for 8 players, 1977; 5 Theatre Poems after Brecht: The Beggar's Opera, realization, 1982; Piano Concerto, 1983; The Duration of Exile, 1984; Saxomphone Concerto, 1985; Sinfonietta, 1986; Aus Subtilior, 1987; Lonely Hearts, 1988; Violin Concerto, 1989-90; On Suicide, for voice and ensemble, 1989; Un Carnival Cubiste for 10 brass players and metronome, 1989; Percussion Concerto, for Evelyn Glennie, 1991; Oboe Concerto, 1992; Trumpet concerto, 1993; Concerto for 4 violins and strings, 1994. *Recordings include:* Piano, Saxaphone and Oboe concertos. *Membership:* APC. *Hobbies:* France. *Current Management:* Cavlin Music Corp. *Address:* c/o National Theatre, London SE1 1PX, England.

MULLER Rufus, b. 1959, Kent, England. Singer (Tenor). *Education:* Choral scholar at New College, Oxford, 1977-81; Studied singing in London with Ronald Murdock. *Career:* Sang Mozart's Bastien with Kent Opera 1985; Winner of English Song Award 1985; Recital repertoire includes medieval monody, renaissance lute song, German Lied, French melodies and 20th century works; Oratorio appearances in Germany, France, Italy, Poland, Denmark, Puerto Rico, and Holland; Recitals at the Utrecht Festival, in Japan, Frankfurt, Munich, Madrid and at the Wigmore Hall, London; Sang First Armed Man and Second Priest in Die Zauberflöte at the 1990 Promenade Concerts, conducted by Roger Norrington. *Recordings:* Bach St John Passion conducted by John Eliot Gardiner (Archiv); Beethoven's Choral Fantasia, and Die Zauberflöte conducted by Norrington (EMI); 18 Englsh Songs (Hyperion) with Emma Kirkby. *Address:* c/o Ron Gonsalves, 10 Dagnan Road, London SW12 9LQ, England.

MÜLLER-LORENZ Wolfgang, b. 24 Nov 1946, Cologne, Germany. Singer (Tenor). *Education:* Studied in Cologne. *Career:* Sang as baritone, at the Mannheim Opera, 1972; Engagements at Munich, Nuremburg, Karlsruhe, Frankfurt and Mannheim as Papageno, Rossini's Figaro and Dvořák's Jacobin; Studied further with Hans Hopf and sang at the Graz Opera from 1980 as Lohengrin, Cavardossi, Calaf, and Loge; Siegmund and Siegfried in a Ring Cycle, 1989; Sang with the Deutsche Oper Berlin on tour to Washington, 1989, and as Bacchus in the original version of Ariadne auf Naxos at the Landestheater, Salzburg, 1991; Other roles have included Otello, Dimitri in Boris Godunov, Pasifal, The Marquis in Lulu, Erik, Herman and Fra Diavolo, Zurich Opera, 1989; Frequent concert appearances, notably in contemporary works. *Address:* c/o Landestheater, Schwarstrasse 22, A-5020 Salzburg, Austria.

MULLER-MOLINARI Helga, b. 28 Mar 1948, Pfaffenhofen, Bavaria, Germany. Singer (Mezzo-soprano). *Education:* Studied with Felicie Huni-Mihaczek in Munich and with Giulietta Simionato in

Rome. *Career:* Sang at Saarbrucken, 1972-73; La Scala Milan, 1975 in L'Enfant et Les Sortileges, Piccola Scala 1979 in Vivaldi's Tito Manlio; Further appearances at the Sanzburg Festival, as Annina 1983, Barcelona, as Cheubino 1984, Turin as Carmen, 1988 and Monte Carlo, Portrait de Manon by Massenet, 1989; Roles in operas by Rossini, Mozart, and other composers at Nancy, Dublin, Pesaro and elsewhere; Trieste, 1991 as Werter. *Recordings include:* Der Rosenkavalier, Ariadne auf Naxos, Mozart Requiem, Bruckner Te Deum, Oronte by Cesti, Monteverdi Madrigals; Handel Partenope; L'Arcadia in Brenta by Galuppi, Rossini's Aureliano in Palmira and La Gazza Ladra. *Address:* Teatro Comunale di Trieste, Riva Novembre 1, 34121 Trieste, Italy.

MULLOVA Viktoria, b. 27 Nov. 1959, Moscow, USSR. Violinist. *Education:* Studied with V Bronin, Central School of Music, Moscow. *Career:* Appearances with many of the World's most renowned orchestras including: Berlin Philharmonic, London Symphony, Royal Philharmonic, Boston Symphony, Pittsburgh and Toronto Symphonies; Worked with conductors including Abbado, Boulez, Haitink, Maazel, Marriner, Masur, Ozawa, Previn and Muti; Appeared at many festivals including Marlboro, Tanglewood, Edinburgh, Lucerne; Appearances with London Symphony Orchestra in Germany, Cleveland Orchestra, Dallas Symphony, Los Angeles Philharmonic, Berlin Philharmonic, Israel Philharmonic etc. *Recordings:* Exclusively for Philips; debut release of Tchaikovsky and Sibelius with Ozawa and the Boston Symphony was awarded the Grand Prix du Disque; Vivaldi's Four Seasons with Abbado and the Chamber Orchestra of Europe; solo works of Bartók, Bach and Paganini; Shostakovich Concerto no 1 and Prokofiev no 2 with André Previn and the Royal Philharmonic; Paganini Concerto no 1 and Vieuxtemps no 5 with Neville Marriner and the Academy of St Martin in the Fields; a programme of Stravinsky, Prokofiev and Ravel with Bruno Canino; J S Bach Violin Sonatas, BWV 1014-1019 with Bruno Canino. *Honours:* 1st Prize, Sibelius Competition, Helsinki, 1981; Gold Medal, Tchaikovsky Competition, Moscow, 1982; International Prize of the Accademia Musicale Chigiana in Siena, 1988. *Current Management:* Harold Holt Ltd. *Address:* c/o Harold Holt Ltd, 31 Sinclair Road, London W14 0NS, England.

MUMMA Gordon, b. 30 Mar 1935, Framingham, Massachusetts, USA. Composer; Performer; Author; Professor of Music. *Career includes:* Composer and Performer of Electroacoustic and Instrumental Music with performances and recordings in North and South America, Europe and Japan; TV and Film Performances, Germany and USA; Visiting Lecturer, various colleges and universities; Composer and Performing Musician, Sonic Arts Union, NYC 1966-74, Merce Cunningham Dance Company, 1966-74; Professor of Music, University of California, Santa Cruz, 1975-; Visiting Professor of Music, University of California, San Diego, 1985-87. *Compositions include:* Music from The Venezia Space Theatre; Dresden Interleaf 13 Feb 1945; Mesa; Hornpipe; Schoolwork; Cybersonic Cantilevers; Pontpoint. *Recordings:* All listed compositions plus performances of music by Robert Ashley, David Behrman, George Cacioppo, John Cage, Mauricio Kagel and Christian Wolff. *Contributions to:* Numerous books and journals including: James Klosty's Merce Cunningham; Appleton and Perera's Development and Practice of Electronic Music; Gilbert Chase's Roger Reynolds: A Portrait; Journal of Audio Engineering Society; Darmstader Beitrage Zur Neue Musik; Neuland I. Major article: Sound Recording in The New Grove Dictionary of American Music, Macmillan, NY 1986. *Memberships:* Society for Ethnomusicology; Broadcast Music Inc. *Current Management:* Artservices, 325 Spring Street, New York, NY 10013, USA. *Address:* Porter College, University of California, Santa Cruz, CA 95064, USA.

MUNDT Richard, b. 8 Sept 1936, Illinois, USA. Singer (Bass). *Education:* Studied in New York and Vienna. *Debut:* Saarbrucken, 1962, as the Commendatore in Don Giovanni. *Career:* Appearances at Kiel, Dortmund, Darmstadt, Graz, Liege and the Spoleto Festival; American engagements at the New York City Opera, San Francisco, Portland, Chicago and Cincinnati; Other roles have included Mozart's Osmin, Don Giovanni, Figaro and Sarastro, Rocco, Arkel in Pelleas et Melisande, Ramphis, King Philip, Padre Guardiano, and Wagner's Marke, Daland, Fasolt, Pogner, Hunding and Landgrave.

MUNI Nicholas, b. 1960, USA. Stage Director. *Career:* Artistic Director, Tulsa Opera, 1988-; Has directed more than 150 opera productions with leading US companies; Season 1989-90 with Il Trovatore at Seattle (transferring to Houston, Toronto and Vancouver); French version of Verdi's opera at Tulsa, with new production of the Juniper Tree by Philip Glass and Robert Moran; New York City Opera debut with La Traviata, 1991; World premiere of Frankenstein the Modern Prometheus, by Libby Larsen, for Minnesota Opera; US premiere of Rossini's Armida at Tulsa, 1992; Complete version of Lulu for Canadian Opera and Ariadne auf Naxos at the Opera Theater of St Louis; World premiere of Moran's The Shining Princess at Minnesota, 1993. *Address:* Atholl Still Ltd, Greystoke House, 80-96 Westow Street, London SE19 3AF, England.

MUNKITTRICK Mark, b. 1951, Boston, Massachusetts, USA. Singer (bass). *Education:* Studied at Fresno State College, California. *Career:* Sang in Carnegie Hall concert performancs of Donizetti's Gemma di Vergy and Puccini's Edgar, 1976-77; New York City Opera, 1977, as Daland and Pogner; Guest appearances in Washington, Los Angeles and Atlanta, as Leporello, Alfonso, Raimondo and Monteverdi's Seneca; Sang at Karlsruhe, 1978-87 as Memphistopheles, Rocco, Basilio, Kecal, Banquo, King Philip, Ramphis, the Landgrave in Tannhäuser and Fafner; Madrid, 1984 as Handel's Giulio Cesare; Dresden Staatsoper 1989, as Morosus in Die Schweigsame Frau; Member of the Stuttgart Staatsoper from 1985; Guest engagements throughout Germany and Europe; Other roles include Arthur in The Lighthouse by Maxwell Davies, Kaspar and Henry VIII in Anna Bolena; Wide concert repertory including bass solo in the Missa Solemnis. *Recordings include:* Gemma di Vergy and Edgar. *Address:* c/o Stuttgart Staatsoper, Oberer Schlossgarten 6, 7000 Stuttgart, Germany.

MUNOZ Daniel, b. 1951, Buenos Aires, Argentina. Singer (Tenor). *Education:* Studied in Buenos Aires. *Career:* Sang at the Teatro Colon Buenos Aires from 1979, Teatro de la Zarzuela Madrid from 1980; Studied further in Milan and sang from 1982 at opera houses in Spain, Portugal, and South America; Nancy Opera 1983 as Cavaradossi, Liege 1986 as Pinkertona and the Berne Stadtheater, 1988; Sang Cornil Schut in Smaregloa's Pittore Fiamminghi at Trieste and Calaf at the Szeged Festival, Hungary, 1991; Other roles include Don Jose, Faust, Werther, Don Carlos and Des Grieux in Manon Lescaut; Frequent concert appearances. *Address:* Teatro Comunale, Riva Novembre 1, 34121 Trieste, Italy.

MUNSEL Patrice, b. 14 May 1925, Spokane, Washington, USA. Singer (Soprano). *Education:* Studied with Charlotte Lange, William Herman and Renato Bellini in New York. *Debut:* Metropolitan Opera 1943, as Philine in Mignon. *Career:* Sang in New York until 1958, as Adele in Die Fledermaus, Offenbach's Périchole, Lucia di Lammermoor, Rosina, Olympia in Les Contes d'Hoffmann, the Queen of Shemakha, Zerlina, Despina and Gilda; European Tour 1948; Starred in 1953 film Melba; Appeared in musical comedy after leaving the Metropolitan.

MURA Peter, b. 21 June 1924, Budapest, Hungary. Conductor. m. Rose Tóth, 1 daughter. *Education:* HS of Music, Budapest. *Debut:* Hungarian State Opera House, 1948. *Career:* Solo repetitor, Hungarian State Opera House, 1945-; Conductor of the Stagione of the Hungarian State Opera House, 1950-53; Director &

Chief Conductor, Miskolc National Theatre Opera Companay, 1953-57; State Opera Conductor, Warsaw, Poland, 1957-58; Conductor, Silesian Opera, Bytom, Poland, 1958-61; Director & Chief Conductor, Miskolc Symphony Orchestra, Hungary, 1961-84; Conductor, Hungarian State Opera, 1984-87; Professor High School of Music, Budapest, 1986-; Wiener Kammeroper (conductor) 1990-91. *Recordings:* (Mozart) Idomeneo Overture & Ballet; Symphony in A K134, Hungaroton, 1974. *Honours:* Liszt Ferenc Prize, 1966; Merited Artist of the Hungarian People's Republic, 1972. *Current Management:* Pentaton Ltd, Budapest, Hungary. *Membership:* Union of Hungarian Musicians. *Address:* Podmaniczky U. 63. H-1064 Hungary, Budapest.

MURADIAN Vazgen, b. 17 Oct 1921, Ashtarak, Armenia. Composer; Viola d'Amore Player. m. Arpi Kirkyasharian, 2 sons. *Education:* Graduate, Benedetto Marcello State Conservatory of Music, Venice, Italy, 1948. *Debut:* Lincoln Center, Alice Tully Hall, New York. *Career:* Composer, Teacher, violin, solfeggio, theory of music, Collegio Armeno, Venice, 1945-50; Violist, various orchestras including New Orleans Philharmonic & Wagner Opera Company; Viola d'Amore soloist, USA & abroad; Extensive performances of Compositions, Europe & America, various artists; Only composer in music history who wrote concerti for all classical intruments and many for lesser known instruments, so far 62 concerti for 35 different instruments; All major compostions are written in Sonata Form, all themes and melodies are his own. *Compositions include:* 62 concerti for all classical & many rare instruments; 24 symphonies; 8 suites for orchestras; 6 sonatas for violin & piano; 7 sonatas for solo violin; 2 sonatas for piano; 4 moto perpetuos for violin or piano & orchestra; 2 quartets; 2 trios for violin, piano & cello; 56 songs with orchestra; 8 songs for chorus & orchestra on works of Shakespeare, Goethe, Dante, Hugo. *Address:* 269 West 72nd Street, New York, NY 10023, USA.

MURAI Hajime Teri, b. 31 July 1953, San Francisco, California, USA. Conductor. *Education:* Aspen School of Music, 1971; Institut des Hautes Etudes Musicales, Crans, Switzerland, 1973; BA Music, 1974, MA Music, 1976, University of California, Santa Barbara; California Institute of the Arts, 1975-76. *Career:* Currently, Ruth Blaustein Rosenberg Director of Orchestral Activities, Peabody Conservatory of Music; Music Director, Peabody Symphony and Concert Orchestras since 1991; Associate Professor of Orchestra and Conducting, College - Conservatory of Music, University of Cincinnati, 1976-91; Music Director and Conductor, Cincinnati Youth Symphony Orchestra, 1978-91; Has conducted the Baltimore Symphony, Cincinnati Symphony, Detroit Symphony, Florida Symphony, Phoenix Symphony, Fort Wayne Philharmonic, San Jose Chamber Orchestra, Indiana Chamber Orchestra, Symphony of the Mountain, Hamilton-Fairfield Symphony; Presented 1st performance in English of Shostakovich's Symphony No 13, Babi Yar, 1983. *Address:* 604 Shelley Road, Towson, Maryland 21286, USA.

MURGATROYD Andrew, b. 1955, Halifax, Yorkshire. Singer (Tenor). *Education:* Studied singing with Barbara Robotham at Lancaster University and with Rudolf Pierney; Lay-Clerk at Christ Church Cathedral, Oxford. *Career:* Concert engagements include Israel in Egypt for John Eliot Gardiner in Stuttgart, Milan, Paris, Rome, East Berlin and Turin; Handel's Esther for WDR in Cologne and Acis and Galatea for Swiss television; Monteverdi Vespers and Alexander's Feast at Aix-en-Provence; Performances of Bach's St John Passion in London, Cambridge and Spain, and the St Matthew Passion at the Festival Hall, 1990; Debussy's Rodrigue et Chimène in London and Manchester; Beethoven's Ninth with the Hanover Band in London and Germany; Contemporary Music Network Tour with Richard Bernas, 1990. *Recordings include:* Beethoven's Missa Solemnis and Ninth Symphony (Nimbus); Monteverdi Vespers with The Sixteen (Hyperion); Campra's Tancrède (Erato); Leclair Scylla et Glaucus; John Tavener, We Shall See Him As He Is, (Chandos); Antonio

Teixeira, Te Deum, (Collins Classics). *Address:* Magenta Music International, 64 Highgate High Street, London N6 5HX, England.

MURGU Corneliu, b. 1947, Timisoara, Romania. Singer (Tenor). *Education:* Studied in Romania and in Florence with Marcello del Monaco. *Debut:* Appearances from 1978 at the Deutsche Oper Berlin Calaf 1989, Munich, Stuttgart, and Hamburg State Operas, Dusseldorf Zurich and Graz; Sang Riccardo, Ballo in Maschera, at Naples, 1982, Bonn, 1983 as Andrea Chenier; Philadelphia and Pittsburgh 1983 and 1987; Season 1989 as Pollione, Norma, at Lyon, Turiddu at Barcelona, Don José and Pinkerton in Vienna; Concert performances of Samson and Calaf in Rio de Janeiro and London, 1989-90. *Recordings include:* Othello. *Address:* c/o Deutsche Oper Berlin, Richard Wagnerstrasse 10, D-1000 Berlin, Germany.

MURIO Jay, b. Louisiana, USA. Concert Artist; Soprano. *Education:* BA, Arkansas College, 1922; BM, 1930, MM, 1932, American Conservatory of Music, Chicago; MA, University of Chicago, 1933. *Career:* Junior and Senior recitals; Soprano Soloist: Century of Progress, Chicago, 1933, 1934, Texas Centennial, 1936; Concerts throughout USA and Latin America; Soloist with various orchestras and opera companies in Chicago and Mexico, 1942-50. *Publications:* La Vida de Don Gregoria Gonzalez y El Siglo Pitagorico by Antonio Enriquez Gomez as a Source of A Journey from This World to the Next and Jonathan Wild by Henry Fielding. *Memberships:* President, Delta Omicron, American Conservatory; President, Chicago Chapter, National Society of Arts and Letters; Board Member, Illinois Opera Guild; Chicago Lyric Opera; RNCC, Washington DC. *Hobbies:* Animal refuge for deer, Harlequin Dane, Chichuhua dogs, Angora cats, Canadian geese, tiger. *Address:* PO Box 678, Oak Park, IL 60303, USA.

MURO Juan Antonio, b. 18 June 1945, Catalonia, Spain. Guitarist; Composer. m. Marja Leena Virtanen, 28 Dec 1968, (dec 1988). *Education:* Conservatorio Superior De Musica, Barcelona; Sibelius Academy, Helsinki. *Debut:* Helsinki 1976. *Career:* Performed as soloist and various chamber music groups in several european countries with appearances in Finnish and Hungarian television; Since 1974, Lecturer and chamber music teacher in the Conservatory of Helsinki, Finland. *Compositions include:* Trilogo odi etamo, 3 guitars; Lettera Amorosa, solo guitar; The Night, guitar ensemble and percussion; Di Pensier in Pensier, 2 guitars and precussion; Relato, for soprano and four guitars. *Recordings include:* With the Finnish Guitar Trio. *Publications:* Basic Pieces, volume I and II, 1992. *Honours include:* Composition Prizes, Hungary, 1986, 1988. *Memberships:* Finnish Composers Society; Catalonian Composers Society; Finnish Art Painters Society. *Hobbies:* Painting. *Address:* Parsitie 6 B, 02620 Espoo, Finland.

MURPHY Suzanne, b. 15 Oct 1941, Limerick, Ireland. Singer (Soprano). *Education:* Studied with Veronica Dunne at the College of Music in Dublin, 1973-76. *Career:* Has sung with Welsh National Opera from 1976 as Constanze, Amelia (I Masnadieri and Un Ballo in Maschera), Elisabeth de Valois, Leonora (Il Trovatore), Elvira (Ernani and I Puritani), Violetta, Norma, Lucia di Lammermoor, and Musetta; Has sung Constanze and Donna Anna for English National Opera; Donna Anna and the soprano roles in Les Contes d'Hoffmann for Opera North, and Constanze for Scottish Opera; German debut 1985, as Norma in a concert performance of Bellini's opera in Munich: returned 1988 for Amelia (Un Ballo in Maschera); Vienna Staatsoper debut 1987, as Electra in Idomeneo: invited to return 1988-89 (Armenian Gala Benefit Concert); Has sung Reiza in Oberon at Lyon and Donna Anna at the Aix-en-Provence Festival; North American engagements include Norma at the New York City Opera, Amelia (Ballo), Elvira (Puritani) and Lucia in Vancouver, Fiordiligi, Ophelia (Hamlet) and Violetta in Pittsburgh; sang Alice Ford in the Peter Stein production of Falstaff for Welsh National Opera (repeated in New York and Milan 1989); Sang

Norma for the Dublin Grand Opera Society 1989, Hanna Glawari in The Merry Widow for Scottish Opera; title role in La Fanciulla del West for Welsh National Opera, 1991; Electra in Idomeneo at the Albert Hall (Proms) and in Wales with WNO, 1991; Season 1992 with Elvira in Ernani and Tosca, in new productions for UNO; Concert appearances in Austria, Sweden, Denmark, Belgium and Portugal; Sang Leonore in Fidelio on South Bank, London, 1989. *Address:* c/o Ingpen & Williams Ltd, 14 Kensington Court, London W8 5DN, England.

MURRAY Ann, b. 27 Aug 1949, Dublin, Ireland. Singer (Mezzo-soprano). m. Philip Langridge. *Education:* Studied at the Royal College of Music in Manchester with Frederick Cox and at the London Opera Centre (1972-74). *Debut:* Aldeburgh 1974, with Scottish Opera as Alceste in the opera by Gluck. *Career:* Wexford Festival 1974-75 as Myrtale in Thaïs by Massenet and Queen Laodicea in Cavalli's Eritrea; English National Opera in Le Comte Ory and as Cenerentola; Covent Garden from 1976, as Cherubino, Siebel (Faust), Ascanio, Tebaldo in I Capuletie i Montecchi, the Child in L'Enfant et les Sortilèges, Idamante and the Composer in Ariadne auf Naxos; Sang Octavian at Covent Garden 1989 and returned 1991 as Sifare in a new production of Mitridate for the Mozart bicentenary; US debut 1979 with the New York City Opera as Sextus in La Clemenza di Tito, repeating the role at the Metropolitan in 1984; Salzburg Festival 1981, as Nicklausse in Les Contes d'Hoffmann; Glyndebourne Festival 1979, as Minerva in Il Ritorno di Ulisse: returned to Salzburg 1985 to sing the role in Henze's version of Monteverdi's opera; Milan La Scala 1983, as Dorabella in Cosi fan Tutte, Returned 1984 as Cecilio in Mozart's Lucio Silla; In 1989 sang Cenerentola at Salzburg; English National Opera 1990 as Berlioz's Beatrice; Sang Cecilio in a new production of Lucio Silla at the Vienna Staatsoper, 1991; Season 1992-93 appeared as Ruggiero in a new production of Handel's Alcina at Covent Garden, Xerxes for ENO, Cecilio at Salzburg and in The Beggar's Opera at Aldeburgh; Title role in Giulio Cesare at Munich, 1994; Many concert appearances including Stravinsky's Pulcinella at the 1993 London Proms. *Recordings include:* St Matthew Passion, Handel and Mozart arias, Roméo et Juliette, Mozart's Requiem (HMV); Haydn's Stabat Mater (RCA); Purcell's Dido and Aeneas (Decca); Les Contes d'Hoffmann (EMI); Così fan Tutte (Deutsche Grammophon), Videos of Xeres, (ENO) and Mitridate (Decca).

MURRAY John Horton, b. 1960, West Berlin, Germany. Singer (Tenor). *Education:* Studied at Curtis Institute in Philadelphia. *Career:* Concert engagements in Beethoven's Ninth with the Atlanta Symphony, Mahler's 8th with Bournemouth Symphony and Janáček's Glagolitic Mass with Royal Philharmonic, 1993; Bach's Magnificat for PBS television in USA; Performances of Salome with Boston Symphony and Idomeneo at Tanglewood; Appearances at Metropolitan Opera from 1991 in Les Contes d'Hoffmann, Lucia di Lammermoor, Die Zauberflöte, Das Rheingold; Sang Max in Der Freischütz with Opera Orchestra of New York and has appeared frequently with Lyric Opera of Chicago; Carnegie Hall debut with Vienna Philharmonic. *Honours:* National Institute for Music Theater Prizes; George London Award 1988; Finalist in 1989 Metropolitanm National Council Auditions. *Address:* c/o IMG Artists, Media House, 3 Burlington Lane, London W4 2TH, England.

MURRAY Niall, b. 22 Apr 1948, Dublin, Ireland. Opera Singer (Baritone). m. Barbara F M Murray, 1 daughter. *Education:* Royal Academy of Music, Dublin. *Debut:* Boy Soprano in Pantomime, Dublin. *Career:* Appearance as Curly in Oklahoma, Dublin, 1970; Opera debut, Bomarzo, Coliseum, London, 1976; Baritone Lead in over 52 musicals including, English National Opera, London; TV and Radio appearances, England and Ireland frequently; Also appeared in Cabarets and Musicals, major opera appearances include, Papageno, Schaunard, Figaro, (Barber of Seville), and Lescaut (Manon); sang Iago at the Basle City Theatre 1988 (under the name Mario di Mario). *Recordings:* Niall Murray

Sings, (Irish Songs); Danilo; The Merry Widow; Robert, La Fille du Régiment. *Address:* c/o English National Opera, London Coliseum, St Martin's Lane, London WC2, England.

MURRAY Sterling Ellis, b. 19 May 1944, Baltimore, Maryland, USA. Professor of Music History. m. Constance M Wright, 16 Aug. 1968. 2 daughters. *Education:* BMus, University of Maryland; MA, Musicology, PhD, Musicology, University of Michigan. *Publications:* Teachers' Manual for Listening by Joseph Kerman, 2nd edition, 1975; Essays on Mannerism in Art and Music, 1979; Seven Symphonies from the Court of Oettingen-Wallerstein 1773-1795, 1981; The Symphonies of Sir William Herschel, 1983; Anthologies of Music: An Annotated Index, 1987, 2nd edition 1992; Five Wind Partitas for the Oettingen-Wallerstein Court, 1989; Numerous reviews. *Contributions to:* The Musical Quarterly; Music and Letters; American Choral Review; Journal of the American Musicological Society; New Grove. *Address:* 513 W Nield Street, West Chester, PA 19382, USA.

MURRAY Thomas (Mantle), b. 6 Oct 1943, Los Angeles, California, USA. Organist. *Education:* Studied with Clarence Mader at Occidental College, BA 1965; Choral conducting with Harold Swan. *Career:* Organist with Immanuel Presbyterian Church at Los Angeles, 1965-73; Organist and choirmaster at St Paul's Episcopal Cathedral at Boston, 1973-81; Faculty of Yale University School of Music from 1981; Repertoire includes works by Saint-Saëns, Franck, Widor, Elgar and Mendelssohn; Concerts as choral conductor in New England and elsewhere in USA. *Recordings:* Albums of 19th Century organ music. *Honour:* Winner, 1966 National Competition of American Guild of Organists. *Address:* c/o Yale University, School of Music (Organ Faculty), Box 2104A, Yale Station, New Haven, CT, USA.

MURRAY William, b. 13 March 1935, Schenectady, New York, USA. Singer (Baritone). *Education:* Studied at Adelphi University and in Rome. *Debut:* Spoleto 1957, in Il segreto di Susanna by Wolf-Ferrari. *Career:* Appearances in Munich, Salzburg, Amsterdam and Frankfurt; Member of the Deutsche Oper Berlin from 1969; Sang Dallapiccola's Ulisse at La Scala in 1970, and took part in the premiere of Nabokov's Love's Labour Lost, Brussels 1973; Other roles include Don Giovanni, Verdi's Macbeth, Luna, Rigoletto and Germont, Puccini's Scarpia and Lescaut, Wagner's Wolfram and parts in We Come to the River by Henze, Orff's Antigonae and Paisiello's Re Theodoro in Venezia. *Honours include:* Fulbright Scholarship, 1956; Kammersänger of the Deutsche Oper Berlin. *Address:* c/o Deutsche Oper Berlin, Richard Wagnerstrasse 10, D-1000 Berlin, Germany.

MURTO Matti, b. 12 July 1947, Tampere, Finland. Composer; Principal of Savonlinna Music School. m. 1s. 1d. *Education:* Diploma of Music Theory at Sibelius Akademy, 1973; Studied Musicology at University of Helsinki, 1988-91. *Career:* Headmaster of Music Schools of Kokkola, 1980-85; General Manager at Tampere Philharmonic Symphony Orchestra, 1985-87; Music Teacher in Hameenlinna and Tampere, 1988-90; Principal of Savonlinna Music School. *Compositions:* Reel Fantasies for Strings; Real Fantasies for two accordians; Concertino for violin and strings; Aurora Borealis for orchestra dur. 10'; Balade and Conjuration fo Kantele; Piano Trio, 1988; Quartet for flute, bassoon; Divertimento; Dancing Suite for violin and accordian. *Recordings:* Recordings of the above. *Membership:* Finnish Composers. *Current Management:* Modus Musiikki Oy, Savonlinna. *Address:* Horsmankatu 4, 57220 Savonlinna, Finland.

MUSACCHIO Martina, b. 11 Feb 1956, Aosta, Italy. Singer (Soprano). *Education:* Studied in Geneva with Ursula Buckel and in Florence, Munich and Zurich. *Career:* Sang at Zurich Opera 1981-82, Lucerne 1982-85; Guest aappearances at Geneva, Dusseldorf, Venice, Mantua, Lausanne and Ravenna; Roles have included

Mozart's Susanna, Zerlina, Despina, Pamina and Papagena, Donizetti's Norina and Adina, Martha, Michaela, Euridice, Orff's Die Kluge and Ismene in Honegger's Antingone; Sang Lisetta in La Rondine at Monte Carlo, 1991; Concert appearances throughout Switzerland and in Hamburg, Munich, Stuttgart, Paris, Venice and Madrid, notably in Baroque repertoire. *Address:* c/o Opera de Monte Carlo, Place du Casino, Monte Carlo.

MUSGRAVE Thea, b. 27 May 1928, Edinburgh, Scotland. Composer m. Peter Mark, 1971. *Education:* Edinburgh University and Paris Conservatoire (under Nadia Boulanger); Hon MUS DOC. *Career:* Lecturer, Extra-Mural Department London University, 1958-65; Visiting Professor, University of California, Santa Barbara, 1970; Distinguished Professor, Queen's College, City University, New York, 1987. *Compositions include:* Chamber concerto 1, 2 and 3, 1966; Concerto for Orchestra, 1967; Clarinet Concerto, 1968; Beauty and The Beast (Ballet), 1969; Night Music, 1969; Horn Concerto, 1971; The Voice of Ariadne (Chamber Opera), 1972-73; Viola Concerto, 1973; Mary Queen of Scots (Opera), 1976-77; A Christmas Carol (Opera), 1978-79; Harriet, A Woman Called Moses, 1980-84; Peripateia for orchestra, 1981; An Occurrence At Owl Creek Bridge (Radio Opera), 1981; Space Play, 1984; The Golden Echo I & II, 1985-86; Rainbow for orchestra, 1990; Wild Winter for ensemble, 1993; Chamber Music; Songs; Choral Music; Orchestral Music. *Honours:* Koussevitzky Award, 1972; Guggenheim Fellow, 1974-75, 1982-83; Hon DMus (Council for National Academic Awards, Smith College and Old Dominion University). *Hobbies:* Cinema; Reading. *Address:* c/o Novello and Co Ltd, 8 Lower James Street, London W1R 4PL, England.

MUSK-CHILVERS Marguerita, b. 11 Apr 1925, Lea, Near Gainsborough, Lincolnshire, England. Singer (Soprano); Music Teacher. m. Norman Chilvers, 19 Aug 1944 (div) 1s. 1d. *Education:* Studied Piano and Singing with E Harpam, E Curtis and E Downes; With Ursula Nettleship, London, Norman Tattersall for Singing and Roy Tead for Piano at Colchester Institute; N Essex Technical College, LRAM; Trent Park Training College, London, College Certificate including A Level Music. *Debut:* Singing Career 1941, engaged professionally. *Career:* Singing Teacher, Piano, Felix School, Southwold, Suffolk, 1960-67; Artistic Director and Founder, Wangford Festival, 1966-74; Class Teacher of Music, Choir Trainer, Conductor, Wymondham School, Norfolk, 1972; Founder and Conductor, Blythburgh Music Society, 1983; Private Teaching Practice, 1979-; Appointed Musical Director and Conductor, Lowecroft Choral Society, 1987-92. *Memberships:* Incorporated Society of Musicians; Elgar Society; Association Teachers of Singing; Association British Choral Directors. *Hobbies:* Gardening; Watching Tennis; Enjoying Grandchildren. *Current Management:* Blythburgh Music Society. *Address:* East Lodge, Henham, Beccles, Suffolk NR34 8AG, England.

MUSKETT Doreen Lydia, (née Taylor), b. 3 June 1931, Cape Town, Republic of South Africa. Performer and Teacher of harpsichord, piano and other early instruments, especially Hurdy-Gurdy. m. Michael P Muskett, 12 Jan 1951, 2 daughters. *Education:* College of Music, Cape Town, with Lili Kraus; Associate, Royal College of Music, London, England; Teachers Diploma, 1958. *Debut:* Purcell Room, London, with husband, 1970. *Career:* Well known for popular children's concerts, Flutes, Reeds and Whistles, with Michael Muskett, touring British Isles, also in USA, France and Federal Republic of Germany; Owns large collection of ancient and ethnic instruments. *Recordings:* Flutes, Reeds and Whistles, Hyperion Records. *Publications:* Method for the Vielle or Hurdy-Gurdy, 1979 and 1982.

MUSKETT Michael Peter, b. 23 June 1928. Musician. m. 12 Jan 1951, 2 daughters. *Education:* Teaching Diploma, Trent Park Teaching College, Hertfordshire, England; Associate, Royal College of Music, London. *Career:* London Philharmonic Orchestra, London Symphony Orchestra, and other orchestras; Clarinet soloist; Duo with wife, Doreen, specialising in early music; Formed chamber ensemble Musique Pastoral, 1983, playing musette, 130 concerts in 17 seasons at London's South Bank concert halls. *Recording:* Flutes, Reeds and Whistles. *Publications:* Method for Hurdy-Gurdy, 1979. *Contributions to:* Recorder and Music Magazine; Hurdy-Gurdy Society Journal. *Memberships:* Society of Recorder Players; Chairman, Hurdy-Gurdy Society; Incorporated Society of Musicians; Galpin Society. *Hobbies:* Music; Musical instruments; Photography. *Address:* Piper's Croft, Chipperfield Road, Bovingdon, Herts HP3 0JW, England.

MUSTONEN Olli, b. 7 June 1967, Helsinki, Finland. Concert Pianist; Composer. *Education:* Studied piano, harpsichord and composition from age 5; later studies with Ralf Gothoni, Eero Heinonen (piano) and Einojuhani Rautavaara (composition). *Career:* From 1984; appearances with most major orchestras in Finland and with the Oslo Philharmonic, City of Birmingham Symphony Orchestra and the Royal Philharmonic Orchestra; Festivals include Helsinki, Berlin, Lucerne and Schleswig-Holstein; US debut 1986 at the Newport Festival; Los Angeles Philharmonic at the Hollywood Bowl and New York recital in Young Concert Artists series; London debut April 1987 at the Queen Elizabeth Hall; concerto performance with the London Philharmonic; Paris debut with the Orchestre de Paris conducted by Kurt Sanderling; 1989- season on Far East tour with the Stockholm Philharmonic and further engagements in the USA; Regular chamber concerts with Heinrich Schiff, Sabine Meyer, Dmitry Sitkovetsky and Steven Isserlis; Soloist in his own two piano concertos; Recital debuts at the Amsterdam Concertgebouw and Chicago's Orchestra Hall, 1990-91; Prom Concerts, London 1991; Beethoven's 1st Concerto, 1993. *Honour:* Prizewinner in 1984 Geneva Competition for Young Soloists. *Recordings include:* Duo recital with Isabelle van Keulen (Philips). *Address:* c/o Harrison/Parrott Ltd, 12 Penzance Place, London W11 4PA, England.

MUTI Riccardo, b. 28 July 1941, Naples, Italy. Orchestra Conductor. m. 3 children. *Education:* Milan Conservatory. *Career:* Principal Conductor, Orchestra Maggio Musicale, Florence, Italy, 1969-81 notably in operas by Rossini, Meyerbeer, Spontini and Verdi; Principal Conductor, 1973-82, Music Director, 1979-82, Philharmonia Orchestra, London, England; Principal Guest Conductor, 1977-80, Music Director, 1980-92, Philadelphia Orchestra, USA; Music Director, La Scala, Milan, 1986-; Guest Conductor, numerous orchestras, Europe, USA; Conductor of Opera, Florence, Milan, London, Vienna, Munich, Salzburg; Covent Garden debut, Aida, 1977; Conducted I Vespri siciliani at the opening of the season at La Scala, 1989, La Clemenza di Tito and La Traviata 1990; Così fan Tutte at the 1990 Salzburg Festival; Season 1992/93 with Parsifal and La Donna del Lago at La Scala, Pagliacci at Philadelphia; engaged for concert performance of Verdi's Nabucco with the Israel Philharmonic. *Recordings:* Symphonic and operatic recordings, EMI, including La Traviata (Scotto) I Puritani (Caballé), Don Pasquale, Attila; Dvořák's Violin Concerto, Scriabin's 1st Symphony; Rigoletto; Guillaume Tell (Studer), Tosca (Vaness). *Honour:* Winner, Guido Cantelli International Contest, 1967. *Current Management:* Columbia Artists Management, New York, USA. *Address:* c/o Columbia Artists Management, 165 West 57th Street, New York, NY 10019, USA.

MUTTER Anne-Sophie, b. 29 Jun 1963, Rheinfeldin, Germany. Concert Violinist. m. Dithelf Wunderlich, 1989. *Education:* Studied in Germany and Switzerland with pupils of Carl Flesch. *Career:* Attracted the attention of Karajan at the 1976 Lucerne Festival and appeared at the 1977 Salzburg Festival; UK debut 1977, at the Brighton Festival with the English Chamber Orchestra under Daniel Barenboim; US debut with the National Symphony Orchestra of Washington; Moscow debut March 1985; several return visits to Russia and Eastern bloc countries; Aldeburgh Festival 1985, playing Beethoven Trios with Rostropovitch and Bruno

Giurrana; UK concerts with the Philharmonia (Tchaikovsky Concerto) and the Royal Philharmonic under Kurt Masur; Gave the premiere of Lutoslawski's Chaine 2 in 1986; Lullaby for Anne Sophie written for her 1988; Chair of Violin at the Royal Academy of Music, London. *Recordings include:* Standard repertoire and works by Stravinsky and Lutoslawski (Partita and Chaine). *Honours:* Citizen of Honour, Wehr, 1989; Bundesverdienstkreuz First Class, awarded by the Bundespraesident; Appointed first holder of the International Chair of Violin Studies, Royal Academy of Music. *Address:* c/o Kaye Artists Management, Barratt House, 7 Chertsey Road, Woking, GU21 5AB, England.

MYERS Helen Priscilla, b. 5 June 1946, Palo Alto, California, USA. Associate Professor of Music, Trinity College, Hartford, Connecticut and Chief Consultant Ethnomusicology, The New Grove Dictionary of Music and Musicians, 1993. m. Robert Julian Woolford, 3 Dec. 1984. 3 sons. *Education:* BMus, Ithaca College, 1967; MM (ed), Syracuse University, 1971; MA, The Ohio State University, 1975; PhD, University of Edinburgh, Scotland, 1984; M. Phil. Columbia University, 1993. *Publications:* Folk Music in the United States: An Introduction (with Bruno Nettl); Ed: Ethnomusicology: An Introduction, 1992; Ethnomusicology: Historical and Regional Studies, 1993; Felicity, Trinidad; Musical Portrait of Hindu Village, 1994; Forthcoming 1994: World Music; Trinidad and Tobago, The New Grove Dictionary of Music, 6th ed; African Music; American Indian Music; Ethnomusicology; Folk Music; South-East Asian Music; The New Oxford Companion to Music, 1983; Ethnomusicology; Sioux; Salish; The New Grove Dictionary of American Music, 1985; East Indian Immigrants in the West Indies: The Universe of Music. *Address:* Department of Music, Trinity College, Hartford, CT 06106, USA.

MYERS Michael, b. 1955, USA. Singer (Tenor). *Education:* Studied at Curtis Institute, Philadelphia. *Debut:* Central City Opera 1977, in The Bartered Bride. *Career:* US appearances in Minnesota, Tulsa, Cleveland, San Francisco, Los Angeles and Des Moines; Season 1981-82 as Belmonte in Ottawa, Alfred in Die Fledermaus for Charlotte Opera, Faust for Providence and Virginia Operas and Jenik in Kentucky and Augusta; Highlights of 1982-83 were debuts at the New York City Opera, as Rodolfo, Santa Fe Opera as Quint (Turn of the Screw), Monteverdi's Nerone with Canadian Opera and the Duke of Mantua for Hawaii Opera Theatre; Sang Nick in the premiere of The Postman always Rings Twice for St Louis Opera (1982) and repeated the role at the 1983 Edinburgh Festival; Scottish Opera debut 1984, as Idomeneo, returning as the Duke in Rigoletto and Cavalli's Orione; Season 1984-85 included Percy to Joan Sutherland's Anna Bolena for Canadian Opera, Flotow's Lionel in Portland and Lord Puff in the US premiere of Henze's The English Cat, at Santa Fe; Season 1985-86 featured debuts with Seattle Opera (Des Griuex in Manon), in Toulouse (Gounod's Romeo), Long Beach Grand Opera (Belmonte), Montpellier (Rimsky's Mozart) and with the Mostly Mozart Festival (Belfiore in La Finta Giardiniera); Active during 1986-87 at Philadelphia (Wagner's Steersman), Pittsburgh (Edgardo in Lucia di Lammermoor), with the Canadian Opera as Dimitri in Boris Godunov and the Mostly Mozart Festival as Ageonore in Il Re Pastore; From 1987 has sung Berg's Painter with the Chicago Opera, the Berlioz Faust with Lyon Opera, Sergei in Lady Macbeth of Mtsensk with Canadian Opera, Boris in Katya Kabanova at Glyndebourne and Ismael in Nabucco in Philadelphia and New York; Season 1992 as Tom Rakewell at Brussels and Percy in Anna Bolena at Santiago; Concert engagements include Rossini's Stabat Mater (Cincinnati May Festival) and Huon in Oberon for Radio France. *Honours include:* First prize 1979 Merola Program of the San Francisco Opera. *Address:* c/o Columbia Artists Inc, 165 West 57th Street, New York, NY 10019, USA.

MYERS Pamela, b. 1952, Baltimore, USA. Singer (Soprano). *Debut:* San Francisco Western Opera 1977

as Mozart's Countess. *Career:* Sang the title role in Stephen Oliver's The Duchess of Malfi, Santa Fe, 1978; Appearances at New York City Opera from 1979, Scottish Opera 1980-81, as Lucia; Giessen 1981 in title role of Menotti's La Loca, Amsterdam 1983 as Mozart's Constanze, Innsbruck Early Music Festival 1984, in Handel's Rodrigo; Sang at Marseille 1988 and 1991 as Desdemona and Ellen Orford; Other roles have included Aennchen in Der Freischütz, Zerlina, Zerbinetta, Micaela, Luisa Miller, Violetta, Liu and Lady Macbeth; Noted concert artist. *Address:* c/o Opera de Marseille, 2 Rue Moliere, F-1321 Marseille, France.

MYERS Rita Koors, b. 29 Sept 1942, Paterson, New Jersey, USA. Pianist; Harpsichordist; Music Educator. m. William Ira Myers. *Education:* BSc 1964, Msc 1965, Eastman School of Music; Juilliard School of Music. *Debut:* Carnegie Hall, 1972. *Career:* Soloist, concerts & chamber ensembles, numerous halls, universities, East coast of USA; Appearances on CBS television network, various New York radio stations. Professor of Music, Department of Fine Arts, Bergen Community College, Paramus, New Jersey. *Recordings:* Sonatas for harpsichord, pianoforte & flute, Johann Christian Bach, complete 4 volume collection, Musical Heritage Society label. *Address:* 73 Oak Drive, Upper Saddle River, NJ 07458, USA.

N

NAAF Dagmar, b. 1934, Munich, Germany. Singer (Mezzo-soprano). *Education:* Studied in Munich. *Career:* Sang in opera at Freiburg 1958-63, Munich 1963-66, Wiesbaden 1963-66 and Hanover 1966-70; Engaged at Cologne 1967-69, Graz 1970-72, Staatsoper Munich 1974-76; Guest appearances at Brussels, Berne, Marseilles, Rio de Janeiro, Amsterdam, Octavian 1965, Barcelona and Vienna 1972; Other roles have included Monteverdi's Ottavia, Handel's Cornelia, Gluck's Paride, Dorabella, Brangaene, Strauss's Composer and Clairon; Verdi's Preziosilla, Azucena, Amneris and Eboli; Noted concert artist. *Address:* c/o Bayerische Staatsoper, Postfach 100148, 8000 Munich 1, Germany.

NADLER Sheila, b. 1945, New York City, USA. Singer (Mezzo-soprano). *Education:* Studied at Manhattan School of Music at the Opera Studio of the Metropolitan Opera and Juilliard School. *Career:* Sang at San Francisco and New York City Opera from 1970, Baltimore from 1972, notably in 1975 premiere of Inez de Castro by Pasatieri; Metropolitan Opera from 1976, Anna in Les Troyens at La Scala, 1982, Clytemnestra in Elektra at Santiago 1984; Further appearances as Fricka and Waltraude in the Ring at Marseilles, Lyon and Brussels and as Erda, Herodias, Jocasta in Oedipus Rex, Azucena, Ulrica, Mistress Quickly, Cornelia, Giulio Cesare and La Cieca in La Gioconda. *Address:* c/o Baltimore Opera Company Inc, 527 North Charles Street, Baltimore, MD 21201, USA.

NAEGELE Philipp Otto, b. 22 Jan 1928, Stuttgart, Germany. Violinist; Violist; Professor. 1 son. *Education:* BA, Queens College, New York, USA, 1949; MA, 1950, PhD, 1955, Princeton University, New Jersey. *Career:* Violinist and Violist, Marlboro Music Festival, Marlboro, Vermont, 1950-; Violinist, Cleveland Orchestra, 1956-64; Member, Resident String Quartet, Kent State University, Kent Ohio, 1960-64; Violin Faculty, Cleveland Institute of Music, 1961-64; Assistant Professor, 1964-68, Associate Professor, 1968-72, Professor, 1972-78, William R Kenan Jr Professor of Music, 1978-, Smith College, Northampton, Massachusetts; Member, Vegh String Quartet, 1977-79; Violist, Cantilena Piano Quartet, concerts USA and abroad, 1980-; Numerous concerts: Music from Marlboro series, USA, independently, Europe; Residences: National Arts Center, Ottawa; Yehudi Menuhin School, England; Freiburg Hochschule fur Music; Banff Center for the Arts; Rubin Academy, Tel Aviv University; Teacher, Chamber Music Ensembles, Musicorda Summer school, Mount Holyoke College, 1987-. *Recordings:* Numerous recordings of violin/viola solos and chamber music for Columbia Records, Marlboro Recording Society, Da Camera Schallplatten (Mannheim), Musical Heritage Society, Nonesuch, Pro Arte, Arabesque, Spectrum, Stradivari Records, Bis Records and Sonny Classical, including 6 LPs as part of complete recorded edition of chamber works of Max Reger for his centennial, Da Camera, 1973. *Publications:* Gustav Mahler and Johann Sebastian Bach; August Wilhelm Ambros in Groves Dictionary of Music and Musicians. *Address:* 57 Prospect Street, Northampton, MA 01060, USA.

NAFE Alicia, b. 4 Aug 1947, Buenos Aires, Argentina. Singer (Mezzo-Soprano). *Education:* Studied in Buenos Aires with Ferruccio Calusio and in Europe with Luigi Ricci and Teresa Berganza. *Career* Sang in Barcelona after winning competition there, debut in Verdi's Requiem; Sang in Toldeo and at the Bayreuth Festival, 1975; Member of the Hamburg Opera, 1977-81; Geneva Opera, 1981, in La Cenerentola; Lyon 1981, in Béatrice et Bénédict by Berlioz; Sang Rosina with the Cologne Opera at the 1981 Edinburgh Festival; La Scala 1984, as Idamante in Idomeneo; Covent Garden 1985, as Rosina; Guest engagements in Spain, South America, France, Germany and China; Other roles include Carmen and Dorabella; Sang Adalgisa at Covent Garden, 1987; Metropolitan Opera debut 1988, as Carmen (conducted by Domingo); Frankfurt Opera 1988, as Sextus in La Clemenza di Tito and Raniro in La Finta

Giardiniera; Sang Massenet's Charlotte at the Teatro Regio Parma, 1990; Also heard in oratorios and as song recitalist. *Recordings:* Mercedes in Carmen and La Vida Breve (Deutsche Grammophon); Monteverdi Madrigals (RCA); Così fan Tutte (Decca). *Address:* c/o Teatro Regio, Via Garibaldi 16, I-43100 Parma, Italy.

NAGANO Kent (George), b. 22 Nov 1951, Morro Bay, California, USA. Conductor. *Education:* University of Oxford, 1969; BA 1974 and studied with Grosvenor Cooper, University of California, Santa Cruz; MM, San Francisco State University, 1976; University of Toronto; Studied piano with Goodwin Sammel; Conducting with Laszlo Varga, San Francisco. *Career:* Opera Company of Boston, 1977-79; Music Director, Berkeley (California) Symphony Orchestra, 1978; Ojai (California) Music Festival, 1984; Chief Conductor, Opéra de Lyon, 1989-; Guest conductor with many orchestras in the USA and Europe; Conducted Madama Butterfly at Lyon, 1990 followed by Dialogues des Carmélites and a French version of Strauss's Salome; Associate Principal Guest Conductor of the London Symphony Orchestra, 1990; Music Director of the Hallé Orchestra from 1992; Season 1992 with Busoni's Turandot at Lyon, Madame Butterfly at Symphony Hall Birmingham (Lyon Company) and The Rake's Progress at Aix-en-Provence. *Recordings include:* The Love for Three Oranges, Dialogues des Carmélites, Salome (Virgin Classics). *Honours:* Co-recipient, Affiliate Artist's Seaver Conducting Award, 1985; Gramophone magazine, Record of the Year Award, for The Love of Three Oranges, 1990. *Address:* c/o Opéra de Lyon, Rue Puits-Gaillot, 69000 Lyon, France.

NAGAO Isaac, b. 14 Mar 1938, Yonago, Tottori, Japan. Professor; Doctor of Miyagi College for Women. m. Kyoko Honda 1 Sept 1968, 3 sons. *Education:* Graduated from Shimane University, BMEd 1963; Tokyo Gakugei University MMEd 1969; Columbia Pacific University, PhD 1990; Tokyo University of Fine Arts and Music, 1960-62. *Compositions:* Nine Preludes; The Seasons; Hosanna! *Recording:* Hosanna! for Organ and Audience. *Publications:* The Seasons, 1981; A Proposition to the Piano Playing of J S Bach, 1986. *Memberships:* ISME; CMS; MENC; Japanese Society for Contemporary Music. *Hobbies:* Travel; Reading. *Address:* 7-37-12 Sakuragaoka, Aoba, Sendai 981, Japan.

NAGY Janos B, b. 1943, Debrecen, Hungary. Singer (Tenor). *Education:* Bartók Conservatory Budapest. *Career:* Sang with Hungarian Territorial Army Choir on tour, 1967-70; Stage debut at Budapest, 1971, as Don José in Carmen; Many performances in operas by Verdi and Puccini; Berlin 1978, in the Verdi Requiem; Warsaw National Opera 1979; Member of Deutsche Oper am Rhein, Dusseldorf, from 1981; Other roles include Puccini's Des Grieux, Cavaradossi and Calaf, Verdi's Manrico, Duke of Mantua, and Macduff, Nemorino in L'Elisir d'Amore and Pollione in Norma; Guest apparances at opera houses in Germany and Switzerland; Sang Radames with the Deutsche Oper am Rhein, Dusseldorf, 1989. *Recordings:* Boito's Nerone (Hungaroton); Kodály's Te Deum, Psalmus Hungaricus and Missa Brevis; Christus by Liszt; Mosé in Egitto; Szokolay's Blood Wedding; Simon Boccanegra. *Address:* c/o Hungarian State Opera House, Nepöztársásay utja 22, 1061 Budapest, Hungary.

NAGY Robert, b. 3 Mar 1929, Lorain, Ohio. Singer (Tenor). *Education:* Cleveland Institute of Music. *Career:* Metropolitan Opera from 1957, as Canio in Pagliacci, Beethoven's Florestan, Herod in Salome and the Emperor in Die Frau ohne Schatten; With the Met and the New York City Opera (from 1969) has sung in 1000 opera performances; Guest appearances in Chicago, Baltimore, San Diego, Seattle, Montreal and New Orleans; Repertoire includes roles in operas by Wagner, Verdi, Barber, Bizet and Puccini.

NAHAY Paul, b. 31 May 1958, Camden, New Jersey, USA. Composer; Music Theorist; Pianist; Music Director;

Professor. *Education:* B.Mus., Composition, University of Maryland, College Park, 1979; M.Mus., Composition, University of Maryland, College Park, 1980; DMA, Composition, Stanford University, 1983. *Career:* Lecturer, General Honours, Associate Music Director, Opera Theater, Music Director, Baroque Ensemble, University of Maryland, 1983-84; Lecturer, Music Theory, Music Director of Alea II, Ensemble for New Music, Stanford University, 1984-86; Music Software Developer. *Publications:* Fanfare for Brass Quintet, 1980; Duet, for Flutes, 1981; Canon for Two Flutes, 1981; Sonnet for Mixed Chorus and Flute Quartet, 1981; For Flute and Tape, 1981; ScoreInput (Music software published by Passport Designs Inc), 1990. *Honours:* 1st Prize, University of Maryland Composition Competition for Etude for Orchestra, 1980; Graduate Fellowship, Stanford University, 1981-83. *Membership:* ASCAP. *Hobbies:* Personal Computer Programming; Racquetball; Puzzle Invention. *Address:* 5117 West Shoreline Drive, Floyds Knobs, IN 47119, USA.

NALLINMAA Eero Veikko, b. 14 Feb 1917, Vanaja, Finland, Conservatory Director (retired). m. Sole Raevuori, 6 Apr 1947, 2 daughters. *Education:* Elementary School Teacher's Certificate, 1941; MA, 1949; Licentiate, 1964; Phil.D, 1970; Musical studies, Helsinki University. *Career:* Director, Tampere Conservatory; Docent, University of Tampere, 1971-74; Compositions performed at concerts, 1977, 1980, 1981, 1986. *Compositions:* Jaakko Ilkka, opera; The Katri Vala Collection; The Son of Man, passion; Songs; Works for symphony orchestra; Piano works. *Recordings:* ENLP 0182; ENCD 0191. *Publications:* Musiikillisen hahmotuksen ongelmia (Problems of the Musical Gestaltung), 1964; Erik Ulrik Spoofin nuottikirja (The Musical Manuscript of Erik Ulrik Spoof), 1969; Barokkimenuetista masurkkaan (From the Baroque Minuet to the Mazurka), 1982. *Contributions to:* Several journals and newspapers. *Honours:* VR 4, 1942; SVR R, 1972; Music Prize, Tampere, 1980; Badge of Merit, Union of Music Schools of Finland, 1982; PHF, 1988. *Memberships:* Pyynikki Rotary Club; Finnish Society of Composers; Musicological Society of Finland. *Hobby:* Genealogy. *Address:* Hämeenpuisto 43-45 A 20, 33200 Tampere, Finland.

NANCARROW Conlon, b. 27 Oct 1912, Texarkana, Arkansas, USA. Composer. *Education:* Studied at the Cincannati Conservatory and with Slonimsky, Piston and Sessions in Boston. *Career:* Fought on the Loyalist side in the Spanish Civil War and subsequently denied passport by the US Government; Lived in Mexico until 1981 (citizen 1956); Attended the New American Music Festival in San Francisco 1981; Composer-in-residence at the Cabrillo Music Festival in Aptos, California, 1982; Awarded grant of $300,000 by the MacArthur Foundation of Chicago, 1983; Gave concert of his works in Los Angeles 1984: music is notated by perforating player-piano rolls. *Compositions:* Sarabande and Scherzo for oboe, bassoon and piano 1930; Blues for piano 1935; Prelude for piano 1935; Toccata for violin and piano 1935; Septet 1940; Sonatina for piano 1940; Trio for clarinet, bassoon and piano 1942; Suite for Orchestra 1943; String Quartet 1945; 44 Studies for Player Piano (1947-); String Quartet No 3, premiered by the Arditti Quartet, Cologne, 1988. *Honours include:* Commission from the European Broadcasting Union (for Study No.39); Letter of Distinction from the American Music Center. *Address:* c/o ASCAP, ASCAP Building, One Lincoln Plaza, New York NY 10023, USA.

NAPIER Marita, b. 16 Feb 1939, Johannesburg, South Africa. Singer (Soprano). *Education:* Studied first in South Africa, then Detmold. *Debut:* Bielefeld 1969, as Venus in Tannhäuser. *Career:* Sang in Essen, Hanover and Hamburg; San Francisco, 1972-75, as Wagner's Sieglinde, Eva and Freia; Covent Garden, 1974; Bayreuth Festival, 1974-75, as Sieglinde and Eva; Verona Festival, 1979; Engagements in Vienna, Frankfurt, Stockholm, Chicago, Philadelphia and Rome; other roles have included Elsa, both Verdi's Leonoras, Santuzza, Ariadne and Elisabeth de Valois; Met Opera New York in Turandot, Hansel and Gretel and The Ring;

Gurrelieder under Boulez and Feuersnot for RAI, Italy; Director of PACT Opera Training Centre at Pretoria, 1992; Sang Isolde at Cape Town, 1992; Guire-liede, Boulez; Feuershot, Rai; Walleüre, Met. *Recordings include:* Beethoven's 9th Symphony (Philips); Das Rheingold (Eurodisc). *Address:* Opera of the Performing Arts Council, Transvaal, PO Box 566, Pretoria 0001, Transvaal, South Africa.

NAPOLI Jacopo, b. 26 Aug 1911, Italy. Composer. *Education:* S. Pietro a Majella Conservatoire of Music, Naples; Obtained diplomas in Composition, Organ and Piano. *Career:* Held Chair of Counterpoint and Fugue at Cagliari Conservatoire, and at Naples Conservatoire; Director. S. Pietro a Majella Conservatoire of Music, Naples 1955, 1962; Director, Giuseppe Verdi Conservatoire of Music, Milan, -1972, then Director, St. Cecilia Conservatory, Rome; Director, Scarlatti Arts Society, 1955-; Works performed in Germany, Spain and on Italian Radio. *Compositions:* (Operas): Il Malato Immaginario, 1939; Miseria e Nobiltà 1946; Un Curioso Accidente, 1950; Masaniello, 1953; I Pescatori, 1954; Il Tesoro, 1958; (Oratorio) The Passion of Christ; Operas Il Rosario, 1962 and Il Povero Diavolo, 1963; Il Barone avaro, 1970; Piccola Cantata del Venerdi Santo, 1964; (Orchestral Works) Overture to Love's Labours Lost, 1935; Preludio di Caccia, 1935; La Festa di Anacapri, 1940. *Address:* 55 Via Andrea da Isernia, I-80122, Naples, Italy.

NASEDKIN Alexei, b. 20 Dec 1942, Moscow, Russia. Concert Pianist. *Education:* Studied at Central Music School and the Conservatoire, Moscow. *Debut:* Public concerts from 1951, aged 9. *Career:* Has toured extensively in Russia and throughout the world, playing works by Haydn, Scarlatti, Mozart, Beethoven, Schubert, Chopin, Prokofiev and Shostakovich; Professor in Piano at Moscow Conservatoire from 1968; Vladimior Ovchinikov has been among his pupils. *Compositions:* Works for piano and orchestra. *Recordings:* Many. *Honours:* Gold Medal at competitions in Vienna and Munich 1967; Prizewinner at Leeds 1966 and Moscow 1962. *Address:* c/o Sonata, 11 Northpark Street, Glasgow G20 7AA, Scotland.

NASH Graham Thomas, b. 21 June 1952, London, England. Conductor. m. Janice Beven, 26 Sept 1981. 1 son. *Education:* LRAM, Royal Academy of Music, 1970-74. *Debut:* Conducting, Royal Albert Hall, 1980; Cracow Radio Symphony Orchestra, Poland, 1988; London Philharmonic Orchestra, 1985. *Career:* Conducting, Victor Hochhauser, Opera Gala Nights at Royal Albert Hall, Royal Festival Hall, Barbican, 1980-89; Guest Conductor, London Festival Ballet; Music Director, London City Ballet, 1986-88; Kuopio Orchestra debut, Finland, 1987. *Composition:* In Memoriam, Lord Mountbatten, for large orchestra, 1979. *Honours:* North London Orchestral Society Prize (conducting), 1974; Blake Memorial Prize (Flute), Ensemble Prize, 1974. *Membership:* Incoporated Society of Musicians. *Address:* 20 Margaret Gardner Drive, Mottingham, London SE9 3LR, England.

NASH Mary Frances Heddle, b. 20 Nov. 1928, Wellington, New Zealand. Accompanist; Repetiteur. Divorced, 3 daughters. *Education:* LRAM; ARCM; FRAM. *Career:* Performances for BBC Radio and TV, CBS, EMI, Polygram; Worked as Repetiteur at, Royal Opera House, Covent Garden, English National Opera, New Opera Company, English Opera Group, English Music Theatre, Scottish Opera, Welsh National Opera, Kent Opera, Harold Holt, Park Lane Group, Chelsea Opera Group, London Opera Centre, Royal Academy of Music, London Symphony Orchestra; Arts Council, Great Britain; London Sinfonietta; London Weekend Television; Fires of London. *Recordings:* Il Segreto di Susanna, CBS; Ian Wallace, A Celebration. Cambra Recording; also several for the BBC. *Contribution to:* Film: Howard's End. *Memberships:* Royal Academy of Music Club; Musicians Union. *Hobbies:* Gardening; Crossword Puzzles; Science Fiction. *Address:* 2 Lyttleton Close, London, NW3 3SR, England.

NASH Pamela Lucille, b. 25 Feb 1959, Bahrain. Performer, Harpsichord, & Early Keyboard Instruments. Piano & Harpsichord Teacher. m. Kevin Malone, 11 May 1985. *Education:* Chetham's School of Music, 1975-77; Trinity College of Music, 1977-81; LTCL, 1979; FTCL, 1980; Schola Cantorum, Paris, Sabbatical, 1980-81; University of Michigan, USA, 1982-85; M.Mus., 1985. *Career:* Edinburgh, Cambridge, Cheltenham and Haslemere Festivals: St Martin-in-the-Fields, Wigmore Hall and South Bank; Harkness Fellowship, 2 Years US Study; French Government Scholarship, 1980; Premieres of New works for Harpsichord; Dolmetsch Festival, 1987; Teacher, Harpsichord, Junior Department, Trinity College of Music, London; Private Teacher. *Recordings:* Scarlatti Sonatas; Alaaddin Label, 1992. *Memberships:* ISM. *Hobbies:* Reading; Films; Cooking; Art Appreciation; Foreign Travel. *Address:* 23 Shelford Road, Trumpington, Cambridge CB2 2LZ, England.

NASH Peter Paul, b. 1950, Leighton Buzzard, Beds., England. Composer. *Education:* Cambridge University, with Robin Holloway. *Career:* Composition Fellow at Leeds University, 1976-78; Composer in Residence at the National Centre for Orchestral Studies, 1983; Producer, BBC Radio 3, 1985-87; Critic and Broadcaster; (presenter of Music Week to Radio 3); Symphony premiered at the 1991 Promenade Concerts, London. *Compositions:* String Trio 1982; Wind Quintet; Insomnia for chamber ensemble; Etudes for Orchestra (On the Beach, Percussion Study, Parting) 1983-84; Figures for harp; Earthquake, scena for narrator and six players, 1985; String Quartet, 1987; Sextet for piano and wind quintet, 1987; Symphony, 1991. *Address:* c/o Faber Music Ltd., 3 Queen Square, London WC1N 3AU, England.

NATANEK Adam Tadeusz (Ted), b. 23 July 1933, Cracow, Poland. Conductor. m. Danuta Florek, 27 July 1966. *Education:* Department of Pedagogy, 1957; Department of Composition and Conducting, 1960; Academy of Music, Cracow, 1960. *Debut:* Cracow Philharmonic Orchestra, 1960. *Career:* Musical Conducting Assistant, 1961-62; Conductor, 1962-69; Director, Artistic manager and Chief Conductor, 1969; Guest Conductor, Warsaw National Philharmonic, The Great Symphony Orchestra of Polish radio and Television, Katowice; The Orchestra of Polish radio and TV, Cracow and USSR, Czechoslovakia, Rumania, The Netherlands, Federal Republic of Germany, Switzerland, Austria, Sweden, Italy, Norway and Spain; Professor of Maria Sklodowska-Curie University, Lublin; Guest Conductor Havana, Cuba; Director, Artistic Manager and Chief Conductor of the Lublin Philharmonics, 1989-90; Artistic Director of the Symphonic Orchestra in Valladulid, Spain, 1990; Guest Conductor in nearly all European countries and in the USA. *Recordings:* Numerous radio and TV recordings. *Contributions to:* Promoter and Reviewer, Maria Sklodowska-Curie University, Lublin and Academy of Music, Warsaw and Poznan. *Address:* ul Szczerbowskiego 13/10, 20-012 Lublin, Poland.

NATRA Sergiu, b. 12 Apr 1924, Bucarest, Romania. Composer. *Education:* MA, National Music Academy, Bucarest, 1952; Studied Composition with Leo Klepper. *Career:* Commissions of Symphony Works, Chamber Music, Stage and Film Music in Romania; major commissions in Israel by the Israel Festival, Israel Philharmonic Orchestra, Israel Radio, Israel Composers Fund; Professor, Composition; Examiner for the higher musical education, Israel Ministry of Education & Culture, 1964-71; commission for Testimonium, 1968. *Compositions:* 3 Corteges in the Street, 1945; Suite for Orchestra, 1948; Sinfonia for Strings, Music for Violin & Harp, Music for Harpsichord & 6 Instruments, 1964; Music for Oboe & Strings, 1965; Sonatina for Harp, 1965; Song of Deborah, 1967; Variations for Piano & Orchestra, 1966; Prayer for Harp, 1972; Sonatina for Trumpet, 1973; Sonatina for Trombone Solo, 1973; Sacred Service, 1976; From the Diary of a Composer, 1978; Variations for Harpsichord, 1978; Hours for mezzo-soprano violin, clarinet and piano, 1981;

Divertimento for harp and strings, 1983; Music for Harp and three Brass Instruments, 1982; Ness Amim, Cantata for solo voices, choir, chamber orchestra with harpsichord, 1984; Sonatina for piano, 1987; Music for Violin & Piano, 1986; Music for NICANOR for Harp Solo and Chamber ensemble, 1988; Developments for viola solo and chamber orchestra, 1988. *Recordings:* Suite for Orchestra, 1948; Music for Harpsichord & 6 Instruments; Song of Deborah; Sonatina for Harp; Sonatina for Harp (Israel Music Anthology, Volume 6); Trio for Violin Violoncello and piano. *Address:* 10 Barth St., Tel-Aviv, 69104, Israel.

NAUHAUS Gerd Ernst Hermann, b. 28 July 1942, Erfurt, Germany. Musicologist. m. Ursula Karsdorf, 15 Aug 1965, 2 sons (1 deceased), 1 daughter. *Education:* Matriculation, 1961; Diploma, Musical Education, 1965, Diploma, Musicology, 1969, PhD, 1980, Martin Luther University, Halle- Wittenberg. *Career:* Dramatizer of Music at Zwickau Opera House, 1967; Musicologist, 1970-, Vice-Director, 1980-, Robert Schumann House, Zwickau; Director, 1993. *Publications:* Robert Schumann, Diaries and Household books, complete scholarly edition, vol III, 1982, vol II, 1987; Clara Schumann 3 part songs after poems by Geibal, 1989; Piano Sonata in G minor, (first editions), 1991. *Honour:* Schumann Prize, Zwickau Town Council, 1986. *Membership:* Vice-Chairman, Scientific Secretary, Robert Schumann Society, Zwickau; Member, German Musicological Society. *Hobbies:* Literature; Architecture; Walking tours; Travel. *Address:* Robert-Schumann-Haus, Hauptmarkt 5, D-08056 Zwickau/Saxony, Germany.

NAYLOR Peter, b. 5 Oct 1933, London, England. Composer. *Education:* MA, Cambridge, 1957; BMus, London, 1961; Fellow of Royal College of Organists, London, 1961; Associate of Royal College of Music, London, 1962. *Career:* Lecturer, City Literary Institute, London, 1963- 65; Lecturer, Harmony and Counterpoint, History, Royal Scottish Academy of Music and Drama, 1965-71; Organist, Ashwell Festival, Herts, 1964-69; Associate Organist, Glasgow Cathedral, 1972-85; Music Associate, Scottish Opera for Youth, 1975-80; Repetiteur, Shepway Youth Opera, Kent, 1982-85. *Compositions:* Symphony in One Movement, Tides and Islands; Beowulf for symphonic wind band; Odysseus Returning, three act opera; Pied Piper, one act opera; The Mountain People, workshop opera; Earth was Waiting, cantata; Wassail Sing We for SA chorus, piano and percussion; A Hero Dies for 22 voices and clarsach; Movement for Organ; Toccata for Organ; Air and Variations for 2 pianos; Clarinet Quintet; Love and Life (5 songs); Carols and anthems. *Recordings:* Eastern Monarchs, carol for SATB; Elizabethan Singers, Louis Halsey; Eastern Monarchs, Choir of St John's College, Cambridge, George Guest; Now the Green Blade Riseth, SATB Choir of Glasgow Cathedral, John R Turner; Clarinet Quintet, Colin Bradbury and the Georgian Quartet. *Address:* "Greenacres" Brady Road, Lyminge, Folkestone, Kent CT18 8HA, England.

NEAMAN Yfrah, b. 13 Feb 1923, Sidon, Lebanon. Concert Violinist. m. 16 Mar 1963, 1 son, 1 daughter. *Education:* 1st Prize, Conservatoire National Superieur de Musique, Paris; Further studies with Carl Flesch, Jacques Thibaud, Max Rostal. *Debut:* Soloist with London Symphony Orchestra, London, 1944. *Career:* Professor, Violin, Head, Advanced Solo Studies, Guildhall School of Music & Drama, London; Recitals; Concerts with Orchestras; Radio & TV Appearances; Masterclasses in Europe, USA, Canada, Japan, China, South America, Africa & Asia; Artistic Consultant, London International String Quartet Competition; Artistic Adviser Wells Cathedral School, England. *Recordings:* Concertos: Roberto Gerhard, Racine Fricker, Don Banks; Sonatas: John Ireland, Franck; Trios: John Ireland; Bloch, Fauré and Ravel. *Publications:* Editions of several Musical Works including Beethoven Violin Concerto, Tartini Devil's Trill Sonata; Beethoven violin and piano sonatas. *Honours:* 1st Prize, Violin, Paris Conservatoire, 1937; FGSM, 1964; Freedom of the City of London, 1980; OBE, 1983. *Memberships:* Freeman,

Worshipful Company of Musicians. *Address:* 11 Chadwell Street, London EC1R 1XD, England.

NEARY Martin Gerard James, b. 28 Mar 1940. Organist and Master of Music, Winchester Cathedral; Organ Recitalist and Conductor; Founder and Conductor, Martin Neary Singers; Conductor, Waynflete Singers. m. Penelope Jane Warren, 1967, 1 son, 2 daughters. *Education:* HM Chapels Royal, St James's Palace; City of London School; Gonville and Caius College, Cambridge (Organ Scholar, MA); FRCO. *Career:* Assistant Organist, 1963-65; Organist and Master of Music, 1965-71; St Margaret's Westminster; Professor of Organ, Trinity College, London, 1963-72; Organ Advisor to Diocesan of Winchester, 1975-; Conductor, Twickenham Musical Society, 1966-72; Founder and Conductor, St Margaret's Westminster Singers, 1967-71; Director of Southern Cathedrals Festival, 1972, 1975, 1978, 1981, 1984, 1987; Organist and Master of Music, Winchester Cathedral, 1972-; Organ Recitalist and Conductor; Founder and Conductor, Martin Neary Singers, 1972-; Conductor, Waynflete Singers, 1972-; Many organ recitals and broadcasts in UK, including Royal Festival Hall and music festivals; Has conducted many premieres of music by British composers including John Tavener's Ultimos Ritos, 1979, Jonathan Harvey's Hymn, 1979, and Passion and Resurrection, 1981; with Martin Neary Singers performing Madrigals and Graces at 10 Downing Street, 1970-74; Toured US and Canada, 1963, 1968, 1971, 1973, 1975, 1977, 1979, 1982, 1984; BBC Promenade Concerts 1979, 1982; Conductor with: ECO, 1978, 1980, 1981; LSO, 1979, 1980, 1981; Bournemouth SO and Sinfonietta 1975-; Many European Tours; Artist-in-Residence, University of California at Davis 1984; President Cathedral Organists Association. *Recordings:* Many recordings including Lloyd Webber's Requiem (Golden Disc). *Hobby:* Watching Cricket. *Address:* 10 The Close, Winchester, Hants, England.

NEATE Ken, b. 28 July 1914, Cessnock, New South Wales, Australia. Singer (Tenor). *Education:* Studied at the University of Melbourne and in New York with Emilio de Gorgoza. *Career:* Appeared in Madama Butterfly and Carmen while at University; After war service sang at Covent Garden 1947-51, as Don José, the Duke of Mantua, Pinkerton and Tamino; Guest appearances in Paris, Bordeaux, Bologna, Turin, Palermo and in Egypt; Madrid 1954; Sang in 1956 premiere of Henri Tomasi's Sampiero Corso; Concert tours of USA, Canada, Australia and England; Bayreuth Festival 1963, as Loge in Das Rheingold; Last stage appearance as Otello, Innsbruck 1975.

NEBE Michael, b. 28 July 1947, Nordenbeck, Waldeck, Germany. Cellist. *Education:* Educational diploma & teaching qualifications, Dortmund Conservatorium; MMus, King's College, University of London, UK (studied under Thurston Dart, Brain Trowell, Antony Milner, Geoffrey Bush); Licentiate, Royal Academy of Music (Studying under Florence Hooton, Colin Hampton). *Debut:* Wigmore Hall, London, 1977. *Career:* Member, London Piace Consort, London Piace Duo, Chamber Music, London; Numerous performances throughout Great Britain; Tours, Federal Republic of Germany, Holland, USA, Canada, Australia; Teacher, freelance musician, soloist, conductor, translator, writer, lecturer and adjudicator; Conductor and Musical Director of Civil Service Orchestra, 1990; Associated Conductor of Surrey Sinfonietta; Conducting private studies in Germany and at Morley College under Lawrence Leonard; Has made numerous recorded radio & television appearances. *Publications:* Translation into German, Eta Cohen's Violin Tutor, 1979; Cello tutor, 1984. *Memberships:* Dvorak Society, Incorporated Society of Musicians, Musicians' Union. *Hobbies:* Reading; Composition; Theatre & opera. *Address:* 24 Thornton Avenue, London SW2 4HG, England.

NEBLETT Carol, b. 1 Feb 1946, Modesto, California. Singer (Soprano). *Education:* Studied with Lotte Lehmann and Pierre Bernac. *Career:* Sang with Roger Wagner Chorale from 1965; Stage debut as Musetta,

New York City Opera 1969: returned as Marietta in Die Tote Stadt, Poppea, and Margherita and Elena in Boito's Mefistofele; Chicago 1975, as Chrysothemis in Elektra; Vienna Staatsoper debut 1976; as Minnie in La Fanciulla del West, Covent Garden 1977; Metropolitan Opera debut 1979, as Senta in Der fliegende Holländer: returned as Tosca, Amelia (Un Ballo in Maschera), Manon Lescaut and Alice Ford in Falstaff; Appearances in Dallas, Turin, Leningrad, Pittsburgh, Baltimore and San Francisco; Other roles include Violetta, Minnie in La Fanciulla del West, Mozart's Countess, Charpentier's Louise and Antonia in Les Contes d'Hoffmann; Salzburg Festival as Vitelia in La Clemenza di Tito (has also appeared as Vitelia in Jean-Pierre Ponnelle's film of the opera); Teatro Regio Turin 1987, in Respighi's Semiramis; Sang Mme Lidoine in Les Dialogues des Carmélites at San Diego, 1990; debut as Norma for Greater Miami Opera, 1990; Aida for Cincinnati Opera; Season 1992 as Tosca for Opera Pacific at Costa Mesa, Queen Isabella in Franchetti's Cristoforo Colombo at Miami and as Amelia in Un Ballo in Maschera at Dublin. *Recordings include:* Die Tote Stadt (RCA); La Fanciulla del West (Deutsche Grammophon); La Bohème (HMV). *Address:* Stafford Law Associates, 26 Mayfield Road, Weybridge, Surrey KT13 8XB, England.

NEDYALKOV Hristo, b. 1 Sept 1932, Dryanovo, Bulgaria. Professor of Choral Conducting, Sofia University. m. Dobrina Nedyalkova, 3 July 1960, 1 son. *Education:* Bulgarian State Conservatory, 1956. *Career:* Artistic Director and Conductor, Children's Choir of Bulgarian Radio and TV, 1960. Numerous Stage appearances, film, TV and Radio in Bulgaria, USSR, USA, Japan, Great Britain, France, Federal Republic of Germany, Austria, Hungary, Mexico, Czechoslovakia, Poland, Greece. Adjudicator: International Competitions: Llangollen (Wales), Cork (Ireland), Neerpelt (Belgium), Varna (Bulgaria), Olomouc (Czechoslovakia); National Competitions. *Compositions:* Numerous Choral Works and Children's Songs. *Recordings:* Numerous. *Publications:* Editor, Musical Collections. *Contributions to:* various professional journals. *Honours:* Honoured Artist of Bulgaria, 1972; People's Artist of Bulgaria, 1980; Bearer of National Medals; Hungarian Medal, Zóltan Kodály, 1984. *Memberships:* Union of Bulgarian Composers; Union of Bulgarian Musicians. *Hobby:* Fishing. *Address:* 5 Malusha Str., Sofia 1421, Bulgaria.

NEE Thomas, b. 25 Oct 1920, Evanston, Ilinois, USA. Conductor; Professor of Music. *Education:* Studied at University of Minnesota and with Krenek at Hamline University, MA 1947; Further study in Vienna with Hans Swarowsky. *Debut:* Vienna Konzerthaus, 1951. *Career:* After study with Robert Shaw at Berkshire Music Center and Herman Scherchen in Zurich, 1951-52, taught at Hamline University, 1947-56 and Macalester College, 1957-67; Assistant Conductor of Minneapolis Symphony Orchestra, 1949-50; Music Director of Civic Orchestra of Minneapolis, 1953-67, New Hampshire Music Festival from 1960, Minnesota Opera, 1963-67, La Jolla Civic Orchestra from 1967; Professor of University of California at San Diego from 1967; Conducted the premiere of Horspfal by Eric Stokes for Minnesota Opera, 1969. *Address:* c/o San Diego State University, Department of Music, 5300 Campanile Drive, San Diego, CA 92182, USA.

NEEVE Robbert Jan de, b. 5 Dec 1943, Rotterdam, Netherlands. Radio Department Head. m. Elisabeth Joriena de Bruyn, 1 son, 1 daughter. *Education:* St Franciscus College, 1962; Musicology, Utrecht University, 1970. *Career:* Producer, 1970, Head of Serious Music, 1976, Deputy Head of Music, 1989; Chairman, Working Party, Serious Music, 1980, NOS Radio, Hilversum. *Composition:* AF (Electronic music, published on Donemus Records). *Honour:* 2nd Prize, Prix Musical, Radio Brno, 1971. *Memberships:* Several board memberships of Dutch musical organisations. *Hobbies:* Tennis; Cycling; Reading. *Address:* 36 Eikbosserweg 1214 AJ Hilversum, Netherlands.

NEGRI Vittorio, b. 16 Oct 1923, Milan, Italy.

Conductor. *Education:* Studied composition, conducting and violin at the Milan Conservatory. *Career:* Assistant conductor to Bernhard Paumgartner at the Salzburg Mozarteum, 1952; Guest conductor with leading orchestras in Europe; Appearances at festivals in Flanders, Salzburg, Montreux, Orange and Versailles; Engagements at La Scala, Milan, and with the Orchestre National de France, the Dresden Staatskapelle and the Boston Symphony Orchestra. *Recordings:* Music by Mozart, Vivaldi and composers of the Venetian Baroque; including the sacred choral works of Vivaldi, with Margaret Marshall, Ann Murray, Linda Finnie, Anne Collins, Felicity Lott, Sally Burgess, Robert Hall and Anthony Rolfe Johnson (Philips). *Honours:* Numerous awards for recordings. *Address:* Chemin des Cuarroz 8, 1807 Blonay, Switzerland.

NEGRIN Francisco Miguel, b. 1963, Mexico. Opera Director. *Education:* Studied in France, notably cinematography at Aix-en- Provence. *Career:* Staff Producer at Theatre Royal de la Monnaie, Brussels; Has assisted such directors as Patrice Chereau, Maurice Bejart, John Cox, Francois Rochaix, and Graham Vick; Associations with the Paris Châtelet, Salzburg Landestheater, Theater an der Wien, Vienna, Grand Théâtre, Geneva, Seattle Opera (The Ring, with Francois Rochaix), Oslo Torshov theatre, Nice and Toulouse Opera and the Aix-en-Provence Festival; Directed the premiere of his version of Debussy's The Fall of the House of Usher in Christ Church, Spitalfields, 1986, and at the London International Opera Festival and Lisbon Opera, 1989; Has produced Werther at the Opera de Nice, 1990; Haydn's Orlando Paladino at Garsington Manor, 1990; La Traviata and the Mozart Pasticcio The Jewel Box at Opera North, 1991; This was also the first production to be invited by Glyndebourne to be performed in its theatre, 1991; Così fan Tutte at Seattle Opera and Don Carlos at Victoria State Opera in Melbourne; L'Heure Espagnole and La Colombe at the Guildhall School of Music, 1993; World premieres of Tourist Variations and Visitatio Sepulchri by James MacMillan at Glasgow's Tramway and at the Edinburgh International Festival, Una Cosa Rara by Martin Soler at the Drottningholm Festival; Handel: Julius Caesar at the Australian Opera in Sydney, 1994. *Current Management & Address:* c/o Diana Mulgan, IMG Artists (Europe), Media House, 3 Burlington Lane, London W4 2TH, England.

NÉGYESY János, b. 13 Sep. 1938, Budapest, Hungary. Violinist. *Education:* State Exam, Franz Liszt Music Academy, Budapest. *Career:* Concertmaster, Berlin Radio Orchestra, West Germany, 1970-74; Professor of Music, University of California, San Diego, USA, 1979-; Soloist in all major European Festivals including Berliner Festwochen, Royan Festival, Donaueschingen, Paris, Witten Chamber Music Festival, Meta Music Festival Berlin, Metz Festival. *Recordings:* All Violin Sonatas by Charles Ives, 1975; Dedications to János Négyesy, 1978, John Cage: Ireeman Etudes I-XVI for solo violin, 1984. *Publications:* New Violin Technique, 1978. *Memberships:* New York Academy of Sciences; American Association of the Advancement of Science, International Platform Association. *Hobbies:* Photo-Montages and Collages (Exhibitions). *Address:* 344 Prospect Street, La Jolla, CA 92037, USA.

NEIGHBOUR Oliver Wray, b. 1 Apr 1923. Retired Music Librarian, Reference Division of the British Library. *Education:* Eastbourne College; BA, Birkbeck College, London, 1950. *Career:* Entered Department of Printed Books, BM, 1946; Assistant Keeper in Music Room, 1951; Deputy Keeper, 1976; Music Librarian, Reference Division of The British Library, 1976-85. *Publications:* (with Alan Tyson) English Music Publishers' Plate Numbers, 1965; The Consort and Keyboard Music of William Byrd, 1978; (Ed) Music and Bibliography: Essays in Honour of Alec Hyatt King, 1980; Article on Schoenberg in New Grove Dictionary of Music and Musicians, 1980; Editor of First Publications of Works by Schumann, Schoenberg and Byrd. *Honours:* Fellow, British Academy. *Hobbies:* Walking; Ornithology.

Address: 12 Treborough House, 1 Nottingham Place, London W1M 3FP, England.

NEIKRUG Marc (Edward), b. 24 Sept 1946, New York City, USA. Composer; Pianist. *Education:* Studied with Giselher Klebe in Detmold, 1964-68; Stony Brook, State University of New York: MM in composition 1971. *Career:* Commissions from the Houston Symphony and the St Paul Chamber Orchestra (Consultant on contemporary music 1978); Los Alamos premiered at the Deutsche Oper Berlin, 1988; Duo partnership with Pinchas Zukerman; Visited London, 1989; British premiere of Violin Concerto at South Bank and duo recital at the Barbican Hall. *Compositions:* Piano Concerto 1966; Solo Cello sonata 1967; Clarinet Concerto 1967; 2 String Quartets 1969, 1972; Viola Concerto 1974; Suite for cello and piano 1974; Rituals for flute and harp 1976; Concertino for ensemble 1977; Fantasies for violin and piano 1977; Continuum for cello and piano 1978; Cycle of 7 for piano 1978; Kaleidoscope for flute and piano 1979; Eternity's Sunrise for orchestra 1979-80; Through Roses, theatre piece 1979-80; Mobile for orchestra 1981; Violin Concerto 1982; Duo for violin and piano 1983; Los Alamos, opera 1988. *Honours:* NEA Awards 1972 and 1974; Prizes for Through Roses at the Besançon Film Festival 1981 and the International Film and Television Festival, New York 1982. *Address:* c/o ASCAP/ASCAP Building, One Lincoln Plaza, New York, NY 10023, USA.

NEJCEVA Liljana, b. 1945, Silistra, Bulgaria. Singer (Mezzo-soprano). *Education:* Studied at the music schools in Ruse and Sofia. *Career:* Sang at the Leipzig Opera 1969- as Amastris in Xerxes, Ulrica, Lady Pamela in Fra Diavolo, Fidalma in Il Matrimonio Segreto and Konschakovna in Prince Igor; Member of Bayerische Staatsoper, Munich, 1973-78, as Azucena, Maddalena, Marina in Boris Godunov and Cherubino; Has sung with Nationaltheater Mannheim, 1981-; Guest appearances include Hamburg (as Eboli), Berlin Staatsoper (Dorabella), Vienna Volksoper (Carmen) and Cologne (Suzuki); Also sings Luisa Miller; Travelled to Japan and Cuba; Concert engagements in Munich, Prague, Rome, Frankfurt and Paris. *Address:* Music International, 13 Ardilaun Road, London N5 2QR, England.

NEL Anton, b. 29 Dec 1961, Johannesburg, South Africa. Pianist; Professor of Piano. *Education:* BMus, University of the Witwatersrand, South Africa, 1983; Performers Diploma, MMus 1984, DMus 1986, University of Cincinnati, USA. *Debut:* Carnegie Recital Hall, New York, 1986. *Career:* Performances with major orchestras including: Chicago, Seattle, Cincinnati, Brooklyn; Recitals and chamber music concerts throughout USA, Canada, Europe, Parts of Africa; Recitals in Alice Tully Hall, NY; Barbican Centre and Queen Elizabeth Hall, London; Many appearances at summer festivals including Aspen, Ravinia; Professor of Piano, Eastman School of Music, Rochester, NY. *Recordings:* Saint-Saëns, Carnival of the Animals; Haydn-4 Sonatas. *Honours:* 1st prize, Walter W Naumburg International Piano Competition; 1st prize, Joanna Hodges International Piano Competition; Prizes at Leeds and Pretoria Int Piano Competition. *Membership:* Pi Kappa Lambda. *Hobbies:* Reading; Board games; Cooking. *Current Management:* Walter W Naumburg Foundation. *Address:* 47 Menlo Place, Rochester, NY 14620, USA.

NELHYBEL Vaclav, b. 24 Sept 1919, Polanka nad Odrou, Czechoslovakia. Composer; Conductor. *Education:* Studied at Prague Conservatory and at Fribourg University. *Career:* Conductor at City Theatre Prague and with Radio Prague, 1939-42, Czech Philharmonic Orchestra, 1945-46, Swiss Radio, 1946-50 and Radio Free Europe, 1950-57; Teacher of Music Theory at Fribourg University from 1947; US citizen from 1962, becoming Lecturer, Conductor and freelance Composer of band works, children's pieces and other music; Teacher at University of Lowell, Massachusetts, 1978-79. *Compositions:* Operas: Legend, 1954, Everyman 1974 and Station 1978; Ballets: Fêtes de feux, 1942, In the Shadow of a Lime Tree, 1946, Cock and the Hangman, 1946; Orchestra: Symphony, 1942; Etude Symphonique, 1949; Sinfonietta Concertante, 1960; Viola Concerto, 1962; Houston Concerto, 1967; Polyphonies, 1972; Polyphonic variations for trumpet and strings, 1976; Slavonic Triptych, 1976; Symphonic band pieces including Sinfonia resurrectionis, 1980; Music for 12 trumpets and winds, 1980; Concerto Grosso, 1981; Clarinet Concerto, 1982; Vocal including Fables for All Time for narrator, chorus and orchestra, 1980; Let There be Music for baritone, chorus and orchestra, 1982; Chamber: 2 String Quartets, 1949, 62; 3 Wind Quintets, 1948, 58, 60; 2 Brass Quintets, 1961, 65; Quintetto Concertante, 1965; Oratorio No 2 for oboe and string trio, 1979; Songs, Anthems, Piano and Organ Music; Concerto for Double Bass and Orchestra, 1990; Toccata in C for Organ and Band, 1991; Concerto for Bass Trombone and Orchestra (or band), 1991; Concertante for Flute, Harp and 13 Instruments, 1992; Toccata in E for Symphonic Band, 1993. Contributions to: Music Theory Series (Folkways). *Address:* c/o ASCAP, ASCAP Building, One Lincoln Plaza, New York, NY 10023, USA.

NELSON Havelock, b. 25 May 1917, Cork, Ireland. Conductor; Accompanist (Piano); Organist; Examiner; Composer; Adjudicator; Broadcaster; Writer. m. Hazel Guthrie Lutton, 2 sons, 1 daughter. *Education:* MA, MSc, PhD, Trinity College, Dublin University; Private Tuition and Royal Irish Academy of Music, Dublin; D.Mus; Licentiate, Royal Academy of Music, Dublin. *Career:* Service in Royal Air Force, 1943; Joined British Broadcasting Corporation, Northern Ireland, 1947; Conductor, Studio Symphony Orchestra; Director, Ulster Singers; Artistic Director, Studio Opera Group; Conductor for various TV Series including: Songs of Praise, The Nelson Touch, Portrait of a Musician, Music for pleasure and Sounding Voices. *Compositions include:* Orchestral Works; Ballet, Choral Suite; Song Cycles; Choral works; works for piano, radio plays, TV plays and films. *Recordings:* Celtic Songs (with Veronica Dunne) Highlights of Irish Opera (as Conductor) Irish Rhythms (Conductor); She Moved Through the Fair (Pianist); Irish Songs of Praise (Conductor); Moore's Melodies (with Bernadette Greevy), 1987. *Hobbies:* Theatre; Cinephotography. *Address:* 30 Rosetta Park, Belfast BT6 ODL, Northern Ireland.

NELSON John, b. 6 Dec 1941, San José, Costa Rica.Conductor. *Education:* Studied at the Juilliard School, N.Y. *Career:* In 1972 conducted the Pro Arte Chorale and Orchestra in a New York concert performance of Berlioz's Les Troyens; engaged for the opera at the Metropolitan in 1973 and has since conducted Cavalleria Rusticana, Pagliacci, Jenůfa and Il Barbiere di Siviglia there; New York City Opera 1972-; Carmen and L'Incoronazione di Poppea; for Santa Fe Opera he conducted the US premiere of Britten's Owen Wingrave; Was Music Director of the St Louis Opera, 1981-91 and the Caramoor Festival, New York; Music Director, Indianapolis Symphony Orchestra 1977-88; tour of Europe Sept. 1987; guest engagements with leading orchestras in North America and Europe; Conducted Werther at St Louis, 1988; Orchestre National de Lyon; production of Benvenuto Cellini Sept. 1989 at the Lyon/Berlioz Festival; Season 1992/93 with Benvenuto Cellini at the Geneva Opera, Hoffmann at the Bastille, Handel's Xerxes and Massenet's Don Quichotte at Chicago, Béatrice et Benedict for Welsh National Opera and Faust at Geneva. *Recordings:* DGG Handel Semele, Arturo Toscanini Award for his recording of works by Ellen Zwillich; Béatrice et Bénédict (Erato); Handel's Semele (DGG). *Honour:* Diapason d'Or Award, for Erato recording of Beatrice and Benedict, 1992. *Address:* c/o IMG Artists, 3 Burlington Lane, London W4 2TH, England.

NELSON Judith, b. 10 Sept 1939, Chicago, Illinois, USA. Singer. m. Alan H. Nelson, 5 Aug 1961, 1 son, 1 daughter. *Education:* BA, Music, St. Olaf College, Northfield, Minnesota, 1961; Studied Piano 12 years; Voice: Principal Teachers: Thomas Wikman, Chicago; James Cunningham, Berkeley; Martial Singher, Santa Barbara. *Debut:* Paris, 1973. *Career:* Radio: BBC, France,

Belgium, Holland, Federal Republic of Germany, Italy, Austria, Scandinavia, BBC several Promenade Concerts; Television: BBC, (Open University Handel's Messiah, Series: Music in Time); ITV; Performances with major symphonies including San Francisco Symphony, Los Angeles Philharmonic, Baltimore Symphony, Atlanta Symphony, St Louis Symphony. *Recordings:* Various recordings including Belinda in Dido and Aeneas (Chandos) Handel's Alceste and La Resurrezione; Haydn: Canzonets and Cantatas, with Koch International. *Honour:* Alfred Hertz Memorial Fellowship, 1972-73; Honorary Doctorate from St Olaf College, 1989. *Current Management:* Christopher Tennant Management, London, England.*Address:* 2600 Buena Vista Way, Berkeley, CA 94708, USA.

NELSON Martin, b. 1950, London. Singer (Bass). *Education:* Studied at Caius College Cambridge and with Tito Gobbi and Peter Harrison. *Career:* Has sung principal roles for Opera North, Kent Opera, English Music Theatre, Travelling Opera, Birmingham Music Theatre and Musica nel Chiostro; Appearances at the Buxton and Wexford Festivals and concerts in Tours, Versailles and Israel; Engagements as Christus in the St John and St Matthew Passions of Bach; Stravinsky's Pulcinella on BBC 2; Has sung in the West End (Sondheim's A Little Night Music) and in music theatre (Royal Opera Garden Venture); Founder of Scrap and Scratch Opera, using recycled materials; With New Israel Opera appeared as Alidoro in La Cenerentola. *Address:* c/o Korman International Management, Crunnells Green Cottage, Preston, Herts SG4 7UQ, England.

NELSON Ron, b. 14 Dec 1929, Joliet, Illinois, USA. Composer; Professor of Music. m. Helen Mitchell (deceased), 1 son, 1 daughter. *Education:* Eastman School of Music, Rochester; BM 1952, MM 1953, DMA 1956; Ecole Normale de Musique, Paris, 1955-56. *Career:* Professor Emeritus, 1993. *Compositions:* Opera The Birthday of the Infanta, 1956; The Christmas Story, 1958; Toccata for Orchestra, 1963; What is Man? 1964; Rocky Point Holiday, 1969; This is the Orchestra, 1969; Prayer for an Emperor of China, 1973; Five Pieces for Orchestra after Paintings of Frank Wyeth, 1975; Four Pieces after The Seasons, 1978; Three Autumnal Sketches, 1979; Mass of LaSalle, 1981; Three Nocturnal Pieces, 1982; Three Settings of the Moon, 1982; Medieval Suite, 1983; Aspen Jubilee, 1984; Te Deum Laudamus, 1985; Danza Capriccio for saxophone, 1988; Three Pieces after Tennyson, 1989; Fanfare for the Hour of Sunlight, 1989; Morning Alleluias, 1989; The Deum Laudamus, 1991; To The Airborne, 1991; Passacaglin (Homage on B-A-C-H), 1992; Lauds (Praise High Day), 1992. *Recordings:* Medieval Suite and Rocky Point Holiday for Golden Great Records; Behold Man, Reference Recordings. Pebble Beach Sojourn, Reference Recordings; Savannah River Holiday, Mercury Records, Morning Alleluas, Kosie Recordings, Passacaglin (Homage on B-A-C-H), EMI Records.*Publications:* Te Deum Laudamus, 1991; To The Airbourne, 1991; Lauds, 1992; Passacaglia (Homage on B-A-C-H), 1993. *Address:* 1606 Shadow Oaks Place, Thousand Oaks, CA 91362, USA.

NELSOVA Zara, b. 23 Dec 1918, Winnipeg, Manitoba, Canada. Concert Cellist. m. Grant Johannesen, 1963. *Education:* Studied at the London Violoncello School with Herbert Walenn; Further studies with Casals. *Debut:* London 1932, in Lalo's Concerto. *Career:* Played in Canadian Trio with two sisters; US debut 1942, New York Town Hall; US Citizen from 1955; Numerous recitals with Grant Johanesen; Appearances in Italy, Spain, Portugal, Switzerland, Holland, Britain, USA, and Scandinavian countries; Performed Bloch's Suites for Solo Cello on the BBC, 1957; Tour of Russia, 1966; Early performances of works by Barber, Hindemith and Shostakovich. *Honours include:* Canadian Centennial Medal of the Confederation, 1967.

NELSSON Woldemar, b. 4 Apr 1938, Kiev, Ukraine. Conductor. *Education:* Studied with his father in Kiev, then at the Novosibirsk Conservatory and in Moscow and Leningrad. *Career:* Assistant to Kyrill Kondrashin at the Moscow Philharmonic, 1972; Conducted leading orchestras in the USSR, with such soloists as Rostropovitch, David Oistrakh and Gidon Kremer; Emigrated to West Germany 1977 and conducted major orchestras in Hamburg, Munich, Berlin, Frankfurt, Vienna, London, Geneva, Amsterdam, Tel Aviv, Jerusalem and Montreal; Directed the premiere of Henze's ballet Orpheus, Stuttgart 1979, and took the production to Washington and the Metropolitan Opera New York; Guest Conductor with Stuttgart Opera from 1980; General Music Director of the State Theatre in Kassel; Has conducted opera productions in Paris, Philadelphia, Japan, Vienna and Barcelona; Bayreuth Festival, 1980-85, Lohnegrin and Der fliegende Holländer; Conducted the world premiere of Penderecki's opera Die schwarze Maske, Salzburg 1986. *Recordings include:* Lohengrin (CBS); Der fliegende Holländer (Philips). *Honours include:* Max Reger Prize. *Address:* c/o Staatstheater Stuttgart, Oberer Schlossgarten 6, D-7000 Stuttgart 1, Germany.

NEMESCU Octavian, b. 29 Mar 1940, Pascani, Rumania. Composer; University Lecturer. m. Erica Nemescu. *Education:* Bucharest Conservatory, D Mus 1978. *Compositions include:* Sonata for clarinet and piano, 1962; Triangle for orchestra 1964; Ego (multi-media performance) 1970; The Play of Senses, music for a pair of ears, of eyes, of hands, a nose and a mouth, 1973-76; Cromosom, imaginary music, 1974; Natural !!!, music in space, 1974; Calendar, permanent music for the environment of a room, 1976; Semantica, metamusic for lovers of music, 1978; Natural-Cultural for chamber ensemble and tape, 1984. *Honours include:* Aaron Copland Composition Prize 1970. *Membership:* Composers' Union of Rumania. *Address:* Bu. Dinicu Golescu 23-25, BL B, Scara 3, Ap 65, Sector VII, Codul 77112, Bucharest, Rumania.

NEMET Mary Ann, b. 10 June 1936, Budapest, Hungary. Violinist. 3 children. *Education:* AMusA, University Conservatorium, Melbourne; Studied with Stella Nemet, Max Rostal and Arthur Grumiaux. *Debut:* Beethoven Violin Concerto with Sydney Symphony Orchestra, 1955. *Career:* Concert tours, radio and TV appearances in Australia and Far East; Toured most European countries with pianist Roxanne Wruble (Duo Landolfi); Appointed to Sydney Conservatorium, 1970; Soloist, East Germany, 1972; Leader of Nemet String Trio and Piano Quartet, London; Chamber Music and solo work throughout Australia; Lecturer in Strings, Victorian College of the Arts. *Recordings:* Numerous recordings. *Memberships:* Australian String Teachers' Association; Musical Society of Victoria. *Address:* 7 Merlin Court, Hodgsonvale, MS 852 Queensland 4352, Australia.

NEMETH Geza, b. 1930, Hungary. Violist. *Education:* Studied at the Franz Liszt Academy, Budapest. *Career:* Violist of the Bartok Quartet from 1957; Performances in nearly every European country and tours to Australia, Canada, Japan, New Zealand and the USA; Festival appearances at Adelaide, Ascona, Aix, Venice, Dubrovnik, Edinburgh, Helsinki, Lucerne, Menton, Prague, Vienna, Spoleto and Schwetzingen; Tour of Britain 1986 including concerts at Cheltenham, Dartington, Philharmonic Hall Liverpool, RNCM Manchester and the Wigmore Hall; Tours of Britain 1988 and 1990, featuring visits to the Sheldonian Theatre Oxford, Wigmore Hall, Harewood House and Birmingham; Repertoire includes standard classics and Hungarian works by Bartók, Durko, Bozay, Kadosa, Soproni, Farkas, Szabo and Lang. *Recordings include:* Complete quartets of Mozart, Beethoven and Brahms; Major works of Haydn and Schubert (Hungaroton); Complete quartets of Bartók (Erato); . *Honours:* (with members Bartók Quartet): Kossuth Prize; Outstanding Artist of the Hungarian People's Republic 1981; UNESCO/IMC Prize, 1981. *Address:* c/o Ingpen and Williams Ltd, 14 Kensington Court, London W8 5DN, England.

NEMETH Pal, b. 31 Dec 1950, Szombathely,

Hungary. Flautist; Conductor; Musical Leader; Professor. m. Agnes Simonyi, 30 Aug 1975, 1 son, 1 daughter. *Education:* Study, flute, Music High School, Györ, 1972; Study, conducting, Music High School, Budapest, 1975. *Career:* Györ Symphony Orchestra, 1970-72; Szombathely Symphony Orchestra, 1975-86; Szombathely Conservatory, 1975-; Leader, Capella Savaria, 1981-. *Recordings:* Approximately 40, with Hungaroton; App. 40, with Hungaroton, Quintana, Harmonia Mundi. *Contributions to:* Various Hungarian music publications. *Honours:* Record of the Year, Hungary, 1985, 1986; Record of the Year, Hungary, 1985-89; Liszt prize, 1991. *Memberships:* Hungarian Music Council; Music Foundation, Budapest. *Current Management:* Musilyre, Paris. *Hobbies:* Research, 17th/18th century Hungarian music; Collecting original instruments. *Address:* H-9700 Szombathely, Batsányi u.20, Hungary.

NENDICK Josephine, b. 1940, Kent, England. Singer (Soprano). *Education:* Studied at the Royal College of Music, the Guildhall School of Music with Audrey Langford. *Career:* Sang first at the Aldeburgh Festival, then premiered works by Boulez and Bo Nilsson at Darmstadt. Has sung with such ensembles as Capricorn, Domaine Musical, Ensemble Musique Nouvelles, Music Group of London, Les Percussions de Strasbourg; Festival engagements at Avignon, Berlin, Cheltenham, London (English Bach), Edinburgh, Prades, Royaun, Warsaw; Conductors include Pierre Boulez, Ernest Bour, Charles Bruck, Colin Davis, Michael Gielen, Norman Del Mar, Bruno Maderna, Manuel Rosenthal; Repertoire includes Berg Der Wein; Berio Magnificat, Chamber Music, Circles; Four Popular Songs, Sequenza; Boulez Improvisations sur Mallarmé, Le Marteau sans Maitre, Le Soleil des Eaux; Birtwistle Entractes and Sappho Fragments; Bussotti Le Passion selon Sade; Ravel Chansons Medécasses and 3 Poèmes de Stéphane Mallarmé; Schoenberg Pierrot Lunaire and Das Buch der Hängeneden Gärten; Webern Songs Op 8 and Op 13; Bartók Village Scenes; Works by Barraqué, Smith Brindle, Finnissy, Dillon, Cage, Crumb, Dallapiccola, Stravinsky, Babbitt, Ives and Satie; sang in Bach's Christmas Oratorio, Berlioz Les Troyens (Ascanius), Delius A Mass of Life; Mahler Das Lied von der Erde, Monteverdi L'Incoronazione di Poppae (Drusilla, at Bremen) and Mozart's Requiem and C minor Mass. *Recordings include:* Boulez Le Soleil des Eaux (EMI); Lutyens Quincunx, with the BBC SO (Argo), Barraqué Sequence and Chant après Chant (Valois).

NENTWIG Franz Ferdinand, b. 23 Aug 1929, Duisburg, Germany. Singer (Bass-Baritone). *Debut:* Bielefeld 1962, as Ottokar in Der Freischütz. *Career:* Sang in Darmstadt and Hanover and at the Vienna Volksoper; Venice 1983, as Amfortas in Parsifal; Wagner performances in Munich, Berlin and Hamburg; Tour of Japan 1984 with the Hamburg Company; Metropolitan Opera 1984, as Telramund in Lohengrin; Barcelona 1986, also in Lohengrin; Further appearances in Cologne, Frankfurt, Karlsruhe, Stuttgart and Mannheim; Other roles include Pizarro in Fidelio, Escamillo, Strauss's Jochanaan and Mandryka, Mozart's Count and Don Alfonso, Verdi's Rigoletto and Amonasro and Wagner's Dutchman, Wotan and Gunther; Sang Hans Sachs with the Berlin Staatsoper on tour to Japan, 1987; Salzburg Festival and Turin 1987, as Schoenberg's Moses and as Wotan; Sang Dr Schön in Lulu and Dr Vigilius in Schreker's Der ferne Klang, 1988; Wotan in the first Polish production of the Ring, 1989; Brussels 1990, as Shishkov in From the House of the Dead; Sang La Roche in a new production of Capriccio at Covent Garden, 1991; Season 1991/92 as Wotan at Brussels and Beckmesser at Spoleto. *Recordings include:* Schreker's Der Schatzgräber (Capriccio). *Address:* c/o Théâtre Royal de la Monnaie, 4 Leopolstrasse, B-1000 Brussels, Belgium.

NERSESSIAN Pavel, b. 26 Aug 1968, Ramenskoye, Moscow, Russia. Concert Pianist. *Education:* Studied at Central Music School, Moscow and at Tchaikovsky Conservatory, Graduated 1987. *Career:* Concert tours of Russia from 1972 and more recent engagements in

Spain, Hungary, Italy, France and Ireland, Season 1992-93 in Cannes and Dublin, tour of Japan and appearances in Austria, Great Britain, Ireland, Canada and the USA; Professor of Piano at Moscow Conservatory. *Honour:* Second Prize, Beethoven Competition in Vienna 1985. *Address:* c/o Ingpen and Williams Ltd, 14 Kensington Court, London W8 5DN, England.

NES Jard van, b. 15 June 1948, Holland. Singer (Mezzo-soprano). *Debut:* Sang in Mahler's 2 Symphony under Bernard Haitink at Concertgebouw 1983. *Career:* Appearances in Bach's St Matthew Passion under Nikolaus Harnoncourt and in Mahler's 8th Symphony; Tour of North America with Minnesota Orchestra and Edo de Waart, 1987-88; Further concerts in Paris, London, Oslo, Montreal and Ludwigsburg; Stage debut with Netherlands Opera 1983, as Bertarido in Rodelinda; Double bill of Hindemith's Sancta Susanna and Mörder, Hoffnung der Frauen 1984; Season 1986-87 with parts in Il Ritorno di Ulisse, Die Meistersinger, Magdalena and Tristan und Isolde, Bragaene. *Recordings:* Mozart Requiem, Brahms Alto Rhapsody, Mahler 2nd Symphony and Zemlinsky Lieder; Messiah; Beethoven's Ninth; Handel's Theodora and Das Lied von der Erde. *Address:* c/o De Nederlandse Opera, Waterlooplein 22, 1011 PG Amsterdam, Netherlands.

NESCHLING John, b. 1945, Rio de Janeiro, Brazil. Conductor. *Education:* Studied in Vienna with Hans Swarowsky; Further study with Leonard Bernstein in the USA. *Career:* Engagements with the London, Vienna and Berlin Radio Symphony Orchestras, New York and Israel Philharmonic, the Tonhalle, Zurich and the Italian Radio at Naples and Milan; Opera appearances at Berlin (Deutsche Oper and Staatsoper), Stuttgart, Hamburg and Stockholm; Principal Conductor of the San Carlo Lisbon 1981-88; Music Director of the Teatro Sao Paulo and at St Gallen in Switzerland (Die Zauberflöte 1989); Engaged for Trovatore, Figaro, Pagliacci and Gianni Schicchi at St Gallen; Lucia di Lammermoor, Butterfly, Andrea Chénier and Il Barbiere di Siviglia as guest conductor at the Vienna Staatsoper. *Honours include:* Winner, International Competition for young conductors in Florence, London Symphony Orchestra International Competition. *Address:* Walter Beloch srl, Artists Management, Via Melzi D'Eril, 26 20154 Milan, Italy.

NESS Arthur J., b. 27 Jan 1936, Chicago, Illinois, USA. Musicologist. m. Charlotte A. Kolczynski, 29 Dec 1982. *Education:* BMus, Music Theory, University of Southern California, 1958; AM, Music, Harvard University, 1963; PhD, Musicology, New York University, 1984. *Career:* Assistant professor, University of Southern California, 1964-76; Associate professor, Daemen College, 1976-83; Visiting lecturer, State University of New York, Buffalo, 1983-87; Editor and Music Engraver, 1990-; General Editor, Monuments of the Lutenist Art, 1992-. *Publications:* Lute Works of Francesco Canova da Milano (1497-1543), 1970; The Herwarth Lute Tablatures, 1984; The Königsberg Manuscript (with John M Ward), 1989. *Contributions to:* Major contributor, New Grove Dictionary of Music, 1980, New Harvard Dictionary of Music, 1986. Also periodicals: Journal of American Musicological Society; etc. Le Luth et sa Musique II, 1985; New Grove Dictionary of American Music, 1986; Music in Context: Essays for John M. Ward, 1985. *Address:* 2039 Commonwealth Avenue, Apt. 10, Boston, MA 02135, USA.

NESTERENKO Evgeny, b. 8 Jan 1938, Moscow, USSR. Singer (Bass). *Education:* Studied at the Leningrad Conservatory. *Debut:* Maly Theatre, Leningrad, 1963, as Gremin in Eugene Onegin. *Career:* Sang at Maly and Kirov Theatres until 1971, when he joined the Bolshoy, Moscow; roles there have included Mussorgsky's Boris Godunov and Dosifey and Borodin's Khan Konchak; Vienna Staatsoper and Metropolitan Opera debuts as Boris Godunov, 1974, 1975; La Scala Milan 1978 as King Philip in Don Carlos; Covent Garden 1978, as Don Basilio; Verona Festival 1978, 1985, 1989, 1991; Barcelona 1984, as Zaccaria in Nabucco; Bregenz Festival 1986; Wiesbaden and Savohinna Festival,

1987, as Boris and Ivan Khovanski; Sang Bartók's Bluebeard at Budapest 1988; Munich and La Scala, Milan 1989, as Konchak in Prince Igor and as Ivan Susanin; Sang Basilio at Munich 1990, King Philip in Don Carlos at the 1990 Orange Festival; Appeared as Verdi's Attila at Antwerp, 1993; Concert engagements in music by Mussorgsky and Shostakovich. *Recordings:* Glinka's Ruslan and Ludmilla and Ivan Susanin; Tchaikovsky's Mazeppa, Iolanta and Eugene Onegin; Rachmaninov's Francesca da Rimini; Songs by Shostakovich and Mussorgsky; Suite on Poems of Michelangelo; 14th Symphony by Shostakovich; Verdi Requiem; Verdi Nabucco; Verdi Trovatore; Gounod Faust; Donizetti Don Pasquale and L'Elisir d'Amore; Verdi - Attila and Bela Bartók, Bluebeard's Castle. *Publication:* Evgeny Nesterenko, Thoughts on My Profession, 1985. *Honours:* People's Artist of the USSR, 1976; Prize City of Vercelly (Italy) Viotti D'Oro, 1981; Prize City of Verona Giovanni Zenatello, Italy, 1986; Golden Disc, Melodia, USSR, 1984. *Address:* Frunzenskaja Nab, 24/1, KV 178, Moscow 119 146, Russia.

NETOLICKA Karel, b. 23 Nov 1929, Vilimovec, Czechoslovakia. Musician (Bass Player). m. Libuse Netolicka, 1 son, 1 daughter. *Education:* Studied bass with Rudolf Tulacek, State Conservatory of Music, Brno, Czechoslovakia, 5 years; Janáček Academy of Music, Brno, 4 years. *Debut:* 1953. *Career:* Principal Bass: Symphony Orchestra SOK B, Brno, 1951-52; Army Opera, Prague, 1953-55; Radio Symphony Orchestra, Prague, 1955-68; Radio Symphony Orchestra, Munich, Federal Republic of Germany, 1968-69; Milwaukee Symphony Orchestra, USA, 1969-70 Assistant Principal Bass, 1972-82; Oslo Philharmony, Norway, 1970-71; Assistant Principal Bass, North Carolina Symphony, USA, 1971-72; Principal Bass Radio Symphony Orchestra, Oslo, 1981-83; Oslo Philharmonic Orchestra, 1983-1994; Played Czech Chamber Orchestra, Prague, 1958-68; Played Orchestra da Camera and Chamber Music Society, 1972-82; Guest artist, Oriana Trio, 1977-81, Fine Artc Quartet, 1981-82; Played in world premieres: Bass Concerto dedicated to him, by Jiri Mindl, 1976; Quintet for Bass and 4 Percussionists, by Burt Levy, 1980; Teacher of Bass, Wisconsin University, Kenosha USA, 1977-81; Musikhögskola Arvika-Sweden 1985-92. *Address:* Tante Ulrikkesvei 48a, 0984 Oslo 9, Norway.

NETTL Bruno, b. 14 Mar 1930, Prague, Czechoslovakia. Musicologist. m. Wanda White. 2 daughters. *Education:* BA 1950, MA 1951, PhD 1953, Indiana University, Bloomington; MALS, University of Michigan, Ann Arbor, 1960. *Career:* Instructor in music, 1953-54, Assistant Professor of music 1954-56, 1959-64, Wayne State University, Detroit, Michigan; Associate Professor of music, 1965-67, Professor of music and anthropology, 1967-, University of Illinois, Urbana. *Publications include:* Music in Primitive Culture, 1956; An Introduction to Folk Music in the US, 1960; Cheremis Musical Styles, 1961; Theory and Method in Ethnomusicology, 1964; Folk and Traditional Music of the Western Continents, 1965, 2nd edition, 1972; Daramad of Chahargan, a study of the performance practice of Persian music, 1972; Contemporary Music and Music Cultures, with C Hamm and R Byrnside, 1975; Eight Urban Musical Cultures, 1978; The Study of Ethnomusicology, 1983; The Western Impact on World Music, 1985; The Radif of Persian Music, 1987, 1992; Blackfoot Musical Thought: Comparative Perspectives, 1989; Comparative Musicology and Anthropology of Music, 1991. *Address:* 1423 Cambridge Drive, Champaign, IL 61821, USA.

NEUBAUER Margit, b. 1950, Austria. Singer (Mezzo-soprano). *Education:* Studied in Vienna. *Career:* Sang at Linz Landestheater, 1975-77, notably in 1976 premiere of Der Aufstand by Helmut Eder; Engagements at Frankfurt Opera from 1977, Zurich, 1978-79, Hamburg, 1980-83, Deutsche Oper Berlin, 1982-85; Bayreuth Festival, 1981-86 as Sigrune in Die Walküre and a Flowermaiden in Parsifal; US tour with Deutsche Opera, 1985; Roles have included Cherubino,

Flosshilde, Brigitte in Korngold's Tote Stadt, Annina, Rosenkavalier and the title role in Miss Jule by Bibalo; Many concert appearances, notably in Baroque music. *Recordings:* Parsifal, Bayreuth, 1985; Bach B minor Mass and Handel Utrecht Te Deum.

NEUBURGER Roberto Pablo, b. 22 Nov 1949, Buenos Aires, Argentina. Singer (Baritone). m. Alicia Del Carmen De Rosa, 27 Feb 1974, 1 son, 1 daughter. *Education:* University of Buenos Aires; Private instruction: Singing and Vocal Technique with Professors Galperín, Souza, Maranca; Piano, Harmony, Counterpoint. *Debut:* Schütz, St Matthew Passion (Evangelist), 1977. *Career:* Regular appearances in chamber music performances or music-theatre presentations from early music (German Renaissance lute songs) to premières of contemporary vocal compositions including Dufour's Jeu Delicieux, Olaizola's Ondo, others, 1977-; 1st performances in Buenos Aires of works by Xenakis, Cage, Stockhausen, Crumb, Kagel, Berio, Roqué Alsina, De Pablo, Bussotti, at Centro Cultural Recoleta, Colón Theatre, other venues. *Recording:* Olaizola, Ondo for solo voice, chorus and percussion, after poem by Oliverio Girondo. *Memberships:* Performs for: Asociacion Argentina de Compositores; Cultrum-Compositores Asociados; Agrupación Nueva Música. *Hobbies:* Tennis; Study of psycho-analytic theory especially Lacanian contributions; Study and practice of languages (English, Spanish, German, French, Italian, Russian, Latin, Modern Greek). *Address:* Tronador 3719, 1430 Buenos Aires, Argentina.

NEUENFELS Hans, b. 1941, Krefeld, Germany. Stage Director. *Debut:* Produced Il Trovatore at Nuremberg, 1974. *Career:* Frankfurt Opera, 1976-80, with Macbeth, Aida, Die Gezeichneten by Schreker and Busoni's Doktor Faust; Productions at Deutsche Oper Berlin, 1982-86 have included La Forza del Destino, Rigoletto and Zimmermann's Die Soldaten; Paris Opera 1989 with the premiere of York Höller's Der Meister und Margarita, the last production at the Palais Garnier.

NEUGEBAUER Hans, b. 17 Nov 1916, Karlsruhe, Germany. Singer (Bass); Stage Director. *Education:* Studied in Mannheim and Hamburg. *Debut:* Karlsruhe 1946, as Bett in Zar und Zimmermann. *Career:* Sang Buffo and other roles at Karlsruhe until 1951, Frankfurt Opera, 1951-60, notable as the King in Aida and Mozart's Figaro; Producer of opera from 1955, first at Frankfurt and Heidelberg, then Kassel, 1962-64; Staged premiere of Zimmermann's Die Soldaten at Cologne, Der Rosenkavalier at Glyndebourne, 1965; Guest engagements as Producer at Dusseldorf, Kassel, Mannheim, Basle, Trieste and Chicago. *Address:* c/o Oper der Stadt Koln, Offenbachplatz, 5000 Cologne, Germany.

NEUHOLD Günter, b. 2 Nov 1947, Graz, Austria. Conductor. m. Emma Schmidt, 1 son. *Education:* Hochschule für Musik, Graz: graduated 1969; Conducting studies with Franco Ferrara in Rome and Hans Swarowsky in Vienna. *Career:* Worked in various German opera houses; 1st Kapellmeister in Hannover and Dortmund, 1980-; Guest conductor of the Vienna Philharmonic, and Radio orchestras in Italy; Orchestra Sinfonica dell'Emilia Romagna in Verdi's Requiem, the Choral Symphony and Mahler's 2nd and 5th Symphonies; Music director of the Teatro Regio in Parma from 1981; Principal guest conductor of the Dresden Staatskapelle: performances of Tannhäuser, Ariadne auf Naxos and Elektra, and the first performance of Strauss's Romance for cello and orchestra (1985); TV engagements in France, Germany, Austria, Spain and Moscow; Beethoven's Missa Solemnis at the Vatican in 1985; Guest appearances at the Vienna State Opera (Fledermaus), La Scala Milan and Philadelphia Opera (Don Giovanni); Opera tours to Moscow, Japan and the USA; Music director and chief conductor of the Royal Philharmonic Orchestra of Flanders, 1986; Music director of the Badisches Staatstheater (Karlsruhe) from 1989; Australian debut 1989, with the Melbourne Symphony Orchestra; Season 1988/89 with Die

Entführung, Tristan, Arabella, Rosenkavalier, Zauberflöte, Die Frau ohne Schatten and at the Karlsruhe Opera followed by Capriccio, Ariadne, Elektra, Salome, Meistersinger, Trovatore, Cav and Pag and The Ring, 1993-; Meistersinger, Falstaff, Tiefland, Staatsoper, Berlin; Il Trovatore, Elktra for Leipzig Opera, 1990; tours of Japan and Britain with the Royal Philharmonic Orchestra of Flanders. *Recordings:* Mahler, 2nd and 5th Symphonies; Bruckner, 4th Symphony; Stravinsky, le Sacre du Printemps; La Damnation du Faust; Brahms 7th Symphony; Rihm, Portraitcouc; Stravinsky The Rite of Spring, Berlioz Faust, Brahms 1st and Tchaikovsky 5th Symphonies; Wagner's Ring. *Honours:* First Prize at conducting competitions in Florence (1976), San Remo (1976) and Salzburg (1977). *Address:* Am Pfinztor 13, 76227 Karlsruhe, Germany.

NEUMAN Daniel M, b. 18 Jan 1944, Lausanne, Switzerland. Ethnomusicologist. m. Arundhati Sen, 12 Feb 1971, 2 sons. *Education:* BA, Anthropology 1965, PhD Anthropology 1974, University of Illinois; Violin Private, Ethnomusicology, University of Illinois. *Career:* Director, University of Washington School of Music, 1984-. *Publications:* The Life of Music in North India, The Organisation of an Artistic Tradition, 1980, 90; Co-Editor, Ethnomusicology and Modern Music History, 1990; Contributor to professional publications. *Honours:* Grants and Fellowships. *Memberships:* Society of Ethnomusicology; American Institute of Indian Studies; Society for Asian Music. *Address:* University of Washington School of Music, DN-10 Seattle, WA 98195, USA.

NEUMANN Dagmar, b. 25 Dec 1961, Bohumin, Czech Republic. Musicologist; Violinist. m. Robert Neumann, 31 Jan 1987, 1 son. *Education:* Conservatory, Czech Republic; Musicology, University of Brno, Vienna. *Career:* Interpretation of 18th Century Music; Founder of Ensemble le Monde Classique, Vienna on original instruments; Repertoire: Archive research in Europe; Concerts, TV Recordings, CD Recording; Emphasis on unknown composers. *Recordings:* First complete recording of Fr V Mica oratorium, Abgesungene Betrachtungen 1727, 1994 (Supraphon); Regular cooperation with Czech TV. *Publications:* Die spieltechnischen Besonderheiten der Violin stimmen in Mozart's Betulia Liberata; Das umbekannte Stimmenmaterial zu Gluck's Don Juan in der Wiener National bibiothek; Das Prinzip der Nachahmung instrumentaler Idiomentaler im 17 und frühen 18 Jahrhundert; Bemerkungen zur Violinskordatur im 18 Jahrhundert; Die Violinskordatur in der Musikaliensammlung des Erzbischofs Carl Liechtenstein-Castelcorn in Kremsier (Diss). *Honour:* Prize granted by Minister of Education of Czech Republic, 1986. *Memberships:* International Gluck Society; Austrian Society for Musical Research. *Hobbies:* Arts; Literature; Botany; Violin Tutor. *Current Management:* Osterreichische Akademie der Wissenschaften, Wien. *Address:* Schottenfelds 55-7, 1070 Wien, Austria.

NEUMANN Václav, b. 29 Sept 1920, Prague, Czechoslovakia. Conductor. *Education:* Prague Conservatoire. *Career:* Former Viola Player, Smetana Quartet; Member of Czech Philharmonic Orchestra; Deputised for Rafael Kubelík, 1948; Later conducted Orchestras in Karlovy Vary and Brno; Conductor, Prague Symphony Orchestra, 1956-63; Czech Philharmonic, 1963-64; Chief Conductor, Komische Oper, Berlin, 1957-60; Conducted first local performance of The Cunning Little Vixen (Janáček); Conductor, Leipzig Gewandhaus Orchestra and General Music Director, Leipzig Opera House, 1964-67; Conductor, Czech Philharmonic Orchestra, 1967-68; Chief Conductor, 1968-; Czech Philharmonic Orchestra; Conductor, Munich Chamber Ensemble in Sweden, 1969; Toured Austria, 1970, 1971, 1972, 1974, Romania 1951, 1971, 1973, Federal Republic of Germany 1962, 1965, 1967, 1971, 1973, 1974, 1975, Yugoslavia 1970, Bulgaria 1975, Belgium 1970, Switzerland 1970, 1975, Spain 1975, Finland 1975, UK 1983. *Recordings include:* Dvořák Cello Concerto, with Julian Lloyd Webber, and

Rusalka, with Gabriela Beňačková Dvořák Symphonies, with the Czech Philharmonic; Mahler symphonies Nos 5, 6, 7 and 9; Janáček's The Cunning Little Vixen and The Excursions of Mr Brouček; Brahms Violin Concerto (Suk), Martinů Violin Concertos; Bach harpsichord concertos (Růžičková); Beethoven overtures, Roussel 3rd symphony. *Honours:* National Prize of German Democratic Republic 1966; Honoured Artist 1967; National Artist 1971; Order of Labour 1980. *Address:* Prague 1-Staře Mesto, Siroká 10, Czech Republic.

NEUMANN Wolfgang, b. 20 June 1945, Waiern, Austria. Singer (Tenor). *Education:* Vocal studies in Essen and Duisburg. *Debut:* Bielefeld 1973, as Max in Der Freischütz. *Career:* Sang at Augsburg from 1978, Mannheim from 1980; Maggio Musicale Florence 1983, as Tannhäuser; Appearances in Zurich, Bologna, Munich and Hamburg; Other roles include Wagner's Erik, Rienzi, Schoenberg's Aron (at Barcelona), Tristan, Lohengrin and Siegfried, Verdi's Otello, the Emperor in Die Frau ohne Schatten, Turiddu in Cavalleria Rusticana, Puccini's Calaf and Edgar in Reimann's Lear; Concert repertoire includes Schoenberg's Gurrelieder and Das Lied von der Erde by Mahler; Metropolitan opera debut as Siegfried in the Met's new production of Siegfried by Otto Schenk/James Levine, 1988; Sang the Cardinal in Mathis der Maler at Munich, 1989; Teatro Colon Buenos Aires 1990 as Rienzi, in a concert performance of Wagner's opera. *Address:* c/o Ingpen and Williams Ltd., 14 Kensington Court, London W8 5DN, England.

NEUNTEUFEL Michael, b. 9 Apr 1958, Vienna, Austria. Pianist; Composer; Pedagogue. m. Corinna Neunteufel, 28 Dec 1978, 2 daughters, 2 sons. *Education:* Music Education Degree, Distinction, Hochschule fur Musik und Darstellende Kunst in Vienna, 1978; Military Service, Gardemusik - Oboe; Further studies, University; Studies continued in instrumental pedagogics (MA degree), Hochschule für Musik und Darstellende Kunst Mozarteum in Salzburg, 1987-1990. *Career:* Music Teacher, Feldkirch and Bregenz, 1978-; Concert Appearances on Piano and Harpsichord; Participation at International Choir and Orchestra Workshops; Lecturer at music-pedagogical courses, juror at music competitions, 1988; Radio Appearances, 1982-. *Compositions:* Chamber Music: Meloi, Kammermusik, Trio, Ohne Titel, Suite in M1, Sonata Longa Vogelstimmen; Piano Music: Fantasia Meditation, Impressionen; Vocal Music: Liederzyklen, Motette for mixed choir, Sacred Music for Men-Choir; Music for String Orchestra: Sonatine, Suite; Music for Children: Wind-instruments and Guitars and Violoncello. *Recordings:* Songs for Soprano and Piano by Joseph Marx and Hugo Wolf; Own Compositions: Ohne Titel; Impressionen. *Honours:* Recipient various honours and awards including Composition Prizes, 1st Prize, Salzburg, 1984; 2nd Prize, Dornbirn, 1986 etc. *Hobbies:* Sports; Hiking; Family; Travel. *Address:* Langenerstrasse 14a, A 6900 Bregenz, Austria.

NEVILLE Margaret, b. 3 Apr 1939, Southampton, Hampshire, England. Singer (Soprano). *Education:* Studied with Ruth Packer and Olive Groves in London, Maria Carpi in Geneva. *Debut:* Covent Garden 1961, in Die Zauberflöte. *Career:* Appearances at Sadler's Wells, Scottish Opera, Welsh National Opera, Barcelona, Aix, Berlin and Hamburg; Glyndebourne 1963- 64, in Die Zauberflöte and L'Incoronazione di Poppea; Roles include Mozart's Zerlina, Despina and Susanna, Verdi's Gilda, Donizetti's Norina and Humperdinck's Gretel; Sang in 1967 BBC production of Cavalli's L'Erismena. *Recording:* Hansel and Gretel (HMV). *Honour:* Mozart Memorial Prize 1962. *Hobby:* Walking with Basset Hound called Henry. *Address:* 15 The Avenue, Bedford Park, Chiswick, London W4, England.

NEWAY Patricia, b. 30 Sept 1919, Brooklyn, New York, USA. Singer (Soprano). m. Morris Gesell. *Eduction:* Studied at Mannes College of Music and with Morris Gesell. *Debut:* Chautauqua 1946, as Fiordiligi in Così fan Tutte. *Career:* New York City Center Opera from 1948, notably as Berg's Marie, in Britten's The Rape of Lucretia and in the 1954 premiere of Copland's The Tender Land; Created roles in Menotti's The Consul (1950) and Maria Golovin (1958); Aix-en-Provence Festival, 1952, in Iphigénie en Aulide; Paris Opéra-Comique, 1952-54, notably as Tosca and as Katiusha in Alfano's Risurrezione; Sang with American companies in works by Poulenc, Hoiby and Weisgall; Formed Neway Opera Company, 1960. *Recordings:* The Consul (Brunswick); Cantatas by Buxtehude; Iphigénie en Tauride.

NEWBOULD Brian Raby, b. 26 Feb 1936, Kettering, Northamptonshire, England. University Professor. m. (1) Anne Leicester, 1960, 1 son, 1 daughter, (2) Ann Airton, 1976, 1 daughter.*Education:* BA, General Arts, Bristol, 1957; BMus 1958, MA 1961, Bristol. *Career:* Lecturer, Royal Scottish Academy of Music, 1960-65; Lecturer, University of Leeds, 1965-79; Professor of Music, University of Hull, 1979-; 3 talks on Schubert's Symphonic Fragments on BBC Radio 3, 1983. *Compositions:* Realisations of Schubert Symphonies No.7 in E D729, No.10 in D D936A; Completion of Schubert Symphony No.8 in B minor D759; Orchestration of Schubert's other symphonic fragments; Patrick, for narrator and small orchestra. *Publications:* Schubert and The Symphony: A New Perspective, 1992; Contributor to 19th Century Music, Current Musicology, Music Review, Musical Times and Music and Letters. *Membership:* Royal Society of Arts. *Hobbies:* Travel; Walking; Badminton. *Address:* Department of Music, University of Hull, Hull HU6 7RX, England.

NEWLAND Larry, b. 24 Jan 1935, Winfield, Kansas, USA. Conductor. m. Paula Kahn, 18 Feb 1977, 2 daughters. *Education:* BM, Oberlin Conservatory, 1955; MM, Manhattan School of Music, 1957. *Career:* Violist and Keyboard Player, New York Philharmonic, 1960-74; Assistant Conductor, New York Philharmonic, 1974-85; Music Director, Harrisburg, Pennsylvania, Symphony, 1978-; Guest Conductor, New York City Ballet and Oerchestras worldwide, 1974-. *Recordings:* Numerous broadcasts with New York Philharmonic and other orchestras. *Publications:* Articles in Apprise. *Honours:* Harold Bauer Award, 1957; Koussevitzky Conducting Prize, 1961; Leonard Bernstein Conducting Fellowship, 1962. *Memberships:* President, Conductors Guild; American Symphony Orchestra League; American Federatioon of Musicians; Chamber Music America. *Hobbies:* Tennis; Hiking; Sailing. *Address:* 300 West End Avenue (G-B), New York, NY 10023, USA.

NEWLIN Dika, b. 22 Nov 1923, Portland, Oregon, USA. Musicologist; Composer. *Education:* Michigan State University, BA 1939; UCLA, MA 1941; Columbia University, PhD 1945; Composition studies with Schoenberg and Sessions. *Career:* Teacher at Western Maryland College, 1945-49; Syracuse University, 1949-51; Drew University, 1952-65; North Texas State University, 1963-75; Virginia Commonwealth University from 1978. *Compositions:* Sinfonia for piano, 1947; Piano Trio, 1948; Chamber Symphony, 1949; Fantasy on a Row for piano, 1958; Study in Twelve Tones for viola d'amore and piano, 1959; Atone for chamber ensemble, 1976; Second-Hand Rows for voice and piano, 1978; Three Operas; Piano Concerto; Symphony for chorus and orchestra. *Publications:* Bruckner-Mahler-Schoenberg, 1947, 1978; Schoenberg Remembered, 1938-76 1980; Translations of Leibowitz's Schoenberg et son Ecole 1949; Schoenberg's Style and Idea 1951; Rufer's Das Werk Arnold Schoenbergs 1962.

NEWMAN Anthony, b. 12 May 1941, Los Angeles, California, USA. Harpsichordist; Organist; Composer; Fortepianist; Conductor. m. Mary Jane Flagler, 10 Sept 1968, 3 sons. *Education:* BS, Mannes College; MA Harvard University; DMA, Boston University; Diplome Superiere, Ecole Normale de Musique, Paris. *Debut:* Carnegie Recital Hall. *Career:* Performing artists, USA and Europe 1967- with Detroit Symphony, Boston Symphony, Los Angeles Symphony, NY Philharmonic, as conductor: LA Chamber, Y Chamber, NY, Scottish

Chamber, St. Paul Chamber; Appearances with: Israel Symphony, Calgary Symphony, Colorado Symphony, New jersey Symphony, Youth Chamber Orchestra, Vienna Boys Choir; St Stephens Cathedral, Vienna, Krakow Festival, 1991, 1992. *Compositions:* Concertino for piano and winds, Concerto for viola and strings, Symphony for string orchestra, Concerto for violin and orchestra, Grand Hymns of Awakening for chorus and orchestra and bagpipes, Works for organ solo, Piano quintet, Quartet for flutes, assorted smaller works; Sinfonia: On Fallen Heroes, 1988 (orchestra), Symphony for strings and percussion, 1987; Adagio and Rondo for piano and orchestra; 12 Preludes and Fugues for piano; Variations and Fugue on Bach for piano, Sonata, piano; Symphony 1 and 2 for organ solo. *Recordings:* Over 100 recordings for CBS, Vox and Newport Classic mainly of Bach, Baroque and Classical repertoire; On Fallen Heroes, NC 60140, Brandenburg Concerti, NC. *Publications:* Bach and The Baroque, Pen Dragon Press 1985; Symphony 1: organ, Symphony 2: organ; Three Preludes and Fugues for organ (published TD Ellis Press 1990, Variationa on Bach; 12 Preludes and Fugues for piano; Sonata for piano, Ellis Press, 1992. *Current Management:* ICM-40 W 57th Street, NY, NY 10019, USA. *Address:* State University, NY, Purchase, NY 10577, USA.

NEWMAN Danny, b. 24 Jan 1919, Chicago, Illinois, USA. Arts Publicist and Administrator; International Audience Building Consultant. m. 18 Aug 1948. *Education:* Attended Wright Junior College, 1937. *Career:* Publicist, Lyric Opera of Chicago, 1954-; Publicist, Chicago Opera Company 1946; Audience Development Consultant for musicial organisations throughout the USA, for Ford Foundation and Theatre Communications Group, 1961-81; for Canada Council 1963-85; Consultant to musical organisations in Australia, New Zealand, England, Scotland, Israel, Philippines, Holland, Republic of China, Finland, also on behalf of theatre companies, symphony orchestras, ballet, modern dance and opera companies. *Publication:* Subscribe Now!, 6th edition 1977, publication re the concept of subscription for all performing and disiplines in use in 31 countries by administrators and marketing in managers of arts organisations. *Address:* c/o Lyric Opera of Chicago, 20 North Wacker Drive, Chicago, IL 60606, USA.

NEWMAN William S, b. 6 Apr 1912, Cleveland, Ohio, USA. Professor of Music; Writer; Pianist. m. 20 Dec 1947. *Education:* Western Reserve University; Cleveland Institute of Music; PhD Musicology; Columbia University, 1939. *Career:* Teacher, Cleveland Public Schools and Western Reserve University, 1935-39; Officer, Army Air Forces Intelligence, WWII; Music Faculty, 1945-55, Professor, 1955-62, Alumni Distinguished Professor of Music, 1962-77, Professor Emeritus, 1977-, University of North Carolina; Courses at Bennington College, Columbia Teachers College, Juilliard School of Music, SUNY in Binghamton, Northwestern University, University of Alberta; Soloist, numerous orchestras; Chamber groups; Recitalist throughout USA. *Publications:* Nine books including: The Sonata in the Baroque Era, Vol I, 1959, 4th ed, 1983; The Sonata in the Classic Era, Vol II, 1963, 3rd ed, 1983; The Sonata Since Beethoven, Vol III, 1969, 3rd ed, 1982; Beethoven on Beethoven-Playing His Piano Music His Way, 1988; Performance Practices in Beethoven's Piano Sonatas, 1971; The Pianist's Problems, 1950, 4th edition 1984; Understanding Music 1953, 2nd ed 1961, paperback 1967. *Address:* c/o Music Department, Hill Hall O 20A, The University of North Carolina, Chapel Hill, NC 27514, USA.

NEWSTONE Harry, b. 21 June 1921, Winnipeg, Canada. Conductor. 1 son. *Education:* With Dr Herbert Howells 1943-45; Guildhall School of Music and Drama, 1945-49; Accademia di Santa Cecilia, Rome, 1954, 56. *Debut:* Chamber Orchestra with Haydn Orchestra at Conway Hall, London, 19 May 1949; Full Orchestra at Royal Festival Hall Philharmonia Orchestra, January 1959, *Career:* Formed Haydn Orchestra, 1949; BBC broadcasts from 1951 with Haydn Orchestra, London Philharmonic Orchestra, London Symphony Orchestra, Philharmonia, RPO, BBC Symphony Orchestra and other BBC Orchestras; Guest appearances in Berlin, Copenhagen, Hamburg, Budapest, Prague, Jerusalem, Toronto, Vancouver, Mexico City, Liverpool Philharmonic, Bournemouth Symphony Orchestra; Music Director, Sacramento Symphony Orchestra, California, 1965-78; Director of Music, University of Kent, 1979-86; Professor of Conducting, Guildhall School of Music, 1979-87; Visiting Lecturer, University of the Pacific, Stockton, California, 1988-89. *Recordings:* Bach Brandenburg Concertos, Clavier Concertos (Mindru Katz), Haydn Symphonies, 49, 73, 46, 52, Haydn and Mozart Arias, (Jennifer Vyvyan, Peter Wallfisch), Mozart Symphony 41 and Serenata Notturna, Stravinsky Dumbarton Oaks Concerto, Mozart Opera Overtures, Clarinet and Orchestral works by Copland, Arnold, Lutoslawski, Rossini. *Publications:* Editions of works by Bach, Mozart and Haydn for Eulenburg Edition Miniature Scores, including new edition of Haydn's 12 London Symphonies from 1983-. *Hobbies:* Photography; Painting. *Address:* 4 Selborne Road, Ilford, Essex IG1 3AJ, England.

NGUYEN (Thuyet) Phong, b. 15 July 1946, Vinh Binh, Vietnam. Professor; Musician. *Education:* BA, Philosophy & Literature, University of Saigon, 1974; PhD, Ethno-Musicology, Sorbonne University, Paris, France, 1982. Studied Vietnamese traditional music & Buddhist chant (voice, stringed instruments, percussion), with Master Tram Van Kien, & Venerable Thien Dao, South Vietnam, from age 5. *Debut:* As professional musician, aged 10. *Career:* Performances, traditional Vietnamese music, Asia, Europe, USA, including: NHK Television, 1975; UNESCO Auditorium, Paris, 1980; Palais du Lac, Vichy, France, 1981; Cosful Theatre, Frankfurt, 1984; Metropolitan Museum of Art, New York, 1985; Memorial Art Gallery, Rochester, USA, 1986; Northwest Folklife Festival, USA, 1988; Approx. 16 American university auditoriums. *Composition:* Dan Tranh: 7 improvisations, 1986. *Recordings:* Traditional Music of Vietnam; Vietnamese Music in France & United States; Dan Tranh: 7 Improvisations, Music for Meditation; Traditional Instrumental & Vocal Music of Vietnam. *Publications:* Ritual Music Ensemble & Traditional Custom in South Vietnam, 1974; From Rice Paddies and Temple Yards: Traditional Vietnamese Music, 1989; Music for Children, 1989; World of Sounds in Vietnam: 12 Contemporary Issues, 1989. *Address:* 717 Avondale Street, Kent, Ohio 44240, USA.

NICA Grigore, b. 14 Oct 1936, Ploiesti, Romania. Composer. m. Constantinescu Anca Rodica, 31 Jan 1970. 1 son, 1 daughter. *Education:* Musical Conservatory, Ciprian Porumbescu, Bucharest. *Career:* Violin Professor, Musical High School, Tulcea; Musical Editor, Radio; Has had Broadcasts of work on Radio and TV, 1968-88. *Compositions:* Symphonic piece for orchestra, Aegyssus Op 28, 1978; Four songs for voice and piano, Op 5, 1965; The Brave Soldier Svejk, sequences for voice and chamber music (and others) Op 13, 1971. *Recordings:* Suite for Orchestra Op 16, 1972-73; Three Sketches for Orchestra Op 9, 1969-70; Cantata The Banner Op 14, 1972. *Membership:* Composers Union of Romania. *Hobbies:* Football; Swimming; Volleyball; Table Tennis; Bicycling. *Address:* 7227 Crest Road, Rancho P-V, CA 90274, USA.

NICHOLAS James, b. 25 Jan 1957, Valley Stream, New York, USA. Cellist. *Education:* BM, Cello Performance 1979, Master of Music, Cello Performance 1982, Master of Early Music 1988, Doctor of Music 1988, Indiana University. *Career:* Freelance Cellist and Baroque Cellist; Announcer-Producer, Public Radio WFIU Bloomington. *Compositions:* Mozart-Horn Concerto in E, K494a (a reconstruction); Mozart-Horn Concerto in Eb, K370b & 371 (a reconstruction); Concerto for Natural Horn (A Romantic Horn) Concerto, 1984; Sonata for Natural Horn and Piano, 1985; Panachida (Mnemosynon) for Unaccompanied Natural Horn. *Publications:* JS Bach-Six Sonatas and Partitas; an Urtext edition for viola, 1986; JS Bach-Six suites for Cello; an attempt at an Urtext for Viola, 1986; JS

Bach-Suite No 6, S1012: a performing version for the 4-stringed cello, 1986; Edition of Horn Concerti from the Lund Manuscript, 1989. *Contributions to:* The Horn Call. *Honour:* Performer's Certificate, Indiana University, 1978. *Hobbies:* Animals; Gardening; Photography; Language study. *Address:* c/o WFIU Radio & TV Building, Indiana University, Bloomington, Indiana 47405, USA.

NICHOLAS Michael, b. 31 Aug 1938, Isleworth, Middlesex, England. Cathedral Organist. m. Heather Grant Rowdon, 20 Sept 1975, 2 sons. *Education:* City of London School, 1950-57; Junior Exhibitioner, Trinity College of Music, London, 1950-56; Organ Scholar, Jesus College, Oxford, 1957-60; Private Organ Lessons with John Webster and C H Trevor. *Career:* Organist and Choirmaster, Louth Parish Church, Lincolnshire, 1960-64; Organist and Choirmaster, St Matthew's Church, Northampton, 1965-71; Organist and Master of the Choristers, Norwich Cathedral, since 1971-94; Part-time Lecturer in Music, University of East Anglia, 1971-94; Conductor, Norwich Philharmonic Chorus; Co-Artistic Director, Norwich Festival of Contemporary Church Music; Chief Executive, Royal College of Organists, 1994-. *Compositions:* From the Rising of the Sun, Cantata for SSA and Organ; Except the Lord Keep the City, Lorenz, USA. *Recordings:* Organ Favourites; Great Cathedral Anthems Vol.II; Morley, Parsley and Inglott; Rejos for Joy; The Psalms of David Vol 7; Te Deums and Jubilates Vol.II. *Publications:* Sight Singing, 1966; The Church Music of Benjamin Britten, English Church Music, 1977. *Hobbies:* Bridge; Reading. *Address:* 53A The Close, Norwich, Norfolk NR1 4EG, England.

NICHOLLS David Roy, b. 19 Nov 1955, Birmingham, England. Musicologist; Composer. m. Tamar Hodes, 28 July 1984, 1 son, 1 daughter. *Education:* St John's College, Cambridge with Hugh Wood, 1975-78, 1979-84. Degrees: BA Honours, 1978; MA, 1982; PhD, 1986, all Cantab. *Career includes:* Keasbey Fellow in American Studies, Selwyn College, Cambridge, 1984-87; Lecturer in Music, Keele University, 1987-; Head of Department of Music, Keele University, 1990-; Senior Lecturer in Music, Keele University, 1992. *Compositions include:* Pleiades, 3 groups of instruments, 1979-80; The Giant's Heart, singers & instrumentalists, 1983; Seascape 1, strings, harp, celeste, percussion, 1984; Theatre Piece 3, dancers & instrumentalists, 1986; 2 Japanese Minatures, 8 instrumentalists, 1988-89; String Quartet (NMC D006, 1992), Bingham String Quartet. *Publications:* American Experimental Music, 1890-1940 (Cambridge University Press, 1990; 253 pp). *Address:* c/o Department of Music, Keele University, Keele, Staffordshire ST5 5BG, England.

NICHOLLS Hyacinth, b. 10 Sept 1956, Trinidad. Singer (Mezzo- soprano). *Education:* Studied at the Guildhall School of Music and the National Opera Studio. *Career:* Sang Cherubino, Octavian, Dorabella, Carmen and Dalilah while a student; Professional debut 1985, Wigmore Hall; Sang in the European premiere of Virgil Thomson's Four Saints in Three Acts, Belgium 1983; Glyndebourne Festival from 1986 in Porgy and Bess, L'Enfant et les Sortilèges, Die Entführung, La Traviata, The Electrification of the Soviet Union (as Natasha, premiere) and Katya Kabanova (Varvara); Tour of Italy 1989, with Albert Herring; Other roles include Carmen (Baylis Education Programme at ENO), Fenina in Nabucco and Humperdinck's Gretel; Sang in the Royal Opera's Garden Venture, 1989; Concert repertoire includes Schumann Lieder (recital at St John's with Iain Burnside), Beethoven's Mass in C, the B minor Mass and the St Matthew Passion. *Honour:* Winner, Maggie Teyte International Competition, 1985. *Address:* Ron Gonsalves Management, 10 Dagnan Road, London SW12 9LQ, England.

NICHOLLS Simon, b. 8 Oct 1951, London, England. Pianist. m. Lorraine Wood, 10 May 1976. *Education:* Junior Exhibitioner, 1963-69, Foundation Scholar, 1969-74, Royal College of Music; Diplomas: GRSM, ARCM, LRAM. *Career:* Performances in London, St

Johns, Smith Square, Wigmore Hall, South Bank; Snape Maltings, Aldeburgh; Music Clubs throughout United Kingdom; Broadcasts on BBC and ITV and Radio; Tours and Broadcasts in France, Holland, Germany, Eire, Greece, USA; Piano Teacher, Yehudi Menuhin School, 1976-86; Professor, Royal College of Music, 1985-. *Publications:* The Young Cellist's Repertoire, Recital Repertoire for Cellists with Julian Lloyd Webber. *Recordings:* Simon Nicholls plays Scriabin. *Contributions to:* Piano Journal, Music and Musicians; Tempo. *Memberships:* Musicians Union; EPTA. *Hobbies:* Languages; Reading; Swimming; Record Collecting. *Address:* 49 Grove Road, London N12, England.

NICHOLSON George Thomas Frederick, b. 24 Septt 1949, Great Lumley, County Durham, England. Composer Pianist. m. Jane Ginsborg, 14 June 1984, 1 son, 1 daughter. *Education:* Bede Grammar School, Sunderland, 1961-68; BA Hons 1971, DPhil, 1979, University of York. *Career:* Freelance Teacher in London, (Guildhall School of Music and Drama, Morley College), 1978-88; Recitals with Jane Ginsborg, Soprano, and also with Philip Edwards, Clarinet, Triple Echo; Associate Composer with Lysis, 1984-; Lecturer, Keele University, 1988-. *Compositions:* Orchestral Works: 1132; The Convergence of the Twain; Blisworth Tunnel Blues, (Soprano and Orchestra); Chamber Concerto; Cello Concerto; Flute Concerto; Chamber works includes: Winter Music; Ancient Lights; Movements; Stilleven; 2 String Quartets; Piano Sonata; Brass Quintet; The Arrival of the Poet in the City (Melodrama for actor and 7 musicians); Vocal Music includes: Aubade; Vignette; Peripheral Visions; Alla Luna (Soprano, Clarinet and Piano). *Contributions to:* Articles in Composer Magazine. *Honours:* Yorkshire Arts Composers' Award, 1977; Young Composer, Greater London Arts Association, 1979-80; Triple Echo, 4th Prize Gaudeamus Competition, Rotterdam, 1982. *Membership:* Association of Professional Composers. *Hobbies:* Photography; Jazz; Winemaking. *Address:* Department of Music, Keele University, Keele, Staffs ST5 5BG, England.

NICHOLSON Linda, b. 1955, England. Fortepiano player. *Career:* Member of the London Fortepiano Trio from 1978; Duo with Hiro Kurosaki, Violin; Solo recitals and concertos; Performances of the Viennese classics on original instruments at major festivals and concert series throughout Europe, including Italy, Belgium, France, Germany, Britain and the Netherlands; 12 concert series of the complete piano trios of Haydn, London 1982, to mark the composer's 250th anniversary; Complete piano trios of Beethoven at the Wigmore Hall 1987; Season 1991 with Mozart trios and quartets in London, tour on the Early Music Network and lunchtime recitals at the Elizabeth Hall; Mozart in Barcelona, Lisbon and Germany; Frequent radio broadcasts. *Recordings:* Complete Trios by Mozart; trios by Haydn and Beethoven (Hyperion); Mozart Concertos (Capriccio); Complete violin sonatas by Mozart with Hiro Kuoselui. *Address:* 21 Clapham Common Northside, London SW4 0RG, England.

NICOLAI Claudio, b. 7 Mar 1929, Kiel, Germany. Singer (Baritone). *Education:* Vocal studies with Clemens Kaiser-Breme in Essen and Serge Radamsky in Vienna. *Debut:* Theater am Gärtnerplatz, Munich, 1954. *Career:* Early engagements as a tenor: Baritone from 1956; Appearances at Bregenz Festival, Vienna Volksoper and in Stuttgart, Hamburg, Brussels, Munich, Berlin, Paris, London, Stockholm, Oslo, Prague, Bucharest, Budapest, Zürich, Amsterdam; Member of the Cologne Opera from 1964: sang in the 1965 premiere of Zimmermann's Die Soldaten and visited London 1969, for the British premiere of Henze's Der junge Lord; Oper der Stadt Köln, from 1966; Roles include Giovanni, Count, Papageno, Guglielmo; Tel Aviv 1984, in Die Zauberflöte; Metropolitan Opera, 1988; sang Don Alfonso at Brussels and Barcelona, 1990; Sang Don Alfonso under John Eliot Gardiner at Amsterdam, 1992; Professor at the Musikhochschule, Cologne. *Recordings:* Der Freischütz, Die Fledermaus and Die Kluge (Eurodisc); Highlights from Die Soldaten.

Address: c/o Staatliche Hochschule für Musik, Degobertstrasse 38, 5000 Köln 1, Germany.

NICOLESCO Marianna, b. 28 Nov 1948, Brasov, Romania. Opera Singer (Soprano). *Education:* From age 6-18 studied music and violin in Romania obtaining Diploma with Bruch Concerto; Voice at Conservatorio Santa Cecilia, Rome with Jolanda Magnoni; With Elisabeth Schwarzkopf and Rodolfo Celletti. *Debut:* Televised Concert for Voci Rossiniane International Award 1972 in Milan. *Career:* Sang Violetta in La Traviata in theatres and at Teatro Comunale in Florence 1976, Metropolitan Opera, 1978, appearing as Gilda in Rigoletto, 1978 and Nedda in Pagliacci, 1986; San Francisco Opera 1991; Donna Elvira in Don Giovanni at Munich Staatsoper and Munich Festival 1986- and at La Scala, Milan, 1987, 88, 93; World premiere of Berio's La Vera Storia and Un Re in Ascolto 1986; Dargomijski's Stone Guest 1983, Mozart's Lucio Silla 1984, Luigi Rossi's L'Orfeo 1985, Jommelli's Fetonte 1988; Elettra in Idomeneo at Salzburg Festival 1990, 91, at Dresden Semper Oper 1991 and in Japan 1990; As true soprano with Bellini's Beatrice di Tenda at La Fenice, Venice 1975; As Donizetti's Maria di Rohan at Martina Franca Festival 1988 and Elisabeth Queen of England in Donizetti's Roberto Devereux, Monte Carlo 1992; Performed in leading opera houses worldwide; Concert appearances at Royal Festival Hall London, Carnegie Hall New York, Musikverein Vienna, Concertgebouw Amsterdam, Boston Symphony Hall, Teattro Real Madrid, Cleveland Symphony Hall, Teatro alla Scala. *Recordings:* Numerous recordings. *Honours:* Chevalier of the Order of Arts and Letters by French Government, 1985; UNESCO Medal for Artistic Accomplishments, 1992; Honorary Citizen of Bucharest, 1991; Honorary Member of Romanian Academy, 1993; Honorary Member of Romanian National Committee for UNICEF, 1993; President and Founder of The Romanian Atheneum International Foundation in New York. *Address:* c/o Wolfgang Stoll, Martius Str 3, 80802 Munich, Germany.

NICOLET Auréle, b. 22 Jan 1926, Neuchâtel, Switzerland. Flautist; Professor of Music. m. Christiane Gerhard. *Education:* Studied in Zurich with André Jaunet and Willy Burkhard; Paris Conservatoire with Marcel Moyse and Yvonne Drapier. *Career:* First flute in Wintherthur Orchestra, 1948-50; Solo flautist with Berlin Philharmonic, 1950-59; Professor, Berlin Musik Hochschule, 1950-65; Later taught in Freiburg and Basle; Concert appearances throughout Europe as soloist with orchestra and with chamber ensembles; Composers who have written for him include Denisov, Takemitsu, Kelterborn and Huber. *Recordings include:* Works by Bach conducted by Karl Richter; Quartets and Concertos by Mozart. *Honours:* First Prize, Paris Conservatoire; First Prize, International Competition, Geneva 1948; Music Critics' Prize, Berlin, 1963.

NICOLL Harry, b. 1952, Coupar Angus, Perthshire, Scotland. Singer (Tenor). *Education:* Studied at the Royal Scottish Academy of Music and Drama. *Career:* Sang with Scottish Opera Go Round from 1979 as Nemorino, Ferrando, Alfredo and Ramiro; Appearances with Welsh National Opera as Valetto in L'Incoronazione di Poppea, Vasek, the Idiot in Wozzeck, and Brighella and the Dancing Master in Ariadne; English National Opera in Pacific Overtures, Street Sceene and The Mikado; Has sung with Scottish Opera in their Rossini Double Bill, as The Lover in the premiere of Judith Weir's The Vanishing Bridegroom, 1990, as Bardolph and as Almaviva; Other engagements with Opera North (Acis and Galatea and L'Heure Espagnole); Park Lane Group (La Finta Semplice); Glyndebourne Touring Opera (Pedrillo in Die Entführung); English Bach Festival in Versailles (Thespis in Platée by Rameau); Kammeroper Berlin (The Lighthouse, Il Re Pastore and Il Matrimonio Segreto); La Fenice Venice (Zaide); Frankfurt and Jerusalem (Roderigo in Otello); Cologne Opera, Vasek, Bartered Bride; Opera Voor Vlaanderen, Pedrillo, Die Entfuhrung; New Israeli Opera, Tel Aviv, Almaviva, Barbiere; Théâtree des Champs Elysées as Medor in Roland (Lully); Has sung in several operas at the

Batignano Festival; Concert appearances in the UK and abroad. *Address:* c/o Ron Gonsalves, 10 Dagnan Road, London, SW12 9LQ, England.

NICOLSON Robina, b. 11 Aug 1940, St Boswells. Musician (Clarinettist). m. Paul Nicolson, 12 Jan 1961, 3 sons, 2 daughters. *Education:* Clarinettist ARCM perf, Royal College of Music; MMus, Reading, 1987. *Career:* Royal Opera House Education Dept; opera in schools and community groups; 7 original music theatre pieces. Royal National Theatre, The Pied Piper, 1986-88, children's director, 1988. Berkshire Young Musicians Trust, Junior Opera: Bendigo Boswell, Smike, The Piper of Hamelin, Brilliant the Dinosaur. National Youth Wind Orchestra, Music Staff, Co-founder with Gail Rosier of Acorn Music Theatre Co. in 1991, original music and theatre for 5-18 year olds. *Honour:* Arthur Somervell Prize for Woodwind, 1960. *Address:* 11 Kings Road, Henley-On-Thames, Oxon RG9 2DW, England.

NICULESCU Stefan, b. 31 July 1927, Moreni, Romania. Composer; Musicologist; Professor. m. Colette Demetrescu, 22 June 1952. *Education:* Conservatory of Music, Bucharest; Studio Siemens for Electronic Music, Munich, Federal Republic of Germany. *Debut:* Bucharest, 1953. *Career:* Professor of Composition and Music Analysis, Bucharest Conservatory of Music, Bucharest, Romania; Guest, Deutscher Akademischer Austauschdienst, Berlin, Federal Republic of Germany, 1971-72. *Compositions:* 3 Symphonies, 1956, 1980 and 1984; 3 Cantatas, 1959, 1960 and 1964; Unisonos for orchestra, 1970; The Book With Apolodor opera for children, 1975; Omaggio a Enescu e Bartók for orchestra, 1981; Recorded: Formants for orchestra; Scenes for orchestra; Symphonies for 15 soloists; Inventions for clarinet and piano; Aphorisms D'Héraclite for choir; Triplum 2 for clarinet, cello and piano; Ison 1 for 14 soloists; Ison 2 concert for winds and percussion; Echoes for violin; Synchronie 1 for 2-12 instruments; Symphony 2; Heteromorphie for orchestra; Tastenspiel for piano. *Publications:* George Enescu, monography, (co-author), 1971; Reflections About Music, 1980. *Contributions to:* Muzica; Revue Roumaine D'Histoire de l'Art; Arta; Studii de Muzicologie; Muzyka. *Address:* Intrarea Sublocotenent Staniloiu 4, 73228 Bucharest 39, Romania.

NIEHAUS Manfred, b. 18 Sept 1933, Cologne, Germany. Composer. *Education:* Studied with Zimmermann at Cologne. *Career:* Dramaturg and Director at Wurttemberg Landesbuhne, Esslingen am Neckar, 1963-65; Editor for Westdeutsche Rundfunk, Cologne from 1967; Freelance Composer from 1989. *Compositions:* Music theatre works Bartleby, Cologne and Berlin, 1967; Die Pataphysiker, Kiel, 1969; Maldoror, Kiel, 1970; Die Badewanne, Bonn, 1973; It Happens, Bonn, 1973; Sylvester, Stuttgart, 1973; Tartarin von Tarascon, Hamburg, 1977; Die Komponiermaschine, Nuremberg, 1980; Das Verlorene Gewissen, Gelsenkirchen, 1981; Das Christbaumbrettl, Cologne, 1983; Die Geschichte vom Riesen und dem kleinen Mann im Ohr, Emmerich, 1984. *Honour:* Cologne Forderpreis, 1966. *Address:* GEMA (Germany), c/o PRS Ltd Member Registration, 29-33 Berners Street, London W1P 4AA, England.

NIEHOFF Beatrice, b. 1952, Mannheim, Germany. Singer (Soprano). *Career:* Sang at Karlsruhe and Darmstadt, 1977-82; Later appearances in Hamburg, Zurich, Berlin and Vienna, notably as Mozart's Constanze, Countess, Pamina and Fiordiligi, Dvořák's Rusalka, Weber's Agathe and Wagner's Elsa; Modern repertory includes roles in operas by Fortner (Bluthochzeit), Zemlinsky (Der Kreidekreis), Hindemith (Mathis der Maler) and Massimilia Doni (Schoeck); In 1988 sang Eva in a new production of Die Meistersinger at Essen and the Protagonist in the German premiere of Berio's Un Re in Ascolto (Dusseldorf); Returned to Dusseldorf, 1989, as Cleopatra in Giulio Cesare by Handel.

NIELSEN Inga, b. 2 June 1946, Holboeke, Seeland,

Denmark. Singer (Soprano). m. Robert Hale, 3 daughters. *Education:* Music Academy Vienna; Musikhochschule Stuttgart. *Debut:* Gelsenkirchen, 1973. *Career:* Sang in Munster, 1974-75; Bern, 1975-77; Member of Frankfurt Opera, 1978-83; Ludwigsburg Festival, 1978, as Zerlina in Don Giovanni; Dusseldorf, 1980, as Blonde in Die Entführung and Norina in Don Pasquale; New York City Opera, 1980, as Johann Strauss's Adele and Nannetta in Falstaff; Schwetzingen, 1983, in the premiere of Henze's The English Cat; Stuttgart, 1984, as Donna Elvira in Don Giovanni; Guest appearances in Hamburg, Aachen and Oslo; has sung Donizetti's Lucia in Pittsburgh, Oslo and Hamburg, 1984-87; Wexford Festival, 1986, as Amenaide in Rossini's Tancredi; Palermo 1987, as Marguerite; sang Mozart's Constanze at Salzburg and Covent Garden, 1987-89; Cologne and Strasbourg, 1989, as Ilia and Fiordiligi; sang Christine in the Italian premiere of Strauss's Intermezzo, Bologna, 1990; Munich Festival, 1990, as Aspasia in Mitridate; Season 1992 as Marzelline at Zurich and Gilda at Oslo. *Recordings:* Zerlina in Don Giovanni, from Luwigsburg; Flowermaiden in Parsifal (Deutsche Grammophon); The Seven Last Words on the Cross by Haydn; Zemlinsky's Der Zwerg (Schwann). *Address:* Pflugstevistr 20, CH-8703 Erleubech, Switzerland.

NIELSEN Svend, b. 20 Apr 1937, Copenhagen, Denmark, Composer. *Education:* Studied music, University of Copenhagen; Music Theory, Royal Academy of Music, Copenhagen. *Career:* Teacher, Royal Academy of Music, Aarhus, 1967-. *Compositions:* Orchestral: Metamorphoses, 1968; Nuages, 1972; Symphony, 1978-79; Nocturne, 1981; Concerto for Violin and Orchestra, 1985; Nightfall for Chamber Orchestra, 1989; Voice and Instruments: Three of Nineteen Poems, 1962; Duets, 1964; Romances, 1970-74; Chamber Cantata, 1975; Sonnets of Time, 1978; Ascent Towards Akseki, 1979; Choral Music: Motets, 1982; Imperia, 1982; Jorden, 1983; Piano Music: Romantic Piano Pieces, 1974; 5 Inventions, 1983; Chamber: Rondo for Flute Quintet, 1986; String Quartet, 1987; Black Velvet, Clarinet Quintet, 1988; Variations for Double Quintet, 1989; Windscapes for Brass Quintet, 1990; Aria for orchestra, 1991. *Honour:* Carl Nielson Prize, 1981. *Address:* Royal Academy of Music, 8210 Aarhus V, Denmark.

NIELSEN Tage, b. 16 Jan 1929, Frederiksberg, Denmark. Professor; Composer. m. Aase Grue-Sorensen, 14 Oct 1950, 1s. 2d. *Education:* Musicology, University of Copenhagen, 1947-55; Additional studies in USA 1974, Israel 1972 and Italy 1975. *Debut:* As Composer 23 Oct 1949, UNM Festival, Stockholm. *Career:* Deputy Head of Music Department, Radio Denmark, 1957-63; Director, Professor, Royal Academy of Music, Aarhus, 1963-83; Chair of Board, Danish State Art Foundation, 1971-74; Director, Accademia di Danimarca, Rome, 1983-89. *Compositions:* Two Nocturnes, piano, 1961; Il gardino magico, orchestra, 1968; Three Character Pieces and an Epilogue, piano, 1972-74; Passacaglia, orchestra, 1981; Laughter in the Dark, opera, 1987-91; Paesaggi, 2 pianos, 1985; Three Opera Fragments, 13 instruments, 1986; The Frosty Silence in the Gardens, guitar, 1990. *Publications:* Fra Palestrina til Berio in Danmark og Italien, 1989; Articles on Langgaard, Alban Berg's Lulu and Lutoslawski a o in Dansk Musiktidsskrift. *Honours:* The Anker Prize, 1975; The Schierbeck Prize, 1992. *Hobby:* Gastronomy. *Current Management:* Managing Director, The Society for Publication of Danish Music. *Address:* Peter Bangsvej 153, 2000 Frederiksberg, Denmark.

NIEMAN Alfred (Abbe), b. 25 Jan 1913, London, England. Composer; Pianist. m. Aileen Steeper, 2 sons. *Education:* RAM; FRAM; ARAM; FGSM. *Career:* Concert appearances in 2 piano team; performances with British Broadcasting Corporation, 5 years; Professor of Composition and Piano, Lecturer, Guildhall School of Music. *Compositions:* (Recorded): 2nd Piano Sonata; 9 Israeli Folk Songs; Chromotempera for cello and piano, Paradise Regained, for cello, piano and Chinese cymbals; Tongs and Bones, for trombone solo. (Other Compositions include): 2nd Symphony; Arie Fantasie for organ; Variations and Finale for piano; 2 Serenades for piano; Adam (cantata) for tenor, 4 trombones, 5 percussion and piano; various songs; Sonata for guitar (commission from Gilbert Biberian through The Arts Council) first performed Purcell Room 2 Feb 1986; Soliloquy for solo cello (commissioned by Stefan Popov, 1st performed, St. John's Smith Square, 16 Apr 1986, also was performed by him six times in Bulgaria); Rilke Song Cycle for string quartet, soprano voice; Chamber Sonatas for violin, cello, piano; Suite for piano; Summer Night, Accordion solo; Three Expressions for Unaccompanied Chorus; Chromotempera, concerto for cello and piano. *Recordings:* Canzona for Quintet, Flute, Oboe, Clarinet, Violin, Piano. *Publications:* Schumann (Symposium); Tension in Music (Symposium); The Earth It Is Your Shoe, Solo Guitar (New). *Contributions to:* A Fresh Look At Webern (The Composer No. 30) Composers Guild of Great Britain. *Honours include:* McFarren Gold Medal. *Memberships:* CGGB; British Association of Music Therapy; Consultant, National Association for Gifted Children. *Hobby:* Cricket. *Address:* 21 Well Walk, London NW3, England.

NIEMELA Hannu, b. 17 Apr 1954, Lohtaja, Finland. Singer (Baritone). *Education:* Graduated Sibelius Academy, Helsinki, 1983. *Debut:* Zurich Opera 1985, as Marullo in Rigoletto. *Career:* Member of Karlsruhe Opera, 1985-89, Staatstheater Mainz from 1989; Further study with Kim Borg and Hans Hotter; Guest engagements at Savonlinna and Schwetzingen Festivals and at Berne, Basle, Mannheim, Dresden, Prague, Leningrad and Strasbourg; Karlsruhe, 1986 in premiere of Der Meister und Margarita by Rainer Kunad; Other roles have included Mozart's Count, Papageno and Don Giovanni, Gluck's Orestes, Escamillo, Wozzeck and Demetrius in A Midsummer Night's Dream; Verdi: Macbeth, Falstaff; Noted concert artist. *Address:* c/o Staatstheater, Gutenbergplatz 7, 6500 Mainz, Germany.

NIEMOTKO Krystyna Anna, b. 22 May 1938, Szczebrzeszyn, Poland. Concert Pianist; Piano Professor. m. 2 June 1968, 2 sons, 1 daughter. *Education:* Frederic Chopin Academy of Music, Warsaw, 1955-61; Master Classes in piano performance; Vacanze Musicale, Venice, Italy, 1964; Bartok Seminar, Budapest, Hungary, 1967; Manhattan School of Music, New York, USA, 1974; Boston University, Boston, 1975. *Debut:* Wroclaw, Poland, 1955. *Career:* Concert pianist, solo and with orchestras in Australia, Bulgaria, Czechoslovakia, Poland, UK and USA; Assistant and Associate Professor of Music, Frederic Chopin Academy of Music, Warsaw, Poland, 1969-; Piano Professor, Ravenswood School for Girls, Sydney, Australia, 1987-; Jury member International Competition for Pianists, Seregno, Italy, 1981; International Competition for Pianist and Singers, Enna, Sicily, 1973, 1979, 1980, 1981. *Recordings:* Recordings for radio in Australia, Germany, Italy, Poland, UK and USA. *Publications:* Co-Editor, Frederic Chopin Works, 1961-67. *Address:* 51 Demetrius Road, Rosemeadow, NSW 2560, Australia.

NIENSTEDT Gerd, b. 10 July 1932, Hanover, Germany. Bass-Baritone. *Education:* Studied with Otto Kuhler in Hanover. *Debut:* Bremerhaven 1954. *Career:* Sang in Gelsenkirchen, 1955-59, Wiesbaden, 1959-61 and Cologne, 1961-72; Vienna Staatsoper, 1964-73; Bayreuth Festival, 1962-75, as Klingsor, Biterolf, Kothner, Donner, Hunding and Gunther; Sang Wozzeck in Wieland Wagner's last production, Frankfurt, 1966 and in the 1965 premiere of Die Soldaten by Zimmermann, Cologne; Intendent of the Landestheater Detmold, 1985-87; Guest appearances in Milan, Berlin, Paris, Buenos Aires, Chicago, San Francisco, Montreal and Zurich; Also heard as concert singer; Worked as Administrator at Bielefeld opera house from 1973; Detmold Landestheater 1985-. *Recordings:* Tannhäuser, Parsifal, Die Meistersinger, Die Walküre and Das Rheingold from Bayreuth (Philips); Mozart's Requiem; Mahler, Das klagende Lied; Salome (HMV). *Address:* c/o Landesheater, 4930 Detmold, Germany.

NIES Otfrid, b. 5 May 1937, Giessen, Germany.

Violinist; Writer on Music. m. Christel Nies-Fermor, 7 Sept 1961, 2 sons, 2 daughters. *Education:* Violin studies with Max Rostal, 1960-64, Chamber Music with Rudolf Kolisch. *Career:* Member, National Theatre Orchestra, Mannheim, 1964-66; Leader, Stadttheaterorchester Hagen, 1966-71; Leader, Staatstheaterorchester Kassel, 1971-; Presentation of music for player piano by Conlon Nancarrow at documenta 7, Kassel, 1982; Founder, Archiv Charles Koechlin, 1984. *Recordings:* Quintets, op 80 piano and strings, op 156 with flute and harp, by Charles Koechlin; Music for violin and player piano by Conlon Nancarrow. *Publications:* Orchestration of Quatre Interludes, op 214 for the Ballet Voyages, op 222 (1947) by Charles Koechlin, 1986. *Contributions to:* Many articles about Charles Koechlin in Das Orchester, Neue Zeitschrift fuer Musik, Fonoforum. *Memberships:* Association Charles Koechlin, Paris; Internationale Schoenberg-Gesellschaft, Vienna. *Hobbies:* Unknown music; Unknown composers; Contemporary music. *Address:* Otfrid Nies, Saengerweg 3, D-3500 Kassel, Germany.

NIGG Serge, b. 6 June 1924, Paris, France. Composer. m. Micheline Nourrit 1950, 1 daughter. *Education:* Paris Conservatory 1941-46, with Messiaen; Studied with Leibowitz 1945-48. *Career:* Freelance composer; Professor of orchestration at the Paris Conservatory. *Compositions include:* 3 sonatas for piano; 1 sonata for violin solo; 1 sonate for violin and piano; 4 Melodies on poems of Paul Eluard; Concerto for viola and orchestra; 2 Piano Concertos; Concerto for flute and strings; Mirrors for William Blake for orchestra; Fulgur for orchestra; Million d'Oiseaux d'Or for orchestra; Du Clair au Sombre song cycle for soprano and orchestra to poems by Paul Eluard; Symponic poems Timour and Pour un poète captif; Violin Concerto; Jérôme Bosch-Symphony; Poème Pour Orchestre. *Recordings:* 1st Piano Concerto (Orchestre National de France); Violin Concerto (Christian Ferras); Visages d'Axel; Le Chant du Depossede; Jérôme Bosch-Symphonie; Arioso for violin and piano; String Quartet; Poème for orchestra. *Honours:* Prix Italia 1958; Grand Prix Musical de la Ville de Paris, 1974; Grand Prix de la Société des Auteurs, Compositeurs et Editeurs de Musique, 1978; Prix Florence Gould, Academie des Beaux-Arts, 1976 and 1983; Prix de la meilleuse crèation contemporian pour le Poèe pour orchestre, SACEM, 1991. Officier des Arts et des Lettres, 1975; Chevalier de l'ordre National du Mérite, 1973; Chevalier de la Legion d'Honneur, 1980; Prix Rene Dumesril, 1987; Six times Grand Prix du Disque. *Memberships:* President de la Societe Nationale de Musique; 1957-89; Elu membre de l'Academie des Beaux-Arts, 1989. *Address:* 15 bis rue Darcel, 92100 Boulogne sur Seine, France.

NIGRO Susan, b. Chicago, Illinois, USA. Contrabassoonist. *Education:* BME, MM, Northwestern University; MA from Roosevelt University. *Career:* Orchestral experience with Civic Orchestra of Chicago and at Tanglewood Music Center; Winner 1993 Pro Musicis Career Development Award; Selected to perform at 1992 South Carolina Arts Commission Showcase and was finalist in the 1991 Chicago Park District Talent Search, performing in the Showcase Concert at the Petrillo Music Shell; Teacher of Bassoon at VanderCook College and at Saint Xavier University; Excerpts from her 1990 recitals were on the air in Australia with 2MBS-FM on 21 June 1991 and March 1993; During the past 4 years she played 20 solo recitals, did solo appearances with several local bands and orchestras, premiered over a dozen new works and was listed on the Artists Rosters in the states of Montana, Alabama, South Carolina, North Dakota, Illinois, Kansas, Nevada and North Carolina; In 1991 & 1993 she was honoured to be featured artist at the 20th & 22nd annual conventions of the International Double Reed Society; In addition to recitals she also offers master classes, workshops and lecture-demonstrations; She has worked with the Chicago Symphony Orchestra, St Paul Chamber Orchestra and Fort Wayne Philharmonic as well as extensive freelancing in the Chicago area; Her current affiliations include the Chicago Chamber Orchestra, Fox River Valley Symphony, Harper Symphony, Illinois

Philharmonic, Lake Forest Symphony, New Philharmonic of DuPage, NW Indiana Symphony, Northbrook Symphony, Oak Park River Forest Symphony and River Cities Philharmonic. Founder and Contrabassoonist of the Chicago Bassoon Quartet. *Publications:* Laffs from the Bottom of the Pit, 1992; More Laffs from the Bottom of the Pit, 1994. *Honour:* Henry B Cabot Prize for Performance, Tanglewood Music Center. *Address:* 179 W Quincy Street, Riverside, IL 60546, USA.

NIJENHUIS Emmie te, b. 11 Nov 1931, Bussum, the Netherlands. Musicologist. 1 son. *Education:* Utrecht Conservatory of Music, Piano, 1955; MA, Western Musicology 1964, PhD, Indian Musicology, 1970, Utrecht University. *Career:* Teacher of Western Musicology, Conservatory, Zwolle, 1958-61; Guest lectures at University of Amsterdam, 1975, Oxford, 1978, Basel, 1984; Reader, Indian Musicology, Utrecht University, 1964-88. *Publications:* Dattilam: A Compendium of Ancient Indian Music, 1970; Indian Music: History and Structure, 1974; The Ragas of Somanatha, 1976; Musicological Literature, 1977; Muttusvami Diksitar's Cycle of Hymns to the Goddess Kamala, 1987; Sangitaśiromani, A Medieval Handbook of Indian Music, 1992. *Contributions to:* Various articles on Indian Musicology in: Journal of Music Academy; Journal of Royal Asiatic Society; Acta Orientalia Neerlandica; Musikgeschichte in Bildern II, 8: W Kaufmann, Alt-Indien; Harmonie en Perspectief (Festschrift Eduard Reeser, Deventer 1988); Journal of Oriental Research, Madras, 1992; Festschrift für Josef Kuuckertz, Salzburg 1992. *Membership:* Royal Dutch Academy of Sciences. *Hobby:* Drawing. *Address:* Verlengde Fortlaan 39, 1412 CW Naarden, The Netherlands.

NIKIPROWETZKY Tolia, b. 25 Sept 1916, Feodosia, Russia. Composer; Ethnomusicologist. m. Ariane Mouren 5 May 1945. *Education:* Studied Harmony at Marseilles Conservatory, 1935-37; Counterpoint and Fugue with Simone Ple-Caunade in Paris; History with Louis Laloy; After the war Composition with Rene Leibowitz. *Career:* Musical Chronicler in Cahiers du Sud, 1947-50; Musical Director, Radio Morocco, Rabat, 1950-55; Head of Record Library with OCORA, 1956-69; Head Associate of Symphonic Department of ORTF Paris, 1969-72; Head of Creation Department of ORTF, then Radio France, 1972-75. *Compositions:* Hommage a Antonio Gaudi for orchestra, 1965; Treize Etudes for piano, 1966; Violin Concerto, 1980; Le Sourire de l'Autre, chamber opera, 1979; Ode Funebre, choir, orchestra, 1985. *Recordings:* Numerous recordings. *Publications:* Trois Aspects de la Musique Africaine, 1967; La Musique dans La Vie, 2 volumes with 21 specialists, Vol 1 1967, Vol 2, 1969. *Address:* 65 Rue La Fontaine, 75016 Paris, France.

NIKKANEN Kurt, b. Dec 1965, Hartford, Conn, USA. Concert Violinist. *Education:* Began violin stuidies aged 3; Boston University Prep Division with Roman Totenberg; Juilliard School New York with Dorothy DeLay: graduated 1986. *Career:* Won first competition 1976; Carnegie Hall debut 1978, playing the Saint-Saëns Introduction and Rondo Capriccioso; 1980 played the Paganini Ist Concerto with the New York Philharmonic; Bruch Ist Concerto with the Boston Pops; Appearances with the Hartford Symphony, Colorado Philharmonic, New Jersey Chamber Orchestra and Aspen Chamber Symphony; European debut 1981, with recital tour of Finland; July 1988 Cleveland Orchestra debut in the Glazunov Concerto; Sept 1988 UK debut playing the Elgar Concerto with the Royal Liverpool Philharmonic conducted by Libor Pesek; toured in Venezuela; debuted at the Kennedy Center in Washington DC; Further engagements with the Helsinki Philharmonic under James DePreist, and an orchestral/recital tour of Japan; Season 1990-91 made debuts in London, Munich and Barcelona; Season 1991-92 engagements with the San Francisco, New Orleans and Portland Symphonies; Recital debuts in Vancouver, Berlin and Paris; Played the Glazunov Concerto at the 1991 Promenade Concerts, London. *Recordings include:*

Tchaikovsky and Glazunov Concertos (Collins Classic). *Hobbies:* Tennis; Physical Fitness.*Address:* c/o Harrison/Parrott Ltd., 12 Penzance Place, London W11 4PA, England.

NIKODEMOWICZ Andrzej, b. 2 Jan 1925, Lvov, Poland. Composer; Pianist. m. Kazimiera Maria Grabowska, 6 July 1952, 1 son, 1 daughter. *Education:* Studied with Adam Soltys, Faculty of Composition, Conservatory of Lvov, 1950; Studied with Tadeusz Majerski, Faculty of Piano, 1954. *Career:* Professor of Composition and Piano, Conservatory of Lvov, 1951-73; Dismissed by reason of religious convictions; 1980-: Professor of Faculty of Music, University of Maria Curie-Sklodowska in Lublin; Professor, Faculty of Church Musicology, Catholic University, Lublin. *Compositions:* Extensive list of compositions including: Piano works, Ekspresje, 66 miniatures for piano solo, 1959-60; Violin works; Songs for voice and piano; Chamber Concerto, 1968; Composizione sonoristica, for violin, violoncello and piano, 1966-71; Musica concertante per tre, for flute, viola and piano, 1966-67; 3 nocturns for trumpet and piano, 1964; Symphonic music, 1974-75; Concertos for violin and symphony orchestra, 1973; choir music, including 500 Polish Christmas carols; Theatre Music, (Pantomime) Glass Mountain, 1969; Magnificat for choir of women and orchestra, 1977-78; Evening Offering for choir and string orchestra, 1980; 5 Lullabies for violin and piano, 1991; 4 songs for soprano, trumpet and organ, text: George Herbert, 1992; Variations, Ave maris Stella, for organ 1993. *Recordings:* Two cantatas, cycle of songs. *Contributions to:* Several reviews in Ruch Muzyczny. *Honour:* Prize of Saint Friar Albert. *Membership:* Polish Composers Society; ZAIKS. *Hobbies:* Astronomy; Painting; Folk music. *Address:* ul Paryska 4/37, 20-854 Lublin, Poland.

NIKOLAJEV Vladimir, b. 15 Dec 1953, Nikolajev Town, Russia. Composer. m. Alparova Nailja, 6 June 1987, 1 son. *Education:* School of Arts, Ufa, 1971-76; Gnesin Musical Institute, Moscow, 1976-81; Aspirant, Moscow Conservatoire, 1982-85. *Debut:* Moscow, 1981. *Career:* Gnesin Concert Hall, Moscow, 1981; Many songs broadcast on radio, 1987-; Art Institute Concert Hall, Ufa, 1984; Participant: Saratov International Competition of Young Composers, 1988; Meeting on Moscow TV, 1989; Participant, Lutoslawski Competition, Warsaw, Apr 1991; Music for The Blue Eye of Siberia, documentary film about Lake Baikal. *Compositions:* Hymn for violin solo, 1987; Cry and Choral for violin and piano, 1988; Serenade capriccio for accordian, 1990; Legend about beautiful maiden Salimakai, 1991. *Recordings:* Ballade for accordian and orchestra, record, 1989; Over 10 song recordings for radio. *Contributions to:* Soviet Musik magazine, 1989; Newspapers. *Honours:* Winner, Magic Cristall, Russia Modern Song Competition, 1989; 4th Place Winner, Concerto for Orchestra, 1st Lutoslawski Competition, 1991; 1st Prize, Lili Boulanger Memory Fund, Boston, USA. *Membership:* Union of Composers, Russia. *Address:* Dirizabielnaja si 24 ap 6, Dolgoprudny, Moscow area, Russia.

NIKOLOV Nikola, b. 1924, Sofia, Bulgaria. Singer (Tenor). *Education:* Studied in Sofia. *Debut:* Varna 1947 as Pinkerton. *Career:* Sang at Varna until 1953 then studied further in Moscow and sang at Sofia National Opera from 1955; Appearances in Moscow and Leningrad throughout the 1950s, La Scala Milan 1958, as Jenik in The Bartered Bride; Season, 1958-60 at Wexford Festival, the Vienna Staatsoper and Covent Garden, Radames; State Operas of Berlin and Hamburg, Naples 1963 as Vasco de Gama in L'Africaine, New York Metropolitan 1960, as Don José; Sang further in Munich, Barcelona, Geneva, Belgrade, Budapest and Bucharest; Other roles included Manrico, Turiddu, Cavaradossi, Calaf and Don Carlos. *Recordings:* Aida and Carmen, Boris Godunov, L'Africaine. *Address:* c/o Bayerische Staatsoper, Postfach 100148, 8000 Munich 1, Germany.

NILES Don William, b. 26 Jan 1955, Chicago, Illinois, USA. Ethnomusicologist. m. Anna Solomon, 2 sons, 3 daughters. *Education:* BMus, Roosevelt University, 1976; MA, University of California at Los Angeles, 1980. *Recordings:* Kovai and Adzera Music, 1981; Music of the Anga, 1983; Sogeri Singsing, 1983. *Publications:* Editor of papers presented at Goroka Ethnomusicology Conference, 1982; Editor, Sound-producing instruments in Oceania, by Hans Fischer, 1983; Compiler, Commercial Recordings of Papua New Guinea Music, 1949-1983, 1984. With Michael Webb, Riwain! PNG Pop Songs, 1986 (with two cassettes) and Papua New Guinea Music Collection, 1988 (with 12 cassettes). *Contributions to:* With Michael Webb, Periods in Papua New Guinea Music History, Bikmaus, 1986; Bikmaus; Ethnomusicology; Wantok; Times of Papua New Guinea; various books concerning Papua New Guinea Music; Co-ordinator for Papau New Guinea; contributions to Garland Encyclopedia of World Music. *Address:* National Research Institute, Box 1432, Boroko, Papua, New Guinea.

NILON Paul, b. 1961, Keighley, Yorkshire. Singer (Tenor). *Education:* Studied with Frederic Cox at the Royal Northern College of Music. *Career:* Appearances with Opera 80 as Don Ottavio, the Duke of Mantua and Sellem in The Rake's Progress; La Fenice, Venice, as Sellem; Musica nel Chiostro in Batignano, Italy, as Jacquino in Beethoven's Leonora; Has sung Strauss's Scaramuccio and Mozart's Belmonte for Opera Northern Ireland, 1987-88; Mario and the Magician, Stephen Oliver, World premiere Batignano, 1988; With the City of Birmingham Touring Opera has sung Fenton in Falstaff and Mozart's Tamino; Has sung with Opera North from 1988 as Hylas in The Trojans, Kudras (Katya Kabanova), Belfiore (La Finta Giardiniera), Leander in Nielsen's Maskarade (British premiere), Ferrando and Don Ottavio; Engagements with New Israel Opera and English National Opera, 1990-92, as Ferrando, Narraboth (Salome) and Telemachus in The Return of Ulysses; Tamino ENO 1992/93, Duel of Tancredi and Clorinda; Tamino Scottish Opera 1992, ENO 1993; Ariodante, ENO, Lurcanio, 1993; Many concert appearances. *Recordings include:* L'Assedio di Calais by Donizetti and Vol. II and III, in One Hundred Years of Italian Opera (Opera Rara); Medea in Corinta by Mayr. *Current Management:* IMG Artists (Europe)*Address:* IMG Artists, Europe, Media Housae, 3 Burlington Lane, London W4 2TH, England.

NILSSON Birgit (Fru Bertil Niklasson), b. 17 May 1918, Karup, Sweden. Opera singer (Soprano). m. Bertil Nicklasson. *Education:* Stockholm Royal Academy of Music. *Career:* With Stockholm Opera 1946-58; Sang at Glyndebourne, England, as Mozart's Electra, 1951; Bayreuth 1953, 1954, 1957-70, Munich 1955, Hollywood Bowl, Buenos Aires and Florence 1956, London (Covent Garden) 1957, 1962, 1963, 1973, as Brünnhilde, Turandot, Elektra and Isolde, Milan (La Scala), Naples, Vienna, Chicago and San Francisco 1958, New York (Metropolitan) 1959, Moscow 1964; Sang in Turandot, Paris 1968, Tosca, New York 1968, Elektra, London 1969; Particularly well-known for her Wagnerian roles (Brünnhilde, Isolde and as Strauss's Elektra, Salome and Dyer's Wife); Last Stage performance 1982; Gala performances at the Metropolitan 1983; Currently gives master classes in England and elsewhere.*Recordings include:* Aida, Der Freischütz (HMV/EMI); Salome, Tristan und Isolde, Un ballo in Maschera, Don Giovanni, Tosca, Der Ring des Nibelungen (Decca); Oberon, Don Giovanni, Tannhäuser and Tristan, Bayreuth 1966 (Deutsche Grammophon); La Fanciulla del West (Columbia). *Honours:* Austrian Kammersängerin, Bavarian Kammersängerin and Hon Member of the Vienna State Opera 1968; First Commander Order of Vasa 1974, Medal Litters et Artibus 1960, Medal for Promotion of Art of Music, Royal Academy of Music, Stockholm 1968 Hon. Member, The Royal Musical Academy, London; Hon. Dr: Andover University, Massachusetts 1970, Manhattan School of Music, New York 1982, East Lansing University of Fine Arts, Michigan 1982; Swedish Golden Medal (CL.18 Illis Quorum). *Address:* c/o Kungliga Teatern, PO Box 16094, S-103 22 Stockholm, Sweden.

NILSSON Bo, b. 1 May 1937, Skelleftehamn, Sweden. Composer. Div; 2 daughters. *Education:* Piano under Micha Pedersen, 1945-50; Audiology under K G St Clair Renard, 1951-54; Counterpoint, instrumentation, under Karl- Birger Blomdahl, 1955-57. *Debut:* Composer, Cologne, 1956. *Career:* Compositions played worldwide. *Compositions:* Variations, clarinet, piano, 1953; For Strings Only, 1954; Four Pieces, bassoon, piano, 1955; Zwei Stucke, flute, bass clarinet, piano, 4 percussionists, 1956; Frequenzen, 8 players, 1956; Bewegungen-Schlagfiguren-Quantitaten, piano, 1956-58; Zwanzig Grupper, woodwind trio, 1957; Audiogramme, electronic music, 1957; Stunde eines Blocks, soprano, 6 players, 1957; Brief an Gosta Oswald, 1958-59; Stenogramme, organ, 1960; Drei Szenen, chamber orchestra, 1960-61; Versuchungen, large orchestra, 1961; Entree, loudspeakers, orchestra, 1962; Vier Prologen, orchestra, 1963; Litanei uber das verlorene Schlagzeug, large orchestra, 1964; Revue, chamber orchestra, 1967; Attraktionen, string quartet, 1967; Ayiasma, mixed choir with flute, 1967; Mass For Christian Unity, mixed choir, organ, 1968; Der gluckliche, mixed choir, soprano, 1968; Reaktionen, 4 percussionists, 1969; Swedenborg Dreaming, electronic music, 1969; Deja vu, woodwind quartet, 1967; Deja connu, deja entendu, wind quintet, 1976; We'll Be Meeting Tomorrow, mixed choir, soprano, celesta, triangles, 1970; Fatumeh, speaker, soloists, mixed choir, electronics, large orchestra, 1973; La Bran, soprano saxophone, mixed choir, orchestra, electronics, 1975; Fragments, marimba, 5 Thai-gongs, 1975; Floten aus der Einsamkelt, soprano, 9 players, 1976; Bass, bass tuba solo, 6 Javanian tuned gongs, Chinese gong, 1977; Plexus, brass instruments, piano, percussion, 1979; Wendepunkt-Infrastruktur-Endepunkt, brass quintet, 1981; Autumn Song, baritone, orchestra, 1984; My Wind Is Yours, baritone, orchestra, 1984; Vagues pour Madame Curie, high soprano, orchestra, 1993; Film music; Songs; Jazz. *Recordings:* Introduction and Midsummer Tune; Quantitaten; Raga Rena Rama; Rendez-vous; You; Illness; Walz in Marjoram; Blue-Black Samba; The Last Lass; To Love; Lidingo Airport; Forward Waltz; The Swinging World of Bo Nilsson; The Missile; In The Loneliness of The Night; Ravaillac; Many others. *Publications:* Spaderboken, 1962; Missilen eller Livet i en mossa, 1993. *Honours:* Christopher Johnson Grand Prize, 1975; Hilding Rosenberg Prize, 1993; State Artist's Salary, 1974-; Freelance Artist, 1976-; Author. *Address:* Kocksgatan 48, 4 tr, 116 29 Stockholm, Sweden.

NILSSON Pia-Marie, b. 1961, Sweden. Singer (Soprano). *Education:* Studied at Stockholm College of Music and the State Opera School. *Debut:* Stockholm Folkoperan 1985 as the Queen of Night. *Career:* Sang at Royal Opera Stockholm and the Drottningholm Theatre 1986-88; Frankfurt Opera from 1989 as Sandrina in La Finta Giardiniera, Servilia, La Clemenza di Tito, Pamina, Oscar, Ballo in Maschera, Gilda and Sophie; French debut 1991 as Donna Anna at Nancy; Concert engagements in Scandinavia, Italy, Switzerland, Germany and Austria; Engaged as Oscar for the Theatre de la Monnaie, Brussels, 1995; Broadcasting commitments in Scandinavia. *Address:* c/o Nordic Artists Management, Sveavagen 76, S-11359 Stockholm, Sweden.

NILSSON Raymond, b. 26 May 1920, Mosman, Sydney, Australia. Singer (Tenor). *Education:* Studied at the New South Wales Conservatorium and at the Royal College of Music, London. *Career:* After early experience in Australia sang with the Carl Rosa Company, the English Opera Group and Sadler's Wells; Royal Opera House Covent Garden from 1952, as Don José, Alfredo Germont and Pandarus in Troilus and Cressida; Guest appearances in Wiesbaden and elsewhere in Germany as concert artist, with further tours to the USA and Holland; Australian tours with the Elizabethan Opera Company 1958 and Sadler's Wells 1960; Other roles included Turiddu, Rodolfo, Narraboth in Salome and Luigi in Il Tabarro; BBC performances of Schoenberg's Gurrelieder, Hindemith's Mathis der Maler, Oedipus Rex and Kodaly's Psalmus

Hungaricus; Sang in Janáček's Glagolitic Mass with ABC, Australia. *Recordings:* Bob Boles in Peter Grimes; Psalmus Hungaricus. *Address:* c/o Australian Opera, PO Box 291, Strawberry Hills, New South Wales 2012, Australia.

NIMPUNO Hannes, b. 5 Mar 1961, Bandung, Indonesia. Managing Director of Chamber Orchestra. *Education:* Studies and degrees in Physics, Geophysics, Informatics and Electronics, University of Karlsruhe, Germany; Private Violin studies with Dusan Pandula, Novak Quartet, 1983 participation in Gidon Kremer's Lockenhaus Festival. *Career:* Founder, Manager, music vera publishing firm (contemporary repertoire), 1986-; Founder, Artistic and Managing Director, International St Gallen Festival of Arts, 1987-; Managing Director, Deutsche Kammerphilharmonie, 1988-; Co-Director, Deutsche Ensemble Akademie, 1991-. *Recordings:* As Record Producer, 1984-: 751, Open Art Band, 1984; Line-Up Arrows, Open Art Band, 1987; Polish Music, Wanda Wilkomirska/Paul Dan, 1988; Brahms, horn trio etc, with Gerd Seifert/Daniel Höxter/Nikolas Chumachenko, 1988; Repertoire for 2 violins, (compositions by Bargielski, Pirchner, Bacewic Knorr), Dagmar Schwalke/Annette Bik, 1989; Music by Telemann and Vivaldi, Tatjana Grindenko/Moscow Academy of Ancient Music, 1990. *Memberships:* Deutscher Musikverlegerverband. *Hobbies:* Modern art; Collecting paintings. *Address:* An den Eichen 37, D-6082 Möhrfelden-Walldorf, Germany.

NIMSGERN Siegmund, b. 14 Jan 1940, St Wendel, Germany. Singer (Baritone). *Education:* Vocal studies with Paul Lohmann and Jakob Staempfli. *Debut:* Lionel in Tchaikovsky's Maid of Orleans, Saarbrucken 1967. *Career:* Sang in Saarbrucken until 1971, Deutsche Oper am Rhein, Dusseldorf, 1971-74; London Promenade Concerts 1972, as Mephistopheles in La Damnation de Faust; La Scala Milan and Paris Opera 1973; Covent Garden 1973, as Amfortas in Parsifal; Paris 1977-82, as the Speaker in Die Zauberflöte, Creon in Oedipus Rex, Telramund in Lohengrin and Beethoven's Pizarro; Metropolitan Opera 1978, as Pizarro; Bayreuth Festival 1983-85, as Wotan in the Peter Hall production of Der Ring des Nibelungen; Often heard as concert singer; Chicago Lyric Opera 1988, as Scarpia; Sang Wotan in Das Rheingold at Bonn 1990; Don Pizarro in Fidelio at La Scala, Milan; Sang Telramund at Frankfurt, 1991. *Recordings:* St John Passion by Bach, Masses by Haydn and Hummel (Electrola); Pergolesi's La Serva Padrona, Cantatas by Bach and Telemann, Bach's Magnificat (Harmonia Mundi); St Matthew Passion and Bach B Minor Mass (CBS); Alberich in Das Rheingold (Eurodisc); Mosè in Egitto (Philips); Die Schöpfung (Decca); Marschner's Der Vampyr. *Address:* c/o Ingpen and Williams Ltd., 14 Kensington Court, London W8 5DN, England.

NIN-CULMELL Joaquin Maria, b. 5 Sep. 1908, Berlin, Germany. American Musician. *Education:* Studied at Schola Cantorum (Paris), Paris Conservatory (class of Paul Dukas) and privately with Manuel de Falla in Granada. *Career:* Instructor, Middlebury College, Vermont, USA, 1938, 1939, 1940, Williams College, 1940-50; Professor, Music, University of California, 1949-74, Emeritus Professor, 1974-; Has appeared as Pianist, Conductor, with San Francisco Symphony and other orchestras in USA and Europe. *Compositions:* Piano Concerto, El burlador de Sevilla (Ballet); Piano Quintet, Sonata Breve, Tonadas (Piano), 12 Cuban Dances; Three Old Spanish Pieces (Orchestra); Diferencias (Orchestra); Concerto for Cello & Orchestra (after Padre Viola); Mass in English (for mixed chorus and organ); La Celestina (Opera); Cantata for voice and harpsichord or piano and strings (after Padre Jose Pradas); Le Rêve de Cyrano (ballet); Incidental music for Shakespeare's Cymbeline, Garcia Lorca's Yerma and Cuban Evocations; songs; choral pieces; guitar and organ pieces; Ragpicker's Song for men's chorus and piano, 1988. *Memberships:* Corresponding member of the Royal Academy of Fine Arts San Fernando, (Madrid). *Publications:* Editor, Spanish Choral Tradition; Prefaces in English and French for Anais Nin's Early Diaries. *Address:* 5830 Clover Drive, Oakland, CA 94618, USA.

NIROUËT Jean, b. 15 Aug 1958, Paris, France. Countertenor; Conductor; Musicologist. *Education:* Baccalauréat of Sciences; Licence, History, Sorbonne University, Paris; Flute, bassoon, piano & theory studies, Music High School/Conservatory, Strasburg until 1964; Harmony & conducting with Claude-Henry Joubert, singing with Jacqueline Bonnardot, Conservatory of Orléans until 1978; Music analysis with Betsy Jolas, singing with Christiane Eda-Pierre, Conservatory of Paris. *Career includes:* Engagements, Opera Houses of Paris, Lyon, Nice, Strasburg, Karlsruhe, Helsinki; Radio France, Germany, Holland; Numerous European festivals; Film for Südwestfunk 2, Pasticcio of Handel/Martinoty, 1985; etc. *Recordings:* Alessandro (Handel); Serse (Cavalli); Vêspres de la Vièrge, (Charpentier); Te Deum, David et Jonathas, (Charpentier); Requiem, (Gilles); H.H. Ulysse, (Prodomidès). *Publications:* Rose et Colas de Monsigny, 1982; L'Irato de Méhul, 1984; La dramaturgie des Opéras de Lully dans l'étude des tempi; Analyse d'Epiphanie d'André Caplet. *Current Management:* Anglo-Swiss London, Rainer/Poilvé Paris, Kempf Munich. *Address:* c/o Anglo-Swiss Artists' Management, PO Box 719, London N6 5UX, England.

NISHIDA Hiroko, b. 17 Jan 1952, Oita, Japan. Singer (Soprano). *Education:* Studied in Tokyo. *Career:* Sang with the Bonn Opera, 1979-81; Appearances at the Zurich Opera as Butterfly, Berne, Mimi, St Gallen, Micaela and the Forza Leonora, Berlin, Munich, Cologne, Frankfurt, Dusseldorf, Stuttgart and Mannheim; Sang Butterfly with Opera de Lyon, 1990; Further guest appearances at San Diego, Enschede and Amsterdam; Other roles include Arminda in La Finta Giarriniera, Pamina, Manon Lescaut, Lauretta, Elisabeth de Valois and Kunigunde in Lortzing's Hans Sachs; Concert repertoire includes works by Bach, Handel, Mozart, Schubert, Beethoven, Bruckner and Mahler. *Address:* c/o Opera de Lyon, 9 Quai Jean Moulin, F-69001 Lyon, France.

NISKA Maralin, b. 16 Nov 1930, San Pedro, California, USA. Singer (Soprano). *Education:* Studied with Lotte Lehmann. *Career:* Sang widely in California from 1955; San Diego Opera 1965, as Mimi in La Bohème; Sang Floyd's Susannah with the Met National Company; New York City Opera 1967, as Mozart's Countess: returned as Turandot, Tosca, Salome and Janáček's Emilia Marty; Metropolitan Opera 1970-77, as Tosca, Musetta and Hélène in Les Vêpres Siciliennes; Italian debut as Marie in Wozzeck, Maggio Musicale Florence 1978; Other roles have included Violetta, Madam Butterfly, Donna Elvira, Manon Lescaut and Marguerite in Faust.

NISSEL Siegmund Walter, b. 3 Jan 1922, Munich, Germany. Musician. m. 5 Apr 1957, 1 son, 1 daughter. *Education:* External Matriculation (Honours Degree) London University; Private Study (Violin); Professor Max Weissgarber until 1938; Professor Max Rostal, London. *Debut:* With Amadeus Quartet. Wigmore Hall, London, 10 Jan 1948. *Career:* Founder Member of Amadeus Quartet; Innumerable BBC Radio and Television appearances, also ITV: International World-wide Concert Career; Quartet disbanded, 1987. *Recordings:* Mozart, Beethoven, Schubert, Brahms Quartets; Benjamin Britten; Brahms Sextets. *Honours:* Honorary Doctor of Music London, York Universities; OBE; Vierdienstkreuz für Musik in Germany Austria; Honorary LRAM. *Memberships:* ISM; ESTA. *Hobby:* Chess. *Address:* 29 The Park, London NW11 7ST, England.

NISSMAN Barbara, b. 31 Dec 1944, Philadelphia, Pennsylvania, USA. Concert Pianist. *Education:* BMus, 1966, MMus, 1966, DMus Arts, 1969, University of Michigan; Studied with pianist, György Sandor. *Debut:* American Orchestral Debut with Philadelphia Orchestra, Ormandy, 1971. *Career:* Appearances with London Philharmonic, Royal Philharmonic, Rotterdam Philharmonic, L'Orchestre de la Suisse Romande, BBC Symphony, Netherlands Chamber, Munich Philharmonic, Bavarian Radio Orchestra, etc; United States; Philadelphia, Pittsburgh, Minnesota Orchestras; Boston Pops; with Ormandy, Muti, Mata, Skrowaczewski, Zinman; Concert tours of the Far East, Latin America and Soviet Union; Presented Dutch Premiere of Ginastera Piano Concerto, 1978 in Concertgebouw; Soloist at Gala 60th birthday concert for Ginastera with Suisse Romande, 1976; Third Piano Sonata, (1982), of Ginastera, dedicated to Ms Nissman. *Recordings:* Music of Alberto Ginastera, CBS/Europe; Music of Franz Liszt, CBS/Globe; American release, Desto-Music of Alberto Ginastera. *Publication:* Alberto Ginastera - Piano Sonata No 3, published by Boosey and Hawkes, 1982. *Contributions to:* Keynote magazine, 1983, Interview with Alberto Ginastera. *Honours:* Stanley Medal, 1966, University of Michigan; Alumnae Athena Award, 1981; Martha Baird Rockefeller Grant, 1971 and 1981. *Current Management:* Thea Dispeker Management, New York City. *Address:* 107 West 86th Street, New York City, NY 10024, USA.

NIXON Marni, b. 22 Feb 1930, Altadena, California, USA. Singer (Soprano); Teacher. *Eucation:* Studied at the University of Southern California with Carl Ebert, Stanford University with Jan Popper and the Berkshire Music Center with Boris Goldovsky and Sarah Caldwell. *Career:* Has sung in musical comedy, programmes for children's television, concerts, opera and film sound tracks: provided the singing voices for Deborah Kerr in The King and I, Natalie Wood in West Side Story and Audrey Hepburn in My Fair Lady; Has appeared in Los Angeles, San Francisco, Tanglewood and Seattle as Mozart's Blondchen, Constanze and Susanna, Philine in Mignon by Thomas, Strauss's Zerbinetta and Violetta; Concert engagements in Cleveland, Toronto, Los Angeles, Israel and London; Modern repertory includes works by Webern, Ives, Hindemith and Stravinsky; Teacher at California Institute of Arts 1969-71; Music Academy of the West, Santa Barbara, from 1980. *Recordings include:* Webern complete works, conducted by Robert Craft. *Address:* c/o Music Academy of the West, 1070 Fairway Road, CA 93109, USA.

NIXON Roger, b. 8 Aug 1921, Tulare, California, USA. Composer. *Education:* Studied at University of California, Berkeley, PhD 1952, notably with Roger Sessions, Arthur Bliss, Bloch and Schoenberg. *Career:* Teacher at Modesto Junior College, 1951-59, San Francisco State University from 1960. *Compositions:* Opera: The Bride Comes to Yellow Sky, 1968; Orchestra: Air for Strings, 1953; Violin Concerto, 1956; Elegaic Rhapsody for viola and orchestra, 1962; Viola Concerto, 1969; San Joaquin Sketches, 1982; California Jubilee, 1982; Golden Jubilee, 1985; Chamber: String Quartet No. 1, 1949; Conversations for violin and clarinet, 1981; Music for clarinet and piano, 1986; Vocal: Christmas Perspectives for chorus, 1980; Festival Mass for chorus, 1980; Chaunticleer for male chorus, 1984; The Canterbury Tales for chorus, 1986; The Daisy for chorus, 1987; Song Cycles including A Narrative of Tides for soprano, flute and piano, 1984. *Honours:* Grants and commissions from the San Francisco Festival of the Masses and American Bandmasters Association. *Address:* c/o ASCAP, ASCAP Bulding, One Lincoln Plaza, New York, NY 10023, USA.

NOBLE Dale Spencer, b. 5 Oct 1958, Barnet, Hertfordshire, England. Flautist; Recorder Player. m. Frances Bell, 13 Aug 1988, 1 daughter. *Education:* Licentiate, Royal Academy of Music (Flute), 1978; Licentiate, Trinity College, London (Recorder), 1977; Guildhall School of Music and Drama, 1979-80; Greek Stage II, Institute of Linguists, 1983. *Debut:* Purcell Room, March 1981. *Career:* Baroque Recital, Fenton House, Hampstead, London, 1979; Televised Vivaldi Concert with l'Orchestre de Chambre de Wallonie, Belgium; BBC lunchtime concert, 1982; Recital, Gordon Craig Theatre, Stevenage, 1983; Has taught in London and Hertfordshire, 1979-; Has played with Steinitz Bach Players and London Orpheus Orchestra. *Honours:* Certificate of Special Merit, Trinity College of Music, 1969; Gold Medal, Royal Schools of Music, 1972.

Memberships: Musicians Union; Incorporated Society of Musicians; Mensa. *Hobbies:* Greek Folk Music; Languages and Linguistics; Travel. *Address:* 13 Hawkins Hall Lane, Datchworth, Nr Knebworth, Hertfordshire SG3 6TF, England.

NOBLE Jeremy, b. 27 March 1930, London, England. Musicologist; Critic; Broadcaster. *Education:* Worcester College, Oxford, 1949-53; Private music studies. *Career:* Music Critic The Times, 1960-63; The Sunday Telegraph 1972-76; Research fellow, Barber Institute, Birmingham, 1964-65; Fellow, Harvard Institute for Renaissance Studies, Florence, 1967-68; Leverhulme Research Fellow, 1975-76; Associate Professor, State University of New York, at Buffalo 1966-70 and from 1976; Many broadcasts for BBC Radio 3. *Publications:* Articles on Joaquin, Debussy and Stravinsky for the Musical Times; Purcell and the Chapel Royal, in Essays on Music ed. I Holst 1959; Mozart: A Documentary Biography, translation of O. Deutsch with E. Blom and P.Branscombe 1965; Entries on Josquin and, jointly with E.W. White, Stravinsky for The New Grove Dictionary of Music and Musicians 1980. *Address:* Department of Music, State University of New York, Buffalo, NY 14260, USA.

NOBLE John, b. 2 Jan 1931, Southampton, England. Singer (Baritone). *Education:* MA, Hons, Cambridge; Privately with Clive Carey CBE and Boriska Gereb. *Career:* Concerts and Oratorio with major orchestras throughout the United Kingdom; Tours in Europe and USA; Guest Artist in opera with Covent Garden and other Companies; Many broadcasts for BBC in wide range of music including several first performances; Professor of Singing at Royal Northern College of Music, Manchester. *Recordings:* Vaughan Williams The Pilgrim's Progress, Title Role, conductor Boult; Britten Albert Herring (Vicar), conductor Britten; Delius Sea Drift, conductor Groves. *Memberships:* Past Chairman, Solo Performers, Incorporated Society of Musicians; Councillor, British Actors Equity Association. *Address:* 185 Syon Lane, Isleworth, Middlesex TW7 5PU, England.

NOBLE Timothy, b. 1956, Indianapolis, Indiana, USA. Singer (Baritone). *Career:* Sang supporting roles in Carmen, Turandot and Wozzeck with San Francisco Opera, 1981; Houston Opera from 1982, as Ping, Leporello and Falstaff; Colorado Springs Festival 1982, as Rigoletto; Fort Worth and Opera-Comique Paris 1983, as Sharpless and Germont; Season 1985-86 at Santa Fe in premiere of John Eaton's The Tempest, as Falstaff in Amsterdam and as Simon Boccanegra at Glyndebourne (returned 1988 as Germont); San Francisco 1987, as Tomsky in The Queen of Spades, Venice 1988 in Verdi's Stiffelio; Sang Shaklovity in Khovanshchina at the Metropolitan 1988 and San Francisco 1990 (returned to New York 1991 as Leporello); Opera Pacific at Costa Mesa and the Santa Fe Festival 1991, as Renato and as Jack Rance in La Fanciulla del West; Other roles include Masetto, Ottokar in Der Freischütz, Macbeth, Schaunard, Abbate in Busoni's Arlecchino and Reimann's Lear; Sang Columbus in the premiere of The Voyage of Philip Glass, New York Metropolitan 1992; Further engagements in musicals and as concert artist. *Address:* c/o Metropolitan Opera, Lincoln Center, New York, NY 10023, USA.

NOBLE Weston H., b. 30 Nov 1922, Riceville, Iowa, USA. Professor of Music. *Education:* BA, Luther College, 1943; MM, University of Michigan, 1953. *Career:* US Army,, Europe, 1943-46; Director, Band & Choir, Luverne High School, Iowa, 1946-48; Professor of Music, Luther College, Decorah, Iowa, current. Also: Guest Director, over 775 music festivals, 48 US States, Canada, Europe; Only Director to conduct All-State groups in all 3 media (over 50 bands, choir, orchestras); 8 concert tours, Europe (Norway to Russia); Conductor, own groups or festival groups, various prestigious venues, Chicago, New York, Washington DC, Los Angeles, Minneapolis, Salt Lake City; Adjudicator, International Festival of 3 Cities (Vienna, Budapest,

Prague); Band Consultant & Guest Director, Association for International Cultural Exchange, Vienna, Austria (39 nations represented); Co-Director of Bridges of Song Festival, Tallinn, Estonia, at which time 25,000 singers from Estonia, and USA participated, 1991. *Memberships include:* Elected, American Bandmasters Association; Charter member, American Choral Directors Association. *Address:* Music Department, Luther College, Decorah, Iowa 52101, USA.

NÖCKER Hans Gunter, b. 22 Jan. 1927, Hagen, Germany. Singer (Bass-Baritone). *Education:* Studied in Brunswick and with Hans-Hermann Nissen and Willi Domgraf-Fassbaender in Munich. *Debut:* Munster 1952, as Alfio in Cavalleria Rusticana. *Career:* Many appearances in Germany, particularly at Hamburg, Munich and Stuttgart; Bayreuth Festival 1958-60; Munich 1963, in the premiere of Egk's Die Verlobung in San Domingo; Schwetzingen 1966, in Gluck's Armide; Deutsche Oper Berlin, in the 1972 premiere of Fortner's Elisabeth Tudor; La Fenice Venice 1983, as Klingsor in Parsifal; Berlin 1984, in the premiere of Reimann's Gespenstersonate; Guest appearances in Florence, Brussels, Palermo, London and Edinburgh; Sang at Munich in the 1986 premiere of D. Kirchner's Belshazzar; Sang in Orff's Trionfo di Afrodite, Munich Festival, 1990. *Recordings:* Orff's Trionfi (BASF); Oedipus der Tyrann (Deutsche Grammophon); Götterdämmerung (Eurodisc). *Address:* c/o Bayerische Staatsoper, Postfach 745, D-8000 Munich 1, Germany.

NODA Ken, b. 5 Oct 1962, New York, USA. Concert Pianist (retired); Musical Assistant to Artistic Director, Artistic Administration/Metropolitan Opera. *Education:* Private studies with Daniel Barenboim. *Career:* London debut 1979 with the English Chamber Orchestra and Daniel Barenboim; later engagements with the Philharmonia, Berlin Philharmonic, Orchestre de Paris, Rotterdam Philharmonic, Israel Philharmonic, New York Philharmonic, Chicago Symphony; conductors include Abbado, Chailly, Andrew Davis, Kubelik, Leinsdorf, Levine, Mehta, Ozawa and Previn; Recitals in London, Toronto, Chicago, Lincoln Center New York, Hamburg and La Fenice Venice; Festival appearances at Mostly Mozart (New York), Ravinia and Tanglewood; 1986 debut with the Vienna Philharmonic in Salzburg; Season 1986-87 concerts with the Berlin Philharmonic the Hallé and the Philharmonia; 1988 concerts with the Rotterdam Philharmonic playing Mozart under James Conlon; Beethoven's Triple Concerto with Pinchas Zukerman and Lynn Harrell at Ravinia; toured Japan with Ozawa and the New Japan Philharmonic. *Recordings include:* Repertoire: Concertos by Beethoven, Chopin, Haydn, Liszt and Schumann. *Address:* c/o Metropolitan Opera, Lincoln Center, New York, NY 10023, USA.

NOEL Rita, b. 21 Nov 1943, Lancaster, South Carolina, USA. Singer (Mezzo-soprano). *Education:* Studied at Eastman School, at Queens College, Charlotte, SC and in New York and Vienna. *Career:* Played violin and viola with the Vienna Chamber Orchestra and the Berlin Symphony; Stage debut with the Metropolitan National Opera Company, 1966, as Flora in Traviata; Further appearances at the Theater am Gartnerplatz Munich, Bielefeld, Amsterdam and Miami; Other roles have included Mozart's Cherubino and Sextus, Cornelia in Giulio Cesare, Carmen, Rosina, Octavian, Nicklausse, Azucena and Santuzza; Frequent concert engagements. *Address:* c/o Staatstheater am Gärtnerplatz, Gärtnerplatz 3, 8000 Munich, Germany.

NOELTE Rudolf, b. 1930, Berlin. Stage Director. *Education:* Studied at Berlin University. *Career:* Assisted Jurgen Fehling, Erich Engel and Walter Felsenstein at the Hebbel Theatre Berlin; Produced Max Brod's adaptation of The Castle by Kafka, 1953; Productions of classic plays in Germany and Vienna; First opera production Lulu in Frankfurt; Has directed Don Giovanni in West Berlin, Eugene Onegin in Munich and The Queen of Spades in Cologne; The Bartered Bride and La Traviata for Welsh National Opera; Der Freischütz in Bremen, Ariadne auf Naxos at the Bayerische

Staatsoper Munich and Otello in Frankfurt; Covent Garden debut 1987, with Massenet's Manon. *Address:* Allied Artists Ltd, 42 Montpelier Square, London SW7 1JZ, England.

NOLAN David, b. 1949, Liverpool, England. Violinist. *Education:* Studied with Yossi Zivoni and Alexander Moskowski at the Royal Manchester College of Music; Study in the Soviet Union, 1972-76. *Debut:* Played the Mendelssohn Concerto, 1965. *Career:* Joined the London Philharmonic Orchestra, 1972, leader from 1976; Many appearances with the LPO and other orchestras in conertos by Bach, Beethoven, Brahms, Bruch, Glazunov, Korngold, Mozart, Paganini, Saint-Saëns, Stravinsky, Tchaikovsky and Walton; Played the Schoenberg Concerto with the BBC Scottish Symphony conducted by Matthias Bamert, 1988. *Recordings:* The Lark Ascending by Vaughan Williams, EMI Eminence; The Four Seasons, Vivaldi, Collins Classics. *Honours:* RMCM performances, diploma, distinction. *Memberships:* Concert Master of Philharmonia Orchestra, since 1992. *Current Management:* Philharmonia Orchestra Ltd.*Address:* 76 Gt Portland Street, London W1N 5AL, England.

NOLEN Timothy, b. 9 July 1941, Rotan, Texas, USA. Singer (Baritone). *Education:* Studied at the Manhattan School of Music and with Richard Fredericks and Walter Fredericks. *Debut:* New Jersey Opera Newark as Rossini's Figaro. *Career:* Sang Marcello in La Bohème with San Francisco Opera, 1968; Appearances in Chicago, Houston, Boston and Minneapolis; European debut Rouen, 1974, as Pelléas; Amsterdam, 1974 in the premiere of The Picture of Dorian Gray by Kox; Sang in Cologne, 1974-78 and Paris, Bordeaux, Aix and Nantes as Mozart's Count, Figaro and Guglielmo, Donizetti's Malatesta and Belcore, Monteverdi's Orpheus, Dandini in La Cenerentola, Puccini's Gianni Schicchi, the Emperor in The Nightingale by Stravinsky and Ford in Falstaff; Sang in the premieres of Carlisle Floyd's Willie Stark and Bernstein's A Quite Place, Houston 1981 and 1983; Further engagements at Florence, Geneva, Miami, New York, City Opera and Philadelphia; Sante Fe Festival, 1992 as Mr Peachum in The Beggar's Opera and Frank in Die Fledermaus. *Address:* c/o Santa Fe Opera, PO Box 2408, Santa Fe, NM 87504, USA.

NOLL Christoph Anselm, b. 2 Jan 1959, Weissenthurm, Germany. Organist. m. Andrea Stenzel, 1991. *Education:* Church Music, Organ, Harpsichord, Oboe, Musikhochschule Koln; Organ, Musikhochschule Stuttgart. *Debut:* Organ Recital, Andernach, 1974. *Career:* Concerts throughout Europe; Since 1981 Church Musician in Andernach; Teacher for Organ at the Gutenberg University of Mainz and the Musikhochschule Detmold. *Recordings:* Organ works of Bach, Krebs. *Honours:* Organ Competitions: 2nd Prize Brugge 1985; 1st Prize Winterthur 1986; 2nd Prize Lausanne 1987; 2nd Prize Nuernberg 1988. *Address:* Karthaeuserstr 18, D-56218 Mueheim-Kaerlich, Germany.

NONI Alda, b. 30 Apr 1916, Trieste, Italy. Singer (Soprano). *Education:* Studied in Trieste and Vienna. *Debut:* Ljubljana 1937, as Rosina in Il barbiere di Siviglia. *Career:* Sang first in Yugoslavia and joined the Vienna Staatsoper, 1942; Sang Mozart's Despina and Verdi's Gilda and Oscar; Appeared as Zerbinetta in a 1944 performance of Ariadne auf Naxos, to celebrate the 80th birthday of Richard Strauss; Sang in Milan, Rome, Venice and Turin from 1945; Cambridge Theatre London, 1946, as Norina in Don Pasquale opposite Marino Stabile; La Scala from 1949 in Cimarosa's Il matrimonio segreto and Piccinni's La buona figliuola; Sang Zerlina, Nannetta and Papagena with the company of La Scala during its 1950 visit to London; Glyndebourne, 1950-54, as Blondchen, Despina and Clorinda in La Cenerentola; Guest appearances in Berlin, Paris (Opéra-Comique), Lisbon, Madrid and Rio de Janeiro. *Recordings include:* Ariadne auf Naxos (Deutsche Grammophon); Don Pasquale, L'Elisir

d'Amore, Lucia di Lammermoor, Il matrimonio segreto and Le nozze di Figaro (Cetra); La Cenerentola (HMV).

NORBERG-SCHULZ Elisabeth, b. Jan 1959, Norway. Singer (Soprano). *Education:* Studied at Accademia di Santa Cecilia, Rome, the Pears- Britten School at Snape and with Elisabeth Schwarzkopf in Zurich. *Career:* Gave Lieder recitals and sang Britten's Les Illuminations at Snape, 1981; Sang supporting roles in Italy and elsewhere at first, then Gilda and Lucia di Lammermoor; Has appeared under such conductors as George Solti, Riccardo Muti and Claudio Abbado, notably at La Scala Milan; Sang Musetta in La Bohème with La Scala on visit to Japan, 1988; Rome Opera 1989, as Barbarina in Le Nozze di Figaro; Maggio Musicale Fiorentino 1989, as Ilia in Idomeneo; Sang Pamina in Die Zauberflöte at the Salzburg Landestheater 1991, as part of the Mozart bicentenary celebrations; Season 1992 as Norina at Naples, Guardian of the Threshold in Die Frau ohne Schatten and Servilia in La Clemenza di Tito, Salzburg. *Address:* c/o Teatro alla Scala, Via Filodrammatici 2, I-20121 Milan, Italy.

NORBORG Ake, b. 18 Aug 1943, Kristianstad, Sweden. Associate Professor (ethnomusicologist). *Education:* Studied at Universities of Lund and Uppsala Sweden, 1963-73; LLB and BA, 1967; PhD, 1970. *Career:* Assistant Professor of Ethnography, 1974-78, Associate Professor, 1978-, University of Copenhagen, Denmark. *Publications:* Musical Instruments from Africa South of the Sahara, 1982; A Handbook of Music and Other Sound-Producing Instruments from Namibia and Botswana, 1987; A Handbook of Mus and Other Sound-Producing Instruments from Equatorial Guinea and Gabon, 1989; The Musical Instruments of the Edo-Speaking Peoples of South Western Nigeria, 1992. *Contributions to:* Articles in Folk; Antropologiska Studier; Chapter in Stockmann (ed) Musikkulturen in Afrika, 1987. *Memberships:* Society for Ethnomusicology; International Council for Traditional Music; the Galpin Society; Society for Asian Music; The American Musical Instrument Society. *Address:* Institute of Anthropology, Frederiksholms Kanal 4, DK-1220 Copenhagen K, Denmark.

NORBY Erik, b. 9 Jan 1936, Copenhagen, Denmark, Composer. *Education:* Basic Music Training, Copenhagen Boys' Choir and Tivoli Band; Conservatory, Copenhagen; Diploma in Composition, 1966. *Career:* Teacher, North Jutland Conservatory, until 1975; Freelance Composer, 1975-. *Compositions include:* Orchestra: Folk Song Suite, 1962; Music for 6 Sextets, 1966; The Rainbow Snake, 1975; Illuminations, Capriccio, 1978; 3 Dances, 1983; Chamber Music: Illustrations, 1965; Schubert variations, 1974; Partita, 1981; Tivoli Collage, 1983; Ravel: Le Tombeau de Couperin, 1984; Solo Instrument: 12 Danish Folk Songs, for piano, 1961; Chromaticon, partita in 8 movements, 1971; Five Organ Chorales, 1976-78; Choral: March, 1972; Winter Twilight, 1973; Nightingale, 1973; Song Near the Depth of Spring, 1973; Festival Contata on the Occasion of the 150th Anniversary of Copenhagen Cathedral, 1979; Edvard Munch Triptych, 1978-79; Solo Voice: Two Songs, 1963; Six Shakespeare Sonnets, 1981; 13 Elizabethan Love Songs; The Ballad About My Life, 1984; Music for Educational Use: Three Suites, 1961; Three Small Suites, 1962; Little Sonatina - Three Humoresques - Evening Song - Suite 2, 1963. *Recordings:* Has made numerous recordings of his work. *Current Management:* Koda, Maltegårdsvej 24, 2820 Gentofte, Denmark. *Address:* Kochsvej 13, 3 tv, DK-1812 Frederiksberg C, Denmark.

NORDAL Jon, b. 1926. Composer; President, Reykjavik College of Music. *Education:* Studied with Arni Kristjansson, Jon Thorarinsson and Dr V Urbancic, Reykjavik College of Music, Reykjavik, Iceland; Studies with W Frey and W Burkhard, Zurich, Switzerland, 1949-51; Further studies in Paris and Rome; Darmstadt summer courses, 1956-57. *Career include:* President, Reykjavik College of Music. *Compositions:* Orchestral works: Concerto Lirico for harp and strings; Epitaphio, 1974; Stiklur, 1970; Canto Elegiaco, 1971; Leidsla,

1973; A Play of Fragments, 1962; Concerto for piano and orchestra, 1956; Adagio for Flute, harp, piano and strings, 1965; The Winter Night, 1975; Twin Song for violin, viola and orchestra, 1979; Sinfonietta Seriosa, 1956; Dedication, 1981; Choralis, 1982; Concerto for cello and orchestra, 1983; Concerto for orchestra, 1949; Chamber Music: Sonata for violin and piano; Fairy Tale Sisters for violin and piano; Chorale Prelude for organ, 1980; Duo for violin and cello, 1983; Choir Music: Seven Songs for male choir, 1955. *Address:* STEF, Laufasveji 40, Reykjavik, Iceland.

NORDEN Betsy, b. 17 Oct 1945, Cincinnati, Ohio, USA. Singer (Soprano). *Education:* Studied at Boston University. *Career:* Member of Metropolitan Opera Chorus from 1969; Solo appearances at the Metropolitan from 1972, in Le Nozze di Figaro, and as Papagena, Elvira in L'Italiana in Algeri, Constane in the Carmelites, Oscar and Despina in Cosi fan Tutte, 1990; Sang in The Cunning Little Vixen at Philadelphia season 1980-81, Constane at San Francisco 1983 and Gretel at San Diego 1985; Many concert appearances. *Address:* c/o Metropolitan Opera, Lincoln Center, New York, NY 10023, USA.

NORDGREN Pehr Henrik, b. 19 Jan 1944, Saltvik, Finland. Composer. *Education:* Studied Composition under Professor Joonas Kokkonen; Musicology, Helsinki University; Composition and Traditional Japanese Music, Tokyo University of Arts and Music, Japan, 1970-73. *Career:* Assistant, Helsinki University. *Compositions include:* Euphonie 1 op 1, 1967; The Turning Point, Op 16, 1972; Symphony Op 20, 1974; Euphonie 3 op 24, 1975; Summer Music Op 34, 1977; Symphony for Strings Op 43, 1978; Concerto No 1 for violin and Orchestra Op 10, 1969; Concerto for clarinet folk instruments and small orchestra, 1970; Autumnal Concerto for Traditional Japanese instruments and Orchestra, 1974; Concerto No 2 for violin and orchestra, 1977; 3 Viola concerts 1970, 1979, 1986; 3 cello concerts, 1980, 1984, 1992; Symphony No.2, 1989; Cronaca for strings, 1991; Streams for small orchestra; Agnus Dei, 1970; 7 string quartets 1967-92; Four Pictures of Death, 1968; Three Enticements, Wind Quintet No 1, 1970; As in a Dream Op 21, 1974; Wind Quintet No 2 Op 22, 1975; Piano Quintet Op 44, 1978; Ten Ballades to Japanese Ghost Stories by Lafcadio Hearn, 1972-77; Butterflies, 1977; In Patches, 1978; In the Palm of the King's Head for soprano, baritone chams and orchestra, 1979; The Lights of Heaven for soprano, tenor, chorus and ensemble 1985. *Recordings:* Hoichi Earless Op 17; Ballades. *Address:* TEOSTO, Lauttasaarentie 1, 00200 Helsinki 20, Finland.

NORDHEIM Arne, b. 20 June 1931, Larvik, Norway, Composer. *Education:* Studied with Conrad Baden and Bjarne Brustad at Oslo Conservatory and with Vagn Holmboe in Copenhagen 1955. *Career:* Critic for Dagbladet of Oslo 1960-68; Lecturer on and Performer of live electronic music. *Compositions:* Epigram for string quartet 1954; String Quartet 1956; Evening Land, song cycle for soprano and chamber ensemble 1957; Canzona for orchestra 1961; Katharsis, ballet on legend of St Anthony for orchestra and tape 1962; Kimare, ballet 1963; Partita for viola, harpsichord and percussion 1963; Epitaffio for orchestra and tape 1963; Favola, musical play 1965; Warsawe, electronic 1968; Three Responses 1967; Eco for soprano, chorus and orchestra 1968; Incidental music for Peer Gynt 1969; Floating for orchestra 1970; Dinosaurus for accordian and tape 1971; Greening and Zimbel for orchestra 1973-74; Doria for tenor and orchestra 1975; Ballets: Strender, Ariadne and The Tempest 1974-79; Be Not Affeared for soprano, baritone and ensemble 1978; Tempora noctis for soprano, mezzo, orchestra and tape 1979; Tenebrae, concerto for cello and orchestra 1982; Aurora for soloists, chorus, 2 percussion and tape 1984; Varder for trumpet and orchestra; Rendez-vous for string orchestra; Maema for Orchestra, 1988; Monolith for Orchestra, 1990; Draumkvede for singers, chorus and orchestra. *Address:* TONO (Norway), c/o PRS Ltd Member Registration, 29-33 Berners Street, London W1P 4AA, England.

NORDIN Birgit, b. 22 Feb 1934, Sangis, Norrbotten, Sweden. Singer (Soprano). *Education:* Studied at the Stockholm Opera School and with Lina Pagliughi in Italy. *Debut:* Stockholm 1957, as Oscar in Un Ballo in Maschera. *Career:* Has sung with the Royal Opera Stockholm on tour to Covent Garden, 1960 and the Edinburgh Festival; Annual visits to the Drottningholm Opera from 1960, notably in operas by Mozart; Wexford Festival 1963 and 1965; Glyndebourne Festival 1968, as Blondchen in Die Entfuhrung; Sang Jenny in Weill's Mahagonny at Copenhagen, 1970; Berlin 1970 as soloist in Bach's St Matthew Passion and Christmas Oratorio; Television appearance as Berg's Lulu, and sang the Queen of Night in Bergman's movie version of The Magic Flute, 1974; Oratorio engagements in Scandinavia, Germany, England and Austria; Other roles include Mozart's Susanna and Pamina, Gilda, Rosina, Sophie in Der Rosenkavalier and Mélisande. *Recordings:* Die Zauberflöte; Madrigals by Monteverdi (Deutsche Grammophon); Virgin-Classics video of Don Giovanni (Donna Elvira). *Honour:* Swedish Court Singer, 1973. *Address:* c/o Kungliga Teatern, P O Box 16094, S-10322 Stockholm, Sweden.

NORDIN Lena b. 18 Feb 1956, Sweden. Singer (Soprano). *Education:* Studied voice and piano at the College of Music in Malmo and Stockholm, and in Salzburg, Florence and Siena. *Career:* Sang title role in the Swedish premiere of Rameau's Hippolyte et Aricie, Swedish Baroque Festival, 1984; Appeared as Verdi's Luisa Miller in 1986 and has since sung at the Royal Opera Stockholm as Handel's Cleopatra, Lauretta, Donna Anna and Maria Stuarda (1990); Wexford Festival and Elizabeth Hall, London 1988-89, as Elisa in Mercadante's Elisa e Claudio and in Mozart's Mitridate; Sang Constanze, Marguerite/Faust and appeared as Christina Gyllenstietna in the modern premiere of Gustav Wase by Naumann at the Royal Opera of Stockholm, 1991; Concert engagements include performances in Paris and Lyon 1988; Beethoven's Ninth with Paavo Berglund and the Stockholm Philharmonic; Mahler's 8th Symphony with the Gothenburg Symphony under Neeme Järvi in Minneapolis; Gala Concert for the opening of the Savonlinna Opera Festival, Finland. *Address:* c/o Allied Artists, 42 Montpelier Square, London SW7 1JZ, England.

NORDMO-LOVBERG Aase, b. 10 June 1923, Malselv, Narvik, Norway. Singer (Soprano); Administrator. *Education:* Studied with Hjaldis Ingebjart in Oslo. *Debut:* Concert debut 1948, opera debut 1952, as Imogen in Cymbeline by Arne Eggens. *Career:* Member of the Royal Opera, Stockholm, 1953-69, debut as Elisabeth in Tannhäuser; Vienna Staatsoper 1957, as Sieglinde in Die Walküre; Concert appearances in London, Phildelphia and Paris, 1957; Metropolitan Opera 1959-61 as Elsa in Lohengrin, Eva, Sieglinde and Leonore; Bayreuth Festival 1960, Elsa and Sieglinde; Sang at the Stora Theater Gothenburg 1963 and 1967, as Elisabeth and Tosca; Engagements at the Drottningholm Court Theatre included Angelica in Handel's Orlando; Professor at the Oslo Music School from 1970; Director of the Oslo Opera 1978-81. *Recordings include:* Excerpts from the 1960 Bayreuth Festival (Melodram). *Honours:* Commander, St Claus Orden, 1981; Commander, Kungl. Nordstjerne orden, 1986; Orde Van Oranje-Nassau, 1963; Officer of L'Ordre de Leopold II, 1964; Harriet Cohen, International Music Award, The Gold medal for singing, 1958. *Address:* Grimeveien 8, 2600 Lillehammer, Norway.

NORDWALL Eva (Marie), b. 4 Oct 1944, Uherské Hradištěk, Czechoslovakia. Harpsichord Soloist. m. Ove Nordwall, 30 Dec 1973, 2 sons. *Education:* Piano Solo, Brno Conservatory, 1959-63; Piano, (Professor Stina Sundell), Harpsichord (Margit Theorell), Swedish Royal High School of Music, 1964-73. *Debut:* As Harpsichord Soloist, Stockholm, 1972. *Career:* Concerts and tours of Sweden, Norway, Denmark, Poland, Austria, Federal Republic of Germany, Canada, USA, Puerto Rico, 1972-; Numerous TV and radio appearances in Sweden and abroad; Solo Harpsichord music written for by some

30 Swedish and International Composers including Ligeti. *Recordings:* Several records (Sweden, Canada, Puerto Rico) of mostly contemporary music, solo harpsichord music. *Honours:* Recipient of several including the Swedish State Award for Artists, 1980, 1981, 1986, 1989. *Memberships:* Swedish Union of Musicians; Musikcentrum; Samtida Musik, Stockholm, Sweden, Member of Board. *Current Management:* Sforzando Produktion, Granvägen 6, S-640 50 Björnlunda, Sweden. *Address:* Österlanggaten 14 I, S-11131 Stockholm, Sweden.

NOREJKA Virgilius, b. 22 Sept 1935, Siauliai, Lithuania. Singer (Tenor); Administrator. *Education:* Studied in Volnius. *Debut:* State Opera of Vilnius 1957, as Lensky in Eugene Onegin. *Career:* Sang in Lithuania as Alfredo, the Duke in Rigoletto, Werther, Don Jose, Almaviva and the Prince in The Love of Three Oranges; Guest appearances in Moscow, Leningrad, Kiev and Kharkov: gave recitals and sang Russian folk songs, in addition to operatic repertoire; Further engagements at the Berlin Staatsoper and in Poland, Bulgaria, Denmark, Finland, Italy, Austria, Hungary, USA and Canada; Hamburg Staatsoper as Radames; Also appeared in operas by Lithuanian composers; Director of the Vilnius Opera, 1975-. *Recordings:* Albums for Melodiya. *Address:* Av. Rómulo Gallegos, Edf Residencias, Santa Rosa, Apt 4-B, Sebucan, Caracas 1071, Venezuela.

NØRGÅRD Per, b. 13 July 1932, Gentofte, Denmark, Composer. *Education:* Degrees in Music History, Music Theory and Composition, Royal Danish Academy of Music, 1952-55; Studied with Nadia Boulanger, Paris, France, 1956-57. *Career:* Teaching Positions, Conservatoire, Odense, 1958-61; The Royal Academy of Music, 1960-65; Royal Academy of Music, Aarhus, 1965. *Compositions include:* Operas: Gilgamesh, 1971-72; Siddharta, 1974-79; The Divine Circus, 1982; Orchestral: Symphony No 1, 1953-55; Luna, 1967; Voyage into the Golden Screen, 1968-69; Dream Play, 1975; Twilight, 1976-77; Symphony No 4, 1981; Symphony No 3 in Two Movements, 1972-75; Symphony No 5, 1990; Spaces of Time, 1991; Night -Symphonies, Day Breaks, 1991; String Orchestra/ Wind Orchestra: Metamorphosis, 1953; Doing, 1968; Modlys, 1970; Chamber Music: Fragment V, 1961; Whirls' World, 1970; Prelude and Ant Fugue (With a Crab Cannon), 1982; Tintinnabulary, string quartet no 6, 1986; Lin for clarinet, cello and piano, 1986; Solo Keyboard: Sonata in One Movement, 1953; 4 Fragments, 1959-60; Canon, 1971; Achilles and the Tortoise, 1983; Choral Works: Evening Land, 1954; Libra, 1973; Frost Psalm, 1975-76; Wie Ein Kind, 1980; Interrupted Hymn, Scream, Drinking Song; Solo instruments and orchestra: Between, 3 Movements for cello and orchestra, 1985; Remembering Child, 2 Movements for viola and chamber orchestra, 1986; Helle Nacht, Violin Concerto, 1987; King, Queen and Ace, harp and 13 instruments, 1989; Perucssion instruments: Iching, solo, 1982. *Recordings:* Has had much of his work recorded; Many works now available on CD. *Honours:* Recipient of numerous honours including: Nordic Council Prize for Music for opera Gilgamesh, 1974; Holds several Honorary posts. *Address:* Koda, Maltegårdsvej 24, 2820 Gentofte, Denmark.

NØRHOLM Ib, b. 24 Jan 1931, Copenhagen, Denmark, Composer. *Education:* The Royal Danish Academy of Music, Copenhagen. *Career:* Music Critic with several major Copenhagen newspapers; Professor of Composition, The Royal Danish Academy of Music; Organist in Copenhagen. *Compositions include:* Stanzas and Fields; Strofer og Marker; Trio Op 22; Fluctuations, The Unseen Pan; Exile - Music for a Composition for Large Orchestra; From my Green Herbarium; September-October-November; After Icarus; Tavole per Orfeo; Invitation to a Beheading, 1965; Den unge Park, 1969-70; The Garden Wall, 1976; Isola Bella, 1968-70; Day's Nightmare, 1973; Decreation, 1979; The Elements; Moralities - or There May Be Several Miles to the Nearest Spider; Ecliptic Instincts; Violin Concerto, 1974; Herectic Hymn, 1975; Apocalyptic Idylls, 1980;

The Funen Cataracts, 1976; Essai Prismatique, 1979; Lys, 1979; Before Silence, 1980; Haven med Steir der deler sig, 1982. *Recordings:* Has had much of his work recorded.*Current Management:* Koda, Maltegårdsvej 24, 2820 Gentofte, Denmark. *Address:* Henningsens Allé 30 B, DK-2900 Hellerup, Denmark.

NORMAN Jessye, b. 15 Sept 1945, Augusta, Georgia, USA. Soprano, Concert and Opera Singer. *Education:* BM cum laude, Howard University, Washington DC; Peabody Conservatory 1967; MMus. University of Michigan 1967-68. *Career:* Operatic debut: Deutsche Oper, Berlin 1969; La Scala, Milan 1972; Royal Opera House, Covent Garden 1972; NY Metropolitan Opera, as Cassandre in Les Troyens, 1983; American debut, Hollywood Bowl, 1972; Lincoln Center, NYC 1973; First Covent Garden Recital, 1980; Debut at Barbican, 1983; Tours include North and South America, Europe, Middle East, Australia, Israel; Many international festivals including: Aix-en-Provence, Aldeburgh, Berlin, Edinburgh, Flanders, Helsinki, Lucerne, Salzburg, Tanglewood, Spoleto, Hollywood, Ravinia; roles include Verdi's Aida, Wagner's Elisabeth and Strauss's Ariadne; Opened the season at Chicago in 1989, as Gluck's Alcestis; Sang Sieglinde in Die Walküre at the Metropolitan 1990 (also televised); Concert repertory includes Les Nuits d'été by Berlioz. *Recordings include:* Le Nozze di Figaro, La Finta Giardiniera, Fidelio, Carmen, Haydn's La Vera Costanza, Ariadne, Verdi's Un Giorno di Regno and Il Corsaro, Schubert Lieder, Das Lied von der Erde (Philips); Alceste, Oedipus Rex, Debussy's La Demoiselle Elue (Orfeo) Mahler's 2nd symphony (CBS); Les Contes d'Hoffmann, Euryanthe (EMI); Fauré's Pénélope (Erato); Die Walküre (Eurodisc); Elektra, conducted by Claudio Abbado (Deutsche Grammophon). *Address:* c/o Shaw Concerts Incorporated, 1995 Broadway, New York, NY 10023, USA.

NORRINGTON Roger Arthur Carver, b. 16 Mar 1934, Oxford, England. Musical Director: London Classical Players, London Baroque Players, Schütz Choir of London. m. Susan Elizabeth McLean May, 1964, divorced 1982, 1 son, 1 daughter, m. Karolyn Mary Lawrence, June 1984. *Education:* Dragon School, Oxford; Westminster; Clare College, Cambridge (BA); Royal College of Music. *Debut:* British 1962; BBC Radio 1964; TV 1967; Germany, Austria, Denmark, Finland 1966; Portugal 1970; Italy 1971; France and Belgium 1972; USA 1974; Holland 1975; Switzerland 1976. *Career:* Freelance Singer 1962-72; Principal Conductor, Kent Opera 1966-84; Principal Conductor, Bournemouth Sinfonietta 1985-89; Musical Director: London Classical Players, 1978-; London Baroque Players, 1975-; Schütz Choir of London 1962-; Guest Conductor for many British, European and American Orchestras; Many Television Specials and Broadcasts at home and abroad; has given weekends of music devoted to authentic performances of work by major composers, Berlioz, Mozart, Beethoven and Purcell, 1993; Conducted British stage premiere of Rameau's Les Boréades, Royal Academy of Music, 1985; Die Zauberflöte at the 1990 Promenade Concerts, London; Series of Beethoven Symphonies on BBC television, 1991; Conducted the London Classical Players in Mozart's Prague Symphony and Requiem, Prom Concerts 1991; Season 1992 with Rossini Bicentenary concert at Fisher Hall, New York. *Recordings:* Extensive catalogue with Argo, Decca and E.M.I. with London Classical Players including Die Zauberflöte, the Symphonie Fantastique, Beethoven's 2nd and 8th symphonies; Schütz St Matthew Passion and Resurrection; Bruckner Mass No 2; Don Giovanni, 1993. *Publications:* Occasional articles in various musical journals. *Contributions to:* Occasional reviews and articles. *Honour:* Order of the British Empire, 1979; Cavaliere, Order al Merito della Repubblica Italiana 1981; Gramophone Award, 1987; Opus Award, 1987; Ovation Award, 1988. *Hobbies:* Reading; Walking; Sailing.

NORRIS David Owen, b. 16 June 1953, Northampton, England. International concert pianist and broadcaster. 2 sons. *Education:* Keble College, Oxford, 1972-75, First Class Honours in Music, Organ Scholar; RAM, 1975-77, Paris, 1977-78. *Career:* Professor, RAM 1978-; Repetiteur at Covent Garden and assistant MD at RSC until 1980; Television appearances across Europe and North America, performances at Henry Wood Promenade Concerts; Chairman of Faculty, Steans Institute for Singers, Chicago, 1992-; Gresham Professor of Music, 1993-; Artistic Director of the Cardiff Festival, 1992-. *Honour:* Fellow of Royal Academy of Music, 1988; first-ever Gilmore Artist, 1991. *Memberships:* Fellow of Royal College of Organists; ISM. *Address:* 60 Old Oak Lane, London NW10 6UB, England.

NORRIS Geoffrey, b. 19 Sept 1947, London, England. Critic; Musicologist. *Education:* ARCM 1967; BA, University of Durham 1969; University of Liverpool 1969-70; 1972-73; Institute of Theatre, Music and Cinematography, Leningrad, 1971. *Career:* Music Critic for The Times Daily Telegraph and The Sunday Telegraph; Lecturer in Music History, Royal Northern College of Music, 1975-77; Commissioning Editor, New Oxford Companion to Music, 1977-83; Music Centre, The Daily Telepgraph, 1983-. *Publications include:* (With others) Enyclopedia of Opera, 1976; Rakhmaninov, 1976, 2nd edition, 1993; Shostakovich: The Man and his Music, 1982; (with Robert Threlfall) A Catalogue of the Compositions of S. Rachmaninoff, 1982. *Contributions to:* New Grove Dictionary of Music and Musicians, 1980; Musical Times; Music Quarterly; Tempo; Music and Letters; BBC Broadcasts. *Membership:* Royal Musical Asssociation; The Critics Circle. *Address:* D44, Du Crane Court, London SW17 7JH, England.

NORTH Nigel, b. 1954, London, England. Lutenist; Guitarist; Professor of Lute. *Education:* Guildhall School of Music, 1964-70; Royal College of Music, 1971-74, Classical guitar with John Williams and Carlos Bonell, Viols with Francis Baines; Postgraduate course in Early Music at the GSM, 1974-75; Baroque lute studies with Michael Schaffer in Germany, 1976. *Career:* Performances from 1973 with the Early Music Consort of London (David Munrow); Academy of Ancient Music (Christopher Hogwood); Schütz Choir of London and Early Opera Project (Roger Norrington); Kent Opera; English Concert (Trevor Pinnock); Taverner Players (Andrew Parrott); London Baroque (Charles Medlam); Trio Sonnerie (Monica Huggett); Raglan Baroque Players (Nicholas Kraemer); The 16 Choir and Orchestra (Harry Christophers); Professor of Lute at the Guildhall School from 1976; Solo debut at the Wigmore Hall 1977, Bach recital on the lute; Bach 300th anniversary concerts in London 1985, with Maggie Cole: all Bach lute works heard in London for the first time; Bach recitals in Holland, Israel, USA, Germany, Poland and York; Visited Poland 1986 to play music by S L Weiss at Wroclaw; Solo recitals and tours from 1977 to USSR, Spain, Canada, Italy, Sweden, Bath and Aldeburgh Festivals; Stuttgart, Madrid, Inndbruck, Moscow, Utrecht, York and London (Lufthansa) Early Music Festivals; Accompanist to such singers as Alfred Deller, Emma Kirkby, Nigel Rogers, Mark Tucker, Stephen Varcoe, Nancy Argenta, James Bowman, Julianne Baird and Michael Chance; Summer Academies with the Lute Society of America 1980-88; Swedish Guitar and Lute Society; French Lute Society and Trio Sonnerie Summer School 1989; Masterclasses, lectures and workshops in Sardinia, Rome, Venice, Vancouver, New York and San Francisco. *Publications:* Lute Music by William Byrd 1976; Lute Music by Alfonso Ferrabosco, 1979; Continuo Playing on Lute, Archlute and Theorbo, 1987. *Recordings:* As soloist, music by Robert de Visee, Dowland, Bach and Vivaldi; Albums of Monteverdi, Handel, Purcell, Corelli and Vivaldi with London Baroque, Taverner Players, The English Concert, Academy of Ancient Music, Raglan Baroque Players, Trio Sonnerie and The 16 Choir and Orchestra (Monteverdi Vespers, 1988).

NORTH Roger Dudley, b. 1 Aug 1926, Warblington, Hampshire, England. Composer; Writer; Tutor. m. Rosamund Shreeves, 3 Apr 1963, 2 daughters. *Education:* Harrow School, 1940-43; Oxford University,

1943-44; RAM, 1947-51; LRAM, 1951. *Career:* Various small choir and orchestra conductorship posts, 1950-56; Evening Institute teaching, 1951-; Morley College, 1963-91; Approximately 100 broadcast talks for BBC, 1960-70. *Composition:* Sonata for Clarinet and Piano, published around 1956 *Recording:* Salle d'Attente Ballet Suite, Chantry Records, 1977. *Publication:* "The Musical Companion' (Book I) Gollancz 1977. *Contributions to:* Thematic Unity in Parsifal (Wagner Society Magazine); The Rhinegold - The Music (ENO Guide) 1985. *Honours:* William Wallace Exhibition (RAM 1948); Oliviera Prescott Gift (composition) (RAM 1949); Battison Haynes Prize (composition) (RAM 1948). *Membership:* Composers Guild. *Address:* 24 Strand on the Green, London W4 3PH, England.

NORTHCOTT Bayan Peter, b. 24 Apr 1940, Harrow-on-the-Hill, Midlesex, England. Music Critic and Composer. *Education:* BA, Dip. ED., University College, Oxford; BMus, University of Southampton. *Career:* Music Critic, New Statesman 1973-76; Sunday Telegraph 1976-86; The Independent 1987-. *Compositions include:* Hymn to Cybele, 1983; Sextet, 1985; instrumental music and songs. *Publications include:* Study of Alexander Goehr. *Contributions to:* New Grove Dictionary of Music and Musicians, 1980; Music and Musicians; The Listener; Musical Times; Daily Telegraph; Guardian; Tempo; Dansk Musiktidsskrift. *Membership:* Music Section, Critics Circle, 1974-. *Address:* 52 Upper Mall, London W6, England.

NORTON Eunice, b. 30 June 1908, Minneapolis, Minnesota, USA. Concert Pianist; Professor of Music. m. Bernard Lewis, 4 May 1934, 1 son, 1 daughter. *Education:* University of Minnesota, 1922-24; Tobias Matthay Pianoforte School, London, England, 1924-31; Private studies with Artur Schnabel, 1931-33. *Debut:* Carnegie Hall, New York, USA. *Career:* Concert Pianist, USA, Europe, 1927-; Recitals, Wigmore Hall and Queens Hall, London; Soloist, London Symphony Orchestra, Queens Hall Orchestra, Birmingham Symphony, BBC Orchestra, and many others; Recitals throughout Europe and USA; Soloist, New York Philharmonic, Boston Symphony, Philadelphia Symphony, Pittsburgh Symphony, Minneapolis Symphony, and many others, USA; Chamber Music Performances, Budapest, Juilliard and Griller String Quartets and American Chamber Orchestra; Performance at the White House, USA; Celebrated Beethoven year with performances of the 32 Piano Sonatas, and Bach tricentennial with performances of the 48 Preludes and Fugues, and numerous other keyboard works; Master Piano Classes at many American universities; Founder and Music Director, Pittsburgh New Fields of Music, Pittsburgh Concert Artists and Peacham (Vermont) Piano Festivals. *Recordings:* 48 Preludes and Fugues (well-tempered clavier), J S Bach; 32 Pianos Sonatas of Beethoven. *Contributions to:* Carnegie Magazine; Clavier. *Address:* 5863 Marlborough Avenue, Pittsburgh, PA 15217, USA.

NORUP Bent, b. 7 Dec 1936, Hobro, Denmark. Singer (Baritone). *Education:* Studied with Kristian Riis in Copenhagen, with Karl Schmitt-Walter in Munich and with Herta Sperber in New York. *Debut:* Copenhagen 1970, as Kurwenal in Tristan und Isolde. *Career:* The Royal Theatre of Copenhagen, 1970-73; Brunswick, 1973-78; Nuremburg, 1978-; Hannover, 1981-; Bayreuth Festival, 1983; San Antonio Festival 1985; Guest appearances in principal roles worldwide: Vienna, London, Paris, Hamburg, Berlin, Düsseldorf, Hannover, France, Spain, Holland, Poland, Ireland and USA; Roles Include: Holländer, Telramund, Kurwenal, Amfortas, Klingsor, Wotan, Sachs, Pizarro, Jochanaan, Iago, Scarpia, Borromeo; Sang Telramund in Lohengrin at Venice, 1990; Klingsor at Aarhus, 1992; Also well known as concert singer. *Recordings include:* Orestes in Elektra (Harmonia Mundi). *Address:* c/o Teatro la Fenice de Veneza, Campos Fantin 2519, I-30124 Venezia, Italy.

NOVOA Salvador, b. 30 Oct 1937, Mexico City,

Mexico. Opera Singer; Tenor, Voice Teacher. m. 16 Aug 1968, 3 sons, 1 daughter. *Education:* School of Music, The University of Mexico, 1957-62; Voice with Felipe Aguilera Ruiz, 1957-66, Kurt Baum, 1972-80. *Debut:* As Pinkerton in Madama Butterfly, Mexico Opera Company, 1960. *Career:* Erik, in Der fliegende Holländer with The Philadelphia Lyric Opera; Several roles in various operas with the New York City Opera including, Don José and Cavaradossi, the title roles in Bomarzo and Don Rodrigo, Faust in Mefistofele and Edgardo in Lucia di Lammermoor; He has appeared with opera companies widely including, San Diego Opera, Houston Grand Opera, Boston Opera, Cincinnati Opera, Teatro Colon, Argentina, Opera Municipal de Marseille, Stuttgart Opera Company, Teheran Opera etc; His repertoire includes, Aida, Radames; Andrea Chenier; Bomarzo, Pier Francesco; Carmen, Don José; Cavalleria Rusticana, Turiddu; Don Rodrigo; Faust; Macbeth, Macduff; Faust in Mefistofele; Pollione in Norma; Samson in Samson and Delilah; numerous other roles in various operas; Symphonic repertoire includes, Beethoven's Ninth Symphony and Verdi's Messa da Requiem. *Recording:* Bomarzo by Alberto Ginastera, CBS Records. *Honour:* 2nd Prize, Metropolitan Opera Regional Auditions, Mexico City, 1959. *Address:* 248 W 88th Street, New York, NY 10024, USA.

NOVOTNY Jan, b. 15 Dec 1935, Prague, Czechoslovakia. Pianist. m. 26 Apr. 1985 2 daughters. *Education:* Conservatory Praha, 1950-55; Academy of Music Arts, Praha, 1955-59. *Debut:* Praha, 1954. *Career:* Concert performances worldwide, frequent appearances at Prague Spring Festival, Festival de Bonaguil, France; Frequent appearances on Radio Prague, Bern, Gothenburg, Brussels, Paris, TV Prague; Chairman of the Jury, Smetana Piano Competition, Czechoslovakia; Head, Piano Classes Department, Prague Conservatory, 1988-. *Recordings:* Beethoven: Sonatas Op 10 No 3, Op 22, Op 28, Op 31, No 1; Smetana: Complete piano works, 10 records; Schumann: Phantasie C major op 17; F X Dussek: Piano Concertos; Jan L Dusik/Dussek: Last piano sonatas; Jaroslav Jezek: Complete piano works; Ignaz Moscheles: Concerto No 5. op. 87 in C minor; J L Dussek: Piano concertos/selection, boith with Prague Radio Symphony Orchestra, (Supraphon, Prague). *Publication:* Smetana: Piano Compositions, 6 volumes, complete edition 1st time in history. *Contributions to:* Gramorevue, Praha. *Honours:* State Prize, 1984; Annual Prize of Panton editor, Praha, 1987. *Membership:* Society Smetana, Chairman of the Committee, 1991. *Address:* Rosickych 6, Prague 5 CS-150 00, Czech Republic.

NOWAK Anna Maria, b. 26 Mar 1953, Bydgoszcz, Poland. Musicologist; Teacher. *Education:* Academy of Music, Gdansk, 1972-77; Postgraduate studies, Academy of Music, Warsaw 1979-81; PhD Theory of Music, 1987. *Career:* Teacher, Academy of Music, Bydgoszcz, 1979-; Lecturer, Pomerania Philharmonic, 1980-; Manager, Music Department, Editor, Pomorze 1990-91; Participation in several scientific sessions, congresses, symposia, e.g. series of sessions on romantic songs, Academy of Music, Cracow. *Publications:* Vocal Lyric of W Friemann; Tadeusz Szeligowski: Studies and Memoirs, co-author, 1985; Chopin and Mostowskis, 1990; Papers on vocal cycles of Wolf, 1989; Messiaen, 1992; Ravel, 1993; and on vocal lyrics of Polish composers, 1978, 1987, 1989; Romance in Europe and in Poland; Oriental motives in the songs of K Szymanowski. *Contributions to:* Encyclopaedia of Music of PWM; Ruch Muzyczny, magazine. *Honours:* Special Prize of Minister of Culture and Art, 1989; Honorary Prize of the President of the Academy of Music, 1983, 1987. *Membership:* Polish Composers' Union. *Hobby:* Tourism. *Address:* ul Igrzyskowa 6 m 20, 85-791 Bydgoszcz, Poland.

NOWAK Grzegorz, b. 1951, Poland. Conductor. *Education:* Studied conducting, violin and composition at the Poznan Academy of Music; later at Eastman School of Music, Rochester, and at Tanglewood with Bernstein, Ozawa, Leinsdorf and Markevitch. *Career:* Music Director Slupsk Symphony Orchestra 1976-80;

won First Prize in 1984 Ansermet Conducting Competition, Geneva; engagements followed with London Symphony, Montreal Symphony and Orchestre National de France; has also appeared with orchestras of Rome, Oslo, Stockholm, Copenhagen, Helsinki, Monte Carlo, Jerusalem, Madrid, Lisbon, Baltimore, Cincinnati, San Diego, Vancouver, Ottawa, Tokyo, Hong Kong, Geneva, Zürich, Baden-Baden, Saarbrücken, Rotterdam, Milan, Florence, Göteborg, Malmö, Birmingham, Bournemouth, Liverpool, Manchester, Belfast and Glasgow; Currently Music Director of the Biel Symphony Orchestra, Switzerland. *Recordings:* Ravel's Daphnis et Chloe and Bartók's Dance Suite with the London Symphony Orchestra. *Honours:* American Patronage Prize 1984; Europaischen Förderpreis für Musik 1985. *Address:* c/o Harrison/Parrott Ltd., 12 Penzance Place, London W11 4PA, England.

NOWAK Lionel (Henry), b. 25 Sept 1911, Cleveland, Ohio, USA. Pianist; Teacher; Composer. m. (1) Isabelle Wood, 30 Jan 1930, 1 son, 1 daughter, (2) Laura Taylor, 1 son, 2 daughters. *Education:* Heidelberg College, 1931-32; Artist Diploma, Piano, 1930; B.Mus., 1933, M.Mus., 1936, Certificate, German Institute of Foreigners, 1929, Cleveland Institute of Music. *Debut:* Soloist, Cleveland Orchestra, 1924. *Career:* Director of Music, Fenn College, Cleveland, 1932-38, Humphrey Weidman Dance Company, 1938-42; Professor, Music, Converse College, 1942-46; Conductor, Spartanburg Symphony Orchestra, 1942-45; Professor, Music, Syracuse University, 1946-48; Bennington College, 1948-; Piano Recitalist, Arts Programme, Association of American Colleges, 1945-63. *Compositions:* Sonata for Solo Violin; Wisdom Exalteth a People, Womens Double Chorus; Diptych for string trio. *Recordings:* Concert Piece for Six Kettledrums, Drums and Strings; Soundscape for Piano; Soundscape for String Quartet; Soundscape for Bassoon and Piano; Soundscape for Three Woodwinds. *Address:* North Bennington, VT 05257, USA.

NUCCI Leo, b. 16 Apr 1942, Castiglione dei Pepoli, Bologna, Italy. Singer (Baritone). m. Adriana Anelli. *Education:* Studied with Giuseppe Marchesi and Ottaviano Bizzarri. *Debut:* Spoleto 1967, as Rossini's Figaro. *Career:* Sang Puccini's Schaunard at Venice 1975; La Scala Milan 1976, as Figaro; Covent Garden 1978, as Miller in Luisa Miller; Metropolitan Opera from 1980, as Renato in Un Ballo in Maschera, Eugene Onegin, Germont, Amonasro and Posa in Don Carlos; Paris Opera 1981, as Renato; Pesaro 1984, in a revival of Rossini's Il Viaggio a Reims; Wiesbaden 1985, as Rigoletto; Salzburg Festival, 1989-90, as Renato in Un ballo di Maschera; Metropolitan Opera, 1988-89, as Rigoletto; Sang Silvio in Pagliacci at Turin, 1990, Di Luna in Il Trovatore at Parma; Sang Iago in concert performances of Otello, Chicago and New York 1991; Season 1992 as Luna at Turin, Tonio at Rome, Iago at Reggio Emilia, the Forza Don Carlo at Florence and Rossini's Figaro at the Festival of Caracalla. *Recordings:* Donizetti's Maria di Rudenz; Aida; Ford in Falstaff; Il Viaggio a Reims (CBS); Aida, Simon Boccanegra Otello and Rigoletto (Decca); Michonnet in Adriana Lecouvreur; Video of Il Barbiere di Siviglia, from the Met, (DGG). *Address:* c/o Allied Artists Agency, 42 Montpelier Square, London SW7 1JZ, England.

NUNEMAKER Richard E., b. 30 Nov 1942, Buffalo, New York, USA. Clarinetist; Saxophonist. m. Lynda Perkins, 15 Aug 1964, 1 son, 1 daughter. *Education:* BS, Education, Clarinet, State University of New York College at Fredonia, 1964; MM, Clarinet, University of Louisville, 1966; Studied with Clark Brody, Jerome Stowell, James Livingston, Allen Sigel, William Wilett. *Career:* Bass Clarinet, Erie Philharmonic, 1963-64; Louisville Orchestra, 1964-66; Clarinet, Chicago Civic Orchestra, 1966-67; Bass Clarinet, Saxophone, Houston Symphony Orchestra, 1967-; Artist-in-Residence, Sewanee Summer Music Centre, 1966; Clarinet, Saxophone, Houston Pops, 1970-85; Music America Chamber Ensemble, 1977-92; Cambiata Soloists, 1970-84; Faculty: Clarinet and Saxophone, Assistant Director, Wind Ensemble, University of St Thomas, Houston,

Texas, 1970-92; Clarinet, Saxophone; Pierrot Plus Ensemble of Rice University, 1987-92; Clarinet and Saxophone concerto appearances with such conductors as Lawrence Foster, Jorge Mester and Sergiu Comissiona. Numerous radio and television performances as recitalist & soloist with various chamber ensembles including many performances of new music; Principal Clarinet, Orquesta Filamonica De La Ciudad De Mexico, 1987; Clarinet and Saxophone Opus 90, New Directions in American Chamber Music, 1990. *Recordings:* America Swings I, II. A Tribute To Benny Goodman; A Tribute to Artie Shaw Pro Arte Records with the Houston Symphony Orchestra; From The Great Land, Bravura Records; Continuum Percussion Quartet, Eugene Kurtz, Logo 1, New World Records; Golden Petals/Richard Nunemaker, Master Musicians Collective Recordings. *Publications:* Author, If The Shoe Fits, 1979. *Honours:* Performers Certificate, Clarinet, State University of New York College at Fredonia, 1964. *Memberships:* International Clarinet Congress; Clarinetwork Inc.; International Saxophone Congress; International League of Women Composers. *Hobbies:* Running; Gardening; Photography. *Current Management:* Lyn-Rich Management. *Address:* 2807 Linkwood, Houston, TX 77025, USA.

NYGAARD Jens, b. 26 Oct 1931, Stephens, Arkansas, USA. Conductor; Pianist. *Education:* Studied with parents, at Louisiana State University and at Juilliard School, MS 1957; *Career:* Conducted Mozart 200th birthday concert, Jan 1956; Conductor of Music In Our Time series concerts at Columbia University 1964-667; Founder of Westchester Chamber Chorus and Orchestra 1965; Beethoven Concerts as Pianist and Conductor, Vienna 1970; Soloist in complete Mozart piano concertos at Washington Heights Young Men's Hebrew Association, New York, 1974-75; Conducted Mozart's I Re Pastore and USA premiere of Pergolesi's La Contadina Astuta; Co-founded the Jupiter Symphony Orchestra in New York 1979; Music Director of the Naumburg Symphony Orchestra 1980; Teacher at Columbia University Teachers College 1981-82; Conductor of Rutgers University Symphony Orchestra 1982. *Address:* c/o Columbia University Teachers College, 703 Dodge, New York, NY 10027, USA.

NYIKOS Markus Andreas, b. 9 Dec 1948, Basel, Switzerland. Cellist. m. Verena Kamber, 8 Dec 1982. 1 daughter. *Education:* Musik-Akademie, Basel with Paul Szabo; Konservatorium Luzern with Stanislav Apolin; Master classes with Zara Nelsova, Pierre Fournier, Sandor Vegh, Janáček Quartet. *Career:* Cellos solo, Festival Strings Lucerne, 1974-79; Cello solo, Philharmonische Virtuosen Berlin, 1983-; Professor, Hochschule der Kunste Berlin, 1979-; Guest Professor, Shanghai Conservatory; Numerous concerts and radio appearances in all continents. *Recordings:* Vivaldi and Cirri: Cello-concerts with Radio-Sinfonie Orchestra Berlin; Brahms Sonatas, E-minor, F-major, with Gerard Wyss Piano; Schubert: Arpeggione-Sonata, A-minor with Gerard Wyss; La Groupe Des Six, compositions by Auric, Poulenc, Honegger, Milhaud with Jaroslav Smykal, piano. *Address:* c/o Robert Gilder, Anglo Swiss Artists Management, 4/5 Primrose Mews, 1A Sharpleshall Street, London NW1 8YW, England.

NYMAN Michael, b. 23 Mar 1944, London, England. Composer. *Education:* Studied with Alan Bush at Royal Academy of Music, 1961-65; King's College, London, 1964-67, with Thurston Dart. *Career:* Writer and Music Critic, 1968-78. *Compositions:* Film music for Peter Greenaway creations The Falls, 1977, The Draughtsman's Contract, A Zed and Two Noughts, Drowning by Numbers and Prospero's Books, Renaissance Masque for cabaret chanteuse, rock singer and opera star; Ballet scores for choreographers Rosemary Butcher and Siobhan Davies; Works for cabaret artist Ute Lemper and the Balanescu Quartet; Concerto and Where the Bee Dances for saxophonist John Harle; Songs for Tony, Saxophone Quartet, premiered 1993; The Kiss, video- duet, 1984; The Man Who Mistook His Wife for a Hat, chamber opera, London, 1986; Vital Statistics, London, 1987; Orpheus'

Daughter, Rotterdam, 1988; La Princesse de Milan, dance opera after The Tempest, Avignon, 1991; Letters, Riddles and Writs, television opera in Not Mozart series, BBC TV, 1991. *Publications:* Experimental Music: Gage and Beyond, 1974; Libretto for Birtwistle's dramatic pastoral Down by the Greenwood Side, 1968-69. *Recordings:* The Michael Nyman Songbook, The Essential Michael Nyman Band, String Quartets Nos. 1-3, Where The Bee Dances, The Man Who Mistook His Wife for a Hat. *Address:* c/o PRS Ltd Member Registration, 29-33 Berners Street, London W1P 4AA, England.

NYSTEDT Knut, b. 3 Sept 1915, Oslo, Norway. Composer; Conductor; Organist. m. Brigit, 20 June 1942, 1 son, 2 daughters. *Education:* Examen, Artium 1935; Studied Organ with Arild Sandvold, Oslo Conservatory of Music and with Ernest White, New York 1947; Studied Composition with Bjarne Brustad, Oslo and Aaron Copland, New York, 1947. *Debut:* As Organist, 1938; As Conductor, Oslo Philharmonic, 1945. *Career:* Conductor of Norwegian Soloist Choir, 1950-90, performances worldwide; Organist at Torshov Church, Oslo, 1946-82; Professor of Choral Conducting at Oslo University, 1964-85. *Compositions:* Piano variations, 1948; Mixed chorus and orchestra: Lucis Creator Optime, for soli, chorus and orchestra, 1968; Masses, Opera: With Crown and Star. Christmas Opera, 1971; Songs of Solomon, church opera, 1989; Chamber Music: Five String Quartets, 1938, 48, 55, 66 and 88; Requiem for nine brass instruments, 1971; Music for Six Trombones, 1980; Orchestra: Symphony for Strings, 1950; Exsultate, 1980; Sinfonia del Mare, 1983; Mountain scenes for concert band, 1981; A Hymn for Human Rights for chorus, organ and percussion, 1982; For a Small Planet, for chorus, harp and string quartet, 1982; Ave Maria for chorus and violin solo, 1986; Ave Christe for women's chorus and orchestra, 1991; Four Grieg Romances, chorus a capella. 1992; The Conch for male quartet with counter tenor, 1993. *Recordings;* Numerous recordings. *Honours:* Knight of the Order of St Olav, 1966; Distinguished Service Citation from Augsburg College, USA, 1975; The Norwegian Council for Cultural Affairs Music Prize, 1980; Professor Honorari, Mendoza University, Argentina, 1991. *Membership:* Society of Norwegian Composers. *Address:* Vestbrynet 25 B, 1160 Oslo, Norway.

O

O'BRIEN Eugene, b. 24 Apr 1945, Paterson, New Jersey, USA. Composer; Teacher. *Education:* Studied at University of Nebraska, MM 1969, with Bernd Alois Zimmermann at Cologne, Indiana University with John Eaton and Iannis Xenakis and with Donald Erb at the Cleveland Institute of Music, DMA 1983. *Career:* Teacher at Cleveland Institute 1973-81, Composer-in-Residence 1981-85; Associate Professor at Catholic University of America in Washington, DC Music Department 1985-87; Associate Professor at Indiana University School of Music, from 1987. *Compositions:* Ballet, Taking Measures, 1984; Orchestra: Symphony 1969; Cello Concerto 1972; Dedales for soprano and orchestra 1973; Rites of Passage 1978; Dreams and Secrets of Origin for soprano and orchestra 1983; Alto saxophone concerto 1989; Chamber: Intessitura for cello and piano 1975; Embarking for Cythera for 8 instruments 1978; Tristan's Lament for cello; Allures for percussion trio 1979; Psalms and Nocturnes for flute, viola da gamba and harpsichord 1985; Mysteries of the Horizon for 11 instruments 1987; Vocal: Requiem Mass soprano, chorus and wind ensemble 1966; Nocturne for soprano and 10 instruments 1968; Elegy for Bernd Alois Zimmermann for soprano and ensemble 1970; Lingual for soprano, flute and cello 1972. *Honour:* Guggenheim Fellowship 1984-85. *Address:* c/o ASCAP, ASCAP Building, One Lincoln Plaza, New York, NY 10023, USA.

O'CONNOR Adam Patrick Joseph, b. 30 Sept 1959, New York City, New York, USA. Editor. *Education:* AB, Philosophy, University of Chicago, 1981. *Career:* Editor, 1989-91, Senior Editor, 1991-93, Editor-in- Chief. 1993-, Abstracts of Music Literature, Repertoire International de Litterature Musicale (RILM), similarly RILM's On-line format Music Literature International on dialogue and RILM's CD-ROM format Muse (music search); Research Associate, Research Center for Music Iconography, 1989- *Address:* RILM, City University of New York, 33 West 42nd Street, New York, NY 10036, USA.

O'HORA Ronan, b. 9 Jan 1964, Manchester, England. Pianist. *Education:* GMus, Honours, Royal Northern College of Music, 1985. *Career:* Recitals and concerts in United Kingdom, USA, Germany, France, Italy, Austria, Switzerland, Spain, Denmark, Norway, Sweden, Belgium, Holland, Portugal, Ireland, Yugoslavia and Czechoslovakia; Concerts with Philharmonia, Royal Philharmonic, BBC Symphony, Hallé, Bournemouth Symphony, Royal Liverpool Philharmonic, BBC Philharmonic, BBC Scottish, Zurich Tonhalle Orchestra, Netherlands Radio Symphony and Chamber Orchestras, Philharmonia Hungaria, Indianapolis Symphony, Florida Philharmonic. *Recordings:* Britten complete muic for two pianos (with Stephen Hough) for Virgin Classics; Numeous radio recordings in UK, USA, France, Holland, Poland, Czechoslovakia, Portugal and Ireland. *Hobbies:* Reading; Theatre; Cinema. *Current Management:* Robert Gilder and Company, London. *Address:* c/o Robert Gilder and Company, Enterprise House, 59-65 Upper Ground, London SE1 9PQ, England.

O'LEARY Thomas, b. 3 Sept 1924, Punxsutawney, Pennsylvania, USA. Singer (Bass). *Education:* Studied with Alexander Kipnis in New York. *Debut:* San Jose 1947 as Kecal in The Bartered Bride. *Career:* Appearances at Boston, Baltimore, New Orleans from 1967, Chicago 1977, San Francisco, Houston and San Diego; Sang at Nuremberg 1960-65, Vienna Volksoper 1962-75, with further engagements at Munich, Hamburg, Rome, Bologna, Berlin, Barcelona, Zurich, Marseilles and Frankfurt; Other roles included Sarastro, Rocco, King Philip, Zaccaria, Arkel, Mephistopheles, Boris and Pimen in Boris Godunov; Wagner's Mark, Daland, Pogner, Hunding, Hagen and Gurnemanz; Frequent concert performances. *Address:* c/o Volksoper, Wahringerstrasse 78, A-1090 Vienna, Austria.

O'NEILL Charles, b. 22 Sept 1930, Ridgefield Park, New Jersey, USA. Singer (Tenor). *Education:* Studied in New York. *Debut:* Fort Worth Opera 1958, as Radames. *Career:* Appearances at opera houses in Santa Fe, Cincinnati, Hamburg, Stuttgart, Berlin, Cologne, Frankfurt, Dusseldorf and Zurich; Member of the Theater am Gartnerplatz Munich, with guest engagements at Toronto, Vancouver, Belgrade and Basle; Other roles have been Florestan, Don Jose, Don Carlos, Alvaro, Manrico, Otello, Turiddu, Samson, Cavaradossi, Rodolfo, Calaf, Andrea Chenier, Oedipus Rex by Stravinsky, Bacchus and Siegmund.

O'NEILL Dennis, b. 25 Feb 1948, Pontarddulais, Wales. Singer (Tenor). *Education:* Studied privately with Frederick Cox, Campogalliani and Ricci. *Career:* State Opera of South Australia, 1975-77, then principal tenor Scottish Opera. *Debuts:* Covent Garden (Norma) 1979, Glyndebourne (Italian Singer, Rosenkavalier) 1980, U.S. (Dallas-Lucia di Lammermoor) 1983, Vienna Staatsoper (Alfredo-Traviata) 1983; Throughout the World including, Hamburg, Berlin, Paris, Brussels, Marseilles, Nice, Munich, Cologne, Oslo, Barcelona, Zurich, Chicago, San Francisco, Metropolitan New York, Vancouver, San Diego, Copenhagen; Long association with Royal Opera House, Covent Garden, many roles including Rodolfo (La Bohème), Duke (Rigoletto), Edgardo (Lucia di Lammermoor), Riccardo (Ballo in Maschera), Foresto (Attila); Season 1992 with British Youth Opera Gala at Covent Garden, Manrico in Munich, Riccardo at the Opéra Bastille, Radames at Tel Aviv. *Recordings include:* Opera Gala Recital, 1991. *Address:* c/o Ingpen and Williams Ltd., 14 Kensington Court, London W8 5DN, England.

O'NEILL Fiona, b. 1958, England. Singer (Soprano). *Education:* Studied at the Royal Northern College of Music; Master Classes at Aldeburgh. *Career:* Solo roles have included: Musetta, Norina, and Donna Anna for Travelling Opera; Mabel in The Pirates of Penzance for New D'Oyly Carte; Serpetta in La Serva Padrona at the Northcutt Theatre Exeter; Salome for the Stockholm Folkopera at the Edinburgh Festival; English National Opera 1990-91 as Papagena and as Gerda in Fennimore and Gerda; Sang the title role in Lakmé and Louise at the Bloomsbury Theatre and Pedrotti's Tutti in Maschera at the Britten Theatre; Concert engagements include Kurt Weill songs at the Cheltenham and Edinburgh Festivals; Premiere of Goehr's Sing Ariel, the 1990 Aldeburgh Festival; Handel's Solomon, Birmingham 1990; Festival Hall debut with the Philharmonia Orchestra, Dec 1990, debut at Barbican and RPO 1991. *Address:* c/o Norman McCann International Artists Ltd, The Coach House, 56 Lawrie Park Gardens, London SE26 6XJ, England.

O'REILLY Brendan, b. 1935, Dublin, Ireland. Violinist. *Education:* Studied at Belvedere College Dublin, with David Martin at the Royal Academy of Music and with Andre Gertler in Brussels. *Career:* Played with the Radio Eireann String Quartet in Cork, then freelanced with the Royal Philharmonic and the English Chamber Orchestra; Co-founded the Gabrieli Quartet 1967 and toured with them to Europe, North America, the Far East and Australia; Festival engagements in Britain, including the Aldeburgh, City of London and Cheltenham; Concerts every season in London participation in the Barbican Centre's Mostly Mozart Festival; Resident Artist at the University of Essex from 1971; Has co-premiered works by William Alwyn, Britten, Alan Bush, Daniel Jones and Gordon Crosse, 2nd Quartets of Nicholas Maw and Panufnik, 1983, 80 and the 3rd Quartet of John McCabe 1979; British premiere of the Piano Quintet by Sibelius 1990. *Recordings:* 5-CDs including early pieces by Britten, Dohnanyi's Piano Quintet with Wolfgang Manz, Walton's Quartets and the Sibelius Quartet and Quintet, with Anthony Goldstone. *Address:* c/o Anglo Swiss Ltd, 3 Primrose Mews, 1a Sharpleshall Street, London NW1 8YW, England.

O'REILLY Graham Henry Meredith, b. 4 Sept 1947, Parkes, New South Wales, Australia. Singer; Conductor; Musicologist. m. Jill Barralet, 2 Sept 1972 (div.), 1 son,

1 daughter; (2) Brigitte Vinson, 27 Dec 1986, 2 daughters. *Education:* BA, Honours, University of Sydney, 1968; Associate, Sydney Conservatorium of Music, 1966; Licentiate, Trinity College, London, 1969; Reading for PhD, London University. *Debut:* Messiah, Sydney Town Hall, 1971. *Career:* Music teacher, Sydney, 1970-73; Concert & session singer, London, 1973-82, member Groupe Vocal de France 1982-86, solo oratorio and ensemble singer specialising in early music, Director, early music ensembles, 1976-; Director, The Restoration Musick 1980-81, Psallite 1981-86, Ensemble William Byrd, 1983-; Researcher, late Restoration stage music 1973-, pitch in Renaissance vocal music, 1979-; Singing teacher, 1980-. *Recordings:* With Psallite: Music by Tallis, Byrd & Gibbons; Collected works of Jon Dixon. With Groupe Vocal de France; Sacred Music of Giacinto Scelsi; With Ensemble William Byrd: English Music of the Seventeenth Century, Volume 1: Orlando Gibbons; Volume 2: Welcome Vicegerent, music of Henry Purcell. *Publication:* Editor, Eccles: Music to Macbeth, Cathedral Music, 1978. *Honour:* Frank Busby Musical Scholarship, Sydney University, 1967. *Hobbies:* Playing with children; Enjoying French cuisine. *Address:* 63A Sunderland Road, London SE23, England.

OAKLEY-TUCKER John, b. 1959, Canada. Opera Singer (Baritone), *Education:* Studied, Guildhall School of Music, Britten-Pears School, Ravel Academy, with Peter Pears, Gerard Souzay, Elisabeth Schwarzkopf and David Pollard. *Career:* Has sung Mozart's Count and Don Giovanni and the title role in Owen Wingrave at Aldeburgh; Glyndebourne Festival in Jenůfa, Arabella and Le Nozze di Figaro (also televised); Papageno in Die Zauberflöte at the Cockpit Theatre, London; Concert performances with the Songmakers' Almanac, Die Schöne Müllerin, Carmina Burana, Messiah, Schubert Masses, Dvořák's Te Deum and Elgar's Apostles; Tour of the UK, Spain and Portugal 1989, singing Mahler's Kindertotenlieder for Ballet Rambert; Other repertoire includes The Creation, Duruflé's Requiem, the Petite Messe Solonnelle, Mozart's C minor Mass and Handel's Dixit Dominus; Lead roles Royal Opera Houses, Garden Venture Project, 1991; Sang Schubert's Winterreise, in the Purcell Room with Nicholas Bosworth, 1992; Tour of Middle East and Far East, sang Marcello in La Boheme, 1992, Belcore in L'Elisir d'Amore, 1993. *Recordings:* TV: Germany 1991, lead role, Tom in Hans Werner Henze's The English Cat, and performances, Italy and Barbican, London for the BBC. *Honours include:* Countess of Munster Musical Trust Scholarship. *Current Management:* Judith Newton, 75 Abedere Gardens, London NW6 3AN, England. *Address:* 18A Wallace Road, London N1 2PG, England.

OBATA Machiko, b. 23 Feb 1948, Sapporo, Japan. Singer (Soprano). *Education:* Studied in Tokyo and Cologne. *Career:* Appearances with the Cologne Opera as Mozart's Pamina and Servilia, Marzelline in Fidelio, Gretel, Liu and Flora in The Turn of the Screw; Sang the Woodbird in Siegfried, 1991; Guest engagements at Strasbourg, Munich and the Opera-Comique in Paris; Salzburg Easter and Summer Festivals 1991 as Barbarina in Le Nozze di Figaro; Frequent concert outings. *Address:* c/o Oper der Stadt Koln, Offenbachplatz, 5000 Cologne, Germany.

OBERHOLTZER William, b. 1947, Bloomington, Indiana, USA. Singer (Baritone). *Education:* Studied at Indiana State University. *Debut:* Indiana 1972 in Herakles by John Eaton. *Career:* Sang Marcello at St Gallen 1976, then sang at Saarbrucken 1978-81, Gelsenkirchen 1981-86, Cassel from 1986, St John in Wolfgang von Schweinitz's Patmos 1990; Engaged at Munster 1986-88 and made guest appearances at Dusseldorf as Marcello, Linz, Krefeld and Hanover; Other roles have included Mozart's Count and Don Giovanni, Valentin, Renato, Rigoletto, Ford, Paolo, Wagner's Wolfram and Amfortas, Strauss's Jochanaan and Mandryka and Wozzeck; Concert engagements include Bach's St John Passion in Berlin and Carmina Burana; Sang in the premiere of Patmos by Schweinitz

at Munich 1990. *Address:* c/o Staatstheater, Friedrichplatz 15, 3500 Kassel, Germany.

OBERLIN Russell, b. 11 Oct 1928, Akron, Ohio, USA. College Professor; Retired Countertenor; Lecturer. *Education:* Artists Diploma, Voice, Juilliard School of Music, 1951. *Career:* Founding Member, New York Pro Musica Antiqua; Soloist with many orchestras including: New York Philharmonic, Chicago Symphony, National Symphony, Buffalo Philharmonic; Little Orchestra Society, Clarion Concerts, Smithsonian Institute Concert Series, CBS Radio Orchestra; Master Classes throughout USA; Opera Appearances in Major Roles at Royal Opera House, Covent Garden (Midsummer Night's Dream); San Francisco Opera; Edinburgh and Vancouver International Festivals; American Opera Society; Solo Recitalist, Concert and Recital Halls, throughout the USA; Radio and TV Appearances; Thomas Hunter Professor of Music, Hunter College and the Graduate Center of the City University of New York, 1966-. *Recordings include:* A Russell Oberlin Recital; Russell Oberlin, Handel Arias; Russell Oberlin, Baroque Cantatas; Soloist with New York Philharmonic, Handel: Messiah; Bach, Magnificat in D; Soloist with New York Pro Musica, The Play of Daniel; Thomas Tallis: sacred Music; Josquin des Prez: Missa Pange Lingua; Walton: Façade with Hermione Gingold; numerous other recordings. *Honours:* Recipient, numerous honours and awards. *Memberships:* National Association of Teachers of Singing; Academia Monteverdiana; Founding Board member, Waverly Consort; Berkshire (Mass) Concert Series; Soho Baroque Opera Company; American Academy of Teachers Singing. *Address:* Hunter College, City University of New York, 695 Park Avenue, New York City, NY 10021, USA.

OBERMAYR Christine, b. 30 May 1959, Wiesbaden, Germany. Singer (Mezzo-soprano). *Education:* Studied in Mainz with Josef Mettrenich. *Debut:* Theater am Gartnerplatz Munich 1983 as Cherubino. *Career:* Sang a Flowermaiden at Bayreuth Festival 1984; Roles in Munich have included Hansel, Flotow's Nancy, Nicklausse and Orlofsky; Engagements at Wiesbaden 1984-89, as Carmen, Emilia, Otello, Olga, Janáček's Fox, the Composer in Ariadne and Ottavia in L'Incoronazione di Poppea; Further appearances at the Theater an der Wien, the Paris Opera and the Teatro Regio Turin; Sang Lyubasha in Rimsky's Tsar's Bride 1985 and Mary in Der Fliegende Holländer at Naples 1992; Many concert and Lieder performances. *Honours:* Prize winner in competitions at Vienna, Wiesbaden and Berlin.

OBERSON René, b. 27 June 1945, La Tour-de-Treme, Fribourg, Switzerland. Composer; Organist; Professor, School of Music, Fribourg. m. 2 sons, 1 daughter. *Education:* Teachers' Training College. Music Education: Schools of Music in Fribourg, Berne and Geneva. *Career:* Organist: Concerts in Switzerland and abroad, notably in Notre-Dame, Paris, France and Symphony Hall, Osaka, Japan. *Compositions:* Latest major works include: L'Exilée (The Exiled Woman), 1983; Concerto for Pan's Pipe, 1984; Le Grand Cercle (The Great Circle), 1985; Homo Somniens, 1988; Au Seuil de l'Ere du Verseau (On the Threshold of the Era of Aquarius), 1988; Jumierè divine, omniprésente, invunerable, for organ 1990; Espoirs, for 2 trumpets, 2 trombones and organ 1990; Numerous works have been recorded by the Lausanne Chamber Orchestra, the Berne Symphony Orchestra, The Netherlands National of Jeunesses Musicales Orchestra. *Recordings:* VDE-Gallo and Jecklin recording companies and radio. *Contributions to:* Has reconstituted the Fourth Concerto for organ or harpsichord and string orchestra by the Swiss composer Meyer von Schauensee (1720-1798) the first 60 bars for the first violin having disappeared. *Memberships:* Association des Musiciens Suisses; Suisa; Société Frank Martin. *Hobbies:* Reading; Chess; Walking; Swimming. *Address:* Pavillon Trobère Miraval, CH-1756 Lovens, Switzerland.

OBRADOVICH Aleksandar, b. 22 Aug 1927, Bled, Yugoslavia. Composer; Professor of Composition. m.

Biljana, 2 Aug 1953. 1 son. *Education:* Academy of Music, 1952; Grant to spec in London, Grant to spec in New York. *Career:* Assistant Professor, Associate Professor, Full Prof, Faculty of Music Art, Belgrade, 1954-; General Secretary of Union of Composers of Yugoslavia, 1962-66; Rector, University of Arts, Belgrade, 1978-83; President of Senate of Union of Yugoslave Universities, 1981-82; President, Union of Yugoslave Universities, 1982-83. *Compositions:* 8 symphonies; 3 concertos; 5 cantatas; Wind of Flame (cycle of songs); Ballet (A Springtime Picnic at Dawn); Many other symphonic works (14); Vocal instrumental works; Chamber works; Film music (7); Music for 8 radio dramas; Electronic music; Chorale works; Compositions performed in 20 different countries. *Recording:* Radio-Televizija Beograd (Belgrade). *Publications:* Orchestration I-II, 1978; III in preparation; Electronic Music and Electronic Instruments, 1978. *Contributions to:* More than 350 articles or music critiques. *Honours:* 24 different prizes including: 7 July prize (1980) for whole work; October Prize of Belgrade (1959 for symphonic epitaph); 4 July Prize (1972 for IV symphony). *Membership:* Society of Composers of Serbia (Sokoj). *Address:* Branka Djonovića 8, Belgrade (Beograd) 11.040, Serbia.

OBRAZTSOVA Yelena Vasilyevna, b. 7 July 1937, Leningrad, USSR. Mezzo-Soprano. m. M. Makarov. *Education:* Leningrad Conservatoire under tuition of Professor Grigoriye. *Debut:* As Marina (Mussorgsky's Boris Godunov) with Bolshoi 1964-65. *Career:* Attached to Staff, Moscow Conservatoire; Soloist with Bolshoi; Many international appearances including: Sofia, Brno, Prague (National and Smetana), Marseilles, Paris, Wiesbaden, Berlin (Komische Oper and Staatsoper), Budapest, Majorca, Barcelona, Kiev, Leningrad, Moscow (Bolshoi and Stanislavsky), Tbilisi, San Francisco, London; Roles include: Azucena, Carmen, Léonore (Donizetti's Favorite), Charlotte (Massenet's Werther), Cherubino, Marina (Boris Godunov), Marfa (Khovanshchina), Hélène (Prokofiev's War and Peace), Dalila, Jocasta (Stravinsky's Oedipus Rex); Countess (Tchaikovsky's Queen of Spades), Amneris, Ulrica (A Masked Ball), Eboli (Don Carlo), Konchakovna (Prince Igor), Lyubashka (Rimsky-Korsakov's The Tsar's Bride), Oberon (Britten's A Midsummer Night's Dream), also song-cycles by Glinka, Tchaikovsky, Rachmaninov and Schumann, and oratorios by Bach and Handel; Sang at the Metropolitan from 1976, as Charlotte, Carmen, Adalgisa, Santuzza, Ulrica and Eboli; Covent Garden and Budapest 1985, 1987, as Azucena; Teatro Colón Buenos Aires 1989, as Amneris; Sang at Madrid in Respighi's La Fiamma, season 1989-90. *Honours:* Glinka Prize 1963; Tchaikovsky International Competition, Moscow 1970; Prizewinner at Francisco Viñas International Competition, Barcelona 1970; People's Artist of RSFSR 1973; Lenin Prize 1976. *Address:* Bolshaya Dorogomilovskaya 21, Moscow, Russia.

OCHMANN Wieslaw, b. 6 Feb 1937, Warsaw, Poland. Singer (Tenor). *Education:* Studied in Warsaw with Gustav Serafin and Sergiusz Nadgryzowski. *Debut:* Bytom 1959, as Edgardo in Lucia di Lammermoor. *Career:* Warsaw Opera from 1964: roles include Jontek in Halka, Tchaikovsky's Lensky, Cavaraddossi, Dmitri in Boris Godunov and Arrigo in Les Vêpres Siciliennes; Guest appearances at the Staatsoper Berlin, Paris Opera, Covent Garden, Hamburg and Prague; Glyndebourne 1968-70, as Tamino, Lensky and Don Ottavio; Metropolitan Opera from 1975, as Henri, Dmitri, Lensky and Golitsin in Khovanshchina; Further appearances in Moscow, Chicago, Vienna, San Francisco and Geneva; Sang Grigory in Boris Godunov at the Metropolitan 1982, Fritz in Schreker's Der Ferne Klang at Brussels, 1988; San Francisco 1987 and 1989, as Hermann in The Queen of Spades and Idomeneo; sang the Shepherd in Szymanowski's King Roger at Buenos Aires 1981 and at the Festival Hall, London, 1990. *Recordings:* Moniusko's Halka and Ghost Castle; Penderecki's Requiem and Te Deum; Idomeneo; Mozart's Requiem; Bruckner's D Minor Mass; Salome; Jenûfa; Rusalka. Labels include: Deutsche Grammophon, HMV and Supraphon. *Address:* c/o San Francisco Opera, War Memorial House, San Francisco, CA 94102, USA.

OCTORS Georges, b. 1940, Zaire, Africa. Conductor. *Education:* Studied violin at first, then composition with Francis de Bourguignon at the Brussels Conservatory; Conducting studies with André Cluytens. *Career:* Founded and conducted the Antwerp Bach Society Chamber Orchestra; Assistant to Cluytens at the National Orchestra of Belgium, 1967: Music Director 1975-83, Resident Conductor 1983-86; Conductor and Musical Adviser of Gelders Orchestra in Arnhem 1986-; Music Director of the Chamber Orchestra of Wallonia 1990; Guest appearances in Amsterdam, Leningrad, London (LSO at the Barbican Hall 1990) and elsewhere; Featured soloists have included Jessye Norman, Yehudi Menuhin, Igor Oistrakh, Uto Ughi, Paul Tortelier, Kyung-Wha Chung and Vladimir Ashkenazy. *Honours include:* Winner of various competitions as violinist. *Address:* Anglo-Swiss Management, 4-5 Primrose Street, Sharpleshall Street, London NW1 8YW, England.

ODNOPOSOFF Ricardo, b. 24 Feb 1914, Buenos Aires, Argentina. Violinist; Educator. m. (1) 1 daughter. (2)Irmtraut Baum, 20 Mar 1965. *Education:* MMus, High Sch Music, Berlin, 1932. *Career:* Violinist, playing in concerts throughout the world, 1932-; Teacher, University of Caracas, Venezuela, 1943-47; Taught summer courses Mozarteum, Salzburg, 1956-60; Internat Summer Acad, Nice, France, 1959-73; Professor, High Sch for Music, Vienna, 1956-, Professor Emeritus, 1975-; Teacher High Sch for Music, Stuttgart, Germany, 1964-; Music High Sch, Zurich, 1975-84. *Honours:* Decorated chevalier des Arts et Lettres, France; chevalier de l'Ordre Rose Blanche, Finland; Comdr Order of Leopold II, Belgium; Grosses Verdienstkreuz des Verdienstordens, Federal Republic of Germany; Mun Hwa Po Chang, Republic of South Korea; Medal for Merit, Argentina; Medal of Honor in Silver, City of Vienna, 1979; Ehrenkreuz fur Wissenshaft und Kunst I Klasse, Austria; Medal of Merit in gold, Govt Baden-Wurttemberg, West Germany. *Memberships:* Freemason. *Address:* 27 Singerstrasse, 1010 Vienna, Austria.

OEHL Kurt, b. 24 Feb. 1923, Mainz, Germany. Musicologist. m. 20 June 1984, 1 son. *Education:* Mainz Gymnasium; University of Mainz, PhD, 1952; Mainz Conservatory. *Career:* Dramaturg, 1952-60; Member, Editorial Staff, Riemann Musiklexikon, 1960-, Brockhaus-Riemann Musiklexikon, Musik-Brockhaus, 1977-78; Member, Musicology Faculty, University of Mainz, 1973-87. *Publication:* Musikliteratur im Überblick, 1988. *Address:* An der Brunnenstube 8, 6500 Mainz-Mombach, Germany.

OELZE Christiane, b. 1965, Cologne, Germany. Singer (Soprano). *Education:* Studied in Cologne 1984-89 and with Elisabeth Schwarzkopf, Mitsuko Shirai, Hartmut Holl and Erna Westenberg. *Career:* Concert engagements at Schleswig-Holstein, Wurzburg Mozart, Berlin and Salzburg Festivals; Sang with Helmuth Rilling and in season 1989-90 with Chamber Orchestra of Europe in Berlin and London under Roger Norrington; English Chamber Orchestra under Leopold Hager; Salzburg Festival recitals 1993, USA debut with Atlanta Symphony under Franz Welser-Moest 1994; Opera debut as Despina at National Arts Centre in Ottawa 1990; Constanze in Die Entführung at Salzburg 1991, conducted by Horst Stein; Promenade Concerts London 1993, in Haydn's Die Jahreszeiten, conducted by Norrington; Glyndebourne debut 1991 as Ann Truelove in Rake's Progress; Autumn 1994 Covent Garden debut Woglinde. *Recordings:* Hansel und Gretel, conducted by Colin Davis; Webern conducted by Boulez; Mozart concert arias under Hartmut Haenchen and Die Jahreszeiten; Pamina in Zauberflöte under John Elliot Gardinez; Goethe-Lieder by Schubert, Wolf with pianist Eric Schneider. *Honour:* Winner, Hugo Wolf Contest 1987. *Address:* Artists Management, Apollolaan 181-1077 AT, Amsterdam, The Netherlands.

OGAWA Noriko, b. 28 Jan 1962, Kawasaki, Japan. Pianist. *Education:* 1977-80 Tokyo College of Music High School; 1981-85 Juilliard School New York; Piano Studies with Benjamin Kaplan 1988-. *Career:* Concerto soloist from 1976 playing works by Mendelssohn, Tchaikovsky, Liszt, Schumann and Chopin; New York recital debut 1982; London Wigmore Hall debut 1988 playing Schumann's Fantasy and Liszt's Sonata; Recitals throughout England and the Republic of Ireland, Northern Ireland. Major appearances worldwide include the Harrogate Festival and the Tokyo and Yokohama Festivals. She has recorded several times for the BBC. Her third recording was of the Tchaikovsky B flat minor and Prokofiev No 3 Concertos with Rozhdestvensky and the State Symphony Orchestra of the USSR Ministry of Culture; Has appeared outside the UK with the Tokyo Symphony, Tokyo Philharmonic, the Yomiuri Nippon Symphony Orchestra (with Jan Pascal Tortelier) and the Singapore Symphony. Formed a duo with the British clarinettist, Michael Collins, 1988 and they have performed at the Wigmore Hall and various festivals; 1991 included performances with Philharmonia Orchestra (Slatkin) at the Festival Hall, The Ulster Orchestra (Yan Pascal Tortelier) and Bournemouth Symphony (Alexandre Myrat); gave world premiere of a work by Lyn Davies at Lower Machen Festival in June and live BBC solo broadcast in July. *Recordings:* Czerny Etudes (Toshiba EMI); Liszt and Prokofiev (NEC); Finzi Bagatelles (Virgin Classics). *Honours:* 1983 2nd Prize at The International Music Competition of Japan; 1984 Gina Bachauer Memorial Scholarship, Juilliard; 1987 3rd Prize Leeds International Piano Competition. *Address:* c/o Clarion/Seven Muses, 64 Whitehall Park, London N19 3TN, England.

OGDON Wilbur L., b. 19 Apr 1921, USA. Composer; Professor of Music Theory, Literature and Composition. m. Beverly Jean Porter, Aug 1958, 1 son, 2 daughters. *Education:* BM, University of Wisconsin, 1942; MA, Hamline University, St Paul, Minnesota, 1947; PhD, Indiana University, 1955; Further study: University of California, Berkeley, 1949-50; Ecole Normale de Musique, 1952-53; Studied composition with Ernst Krenek, Roger Sessions, Rene Leibowitz. *Career:* Professional positions and teaching: University of Texas, 1947-50; College of St Catherine, St Paul, 1956-57; Illinois Wesleyan University, 1957-65; Music Director, Pacifica Foundation, Berkeley, 1962-64. University of Illinois, 1965-66; University of California, San Diego, 1966-; Founding Chair, Music Department, 1966-71; Emeritus, UCSD, 1990-. *Compositions:* 3 Piano Pieces, 1950; Capriccio for Piano, 1952; Seven Piano Pieces, 1987; Voice: 3 Baritone Songs, 1950/56; Two Ketchwa Songs, 1955; Le Tombeau de Jean Cocteau, I, II and III, 1964, 1972, 1976; By the ISAR, 1969; Winter Images; Summer Images, 1981; The Awakening of Sappho (chamber opera), 1980; Chorus: Statements; 3 Sea Songs; Instrumental: 7 Pieces and a Capriccio for violin and piano, 1988/89; 6 Small Trios, trumpet, marimba, piano, 1980; 5 Preludes, violin, piano, 1982; 5 Preludes, violin, chamber orchestra, 1985; Capriccio and 5 Comments, symphony orchestra, 1979; Serenade No.1 for Wind Quintet, 1987; Serenade No.2 for Wind Quintet, 1990; Palindrome and Variations, string quartet, 1962; 3 Trifles, cello, piano, 1958; Two Sea Chanteys, soprano, baritone and two percussionist, 1988; Four Chamber Songs, soprano with viola, cello, flute, oboe and harp, 1989; Four Tonal Songs, 1988-90; A Modern Fable, 2 soprano, baritone with violin, cello, clarinet, bass clarinet and percussion. *Publications:* Series and Structure, 1955; Horizons Circled (with Ernst Krenek and John Stewart), 1974; How Tonality Functions in Webern's Opus 9, Ex tempore 1990. *Contributions to:* On Weberns's op 27 II, in Journal of Music Theory; Journal of Schoenberg Institute: An Unpublished Treatise by Rene Leibowitz; How Tonality Functions in Schoenberg's op 11, No. I. *Address:* 482 15th Street, Del Mar, CA 92014, USA.

OGNIVTSEV Alexander Pavlovich, b. 27 Aug 1920, Petrovoskoy, USSR. Singer (Bass). *Education:* Studied at the Kishinev Conservatory. *Debut:* Bolshoi Theatre, Moscow, 1949, as Dosifey in Khovanshchina. *Career:* Has sung major roles in the Russian bass repertory, such as Rimsky-Korsakov's Ivan the Terrible and Tchaikovsky's Prince Gremin and Renée (Iolanta); Has also performed Philip II in Don Carlos, Mephistopheles, Don Basilio and the General in The Gambler by Prokofiev (also on the Bolshoy's visit to the Metropolitan, 1975); Sang in the premieres of Shaporin's The Decembrists (1953) and Kholminov's An Optimistic Tragedy (1967); Guest appearances in Italy (La Scala), Austria, France, Rumania, Canada, Poland, India, Turkey, Hungary and Japan; Appeared in 1953 film version of the life of Shalyapin and sang Aleko in a film of Rachmaninov's opera. *Honours include:* People's Artist of the USSR, 1965.

OHANESIAN David, b. 6 Jan 1927, Bucharest, Rumania. Singer (Baritone). *Education:* Studied in Budapest with Aurel Costescu-Duca and in Cluj with Dinu Badescu. *Debut:* Cluj 1950, in Pagliacci. *Career:* Sang Tonio at Bucharest in 1952 and remained at the National Opera until 1977 as Verdi's Iago, Rigoletto, Amonasro and Luna, Eugene Onegin, Telramund, Scarpia, Escamillo and Rossini's Figaro, in Meyerbeer's Margherita d'Anjou and Tchaikovsky's Mazeppa; Noted as Enesco's Oedipe, which he sang in Bucharest and as guest abroad; Engagements in Hamburg, Moscow, Prague, Lyon, Paris, Barcelona, Budapest, Leningrad, Warsaw and Tel Aviv. *Recordings include:* Oedipe and Cavalleria Rusticana (Electrecord). *Publication:* Passion of Music (Bucharest 1986, with I Sava).

OHLSSON Garrick, b. 3 Apr 1948, Bronxville, New York, USA. Pianist. *Education:* Westchester Conservatory; Juilliard School with Sascha Gorodnitsky; Later with Olga Barabini & Rhosa Lhevinne. *Career includes:* Nearly a dozen tours of Poland, appearances with major symphony orchestras in Europe, USA, Japan, New Zealand. Recent appearances with Cleveland, Chicago, Philadelphia, Pittsburgh, San Francisco Orchestras, USA; European engagements with Munich Philharmonic, North German Radio, Rotterdam Philharmonic, all major London orchestras; City of London Festival, South Bank Summer Music, Promenade Concerts with BBC Symphony Orchestra; Festivals, recitals, concerts, Bergen, Prague, Sofia, Dubrovnik, Tivoli. *Recordings:* Brahms Concerto No 1 (LPO/Tennstedt); Liszt Concerti & solo works by Chopin (EMI); Scriabin Piano Concerto with Czech Philharmonic (Supraphon). *Honours:* Prizes: Busoni Piano Competition, Italy, 1966; Chopin International Piano Competition, Warsaw, 1970; Montreal International Piano Competition, 1970. *Current Management:* Harold Holt Ltd. *Address:* Harold Holt Ltd, 31 Sinclair Road, London W14 0NS, England.

OHYAMA Heiichiro, b. 31 July 1947, Kyoto, Japan. Violinist; Violist; Conductor. m. Gail J, 1 son. *Education:* Toho Music High School; Toho College of Music; Guildhall School of Music and Drama; AGSM, Indiana University, USA. *Debut:* New York City, USA. *Career:* Professor of Music, University of California, Santa Barbara; Assistant Conductor and Principal Violist, Los Angeles Philharmonic; Music Director, Santa Barbara Chamber Orchestra; Music Director, Crossroads Chamber Ensemble; Music Director, Artistic Director, La Jolla Chamber Music Festival. *Recordings:* Columbia; Nonesuch; Sonic Arts. *Contributions to:* Marlboro Music Festivals; Santa Fe Chamber Music Festivals; Round Top Music Festivals. *Honours:* Winner, Young Concert Artist, 1975; Carl Flesch International Competition, 1968; Indiana University, 1971. *Membership:* Musicians Union, England. *Hobbies:* Skin Diving; Kendo. *Address:* 2878 Angelo Drive, Los Angeles, CA 90077, USA.

OISTRAKH Igor Davidovich, b. 27 Apr 1931, Odessa, USSR. Violinist. *Education:* Music School and State Conservatoire, Moscow; Student, State Conservatoire 1949-55. *Career:* Many foreign tours, several concerts with father, David Oistrakh, notably in music by Spohr, Leclair and Bach; 60th Birthday Concert at the Barbican Centre, London, April 1991 (concertos by Mozart and Mendelssohn). *Honours:* 1st Prize, Violin competition, Budapest 1952, Wieniawski Competition, Poznán; Honoured Artist of RSFSR.

Address: State Conservatoire, 13 Ulitsa Herzen, Moscow, Russia.

OKADA Yoshiko, b. 5 Oct 1961, Japan. Pianist. m. Grzegorz Cimoszko (Polish flautist of Warsaw Philharmonic Orchestra), 1 son.*Education:* Ecole Normale de Musique, Paris, 1976-80; Studied in Paris with Yvonne Loriod, 1980-82; in London with Maria Curcio, in Switzerland with Nikita Magaloff. *Debut:* Carnegie Hall, New York, 1991. *Career:* Touring in recital and as soloist with orchestras throughout USA, Canada, Poland, Denmark, Belgium, Switzerland and France. *Recordings:* Pony Canyon Label Japan: CDs of Mozart Sonatas and Concertos with Warsaw Chamber Orchestra. *Hobbies:* Literature; International Cuisine; Fashion Designing. *Current Management:* Albert Kay Associates, Inc., Concert Artists Management, 58 West 58th Street, New York NY 10019-2510, USA.

OKAMOTO Tsunenori, b. 14 Nov 1939, Tokyo, Japan. Composer; Educator. m. Yoshiko Tanaka, 23 Mar 1985. 1 son, 1 daughter. *Education:* BFA, Tokyo University of Arts, 1963; US Fulbright study grant recipient, 1965-70; MA, The New England Conservatory, Boston, 1967; Berkshire Music Center fellow, 1967-68; Indiana University, 1967-69; State University of New York at Buffalo, 1969-73; Edward MacDowell Colony residence fellow, 1970; Columbia University, 1970; Fontainebleau American Conservatory of Music, 1970. *Career:* Professor of Piano, Tsuru University, Yamanashi, Japan; Lecturer, Music Theory and Composition, Tohogakuen School of Music, Tokyo, Japan. *Publication:* J Banowetz: The Pianist's Guide to Pedaling, translated to Japanese, 1989. *Memberships:* International Society for Contemporary Music; American Musicological Society. *Hobby:* Photography. *Address:* 3450-119 Honmachida, Machida-Shi, Tokyo 194, Japan.

OKE Alan, b. 1956, London, England. Singer (Baritone). *Education:* Studied at the Royal Academy of Music, Glasgow, and in Munich with Hans Hotter. *Career:* Sang first in concert and in oratorios; Stage debut with Scottish Opera: roles include Papageno in Die Zauberflöte, Schaunard in La Bohème and Olivier in Capriccio; Sang in Cavalli's L'Egisto in Frankfurt, Venice and Schwetzingen, 1983; Covent Garden 1984, in Taverner by Maxwell Davies; Took part in the British premiere of Weill's Street Scene, Glasgow 1989; Guest appearances with English National Opera and Opera North; Sang Malatesta in Don Pasquale with Travelling Opera at Stratford-Upon-Avon, 1990; Macheath in The Threepenny Opera at Leeds, 1990; Season 1992 with Pluto in Orpheus in the Underworld for Opera North. *Recordings include:* Giuseppe in The Gondoliers, (TER). *Address:* c/o Opera North, The Grand Theatre, 46 New Briggate, Leeds, Yorkshire, LS1 6NU.

OLAFIMIHAN Tinuke, b. 1961, London (Nigerian/Welsh parentage). Singer (Soprano). *Education:* Studied at the Colchester Institute, at Morley College and the National Opera Studio, London. *Debut:* Despina at the Elizabeth Hall 1989, with the National Opera Studio; Further study with Elisabeth Schwarzkopf; Has sung Zerlina in Don Giovanni at the Snape Maltings; Messiah with The Sixteen under Harry Christophers; Appearances with the Vivaldi Concertante at St John's Smith Square and in the St John Passion at Belfast; Susanna in a production of Figaro by Colin Graham and Barbarina for Opera Northern Ireland and in Aix-en-Provence; Carmina Burana at the Elizabeth Hall, Dec 1990; Sang Clara in the Covent Garden premiere of Porgy and Bess, 1992. *Honours include:* Peter Stuyesant Foundation Scholarship; Walter Legge/Elisabeth Schwarzkopf Society Award; Finalist, 1988 Richard Tauber Competition. *Address:* Magenta Music International, 64 Highgate High Street, London N6 5HX, England.

OLAH Tiberiu, b. 2 Jan 1928, Arpasel, Transvylvania, Romania. Composer. m. Yvonne, 28 Mar 1959. *Education:* Academia de Musica, Cluj, 1946-49;

Tchaikovsky Conservatory, Moscow, 1949-54; Composition Diploma, (magna cum laude), *Debut:* Trio, Cluj, 1955. *Career:* Performer of Cantata for women choir and ensemble, Prague 1962, Warsaw 1963, Budapest 1963; Warsaw 1966, W Berlin STB Orchestra 1967; Darmstadter Ferienkurse 1968; Performer of Columna Infinita Orchestra; World's First Performance and Commissioned Works: W Berlin 1971, Perspectives, Paris 1971, Ed Salabert's ORTF orchestra Translations for 16 Strings, New York Lincoln Center, Washington Kennedy Center 1974; Time of Memory to the Memory of N and S Koussevitsky Berlin Festwochen 1988; Concerto delle Coppie; Bucharest: The International Week of New Music 1991; Obelisque for Wolfgang Amadeus, saxophone and orchestra; Karlsruhe, Germany 1992 Concertante commissioned by Land Baden, Wurttemberg. *Recordings:* Numerous. *Publications:* Editor: Muzicale, Bucharest; Salabert, Paris; Schott, Germany; Muzyka, Moscow. *Hobby:* Travel. *Address:* Bulevard Dacia 11, 70185 Bucharest, Romania.

OLCZAK Krzysztof Robert, b. 26 May 1956, Lodz, Poland. Composer; Solo Concert Accordionist. m. 21 June 1980, 1 son, 1 daughter. *Education:* Diploma, Accordion, Fr Chopin Academy of Music, Warsaw, 1979; Diploma, hon mention, Composition, Academy of Music, Gdansk, 1986. *Career:* Solo & chamber concerts, Poland, 1978-; Played with National Philharmonic, 1985, 1986; Philharmonics: Bialystok, Gdansk, Koszalin, Lodz, Opole, Poznan, Wroclaw, Austria, Finland, Germany, Italy, Norway, Sweden, USSR; Contemporary Music Festivals, Styrian Autumn, Austria, 1978, Warsaw Autumn, 1979, 1987, 1988, 1989, Poznan Spring, 1979, 1985, 1987, Gdansk Encounters of Young Composers, 1987, 1989, 1991; Conservatorium Legnica, 1987, 1991, Musik Biennale, Berlin, 1987, Musica Polonica Nova, Wroclaw, 1988, Internationale Studienwoche, Bonn, 1991; Scandinavia tour with American Waterways Wind Orchestra, 1990; Currently Lecturer, Gdansk Academy of Music. *Compositions include:* Accordion solos: Manualiter, 1977; Phantasmagorien, 1978; Winter Suite, 1980; Fine Pluie, 1980; Berceuse, 1984; Rondino, 1985; Pozymk, 4 performers, 1982; Sea Spaces, strophes for soprano, prepared piano, 1982; Cantata, soprano, 2 accordions, 1984; Sinfonietta Concertante, percussion, orchestra, 1985-86; Belt the Bellow, tuba, accordion, 1986; Trio, homage to Karol Szymanowski, 1987; Intervals, organ, 2 accordions, 1987; Concerto for accordian and orchestra, 1989; Concerto Grosso for wind orchestra, 1990. *Hobby:* Tennis. *Address:* 11 Listopada 79, 80-180 Gdańsk, Poland.

OLDFIELD Mark, b. 1957, Sheffield, England. Singer (Baritone). *Education:* Studied at School of Music, Colchester with Rae Woodland and at Royal College of Music. *Career:* Operatic work has included Metcalf's Tornrak at Banff Center in Canada, and Papageno for London Opera Players; London International Opera Festival 1989 in The Fisherman by Paul Max Edlin; Purcell's Aeneas and Eugene Onegin at the Royal College of Music; Further study with Kenneth Woollam; Concert repertoire includes the Brahms Requiem, Snape Maltings, Bach's Magnificat, Las Palmas and Cantata No.11, Handel's Chandos Anthems with the English Chamber Orchestra under Charles Mackerras; Vaughan Williams Five Mystical Songs; Carmina Burana; Monteverdi Madrigals and the Brahms Liebeslieder in Northern Italy; Sang Mercurio in Cavalli's La Calisto in Provence. *Address:* c/o Anglo Swiss Ltd, 3 Primrose Mews, 1a Sharpleshall Street, London NW1 8YW, England.

OLDHAM Arthur, b. 6 Sept 1926, London, England. Composer; Chorus Master. 2 sons, 2 daughters. *Education:* Royal College of Music; Private Pupil of Benjamin Britten, 8 years. *Debut:* Mercury Theatre, London, 1946. *Career:* Conductor, Ballet Rambert, 1946-47; Director of Music, St Mary's Catholic Cathedral, Edinburgh, 1956; Chorus Master, Scottish Opera; Chorus Master, Edinburgh Festival Chorus, 1965-; Chorus Master, London Symphony Orchestra

Chorus; Chorus Master, Concertgebouw Orchestra; Chorus Master, Orchestre de Paris; Trained the Festival Chorus in Moses and Aron by Schoenberg at Edinburgh, 1992. *Compositions:* Opera: Love in a Village; Song Cycles: Five Chinese Lyrics, The Commandment of Love, Psalms in Time of War (premiered at Edinburgh Festival 1977). *Recordings:* Major portion of choral and operatic repertoire. *Honours:* Officier de l'Ordre des Arts et des Lettres, France, 1986; Three Grammy Awards; OBE 1989. *Membership:* ISM. *Hobbies:* Gardening; Golf. *Address:* Fontaine Melon, 58230 Gouloux, France.

OLEDZKI Bogdan, b. 25 June 1949, Stupsk, Poland. Conductor. m. Ewa Gtowacka, 12 Aug 1981. *Education:* Warsaw Musical Academy, 1974. *Debut:* National Philharmonic Orchestra, Warsaw, 1974. *Career:* Conductor, Warsaw, Radom, Poznan, 1974-82; Principal Conductor, Rzeszow Philharmonic Orchestra, 1982-84; Conductor, Great Opera, Warsaw, 1984-; Guest Conductor with Philharmonic Orchestra, Poland, and Salzburg-Aspecte, Edinburgh, and Skopje Festivals. *Current Management:* Polish Artistic Agency (PAGART), Warsaw, Poland. *Address:* Bandrowskiego 8 m 60, 01-496 Warszawa, Poland.

OLEFSKY Paul, b. 4 Jan 1926, Chicago, Illinois, USA. Cellist; Teacher. *Education:* Studied at Curtis Institute with Gregor Piatigorsky 1943-47, with Pablo Casals and with Karajan and Monteux (Conducting). *Career:* Former First Cellist of Philadelphia Orchestra and Detroit Symphony Orchestra; Concert soloist with leading orchestras in USA and abroad; Recitalist in North America and Europe with solo works by Kodaly and Bach and the premieres of works by Milhaud, Tcherepnin, Virgil Thomson and Shapleigh; Professor of Cello and Chamber Music at University of Texas at Austin, since 1974; Solo recordings with the English Chamber Orchestra as Cellist/Conductor. *Honours:* Naumburg Award, 1948; Michaels Memorial Award of the Young Concert Artists, 1953. *Address:* University of Texas at Austin, Department of Music, Austin, TX 78712, USA.

OLEG Raphael, b. 8 Sept 1959, Paris, France. Concert Violinist. *Education:* Paris Conservatoire from 1972: first prizes for violin and chamber music 1976. *Career:* International reputation as recitalist and with Europe's major symphony orchestras; Lucerne Festival 1986 with the Czech Philharmonic and Vaclav Neumann; First Prize in Tchaikovsky International Competition 1986; British debut 1987, playing the Brahms Concerto with the London Symphony Orchestra conducted by Jeffrey Tate; 1987 tour of European Festivals with the Orchestra National de France and Lorin Maazel; Engagements with the Concertgebouw under Chailly, Orchestre de Paris under Bychkov, the Philadelphia Orchestra under Maazel and the Munich Staatsorchester under Sawallisch; UK appearances with the Philharmonia, English Chamber Orchestra, Northern Sinfonia, Scottish Chamber Orchestra and City of London Sinfonia; Japanese debut at Suntory Hall July 1989; Engagements in 1989-90 season included tour of Italy with ECO and Tate and a tour of France and Switzerland with the Academy of St. Martin-in-the-Fields and Marriner; gave recitals in Prague Spring Festival and Paris, concerts with the Orchestre National de France, Polish Chamber Orchestra; 1990-91, toured Germany with Chamber Orchestra of Europe and Berglund, and Japan with the Nouvel Orchestre Philharmonique. *Address:* Van Walsum Management Ltd., 26 Wadham Road, London SW15 2LR, England.

OLEKSA Michael John, b. 2 May 1950, Youngstown, Ohio, USA. Musician (Flute, Saxophone). *Education:* BMus Performance (Flute) Cum Laude, Dana School of Music of Youngstown State University, 1989; Graduate US Navy School of Music, 1969. *Career:* Currently performing with Easy Street Productions, Uptown Little Big Band, recording with original rock group, The Sharkbites, and teaching privately; Travelled with show group Rich Mauro Revue, 1979-85, including USO European Tour, 1981-82; Tester and final adjuster for Yamaha Musical Products, 1974-76; Freelance work includes John Davidson with Angelo Lacivita Orchestra, Maureen McGovern with Youngstown Symphony, Art Mooney Orchestra, and Jimmy Dorsey Orchestra (dir Lee Castle); US Navy Musician, 1968-72. *Compositions:* As a member of The Sharkbites, Album, Fork it Over, on minor Details. *Recordings:* Label, Published by Phistosongs (ASCAP); Published by After Hours Music. *Publications:* Album Nowhere Fast, E.P, Wait for Me, compilation album Rustbelt Vibrations, and singles Keep it in Mind and Gimme Back my Smokestack (about an out-of-work Youngstown Steelworker). *Honours:* International Association of Jazz Educators Special Citation for Outstanding Musicianship, 1977 and 1986; JFK High School Band Outstanding Senior, 1968; American Biographical Insititute World Decoration of Excellence, 1989. *Memberships:* President of YSU Jazz Society, 1978-1979; National Flute Association; American Federation of Musicians; Chamber Music American; Golden Key National Honor Society. *Address:* 419 Garfield Avenue, McDonald, Ohio 44437, USA.

OLESCH Peter Otto, b. 10 Sept 1938, Andreashutte, Oberschlesien, Germany. Singer (Bass-baritone). *Education:* Studied in Dresden with Rudolf Bockelmann. *Debut:* Berlin Staatsoper 1963 as a Flemish Deputy in Don Carlos. *Career:* Sang at the Staatsoper until 1982 in such roles as Masetto, Monterone, Bartolo, Pistol, Falstaff, Alberich, Alfio, Cavalleria Rusticana, Varlaam and Rangier in The Devils of Loudun by Penderecki; Leipzig Opera 1989 as Don Pasquale; Many concert performances. *Recording:* Puntila by Dessau. *Address:* c/o Stadtische Theater, 7010 Leipzig, Germany.

OLIPHANT Naomi Joyce, b. 24 Jan 1953, Toronto, Ontario, Canada. Professor of Music; Concert Pianist; Chamber Musician. *Education:* ARCT, Piano, 1967; ARCT, Voice, 1973; Royal Conservatory of Music, Toronto; Mus.B, 1975, MusM, 1976, University of Toronto; DMA, University of Michigan, USA, 1982. *Debut:* Soloist with Toronto Symphony Orchestra, 1965. *Career:* Solo recitals and chamber music appearances in Canada, USA, Europe and the Orient on piano and harpsichord; Appearances on radio and television in Canada, USA and Europe; Soloist with orchestras including: Toronto Symphony Orchestra; Louisville Orchestra; Hamilton Philharmonic; Niagara Symphony; European Debut recital tour, Apr. 1987; Recital tours of Europe since 1987; Professor, University of Louisville, 1983-; Former Teacher: Brock University, University of Toronto and Banff School of Fine Arts; Chairman University of Louisville and Director, Louisville Suzuki Piano Association; Guest Clinician, Speaker and Adjudicator in Canada, USA, Europe and Orient. Author of published articles on piano pedagogy. *Honours:* Master Teacher, Music Teachers National Association, 1984; Distinguished Teacher of School of Music, University of Louisville, 1985-86; Numerous scholarships and grants from National organizations. *Hobbies:* Needlework; Walking; Swimming; Reading. *Address:* School of Music, University of Louisville, Louisville, KY 40292, USA.

OLIVEIRA Elmar, b. 28 June 1950, Waterbury, Connecticut, USA. Violinist. *Education:* Hart College of Music, Hartford, Coonecticut; Manhattan School of Music. *Career:* Appearances with orchestras including New York Philharmonic, Cleveland, Baltimore, Chicago Symphony, Dallas, Montreal, Moscow Philharmonic. *Recordings include:* Sonata by Husa. *Honours:* First Prize, Naumburg Competition 1975; Gold Medal, Tchaikovsky International Competition, 1978. *Hobbies:* Antiques; Art; String Instrument Collection; Pool; Billiards.

OLIVER Alexander, b. 27 June 1944, Scotland. Singer (Tenor). *Education:* Royal Scottish Academy; Further studies in Vienna and with Rupert Bruce-Lockhart. *Career:* Netherlands Opera from 1971, in The Love for Three Oranges, Intermezzo, Peter Grimes, L'Ormindo and The Turn of the Screw; Scottish Opera in A Midsummer Night's Dream, Wozzeck, The Bartered Bride, Eugene Onegin and Mahagonny; Opera North as Nemorino in L'Elisir d'Amore; Glyndebourne Opera in Il Ritorno d'Ulisse, Ariadne auf Naxos and Albert Herring (1985); Covent Garden in Eugene Onegin, Le Nozze di Figaro, Andrea Chénier, Manon and Albert Herring (1989); Zurich Opera from 1978, in L'Incoronazione di Poppea and Les Contes d'Hoffmann; Brussels Opera 1982, as Arbace in Idomeneo: returned for the world premiere of Gilles des Rais by Boesmans; Antwerp Opera and Canadian Opera debuts 1983, in Death in Venice and Poppea; La Fenice Venice in Curlew River; La Scala Milan in the premiere of Riccardo III by Flavio Testi; Sang Mime in a new production of Siegfried at Covent Garden, 1990; Shapkin in From the House of the Dead at Brussels, 1990; Salzburg 1991, in Le Nozze di Figaro; Concert engagements with the Concertgebouw Orchestra in the St John and St Matthew Passions of Bach and Stravinsky's Pulcinella; Houston Symphony and Chicago Symphony; Frequent appearances with the Songmakers' Almanac. *Recordings include:* Videos of Gilbert and Sullivan's The Sorcerer and Pirates of Penzance. *Address:* c/o Harrison/Parrott Ltd., 12 Penzance Place, London W11 4PA, England.

OLIVER John Edward, b. 21 Sept 1959, Vancouver, Canada. Composer. *Education:* MMus 1984, DMus 1992, Composition, McGill University, Montreal; BMus, Composition, University of British Columbia; Studies: Composition, Guitar, Piano, Voice, San Francisco Conservatory of Music 1977-79. *Career:* Works performed by: New Music Concerto, Toronto 1982, 87, Vancouver New Music 1982, 90, Societe de Musique Contemporaine de Quebec 1989, Canadian Opera Company 1991;' Composer-in-Residence, Banff Centre, Leighton Artist Colony, 1989, 90 and Music Department, 1990, 91, Canadian Opera Company, 1989, 91, Vancouver Opera 1992-. *Compositions:* Gugcamayo's Old Song and Dance, Canadian Opera Company 1991; El Reposo del Fuego, 1987; Aller Retour 1988; Marimba Dismembered 1990; Before the Freeze 1984. *Recordings:* El Reposo del Fuego; Marimba Dismembered; Before the Freeze. *Publication:* New Music in British Columbia in Soundnotes, Fall 1992. *Honours:* Canada Council Arts Awards, 1984-87, 91; 8th CBC National Radio Competition for Young Composers, 1988; Two prizes, 1989 PROCAN Young Composers Competition. *Memberships:* Society of Composers, Authors and Music Publishers of Canada; American Federation of Musicians; Canadian Electroacoustic Community. *Hobbies:* Reading; Skiing; Hiking; Dining. *Address:* 1640 Alma Street, Vancouver, British Columbia, Canada V6R 3P4.

OLIVER Lisi, b. 13 Dec 1951, Frankfurt AM, Germany. Stage Director, Translator. *Education:* BA Smith College, 1973; Harvard University ALM, 1988; PhD in Medieval Philology, 1994. *Career:* Stage Manager, Bolshoi Opera US Tour, 1974; Inaugural Gala for President Carter, 1978; Production Stage Manager, Assistant Director, Opera Company of Boston, 1975-78; Assistant Director, Komische Oper, Berlin, 1979-80; Director, Opera Company of Boston, Opera New England, Skylight Comic Opera, Des Moines Metro Opera, Atlanta Opera, Baldwin-Wallace Conservatory, Opera Company of the Philippines, Massachusetts Institute of Technology, Wolftrap Farm Park, City of Boston First Night, 1980-90; Director Opera Studio, New England Conservatory, 1988-90; First projected titles at Bolshoi Opera, 1991; Director, Atlanta Opera Studio, 1989-; Title supervisor, Atlanta Opera, Boston Lyric Opera; Director of Raymond Street Translations, Titles Rental Company. *Publications:* Translations or Surtitles used by Opera Company of Boston, Opera New England, Atlanta Opera, San Diego Opera, Youngstown Symphony, Syracuse Opera, Memphis Opera, Indianapolis Opera, Florida Opera; Boston Rouge Opera, Opera Northeast, The Juilliard School; Edmonton Opera; Dayton Opera; Anchorage Opera; West Palm Beach Opera. *Honours:* Yvonne Burger Award, Smith College, 1973; Merit Award, Komische Oper, 1980; National Opera Institute Grant, 1978-80. *Hobbies:* Linguistic Research; Golf; Tennis; Sailing. *Address:* 157 Raymond Street, Cambridge, Mass. 02140, USA.

OLIVERO Alberto, b. 8 Oct 1952, Turin, Italy. Composer; Music Teacher. *Education:* Diploma, Vocal Composition, Conservatory of Music of Milan, 1977; Specialisation courses in Medieval Musicology, 1981. *Debut:* 1973. *Career:* Medieval harp and recorder player with early music consorts: Studio di Musica Antica, 1973-77; Ars Antiqua, 1978-; Lyocorne Early Music Consort, 1980-; Teacher, Choral Practice and Music Theory. *Compositions:* Chromophonie (for solo recorder); Scharade (for 3 recorders); Kryptographie (for recorder and harpsichord); Song for Faith (for soprano and guitar); Madrugada (for tenor and piano); Vide-runt Omnes (for 3 choirs and 3 mixed instrumental groups). *Recording:* Medioevo & Rinascimento, Lyocorne Early Music Consort. *Publications:* Carissimi- Judicium Salomonis-Revision, 1986; Anon Sec XII-Ordo ad representandum Herodem-Transcription; Anon Sec XIII-Laude del Cod Magh II.I.122 & Cortona 91, 1985. *Contributions to:* Concert programmes for Settembre Musica - Festival di Aosta-Accademia Stefano Tempia and many other concert societies. *Memberships:* American Musicological Society; Società Italiana di Musicologia; Internationale Musikwissenschaftsgesellschaft; Sociedad Espanola de Musicologia. *Address:* Via Meucci 2, 10121 Torino, Italy.

OLIVERO Magda, b. 25 Mar 1912, Saluzzo, Turin, Italy. Singer (Soprano). *Education:* Studied in Turin with Luigi Gerussi, Luigi Ricci and Ghedini. *Debut:* Turin 1933, as Lauretta in Gianni Schicchi. *Career:* La Scala 1933, in Nabucco; Sang widely in Italy as Adriana Lecouvreur, Puccini's Liu, Suor Angelica and Minnie, Violetta, Zerlina, Poppea and Sophie in Der Rosenkavalier; Retired 1941, but returned to stage 1951, to sing Adriana at the composer's request; Stoll Theatre, London, as Mimi, 1952; Further appearances in Edinburgh, Paris, Brussels, Amsterdam and Buenos Aires; Other roles included Fedora, Mascagni's Iris, Zandonai's Francesca, Puccini's Giorgetta and Tosca and parts in operas by Poulenc and Menotti; US debut Dallas 1967, as Medée; Metropolitan Opera 1975, as Tosca. *Recordings:* Turandot; Fedora; Francesca da Rimini; La Fanciulla del West; Il Tabarro; Risurrezione by Alfano; Medée; Madama Butterfly.

OLIVEROS Pauline, b. 30 May 1932, Houston, Texas, USA. Composer; Performer. *Education:* BA, San Francisco State College, 1957. *Career:* Director, San Francisco Tape Music Center, 1966; Expo '67, Montreal, Canada, 1967; Expo '70, Osaka, Japan, 1970; Full Professor of Music, University of California, San Diego, 1970; Summer Olympics, Los Angeles, 1984; Works performed and solo performances worldwide and with numerous orchestras. *Compositions:* Roots for the Moment; Tara's Room; The Well and the Gentle; Tashi Gomang; Rose Moon; Sonic Meditations; Horse Sings from Cloud; Rattlesnake Mountain; Lullaby for Daisy Pauline; Spiral Mandala; Bonn Feier; Double Basses at 20 Paces; 3 Songs for Soprano and Piano; To Valerie Solanas and Marilyn Monroe; Jar Piece; Sound Patterns. *Recordings:* The Well and the Gentle (Hat Art); The Wanderer (Lovely Music); Accordion and Voice (Lovely Music); Vor der Flüt (Eigelstein). *Publication:* Software for People, 1984. *Contributions to:* Numerous. *Honours:* Foundation Gaudeamus Prize, 1962; Guggenheim award, 1973; Beethoven Prize, Bonn, Federal Republic of Germany, 1977; Pauline Oliveros Day and 30-year Retrospective, Houston, Texas, 1983; Retrospective at J.F. Kennedy Center for Performing Arts, Washington DC, 1985; Honorary DMA, University of Maryland, 1986. *Memberships:* Founding Director, Pauline Oliveros Foundation; American Music Center (Board of Directors); Founding Co-Director, Good Sound Foundation; New York Foundation for Arts (Board of Governors). *Current Management:* Stidfole and Pratt Associates. *Address:* ASCAP, ASCAP Building, One Lincoln Plaza, New York, NY 10023, USA.

OLIVIERI Luis Arturo, b. 21 Apr 1937, Puerto Rico. Professor; Clergyman; Musician. m. Evelyn Robert, 30 June 1961. 2 sons. *Education:* Bachelor of Music Education, Conservatory of Music of Puerto Rico, 1972; Master of Sacred Music, Boston University, 1976.

Career: Minister, Puerto Rico Baptist Churches, 1958-72; Director of Music, Baptist Church of San Juan, 1967-72; Organist, Episcopal Cathedral of San Juan, 1982-; Professor of Music, Interamerican University; Professor of Music and Liturgy, Evangelical Seminary of Puerto Rico, 1965-; Director of Interdenominational Chorale of Puerto Rico, 1971-; Co-founder and assistant conductor, Coro Sinfonico de Puerto Rico, 1984; Choral conductor for Opera APTEL, 1978; Co- founder and Dean of Puerto Rico Institute of Sacred Music; Conductor, International Festival of Evangelical Choirs, Mexico; Conductor, Interamericana-Metro Chorus; Conductor, Choral Concerts, Puerto Rican Institute of Culture; Production of choral programmes, Public Television of Puerto Rico. *Recordings:* Villancicos Corales de Navidad; Coro de Seminaristas. *Publications:* Himnos y Cantos Puertorriquenos de la Fe Cristiana, 1980; Musica Coral Puertorriquena: Coleccion Navidena, 1978; Arreglos Corales de Dr Bartolome Bover, 1981; Musica Coral Sagrada para coros SAB, 1982; Con Profetica Voz: Himnos, 1984. *Contributions to:* Editor, choir magazine, Coral. *Memberships:* Founder, Puerto Rican Choral Directors Society, 1979; New Spanish Methodist Hymnal Committee, 1992. *Address:* 1745 Colorado St, Urbanizacion San Gerardo, San Juan, Puerto Rico 00926.

OLLESON (Donald) Edward, b. 11 Apr 1937, South Shields, England. University Lecturer; Writer on Music. m. Eileen Gotto, 2 sons, 1 daughter. *Education:* BA, Hertford College, Oxford, 1959; MA 1963; DPhil 1967. *Career:* Assistant Lecturer, Hull University, 1962-63; Research Lecturer, Christ Church, Oxford, 1963-66; Faculty Lecturer, Oxford University, 1966-72; University Lecturer in Music 1972-; Fellow, Merton College, 1970-. *Publications:* Editor, Proceedings of the Royal Musical Association, volumes 94-100; Essays on Opera and English Music in honour of Sir Jack Westrup (with Nigel Fortune and F.W. Sternfeld) 1975; Participation in Everyman Dictionary of Music, 5th Edition, 1975; Modern Musical Scholarship 1978; Co-editor of Music and Letters 1976-86. *Hobbies:* Gardening; Cooking. *Address:* Faculty of Music, St Aldate's, Oxford OX1 1DB, England.

OLLMANN Kurt, b. 19 Jan 1957, Racine, Wisconsin, USA. Singer (Baritone). *Education:* Studied with Gerard Souzay, among others. *Career:* Sang with the Milwaukee Skylight Opera 1979-82; Engagements in Santa Fe, Washington DC, Milan and Brussels in operas by Debussy and Mozart; Pepsico Summerfare New York 1987, as Don Giovanni, in the Peter Sellars version of Mozart's opera; Sang under Bernstein in the Viennese premiere of A Quiet Place (1986) and as Maximilian in a concert performance of Candide at the Barbican, London 1989; Seattle Opera 1988, as Mercutio in Gounod's Roméo et Juliette; St Louis Opera 1989-90, as Purcell's King Arthur and Mozart's Count; Many concert appearances; Season 1992 in On the Town at the Barbican Hall and the title role in the US premiere of Bose's The Sorrows of Young Werther, (Santa Fe). *Recordings:* Count Paris in Roméo et Juliette, conducted by Michel Plasson; Candide and West Side Story, conducted by the composer. *Address:* Opera Theater of St Louis, P O Box 13148, St Louis, MO 63119, USA.

OLMI Paolo, b. 1953, Italy. Conductor. *Education:* Studied with Massimo Pradella and Franco Ferrara in Rome. *Career:* Frequent appearances with major orchestras in Italy and abroad from 1979; Opera debut at Teatro Communale di Bologna, 1986; Conducted Rossini's Mosé in Egitto at Rome 1988, later at the Bayerische Staatsoper, Munich; Deutsche Oper am Rhein Dusseldorf with Traviata, Theatre des Champs Elysees with Rossini's Guillaume Tell; British debut 1991 with Royal Philharmonic in a concert performance of Nabucco; Bellini's Zaira at Catania, 1990; Concerts at the Schleswig-Holstein Festival, the Philharmonic Berlin, the Frankfurt Alte Oper and the Philharmonie in Munich; English Chamber Orchestra with Rostropovitch as soloist; Appointed Principal Conductor of the RAI Rome 1991; Deutsche Oper Berlin 1992 with La Forza del Destino, tour of Italy with the Royal

Philharmonic 1993, Verdi Requiem at the Festival Hall 1994; Engagements with Liverpool Philharmonic in season 1992-93 and invited to conduct Mosè at Covent Garden 1994. *Address:* c/o IMG Artists, Media House, 3 Burlington Lane, London W4 2TH, England.

OLOF Theo, b. 5 May 1924, Bonn, Germany. Violinist. *Education:* Studied with Oskar Back in Amsterdam. *Debut:* Amsterdam 1935. *Career:* Tours of Europe, the United States and Russia from 1945 as soloist; Leader of the Hague Residentie Orchestra 1951-71; Duo partnership with Hermann Krebbers included premieres of Concertos written for them by Henk Badings (1954), Geza Frid (1952) and Hans Kox (1964); Leader of the Concertgebouw Orchestra 1974-85; Recitals with pianist Janine Dacosta, Gérard van Blerk until 1985 and teacher at the Hague Conservatory; Has given first performances of works by Bruno Maderna and Hans Henkemans. *Address:* de Lairessestraat 12 B, 1071 PA Amsterdam, Holland.

OLSEN Derrick, b. 30 Mar 1923, Berne, Switzerland. Singer (Bass- baritone); Administrator. *Education:* Studied in Berne, Geneva and Lucerne. *Career:* Sang at Grand Théâtre Geneva 1944-69; Basle 1950-55, with guest engagements at Holland and Schwetzingen Festivals, Buenos Aires, Milan, Berlin Staatsoper, Zurich, Lucerne and Marseilles; Roles included Mozart's Count, Masetto and Alfonso, Pizarro, Rossini's Basilio and Bartolo, Tago, Germont and Melitone, Wagner's Dutchman, Telramund and Klingsor, Jochanaan, Malatesta and Achilles in Penthesilea by Schoeck; Basle Opera 1952 and 1958 in the premieres of Leonore 40-45 by Liebermann and Titus Feuerfuchs by Sutermeister; Concert premieres of oratorios by Honegger, Cantate de Noel 1953, Kelterborn and Frank Martin, Mystère de la Nativité 1958 and Martinů, Gilgamesh 1958; Sang in the British premiere of Schoenberg's Von Heute auf Morgen, Festival Hall 1963; Member of the Quatuor Vocale de Geneve and Artistic Director of the Radio Orchestra Beromunster at Zurich 1958-70. *Recordings:* Pelléas et Mélisande, Monteverdi's Combattimento, Sutermeister's Schwarze Spinne, Martin's Le Vin Herbe and Handel's Apollo e Dafne. *Address:* c/o Opernhaus Zurich, Falkenstrasse 1, CB-8008 Zurich, Switzerland.

OLSEN Frode, b. 10 Apr 1952, Oslo, Norway. Singer (Bass). *Education:* Studied at Opera State Conservatory, Oslo and in Dusseldorf. *Debut:* Music Festival in Aix in Prevence, as King Ludwig in Euryanthe, 1993. *Career:* Sang at Deutsche Oper am Rhein Dusseldorf 1982-86, notably as Mozart's Masetto and Don Alfonso; Badisches Staatstheater Karlsruhe from 1986, as Sarastro, Pimen, Gremin, Zaccaria, Wagner's Pogner, King Mark and Landgrave, Orestes and Basilio; Guest engagements at Dresden, Leipzig, Strasbourg, Dortmund, Berne, Vienna, Volksoper and Oslo; Fasolt in The Ring at Brussels, 1991; Salzburg Festival debut 1992 as a Soldier in Salome; Further appearances as Sarastro at Brussels 1992, the Doctor in Wozzeck at Frankfurt and Gremin in Eugene Onegin at the reopened Glyndebourne Opera House 1994; Other roles include Raimondo, the Commendatore in Don Giovanni, Coline, Timur and Elmiro in Rossini's Otello; Concert repertoire includes the Verdi Requiem, Rossini's Petite Messe solennelle and Stabat Mater, Messiah, Bach's Christmas Oratorio and St Matthew Passion, Elijah and Die Schöpfung. *Address:* c/o Atholl Still Ltd, 80-86 Westrow Street, London SE19 3AF, England.

OLSEN Keith, b. 1957, Denver, Colorado, USA. Singer (Tenor). *Education:* BM San Francisco Conservatory; MM University of Tennessee and Professional Studies, The Juilliard School of Music. *Debut:* US Debut: New York City Opera 1982, in Die Lustige Witwe. European Debut: Staatstheater Karlsruhe, as Rodolfo, 1987. *Career:* San Francisco (Capriccio), Helsinki, Los Angeles, Barcelona as Alfredo, Pretoria (Hoffmann) with Rodolfo in Hamburg, London, Arena di Verona, Frankfurt, Düsseldorf, Wiesbaden, Hannover and Toronto with Manrico in Berlin and Leipzig with Hans in Stuttgart and MacDuff in Bologna.

Other guest appearances include Radamés in Rome and Radio France with Dick Johnson, Turiddú and Hoffmann in Bonn. Film credits include Des Grieux (Puccini's) 100th anniversary performance, RAI, Turiddu, SABC (South African Broadcasting Corp) and Beethoven's Ninth Symphony with Kurt Masur, MDR (Mittel Deutsche Rundfunk). For three consecutive years he has sung at the Royal Opera House; Covent Garden debuting as Rodolfo and subsequently Pinkerton and Boris in Katà Kabanová.*Recording:* Giuliano in Handel's Rodrigo. *Address:* c/o San Francisco Opera, War Memorial Opera House, San Francisco, CA 94102, USA.

OMACHI Yoichiro, b. 22 Aug 1931, Tokyo, Japan. Conductor. *Education:* Studied at Tokyo Academy of Music 1948-54, with Akeo Watanabe and Kurt Woss; Academy of Music Vienna with Karl Bohm, Franco Ferrara, Herbert von Karajan. *Career:* Toured Japan 1957 with Karajan and the Berlin Philharmonic; Guest conductor with the Berlin Philharmonic, Tonkunstler Orchestra, Vienna, 1959; Chief Conductor, Tokyo Philharmonic Orchestra 1961; Founded Tokyo Metropolitan Symphony 1964; Guest Conductor Vienna Symphony Orchestra 1964-67; Permanent conductor of the Dortmund Opera 1968-73; East Asian tour with the Tokyo Philharmonic, 1973; Season 1976-77 conducted Aida at Mannheim, Fidelio in Prague, Madama Butterfly at the Berlin Staatsoper and The Merry Widow in Tokyo; Concerts in Japan, South America 1978-79; Madame Butterfly at the Vienna Staatsoper 1980, Permanent Conductor 1982-84, including Attila on Austrian TV and ballet performances; Professor in the Opera Faculty at the Tokyo Academy of Music. *Recordings:* Albums for CBS/Sony with the Tokyo Philharmonic.

OMAN Julia Trevelyan, b. 11 July 1930, London, England. Stage Designer. *Education:* Studied at Royal College of Art with Hugh Casson. *Career:* Television Designer with the BBC 1955-67; Royal Opera House Covent Garden with designs for Eugene Onegin 1971, La Bohème 1974 and Die Fledermaus 1977; Hamburg Staatsoper 1973 in Un Ballo in Maschera, Royal Opera Stockholm 1982, Otello, The Consul for Connecticut Opera 1985; Designed Arabella at Glyndebourne 1984. *Honours:* Royal Designer for Industry 1977; CBE 1986. *Address:* c/o Royal Opera House, Covent Garden, London WC2, England.

ONAY Gülsin, b. 1954, Istanbul, Turkey. Concert pianist. *Education:* Studied at the Paris Conservatoire with Pierre Sancan and Nadia Boulanger and with Monique Haas and Bernhard Ebert. *Career:* Solo appearances with the Berlin Radio Symphony Orchestra, Austrian, Bavarian and North German Radio orchestras; Copenhagen Symphony, Staatskapelle Dresden, Mozarteum Orchestra Salzburg and the Tokyo Symphony; Repeated tours of West and East Europe, the Far East, in particular Japan; International Festival appearances: Steirischer Herbst, Warsaw autumn, Berliner Festtage, Mozartfest Würzburg, Istanbul Festival, Schleswig-Holstein Festival; Repertoire includes all the concertos of Beethoven, Brahms, Chopin, Liszt, Grieg, Schumann and Rachmaninov and A.A. Saygun; Mozart K414, K466, K467, K488, K491, K503 and K595 and for 2 pianos and orchestra; Saint-Saëns 2, Tchaikovsky 1, Bartók 2 and 3, Prokofiev 1 and 3, Ravel and Weber F minor; Dvořák piano concerto, de Falla (Nights in Gardens of Spain). *Recordings include:* Solos by Franck, Schubert (Harmonia Mundi); Chopin; Debussy, Ravel (KLAVINS); Bartók. *Address:* Schlossgasse 20, 79112 Freiburg, Germany.

ONCINA Juan, b. 15 Apr 1925, Barcelona, Spain. Singer (Tenor). *Education:* Studied in Oran, Barcelona with Mercedes Caspir and in Milan with Augusta Oltrabella. *Debut:* Barcelona 1946, as Des Grieux in Manon. *Career:* Sang opposite Tito Gobbi in Il Barbiere di Siviglia at Barcelona; Paris 1949 in Il Matrimonio Segreto; Florence 1949-50, in Cherubini's Osteria Portoghese and Lully's Armida; Glyndebourne 1952-65, as Don Ramiro in Cenerentola, Ferrando, Comte Ory, Scaramuccio in Ariadne auf Naxos, Rossini's Almaviva,

Fenton in Falstaff, Don Ottavio, Lindoro in L'Italiana in Algeri and in Anna Bolena; Palermo 1959, in Bellini's Beatrice di Tenda; Verdi and Puccini roles from 1963; Guest appearances in Monte Carlo, Venice, Triste and Florence; Vienna Staatsoper 1965; Hamburg 1971-74. *Recordings:* Le Comte Ory and La Cenerentola from Glyndebourne (HMV); Don Pasquale (Decca); L'Arlesiana by Cilea; Un Giorno di Regno by Verdi; Donizetti's Roberto Devereux; Sacchini's Oedipe a Colonne. *Address:* c/o Hamburgische Staatsoper, Grosse-Theaterstrasse 34, D-2000 Hamburg 36, Germany.

ONISHI Aiko, b. 26 Nov 1930, Tokyo, Japan. Pianist; Professor. *Education:* BM, Performers Certificate, 1953; Artists Diploma, 1956, Eastman School of Music, USA; Study with Cecile Genhart, Frank Mannheimer, Dame Myra Hess. *Debut:* Tokyo 1956. *Career:* Performed, all major cities in Japan, over 60 cities in USA; Numerous Lectures & Workshops, at Universities, Conventions, Music Festivals throughout USA. *Publications:* Basics of Pianism in process. *Contributions to:* Professional journals. *Memberships:* American Matthay Association; Music Teachers' Association of Cal. *Hobbies:* Photography; Hiking; Reading; Sewing. *Address:* 53 Citation Dr., Los Altos, CA 94024, USA.

OPALACH Jan, b. 2 Sept 1950, Hackensack, New Jersey, USA. Singer (Bass-baritone). *Education:* Studied at Indiana State University. *Career:* Sang at various regional USA operatic centres, New York City Opera from 1980 as Dulcamara, Papageno, Taddeo, Italiana in Algeri, Pistol and Leporello; Caramoor Festival 1980, as Vilotolla in the USA premiere of Haydn's La Vera Costanza; St Louis 1986 in USA premiere of Rossini's Il Viaggio a Rheims; Sang at Seattle Opera 1991-92, as the Music Master in Ariadne auf Naxos and Guglielmo in Cosi Fan Tutte; New York City Opera 1991 as the Forester in The Cunning Little Vixen, Mozart's Figaro at Toronto; Sang in Rossini Gala Concert at New York's Fisher Hall, 29 Feb 1992. *Address:* c/o New York City Opera, Lincoln Center, New York, NY 10023, USA.

OPIE Alan, b. 22 Mar 1945, Redruth, Cornwall, England. Singer (Baritone). *Education:* Guildhall School of Music, London; London Opera Centre with Vera Rozsa. *Debut:* Sadler's Wells Opera 1969, as Papageno in Die Zauberflöte; Appearances with English National Opera, Welsh National Opera, Aldeburgh Festival and Santa Fe Opera; Other roles include Mozart's Guglielmo, Rossini's Figaro, Verdi's Germont, Britten's Demetrius and Charles Blouth (Gloriana) and Massenet's Lescaut; Sang Wagner's Beckmesser with English National Opera 1984 and at Bayreuth 1988; sang Germont with ENO, 1990 and the title role in Busoni's Doctor Faust; Glyndebourne Festival 1990, as Sid in Albert Herring; Season 1992 as The Fiddler in Königskinder for ENO, The Traveller in Death in Venice at Covent Garden, Balstrode in Peter Grimes at Glyndebourne, Melitone in The Force of Destiny and Papageno at the Coliseum. *Recordings include:* Maria Stuarda by Donizetti (EMI). *Address:* c/o Allied Artists Agency, 42 Montpelier Square, London SW7 1JZ, England.

OPPENHEIM David J, b. 13 Apr 1922, Detroit, Michigan, USA. Musician (Clarinettist); University Dean. m. (1) Judy Holiday, 1948, (2) Ellen Adler, 1957, 2 sons, 1 daughter. *Education:* Interlochen National Music Camp, Michigan; Juilliard School of Music, New York, 1939-40; University of Rochester Eastman School of Music, 1940-43. *Career:* Director, Master Works Division, Columbia Records, 1950-59; Producer, Director, Writer, Network News, CBS Television, 1962-68; Executive Producer, Public Broadcasting Laboratory, 1968-69; Co-Producer of Saul Bellow's Last Analysis, Broadway, New York, 1962; Producer of documentary films on Stravinsky and Casals, CBS; Executive Producer, Cultural Programming, Public Broadcasting Laboratory; Clarinet soloist, Prades, France, 1957, San Juan, Puerto Rico, 1959; Performed under Koussevitsky, Toscanini, Leinsdorf, Steinberg, Bernstein, Stokowski, Stravinsky; Performed chamber music with Casals, Serkin, and Casadesus; Tony Awards Nominating

Committee, 1983-87; Artist-in-Residence, New Mexico, Music Festival. *Recordings:* Brahms Clarinet Quintet with Budapest Quartet; Mozart Clarinet Quintet in A Major with Budapest Quartet; L'histoire du Soldât, Octet, Septet, conducted by Stravinsky; Bernstein Sonata, Clarinet and Piano (dedicated to David Oppenheim); Copland Sextet with Juilliard Quartet; Douglas Moore Quintet with New Music Quartet. *Hobbies:* Mycology; Gardening; Theatre; Literature; Travel. *Address:* 1225 Park Avenue, No. 6A, New York, NY 10128, USA.

OPPENS Ursula, b. 2 Feb 1944, New York City, USA. Concert Pianist. *Education:* BA, Radcliffe College, 1965; Juilliard School 1966-69, with Rosina Lhevinne, Guido Agosti and Leonard Shure. *Debut:* New York, 1969. *Career:* Performances with Boston Symphony, New York Philharmonic and other leading American orchestras; Recitals at Tully Hall, Kennedy Center; Appearances at Aspen, Berkshire and Marlboro Festivals; Tours of Europe and US as soloist and as member of Speculum Musicae: performances of contemporary music; Engagements with the Chamber Music Society of Lincoln Center and the Group for Contemporary Music; Composers who have written for her include Rzeweski, Wolff, Carter and Wuorinen; Teacher at Brooklyn College, City University of New York. *Recordings include:* Stravinsky 2 Piano Music and Petrushka; Music by Busoni, Mozart and Rzewski. *Honours:* Winner, Busoni International Piano Competition, 1969; Avery Fisher Prize, 1976. *Current Management:* Colbert Artists Managament, 111 West 57, New York, NY 10019,USA. *Address:* 777 West End Avenue, New York, NY 10025, USA.

ORBÁN Gyorgy, b. 12 July 1947, Tirgu-Mures, Romania. Hungarian composer. *Education:* Studied at Cluj Conservatory 1968-73. *Career:* Teacher of Theory at Cluj Conservatory until 1979; Moved to Hungary and became Editor of the Editio Musica Budapest; Teacher of Composition at Music-Academy, Budapest. *Compositions:* Orchestra: Five Canons to Poems by Attile Joszef for soprano and chamber ensemble 1977; Triple Sextet 1980; 2 Serenades 1984, 85; 4 Duos with soprano and clarinet 1979, soprano and double bass 1987; Soprano and Violoncello, 1989; Soprano and Violin, 1992; Sonata Concertante for clarinet and piano 1987; Wind Quintet, 1984; Brass Music for Quintet Nr.1, 1987; Sonata for bassoon and piano 1987; Sonata for violin 1970; 2 Sonatas for Violin and Piano, 1989, 1991; Suite for piano 1986; 4 Piano Sonatas 1987, 1988, 1989; Chorus and Orchestra: Rotate Coeli, orartorio, 1992; Regina Martyrum, oratorio, 1993; Missa No.2, 1990, No.4, 1991, No.6, 1993; Chorus and Chmaber Ensemble: Missa No.1, 1990, No.3, 1991, No.5, 1992. Choral: Missa No.7, 1993; Flower Songs for Female Choir 1978; Chorus Book in Memory of S A No.1 1984; Chorus Book No.2; Book of Medallions, cycle of 9 choruses 1987; Stabat Mater 1987; About 40 little latin motets for mixed and female chorus. *Address:* ARTISJUS (Hungary), c/o PRS Ltd Member Registration, 29-33 Berners Street, London W1P 4AA, England.

ORDONEZ Antonio, b. 27 Oct 1948, Madrid, Spain. Singer (Tenor). *Education:* Studied in Madrid with Miguel Garcia Barrosa. *Career:* Concert appearances in Spain and USA from 1980; Opera debut at Teatro Zarzuela Madrid 1982, as Pinkerton; Sang Don Carlos at Liege 1986 and at Deutsche Oper Berlin 1988; Teatro Liceo Barcelona 1986, in Paccini's Saffo, with Montserrat Caballe; Further guest appearances as Cavaradossi at Dallas 1987, Calaf at Ravenna Festival 1988 and as Alvaro in La Forza del Destino at Washington 1989; San Francisco Opera 1991 as Foresto in Attila; Other roles include Rodolfo, Deutsche Oper 1989, Alfredo, Riccardo, Gabriele Adorno and Edgardo in Lucia di Lammermoor, Liège 1987; Sang Don José in Carmen at Earl's Court, London 1991. *Address:* c/o San Francisco Opera, War Memorial Opera House, San Francisco, CA 94102, USA.

ORE Cecilie, b. 1954, Oslo, Norway. Composer. Education: Piano Studies at Norwegian State Academy of Music and in Paris; Studied Composition with Ton de Leeuw at Sweelinck Conservatory, Amsterdam and at Institute of Sonology in Utrecht. *Career:* Since 1985 her instrumental, vocal and electro-acoustic compositions have been regularly performed at Nordic and international festivals for contemporary music. In 1988 she received the Norwegian State Guarantee Income for Artists. *Compositions:* Instrumental Music: Helices for wind quintet, 1984; Prophyre for orchestra, 1986; Contracanthus for double-bass solo, 1987; Praesens Subitus for amplified string quartet,1989; Erat Erit Est for amplified chamber ensemble, 1991; Lex Temporis for string quartet 1992; Futurum Exactum for amplified string ensemble, 1992; Vocal Music: Ex Oculis for 4 male voices, 1985; Electro-acoustic Music; Etapper, 1988; Multi- Media: Im-Mobile I, II, III, music for exhibition, 1984; Video: Contracanthus for double-bass solo, 1988; Im-Mobile, 1984; Film Music: Kald Verden, 1986. *Address:* Ullevålsvn 61, 0171 Oslo, Norway.

ORGA Hüsnü Ates, b. 6 Nov 1944, Kingston-on-Thames, England. Record Producer; Consultant; Writer; Critic. m. Josephine Prior, 23 Nov 1974, divorced Dec 1991, 1 son, 1 daughter. *Education:* ATCL, 1964, LMus TCL, 1966, FTCL, 1972, Trinity College of Music; BMus, University of Durham, 1968. *Career:* Music Information/Presentation Assistant, BBC Radio 3, 1971-74; Lecturer in Music, Concert Director, University of Surrey, 1975-90; Artistic Director, Institute of Armenian Music, 1976-80; Member, various competition juries, 1976-, including Charles Heidsieck Champagne Music Awards, Royal Philharmonic Society, 1990; Artistic Director, Music Armenia, 1978; Examiner, Associated Board of Royal Schools of Music, 1981-; Artistic Director, Guildford International Music Festival, 1991. *Recordings:* Record Producer for Conifer, Hyperion, Unicorn-Kanchana, RPO/ASV, JCV, Collins Classics: Orchestral, chamber, piano and vocal repertoire. *Publications:* The Proms, 1974; Records and Recording Classical Guides, 1977, 1978; Chopin: His Life and Times, 1976; Beethoven: His Life and Times, 1978; Portrait of a Turkish Family (afterword), 1988. *Contributions to:* Classical Music; H-Fi News and Record Review; The Listener; The Literary Review; Music and Musicians; Records and Recording; Books and Bookmen; Radio Times; The Musical Times; Programme Annotator: London Sinfonietta, 1968-73; London Symphony Orchestra, 1976-81; Sutton Place Heritage Trust, 1983-86; Sleeve notes: CBS, Decca, DGG, Hyperion, RCA, Collins Classics, Conifer, EMI. *Address:* 102 Glisson Road, Cambridge CB1 2HQ, England.

ORGAD Ben Zion, b. 1926, Germany. Composer. *Education:* Academy of Music, Jerusalem, Israel; Brandeis University; Private instruction in composition. *Career:* Superintendent of Musical Education, Israel Ministry of Education and Culture, Tel-Aviv, 1950-. *Compositions:* Cantatas: The Story of the Spies; Isaiah's Vision; Orchestral Works: Building a King's Stage; Choreographic Sketches; Movements on A; Kaleidoscope; Music for Horn and Orchestra; Ballad for Orchestra; Dialogues on the First Scroll; Suffering for Redemption, for mezzo-soprano, choir and orchestra; Out of the Dust, soloist and instruments; Ballada, for violin; Taksim, for harp; Monologue, for viola; Numerous works for soloists and orchestra; Piano pieces. *Honours:* Recipient of various awards for compositions including: UNESCO Koussevitsky Prize, 1952. *Membership:* Chairman, Israel Composers' League. *Address:* Israel Ministry of Education and Culture, Tel-Aviv, Israel.

ORGONASOVA Luba, b. 22 Jan 1961, Bratislava, Czechoslovakia. Singer (Soprano). *Education:* Studied at Bratislava Conservatory. *Career:* Concert and operatic engagements in Czechoslovakia 1979-83; Hagen Opera, West Germany, 1983-88 as Mozart's Ilia and Pamina, Gilda and Violetta, Lauretta and Sophie in der Rosenkavalier; Guest appearances in Nuremberg, Essen, Hamburg and Zurich; Vienna Volksoper 1988-89; Sang Pamina and Donna Anna at Aix-en-Provence Festival, 1988-89; Opera de Lyon 1988 as Madame Silberklang in Der Schauspieldirektor; Sang Constanze at Deutsche Oper Berlin and in Lisbon 1991, with concert performances of Die Entführung under John Eliot Gardiner in London and Amsterdam; Other roles include Susanna, Atalanta in Handel's Serse, Marzelline, Cendrillon and Antonio, Les Contes d'Hoffmann; Concert repertoire includes Janáček's Glagolitic Mass, Bruckner's Te Deum and the Missa Solemnis, all at Zurich, Haydn's Harmonie Mass, Bremen and Oratorios by Bach, Handel and Dvořák. *Recording:* Die Zauberflote.

ORKIS Lambert Thomas, b. 20 Apr 1946, Philadelphia, Pennsylvania, USA. Pianist; Chamber Music Artist; Soloist; Educator. m. Janice Barbara Kretschmann, 19 Feb 1972. *Education:* Diploma and BM, Piano Performance, Curtis Institute of Music. *Career:* Chamber music artist, soloist, performer on historical instruments; Worldwide performances; Premiered solo works of George Crumb, Richard Wernick, Maurice Wright and James Primosch, including Richard Wernick's award-winning Piano Concerto in Washington, DC and Carnegie Hall, New York, with the National Symphony Orchestra, Mstislav Rostropovich conducting, 1991; Recitals with cellist Mstislav Rostropovich, 1981-; Principal Keyboard, National Symphony Orchestra, Washington, DC, 1982-; Faculty, Temple University, Philadelphia, currently: Professor of Piano, Co-ordinator of Master of Music Programme in Piano Accompanying and Chamber Music, 1968-; Recitals with soprano Lucy Shelton, 1981-; Recitals with soprano Arleen Augér, 1987-90; Recitals with violinist Anne-Sophie Mutter, 1988-; Founding Member and fortepianist, Castle Trio, 1988-; Pianist, Smithsonian Chamber Players, 1983-; Pianist, Library of Congress Summer Chamber Festival, 1986-89; Pianist, American Chamber Players, 1986-89; Pianist, 20th Century Consort, 1976-87; Judge, Carnegie Hall International American Music Competition for Pianists, 1985; Judge, Kennedy Center Friedheim Awards, 1991; Nationwide telecast: Soloist with National Symphony Orchestra, Great Performances, Public Broadcasting System, 1983; Soloist, In Residence, 1983. *Recordings:* Schubert Impromptus, Virgin Classics, 1990. *Hobbies:* Travel; Photography. *Current Management:* Smithsonian Artists. *Address:* c/o Smithsonian Artists, NMAH/Room 4123, Smithsonian Institution, Washington, DC 20560, USA.

ORLANDI MALASPINA Rita, b. 28 Dec 1937, Bologna, Italy. Singer (Soprano). m. Massimiliano Malaspina. *Education:* Studied with Carmen Melis in Milan. *Debut:* Teatro Nuovo Milan 1963, as Verdi's Giovanna d'Arco. *Career:* Sang widely in Italy, and at Covent Garden, London, Munich, Hamburg, Paris, Nice, Barcelona, Vienna and Buenos Aires; Metropolitan Opera debut 1968; Other roles include Puccini's Tosca and Suor Angelica, Wagner's Elsa, Giordano's Maddalena and Verdi's Aida, Odabella, Leonora, Amelia, Abigaille, Desdemona, Luisa Miller, Elisabeth and Lucrezia (I Due Foscari); Also heard in concert. *Address:* c/o Teatro alla Scala, Via Filodrammatici 2, Milan, Italy.

ORLOFF Claudine, b. 6 Jan 1961, Brussels, Belgium. Pianist. m. Burkard Spinnler, 1 Oct 1983, 2 sons. *Education:* Diplome superieur, Piano, class of J C Vanden Eunden, 1985, Diplome superieur, Chamber Music, class of A Siwy, 1987, Conservatoire Royal de Musique, Brussels; Private studies with B Lemmens, 1985-88. *Career:* Recording for RTB, 1978; Regular appearances as soloist and in chamber music; Often includes contemporary works in recital programmes, including Van Rossum's 12 preludes, 1986; Many concerts on 2 pianos (with Burkard Spinnler), Belgium, France, Germany, including Musique en Sorbonne, Paris, July 1991; Radio engagement, Hommage à Milhaud, live, RTB Brussels, Oct 1992. *Honours:* Ella Olin Prize, Brussels, 1985. *Current Management:* F E de Wasswige Music Management. *Address:* 82 rue des Garonnes, 1170 Brussels, Belgium.

ORMAI Gabor, b. 1950, Hungary, Violist. *Education:* Studied with András Mihaly at the Franz Liszt Academy,

Budapest, with members of the Amadeus Quartet and Zoltán Szekely. *Career:* Founder member of the Takacs Quartet, 1975; Many concert appearances in all major centres of Europe and the USA; Tours of Australia, New Zealand, Japan, South America, England, Norway, Sweden, Greece, Belgium and Ireland; Bartók Cycle for the Bartók-Solti Festival at South Bank, 1990; Great Performers Series at Lincoln Center and Mostly Mozart Festival at Alice Tully Hall, New York; Visits to Japan 1989 and 1992; Mozart Festivals at South Bank, Wigmore Hall and Barbican Centre 1991; Bartók Cycle at the Théâtre des Champs Elysées 1991; Beethoven Cycles at the Zurich Tonhalle, in Dublin, at the Wigmore Hall and in Paris, 1991-92; Resident at the University of Colorado, Resident at the London Barbican 1988-91, with master classes at the Guildhall School of Music; Plays Amati instrument made for the French Royal Family and loaned by the Corcoran Gallery, Gallery of Art, Washington DC. *Recordings:* Schumann Quartets Op 41, Mozart String Quintets (with Denes Koromzay), Bartók 6 Quartets, Schubert Trout Quintet (with Zoltán Kocsis) Hungaroton; Haydn Op 76, Brahms Op 51 nos 1 and 2, Chausson Concerto (with Joshua Bell and Jean-Yves Thibaudet); Works by Schubert, Mozart, Dvořák and Bartók (Decca). *Honours:* Winner, International Quartet Competition, Evian 1977; Winner Portsmouth International Quartet Competition, 1979. *Address:* c/o Lies Askonas, 6 Henrietta Street, London WC2E 8LA, England.

ORNSTEIN Doris Lee, b. 7 Aug 1930, New York, USA. Harpsichordist; Teacher of Baroque Performance Practices. m. Robert Ornstein, 19 Aug. 1951, 1 son, 2 daughters. *Education:* University of Illinois, 1958-59; Mannes College of Music, 1961-62. *Debut:* Severance Chamber Hall, Cleveland, Ohio, 1966. *Career:* Master Classes and Recitals throughout United States; Director and Harpsichordist, Cleveland Baroque Soloists; Soloist at Baldwin Wallace Bach Festival, American Shakespeare Festival, Matrix-Midland Festival, Boulder Bach Festival, Los Angeles Harpsichord Centre; Faculty, Oberlin Conservatory, 1971-72; Artist-In-Residence, Case Western Reserve University; Director of Early Music Studies, Cleveland Institute of Music; Solo Harpsichordist and Faculty Member, Aspen Music Festival, 1972-84; Soundtracks for 2 films sponsored by National Endowment for the Humanities, Harpsichord Building in American and The Staging of Shakespeare; Radio appearances on National Public Radio; 2 Recitals in New York sponsored by the Carnegie Hall Corporation. *Recordings:* The Three Sonatas for Viola da Gamba and Harpsichord by JS Bach, Gasparo Records with Catharine Meints; The Cleveland Baroque Soloists, Gasparo Records. *Contributions to:* First complete edition of Handel's Cantata, Mi Palpita il Cor, with realization and accompanying article in Bach Magazine, 1979. *Hobbies:* Reading English literature; Tennis; Mountain hiking. *Current Management:* Beverly Simmons Artist Management. *Address:* 3122 Woodbury Road, Shaker Heights, OH 44120, USA.

OROZCO Rafael, b. 24 Jan 1946, Cordoba, Spain. Concert Pianist. *Education:* Studied at the Cordoba Conservatory and the Madrid Conservatory, 1960-64; Studied in London with Maria Curcio. *Career:* Won Leeds International Competition 1966; Many appearances with leading orchestras in the USA and Europe: London Symphony, Royal Philharmonic, Berlin Philharmonic, Orchestre de Paris, New York and Los Angeles Philharmonics and the Cleveland Orchestra; Conductors include Chailly, Maazel, Previn, Muti, Bychkov and Andrew Davis; Engagements at the Prague, Granada, Santander, Bath and Aldeburgh fesitivals. *Recordings include:* Rachmaninov Concertos with Edo de Waart and the Royal Philharmonic; Mozart's Concertos K537 and K595 with the English Chamber Orchestra and Charles Dutoit; the Liszt Sonata; the complete Iberia by Albeniz. *Address:* c/o Terry Harrison Ltd., 3 Clarendon Court, Park Street, Charlbury, Oxon OX7 3PS, England.

ORR Buxton Daeblitz, b. 18 Apr 1924, Glasgow, Scotland, Composer; Conductor. m. (1) Isobel Roberts,

1954, (2) Jean Latimer, 1968. *Education:* University College School, London; Middlesex Hospital, BSc Physiol 1st Class honours 1946, MBBS 1948; Guildhall School of Music and Drama, FGSM 1971. *Career:* Film and Theatre Music, 1955-61; Conductor, London Jazz Composers Orchestra, 1970-80; Founder and Director, Guildhall New Music Ensemble, 1975-91; Conductor, Guildhall New Music Ensemble, 1975-91; Composer in Residence, Banff, Alberta, Canada, 1984-85. *Compositions:* Opera, The Wager, 1961; Music Theatre, Unicorn, 1981; The Last Circus, 1984, Ring in the New, 1986; Chamber, vocal and orchestral music; Works for brass and wind ensembles including concertos for trumpet, trombone and A John Gay Suite for symphonic wind band; Sinfonia Ricercante, 1988; Refrains VI for chamber orchestra, 1992-. *Recordings:* Apollo Records, vocal and piano music. *Contributions to:* Composer; The Listener; New Grove Dictionary; ENO Opera Guides; BBC Talks. *Honours:* Commissions from McEwen, Glasgow, BBC London and Scotland, City of London Festival, Merseyside Arts; Seagrams Award, American National Music Theater Network, 1988. *Memberships:* Executive Council, Composers Guild; Park Lane Group; Editorial Board, Composer Magazine; Reading Panels, SPNM, BBC; Association of Profesional Composers. *Address:* Church House Barn, Llanwarne, Hereforrd HR2 8JE, England.

ORR Robin (Robert Kemsley), b. 2 June 1909, Brechin, Scotland. Composer. m. (1) Margaret Ellen Mace, 29 Dec 1937, 1 son, 2 daughters. (2) Doris Ruth Winny-Meyer, 14 July 1979. *Education:* Royal College of Music, London; Organ Scholar, Pembroke College, Cambridge University; MA, MusD; Studied with Casella in Siena; Boulanger in Paris. *Career:* Organist, St John's College, Cambridge, 1938-51; RAFVR, Flight Lieutenant, 1939-45; University Lecturer in Music, 1947-56, Professor of Music 1965-76, Cambridge University; Professor of Music, Glasgow University, 1956-65; Chairman, Scottish Opera, 1962-76; Director, Welsh National Opera, 1977-83; Director, Art's Theatre, Cambridge, 1970-76. *Compositions include:* Symphony in One Movement, 1963 (Edinburgh Festival and Promenade Concerts); Symphony No 2, 1971 (Edinburgh festival); Symphony No 3 (Llandaff Festival Commission 1978—); Full Circle, opera in 1 act (Scottish Opera, 1967 and 1968); Hermiston, opera in 3 acts (Scottish Opera, Edinburgh Festival, 1975); On the Razzle, opera in 3 acts (RSAMD Glasgow, 1988) Libretto by composer after the play by Tom Stoppard; Sinfonnietta Helvetica (BBC Commision 1990); Numerous other works including Church music. *Honours:* CBE, 1972; Hon DMus, Glasgow, 1972; Hon LLD, Dundee, 1976; FRCM, 1965; Hon RAM, 1966; Hon FRSAMD, 1985; Honorary Fellow, St John's College, Cambridge, 1987; Honorary Fellow, Pembroke College, Cambridge, 1988. *Address:* 16 Cranmer Road, Cambridge CB3 9BL, England.

ORREGO-SALAS Juan A., b. 18 Jan 1919, Santiago, Chile, South America. Composer; Professor of Music; Architect. m. Carmen Benavente 1943, 4 sons, 1 daughter. *Education:* BA 1938, MA 1943, State University of Chile. *Career includes:* Conductor, Catholic University Choir, 1938-44; Professor of Musicology, Faculty of Music, State University of Chile, 1942-61; Editor, Revista Musical Chilena, 1949-53; Music Critic, El Mercurio, 1950-61; Director, Instituto de Extension Musical, Chile, 1957-59; Chairman, Music Department, Catholic University, Chile, 1951-61; ; Professor of Music, Director of Latin American Music Centre, Indiana University, USA, 1961-. *Compositions include:* Orchestral: Variaciones serenas for strings 1971; Volte for chamber orchestra 1971; Symphony No. 4 1966; Violin Concerto 1983; Second Piano Concerto, 1985; Cello Concerto, 1992; Chamber music: Trio No 2 1977; Presencias 1972; Tangos 1982; Balada for cello and piano 1983; Partita, 1988; Vocal music: Missa in tempore discordige 1969; The Days of God 1974-76; Bolivar for narrator, chorus and orchestra 1982; The Celestial City, 1992; Stage Music: The Tumbler's Prayer (ballet) 1960; Widows (opera) 1989. *Publications include:* Latin American Literary Review 1975; Music of the Americas (co-editor) 1967; Encyclopedia Americana 1970. *Contributions to:* Musical Quarterly;

Tempo; Revista Musical. *Address:* 490 S Serena Lane, Bloomington, IN 47401, USA.

ORTEGA Ginka Gerova, b. 18 Mar 1946, Preslav, Bulgaria. Flautist. m. Dr. Jesus Ortega, 3 Aug 1969, 1 son, 1 daughter. *Education:* Diploma in Performance, Varna State School of Music, Bulgaria, 1962; BM, Oberlin Conservatory of Music, 1967; MMus, Wayne State University, Detroit, Michigan, 1969; Postgraduate: University of Michigan School of Music, 1971; Masterclasses: J. P. Rampal, L. Moyse. *Debut:* Carnegie Hall, New York, 1983. *Career:* Radiotelevizione Italiana Castres Culturas, Spain; Carnegie Hall, New York; St Laurence Center, Toronto, Ontario, Canada, Palazzo de Compidoglio, Rome, Italy; Macomb Theatre for the Performing Arts, Michigan; Juventudes Musicales Concerts, Spain; University of Mexico, Mexico; Biblioteca Angel, Bogotà, Colombia; Music from Oberlin Radio Broadcasts; Sofia Concert, Bulgaria; Orchestra Hall, Detroit, Michigan; Duquesne University, Pittsburgh, Pennsylvania; Palacio Benacazon, Toledo, Spain; Yale University Schools of Music; Columbia University; Art Museum, Detroit; Art Gallery, Windsor, Canada; Ontario Science Center, Toronto; Satellite Cable TV, New York City; Educational Programs; Artist-in-Residence, Wayne State University School of Fine and Performing Arts, Detroit; Flute, Piano, The Michigan Duo. *Hobbies:* Travel; Literature; Art; Flamenco.

ORTH Norbert, b. 1939, Dortmund, Germany. Singer (Tenor). *Education:* Studied in Hamburg and Cologne and at the Dortmund Opera House school. *Career:* Sang in Enschede, Holland, then at opera houses in Dusseldorf, Nuremburg, Munich, Paris, Berlin and Stuttgart; Metropolitan Opera 1979, as Pedrillo in Die Entführung; Augsburg 1981, as Max in Der Freischütz; Appearances at the Salzburg and Bayreuth Festivals: Loge in Das Rheingold 1984; Sang Walther in Die Meistersinger at Hanover, 1986; Sang Tannhaüser at Kassel 1988, Lohengrin at Hanover and Wiesbaden; Walther in Die Meistersinger at the rebuilt Essen Opera, 1988; Théâtre du Châtelet, Paris, 1990, as Walther; Season 1992 as Berg's Alwa at Dresden and Parsifal at Turin; Also heard in the concert hall, as Lieder and oratorio singer. *Recordings:* Die Entführung (Eurodisc); Paer's Leonore (Decca); Les Contes d'Hoffmann (HMV); Schubert's Die Freunde von Salamanka (Deutsche Grammophon); Augustin Moser in Die Meistersinger, Bayreuth 1974, (Philips). *Address:* c/o Niedersächsische Staatsheater, Opernplatz 1, D-300 Hannover 1, Germany.

ORTIZ Cristina, b. 17 Apr 1950, Bahia, Brazil. Pianist. *Education:* Studied at the Conservatory in Rio de Janeiro, then with Magda Tagliaferro in Paris; After becoming first woman to win the Van Cliburn Competition (1969) resumed studies at the Curtis Institute, Philadelphia, with Rudolf Serkin. *Career:* New York recital debut 1971; moved to London 1972 and has since played with most of the world's leading orchestras: Vienna Philharmonic, Berlin Philharmonic, New York Philharmonic, Concertgebouw, Chicago Symphony, Israel Philharmonic and Los Angeles Philharmonic; tours with Royal Philharmonic and Philharmonia Orchestras in Europe and Latin America; conductors include Previn, Mehta, Kondrashin, Ashkenazy, Leinsdorf, Chailly, Masur, Salonen, Colin Davis, Janssons, Fedoseyev. *Recordings:* Extensive repertoire with EMI, Decca, Pantheon, Pickwick, BIS, RPO Records and Collins. *Address:* c/o Harrison/Parrott Ltd., 12 Penzance Road, London W11 4PA, England.

ORTIZ Francisco, b. 1948, Spain. Singer (Tenor). *Education:* Studied in Barcelona and Madrid. *Debut:* Barcelona 1973 as Foresto in Attila. *Career:* Further appearances as Foresto in London, Paris, 1974, Madrid and Venice 1976, Toulouse 1979; New York City Opera 1973 as Turiddu, Nice 1974 as Radames, Geneva 1975 as Puccini's Des Grieux; Sang Pollione in Norma at Amsterdam, Barcelona and Vienna 1978-80; Theatre de la Monnaie Brussels 1981 as Cavaradossi, Sydney Opera 1982 as Manrico; Further engagements at Hamburg, Santiago, Ernani 1979, Paris, Rio de Janeiro and the Vienna Staatsoper, Alvaro in La Forza del Destino; Appeared with Canadian Opera Company at Toronto as Pollione 1991; Performances in Zarzuela and as concert artist. *Address:* c/o Canadian Opera Company, 227 Front Street East, Toronto, Ontario MFA 1E8, Canada.

ORTIZ William, b. 30 Mar 1947, Salinas, Puerto Rico. Composer. m. Candida, 26 Mar 1988, 2 daughters. *Education:* Puerto Rico Conservatory of Music; MA, PhD, State University of New York, Stony Brook. *Career:* Approximately 100 works for orchestra, chamber ensembles, solo works, songs, opera and electronic music. *Compositions:* Unknown Poets from the Full-Time Jungle; Loaisai; Nueva York Tropical; Caribe Urbano; Garabato; A Sensitive Mambo in Transformation; Suspension de Soledad en 3 Tiempos. *Recordings:* 1245 E 107th Street; Amor, Cristal y Piedra; William Ortiz Chamber Music; Abrazo New Music for Four Guitars. *Publications:* Du-Wop and Dialectics, Perspectives of New Music, Winter 1988; Musical Snobbism, Latin American Music Conference 1882; Music Critic to San Juan Star. *Honours:* Music Composition Prize, Ateneo Puertorriqueno, 1989; Guest Composer, Latin American Music Festival, Caracas, Venezuela, 1991-92. *Memberships:* American Composers Alliance; American Music Center; Composers Forum. *Address:* Calle Jaguey D-43, El Plantio, Toa Baja, Puerto Rico 00949.

ORTON Richard Henry, b. 1 Jan 1940, Derby, England. Composer; University Teacher. m Diane Helm, 12 Apr 1973, 3 sons, 1 daughter. *Education:* Birmingham School of Music, 1958-60; St John's College, Cambridge, 1961-67. *Compositions:* Cycle for 2 or 4 Players, 1968; Timescape for York Minster, 1984; Tabula Vigilans Studies, 1992-93. *Recordings:* Cycle; Icarus. *Publications:* Electronic Music for Schools, Editor, 1981; Companion to Contemporary Musical Thought, Editor, 1992. *Memberships:* SPNM; APC; ICMA. *Address:* 21 West Moor Lane, Heslington, York YO1 5ER, England.

OSBORNE Charles, b. 24 Nov 1927, Brisbane, Australia. Critic; Author. *Education:* Studied piano with Archie Day and Irene Fletcher and voice with Vido Luppi and Browning Mummery. *Career:* Assistant Editor, London Magazine, 1957-66; Assistant Literary Director, Arts Council of Great Britain, 1966-71, Literary Director 1971-86; Member of Editorial Board, Opera Magazine; Broadcaster on musical subjects on BBC Radio 3; Currently Theatre Critic for the Sunday Telegraph. *Publications:* Opera 66, 1966; The Complete Operas of Verdi, 1969; Editor, Letters of Giuseppe Verdi, 1971; The Concert Song Companion, 1974; Wagner and his World, 1977; The Complete Operas of Mozart. 1978; The Dictionary of Opera, 1983; The Operas of Richard Strauss, 1988. *Contributions to:* Opera; London Magazine; Spectator; Times Literary Supplement; Encounter; New Statesman; Observer; Sunday Times. *Hobby:* Travel. *Address:* Richard Scott Simon Ltd., 36 Wellington Street, London WC2, England.

OSBORNE Conrad L(eon), b. 22 July 1934, Lincoln, Nebraska, USA. Music Critic; Vocal Coach. *Education:* Studied at Columbia University, Singing with Cornelius Reid and Acting with Frank Corsaro. *Career:* Private Teacher of Singing and Arts; Management Consultant; Former actor in theatre and on television, former baritone with minor opera companies in the New York area; Chief Critic of vocal music of High Fidelity, 1959-69; New York Music Critic for the Financial Times, 1962-69; Advisory Editor of the Musical Newsletter, 1970-77. *Publications:* Discographies for the operas of Verdi, Mozart and Wagner for High Fidelity; Articles and reviews for Opus Magazine from 1984. *Address:* Financial Times Ltd (Arts), Bracken House, Cannon Street, London EC4, England.

OSBORNE Nigel, b. 23 June 1948, Manchester, England. Composer.*Education:* Oxford University, with Kenneth Leighton and Egon Wellesz; Warsaw, with

Witold Rudzinski, 1970-71. *Career:* Swiss Radio Prize 1971 for Seven Words; 1978- Lecturer at Nottingham University; Conducted the premiere of The Sun of Venice at the Festival Hall, London, 1992. *Compositions:* Seven Words, cantata 1971; Heaventree for chorus, 1973; Remembering Esenin for cello and piano, 1974; The Sickle for soprano and orchestra, 1975; Chansonier for chorus and ensemble, 1975; Prelude and Fugue for ensemble, 1975; Passers By for trio and synthesizer, 1976; Cello Concerto, 1977; I am Goya for baritone and quartet, 1977; Vienna.Zurich.Constance for soprano and quintet, 1977; Figure/Ground for piano, 1978; Kerenza at the Zawn for oboe and tape, 1978; Orlando Furioso for chorus and ensemble, 1978; Songs from a Bare Mountain for women's chorus, 1979; In Camera for ensemble, 1979; Under the Eyes for voice and quartet, 1979; Quasi una fantasia for cello, 1979; Flute Concerto, 1980; Gnostic Passion for chorus, 1980; Poem without a Hero for four voices and electronics, 1980; Mythologies for sextet, 1980; The Cage for tenor and ensemble, 1981; Piano Sonata, 1981; Choralis I-III, for six voices, 1981-82; Sinfonia I, 1982; Sinfonia II, 1983; Cantata piccola for soprano and string quartet; Fantasia for ensemble, 1983; Wildlife for ensemble, 1984; Alba for mezzo-soprano, ensemble and tape, 1984; Zansa for ensemble, 1985; Hell's Angels, Chamber Opera 1985; Pornography for mezzo-soprano and ensemble; The Electrification of the Soviet Union, opera after Pasternak, 1986; Lumiere for string quartet and 4 groups of children 1986; The Black Leg Miner for ensemble 1987; Esquisse I and II for strings 1987; Stone Garden for Chamber Orchestra 1988; Zone for oboe, clarinet and string trio 1989; Tracks for 2 choirs, orchestra and wind band 1990; Eulogy (for Michael Vyner) 1990; Canzona for brass 1990; Violin Concerto 1990; The Sun of Venice (after Turner's visions of Venice), 1991; Terrible Mouth, opera, 1992. *Address:* c/o Universal Edition Ltd., 2 Fareham Street, London W1, England.

OSBORNE Tony Roy Stuart, b. 10 Nov 1947, Slough, Berkshire, England. Double Bass Player; Composer; Arranger; Teacher; Bass Guitarist. m. Jocelyn S Levy 1971, 2 sons. *Education:* Blyth Major, Royal Academy of Music, London, 1966-69 with John Walton, double bass and Richard Stoker, composition; LRAM 1969. *Career:* Freelance Bassist; Symphony orchestras including BBC Proms; Opera, Light Music; Seasons at Covent Garden, Royal Ballet; Theatre Royal Windsor; D'Oyly Carte; West End Theatre; The Ritz Hotel, including 1981 BBC Documentary; Orchestral Assistant, Royal Academy of Music, 1972-75; Tutor and Assistant on many courses and seminars, including The Yorke Mini-Bass Project; Teacher: Leighton Park School, 1978-, Bradford College, Berkshire, 1986-, St Joseph's College, 1987-, Bulmershe College, University of Reading, 1984-; Royal County of Berkshire (Now Berkshire Young Musicians Trust); Appearances in several films for Cinema and TV. *Compositions:* Commissions; Piano trio; Fantasia for Cello and Piano; Essay for Orchestra; 3 pieces for Orchestra; Elegy for Chorus and Orchestra; Sonatina for Oboe and Bassoon; Suite for String Orchestra; Songs; Instrumental Jingles; Double Bass trios and quartets; Concertina for double bass and strings; Elegie for double bass and piano; pieces for Brass Quintet; Ubi Caritas, SATB; 3 Nonsense songs for soprano, cello and double bass, 1992; 3 Melodic Portraits for double bass and string orchestra, 1992. *Recordings:* Numerous. *Publications:* The Double Bass Sings, 17 pieces for Double Bass and Piano, 1983; Strings Together Series, 1986; Contributor to Bass is Best, Caroline Emery, Yorke, Editor, 1988; Stringsets Series; The Really Easy Bass Book, 1990; The Really Easy Electric Bass Book, 1992. *Address:* 42 Parkland Avenue, Slough, Berkshire SL3 7LQ, England.

OSIECK Hans (Hendrik Willem), b. 25 Jan 1910, Amsterdam, Netherlands. Pianist; Composer; Music Teacher. *Education:* Piano soloist cum laude, Musikhochschule, Stuttgart, Germany, 1930-34. *Debut:* As Pianist and Composer, The Hague, Netherlands, 1934. *Career:* Many performances with Dutch orchestras including Concertgebouw Orchestra; Many radio performances; Played 1st piano concertino with Berlin Philharmonic Orchestra, Berlin, Federal Republic of Germany, 1949; Performances for radio in East and in West Berlin; Series of tours and radio performances, Federal Republic of Germany; Tours of Curaççao, Aruba, Venezuela and Republic of South Africa, 1949-51; Several radio recitals in Denmark and Sweden; Concert of 2nd piano concertino with Malmo Orchestra, broadcast by Stockholm Radio; Teacher of piano, in several Towns in the Netherlands. Currently piano recitals in Netherlands, Germany, France, Italy. *Compositions:* About 100 including: In een Blauw Geruite Kiel; Concerto for 2 pianos; Piano Concerto for piano and orchestra; 3 Piano Concertinos; 8 character sketches for 4-handed piano; Variations on De Vier Weverkens for flute, hobo and piano. *Recordings:* The Seasons, Tchaikovsky, 1953; Berceuse Antique (own composition). *Honours:* Dannenberg Order, Denmark; Order Ridder Oranje Nassau, Netherlands. *Memberships:* Genootschap Nederlandse Componisten and Donernus. *Hobbies:* Travelling; Walking; Cycling; Cooking; Reading; Architecture. *Address:* De Rÿp flat 217, Bloemendaalseweg 136, 2061 SE Bloemendaal, Netherlands.

OSTEN Sigune von, b. 8 Mar 1950, Dresden, Germany. Singer (Soprano). *Education:* Studied in Hamburg and Karlsruhe and with Elisabeth Grümmer and Eugen Rabine. *Debut:* Sang John Cage's Aria at Hanover 1973. *Career:* Noted interpreter of 20th century repertoire at the Dresden and Salzburg Festivals, the Bonn and Vienna Festivals, at Venice, Berlin, Donaueschingen, Madrid, Strasbourg, Peterburg, Moscow and Tokyo; Concert tours, radioi and television recordings of Europe, the USA, Japan and South America and opera engagements at Stuttgart, Wiesbaden, Paris, Venice and Lisbon; Repertoire includes Berg's Marie and Lulu and the Woman in Schoenberg's Erwartung; Schostakowitsch, Lady Macbeth; Sang Fusako in Henze's Des verratene Mees Wiesbaden, 1991 and the Mother in the German premiere of Turnage's Greek, Wuppertal 1992; Worked with composers such as Halffter, Penderecki, Denisov, Messiaen Cage and Scelsi, Nono. *Recordings:* Penderecki Luke Passion; Messiaen, Harawi; Noche pasiva by Halffter and Dittrich's Engführung; Songs by Ives, Satie, Cage. *Address:* c/o Hessisches Staatstheater, Postfach 3247, 8200 Wiesbaden, Germany.

OSTENDORF John, b. 1 Nov 1945, New York, USA. Singer (Bass- baritone). *Education:* Studied at Oberlin College and with Margaret Harshaw. *Debut:* Chautauqua Opera 1969, as the Commendatore in Don Giovanni. *Career:* Appearances at San Francisco, Houston, Baltimore, Toronto and Philadelphia; Amsterdam 1979 in the premiere of Winter Cruise by Henkeman; Repertoire includes Don Alfonso, Basilio, Escamillo, Ramphis in Aida and Handel's Julius Caesar; Many concert performances, notably in the Baroque repertoire. *Recordings:* Bach's St John Passion and Handel's Sirce, Imeneo, Joshua and Acis and Galatea. *Address:* c/o San Francisco Opera, War Memorial Opera House, San Francisco, CA 94102, USA.

OSTHOFF Wolfgang, b. 17 Mar 1927, Halle Saale, Germany. Musicologist. m. Renate Göetz, 3 sons. *Education:* Frankfurt Conservatory with Kurt Hessenburg and others; Universities of Frankfurt and Heidelberg with H. Osthoff, T. Georgiades and others. *Career:* Assistant Lecturer, Munich University, 1957-68; Professor, Wurzburg University, 1968-. *Publications:* Das dramatische Spätwerk Claudio Monteverdis 1960; Beethoven Klavier Konzert c-moll 1965; Theatergesang und darstellende Musik in der Italienischen Renaissance, 2 volumes 1969; Heinrich Schütz 1974; Stefan George and 'les deux Musiques', 1989; Briefwechsel Hans Pfitzner-Gerhard Frommel, 1990. *Contributions to:* Musicology journals. *Memberships:* International Musicology Society and others. *Address:* Institute für Musikwissenschaft, University of Würzburg, Residenzplatz 2, D-97070 Würzburg, Germany.

ÖSTMAN Arnold, b. 24 Dec 1939, Malmo, Sweden. Conductor; Musical Director. *Education:* Studied art history at Lund University, history of music at the Paris and Stockholm Universities. *Career:* Taught at State Academy for Music and Drama in Stockholm; appointed artistic director of the Vadstena Academy, Stockholm, 1969, and researched and conducted operas by Provenzale, Stradella, Leo, Abbatini, Monteverdi, Cimarosa and Purcell; in 1979 appointed musical director of the Court Theatre at Drottningholm in Sweden; productions there on period instruments include Mozart's Don Giovanni, Così fan Tutte, Nozze di Figaro and Die Zauberflöte, La Clemenza di Tito, Idomeneo, Entfuhrung aus dem Serail, La Finta Giardiniera, Krauss's Proserpin, Cimarosa's Il Matrimonio Segreto and Gluck's Iphigénie en Aulide; conducted Mozart's oratorio La Betulia Liberata at La Fenice, Venice, 1982; series of Purcell's The Fairy Queen throughout Italy; Il Matrimonio Segreto at Cologne Opera, at Washington Opera and at Sadler's Wells Theatre, London, 1983, gaining Society of West End Theatres Award; Covent Garden debut 1984, Don Giovanni; Il Barbiere di Siviglia for Kent Opera, 1985; Rossini's Tancredi in a new production at the 1986 Wexford Festival, also heard in London that year; performances of Don Giovanni and Idomeneo with the Drottningholm ensemble at the 1987 Brighton Festival; Le Siège de Corinth/Rossini, Paris Opera, 1985; Semiramide/Rossini, Opéra de Nice, 1987 and Théatre du Capitole Toulouse, 1989; The Creation/Haydn, Residentie Orkest, The Hague, 1989; Armida/Haydn, Dutch Radio, Concertgebouw Amsterdam, 1989; Faust/ Gounod, Norrlands Operan Umeå, 1989; Conducted Mozart's Lucio Silla at the Vienna Staatsoper, 1990; Concerts from 1990 with the Netherlands Radio Chamber Orchestra, Stuttgart Philharmonic, Cologne Orchestra of WDR and Dusseldorf Symphony; Season 1992 with Rossini's La Donna del Lago at the Concertgebouw and Orfeo ed Euridice at Drottningholm; *Recordings:* Audio recordings of Così fan Tutte, Le Nozze di Figaro, Don Giovanni and Zauberflöte for Decca Records/Florilegium Label and video recordings of Mozart's operas, based on performances at Drottningholm. *Honours:* Received the Edison Prize in Holland, and the Cecilia Prize of the Belgian critics for his recording of Le Nozze di Figaro (recorded at Drottningholm for Decca). *Address:* c/o Haydn Rawstron Ltd, PO Box 654, London SE26 4DZ, England.

OSVALD Miloslav, b. 12 Oct 1946, Prague, Czech Republic. *Education:* Conservatoire Prague, Graduation 1966; Academy of Fine Arts, Faculty of Music, Diploma 1985. *Debut:* Trio for flute, violin and violoncello, Pilsen 1974. *Career:* Violinist in various symphony orchestras, Karlovy Vary, Pilsen, 1968-85; Editor of music publishing company Panton in Prague, 1986-90. *Compositions:* Radio recordings: Sonata for viola and piano, 1983; Concerto grosso for orchestra, 1985; Sonata for viola and piano, 1986. *Recording:* String quartet No. 1, 1976. *Memberships:* Association of Music Artists and Scientists; Society of Composers, Prague. *Hobbies:* Jogging; Tourism. *Address:* U Uranie 12-1362, 170 00 Prague 7, Czech Republic.

OTAKA Tadaaki, b. 8 Nov 1947, Kamakura, Japan. Orchestra Conductor m. Yukiko Otaka, 23 Nov 1978. *Education:* Toho-Gakuen School of Music, Japan; Hochschule für Musik, Vienna, Austria. *Career:* Music Faculty, Toho-Gakuen School of Music, 1970-; Principal Conductor, Tokyo Philharmonic Orchestra, 1974-; Principal Conductor, Sapporo Symphony Orchestra, 1981; Principal Conductor of the BBC Welsh Symphony Orchestra: Promenade Concerts London 1991, with Tchaikovsky's Violin Concerto, excerpts from Romeo and Juliet, Tippett's Piano Concerto and Ein Heldenleben. *Address:* c/o BBC Welsh Symphony Orchestra, Broadcasting House, Llandaff, Cardiff CF5 2YQ, Wales.

OTT Karin, b. 13 Dec 1945, Wädenswil, Zurich, Switzerland. Singer (Soprano). *Education:* Studied in Zurich and Germany. *Career:* Sang first with the opera house of Biel-Solothurn; Appeared in Mussorgsky's Sorochintsy Fair at Brunswick 1970; Zurich 1970, as Tove in Schoenberg's Gurrelieder; Paris Opéra as the Queen of Night in Die Zauberflöte; Salzburg Festival

1979-81; Venice 1981, in the premiere of Sinopoli's Lou Salomé; Engagements at Stuttgart, Berlin, Zurich, Amsterdam amd Vienna. *Recordings include:* Die Zauberflöte, conducted by Karajan (Deutsche Grammophon). *Address:* c/o Opernhaus Zurich, Falkenstrasse 1, CH-8008 Zurich, Switzerland.

OTTENTHAL Gertrud, b. 1957, Bad Oldesloe, Schleswig-Holstein, Germany. Singer. *Education:* Studied in Lubeck. *Career:* Sang at Wiesbaden Opera 1980, Hamburg 1981-82; Engagements at Vienna Volksoper 1982, Salzburg Festival 1984, Vienna Festival 1986-88; Sang Mozart's Countess at Klagenfurt 1984, Komische Oper Berlin 1986, returned to Berlin 1990 as Mimi; Further appearances at Theater am Gartnerplatz Munich, Barcelona and the Schwetzingen Festival; Other roles include Agathe, Fiordiligi, Sandrina in La Finta Giardiniera, Rosalinde, Antonio and Arianna in Giustino by Handel; Concert repertoire includes works by Bach, Handel, Mozart, Bruckner and Schubert. *Recordings:* Werther, Der Rosenkavalier and Der Wildschütz; Mrs Ma in Der Kreiderkreis by Zemlinsky; Donna Elvira in Don Giovanni, conducted by Neeme Järvi. *Address:* c/o Komische Oper Berlin, Behrenstrasse 55-57, 1086 Berlin, Germany.

OTTER Anne Sofie von, b. 9 May 1955, Stockholm, Sweden. Singer (mezzo-soprano). *Education:* Stockholm Royal Conservatory; and Guildhall School of Music and Drama, London; vocal studies since 1981 with Vera Rozsa. *Career:* Basle Opera from 1982 as Hansel, Alcina in Haydn's Orlando Paladino, Mozart's Sextus and Cherubino (Le Nozze di Figaro) and Gluck's Orpheus; Aix-en-Provence Festival (La Finta Giardinioera-Don Ramiro) 1984; in 1985 sang Mozart's Dorabella (Così fan tutte) in Geneva and Cherubino at Covent Garden; US debut 1985, with the Chicago Symphony; Bach's B Minor Mass in Philadelphia; Cherubino at the Metropolitan Opera; Guest appearances in Milan, Berlin, Munich, Stockholm, Geneva and Lyon; La Scala Milan 1987; Season 1992 as Romeo in I Capuleti e i Montecchi at Covent Garden, Ramiro in La Finta Giardiniera at Salzburg; Conductors include John Eliot Gardiner, Solti, C Davis, Giulini, Levine, Sinopoli and Muti. *Recordings:* Così fan tutte; Orfeo ed Euridice, Idomeneo and La Clemenza di Tito conducted by Gardiner, Olga in Eugene Onegin and Cherubino in Figaro under Levine; Les Contes d'Hoffmann and Hansel and Gretel with Tate, Der Rosenkavalier under Haitink; Mozart and Verdi Requiem (Gardiner) and C minor Mass (Marriner), Bach Matthew Passion and Christmas Oratorio (Gardiner) and B minor Mass (Solti) Messiah and Dido and Aeneas (Pinnock); Brahms Alto Rhapsody (Levine) Messiah and Elijah (Marriner); Songs by Grieg, Mahler, Brahms (DGG), Sibelius (BIS) and Stenhammar; Handel's Jephtha, Gluck's Le Cinesi, Schubert's Rosamunde and A Berg Songs with Abbado. *Address:* IMG Artists, 3 Burlington Lane, Chiswick, London W4 2TH, England.

OTTO Lisa, b. 14 Nov 1919, Dresden, Germany. Singer (Soprano). m. Albert Blind. *Education:* Dresden Musikhochschukle, with Susanne Steinmetz-Pree. *Debut:* Beuthen 1941, as Sophie in Der Rosenkavalier. *Career:* Sang in Beuthen 1941-44; Nuremburg 1945-46; Dresden 1946-51; Städtische (later Deutsche) Oper Berlin from 1951: took part in the 1965 premiere of Henze's Der junge Lord; Salzburg 1953-57, as Blondchen and Despina; Glyndebourne 1956, as Blondchen in Die Entführung; Guest appearances in Vienna, Milan, and Paris; Other roles include Mozart's Papagena and Susanna, Beethoven's Marzelline, and Ighino in Palestrina; Many engagements as concert singer. *Recordings:* St John Passion by Bach (HMV); Der junge Lord (Deutsche Grammophon); Die Zauberflöte; Cosi fan Tutte.

OUNDJIAN Peter, b. 21 Dec 1955, Toronto, Ontario, Canada. Violinist. Studied at the Juilliard School with Ivan Galamian and Dorothy DeLay. *Career:* Leader of the Tokyo Quartet from 1981; Regular concerts in the USA and abroad; First cycle of the complete quartets of Beethoven at the Yale at Norfolk Chamber Music Festival, 1986; Repeated cycles at the 92nd Street Y (New York), Ravinia and Israel Festivals and Yale and Prinecton Universities; Season 1990-91 at Alice Tully Hall and the Metropolitan Museum of Art, New York, Boston, Washington DC, Los Angeles, Cleveland, Detroit, Chicago, Miami, Seattle, San Francisco, Toronto; Tour of South America, two tours of Europe including Paris, Amsterdam, Bonn, Milan, Munich, Dublin, London, Berlin; Quartet-in-residence at Yale University, University of Cincinnati College-Conservatory of Music. *Recordings:* Schubert's major Quartets; Mozart Flute Quartets with James Galway and Clarinet Quintet with Richard Stolzman; Quartets by Bartók, Brahms, Debussy, Haydn, Mozart and Ravel; Beethoven Middle Period Quartets (RCA). *Honours:* Grand Prix du Disque du Montreux; Best Chamber Music Recording of the Year from Stereo Review and the Gramophone; Four Grammy nominations. *Address:* Intermusica Artists' Management, 16 Duncan Terrace, London N1 8BZ, England.

OUSSET Cécile, b. 23 Jan 1936, Tarbes, France. Concert Pianist. *Career:* Studied Paris Conservatoire with Marcel Ciampi; Graduated 1950 with First Prize in piano; British debut at Edinburgh Festival 1980; Many appearances with leading orchestras in Britain and abroad; French debut with the Orchestre de Paris, followed by appearances with all major French orchestras; First recital at the Théâtre des Champs-Elysées in season 1987-88; US debut with the Los Angeles Philharmonic Orchestra, 1984: later engagements with the Minnesota and Boston Symphony Orchestras; Debut tour of Japan 1984; Repertoire includes Brahms, Beethoven, Rachmaninov and French music; Played Debussy's Preludes on BBC TV 1988. *Recordings:* Brahms 2nd Concerto, with the Leipzig Gewandhaus Orchestra; Concertos by Rachmaninov, Liszt, Saint-Saëns, Grieg, Ravel and Mendelssohn; Recitals of Chopin, Liszt and Debussy (EMI). *Honours include:* Prizewinner at Van Cliburn, Queen Elisabeth of Belgium, Busoni and Marguerite Long-Jacques Thibaud Competitions; Grand Prix du Disque for Brahms Concerto recording. *Address:* c/o Intermusica Artists' Management, 2-3 Golden Sqaure, London W1 3AD, England.

OVCHINIKOV Vladimir, b. 1960, Belebey, USSR. Concert Pianist. *Education:* Studied in Moscow with Anna Artobolevskaya and Alexey Nazedkin. *Career:* International engagements from 1980, including Aldeburgh, Cheltenham, Edinburgh, Lichfield and Schleswig Holstein Festivals; Recitals in London (debut at the Barbican Hall, 1987), Chicago, Toronto, Munich and Rotterdam; Season 1989- includes tour of Japan and London concerto debut with the Philharmonia Orchestra at the Festival hall; Glyndebourne recital for the Brighton Festival; Western debut in Trio with Alexander Vinnitsky and Alexander Rudin at the Wigmore Hall, May 1989. *Recordings include:* Trios by Rachmaninov and Shostakovich; Tchaikovsky's 1st Piano Concerto, with the London Philharmonic conducted by Yuri Simonov (Collins Classics). *Honours:* Runner up (to Ivo Pogorelich) Montreal Competition 1980; Joint Silver Medal (with Peter Donohoe) Tchaikovsky Competition Moscow 1982; Winner, Leeds International Piano Competition 1987. *Address:* Artist Management International, 12/13 Richmond Buildings, Dean Street, London, W1V 5AF, England.

OVENS Raymond, b. 14 Oct 1932, Bristol, England. Violinist. m. Sheila Margharet Vaughan Williams, 1 son, 1 daughter. *Education:* Royal Academy of Music; ARAM. *Debut:* Wigmore Hall, London, 1950. *Career:* Leader, London Symphony Orchestra 1951; Principal 2nd Violin, Royal Philharmonic Orchestra, 1956: Assistant leader 1972; Leader until 1980, BBC Scottish Symphony Orchestra; Leader, Philharmonia Orchestra 1980-85, orchestra of the English National Opera from 1985; Has played concertos with the BBC Scottish Symphony, the Vancouver Symphony and the Philharmonia Orchestra; Concerts and Recitals for BBC; Leader, Lyra String Quartet; Leader, Ceol Rosh Chamber Group. *Honours:* FRAM. *Hobbies:* Painting; Golf.

OWEN Barbara, b. 25 Jan 1933, Utica, NY, USA. Organist and Musicologist. *Education:* Mus.B., Westminster Choir College 1955; Mus.M., Boston University 1962; Additional study at North German Organ Academy and Academy of Italian Organ Music. *Career:* Music Director of First Religious Society, Newburyport, MA 1963-; Freelance Researcher, Lecturer, Recitalist, Teacher and Organ Consultant. *Publications:* Editions of Music published: A Century of American Organ Music, 4 Volumes, 1975, 1976, 1983, 1991; A Century of English Organ Music 1979; English Romantic Classics 1984; Carol Preludes, 2 Volumes, 1983 and 1984; A Handel Album 1981; The Candlelight Carol Book 1982 and several other editions of organ and choral music by various composers. Books written: The Organs and Music of King's Chapel 1965; The Organ in New England 1979; E. Power Biggs, Concert Organist 1987; Co-editor: Charles Brenton Fisk, Organ Builder 1986; The Mormon Tabernacle Organ, 1990. *Contributions to:* Articles for Grove's Dictionary, 6th Edition, Grove's Dictionary of Musical Instruments; New Grove Dictionary of American Music; Harvard Dictionary of Music; The Diapason; The American Organist; Journal of Church Music (Contributing Editor), The Tracker, etc.; Written jacket notes for 6 recordings. *Hobbies:* Gardening; Cats. *Address:* 28 Jefferson Street, Newburyport, MA 01950, USA.

OWEN Blythe, b. 26 Dec 1898, Bruce, Minnesota, USA. Professor of Music; Composer. m. 29 Aug 1921, divorced 1954. *Education:* B.Mus., Chicago Musical School, 1941; MMus., Northwestern University, 1942; PhD, Eastman School of Music, 1953; Ecole des Americaines, Fontainebleau, France, 1949. *Debut:* Young American Artists, Chicago, 1927. *Career:* Appearances, Western Artists Series, Portland, Oregon, Kimball Hall, Chicago, Illinois, Chamber Music Series, Andrews University, WNYC, New York; Professor of Music, Emeritus. *Compositions:* Serially Serious; Go Lovely Rose; Easter SATB; Trio for Oboe, Clarinet, Bassoon; Inventions for WW; Fanfare and Processional, organ & brass; Choral Prelude on Rothwell; 5 Youthful pieces for piano. *Recordings:* Festival Te Deum; Festal Prelude for organ dedication; How Lovely are Thy Dwellings; Programme of American Composers for Piano. *Publications include:* A Sunny Day; A Little Ballard, 1984; Sonatinetta Op 66 1986; Nativity Suite, piano, 1987; Fairest Lord Jesus, SAB, 1984; The Trinity SATB. *Hobbies:* Gardening. *Address:* 9138 Kephart Lane, Berrien Springs, MI 49103, USA.

OWEN (Rasmussen), Lynn, b. 1936, Kenosha, Wisconsin, USA. Concert and Opera Singer; Voice Teacher, Barnard College and privately. m. Richard Owen, 4 June 1960, 3 sons. *Education:* Northwestern University; BS, MS with honours 1958, Juilliard School of Music; Diplomas in Voice and Opera (highest honours), Vienna Academy of Music, Austria, 1960. *Debut:* Constanza in Abduction from the Seraglio, New Orleans Opera, USA. *Career:* La Fanciulla del West (Minnie), Fliegende Holländer (Senta), Metropolitan Opera, New York; Don Carlos (Elisabetta), Forza del Destino (Leonora), Il Trovatore (Leonore), Prince Igor (Jaroslavna), Zurich, Switzerland; Il Trovatore, Turandot, Fidelio (Leonora), Krefeld Opera, Hamburg, and Frankfurt, Germany; Fanciulla del West, Central City, Fliegende Holländer, Aspen, USA; Ballo in Maschera, Othello, Calgary, Canada; Il Trovatore, Caracas, Venezuela; Siegfried (Brünnhilde), Art Park, New York; Isolde, Mexico City Opera; Concerts and recitals throughout USA and Europe. *Recordings:* Serenus Records; Vanguard Records. *Contributions to:* Music Journal. *Hobbies:* Tennis; Skiing; Sailing. *Address:* 21 Claremont Avenue, New York, NY 10027, USA.

OWENS Anne-Marie, b. 1955, Tyne and Wear, England. Singer (Mezzo-soprano). *Education:* Studied at the Newcastle School of Music, the Guildhall School and the National Opera Studio. *Career:* Sang Gluck's Orpheus, Dido, Dalila and Angelina (La Cenerentola) while a student; Professional debut as Mistress Quickly on the Glyndebourne Tour; For English National Opera has sung Charlotte, Rosina, Maddalena, Suzuki (Madame Butterfly), Bianca (The Rape of Lucretia), Solokha in the British premiere of Rimsky-Korsakov's Christmas Eve, 1989, and Magdalene; Covent Garden 1989, as Third Lady in Die Zauberflöte and Rossweise in a new production of Die Walküre; Visit to the Vienna Staatsoper with the company of the Royal Opera, 1992; Sang Jocasta in Oedipus Rex for Opera North, followed by the title role in Ariane and Bluebeard by Dukas, 1990; Season 1992 in Les Contes d'Hoffmann at Covent Garden, as Baba the Turk in The Rake's Progress at Brussels and Preziosilla in The Force of Destiny for ENO; Other roles include Arnalta in Monteverdi's Poppea (Glyndebourne Festival); Clotilde in Norma and the Hostess in Boris Godunov (Royal Opera); Baba the Turk (Brussels); Fidalma in Il Matrimonio Segreto (Lausanne); Concert appearances with the City of Birmingham Symphony, BBC Symphony, London Mozart Players, Royal Liverpool Philharmonic; Has sung at the London Proms, Aix-en- Provence, San Sebastien, Rouen and Detroit (US debut, with Messiah). *Address:* Athole Still Man Ltd, Greystoke House, 80/86 Weston Street, London SE19 3AF, England.

OWENS David Bruce, b. 16 Oct 1950, USA. Composer. m. 23 June 1974, 1 son, 2 daughters. *Education:* Eastman School, Rochester, New York; Manhattan School, New York City. *Compositions:* Sonatina for Percussion Solo, 1969; Quartet for Strings, 1969; Encounter, for orchestra, 1970; Gentle Horizon, chamber ensemble, 1972; Ricercar for Band, 1978; Concerto for Viola and Orchestra, 1982; The Shores of Peace, for chorus and chamber orchestra, 1984; Fantasy on a Celtic Carol, for viola and piano, 1985; Jonah, opera in 3 acts, 1986-89; Choral, piano, organ pieces, songs. *Contributions to:* Columns and articles on 20th century music, also reviews of many books in music, The Christian Science Monitor, Ovation, Musical America. *Honour:* ASCAP/Deems Taylor Award for Distinguished Criticism (for Christian Science Monitor column Inside 20th-century music) 1983. *Membership:* American Society of Composers, Authors and Publishers. *Address:* 75 Travis Road, Holliston, MA 01746, USA.

OXENBOULD Moffatt, b. 18 Nov 1943, Sydney, New South Wales, Australia. Administrator; Stage Director. *Education:* Studied at the National Institute for Dramatic Art. *Career:* Stage Manager with Elizabethan Trust Opera 1963-65 and at Sadler's Wells, London, 1966-67; Planning Coordinator with Elizabethan Trust Opera-Australian Opera, 1967-73; Artistic Administrator, Australian Opera, 1974-84, Artistic Director from 1984; Productions include The Rape of Lucretia 1971, Il Trittico 1978, La Clemenza di Tito, 1991; Idomeneo, 1994. *Address:* Australian Opera, PO Box 291, Strawberry Hills, New South Wales, 2012, Australia.

OZAWA Seiji, b. 1 Sept 1935, Shenyang, China. Conductor, Music Director, Boston Symphony Orchestra. m. Vera Motoki-Ilyin, 1 son, 1 daughter. *Education:* Student, Toho School of Music, Tokyo, Japan, 1953-59; Studied with Hideo Saito, Eugene Bigot, Herbert von Karajan, Leonard Bernstein, at the invitation of Charles Munch studied at Tanglewood, 1960. *Career:* One of three assistant conductors, NY Philharmonic, 1961-62 season; Music Director, Ravinia Festival, 1964-68; Music Director, Toronto Symphony Orchestra, 1965-69; Music Director, San Francisco Symphony Orchestra, 1970-76; Artistic Advisor, Tanglewood Festival, Tanglewood, 1970-73; Music Director, Boston Symphony Orchestra, 1973-; Guest Conductor, major orchestras throughout the world including Philadelphia, Chicago Symphony Orchestras, NY Philharmonic, Berlin Philharmonic, Orchestre de Paris, New Philharmonia, Paris Opéra, Orchestre National de France, La Scala, New Japan Philharmonic, Central Peking Philharmonic, Vienna Philharmonic; Led Boston Symphony Orchestra Cultural Exchange in Peking and Shanghai, China, 1979; Conducted the world premiere of Olivier Messiaen's St Francis of Assisi, Nov. 1983, at Paris Opéra, which was subsequently awarded the Grand Prix de la Critique, 1984, in the category of French world premieres; Conducted the Boston Symphony in Beethoven's 8th and the Symphonie Fantastique at the 1991 Promenade Concerts, London. *Recordings:* Philips, Telarc, CBS, Deutsche Grammophon, Angel/EMI, New World, Hyperion, Erato and RCA Records, including the Berg and Stravinsky Violin Concertos (Perlman); Saint François d'Assise; Schoenberg's Gurrelieder; Messiaen Turangalilâ Symphony; Stravinsky Firebird, Rite of Spring and Petrushka; Ives 4th Symphony; Orff Carmina Burana; Mahler 8th Symphony; The Queen of Spades (RCA). *Honours:* Recipient Emmy Award for Outstanding Achievement in Music Direction for Boston Symphony's Evening at Symphony PBS TV Series; Grand Prix du Disque for recording of Berlioz Romeo et Juliette; 1st Prize, International Competition of Orchestra Conductors, France, 1959. *Current Management:* Columbia Arts Management Inc., 165 W. 57th Street, New York, NY 10019, USA. *Address:* Music Director, Boston Symphony Orchestra, Symphony Hall, 301 Massachusetts Avenue, Boston, MA 02115, USA.

OZIM Igor, b. 9 May 1931, Ljubljana, Yugoslavia, Violinist; Professor of Violin. m. Breda Volovsel, 1963, 1 son, 1 daughter. *Education:* State Academy of Music, Ljubljana, Yugoslavia; Diploma RCM, London; Private study with Max Rostal, London. *Debut:* Ljubljana, 1947. *Career:* Tours of Europe, USA, South America, Australia, New Zealand and Japan; Broadcasts in all European countries; Numerous recordings. *Publications:* Editor, numerous contemporary violin works; Editor, Pro Musica Nova, 1974. Editor Complete Violin Concertos by Mozart, for Neue Mozart Ausgabe, Bärenreiter Edition. *Honours:* Carl Flesch Medal, International Competition, London, 1951; 1st Prize, German Broadcasting Stations International Competition, Munich, 1953. *Hobbies:* Photography; Table Tennis. *Current Management:* Konzertdirektion Hörtnagel, Munich. *Address:* Breibergstr 6, D-50939 Köln 41, Germany.

OZOLINS Arthur Marcelo, b. 7 Feb 1946, Lübeck, Germany. Concert Pianist. *Education:* Faculty of Music, University of Toronto, Canada, 1962-63; BSc., Music, Mannes College of Music, New York, USA, 1964-67; Studies with: Pablo Casals, Jacques Abram, Nadia Boulanger, Nadia Reisenberg, Vlado Perlemuter. *Debut:* Toronto Symphony Orchestra, Toronto, 1961. *Career:* Soloist with Royal Philharmonic, Hallé Orchestra, Stockholm and Oslo Philharmonic, Leningrad Philharmonic, Montreal Symphony, Toronto Symphony; Recitals, New York, London, Paris, Moscow, Leningrad, Buenos Aires, Sydney, San Paulo; 7 Tours, USSR; TV and Radio Performances, CBC, BBC, Swedish Radio; Concerto repertoire included works by Bach, Brahms, Beethoven, Mozart (K414, K466 and K503), Rachmaninov, Prokofiev, Tchaikovsky and Tippett (Handel Fantasy). *Recordings:* The complete Piano Concerti and Paganini Rhapsody of Rachmaninov with Mario Bernardi and the Toronto Symphony plus Dohnányi's Variations on a Nursery Song, Healey Willan's Piano Concerto and Strauss Burleske: all on CBC Records. Numerous solo recordings with CBC, Kaibala & Aquitane. *Honours:* Juno Award, Best Classical Record, 1981; 7 Canada Council Awards; 1st Prizes, Edmonton Competition, 1968, CBC Talent Festival, 1968. *Memberships:* AFM; English Speaking Union. *Hobbies:* Swimming; Study of Philosophy & Psychology. *Current Management:* Richard von Handschuh, Toronto; Robert Gilder & Co. London. *Address:* 159 Colin Avenue, Toronto, Canada M5P 2C5.

OZOLINS Janis Alfreds, b. 29 Sept 1919, Riga, Latvia. Violoncellist; Concert Singer; Orchestral Conductor. m. Adine Uggla, 15 May 1951, 2 sons, 1 daughter. *Education:* Dip Solo Violoncello, Conservatory of Latvia, 1944; Studied with Professor E. Mainardi, Rome, Italy, 1947-48; Studied Composition, Riga and Royal Academy of Music, Stockholm, Sweden; Singing Teachers Examination, Stockholm, 1958; Examinations in Musicology, University of Uppsala, 1962. *Debut:* (Violoncello) Riga, 1933. *Career:* Concert Radio Recitals, Solo Performances with orchestra, Latvia, Sweden, Denmark, UK, Italy, Switzerland; Music Master, 1956-; Conductor, Landskrona Symphony Orchestra, 1957;

Bass Soloist, Beethoven's 9th Symphony with H. Blomstedt, Norrkoping, 1961; Director, Vaxjo Municipal School of Music and Municipal Music Dor, Vaxjo, 1964-84; Conductor, Operas and Ballets, Vaxjo. *Contributions to:* Sohlmans Musiklexikon, Sweden. *Honours:* National Prize of Latvia, 1944; Culture Prize, Vaxjo Lions Club, 1976; Royal Gold Medal, Swedish Orchestra National Federation, 1977, 1984. *Hobbies:* Languages; Globetrotting; Gastronomy. *Address:* Via Sicilia 1, I-63039 Italia, San Benedetto Del Tronto, (AP).

P

PABST Michael, b. 1955, Graz, Austria. Singer (Tenor). *Education:* Studied in Graz and Vienna. *Career:* Principal Tenor at Vienna Volksoper 1978-84, singing operetta and lyric opera roles; Dramatic repertoire from 1985, including Max in Der Freischütz ty Munich, Bacchus in Philadelphia, Stuttgart, Frankfurt and Houston, Lohengrin at Hamburg and Zurich, Walther at Cape Town and Trieste, Erik at La Scala and Buenos Aires, Huon, Oberon at La Scala, Florestan at the Savonlinna Festival and Siegmund in Liège; Guest appearances at Vienna Staatsoper from 1991, with Florestan, the Drum Major in Wozzeck, Max, Jenik, The Bartered Bride and Erik; Other roles include Hoffmann, Pedro, Tiefland, Luigi, Il Tabarro, Schubert's Fierabras, Sergei in Lady Macbeth; Strauss's Matteo, Aegisthus, Burgermeister in Friedenstag and Apollo. *Address:* c/o Atholl Still Ltd, Greystoke House, 80-86 Westrow Street, London SE19 3AF, England.

PACCAGNINI Angelo, b. 17 Oct 1930, Castano Primo, Milan, Italy. Composer. *Education:* Studied at Milan Conservatory 1949-53 and with Berio and Maderna. *Career:* Teacher of electronic music at the Milan Conservatory 1969-80; Former Director of the Mantua and Verona Conservatories. *Compositions:* Le Sue Ragioni, opera in 1 act, Bergamo, 1959; Mose, radio opera, 1963; Il Dio, radio opera, 1964; Tutta la Vogliono, Tutti la Spogliano, opera in 3 acts, Venice; Un Uomo da Salvare, Milan 1969; Partner, electronic scena, Turin, 1969; E L'Ora, radio opera, 1970; La Misura, il Mistero, Milan, 1970 ; C'Era una Volta un re, television opera, 1974; Olivo Verdevivo, television opera, 1977. *Honour:* Prix Italia 1964 for Il Dio di oro. *Address:* SIAE (Italy), c/o PRS Ltd Member Registration, 29-33 Berners Street, London S1P 4AA, England.

PACE Carmelo, b. 17 Aug 1906, Valletta, Malta. Music Teacher; Composer. *Education:* Fellow, London College of Music, England; Licentiate, Royal Schools of Music. *Career:* Founder and Conductor, Malta Cultural Institute Concerts, 1948-; Lecturer of history and theory of music. *Compositions include:* Works for pianoforte, solo and various other instruments; Orchestral, choral and vocal solos and chamber music; Operas including Caterina Desguanez, 1965, I Martiri, 1967, Angelica, 1973 and Ipogeana, 1976; Incidental music for stage works includes: La Predestinata, 1954; Il Natale di Cristo, 1955; San Paolo, 1960; Space Adventure, 1962; Il-Kappella tal-Paci, 1973; Il-Francizi f'Malta, 1978; Oratorios and Cantatas include: Alba Dorata (opera oratorio in 3 parts), 1964; Eternal Triumph, 1966; The Seven Last Words, 1978; Cantico di Salomone, 1982; Cantate Domino, 1982; Stabat Mater, 1982; Te Deum, 1983; Sultana tal-Vittorji, 1985; Sejha, 1986; Alter Christus - San Frangisk, 1986; Gloria, 1989; Ballet: Ballet Hongrois, 1940; Ruth, 1979. *Publications:* Carmelo Pace - A Maltese Composer who collected some Maltese Folk Music. His Fantasia Maltesina was premiered in 1931. *Membership:* Performing Right Society, London. *Hobbies include:* Reading. *Address:* 14 St Dominic Street, Sliema, SLM 06, Malta.

PACE Patrizia, b. 1963, Turin, Italy, Singer (Soprano). *Education:* Studied at Turin Conservatory. *Debut:* La Scala 1984 as Celia in Mozart's Lucio Silla. *Career:* Has appeared in Milan as Micaela, Mozart's Despina, Susanna and Zerlina, Oscar, Lisa in La Sonnambula and in premiere Il Principe Felice by Mannino, 1987; Guest appearances at Deutsche Oper Berlin, Spoleto Festival and the Vienna Staatsoper as Oscar and Rossini's Elvira, 1986 and 1988 Gilda, Nannetta in Falstaff and Yniold; Further engagements at Hamburg Staatsoper as Liu, Florence, Genoa, Palermo and Covent Garden 1991 and 1993 as Gilda and Yniold in Pelléas et Mélisande; Other roles include Rosina and Sofia in Il Signor Bruschino. *Recordings:* Barbarina in Le Nozze di Figaro and Mozart's Requiem; Mozart's C minor Mass. *Address:* c/o Teatro alla Scala, Via Filodrammatici 2, Milan, Italy.

PACIOREK Grazyna, b. 11 Dec 1967, Zyrardow,

Poland. Composer. *Education:* Degree in Violin, State School of Music, Warsaw, 1987; Currently studying Composition under Professor M Borkowski, Academy of Music, Warsaw; International courses for young composers, Polish Section, ISCM, Kazimierz Dolny, Poland, 1989, 1990, 1991. Computer course and workshops, Studio of Electroacoustic Music, Academy of Music, Cracow, 1991. *Career:* Many performances at the composers concerts in Warsaw (Academy of Music, Royal Castle) and in Cracow, 1987-91; Composed music for film aired on Polish TV 1991; Works presented in radio programme, at Gdańsk Meeting of Young Composers, Oct 1991 and 5th Laboratory of Contemporary Chamber Music, 1991. *Compositions include:* Monologue for Oboe Solo; Te-qui-la for 6 percussion group; Toccata for violin, cello and piano; string quartet; muzyka mapothana for oboe and accordiov; Concert for viola and orchestra; electronic music, film music. *Honours:* June 1991 Academy of Music in Warsaw applied to Minister of Culture and Fine Arts for her artistic scholarship in 1991. *Memberships:* Polish Society for Contemporary Music; Polish Composers' Union, Youth Circle. *Hobbies:* Sailing; Dancing. *Address:* ul Sienkiewicza 28/4, 05-825 Grodzisk Maz., Poland.

PACKFORD Vincent Hubert, b. 26 Sept 1922, Oxford, England. Pianist; Teacher; Organist; Choral Director. m. Diana Grace Knott, 19 Sept 1946, 1 daughter. *Education:* City of Oxford School, 1929-39; BA 1944, MA 1947, Oxford University; Studied with Victor Booth and Harold Craxton, Royal Academy of Music; Associate, Royal College of Music; Fellow, Royal College of Organists. *Career:* Director of Music,. Christ Church, Cathedral School, Oxford, 1955-72; Director of Music, Chiltern Edge School, 1972-79; Organist and Choir Director, St Mary Magdalen, Oxford; Teacher and Adjudicator, 1979-. *Compositions:* Various choral works, motets and carols. *Membership:* Honorary Local Secretary, Incorporated Society of Musicians 1957-67. *Address:* 7 Burlington Crescent, Headington, Oxford OX3 8DY, England.

PACLT Jaromir, b. 24 Feb 1927, Hradec Kralove, Bohemia. Musicologist; Violinist. *Education:* Ph, Dr, University of Prague, 1953, CSc, University of Prague, 1966; DrSc, Doctor of Science, 1993. *Career:* Editor, Kniznice Hudebnich rozhledu, 1955-60; Director, Exposition Hall, Theatre of Music, Prague, 1961-63; Czechoslovakian Academy of Sciences, 1963-. *Publications:* Editor, Tri Kapitoly o Z. Nejedlem, 1957; Editor, Stravinsky u nas, 1957; Editor, Tvurci moderní hudby, 1965; Editor, Kresba a zvuk, 1969; Editor, Hudba v ceském divadle a cinohre, 1972; Editor, Slovnik svetovych skladatelu, 1971; Editor, E. F. Burian, 1981; Redactor and editor of the synthetic work: History of the Czech Musical Theatre (1848-1945); Editor, Conception of colour-music in the work of Czech modern composer M Ponc (1902-1976), 1986; Editor, The Artists of the Czech Musical Theatre (dictionary); Editor, M Ponc (monograph), 1990; Editor, Tableaux vivants, 1990; Editor, Musical Theatre of Horror, 1991; Editor, V. Talich in Sweden, 1992; Editor, Prag als Asylstadt, (1918-1938), 1993, (Germany). *Honours:* 1st Prize, Czechoslovakian Radio, 1967; 2nd Prize, International Music Competition, Radio Brno, 1970; Prize Supraphon, 1982. *Hobbies:* Painting; Motoring. *Address:* 19 U Nesypky, 150 00 Prague 5, Czech Republic.

PADMORE Elaine Marguirite, b. 1945, Haworth, Yorkshire, England. Festival Director; BBC Producer and Presenter; Singer. *Education:* BMus, MA, University of Birmingham, 1965-69; LTCL Piano Diploma; Scholarship for Piano Accompaniment, Guildhall School of Music; Studied singing privately with Helen Isepp. *Career:* Editor with Oxford University Press; BBC Producer, music programmes and major series for Radio 3; BBC Chief Producer, opera, 1976-82; Artistic Director, Wexford Festival, 1982-94; Radio Broadcaster and Singer appearing in concerts and opera; Lecturer in Opera, Royal Academy of Music, London; Artistic Director, Dublin Grand Opera, 1989-93; Artistic Director, Classical Productions, London, 1990-92,

(Tosca, 1991, Carmen, 1992); Artistic Consultant, London International Opera Festival, 1991-; Director Royal Danish Opera, Copenhagen, 1993-. *Publications:* Author of Wagner (in series The Great Composers), 1970; Chapter on Germany in Music in the Modern Age, 1973. *Contributions to:* Grove's Dictionary; Various British professional journals. *Honours:* Pro Musica Prize, Hungarian Radio, 1975; Prix Musical de Radio Brno, 1976; Honorary Associate, Royal Academy of Music, 1981; Sunday Independent Arts Award for services to music in Ireland, 1985. *Membership:* Incorporated Society of Musicians. *Address:* 11 Lancaster Avenue, Hadley Wood, Herts, England.

PADROS David, b. 22 Mar 1942, Igualada, Barcelona, Spain. Composer and Pianist. *Education:* Municipal Music School, Barcelona, 1966; Musikhochschule Trossingen, Freiburg, Germany, 1966-69; Konservatorium, Basel, 1969-72; Zurich, Switzerland, 1972-75. *Compositions:* Styx (Cham ensemble); Heptagonal (Piano); Crna Gora (Chamb ens); Khorva (Orch); Cal.ligrama I (Fl in G, Piano); 2 Legendes (Organ); Batalla (Piano, harpsichord, strings); Musik im Raum (Chamb ens); Jo-Ha-Kyu (Orch); Arachne (Chamb ensemble); Maqam (Piano); Trajectories (Violin); Confluencies (Brass ensemble, percussion, tape); Chaconne (String Quartet, Harpsichord); El Sermo de R Muntaner (4 mixed voices, 4 old wind instruments, organ); Ketjak (Pianists Quartet); Recordant W A M (Clarinet, organ). *Recordings:* Musik im Raum (Association of Catalan Composers); Arachne (Catalunya Musica); Confluencies (AS). *Contributions to:* Revista Musical Catalana. *Honours:* Hans-Lenz-Preis, (GFR), 1969; Komposition-Preis der Stiftung Landis & Gyr (Switzerland), 1976. *Membership:* Associacio Catalana de Compositors. *Address:* Rossello 213, 1-1, E-08008 Barcelona, Spain.

PADRÓS Jaime, b. 26 Aug 1926, Igualada, Spain. Composer; Pianist. m. Eva Marie Wolff, 1962. 1 son, 2 daughters. *Education:* Baccalaureat, Monastery of Montserrat, Barcelona; Formation, Escolania de Montserrat, 1939-; Piano, organ and musical studies with Dom David Pujol; Piano studies with Frank Marshall & Alicia de Larrocha, Academia Marshall, 1941; Composition with Josep Barberà, Cristóbal Taltabull, Barcelona, Darius Milhaud, Paris. *Debut:* As composer: Ballet Fantasia de circo, 1954. *Career:* Concerts in all major cities and radio stations in Spain, Paris, Prague and many German cities; First pianist to rediscover several of the works of the 18th Century Spanish Composers Antonio Soler and Narcis Casanoves; First to play complete piano works of Arnold Schoenberg, Alban Berg, Anton Webern and other contemporary composers in Spain; Piano Teacher, Academy of Music, Trossingen, West Germany, 1964-94; Numerous commissioned works, 1954-. *Compositions:* Chamber music for different casts of instruments: Tannkas del somni, 1950; Sonata para piano, 1954; Quintet per a quartet d'arc i piano, 1962; Planctus, 1977; Cancionero del lugar, 1978; Policromies, 1980; several settings of folk songs for choir; Poemas de fragua, 1984; Música cambiante (piano solo and string orchestra), 1986. *Recordings:* Contrapuntos sobre canciones populares castellanas, 1962; Sternverdunkelung, 1960; Llibre d'alquimíes I, 1967; Serenata, 1978; Trama concèntrica, 1982; Paseo y contradanza, 1985. *Honours:* Premio Juventudes musicales, 1954; Premi Orfeó català, 1962. *Address:* Seelengraben 30, 89073 Ulm, Germany.

PAETZOLD-HRDLIČKOVÁ Nadja, b. Sofia, Bulgaria. Harpist. Divorced, 1 d. *Education:* Studied at Prague State Conservatory, Czech. *Career:* Appointments with The State Opera Slask-Katowice Poland, 1956-59; State Symphony Orchestra, Poznan Poland, 1959-61; Radio & Film Symphony Orchestra, Prague, Czech, 1961-65; Konzertverein St Gallen, Switzerland, 1966-69; Stadttheater Biel, Switzerland, 1969-71; Allgemeine Musikgesellschaft, Lucerne, Switzerland, 1971-81; Harp Teacher, Founder, Director, First Hrp School of Switzerland, 1989; Formed Harp Duo of Lucerne together with her Daughter, 1977; Founded Childrens Harp Ensemble of Lucerne, 1982-; Founded Adult Harp

Ensemble, 1987-. *Memberships:* Janáček Society, Zurich; Schweizerischer Musik Verband; Schweizerscher Musikpaedagogischer Verband; Deutscher Harfen Verband, Schweizerischer Harfen Verband. *Hobby:* Adapting and performings Works of old, unknown composers. *Address:* Zahringerstr 1, CH-6003 Lucerne, Switzerland.

PAGANUZZI Enrico, b. 18 Jan 1921, Asmara, Eritrea. Professor of Literature. *Education:* Musical studies with David Begalli and Arrigo Pedrollo; Diploma, Musical Paleography, Cremona; Graduate in Humanities. *Publications:* Medioevo e Rinascimento in La Musica a Verona, 1976. *Contributions to:* Rivista Musicale Italiana; Convivium; Cultura neolatina; Vita Veronese; Enzyclopädie Die Musik in Geschichte und Gegenwart; Enciclopedia della Musica (Rizzoli-Ricordi); New Grove Dictionary of Music and Musicians, 6th edition. *Memberships:* Libn Accademia Filarmonica, Verona; Italian Society of Musicology; Veronese Academy of Agriculture, Science and Letters; Veronese Academy Cignaroli. *Address:* Lungadige Matteotti 9, 37126 Verona, Italy.

PAGE Christopher Howard, b. 8 Apr 1952, London, England. Medievalist. m. Régine Fourcade, 15 Sept 1975. *Education:* BA, English, Oxford University; D.Phil., York University. *Career:* University Lecturer in Medieval English, University of Cambridge; Frequent Broadcaster on BBC Radio 3, both as Lecturer and as Director of his Ensemble, Gothic Voices; Presenter of Radio 4 Arts programme, Kaleidoscope. *Recordings:* Directed Gothic Voices in Sequences and Hymns by Abbess Hildegard of Bingen; The Mirror of Narcissus: Songs by Guillaume de Machaut; The Garden of Zephirus: Courtly Songs of the Early 15C; The Castle of Fair Welcome: Courtly Songs of the late 15C; The Service of Venus and Mars; A Song for Francesca; Music for the Lionhearted King. *Publications:* (Book) Voices and Instruments of the Middle Ages; Sequences and Hymns by Abbess Hildegard of Bingen; The Owl and the Nightingale: Musical Life and Ideas in France, 1100-1300. *Contributions to:* Many academic and scholarly contributions to Early Music; Galpin Society Journal; Proceedings of the Royal Musical Association; New Oxford History of Music; Cambridge Guide to the Arts in Britain; Early Music History; The Historical Harpsichord. *Honours:* British Entrant and Prizewinner, Innsbruck International radio Prize, 1981; several awards for record of Hildegard; Grammophone Awards for three records; Fellow, Fellowship of Makers and Restorers of Historical Instruments; Senior Research Fellow in Music, Sidney Sussex College, Cambridge. *Hobbies:* Research & Performance. *Address:* Sidney Sussex College, Cambridge University, Cambridge, England.

PAGE Kenneth, b. 8 Dec 1927, Birmingham, England. Musician; Violinist; Violist; Conductor. m. Brenda Gane, 10 Oct 1953. *Education:* Birmingham Conservatoire, Studied with Ernest Element, YFRAH Neaman, Max Rostal. *Career:* BBC Radio 3 & 4; BBC TV; Amati Quartet, 1951-53 (violin); Element Quartet, 1953-60 (violin and viola); Archduke Trio 1961 (violin); Voces Intimae Quartet 1960- (violin, viola); Orchestra da Camera, Founder and Music Director, Conductor; Birmingham Philharmonic Orchestra, 1959-86, Conductor. *Recordings:* Wilfred Josephs Piano Concerto 2; Christmas Music Hereford Cathedral. *Honours:* Hon.MMus Leicester University, 1975; Hon.MSc, University of Aston, 1983. *Hobbies:* Photography; Model Railways. *Address:* 41 Fishponds Road, Kenilworth, Warwickshire CV8 1EY, England.

PAGE Paula, b. 24 Sept 1942, Corinth, Mississippi, USA. Singer (Soprano). *Education:* Studied at Indiana University, Bloomington, and on a Fulbright Scholarship in Europe. *Debut:* Inez in II Trovatore, Hamburg, Staatsoper, 1968. *Career:* Hamburg Staatsoper 1968-72; Appearances at Wuppertal, Aachen, Bremen, Santa Fe, Norfolk, Antwerp, Liège, Bordeaux, Lisbon, Venice, Dusseldorf; Berlin, Frankfurt-am-Main Opera from 1983; Repertory includes lyric roles and parts in modern operas; Presently Professor of Voice, Staatliche Hochschule für Musik. *Honours:* Prizewinner, New York Metropolitan Auditions of the Air 1967; WGN Auditions of the Air, 1967; Geneva International Competition, 1968; 's-Hertogenbosh Holland, 1968; Martha B Rockefeller Grant, 1977. *Address:* Königsberger Straße 25, D-6239, Germany.

PAGE Robin Gregory, b. 7 Mar 1954, Ipswich, Suffolk. Conductor. m. 4 Jan 1980, 1 son, 4 daughters. *Education:* Magdalen College School, Oxford; Gonville and Caius College, Cambridge; Royal Academy of Music, London. *Career:* Conductor, Hounslow Symphony Orchestra 1977-85; Conductor, Thames Sinfonia 1979-85; Musical Director, Surbiton Oratorio Society; Principal Conductor, Purcell Orchestra 1982-; Musical Director, West Sussex Philharmonic Choir 1984-; Musical Director, Kingston Choral Society 1985-; Principal Conductor, Birmingham Philharmonic Orchestra 1985-; Semi-Finalist, MTV Hungarian International Conductors Competition 1986; BBC recordings Ulster Orchestra 1989; Junior Professor, Royal Academy of Music 1980-. *Contributions to:* Composer Magazine; Classical Music Magazine. *Hobbies:* Ipswich Town Football Club; The Arts and Literature. *Address:* 86 Park Hill, Carshalton, Beeches, Surrey, England.

PAGE Steven, b. 1950, England. Singer (Baritone).*Education:* Studied with Margaret Hyde and at the National Opera Studio, London. *Career:* Sang Don Alfonso and Nick Shadow with Opera 80, the Arts Council's touring company; Appearances with English National Opera as Tarquinius in The Rape of Lucretia, Don Giovanni, Albert in Werther and Paolo in Simon Boccanegra; invited to return as Valentine in Faust and as Count Almaviva; Engagements with Kent Opera and at the Buxton Festival (from 1986); With Scottish Opera has sung Guglielmo and Marcello, in new productions of Così fan Tutte and La Bohème; Sang Don Giovanni with English National Opera, 1989; Milord Arespingh in Cimarosa's L'Italiana in Londra, Buxton Festival 1989; Scottish Opera 1989 as Count Almaviva; debut as Gounod's Valentin with ENO 1990 (Almaviva, 1990); Sang Chorebus in Les Troyens at Glasgow and London; Season 1992 as Mozart's Count Don Giovanni for Scottish Opera, Nick Shadow in The Rake's Progress for the Glyndebourne Tour. *Address:* c/o Stafford Law Associates, 26 Mayfield Road, Weybridge, Surrey KT13 8XB, England.

PAIK Byung-dong, b. 26 Jan 1936, Seoul, Korea. Professor. m. Wha-ja Woo, 4 Oct 1969. *Education:* Graduated, Shin-Heung High School, Jeon-joo; Department of Composition, College of Music, Seoul National University, 1961-63; Stadtliche Hochschule fuer Musik, Hanover, Federal Republic of Germany, 1971-79. *Debut:* Annual Korean New Composers Prize with Symphonic Three Chapters, 1962. *Career:* 6 composition recitals since 1st recital, 1960-; Has presented his works several times with National Symphony Orchestra, Seoul Philharmonic Orchestra and other ensembles; Professor, Personnel Management Member, College of Music, Seoul National University; President, Perspective Composers Group. *Compositions:* Major works: Symphonic Three Chapters, 1962; Un I, II, III, IV, V, VI for Instrumental Ensemble; Drei Bagetellen fur Klavier, 1973; Concerto for Piano and Orchestra, 1974; Veranderte Ehepaar, 1986; In September for Orchestra, 1987; Contra, 1988. *Recordings:* Ein kleine Nachtlied fur Violine und Klavier, SEM, Seoul, 1978; Guitariana for two Guitars, SEM, 1984; Byul-Gok 87, Jigu Record Corporation, Seoul, 1987. *Publications:* Musical Theory, 1977; Essays: Seven Fermatas, 1979; Essays: Sound, or Whispering, 1981; Harmony, 1984; Music for Culture, 1985; College Musical Theory, 1989; The Streams of Modern Music, 1990. *Address:* 214-1 Sangdo 1 dong, Dongjakgu, A-202 Sangdo villa, Seoul, Korea.

PAIK Kun-Woo, b. 10 May 1946, Seoul, South Korea. Classical Pianist. m. Mi-Ja Son, 14 Mar 1976, 1 daughter. *Education:* High School of Performing Arts,

New York City, USA, 1965; Diplomas, Juilliard School of Music, New York, 1965-71; Studied with Rosina Lhevine; Further studies with Ilona Kabos, London, with Wilhelm Kempff and Guido Agosti, Italy. *Debut:* As soloist, Grieg Concerto with National Orchestra of Korea, Seoul, at age 10; New York orchestral debut with James Conlon and National Orchestra, Carnegie Hall, 1972; London debut, 3 recitals, Wigmore Hall, 1974. *Career:* Recitalist, Alice Tully Hall, New York city, 1971; Recitals, concerts, USA, Europe, South Korea, 1971-; Performed at numerous major festivals, USA and Europe including Berlin, Spoleto, Edinburgh, Paris, Aix-en-Provence; Appearances with major orchestras include: London Philharmonic; Paris Orchestre Nationale; Berlin Radio; Suisse Romande; Frankfurt Radio Symphony; US West Coast solo debut with recitals, Los Angeles and San Francisco. *Recordings:* Ravel's complete solo works and 2 concerti, Orfeo and Seon; Moussorgsky's complete piano solo works, RCA; Sonata D960, Schubert, Seon. *Honours:* Special prize, Dmitri Mitropoulos Competition, New York, at age 15; Gold Medal, Busoni Competition, 1969; 1st prize, Walter Naumburg Piano Competition, New York, 1971; Finalist, Leventritt Competition, 1971; Joseph Lhevine Award; Franz Listzt Award. *Hobbies:* Photography; Cinema; Travel; Food; Drawing; Reading. *Address:* 7 rue Villebois-Mareuil, 94300 Vincennes, France.

PAIK Nam June, b. 20 July 1932, Seoul, South Korea. *Education:* Studied at University of Tokyo; Music theory with Thrasybulos Georgiades in Munich and with Wolfgang Fortner in Munich. *Career:* Worked with Stockhausen at Electronic Music Studio in Cologne 1958-60; Summer seminars for new music at Darmstadt, 1957-61; Moved to New York 1964, Los Angeles 1970; Performance of music involves total art, including duo recitals with topless cellist Charlotte Moorman in which composer's spine serves as cellist's fingerboard. *Compositions:* Ommaggio a Cage, involving the destruction of pianos and raw eggs, and the painting of hands in jet black, 1959; Symphony for 20 Rooms 1961; Global Groove, high-velocity collage using video tape 1963; Variations on a Theme of Saint-Saëns for piano and cellist in oil drum; Performable Music, in which performer is required to cut left forearm with a razor, 1967; Opera Sextronique, 1967; Opera Electronique, 1968; Creep into a Whale; Young Penis Symphony, 1970; Earthquake Symphony, with grand finale, 1971. *Address:* c/o ASCAP, ASCAP Building, One Lincoln Plaza, New York, NY 10023, USA.

PAILLARD Jean-François, b. 28 Apr 1928, Vitry-le-Francois, France. Conductor; Musicologist. m. Anne Marie Beckensteiner, 3 sons. *Education:* First Prize in Music History, Paris Conservatoire; Studied conducting with Igor Markevitch, Salzburg; Graduated from the Sorbonne in mathematics. *Career:* Founded the Jean-Marie Leclair Instrumental Ensemble 1953; Many tours of Europe, USA and the Far East with the Jean-Francois Paillard Chamber Orchestra, notably in French music of the 17th and 18th centuries; Organiser and Teacher of Conducting Courses, Spring and Summer, France. *Publications:* La Musique Française Classique 1960, 1973; Archives de la Musique Instrumentale; Archives de la Musique Religieuse. *Recordings include:* Bach, Brandenburg Concertos, Suites for Orchestra, Harpsichord Concertos and Musical Offering; Handel Alexander's Feast, Water and Fireworks Music, Dettingen Te Deum, Concertos for oboe, organ and harp; Couperin Les Nations; Delalande Symphonies; Charpentier Te Deum, Magnificat and Messe de Minuit, Baroque trumpet concertos (Maurice André); Rameau Les Indes Galantes; Mozart Divertimenti; Flute and Violin concertos, concerto K 299. *Honours:* Many Grand Prix du Disque (Academie Charles Cros, Disque Français, Disque Lyrique); Prix Edison, Holland; German Record Prize; Gold Record, Japan. *Memberships:* French Musicological Society; French Society of the 18th Century. *Hobbies:* Piloting Aircraft; Sailing; Mountaineering. *Address:* 23 Rue de Marly, 7860 Etang la Ville, France.

PAITA Carlos, b. 10 Mar 1932, Buenos Aires,

Argentina. Conductor m. Elisabeth de Quartbarbes, 7 children. *Education:* Studied with Juan Neuchoff and Jacobo Fischer. *Debut:* Teatro Colon, Buenos Aires. *Career:* Conducted the National Radio Orchestra in Argentina; Verdi Requiem, 1964, Mahler's 2nd symphony, 1965; Stuttgart Radio Symphony from 1966; Appearances in London, Paris, Edinburgh and the USA (debut 1979, with the Houston Symphony Orchestra). *Recordings:* Festival Wagner; Grands Overtures; Verdi Requiem; Beethoven's Eroica Symphony; Rossini Overtures; Mahler's 1st Symphony; Symphonie Fantastique by Berlioz. *Honours:* Grand Prix Academie Charles Cros, Paris, 1969; Grand Prix de L'Academie Française, 1978. *Address:* 15 Chemin du Champ D'Anier, 1209 Geneva, Switzerland.

PAL Tamas, b. 16 Sept 1937, Gyula, Hungary. Conductor. *Education:* Studied with Janos Viski and Andreas Korody at the Franz Liszt Academy Budapest. *Career:* Conducted the Budapest State Opera 1960-75, notably at the Edinburgh Festival (1973) and the Wiesbaden May Festival (1974); Principal Conductor of the Szeged Symphony Orchestra and Opera 1975-83; Permanent Conductor of the Budapest Opera 1983-85; Artistic Director of the open air summer music festival at Budapest, 1987; Has conducted operatic rarities such as Salieri's Falstaff, Liszt's Don Sanche and Il Pittor Parigino by Cimarosa. *Recordings include:* Liszt Piano Concerto no 2 with the Hungarian State Orchestra; Brahms Symphony no 3 and Academic Festival Overture, with the Budapest Symphony Orchestra; Il Pittor Parigino (premiere recording). *Address:* c/o Hungarian State Opera House, Nepoztarsasag uta 22, 1061 Budapest, Hungary.

PALACIO Ernesto, b. 19 Oct 1946, Lima, Peru. Singer (Tenor). *Education:* Studied in Peru and Milan, Italy . *Debut:* Sang Almaviva in San Remo, Italy 1972. *Career:* Sang lyric roles in Milan, Rome, Venice, Trieste, Bologne, Turin, Genoa, Palermo, Naples, Parma, Catania; Guest appearances in London (Covent Garden), New York (Metropolitan and Carnegie Hall), Buenos Aires (Colon), Berlin (Philharmonic), Edinburgh, Marseilles, Bordeaux, Lille, Nancy, Lyon, Strasbourg, Houston, Dallas, Zurich, Dusseldorf, Munich, Caracas, Chile; Other roles include 18 operas of Rossini; Don Giovanni, Così fan Tutte, Re Pastore, Die Zauberflöte, Finta giardiniera, Finta Semplice (Mozart); Elisir d'amore, Don Pasquale, La fille du Régiment, Esule di Roma, Torquato Tasso (Donizetti); Sang in a revival of Ciro in Babilonia of Rossini at Savona, 1988; Appeared as Argirio in Tancredi opposite Marilyn Horne at Barcelona, May 1989, Bilbao, Jan 1991; Bonn Opera 1990, as Almaviva. *Recordings:* Mosè in Egitto (Philips); Il Turco in Italia (CBS); Miserere by Donizetti (Voce); Adelaide di Borgogna by Rossini; Vivaldi's Serenata a Tre (Erato); Torquato Tasso; Catone in Utica by Vivaldi (RCA); Unpublished arias by Rossini, conducted by Carlo Rizzi; Prince Giovanni in Una Cosa Rara (Astrée/Auvidis). *Address:* c/o Via Del Gelso 1, 20070 Dresand, Milan, Italy.

PALASZ Bogumil, b. 18 Apr 1931, Warsaw, Poland. Historian. m. Maria Rodziewicz, 29 July 1957, 1 daughter. *Education:* Master's degree, Diploma Historian, University of Warsaw. *Career:* Film on Warsaw; History Consultant; Historian; Currently: General Director, F Chopin Society, Warsaw; Secretary General and President of the Board, International F Chopin Foundation. *Contributions to:* Warsaw Chronicle. *Honours:* Cross of the Polonia Restituta Order, 1976; Many other high distinctions of the Polish State. *Hobbies:* Classical music; Old prints; Angling. *Address:* The Fryderyk Chopin Society, ul Okolnik 1, 00-368 Warsaw, Poland.

PALAY Elliot, b. 18 Dec 1948, Milwaukee, Wisconsin, USA. Singer (Tenor). *Education:* Studied at Indiana University, Bloomington, with Charles Kullmann; Further study with Clemens Kaiser-Breme in Essen. *Debut:* Lubeck 1972, as Matteo in Arabella. *Career:* Sang in Freiburg, Dusseldorf, Munich and Stuttgart; Komische Oper Berlin 1977, in Aufstieg und

Fall der Stadt Mahagonny; Returned to USA and sang at the New York City Opera; Santa Fe and Seattle 1983, as Siegfried in Der Ring des Nibelungen; Antwerp and Ghent 1983, as Siegmund in Die Walküre; Dresden 1984, in Wozzeck; Other roles include Wagner's Tristan and Walther, Verdi's Radames and Ismaele, the Emperor in Die Frau ohne Schatten and Boris in Katya Kabanova; Sang Siegfried with the Jutland Opera at Aarhus, 1987. *Address:* c/o Den Jydske Opera, Musikhuset Ärkus, Thomas Jensens Alle, DK-8000 Aarkus, Denmark.

PALEY Alexander, b. 9 Jan 1956, Kishinev, USSR. Concert Pianist. m. 29 July 1978, 1 daughter. *Education:* Master's degree, PhD, Moscow Conservatory. *Debut:* Kishinev, 2 Apr 1969. *Career:* Performed with Moscow Virtuosi (U Spivakov), 1985-90; Bolshoi Theatre Orchestra, 1986; with Monte Carlo Philharmonic, 1989; with Colorado Symphony, 1991; Recitals, Chatelet, Paris, 1990, Auditorium de Halles, 1991, Strasbourg, Moscow, Prague, Berlin, Sofia, Appeared with National Symphony Orchestra, Wolf Trapp Festival, 1991 and Boston Pops, 1991; Chamber music with Fine Arts Quartet, New York Chamber Soloists also with V Spivakov, Bella Davidovich, Oleg Krysa, D Sitkovetsky and B Pergamentshikov; Musical Director, Cannes-sur-Mer Festival, France. *Recordings:* Talent, Belgium; Liszt, all 4 Mephisto valses, other pieces; National Public Radio, USA; Radio France; Melodia, Moscow, 1990. *Honours:* Bach International Competition, Leipzig, 1984; 1st Prize, Vladigekov International Competition, Bulgaria, 1986; Grand Prix, Young Artist Debut, New York, 1988; 1st Prize, Aiex de Vries Prize, Belgium, 1990. *Hobbies:* Reading classical and philosophical literature; Museums; Theatre, opera and ballet. *Current Management:* Melvin Kaplan Inc. *Address:* 850 West 176th Street, Apt 4 D, New York, NY 10033, USA.

PALISCA Claude Victor, b. 24 Nov 1921, Rijeka, Croatia. Professor of History of Music. m. (1) Jane Pyne, 1 son, 1 daughter, (2) Elizabeth Keitel, 1987. *Education:* BA, Queens College, Flushing, New York, 1943; MA, Harvard University 1948; PhD, Harvard University, 1954; MA (Honorary), Yale University 1964. *Career:* Instructor, Assistant Professor in Music, University of Illinois, 1953-59; Associate Professor of History of Music 1959-64; Professor of History of Music, 1964-; Director of Graduate Studies in Music, 1967-70; Chairman, Department of Music, 1969-75, Yale University. *Publications:* Girolamo Mel: Letters on Ancient and Modern Music to Vincenzo Galilei and Giovanni Bardi, 1960; 17th Century Science and the Arts (with 3 others), 1961; Musicology (with others), 1963; Baroque Music 1968; Translated with Guy Marco, Zarlino, The Art of Counterpoint, Le istitutioni harmoniche, 1558, Part III, 1968; Norton Anthology of Western Music, 1980, 2nd edition, 1988; History of Western Music (with D.J. Grout), 3rd edition, 1980, 4th edition 1988; Humanism in Italian Renaissance Musical Thought, 1985; The Florentine Camerata, 1989. *Honours include:* Guggenheim Fellowships, 1960-61, 1980-81; Prize of International Musicological Society for Humanism, 1987; Fellow, American Academy of Arts and Sciences, Academia Filarmonica of Bologna. *Memberships include:* President, National Council of the Arts in Education, 1967-69; Vice-President, New Haven Symphony Incorporated, 1969-; President, American Musicological Society, 1970-72; Vice President, International Musiicological Society, 1977-82. *Address:* 954 Prospect Street, Hamden, CT 06517, USA.

PALM Siegfried, b. 25 Apr 1927, Barmen, Germany. Cellist; Professor of Music; Administrator. m. Brigitte Heinemann. *Education:* Studied with father and in Enrico Mainardi's master classes at Salzburg. *Career:* Principal Cellist, Lubeck City Orchestra 1945-47, Hamburg Radio Symphony 1947-62, Cologne Radio Sympony 1962-67; Played with Hamann Quartet 1950-62; Formed Duo with Aloys Kontarsky 1965; Joined Max Rostal and Heinz Schroter in Piano Trio, 1967; Professor at Cologne Musikhochschule 1962, Director from 1972; Teacher at Darmstadt from 1962; Has also taught at the Royal Conservatory Stockholm, Dartmouth College USA, Marlboro USA and the Sibelius Academy Helsinki;

Intendant of the Deutsche Oper Berlin 1977-81; Many recitals and appearances with leading orchestras; Engagements at Holland Festival, Warsaw Autumn Festival, Prague Spring Festival and Barcelona Festival; First performances of works by Stockhausen, Zimmermann, Penderecki, Xenakis, Zillig, Blacher, Feldman, Ligeti, Fortner, Yun, Kelemen and Kagel. *Publication:* Pro musica nova: Studien zum Spielen neuer Musik für Cello 1974. *Honours include:* German Record Prize 1969. *Address:* c/o Ingpen and Williams Ltd., 14 Kensington Court, London W8 5DN, England.

PALMER Cedric King, b. 13 Feb 1913, Eastbourne, Sussex, England. Composer; Conductor; Author; Teacher. m. Winifred Henry (dec), 2 May 1947, 1 son, 1 daughter. *Education:* Royal Academy of Music; Trinity College of Music; ARAM; LRAM; FRSA. *Debut:* Queens Hall, London Conducting Royal Academy of Music Symphony Orchestra, 1920. *Career:* Conductor and Lecturer, City Literary Institute, 1939; Conductor: King Palmer Light Orchestra (BBC) 1939; N London Orchestra; Sevenoaks Choral Society; West End Theatrical Production, Film Orchestras. *Compositions:* Film Scores for Dark Eyes of London; Cockney Kids Adventure; Secrets of the Stars; Rhythm of the Road; Holiday Tims; Signs of the Times; Operettas: Gay Romance; The Snow Queen; The Film Opens. *Recordings:* 11th Hour Melody; With Pomp and Pride; Sousa on Parade; Galopade; 3 Atonal Studies; Jogging Along; 300 recorded pieces of mood music. *Publications:* Teach Yourself Music, 1946 (also in Spanish); Teach Yourself Piano, 1957 (also in Spanish); Teach Yourself Composition, 1947; Teach Yourself Orchestration, 1968; ABC of Church Music, 1921; The Musical Production, 1953; Your Music and You, 1938. *Honours:* Freeman of the City of London, 1963; Justice of the Peace, 1968. *Memberships:* ISM (PTR); EPTA; IPTEC; Royal Society of Arts; Royal Musical Association. *Hobbies:* Concerts; Books. *Address:* Clovelly Lodge, 2 Popes Grove, Twickenham TW2 5TA, England.

PALMER Felicity Joan, b. 6 Apr 1944, Cheltenham, England. Mezzo-Soprano. *Education:* Erith Grammar School; Guildhall School of Music and Drama; AGSM (Teacher/Performer); FGSM. *Debut:* Purcell's Dido with Kent Opera, 1971; US Operatic debut, Marriage of Figaro, Houston, USA, October 1973; Chicago Lyric Opera as Kabanicha in Janáček's Katya Kabanova, November 1986; Debut La Scala, Milan in World Premiere of Riccardo III, January 1987. *Career:* Major appearances at concerts in Britain, America, Belgium, France, Germany, Italy, Russia and Spain. Operatic appearances include: The Magic Flute, London 1975; Don Giovanni, London 1976; Alcina, Bern 1977; Julius Caesar, Frankfurt 1978, Idomeneo, Zürich, 1980; Tristan and Isolde, ENO 1981; Rienzi, ENO, 1983; Orfeo, Opera North, 1984; King Priam, Royal Opera 1985; Mazeppa, ENO, 1984; Albert Herring, Glyndebourne 1985; Tamburlaine, Opera North 1985; Recitals in Amsterdam, Paris, Vienna 1976-77; Concert Tours with BBC SO, Europe 1973, 1977 and 1984; Australasia, Far East and Eastern Europe 1977-; ABC Tour of Australia 1987; Sang in Flavio Testi's Riccardo III at Milan, 1987; Glyndebourne Festival 1990, in Falstaff as Mistress Quickly (Countess in The Queen of Spades 1992); Chicago Lyric Opera 1990, as Gertrude in Thomas' Hamlet; Has sung Kabanicha at Chicago and Glyndebourne; Sang the title role in the stage premiere of Roberto Gerhard's The Duenna, Madrid 1992; Season 1992 as Clytemnestra for Welsh National Opera and the Countess in The Queen of Spades at Glyndebourne. *Recordings:* Many recordings which include: Messiaen's Poèmes pour Mi, with Pierre Boulez; Sea Pictures, Elgar, with LSO, Richard Hickox for EMI; Title Role in Gluck's Armide; Elektra in Idomeneo, with Nikolaus Harnoncourt; Recitals with John Constable of Songs by Poulenc, Ravel and Fauré, and of Victorian Ballads. *Honour:* Kathleen Ferrier Memorial Prize 1970. *Address:* Tom Graham, c/o IMG Artists Europe, Media House, 3 Burlinton Lane, London W4 2TH, England.

PALMER Larry, b. 13 Nov 1938, Warren, Ohio, USA. Harpsichordist; Organist. *Education:* Studied at Oberlin College Conservatory and Eastman School at Rochester, DMA 1963; Harpsichord with Isolde Ahlgrimm at Salzburg Mozarteum and with Gustav Leonhardt at Haarlem. *Career:* Recitalist on Harpsichord and Organ throughout the USA and Europe, with premieres of works by such composers as Vincent Persichetti and Ross Lee Finney; Harpsichord Editor of The Diapason from 1969; Professor of Harpsichord and Organ at Southern Methodist University in Dallas, 1970. *Publications:* Hugo Distler and his Church Music, 1967; Harpsichord in America: A 20th Century Revival, 1989 (2nd Ed. 1992). *Recordings:* Organ works of Distler and harpsichord pieces from the 17th to the 20th centuries. *Address:* c/o Southern Methodist University, Meadows School of the Arts, Dallas, TX 75275, USA.

PALMER Peter, b. 7 Mar 1945, West Bridgford, Notts. Writer on Music; Opera Director. *Education:* Exhibitioner in modern languages, Gonville & Caius College, Cambridge 1963-66, MA; Apprentice stage director, International Opera Studio, Zurich 1967-69. *Career:* Founder and artistic director, East Midlands Music Theatre: first British stage productions of works by Janáček, Krenek, John Ogdon and Schoeck. *Publications:* Translations include: From the Mattress Grave, Heine song cycle by David Blake, 1980, and Wagner and Beethoven by Klaus Kropfinger, 1991; Essays on the Philosophy of Music by Ernst Bloch 1985; Johann Faustus, libretto by Hanns Eisler. *Contributions to:* Reviews and articles in Die Tat, Zurich; Music and Musicians; German Life and Letters; Tempo; The Singer; talks for BBC Radio 3. *Honour:* Music & Letters Award, 1991. *Memberships:* Founding Member, Carl Nielsen Society of Gt Britain; Life Member, Othmar Schoeck Gesellschaft. *Hobbies:* Cats; Crosswords. *Address:* 2 Rivergreen Close, Beeston, Nottingham NG9 3ES, England.

PALMER Rudolph Alexis, b. 5 Aug 1952, New York City, New York, USA. Conductor; Composer; Pianist. m. Madeline Rogers, 21 June 1981. *Education:* BA, Russian, French, Bucknell University, 1973; BS, Composition, Mannes College of Music, 1975; MM, Juilliard, Composition, 1977; DMA, Juilliard, Composition, 1982. *Career:* Conducting and Composition Faculty, Mannes College of Music, 1982- ; Director, Great Neck Choral Society, 1983-84; Orchestra Director, Horace Mann School; Associate Conductor: Amor Artis Chamber Choir, Fairfield County Chorale; Conductor, North Jersey Music Educators Orchestra, Brewer Chamber Orchestra; Palmer Chamber Orchestra; Palmer Singers. *Compositions:* Contrasts for Four Bassoons (recorded Leonarda Records); O Magnum Mysterium (Albany Records) Commissions: Songs of Reflection; The Vision of Herod; The Immortal Shield; Orchestration of Leonard Bernstein's Touches; Numerous other works for chamber groups, chorus and orchestra, including 3 string quartets, 1 symphony, orchestral overtures and several dramatic cantatas. *Recordings:* Accompanist: Lieder, (by women composers), Leonarda; The Unknown Dvořák, Spectrum; Conductor: Baroque Cantatas of Versailles, Spectrum; The Romantic Handel, Leonarda; Handel's Imeneo, Vox Cum Laude; Telemann's Pimpinone, Newport Classic; Handel's Siroe, Newport Classic; Pergolesi's La Serva Padrona, Omega; Handel's Joshua, Newport Classics; Handel's Muzio, Newport Classics; A Scarlatti's, Ishmael, Newport Classics; F Joseph Haydn's La Canterina, Newport Classics; Handel Arias, Julianne Baird, Newport Classics; Chorusmaster: Bach, St John Passion, Newport Classic. *Hobbies:* Theatre; Concerts; Avid baseball fan (New York Yankees); Travel; Wine collector. *Address:* 215 West 88th Street Apt 7E, New York, NY 10024, USA.

PALMER Willard Aldrich, Jr, b. 31 Jan 1917, McComb, Mississippi, USA. Senior Keyboard Editor. m. Ruby Lenora Touchstone, 28 Feb 1941, 2 sons, 1 daughter. *Education:* BS Millsaps College, Jackson, Mississippi, 1940; Postgraduate Music Studies, University of Houston; 2-year scholarship to Leipzig Conservatory; PhD, Music Education, PhD, Musicology. *Career:* Concert Pianist; Harpsichordist and

Accordionist; Contributed improvements in accordion construction, extending range and capabilities of the basses; Member, Music Faculty, University of Houston, Texas, 1946-64; Director, Memorial Lutheran Church Choir, Houston, 1969-77, 1986-90; Lectured at Royal Conservatory and University of Toronto, Baldwin-Wallace University, Oberlin School of Music, Eastman College and many other institutions; Currently Senior Keyboard Editor, Alfred Publishing Company, Van Nuys, California. *Compositions:* Numerous sacred and secular choral compositions; Piano works include A Contemporary Album for the Young, 1980; Hundreds of educational piano compositions. *Publications:* Palmer-Hughes Accordion Course (with William H Hughes Jr), 75 volumes 1952-64; Piano Courses (with Amanda Vick Lethco and Morton Manus), 1982-99; Alfred's Basic Piano Library, Instructions Books for Children and Adults, over 90 volumes; Alfred Masterwork Editions, over 100 scholarly piano editions, Editor, over 550 volumes. *Honours:* Doctor of Humanities, Whitworth College, 1971; Honorary DMus, Millsaps College 1983. *Memberships:* American Society of Composers, Authors and Publishers; Advisory Board, Houston Harpsichord Society; Advisory Board, Riemenschneider Bach Institute, Berea, Ohio. *Hobbies:* Philately; Walking. *Address:* 9602 Winsome Lane, Houston, TX 77063, USA.

PALMIERI Robert Michael, b. 30 Oct 1930, Milwaukee, Wisconsin, USA. Professor Emeritus of Kent State University, Kent, Ohio, USA; Research Associate at Western Washington University, Bellingham, Washington. m. Margaret Walsh, Soprano, 27 July 1957, 3s. 1d. *Education:* Piano study with Norbert Schneider of Wisconsin Conservatory of Music, BM, 1953; Study with Jose Echaniz, Eastman School of Music, MM, 1954; Additional study with Carlo Vidusso, Milan and Robert Goldsand, New York City. *Career:* Pianist; Author; Concerts: Milwaukee Civic Music Association Artist Series Concerts 1954-55, 1960-61; in Hamburg, Stuttgart, Heidelberg and Milan; Various centers in USA; Adjudication for various competitions such as British Language Centre in Taipei, Taiwan; Lectures on Russian musical studies and history of the pianoforte. *Compositions:* Twenty Piano Exercises, 1971. *Publications:* Artist and Artisan, American Music Teacher, July-Aug 1963; Sergei Vasil'evich Rachmaninoff: A Guide to Research, 1985; Piano Information Guide: An Aid to Research, 1989; Encyclopedia of Keyboard Instruments, General Editor, 1993. *Address:* 2904 Heights Drive, Bellingham, Washington 98226, USA.

PALSSON Pall, b. 30 Aug 1912, Reykjavik, Iceland. Organist; Conductor; Musical Director. m. (1) Margret Arnadottir, 1934 (divorced) (2) Kristin Juliusdottir 1957. *Education:* Reykjavik Music School, Piano and Theory, 1930-32; Studied Organ with P Isolfsson 1937-38, Counterpoint with Dr V Urbancic, 1940-42, Organ with T Hultstrand, Stockholm, 1946 and P Thomsen, Copenhagen 1947; Organ with Herrick Bunney and Composition with Dr Hans Gal in Edinburgh 1947-48. *Debut:* St Giles, Edinburgh, December 1948. *Career:* Organist at Hafnarfjordur Church and President's Chapel 1950-74; Principal, Hafnarfjordur Music School 1950-71; Teacher of Organ and History at Tonskoli Sigursveinn D Kristinsson's 1972-82; Music Librarian at Hafnarfjordur Town Biblioteca, 1962-. Co-founder of Iceland Society of Organists 1951, Chairman 1965-71, organ recitals home and abroad, representative at various meetings concerned with music including member of jury of Scandinavian Chambers bi-annual awards to composers 1968-85. *Address:* Alfaskeid 64, 220 Hafnarfjordur, Iceland.

PAMPUCH Helmut, b. 1939, Grossmahlendorf, Oberschlesien, Germany. Singer (Tenor). *Education:* Studied at Nuremberg with Willi Domgraf- Fassbaender, 1957-62. *Career:* Sang at Regensburg from 1963; Appearances in Brunswick, Wiesbaden and Saarbrucken; Member of the Deutsche Oper am Rhein Dusseldorf 1973-, notably in character and buffo roles; Bayreuth debut 1978, later appeared as Mime in Das

Rheingold (1990); Paris Opera 1979, in the premiere of the full version of Berg's Lulu, conducted by Pierre Boulez; Has sung Mozart's Monostatos at La Scala (1985) and Mime in Ring cycles at San Francisco 1984-90 and Zurich 1989; Further engagements at the State Operas of Hamburg, Munich and Stuttgart; Deutsche Oper Berlin and the Grand Théâtre Geneva; Sang Mime in Das Rheingold at Bayreuth, 1992; Many concert appearances. *Recordings include:* Lulu (Deutsche Grammophon); Das Rheingold (Philips). *Address:* c/o Deutsche Oper am Rhein, Heinrich-Heine Allee 16, D-4000 Dusseldorf, Germany.

PANENKA Jan, b. 8 July 1922, Prague, Czechoslovakia. Pianist. *Education:* Studied with Frantisek Maxian in Prague and with Serebryakovv in Leningrad. *Debut:* Prague 1944. *Career:* Member of the Suk Trio 1957-; Duo recitals with Josef Suk; Chamber concerts with the Smetana Quartet; Soloist with the Czech Philharmonic Orchestra from 1959; Performances in Eastern Europe, West Germany, England and Australia; Professor of Piano at the Prague Academy. *Recordings:* Beethoven Concertos; Dvořák Piano Trios; Violin Sonatas by Suk and Debussy. *Honours:* Winner, International Piano Competition Prague 1951; Grand Prix du Dusque 1959; Artist of Merit 1972.

PANERAI Rolando, b. 17 Oct 1924, Campi Bisenszio, Florence, Italy. Singer (Baritone). *Education:* Studied in Florence with Raoul Frazzi and in Milan with Armani and Giulia Tess. *Debut:* Naples 1947, as Faraone in Rossini's Moses. *Career:* Sang at La Scala from 1951, debut in Samson et Dalila; Venice 1955, in the stage premiere of Prokofiev's The Fiery Angel; Aix 1955, as Mozart's Figaro; Salzburg from 1957, as Ford in Falstaff; Masetto in Don Giovanni, Guglielmo in Così fan Tutte and Paolo in Simon Boccanegra; Sang in the Italian premiere of Hindemith's Mathis der Maler, Milan 1957; Covent Garden debut 1960, as Rossini's Figaro; Other roles include Verdi's Luna and Giorgio Germont, Henry Ashton in Lucia di Lammermoor and Marcello in La Bohème; Appearances in Verona, Florence, Rome, San Francisco (1958), Moscow, Rio de Janeiro, Athens, Berlin, Munich and Johannesburg; Returned to Covent Garden 1985, as Dulcamara in L'Elisir d'Amore; Maggio Musicale Florence 1988, as Puccini's Gianni Schicchi; Sang Michonnet in Adriana Lecouvreur at the 1989 Munich Festival; Douglas in Mascagni's Guglielmo Ratcliff at Catania, 1990; returned to Covent Garden, March 1990, as Dulcamara. *Recordings:* I Puritani; Così fan Tutte; Il Trovatore; Falstaff; Il Barbiere di Siviglia; La Bohème; Aida; Verdi's Oberto; Parsifal with Maria Callas; Labels include Columbia, HMV, Philips, Cetra, Decca and Deutsche Grammophon. *Address:* c/o Royal Opera House, Covent Garden, London WC2, England.

PANHOFER Walter, b. 3 Jan 1910, Vienna, Austria. Pianist. m. Getraut Schmied 1956, 2 sons. *Education:* Vienna State Academy of Music and Dramatic Art. *Career:* Concert tours throughout Europe and overseas, as soloist and as chamber music performer; Professor of Music, University of Vienna, 1971-. *Recordings:* Various works, including Schubert's Trout Quintet, with members of the Vienna Octet on the Decca label. *Honour:* Austrian Cross of Honour, for science and art. *Hobbies:* Books; Skiing; Mountains. *Address:* Erdbergstrasse 35, A-1030 Vienna, Austria.

PANNELL Raymond, b. 25 Jan 1935, London, Ontario, Canada. Composer; Pianist. *Education:* Studied piano with Steuermann and composition with Wagenaar and Giannini at Juilliard. *Career:* Taught at Toronto Royal Conservatory from 1959, Directed opera workshop at Stratford Festival, Ontario, 1966; Assistant Director and Resident Conductor at Atlanta Municipal Theater, 1960 and Director of Youth Experimental Opera Workshop, 1969; Co-founder and General Director of Co-Opera Theatre in Toronto 1975. *Compositions:* Stage works: Aria da Capo, opera in 1 act, Toronto 1963; The Luck of Ginger Coffey, opera in 3 acts, Toronto 1967; Exiles, opera in 1 act, Stratford 1973; Go, children's opera 1975; Midway 1975; Push, developmental opera in 1 act, Toronto 1976; Circe, masque, Toronto 1977; Aberfan, video opera, CBC 1977; N-E-U-S, radio opera 1977; Souvenirs, opera in 1 act, Toronto 1979; Refugees, vaudeville, Little Rock, Arkansas 1986 (revised version); The Downsview Anniversary Song-Spectacle Celebration Pageant 1979; Harvest, television opera, CBC 1980; The Forbidden Christmas, musical 1990. *Honour:* Salzburg Television Opera Prize for Aberfan, 1977. *Address:* SACEM (Canada), c/o CAPAC (Canada), PRS Ltd Member Registration, 29-33 Berners Street, London W1P 4AA, England.

PANNI Marcello, b. 24 Jan 1940, Rome, Italy. Composer/Conductor. m. Jane Colombier, 3 Dec 1970, 1 daughter. *Education:* Roma Liceo Classico; Roma Accademia Santa Cecilia, 1961-65; Paris Conservatoire National Superieur, 1965-68. *Debut:* Venice 1969. *Career:* Teacher, (Milhaud Chair), Composition and Conducting, Mills College, Oakland, California, USA, 1979-85; Guest Conductor, major stages in Italy: Rome Opera; La Scala, Milan; San Carlo, Naples; La Fenice, Venice; Paris Opera, 1985; Vienna Staatsoper, 1986; Hamburg Staatsoper, 1977; Zurich, 1986; Berlin Deutsche Oper, 1988; New York Metropolitan Opera House, 1988; London Covent Garden, 1989; Concerts: Roma Accademia Santa Cecilia, 1970-; Radio Symphony Orchestras, Italy; Season 1992 with L'Elisir d'amore at Barcelona and The Fall of the House of Usher by Philip Glass at Florence; Season 1993, Trittico by Puccini; Wildschütz by Lortzing at the opera of Bonn; First Guest Conductor, Bonn Opera, 1993. *Compositions:* Klangfarbenspiel, performed at Milan Piccola Scala, in conjunction with director Mario Ricci and painter Piero Dorazio, 1973; La Partenza dell'Argonauta, directed by Memé Perlini, performed at Florence Maggio Musicale, 1976.*Current Management:* Stage Door, Via Giardini 941, Modena 41040, Italy. *Address:* 3 Piazza Borghese, 00186 Rome, Italy.

PANOCHA Jiri, b. 1940, Czechoslovakia. Violinist. *Education:* Studied at the Prague Academy of Arts. *Career:* Leader of International Student Orchestra in Berlin, under Karajan; Co-founded the Panocha Quartet 1968; Many concert appearances in Europe, the USA, Canada, Iraq, Mexico, Cuba and other centres; Repertoire includes works by Smetana, Janáček, Dvořák, Martinů, Haydn, Mozart, Beethoven, Schubert, Bartók and Ravel. *Recordings include:* Dvořák late quartets and Terzetto; Haydn Op 33 nos 1-6, D Major Op 64; Martinů Complete Quartets; Mendelssohn Octet (with Smetana Quartet); Mozart Oboe Quartet, Clarinet Quintet and Horn Quintet; Schubert Quartettsatz D703 (Supraphon). *Honours include:* Prize winner (with members of Panocha Quartet) at Kromeriz 1971; Weimar 1974; Prague 1975; Bordeaux 1976; Grand Prix du Disque, Paris, 1983 for Martinů recordings. *Address:* Pragokoncert, Maltezska nam 1, 118 13 Prague 1, Czech Republic.

PANTILLON Christophe David, b. 26 Jan 1965, Neuchâtel, Switzerland. Cellist. *Education:* Baccalaureat es Lettres, Humanities, Neuchatel, Switzerland, 1983; Studied with Heinrich Schiff, Conservatory, Basle, 1984-88; Diploma of Cello, 1988; Studied with Valentin Erben, Hochschule für Musik, Vienna. *Career:* Numerous appearances as soloist or chamber player; Member, Trio Pantillon (with 2 brothers); Concerts in Geneva, Zurich, Bern, Vienna, Paris, Rome, Great Britain, France, Germany, Holland; Appeared on Swiss television and radio. *Recording:* Kabalevsky: Cello Concerto No 1 in G Minor. *Honour:* 2nd prize, Swiss Youth Competition, Lucerne, 1983. *Membership:* ESTA. *Current Management:* Music Management International. *Address:* La Chanterelle, CH-2022 Bevaix, Switzerland.

PANTILLON Pierre Louis, b. 28 May 1960, Austin, Texas, USA. Violinist. *Education:* Baccalaureat, Humanities, Neuchâtel, Switzerland, 1979; Diploma with highest honours, Conservatory Bern, 1983; Studied with Yuval Yaron, Josef Gingold and Franco Gulli, Indiana University, USA. *Career:* Numerous appearances as soloist or chamber player in

Switzerland, France, Italy, Holland, Great Britian, USA; Member of Trio Pantillon; Numerous appearances on Swiss radio and television. *Honour:* Kiwanis Music Prize, Bern, 1984. *Memberships:* ESTA (European String Teachers' Association); SSPM (Societe Suisse de Pedagogie Musicale). *Current Management:* Music Management Int. *Address:* La Chanterelle, 2022 Bevaix/NE, Switzerland.

PANULA Jorma, b. 10 Aug 1930, Kauhajoki, Finland. Composer; Conductor; Professor of Conducting. *Education:* Studied at the Helsinki School of Church Music, at the Sibelius Academy and with Dean Dixon in Lund; Further study with Franco Ferrara at Hilversum, and in Austria and France. *Career:* Conducted at theatres in Lahti and Tampere 1953-58, Helsinki 1958-62; Founded the chamber orchestra of the Sibelius Academy and conducted the Helsinki Philharmonic Orchestra 1965-67 and the Aarhus City Orchestra in Denmark, 1973; Guest appearances in the USSR, USA and Europe; Notable for his interpretations of late Romantic and early 20th Century music; Professor of Conducting at the Sibelius Academy 1973-; Stockholm Musik Hógskolen, 1981-88; Copenhagen Royal Conservatorium, 1988-91; Professor for many summer courses in conduction including Yale University and Bartok Seminar in Hungary. *Compositions include:* Violin Concerto 1954; Jazz Capriccio for piano and orchestra 1965; Steel Symphony 1969; Choral and vocal works. *Recordings include:* Madetoja's Symphony no 3 and opera Pohjalaisia; Englund's Piano Concerto and Palmgren's Piano Concerto no 2, with the Helsinki Philharmonic (EMI). *Address:* c/o Sibelius Academy, P Rautatiekatu 9, 00100 Helsinki 10, Finland.

PAPE Gerard Joseph, b. 22 Apr 1955, Brooklyn, New York, USA. Composer; Psychoanalyst. m. Janet Smarr Pape, 23 Aug 1981, 2 sons. *Education:* BA, Columbia University, 1976; MA, 1978, PhD, 1982, University of Michigan; Studied composition with George Cacioppo and William Albright. *Career:* Director, Composer-in-Residence, Sinewave Studios, 1980-91; Music presented in over 25 concerts in Ann Arbor, Michigan; produced Twice Festival, annual festival of contemporary orchestral, ensemble, and electronic music, Ann Arbor, 1986-91; Since 1991, Director, Les Ateliers, UPIC, Paris, France (Electronic Music Studio). *Compositions:* Pour un Tombeau d'Anatole for soprano, percussion and saxophone orchestra, 1984; Ivan and Rena for 4 vocal soloists and orchestra, 1984; Cosmos for large orchestra, 1985; The Sorrows of the Moon for baritone and tape, 1986; Folie à Deux for violin and piano, 1986; Exorcism for baritone and orchestra, 1986; Catechresis for soprano and orchestra ,1987; Cerberus for organ and tape, 1987; String Quartet 2, 1988; Three Faces of Death, for orchestra, 1988; Piano Concerto, 1988; That Burning Thing, for flute and tape, 1989; 5 Pieces for Saxophone and Piano, 1989; A Piece of Monologue for Baritone and tape, 1990; Prélude Electrouque (for tape), Xstasis (for ensemble and tape), Varesia Variations, (for tape), 1992; Two Electro-Acoustic songs (for voice, flute, tape), 1993.*Recordings:* Mode 26, Music of Gerard Pape (six pieces of Pape), 1992. *Honours:* Various grants to produce the Sinewave series of concerts, Michigan Council for the Arts; Meet The Composer, 1989; ASCAP Standard Award, 1992, 1993. *Membership:* ASCAP. *Address:* 62 rue Michel-Auge, 75016 Paris, France.

PAPE Rene, b. 4 Sept 1964, Dresden, Germany. Singer (Bass-baritone). *Education:* Member of Dresden Kreuzchor 1974-81, tours to Japan and Europe; Dresden Musikhochschule from 1981. *Debut:* Berlin Staatsoper 1987 as the Speaker in Die Zauberflöte. *Career:* Sang in 1989 premiere of Siegfried Matthus's Graf Mirabeau at Berlin Staatsoper and has appeared there and elsewhere in Germany as Mozart's Figaro and Alfonso, Verdi's Banquo, Procida and King in Aida, Gremin in Eugene Onegin and Galitzky in Prince Igor; Guest engagements at Frankfurt and Vienna Staatsoper; Salzburg Festival 1991 as Sarastro in Die Zauberflöte; Many concert appearances, notably in Mozart's Requiem for the bi-centenary performances in 1991.

Address: c/o Berlin Staatsoper, Unter den Linden 7, 1086 Berlin, Germany.

PAPERNO Dmitry, b. 18 Feb 1929, Kiev, USSR. Concert Pianist; Professor of Piano. m. Ludmila Gritsay, 21 May 1966, 2 daughters. *Education:* Graduated, Central School of Music for Especially Gifted Children (Affiliated with Tchaikovsky Conservatory), Moscow, 1946; Honours degree, Moscow Tchaikovsky Conservatory, 1951; Postgraduate (Aspiranture), 1955; Studied with Professor Alexander Goldenweiser. *Debut:* Recital, Moscow, 1955. *Career:* Concert career: Pianist-Soloist, Mosconcert; About 1500 solo recitals and performances in USSR, Eastern and Western Europe, and Cuba including The USSR State Orchestra (Moscow, Leningrad and Brussels, Belgium EXPO 1958), Gewandhaus Orchestra, Leipzig 1960, Hallé Orchestra, Manchester 1967; many others, 1955-76. Many concerts in Holland, France, Belgium, Majorca, and Portugal, 1985-; Sonata recital with Mstislav Rostropovich, Pasadena, CA, 1989. Teaching: Moscow State Gnesin Institute 1967-73; DePaul University, Chicago, 1977-; Full Professor of Piano, 1985. *Recordings:* Melodia, USSR - 5 recordings: works by Chopin, Liszt, Grieg, Schumann, Bach-Busoni, Debussy, Medtner; also 2 videotapes for Moscow TV - piano recital and Chopin F-minor Concerto with Moscow Radio and TV Orchestra, under Gennady Rozhdestvensky. Musical Heritage Society, USA - 2 recordings: Selected works by Scriabin, 1978 and Tchaikovsky's The Seasons, 1982; 3 Compact discs: Cedille Records, USA; Russian Piano Music, 1989; Works of Bach-Busoni, Beethoven, Schubert, Brahms, 1990; and Uncommon Encores (16 miniatures of different composers), 1991. *Publications:* Several articles and reviews both in USSR and USA; 2 books in Russian, Notes of a Moscow Pianist (illustrated, preface by Vladimir Ashkenazy), 1983, Post Scriptum (afterword by Mstislav Rostropovich), 1987. *Hobbies:* Books; Chess; Stamps. *Address:* 2646 North Wayne, Unit A, Chicago, IL 60614, USA.

PAPINEAU-COUTURE Jean, b. 12 Nov 1916, Outremont, Québec, Canada. Composer. m. Isabelle Baudouin, dec. 1987. *Education:* Studied with Francis Findley (conducting), Quincy Porter (composition), and Beveridge Webster (piano); BMus. degree 1941, Boston's New England Conservatory of Music 1941; studied composition and harmony under Nadia Boulanger at Madison, Wisconsin, Lake Arrowhead and Santa Barbara, California. *Career:* Teaching piano, Jean-de-Brebeuf College, Montreal 1943-44; Teacher of music, Conservatoire de Musique et d'Art Dramatique de la Province de Québec, Montreal 1946-52; Professor 1951-; Secretary of Faculty 1952-67; Vice-Dean 1967; Dean 1968-73; Faculty of Music, University of Montreal; compositions have been commissioned by Canadian Broadcasting Corporation, Montreal Symphony Orchestra and others. *Compositions include:* Orchestral: Aria 1949, Concerto Grosso 1943, revised 1955; March de guillaumet 1952; Oscillations 1969; Papotages 1949; Piece concertante No.5 1963; Poeme 1952; Prelude 1953; Suite Lapitsky 1965; Symphonie en do Majeur 1948, revised 1956; Trois pieces 1961. Soloist with Orchestra. Instrumental Ensemble: Canons 1964; Dialogues 1967; Fantaisie pour quintette a vent 1963; Nocturnes pour sept instruments 1969; Obsession 1973; Sectuor 1967; Slano 1975; Sonate en sol 1944, revised 1953; Suite 1947; Trio en quatre mouvements 1974; Trois Caprices 1962. Voices with Instrumental Ensemble: Chanson de rahit 1972; Le debat du coeur et du corps de villon 1977; Eglogues 1942; Paysage 1968; Psaume CI 1954. Chorus: Te Mater 1958; Viole d'amour 1966; Prouesse, viola, 1986; Nuit Polaire, contralto and ten instruments, 1986; Thrène, violin and piano, 1988; Les arabesques d'Isabelle, flute, English horn, clarinet, basson and piano, 1989; For Organ: Vers l'Extinction, 1987; Courbes, 1988; Quasipassacaille, C'est bref, 1991; Tournants, 1992; For woodwinds, 5 brass percussions, piano and strings, Celebrations, 1990; For flute, oboe, clarinet, basson, horn and string quintet, Automne, 1992; For flute, oboe, clarinet, basson and piano, Vents capricieux sur le clavier, 1993. *Recordings:* Many recordings on various labels.

Address: 4694 Lacombe, Montreal, Quebec, H3W 1R3, Canada.

PAQUETTE Daniel, b. 1930, Morteau, Doubs, France. Professor Emerite of History of Music. m. Madeleine Mougel, 22 Aug 1957, 1 son, 1 daughter. *Education:* Licence, Degree in History of Art and Archaeology, University of Dijon, 1962; Doctorate, 3rd cycle, University of Dijon, 1969; Doctor of Letters, University of Paris IV, Sorbonne, 1978; 1st prize in Musical Composition, National Conservatoire of Dijon, 1961; 1st prize for Violincello and History of Music, National Conservatoire of Saint Etienne, 1951. *Career:* Teacher of Musical Education, Lycees in Angiers, 1952, Dijon, 1953-64; Assistant, Institute of Musicology, University of Strasbourg, 1964-69; Lecturer, University of Dijon, 1970-72; Professor, University of Lyon, 1972-; Head, Musicology Section, Universities of Besancon and Dijon (Audio-visual education), St Etienne; Leader, Philharmonic Choirs of Dijon and Voix Amies Dijon, 1953-64; Leader, University Orchestra, Strasbourg, 1964-69. *Compositions:* Les Dames des Entreportes, symphonic poem; Operetta for children: Les Fantomes du Val au Faon; A cappella choral music based on ancient music of 16th-18th century; Film and chamber music. Films: J. J. Rousseau et la musique; J. Ph. Rameau, musicien sensible et savant rigoureux. *Publications:* L'Instrument de musique dans la Grece Antique, 1984; Jean Phillipe Rameau musicien bourguignon, 1983; Musique baroque, Aspects dela musique en France et a Lyon au XVIII, since 1990; Articles in Dictionaire de la Musique, 1976-86 and Die Musik in Geschichte und Gegenwart, 1970. *Address:* Les Furtins, 71960 Berze-la-Ville, France.

PARADISE Paul L, b. 12 May 1927, San Francisco, California, USA. Violist; Teacher; Author. m. Anna Ho, 19 June 1949, 2 sons, 1 daughter. *Education:* BS, Juilliard, 1950; MA, Columbia, 1951; Doctoral, Boston University, 1961; MED, Northeastern University, 1963. *Career:* Performances in Boston Pops, New Jersey Chamber Orchestra, Rutgers Cont. Music Ensemble, New Jersey State Orchestra, Showcase String Quartet; Executive Vice-President, Paganiniana Publications; Manager, St Peter by the Sea Orchestra. *Compositions:* The Best of Haydn (with Applebaum); The Best of Mozart (with Applebaum); Best of Schubert; Best of Beethoven; Best of Johann Strauss, Jr Waltzes, 1992; Best of Vivaldi, 1994. *Recordings:* Music Minus One, T.P. 1, 2, 3, 4, 5, 6; Paganiniana, Pleyel Duets UPC 245. *Publications:* Editor: The Way They Play, Vols. 1-13, 1975-84; Heifetz, 1981; Ysaÿe, 1980; Tartini, 1981. *Address:* 509 Sunset Avenue, Asbury Park, NJ 07712, USA.

PARATORE Anthony, b. 17 June 1946, Boston, Massachusetts, USA. Concert Pianist. *Education:* BM, Boston University, 1966; BM, MS, Juilliard School, New York, 1970. *Debut:* Metropolitan Museum, 1973. *Career:* Guest appearances with New York Philharmonic, Chicago, San Francisco, Detroit, Washington National, Denver, Indianapolis, Atlanta, San Diego, BBC London, Vienna Philharmonic, Berlin Philharmonic, Vienna Symphony, RAI Orchestra, Nouvel Philharmonique, Warsaw Philharmonic, Amsterdam Philharmonic, Rotterdam Philharmonic; Norwegian Chamber Orchestra, English Chamber Orchestra, Prague Chamber Orchestra, Bavarian Radio Orchestra; Festival appearances (mainly Mozart), Salzburg, Berlin, Lucerne, Istanbul, Adelaide Festival in Australia and Spoleto; PBS television special, The Paratores, Two Brothers, Four Hands; NPR radio, All Things Considered, and A Note To You. *Recordings:* CBS Masterworks; Pictures at an Exhibition (Mussorgsky); Opera Festival for Four Hands; Also recordings for New World Records, Schwann Musica Mundi, and Orion; CBS Masterworks Mendelsshon Concerti for two pianos and orchestra; Koch International, Variations for Four Hands; Koch International, Schoenburg Chamber Symphony, op. 9; Stravinsky, Sacred du Printemps, Koch International; Ravel, Bolero, Ma Mere L'Oye, Rapsodie Espagnole, Koch International; Gershwin, Rhapsody in Blue, Concerto in F, Koch International. *Contributions to:*

Keyboard Classics; Clavier. *Honour:* 1st Prize, Munich International Music Competition, 1974. *Address:* 142 Chilton Street, Belmont, MA 02178, USA.

PARATORE Joseph D, b. 19 Mar 1948, Boston, Massachusetts, USA. Concert Pianist. *Education:* BM, Boston University, 1970; Master of Science, Juilliard School, 1972. *Debut:* Metropolitan Museum of Art, December 1973. *Career:* Guest appearances: with New York Philharmonic, Chicago Symphony, San Francisco, Detroit, Indianapolis, Atlanta, Washington National, Denver, San Diego, BBC, Vienna Philharmonic, Berlin Philharmonic, Vienna Symphony, RAI, Nouvel Philharmonique, Warsaw Philharmonic, Amsterdam Philharmonic, Rotterdam Philharmonic; Norwegian Chamber Orchestra, English Chamber Orchestra, Prague Chamber Orchestra, Bavarian Radio Orchestra, Festival appearances: Lucerne, Istanbul, Adelaide Festival, Australia; Salzburg, Berlin, Spoleto - mostly Mozart; Television: WGBH-PBS Television Special The Paratores, Two Brothers/Four Hands; Radio: NPR All Things Considered and A Note to You. *Recordings:* CBS Masterworks: Mussourgsky - Pictures at an Exhibition and Opera Festival for Four Hands; New World Records - Schwann Musica Mundi, Orion; CBS Masterworks, Mendelssohn Concerti for Two Pianos and Orchestra; Koch International, Variations for Four Hands; Schoenburg, Chamber Symphony, op. 9; Stravinsky, Sacred du Printemps, Koch International; Ravel, Bolero, Ma Mere L'Oye, Rapsodie Espagnole, Koch International; Gershwin, Rhapsody in Blue, Concerto in F, Koch International. *Contributions to:* Keyboard Classics - The Art of Transcribing Mussorgsky; Clavier Magazine - Master Class - Ravel Ma Mere L'Oye. *Honour:* First Prize, Munich International Music Competition, 1974. *Address:* 142 Chilton Street, Belmont, MA 02178, USA.

PARDEE Margaret, b. 10 May 1920, Valdosta, Georgia, USA. Violinist; Violist; Teacher of violin and viola. m. Daniel R Butterly, 5 July 1944. *Education:* Diploma, 1940, Post Graduate Diploma, 1942, Institute of Musical Art, Juilliard School; Diploma, Juilliard Graduate School, 1945; Studied with Sascha Jacobsen, 1937-42, Albert Spalding, 1942-44, Louis Persinger, 1944-46, and Ivan Galamian, 1948-56. *Debut:* New York Town Hall, New York, 1952. *Career:* Toured as soloist and in String Quartet and Duo recitals as violinist and violist, USA; Soloist, with Symphony Orchestra; Concert Master, Great Neck Symphony, New York, 1954-85; Faculty Member and Director, Meadowmount School of Music, 1956-85, 1988-; Faculty Member, Juilliard School, 1942-; Adjunct Professor, Queens College, New York City, 1978-, State University of New York, Purchase, New York, 1980-; Jury Member, National and International Competitions; Faculty Member, Estherwood Festival and School, Dobbs Ferry, New York, 1984-85, Estherwood Festival and Summer School, Oneonta State University, 1986; Faculty, Bowdoin Summer Music Festival, Bowdoin College, Brunswick, Maine, 1987; Taught in Conservatory of Music of the Simon Bolivar Orchestra in Caracas, Venezuela, 1988, 1989; Invited to teach in Caracas, Venezuela for Municipal Orchestra and Symphonica, 1991, 1992, 1993; On Faculty at Killington Chamber Music Festival, Killington, 1993. *Honour:* Received Andres Bello Primiera Clase Award for Education, Caracas, 1993. *Address:* c/o Juilliard School, Lincoln Center Plaza, New York, NY 10023, USA.

PARIK Ivan, b. 1955, Czechoslovakia. Conductor. *Education:* Studied with Hans Swarowsky in Vienna and with Arvid Jansons and Kurt Masur in Weimar; Munich Staatsoper with Wolfgang Sawallisch. *Career:* Has appeared with leading orchestras in Czechoslovakia and elsewhere in Eastern Europe; Conductor at Ostrava Opera from 1980, leading works by Mozart, Verdi, Puccini, Weber, Gounod, Wagner, Bizet, Strauss, Shostakovich and Czech composers; Guest conductor at Vienna Volksoper, notably with The Bartered Bride, Die Entführung, Die Zauberflöte and Dvořák's Jacobin; Guest appearance in Dresden with Rusalka and Lohengrin; Bilbao and Prague with Così fan Tutte;

Conducted Rigoletto at Gars am Kamp, Austria, 1992; Musical Director of the Klagenfurt Opera from 1992; Concert engagements in works by Mozart, Schubert, Berlioz, Brahms, Dvořák, Janáček, Debussy, Stravinsky and Strauss. *Address:* c/o Pragokoncert, Maltezske nam 1, 118 13 Prague 1, Czech Republic.

PÂRIS Alain, b. 22 Nov 1947, Paris, France. Conductor. m. Marie-Stella Abdul Ahad, 23 June 1973. *Education:* Licence in Law, Paris, 1969; studied piano with Bernadette Alexandre-Georges, Ecriture with Georges Dandelot; Conducting with Pierre Dervaux (Licence de concert, Ecole Normale de Musique, 1967), Louis Fourestier, Paul Paray. *Debut:* 1969. *Career:* Guest Conductor, with major French orchestras including, Orchestre de Paris, Orchestre National, Orchestre de Lyon, Toulouse, Strasbourg; performed with various orchestras abroad including, Dresdner Philharmonic, Philharmonie Slovaque, Orchestre de la Suisse Romande, Philharmonia Hungarica, Philharmonie George Enesco (Bucarest), Orchestra de la BRT (Brussels), Milan, Germany, Luxembourg, Greece, Iraq, etc; Assistant Conductor, Orchestre du Capitole de Toulouse, 1976-77; Associate Conductor, 1983-84, Permanent Conductor, 1984-87, Opéra du Rhin, Strasbourg; Producer, Musical Broadcasts for French Radio, 1971-; Professor of Conducting, Strasbourg Conservatory, 1986-89. *Publications:* Dictionnaire des interprètes et de l'interprétation musicale, Paris, Robert Laffont ed, 1982, 4th edition, 1994; Spanish Translation, Turner ed, Madrid, 1989; German Translation, Bärenreiter/dtv, Kassel-Munich, 1991; Les Livrets d'opéra, Paris, Robert Laffont, ed, 1991; editor, French edition of the New Oxford Companion to Music (Dictionnaire encyclopedique de la musique, Robert Laffont, 1988) and Baker's Biographical Dictionary of Musicians (Robert Laffont, 1994). *Contributions to:* Encyclopaedia Universalis; Retz; Quid; Scherzo; Courrier musical de France. *Honours:* Licence de concert. Ecole Normale de Musique, Paris, 1967; 1st Prize, concours international de Besancon, 1968. *Membership:* Société Française de Musicologie. *Hobby:* Tennis. *Address:* 33 rue de Constantinople, 75008 Paris, France.

PARISOT Aldo (Simoes), b. 30 Sept 1920, Natal, Brazil, Cellist. *Education:* Studied with Thomazzo Babini and with Ibere Gomes Grosso; Further study at Yale University. *Debut:* With the Boston Sumphony at the Berkshire Music Center, 1947. *Career:* Principal cellist, Pittsburg Symphony 1949-50; Tours to Europe, Asia, Africa, South America and throughout the USA from 1948; Plays solo works by Bach and the sonatas of Brahms and Beethoven in recital; Joined faculty of Peabody Conservatory 1956-58, Yale University 1958; Mannes College 1962-66, New England Conservatory 1966-70; Music Director of Also Parisot International Cello Course and Competition in Brazil, 1977; Artist-in-residence at the Banff Center for the Arts, Canada, 1981-83; Has given the premieres of works by Quincy Porter, Villa-Lobos (concerto no 2, 1955), Claudio Santoro (Concerto, 1963), Leon Kirchner (Concerto for violin, cello and orchestra, 1960), Alvin Etler (Concerto, 1971), Yehudi Wyner (De novo, 1971) and Donald Martino.

PARKER Jon Kimura, b. 25 Dec 1959, Vancouver, British Columbia, Canada. Concert Pianist. *Education:* Doctor of Musical Arts, Juilliard School, 1989; Master's Music, Juilliard School, 1983; Teachers: Adele Marcus, Lee Kum-Sing, Edward Parker, Marek Jablonski. *Debut:* New York, May, 1984; London, Dec. 1984. *Career:* Performed with London Symphony, London Philharmonic, Toronto Symphony, Cleveland Orchestra, Minnesota Orchestra, Los Angeles Philharmonic, Scottish National Orchestra, Berlin Radio Symphony, NHK Orchestra, (Japan), all Canadian Orchestras; Recital Tours in Europe, Canada, USA, South America, Far East and Australia; Featured on CBC-TV documentary show The Journal, Local Boy Makes Great, 1985; Command Performance for Queen Elizabeth II and Prime Minister of Canada, 1984. *Recordings:* Tchaikovsky Piano Concerto No. 1, Prokofiev Piano Concerto No. 3 with André Previn and Royal

Philharmonic Orchestra, 1986, Label: Telarc; Solo Piano Music of Chopin, 1987, Label: Telarc. *Honours:* 1st Prize and Princess Mary Gold Medal, Leeds International Piano Competition, 1984; numerous other first prizes in Competitions in Canada, USA and Chile. *Hobbies:* Old Jazz Recordings; Producing Home Videos with original plots. *Current Management:* Harrison/Parrott Ltd, North America; ICM Artists Ltd, Japan, Kambara. *Address:* c/o ICM Artists Ltd, 40 West 57 Street, New York, NY 10019, USA.

PARKER Moises, b. 1945, Las Villas, Cuba. Singer (Tenor). *Education:* Studied in Munich, at Juilliard School and Verdi Conservatory Milan; Teachers included Tito Gobbi, Richard Holm and Hermann Reutter. *Debut:* New York City Opera 1976 as Don José. *Career:* Sang at Strasbourg Opera 1978-80 as Tamino, Hoffmann and Ratansen in Roussel's Padmavati; Season 1981-82 with Welsh National Opera and Scottish Opera as Rodolfo and Alvaro; Brunswick and Augsburg 1982-83 as Don José and Alvaro; Deutsche Oper Berlin as Pinkerton; Sang Otello at Coburg 1984 and at Stuttgart and Klagenfurt 1989; Theater des Westens Berlin 1988-89, as Gershwin's Porgy, Wurzburg 1990 as Bacchus; Member of Kiel Opera from 1988, notably as Turiddu in Cavalleria Rusticana and Win-San-Lui in Leoni's L'Oracolo, 1990; Concert repertoire includes Messiah, Beethoven's Ninth and the Missa Solemnis, Elijah, Rossini's Stabat Mater and Messe Solennelle, Verdi's Requiem. *Honours:* Prize winner at 1974 Voci Verdiane Competition at Bussetto, 1975 Francisco Vinas at Barcelona. *Address:* c/o Buhnen des Landeshaupt, Rathausplatz, 2300 Kiel, Germany.

PARKER Robert LeRoy, b. 4 Sept 1929, Lovington, New Mexico, USA. Professor of Musicology; Graduate Music Dean. *Education:* BA, Baylor University, 1952; MMus 1956, PhD, Musicology 1963, The University of Texas. *Career:* Assistant Professor of Music, Corpus Christi University, 1956-60; Professor of Music, Houston Baptist University, 1963-73; Assistant Dean 1979-, Professor of Musicology 1973-, University of Miami School of Music. *Publications:* Editor, Collected Works of Adam Rener (c 1485-c 1520) Vols I & II, 1964, 1976; Carlos Chávez: Mexico's Modern-day Orpheus, 1983; Officia Paschalia (1539), new edition, 1988. *Contributions to:* Latin American Music Review; Pauta; Heterfonía; American Music; Dance Chronicle. *Hobbies:* Travel; Tennis; Woodworking. *Address:* 1540 San Remo Ave, Apt 6, Coral Gables, Florida 33146, USA.

PARKER Roger, b. 2 Aug 1951, London, England. Writer on Music. *Education:* Studied at London University with Margaret Bent and Pierluigi Petrobelli. *Career:* Professor at Cornell University 1982; Coordinating Editor of Donizetti Critical Edition 1988; Founding Co-editor of the Cambridge Opera Journal 1989. *Publications:* Critical Edition of Verdi's Opera with Nabucco, 1987; (with A Groos) Giacomo Puccini; La Bohème, 1986 and Reading Opera, 1989; Studies in Early Verdi, 1989; (with C Abbate) Analyzing Opera: Verdi and Wagner, 1989; Articles on Verdi and his Operas in The New Grove Dictioonary of Opera, 4 volumes, 1992. *Address:* Faculty of Music, St Aldate's, Oxford OX1 1DB, England.

PARKER William, b. 5 Aug 1943, Butler, Pennsylvania, USA. Concert and Opera Singer (Baritone). *Education:* BA, Germanic Languages and Literatures, Princeton University; Studied with Pierre Bernac, Rosa Ponselle and John Bullock. *Recordings:* 3 recordings of American Songs for New World Records; EMI, Poulenc: Mélodies; Centaur Records: Songs of Brahms and Copland; Harmonia Mundi, USA; Pergolesi La Serva Padrona, Uberto, 1987; Connecticut Early Music Festival with Igor Kipnis. *Honours:* First Prize in Competitions in Paris, 1971, Barcelona, 1975, Baltimore, 1970; Opera Competition, Toulouse, 1970; First Prize, US National Association of Teachers of Singing, 1970; First Place, American International Music Competition for Singers. *Current Management:* CAMI: Elizabeth Crittenden, New York. *Address:* 290 6 Avenue 6-C, New York, NY 10014, USA.

PARKIN Simon, b. 3 Nov 1956, Manchester, England. Composer; Pianist; Teacher. *Education:* Yehudi Menuhin School, 1967-74; MusB, University of Manchester, 1977; Graduate, Royal Northern College of Music, 1978; Associate, Royal College of Music, 1973. *Career:* Performances in St. John's, Smith Square, London, Wigmore Hall and Queen Elizabeth Hall, London; Performances as duo-partner in Budapest, Liszt Academy and Berlin (Otto Braun Saal); Resident Pianist at ISM, LDSM and Lenk courses; Compositions performed in London, New York, Frankfurt, Germany; Broadcasts on German radio; Teaching Posts: Royal Northern College of Music; Yehudi Menuhin School. *Compositions:* Ted Spiggot and the Killer Beans (Opera); Le Chant des Oiseaux (choral work); Laughter and Tears (Requiem, choir and orchestra); Piano trio, string quartet, chamber concerto; Composer of several sonatas for solo instruments and piano. *Honours:* Recipient various university and college prizes; Morley College Centenary Concerto Prize for chamber concerto. *Hobbies:* Reading; Writing; Giraffes. *Address:* 39 Crompton Road, Burnage, Manchester M19 2QT, England.

PARKINSON Del R, b. 6 Aug 1948, Blackfoot, Idaho, USA. Pianist; University Professor. m. Glenna M. Christensen, 6 Aug 1986. *Education:* BM, 1971, MM, 1972, Performers Certificate 1972, DM, 1975, Indiana University; Postgraduate Diploma, The Juilliard School, 1977; Fulbright-Hays grant for graduate study in London, England, 1974-75. *Debut:* London, Wigmore Hall, 1976; New York, Carnegie Recital Hall, 1981. *Career:* Concerto appearances with Chicago Civic Orchestra, Utah Symphony, Boise Philharmonic and Guadalajara Symphony; Solo recitals in USA, England and Mexico; Chamber music in USA and aboard Royal Viking Cruise Line. Teaching career: Assistant Professor, Furman University, 1975-76; Piano Co-ordinator, Ricks College, 1977-85; Professor, Boise State University, 1985-; Joined the American Piano Quartet, 1989, which has since performed through USA and Europe. *Recording:* American Piano Quartet, 1992. *Publication:* Selected Works for Piano and Orchestra in One Movement, 1821-53, Indiana University Doctoral Dissertation, 1975. *Contributions to:* Record review for Journal of American Liszt Society (Charles Koechlin piano music) 1984. *Honours:* Winner of concerto competitions in Indiana, Illinois and Ohio, 1973; Winner, New Era International Young Artists Competition, 1975; Finalist, Gina Bachauer International Piano Competition, 1976; Distinguished Teaching Award, Ricks College, 1984; Distinguished Teaching Award, Boise State University, 1991. *Address:* Music Department, Boise State University, Boise, ID 83725, USA.

PARKINSON John Alfred, b. 2 Feb 1920, Croydon, England. Music Librarian. m. Marie Hupka, 3 sons. *Education:* Jesus College, Cambridge, 1939-40, 1946-49; MA (Cantab); Royal Academy of Music, 1945-46; ARCM. *Career:* Director of Music, Trinity School, Croydon, 1949-64; Research Assistant, British Library, 1964-81; Since Retirement, engaged as a Dealer in Antiquarian Music. *Publications:* Editor: Oxford Book of Carols, 1964; Renaissance Song Book, 1971; Index to the Vocal Works of T A Arne and M Arne, 1972; Polyglot Dictionary of Musical Terms, 1978; Victorian Music Publishers, 1990; Many Editions of renaissance and baroque vocal and instrumental music including works by Arne, Boismortier, Handel and Senallie. *Contributions to:* The New Grove Dictionary; Musical Times; Music and Letters; Monthly Musical Record; New Grove Dictionary of Opera, 1992. *Honour:* C B Oldman Prize for musical bibliography, 1990. *Membership:* Conductor, British Museum Choral Society, 1965-90. *Hobby:* Victorian Music Covers. *Address:* 130 Farley Road, Selsdon, South Croydon CR2 7NF, England.

PARKINSON Paul Andrew, b. 26 Mar 1954, Wallasey, Cheshire, England. Composer. *Education:* Royal Academy of Music, 1973-78; Mendelssohn Scholar, 1978-79; Studies with Nadia Boulanger, Paris, France, and Peter Racine Fricker, Santa Barbara, California, USA. *Career:* Lecturer, Royal Academy of Music, London, England, 1979-83; Composer-in-

Residence, Lincolnshire and Humberside Arts, 1984; Freelance Composer/Lecturer, 1985-. *Compositions:* Oboe Sonata, 1976; Sinfonia for Orchestra, 1977; String Trio, 1977; Wind Quintet, 1978; Four Love Songs, 1979; Transit One (flute, oboe and piano), 1979; Dance Poems for Chamber Orchestra, 1982; String Quartet, 1982; Capriccio (harp), 1983; Dream Gold (cantata), 1984; Prayer Before Birth, 1984; Brass Reflections, 1984; Three Donne Songs, 1985; Hymn, 1985; Piano Sonata, 1986; Passion for Double String Orchestra, 1989; Release for Orchestra, 1991. *Address:* 37e Allen Road, Stoke Newington, London N16 8RX, England.

PARNAS Leslie, b. 22 Nov 1932, St. Louis, Missouri, USA. Concert Cellist; Professor of Music. m. Ingeburge Parnas, 2 sons. *Education:* Curtis Institute of Music, Philadelphia, with Piatigorsky. *Debut:* New York Town Hall, 1959. *Career:* Solo cellist, annual world wide concert tours with leading orchestras; Director Kneisal Hall Summer Music School, Blue Hill, Maine; Teacher at the St. Louis Conservatory of Music, from 1982. *Recordings:* Has recorded for Columbia and Pathé-Marconi records. *Honours:* Pablo Casals Prize, Paris, 1957; Primavera Trophy, Rome, 1959; Prizewinner, International Tchaikovsky Competition, Moscow, 1962. *Memberships:* Chamber Music Society of Lincoln Center, New York. *Hobbies:* Languages; Photography; Tennis. *Address:* c/o Columbia Artists Management, 165 West 57th Street, New York, NY 10019, USA.

PARNELL Andrew, b. 17 Feb 1954, Stockport, Cheshire, England. Organist; Teacher. m. Sally, 31 July 1976, 2 sons, 1 daughter. *Education:* BA, 1975, MA, 1976, PGCE, 1976, Christs College, Cambridge; Associate, 1972, Fellow, 1974, Royal College of Organists. *Career:* Organist, St Albans Abbey, 1976-; Director of Music, St Albans School, 1978-91; Music Master and Choir Director, 1991-; Conductor, St Albans Symphony Orchestra, 1984-; Regular Accompanist for BBC Radio daily service; Director of organ and choral courses. *Compositions:* Editor, I Love All Beauteous Things by Herbert Howells. *Recordings:* Accompanist on In Honour of St Alban; Psalms from St Albans; Anthems by S S Wesley; Continuo Organist on Magnificat, Fayrfax Consort of St Albans; Accompanist for English Music of 20th Century, Carols from St Albans, Berkeley and Elgar; Accompanist and Soloist on A Crown of Light and Christmas at St Albans; Chorus Master on Carmina Burana with L P O Welser-Möst. *Honours:* Fellow, Royal College of Organists. *Hobbies:* Walking; Television. *Address:* 16 Glenferrie Road, St Albans, Hertfordshire, AL1 4JU, England.

PARR Patricia Ann, b. 10 June 1937, Toronto, Canada. Musician (pianist); Educator. 2 sons. *Education:* Curtis Institute of Music, Philadelphia, Pennsylvania, USA; studied piano with Isabelle Vengerova; composition with Gian-Carlo Menotti; Diploma, 1957; Postgraduate studies with Rudolf Serkin. *Debut:* Toronto Symphony age 9. *Career:* Soloist with Philadelphia, Cleveland, Pittsburgh, Toronto Orchestras and others; New York Town Hall debut; Soloist and Chamber musician appeared extensively in Canada and USA; In Trio Concertante toured Australia, 1975 and 1978; Festival appearances include: Marlboro, Stratford, Fontana, Marin County, Festival of the Sound; Founding member, Amici (a chamber ensemble); Faculty: Duqueshe University, 1967-74; University of Toronto, 1974-; Royal Conservatory of Music, 1982-90. *Recordings:* Summit Records with AMICI; Musica Viva Series with Clarinettist Joaquin Valdepenas; Arbor Discs with violinist Lorand Fenyves; CBC records with hornist Eugene Rittich; Centrediscs with Marc Dubois tenor. *Address:* 57 Woodlawn Ave W, Toronto, Ontario, Canada M4V 1G6.

PARRIS Robert, b. 21 May 1924, Philadelphia, Pennsylvania, USA. *Education:* Studied at University of Pennsylvania (MS 1946), with Peter Mennin and William Bergsma at Juilliard (BS 1948), with Ibert and Copland at Berkshire Music Center and with Honegger at the Ecole Normale in Paris. *Career:* Has taught at Washington State College and University of Maryland;

George Washington University, 1963, Professor, 1976-. *Compositions include:* Orchestra: Symphony, 1952; Piano Concerto, 1953; Concerto for 5 kettledrums and orchestra, 1955; Viola Concerto, 1958; Violin Concerto, 1958; Flute Concerto, 1964; Concerto for trombone and chamber orchestra, 1964; Concerto for percussion, violin, cello and piano, 1967; The Phoenix, 1969; The Messengers, 1974; Rite of Passage, 1978; The Unquiet Heart for violin and orchestra, 1981; Chamber Music for orchestra, 1984; Vocal: Night for baritone string quartet and clarinet, 1951; Alas for the Day, cantata, 1954; Hymn for the Nativity for chorus and brass ensemble, 1962; Dreams for soprano and chamber orchestra; Cynthia's Revell's for baritone and piano, 1979; Chamber: 2 String Trios, 1948, 1951; 2 String Quartets, 1951, 1952; Sonata for solo violin, 1965; The Book of Imaginary Dreams, Parts I and II for ensemble, 1972, 1983; Three Duets for electric guitar and amplified harpsichord, 1984. *Honours include:* NEA Grants, 1974, 1975; Commissions from Detroit Symphony Orchestra and the Contemporary Music Forum. *Address:* c/o ASCAP, ASCAP Building, One Lincoln Plaza, New York, NY 10023, USA.

PARRISH Cheryl, b. 6 Nov 1954, Pasadena, Texas, USA. Singer (Soprano). *Education:* Graduated Baylor University, 1977, and studied at Vienna Musikhochschule, 1978-79. *Career:* Has sung at San Francisco Opera from 1983, as Sophie in Rosenkavalier and Werther, and Mozart's Blondchen and Susanna (season 1990-91); Miami Opera, 1987 and 1991, as Ophelia in Hamlet and as Despina; Sang Adele in Die Fledermaus at Toronto, 1987, and San Diego, 1991; Sophie in Der Rosenkavalier at Zurich Opera, 1988, and has guested further at Florence and Santa Fe; Frequent concert appearances. *Address:* c/o San Francisco Opera, War Memorial Opera House, San Francisco, CA 94192, USA.

PARROTT Andrew, b. 10 Mar 1947, Walsall, England. Conductor. *Education:* Merton College Oxford (Director of Music and research into performance practice of early music). *Career:* Formed Taverner Choir at the invitation of Michael Tippett for a 1973 Bath Festival concert; subsequently founded Taverner Consort and Players; Promenade Concert debut 1977 with Monteverdi's Vespers; Guest conductor with English and Scottish Chamber Orchestras, London and Bournemouth Sinfoniettas, the BBC Philharmonic and orchestras in Canada, Czechoslovakia, Holland, Norway, Switzerland, USA and Austria; Conducted world premiere of Judith Weir's A Night at the Chinese Opera for Kent Opera 1987; performances of music by Britten, Nono, Henze, Stravinsky and Varèse; He has been musical assistant to Tippett and a member of Electric Phoenix. Season 1992/93 Figaro for Opera North, Monteverdi's Orfeo in Boston, Die Zauberflöte at Covent Garden (debut), the premiere of a symphony by Vladimir Godár and music by Tippett in Norway. *Recordings:* Orchestral music, opera and major choral masterpieces for EMI and other companies including CDs of Bach B Minor Mass and St Johns Passion, Monteverdi Vespers, Purcell Dido and Aeneas, Handel Carmelite Vespers, Vivaldi concertos; Choral music by Gabrieli, Josquin, Mozart, Schütz, Tallis and Taverner. *Contributions to:* Early Music, New Oxford Companion to Music, 1983, New Oxford Book of Carols (co-editor), 1992. *Address:* c/o Allied Artists Ltd., 42 Montpelier Square, London SW7 1JZ, England.

PARROTT Ian, b. 5 Mar 1916, London, England. Professor of Music (retired). m. Elizabeth Olga Cox, 2 sons. *Education:* Royal College of Music, 1932-34; New College, Oxford University, 1934-37; Associate, Royal College of Organists, 1936; DMus, Oxford University, 1940; MA, 1941. *Compositions include:* The Black Ram (opera), 1957; Several orchestral works including 5 symphonies; Chamber music and songs; Ceredigion for Harp, 1962; Flamingoes (song); Soliloquy and Dance (harp); Welsh Folk Song Mass, 1973-74; Duo Fantastico No.2 for violin and piano, 1990. *Recordings include:* Contemporary Welsh Choral Music, 1969; Contemporary Music for Harp and Flute, 1969-70;

Contemporary Welsh Chamber Music, 1971; Trombone Concerto, 1974. *Publications include:* Elgar, 1971; The Music of Rosemary Brown, 1978; Cyril Scott and His Piano Music, 1991. *Contributions to:* Various professional journals. *Honours include:* 1st Prize for Luxor, Royal Philharmonic Society, 1949; Harriet Cohen International Musicology Medal, 1966. *Memberships include:* Vice-President, Elgar Society; Vice-President, Peter Warlock Society. *Address:* Henblas Abermad, near Aberystwyth, Dyfed SY23 4ES, Wales.

PARSONS Geoffrey Penwill, b. 15 June 1929, Sydney, Australia. Concert Accompanist. *Education:* Canterbury High School, Sydney; State Conservatorium of Music (with Winifred Burston) Sydney. *Career:* First tour of Australia 1948; Arrived England 1950. Has made 29 tours of Australia; Made 25th Tour of Australia 1983; Has accompanied many of world's greatest singers and instrumentalists, including Elisabeth Schwarzkopf, Victoria de Los Angeles, Janet Baker, Jessye Norman, Olaf Bär, Thomas Hampson, in 42 countries of world on all continents. Master Classes: South Bank Summer Festival 1977 and 1978; Sweden annually; Austria 1985; Australia 1985; USA 1987; 1990, Geoffrey Parsons and Friends, International Song Recital Series, Barbican Concert Opening Season 1982, 1983, 1984. *Honours:* Hon. RAM 1975; OBE 1977; Hon. GSM 1983; FRCM, 1988; AO, 1990. *Address:* 176 Iverson Road, London NW6 2HL, England.

PÄRT Arvo, b. 11 Sept 1935, Paide, Estonia. Composer. *Education:* Studied at the Tallinn Conservatory, with Heino Eller. *Career:* Music Division of Estonian Radio 1958-67; Settled in West Berlin 1981. *Compositions:* Orchestral: Nekrolog 1959; 3 Symphonies: 1963, 1966, 1971; Perpetuum Mobile 1963; Collage on the Theme B-A-C-H 1964; Pro et Contra for cello and orchestra 1966; Wenn Bach Bienen gezüchtet hätte 1977; Cantus in Memory of Benjamin Britten 1977; Tabula Rasa, for 2 violins, strings and prepared piano 1977; Introductory Prayers for string orchestra, 1992; Fratres for String Orchestra, 1980; Festina lente, for String Orchestra, 1989; Summa, for String Orchestra, 1991. Vocal: Our Garden, cantata, 1959; Credo, for Solo Piano, Choir and Orchestra, 1968; Missa Sillabica, 1977; Summa, for Vocal Quartet, 1978; De Profundis, for Mens Voices and Organ, 1981; St. John Passion, 1981-82; Stabat Mater, for Vocal and String Trios, 1985; Te Deum, for 3 Choirs, String Orchestra and Tape, 1985; Es Sang for langen Jahren, for Alto, Violin and Viola, 1985; Miserere, for 5 solo voices, Chorus and Orchestra, 1989; The Beatitudes for chorus and organ, 1989; Berlin Mass, for chorus and string orchestra, 1990; Statuit ei Dominus 1990; Beatus Petronuis for 2 choruses and 2 organs 1990; Mother of God and Virgin for Chorus 1990. Chamber Music: Quintettino, for Wind Quintet, 1964; Arbos, for 7 Wind Instruments, 1977; Fratres, for Violin and Piano, 1977; Fratres, for 4-12 Cello, 1981; Fratres, for String Quartet, 1982; Summa, String Quartet, 1991; Psalom, String Quartet, 1991; Sarah was ninety years old, for 3 voices, percussion and organ, 1990; Mirror in Mirror, for Violin and Piano, 1978; Magnificat Antiphons 1988; Magnificat for chorus 1989. Adagio, for Piano Trio, 1992; Piano and Organ Music. *Memberships:* Ehrendoktor of the Tallinn Conservatory; Member of the Swedish Royal Music Academy. *Address:* c/o Universal Edition (London) Ltd, Warwick House, 9 Warwick Street, London W1R 5RA, England.

PARTRIDGE Ian (Harold), b. 12 June 1938, England. Concert Singer (Tenor). m. Ann Glover, 1959, 2 sons. *Education:* Chorister, New College, Oxford; Music scholar, Clifton College; Royal College of Music; LGSM, singing & teaching, Guildhall School of Music. *Career:* Began as piano accompanist, although sang tenor in Westminster Cathedral Choir, 1958-62; Full-time concert singer, 1963-; Performs in England and abroad with many leading conductors including Stokowski, Boult, Giulini, Boulez, Colin Davis. Opera debut at Covent Garden, Iopas in Berlioz' Les Troyens, 1969; Title role, Britten's St. Nicolas, Thames Television, 1977. *Recordings:* Over 100 including: Schubert, Die Schöne

Müllerin; Schumann, Dichterliebe; Beethoven, An die ferne Geliebte; Vaughan-Williams, On Wenlock Edge; Warlock, The Curlew; Fauré & Duparc songs; Britten, Serenade, Winter Words. Innumerable radio broadcasts, many TV appearances. Governor, Clifton College, 1981- . *Honours:* Prix Italia, 1977; CBE 1991. *Hobbies:* Bridge; Horse racing; Theatre; Cricket. *Address:* 127 Pepys Road, London SW20 8NP, England.

PARTRIDGE Jennifer, b. 17 June 1942, New Malden, Surrey, England. Accompanist. m. David Smith. *Education:* Guildhall School of Music; LRAM. *Career:* Recitals, Concerts, TV and Radio appointments with singers and instrumentlists; Duo with brother Ian Partridge. *Recordings include:* Music all Powerful, with Purcell Consort; Vaughan Williams Songs; Die schöne Müllerin; Dichterliebe; Schubert Lieder; An Album of English Songs; French Songs; English Part Songs; Schubert Part Songs with Baccholian Singers. *Honour:* Eric Rice Memorial Prize for Accompanists, Overseas League, 1964. *Hobbies:* Dogs; Sport. *Address:* 50 Howberry Road, Thornton Heath, Surrey, CR4 8HY, England.

PASATIERI Thomas, b. 20 Oct 1945, New York, USA. Composer. *Education:* Studied with Giannini and Persichetti at Juilliard and with Darius Milhaud at the Aspen Music School. *Career:* Freelance composer 1965- ; Commissions from National Educational Television, Houston Grand Opera, Baltimore Opera, Michigan Opera Theater, University of Arizona, Evelyn Lear and Thomas Stewart. *Compositions:* Operas: The Women, Aspen 1965; La Divine, New York, 1966; Padrevia, New York, 1967; The Trial of Mary Lincoln, NET 1972; Black Widow, Seattle, 1972; The Seagull, Houston, 1974; Signor Deluso, Vienna 1974; The Penitentes, Aspen 1974; Inez de Castro, Baltimore, 1976; Washington Square, Detroit, 1976; Three Sisters, 1979; Before Breakfast, New York, 1980; The Goose Girl, Fort Worth, 1981; Maria Elena, Tucson 1983; Invocations for orchestra, 1968; Heloise and Abelard for soprano, baritone and piano, 1971; Rites de passage for low voice and chamber orchestra, 1974; Three Poems of James Agee, 1974; Far from Love for soprano, clarinet and piano, 1976; Permit me Voyage, cantata 1976; Mass for 4 solo voices, chorus and orchestra, 1983; Piano music; 400 songs. *Address:* ASCAP, ASCAP Building, One Lincoln Plaza, New York, NY 10023, USA.

PASCAL Claude, b. 19 Feb 1921, Paris, France. Composer; Critic; Director of Studies. m. Gwendolen Rooke, 1 daughter. *Education:* Conservatoire National Supérieur de Musique, Paris. *Career:* Director of Studies, Conservatoire National Supérieur de Musique, Paris. *Compositions:* Concertos for cello and orchestra, piano and chamber orchestra, harp and orchestra; Octet for wind; 2 Sonatas and Sonatina for violin and piano; Suite and Sonatina for piano; Saxophone quartet; Framboise and Amandine, Twins in Space, children's opera; Patchwork, ballet for ensemble of 12 saxophones, 1992. *Recordings:* 2nd Sonata for violin and piano; Saxophone quartet; Orchestration with Marcel Bitsch of Bach's Art of Fugue. *Contributions to:* Le Figaro, 1969-79. *Address:* 10 rue Darcet, 75017 Paris, France.

PASCANU Alexandru, b. 3 May 1920, Bucharest, Romania. Composer; Professor. *Education:* Faculty of Law; Academy of Music. *Debut:* 1947. *Career:* Assistant, Theory and Solfeggi, 1952-55, Lecturer, Score Reading and Theory of Instruments, 1955-60, Reader, Harmony and Orchestration, 1960-66, Professor of Harmony, 1966-, Music Conservatoire of Bucharest; Councillor Direction Creative People, 1952; Councillor, Electrecord, 1971-. *Compositions:* Choral Music (Old Laments, Kyndya, Festum, Hibernum); Chamber Music (Suite for Piano, Nocturnes for Piano, Horn, Cello, Balade for Clarinet); Symphonic Music: Poem of the Carpatians; In Memoriam; Black Sea; Toccata for Orchestra. *Recordings:* Suite, Diptich for string orchestra; Pro Humanitate. *Publications:* Principles of Harmony (in collaboration); About the Musical Instruments, 3 editions, 1959, 66, 80; Armonia (Harmony), 2 volumes, 1974, 75, 77, 82. *Contributions to:* Muzica;

Contemporanul; Cronica; Essays; Educational Broadcasting cycles. *Hobbies:* Humourist; Photography. *Address:* str. 0, Cocarascu 102, 78182 Bucharest, Romania.

PASCHER Hartmut, b. 1956, Vienna, Austria. Violist. *Education:* Studied at the Vienna Academy of Music. *Career:* Member of the Franz Schubert Quartet from 1979; Many concert appearances in Europe, the USA and Australia, including the Amsterdam Concertgebouw, the Vienna Musikverein and Konzerthaus, the Salle Gaveau Paris and the Sydney Opera House; Visits to Zurich, Geneva, Basle, Berlin, Hamburg, London, Rome, Rotterdam, Madrid and Copenhagen; Festival engagements include Salzburg, Wiener Festwochen, Prague Spring, Schubertiade at Hohenems, the Schubert Festival at Washington DC and the Belfast and Istanbul Festivals; Tours of Australasia, USA; Frequent concert tours of Britain: Frequent appearances at the Wigmore Hall and Cheltenham Festival; Teacher at the Graz Musikhochschule; Masterclasses at the Royal Northern College of Music and at Lake District Summer Music. *Recordings include:* Schubert's Quartet in G, D877; Complete quartets of Dittersdorf; Mozart: String quartet in D, K575, String quartet in B Flat, K589, Tschaikowsky string quartets No 1 and 3 op. 11 D major and op. 30 E flat minor. *Address:* Unit 2, 39 Tadema Road, London SW10 0PY, England.

PASCOE John, b. 1949, Bath, England. Artistic Director and Founder of Bath and Wessex Opera. *Debut:* Designed Julius Caesar for English National Opera, (also seen in San Francisco, Geneva, the Metropolitan and television), 1979. *Career:* Designed Lucrezia Borgia at Covent Garden and Alcina at Sydney, both with Joan Sutherland, Tosca for Welsh National Opera, 1980; As Producer/Designer, La Bohème in Belfast, Solomon Goettingen Festival, 1984; Producer and Designer, Rameau's Platée in Spoleto Festival USA (also seen in BAM, New York), Designer, Orlando at San Francosco and Chicago, Così fan Tutte in Dallas and Anna Bolena with Joan Sutherland in Toronto, Chicago, Detroit, Houston and San Francisco, 1985/86; Designer, Amahl and the Night Visitors at Covent Garden and Norma in Santiago, 1987; Producer and Designer, Anna Bolena at Covent Garden and Norma in Los Angeles and Detroit, both with Joan Sutherland, 1988; Producer and Designer, La Bohème in Bath, Designed Tosca in Nice, Apollo and Hyacinthus in Cannes Festival, Madrid, Paris, 1992; Producer and Designer, La Traviata in Bath, Designer, Anna Bolena in Washington DC, 1993. *Honours include:* Evening Standard Award for Julius Caesar, 1979. *Address:* c/o Atholl Still Ltd, 80-86 Westrow Street, London SE19 3AF, England.

PASCOE Keith, b. 1959, England. Violinist. *Career:* Founder member of the Britten Quartet, debut concert at the Wigmore Hall, 1987; Quartet in Residence at the Dartington Summer School, 1987, with quartets by Schnittke; Season 1988-89 in the Genius of Prokofiev series at Blackheath and BBC Lunchtime Series at St John's Smith Square; South Bank appearances with the Schoenberg/Handel Quartet Concerto conducted by Neville Marriner, concerts with the Hermann Prey Schubertiade and collaborations with the Alban Berg Quartet in the Beethoven Plus series; Tour of South America 1988, followed by Scandinavian debut; Season 1989-90 with debut tours of Holland, Germany, Spain, Austria, Finland; Tours from 1990 to the Far East, Malta, Sweden, Norway: Schoenberg/Handel Concerto with the Gothenburg Symphony; Festival appearances at Brighton, the City of London, Greenwich, Canterbury, Harrogate, Chester, Spitalfields and Aldeburgh; Collaborations with John Ogdon, Imogen Cooper, Thea King and Lynn Harrell; Formerly resident quartet at Liverpool University; Teaching role at Lake District Summer Music 1989; Universities of Bristol, Hong Kong 1990. *Recordings:* Beethoven Op 130 and Schnittke Quartet no 3 (Collins Classics); Vaughan Williams On Wenlock Edge and Ravel Quartet (EMI); Britten, Prokofiev, Tippett, Elgar and Walton Quartets (Collins Classics); Exclusive contract with EMI from 1991.

Address: c/o Ingpen and Williams Ltd, 14 Kensington Court, London W8 5DN, England.

PASHLEY Anne, b. 5 June 1937, Skegness, England. Singer (Soprano). m. Jack Irons, 1 son, 1 daughter. *Education:* Guildhall School of Music, London. *Career:* Took part as sprinter in 1956 Olympic Games, at Melbourne; Stage debut in Semele, with Handel Opera Society, 1959; Glyndebourne debut 1962, in Die Zauberflöte; Covent Garden debut 1965, as Barbarina in Le Nozze di Figaro; Guest appearances with English National Opera, Scottish Opera, Welsh National Opera and at Edinburgh and Aldeburgh Festivals; Foreign engagements in France, Germany, Portugal, Spain, Belgium Italy, Israel; Leading roles in 8 BBC TV operas and numerous radio broadcasts; New Opera Company, London, in the British premiere of Hindemith's Cardillac (1970). *Recordings include:* La Morte de Cléopâtre, Berlioz; Magnificat, Bach; Albert Herring and Peter Grimes, Britten. *Contribution to:* The Listener. *Membership:* Equity. *Hobbies:* Winemaking; Table Tennis; Tennis; Art Collecting; Interior Design. *Address:* 289 Goldhawk Road, London W12, England.

PASKALIS Kostas, b. 1 Sept 1929, Levadia, Boeotia, Greece. Singer (Baritone). m. Marina Krilovici. *Education:* Studied at the National Conservatory Athens. *Debut:* Athens 1954, as Rigoletto. *Career:* Vienna Staatsoper from 1958, debut as Renato in Un Ballo in Maschera; Tour of North America 1960; Glyndebourne 1964-72, as Macbeth and Don Giovanni; Metropolitan Opera debut 1965, as Don Carlos in La Forza el Destino; Rome Opera 1965-66 as Rigoletto and Posa, in Don Carlos; Salzburg Festival 1966, as Pentheus in the premiere of Henze's The Bassarids; La Scala Milan 1967, as Valentin in Faust; Guest appearances in Leningrad, Kiev, Berlin and Moscow; Sang Nabucco at Brussels 1987; New Jersey Opera 1988, as Don Giovanni; Director of the National Opera of Greece from 1988. *Recordings:* Escamillo in Carmen (HMV); Alfonso in Donizetti's Lucrezia Borgia. *Address:* National Union of Greece, 18-A Harilaou Trikoupi Street, 106 79 Athens, Greece.

PASKUDA Georg, b. 7 Jan 1926, Ratibor, Germany. Singer (Tenor). *Career:* Sang small roles in various German theatres from 1951; Bayreuth Festival from 1959, notably as Froh and Mime; Paris Opéra 1960; Bavarian State Opera Munich from 1960, notably in operas by Strauss, Puccini, Lortzing, Wagner, Verdi and Mozart; Munich 1967, as Don Carlos, and 1986 in the premiere of V.D. Kirchner's Belshazzar. *Recordings:* Parsifal, Tannhäuser and Arabella; Die Frau ohne Schatten; Das Rheingold and Der fliegende Holländer, from Bayreuth. *Address:* c/o Bayerische Staatsoper, Postfach 745, D-8000 Munich 1, Germany.

PASQUIER Bruno, b. 10 Dec 1943, Neuilly-sur-Seine, France. Violist. *Education:* Studied at the Paris Conservatoire 1957-63 with Etienne Ginot and his father, Pierre Pasquier. *Career:* Member of the Bernede Quartet 1963-67; Violist of the Orchestre de la Garde Republicaine and soloist at the Concerts Colonne; Sub-leader (1969) then leader (1972) of the viola section in the orchestra of the Paris Opéra; With Regis Pasquier and Roland Pidoux founded the New Pasquier Trio, 1970; Solo performances with leading orchestras in France and abroad; Professor of Viola and of Chamber Music at the Paris Conservatoire, 1983; Soloist with the Orchestre National de France 1984; Plays a Magini viola, ca 1620. *Address:* Conservatoire National Superieur de Musique, 14 Rue de Madrid, 75008 Paris, France.

PASQUIER Regis, b. 10 Oct 1945, Fontainebleau, France. Violinist. *Education:* Studied at the Paris Conservatoire, gaining first prize in violin and chamber music aged 12; Further study with Isaac Stern. *Career:* Concert tours of Belgium, Holland and Luxembourg 1958; New York recital 1960; Many concerts with leading orchestras in Europe and America; Soloist with the Orchestre National de France, 1977-86; With Bruno

Pasquier and Roland Pidoux formed the New Pasquier Trio, 1970; Sonata recitals with pianist Jean-Claude Pennetier; Concerto repertoire ranges from standard classics to works by Xenakis and Gilbert Amy (Trajectoires); Plays a Montagnana instrument; Professor of Violin and of Chamber Music at the Paris Conservatoire, 1985. *Address:* Conservatoire National Superieur de Musique, 14 Rue de Madrid, 75008 Paris, France.

PASTILLE William, b. 30 Apr 1954, Providence, Rhode Island, USA. Musicologist. m. Janice M. Macaulay, 31 May 1986. *Education:* AB Music, Brown University, 1976; MA Musicology, 1979, PhD Musicology, 1985, Cornell University. *Career:* Visiting Professor of Music History, University of Wisconsin, Madison, 1985-86; Faculty, St John's College, Annapolis, Maryland, 1986-. *Publication:* Ursatz: The Musical Philosophy of Heinrich Schenker, 1985. *Contributions to:* Heinrich Schenker, Anti-Organicist, in 19th-Century Music, 1984; (translation) Franz Schubert: Ihr Bild by Heinrich Schenker, Sonus 6, 1986; Review of Federhofer, Heinrich Schenker, Journal of the American Musicological Society, 1986; Schenker's Brahms, The American Brahms Society Newsletter, 1987; Counterpoint and Free Composition, Theoria, 1988; The Spirit of Musical Technique by Heinrich Schenker (a translation), Theoria, 1988; Music and Morphology: Goethe's Influence on Schenker's Ontology in Schenker Studies, 1990; The Development of the Ursatz in Schenker's Published Works, forthcoming in Trend in Schekerian Research, 1990; Johannes Brahms by Heinrich Schenker, The American Brahms Society Newsletter, 1991. *Honour:* National Endowment for the Humanities Summer Stipend, 1986. *Memberships:* American Brahms Society; American Musicological Society; Society for Music Theory. *Address:* St John's College, PO Box 2800, Annapolis, MD 21404-2800, USA.

PATACHICH Ivan, b. 3 June 1922, Budapest, Hungary. Composer. m. Ibolya Markovics, 10 Nov. 1951, 1 daughter. *Education:* Ferenc Liszt Academy of Musik, 1941-47; Composition: A Siklos; Conducting; J Ferencsik. *Debut:* Opera House, Budapest. *Career:* Musical Director, MAFILM, Budapest, 1952-. *Compositions:* Concerto per Arpa, 1956; Tre pezzi, 1961; Petite Suite, 1961; Theomachia, 1 Act Opera, 1962; Fuente Ovejuna, 3 Act Opera, 1971; Symphonietta Savariansis, 1965; Contorni per Arpe, 1968; Concerto per Violino per Pianoforte, 1969; Concerto per Organo, 1973; Spettri, electronic music, 1974; Ritmi Dispari, 1966; Music of the Bible, Cantata, 1968. *Recordings:* Quartettino per Sassofoni, 1972; Musical Electroalchemy, 1981; Sonata per Zymbalum, 1975; ludi Spaziali, 1986; Funzione Acustica, 1979; Ta Foneenta, 1979; Metamorphosi per Marimba, 1981; On Filmmusic, 1972; MELOS, 1978 Eine neue Notation electronischer Musik. *Honours:* International Electroacoustic Prize, Bourges, 1978; World Youth Festival Prize, Moscow, 1957; Niveau Prize, Hungarian TV, 1972; CIME Grand Prix, France, 1984. *Memberships:* Hungarian Artisjus; Computer Music Association, San Francisco, USA. *Address:* 1016 Budapest, Naphegy tér 9, Hungary.

PATAKI Eva, b. 19 Oct 1941, Budapest, Hungary. Pianist. m. T Batny, 27 Aug 1971. *Education:* Diploma, Concert Performance, Pedagogy, Academy of Music, Budapest; Studied with Carlo Zecchi in Salzburg. *Debut:* Recital, Budapest, 1965. *Career:* Assistant, Mozarteum, Salzburg, 5 years; Coach, Royal Opera, Stockholm, 1967-; Concerts, radio and TV, with Helena Doese, Catarina Ligendza, C-H Ahnsjo, Nicolai Gedda, Gosta Winbergh, others, all over Europe and in Moscow, St Petersburg and other venues, 1967-; Producer, concerts at Royal Opera, Stockholm, 1985-. *Recordings:* Several. *Hobby:* Psychology. *Address:* Artistsekretariat Ulf Tornqvist, Sankt Eriksgatan 100 2 tr, S-113 31 Stockholm, Sweden.

PATCHELL Sue, b. 1948, Montana, USA. Singer (Soprano). *Education:* Studied in Montana and at

University of California t Los Angeles. *Career:* Engaged at Graz Opera, 1974, Gelsenkirchen, 1979-86; Wiesbaden, 1986-, notably as Elsa in Lohengrin, 1988, and Elisabetta in Don Carlos at Wiesbaden Festival, 1990; Hamburg Staatsoper as Tatiana in Eugene Onegin, Barcelona, 1989 and 1990, as Eva and Chrysothemis, Antwerp Opera as Elisabeth in Tannhäuser and Ariadne; Other roles include Marguerite, Mozart's Countess and Donna Elvira, Frau Fluth and Rosalinde; Concert repertoire includes Das Buch mit Sieben Siegeln by Franz Schmidt. *Recordings include:* Das Dunkle Reich by Pfitzner. *Address:* c/o Hessisches Staatstheater, Postfach 3247, 6200 Wiesbaden, Germany.

PATHAK Ashok Pandit, b. 12 Aug 1949, Budha Gaya, India. Traditional Musician. m. 12 Feb 1982, 2 daughters. *Education:* 32 years training in West Bengal in Calcutta - Balram Pathak-Music School on Sitar and Base Sitar; M Mus, Allahabad Music University, 1976-78. *Debut:* Calcutta Music Festival, 1965. *Career:* Solo performances and lectures at major music conferences and festivals throughout India and abroad; Radio and TV appearances in India and abroad 1972-. *Compositions:* Composer of new ragas, such as Gayankali, Kushum Kedara, Hindolbahar, Guorishankara. *Recordings:* Live in Amsterdam, 1986 CD Recording, 1990, Live in Congress Centre, The Hague, Melodical Sitar Recitals. *Publication:* Pathak Gharana's Finger Techniques on Sitar, to be published in 1992. *Contributions to:* Video Text 1991, LIW (Rural Indian work) in Holland. Director of Maharishi Gandharva Veda Music, 1989; Director, Cultural Organisation of Indian Art. *Hobbies:* Photography; Gardening; Music Therapy. *Address:* Van Leeuwenhoekstraat 85, 25 16 GE, The Hague, Holland.

PATON Iain, b. 1960, Scotland. Singer (Tenor). *Education:* Studied at Royal Scottish Academy and with David Keren in London. *Career:* Appearances with Glyndebourne Festival and Touring Opera in Capriccio, Death in Venice and Le Nozze di Figaro (Don Curzio); Sang in Judith Weir's The Vanishing Bridegroom for Scottish Opera at Glasgow and Covent Garden; Season 1992-93 as Pedrillo in Die Entführung and in The Makropoulos Case, season 1993-94 as Vanya in Katya Kabanova, Tamino and the Shepherd in Tristan und Isolde; Sang Leicester in Maria Stuarda for Scottish Opera-Go- Round, 1992; City of Birmingham Touring Opera in Mozart's Zaid; Concert repertoire includes Liszt's Faust Symphony and appearances with Scottish Early Music Consort in Northern Ireland, Germany and Poland; Sang Eurimachos in Dallapiccola's Ulisse for BBC, 1993. *Honours include:* Eric Vertier Award, at Glyndebourne. *Address:* c/o John Coast Ltd, 31 Sinclair Road, London W14 0NS, England.

PATRICK David Michael, b. 8 Dec 1947, Exeter, Devon, England. Concert Organist; Teacher. *Education:* Royal College of Music, 1966-70. *Career:* Concerts in Cathedrals, Abbeys, and parish churches in Great Britain, America and Canada; regular organ recitals on BBC Radio 3, 1972-; Director of Music, St Michaels School, Tawstock, North Devon, 1972-80; Director of Music, Chelmsford Hall School, Eastbourne, Sussex, 1980-85; Music Master, St Bedes School, Eastbourne, Sussex, 1986-; Director of Music, 1990-93. *Recordings:* Duruflé, Suite op 5; Vierne, Symphony No 6, Symphony No 2; Widor, Symphony No 6, Symphony No 4; Parisian Splendour, French virtuoso organ works; Great European Organs, Blackburn Cathedral. *Honours:* Stuart Prize for Organ, 1967; Walford Davies prize for Organ, 1968, Royal College of Music, London. *Membership:* Incorporated Society of Musicians. *Hobby:* Sailing. *Address:* 12, Matford Avenue, Exeter, Devon EX2 4PW, England.

PATTERSON Jeremy (David Kyle), b. 15 June 1934, Solihull, Warwickshire, England. Educator; Conductor; Adjudicator; Examiner; Director. *Education:* Birmingham School of Music, 1954-58; Associate, Violin and Viola Teaching, 1956; Graduate and Qualified Teacher Status, 1957. *Career:* Junior School Generalist Teacher, 1958-

60; Secondary School Specialist Music Teacher, 1960-65; Senior Lecturer, Faculty of Education, Birmingham Polytechnic, 1965-86: PGCE Music in Education Course Director and DipSE Music in Education Course Director; Speaker, Conductor, BBC Radio; Choirmaster, St Mark's, Smethwick, 1958-63; Conductor: Birmingham Anglo-Orthodox Choir, 1963-69, Bromsgrove String Orchestra, 1966-72, Clent Hills Choral Society, 1972-76; Music Director, Birmingham Festival Choral Society, 1969-; Chairman, Birmingham Conservatoire Association, 1986-; Editor, Birmingham Conservatoire Fanfare II magazine; Major commissions and premieres: Gunilla Lowenstein's Music for Strings, 1972, Malcolm Dedman's Christmas Cantata, 1975, Patric Standford's Ancient Verses, 1979, Andrew Downes' The Temple of Solomon, 1980, John Joubert's For the Beauty of the Earth, 1989, Malcolm Carlton's A Gift from a Child, 1990, and Elis Pehkonen's Russian Requiem, 1986, The Harvest of the Sea, 1992, and The First Coming, 1994. *Recording:* Russian Requiem, 1988. *Honours:* Fellowship of Birmingham Conservatoire, 1993. *Membership:* Incorporated Society of Musicians. *Address:* Fishers Castle, Sandy Lane, Harvington, Nr Kidderminster, Worcestershire DY10 4NF, England.

PATTERSON Paul Leslie, b. 15 June 1947, Chesterfield, England. Composer; Educator. m. Hazel Wilson, 1981, 1 daughter, 1 son. *Education:* Royal Academy of Music; FRAM, FRSA, 1980. *Career:* Freelance composer, 1968-; Art Council Composer-in-Association, English Sinfonia, 1969-70; Director, Contemporary Music, Warwick University, 1974-80; Composer-in-residence, SE Arts Association, 1980-82, Bedford School, 1984-85; Professor of Composition, 1970-, Head of Composition/20th Century Music, 1985-, Royal Academy of Music; Artistic Director, Exeter Festival, 1991; Composer-in-residence, 1990-91. *Compositions:* Te Deum, 1988; Symphony, 1990; The Mighty Voice, 1991; Performances widely by leading orchestras, soloists, ensembles, also film & television music. *Publications:* Rebecca, 1968; Trumpet Concerto, 1969; Time Piece, 1972; Kyrie, 1972; Requiem, 1973; Comedy for 5 Winds, 1973; Requiem, 1974; Fluorescences, 1974; Clarinet Concerto, 1976; Cracowian Counterpoints, 1977; Voices of Sleep, 1979; Concerto for Orchestra, 1981; Canterbury Psalms, 1981; Sinfonia, 1982; Mass of the Sea, 1983; Deception Pass, 1983; Duologue, 1984; Mean Time, 1984; Europhony, 1985; Missa Brevis, 1985; Stabat Mater, 1986; String Quartet, Harmonica Concerto, Magnificat & Nunc Dimitus, 1986; Te Deum, 1988; Tonnell of Time, 1988; The End, 1989. *Honours:* Medal of Honour Polish Ministry of Culture, 1986. *Hobbies:* Sailing; Croquet. *Current Management:* Sykes. *Address:* 31 Cromwell Avenue, Highgate, London N6 5HN, England.

PATTINSON John Gilbert, b. 10 Aug 1938, Ormesby, Yorkshire, England. University Lecturer. m. Judi Sutton, 1 Aug 1978, 2 sons. *Education:* BMus, University of Manchester; Royal Manchester College of Music (Associate) Graduate, Royal Schools of Music; Associate, Royal College of Organists. *Career:* Teacher, Ernest Bailey Grammar School, Matlock; Director of Music, St Alban's Boys Grammar School; Head of Music and Performing Arts, North Staffordshire Polytechnic; Currently Senior Lecturer, Department of Continuing Education, University of Canterbury, Christchurch, New Zealand; Examiner, JMB and University of London; Adjudicator; Conductor, various orchestras in UK including: Shrewsbury Orchestral Society, Janus Contemporary Music Ensemble, University of Keele Ives Choir; in New Zealand including: Christchurch Symphony Orchestra; Amici Chamber Orchestra, Harmonic Chorale, Jubilate Singers, Canterbury Regional Opera, University Chamber Orchestra; Pianist and Accompanist, Broadcasting Artist for Broadcasting Corporation of New Zealand; Several 1st performances of works by British and New Zealand composers. *Hobbies:* Walking; Skiing; Building miniature steam locomotives. *Address:* 53 Marine Drive, Diamond Harbour, Christchurch, New Zealand.

PAUER Jiri, b. 22 Feb 1919, Libusin, Kladno,

Czechoslovakia. Composer; Administrator. *Education:* Studied with Alois Haba at Prague Conservatory, 1943-46, and at Academy of Musical Arts. *Career:* Professor of Composition at Prague Academy, 1965-89; Head of Opera at Prague National Theatre, 1951-55, 1965-67, Director, 1979-89; Director of Czech Philharmonic, 1958-79. *Compositions include:* Operas: Prattling Slug, for children, Prague, 1958; Zuzana Vojirova, Prague, 1958; Little Red Riding Hood, Olomouc, 1960; Matrimonial Counterpoints, Ostrava, 1962; The Hypochondriac (after Moliere), Prague, 1970, revised version, Prague, 1988; Swan-Song, monodrama, Prague, 1974; Ballet: Ferdy the Ant, 1975; Orchestral: Comedy Suite, 1949; Bassoon Concerto, 1949; Rhapsody, 1953; Oboe Concerto, 1954; Horn Concerto, 1958; Symphony, 1963; Commemoration, 1969; Trumpet Concerto, 1972; Initials, 1974; Symphony for Strings, 1978; Marimba Concerto, 1984; Suite, 1987; Chamber: Divertimento for 3 clarinets, 1949; Violin Sonatina, 1953; Cello Sonata, 1954; 4 String Quartets, 1960, 1969, 1970, 1976; Divertimento for Monet, 1961; Wind Quintet, 1961; Piano Trio, 1963; Characters for brass quintet, 1978; Episodes for string quartet, 1980; Trio for 3 horns, 1986; Violin Sonata, 1987; Nonet No 2, 1989; Piano music, cantatas and songs. *Address:* c/o National Theatre, PO Box 865, 112 30 Prague 1, Czech Republic.

PAUK György, b. 26 Oct 1936, Budapest, Hungary. Concert Violinist. m. 19 July 1959, 1 son, 1 daughter. *Education:* Franz Liszt Music Academy, Budapest, youngest pupil of Professors Zathureczki, Weiner and Kodály. *Career:* Many concerts in Hungary and throughout Eastern Europe; In 1961 he made his home in London, England and gave both his recital and orchestral debuts there the same year; He has performed throughout the world with all major orchestras of London and on the Continent under such conductors as Pierre Boulez, Colin Davis, Antal Dorati, Kondrashin, Lorin Maazel, Rozhdestvensky, Haitink, Tennstedt, Georg Solti, Simon Rattle, Charles Dutoit and Sergiu Comissiona; American debut was with Chicago Symphony Orchestra; He has played with the Cleveland, Philadelphia, Los Angeles Philharmonic and Boston Symphony Orchestras; Appearances at such festivals as Aspen, Ravinia, Hollywood Bowl and Saratoga; Formed a trio with Peter Frankl and Ralph Kirshbaum which has achieved world-wide acclaim; Conductor and Soloist with the English Chamber Orchestra, London Mozart Players and Academy of St Martin-in-the-Fields; Teacher of Masterclasses. From Sept 1987 Professor at Royal Academy of Music, London; Director, Mozart Bicentenary Festival, 1991. *Recordings include:* Alban Berg's Chamber Concerto, a Bartók Album and Tippett's Triple Concerto (Record of the Year, 1983); Complete Sonatas by Handel; Complete Violin Concertos by Mozart; 3 Brahms Sonatas, Mozart Quintets (viola part), in preparation: all Bartók works for violin, piano and solo violin. *Honours include:* Honorary Fellow, Guildhall School of Music; Hon RAM, 1990. *Hobbies:* Sport; Family. *Current Management:* Clarion Seven Muses, 47 Whitehall Park, London N19 3TW, England. *Address:* 27 Armitage Road, London NW11 8QT, England.

PAUL Steven Everett, b. 6 Dec 1937, Atlanta, Georgia, USA. Producer; Editor; Musicologist; Broadcaster; Flautist. m. Sophie Arbenz, 6 Oct 1981, 2 sons. *Education:* BA, Columbia, 1958; MA, Yale, 1959; PhD, Musicology, King's College, Cambridge, England, 1981; Juilliard School of Music; Trinity College of Music, London, England; Harvard Law School, USA. *Career:* Performances in chamber ensembles and orchestras in New York, Boston, London, Cambridge, Hamburg; Producer, CBS Records, New York, 1966-72; Editor, Deutsche Grammophon (Polydor), Hamburg, 1975-79; Executive Producer, Deutsche Grammophon, 1979-; Broadcasts on BBC Radio 3, WNCN (NY), WFMT (Chicago), NPR (National Public Radio, USA), NDR (Norddeutscher Rundfunk, Hamburg), DLF (Deutschlandfunk Cologne); Lectures at International Music Conferences (Washington, 1975, Vienna, 1982), and Universities (Cambridge, Oxford, Warwick, England and Minnesota, USA). *Publications:* Author of sleeve notes for CBS, DGG and RCA Recordings; Introduction and Notes for The Scatological Songs and Canons of W A Mozart, 1969; The Musical Surprise; A Discussion of the Element of the Unexpected in the Humour of Haydn, 1975; Comedy, Wit and Humour in Haydn's Instrumental Music, in Haydn Studies, 1981; Wit and Humour in the Operas of Haydn in Proceedings of the International Joseph Haydn Congress, 1986; Several published interviews with musicians; Music Arrangements (Chappell/Intersong). *Contribution to:* Professional publications and concert programmes. *Address:* c/o Polygram, Alte Rabenstrasse 2, D-2000 Hamburg 13, Germany.

PAUL Thomas, b. 22 Feb 1934, Chicago, Illinois, USA. Singer (Bass). *Education:* Studied at the Juilliard School with Beverly Johnson and Cornelius Reid. *Debut:* New York City Opera 1962, as Sparafucile in Rigoletto. *Career:* Sang in New York, Pittsburgh, Washington, Vancouver, San Francisco and Montreal as Mozart's Figaro and Sarastro, Pogner in Die Meistersinger, Bartok's Duke Bluebeard, Padre Guardiano (La forza del destino) and Ptolemy in Giulio Cesare by Handel; Sang at Central City Colorado in the premiere of Robert Ward's Lady from Colorado, 1964; Many concert performances; Teacher at the Eastman School, Rochester, and the Aspen School, Colorado. *Recording include:* Brander in La Damnation de Faust (Deutsche Grammophon).

PAULI Hansjörg, b. 14 Mar 1931, Winterthur, Switzerland. Musicologist; Writer; Filmmaker. m. Federica Staub, 22 Sept 1960. 1 son, 1 daughter. *Education:* Abitur Oberrealschule, Winterthur, 1949; Winterthur Conservatory of Music, 1953-56; Private studies with Hans Keller, London, 1956-57; Drphil, University of Osnabrück, Germany, 1987. *Career:* Producer, 20th Century music, Zurich radio, 1960-65; Music producer, Hamburg Television, 1965-68; Freelance, 1968-; Teaching: Filmhochschule Munchen, 1969-; Accademia di musica della Svizzera italiana, 1980-; Filmakademie Berlin, 1981-; Zurich University, 1984; Musikhochschule Freiburg, 1987; Bern Conservatory, 1988; Frankfurt University, 1989. *Compositions:* As writer/director some 30 TV-films on contemporary music, art, literature; Some 200 radio broadcasts; 2 major exhibitions on Hermann Scherchen, Berlin, 1986; on Stravinsky/Schlemmer/Scherchen Les Noces, Lugano, 1988. *Publications:* Für wen komponieren Sie eigentlich?, 1971; Filmmusik: Stummfilm, 1981; Hermann Scherchen, Musiker 1891-1966, with Dagmar Wünsche, 1986. *Contributions to:* Numerous articles in worldwide publications; contributions to various anthologies. *Address:* Sentiero al Calvario 20, CH 6644 Orselina, Switzerland.

PAULUS Stephen Harrison, b. 24 Aug 1949, Summit, New Jersey, USA. Composer. m. Patricia Ann Stutzman, 18 July 1975, 1 son. *Education:* Alexander Ramsey High School, 1967; BA, 1971, MA, Music Theory and Composition, 1974, PhD, Music Theory and Composition, 1978, University of Minnesota. *Career:* Co-founder, Minnesota Composer's Forum, 1973-85; Composer-in-Residence, Minnesota Orchestra, 1983-87; Vice-President, Minnesota Composer's Forum, 1983-. *Compositions:* The Village Singer, The Postman Always Rings Twice, The Woodlanders, Operas; Orchestral, Suite from The Postman Always Rings Twice, Symphony in Three Movements, Reflections, Ordway Overture, Concerto for Orchestra, Spectra; Chorus and Orchestra, So Hallow'd Is The Time, Letter For The Times, Canticles, North Shore; Chorus, Too Many Waltzes, Jesn Carols, Echoes Between the Silent Peaks; Chamber Ensembles, Partita for Violin and Piano, Music for Contrasts, (String Quartet), Courtship Songs (Flute, oboe, cello, piano), Wind Suite (WW Quartet), Voice, Letters from Colette (Soprano and Chamber Ensemble), All My Pretty Ones, (Soprano and piano), Artsongs, (Tenor and piano), Mad Book, Shadow Book, (Tenor and pf), Three Elizabethan Songs (Soprano and pf). *Recordings:* So Hallow'd Is The Time (Pro-Art), for Chorus, Orchestra and Soloists; Symphony in Three Movements (Nonesuch), Neville Marriner/Minnesota Orchestra. *Memberships:* American Society of Composers, Authors and Publishers; Minnesota

Composers' Forum. *Hobbies:* Tennis; Hiking; Reading. *Address:* c/o Opera Theater of St Louis, PO Box 13148, St Louis, MO 63119, USA.

PAUSTIAN Inger, b. 1937, Denmark. Singer (Mezzo-soprano). *Education:* Studied in Copenhagen. *Career:* Engaged at Kiel Opera, 1965-67, Hanover, 1967-69, Frankfurt, 1969-78; Guest appearances at Hamburg, 1970, Munich, 1971, and Valencia, 1976, as Ortrud in Lohengrin; Bayreuth Festival, 1968-71, as Siegrune, Wellgunde and a Flowermaiden; Sang at Zurich Opera, 1976-77; Other roles included Monteverdi's Penelope, Mozart's Marcellina, Magdalene, Brangaene, Herodias and the Nurse in Die Frau ohne Schatten; Verdi's Azucena, Amneris and Eboli, Giulietta in Les contes d'Hoffmann, Larina in Eugene Onegin and Agave (The Bassarids by Henze); Frequent concert performances. *Address:* c/o Opernhaus Zurich, Falkenstrsse 1, CH-8008 Zurich, Switzerland.

PAUTZA Sabin, b. 8 Feb 1943, Calnic, Rumania. Composer; Conductor. m. Corina Popa, 2 Oct 1974, 2 daughters. *Education:* Conducting, Bucharest Academy of Music, 1964; Composition, Accademia Musicale Chigiana, Siena, Italy, 1970. *Debut:* Rumanian Athenee, Rumania, 1964. *Career:* Professor of Harmony and Conducting, Iassy Academy of Music, 1965-84; Conductor, Iassy Academy of Music Orchestra, 1969-84; Appearances, Bayreuth Wagner Youth Festival, 1974, 1977, 1978, Carnegie Hall, New York, 1984; Music Director, Conductor, Plainfield Symphony Orchestra, New Jersey, USA, 1987-. *Compositions:* Symphony No 1, In Memoriam; Symphony No 2, Sinfonia Sacra; Offering to the Children of the World for double choir; Games I, II, III and IV for orchestra; 3 String Quartets; Double Concerto for viola, piano and orchestra; Ebony Mass for choir, organ and orchestra; Another Love Story, opera for children; Laudae for chamber orchestra; Five Pieces for large orchestra; Nocturnes for soprano and orchestra; Haiku for soprano and chamber orchestra. *Hobbies:* Gardening; Carpentry. *Address:* 40 Locust Avenue, Locust, NJ 07760, USA.

PAVAROTTI Luciano, b. 12 Oct 1935, Modena, Italy. Opera Singer (Tenor). m. Adua Veroni 1961, 3 daughters. *Education:* DMus; Istituto Magistrale; Tenor Range. *Debut:* As Rodolfo in La Bohème at Reggio nell'Emilia 1961; As Edgardo in Lucia di Lammermoor in USA (Miami) 1965. *Career:* Appearances include: Staatsoper Vienna, Royal Opera House of London 1963, La Scala 1965, Metropolitan Opera House, New York 1968, Paris Opèra and Lyric Opera of Chicago 1973; La Scala Tour of Europe 1963-64; other roles include Mozart's Idamante and Idomeneo, Donizetti's Ernesto, Tonio and Nemorino, Verdi's Radames, Alfredo and Riccardo, Puccini's Cavaradossi, Calaf and Pinkerton, Bellini's Arturo and Ponchielli's Enzo; Recitals and Concerts abroad including in the USA and Europe 1973-; Appeared in MGM film Yes, Giorgio 1981; Sang Manrico in TV simulcast from the Met, 1988, Rigoletto in a new production of the opera, 1989; Nemorino in L'Elisir d'Amore at Covent Garden, 1990; Concert at Glasgow, 1990; Sang Manrico at the 1990 Maggio Musicale Florence and appeared with two other tenors at World Cup Concert, Caracalla; Concert performances of Otello at Chicago, 1991; Sang Otello and Nemorino in New York, 1991-92; debut as Verdi's Don Carlos at the opening of the 1992-93 Season at La Scala, Milan; Returned to Covent Garden 1992 as Cavaradossi; Metropolitan Opera, 1994 as Arvino in I Lombardi. *Recordings include:* La Bohème, Madame Butterfly, Beatrice di Tenda, Lucia di Lammermoor, Elisir d'Amore, La fille du régiment, Maria Stuarda, Un ballo in maschera, Luisa Miller, Macbeth, Rigoletto, Mefistofele, Idomeneo, Aida, Norma, Tosca, Otello (Decca). *Publication:* Pavarotti: My Own Story (with William Wright). *Honours:* Hon degree, Pennsylvania 1979; Grand Officer, Italian Republic, Noce d'Oro Nat. Prize, Luigi Illica International Prize, First Prize Gold Orfeo (Academie du Disque Lyrique de France), many other prizes. *Hobbies:* Painting; Equitation. *Address:* Via Giardini 941, 41040 Saliceta, Modena, Italy.

PAWLAK Ireneusz Jakub, b. 22 Mar 1935, Wrzesnia, Poland. Catholic priest; Scholar; Composer. *Education:* Theology, Seminary of Gniezno, 1960; Master of Art 1964, Music and Musicology 1965, Doctorate 1976, Privatdocent 1990, Catholic University, Lublin. *Appointments:* Choirmaster in Gniezno, 1965; Director of Schola Gregoriana in Lublin, 1974-; Director of chair od Gregorian Chant, Catholic University of Lublin. *Compositions:* Two liturgical Masses, some liturgical songs for common use. *Publications:* Petricovian Graduals as document of Polish Gregorian Chant after Trient Council, 1988; Spiewy Uwielbienis (Cantica Laudis), 1993. *Contributions to:* About 100 articles on Music in Polish periodicals: Studia Gnesnensia, Msza Swieta, Homo Dei, Ruch Biblijny i Liturgicsny, Encyklopedia Katolicka; Encyklopedia Muzyczna PWM. *Memberships:* Zwiazek Kompozytorow Polskich; Towarzystwo Naukowe KUL; Society of Church Music Lecturers; Episcopal Commission of Church Music. *Address:* ul Niecała 8/93, 20-080 Lublin, Poland.

PAYNE Anthony Edward, b. 2 Aug 1936, London, England. Composer. m. Jane Manning, 24 Sept 1966. *Education:* Classics, Dulwich College, London; Music Durham University, 1958-61. *Career:* Freelance Writer, Musicologist, Lecturer, 1962-73 (Composing part-time); Composer, 1973-. *Compositions:* Paraphrase and Cadenzas, 1969; Paean for solo Piano, 1971; Concerto for Orchestra, 1974; World's Winter, Soprano and Ensemble, 1976; String Qtet., 1978; The Stones and Lonely Places Sings, Septet, 1979; Song of the Clouds, Oboe and Orchestra, 1980; A Day in the Life of a Mayfly, Sextet, 1981; Evening Land, Soprano and Piano, 1981; Spring's Shining Wake, Orchestra, 1982; Songs and Dances, Strings, 1984; The Spirits Harvest, Full Orchestra, 1972-85; The Song Streams in the Firmament, Septet, 1986; Half Heared in the Stillness, Full orchestra, 1987; Consort Music, String Quintet, 1987; Sea-Change, Septet, 1988; Time's Arrow, Full Orchestra, 1990; The Enchantress Plays, Bassoon and Piano, 1990; Symphonies of Wind and Rain, chamber ensemble, 1992. *Recordings:* The Worlds Winter; Paean; Phoenix Mass; The Music of Anthony Payne, BBC Records. *Publications:* Schoenberg, 1968; The Music of Frank Bridge, 1984. *Contributions to:* Musical Times; Tempo; Music and Musicians; The Listener; Daily Telegraph; The Times; The Independent. *Honours:* Radcliffe Prize, 1975; Concerto for Orchestra chosen for ISCM Festival, Boston, 1976. *Memberships:* Composers Guild; Association of Professional Composers; Society for the Promotion of New Music. *Hobbies:* English Countryside; Films. *Current Management:* J W Chester. *Address:* 2 Wilton Square, London N1 3DL, England.

PAYNE Nicholas, b. 1945, Kent, England. Administrator. m. 2 sons. *Education:* Eton (King's Scholar) 1958-63; Trinity College, Cambridge, 1963-66. *Career:* Paterson Concert Management 1967; Arts Council Administration Course 1967-68; Finance Department, Royal Opera House, Covent Garden, 1968-70; Subsidy Officer, Arts Council, 1970-76; Financial Controller, Welsh National Opera, 1976-82; General Administrator, Opera North, 1982-93; Director of the Royal Opera at Royal Opera House, Covent Garden, from 1993. *Address:* c/o Royal Opera House, Covent Garden, London WC2E 9DD, England.

PAYNE Patricia, b. 1942, Dunedin, New Zealand. Singer (Mezzo- Soprano). *Education:* Studied in Sydney and London. *Debut:* Covent Garden 1974, as Schwertleite in Die Walküre; returned as Ulrica in Un Ballo in Maschera, Azucena, Erda in Das Rheingold, First Norn in Götterdämmerug and Filippyevna in Eugene Onegin (1989); Barcelona 1974-75, as La Cieca in La Gioconda and as Erda; Bayreuth Festival and San Francisco Opera 1977; La Scala Milan 1978, as Ulrica; Verona Festival 1980; Guest appearances at Frankfurt Opera and the Metropolitan, New York (debut 1980 as Ulrica, sang in La Gioconda 1983); has sung Gaea in the British premiere of Strauss's Daphne (Opera North, 1987); appearances with English National Opera in The Love for Three Oranges, Salome and The Magic Flute; Sang Prokofiev's Princess Clarissa with Opera North at the 1989 Edinburgh Festival; Season 1992 as Herodias in Salome at Wellington; Concert repertoire includes the Wesendonck Lieder, Bach's St John Passion (in Paris), the Alto Rhapsody and Beethoven's 9th (Spain), Alexander Nevsky and the Mozart Requiem (London, Festival Hall). *Recordings include:* Un Ballo in Maschera and Peter Grimes (Philips); Beethoven's Missa Solemnis. *Honour:* Sydney Sun Aria Winner, 1966; Prize winner, s'Hertogenbosch Competition, 1972. *Address:* c/o Harrison/Parrott Ltd., 12 Penzance Place, London W11 4PA, England.

PAYNTER John Frederick, b. 17 July 1931, England. University Professor. m. Elizabeth Hill, 1956, 1 daughter. *Education:* GTCL, Trinity College of Music, London, 1952; DPhil, York, 1971. *Career:* Teacher, primary & secondary schools, 1954-62; Lecturer, Music, C.F. Mott College of Education, Liverpool, 1962-65; Principal Lecturer/Head, Department of Music, Bishop Otter College, Chichester, 1965-69; Lecturer 1969, Senior Lecturer 1974-82, Professor of Music Education/Head, Department of Music, University of York, 1982-. *Compositions:* Choral & instrumental works including: Landscapes, 1972; The Windhover, 1972; May Magnificat, 1973; God's Grandeur, 1975; Sacraments of Summer, 1975; Galaxies for Orchestra, 1977; The Voyage of Brendan, 1978; The Visionary Hermit, 1979; The Inviolable Voice, 1980; String Quartet, No 1. 1981; Cantata for the Waking of Lazarus, 1981; The Laughing Stone, 1982; Contrasts for Orchestra, 1982; Variations for Orchestra & Audience, 1983; Conclaves, 1984; Piano Sonata, 1987; Three Sculptures of Austin Wright, for Orchestra, 1991; String Quartet, No. 2; Time After Time, 1991. *Publications include:* Sound & Silence, with P. Aston, 1970; Hear & Now, 1972; The Dance & the Drum, with E. Paynter, 1974; All Kinds of Music, volumes 1-3, 1976, volume 4, 1979; Sound Tracks, 1978; Music in the Secondary School Curriculum, 1982; Sound and Structure, 1992. Editor, series, Resources of Music; Joint editor, British Journal of Music Education; Companion to Contemporary Musical Thought, (Ed and Contr.). *Honours:* OBE, 1985; Hon GSM, 1986. *Membership:* FRSA. *Address:* Westfield House, Newton upon Derwent, York YO4 5DA, England.

PAZDRO Michel Wojciech, b. 30 Mar 1948, Katowice, Poland. Musicologist; Editor. m. Anna Mendychowska, 31 Mar 1973. *Education:* Musicology, University of Warsaw, 1966-71. *Career includes:* Chief Editor, 1986-, Director, 1989-, L'Avant-Scene Opera magazine; Director, Editions Premieres Loges, Paris, 1989-. *Publications:* Guide des opéras de Wagner, 1988; F Chopin, biographie, 1989. *Honours:* Medaille Beaumarchais, Priz SACD, Paris, 1990. *Address:* L'Avant-Scene Opera, 15 rue Tiquetonne, 75002 Paris, France.

PEACOCK Lucy, b. 21 June 1947, Jacksonville, Florida, USA. Singer (Soprano). *Education:* North West University, USA, and at the Opera Studio of the Deutsche Oper Berlin. *Debut:* Berlin 1959, in Der Rosenkavalier. *Career:* Sang in Berlin as Flotow's Martha, Mozart's Pamina, Countess and Servilia, Cavalli's Calisto, Micaela in Carmen and Rosina in Il Barbiere di Siviglia; Guest appearances in Dusseldorf, Vienna, Munich, Hamburg, Turin, Geneva, Paris and London; Bayreuth 1985, as Freia in Das Rheingold and in Die Walküre and Götterdämmerung; Sang Eva in Die Meistersinger at the 1988 Festival; Sang Mathilde in Guillaume Tell at Catania, 1987; Deutsche Oper Berlin as Marenka in The Bartered Bride and as Myrtocle in Die toten Augen by d'Albert; Created the title role in Desdemona and ihre Schwestern by Siegfried Matthus, Schwetzingen 1992; Television appearances include Martha, in Flotow's opera. *Address:* Ingpen and Williams Ltd., 14 Kensington Court, London W8 5DN, England.

PEARCE Alison Margaret, b. 5 Aug 1953, Bath, England. Soprano. *Education:* AGSM (Distinction in Performance), Guildhall School of Music and Drama, 1972-77; Pierre Bernac, Paris, 1977-78; Gerhard

Husch, Munich, 1980-81. *Debut:* Wigmore Hall, London. *Career:* International career in Oratorio, Concert and Opera; Performances with leading British Orchestras including: Halle, Bournemouth, RPO, RLPO, BBC Welsh, under Charles Groves, Jane Glover, Sylvain Cambreling, Stanislav Skrowaczewski, Laszlo Heltay, Libor Pešek; Major Festivals: Three Choirs; Cheltenham; Fishguard; Llandaff; Brighton and Choral Societies; Soloist in world premieres: Sinfonia Fidei, A Hoddinott; Six Psalms, D Muldowney; Music's Empire, J McCabe; Numerous recitals for BBC and Netherlands radio; TV Debut, Hallé Orchestra 1982; Opera debut, title role of Lucia in Lucia di Lammermoor, England, 1982, Roles performed include: Violetta in La Traviata, 1984; Adina in L'elisir d'amore, 1985; Leila in Les Pêcheurs de perles, 1986; Giselda in I Lombardi, 1987; Abigaille in Nabucco, 1988; Manon Lescaut, 1991; Season 1992/93 in Macbeth for ENO, RLPO tour of Spain with Mahler 8, Verdi and Wagner opera in the Philippines and festival appearances in Norway and the Netherlands. *Recordings:* Songs of the Hebrides 1977 and 1981; Songs of Ireland 1981; Haydn's Welsh Folk Song Arrangements, 1983; Renaissance and Mediaeval Music, Vaughan-Williams, Serenade to Music. *Memberships:* Equity; Incorporated Society of Musicians; Royal Overseas League. *Honours include:* Arts Council of Great Britain, Miriam Licette Scholarship, 1977; 2nd Kathleen Ferrier Memorial Competition, 1977; Greater London Arts Association Young Musician, 1978-79; Incorporated Society of Musicians, National Westminster Bank Prize, 1979; Arts Council of Great Britain, Henry and Lily Davis Award, 1979; 1st Prize, Great Grimsby International Competition, 1980-83; Premier Soprano Awards, Hertogenbosch, Netherlands, 1983-84; 1st Prize for Concert Singing, Rio, 1985. *Hobbies:* Theatre; Travel; Continental Cuisine. *Current Management:* Ariette Drost, The Netherlands. *Address:* P O Box 223, 27 Endell Street, Covent Garden, London WC2H 9BY, England.

PEARCE Michael, b. 1945, England. Singer (Baritone). *Education:* Choral Scholar at St John's College, Cambridge; Study with Otakar Kraus and Elizabeth Fleming. *Career:* Concerts throughout Britain and Europe from 1977, and in Israel, Canada and China; Sang in Bach's B minor Mass at the 1990 Edinburgh Festival and in Poland; Lieder eines fahrenden Gesellen by Mahler and Rihm's Dies on South Bank; Elgar's Kingdom and Apostles in Scotland; Messiah in Belgium and Mozart's Requiem in Milan; more recently: Britten's War Requiem in France; Bach's St Matthew Passion in Spain; Concert of Brazilian music in London with The Sixteen Choir and Orchestra. Engagements in opera and oratorio for BBC Radio 3 and for television; Has sang Old Sam in the British premiere of Bernstein's A Quiet Place, The Herald in The Burning Fiery Furnace for Kent Opera and Becket in Bergen Opera's Murder in the Cathedral (Pizzetti); Covent Garden 1991, in Capriccio; Season 1992/93 as Emperor Claudius in Handel's Agrippina for Midsummer Opera, in Salome and Meistersinger at Covent Garden and in Nyman's; The Man Who Mistook his Wife for a Hat with Music Theatre Wales; Future engagements: Brahms's Requiem in the Queen Elizabeth Hall, Berio's Canticum Novissimi in Boston and a series of concerts and recitals in the Philippines. Recordings: Handel's Coronation Anthem (Archive).*Honours include:* English Song Award, 1984. *Address:* Woolmer Croft, Critchmere Hill, Haslemere, Surrey, England.

PEARCE Tony Scot, b. 31 Oct 1955, Santa Monica, California, USA. Alaskan Ethnomusicologist; Researcher; Teacher; Equistrian; Outdoor Adventure; Private Businessman. *Education:* BM, MMus, Alaskan Ethnomusicology, 1985, University of Alaska, Fairbanks. *Career:* Founder and President, Alaskan Folk and Traditional Arts Association; State contact for Congress on the Research in Dance (CORD); USA National Endowment for the Arts on site observer for 5th Annual Alaksan Old Time Fiddling Festival; Board Member of Education Committee for the Society of Ethnomusicology. *Composition:* Musical Characteristics of Tanana Athabascan Dance Song, 1985. *Publication:* Heartbeat: World Eskimo Indian Olympic Games/The story of Alaskan Native Music & Dance and Sport, 1985. *Hobbies:* Alaskan native music and dance research; Whitewater action; Dancing; Concertina Playing. *Address:* P O Box 84195, Fairbanks, AK 99708, USA.

PEASLEE Richard Cutts, b. 13 June 1930, New York City, USA. Composer. m. Mary Dixon Palmer, 10 Nov 1962, 1 son, 1 daughter. *Education:* BA, Yale University, 1952; Phi Beta Kappa, Diploma, 1956, MSc, 1958, Juilliard School of Music; Private study with, Nadia Boulanger and Wm Russo. *Career:* Composer of music for the Royal Shakespeare Company, The National Theatre, London, Broadway, Off-Broadway, The New York Shakespearean Festival, The Guthrie Arena Stage, ART, The Yale Repertory, Music Theater Group, Joffrey Ballet, London Jazz Orchestra, The Open Theater, American Place Theatre and many others. *Compositions:* Animal Farm, The Marat/Sade Music, The Garden of Earthly Delights, Vienna Lusthaus, Stonehenge, The Devil's Herald, Nightsongs, Divertimento for Brass and Percussion, October Piece, Chicago Concerto, Housman Choruses, Duets for Young Pianists, Music for a Summer Evening in Charlemont, Afterlight, Miracolo D'Amore, The Snow Queen. *Recordings:* Stonehenge, Passage, The Garden of Earthly Delights, Music for a Summer Evening in Charlemont, The Marat/Sade, Miracolo D'Amore.*Honours:* Recipient of OBIE and American Institute of Arts and Letters awards. *Hobbies:* Backpacking; White water canoeing. *Address:* 90 Riverside Drive, New York, NY 10024-5322, USA.

PECCHIOLI Benedetta, b. 1949, Italy. Singer (Mezzo-soprano). *Debut:* Piccola Scala, as Clarina in La Cambiale di Matrimonio, 1973. *Career:* Appearances at Monte Carlo from 1974, Rouen, 1974-75, Maggio Musicale, Florence, 1976-77, in Henze's Il Re Cervo and as Fenena in Nabucco; Spoleto Festival, 1976, as Cenerentola, Geneva, 1980 and 1986, Brussels, 1982 and 1987; Metropolitan Opera debut, 1983, as Rosina; Further engagements at Teatro Reggio Turin, Bilbao Festival, Teatro Massimo Palermo and Aix-en- Provence Festival (Meg Page, 1971); Concert appearances in the Ring at Paris, and at Carnegie Hall, New York; La Scala, Milan, 1989, in Rossi's Orfeo; Other roles include Fidalma in Il Matrimonio Segreto, Lisetta in Il Mondo della Luna, Erilda in Le Pescatrici by Haydn, Maddalena, Federica in Luisa Miller, Donizetti's Smeton in Anna Bolena and Orsini in Lucrezia Borgia, and Genevieve in Pelléas et Mélisande. *Recordings include:* Il Guiramento by Mercadante; Demetrio e Polibio by Rossini; Donizetti's Pia de' Tolomei. *Address:* c/o Tetro alla Scala, Via Filodrammatici 2, Milan, Italy.

PECH ANSHUTZ Joyce Kay, b. 27 June 1940, Cedar Rapids, Iowa, USA. Musician; Music Educator. m. Richard Anshutz, 7 June 1989, 3 sons. *Education:* BMusEd cum laude, Morningside College, 1962; MA magna cum laude, University of Iowa, 1968. *Career:* Violinist/Violist as soloist, chamber music player and with orchestras; Suzuki Festival Coordinator: State of New Jersey, 1971-77, Orange County, California, 1977-86; Associate Professor of Chamber Music, Saddleback College, 1979-; Music Director of Chamber Players; Principal Violist of Downey Symphony and Disneyland Orchestra; Chamber Music Coach for California American String Teachers Association Summer Institute of Chamber Music, 1986-. *Publications:* Music Teachers Association of California: Syllabus for Violin/Viola Teaching Literature, 1990; Syllabus for Cello Teaching Literature, 1990. *Contributions:* Editor: SMAC-OC Newsletter to Suzuki Teachers, 1992-, MTAC-LB Newsletter to Music Teachers, 1993-. *Honours:* Sioux City Symphony Scholar, Aspen Music Festival, 1960. *Memberships:* Music Teachers Association of California, Past State Chair for Strings; American String Teachers Association, Saddleback College Chapter Founder; Suzuki Association of the Americas. *Hobbies:* Golf; Cycling. *Address:* 10711 Ashworth Circle, Cerritos, CA 90701, USA.

PECK Russell James, b. 25 Jan 1945, Detroit, Michigan, USA. Composer. m. 2 Aug 1982, Cameron

Gordon Peck, 1 daughter. *Education:* Eastman School of Music, 1962-63; B.Mus., 1966, M.Mus., 1967, D.Mus. Arts, 1972, University of Michigan. *Career:* Composer in Residence, Indianapolis Symphony, 1971-73; Performances with Pittsburgh, Detroit, Milwaukee, Buffalo, Dallas, Cincinnati, Minnesota, Atlanta, London Symphony, Royal Philarmonic, many other orchestras. *Compositions:* The Glory and the Grandeur, (percussion concerto); Peace Overture, The Upward Stream, (tenor saxaphone concert); Signs of Life (strings), The Thrill of the Orchestra, (orch/narr); The Phoenix (trumpet concerto), Song of the Little Robin (orch/narr); Playing with Style (orch/narr); Jack and Jill at Bunker Hill (orch/narr). *Recordings:* The Upward Stream, The Glory and The Grandeur, Signs of Life, Peace Overture (Albany Records), Drastic Measures (Koch International), Automobile (CRI), Lift-Off (Opus One). Video: The Thrill of the Orchestra (SIRS). *Current Management:* Stanton Consulting & Management, 45-05 Newtown Road, Astoria, NY 11103, USA. *Address:* 3605 Brandywine Drive, Greenboro, NC 27410, USA.

PECKOVA Dagmar, b. 4 Apr 1961, Chrudim, Czechoslovakia. Singer (Mezzo-soprano). *Education:* Studied at Prague Conservatory and in Dresden, *Career:* Sang at Dresden Staatsoper, 1987-, as Cherubino, Rosina and a Dryad in Ariadne auf Naxos; Berlin Staatsoper, 1989-, as Dorabella, Konchakovna in Prince Igor, Hansel, and in Der Kaiser von Atlantis by Ullmann; Guest appearances elsewhere in Germany and in Czechoslovakia; Season 1992 as Jenny in Aufstieg und Fall der Stadt Mahagonny at Stuttgart Staatsoper and Olga in Eugene Onegin at the Théâtre du Châtelet, Paris; Concert repertoire includes Requiems by Mozart, Dvořák and Verdi, Mahler's 2nd Symphony and Debussy's Le Martyre de St Sebastien. *Address:* c/o Stuttgart Staatsoper, Oberer Schlossgarten 6, 7000 Stuttgart, Germany.

PEDANI Paolo, b. 1930, Italy. Singer (Bass). *Education:* Studied in Milan. *Career:* Sang in Cherubini's L'Osteria portoghese and Falla's Vida Breve at La Scala, 1950-51; Appearances at Bologna, Genoa, Trieste and Venice from 1954, Wexford Festival, 1956-59, Spoleto, 1961; Aix- en-Provence Festival from 1959, in Haydn's Mondo della Luna and as Masetto; Venice, 1966, in premiere of La metamorfosi di Bonaventura by Malipiero, Florence, 1976, in the Italian premiere of Henze's Il Re Cervo; Guest appearances at Barcelona, Catania, Mexico City and Antwerp; Other roles included Rossini's Alidoro, Don Magnifico, Taddeo and Basilio, Don Pasquale, Don Alfonso, Melitone in La Forza del Destino and Paisiello's Basilio; Character roles from 1970. *Address:* c/o Tetro Comunale di Firenze, Via Solferino 15, 50123 Florence, Italy.

PEDERSEN Paul, b. 1935, Camrose, Alberta, Canada. Composer. *Education:* BA, University of Saskatchewan; Studied under Murray Adaskin and John Weinzweig, MMus Degree 1961, PhD, Musicology, 1970, University of Toronto; Studied electronic music with Myron Schaeffer. *Career:* Music Director, Camrose Lutheran College, Alberta, 1962; Teacher, 1966; Director of Electronic Music Studio 1971-74, Chairman, Theory Department 1970-74, Associate Dean 1974-76, Dean 1976-86, Faculty of Music, McGill University, Montreal; Director, McGill Records, 1976-. *Compositions include:* De Profundis for Choir, Soprano Solo and Orchestra, 1987. *Memberships:* Associate Member, Canadian Music Centre; Canadian League of Composers; Canadian Association of University Schools of Music.

PEDERSON Monte, b. 1960, Sunnyside, Washington, USA. Singer (Bass-baritone). *Education:* Studied in USA and with Hans Hotter in Munich. *Debut:* San Francisco Opera, as M Gobineau in Menotti's The Medium, 1986. *Career:* Engaged at various opera houses in USA and at Bremen, 1987-88, notably as Szymanowski's King Roger; Montpellier and Bregenz, 1988-89, as Wagner's Dutchman; Minister in Fidelio at Orange, Deutsche Oper Berlin and Stuttgart, 1989-90; Sang Pizarro in a new production of Fidelio at Covent

Garden, 1990, followed by concert performance at the Festival Hall, conducted by Lorin Maazel; Season 1990-91 as Shishkov in From the House of the Dead at Cologne, Orestes in Elektra at San Francisco and Amfortas at La Scala; Salzburg Festival, 1992, as Shishkov, Houston Opera, 1992, as Amfortas in a production of Parsifal by Robert Wilson; Other roles include Jochanaan in Salome (Basle, 1989) and Angelotti. *Recordings include:* Video of Covent Garden Fidelio.

PEDICONI Fiorella, b. 1950, Italy. Singer (Soprano). *Education:* Studied at Conservatorio Giuseppe Verdi, Milan. *Career:* Appeared at first in Il Barbiere di Siviglia and I Puritani at opera houses in Italy; Sang Violetta at Glyndebourne, 1988, Gilda at Covent Garden, 1989; Appeared in Bussotti's L'Inspirazione at Turin, 1991, as Sandrina in La Finta Giardiniera at Alessandria; Has also sung in operas by Haydn, Pergolesi, Rossini, Respighi, Cimarosa and Donizetti at such opera centres as La Scala, Milan, San Carlo, Naples, La Fenice, Venice, Teatro dell'Opera, Rome, Grand Théâtre, Geneva, Theatre des Champs Elysées, Paris, and the Gran Liceo, Barcelona.

PEDUZZI Richard, b. 28 Jan 1943, Argentan, France. Stage and Costume Designer. *Education:* Studied sculpture at Academie de Dessin, Paris. *Career:* Collaborations with producer Patrice Chereau have included L'Italiana at Spoleto, 1969, and Les contes d'Hoffmann and Lulu at the Paris Opera, 1974, 1979; Der Ring des Nibelungen at Bayreuth, 1976; Lucio Silla for La Scala, Theatre des Amandiers in Nanterre and Theatre de la Monnaie, Brussels, 1984-85; Co-Artistic Director with Chéreau of Théâtre des Amandiers, 1982-89; Stage designs for Tony Palmer's production of Les Troyens at Zurich, 1990, Don Giovanni at Rome, 1991; Costume designs for War and Peace at San Francisco, 1991. *Address:* c/o Teatro dell'Opera, Piazza B Gigli 8, 00184 Rome, Italy.

PEEBLES Anthony Gavin Ian, b. 26 Feb 1946, Southborough, England. Concert Pianist. m. Frances Clark 1982, 1 son, 2 daughters. *Education:* Westminster School; Trinity College Cambridge; Piano with Peter Katin. *Debut:* Wigmore Hall, London, 1969. *Career:* Has given concerts in 100 countries; Many BBC recordings; Soloist with London Symphony, Royal Philharmonic, Philharmonia, Halle, Royal Liverpool Philharmonic, City of Birmingham Symphony and BBC Welsh Symphony Orchestras. *Recordings:* Unicorn Records: Copland Fantasy; Bartók Studies; Dallapiccola Quarderno Musicale di Anna Libera; Meridian Records: Ravel Gaspard de La Nuit, Miroirs, Sonatine, Pavane. *Honours:* First prize, BBC Piano Competition 1971; First prize, Debussy Competition 1972. *Hobbies:* Tennis. *Address:* 18 Geneva Road, Kingston upon Thames, Surrey KT1 2TW, England.

PEEBLES Charles Ross, b. 31 Aug 1959, Hereford, England. Conductor. *Education:* ARCM, 1977; MA (Cantab) Trinity College, Cambridge, 1980; Guildhall School of Music and Drama, 1980-81; Conducting Fellow, Tanglewood, 1982. *Debut:* Will make Debut with Vienna Chamber Orchestra. *Career:* Performances since 1979 include appearances in Italy, Germany, USA and most major UK venues since South Bank debut in 1982; Orchestras worked with include: Southern Pro Arte; City of London Sinfonia; London Concert Orchestra; London Sinfonietta; City of Birmingham Symphony Orchestra; Nash Ensemble; Bournemouth Sinfonietta; European Community Chamber Orchestra; Opera 80; London Mozart Players; English Touring Opera, Royal Opera House Garden Venture, Garsington Opera. *Recordings:* Orchestral Works by Kenneth Leighton and Michael Berkeley with Southern Pro Arte on Hyperion (A66097). *Honours:* Winner 1st Prize, 1st Cadaques International Conducting Competition, Spain, 1992. *Hobbies:* Cinema; Cricket; Literature. *Current Management:* Norman McCann International Artists, The Coach House, 56 Lawrie Park Gdns, London SE26 6XJ, England. *Address:* 71 Bartholomew Road, London NW5 2AH, England.

PEETERS (Jan Willem) Paul, b. 22 June 1953, Weert, The Netherlands. Musicologist; Organist. *Education:* Private Studies, Piano 1961-71; Organ, 1971-73, School of Music, Weert; Student of Musicology, Utrecht State University, 1972-88; Organ, Utrecht Conservatory, 1976-78; Private Cembalo study with Martine Visser, 1980-; Private Organ study with J Van Oortmerssen, 1983-86; BA Musicology 1986, MA Musicology 1988. *Career:* Organist, St Mathias, Weert, 1968-72; Chapel of Nunnery of Ursulines, 1970-72; Bodegraven, St Willibrordus, 1975; Werkhoven, OLV ten Hemelopneming, 1977-79; Utrecht, St Gertrudis, 1979-80; Utrecht, Chapel of St Anthoniushospital, 1980; Choir Director, Werkhoven and Utrecht, 1979-80; Some organ concerts; Organist, Utrecht OLV ten Hemelopneming, 1980-92; H Aloysiuskerk Utrecht, 1992-; General Editor, HET ORGEL, 1984-91; Member of editorial staff of Communications of the Central Organ Archives, Brussels, 1985-90, and Kerkmuziek & Liturgie, Utrecht, 1987-; Member Congress Committee, International Bach-Congress of the Netherlands Society of Organists, 1985; Member Congress Committee, Internationale Orgeltagung der Gesellschaft der Orgelfreunde, 1985. *Publications:* 3 chapters in 250 jaar Orgelmakers Vermeulen 1730-1980, Alkmaar Weert, 1980; Orgeln in der alten Grafschaft Flandern, Berlin 1985 with Luc Lannoo. *Hobbies:* History of organ building; Cycle-racing; Cooking. *Address:* Hommelseweg 343, NL-6821 LJ Arnhem, The Netherlands.

PEGG Carole Anne, b. 19 Sept 1944, Nottingham, England. Ethnomusicologist; Musician (Singer, Fiddle Player). 1 daughter. *Education:* BA, Social Anthropology, 1979, PhD, Social Anthropology, 1985, Cambridge University; Traditional English Folk Fiddle learned in the field; Mongolian Horse-Head Fiddle from Mongolian musicians. *Debut:* Queen Elizabeth Hall. *Career:* As Mr Fox, Queen Elizabeth Hall; As Carolanne Pegg, The Roundhouse half-hour TV programme Sounding Out; Many TV and radio performances; Currently Ethnomusicologist specialising in Mongolian traditional music, song and dance; Compiled and introduced half-hour programme on Mongolian music, Radio 3; Co-Editor, The British Journal of Ethnomusicology, 1993. *Compositions:* Recorded: The Gay Goshawk, 1970; Mendle, 1971; Clancy's Song, Man of War, Winter People, The Lizard, Wycoller, The Lady and The Well, Fair Fortune's Star, The Sapphire, Mouse and the Crow, A Witch's Guide to the Underground, 1973. *Publications:* Book on Mongolian Music and Ethnicity, in preparation. *Address:* Mongolia & Inner Asia Studies Unit, University of Cambridge, Faculty of Oriental Studies, Sidgwick Avenue, Cambridge CB3 9DA, England.

PEHRSON Joseph Ralph, b. 14 Aug 1950, Detroit, Michigan, USA. Composer; Pianist. m. Linda Past, 13 July 1985. *Education:* BA 1972, MM 1973, DMA 1981, University of Michigan; Graduate studies, Eastman School of Music. *Career:* Recent performances include: Concertino for Horn, 8 Instruments, Francis Orval, horn at the University of Delaware, 1987; Harmonic Etude for solo horn, at Merkin Concert Hall, New York, 1988 performed by Francis Orval; Hornucopia, by the Francis Orval horn ensemble, Budapest, Hungary, 1989; Concertino for Horn, 8 Inst, performed by North/South Consonance Inc, 1991, Max Lifchitz, conducting, Lincoln Center, New York City. *Compositions:* Works for Orchestra: Sinfonia Concertante, 1980; Manhattan Plazza Orchestral Painting No. 1, 1988. Chamber Ensemble: Works include: Concerto for Horn and Eight Instruments, flute, oboe, clarinet, bassoon, solo horn, violin, viola, cello, contrabass, 1987; Windwork No. 1, for woodwind quintet, 1990; Confessions of the Goliards for tenor voice, flute, violin and cello, 1992; Lustpiel, clarinet, violin, cello, piano, 1993. Duos and Trios: include: Areciba, piano and percussion, 1976; Caprice, flute and piano, 1984; Violarimba, viola and marimba, 1988; Lewis Carroll Songs, for soprano and piano, 1986/90; Piercing Phrenetics, for clarinet, cello and piano, 1993. Works for Solo Instruments: Etude Moderne, harp solo, 1981; Three Pianipieces, 1991; Panoply, for solo flute, 1992; Lake Fantasy, for solo oboe, 1993. *Publications:* See compositions. Seesaw Music

Inc, New York. *Honours:* Standard Awards, 1976-, American Society of Composers Authors and Publishers. *Membership:* Co-Director, Composers' Concordance, Manhattan. *Hobbies:* Reading; Visual arts; Chess; Computer Interests. *Address:* 484 W 43rd Street No 35H, New York, NY 10036, USA. 6.

PEINEMANN Edith, b. 3 Mar 1939, Mainz, Germany. Violinist; Professor. *Education:* Guildhall School of Music, London; Violin lessons with father, Robert Peinemann, Heinz Stanske, Max Rostal. *Career:* 1st Prize at ARD Competition, Munich; Appearances resulting with Solti, Szell, Steinberg, Karajan, Herbig, Tennstedt, Dohányi, Boulez, Yan Pascal Tortelier, Kempe, Keilberth, Munch, Barbirolli, Sargent with leading orchestras worldwide; Carnegie Hall debut with Szell and Cleveland Orchestra, 1965; Festivals including Salzburg, Luzern, Marlboro Chamber Music; Professor, Academy of Music, Frankfurt, 1976-; performances of the Beethoven Concerto with the Detroit Symphony, the Mendelssohn in Chicago, and the Pfitzner in Cleveland and with the BBC Philharmonic, 1991. *Recordings:* with DGG. *Honour:* Plaquette Eugene Ysaÿe, Liège. *Hobbies:* Reading; Hiking; Fine arts; Cooking; Cross country skiing. *Address:* c/o Pro Musicis, Ruetistrasse 38, CH-8032 Zurich, Switzerland.

PELINKA Werner, b. 21 Jan 1952, Vienna, Austria. Composer; Pianist; Teacher. m. Liliane Flühler, 26 Mar 1976, 2 daughters. *Education:* Hochschule fur Welthandel, Vienna; University of Michigan; Konservatorium der Stadt Wien; MA, Hochschule für Musik und darstellende Kunst, Wien, 1985; D Phil, University of Vienna, 1985. *Career:* Concerts with horn player Roland Horvath (member of Vienna Philharmonic) as Ensemble Wiener Horn; His own compositions played in Großer Musikvereinssaal and Großer Konzerthaussaal in Vienna and on television; Teaching, Toho-Vienna Music Academy. *Compositions:* Op 1-26 e.g. Op 1: Pater Noster; Op 5: Sinfonietta con Corale; Op 9: Trio Reflexionen; Op 14: Passio Silvae; Op. 24: Concerto for Jon. *Recordings:* Horn und Klavier 4, Aricord 18712 Vienna (with op 2, op 5, and op 8) Werner Pelinka (piano) and Roland Horvath (horn); Österreichische Komponisten der Gegenwart - KKM, Vienna (with op 12) Brigitte Hubner (contralto), Werner Pelinka (piano); Passio Silvae, Aricord Vienna (with op. 14) with Johannes Jokel (bass voice), Roland Horvath (horn) and Werner Pelinka (piano). *Publication:* Die Vertonungen des lateinischen Paternoster der nachklassischen Zeit (Diss 1985, Vienna). *Contributions to:* Gebet und Kunst (in Singende Kirche 1985); Eine Atom-Oper als Warnung (in Morgen, 1986). *Address:* Gusenleithnergasse 30, A-1140 Vienna, Austria.

PELL William, b. 1946, USA. Singer (Tenor). *Education:* Studied in Baltimore and at Manhattan School of Music. *Career:* Sang at first as baritone, notably, Don Giovanni, Mozart's Figaro (Toronto) and Germont (San Francisco); Tenor roles, 1975-, debut as Rodolfo; Sang in Amsterdam, 1983, Spoleto, 1987, as Parsifal; Deutsche Oper Berlin, 1982, notably in the 1987 premiere of Rihm's Oedipus; As Siegfried, 1988, and Kudriash in Katya Kabaova; Trieste and Hanover, 1988, as Bacchus and as Alwa in Lulu; Bayreuth Festival, 1989-91, as Parsifal and Walter von der Vogelweide; Frankfurt Opera, 1990, as Jimmy in Mahagonny, Cologne, 1991, in From the House of the Dead; Other roles include Gounod's Romeo, Matteo in Arabella, Andres (Wozzeck), Desportes (Die Soldaten) and Jean in Miss Julie by Bibalo. *Recordings include:* Walther von der Vogelweide in Tannhauser. *Address:* c/o Deutsche Oper Berlin, Richard Wagnerstrasse 10, D-1000 Berlin, Germany.

PELLEGRINI Maria, b. 15 July 1943, Pescara, Italy. Singer (Soprano). *Education:* Studied at the Opera School of the Royal Conservatory in Toronto. *Debut:* With the Canadian Opera Company as the Priestess in Aida, 1963. *Career:* Sang Gilda 1965; Appearances in Montreal, Toronto and Vancouver; Sadler's Wells Opera from 1967, Covent Garden from 1968, notably as Violetta, Micaela in Carmen and Madama Butterfly;

Guest appearances in Genoa, Bologna, Parma and Trieste and with the Welsh National Opera; US debut Pittsburgh 1975. *Recordings include:* Carmen (Decca).

PELLEGRINO Ron(ald Anthony), b. 11 May 1940, Kenosha, Wisconsin, USA. Composer; Performer. *Education:* Studied at Lawrence University (BM, 1962) and with Rene Leibowitz and Rudolph Kolisch at University of Wisconsin (PhD, 1968). *Career:* Electronic music studio at University of Wisconsin from 1967; Director of the electronic music studios at Ohio State University, 1968-70, and Oberlin Conservatory, 1970-73; Associate Professor at Texas Tech University, Lubbock, 1978-81; Founded electronic music performance ensembles Real Electric Symphony and Sonoma Electro-Acoustic Music Society. *Compositions include:* Electronic and mixed media: S&H Explorations, 1972; Metabiosis, 1972; Figured, 1972; Cries, 1973; Kaleidoscope, electric rags, 1976; Setting Suns and Spinning Daughters, 1978; Words and Phrases, 1980; Siberian News Release, 1981; Spring Suite, 1982; Laser Seraphim and Cymatic Music, 1982; Tape and instruments: The End of the Affair, 1967; Dance Drama, 1967; Passage, 1968; Markings, 1969; Leda and the Swan, 1970; Phil's Float, 1974; Wavesong, 1975; Issue of the Silver Hatch, 1979. *Publications include:* An Electronic Music Studios Manual, 1969. *Honours include:* National Endowment for the Arts and National Endowment for the Humanities grants for founding the Leading Edge contemporary music series. *Address:* c/o ASCAP, ASCAP Building, One Lincoln Plaza, New York, NY 10023, USA.

PELLERIN Louise Marie Eva, b. 19 Oct 1957, Sherbrooke, Canada. Oboist. m. Christoph Schiller, 29 Dec 1981, 1 son. *Education:* College Marie-de-l'Incarnation, Trois Rivieres, Canada; Conservatoire de Musique du Quebec, Trois-Rivieres and Montreal; Musikhochschule Freiburg im Breisgau, Germany, 1977-80. *Career:* Oboe Soloist and Chamber Musician throughout Europe and North America; member, Ensemble Mobile; Professor, Conservatories of Winterthur and Zurich. *Recordings:* Mozart, Wind Serenades, Philips; Vivaldi, Concerto, Philips; Mozart, Concertone kv 190; Marcello, La Cetra, Deutsche Grammophon; Telemann, Wind Concertos, with Heinz Holliger, Deutsche Grammophon. *Honours:* Orchestra Symphonique de Montreal, 1976; Belgrade, 1981; La Chaux-de-Fonds, 1982. *Hobbies:* Family; Reading; Interior decoration; Hiking; Gardening.

PELTZ Charles Harvey Jones, b. 30 July 1959, Bath, New York, USA. Conductor; University Professor. 1 son, 2 daughters. *Education:* BM, Ithaca College; MM, Conducting Performance, New England Conservatory. *Debut:* Rome, 1982; Boston, 1986, New York, 1987; Hamilton, Ontario, 1989. *Career:* Broadcasts on NPR, APR and Euroradio; Guest Conductor: New Jersey Ballet, 1988, Pacific Symphony, 1992, Buffalo Philharmonic, 1993; Appeared: Musicisti Americani, Italy, 1984-87, North American New Music Festival, 1988, 1993, Hamilton Philharmonic, 1989, Buffalo Opera Sacra, 1991-; Faculty, State University of New York, Buffalo. *Recordings:* World Premiere Recording: Honneger, Christoph Colomb '93, Opera Sacra. *Honours:* Plesur Excellence in Teaching Award; Distinction in Performance, New England Conservatory; Pi Kappa Lambda. *Membership:* Conductors Guild. *Hobby:* Equestrian. *Address:* 222 Baird Hall, SUNY at Buffalo, Buffalo, NY 14260, USA.

PEMBERTON JOHNSON Anne, b. 3 Sept 1958, New York City, New York, USA. Singer (Soprano). *Education:* Studied at New England Conservatory and Peabody Institute. *Career:* Sang in Heinz Holliger's Not I at Frankfurt, Paris and Almeida Festival, London; Appearances at Munich in George Crumb's Star Child conducted by Paul Daniel and at Salzburg Festival with the Ensemble Modern under Hans Zender; Premieres of works at Library of Congress and Kennedy Center, Washington DC; Recent engagements of Pli selon Pli by Boulez and Berg's Altenberg Lieder with RAI Milan and BBC Philharmonic Orchestras; Season 1992-93

with Stravinsky's Rossignol in The Hague, conducted by Edward Downes, and opening concert of Luigi Nono Festival of the Venice Biennale, 1993; Other conductors include Matthias Bamert and Peter Eötvös. *Address:* c/o Ingpen and Williams Ltd, 14 Kensington Court, London W8 5DN, England.

PENA Peco, b. 1 June 1942, Spain. Musician; Flamenco Guitar Player. m. Karin Vaessen, 1982, 2 daughters. *Education:* Cordoba, Spain. *Career:* Flamenco guitar player, 1954-; Founded Paco Pena Flamenco Company, 1970; Founded Centro Flamenco Paco Pena, Cordoba, 1981. *Honour:* Ramon Montoya Prize, 1983. *Address:* c/o Heatherington Seelig, Queen's Theatre, 51 Shaftesbury Avenue, London W1V 8BA, England.

PENBERTHY James, b. 3 May 1979, Melbourne, Victoria, Australia. Composer. *Career:* Musical Director of Australian National Ballet, 1947-50; Studied further in Europe and returned to Australia, 1952; Performances of stage works in Hobart, Perth and Canberra. *Compositions include:* Operas: The Whip, 1952; Larry, 1955; Ophelia of the Nine Mile Beach, Hobart, 1965; The Earth Mother, 1957; The Bullock Driver, 1958; Dalgerie, Perth, 1959; The Miracle, Perth, 1964; The Town Planner, 1965; Swy, Canberra, 1975; Stations, 1975; Henry Lawson, 1989; The Creation of the World, 1990; Ballets and concert music. *Address:* c/o Western Australia Opera Company, PO Box 7052, Cloisters Square, Perth, WA 6000, Australia.

PENDACHANSKA Alexandrina, b. 1970, Bulgaria. Singer (Soprano). *Education:* Studied with her mother Valeri Popova. *Debut:* Sang in concert at Sofia 1987, with Violetta's Act 1 aria. *Career:* Concert tour of West Germany 1989; Performances of Traviata in Sofia and Bilbao; Performances of Lucia in Cairo and Sofia; Performances of Gilda in a new production of Rigoletto for Welsh National Opera, 1991; Concert engagements with the Sofia Philharmonic and other orchestras in Bulgaria, Moscow and Kiev; Lucia di Lammermoor (title role) in Dublin, Ophelia in Hamlet with Monte Carlo Opera, 1991-92. *Recording:* Antonida in A Life for the Tsar by Glinka (CBS). *Honours:* Second prize, International Competition, Bilbao, 1988; Winner, 23rd International Dvořák Competition in Prague, 1988; Pretoria Music Competition, 1st Prize, 1990. *Address:* John Coast Ltd, 31 Sinclair Road, London W14 0NS, England.

PENDERECKI Krzysztof, b. 23 Nov 1933, Debica, Poland. Composer; Educator. m. Elzbieta Solecka, 1965. 1 son, 1 daughter. *Education:* State Academy of Music, Cracow, Poland. *Career:* Professor, Higher School of Music, Essen, Federal Republic of Germany, 1966-68; Rector, Professor Docent, State Academy of Music, Cracow. *Compositions:* Dimensions du temps et du silence, 1960; Quatuor a cordes, 1960; Anaklasis, 1960; Threnes aux victimes d'Hiroshima, 1961; Polymorphie, 1961; Canon, 1961; Stabat Mater, 1962; Capriccio for oboe and strings, 1965; Passio et Mors Domini Nostri Jesu Christi, secundum Lucam, 1966; De natura sonoris I, 1966; Dies Irae, 1967; Capriccio for violin and orchestra, 1967; Pittsburgh Overture, 1967; Capriccio for cello, 1968; The Devils of Loudun (opera), 1969; Quartetto per archi No 2, 1968; Kosmogonia, 1970; Utrenja, Grablegung and Auferstehung Christi, for 5 soloists, 2 choirs, orchestra, 1971; De natura sonoris no 2, 1971; Concerto violoncello and orchestra, 1972; Partita for harpsichord and orchestra, 1972; Ecloga VIII, for 6 singers, 1972; Canticum canticorum Salominis for 16 part chorus and chamber orchestra, 1973; Symphonie, 1973; Magnificat, 1974; Awakening of Jacob, for orchestra, 1974; Violin concerto, 1977; Paradise Lost (Rappresentazione), 1978; (Christmas) Symphony No 2, 1980; Te Deum, 1980; Lacrimosa, 1980; Cello Concerto, 1982; Viola Concerto, 1983; Polish Requiem, 1983-84; The Black Mask (Opera), 1986; Ubu Rex (opera), 1991. *Honours:* North Rhine-Westphalia Award, 1966; Sibelius Award, 1967; Prix d'Italie, 1967, 1968; 1st class State award, 1968; Gustav Charpentier Prize, 1971; Gottfried von Herder Prize,

1977; Arthur Honegger Music Award for Magnificat 1978; Grand Medal of Paris, 1982; Dr L C Mult, Wolf Prize, 1987; others. *Address:* Cisowa 22, Wola Justowska, Cracow, Poland.

PENDLEBURY Sally, b. 1960, England. Cellist. *Education:* Studied at Chetham's School of Music, in Dusseldorf and at New England Conservatory. *Career:* Led cello section of the European Community Youth Orchestra, 1982-85; Currently member of the Chamber Orchestra of Europe; Recitals with Natalia Gutman and Yuri Bashmet; Co-founded Vellinger String Quartet, 1990; Participated in master classes with Borodin Quartet at Pears- Britten School, 1991; Concerts at Ferrara Musica festival, Italy and debut on South Bank with London premiere of Robert Simpson's 13th Quartet; BBC Radio 3 debut, Dec 1991; Season 1992-93 with concerts in London, Glasgow, Cambridge, at Davos Festival Switzerland and Crickdale Festival Wiltshire; Wigmore Hall with Haydn (Op 54 no 2), Gubaidulina and Beethoven (Op 59 no 2), Purcell Room with Haydn's Last Seven Words. *Recordings include:* c/o Georgina Ivor Associates (Vellinger Quartet), 66 Alderbrook Road, London SW12 8AB, England.

PENHERSKI Zbigniew, b. 26 Jan 1935, Warsaw, Poland. Composer. m. Malgorzata, 1 son. *Education:* Composers Diploma, Warsaw Conservatory of Music, 1959. *Compositions include:* Musica Humana for baritone, choir and symphony orchestra, 1963; Missa Abstracta for tenor, reciting voice, choir and symphony orchestra, 1966; Street Music, chamber ensemble, 1966; Samson Put on Trial, radio opera, 1968; .3 Recitativi for soprano, piano and percussion, 1968; 3M-H1, electronic piece, 1969; Instrumental Quartet, 1970; Incantationi 1 Sextet for Percussion Instruments, 1972; The Twilight of Peryn, opera in 3 parts, 1972; Masurian Chronicles 2, for symphony orchestra and magentic tape, 1973; Radio Symphony for 2, 1975; Amammesis for symphony orchestra, 1975; String Play for string orchestra, 1980; Edgar: The Son of Walpor, opera in 3 parts, 1982; Jeux Partis for saxophone and percussion, 1984; 3 impressions for soprano, piano and four percussions, 1985; Scottish Chronicles for symphony orchestra, 1987; The Island of the Roses, chamber opera, 1989; Signals for Symphony orchestra 1992; Cantus for mixed choir, 1992. *Address:* Al Wojska Polskiego 20, 01-554 Warsaw, Poland.

PENKOVA Reni, b. 28 Oct 1935, Tarnovo, Bulgaria. Singer (Mezzo- Soprano). *Education:* Studied with Nadia Aladjem and Elena Doskova-Ricardi in Sofia. *Debut:* Burgass 1960, as Olga in Eugene Onegin. *Career:* Member of the National Opera Sofia from 1964; Guest appearances in Holland and England; Glyndebourne Festival 1971-77, as Olga, Pauline in The Queen of Spades, Dorabella in Così fan Tutte and Meg Page in Falstaff; Other roles include Gluck's Orpheus, Cherubino, Octavian in Der Rosenkavalier, Amneris and Angelina in La Cenerentola; Also heard in concert and oratorio; member of the Bulgarian National Opera, Sofia till 1991; Presently, Vocal Professor, State Musical Academie, Sofia. *Compositions include:* Further roles include: B Bartok, Bluebeard's Castle, Judith, 1975; B Britten, Midsummer Night's Dream, Oberon, 1982; Verdi, Nabucco, Fenena, 1976; Bellini, Norma, Adalgisa, 1984; Donizetti, La Favorita, Leonora, 1985; Cilea, Adriana Lecouvreur, La Princessa de Bouillon, 1987. *Recordings include:* Prince Igor by Borodin (HMV). *Address:* 1202 Bulgaria Blvd, Slivnitza, 212-A, Sofia, Bulgaria.

PENN William (Albert), b. 11 Jan 1943, Long Branch, New Jersey, USA. Composer. *Education:* Studied with Henri Pousseur and Mauricio Kagel at the State University of New York at Buffalo (MA, 1967) and at Michigan State University (PhD, 1971); Further study at Eastman School with Wayne Barlow. *Career:* Faculty member of Eastman School, 1971-78; Staff composer at New York Shakespeare Festival, 1974-76; Folger Shakespeare Theatre and Sounds Reasonable Records in Washington from 1975. *Compositions include:* String Quartet, 1968; At Last Olympus, musical, 1969;

Spectrums, Confusions and Sometime for orchestra, 1969; The Pied Piper of Hamelin, musical, 1969; Chamber Music no 1 for violin and piano, 1971, for cello and piano, 1972; Symphony, 1971; The Boy who cried 'Wolf' is Dead, musical, 1971; Ultra Mensuram 3 Brass Quintets, 1971; The Canticle, musical, 1972; Inner Loop for band, 1973; Niagara 1678 for band, 1973; Night Music for flute and chorus, 1973; Miroirs sur le Rubaiyat for piano and narrator, 1974; Incidental music and songs. *Honours include:* American Society for Composers, Authors and Publishers awards and National Endowment for the Arts fellowships. *Address:* c/o ASCAP, ASCAP Building, One Lincoln Plaza, New York, NY 10023, USA.

PENNARIO Leonard, b. 9 July 1924, Buffalo, New York, USA. Concert Pianist. *Education:* Studied with Guy Maier, Olga Steeb and Ernest Toch. *Debut:* With the Dallas Symphony Orchestra 1936, playing the Grieg Concerto. *Career:* Soloist with the Los Angeles Philharmonic 1939; Played Liszt's E flat Concerto with the New York Philharmonic under Artur Rodzinski, 1943; Tour of Europe 1952, in the popular Romantic repertory; Chamber concerts with Jascha Heifetz and Gregor Piatigosky in Los Angeles; Premiered the Concerto by Miklos Rozsa with the LA Philharmonic under Zubin Mehta, 1966. *Address:* Columbia Artists Management Inc., 165 West 57th Street, New York, NY 10019, USA.

PENNETIER Jean-Claude, b. 16 May 1942, Chatellerault, France. Pianist; Conductor. *Education:* Studied at Paris Conservatoire. *Career:* Numerous solo appearances in Europe and elsewhere 1968-; Chamber musician with Regis Pasquier (violin) and Trio with E Krivine and F Lodeon; Recitals with piano four hands; Duo with clarinettist Michel Portal 1979-80; Member of such ensembles as Domaine Musical, Musique Vivante, Ars Nova, Itineraire and Musique Plus; Performer of contemporary music at the Roayn and La Rochelle festivals; Has conducted the Ensemble InterContemporain and the orchestras of French Radio; Premiered Maurice Ohana's 24 Preludes (1973) and Piano Concerto, 1981; Nikiprovetski's Piano Concerto 1979; Professor of Chamber Music at the Paris Conservatoire 1985-. *Honours include:* Winner, Prix Gabriel Fauré and International Competition Montreal, 2nd Prize, Long-Thibaud Competition; Winner, Geneva International Competition, 1968. *Address:* Conservatoire National Superieur de Musique, 14 Rue de Madrid, 75008 Paris, France.

PENRI-EVANS David, b. 18 Jan 1956, Wrexham, Wales. Composer. *Education:* BMus, Centenary College of Louisiana, 1978; PGCE, University of Wales, 1979; MMus, DMA, Louisiana State University, 1981-86; FTCL, Trinity College, London, 1989; Composition Teacher, Dinos Constantinides. *Career:* Teacher, Victoria College, Jersey, Channel Islands, 1979-81; Teacher, Portsmouth Grammar School, England, 1987-; Assistant Professor, American University of London, 1987-; Founder, Coordinator, Tempo new music festival, 1987-; Many commissions, UK and USA. *Compositions:* Symphony; Study in Grey, opera; String Quartet - Dinas Bran; Brown Studies; Textures; Night Music; Song of Ajax; Death in the Surf; Bayou Blues. *Contributions to:* Compiles First Performances, annual list of premieres of British works for Composers Guild of Great Britain. *Address:* Portsmouth Grammar School, High Street, Portsmouth PO1 2LN, England.

PENROSE Timothy Nicholas, b. 7 Apr 1949. Singer, Farnham, Surrey, England. m. (1) Shirley Margaret Bignell, (2) Carol Heather Oake, 15 Nov 1986. *Education:* Licentiate and Fellow, Trinity College, London. *Debut:* Opera - Holland Festival, 1974. *Career:* Numerous solo concert appearances throughout UK and most European countries; Visits to North and South America; Tours with Pro Cantione Antique of London, Solo recitals for BBC and European radio Stations; Concerts with Medieval Ensemble of London and London Music Players. *Recordings:* Handel's Semele; Purcell's The Fairy Queen, with John Eliot Gardiner; Others with Pro Cantione Antiqua, Medieval Ensemble of London,

London Music Players and London Early Music Group. *Honour:* Recipient, Greater London Arts Association, Young Musicians Award, 1975. *Memberships:* Gentlemen-in-Ordinary, Her Majesty's Chapel Royal, 1972-75; City Glee Club, London. *Hobbies:* Motorcycling; Organ playing. *Address:* 83 Langdale Avenue, Mitcham, Surrey CR4 4AJ, England.

PENTLAND Barbarba, b. 2 Jan 1912, Winnipeg, Canada. Composer. *Education:* Studied composition with Cecile Gauthiez, Paris; Studied under Frederick Jacobi and Bernard Wagenaar at Juilliard School of Music, New York and Aaron Copland at Berkshire Music Centre. *Career:* Instructor, Royal Conservatory of Music, Toronto 1942; Worked at MacDowell Colony 1947-48; Taught theory and composition, Music Department, University of British Columbia, Vancouver 1949-63; performed as pianist throughout Canada, USA and Europe and in broadcasts for CBC and BBC; has composed music and has received commission from Canadian Broadcasting Corporation, Winnipeg Symphony Orchestra, University of British Columbia, Purcell String Quartet, International Institute of Music of Canada, Vancouver New Music Society, New Music Concerts, among others. *Compositions include:* Stage Works: Beauty and The Beast 1940, The Lake 1952. Orchestral: Arioso and Rondo 1941; Ave Atque Vale 1951; Cinescene 1968; Symphony No. 1, 1945-48, No. 2, 1950; Symphony For Ten Parts, No. 3, 1957; Symphony No. 4, 1959; Variations on a Boccherini Tune 1948. String Orchestra: 5+, Simple Pieces for Strings 1971; Res Musica 1975; Ricercar for Strings 1955; Strata 1969. Soloist with Orchestra: Colony Music 1947; Concerto for Organ and Strings 1949; Concerto for Piano and Strings 1956; News 1970; Variations Concertantes 1970; Instrumental Ensemble: Canzona 1961; Cavazzoni for Brass 1961; Duo for Viola and Piano 1960; Eventa 1979; Interplay 1972; Mutations 1972; Occasions 1974; Septet 1967; Sonata for Cello and Piano 1943; Sonata for Violin and Piano 1946; String Quartet No. 1, 1945, No. 2, 1953, No. 3, 1969, No. 4, 1980, No. 5, 1985; Triance 1978; Trio Con Alea 1966. Instrumental Solo: Phases for Solo Clarinet 1977; Reflections 1971; Solo Violin Sonata 1950; Sonata for Solo Flute 1954; Variations for Viola 1965. Chorus: Epigrams and Epitaphs 1952; Salutation of The Dawn 1954; Three Sung Songs 1965; What Is Man 1954. Solo Voice: At Early Dawn 1945; Disasters of The Sun 1976; Sung Songs 1-3, 1964, 4-5, 1971. Keyboard: Aria 1954; Arctica 1971-73; Caprice 1965, revised 1977; Dirge 1948; Echoes I and II; Ephemera 1974-78; Fantasy 1962; From Long Ago, 3 Little Pieces 1946; Hands Across the C 1965; Maze/Labyrinthe and Casse-Tete/Puzzle 1968, 1964; Music of Now 1969-70; Tenebrae 1976; 3 Pairs 1964; Toccata 1958; Variations 1942; Vita Brevis 1973. *Recordings:* Many recordings on various labels. *Address:* Performing Rights Organisation of Canada Ltd, 41 Valley brook Drive, Don Mills, Ontario, M3B 2S6, Canada.

PEPPERCORN Lisa Margot, b. 2 Oct 1913, Frankfurt/Main, West Germany. Brazilian Citizen of German Origin. Musicologist. m. Lothar Bauer, 9 Apr 1938. *Education:* Abitur; Degree, History of Music, Royal Conservatory, Brussels. *Debut:* London. *Career:* Worked in London until 1938, Since 1938, Rio de Janeiro, Music Correspondent, for New York Times, 1939-46, Musical America, 1940-47, Market Researcher, RCA Victor, Camden, New Jersey, and other US Companies, 1946-52; Agent for English Piano export company, 1946-52; Researching, The Villa-Lobos biography, Travels in Latin America and the United States, 1959-60; Research work, Villa-Lobos, Zurich, Switzerland, 1961-. *Publications:* Numerous studies on Villa-Lobos including, A Villa Lobos Opera, 1940, Violin Concerto by Villa-Lobos, 1941, New Villa-Lobos Works, 1942, Musical Education in Brazil, 1940, Villa-Lobos in Paris, Vol 6, 1985, all published in USA; H. Villa-Lobos, Leben und Werk des Brasilianischen Komponisten. Atlantis, Zurich, 1972 (out of print); various other studies on Villa-Lobos published in Brazil, West Germany, Italy, Holland, Switzerland and Belgium; Published in Great Britain: Villa-Lobos in The Illustrated Lives of the Great Composers, 1989; Villa-Lobos, the Music, Kahn &

Averill, 1991; Villa-Lobos: Collected Studies, 1992; Letters, Toccata Press, 1994, also in preparation in Chinese and Portuguese. *Address:* Schulhaus Strasse 53, 8002 Zurich, Switzerland. 138.

PERAGALLO Mario, b. 25 Mar 1910, Rome, Italy. Composer. *Education:* Studied with Vincenzo di Donato and Alfredo Casella. *Compositions include:* Ginerva degli Almieri, melodrama, Rome, 1937; Lo stendardo di San Giorgio, melodrama, Genoa, 1941; La Collina, madrigale scenico, Venice, 1947; La Gita in Campagna, opera in 1 act, Milan, 1954; La Parrucca dell'Imperatore, rondo scenico, Spoleto, 1959; Concerto for Orchestra, 1939; 2 Piano Concertos, 1949, 1951; Violin Concerto, 1954; Fantasia for orchestra, 1950; Forme sovrapposte for orchestra, 1959; Emircal for orchestra and tape, 1980; 3 String Quartets, 1933-37; Perclopus, chamber concerto for ensemble and tape, 1982; Piano and organ music, choral works and songs. *Address:* c/o SIAE (Italy), PRS Ltd, Member Registration, 29-33 Berners Street, London W1P 4AA, England.

PERAHIA Murray, b. 19 Apr 1947, New York City, New York, USA. Pianist; Conductor. *Education:* Graduate, Mannes College; Studied with Jeanette Haien, Artur Balsam, Mieczyslaw Horszowski. *Career:* Debut: Carnegie Hall 1968 won Leeds International Competition 1972; London debut 1973. Guest Pianist and Conductor, all major orchestras including: New York, Boston, Chicago, Philadelphia, Cleveland, Los Angeles, London, Paris, Berlin, Amsterdam symphony orchestras; Performed with Budapest, Guarneri and Galimir string quartets; Participant, Marlboro Music Festival, Aldeburgh, Edinburgh and Vienna music festivals; Recitaltours, USA, Canada, Europe, Japan; From 1982 through 1989 he was co-artistic director of the Aldeburgh Festival, England. *Recordings:* Sony Classical, Masterworks; including all Mozart concertos as pianist-conductor with English Chamber Orchestra; Beethoven Concerti with Concertgebouw Orchestra, Chopin with the Israel Philharmonic, concertos by Mendelssohn, Schumann and Grieg; solo works by Schubert, Schumann, Mendelssohn, Chopin, Beethoven and Bartók (Sonata for two pianos and percussion, with Georg Solti); Schubert's Winterreise with Dietrich Fischer-Dieskau. *Honours:* Avery Fisher Artist Award, 1975; Kosciusko Chopin Prize. *Current Management:* Peter Gelb, c/o 165 West 57th Street, New York, NY 10019, USA. *Address:* Frank Salomon Associates, 201 West 54th Street Suite 1C, New York, NY 10019, USA.

PERDIGAO Maria Madalena Azeredo, b. 28 Apr 1923, Figueira Da Foz, Portugal. Director of The Department of Artistic Creation and Art Education of The Calouste Gulbenkian Foundation.m. Dr. José De Azeredo Perdigão, 1 son. *Education:* Graduate in Mathematics, Coimbra University 1944; Graduate in Piano, Conservatorio Nacional, Lisbon 1948; studied in Paris with Marcel Ciampi, Professor of National Conservatory of Paris. *Career:* Lectures on musical subjects; Head of Music Department, Calouste Gulbenkian Foundation, 1958-74; Created The Gulbenkian Orchestra 1962, The Gulbenkian Choir 1964, The Gulbenkian Ballet 1965 and organised The Gulbenkian Music Festivals 1958-70; President, International Music Festival of Lisbon 1987; Piano Recitals and Concert Performances; Assessor to the Ministry of Education for Artistic Education, Lisbon, Portugal 1978-84; Director of The Department of Artistic Creation and Art Education of The Calouste Gulbenkian Foundation. *Address:* R. Marques de Fronteira, 8, 2° D, 1000 Lisbon, Portugal.

PEREIRA Paulo Sergio de Graca Torres, b. 28 Nov 1954, Castro, Paraná, Brazil. Conductor; Violinist; Professor. m. Maria Alejandra Silva Orozco, 10 Mar 1985, 2 daughters. *Education:* Paraná School of Music and Fine Arts Conservatory, 1972; BSEd, Music Education, Tennessee Technological University, 1978; MM, Applied Music, Andrews University, 1990; DMA, Applied Music, Michigan State University, 1992. *Debut:* Soloist, Teatro Nacional, Brasília, 1967; Conductor, St

Michael the Great Orchestra, England, 1992; Brazilian Chmaber Orchestra, 1994. *Career includes:* Concertmaster and/or Assistant Concertmaster: Curitiba Opera Company, Campos do Jordao I International Music Festival, Paraná State Symphony (and Assistant Conductor), Paraná State Chamber and Londrina VIII Music Festival Orchestras, Paraná Soloists, Brazil; Caracas and Mérida Philharmonics, Mérida Chamber Orchestra, Venezuela; St Joseph Pro Musica Chamber, Michiana Symphony (and Assistant Conductor, Guest Conductor), Michigan State University Symphony (and Assistant and Guest Conductor); Newbold Summer Music Festival Orchestra; ASTA International Workshop String Orchestra, Switzerland; St Michael the Great Symphony and Chamber Orchestras; Assistant Concertmaster, 1st Violinist: Sao Paulo State Symphony, Paraná Federal University Symphony, Camerata Antiqua of Curitiba (and Music Director, Guest Conductor); Tennessee Technological Community, Nashville, Virginia Commonwealth University, Richmond and Greater Lansing Symphonies, Renaud Chamber Orchestra; Music Director, Conductor, Venezuelan National Youth Symphony; Guest Conductor: Curitiba Chamber Orchestra, Michigan New Music Ensemble; Music Director, Early Music Ensemble, Berrien Springs, Michigan; Assistant Conductor, Andrews University Symphony; Conductor, 5th and 6th Annual International Music Festivals, Andrews University; Musical Director: School of Music and Fine Arts Symphony (Paraná), Paraná State University Youth Philharmonic. *Honours:* Honorary Citizen, State of Tennessee, 1975; Nominated Bicho do Paraná, 1992. *Memberships:* American String Teachers Association; American Symphony Orchestra League; Circulo Militar do Paraná; Conductors Guild; Parana State Symphony Orchestra Board of Directors; Kappa Delta Pi; Phi Kappa Phi; Phi Kappa Lambda; Phi Beta Delta. *Hobbies:* Drawing; Sports. *Address:* R Cons Laurindo 41, apto 84, Curitiba, PR 80060-100, Brazil.

PERERA Ronald (Christopher), b. 25 Dec 1941, Boston, Massachusetts, USA. Composer. *Education:* Studied with Leon Kirchner at Harvard (MA, 1967) and at the electronic music studios of Utrecht University. *Career:* Teacher at Syracuse University, 1968-70, Dartmouth College, 1970, Smith College, Northampton, 1971. *Compositions include:* Ch teys for orchestra, 1976; Instrumental: Suite for piano, 1966; Improvisation for loudspeaker, tape, 1968; Reverberations for organ and tape, 1970; Alternate Routes for electronics, 1971; Reflex for viola and tape, 1973; Fantasy Variations for piano and electronics, 1976; Bright Angels for organ, percussion and tape, 1977; Tolling for 2 pianos and tape, 1979; Choral: Mass, 1967; Did you Hear the Angels Sing?, 1968; Three Night Pieces, 1974; Everything that has Breath, 1987; Songs: Dove sta amore for soprano and tape, 1969; Five Summer Songs for soprano and piano, 1972; Apollo Circling, 1972; Three Poems of Gunther Grass for mezzo, chamber ensemble and tape, 1974; Children of the Sun for soprano, horn and piano, 1979; The White Whale for baritone and orchestra, 1981; *Recordings:* Albums. *Publications include:* Developments and Practice of Electronic Music (co-editor), 1975. *Address:* c/o ASCAP, ASCAP Building, One Lincoln Plaza, New York, NY 10023, USA.

PERESS Maurice, b. 18 Mar 1930, New York, USA. Conductor; Trumpeter. *Education:* Studied at New York University and Mannes College (conducting with Philip James and Carl Bamberger). *Career:* Played trumpet before appointed by Bernstein as assistant conductor of the New York Philharmonic, 1961; Conducted revivals of Candide, Los Angeles 1966, and West Side Story, New York, 1968; Music Director of the Corpus Christi Symphony Orchestra 1962-75, the Austin Symphony 1970-73 and the Kansas City Philharmonic 1974-80; Guest conductor in Brussels, Hong Kong, Vienna, Jerusalem and Mexico City; Conducted the premiere of Bernstein's Mass at the opening of the Kennedy Center, Washington DC 1971, and at the Vienna Staatsoper 1981; Led the US premiere of Einem's Der Besuch der alten Dame at the San Francisco Opera, 1972; Has orchestrated, edited and conducted jazz music by Duke Ellington, Eubie Blake and Gershwin (60th anniversary concert of the Rhapsody in Blue, New York, 1984); Has taught at New York University, the University of Texas at Austin and Queens College, New York. *Recordings include:* Bernstein's Mass (musical director); Organ Concertos 1 and 2 by Rheinberger, with E Power Biggs and the Columbia Symphony Orchestra. *Memberships include:* President, Conductors' Guild of the American Symphony Orchestra League. *Address:* Music Faculty, Queen's College, City University of New York, NY, USA.

PEREZ-GUTIERREZ Mariano, b. 11 Sept 1932, Palencia, Spain. Professor; Principal Director; Director of Orchestra and Choirs. m. Mary Cruz Bianco. *Education:* Licentiate, Doctorate Arts, University of Sevilla; Diploma, 1st Class, Graduate Awards, Conservatorio of Madrid, piano, conterpoint and fugue, composition, organ; Licentiate in Chant Gregorian & Musicological Studies, Paris, 1963, 1964. *Career:* Canon, Cathedral of Santiago de Compostela, 1964; Choir Master, 1964; Director of Orchestra, Choirs, Chapel of the Cathedral; Professor, Aesthetics & History of Music, Higher Conservatory of Music of Sevilla, 1969, Head of Studies, 1972, Vice Principal, 1974, Principal Director, 1978; Professor, History of Music, Royal Higher Conservatory of Music, Madrid, 1985; Vice-Principal, National Musicological Society, 1984; President, International Society for Music Education, 1986; Editor of Journal Musica and Educacion, from 1988-. *Compositions include:* Elegia Cromatica for violin and piano; Secuencias ciclicas for orchestra; Canto a Santiago for choir organ and orchestra. *Recordings:* Misa Jubilar. *Publications include:* Musica Sagrada y Lenguas Modernas, 1967; Origen y Naturaleza del Jubilus Alelyuatico, 1972; Comprende y ama la Musica, 1979; El Universo de la Musica, 1980; Falla y Turina, 1982; Diccionario de la Musica y los Musicos, 3 volumes, 1985; Estética Musical de Ravel, 1987; Falla y Paris; A Si Canta Palencia, 1994; Asi Canta Espana, 1994; Ed. zarzuela Gran Via, by F Chuecos, 1994. *Hobbies:* Private Collection of Ancient and Exotic Instruments. *Address:* Revisrie Musica y Educacion, Escosora 27-50, 28015 Madrid, Spain.

PÉRISSON Jean-Marie, b. 6 Sept 1924, Arcachon, France. Conductor. *Education:* Studied with Jean Fournet in Paris and with Igor Markevitch in Salzburg. *Career:* Conducted the orchestra of the Salzburg Mozarteum in Austria and Germany then led the Orchestra of French Radio at Strasbourg, 1955-56; Permanent conductor at the Orchestre Philharmonique of Nice and musical director of the Nice Opera: conducted cycles of the Ring and the French premieres of Katerina Ismailova by Shostakovich (1964), Elegy for Young Lovers by Henze (1965) and Prokofiev's The Gambler (1966); Gave Janáček's Katya Kabanova at the Salle Favart, Paris, and conducted the Monte Carlo Opera 1969-71; Directed the Presidential Symphony Orchestra 1972-76 and worked in the French repertory at the San Francisco Opera; Conducted Carmen at Peking in 1982. *Address:* c/o San Francisco Opera, War Memorial Opera House, San Francisco, CA 94102, USA.

PERKINS John MacIvor, b. 2 Aug 1935, St Louis, Missouri, USA. Composer; Teacher. *Education:* Studied at Harvard University (BA, 1958) and New England Conservatory (BMus, 1958); Further study with Nadia Boulanger in Paris, Roberto Gerhard and Edmund Rubbra in London and Arthur Berger and Irving Fine at Brandeis University. *Career:* Teacher at University of Chicago, 1962-65, Harvard, 1965-70, and Washington University at St Louis (Chairman of Music Department), from 1970. *Compositions include:* Divertimento, chamber opera, 1958; Andrea del Sarto, music theatre, 1980; Instrumental: Canons for 9 instruments, 1958; Intermezzo, Variations for piano, 1962; Five Miniatures for string quartet, 1962; Quintet Variations, 1962; Music for Orchestra, 1964; Music for Brass, 1965; Music for 13 Players, 1966; Cadenza, 1978; Eight songs, 1956-62; Three Studies for chorus, 1958; Alleluia, 1971; After a Silence-Alph, 1976. *Honours include:* Commissions from the Fromm Foundation, St Louis Bicentennial and the Smithsonian

Bicentennial. *Address:* c/o ASCAP, ASCAP Building, One Lincoln Plaza, New York, NY 10023, USA.

PERL Alfredo, b. 1965, Santiago, Chile. Concert Pianist. *Education:* Studied at the Universidad de Chile with Carlos Botto; Cologne Musikhochschule with Günter Ludwig; with Maria Curcio in London. *Career:* Concerts throughout South America and Europe, with the Filarmonica de Santiago and the Zagreb Symphony; Liszt Années de Pelerinage for the BBC, 1990; Season 1990-91 with Amsterdam recital and London debut at the Purcell Room, Beethoven and Liszt; Schumann and Mendelssohn for Radio France, Schubert at the Bishopgate Institute, London; recitals at the Herkulessaal, Munich, May 1991; Recital, Queen Elizabeth Hall, London as part of the International Piano series, 1992; Concerts with the Royal Philharmonic and the Noord-Nederkands Orchestra, 1992; Beethoven 5th Concerto with the Residentie Orchestra at the Hague, 1991-92 season; Leipzig Gewandhaus recital and in Prague 1993, also US debut with the Florida Philharmonic, a recital at Ravinia. *Recordings:* Mozart Concerto K365 with Carmen Piazzini; Fantasias by Schumann, Liszt and Busoni (Collegno-Fine Arts); Brahms Sonatas for clarinet and piano (with Ralph Manno). *Honours:* Prizewinner at such competitions as Vina del Mar (Tokyo), Ferruccio Busoni at Bolzano and the Beethoven in Vienna; First Prize, International Piano Competition in Montevideo, 1985. *Address:* c/o Harold Holt Ltd, 31 Sinclair Road, London W14 0NS, England.

PERLE George, b. 6 May 1915, Bayonne, New Jersey, USA. Composer; Author. m. (1) Laura Slobe, 1940, (2) Barbara Phillips, 1958, 2 daughters, (3) Shirley Gabis Rhoads, 6 June 1982. *Education:* B.Mus., DePaul University, 1938; M.Mus., American Conservatory of Music, 1942; PhD, New York University, 1956. *Career:* Professor Emeritus, City University of New York; Major Compositions performed by Chicago Symphony, Boston Symphony, BBC Symphony, Royal Philharmonic Orchestra, Philadelphia Symphony, San Francisco Symphony, Juilliard Quartet; Bavarian State Radio Orchestra; Da Capo Chamber Players; Cleveland Quartet; Dorian Wind Quintet; Goldman Band. *Compositions include:* Quintet for Strings, 1958; Serenade No. 1 for Viola & Chamber Orchestra, 1962; Six Bagatelles for Orchestra, 1965; Solo Partita for Violin and Viola, 1965; Concerto for Cello and Orchestra, 1966; Songs of Praise and Lamentation for soloists, chorus, and orchestra, 1974; Sonnets to Orpheus, for chorus, 1974; A Short Symphony, 1980; Sonata for Cello and Piano, 1985; Sonata a Cinque, 1986; Dance Fantasy for orchestra, 1986; Sinfonietta I, 1987; Windows of Order (String Quartet No.8), 1988; Concerto for Piano and Orchestra, 1990; Sinfonietta II, 1990. *Recordings include:* Two Rilke Songs, 1941; Fifth String Quartet, 1960; Three Movements for Orchestra, 1960; Short Sonata, piano, 1964; Four Wind Quintets, 1967; Toccata for piano, 1969; Suite in C for piano, 1970; Fantasy Variations for piano, 1971; 7th string quartet, 1973; Sonnets to Orpheus, for a cappella, 1974; Six Etudes for piano, 1976; 13 Dickinson Songs, 1978; Concertino for Piano, Winds and Timpani, 1979; Ballade for Piano, 1980; Sonata a quattro, 1982; Serenade No. 3 for Piano and Chamber Orchestra, 1983; 6 New Etudes for piano, 1984. *Publications:* Serial Composition & Atonality, 1962, 6th Edition 1991; Twelve-Tone Tonality, 1977; The Operas of Alban Berg, Volume 1, Wozzeck, 1980, Volume II, Lulu, 1985; Co-author, New Grove Second Viennese School, 1983; The Listening Composer, 1990. *Contributions to:* Professional journals. *Honours:* Guggenheim Fellowships, 1966, 1974; Pulitzer Prize for Wind Quintet IV, 1986; MacArthur Fellowship, 1986; Elected to American Academy & Institute of Arts & Letters, 1978, American Academy of Arts & Sciences, 1985. *Memberships:* Various professional organisations. *Current Management:* E C Schirmer, Boston . *Address:* 138 Ipswich Street, Boston, MA 02215, USA.

PERLEMUTER Vlado, b. 26 May 1904, Kowno, Poland. Pianist; Professor. m. Jacqueline Deleveau. *Education:* Studied with Moszkowski and Cortot. *Career:* Learnt Ravel's Piano Music 1925-27 and played it to the composer; Notable exponent of French music and of Chopin; Professor at the Paris Conservatoire from 1950; Appearances in all major European cities; Tours of Canada, USA and Japan; Master classes in Canada and Japan and at the Dartington Summer School. *Recordings include:* Complete piano works of Ravel; Chopin's 24 Etudes; 12 Nocturnes, Piano Sonatas, 4 Ballards. *Publication:* Ravel d'après Ravel (with Helene Jourdan-Morhange) 1953. *Honours:* 1st Prize, Paris Conservatoire; Grand Prix du Disque for Chopin Recital, 1972; Grand Prix de l'Academie du Disque Charles-Cros, for Chopin Etudes 1981; Commander of the Légion d'Honneur 1987. *Address:* c/o Basil Douglas Services, 8 St George's Terrace, Regent's Park Road, London NW1 8XJ, England.

PERLMAN Itzhak, b. 31 Aug 1945, Tel Aviv, Israel. Violinist. *Education:* Shulamit High School, Tel Aviv; Juilliard School, New York. *Debut:* In USA, at Carnegie Recital Hall, 1963, in London, with London Symphony Orchestra, 1968. *Career:* Tours extensively in Europe and USA; Masterclasses at Meadowbrooks Festival, USA, 1970. *Recordings:* Records for EMI, CFP and DG, Most Major Concertos including, Bartók, Berg, Stravinsky; Chamber music including, Beethoven Piano Trios. *Honours:* Honorary MusD, University of South Carolina, 1982; Medal of Liberty, 1986. *Address:* c/o Sheldon Gold, ILM Artists Limited, 40 West 57th Street, New York, NY 10019, USA.

PERNEL Orrea, b. 9 July 1906, St Mary's Platt, Kent, England. (US citizen, 1949). Solo Violinist. *Education:* Private studies, violin, Venice, from age 6; Further studies, Adila Fachiri, London; Chamber music, Lily Henkel; Edouard Nadaud, Paris Conservatoire. *Career includes:* Tours, recitals, soloist with all major orchestras, UK & Europe. Represented England, ISCM Festival, Prague, & Soloist, Helsinki Philharmonic & Radio Orchestras (also played to Sibelius by invitation), 1935; 1st US tour, 1937; Tours, Holland, Belgium, USA (including series, Beethoven sonatas, with Dean Bruce Simonds, Yale), 1939; Concerts & teaching (including Bennington College), USA, 1940-68; Bach Festival, Prades (sent by Pablo Casals's US Committee), 1950, 1953; Sonata recitals, Finland, 1951; Various European tours, 1950's; Teacher, Royal College of Music, London, 1966-67; BBC broadcasts, Promenade Concerts, various chamber groups, UK, 1960's-70's; Dartington Hall Summer School; Master classes, Dartington, London, Glasgow, International Cello Centre, UK, 1968-; *Honour:* Premier Prix, Paris Conservatoire (1st Briton), 1924. *Membership:* Emeritus member, International Society of Musicians. *Address:* 34 High Street, Bideford, North Devon EX39 2AN, England.

PERRIERS Danièle, b. 24 June 1945, Beaumont-le-Roger, Eure, France. Singer (Soprano). *Education:* Studied in Paris with Janine Micheau, Roger Bourdin and Fanely Revoil. *Debut:* Marseille 1968, as Sophie in Werther. *Career:* Has appeared in France at the Paris Opéra and the Opéra-Comique, and in Nice, Bordeaux, Lyons, Rouen, Toulouse and Strasbourg; Also engaged at the Grand Théâtre Geneva, Théâtre de la Monnaie, Brussels and in Liège and Monte Carlo; Glyndebourne Festival 1972-73 and 1976, as Despina and Blondchen; Widely known in the Coloratura and light lyrical repertory and in operettas; Sang also in works by Bizet, Boieldieu, Lecocq, Offenbach, Rossini and Richard Strauss. *Recordings:* Les Brigands by Offenbach; Scenes from Die Entführung, Glyndebourne 1972 (Classics for Pleasure); L'Amant jaloux by Grétry.

PERRY Elisabeth, b. 1955, England. Concert Violinist. *Education:* Graduated, Menuhin School, 1972, and studied further with Dorothy DeLay and Oscar Shumsky at Juilliard. *Debut:* South Bank, London, 1978. *Career:* Concerts in Cincinnati, Florida, Chicago, Colorado and San Francisco and showings at Carnegie Hall with Alexander Schneider; Bartok's Second Concerto in Chicago; Further engagements in France, Switzerland, Italy and Germany; Leader of Deutsche Kammerakademie, 1987; Concerts in Sviatoslav

Richter's Festival of British Music at Moscow and Leningrad, 1987; US premiere of Schnittke's Quasi una Fantasia at Alice Tully Hall and the Berg Chamber Concerto at Elizabeth Hall under Lionel Friend; Recital tour of New Zealand, 1990, and the Berg Violin Concerto in London; Plays a Giovanni Grancini violin on loan from Yehudi Menuhin. *Recordings include:* Bach's Double Concerto, with Menuhin; Kirschner's Duo for violin and piano. *Honours include:* Winner, Concert Artists Guild Competition, New York. *Address:* c/o Anglo Swiss Ltd, 3 Primrose Mews, 1a Sharpleshall St, London NW1 8YW, England.

PERRY Eugene, b. 1955, New York City, New York, USA. Singer (Baritone). *Education:* Studied in New York. *Debut:* Sang St Ignatius in Four Saints in Three Acts by Virgil Thomson, with the Opera Ensemble of New York, 1986. *Career:* Sang Tarj in premiere of Under the Double Moon, by Anthony Davis, St Louis, 1989; Don Giovanni in the Peter Sellars production of Mozart's opera at Purchase and elsewhere; European debut as Alidoro in La Cenerentola at Nice, 1989; Season 1990-91 at New York City Opera, as Shiskov in US stage premiere of From the House of the Dead and as Stolzius in Die Soldaten by Zimmermann; Appeared as the Devil in Dvořák's Devil and Kate at St Louis, 1990; Théâtre de la Monnaie, Brussels, 1991, as Mamoud in premiere of The Death of Klinghoffer by John Adams (repeated at Brooklyn Academy of Music, New York). *Recordings include:* Video of Don Giovanni; The Death of Klinghoffer. *Honours include:* George London Award from National Institute of Music Theater, 1986. *Address:* c/o New York City Opera, Lincoln Center, New York, NY 10023, USA.

PERRY Janet, b. 27 Dec 1947, Minneapolis, Minnesota, USA. Singer (Soprano). m. Alexander Malta. *Education:* Curtis Institute, Philadelphia, with Euphemia Gregory. *Debut:* Linz 1969, as Zerlina in Don Giovanni; Appearances in Munich and Cologne as Norina (Don Pasquale), Adina (L'Elisir d'Amore), Blondchen (Die Entführung), Zerbinetta (Ariadne auf Naxos) and Olympia (Les Contes d'Hoffmann); Guest engagements in Vienna, Frankfurt, Stuttgart and at the Aix-en-Provence Festival; Glyndebourne 1977, as Aminta in Die schweigsame Frau; Numerous opera and operetta films for German TV; Salzburg Festival; Sang Zerbinetta in Ariadne auf Naxos, RAI Turin 1989; Violetta at the 1990 Martina Franca Festival; Season 1992 as Gluck's Eurydice at Bonn and Cleopatra in Giulio Cesare at the Halle Handel Festival. *Recordings:* Papagena in Die Zauberflöte, conducted by Karajan (Deutsche Grammophon); Falstaff, Der Rosenkavalier, Beethoven's Ninth, Bruckner Te Deum; Nannetta in Falstaff (Philips); Egk's Peer Gynt. *Address:* c/o Harrison/Parrott Ltd., 12 Penzance Place, London W11 4PA, England.

PERRY-CAMP Jane, b. 5 Oct 1936, Durham, North Carolina, USA. Professor; Pianist. m. Harold Schiffman, 10 June 1978, 1 stepson. *Education:* AB, magna cum laude, Duke University, 1958; MMus, 1960, PhD, 1968, Florida State University; Advanced piano studies with Edward Kilenyi; Piano repertoire with Ernst von Dohnanyi. *Debut:* Salle Chopin-Pleyel, Paris, 1973; Wigmore Hall, London, 1974; Alice Tully Hall, Lincoln Center, New York, 1981. *Career:* Performances throughout USA, centering on Southeast; Performances, solo and chamber music, in Europe; Professor of Music, Brevard Community College and St. Petersburg Junior College, Florida; Sweet Briar College, Virginia; Florida State University; Advisory Editor for Musicology, Eighteenth Century Studies; Research: Mozart autograph manuscripts; Musical time and temporal proportioning. *Recordings:* Harold Schiffman: Fantasy for Piano; Concertino for Piano and Wind Ensemble. *Publications:* Madamina! A Few of Mozart's Females or Fanno così tutte? in Man, God and Nature in the Enlightenment, 1988; Mozart's Magic Flute: Dialogues of Life, for Compendious Conversations: The Method of Dialogue in the Early Enlightenment, ed Kevin L Cope; Frankfurt: Verlag Lang International (forthcoming). *Contributions to:* Mozart-Jahrbuch, 1984-85; Eighteenth Century Life; Musick; Journal of

Musicological Research; College Music Symposium; Eighteenth-Century Studies; Studies in Eighteenth-Century Culture 14; Theoretically speaking. *Address:* The School of Music, Florida State University, Tallahassee, FL 32306-2098, USA.

PERTUSI Michele, b. 1965, Parma, Italy. Singer (Bass). *Education:* Studied in Parma with Carlo Bergonzi. *Debut:* Modena, as Silva in Ernani, 1984. *Career:* Appearances at Teatro Donizetti, Bergamo, Ravenna Festival and Teatro Comunale, Bologna; Teatro Regio, Parma, 1987-, notably as Dulcamara, 1992; Season 1992 as Mozart's Count at Orchestra Hall, Chicago, and Figaro at Florence; Sang Talbot in Maria Stuarda at Barcelona, Assur in Semiramis at Pesaro; Other roles include Raimondo in Lucia di Lammermoor, Pagano in I Lombardi, and Rossini's Maometto. *Recordings include:* Mozart's Figaro, Assur, Alidoro, Silva, Lodovico in Otello; La Wally by Catalani. *Address:* c/o Teatro Regio, Via Garibaldi 16, 43100 Parma, Italy.

PERUSKA Jan, b. 1954, Czechoslovakia. Violist. *Education:* Studied in Prague with members of the Smetana Quartet. *Career:* Co-Founder and violist of the Stamic Quartet of Prague 1977; Performances at the Prague Young Artists and the Bratislava Music Festivals; Tours to Spain, Austria, France, Switzerland, Germany and Eastern Europe; Tour of the USA 1980, debut concerts in Britain at London and Birmingham 1983; further British tours 1985, 1987, 1988 (Warwick Arts Festival) and 1989 (20 concerts); Gave the premiere of Helmut Eder's 3rd Quartet, 1986; Season 1991-92 with visit to the Channel Islands (Festival of Czech Music), Holland, Finland, Austria and France, Edinburgh Festival and debut tours of Canada, Japan and Indonesia. *Honours:* (with members of Stamic Quartet): Prize winner, International Festival of Young Soloists, Bordeaux 1977; Winner, 1986 ORF (Austrian Radio) International String Quartet Competition (followed by live broadcast from the Salzburg Mozarteum); Academie Charles Cros Grand Prix du Disque 1991, for Dvořák quartets. *Recordings:* Shostakovich No 13, Schnittke No 4 (Panton); Mozart K589 and K370 (Lyrinx); Dvořák, Martinů and Janáček complete quartets (Cadenza). *Address:* c/o Anglo-Swiss Management, 4-5 Primrose Mews, Sharpeshall Street, London NW1 8YW, England.

PERUSSO Mario, b. 16 Sept 1936, Buenos Aires, Argentina. Conductor; Composer. *Career:* Deputy Conductor at Teatro Colon, Buenos Aires, giving his own opera Escorial in 1989 and Puccini's La Rondine, 1990; Conducted Otello and Turandot at La Plata, season 1990-91. *Compositions include:* Operas: La Voz del silencio, 1 act, Buenos Aires, 1969; Escorial, 1 act, Buenos Aires, 1989; Sor Juana Ines de la Cruz, 1991-92, premiered, 1993. *Recordings include:* La Voz del silencio. *Address:* c/o Teatro Colon, Buenos Aires, Cerrito 618, 1010 Buenos Aires, Argentina.

PERUZZI Elio, b. 14 Oct 1927, Malcesine, Verona, Italy. Clarinettist; Conservatory Teacher. *Education:* Canneti Institute, Vicenza; B. Marcello Conservatory, Venice. *Debut:* Olympic Theatre, Vicenza. *Career:* Soloist with: Virtuosi di Roma, Solisti Veneti, Solisti di Milano, 1950-; String quartets of Milan, Ostrava, Brno, Prague & Zagreb, Brno Philharmonic Orchestra, Bozen Orchestra, Padua Chamber Orchestra, Filarmonici di Bologna, 1960-. Founder, Bartók Trio (clarinet, violin, piano) 1958, Piccola Camerata Italiana (medieval, renaissance & baroque instruments) 1967. Performances, Europe, USA, South America, USSR, Canada, 1960-. *Recordings:* Mozart Clarinet Quintet with Moravo Quartet; 18th & 19th century music with Virtuosi di Roma. *Publications:* Esercizi e Studi Method for Recorder, 1972. Editor, various works including: Sonatas by Robert Valentine for 2 recorders, 1973; G. Rossini Variations for Clarinet & Orchestra, 1968; A. Ponchielli's Il Convegno for 2 Clarinets & Piano, 1988. *Honour:* Accademia Tiberina, Rome. *Hobby:* Photography. *Current Management:* Francesca Diano, Via Vallisnieri 13, 35100 Padova, Italy. *Address:* Via Monte Solarolo 9, 35100 Padova, Italy.

PEŠEK Libor, b. 22 June 1933, Prague, Czechoslovakia. Conductor. *Education:* Graduate, Academy of Musical Arts, Prague, 1956. *Career:* Founder, Prague Chamber Harmony, 1959; Founder, Sebastian Orchestra, Prague, 1965; Musical Director, State Chamber Orchestra, Czechoslovakia, 1969-77; Frysk Orkest, NL 1969-75, Overijssels Philharmonic Orkest, NL, 1975-79, Slovak Philharmonic Orchestra, 1981-82; Conductor in Residence, Czech Philharmonic Orchestra, Prague, 1982-; Principal Conductor, Musical Advisor, Royal Liverpool Philharmonic Orchestra, England, 1987-; Regular Guest appearances with Philharmonia Orchestra, London, England; Films include: Dvořák's Rusalka, Munich, 1976; Stravinsky's Pulcinella, Television, Prague, 1983; Stravinsky's L'Histoire du soldàt, Television, Prague, 1982; Benda's Medea, 1975; Tchaikovsky's Swan Lake, 1970; Guest Conductor with orchestras in Paris, Naples, Brussels, Berlin, Amsterdam, Vienna, Warsaw, Basel, Lisbon, USA, USSR, Montreal; Conducted the RLPO at the 1991 Promenade Concerts, London; Elgar's Cello and Beethoven's C Minor Concerts; Suk's Asrael Symphony and Tchaikovsky's Pathétique. *Recordings:* B. Martinů's Greek Passion - complete opera; W.A. Mozart's Don Giovanni - complete opera; M. Ravel's Daphnis et Chloe, Bolero; J. Suk's Praga, Fairy-Tale, Serenade for Strings & A Summer Fairy Tale; A. Honegger's Christmas Cantata; F. Poulenc's Stabat Mater; B. Martinů's A Bouquet of Flowers; J. Haydn's 6 Paris Symphonies; Strauss' Vier Letzte Lieder; Wagner's Wesendonck Lieder; Schmidt's 3rd Symphony; Massenet, Werther - complete opera; Bruckner, 7th Symphony; complete Symphonies of Dvořák (Virgin Classics). *Memberships:* Union of Czech Composers & Performing Artists. *Address:* IMG Artists Europe, Media House, 3 Burlington Lane, Chiswick, London W4 2TH, England.

PESKO Zoltán, b. 15 Feb 1937, Budapest, Hungary. Composer; Conductor. *Education:* Diploma, Liszt Ferenc Music Academy, Budapest, 1962; Master Courses in Composing with Goffredo Petrassi, Accademia di S Cecilia, Rome, Italy and in conducting, Pierre Boulez, Basel, Switzerland and Franco Ferrara, Rome, Italy, 1963-66. *Debut:* As Composer and Conductor, Hungarian TV, 1960. *Career:* Work with Hungarian TV, 1960-63; Assistant Conductor to Lorin Maazel, West Berlin Opera and Radio Orchestra, West Berlin, 1969-73; Performances at Teatro alla Scala, 1970; Professor, Hochschule, West Berlin, 1971-74; Chief Conductor, Teatro Communale, Bologna, Italy, 1974-; conducted Wagner's Ring at Turin, 1988; Concert performance of Mussogsky's Salammbô at the 1989 Holland Festival; Teatro Lirico Milan 1990, premiere of Blimunda by Azio Corghi; has also led the premieres of Bussotti's Il Catalogo è questo 1960; Donatoni's Voci 1974, In Cauda 1982, Tema 1982, Atem 1985; Jolivet's Bogomile suite 1982; Dies by Wolfgang Rihm 1985; Fünf Geistliche Lieder von Bach by Dieter Schnebel 1985; Season 1992 with der fliegende Holländer at Naples and Le Grand Macabre at Zurich. *Compositions:* Tensions, string quartet, 1967; Trasformazioni, 1968; Bildinis einer Heligen, soprano and children's choir, Chamber Ensemble, 1969; Jelek, 1974. *Recordings:* Various for CBS Italiana. *Contributions to:* Melos. *Honours:* Prize for Composition, Academia di S Cecilia, Rome, Italy, 1966; Premio Discografico, for recording debut as conductor, Italian Critics, 1973. *Current Management:* Musart, 20121 Milan, Via Manzoni 31, Italy. *Address:* 40125 Bologna, Teatro Communale, Largo Respighi, Italy.

PESKOVA Inna, b. 1960, Moscow, Russia. Violist. *Education:* Studied at Moscow Conservatoire with Alexei Shislov. *Career:* Co-founded the Glazunov Quartet, 1985; Many concerts in former Soviet Union and recent appearances in Greece, Poland, Belgium, Germany and Italy; Works by Beethoven and Schumann at Beethoven Haus in Bonn; Further engagements in Canada and Netherlands; Teacher at Moscow State Conservatoire and Resident at Tchaikovsky Conservatoire; Repertoire includes works by Borodin, Shostakovich and Tchaikovsky, in addition to the standard works. *Recordings include:* CDs of the six quartets of Glazunov. *Honours:* With Glazunov Quartet:

Prizewinner of Borodin Quartet and Shostakovich Chamber Music Competitions. *Address:* c/o Sonata (Glazunov Quartet), 11 Northpark Street, Glasgow C20 7AA, Scotland.

PETCHERSKY Alma, b. 1950, Argentina. Concert Pianist. *Education:* Studied with Bruno Caamano in Buenos Aires; Maria Curcio in London and with Magda Tagliaferro and Bruno Seidlhofer at the Vienna Academy. *Debut:* Teatro Colon Buenos Aires, with Bartók's 3rd Concerto. *Career:* Concert and broadcasting engagements in Russia, USA, Canada, Spain, Germany, Brazil, Czechoslovakia, Mexico and the Far East; London appearances at the Wigmore Hall. *Recordings:* Works of the German, French and Russian schools, Latin-American and Spanish Romantic composers; Complete piano music by Grinastera, including Concerto No 1, which she has performed worldwide (ASV). *Address:* c/o M Gilbert Management, 516 Wadsworth Avenue, Philadelphia, PA 19119, USA.

PETER Fritz, b. 7 Nov 1925, Camorino, Switzerland. Singer (Tenor). *Education:* Studied in Winterthur, Zurich and Stuttgart, 1945- 55. *Career:* Sang at Ulm Stadttheater, 1955-61, Zurich Opera from 1961, notably in premieres of Martinu's Greek Passion, 1961, Sutermeister's Madame Bovary, 1967, and Kelterborn's Ein Engel kommt nach Babylon, 1977; Guest appearances at Geneva, Lucerne, Munich, Hamburg, Frankfurt, Cologne, Nice, Milan, Helsinki, Vienna and Edinburgh, as Ernesto, Max and Tristan; Many concert performances. *Recordings include:* Monteverdi's Poppea and Ulisse conducted by Nikolaus Harnoncourt. *Address:* Opernhaus Zurich, Falkenstrasse 1, CH-8008 Zurich, Switzerland.

PETERS Johanna McLennan, b. 1932, Glasgow, Scotland. Singer (Mezzo-Soprano); Professor of Singing; Head of Opera Studies, 1978-86. *Education:* National School of Opera, London. *Debut:* Glyndebourne 1959, as Marcellina in Le Nozze di Figaro. *Career:* Sang at Royal Opera House, Covent Garden, Sadler's Wells Opera, Welsh National Opera, Scottish Opera, Glyndebourne Festival Opera, English Opera Group, Phoenix Opera; Professor of Singing, Head of Vocal Studies at the Guildhall School of Music, London, 1989- . *Recordings include:* Albert Herring by Britten. *Hobbies:* Travel; Archaeology; Cooking. *Address:* c/o Music International, 13 Ardilaun Road, London N5 2QR, England.

PETERS Reinhard, b. 2 Apr 1926, Magdeburg, Germany. Conductor. *Education:* Studied at the Hochschule fur Musik in Berlin and in Paris with Enescu, Thibaud and Cortot. *Career:* Repetiteur at the Berlin Staatsoper 1946-49; Conducted the Berlin Stadtische Oper from 1952 (debut with Rigoletto); Concerts with the Berlin Philharmonic from 1952; Conductor of the Deutsche Oper am Rhein Dusseldorf, 1957-60; Generalmusikdirektor at Munster 1961-70; Permanent guest conductor at the Deutsche Oper Berlin from 1970; Musical Director of the Philharmonia Hungarica 1975-79; Guest conductor with orchestras in Europe and the Americas; Salzburg, Spoleto, Edinburgh and Glyndebourne Festivals; Conducted the first performances of Blacher's Zwischenfalle bei einer Notlandung, 1966, Sutermeister's Madame Bovary, 1967, Reimann's Melusine, 1970, Derives by Grisey, 1974 and Symphony no 1 by Isang Yun, 1984. *Recordings:* Suites from Dardanus, Amadis de Gaule and King Arthur, with the Collegium Aureum (RCA); Handel Organ Concerto, Praise of Harmony and Look Down, Harmonius Saint, with Theo Altmeyer, and three Italian cantatas, with Elly Ameling; Symphonies by Haydn and Mozart; Viola Concertos by Paganini, Stamitz and Hoffmeister, with the Philharmonica Hungarica; Le Postillion de Lonjumeau by Adam (Eurodisc). *Address:* c/o Deutsche Oper Berlin, Richard Wagnerstrasse 10, D-1000 Berlin, Germany.

PETERS Roberta, b. 4 May 1930, New York City, USA. Singer (Soprano). *Education:* Studied with William

Herman in New York. *Debut:* Metropolitan Opera 1950, as Zerlina in Don Giovanni: remained with the company until 1985 as the Queen of Night, Rosina, Mozart's Barbarina, Despina and Susanna, Verdi's Oscar, Nannetta and Gilda, Donizetti's Norina, Lucia and Adina, Strauss's Sophie and Zerbinetta, and Olympia in Les Contes d'Hoffmann; Covent Garden 1951, in The Bohemian Girl, under Beecham; Salzburg Festival 1963-64, as the Queen of Night; Sang in Leningrad and Moscow, 1972; Other roles included Violetta, Mimi and Massenet's Manon; Sang on Broadway in The King and I, 1973; appeared with Newark Opera 1989, as Adina in L'Elisir d'amore. *Recordings:* Il Barbiere di Siviglia; Un Ballo in Maschera; Ariadne auf Naxos; Così fan Tutte; Die Zauberflöte; Lucia di Lammermoor; Orfeo ed Euridice; Labels include RCA, Decca, CBS and Deutsche Grammophon. *Publication:* Debut at the Met, 1967. *Address:* c/o Metropolitan Opera, Lincoln Center, New York, NY 10023, USA.

PETERSEN Dennis, b. 1960, Iowa, USA. Singer (Tenor). *Education:* Studied at University of Iowa and with San Francisco Opera's Merola Programme. *Career:* Concert appearances in Mozart's Requiem with St Paul Chamber Orchestra (also Messiah and Bach's Magnificat), Haydn's Theresienmesse at Spoleto Festival in Charleston; Tippett's A Child of our Time at Carnegie Hall and concerts with New Jersey Symphony, Baltimore Symphony under David Zinman and Calgary Philharmonic under Mario Bernardi; Engagements with San Francisco Opera, 1985-, in Il ritorno di Ulisse, Don Quichotte, Capriccio (Flamand), Wozzeck (Captain), Der Ring des Nibelung (Mime), Le nozze di Figaro (Basilio), Die Meistersinger, The Queen of Spades and Roméo et Juliette (Tybald); Lyric Opera of Chicago debut in season 1992-93, as Mime in Das Rheingold conducted by Zubin Mehta; Spoleto Festival as Carlo in Donizetti's Il Duce d'Alba. *Address:* c/o IMG Artists, Media House, 3 Burlington Lane, London W4 2TH, England.

PETERSEN Gunilla, b. 13 Dec 1942, Kristianstad, Sweden. Writer on Music; Editor. widowed, 1988, 1 daughter. *Education:* BA (Fil kand), Music History, Theatre History, Art History, Stockholm University, 1968; Graphic Education, Graphic Institute, Stockholm. *Career:* Editor, Tonfallet magazine, National Swedish Institute for Concerts, 1970-81; Editor, Musiklivet Var Sang choir magazine, 1977-89; Programme Editor, Royal Opera, Stockholm, 1981-. *Contributions:* Several articles on music in various newspapers, Royal Opera magazine and music publications; Record sleeves and commentaries for Royal Philharmonic Orchestra, Stockholm; Several music programmes in the Swedish Broadcast P2: Opp Amaryllis, 1992-93. *Memberships:* Swedish Journalists Union; Swedish Theatre Union. *Hobby:* Choir singing in Royal Philharmonic Choir, Stockholm. *Address:* Lagerlofsgatan 4 V, 112 60 Stockholm, Sweden.

PETERSEN Nils Holger, b. 27 Apr 1946, Copenhagen, Denmark. Composer; Minister of the Danish Church. m. Frances Ellen Hopenwasser, 11 Sept 1971, divorced 1989, 1 son, 1 daughter. *Education:* Degree in Mathematics, University of Copenhagen, 1969; Postgraduate studies in Mathematics, Universities of Copenhagen and Oslo; Studies in Theology, Copenhagen University; Minister of the Danish Church 1974-; Research Fellow, University of CPH, 1990-; Piano studies with Elisabeth Klein; Composition studies with Ib Nørholm. *Career:* Compositions performed on Danish, Swedish, Norwegian and Dutch radio and on Danish TV, at Nordic Music Days and various concerts in many countries. *Compositions:* Piano and guitar solo works published and available on cassette tape at The Society for Publishing Danish Music where other works are also obtainable. Major works: Opera: Fools Play, 1970 first performed 1985; Liturgical Opera: Vigil for Thomas Beckett, 1989; Church Cantatas 1971, 1974, 1976; Antiphony for Good Friday (9 instruments and vocal); 2 Wind Quintets; Solo works for violin, for piano and for organ; Liturgical Opera: The Lauds of Queen

Ingeborg, 1991. *Publications:* Kristendom i Musikken, (On connection and separation between the music of western societies and Christendom - from Gregorian chant to post-modernism) 1987. *Contributions to:* Various articles on theologico-musical aspects of the western culture in musical and theological papers. *Hobby:* Mountain Hiking. *Address:* Brødrene Reebergs vej 5, DK-2000 Frederiksberg, Denmark.

PETERSON Claudette, b. 15 July 1953, Lakewood, Ohio, USA. Singer (Soprano). *Education:* Studied at San Francisco Conservatory. *Career:* Sang at San Francisco Opera from 1975; Washington Opera, 1979, as Blondchen in Die Entfuhrung, Boston, 1980, as Dunyasha in War and Peace, Chicago, 1982, as Adele in Fledermaus; New York City Opera, 1985-86, as Manon and Lisette in La Rondine; Sang Yum-Yum in The Mikado for Canadian Opera at Toronto, 1986; Other roles have included Lucia (Arizona Opera) and Gilda (Shreveport); Further engagements at Buffalo, Houston, Geneva and Honolulu; Frequent concert appearances. *Recordings include:* Musgrave's A Christmas Carol. *Address:* c/o New York City Opera, Lincoln Center, New York, NY 10023, USA.

PETERSON Glade, b. 17 Dec 1928, Fairview, Utah, USA. Singer (Tenor). *Education:* Studied with Carlos Alexander in Salt Lake City and with Enrico Rosati and Ettore Verna in New York. *Debut:* NBC Opera New York 1957, as Pinkerton. *Career:* Sang at such American centres as Dallas, Baltimore, San Francisco, Houston, Pittsburgh, San Antonio and Santa Fe; European engagements at Brussels, Amsterdam, Basle, Bordeaux, Geneva, Munich, Hamburg, Stuttgart and Milan; Many appearances at the Zurich Opera, including the premiere of Martinů's Greek Passion, 1961; Metropolitan Opera 1973; Other roles have included Florestan, Riccardo, Don Alvaro (La Forza del Destino), Walther, Loge, Cavaradossi, Don José and Hermann in The Queen of Spades; Lyric roles have been Mozart's Ferrando, Belmonte and Tamino; Puccini's Rodolfo and Rinuccio; Edgardo in Lucia di Lammermoor and Tonio in La Fille du Régiment; Massenet's Des Grieux and Bizet's Nadir; Verdi's Fenton and Alfredo; Many concert appearances. *Recordings include:* Duets from Madama Butterfly and Manon, with Felicia Weathers.

PETIT Jean-Louis, b. 20 Aug 1937, Favrolles, France. Conductor; Harpsichordist; Composer. *Education:* Studied in Paris with Igor Markevitch, Pierre Boulez and Olivier Messiaen. *Career:* Organised and conducted various ensembles in the regions of Champagne, 1958-63 and Picardy, 1964-70; Performances on radio and television, tours of Europe and the United States; Co-directed the Paris Summer Festival 1972-77; Founder member of the contemporary music group Musique Plus; Director of the Association musicale internationale d'echange (AMIE); Director of the Ecole Nationale de Musique of Ville-d'Avray. *Compositions include:* Au-dela du signe for orchestra; De quelque part effondree de l'homme for quartet; Continuelles discontinues for percussion; (82 opus) Transcriptions of early music. *Recordings include:* Works by Boismortier, Leclair, Marais, Rameau, Lully, Mouret, Devienne, Campra, Francoeur, Couperin and Mondonville (Decca); Roussel's Sinfonietta; Les Troqueurs by d'Auvergne (Decca); 2nd Symphonie of Gounod (Arion); chamber music by Saint-Saëns; Compact Disques (REM) music by Jolivet, Ancelin, Casterède, Roizemblat, Tisné, Chaynes, Condé, Makimo, Petit, Ibert, Philippot, Gaussin. *Memberships:* Secrétaire Général de l'Union Nationale des Compositeurs, Director Artistique de la Société Française de Musique Contemporaine.

PETIT Pierre, b. 21 Apr 1922, Poitiers, France. m. (3) Liliane Fiaux 1974; 4 sons, 1 daughter from previous marriages. *Education:* Lycée Louis-le-Grand, Université de Paris à la Sorbonne and Conservatoire de Paris. *Career:* Head of Course, Conservatoire de Paris 1950; Director of Light Music, Office de Radiodiffusion et Télévision Française (ORTF) 1960-64, Director of Music Productions, ORTF 1964-70, Chamber Music 1970-; Producer, Radio-Télévision Luxembourgeoise (RTL)

1980; Director- General, Ecole Normale de Musique de Paris 1963; Music Critic, Figaro. *Compositions include:* Suite for 4 cellos 1945, Zadig (Ballet) 1948, Ciné-Bijou (Ballet) 1952, Feu Rouge, Feu Vert 1954, Concerto for Piano and Orchestra 1956; Concerto for Organ and Orchestra 1960, Furia Italiana 1960, Concerto for 2 guitars and orchestra 1965. *Publications:* Verdi 1957, Ravel 1970. *Honours:* Chevalier, Légion d'honneur, Officier des Art et Lettres, Ordre nationale du Mérite, Officier de l'Ordre du Cèdre du Liban; Premier Grand Prix de Rome 1946. *Membership:* Gov. Council Conservatoire de Paris. *Address:* 28 Rue Cardinet, 75017 Paris, France.

PETKER Allan Robert, b. 24 Jan 1955, Bakersfield, California, USA. Composer; Publisher; Conductor. m. Ann Louise Steinberg, 18 June 1977, 1 son, 1 daughter. *Education:* BA cum laude, Viola, 1977, MA, Choral Conducting, 1981, California State University, Northridge. *Career:* Director of Publications, Fred Bock Music Company and Gentry Publications, 1977-89, later also The Raymond A Hoffman Company and H T FitzSimons Company, to 1989; Established own company, Pavane Publishing, 1989; Orchestrator, Violist, Guitarist, Conductor; Guest Clinician or Conductor for publishers, choral societies, churches, colleges; Formerly Director of Music, Lutheran and Presbyterian Churches; Freelance studio work and occasional concert playing; Works performed throughout USA. *Compositions:* Over 130 choral works mainly of religious nature including: Canticle of St Augustine, 5- movement cantata for choir and orchestra; Speak of Peace, SATB; Canon of Praise for Easter Morning; Sing Merry Christmas; Behold the Lamb of God, SATB; All Praise to God in Heaven, 2-part; Sing a Merry Madrigal, SATB; After the Rain, SA; Springtide Is Come, SATB; Easter Fantasia, for handbells. *Recordings:* Canticle of St Augustine, Gentry Publications. *Publications:* Choral Questions and Answers, 1990; Choral Questions and Answers, Vol II, for Young Voices, 1991. *Hobby:* Camping. *Address:* 28 Hooper Lane, San Anselmo, CA 94960, USA.

PETKOV Dimiter, b. 5 Mar 1939, Sofia, Bulgaria. Singer (Bass). m. Anne-Lise Petkov. *Education:* Sofia Music Academy with Christo Brambarov. *Debut:* Sofia as Ramfis and Zaccaria, 1964. *Career:* Guest appearances, Glyndebourne Festival, 1968, 1970, as Osmin and Gremin; Rostropovich Festival, Aldeburgh, 1983; Earl's Court, London, 1988; Birmingham Arena, 1991; Daytona Festival with London Symphony Orchestra, 1993; Arena di Verona as Philipp II, 1969, as Zaccaria, 1981, as Ramfis, 1986, 1987; Appearances: Vienna State Opera, 1972-86, 1990, as Philip II, Ramfis, Boris, Khovansky, Mephisto; Madrid, Barcelona, 1978-86, 1990; Chicago, 1980; Bologna, 1980-83, 1988; Catania, Palermo, Lecce, 1981, 1984, 1986; La Scala, Milan, 1981, 1984, 1989; Washington DC, 1982, 1984; Carnegie Hall, New York City, 1982, 1984, 1989; Zurich, Hamburg, Bonn, 1984-85, 1990; Naples, 1984, 1991; Rome, 1987, 1992; Florence, 1986, 1987, 1989, 1991; Monte Carlo, 1986, 1989; Paris, 1986, 1988; Deutsche Oper Berlin, 1988-89, 1990, 1992, 1993; Dallas, 1989, 1993; Opera Bastille, Paris, 1990, 1991, 1993; Appeared with Berlin Philharmonic, London Symphony Orchestra, National Symphony Washington DC, Boston Symphony Orchestra at Tanglewood, Israel Philharmonic (Zubin Mehta) at Tel-Aviv, Montreal Symphony Orchestra, RAI Orchestras in Milan, Rome, Naples, Orchestre de Paris, Orchestre National de France, Concertgebouw Amsterdam, St-Petersburg Philharmonic Jerusalem Symphony, San Francisco Symphony; In demand for all the Verdi roles: Philipp, Zaccaria, Fiesco; Bellini, Rossini, Donizetti; Mephisto by Gounod in French repertoire; All main roles in Russian repertoire: Boris Godunov, Ivan Khovansky, Ivan Susanin, others. *Recordings:* EMI, Lady Macbeth of Mtsensk; EMI, Shostkovich 13th Symphony with London Symphony Orchestra; Aleko by Rachmaninov; Khovanshchina by Mussorgsky; Erato, Yolanta by Tchaikovsky, Mussorgsky cycles and Boris arias, 1989; Koch, Shostakovich cycles, 1993; Sony, Boris Godunov, 1992; Verdi Requiem at Eckphrasis Records, New York, 1994; Sings with such conductors as Abbado, Mehta,

Bartoletti, Previn, Molinari-Pradelli, Rostropovich, Ozawa, Rozdestvensky, Pretre, Bernstein, Pritchard, Maazel, Giulini; Werner Herzog's Fitzcarraldo sing Ernani in Manaus. *Address:* Rue Du Conseil-Général 6, 1205 Geneva, Switzerland.

PETRASSI Goffredo, b. 16 July 1904, Zagarolo, Italy. Composer. m. Rosetta Acerbi 1962, 1 daughter. *Education:* Conservatorio S. Cecilia, Rome. *Career:* Supt. Teatro Fenice, Venice 1937-40; President, International Society for Contemporary Music 1954-56; Professor of Composition, Accadamie S. Cecilia. *Compositions include:* Orchestral: Partita 1932, First Concerto 1933, Second Concerto 1951, Recreation Concertante (Third Concerto) 1953, Fourth Concerto 1954, Fifth Concerto 1955, Invenzione Concertata 1957, Quartet 1957; Operas and Ballets: Follia di Orlando 1943, Ritratto di Don Chisciotte 1945, Il Cordovano 1948 Morte dell'Aria 1950; Choral Works: Salmo IX 1936, Magnificat 1940, Coro di Morti 1941, Noche Oscura 1951, Mottetti 1965; Voice and Orchestra Quattro Inni Sacre 1942; Chamber Music: Serenata 1958, Trio 1959, Suoni Notturni 1959, Propos d'Alain 1960, Concerto Flauto 1960, Seconda Serenata-Trio 1962, Settimo Concerto 1964, Estri 1966-67, Beatitudines 1968, Ottetto di Ottori 1968, Souffle 1969, Ottavo Concerto 1970-72, Elogio 1971, Nunc 1971, Ala 1972, Orationes Christi 1975, Alias 1977, Grand Septuor 1978, Violasola 1978, Flou 1980, Romanezetta 1980, Poems 1977-80, Sestina d'Autunno 1981-82, Laudes Creaturarum 1982; Duetto for violin and viola, 1985. *Address:* Via Ferdinando di Savoia 3, 00196 Rome, Italy.

PETRE Leonardus Josephus, b. 27 Jan 1943, Sint Triniden, Belgium. Professor of Trumpet. m. Maes Arlette, 24 July 1965, 2 sons. *Education:* Bachelor of Medicine, University of Leuven, 1962; Music schools of St. Trinden en Hasselt, First prizes in Music-Reading and Trumpet; Royal Music Academy (Conservatoire Royal) Brussels, First Prizes in Music Reading, Transposition, Trumpet and Musical History. *Career:* Teacher of trumpet and several other brass instuments in several music schools; Professor of Trumpet at the Lemmens Institute, Leuven; Many appearances as member of orchestra or soloist on the Belgian and German radio and TV; Soloist at many classical concerts in Belgium, France, Holland and Germany; Trumpet-soloist with The New Music Group, and Collegium Instrumentale Brugense; Member of the Xenakis ensemble, Holland; Creator and leader of The Belgian Brass Quintet 2 1973-79; Conductor of brassband and fanfare; Specialist in playing Bach-trumpet (piccolo) and copies of very old trumpets. *Recordings:* Several cantatas of J.S. Bach with La Chapelle des Minimes, Brussels. *Contributions to:* Several articles concerning the trumpet and brass playing in local music magazines. *Membership:* International Trumpet Guild. *Hobbies:* Gardening; Reading about natural healing methods. *Address:* Smoldersstraat 44, 3910 Herk de Stad, Belgium.

PETRI Michala, b. 7 July 1958, Copenhagen, Denmark. Recorder Player. *Education:* Studied with Professor Ferdinand Conrad, Staatliche Hochschule für Musik und Theater, Hanover, Germany. *Debut:* Danish Radio, 1964. *Career:* Appearances as Soloist with Orchestra Tivoli, Copenhagen, 1969; Over 1,200 concerts in Denmark, Norway, Sweden, Germany, Switzerland, Belgium, Finland, Italy, Iceland, England, Israel, Colombia, Mexico, Haiti, Canada, Turkey, France, Taiwan, USA, Portugal and Japan. Numerous appearances at Festivals and performances on TV and radio. *Recordings include:* Music by Henning Christiansen, Berio, Handel, Telemann, van Eyck, Sammartini, Vivaldi; 12 records with The Academy of St Martins-in-the-Fields, Holliger and George Malcolm; 30 LPs in all, most of them for Philips. *Honours:* Jacob Gade Prize, 1969, 1975; Critics Prize of Honour, 1976; Nording Radio Prize, 1977; Niels Prize, 1980; Tagea Brandts Prize, 1980; Maarum Prize, 1981; Schroder Prize, 1982. *Address:* Noddehegnet 30, 3480 Fredensborg, Denmark.

PETRIC Ivo, b. 16 June 1931, Ljubljana. Musician; Composer; Conductor. *Education:* Music Academy Ljubljana. *Debut:* First performances, piano trio, May 1952. *Career:* Conductor of Slavko Osterc Ensemble (for contemporary music), 1962-82; Editor-in-Chief of Composers Editions, 1970-; Artistic Director, Slovenian Philharmonic, 1979-. *Compositions:* Orchestral music; Concertos for various instruments; Chamber Music; Sonatas for various instruments with piano. (3 Symphonies 1954, 1957, 1960); Trumpet Concerto 1986; Dresden Concerto for strings 1987; Trois Images, 1973, Dialogues Entre Deux Violons, 1975, Jeux Concertants for Flute and Orchestra, 1978, Toccata Concertante for 4 Percussionists and Orchestra 1979, Gallus Metamorphoses, 1992. *Recordings:* Several works of orchestral, chamber and solo music. *Honours:* Slovene State Preseren Foundation Prize, 1971; 1st Prize, Wieniawski International Composition Competition for violin, 1975; Ljubljana Prize for Artists, 1977; Oscar Espla International Competition, First Prize, 1984. *Membership:* Association of Slovene Composers. *Address:* Bilecanska 4, 61000 Ljubljana, Slovenia.

PETRINJAK Darko, b. 1 Dec 1954, Zagreb, Yugoslavia. Concert Guitarist, Lutenist, Double Bassist; Guitar Pedagogue. m. Jasna Kos, 16 July 1983, 1 son, 1 daughter. *Education:* Diploma, Double Bass, Zagreb Academy of Music, 1975; Recital Diploma, Guitar, 1978, Lute, 1980, London Royal Academy of Music, England. *Debut:* 11 Nov. 1971. *Career:* Double Bass Player, Philharmonic Orchestra, Zagreb, 1974-75; Visiting Guitar Teacher, Birmingham School of Music, 1978-81; Professor, Guitar, Zagreb Academy of Music, 1982-; As Concert Guitarist played in Great Britain, Soviet Union, Chile, Czechoslovakia, Yugoslavia; Founder, Zagreb Guitar Trio, 1984-. *Recordings:* 3 Solo LP's; Double LP with Singer Dunja Vejzovic; LP with Violinist Tonko Ninic; LP with Cellist Valter Despalj; 2 LP's with Zagreb Guitar Trio. *Honours:* Julian Bream Prize, London, 1977; 1st Prize, Yugoslav Competition of Music Artists, 1979. *Current Management:* Zagreb Concert Management. *Address:* c/o Zagreb Concert Management, Trnjanska bb, 41000 Zagreb, Slovenia.

PETRO Janos, b. 5 Mar 1937, Repceszemere, Hungary. Conductor; Chief Music Director. m. 27 Aug 1959, 1 son, 1 daughter. *Education:* Conductor and Composer, Academy of Music, Budapest, 1959. *Debut:* As Composer, Vienna, 1959. *Career:* Opera and Concerts in Budapest, Vienna, Berlin, Dublin, Bratislava, Frankfurt, Hamburg, Graz; Radio Budapest; Vienna Symphonic Record Register; Television Budapest and Vienna. *Recordings include:* Goldmark: Concerto for Violin and Orchestra; Mendelssohn: Concerto for Violin and Orchestra; Haydn: Scena di Berenice and Concert arias; P Karolyi: Epilogus; P Karolyi: Consolatio; Bizet: Symphony C-major; Bizet: Suite L'Arlesienne; Beethoven: Egmont Overture; Liszt: Les Préludes; Haydn: Symphony No. 104. *Honours:* F Liszt Prize, Conductor, Budapest, 1983; World Young Composer Prize, Vienna, 1959; State Prize, Budapest, 1982. *Membership:* Musicians Alliance, Budapest, President and Member. *Hobby:* Stamp Collecting. *Current Management:* Interkoncert Budapest, Vorosmarty ter 1; Austrokonzert, Vienna. *Address:* Martirok tere 8, H-9700 Szombathely, Hungary.

PETROBELLI Pierluigi, b. 18 Oct 1932, Padua, Italy. Musicologist; University Teacher. *Education:* Studied Composition with A Pedrollo, Padua, 1954-57; Laurea in Lettere, University of Rome, 1957; MFA, Musicology (under O Strunk and A Mendel), Princeton University, 1961; Studied Musicology under W Waite, Harvard Summer School. *Career:* Librarian, Archivist, Verdi Institute, Parma, 1964-69; Librarian, G Rossini Conservatory, Pesaro, 1970-73; Teacher of Music History, Parma University, Cremona extension, 1970-72; Lecturer in Music, 1973-75, Reader in Musicology, 1976-80, King's College, University of London; Member of Organising Committee for Xth Congress of International Society of Musicology in Copenhagen, 1972; Director, Istituto nazionale di studi verdiani, Parma, 1980-; Professor of Music History, University of Perugia, 1981-83; Professor of Music History, La Sapienza University of Rome, 1983-. *Publications:* Giuseppe Tartini: le fonti biografiche, 1968; Tartini, le sue idee e il suo tempo, 1992; Music in the Theater - Essays on Verdi and other composers, 1994; Studi verdiani, yearbook (editor), 1981-; Critical edition of Mozart's Il re pastore (with Wolfgang Rehm), 1984; Carteggio Verdi-Ricordi 1880-1881, (co-editor), 1988. *Contributions to:* Acta Musicologica; Nuova Rivista Musicale Italiana; Tempo; Mozart Jahrbuch; Studi Verdiani; Chigiana. *Address:* 34 Via di S Anselmo, I-00153 Rome, Italy.

PETROFF-BEVIE Barbara, b. 2 June 1934, Hamburg, Germany. Lyric Artist; Professor of Music. m. Joseph Petroff, 17 May 1973, 1 son, 1 daughter. *Education:* University; Master classes, Hochschule fur Music, Hamburg; Opera classes, Bern and Geneva Conservatories; Diploma. *Debut:* As Constance in Entführung aus dem Serail, Stadttheaart Luneburg, 1959, and as Clarice in Haydn's Il mondo della luna, Stadttheater Bern, 1960. *Career includes:* Main appearances: Aarhus, Denmark; Bern and Geneva, Switzerland; The Hague, Netherlands; Gent, Belgium; Linz, Austria; Kiel, Germany; Grand Theatre Geneva and Kgl Opera at Stockholm; Sang as Carolina in Il matrimonio segreto, Gilda in Rigoletto, Blondchen and Constance in Entfuhrung, Musetta, Sophie in Der Rosenkavalier, Aennachen in Freischutz, Susanna in Figaro, Despina in Cosi fan tutte, Adele in Die Fledermaus, Rosina in Barbier de Sevilla and Adina in L'Elisir d'amore; Operettes: Maritza in Grafin Mariza, Evelyne in Graf von Luxemburg and Viktoria in Viktoria und ihr Husar; Also sang Es lebe der Konig by Grandis; Radio Linz, Songs to words by Else Lasker, school music by J Petroff; Radio Genf, Songs to words by Therese Loup, music by Josef Petroff. *Membership:* Schweizerischer Tonkunstler Verband. *Hobbies:* Dogs; Writing. *Address:* 12 rue de Chêne-Bougeries, CH 1224 Geneva, Switzerland.

PETROV Andrey Pavlovich, b. 2 Sept 1930, Leningrad, Russia. Composer. *Education:* Studied at Leningrad Conservatory, 1949-54. *Career:* Editor at Muzgiz music publishers, teacher at Leningrad Conservatory, 1961-63, Chairman of Leningrad/St Petersburg Composers Union from 1964. *Compositions include:* Operas: Peter the First, Leningrad, 1975; Mayakovsky Begins, Leningrad, 1983; Ballets: The Magic Apple Tree, 1953; The Station Master, 1955; The Shore of Hope, 1959; The Creation of the World, 1971; Pushkin: Reflections on the Poet, 1978; Orchestral: Pioneer Suite, 1951; Sport Suite, 1953; Radda and Lioko, symphonic poem, 1954; Songs of Today, 1965; Poem, in memory of the siege of Leningrad, 1965; Patriotic vocal music; Film music and popular songs. *Honours:* USSR State Prizes. *Address:* c/o RAIS (CIS), PRS Ltd, Member Registration, 29-33 Berners Street, London W1P 4AA, England.

PETROV Ivan, b. 23 Feb 1920, Irkutsk, USSR. Singer (Bass). *Education:* Glazunov Music College Moscow 1938-39, with A. Mineyev. *Career:* Sang with Ivan Kozlovsky's opera group from 1939; Concert engagements with the Moscow Philharmonic 1941; Bolshoy Theatre, Moscow, from 1943: sang there in the 1953 premiere of Shaporin's The Decembrists; Paris Opéra 1954, as Boris Godunov; Concert tour of Europe 1954-55; Other operatic roles include Glinka's Ruslan, Dosifey in Khovanshchina, Mepistopheles in Faust, Verdi's King Philip and Basilio in Il Barbiere di Siviglia. *Recordings:* Eugene Onegin; Rachmaninov's Aleko; Prince Igor; Ruslan and Ludmilla; Boris Godunov; Verdi Requiem (Philips); The Tale of Tsar Saltan by Rimsky-Korsakov, Tchaikovsky's Mazeppa and Roméo and Juliette (Melodiya). *Address:* c/o Bolshoi Theatre, Pr Marxa 8/2, 103009 Moscow, Russia.

PETROV Marina, b. 27 Dec 1960, Kiev, USSR. Recital Pianist; Piano Lecturer. *Education:* Central Music School for Gifted Children, Belgrade, 1966-76; Central Music School for Gifted Children, Kiev, 1976-77; College of Music, Belgrade, 1977-79; Graduate course in

Performance, Teaching, Accompaniment, Moscow Conservatoire, 1979-84; Advanced solo studies, Belgrade Academy of Music, 1985-87. *Debut:* In Belgrade, 1969. *Career:* Recital pianist, 1969-; First appearance on TV and radio, Belgrade, 1969; Subsequently played in Kiev and Moscow, USSR; Tours in Yugoslavia; Has also played in Norway and in UK at venues including London, Dartington Hall and Bristol, 1990-; Lecturer in Piano. *Contributions to:* The Times; Rutland and Stamford Mercury; West Country Tribune; Politica, Yugoslavia. *Honours:* 1st Prize, Republican Festival for Gifted Children, Yugoslavia, 1970, 1972, 1973; 1st Prize, 1972, 3rd Prize, 1973, 2nd Prize, 1978, Federal Competition for Young Pianists; 1st Prize, Republican Competition for Young Pianists, 1978. *Membership:* Incorporated Society of Musicians. *Hobbies include:* Reading; Swimming; Theatre; Arts. *Address:* 53A Berriman Road, London N7 7PN, England.

PETROV Nikolai, b. 14 Apr 1943, Moscow, USSR. Pianist. *Education:* Graduated Moscow Conservatory 1967; Postgraduate studies with Yakov Zak. *Career:* Public career from 1962: many appearances with leading orchestras in Europe, Turkey, Canada, Japan, Mexico, the USA and USSR; Soloist with the Moscow Philharmonic Orchestra from 1968; Often heard in Tchaikovsky and Rachmaninov. *Honours:* Second Prize Van Cliburn International Competition, 1962; Second Prize Queen Elisabeth of the Belgians Competition, 1964. *Address:* c/o The Entertainment Corporation, 9 Great Newport Street, London WC2H 7JH, England.

PETROV Petar Konstantinov, b. 23 June, 1961, Stara Zagora, Bulgaria. Composer and Pianist. *Education:* Musical School, St Zagora, 1975-80, State Musical Academy, Sofia, 1983-88. *Debut:* New Bulgarian Music, 1984. *Career:* Manager and pianist in Chilorch-choire, Gouslartche, Sofia, 1988-; Piano Teacher, Blagoevgrad University, 1988-90; Composition Teacher, Music School, St Zagora 1989-90; Honorary Professor of contrapunjct in Bulgarian State Academy 1990-; Many appearances as chamber pianist with Rosen Idealov - clarinet. *Compositions:* Lamento for string orchestra, 1987, BR; Concert for violin and orchestra, 1987 BR, BTV; Improvisions of concert for piano, 1990, BTV; Katarsis for chamber orchestra, 1990, BR. *Recordings:* Sonata-Partita for violin solo 1986, BTV; Concerto piccolo for flute violin and piano, 1987, BR; Studium 2 for flute solo, 1989, BR. *Address:* ul Chr. Morfova No 2 ych, V Et 3 m, Ap 42, Stara Zagora, 6000 Bulgaria.

PETROVIC Danica, b. 2 Dec 1945, Belgrade, Yugoslavia. Musicologist. m. Dr. Milan D Petrovic, 27 Dec 1970, 2 daughters. *Education:* Piano and Theory, Secondary Music School; Musicology and Ethnomusicology, Faculty of Music; PhD, University of Ljubljana, 1980. *Career:* Institute of Musicology, Serbian Academy of Science and Arts; Research Fellow, Institute of Musicology, Belgrade; Professor, Balkan Music History, University of Arts, Novi Sad. *Publications:* Octoechos in the Musical Tradition of Southern Slavs (2 volumes), 1982. *Contributions to:* Editions of Serbian Academy of Sciences and Arts; Studies in Eastern Chant (New York); Musica Antiqua, (Poland)); Musicological Annual (Ljubljana); Arti Musices (Zagreb); Review of the Aesthetics and Sociology of Music (Zagreb). *Memberships:* International Musicological Society. *Address:* Institute of Musicology, Knez Milahilova 35, 11000 Belgrade, Serbia.

PETROVICS Emil, b. 9 Feb 1930, Nagybecskerek, Yugoslavia. Composer; Professor of Composition. 1 daughter. *Education:* Studied with Ferenc Farkas, Liszt Ferenc Academy of Music, Budapest, Hungary. *Career:* Professor, Academy of Dramatic and Film Arts; Professor of Composition, Head of Composition Faculty, Liszt Academy of Music; Director, Hungarian State Opera, 1986-. *Compositions:* Opera: c'est la guerre; Lysistrata; Crime and Punishment; Ballet: Salome; Oratorio: The Book of Jonah, 6 cantatas; Symphonic works: Symphony for String Orchestra; Concerto for Flute and Orchestra; Chamber works: String Quartet: Wind Quintet;

Cassazione, for 5 brass; Passacaglia in Blues, for bassoon and piano; Nocturne; Mouvement en Ragtime, for 1 and 2 cymbals; All above works recorded Hungaraton; Hungarian Children's Songs, for flute and piano, recorded in Canada; Four Self-Portraits in Masks, for harps. *Address:* Attila út 39, Budapest H-1013, Hungary.

PETRUSHANKY Boris, b. 3 June 1949, Moscow, Russia. Concert Pianist. *Education:* Studied at Central School of Music and Moscow Conservatoire. *Career:* Many concert tours of Russia and appearances in Italy, Hungary, UK, Germany, France, Japan and Australasia; Repertoire includes works by Beethoven, Brahms, Liszt, Prokoviev, Shostakovich, Schnittke and Gubaidullina; Professor at Academica Pianistica in Italy. *Recordings include:* Works by Schnittke and Gubaidullina. *Honours include:* Prizewinner in competitions at Leeds, 1969, Moscow, 1970, Munich, 1971, and Casagrande, 1975. *Address:* c/o Sonata, 11 Northpark Street, Glasgow G20 7AA, Scotland.

PETRUSHKA Shabtai Arieh, b. 15 Mar 1903, Leipzig, Germany. Composer; Arranger; Conductor. m. Pnina Dogar, 11 Oct 1977, 1 step-son from former marriage. *Education:* Technical University, Berlin-Charlottenburg; Leipzig Conservatory of Music; Stern's Conservatory, Berlin. *Career:* Orchestra Leader in various theatres, Berlin, 1928-33; Arranger, DGG, Berlin-UFA Film Company, 1933-37; Arranger and Conductor, Palestine Broadcasting Service, Jerusalem, 1938-48; Assistant Director of Music, 1948-58, Head, Music Division, 1958-68, Israel Broadcasting Service; Senior Lecturer, Orchestration and Score Reading, Rubin Academy of Music, Jerusalem, 1969-81. *Compositions include:* (Recorded and published) 5 Oriental Dances; 4 Movements for Band; 3 Movements for Orchestra; Piccolo Divertimento for Symphonic Band; various choral settings of Israeli folk tunes; 3 Jewish Melodies for String Orchestra; Hebrew Suite for Band; Various chamber music for woodwind and brass; Sonatina for Horn and String Quartet; Little Suite for Symphonic Band (3 Prize, Competition Rothschild Foundation); 3 Sephaidic Romances for 3 equal voices. *Hobbies:* Photography. *Current Management:* Petrushka, Shabtai Arieh. *Address:* 328 Nofei Yerushalain, 25 Shachri St, Bayit Vagan, 96470 Jerusalem, Israel.

PETTAWAY Charles Henry Jr., b. 7 June 1951, Philadelphia, Pennsylvania, USA. Concert Pianist; Educator. m. Terri Lynn, 5 Oct 1985, 1 son, 1 daughter. *Education:* BMus cum laude, Philadelphia Musical Academy; MMus cum laude, Temple University; Private studies, master classes, various teachers. *Debut:* Orchestral, Guest soloist, Capital Orchestra, Toulouse, France, 1974. *Career includes:* Performances, Washington DC; Philadelphia; New York; Israel; France; USSR; Tour, Switzerland, 1981. Guest soloist, numerous major & community orchestras throughout USA; Radio & TV performances; Master classes, various colleges; Visiting Lecturer, Piano, Lincoln University, Pennsylvania, 1988-89; Assistant Professor of Music, Lincoln University, Pennsylvania. *Recording:* Charles Pettaway Performs Russian Piano Music. *Honours include:* Selected participant, Tchaikovsky International Competitions, USSR, 1974, 1978; 1st prize, Robert Casadesus International Competition, Paris, France. *Current Management:* Lumaria Ricks Blakeney. *Address:* 1267 Cox Road, Rydal, PA 19046, USA.

PETTIT David Robin, b. 10 Oct 1936, Romford, Essex, England; Lecturer in Music; Professional Pianist. m. Angela Malsbury, 24 July 1965, 1 son. *Education:* Junior Exhibitioner, Guildhall School of Music, London, 1949-55; LGSM, Piano Performers; FRCO; MA, 1959, B.Mus., 1960, Keble College, Oxford. *Career:* Director of Music, Beauchamp School, 1960-63; Organist, St Peter's, Leicester and Assistant Conductor, Leicestershire County Youth Orchestra; Director of Music, St Edward's School, Oxford, 1963-66; Director of Music, Organist, Clifton College, Bristol, 1967-81; Assistant Director of Studies, Trinity College of Music, London, 1981-85; Vice Principal and Director of Studies, Trinity College of

Music, 1985-91; Hon Secretary, Royal College of Organists, London; Graduate and Performers Course Tutor, Royal Academy of Music, London, 1991-. *Recordings:* Organs of Clifton College; Richard Baker's Musical Menagerie. *Honour:* Dr August Mann Memorial Prize for Organ, 1955; Hon. FTCL, 1987. *Memberships:* Member of Council and Executive Committee; Royal College of Organists; Music Masters Association; Musicians Union; Royal Society of Musicians. *Hobbies:* Motoring; Swimming; Gardening; Cooking. *Address:* 40 Greenford Avenue, Hanwell, London W7 3QP, England.

PETTITT Maxwell Wayne, b. 10 Sept 1948, Newcastle-under-Lyme, Staffordshire, England. Composer; Academic. m. Maureen Tully, 22 Dec 1989. *Education:* Studied musical subjects privately during school years; ARCM, Piano Performance, 1965; BMus, 1971, MMus, 1972, University of Wales, Bangor. *Career:* Assistant Head of Music, Notre Dame High School, London, 1973; Director of Music, Rydal School, North Wales, 1974-78; Director of Music, South Wiltshire Grammar School, Salisbury, 1978-82; Tutor with Open University, 1979-; Head of Music (BA and PGCE), Nene College of Higher Education, Northampton, 1982-; Examiner/Moderator with London College of Music, Oxford University A Level and Cambridge University GCSE; Adjudicator in festival movement; Piano Lecturer/Recitalist; Organist. *Compositions:* Orphan of Chao, opera, 1977; Missa Solemnis, 12 part a cappella, 1980; Piano Concerto, 1982; Russian Folk Cantata, 1985; Various piano, choral and chamber works. *Contributions to:* Articles on Victorian Musical Life to various journals especially British Music Society. *Honours:* Scholarship, 1968; Finalist, Grand Prix Arthur Honegger, Paris, 1984. *Memberships:* Fellow, Royal Society of Arts; RMA; International Society for Music Educators; IMS; Victorian Society; British Music Society. *Hobbies:* Cats; Antiques; Natural history; Travel. *Address:* The Old Bakehouse, 14 Chapel Brampton, Northants NN6 8AF, England.

PETUKHOV Mikhail, b. 24 Apr 1954, Varna, Bulgaria. Concert Pianist. *Education:* Studied in Kiev and at Moscow Conservatoire with Tatiana Nikolayeva. *Career:* Many concerts in the former Soviet Union and, since its dissolution, in Italy, Belgium, Netherlands, Czechoslovakia and Germany; Played with Royal Scottish Orchestra, 1992, followed by Tchaikovsky First Concerto with City of Birmingham Symphony under Yuri Simonov; Repertoire has also included works by Purcell, Ravel, Handel, Stravinsky, Mendelssohn, Schumann, Schoenberg and Ives; Professor in Piano at Moscow Conservatoire. *Honours include:* 3rd Prize at J S Bach Competition, Leipzig, 1972, and Queen Elisabeth Competition at Brussels, 1975. *Address:* c/o Sonata, 11 Northpark Street, Glasgow G20 7AA, Scotland.

PEYREGNE André b. 6 Feb 1949, St Brieuc, France. Conservatory Principal. m. Agata Krzeminska, 3 Mar 1977, 1 son, 1 daughter. *Education:* Licence de Mathématiques, University of Nice; Studied piano and conducting, Conservatoire de Nice. *Career:* Vice-Principal, 1971-81, Principal, 1981-, Conservatoire de Nice; Music Critic, Nice-Matin, 1971-; Author of programmes, Radio-France and various French television channels. *Contributions to:* Articles on music in specialist French periodicals; Reviews. *Honour:* 1st Prize for Piano and Orchestral Conducting, Conservatoire de Nice. *Address:* 8 av. Roi Albert 1, 06700 Nice, France.

PFAFF Graham, b. 11 Aug 1948, Ipswich, England. Oboist; Orchestra Manager. m. Regina Diniz Schlaepfer, 17 Dec 1977. *Education:* Royal College of Music under Professor Terence MacDonagh. *Career:* Freelance Orchestral Oboist with London Symphony Orchestra, Philharmonia, BBC and others, 1969-72; Oboist, London Mozart Players, 1972-75; Oboist, 1974-91, General Manager, 1984-, English Sinfonia. *Publication:* Revision of A Tune A Day for Oboe, 1966. *Membership:* Musicians Union. *Hobbies:* Chess; Bridge; Soccer referee. *Address:* The Barn, Layston Park, Royston, Herts SG8 9DS, England.

PFAFF Luca, b. 25 Aug 1948, Olivone, Switzerland. Conductor. m. Dominique Chanet, 1986, 2 sons. *Education:* Basel University; Conservatorio G Verdi, Milan; Musikakademie, Vienna; Accademia Santa Ceàlia, Rome. *Career:* Director, Orchestre Symphonique du Rhin, France; Director, Carme, Milan; Founder, Ensemble Alternance, Paris; Guest Conductor, major orchestras, Europe. *Recordings:* Scelsi, RCA; Donatoni, Harmonic Records; Dusapin, Opera Romeo et Juliette, Accord; Mozart, Gran Partita, Nuova ERA. *Contributions to:* Monde de la Musique; Harmonie; Rivista Musicale. Diapason d'Or, 1985; Best CD of 1988, Donatoni, CHOC, Monde de la Musique. *Hobbies:* Himalayas; Skiing; Driving collection cars. *Current Management:* Valmalete, Paris, France. *Address:* Aeschenvorstadt 15, CH-4051 Basel, Switzerland.

PFISTER Daniel, b. 6 Nov 1952, St Gallen, Switzerland. Composer. *Education:* Teachers' Training College, 1970-74. Music Education: Konservatorium Winterthur (Conservatoire), 1974-78; Teachers' Diploma piano, 1978; Musikhochschule Zurich, music theory with Hans Ulrich Lehmann, 1977-78; Hochschule für Musik und darstellende Kunst in Wien, composition with Prof. Alfred Uhl, 1978-84; Diploma composition, 1984; Hochschule für Musik und darstellende Kunst in Wien, conducting with Prof. Otmar Suitner, 1984-87. *Career:* Freelance Composer; Private teacher for music theory composition and piano, 1982-. *Compositions:* Saitenspiel, 1982 for 2 guitars; Concerto for String orchestra, 1982-87; Aeon for sporano and piano, 1983; Aeon for soprano and orchestra, 1983-84; Canto for soprano or flute or saxophone, 1985-88; Canto for soprano (flute), clarinet and vibraphone, 1986; Neun und Zehne auf einen Streich, for guitar, 1988; Touches for flute, oboe, clarinet, bassoon, horn, trumpet, snare drum, gong, xilorimba, vibraphone, guitar, piano, violin, viola, violincello, 1988-89; Bruchstuecke aus Touches, 1988; 880 un satiesme, instrument is free, 1988; Piano Trio for violin, violoncello and piano, 1988-89; 12 kleine Odien for flute and guitar, 1987-89; Max and Moritz for reciter and guitar, 1990-91. *Memberships:* SMPV Schweizerischer Musikpaedagogischer Verband; SUISA. *Address:* Lehnstrasse 33 CH-9014, St Gallen, Switzerland.

PHARR Rachel Elizabeth Caroline, b. 15 Apr 1957, Picayune, Mississippi, USA. Harpsichordist. m. Bernard Gerard Kolle, 1 Jan 1989. *Education:* BMus summa cum laude, Piano Performance major, 1978, MMus, Piano Performance major, 1980, University of Southwestern Louisiana, Lafayette; Aspen Music School, Aspen Festival, 1980, 1981; MMus, Harpsichord Performance major, Arizona State University, Tempe, 1982; Banff Centre School of Fine Arts, Canada, 1987-89. *Career:* Harpsichordist with Houston Baroque Ensemble, 1983-87, with Texas Chamber Orchestra in Houston, Texas, 1985-87; Numerous concerts, Banff Centre, Banff, Alberta, Canada, 1987-89; Performed at Aspen Music Festival, 1981, Breckenridge Music Institute, 1982, 1983; Featured Soloist in Houston Harpsichord Society's presentation of the entire J.S.Bach Well-Tempered Clavier for Bach Tercentenary, 1985; New Music America concerts, 1986; Tours as Solo Harpsichord, 1986, with Liedermusik Ensemble, 1987; Harpsichord Accompanist, Banff Centre, 1988-89; Radio performances, KLEF, Houston and WWNO, New Orleans; TV performance, NBC-Channel 4, Denver. *Hobbies:* Studying French; Reading; Jogging; Cross-country skiing. *Address:* c/o Newton T.Pharr, 314 Dodson Street, New Iberia, LA 70560, USA.

PHILIP Robert Marshall, b. 22 July 1945, Witney, Oxfordshire, England. Freelance Music Critic; BBC Television Producer. m. Maria Lukianowicz, 3 Jan 1976, 2 daughters. *Education:* Royal College of Music, 1962-64; Peterhouse, Cambridge, 1964-68; University (now Wolfson), College, Cambridge, 1968-72; ARCM; MA; PhD. *Career:* Junior Research Fellow at University Wolfson College, Cambridge, 1972-74; Producer, BBC Television, Open University Department, 1976-; Freelance Music Critic and Broadcast Talks. *Publications:* PhD Thesis, unpublished, on Orchestral

Style on Gramophone Records, 1920-50; Early Recordings and Musical Style, 1992. *Contributions to:* Records and Recording; BBC Record Review; Broadcast series includes: The Long Playing Era (Radio 3); The Developing Musician (Radio 3); Composer and Interpreter (BBC World Service); Musical Yearbook (BBC World Service); Vintage Years, Radio 3. *Honour:* Organ Scholarship, Peterhouse, Cambridge, 1964. *Membership:* Royal Musical Association. *Address:* BBC Open University Production Centre, Walton Hall, Milton Keynes, England.

PHILIPS Daniel, b. 1960, USA. Violinist. *Career:* Winner of Young Concert Artists International Auditions and recitalist at Lincoln Center's Alice Tully Hall, 92nd Street 'Y' and appearances with major orchestras; Chamber musician at Santa Fe Festival, Spoleto Festival, Lockenhaus Kammermusikfest and the International Musicians Seminar in Prussia Cove; Co-founded the Orion Quartet and has given concerts at Kennedy Center, Washington DC, at Gardner Museum, Boston and throughout USA; Carnegie Hall recital, 1991, as part of the Centennial Celebration tribute to next 100 years of music making; Concerts at Turku Festival in Finland; Professor of Violin at State University of New York and Faculty member at Aaron Copland School of Music. *Address:* c/o Ingpen and Williams Ltd, 14 Kensington Court, London W8 5DN, England.

PHILIPS Leo, b. 1960, England. Violinist. *Education:* Studied at Yehudi Menuhin School and with Sando Vegh, Dorothy DeLay and Shmuel Ashkenasi. *Career:* Concerts as chamber musician and soloist; Former member of the Chamber Orchestra of Europe; Currently Leader and Principal Director of East of England Orchestra; Co-founder Vellinger String Quartet, 1990; Participated in master classes with Borodin Quartet at Pears- Britten School, 1991; Concerts at Ferrara Musica festival, Italy and debut on South Bank with London premiere of Robert Simpson's 13th Quartet; BBC Radio 3 debut, Dec 1991; Season 1992-93 with concerts in London, Glasgow, Cambridge, at Davos Festival, Switzerland and Crickdale Festival, Wiltshire; Wigmore Hall with Haydn (Op 54 no 2), Gubaidulina and Beethoven (Op 59 no 2), Purcell Room with Haydn's Last Seven Words. *Recordings include:* Elgar's Quartet and Quintet, with Piers Lane. *Address:* c/o Georgina Ivor Associates (Vellinger Quartet), 66 Alderbrook Road, London SW12 8AB, England.

PHILLIPS Elizabeth Ann, b. 3 Mar 1958, Swansea, Wales. Teacher; Director of Music; Soprano. m. Eric Wyn Phillips, 3 Apr 1986. *Education:* BA (Hons), Cardiff University; Postgraduate study, Advanced Certificate, Welsh College of Music and Drama. *Career:* Assistant Music Teacher, Heathfield House, Cardiff, 1980-81; Assistant Music Teacher, Radyr Comprehensive, Cardiff, 1981-87; Head of Music, Bryn Hafren Girls School, Barry, 1987-91; Currently Director of Music, Howell's School, Llandaff, Cardiff; Founder Tutor and Assistant Conductor, South Glamorgan High Schools' Choir; Member of BBC Welsh Chorus. *Honours:* Pernod Prize; Silver Medal, Worshipful Company of Musicians; Scholarship to study Voice, Welsh Arts Council. *Memberships:* Incorporated Society of Musicians; ATL; ABCD. *Hobbies:* Choral singer and soloist; Gardening. *Address:* 7 Apremont, 34 LLantrisant Road, LLandaff, Cardiff.

PHILLIPS Jean Susan, b. 24 May 1942, London, England. Concert Pianist; Harpsichordist; Teacher. div., 2 daughters. *Education:* Junior Exhibitioner, 1952-58, Senior Exhibitioner, 1958-63, ARCM, 1961, Royal College of Music. *Debut:* Wigmore Hall, London, 1965. *Career:* Concert Pianist, concerts at Queen Elizabeth Hall, Purcell Room, Wigmore Hall and major venues in England; Founder, Concerts for Children and Parents, Purcell Room, South Bank, London, 1971, giving concerts with Gerard Benson for 19 years; Television performances for ITV and national and local radio; Visiting Lecturer in piano and harpsichord, Christchurch College, Canterbury; Concert tours abroad, Belgium, France, Kenya, Cyprus and Jersey, 1988; Concerts in

Iceland and Australia including 2 broadcasts for ABC, 1990. *Recording:* For National Trust on Broadwood Square piano 1788, 1992. *Current management:* Don Goodsell. *Address:* Gothic Cottage, 22 Orchard St, Canterbury, Kent CT2 8AP, England.

PHILLIPS John Alan, b. 14 Apr 1960, Adelaide, South Australia, Australia. Musicologist. *Education:* BMus (Hons), 1983, PhD Musicology, in progress, University of Adelaide; Conducting, Composition, Vienna Konservatorium and Hochschule, 1983-85. *Career:* Active as Choral Conductor, Adelaide; Involved on major research project concerning Bruckner's 9th Symphony finale, 1989-; New Performing Version of finale completed in Rome with Nicola Samale, May 1991, first performed in Linz, Austria by Bruckner Orchestra, Dec 1991, first recorded by same orchestra, 1993; Lectures, conference papers, Australia, Europe; Press conferences, Australian, German, Austrian, US newspapers; Interviews, Australian, German, Austrian Radio. *Compositions:* Numerous unpublished works; Choral arrangements. *Recording:* 2- piano recording of Finale of Bruckner Ninth Symphony with Edward Kriek for ABC Radio, Dec 1990. *Publications:* Bruckner's Ninth Symphony Revisited. Towards the re-evaluation of a four-movement symphony, dissertation, 1994; Editor: Anton Bruckner: Ninth Symphony in D Minor: Finale: Reconstruction of the Autograph Score from the Surviving Manuscripts: Performing Version by Nicola Samale, John A Phillips and Giuseppe Mazzuca, with the assistance of Gunnar Cohrs, 1992; Anton Bruckner Gesamtausgabe: Zu Band IX; Finale: Rekonstruktion der Autograph-Partitur nach den erhaltenen Quellen. a): Studienpartitur; b) Textband, 1994; Anton Bruckner: Faksimile-Ausgabe aller dem Finale der IX. Symphonie zugehörigen Manuskripte, 1994. *Contributions include:* Neue Erkenntnisse zum Finale der Neunten Symphonie Anton Bruckners, in Bruckner Jahrbuch, 1989-90; The Finale of Bruckner's Ninth Symphony: new light on an old problem, in Miscellanea Musicologica. Adelaide Studies in Musicology, 1990; Zum leidigen Thema 'Finale der Neunten Symphonie Anton Bruckners' in Österreichische Musikzeitschrift, 1992. *Memberships:* Internationale Bruckner Gesellschaft; Österreichische Gesellschaft fur Musikwissenschaft; American Musicological Society. *Hobby:* Body-building. *Address:* 107 Fourth Avenue, Joslin, SA 5070, Australia.

PHILLIPS Margaret Corinna, b. 16 Nov 1950, Exeter, Devon, England. Concert Organist; Harpsichordist. *Education:* Royal College of Music, 1968-72; FRCO; GRSM; ARCM (organ performing with honours); Studied privately with Marie-Claire Alain in Paris, France, 1972-73. *Debut:* Royal Festival Hall, 1972. *Career:* Director of Music, St Lawrence Jewry next Guildhall, London, 1976-85; Professor of Organ and Harpsichord, London College of Music, 1985-91; Tutor in organ studies, Royal Northern College of Music, 1993-; Recitals throughout Europe, USA, Mexico and Australia; Radio broadcasts in UK, Sweden, Denmark, Netherlands and Australia; Performances with London Choral Society, BBC Singers, The Sixteen and London Mozart Players; Lecturer, English church and organ music. *Recordings:* Festliche Orgelmusik; English Organ Music from Queen Elizabeth I to Queen Elizabeth II; D Buxtehude; Orgelmusik i Karlskoga kyrka; Klosters Orgel; Organ Music of Saint-Saens; 18th Century English Organ Music; 19th Century English Organ Music; Wesley, Music for Organ. *Hobbies:* Reading; Walking; Playing the violin. *Address:* 54 Priory Road, Richmond, Surrey TW9 3DH, England.

PHILLIPS Paul Schuyler, b. 28 Apr 1956, New Jersey, USA. Conductor. m. Kathryne Jennings, 23 Nov 1986, 1 daughter. *Education:* BA cum laude, Music, Columbia College, 1978; MA, Composition, Columbia University, 1980; MM, Conducting, College-Conservatory of Music, University of Cincinnati, 1982; Eastman School, 1974-75; Mozarteum, Salzburg, 1977; Aspen, 1979, 1980, 1981; LA Philharmonic Institute, 1982; International Conductors Course, NOS, Netherlands, 1983; Tanglewood, 1985; New York Philharmonic Conductors Symposium, 1987; Music Academy of the West, 1986; Workshops, 1987, 1991,

1992, Masterclass, 1992, American Symphony Orchestra League; Weiner Meisterkurse, 1990. *Debut:* Conducting Brown Orchestra (with Dave Brubeck Quartet), Carnegie Hall, 1990, (with Itzhak Perlman), Avery Fisher Hall, 1992. *Career:* Frankfurt Opera, 1982-83; Kapellmeister, Luneberg Stadttheater, 1983-84; Associate Conductor: Greensboro Symphony, 1984-86, Savannah Symphony, 1986-89, Rhode Island Philharmonic, 1989-92; Assistant Conductor, Greensboro Opera, 1984-86; Music Director: Young Artists Opera Theatre, 1984-85, Brown University Orchestra, 1989-, University of Rhode Island Opera Ensemble, 1990-91, Worcester Youth Symphony, 1991-, Holy Cross Chamber Orchestra, 1993-; Youth Concert Conductor, Maryland Symphony, 1985-; Director, Savannah Symphony Chorale, 1987-89; Artistic Director, Brown Opera, 1992-; Guest Conductor, Netherlands Radio Chamber Orchestra and Choir, Pro Arte Orchester of Vienna, US orchestras. *Compositions:* For orchestra, chamber ensembles, voice, piano, theatre, film, TV. *Contributions to:* The Enigma of Variations: A Study of Stravinsky's Final Work for Orchestra, Music Analysis, 1984. *Address:* Brown University, Box 1924, Providence, RI 02912, USA.

PHILLIPS Peter, b. 15 Oct 1953, Southampton, England. Choral Director. *Education:* Studied at Winchester College and St John's College, Oxford. *Career:* Has taught at Oxford University and at Trinity College of Music and the Royal College of Music; Founded the Tallis Scholars 1978; Regular concerts in Britain and abroad, including the USA from 1988 and Australia from 1985 (Byrd's Five-part Mass at the Sydney Opera House); Substantial tours of the Far East (Japan, Taiwan and Korea Jan 1991); Promenade Concert debut 1988, with Victoria's Requiem; Documentary feature on ITV South Bank Show Dec 1990; UK concerts 1990-91 at Greyfriars Church Edinburgh, St John's Smith Square and the Grand Theatre, Blackpool; Author of English Sacred Music, 1549-1649, 1991. *Recordings include:* Lassus Music for Double Choir; Sarum Chant; John Sheppard Media Vita; Gesualdo Tenebrae Responsories; Corynysh Stabat Mater, Salve Regina and Magnificat; Clemens non Papa Missa Pastores quid am vidistis; Victoria Requiem and Tenebrae Responsories; Cardoso Requiem; Josquin Masses; Byrd The Great Service and Three Masses; Medieval Christmas Carols and Motets; Palestrina Masses (4 CDs); Tallis Complete English Anthems and Spem in Alium; Allegri Miserere and Mundy Vox Patris caelestis; Taverner Missa Gloria Tibi Trinitas; Russian Orthodox Music; Ikon of Light by John Tavener; CD based on South Bank TV feature; Isaac Missa de Apostolis; Tomkins The Great Service; Tallis Lamentations of Jeremiah; All recordings produced by Gimell Records, co-founded by Peter Phillips and Steve Smith in 1981. *Honours:* (with Tallis Scholars) include: Record of the Year, Gramophone Magazine, 1987 (for Josquin Masses); Diapason d'Or 1989, for Lassus and Josquin Masses. *Contributions to:* Music and Letters; The Listener; Spectator. *Memberships:* Athaeneum; Chelsea Arts Club; MCC. *Hobby:* Cricket; Arabic Studies. *Address:* c/o The Administrator, Tallis Scholars Trust, Fenton House, Banbury Road, Chipping Norton, Oxon OX7 5AW, England.

PIAN Rulan Chao, b. 20 Apr 1922, Cambridge, Massachusetts, USA. Professor Emerita of East Asian Languages and Civilisations and of Music. m. Theodore Hsueh-huang Pian, 1 daughter. *Education:* BA, Music, 1944, MA, Music, 1946, PhD, Musicology, Far Eastern Languages, 1960, Radcliffe College; Private lessons in Piano, Cello, Japanese Court Music, Chinese Zither. *Career:* Teaching Assistant, Chinese, 1947-58, Instructor, Chinese, 1959-61, Lecturer, Chinese, 1961-74, Professor, East Asian Languages and Civilisations, Music, 1974-92, Departments of East Asian Languages and Civilisations, and of Music, Master of South House, 1975-78, Harvard University; Numerous field trips on Music to Far East, 1958-; Visiting Professor, Music, Chung Chi College, Chinese University of Hong Kong, 1975, 1978-79, 1982, 1994; Visiting Professor, Taiwan, ROC: Tsing Hua University, 1990, Central University, 1992. *Publications:* A Syllabus for the Mandarin Primer,

1961; Sonq Dynasty Musical Sources and Their Interpretation, 1967; Complete Musical Works of Yuen Ren Chao (compiler), 1987. *Contributions to:* Numerous articles to music publications. *Honours:* Caroline I Wilby Prize for dissertation, Radcliffe College, 1960; PBK, 1961; O Kinkeldy Award for book, American Musicological Society, 1968; Medal for Distinguished Achievement, Radcliffe Graduate Society, 1980; Various grants, 1958-79; Honorary Professor: Central China University of Science and Technology, Wuhan, 1990, Central-South University of Science and Technology, Changsha, Hunan, 1991; Academician, Academia Sinica, Taiwan, 1990; Honorary Research Fellow, Institute of Music Research, Shanghai Conservatory of Music, 1991; Research Institute of Music, China Academy of Arts, Beijing, 1994. *Memberships:* Past Council Member Society of Ethomusicology; Council Member, American Musicological Society; International Musicological Society; Past Advisor, Society for Asian Music, Shanghai; Past President, Conference on Chinese Oral and Performing Literature; Association for Asian Studies; International Council for Traditional Music; Past Executive Board Member, Chinese Language Teachers Association; Editorial Boards: Musicology in China, Beijing, and Chinese Theatrical Forum, Lanzhou. *Address:* 14 Brattle Circle, Cambridge, MA 02138, USA.

PIANA Dominique, b. 5 July 1956, Eupen, Belgium. Harpist; Teacher; Performer; Musical Director. m. Will Joel Friedman, 26 May 1985, 1 son. *Education:* Royal Conservatory of Music, Brussels, 1974-80; Claremont Graduate School, California, 1982-85; Special training in Music Education Methods, Music & Movement, and the Concept of Life Energy in Music. *Career:* Professor of Harp, La Sierra University, Riverside, California, USA, 1982-; Professor of Harp, University of Redlands, California, 1985-; Director, Inland Empire Harp Ensemble; As performer: Solo and lecture recitals, chamber music, concerti. *Recordings:* Harpiana Productions: Fancy, entertaining music for harp, 1984; Lulling the Soul, Cardis of Love and Wonder, 1992; The Harp of King David, Ballads of Longing and Hope, 1994; Dreams & Passion, 19th Century Music for Harp, in preparation. *Contributions to:* Revue Musicale Belge, Belgium; Lumiere, France. *Memberships:* American Harp Society, Programme Chairman, 1992 National Conference; Music Teachers Association of California; American String Teachers Association; World Harp Congress; American Musicological Society. *Hobbies:* Creative writing; Linguistics; Nature; Healing. *Address:* 30765 Palo Alto Drive, Redlands, CA 92373, USA.

PICHLER Guenther, b. 9 Apr 1940, Austria, Violinist. *Education:* Studied in Vienna. *Career:* Leader of the Vienna Symphony Orchestra, 1958, Vienna Philharmonic, 1961; Professor, Hochschule für Musik, Vienna, 1963-; founder, leader of the Alban Berg Quartet from 1971; All over the World concert engagements, including complete cycles of the Beethoven Quartets in 15 Major European cities, 1987-88, 1988-89 seasons; Bartók/Mozart cycle in London, Vienna, Paris, Frankfurt, Munich, Geneva and Turin, 1990-91; Annual concert series at the Vienna Konzerthaus, the QEH London, Théâtre des Champs Elysées Paris, Opera Zurich, and festival engagements worldwide; Associate Artist at the South Bank Centre, London; US appearances in Washington DC, San Francisco and New York (Carnegie Hall). *Recordings include:* Complete quartets of Beethoven, Brahms, Berg, Webern and Bartók; Late quartets of Mozart, Schubert, Haydn and Dvořák; Ravel, Debussy and Schumann quartets; Live recordings from Carnegie Hall (Mozart, Schumann); Konzerthaus in Vienna; Complete Beethoven; Brahms, Dvořák, Smetana, Rihm, Schnittke, Janacek, Opéra-Comique Paris, (Brahms). *Honours include:* Grand Prix du Disque; Deutscher Schallplatenpreis; Edison Prize; Japan Grand Prix; Gramophone Magazine Award; International Classical Music Award, 1992; Honorary Member of the Vienna Konzerthaus. *Address:* Intermusica Artists' Management, 16 Duncan Terrace, London N1 8BZ, England.

PICHT-AXENFELD Edith Maria, b. 1 Jan 1914, Freiburg, Germany. Pianist; Organist; Harpsichordist; Educator. m. Dr Georg Picht, 4 sons, 1 daughter. *Education:* Studied piano with Paula Roth-Kastner, 1920-32, 1932-34 with Anna Hirzel-Langenhan, Rudolph Serkin, 1934-35; Abitur, Freiburg, 1931; Private Music teaching Examination, 1932; Studied organ with Albert Schweitzer. *Debut:* Freiburg 1927. *Career:* Piano and Harpsichord Concerts throughout Europe, Britain, South America, South Africa and Asia, 1935-; Participant, International Festivals including English Bach Festival; Chamber music partnership with Aurele Nicolet and Heinz Holliger; Piano Trio with Nicolas Chumachenco and Alexandre Stein; Professor, Staatliche Hochschule für Musik, Freiburg, 1947-. *Recordings include:* Bach, Goldberg Variations and Six Partitas; Baroque Sonatas for oboe and basso continuo; Bach Wohltemperiertes Klavier Books I and II, English Suites. *Honour:* Chopin Prize, Warsaw, 1937. *Memberships:* Deutscher Musikrat; European Piano Teachers Association. *Current Management:* Konzertdirektion Franz Günther Büscher, Heidelbreg, Germany. *Address:* Altbirkelhof, D-7824 Hinterzarten, Germany.

PICK Karl-Heinz, b. 18 Aug 1929, Rothenburg/Lausitz, Germany. Pianist; Composer; Piano Teacher. m. Elisabeth Buckisch, 3 Sept 1949, 2 daughters. *Education:* Felix Mendelssohn Bartholdy College of Music, Leipzig. *Career:* Professor of Piano, F. M. Bartholdy College of Music, Leipzig; Concert Pianist in Europe, Asia, Near East; Composer of Songs, Cantatas, Chamber Music, Violin Concerto, numerous piano works (see also Compositions); His 2 Concertos for piano and orchestra performed in Leipzig; Director, Piano Department, Leipzig College; Hon. Guest of USSR, Ministry of Culture to International Tchaikovsky Competition in Moscow, 1958; Elected President of Chopin Society, GDR, 1986; Jury Member: Sofia Festival Competition, 1969; J. S. Bach Competition, Leipzig, 1977 and 1980; Tchaikovsky Competition, Moscow, 1978; Vianna da Motta Competition, Lisbon, 1979; Viotti Competition, Vercelli, 1979, 1980, 1981, 1984; Robert Schumann Competition, Zwickau, 1981; Queen Elizabeth Competition, Brussels, 1983; Marguerite Long-Jacques Thibaud Competition, Paris, 1983; Maria Callas Competition, Athens, 1985; Frédéric Chopin Competition, Warsaw, 1985. *Compositions include:* Piano Works: Toccata; Vier tänzerische Stücke für Klavier; Huldigungen; Trois pièces pour piano; Erste Sonate; Suite zu dritt; Fantastisches Nocturne; Klaviergeschichten des Burattino; President, Piano Jury, J. S. Bach Competition for Students. *Address:* Heinrich-Buchner-Str. 2, Leipzig 7024, Germany.

PICK-HIERONOMI Monica, b. 1940, Cologne, Germany. Singer (Soprano). *Education:* Studied at Rheinisches Musikschule with Diether Jakob. *Career:* Sang first in Oberhausen, then Gärtnerplatztheater Munich; Sang at Nationaltheater Munich 1977-88; has appeared elsewhere in Germany, and in Holland, Belgium, Austria and Switzerland; British appearances with Welsh National Opera and Opera North and at Buxton Festival; Roles have included Mozart's Constanze, Donna Anna, Electra, Vitellia and Countess; Verdi's Leonora (Il Trovatore), Luisa Miller, Violetta and Desdemona; Ariadne, the Marschallin, the Empress in Die Frau ohne Schatten and Elektra; Mathilde in Guillaume Tell (Zurich); Prima Donna in Donizetti's Viva la Mamma, Amelia (Ballo in Maschera) and Leonora (Forza del Destino); Concert engagements include Christ at the Mount of Olives by Beethoven, with the Orchestre de Lyon, under Serge Baudo; Season 1988-89 included Donna Anna in Liège and Handel's Belshazzar in Karlsruhe; Puritani at Brescia and Aida at the Verona Arena. *Address:* Music International, 13 Ardilaun Road, London N5 2QR, England.

PICKENS Jo Ann, b. 1955, USA. Singer (Soprano). *Education:* Studied in the US and Europe. *Career:* Concert appearances with the Chicago Symphony under Solti, the Los Angeles Philharmonic conducted by Kurt Sanderling and the Baltimore Symphony; Toured France

1987 with the Orchestra Symphonique de Paris in Verdi's Requiem; German debut 1984, appearing later in Porgy and Bess; British appearances with the Scottish Chamber, Scottish National, Royal Philharmonic, Ulster, Royal Liverpool Philharmonic Orchestras; London Mozart Players, English Chamber and Halle Orchestras; Conductors include Antal Dorati, Penderecki, Rattle, Norrington and Libor Pešek; Sang in Liszt's Christus at the Festival Hall 1990, conducted by Brian Wright; A Child of our Time under Richard Hickox at the City of London Festival; Concert performance of Nabucco with the Chorus and Orchestra of Welsh National Opera at St David's Hall; Sang in Les Troyens at the Berlioz Festival Lyon with Serge Baudo, Armide at the Buxton Festival and as Purcell's Dido in France; Other appearances with the Chicago Lyric Opera and in Spain. *Recordings include:* Verdi Quattro Pezzi Sacri with the Chicago Symphony. *Honours:* Winner, Concours International de Chant, Paris; Benson and Hedges Gold Award for Concert Singers; Metropolitan Regional Auditions, Paris. *Address:* c/o Norman McCann International Artists Ltd, The Coach House, 56 Lawrie Park Gardens, London SE26 6XJ, England.

PICKER Martin, b. 3 Apr 1929, Chicago, Illinois, USA. Professor/Musicologist. m. Ruth Gross, 21 June 1956, 1 son, 2 daughters. *Education:* PhB 1947; MA 1951; University of Chicago; PhD, University of California, Berkeley 1960. *Career:* Instructor, University of Illinois 1959-61; Assistant Professor 1961-65; Associate Professor 1965-68; Professor 1968-; Rutgers University; Music Department, Rutgers College, 1973-79. *Publications:* The Chanson Albums of Marguerite of Austria 1965; Introduction to Music (With Martin Bernstein), 3rd Edition 1966, 4th Edition 1972; Fors Seulement: 30 Compositions 1981; The Motet Books of Andrea Antico, 1987; Johannes Ockeghem and Jacob Obrecht: A Guide to Research, 1988; Henricus Isaac, A Guide to Research, 1991. *Address:* Music Department, Mason Gross School of The Arts, Douglass Campus, Rutgers University, New Brunswick, NJ 08903, USA.

PICKETT Philip, b. 17 Nov 1950, London, England. Director; Performer of Early Wind Instruments. *Education:* Introduced to variety of early wind instruments by Anthony Baines and David Munrow; experienced on recorder, crumhorn, shawm, rackett and others; Professor of Recorder at the Guildhall School of Music 1972, helping to organise the School's early music department; Fellow of the GSM 1985; Soloist with leading ensembles, including the Academy of St Martin in the Fields, Polish Chamber Orchestra, London Mozart Players, City of London Sinfonia, London Bach Orchestra and the English Concert; As Director of the New London Consort has appeared at major festivals and concert halls in Finland, France, Germany, Greece, Holland, Hong Kong, Israel, Belgium, Spain, Italy, Latin America, Switzerland, USSR and Yugoslavia; British appearances include five Early Music Network tours; Medieval Christmas Extravaganza on the South Bank and concerts for the 21st anniversary of the Elizabeth Hall; Director of the South Bank Summerscope Festival of Medieval and Renaissance Music (Pickett's Pageant) 1988; Regular engagements at the Bath, Edinburgh, King's Lynn, Edinburgh and City of London Festivals; BBC Programmes include music for half the complete Shakespeare play series, BBC2; Music in Camera showings and regular concerts on Radio 3; Composed music for A Meeting in Vallodolid (Shakespeare and Cervantes) for Radio 3, 1991; Promenade Concerts include Bonfire of the Vanities (Medici Wedding Celebrations of 1539) 1990. *Recordings include:* Dances from Terpsichore by Michael Praetorius; Medieval Carmina Burana; The Delights of Posilipo (Neapolitan Dances); Instrumental music by Biber and Schmelzer; Monteverdi Vespers and Orfeo; Cantatas and concertos by Telemann and Vivaldi; Medieval pilgrimage to Santiago; CD of Virtuoso Italian Vocal Music with Catherine Bott: de Rore, Cavalieri, Luzzaschi, G Caccini, Rasi, Gagliano, Marini, Frescobaldi, Monteverdi, F Caccini, Bernardi, Rossi and Carissimi (Il lamento in morte di Maria Stuarda) (Decca Florilegium); Biber Requiem. *Address:* c/o Jessica Atkinson, Polygram

Classics (publicity), P O Box 1420, 1 Sussex Place, Hammersmith, London W6 9XS, England.

PIDOUX Roland, b. 29 Oct 1946, Paris, France. Cellist. *Education:* Studied at the Paris Conservatoire from 1960, with André Navarra, Jean Hubeau and Joseph Calvet. *Career:* Co-founded the Ensemble Instrumental de France; Played with the orchestra of the Paris Opéra from 1968; Member of the Via Nova Quartet, 1970-78; Joined Regis and Bruno Pasquier, 1972, to form the Pasquier Trio; Directed the record collection Les Musiciens for Harmonia Mundi, 1979; Soloist with the Orchestre National of France, 1979-87; Professor of Cello at the Paris Conservatoire, 1987; Plays a Stradivarius of 1692. *Address:* Conservatoire National Superieur de Musique, 14 Rue de Madrid, 75008 Paris, France.

PIECZONKA Adrianne, b. 1963, Canada. Singer (Soprano). *Education:* Studied in Canada and with Vera Rosza in London. *Career:* Concert engagements include Mozart's C minor Mass at the opening of the 1991 Edinburgh Festival (also at Gstaad, both conducted by Menuhin); Concerts with orchestras in Vienna, Amsterdam, Warsaw and Toronto; Recitals in UK, Switzerland, France, Brazil, USA and Canada; Appearances at Vienna Volksoper and Staatsoper include Tatyana in Eugene Onegin, Donna Elvira, Agathe, Laura in Der Bettelstudent, Micaela, Countess Almaviva, and Freia in new production of Das Rheingold, 1992; Other performances of the Countess at Deutsche Oper Berlin and Staatsoper Dresden; Sang in premiere of Reimann's Das Schloss (after Kafka), 1992; Productions of Gounod's Faust (Volksoper) and Hindemith's Cardillac (Staatsoper) in Vienna. *Recordings include:* First Lady in Die Zauberflöte, conducted by Solti. *Honours include:* Winner, 's Hertogenbosch, Netherlands, and Pleine-sur-Mer, France, International Vocal Competitions. *Address:* c/o IMG ARtists, Media House, 3 Burlington Lane, London W4 2TH, England.

PIERCE Judith, b. 21 Nov 1930, St Helens, Lancashire, England. Opera Singer. m. Theo Barker, 2 Aug 1955. *Education:* Royal Manchester College of Music, ARMCM; Royal College of Music, Opera School; Private Study with Edith Lukaschik in Munich and Audrey Langford in London. *Debut:* Sadler's Wells, 1952. *Career:* Sadler's Wells; Royal Opera House; Aldeburgh Festival; Scottish Opera; Opera North; BBC TV and ITV and Canadian TV; Performances in Germany, Italy, Portugal, Canada, Iceland, Austria, South Africa, Yugoslavia and Poland; Singing Teacher. *Honours:* Queen's Prize, Royal College of Music, 1960. *Hobbies:* Keeping open house; 2 cats. *Address:* Minsen Dane, Brogdale Road, Faversham, Kent, ME13 8YA, England.

PIERRET Florencia, b. 11 Sept 1932, Puerto Plata, Dominican Republic. Pianist; Music Educator. m. Jorge Betancur, 20 Aug 1983. *Education:* Pianist Diploma 1954, National Conservatory of Music, Santo Domingo, 1950-56; Postgraduate studies, Inter-American Institute of Music Education INTEM, University of Chile-OAS, Santiago, Chile, 1963-64. *Debut:* Graduation recital, 1954. *Career includes:* Technical Coordinator and Professor, Inter-American Institute of Music Education INTEM, University of Chile-OAS, 1965-69; Assistant Dean and Professor, 1965-68, Director of Music Education Department, 1969-72, Catholic University of Chile; Member of Ancient Music Ensemble of Chile, 1968-74; Founder, First Director, Music Education Department, Ministry of Education, Dominican Republic, 1976; Organizer and Director, Superior Centre for Musical Studies, Caracas, Venezuela, 1977-78; Organizer and Director, Regional Program of Musicology, Bogotà, Colombia, 1979-82; Director General of Fine Arts, Dominican Republic, 1984-85; Harpsichord and piano soloist; Recitalist, Dominican Republic and Chile. *Publication:* Cancionero Juvenil Dominicano, 1966. *Address:* Benigno Filomeno Rojas 54, Santo Domingo, Republica Dominicana.

PIETRZAK Rajmund Michak, b. 10 Dec 1965, Posnan, Poland. Musican: Composer, Violoncellist, Organist. *Education:* Violoncello studies, 1984-89, Composition studies, 1985-90, Organ studies 1991-, Academy of Music, Poznan. *Debut:* Performance of her work at Moskva, 1990. *Appointment:* Organist of St Stanislaw Kostka Church in Poznan. *Compositions include:* Gloria per 2 cori missti Ed Orchestra, 1990; Psalmus 66 per Coro Missto Ed Orchestra, 1989; Glorificamus Te per Organo, 1989. *Membership:* Polish Composers' Association. *Honours:* 2nd Prize, Polish Competition of Composition, Krakow, 1988. *Address:* ul Stowianska 24A/10, 60-651 Poznan, Poland.

PIGNEGUY John Joseph, b. 8 July 1945, Shoreham-by-Sea, Sussex, England. Freelance Horn Player. m. Ruth Smith, 16 June 1973. *Education:* Royal Academy of Music, 1963-66; Studied with James Brown OBE. *Career:* 1st Horn, London Mozart Players, 1968-70; 1st Horn, Royal Opera House, Covent Garden, 1972-74; Member of Merlot Trio; Founder-Member, Nash Ensemble, broadcasting on radio and TV and Promenade Concert appearances; 1979-83, member, Philip Jones Brass Ensemble; Regular adjudicator for BBC TV Young Musician of the Year, competition; Musical Director, Sound of Horns and Horns Unlimited; Invited by Yehudi Menuhin to appear with Merlot Trio, Gstaad Festival, Switzerland, 1978; Extensive studio work for films, TV, records; Former Professor of Horn, Trinity College of Music, London. *Recordings:* Numerous records with Nash Ensemble, Philip Jones Brass Ensemble, Locke Brass, Sound of Horns.*Memberships:* Associate of the Royal Academy, 1990. *Hobbies:* Archaeology; Cycling; Walking holidays; Gardening; General interest in sport. *Address:* 21 Brechin Place, London, SW7 4QD, England.

PIKE Jeremy, b. 20 Nov 1955, London, England. Composer. m. Teresa Majcher, 15 Aug 1981, 1 daughter. *Education:* Abingdon School, 1966-73; MA, King's College, Cambridge, 1973-76; Junior Exhibitioner, Royal Academy of Music, 1969-73; Post-graduate composition and conducting, RAM, 1976-77; LRAM, Piano, 1979. *Career:* British Council Scholarship to study composition with Henryk Gorecki in Poland, Katowice Academy of Music, 1978-79, and with Tadeusz Baird at the Warsaw Academy, 1979; Director of Contemporary Music, University of Warwick, 1981-; Teaching posts held at, Bedford School, 1981-82 and Stamford School, 1982-. *Compositions include:* Time and Tide (Chorus and Orchestra); 2 Piano Concertos; 2 Chamber Symphonies; Shorter Orchestral works include, The Voice; Overture; Fugue; 5 String Quartets; Oboe Quartet; Clarinet Quartet; Quintet for 5 Clarinets; Fantasy for Nonet; 6 Piano Sonatas and other piano works; Guitar Sonata; Vocal works. *Hobbies:* Photography; Walking; Railways. *Address:* University of Warwick, Coventry, West Midlands, CV4 7AL, England.

PIKE Julian, b. 1958, England. Singer (Tenor). *Education:* Studied at the Royal College of Music and with Pierre Bernac in France. *Career:* Sang Don José in Peter Brook's version of Carmen in Paris, Zurich, Stockholm, Copenhagen and New York, 1982-84; Sang Michael in productions of Stockhausen's Donnerstag aus Licht in Holland, Germany, Italy and London (Covent Garden, 1985); Tour with the European Community Youth Orchestra under Matthias Bamert 1985; Wexford Festival 1985, in Mahagonny; Appearances with Kent Opera in Poppea and Rameau's Pygmalion; Has sung in Henze's English Cat in Frankfurt, at the Edinburgh Festival and for the BBC; Premiere productions of Montag aus Licht in Milan, Amsterdam, Frankfurt and Paris, from 1988; Sang Roderick in The Fall of the House of Usher by Glass with Music Theatre Wales, 1989; Ligeti Festival at the South Bank, 1989; Other roles include the Dancing Master in Ariadne and Piet the Pot in Le Grand Macabre (Stockholm 1991); Season 1992 as Michael in the premiere of Stockhausen's Dienstag aus Licht as Lisbon and later at Amsterdam; Recitals at the Bath, City of London, Camden and Aldeburgh festivals: repertoire includes, Bach, Monteverdi and contemporary music; Tours of France, Germany, Belgium, Holland, Poland, Finland, and

Austria (Salzburg); Appearances with the Songmakers' Almanac and Fortune's Fire Lute Song Ensemble. *Address:* Allied Artists, 42 Montpelier Square, London SW7 1JZ, England.

PILAND Jeanne, b. 3 Dec 1945, Raleigh, North Carolina, USA. Singer (Mezzo-soprano). *Education:* Studied in North Carolina and in New York. *Career:* New York City Opera, 1974-77; Sang at the Deutsche Oper am Rhein from 1977 as Cherubino, Composer, Ariadne, Octavian, Der Rosenkavalier, Silla in Palestrina and the Child in L'Enfant et les Sortilèges; Hamburg from 1981, Munich from 1985; Ludwigsburg Festival 1984, as Dorabella, Vienna Staatsoper, 1984, 1987, 1991 as Composer and Dorabella; Sang the Composer in Paris, Dresden, Hamburg, Vienna, Nice, Monte Carlo, Amsterdam, 1987, Ariadne auf Naxos at Covent Garden and Aix-en-Provence, 1985; returned to Aix 1986 and 1988, as Mozart's Idamante and Sextus, Composer and Octavian; has appeared as Octavian at Dresden 1986 for 75th Anniversary of World Premiere, Köln, Zurich, Nice 1986, and Monte Carlo 1987, Santa Fe, 1988; Aix en Provence, Munich, Hamburg 1988, as Idamante and Octavian; Sang Octavia in L'Incoronazione di Poppea Annius, La Clemenza, at Geneva, 1989; other roles include Rosina and Cenerentola, Preziosilla, Smeaton (Anna Bolena), Zerlina and Massenet's Charlotte; Rosina, Concepcion, L'Heure Espagnole, Elena, La Donna del Lago, Clytemnestra, Iphigenia in Aulis; La Scala Milano, Cherubino, 1981; Houston, Dorabella; Los Angeles, Dorabella; Vancouver, Adalgisa, Norma, 1991 - Carmen. *Address:* c/o Grand Théâtre de Geneve, 11 Boulevard de Theatre, CH-1211 Geneva 11, Switzerland.

PILARCZYK Helga, b. 12 March 1925, Schoningen, Brunswick, Germany. Singer (Soprano). *Education:* Studied in Brunswick and Hamburg. *Career:* Brunswick, 1951-54, debut as Irmentraud in Lortzing's Der Waffenschmied; Hamburg Staatsoper, 1954-68, notably as Berg's Marie and Lulu, the Mother in Dallapiccola's Il Prigioniero, Jocasta in Oedipus Rex, Renata in The Fiery Angel; Städtische Oper Berlin, 1956, in the premiere of Henze's Il Re Cervo; Glyndebourne, 1958, 1960, as the Composer in Ariadne auf Naxos and Columbina in Arlecchino; Covent Garden, 1959, as Salome; US debut Washington, 1960, as the Woman in Erwartung; Metropolitan Opera, 1965, as Marie in Wozzeck. *Publication:* Kann Man die Moderne Opern Singen?, 1964. *Recordings:* Erwartung (Westminster); Pierrot Lunaire (Columbia). *Address:* c/o Hamburgische Staatsoper, Grosse-Theaterstrasse 34, D-2000 Hamburg 36, Germany.

PILBERY Joseph, b. 30 March 1931, London, England. Conductor; Orchestral Administrator. m. 1970, 1 son. *Education:* Royal Academy of Music, with Ernest Read; Trinity College of Music, with Trevor Harvey, Peter Gellhorn and Harry Blech. *Debut:* Royal Albert Hall, Dec. 1954. *Career:* Has given concerts in all major London concert halls, notably with the London Mozart Players and the Royal Philharmonic Orchestra; Has conducted all 10 Mahler Symphonies, including the Resurrection Symphony at the Festival Hall; Lectures for the University of Maryland, the Elgar Society and the London Symphony Orchestra Club; Foreign engagements in Zurich, Vienna and the Salzburg Festival (1982); Repertoire includes Carmina Burana, Sullivan's Golden Legend and Ivanhoe, Aida, La Bohème, Die Meistersinger, The Bartered Bride, Holst's The Perfect Fool, and Tosca; Founded the Vivaldi Concertante 1983. *Recordings include:* Serious music by Arthur Sullivan, Music Rara 1975. *Contributions to:* Music and Musicians; Classical Music. *Honours:* Diploma, Services to Italian Music 1989. *Hobbies:* History; Cinema. *Address:* Allegro 35 Laurel Avenue, Potters Bar, Herts. EN6 2AB, England.

PILGRIM Shirley, b. 1957, London. Singer (Soprano). *Education:* Studied at the Royal Academy of music with Ilse Wolf and Patricia Clark; Further study at the National Opera Studio. *Career:* Sang with the Glyndebourne Festival and Touring Opera choruses; Solo debut as

Helena with the Touring Opera, in A Midsummer Night's Dream; Appearances in Hong Kong (1986) and at the Buxton and Wexford Festivals; With Opera East has sung Mimi, and the Female Chorus in The Rape of Lucretia (1991); Scottish Opera as Despina, and cover for various roles; New D'Oyly Carte Opera Carte 1988, in Yeoman of the Guard and Iolanthe; Oratorio and concert engagements, notably at the Barbican Hall, London, and recitals including lighter American music; Sang in Born Again at the 1990 Chichester Festival; Other recent roles include: Countess in The Marriage of Figaro, Fiordiligi in Cosí fan Tutte, Tosca in Tosca. *Address:* 85 Chichester Road, Edmonton Green, London, N9 9DH, England.

PILKOVÁ Zdeňka, b. 15 June 1931, Prague, Czechoslovakia. Musicologist. m. Dr Jiří Pilka, 27 June, 1951, 2 daughters. *Education:* Diploma, Charles University, Prague, 1955; PhD 1969; Private piano studies 1938-53. *Career:* Editor in Music Department of Czechoslovak Radio Broadcasting, Prague, 1954-64; Research Worker, Musicological Institute, Czechoslovak/Czech Academy of Sciences, Prague, 1964-94; Visiting Lecturer, Charles University, Prague, 1987-88; Specializes in 18th century music; Lectures and seminars at foreign universities. *Publications include:* Dramatická tvorba Jiřího Bendy (Dramatic Works of Georg Benda) 1960; co-author of Hudba v ceských dejinách (Music in Czech History), 1983, 1988, (co-author), Hudební věda (Musicology) I-II 1988 (co-author); Böhmische Musiker am Dresdner Hof 1710-1840; Various score editions as editor or co-editor including Böhmische Violinsonaten I, II 1982, 1985. *Contributions to:* Various music Lexica, congress reports and journals including: New Grove Dictionary of Music and Musicians; Musikforschung, Haydn Studies; Bachstudien Zelenka-studien; Series of programmes for broadcasting. *Memberships include:* International Musicological Society; Czech Early Music Society (Board Member); Member of editorial board of the series Thesaurus Musicae Bohemiae; Gesellschaft für Musikforschung. *Hobbies:* Gardening. *Address:* Nám J Machka 9, 15800 Prague 5, Czech Republic.

PILOU Jeannette, b. July 1931, Alexandria, Egypt. Singer (Soprano). *Education:* Studied with Carla Castellani in Milan. *Debut:* Milan 1958, as Violetta. *Career:* Sang widely in Italy as Mélisande, Mimi, Liu, Susanna, Manon, Nedda, Micaela, Marguerite and Nannetta; Appearances in Barcelona, Buenos Aires, Hanover, Hamburg and Wexford; Vienna 1965, as Mimi; Metropolitan Opera from 1967-86, debut as Gounod's Juliette; Covent Garden 1971, as Madama Butterfly; Monte Carlo 1973, in the premiere of Rossellini's La Reine Morte; Other roles included the female leads in Von Einem's Der Prozess, Gluck's Euridice, Marzelline in Fidelio and Magda in La Rondine; US appearances in Houston, Chicago, San Francisco, New Orleans and Philadelphia. *Recordings include:* Micaela in Carmen (Erato). *Address:* c/o Metropolitan Opera, Lincoln Center, New York, NY 10023, USA.

PILZ Gottfried, b. 1944, Salzburg, Austria. Stage and Costume Designer. m. Isabel Ines Glathar, 1 son.*Education:* Academy of Arts, Vienna, 1962-1966; Assistant at the Vienna State Opera to Wieland Wagner, Luchino Visconti, Teo Otto, Luciano Damiani, Rudolf Heinrich and others, 1965-1969, Assistant to Filippo Sanjust, 1969-1972. *Debut:* Reimann's Melusine world premiere at Berlin, Edinburgh and Schwetzingen Festival, staged by Gustav Rudolf Sellner. *Career:* Operas, dramatic theatre and Ballets in Austria, Belgium, Great Britain, Netherlands, USA and Switzerland, principal in Germany; Exhibitions in Berlin, Kunsthalle Bielefeld, Düsseldorf, Kunsthalle Kiel and Wuppertal (Reflexe I-III, Aus-Grenzen I-III); Debut as a Producer with Rameau's Hippolyte et Aricie at Oper Leipzig, 1993; Collaborations with John Dew, 1979-1992 (Wagner's Ring, Krefeld, 1981-1985, The Unknown Repertory at Bielefeld, 1983-1991, Les Huguenot's Deutsche Oper Berlin, 1987 as well as Royal Opera House, Covent Garden, 1991 and others); with Götz Friedrich (Der Rosenkavalier, Un Ballo in Maschera,

Deutsche Oper Berlin, 1993) with Gunter Krämer since 1990 at Kölner Schauspiiel, with Nikolaus Lenhoff at Oper Frankfurt and Leipzig, at Munich as well as at Zürich Henze's new Version of, Der Prinz von Homburg, 1992 and 1993; with Christine Mielitz, Rienzi at Komische Oper Berlin, 1992, engaged Henze's The Bassarids at Hamburg Oper, 1994 and also for 1994 at Oper Leipzig, Moses and Aron staged by George Tabori.

PILZ Janos, b. 1960, Hungary. Violinist. *Education:* Studied at the Franz Liszt Academy of Budapest and with Sandor Devich, György Kurtág and András Mihaly. *Career:* Member of the Keller String Quartet from 1986, debut concert at Budapest March 1987; Played Beethoven's Grosse Fuge and Schubert's Death and the Maiden Quartet at Interforum 87; Series of concerts in Budapest with Zoltán Kocsis and Deszö Ranki (piano) and Kalman Berkes (clarinet); Further appearances in Nuremberg, at the Chamber Music Festival La Baule and tours of Bulgaria, Austria, Switzerland, Italy (Ateforum 88 Ferrara), Belgium and Ireland; Concerts for Hungarian Radio and Television. *Recordings:* Albums for Hungaroton (from 1989). *Honour:* 2nd Prize, Evian International String Quartet Competition, May 1988. *Address:* c/o Artist Management International, 12/13 Richmond Buildings, Dean Street, London W1V 5AF, England.

PIMLOTT Steven Charles, b. 18 Apr 1953, Manchester, England. Director of Opera, Theatre, Musicals. m. Daniela Bechly, 27 July 1991, 1 son. *Education:* Manchester Grammar School; MA, English Cambridge University. Studied the oboe. *Career:* Staff Producer ENO, 1976; Began long working relationship with Opera North, 1978, including productions of Nabucco, The Bartered Bride and Prince Igor; Other opera works include Samson and Delila in Bregenz, 1988, Carmen at Earls Court, 1989. Musicals: Carousel, Royal Exchange Theatre, 1985, Carmen Jones, 1986, Sheffield Crucible, Sunday in the Park with George, National Theatre 1990; Also directs straight theatre including, most recently, Molière's The Miser, National 1991, Julius Ceasar, RSC, 1991, and was Associate Director at Sheffield Crucible Theatre 1987-88; Season 1992 with Un Ballo in Maschera for Flanders Opera and Eugene Onegin for New Israeli Opera. *Hobby:* Playing the oboe. *Current Management:* Harriet Cruickshank. *Address:* 97 Old South Lambeth Road, London SW8 1XU, England.

PINEL Stephen Leigh, b. 25 June 1956, Syracuse, New York, USA. Organist and Musicologist. *Education:* BM 1978, MM 1982 with high honours, Westminster Choir College, Princeton; PhD, New York University, currently; Rutgers College, New Brunswick and Union College, Schenectady. *Career:* Artistic Director, Community Concerts, Burnt Hills, NY, 1972-82; Artistic Director, St Joseph's Church, New York, 1981-84; Music Commission, Archdiocese of NY, 1981-84; Archivist, The Organ Historical Society, 1984-; American Guild of Organists; Central NJ Chapter, Dean, 1985-87; Music Director, St Francis de Sales Church, NY, 1987-. *Recordings:* Several on Classic Masters, Raven Recordings, The Organ Historical Society labels with the Metropolitan Chamber Orchestra, Metropolitan Museum of Art, NY and Round Lake Festival orchestra. *Publications:* Old Organs of Princeton, 1989; Ferris & Stuart, Organbuilders in Nineteenth Century New York, 1990. *Contributions:* Numerous articles on organ history in organ journals in USA and abroad. *Address:* 629 Edison Drive, East Windsor, New Jersey 08520, USA.

PINKHAM Daniel, b. 5 June 1923, Lynn, Massachusetts, USA. Composer. *Education:* AB 1943; MA 1944; Harvard University; The following degrees honoris causa: Litt D, Nebraska Wesleyan University 1976; Mus D, Adrian College 1977; Mus D, Westminster Choir College, 1979; Tanglewood; Mus D, New England Conservatory, 1993; Private studies with Nadia Boulanger. *Career:* Faculty Member, New England Conservatory 1957-; Music Director of King's Chapel, Boston 1958-. *Compositions:* 4 Symphonies, Concertos

for Trumpet, Violin, Organ, Piano, Piccolo; Theatre Works and Operas, Chamber Music, Songs, Electronic Music, Television Film Scores. *Recordings:* Christmas Cantata; Signs of The Zodiac; Symphony No. 2; Serenades; Miracles; Epiphanies; Magnificat; Proverbs; Diversions; Concertante for Violin and Harpsichord Soli, Strings and Celesta; inter alia; Advent Cantata; Wedding Cantata; String Quartet; Versets; Holland Waltzes. *Honour:* Ford Foundation Fellowship, 1962. *Memberships:* Past Dean, Boston Chapter, American Guild of Organists; American Academy of Arts and Sciences; Honorary Member Phi Mu Alpha Sinfonia; Signet Society. *Address:* 150 Chilton Street, Cambridge, Massachusetts, MA 02138-1227, USA.

PINNOCK Trevor (David), b. 16 Dec 1946, Canterbury, Kent, England. Musician; Conductor/Harpsichordist. *Education:* Canterbury Cathedral Choir School; Simon Langton Grammar School, Canterbury; Foundation Scholarship, Royal College of Music, 1966-68. *Debut:* London Solo Debut: Purcell Room, 1968. *Career:* Galliard Harpsichord Trio, (with Stephen Preston, flute; Anthony Pleeth, cello) 1966-71; Founder/current Musical Director, The English Concert, 1972-; Recitals throughout Europe, Canada, USA and Japan; Recordings (CRD 1974-1978, DG Archiv 1978-); Artistic Director & Principal Conductor of the National Arts Centre Orchestra of Canada, 1991-. *Recordings include:* Complete Keyboard Works of Rameau; Bach, Partitas, Goldberg Variations; Handel Harpsichord Suites; Bach Complete Orchestral Works and Harpsichord Concerti; Orchestral Works of CPE Bach, Handel, English Composers, Vivaldi, Messiah, Purcell: Dido and Aeneas; Haydn: Nelson Mass; Handel Concerti Grossi Op.3, Op.6 and organ concertos; Boyce Symphonies; Haydn Symphonies 6, 7, 8; Scarlatti Sonatas; Vivaldi Concertos; Handel: Acis & Galatea and Purcell: King Arthur with The English Concert, 1992; Currently recording all Mozart Symphonies for DGG. *Honours:* Grand Prix du Musique, Edison Pries, Deutsche Schallplattenpreis, The Gramophone Prize; CBE, 1992. *Current Management and address:* c/o Ms Jan Burnett, 8 St. George's Terrace, London, NW1 8XJ, England.

PINSCHOF Thomas, b. 14 Feb 1948, Vienna, Austria. Musician (Flautist). *Education:* Artist and Teacher Diploma, Conservatorium of Vienna with Camillo Wanausek; Studies with Aurèle Nicolet; Master Classes with Karl-Heinz Zöller, Jean-Pierre Rampal, Severino Gazzelloni; Postgraduate studies, Indiana University, USA. *Debut:* Wiener Musikverein, Brahms-Saal, 1965. *Career:* Member, Vienna Symphony Orchestra, 1971-72; Berkshire Music Festival, Tanglewood, USA (with Scholarship Boston Symphony Orchestra), 1969; Founder, ENSEMBLE I, 1971-; Artist-in-Residence, with ENSEMBLE I, Victorian College of The Arts, Melbourne, Australia, 1976; Acting Head, Woodwind Department, Lecturer in flute and chamber music, Victorian College of Arts, Melbourne; Lecturer, Canberra School of Music, Melbourne University and Vienna Conservatory. *Recordings:* Deutsche Grammophon, Adel-Cord, Philips. *Publications:* Music editions for various publishers including, own series, Pinschofon, with Zimmermann. *Contributions to:* The Flautist; Flutenotes; Musikerzeitung; Osterreichische Musikzeitschrift; Kunst und Freie Berufe. *Honours:* 2nd Prize, international flute competition, Severino Gazzelloni, 1975; Alban Berg Foundation Award, 1971; Australia Council Music Board Grantee, 1984-85 for project with Prof. Nikolaus Harnoncourt. *Hobbies:* Flying; Tennis; Swimming; Skiing. *Address:* 100 Woodhouse Road, Donvale, VIC 3111, Australia.

PIPE Daniel, b. 18 Sept 1955, London, England. Concert Pianist. *Education:* Central Tutorial School for Young Musicians (now called The Purcell School), 1970; Guildhall School of Music; Tanya Polunin School of Pianoforte Playing, 1970; Royal College of Music, 1972; ARCM (perf.), LRAM (Perf.), 1974. *Career:* Concerts in Great Britain including performances at The Purcell Room, Local Radio, and as Orchestra Soloist, 1974-82; Visiting Lecturer, Piano, Avery Hill College, London,

1985; Tour of Hong Kong, including City Hall and Broadcasts for Radio Television Hong Kong. *Recordings:* Radio Television Hong Kong: Chopin: 12 Studies Op 10, Fantasy in F Minor Op. 49, Liszt: Mephisto Waltz No 1, Sonetto 123 Del Petrarca, Hungarian Rhapsody No 12, 1985. *Memberships:* Solo Performers Section, Incorporated Society of Musicians; European Piano Teachers Association. *Hobbies:* Swimming; Cooking. *Address:* 2 Dersingham Avenue, Manor Park, London E12 5QE, England.

PIRES Filipe, b. 26 June 1934, Lisbon, Portugal. Composer. m. Ligia Falcao, 29 Mar. 1958. *Education:* Piano Superior Course 1952, Composition Superior Course 1953, National Conservatory, Lisbon; Piano and Composition, Hannover Music High School, 1957-60. *Career:* Professor of Composition, Porto National Conservatory, 1960-70; Professor of Composition, Lisbon National Conservatory, 1972-75; Music Specialist, UNESCO, Paris, 1975-79; Concert Tours in Europe (Pianist and Composer). *Compositions:* Figurations I - flute (Oficina Musical - Porto, Portugal); Sonatine, violin and piano, Piano Trio, Figurations II - Piano (Edizioni Curci, Milan); Figurations III - 2 Pianos (Oficina Musical - Porto); 3 Poems by Fernando Pessoa - High Voice and Piano (Oficina Musical - Porto); String Quartet (Gulbenkian Foundation - Lisbon); Ostinati - 6 percussionists (Zimmermann - Frankfurt). *Recordings:* Educo (Ventura, California, USA): Sonatine (violin and piano), Piano Trio, Figurations I (flute), Figurations IV (harp), Sonatine (cello and piano), Ostinati (6 percussionists), Figurations III (2 pianos), String Quartet; Ministry of Culture, Lisbon: Canto Ecumenico (tape music), Litania (tape music), Homo Sapiens (tape music); Ministry of Culture, Lisbon: 20 Choral Songs; Ministry of Culture, Lisbon: Portugaliae Genesis (Baritone, Mixed Choir and Orchestra), Sintra, (Orchestra) and Akronos (Strings); Are, Wolfsburg: Sonata 1954 (Piano). *Publication:* Theory of Counterpoint and Canon, Gulbenkian Foundation, Lisbon, 1981. *Address:* R. Costa Cabral, 2219-4D, 4200 Porto, Portugal.

PIRES Maria Joao, b. 23 July 1944, Lisbon, Portugal. Concert Pianist. *Education:* Lisbon Academy of Music with Campos Coelho; Studied composition and theory with Francine Benoit; Further study with Rosl Schmid in Munich and Karl Engel in Hanover. *Career:* First recital aged 5; Concerto debut in Mozart aged 7; Early concert tours of Portugal, Spain and Germany; International career from 1970, with performances in Europe, Africa and Japan; Career interrupted by ill-health; British debut 1986, at the Elizabeth Hall, London; Canadian debut 1986, with the Montreal Symphony conducted by Charles Dutoit; Debut tour of North America 1988, appearing with the New York Philharmonic, Houston Symphony, Toronto Symphony and the National Arts Centre Orchestra, Ottawa; Season 1988-89 with concerts in Vienna with Claudio Abbado; Munich with Carlo Maria Giulini; Carnegie Hall debut recital; Repertoire includes Mozart, Schubert, Schumann, Beethoven and Chopin. *Recordings include:* Complete Mozart Piano Sonatas. *Honours:* First Prize, Beethoven International Competition, Brussels 1970; Edison Prize, Prix de l'Academie du Disque Français and Prix de l'Academie Charles Cros for Mozart Sonata Recordings. *Address:* Harrison/Parrott Ltd., 12 Penzance Place, London W11 4PA, England.

PIRONKOFF Simeon (Angelov), b. 18 June 1927, Lom, Bulgaria. Composer. *Education:* Graduated from State Music Academy at Sofia, 1953. *Career:* Violinist at National Youth Theatre, Sofia, 1947-51, later working as conductor; Bulgarian Film Studios from 1961, Vice-President of Union of Bulgarian Composers, 1980. *Compositions include:* Opera: Socrates' Real Apology, Sofia, monodrama, 1967;The Good Person of Szechwan (after Brecht), Stara Zagora, 1972; The Life and Suffering of Sinful Sophronius, oratorio, Sofia, 1977; The Motley Bird, Ruse, 1980; Oh, My Dream, Ruse, 1987; Orchestral: Symphony for Strings, 1960; Movements for strings, 1967; Night Music, 1968; Requiem for an Unknown Young Man, 1968; A Big Game, 1970; Ballet Music in Memory of Igor Stravinsky, 1972; Music for

two Pianos and Orchestra, 1973; Concerto Rustico for cello and orchestra, 1982; Entrata and Bulgarian Folk Dance, 1983; Lyric Suite for strings, 1983; In the Eye of the Storm for tenor and orchestra, 1986; Symphonic Sketch on a Popular Melody, 1986; Flute concerto, 1987; Passaglia for Symphonic Orchestra, 1991; Chamber: 3 Trios, 1949, 1950, 1987; 3 String Quartets, 1951, 1966, 1985; Sonato for solo violin, 1955; Berceuse for clarinet and piano, 1983; Theme and Variations for violin and piano, 1985; Symphony for 11 Soloists, 1990; Songs of Life, poetry E Dickinson for woman's voice and chamber assembly, 1988; Songs of Death, poetry E Dickinson for woman's voice and chamber assembly, 1988; Tree Movements for Harp Solo, 1992; Piano music, choruses and songs; Film and theatre music. *Address:* Union of Bulgarian Composers, Sofia, Bulgaria.

PISCHNER Hans, b. 20 Feb. 1914, Breslau, Germany. Teacher; Harpsichordist; Musicologist; Intendant; Retired. *Education:* Musicology studies at University of Breslau; Keyboard studies with Bronislav von Pozniac and Gertrud Wertheim; Professor 1949, PhD 1961. *Career:* Head, Radio Music Department, 1950-54, Head, Music Department, 1954-56, Ministry of Culture; Representative, Ministry of Culture, 1956-62; Intendant, Deutsche Staatsoper, Berlin, 1963-89; Numerous appearances as soloist and accompanist, Europe, America and Japan; Retired. *Recordings:* Numerous works of Bach, both as soloist and continuo player. *Publications:* Music in China, 1955; Die Harmonielehre Jean-Philippe Rameaus 1967; Several articles for professional journals. *Publications:* Premier en eines Lebens, Autobiography, 1986. *Honours include:* Handel Prize, Halle, 1961; National Prize, 3rd class, 1961; Johannes R Becher, 1962; National Prize, 1st class. *Memberships:* Chairman, Neue Bach-Gesellschaft, Leipzig. *Address:* 0-1040 Berlin, Friedrichstr, 105c, Germany.

PITFIELD Thomas Baron, b. 5 Apr 1903, Bolton, Lanchashire, England. Composer; Artist; Author. m. 26 Dec 1934. *Education:* Royal Manchester College of Music, 1924-25. *Career:* Engineering, 1917-24; Tettenhall College, 1935-45;, RMCM, 1947-72; RNCM, 1972-73. *Compositions include:* Numerous compositions for Orchestra; Brass Band; Choral; Chamber Music; Piano solo; Stage works. *Publications:* The Poetry of Trees; No Song, No Supper (Autobiography), 1986; Recording a Region, 1987; My Words, 1988; A Song After Supper (vol.2 of autobiography); A Cotton Town Boyhood, 1991; A Wayfarers Chronical, 1991; 26 Songs British Heritage Series. *Contributions to:* Musical Times; Listener; Country Life; The Countryman; The Artist. *Honours:* Hon Fellow (FRMCM), 1943; OUP Choral Prize, 1943; Welsh National Chamber Music Prize. *Memberships:* Composers' Guild of Gt Britain; Hon Member, the Assoc of Professional Composers, 1993. *Hobbies:* Crafts; Nature study, especially trees and bird-song. *Address:* Lesser Thomas, 21 East Downs Road, Bowdon, Altrincham, Cheshire WA14 2LG, England.

PITTI Katalin, b. 1953, Hungary, Soprano. *Education:* Béla Bartók Conservatory, 1972; Studied under Professor Jeno Sipos, department of Singing, Ferenc Liszt Academy of Music, Budapest; Master Course with Irmgard Seefried, Vienna, Austria, 1975. *Career:* Desdemona in Othello, 1977; Budapest State Opera, 1977-. *Honours:* 2nd Prize, Leipzig International Bach Competition, 1976; Graduate with Distinction, Budapest Academy of Music, 1977; Co-Recipient, 4th Prize, Tchaikovsky International Singing Concours, Moscow, USSR, 1978.

PITTMAN Richard Harding, b. 3 June 1935, Baltimore, Maryland, USA. Conductor. m. 10 Sept 1965, 1 son. *Education:* BMus, Peabody Conservatory, 1957; Private Study of Conducting with Laszlo Halasz, NY, 1960-63; Conducting, Sergiu Celibidache, Accademia Musicale Chigiana, Siena, Italy, 1962; Conducting, W. Brueckner-Ruggeberg, Hamburg, 1963-65; Conducting,

Pierre Boulez, Basel, Switzerland, 1970. *Career:* Music Director, The Little Chorus, Washington, DC, 1961-62; Music Director, Die Kammeropern-Gruppe, Hamburg, 1964-65; Instructor of Conducting and Opera, Eastman School of Music, 1965-68; Teacher of Orchestral Conducting, New England Conservatory, 1968-85; Conductor, Concord Orchestra, Massachusetts, 1969-; Music Director, Boston Musica Viva, 1969-. Guest Conducting: National Symphony, Washington, DC; BBC Symphony, London; BBC Philharmonic, Manchester; BBC Scottish Symphony, Glasgow; BBC Welsh Symphony, Cardiff; London Sinfonietta; Frankfurt Radio Symphony, Germany; Hamburg Symphony, Germany; BBC Concert Orchestra, London; Virginia Philharmonic, Norfolk; Chattanooga Symphony, Tennessee; American Repertory Theatre, Cambridge, Massachusetts; Hartford Chamber Orchestra; Connecticut; Boston Lyric Opera; Tulsa Opera; Opera Omaha; Huntingdon Theatre Company Boston; City of London Sinfonia, Ulster Orchestra Belfast, Nebraska Chamber Orchestra, Lincoln; Dutch Ballet Orchestra Amsterdam; Assistant Conductor, New York Philharmonic. *Recordings:* Music by, Ives, Berio, Davidovsky, Harris, Schwantner. *Address:* 41 Bothfeld Road, Newton Centre, MA 02159, USA.

PIZARRO Artur, b. 1968, Portugal. Concert Pianist. *Education:* Studied with Sequeira Costa in Lisbon and at the University of Kansas; National Conservatory of Music in Lisbon. *Career:* Numerous concert performances in Europe from 1987; London debut 1989, at the Wigmore Hall, followed by concerts with the London Mozart Players at the Elizabeth Hall; Has also played with the RAI-Torino Symphony, the Gulbenkian Orchestra and the Moscow Philharmonic; Rachmaninov's 3rd Concerto with the City of Birmingham Symphony in Leeds and the BBC Symphony under Andrew Davis in London, 1990; Further engagements with the London Symphony (de Burgos), Royal Liverpool Philharmonic (Pešek), Los Angeles Philharmonic at Hollywood Bowl, English Chamber Orchestra, City of London Sinfonia, Hallé and BBC Symphony (Proms 1991); Recitals in Britain, Japan, Australia and the USA; Played the Ravel Concerto in G at the 1991 Promenade Concerts, London. *Honours:* Winner 1987 International Vianna da Motta Competition, Lisbon; Greater Palm Beach Symphony Invitational Piano Competition, Florida, 1988; First prize, 1990 Harvey Leeds International Pianoforte Competition. *Address:* Harrison/Parrott Ltd, 12 Penzance Place, London W11 4PA, England.

PIZER Elizabeth Faw Hayden, b. 1 Sept 1954, Watertown, New York, USA. Composer; Musician. m. Charles Ronald Pizer, 10 July 1974. *Education:* High School Diploma, New York State Regents Diploma, Watertown High School, 1972; Boston Conservatory of Music, Boston, Massachusetts, 1972-75. *Career:* Numerous major concert performances of her compositions internationally including, San Jose State University Symphonic Band, 1979; members of Honolulu Symphony Orchestra, String Quartet, 1980; Lincoln Centre, New York, Charleston South Carolina; Jacksonville, Florida, Donne in Musica Festival, Rome, 1982; Institute of Sonology, Utrecht, Netherlands, 1982; San Francisco Chamber Singers, Nevada City, San Francisco, Berkeley and Ross, California, 1982; Piccolo Spoleto Festival, 1983; University of Michigan, 1983; Mexico City, 1984; Heidelberg, West Germany, 1985; Oakland, California, 1986; Many major broadcasts of compositions, throughout the USA, 1979-86 and a live concert broadcast including pre-recorded material in Australia, 1986. *Compositions:* Expressions Intimes, for solo piano, 1975; Quilisoly, for flute and piano, or violin and piano, 1976; Look Down, Fair Moon, for voice and piano, 1976; Elegy, (formerly known as Interfuguelude) for string orchestra, or string quartet or wind quartet, 1977; Fanfare Overture, symphonic band, 1977-79; Five Haiku, for soprano and chamber ensemble, 1978; Five Haiku, II, for Mezzo-soprano and piano, 1979; Madrigals Anon, A Capella choir, 1979; Sunken Flutes, electronic tape, 1979; String Quartet, 1981; Lyric Fancies, solo piano, 1983; Kyrie Eleison, A Capella chorus, 1983; numerous other compositions. *Address:* Southshore

Road, Point Peninsula, PO Box 42, Three Mile Bay, NY 13693, USA.

PIZZI Pier Luigi, b. 15 June 1930, Milan, Italy. Stage Director and Designer. *Education:* Studied architecture at Milan Polytechnic. *Debut:* Designed Don Giovanni at Genoa, 1952. *Career:* Designs and productions for such Baroque operas as Handel's Orlando (Florence, 1959) and Rinaldo (seen at Reggio Emilia, Madrid and Lisbon); Rameau's Hippolyte et Aricie and Castor et Pollux (Aix-en-Provence, 1983, 1991); Gluck's Alceste for La Scala, 1987; Other work has included Les Troyens, to open the Opera Bastille at Paris in 1990, followed by Samson et Dalila, 1991; I Capuleti e i Montecchi at Covent Garden, 1984, Don Carlos at Vienna, 1989; Rigoletto in Chicago, La Traviata seen at Monte Carlo, Venice and Lausanne; Rossini productions at Pesaro include Otello and Tancredi (1991). *Address:* c/o Opera de la Bastille, 120 Rue de Lyon, F-75012 Paris, France.

PLAIN Gerald Hayes, b. 30 Nov 1940, Sacramento, Kentucky, USA. Composer. m. Marilyn Van Wienen, 29 Dec 1966. *Education:* BME, Murray State University, 1963; MM, Butler University, 1966; Doctoral Study in Composition, University of Michigan, 1966-70. *Career:* Visiting Assistant Professor, Texas Tech University, 1971-72; Part-time Instructor, DePaul University, 1973-74, Chicago Musical College, Roosevelt University, 1974; Instructor, University of Wisconsin at Stevens Point, 1977-78; Assistant Professor, Eastman School of Music, 1978-81. *Compositions:* Violin Concerto (violin and orchestra); Three Pieces (12 instruments and percussion); Raccoon Song (solo cello); Ripsnorter (magnetic tape); Showers of Blessings (clarinet and magnetic tape); Golden Wedding (magnetic tape); Arrows (orchestra); Portrait 1: Sally Goodin (flute, harp, violin and cello); Portrait 2: Pretty Polly (Orchestra); Llawhammer (Orchestra); Portrait 1: Sally Goodin (Orchestra), new version; Antics (for soprano and piano). *Address:* 30 Doncaster Road, Rochester, NY 14623, USA.

PLAISTOW Stephen, b. 24 Jan 1937, Welwyn Garden City, England. Pianist; Critic; Administrator. *Education:* ARCM, Clare College, Cambridge. *Career:* Freelance Journalist from 1961; BBC Music Producer, 1962-74; Chairman British Section of ISCM and Music Section of ICA, 1967-71; Member, Music Panel, Arts Council of Great Britain, 1972-79; Chief Assistant to Controller of Music, BBC, 1974-79; Chairman, British section of ISCM and Arts Council Contemporary Music Network, 1976-79; Editor, Contemporary Music, BBC, 1979-; Deputy Head of Radio 3 Music Department, BBC, 1989-. *Contributions to:* The Gramophone; Musical Times; Tempo. *Membership:* Critics' Circle. *Hobby:* Travel in France. *Address:* c/o BBC Radio 3 Music Department, Broadcasting House, Portland Place, London W1, England.

PLANCHART Alejandro Enrique, b. 29 July 1935, Caracas. Music Historian; Composer. Divorced, 1 daughter. *Education:* MusB, 1958, MusM, 1960, Yale University School of Music; PhD, Harvard University, 1971. *Career:* Freelance arranger, composer, New York and New Haven, 1960-64; Instructor/Assistant Professor, Yale, 1967-75; Associate Professor, University of Victoria, 1975-76; Associate/Professor, University of California at Santa Barbara, 1976-; Visiting Professor, Brandeis, 1982-83. *Compositions:* Divertimento for Percussion Trio; Five Poems of James Joyce for Soprano and Piano. *Recordings:* 20 recordings of mediaeval and renaissance music with the Cappella Cordina, Lyrichord and Musical Heritage Society. *Publications:* The Repertory of Tropes at Winchester, 2 volumes, Princeton, 1977; Beneventanum Troporum Corpus, with John Boe co-editor, 10 volumes, in press. *Contributions to:* Guillaume Dufay's Masses: Notes and Revisions, in Musical Quarterly, 1972; Fifteenth-Century Masses: Notes on Chronology and Performance, in Study Musicali 10, 1983; About 50 other titles. *Address:* 1070 Via Regina, Santa Barbara, CA 93111, USA.

PLASSON Michel, b. 2 Oct 1933, Paris, France. Conductor. *Education:* Studied at the Paris Conservatoire and in the USA with Leinsdorf, Monteux and Stokowski. *Career:* Musical Director in Metz 1966-68; Director of the Orchestra and of the Théâtre du Capitole in Toulouse, 1968-83; Operatic performances in Toulouse include Salome, Aida, Die Meistersinger, Faust, Parsifal, Carmen and Montségur by Landowski (world premiere 1985); Conductor of the Orchestre National du Capitole de Toulouse from 1983; At the Palais Omnisport de Paris-Bercy has conducted Aida, Turandot, the Verdi Requiem and Nabucco, 1984-87; Guest engagements with the Berlin Philharmonic Orchestra, London Phillharmonic, Orchestre of the Suisse Romande, and the Gewandhaus Orchestra Leipzig; Paris Opéra, Geneva Opera, State Operas of Vienna, Hamburg and Munich, Zurich Opera, Covent Garden, Metropolitan Opera, Chicago and San Francisco; Principal Guest Conductor of the Zurich Tonhalle Orchestra from 1987, Conducted new production of Guillaume Tell at Covent Garden, 1990; Il Trovatore at the Halle aux Grains, Toulouse, 1990; Faust at the 1990 Orange festival; Returned to Covent Garden, 1991, Tosca; Season 1991-92 with Lucia di Lammermoor at Munich, Guillaume Tell at Covent Garden, Don Quichotte at Toulouse and Carmen at Orange. *Recordings include:* La Vie Parisienne (EM); La Grande Duchesse de Gérolstein (CBS); Chausson's Symphony; Saint-Saëns Piano Concertos (Entremont); premiere pressings of Roussel's Padmâvatî, Magnard's Symphonies and Guercoeur, Symphonic poems by Chausson; Les Pêcheurs de perles (EMI); Faust (Sony) *Address:* c/o SA Gorlinsky Ltd., 33 Dover Street, London W1X 4NJ, England.

PLATT Ian, b. 1959, Fleetwood, England. Singer (Baritone). *Education:* Studied with John Cameron at Royal Northern College of Music. *Career:* Sang Rossini's Figaro, Guglielmo, Papageno and Junius in The Rape of Lucretia for Royal Northern College of Music; Professional debut for Kent Opera, in La Traviata, and Il Barbiere di Siviglia; Engagements with Opera 80 as Don Magnifico in La Cenerentola and Baron Zeta in The Merry Widow; New Sadler's Wells Opera as Agamemnon in La Belle Helene; Sang Tom in Henze's The English Cat at Hebbel Theatre, Berlin, and toured with Travelling Opera as Schaunard and Mozart's Figaro; Welsh National Opera and Scottish Opera, 1991, in La Traviata; Alcindoro in La Bohème for Glyndebourne Touring Opera, 1991; Pirate King, D'Oyly Carte, 1993; Don Magnifico, Welsh National Opera, 1993/94. *Recordings include:* Il Crociato in Egitto by Meyerbeer, Opera Rara. *Address:* Robert Gilder & Co, 59/65 Upper Ground, London, SE1 9PQ, England.

PLATT Norman, b. 29 Aug 1920, Bury, Lancashire, England. Singer; Opera Director. m. (1) Diana Franklin Clay, 1942, 1 son, 1 daughter. (2) Johanna Sigrid Bishop, 1963. 1 son, 2 daughters. *Education:* BA, King's College, Cambridge, 1939-41; Music Education: Studied singing with Elena Gerhardt and Lucy Manen. *Career:* Principal, Sadler's Wells, 1945-47; English Opera Group, 1948; Vicar Choral, St Paul's Cathedral, 1948-52; Freelance Recitalist, Actor, Opera Singer and Broadcaster in Britain and Europe; Member of Deller Consort, 1950-64; Visiting Instructor in Vocal Studies, Morley College, Goldsmiths' College and Royal School of Church Music, 1956-76; Founder, Artistic Director and Principal Producer, Kent Opera, 1969-89, Refounded Kent Opera, 1992. Productions for Kent Opera include, The Return of Ulysses, The Marriage of Figaro, Iphigenia, Agrippina, Dido and Aeneas and Peter Grimes; Director of first Acting in Opera course, 1989. *Recordings:* Recordings for Deutsche Grammophon and Harmonia Mundi. *Publications:* Translations of songs and operas including: Don Giovanni, Fidelio and The Coronation of Poppea. *Contributions to:* Author of numerous articles on music. *Honours:* OBE, 1985; Honorary Doctorate, University of Kent, Canterbury, 1980. *Address:* Pembles Cross, Egerton, Ashford, Kent, England.

PLATT Richard Swaby, b. 14 May 1928, London, England. Musicologist. m (1). 2 sons, 1 daughter. m.

(2) Diane Ibbotson, 3 Dec 1977, 1 son, 1 daughter. *Education:* Associate, Royal College of Art, 1953; Studied privately with Walter Bergmann, 1965-, Hugh Wood, 1966-68. *Career:* Painter, Printmaker, exhibiting at Royal Academy, London, Group and others, 1953-61; One man show of works, Leicester Galleries, 1956; Musicologist, specialising in 18th Century English Music, 1969. *Compositions include:* Editions: William Boyce, 12 Overtures; Thomas Arne, 4 Symphonies; Works by Croft, Roseingrave, Mudge, Fisher; Semele by John Eccles; Comedy of Errors, by Stephen Storace, Peleus and Thetis by William Boyce. *Recordings:* Editions: Boyce Solomon, Arne Symphonies, Roseingrave. *Publications:* Contributor of chapters, New Grove, 1980 and Grove Opera, 1992; Theatre Music 1700-1760 in Blackwell's History of Music in Britain volume 4; The Symphony, 1720-1840, 1983; Eccles, Judgment of Paris, 1984. *Membership:* Royal Musical Association. *Address:* 3 Stratton Place, Falmouth, Cornwall TR11 2ST, England.

PLATT Theodore, b. 8 Sept 1937, Moscow, Russia. Conductor; Composer; Double Bassist; Harpsichordist. *Education:* Degree in Double Bass Performance, Composition and Music Education, Ippolitov-Ivanov Conservatory of Music, 1956; Doctorate, Moscow Conservatory of Music, 1962. *Career:* Founder and Director, 4 chamber ensembles including first baroque and classical ensembles in USSR (Moscow), 1968-81, and New York Concertino Ensemble, 1981; Live concerts on major classical music radio stations in US; 8 years as Double Bass Soloist of Moscow Chamber Orchestra under Rudolf Barshay (performances with Gilels, Menuhin, Oistrakh, Rostropovich, others); Discovered and premiered lost baroque works; Teacher and Coach of string instruments and voice. *Compositions:* 2 symphony concertos; Cycles of vocal compositions; 1 quartet. *Recordings:* Baroque, Romantic and modern works as Double Bass Soloist of Moscow Chamber Orchestra under Rudolf Barshay; Baroque-Early Romantic repertoire (Mozart, Boccherini, Bach, Schubert, others) as Music Director and Soloist with New York Concetino Ensemble. *Memberships:* Conductors Guild; College Music Society. *Hobbies:* Film; Current events; Cooking. *Current Management:* Ishikawa Foundation. *Address:* Sai Wai-Cho 5-7, Kanazawa-shi, Ishikawa-ken, Japan 920.

PLATZ Robert H P, b. 16 Aug 1951, Baden-Baden, Germany. Composer; Conductor. *Education:* Studies with Wolfgang Fortner, Karlheinz Stockhausen, Francis Travis; IRCAM computer workshop for composers. *Career:* Founded new music group Ensemble Köln, 1980; Own concert series with Ensemble Köln, 1982; Appeared in new music festivals such as Musik der Zeit WDR and Musica Viva series of Munich, Donaueschingen and La Rochelle; Performed at Salzburg Festival, Metz; All works recorded by radio stations in Germany. *Compositions:* Schwelle, full orchestra and tape; Chlebnicov, ensemble and tape; Maro & Stille, soprano, violin and piano solos, plus ensembles and choirs; Raumform, clarinet solo; Flotenstücke - 7 pieces for flute and ensemble; Requiem for tape; Pianopiece 2; Closed loop, guitar; Verkommenes ufer, opera (texts Heiner Müller); Quartett (Zeitstrahl) for string quartet, 1986. *Publications:* Musikalische Prozesse, 1979; Uber Schwelle, 1980; Uber Schwelle III, 1981; Über Tasten, 1983; Versuch einer Asthetik des Kleinen, 1984; Blumroder, Nicht einfach, aber neu, 1980; Formpolyphone Musik, 1981; Stegen: Robert HP Platz, 1982; Van den Hoogen: Komplizierte Horbarkeit, 1982; Blumröder: Maro, 1984; Van den Hoogen: Raumform, 1984; Allende-Blin: Uber Chielnicov, 1984; Record (EMI) Maro, Irvine Arditti, violin. *Address:* Johannes-Müllerstr 26, D-5000 Köln, Germany.

PLAVIN Zecharia, b. 7 June 1956, Vilnius (Vilna), Lithuania. Pianist. m. 12 June 1984, 1 son; 1 daughter. *Education:* BMus, MMus, Ciurlionis School of Arts, S. Rubin Academy of Music, University of Tel Aviv, Israel. *Career:* Concerts with Israel Philharmonic Orchestra, Jerusalem Symphony Orchestra, Symponietta of Beer-

Sheva, Haifa Symphony Orchestra etc; Recitals on all major stages in Israel; Concerts in Western Europe from 1988; Numerous recordings for Israel Broadcasting Authorities; Work for Israel Concert Bureau Omanuth Laam. Records: For Sound-Star-Ton Label (W. Germany). *Publication:* The Metamorphoses by O. Partos. *Honours:* 1st prize, S. Rubin Academy of Music Competition, 1978; National François Shapira Prize, 1980; Diploma, Israel Broadcasting Competition, 1985. *Current Management:* International Music Consultants. *Address:* c/o Willyam Elyas, President, International Music Consultants, IBN-GVIROL Str 176, Tel-Aviv, Israel.

PLAZAS Mary, b. 9 Sept 1966, Wallingford, England. Singer (Soprano). *Education:* Studied at Royal Northern College of Music with Ava June and at National Opera Studio. *Career:* Solo recitals at Wigmore Hall, Purcell Room, Birmingham Town Hall and Royal Exchange Theatre, Manchester; Concerts at Cheltenham and Aldeburgh Festivals; Opera engagements include Poulenc's La Voix Humaine at Aix-en-Provence, Nannetta at Aldeburgh and Despina for Mid-Wales Opera; English National Opera debut, 1992, as Heavenly Voice in Don Carlos; Opera North, 1992-, as the Gypsy in UK premiere of Gerhard's The Duenna, Barbarina and Susanna in Figaro and Tebaldo in Don Carlos; Sang in Opera Factory's Nozze di Figaro for Channel 4 Television and appeared as Echo in Ariadne auf Naxos for Garsington Opera. *Honours include:* Winner, Kathleen Ferrier Memorial Scholarship, 1991. *Address:* c/o Owen/White Management, 14 Nightingale Lane, London N8 7QU, England.

PLEASANTS Henry, b. 12 May 1910, Wayne, PA, USA. Writer on Music. *Education:* Philadelphia Musical Academy; Curtis Institute of Music. *Career:* Music critic, Philadelphia Evening Bulletin, 1930-42; Central European Music Correspondent for the New York Times, 1945-55; London Music Critic for the International Herald Tribune (Paris), 1967-; London Editor for Stereo Review (New York), 1967-; Guest lecturer at numerous institutions in the USA and UK; Participant in musical TV and radio programmes for the BBC and in the USA, Canada and Europe. *Publications:* The Agony of Modern Music, 1955; Death of a Music, 1961; The Great Singers, 1966; Serious Music- and All that Jazz ! 1969; The Great American Popular Singers, 1974; Translator and editor of Vienna's Golden Years of Music (Eduard Hanslick), 1950; The Musical Journeys of Louis Spohr, 1961; The Musical World of Robert Schumann, 1965; The Music Critiicsm of Hugo Wolf, 1979; Piano and Song (Friedrich Wieck), 1988; Opera in Crisis, 1989. *Contributions to:* Major US and UK music magazines; Encyclopedia Britannica; New Grove Dictionary of Music and Musicians 1980. *Address:* 95 Roebuck House, London SW1E 5BE, England.

PLECH Linda, b. 1951, Vienna, Austria. Singer (Soprano). *Education:* Studied in Vienna and at Salzburg Mozarteum. *Career:* Sang as mezzo at Klagenfurt Opera, 1976-77, Oldenburg, 1980-84; Soprano roles at Kaiserslautern, 1985-86, Hamburg Staatsoper, 1987-88, as Donna Anna and Elisabeth de Valois; Cologne, 1989, as Jenufa, Bregenz Festival, 1988-89, as Senta in Fliegende Hollander; Sang the Trovatore Leonore at Deutsche Oper Berlin, 1989, Ariadne auf Naxos at Antwerp; Season 1991-92 as Senta at Geneva, Elisabeth in Tannhauser at Barcelona; Other roles include Marenka in The Bartered Bride and Giulietta in Les contes d'Hoffmann. *Address:* c/o Grand Theatre de Geneve, 11 Boulevard du Theatre, CH-1211 Geneva, Switzerland.

PLEETH William, b. 12 Jan 1916, London, England. Cellist; Professor. m. Margaret Good, 1 son, 1 daughter. *Education:* London Academy; London Cello School; Leipzig Conservatory with Julius Klengel. *Debut:* Leipzig, 1932. *Career:* Played at Grotrian Hall, London, 1933; Performances on BBC TV and Radio ; Concerts in London, Britain, Netherlands, Germany, France, Italy, Australia and New Zealand; Sonatas with Margaret Good; Member of Blech Quartet 1936-41, Allegri

Quartet 1952-67; Additional cellist for Amadeus and other String Quartets; Professor of Cello at the Guildhall School of Music, London, from 1948-78: Anthony Pleeth and Jacqueline du Pré were among his pupils. *Recordings:* Cello and piano sonatas by Brahms, Grieg and Mendelssohn; Schubert's String Quintet; Messiaen's Quatuor pour le fin du Temps; Brahms Sextets. *Memberships:* ISM; ESTA. *Honour:* OBE, 1989. *Hobbies:* Gardening; Collecting Early English Furniture. *Address:* 19 Holly Park, London N3 3JB, England.

PLESHAK Victor Vasilievich, b. 13 Nov 1946, Leningrad, Russia. Composer. 2 sons. *Education:* Choral College of Chapel; Choir Conductors Department, St Petersburg Conservatoire (with B Tishchenko). *Debut:* Many-coloured Balls, song cycle for children, verses by Akimya, Leningrad Radio. *Compositions:* Over 17 musicals and operas including: The Red Imp, musical, 1980; The Knight's Passions, 1981; The Glass Menagerie, opera, 1987; A Tale of a Blot, New Year operetta, 1988; Caution Baba-Yaga, ecological opera; Inspector, an opera after Gogol, 1993; Choral cycle, About Friendship, Love and Brotherhood, to verses by R Burns, 1983; Over 100 published songs including: V Pleshak, Songs for voice and piano (guitar, accordion), in Soviet Composer, 1988. *Recordings:* The Tale of a Dead Tsarevna and Seven Epic Heroes, opera in 2 acts; The Wodow of Valencia, musical after the play by Lope de Vega; Oh These Pretty Sinners, musical farces after Lasage and Rabelais; The Booted Cat, musical after the play by Pierrot. *Honours:* All-Union Competition of Songs for Students Choir, 1972; Winner, Leninsky Komsomol Prize, All-Union Songs Competition, All-World Festival of Youth and Students, 1985. *Memberships:* Composers Union of St Petersburg. *Hobby:* Football. *Address:* Gorokhovaya St (formerly Dzerzhinskaya) 53 kv 29, 190031 St Petersburg, Russia.

PLETNEV Mikhail, b. 1957, USSR. Concert Pianist; Composer; Conductor. *Career:* Performs throughout Russia, Europe, Japan and the USA with the world's leading orchestras; Season 1993/94 includes recitals in London, Berlin, Vienna, Amsterdam, Geneva, Munich and Basle; Founded Russian National Orchestra in 1990 and now tours with them as conductor in Europe, Japan, North and South America; Also conducts the Philharmonia Orchestra, the Deutsche Kammerphilharmonie, Norddeutsche Rundfunk Symphony Orchestra, the London Symphony Orchestra. *Recordings include:* Virgin Classics as pianist include Rachmaninov's 1st Concerto and Paganini Rhapsody, works by Haydn, Beethoven, Chopin, Tchaikovsky, Mussorgsky and clarinet sonatas with Michael Collins, and Tchaikovsky's 6th Symphony as conductor with Russian National Orchestra which was voted runner-up in orchestral category of 1992 Gramophone Awards; Now signed with Deutsche Grammophon to record as conductor with RNO. *Honours:* Gold Medal, Tchaikovsky International Piano Competition, Moscow, 1978. *Address:* c/o Columbia Artists Management Ltd, 28 Cheverton Road, London N19 3AY, England.

PLISHKA Paul, b. 28 Aug 1941, Old Forge, Pennsylvania, USA. Singer (Bass). *Education:* Studied at Montclair State College and with Armen Boyazjian. *Debut:* Paterson Lyric Opera 1961. *Career:* Metropolitan Opera from 1967, as King Marke in Tristan, Procida in Les vêpres Siciliennes, Varlaam and Pimen in Boris Godunov, Oroveso in Norma, Leporello and the Commendatore in Don Giovanni, Banquo in the Peter Hall production of Macbeth, and Philip II in Don Carlos; La Scala 1974, in La Damnation de Faust; San Francisco 1984, as Silva in Ernani; Teatro Liceo Barcelona 1985; Orange Festival 1987, as Phanüel in Massenet's Hérodiade; sang Daland in Der fliegende Holländer at the Metropolitan, 1989; Procida at Carnegie Hall 1990; Opera Company of Philadelphia 1990, as the Mayor in La gazza ladra, Fiesco in Simon Boccanegra at the Metropolitan; Grant Park concerts Chicago, in Prince Igor; Season 1991/92 as Giorgio in Puritani at Chicago, the Pope in Benvenuto Cellini at Geneva and Zaccaria at Montreal. *Recordings:* Crespel in Les Contes d'Hoffmann and Henry VIII in Anna Bolena (Decca);

Norma (HMV); Le Cid and Donizetti's Gemma di Vergy (CBS); Faust (RCA); Wurm in Luisa Miller (Sony). *Address:* c/o Ingpen and Williams Ltd., 14 Kensington Court, London W8 5DN, England.

PLOWRIGHT Rosalind Anne, b. 21 May 1949, Worksop, England. Soprano. *Education:* LRAM, Royal Northern College of Music, Manchester. *Debut:* As Page in Salome, English National Opera, 1975. *Career includes:* Miss Jessell, Turn of the Screw, ENO, 1979; Debut, Covent Garden as Ortlinde, Die Walküre, 1980; With Bern Opera, 1980-81, Frankfurt Opera & Munich Opera, 1981; US debuts, Philadelphia, San Diego, also Paris, Madrid, Hamburg, 1982; La Scala, Milan, Edinburgh Festival, San Francisco, New York, 1983; With Deutsche Opera, Berlin, 1984; Houston, Pittsburgh, Verona, 1985; Teatro Communale, Florence 1986; Tulsa, Lyon, Buenos Aires, Israel 1987; Lausanne, Geneva, Bonn 1988; Copenhagen, Lisbon 1989; sang Wagner's Senta at Covent Garden 1986, Gluck's Alceste at La Scala Milan 1987 (followed by Desdemona in London); season 1988 as Médée in Lausanne, Elisabeth de Valois in Geneva and Norma in Bonn; 1988/89 as Médée and the Trovatore Leonora at Covent Garden; Vienna Staatsoper debut 1990 as Amelia (Un Ballo in Maschera); season 1990/91 as Lady Macbeth in Frankfurt and Israel, Desdemona in Munich and Tchaikovsky's Tatyana at Pittsburgh; Tosca at Torre del Lago, Italy; Recitals, concerts, UK, Europe, USA; Featured Artist (People, no. 180) Opera Magazine, 1992; Season 1992/93 as Elisabeth de Valois at the London Coliseum and Nice, Gioconda for Opera North; Other Roles: Ariadne; Elizabeth I, Maria Stuarda; Elena, Sicilian Vespers; Manon Lescaut; Aida; Suor Angelica; Giorgetta, Il Tabarro; Violetta, La Traviata; Norma; Madama Butterfly; Maddalena, Andrea Chénier; Leonora, La Forza del Destino. *Honours include:* SWET Award, 1979; 1st prize, 7th International Competition for Opera Singers, Sofia, 1979; Prix, Fondation Fanny Heldy, Academie Nationale du Disque Lyrique, 1985. *Address:* c/o Barratt House, 7 Chertsey Road, Woking, Surrey, GU21 5AB, England.

PLUISTER Simon, b. 12 Nov 1913, Obdam, The Netherlands. Composer; Conductor; Organ and Piano Teacher. m. Jacoba Maria Leentvaar, 1943, 1 son, 1 daughter. *Education:* Studied Composition with Daniel Ruyneman, and at Amsterdam Conservatory with Hendrik Andriessen and Ernest W. Mulder; Studied Pianoforte with André Jurres. *Debut:* As Composer, Amsterdam, 1936. *Career:* Composer for Dutch Broadcasting (NCRV), 1950-57; Conductor, The Harold Shamrock Concert Orchestra, Radio Tivoli Orchestra and Vocal Ensemble with instruments, 1955-66; Organ Teacher, Music School, Emmeloord, 1969-79. *Compositions:* For Orchestra: 15 Psalms and Hymns, 3 Suites, Punch-and-Judy Show, 3 Cascades, Rhapsody in Beer- tonality; For Solo, Choir and Orchestra: Psalm 65, 121, 137, 138, Cantata St Luke 24, Concerto da chiesa The Acts II; 3 Operettas; 2 Works, voice with orchestra; 3 Works for String-Orchestra; 75 Works for Small-Orchestra (Short pieces and suites); Concertino for Piano and Orchestra, Ricercare and Ciga for Organ and String-Orchestra; Chamber Music, Donemus, Amsterdam, Holland; Music for Pianoforte 2 hds, 4 hds and for 2 Pianofortes; Calvinus Sinfonia for Strings 1987. Commission N.C.R.V.; To Silvestre Revueltas, from Mexico, at his death, for Choir (mixed voices) and orchestra, 1987, (choir singing and speaking); Five Brown Songs, for soprano, Flute, Alto Saxophone and pianoforte, 1988; Larghetto for Strings, 1988; The days after the Crucifixion, prologue from the opera Bar Abbas, for soli, female-choir and orchestra, 1986, (also as cantata); Opera Bar Abbas, for soli, and orchestra, 1986-88; Concerto da Chiesa for 2 recorders, V-cello and Organ, 1990; Ant Brothers (fruit nursery) Musical for soli, choir and Orchesta, 1990-1991; Chronicle of an eyewitness, electronic music for a Broadcast-play; Super Flumina Babylonis for soprano-solo, male-choir and pianoforte, 1992; Ave Verum Corpus and Gloria for baritone-solo, male choir and Organ, 1992; Duo Facile for Violin, V-cello; Fantasia for trio (Violin, viola and V-cello), 1993. *Membership:* GENECO (Society of

Dutch Composers). *Address:* Zwartemeerweg 23, 8317 PA Oud-Kraggenburg, Nop, The Netherlands.

PLUSH Vincent, b. 1950, Adelaide, South Australia. Composer. *Education:* BM, University of Adelaide; Studied computer music, University of California, San Diego, USA. *Career:* Staff, Music Department, Australian Broadcasting Commission; Teacher, NSW State Conservatorium of Music, 1973-80; Tutor, Music Department, University of NSW, 1979; Founder, The Seymour Group, University of Sydney, 1976; Consultant for many arts bodies on Federal, State and municipal levels; Composer-in-Residence, Musica Viva, 1985; Artistic Director, The Braidwood Festival, 1989 and 1991; Composer-in-Residence, ABC Radio, 1987. *Compositions:* Work for Orchestra, Pacifica, 1986, rev 1987; Works for Ensemble: On Shooting Stars-Homage to Victor Jara, 1981; Facing the Danger, 1982; The Wakefield Convocation, 1985; Helices, from The Wakefield Chronicles, 1985; The Love Songs of Herbert Hoover, 1987. Works for Solo Instrument and Ensemble: Aurores, from O Paraguay!, 1979; Bakery Hill Rising, 1980; Gallipoli Sunrise, 1984; FireRaisers, 1984. Works for Brass Band: The Wakefield Chorales, 1985- 86; March of the Dalmatians, 1987. Works for Narrator and Accompaniment: The Wakefield Chronicles, 1985-86; the Maitland and Morpeth String Quartet, 1979- 85; The Musie of Fire, 1986-87. Instrumental Works: Chu no mai, 1974-76; Encompassings, 1975; Chrysalis, 1977-78; Stevie's Wonder Music, 1979; The Wakefield Invocation, 1986; The Wakefield Intrada, 1986; Works for Tape; Vocal Works; Choral Works; Music Theatre Works and Arrangements. *Address:* c/o Australian Music Centre, P O Box 49, Broadway 2007, Australia.

PLUYGERS Catherine, b. 20 Nov 1955, Colchester, Essex, England. Oboist; Artistic Director. *Education:* BMus (Honours), University of London, 1978; ARCM, Performance, 1978, ARCM, Teaching, 1979, Royal College of Music; Banff Centre School of Fine Arts, Canada, 1984; Goldsmiths College, 1991. *Career:* Freelance orchestral player with BBC, Royal Ballet Orchestra, Ulster Orchestra; Founder Member, Thomas Arne Players, with Purcell Room debut, 1985, Wigmore Hall debut, 1986; Recital tour, oboe and organ music, South Norway, sponsored by Norwegian Arts Council, 1982; Formed New Wind Orchestra (NEWO), 1985 and New Wind Summer School (NWSS) 1988; Premiered Sonata No 2, opus 64, oboe and piano, dedicated to self by Dr Ruth Gipps, 1986; BBC World Service broadcast, 1986; NEWO South Bank premiere, Queen Elizabeth Hall, 1986. *Compositions:* Gloryland, Mixed Media one woman show on subject of War and The Square, A Mixed Media piece performed in Purcell Room, 1990, by the Group Interartes and Hong Kong City Hall, 1990. *Recordings:* English Music for Oboe and Piano, with accompanist Matthew Stanley, Redbridge Recordings, 1984. *Current Management:* Self: New Wind Management Ltd. *Address:* 119 Woolstone Road, Forest Hill, London SE23 2TQ, England.

PODHAJSKI Marek, b. 7 Apr 1938, Nowogodek, Poland. *Education:* Academy of Mucik, Gdansk, Academy of Music, Warsaw. *Career:* Musical Career Started in 1958, From 1961-90 He Worked at the Academy of Music, Gdansk He Held teaching Positions Ranging From Assistant to Prorector. He is also the Founder of the Institute; Since 1990 He Has Worked at the Akureyri Music School, Iceland; He Has 4 Books and About 80 Printed Papers Published; Organiser, Iniator and Scientific Manager of International Scientific Conferences in Poland and 1st Festival of Icelandic Piano Music in Akureyri. *Publications Include:* Interpretacia Matematyczno Logiczna Elementarnych Pojec Harmonii Funkcyjnej; Formy Muzyczne; Nowy System Muzyki. *Contributions to:* Zeszyty Naukowe; Prace Specjalne. *Honours include:* Whos Who Listings; International Man of the Year; Silver Shield of Valour. *Memberships:* Polish Composers Union; Internationa Musicological Society; American Biographical Institute Research Association. *Hobbies:* Methodology; Hindu Music; Contemporary

Polish History; Photography; Travel. *Address:* ul Komandorska 6, 80-299 Gdansk-Osowa, Poland.

POGACNIK Miha, b. 31 May 1949, Kranj, Yugoslavia. Concert Violinist; Music Director; President of Idriart. m. Judith Csik, 31 Jan 1974, 1 son, 1 daughter. *Education:* Artist's Diploma with distinction, DAAD Scholar, Cologne Conservatory of Music (Musikhochschule), 1967-72; Fulbright Scholar, Indiana University School of Music, 1973-74; Professors: Veronek, Ozim, Gingold, Rostal, Szeryng. *Career:* Over 100 Concerts per season 1977- in: USA, Canada, Mexico, South America, Australia, New Zealand, China, Scandinavia, Western and Eastern Europe; Music Director of Chartres Festival d'Ete, 1981-; President and Founder, IDRIART International, Geneva (Institute For The Development of Intercultural Relations Through The Arts) now represented in 30 countries, 1983-; Music Director of past 20 IDRIART Festivals on 5 continents. *Recordings:* Have chosen to refuse all offers to record in order to further live communication with audiences.

POGORELICH Ivo, b. 20 Oct 1958, Belgrade, Serbia. Pianist. m. Aliza Kezeradze 1980. *Education:* Studied with Aliza Kezeradze at the Moscow Conservatory. *Career:* International success from 1980, after elimination from the Chopin International Piano Competition; Solo recitals and appearances with major orchestras in Europe, USA, Japan, Australasia; Plays Chopin, Rachmaninov and other Romantics; Records exclusively for Deutsche Grammophon; Settled in England 1982. *Recordings include:* CD of Prokofiev's 6th Sonata and Gaspard de La Nuit by Ravel (Deutsche Grammophon); Works by Chopin. *Honours:* First Prize Casagrande Competition at Terni, 1978; First prize Montreal International Competition 1980; Created Ambassador of Goodwill at UNESCO in 1987 (only musician to be bestowed this honor). *Address:* c/o Kantor Concert Mgmt & PR, 67 Teignmouth Road, London NW2 4EA, England.

POHL Carla, b. 1942, Johannesburg, South Africa. Singer (Soprano). *Education:* Studied in South Africa and at the Wiesbaden Conservatory. *Career:* Sang at Pforzheim from 1970; Freiburg from 1979, notably as Tosca, Maddalena in Andrea Chenier, Marenka in The Bartered Bride and Stauss's Chrysothemis; Wiesbaden, 1979-81; Deutsche Oper am Rhein Dusseldorf from 1981, as Wagner's Elisabeth, Eva and Sieglinde, the Empress in Die Frau ohne Schatten, Strauss's Ariadne and Marschallin, and Leonore in Fidelio; Guest apparances in Mannheim, Berlin, Nancy, Karlsruhe, Stuttgart, Vienna State Opera, Munich State Opera, Milan, Rome and Brunswick; Tour of South Africa, 1985; Deutsche Oper am Rhein 1987, as Rezia in Oberon; Deutsche Oper Berlin and Santiago Chile 1988, as Chrysothemis and Elsa. *Address:* c/o Deutsche Oper am Rhein, Heinrich-Heine Allee 16, D-4000 Dusseldorf, Germany.

PÓKA Balázs, b. 1955, Hungary, Baritone. *Education:* University of Medicine, 1976. *Career:* Hungarian State Opera House; Has made several films on television in works of Rossini, Menotti, Lortzing and Puccini; Sang role of Schaunard in Puccini's La Bohème; Participant in concert and opera performances broadcast by Hungarian Radio; Numerous appearances on concert stage in oratorios; Has performed in numerous countries including, Federal Republic of Germany; France, Belgium, The Netherlands, Czechoslovakia, Bulgaria, Austria, Ireland and Italy; Roles include: Dandini in La Cenerentola; Valentin in Faust, Silvio in Pagliacci; Malatesta in Don Pasquale; Albert in Werther; Igor in Prince Igor; Di Luna in Il Trovatore; Carlos in La Forza del Destino; Germont in La Traviata; Renato in Un Ballo in Maschera; Onegin in Onegin; Ping in Turandot; Figaro in Il Barbiere di Siviglia; Rodrigo in Don Carlos; Escamillo in Carmen; Marcello in La Bohème. *Honours:* Silver Diploma, Pula International Opera Competition.

POL Wijnand van de, b. 14 Feb 1938, Alkmaar, Holland. Organist Conductor. m. Marina Amadessi, 16

Sept 1984, 2 sons. Diploma in Organ, St Cecilia Conservatoire, Rome, Italy; Doctoral Degree in Modern Languages, University of Rome. *Career:* Concerts as organist in all countries in Europe and USA; Master Classes in various universities; Organist, English Anglican Church of All Saints, Rome, 1960-; Organ Professor, Conservatoire of Music, Perugia. *Recordings:* 6 Records of Organ Music; Recordings with radio stations in various countries in Europe and USA. *Publication:* Book: La registrazione organistica dal 1500 al 1800, Paideia - Editor, 1992. *Contributions to:* Articles for: Piano-Time (Rome); Il Bolletino degll Amici de;;'Organo, Rome; Ass. Pro-Musica Antiqua, Perugia; Strumenti e Musica, Ancona. *Honours:* Diocesan Certificate of Honour of the Diocese of Gibraltar in Europe for 25 years as Organist and Choir Master in All Saints' Church, Rome, 1985; Zilveren-meiboom award of Dutch Embassy, Rome. *Memberships:* Ispettore Onorario for the Ministry of Culture and Art for the Restoration and Conservation of antique organs in the regione of Umbria; President of Music Associations in Perugia and Rome. *Address:* via Pereira 14, 005022 Amelia, (Terni), Italy.

POLAKOVICOVA Viera, b. 25 Aug 1953, Zilina, Czechoslovakia. Musicologist. m. Jozef Polakovic, 27 Nov 1976, 1 son. *Education:* Graduate 1976, Doctor 1979, Candidate of Sciences 1982, Musicology, Philosophical Faculty, Commenius University, Bratislava. *Career:* Stipendium on Philosophical Faculty, Commenius University; Responsible for the International Rostrum of Young Performers UNESCO at the Bratislava Music Festival, 1980-85; Secretary, International Rostrum of Young Performers, UNESCO, 1980-85; Head of the Music Information Centre, Slovak Music Fund, 1985-. *Recordings:* Editor, Franz Paul Rigler Sonatas, Marica Dobiasova harpsichord, 1986. *Publications:* Editor of Sonatas from Franz Paul Rigler, in Old Music in Slovakia OPUS, 1981; Franz Paul Rigler in the Light of the latest researche, in Lusicologica Slovaca 1985. *Current Managment:* Head of the Slovak Music Information Centre. *Address:* Music Information Centre, Medená 29, 811 02 Bratislava, Slovakia.

POLANSKY Larry, b. 16 Oct 1954, New York City, USA. Composer; Theorist; Writer; Performer; Software Systems Designer (music). m. Jody Diamond, 6 Jan 1985. *Education:* Various studies. *Career includes:* Staff Member, Centre for Contemporary Music, Mills College, 1981-; Assistant Professor, Music, Mills College, 1981-; Composer, several dance companies including: Ann Rodiger, Anita Feldman, Toronto Independent Dance Ensemble, Barbara Roesch, etc; Founder and Director, Frog Peak Music, (A composers collective); Music Advisory Editor, Leonardo, The International Journal of Arts, Sciences and Technology; Guest Composer, Darmstadt and Telluride Festivals; Currently Professor of Music, Dartmouth College; Record Reviewer; Editor; Publisher. *Compositions include:* Three Rimbaud Settings, 1986; Will You Miss Me, 1986; Sh'Ma: Fuging Tune in G, 1980; Movement for Andrea Smith, 1977; Cocks Crow, Dogs Bark, 1987; Piano Studies, 1978; Here to Stay, 1984; Another You, 17 variations for Solo Harp; Lonesome Road (51 Variations for solo piano); 3 studies (for computer and performer); Many other works for computer and performer. *Recordings include:* Hensley Variations, 1985; Four Voice Canon, 1986. *Address:* Music Department, Dartmouth College, Hanover, NH 03755, USA.

POLASKI Deborah, b. 26 Sept 1949, Richmond Centre, Wisconsin, USA. Singer (Soprano). *Education:* Conservatory of Music Ohio; American Institute of Music Graz. *Career:* Sang at Gelsenkirchen, Karlsruhe and Ulm from 1976; Further appearances at opera houses in Hanover, Munich, Hamburg and Freiburg; Festival of Waiblingen 1983, in a revival of Croesus by Reinhard Keiser; Oslo 1986, as Elektra; Other roles include Leonore in Fidelio, Wagner's Isolde and Sieglinde and Marie in Wozzeck; Bayreuth Festival, 1988, as Brünnhilde in the Ring cycle directed by Harry Kupfer; Sang Brünnhilde at Rotterdam 1988, Cologne 1990; Stuttgart Staatsoper 1989, as Elektra (also at the Teatro

Nuovo Spoleto, 1990); Season 1992 as the Dyer's Wife in Die Frau ohne Schatten at Amsterdam and Brünnhilde at Bayreuth. *Recording:* Wolf-Ferrari's Sly (RCA); Brünnhilde's Immolation with the Chicago Symphony (Erato). *Address:* Oper der Stadt Köln, Offenbachplatz, D-5000 Cologne, Germany.

POLGAR Laszlo, b. 1 Jan 1947, Somogyszentpal, Hungary. Singer (Bass). *Education:* Studied at the Franz Liszt Academy of Music, Budapest. *Career:* Sang at the Budapest Opera from 1972, as Rocco, Osmin, Sarastro and Leporello; Professor of Singing at the Liszt Academy from 1978; Brussels debut 1981, as Colline in La Bohème; Covent Garden debut 1982, as Rodolpho in La Sonnambula; Hamburg Staatsoper as Osmin and Basilio; US debut Philadelphia 1982, as Colline; Has sung Gurnemanz (Parsifal) in Budapest and Berlin; Concert appearances as Bartók's Bluebeard in Hungary, Ireland, the USSR, Italy, France and Canada; Promenade Concerts London 1984, 1987, as Bluebeard and in Pulcinella by Stravinsky; Carnegie Hall New York 1987, in the Choral Symphony; Die Schöpfung and the Dvořák Requiem at La Scala, Milan; Operatic engagements in Paris (Varlaam in Boris Godunov), Vienna, Munich (Leporello, 1984) and Zurich; sang Padre Guardiano in La Forza del destino at Budapest, 1990; Member of the Zurich Opera from 1991; Season 1992 as Rosini's Basilo at Brussels and Vienna, Bartók's Bluebeard at the Prom Concerts London. *Recordings include:* Il Barbiere di Siviglia and works by Haydn and Liszt (Deutsche Grammophon); Alphonse in La favorita by Donizetti. *Honours:* Winner, Dvořák International Singing Competition, 1974; Winner, Hugo Wolf Competition Vienna (1980) and Pavarotti Conmpetition Philadelphia (1981); Liszt Prize, Hungary, 1982. *Address:* c/o Hungarian State Opera House, Népöztársaság utja 22, 1061 Budapest, Hunagry.

POLGAR Tibor, b. 11 Mar 1907, Budapest, Hungary. Composer; Conductor; Pianist; Professor of Music. m. Ilona Nagykovacsi, 10 July 1947. *Education:* University degree in philosophy; Diploma in composition, Royal Academy of Music, Budapest, 1925. *Debut:* Concerts and radio Broadcasts, Budapest, 1925. *Career:* Conductor, Composer in residence, Hungarian Broadcasting Corporation, 1925-48; Artistic Director, Hungarian Radio, 1948-50; Associate Conductor, Philharmonia Hungarica, Marl-Westphalen, Germany, 1962-64; Teaching Staff, Opera Department, University of Toronto, Canada, 1966-75; Course Director, York University, Toronto, 1976-77. *Compositions include:* A European Lover, musical satire in one act; The Glove, one act opera; The Troublemaker, comic opera; The Suitors, opera; A Strange Night, opera; The Last Words of Louis Riel, cantata from Canadian history; Notes on Hungary, suite concert band; Ilona's Four Faces, for Clarinet; Lest We Forget the Last Chapter of Genesis, Cantata; Pentatonia; Festive Fanfare; Passacaglia; Concerto romantico for Harp; Concertino for Trumpet with Symphonies Orchestra, Two Symphonic Dances in Latin Rhythum for Trumpet solo and Concert Band; The Voice of the Soul, A Fantasy in 3 movements for Concert Band; 200 feature and documentary film scores; music for CBC radio and television plays. *Address:* 21 Vaughan Road, Apt. 1903, Toronto, Ontario, Canada, M6G 2N2.

POLIANSKY Valerig K, b. 19 Apr 1949, Moscow, USSR. Conductor. m. Olga P Lapuso, 29 Sept 1976, 1 son, 1 daughter. *Education:* State Conservatoire Tchaikowsky, Moscow, graduated in Choir Conducting, 1971, Orchestra Conducting, 1974. *Debut:* Moscow Operetta. *Career:* Conducted, Shostakovich's Katerina Ismailowa at Bolshoi Theatre; Leading conductor in Moscow Operetta Theatre. *Recordings:* Rachmaninov Vespers, Liturgia of St John Chrysostom, A Schnittke, Choir Concert; A Bruckner, Geistliche motetten, L Cherubini, Requiem in c, P Tchaikowsky, Liturgia of St Joaum Christosamus, Various chorus; Orchestral Serenade. *Contributions to:* Soviet Music; Music LIfe; Music in the USSR. *Honours:* Arezzo Prize for best conductor, 1975. *Hobbies:* Skiing; Volleyball; Walking.

Address: M Kolchosnaia Square 3-106, 129090 Moscow, Russia.

POLISI Joseph W., b. 1944, USA. President, The Juilliard School. *Education:* BA, Political Science, University of Connecticut, 1969; MA, International Relations, Fletcher School of Law and Diplomacy, Tufts University, 1970; MMus, 1973, MMA, 1975, DMA, 1980, Yale University; Studies with Maurice Allard, Conservatoire National de Paris, 1973-74. *Career:* Currently President, The Juilliard School, New York City; Extensive solo and chamber bassoon performances throughout USA; Chairman, Seaver Institute/National Endowment for the Arts Conductors Program; Member, National Committee on Standards in the Arts; Scholarship Committee, Presser Foundation; Co-Chair, Music Professional Training Panel, National Endowment for the Arts, 1984-87; Former Accreditation Evaluator for National Association of Schools of Music. *Recording:* A Harvest of 20th Century Bassoon Music, Crystal S341, 1979. *Contributions to:* Doctor of Music, Curtis Institute of Music, Philadelphia, PA, 1990; Honorary Member, Royal Academy of Music, London, England, 1992. *Address:* The Juilliard School, 60 Lincoln Center Plaza, New York, NY 10023, USA.

POLIVNICK Paul, b. 7 July 1947, Atlantic City, New Jersey, USA. Conductor. m. Marsha Hooks, 20 June 1980. *Education:* BM, Juilliard School of Music, New York, 1969; Aspen (Colo) Music School summers 1961, 1968, 1970, 1972; Berkshire Music Center, Tanglewood, Massachusetts, summers 1965, 1966 and 1971; Accademia Musicale Chigiana, Siena, Italy, summer 1969. *Career:* Conductor, Debut Orchestra, Los Angeles, 1969-73; Associate Conductor, Indianapolis Symphony Orchestra, 1977-80; Associate Principal Conductor, Milwaukee Symphony Orchestra, 1981-85; Music Director, Alabama Symphony Orchestra, Birmingham, 1985-. *Recordings:* For KKM; Nonesuch. *Honour:* Honorary Doctorate, Montevallo University, 1986. *Membership:* American Symphony Orchestra League. *Hobbies:* Working out; Reading; Backpacking; Cooking; Travelling. *Current Management:* Maxim Gershunoff Attractions Inc. *Address:* c/o Alabama Symphony Orchestra, 1814 First Avenue North, Birmingham, AL 35209, USA.

POLLACK Howard Joel, b. 17 Mar 1952, Brooklyn, New York, USA. Associate Professor. *Education:* BM, University of Michigan, 1973; MA, PhD, Cornell University, 1981. *Career:* Taught at Cornell University, RIT, Hochstein School; Assistant Professor, 1987-1992, currently Associate Professor, University of Houston, Texas. *Publications:* Walter Piston, 1982; Harvard Composers: Walter Piston and his Students from Elliott Carter to Frederic Rzewski, 1992; An Aesthetic Fusion: German Literature and Music 1890-1989 (co-editor), 1992; Forthcoming: Skyscraper Lullaby: The Music of John Alden Carpenter. *Contributions to:* American Music, College Music Symposium, Current Musicology, Journal of Musicology, Notes, Opera Quarterly. *Memberships:* American Musicological Society; Sonneck Society; Pi Kappa Lambda, Zeta Tau. *Address:* School of Music, University of Houston, Houston, TX 77204, USA.

POLLAK Anna, b. 1 May 1912, Manchester, England. Singer (Mezzo- Soprano). *Education:* Studied with Lawrance Collingwood, Joseph Hislop and Joan Cross. *Debut:* Sadler's Wells 1945, as Dorabella in Cosí fan Tutte. *Career:* Sang at Sadler's Wells until 1962, notably as Carmen, Cherubino, Siebel in Faust, Orlofsky and Hansel; Created roles in The Rape of Lucretia (1946), Berkeley's Ruth (1954) and Nelson (1956), Gardner's The Moon and Sixpence and Williamson's English Eccentrics (1964); Holland Festival, 1950, as Fatima in Oberon; Covent Garden, 1952, as Cherubino; Glyndebourne Festival, 1952-53, Dorabella; Sang Public Opinion in Offenbach's Orpheus in the Underworld at the London Coliseum in 1968; Appearances at concerts and on radio and TV. *Recordings:* The Rape of Lucretia, conducted by Ansermet; Semele (London). *Honour:* Order of the British Empire, 1962. *Hobbies:* Gardening;

Swimming; Driving; Literature. *Address:* Hawthorn House, Stanford, Ashford, Kent, England.

POLLARD Anthony Cecil, b. May 1929, London, England. Publisher. m. Margaret Cleveland, 1 son, 1 daughter. *Education:* John Lyon School, Harrow, England. *Career:* Joined Gramophone, 1946, rejoined 1949; Served in British Army, 1946-49; London Editor, 1959-61, Editor, 1961-72, Managing Editor, 1972-89, Publisher 1972-; Gramophone. *Hobbies:* Music; Literature; Gardening; Golf. *Address:* The Barn House, Layter's Green Lane, Gerrards Cross, Buckinghamshire, SL9 8TH, England.

POLLASTRI Paolo, b. 12 July 1960, Bologna, Italy. Oboist. m. Christine Dechaux, 24 Sept 1988. 1 daughter. *Education:* Scientific Diploma, Bologna, 1979; Oboe Diploma, Bologna, 1977; Oboe Diploma 1982, Baroque Oboe Diploma 1982, Brussels; Diploma D'Onore (Accademia Chigiana, Siena), 1977. *Career:* 1st Oboe, Orchestra Giovanile Italiana, 1977; Genova, 1979; Rai Roma, 1981; Orchestra Regionale Toscana-Firenze, 1982-89; Accademia di S Cecilia, Roma, 1989; Solisti Veneti, 1984-89; TV and Radio appearances with RAI 1, 2, 3 (Solisti Veneti); TV Australiana (Solisti Veneti); Radio Israeliana (Accademia Bizzantina); BBC (Solisti Veneti); Played at Festivals in Montreux, Salzburg, Zagreb and Belgrade, Martigny and Vevey, Toulouse, Paris, Stuttgart, Edinburgh, Sydney, Melbourne and Canberra. *Recordings:* Respighi, Solisti Veneti, Erato; Vivaldi, Oboe concertos, Accademia Bizantina, Frequenz; Malipiero, Respighi, Ghedini, Rota, Woodwind Quintet, Fonè. *Contributions to:* Il Dopo Concerto, 1980-81; The Italian Academy of Woodwinds, 1988-89. *Current Management:* Modena International Music. *Address:* Paolo Pollastri, Via di Mugnana 3, 50027 Strada in Chianti, Firenze, Italy.

POLLET Francoise, b. 10 Sept 1949, Boulogne Billancourt, near Paris, France. Singer (Soprano). *Education:* Studied at Versailles Conservatory and in Munich. *Debut:* Lubeck, as the Marschallin, 1983. *Career:* Sang at Lubeck until 1986, as Santuzza, Fiordiligi, Donna Anna, Elisabeth in Tannhäuser, Amelia in Ballo in Maschera, Alice Ford, Giulietta, Ariadne and Arabella; Appearances as Agathe at Marseilles, Vitellia in La Clemenza di Tito at Opera-Comique, Paris, and Dukas' Ariadne at Theatre du Chatelet in a production by Ruth Berghaus, 1991; At Montpellier has sung Reizia in Oberon, Meyerbeer's Valentine, Catherine of Aragon in Saint-Saens's Henry VIII, Elisabeth and Magnard's Berenice; Hamburg, 1990, in premiere of Liebermann's Freispruch fur Medea; Covent Garden, 1991, as Valentine; Other roles include Cassandra in Les Troyens, at Brussels, and Mozart's Countess; Concert repertoire includes Schumann's Liederkreis and Les Nuits d'Ete by Berlioz. *Recordings include:* 4th Symphony by Guy Ropartz; La Vierge in Jeanne d'Arc au Bucher by Honegger, conducted by Ozawa. *Address:* c/o Opera de Montpellier, 11 Boulevard Victor Hugo, F-34000 Montpellier, France.

POLLETT Patricia Engeline Maria, b. 13 Oct 1958, Utrecht, Holland. Violist (Lecturer/Musician in Residence at University of Queensland). m. Dr Philip Keith Pollett, 28 Jan 1978, 1 son. *Education:* B Mus (Hons), University of Adelaide, 1979; ARCM, Royal College of Music, 1980; Hochschule der Kunst, West Berlin, 1988; Teachers: Beryl Kimber, Peter Schidlof, Margaret Major, Bruno Giuranna. *Career:* Member, I Solisti Veneti, 1983-84; Founder-member of contemporary ensemble Perihelion; Resident at University of Queensland, 1988-; Concerto soloist with: Gulbenkian Orchestra, Lisbon, 1984; Queensland Philharmonic Orchestra, 1989; Queensland Symphony Orchestra, 1990, 1991; Sydney Symphony Orchestra, 1991; Mozart Symposium, University of Otago, New Zealand, 1991. *Compositions:* Commissioned new works for viola by: Colin Spiers, Andrew Schultz, Nigel Sabin, Philip Bracanin (World premiere performances of these), Ross Edwards, Colin Brumby, Moya Henderson. *Address:* 21 Almay Street, Kenmore, Queensland 4069, Australia.

POLLINI Maurizio, b. 5 Jan 1942, Milan, Italy. Pianist; Conductor. *Education* Studied with Carlo Lonati, and with Carlo Vidusso at the Milan Conservatory. *Career:* Has played with Berlin and Vienna Philharmonic Orchestras, Bayerischer Rundfunk Orchestra, London Symphony Orchestra, Boston, New York, Philadelphia, Los Angeles and San Francisco Orchestras; Has played at Salzburg, Vienna, Berlin, Prague Festivals; Plays Boulez, Nono and Schoenberg, in addition to the standard repertory; Has conducted operas by Rossini at Pesaro from 1981 (La Donna del Lago); World tour with Bach's Well-Tempered Clavier, 1985; Played the 2nd Sonata of Boulez and Beethoven's Diabelli Variations, London 1990. *Recordings:* For Polydor International, including CDs of Bartók Piano Concertos 1 and 2 (Chicago Symphony/Abbado); Chopin 1st Concerto (Philharmonic/Kletski) and Sonatas Op.35, Op.58; Beethoven Late Sonatas; Brahms Piano Quintet (Quartetto Italiano); Schoenberg piano music; Stravinsky Petrushka Three Movements, Webern Variations, Boulez 2nd Sonata, Prokofiev 7th Sonata. *Honour:* First Prize, International Chopin Competition, Warsaw 1960. *Address:* c/o Harrison/Parrott Ltd., 12 Penzance Place, London, W11 4PA, England.

POLOZOV Vyacheslav M, b. 1950, Mariupol, Ukraine, USSR. Singer (Tenor). *Education:* Studied at the Kiev Conservatory. *Debut:* Liev Opera 1977, as Alfredo in La Traviata. *Career:* Leading tenor at the Saratov Opera 1978; Leading tenor at the Minsk Opera 1980; Bolshoi Opera Moscow 1982, Alfredo and Turiddu, opposite E. Obraztsova; Sang Pinkerton at La Scala 1986; US debut with Pittsburgh Symphony Orchestra 1986, as Cavaradossi, opposite R. Scotto (Great Wood Festival), conductor M.Tilson Thomas; US stage debut the Chicago Lyric Opera 1986, as Rodolfo in La Bohème, opposite K. Ricciarelli; Further appearances at Washington DC (1986, as Lykov, under M. Rostropovich, director-G. Vishnevskya), New York (Met 1987, as Pinkerton, opposite R Scotto); Palm Springs, as Cavaradossi with R. Scotto; San Antonio (as Cavaradossi under Julius Rudel); Met (as Rodlofo, 1987, summer park concerts); Washington DC, as Dimitri in Boris Godunov, under M. Rostropovich; season 1987/88 with Calaf in New City Opera, repeated at the Bayerische Staatsoper Munich under the late Giuseppe Patanè; Rome Opera as Lykov and the Metropolitan as Verdi's Macduff; Michigan Opera Theatre as Rodolfo in La Bohème, (1988, debut); Further debuts at the San Francisco Opera (1988, as Enzo, opposite E Marton in La Gioconda), Carnegie Hall (1988, as Andrea Chénier, opposite A. Millo, conducted by Eve Queler), Canadian Opera Company (1989, as Cavaradossi), Greater Miami Opera (1989, as Alvaro in La Forza); Sang Pinkerton in San Francisco, 1989, Lyon Opera (debut, 1990), as Pinkerton, repeated in the Greater Miami Opera, director R. Scotto; appearance, at the 1990 Caracalla Festival, Rome, and Turiddu and Lensky with the Chicago Lyric Opera, 1990; Calaf with the Greater Miami Opera; Cavaradossi in the Houston Grand Opera, 1991, opposite E. Marton; as Lensky in Hamburg; as Don Carlo in Denver at the Opera Colorado.*Recordings include:* Aleko by Rachmaninov (Melodia, under D. Kitaneko); Boris Godunov (Erato, under M. Rostropovich), TY broadcast.Canadian Opera Company, Tosca. *Honours:* Winner, All-Russia Glinka Competition 1981; Sofia Competition, Bulgaria, 1984 (for the Duke of Mantua); Madam Butterfly Competition, Tokyo, 1986. *Address:* 367 Columbus PKWY, Mineola, New York, 11501, USA.

POLSTER Hermann Christian, b. 8 Apr 1937, Leipzig, Germany. *Education:* Studied with his father and at the University of Leipzig. *Career:* Sang with the Dresden Kreuzchor while a boy; Many engagements with the Leipzig Bach Soloists, the chorus of St Thomas's Leipzig and the Leipzig Gewandhaus Orchestra; Guest appearances Berlin; Munich, Frankfurt, Hamburg, Roma, Milano, Torino, Amsterdam (St Matthew Passion); Halle (Shostakovich 14th Symphony); Tokyo, Osaka (Bach: St Matthew and St John Passion, Beethoven's Ninth); Paris (Fidelio), Moscow, Buenos Aires, Rio de Janerio, Aix-en-Provence, Venezia, Dubrovnik, Prague (Beethoven's Ninth). Other repertoire includes Monteverdi's Vespers; Buxtehude Cantatas Telemann Cantatas, Psalms, Serenades and Messiah; Handel Saul, Acis and Galatea, Samson, Belshazzar, Judas Maccabeus, Solomon, Jeptha, Hercules and Messiah; Bach Cantatas and Oratorios; Haydn Oratorios; Mozart Masses, Requiem, Solemn Vespers and Die Zauberflöte (Sarastro); Beethoven Missa Solomnis, Mass in C and Christus am Ölberg; Mendelssohn Elijah, St Paul, Erste Walpurgisnacht; Schumann Paradies und die Peri; Verdi Requiem; Brahms Ein Deutsches Requiem; Mahler 8th Symphony; Janácek Glagolitic Mass; Stravinsky Oedipus Rex; Wagner Die Meistersinger (Pogner); Tchaikovsky Eugene Onegin (Gremin); Blacher The Grand Inqisitor; Shostakovich 13th Symphony, Songs of Michelangelo; Professur für Gesang Musikhochschule Leipzig, International Masterclasses, Juror by international competitions (Brussels, Moscow, Berlin, Leipzig). *Recordings:* St Matthew Passion and Bach Cantatas (Eurodisc); Elijah and Orff's Die Kluge (Philips); Beethoven: Fidelio (1804 version), Missa solemnis (Eterna); Shostakovitch Michelangelo Sings (Eterna); Mozart: Litaneien (Philips); Concert works conducted by Karl Böhm, Karajan, Herbert Kegel, Neville Marriner, Wolfgang Sawallisch and Kurt Masur. *Honours:* Kammersänger, Kunstpreisträger. *Memberships:* Deutscher Musikrat, Bundesverband Deutscher Gesangspädagogen (Vizepräsident); Neue Detusche Bachesellschaft. *Address:* c/o Gewandhausorchester, Augustusplatz 8, 0-4109, Leipzig, Germany.

POLYAKOV Vladimir, b. 19 Jan 1953, Omsk, USSR. Pianist; Professor. m. Ksenia Blyakova, 22 June 1975, 1 son. *Education:* MA, St Petersburg Conservatory, 1978; Postgraduate course, 1978-81. *Debut:* Appearance with Omsk Symphony Orchestra, 1969. *Career:* Appearance in Dresden, 1975; Participation in All-Russian Competition, Kazan, 1977; Regular appearances at concerts, festivals, recitals, 1969-; Radio and TV appearances, 1969-; Professor, St Petersburg Conservatory, 1986-. *Recordings:* Radio recordings: S Rakhmaninov, Etudes-Tableaux, op 39, No 109, 1990; B Tishchenko, Sonata No 8, op 99. *Membership:* Performers Union of Russia. *Address:* Torzhkovskaya St 2-1-11, St Petersburg 197342, Russia.

POMERANTS-MAZURKEVICH Dana, b. 11 Oct 1944, Kaunas, USSR. Concert Violinist; Professor of Violin. m. Yuri Mazurekvich, 4 July 1963, 1 daughter. *Education:* MMus, 1961-65, Artist Diploma 1965-68, Moscow State Conservatory. *Career:* Performed as the Mazurkevich Violin Duo member and also as a soloist in: USSR, Poland, USA, Canada, Australia, England, France, Belgium, East and West Germany, Hong Kong, Taiwan, Switzerland, Italy, Roumania, Mexico and other countries; Recorded for Radio Moscow, France, ABC (Australia), WGBH (Boston); CBC (Canada); BBC (England); Sender Freies (W Berlin), and others. *Recordings:* Works by Telemann, Prokofiev, Honegger, Sarasate, Spohr, Rawsthorne, Wieniawski, Shostakovich, Leclair, Handel and others; Masters of the Bow, Toronto, Canada; SNE, Montreal, Canada. *Current Management:* Robert M Gewald Management. *Address:* School of Music, Boston University, 855 Commonwealth Ave, Boston, MA 02215, USA.

POMMIER Jean-Bernard, b. 17 Aug. 1944, Beziers, France. Concert Pianist; Conductor. *Education:* Began piano studies aged 4; later studied with Yves Nat, Eugene Istomin and Eugen Bigot (conducting); 1958-61 Paris Conservatoire. *Career:* Has performed widely from 1962, notably in Europe, the USA, Far East, the USSR, Israel and Scandinavia; Salzburg debut with Karajan 1971; Berlin Philharmonic 1972; US debut in season 1973-74 with the New York Philharmonic and the Chicago Symphony; Engagements with the Concertgebouw under Haitink, the Orchestre de Paris under Barenboim, the St Paul Chamber Orchestra and Zukerman; Festival appearances at Edinburgh, South Bank Summer Music, Ravinia and Mostly Mozart (New York); Director/soloist with English Chamber Orchestra in Salzburg and Vienna and with Scottish Chamber Orchestra in France, Belgium and Holland; Season

1987-88 solo appearances with the London Philharmonic, the Hallé and Royal Philharmonic; conducting Bournemouth Symphony and Ulster Orchestras and the Northern Sinfonia on a tour of Spain; Appointed Music Director of the Melbourne Summer Music Festival for 1990; Chamber music with Casals, Schneider, Richter, Oistrakh and Stern and with the Guarneri and Vermeer Quartets; Season 1991-92 appearances with the Northern Sinfonia in North America, Bournemouth Symphony, the Philharmonia and Ulster Orchestra and conducted the Hallé and Royal Liverpool Philharmonic. *Recordings:* Poulenc's Piano Concerto with the City of London Sinfonia and Sonatas by Brahms with Leonard Rose and Jaime Laredo (Virgin). *Honour:* First Diploma of Honour at the 1962 Tchaikovsky Competition Moscow. Poulenc's Piano Concerto with the City of London Sinfonia and Sonatas by Brahms with Leonard Rose and Jaime Laredo (Virgin). *Address:* c/o Harold Holt Ltd., 31 Sinclair Road, London W14 ONS, England.

POND Celia Frances Sophia, b. 5 Jan 1956, London, England. Cellist. m. Ambrose Miller, 4 Apr 1981. *Education:* BA, 1974-77, MA, 1981, Girton College, Cambridge University; LRAM, Royal Academy of Music, London, 1977-78; Staatliche Hochschule für Musik, Rheinland, 1978-81. *Career:* Principal Cello, European Community Chamber Orchestra, 1981-; Artistic Adviser; Many recitals throughout Europe with Trio Gardellino, 1983-86; Cello and Piano Duo, Celia and Mary Pond; Recitals in Britain and Far East including Hong Kong and Peking. *Recordings:* Antonio Duni; Cantate da Camera Dedicate Alla Maesta di Giovanni V. *Contributions to:* Early Music, 1978; Solo Bass Viol Music in France. *Honours:* Edith Helen Major Prize, Cambridge, 1976; West German Government Scholarship, 1978. *Membership:* Incorporated Society of Musicians. *Hobbies:* Cooking; Eating; Travel. *Address:* Fermain House, Dolphin Street, Colyton, Devon EX13 6LU, England.

PONDER Michael, b. 28 July 1948, London, England. Musician (Viola Player). m. twice, 4 sons, 1 daughter. *Education:* Royal Academy of Music, 1966-70. *Debut:* St John's, Smith Square, London, 1972. *Career:* Performed with Philarmonia, 1973-86; Solo career, UK and USA; Feature Writer; Record Producer for ASV and Pickwick. *Contributions to:* The Guardian; Features to Strad and Music and Musicians. *Honours:* ARAM. *Address:* 55 Lincoln Road, London, N2 9DJ, England.

PONE Gundaris, b. 17 Oct 1932, Riga, Latvia. Conductor; Composer. div., 2 sons. *Education:* BA, 1954, MA, 1956, PhD, 1962, University of Minnesota, USA. *Debut:* Carnegie Recital Hall, New York City, 1966. *Career:* Appearances as conductor and composer, USA, Italy, West Germany, UK, Sweden, Belgium, Canada, USSR, 1967-; Numerous works performed, international festivals including Spoleto, Tanglewood, Cologne, Inter-American; Music Director, Music in the Mountains Festival, USA, 1982-. *Compositions include:* 10 major orchestral works; Numerous chamber works. *Recordings:* De Mundo Magistri Ioanni, West Germany; La Serenissima, USA. *Contributions to:* Jauna Gita; Music Review; Perspectives of New Music. *Current Management:* Mariolina Russo Enterprises. *Address:* 144 Main Street, Apt 202, New Paltz, NY 12561, USA.

PONIATOWSKA Irena, b. 5 July 1933, Góra Kalwaria, near Warsaw, Poland. Musicologist. m. Andrzej Poniatowski, 14 Nov 1953, 1 daughter. *Education:* Diploma, Musicology, Warsaw University, 1962; PhD, 1970; Qualification to Assistant Professor, 1983; Habil; Extraordinary Professor, 1991; Music School, Middle Degree, 2 Diplomas: Eurhythmy, 1956; Piano, 1958. *Career:* Tutor, 1970, Assistant Professor, 1984, Vice Director, 1974-79, Institute of Musicology, Warsaw University; President, Council, Chopin Society, 1976-86; Vice-President of Society, 1986-91; President of the Congress, Musica Antique Europae Orientalis, Budgoszcz (Poland), 1988, 1991; Editor of many Encyclopaedias including Polish Encyclopaedia of Music, Vol I, 1979, Vol II, 1984, Vol III, 1987-, Vol IV,

1993-; Various offices in Union of Polish Composers, Section of Musicologists; One of Deans, Faculty of History, Warsaw University, 1988-90 and 1993-. *Publications:* Author, Beethoven Piano Texture, 1972; The Chronicle of the Important Musical Events in Poland 1945-72, 1974; Piano Music and Playing in XIX Century Artistic and Social Aspects, 1991; Dictionary of Music for the Schools, 1991; History and Interpretation of Music, 1993; Editor, Musical Work: Theory, History, Interpretation, 1984; Many articles in collective works, about piano music, interpretation of piano music and reception of music. *Contributions to:* Muzyka; Ruch Muzyczny; Rocznik Chopinowski; Hudobný život, Bratislava; Quadrivium, Bologna. *Honours:* Golden Cross of Merit, 1979; Prize of the Minister of National Education in Poland, 1992. *Memberships:* International Musicological Society; Union of Polish Composers; Polish Society of Contemporary Music; Chopin Society; Antiquae Musicae Italicae Studiosi, Como. *Address:* Filtrowa 63-38, 02-056 Warsaw, Poland.

PONKIN Vladimir, b. 1951, Irkutsk, Siberia. Conductor. *Education:* Studied at Gorky Conservatoire and with Rozhdestvensky in Moscow. *Career:* Assistant Conductor at Bolshoy Theatre and at Moscow Chamber Theatre; First full appointment with Yaroslavl Philharmonic Orchestra, later with USSR State Cinema Orchestra; Guest engagements with St Petersburg Philharmonic and USSR State Academic Symphony Orchestra; Chief Conductor and Music Director of Russian State Maly Symphony from 1991; Currently Music Director of New Moscow State Symphony Orchestra; Has toured to Italy, Hungary, Germany, Austria, Spain and Denmark; Repertoire has included much contemporary music, as well as standard works. *Recordings include:* CDs on the Chant du Monde. *Honours include:* Winner, 1990 Rupert Foundatin conducting Competition, London. *Address:* c/o Sonata, 11 Northpark Street, Glasgow G20 7AA, Scotland.

PONMAN James Jeremy, b. 6 May 1953, London, England. Piano Accompanist; Repetiteur; Conductor. *Education:* Graduate, Guildhall School of Music, London; London Opera Centre. *Debut:* As Pianist with Bach's Brandenburg Concerto No 5, London, 1970; As Conductor with Lehar's Der Zarewitsch, Giessen, Germany, 1978. *Career:* Repetiteur and Conductor: Giessen, 1978-80, Heidelberg, 1980-82, Aachen, 1982-84, National Theatre, Mannheim, 1984-87 (conducted Bellini's Norma, 1984, 1986); Presently Repetiteur in Opera Schools of Mannheim and Karlsruhe; Duo Pianist in ballet The Green Table (Cohen), Zurich Opera House and Royal Festival Hall, 1978; Also conducted for South German Radio. *Publication:* Dvořák Requiem piano score, 1991. *Hobbies:* Good food; Cinema; Travel; Reading. *Address:* Eichendorffstr 9, 69207 Sandhausen, Germany.

PONS Juan, b. 1946, Ciutadella, Menorca. Singer (Baritone). *Education:* Studied in Barcelona. *Career:* Sang at the Teatro Liceo Barcelona, at first as a tenor; Covent Garden 1979, as Alfio in Cavalleria Rusticana; Barcelona 1983, Herod in Massenet's Hérodiade; Paris Opéra 1983, as Tonio in Pagliacci; Guest appearances in Munich, Madrid and at the Orange festival; Verona Arena 1984-85, Amonasro; La Scala Milan 1985, as Rigoletto and as Sharpless in Madama Butterfly; Metropolitan Opera 1986, as Scarpia in Tosca; Well known as Verdi's Falstaff; (Munich Staatsoper 1987); San Francisco and Rome 1989; Also sings Renato in Un Ballo in Maschera and roles in operas by Donizetti; sang Verdi's Germont at Chicago 1988; Sharpless in Madame Butterfly at La Scala, 1990; Barcelona 1989, as Basilio in Respighi's La Fiamma (also at Madrid); Season 1992 as Tonio in Pagliacci at Philadelphia, Scarpia at San Francisco and Luna at Madrid. *Recordings:* Aroldo by Verdi (CBS); Pagliacci (Philips). *Address:* c/o Teatra alla Scala, Via Filodrammatici 2, Milan, Italy.

PONSONBY Robert Noel, b. 19 Dec 1926, Oxford, England. Arts Administrator. m. Lesley Black, 23 Apr 1977. *Education:* MA Hons, Trinity College, Oxford,

1948-50. *Career:* Staff Member, Glyndebourne Opera, 1951-55; Artistic Director, Edinburgh Festival, 1956-60; General Administrator, Scottish National Orchestra, 1964-72; Controller Music, BBC, 1972-85; Artistic Director, Canterbury Festival, 1986-88; Administrator, Friends of Musicians Benevolent Fund, 1987-. *Publications:* Short History of Oxford University Opera Club, 1950. *Contributions to:* Numerous magazines and journals. *Honours:* CBE, 1985; HonRAM, 1975; Czech Government Janáček Medal, 1980. *Membership:* Fellow, Royal Society of Arts; Royal Society of Musicians; Chairman, London Choral Society. *Hobbies:* Music; Fell walking; English painting. *Address:* 11 St Cuthbert's Road, London NW2 3QJ, England. 1.

PONTES-LEÇA Carlos de, b. 26 Nov 1938, Coimbra, Portugal. Writer on Music and Music Manager. *Education:* Law Graduate, Coimbra University; Journalist Graduate, University of Navarra, Spain; Piano and Composition, Music Conservatories of Lisbon and Coimbra, with Croner de Vasconcellos and M Lourdes Martins, among other teachers. *Career:* Assistant Director of the Music Department, Calouste Gulbenkian Foundation; Associated Editor (for Music and Dance) of the cultural magazine Coloquio-Artes, Lisbon; Author of musical Programmes on Portuguese Television and Broadcasting, Essays on History of Music and Musical Aesthetics and programme notes for Gulbenkian Foundation, San Carlos Theatre (Lisbon National Opera) and the record Collection of the Portuguese Ministry of Culture; Commentator of Opera Performances on Radio and Television; Artistic Director of the Leiria Music Festival. *Contributions to:* The New Grove Dictionary of Music and Musicians, London; Gulbenkian Dictionary of Portuguese Music and Musicians, Lisbon; Verbo Encyclopedia, Lisbon. *Address:* Calouste Gulbenkian Foundation, 1093 Lisbon, Portugal.

PONTINEN Roland, b. 1963, Stockholm, Sweden. Concert Pianist. *Education:* Studied at Stockholm Music Academy and with Menahem Pressler, Gyorgy Sebok and Elisabeth Leonskaya. *Debut:* Stockholm, with Bartok's 2nd Concerto, 1983. *Career:* Many appearances with leading orchestras, including all major Swedish ensembles, Oslo Philharmonic, Jerusalem Symphony, BBC Symphony, Slovak Philharmonic and Accademia Santa Cecilia, Rome; Festival engagements include Bergen, Schleswig-Holstein, Ludwigsburg, Ravenna, Edinburgh and Newport, USA; Promenade Concerts, London, 1989; and Aldeburgh Festival; Recitals throughout Scandinavia, Western Europe, Australia and New Zealand; Chamber concerts and Lieder evenings with Hakan Hardenberger, Nobuko Imai, Christian Lindberg, Arve Tellefsen, Barbara Hendricks and Sylvia Lindenstrand. *Recordings include:* Albums as accompanist to singers and instrumentalist and Concertos by Grieg and Tchaikowsky, with Bamberg Symphony Orchestra conducted by Leif Segerstram. *Address:* c/o Anglo/Swiss Ltd, 3 Primrose Mews, 1a Sharpleshall St, London NW1 8YW, England.

POOLE Penelope Jane, b. 12 Nov 1961, Aberystwyth, Wales. Violinist. m. Andrew Littlejohns, 18 Aug 1984. *Education:* Studies with Hugh Maguire and Winifred Roberts 1980-84, Licenciate 1982, Royal Academy of Music, London, England; Graduate, Royal Schools of Music, 1983. *Debut:* Queen Elizabeth Hall, 1986. *Career:* Numerous solo recitals; Leader, Leri String Quartet; Mercury Ensemble; Member, Sadler's Wells Royal Ballet Orchestra; Freelance work with several chamber orchestras including solo appearances at Queen Elizabeth Hall. *Honours:* Ceredigion Music Prize, 1980. *Memberships:* Incorporated Society of Musicians; European String Teachers Association. *Address:* 115A Burnt Ash Rd, Lee, London SE12 8RA, England.

POOT Sonja, b. 3 Dec 1936, Gravenzande, Netherlands. Singer (Soprano). *Education:* Studied in Salisbury (Rhodesia), Amsterdam and Vienna. *Career:* Sang at Bonn Opera, 1964-71, notably as Constanze in Entführung, and Donizetti's Lucia and Maria de Rohan; Nuremberg, 1971-73, Stuttgart Staatsoper, 1973-78; Guest engagements at Basle, Amsterdam

(Elsa, 1978), Vienna Volksoper, Rome, Geneva (Elettra in Idomeneo, 1973), Barcelona and Ottawa; Other roles have included Mozart's Donna Anna, Queen of Night and Pamina, Anna Bolena, Lucrezia Borgia, Violetta, Amelia in Ballo in Maschera and Norina in Don Pasquale; Many concert performances. *Address:* c/o Staatsoper Stuttgart, Oberer Schlossgarten 6, 7000 Stuttgart, Germany.

POPE Cathryn, b. 1960, England. Singer (Soprano). *Education:* Studied with Ruth Packer at the Royal College of Music; Further study at the National Opera Studio. *Career:* With English National Opera has sung Papagena and Pamina in The Magic Flute, Anna (Moses), Susanna, Zerlina, Sophie (Werther), Leila (The Pearl Fishers), Gretel and Werther; Sang Oksana in the first British production of Christmas Eve by Rimsky-Korsakov, 1988; Sang Amor in Orpheus and Euridice for Opera North; Royal Opera Covent Garden as Gianetta (L'Elisir d'Amore), Frasquita (Carmen) and a Naiad (Ariadne auf Naxos). *Recordings include:* Anne Trulove in The Rake's Progress; Barbarina in Le Nozze di Figaro; Sang Gretel with Netherlands Opera 1990, Pamina at the London Coliseum; Sang in new productions of The Marriage of Figaro and Königskinder at the Coliseum, 1991-92; Gilda in a revival of Rigoletto, 1992/93; Featured Artist, Opera Now magazine, Feb. 1992. *Recordings include:* Video of Rusalka (as Wood Nymph). *Address:* c/o Stafford Law Associates, 26 Mayfield Road, Weybridge, Surrey KT13 8XB, England.

POPE Michael Douglas, b. 25 Feb 1927, London, England. Musician; Radio Producer; Choral Conductor; Writer. m. (1) Margaret Jean Blakeney, 1954, 1 son, (2) Gillian Victoria Peck, 1967, 1 son, 1 daughter. *Education:* Wellington College; Guildhall School of Music & Drama, 1949-53. *Career:* Served in Army, 1945-48; Joined BBC, 1954, Assistant, Music Division, 1960; Producer, music programmes and music talks, 1966-80; productions include Omar Khayyám trilogy, Boyce's Solomon, Prometheus Unbound and other revivals; Musical Director, London Motet & Madringal Club, 1954-93; Guest Conductor, RTE; Freelance musician, lecturer and writer on English musical heritage, 1981-; Hon Secretary, Royal Philharmonic Society, 1983-85. *Publications:* King Olaf and The English Choral Tradition in Elgar Studies; Various Other Essays. *Contributions to:* Dictionary of National Biography, 1981-1985. *Memberships:* Royal Musical Association; Incorporated Society of Musicians; Association of British Choral Directors; Elgar Society, Chairman 1978-88, Vice-President 1988. *Hobbies:* Reading; Theatre; Athletics history. *Address:* 11 Westbury Road, Warminster, Wiltshire BA12 0AN, England.

POPLE Ross, b. 11 May 1945, Auckland, New Zealand. Conductor; Cellist. m. (1) Anne Storrs, 25 June 1965, div, 3 sons, 1 daughter, (2) Charlotte Fairbairn, July 1992. *Education:* Royal Academy of Music, London; Recital Medal, Hon RAM: Paris Conservatoire. *Debut:* London, 1965. *Career:* Principal Cello, Menuhin Festival Orchestra; BBC Symphony Orchestra, 1976-86; Director of London Festival Orchestra, 1980-; Founder Cathedral Classics, Festival of Music in Cathedrals, UK, 1986-; London South Bank series, Birthday Honours, 1988-. *Recordings:* EMI, Hyperion, Nimbus, Enigma, Deutsche Grammophon, ASV: Haydn, Boccherini, Mozart, Mendelssohn, Schoenberg, Vaughan Williams, Holst, Strauss, Arnold, Franck, Bach and others. *Hobbies:* Tennis; Golf; Sailing; Farming. *Address:* Sellet Hall, Stainton, Kendal LA8 0LE, England.

POPOV Stefan, b. 1940, Bulgaria. Cellist. *Education:* Studied in Sofia, the Moscow Conservatory with Sviatos av Knushevitsky and Mstislav Rostropovitch, 1961-66. *Debut:* Sofia 1955. *Career:* Many concert appearances in Europe, North America, Asia notably at London, Moscow, Boston, Florence, Geneva, Dublin, Genoa, Milan, Budapest; Concerto repertoire includes works by Vivaldi, Haydn, Boccherini, Beethoven, Schumann, Dvořák, Brahms, Elgar, Hindemith, Milhaud, Honegger, Kabalevsky and Shostakovich; Don Quixote by Strauss;

Respighi Adagio with Variations; Prokofiev Symphonie Concertante; Bloch Schelomo; Sonata collaborations with the pianist Allan Schiller; Has taught at Boston University, the New England Conservatory of Music. *Honours:* Winner of competitions in Moscow 1957, Geneva 1964, Vienna 1967, Florence 1969; Winner, 1966 Techaikovsky International Competition, Moscow 1966. *Address:* Sofia-concert, Bulgarian Artistic Agency, 3 Volov Street, Sofia, Bulgaria.

POPOV Vladimir, b. 29 Apr 1947, Moscow, Russia. Singer (Tenor). *Education:* Studied at Tchaikovsky Conservatory, Moscow. *Career:* Sang at Bolshoi Opera, Moscow, 1977-81; Studied further in Milan and emigrated to USA, 1982, singing Ramirez in La Fanciulla del West at Portland; Metropolitan Opera debut, 1984, as Lensky in Eugene Onegin; Further engagements as Calaf at Houston, 1987, as Cavaradossi at Philadelphia, 1987, as Dimitri in Boris Godunov at Covent Garden, 1988, and Hermann in The Queen of Spades at Washington, 1989; Sang Calaf with Covent Garden Company at Wembley Arena, 1991, Samson at Detroit and Canio in Pagliacci at Buenos Aires, 1992; Other roles include Ernani, Gabriele Adorno, Don José and Radames (San Francisco, 1989).

POPOVA Valeria, b. 1945, Bulgaria. Singer (Soprano). *Education:* Studied with father Sacha Popov, in Sofia and with Gina Cigna. *Debut:* Sang Lauretta in Gianni Schicchi at National Theatre, Belgrade. *Career:* Sang at Plovdiv Opera, 1971-76, Sofia from 1976; Guest engagements in former Soviet Union, Germany, Rumania and cuba; Other roles include Violetta, Manon, Mozart's Countess, Jenufa, Fiordiligi, Marguerite, Donna Anna, Pamina and Leonora in La Forza del Destino; Sang Amelia in Ballo in Maschera at Milwaukee, 1990; Also teacher of singers: daughter Alexandrina Pendachanska has been among her pupils. *Recordings include:* Arias by Puccini, Verdi, Massent and Bellini. *Address:* c/o Alexandrina Pendachanska, John Coast Ltd, 31 Sinclair Road, London W14 0NS, England.

POPOVICI Doru, b. 17 Feb 1932, Resita, Rumania. Composer. *Education:* Studied in Timosoara, 1944-50, at Bucharest Conservatory, 1950-55, and Darmstadt, 1968. *Career:* Editor of Rumanian Radio and Television, 1968. *Compositions:* Operas: Prometheu, Bucharest, 1964; Mariana Pineda, Iasi, 1969; Interrogation at Daybreak, Galati, 1979; The Longest Night, Bucharest, 1983; Firmness, composed 1989; Orchestral: Triptyque, 1955; 2 Symphonic Sketches, 1955; Concertino for strings, 1956; Concerto for orchestra, 1960; 4 Symphonies, 1962, 1966, 1968, 1973; Poem Bizantin, 1968; Pastorale Suite, 1982; Chamber: Cello sonata, 1952; Violin sonata, 1953; String Quartet, 1954; Fantasy for String Trio, 1955; Sonata for 2 cellos, 1960; Sonata for 2 violas, 1965; Quintet for piano, violin, viola, cello and clarinet, 1967; Piano Trio, 1970; Madrigal for flute, clarinet, string trio and trombone; Cantatas, piano music, choruses, songs. *Address:* Union of Rumanian Composers, Bucharest, Rumania.

POPPLEWELL Richard John, b. 18 Oct 1935, Halifax, England. Organist; Choirmaster; Recitalist; Composer; Accompanist; Teacher. m. Margaret Conway, 1 son. *Education:* Chorister, organ scholar, Kings College, Cambridge; Clifton College, Bristol; Royal College of Music. FRCO, FRCM. *Career includes:* Regular broadcasts; Soloist, Henry Wood Promenade Concert, 1965; Recitalist, Great Britain; Tours, Canada, Netherlands, France, Portugal; Assistant organist, St. Paul's Cathedral, 1958-66; Director of Music, St. Michael's, Cornhill, 1966-79; Professor of Organ, Royal College of Music, 1962-; Assistant conductor/accompanist, Bach Choir, 1966-79; Organist, choirmaster & composer, Her Majesty's Chapels Royal, St. James' Palace, 1979-; A conductor, various royal weddings. *Compositions include:* Organ Suite; Puck's Shadow; Trio Sonata; Chorale Preludes; Easter Hymn & Down Ampney; Elegy; Aria, The Time of the Singing; Variations on a New Year's Carol There is No Rose (Carol) Concerto in D, full orchestra & organ; Christening

Anthems for Royal Occasions; Romance (organ); Jubilee March (organ); Prelude Under One Note (organ); Concerto of F, full orchestra & organ; Anthem, 250th Anniversary, Royal Society of Musicians; Further choral & organ works; National Anthem, dedicated by Gracious Permission to HM Queen Elizabeth II; O How Amiable (SATB & Organ). *Recordings:* Own compositions; Carols with Bach Choir; Organ music from St. Michael's, Cornhill. *Publications:* Triumphal March for Organ (Banks); Two Amens (SSAATTBB) (Banks). *Honours:* ARCO Sawyer Prize, aged 14; Prizes, Royal College of Music, 1955, 1956; Fellow, ibid, 1982; M.V.O., 1990. *Memberships:* Royal College of Organists; Incorporated Society of Musicians; Musicians Union. *Hobbies:* Reading; Swimming; Walking. *Address:* 23 Stanmore Gardens, Richmond, Surrey TW9 2HN, England.

POREBSKA Maria, b. 20 May 1959, Nowa Sol, Poland. Violinist; Violin Maker. *Education:* Music High School, Poznan, 1974-78; Music Academy, Poznan, 1979-84; Violin and Violin Maker including Pedagogic studies, 1981-83; MA and Music Teachers Diploma, both with outstanding examinations. *Debut:* Theatre and Radio Orchestra, Poznan. *Career:* Has played in several chamber and symphony orchestras in Germany, Spain, France, Austria and USA, 1985-; Also work as Violin Maker, especially as expert for sound adjustment of violins; Repair and sales of string instruments (own studio, 1993-). *Honours:* Document of Minister of Hesse for Science and Art, 1986. *Membership:* Polish Violin Maker-Artist Association. *Hobby:* Restoring old Italian violins. *Address:* August-Bebel Str 19, 65199 Wiesbaden, Germany.

PORTER Andrew, b. 26 Aug 1928, Cape Town, South Africa. Writer on Music. *Education:* MA, Oxford University, England. *Career:* Wrote for Manchester Guardian 1949, and The Times 1951; Music Critic, Financial Times 1953-74, The New Yorker 1972-92 and The Observer, 1992-; Editor, The Musical Times, 1960-67; Visiting Fellow, All Souls College, Oxford, 1973-74; Bloch Professor, University of California, Berkeley, California, USA, 1980-81. Opera translation performances include: Verdi, Don Carlos, Rigoletto, Othello, Falstaff, Macbeth, The Force of Destiny, Nabucco, King for a Day; Wagner, The Ring, Tristan and Isolde, Parisfal; Handel, Ottone; Haydn, Deceit Outwitted, The Unexpected Meeting; Mozart, Mithradates, Lucio Silla, The Abduction from the Seraglio, Idomeneo, The Impresario, Figaro's Wedding, Cosí fan tutte, Don Giovanni, The Magic Flute; Gluck, Orpheus; Richard Strauss, Intermezzo; Rossini, The Turk in Italy, The Voyage to Rheims; Puccini, La Bohème. *Recordings:* The Ring; Othello, (English translation). *Publications:* A Musical Season, 1974; Music of Three Seasons, 1978; Music of Three More Seasons, 1980; Musical Events: A Chronicle, 1986 and 1991; Verdi's Macbeth: A Sourcebook (editor with David Rosen), 1984. *Contributions to:* Music and Letters; Musical Quarterly; Musical Times; Proceedings of the Royal Musical Association; Atti del Congresso Internazionale di Studi Verdiani, and others. *Honours:* Deems Taylor Award, American Society of Composers, Authors and Publishers, 1975, 1978 and 1981. *Memberships:* Vice-President, Donizetti Society; American Society of Composers, Authors and Publishers; Royal Musical Association; American Musicological Society; American Institute of Verdi Studies. *Address:* c/o The Observer, 119 Farringdon Road, London EC1R 3ER, England.

PORTER Cecelia Hopkins, b. Washington DC, USA. Musicologist; Critic; Organist. m. Douglas R Porter, 8 June 1963, 2 sons, 2 daughters. *Education:* Studied at Harvard University, Columbia University, University of Maryland and Hochschule Fur Musik, Germany. *Career:* Professor, Lecturer, George Washington University, Maryland University; Soloist, Piano Concerto; Freelance Organist, Pianist, Flutist. *Publications include:* Music Criticism, The Washington Post; The Rheinlieder Critics; Lower Rhine Music Festivals; Schubert and This Circle. *Honours:* Radcliffe Scholarship; Faculty scholar, Columbia University; National Defense Education Act Fellowship. *Memberships:* American Musicological

Society; American Guild of Organists. *Hobbies:* Flower Gardening; Painting; Photography; Travel. *Address:* 5406 Trent Street, Chevy Chase, MD 20815, USA.

PORTER David Gray, b. 10 June 1953, Los Angeles, California, USA. Musician, Editor, Sound Engineer, Musicologist. m. Melinda Niekum, 11 June 1984. *Education:* Music Composition, Bmus, 1975, MA, Composition and Musicology, 1980, California State University at Fullerton. *Debut:* California State University at Fullerton. *Career:* Studied composition with Donal Michalsky, Lloyd Rodgers, Gail Kubik, Nicolas Slonimsky, 1973-76; Performed with New Music Company, 1975-78, Cal. St. University, Fullerton and The Claremont College; Played with Pacific Symphony, 1982-84 and under John Cage, 1980; Member and Co-Founder, Associate Image Director, Direct Image Ensemble, 1974; and New Music Co; Sound Engineer, 1980-; Producing 38-hour radio program (KPFK) on the complete published writings and music of Charles Ives (by permission of W.W. Norton, N.Y.); scheduled completion 12-hour version broadcast, 1991. *Compositions:* Events for 2 pianos, 1974; Chamber Pieces, 1973-78, various ensembles; Music for Harp or Piano, 1982; Percussion Music for 12 players, 1977-82; Tape Compositions, 1977-87, including Walking Bells, 1981; Machaut Variations (percussion), 1989. *Recordings:* Recordings of Ives, chamber music editions by Ensemble Modern, EMI Classics (A Portrait of Charles Ives), Ingo Metzmacher, conductor and by Music Projects/London, Argo records, Richard Bernas, conductor, 1991 & 1993; EMI album (Ensemble Modern) recorded 10 editions & Music Projects/London recorded 13 editions; Privately-issued cassette of 7 tape pieces released in 1990, titled First He'll Tell You What Happened While He Was Dead! *Publications:* Pending, Commentary to C.E. Ives, Universe Symphony; Chamber Set No 1 by Ives; Other Ives projects, mostly chamber music and unfinished pieces, 1978-. *Address:* 218 S. Knott Avenue, No.3, Anaheim, CA 92804, USA.

PORTER David Hugh, b. 29 Oct 1935, New York, NY, USA. Pianist and Harpsichordist; Educator; College President. m. Laudie E. Dimmette, 21 June 1958, deceased, 3 sons, 1 daughter, (2) Helen L Nelson, 24 Aug 1987. *Education:* BA, summa cum laude, Swarthmore College, 1958; PhD, Princeton University, 1962; Philadelphia Conservatory of Music, 1955-61; Private Piano Study with Edward Steuermann, 1955-62; Harpsichord with Gustav Leonhardt, 1970, 1977. *Debut:* Philadelphia, 1955. *Career:* Piano and Harpsichord Recitals and Lecture-Recitals throughout USA, 1966-; In London and Edinburgh, 1977; Performances on Radio and TV, 1967-; Professor of Classics and Music, Carleton College, 1962-; President, Carleton College, 1986-87; President, Skidmore College, 1987-; Author: Only Connect: Three Studies in Greek Tragedy, Horace's Poetic Journey, The Not Quite Innocent Bystander: Writings of Eduard Steuermann. *Contributions to:* Articles in Music Review and Perspectives of New Music; numerous articles in classical journals. *Honours:* Steuermann Scholarship, Philadelphia Conservatory of Music, 1955-. *Address:* Skidmore College, Saratoga Springs, NY 12866, USA.

PORTMAN Rachel Mary Berkeley, b. 11 Dec 1960, Haslemere, Surrey, England. Film Composer. *Education:* Worcester College, Oxford; BA Hons, Music, Oxford; Studied Piano, Organ, Viola; Studied Composition with Roger Steptoe at Charterhouse. *Debut:* Film score for Experience Preferred But Not Essential. *Compositions:* Fantasy for Cello and Piano, Salisbury Festival commission, 1985; Film scores: Benny and Joon; Used People; Life Is Sweet; Oranges Are Not The Only Fruit; Where Angels Fear To Tread; Friends; Elizabeth R; The Storyteller; Shoot To Kill; Precious Bane. *Recordings:* Benny and Joon; Used People; Where Angels Fear To Tread. *Honours:* Composer of the Year, British Film Institute, 1988. *Membership:* APC. *Current Management:* Tim Corrie, Peters Fraser Dunlop. *Address:* 13 Ascham St, London NW5 2PB, England.

POSCHNER-KLEBEL Brigitte, b. 1957, Vienna,

Austria. Singer (Soprano). *Education:* Studied in Vienna with Gerda Scheyrer and Gottfried Hornik. *Career:* Sang with Vienna Staatsoper, 1982-, Volksoper, 1983-; Guest appearances at Aix-en-Provence Festival, 1988-89, Fiordiligi, La Scala, Milan as Pamina, 1986, Venice, Amsterdam and Tokyo; Sang Susanna in Khovanshchina at Vienna Staatsoper, 1989; Other roles include Hansel, Rosalinde, Esmerelda in The Bartered Bride, Aennchen in Der Freischütz, Sophie in Der Rosenkavalier, Xenia in Boris Godunov and Lucy in The Beggar's Opera; Frequent concert appearances. *Recordings:* Khovanshchina; Video of Elektra conducted by Abbado, as a Maidservant. *Address:* c/o Staatsoper, Opernring 2, A-1010 Vienna, Austria.

POSPISIL Miloslav, b. 25 Nov 1947, Prague, Czechoslovakia. Professor and Teacher of Singing; Opera Singer; Musicologist. *Education:* Absolutory of Piano, 1970, Singing, 1962, State Conservatory, Prague; Absolutory of Art, Academy of Music, Bucharest, Rumania; Postgraduate study, Accademia di Santa Cecilia, Rome; MA, Musicology and Teatrology, Faculty of Philosophy, Charles University, Prague; PhDr. *Debut:* As Silvio in Pagliacci's Leoncavallos, National Theatre of Prague, 1974. *Career:* Opera and concert activity in Czechoslovakia; Educational musicology courses (Biography of World and Czech Opera Singers) in Music Theatre, Prague; Main parts of courses also broadcast on Czech Radio-Prague; Professor of Singing, Prague Conservatory. *Recordings:* Recitals of songs from romantic composers at Radio Prague. *Publications:* Critical monograph on Emmy Destinn, 1974, 2nd Edition, 1980; Critical monograph of Czech dramatic soprano Marie Podvalova (main member of the Czech National Theatre); Textbooks for editions of complete licensed operas. *Contributions to:* Numerous sleeve notes; Bertramka, historical studies, in Magazine of Prague Mozart Society; Critical studies in Gramorevue Magazine, Music View Magazine and Czechoslovakina Radio Magazine. *Honours:* 1st Prize, Chopin Composition, Marianske Lazne (Marienbad), 1967; 1st Prize, Smetana Competition, Hradec Kralove, 1969. *Memberships:* Smetana Society; Society of Emmy Destinn; Prague Mozart Society. *Hobbies:* Art drawing; Zoology; Collecting records of famous opera and concert singers. *Address:* Budejovicka 36/479, 140 00 Prague 4, Czech Republic.

POSSEMEYER Berthold, b. 1950, Gladbeck, Westfalen, Germany. Singer (Baritone). *Education:* Studied in Cologne with Josef Metternich. *Career:* Sang at first in concert and gave Lieder recitals, notably at Paris, New York, Jerusalem, Hamburg, Turin and Venice; Stage career from 1978, at first at Oldenburg, then from 1979 at Essen, as Rossini's Figaro, Papageno, Guglielmo, Eugene Onegin and Silvio in Pagliacci; Sang at Gelsenkirchen Opera, 1984-86, then returned to concerts; Repertoire includes works by Bach, Mozart, Mendelssohn and Distler. *Address:* c/o Musiktheater im Rivier, Kennedyplatz, 4650 Gelsenkirchen, Germany.

POSTNIKOVA Viktoria, b. 12 Jan 1944, Moscow, USSR. m. Gennadi Rozhdestvensky 1969. Concert Pianist. *Education:* Studied at the Moscow Central School of Music with E B Musaelian, 1950-62; Further study with Yakov Flier at the Moscow Conservatoire. *Career:* Many concert appearances in Europe, Russia and the USA from 1966; Repertoire includes music by Bach, Handel, Scarlatti, Haydn, Mozart, Liszt, Chopin, Mendelssohn, Schumann, Brahms and Rachmaninov; Modern repertoire includes music by Busoni, Ives, Britten and Shostakovich; Played in the UK premiere of Schnittke's Concerto for piano duet and orchestra in London 1991. *Recordings:* Tchaikovsky Concertos (Decca); Busoni Concerto and complete piano works by Janáček and Tchaikovsky (Erato); Violin sonatas by Busoni and Strauss (Chandos); Complete piano concertos of Brahms, Chopin and Prokofiev (Melodiya). *Honours include:* Prize winner at competitions in Warsaw (1965), Leeds (1966), Lisbon, (1968) and Moscow, (1970). *Address:* Allied Artists, 42 Montpelier Square, London SW7 1JZ, England.

POTT Francis John Dolben, b. 25 Aug 1957, Oxfordshire, England. Composer; Pianist; Baritone; University Lecturer. m. Virginia Straker, 19 Sept 1992. *Education:* Chorister, New College, Oxford; Music Scholar, Winchester College and Magdalene College, Cambridge; Composition with Robin Holloway, Hugh Wood; Piano with Hamish Milne, London; MA, MusB, University of Cambridge. *Career:* Assistant Director of Music, Exeter School, 1980; Director of Music, New College School, Oxford, 1982; Acting Assistant Director, Abingdon School, 1986; Freelance composition/performance; Tutor in Compositional Techniques, Oxford University, 1987-89; Lecturer in Music, St Hugh's College, 1988; Lecturer in Music, Director of Foundation Studies, West London Institute, 1989-91; John Bennett Lecturer in Music, St Hilda's College, Oxford, 1991-; Visiting Tutor in Composition, Winchester College, 1991-; Piano recitalist and accompanist; Toured Brazil with Winchester Cathedral Choir, 1991. *Compositions:* Organ: Mosaici di Ravenna, 1981; Empyrean, 1982; Fenix, Music for Lincoln Minster, Organ, Brass, Percussion, Timpani, 1985; Passion Symphony, Christus, 1986-90, premiered Westminster Cathedral, 1991; Piano, chamber, choral (church) and other works; Piano Quintet, premiered by The Twentieth Century Consort, Smithsonian Institute, USA, 1993; Piano Concerto, in progress; Many TV and radio broadcasts; Works performed in 15 countries worldwide. *Address:* 15 Canute Road, Winchester, Hampshire SO23 8PW, England.

POTTER Andrew John, b. 8 Apr 1949, London, England. Music Publisher. m. Frances Hillery, 16 July 1970, 3 daughters. *Education:* Chorister School, Durham, England, 1958-62; Clifton College, Bristol, England, 1962-68; BA, University College, Durham, 1970; Diploma in Arts Administration, Polytechnic, Central London, England, 1970-71; Choral Scholar, Durham University. *Career:* Publicity Secretary, London Symphony Orchestra, 1971; Promotion Manager, Oxford University Press, Music Department, 1972-75; General Administrator, Wexford Festival and Arts Centre, Ireland, 1975-77; General Administrator, National Operatic and Dramatic Association, England, 1977-79; Deputy Head of Music Publishing, 1979-85; Head of Music Publishing, 1985-; Director, Music and Bibles Publishing, 1989; Oxford University Press; Deputy Chairman, Performing Right Society, 1989-; Director, Association British Choral Directors, 1986-. *Hobbies:* Singing; Fishing; Gardening; Laughing. *Address:* Oxford University Press, Walton Street, Oxford, OX2 6DP, England.

POTURLJAN Artin Bedros, b. 4 May 1943, Kharmanli, Bulgaria. Composer. m. Akopjan Anahid Aram, 28 June 1974, 2 sons. *Education:* Graduated, Secondary School, St Kiriland Methody, Sofia, 1961; State Academy of Music, Sofia, Theoretical Faculty with speciality in Musical Pedagogy, 1967; Yerevan State Conservatoire Komitas, with speciality in Composition, 1974. *Career:* First public performances of compositions in Yerevan, Moscow and Tbilissi, 1970-74; Performances of Symphonies No 1 and No 2 in Sofia 1976, 1978; Member of Bulgarian Composers Union, 1978; Regular appearances in New Bulgarian Music festival, 1980-93; Authorial recital of Chamber compositions, Yerevan, Armenia, 1987 and Sofia, 1991; Performances of Four spiritual songs for organ in Austria (Vienna, Klagenfurt, Anif), 1991; Participation in Holland - Bulgarian Music Festival, Sofia, 1992; Teacher of Polyphony in State Musical Academy, Sofia. *Compositions:* Concerto for Violin and Symphony Orchestra; Music for 3 flutes, 2 pianos, tam-tam and strings; Klavier-Quintet, Sonata for Violin and Piano; Four spiritual songs on Themes by Nerses Shanorhali for organ and others; Opera Woman's Cry (in one act), 1979; Fantasia for piano and Symphony Orchestra, 1990; Songs for others. *Recordings:* Arabesques for piano; The Confessions for piano; Fantasia, Worlds for two pianos; Symphony No 2 (documentary); Concerto for Violin and Symphony Orchestra (documentary) and others on Bulgarian Radio. *Hobby:* Chess. *Address:* Iztok Bl. 4, vch B, 1113 Sofia, Bulgaria.

POTVLIEGHE Ghislain Hugo, b. 5 Apr 1936, Bruges, Belgium. Organ and Keyboard Instrument Builder. m. Gisella De Maeyer. *Education:* Royal Conservatorium of Music, Ghent. *Career:* Lecturer in Organology (History and construction of Flemish organs, the clavichord), conservatoria in Antwerp, Brussels and Ghent, 1969- ; Music Reviewer, various newspapers and Belgian Radio and Television (BRT), 1963-75); Researcher for Royal Commission for Monuments and Landscapes, 1970-73; Currently Director, Potvlieghe-De Maeyer (keyboard instrument building firm, producing clavichords, tangent pianos, pipe organs, restoring historic organs); Member, Editorial Board of Orgelkunst quarterly journal of organ culture. *Publication:* Orgelkunst in de Nederlanden (co-author), 1971; Biographical articles of organ builders in Winkler Prins Vlaanderen Encyclopaedia; Het Historisch Orgel in Vlaanderen (1974), Mozart in België (co-author), 1991; Art Director Mozarteum Belgicum, 1992; Executive Producer, PHI compact disc. *Address:* Linkebeek 26, 9400 Ninove, Belgium.

POULENARD Isabelle, b. 5 July 1961, Paris, France. Singer (Soprano). *Education:* Studied at L'Ecole de l'Opera de Paris. *Career:* Sang at Tourcoing in operas by Mozart, Paisiello, Monteverdi, Scarlatti and Vivaldi, conducted by Jean-Claude Malgoire; Has performed in operas at the festivals of Carpentras and Avignon; Hippolyte et Aricie under William Christie at the Opéra-Comique; Les Dialogues des Carmélites at the Opéra du Rhin; Cesti's Orontea at the Innsbruck Festival, under René Jacobs; Sang Gluck's Iphigénie en Aulide with the City of London Sinfonia at the Spitalfields Festival; Other repertoire includes Paisiello's Il Re Teodoro in Venezia, Handel's Alessandro and Massenet's Grisélidis; Concert appearances throughout France and in Venice, Flanders, Innsbruck and Stuttgart; British engagements at the Barbican, London and for Music at Oxford; Season 1992 as Teutile in the Vivaldi pastiche Montezuma at Monte Carlo and in Conti's Don Chisciotte at the Innsbruck Festival of Early Music. *Recordings:* Music by Cesti, Rameau, Couperin, Schütz, Cavalli, Bach and Vivaldi; Monteverdi's Il Combattimento di Tancredi e Clorinda; Lully's Armide, La Malade imaginaire by Charpentier and Die Zauberflöte (Erato); Handel's Tamerlano (CBS); Le Cinesi by Gluck and Les Indes Galantes by Rameau, (Harmonia Mundi). *Address:* Magenta Music International, 64 Highgate High Street, London N6 5HX, England.

POULET Michel, b. 1960, France. Cellist. *Education:* Studied at the Paris Conservatoire with Jean-Claude Pennetier and with members of the Amadeua and Alban Berg Quartets. *Career:* Member of the Ysaÿe String Quartet from 1986; Many concert performances in France, Europe, America and the Far East; Festival engagements at Salzburg, Tivoli (Copenhagen), Bergen, Lockenhaus, Barcelona and Stresa; Many appearances in Italy, notably with the 'Haydn' Quartets of Mozart; Tours of Japan and the USA 1990 and 1992. *Recordings:* Mozart Quartet K421 and Quintet K516 (Harmonia Mundi); Ravel, Debussy and Mendelssohn Quartets (Decca). *Honours:* Grand Prix Evian International String Quartet Competition, May 1988: special prizes for best performances of a Mozart quartet, the Debussy quartet and a contemporary work; 2nd Prize, Portsmouth International String Quartet Competition, 1988. *Address:* c/o Lies Askonas Ltd, 6 Hennrietta, London, WC2E 8LA, England.

POULSON Lani, b. 7 Mar 1953, Tremonton, Utah, USA. Singer, *Career:* Sang as Charlotte, Ramiro, Carmen, Octavian and the Composer; From 1986 at Brussels as Octavian, Ramiro and the Countess Geschwitz in Lulu; Has sung at the Hamburg Staatsoper as Cherubino; Court Theatre at Drottningholm as Sextus in La Clemenza di Tito; Montpellier, 1988 as Dorabella; Sang Andromeda in Perseo ed Andromeda by Sciarrino, Stuttgart 1991; Appearances at Essen, Lausanne, Stavanger, Frankfurt, Orleans and Munich; Capricco, Opera du Rhin Strasbourg; Der Rosenkavalier, Mannheim; concert Repertory Includes the St Matthew Passion; Mozart's Requiem and Beethoven's Mass in

C; Future engagements include performances of Sesto/ Titus at Dresden Staatsoper and World Premiere of Rihm's Das Schweigen des Serenas & Sirenen in Stuttgart. *Address:* c/o Haydn Rawstron Management, PO Box 654, London, SE26 4DZ, England.

POULTER Eileen Margaret, b. 29 Apr 1928, London, England. Singer. m. Clifton Bell, 1951, 1 son. *Career:* Oratorio peformances, recitals and broadcasts; Formerly member of vocal groups including Deller Consort; Adjudicator at Competitions and Festivals; Teaching Colchester Institute, 1967-81; Private Teacher, Church Organist and Choir Trainer. *Honour:* FTCL. *Membership:* ISM. *Hobbies:* Gardening; Dressmaking; DIY. *Address:* Golf Cottage, Church Path, Friston, Saxmundham, Suffolk IP17 1PY, England.

POULTON Robert, b. 1960, Brighton, England. Singer (Baritone). *Education:* Studied with Rudolf Piernay at the Guildhall School of Music and Drama; Further study at the European Opera Centre in Belgium and at the National Opera Studio London. *Career:* Sang The Ferryman in Britten's Curlew River for Nexus Opera at the 1986 Bath Festival: repeated at the Promenade Concerts; With Glyndebourne Touring Opera has appeared in L'Heure Espagnole, L'Enfant et Les Sortilèges, La Traviata and Le Nozze di Figaro (Figaro, 1989); Glyndebourne Festival, 1988-89, in Katya Kabanova and Jenůfa (also televised); Oratorio repertoire includes Purcell, Haydn (Creation), Vaughan Williams, Bach (St John Passion), Handel (Messiah), Elgar (The Kingdom) and Finzi; Concerts in Singapore, Italy, Belgium and Israel; Created roles of Doctor, Policeman, Stranger in Judith Weir's The Vanishing Bridegroom, Scottish Opera, 1990; Created title role in Gassir The Hero, by Theo Logvendie for Netherlands Opera 1991; ENO Debut, Leander (Love for 3 Oranges) 1991; Engaged as Figaro (Mozart) Scottish Opera; Ned Keene, Peter Grimes, Glyndebourne Festival 1992; Sang Punch in Birtwistle's Punch and Judy for Netherlands Opera, 1993. *Honours include:* Silver Medal for Singing and the Lord Mayor's Prize at the GSM. *Address:* c/ o Ron Gonsalves Management, 10 Dagnan Road, London SW12 9LQ, England.

POUNTNEY David, b. 10 Sept 1947, Oxford, England. Opera Producer. *Education:* Radley College and Cambridge University. *Career:* First opera production Cambridge 1967, Scarlatti's Trionfo dell'Onore; Wexford Festival 1972, Katya Kabanova; Director of Productions for Scottish Opera 1975-80, notably with Die Meistersinger, Eugene Onegin, Jenůfa, The Cunning Little Vixen, Die Entführung and Don Giovanni; Australian debut 1978, Die Meistersinger; Netherlands Opera 1980, world premiere of Philip Glass's Satyagraha; Principal Producer and Director of Productions, English National Opera from 1982: work includes The Flying Dutchman, The Queen of Spades, Rusalka, The Valkyrie and Lady Macbeth of Mtsenk; American debut with Houston Opera, Verdi's Macbeth: returned for the world premiere of Bilby's Doll by Carlisle Floyd, Katya Kabanova and Jenůfa; Produced Weill's Street Scene for Scottish Opera, 1989; Other productions include From the House of the Dead in Vancouver, Dr Faustus in Berlin and Paris, and The Fiery Angel at the State Opera of South Australia, Adelaide; Produced The Gambler, Macbeth and Wozzeck for English National Opera 1990-91 (Macbeth seen on tour of USSR); Season 1992 with new productions of Don Carlos at the Coliseum and The Voyage by Philip Glass (premiere) at the Metropolitan. *Contributions to:* Opera Magazine: Sense, Condoms and Integrity, 1992. *Address:* c/o Harrison/Parrott Ltd., 12 Penzance Place, London W11 4PA, England.

POUSSEUR Henri, b. 23 June 1929, Malmedy, Belgium. Composer. *Education:* Studied at the Liège Conservatory, 1947-52, Brussels Conservatory 1952-53. *Career:* Worked at the Cologne and Milan electronic music studios, notably with Stockhausen and Berio; Taught music in Belgian schools 1950-59; Founded 1958 and directed the Studio Musique Electronique APELAC in Brussels; Lecturer in courses of new music

Darmstadt 1957-67, Cologne 1962-68, Basle 1963-64, and the State University of New York at Buffalo 1966-69; Lecturer at the Liège Conservatory, Professor of Composition from 1971, Director of this Institution since 1975, Teacher also at Liège University, 1983-1987, directed the organisation of the New Institut de Pedagogie Musicale in Paris. *Compositions include:* Seismogrammes for tape 1953; Symphonies for 15 instruments 1955; Quintet to the Memory of Webern 1955; Mobile for 2 pianos 1958; Rimes pour différentes sources for 3 orchestral groups and tape 1959; Electra 1960; Répons for 7 players 1960-65; Ode for String Quartet 1961; 3 Visages de Liège for tape 1961; Votre Faust opera 1961-67; Portrait de Votre Faust; Miroir de Votre Faust; Apostrophe et 6 Reflexions for piano 1966; Phonèmes pour Cathy 1966; Echos de Votre Faust 1969; Couleurs croisées for orchestra 1967; Mnemosyne, monody 1968; Crosses of Crossed Colors 1970; Icare apprenti 1970; Les Ephemerides d'Icare 2 for pianos and 19 instruments 1970; Invitation a L'Utopie 1971; L'Effacement du Prince Igor, scene for orchestra 1971; Le Temps de paraboles 1972; Die Erprobung des Petrus Hebraicus, chamber opera 1974; Vue sur les jardins interdits 1974; Chronique berlinoise for baritone and piano quintet 1976; Chronique illustrée for baritone and orchestra 1976; Tales and Songs from the Bible of Hell 1979; Agonie for voices and tape 1981; Les Léchainées for jazz ensemble, quartet of symthesizers and symphonic orchestra, 1980; La Seconde Apothéose de Rameau, for chamber orchestra 1981; La Prose des voix, for 4 speakers, 4 vocal quartets, 4 choirs and 8 instruments, 1982; Trajets dans les apents du ciel, for solo-instrument and orchestra 1983; Sur le qui-vive, for voice and 5 instruments, 1985; Nuit des Nuits, for orchestra, 1985; Traverser La Forêt, canata for speaker, Mezzo, Baritone, Choir and 12 instruments, 1987; Methodicare, large collection of more or less easy pieces, in several volumes, specialised for various instruments or groups, still in development, 1988-; 5 volumes published 1991; Mnemosyne Doublement Obstinee for string quartet with female voice ad libitum, 1988; Déclarations d'Orages, for speaker, 2 solo-singers, 3 solo-instruments, large orchestra and tape, 1989; L'écloe N'Orphée, for organ with speaker and electronic equipment ad lib, 1989; Leçons d'enfer, chamber opera for the 100th anniversary of the death of Arthur Rimbaud, for actors, singers, solo-instruments and tapes, 1989-91. *Publications:* Books: Ecrits d'Alban Berg, seleted and translated with commentary, 1956; Fragments théoriques I Sur la musique experimentale, 1970; Musique sémantique Société, 1972; Numerous Theoretical Articles.*Address:* c/o SABAM, Rue d'Arlon 75-77, 1040 Brussels, Belgium.

POWELL Ardal Kieran, b. 22 Apr 1958, Bournemouth, England. Baroque Flute Maker and Player; Editor. m. Catherine Folkers, 27 Dec 1984. *Education:* Westminster Cathedral Choir School, 1970; Magdalene College, Cambridge; BA, 1980, MA, 1989; Royal Conservatory, The Hague, 1983. *Career:* Co-Founder, Folkers and Powell, Makers of Historical Flutes, 1984-; Soloist with Tregye Festival Players, Handel and Haydn Society Chamber Ensemble; Appearances on US Public Radio; Editor, Traverso, baroque flute newsletter, 1989-. *Publications:* The Virtuoso Flute-Player by Johann George Tromlitz (translator, editor), 1991. *Contributions to:* The Flutist Quarterly; Boston Early Music News; Early Music, Tibia. *Hobbies:* Brewing; Gardening; Weightlifting; Cooking. *Address:* RD 3, Box 56, Hudson, NY 12534, USA.

POWELL Claire, b. 1954, Tavistock, Devon, England. Singer (Mezzo-Soprano). *Education:* Royal Academy of Music; London Opera Centre. *Career:* Sang Alceste and Cherubino at Sadler's Wells while with London Opera Centre; London debut recital Wigmore Hall, 1979; Early appearances with Glyndebourne Festival Opera; Has sung in Il Ritorno d'Ulisse, Falstaff, La Fedeltà Premiata and A Midsummer Night's Dream; Appearances with Welsh National Opera, Scottish Opera, Opera North and English National Opera: roles include Berlioz, Didon, Beatrice & Marguerite, Carmen, Verdi's Ulrica and Preziosilla, Mussorgsky's Marina, Mozart's Cherubino

and Idamante, Gluck's Alceste and Orfeo, Handel's Cornelia and Cyrus, Ponchielli's Laura, Saint-Saens's Dalila, Ravel's Concepcion and Tchaikovsky's Pauline; Covent Garden from 1980, Les Contes d'Hoffman, Midsummer Night's Dream, Otello, Lulu, Rigoletto, Die Zauberflöte, Ariadne auf Naxos, A Florentine Tragedy, Don Carlos (Eboli 1989); Medée (Neris), Rigoletto (Maddalena) and Samson et Dalila; US debut 1990, as Maddalena at San Francisco; Sang Pauline in The Queen of Spades at Madrid, 1990; Guest appearances in Frankfurt, San Francisco, Barcelona, Madrid, Toronto, Paris, Rome, Brussels, Liège and Lisbon; Sang Eboli in a new production of Don Carlos for Opera North, 1993; concert repertoire includes Berlioz Mort de Cléopâtre, Oedipus Rex, Elijah and Mahler 2 symphony (in Barcelona); Haydn's Paukenmesse, St. Matthew Passion, Messiah, La Damnation de Faust, Verdi Requiem, Missa Solemnis, Mahler 3, Bach B minor mass, Bruckner Te Deum and Mahler Das Lied von der Erde (Royal Ballet at Covent Garden); Mistress Quickly (Verdi, Falstaff), sung both in Paris and in 1993 in Peter Stein's WNO production and also in a new production in Toulouse.*Recordings include:* Video of Les Contes d'Hoffmann (as Nicklausse) and A Midsummer Night's Dream; El amor Brujo, Der Rosenkavalier, Il Ritorno di Ulisse in Patria; Der Rosenkavalier conducted by Bernard Maitink. *Honour:* Richard Tauber Memorial Prize 1978. *Recordings include:* El Amor Brujo by Falla. *Address:* John Coast Ltd., 31 Sinclair Road, London W14 0NS, England.

POWELL Kit (Christopher Bolland), b. 2 Dec 1937, Wellington, New Zealand. Composer; Lecturer in Music. m. Brigitte Bänninger, 14 Dec 1966, 1 son, 1 daughter. *Education:* MSc, Diploma of Teaching; BMus. *Career:* Teacher, Mathematics and music, New Zealand High School, 1962-75; Lecturer, Christchurch Teachers College, 1975-84; Studied in Europe, 1980-81; Has written experimental music for choruses and percussion and 5 song cycles settings of poems by Michael Harlow and 3 major works of experimental music, theatre; Computer Music, Swiss Computer Music Centre, 1985; Atelier UPIC, Paris, 1987. *Compositions:* 4 Carols on 4 Notes, 1980; Galgenlieder, 1982; Pied Beauty, 1983; Concerto for 2 violins, string and percussion, 1989; Gargantua for Wind Orchestra, 1990. *Recordings:* Devotion to the Small, 1980; The Evercircling Light, 1982; Hubert the Clockmaker, 1982. *Publications:* Workbook for University Entrance Prescription, 1973; Musical Design, 1975; Musik mit gefundenen Gegenständen, 1982; Suite for solo trombone. *Hobby:* Arts. *Address:* Nigelstrasse 11, 8193 Eglisau, Switzerland.

POWELL Mel, b. 12 Feb 1923, New York, New York, USA. Composer. m. Martha Scott, 23 July 1946, 1 son, 2 daughters. *Education:* MusB, MA, Yale University, 1952; Studied piano with Sara Barg and Nadia Reisenberg; Composition with Paul Hindemith. *Career:* Chairman, Yale University Composition Faculty, 1954-69; Dean, California Institute of the Arts School of Music, 1969-72, Provost, (CalArts), 1972-76, Professor and Fellow of the Institute, 1976-. *Compositions:* Filigree Setting for String Quartet; Haiku Settings for voice and piano; String Quartet, 1982; Woodwind Quintet; Modules for Chamber Orchestra; Strand Settings for mezzo soprano & Electronics; Duplicates: a concerto for Two Pianos and Orchestra 1990; many other orchestral pieces, vocal, chamber music and electronic works (Computer Prelude, 1988). *Recordings:* The Music of Arnold Schoenberg and Mel Powell, Nonesuch; The Music of Milton Babbitt and Mel Powell, Nonesuch; The Chamber Music of Mel Powell, CRI; Mel Powell: Six Recent Works (Musicmasters). *Publications:* Compositions published by G. Schirmer, Inc.; Essays and articles. *Contributions to:* Perspectives of New Music; Journal of Music Theory; American Scholar. *Honours:* Guggenheim Fellowship, 1960; National Institute Arts and Letters Grant Award, 1964; Works chosen to represent US in International Society for Contemporary Music festivals, 1960 and 1984; Politzer Prize 1990. *Memberships:* President, American Music Center, 1957-60; Consultant, National Endowment for the Arts, 1970-73; Awarded Honorary Life Membership in Arnold Schoenberg Institution. *Address:* c/o California Institute of the Arts, Valencia, CA 91355, USA.

POWER Patrick, b. 6 June 1947, Wellington, New Zealand. Singer (Tenor). *Education:* Studied at Universities of Otago and Auckland, New Zealand and the Studied at the University of Perugia, Italy. *Career:* Principal lyric tenor with the Norwegian Opera in Oslo, at the Gärtnerplatz in Munich and in Krefeld; Covent Garden debut 1983, as the Simpleton in Boris Godunov, followed by Britten's Serenade for the Royal Ballet; Has sung Alfredo for Kent Opera, Rodolfo and Almaviva for Scottish Opera; Glyndebourne Festival as Flute and Des Grieux in Manon for Opera North; Wexford Festival in the title role of Massenet's Le Jongleur de Notre Dame; Overseas engagements as The Italian Tenor in Rosenkavalier and Fenton for the Royal Danish Opera; Don Ottavio, Tamino and Rodolfo in Cologne; Belmonte in Drottningholm and New Zealand; Le Comte Ory and Huon (Oberon) in Lyons and Alceste in Paris; Alfredo, Tamino and Don Ottavio in Canada; Almaviva in San Francisco; Season 1988-89 as Nadir (Les Pêcheurs de Perles) in Pisa and Faust with Victorian State Opera; Has returned to Australia as Pinkerton, Hoffmann, Rodolfo and the Duke of Mantua. *Recordings include:* Beethoven's Ninth Symphony conducted by Roger Norrington (EMI); Balfe's Bohemian Girl conducted by Richard Bonynge (Decca). *Address:* c/o Athole Still Ltd., Greystoke House, 80-86 Westow Street, London, SE19 3AF, England.

POWERS Anthony, b. 1953, London, England. Composer. *Education:* Studied with Nadia Boulanger in Paris and with David Blake and Bernard Rands at York. *Career:* Composer-in-residence, Southern Arts; Composer-in-residence, University of Wales, Cardiff College. *Compositions include:* Piano Sonata No 2, 1985-86; Stone, Water, Stars, 1987; Horn Concerto, 1989; Cello Concerto, 1990; String Quartet No 2, 1991. *Current management:* Oxford University Press, London, England. *Address:* Oxford University Press, Music Department, 3 Park Road, London NW1 6XN, England.

PRABUCKA-FIRLEJ Anna, b. 8 Mar 1950, Elblag, Poland. Solo, Chamber Pianist; Teacher. m. Jan Firlej, 27 Mar 1971, divorced 1991, 1 son. *Education:* Diploma, with distinction, Music Lyceum, Gdansk, 1969; MA 1974, Doctorate (Adjunct qualification), 1980, Academy of Music, Gdansk; Habilitation (Docent qualification) Academy of Music, Lodz, 1987. *Debut:* Piano soloist with orchestra at age 11 in Elblag, Poland. *Career:* Piano soloist (symphony concerts, recitals) and Chamber Pianist, performed: Poland, Finland, Sweden, UK, Germany, Iceland, Austria, Greece, Czechoslovakia, Hungary, Bulgaria, USSR, Italy, Switzerland; as accompanist appearances with Eduard Melkus (Austria)-violin, Peter Damm (Germany)-horn, Marina Tschaikovskaja Russia-cello, Peter Leisegang (Switzerland)-cello, Siegfried Palm (Germany)-cello; Radio and TV recordings; Teaching: Professor of Chamber Music, Academy of Music, Gdansk; Guest Professor and Accompanist: Music Master Classes Mynamaki, Finalnd, 1976, Internationale Musikseminar Weimar, Germany, 1984-91, Mattheiser Sommer-Akademie Sobernheim, Germany, 1988, 1991, Chamber Music Seminar, Kozani, Greece, 1990, 1991, 1992. *Publications:* Realisation of the piano part of instrumental baroque sonatas on basis of selected contemporary editions, 1988; Remarks on realisation accompaniement for piano extract from the selected works of vocal-instrumental scores by J S Bach, 1989. *Hobbies:* Painting; Literature; History; Languages. *Address:* ul Leszczynskich 1g 24, 80-464 Gdansk, Poland.

PRANDELLI Giacinto, b. 8 Feb 1914, Lumezzane, Brescia, Italy. Singer (Tenor). *Education:* Studied with Fornarini in Rome and with Grandini in Brescia. *Debut:* Bergamo 1942, as Rodolfo in La Bohème. *Career:* Sang at La Scala in May 1945, in a performance of the Choral Symphony conducted by Toscanini; Appeared in Milan 1947 and 1954, in the local premieres of Peter Grimes

and Menotti's Amelia al ballo; Engagements at the Verona, Edinburgh and Florence Festivals; Metropolitan Opera 1951; London debut 1957 as Edgardo in Lucia di Lammermoor at the Stoll Theatre. *Recordings include:* Amelia al ballo and La Bohème (Decca); Adriana Lecouvreur, Fedora and Francesca da Rimini (Cetra); Mefistofele and Il Tabarro (HMV); Lodoiska by Cherubini (MRF).

PRANTL Pavel, b. 21 Apr 1945, Susice, Czechoslovakia. Concertmaster; Professor of Violin. m. Martina Maixnerova, Concert Pianist and Professor of Piano, 24 June 1972. 2 sons. *Education:* Conservatory of Music, Kromeriz, 1960-65; Master's Degree with Distinction, Academy of Musical Arts, Prague, 1965-72; Master classes with Maestro David Oistrakh, 1966, 1971. *Debut:* Czechoslovak Broadcasting Corporation, 1956. *Career:* Member, First violin Group 1967-76, Assistant Concert Master 1976-78, Czech Philharmonic Orchestra; Concert Master and Artistic Director, Prague Chamber Orchestra Without a Conductor, 1978-80; Founder and Artistic Leader, Prague Baroque Ensemble, 1973-80; Concert Master, Singapore Symphony Orchestra, 1980-; Guest soloist with: Prague Symphony Orchestra 1968; Moravian Philharmonic Orchestra 1975; Radio Pilsen Symphony Orchestra 1977; Singapore Symphony Orchestra, 1981-87; Numerous tours abroad including festivals in: Salzburg, Montreux, Edinburgh, Wurzburg. *Recording:* Ivo Blaha's Violin Concerto (Supraphon), 1970. *Address:* 110 Wishart Road, No 03-07 Pender Court, Singapore 0409, Republic of Singapore.

PRATLEY Geoffrey Charles, b. 23 Mar 1940, Woodford, Essex, England. Accompanist. m.(1) Wendy Eathorne, 27 Mar 1965, 1 daughter, (2) Vija Rapa, 20 June 1987, 1 daughter. *Education:* Royal Academy of Music, 1958-63; LRAM, ARCM, 1960; GRSM, 1961; BMus, Dunelm, 1969. *Career:* Numerous Concerts throughout the World with many international artists including Baker, Domingo, Tortelier, Goossens, Brymer, Holmes, Streich and Milanova; Professor, Royal Academy of Music, from 1965-; Professor, Trinity College of Music, 1990-.*Compositions:* Dorothy Parker Poems for female voice and piano; Five Irish Folk-Songs; Five English Folk-Songs. *Recordings:* Ivor Gurney Songs with C. Keyte; numerous BBC Recordings for Radio and TV.*Publications:* Handel Operatic Repertory BK.2: Arias for tenor and piano (Stainer and Bell); Concert Master Series: Book 1 - Tchaikovsky Violin solos with piano (Faber); William Walton's Viola Concerto, new viola/piano score (OUP). *Honours:* ARAM, 1967; FRAM, 1977.*Memberships:* Incorporated Society of Musicians; Royal Society of Musicians; R.A.M. Club; R.A.M. Guild. *Address:* The Willows, Bambers Green, Takeley, Essex CM22 6PE, England.

PRATS Jorge Luis, b. 3 July 1956 Camaguey, Cuba. Pianist. *Education:* Graduate, National School of Arts, La Habana, Cuba; Graduate, Moscow Conservatory, (under Rudolph Kerer), USSR; Private study, Magda Tagliaferro (Paris), Badura-Skoda (Vienna). *Debut:* Soloist, National Symphony Orchestra, Habana. *Career:* Recitals & concerts, major orchestras, France, Germany, Austria, Poland, Mexico, England (BBC, London), Japan, USSR, USA, numerous countries in South America & Eastern Europe. TV & radio broadcasts, worldwide. Specialist, Cuban & Latin American music. *Recordings:* Deutsche Grammophon, EMI, Egrem. *Honours:* 1st prize, & various special awards, Marguerite Long-Jacques Thibaud Grand Prix Competition, Paris; Awards, best interpretations, Ravel, & contemporary music. *Hobbies:* Medicine; Cooking. *Current Management:* Mme. Valmalett, Bureau de Concerts, Paris, France. *Address:* E 158, Apartamento 25B, Vedado, La Habana, Cuba.

PRATT George Malcolm, b. 11 Feb 1935, Cheshire, England. Professor of Music, Univ of Huddersfield. m. Mary Margaret, 9 Aug 1961, 2 sons. *Education:* Birkenhead School, 1946-54; National Service, 1954-56; St Peter's College, Oxford University, Organ Scholar, 1956-60; BA, Class I (Oxon), 1959; BMus (Oxon), 1960;

ARCO. *Career:* Director of Music, Abingdon School, 1960-64; Director of Music, University of Keele, 1964-74; Senior Lecturer, 1974-85; Head of Department, 1984-85; Head of Department of Music, Huddersfield Polytechnic, 1985-91; Professor, 1985-; Director of Unit for Research into Applied Musical Perception (RAMP). *Compositions:* Four Anthems; John Stanley's Solos Opus, 1972; John Stanley's Solos, Opus 4, 1975; William Babell Sonatas 2 and 11, 1978; J. S. Bach Cello Suites (Edition), 1978; Thomas Vincent Solos for Oboe and Continuo (Edition), 1984; A Gyrowetz - Parthia in E Flat, Opus 3 No. 1 (Edition), 1984. *Recordings:* Organ of University of Keele, 1966; Come Living God, 1975. *Publications:* The Dynamics of Harmony: Principles and Practice, 1984; Aural Awareness: Principles and Practice, 1990. *Address:* Department of Music, The Polytechnic, Huddersfield HD1 3DH, England.

PRATT Stephen Philip, b. 15 June 1947, Liverpool, England. Composer; Lecturer; Broadcaster; Conductor. m. Monica Mullins, 14 Oct 1972, 1 son, 3 daughters. *Education:* Certificate of Education, Christ's College, Liverpool, 1965-68; Royal Manchester College of Music, 1968-69; BA Honours, University of Reading, 1969-71; BMus, University of Liverpool, 1971-72. *Career:* Broadcaster, BBC Radio Merseyside, 1971-; Senior Lecturer in Music, 1972-, Head of Music, 1991-, Liverpool Institute of Higher Education; Fellow, University of Liverpool, 1993-; Freelance Conductor, 1975-; Part-time Lecturer, Open University, 1976-78; Part-time Lecturer, Lancashire Polytechnic, 1983-; Part-time Lecturer, Liverpool University, 1984-86. *Compositions include:* Star and Dead Leaves, (recorded by Pro Viva ISPV 132), 1977; Winter's Fancy, 1978; Some of Their Number for orchestra, 1980; Fruits of the Ground for horn trio, 1982; The Judgement of Paris for orchestra, 1985; Strong Winds, Gentle Airs, for concert band 1987; String Trio, 1988; Uneasy Vespers, for mixed choir, soloists and orchestra, 1991. *Contributions to:* Arts Alive, 1972-; Reviewer 1976-78, The Guardian; Classical Music, 1975-78. *Honours:* Chandos Composition Prize, Musica Nova, Glasgow, 1981. *Hobbies:* Football; Painting. *Address:* 43 Hallville Road, Mossley Hill, Liverpool, L18 0HP, England.

PRAUSNITZ Frederik William, b. 26 Aug 1920, Cologne, Germany. Conductor. m. Margaret Britten Grenfell, 1 son, 1 daughter. *Education:* Juilliard Graduate School 1945. *Debut:* Conducted Detroit Symphony Orchestra 1944. *Career:* Guest conductor with BBC Symphony Orchestra, London Symphony, New Philharmonia, London Philharmonic, Royal Philharmonic, English Chamber Orchestra and many orchestras on the continent; First European performances of music by Carter, Schuman, Sessions and Wolpe; Associate director, Public Activities, Juilliard School of Music, 1947-49; Assistant Dean at Juilliard 1949-61; Conductor, New England Conservatory Symphony Orchestra, Boston, 1961-69; Music Director, Syracuse Symphony 1971-74; First US performances of works by Schoenberg, Stockhausen, Varèse, Webern and Dallapiccola; Director of the Peabody Conservatory Symphony Orchestra 1976-80; Director of Conducting Programs, 1980-; Conductor Laureate; Director of the Contemporary Music Ensemble at Peabody; Visiting lecturer at Harvard, and Sussex University. *Recordings:* Walton's Façade; Works by Roger Sessions and other modern composers. Labels include Columbia, EMI, Angel, Philips and Argo. *Publications:* Score and Podium: a Complete Guide to Conducting, 1983; Roger Sessions: a Critical Biography, 1990; reprint forthcoming, for the centenary of the birth of Sessions. *Honours include:* Honorary Fellow, University of Sussex, 1970; Gustav Mahler Medal of Honor of the Bruckner Society of America 1974. *Address:* c/o Peabody Conservatory of Music, 1 E. Mt. Vernon Place, Baltimore, Maryland 21202, USA.

PRECHT Ulrika, b. 1959, Sweden. Singer (Mezzo-soprano). *Education:* Studied at Opera Studio 67 and Stockholm State Opera, Stockholm. *Debut:* Royal Opera, Stockholm, as Cherubino, 1990. *Career:* Sang Dalila with Folkoperan Stockholm, 1991, and Nancy in Marthe for Dublin Opera, 1992; Season 1992-93 in Rossini's Il Signor Bruschino at Frankfurt, Eboli in Don Carlos at Stockholm and title role of Carmen at Sodertaleoperan; Concert engagements throughout Scandinavia. *Address:* Nordic Artists Management, Svervagen 76, S-11359 Stockholm, Sweden.

PREECE Isobel Paterson (Woods), b. 1 Jan 1956, Giffnock, Renfrewshire, Scotland. Musicologist; Conductor. m. Dr. Clive Preece, 31 Mar 1990. *Education:* Royal Scottish Academy of Music and Drama, 1971-73; University of Glasgow, 1973-79; BSc, Glasgow, 1977; BMus (Hons), Glasgow, 1978; Princeton University, 1979-83; MFA, 1981; PhD, 1984. *Career:* Assistant in Instruction and Assistant Conductor of Choruses, 1980-83, Visiting Lecturer in Music, 1984, Princeton University, USA; Haswell Ellis Music Fellow, 1984-86, Lecturer in Music and Conductor, 1986-, University of Newcastle-upon-Tyne, England; Broadcasts for Kansai TV, NHK, BBC Radio Newcastle, BBC Radio Scotland. *Publications:* The Carver Choirbook, 1984; Conference Editor, Journal of the Royal Musical Association, 1989-. *Address:* Department of Music, The University, Newcastle-upon-Tyne NE1 7RU, England.

PRÉGARDIEN Christoph, b. 18 Jan 1956, Limburg, Germany. Singer (Tenor). *Education:* Studied at the Frankfurt Hochschule für Musik and in Milan and Stuttgart. *Career:* Sang first with the Limburg Cathedral Choir; Operatic engagements in Frankfurt, Gelsenkirchen, Stuttgart, Ludwigshafen, Hamburg, Antwerpen and Karlsruhe; parts include Almaviva, Tamino, Fenton and Don Ottavio; Concert appearances in the festivals of Flanders, Holland, Israel, Paris, Aix, Ansbach, Innsbruck and Göttingen; Conductors include Sigiswald Kuijken, Gustav Leonhardt, Ton Koopman, Philipe Herreweghe, Roger Norrington, Ivan Fischer, Hans-Martin Linde, Wolfgang Gönnenwein, Frans Brueggen, Helmuth Rilling, Ferdinand Leitner and Michael Gielen; Sang in production of the St Matthew Passion for Belgian television; Towards Bach and Haydn concert series on London's South Bank, 1989; sang in L'Infedeltà Delusa by Haydn for Flanders Opera 1990; Debut recital at the Wigmore Hall, London, 1993. *Recordings include:* St John and St Matthew Passion conducted by Leonhardt; St John Passion, Bach's Magnificat; L'Infedeltà Delusa by Haydn; Mozart Concert Arias conducted by Kuijken; Buxtehude Cantatas and Mozart Requiem under Ton Koopman; Bach Lutheran Masses under Herreweghe; Symphoniae Sacrae by Schütz; Grimoaldo in Rodelinda (Harmonia Mundi). *Address:* c/o Opera voor Vlaanderen. Schouwburgstrasse 3, B-9000 Ghent, Belgium.

PREIN Johann Werner, b. 3 Jan 1954, Trofaiach, Leoben, Austria. Singer (Bass-baritone). *Education:* Studied with Herma Handl- Wiedenhofer in Graz. *Career:* Sang in concerts and recitals from 1979; Stage career from 1984, notably at Graz and Vienna; Bayreuth Festival, 1984-85, as Donner in Das Rheingold; Engaged at Gelsenkirchen from 1986; Guest appearances at the Vienna Staatsoper, Dusseldorf and Barcelona; Wiesbaden 1988, as King Henry in Lohengrin; At Gelsenkirchen in 1989 sang Wagner in the first German production of Busoni's Doktor Faust, in the completion by Antony Beaumont; Other roles include: Mephistopheles (Faust); 4 villains in Les Contes d'Hoffmann; the Speaker in Die Zauberflöte; Biterolf and the Landgrave in Tannhäuser; Wotan in Der Ring des Nibelungen; Achilles in Penthesilea by Schoeck. *Recordings include:* Lieder by Joseph Mathias Hauer (Preiser). *Address:* Musiktheater im Revier, Kennedyplatz, D-4650 Gelsenkirchen, Germany.

PREMRU Raymond Eugene, b. 6 June 1934, Elmira, New York, USA. Composer; Musician. Divorced, 2 daughters. *Education:* BMus., Composition (Performers), Certificate of Trombone, Eastman School of Music, University of Rochester, New York, 1956. *Career:* Member, Phillip Jones Brass Ensemble, 1960-; Commissions from Cleveland Orchestra (Lorin Maazel), Pittsburgh Symphony (André Previn), Philadelphia

Orchestra (Riccardo Muti), Philharmonia Orchestra (Lorin Maazel), London Symphony Orchestra (Previn), Royal Choral Society (Meredith Davies), International Trumpet Guild, York Festival, Cheltenham Festival, Camden Festival, Philip Jones Brass Ensemble; Visiting Professor, Trombone, Guildhall School of Music, Eastman School of Music, Rochester, 1987. *Compositions:* Music from Harter Fell; Quartet for 2 Trumpets, horn and Trombone; Divertimento for Ten Brass; Concertino for Trombone, flute, oboe, clarinet and bassoon; Tissington variations. *Recordings:* Easy Winner, Argo/Decca Records; Modern Brass, Philip Jones Brass Ensemble. *Contributions to:* International Trombone Association Journal; Instrumentalist Magazine. *Hobby:* Tennis. *Address:* Eastman School of Music, University of Rochester, 26 Gibbs Street, Rochester, NY 14604, USA.

PRESCOTT Duncan, b. 1964, England. Clarinettist. *Education:* Studied at the Royal Academy of Music with Anthony Pay, and with Karl Leister. *Career:* Recitals at the Wigmore Hall and on the South Bank; Member of the Nash Ensemble, with whom he has broadcast the Brahms, Reger and Weber Clarinet Quintets; Mozart Clarinet Concerto with the London Sinfonietta and the English String Orchestra; Performances at many jazz venues, including Ronnie Scott's; Member of the Boronte Ensemble and duo partnership with pianist Scott Mitchell; Further engagements in Germany, America, Israel, Russia, Japan, Hong Kong and Italy. *Recordings:* Virtuoso pieces with Scott Mitchell (Chandos). *Honours:* Capitol Radio Music Prize; Lambeth Music Award; Frank Britton Award; Malcolm Sargent Music Award; Scholarships from the Myra Hess Trust, Countess of Munster Trust and the English Speaking Union. *Address:* c/o Anglo-Swiss Management, 4-5 Primrose Mews, Sharpeshall Street, London NW1 8YW, England.

PRESCOTT Thomas Mayhew, b. 11 May 1951, Beckley, West Virginia, USA. Maker of Historical Flutes & Recorders. m. 19 Aug 1978, 1 son. *Education:* BA, Lake Forest College, Illinois, 1973. *Career:* Apprentice to Friedrich von Huene, 1973-75; Produced 1st instrument, 1975; Instruments produced are classical & baroque flutes, baroque & Renaissance recorders, owned by many noted performers of early music. *Contributions to:* The American Recorder. *Memberships:* Boston Early Music Festival & Exhibition, offices; American Musical Instrument Society; American Recorder Society. *Hobbies:* Gardening; Playing early instruments; Board sailing.

PRESSLER Menahem, b. 16 Dec 1923, Magdeburg, Germany. Pianist; Professor of Music. m. Sara Szerszen, 1 son, 1 daughter. *Education:* Educated in Israel; Studied with Petri and Steuermann. *Career:* Distinguished Professor, Indiana University, USA, 1955-; Soloist under Stokowski, Dorati, Ormandy, Mitropoulos; Co-founder, The Beaux Arts Trio, 1955, which performs yearly in the Capitals of Europe and Americas; Appearances at Festivals in Edinburgh, Salzburg, Paris; Since 1984 in Residence at the Library of Congress in Washington, DC; Subscription concerts in New York, Metropolitan Museum and at Harvard University. *Recordings:* Most of the Trio Repertoire; More than 50 records for Philips. *Publications:* Several publications. *Honours:* Winner of Debussy Prize in San Francisco; 3 Grand Prix du Disques, Grammophone Record of the Year Award; Prix d'honneur Montreux Prix Mondial Du Disques. *Current Management:* Columbia Artists Management, New York. *Address:* 1214 Pickwick Place, Bloomington, IN 47401, USA.

PRESTON Katherine Keenan, b. 7 Dec 1950, Hamilton, Ohio, USA. Music Historian. m. Daniel F. Preston, 8 Oct 1971, 1 son. *Education:* University of Cincinnati, 1969-71; BA, The Evergreen State College, Olympia, Washington, 1974; MM, Musicology, University of Maryland, 1981; PhD, Musicology, Graduate Center, City University of New York, 1989. *Career:* Taught at University of Maryland, Catholic University, and Smithsonian Institution; Currently

Assistant Professor, College of William and Mary, Williamsburg, Virginia, 1989-. *Publications:* Books: Scott Joplin, juvenile biography, 1987; Music for Hire: The Work of Journeymen Musicians in Washington DC 1875-1900, 1992; Opera on the Road: Traveling Opera Troupes in the United States, 1820-1860, 1993; The Music of Toga Plays (Introduction) in Playing Out The Empire: Ben Hur and other Toga Plays and Films, 1883-1908, edited by David Wagner, forthcoming 1994. *Contributions include:* Various articles including: The 1838-40 American Concert Tour of Jane Shirreff and John Wilson, British Vocal Stars in Studies in American Music, forthcoming; Popular Music in the Gilded Age: Musicians' Gigs in Late Nineteenth-Century Washington DC, in Popular Music, 1985; Music and Musicians at the Mountain Resorts of Western Virginia, 1820-1900, in A Celebration of American Music, 1989; Numerous articles in The New Grove Dicitonary of American Music, 1986 and The New Grove Dicitonary of Opera, 1992. *Address:* 137 Pintail Trace, Williamsburg, VA 23188, USA.

PRESTON Simon John, b. 4 Aug 1938, Bournemouth, England. Musician; Organist; Conductor. *Education:* BA 1961, MusB 1962, MA 1964, King's College, Cambridge University; Associate, Royal College of Music; Fellow, Royal Academy of Music. *Career:* Suborganist, Westminster Abbey, 1962-67; Acting organist, St. Albans Abbey, 1968-69; Organist and Tutor in Music, Christ Church, Oxford, 1970-81; C.U.F. Lecturer in Music at Oxford University, 1972-1981; Organist/Master of Choristers, Westminster Abbey, London, 1981-87. *Recordings:* Organ Music by Handel and Liszt and Masses by Haydn with the Christ Church Choir; Handel: Choral Works with Westminster Abbey Choir; Series of Bach's Organ Works; Liszt Fantasia on Ad nos, ad Salutaren Undam, Reutske Sonata on the 94th Psalm; Choral works for Palestrina, Allegri, Anerio, Nanino and Giovannelli. *Honours:* Dr Mann Organ Student, King's College, Cambridge; Honorary Fellow, Royal College of Organists; Edison Award, 1971; Grand Prix du Disque, 1979; International Performer of the Year (New York Chapter of the American Guild of Organists), 1987. *Memberships:* Member of the Jury for Organ Competitions at: St Albans 1983, Lahti Finland 1985, Bruges Belgium 1986, Dublin Ireland 1990, Calgary Canada 1990; Chairman, Performer of the Year Award (Royal College of Organists), 1988; Patron of the University of Buckingham; Member, Music Panel of the Arts Council, 1968-72; Member, BBC Music Advisory Committee, 1965-67; Royal Society of Musicians; Vice President, Organ Club; Vice President, Organists' Benevolent League; Chairman, Herbert Howells Society; Fellow of the Royal Society of Arts. *Hobbies:* Theatre; Croquet. *Address:* Little Hardwick, Langton Green, Kent TN3 0EY, England.

PRÊTRE Georges, b. 14 Aug 1924, Waziers, France. Conductor. m. Gina Marny 1950, 1 son, 1 daughter. *Education:* Lycée and Conservatoire de Douai, Conservatoire national supérieur de musique de Paris and Ecole des chefs d'orchestre. *Career:* Director of Music, Opera Houses of Marseilles, Lille and Toulouse 1946-55, Director of Music, Opéra-Comique, Paris, 1955-59, at l'Opéra 1959-; Director-General of Music at l'Opéra, 1970-71; Conductor of the symphonic associations of Paris and of principal festivals throughout the world; also conducted at La Scala, Milan and major American orchestras; Conductor, Metropolitan Opera House, New York, 1964-65, La Scala, Milan, 1965-66, Salzburg, 1966; Appointed First Guest Conductor, Wiener Symphoniker, Vienna, 1986. *Recordings:* several complete opera sets with Maria Callas; Lucia di Lammermoor, La Traviata, Tosca, Iphigénie en Tauride; Poulenc Sinfonietta, Les Biches, Suite Française, and piano concerto; La Damnation de Faust; Saint-Saëns 3rd Symphony; Berg Chamber Concerto and Violin Concerto (Christian Ferras); Symphonie Fantastique; Franck Psyché et Eros; Faust (Domingo/Freni); Samson et Dalila. (Vickers/Gorr). *Honours:* Chevalier, Légion d'honneur, 1971; Haute Distinction République Italienne, 1985, Commdr. République Italienne, 1980; Officer, Légion d'honneur,

1984. *Address:* Château de Vaudricourt, à Navés, par Castres, 81100 France.

PREVIN André George, (Andreas Ludwig Priwin) b. 6 Apr 1929, Berlin, Germany. Conductor/Composer/Pianist. m. 4 Jan 1982, 4 sons, 3 daughters. *Education:* Berlin Conservatory; Conductor - Pierre Monteux; Composition - Mario Castelnuovo-Tedesco. *Career:* Music Director: Houston Symphony, 1967-69; London Symphony, 1968-79; Pittsburgh Symphony 1976-84; Royal Philharmonic, 1985-91; Los Angeles Philharmonic, 1985-89; Guest Conductor, Salzburg and Edinburgh Festivals, all major orchestras in Europe and USA; Concert performances of Fledermaus on South Bank, 1990; Conductor Laureate, London Symphony Orchestra, 1992-. *Compositions:* Piano Concerto, Cello Sonata, Guitar Concerto; Principals (orchestra), Reflections (orchestra); Triolet for Brass; Outings for Brass; Song Cycle, Piano Preludes, Invisible Drummer (piano); Serenades (violin); Every Good Boy Deserves Favour (Orchestra and Actors - play by Tom Stoppard). *Recordings:* Over 150 recordings as conductor; 25 Recordings as Pianist, including CDs of Elgar 1st Symphony; Orff Carmina Burana; Prokofiev 1st and 5th Symphonies; Debussy Images and Prelude; Maxwell Davies Violin Concerto (Stern); Prokofiev Piano Concertos (Ashkenazy) and Alexander Nevsky; Shostakovich 6th Symphony; Ravel Ma mère l'oye; Vaughan Williams Pastoral and 4th Symphonies; Walton 1st Symphony; Die Fledermaus, with the Vienna Philharmonic (Philips). *Publications:* Orchestra, 1979; Guide to Music, 1983; Face To Face, 1971; No Minor Chords (autobiography) 1992. *Honours:* Academy Award (4 times); Grammy Awards (6 times); Honorary Fellow Royal Academy and Guildhall; Honorary Doctorates in various US Universities. *Address:* c/o Harrison-Parrott, 12 Penzance Place, London W11, England.

PRÉVOST André, b. 30 July 1934, Hawkesbury, Ontario, Canada. Composer. *Education:* Conservatoire de Musique de Montréal; Studied under Olivier Messiaen at Paris Conservatoire and Henri Dutilleux at Ecole Normale, Paris; Studied electronic music under Michel Philippot, ORTF; Studied under Aaron Copland, Zoltán Kodály, Gunther Schuller and Elliott Carter at Berkshire Music Center, Tanglewood, Massachusetts. *Career:* Professor of composition and analysis, Faculty of Music, University of Montreal; composed music played throughout Canada and also France, USA, England, Yugoslavia, India and New Zealand; commissions have been received from Jeunesse Musicales du Canada, Quintette de Cuivres de Montreal, Charlottetown Festival, Ten Centuries Concerts, Canadian Broadcasting Corporation, National Arts Centre Orchestra, McGill Chamber Orchestra, l'Orchestre symphonique de Quebec, Communaute Radiophonique des Pays de Langue Française, London (Ontario) Symphony Orchestra, Société de Musique Contemporaine du Québec, Canadian Music Centre among others. *Compositions Include:* Orchestral: Célébration 1966; Chorégraphie I, 1972, II, 1976, III, 1976, IV, 1976; Cosmophonie 1985; Diallele 1968; Evanescence 1970; Fantasmes 1963; Hommage 1970-71; Ouverture 1975; Scherzo 1960. Soloists with Orchestra: Concerto pour Violoncelle et Orchestre 1976; Le Conte de l'Oiseau 1979; Hiver dans l'Ame 1978; Paraphrase 1980. Chamber Music: Improvisation Pour Violon Seul 1976; Improvisation pour Violoncelle Seul 1976; Improvisation pour Alto Seul 1976; Mobiles 1959-60; Mouvement pour Quintette de Cuivres 1963; Musique pour l'Ode au St-Laurent 1965; Mutations 1981; Quatuor 1958, No. 2 1972; Sonate pour Alto et Piano 1978; Sonate No. 1 pour Violoncelle et Piano 1962; No. 2 Pour Violoncelle et Piano 1985; Suite pour Quotuor a Cordes 1968; Triptyque 1962; Trois Pieces Irlandaises 1961. Solo Voice: Geôles 1963; Improvisation pour Voix et Piano 1976; Musique Peintes 1955. Chorus: Ahimsâ 1984; Missa de Profundis 1973; Psalm 148 1971. Keyboard: Cinq Variations sur un Thème Grégorien 1956; Improvisation pour piano 1976; Variations en passacaille 1984. *Address:* SOCAN (Canada), Member Regisbration PRS Ltd, 29/33 Berners Street, London W1P 4AA, England.

PREY Claude, b. 30 May 1925, Fleury-Sur-Andelle, France. Composer. *Education:* Studied with Milhaud and Messiaen at the Paris Conservatoire, with Migone in Rio de Janiro and at the Laval University. *Compositions include:* Lettres Perdues, Opera Episolaire, RFT, 1961; Le Coeur Revelateur, Chamber Opera After Poes Tel Tale Heart, Paris, 1964; L'Homme Occis, Opera Clinique composed, 1963, Staged Rouen, 1978; Jonas Opera Oratorio, ORTF, 1966; Les Mots Croises, composed, 1965, Staged Paris, 1978; Donna Mobile, Opera d'Appartement, composed 1965, Staged Tours 1985; Metamorphose D'Echo Opera de Concert, Prague, 1967; La Noirceur Du Lait, Opera Test, Strasbourg, 1967; On Veutt La Lumiere, Allonsy, Opera Parodie, Angers, 1968; Fetes de la Faim, Opera Pour Comediens, Avignon, 1969; Donna mobile 2, Opera Pour Dames, Avignon, 1972; Les Liaisions Dangereuses, Strasbourg, 1974; Young Libertad, Opera Study, Lyons, 1976; La Grand Mere Francaise, Opera Illustre, Avignon, 1976; Utopopolis, Opera Chanson, Paris, 1980; L'Escalier de Chambord, Dramma Melodico, Tours, 1981; Lunedi Blue, Opera Breve, Paris, 1982; Pauline, Chamber Opera, Touring, 1983; O Commeeau, Opera Madrigalesque, Paris, 1984; Le Rouge at le Noir, Opera in 2 Acts After Stendhal, Aix en Provence, 1989; Sommaire Soleil, Opera Composed, 1990; Theatrephonie for 12 Voices and Piano, 1971. *Address:* SACEM, PRS Ltd, Member Registration, 29/33 Berners Street, London W1P 4AA, England.

PREY Florian, b. 1959, Hamburg, Germany. Singer (Baritone). *Education:* Studied with father, Hermnn Prey, and at Munich Musikhochschule. *Career:* Gave Lieder recitals and appeared in concert from 1982; Opera debut as the Count in Schreker's Der ferne Klang, Venice, 1984; Sang in a staged version of St Matthew Passion at Teatro La Fenice, 1984, Silvio for Vienna Kammeroper, 1986; Stadttheater Aachen, 1988-, as Harlekin in Ariadne auf Naxos, Falke and Papageno; Writer of stage pieces and film scripts (Montag eine Parodis, 1985). *Address:* c/o Stadttheater, Theaterstrasse 1-3, 5100 Aachen, Germany.

PREY Hermann, b. 11 July 1929, Berlin, Germany. Opera and Concert Singer (Baritone). m. Barbara Pniok 1954, 1 son, 2 daughters. *Education:* Humanistisches Gymnasium Zum Grauen Kloster Berlin and Staatlich Musikhochschule, Berlin. *Career:* Appeared at State Opera, Wiesbaden 1952, also Hamburg, Munich, Berlin, Vienna; Created Meton in Krenek's Pallas Athene Weint, Hamburg, 1955; Guest Appearances at La Scala, Milan, Metropolitan Opera, New York, Teatro Colón, Buenos Aires, San Francisco Opera; New York debut, 1960; Covent Garden debut, 1973, Rossini's Figaro; Has sung at Festivals at Salzburg, Bayreuth, Edinburgh, Vienna, Tokyo, Aix-en-Provence, Perugia, Berlin, etc.; now with Munich State Opera; best known as Mozart's Papageno, Figaro and Guglielmo, and Wagner's Wolfram and Stauss's Storch (Munich 1990); returned to Metropolitan 1987, in Ariadne auf Naxos; sang Beckmesser at Covent Garden 1990 and at the 1990 Munich Festival; Appeared as Beckmesser in a new production of Die Meistersinger at the Metropolitan, 1993; Noted recitalist, in Lieder by Schubert, Brahms and Schumann. *Publication:* Premierenfieber (memoirs) 1981. *Honours include:* Winner Meistersänger-Wettbewerb, Nuremberg 1952. *Hobbies:* Riding; Films. *Address:* 8033 Krailling vor München, Fichtenstrasse 14, Germany.

PRICE Curtis (Alexander), b. 7 Sept 1945, Springfield, Missouri, USA. Musicologist. *Education:* Studied at Southern Illinois University, 1963-67, and at Harvard with John Ward and Nino Pirotta (PhD, 1974). *Career:* Teacher at Washington University, St Louis, Missouri, 1974-81, and at King's College, London: Reader, 1985, Professor, 1988. *Publications include:* The Critical Decade for English Music Drama, 1700-1710, Harvard, 1978; Music in the Restoration Theater: with a Catalogue of Instrumental Music in the Plays, 1665-1713, Ann Arbor, 1979; Henry Purcell and the London Stage, Cambridge, 1984; H Purcell: Dido and Aeneas (editor), New York, 1986; Italian Opera and

Arson in Late Eighteenth-Century London, 1989; The Impresario's Ten Commandments: Continental Recruitment for Italian Opera in London 1763-4 (with J Milhons and R D Hume), London, 1992; Man and Music: The Early Baroque Era (editor), London, 1993. *Address:* Department of Music, King's College, University of London, Strand, London WC2R 2LS, England.

PRICE Gwyneth, b. 1945, Bath, England. Singer (Soprano). *Education:* Studied in London with E Herbert-Caesari. *Career:* Many appearances at opera houses throughout the UK; Royal Opera, Covent Garden, as the Priestess in Aida, Fortune Teller in Arabella, Milliner and Duenna in Rosenkavalier, Villager in Jenůfa, 1993; Title role in Menotti's The Old Maid and the Thief, Norfolk Festival, 1992; Concert repertoire includes Verdi's Requiem, conducted by Colin Davis; Council member of Friends of Covent Garden. *Address:* c/o Royal Opera House, Covent Garden, London WC2, England.

PRICE Janet, b. 1938, Abersychan, Pontypool, Gwent, South Wales. Singer (Soprano). m. Adrian Beaumont. *Education:* University College of Cardif, S. Wales; B.Mus. (First class honours) & M.Mus. (Wales); LRAM (singing performer); ARCM (piano performer); LRAM (piano accompanist); Special study of French Music with Nadia Boulanger, Paris; Studied singing with Olive Groves, Isobel Baillie and Hervey Alan. *Career:* Singer in concerts with leading orchestras and conductors throughout Britain and Western Europe; Numerous premieres, including the Belgian premiere of Tippett's Third Symphony, Festival of Flanders 1975; Has sung opera with Glyndebourne Festival Opera, Welsh National Opera Company, Kent Opera Company, Opera Rara, Handel Opera Society, San Antonio Grand Opera (Texas), BBC TV; Has made a speciality of resurrecting neglected Heroines of Bel Canto period, being the first person to sing a number of these roles in the modern era; Highlights include: live commercial recording of Beethoven's 9th Symphony with Haitink and the Concertgebouw Orchestra and Chorus; Tippett's 3rd Symphony with Haitink and The London Philharmonic Orchestra; Stravinsky's Les Noces, with Rozhdestvensky and the BBC Symphony Orchestra and Chorus; Sang role of Hecuba in Kent Opera's; King Priam (video). *Recordings:* For EMI, Philips, Decca, Argo and Opera Rara. *Contributions to:* The Haydn Yearbook 1983, with article entitled Haydn's Songs From A Singer's Viewpoint. *Honour:* Winner of British Art Council's First Young Welsh Singers' Award. *Hobbies:* Fell-Walking; Tapestry-work; Gardening. *Address:* 73 Kings Drive, Bishopston, Bristol BS7 8JQ, England.

PRICE Leontyne, b. 10 Feb 1927, Laurel, Mississippi, USA. Soprano Singer. *Education:* Central State College, Wilberforce, Ohio and Juilliard School of Music. *Career:* Appeared as Bess (Porgy and Bess), Vienna, Berlin, Paris, London, New York, 1952-54; Recitalist, Soloist, 1954-; Soloist, Hollywood Bowl, 1955-59, 1966; Opera Singer NBC-TV, 1955-58, San Francisco Opera Co, 1957-59, 1960-61, Vienna Staatsoper, 1958, 1959-60, 1961; Recording Artist RCA-Victor, 1958-; Appeared Covent Garden, 1958-59, 1970, Chicago, 1959, 1960, 1965, Milan, 1960-61, 1963, 1967, Metropolitan Opera, New York, 1961-62, 1963-70, 1972, as both Leonoras of Verdi, Madame Butterfly, Fiordiligi, Puccini's Tosca, Minnie, Liu and Manon, Ariadne and Pamina; Paris Opéra as Aida, 1968, Metropolitan Opera as Aida, 1985 (Retired). *Recordings:* Numerous recordings. *Honours:* Fellow, American Acad. of Arts and Sciences; Hon. DMus (Howard University, Central State College, Ohio); Hon DHL (Dartmouth); Hon. Dr of Humanities (Rust College, Mississippi); Hon. DHum Litt (Fordham); Presidential Medal of Freedom, Order of Merit (Italy), National Medal of Arts, 1985. *Address:* c/o Columbia Artists Management Inc., 165 West 57th Street, New York, NY 10019, USA.

PRICE Margaret Berenice, (Dame), b. 13 Apr 1941, Tredegar, Wales. Opera Singer (Soprano). *Education:* Pontllanfraith Grammar School and Trinity College of Music, London. *Debut:* Operatic debut with Welsh National Opera in Marriage of Figaro. *Career:* Renowned for Mozart Operatic Roles; Has sung in world's leading opera houses and festivals; many radio broadcasts and television appearances; Major Roles include: Countess in Marriage of Figaro, Pamina in The Magic Flute, Fiordiligi in Così fan Tutte, Donna Anna in Don Giovanni, Constanze in Die Entführung, Amelia in Simon Boccanegra, Agathe in Freischütz, Desdemona in Otello, Elisabetta in Don Carlo, Aida and Norma; Sang Norma at Covent Garden 1987; Adriana Lecouvreur at Bonn 1989; Elisabeth de Valois at the Orange Festval; sang Amelia Grimaldi in a concert performance of Simon Boccanegra at the Festival Hall, 1990; Season 1992/93 as Adriana Lecouvreur at the Concertebouw and Giovanna d'Arco at Salzburg (concerts). *Recordings:* Many recordings of Opera, Oratorio, Concert Works and Recitals, including Tristan und Isolde (Deutsche Grammophone); Le Nozze di Figaro and Elgar's The Kingdom, Don Giovanni, Così fan Tutte (EMI); Judas Maccabeus; Berg's Altenberglieder (LSO/Abbado); Mozart's Requiem (Philips) and Die Zauberflöte (Philips). *Honours:* CBE; Hon. Fellow, Trinity College of Music; Elisabeth Schumann Prize for Lieder, Ricordi Prize for Opera, Silver Medal of The Worshipful Company of Musicians; D.Mus, University in Wales, 1989; DBE, 1993. *Memberships:* Fellow of the College of Wales, 1991; Fellow of the College of Music and Drama of Wales, 1993. *Hobbies:* Cookery; Reading; Walking; Swimming. *Address:* c/o Bayerische Staatsoper, Postfach 100148, D-80075, Munich, Germany.

PRICE Perry, b. 13 Oct 1942, New York, Pennsylvania, US. Singer (Tenor). m. Heather Thomson. *Education:* Studied at University of Houston, in London with Otakar Kraus, and in New York. *Debut:* San Francisco, as Des Grieux in Manon, 1964. *Career:* Appearances at such US opera centres as New York (City Opera), Houston, Philadelphia, San Diego and Portland; Sang further at Montreal, Vancouver, Toronto, Lisbon and Stadttheater Augsburg; Other roles have included Mozart's Ferrando, Don Ottavio and Tamino, Rossini's Almaviva and Lindoro, the Duke of Mantua, Edgardo, Nemorino, Faust and Hoffmann; Active in concert and as teacher.

PRICK Christof, b. 23 Oct 1946, Hamburg, Germany. Conductor. *Education:* Studied in Hamburg with Wilhelm Bruckner-Ruggebourg. *Career:* Assistant at the Hamburg Staatsoper; Permanent conductor at Trier Opera, 1970-72, Darmstadt, 1972-74; Musical Director at Saarbrucken, 1974-77, Karlsruhe, 1977-84; Staatskapellmeister at the Deutsche Oper Berlin, 1977-84 (returned to conduct the premiere of Wolfgang Rihm's Oedipus, 1987); Conducted Così fan Tutte at Los Angeles 1988 and Arabella at Barcelona, 1989; Music Director, Los Angeles Chamber Orchestra, 1992-; Conducted Fidelio and Tannhäuser at the Metropolitan, 1992; Engaged as Music Director City of Hannover, Germany, as of 1993-94 Season. *Address:* Los Angeles Chamber Orchestra, 315 W 9th Street, Suite 801, Los Angeles, CA 90015, USA.

PRIDAY Elisabeth, b. 1955, Buckingham, England. Singer (Soprano). *Education:* Studied at the Royal Academy of Music. *Career:* Joined the Monteverdi Choir 1975: concerts at the Aix Festival, and BBC Promenade; Sang in Handel Opera's Giustino 1983 and Hasse's L'Eroe Cinese at the 1985 Holland Festival; Appearances with Roger Norrington for the Maggio Musicale Florence (Speranza in Orfeo) and Amor in Gluck's Orfeo with the Scottish Chamber Orchestra; Dido and Aeneas with the English Concert in Germany, London and the Brighton Festival Concert performances of Bach's B minor Mass in King's College, Cambridge, Handel's Carmelite Vespers with the European Baroque Orchestra, Alexander's Feast for RAI in Italy and Messiah at the Festival de Beaune in France and also QEH; Monteverdi Vespers in St. Johns Smith Square, Bristol, St Albans; Concerts in France and England with Chiaroscuro and Clímene in Gluck's La Corona at the City of London Festival; Paris 1991 with the Deller Consort. *Recordings:* Bach Motets with the Monteverdi Choir; Purcell's King Arthur, Music for the Chapels Royal and the Fairy Queen; Handel's Israel in Egypt, Semele and Dixit Dominus with the Winchester Cathedral Choir; Motets by Schütz and Monteverdi; Rameau's Les Boréades; Vivaldi Glorias (Nimbus); Dido and Aeneas with Trevor Pinnock and also with John Elliot Gardiner. *Address:* Magenta Music International, 64 Highgate High Street, London N6 5HX, England.

PRIESTMAN Brian, b. 10 Feb 1927, Birmingham, England. Conductor; Music Director; Professor. m. Ford McClave, 2 Mar 1972, 1 daughter. *Education:* BMus, 1950, MA, 1952, University of Birmingham; Dipl Sup, Brussels Conservatoire, 1952. *Career:* Has held Musical Directorships of Royal Shakespeare Theatre, and with Symphony Orchestras in Edmonton, Canada; Baltimore; Denver & Miami; USA; Principal Conductor, New Zealand Symphony Orchestra & Malmö, SO; Former, Dean and Professor, University of Cape Town; Currently Artist-in-Residence, University of Kansas, USA. *Recordings:* for Westminster, RCA and Musique en Wallonie. *Honour:* DHL, University of Colorado, 1972. *Hobbies:* Cooking; Reading. *Address:* 3700 Clinton Parkway No 1307, Lawrence, KS 66047, USA.

PRIETO Carlos, b. 1 Jan 1937, Mexico City, Mexico. Concert Cellist. m. Maria Isabel, 28 Dec 1964, 2 sons, 1 daughter. *Education:* BS, Metallurgical Engineering, 1958, BS, Economics, 1959, Massachusetts Institute of Technology, USA; Russian, Lomonosov University, Moscow, USSR, 1962; Master of Engineering, CESSID, Metz, France, 1963; Mexico City Conservatory of Music, under Imre Hartman, 1942-54; Studied with: Pierre Fournier, Geneva, 1978; Leonard Rose, New York, USA, 1981, 82. *Career:* Member of Trio Mexico, 1978-81; International career as Concert Cellist. Many world tours, USA, Canada, Western and Eastern Europe, USSR, Latin America, China, Japan, India, 1981-; Performances in Carnegie Hall and Lincoln Center, New York; Kennedy Center, Washington; Salle Pleyel and Salle Gaveau, Paris; Philharmonic Hall, Leningrad; Concertgebouw, Amsterdam; Has performed at international music festivals; Played at world premieres of many cello concerti including those of Carlos Chavez, Joaquin Rodrigo. *Recordings include:* Complete Bach Suites for Cello Solo, 1985; Works by Paganini, Ponce, Rachmaninov, Fauré, Mendelssohn, Tchaikovsky. *Publications:* Alrededor del Mundo con el Violonchelo (Around the World with the Cello), autobiography, 1987; Russian Letters, 1965. *Honour:* Outstanding Soloist of 1981 given by Mexican Association of Music Critics, 1982. *Current Management:* Gurtman & Murtha Associates Inc., New York City, USA; Choveaux Management, Mancroft Towers, Oulton Broad, Lowestoft, Suffolk, England. *Address:* c/o Gurtman and Murtha, 162 West 56th Street, New York, NY 10019, USA.

PRIMROSE Claire, b. 2 Oct 1957, Melbourne, Victoria, Australia. Singer (Soprano). *Education:* Studied at Victorian College of Arts, with Joan Hammond in Melbourne and Gerard Souzay in Paris. *Career:* Sang as a mezzo in Australia from 1982, as Nicklausse, Siebel, Olga, Suzuki, Krista in The Makropoulos Case, Meg Page, Mercedes, and Cornelia in Guilio Cesare; European engagements from 1985, including Massenet's Cendrillon at Wexford and Charlotte at Montpellier, Giulietta in Lille, Salud (La Vida Breve) at Liège and Mozart's Dorabella and Sesto for Opera Forum, Netherlands; Soprano roles, 1988-, including Leonora for Kent Opera, Medea in Handel's Teseo at Athens Festival and Sadler's Wells, Dido at Bologna and Gluck's Alceste at Monte Carlo and Covent Garden; English National Opera debut, 1990, in the premiere of Holloway's Clarissa; Valencia Festival, 1991, as Elettra in Idomeneo; Season 1991-92 as Strauss's Chrysothemis at Festival of Melbourne and Alceste at Théâtre du Châtelet, Paris; Recent engagements as Leonore for Australian Opera, Elettra at Helsinki and Tel Aviv and Fiordiligi for the Lyric Opera of Queensland; Concert appearances include Wigmore Hall recital with Roger Vignoles and the Berlioz Romeo et Juliette at Salle Pleyel, Paris; Leonore in La Forza del Destino for Scottish Opera. *Honours include:* Winner of

Metropolitan Opera Auditions and Pavarotti International Competition at Philadelphia. *Address:* c/o Atholl Still Ltd, 80-86 Westrow Street, London SE19 3AF, England.

PRINCE-JOSEPH Bruce, b. 30 Aug 1925, Beaver Falls, Pennsylvania, USA. Conductor; Composer; Organist; Harpsichordist; Pianist. *Education:* BMusA, Yale University, 1946; MMus A, University of Southern California, 1952; Conservatoire Nationale de Musique, Paris, France, 1953. *Career:* Staff pianist, Organist and Harpsichordist, New York Philharmonic, 1955-74; Professor and Chairman, Department of Music, Hunter College of the City University of New York, 1955-78. *Recordings:* 6 Sonatas for Violin and Harpsichord, RCA, 1965; Glagolitic Mass, Janáček, 1967, Ode to St Cecilia, Handel, 1958, Columbia Records. *Honours:* Grammy Nomination, 1965 for 6 Sonatas for Violin and Harpsichord; Associate Fellow, Berkeley College, Yale University, 1978-83. *Memberships:* Knight Officer, The Order of the Cedars, Lebanon, 1974, Commandeur, and Grand Officer and Grand Cross, The Sovereign Military Order of the Temple at Jerusalem, Prior, St. Mary the Virgin, 1989. *Address:* 6540 Pennsylvania Ave, Kansas City, MO 64113, USA.

PRING Katherine, b. 4 June 1940, Brighton, England. Singer (Mezzo-Soprano). *Education:* Studied at the Royal College of Music with Ruth Packer; Further study with Maria Carpi in Geneva and Luigi Ricci in Rome. *Debut:* Geneva 1966, as Flora in La Traviata. *Career:* Sang at Sadler's Wells from 1968, notably as Carmen, Dorabella, Poppea, Eboli, Azucena and Waltraute; Sang in the 1974 British stage premiere of Henze's The Bassarids; Covent Garden debut 1972, as Thea in The Knot Garden; Bayreuth 1972-73, as Schwertleite in Die Walküre; Glyndebourne 1978, as Baba the Turk in The Rake's Progress; Other modern roles include Kate in Owen Wingrave and Jocasta in Oedipus Rex. *Recordings:* Fricka and Waltraute in The Ring conducted by Reginald Goodall (EMI); The Magic Fountain by Delius (BBC Artium). *Address:* c/o Trafalgar Perry Ltd., 4 Goodwin's Court, St Martin's Lane, London WC2N 4LL, England.

PRING Sarah, b. 1962, England. Singer (Soprano). *Education:* Studied at Guildhall School, in Florence with Suzanne Danco, and with Johanna Peters. *Career:* Sang Norina, Susanna, Concepcion and Martinů's Julietta while a student in London, the Trovatore Leonora in Belgium; Professional debut at Glyndebourne, 1988, as Alice in Falstaff, returning as Barena in Jenůfa; Glyndebourne Touring Opera as Glasha in Katya Kabanova, First Lady in Die Zauberflöte and Dorabella; Opera North debut, 1989, as Concepcion, Scottish Opera, 1991, as Mimi; Concert appearances at Festival Hall (Jenůfa), Greenwich Festival (Judas Maccabeus), Belfast (Beethoven's Ninth) and Purcell Room; Sang Gluck's Euridice for Opera West, 1991; English National Opera debut, 1993, Princess Ida, Don Paquale; ENO, 1993, Norina, Don Pasquale; ENO, 1994, Nannetta, Falstaff, also Glyndebourne Touring Opera, Second Niece, Peter Grimes; Debut 1995, Second Niece, Paris Châtelet. *Honours include:* Joint winner, 1990 John Christie Award. *Address:* Little Easthall Farmhouse, St Paul's Walden, Nr Hitchin, Hertfordshire, SG4 8DH, England.

PRINGLE John, b. 17 Oct 1938, Melbourne, Victoria, Australia. Singer (Baritone). *Education:* Studied in Melbourne and with Luigi Ricci in Rome. *Debut:* Australian Opera, as Falke in Die Fledermaus, 1967. *Career:* Many appearances with Australian Opera as Mozart's Don Giovanni, Count and Papageno, Verdi's Renato, Posa, Don Carlo, Ford, the Lescauts of Puccini and Massenet; Nick Shadow in The Rake's Progress, Andrei in War and Peace, Janáček's Forester and Robert Storch in Intermezzo (Glyndebourne, 1984); Also sings Olivier in Capriccio and appeared at Paris, Brussels and Cologne, 1980-85; Sang Beckmesser in Meistersinger for Australian Opera, 1988-89, Comte de Nevers in Les Huguenots, 1990. *Recordings include:* Video of Les Huguenots. *Address:* c/o Australian Opera, PO Box 291, Strawberry Hills, NSW 2012, Australia.

PRIOR Claude, b. 8 June 1918, Geneva, Switzerland. Composer. m. Anne-Marie Pharabod, 1 Aug 1940, 1 son, 3 daughters. *Education:* Universitat Munich; Conservatoire, Paris. *Career:* Radiodiffusion Francaise, Club d'essai, Concerts of UNESCO, 1948; Club Francais du disque, 1953; Resonances, 1957; Teaching, 1967; Director, Music School and Festival of St Malo, 1968; Director of Studies, Dijon, 1972; Independent conducting and teaching, 1984-. *Compositions include:* Uniting Messiaen's Harmony and Stravinsky's Counterpoint: Melodies, Choir and Orchestra; Bateau Ivre, Paris, 1957; Song of songs, Koln, 1957; Symphonie Concertante-Organ Concertino-Musical Tales, Sydney 59; The Snow Queen-La petite Sirene-Magnificat, soloists, choir & Orchestra or soloists, choir & Organ Trio and 5 instruments; Seagulls, Concerto for Saxophone and Wind Operas; L'heure sicilienne-No Orchids-Wuthering Heights-Concertos; Piano-Orch-Violin-Orch; Piano Preludes. *Recordings:* La Petite Sirene; Petit Poucet; Musical Tales. *Address:* 38 rue de Vaugirard, 75006 Paris, France.

PRITCHARD Edith, b. 1962, Vancouver, Canada. Singer (Soprano). *Education:* Studied at University of Toronto and Royal Northern College of Music. *Career:* Represented Canada at the 1991 Cardiff Singer of the World Competition; Sang Fiordiligi at the 1991 Glyndebourne Festival and the Countess in Cornet Rilke by Siegfried Matthus with the 1933 Glyndebourne Tour; Other roles include First Lady in Die Zauberflöte at Covent Garden 1992-93, Licenza in Mozart's Sogno di Scipione at Buxton Festival and the Heavenly Voice in Don Carlos for Opera North. *Honours include:* Brigitte Fassbaender Prize for Lieder, Royal Northern College of Music, and 1992 John Christie Award, Glyndebourne. *Address:* c/o John Coast Ltd, 31 Sinclair Road, London W14 0NS, England.

PRITCHARD Gwyn Charles, b. 29 Jan 1948, Richmond, Yorkshire, England. Composer; Conductor; Cellist. m. Claudia Klasicka, 23 June 1967, 2 daughters. *Education:* Royal Scottish Academy of Music and Drama, 1966-69; Studied Cello with Joan Dickson, Composition with Dr Frank Spedding; DRSAM. *Career:* Director of Music, Salisbury Cathedral School, 1969-70; contract for documentary Young Composer, 1972-73; Cellist with Medusa Ensemble, 1976-78; Artistic Director and Conductor, Uroboros Ensemble, 1981-; Compositions performed worldwide, including Warsaw Autumn Festival, Mexico Festival, International Composers Forum, USA, Eastern and Western Europe, and Australia; Featured composer at Southampton International New Music Week, 1989. *Compositions:* Concerto for Viola and Orchestra, 1967 (revised 1984); Tangents, 1970; Spring Music for Chamber Orchestra, 1972; Enitharmon, 1973; Becoming, 1974; Five pieces for Piano, 1975; Ensemble Music for Six, 1976; Nephalauxis, 1977; Strata, 1977; To Jardenna, 1978; Objects in Space, 1978; Mercurius, 1979; Duo, 1980; Earthcrust, 1980; Visions of Zosimos, 1981; Sonata for Guitar, 1982; Moondance, 1982; Lollay, 1983; Dramalogue, 1984; Chamber Concerto, 1985; Madrigal, 1987; La Settima Bolgia, 1989; Eidos, 1990; Janus, 1991; Wayang, 1993. *Membership:* Society for the Promotion of New Music. *Current Management:* Classical Artists Management, 63 Charles Street, Epping, Essex, CM16 7AX. *Address:* 13 Nevil Road, Bishopston, Bristol, BS7 9EG, England.

PROBST Dominique Henri, b. 19 Feb 1954, Paris, France. Percussionist; Composer; Conductor. *Education:* Baccalaureat, Philosophy Studies, La Sorbonne, Paris, 1971; Paris Conservatoire National Superieur De Musique, 1st Prize Percusion, 198; Prize, Composition, Lili & Naida Boulanger Foundation, 1979. *Career:* As Musician at La Comedie Française, and many other great Parisian theatres, 1974-; Titulary Member, Concert Colonne & Ensemble Percussion 4; Assistant, CNSM, Paris, 1978-; Professor, Levallois Conservatory of Music, 1984-. *Compositions:* Numerous pieces for Theatre: King Lear, 1978; Dom Juan, Tete d'or, Berenice, 1979; Macbeth; Les Caprices de Marianne, Les Plaisirs de L'Ile Enchantée, 1980; Les Cenci, 1981; Marie Tudor,

1982; L'Esprit des Bois; Dialogue des Carmélites, 1984; La Mouette, L'Arbre des Tropiques, Le Cid, 1985; L'Hote et le Renegat; Thomas More' Richard de Gloucester' Bacchus, 1987; Ascese-A-Seize, 6 percussion players; Les Plaisirs de l'Ile Enchantée, for recorder, violin, guitar & percussion; Coda & Variation IV, guitar. *Contributions to:* Professional journals including La Revue Musicale. *Honours:* Prize Marcel Samuel Rousseau, Académie des Beaux-Arts of Paris, 1986, for Opera, Maximilien Kolbe. *Hobby:* Chess. *Address:* 39 Rue Durantin, 75018 Paris, France.

PROCTER Michael Robert, b. 1 Apr 1951, Chichester, West Sussex, England. Choral Conductor. *Education:* Christ's Hospital, 1960-69; Bristol University; MA, City University; Royal Academy of Music, 1972-76; LRAM; ARCM. *Career:* Singer with St Paul's Cathedral Choir, 1974-80; Choir Trainer, frequent workshops/clinics in Renaissance music and vocal training; Director, Orpheus Choir, 1983-89; Founder, Early Music News, Juniper Arts Music; Director Euromusica, Renaissance Society, Renaissance Singers, Campion Singers, Venice Academy of Sacred Music; Director, Benslow Music Trust, 1983-93. *Recordings:* Music in Pictures (National Gallery); BBC recordings; Schola Polyphonica (Director); Renaissance Singers/Octave Recordings. *Publications:* Singing for Choirs, series of articles in Vocal Lines, 1983-88, for re-issue in book form; Byrd Gradualia 20 vols (Ed.): JOED Music Publishers; Boismortier Don Quixote (translator), King's Music, 1993; Co-Editor Early Music Yearbook, 1993. *Honour:* FRSA, 1985. *Memberships:* ISM. *Hobbies:* Liturgiology; Languages. *Address:* 2a Bridge Street, Hitchin, Herts, SG5 2DN, England.

PROCTER Norma, b. 15 Feb 1928, Cleethorpes, Lincolnshire, England. *Career includes:* International Concert Singer (Contralto), now retired; Vocal studies with Roy Henderson; Musicianship with Alec Redshaw, Lieder with Hans Oppenheim & Paul Hamburger; London debut at Southwark Cathedral, 1948; Specialist in concert work, oratorio & recitals; appeared with all major festivals in UK & Europe; Operatic debut as Lucretia in Britten's, Rape of Lucretia, Aldeburgh Festival, 1954, 1958; Covent Garden debut in Gluck's Orpheus, 1960; Performed in Germany, France, Spain, Portugal, Norway, Sweden, Denmark, Finland, Holland, Belgium, Austria, Israel, Luxemborug, South America. *Recordings include:* Messiah, Elijah, Samson, Mahler's; 2nd, 3rd, 8th Symphonies, Das Klagende Lied; Hartmann 1st Symph; Julius Caeser Jones-Williamson; Nicholas Maws Scenes & Arias; BBC, Last Night of the Proms; Prelude recording Brahms, Mahler, Ballads; Conductors include: Bruno Walter, Bernstein, Rafael Kubelik, Karl Richter, Pablo Casals, Sirs: Malcolm Sargent, Charles Groves, David Willcocks; Alexander Gibson, Charles Mackerras, Norman del Mar. *Memberships:* President, Grimsby Phil Society. *Honour:* Honorary RAM, 1974. *Hobbies:* Sketching; Painting; Tapestry. *Address:* 194 Clee Road, Grimsby, Lincolnshire, England.

PROFETA Laurentiu, b. 12 Jan 1925, Bucharest, Romania. Composer. m. Nicole Profeta, 6 Nov 1956. *Education:* Philosophical Degree, 1948; Bucharest and Moscow Conservatories, 1955. *Debut:* Puppet Suite, awarded Enescu Prize, 1946. *Compositions include:* Songs for Children and Youth, 1968; Prince and Pauper, Ballet, 1970; Gypsy Songs, 1971; Adventure in the Garden, Oratorio for children's choir and symphony orchestra, 1973; 6 Humorous Pieces, suite for children's choir and small orchestra, 1974; madrigal, for choir and small orchestra, 1975; Songs, 1982; The Triumph of Love, ballet, 1983; Chosen Melodies, 1983; Music for Artistic pictures; The Story of Peter Pan, opera for children, 1984; Rica's, one-act Ballet, 1986; The Loosers, Musical, 1990; Hershale, Musical, 1989; Of The Carnival, Ballet, 1991; Turandot, musical, 1992; Maria Tanase, musical, 1992; Eva-Now, musical, 1993. *Recordings:* 7 Long playing records; The Story of Peter Pan, 1986; Adventure in the Garden, 1984. *Contributions to:* Muzica Review and other professional publications. *Address:* Str Take Ionescu no 8, 70154 Bucharest, Romania.

PROKINA Elena, b. 1960, Odessa, Russia. Singer (Soprano). *Education:* Studied in Odessa and at the Leningrad Theatre Institute and Leningrad Conservatory. *Career:* Kirov Theatre Leningrad from 1988 as Emma in Khovanshchina, Violetta, Marguerite, Natasha in War and Peace (seen on BBC TV), Tatyana, Desdemona, Pauline in The Gambler, Jaroslavna in Prince Igor, Iolanta and Maria in Mazeppa; tours with the Kirov companny in Europe and Kirov Gala at Covent Garden, 1992; Shostakovich Symphony No. 14 with the LSO under Rostropovitch, 1993; Covent Garden debut, 1994 as Katya Kabanova in production by Trevor Nunn. *Address:* c/o Royal Opera, Covent Garden (Contracts), London WC2, England.

PROMONTI Elisabeth, b. 9 July 1942, Budapest, Hungary. Opera and Concert Singer; Music Educator. 1 son. *Education:* Diploma, Choir Conducting Faculty, Franz Liszt Music Academy, Budapest; Diploma, Opera, Song, Oratorio, Akademie Mozarteum, Salzburg, 1st Class Honours; Studied with Zoltan Zavodszky, Viorica Ursuleac, Friederike Baumgartner, Denes Bartha, Paul von Schilhawsky, Cecilia Vajda; Diploma (1st Class Honours), International Opera Studio, Opera Zurich, 1970-71. *Debut:* As Aida, Bielefeld Municipal Theatre, 1967. *Career:* Opera Singer, Bielefeld, Oberhausen, Kiel, Bremen, Heidelberg, Bordeaux, Vienna, Zurich, 1967-75; Concert Singer, also Music Educator adapting the Zoltan Kodály Music Education Concept in Switzerland, 1975-81; Music Educator (solo singing), international Solo Singer, appearances on radio and TV, 1981-; Director, Swiss Kodály Institute, 1983-; Co-Editor, Swiss Kodaly Bulletin. *Recordings:* Kodály Zoltan, Epigrammes, MAFILM, Budapest, 1991; Folk Songs arranged by Great Composers, Urai-Vamosi Ltd, Budapest, 1993. *Publications:* Musik auf der Elementarstufe 1/2, adaptation of the Kodály Music Education Concept based on Swiss Folk Songs (editor), 1985. *Address:* PO Box 4051, CH-6002 Lucerne, Switzerland.

PROSZYNSKI Stanislaw Tadeusz Konrad, b. 31 Jan 1926, Warsaw, Poland. Composer; Teacher; Musical Writer. *Education:* Baccalaureat, High School Lyceum, Lodz, 1945; MA, Composition, 1953, Postgraduate Studies, 1954-58, State Academy of Music, Warsaw. *Debut:* Theatre Music, Lodz, Poland, 1945. *Career:* Director of Music, various theatres, Lodz and Warsaw, 1945-48; Teacher, High School Music Schools, Warsaw, 1954-60; Faculty Member, State Academy of Music, Warsaw, 1960-; Chairman, Department of Problems in Music Education, 1968-71; Docent/Senior Lecturer, 1970-84; Extraordinary Professor, 1984-, State Academy of Music, Warsaw; Docent, High School of Education, Olsztyn, 1974-79; Numerous interviews for radio and television documentaries with his collection of music boxes and others; Dean of the Faculty of Composition, orchestra conducting and Music Theory, 1987-. *Compositions:* The Red Lion, Opera, 1953-61; Seven Girls Under Arms, Musical Comedy, 1968-69; Olympic Pictures, 1952; String Quartet I, 1954; Lyrical Constructions, 1962; String Quartet II, Music in Two Pitches, 1973; Choir and Piano Works, Solo Songs, Theatre, Radio and Film Music. *Recordings:* Numerous Radio Recordings. *Publications:* Tosca by G. Puccini, 1956; Aida by G. Verdi, 1958; Gyganeria, La Bohème by G. Puccini, 1961; The World of the Music Mechanisms, 1986 (in preparation). *Contributions to:* professional journals. *Hobbies:* Collecting Music Boxes and Barrel Organs (Collection contains over 80 specimens). *Address:* ul. Lowicka 58/5A, 02-531, Warsaw, Poland.

PROTERO Dodi, b. 13 Mar 1935, Toronto, Canada. Opera Singer; Teacher. m. Alan Paul Crofoot, 23 Mar 1961, divorced. *Education:* Toronto Conservatory, 1945; Sienna Academy, 1958; Mozarteum Salzburg, 1956-57. *Debut:* San Carlo Opera, Naples, Italy, 1956. *Career:* Sang with major companies in Austria, Canada, United Kingdom, Italy, and USA; Roles included: Adele, Fledermaus; Oscar, Ballo in Maschera; Gilda, Rigoletto; Violetta, La Traviata; Video and Film Broadcasts; Private Voice Teacher, New York City, 1974-; Voice Teacher,

Banff School of Fine Arts, 1975-82; Professor of Voice, University of Illinois, Champaign, Urbana, 1976-87; Director pf Voice, New Jersey Opera Musical Theatre International Institute, 1987-. *Recordings include:* Philips; Tiefland; Serva Padrona; Finta Giardiniera. *Honours:* Canada Council Fellowships, 1967, 1968, 1973; Scholarship Award, Mozarteum, Salzburg, 1956-57; Scholarship Award, Accademy Chigianna, Siena, 1955. *Address:* 50W 67 street, Apt. 8D, New York, NY 10023, USA.

PROTSCHKA Josef, b. 5 Feb 1946, Prague, Czechoslovakia. German Singer (Tenor). *Education:* Studied Philology and Philosophy at Universities of Tubingen and Bonn; Studied at Cologne Musikhochschule with Erika Köth and Peter Witsch. *Career:* Giessen, 1977-8, Saarbrücken, 1978-80, leading tenor at Cologne Opera from 1980 singing all main tenor parts in Ponnelle's Mozart cycle and Lionel (Martha), Tom Rakewell, Faust, Max, Lensky, Hans, José, Hermann (Queen of Spades), Loge, Erik, Eisenstein; Freelance from 1987; Important debuts: Salzburg Festival and Vienna State Opera (Hans), 1985; La Scala and Semperopera Dresden (José), 1986; Bregenz Festival (Hoffmann), Maggio Musicale, Florence (Flamand) and Zürich Opera, 1987; Hamburg State Opera (Florestan/Elis in Schrekers Schatzgräber, 1989/Idomeneo, 1990) and Wiener Festwochen (Fierrabras-Schubert), 1988; Royal Opera, Brussels (Florestan/Lohengrin, 1990), 1989; Covent Garden (Florestan) and Tokyo NHK (Florestan), 1990; US debut in Houston (Song of the Earth), 1991; Now regularly appearing on stage at all famous festivals and opera houses working with leading conductors and producers; Is also heard in lieder recitals, concerts, broadcast and TV productions. *Recordings include:* Haydn's Die Schöpfung; Schubert's Fierrabras; Schubert's Schone Mullerin; Mendelssohn's Lieder, complete; Fidelio (Florestan) and Flying Dutchman (Erik) with Vienna Philharmonic with Dohnanyi; Mozart Lieder, complete; Videos: Fidelio, Covent Garden; Tales of Hoffmann, Bregenz Festival; Fierrabras, Theater an der Wien; Schatzgräber, Hamburg Opera; Missa solemnis, Uracher Musiktage; Lieder recital, Urach. *Address:* Ringstrasse 17B, 50765 Köln, Germany.

PROTTI Aldo, b. 19 July 1920, Cremona, Italy. Singer (Baritone). m. Masako Tanaka. *Education:* Studied at the Parma Conservatory. *Career:* Pesaro 1948, as Rossini's Figaro. *Career:* Sang at Livorno from 1948, La Scala Milan from 1949; Mantua 1950, as Amonasro; Palermo 1951, in La Forza del Destino; Verona Arena 1950-61 and 1974; Guest appearances at the Vienna Staatsoper from 1957; Other engagements at Rome and Paris, and in Spain, the USA, Belgium, Germany, France and Switzerland. *Recordings:* Pagliacci, Cavalleria Rusticana, Aida, Otello, Rigoletto, La Traviata (Decca). *Address:* c/o Teatro alla Scala, Via Filogdrammatici 2, Milan, Italy.

PROUVOST Gaetane, b. 21 July 1954, Lille 59, France. Violinist. m. Charles de Couessin, 6 July 1985, 2 sons. *Education:* Baccalaureat; 1st Prize, Violin and Chamber Music, Cycle de Perfectionnement, Conservatoire National Superieur, Paris; Studied: With Ivan Galamian, Juilliard School of Music, New York; Chigiana, Siena, Italy; With D.Markevitch, Institut des hautes etudes musicales, Montreux; Pupil of Zino Francescatti. *Debut:* Carnegie Hall, 1974. *Career:* Soloist with Radio-France Orchestra, Orchestre Lamoureux, Bucharest Philharmonic; Gdansk Philharmonic, Ensemble Intercontemporain, Ensemble Forum; Performed under conductors J.Conlon, K.Nagano, G.Bertini, P.Boulez, A.Tamayo, S.Baudo, R.Kempe; Recitals with M.Dalberto, N.Lee, P.Barbizet, B.Rigutto, A.Queffelec; Premiered: Olivier Greif's Sonate; M.Rateau's Offrande lyrique, Paris, 1984; Participated in Etienne Perrier's film Rouge Venitien; Professor, Conservatoire National Superieur de Musique, Paris. *Recordings:* Prokofiev, Sonatas op 80 and 94 for violin and piano (with A.R.el Bacha); Szymanowski, Complete works for violin and piano. *Honours:* Prizewinner, Carl Flesch International Competition, London; Award for

Best Record, France, 1987. *Current management:* E.Ribet, 9 rue Ledion, 75014 Paris, France. *Memberships:* Alumni Association of Conservatoire National Superior de Musique, Paris. *Address:* 7 rue des Volontaires, 75015, Paris, France.

PROUZA Zdenek, b. 3 Aug 1955, Prague, Czechoslovakia. Cellist. m. Katherine H Allen, 25 Apr 1987. *Education:* Conservatory of Music, Prague; Academy of Performing Arts, Prague; Hochschule für Musik, Wien; Mozarteum, Salzburg; Accademia Musicale Chigiana, Siena. *Debut:* Recital debut: Prague, 1973. *Career:* Principal Cellist with Czechoslovak Chamber Orchestra and Nurnberg Symphony Orchestra; Co-principal with Vienna Chamber Orchestra and Munich Chamber Orchestra; Solo appearances in: Czechoslovakia, West Germany, Belgium, Italy, France, Austria, USA, Canada. *Recordings:* Radio Prague (Pauer); Czechoslovak Television (Suk); ORTF (Suk); RAI (Vivaldi); Colosseum (Saint-Saëns); Musical Heritage Society. *Honours:* Contemporary Performance Award, 1977 and 1978, Czechoslovak Music Foundation; Czechoslovak Cello Competition, 1976; Beethoven Cello Competition, 1972; Concertino Praga, 1970. *Membership:* American Cello Society. *Hobby:* Computers; Financial markets. *Current Management:* The Added Staff. *Address:* 820 West End Avenue, Suite 3C, New York, NY 10025, USA.

PROVOST Serge, b. 1952, Saint-Timothée de Beauharnois, Quebec, Canada. Composer, Performer, Professor. *Education:* Studied composition and analysis under Gilles Tremblay, organ with Bernard Lagacé; Studied writing, electroacoustics, orchestration, piano and harpsichord, Conservatoire de Musique, Montréal 1970-79; Studied composition and analysis under Claude Ballif, Paris 1979-81. *Career:* Professor of analysis, Trois-Rivières and Hull Conservatories; took part in Banff Centre's Composers Workshop 1979 and Rencontres Internationales de la Jeunesse at Bayreuth Festival; given organ recitals in France, Germany and Canada. *Compositions include:* Les Isle du Songe, for choir, orchestra and percussion; Cretes, a piece for 2 harpsichords which Swiss duo Esterman-Gallet commissioned and played in 1980; Tetrarys, 1988, saxophone, harp, flute, piano; Les Jardins Suspendus, 1989, 4 ondes martenots, piano. *Honours:* Won 1st Prize in composition for choir, orchestra and percussion with Les Isle du Songe, 1979; Won First Prize in analysis at Conservatoire de Paris 1981. *Address:* c/o CAPAC (Canada) PRS Ltd, Member Registration, 29/33 Berners Street, London W1A 4AA, England.

PROWSE Philip, b. 29 Dec 1937, Worcestershire, England. Stage Director and Designer. *Education:* Studied at Slade School of Fine Art, London. *Career:* Teacher at Birmingham College of Art and Slade School of Fine Art; Designed ballets for Covent Garden, followed by Orfeo ed Euridice, 1969, and Ariadne auf Naxos, 1976; Director of Citizens Theatre, Glasgow, 1970-; Produced and designed Handel's Tamerlano for Welsh National Opera, 1982, and Les Pecheurs de Perles for English National Opera, 1987; Designs for Jonathan Miller's production of Don Giovanni at English National Opera, 1985 and The Magic Flute, Scottish Opera; Work for Opera North includes Die Dreigroschenoper, Aida (1986), UK premiere of Strauss's Daphne, 1987, and La Gioconda, 1993. *Address:* c/o The Citizens Theatre, Gorbals Street, Glasgow, G5 9DS, Scotland.

PRUETT James, W(orrell), b. 23 Dec 1932, Mount Airy, North Carolina, USA. Music librarian; Musicologist. *Education:* PhD University of North Carolina 1962. *Career:* Reference assistant at North Carolina University Library 1955, Music librarian 1961-76; Music Department 1963, Professor of Music and Chairman 1976; Chief of Music Division, Library of Congress, 1987. *Memberships:* Member, American Musicological Society; Member, Music Library Association (President 1973-75), Editor of Notes (Journal of the Music Library Association) 1974-77. *Publications include:* Studies in Musicology, 1969; Many journal and encyclopaedia articles, book and music reviews. *Address:* 325 6th Street SE, Washington DC 20003, USA.

PRUETT Jerome, b. 22 Nov 1941, Poplar Bluff, Missouri, USA. Singer (Tenor). *Education:* Studied with Thorwald Olsen in St Louis and with Boris Goldovsky in West Virginia. *Debut:* Carnegie Hall New York 1974, in a concert performance of Donizetti's Parisina d'Este. *Career:* Sang with New York City Opera then followed a career in Europe: Vienna Volksoper, 1975, in the premiere of Wolpert's Le Malade Imaginaire; Théâtre de la Monnaie Brussels, 1983, as Julien in Louise and as Boris in Katya Kabanova; Geneva Opera, 1984, as Debussy's Pelléas; Sang at Nancy, 1984, in Henze's Boulevard Solitude; Other roles include Mozart's Belmonte and Tamino, Nicolai's Fenton, Tonio in La Fille du Régiment and Ernesto in Don Pasquale; Amsterdam and Paris, 1988, as Boris in Katya Kabanova and Faust; Sang Ferrando in Così fan Tutte at the Gran Teatre del Liceu Barcelona 1990. *Recordings:* Louise (Erato). *Address:* c/o Harrison/Parrott Ltd, 12 Penzance Place, London, W11 4PA.

PRUSLIN Stephen (Lawrence), b. 16 Apr 1940, Brooklyn, New York, USA. Pianist; Writer on Music. *Education:* Studied at Brandeis University (BA, 1961) and Princeton (MFA, 1963); Piano studies with Eduard Steuermann. *Career:* Taught at Princeton until 1964, then moved to London; Recital debut as pianist at Purcell Room, South Bank, 1970; Concert appearances with BBC Symphony and Royal Philharmonic; Recital accompanist to Bethany Beardslee, Elisabeth Söderström and the late Jan DeGaetani; Appearances with London Sinfonietta and the Fires of London (co-founder), 1970-87; Repertoire has included works by Elliott Carter, Maxwell Davies (premiere of Piano Sonata), late Beethoven, Bach and John Bull; Collaborated with Davies on music for Ken Russell's film The Devils and has written other film and theatre music, including Derek Jarman's The Tempest; Articles on contemporary music, translation of Schoenberg's Pierrot Lunaire and librettos for Birtwistle's Monodrama, 1967, and Punch and Judy, 1968.*Recordings include:* Award-winning albums as solo and ensemble pianist. *Publications include:* Peter Maxwell Davies: Studies from Two Decades (editor), London, 1979. *Address:* c/o Universal Edition, Warwick House, 9 Warwick Street, London W1R 5RA, England.

PRYCE-JONES John, b. 1946, Wales. Conductor. *Education:* Studied in Penarth and Worcester and at Corpus Christi College, Cambridge (Organ Scholar). *Career:* Assistant Chorus Master and Conductor at Welsh National Opera 1970-; Freelance conductor in the United Kingdom and abroad until 1978; Chorus Master and Conductor with Opera North 1978-; Head of Music Scottish Opera 1987; Debut with English National Opera in The Mikado; Music Director of the New D'Oyly Carte Opera 1990: first US visit of the company with The Mikado and The Pirates of Penzance; Artistic Director of The Halifax Choral Society; Has conducted the Oslo Philharmonic, the Bergen Symphony and the Norwegian Broadcasting Orchestra; Debut with Icelandic Opera 1991, Rigoletto; Principal Conductor Northern Ballet Theatre, 1992; Rigoletto Opera North, 1992; La Bohème, Welsh National Opera, 1993; Conducted CBSO, BBC Welsh Symphony Orchestra. *Recordings:* Pirates of Penzance; Mikado, Iolanthe, Gondoliers. *Honours:* ARCO; MA. *Current Management:* Stafford Law. *Address:* 4 Croft Way, Menston, W.Yorks, CS29 6LT, England.

PRYOR Gwenneth, b. 7 Apr 1941, Sydney, New South Wales, Australia. Concert Pianist. m. Roger Stone, 10 Dec 1972, 1 son, 1 daughter. *Education:* Diploma, New South Wales State Conservatorium of Music; ARCM, Royal College of Music. *Debut:* Wigmore Hall, London. *Career:* Recitals and concerts in major cities, UK, Europe, North and South America and Australia; Many records and radio broadcasts, both solo and chamber music; Teaching, Morley College. *Recordings:* Moussorgsky's Pictures at an Exhibition; Schumann's Carnaval and Papillons; Gershwin's Rhapsody in Blue and Concerto; Several discs with clarinettist Gervase de Peyer; Malcolm Williamson Concertos. *Hobbies:* Cooking; Reading. *Current Management:* Roger Stone Artist Management. *Address:* West Grove, Hammers Lane, London NW7 4DY, England.

PRYTZ Holger, b. 22 May 1928, Copenhagen, Denmark. Composer. *Education:* Private education with Professor Anders Rachlev, piano, 1946-50; Professor Vagn Holmboe, composition, 1950-53; Studied with Professor Bruno Seidlhofer, piano; Professor Felix Retyrek, composition, Vienna; Professor Antonio Cece, Naples, 1963-65. *Debut:* As pianist, Copenhagen, 1950. *Career:* Danish Radio, Compositions Songs op 4 and op 12, Sonata for Flute and Piano op 7, 1950-63; Sinfonietta for orchestra op 21, performed on Danish Radio 1967 and Norwegian Radio, 1986; Second Symphony for orchestra recorded for broadcasting on Norwegian Radio, 1987. *Compositions:* 38 compositions for piano solo, vocal, chamber music, orchestral works; Quadrillo op 8 for alto voice, clarinet, cello and piano, 1974. *Honours:* 2nd prize, Danish Radio Competition, 1958; 3rd prize, Competition of Flemish Musicala, Danish Section. *Hobbies:* Philosophy; Runic cosmology; Literature. *Address:* Rubjergrej 73, Lonstrup, DK 9800 Hjorring, Denmark.

PTASZYNSKA Marta, b. 29 July 1943, Warsaw, Poland. Composer; Percussionist; Teacher. m. Andrew Rafalski, 9 Nov 1974, 1 daughter. *Education:* Warsaw Lyceum and Academy of Music - MA in Music Theory 1967; Composition 1968, and Percussional 1967 (all 3 diplomas with distinction); Studied composition with Nadia Boulanger in Paris and l'ORTF music concrete; Artist Diploma Degree, The Cleveland Institute of Music, Cleveland, USA 1974. *Career:* Performances at International Festivals: ISCM World Music Days, International Festival of Continuous Music Warsaw Autumn, Aspen Music Festival Percussive Arts Society International Conventions, Foundation Gulbenkian Contemporary Music Festival (Portugal) and many others, Radio and TV appearances in Poland and USA; Teacher of Composition and percussion: Warsaw Higher School of Music and in USA, successively at The Bennington College in Vermont, at The University of California in Berkeley and in Santa Barbara and at The Indiana University in Bloomington, 1970-. *Compositions:* Composed many works which include: Symphonic Music; Chamber Music; Instrumental Solo Pieces; Music for Children; Television opera, Oscar of Alva 1972; Madrigals for chamber ensemble 1971; Spectri Sonori for orchestra 1973; Siderals for 10 percussionists and light projection 1974; Space Model for 1 percussionist 1975; Epigrams 1976-77; Dream Lands, Magic Spaces for violin and percussion ensemble 1979; Sonnets to Orpheus for mezzo-soprano and chamber orchestra 1981; La Novella d'inverno for string orchestra 1984; Concerto for Marimba and orchestra 1985; Moon Flowers for cello and piano 1986. *Recordings:* Polskie Nagraina, MUZA: Un Grand Somnieil noir 1979; La Novella d'inverno 1985; Moon Flowers 1986; Sonoton - Pro Nove: Space Model, Epigrams, Moon Flowers 1987; many archive recordings at Polish Radio and also Moon Flowers at BBC 1986. *Publications:* Many works published. *Contributions to:* Articles to Ruch Muzyczny in Poland, also to Cum Notis Variorum of University of California in Berkeley. *Hobbies:* Art (Paintings) and Theatre. *Address:* 48 Aspen Way, Brookfield, CT 06804, USA.

PUCHNOWSKI Wlodzimierz Lech, b. 28 Feb 1932, Warsaw, Poland. Musician; Concert artist. m. Agnieszka Mria Sikorzyńska, 14 Sept 1958, 2 daughters. *Education:* MA, Warsaw University, 1955; Graduate in conducting, music theory, accordion, Franz Liszt Music Academy, Weimar, 1959; World University, Benson, Arizona, Doctorate in Philosophy of Music, 1988. *Debut:* Concert Hall, Reytan College, Warsaw, 1945. *Career:* Prizewinner, national & international music competitions; Trossingen College of Music, Gastdozent, Federal German Republic, 1965-70; Professor of Music, Leader of music seminars, Denmark, Norway, Sweden, Finland, Germany, Yugoslavia, Poland, Holland; Vice

President of National Council for University Level Music Education, 1985-90; Over 2000 concerts all over Europe & Asia; Numerous radio & television appearances, Poland, Finland, Italy, German Democratic Republic & Korea. Currently: Leader of Warsaw Accordion Quintet; Professor/Head of Accordion Chair, Frederick Chopin Academy of Music, Warsaw; Vice president, 1981-84, ibid. *Recordings:* Warsaw Accordion Quintet Plays Bach, Mendelssohn & Khachaturian, 1975; Warsaw Accordion Quintet, Finland, 1979; Contemporary Music Festival, Warsaw, Alkagran, Asteroeides, 1981. *Hobbies:* Fishing. *Address:* ul. Zimowa 1, 04-823 Warsaw, Poland.

PUDDY Keith, b. 27 Feb 1938, Wedmore, England. Clarinettist. *Education:* Studied at the Royal Academy of Music, London. *Career:* Played principal clarinet with Hallé Orchestra, under John Barbiroli; appeared frequently for the BBC and appeared in chamber concerts; member of London Wind Trio and the Music Group of London; Founder member of the Gabrieli Ensemble; awarded Leverhulme Trust Fellowship 1983 to study early clarinets and the basset horn; further Fellowship 1987 to study the work of early clarinet virtuosi; Professor of Clarinet and Classical Clarinet at the Royal Academy of Music, 1985-; Professor, Trinity College, London; Performs regularly in North and South America, Europe and the Far East. *Recordings:* Works by Beethoven, Weber, Schubert, Brahms, Prokoviev for various labels; music by Vanhal, Danzi, Molter, Lefevre and Devienne on historical instruments. *Address:* The Secretary, 20 Courtnell Street, London W2 5BX, England.

PUFFETT Derrick Robert, b. 30 Nov 1946, Oxford, England. Musicologist. *Education:* BA, New College, Oxford, 1968; DPhil, 1977, Wolfson College, Oxford. *Career:* Research Fellow, Wolfson College, Oxford, 1973-84; Member, Oxford University Music Faculty, 1978-84; Lecturer: Hertford College, Oxford, 1978-81; St. Hilda's College, 1979-84; St. Edmund Hall, 1979-84; Christ Church, 1981-84; Lecturer: Cambridge University Music Faculty, 1984-; Fellow and Lecturer of St. John's College, Cambridge, 1984-; Associate Editor, Music Analysis Journal, 1984-86; Editor, 1986-. *Publication:* The Song Cycles of Othmar Schoeck, 1982. *Contributions to:* Articles to professional journals. *Memberships:* British Royal Music Association; Advisory Board, Music Analysis Journal.

PULIEV Michael, b. 27 Mar 1958, Sofia, Bulgaria. Singer (Bass-baritone). *Education:* Studied in Sofia with Boris Christoff. *Career:* Sang at the National Opera, Sofia, 1984-86, then gave concerts in Bulgaria, China, Korea, Germany and Switzerland; Sang at Stadttheater Bern, 1986-87, Liège, 1987-, as Mars in Orphée aux Enfers, Frère Laurent in Roméo et Juliette and roles in Mascagni's Nerone, Die Zauberflöte, Le nozze di Figaro, La Traviata and Andrea Chenier. *Honours:* Winner, Bulgarian young singers competitions; Prize winner, Maria Callas Competition at Athens, 1984, Geneva International, 1987.

PURCELL Patricia (Elizabeth Harley), b. 7 Sept 1925, Egham, Surrey, England. Pianist; Teacher. *Education:* Royal College of Music, London, 1944-47; ARCM, 1945; Pupil of Frank Merrick; Disciple of Leschetizky & Viennese School. *Debut:* Royal Albert Hall, London, 1958. *Career:* Various recital/concerto appearances including Wigmore Hall, London, 1969; Polish Tour, Frederic Chopin Society, 1972, including Chopin's birthplace, 27th Chopinowski International Festival at Duszniki, and appearances on Polish Radio and TV; Private Teacher. *Honour:* Winner, 1st Prize, Piano Concerto Class, London Musical Competition Festival, 1956. *Membership:* Incorporated Society of Musicians. *Hobbies:* Cooking; Psychology; Nature. *Address:* c/o National Westminster Bank plc, 81 Aldwick Road, West Bognor Regis, West Sussex, PO21 2NS, England.

PURSER John Whitley, b. 10 Feb 1942, Glasgow, Scotland. Composer; Writer. 1 son, 1 daughter.

Education: Fettes College, 1955-60; RSAMD, 1960-63; Caird Scholar with Sir Micahel Tippett and Dr Hans Gal, 1963-66; Glasgow University, 1976-80 and 1980-83. *Career:* Freelance Composer, Poet, Playwright, Lecturer, Critic, Cello Teacher; Manager of the Scottish Music Information Centre, 1985-88. *Compositions:* Wide range of orchestral and chamber music. *Recording:* Circus Suite (SSC 002). *Publication:* Is the Red Light On? 1986 (The story of the BBC SSO); Clavier Sonata, Prelude and Toccata for Guitar; Scotland's Music, 1992; Carver, 1992. *Hobbies:* Sailing; Climbing. *Address:* 29 Banavie Road, Glasgow G11 5AW, Scotland.

PUSAR Ana, b. 1954, Celje, Yugoslavia. Singer (Soprano). *Education:* Studied in Celje and at the School of Music in Ljubljana. *Career:* Sang in Ljubljana from 1975 as Rosina, Manon, Tatiana, Dido, Nedda, Micaela, Desdemona and Poppea; Berlin Komische Opera, 1979-85; Appearances at the State Operas of Berlin and Dresden; Guest appearances in Japan, Prague, Moscow, Leningrad, Edinburgh, Venice and Madrid; Roles have included Mozart's Fiordiligi and Countess, Agathe, Ariadne, Elsa, Madama Butterfly and Ellen Orford; Sang the Marschallin at the reopening of the Dresden Semper Oper, 1985; Vienna Staatsoper from 1986 as Donna Anna, Arabella, Agathe and the Marschallin; Munich Staatsoper in Daphne, as the Countess in Figaro and Capriccio and Donna Anna; Has also sung in Barcelona, Venice (Elsa), Hamburg (Leonore and Marguerite), Montreal, Geneva, Stuttgart, Lisbon, Toulouse, Graz and Cologne; Season 1992 with Sieglinde in Die Walüre at Bonn; Concert appearances in most major European centres; Has worked with such conductors as Sawallisch, Peter Schneider, Gustav Kuhn, George Prêtre, Riccardo Chailly, Gerd Albrecht, John Pritchard, Nikolaus Harnoncourt and Lorin Maazel. *Recordings include:* Der Rosenkavalier (from the Semper Oper); Bontempi Requiem; Dvořák Stabat Mater; Cosi fan Tutte. *Honours include:* Winner, Toti dal Monte Competition, and Mario del Monaco Competition, 1978; National Award of Slovenia 1979. *Address:* Music International, 13 Ardilaun Road, London N5 2QR, England.

PUTNAM Ashley, b. 10 Aug 1952, New York, USA. (Singer) Soprano. *Education:* University of Michigan, with Elizabeth Mosher and Willis Patterson. *Career:* Norfolk Opera, Virginia, from 1976 as Donizetti's Lucia and the title role in the US premiere of Musgrave's Mary Queen of Scots; New York City Opera debut 1978, as Violetta: later sang Bellini's Elvira, Verdi's Giselda, Thomas' Ophelia and Donizetti's Maria Stuarda; European debut 1978 as Musetta at Glyndebourne; returned for Arabella 1984; Lucia with Scottish Opera; Mozart's Fiordiligi at Venice and for BBC TV, Sifare in Mitridate at Aix, Donna Anna in Brussels and Countess Almaviva in Cologne; Covent Garden debut 1986, as Janáček's Jenůfa; Appearances at Santa Fe in Thomson's The Mother of us All and in the title role of Die Liebe der Danae, 1985; Metropolitan Opera debut 1990, as Donna Elvira; Florence 1990, as Katya Kabanova; sang Ellen Orford in Peter Grimes at the Geneva Opera and Vitellia in La Clemenza di Tito at the 1991 Glyndebourne Festival; Season 1991/92 as Fusako in the US premiere of Henze's Das Verratere Meer, at San Francisco, and the Marschallin at Santa Fe; Concert engagements with the Los Angeles Philharmonic, New York Philharmonic and Concertgebouw Orchestras; Regular concerts at Carnegie Hall. *Recordings:* The Mother of us All, New World Records; Mary Queen of Scots, MMG; Musetta in La Bohème, Philips. *Address:* c/o Lies Askonas Ltd., 186 Drury Lane, London WC2B 5RY, England.

PÜTZ Ruth-Margret, b. 26 Feb. 1931, Krefeld, Germany. Singer (Soprano). *Education:* Studied with Bertold Putz in Krefeld. *Debut:* Cologne 1950, as Nuri in Tiefland by d'Albert. *Career:* Sang at Hanover 1951-57; Stuttgart from 1957, notably as Gilda and Zerbinetta; Bayreuth Festival 1960, as Waldvogel; Salzburg Festival 1961, as Constanze in Die Entfuhrung; Russian Tour with the Capella Coloniensis 1961; Hamburg Staatsoper 1963-68; Guest appearances in Buenos Aires, Helsinki,

Frankfurt, Munich, Nice, Rome, Venice, Naples and Barcelona. *Recordings:*, Bach's Magnificat; Die Lustigen Weiber von Windsor; Lortzing's Undine; Il Barbiere di Siviglia; Queen of Night in Die Zauberflöte; Trionfo by Orff (BASF). *Address:* c/o Bayerische Staatsoper, Postfach 745, D-8000 Munich 1, Germany.

PUYANA Rafael, b. 4 Oct 1931, Bogotá, Colombia. Harpsichordist. *Education:* Studied under Wanda Landowska. *Career:* Now lives in Spain but gives performances throughout the world; Fesitval appearances at Berlin, Ansbach, Holland, Aldeburgh, Harrogate, Besançon and Aix-en-Provence; BBC tv 1985, with sonatas by Scarletti. *Recordings:* Records for Philips and CBS Labels. *Hobbies:* Collecting Old Keyboard Instruments. *Address:* c/o Basil Douglas Artists Management, 8 St George's Terrace, London NW1 8XJ, England.

PY Gilbert, b. 9 Dec 1933, Sete, France. Singer (Tenor). *Debut:* Verviers, Belgium, 1964 as Pinkerton in Madama Butterfly. *Career:* Paris Opera from 1969, notably as Manrico, Don José, Samson, Florestan, Tannhäuser, Lohengrin and in La Damnation de Faust; Paris Opéra-Comique 1969, in the title role of Les Contes d'Hoffmann; Nice Opéra in the local premiere of Sutermeister's Raskolnikov; Toulouse 1970, in Gounod's La Reine de Saba; Guest appearances in Vienna, Munich, Verona, Florence, Barcelona, New Orleans and Budapest; Turin 1973, as Lohengrin; Sang at the 1987 Orange Festival as Jean in Massenet's Hérodiade; Aeneas in Les Troyens at Marseilles 1989. *Recordings include:* Carmen (RCA); La Vestale by Spontini. *Address:* Opéra de Marseille, 2 Ruè Moliére, F-1323 Marseille Cedex 01, France.

PYPER George Earl, b. 5 June 1927, Toronto, Ontario, Canada. Violinst (Orchestral & Soloist); Instructor; Journalist-Music, Theatre & Arts Critic. *Education:* Graduate, Jarvis Collegiate Institute, Toronto, 1945; Studied, Ontario College of Art with Eric Friefeld & Harley Parker, 1948; Acting with Burton James, Banff School Fine Arts; Toronto Conservatory of Music, Jack Montague, Kathleen Parlow Chamber Music; Alexander Brott, McGill Conservatorium, Montreal; Violin: Alexander Chuhaldin, Toronto, Dr Healey Willan, Counterpoint. *Debut:* Soloist, Tomorrow's Concert Stars, CBC, 1944. *Career:* Resident Concertmaster, Royal Alexandra Theatre, Toronto, 1947-54; Performing Member, London Symphony Orchestra, London, 1956-57; Toronto Symphony Orchestra, 1958-63; Violin Instructor, Lakefield College School, 1970-74; Concertmaster, Peterborough Symphony Orchestra, 1972-77, also Soloist, Trent University; Instructor, Sir Sandford Fleming College, Peterborough, Ontario; Solo Violin Concertsin British Columbia, Canada, Gabriola, Victoria, Surrey and at most LDS Chapels, Vancouver Island; Member, First American Violin Congress, Yehudi Menuhin, Washington, DC, 1987; Solo Engagements, West Coast featuring Bach Partitas for Solo Violin. *Hobbies:* Landscape painter; All arts. *Address:* 320-3120 North Isle Hwy, Campbell River, British Columbia, Canada V9W 2H7.

Q

QUARTARARO Florence, b. 31 May 1922, San Francisco, USA. Singer (Soprano). *Education:* Studied with Elizabeth Wells in San Francisco and Pietro Cimini in Los Angeles. *Debut:* Hollywood Bowl 1945, as Leonora in Il Trovatore. *Career:* Metropolitan Opera from 1946, as Micaela (Carmen), Pamina, Verdi's Violetta and Desdemona and Nedda (Pagliacci); San Francisco 1947, as Donna Elvira in Don Giovanni; Guest appearances at Philadelphia and elsewhere in the USA; Arena Flagrea, Naples, 1953 as Margherita in Mefistofele; Many concert appearances.

QUEFFELEC Anne, b. 17 Jan 1948, Paris, France. Concert Pianist. m. 2 children. *Education:* Studied at the Paris Conservatoire and in Vienna with Paul Badura-Skoda, Jörg Demus and Alfred Brendel. *Career:* Solo recitals and orchestral concerts from 1969 in Europe, Japan, USA, Israel and Canada; Conductors include James Conlon, Rudolf Barshai, Colin Davis, Pierre Boulez, Theodor Guschlbauer, Charles Groves, Heinz Holliger, Armin Jordan, Raymond Leppard, David Zinman, Neville Marriner, Jerzy Semkov and Stanislav Skrowaczewski; British appearances with all the BBC Symphony Orchestras, the Royal Liverpool Philharmonic, Bournemouth Symphony, Hallé, Scottish Chamber, Northern Sinfonia, Royal Philharmonic, City of Birmingham Symphony and the London Symphony; Concerts at the Proms in London, Cheltenham, Bath, King's Lynn Festivals; Chamber music recitals with Pierre Amoyal, Augustin Dumay, Regis Pasquier, Frederic Lodeon, the Chilingrian Quartet and Imogen Cooper (piano duo). *Recordings:* Works by Scarlatti, Chopin, Schubert, Liszt, Ravel, Bach, Mendelssohn, Fauré, Hummel and Debussy (Erato); Complete solo works of Satie and Ravel, Poulenc's Concerto for Two Pianos (Virgin Classics). *Honours:* First prizes for piano and for chamber music at the Paris Conservatoire, 1965, 1966; Winner, Munich International 1968; Fifth Prize, Leeds International 1969; Victoire de la Musique Awards, Best French Classical Artist of the Year, 1990. *Hobbies:* Reading; Philosophy, Cooking; Friends; Cycling; Jogging. *Address:* c/o Christopher Tennant Management, Unit 2, 39 Tadema Road, London SW10, England.

QUELER Eve, b. 1 Jan 1936, New York. Conductor/ Director of Opera Orchestra of New York. m. Stanley N. Queler, 1 son, 1 daughter. *Education:* High School of Music and Art, New York, NY; City University of New York, New York, NY; Mannes College of Music, New York, NY; Graduate Conducting Studies with Joseph Rosenstock; at American Institute of Conducting (auspices of St Louis Symphony) with Walter Susskind and Leonard Slatkin; and at Concours de Monte Carlo with Igor Markevitch and Herbert Blomstedt; Accompanying Studies with Paul Ulanovsky and Paul Berl; Analysis with Paul Emerich. *Career:* Musical Assistant, New York City Opera; Musical Assistant, Metropolitan Opera National Company; Founder/ Director/Conductor of Opera Orchestra of New York, 1968-; National Opera Orchestra Workshop created for her by University of Maryland, 1978; Guest Conductor: Cleveland Orchestra; Philadelphia Orchestra; Symphonies of Jacksonville, Edmonton, Toledo, Kansas City, New Jersey, Hartford, Chautauqua, Montreal, Puerto Rico and Colorado Springs, Michigan Chamber Orchestra, Fort Wayne Philharmonic; Opera Companies of: Las Palmas, Gran Teatro Liceo (Barcelona), St Louis, Chattanooga, Providence, Shreveport, Lake George, San Diego, Sydney (Australia) Opera South, Opera de Nice, Oberlin Opera Festival in Lyon, Opera Metropolitan in Caracas, National Theatre of Czechoslovakia, Orchestra Lyrique on Radio France and New York City Opera. *Recordings:* Puccini's Edgar; Donizetti's Gemma di Vergy; Massenet's Le Cid; Verdi's Aroldo; on Columbia Masterworks label; Boito's Nerone; Strauss' Guntram on Hungaroton label. *Contributions to:* An American Conductor in Prague; Musical America/High Fidelity, 1984. *Honours:* Martha Baird Rockefeller Fund for Music Study Grant, 1970; Musician of Month, Musical America Magazine, 1971; Honorary Doctorates from Russell Sage College, 1978 and Colby College, 1983.

Current Management: Herbert Barrett Management, 1776 Broadway, Suite 504, New York, NY 10019, USA. *Address:* Edgar Vincent-Cynthia Robbins Associates, 124 East 40th Street, Suite 304, New York, NY 10016, USA.

QUILICO Gino, b. 29 Apr 1955, New York, USA. Singer (Baritone). *Education:* Graduated University of Toronto 1978; Further vocal studies with Lina Pizzolongo and his father. *Career:* Canadian debut 1978, in a TV performance of The Medium; Sang Mozart's Papageno and Count, Bizet's Escamillo and Verdi's Paolo in the USA; Guest appearances in Dallas, Toulouse and Toronto (Gershwin's Porgy); Member of the Paris Opéra from 1980, in operas by Messager, Britten, Poulenc, Puccini, Gounod, Massenet and Gluck; UK debut with Scottish Opera at the 1982 Edinburgh Festival, as Puccini's Lescaut; Covent Garden debut 1983, as Valentin in Faust; later London appearances as Puccini's Marcello, Donizetti's Belcore, Escamillo and Posa in Don Carlos (1989); Aix-en-Provence Festival 1985 and 1986, as Monteverdi's Orfeo and Mozart's Don Giovanni; Metropolitan Opera debut 1987, as Massenet's Lescaut; Sang Rigoletto in New York 1989; Malatesta in Don Pasquale at Lyon; Sang Dandini in La Cenerentola at the 1988 Salzburg Festival; Rome Opera 1990, as Riccardo in I Puritani. *Recordings include:* Lescaut in Manon (EMI); Dancairo in Carmen (Deutsche Grammophon); Mercutio in Roméo et Juliette (EMI); Monteverdi's Orfeo and Marcello in La Bohéme and Malatesta in Don Pasquale (Erato); Video of 1988 Salzburg Cenerentola. *Address:* c/o Lies Askonas Ltd., 186 Drury Lane, London WC2B 5RY, England.

QUILICO Louis, b. 14 Jan 1929, Montreal, Canada. Opera Singer (Baritone); University Professor. m. 29 Oct 1949, 1 son, 1 daughter. *Education:* Quebec Conservatory; Maness School of Music, New York, USA. *Debut:* New York City Opera. *Career:* New York City Opera, 1949; Spoleto Festival, 1959; San Francisco Opera, 1953; Metropolitan Opera Audition of the Air, 1953; Covent Garden Opera, London, England, 1960; Paris Opera, France, 1962; Vienna Opera, Austria, 1964; Canadian Opera Company, 1959; CBC TV, Canada, Television France, Live from the Metropolitan Opera House of New York, 1982, 1983, 1984, 1985 (New York roles included Golaud, Rigoletto, Iago, Macbeth, Posa, Falstaff, Scarpia, Renato and Germont; Professor, Toronto University; Sang Mickonnet in Adriana Lecouvreur for L'Opéra de Montréal, 1990. *Recordings:* CBC 5000; Pioneer; Video Disk. Live from the Met.; Un Ballo in Maschera (Renato). *Honours:* Honorary Doctor Immeritum, Quebec University; Campanion, Order of Canada. *Hobbies:* Building Model Radio Control Aeroplanes; Electric Trains; Photography; Video Recording. *Current Management:* Columbia Artists Management, New York City, USA. *Address:* 31 Clever Ave., Toronto, Ontario M6B 2V7, Canada.

QUINN Gerard, b. 1962, Irvine, Scotland. Singer (Baritone). *Education:* Studied flute at Napier College, Edinburgh; Singing at the Royal Northern College of Music, Manchester; The National Opera Studio, London; In Vienna with Otto Edelmann and presently with Iris Dell'Acqua. *Career:* Early appearances as Golaud, Pelleas et Mélisande, Escamillo, Mozart's Count and Junius, The Rape of Lucretia; Buxton Festival Opera 1985; Glyndebourne Festival debut 1987, in Capriccio; Glyndebourne Tour, 1988, in La Traviata; Scottish Opera debut 1989, Donner, Das Rheingold; English National Opera debut 1990, as Pantaloon, The Love for Three Oranges; Royal Opera, Covent Garden debut Flemish Deputy, Don Carlo, 1989, Meru, Les Huguenots, 1991 and in 1994 Le Comte in the British premiere of Massenet's Cherubin, and sang various roles with the new Garden Venture in world premieres of Biko Survival Song and The Menaced Assassin; Welsh National Opera debut, 1993, Enrico, Lucia di Lammermoor; English Touring Opera, 1994, Marcello, La Boheme; European Chamber Opera 1993, Count di Luna, Il Trovatore (also recorded), 1994 Count Alamaviva, Le Nozze di Figaro and Rigoletto; Other roles performed include Germont, La Traviata, Ford, Falstaff, Michele, Il Tabarro, Zurga,

The Pearl Fishers, Malatesta, Don Pasquale, Danilo, The Merry Widow, Don Giovanni and Eugene Onegin; Concert repertoire includes Elijah, Carmina Burana, Sea Symphony, Dream of Gerontius, Brahms Requiem and Britten's War Requiem. *Honours include:* International Opera and Bel Canto Duet Competition, Antwerp, with his wife, the soprano, Heather Lorimer; South East Arts Young Musicians Platform; Sir James Caird Travelling Scholarship; Awards from the Vaughan Williams Trust, Countess of Munster and The Peter Moores Foundation. *Address:* c/o International Opera and Concert Artists, 75 Aberdare Gardens, London, NW6 3AN, England.

QUINN James Joseph, b. 30 Apr 1936, Chicago, Illinois, USA. Composer; Lyricist; Professor of Humanities. m. 18 Oct 1958, 3 sons, 2 daughters. *Education:* BMus, 1958, MMus, 1963, DePaul University, Chicago; PhD, Northwestern University, Evanston, Illinois, 1971. *Career:* Professional Musician, 1954-; Published Composer, 1958-; Professor, City College of Chicago, 1965-. *Compositions:* Portrait of the Land, 1958; Chorale of Winds, 1960; Requiem for a Slave, 1966; Ritual D, 1970; Shoes, Symphonic Song Set, Chicago Symphony Orchestra, 1983; Rhapsody for Piano and Orchestra, Chicago Symphony Orchestra, 1984. *Recordings:* Do Black Patent Leather Shoes Really Reflect Up, premiere, 1979; Recording CBS, 1985. *Honours:* American Society of Composers, Authors and Publishers Awards, 1965-; American Bandmaster's Ostwald Award, 1959; Emmy, Chicago, Requiem for a Slave, 1966. *Membership:* American Society of Composers, Authors and Publishers. *Address:* 4 Aberdeen Road, Hawthorn Woods, IL 60047, USA.

QUITTMEYER Susan, b. 1955, USA. Singer (Mezzo-soprano). m. James Morris. *Education:* Studied at Wesleyan University, Illinois, and at the Manhattan School of Music. *Career:* Sang with the America Opera Project, notably in the premiere of John Harbison's A Winter's Tale, at San Francisco, 1979; Guested at St Louis (debut in a revival of Martin y Soler's L'Arbore di Diana, 1978), and sang further at San Francisco from 1981; Sang in Montreal from 1983, Los Angeles 1984; Santa Fe 1984-88, notably in the US premiere of Henze's We Come to the River; Further US appearances in Philadelphia, Cincinnati and San Diego; Sang the Messenger in Monteverdi's Orfeo at Geneva (1986) and Sesto in Giulio Cesare at the Paris Opera, 1987; Further European engagements as Octavian for Netherlands Opera, Cherubino and Annius at Munich and Zerlina at the Vienna Staatsoper; Salzburg Festival debut 1991, as Idamantes in Idomeneo; Concerts with the Los Angeles Philharmonic and the Symphony Orchestras of Oakland, Sacramento and San Francisco; Metropolitan Opera from 1987 as Nicklausse in Les Contes d'Hoffmann and Dorabella; Sang Varvara in Katya Kabanova and Siebel with James Morris, 1991; Other roles include Meg Page, Cherubino, the Composer in Ariadne, Carmen, Pauline (The Queen of Spades) and Zerlina (Miami 1988); Many concert appearances. *Address:* c/o Metropolitan Opera, Lincoln Center, New York, NY 10023, USA.

QUIVAR Florence, b. 3 Mar 1944, Philadelphia, USA. Singer (Mezzo-Soprano). *Education:* Philadelphia Academy of Music; Juilliard School New York. *Career:* Concert appearances with the New York, Los Angeles and Israel Philharmonics, the Cleveland, Philadelphia and Mostly Mozart Festival Orchestras and the Boston Symphony; Conductors include Mehta, Bernstein, Leinsdorf, Boulez, Muti and Colin Davis; Metropolitan Opera debut 1977, as Marina in Boris Godunov; returned to New York for Jocasta (Oedipus Rex), Isabella (L'Italiana in Algeri), Fides (Le Prophète) and Serena in Porgy and Bess; Guest appearances in Berlin, Florence, Geneva, Montreal and San Francisco; Recent engagements include La Damnation de Faust in Geneva, the Wesendonk Lieder in Madrid and London, the Verdi Requiem with the Philharmonia Orchestra, Mahler's 3rd Symphony with the New York Philharmonic and peformances with the Berlin Philharmonic under Giulini; Festival appearances with the Israel Philharmonic in Salzburg, London, Lucerne, Florence and Edinburgh; Sang Ulrica in Un ballo in maschera at the 1990 Salzburg Festival (also televised); Season 1990/91 with Mahler's 2nd and 3rd symphonies (La Scala and New York, and in Japan); Met Opera as Federica in Luisa Miller; Gurrelieder under Zubin Mehta; London Proms 1991, in The Dream of Gerontius. *Recordings:* Rossini's Stabat Mater (Vox); Mahler's 8th Symphony under Seiji Ozawa (Philips); Mendelssohn's Midsummer Night's Dream (Deutsche Grammophon); Berlioz's Romeo and Juliet (Erato); Virgil Thomson's Four Saints in Three Acts (Nonesuch); Verdi Requiem; Un ballo in maschera conducted by Karajan (Deutsche Grammophon); Luisa Miller (Sony); Schoenberg's Gurrelieder. *Address:* Kaye Artists Management, Barratt House, 7 Chertsey Road, Woking, Surrey GU21 3AB, England.

R

RAAD Virginia, b. 13 Aug 1925, Salem, West Virginia, USA. Concert Pianist; Musicologist. *Education:* BA, Wellesley College; New England Conservatory; Diploma, Ecole Normale de Musique, Paris; Doctorate, highest honours, University of Paris. *Career:* Numerous concerts, lectures, master classes, including: Alliance Francaise, Pittsburgh and University of Pittsburg; Walsh College, Ohio; Special Summer Artist, Middlebury College, Vermont; Wellesley College, Massachusetts; University of Michigan-Dearborn; Elmira College, Manhattanville College, New York; Rollins College, Florida; College of William and Mary, Virginia; University of Notre Dame, Indiana; Marietta College, Ohio; Huntington Galleries, West Virginia; Music Teachers Association Convention, Houston, Texas; North Carolina Arts Council and Community Colleges; Mount Mary College, Wisconsin; Portland State University, Oregon; Seton Hill College, Pennsylvania; Mount Union College, Ohio; Berea College, Kentucky; Community concerts, music clubs, TV, radio, USA, Europe; Adjudicator: West Virginia Music Teachers Association; Grant Reviewer, National Endowment for the Humanities, American Society for Aesthetics; West Virginia Federation of Music Clubs; National Guild of Piano Teachers; Grant Reviewer. *Publications include:* L'Influence de Debussy; Amerique (Etats-Unis) in Debussy et l'evolution de la musique au XXe siècle, Paris, 1965; The American Music Teacher, Sketches of Claude Debussy Pianist, 1971; Piano Guild Notes. Notes of a Musician-in-Residence, 1973; The American Music Teacher, 1976, 1977; Clavier, Debussy and the Magic of Spain, 1979; The Piano Sonority of Claude Debussy, NY, 1994. *Address:* 60 Terrace Avenue, Salem, WV 26426, USA.

RABE Folke, b. 28 Oct 1935, Stockholm, Sweden. Composer; Head of Radio Production Department. m. Eva Rehnstrom, 1 May 1992, 1 son, 2 daughters. *Education:* Composition, Trombone, Music Pedagogy, Royal College of Music, Stockholm, 1957-64; Music Teachers' Examination; Community School Leader's Examination. *Career:* Jazz Musician, 1950-; Composer, 1957-; Writer on Musical Subjects, 1959-; Assistant, Royal College of Music, Stockholm, 1964-68; Staff Member, 1968-80, Programme Director, 1977-80, Institute for National Concerts, Stockholm; Member: Culture Quartet, 1963-73, New Culture Quartet, 1983-; Music Producer, 1980-92, Head of Production Department, 1992-, Swedish National Radio. *Compositions include:* Bolos for 4 trombones (with J Bark), 1962; Rondes for choir, 1964; Eh??, electronic music, 1967; Joe's Harp for choir, 1970; Basta for solo trombone, 1982; To Love for choir, 1984; Shazam for solo trumpet, 1984; Escalations for brass quintet, 1988; All the Lonely People, trombone concerto, 1990; Nature, Herd and Relatives, French horn concerto, 1991. *Recordings:* Bolos; Joe's Harp; Rondes; Eh??; Basta; Shazam; No Hambones on the Moon, film with Culture

RABES C-A. Lennart, b. 1938, Eskilstuna, Sweden. Pianist; Harpsichordist; Organist; Conductor; Lecturer; Editor; Examiner. *Education:* Music Academy, Zurich, Switzerland; Accademia Chigiana, Siena, Italy; ARCM (London); Studied piano with Professor S. Sundell, Stockholm, E. Cavallo, Milan, B. Siki, Zurich, M. Tagliaferro, Paris, J. von Karolyi, Munich; Studied conducting with C. von Garaguly, Stockholm, P. von Kempen, Siena, Sir Adrian Boult, London; BA Music, by the Pacific Western University, Los Angeles, CA, USA, 1992. *Debut:* As pianist and conductor, Stockholm, 1951. *Career:* Performances in major cities of Europe and USA; Many recordings for Swedish, Austrian, French, Swiss and German broadcasting companies; Musical Director, International Liszt Centre, Stockholm; Organist, various churches in Munich, 1960-66, Swiss Church, London, 1966-78; Founder, Musical Director, Deal Summer Music Festival, Deal, Kent, England, 1981-83, Säbylund Festival, Sweden, 1985-; Repetiteur at Norrlandsoperan, Umeå, Sweden, 1985-88; Has given concerts at historical places including On Wagner's Erard at the Wagner Museum, Tribschen, Lucerne, Switzerland, 1985; Lecturer for research associations, Universities radio and conservatories;

Examiner for Associated Board, Royal Schools of Music, London; Currently working at Operastudio 67 and Roslagsoperan, Stockholm. *Recordings:* Piano works by Liszt, (Delysé). *Address:* Synålavägen 5, S-161 49 Bromma, Sweden.

RABIN Shira, b. 1 April 1970, Tel-Aviv, Israel. Violinist. *Education:* Studied at the Juilliard School with Dorothy DeLay. *Debut:* Played with the Israel Philharmonic 1979. *Career:* Appeared in the International Huberman Week with Isaac Stern and the Israel Philharmonic 1983; Toured Europe 1983, Canada coast-to-coast tour 1985; Played with Henryk Szeryng during Israel Philharmonic Jubilee Season 1987; Soloist in the Stradivarius Year in Cremona; Israel representative in Italian Nights of Music with Zubin Mehta; Gala concert at Carnegie Hall with Isaac Stern; Musical Discovery of 1989 in Italy, after recital debut in Milan; German debut Feb. 1991, with the Bavarian Radio Symphony Orchestra; US debut 1992 with the Philadelphia Orchestra under Riccardo Muti; Further concerts with the Pittsburgh Orchestra under Lorin Maazel. *Address:* IMG Artists Europe, Media House, 3 Burlington Lane, Chiswick, London, W4 2TH, England.

RABSILBER Michael, b. 8 Sept 1953, Stassfurt, Magdeburg, Germany. Singer (Tenor). *Education:* Studied at Leipzig Musikhochschule. *Debut:* Stadtheater Halle 1980 in Wagner-Régeny's Die Burger von Calais. *Career:* Sang at Halle until 1984 then joined the Komische Oper Berlin, with guest appearances in Leipzig and Dresden; Roles have included Mozart's Melmonte and Don Ottavio, Lensky, Ferrando Tamino, Max in Der Freischutz, Nicolai's Fenton and Pinkerton; Sang Zhivny in a production by Joachim Herz of Janáček's Osud, Dresden 1991; Frequent concert engagements. *Address:* c/o Komische Oper Berlin, Behrenstrasse 55-57, 1086 Berlin, Germany.

RADIGUE Eliane, b. 24 Jan 1932, Paris, France. Composer. m. Arman, 17 Feb. 1953 (div. 1971), 1 son, 2 daughters. *Education:* Studied with Pierre Schaeffer, Pierre Henry; School of the Arts, New York University, University of Iowa, California Institute of the Arts, USA. *Career includes:* Work with electronic sounds on tape. Recent performances: Salon des Artistes Decorateurs, Paris; Foundation Maeght, St Paul de Vence; Albany Museum of the Arts, New York; Gallery Rive Droite, Paris; Gallery Sonnabend, New York; Gallery Yvon Lambert, Paris; etc. Festivals including: Como, Italy; Paris Autumn; Festival Estival, Paris; International Festival of Music, Bourges, France; etc. Also: New York Cultural Center; Experimental Intermedia Foundation, New York; Vanguard Theater, Los Angeles; Mills College, Oakland, California; University of Iowa; Wesleyan University; San Francisco Art Institute. *Compositions include:* Environmental Music, 1969; OHMNT-Record Object, 1971; Labyrinthe Sonore, tape music, 1971; Chry-ptus, 1971; Geelriandre, 1972; Biogenesis, 1974; Adnos, 1975; Adnos II, 1980; Adnos III, 1982; Prelude a Milarepa, 1982; 5 songs of Milarepa, 1984; Jetsun Mila, 1986. *Recordings:* Songs of Milarepa, New York; Mila's Journey Inspired by a Dream; Jetsun Mila, cassette, New York. *Contributions to:* Musique en Jeu, 1973; Art Press, 1974, Guide Musical, 1975. *Address:* 22 rue Liancourt, 75014 Paris, France.

RADNOFSKY Kenneth Alan, b. 31 July 1953, Bryn Mawr, Pennsylvania, USA. Saxophonist. m. Nancy Abramchuk, 1 May 1977. 2 daughters. *Education:* BM cum laude, University of Houston, Texas; MM, with honours, New England Conservatory of Music, Boston. *Career:* Carnegie Hall Debut, 1985 performance of Gunther Schuller Saxophone Concerto written for Radnofsky; European debut, 1987 with Leipzig Gewandhaus Orchestra as first ever Saxophone Soloist, under direction of Kurt Masur; First ever saxophone soloist with Dresden Staatskapelle Orchestra and Pittsburgh Symphony Orchestra; Solo works premiered or dedicated to Radnofsky by: Milton Babbitt, Donald Martino, Gunther Schuller, Morton Subotnick, Lee Hoiby, David Amram, Alan Hovhaness; Saxophonist with Boston Symphony, 1977-; Soloist with BBC, Boston

Pops and numerous USA orchestras. *Recordings:* With Boston Symphony as saxophone in Berg Violin Concerto; Bass clarinet in Schoenberg Kammersymphonie with Felix Galimir; Soprano Sax in works by Roger Bourland. *Contributions to:* Numerous articles in Saxophone Journal. *Honours:* Appointed youngest member of Faculty, New England Conservatory, 1976. *Current Management:* Jecklin Associates. *Address:* P O Box 1016, E Arlington, Massachusetts 02174, USA.

RADOVAN Ferdinand, b. 26 Jan 1938, Rijeka, Yugoslavia. Singer (Baritone). *Education:* Studied in Belgrade. *Debut:* Belgrade National Opera 1964 as Germont. *Career:* Sang at Ljubljana 1965-67, Graz 1967-74, Dortmund 1974-77; Guest appearances at Vienna Volksoper, Dusseldorf, Essen, Bordeaux and Prague and the States Operas of Hamburg and Munich; Returned to Yugoslavia 1977; Other roles have included Escamillo, Mozart's Count and Don Giovanni, Verdi's Rigoletto, Nabucco, Amonasro, Renato, Luna and Iago; Prince Igor, Scarpia, Barnaba in La Gioconda, Nelusko in L'Africaine, Jochanaan, Enrico, Gerard and Milhaud's Christophe Colombe; Concert and oratorio engagements. *Address:* Slovensko Narodno Gledalisce, Zupancicava 1, 61000 Ljubljana, Yugoslavia.

RAE Caroline Anne, b. 1960, Leeds, Yorkshire, England; Pianist; Writer on Music; Lecturer. *Education:* BA, Oxon, 1982, MA, Oxon, 1986, D.Phil, Oxon, 1990, Somerville College, Oxford; ARCM (P.pf) 1984; Diploma Music, Hochschule für Musik und Theater, Hannover, FRG, 1988. *Debut:* 1982. *Career:* As pianist: solo recitals, lecture-recitals, chamber music, master-classes, UK, Germany & France; 2 piano duo with Robert Sherlaw Johnson; appearance on TV and BBC radio. As lecturer: Tutor in Music at Oxford University, 1984-88; Temporary Lecturer in piano at Oxford Polytechnic, 1984 & 1988; Lecturer in Music at University of Wales, College of Cardiff 1989-. *Publications:* Monograph: The Music of Maurice Ohana, to appear.*Contributions to:* New Grove Dictionary of Opera; Die Neue Zeitschrift für Musik; The Musical Times; Les Cahiers du Centre International de Recherches en Esthétique Musicale. *Address:* Department of Music, University of Wales, College of Cardiff, Corbett Road, Cardiff CF1 3EB.

RAE (John) Charles Bodman. b. 10 Aug 1955, Catterick, England. Composer. m. Dorota Kwiatkowska, 14 Apr 1984. *Education:* Cambridge University, 1974-78; Chopin Academy of Music, Warsaw, 1981-83; Piano Studies with Miss Fanny Waterman, Composition Studies with Edward Cowie, Robert Sherlaw Johnson and Robin Holloway; MA (Cantab); PhD (Leeds); ARCM; FRSA. *Career:* Broadcaster: Contributions as Writer, Presenter for BBC Radio 3 including Glocken, Cloches, Kolokola (6 hour series on European Bells); An Affair with Romanticism, features on Penderecki and Lutoslawski's; Lecturer, Composition and Analysis 1979- 81, 1983-92, Head of School of Creative Studies 1992-, City of Leeds College of Music; Visiting Composer, University of Cincinnati College-Conservatory of Music, Ohio, USA 1993. *Compositions:* Six Verses of Vision, 1976; String Quartet, 1981; Jede Irdische Venus, 1982; Fulgura Frango, 1986; Donaxis Quartet, 1987. *Publications:* The Music of Lutoslawski, (Faber and Faber), 1994; Bells in European Music (in progress); Many articles on Music of Lutoslawski. *Memberships:* Royal Musical Association; Fellow of Royal Society of Arts; Composers Guild of Great Britain. *Address:* Crossbeck House, Crossbeck Road, Ilkley LS29 9JN, West Yorkshire.

RAE-GERRARD Colleen Margaret, b. 7 Jan 1938, Auckland, New Zealand. Pianist; Fortepianist. m. Ronald Joseph Gerrard, 16 Sept 1961, 1 son, 1 daughter. *Education:* Licenciate, Royal School of Music, 1958; BMus, 1972; B Mus Honours, 1977. *Debut:* Auckland, 1955. *Career:* Appearances as recitalist, concerto soloist, accompanist and chamber music player in New Zealand, Australia, UK and Vienna, Austria; Network artist for radio New Zealand and ABC Australia; Appearances for TVNZ - Television New Zealand; Specializes in early pianos and has given many concerts

on a Stein copy in Australia and New Zealand; Toured for New Zealand Music Federation, 1981 and 1982; Concerts also in Brussells, Greece, Holland. *Recordings:* Solo piano, Haydn, Debussy, Villa-Lobos, Ode Record, 1972; The Colonial Piano, played on 2 historic pianos, 1978; On Wenlock Edge with tenor Anthony Benfell and a string quartet of NZSO players, 1981; Romanza with soprano Anna Langston and clarinettist Deborah Rawson, 1983; Arianna a Naxos with contralto Flora Edwards. *Honours:* Auckland Star Piano Concerto, 1959; Waikato Times Piano Concerto Contest, 1959; Queen Elizabeth II Arts Council Study Awards, 1977 and 1983. *Hobby:* Yachting. *Address:* 91 Fox Street, Ngaio, Wellington, New Zealand.

RAEKALLIO Matti Juhani, b. 14 Oct 1954, Helsinki, Finland. Pianist; Lecturer. m. Sinikka Alstela, 7 May 1977, 1 son, 1 daughter. *Education:* Turku Institute of Music, 1967-72; Private lessons with Maria Diamond Curcio, London, England, 1972-73; With Dieter Weber, Vienna Music Academy, Austria, 1974-76; Leningrad Conservatory, USSR, 1977-78; Diploma, Sibelius Academy, Finland, 1978. *Debut:* As orchestra soloist, Turku, 1971; Solo, Helsinki, 1975. *Career:* Extensive tours with every professional Finnish symphony orchestra 1971-, Recitals in Nordic countries 1971-, in Finland 1975-, in Central Europe 1979-; Recitals in USA, 1981-; First American tour as orchestra soloist with Helsinki Philharmonic Orchestra, 1983; Visiting Professor, Western Michigan University, 1984-85; Lecturer, Sibelius Academy, Finland; Recitals in the USA, 1988, Helsinki Festival, 1981-87, Savonlinna Opera Festival, 1988; Beethoven Complete Sonatas in five Finnish cities, 1989-90; Concerto repertoire includes over 40 works for Piano and Orchestra. *Recordings:* For Fuga, Finlandia, Melodiya and Ondine labels including e.g. Complete Prokofiev Sonatas; Numerous for the archives of the Finnish Broadcasting Company. *Contributions to:* Music Critic, Turun Sanomat newspaper, 1977. *Current Management:* Jonathan Wentworth Associates, Ltd, USA. *Membership:* Board of Directors, Society for Finnish Concert Soloists. *Hobbies:* Chess; Literature. *Address:* Kauppiaankatu 8-10 A2, 00160 Helsinki, Finland.

RAES Godfried-Willem, b. 3 Jan 1952, Ghent, Belgium. Musicmaker. m. Moniek Darge, 15 Sept 1973. *Education:* Masters Degree in Musicology 1973, Ghent University; Masters Degree in Philosophy 1975; Doctors Degree in Musicology 1993; Piano, Clarinet, Composition, Avant-Garde Music, Royal Conservatory of Music, Ghent. *Debut:* With Logos-ensemble 1968. *Career:* Concert Manager for Philharmonic Society, Brussels 1973-88; Leader of The Logos-Ensemble 1968-; Director of The Logos-Foundation 1977-; Professor of Experimental Music Composition and Performance at The Ghent Royal Conservatory 1982-. *Compositions:* Bellenorgel; Attitudes; Epitafium; Cues; Fortepiano; Holosound; A Book of Fugues; A Book of Chorals; Symphony for Singing Bicycles; Compositions for traditional and newly invented instruments: Pneumafoon, Junks, Sirene; Sound sculptures Radar-harps and automats; Hex (a concerto for violin and full automated orchestra), A Book of Moves, for non-impact instruments of his own design. *Recordings:* All major international radio and television stations; Records on IGLOO Label: Bellenorgel, Improvisation/Composition, Pneumafoon. *Publications:* Creative Music Making in an Anti-Creative Society? (Essay 1976); Improvisation 1981-93; An Invisible Musical Instrument, (doctoral dissertation, 1993).*Honours:* Louis Paul Boon Prize, 1982; Tech-Art Prize, 1990. *Hobbies:* Digital and analog microelectronics, computer, programming and architecture. *Address:* c/o Logos Foundation, Kongostraat 35, B-9000 Ghent, Belgium.

RAFFAELLI Piero, b. 8 Apr 1949, Cesena, Italy. Violin Teacher and Concertist. m. Santarelli Mariangela, 18 May 1975, 2 daughters. *Education Includes:* Violin Studies, Diploma, Conservatory of Music, G.B. Martini, Bologna, 1971, Viola Studies; Primary School Teachers Diploma, 1968; Master Courses with various teachers: *Debut:* 7 February 1968, Italy. *Career:* Radio appearances in Italy and Norway; Italian and European Concerts wth Ensemble I Cameristi di Venezia; Solo Concerts with Capella Academica of Vienna, Italy; Chamber Music Group Layer & Soloist, Italy, Europe, North America with Italian Ensembles, 1971-73; Leader, Guitar Trio Paganini, (also as viola player); Duo Recitals with Main M. Halls Barcelona, Vienna, Berlin W, Oslo, Trondheim, Greece, Italy; Violin Teacher, Conservatory of Music, Bologna, 1978-. *Recordings:* With Ensemble E. Melkus; Wien; Solo Violin Works by M. Kich, (Yugoton) dedicated to him, 1981; Contemporary Violin Chamber Music Recording, 1982. *Publications:* Revisions of Violin Works in First Printing for Zanibon/Padova, Italy; A Corelli 2 Sonate for Violin and Violoncello, 1979; A. Vivaldi Concerto F. 1 n 237 in D for violin, strings, cembalo, 1980; N. Paganini 3 Duetti Concertanti for Violin and Violoncello, 1982. *Address:* Via Filli Latini 112, I -47020, S. Giorgio di Cesena, Italy.

RAFFANTI Dano, b. 5 Apr 1948, Lucca, Italy. Singer (Tenor). *Education:* Studied at the La Scala School. *Debut:* Scala School 1976, in Bussotti's Nottetempo. *Career:* Verona 1978, in Orlando Furioso: Dallas 1980, in the US premiere of Vivaldi's opera; San Francisco 1980, as Almaviva in Il Barbiere di Siviglia; Houston 1981-82, as Giacomo in La Donna del Lago by Rossini; Metropolitan Opera from 1981, as Alfredo, Rodolfo, the Duke of Mantua, Edgardo, Goffredo in Handel's Rinaldo and the Italian Singer in Der Rosenkavalier; Teatro San Carlo Naples and Covent Garden, 1983 and 1984, as Tebaldo in I Capuleti e i Montecchi by Bellini; Guest appearances in Hamburg, Berlin, Santiago, Bilbao and at the Landestheater Salzburg; Maggio Musicale Florence 1989, as Idomeneo; Sang the Duke of Mantua at Turin, Dec 1989; Florence 1990, as Ugo in Donizetti's Parisina; Season 1992 as Cléomène in La Siège de Corinthe by Rossini at Genoa. *Recordings include:* Fra Diavolo (Cetra); I Capuleti e i Montecchi (EMI); La Donna del Lago (CBS). *Address:* c/o Harrison/Parrott Ltd., 12 Penzance Place, London W11 4PA, England.

RAFFEINER Walter, b. 8 Apr 1947, Wolfsberg, Germany. Singer (Tenor).*Education:* Studied in Vienna and Cologne. *Debut:* Sang at Hagen in Germany as a baritone. *Career:* Sang at Darmstadt as a tenor 1979 and appeared in Frankfurt from 1980 as Max, Parsifal, Florestan, Stolzius in Die Soldaten and the Painter and Negro in Lulu; Sang at Rouen and the Paris Opera 1982 as Siegmund and Lohengrin; Guest appearances in Hamburg, Freiburg, Vienna, Dusseldorf and Munich; Salzburg Festival 1986 as Silvanus Schuller in the premiere of Penderecki's Schwarze Maske; Appeared as Siegmund with the Kassel Opera at the restored Amsterdam Opera House; Other roles have included Tristan, Pedro in Tiefland, Ivanovich in The Gambler, Sergei in Katerina Ismailova, Shuisky, Herod, Yannakos in Martinů's Greek Passion and Tichon in Katya Kabanova. *Recording:* Drum Major in Wozzeck. *Address:* c/o Staatstheater, Friedrichplatz 15, 3500 Kassel, Germany.

RAFFELL Anthony, b. 1940, London. Singer (Baritone). *Career:* Sang first with a touring company with the works of Gilbert and Sullivan; Opera debut Glyndebourne 1966, in Werther by Massenet; Sang at Gelsenkirchen, Karlsruhe and Bremen; Member of the Stuttgart Opera from 1985; Metropolitan Opera debut 1983 as Kurwenal in Tristan and Isolde, returning as Hans Sachs 1985; Appearances in Ring cycles with the English National Opera and in Seattle; Further appearances in Turin (Klingsor), Rome (Wotan), Rio de Janeiro (Jochanaan), Lisbon (Falstaff), Parma, Trieste and Nancy; Metropolitan Opera 1989, as Gunther in Götterdämmerung; Sang Telramund at Buenos Aires, 1991; Regularly at Vienna State Opera, Hamburg, Berlin and Stuttgart; More recently in Buenos Aires, Tales of Hoffmann, as a guest, 1993. *Recordings include:* Der Ring des Nibelungen, conducted by James Levine, also on video (Deutsche Grammophon). *Address:* 14 Stevenson Drive, Abington, Oxon OX14 1SN, England.

RÁFOLS Alberto Pedro, b. 7 July 1942, Guantanamo, Cuba. Pianist/Professor of Music.

Education: BM 1967; MM 1969; University of Illinois; DMA, University of Washington 1975; Fulbright Scholar: Academia Marshall, Barcelona, Spain 1970-72; Academia Chigiana, Siena, Italy, Summer 1971; Teachers: Alicia de Larrocha, Bela Siki, Howard Karp. *Career:* Performances: Throughout the United States, Canada, Peru, Bolivia, Portugal, Spain and Colombia including Alaska, Hawaii and Azores Islands. Academic Appointments: University of Illinois 1969-70; University of Washington, Seattle 1975-84; University of Alaska (part-time) 1982-84; University of Texas in San Antonio 1984-. *Recordings:* Live Broadcasts, Nationwide; Radio Television: Espanola, Madrid 1981; Barcelona 1984. *Hobbies:* Visual Arts/Literature. *Address:* Division of Music, The University of Texas at San Antonio, San Antonio, TX 78285, USA.

RAFTERY J Patrick, b. 4 Apr 1951, Washington DC, USA. Singer (Baritone). *Education:* Studied with Armen Boyajian. *Debut:* Chicago Lyric Opera 1980, as Shchelkalov in Boris Godunov. *Career:* European debut 1982, at the Théâtre du Châtelet, Paris, as Zurga in Les Pêcheurs de Perles; Glyndebourne 1984, as Guglielmo; Santa Fe, New Mexico, 1984 in Verdi's Il Corsaro and Gwendoline by Chabrier; Covent Garden debut 1985, as Mozart's Count; Further appearances with the New York City Opera and in Hamburg, Brussels, and Cologne; Santiago 1988, as Luna in Il Trovatore; Rome Opera 1988, as Puccini's Lescaut; Sang Belcore in L'Elisir d'Amore at Genoa in 1989; Other roles include Escamillo, Mercutio (Roméo et Juliette), Eugene Onegin, Valentin (Faust), Yeletsky in The Queen of Spades and Rossini's Figaro; Sang Rossini's Figaro at Vancouver, 1991.

RAGACCI Susanna, b. 1959, Stockholm, Sweden. Singer (Soprano). *Education:* Studied in Florence. *Career:* Sang first at Rome as Rossini's Rosina, then appeared at Florence, Venice, Palermo, Turin and La Scala Milan; Sang Gilda in Dublin and at the Wexford Festival in Cimarosa's Astuzie Femminili; Opera de Wallonie at Liège 1987-88 as Rosina and as Egloge in Mascagni's Nerone; Sang at Bologna in the 1987 Italian premiere of Henze's English Cat and at Florence as the Italian Singer in Capriccio; Théâtre du Châtelet Paris 1992 as Sofia in Il Signor Bruschino. *Recordings:* Vivaldi's Catone in Utica and La Caduta di Adamo by Galuppi; I Pazzi per Progresso by Donizetti; L'Elisir d'amore.

RAGIN Derek Lee, b. 17 June 1958, West Point, New York, USA. Singer (Counter-tenor). *Education:* Arts High School, Newark, New Jersey; Newark Boys Chorus School, 1969-72; Piano Scholarship, Newark Community Center of Arts, 1970-75; Piano, BM, MMT, Oberlin Conservatory of Music, 1980. *Debut:* Opera - Festwoche der Alten Musik, Innsbruck, Austria, 1983. *Career:* Recital Debut, Wigmore Hall, London, 1984; Debut Recital, Aldeburgh Festival, 1984; Sang title role in Handel's Tamerlano, both at Lyon Opera, France and at Göttingen Handel Festival; BBC Debut Recital, 1984; Debut at the Metropolital Opera in Handel's Giulio Cesare, September 1988; Recitals and Oratorio continued in Frankfurt, Munich, Stuttgart, Cologne, Venice, Milan, Bologna, New York, Amsterdam, Maryland Handel Festival, London, Washington DC, Atlanta, Boston, San Francisco; Made Salzburg debut in Gluck's Orfeo, 1990; Gluck's Orfeo in Budapest, 1991; Season 1992 in Conti's Don Chisciotte at Innnsbruck and as Britten's Oberon at Saint Louis. *Recordings:* Role of Spirit in Purcell's Dido and Aeneas (Philips Label), 1985; Title role in Handel's Tamerlano (Erato Label), 1985; Handel's Flavio and Tolomeo in Giulio Cesare, Harmonia Mundi; Handel's Saul, Philips Label; Vivaldi Cantatas, Etcetera Label and CCS. *Hobbies:* Dancing; Movie-goer; Reader of all kinds of magazines *Current Management:* Colbert Artists Management, New York, USA. *Address:* 106 1/2 9th Avenue, Newark, NJ 07107, USA.

RAGNARSSON Hjalmar Helgi, b. 23 Sept 1952, Isafjordur, Iceland. Composer. m. Sigridur Asa Richardsdottir, 2 sons, 1 daughter. *Education:* Isafjordur

School of Music, 1959-69; Reykjavik College of Music, 1969-72; BA 1974, Brandeis University, USA, 1972-74; Rijksuniversiteit Utrecht-Instituut voor Sonologie, 1976-77; MFA 1980, Cornell University, USA, 1977-80. *Career:* Conductor, The University Choir of Iceland, 1980-83; Compositions performed in Eastern and Western Europe, USA and Canada; Nordic Music Days, 1976, 1978, 1984 and 1986; International Rostrum of Composers, UNESCO, 1979 and 1983; Works at ISCM Festivals, 1980, 1985 and 1988; Co-Director, Iceland Music Information Centre; President of the Composers Society of Iceland, 1988-92 and President of the Union of Icelandic Artists since 1991. *Compositions include:* Six Songs to Icelandic Poems for voice and chamber ensemble, 1978-79; Romanza for flute, clarinet and piano, 1981; Trio for clarinet, cello and piano, 1983-84; Canto for mixed choirs and synthesizer, 1982; Five Preludes for piano, 1983-85; Music for theatre including Icelandic National Theatre and Reykjavik Municipal Theatre; Music for television films, Icelandic State Television Service and Swedish State Television; Mass, for mixed choir 1982-89; Tengsl for voice and string quartet, 1988; Spjotalög for orchestra, 1989; Raudur Thradur-ballet music for orchestra, 1989; Rhodymenie Palmata, chamber opera, 1992. *Recordings:* Conductor, Icelandic Choral Works with the University Choir of Iceland. *Publications:* Jon Leifs, Icelandic Composer: Historical Background, Biography, Analysis of Selected Works, MFA thesis, 1980; A Short History of Icelandic Music to the Beginning of the Twentieth Century, 1985. *Memberships:* Composers Society of Iceland. *Address:* Laekjarhjalli 22, 200 Kopavogur, Iceland.

RAICHEV Rouslan, b. 2 May 1924, Milan, Italy. Conductor. *Education:* Studied the piano in Milan, then with Leopold Reichwein, Emil Sauer and Karl Bohm in Vienna (until 1944). *Career:* Assistant at the Vienna Staatsoper 1942-43; Chief Conductor at the Konigsberg Opera 1943- 44; Conductor of the Varna Opera, Bulgaria, 1946-48; Conductor of the Sofia Opera 1948-89 (Musical Director 1981-89); Conducted the State Orchestra of Plovdiv 1968 and directed stage works at the Schleswig-Holstein Festival 1974-78; Guest conductor at the Vienna Staatsoper, La Scala Milan and the Paris Opéra. *Recordings include:* Rachmaninov Aleko (AVM).

RAILTON Ruth, b. 14 Dec 1915, Folkestone, England. Musician; Pianist; Conductor. m. Cecil Harmsworth King, 1962. *Education:* Royal Academy of Music, London; Pupil of Rachmaninov, Myra Hess and Schnabel; Conducting with Sir Henry Wood; LRAM; ARAM; FRAM. *Career:* Director of Music or Choral Work for many schools and societies 1937-48; Founder and Musical Director of the National Youth Orchestra, 1946-66; Adjudicator, Federation of Music Festivals; Governor Royal Ballet School, 1966-74; Director of National Concert Hall, Dublin, 1981-86; President, Ulster College of Music; Chairman, National Children's Orchestra, 1989. *Publication:* Daring to Excel, 1992. *Honours:* OBE, 1954; DBE, 1966; Honorary LLD, Aberdeen University; Honorary FRCM, FTCL and RMCM; Professor, Chopin Conservatoire, Warsaw; Professor Conservatoire of Azores. *Memberships:* ISM; University Womens Club. *Hobbies:* Interested in everything. *Address:* Ardoyne House, Pembroke Park, Dublin 4, Republic of Ireland.

RAIMONDI Gianni, b. 13 Apr 1923, Bologna, Italy. Singer (Tenor). *Education:* Studied with Gennaro Barra-Caracciolo and with Ettore Campogalliani in Milan. *Debut:* Bologna 1947, as the Duke of Mantua. *Career:* Sang Pinkerton at Budrio, 1947; Bologna 1948, as Ernesto in Don Pasquale; Florence 1952, in Rossini's Armida, with Callas; London, Stoll Theatre, 1953; Naples 1955, in the premiere of Madame Bovary by Pannain; La Scala Milan from 1956, notably as Alfredo and as Lord Percy in Anna Bolena, opposite Callas, and in Mosè and Semiramide (1958, 1962); US debut San Francisco 1957; Verona Arena from 1957; Guest appearances in Vienna from 1959, Munich from 1960; Metropolitan Opera from 1965, as Rodolfo, Cavaradossi and Faust; Hamburg Staatsoper 1969-77; Other appearances in Paris 1953, Chicago, Dallas, Lisbon, Edinburgh, Geneva,

Zurich and Helsinki; Other roles included Gabriele Adorno, Ismaele (Nabucco), Arrigo in Les Vêpres Siciliennes, Pollione, and Edgardo. *Recordings:* La Favorita (Cetra); La Traviata (Deutsche Grammophon); Linda di Chamounix; Maria Stuarda, with Callas; I Puritani; Armida. *Address:* c/o Teatro alla Scala, Via Filodrammerici 2, Milan, Italy.

RAIMONDI Ruggero, b. 3 Oct 1941, Bologna, Italy. Bass. m. Isabel Maier. *Education:* Student, Teresa Pediconi, Rome, 1961-62; Maestro Piervenanzi, 1963-65. *Debut:* Spoleto 1964. *Career:* Appeared Rome Opera, Principal opera houses in Italy; Metropolitan Opera, 1970; Munich; La Scala; Lyric Opera, Chicago; Paris Opera; Sang Don Giovanni at Glyndebourne, 1969; Covent Garden 1972, as Fiesco in Simon Boccanegra; Vienna Staatsoper 1982, as Don Quichotte, Hamburg, 1985, as Gounod's Mephistopheles; Sang Selim in Il turco in Italia; Chicago 1987, as Mozart's Count; Pesaro 1985 and Vienna as Don Profondo in Il Viaggio a Reims; Sang in the opening concert at the Bastille Opéra 1989, leukaemia relief with José Carreras, 1991; 25th Anniversary Celebration at the Barbican Hall 1990; Sang Attila in a new production of Verdi's opera at Covent Garden, Oct 1990; Don Giovanni at the Theater an der Wien, Vienna, 1990; Season 1992 as Massenet's Don Quichotte at Florence and Monte Carlo, Scarpia in a televised Tosca from Rome, Rossini's Basilio at Madrid and Caracalla; Engaged as Rossini's Mosè at Covent Garden, 1994. *Recordings:* 2 Verdi Requiems; complete operas Attila, I Vespri Siciliani, La Bohème, Aida, Don Carlos, Forza del Destino, Il Pirata, Norma, Don Giovanni, Carmen, Nozze di Figaro, Mose, Italiana in Algeri, Boris Godunov; sang Don Giovanni in Joseph Losey's film of Mozart's opera; sang Escamillo in Francesco Rosi's Carmen; Maurice Béjart's 6 Characters in Search of a Singer; Boris in Zulawsky's film Boris Godunov; played in Alain Resnais' Life is a Bed of Roses. *Honour:* Recipient Competition Award Spoleto; Officier des Arts et Lettres in France; Commendatore Della Republica in Italy; Chevalier de l'ordre de Malte. *Address:* c/o Columbia Artists Management Incorporated, 165 W. 57th Street, New York, NY 10019, USA.

RAINER Alice and Clarice (Twins), b. 28 Aug 1932, Opp, Alabama, USA. Concert Piano-Duettists. *Education:* Diploma, Opp High School 1950; BMus. Degree, University of Montevallo School of Music 1954; Aspen Music School, Aspen, Colorado 1958-59; Private Study with Vronsky and Babin, Duo-Pianists 1960-61. *Debut:* Judson Hall, New York City. *Career:* Concert also broadcast, National Gallery of Art, Washington DC; Haarlem Philharmonic Society of New York City; Woman to Woman, National TV, Los Angeles, California; Philadelphia, PA; Chicago, IL; Minneapolis, MN; Oklahoma, OK; Mobile, AL; Jackson, MS; Memphis, TN; Charleston, SC; West Palm Beach, FL; Richmond, VA; Ft. Wayne, IN; Colorado Springs, CO; Winston-Salem, NC. *Contributions to:* Music Journal, Viva le Piano Duet!; Music Journal, Piano Duet Treasure Chest; Piano Technicians Journal, The Unseen Artist. *Hobbies:* Constant Research into Original Piano Duet Repertoire and Little Known Duets; Twin Toy Poodles; Flowers and Plants. *Current Management:* The Alkahest Agency, Atlanta, GA, USA. *Address:* 409 Sellars Drive, Opp, AL 36467, USA.

RAITIO Pentti, b. 4 June 1930, Pieksamaki, Finland. Composer; Music Educator. *Education:* Studied composition with Joonas Kokkonen, 1961-63; Erik Bergman, 1963-66; diploma, Sibelius Academy, Helsinki, 1966. *Career:* Director, Hyvinkaa School of Music, 1967-; Chairman, Lahti Organ Festival, 1981-85; Association of Finnish Music Schools, 1986-. *Compositions:* Orchestral: 13, 1964; Audiendum, 1967; 5 Pieces for String Orchestra, 1975; Petandrie, 1977; Noharmus, 1978; Noharmus II, 1980; Canzone d'autunno, 1982; Flute Concerto, 1983; Due figure, 1985; Yoldia arctica, 1987; Chamber: Small Pieces for Brass Instruments, 1974; Wind Quintet, 1975; Nocturne for Violin and Piano, 1977; Vocal: 3 Songs for Soprano, 1962; the River, 7 Songs for Soprano and 7 Instruments, 1965; Along the Moonlit Path, 3 songs for Soprano and

4 Instruments, 1965; Orphean Chorus, 3 songs for Baritone and Men's Chorus, 1966; 3 Songs for Baritone and String Quartet, 1970; One Summer Evening for Men's Chorus, 1971; Song for Men's Chorus, 1972; Song for a Rain Bird for Baritone and Piano, 1974; I'm Looking at the River, 6 songs for Women's or Youth Chorus, 1986. *Address:* c/o Hyvinkaa School of Music, 05800 Hyvinkaa, Finland.

RAJNA Thomas, b. 21 Dec 1921, Budapest, Hungary. Pianist; Composer; Lecturer. *Education:* 1944-47 Liszt Academy of Music with Kodály, Sandor Veress and Leo Weiner; Royal College of Music with Herbert Howells and Angus Morrison. *Career:* Professor of Piano and Composition, Guildhall School of Music, 1963; Lecturer, Keyboard History and Studies, University of Surrey, 1967; Senior Lecturer at Cape Town University from 1970; Appointed Associate Professor, 1989; Numerous performances as pianist in Europe and South Africa of music by Stravinsky, Messiaen, Scriabin, Liszt, Granados and Rajna. *Compositions include:* Dialogues for clarinet and piano 1947; Music for cello and piano 1950; Music for violin and piano 1957; Capriccio for keyboard 1960; Piano Concerto No 1 1962; Movements for strings 1962; Cantilenas and Interludes for orchestra 1968; Three Hebrew Chorus, 1972; Four African Lyrics for high voice and piano 1976; Piano Concerto No 2, 1984; Concerts for Harp and Orchestra, 1990. *Recordings:* Complete piano works of Stravinsky and Granados; works by Messiaen, Bartók, Scriabin, Liszt and Schumann; Rajna: Piano Concerto No. 1; Music for Violin and Piano; Preludes for Piano; Serenade for 10 Wind Instruments, Piano and Percussion; Divertimento Piccolo for Orchestra. *Contributions to:* The Composer. *Honours:* Liszt Prize, Franz Liszt Academy, 1947; Dannreuther Prize, Royal College of Music, 1951; ARTES Award (S.A. Broadcasting Corp), 1981; Fellow of the University of Cape Town, 1981; Doctor of Music (UCT), 1985. *Address:* S. African College of Music, Main Road, Rosebank, Cape Town, South Africa, 7700.

RAJTER Ludovit, b. 30 July 1906, Pezinok, Slovakia. Conductor; Composer. m. Elisabeth Rajter, 14 July 1967, 1 son, 1 daughter. *Education:* Studied with Franz Schmidt, Joseph Marx (Composition), Clemens Krauss, Alexander Wunderer (Conducting), Academy of Music, Vienna, 1929; Study with E.von Dohnányi, Liszt Academy, Budapest. *Debut:* Vienna, 1929. *Career:* 1st Conductor, Hungarian Radio, Budapest, 1933-45; Chief Conductor, CS Radio Bratislava, 1945-50, 1968-77; 1st Conductor, Slovak Philharmonic, Bratislava, 1949-76; Guest Conductor, Radio Basel, 1969-70; Professor, Ferenc Liszt Academy of Music, 1938-45; Professor, Academy of Music, Bratislava, 1949-76. *Compositions:* Sinfonietta, 1929; Divertimento for orchestra, 1932; Balett (Maiales), Budapest, 1938; String Quartet No 1, Vienna; Quintet (Serenade) for flute, oboe, clarinet, horn and bassoon; Sonata per contrabbasso e pianoforte; Suite for violoncello solo Nos 1 and 2; Divertimento for winds; several works for choir; Suite for violin, solo, 1992; Sinfonietta, Bratislava, 1993. *Recordings:* Brahms: Symphonies 1- 4; Franz Schmidt: Symphonies 1-4; Several other compositions, Mozart, Dvořák, Berlioz, Brahms, Kodály, Svendsen, Wolf-Ferrari, Haydn; Suchoň, Cikker and other Slovak composers; A von Zemlinsky: Symphony d minor; Franz Schmidt: Piano concerto E flat major; Variations on a Theme by Beethoven. *Contributions to:* Hudobny Zivot, Slovak Music, Bratislava. *Current Management:* Slovkoncert, Bratislava. *Address:* Fandlyho 1, SK-81103 Bratislava, Slovak Republic.

RAKOWSKI Andrzej, b. 16 June 1931, Warsaw, Poland. Professor of Music Acoustics. m. Magdalena Jakobczyk, 1 son, 2 daughters. *Education:* MSc, 1957, PhD, Acoustics, 1963, Technical University, Warsaw, Poland. MA, Theory, Warsaw Academy of Music, Poland, 1958; Doctor Habil, Musicology, Warsaw University, 1977. *Publications:* Selected Topics on Acoustics, 1959; Categorical Perception of Pitch in Music, 1978; Co-Editor, Short Music Encyclopaedia, 1981; Reiss Music Encyclopaedia, 1960; Music Encyclopaedia of PWM, 1979-. *Contributions to:*

Acustica; Archives of Acoustics; Journal of the Acoustical Society of America; Muzyka; Musique en Pologne; Das Musikinstrument; Folia Phoniatrica; Musical Lexicons. *Hobbies:* Touring; Skiing. *Address:* Pogonowskiego 20 m 2, 01-564 Warszawa, Poland.

RAMBALDI José Ariel, b. 16 May 1931, Chivilcoy, Argentina. Composer; Conductor; Pianist; Teacher. 1 daughter. *Education:* Teachers Certificate; BM, Cleveland Institute of Music, 1959; MM, Michigan State University, 1965; Special Studies in Conducting with Richard Lert, USA, Hans Swarowsky, Hochschule für Musik, Vienna. *Career:* Conductor, with Seattle Opera Co., Assistant in The Ring of the Nibelung, Seattle, 1976; Summer Opera Workshop, Cleveland, 1957, 1959; Walla Walla Symphony, 1968-76; Whitman College Chamber Orchestra & Opera Productions; Teacher, Cleveland Institute of Music, 1961; Michigan State University, 1964-65; Professor, Music, Whitman college, 1965-; Piano Performances from age 12; Premiere Sessions's Second Sonata and Carter's Piano Sonata in Cleveland; Toured Europe, 1960, Argentina and Brazil, 1963; Carnegie Hall Recital, 1966; Soloist wih orchestra in Northwest USA, Radi & TV appearances. *Composition:* The Tigress, Opera, premiered 1984. *Address:* Dept. of Music, Whitman College, Walla Walla, WA 99362, USA.

RAMEY Samuel, b. 28 March 1942, Kolby, Kansas, USA. Singer (Bass- Baritone). *Education:* Wichita State University, with Arthur Newman; New York with Armen Boyajian. *Debut:* New York City Opera 1973, as Zuniga in Carmen: returned as Mephistopheles (Gounod and Boito), Attila, Don Giovanni, Henry VIII (Anna Bolena) and Massenet's Don Quichotte; Glyndebourne debut 1976, as Mozart's Figaro; Nick Shadow in The Rake's Progress 1977; Guest appearances in Hamburg, San Francisco, Chicago and Vienna, as Colline in La Bohème, Figaro and Arkel, in Pelléas et Mélisande; Covent Garden debut 1982: returned to London for a concert performnce of Semiramide, 1986 and as Philip II in Don Carlos, 1989; Metropolitan Opera debut 1984, as Argante in Rinaldo; 1986-87 as Walton in I Puritani and Escamillo; Pesaro 1984, in a revival of Rossini's Il Viaggio a Reims; Bartók's Bluebeard 1989, at the Met; Pesaro Festival 1986 (Maometto II) and 1989 (La gazza ladra); Munich 1988, as Mephistopheles; Don Giovanni at Salzburg from 1987, Metropolitan and Maggio Musicale, Florence 1990; Season 1992/93 as Attila at San Francisco and Geneva, Rossini's Basilio at the Met, Philip II in Venice and New York, the Hoffmann Villains and Berlioz Mephistopheles at Covent Garden and Nick Shadow at Aix-en-Provence; Other roles include the villains in Les Contes d'Hoffmann, Verdi's Renato and Banquo, and Mozart's Leporello. *Recordings:* Bach B Minor Mass, I Due Foscari, Un Ballo in Maschera, Ariodante, Lucia di Lammermoor, Maometto II, Petite Messe solennelle, Haydn's Armida (Philips); Le Nozze di Figaro, The Rake's Progress (Decca); Il Turco in Italia, La Donna del Lago (CBS); Il Viaggio a Reims, Don Giovanni (Deutsche Grammophon). *Address:* c/o Harrison/Parrott Ltd., 12 Penzance Place, London W11 4PA, England.

RAMICOVA Dunya, b. 1950, Czechoslovakia. Costume Designer. *Education:* Studied at Yale School of Drama. *Career:* Has collaborated with Director Stephen Wadsworth on Jenůfa and Fliegende Holländer for Seattle Opera, Fidelio for Scottish Opera and La Clemenza di Tito for Houston Grand Opera; Costume designs for Peter Sellars production of Die Zauberflöte and The Electrification of the Soviet Union at Glyndebourne, Tannhäuser at Chicago, Nixon in China for Houston and St François d'Assise at Salzburg 1992; Premiere of The Voyage by Philip Glass at the Metropolitan 1992, production by David Pountney; Covent Garden 1992, costumes for Alcina.

RAMINSH Imant Karlis, b. 18 Sept 1943, Ventspils, Latvia. Composer; Conductor; Teacher. m. Becky Benita Strube, 21 June 1975, 1 daughter. *Education:* Jarvis Collegiate Institute, Toronto, 1961; Royal Conservatory of Toronto, Diploma 1962; University of Toronto, B.Mus

1966; Akademie Mozarteum, Salzburg, 1966-68; University of British Columbia, 1968-69; University of Victoria, 1975-77. *Career:* Established Music Department, College of New Caledonia, Prince George, British Columbia, 1969-71; Founding Conductor, New Caledonia Chamber Orchestra (now Prince George Symphony), 1970-75; Choral Director, Okanagan Symphony Choir, 1978-82; Founding Conductor, Aura Chamber Choir, 1979-; Nova Children's Choir, 1983-86; Youth Symphony of the Okanagan, 1989-. *Compositions:* Ave, Verum Corpus; Magnificat; The Great Sea; Songs of the Lights; Gloria; Veni, Sancte Spiritus; Stabat Mater. *Recordings:* Songs of the Lights; Love Songs for a Small Planet; Simple Gifts including Northwest Trilogy. *Publications:* Many works. *Honours:* National Choral Award, Association of Canadian Choral Conductors for Magnificat, 1990; First Prize in Melodious Accord Biennial Choral Literature Search, 1992. *Memberships:* American Choral Directors Association; Associate Composer, Canadian Music Centre; Canadian League of Composers; Association of Canadian Choral Conductors; British Columbia Choral Federation. *Hobbies:* Natural History; Hiking; Canoing; Skiing; Photography; History; Languages. *Address:* 11600 Upper Summit Drive, Vernon, British Columbia, Canada V1B 2B4.

RAMIREZ Alejandro, b. 2 Sept 1946, Bogota, Columbia. Singer (Tenor). *Education:* Qualified as Doctor of Medicine, then studied singing at the Conservatory of Bogota; Further study at the Musikhochschule Freiburg, 1973-75; Completed studies with the late Annelies Kupper in Munich and with the late Gunther Reich in Stuttgart. *Career:* Sang in Pforzheim 1975-77, Kaiserslautern 1977-80; Member of the Mannheim Opera 1980-82, Frankfurt from 1982; Covent Garden, London, 1984 as Nemorino in L'Elisir d'Amore; Vienna Staatsoper 1985, as Alfredo; Salzburg Festival 1985, in the Henze-Monteverdi Il Ritorno d'Ulisse; Other roles include Belmonte, Don Ottavio, Tamino, Ferrando; Jacquino (Berlin 1984); Elvino (La Sonnambula); Rossini's Almaviva and Lindoro; Strauss's Narraboth and Flamand; Rodolfo and Edgardo; Concert repertoire includes the Evangelist in the Bach Passions, and works by Handel, Bruckner, Schumann, Dvořák, Beethoven and Verdi; Bavarian State Opera as Don Ottavio, Frankfurt, 1980-85; Scala di Milano, 1988 as Henry Morosus in R Strauss Schweigsame Frau, Oct. 1990; Season 1992 as Rodolfo at Bonn and Tamino at Dusseldorf; Professor of singing at the Musikhochschule of Mannheim, Germany. *Recordings include:* Schumann's Manfred; St John Passion and Christmas Oratorio by Bach; Sacred music by Schubert, Mendelssohn and Charpentier (Erato); The Seven Last Words by Schütz; Nozze di Figaro by Mozart under Riccardo Muti. *Address:* Ludwigstr 73, D-6751 Mehlinger, Germany.

RAMOVS Klemen, b. 20 Mar 1956, Ljubljana, Slovenia. Musician. *Education:* Artistic Diploma, Recorder, Music Academy of Graz, Austria, 1979; Studied with Hans Florey; Postgraduate studies with Hans-Martin Linde and Ferdinand Conrad. *Career:* Concerts, as soloist, with various orchestras, in several chamber music groups, throughout Europe, Israel, and South America, 1976-; Leader, international master classes, Leader, Festival Radovljica; Founder, ensembles for early music in Slovenia: Ramovs Consort; Director and Owner of the Klemen Ramovs Management Lts Concert Agency; International Summer Academy for Early Music in Radovljica, Radovljica Festival, various concert series; Introduction of Slovene soloists and ensembles to audiences at home and abroad and of foreign soloists and ensembles to Slovenia. Initiated numerous compositions for recorder written by Slovenian Composers; Baroque specialist, using authentic instruments. *Recordings:* Radio, TV and LPs. *Hobby:* Mountaineering. *Address:* Slovenska 1, SLO-61000 Ljubljana, Slovenia.

RAMOVS Primoz, b. 20 Mar 1921, Ljubljana, Yugoslavia. Composer; Librarian. m. Stefanija Schubert, 17 Jan 1955, 2 sons, 1 daughter. *Education:* Diploma,

Conservatory, Music Academy, Ljubljana, 1941; Corse di perfezionamento, Accademia Musica, Siena, Italy; Private study with Alfredo Casella, Rome. *Debut:* 1938. *Career:* Librarian 1945-52, Librarian-in-Chief 1952-87, Slovene Academy of Sciences and Arts; Professor, Conservatory Ljubljana, 1948-52 and 1955-64. *Compositions:* 5 symphonies; 13 symphonic Poems, over 400 opuses; 29 concertos; Symphonic, chamber and instrumental works; Many recordings of his works. *Honours:* Philharmonic Society Ljubljana, 1944; Festival Ljubljana, 1958; Preseren's Foundation, Ljubljana, 1962; Cop's Diploma 1971, Yugoslav Radio Beograd, 1967, 1969, 2 awards 1970, 2 awards 1976; Slovene Philharmony Ljubljana, 1978; Slovene Academy of Sciences and Arts, Ljubljana, 1978; Order of the Work with Golden Wreath, 1981; Preseren's Prize, Ljubljana, 1983; Cultural Doctorate, World University Tucson, USA, 1982; The International Cultural Diploma of Honor, 1988; Doctor of Music (Honoris Causa), 1988; World Decoration of Excellence, 1989; Order of the White Cross International, 1990; Doctor of Philosophy in Music Honoris Causa, 1990; Order of the Lyre Bird in the Class of Gold, 1990; Order of SS Cyrille and Methode, 1991; Decoration of the town of Ljubljana, 1991. *Memberships:* Slovene Academy of Arts and Sciences; Secretary 1953-65, Vice-President 1967-71, Association of Slovene Composers; Association of Slovene Librarians; Slovene Alpine Association; Slovene Literary Society; Member of Honor, Slovene Philharmony; Member World Institute of Achievement; Doctoral Member, World University Roundtable; Life Membership of Merit, Confederation of Chivalry; Croatian Academy of Sciences and Arts; Academia Scientiarum et Artium Europaea. *Hobby:* Mountaineering. *Address:* Alovenska Cesta 1, 61101 Ljubljana, Slovenia.

RAMPAL Jean-Pierre Louis, b. 7 Jan 1922, Marseille, France. Flautist. m. Françoise-Anne Bacqueyrisse, 1947, 1 son, 1 daughter. *Education:* University of Marseille. *Career:* World-wide tours, 1945-; Participant in major festivals including in Rio de Janeiro, Aix, Menton, Salzburg, Edinburgh, Prague, Athens, Zagreb, Granada and Tokyo; Editor for Ancient and Classical Music, International Music Company, New York City, USA, 1958-; Professor, Conservatoire National Superieur de Musique de Paris, France, 1969-82; Has premiered concertos by Jolivet (1950), Martinon (1971), Rivier (1956), Françaix (1967) and Nigg (1961). *Publications:* La Flûte, 1978; Music, My Love. *Honours:* Officer, Legion d'honneur; Officer de l'Ordre des Arts et Lettres de France; Grand Prix du Disque, 1954, 1956, 1959, 1960, 1961, 1963, 1964 and 1978; Oscar du Premier Virtuose Français, 1956; Prix Edison, 1969; Léonie Sonning Danish Music Prize, 1978; Prix d'honneur du Prix Mondial du Disque de Montreaux, 1980; Commandeur De L'Ordre National Du Merité. *Memberships:* French Musicological Society; President, Association Musique et Musiciens, 1974-. *Hobbies:* Tennis; Deep sea diving; Movie making. *Current Management:* Bureau de Concerts, M De Valmalete, 11 Av Delcassé, 75008 Paris, France. *Address:* 15 Avenue Mozart, 75016 Paris, France.

RANACHER Christa, b. 12 Dec 1953, Dollach in Karnten, Germany. Singer (Soprano). *Education:* Studied in Vienna and attended master classes by Mario del Monaco and Elisabeth Schwarzkopf. *Career:* Sang at Regensburg 1984-85, Monchengladbach from 1985, Leonore in Fidelio 1989; Further appearances at Gelsenkirchen, Mannheim, Munster, Hanover, the Deutsche Oper Berlin, Staatsoper Munich and Zurich; Season 1992 as Salome at Dusseldorf and Shostakovich's Katerina Ismailova at Berne; Other roles include Mozart's Countess and Donna Anna, Agathe, Marenka in The Bartered Bride, Senta, and Ada in Wagner's Die Feen; Tosca, Santuzza, Zdenka, Arabella, Judith in the opera by Siegfried Matthus, Sophie in Cerha's Baal and Andromache in Troades by Reimann; Noted concert performer. *Address:* c/o Deutsche Oper am Rhein, Heinrich Heine Allee 16, 4000 Dusseldorf, Germany.

RANDALL Bruce Allan, b. 2 Nov 1958, Haverhill, Massachusetts, USA. Performer; Editor; Instrument maker. *Education:* BMus, University of Lowell, 1981. *Career:* Member, Norumbega Harmony; Collegium Josquinium; Revels; Lancaster Brass Quintet; Principal Trombone, Merrimack Valley Philharmonic; Conductor and Trombonist, Haverhill City Band; Maker of instruments for traditional and early music; Music researcher/editor for New England and the Constitution. *Compositions:* Editor and arranger of music for brass ensemble; Choral work, Mount Desert, revision of The Sacred Harp, 1991. *Recordings:* Norumbega Harmony; University of Vermont; Revels; Hancock Shaker Village. *Publication:* Political and Religious Songs from the Constitutional Era, 1987. *Contributions to:* Boston Early Music News; National Sacred Harp Newsletter; Historical Performance. *Memberships:* Founder Member: Early Music America; Historical Brass Society; American Federation of Musicians. *Address:* 218 Broadway, Haverhill, MA 01832, USA.

RANDLE Thomas, b. 21 Dec 1958, Hollywood, USA. Singer (Tenor). *Education:* Studied at the University of Southern California. *Career:* Concert appearances in the USA and Europe with the London Philharmonic Orchestra, Boston Symphony Orchestra and the Leipzig Radio Symphony Orchestra; Conductors include Helmuth Rilling, Ghennadi Rozhdestvensky, Michael Tilson Thomas and André Previn; Has sung Berg and Stravinsky, and the US and world premieres of works by Tippett, Heinz Holliger and William Kraft with the Los Angeles Philharmonic; Often heard in Bach, Handel and Mozart: Bach's Christmas Oratorio in Leipzig; Operatic repertoire includes all the major tenor roles of Mozart, Rossini and Donizetti, and French roles of Massenet and Thomas; British debut as Tamino in Nicholas Hytner's production of The Magic Flute (English National Opera 1988; returned 1989); European opera debut at the Aix-en-Provence Festival, France in Purcell's The Fairy Queen; Sang Monteverdi's Orfeo at Valencia, 1989; Ferrando in Brussels and with Scottish Opera; Sang Tamino at Glyndebourne, 1991; Sang Dionysus in the premiere of John Buller's The Bacchae and as Pelléas, English National Opera, 1992; Sang title role in new production of Pelléas et Mélisande with Peter Brook in Paris and European Tour, Netherlands Opera in world premiere of Peter Schaat's Opera, Symposion, based on Life of Tchaikovsky in 1994; Season 1994 returns to ENO to sing Tippett's King Priam, and to appears in Britten's Gloriana at Covent Garden. *Recordings:* Purcell's Fairy Queen with Les Arts Florissants (Harmonia Mundi); Tippett's The Ice Break with London Sinfonietta (Virgin Classics). *Address:* c/o IMG Artists Europe, Media House, 3 Burlington Lane, Chiswick, London W4 2TH, England.

RANDOLPH David, b. 21 Dec 1914, New York City, New York, USA. Conductor; Author; Lecturer; Broadcaster. m. Mildred Greenberg, 18 July 1948. *Education:* BS, City College of New York; MA, Teachers College, Columbia University. *Career:* Conductor, The Masterwork Chorus and Orchestra, St Cecilia Chorus and Orchestra, Carnegie Hall and Avery Fisher Hall, Kennedy Center, Washington DC, numerous choral works including Bach's B Minor Mass, Christmas Oratorio, St Matthew Passion and St John Passion, Brahms' Requiem, Mozart's Requiem, Berlioz's Requiem, Vaughan Williams' A Sea Symphony, Haydn's Mass in Time of War, Orff's Carmina Burana, Beethoven's Mass in C and Missa Solemnis, Mozart's Mass in C Minor, Mendelssohn's Symphony No 2 and Elijah, Poulenc's Gloria, Kodály's Te Deum, and 166 complete performances of Handel's Messiah; Guest Conductor: The Philharmonia Orchestra, Barbican Centre, London, in Brahms' Requiem, under auspices of MidAmerica Productions, 1988; Pre-concert Lecturer: The New York Philharmonic, The Cleveland Orchestra, Vienna Symphony Orchestra; Conductor, David Randolph Singers; Radio broadcasts, The David Randolph Concert, WNYC radio, 1946-79: Guest Critic, First Hearing, WQXR radio and 60 stations throughout USA, 1986-; Host, Lincoln Center Spotlight, WQXR radio; Lecturer, New York University, The New School;

Professor of Music, State University of New York, College at New Paltz; Fordham University; Montclair State College, New Jersey; Conductor, Concert Tour of Spain, with four American choruses and The Radio-Television Orchestra of Moscow, Russia, 1992. *Compositions:* A Song for Humanity. *Recordings:* works by Monteverdi, Schütz and Handel's Messiah. *Publications:* This Is Music: A Guide to the Pleasures of Listening, (McGraw-Hill), 1964. *Address:* 420 East 86th Street, Apt 4C, New York, NY 10028, USA.

RANDOVA Eva, b. 31 Dec. 1936, Kolin, Czechoslovakia. Singer (Mezzo-Soprano). *Education:* Studied with J. Svabova at Usti nad Labem, and at the Prague Conservatory. *Career:* Sang first at Ostrava, as Eboli, Carmen, Amneris, the Princess in Rusalka, and Ortrud; Prague National Opera from 1969; Nuremberg and Stuttgart from 1971; Bayreuth Festival from 1973, as Gutrune, Fricka and Kundry; Salzburg Festival 1975, Eboli in Don Carlos, conducted by Karajan; Covent Garden debut 1977, as Ortrud: has returned to London as Marina, Venus, the Kostelnička in Jenůfa 1986 and Azucena in a new production of Il Trovatore 1989; Metropolitan Opera 1981, 1987, as Fricka and Venus; Orange festival 1985, as Marina in Boris Godunov, Vienna 1987, in Rusalka; Sang Ortrud at San Francisco 1989, Stuttgart 1990; Sang Marina in Boris Godunov at Barcelona, 1990; Season 1992 as Clytemnestra at Athens; Covent Garden 1994, as Kabanicha in Katya Kabanova; Frequent concert engagements. *Recordings:* Bach cantatas; Santuzza in Cavalleria Rusticana (EMI); Mahler's Resurrection Symphony, Glagolitic Mass by Janáček, Sarka by Fibich (Supraphon); The Cunning Little Vixen and Jenůfa, conducted by Charles Mackerras (Decca). *Address:* c/o Lies Askonas Ltd., 186 Drury Lane, London WC2B 5QD, England.

RANDS Bernard, b. 2 Mar 1935, Sheffield, Yorks, England. Composer; Conductor. *Education:* University of Wales, Bangor: BMus 1956, MMus 1958; Study in Italy with Dallapiccola, Boulez, Maderna and Berio. *Career:* 1968-74 instructor at the music department of York University; Fellowship in Creative Arts at Brasenose Colege Oxford 1972-73; Professor of Music at the University of California, San Diego, from 1976; Visiting professor at the California Institute of the Arts in Valencia 1984- 85; Has worked at electronic music studios in Milan, Berlin, Albany (New York) and Urbana; Appearances as conductor of new music, notably with the London Sonor ensemble; Founder-member of music-theatre ensemble C.L.A.P. *Compositions:* Serena, music theatre 1972/78; Orchestral: Per Esempio 1968; Agenda 1970; Wildtrack I-III 1969-75; Mesalliance 1972; Ology for jazz group 1973; Aum 1974; Serenata 75b for flute and chamber orchestra 1976; Instrumental: Series of piano pieces Espressioni 1960-70; Actions for Six 1962; Formants 1 and II 1965-70; Tableau 1970; Deja 1 1972; as all get out 1972; etendre 1972; Scherzi 1974; Cuaderna for string quartet 1975; Memo 1-5, solo pieces 1971-75; Response for double bass and tape 1973; Madrigali 1977; Obbligato for string quartet and trombone 1980; Vocal: Ballad 1-3 1970-73; Metalepsis 2 for mezzo 1971; Lunatici for soprano and ensemble 1980; Deja 2 for soprano and ensemble 1980; Sound Patterns 1-5 for various combinations with voices; Canti del Sole for tenor and orchestra 1983, London Serenade, 1984; Le Tambourin, suite 1 and 2 1984; Ceremonial 1 and 2 1985-86; Serenata 85 1985; Requiescant for soprano, chorus and ensemble 1985-86; Hirath for cello and orchestra, 1987; ...In The Receding Mist... for flute, harp and string trio 1988; ...Among The Voices... for chorus and harp,. 1988; ...Body and Shadow... for orchestra, 1988. *Honours include:* 1984 Pulitzer Prize for Canti del Sole. *Address:* c/o Universal Edition, 2/3 Fareham Street, London W1, England.

RANKI Dezsö, b. 8 Sept 1951, Budapest, Hungary. *Education:* Béla Bartók Conservatory; Ferenc Liszt Academy of Music; Graduated with Distinction, 1973. *Career:* Has made numerous guest performances including: Kremlin Congress Palace, Moscow, USSR; Royal Festival Hall, London, England; Deputized for Rubinstein in Milan and for Benedetti-Michelangeli at

Menton; Appearances at International festivals of Antibes, Helsinki, Lucerne, Menton, St Moritz, Paris and Prague; Carinthian Summer Festival, Ossiach, Villach; Solo Part, Bernstein's The Age of Anxiety, Carinthian Festival, 1975; Regular appearances worldwide. *Honours:* Kossuth Prize; Liszt Prize; 1st Prize, Zwickau Robert Schumann International Piano Competition, 1969; Recipient, 1st prizes, national piano competitions, 1965, 1967, 1969.

RÁNKI György, b. 30 Oct 1907, Budapest, Hungary. Composer. m. Anna Dékány, 13 Nov 1940, 1 son, 1 daughter. *Education:* Ferenc Liszt Academy of Music, Budapest; Studied Composition under Zoltán Kodály. *Career:* World Publicity on some compositions: King Pomade Suite; Pentaerophonia; Serenade of the Seven Headed Dragon; The Ballet Comedy: Magic Drink has been world premiered in Wiesbaden. *Compositions:* 3 Operas: King Pomade's New Clothes 1953; The Tragedy of Man 1970; The Boatman of the Moon 1979; 5 Ballets including: The Circus 1965; The Magic Drink 1975; 4 Oratorios including: 1944; Cantus Urbis; Cain and Abel, 1989; 12 Symphonic Scores including: 2 Symphonies; Concertos; Suites etc. Chamber Music including: Pentaerophonia (woodwind quintet); Serenade (Brass septet); String Quartet; Two Wonder Oxen (Story with Music); Vocal and Instrumental; Theatre and Film Music. *Recordings:* King Pomade's New Clothes I Suite (Louisville Symphony Orchestra); The Tragedy of Man; 1st Symphony Concertos; Historical Tableaux; Three Nights (Hungaroton); Don Quixote (Melodia); Cain and Abel, Hungaroton, 1989. *Honours:* Kossuth Prize, 1954; Erkel Prize; Named Merited Artist (Pro Arte), 1950-77. Bartók-Pasztory Prize, 1987. *Current Management:* Artisjus, Vörösmarty-Tér 1, Budapest, 1051, Hungary. *Hobbies:* Yoga; Swimming; Gardening. *Address:* 36 Gülbaba-Utca, 1023 Budapest, Hungary.

RANKIN Nell, b. 3 Jan 1926, Montgomery, Alabama, USA. Singer (Mezzo-Soprano). *Education:* Studied with Jeanne Lorraine at the Birmingham Conservatory and with Karin Branzell in New York. *Debut:* Sang in concert, New York 1947. *Career:* Stage debut Zurich 1949, as Ortrud in Lohengrin; Sang 1949-50 in 126 performances; La Scala Milan 1951, in the Verdi Requiem; Metropolitan Opera from 1951, as Amneris, Laura, Marina, Azucena, Ulrica, Gutrune and Ortrud; Covent Garden 1953-54, as Carmen, Amneris and Ortrud; Sang at Cincinnati 1956, in the US premiere of Britten's Gloriana; Appearances at San Francisco 1955 and Vienna; La Scala Milan 1960, as Cassandre in Les Troyens. *Recordings include:* Suzuki in Madama Butterfly (Decca); Les Troyens; Lieder recital (Capitol). *Address:* c/o Metropolitan Opera, Lincoln Center, New York, NY 10023, USA.

RANS Paul, b. 20 Dec 1946, Louvain, Belgium. Singer and Lutenist. m. Nell Race, 9 Jan 1976, 2 daughters. *Education:* Latin/Greek Secondary Education, Louvain; Higher Institute for Translators, Brussels, 1965-68; Classical Guitar, Royal Conservatoire, Brussels, 1969-72; Lute Studies with Michael Schäffer, Cologne, 1973-74. *Career:* Member of Trio, Rum, 1969-78; TV/Radio and Concerts in Belgium, Holland, France, Germany, Switzerland, Ireland, England; Duo with L. Misschaert, 1977-83; Solo Appearances in Britain, France, Belgium including Festival of Flanders, 1987 and BRT Radio and TV, 1987. *Recordings:* RUM 1, 1972; RUM 2, 1974; RUM 3, 1975; on Philips Label; RUM 4, 1978, WEA Label; Die Nachtegael Int Wilde - with L. Misschaert, 1979, on Philips Label; Blame Not My Lute, Solo Voice and Lute, 1987, on Pavane Label; Vive Le Geus, BRT Label, 1988; CD Medieval Christmas Songs, Paul Rans Ensemble, on BRT Label, 1989; CD Gruuthuse Manuscript, Paul Rans Ensemble, 1992; CD: Antwerp Songbook (1544) - Paul Rans Ensemble. *Contributions to:* Weekly Programme, Music from Flanders, in English, for Radio Vlaanderen International and Producer Traditional Music BRTN Radio 3. *Hobbies:* Lute Making. *Address:* Schavolliestraat 71, B-1755 Oetingen-Gooik, Belgium.

RAPER Marion Eileen, b. 18 Feb 1938, Birmingham,

England. Pianist; Accompanist. m. 28 July 1962, divorced 1979. *Education:* Licentiate, Royal Academy of Music, 1957-59; University of London Teaching Certificate, Goldsmiths' College, University of London, 1959-61. *Career:* Recitals throughout England with singers and instrumentalists, Broadcasts for BBC and Capital Radio; Teaching, Guildhall School of Music; Master Classes in London; Tour of Canada with Jennifer Hillman, piano duo, 1987; Appearances on television (ITV and Channel 4); Member of the Ridings Piano Quartet; Second tour of Canada with Jennifer Hillman, 1989. *Membership:* Incorporated Society of Musicians. *Address:* 3 Cavendish Drive, Guiseley, Leeds, LS20 8DR, England.

RAPF Kurt, b. 15 Feb 1922, Vienna, Austria. Conductor; Musician; Composer. m. Ellen Rapf, 2 Dec 1961, 1 daughter. *Education:* Graduate in Piano, Organ and Conducting, Music Academy, Vienna. *Career:* Founder and Conductor, Collegium Musicum Wien (Vienna String Symphony), 1945-56; Assistant Conductor to Hans Knappertsbusch, Opera House Zurich, Switzerland; Accompanist to famous singers and instrumentalists; Director of Music, Innsbruck, Austria, 1953-60; Broadcast and television activities; Numerous tours in Europe, USA, Canada, Middle and Far East; Many appearances at festivals in Europe; Professor, Chief of Music Department, City of Vienna, 1970-87; Head of Austrian Composers Guild, 1970-83; Founder and Music Director of Vienna Sinfonietta, 1986. *Compositions:* Over 140 Works for orchestra, choir, chamber orchestra, organ and piano solo, chamber music and vocalworks. *Recordings:* Over 70 records as conductor, harpsichordist, organist, pianist, and composer. *Hobby:* Swimming. *Address:* Bossigasse 35, A-1130, Vienna, Austria.

RAPHANEL Ghilaine, b. 19 Apr 1952, Rouen, France. Singer (Soprano). *Education:* Studied at the Rouen Conservatory and at the Paris Conservatoire with Janine Micheau. *Career:* Sang Rosina in Il Bariere di Siviglia at the Opera Studio of the Paris Opera; Stadttheater Basle from 1980 as Gilda, Constanze, Juliette, Manon, and Titania in A Midsummer Night's Dream; Guest appearances in Lyon and Nantes; Hamburg Staatsoper 1985, as the Queen of Night and Zerbinetta; Aix-en-Provence Festival 1985, Zerbinetta; Sang at Mézières 1988 as Amor in Orfeo ed Euridice; at Nancy 1989, as Susanna. *Recordings include:* Pousette in Manon, L'Etoile by Chabrier (EMI); Fiorella in Les Brigands by Offenbach (EMI); Marguerite de Valois in Les Huguenots (Erato). *Address:* c/o Opéra de Nancy et de Lorraine, Rue Ste, Catherine, F-54000 Nancy, France.

RASCH Rudolf Alexander, b. 15 Dec 1945, Borger, Netherlands. Musicologist. *Education:* Doctorandus Musicology, Universiteit van Amsterdam, 1968; Doctorate in Social Sciences (Experimental Psychology), 1981; Doctorate in Humanities (Musicology), 1985. *Career:* Research Assistant, Institute for Perception, TNO, Soesterberg, Netherlands, 1975-78; Lecturer in Music Theory and Acoustics, Institute of Musicology, University of Utrecht, 1977-; Hoofddocent (Associate Professor), Department of Musicology, University of Utrecht, 1988. *Publication:* The cantiones natalitiae and the Church Music of the Southern Netherlands during the Seventeenth Century (in Dutch), 1985. *Contributions to:* Articles on Dutch music history, mostly 17th century, musical psychoacoustics, musical acoustics, psychology of music, music theory, tuning and temperament; Prefaces for re-editions, contributions to encyclopaedias, modern editions of early Dutch music. *Address:* Department of Musicology, University of Utrecht, Kromme Nieuwe Gracht 29, 3512 HD Utrecht, Netherlands.

RASMUSSEN Karl Aage, b. 14 Dec 1947, Kolding, Denmark. Composer; Conductor; Professor of Music. m. Charlotte Schiøtz, 7 May 1975. *Education:* Academy of Music, Aarhus, studied composition with Per Noergaard, Degrees in Music History, Theory and Composition. *Career:* Teacher, Academy of Music, Aarhus 1970-; Teacher, Royal Academy in Copenhagen 1980-;

Director/Conductor of Chamber Ensemble, The Elsinore Players 1975-; Other activities include numerous obligations at The New Music Department of The Danish Radio, co-editing The Danish Music Magazine; Lectures in many European countries and USA; Artistic Director, NUMUS Festival in Aarhus. *Compositions include:* Stage Works: Jephta, Opera in 2 Acts 1976-77; Majakovskij, Scenic concert piece in 2 Acts, 1977-78; Jonas, Musical Play for radio, 1978-80. Orchestral Works: Symphony for Young Lovers 1967; Recapitulations 1968; Symphonie Classique 1969; Symphony Anfang und Ende 1973; Contrafactum, concerto for cello and orchestra 1980; A Symphony In Time 1982. Chamber Works: Protocol and Myth 1971; Genklang (Echo) 1972; A Ballad of Game and Dream 1974; Lullaby 1976; Berio Mask 1977; Le Tombeau de Pere Igor 1977; Parts Apart 1978; Capricci e Dance 1979; Italiensk Koncert (Italian Concerto) 1981; Ballo In Maschera 1981; Pianissimo Furioso 1982; A Quartet of Five 1982; Solos and Shadows 1983; Fugue/Fuga (Encore VIII) 1984; Surrounded by Scales 1985. Solo Instrument: Aria Grigia 1966; My Spring Diary I-II (1967-68); Invention 1972; Antifoni 1973; Paganini Variations 1976; Fugue/Fuga 1984; Triple Tango 1984. Vocal: This Moment 1966; When I Was Happy I Wrote No Songs 1967; Love Is In The World 1974-75; One And All 1976; Encore Series, I-XI (1977-85). *Membership:* Danish Music Council. *Address:* Brokbjerggaard, DK-8752 Oestbirk, Denmark.

RASMUSSEN Paula, b. 1965, California, USA. Singer (Mezzo-soprano). *Career:* Concert appearances with San Francisco Symphony under Nicholas McGegan in Bach Cantatas, the Los Angeles Master Chorale in Messiah, Bruckner's Te Deum and Pergolesi's Magnificat and with Jose Carreras in Dublin 1992; Opera engagements as Nancy T'ang in the Peter Sellars production of Nixon in China in Los Angeles, Paris and Frankfurt; Iola in Cavalleria Rusticana with Long Beach Opera; Nancy in Albert Herring, Hansel, Anna in Les Troyens, Hippolyta in Midsummer Night's Dream and the Composer in Ariadne auf Naxos with the Los Angeles Music Center Opera. *Honour:* Regional Winner 1992 Metropolitan Opera Competition. *Address:* c/o IMG Artists, Media House, 3 Burlington Lane, London W4 2TH, England.

RASTALL George Richard, b. 5 Dec 1940, Nottingham, England. University Senior Lecturer. m. Jane Elizabeth Oakshott, 11 Aug 1978, 2 sons, 1 daughter. *Education:* BA 1963, MusB 1964, MA 1967, Christ's College, Cambridge; PhD, Manchester University, 1968. *Publications:* Editor, Benjamin Rogers: Complete Keyboard Works, 1972; Editor, all publications of Boethius Press, 1973-82; The Notation of Western Music, 1983. *Contributions to:* Music and Letters; RMA Research Chronicle; Musical Times; Music Analysis; Early Music; Medieval English Theatre. *Memberships:* Royal Music Association; Plainsong and Mediaeval Music Society. *Address:* Department of Music, Leeds University, Leeds, LS2 9JT, England.

RATH John Frédéric, b. 10 June 1946, Manchester, England. Opera and Concert Singer, Bass. *Education:* BA (Hons.), Drama, Manchester University; RNCM, Opera School, Basle; Studied with Elsa Cavelti, Max Lorenz, Otakar Kraus. *Debut:* Ramphis in Aida, RNCM. *Career:* Appeared with English Music Theatre Company, The Northern Ireland Opera Trust, Glyndebourne Festival and Touring Company Royal Opera House, Covent Garden, in Paris at the Châtelet, Lille with Opera du Nord, at La Monnaie in Brussels, La Fenice, Venice with Handel Opera Society and Chelsea Opera Group and Maggio Musicale in Florence; Roles include: Guglielmo and Don Alfonso in Cosi; Masetto in Don Giovanni; Colline in La Bohème; Argante in Handel's Rinaldo; Ramphis in Aida; Sparafucile in Rigoletto; Melibeo in Haydn's La Fedeltà Premiata; Escamillo and Zuniga in Carmen; the Narrator in Stravinsky's Soldier's Tale; Most recently in Peter Brook's La Tragédie de Carmen in Paris; its European tour and New York as Escamillo; also in film version; For Kent Opera - Rocco in Fidelio, For Nexus Opera - Azarius in Britten's The Burning Fiery Furnace; The Traveller in Britten's Curlew River, at Wells Cathedral and filmed by BBC 2 also at the Proms; For Edinburgh Festival Jochanaan in Salome; For English Bach Festival Polyphemus in Acis and Galatea, Aeneas in Dido and Aeneas and Charon in Alceste (Handel); Bach's Coffee Cantata (staged), Don Quichotte in Master Peter's Puppet Show (Falla); Mahomet in Le Siège de Corinthe (Rossini) in Madrid; Florence Festival bass roles in The Fairy Queen; Wexford Festival as Angelo in Stephen Storace's Comedy of Errors and Il Capitano in Mascagni's Il piccolo Marat; Principal bass with D'Oyly Carte Opera Co. roles: Private Willis in Iolanta, Grand Inquisitor in Gondoliers, The Mikado, Sergeant of Police in Pirates of Penzance, Dick Deadeye in HMS Pinafore, 1990-92; For Opera North the Doctor in Berg's Wozzeck and Sarastro in The Magic Flute; Concert and Oratorio work throughout Europe including notable performances of Messiah and St Matthew Passion in Paris, Handel's Theodora in London, Spain and Italy, Bach Cantatas in New York, and concert performances as Gurnemanz in Parsifal, King Mark in Tristan und Isolde, and Wotan in Das Rheingold and Die Walküre. *Recording:* Private Willis and Grand Inquisitor. *Hobbies:* Farming and Living in Mid-Wales. *Current Management:* Athole Still International Management. *Address:* Cwmllechwedd Fawr, Llanbister, Powys LD1 6UH, Wales.

RATTAY Evzen, b. 1945, Czechoslovakia. Cellist. *Education:* Studied at the Prague Academy of Arts. *Career:* Cellist of the Talich String Quartet from 1962; Tours to most European countries, Egypt, Iraq, North America, Japan, Indonesia; Chamber Ensemble of the Czech Philharmonic from 1975; Annual visits to France from 1976; Tours of Britain 1990-91, with concerts at the Wigmore Hall, appearances at the Bath, Bournemouth Festivals, Elizabeth Hall and on BBC2's Late Show, with Janáček's 2nd Quartet; Also played Beethoven's quartet Op 74, the Brahms A minor, Smetana D minor and works by Mozart in England; Festival appearances in Vienna, Besancon, Lucerne, Helsinki, Amsterdam, Prague and Salzburg; Repertoire also includes works by Debussy, Bartók (complete quartets recorded with Supraphon), Shostakovich, Ravel and Dvořák. *Recordings include:* For the French companies Sarastro and Calliope, with the complete quartets of Beethoven; Albums for Collins Classics. *Honours include:* Grand Prix Charles Cros. *Address:* c/o Clarion/Seven Muses, 64 Whitehall Park, London N19 3TN, England.

RATTI Eugenia, b. 5 Apr 1933, Genoa, Italy. Singer (Soprano). *Education:* Studied with her mother. *Career:* Concert tour with Tito Schipa 1952; Stage debut 1954, in Sestri Levante; La Scala Milan from 1955, as Lisa in La Sonnambula, and in the premieres of Milhaud's David 1955 and Dialogues des Carmélites 1957; Holland Festival 1955, in L'Italiana in Algeri; Glyndebourne Festival 1955, 1961, as Nannetta and Adina; Edinburgh Festival 1957, Il Matrimonio di Segreto; Holland Festival 1970, in Haydn's Le Fedeltà Premiata; Returned to Glyndebourne 1973 and 1976, as the Italian Singer in Capriccio; Other roles include Zerlina in Don Giovanni, Susanna, Rosina, Musetta and Oscar. *Recordings:* Un Ballo in Maschera, Il Matrimonio Segreto, Aida, La Sonnambula (Columbia); Don Giovanni, conducted by Leinsdorf (RCA). *Address:* c/o Glyndebourne Festival Opera, Lewes, Sussex.

RATTLE Simon, b. 19 Jan 1955, Liverpool, England. Conductor. m. 1980, Elise Ross, 1 son. *Debut:* Queen Elizabeth Hall, London, 1974; Royal Festival Hall, London, 1976; Royal Albert Hall, London, 1977; Glyndebourne, 1977, The Cunning Little Vixen. *Career:* Has conducted Bournemouth Symphony Orchestra, Bournemouth Sinfonietta, New Philharmonia (now Philharmonia) Orchestra, Northern Sinfonia, London Philharmonic, London Sinfonietta, Los Angeles Philharmonic, Stockholm Philharmonic, Toronto Symphony, Boston, Cleveland, Chicago, San Francisco, Montreal, Israel Philharmonic, Amsterdam Concertgebouw, etc; Assistant Conductor, BBC Scottish Symphony Orchestra, 1977-80; Associate Conductor,

Royal Liverpool Philharmonic Society, 1977-80; Principal Conductor, London Choral Society, 1979-84; Artistic Director, Aldeburgh Festival, 1982-; Principal Guest Conductor, Los Angeles Philharmonic, 1981-, Rotterdam Philharmonic, 1981-84; Principal Conductor and Artistic Director, City of Birmingham Symphony Orchestra, 1980-1991; Music Director City of Birmingham Symphony Orchestra, 1991-; Salzburg Festival debut with City of Birmingham Symphony Orchestra, 1992; conducted Katya Kabanova at the London Coliseum 1985, Porgy and Bess at Glyndebourne 1986; US opera debut 1988, Wozzeck at Los Angeles; Covent Garden debut 1990, The Cunning Little Vixen; Season 1990-91 with the Berlin Philharmonic; London Philharmonic Brahms Cycle; CBSO tour to Hong Kong and Japan; Così fan Tutte at Glyndebourne; opening of Symphony Hall at Birmingham; Promenade Concerts, London; Gubaidulina's Offertorium, Prokofiev 5th and Mahler 9th Symphonies; Season 1991-92 with CBSO tours to Scandinavia and the USA; appearances with Berlin, London and Rotterdam Philharmonic Orchestras; Season 1992/93 included Berlin Philharmonic at Berlin Festival; Boston Symphony & Los Angeles Philharmonic, Netherlands Opera debut (Pelléas & Mélisande) and Tanglewood; Season 1993/94 includes Vienna Philharmonic and Philadelphia Orchestra debuts; Glyndebourne Festival 1994, Don Giovanni. *Recordings include:* The Dream of Gerontius, Mahler 2, Turangalîla Symphony, Porgy and Bess, music of the Second Viennese School. *Honours:* Winner, Bournemouth John Player International Conducting Competition, 1973; ISM Distinguished Musician Award; Hon Doctorate, Birmingham University, City of Birmingham Polytechnic; CBE, 1987. *Current Management:* Harold Holt Limited, London. *Address:* c/o Harold Holt Limited, 31 Sinclair Road, London W14 0NS, England.

RAUCH Wolfgang, b. 27 Jan 1957, Cologne, Germany. Singer (Baritone). *Education:* Studied in Cologne with Josef Metternich and in Italy with Mario del Monaco. *Career:* Sang with the Deutsche Oper am Rhein Dusseldorf from 1984, member of the Bayerische Staatsoper Munich from 1987; Guest appearances at La Scala Milan, the State Operas of Vienna and Hamburg and the Deutsche Oper Berlin; Sang Papageno in Mozart bicentenary performances of Die Zauberflöte at Barcelona and Bonn, 1991; Other roles include Lortzing's Tsar, Marcello, Mozart's Guglielmo and Figaro, Count Perruchetto in Haydn's La Fedelta Premiata, Silvio, Lionel in Tchaikovsky's The Maid of Orleans, Strauss's Count, Capriccio and Harlekin and the Herald in Lohengrin; Frequent concert and broadcasting engagements. *Address:* Bayerische Staatsoper, Postfach 100I48, 8000 Munich 1. Germany.

RAUHE Hermann Wilhelm, b. 6 Mar 1930, Wanna, Niederelbe, Germany. Musicologist. m. 16 Aug 1963, Annemarie Martin, 1 daughter. *Education:* Academy of Music and University of Hamburg, Federal Republic of Germany, 1951-55; MA, University of Hamburg, 1955; PhD, Musicology, 1959. *Career:* Music Teacher, Wilhelm Gymnasium, Hamburg, 1960-62; Lecturer, Academy of Music of Hamburg, 1962-64, Assistant Professor, Musicology and Music Education, 1964-65, Professor, 1965-68, Dean, Department Music Education, 1968-; Professor, Musicology, Music Education, University of Hamburg, 1970-; President, Academy of Music and Theatre, Hamburg, 1978. *Publications:* Author of books including: Horen und Verstehen, 1975; Jugend zwischen Opposition und Identifikation, 1975; Musik in der Umwelt; Hilfe oder Bedrohung?, 1978; Author, radio and TV series; research; numerous articles on musicology, Music-sociology and psychology, music education, music therapy; Editor, book series: Beitrage zur Schubmusik, 1962-; Musikalische Formen in historischen Reihen, 1962-; Schriften zur Musikpadagogik, 1975-; Editor, rec. series. *Honour:* Gold Medal, Society Musicians and Music Educators, 1974. *Memberships:* Member, Deputation at State Department of Education and Science, Hamburg; Vice-President, Landesmusikrat Hamburg; Society Research in Music Education,

President, 1971-74. *Address:* 18 Bredengrund D-2104, Hamburg 92, Germany.

RAUTAVAARA Einojuhani, b. 9 Oct 1928, Helsinki, Finland. Composer. m. Sini Koivisto, 18 Aug 1984. *Education:* MA, University of Helsinki; Sibelius Academy, 1950-57; Juilliard School of Music (with Vincent Persichetti), New York, USA, 1955-56; Tanglewood Music Center (with Aaron Copland, and Roger Sessions), 1955-56; Kölner Musikhochschule (with Rudolf Petzold), Federal Republic of Germany, 1958; Ascona (with Wladimir Vogel), 1957. *Career:* Art Professor, Finland, 1971-76; Professor of Composition, Sibelius Academy, 1976-90. *Compositions:* 6 operas; 2 choir-operas; 7 symphonies; Concerti for cello, piano, flute, violin, organ, double bass; Cantus Arcticus (concerto for birds and orchestra); 4 string quartets, cantatas, chamber music, piano music, songs, and other works. *Recordings include:* Thomas (opera), Vincent (opera), 6 symphonies, Ondine Company; Angel of Dusk (concerto for double bass and orchestra), Finlandia; Vigilia (orthodox mass), EMI-HMV; Cantus Arcticus, Ondine, Bis and Finlandia; Piano concertos 1 & 2, Ondine; symphony 6, cello concerto, Ondine. *Hobbies:* Painting; Literature. *Current Management:* Faber Music Inc. and Finnish Music Information Centre, Runeberginkatu 15A, 00100 Helsinki. *Address:* Bertel Jungin tie 3, Helsinki 57, Finland.

RAUTIO Erkki Ilmari, b. 5 Oct 1931, Helsinki, Finland. Professor of Cello. m. Aldelheid Mörike, 5 children. *Education:* Studies with Yrjo Selin, Enrico Mainardi and Pierre Fournier. *Career:* Concerts in USA, Canada, Japan, Russia and in most European countries; Professor of Violoncello, Sibelius Academy, Helsinki, Finland; Rector of The Sibelius-Academy, 1990-. *Recordings:* EMI; Camera. *Honours:* Violoncello Prize, Harriet Cohen International Music Awards, London, 1968; Pro Finlandia Medal, 1968. *Hobbies:* Lappland rambling; Chess. *Current Management:* Music Fazer, Helsinki. *Address:* Maamiehentie 8, 01630 Vantaa 63, Finland.

RAUTIO Nina, b. 21 Sept 1957, Bryamsk, Russia. Singer (Soprano). *Education:* Studied at Leningrad Conservatoire. *Career:* Sang first at the Leningrad State Theatre 1981-87; Bolshoi Opera from 1987; Western debut with Bolshoi Company at Metropolitan and the Edinburgh Festival 1991, as Tatiana and as Oksana in Rimsky's Christmas Eve; Season 1992 as Manon Lescaut at La Scala, conducted by Lorin Maazel, Verdi Requiem at Rome, Aida at the Savonlinna Festival and in concert performances conducted by Zubin Mehta; Sang with the Pittsburgh Symphony on tour to Seville Expo 92 and as Elisabetta in Don Carlo to open the season at La Scala; Season 1993-94 as Lisa in The Queen of Spades at the Opera Bastille Paris, Ballo in Maschera and Aida at Covent Garden, Verdi Requiem at Florence and the Festival Hall, Beethoven and Mahler in Pittsburgh, Desdemona at the Orange Festival, the Glagolitic Mass at La Scala and Amelia Boccanegra at Florence; Season 1994-95 as the Forza Leonora at the Staatsoper Berlin and Amelia Boccanegra at Covent Garden. *Recordings:* Manon Lescaut; Verdi Requiem; Guillaume Tell; Norma. *Address:* c/o Atholl Still Ltd, 80-86 Westow Street, London SE19 3AF, England.

RAWLINS Emily, b. 25 Sept 1950, Lancaster, Ohio, USA. Opera and Concert Singer. m. 18 Apr 1982. *Education:* BMus, Voice, Indiana University; Artists Diploma, Curtis Institute of Music; Diploma, Hochschule für Musik, Vienna. *Debut:* Basel, Switzerland. *Career:* Basel Stadttheater, 1973-77; Deutsche Oper am Rhein, 1977-82; Debuts: Theater de Stadt, Bonn, 1975; National Theater, Mannheim, 1976; Theater der Stadt, Köln, 1977; Städtische Bühnen, Dortmund, 1979; Städtische Bühnen, Augsburg; San Francisco Opera, 1980; American premiere, Lear, Salzburg Festival, world premiere Baal, 1981; Vienna Staatsoper, 1981; Teatro Nacional de Sao Carlos, Lisbon, 1982; Grand Théâtre du Genève, 1982; Houston Grand Opera, 1983; Anna Karenina, American Premiere, Los Angeles Opera Theater, 1983; ZDF, German Television, 1981 and 1982;

ORF Austrian Television, 1981; 2 Films, Bartered Bride and Fra Diavolo, 1983; 1 Film, Baal, 1984; Vienna State Opera, 1985; ORF, Wiener Symphoniker; Concert Opera Association, 1986; World Premiere, Das Schloss, Opera National, Brussels, 1986. *Recordings:* Part of Sophie in Baal, Classico Amadeo Label, 1985. *Address:* c/o California Artist's Management, 1182 Market Street, Suite 311, San Francisco, CA 94102, USA.

RAWNSLEY John, b. 14 Dec 1949, England. Singer (Baritone). *Education:* Royal Northern College of Music. *Debut:* Glyndebourne Touring Opera 1975: later sang Verdi's Ford and Stravinsky's Nick Shadow on tour, Mozart's Masetto, Rossini's Figaro and Puccini's Marcello at Glyndebourne; Covent Garden debut 1979, as Schaunard in La Bohème; French debut at Nancy in 1980, as Tonio in Pagliacci; English National Opera from 1982, as Amonasro and as Rigoletto in Jonathan Miller's production of Verdi's opera: tour to the USA 1984; Italian debut 1985, as Verdi's Renato in Trieste; La Scala Milan 1987, as Tonio; Guest engagements at the Vienna Staatsoper, San Diego, Barcelona, Bilbao, Brussels and Geneva: roles include Paolo Albiani (Simon Boccanegra), Macbeth, Papageno, Don Alfonso and Taddeo in L'Italiana in Algeri; Sang Rigoletto at Turin, 1989; Simon Boccanegra in a concert performance at the Festival Hall, 1990; Season 1992 as Rigoletto at Oslo and the Coliseum, and in The Beggar's Opera at the Aldeburgh Festival. *Recordings:* Rigoletto, and Masetto in Don Giovanni (EMI); Videos of Così fan Tutte, Il Barbiere di Siviglia, La Bohème and Rigoletto. *Address:* c/o Kaye Artists Management, Barratt House, 7 Chertsey Road, Woking, Surrey GU21 5AB, England.

RAYAM Curtis, b. 4 Feb 1951, Belleville, Florida, USA. Singer (Tenor). *Eucation:* Studied at the University of Miami with Mary Henderson Buckely. *Debut:* Miami 1971, in Manon Lescaut. *Career:* Appearances in Dallas, Houston and Jackson Opera/South. European debut at the Wexford Festival 1976, in Giovanna d'Arco by Verdi, returning as the Sultan in Mozart's Zaide and as Wilhelm Meister in Thomas' Mignon; Boston 1979, as Olympion in the US premiere of Tippett's The Ice Break, conducted by Sarah Caldwell; Amsterdam 1981, as Massenet's Werther; Further engagements at Salzburg, Paris, Frankfurt and Venice; La Scala 1985, in Handel's Alcina, returning 1988 as Orcane in Fetonte by Jommelli; Spoleto 1988 as Creon in Traetta's Antigone; Other roles include Rossini's Otello and Cleomene (L'Assedio di Corinto), Mozart's Idomeneo, Belmonte and Mitridate, Irus in Il Ritorno di Ulisse, Nemorino and Puccini's Pinkerton and Rodoldo. *Honours include:* Finalist Metropolitan Auditions 1972; Winner Dallas Competition 1974. *Recordings include:* Treemonisha by Scott Joplin (Deutsche Grammophon); Da-ud in Die Aegyptische Helena by Strauss (Decca).

REA John, b. 14 Jan 1944, Toronto, Canada. Composer. *Education:* Studied with John Weinzweg at University of Toronto and Milton Babbitt at Princeton. *Career:* Teacher at McGill University 1973, Dean of the Faculty of Music 1986-91; Composer-in-Residence at Mannheim 1984; Founder Member of the Montreal Music Society Les Evements du neuf. *Compositions:* Music theatre pieces Les Jours, ballet 1969; The Prisoner's Play, opera 1973; Hommage a Richard Wagner 1977; Com-possession 1980; Le Petit Livre des Ravalet, opera 1983; Offenes Lied, operatic scenes 1986; Operatic scenes based on Dante's Inferno and Poe's Morella, 1990-93; Orchestral: Hommage a Vasarely 1977; Vanishing Points 1983; Over Time 1987; Time and Again 1987; Chamber: Clarinet Sonatina 1965; Sestina 1968; Prologue, Scene and Movement for soprano, viola and 2 pianos 1968; Tempest 1969; What You Will for piano 1969; La Derniere Sirene for ondes martenot, piano and percussion 1981; Les Raisons des Forces Mouvantes for flute and string quartet 1984; Some Time Later for amplified string quartet 1986; Vocal: Litaneia for chorus and orchestra 1984. *Address:* c/o McGill University, Faculty of Music, Strathcona Music Building, 555 Sherbrooke Street West, Montreal, Quebec H3A 1E3, Canada.

READ Gardner, b. 2 Jan 1913, Evanston, Illinois, USA. Composer; University Professor. *Education:* BMus., 1936, MMus., 1937, Eastman School of Music; studied composition with various masters including Jan Sibelius, Finland, 1939, Aaron Copland, Tanglewood, Summer 1941; studied piano, organ, conducting, theory with various masters. *Career:* Teacher, Composition and Theory, various institutions, 1940-; Professor, Composition & Music Theory and Composer-in-Residence, School of Fine & Applied Arts, Boston University, Massachusetts, 1948-, Professor Emeritus, 1978-; Guest Conductor, major orchestras including: Boston Symphony, 1943, 1954, and Philadelphia Orchestra, 1964; Originator and Host, weekly educational radio series, Our American Music, 1953-60. *Compositions to:* Numerous commissioned works including Passacaglia and Fugue, Ravinia Festival, Chicago, 1938, and A Bell Overture, Cleveland Orchestra, 1946; numerous other orchestral works performed by major orchestras in USA and abroad; works for chamber or string orchestras and solo instruments; Toccata Giocosa and Night Flight; Choral and vocal music; opera Villon 1967; Chamber Music; Organ and Piano Music; Five Aphorisms, 1991. *Recordings:* Los Dioses Aztecas, 1982; De Profundis, 1985, 1991; Preludes on Old Southern Hymns, 1985, 1990; Symphony No. 4, 1986; Sonata Brevis, 1986; Works for Organ, 1989; Night Flight, 1962; Toccata Giocosa, 1954; Fantasy-Toccata, 1993; String Quartet No.1, 1993; Five Aphorisms, 1993; Sonata da Chiesa, 1993; Soronic Fantasia No 1, 1993. *Publications include:* Thesaurus of Orchestral Devices, 1953; Source Book of Proposed Music Notation Reforms, 1987; Music Notation, 2nd edition, 1972; Contemporary Instrumental Techniques, 1975; Modern Rhythmic Notation, 1978; Style and Orchestration, 1979; 20th-Century Microtonal Notation, 1989; Compendium of Modern Instrumental Techniques, 1993. *Contributions to:* Professional journals. *Honours:* Recipient, numerous scholarships, Fellowships, prizes and musical honours including: DMus., Doane College, Nebraska, 1962; Achievement Award, Eastman School of Music, 1982; National Association of Teachers of Singing Art Song Competition, 1986. *Membership:* ASCAP. *Address:* 47 Forster Road, Manchester, MA 01944, USA.

REANEY Gilbert, b. 11 Jan 1924, Sheffield, England. Professor. *Education:* Licentiate, Royal Academy of Music, 1946; BA 1948, BMus 1950, MA 1951, Sheffield University; Sorbonne University, Paris, France, 1950-53. *Career:* Performer, BBC, & tours, Britain & continent, 1952-88; Research Fellow, Reading University 1953-56, Birmingham 1956-59; Director, London Medieval Group, 1958-; Visiting Professor, Hamburg University, Germany, 1960; Associate Professor, University of California, Los Angeles, 1960-62, Full Professor, 1963-93. *Publications:* Early 15th Century Music, 8 volumes, 1955-83; Catalogue, Medieval Polyphonic Manuscripts to 1400, 2 volumes, 1966, 1969; 7 volumes for Corpus Scriptorum de Musica. *Contributions to:* Assistant and co-editor, numerous articles, Musica Disciplina, 1956-93; General Editor, Corpus Scriptorum de Musica. *Honour:* 1st Dent Medal, Royal Musical Association, 1961. *Memberships:* Royal Musical Association; American Musicological Society; Council, Plainsong & Medieval Music Society. *Hobbies:* Walking; Reading; Travel. *Address:* 1001 Third Street, Santa Monica, California 90403, USA.

REARICK Barbara, b. 1960, USA. Singer (Mezzo-soprano). *Education:* Studied at Manhattan School of Music and at Britten-Pears School with Nancy Evans and Anthony Rolfe Johnson. *Career:* Concert and opera performances in Britain and USA; British debut 1987 at Aldeburgh Festival as Britten's Lucretia; Sang Copland's Old American Songs with Lukas Foss, piano at the Snape Concert Hall; Other repertoire includes Messiah, Lieder eines fahrenden Gesellen, L'Enfance du Christ and Britten's Charm of Lullabies orchestrated by Colin Matthews, all at Snape; Ravel's Chansons Madecasses, Haydn Masses with the Orchestra of St John's Smith Square and Handel's Dixit Dominus at the Norfolk and Norwich Festival, American popular songs there 1992, with Richard Rodney Bennett;

Operatic repertoire includes Meg Page, Chautauqua Opera, Suzuki in Opera Delaware and Annina in Rosenkavalier in New York City Opera; Member of the Britten-Pears Ensemble, with performances throughout Britain and USA. *Address:* c/o Owen-White Management, 14 Nightingale Road, London N8 7QU, England.

REBER William Francis, b. 3 Dec 1940, Oakland, California, USA. Conductor; Vocal Coach; Accompanist. m. Margaret Moffatt, 24 June 1986, 1s. 1d. *Education:* BMus, magna cum laude, Theory and Composition, 1964, MMus, Conducting, 1966, University of Utah; Doctor of Musical Arts, University of Texas, Austin, 1977. *Debut:* Music Director and Conductor for Candide, Minnesota Opera, 1977. *Career:* Conductor, 17th Air Force Men's Chorus, Germany, 1969; Music Director for production of Curlew River, telecast internationally, 'Britten in Texas'; Music Director, Minnesota Opera Company Studio, 1976-77; Conductor, University of Texas Opera Theatre, 1978-90; Conductor, Corpus Christi Ballet, Texas, 1986-; Conductor, Corpus Christi Symphony for Education concerts, 1986-91; Music Director, Chamber Orchestra, Associate Conductor, Symphony, University of Texas; Music Director, California State University, Fullerton Symphony and Opera Theatre, 1990-91; Director and Principal Conductor, Lyric Opera Theatre, Arizona State University, Tempe, 1991-; Also affiliated as Conductor, Vocal Coach and accompanist with American Institute of Musical Studies, Graz, Austria and Altenburg Musiktheater Akademie, Altenburg, Germany. *Publications:* The Operas of Ralph Vaughan Williams, 1977; English version of Hans Pfitzner's Das Christelflein, 1977. *Memberships:* American Symphony Orchestra League; Conductors Guild; Opera America; National Opera Association. *Hobbies:* Private Pilot; Chess. *Address:* 2025 E Campbell No.331, Phoenix, AZ 85016, USA.

RECHBERGER Herman, b. 14 Feb 1947, Linz, Austria. Composer; Performer. m. (1) Ilse Maier, 1966, 1 son, 1 daughter, (2) Soile Jaatinen, 1972, 1 son, 2 daughters. *Education includes:* Graphic Arts, Linz, 1967; Teaching degree, Classical Guitar, Recorder, 1973, Diploma, Composition, 1976, Sibelius Academy, 1971-76. *Career:* Music Teacher and Choir Conductor, 1975-79; Producer of Contemporary Music, Artistic Director of Experimental Studio, Finnish Broadcasting, 1979-84; State Grant, 1985-; Recitals of new recorder music, most European countries, Russia, Cuba, USA; Performed own works, ISCM Music Days, Helsinki/Stockhom, 1978, Athens, 1979, Warsaw, 1992, and Helsinki Biennale, 1981, 1983; Frequent performances and tours with ensembles Poor Knights and Sonores Antiqui, specialised in early music and scenic performances of contemporary music; Guest Composer, for Hungarofilm at Hungarian Broadcasting Companies Electronic Music Studio, 1985, and Slovak Radio, 1986 (Rustle of Spring); Currently Composer-in-Residence; Finnish citizen, 1974-. *Compositions include:* Orchestra: Consort Music 1, 2, 4, 5; The Garden of Delights; Venezia; 3 Guitar Concertos; Songs from the North; Goya; 2 Operas; The Nuns; Laurentius; Radiophonic works: The Rise of Mr Jonathan Smith; Magnus Cordius, entries in a diary; Vocal music: Vanha Linna; Hades; Dunk; Rhythm & Blues; Notturno inamorata; Seis Canciones de anochecer; Musica Picta for small children; Tape music; Cordamix; Narod; KV- 622bis; Moldavia; Rustle of Springs; Multimedia: Zin Kibaru; lSmo..; Firenze 1582; Survol; La Folia; Chamber music: Consort Music 3 for brass nonet; El Palacio del Sonido for 3 guitars; Consort music 6 for 12 recorders; Musical Graphics and pictographic scores for educational purposes; Many arrangements and reconstructions of early music and Ancient Greek Music, e.g. the world's first opera: Peri Jacopo's Euridice . *Recordings include:* The King's Hunt, (Esa-Pekka Salonen - french horn); Cordamix; Rasenie jari - Rustle of Spring; The Garden of Delights, Austrian RSO, conductor Leif Segerstam; Consort Music I, Clas Pehrson-recorders, Swedish RSO, conductor Leif Segerstam. *Hobbies:* Graphic arts; Languages; Chinese calligraphy; Computer art. *Address:* Laajavuorenkuja 5 B 11, 01620 Vantaa, Finland.

RECTANUS Hans, Professor Dr. b. 18 Feb 1935, Worms, Germany. Professor. m. Elisabeth Zilbauer, 1 son, 1 daughter. *Education:* Civic Music Academy and University, Frankfurt/Main; Academy of Music and Interpretive Art, University of Vienna, Vienna; School for Protestant Church-Music, Schluechtern/Hesse; PhD, University of Frankfurt, 1966. *Career:* Teacher (Music, German Literature) for Gymnasium, 1960-63; Lecturer and Assistant, University of Frankfurt/Main, 1963-66; Lecturer, Teachers College, Heidelberg, 1966-71; Professor at Heidelberg, 1971-. *Compositions:* Edited: Hans Pfitzner String Quartet, D Minor; Trio for Violin, Violoncello, Piano. *Publications:* Leitmotivik und Form in den Musikdramatischen Werken Hans Pfitzners, 1967; Neue Ansaetze im Musikunterricht, 1972; Hans Pfitzner, Saemtliche Lieder mit Klavierbegleitung, Volume I, 1980, Volume II, 1983. *Contributions to:* Die Musikforschung; Riemannmusiklexikon; Studien zur Musikgeschichte des 19 Jahrhundert; Mitteilungen der Hans Pfitzner - Gesellschaft; Festschrift H. Osthoff - Renaissance - Studien; Zeitschrift für Musik - Pädagogik, Lexikon der Musikpädagogik, Pfitzner - Studien. *Honours:* Kritiker-Preis, 1956; Recipient, Music Director, Organist. *Memberships:* Praesidium Hans Pfitzner Society, Munich; Society for Music Research, Cassel; Member of The Society of Professional Choirmasters. *Current Management:* Pädagogische Hochschule, Heidelberg, W. Germany. *Address:* D-6905 Schriesheim/Bergstr., Schlittweg 31, Germany.

REDEL Kurt, b. 8 Oct 1918, Breslau, Germany. Conductor; Flautist. *Education:* Studied flute, conducting and composition at the Breslau Hochschule fur Musik. *Career:* Conductor and flute soloist from 1938; Professor at Salzburg Mozarteum 1938; Professor at the Music Academy Detmold, 1943; Debut as flautist outside Germany at Menton 1950; Founded the Munich Pro Arte Orchestra 1952; Conducted at Festival de Royaumont and the Semaines Musicales in Paris 1953; Founder and Artistic Director of the Easter Festival at Lourdes; Conductor of the Mozart Chamber Orchestra of Salzburg. *Recordings include:* Bach's Brandenburg Concertos, Orchestral Suites, Die Kunst der Fuge, Musikalisches Opfer, Harpsichord and Violin Concertos, Magnificat, Masses and Cantatas; Telemann Concertos for Flute, Oboe, Trumpet, Viola and Violin, St Mark Passion and St Matthew Passion; Vivaldi Four Seasons and other concertos; Concerti Grossi by Handel, Torelli, Corelli, Scarlatti, Stolzel; Music by Marais, Couperin, Caldara, Carissimi and Marcello; Mozart Symphonies, Divertimenti, and Concertante K364; Solo flautist in Mozart Sonatas, Quartets and Concertos; Schubert 4th Symphony with the Czech Philharmonic. Labels include Philips, Vox, Decca, Telefunken and Supraphon.

REDGATE Christopher Frederick, b. 17 Sept 1956, Bolton, Lancashire, England. Musician (Oboist). m. Celia Jane Pitstow, 3 Oct 1981, 2 sons. *Education:* Chethams School of Music, Manchester; Royal Academy of Music, London. *Career:* Solo & chamber performances, England & Europe; Performer-in-residence, courses for composers, York University, Aldeburgh School for Advanced Musical Studies, Dartington Summer School; Artist-in-residence, Victorian College of the Arts, Melbourne, Australia, including recitals, lectures, recordings, 1983; Toured Canada, 1985; American debut, Pittsburgh International Festival of New Music, 1986; Professor of Oboe, Darmstadt International School for Contemporary Music, 1986. Performed regularly with the Phoenix Wind Quintet, Krosta Trio, Exposé, Lontano; Broadcasts, radio in UK & Netherlands, television; Performed British premiere, Penderecki's Capriccio for Oboe & Strings, conducted by composer; Performed works by Strauss, Martinů, Bennett, collaborated with choreographer Ian Spink and worked for Thames TV; Now regular Professor of Oboe, Darmstadt International School for Contemporary Music. *Contributions to:* Series of articles on Woodwind instruments in Worship for Christian Music Magazine; Articles on Christianity and the Arts for Kerygma Magazine. *Membership:* Member of the Worship Group Wellspring, 1987-; Co-ordinator of the Musicians' Christian Fellowship. *Hobby:* Christianity. *Address:* 7 Glemsford Drive, Harpenden, Herts AL5 5RB, England.

REE Jean van, b. 7 Mar 1943, Kerkrade, Holland. Singer (Tenor). *Education:* Studied with Else Bischof-Bornes in Aachen and Franzika Martienssen-Lohmann in Dusseldorf. *Debut:* Mainz 1963, in Zar und Zimmermann. *Career:* Sang in Basle, Augsburg and Cologne; Guest appearances in Amsterdam, Hamburg, Hanover, Salzburg and Frankfurt; Augsburg 1971, in the premiere of Rafael Kubelik's opera on the life of Titian, Cornelia Faroli; Teatro Reggio Turin 1983, in Lulu; Antwerp and Ghent 1984, as Matteo in Arabella; Other roles include Don Ottavio, Hoffmann, Count Almaviva, Alfredo, and Mephistopheles in Doktor Faust by Busoni; Metropolitan Opera 1978, as Bicias in Massenet's Thäis; Sang Berg's Alwa at Barcelona and Vienna 1987. *Recordings include:* Les Brigandes, by Offenbach (RCA). *Address:* c/o Staatsoper, Opernring 2, A-1010, Vienna, Austria.

REECE Arley, b. 27 Aug 1945, Yoakum, Texas, USA. Singer (Tenor). *Education:* Studied at North Texas State University with Eugene Conley and at Manhattan School of Music. *Debut:* Sang Assad in Die Königin von Saba by Goldmark with the American Opera Society at Carnegie Hall, 1970. *Career:* Sang with Dallas Civic Opera, Shreveport Symphony, Philadelphia Lyric Opera, Kentucky and Connecticut Opera Associations, Opera Society of Washington and at the Lake George Festival; European debut in Prokofiev's The Gambler at Wexford Festival, Ireland, 1973; New York City Opera debut 1974, as Bacchus; European engagements in Netherlands, Belgium, France including Berlioz Festival, Germany including East and West Berlin, Spain, Italy, Austria, Poland and Switzerland, appearances in Canada and Iran; British appearances with the Northern Ireland Trust, Scottish Opera, Welsh National Opera and at Edinburgh and Wexford Festivals; Broadcasts: Cardillac (RAI Italy), The Gambler (BBC), Oberon, Ariadne auf Naxos and Wozzeck (Radio France), Macbeth (Netherlands Radio), From the House of the Dead, Schmidt's Das Buch mit Sieben Siegeln and Dallapiccola's Job (WDR), From the House of the Dead (CBC Canada), Turandot (Radio Warsaw), Tannnhäuser (Spanish Radio, Barcelona), Wozzeck (BBC Scotland), Lohengrin (Radio Espana); TV appearances: Lohengrin (Spanish TV), Concert celebrating the 100th Anniversary of Richard Wagner (Polish TV), Das Kleine Mahagonny and Il Ritorno d'Ulisse in Patria (TV Schweiz); Season 1989-90 sang Siegmund and Siegfried in Ring cycles for Warsaw Opera, Saint François d'Assise for Polish radio and TV; Lohengrin, Calaf and Samson at Wiesbaden. Other roles include Otello, Canio and Manrico. *Recordings include:* Il Ritorno di Ulisse. *Address:* Martin Luther 63, 46284 Dorsten, Germany.

REED H(erbert) Owen, b. 17 June 1910, Odessa, Missouri, USA. Composer; Author; Conductor. m. (1) Esther Reed, deceased 1981; (2) Mary Arwood, 12 Aug 1982; 2 daughters. *Education:* University of Missouri, Columbia 1929-33; BMus, La State University, Baton Rouge 1934; MMus at the same place 1936; BA 1937; PhD, Eastman School of Music, University of Rochester, NY 1939. *Career includes:* Chairman of Theory and Composition, Michigan State University 1939-67; Acting Head Music Department at the same place 1957-58; Chairman of Music Composition at the same place 1967-75; Professor Emeritus, at the same place 1976-; Guest Professor, Lecturer, Guest Conductor at many Universities. *Compositions include:* (Orchestral): La Fiesta Mexicana 1964; The Turning Mind 1968; (Band): La Fiesta Mexicana, For The Unfortunate 1972; The Awakening of the Ents, for Wind Ensemble 1986; Of Lothlorien, for wind ensemble, 1987; (Stage): Earth Trapped 1960; Living Solid Face 1974; Butterfly Girl and Mirage Boy 1980; Peter Homan's Dream 1955 Opera; (Chamber): El Muchaco 1963; (Choral and Orchestra); Tabernacle for the Sun 1963; Works also recorded, Kinescoped and videotaped. *Recordings:* La Fiesta Mexicana, recorded by the Tokyo Kosei Wind Orchestra, Fredrick Fennell, Conductor on Kosei Stereo Label. *Publications include:* Basic Music, 1954, and Basic Music Workbook, 1954; Basic Contrapuntal Techniques (with Paul Hardes), 1964, and Basic Contrapuntal Workbook, 1964; The Materials of Musical Composition (with Robert G. Sidnell) 3 Volumes (in preparation), Volume I Fundamentals 1978; Scoring for Percussion 1978. *Recordings:* La Fiesta Mexicana, Dallas (TX), Wind Symphony, Howard Dunn, conducting, Reference Recordings (RR38CD), 1991. *Memberships:* Professional Organisations. *Honours include:* Guggenheim Fellowship; Neil A. Kjos Memorial Award For The Unfortunate 1975. *Hobbies:* Fishing. *Address:* 7805 W. Lake Drive, Canadian Lakes Club, Stanwood, MI 49346, USA.

REED John, b. 30 May 1909, Aldershot, England. Broadcasting Official, BBC, retired; Writer on Music. m. Edith Marion Hampton, 30 Oct. 1936, 2 sons, 2 daughters. *Education:* BA, Honours, English Language and Literature, London University, 1927-30, 1934-35. *Publications:* Schubert: The Final years, 1972; Schubert, Great Composer Series, 1978; The Schubert Song Companion, 1985, (Vincent H. Duckles Award); Schubert (The Master Musicians Series) 1987. *Contributions to:* Music Critic, Guardian Newspaper, 1974-80; Musical Times; Music and Letters; Radio 3 Magazine. *Memberships:* Royal Musical Association; Hallé Society; Victorian Society; Ehrenmitglied, International Franz Schubert Institute of Vienna, 1989; Chairman, Schubert Institute (UK). *Hobbies:* Gardening; Cricket; Reference Books. *Address:* 130 Fog Lane, Manchester M20 0SW, England.

REES Jonathan, b. 1963, England. Violinist; Director. *Education:* Studied at the Yehudi Menuhin School and with Dorothy Delay at Juilliard. *Career:* Student engagements at the Windsor, Gstaad and Llandaff Festivals and three tours of the Netherlands; Later recitals at the Bath, City of London, Brighton, Henley and Salisbury Festivals; Concerto soloist with the Bournemouth Sinfonietta, Philharmonia, London Soloists Chamber Orchestra and the Royal Philharmonic; Concerts with the Academy of St Martin in the Fields at Carnegie Hall, the Festival Hall and at St Martin's Church; Beethoven's Concerto with the Bournemouth Sinfonietta, 1990; Director of the Scottish Ensemble: concerts in Edinburgh, elsewhere in Scotland and in Austria, Belgium, France, Germany, the Netherlands, Norway and North and Central America; Festivals include Berlin, Guelph, Spoleto, Prague, Sofia, Cheltenham and Edinburgh; Royal Command Performances at the Palace of Holyrood House and at Balmoral. *Honours:* Prize winner 1978, BBC Young Musician of the Year competition; First prize, Royal Overseas League Competition, 1979. *Address:* c/o Anglo-Swiss Management, 4-5 Primrose Mews, Sharpeshall Street, London NW1 8YW, England.

REES-WILLIAMS Jonathan, b. 10 Feb 1949, St Helier, Jersey. Organist; Master of Choristers. m. Helen Patricia Harling, 25 May 1985, 1 son, 2 daughters. *Education:* Royal Academy of Music, 1967-69; ARCO, 1966; FRCO, 1968; LRAM, 1968; Organ Scholar, New College, Oxford, 1969-72; MA. *Career:* Numerous recitals with specialization in 20th century Polish Organ Music; Radio broadcasts as Organists and Director; BBC TV Pebble Mill at One, 1982; ATV England Their England, 1980; Central News, 1981; Acting Organist, New College Oxford, 1972; Assistant Organist, St Clement Danes and Hampstead Parish Church, London, 1972-74; Assistant Organist, Salisbury Cathedral, 1974-78, and Director of Music, Salisbury Cathedral School; Chorusmaster, Portsmouth Festival Choir, 1974-78; Organist and Master of the Choristers, Lichfield Cathedral, 1978-1991; Organist and Master of the Choristers, St Georges Chapel, Windsor Castle, 1991-. *Recordings:* Evensong from New College; In Quires and Places; Music from Salisbury; Lichfield Composers; From Darkness to Light; Evensong for the Feast of St Chad; Hear My Prayer; Bist du bei mir; Producer for recordings by New College Choir, Westminister Cathedral, Ex Cathedral, Exon Singers, St Mary, Warwick; The King and The Kingdom; The Psalms of David (Priory), 1991; Organ Music from Lichfield Cathedral, 1990, Abbey; Christmas Music from Lichfield Cathdral, 1990, Abbey; The Organ of St George's Hall, Windsor Castle, 1991, Heritage. *Memberships:* Member of the Royal Society of Musicians, 1993. *Hobbies:*

Railways and Vintage model Railway Collecting; Cycling; Walking; Wine. *Address:* 25, The Cloisters, Windsor Castle, Berks, SL4 1NJ, England.

REEVE Joyce Doreen May, b. 28 Sept 1919, Norwich, England. Retired Business Executive; Private Piano Teacher. *Education:* Private Tuition from 4 1/2 years to 72 years; LTCL Diploma in Piano teaching; Basic skills in Church Organ playing. *Career:* Piano teacher; Accompanist for choirs, (Piano rather than church organ playing). *Honour:* Runner-up certificate, Daily Express Piano Competition, 1928. *Membership:* ISM. *Hobbies:* Embroidery; Art (Painting). *Address:* 55 Aster Drive, Werrington, Peterborough, Cambridgeshire PE4 7RY.

REEVE Stephen, b. 15 Mar 1948, London, England. Composer. *Education:* Composition class of Henri Pousseur, Liège Conservatoire, 1971-72. *Career:* Major Commissions, BBC So, 1975, IRCAM, 1980, Institute of Contemporary Arts, London, 1985. *Compositions:* The Kite's Feathers, 1969-70; Japanese haikai for mezzo & Ensemble; Colour Music, 1970, for woodwind quartet; Poème: Couleurs du Spectre, 1972-73, for orchestra with optional light projection; Summer Morning by a lake full of colors, 1974, an expansion of Schoenberg's Farben, for large orchestra; aux régions éthérées, 1975-76, for three chamber groups; Grande thèse de la petite-fille de Téthys, 1980-87 an ethnic encyclopaedia for solo cello; L'Oracle de Delphes, 1985, music-theatre for brass quintet; Strophe, 1985-86, for solo rock and 4 classical guitars; Les fées dansent selon la mode double, 1988-89, scene for 3-5 dancer-percussionnists & 6-10 or more actor extras; Ô que Zeus apparaisse à l'horizon, 1989-90, for gamelan ensemble & tape. *Memberships:* PRS; Association of Professional Composers. *Address:* 73 Knightsfield, Welwyn Garden City, Herts, AL8 7JE, England.

REHER Sven Helge, b. 6 Sep. 1911, Hamburg, Germany. Musician (Violist); Composer; Lecturer. m. Anne Sullivan, 11 Apr. 1942, 3 sons, 2 daughters. *Education:* AB, University of California, Los Angeles, USA, 1940; MA, Music, 1948; Studies at University of Southern California; Certificate, Hochschule für Musik, Berlin. *Career:* Los Angeles Philharmonic Orchestra, 8 seasons; principal Violist, California Chamber Symphony; Principal Violist, San Luis Obispo Mozart Festival; member, Pasadena Symphony, Santa Barbara Symphony Orchestra. *Compositions:* 12 Studies for Viola; Sonata for Solo Viola (Enigma); Cuenca Rapsodia Para Flauta y Viola; Essay for Solo Viola and String Orchestra; several transcriptions, arrangements and editions. *Recordings:* Eric Zeisl, Sonata for Viola and Piano; Leon Levitch, Viola Sonata with Composer; Hindemith: Duet for Viola and Cello, with Kurt Reher, Solo Sonata Op 25 1. *Contributions to:* Viola Society of America; Modern Language Form. *Memberships:* Phi Mu Alpha (Sinfonia), UCLA; American String Teachers Association. *Hobbies:* Travel; Natural History; Politica - World-wide; Study of Foreign Languages. *Address:* 258 West Alamar Avenue 2, Santa Barbara, CA 93105, USA.

REICH Steve, b. 3 Oct 1936, New York, USA. Composer. m. Beryl Korot, 30 May 1976, 1 son. *Education:* BA, Honours, Philosophy, Cornell University, 1957; Studied Composition with: Hall Overton, 1957-58, Juilliard School of Music with William Bergsma, Vincent Persichetti, 1958-61; MA, Music, Mills College, California (study with Darius Milhaud, Luciano Berio, 1963); Studied African drumming (1970); Balinese Gamelan Semar Pegulingan (1974); Hebrew Cantillation (1976). *Career:* Formed own ensembele with 3 musicians, 1966, which has grown to 18 or more musicians, and performs throughout the world; More than 300 concerts 1971-87; Composer of music, played by major orchestras throughout USA and Europe, also choreographed by leading dance companies. *Compositions include:* (Recorded) Come Out, 1966; It's Gonna Rain, 1965; Four Organs, 1970; Drumming, 1971; Music for 18 Musicians, 1976; Variations for Winds, Strings and Keyboards, 1980; (Published) The Desert Music, 1984; Sextet, 1985; Octet, 1979; The Four Sections, 1987; Electric Counterpoint for guitar and tape 1987; Different Trains for string quartet and tape 1988; Co-Commission in 1993 by Vienna Festival, Holland Festival, Hebbel Theater, Berlin, Serious Speakout & The South Bank Centre, London, Festival d'Actomne a Paris, Theatre de la Monnaie, Brussels and Brooklyn Academy of Music Next Wave Festival for The Cave, a new form of opera with video. A collaboration with video artist Beryl Korot. *Publications:* Writing About Music, 1974, translated into French, 1981. *Contributions to:* New York Times; Notations; Source Magazines; Aspen Managazine; Interfuntionen: VH-101; Attitudes. *Honours:* Guggenheim Fellow, 1978; Rockfeller Foundation Awards, 1975, 1981, 1982; Grants, national Endowment for the Arts, 1974, 1976; Artist in Residence, Berlin, 1974; Grammy Award, for Best New Composition, Different Trains, 1990. *Current Management:* Allied Artists Management, London and Elizabeth Sabal, IMG Artists, 22 East 71st St. New York, NY 10021, USA. *Address:* c/o Allied Artists Agency, 42 Montpelier Square, London SW7 1JZ, England.

REICHERT Manfred, b. 5 May 1942, Karlsruhe, Germany. Conductor. *Education:* Studied at the Karlsruhe Hochschule, 1961-65; Musicology at the University of Fribourg/Brisgau, 1966-67. *Career:* Producer at South West German Radio, Baden-Baden, 1967-83; Founded the chamber group Ensemble 13, 1973; Directed the festivals Wintermusik and Musik auf den 49ten at Karlsruhe, 1980 and 1983; Artistic Director of the Festival of European Culture at Karlsruhe, 1983-87; Teacher at the Hochschule für Musik at Karlsruhe from 1984; Has conducted the premieres of Hans-Jurgen von Böse's Variations for Strings, 1981, Wolfgang Rihm's Chiffre-Zyklus, 1988 and Gejagte Form, 1989.

REIMANN Aribert, b. 4 March 1936, Berlin, Germany. Composer; Pianist. *Education:* 1955-59 Berlin Hochschule für Musik with Boris Blacher (composition), Ernst Pepping (counterpoint) and Rausch (piano); Musicological studies in Vienna 1958. *Career:* Freelance composer, notably of operas, and accompanist in Lieder recitals to Dietrich Fischer- Dieskau. London premieres of Lear and the Ghost Sonata 1989; Opera Das Schloss (The Castle) premiered at the Deutsche Oper Berlin, 1992. *Compositions:* Operas: A Dream Play, after Strindberg, 1964; Melusine, 1970; Lear, after Shakspeare, 1978; The Ghost Sonata, after Strindberg, 1984; Troades, after Euripides, 1986; The Castle, after Kafka, 1992; Ballet: Stoffreste 1957; rev. as Die Vogelscheuchen, The Scarecrows, 1970; Orchestral: Violin Concerto 1959; Piano Concerto No.1 1961; A Dream Play suite 1965; Rondes for strings 1968; Loqui 1969; Piano Concerto No. 2 1972; Variations 1975; Sieben Fragmente 1988; Concerto for violin, cello and orchestra 1988/89. Vocal: Ein Totentanz for baritone and chamber orchestra 1960; Hölderlin-Fragments for soprano and orchestra 1963; 3 Shakespeare Sonnets for baritone and piano 1964; Epitaph for tenor and 7 instruments 1965; Verra la Morte, cantata 1966; Inane for soprano and orchestra 1968; Zyklus for baritone and orchestra 1971; Lines for soprano and strings 1973; Wolkenloses Christfest, Cloudless Christmas, Requiem for baritone, cello and orchestra 1974; Lear, Symphony for baritone and orchestra 1980; Unrevealed for baritone and string quartet; Tre Poemi di Michelangelo 1985; Neun Sonette der Louize Labé 1986; Chacum sa Chimère for tenor and orchestra 1981; Three Songs for poems by Edgar Allan Poe 1982; Apocalyptic Fragment for mezzo, piano and orchestra, 1987; Requiem for soprano, mezzo, baritone and orchestra 1982; orchestration of Schumann's Gedichte der Maria Stuart, 1988. Chamber: Piano Sonata 1958; Canzoni e Ricercare for flute, viola and cello 1961; Reflexionen for 7 instruments 1966; Cello Sonata 1963; Invenzioni for 12 players 1979; Trio for violin, viola and cello, 1987; More recent works include: Das Schloß, 1990/91; Ladt Lazarus, 1992; Eingedunkelt, 1992; Nightpiece (James Joyce) for Soprano and Klavier, 1992. *Honours include:* Rome Prize 1963; Schumann Prize of Dusseldorf 1964; Prix de composition musicale de la Fondation Prince Pierre de Monaco, 1986; Frankfurt Music Award, 1991. *Current Management:* B.Schott's Soehne, Weihergarten 5, Postfach 3640, 6500 Mainz, Germany.

Address: c/o Schott and Co. Ltd., 48 Great Marlborough Street, London W1, England.

REIMERS K Lennart, b. 31 Mar 1928, Algutsbode, Sweden. Music and Book Publisher; Ord. Professor in Music Pedagog. m. Gerd Wadelius, 1 son, 1 daughter. *Education:* Degree in Musicology, Literature and Philosophy, University of Uppsala; Director of Music Diplomas, Royal College of Music, Stockholm; PhD Fil dr, University of Göteberg, 1983. *Career:* Managing Director, Nordiska Musikförlaget, Stockholm, 1961-71; Director, Universal Edition, Vienna, 1971-75; Founder and Proprietor, Edition Reimers, Stockholm, 1975-; Lecturer and Researcher, Institute for Musicology, University of Stockholm and College of Music, Stockholm; Director of Center for Research in Music Education, Stockholm, 1989-1993. *Publications:* A Swedish St John Passion, 1957; Mozart och Sverige, 1961; Konst-och Musik historia, (with Gerd Reimers), 1966; Tio Musikanalyer, 1971; Wienervalsen och Familien Strauss, (with Gerd Reimers), 1975; Alice Tegners Barnvisor, 1983. *Contributions to:* Several musical journals, Music in Sweden (MIS), 1993-94 together with Bo Wellner Choral Music Perspectives, 1993. *Honours:* Recipient, several decorations. *Memberships:* Swedish Royal Academy of Music; President, for Music Education Commission; International Society for Music Education, 1968-72; Editor, International Music Educator, 1968-72 and Musikkultur, Stockholm, 1959-72; President, Swedish Section, International Society for Contemporary Music, 1975-78; President, Electro-acoustic Music, (EMS), 1991-94. *Hobbies:* Travel; Vinology. *Address:* Mårdvägen 44-46, S-16137 Bromma- Stockholm, Sweden.

REINEMANN Udo, b. 6 Aug 1942, Lubeck, Germany. Singer (Baritone). *Education:* Studied at Krefeld, the Vienna Academy of Music and with Erik Werba and W Steinbruck at the Salzburg Mozarteum, 1962-67. *Debut:* Song recital at Bordeaux, 1967. *Career:* Gave more recitals then studied further with Germaine Lubin in Paris and with Otakar Kraus in London; Many performances in Lieder, opera and oratorio; Founded a vocal quartet 1975 with Ana-Maria Miranda, Clara Wirtz and Jean-Claude Orliac (Lieder Quartet); Sang in the premiere of Adrienne Clostre's opera Nietzsche, 1978; My Chau Trong Thuy by Dao, 1979. *Recordings include:* Vocal quartets by Haydn; Lieder by Clara Schumann and Richard Strauss; Posthumous Lieder by Hugo Wolf. *Honours include:* First Prize for concert singing, Vienna Academy of Music, 1967.

REINHARD Johnny, b. 29 Apr 1956, Geneva, New York, USA. Director; Bassoonist; Scholar; Vocalist; Recorder Player; Educator. *Education:* North Carolina School of the Arts; Manhattan School of Music; Columbia University. *Career:* Founder, Director, American Festival of Microtonal Music Inc., 1981- in 70 different concerts; Host, Aspects of Microtonality on WKCR FM Radio, 6 Years; Directed, Performed, 2 Concerts in Futurimo Festival in Venice, Italy; Directed, Performed M A N C A, in Nice, France, 1986; Filmed as a Conductor in Nova, Childs Play, 1986, on PBS. *Recordings include:* Between the Keys on Newport-Classic Premier, Cowpeoples on M Tone Records with the Microtones Band. *Publications:* Pitch for the International Microtonalist; The Microtonal Bassoon; Ear Microtonal Issue. *Address:* 318 East 70th Street 5FW, New York, NY 10021, USA.

REINHARDT Rolf, b. 3 Feb 1927, Heidelberg, Germany. Conductor. *Education:* Studied piano with Kwast-Hodapp and composition with Wolfgang Fortner. *Career:* Conducted at the Stuttgart Opera 1945, in Heidelberg from 1946; Assistant at Bayreuth 1954-57; Conducted opera at Darmstadt, Generalmusikdirektor at the Pfalztheater Kaiserslautern 1958; Trier Opera 1959-68; Professor at the Hochschule für Musik Frankfurt from 1968. *Recordings:* Bach's Magnificat, Cantatas and Concertos for harpsichord and violin; Haydn Sinfonia Concertante and Concertos for trumpet, Horn and oboe; Mozart Violin Concertos, Concertante

K297b, Thamos King of Egypt and Litaniae Lauretanae; Handel Organ Concertos and Silete Venti; Stamitz Viola Concerto, Sinfonia Concertante; Bartók 1 and Brahms 2 Piano Concertos, with György Sandor; Mozart Bastien and Bastienne, La Finta Giardiniera; Bartók Music for Strings, Percussion and Celesta, Wooden Prince and Miraculous Mandarin; Beethoven Egmont; Schumann Cello Concerto, Violin Fantasia, Konzertstück for four horns and D minor Introduction and Allegro; Dvořák and Goldmark Violin Concertos, with Bronislav Gimpel; Lieder accompanist for Fritz Wunderlich. *Address:* Staatliche Hochschule für Musik, Escherheimer Landstrasse 33, Postfach 2326, Frankfurt, Germany.

REINHARDT-KISS Ursula, b. 3 Nov 1938, Letmathe, Sauerland, Germany. Singer (Soprano). *Education:* Studied with Ellen Bosenius in Cologne and Irma Beilke in Berlin. *Debut:* Saarbrücken 1967, as Marie in Der Waffenschmied. *Career:* Sang in Saarbrücken until 1969, Aachen 1969-71; Guest appearances in Lubeck, Cologne, Zurich, Antwerp, Milan, Copenhagen and Rome; Drottningholm 1983, in Il Fanatico Burlato by Cimarosa; Komische Oper Berlin as Susanna and Lulu; Dresden Staatsoper as Aminta in Die schweigsame Frau; Sang at Graz 1985, in Angelica Vincitrice di Alcina, by Fux; returned 1987, in the premiere of Der Rattenfänger by Cerha; Also sings Salomé in Hérodiade by Massenet. *Recordings:* Sacred music by Mozart (Philips); Lazarus by Schubert (Eterna); Epitaph for Garcia Lorca, by Nono.*Address:* c/o Voreinigte Bühnen, Kaiser Josef Platz 10, A-8010 Graz, Austria.

RELTON William, b. 1 Apr 1930, Halifax, Yorkshire, England. Symphony Administrator. m. Elisa De Paola, 18 Jan 1966, 2 children. *Education:* Saltley College; Royal College of Music. *Career:* Served with Royal Air Force, 1948-49; Freelance Trumpeter, London, 1952-55; Trumpeter, Sadler's Wells Opera, London, 1955-57; Trumpeter, BBC Concert Orchestra, London, 1957-60, Music Producer, 1960-70, Orchestra Manager, 1970-75, General Manager, BBC Symphony Orchestra, 1975-86; General Manager, Eastern Orchestral Board, 1986-; Assessor, Conservatoire de Lausanne; Birmingham School of Music, Royal Academy of Music, Bergen Conservatoire; National Band Festivals; Composer; International Adjudicator; Chairman, National Brass Band Championships; Composer for brass bands; Lecturer, music in Britain. *Address:* EOB, 10 Stratford Place, London, W1N 9AE, England.

REMEDIOS Alberto, b. 27 Feb 1935, Liverpool, England. Singer (Tenor). *Education:* Studied in Liverpool with Edwin Francis and at the Royal College of Music. *Debut:* Sadler's Wells Opera 1957, as Tinca in Il Tabarro. *Career:* Has sung at Sadler's Wells/English National Opera as Alfredo, Max, Erik, Bacchus, Walther, Siegmund, Siegfried, Lohengrin, Massenet's Des Grieux and the Berlioz Faust; Toured Australia with Joan Sutherland 1965, singing Edgar in Lucia di Lammermoor, Alfredo, Lensky in Eugene Onegin and Gounod's Faust; Covent Garden from 1965, as Dimitri (Boris Godunov), Erik, Florestan, Mark in The Midsummer Marriage, Siegfried, Bacchus and Max; Camden Town Hall 1968, in the British premiere of L'Arlesiana by Cilea; BBC radio 1970, as Huon in Oberon; Sang Mozart's Don Ottavio in South Africa, 1972; US debut 1973 as Dimitri and Don Carlos, at San Francisco; Siegfried in Los Angeles, San Diego and Seattle; Boston Opera as Faust; Metropolitan Opera debut 1976, Bacchus; Scottish Opera 1983, as Walther in Die Meistersinger; English National Opera 1981,1985 and 1989, Tristan and Walther; Performances of Otello, Siegmund, Florestan and Radames for Australian Opera; sang in Schoenberg's Gurrelieder at Melbourne, 1988; Das Lied von der Erde at Adelaide; Concert repertoire also includes Mahler's 8th Symphony (Promenade Concerts, London); Returned to Scottish Opera, 1989, as Stravinsky's Oedipus; Sang Erik in Der fliegende Holländer at Brisbane, 1990; Second Armed Man in Die Zauberflöte at Covent Garden, 1991; Sang in Reginald Goodall memorial concert, London, 1991; Appeared in Janáček's The Excursions of Mr Broucek at the London Coliseum, 1992 and sang Tristan in concert performances of Wagner's Opera at Nashville, Tennessee, 1993. *Recordings include:* The Ring of the Nibelung, conducted by Reginald Goodall (EMI). *Honours:* Prizewinner, Sofia International Competition, 1963; Commander of the British Empire, 1981. *Address:* Royal Opera House, Covent Garden, London WC2, England.

REMEDIOS Ramon, b. 9 May 1940, Liverpool, England. Singer (Tenor). *Education:* Studied at the Guildhall School of Music, the National School of Opera and the London Opera Centre. *Career:* Sung with Opera For All, Scottish Opera and European companies and Welsh National Opera; Notably as Alfredo, Macdaff, Ismaele in Nabucco, Grigory/Dimitri, Don Ottario, the Duke of Mantua, the Painter in Lulu, Skuratov (From the House of the Dead), Tamino and Almaviva; English National Operas: Alfredo, Rodolfo, Don José, Pinkerton, Paris in La Belle Hélène, Smith in the British premiere production of Christmas Eve (1988) and Lensky in Eugene Onegin, Covent Garden 1990, as Uldino in a new production of Attila; Television appearances in Top C's and Tiaras, and The Word by Rick Wakeman; Season 1992 as Sir Bruno Robertson in I Puritani at Covent Garden; Concert engagements include operatic arias in Glasgow, a Viennese Evening at the Festival Hall and Verdi's Requiem (Royal Festival Hall, Mar 1991). *Recordings include:* The Word, with the Eton College Choir; Kalman's Countess Maritza with New Sadler's Wells Opera; A Suite of Gods, songs by Rick Wakeman. *Honours:* School Tenor Prize, Ricordi Prize and Countess of Munster Trust (GSM); Finalist, Kathleen Ferrier Competition. *Address:* c/o Norman McCann International Artists Ltd, The Coach House, 56 Lawrie Park Gardens, London SE26 6XJ, England.

REMENIKOVA Tanya, b. 31 Jan 1946, Moscow, USSR. Cellist - performer and teacher. m. Alexander Braginsky, 15 Sept 1967. *Education:* Moscow Conservatoire, studied with Professor Rostropovich. *Career:* Regular appearances in recitals and with various orchestras, including Israel Philharmonic, Orchestre National de Belgique; Foreign tours - Europe, Taiwan, People's Republic of China, New York debut, 1979; Radio - BBC, RTB (Belgium), WFMT (Chicago), WQXR, New York; North American tours - Chicago, New York, Washington DC, Minneapolis, Los Angeles, among others. Professor of Cello, School of Music, University of Minnesota; Artist-in-Residence, Churchill College, Cambridge, 1981, 1986; Premieres of Stephen Paulus, American Vignettes, 1988. *Recordings:* DDF - Belgium - Stravinsky, Suite Italienne, Prokofiev - Sonata op 119; Sound Star Ton, Germany, Shostakovich - Sonata op 40, Britten - Sonata in C. *Memberships:* College Music Society; American String Teachers Assoication. *Honours:* Eugene Ysaÿe award for musical contribution, Brussels, 1979; Gold Medal, Gaspar Cassado Cello Competition, 1969. *Hobbies:* Playing with dog; Reading books; Walking around the lakes. *Current Management:* Richard Berg. *Address:* 4141 Dupont Avenue South, Minneapolis, MN 55409, USA.

REMES Vaclav, b. 1950, Czechoslovakia. Violinist. *Education:* Studied at the Prague Conservatory. *Career:* Founder member of the Prazak String Quartet, 1972; Tour of Finland 1973, followed by appearances at competitions in Prague and Evian; Concerts in Salzburg, Munich, Paris, Rome, Berlin, Cologne and Amsterdam; Tour of Britain 1985, including Wigmore Hall debut; Tours of Japan, the United States, Australia and New Zealand; Tour of UK 1988 and concert at the Huddersfield Contemporary Music Festival 1989; Recitals for the BBC, Radio France, Dutch Radio, the WDR in Cologne and Radio Prague; Appearances with the Smetana and LaSalle Quartets in Mendelssohn's Octet. *Recordings:* Albums for Supraphon, Panton and Orfeo. *Honours:* First Prize, Chamber Music Competition of the Prague Conservatory, 1974; Grand Prix International String Quartet Competition, Evian Music Festival, 1978; First Prize, National Competition of String Quartets in Czechoslovakia, 1978; Winner, String Quartet Competition of the Prague Spring Festival,

1978. *Address:* c/o Ingpen and Williams Ltd, 14 Kensington Court, London W8 5DN, England.

RENDALL David, b. 11 Oct 1948, London, England. Singer (Tenor). *Education:* Studied at the Royal Academy of Music and at the Salzburg Mozarteum. *Debut:* Glyndebourne Touring Company 1975, as Ferrando in Così fan Tutte. *Career:* Covent Garden from 1975, as the Italian Tenor in Der Rosenkavalier, Almaviva, Matteo, Rodolfo, Des Grieux in Manon and Rodrigo in a new production of La Donna del Lago by Rossini (1985); Glyndebourne Festival 1976, Ferrando; has returned as Belmonte and Tom Rakewell (1989); English National Opera from 1976, as Leicester in Mary Stuart, Rodolfo, Alfredo, Tamino and Pinkerton; European debut at Angers 1975, as the High Priest in Idomeneo; North American debut Ottawa 1977, as Tamino; New York City Opera 1978, Rodolfo and Alfredo; San Francisco debut 1978, Don Ottavio; Metropolitan Opera from 1980, as Ottavio, Ernesto, Belmonte, Idomeneo, Lenski, Ferrando, Alfred in Die Fledermaus and Mozart's Titus; Lyon Opera 1983, in the title role of La Damnation de Faust by Berlioz; Further engagements in Amsterdam, Berlin, Paris, Milan, Hamburg, Tel Aviv, Turin, Washington, Vienna, Dresden, Chicago, Santa Fe and Munich; Other operatic roles include Gounod's Faust (Palermo) and the Duke of Mantua; Many concert appearances in Europe and the USA; Sang the Duke of Mantua and Matteo at Covent Garden 1989/90; Cavaradossi with ENO, 1990; Season 1992 as Don Antonio in the stage premiere of Gerhard's The Duenna (Madrid), Pinkerton at the Coliseum and for WNO. *Recordings:* Maria Stuarda; Ariodante; Così fan Tutte; the Mozart Requiem; Beethoven's Missa solemnis; Madama Butterfly, and the Bruckner Te Deum. *Honours:* Young Musician of the Year Award 1973; Gulbenkian Fellowship 1975. *Address:* Stafford Law Associates, 26 Mayfield Road, Weybridge, Surrey KT13 8XB, England.

RENICKE Volker, b. 3 July 1929, Bremen, Germany. Conductor; Professor. m. Rey Nishiuchi, 5 Apr 1975. *Education:* Nordwestdeutsche Musikakademie, Detmold, 1950-54; Academia Chigiana, Siena with Paul van Kempen. *Career:* In Korea 1991 with Korean Symphony Orchestra in the Korean Orchestral Festival; Tokyo Mozart 200 Anniversary of Death, Idomeneo, 1991; In Seoul Opera Favorita and Fidelio at National Theatre, 1992; International Festival in Tsuyama, Japan, Mozart Tito, 1993; Salzburg Mozart Requiem, 1993; Guest conducting and concerts in England, France, Germany, Netherlands, Luxembourg, Switzerland, Italy, Yugoslavia and Korea; Concerts with Kuyshu Symphony Orchestra, Yomiuri Orchestra, Tokyo Metropolitan Orchestra, Tokyo Philharmonic Orchestra, Tokyo Symphony Orchestra, Japan Philharmonic Orchestra, New Japan Philharmonic Orchestra, Shinsei Orchestra, Osaka Philharmonic Orchestra, Kansai Philharmonic Orchestra, Teleman Orchestra, Sapporo Symphony Orchestra; In Korea: Seoul Philharmonic Orchestra and Korean Symphony Orchestra. *Recordings:* With Jorg Demus and NHK Orchestra Member; Piano concerts of Bach, Haydn, Mozart, Debussy, Frank, Fauré; With Karl Suske, Violin and NHK Orchestra Member; Recordings of Vivaldi and Bach; Humperdinck's Hänsel and Gretel, in Japanese, with Yomiuri Orchestra. *Membership:* Kojimachi Rotary Club, Tokyo. *Hobby:* Philosophy. *Address:* 5-26-15 Okuzawa, Setagaya-Ku, 158 Tokyo, Japan.

RENNERT Jonathan, b. 17 Mar 1952, London, England. Organist; Conductor; Writer. *Education:* St Paul's School, London; Foundation Scholar, Royal College of Music; Organ Scholar, St John's College, Cambridge; Stewart of Rannoch Scholar in Sacrad Music, Cambridge Univ; MA, Cantab; FRCO; FRCCO (h.c); ARCM; LRAM. *Career:* Numerous organ recitals, radio and TV appearances in UK, France, Belgium, Luxemburg, Netherlands, Sweden, Denmark, Hungary, Germany, Switzerland, West Indies, USA, Canada, Australia and Japan; Director of Music, Holy Trinity Church, Barnes, London, 1969-71; Director of Music, St Jude's, Courtfield Gardens, London, 1975-76; Acting Director of Music, St Matthews, Ottawa, Canada, 1976-

78; Director of Music, St Michael's Cornhill, London, 1979-; Musical Director, Cambridge Opera, 1972-74; Conductor, American Community Choirs in London and St Jude's Singers, 1975-76; Musician-in-Residence, Grace Cathedral, San Francisco, 1982; Musical Director, St Michael's Singers, 1979-; Conductor, Elizabethan Singers, 1983-88; Conductor, English Harmony, 1988-; Music Adjudicator for Thames TV; Home and Overseas Examiner and Moderator to the Associated Board, Royal Schools of Music; Artistic Director, Cornhill Festival of British Music; Course Director and Assessor Royal School of Church Music; Administrator, International Congress of Organists, Cambridge, 1987. *Recordings:* Several as solo organist, conductor, organ accompanist & harpsichord continuo player. *Publications:* William Crotch (1775-1847): composer, teacher, artist, 1975; George Thalben-Ball: a biography, 1979. *Contributions to:* various musical journals and publications. *Memberships:* Royal College of Organists (Council Member & Examiner); Incorporated Society of Musicians (Performers/Composers Section Committee Member); Organists Benevolent League (Council Member); Sir George Thalben-Ball Memorial Trust (Hon Secretary and Trustee); The Organ Club (Past President); Worshipful Company of Musicians (Liveryman). *Address:* 74 Pembroke Road, Kensington, London W8 6NX, England.

RENNERT Wolfgang, b. 1 April 1922, Cologne, Germany. Conductor. m. (1) Anny Schlem 1958 (2) Ulla Berkewicz 1971, divorced 1975, 1 daughter. *Education:* Mozarteum Salzburg 1940-43, 1945-47. *Debut:* Dusseldorf Opera 1948, Un Ballo in Maschera. *Career:* Conducted Dusseldorf Opera 1947-50, Kiel 1950-53; Assistant Conductor Frankfurt Opera 1953-67; Music Director, Staatstheater am Gärtnerplatz, Munich, 1967-72; General Music Director and Opera Director National Theatre Mannheim 1980-85; Conducted Mozart's Il Rè Pastore at Rome, 1988, Die Zauberflöte at Dallas; Teatro Sao Carlos, Lisbon, 1989; Die Walküre; Staatsoper, Berlin, 1990; Semperoper, Dresden, 1991; Komische Oper Berlin, 1990; Season 1992 with Arabella at Dresden. *Recordings:* Elektra; Arabella; Wozzeck; Die Dreigroschenoper. *Current Management:* Allied Artists Agency, 42 Montpelier Square, London SW7 1JZ, England.

RENTOWSKI Wieslaw Stanislaw Vivian, b. 23 Nov 1953, Bydgoszcz, Poland. m. Magdalena Kubiak, 5 Sept 1985, 1 son. *Education:* MA, Psychology, University of Lodz, 1978; MA, Organ, Academy of Music, Lodz, 1985; MA, Composition, Fr. Chopin Academy of Music, Warsaw, 1987; M Mus, Composition, Louisiana State University, School of Music, 1991. *Debut:* Carnegie Hall, Lagniappe for 8 instruments, 1991. *Career:* Composition: International Festival of Contemporary Music, Warsaw Autumn 1984, 86, 87, 89; Internationale Sinziger Orgelwoche, Bonn 1989, 1990; Festival International de Lanaudière, Canada, 1989; International Festival of Contemporary Music, Baton Rouge, USA 1990, 1991; Organ: Many performances and recordings including solo recitals and chamber concerts in Warsaw, Banff, Toronto, Bayreuth, Baton Rouge, New Orleans. *Compositions:* Chorea minor by Authors' Agency, Warsaw, Poland, 1989; Por dia de anos by Pomorze, Bromberg, Poland, 1989 and Edition Pro Nowa, Sonoton, Munich, West Germany, 1987. *Recordings:* 11 compositions recorded by Polish National Public Radio; Records: Anagram 1986 and Wayang, 1989 by Polskie Nagrania, Muza, Poland; Por dia de anos '90 by Sonoton, Proviva, Munich, West Germany. *Contributions to:* Intellectual music harmony by W Rentowski, Ruch Muzyczny, Polish National Musical Magazine, No 27, 1989. *Hobbies:* Architecture; Historic landmarks; Swimming; Driving. *Address:* Louisiana State University School of Music, Baton Rouge, LA 70803, USA.

RENZETTI Donato, b. 30 Jan 1950, Milan, Italy. Conductor. *Education:* Studied at the Conservatorio Giuseppe Verdi, Milan. *Career:* Assisted Claudio Abbado in Milan then conducted the Verdi Requiem in Salzburg; Gave Rigoletto at Verona in 1981 and has since worked at most Italian opera houses: conducted the premiere of Corghi's Gargantua at Turin, 1984; Paris Théâtre Musical, Macbeth; Conducted La Sonnambula at the Chicago Lyric Opera 1988 and Le Nozze di Figaro at Rome, 1989; Bonn Opera and Teatro Fenice, Venice, 1990 with Il Barbiere di Siviglia and Ernani; Has given orchestral concerts in Italy and elsewhere. *Honours include:* Prize winner at the Gino Marinuzzi International Competition 1976; Bronze Medal, Ernest Ansermet Competition at Geneva, 1978; Guido Cantelli Prize at Milan, 1980. *Address:* c/o Teatro dell' Opera, Piazza Beniamino Gigli 8, 1-00184 Rome, Italy.

RENZI Emma, b. 8 April 1937, Heidelberg, Transvaal, South Africa. Singer (Soprano). *Education:* Studied at the College of Music in Kapstad, at the London Opera Centre, with Santo Santonocito in Catania and with Virginia Borroni in Milan. *Debut:* Karlsruhe 1961, as Sieglinde. *Career:* Has sung in Milan, Genoa, Lisbon, Buenos Aires, Barcelona, Edinburgh, Mexico City, Johannesburg, Naples, Rome and Munich; Italian Radio 1977, in Parisina by Mascagni; Verona Arena 1979; Other roles include Norma, Aida, Amelia (Un Ballo in Maschera), Tosca, Leonora (Il Trovatore), Turandot, the Duchess of Parma in Doktor Faust, Elisabeth, and Countess Almaviva. *Address:* c/o Johannesburg Operatic and Dramatic Society, PO Box 7010, Johannesburg 2000, Transvaal, South Africa.

REPAS GONCALVES Maria, b. 30 July 1957, Almada, Portugal. Singer. m. Joao Repas Goncalves, 15 June 1976, 1 s, 3 d. *Education:* Studied Voice & Composition at Lisbon Conservatory and Music at Indiana University. *Debut:* Solist with Indiana University Borrague Orchestra. *Career:* Recitals in UK, 1990; Norwich Festival, Glasgow University, Apsley House, London, 1992; Purcell Room, Leading Role in the Balad Opera, The Voyage of the Catanineta, Concerts in USA, 1992; Holland, 1992, Paris, 1993; Recordings for BBC Radio 3, 1992; Concerts All Over Portugal and Portugues TV and Radio. *Recordings:* Laude; Focus Records. *Honours:* 1st Prize, Erwin Bodky Early Music Competition. *Hobbies:* Swimming; Cooking; Handicrafts. *Address:* Rua Soares Des Reis N5, 2D 1000 Lisbon, Portugal.

REPPA David, b. 2 Nov 1926, Hammond, Indiana, USA. Scenic Designer. *Education:* Professional training at the Metropolitan Opera, 1957-58. *Debut:* Designed Le Nozze di Figero for North Shore Opera, New York, 1960. *Career:* Has worked with Sarah Caldwell's Opera Company of Boston and in Miami and San Francisco; Debut with the Metropolitan Opera 1974, Duke Bluebeard's Castle and Gianni Schicchi; Other designs include Aida 1976, Dialogues des Carmélites 1977 and Don Carlos 1979; As staff scenic designer has worked with most Metropolitan Opera scenic designers, supervising painting and construction of sets and adapting productions for the company's former spring tours. *Address:* c/o Metropolitan Opera, Lincoln Center, New York, NY 10023, USA.

REPPEL Carmen, b. 27 April 1941, Gummersbach, Germany. Singer (Soprano). *Education:* Studied at the Hamburg Musikhochschule with Erna Berger. *Debut:* Flensburg 1968, as Elisabeth de Valois. *Career:* Has sung in Hanover, Hamburg, Frankfurt, Cologne, Mannheim, Wiesbaden and Kassel; Bayreuth Festival 1977-80, as Freia and Gutrune, and in Die Walküre and Parsifal; Wuppertal 1983, in a concert performance of Schwarzschwanenreich by Siegfried Wagner; San Francisco 1983, as Ariadne auf Naxos; Sang Mozart's Electra at Stuttgart, 1985; Hamburg and Vienna 1985, as Leonore and Chrysothemis; Munich Opera 1986, as Andromache in the premiere of Troades by Reimann; Zurich Opera 1986, Salome; Further appearances in Berlin, Zurich, Barcelona, Milan, and Tokyo; Other roles include Fiordiligi, Donna Anna, Mélisande, Mimi, Liu, Marenka in The Bartered Bride; Violetta, Desdemona, Leonora in Il Trovatore, Ariadne, Salome, Elsa, and Sieglinde; Sang in Flavio Testi's Riccardo III at La Scala, 1987; Sieglinde in Die Walküre at Bologna 1988; Strauss's Ariadne and Salome, Turin, 1989; Salome at the Torre del Lago festival, 1989. *Recordings include:*

Freia and Gerhilde in Der Ring des Nibelungen, from Bayreuth (Philips); Les Troyens by Berlioz (EMI);Chrysothemis in Götz Friedrich's film version of Elektra. *Address:* Ingpen & Williams Ltd., 14 Kensington Court, London W8 5DN, England.

RESA Neithard, b. 1954, Berlin, Germany. Violist. *Education:* Studied in Berlin with Michel Schwalbe, Cologne with Max Rostal, USA with Michael Tree. *Career:* Prizewinner of German Music Foundation, 1978; Principal Viola of Berlin Philharmonic, 1978; Co-founded the Philharmonia Quartet, Berlin, giving concerts throughout Europe, USA and Japan; British debut 1987 playing Haydn, Szymanowski and Beethoven at Wigmore Hall; Bath Festival 1987 playing Mozart, Schumann and Beethoven; Other repertoire includes quartets by Bartók, Mendelssohn, Nicolai, Ravel and Schubert; Quintets by Brahms, Weber, Reger and Schumann. *Address:* c/o Anglo- Swiss Ltd, 3 Primrose Mews, 1a Sharpleshall Street, London NW1 8YW, England.

RESCIGNO Nicola, b. 28 May 1916, New York City, USA. Opera Conductor; Artistic Director. *Education:* Italian Jurisprudence Degree, Rome. *Debut:* Brooklyn New York Academy of Music, 1943. *Career:* Co-Founder, Artistic Director, Chicago Lyric Opera, 1954-56; Presented American Debut of Maria Callas; Co-Founder, Artistic Director, Dallas Civic Opera (currently The Dallas Opera), 1957-; Regularly presents American debuts, past debuts include Sutherland, Vickers, Berganza, Montarsolo, Caballé, Knie, Domingo, Olivero, Dimitrova, W. Meier; Instrumental in presenting baroque opera including American stage premieres of Handel's Alcina, Monteverdi L'Incoronazione di Poppea, Samson, Giulio Cesare, and Vivaldi's Orlando Furioso; Guest Conductor: San Francisco, Metropolitan, Chicago Lyric, Cincinnati, Philadelphia, Washington, Tulsa, Houston, at the Metropolitan Opera has conducted Donizetti's Don Pasquale and L'Eisir d'Amore, Rossini's Italiana in Algeri and Verdi's La Traviata; Guest Conductor in Canada, South America, Italy, Portugal, UK, Switzerland, Austria and France; Conducted the premiere of Argento's The Aspern Papers, Dallas, 1988; Werther at Rome, 1990; Aida at the 1990 Caracalla Festival, Rome; Season 1991 with Il Barbiere di Siviglia at Philadelphia. *Current Management:* CAMI Conductors Division. *Address:* Dallas Opera, 1925 Elm Street, Suite 400, Dallas, TX 75201, USA.

RESNIK Regina, b. 30 Aug 1924, New York, USA. Mezzo-soprano Singer. m. (1) Harry W Davies, 1947, 1 son, (2) Arbit Blatas, 1975. *Education:* Hunter College, New York, USA. *Debut:* Concert, Brooklyn Academy of Music, 1942. *Career:* Appeared as Leonora in Fidelio, Mexico City, Mexico, 1943; With New York City Opera, USA, 1944-45; Debut as Leonore in Il Trovatore 1944, with company 1946-; Metropolitan Opera, New York, Conducted seminars on opera, New School for Social Research; Subsequently sang at venues including Chicago Opera Theatre and San Francisco Opera; Bayreuth debut, as Sieglinde, 1953; London debut, 1957; Has sung at Vienna, Berlin, Stuttgart, Buenos Aires, Paris, Marseilles and Sazburg; Directed Carmen, Hamburg State Opera, 1971; San Francisco, 1972, as Claire in the US premiere of Der Besuch der alten Dame by Einem; returned 1982, as the Countess in The Queen of Spades; Produced and acted in Falstaff, Teatr Wielki, Warsaw, Poland, 1975. *Honours:* President's Medal, Commandeur, Arts et Lettres, France. *Address:* 50 West 56th Street, New York, NY 10019, USA.

RESS Ulrich, b. 29 Oct 1958, Augsburg, Germany. Singer (Tenor). *Education:* Studied at Augsburg Conservatory 1975-78, with Leonore Kirchstein from 1979. *Career:* Sang at Stadttheater Augsburg 1979-84, notably as Idamante and Rossini's Almaviva; Engaged at Bayerische Staatsoper from 1984, as Mozart's Pedrillo and Monostatos, Verdi's Bardolph and Macduff, Beppe in Pagliacci and Pong in Turandot; Sang the Steersman and Strauss's Truffaldino at Munich 1991; Guest appearances at Bayreuth and Barcelona 1988-89, as David in Meistersinger, Strasbourg and Nice,

Jacquino 1989. *Recordings:* Young Servant in video of Elektra conducted by Abbado; Bardolph in Falstaff conducted by Colin Davis; Massimilia Doni by Schoeck. *Address:* c/o Bayerische Staatsoper, Postfach 100184, 8000 Munich 1, Germany.

RETHY Ester, b. 22 Oct 1912, Budapest, Hungary. Singer (Soprano). *Eucation:* Studied in Budapest and Vienna. *Debut:* Budapest 1934, as Micaela in Carmen. *Career:* Sang at the Vienna Staatsoper until 1949 in operas by Mozart and Strauss; Salzburg Festival 1937-39, as Susanna and Sophie (Der Rosenkavalier); Vienna Volksoper from 1948, notably in Der Zigeunerbaron and Eine Nacht in Venedig by Johann Strauss and in operettas by Kalman and Lehar; Returned to Salzburg 1950 and 1952, as Donna Elvira and as Europa in the first public performance of Richard Strauss's Die Liebe der Danae; Other roles included Handel's Rodelinda and Wagner's Eva. *Recordings include:* Der Bettelstudent by Millöcker; Le Nozze di Figaro and Die Liebe der Danae from Salzburg.

REUTER Rolf, b. 7 Oct 1926, Leipzig, Germany. Conductor. *Education:* Studied at the Dresden Hochschule für Musik, 1958-61. *Career:* Repetiteur and conductor at Eisenach 1951-55; Musical Director at Meinigen 1955-61; Leipzig Opera 1961-73 (Generalmusikdirektor from 1963); Music Director at Weimar 1979-80, Komische Oper Berlin from 1981; Professor of Music and Conductor of the orchestra at the Hanns Eisler Hochschule, Berlin; Guest conductor in Cuba, France, Germany, Yugoslavia, Czechoslovakia, Tokyo, Houston, Rome, Buenos Aires, Copenhagen, Moscow and Prague; Gave Der Ring des Nibelungen at the Paris Opéra 1978 and Tristan und Isolde at the Berlin Staatsoper; Gave the premieres of Guayana Johnny by Alan Bush (1966) and Judith by Siegfried Matthus (1985); Visited Covent Garden and Wiesbaden 1989 with the company of the Komische Oper, conducting The Bartered Bride and Judith; Conducted a new production of Der Freischütz at the Komische Oper 1989; Le Nozze di Figaro for New Israeli Opera, 1992. *Recordings include:* Beethoven's incidental music for Egmont; Handel: Oratorio L'Allegro, Il Moderato ed il Penseroso. *Address:* Komische Oper, Behrenstrasse 55/57, D-1080 Berlin, Germany.

REVERDY Michele, b. 12 Dec 1943, Alexandria, Egypt. Composer. 1 daughter. *Education:* Literature, Sorbonne, Paris; Counterpoint with Alain Weber, Analysis with Claude Ballif, Composition with Olivier Messiaen, Paris Conservatory; Casa de Velazquez, Madrid. *Career:* Professr, lycees, 1965-74; Professor, Analysis, regional and municipal conservatories, 1974-83; Producer, Radio-France, 1978-90; Professor, Class of Analysis, Paris Conservatory, 1983-. *Compositions include:* Kaleidoscope for harpsichord and flute, 1975; Number One for guitar, 1977; Meteores for 17 instruments, 1978; L'Ile aux Lumieres for solo violin and string orchestra, 1983; Scenic Railway for 16 instruments, 1983; La Nuit Qui Suivit Notre Dernier Diner, chamber opera, 1984; Triade for guitar, 1986; Trois Fantaisies de Gaspard de la Nuit for choir or 12-voice ensemble, 1987; Sept Enluminures for soprano, clarinet, piano, percussion, 1987; Propos Felins for string orchestra and children's choir, 1988; Le Cercle du Vent for orchestra, 1988; Vincent, opera based on the life of Vincent Van Gogh, 1984-89; Le Precepteur, opera (Jakoblent), for coloratura soprano, soprano, mezzo-soprano, contralto, 3 tenors, 2 baritones, 3 basses and 20 instruments. *Recordings:* CD, Michele Reverdy (Scenic Railway, Sept Enluminures, Meteores, Figure, Kaleidoscope), MFA-Salabert; Triade, CD Rafael Andia, guitar; Il Chateau, 1980-86, Opera for 9 singles, 2 choirs (men and children), orchestra, text from Franz Kafka. *Publications:* L'oeuvre pour piano d'Olivier Messiaen, 1978; Histoire de la Musique Occidentale, 1985; L'oeuvre pour orchestre d' Olivier Messiaen, 1988. *Address:* 75 rue des Gravilliers, 75003 Paris, France.

REVEYRON Joseph. b. 2 Sept 1917, Lyon, France. Composer. m. 27 July 1950, 2 sons, 2 daughters.

Education: Studied organ, harmony, counterpoint and composition with Edouard Commette. *Debut:* 1934. *Career:* Organist, Notre Dame de la Mulatiere, near Lyon, 1934-54; Assistant Organist, then Organist, St Jean's Cathedral, Lyon; Jury member, School of Music, Lyon and other cities; Various recitals, France and abroad, including Notre Dame in Paris, Chartres Cathedral, St Thomas in Leipzig, and Lausanne, Switzerland; Various radio and TV programmes, France and abroad; Works performed by international artists and groups. *Compositions:* Published: Fantaisie-Choral, organ pedals only; Anamnese, organ 4 hands; Toccato, organ; Interludes Gregoriens, organ; Messe breve, choir a capella; Exsultet, choir a capella; Les vivants et les morts, choir a capella; Chants pour Eurydice Fleurie, choir a capella; Les douze portes, orchestra; Shema, voice, orchestra; Le chant des noces, voice, orchestra; Concertino da chiesa, trumpet; Tiento, trumpet; Chanson des gitanes, voice, piano; Recorded: Les sept sceaux, organ; Extraits de la Bible, organ; Les Lauretanes, organ; Versets pour un orgue ancien, organ; Oi Nekroi, oratorio; Psaume du Berger, choir, orchestra; La Dormition, oratorio; Jean le Baptiste, oratorio, 1984; Au milieu de la vie, choir a capella; Ayez en vous meme sentiment, choir a capella; Tous les peuples, choir, organ; Communion de la Messe de Minuit, choir, organ; Concertino da chiesa; Matinées du samedi saint, voice, organ; Prelude, Tiento et Ronde, 2 pianos; Villancico, violin, piano. *Hobbies:* Painting; Sculpture. *Address:* 336 Route de Cailloux, Les Echets, F-01700 Miribel, France.

REYMOND Valentin, b. 1954, Neuchâtel, Switzerland. Conductor. *Education:* Studied at Conservatories of Bienne and Zurich. *Career:* Assistant at the Grand Théâtre Geneva; Has assisted such conductors as Jean-Marie Auberson, Horst Stein, Armin Jordan and Roderick Brydon; Music Director of Opéra Decentralisé. Concert and Broadcast appearances with: Orchestra de la Suisse Romande Orchestra de la Radio Suisse Italienne; Orchestra de Chambre de Toulouse, Orchestre Symphonique de Krasnoiarsk, (Siberia); Orchestra Symphonique d'Etat de Russie. Operatic appearances: Traviata (Opéra de Lucerne); Rape of Lucretia (Opéra Décentrativé and Opéra de Lausanne); Albert Herring, (Opéra de Berne/Opéra de Lausanne/Opéra de Nantes); Les Pêcheurs de Perles, (Opéra de Dublin); Les Mamelles de Tiresias, Das Rheingold, Die Walküre, Le Roi Malgre Lui (Opéra de Nantes), L'Etoile (Opéra North). *Address:* Music International, 13 Ardilaun Road, London N5 2QR, England.

REYNOLDS Anna, b. 5 June 1931, Canterbury, England. Opera and Concert Singer. *Education:* Benenden School; Royal Academy of Music (FRAM); Studied with Professoressa Debora Fambri. *Career:* Italy from 1958 in Operas by Rossini, Donizetti and Massenet; Appearance at many international festivals including Spoleto, Edinburgh, Aix-en-Provence, Salzburg Easter Festival, Vienna, Tanglewood; Bayreuth Festival 1970-75, as Fricka, Waltraute and Magdalene. Has sung with leading orchestras all over the world including Chicago Symphony, New York Philharmonic, Berlin Philharmonic, London Symphony; Appearances in opera performances in New York Metropolitan, La Scala, Milan, Covent Garden, Bayreuth, Rome, Chicago Lyric Opera, Teatro Colon, Buenos Aires, Teatro Fenice, Venice and many others; Currently a teacher of singing. *Recordings:* Recordings for Decca, EMI, Polydor and Philips, notably of cantatas by Bach. *Hobbies:* Reading; Piano; Travel; World-wide correspondence. *Address:* 37 Chelwood Gardens, Richmond, Surrey TW9 4JG, England.

REYNOLDS Roger Lee, b. 18 July 1934, Detroit, Michigan, USA. Composer. m. Karen Jeanne Hill, 11 Apr 1964, 2 daughters. *Education:* BSE, Physics, University of Michigan; BM, MM in Composition, University of Michigan. *Career:* Associate Professor, University of California, San Diego, 1969-73; Professor UCSD, 1973-; Founding Director, Center for Music Experiment and Related Research, 1971-77; Director, CME, 1988. *Compositions:* Approximately 60 works published by C. F. Peters, New York; Approximately 20 recordings on CRI, Neume, Nonesuch, Wergo, Lovely Music, New World; GM, Vanguard - Selected works: The Emperor of Ice Cream; Ping; Visions, Transfigured Wind, Voicespace; Versions/Stages, Dreaming, Symphony (Myths). *Publications:* Mind Models: New Forms of Musical Experience, 1975; A Searcher's Path: A Composers' Ways, 1987; A Jostled Silence: Contemporary Japanese Musical Thought, 1992-93; Articles in: The Musical Quarterly; Perspectives of New Music; New York Times Review; Musical America. *Honours:* Pulitzer Prize in Music, 1989; Rockefeller, Ford, Koussevitzky, Guggenheim, Suntory Foundations; National Endowment for the Arts. *Memberships:* Meet The Composer (Board); Institute of Current World Affairs (Trustee); Fromm Music Foundation (Board); American Music Center (Board); Center for Research in Computing and the Arts (Board). *Address:* 624 Serpentine Drive, Del Mar, CA 92014, USA.

REZITS Joseph, b. 16 June 1925, New York City, USA. Concert Pianist; Professor; Writer; Lecturer; Bibliographer. m. Roberta Weingart, 2 sons. *Education:* Artist Diploma, Curtis Institute of Music; BMus, MMus, University of Illinois; Professional Diploma, Columbia University; DMA, University of Colorado. *Debut:* With Philadelphia Orchestra, 1950. *Career:* Tours in USA, Canada, Australia, Brazil, UK, China, Japan, Hong Kong, Malaysia, Singapore and Finland, as soloist, ensemble player, lecturer; Adjudicator; Reviewer; Faculty, School of Music, Indiana University. *Recordings:* Numerous. *Publications:* Source Materials for Piano Techniques, 1965; Teachers Guide to the New Scribner Music Library, 1973; The Pianist's Resource Guide, 1974 (revised 2nd edition, 1978); Source Materials for Keyboard Skills, 1975; The Guitarist's Resource Guide, 1983; Source Materials for Keyboard Skills (revised 2nd edition, 1986). *Contributions to:* Numerous professional journals. *Honour:* Winner, Philadelphia Orchestra Youth Auditions, 1949. *Hobbies:* Photography; Walking. *Address:* School of Music, Indiana University, PO Box 2226, Bloomington, IN 47402, USA.

RHEE Heasook, b. 1950, Korea. Pianist; Accompanist. *Education:* BM summa cum laude, Piano, Seoul National University; Diploma in Piano, Professional Programme in Piano Accompanying, Juilliard School of Music; Menahem Pressler Chamber Music Seminar, University of Indiana, Bloomington; MM, DMA, Piano Music, Accompanying, University of Michigan, Ann Arbor; Student of Soonyul Kim, Jacob Lateiner, Rosina Lhevine, Samuel Sanders, Eugene Bossart. *Career:* Appeared as Recitalist or Accompanist with Simon Estes, Ilya Grubert, Tilmann Wick, Peter Zazofsky, Julius Baker, Samuel Mayes, Jeffrey Solow, Charles Curtis; Has toured throughout USA; Played at Berlin Festival, Munich, Alte Oper Frankfurt, Stuttgart and Hanover, Germany, also in Brussels, Tonhalle Zurich in Switzerland, Italy, Spain, Norway, Australia, Central America and Far East; Accompanist, 5 consecutive Piatgorsky Seminars, Los Angeles; Congress Pianist, American Cello Congress, 1990; Chamber music with Lake George Chamber Orchestra, Muse Woodwind Chamber Ensemble; Seoul Philharmonic Piano Trio, and at Sandpoint Festival; Solo recitals, Pirmasens, Germany, Shoreham, New York, Ann Arbor, Michigan, Seoul; Radio broadcasts, Germany, Zurich and Boston; Faculty, Choong-Ang and Han-Yang Universities, Choogye Conservatory, Seoul; Piano Instructor, Rose Music Foundation, Melbourne, Australia; Private studio, New York City. *Recordings:* CD, Carter, Poulenc, Miaskovsky Cello Sonatas. *Address:* 160 West End Avenue Apt 20U, New York, NY 10023, USA.

RHODES Cherry, b. 28 June 1943, Brooklyn, New York, USA. Educator; Concert Organist; Adjunct Professor, Organ Department, University of Southern California. m. Professor Ladd Thomas. *Education:* BMus, Curtis Institute of Music, Philadelphia, Pennsylvania, 1964; HS Music, Munich, studied with Karl Richter, 1964-67; Private study with Marie-Claire Alain and Jean Guillou, Paris, 1967-69; Summer Schools, Harvard and University of Pennsylvania, 1961, 1962, 1963. *Career:*

Soloist, Philadelphia Orchestra, South German Radio Orchestra, Chamber Orchestra of French National Radio, Pasadena Chamber Orchestra, Phoenix Symphony Orchestra; Los Angeles Philharmonic; First American to win an international organ competition, Munich; Recitals, Lincoln Center, New York City, Notre Dame, Paris, Royal Festival Hall, London, Los Angeles Music Center, Milwaukee Performing Arts Center, Meyerson Symphony Center; Number of appearances at national and regional conventions of AGO; Performances, several Bach festivals and festivals, Bratislava, Nurnberg, Paris, St Albans, Luxembourg and Vienna; Gave opening recital on new organ at John F Kennedy Center in Washington DC; Broadcast performances in US, Canada and Europe; Adjudicator for National and International Organ-Playing Competitions. *Recordings:* Everyone Dance, CD of Music of Calvin Hampton on Pro Organ label. *Address:* School of Music, University of Southern California, Los Angeles, CA 90089-0851, USA.

RHODES Jane, b. 13 March 1929, Paris, France. Singer (Soprano). m. Roberto Benzi 1966. *Debut:* Marguerite in La Damnation de Faust, Nancy 1953. *Career:* Sang Renata in the first (concert) performance of The Fiery Angel by Prokofiev; Sang in the 1956 premiere of Le Fou by Landowski; Paris Opéra from 1958, as Marguerite, Carmen, Salome and Kundry 1974; Metropolitan Opera 1960, Carmen; Aix-en-Provence 1961, in L'Incoronazione di Poppea; Paris Opéra-Comique 1968, in L'Heure Espagnole and La Voix Humaine; Also sang in Duke Bluebeard's Castle, by Bartók. *Recordings:* Carmen; La Juive by Halévy; Mireille by Gounod; Margared in Le Roi d'Ys by Lalo; The Fiery Angel; Public Opinion in Orphée aux Enfers (EMI).

RHODES Samuel, b. 13 Feb 1941, Long Beach, New York, USA. Violist. m. 30 Dec 1968, 2 daughters. *Education:* BA, Queens College, New York City; MFA, Princeton University. *Debut:* Carnegie Recital Hall, 1966. *Career:* Juilliard String Quartet, 1969-; Great Performances, PBS TV 1977; Hindemith: The Viola Legacy 3 Concert Series, Carnegie Recital Hall, 1985; CBS Sunday Morning, 1986. *Compositions:* Quintet for string quartet & Viola. *Recordings:* Schoenberg Quartets; Complete Beethoven Quartets; Mozart-Haydn Quartets; Bartók Quartets (complete); Schubert and Dvořák Quartets; Guest Artist with Beaux Arts Trio. *Honours:* 3 Grammy Awards, 1971, 1976, 1985; Honorary Doctorates: Michigan State University, 1984, University of Jacksonville, 1986; Edison Award, The Netherlands, 1974. *Memberships:* Viola Society; The Bohemians; Board Member, Chamber Music America. *Hobbies:* Running; Baseball. *Current Management:* Naomi Rhodes Associates Inc., New York City. *Address:* c/o The Juilliard School, 144 West 66th St., Lincoln Center, New York, NY 10023, USA.

RHYS-DAVIES Jennifer, b. 8 May 1953, Panteg, Gwent, Wales. Singer (Soprano). *Education:* Studied at Trinity College of Music, London. *Career:* Appearances with Welsh National Opera as the Forester's Wife in Cunning Little Vixen, Fortune in Poppea, Miss Jessel in Turn of the Screw, also in Dresden and Leipzig, First Lady in Die Zauberflote and Donna Elvira; Further appearances as Constanze for Opera 80 and Donna Anna for Kent Opera on tour to Valencia; Opera North as Sandrina in La Finta Giardiniera, Aloysia in the Mozart-Griffiths pastiche; Sang Semiramide and Sieglinde at Nuremberg, Queen of Night for Dublin Grand Opera and Scottish Operas, 1993; Covent Garden and English National Opera debut 1993, as Berta in Barbiere di Siviglia and Mrs Fiorentino in Street Scene; Concert engagements in Beethoven's Mount of Olives and Haydn's Seasons at Dublin, Handel's Dixit Dominus and Polenc's Gloria for Stuttgart Radio; Garsington Hall in Haydn's Orlando Paladino. *Honours:* Kennedy Scott Prize and Rowland Jones Memorial Award, Trinity College. *Address:* IMG Artists , Media House, 3 Burlington Lane, Chiswick, London W4 2TH, England.

RIBARY Antal, b. 8 Jan. 1924, Budapest, Hungary. Composer. *Education:* Diploma in Art History, Pazmany Peter University of Budapest; Diploma Composition, Academy of Music, Budapest. *Debut:* 2 Michelangelo songs, 1947. *Career:* 6 interviews with Radio Budapest; 1 interview tih Radio Bruxelles; 1 interview with Radio Stockholm; The Divorce of King Louis (1 act opera), Hungarian State Opera House, 1959. *Compositions include:* Pantomime Suite; Hellas Cantata; Requiem for the Lover; 6 Lines from the Satyricon; Concerto Grosso; 5 Quartets; 4 Violin and Piano Sonatas; King Louis Divorces/Opera; 2 Michelangelo songs; 5 Shakespeare Sonnets; 5 Villon songs; I-VII Symphonies, 1960-84; De Profundis/Motetta; 2 poems for choirs; Rest C G Rossetti; Chant pour 8 Ligne/Baudelaire; 2 Piano Concertos 1979-80; In manuscript: V-VIII Symphonies; In Memoriam Charles Beaudelaire; Six portraits imaginaire de Charles Moreas; 4 Piano Concertos; V-XII Symphonies; Masks and Churches in Spain (suite for orchestra); Two Spanish Songs (voice and piano). *Recordings:* The Music of Antal Ribary, Volumes 1, 2 and 3; Sonata for Alto and Piano, (Melodia); Six Staves from Satyricon (by Hungaroton Composers Album) 1980. *Publications:* Music Criticism 1960-70. *Hobbies:* Pictures, Churches. *Address:* 1136 Budapest, Felka 3, Hungary.

RICCI Ruggiero, b. 24 July 1918, San Francisco, California, USA. Violinist. m. (1) Ruth Rink, 1942, (2) Valma Rodriquez, 1957, (3) Julia Whitehurst Clemenceau, 1978; 2 sons, 3 daughters. *Education:* Under Louis Persinger, Mischel Piastro, Paul Stassévitch and Georg Kulenkampff. *Debut:* With Manhattan Symphony Orchestra, New York, 1929. *Career:* 1st tour of Europe, 1932; Served USA Air Force, 1942-45; over 5000 concerts in 60 years worldwide; played the first performances of the Violin concertos of Ginastera, Von Einem and Veerhoff; Specializes in violin solo literature; Professor of Violin at the Hochschule für Musik; Mozarteum, Salzburg, Austria.*Recordings:* 1st recording of Paganini Caprices on the Composer's violin, lent by city of Genoa; over 500 recordings in discography. *Publications:* Left Hand Violin Technique, 1987. *Honours:* Cavaliere, Order of Merit, Italy. *Current Management:* Intermusica, 16 Duncan Terrace, London N18 BZ. *Address:* c/o Hochschule für Musik Mozarteum, Mirabellplatzl, A-5020 Salzburg, Austria.

RICCIARELLI Katia, b. 16 Jan 1946, Rovigo, Italy. Singer (Soprano). m. Pippo Baudo 1986. *Education:* Studied at the Benedetto Marcello Conservatory, Venice. *Debut:* Mantua 1969, as Mimi in La Bohème. *Career:* Sang Leonora in Il Trovatore at Parma in 1970; After winning the 1971 New Voices Competition on TV appeared throughout Italy; US debut at the Chicago Lyric Opera 1972, as Lucrezia in I Due Foscari; Covent Garden 1974, La Bohème and as Amelia in Un Ballo in Maschera 1975; Metropolitan Opera from 1975, as Mimi, Micaela in Carmen, Desdemona, Luisa Miller and Amelia; Guest appearances in Moscow, Barcelona, Berlin, New Orleans and Verona; At Pesaro she has sung in revivals of Rossini's Il Viaggio a Reims and Bianca e Falliero (1985-86); Other roles include Donizetti's Caterina Cornaro, Maria di Rohan and Lucrezia Borgia, and Bellini's Imogene (Il Pirata) and Giulietta (I Capuleti e i Montecchi); Returned to Covent Garden 1989, as Elisabeth de Valois in Don Carlos; Théâtre du Châtelet, Paris 1988, as Gluck's Iphigénie en Tauride; Pesaro Festival 1988, as Ninetta in La gazza ladra; Sang Desdemona at the Met and Covent Garden 1990, Maria Stuarda at Reggio Emilia; Geneva 1990 as Amenaide in Rossini's Tancredi; Season 1992/93 as Wolf-Ferrari's Susanna at Monte Carlo and Rosalinde in Fledermaus at Catania. *Recordings:* Roles in Suor Angelica and Simon Boccanegra (RCA); I Due Foscari, Tosca, Il Battaglia di Legnano, Il Trovatore, La Bohème (Philips); Luisa Miller, Tosca, Falstaff, Un Ballo in Maschera, Don Carlos, Aida, Turandot, Carmen, Il Viaggio a Reims (Deutsche Grammophon); La Donna del Lago (CBS); I Capuleti e i Montecchi (Nuova Era); Anacréon, Tancredi and I Lombardi on various minor labels; Appears as Desdemona in the video of Otello directed by Franco Zefffirelli. *Address:* c/o John Coast Ltd, 31 Sinclair Road, London, W14 0NS, England.

RICH Alan, b. 17 June 1924, Boston, Massachusetts, USA. Music Critic; Editor; Author. *Education:* AB, Harvard University, 1945; MA, University of California, Berkeley, 1952; Vienna, Austria, 1952-53. *Career:* Assistant Music Critic, Boston Herald, 1944-45; New York Sun, 1947-48; Contributor, American Record Guide, 1947-61; Saturday Review, 1952- 53; Musical America, 1955-61; Teacher of Music, University of California, Berkeley, 1950-58; Programme and Music Director, Pacifica Foundation FM Radio, 1953-61; Assistant Music Critic, New York Times, 1961-63; Chief Music Critic and Editor, New York Herald-Tribune, 1963-66; Music Critic and Editor, New York World-Journal-Tribune, 1966-67; Contributing Editor, Time magazine, 1967- 68; Music and Drama Critic and Arts Editor, 1979-83, Contributing Editor 1983- 85, California magazine; General Editor, Newsweek magazine, 1983-87; Music Critic, Los Angeles Herald-Examiner, 1987-; Teacher, New School for Social Research, 1972-75, 1977-79; University of Southern California School of Journalism, 1980-82; California Institute of the Arts, 1982-; Artist-in- Residence, Davis Center for the Performing Arts, City University of New York, 1975-76. *Publications:* Careers and Opportunities in Music, 1964; Music: Mirror of the Arts, 1969; Simon & Schuster Listener's Guide to Music, 3 volumes, 1980; The Lincoln Center Story, 1984. *Contributions to:* Numerous articles and reviews in various journals. *Address:* c/o Los Angeles Herald-Examiner, 1111 S Broadway, Los Angeles, CA 90015, USA.

RICH Elizabeth, b. 8 Feb 1931, New York City, USA. Concert Pianist. m. Joel Markowitz, 30 June 1952, 2 sons, 1 daughter. *Education:* Juilliard School of Music, Scholarships, Ages 7-18; etc. *Debut:* New York Philharmonic Auditions, Young People's Concert, Carnegie Hall, 1949. *Career:* English Premiere, Clara Schumann Piano Concerto, Beethoven Choral Fantasy, Queen Elizabeth Hall, London, 1985; Complete Cycle, Mozart Piano Sonatas, New York, 1984-85; Guest artist, Mt Desert Festival of Chamber Music, 1987-91 and 1993; 4th Recital, Alice Tully Hall, Lincoln Center, 1993; Mozart Concerto & Bach Concerto, St Martin's in The Field, London Chamber Soloists Orchestra, 1993. *Recordings:* for Dutch Radio; Schumann CD for Connoisseur Society, 6 Noveletten and Carnaval, released 1992. *Memberships:* Private Lesson Faculty, SUNY, Purchase. *Current Management:* Liegner Management. *Address:* c/o Liegner Management, PO Box 884, New York, NY 10023, USA.

RICHARDS Denby, b. 7 Nov 1924, London, England. Music Critic; Author; Lecturer. m. Rhondda Gillespie, 29 May 1973. *Education:* Forest School and Regent Street Polytechnic, London; Self-taught Piano and 40 years attending concerts and studying scores. *Career:* Early writing on Kensington News, then Music Critic to Hampstead and Highgate Express for 30 years; Contributor to Music and Musicians from first issue, 1952; Editor, 1981-84; Opera Editor, 1984-; Editor Musical Opinion, 1987-; Many radio and TV appearances in UK, USA, Scandinavia, Australia; Lecturer including Seminar Course on History and Function of Western Musical Criticism at Yale University, USA; Programme Notes and Record Sleeves, etc. *Publication:* The Music of Finland, London, 1966. *Contributions to:* Music and Musicians; Records and Recording; Musical Opinion; New Film Review; Parade and other journals in UK and internationally. *Memberships:* The Critics Circle; Savage Club; Zoological Society of London. *Hobbies:* Musical Oddities; Puns; Exotic Food and Vintage Wine. *Address:* 2 Princes Road, St Leonards-on-Sea, East Sussex TN37 6EL, England.

RICHARDS Goff, b. 18 Aug 1944, St Minver, Cornwall, England. Composer; Arranger; Conductor; Adjudicator. m. Sue Tinkley, 2 June 1975, 3 sons. *Education:* ARCM, GRSM, Royal College of Music, 1962-65; Teaching Certificate, Reading University, 1966. *Career:* Head of Music, Fowey School, 1966-70; Head of Music, Newquay School, 1972-75; Lecturer in Music, Salford College of Technology, 1976-81; Freelance Composer, Arranger and Conductor, 1981-; Regular contribution to BBC Radio and TV; Extensive travel including New Zealand, Norway, USA, Lithuania. *Compositions:* Jaguar, 1983; Continental Caprice, 1984; Country Scene, 1985; Oceans, 1986; Cornish Fantasia, 1987; Lord Lovelace, 1987; Momentary, 1992; Homage to the Noble Grape, 1989; Cross Patonce, 1990; Counting the Days to Christmas, 1990; The Aeronauts; Saddleworth Festival Overture A; Higgyjig, E flat horn; Pastorale, cornet with piano Rhumba, tenor trombone with piano; Little Swiss Suite, 2 cornets, E flat horn, euphonium; Others. *Recordings:* Burnished Brass, 1986; Compositions and Arrangements on many recordings by The King's Singers, leading Brass and wind Bands, Choirs; Calling Cornwall, 1992; Midnight Cuphonium, 1992; Celebration, 1993; A Cycle Round Britain, 1992. *Address:* Caxton, 131 Walton Road, Stockton Heath, Warrington, Cheshire WA4 6NT, England.

RICHARDS Leslie, b. 19 Feb 1950, Los Angeles, California, USA. Mezzo-soprano. m. Alexander Pellegrini, 11 Dec 1982. *Education:* San Francisco Conservatory of Music. *Debut:* San Diego Opera, 1979. *Career:* San Francisco Opera, 1980; Hawaii Opera Theater 1983; Festival Autunno Musicale a Como, 1984; Fort Worth Opera, 1985; Canadian Opera Company, 1985; Metropolitan Opera Company, 1986; Spoleto Festival, USA, 1986; Anchorage Opera, 1986; Opera Company of Philadelphia, 1986; Milan, 1986, Teatro Piccolo; New York City Opera, 1988; Seattle Opera, 1989; Washington Opera, 1991; Opera Company of Philadelphia, 1991; Connecticut Opera, 1991; Cleveland Opera, 1991. *Recordings:* Mozart: Opera Arias, Midsummer Mozart Festival Orchestra, G. Cleve conducting, (Sonic Arts Recordings). *Hobbies:* Painting; Walking; Fashion. *Current Management:* Robert Lombardo, 61 West 62nd Street, Suite 67, New York, NY 10023, USA. *Address:* 1176 Chestnut Street, San Francisco, CA 94109, USA.

RICHARDSON Carol, b. 1948, California, USA. Singer (Mezzo- soprano). *Education:* Studied at Occidental College, Los Angeles, with Martial Singher in Philadelphia and in New York. *Debut:* Klagenfurt 1973 as Nicklausse in Hoffmann. *Career:* Sang at Kiel from 1975, Bayreuth Festival 1976-81, in Parsifal; Engagements at Bern Stadttheater until 1984, Cenerentola at Bielefeld 1988; Other roles have included Dorabella and Cherubino, Rosina, Orlofsky, Nancy in Martha, Lola and Zerlina; Further guest appearances at Hamburg, Gelsenkirchen, Karlsruhe and Hanover; Noted concert performer. *Address:* c/o Städtische Buhnen, Brunnenstrasse 3, 4800 Bielefeld 1, Germany.

RICHARDSON David Vivian, b. 7 June 1941, London, England. Orchestra Manager. m. Janet Lesley Hilton, 6 July 1968, 1 son, 1 daughter. *Education:* BMus, Manchester University, 1964; ARMCM, 1963; GRSM, 1964, Royal Manchester College of Music; Caius College, Cambridge, Diploma in Education, 1965. *Career:* Professional Trumpet Player; Music Producer, BBC Manchester, 1966-70; Concerts Manager, New Philharmonia Orchestra, London, 1970-72; General Administrator, Scottish National Orchestra, 1972-80; Managing Director, St Paul Chamber Orchestra, Minnesota, USA, 1980-82; Chief Executive, Western Orchestral Society, Bournemouth, England, 1983-91; Chief Executive, Hallé Concerts Society, Manchester, England, 1991-. Member, Board of Directors, Association of British Orchestras, 1984-; Deputy Chairman, National Youth Orchestra of Great Britain, 1985-; Chairman, Association of British Orchestras, 1987-90; Member Gowrie Committee on London Music Conservatoires, 1989. *Honours:* Winston Churchill Memorial Fellowship, 1976. *Hobbies:* Theatre; Photography; Paintings. *Address:* Hallé Concerts Society, Heron House, Albert Square, Manchester M2 5HD, England.

RICHARDSON Marilyn, b. 10 June 1936, Sydney, New South Wales, Australia. Singer (Soprano). m. (1)

Peter Richardson, 3 children, 1954, (2) James Christiansen, 1974, 3 stepchildren. *Education:* Studied at the New South Wales Conservatorium of Music, with Pierre Bernac in Paris and Conchita Badia in Barcelona. *Debut:* Schoenberg's Pierrot Lunaire, ISCM concert, Sydney, 1958. *Career:* Debut with Basler Theater, Switzerland, 1972, Lulu; Salome, debut with The Australian Opera, 1975, Aida; Roles and operas include: Four Sopranos in Tales of Hoffmann, Marschallin, Countess, Donna Anna, Katya Kabanova, Queen of Spades, Otello, Eva, Sieglinde, Elsa, Mimi, Rosalinda, Merry Widow, Laura in Voss, Leonore (Fidelio), Isolde, 1990 and Tosca, 1992; Has appeared with all State Companies: Leading roles and opera such as, The Excursions of Mr Brouček, Fiordiligi, La Traviata, Madame Butterfly, Midsummer Marriage, Mistress Ford, Senta, Alcina, Cleopatra; Soloist in a huge range of concert music, including Australian Premieres of about 400 songs and vocal works. *Honours:* Churchill Fellowship, 1969; Australia Council Creative Fellowship, 1991. *Address:* Australian Opera, PO Box 291, Strawberry Hills, NSW 2012, Australia.

RICHTER Sviatoslav Teofilovich, b. 20 March 1915, Zhitomir, Ukraine, Russia. Pianist. *Education:* Self-taught at first, then entered the Moscow Conservatory 1937, studying under Heinrich Neuhaus. *Career:* Repetiteur at the Odessa Opera 1930, chief assistant conductor 1933; Gave the premieres of Prokofiev's 6th, 7th and 9th piano sonatas and conducted the first performance of the Symphony-Concerto for cello and orchestra (1952); Played in USSR and Eastern Europe in the 1950s; Western debut Finland May 1960; US debut Chicago and New York October 1960; Appearances at the Spoleto and Aldeburgh Festivals, in partnership with Britten and Rostropovitch; From 1964 visits to the Fêtes Musicales at the Grange de Meslay, near Tours; Most often heard in Schubert, Schumann, Liszt, Beethoven, Debussy, Prokofiev and Ravel; Also heard as chamber musician with the Borodin Quartet and as accompanist to leading singers; Returned to London 1989, to perform Schubert, Chopin, Mozart and Prokofiev. *Recordings:* Most of solo repertory, as well as duets with Britten and song recitals with Schwarzkopf and Fischer- Dieskau; CDs of Liszt Concertos (LSO, Kondrashin), Schubert Winterreise (Schreier); Beethoven Triple Concerto (Karajan) and Diabelli Variations; Britten Piano Concerto; Prokofiev 5th Concerto (Rowicki); Shostakovich Piano Quintet (Borodin Quartet); Prokofiev Sonatas; Mussorgsky Pictures at an Exhibition. *Publication:* S.S. Prokofiev 1961. *Honours:* USSR Music Competition 1945; Stalin Prize 1949; Order of Lenin. *Address:* c/o Moscow State Philharmonic Society, 31 Ulitsa Gorkogo, Moscow, Russia.

RICKARDS Steven, b. 1955, United States. Singer (Countertenor). *Education:* Studied at Indiana University, Bloomington, with Russell Oberlin and at the Aspen Music Festival; Further study at the Guildhall School and with Peter Pears and Robert Spencer. *Career:* Concert engagements with the Waverly Consort (New York), Chicago's Music of the Baroque, Concert Royal, Ars Musica and Chanticleer; British appearances with the Ipswich Bach Choir and at the East Cornwall Bach Festival; Tour of Ireland with the Gabrieli Consort and worldwide recitals with lutenist Dorothy Linell; Has toured France and Michigan with Messiah 1981-82; Carnegie Hall debut 1987, with the Oratorio Society of New York; Boston Early Music Festival in Handel's Teseo and Santa Fe Opera as Ariel in the premiere of John Eaton's The Tempest (1985); Sang with the Opera Company of Philadelphia as Apollo in Death in Venice; Recent revivals of Handel's Siroe in New York, Locke's Psyche on London, Hasse's L'Olimpiade in Dresden and Mondonville's De Profundis at Harvard. *Recordings include:* Bach Cantatas 106 and 131 with Joshua Rifkin (Decca); St John Passion by Bach; Gradualia by Byrd with Chanticleer (Harmonia Mundi); Medarse in Siroe by Handel (Newport Classic). *Address:* 250 Hartford Avenue, Daytona Beach, FL 32118, USA.

RICKENBACHER Karl Anton, b. 20 May 1940,

Basle, Switzerland. Conductor. *Education:* Studied at the Berlin Conservatory 1962-66 and took courses with Herbert von Karajan and Pierre Boulez. *Career:* Assistant Conductor at the Zurich Opera 1966-69; Principal Conductor of Freiburg Opera 1969-74; General Music Director of the Westphalean Symphony Orchestra from 1976; Principal Conductor of the BBC Scottish Symphony in Glasgow, 1977-80; Debut with the Berlin Philharmonic and the Deutsche Oper Berlin 1983; Debut with Royal Philharmonic and Philharmonia Orchestras 1987; North American debut season 1987-88, Numerous TV and Radio appearances; Since 1985 Guest Conductor with major European and North American Symphony Orchestras. Discography includes productions with London Philharmonic, Bavarian Radio and Berlin Rundfunk Symphony Orchestras, Bamberg and Budapest Symphony Orchestras (EMI, ORFEO, KOCH-Schwann and VIRGIN Classics). *Address:* Villa Oriole, CH-1822, Chernex-Montreux, Switzerland.

RICQUIER Michel, b. 2 Oct 1949, France. Professor of Trumpet. m. 2 children. *Education:* National Conservatory of Music, Douai; Conservatoire National Superieur de Musique, Paris; Teaching Certificate; Diplomas: Ecole d'Hypnologie et de Psychologie Appliquee, Paris; Heilpraktiker Fachschule, Sarrebruck; Hong Kong Institute of Chinese Acupuncture; New Medicine Institute of Hong Kong. *Career:* Professor of Trumpet, National Conservatory of Music, Chambery, 1969-; Participant, numerous national and international conferences. *Publications:* La Lecture musicale par l'education de l'oeil; L'utilisation do vos ressources intérieures dans votre activité artistique, with accompanying exercises; Traite methodique de pedagogie instrumentale; J'apprends la trompette, method for beginners; Méthode Arban (with Maurice Andre); Je ne manque pas de souffle. *Address:* 240, Rue des Cigales, F-73230 Barby, France.

RIDDER Anton de, b. 13 Feb 1929, Amsterdam, Holland. Singer (Tenor). *Education:* Studied at the Amsterdam Conservatory with H. Mulder and J. Keyzer. *Career:* After Dutch stage debut in 1952 sang in Karlsruhe from 1956; Munich Theater am Gärtnerplatz 1962-66; Sang with Cologne Opera in the premiere of Zimmermann's Die Soldaten 1965, and at the Edinburgh Festival, 1972; Guest appearances in London, East Germany and Amsterdam; Bregenz Festival 1974, as Don José; Glyndebourne Festival 1979, as Florestan in the Peter Hall production of Fidelio, conducted by Haitink; Salzburg Festival 1985, in Capriccio. *Recordings:* Busoni's Doktor Faust and Capriccio (Deutsche Grammophon); La Traviata (HMV); Lucia di Lammermoor (Eterna).

RIDDERBUSCH Karl, b. 29 May 1932, Recklinghausen, Germany. Singer (Bass). *Education:* Studied with Rudolf Schock and in Essen. *Debut:* Munster 1961. *Career:* Member of the Essen Opera 1963-65, hen the Deutsche Oper am Rhein Dusseldorf; Bayreuth Festival 1967-77, as King Henry, Hans Sachs, Pogner, Daland, Titurel and Fasolt; Metropolitan Opera 1967-76, as Hunding, Fafner and Hans Sachs; Paris Opéra 1967, 1978, as King Marke and Baron Ochs; Sang Fasolt, Hunding and Hagen at Covent Garden, 1971; Salzburg Easter Festival 1974-75, as Pogner in Die Meistersinger, conducted by Karajan; Guest appearances in Berlin, Mannheim, Stuttgart, Buenos Aires, Vienna, Hamburg and Chicago; Sang Podestà in Schreker's Die Gezeichneten at the 1989 Vienna Festival, with the company of the Deutsche Oper am Rhein. *Recordings:* Fidelio, Die Meistersinger, Tristan und Isolde, Die Königskinder (Electrola); Palestrina, Der fliegende Holländer, Lohengrin, Der Ring des Nibelungen, Parsifal, Capriccio (Deutsche Grammophon); Der Barbier von Bagdad, Martha, Verdi Requiem (Eurodisc); Missa Solemnis by Beethoven (Philips); Die Lustigen Weiber von Windsor (Decca). *Address:* c/o Staatsoper, Opernring 2, A-1010 Vienna, Austria.

RIDOUT Alan, b. 9 Dec 1934, West Wickham, Kent, England. Composer. *Education:* Studied with Gordon

Jacob and Herbert Howells at the Royal College of Music, privately with the late Peter Racine Fricker and Henk Badings. *Career:* Teacher of Composition at London, Oxford, Cambridge and Birmingham Universities; Professor at Royal College of Music, 1961-84. *Compositions:* Stage works: The Greek Islands, children's opera, Tunbridge Wells 1956; The Rescue, chamber opera, Hastings 1963; The Boy from the Catacombs, church opera, Canterbury Cathedral 1965; Children's Crusade, church opera, Canterbury Cathedral 1968; The Pardoner's Tale, Canterbury 1970; Angelo, chamber opera, Canterbury 1971; The Cat, Berkshire, New York 1971; The Gift, children's opera, Canterbury Cathedral 1971; Creation, church opera, Ely Cathedral 1973; Phaeron, radio opera, BBC 1974; A Vision, monodrama, Manchester 1974; The Selfish Giant, chamber opera, Wye Church 1977; Wenceslas, church opera, Bournemouth 1978; The White Doe, church opera, Ripon Cathedral 1987; 8 Cantatas; Christmas Oratorio; 12 Melodramas with narrator; 8 Song Cycles; 8 Symphonies; Flute Concerto 1973; Double Bass Concerto 1974; 13 Concertinos with strings 1975-79; Flute and Harp Concerto 1979; Organ: The Seven Last Words 1965; Dance Suite 1969; Resurrection Dances 1970; 6 Studies 1976; 14 Stations of the Cross 1978; Piano and Chamber Music. *Address:* 3 Stourvill, Canterbury, Kent CT1 2PB, England.

RIEBL Thomas, b. 1956, Vienna, Austria. Violist. *Education:* Studied at the Vienna Academy of Music and with Peter Schidlof and Sandor Vegh. *Career:* Led the violas of the World Youth Orchestra, 1972; Solo debut at the Vienna Konzerthaus 1972 and has since appeared with leading orchestras in Europe and North America: Chicago Symphony, Helsinki Radio, Vienna and Berlin and Bournemouth Symphony Orchestras; Royal Liverpool Philharmonic; Los Angeles and Vienna Chamber Orchestras; Conductors include Abbado, Walter Weller, Andrew Davis, Horst Stein, Erich Bergel and Edo de Waart; Festival appearances at Salzburg, Vienna, Aspen, Ravinia, New York, Munich, Lockenhaus and Carinthian Summer; Concerts with the Juilliard Quartet, Gidon Kremer and Jessye Norman (Brahms Lieder Op 91); Founder member of the Vienna Sextet; Professor of Viola at the Musikhochschule, Mozarteum, at Salzburg from 1983. *Honours include:* Prizewinner at international competitions in Budapest 1975 and Munich, 1976; Ernst Wallfisch Memorial Award at the International Naumburg Viola Competition in New York, 1982. *Recordings include:* Brahms Lieder Op 91 with Brigitte Fassbaender and Irwin Gage (Fonoteam); Albums for RCA and Musical Heritage Society, New York.

RIEDEL Deborah, b. 31 July 1958, Sydney, Australia. Singer (Soprano). *Education:* Studied at the Sydney Conservatorium and in London with Audrey Langford and Paul Hamburger. *Career:* Sang Hansel with Western Australian Opera 1986, followed by Meg Page and Thomas' Mignon, Mimi and Norina; The Australian Opera from 1988 as Zerlina, Micaela, Juliette and Susanna; Appearances with the Victorian State Opera as the Drummer in Ullmann's Emperor of Atlantis, Nayad in Ariadne auf Naxos, Leila (Les Pêcheurs de Perles); London engagements as Marguerite with English National Opera and Freia in Das Rheingold at Covent Garden; Concert engagements as Mariana in Il Signor Bruschino at the Festival of Flanders; Jemmy in Guillaume Tell and Rossini's Petite Messe Solonnelle; Scarlatti's St Cecilia Mass and frequent appearances with the Australian Pops Orchestra; Mozart's Vespers for the Rantos Collegium and Messiah for the ABC in Melbourne and Sydney; Mendelssohn's Midsummer Night's Dream with the Sydney Symphony Orchestra and Strauss's Four Last Songs for the Australian Ballet; Geneva Opera 1992, as Teresa in Benvenuto Cellini, Gounod's Juliette at Geneva. *Honours:* Winner, Australian Regional final of the Metropolitan Opera Auditions; Dame Sister Mary Leo Scholarship; Dame Mabel Brookes Fellowship; 1986 Sydney Sun Aria Award. *Address:* c/o Lies Askonas Ltd., 186 Drury Lane, London WC2B 5RY, England.

RIEDEL Friedrich Wilhelm, b. 24 Oct 1929, Cuxhaven, Germany. Professor of Musicology. m. Almuth Keller, 4 children. *Education:* Christian Albrechts University, Kiel; PhD, 1957; Qualified in Musicology, Johannes Gutenberg University, Mainz, 1971; Training as Organist and Choirmaster, Landesmusikschule, Luebeck; Qualified in Church Music. *Career includes:* Musicology Assistant, Institute of Musicology, Mainz University; University Lecturer, Johannes Gutenberg University, Mainz, 1971-; Director, Capella Moguntina (ensemble for old music), Mainz, 1972; Chief of Central Secretariat of the International Inventory of Musical Sources, Kassel, 1960-67; Expert for Historical Organs, Landesamt fuer Denkmalpflege Rheinland-Pfalz, 1978-. *Recordings include:* Kurmainzer Chamber Music from Rokoko, 1975; Organ and Bells der Basilika zum Heiligen Blut in Wallduern, 1976; Editor of several musical works. *Publications:* Quellenkundliche Beitraege zur Geschichte der Musik fuer Tasteninstrumente, 1960, 1990; Kirchenmusik am Hofe Karls VI, 1977; Joseph Martin Kraus und Italien, 1987; Der Goettweiger Thematische Katalog von 1830, 1979; Musikalische Schaetze aus neun Jahrhunderten, 1979; Joseph Martin Kraus in seiner Zeit, 1982; Musik und Geschichte, 1989; Geistliches Leben und geistliche Musik im fraenkischen Raum am Ende des alten Reiches, 1990; Das Himmlische lebt in seinen Toenen. Joseph Martin Kraus, ein Meister der Klassik, 1992; Die Orgel als sakrales Kunstwerk, 1992. *Contributions to:* Professional journals. *Memberships:* President, International Joseph Martin Kraus Society, 1982-; Gesellschaft fuer Musikforschung (Chairman of the Commission for Church Music, 1982-); Gesellschaft der Orgelfreunde. *Address:* Im Muenchfeld 7, D-55122 Mainz, Germany.

RIEGEL Kenneth, b. 19 April 1938, Womelsdorf, Pennsylvania, USA. Opera Tenor. *Education:* Manhattan School of Music; Berkshire Music Center; Metropolitan Opera Studio. *Debut:* Santa Fe Festival, 1965, as the Alchemist in the US premiere of Henze's König Hirsch. *Career:* San Francisco Opera, 1971; Metropolitan Opera, New York, 1973; Vienna State Opera, 1977; Paris Opera, 1979 as the Painter in the premiere of the 3-act Version of Lulu; La Scala, 1979; Hamburg State Opera, 1981; Geneva Opera, 1981; Deutsche Opera, West Berlin, 1983; Bonn Opera, 1983; Sang the Leper in the premiere of Messiaen's St François d'Assise, Paris, 1983; Brussels Opera, 1984; Royal Opera, Covent Garden, 1985, in Der Zwerg by Zemlinsky; appeared in film, Don Giovanni; Bavarian State Opera, Munich, 1988; Sang at Stuttgart 1989, as Dionysos in The Bassarids by Henze; Season 1992 as Herod in Salome at Covent Garden and Salzburg. *Recordings:* Der Zwergh; Damnation of Faust; Florentinische Tragoedie; Don Giovanni; Lulu; Mahler Symphony No. 8; Berlioz Requiem. *Honours:* Nominated for Sir Laurence Oliver Award for Best Individual Performance in an Opera, 1985. *Hobbies:* Cooking; Gardening. *Current Management:* SAFIMM Corporation. *Address:* c/o SAFIMM Corp, 250 West 57th Street, Suite 1018, New York, NY 10107, USA.

RIFKIN Joshua, b. 22 April 1944, New York, USA. Musicologist; Conductor; Composer. *Education:* Juilliard School of Music with Persichetti (BS 1964); New York University 1964-66 with Gustave Reese; University of Göttingen 1966-67; Princeton University with Lewis Lockwood, Arthur Mendel and Milton Babbitt. *Career:* Nonesuch Records, New York, 1964-75; Brandeis University 1970-82; Visiting lecturer to various Eastern US Universities; As a musicologist has researched Renaissance and Baroque music; Performances as Director of the Bach Ensemble; Guest appearances as conductor with St. Louis and San Francisco Symphony Orchestras, and with the St. Paul, English and Scottish Chamber Orchestras; Major contribution to the revival of interest in the ragtime music of Scott Joplin; 1989 at Melbourne Summer Festival, playing Joplin and conducting Copland, Stravinsky and Weill; Conducted St John Passion by Bach at the Lufthansa Early Music Festival, London 1989. *Recordings:* Bach Cantatas and Mass in B Minor in an attempt to recreate early performance practice (Nonesuch, L'Oiseau Lyre), Music by Scott Joplin; Fanfares and sonatas by Pezel and Hammerschmidt; Sonatas by Biber; Vocal music by Busnois and Josquin. *Publications:* Articles on Haydn, Schütz, Bach and Josquin in the Musical Times, Musical Quarterly and other journals. *Address:* c/o Clarion/Seven Muses, 47 Whitehall Park, London N19 3TW, England.

RIGACCI Bruno, b. 1921, Florence, Italy. Conductor; Composer; Pianist. *Education:* Studied conducting with Antonio Guarneri. *Career:* Early appearance as a pianist in Italy and abroad; Founded and became permanent conductor of the Chamber Orchestra of Florence; Conductor at the Royal Opera in Stockholm and permanent orchestral conductor at Accademia Chigiana in Siena; Music director of the Festival Settimane Musicali Senesi, 1966; Member of the faculty, Philadelphia Musical Academy 1970; Musical Director of the Philadelphia Music Theatre 1974; Appearances with major Italian orchestras and in leading opera houses; Maggio Musicale Florence, with La Bohème and Lucia di Lammermoor; Principal conductor of the San Diego Opera 1980-84; Guest conductor at Teatro Rossini in Lugo, 1987; Currently artistic director of the Festival Opera at Barga, Italy; Engagements 1986-89 included Hamlet by Thomas at San Diego (with Sherrill Milnes and Ashley Putnam); Macbeth at Pittsburgh (Carlo Bergonzi, Ghena Dimitrova, Justino Diaz); Rossi's Orfeo at La Scala; Turandot (Eva Marton) and Semiramide (June Anderson and Kathleen Kuhlmann) at the Bilbao Festival; Canadian Opera in Toronto 1989, La Bohème and Il barbiere di Siviglia; Opera School of the Royal Opera, Stockholm, from 1988 as visiting consultant in Italian repertoire. *Compositions include:* Chamber music; Symphonies; Ecuba, Professor Tkimg and three other operas. *Honours:* First prize at the Teatro del'Opera in Rome for Ecuba; Orfeo d'Argento for conductors. *Recordings:* Bohème and Lucia di Lammermoor from the Maggio Musicale; Demetrio e Polibio (Rossini); Andrea Chenier; Donizetti's Pia de Tolomei, Parisina d'Este, Olivo e Pasquale, Betly, Le Convenienze teatrali and I pazzi per progetto; Mascagni's I Rantzau. *Address:* Via Giambologna 3a, 50132 Firenze, Italy.

RIGBY Jean, b. 22 Dec 1954, Fleetwood, Lancashire, England. Singer (Mezzo- Soprano). m. J Hayes, Producer, 1987. 2 sons. *Education:* Birmingham School of Music with Janet Edmunds; Royal Academy of Music with Patricia Clark; National Opera Studio, London. *Career:* Member of English National Opera from 1982: roles include Mercedes in Carmen, Maddalena in Rigoletto, Marina in Boris Godunov, Blanche in The Gambler, Britten's Lucretia and Magdalena in The Mastersingers; Concert performance of Lady Essex in Gloriana with Chelsea Opera Group; Festival Hall debut in the Verdi Requiem; Covent Garden debut as Thibault in Don Carlos, 1983; Glyndebourne Festival 1985, as Mercedes in Carmen; Zurich 1986, as Cornelia in Handel's Giulio Cesare; Sang Penelope in The Return of Ulysses with ENO (1989 and 1992), Ursula in Beatrice and Benedict 1990; Glyndebourne 1990 as Nancy in Albert Herring; Season 1992/93 as Amastris in Xerxes, Rossini's Isabella at Buxton and Nicklausse in Les Contes d'Hoffmann at Covent Garden. *Recordings include:* Video of English National Opera Rigoletto. *Honours:* Friends of Covent Garden Bursary; Countess of Munster Scholarship; Worshipful Company of Musicians' Medal; Royal Overseas League Competition 1981; Young Artists competition, ENO, 1981. *Address:* 31 Sinclair Road, London W14 0NS, England.

RIHM Wolfgang, b. 13 March 1952, Karlsruhe, Germany. Composer. *Education:* 1968-72 Hochschule für Musik Karlsruhe, with Eugen W. Velte; Later studies with Stockhausen in Cologne and with Klaus Huber in Freiburg. *Career:* Teacher at the Karlsruhe Hochschule für Musik 1973-78; Freelance composer; since 1985: Professor of Composition at the Musikhochschule Karlsruhe; British premiere of Jakob Lenz London 1987; Die Eroberung von Mexiko Premiered at the Hamburg Staatsoper, 1992. *Compositions:* Operas: Deploration 1974; Faust und Yorick 1977; Jakob Lenz 1978; Hamlet-

Machine,1986; Oedipus 1987, Die Eroberung von Mexico, 1987/89. Orchestral: 3 Symphonies: 1969, 1975, 1976 (No. 3, after Rimband and Nietzsche); Dis-Kontur 1975; Sub-Kontar 1975/76; Cuts and Dissolves 1977; La Musique Creuse le Ciel for 2 pianos and orchestra 1979; Doppelgesang II for clarinet, I: for viola, violoncello and orchestra, 1980, cello and orchestra 1983; Monodram for cello and orchestra 1983; Klangbeschreibung I-II 1982-87; Medea-Spiel 1988; Urbenannt III 1989; Passion 1989; Ungemaltes Bild, 1990; Schwebende Begegnung, 1989; Abgewandt, 1989; Dunkles Spiel, 1990. Vocal: Hervorgedunkelt for mezzo and ensemble 1974; Abgesangsszenen Nos. 1-5 1979-81; Umhergetrieben aufgewirbelt, Nietzsche Fragments for baritone and mezzo, chorus and flute 1981; Wölfi-Lieder for baritone and piano or orchestra 1982; Lowry-Liede (Wondratschek), 1987; Mein Tod (Wondratschek), 1988, song cycles for Soprano and orchestra; Geheimer Block for voices and orchestra, 1989; Frau/Stimme for soprano and orchestra, 1989; Engel for men's voices and 20 instruments, 1989; Mein Tod: Requiem in Memoriam Jane S 1990. Chamber: Paraphrase for cello, percussion and piano 1972; Deploration 1974; Ländler for 13 strings 1979; 8 String Quartets 1970-1980; Chiffre I-VII 1982-88; Gebild for trumpet, strings and percussion 1983; Canzona for 4 violas 1983; Fremde Szene I-III 1982-83, 1988; Duomonolog for violin and cello, 1989. Music for voice and piano; Organ and piano music. *Address:* c/o Universal Edition Ltd., 2 Fareham Street, London W1, England.

RILEY Dennis Daniel, b. 28 May 1943, Los Angeles, California, USA. Composer. *Education:* BMus, University of Colorado, 1965; MMus, University of Illinois, 1968; PhD, University of Iowa, 1973. *Career includes:* Assistant professor of music, Columbia University. *Compositions:* Theme & Variations for Orchestra; Viola Concerto; Elegy for Violoncello & Orchestra; Symphony for Large Orchestra; Noon Dances for Chamber Orchestra; Rappaccini's Daughter, opera; Cat's Concert, children's opera; Piano Pieces I-III; Cantatas I-V; Viola Variations; Clarinet Variations; Concertino; Canzona; Winter Music; Cloud Songs; 5 Haiku; Summer Music; 7 Dickinson Songs; Liebeslied; Elegy for September 15, 1945; Psalm 83; Winter Settings; Masques, woodwind quintet; Apparitions; Fantasia, after Orlando Gibbons; 6 Preludes for Harp; 2 Roethke Songs; 5 Poems of Marilyn Hacker; Improvisations for guitar; Bagatelles for violin; Dances and Interludes; in Eius Memoriam for winds, piano, percussion. *Recordings:* Beata Viscera; String Trio; Cantata II; Magnificat. *Address:* c/o C.F. Peters Corporation, 373 Park Avenue South, New York, NY 10016, USA.

RILEY Howard, b. 16 Feb 1943, Huddersfield, England. Pianist; Composer. *Education:* BA 1964, MA 1966, University of Wales; M Mus, Indiana University, USA, 1967; M Phil, York University, England, 1970. *Career:* Concerts as solo/group pianist, 1967-; Broadcasts throughout Europe, USA and Canada; Festival appearances include: Berlin, Paris, New York, Debrecen, Leipzig; Creative Associate, Center of the Creative and Performing Arts, Buffalo, New York, USA, 1976-77. *Compositions include:* The Contemporary Piano Collection, portfolio of piano compositions published 1982; Many compositions recorded including: Angle; Zones; Trisect for 3 pianos. *Recordings include:* 20 LP recordings of own music including: Facets, 3 LP box set, 1983; For Four on Two Two, 1984; In Focus, 1985; Live At The Royal Festival Hall, 1985; Feathers, 1988; Procession, 1990. *Contributions to:* The Musical Times, 1966; The Music Review, 1966 and 1972; Jazz Monthly, 1969. *Honour:* UK/USA Bicentennial Fellowship in the Arts, 1976-77. *Hobbies:* Football; Walking. *Address:* Flat 2, 53 Tweedy Road, Bromley, Kent BR1 3NH, England.

RILEY Terry, b. 24 June 1935, Colfax, California, USA. Composer. *Education:* Studied at San Francisco State College 1955-57 and the University of California (MA 1961). *Career:* Member of the San Francisco Tape Music Center; Studios of ORTF Paris 1963; Creative

Associate at the Center for Creative and Performing Arts, Buffalo, 1967; Studied raga singing in India, 1970; Associate Professor at Mills College, 1971-80; Works include string quartets (Kronos Quartet) and Indian instruments from 1981. *Compositions:* Trio for violin, clarinet and cello 1957; Spectra for 3 wind and 3 strings 1959; Concert, for 2 pianos and tape 1960; String Quartet 1960; String Trio 1961; I Can't Stop No, Mescalin Mix and She Moves, for tape 1962-63; Keyboard Studies 1963; Dorian Reeds for ensemble 1964; Poppy Nogood and the Phantom Band, for saxophone, keyboard and tape delay 1967; A Rainbow in the Curved Air 1968; Persian Surgery Dervishes, for electronic keyboard 1971; Happy Ending 1972; Descending Moonshine Dervishes 1975; Shri Camel for electronic organ and tape delay 1976; Cadenza on the Right Plain for string quartet, 1984; Works with synthesizer include Chorale of the Blessed Day, Eastern Man, Emroidery, Song from the Old Country, G-Song, Remember this oh Mind, Sunrise of the Planetary Dream Collector, The Ethereal Time Shadow, Offering to Chief Crazy Horse, Rites of the Imitators, The Medicine Wheel, Song of the Emerald Runner 1980-83; Do you know How it Sounds? for low voice, piano and tabla 1983. *Honours include:* Guggenheim Fellowship 1979. *Address:* c/o ASCAP, ASCAP Building, One Lincoln Plaza, NY 10023, USA.

RILEY-SCHOFIELD John, b. 1954, England. Singer (Baritone). *Education:* Studied at Huddersfield School of Music 1972-75 and at Royal Academy of Music 1975-78 with Raimund Herincx. *Career:* Sang with English National Opera 1978-85, and as Cascada in The Merry Widow, many small roles; Gelsenkirchen Opera from 1986, as Germont, Mozart-Count, Giovanni and Guglielmo, the Speaker in Die Zauberflöte, the Count in Capriccio and in Matrimonio Segreto, and Mel in The Knot Garden by Tippett; Bregenz Festival 1988, in Les Contes d'Hoffmann; Further guest appearances in Cologne, Mainz, Amsterdam, New York, London, Portugal and Austria; Other roles have included Valentin, Papageno and Rossini's Figaro; Concert repertoire includes Bach's Passions and B minor Mass, Handel's Messiah, Samson and Saul, Ein Deutsches Requiem, Haydn's Oratorios, Elijah, the Requiems of Mozart and Fauré, Carmina Burana. *Address:* c/o Musiktheater im Revier, Kennedyplatz, 45881 Gelsenkirchen, Germany.

RILLING Helmuth, b. 29 May 1933, Stuttgart, Germany. Conductor; Chorus Master; Organist. *Education:* Studied at the Musikhochschule Stuttgart 1952-55 (composition with Johann Nepomuk David); Further organ studies with Fernando Germani in Rome and conducting with Bernstein in New York. *Career:* Founded the Gächinger Kantorei 1954: tours of Europe, Asia and North and South America; Organist and choirmaster at the Gedächtniskirche, Stuttgart, 1957; Re-formed the Spandauer Kantorei while teaching at the Spandau Kirchenmusikschule (1963-66); London debut, as organist 1963; Founded the Bach-Collegium of Stuttgart 1965: tours to USA 1968, English Bach Festival 1972 and Japan 1974; Professor at the Frankfurt Musikhochschule from 1969; Director of the Frankfurt Kantorei; Performances of works by Pepping, Bach, Handel, Verdi and Reger. *Recordings:* Cycle of Bach Cantatas from 1972 with the Frankfurter Kantorei, the Gächinger Kantorei and the Figuralchor of Stuttgart; Motets, Lutheran Masses, Choral Preludes and Orgelbüchlein by Bach; Magnificats by Schütz, Bach, Monteverdi and Buxtehude; Carissimi's Jephte and Judicum Salomonis; Handel's Belshazzar; Telemann's Ino and Pimpinone; Mozart's Concertos K364 and K190, Mass K317 and Vesperae solennes de confessore; Geistliche Chormusik, St Matthew Passion, Symphoniae Sacrae and Cantiones Sacrae by Schütz; Messiaen's Cinq Rechants. *Address:* c/o Staatliche Hochschule für Musik, Escherheimer Landstrasse 33, Postfach 2326, Frankfurt, Germany.

RINALDI Alberto, b. 6 June 1939, Rome, Italy. Singer (Baritone). *Education:* Studied at the Accademia di Santa Cecilia, Rome. *Debut:* Spoleto 1963, as Simon Boccanegra. *Career:* Teatro Fenice Venice 1970, as Rossini's Figaro; Appearances in Milan, Rome, Naples, Paris, Rio de Janeiro, Ghent, Florence and Aix-en-Provence; Edinburgh Festival 1973; Glyndebourne Festival 1980, as Ford in Falstaff; Sang Mozart's Count on tour to Japan with the company of the Vienna Staatsoper, 1986; Sang at the Berlin Staatsoper, 1987 as Dandini in Cenerentola; Pesaro and Cologne 1988/89, in Il Signor Bruschino and Il Cambiale di matrimonio; Bonn Opera 1990, as Rossini's Figaro; Sang Blansac in La Scala di Seta at the 1990 Schwetzingen Festival; Season 1992 as Blansac at Cologne and Paris; *Recordings:* Masetto in Don Giovanni (EMI); Il Matrimonio Segreto, Il Campanello (Deutsche Grammophon); Pagliacci (Philips); Video of La Scala di Seta (Warner Classics). *Address:* c/o Oper der Stadt Köln, Offenbachplatz, D-5000 Cologne, Germany.

RINALDI Margarita, b. 12 Jan 1933, Turin, Italy. Singer (Soprano). *Education:* Studied in Rovigo. *Debut:* Spoleto 1958, as Lucia di Lammermoor. *Career:* La Scala Milan 1959, as Siaide in Mose by Rossini; Dublin 1961, as Carolina (Il Matrimonio Segreto) and Gilda; Verona Arena 1962, 1969; US debut Dallas 1966, as Gilda; Glyndebourne Festival 1966, Carolina; Bregenz Festival 1974 and 1980, in Un Giorno di Regno, and as Alice Ford; Further appearances in Barcelona, Chicago, San Francisco, Wexford, Rome, Naples and Turin; Other roles include Amina, Norina, Linda di Chamounix, Marie in La Fille du Régiment, Bertha in La Prophète, Sophie, Ilia, Fiordiligi, Violetta, Oscar, and the Marschallin; Maggio Musicale Florence 1977-78 as Amenaide in Tancredi and Helena in A Midsummer Night's Dream; Retired from stage, 1981; Many concert engagements. *Recordings:* Lucia di Lammermoor; Rigoletto; Le Prophète; La Scala di Seta (RCA); L'Africaine; Ilia in Idomeneo (Philips).

RINGART Anna, b. 15 Jan 1937, Paris, France. Singer (Mezzo-soprano). *Education:* Studied with Irene Joachim and Marguerite Liszt in Paris; Hamburg Musikhochschule with Frau Anders-Mysz-Gmeiner. *Career:* Sang at such German opera centres as Lubeck, Koblenz, Dusseldorf and Hamburg; Sang at the Paris Opéra from 1973 under Karl Böhm, Pierre Boulez, Seiji Ozawa and Georg Solti, in a repertoire extending from Mozart to Schoenberg (Moses und Aron); Appeared in the 1985 premiere of Docteur Faustus by Konrad Boehmer; Opéra-Comique 1988, as the Nurse in Boris Godunov; Has sung at many festivals of contemporary music, notably with the group Contrasts. *Address:* c/o Théâtre National de Paris, 8 Rue Scribe, F-75009 Paris, France.

RINGBORG (Hans) Patrik Erland, b. 1 Nov 1965, Stockholm, Sweden. Conductor. *Education:* Stockholm Institute of Music, 5 years; Royal College of Music, Stockholm, 4 years; Further studies in Vienna and London. *Debut:* Ystad Summer Opera, Akhnaten, Ph.Glass, 1989; Städtische Bühnen, Freiburg, Carmen, Bizet, 1992; Royal Opera, Stockholm, 3 bill with Scheherazade 1993. *Career:* Conductor and Coach since 1987, Swedish Radio Choir 1988, Sächsische Staatsoper, Dresden 1988, Royal Opera, Stockholm 1989-93 (including TV), Canadian Opera Company 1992, 2 Kapellmeister and Studienleiter, Städtische Bühnen, Freiburg, since 1993. *Honours:* British Council Fellow, 1987; Major Scholarship, Royal Academy of Music, Stockholm, 1987; Music Fellowship, Swedish-American Foundation, 1990; 1st R-U, First Competition for Opera Conductors, Royal Opera, Stockholm. *Hobbies:* Computers; Tennis. *Current Management:* Nordic Artist Stockholm. *Address:* Städtische Bühnen, Postfach 1569, D-79075 Freiburg im Breisgau, Germany.

RINGHOLZ Teresa, b. 30 Dec 1958, Rochester, New York, USA. Singer (Soprano). *Education:* Studied at the Eastman School Rochester and in San Francisco. *Debut:* Western Opera Theater San Francisco 1982, as Gilda. *Career:* Toured in the USA then sang in Europe from 1985 (debut at Strasbourg as Zerbinetta); Cologne Opera from 1985, as Liu, Sophie, Susanna, Despina, Pamina and Sandrina (La Finta Giardiniera); Sang at the

Salzburg Festival 1987-88 and at Tel-Aviv with the company of Cologne Opera; Further appearances in opera and concert throughout Germany, France and Switzerland; Other roles include Gretel, Oscar, Lauretta, Micaela, Marzelline and Adele in Die Fledermaus; Season 1992 as the Wife in the premiere of Schnittke's Life with an Idiot (Amsterdam) and as Fanny in Rossini's La Cambiale di Matrimonio at Paris. *Address:* Oper der Stadt Köln, Offenbachplatz, D-5000 Cologne, Germany.

RINKEVICIUS Gintaras, b. 20 Feb 1960, Vilnius, Lithuania. Conductor. *Education:* Studied at St Petersburg and Moscow Conservatoires. *Career:* Assistant Conductor of Lithuanian Philharmonic Orchestra 1979; Music Director of Lithuanian State Symphony Orchestra from 1988; Tours with Moscow Radio Orchestra to Italy, Spain, Austria, Finland and Yugoslavia and has worked with such soloists as Natalia Gutman, Peter Donohoe, Oleg Kagan and Vladimir Ovchinikov; Repertoire includes music by Dvorak, Mahler, Poulenc, Orff, Honegger, Prokoviev, Elgar and John Adams in addition to the standard works; Appearances with Lithuanian State Opera, notably conducting Nabucco in Paris 1992; Guest engagements with Russian State Symphony, Moscow Philharmonic and St Petersburg Philharmonic Orchestras. *Honours:* Winner, All-Union Conducting Competition at St Petersburg Conservatoire; Third Prize, Herbert von Karajan Conducting Competition, 1985; Second Prize in Janos Ferencsik Competition, Budapest, 1986. *Address:* c/o Sonata, 11 Northpark Street, Glasgow G20 7AA, Scotland.

RINTZLER Marius, b. 14 March 1932, Bucharest, Rumania. Singer (Bass). *Education:* Studied at the Bucharest Conservatory with A. Alexandrescu. *Debut:* Bucharest 1964, as Basilio in Il Barbiere di Siviglia. *Career:* Member of the Deutsche Oper am Rhein Dusseldorf; Has sung also at Covent Garden, Drottningholm, Edinburgh (Die Soldaten, 1972), and Cologne; Glyndebourne Festival 1967-79, as the Commendatore, Enrico in Anna Bolena, Osmin, Bartolo, La Roche in Capriccio, and Morosus in Die schweigsame Frau; Metropolitan Opera 1973-74, as Alberich; Geneva 1974, as Osmin; Further appearances in Rio de Janeiro, San Francisco, Stockholm and Oslo; Sang in the US premiere of Penderecki's Die schwarze Maske, Santa Fe 1988; Concert engagements in sacred music by Bach. *Recordings:* Bruckner F Minor Mass, Beethoven Mass in C (EMI); Bach Cantatas, Madama Butterfly, Shostakovich 13th Symphony (Decca); Orlando by Handel (RCA); Tamerlano by Handel (Cambridge); Video of Il Barbiere di Siviglia (Topaz). *Address:* c/o Norman McCann Artists Ltd, The Coach House, 56 Lawrie Park Gardens, London SE26 6XJ, England.

RIPPON Michael George, b. 10 Dec 1938, Coventry, Warwickshire, England. Singer (Bass-Baritone). *Education:* MA (Cantab), St John's College, Cambridge, 1957-60; Royal Academy of Music, 1960-63; ARAM. *Debut:* Handel Opera Society, 1963, as Nireno in Giulio Cesare; Sang in the 1967 London premiere of Puccini's Edgar. *Career:* Covent Garden Opera 1969; Sang Leporello with Welsh National Opera 1969; Glyndebourne Festival 1970-73, in Die Zauberflöte, Le Nozze di Figaro, The Queen of Spades, and The Visit of the Old Lady; Has also sung with English National Opera, Scottish Opera, Handel Opera, Boston Opera, New York City Opera; PACT, Johannesburg; Most leading music festivals and societies in UK and abroad; Sang in the premieres of Maxwell Davies's Martyrdom of St Magnus (1977) and The Lighthouse (1989); Merlin in Hamilton's Lancelot (1985). *Recordings:* Belshazzar's Feast (Classics for Pleasure); Bach Cantatas and B Minor Mass, Mozart Requiem (Vanguard); Purcell's Ode to St Cecilia, Israel in Egypt by Handel (Deutsche Grammophon); Moses und Aron by Schoenberg, Hugh the Drover by Vaughan Williams, The Wandering Scholar by Holst (EMI); This Worlds Joie by Mathias (Argo); Salome (RCA). *Hobbies:* Reading; Walking; Swimming.

RISA Neithard, b. 1958, Berlin. Violist. *Education:*

Studied with Michel Schwalbe in Berlin, Max Rostal in Cologne and with Michael Tree of the Guarneri Quartet. *Career:* Leader of the viola section of the Berlin Philharmonic Orchestra from 1978; Co-founded the Philharmonia Quartet Berlin 1980; Many concerts in Europe, notably at the Salzburg Festivals, Bath Festival (1990), Wigmore Hall, London and the Berlin Festival 1991, with works by Mozart; Annual visits to Japan from 1986; International career as solo violist. *Recordings include:* CD of quartets by Beethoven (Camerata/Tokyo). *Address:* c/o Anglo-Swiss Management, 4-5 Primrose Mews, Sharpeshall Street, London NW1 8YW, England.

RISELING Robert Allen, b. 4 Sept 1937, Aurora, Illinois, USA. Professor; Free-lance Clarinetist. m. Judy Johnson, 11 June 1961, 1s. 2d. *Education:* MM, Composition, University of Texas, Austin, 1961; DMA, Performance-Clarinet, University of Michigan, 1978. *Career:* Teacher: Albion College, Michigan 1964-66, Eastern Kentucky University 1966-69, Wichita State University 1969-70, University of Western Ontario, 1970-; Aacadia University, 1981-82, Universite Canadienne en France, Fall 1992; Conducting: Fanshawe Community Orchestra, London, Ontario, Music Director and Conductor 1981-82; Orchestra London Canada, Assistant Conductor 1983-85; Royal Conservatory Toronto, Guest Conductor, Orchestral Training Programme, 1985; Clarinet: 100's recitals in USA, Canada; Over 30 solo works commissioned and premiered; Invitations to perform at International Clarinet Festival: Denver, Colorado 1979; Champaign, Illinois, 1987; Richmond, Virginia, 1988; Quebec, Canada, 1990; Concert tour 1985-86: USA, Canada, Europe, Iceland; Radio: CBS Radio Canada, 1978-; Magyar Radio, Hungary, 1976, 86; Icelandic Radio, 1986. *Recordings:* With Stratford Canada Chamber Ensemble, Cantabile, CBC 5000; Spells, Bear Lake Music Festival, Utah, Idaho, Principal Clarinetist 1992, 93; Domaine Forget, 1993 Sichuan Conservatory, China; Master classes, Chamber, Performer, 1993. *Publication:* Paul A Pisk: Essays in His Honor. Motivic Structures in Beethoven's Late Quartets, 1966. *Address:* 79 Deer Park Circle, London, Ontario, Canada N6H 3B7.

RISHTON Timothy John, b. 14 Aug 1960, Lancashire, England. Organist; Musicologist. m. Tracy Jane Hogg, 11 July 1987. *Education:* BA Music, University of Reading; Certificate in Welsh, University of Wales; MusM, University of Manchester, England; Associate, Royal College of Organists. *Career:* Numerous recitals worldwide including complete Stanley series, London, 1981 and complete Bach Trio Sonatas, London and Salford, 1983; complete Bach organ works, Norway, 1988-89; concerts in Belgium and Central Europe; 3 week tour of Arctic and Scandinavia, 1986; subsequent tours 1987-89 including Bodo Cathedral and Nordlands Musikkfestuke; tours in Far East and USA; 1st performance of Smethergell Harpsichord Concerto, Tadley, 1983; Lectures, Boxhill Summer School annually since 1985, University of Oxford 1986 and 1987; University of Reading 1988; Many public lectures in English and in Welsh, some broadcast; Many television broadcasts for HTV and BBC; Tutor, University College of North Wales, Bangor, Wales, 1987; Organist and Master of Choristers, Collegiate Church of St Cybi, Holyhead and Parish Churches of Holy Island, Anglesey, 1984-1987; Director, North Wales Organ Music Foundation, 1989- . *Recordings:* with Aled Jones, 1985; Organ Works of the Eighteenth-Century (Wealden WSC 229), 1986; Music for Harp and Organ with Eleri Davies, 1989.*Current Management:* (USA) Steve Cram Management, 1080 Eddy Street, Suite 607, San Francisco, CA 94109, USA. *Address:* Parc Uchaf, Rhosmeirch, Llangefni, Gwynedd LL77 7NQ.

RISINGER Karel, b. 18 June 1920, Prague, Czechoslovakia. Musical Theorist; Composer. m. Vlasta Karasova, 5 Oct 1948, 1s. 1d. *Education:* The Realgymnasium, The Faculty of Arts, Charles University, Prague; Composition at Conservatoire of Prague and at Senior School in Music, Prague. *Debut:* The Faculty of Music, The Academy of Music and Dramatic Arts. *Career:* Professor: Faculty of Arts of Charles University, Institute of Musicology at Czechoslovak Academy of Sciences, Faculty of Music of the Academy of Music and Dramatic Arts. *Compositions:* Sonatine for Oboe and Piano, 1953; Puppet Suite for Clarinet and Piano, 1957, 86; Concertino for Clarinet and Piano, 1981. *Recording:* Concertino for Clarinet and Piano. *Publications:* The Hierarchy of Musical Totals in the Modern European Music, 1969; The Textbook of the Harmony of the XX Century, 1978; The Textbook of the Contrapunt of the XX Century, 1984; Contributor to The Methodology of the Practical Teaching the European Musical Tectonics of the XX Century, 1986. *Honours:* Prize of the Union of the Czech Composers and Concert Artists, 1979; The National Prize of the Czech Republic, 1987. *Memberships:* Association of the Musical Artists and Scientists; The Czech Musical Society; Present Time. *Hobbies:* Astronomy; Relativistic Cosmology; Mathematics. *Address:* Plzenska 216, 150 00 Praha 5, Czech Republic.

RITCHIE Elizabeth Nicol, b. 27 Apr 1929, Ayr, Scotland. Teacher of Singing; Examiner Music-Voice Therapist; Adjudicator. m. James Ritchie, 1957, 2s. *Education:* Ayr Academy; RSAMD; Jordanhill College, Glasgow; RSAMD, Glasgow, Graduate Course; Singing, Winifred Busfield, Norman Allin; Music Therapy Diploma, Roehampton Institute; RIHE; Music Therapy Diploma, Nordoff- Robbins. *Career:* BBC Singers, London, 1956-62; Lecturer in Voice, Berkshire College of Education and Luton College of Higher Education; Lecturer in Music, Later Head of Music, Luton College of Higher Education, 1969-79; Lecturer in Singing, City Lit. Institute, 1969-; Music Therapist, St Thomas's Hospital; Harborough Autistic School, 1979-87. *Honour:* CAIRD Singing Award, 1954. *Memberships:* ISM; AOTOS; NATFHE; Ass.MT (Nordoff-Robbins); Equity; Voice Research Society; BFMF, Adjudicator Member. *Hobbies:* Sketching; Water Colour Painting; Writing. *Address:* Flat 40, The Drive Mansions, Fulham Road, London SW6 5JD, England.

RIVA Douglas, b. 16 Aug 1951, Jacksonville, Illinois, USA. Pianist. m. Karen E. Riley, 9 Nov 1974. *Education:* BM 1974, MM 1975, Juilliard School of Music; PhD, New York University, 1983. *Debut:* Town Hall, New York, May 1982. *Career includes:* World premiere, Granados' Serenata for 2 violins & piano, 1987; American premiere, Scarlatti's Sonata in G major, 1987; World premiere, Granados, 15 solo piano works & duet En la Aldea, 1984; World premiere, John Corigliano's Gazebo Dances, 1984; Concerts at White House, Carnegie Hall, US National Gallery of Art, New York Museum of Modern Art, 1993; Radio Nacional de España, Catalunya Radio, Barcelona TV; Principal flutist, El Paso Symphony Orchestra, Texas, 1967-68; World premiere, Farfalle by Xavier Turull, Barcelona, 1991; Inaugural Recital, Sala Fernando Coelho, Belo Horizonte, Brazil, 1992. *Recordings:* Centaur Records, Musical Heritage Society, Keystone Music Roll Co. (Piano Roll Recordings, 1987); Documentary, Nos Dutch Television, 1991; Brazil Television, 1992. *Publications:* The Goyescas for Piano by Enrique Granados: A Critical Edition, 1982; The 20 Minute Piano Workout, 1987. *Current Management:* Conciertos Daniel, Los Madrazo 16, 28014 Madrid, Spain. *Address:* 393 Bergen Street, Brooklyn, NY 11217, USA.

RIVENO Nicolas, b. 1958, London, England. Singer (Baritone). *Education:* Studied with Mdme Bonnardo in Paris, at the Orleans Conservatory and with Michel Senechal at the School of the Paris Opera; Further study with Nicola Rossi-Lermeni at Indiana University. *Career:* Sang major roles in such operas as Boris Godunov, La Traviata and Don Giovanni at Indiana; 1984-85 season as Sulpice in La Fille du Regiment, Guglielmo, Marcello and Jupiter in Orphée aux Enfers; Christus in Bach's St Matthew Passion; Recitals in Moscow and Leningrad 1984; Bach Cantatas with English Chamber Orchestra in London and Edinburgh; Sang in Lully's Atys under William Christie at the Paris Opera 1986 and on tour to Tourcoing Versailles and New York 1988;

Schwetzingen and Karlsruhe Festivals 1988 with Tarare by Salieri under Jean-Claude Malgoire, Paris Opera 1989; Season 1989 with Rameau's Platée at Montpellier and Don Giovanni for Opera Northern Ireland; 1990-91 included Osman and Adario in Les Indes Galantes at Aix, Mozart's Count in Toulouse and performances of La Clemenza di Tito by Gluck at Tourcoing; Cherubini's Anacreon with the Orchestra of the Age of Enlightenment, 1992. *Address:* c/o Anglo-Swiss Ltd, 3 Primrose Mews, 1a Sharpleshall Street, London NW1 8YW, England.

RIVERS Malcolm, b. 1940, England. Baritone. *Education:* Studies at Royal College of Music and is a Member, RSC. *Career:* Appearances with English National Opera in various roles including, Alberich (The Ring); Escamillo (Carmen), Marullo (Rigoletto); Played in Troilus and Cressida and La Fanciulle del West at Covent Garden, Germont (La Traviata) and Alberich in Seattle, numerous other appearances; Sang Sullivan's Pirate King and Pooh-Bah with the D'Oyly Carte Company, 1989. *Address:* c/o D'Oyly Carte Opera Company, Africa House, 64/68 Kingsway, London, WC2B 6BD, England.

RIZZI Carlo, b. 1950, Milan, Italy. Conductor. *Education:* Studied at the Milan Conservatoire, with Vladimir Delman in Bologna and at the Accademia Chigiana with Franco Ferrara. *Debut:* Milan Angelicum 1982, Donizetti's L'Aio nell'imbarrazzo. *Career:* Conducted Falstaff in Parma, 1985 and has since appeared widely in Italy with Rigoletto, La Traviata, Tancredi, Torquato Tasso (Donizetti), Beatrice di Tenda, La Voix Humaine, Don Giovanni, L'Italiana in Algeri and Salieri's Falstaff; British debut Buxton Festival 1988, Torquato Tasso; Australian Opera 1989-90, Il Barbiere di Siviglia and Lucrezia Borgia; Tosca for Opera North 1990 and La Cenerentola at Covent Garden; Netherlands Opera debut 1989, Don Pasquale; Productions of Fra Diavolo and Norma at Palermo, 1989; Concert repertoire includes symphonies by Tchaikovsky and works by Haydn, Mozart, Beethoven and French composers; Regular guest in Italy and in Holland with the orchestras of The Hague, Arnhem and Haarlem; Royal Philharmonic debut May 1989, London Philharmonic Oct 1990 and Philharmonia Mar 1991; Le Comte Ory, Elektra and Rigoletto with Welsh National Opera and Il Viaggio a Rheims at Covent Garden, 1991/92; US opera debut 1994, with Il barbiere di Siviglia. *Recordings:* L'Italiana a Londra (Cimarosa); Il Furioso sull'Isola di San Domingo (Donizetti); Ciro in Babilonia (Rossini); La Scuffiara (Paisiello); La Pescatrice (Piccinni); Arias for tenor and orchestra by Rossini, with Ernesto Palacio; Schubert, Liszt and Debussy with the London Philharmonic and Philharmonia Orchestras (Collins Classics). *Address:* Allied Artists, 42 Montpelier Square, London SW7 1JZ, England.

RIZZO Francis, b. 8 Nov. 1936, New York, New York, USA. Stage Director; Administrator. *Education:* BA, Hamilton College, 1958; Yale University School of Drama, 1958-60. *Career:* American Director, Spoleto Festival of Two Worlds, 1968-71; Artistic Administrator, Wolf Trap Farm Park for the Performing Arts, 1972-78; Artistic Director, The Washington Opera, 1977-87; As Director staged productions for New York City Opera, Houston Grand Opera, Washington Opera, Wolf Trap, Opera Theater of St Louis, Santa Fe Opera, Baltimore Opera, Teatro Verdi, Trieste, Michigan Opera Theater, Théâtre Municipal, Marseilles. *Contributions to:* Opera News. *Membership:* American Guild of Musical Artists. *Address:* 590 West End Avenue, New York, NY 10024, USA.

ROADS Curtis Bryant, b. 9 May 1951, Cleveland, Ohio, USA. Composer; Author; Producer; Editor. *Education:* Experimental Music Studio, University of Illinois, 1970-71; California Institute of the Arts, 1972-74; University of California, San Diego, 1974-77. *Career:* Associate Fellow, Center for Music Experiment, University of California, San Diego, 1977; Editor, Computer Music Journal, The Massachusetts Institute of Technology Press, 1978-1989; Research Associate,

Experimental Music Studio, Massachusetts Institute of Technology, 1980-1986; Visiting Professor, University of Naples, 1988; Visiting Lecturer, Harvard University, 1989; Co-founder Cahill Society, 1990, Professor in Dept. of Pedagogy IRCAM, Paris; 1991-93; Currently: Professor of Les Ateliers, UPIC. *Compositions:* Construction, 1976; Objet, 1977; Nscor, 1980; Field, 1981; Message, 1987. *Recordings:* Music for Instruments and Computer (compact disc), Experimental Music Studio, Massachusetts Institute of Technology; New Computer Music (compact disc), Wergo Schallplatten GmbH, Mainz, Germany; Clang-tint, 1991-92. *Publications:* Foundations of Computer Music, 1985; Composers and the Computer, 1985; The Music Machine, 1988; Representations of Musical Signals, Computer Music Tutorial, 1994; Representations of Musical Signals, 1991. *Contributions to:* Proceedings of the International Computer Music Conference, 1977 and 1978. *Address:* Department of Pedagogy, Les Ateliers UPIC, 5 allée de Nantes, Massy, France.

ROAR Leif, b. 31 Aug 1937, Copenhagen, Denmark. Singer (Baritone). *Education:* Studied in Copenhagen. *Career:* Sang in Kiel and Dusseldorf from 1967; Schwetzingen Festival 1969, in the premiere of Klebe's Märchen von der Schönen Lilie; Munich Opera from 1971, as Wotan and Jochanaan; Salzburg Easter Festival 1973-74, as Donner and Kurwenal; Stuttgart 1974, as Escamillo; Bayreuth Festival from 1976, as Telramund and Klingsor; Metropolitan Opera debut 1982 as Pizarro in Fidelio; Other roles include: Mozart's Count and Don Giovanni, Hindemith's Mathis, Scarpia, Nick Shadow in The Rake's Progress and Hans Sachs; Guest engagements in Moscow, Milan, Buenos Aires, Hamburg, Mannheim, Bregenz and Stockholm; Sang Orestes in Elektra at Copenhagen 1986; Wotan in the Ring at Århus, 1987; Also heard in concerts and as oratorio singer. *Recordings include:* Telramund in Lohengrin, Bayreuth 1982 (CBS); Video of Die Meistersinger in production from Royal Opera, Stockholm. *Address:* c/o Der Jydske Opera, Musikhuset Århus, Thomas Jensens Alle, DK-8000 Århus, Denmark.

ROARK-STRUMMER Linda, b. 1952, Tulsa, Oklahoma, USA. Singer (Soprano). *Education:* Studied at Tulsa University. *Career:* Sang Dorabella at St Louis 1977; Engaged at Hanover 1979-80, Linz 1980-86, as Regina in the 1983 Austrian premiere of Lortzing's opera and in the 1984 premiere of In Seinem Garten Liebt Don Perlimplin Belinda, by B Sulzer; New York City Opera 1985 as Giselda in I Lombardi; More than 150 performances of Verdi's Abigaille, notably at the Deutsche Oper Berlin 1987, Ravena 1988 and Montreal and Verona 1992; La Scala Milan 1988, as Lucrezia in I Due Foscari; Sang Krasava in a concert performance of Smetana's Libuse in New York; Other roles include Lina in Stiffelio, the Forza and Trovatore Leonoras, Arabella, Jenůfa and Antonio; Guest engagements at Hamburg, Krefeld, Milwaukee and Venice; Sang Norma for Opera Hamilton at Toronto 1991. *Address:* Opera Hamilton, 2 King Street West, Hamilton, Ontario L6P 1A1, Canada.

ROBBIN Catherine, b. 1960, Toronto, Canada. Singer (Mezzo-Soprano). *Career:* Many appearances in baroque music: Messiah with the English Baroque Soloists conducted by John Eliot Gardiner; Bach's B Minor Mass with the Monteverdi Choir and Handel's Orlando at the 1989 Promenade Concerts; Opera performances as Olga in Eugene Onegin at the Opéra de Lyon, Handel's Alessandro at the Kennedy Center Washington; Purcell's Dido and Handel's Caesar with the Academy of Ancient Music; Collaborations with Trevor Pinnock, Hogwood, Andrew Davis, Robert Shaw, Boris Brott and Charles Dutoit: repertoire includes Les Nuits d'Été by Berlioz, Mahler's Lieder eines fahrenden Gesellen and Des Knaben Wunderhorn, Sea Pictures by Elgar and the Brahms Alto Rhapsody; Many recitals in Canada and the USA; Appearances at the Aldeburgh Festival and with the Songmakers' Almanac; Sang the title role in the North American premiere of Handel's Floridante, Toronto 1990; Annius in La Clemenza di Tito at the

Elizabeth Hall, London, 1990. *Recordings include:* Beethoven's Mass in C and Missa Solemnis (Archiv); Messiah, conducted by Gardiner; Les Nuits d'Été (Erato); Haydn's Stabat Mater with Trevor Pinnock and the English Concert (Archiv); Orlando conducted by Hogwood (EMI); Mahler Song Cycles. *Honours include:* Gold Award at the International Benson and Hedges Competition, Aldeburgh, England. *Address:* c/o Ron Gonsalves Management, 10 Dagnan Road, London SW12 9LQ, England.

ROBBINS Julien, b. 14 Nov. 1950, Harrisburg, Pennsylvania, USA. Singer (Bass). *Education:* Studied at the Philadelphia Academy of Vocal Arts, and with Nicola Moscona in New York. *Debut:* Philadelphia 1976, in Un Ballo in Maschera. *Career:* Engagements at Santa Fe, Miami, Washington and Chicago; Metropolitan Opera from 1979, as Ramphis, Colline, Gremin, and Don Fernando in Fidelio; Deutsche Oper Berlin 1990, as Abimelech in Samson et Dalila; Sang Masetto at the Metropolitan, 1990; world premiere, The Voyage, by Philip Glass, Metropolitan Opera (Second Mate and Space Twin), Nightwatchman in Meistersinger, 1993; Deutsche Oper Berlin, Don Giovanni, 1992, 1993, Carmen Escamillo, 1993, Turandot, Timur, 1992; Staatsoper Berlin, Barber of Seville, Basilio, 1992. *Recordings:* Doctor, La Traviata, Metropolitan Opera, 1992; Salome, First Soldier, Berlin Philharmonic, 1991. *Current Management:* Herbert Barrett, 1776 Broadway, New York, NY 10019, USA. *Address:* c/o Etzel, 1104 Harris Drive, Emmaus, PA 18049, USA.

ROBBOY Ronald, b. 17 Feb. 1950, Cleveland, Ohio, USA. Musician. m. Susan Severtson Hintz, 29 May 1986. *Education:* Studied Art, Ethnopoetics, Chinese, Musical Composition and Performance, University of California, San Diego 1967-68, 1970-72. Composition with Kenneth Gaburo and Pauline Oliveros; Cello and Chamber Music with Gabor Rejto and Rafael Druian; Research Fellow, Center for Music Experiment, University of California, San Diego, 1974. *Career:* Cellist; Oregon Symphony 1969-70; San Diego Symphony 1970-; San Diego Opera 1971-; Founder: Fatty Acid (Experimental Ensemble) 1973-75; The Big Jewish Band (Post-Electronic Klezmer) 1980-84; Experimental Violinist: Museum of Modern Art (New York) New Music America, Pacifica Radio (Los Angeles and Berkeley), The Kitchen Centre (New York), Los Angeles Institute of Contemporary Art; Director, Robboy's Jewish Orchestra, 1987-. *Compositions:* Lesbians Removing Linoleum, Rupert Centre International Music Exhibition (Paris, Berlin, NY, Los Angeles) 1975; Custommusic, commissioned by Melbourne International Electronic Music Festival 1975; Sudden Loss of Hearing, Radio Composition, commissioned by University of New Mexico for National Public Radio 1979; Der Yiddisher Cowboy (with Warren Burt), Conceptual Opera on film 1979; Blue Moon For Susan, commissioned by Australia Broadcasting Corporation 1985. *Address:* ASCAP, ASCAP Building, One Lincoln Plaza, New York, NY 10023, USA.

ROBERTI Margherita, b. 1930, Davenport, Iowa, USA. Singer (Soprano). *Education:* Studied at Hunter College and the Mannes School of Music, New York; Further study in Italy, 1956. *Debut:* Teatro Alfieri Turin 1957, as Leonora in Il Trovatore. *Career:* Appeared at Covent Garden 1959 as Tosca; La Scala debut 1959, as Abigaille in Nabucco; Engagements at the Verona Arena from 1959; Metropolitan Opera debut 1962, as Tosca; Edinburgh Festival 1963 as Luisa Miller and Glyndebourne Festival 1964, as Lady Macbeth; Other roles included Elisabeth de Valois, Amelia (Un Ballo in Maschera), Hélène (Les vêpres Siciliennes) and Odabella in Atilla; Guest appearances as concert artist in England and North America. *Recordings include:* Elena in Donizetti's Marino Faliero (OPR).

ROBERTS Brenda, b. 16 Mar 1945, Lowell, Indiana, USA. Singer (Soprano). *Education:* Studied at Northwestern University, Evanstown with Hermann Baer; Further study with Lotte Lehmann, Gerald Moore and Josef Metternich in Germany. *Debut:* Staatsteater

Saarbrucken 1968, Sieglinde in Die Walküre. *Career:* German appearances at Dusseldorf, Essen, Frankfurt, Nuremberg, Wiesbaden and Wuppertal; Member of the Hamburg Staatsoper; Bayreuth Festival 1974, as Brünnhilde in Siegfried; Sang Isolde at Kassel 1983; American engagements in Baltimore, Chicago, Baltimore and San Francisco; Metropolitan Opera debut 1982, as the Dyer's Wife in Die Frau ohne Schatten; Other roles include Salome (Vienna 1984) and Salome (Bremen 1986), Wagner's Senta and Elsa; Verdi's Elisabeth de Valois, Aida, Lady Macbeth, Leonora and Violetta; Mozart's Donna Elvira and Countess; Puccini's Tosca, Giorgetta and Turandot; Santuzza and Lulu; Sang in a concert performance of Die Bakchantinnen by Egon Wellesz at Vienna, 1985; Kiel Opera 1990 as Elektra and the title role in the premiere of Medea by Friedhelm Dohl. *Address:* Buhnen des Landeshaupstadt, Rathausplatz, D-2300 Kiel, Germany.

ROBERTS David Thomas, b. 16 Jan 1955, Moss Point, Mississippi, USA. Composer; Pianist; Writer; Painter. *Education:* Began piano lessons at age eight; Started composing the same year. *Debut:* Tulane University, New Orleans, 1977. *Career:* First performance in New Orleans, 1977; Radio debut in Lawrence, Kansas, 1980; Concertized all over USA mainly in West and Middle West; European debut in Oslo 1988. *Compositions:* Pinelands Memoir 1978; Camille 1979; Roberto Clemente 1979; Frederic and the Coast 1979; Through the Bottomlands 1980; New Orleans Streets, suite for piano, 1981-85; Memories of a Missouri Confederate, 1989; Washington County Breakdown, 1992. *Recordings:* Video of Music by David Thomas Roberts, 1989; An Album of Early Folk Rags, 1982; Pinelands Memoirs, 1983; Through the Bottomlands, 1984; New Orleans Streets, 1992; Various works by Nazareth, Joplin, Lamb and other Pan American composers. *Publications:* Ragtime Compositions of David Thomas Roberts, Volume I, 1992, Volume II, 1993; Contributor to The New Grove Dictionary of American Music and Notes of a Terrain Wrangler in Southern Reader, 1993. *Hobbies:* Travel; Collecting obscure periodicals. *Current Management:* Ann Fails Westerberg, Littleton, Colorado. *Address:* PO Box 5243, Kreole Station, Moss Point, MS 39563, USA.

ROBERTS Deborah, b. 1952, England. Singer (Soprano). *Education:* Studied at Nottingham University (editing and interpreting Renaissance Baroque music); Further study with Andrea von Ramm in Basle. *Career:* Has sung with the Tallis Scholars on tours to Europe, Australia and the USA, appearing at most major festivals; Guest concerts with the Deller Consort and the Consort of Musicke; Frequent engagements with Musica Secreta, notably in the Early Music Centre Festival, the Lufthansa Festival of Baroque Music, and at the National Gallery; Early Music Network tour of Britain with programme Filiae Jerusalem (sacred music for women's voices by Monteverdi, Carissimi, Cavalli, Viadana, Grandi and Marco da Gagliano); Other repertoire includes works by Marenzio, Wert, Luzzaschi, Luigi Rossi and the women composers Francesca Cacini and Barbara Strozzi; Participation in lecture-recitals and workshops on performance practice and ornamentation. *Recordings:* With Musica Secreta (as musical Director), Luzzaschi Madrigals for 1-3 Spranos; Ensemble music of Barbara Strozzi, 1994; Over 30 recordings with Tallis Scholars. *Honours:* Prize winner, Brugts Early Music Competition, 1981. *Address:* Robert White Management, 182 Moselle Avenue, London N22 6EX, England.

ROBERTS Eric, b. 16 Oct 1944, Conway, North Wales. Singer (Baritone). *Career:* Opera debut as Papageno with Welsh Natioanl Opera; Has sung with various British companies as Guglielmo, Falke, Mozart's Figaro and Count and Trinity Moses in Mahagonny, Scottish Opera; English National Opera in Pacific Overtures and the British premiere of Rimsky's Christmas Eve, 1988; D'Oyly Carte Opera Company, 1988-90; Further appearances as Don Alfonso for Opera North, Bartolo and Britten's Redburn for Scottish Opera, Don Isaac in the British premiere of Gerhard's The

Duenna, Haly in L'Italiana in Algeri at Dublin and Eugene Onegin for Opera Omaha, Nebraska, 1993; Australian debut as Bartolo for the Lyric Opera of Queensland, 1992; Concert engagements in Britten's War Requiem at Belgrade and L'Enfant et les Sortilèges at Rotterdam. *Address:* c/o Atholl Still Ltd, Greystoke House, 80-86 Westrow Street, London SE19 3AF, England.

ROBERTS John Peter Lee, b. 21 Oct 1930, Sydney, New South Wales, Australia. Cultural Advisor; Administrator; Writer. m. Christina van Oordt, 1 son, 2 daughters. *Education:* MA, Carleton University, 1988. *Career includes:* National Supervisor of Music, 1965-71, Head of Radio Music and Variety, CBC Radio Toronto, Canada, 1971-75; Member, Executive Committee, International Music Centre, Vienna, Austria, 1968-72; Member, Executive Committee, 1973-, Vice President, 1975, President, 1978-79, International Music Council, Paris, France; President 1971-73, Director-General 1977-81, Canadian Music Centre; Special Advisor, Chairman, Canadian Radio Television Telecommunications Commissions 1981-83; Senior Advisor Cultural Development, CBC, Ottawa, 1983-87; Dean, Faculty of Fine Arts, The University of Calgary, 1987-; Chairman, Canadian Association of Fine Arts Deans, 1989-; Chairman, International Vocal Competition, Rio de Janeiro, Brazil, 1979; Vice-President, International Institute of Audio-Visual Communication and Cultural Development, Vienna, 1976-, President, 1987-; President, Les Jeunesses Musicales du Canada, 1980-83; President, The Glenn Gould Foundation, Toronto, 1983. *Address:* Faculty of Fine Arts, University of Calgary, 2500 University Drive NW, Calgary, Alberta, Canada T2N 1N4.

ROBERTS Kathleen, b. 9 Oct 1941, Hattiesburg, Mississippi, USA. Singer (Soprano). *Education:* Studied at Mississippi College, at Texas Christian University and in Zurich and Darmstadt. *Debut:* St Gallen, 1967, as Violetta. *Career:* Appearances at opera houses in Zurich, Geneva, Cologne and Frankfurt; Member of the Darmstadt Opera as Marzelline in Fidelio, Micaela, Aennchen (Der Freischütz), Mozart's Pamina, Susanna and Constanze, Gretel, Martha and Mimi; Modern repertoire has included Luise in Henze's Der junge Lord and Laetita in The Old Maid and the Thief by Menotti; Many concert appearances; Teacher of singing in Darmstadt and elsewhere. *Address:* Staatstheater Darmstadt, Postfach 111432, D-6100 Darmstadt, Germany.

ROBERTS Ken, b. 16 Oct 1953, Hastings, England. Conductor; Composer; Pianist. *Education:* BA, Music (Hons), MA, Music, York University. *Career:* Head of Music, Borden Grammar School 1980-88; Subsequently freelance; Musical Director: First Act Opera 1991-; Hastings Opera 1983-; Entr'acte 1988-91; Cameo Opera 1991-; Radio appearances for Classic FM and BBC; Lectures; Recitals; Guest Conductor, Sussex Concert Orchestra. *Compositions:* Five Chinese Poems 1978; Mass 1982; Embers 1983; Quel Weekend 1991; Mr Butterfly 1993. *Hobbies:* Cricket; Photography. *Address:* Chestnuts, Canterbury Road, Challock, Ashford TN25 4DF, England.

ROBERTS Paul Anthony, b. 2 June 1949, Beaconsfield, England. Concert Pianist. 2 sons. *Education:* BA Honours, University of York, 1970; Royal Academy of Music, London. *Career:* Juror, International Debussy Piano Competition, France, 1982, 1984; Cycle, complete Debussy piano music, Purcell Room, London, 1984; World premiere, Maurice Ohana piano etudes, live broadcast, Radio France, 1986; Premieres, Ohana, BBC, 1984, 1986, 1988; World premiere (original piano score), Debussy unpublished opera, Rodrigue et Chimène, BBC Radio 3, 1988. Lecturer, Professor, Piano, Guildhall School of Music, London, 1985-; Director International Piano Summer School, SW France: Music at Ladevie. *Publications:* Book reviews: Times Educational Supplement; Composer; Revue Musicale (Paris). *Hobbies:* Theatre; Reading. *Current Management:* Management USA, Pat Zagelow, 3420

NE 21st Avenue, OR 97212, USA. *Address:* 10 Montague Road, London E8 2HW, England.

ROBERTS Richard, b. 19 May 1946, Charleston, West Virginia, USA. Violinist; Concertmaster. m. Janet Louise Marston, 9 Dec 1972, 3 sons. *Education:* Bachelor of Music, Performance, Indiana University, 1968; Violin studies with Josef Gingold, Chamber Music with Janos Starker and William Primrose. *Debut:* Soloist with Minneapolis Symphony Orchestra in Lalo's Symphonie Espagnole, S Skrowaczewski conducting, February, 1964. *Career:* Member, Minneapolis Symphony Orchestra 1968-71; Associate Concertmaster, Toronto Symphony 1971-73; Assistant Concertmaster, Cleveland Orchestra, 1974-82; Concertmaster, Montreal Symphony Orchestra 1982-; Soloist with Minneapolis, Toronto, Detroit, Cleveland, Montreal and Melbourne (Australia) Symphony Orchestras; Master Classes given at University of Minnesota, Oberlin College and Indiana University; Jurist for Montreal International Violin Competition, 1987. *Recordings:* Solo violin, Rimsky-Korsakov's Scheherazade and Capriccio Espagnol, London - Decca Records; Chamber Music recordings for Crystal Records, Coronet Records, CBC Records. *Honour:* Performer's Certificate from Indiana University, 1967. *Address:* 204 Seigniory Avenue, Pointe Claire, Quebec, Canada H9R 1E2.

ROBERTS Stephen Pritchard, b. 8 Feb 1949. Singer (Baritone). *Education:* Scholar, Associate 1969, Royal College of Music; Graduate, Royal Schools of Music, 1971. *Career:* Professional Lay-Cleric, Westminster Cathedral Choir, 1972-76; Sings regularly in London, UK and Europe, with all major orchestras and choral societies; Has sung in USA, Canada, Israel, Hong Kong, Singapore and South America; Opera roles include: Count in Marriage of Figaro, Falke in Die Fledermaus, Ubalde in Armide, Ramiro in Ravel's L'Heure Espagnole, Aeneas in Dido and Aeneas, Don Quixote in Master Peter's Puppet Show; Mittenhofer in Elegy for Young Lovers (Henze); Television appearances include Britten's War Requiem, Weill's Seven Deadly Sins, Delius' Sea Drift, Handel's Jephtha and also Judas Maccabaeus, Penderecki's St. Luke Passion at 1983 Proms, Walton's Belshazzar's Feast at 1984 Proms; Sang in Bach's Magnificat at the 1989 Proms, Fauré's Requiem 1990; Season 1990-91 with Israel in Egypt (Royal Choral Society), Mozart C Minor Mass (Washington), Brahms's Requiem (Ulster Orchestra); Mahler 8 and the St Matthew Passion (Bach Choir). *Recordings include:* Tippett's King Priam; Birtwistle's Punch and Judy; Gluck's Armide; Orff's Carmina Burana; Vaughan Williams' Five Mystical Songs and Sea Symphony and Hodie; Works by J.S. Bach, C.P.E. Bach, Duruflé and Walton. *Address:* 144 Gleneagle Road, London SW16 6BA, England.

ROBERTS Susan, b. 1960, USA. Singer (Lyric-Coloratura Soprano). m. Dmitry Sitkovetsky (qv) 26 July 1983. *Career:* Sang at first at the Frefeld Opera, then in Wiesbaden and Frankfurt; Has sung Blondchen in productions of Die Entführung by Ruth Berghaus (Frankfurt), Giorgio Strehler (Bologna), Jean-Pierre Ponnelle (Cologne) and Giancarlo del Monaco (Bonn); Sang Minette in the premiere of Henze's English Cat (Frankfurt) and repeated the role in Edinburgh and for the BBC; Further appearances at the Bayreuth and Orange Festivals and other German theatres; Paris Opera, 1988, in the premiere of La Celestina by Maurice Ohana; Season 1990-91 as Blondchen for Netherlands Opera and Zan in Blitzstein's Regina for Scottish Opera; Concert engagements with radio orchestras in Vienna, Turin and Berlin, the National Orchestra of Spain, Orchestre Philharmonique Paris, Orchestre de Lyon and the Dusseldorf Symphonic; Recitals at the Vaasa, Lockenhaus and Schleswig-Holstein Festivals; Season 1992 as Handel's Agrippina at the Buxton Festival. *Honours include:* Martha Baird Rockefeller Foundation Grant; Laureate Winner, Concours International Musicale, Geneva. *Address:* Music International, 13, Ardilaun Road, London N5 2QR, England.

ROBERTS Winifred, b. 1920, Lismore, New South Wales, Australia. Violinist. m. Geraint Jones. *Education:* Royal College of Music; studied with Antonio Brosa, Albert Sammons. *Career:* National Gallery Concerts, England; Promenade Concerts; 3 Choirs Festival; Lake District Festival; Salisbury Festival; Manchester Festival; Soloist, Festival Hall and Queen Elizabeth Hall; Tours of Italy, Spain and USA; BBC Radio and TV appearances; Professor of Violin, Royal Academy of Music (now retired); Advanced Performers Class, Morley College, London and private teaching. *Recordings:* EMI History of Music; Biber Sonata; Vivaldi Double Concerto; Harpsichord and Violin Sonatas with husband. *Honours:* Tagore Gold Medal, 1st Prize, Violin Playing, Royal College of Music; Hon RAM, 1983. *Hobbies:* Reading; Cooking; Gardening; Walking. *Address:* The Long House, Arkley Lane, Barnet, Hertfordshire, EN5 3JR, England.

ROBERTSON Duncan, b. 1 Dec 1924, Hamilton, Scotland. Tenor. m. Mary Dawson, 24 June 1950, 1 son, 1 daughter. *Education:* Dip SNAM (Gold Medal) 1945, Scottish National Academy of Music; LRAM 1946, Royal College of Music, London; FGSM, 1975; Fellow Emeritus GSM, 1979. *Career:* Varied career in Oratorio including appearances in most European countries; Opera mostly at Glyndebourne and Scottish Opera, also Covent Garden, Sadler's Wells, English Opera Group, Welsh Opera and Handel Opera; Many broadcasts ranging from light music to Radio 3; Some television, recordings and recital work; Sang in Canticum Sacrum, by Stravinsky, 1st performance in Britain conducted by Robert Craft, 1956; Appeared in Oedipus Rex, Stravinsky, with Jean Cocteau as narrator and conducted by Stravinsky, 1959; Sang in Benjamin Britten's 50th Brithday Concert, 1963; Sang with Giulini conducting, performance of Schubert's Mass in E Flat, televised from the Edinburgh Festival, 1968; Professor of Singing, Guildhall School of Music & Drama, London, 1966-77; Lecturer in Singing, Royal Scottish Academy of Music & Drama, Glasgow, 1977-88. *Address:* 13 Priory Park, Bradford on Avon, Wiltshire BA15 1QV, England.

ROBERTSON Ian Robert, b. 3 Dec 1947, Glasgow, Scotland. Music Critic. *Education:* MA, Glasgow University, 1970; Royal Scottish Academy of Music, 1960-64; Private Composition Pupil of John Maxwell Geddes & Thomas Wilson, 1962-71. *Debut:* Composition, RSAM, 1964. *Career:* Composition, Variations, BBC SSO (Loughran), 1966; Five Piano Pieces, played by Composer on BBC Scotland, 1968; Assistant Music Critic, The Glasgow Herald, 1977-82; Music Critic, The Times Educational Supplement, Scotland, 1977-, Scottish Music Critic, Classical Music Magazine, 1977-81. *Contributions to:* Criticism in: The Glasgow Hearld; The Scotsman; The Times; Times Education Supplement, Scotland; Classical Music; Stretto. *Hobbies:* BBC Radio Scotland Young Composer Competition, 1968. *Address:* 311 West Princes St., Glasgow G14 9DR, Scotland.

ROBERTSON John, b. 20 Sept 1938, Galashiels, Scotland. Singer (Tenor). *Education:* Studied at Sedbergh and Edinburgh Universities. *Career:* Regular appearances with Scottish Opera: 850 performances in 50 roles include Ferrando, Tamino, Ottavio, Albert Herring and Almaviva; Has toured with the Company to Austria, Germany, Switzerland, Yugoslavia, Poland, Portugal and Iceland in The Turn of the Screw, The Rape of Lucretia and A Midsummer Night's Dream; Appearances at Edinburgh as Tannhäuser and in Le Nozze di Figaro; Has directed the Edinburgh Opera Company in La Traviata, L'Elisir d'Amore and La Sonnambula; Oratorio and concert work throughout Scotland and on BBC and Scottish Television; Teaches voice in Glasgow and Edinburgh; Teacher at the School of Vocal Studies at the Royal Northern College of Music, Manchester. *Recordings include:* Le Nozze di Figaro (EMI). *Address:* c/o Christopher Tennant Artists' Management, 11 Lawrence Street, London SW3 5NB, England.

ROBERTSON Stewart John, b. 22 May 1948,

Glasgow, Scotland. Conductor; Pianist; Music Director. *Education:* General - Penilee Secondary School, Glasgow; Musical - Royal Scottish Academy of Music, 1965-69; Bristol University, 1969-70; Vienna Academy, 1975; Mozarteum, Salzburg, 1977; Teachers: Otmar Suitner and Hans Swarowsky (Conducting), Denis Matthews (Piano). *Career:* Assistant Chorus Master, Scottish Opera, Edinburgh Festival Chorus, 1968-69; Chorus Master, London City Singers, 1970-72; Conductor, Cologne Opera, 1972-75; Music Director, Tanz Forum, Zurich Opera, 1975-76, Scottish Opera Touring Company, 1976-79; Music Director, Hidden Valley Chamber Orchestra, California, 1979-82; Associate Conductor and Director of Appn Artists Programme, Des Moines Metro Opera, 1980-88; Music Director, Mid-Columbia Symphony Orchestra, 1984-85; Assistant Conductor, Oakland Symphony Orchestra, 1985-86; Music Director, Santa Fe Symphony Orchestra 1986-; Music Director/Principal conductor, Glimmerglass Opera, New York, 1987-; Guest Conductor, SNO, BBC Scottish Symphony Orchestra; CBSO Swiss-Italian Radio S.O; San Jose Symphony Orchestra; Utah Symphony Orchestra; Britt Festival, Long Beach, Portland, Sacramento, Kentucky Opera, Arkansas Opera and Montreal Opera Companies. *Current Management:* John Miller, Robert Lombardo Associates, New York. *Address:* 81 Poppy Road, Carmel Valley, CA, 93924, USA.

ROBERTSON-WILSON Alice Marian. b. 20 Aug 1926, Morgan, Utah, USA. Cellist; Musicologist. m. W Keith Wilson, 13 Feb 1979. *Education:* AB, Brigham Young University 1948; MA 1952, PhD, French and Music, 1960,PhD, Arabic 1970, University of Utah; Private theory and composition with Leroy Robertson since age 10; Private cello studies with Joseph Wetzels, Maurice Marechal at Conservatory of Paris; Zara Nelsova at San Francisco and Aspen; Pablo Casals, University of California, Berkeley. *Career:* Cellist, Utah Symphony 1947-61; Assistant Solo Cellist 1953-61; Assistant Professor of Music, Utah State University 1968-74; Music Editor, Coptic Encyclopedia 1982, 91; Consultant in Coptic Music to Library of Congress 1991- . *Compositions:* Vocal: Golgotha, Anthem for SATB chorus and keyboard, based on an ancient Coptic hymn; Old Things Are Done Away, arranged for SATB chorus and keyboard from original SA Score of Leroy Robertson; Instrumental: Fugue for String Quartet; Fugue, Adagio and Gigue for String Quartet; Canon (four part) for String Quartet. *Publications:* Several papers concerning coptic music; Register of the papers of Leroy Robertson, 1980; Register of the Annotated Bibliography of the Compositions of Leroy J Robertson, 1985; A Guide to the Ragheb Moftah Collection of Coptic Music Recordings in the Library of Congress (in progress). *Honours:* Several Scholarships and Fellowships. *Memberships:* American Musicological Society; International Association of Coptic Studies; American Research Center in Egypt. *Hobby:* Playing String Quartets with Friends. *Address:* 3631 Wellington Street, Salt Lake City, UT 84106, USA.

ROBINSON Christopher John, b. 20 Apr 1936, Peterborough, England. Organist; Conductor. m. Shirley Churchman, 6 Aug 1962, 1 son, 1 daughter. *Education:* Rugby School; Christ Church, Oxford; FRCO 1954; MA B.Mus, Oxon. *Career:* Organist, Worcester Cathedral, 1963-74; Organist, St George's Chapel, Windsor Castle, 1975-91; Conductor, City of Birmingham Choir, 1963-; Conductor, Oxford Bach Choir, 1977-; President Royal College of Organists, 1982-84. *Recordings:* Elgar Sacred Music; Tomkins Sacred Music; Parry Cathedral Music; Tavener Church Music. *Honours:* Hon M.Mus, Birmingham University, 1987; CVO, 1992; Hon.Fellow University of Central England, 1989; Hon RAM, 1980. *Membership:* Vice-President, Royal College of Organists. *Hobby:* Watching cricket. *Current Management:* ssa 00Stephannie Williams Artists. *Address:* St John's College, Cambridge CB2 1TP, England.

ROBINSON David Peter Francis, b. 2 Apr 1937, Croydon, England. Pianist; Organist; Conductor. m.

Mary, 22 Dec 1978, 3 sons, 3 stepchildren. *Education:* Scholar, Royal Academy of Music. *Career:* Director of Music, St Paul's, 1963-73; Professor and Course Tutor, Royal Academy of Music, 1973-91; Director of Music, Ardingly College, 1991-; Conductor, Ardingly College Choral Society; Organ Recitalist in Westminster Abbey, St Paul's Cathedral and Churches in Germany and Europe. *Honours:* FRAM: B.Mus London; FRCO; Hon. RCM. *Membership:* Royal College of Organists; ISM. *Hobbies:* Gardening; Cycling; Reading; Sports. *Address:* 29 Holmans, Street Lane, Ardingly, West Sussex RH17 6UQ, England.

ROBINSON Faye, b. 2 Nov 1943, Houston, Texas, USA. Singer (Soprano). *Education:* Studied with Ruth Stewart at Texas Southern University and with Ellen Faull in New York. *Debut:* New York City Opera, 1972, as Micaela. *Career:* Has sung Violetta, the Queen of Shemakhan and Liu in New York; Washington Civic Opera, 1973, as Violetta and Juliette; Jackson, Florida, 1974-75, as Desdemona and Adina; Aix-en-Provence, 1975, in Der Schauspieldirektor and La Serva Padrona; Engagements in Houston, Barcelona, and Frankfurt; Buenos Aires, 1980, in Les Contes d'Hoffmann; Schwetzingen Festival, 1981, as Electra in Idomeneo; Paris Opéra and Bordeaux, 1982, as Juliette and Luisa Miller; Other roles include Constanze, Norina, and Oscar; Sang in the premiere of The Mask of Time, Boston, 1984, and in the first British performance of Tippett's oratorio; Cologne, 1988, as Constanze. *Recordings:* Mahler's 8th Symphony (CBS); The Mask of Time. *Address:* c/o Oper der Stadt Köhn, Offenbachplatz, D-5000 Cologne, Germany.

ROBINSON Gail, b. 7 Aug 1946, Meridian, Mississippi, USA. Singer (Soprano). *Education:* Studied at Memphis State University and with Robley Lawson. *Debut:* Memphis, 1967, as Lucia di Lammermoor. *Career:* Appearances in Berlin, Munich and Hamburg; Metropolitan Opera from 1970, in Die Zauberflöte, and as Gilda, Adina, Oscar, Marie in La Fille du Régiment, Rosina, and Gretel. *Address:* c/o Metropolitan Opera, Lincoln Center, New York, NY 10023, USA.

ROBINSON Kenneth, (Sir). b. 19 Mar 1911. Music Administrator. m. Elizabeth Edwards, 18 Apr 1941, 1 daughter. *Education:* Oundle School, 1923-26; Hon.D.Litt. (Liverpool), 1980. *Career:* Chairman, English National Opera, 1972-77; Chairman, Arts Council of Great Britain, 1977-82; Member, London Orchestral Concert Board, 1977-86; Member, UK Committee for European Music Year, 1982-86; Chairman of Opera Sub- Committee; Chairman, Young Concert Artists Trust, 1983-90. *Membership:* Council Member, Royal Society of Arts, 1978-88. *Hobbies:* Listening to Music, especially Opera; Reading; Travel. *Address:* 12 Grove Terrace, London NW5 1PH, England.

ROBINSON Michael Finlay, b. 3 Mar 1933, Gloucester, England. University Professor. m. Ann James, 28 Dec 1961, 2 son. *Education:* BA (Oxon), 1956; BMus (Oxon), 1957; MA (Oxon), 1960; DPhil (Oxon), 1963. *Career:* Teacher, Royal Scottish Academy of Music, 1960-61; Music Lecturer, Durham University, 1961-65; Assistant Professor, 1965-67, Associate Professor, 1967-70, McGill University, Montreal; Music Lecturer, 1970-75, Senior Lecturer in Music, 1975-91, Head of Music Department, 1987-, Professor of Music, 1991-, University of Wales College of Cardiff, Wales. *Publications:* Opera Before Mozart, 1966, 2 later editions; Naples and Neapolitan Opera, 1972, American Reprint 1984, Italian Edition 1985; Giovanni Paisiello, a thematic catalogue of his works, Volume 1 1990, Volume 2 1993; Contributor to Proceedings of the Royal Musical Association, New Grove. Chigiana, Studi Musicali, Soundings, Music and Letters. *Memberships:* Royal Musical Association; American Musicological Society; International Musicological Society. *Hobbies:* Gardening; Walking; Watercolour Painting. *Address:* Department of Music, University of Wales College of Cardiff, Cardiff CF1 3EB, Wales.

ROBINSON Peter, b. 1949, England. Conductor. *Education:* Studied music at Oxford. *Career:* Assistant organist at Durham Cathedral; Associated with the Glyndebourne Festival Opera, 1971-73; Head of Music Staff and resident conductor at Australian Opera, 1973-80; Assistant music director at English National Opera 1981-89, conducting Le Nozze di Figaro, Don Giovanni, Die Zauberflöte, Così fan Tutte, Otello, Rigoletto, The Mastersingers, Madame Butterly, Orfeo, Maria Stuarda, The Mikado, Carmen, Werther, Hansel and Gretel, Simon Boccanegra, and The Turn of the Screw; Appearances for Kent Opera with The Beggar's Opera and Don Giovanni, and for Scottish Opera with the Pearl Fishers; Conducted Così fan Tutte in a production for BBC TV; Has conducted in Australia: Le Nozze di Figaro, Victoria State Opera, 1987; Die Entführung, VSO, 1989; Così fan Tutte, The Australian Opera, 1990; Don Giovanni, State Opera of South Australia, 1991; Engagements with Opera Factory (Marriage of Figaro, also for TV), 1991; Symphony concerts with the London Symphony, London Mozart Players and London Sinfonietta; Concerts with the Melbourne and Sydney Symphony Orchestras, 1988-90. *Address:* c/o Athole Still Ltd, Greystoke House, 80-86 Westrow Street, London, SE19 3AF, England.

ROBINSON Ray E, b. 26 Dec 1932, San Jose, California, USA. Professor of Music; President of Westminster Choir College. m. Ruth Aleen Chamberlain, 12 Mar. 1954, 4 sons, 1 daughter. *Education:* BA, San Jose State University, 1956; MM, 1968, DMA, 1969, Indiana University. *Career:* Instructor, Indiana University School of Music, 1958-59; Associate Professor, Cascade College, 1959-63; Dean, Peabody Conservatorium of Music, 1963-69; President and Professor, Westminster Choir College, Princeton, New Jersey, 1969-87; Visiting Fellow, Wolfson College, Cambridge University, 1987-89 *Compositions:* The Choral Tradition Series; Choral Music at Westminster; Westminster Fiftieth Anniversary Series. *Publications:* The Choral Experience, 1976; Choral Music, 1978; Krzysztof Penderecki, 1983; A Study of the Penderecki St Luke Passion, 1983; John Finley Williamson: A Centennial Appreciation, 1987. *Hobbies:* Travel; Golf; Tennis. *Address:* 55 Spruce Street, Princeton, NJ 08540, USA.

ROBINSON Sharon, b. 2 Dec 1949, Houston, Texas, USA. Concert Cellist. m. Jaime Laredo, 23 Nov 1976. *Education:* Graduated, North Carolina School of the Arts, 1968; University of Southern California, 1968-70; BM, Peabody Conservatory of Music, 1972. *Debut:* New York, 1974. *Career:* Member of Kalichstein-Laredo-Robinson Trio from 1976; Soloist at Marlboro Music Festival, Mostly Mozart Festival, South Bank Festival (London), Edinburgh Festival, Madeira Bach Festival, Helsinki Festival and Tivoli Gardens; Commissioned and premiered Ned Rorem's After Reading Shakespeare, for solo cello, and premiered Alan Shulman's Kol Nidrei for cello and piano, William Bland's Rhapsody for cello and piano and Robert Blake's Cello Sonata. *Recordings:* Vivaldi Sonatas (Moss Music); Fauré Elegy and Debussy Sonata; Rorem's After Reading Shakespeare, (Grenadilla Records); Beethoven Triple Concerto (Chandos); Mendelssohn and Brahms Trios with Kalichstein-Laredo-Robinson Trio; Duos for violin and cello with Jaime Laredo. *Honours:* Avery Fisher Award, 1979; Levintritt Award, 1975; Pro Musicis Foundation Award, 1974. *Membership:* Violoncello Society of America. *Hobbies:* Gardening; Hiking; Swimming. *Current Management:* Harold Shaw Concerts. *Address:* c/o Shaw Concerts, 1900 Broadway, New York, NY 10023, USA.

ROBISON Paula, b. 8 June 1941, Nashville, Tennessee, USA, Flautist. m. Scott Nickrenz, 1 daughter. *Career:* Founding Artist-Member, Chamber Music Society of Lincoln Center; Joint Recitalist with pianist Ruth Laredo and guitarist Eliot Fisk; Soloist, New York Philharmonic, Atlanta, American and San Francisco Symphony Orchestra; Recitalist at numerous venues including Carnegie Hall and Kennedy Center and Wigmore Hall in January 1990; Commissioned and premiered Kirchner's Music for Flute and Orchestra with

the Indianapolis Symphony, Toru Takemitsu's I Hear the Water Dreaming, Robert Beaser's Song of the Bells; Numerous television appearances including Live from Lincoln Center, 1984-85; Christmas at the Kennedy Center; Sunday Morning, CBS Television; For 10 years (1978-1988) Co-Director of Chamber Music, Spoleto Festival at Charleston, South Carolina, and Spoleto, Italy; Blue Ridge Airs II, flute and orchestra, Kenneth Frazelle, 1991. *Recordings:* Has made many recordings including, Flute Music of the Romantic Era; The Sonatas for Flute and Harpsichord by J.S. Bach (complete) and G.F. Handel (complete) with Kenneth Cooper; Release for Music Masters: American Masterworks for flute & piano; Omega, Brasileirinho, Choros of Brazil, 1993; Musicmasters, French Master pieces with Ruth Laredo, piano, 1990. *Publications:* The Paula Robison Flute Warmups Book, European American Publishers, 1990. *Honours:* First American to win 1st Prize, Geneva International Competition; Adelaide Ristori Prize, 1987; House Musician: Isamu Noguchi Garden Museaum, 1988. *Memberships:* British Flute Association; The National Flute Assiciation, (NSA). *Current Management:* Shaw Concerts. *Address:* c/o Shaw Concerts Inc., 1900 Broadway, New York, NY 10023, USA.

ROBLES Marisa, b. 4 May 1937, Madrid, Spain. Concert Harpist. m. David Bean 29 Oct 1985, 2 sons, 1 daughter. *Education:* Real Conservatorio de Musica, Madrid (Honours 1953). *Career:* Debut in Spain 1954; Settled in Britain and appeared on many TV programmes; London concert debut 1963; Solo recitals and major orchestral appearances in UK, Europe, Japan, Australia, Canada, United States, South America with most London orchestras, New York Philharmonic; Professor Real Conservatorio de Musica Madrid 1958-63; Professor, Royal College of Music London 1973-; Artistic Director, World Harp Festival, Cardiff, Wales, 1991; Artistic Director, World Harp Festival II, 1994. *Compositions:* Narnia Suite; Music for Narnia Chronicles; Irish Suite; Basque Suite for flute and harp. *Recordings:* Argo Records; Decca; RCA; Collins Classics, BMG, Harper Collins; Academy Sound and Vision. *Honour:* Fellow, Royal College of Music 1983. *Memberships:* International Harp Association; Royal Overseas League; United Kingdom Harp Association; Vice-President Spanish Association of Harpists. *Hobbies:* Gardening; Theatre. *Current Management:* Clarion/Seven Muses, 47 Whitehall Park, London N19 3TW, England. *Address:* 38 Luttrell Avenue, London SW15 6PE, England.

ROBOTHAM Barbara, b. 15 Jan 1936, Blackpool, Lancashire, England. Musician; Singer. m. Eric Waite, 30 Aug 1958, 1 son. *Education:* ARMCM Teachers Diploma with distinction, 1957. Performers Diploma with distinction, 1959, Royal Manchester College of Music. *Career:* Appearances with all major British Orchestras; Festivals include: Three Choirs Festival, Harrogate, Cheltenham, Haydn-Mozart Festival, N Italy; Gulbenkian Lisbon, Santander Spain, Bordeaux, France; Concerts in Paris, Madrid, Barcelona, Prague, Frankfurt etc. Broadcasts; Teaching appointments: Senior Lecturer, Royal Northern College of Music and Professor of Voice, Lancaster University. *Recordings:* Stravinsky - Cantata on Old English Texts - Supraphon; Walton, Gloria. *Honours:* Imperial League of Opera Prize and Curtis Gold Medal, 1958; 1st Prize, Liverpool Philharmonic International Singers Competition, 1960; 2nd Prize Concours International de Geneva, 1961; Honorary Fellowship, Royal Northern College of Music, 1992. *Memberships:* Incorporated Society of Musicians. *Hobbies:* Reading; Sewing; Sailing. *Address:* 49 Blackpool Road North, St Annes on Sea, Lancashire, England.

ROBSON Christopher, b. 9 Dec 1953, Falkirk, Scotland. Opera and Concert Singer (counter-tenor). m. Laura Carin Snelling, 18 May 1974, divorced 1984. *Education:* Cambridge College of Arts and Technology, 1970-72; Singing with James Gaddarn Trinity College of Music, London, 1972-73; Private studies with Paul Esswood and Helga Mott. *Debut:* Handel's Samson, Queen Elizabeth Hall, London, 1976. *Career:* Operatic debut in Handel's Sosarme, Barber Institute, Birmingham, 1979; Principal roles with Kent Opera, Phoenix Opera, Handel Opera Society, Royal Opera Covent Garden 1988- (Semele); English National Opera (Orfeo, Xerxes, Julius Caesar title role, Akhnaten title role, Lear), Frankfurt State Opera, Berliner Kammeroper (Orlando title role), Houston Grand Opera, New York City Opera, Opera Factory Zurich, Opera Factory-London Sinfonietta, Nancy Opera, Innsbruck Tirolertheater; Appeared at festivals: Aix-en-Provence, Montpellier, Tourcoing, Saintes, Barcelona, Edinburgh, Three Choirs, Greenwich, Oxford, Innsbruck, Vienna, Paris, Chaises-Dieux, London (Camden Festival) Den Haag, Bilbao, Utrecht, New York, Chichester, Junifestwoche Zurich, Stuttgart, BBC Proms, Wroclaw, Warsaw; Concerts throughout UK and Europe; Broadcasts, BBC, SFB, WDR, ORF, DRS, Radio France Musique; Member: Monteverdi Choir, 1974-84; London Oratory Choir, 1974-80; The Spieglers, 1976-82; St George's Theatre Company, 1976; Kings Consort, 1981-86; Westminster Cathedral Choir, 1980-85; New London Consort, 1986-; Sang in Xerxes on ENO tour of Russia, 1990; Season 1992/93 sang Ptolemy (Julius Caesar) for Scottish Opera, Polinesso (Ariodante) for ENO, Andronicus (Tamerlano) for Karlsruhe, and Ezio (title role) for Berliner Kammeroper; Season 1993/94 sang Tamerlano (title role) for Opera North, Arsamenes (Xerxes) for ENO, Apollo (Death in Venice) for Liege, Oberon (Midsummer Nights Dream) for Covent Garden Festival, Tolomeo (Giulio Cesare) for Bayerische Staatsoper Munich. *Recordings:* Missa Scala Aretina, Valls, CRD; Nisi Dominus, Vivaldi, Meridien; 1610 Vespers, Monteverdi, Decca-Florilegium; Vespers, Biber, Harmonia Mundi; Orontea, Cesti, Austrian TV; Xerxes, Handel, Channel 4 and RM Arts: Hail Bright Cecilia, Purcell, EMI and Channel 4; Messiah, Handel, Chandos; Orfeo, Monteverdi, Florilegium-Decca; The Ice Break, Tippett, Virgin; Golem, Casken, Virgin; Auferstehungs Historia, Schutz, Sony; Come ye Sons of Art, Purcell, Virgin; BBC; La Calisto, Cavalli; Euridice, Caccini; Telemaco, Gluck; Akhnaten, Glass; Messiah, Handel, Chandos; Orfeo, Monteverdi, Florilegium/Decca; The Ice Break, Tippett, Virgin; The Delights of Posilipo, Various, Florilegium/Decca; Verse Anthems, Purcell, Argo; Requiem, Biber, Florlegium-Decca. BBC: La Calisto, Cavalli; Euridice, Caccini; Telemaco, Gluck; Akhnaten, Glass; Xerxes, Handel: St John Passion, Bach; Ode on the Death of Purcell, Blow. *Hobbies:* Wine and food; Theatre; Cinema; Driving; Television; Photography; Travel. *Address:* c/o Music International, 13 Ardilaun Road, London, N5 2QR, England.

ROBSON Elizabeth, b. 1938, Dundee, Scotland. Singer (Soprano). m. Neil Howlett. *Education:* Studied at Royal Scottish Academy of Music and in Florence. *Debut:* Sadler's Wells 1961 as Micaela. *Career:* Appearances at Covent Garden throughout the 1960s as Musetta, Zdenka, Sophie, Susanna, Pamina, Marzelline and Nannetta in Falstaff; Guest appearances with Scottish Opera as Zerlina and at the 1967 Edinburgh Festival as Anne Trulove in The Rake's Progress; Sang also at Aix-en-Provence and La Scala Milan; Noted concert artist. *Recording:* Marzelline in Fidelio.

ROBSON Nigel, b. 1955, Argyllshire, Scotland. Singer (Tenor). *Education:* Studied at the Royal Northern College of Music with Alexander Young. *Career:* Sang with the Glyndebourne Festival Chorus; English National Opera from 1981, as Monteverdi's Orfeo and in the premiere of Birtwistle's The Mask of Orpheus (1986); British stage premiere of Weill's Der Protagonist; Ferrando in David Freeman's production of Falstaff; Sang in the premiere of Michael Finnissy's The Undivine Comedy and in Tippett's Songs for Dov conducted by the composer; La Finta Giardiniera for Opera North and Don Ottavio in Don Giovanni for Opera Factory; Appearances with the Monteverdi Choir and Orchestra include tours of Italy, Germany and France; Performances of Monteverdi's Vespers in Venice and Orfeo in Spain as well as Idomeneo in Lisbon, Paris, Amsterdam and London; Handel's Jephtha at the Handel Festival in Göttingen and at the Holland Festival; Sang the Anonymous Voice in the British premiere of Tippett's

New Year at Glyndebourne, 1990; Concerts at the Festival Hall (Janáček's Glagolitic Mass), with the Ensemble Intercontemporain in Paris and with the London Sinfonietta (Henze's Voices, 1991); Season 1992 as Claggart in Billy Budd for Scottish Opera and Nero in The Coronation of Poppaea for Opera Factory. *Recordings include:* Handel's Tamerlano, Alexander's Feast and Jephtha (Philips); Tippett's Songs for Dov (Virgin Classics); Stravinsky's Renard (Sony Classics); Arbace in Idomeneo (Deutsche Grammophon Archiv). *Address:* c/o Ingpen and Williams Ltd., 14 Kensington Court, London W8 5DN, England.

ROCHAIX Francois, b. 2 Aug 1942, Geneva, Switzerland. Stage Director. *Education:* Studied at University of Geneva and at Berliner Ensemble, East Berlin. *Career:* Founded the Atelier de Genève 1963, Actor and Director; Director of the Théâtre de Carouge 1975-81; Produced The Turn of the Screw and Death in Venice at Geneva 1981 and 1983; La Traviata for Opera North 1985, Cardillac and Parsifal at Berne 1988-89; Der Ring des Nibelungen 1985-87 and Die Meistersinger 1989 at Seattle; Production of Tristan und Isolde for Opera Lyon 1990. *Address:* c/o Seattle Opera Association, PO Box 9248, Seattle, WA 98109, USA.

ROCHBERG George, b. 5 July 1918, Paterson, New Jersey, USA. Composer. m. Gene Rosenfeld, 18 Aug. 1941, 1 son, 1 daughter. *Education:* BA, Montclair Teachers College, 1939; Mannes School of Music, 1939-42; BM, Curtis Institute of Music, 1948; MA, University of Pennsylvania, 1949. *Career:* US Army, World War II, Purple Heart; Faculty, Curtis Institute; Director of Publications, Theodore Presser Company, 1951-60; Music Department Chair 1960-68, Professor of Composition 1960-1979, Annenberg Professor of Humanities 1979-, University of Pennsylvania; Work in progress: Chromoticism: Symmetry in Atonal and Tonal Music. *Compositions:* 6 symphonies; 5th Symphony, commissioned for and premiered by Georg Solti and the Chicago Symphony; 6th Symphony, commissioned for and premiered by Lorin Maazel and the Pittsburgh Symphony and was given by the same in Leningrad, Moscow and Warsaw, Oct. 1989; 7 string quartets; Violin and oboe concertos; Piano solos, trios, quartet & quintet; Various other chamber works, The Confidence Man, opera, libretto by Gene Rochberg. *Recordings:* Violin Concerto, recorded by Isaac Sterm, violinist, and André Previn conductor; Oboe Concerto, soloist Joseph Robinson, conductor Zubin Mehta, NY Philharmonic; Black Sounds; Blake Songs; Caprice Variations; Chamber Symphony; La Bocca della Verita; Serenate d'Estate; Tableaux; 12 Bagatelles. Columbia; RCA; Deutsche Grammophon, CRI. *Publication:* Aesthetics of Survival, 1984. *Contributions to:* Critical Inquiry; New Literary History. *Honours include:* 1st prize, Kennedy Friedheim Awards, 1979; Honorary doctorates, University of Michigan, Philadelphia Musical Academy, Montclair State University; Numerous fellowships, grants, awards. *Memberships:* American Academies, Arts & Letters, Arts & Sciences; American Society of Composers, Authors & Publishers. *Hobbies:* Reading philosophy theory & sciences. *Address:* 285 Aronimink Drive, Newtown Square, Pennsylvania 19073, USA.

ROCHE Jerome Laurence Alexander, b. 22 May 1942, Cairo, Egypt. Musicologist. m. Elizabeth Nicholls, 20 Sept. 1969, 1 daughter. *Education:* ARCO, 1959; MA, MusB, PhD, St John's College, Cambridge University, UK. *Career:* Lecturer, Senior Lecturer, Reader, Music, University of Durham, 1967-. *Publications:* Palestrina, 1971; The Madrigal, 1972; Penguin Book of Italian Madrigals, 1974; Dictionary of Early Music, with Elizabeth Roche, 1981; Lassus, 1982; North Italian Church Music in Age of Monteverdi, 1984; The Flower of Italian Madrigals, 1988; Editions of 17th Century Italian Church Music. *Contributions to:* Musical Times; Music & Letters; Early Music; Proceedings and Journals, Royal Musical Association (RMA); Review Editor, RMA Journal, 1987-91. *Memberships:* Northern Chapter Secretary 1976-80, Council 1979-84, RMA; International Musicological Society; Royal College of Organists. *Hobbies:* Meteorology; Railways; Political statistics. *Address:* The Music School, Palace Green, Durham DH1 3RL, England.

ROCHESTER Marc Andrew, b. 28 Apr. 1954, London, England. Music Journalist; Organist; Conductor; Adjudicator. *Education:* BMus, MA, PhD, University of Wales, 1972-77; FTCL; ARCM; LRAM. *Career:* Music critic, Western Mail, 1975-80; Correspondent, Organists Review, Musical Times, 1980-89, Independent, 1987-, Gramophone, 1989; Sub-Organist, Bangor Cathedral, 1978-80; Organist & Master of Choristers, Londonderry Cathedral, 1980-82; Music Tutor, New University of Ulster, Northern Ireland, 1980-84; Solo recitalist; Choral conductor; Examiner, Associated Board, Royal Schools of Music, Northern Ireland Schools Examinations Council; University of London. *Compositions:* Hymn tunes; Various church music. *Recordings:* Soloist, 20th Century British Organ Music, 1983; Conductor, Hymns of C. F. Alexander, Derry Cathedral Choir, 1981; Accompanist: Beaufort Male Voice Choir 1977, 1978, Leila Carewe (soprano) 1980. *Publications:* Frank Martin at Golgotha, 1977; Articles, 20th century music; Editor, catalogue, Traditional Welsh Musical Instruments. *Hobbies:* Croquet; Sailing; Rugby; Bus driving. *Address:* Bow Anchor, Squires Hill Lane, Tilford, Farnham, Surrey GU10 2AD, England.

ROCKWELL John Sargent, b. 16 Sept. 1940, Washington DC, USA. Music Critic. *Education:* BA, Harvard College, 1962; MA 1964, PhD 1972, University of California, Berkeley. *Career:* Music & Dance Critic: Oakland Tribune (California) 1969, Los Angeles Times 1970-72; Music Critic, New York Times, 1972-. *Publications:* Sinatra: An American Classic, 1984; All American Music: Composition in Late 20th Century, 1983. *Contributions to:* Numerous books & magazines. *Membership:* Past Treasurer, US Music Critics Association. *Address:* Music Department, New York Times, 229 West 43rd Street, New York, NY 10036, USA.

RODAN Mendi, b. 17 Apr. 1929, Jassy, Romania. Conductor; Professor. m. Judith Calmanovici, 2 children. *Education:* BMus, MA, Academy of Music, Arts Institute. *Career:* Permanent Conductor, Radio & Television Orchestra, Bucharest, 1953-58; Founder, Permanent Conductor, Jerusalem Chamber Orchestra; Chief Conductor, Music Director, Jerusalem Symphony (IBA), 1963-72; Music Director, Israel Sinfonietta, 1977-91; Music Director, Permanent Conductor, Orchestre National Belge, 1983-89; Music Director, IDF Educational Corp Chamber Orchestra, 1990-; Laureate Conductor: Israel Sinfonietta, 1991-; Associate Conductor, Israel Philharmonic Orchestra, 1993; Guest Conductor, Israel Chamber Ensemble, Jerusalem Symphony; Concert tours worldwide, orchestras including Oslo Philharmonic, Vienna Symphony, Berlin Radio Symphony, London Symphony, Pasdeloup Paris, Frankfurt Radio, Stockholm Philharmonic; Adviser, Jerusalem International Music Centre; Head, Jerusalem Academy of Music & Dance. *Recordings:* Numerous, various labels. *Contributions to:* Editorial Advisory Committee, Ariel. *Honours:* M. Rodan Stipendium, Hebrew University, Jerusalem; Member, Council for Music, Ministry of Culture & Education; Medal of Distinction, Republic of Italy; Honorary Citizen, Tucson, Arizona, USA. *Memberships:* Several international professional organisations & juries. *Hobbies:* Music; Driving; Reading. *Current Management:* R. Shahar, Tel Aviv. *Address:* 6 Shiler Street, Jerusalem 96227, Israel.

RODDE Anne-Marie, b. 21 Nov. 1946, Clermont-Ferrand, France. Singer (Soprano). *Education:* Studied at the Conservatory of Clermont-Ferrand, and at the Paris Conservatoire with Irene Joachim and Louis Nougera. *Career:* Aix-en-Provence 1971, as Amor (Orfeo ed Euridice), Yniold (Pelléas et Mélisande) Paris 1972, in Cantate Nuptial by Milhaud and The Nightingale by Stravinsky; Hippolite et Aricie, Covent Garden; Falstaff, Médée (Cherubini), Rosenkavalier, Paris Opera House; Pelléas et Mélisande, Roma Opera House; Pearl Fishers, Stockhólm Opera; Magic Flute, debut, 1991, La Bastille

Opera; Magic Flute, Montreal Opera, Bonn Opera House; Appearances in Amsterdam, Nozze di Figaro; Zurich and Barcelona; Many appearances in the Baroque repertory: London Bach Festival in Les Boréades by Rameau; Other roles include Zerbinetta, Oscar, Nannetta, Ravel's Child and Dirce in Médée; Paris Opéra 1986, in Cherubini's Médée. *Recordings:* Les Indes Galantes by Rameau, Handel's Xerxes, Le Triomphe d'Alcide by Lully (CBS); Les Boréades (Erato); Honegger's Jeanne d'Arc au Bûcher (Eurodisc); Messiah; Songs by Debussy (Etcetera); Avietta di Camera by Rossini; Songs by Widor (Etcetera); Bellini and Donizetti (Etcetera); Gluck: Pèlerins de La Mecque (Orfeo). *Address:* c/o Christophe Delhoume, Opéra et Concerts, Rue Vignon 19, 75008 Paris, France.

RODEN Anthony, b. 19 Mar. 1937, Adelaide, Australia. Opera & Concert Singer (Tenor). m. Doreen. *Education:* Associated Australian Insurance Institute; Licenciate, Adelaide Conservatory. *Debut:* Glyndebourne, England. *Career:* Appearances: London Opera Centre, Glyndebourne, Netherlands festivals; English, Welsh, Scottish National Operas; Opera North; Prague National Opera; Krefeld Opera; Victorian State Opera; Royal Opera Covent Garden in Peter Grimes, Freiburg Opera; Numerous concerts, BBC, British, Italian and Dutch Orchestras; Sang Samson and Tannhäuser in Melbourne, 1992; Mahler 8th Symphony RLPO; Florestan Glyndebourne, 1993. *Recordings:* Various labels. *Honours:* John Christie Award, 1971; Opera Prize, Adelaide Conservatory. *Hobbies:* Antiques; Golf. *Current Management:* Patricia Greenan. *Address:* 33 Castlebar Road, Ealing, London W5 2DJ, England.

RODERICK JONES Richard Trevor, b. 14 Nov. 1947, Newport, Gwent, Wales. Composer; Conductor; Pianist; Musicologist. m. Susan Anne Thomason, 1992. *Education:* Associate, Royal College of Music, 1967; Graduate, Royal Schools of Music 1969; MMus, University of Bristol, 1989. *Career:* Head of Music, South Warwickshire College, Stratford-upon-Avon, 1970-79; Extramural Tutor, University of Birmingham, 1971-79; Musical Director, National Youth Theatre, Wales, 1978-87; Tutor, Welsh College of Music & Drama, 1979-93; Extramural Tutor, University College, Cardiff, 1980-93; External Tutor, University of Oxford, 1993-. *Compositions:* Piano concerto; 3 symphonies; 3 chamber concertos; 3 sinfoniettas; Numerous choral works including oratorio, Altus Prosator; Numerous chamber works including 2 piano trios. Stage works including: Opera, Me & My Bike (BBC commission); Chanticleer, church opera; Altar Fire, scenic celebration; Game Circle, scenic cantata; Over 30 scores, TV & stage. *Hobbies:* Fishing; Reading; Walking; Record collecting. *Address:* 2 Primrose Court, Moreton-in-Marsh, Glos GL56 0JG, England.

RODESCU Julian, b. 1 May 1953, Bucharest, Romania. Opera Singer (Bass). m. Barbara Govatos, 4 June 1983. *Education:* Bachelor and Master of Music, Juilliard School; Teachers: Giorgio Tozzi, William Glazier, Jerome Hines, Hans Hotter and Daniel Ferro. *Debut:* Plutone in Monteverdi's Il Ballo delle Ingrate with Brooklyn Opera 1980. *Career:* Teatro alla Scala with Riccardo Muti, 1991; Boston Symphony with Seiji Ozawa in Boston Symphony Hall, Carnegie Hall and Tanglewood; Carnegie Hall debut in 1989 with Rostropovich in World premiere of Shostakovich's Rayok; Miami Opera, New York City Opera, Knoxville Opera, Aachen Stadttheater, Kennedy Center in Washington DC, Alice Tully Hall, WHYY-TV Philadelphia, WQXR, WNCN New York, Central City Opera, Opera Delaware. *Recordings:* Shostakovich, Rayok; Tchaikovsky, Pique Dame; Bortniansky, Complete Vocal Concerti. *Honour:* Winner of Luciano Pavarotti Competition 1988. *Hobbies:* Tennis; Ping Pong; Photography; Cooking. *Current Management:* Ann Summers International. *Address:* 1420 Locust Street, Philadelphia, PA 19102, USA.

RODGERS Joan, b. 1960, Cumbria. Singer (Soprano). m. Paul Daniel. *Education:* Studied at the Royal Northern College of Music with Joseph Ward, and with Audrey Longford. *Career:* Opera debut as Pamina at the 1982 Aix-en-Provence Festival; Engagements at the Ponnelle-Barenboim Mostly Mozart Festival in Paris as Zerlina, and with the English National Opera as Nannetta in Falstaff; Israel Mozart Festival as Susanna and Despina; Turin Opera as Ilia in Idomeneo; Covent Garden debut 1983, as the Princess in L'Enfant et les Sortligès: has returned for Xenia (Boris Godunov), Echo (Ariadne auf Naxos), Zerlina in Don Giovanni 1988 and Servilia in La Clemenza di Tito 1989; Glyndebourne debut 1989, as Susanna in an authentic version of Le Nozze di Figaro conducted by Simon Rattle; Promenade Concerts 1989, as soloist in Mahler's 4th Symphony (Feature on BBC TV Omnibus programme); Munich Opera and Covent Garden, 1990-91, as Pamina, Mélisande in a concert performance at Madrid; Susanna and Despina at the Maggio Musicale, Florence and with the Chicago Symphony Orchestra; Mozart's Countess for English National Opera and Handel's Cleopatra for Scottish Opera, 1992; Season 1992 as Yolanta in Tchaikovsky's opera for Opera North at the Edinburgh Festival and as Susanna at Florence; Many recitals and concert appearances in Great Britain. *Honours include:* Kathleen Ferrier Memorial Scholarship 1981; Peter Moores Foundation Scholarship. *Address:* c/o Ingpen & Williams Ltd., 14 Kensington Court, London W8 5DN, Engalnd.

ROE Richard Allen, b. 25 Sept 1960. Church Musician; Conductor. *Education:* BA, University of North Texas, Denton; MMus Southern Methodist University, Dallas; DMus, Indiana University; Principal teachers: Helmuth Rilling, choral conducting, Anshel Brusilow, orchestral conducting; Additional studies at Westminster Choir College, Staatliche Hochschule für Musik und Darstellende Kunst, Frankfurt, Germany, International Bachakademie Stuttgart and the University of Iowa. *Debut:* Conductor with performances of Verdi Requiem and various Bach Cantatas from 1986 Sommeracademie Johann Sebastian Bach in Stuttgart, Germany, broadcast over South German Radio. *Career:* Director of Music, Spencer Presbyterian Church, Spencer, Indiana. *Address:* c/o Spencer Presbyterian Church. 156 North Main Street, Spencer, IN 47460, USA

ROESEL Peter, b. 2 Feb 1945, Dresden, Germany. Pianist. m. Heidnun Bergmann, 1 son, 1 daughter. *Education:* Completed study, with Bazkirov and Oborin, Moscow Conservatory, 1964-69. *Debut:* With Berlin Symphony, 1964. *Career:* Regular appearances with leading European and American orchestras, 1966-; Performances at major festivals including Salzburg, Berlin, Edinburgh, Prague, London Proms, Hollywood Bowl. *Recordings:* Over 50 records for Deutsche Schallplatten, EMI, Capriccio, Tokuma, Ars Vivendi including complete concerti by Weber, Beethoven, Schumann, Rachmaninoff, complete piano works by Brahms, major piano sonatas by Mozart, Beethoven, Schubert, Schumann, various chamber music works; Played a concerto by Weber with the BBC Philharmonic, 1991. *Honours:* Prizewinner of competitions: Schumann, 1963, Tchaikovsky, 1966, Montreal, 1968; Honorary Citizen of Minnesota, USA. *Memberships:* Committee Member, New Saxonian Arts Association; Committee Member, Friends of Dresden Music Festival. *Hobbies:* Reading; Gardening. *Current Management:* Interartists Holland BV, 584 Keizersgracht, NL-Amsterdam, Netherlands. *Address:* Kruegerstrasse 20, D-01326 Dresden, Germany.

ROGALA Jacek Wojciech, b. 22 Apr 1966, Brzeg, Poland. Composer, Conductor, Journalist. *Education:* Diploma in Horn, State Lyceum of Music, Wroclaw; Diploma, Composition, 1990, Diploma in Conducting, 1992, Academy of Music, Wroclaw. *Career:* Regular performances in Poland, Germany, Spain, 1985-; Participation in summer workshops of Polish Section ISCM, 1986-89; Teacher of choirs in Wroclaw, 1988-92; Co-organizer, Young Composers Meetings, Musica Nova in Brzeg (Poland) 1989, 1990; Journalist in Polish Radio, Wroclaw, Chief of Redaction of Music, 1990-91, 1990-1992; Scholarship in Konservatorium

Enschede, Holland, 1989; Regular concerts as a orchestra-conductor, 1990; Assistant Conductor, State Opera in Wroclaw, 1991-92; Adviser of Minister of Cultural and Fine Arts for Musical Affair, 1992-. *Memberships:* Youth Section, Polish Composer's Union, 1986-, Board Member 1988-90; Polish Section of ISCM, 1986-. *Address:* ul. Trebacka 3 m 600-074 Warszawa, Poland.

ROGÉ Pascal, b. 6 Apr 1951, Paris, France. Concert Pianist. *Education:* Studied at the Paris Conservatoire from 1962, piano with Lucette Descaves, chamber music with Pierre Pasquier; Further study with Julius Katchen 1966-69. *Career:* First orchestral appearance Paris 1962; Many solo recitals and concerto engagements in France, elsewhere in Europe, the Far East, Australia and the USA; Noted for interpretations of Ravel, Fauré, Debussy and other French composers; Duo partnership with violinist Pierre Amoyal includes recital at the 1990 Bath Festival, with works by Fauré, Schubert amd Brahms. *Recordings include:* CDs of Satie, Poulenc and Fauré and Brahms piano works (Decca); Saint-Saëns Piano Concertos, conducted by Charles Dutoit; Sonatas by Brahms, with Pierre Amoyal (Decca). *Honours:* Premiers prix for piano and chamber music at the Paris Conservatoire, 1966; 1st prize, Long-Thibaud Competition, 1971. *Honours:* Premiere Prix for piano and chamber music at the Paris Conservatoire, 1966; Grand Prix du Disque and Edison Award, 1984, Gramophone Award Best Instrumental Recording, 1988. *Address:* Balmer and Dixon Management AG, Granitweg 2, CH-8006 Zurich, Switzerland.

ROGER David, b. 1950, England. Stage Designer. *Career:* For Opera Factory (London) has designed La Calisto; The Knot Garden; Hell's Angels (Osborne, premiere); Eight Songs for a Mad King (Maxwell Davies); Yan Tan Tethera (Birtwistle, premiere, 1986); A conflation of Gluck's Iphigenia operas; Aventures/Nouvelles Aventures (Ligeti); Mahagonny Songspiel; Cosi Fan Tutte; Don Giovanni; The Ghost Sonata (Reimann); The Marriage of Figaro (1991); Other work has included La Grand Macabre (Ligeti, at Freiburg); Akhnaten by Philip Glass and The Return of Ulysses at English National Opera; La Bohème for Opera North and Manon Lescaut for the Opéra-Comique, Paris; Has designed plays at the Traverse Theatre, Soho Polytechnic, the Royal Court, the RSC and for the Lyric Hammersmith (Faust and Morte d'Arthur). *Address:* c/o Opera Factory, 8a The Leather Market, Weston St, London SE1 3ER, England.

ROGERS Lesley-Jane, b. 25 Apr 1962, Bristol, England. Soprano. m. Robin Daniel, 3 June 1988, 1 stepson, 1 stepdaughter. *Education:* Royal Academy of Music, 1981-85; LRAM (Pianoforte Teachers), 1983; GRSM Honours, 1984; LRAM (Singing Teachers) 1985. *Career:* Performed extensively in the fields of oratorio and solo cantatas, especially baroque and classical music; Opera includes The Milliner in Strauss's Der Rosenkavalier, Aix-en- Provence Festival, 1987; Asteria in Handel's Tamerlano (authentic instruments) 1990. *Recordings:* Two rare Telemann cantatas, Lecosaldi Ensemble. Director Peter Lea-Cox, 1988. Highlights from Handel's Tamerlano, ECBO, Director Roy Goodman, 1990; Caldara Madrigals and Cantatas, Wren Baroque Soloists (authentic instruments), (Unicorn-Kanchana), 1992. *Hobbies:* Dressmaking; Sports; Riding. *Current Management:* Norman McCann International Artists. *Address:* 60 Church Crescent, Finchley, London N3 1BJ, England.

ROGERS Nigel David, b. 21 Mar. 1935, Wellington, Shropshire, England. Singer (Tenor); Conductor; Teacher. *Education:* Choral Scholar, King's College, Cambridge, 1953-56; BA, 1956, MA, 1960, Cantab; Private musical tuition, Rome and Milan; Hochschule für Musik, Munich, 1959-61. *Career:* Began professional career with group Studio der Frühen Musik (quartet), 1961; Resident in England, 1965-; Operatic debut, Amsterdam, 1969; Sang in Monteverdi's Ulisse and Orfeo under Harnoncourt at Vienna and Amsterdam, 1971, 1976, Poppea at Amsterdam under

Leonhardt, 1972 and II Combattimento at Milan under Berio, 1973; British premiere of Arden must Die by Goehr, Sadler's Wells 1974; Sang the title role in Handel's Teseo at Warsaw, 1977; Conducting, 1985-. *Recordings:* Some 70 from Machaut to Schubert, especially Monteverdi-including 1610 Vespers and Orfeo; John Dowland lute songs, Virgin Classics, 1988; Sigismondo d'India, Virgin Classics, 1991; Florentine Intermedi of 1589; Dido and Aeneas, Hippolyte et Aricie and Billy Budd. *Contributions to:* Various magazines, academic publications; Chapter on Voice, Companion to Baroque Music, editor Julie Anne Sadie, 1991. *Honour:* Honorary RCM, Royal College of Music, 1980. *Hobbies:* Walking; Country pursuits; Wine; Travel. *Address:* Chestnut Cottage, East End, East Woodhay (Hants), Nr Newbury, Berks RG15 0AF, England.

ROGERS Patrick John Francis, b. 15 Dec. 1948, Eureka, California, USA. Musicologist; Musician. m. Susan Beth Smalakis, 10 Sept. 1982. 1 son. *Education:* BA, Humboldt State University, 1971; MA, University of California Santa Barbara, 1977; PhD, Claremont Graduate School, 1986; University of Maryland, UCLA. *Career:* Director, Fiske Museum of Musical Instruments, 1986-89, Honorary Director, 1989-; Organist, St Denis Church, 1986-; Fletcher Jones Foundation Fellow, Huntington Library, 1991-92; Performed regularly with Early Music Ensemble of Los Angeles; I Cantori; Los Angeles Baroque Orchestra; Santa Barbara Chamber Orchestra; Has worked with Martial Singher; Max van Egmond; Specialist in continuo accompaniment; Soloist on Harpsichord, organ and clavichord. *Recordings:* Soundtrack for film Foes. *Publications:* Continuo Realization in Handel's Vocal Music, 1989; Continuo Realizations of Baroque Cello Sonatas; American Handel Society Newsletter, Performance Practice Review, Göttinger Händel-Beiträge. *Contributions to:* Musical Times; Early Music; The 18th Century; American Musical Instrument Society Newsletter. *Hobbies:* Weight training; Hiking; Duplicate bridge. *Address:* 112 Harvard Ave No 118, Claremont, CA 91711, USA.

ROGG Lionel, b. 21 Apr. 1936, Geneva, Switzerland. Organist; Composer. m. Claudine Effront, 1957, 3 sons. *Education:* Geneva Conservatory; Piano, Nikita Magaloff; Organ, Pierre Segond. *Career includes:* Complete Bach organ works in 10 recitals, Victoria Hall, Geneva, 1961; Concerts (organ, harpsichord) worldwide; Interpretative courses, USA, UK, Switzerland, Austria, Japan, Italy. *Compositions include:* Organ: 12 chorales; Variations, Psalm 91, 1983; Introduction, ricercare, toccata; Cantata, Geburt der Venus. Also: Face à face, 2 pianos; Missa Brevis, chorus & orchestra; Concerto for organ and orchestra, 1992. *Recordings:* Complete Bach organ works; Art of Fugue; Complete Buxtehude organ works; Rogg Plays Reger; Rogg Plays Rogg (organ compositions); Du Mage, Clérambault. *Publication:* Improvisation Course for Organists. *Honours include:* Grand Prix du Disque, 1970; Deutscher Schallplatten Preis, 1980; Doctor honoris causa, University of Geneva, 1989. *Hobbies:* Mountain climbing; Japanese culture. *Address:* 38A route de Troinex, CH-1234 Vessy, Geneva, Switzerland.

ROGNER Heinz, b. 1929, Leipzig, Germany. Conductor. *Education:* Studied composition and piano with Egon Boelsche and Hugo Steurer in Leipzig. *Career:* Repetiteur and Conductor at the German National Theatre in Weimar; Teacher at the Leipzig Musikhochschule 1954-58; Principal Conductor, Great Leipzig Radio Orchestra, 1959-63; General Musical Director, Deutsche Staatsoper Berlin, 1962-73; Chief Conductor of the Berlin Radio Symphony Orchestra, 1973, tours to Eastern Europe, Austria, Sweden, France, Belgium, Switzerland, Germany and Japan; Regular Guest Conductor, Yomiuri Nippon Symphony Orchestra from 1978, Principal Conductor 1984. *Recordings:* Strauss Horn Concertos; Abu Hassan by Weber and Eine Nacht in Venedig, with the Dresden Staatskapelle; Trumpet Concertos by Torelli, Grossi, Fasch and Albinoni; Schubert's 7th Symphony (arranged by Weingartner) and 9th Symphony; Reger's Romantic Suite and Symphonic Prologue; Beethoven's Cantata

on the Accession of Leopold II, Die glorreiche Augenblick and Vestas Feuer; Strauss's Duet Concertino and Preludes to Palestrina by Pfitzner (Eterna). *Honours:* National Prize of the GDR 1975; Gerhardt Eusler Gold Plakette 1979; Professor 1981. *Address:* Norman McCann International Artists Ltd, The Coach House, 56 Lawrie Park Gardens, London SE26 6XJ, England.

ROGOFF Ilan, b. 1950, USSR. Concert Pianist. *Education:* Studied with Karol Klein, Stefan Askenase, Leonard Shure and Claudio Arrau. *Career:* Has appeared as soloist with such conductors as Rudolf Barschai, Antal Dorati, Charles Groves, Gunther Herbig, Kurt Sanderling, Walter Weller and Zubin Mehta; Concerts with most major British orchestras including 1983 engagements with the BBC Philharmonic (Prokofiev's Third Concerto), Royal Liverpool Philharmonic and the Bournemouth Symphony; Gave the premiere of John McCabe's Third Concerto 1978; Tours to America and the Far East, 1983-85; Performances of Beethoven's Piano Concertos directed from the keyboard in South America and Germany, 1984; Repertoire also includes Beethoven, Brahms and Liszt Sonatas; Schumann and Schubert C major Fantasies; Bach/Busoni Chaconne; Chopin Ballades and Etudes. *Address:* c/o Norman McCann Ltd, The Coach House, 56 Lawrie Park Gardens, London SE26 6XJ, England.

ROHLFS Eckart, b. 23 Dec 1929, Tuebingen, Germany. General Secretary, Editor. m. 1959, 4 d. *Education:* University of Munich. *Career Includes:* Generaly Secretary, Jeunesses Musicales Germany, 1959-74; President, Gewerkschaft Dt Musikerzieher u Konzert Kunstler, 1975-84; President, Romain Rolland Sociation, Germany, 1992; General Secretary, European Union of Music Competition for Youth, Brussels, Since 1988; General Secretary National Competition, Jugend Musiziert, since 1963; Editor, Neue Musikzeittung since 1952; Kuratorium Institute für Musikalische Begabungs Forschung Begabtenforderung, Paderborn, Since 1992. *Publications include:* Musik Almanach German Musiklife; Invention und Durchfuehrung Jugend Musiziert. *Contributions to:* Numerous to Books and Journals Including, Neue Musikzeitung; Handbuch fur Musikberufe. *Memberships:* Numerous Professional Organizations. *Hobby:* Gardening. *Address:* D-82166 Lochham b Muenchen, Jahnstrasse 31a, Germany.

ROHNER Ruth, b. 18 Sept 1935, Zurich, Switzerland. Singer (Soprano). *Education:* Studied in Winterthur and Amsterdam. *Career:* Sang at the Opera of Biel-Solothurn 1960-61, Vienna Kammeroper 1960-62; Engaged at Zurich Opera since 1962, notably in premieres of Sutermeister's Madame Bovary 1967 and Kelterborn's Ein Engel Kommmt Nach Babylon 1977; Many performances in the lyric and coloratura repertory and in the first local performances of Burkhard's Ein Stern Geht Auf Jakob and Karl V by Krenek; Guest engagements at Berne, Basle, the State Operas of Hamburg and Munich, Dusseldorf, Strasbourg, Helsinki and Châtelet Paris; Festival appearances at Lausanne, Wiesbaden and Athens; Noted concert artist in oratorio and lieder. *Address:* c/o Zurich Opera, CH-8008 Zurich, Switzerland.

ROHRL Manfred, b. 12 Sept. 1935, Augsburg, Germany. Singer (Bass). *Education:* Studied at the Augsburg Conservatory and with Franz Kelch and Margarethe von Winterfeld. *Debut:* Augsburg 1958, as Masetto. *Career:* Member of the Deutsche Oper Berlin, notably in the 1965 premiere of Der junge Lord by Henze; Guest appearances in Brussels, Nancy, Dusseldorf, Geneva, Zurich, Zagreb and Rotterdam; Netherlands Opera Amsterdam 1984, as Leporello; Sang Waldner in Arabella at the Deutsche Oper, Berlin 1988, Dr Kolenaty in The Makropoulos Case, 1989; Many performances in the buffo repertory; Sang Taddeo in L'Italiana in Algeri with the Deutsche Oper, 1992. *Recordings:* For Deutsche Grammophon and Eurodisc.

Address: c/o Deutsche Oper Berlin, Richard Wagnerstrasse 10, D-1000 Berlin 1, Germany.

ROHWER Jens, b. 6 July 1914, Neumunster, Germany. Composer; Musicologist; Professor. m. Gabriele Zimmermann, 3 sons, 3 daughters. *Education:* PhD, University of Kiel, 1958. *Career:* Instructor, Posen Regional Music School 1943, Lubeck State Music School 1946; Director, Schleswig-Holstein Music Academy, Lubeck, 1955-72; Professor, Musikhochschule, Lubeck, 1972-80. *Compositions:* Orchestral, chamber, instrumental, vocal & choral works including: Concerto, piano & orchestra, 1952; Chamber Concerto, violin, viola & string orchestra, 1967; Chelion, pantomime ballet, 1967; String Quartet, 1968; Webmuster, piano, 1970; Sonata, flute & piano, 1971; Nachhall, 4 organ pieces, 1975; Paulusbrief, oratorio, 1976; Miniatures, female voice & orchestra or piano, 1976; Quartet, 2 parts, flute, recorder, violin & violoncello, 1978; 3 cycles, voice & piano, 1980; Fantasie, violin solo, 1981; Triostuck, Ophelia, 2 violins & piano, 1981; 224 Begleitsatze zum Evangelische Kirchengesangbuch, 1982; There Was A Star With The Name Earth, cassette & 2 records. *Publications include:* Tonale Instruktionen und Beitrage zur Kompositionslehre, 1951; Neueste Musik, ein Kritischer Bericht, 1964; Sinn und Unisinn in der Musik, 1969; Harmonische Grundlagen der Musik, 1970; Revolution zur Guten Kultur; Studien und Fantasien zu einer Individualsozialen Herrschaftsfreien Gesellschaftsordnung, 1980. *Honours include:* Schleswig-Holstein Art Prize, 1952. *Memberships include:* Society of Musicology; Amnesty International; Lions Club. *Address:* Lutherstrasse 16, 24 Lubeck, Germany.

ROKOVIC Borislav, b. 19 July 1925, Zrebjanin, Yugoslavia (Serbia). Musician; Pianist; Composer. m. Nona 14 Mar 1954, 1d. *Education:* College, Matura 1944; Academy of Music, Belgrade; Private Teachers; Piano and Trumpet Classes. *Debut:* Arranger and Composer, Budapest, Hungary 1942. *Career:* Radio Belgrade, 1948-54; West Germany since 1954; Radio and TV appearances; Since 1957 on Staff WDR-KOLN; Orchestra Kurt Edelhagen; Since 1962 permanent radio, TV and concert appearances; Several European World Tours. *Compositions:* Permanent Arranger of WDR-KOLN; Several jazz oriented tunes including Velvet Lady 1978, My Big Brother 1992, Love, Last Call 1991; Sugar Box 1975; Bora's Blues 1977; Showdown 1990; Mara's Dance 1992. *Recordings:* Ultranative 1971; 1400 recordings in WDR-KOLN. *Honours:* Several prizes from Radio Televizija Beograd. *Hobbies:* Reading Science, Philosophy, History in Five Languages. *Address:* Overstolzen Str 19, 5000 Cologne 1, Germany.

ROLAND Claude-Robert, b. 19 Dec 1935, Pont-de-Loup, Belgium. Conductor; Organist; Composer. m. Anne-Marie Girardot, 6 Sept 1963, 1s. *Education:* Athenee Royal; Academy of Music, Chatelet; Conservatories, Liege, Paris, Brussels, Bernier, Froidebise, Mawet, Demessieux, Messiaen, Defossez. *Career:* Organist, Notre Dame Church, Wasmes, 1955-63, Basilica Charleroi 1963-67; Professor, Brussels Copnservatory 1972-; Weekly contribution RTB 1968-70; Musical Director, Amis de la Musique, 1974-; *Performances:* works of Prokofiev, Guillaume, Quatrefages, RTBF. *Compositions:* Over 100 works including Piano preludes (Marie-Madeleine petit, ORTF); Voya Toncitch, All Over the World; Rossignolet du Bois 1974; Chants de Mort et de Vie, Fabienne Petris and Georges Deppe 1985. *Recordings:* Compositeurs Liegeois, Alpha-Organ; Musique au Chateau, Musica Magna, Organ and Brass; Sinfonietta Prokofiev (RTBF). *Publication:* Orgues en Hainaut, 1966; Contributor to Musique Vivante, Feuillets du Spantole; Hainaut-Tourism, UWO. *Honours:* Composers Prize, JMB, 1955; Prix Koopal, 1968; Prix Doehaerd, 1971. *Memberships:* President, Founder, Musique Vivante; Societe Liege Musicologie; Orgue Pour Notre Temps. *Hobbies:* Martial Arts; Athletics; Poetry. *Address:* 59 Rue Lebeau, B-1000 Brussels, Belgium.

ROLANDI Gianna, b. 16 Aug. 1952, New York, USA. Singer (Soprano). *Eucation:* Studied with her mother and with Ellen Faull and Max Rudolf. *Debut:* Sang Offenbach's Olympia in Les Contes d'Hoffmann at the New York City Opera, 1975. *Career:* Metropolitan Opera 1979, as Sophie, later singing Olympia, the Nightingale in the opera by Stravinsky and Zerbinetta; Glyndebourne debut 1981, as Zerbinetta, returning 1984 as Zdenka (Arabella) and Susanna; English National Opera 1983 as Cleopatra in Giulio Cesare; San Diego 1984, as Ophelia in Hamlet by Thomas; Sang Lucia di Lammermoor at San Francisco in 1986; At the Rome Opera in 1989 sang Curiazio in a performance of Cimarosa's Gli Orazi e i Curizai, to mark the 200th anniversary of the French Revolution; Other roles include Gilda, the Queen of Night and parts in operas by Donizetti (at the New York City Opera). *Address:* c/o Teatro dell'Opera, Piazzo Beniamino Gigli 8, 1-00184 Rome, Italy.

ROLFE JOHNSON Anthony, b. 5 Nov. 1940, Tackley, Oxon., England. Singer (Tenor). *Education:* Guildhall School of Music, London. *Debut:* With the English Opera Group 1973, in Tchaikovsky's Iolanta. *Career:* Glyndebourne 1974-76, as Storch (Intermezzo), Lensky (Eugene Onegin) and Fenton (Falstaff); European career from 1977: Lensky and Mozart's Titus with Netherlands Opera; Hamburg State Opera, La Scala Milan (as Mozart's Lucio Silla); Aschenbach in Death in Venice, seen in Geneva and at the Edinburgh Festival; With English National Opera he has sung Mozart's Don Ottavio, Tamino and Ferrando, Monteverdi's Ulysses, Britten's Male Chorus and Essex and Monteverdi's Orfeo; Jupiter in Semele at Covent Garden; US concerts with the Chicago Symphony under Solti, the Boston Symphony Orchestra under Ozawa, the New York Philharmonic under Rostropovitch and the Cleveland Orchestra under Rattle; Other conductors include Giulini, Marriner, Norrington, Gardiner, Tennstedt, Boulez, Haitink, Masur and Abbado; Salzburg debut 1987, in Schmidt's Das Buch mit sieben Siegeln, returned to Salzburg in 1991 for the title role in Idomeneo; Season 1992/93 as Monteverdi's Ulisse and Orfeo for ENO, Lucio Silla at Salzburg; Oronte in a new production of Handel's Alcina at Covent Garden, Peter Grimes in the first season of the reopened Glyndebourne Opera and Aschenbach in Death in Venice at the Met, 1994. *Recordings:* Handel's Acis and Galatea, Saul, Hercules, Jephtha, Alexander's Feast, Esther, Solomon, Semele and Messiah; Haydn's Il Sposo deluso, Il Mondo della Luna and Stabat Mater; Mozart's Apollo et Hyacinthus and La Finta Semplice, from the Salzburg Mozartwoche; Bach's St John and St Matthew Passion; Mozart's Zauberflöte, La Clemenza di Tito, Idomeneo; Haydn's Creation, Seasons; Peter Grimes; Samson; Oedipus Rex; Orfeo; War Requiem. *Address:* c/o Lies Askonas Ltd. 6 Henrietta Street, London WC2E 8LA, England.

ROLL Michael, b. 17 July 1946, Leeds, England. Pianist. m. Juliana Markova, 1 son. *Education:* Piano studies with Fanny Waterman. *Career:* Debut 1958 at the Royal Festival Hall playing the Schumann Concerto with Malcolm Sargent; First Prize at 1963 Leeds International Pianoforte Competition; Regular appearances with major UK orchestras; Visited first Hong Kong Festival with the London Philharmonic and toured Japan with the BBC Symphony; Tour of Holland with the English Chamber Orchestra, Germany and Switzerland with the BBC Symphony, Spain with the Royal Philharmonic and Eastern Europe with the Scottish Chamber Orchestra; Tours of the USSR and Scandinavia in recital and with orchestra; Engagements with the conductors Barbirolli, Boulez, Giulini, Leinsdorf, Previn and Kurt Sanderling; Visits to Aldeburgh, Bath, Edinburgh, Granada and Vienna Festivals; US debut 1974 with the Boston Symphony Orchestra conducted by Colin Davis; 1987-88 season with recitals in Milan, East Berlin, Dresden, Leipzig and London; Royal Philharmonic concerts conducted by Kurt Masur; 1988-89 season with the London Symphony, Scottish National, Hallé, Bournemouth Symphony, Helsinki Philharmonic and Hong Kong Philharmonic Orchestras; Recitals in London, Milan, Leipzig, Berlin and Dresden;

Concertos in the 1990 Henry Wood Proms, with Kurt Masur in Leipzig and London and Valery Gergiev in Leningrad and the UK; 1991-92 season concertos with Skrowaczewski and the Hallé, BBC Philharmonic, BBC Scottish Orchestras and Leipzig Gewandhaus, recitals in the International Piano Series at the Queen Elizabeth Hall and at the Klavierfestival Ruhr in Germany with Helsinki Philharmonic under Comissiona, 1992; for the English Chamber Orchestra at the Barbican and his New York debut recital, 1992. *Address:* c/o Harold Holt Ltd., 31 Sinclair Road, London W14 0NS, England.

ROLLA Janos, b. 1944, Hungary. Violinist. *Education:* Violin, from age 5; Graduate, Ferenc Liszt Academy of Music, Budapest, 1969. *Career:* Leader, Ferenc Liszt Chamber Orchestra, 1963-; Chamber musician, concert halls throughout Europe. *Honours:* 3rd prize, violin competition, Hungarian Radio, 1969; Merited Artist, Hungarian People's Republic, 1981.

ROLLAND Sophie, b. 18 Jul 1963, Montreal, Canada. Solo Concert Cellist. *Education:* Studied with Walter Joachim, Conservatoire de Musique du Québec, Montreal; Further study with Nathaniel Rosen in New York, Pierre Fournier in Geneva and William Pleeth in London. *Debut:* Montreal Symphony Orchestra under Charles Dutoit, 1982. *Career:* Regular appearances throughout Canada with every major orchestra including the Montreal, Toronto and Vancouver Symphony Orchestras Toured in USA, France, Spain, England, Wales, Germany, Switzerland, Bulgaria, Hungary, Yugoslavia, Finland and China; Frequent guest at international chamber music festivals including Kuhmo, Dubrovnik and Parry Sound; Duo partnership with pianist Marc-Andre Hamelin since 1988-; 1990-91 season: Beethoven cycle in New York (Carnegie Hall, May 1991), Washington DC, Montreal (broadcast CBC) and London (Wigmore Hall, Mar 1991, broadcast BBC); Plays a 1674 cello by Petrus Ranta of Brescia. *Honours include:* Premier Prix à l'Unamanité, Montreal; Study awards from the Canadian and Quebec governments; Prix d'Europe, Canada; First prize, Du Maurier Competition; Virginia P Moore Prize, Canada Arts Council, 1985. *Address:* 27 Cleveland Avenue, London W4 1SN, England.

ROLLER Elisabeth, b. 27 Nov 1934, Salzburg, Austria. Harpsichordist. m. Wilfrid Junge, 10 Dec 1955, 4 sons, 1 daughter. *Education:* Piano, 1955, Graduation Diploma, Harpsichord, 1978, MA, Harpsichord, 1989, Mozarteum, Salzburg; Licenciatura, Harpsichord, Concepcion, Chile, 1975. *Career:* Concerts as Soloist and participating in various chamber music ensembles, USA, Austria, Chile, Italy, Germany; Teaching: Harpsichord, Universidad de Concepcion, Chile; Harpsichord, Landesmusikschulwerk, Linz, Austria; Conductor, Camerata Antica. *Recordings:* Chilean Contemporary Music for Harpsichord, compositions by Roberto Escobar. *Address:* Keplerstrasse 3-1-12, A-4560 Kirchdorf-Kr, Austria.

ROLNICK Neil B., b. 22 Oct. 1947, Dallas, Texas, USA. Composer; Professor. m. Wendy Goodale, 28 Oct. 1972, 1 daughter. *Education:* AB, English Literature, Harvard College, 1969; San Francisco Conservatory of Music, 1973-74; Computer music, Stanford University, summer 1976; MA 1976, PhD 1980, University of California, Berkeley; *Career:* Researcher, IRCAM, Paris, 1977-79; Assistant Professor 1981-86, Associate Professor 1986-, Music, Rensselaer Polytechnic Institute, Troy, New York; Soloist, synthesiser & computer music, 1982-; Performances, throughout USA & Europe. *Compositions include:* A la Mode, 8 instruments & digital synthesiser; Real Time, 13 instruments & digital synthesiser; Wonderous Love, trombone & tape; Ever-Livin Rhythm, percussion & tape; Blowin, solo flute; Loopy, Solo Synclavier II; Roberet Johnson Sampler, Balkanization, What Is the Use?, Macedonian Air Drumming and Sanctus, all computer music; Drones and Dances, for chamber orchestra and synthesiser; I Like It, for 2 singers and Digital processing; Vocal Chords, for voice and digital processing; The Original Child Bomb Song, for voices and synthesisers.

Address: 152 Wittenberg Road, Bearsville, New York 12409, USA.

ROLOFF Elisabeth, b. 18 Feb. 1937, Bielefeld, Germany. Organist. *Education:* Berlin High School of Music, 1958-60; BM, Bremen Conservatory of Music, 1960-61; BA 1965, Artist's Diploma 1966, Cologne High School of Music; Royal College of Music, London, UK, 1966-67. *Honours:* Scholarship, British Council, 1966-67. *Career:* Organist & Choirmaster, Christ Church, Hannover, West Germany, 1968-74; Titular Organist, German Church, Paris, France, 1974-82; Concerts throughout Europe, Israel & USA; Faculty, Rubin Academy of Music, Jerusalem, Israel, 1983-; Titular Organist, Redeemer Church, Jerusalem, 1983-. Appearances: International Organ Festival, Sorø, Denmark; Royal Festival Hall, London, UK; King's College Chapel, Cambridge, UK; St Ouen, Rouen, France; Notre-Dame, Paris; Chartres Cathedral, France; Kaiser-Wilhelm-Gedächtniskirche, Berlin; Marburg University; Cathedral & St Jacobskirche, Lubeck; Liturgica, Israel; Bach Organ Festival, Israel, 1985; Radio appearances, Belgium, Denmark, West Germany, Israel, Norway, Switzerland. *Recordings:* Musica Sacra at the Redeemer Church, Jerusalem; Organ works, Pachelbel, Buxtehude, J. S. Bach, Mozart (integral). *Hobby:* Reading. *Current Management:* International Music Consultant, PO Box 45401, Tel Aviv 61453. *Address:* PO Box 14076, Jerusalem, Israel.

ROLOFF Roger Raymond, b. 22 Feb. 1947, Peoria, Illinois, USA. Baritone Singer. m. Barbara A. Petersen, 19 Mar. 1982. *Education:* BA magna cum laude, English, Illinois Wesleyan University, 1969; MA, Illinois State University, 1972; Graduate study, English, State University of New York, Stony Brook; Private voice study, Sam Sakarian, New York City, 1975-; Vocal & dramatic coaching, various teachers including Hans Hotter. *Debut:* Deertrees Opera Theatre, Maine, 1975. *Career:* Operatic roles (baroque to comtemporary) including: Wotan & Wanderer, The Ring; Jochanaan, Salome; Ruprecht, Prokofiev's Fiery Angel. Appearances with: English National Opera; Deutsche Oper, Berlin; Seattle, Kentucky, Dallas, San Diego, New York City Operas; Niederschsische Staatsoper Hannover; Hawaii Opera Theater; Houston Grand Opera; Major orchestras, USA & Canada. Concert appearances, Milwaukee, Boston, Los Angeles, Germany, Switzerland; Sang the Dutchman in a concert performance of Der fliegende Holländer, Boston 1990; Telramund in Lohengrin at Nice, 1990. *Contributions to:* Interviews, features, Ovation magazine. *Honours:* Prizes, Montreal International Competition, & awards, William M. Sullivan Foundation, 1981; 1st prize, Wagnerian voices, Liederkranz Foundation, 1982; Richard Tucker Award, 1984. *Hobbies:* Hiking; Cycling; Walking; Chopping wood; Old recordings; Humour; Art; Museum-going, home & abroad; Writing German poetry. *Address:* International Music Consultants, PO Box 45401, Tel Aviv 61453, Israel.

ROLTON Julian, b. 1965, England. Pianist. *Career:* Co-founded the Chagall Piano Trio at the Banff Centre for the Arts in Canada, currently Resident Artist; Debut concert at the Blackheath Concert Halls in London 1991; Further appearances at Barbican's Prokofiev Centenary Festival, the Warwick Festival and the South Place Sunday Concerts at the Conway Hall, London; Purcell Room London recitals 1993 with the London premiere of Piano Trios by Tristan Keuris, Nicholas Maw and Dame Ethel Smyth, composed 1880; Premiere of Piano Trio No. 2 by David Matthews at Norfolk and Norwich Festival 1993; Engaged for Malvern Festival 1994. *Address:* South Bank Centre, c/o Press Office (Pamela Chowhan Management), London SE1, England.

ROMANIUK Jerzy, b. 26 Mar 1943, Skierniewice, Poland. Pianist. m. Jolnta Latkowska, 12 Oct 1968, 1s. 1d. *Education:* Music School in Lodz; Chopin's High Music School in Warsaw; Warsaw Conservatory. *Debut:* With Warsaw Philharmonic Orchestra, 26 June 1968. *Career:* Concerts in England, France, Denmark, Germany, Hungary, Spain, Holland, Cuba, UAE, Italy,

Poland, Yugoslavia. *Recordings:* Chopin, Liszt. *Memberships:* Chopin Society; Symphony Society. *Hobbies:* The Universe; Jogging. *Address:* Ul Roztogi 48, 01-310 Warsaw, Poland.

ROMANOVA Nina, b. 1946, Leningrad, Russia. Singer (Mezzo- soprano). *Education:* Studied with Vera Sopina at Leningrad Aacademy of Music. *Career:* Performed at Pushkin Theatre in Kishinov then from 1976 member of the Maly Theatre Leningrad, now St Petersburg; Roles have included: Barber of Seville, by Rossini - Rosina; Il Trovatore by Verdi - Azucena; Don Carlo by Verdi - Eboli; Macbeth - Lady Macbeth; Carmen by Bizet - Carmen; Eugene Onegin by Tchaikovsky - Olga; Dame Pique by Tchaikovsky - The Countess and Polina; Boris Gudunov by Musorgsky - Marina; Khovanshchina by Mussorgsky - Marfa; Also Alexandr Nevsky by Prokofiev (in Verona also); Ivan Grozny by Prokofiev (in Paris also); St Matthew Passion, St John, Messa B-mionor by Bach; Requiem by Mozart; Requiem by Verdi; 2nd and 8th Symphonies by Mahler; Guest performances with St Petersburg M Mussorgsky State Academic Opera and Ballet Theatre (formerly Leningrad Maly Theatre); as member of Opera Company; Italy (Palermo, Modena, Reggio, Emilia, Parma, Ferrara, Ravenna, Catania), France (Paris, Cannes, Nantes), USA (New York), Japan (Tokyo, Osaka, Hiroshima, Iokogama), Greece, Portugal, The Netherlands. *Address:* Maly Opera and Ballet Theatre, St Petersburg, Russia, CIS.

ROMANUL Myron, b. 21 Mar 1954, Baltimore, Maryland, USA. Musician; Conductor; Pianist. m. Gabriele Weber, 8 June 1990. *Education:* New England Conservatory of Music, Boston 1972-75; Boston University School of Music, BM, Piano, 1978-81; Kneisel Hall, Blue Hill, Maine, 1978-79; Berkshire Music Center at Tanglewood 1973; Andre Watts Piano Seminar, 1984 Conductors' Seminar. *Debut:* Soloist with Boston Symphony Orchestra in Weber Konzertstück as youngest winner of Harry Dubbs Memorial Award 1965. *Career:* Performed and toured as Piano Soloist with Arthur Fiedler and Boston Pops and with orchestras in America and Canada 1973-79; Formed with three younger brothers Romanul Chamber Players and performed concerts, on radio and TV; Original Pianist of New England Conservatory Ragtime Ensemble 1972-76; Performances as Pianist and Zimbalist with Boston Symphony Orchestra, Speculum Musicae and Chamber Music Society of Lincoln Center; Principal Conductor of Boston Ballet 1984-86; Conductor and Solo Pianist with Stuttgart Ballet 1985-90; Music Director of Fairbanks Summer Arts Festival 1985-; Second Kopellmeister and Assistant Music Director at Badisches Staatstheater Karlsruhe 1990-94; First Kapellmeister and Associate Music Director at Staatstheater Mainz, 1994-. *Recordings:* As featured Pianist and Zimbalist. *Honours:* Numerous honours and awards. *Memberships:* American Symphony Orchestra League; Conductors Guild. *Hobbies:* Walking; Cooking; Travelling; Magic; Chamber Music. *Address:* Kremmlerstrasse 53, D-70597 Stuttgart, Germany.

ROMERO Patricia, b. 20 Sept 1953, Mexico City. Concert Pianist. m. David Hanesworth, 1 son. *Education:* Instituto Pedagogico Anglo Espanol, Mexico City; Conservatorio Nacional de Musica, Mexico City 1965-72; Trinity College, London 1972-76; Studies with Louis Kentner 1976-85. *Debut:* Wigmore Hall, London, June 1976. *Career:* Concerts in Spain and Switzerland; Concert tours in Mexico and UK; London appearances: Purcell Room, Wigmore Hall, Fairfield Halls, St John's Smith Square, Leighton House; Performances with Orquesta Sinfonia del Bajio, Orquesta de la Universidad de Guadalajara, Orquesta Sinfonia de Coyoacan; Radio Broadcasts in Mexico City and Guadalajara and BBC. *Honours:* First Prize, Yamaha National Piano Competition 1971; Third Prize National Sala Chopin Competition 1972; Maud Seton Prize, London 1975. *Memberships:* Incorporated Society of Musicians; Mexico Amigo. *Hobbies:* Archaeology; Food and Wine; Opera; Gardening. *Current Management:* Manygate Management, 13 Cotswald Mews, 30 Battersea Square,

London SW11 3RA, England. *Address:* 57 Osmond Gardens, Wallington, Surrey SM6 8SX, England.

ROMERO Pepe, b. 8 Mar 1944, Malaga, Spain, Classical Guitarist. *Education:* Studied classical and flamenco styles with his father. *Career:* Moved to USA 1958 and joined family guitar quartet, giving 3,000 concerts in USA, Australia, South America and Europe, from 1970; Solo European tour 1982, followed by performances in Rome, Madrid, Budapest, Stockholm, Amsterdam, Paris, Vienna, Berlin, London and Copenhagen; Festival appearances at Osaka, Bergen, Istanbul, Rome and Luxembourg; Has premiered the Concerto Andalou and the Concierto Para una Festa by Rodrigo, 1967, 73, and the Concerto Iberico by Torroba; Professor of the Guitar Department of the University of Southern California, Los Angeles; San Diego from 1982. *Recordings:* Five Rodrigo Concertos with the Boccherini Guitar Quintets and the Giuliani Concerti Op. 65 and Op. 70; Spanish Songs with Jessye Norman. *Address:* c/o Anglo Swiss Ltd, 3 Primrose Mews, 1a Sharpleshall Street, London NW1 8YW, England.

ROMERO Raul R., b. 25 Dec. 1953, Lima, Peru. Musicologist. m. 8 Sept. 1988. *Education:* BA, Sociology, Catholic University, Peru, 1978; MA, Ethnomusicology, Columbia University, New York, USA, 1983. *Recordings:* Editor, record series, Archivo de Musica Tradicional, titles include: Musica Tradicional del Valle del Mantaro, 1986; Musica Andina del Peru, 1987; Musica Tradicional de Cajamarca, 1988. *Publication:* Co-author, Music of Peru, 1985. *Contributions to:* Yearbook of Traditional Music; Latin American Music Review. *Honours:* Grant, OAS, 1977; Fulbright-Hayes grant, 1979-81. *Memberships:* Liaison Officer, Peru, International Council for Traditional Music. *Address:* Instituto Riva Aguero, Universidad Catolica del Peru, Jr. Camana 459, Lima 1, Peru.

ROMMES Rita, b. 1 July 1962, Turnhout, Belgium. Teacher. *Education:* Conservatory Antwerp. *Career:* Radio 1 Fred Broumets Solist with BRT Orchestral Philharmonic; Solist with Antwerp Philharmonic Orchestra. *Recordings:* A Taste of Percussion; Gemmini Ensemble. *Honours:* 1st Prize Namut; Jeunes Solist 1st Prize; Tenuto BRT. *Hobby:* Reading. *Address:* Broekstraat 1, 2480 Dessel, Belgium.

RONCONI Luca, b. 8 Mar 1933, Susah, Tunisia. Stage Director. *Education:* Graduated the Accademia d'Arte Drammatica Rome 1953. *Career:* Began as an actor then directed plays; Opera debut 1967, with Jeanne d'Arc au Bucher by Honegger and Busoni's Arlecchino, at Turin; Later work has included revivals of neglected operas by Purcell, Jommelli, Cimarosa and Rimsky-Korsakov, The Tsar's Bride; Founding Director of theatre laboratory at the Teatro Metastasio, Prato 1977; Produced Così fan Tutte at Teatro La Fenice, Venice 1983, Piccinni's Iphigénie en Tauride at Bari 1985, seen also in Paris and Rome; Teatro alla Scala with Rossi's Orfeo 1985 and Cherubini's Lodoiska 1990; Productions of Don Giovanni 1990 and I Vespri Siciliani at Bologna, Rossini's Ricciardo e Zoraide at the 1990 Pesaro Festival; Modern repertory includes stagings of works by Stockhausen, Berio and Globokar; Director of the Teatro Stabile at Turin from 1989. *Address:* c/o Teatro alla Scala, Via Filodrammatici 2, Milan, Italy.

RONGE Gabriela Maria, b. 3 July 1957, Hanover, Germany. Singer (Soprano). *Career:* Sang in opera at Heidelberg from 1982, Osnabruck from 1983 notably as Fiordiligi and Hanna Glawari; Further engagements at Hanover 1985-87, Cologne 1989, Frankfurt, Bonn, the Deutsche Oper Berlin and Brunswick; Bayerische Staatsoper Munich from 1987 as the Marschallin, Elsa, Eva and Agathe; Frankfurt 1987 as Gluck's Iphigénie, en Tauride, Paris Opera 1989, as Eva; Sang Isabella in Wagner's Das Liebesverbot at Palermo 1991; Noted interpreter of Lieder. *Address:* c/o Bayerische Staatsoper, Postfach 100148, 8000 Munich 1, Germany.

RONI Luigi, b. 22 Feb. 1942, Vergemoli, Lucca, Italy. Singer (Bass). *Education:* Studied with Sara Sforni Corti in Milan. *Debut:* Spoleto 1965, as Mephistopheles in Faust. *Career:* Sang in Milan, Rome, Turin, Venice, Palermo, Florence and Naples; Moscow 1973, with the La Scala company; Guest appearances in Vienna, Munich, Berlin, London, Paris, New York (City Center), Chicago, Dallas and Houston; Orange Festival 1984, as the Grand Inquisitor in Don Carlos; Other roles include Mozart's Commendatore and Mussorgsky's Dosifey; La Scala 1987, as Lodovico in Otello; Sang MacGregor in Mascagni's Guglielmo Ratcliff at Catonia, 1990; Rossini's Basilio at Bonn; Festival d'Orange 1990, as the Grand Inquisitor in Don Carlos. *Recordings include:* Aida (HMV); Don Giovanni (Philips); Fernand Cortez by Spontini; Zaira by Bellini; Otello. *Address:* c/o Teatro Massimo Bellini, I-95100 Catonia, Italy.

RONTGEN Joachim, b. 27 Oct. 1906, Amsterdam, Netherlands. Violinist. m. Annemarie Tutsch, 8 Apr. 1930. *Education:* With Telice Togni, Music School, Amsterdam, 1915-24; Professor B. Eldering, Hochschule Cologne, Germany, 1924-28; Studies with Professor Carl Flesch, Baden-Baden, 1929-30. *Career:* Concert Master, Winterthur Town Orchestra; Violin teacher, Winterthur Music School; Leader, Winterthur String Quartet, 1928-39; Violin teacher, Royal Conservatory, The Hague, 1939-71; Leader, Rontgen Quartet, 1940-68, 1973-85. Also: Violinist: Elite orchestra (conductor, Arturo Toscanini), Luzern, Switzerland 1938-39, Festival Orchestra (conductor, Pablo Casals), Prades, France 1951, 1953. *Compositions include:* Scales for violin. *Recordings:* Elite (Turicaphon, Zurich); String Quartets, Haydn, Mozart, Schubert, Dvorák. *Publication:* Memoirs: Music Is My Life, 1988. *Hobbies:* Walking; Reading. *Address:* Rosa Spier Huis, Laren NH, Netherlands.

ROOCROFT Amanda, b. 1966, Coppull, Lancashire, England. Singer (Soprano). *Education:* Studied at the Royal Northern College of Music with Barbara Robotham. *Career:* Sang Fiordiligi and Handel's Alcina while at the RNCM, 1988-98; Frequent appearances with the RNCM Chamber and Symphony Orchestras; Gave concerts at the Aix-en-Provence, Buxton and Greenwich Festivals, 1989; Professional operatic debut as Sophie in Der Rosenkavalier with Welsh National Opera, conducted by Charles Mackerras; Glyndebourne Touring Opera 1990 as Pamina, Fiordiligi at the Festival 1991; Covent Garden, 1991, as Pamina; Fiordiligi in Paris, Amsterdam and Lisbon with John Eliot Gardiner, 1992; Returned to Covent Garden for Giulietta/I Capuleti e I Montecchi, 1992; Debut at Bayerische Staatsoper, Munich, Fiordiligi/Così Fan Tutte, 1993; Debut at English National Opera, Ginevra in Ariodante, 1993; Covent Garden as Pamina in new production, 1993-94 season; Engaged by Glyndebourne as Donna Elvira in Don Giovanni for 1994 season (new production); Concert engagements include Mahler's 4th Symphony in Spain, Messiah in Porto and Lisbon and the Choral Symphony in Nottingham; Britten's Les Illuminations at the Greenwich Festival and in Antwerp; Mozart concerts conducted by Simon Rattle; Berg's Seven Early Songs with the Scottish Chamber Orchestra, 1991. *Recordings include:* Così fan Tutte (Deutsche Grammophon). *Honours include:* Various awards and prizes at the RNCM; Decca-Kathleen Ferrier Prize, 1988; Silver Medal of the Worshipful Company of Musicians, 1988; A Royal Philharmonic Society, Charles Heidsieck Award, 1991. *Current Management:* c/o Ingpen and Williams Ltd. *Address:* c/o Ingpen and Williams Ltd., 14 Kensington Court, London W8 5DN, England.

ROOLEY Anthony, b. 10 June 1944, Leeds, Yorkshire, England. Musician (Lutenist); Director; Lecturer. *Education:* Studied guitar at the Royal Academy of Music, 1965-68. *Career:* Teacher of guitar and lute at the RAM 1969-71; With James Tyler founded the Consort of Musicke 1969; As dirctor and lutenist has given many concerts of early music, in Europe, the Middle East and the USA; Sole director from 1972, often giving concerts with a Renaissance theme; Appearances on BBC TV and Radio; French and German TV and radio; International Festivals in Europe, Scandinavia and USA; Concerts with the sopranos Emma Kirkby and Evelyn Tubb, bass David Thomas, alto Mary Nichols, tenors Andrew King and Paul Agnew, and other early music specialists; Music-theatre activities include a staging of Le Veglie di Siena, Copenhagen and London 1988, with music by Orazio Vecchi; Collaboration with the troupe of Italian commedia dell'arte actors, La Famiglia Carrara, in The Marriage of Pantelone; Promenade Concert 1988, based on settings of the poet Torquato Tasso; Concerts in Tel-Aviv and New York, 1988; Joint Director with Arjen Terpstra of new record label Musica Oscura; Teacher in Japan, Padova (Italy), Basle and Dartington, promoting Renaissance Attitudes to Performance; Joint Director, with Don Taylor of film Banquet of the Senses. *Recordings include:* Complete works of John Dowland 21 record cycle; Grabbe, First Book of Madrigals; Music from the time of Christian IV; D'India, Il Terzo Libro di Madrigali (EMI); Music Dedicated to the House of Fugger (EMI); Monterverdi Solos and Duets (Pickwick); Welcome Every Guest (Nonesuch); Lamento d'Arianna (EMI); Madrigals by Monteverdi, de Rore, Marini, Porter, Marenzio (Musica Oscura). *Publications include:* A New Varietie of Lute Lessons (record and book), 1975; The Penguin Book of Early Music (record and book), 1979; Performance: Revealing the Orpheus Within (Element 1990). *Contributions to:* Lute Society Journal; Early Music Magazine; Guitar Magazine. *Memberships:* Viola da Gamba Society; Galpin Society; Wine Society. *Hobbies:* Renaissance Philosophy; Wine. *Address:* 54a Leamington Road Villas, London W11 1HT, England.

ROOT Deane Leslie, b. 9 Aug 1947, Wausau, Wisconin, USA. Musicologist; Museum Curator; Teacher; Librarian; Editor; Author. m. Doris J Dyen, 27 Aug 1972, 2 d. *Education:* New College, Sarasota, Florida; University of Illinois. *Career:* Research Associate, 1976-80, University of Wisconsin; Editorial Staff, New Grove Dictionary of Music and Musicians, 1974-76; Visiting Research Associate, Florida State University, 1981-82; Curator, Stephen Foster Memorial and Adjunct Assistant Professor in Music, 1982; Heinz Chapel Administrator, 1983-, University of Pittsburgh; Director of Cultural Resources, 1990, Adjunct Associate Professor, 1992, University of Pittsburgh. *Recordings:* Proud Traditions; Musical Tribute to Pitt. *Publications:* American Popular Stage Music 1860-1880; Music of Florida Historic Sites; co Author, Resources of American Music History; Co-Editor, Music of Stephen C Foster. *Contributions to:* New Grove Dictionary of Music and New Grove Dictionary of American Music; Various Journals, Yearbooks, Conference Proceedings. *Hobbies:* Singing: Shape - Note Music; Trumpet in Klezmer Music; Helping non Profit Cultural Organisations. *Address:* Foster Hall Collection, University of Pittsburgh, PA 15260, USA.

ROOTERING Jan-Hendrik, b. 18 Mar 1950, Flensburg, Germany. Singer (Bass). *Education:* Musikhochschule Hamburg. *Debut:* Gelsenkirchen 1980, in La Bohème; Sang in Hamburg and Munich from 1982; Frankfurt 1983, as Marke in Tristan und Isolde; Other roles include Wagner's Daland, Landgrave and Colonna (Rienzi), Verdi's Falstaff, Sparafucile and Banquo, Mozart's Commendatore and Osmin, and Tchaikovsky's Gremin; Season 1987 as Orestes at Geneva, King Marke at Amsterdam, Sarastro at Covent Garden and as Marcel in Les Huguenots at the Deutsche Oper Berlin; Metropolitan Opera 1987-90, as the Landgrave, Claggart, Sparafucile and Fasolt; Season 1988-89 as Sarastro in Vienna Riedinger in Mathis der Maler and Baron Ochs at Munich and the Landgrave (Tannhäuser) in Chicago; Sang Pogner in Die Meistersinger at La Scala, 1990 and at the Metropolitan, 1993; Often heard in oratorios. *Recordings include:* Dvořák's Requiem and Stabat Mater, Rigoletto, Don Giovanni (Eurodisc); Verdi's Alzira (Orfeo); La Bohème (HMV); Masses by Weber (Electrola). *Address:* c/o Bayerische Staatsoper, Postfach 745, D-8000 Munich 1, Germany.

ROOŸ DE Dorothy M. G., b. 21 Apr. 1946, Nuenen, Netherlands. Organist; Professor. *Education:* Sweelinck Conservatory, Amsterdam; Soloist Certificate, summa cum laude, 1969; Studies, Maurice Duruflé, Paris, France; Old Italian music, Professor Luigi Tagliavini, Bologna, Italy; Iberian music, Professor Macario Kastner, Lisbon, Portugal; Master classes, Anton Heiller, Marie-Claire Alain, Gustav Leonhardt. *Career:* Numerous solo recitals, Europe, USA, Canada; TV & radio appearances.Recitals, international music festivals; Lectures, master classes. Current appointments: Professor of Organ Music, Maastricht Conservatory Superior; Titular Organist, Augustinian Church, Eindhoven. *Recordings:* Christian Muller organ, St Bavo, Haarlem; Dutch historical instruments, Neerloon; Historical organ, Oudshoorn; Portuguese music, Capela da Universidade, Coimbra; 7 Historical Organs Portugal. *Contributions to:* Articles, music reviews. *Honours:* 1st prize, Stad Eindhoven, 1971; Prix d'Excellence (unanimous verdict, international jury), St Bavo, Haarlem, 1972. *Membership:* Toonkunstenaarsvereniging; Soroptimists. *Hobbies:* Philosophy; Art; History. *Address:* Het Puyven 25, 5672 RA Nuenen NBr, Netherlands.

ROPEK Jiří, b. 1 July 1922, Prague, Czeckoslavakia. Professor of Organ; Organist. m. Jirina Kupkova, 1 daughter. *Education:* Conservatory of Music, Prague; Charles University, Prague; Academy of Music, Prague. *Career:* Recitals, Czechoslovakia, 1950-; Most European Countries, 1960-; Regular Performances, USSR, Holland, Germany, UK; 1st Czechoslovakian Organist to Play in Royal Festival Hall, Westminster Cathedral; Professor of Organ, Prague Conservatory; Organist, St Jacobs Church, Prague; TV & Radio Appearances. *Compostitions Include:* Organ Variations on Victimae Pashali Laudes; Christmas Fantasy, For Choir, Orchestra and Organ; Toccata & Fugue for Organ and Toccata for John Scott, premiered at St Paul's Cathedral, 1993, published by Cathedral Music, 1993; Music for Brass and Organ, Partita on Adoro Te Devote, Sonatas for various solo instruments, flute, trumpet, oboe, violin, with organ, Mozart: Strahover Improvisation/historical torso completed 1983 by J Ropek, all published by Musikverlag P E Muster, Switzerland. *Recordings:* Numerous, Various Labels. *Address:* U Plátenice 2, 150 00 Prague 5, Czech Republic.

ROREM Ned, b. 23 Oct. 1923, Richmond, Indiana, USA. Composer. *Education:* American Conservatory Chicago with Leo Sowerby; 1940-42 Northwestern University; 1943 Curtis Institute Philadelphia; 1946 Juilliard School New York; Masters Degree, Juilliard, 1948; Private studies with Thomson and Copland. *Career:* Lived in Morocco 1949-51; France 1951-57; Composer-in-residence University of Buffalo 1959-61, University of Utah 1966-67; Curtis Institute from 1980. *Compositions:* 3 Symphonies, 1951, 1956, 1959; Design for orchestra 1953; A Childhood Miracle, opera 1955; The Poet's Requiem 1955; The Robbers, opera 1958; Eleven Studies for Eleven Players 1960; Ideas for orchestra 1961; Lift up your Heads for chorus and wind 1963; Lions (A Dream) for orchestra 1963; Miss Julie, opera 1965; Letters from Paris for chorus and orchestra 1966; Sun, 8 poems for high voice and orchestra; Water Music for clarinet, viola and orchestra 1966; Bertha, 1-act opera 1968; 3 Piano Concertos, 1950, 1951, 1969; Little Prayers for soprano, baritone and orchestra 1973; Air Music, variations for orchestra 1974; Serenade on Five English Poems 1975; Hearing, 5 scenes for singers and 7 instruments 1976; Sunday Morning for orchestra 1977; The Nantucket Songs 1979; Remembering Tommy, concerto for piano, cello and orchestra 1979; After Reading Shakespeare for solo cello 1980; After Long Silence for soprano, oboe and strings 1982; An American Oratorio 1983; Winter Pages, for 5 instruments, 1982; Whitman Cantata 1983; Violin Concerto 1984; Septet, Scenes from Childhood, 1985; Organ Concerto 1985; End of Summer, for violin, clarinet and piano 1985; String Symphony 1985; Homer (Three Scenes from the Iliad) for chorus and 8 instruments 1986; Goodbye My Fancy chorus, soloists, orchestra, 1988-89; The Auden Poems, Tenor and Piano Trio, 1989. *Publications:* Paris Dairy 1966; Music From

Inside Out, 1966; Music and People, 1968; New York Diary 1967; Critical Affairs 1970; The Later Diaries, 1974; Pure Contraption, 1974; Setting the Tone, 1980; The Nantucket Diary, 1985; Settling the Score, 1988. *Address:* c/o ASCAP,ASCAP Building, One Lincoln Plaza, New York, NY 10023, USA.

RORHOLM Marianne, b. 1960, Denmark. Singer (Mezzo-soprano). *Education:* Studied at the Opera Academy in Copenhagen. *Debut:* Royal Opera, Copenhagen, as Cherubino. *Career:* During season 1984-85 sang Olga, Lola and Rosina at Copenhagen and appeared as the Sorceress in Dido and Aeneas at the Paris Opéra; Frankfurt Opera, 1985-88, as Rosina, Dorabella, Sextus (La Clemenza di Tito), Nicklausse and Octavian; Sang Cherubino with the Israel Philarmonic under Daniel Barenboim and at the 1987 Ludwigsburg Festival; Bayreuth Festival 1988, as a Flowermaiden in Parsifal; Season 1988-89 included US debut with the Indianapolis Symphony under Raymond Leppard, a concert at Carnegie Hall, Cherubino at Glyndebourne and Isolier in Le Comte Ory for Netherlands Opera; Regular appearances with the Dusseldorf (Deutsche Oper am Rhein) and Basle Operas; Season 1992 as Annius in La Clemenza di Tito at Toulouse, Varvara in Katya Kabanova at Bonn, Purcell's Dido at Brussels, the Berlioz Marguerite at Amsterdam; Concert repertory includes Mahler's Das Lied von der Erde. *Recordings include:* Kate Pinkerton in Madame Butterfly, and Salome, conducted by Giuseppe Sinopoli (Deutsche Grammophon); Dryad in Ariadne auf Naxos (Philips). *Honours include:* Carl Nielsen Scholarship, 1984; Elisabeth Dons Memorial Prize, 1985. *Address:* c/o Ingpen and Williams Ltd., 14 Kensington Court, London W11 4PA, England.

ROS MARBA Antoni, b. 2 Apr 1937, Barcelona, Spain. Conductor. *Education:* Barcelona Conservatory; Studied Orchestral conducting with Eduard Toldra, with Celibidache, Accademia Chigiana, Siena, with Jean Martinon, Dusseldorf. *Debut:* Barcelona, 1962. *Career:* Principal Conductor: Spanish Radio and Television Orchestra, 1965-68, City of Barcelona Orchestra, 1967-77, Spanish National Orchestra, 1978-81, Netherlands Chamber Orchestra, 1979-86; Principal Guest Conductor and Artistic Consultant, Spanish Radio and Television Orchestra; Principal Guest Conductor, Netherlands Chamber Orchestra since it joined with Netherlands Philharmonic Orchestra, 1986-; Further appearances and tours worldwide, including principal cities and music centres in Europe, North and South America, Japan, China, and orchestras such as Berlin Philharmonic Orchestra; Apart from career as symphonic conductor has recently developed international career as opera conductor to great acclaim, with special success at Teatro de la Zarzuela, Madrid, Gran Teatro del Liceu, Barcelona; Appointed Musical Director, National Opera Theatre Teatro Real, Madrid, 1989; Season 1992 with the stage premiere of Gerhard's The Duenna at Madrid, repeated for Opera North. *Recordings include:* Haydn's Seven Last Words on the Cross; Recordings with Victoria de los Angeles, Teresa Berganza, English Chamber Orchestra, Netherlands Chamber Orchestra. *Honours:* National Music Prize of Spain, Ministry of Culture, 1989; Arthur Honneger International Recording Prize for Seven Last Words in the Cross; The Cross of St Jordi Generalitat de Cataluna. *Address:* c/o Teatro Real, Plaza de Isabel II s/n, 28013 Madrid, Spain.

ROS-FABREGAS Emilio, b. 31 Dec. 1955, Barcelona, Spain. Musicologist; Pianist; Conductor. *Education:* Piano studies, Conservatorio Superior Municipal de Musica, Barcelon, 1968-78, graduating as Profesor de Solfeo; Universidad Autonoma, Barcelona, 1973-75; Staatliche Musikhochschule, Freiburg, Germany, 1979; BM Piano Performance, 1981, MM Piano Performance 1983, Hartt School of Music, University of Hartford, USA; MPh 1987, PhD Candidate, Musicology, Graduate School, City University of New York. *Career:* Soloist, Escolania Colegio Balmes, 1962-70; Opera performances, Teatre del Liceo; Participated in Spanish premieres of Britten's War

Requiem and Penderecki's St Luke Passion; Conductor, Children's Choir Orfeo Atlantida, Barcelona, 1976-78; Graduate Music History Assistant, Hartt School of Music, USA, 1981-83; Assistant Conductor, Hartt Wind Ensemble and Contemporary Players, 1982-83; Freelance pianist, New York, 1983-; Performed with San Francisco New Music Ensemble of New York; Graduate Fellow, Brooklyn College, City University of New York, 1986-; Assistant Conductor, Brooklyn College Chorus and Chamber Chorus. *Publications:* Repertoire International de Litterature Musical (editorial assistant) 1983-; RIdIM/RCMI Inventory of Music Iconography (assistant editor) 1986, 1987; French Opera of the 17th and 18th Centuries (production editor), 1987-. *Hobbies:* Reading; Languages; Travel. *Address:* Graduate Center, City University of New York, Department of Music, 33 West 42nd Street, New York, NY 10036, USA.

ROSAND Aaron, b. 15 Mar 1927, Hammond, Indiana, USA. Violinist; Teacher. *Education:* Studied with Marinus Paulsen 1935-39 and Leon Samenti 1940-44, and Efrem Zimbalist 1944-48. *Debut:* With the Chicago Symphony under Frederick Stock playing the Mendelssohn Concerto, 1937. *Career:* Played at New York Town Hall, 1948; European debut at Copenhagen 1955; Tours of Europe, the Far East, and the USSR; Appearances with leading orchestras in the United States; Repertoire includes concertos by Lalo, Ries, Vieuxtemps, Joachim, Hubay and Wieniawski; Taught at the Academie Internationale d'Ete in Nice from 1971; Peabody Conservavtory, Baltimore and Mannes College, New York; Curtis Institute, Philadelphia 1981-; Plays a Guarneri del Gesù of 1741. *Recordings:* 15 CDs for Vox, Biddulph of London, Sony Harmonia Mundi, and Audiofon Record Co.*Honours include:* Chevalier pour Merite Cultural et Artistique, 1965; Gold Medal of the Fondation Ysaye, Belgium, 1967. *Current Management:* Jacques Leiser Artist Management*Address:* Jacques Leiser Artists Management, The Del Prado, 666 L/Pas Street, Suite 602, San Diego, CA 92103, USA.

ROSCOE Martin, b. 3 Aug. 1952, Halton, Cheshire, England. Pianist. *Education:* Royal Manchester College of Music (Marjorie Clementi, Gordon Green). *Career:* Appearances: Cheltenham, Bath, Leeds, South Bank Summer Music Festivals; Performances: Royal Festival Hall, Queen Elizabeth Hall, Royal Albert Hall, Wigmore Hall (London), with Hallé, City of Birmingham, Royal Philharmonic, Royal Liverpool Philharmonic, Northern Sinfonia, London Mozart Players, BBC Philharmonic Orchestras; Tours, Australia, Middle East, South America; Appearances: Harrogate Festival, with Scottish National Orchestra, BBC, Welsh Symphony Orchestras; Promenade Concerts, BBC Symphony Orchestra, 1987; French Philharmonic Orchestra, 1989. *Recordings:* Many for BBC Radio 3, including: Piano Concertos, Berwald, Liszt, Beethoven, Stravinsky, Fauré, Vaughan Williams, Shostakovich; Solo works, Beethoven; Complete sonatas of Schubert, Debussy, Liszt, Bartók; Concertos, Strauss, Szymanowski. Solo commmercial recordings, Liszt. *Honours:* Davas Gold Medal, 1973; Silver Medal, Worshipful Company of Musicians, 1974; British Liszt Piano Competition, 1976; Sydney International Piano Competition, 1981. *Memberships:* Incorporated Society of Musicians; Musicians Union. *Hobbies:* Fell walking; Reading; Cinema. *Current Management:* Hazard Chase Ltd, 25 City Road, Cambridge, England. *Address:* 225 Revidge Road, Blackburn, BB2 6DT, England.

ROSE Barry Michael, b. 24 May 1934, London, England. Organist; Choirmaster; Music Adviser. m. 21 Apr. 1965, 1 son, 2 daughters. *Education:* FRSCM, FRAM, Royal Academy of Music, 1958-50. *Career:* Organist, St Anne's, Chingford, 1946-56; Bass chorister, Hampstead Parish Church, 1956-58; Organist & Master of Choristers, Guildford Cathedral, 1960-74; Music adviser to Head of Religious Broadcasting, BBC, 1971-; Sub-Organist 1974-77, Master of the Choir, 1977-84, St Paul's Cathedral, London; Master of Choirs, King's School, Canterbury, 1984-88; Master of Music, St Alban's Abbey, 1988-. *Compositions:* Original

compositions & arrangements for radio and television. *Recordings:* Organist & conductor, various labels. *Publications:* Hymns, carols, song arrangements, for several published collections. *Honours:* 1 Platinum; 3 Gold Discs; 1 Silver Disc; D Mus. (Honoris Causa), City University, 1991; M. Univ, University of Surrey, 1992. *Hobbies:* Running a record company (Guild Records), founded 1967. *Address:* 31 Abbey Mill Lane, St Albans, Hertfordshire AL3 4HA, England.

ROSE Bernard William George, b. 9 May 1916, Little Hallingbury, Hertfordshire, England. Composer; Conductor; Organist; University Teacher; Editor. m. Molly Daphne Marshall OBE, JP, DL, 23 Dec. 1939. 3 sons. *Education:* Cathedral School, Salisbury, 1925-31; Royal College of Music, 1933-35; BMus 1938, BA 1939, St Catharine's College, Cambridge University; MA (Oxon et Cantab), 1946; DMus (Oxon), 1951; OBE, 1980. *Career:* Organist, Conductor, Eaglesfield Musical Society 1939-57, Fellow 1949-57, The Queen's College, Oxford; Lecturer in Music, Oxford University, 1950-81; Organist, Informator Choristarum and Fellow 1957-81, Vice President 1973-75, Magdalen College, Oxford; Conductor, Cambridge University Musical Society, 1938, The Bodley Singers 1947-52 and Oxford Symphony Orchestra 1971-73. *Published Compositions include:* Te Deum Laudamus, Jubilate Deo, Benedictus for Trebles and Organ, 1956; Versicles, Responses and Lord's Prayer, 1961; Magnificat and Nunc Dimittis in C Minor, 1968; According to His Promise, 1969; Praise ye the Lord, 1973; 3 Addison anthems, 1979; Author of Divine Life, 1980; Who are these? 1981; Surely thou hast tasted, 1981; Chimes for Organ, 1982. *Recordings include:* History of Music in Sound; English Polyphonic Church Music; Music at Magdalen (1 and 2); Music at Magdalen, Stainer; Music at Magdalen, Early English Music; Music from Venice; Music for Evensong, Pergolesi Miserere II. *Publications:* Tomkins Musica Deo Sacra, 1965, 1968, 1973, 1982, 1991, 1992; Proceedings of the Royal Musical Association, 1955-56; Handel's Susanna, 1967. *Contributions to:* The Musical Times; Music and Letters; Early Music; Oxford Magazine. *Hobbies:* DIY; Reading; Harpsichord; Bowls. *Address:* Bampton House, Bampton, Oxford OXI8 2JX, England.

ROSE Gregory, b. 18 Apr. 1948, Beaconsfield, England. Conductor. *Education:* BA, Magdalen College, Oxford University, 1967-70; Trained violinist, pianist and singer. *Career:* Conductor, Founder of Singcircle, Circle, 1977-; Music Director, London Jupiter Orchestra, 1986-; Conductor, Reading Festival Chorus, 1984-88; Conductor, London Concert Choir, 1988-; Conductor, Reading Symphony Orchestra, 1986-91; Conductor, National Youth Choir of Wales, 1986-89; Guest Conductor, BBC Concert Orchestra, Ulster Orchestra, Estonian National Symphonies Orchestra, Netherlands Radio Chamber Orchestra, BBC Singers, Nederlands Kamerkoor, Groupe Vocal de France, WDR Choir, Steve Reich and Musicians; Series Director, Cage at 70, Almeida Festival 1982 and Reich at 50, Almeida Festival, 1986. *Recordings:* Hyperion, Mouth Music, Stockhausen's Stimmung; Wergo: Son Entero by Alejandro Vinao: Continuum, music by Simon Emmerson; October Music, music by Trevor Wishart; Chandos, music by Janáček. Numerous recordings for BBC radio, television, Channel 4, ITV and European radio stations. *Publications:* Various compositions, Novello, Boosey & Hawkes, OUP. *Address:* 57 White Horse Road, London E1 0ND, England.

ROSE John Luke, b. 19 July 1933, Northwood Hills, Middlesex, England. Composer; Pianist; Lecturer; Teacher; Writer. *Education:* University of London, Trinity College of Music, 1954-58; BMus, London, 1957; LMus TCL, 1957; PhD, London, Wagner's Musical Language, 1963. *Debut:* 1958. *Career:* Extension Lecturer in Music, University of Oxford, 1958-66; Lecturer, Teacher and Examiner, Trinity College of Music, 1960-; (UK; USA; Newfoundland; Canada; Fiji; New Zealand; Australia; India); Part-time Teacher, St Marylebone Grammar School, 1960-66; Staff Tutor, University of London, Department Extra-Mural Studies, 1966-84.

Compositions: Symphony No 1, The Mystic, BBC Philharmonic, 1982; Piano Concerto, BBC Northern and Scottish Orchestras, 1977; Overture Macbeth, BBC Scottish Symphony Orchestra, 1977; Symphony No 2, 1985; Symphonic Dances, Halle Orchestra; String Quartet; Part-songs; 2 Piano Sonatas; Various Piano works; Violin Concerto, BBC Philharmonic, 1987; Blake's Songs of Innocence; Cantata The Pleasures of Youth; Hymns and Anthems; Apocalyptic Visions for piano; Musical play, St Francis, 1985; Opera, Odysseus, 1987. *Publications:* Wagner's Triston and Isolde: A Landmark in Musical History (introductory essay to libretto book: English National Opera Guide, No 6, 1981); Essay and Lecture: Ludwig, Wagner and the Romantic View (Victoria and Albert Museum Exhibition); BBC Interviews. *Address:* Kalon, 113 Farnham Road, Guildford, Surrey GU2 5PF, England.

ROSE Jurgen, b. 25 Aug 1937, Bernburg, Germany. Stage Designer. *Education:* Studied Acting and Painting in Berlin. *Career:* Ballet Designs for the Stuttgart Ballet, 1962-73; Collaborations with Director Otto Schenk for Don Carlos and Die Meistersinger in Vienna, Simon Boccanegra and Der Rosenkavalier at Munich and Così fan tutte in Berlin; Bayreuth Festival, 1972 and 1990, Tannhäuser and Der Fliegende Holländer, in productions by Götz Friedrich and Dieter Dorn; Salome and Die Entführung in Vienna, Lucia di Lammermoor and Lohengrin in Hamburg; Designed Die Zauberflöte for the Munich opera and the 1981 Ludwigsburg Festival; Premiere Isang Yun's Sim Tjong at Munich, 1972. *Recordings Include:* Video of Munich production of Die Zauberflöte. *Address:* c/o Bayerische Staatsoper, Postfach 100148, 8000 Munich 1, Germany.

ROSE Peter, b. 1961, Canterbury, Kent, England. Singer (Bass). *Education:* University of E. Anglia, Guildhall School of Music with Ellis Keeler; National Opera Studio. *Career:* Debut as Commendatore in Don Giovanni with Glyndebourne Opera in Hong Kong 1986 and on tour; Welsh National Opera, 1986-89, as Bartolo, Basilio, Prince Gremin in (Eugene Onegin), Angelotti (Tosca) & Osmin; Glyndebourne Touring Opera as Don Inigo in (L'Heure Espagnole), Osmin in (Die Entführung) and Basilio (Barbiere); Maggio Musicale Florence, as the Commendatore; Scottish Opera as Narbal in Les Troyens; Sang in La Damnation de Faust in Chicago, BBC Proms and Salzburg Festival with the Chicago Symphony under Solti. ENO: Angelotti; Covent Garden debut 1988, as Lord Rochefort in Anna Bolena; then Cadmus (Semele), Bonze (Butterfly), Lodovico (Otello), Nightwatchman (Meistersinger); Engaged as Kecal in The Bartered Bride, 1992; Commendatore, Gesler (Guillaume Tell) and Basilio at San Francisco, 1991-92; 1991, Amsterdam; Walther (Luisa Miller), Tutor, (Count Ory) and Marke (Tristan); 1992, Salzburg 1st Nazarene (Salome); Aix-en-Prevence, Bottom (Midsummer Night's Dream); 1993, Commendatore, Covent Garden. *Recordings include:* Nozze di Figaro with Barenboim and Berlin Philharmonic; Kurt Weill: Seven Deadly Sins (Also on Video); Video of Clemenza di Tito, Mozart, for Glyndebourne. Other roles include: Ramfis (Aida), Berlin Staatsoper, 1993; Hunding (Walküre), Berlin Staatsoper, 1994; Dosifei (Khovanshchina), Hamburg Staatsoper. *Address:* IMG Artists, 3 Burlington Lane, London W4, England.

ROSEBERRY Eric Norman, b. 18 July 1930, Sunderland, England. Musician; Writer. m. (1) Elspeth Mary Campbell, 20 Aug 1952, 4 daughters. (2) Frances Jill Sharp, 21 Aug. 1969. *Education:* Pocklington School, York, 1941-48; BA, BMus, University of Durham; PhD, University of Bristol, 1982. *Career:* Director of Music, Stand Grammar School for Boys, Manchester, 1953-58; County Music Organiser, Huntingdonshire, 1958-64; Music Assistant, BBC London, 1964-69; Radcliffe Lecturer in Music, University of Sussex, 1969-72; Lecturer for University of Bristol Extra-Mural Department, 1972-; Senior Lecturer in Music, Bath College of Higher Education, 1972-85; Director of Music, Bath Symphony Orchestra, 1977-1989; Founder Director of Apollo Ensemble of Bath, 1989. *Publications:* Faber Book of Christmas Carols and Songs, 1969; Dmitri

Shostakovich-His Life and Times (Midas), 1982; Essays appearing in Of German Music (Wolff), 1976; The Britten Companion (Faber), 1984; Benjamin Britten Death in Venice, Cambridge Opera Handbooks (CUP), 1987; Shostakovich's Musical Style (Garland USA), 1990. *Contributions to:* Articles, Reviews appearing in Tempo; The Listener; Music and Musicians; Music and Letters, Musical Times, CD Review; Programme Notes for BBC Symphony Concerts Aldeburgh Festival and Proms; Broadcast talks on BBC Radio 3. *Hobbies:* Gardening; Swimming; Walking; Cooking; Victorian book illustrations. *Address:* The Toll House, Marshfield, Chippenham, Wiltshire SN14 8JN, England.

ROSEN Albert, b. 14 Feb 1924, Vienna, Austria. Conductor. *Education:* Studied piano, composition and conducting at the Prague Conservatory and the Vienna Music Academy. *Career:* First operatic engagement at Pilsen; Has conducted many performances at the Prague National Theatre; First Conductor at the Smetana Theatre Prague 1964; Permanent Guest Conductor with the Prague Symphony Orchestra; Chief Conductor of the RTE Symphony Orchestra Dublin from 1969; Wexford Festival from 1972, Katya Kabanova, The Gambler, The Turn of the Screw, Hans Heiling, The Kiss, Königskinder, La Cena delle Beffe, The Devil and Kate and Der Templer und die Jüdin (Marschner) 1989; US debut San Francisco 1980, Jenůfa; Has conducted The Cunning Little Vixen in Strasbourg, Medée in Milan and The Greek Passion in Paris; With English National Opera has conducted Tosca, the British premiere of Rimsky-Korsakov's Christmas Eve 1988 and Katya Kabanova 1989; Conducted Carmen at Dublin, 1989; Salome at Vancouver, 1991; Currently Chief Conductor of the Western Australia Symphony Orchestra in Perth; Season 1992 with L'Italiana in Algeri for the Prague State Opera. *Address:* c/o Allied Artists, 42 Montpelier Square, London SW7 1JZ, England.

ROSEN Charles, b. 5 May 1927, New York City, USA. Pianist; Writer on Music.*Education:* Juilliard School 1934-38; Piano studies with Moritz Rosenthal and Hedwig Kanner-Rosenthal; Studied Romance languages at Princeton, PhD 1951. *Debut:* New York, 1951. *Career:* Recitalist and orchestral soloist in Europe and America; With Ralph Kirkpatrick premiered Elliott Carter's Double Concerto, New York 1961; Frequent performances of Beethoven, Bach, Boulez and Debussy; On faculty of SUNY, Stony Brook, 1971-; Gave Messenger Lectures, Cornell University, 1975. *Recordings:* First complete recording of Debussy's Etudes, 1951; Stravinsky's Movements with the composer conducting, 1961; Beethoven's last 6 sonatas, 1972; Boulez Piano Music, Vol. 1. *Publications:* The Classical Style: Haydn, Mozart, Beethoven, 1971; Schoenberg 1975; Sonata Forms 1980, (revised second edition, 1988). *Contributions to:* New York Review of Books and other journals. *Honours include:* National Book Award, 1972. *Address:* 101 W 78th Street, New York, NY 10024, USA.

ROSEN Jerome William, b. 23 July 1921, Boston, Massachusetts, USA. Composer; Clarinettist; Professor of Music. m. Sylvia T. Rosen, 1 son, 3 daughters. *Education:* MA, University of California, Berkeley, 1948; Special student at National Conservatory of Paris; Studied with Darius Milhaud, 1949-50; Professor of Music and director of electronic studio at University of California, Davis, from 1963. *Compositions include:* Sonata for clarinet and cello, 1954; 2 String Quartets, 1953, 1965; Suite for 4 Clarinets 1962; Three Songs for Chorus and Piano 1968; Clarinet Concerto 1973; Serenade for clarinet and violin 1977; Calisto and Melibea, chamber opera 1978; Campus Doorways for chorus and orchestra 1978; Music for 2 clarinets 1980; Fantasy for violin 1983; Concertpiece for clarinet and piano 1984. *Contributions to:* Various musical journals, and articles in Grove's Dictionary of Music and Musicians. *Honours:* George Ladd Prix de Paris, 1949-51; Fromm Foundation, 1952; Guggenheim Fellowship, 1958. *Memberships:* American Composers Alliance; Musicological Society. *Address:* Department of Music, University of California, Davis, CA 95616, USA.

ROSEN Jerome, b. 16 Nov. 1939, Detroit, USA. Violinist; Pianist. *Education:* Studied violin and piano from age 6; Violin with Josef Gingold in Cleveland and Ivan Galamian at the Curtis Institute, Philadelphia, 1955-58; Composition with Herbert Elwell in Cleveland and Wallingford Riegger in Stockridge; Studied chamber music with Alexander Schneider and conducting with George Szell and James Levine in Cleveland. *Career:* Joined Cleveland Orchestra as violinist and pianist, 1959-66; Detroit Symphony Orchestra 1968-72; Joined Boston Symphony Orchestra as violinist and keyboard player 1972; Chairman of chamber music studies at Berkshire Music Center; Rehearsal pianist for Ozawa, Rostropovich and Szell; Has also composed and written light verse. *Address:* c/o Boston Symphony Orchestra, Symphony Hall, 301 Massachusetts Avenue, Boston, MA 02115, USA.

ROSEN Nathaniel Kent, b. 9 June 1948, Altadena, California, USA. Cellist. m. Margo Shohl. *Education:* Studied with Eleonore Schoenfeld in Pasadena and with Piatigorsky at the University of Southern California, Los Angeles. *Career:* Assistant to Piatigorsky 1966-76; Solo debut with the Los Angeles Philharmonic 1969; New York debut 1970, Carnegie Hall; Principal cellist Los Angeles Chamber Orchestra 1972-76; Pittsburgh Symphony Orchestra 1977-79; Professor, University of Illinois at Champaign-Urbana, 1988; Appearances with leading American orchestras and as recitalist and in chamber music. *Recordings include:* Complete music for Cello and Piano by Chopin. *Contributions to:* American String Teacher. *Honours:* First Prize, Naumburg Competition, 1977; First Prize, Tchaikovsky Competition, Moscow, 1978. *Memberships include:* New York Violoncello Society; Century Association, New York. *Address:* 612 W Oregon, Urbana IL 61801, USA.

ROSEN Robert Joseph, b. 20 May 1956, Melfort, Saskatchewan, Canada. Composer; Performer. m. Deborah Alpaugh, 18 Aug. 1979. 2 sons, 1 daughter. *Education:* BMus with distinction, University of Alberta, 1977; Advanced Music Studies Programme of Banff Centre, 1979-81; Darmstadt Summer Course, 1982; Studied Composition with Violet Archer and Bruce Mather; Worked for short periods with John Cage, R Murray Schafer, Witold Lutoslawski, Iannis Xenakis and Morton Feldman; National Choreographic Workshop, Vancouver, 1985. *Career:* Broadcasts as performer on CBC National Radio; Compositions performed in Canada, Sweden, Netherlands, Germany, France, Spain, USA, Italy and Australia by such notable performers as Robert Aitken, Jean-Pierre Drouet and Alan Hacker; Founding Member, Performing ensemble, Fusion 5; Created film scores for documentaries produced by Helios Pictures for the National Film Board of Canada; Recordings on RCI and Centredisc Labels; Assistant Director, Music Programs at the Banff Centre for the Arts since 1991; Musical Director of Kokoro Dance. *Compositions:* From Silence, piano and orchestra; String Quartet, 1979; Krikos 1, 1980; Krikos, 11, 1982; Enigmas from the Muse; Meditation No 1, flute, violin and cello; Meditation No 2, small orchestra; Meditation No 4, two pianos; Meditation No 5, Mosaic, flute and piano; Meditation No 6, piano; Meditation No 7, Coro for 24 voices; In Anticipation of Beautiful Shadows, seven cellos; Mi istakistsi for flute, percussion and string quartet; Zero to the Power for violin, cello, taiko percussion and electronics; Stones, for 2 sopranos, tuba and percussion; Canyon Shadows: Stones; Animals, 1993 for 2 sopranos, alpenhorn and tuba. *Publications:* Canadian Composers at Banff, Celebration, Canadian Music Centre. *Address:* PO Box 1726, Canmore, Alberta, Canada T0L 0M0.

ROSENBAUM Harold, b. 24 Jan. 1950, Danville, Pennsylvania, USA. Conductor. *Education:* BA 1972, MA, Aaron Copland School of Music, 1974, Queens College, City University of New York. *Career:* Founder, Conductor, Canticum Novum Singers, New York, appearing Carnegie Hall, Alice Tully Hall, 92 St Y, also Madeira Bach Festival, Portugal (Broadcast Europe and America); Appearances on several radio stations, New York City, also WOR TV; Guest Conductor, Avery Fischer

Hall, Lincoln Center, with The Village Singers, New York Choral Society, The Pleasantville Cantata Singers; Has conducted American and New York premieres of works of Ravel, Fauré, others; Currently Assistant Professor, Queens College, City University of New York, Flushing. *Compositions:* Arrangements: In Darkness Let Me Dwell (John Dowland), 1980; Flow My Tears (John Dowland), 1980. *Recording:* From Schütz to Schoenberg, with The Canticum Novum Singers. *Honours:* Karol Rauthaus Memorial Award, 1972; Winston Churchill Travelling Fellowship, New York branch, English-Speaking Union, 1983. *Memberships:* Association of Professional Vocal Ensembles; Past Member, Association of Choral Conductors.

ROSENBAUM Victor, b. 19 Dec. 1941, Philadelphia, Pennsylvania, USA. Musician; Pianist; Conductor; Administrator. 2 daughters. *Education:* BA (Hons), Brandeis University, 1964; MFA, Princeton University, 1967; Aspen Music School, 1957-60; Piano with Leonard Shure, Rosina Lhevinne; Composition with Roger Sessions, Earl Kim, Edward T Cone; Chamber Music with Robert Koff, Eugene Lehner. *Career:* Solo performances in USA, Japan, Brazil, Israel and the Soviet Union; Chamber performances with artists Leonard Rose, Laurence Lesser, Roman Totenberg, Arnold Steinhardt; Cleveland, Vermeer, New World Quartets; Tully Hall; Town Hall (New York); Jordan Hall, Boston; Conductor, Concerto Company (chamber orchestra); Former Faculty Member: Eastman School of Music, Brandeis University; Faculty Member, New England Conservatory; Director, Longy School of Music, Cambridge, Massachusetts. *Compositions:* For voice, piano, chorus, chamber ensemble and theatre pieces. *Recordings:* John Harbison Trio, CRI. *Contributions to:* College Music Society Symposium. *Honours:* Young Composers' Award; Indiana Young Artists Award. *Memberships:* College Music Society; Music Teachers National Association. *Address:* Longy School of Music, 1 Follen Street, Cambridge, MA 02138, USA.

ROSENBOOM David, b. 9 Sept 1947, Fairfield, Iowa, USA. m. Jacqueline Humbert, 17 July 1981, 1 s, 1 d. *Education:* Studied at the University of Illinois. *Career:* Dean of the School of Music, California Institute of the Arts; Darius Milhaud Professor of Music at Mills College; Teacher Interdisciplinary Subject, San Francisco Art Institute and the California College of Arts & Crafts; Guest Faculty Member at Many Institutions; Founder of the Department of Music and Interdisciplinary Graduate Studies Programme, York University in Toronto; Creative Associate, Centre for Creative and Performing Arts at SUNY. *Recordings include:* Brainwave Music; On Being Invisible; Future Travel; Suitable Framing; And Out Come the Night Ears; Systems of Judgement; A Precipice in Time. *Publications:* Two Books: Biofeedback and the Arts; Extended Musical Interface With the Human Nervous System. *Address:* School of Music, California Institute of the Arts, 24700 McBean Parkway, Valencia, CA 91355, USA.

ROSENFELD Gerhard, b. 10 Feb 1931, Königsberg, Germany. Composer. *Education:* Studied Musicology at the Humboldt University, East Berlin and Composition with Rudolf Wagnar Regeny. *Career:* Worked in Berlin, 1961-64, the Moved to Potsdam as Freelance Composer. *Compositions include:* Operas Das Alltagliche Wunder, Stralsund, 1973; Der Mantel, after Gagol, Weimar, 1978; Das Spiel Von Liebe und Zufall, Potsdam, 1980; Die Verweigerung, after Gogol, Osnabruck, 1989. *Address:* c/o Stadtische Buhnen, Domhof 10-11, 4500 Osnabruck, Germany.

ROSENKRANZ Helge, b. 1962, Austria. Violinist. *Career:* Member, Franz Schubert Quartet, Vienna, 1989-; Many concert engagements, Europe, USA, Australia, including appearances at Amsterdam Concertgebouw, Vienna Musikverein and Konzerthaus, Salle Gaveau, Paris and Sydney Opera House; Visits to Zurich, Geneva, Basle, Hamburg, Rome, Rotterdam, Madrid and Copenhagen; Festival engagements include Salzburg, Wiener Festwochen, Prague Spring, Schubertiade at

Hohenems, Schubert Festival in Washington DC. Belfast Festival, Istanbul Festival; Tours of Australasia, USSR, USA; Frequent concert tours, UK; Featured in Concerto by Spohr with Royal Liverpool Philharmonic, Liverpool and Festival Hall, London; Many appearances, Wigmore Hall and Cheltenham Festival; Masterclasses, Royal Northern College of Music, Lake District Summer Music. *Recordings include:* Schubert's Quartet in G, D877; Complete quartets by Dittersdorf. *Address:* c/o Christopher Tennant Artists Management, 11 Lawrence Street, London SW3 5NB, England.

ROSENSHEIN Neil, b. 27 Nov 1947, New York, USA. Singer (Tenor). *Education:* Studied in New York. *Debut:* Florida Opera 1972, as Almaviva in Il barbiere di Siviglia. *Career:* Sang in Washington, Dallas, Boston and Santa Fe; European debut Vaison-la-Romaine 1980 as Almaviva; Further appearances in Geneva, Zurich and Paris; Covent Garden debut 1986, as Lensky in Eugene Onegin; Chicago Lyric Opera 1988, as Alfredo in La Traviata; Sang in the premiere of The Aspern Papers by Dominick Argento, Dallas 1988; Berlioz Festival Lyons 1989, as Benvenuto Cellini; Other roles include Mozart's Tamino and Belmonte, Verdi's Fenton and Don Carlos, Massenet's Des Grieux and Werther (Turin and Sydney, 1989), (Metropolitan 1989) and Steva in Jenůfa; Season 1992/93 at the Met as Faust, Werther, Traviata (Alfredo), and Léon in the premiere of Corigliano's The Ghosts of Versailles; Sang the Berlioz Faust at Turin, 1992, Peter Grimes at Sydney. *Recordings:* Onegin, (EMI).*Address:* c/o Metropolitan Opera, Lincoln Center, New York, NY 10023, USA.

ROSENTHAL Manuel, b. 18 June 1904, Paris, France. Conductor; Composer. m. Claudine Verneuie, 2 sons. *Education:* Studied with Ravel at the Paris Conservatory, 1918-23. *Career:* Conducted French Radio Orchestra 1934-47; Musical Director and Conductor, Orchestre National de Paris 1945-48; Conducted Seattle Symphony Orchestra 1949-51; Royal Orchestra of Liège, Belgium, 1964-67; Composer-in-Residence, College of Puget Sound, Washington, 1948-49; Guest conductor with various orchestras in the USA; Conducted Oedipus Rex and Carmina Burana at New York City Opera 1977; French repertory, including Dialogues des Carmélites and Manon at the Metropolitan from 1981; Conducted The Ring at Seattle 1986; Has conducted the French premieres of works by Bartók, Stravinsky, Strauss, Prokofiev and Britten. *Compositions:* Sonata for 2 violins and piano; La Fête du Vin for orchestra; Musique de Table for orchestra; Magin Manhattan; Desese Deo Gratias; La Poule Noire; Les Femmes au Tombeau.*Recordings include:* Violin Concertos by Saint-Saëns and Vieuxtemps, Lalo Symphonie Espagnole (Grumiaux); Chopin 1st Concerto Cziffra; Debussy La Demoiselle Elue. *Honours:* Knight, Legion of Honour; Officer of Arts and Letters. *Address:* c/o Seattle Opera Association, PO Box 9248, Seattle, WA 98109, USA.

ROSKELL Penelope, b. 1960, Oxford, England. Pianist. m. Richard Griffiths, 26 Oct. 1985. *Education:* GMus (RNCM) Hons, PPRNCM, Royal Northern College of Music; Private study with Guido Agosti, Rome, Italy. *Career:* Solo pianist, tours worldwide at invitation of the British Council; Concerts regularly Western and Eastern Europe, Scandinavia, USA, Africa, Asia, Middle and Far East; 1988, First Prize Winner, British Contemporary Piano Competition and Formerly Piano Tutor at Keele University; Broadcasts: BBC Radio 3, WFMT Radio Chicago, British and Polish Television; Professor of Piano, London College of Music; Recitals, Wigmore Hall, Purcell Room; Concerto engagements include recording with Oxford Pro Musica; Tours with Manchester Camerata and the Bournemouth Sinfonietta under Simon Rattle. *Current Management:* Helen Sykes Artists' Management. *Address:* c/o Helen Sykes' Artists Management, 79 Bickenhall Mansions, Bickenhall Street, London W1, England.

ROSS Elinor, b. 1 Aug. 1932, Tampa, Florida, USA. Singer (Soprano). *Education:* Studied with the late Zinka Milanov in New York. *Debut:* Cincinnati Opera 1958, as Leonora in Il Trovatore. *Career:* Guest appearances in Boston, Chicago, Baltimore and Philadelphia; New York, Carnegie Hall, in the 1968 US premiere of Verdi's Alzira; Metropolitan Opera from 1970, debut as Turandot; European engagements at La Scala, Bologna, Palermo, Vienna, Budapest, Zagreb, Verona and Florence; Other roles include Bellini's Norma, Verdi's Aida, Elisabetta, Amelia, Lady Macbeth and Abigaille, Mozart's Donna Anna, Puccini's Tosca and Giordano's Maddalena; Sang Tosca at the Metropolitan 1973, the Trovatore Leonora at Buenos Aires, 1974; Frequent concert appearances. *Address:* c/o Metropolitan Opera, Lincoln Centre, New York, NY 10023, USA.

ROSS Elise, b. 28 April 1947, New York, USA. Singer (Soprano). m. Simon Rattle. *Career:* Sang with the Juilliard Ensemble New York and the Los Angeles Philharmonic Orchestra from 1970; Performances of music by Berio in USA and Europe (Passagio in Rome); Tour of Europe with the London Sinfonietta; Appearances at Royan and Bath Festivals and in Venice and Warsaw; Sang in Bussotti's Passion selon Sade and Le Racine (La Scala 1981); Concerts with the Ensemble Intercontemporain, Paris, from 1976; Repertoire includes Berlin Cabaret songs, Lieder by composers of the Second Viennese School, Chansons by Ravel and Debussy and Lieder by Mozart, Schumann and Strauss; Shostakovich Symphony 14 with the L.A. Philharmonic and Ensemble Intercontemporain; Has sung Cherubino for Opera SO, Opera North and for Long Beach Opera; Marie in Wozzeck at Los Angeles (1989) and Mélisande with Netherlands Opera and Berlioz Romeo and Juliette, Rotterdam, 1993. *Address:* c/o John Coast, 31 Sinclair Road, London W14 0NS, England.

ROSS Glynn (William), b. 15 Dec 1914, Omaha, Nebraska. Administrator; Stage Director. *Career:* Stage Director at the Teatro San Carlo Naples, 1945-47 and 1960-63; Stage Producer, San Francisco Opera, 1948-60, Los Angeles Opera Theatre, 1948-60, Fort Worth Opera, 1948-56, New Orleans Opera Association, 1949-62; Has also produced opera in Philadelphia; Founded the Seattle Opera Association, 1963, Presenting the World Premieres of Floyd's of Mice and Men, 1972 and Pasatieri's Black Widow, 1972; Instituted the Pacific North West Wagner Festival, 1975, with Ring Cycles in German and English; General Director of Arizona Opera Company at Phoenix From 1983.

RÖSSEL-MAJDAN Hildegard, b. 30 Jan. 1921, Moosbierbaum, Austria. Singer (Contralto). m. DDDr, Karl Rossel-Majdan. 1 daughter. *Education:* HS for music and dramatic art, Vienna. *Career:* Concert and Oratorio singer under leading Austrian and foreign conductors, 1948-; Member, Vienna State Opera, 1951-71; Professor, University for Music and Dramatic Art, Vienna, 1971-1991; Concerts, opera and oratorio in Europe, USA and Japan; Lecturer in Austrian, seminaries and in Japan; President of Goetheanistic Konservatory and Waldorfpedagogical Akademy. *Recordings:* Westminster, USA. *Address:* Agnesgasse 13, Vienna, Austria.

ROSSELLI John, b. 8 June 1927, Florence, Italy. Writer on Music. *Education:* Studied at Swarthmore College, Pennsylvania; Research student at Peterhouse, Cambridge. *Career:* Leader Writer, and Deputy London Editor, The Manchester Guardian; Teacher, Reader in History at Sussex University, 1964-89. *Publications include:* The Opera Industry in Italy from Cimarosa to Verdi, Cambridge, 1984; Music and Musicians in Nineteenth Century Italy, London, 1991; Singers of Italian Opera; The History of a Profession, Cambridge, 1992. *Address:* c/o Cambridge University Press, Edinburgh Building, Shaftesbury Road, Cambridge CB2 2RU, England.

ROSSI Luke, b. 17 Sept. 1947, Argentia. Clarinettist. *Education:* National Music Teacher Degree, Degree in Music Interpretation, Clarinet, Liceo Cervantes, National

Conservatoire, Buenos Aires, 1968; Clarinet with Guy Deplus, Paris, France, 1970; Postgraduate studies Royal College of Music, 1975; Music Degree, clarinet, University of Chile, 1978. *Debut:* Teatro Colón, Buenos Aires, Argentina, 1973. *Career includes:* Principal Clarinet, National Symphony Orchestra, Lima, Peru, 1968-70; Principal Clarinet, San Juan Symphony Orchestra, Argentina, 1974-77; Soloist with Ensemble Musical, 1976; Tour with Thomas Tichauer and Monica Cosachov, Switzerland, 1977; Principal Clarinet 1978-80, Soloist 1980, Chile Symphony Orchestra; Principal Clarinet 1981-82, European tour soloist, 1981, Venezuela's Symphony Orchestra; Principal Clarinet, Chile Philharmonic Orchestra, 1982-86; Soloist, Buenos Aires Philharmonic Orchestra, Teatro Colón, Argentina, 1983; Soloist, Venezuelan National Youth Orchestra and Chilean Chamber Orchestra, 1987; Recitals throughout South America; Master courses, Organization of American States, Costa Rica. *Recordings:* Stravinsky, Schumann, Bruch and Vanhal. *Publication:* Single Reed Instruments, 1st volume, 1987. *Address:* Instituto de Musica, Universidad Catolica de Chile, Pdte Battle y Ordonez 3300, Santiago, Chile.

ROSSI Nick, b. 14 Nov. 1924, San Luis Obispo, California, USA. Opera Administrator; Author. *Education:* BMus 1948, MMus 1952, University of Southern California; PhD, Sussex College of Technology, 1971. *Career:* Supervisor of Music, Los Angeles City Schools, 1948-68; Senior Professor of Music, City University of New York, 1973-83; Administrative Director, Studio Lirico 1983-, Fiesta Musicale Stiana 1985-88, Italy. Producer: 4 Saints in 3 Acts (Thomson), US West Coast premiere, 1962; Liberty? (Roy Harris), 1963; Virgil Thomson Festival, 1971; Castelnuovo-Tedesco (C-T) Festival, 1974; Carmen Moose Festival, 1976; Women in Music Festival, 1978; Song of Songs (C-T) world premiere, 1973; L'Importanza de esse Franco (C-T), European premiere, 1984; Imeneo (Handel), New York premiere, 1984. *Recordings:* As producer, & author of programme notes, various labels, UK, Holland, USA. *Publications:* Music Through the Centuries, 1963; Music of Our Time, 1969; Pathways to Music, 1970; Musical Pilgrimage, 1971; Electronic Music, 1971; 20th-Century Music & Art, 1972; Hearing Music, 1981; J. S. Bach: Biography in Pictures, 1985; Opera in Italy, in progress. Italian/European correspondent, various journals. *Address:* Via Pian delle Macchie 100, I-50063 Figline Valdarno, Italy.

RÖSSLER Almut, b. 12 June 1932, Beveringen, Germany. Organist; Choral Director. *Education:* Studied organ with Michael Schneider at Detmold and Gaston Litaize in Paris; Piano with Hans Richter-Haaser and choral direction with Kurt Thomas. *Career:* Performances of music by such contemporary composers as André Jolivet, Giselher Klebe (Organ Concerto, 1980) and Olivier Messiaen: premieres of Le Mystère de la sainte Trinité (1972) and Le Livre du saint Sacrement (1986); Kantor at the Johanneskirche Dusseldorf and Professor of Organ at the Robert Schumann Conservatory; Founder and director of the Johannes-Kantorei, giving a capella work and performing in oratorios; Director of Messiaen festivals at Dusseldorf 1968, 1972, 1979 and 1986; Master classes in Japan and at Yale University. *Honours include:* Organist of the Year, Yale University, 1986. *Address:* Staatliche Hochschule für Musik Rheinland, Robert Schumann Institut, Fischerstrasse 110, D-4000 Dusseldorf, Germany.

ROSSMANITH Gabriele, b. 1960, Stuttgart, Germany. Singer (Soprano). *Education:* Started violin studies at the Staatliche Hochschule für Musik Trossingen which finished with an artistic exanination in violin, Music Teacher; Studies in singing with Professor Sylvia Geszty up to 1984; Final examination at the Hochschule für Darstellende Kunst Stuttgart, 1985. *Career:* Sang at the Badisches Stadttheater Karlsruhe, 1985-88; Hamburg Staatsoper from 1988, Notably as Susanna (Le Nozze di Figaro), Sophie (Rosenkavalier), Marzelline (Fidelio), Gretel (Hänsel and Gretel), Musetta (La Bohème), Despina (Così fan tutte),

Pamina (Zauberflöte). Various performances at important opera houses in München, Frankfurt, and Barcelona. Guest contracts with Dresdner Staatsoper (Semperoper), Opernhaus Leipzig, Theatre Royal de la Monnaie Brüssel and Komische Oper Berlin. Various tours included USA, South America in 1991 and Japan in 1992. *Honours include:* Scholarship for Study in Japan; 1st Prize, Mozartfest-Wettbewerb Würzburg. *Current Management:* Artists Management Hartmut Haase, Lister Meile 78, D-30161 Hannover, Germany. *Address:* c/o Staatsoper Hamburg, Grosse-Theatrestrasse 34, 2000 Hamburg 36, Germany.

ROSTROPOVICH Mstislav, b. 27 Mar. 1927, Baku, USSR. Cellist; Pianist; Conductor. m. Galina Vishnevskaya 15 May 1955. 2 daughters. *Education:* Moscow Conservatory. *Debut:* USSR, 1941; International, 1948. *Career:* Professor, Moscow, Leningrad Conservatories; Music Director, National Symphony Orchestra, Washington DC, USA, 1977; Conducting Debut, 1961; Artistic Director, Aldeburgh Festival, Evian Festival; Over 30 Honorary Degrees including: Oxford, Cambridge, Yale, Harvard, Trinity University (Dublin), St Andrews University (Scotland); Prokofiev and Shostakovich wrote concertos for him, Britten the 3 Cello suites and Cello Symphony; has also premiered the Shostakovich cello sonata, concertos by Bliss, Lutoslawski, Christobal Halffter, 1986 and Panufnik, 1992; Tout un Monde Lointain by Dutilleux and Walton's Passacaglia; as conductor has premiered works by Bernstein, Landowski, Mennin (9th Symphony), Walton (Prologue and Fantasia), Schnittke (Seid nüchtern und Wachet) and Penderecki (Polish Requiem); Opera engagements include, The Queen of Spades at San Francisco, 1975 and Eugene Onegin at Aldeburgh, 1979; Tsar's Bride, Washington DC, 1986; Conducted Prokofiev's The Duenna at the Royal Academy of Music, London, 1991; Season 1992 with the premieres of Gubaidulina's opera-oratorio-ballet Orazione per l'era di Acquario, at Genoa, and Schnittke's Life With an Idiot at Amsterdam; Conducted The Golden Cockerel at the Barbican Hall, London, 1992. *Recordings include:* CDs of Beethoven's Triple Concerto and Dvořák Cello Concerto, Berlin PO; Britten's Cello Symphony, Debussy and Schubert Sonatas (Decca); Dutilleux and Lutoslawski Concertos (EMI); Mozart Flute Quartets (CBS); Boris Godunov (Erato). *Honours:* Stalin Prize, Lenin Prize, People's Artist of USSR; Officier Legion of Honor, France; Decorations - Medal of Freedom, Germany Russia USA, Spain, Portugal, Sweden, Denmark, Greece, Lebanon, Venezuela; Fellow, Royal College of Music; KBE, 1987. *Memberships:* Academy of Arts and Sciences, USA; Academy of St Cecilia, Rome: Royal Swedish Academy; Royal Academy of Music, England. *Current Management:* Ronald A Wilford, Columbia Artists Management, Inc. *Address:* National Symphony Orchestra, Kennedy Center, Washington DC 20566, USA.

ROTENBERG Sheldon, b. 11 Apr. 1917, Attleboro, Massachusetts, USA. Concert Violinist. m. 29 Jan. 1950. 1 son, 1 daughter. *Education:* AB, Tufts Unviersity, 1939; Graduate School, 1940; Student of Felix Winternitz, Boston, Georges Enesco, Maurice Hewitt, Paris; Faculty, Boston University Tanglewood Institute. *Debut:* Boston Pops, 1939, 1941. *Career:* Member, Boston String Quartet, New England Conservatory; Concerts throughout New England and at Library of Congress, Washington, 1948-57; First Violin Section, Boston Symphony Orchestra, 1948-. *Recordings:* With Library of Congress-Boston String Quartet, Mozart D Minor Quartet, Barber (Opus 11) Quartet, Debussy String Quartet. *Honours:* Cultural Exchange Representative, Boston Symphony in State Department Programme with Japan Philharmonic, Tokyo, 1969, as Teacher Soloist & member of orchestra. *Hobbies:* Reading; Tennis. *Address:* 60 Browne St, Brookline, MA 02146, USA.

ROTH Daniel, b. 31 Oct 1942, Mulhouse, France. Organist. *Education:* Studied at the Paris Conservatoire 1960-70, with Maurice Durufle. Further study with Marie Claire Alain. *Career:* Organist at Sacre-Coeur

Paris 1963-85; Professor of Organ, Marseille Conservatoire 1973-79, later at Strasbourg Conservatoire; Visiting Professor at the Summer Academy, Haarlem, Holland; Professor, Catholic University and resident artist at the National Shrine, Washington DC, 1974-76; Organist at Saint-Sulpice, Paris, since 1985; Professor at the Saarbrücken Musikhochschule 1988. *Compositions:* Final Te Deum (Bärenreiter 1993), Hommage à César Franck (Leduc 1993), Joie, Douleur et Gloire de Marie (Novello 1990). *Recordings:* C Franck: Les 12 Pièces et Pièes choisies pour orgue; C M Widor: Symphonies V and X, Symphonies III and VII (Motette-Ursina, Düsseldorf). *Honours include:* Premier Prix in harmony, improvisation, counterpoint, fugue organ and accompaniment at the Paris Conservatoire; SACEM Prize Nice, 1964; Interpretation Prize at Arnhem 1964; Improvisation Prize, Amis de l'Orgue, Paris, 1966; First Prize, International Competition, Chartres 1971; Chevalier de l'ordre des Arts et des Lettres, 1986. *Address:* Musikhochschule des Saarlandes, Bismarckstrasse 1, 66 Saarbrücken, Germany.

ROTH David Robert, b. 9 Mar. 1936, Stockton-on-Tees, County Durham, England. Violinist. m. Ruth Elaine West, 22 July 1963. 2 sons. *Education:* University of Edinburgh, 1953-54; Royal Academy of Music, 1954-59; LRAM. *Debut:* West Linton, Peebles, Scotland, 1954. *Career:* With Netherlands Chamber Orchestra, Amsterdam, 1960-64; Played Bloch Sonata No 1, KOT Israel Radio, Tel Aviv, 1962; Deputy Leader, Northern Sinfonia Orchestra, Newcastle-upon-Tyne, 1966-68; 2nd violin, Allegri String Quartet, 1969-. *Recordings:* With Allegri String Quartet for Open University. *Honours:* MMus, Hull, 1975; ARAM. *Memberships:* Incorporated Society of Musicians; Musicians Union. *Hobbies:* Chess; Theatre; Reading. *Current Management:* Dominic Barrington, 61 Lime Grove, New Malden, KT3 3TP. *Address:* 16 Oman Avenue, London NW2 6BG, England.

ROTHENBERGER Anneliese, b. 19 June 1924, Mannheim, Germany. Singer (Soprano). m. Gerd Dieberich 1954. *Education:* Mannheim Musikhochschule with Erika Muller. *Debut:* Koblenz 1943. *Career:* Hamburg Staatsoper 1046-73, notably as Blonde in Die Entführung, Verdi's Oscar and Lulu: visited Edinburgh with the company in 1952, for the British premiere of Hindemith's Mathis der Maler; Vienna Staatsoper from 1953; Salzburg from 1954, in the premiere of Liebermann's Penelope and Die Schule der Frauen: also sang Papagena in Die Zauberflöte, Zdenka in Arabella, Sophie in Der Rosenkavalier and Flaminia in Haydn's Il Mondo della Luna; Glyndebourne 1959-60, as Sophie; Metropolitan Opera debut 1960: returned as Susanna, Oscar and Sophie; Zurich 1967, in the premiere of Sutermeister's Madame Bovary; Tour of Russia 1970. *Recordings:* Le Nozze di Figaro; Die Fledermaus; Martha; Der Wildschütz; Die Entführung; Arabella; Gluck's Le Cadi Dupé; Sophie in 1960 film version of Der Rosenkavalier. *Publication:* Melodie meines Lebens (autobiography) 1972. *Address:* c/o Hamburgische Staatsoper, Grosse-Theaterstrasse 34, D-2000 Hamburg 36, Germany.

ROTHFUSS Earl Levering, b. 20 Apr. 1952, Hannibal, Missouri, USA. Pianist; Accompanist. *Education:* BM, Piano, magna cum laude, University of Missouri, Columbia, 1974; MM, Accompanying, University of Southern California, Los Angeles, 1976. *Career:* Numerous recitals throughout USA, Canada and Europe with artists such as Marilyn Horne, Carol Neblett, John Alexander, Stephen Dickson, William Parker, Janice Taylor, Kathleen Battle, Spiro Malas, James Atherton, Jennifer Jones, Brenda Boozer, Licia Albanese and others; Numerous TV appearances on The Tonight Show, 1978-80; Musical Assistant, Chautauqua Opera, 1981; Musical Assistant, Glimmerglass Opera, 1984; Musical Assistant, Glimmerglass Opera and Festival Aix-en-Provence, 1985; Instructor of Piano, Pepperdine University, Malibu, California, 1977. *Membership:* Pi Kappa Lambda. *Address:* 315 W 104th Street, New York, NY 10025, USA.

ROTZSCH Hans-Joachim, b. 25 April 1929, Leipzig, Germany. Singer (Tenor); Educator. *Education:* Institute for Church Music at the Musikhochschule Leipzig, 1949-53; Organ with Gunter Ramin; Vocal studies with P. Losse and P. Polster in Leipzig. *Career:* Many concerts and recordings of sacred music in East and West Germany, Switzerland, Austria, Poland, USSR and Czechoslovakia; Appearances at the Leipzig Opera from 1961; Kantor at St Thomas' School, Leipzig, from 1972; President of Bach-Committee, East Germany, 1983. *Recordings:* Bach Cantatas and the St Luke Passion by Schütz (Deutsche Grammophon); Dessau's Das Verhör des Lukullus (Telefunken); Mendelssohn's Elijah (Philips).

ROUCHON Jean-Philippe, b. 20 Oct 1957, Paris, France. Conductor. m. Claire Bertin, 9 July 1983, 1 son. *Education:* Maitrise, Musicology, Diploma of Conductor, Paris. *Debut:* 1977. *Career:* Regular appearances with French Youth Orchestra, 1977-84; Foundation of Maurice Ravel Orchestra, Vienna, 1985; Salzburg Theatre, 1987; Schubert Opera, Styriarte Graz, 1990. *Recordings:* 3 CDs: Rameau, Haydn; Wiener Walzer; Milhaud. *Publications:* Maitrise: Conductor Experience of Youth Orchestras in France, 1982. *Hobbies:* Aerobics; Jazz dance. *Current Management:* The Agency, Austria. *Address:* The Agency, Sandleitengasse 15-17, 1760 Vienna, Austria.

ROULEAU Joseph, b. 28 Feb. 1929, Matane, Quebec, Canada. Singer (Bass). *Education:* Montreal Conservatory with Pauline Donalda; New York with Martial Singher; Milan with Mario Basiola and Rachaele Mori. *Debut:* Montreal Opera Guild 1951 in Un Ballo in Maschera. *Career:* Montreal 1955 as King Philip in Don Carlos; New Orleans 1956; Covent Garden from 1957 in more than 1000 performances: debut as Colline; Sang in 1957 production of Les Troyens and in Turandot, Aida, Rigoletto, Simon Boccanegra, Don Giovanni and Billy Budd; Sang the Grand Inquisitor in Don Carlos 1983; Paris Opéra 1960 as Raimondo in Lucia di Lammermoor: returned as Gurnemanz in Parsifal 1974; Guest appearances Berlin, Amsterdam, Munich, Moscow, Leningrad, Boston, Chicago and New York; Toronto 1967, in the premiere of Harry Sommers's Louis Riel; Festivals of Edinburgh, Aldeburgh and Wexford; Other roles include Arkel (Pelléas et Mélisande), Sarastro, Boris Godunov, Osmin in Die Entführung, Daland in Der fliegende Holländer and Oroveso in Norma; sang Don Marco in Menotti's The Saint of Bleecker Street, at Philadelphia, 1989; Trulove in The Rake's Progress for Vancouver Opera, 1989, the Prince in Adriana Lecouvreur for L'Opéra de Montreal, 1990; Sang Mozart's Bartolo with Vancouver Opera, 1992. *Recordings include:* Semiramide; Roméo et Juliette by Gounod; L'Enfance du Christ; Lucia di Lammermoor; Don Carlos; Marie-Magdalene by Massenet. *Honours include:* Order of Canada 1977. *Address:* c/o L'Opéra de Montreal, 1157 Rue Sainte, Catherine E., Montreal, Province Quebec, H2L 2GB, Canada.

ROURKE Sean Timothy, b. 16 Sept 1960, Bradford, England. Music Marketing Consultant; Composer. *Education:* BA (Hons), Music and English, Keele University; MPhil, Royal Holloway College, University of London; Informal compositional guidance from Malcolm Williamson, Roger Marsh and Justin Connolly. *Career:* Worked in Promotion Departments of Weinberger and Novello Publishing Houses, 1982-90; Compositions featured at Tivoli Gardens, Cornhill Festival, Forward Music Nights; Created Novello Youth Orchestra Award, 1989; Set up Forward Music Publishing house; Set up STR Music Marketing and Management, 1990. *Compositions:* Published: Nocturne for Organ; In Deed Pure Sky, for piano solo; Recorded (BBC broadcast): Berberis Darwinii or 4 Horns. *Publications:* Thematic Catalogue of Franz Lehar (compiler), 1985. *Contributions to:* Occasional reviews, Musical Times; New Routes in Music Education, Music Teacher, 1986; Ligeti's Early Years in the West, Musical Times, 1989. *Hobbies:* Football; Cooking; Steam railways. *Address:* 32 Knights Park, Kingston-upon-Thames, Surrey KT1 2QN, England.

ROUSE Christopher Chapman, b. 15 Feb. 1949, Baltimore, Maryland, USA. Composer. m. Ann Jensen, 28 Aug. 1983. 2 daughters. *Education:* BMus, Oberlin Conservatory, 1967-71; Private Study with George Crumb, 1971-73; MFA, DMA 1977, Cornell University, 1973-77. *Career:* Assistant Professor, University of Michigan, 1978-81; Assistant Professor 1981-85, Associate Professor 1985-91, Professor, 1991-, Eastman School of Music; Composer-in-Residence, Indianapolis Symphony Orchestra, 1985-86; Composer-in-Residence, Baltimore Symphony Orchestra, 1986-88. *Compositions:* Ogoun Badagris, 1976; Ku-Ka Ilimoku, 1978; Mitternachtlieder, 1979; Liber Daemonum, 1980; The Infernal Machine, 1981; String Quartet, 1982; Rotae Passionis, 1982; Lares Hercii, 1983; the Surma Ritornelli, 1983; Gorgon, 1984; Contrabass Concerto, 1985; Phantasmata, 1985; Phaethon, 1986; Symphony No 1, 1986; Jagannath, 1987; String Quartet No 2, 1988; Bonham 1988; Iscariot, 1989; Concerto per Corde, 1990; Karolju, 1990; Violin Concerto, 1991; Trombone Concerto, 1992; Violloncello Concerto, 1992; Flute Concerto, 1993; Symphony No. 2, 1994. *Honours:* Guggenheim Fellowship, 1990; American Academy of Arts and Letters Award, 1993; Kennedy Center Friedheim Award, 1988; Pulitzer Prize, 1993. *Address:* 162 Selborne Chase, Fairport, NY 14450, USA.

ROUTH Francis John, b. 15 Jan. 1927, Kidderminster, England. Composer; Pianist; Writer. m. (1) Virginia Anne Raphael, 1 Sept 1956, (2) Diana Florence Elizabeth Cardell Oliver, 1 Nov 1991. 2 sons, 2 daughters. *Education:* BA 1951, MA 1954, King's College, Cambridge; FRCO, LRAM, Royal Academy of Music; Private study with Matyas Seiber. *Career:* Appeared as pianist, occasionally conducted in London and elsewhere, South Bank, Radio broadcasts; Founder-Director, Redcliffe Concerts, 1963-64. *Compositions:* A Sacred Tetralogy, 1959-74; Dialogue for Violin and Orchestra, 1968; Double Concerto, 1970; Sonata for Solo Cello, 1971; Spring Night, 1971; Symphony, 1972; Cello Concerto, 1973; Mosaics, 1976; Oboe Quartet, 1977; Fantasy for Vio and Pf, 1978; Scenes for Orch, 1978; Vocalise, 1979; Concerto for Ensemble I, 1982, II 1983; Tragic Interludes for Oboe, 1984; Celebration for Piano, 1984; Elegy for Piano, 1986; Oboe Concerto, 1986; Poeme Fantastique for Piano and Orchestra, 1986-88; Four Marian Antiphons for Organ, 1988; Romance, 1989; Woefully Arranged, for Soloists, Choir and Orchestra, 1990; Fantasy Duo for Violin and Piano, 1990; Romanian Dance, 1990; Concerto for Ensemble III, 1991; Suite for String Orchestra, 1992. *Recordings:* A Sacred Tetralogy, Organ, Christopher Bowers-Broadbent, 1984; Celebration, Elegy, piano, Jeffrey Jacob, 1986; Oboe Quartet, Tragic Interlude, Oboe Robin Canter with Redcliffe Ensemble, 1992. *Publications:* The Organ, 1958; Contemporary Music, 1968; The Patronage and Presentation of Contemporary Music, 1970; Contemporary British Music, 1972; Early English Organ Music, 1973; Stravinsky, 1974. *Contributions to:* Various journals including: Records and Recording; Performance; Editor of Composer, 1980-88. *Honours:* Jasper Ridley prize, Cambridge, 1951; Limpus Prize, 1954; Bach Choir Prize, 1963; Composers Guild Award, 1974; ARAM, 1991. *Memberships:* Composers Guild of Great Britain; Performing Right Society. *Address:* 68 Barrowgate Road, Chiswick, London W4 4QU, England.

ROUX Michel, b. 1 Sept. 1924, Angouleme, France. Singer (Baritone). *Education:* Conservatories of Bordeaux and Paris. *Career:* Sang in Paris from 1948, at the Opéra and the Opéra-Comique; Sang in the 1950 premiere of Milhaud's Bolivar; La Scala Milan 1953, as Golaud in Pelléas et Mélisande; Glyndebourne Festival 1956-64, as Golaud, the Count in Le Nozze di Figaro and Il Segreto di Susanna, Don Alfonso and Macrobio in La Petra del Paragone: returned 1970, in Il Turco in Italia; Mozart performances at Aix-en-Provence; Chicago 1959, as Athanael in Massenet's Thais; Guest apparances in Vienna, Berlin, Geneva, Brussels, Amsterdam, Barcelona and Prague. *Recordings:* Le Comte Ory (HMV); Thaïs and Werther (Nixa); Pelléas et Mélisande (Philips); Rousseau's Le Devin du Village and Stravinsky's Le Rossignol (Columbia).

ROWLAND Christopher Selwyn, b. 21 Dec. 1946, Barnet, Hertfordshire, England. Violinist; Teacher; Quartet Leader. m. Elizabeth Attwood, 18 Dec. 1982. 1 son. *Education:* BA, MA, Trinity College, Cambridge, 1965-68; Associate, Royal Academy of Music, 1980; DMus, Bucknell University, Pennsylvania, 1981. *Career:* Performed live on radio throughout UK and Europe and regularly in North America; Supervisor of Chamber Music; Tutor in Violin, Royal Northern College of Music, Manchester; Violinist, contemporary music group, Lumina; Leader of Sartori Quartet, 1970- 74 and Fitzwilliam Quartet, 1974-84; Tours to USSR in 1976 and 1978. *Recordings:* Many recordings, exclusive Decca recording artist. *Publication:* Shostakovich-Man and Music, 1982. *Contributions to:* Music Times; Soviet Music; Berlioz Bulletin. *Honours include:* Numerous prizes at Royal Academy of Music and Cambridge University; Grammy Awards and Grand Prix du Disque. *Membership:* Communicant Member of the Church of England. *Hobbies:* Christianity; Soccer; Golf. *Address:* Fountain House, Low Street, Burton-in-Lonsdale, via Carnforth, Lancashire, England.

ROWLAND Joan Charlotte, b. 7 May 1930, Toronto, Ontario, Canada. Pianist; Teacher. m. John Michael Thornton, 5 May 1956. 3 sons, 1 daughter. *Education:* BA, English, Columbia University, New York, USA, 1970; Piano study with Mona Bates, Toronto, 1938-48; Theoretical Studies, Royal Conservatory of Music, 1940-46; Piano Study with Eduard Steuermann, Juilliard School, New York, 1952-56. *Debut:* With the Toronto Symphony under Sir Ernest MacMillan, 1942; Recital debut, New York, USA, 1948. *Career:* Solo recitals in Canada, USA and Europe; Canadian Broadcasting Corporation recitals since, 1942; Tours of USA and London with Columbia Canadian Trio, twice; Toured with Reginald Kell Players; Soloist, various orchestras including Toronto Symphony, Wiesbaden Orchestra, Mozarteum Orchestra, Mozart Festival Orchestra, San Francisco and Buffalo Symphonies; Toured with Piano Duo Schnabel, USA and Europe, 1981-84. *Recordings:* Schubert Grand Duo and B Flat variations with Piano Duo Schnabel: Mozart Sonata F major and Schubert E minor sonata with Piano Duo Schnabel; Schubert Fantasy in F minor and variations in A flat with Piano Duo Schnabel; Solo recording of Schumann Fantasy and Schumann Carnaval. *Publication:* Playing Four-Hands: A Pilgrim's Progress, The Piano Quarterly, Winter 1986-87. *Honours:* 1st Prize, Kranichsteiner Modern Music Competition, Darmstadt, Germany, 1954; 1st Prize, Mozarteum Piano Competition, Salzburg, Austria, 1955. *Hobbies:* Outdoor sports; Swimming; Canoeing; Mountain climbing. *Address:* 285 Riverside Drive, No.4A, New York, NY 10025, USA.

ROWLAND-JONES Simon Christopher, b. 8 Sept 1950, Colchester, England. Violist; Composer. *Education:* Studied at the Royal College of Music. *Debut:* Carnegie Hall, 1979. *Career:* Chilingirian String Quartet, 1971-78, 1992-; Nash Ensemble; Villiers Piano Quartet; Chamelson; Arenski Ensemble; Professor and Chamber Music Co-Ordinator at Royal College of Music. *Compostitions:* String Quartet; Piano Quartet; String Trio; Rivers Gods; Seven Pieces for Solo Viola. *Recordings include:* Dale, Phantasy & Suite; Bloch, Suites; Schubert Schumann and Beethoven; Bach Solo cello Suites, Vol 1. (Suites 1-3) after own edition/ transcription. *Memberships:* Musicians Union; Performing Rights Society. *Address:* 77 The Vineyard, Richmond, Surrey TW10 6AS, England.

ROWLANDS Carol, b. 1960, Newcastle upon Tyne. Singer (Mezzo- soprano). *Education:* Studied at the Royal Northern College of Music. *Career:* Appeared with Scottish Opera 1982-90 in L'Egisto, The Magic Flute, Le Nozze di Figaro, Oberon, Rigoletto, Il Trovatore, Lulu, Madame Butterfly and Salome; Has also understudied Mozart's Cherubino, Puck in Oberon, Wellgunde in Das Rheingold, Clairon in Capriccio, and Judith in Bluebeard's Castle (1990), also understudied, Didon in

Berlioz's The Trojans, Scottish Opera; Performed Santuzza in Scottish Opera Go Round's autumn tour of Pagliacci/Cavalleria Rusticana, 1989; For University College sang Tigrana in Edgar by Puccini, also performed Regina, title role, Scottish Opera; Santuzza in Cavalleria Rusticana, Opera South; The Mother in Amahl and the Night Vistors, Opera West; Suzuki in Madame Butterfly, Isle of Man; Orfeo title role, concert performances, John Currie Singers; Season 1992/93 as Cherubino in Marriage of Figaro, Malta; Waltraute in Die Walküre, Scottish Opera; Marcellina in Marriage of Figaro, Scottish Opera; Second Lady in Magic Flute, Scottish Opera; Marcellina in Figaro, Opera Factory; Title Role: Carmen, Regency Opera. *Current Management:* 6 Hurlingham Mansions, 218-220 New King's Road, London SW6 4PA, England.

ROY Will, b. 9 Oct. 1937, Schenectady, new York, USA. Singer-Basso (Opera, Concert, Recital). m. (1) Nancy Honegger, 1959, deceased, 1 daughter. (2) Marilyn Brustad, 4 July 1981. *Education:* Hope College, Holland, Michigan; Alumnus, The Curtis Institute of Music; The Manhattan School of Music. *Career:* Over 60 leading Bass roles, The New York City Opera; Houston Grand Opera; Grand Théâtre de Genéve; French National Radio Opera Broadcast; Teatro Communale di Firenze; Dallas Opera; Philadelphia Opera; Pittsburgh Symphony; Washington Opera; NJ State Opera; Handel and Haydn Society of Boston; Hartford Opera; Minnesota Opera; Connecticut State Opera; Long Island Symphony; Pittsburgh Opera; Cincinnati Opera; Cleveland Opera; Columbus Opera; Opera Classics of New Jersy; Mostly Mozart Festival at Lincoln Center; Mexican Television Opera Broadcast; Leon Opera Mexico; Bravo Cable TV Network. *Recordings:* The Three Sisters by Thomas Pasatieri on Painted Smiles Records; The Abduction of Figaro by PDQ Bach, Videorecording on Video Arts Internation. *Current Management:* Ace In The Hole Productions Inc., *Address:* Ace In The Hole Productions Inc., 25 Cedarhurst Avenue, West Paterson, NJ 07424, USA.

ROZARIO Patricia, b. 1960, Bombay, India. Singer (Soprano). m. Mark Troop, 1 daughter. *Education:* Guildhall School of Music with Walter Gruner; in St Jean de Luz Pierre Bernac; National Opera Studio; Studies with Vera Rozsa from 1980. *Career:* Concerts with the Songmakers' Almanac, including a tour to the USA; Solo Recitals on South Bank, London, and elsewhere; Frequent performances of Bach, Handel and Mozart; Vaughan Williams Serenade to Music at the 1988 Promenade Concerts; Schumann's Paradies und der Peri in Madrid with Gerd Albrecht; Appearances at the Bath and Edinburgh Festivals; Operatic roles include Giulietta in Jommelli's La Schiava Liberata with Netherlands Opera; Gluck's Euridice for Opera North; Mozart's Bastienne and Pamina, Kent Opera; Ilia, Glyndebourne Tour, Ismene in a Lyon production of Mitridate and Zerlina, Aix; Statue in Rameau's Pygmalion and Purcell's Belinda, Kent Opera; Florinda in Handel's Rodrigo, Innsbruck; Nero in L'Incoronazione di Poppea and Massenet's Sophie; Concert performance of Il Re Pastore at the Elizabeth Hall; Opera: world premiere of John Casken's Golem, singing Miriam at the Almeida Festival, London; Wexford Festival, 1989, as Mozart's Ismene; Created the title role in the premiere of Tavener's Mary of Egypt, Aldeburgh 1992; Pasagena at the Ludwigsburg Festival. *Recordings:* Mahler Symphony No.4 with the London Symphony; Songs of the Auvergne conducted by John Pritchard; Haydn-Stabat Mater conducted by Trevor Pinnock for Deutsche Grammophon. *Honours:* British Song Prize in Barcelona; Maggie Teyte Prize; Sängerforderungspreis at the Salzburg Mozarteum; Gold Medal at Guildhall School. *Address:* c/o Lies Askonas Ltd., 186 Drury Lane, London WC2B 5RY, England.

ROZHDESTVENSKY Gennady Nikolayevich, b. 4 May 1931, Moscow, USSR. Conductor. m. Viktoria Postnikova 1969. *Education:* Moscow Conservatory, with Nikolay Rozhdstvensky and Lev Oborin. *Debut:* Bolshoy Theatre 1951, The Nutcracker. *Career:* Conducted at the Bolshoy 1951-70 (Principal Conductor 1964-70); productions included Spartacus, Prokofiev's War and Peace and A Midsummer Night's Dream; London debut 1956; Principal Conductor of the Symphony Orchestra of All-Union Radio and TV 1961-: gave works by Prokofiev, Hindemith, Berg, Martinů and Sergei Slonimsky; Conducted Boris Godunov at Covent Garden 1970; Artistic Director of Stockholm Philharmonic Orchestra 1974; Chief Conductor BBC Symphony Orchestra 1978-81; Vienna Symphony Orchestra 1981-; Conducted the premiere of Smirnov's Jacob's Ladder at the Elizabeth Hall 1991 (London Sinfonietta); returned to Covent Garden 1991, Boris Godunov; Idomeneo at the Finlandia Hall, Helsinki, 1991. *Honours include:* People's Artist of the RSFSR 1966; Lenin Prize 1970. 21. *Address:* c/o Royal Opera House, (Contracts), Covent Garden, London WC2, England.

ROZSA Miklos, b. 18 Apr. 1907, Budapest, Hungary. Composer. m. Margaret Finlason, 30 Aug. 1943. 1 son, 1 daughter. *Education:* Leipzig Conservatory, 1929. *Debut:* Violin Concerto, Leipzig, 1929. *Appointments:* Musical Director, Alexander Korda Films, 1938-42; Musical Scores for 100 films; Thief of Baghdad, The Jungle Book, Lady Hamilton, Spellbound, The Lost Weekend, Ivahoe, Quo Vadis, King of Kings, Ben Hur. *Compositions:* String Trio Op 1, Piano Quintet, Op 2; Duos; Theme Variations and Finale Op 13; Concerto for String Orchestra; Piano Sonata; Flute Sonata; Clarinet Sonata; Violin Concerto; Piano Concerto; Cello Concerto; Sinfonia; Solo Violin Sonata. *Recordings:* Nearly all works recorded. *Publication:* Double Life, autobiography, 1982. *Contributions to:* Various professional journals. *Honours:* Frans Joseph Prize, Budapest, 1937-38; Academy Awards (Oscars) for Spellbound, 1946, A Double Life, 1948, Ben Hur, 1959. *Hobby:* Collector of 17th Century Dutch Paintings. *Address:* c/o ASCAP, ASCAP Builders, One Lincoln Plaza, New York, NY 10023, USA.

RUAN Joshua, b. 21 Feb 1964, Winnipeg, Canada. Composer. *Education:* Rowland School of Music, Canada; BA (Hons) Music, Composition with Dudley Hyams and Jonathan Harvey, Sussex University, England; Piano with Leslie Murchie, Postgraduate Composition with Robert Saxton, Guildhall School of Music. *Career:* Came to England, 1975; Commissions from various ensembles including The Ensemble Notturno; Works regularly performed and broadcast in UK; His life and work featured in Kathryn Taylor's article Snakes and Ladders, in several European journals. *Compositions:* Over thirty solo, chamber, vocal, theatrical and orchestral works including: L'Hotel Dieu, double bass solo, 1986, published 1992; Serenissima Variations for viola and piano, 1988, published 1992; Lolita, masque in 3 acts for piano, actors and dancer, 1989; Phosphate Sugar and Basses for viola, cello, double bass and piano, 1990, published 1992; Once Five Years Pass, piano solo, 1991, published 1992; The Girl, the Goldwatch and Everything for alto flute, clarinet, bassoon, horn, harmonium, mandolin, violin, viola, cello and double bass, 1992; Caravaggio, chamber opera, 1993. *Honours:* South East Arts Award, 19987. *Memberships:* Composers Guild of Great Britain; Performing Rights Society; Society for the Promotion of NBew Music; MCPS. *Hobbies:* Chess; Cooking; Collecting paintings. *Address:* Ricordi, The Bury, Church Street, Chesham, Bucks HP5 1LR, England.

RUBENSTEIN Bernard, b. 30 Oct. 1937, Springfield, Missouri, USA. Conductor. m. Ann Warren Little, 28 Aug. 1961. 1 son, 1 daughter. *Education:* BMus 1958, Eastman School of Music, 1958; MMus, Yale University, 1961. *Career:* Assistant Conductor, Rhode Island Philharmonic Orchestra, 1961-62; Music Director, Santa Fe Symphony Orchestra, 1962-64; Assistant Conductor, Wurttemberg State Theater, Stuttgart, 1966-68; Associate Professor of Conducting and Director of Orchestras, Northwestern University, 1968-80; Conductor, Greenwood Chamber Orchestra, Cummington, Massachusetts, 1968-79; Music Director, Music for Youth, Milwaukee, 1970-80; Associate Conductor, Cincinnati Symphony Orchestra, 1980-86;

Music Director, Tulsa Philharmonic Orchestra, 1984-; Guest Conductor of many orchestras in USA and Europe. *Current Management:* Herbert Barrett Management, New York City.*Address:* c/o The Tulsa Philharmonic, 2901 S. Harvard, Tulsa, OK 74114, USA.

RUBIN Henry Park, b. 12 May 1943, Philadelphia, Pennsylvania, USA. Violinist; Associate Professor of Violin. 1 son. *Education:* Oberlin College, 1961-63; BM Indiana University, 1965; Studied with Josef Gingold; MS, Juilliard School of Music, 1967; Studied with Oscar Shumsky, Rye, NY 1968-69, Ivan Galamian; Private studies with Szymon Goldberg, London, 1973-76. *Debuts:* Wigmore Hall, London, 1978; Philips Collection, Washington, 1983; American Church in Paris, 1985. *Career:* Violin Soloist, US Army Band, Washington DC, 1967-70; Co-Concertmaster, Concerto Soloists of Philadelphia, 1970-71; Solo Violinist, Center for the Creative and Performing Arts, State University of New York, Buffalo, 1971-73; Taught violin, Villa Maria Institute of Music, Buffalo, 1972-73; Violin Tutor, University College, London University and Young Musicians Centre, London, 1976-77; Associate Professor of Violin, Violinist, Cadek Piano Trio, University of Alabama, 1977-91; Conductor, Red Mountain Chamber Orchestra, Birmingham, 1980-82; Masterclasses, USA, Central America, England; Recitals, London, Paris, Guatemala, Panama, Mexico, throughout USA; Festival appearances: Chautauqua, 1979; Spoleto, USA, 1979, 1983; International Musicians Seminar, Cornwall, England, 1982; Associate Professor of Violin, School of Music, University of Houston, 1991-. *Honours:* First Governor's Arts Award (Alabama) 1980. *Address:* University of Houston, School of Music, Houston, Texas 77204-4893, USA.

RUDEL Julius, b. 6 Mar. 1921, Vienna, Austria. Conductor. *Education:* Vienna; Mannes School of Music, USA. *Career:* Rehearsal Pianist, New York City Opera; Conductor, Johann Strauss' The Gypsy Baron, New York, 1944, overall command 1957 and was responsible for premieres of an unparalleled number of works by American and foreign composers, revivals of many neglected operas. Guest, Milan's La Scala, London's Covent Garden, Buenos Aires Teatro Colon, Vienna State Opera and the opera houses of Berlin, Munich, Paris and Hamburg; Conducted Rigoletto at the Metropolitan, 1989, Hamlet by Thomas at Chicago, 1990; Der Rosenkavalier at Toronto, 1990; (follow Toronto 1990 with) Season 1992 conducted La Bohème at Bonn, Don Carlo at Nice and Tosca at Buenos Aires. *Recordings include:* Julius Caesar by Handel for RCA; The Merry Widow by Lehar for Angel and Kurt Weill's Silverlake for Nonesuch; Columbia recordings include: Ginastera's Bomarzo; Freelance recordings include: Massenet, Donizetti, Offenbach, Verdi, Bellini, Boito, Charpentier; Many television recordings; Julius Rudel Award established in his honour for Young Conductors, 1969. *Current Management:* Edgar Vincent-Cynthia Robbins Associates. *Address:* c/o Edgar Vincent-Cynthia Robbins Associates, Suite 304, 124 East 40th Street, New York, NY 10016, USA.

RUDENKO Bela Andreyevna, b. 18 Aug. 1933, Bokovo-Antratsit, Ukraine, USSR. Singer (Soprano). *Education:* Studied at the Odessa Conservatory with Olga Blagovolina. *Debut:* Odessa 1955 as Gilda in Rigoletto; Sang at Kiev from 1956, notably as Glinka's Ludmila, Rosina (Il barbiere di Siviglia), Lakmé, and Natasha in War and Peace; Bolshoy Theatre Moscow from 1972; Also successful in operas by Ukrainian composers. *Recordings include:* Ruslan and Ludmila and A life for the Tsar, by Glinka. *Address:* c/o TG Shevchenko Theatre, Ul Vladimirskaya 50, Kiev, Ukraine, CIS.

RUDERS Poul, b. 27 Mar. 1949, Ringsted, Denmark. Composer. *Education:* Mainly self-taught in Composition; Final degree in organ from The Royal Danish Music Academy. *Career:* Performances with all major Danish Symphony Orchestras. Performance by London Sinfonietta, Ensemble Intercontemporain, Speculum Musicae, New York Philharmonic, Philharmonia, Capricorn, Lontano; Psalmodies (guitar and ensemble), 1990. *Compositions:* Major Orchestral Pieces; Capriccio Pian E Forte, 1978; Manhattan Abstraction, 1982; Thus Saw St John, 1984; The Drama-trilogy: Dramaphonia, Monodrama, Polydrama, 1987-88; Symphony, Himmelhoch Jauchzendzum Tode betrübt, 1989; Violin Concerto No. 2, 1991; Gong for orchestra, 1992; Major Chamber works: Four Compositions, 1980; Greeting Concertino, 1982; 4 Dances in One Movement, 1983; String Quartet No 1, 1971; No 2, 1979; Vox in Rama, 1983. *Recordings include:* Recorded on Paula Label with London Sinfonietta, conductor Oliver Knussen, Four Dances, 1983-89; Commissioned by London Sinfonietta; Corpus Cum Figuris, 1984-90; Commissioned by Ensemble Intercontemporain; Corpus Cum Figuris: Point PCD 5084; Violin Concerto, No.1 Unicorn-Kanchana, 9114; Psalmodies: Bridge 9037; Symphony: Chan 9179. Other recordings on various labels; Numerous solo pieces for various instruments; Frequent performances at several international festivals. *Honours:* Royal Philharmonic Charles Heidsieck Prize, Symphony, London, 1991. *Membership:* Danish Composers' Guild, SPNM, England. *Current Management:* Denmark: Edition WH England; Chester Music, USA; Bridge Management. *Address:* c/o Chester Music, 8-9 Frith Street, London W1 5TZ, England.

RUDIAKOV Michael, b. 9 Aug. 1934, Paris, France. Cellist; Conductor; Artistic Director. m. Judith Peck, 12 June 1964. 1 son, 1 daughter. *Education:* Studies with Father Eliahu Rudiakov; BMus, Manhattan School of Music, New York City, 1956-61. *Career:* Concert Cellist, Solo & Chamber Music, Tours of Europe, USSR, 1972, India 1975, Australia 1976, Canada, Israel, People's Republic of China, 1981, USA; Member, Composers String Quartet, 1969-76; Guest, Fine Arts Quartet, 1977-78; Artistic Director, Chamber Music, Sarah Lawrence, 1969-80; Musical Director, Manchester Music Festival, Vermont, USA, 1983-; TV Programmes for CBS and National Euducational TV; Radio Programme, Bern, Zurich, Paris, Rome, Jerusalem, Hamburg, Berlin, New Delhi, BBC London and Manchester; Principal Cellist, Indianapolis, 1963-65; Jerusalem Symphony, 1965-66; Faculty, Manhattan School of Music, New York City, 1981; Faculty, Lehman College, (Cuny), New York City, 1993; Founder, Manchester Festival Orchestra, 1988. *Recordings:* Over 25. *Contributions to:* Musical America, 1982. *Honours:* Harold Bauer Award, American Society of Composers, 1971; Grammy Nomination, 1972. *Memberships:* Violoncello Society of New York; Local 802 Musicians Union, New York City; Bohemians. *Current Management:* Arilisa Concerts Inc. *Address:* 93 Franklin Ave, Yonkers, NY 10705, USA.

RUDOLF Max, b. 15 June 1902, Frankfurt-am-Main, Germany. Symphony and Opera Conductor. m. Liese Ederheimer, 4 Aug. 1927. 1 son, 1 daughter. *Education:* Student, Goethe-Gymnasium, Frankfurt; Hochschule Conservatory of Music, Frankfurt University; Private Music Instruction; DMus (Honours) Cincinnati Conservatory of Music; LHD, (Hons) University of Cincinnati, 1960, Miami University 1963, Curtis School of Music 1972; DMus, Baldwin-Wallace College 1973, Temple University, 1975. *Career:* Assistant Conductor, Freiburg, Germany, Municipal Opera, 1922-23; Conductor, State Opera of Hesse, Darmstadt, Germany, 1923-29, German Opera, Prague, 1929-35; Guest Conductor, Gothenburg, Sweden, Orchestral Society, also Choral Director, radio concerts, Swedish Broadcasting Corp, 1935-40; Faculty, Central YMCA Colelge, Chicago, 1941-43; Conductor, New Opera Co, New York City, 1944; Member, Musical Staff, Metropolitan Opera Association, New York City, 1945-58, Artistic Administrator, 1950-58; Administrator, Kathryn Long Opera courses, Metropolitan Opera, New York, 1949-58; Musical Director, Cincinnati May Festival, 1963-70; Music Director, Conductor, Cincinnati Symphony Orchestra, 1958-70, world-wide concert tour, 1966; Conductor, Metropolitan Opera Association, New York City, 1973-75; Member Faculty, Curtis Institute of Music, Philadelphia, 1970-73, 1981-; Teacher, Conducting, Ford Foundation Project,

Baltimore, 1962-64; Tanglewood, 1964; Distinguished Service Profesor, University of Cincinnati, 1966-68; Conductor, Columbia Records, Book of Month Club Music Appreciation Series, Cetra, Italy, Decca; Guest Conductor, Symphony orchestras throughout USA, Italy; Panel Member, National Endowment for the Arts, Washington, 1970-73; Artistic Advisor, Dallas Symphony Orchestra, 1973, New Jersey Symphony Orchestra, 1976-77; Detroit Symphony Orchestra, 1983, Exxon/Art Endowment Conductors Programme, 1977-. *Publication:* Author, The Grammar of Conducting 1950, 2nd edition 1980. *Honours include:* Alice M Ditson Award, 1964; Phi Kappa Lambda. *Address:* 220 W Rittenhouse Square, Philadelphia, PA 19103, USA.

RUDY Mikhail, b.3 April, 1953, Tashkent, USSR. Concert pianist. *Education:* Moscow Conservatory with Jakov Flier. *Career:* After winning prizes at competitions in Leipzig and Paris he made his western debut in 1977, playing Beethoven's Triple Concerto in Paris with Rostropovitch and Stern; Guest appearances with the Berlin Philharmonic, Orchestre de Paris, Concertgebouw, Boston Symphony, Montreal Symphony Orchestra, London Philharmonic and Toronto Symphony; US debut 1981, with the Cleveland Orchestra conducted by Lorin Maazel; Festivals include Berlin, Tanglewood, Lockenhaus and Vienna; Salzburg Easter Festival 1987, with Karajan; Chamber music concerts with the Amadeus Quartet, until 1987, Guarneri Quartet and Vienna Philharmonic Wind Ensemble; London debut with the LSO under Michael Tilson Thomas, 1988; Promenade Concerts 1989, Prokofiev's 2nd Concerto; subject of French TV Documentary Le Grand Echiquier, 1989; debut with Dresden Staatskapelle, 1991; season 1991-92 with concerts in Cleveland and Munich; returned to Russia 1990, concerts with the St Petersburg, Philharmonic. *Recordings:* Grand Prix Academie Charles Cros for Scriabin album; Brahms and Ravel recital EMI; Music by Mussorgsky, Liszt and Janáček; Concertos by Rachmaninov and Tchaikovsky with the St Petersburg Philharmonic. *Honours:* Prize winner at 1971 Bach Competition in Leipzig; First Prize Marguerite Long Competition Paris 1975. *Current Management:* IMG Artists (Europe). Address: c/o IMG Artists, Europe, Media House, 3 Burlington Lane, London, W4 2TH, England.

RUDZINSKI Witold, b. 14 Mar. 1913, Siebiez. Composer; Musicologist; Pedagogue. m. Nina Rewienska, 26 Dec. 1958. 1 son, 2 daughters. *Education:* Phil Mag, University of Wilno, 1936; Conservatory M Karlowicz Wilno, 1937; Studies with Nadia Boulanger and Charles Koechlin, Institut Gregorien, Paris, France, 1938-39. *Debut:* 1936. *Career:* Head, Music School Swieciany, Poland, 1937-38; Conservatory Wilno, 1939-42; Professor, Cons Lodz, 1945-47; Director of Music Department, Ministry of Culture, Warsaw, 1947-48; Academy of Music, Warsaw, 1957-. *Compositions:* Operas: Janko Muzykant (Janko The Fiddler), 1951; Commander of Paris, 1957; The Dismissal of Grecian Envoys, 1962; Sulamith, 1964; The Peasants, 1972; The Ring and The Rose, 1982; The Yellow Nightcap, 1969; Oratorios: The Roof of The World, 1960; Gaude mater Polonia, 1966, The Circle of Psalms 1987, Madonna, 1991; Symphonic Music: Musique Concertante for Piano and Orchestra, 1958; Pictures from Holy Cross Mountains, 1965; Concerto Grosso for Percussion and with String Orchestra, 1970; Chamber Music: Sonata for Viola and Pianoforte, 1946; Flute Quintet, 1954; Deux Portraits des Femmes for Voice and String Quartet, 1960; To Citizen John Brown, Voice and Chamber Ensemble, 1972; Duo Concertante for Percussion, 1976; Sonata Pastorale for Violin and Pianoforte, 1976; Instrumental: Variations and Fugue for Percussion, 1966; Quasi una sonata for Pianoforte, 1975; Sonata per clavicembalo, 1978; Dialogue for saxophone and piano, 1987; Pleiades, sonata for clarinet and piano, 1987; Songs; Incidental music. *Recordings:* Sonata for Viola and Pianoforte; Janko Muzykant Muza; Musique Concertante for Pianoforte and orchestra; The Roof of the World and Pictures from Holy Cross Mountains; Odprawa poslow greckich; Gaude mater Polonia; Children Songs. *Publications:* Music for

Everybody, 1948, 1966; Stanislaw Moniuszko, Principal Biography in 2 volumes, 1954-61; Moniuszko's Correspondence, 1969; Moniuszko, Popular Mongr, 1978; What Is Opera? 1960; Béla Bartók Musical Technique, 1965; How To Listen To Music, 1975; Treatise on Musical Rhythm, 2 volumes, 1987. *Hobbies:* History; Biography. *Address:* PL - 02541. Warszawa, Narbutta 50 m 6, Poland.

RUDZINSKI Zbigniew, b. 23 Oct. 1935, Czechowice, Poland. Composer. m. Ewa Debska, 13 July 1965. 1 daughter. *Education:* Warsaw University, 1956; MA, Composition Diploma with Distinction, State High School (Music), 1956-60. *Career:* Professor of Composition, 1973-, Head, Composition Department 1980-81, Rector (Director) 1981-84, Academy of Music, F Chopin, Warsaw, Poland. *Compositions include:* orchestral works: Sonata for two string quartets, piano and kettle drums, 1960; Contra Fidem, 1964; Moments Musicaux I, II, III, 1965-68; Music by Night, 1970; Vocal Instrument works: Epigrames for flute, choir and percussion, 1962; Three Songs for tenor and two pianos, 1968; Symphony for mens' choir and orchestra, 1969; Requiem for the Victims of Wars for choir and orchestra, 1971; Tutti E Solo for soprano, flute, French horn and piano, 1973; Chamber works: Quartet, for 2 pianos and percussion, 1969; Sonata for piano, 1975; Campanella for percussion Ensemble, 1977; Tritones for percussion Ensemble, 1979; Opera: The Mannequins, 1981; The Book of Hours, songs for mezzo-soprano and piano trio, 1983; Das sind keine Träume - songs for mezzo-soprano and piano, 1986. *Membership:* President, Warsaw District, Polish Composers Union, 1983-85, Secretary General, 1985-. *Hobbies:* Old and folk instruments; Musical pictures. *Address:* ul Poznanska 23 ul 26, 00-685 Warszawa, Poland.

RUFO Bruno, b. 1941, Italy. Singer (Tenor). *Debut:* Spoleto 1965, as Pinkerton. *Career:* Many Appearances at La Scala Milan, Rome, Naples, and Verona Arena, (Radames 1981); Further Engagements at Bologna, Parma, Hamburg, Munich, Vienna, the Deutsche Oper Berlin and Dusseldorf; Sang Manrico at Liège, Samson in Season 1986/87; TV Appearances have included Verdi's Ernani. *Address:* c/o Opera Royal de Wallonie, 1 Rue des Domincains, B-4000 Liège, Belgium.

RUGSTAD Gunnar, b. 5 Sept. 1921, Gjerpen, Norway. Musicologist; Musician (Trombone). m. Ingeleiv Ramberg, 2 children. *Education:* MA, Musicology, University of Oslo; PhD, Musicology 1977; Lecturer's Degree, Conservatory of Oslo. *Career:* Trombonist, Norwegian Broadcasting Orchestra until 1968; Research Work, University of Bergen, 1968-74; Head of Music Department, Norwegian Broadcasting TV, 1974-. *Publications:* Christian Sinding; Biographic & Stylistic Study 1856-1941. *Contributions to:* Professional Journals. *Memberships:* Musicians Union, Norway; International Society for Contemporary Music; Board Member, Norwegian Culture Fund; Norwegian Society of Artists in Music. *Address:* Hafrsfjordsgt 7, 0273 Oslo 2, Norway.

RUK-FOCIC Bozena, b. 31 Oct. 1937, Zagreb, Yugoslavia. Singer (Soprano). *Education:* Studied with Zlatko Sir in Zagreb. *Debut:* Basle 1960, as Micaela in Carmen. *Career:* Member of Croatian National Opera, Zagreb; Guest appearances in Bucharest/Athens, Roma, Palermo, Napoli, Trieste, Genova, Luxembourg, Holland, Graz, Bern, Belgrade, Vienna, Berlin, Stuttgart, Hamburg and at Covent Garden (Eva in Die Meistersinger); La Scala Milan-Walküre Sieglinde 1970, and in the Italian premiere of Dallapiccola's Ulisse; Further engagements in Kiev, Budapest, Houston, Pittsburgh, Seattle, Washington, Zurich, Geneva, Barcelona and Salzburg; Other roles include Jaroslavna in Prince Igor, Alceste, Madama Butterfly, Mozart's Countess, Verdi's Leonora and Aida, Wagner's Elsa, Elisabeth and Sieglinde, Strauss's Ariadne and Weber's Agathe, Desdemona (Otello), Tosca, Elisabetta (Don Carlos), Manon (Manon Lescaut), Arabella, Ariadne, Margareta (Faust), Amelia (Simone Bocanegra); Many appearances as concert singer.

RUNDGREN Bengt, b. 21 April 1931, Karlskrona, Sweden. Singer (Bass-Baritone). *Education:* Studied with Arne Sunnegaard and Ragnar Hulten in Stockholm. *Career:* Sang in operetta, then made opera debut as the Commendatore, Stockholm 1962; Member of Royal Opera, Stockholm, until 1969; Sang Osmin in Die Entführung at Drottningholm, 1965-67; Member of Deutsche Oper, Berlin, from 1969: often heard as Leporello in Don Giovanni; Metropolitan Opera 1974, as Hagen; Sang Hagen at Bayreuth, in the 1976 centenary production of The Ring; sang the Commendatore in Don Giovanni at Stockholm, 1988; Also heard as concert singer. *Honours include:* Swedish Court Singer 1975. *Address:* Kunglica Teatern, PO Box 16094. S-10322 Stockholm, Sweden.

RUNGE Peter-Christoph, b. 12 April 1933, Lubeck, Germany. Singer (Baritone). *Education:* Studied with Lilly Schmitt di Giorgi in Hamburg and with Prof. Cl. Kaiser-Breme. *Debut:* Flensburg 1958, as Guglielmo in Così fan Tutte. *Career:* Sang in Wuppertal 1959-64; Deutsche Oper am Rhein, Dusseldorf, from 1964: roles include Mozart's Papageno and Figaro; Glyndebourne Opera 1966-73, 82, 83 as Papageno and Pelléas and in the Leppard/Cavalli L'Ormindo; Edinburgh Festival 1972, in the British premiere of Zimmermann's Die Soldaten; Guest appearances in Vienna, Brussels, Stockholm, Amsterdam, Warsaw, Bolshoi, Berlin, Hamburg and Zürich; Paris, as Barber in Schweigsame Frau, Buenos Aires, as Harlekin in Ariadne auf Naxos, Berlin 1986 as Beckmesser and Salzburg 1983 in the Vocal Symphony Die Soldaten by Zimmermann; Sang the premieres of Goehr's Behold the Sun, Duisburg 1985, and Reimann's Das Schloss, Dusseldorf, Berlin 1992; Nice Opera 1986, as Beckmesser in Die Meistersinger and Wozzeck; Duisburg 1988, as Alfons in Der Jüngste Tag by Klebe; Wexford Festival 1990, as Major Max von Zastrow in The Rising of the Moon by Maw; As concert artist, often heard in Bach, Schubert, Schumann, Brahms, Strauss, Mozart and Monteverdi. *Recordings include:* L'Ormindo (Decca); Music by Monteverdi and Bach (Telefunken); Auber's Manon Lescaut (EMI).*Honours:* The title of Kammersänger, 1990.*Current Management:* Athole Still, London. *Address:* c/o Deutsche Oper am Rhein, Heinrich-Heine Allee 16, D-4000 Dusseldorf, Germany.

RUNKEL Reinhild, b. 25 Dec 1943, Volkach am Main, Germany. Singer (Mezzo-soprano). *Education:* Studied in Wuppertal. *Career:* Sang at the Nuremberg Opera, 1975-82; Guest engagements at Lisbon, Regio Emilia, Paris and San Francisco, 1985, and Florence (Magdalene in Meistersinger), 1986; Salzburg Festival 1987, in Moses and Aron by Schoenberg; Sang Fricka in Ring performances at Bologna, Stuttgart and Cologne, 1987-88; Appearances at the Zurich Opera from 1985, as Herodias, Fricka and Clytemnestra in a Ruth Berghaus productioon of Elektra, 1991; Stuttgart Staatsoper 1992, as Begbick in Aufstieg und Fall der Stadt Mahagonny; Other roles include Erda, Waltraute, Brangaene, Lyon 1990, Jocasta in Oedipus Rex and the Nurse in Die Frau ohne Schatten; Frequent concert appearances. *Recordings include:* Fortune Teller in Arabella and Nurse in Die Frau ohne Schatten, conducted by Solti (Decca); Beethoven's Ninth, (Deutsche Grammophon). *Address:* c/o Zurich Opera, Falkenstrasse 1, Ch-8008 Zurich, Switzerland.

RUNNICLES Donald, b. 16 Nov. 1954, Edinburgh, Scotland. Conductor. *Education:* Studied at Edinburgh and Cambridge Universities and at the London Opera Centre. *Career:* Repetiteur at the Mannheim National theater from 1980, debut with Les Contes d'Hoffmann; Kapellmeister from 1984, conducting Fidelio, Le Nozze di Figaro, Un Ballo in Maschera, Die Walküre and Parsifal; Principal conductor at Hanover from 1987, leading Salome, Jenůfa, Tosca, Don Giovanni and Werther; Regular engagements with the Hamburg Staatsoper: Turandot, The Bartered Bride, Die Zauberflöte, Manon Lescaut, Carmen, Don Carlos, Zar und Zimmermann, Il Trovatore, Il Barbiere di Siviglia, L'Elisir d'Amore and Lady Macbeth of Mtsensk; General Music Director at Freiburg from 1989: Lady Macbeth,

Billy Budd and Peter Grimes; Assisted James Levine at Bayreuth, then conducted Lulu at the Metropolitan (1988) followed by Der fliegende Holländer (1990) and Die Zauberflöte; Conducted The Ring at San Francisco, Summer 1990; Vienna Staatsoper from season 1990-91, with Il barbiere di Siviglia, Don Giovanni, Madame Butterfly and La Traviata; Prince Igor at the Vienna Staatsoper; Glyndebourne debut 1991 with Don Giovanni; Musical Director of San Francisco Opera from 1992; Season 1992/93 with Lady Macbeth of the Mtsensk District at the Vienna Volksoper and The Fiery Angel, Guillaume Tell and Boris Godunov at San Francisco, Don Giovanni at Munich, Tannhäuser at Bayreuth and Der Ring des Nibelungen at Bayreuth; Other repertory includes Idomeneo (Hanover) and Der Freischütz; Symphonic engagements in Darmstadt, Odensee, St Gallen, Copenhagen and with the NDR Orchestra, Hamburg. *Address:* c/o Athole Still Ltd., Greystoke House, 80-86 Westow Street, London SE19 3AF, England.

RUNSWICK Daryl, b. 12 Oct 1946, Leicester, England. Composer; Musician; Singer. *Education:* Choral Exhibitioner, Corpus Christi College, Cambridge; MA (Cantab), Music. *Career:* Musical Director, Footlights Club, 1966-67; Jazz Bass Player, especially with C Laine/J Dankworth, 1968-82; Concert Bass Player, especially with London Sinfonietta, 1970-82; Session Player, bass, bass guitar, keyboards, 1970-81; Arranger, Record Producer, especially King's Singers, 1971-; Composer of film and TV music, 1976-; Tenor Singer in Electric Phoenix, 1983-; Musical Director, Green Light Theatre Company, 1990-. *Compositions:* One More Day; Cool-Warm- Hot; I Sing The Body Electric; Lady Lazarus; Patents Pending; Taking The Air; Dialectic I; Main-Lineing; Needs Must When The Devil Drives; I Am A Donut; 4 Nocturnes; Zuppa Inglese. *Recordings:* With Electric Phoenix including Berio, Cage, Nordheim, Wishart; With London Sinfonietta including Songs for Dov, Agon, King Priam; With Nash Ensemble including The Soldier's Tale; Many jazz records including Cleo Laine at Carnegie Hall. *Hobbies:* Touring; Theatre; Cinema; Collecting Art; Visiting gardens. *Address:* 34A Garthorne Road, London SE23 1EW, England.

RUNZE Klaus, b. 20 July 1930, Berlin, Germany. Pianist; Pedagogue; Composer. m. Bonn, 1972. 1 son, 1 daughter. *Education:* Piano Studies, Konservatorium Klindworth-Scharwenka, Berlin, 1946-48; Piano Studies 1948-50, Harpsichord Studies 1952-55, Rhythmische Erziehung 1959-61, Hochschule für Musik, Berlin. *Career:* Akademie der Kunste, Exposition and performances about experiences with children, Berlin 1972; Seminars about Piano-pedagogical questions, Institut für Neue Musik and Musikerziehung, Darmstadt, 1973, Konservatorium Winterthur, Switzerland 1974 and Musikakademie Basel 1976, 1977; Lecture and exposition, World Congress Paris 1975, also ISME World Conference, Innsbruck 1986; Other lectures at seminars on research of musical creativity of children; Seminars and contributions at conferences at music schools, colleges and professional musical societies in Germany, Switzerland and Austria 1977-85; England 1982; Japan 1986; Goethe-Institut, Tokyo 1986; Concerts, Performances; IGNM Basel 1980; Cologne 1982-83; Darmstadt 1983; Munich 1983-84; Belgrade 1984; Max Mueller Bhavan (Goethe-Institut) Bombay, New Delhi, Calcutta, 1985, Tage Neuer Musik, Bonn, 1984-85; Radio: DRS, Studio Zurich, Proposal: Radio DRS, Studio Zurich Ruckkehr zur utopie, A Portrait as Piano-Pedagogue and Piano-Improvisator, Nov 1986; Lecturer, State College of Music, Cologne. *Publications:* Piano-Pedagogical Work Zwei Hände-Zwolf Tasten, Volume I 1972, 2nd edition 1982, Volume II, 1973, 2nd edition 1985, English edition 1977, Japanese edition 1986, Lehrerheft, 1984; Klavierspiel als Improvisation, Basel 1979. *Address:* Beethovenstrasse 51, D-5300 Bonn 1, Germany.

RUOFF Axel D, b. 24 Mar. 1957, Stuttgart, Germany. Composer. *Education:* State University for Music, Stuttgart and Academy for Music, Kassel, West Germany 1975-84; Diplomas, piano and music theory, cum laude, 1979; Diploma for Composers 1984; National University for Fine Arts and Music, Tokyo, Japan, 1985-87. *Career:* Head of Department, Stuttgart Music School, West Germany 1981-88; Lecturer, State University for Music, Trossingen, 1985-87; Concurrently Guest-Professor in Composition at Morioka College 1988, sected for the Forum for Young Composers, Berlin; Fellowship from the Art Foundation of Baden, Württemberg; Fellowship from the Japanese Ministry of Culture, for study at the National University for Fine Arts and Music in Tokyo; Professor at State University for Music, Stuttgart, 1992. *Compositions:* Prozession for orchestra, 1983; Concerto for flute and orchestra, 1984; Correlations, cello solo, 1983; Jemand in Vorbeigehen, voice and piano, 1984; Via Dolorosa, organ, 1985; Fassaden, violin solo, 1985; String Quartet, 1986; Salomo-Variations, choir, 1986; String quartet No 2, 1988; Piano concert, 1989; Nacht und Träume, 1987-88, for Orchestra. *Recordings:* First records release, with Aulos Recrds; Broadcating Stations in Germany, other European countries and Japan. *Publications:* Publishing Contracts with Edition Moeck, Con Brio (Berlin), (Celle) and Mieroprint (Münster). *Honours:* Valentino Bucchi, Rome, 1985, 1987; 1st Prize, ICONS, Torino, 1988; 2nd Prize Ensemblia, Mönchengladbach, 1986; 1st Prize, Corciano (Perugia), 1991. *Address:* Möhringer Land Str 53, 7000 Stuttgart 80, Germany.

RUOHONEN Seppo, b. 25 April 1946, Turku, Finland. Singer (Tenor). *Education:* Studied in Helsinki, with Luigi Ricci in Rome and with Anton Dermota in Vienna. *Debut:* Helsinki 1973, as Alvaro in La forza del destino. *Career:* Appearances with Finnish National Opera as Verdi's Duke and Manrico, Tchaikovsky's Lensky and Hermann, and Don Ottavio; Savonlinna 1977 in The Last Temptations by Kokonnen, with Sallinen's The Red Line, repeated at the Metropolitan, New York, 1983; San Diego Opera as Riccardo in Un ballo in maschera; Returned to Savonlinna 1983 as Don Carlos and as Erik in Der fliegende Holländer; Has sung at Frankfurt from 1978 and made guest appearances in Berlin, Dresden, Leeds, Glasgow, Stuttgart and Wiesbaden as the Duke of Parma in Doktor Faust, Puccini's Cavaradossi, Luigi and Pinkerton and Jenik in The Bartered Bride; Sang Florestan at the 1992 Savonlinna Festival. *Recordings Include:* The Last Temptations (Deutsche Grammophon). *Address:* c/o Städtische Buhnen, Untermainanalage 11, D-6000 Frankfurt am Main, Germany.

RUSHBY-SMITH John, b. 28 Sept. 1936, Redcar, Yorkshire, England. Record Producer; Composer; Writer. m. Margaret Field, Soprano, 25 Apr 1986, 2 sons (1st M.). *Education:* Southwell Minister Grammar School; St Edmund Hall, Oxford. *Career:* Music Studio Manager, BBC, 1962-; Senior post 1967-; i/c BBC SO Broadcasts and recordings 1971-90; Technical Director, Stockhausen Music & Machines, Barbican, 1985; Steve Reich Festival, RFH, 1988. *Compositions:* Violin sonata; Piano duet Aspects of Night; Syzygy for flute and piano; Piano sonata; Saxophone Quartet; Concerto Grosso for strings; Monologue for oboe; Reverie & Valse Seriale for Orchestra. *Recordings:* Production of Schoenberg series for CBS; Various recordings for Erato, including Boulez series, Rameau's Naïs (McGegan), Gluck's Orfeo (Leppard/Baker); Tippett's Mask of Time and Enesco's Oedipe for EMI; Further productions for Erato, Fonit Cetra, Kiwi Pacific, RCA, RPO Records, Transatlantic Records and others. *Contributions to:* On broadcasting Wagner's Ring Cycle for Studio Sound; On broadcasting The Proms for Proms Prospectus; The Cave of Harmony, Talk for BBC Radio; Concert Hall acoustical design, paper for Institute of Acoustics, 1988; The Production of Enesco's Oedipe for Classic CD, 1991. *Honours:* Gramophone Awards: Best Contemporary Recording 1984, (Boulez's Pli selon pli) 1987 (Tippett's Mask of Time); Prix du Disque France Opera, 1982 (Rameau's Naïs); Grand Prix Charles Cros, 1987 (Tippett's Mask of Time) 1991 (Enesco's Oedipe); Diapason d'or, Grand Prix du Disque Lyrique, Grand Prix de la Nouvelle Academie du Disque Française, 1991 (Enesco's Oedipe). *Memberships:* Institute of Acoustics; Composers' Guild; Sonic Arts Network; PRS. *Hobbies:* Watercolour painting; Fungi; Walking. *Address:* The Folly, Lower Soudley, Cinderford, Glos GL14 2UB, England.

RUSHTON Julian Gordon, b. 22 May 1941, Cambridge, England. University Professor. m. Virginia Susan Medlycott Jones, 16 Mar 1968, 2 s. *Education:* Studied at Trinity College, Cambridge and Magdalen College, Oxford. *Career:* University Lecturer, University of East Anglia, 1968-74; University of Cambridge, 1974-81; West Riding professor and Head of Department, University of Leeds, 1982-. *Publications:* Berlioz, Huit Scenes de Faust; La Damnation de Faust; The Musical Language of Berlioz; Classical Music: A Concise History; WA. Mozart: Don Giovanni; WA, Mozart: I Domeneo. *Contributions to:* New Grove Dictionary of Music and Musicians; Various Professional Journals; New Grove Dictionary of Opera. *Memberships:* Musica Britannica; Council of Royal Musical Association; American Musicological Society. *Hobbies:* Literature; Walking. *Address:* Department of Music, University of Leeds, Leeds, LS2 9JT, England.

RUSSELL James Reagan, b. 2 Apr. 1935, Alameda, California, USA. Clarinettist; Conductor. *Education:* BA, University of California, Berkeley; MMus, State University of New York, Stony Brook; Studies with Jack Brymer and Stephen Trier, London, David Glazer, New York and Rudolf Jettell, Vienna. *Career:* Assistant Conductor, University Symphony Orchestra, University of California, Berkeley, 1958-65; Solo Clarinettist, Golden Gate Park Band, San Francisco, 1963-71; Lecturer in Music-Clarinet, University of California, Berkeley, 1969-; Bassethorn, San Francisco Opera Orchestra, 1980-81; Formed Russell-Graber Duo, with pianist Miles Graber, 1983-; Concert series of recitals surveying development of Clarinet Sonata in England, France and Germany. *Recordings:* Music of Macedonia and Bulgaria. *Contributions to:* MLA Notes. *Honours:* Alfred Hertz Travelling Scholarship in Music, 1965-66 and 1966-67. *Memberships:* San Francisco Single Reed Society; International Clarinet Society. *Hobby:* Photography. *Address:* 2310 Ellsworth Street No 6, Berkeley, CA 94704, USA.

RUSSELL Ken, b. 3 July 1927, Southampton, England. Stage Producer. *Education:* Nautical College, Pangbourne; Choreography with Nicolai Sergueff of the Marinsky Ballet St Petersburg. *Career:* Films for the BBC, 1959-70, including studies of Elgar, Debussy, Prokofiev, Delius, Vaughan Williams, Martinů and Richard Strauss; Feature films include The Music Lovers (Tchaikovsky), Mahler, and The Devils (music by Peter Maxwell Davies); First opera production The Rake's Progress at the 1982 Maggio Musicale in Florence; Other productions include Zimmermann's Die Soldaten for Opéra de Lyon (1983), Madama Butterfly (Spoleto, 1983), L'Italiana in Algeri (Geneva 1984), La Bohème (Macerata Festival 1984), Faust (Vienna 1985) and Mefistofele (Genoa 1987); He has directed his production of Butterfly in Houston and Melbourne; Gilbert and Sullivan's Princess Ida at the London Coliseum, 1992 (a production of Wagner's Tannhäuser had earlier been withdrawn). *Honours include:* 1985 Prix Italia for his Symphonic Portrait of Vaughan Williams. *Address:* Barratt House, 7 Chertsey Road, Woking, Surrey GU21 5AB, England.

RUSSELL Lynda, b. 1963, Birmingham, England. Singer (Soprano). *Education:* Studied in London with Meriel St Clair and in Vienna with Eugenie Ludqig. *Career:* Has sung with Glyndebourne Opera as the Queen of Night, Fortuna in Monteverdi's Ulisse and Marzelline in Fidelio; Opera engagements at Barcelona, Madrid, Nice, Venice, Vicenza, Rome, Bologna and Strasbourg; British appearances as Handel's Partenope and with Opera North and English National Opera; Trieste 1990 as Donna Elvira; Concert showings at the festivals of Athens, Barcelona, Granada, San Sebastian, Cuence, Venice, Berne, Munich and Siena; Brahms Requiem under Jesus Lopez-Cobos and Beethoven's Ninth with Walter Weller; Has sung Mozart's oratorios Davidde Penitente and Betulia Liberata in Italy; Further repertoire includes Wolf's Italienisches Liederbuch,

Beethoven's Missa Solemnis (Weller) and Ah, Perfido; Mozart's Exsultate and Coronation Mass: Mozart bicentenary concerts in London, Birmingham, Winchester and Lahti (Finland) 1991. *Recordings:* Handel Dixit Dominus, with The Sixteen; Missa Solemnis, with the City of Birmingham Symphony. *Address:* Magenta Music International, 64 Highgate High Street, London N6 5HX, England.

RUSSO William, b. 25 June 1928, Chicago, IL, USA. Composer. *Education:* Studied with Lenni Tristano, 1943-46, John Becker, 1953-55 and Karel Jirak, 1955-57. *Career:* Trombonist and Chief Composer, Arranger with the Stan Kenton Orchestra, 1950-54; Taught at the Manhattan school of Music, 1958-61 and Formed and Conducted the Russo Orchestra; Columbia College Chicago, 1965-67, Antioch College, 1971-72; Founded and Directed the Center for New Music and Free Theatre at Columbia College, 1965-75, Returned to teaching at Columbia, 1979. *Compositions include:* Operas John Hooten, BBC 1963; The Island, BBC 1963; Land of Milk and Honey, Chicago 1967; Antigone, Chicago 1967; A Cabaret Opera, New York 1970; Aesop's Fables, Chicago 1971; The Shepherds' Christmas, Chicago 1979; Isabella's Fortune, New York 1974; Pedrolino's Revenge, Chicago 1974; A General Opera, Chicago 1976; The Pay Off, Chicago 1984; Talking to the Sun, Chicago 1989; Ballets The World of Alcina 1954, Les Deux Errants, Monte Carlo 1956 and The Golden Bird, Chicago 1984; 2 Symphonies 1957 and 1958; Music for Blues and Jazz Bands, Rock Cantatas and Sonata for violin and piano 1986. *Publications include:* Composing Music: A New Approach, Chicago 1988. *Address:* c/o ASCAP, ASCAP Building, One Lincoln Plaza, New York, NY 10023, USA.

RUT Josef, b. 21 Nov. 1926, Kutná Hora, Czechoslovakia. Violinist; Composer. m. Dr. Milada Rutová, 14 Feb. 1953, 1 son. *Education:* Studied with Prof. Bedrich Voldan; State Conservatory of Music, Prague. *Debut:* Prague, 1951. *Career:* Violinist, Radio Prague Symphony Orchestra, 1953-83, Composer, 1983-. *Compositions:* 32 Compositions based on own 12 Note Tonal Theory. *Recordings:* Sonata for Double Bass and Strings; String Quartet; Symphony No. 2; Sonate for Winds; Wind Quintet; Concerto for Violin and Orchestra; Duo for Violin and Violoncello; Concerto for Horn and Strings; Variations for Orchestra, Sonate for Piano. *Publications:* Studies for Two Violins; Small Dialogues for Trumpet and Trombone; Five Little Pieces for Flute and Piano; 12 Note Tonal Theory, 1969; Die Musik und ihre Perspektive vom Gesichtspunkt der Relativitätstheorie (International Review of the Aesthetics and Sociology of Music), 1980; Manual of Rhythm with Jan Dostal, 1979 and 1984; Beitrag zur übersichtlicheren Notierung des Rhythmus, 1982; The Relativist Theory of Musical Motion, Prague 1990. *Membership:* Society of Czech Composers. *Hobbies:* Scoring and Revising 18th Century Music; Touring. *Address:* Zborovská 40, 15000 Prague 5, Czech Republic.

RUTENBERG Peter, b. 27 July 1951, St Louis, MO, USA. Conductor; Composer; Producer. m. Sara Jan Berman, 13 Aug 1972, 1 s, 1 d. *Education:* Studied at UCLA and California State University, Fullerton. *Career:* Founder, Music Director, Los Angeles Chamber Singers; Program & Production Director, KUSC FM Los Angeles; Composer, Harry and the Hendersons, TV Series. *Compositions include:* Ballad of the Buffalo Skinners. *Recordings Include:* Shenandoah: An American Chorister. *Memberships:* ASCAP; Conductors Guild; Pacific Composers Forum. *Hobbies:* Wine; Cooking; Architecture. *Address:* 2055 Kelton Avenue, Los Angeles, CA 90025, USA.

RUTKOWSKI Joseph Richard, b. 13 June 1954, New York City, USA. Professional Clarinettist; Educator. m. Lisa N. Binder, 24 June 1984, 2 sons. *Education:* BMus, Mannes College of Music, New York City, 1977; MA, Music, Queens College, New York City, 1982; Post Masters Degree, Educational Administration & Supervision, 1987; Studied Clarinet Privately, with L.

Sobol, E. Simon, G. Cioffi, H. Geuser. *Debut:* Carnegie Recital Hall, New York City, 1978. *Career:* As Soloist and Member of Alaria, L'Arema Chamber Ensemble, & Norwegian Chamber Orchestra, at Carnegie Recital Hall, Lincoln Centre, Robert Todd Lincoln Estate,USA, Musikhochschule, Bonn, Germany, and a tour of Caribbean Islands; Solo Concerto appearances in Tully, Avery Fisher and Carnegie Halls; Appearances on major Radio & TV Shows including: Robert Sherman's, The Listening Room, WQXR, New York, and CBS TV; Teacher of Music, Conductor of Symphony Orchestra, Stuyvesant Science High School, New York, 1984-91; Teacher, Clarinet, & Chamber Music, Mannes College of Music, 1976-; Assistant Conductor, All-City Concert Band of New York, 1987-91; Teacher of Music Director of Instrumental Music, Great Neck (New York), North Secondary Schools, 1991-. *Recordings:* The Shepherd on the Rock, Franz Schubert; Chorale & Rondo, Jeffrey Kaufman. *Publications:* Transcriptions and arrangements for Woodwinds include: Four Anniversaries, Leonard Bernstein; Joplin for Winds, Scott Joplin. *Address:* 309 Avenue 'C' New York, NY 10009, USA.

RUTMAN Neil, b. 12 July 1953, California, USA. Pianist. *Education:* BMus, San Jose State University 1976, Student of Aiko Onishi; MMus, Piano Performance, Eastman School of Music, University of Rochester 1977; Student of Cecile Genhart; DMA, Piano Performance, Peabody Institute of The Johns Hopkins University 1983, Student of Ellen Mack; Private Piano Studies with Leon Fleisher, Frank Mannheimmer and Gaby Casadesus. *Debut:* NY debut, Carnegie Recital Hall 1985; London debut, Wigmore Hall 1985; Washington DC debut, Phillips Gallery 1985. *Career:* Associate Professor, Piano, Goucher College, Baltimore 1983-; Master Classes: Chateau de la Gesse, Toulouse France and University of Colorado, Denver 1986; Master Class: Fauré, Debussy, Ravel: Interpretation of French Piano Music, Wright State University, Dayton, Ohio, 1986; Recitalist, Chateau de la Gesse, Toulouse, France 1985; Soloist, Denver Symphony, Denver 1986; Recitalist, Cheltenham International Festival of Music, England 1986; US State Department Recital Tour, Yugoslavia 1986; Soloist, Metropolitan Orchestra of NY, Carnegie Hall 1986; Recitalist, Merkin Hall, NYC, 3 Recitals of the music of Ravel, Debussy, Fauré and Poulence with American premiere each evening 1987. *Recordings:* 3 movements of Petrouchka, Stravinsky; 2 Mozart Piano Concerti, K 482 and K 414; Academy of London Orchestra, Richard Stamp, conducting; Preludes Book 1 and 2, Debussy. *Current Management:* Thea Dispeker, NYC, USA. *Address:* 1465 Mary Avenue, Sunnyvale, CA 94087, USA.

RUTTER John, b. 24 Sept. 1945, London, England. Composer; Conductor. m. Joanne Redden, 1980, 2 sons, 1 daughter. *Education:* MA, MusB, Clare College, Cambridge. *Career:* Director of Music, Clare College, Cambridge, 1975-79; Lecturer, Open University, 1975-88; Honorary Fellow, Westminster Choir College, Princeton, 1980; Founder and Director, Cambridge Singers. *Compositions include:* The Falcon, 1969; Gloria, 1974; The Piper of Hamelin, 1980; Requiem, 1985; Magnficat, 1990; Many carols, anthems and songs; Edited and recorded original version of Fauré's Requiem, 1984. *Recordings include:* Many including his own Requiem with Cambridge Singers and City of London Sinfonia. *Address:* Old Lacey's, St John's Street, Duxford, Cambridge, England.

RÜTTI Carl, b. 24 Mar. 1949, Fribourg, Switzerland. Musician, (Pianist; Composer). m. Marie-Louise Studer, 29 June 1973, 2 sons. *Education:* Zurich Conservatoire, 1970-75; Piano with Sava Savoff, organ with Erich Vollenwyder, Concert Diploma, both instruments, 1975; Further studies with Kendall Taylor (piano), Richard Latham (Organ), London, UK, 1976. *Career:* Pianist: Tonhalle Zurich, Schauspielhaus Berlin: Gewandhaus Leipzig, 1987. Piano teacher, Zurich Conservatoire. *Publications:* Alpenhorn concerto, 1989. *Compositions include:* Veni Cretor Spiritus, organ; Vater unser/Wach auf, 4-voice choir a capella; Michaels-Vesper, 4-voice choir, organ & orchestra; Concerto for Alpenhorn and Strings. *Recordings:* Pianist, Debussy, Preludes Vol. 2; Composer, pianist, Das Stundenbuch; Composer, 7 motets (10 voices), poems by Rilke, BBC Singers, Brompton Oratory Choir. *Memberships:* Tonkünstlerverein Schweiz; SMPV. *Hobbies:* Jogging; House & Garden. *Address:* Weststrasse 77, CH-6314 Unterägeri, Switzerland.

RUUD Ole Kristian, b. 1958, Lillestrom, Norway. Conductor. *Education:* Studied at the Norwegian State Academy of Music and at the Sibelius Academy in Helsinki under Jorma Panula. *Career:* Has appeared widely in Norway and Europe from 1985; Principal Guest Conductor of the Trondheim Symphony then Chief Conductor and Artistic Director (1987); Regular engagements with the Oslo Philharmonic and Bergen Philharmonic; Principal Guest Conductor of the Stavanger Symphony Orchestra; Led the Yomiuri Nippon Symphony Orchestra in Japan, 1990; Engagements with the Bergen Philharmonic in Germany, with the Trondheim Symphony in Spain and the Baltic States of the former USSR with the Stavanger Symphony; Further appearances with the Gothenburg Symphony, Stockholm Chamber, Norrkoping Symphony and Belgian National Orchestras. *Address:* c/o Van Walsum Management Ltd., 26 Wadham Road, London SW15 2LR, England.

RUZICKA Rudolf, b. 25 Apr 1941, Brno, Czech Republic. Composer; Teacher. m. Bozena, 7 July 1967, 2 s. *Education:* Compositions Studies, Brno Conservatory & Janacek Academy of Performing Arts. *Career:* Composer; Professor of Composition & music thoery, Brno & Kromeriz Conservatories, Brno State University, Janáček Academy. *Compositions:* Over 90 Instrumental, Vocal, Electroacoustic and Computer Compositions. *Recordings:* Approx 50 Compositions Recorded, Radio, TV, Gramophone. *Publications:* Use of Computers in Creating Works of Art; Numerous Articles, Music Theory of Computer Composition and Automatic Notation. *Honours:* 1st Prize Electroacoustic & Computer Music; Various International Competitions. *Memberships:* Newcomp International Computer Music Competition; Electro Acoustic Music Association of Great Britain; Computer Music Association. *Hobbies:* Theoretical Research & Practical Composition of Contemporary Serious Music; Electroacoustic Music; Computer Music & Automatic Note Printing. *Address:* Serikova 32, 637 00 Brno, Czech Republic.

RUZICKOVÁ Zuzana, b. 14 Jan. 1928, Plzeň, Czechoslovakia. Harpsichordist. m. Viktor Kalabis. *Education:* Prague Academy of Music. *Career:* Has appeared widely in Europe from 1956; Co-founder with Vaclav Neumann of the Prague Chamber Soloists: performances 1962-67; Formed duo with violinist Josef Suk 1963; Teacher at Prague Academy from 1962; Chairman International Competitions Prague Spring festival. *Recordings:* Complete keyboard works of JS Bach; Concertos by Benda; CD: Sonatas D. Scarlatti (ORFEO) B. Martinů: Concert pour Clavecin (Supraphon), Bach and his Predecessors (Sopraphon) J.S. Bach: Concerti (V.Neumann-Supraphon). *Memberships:* Member Directories, Neue Bachgesellshaft Leipzig; Honorary member for Life, British National Early Music Association (NEMA). *Honours:* Winner, Munich International Competition, 1956; Grand Prix du Disque 1961; Supraphon Grand Prix 1968, 1972; Artist of Merit, 1968; State prize Czechoslovak Republic 1970; National Artist, 1989. *Address:* Prague Academy of Arts, Korunni 98, 12000 Prague 2, Czech Republic.

RYBAR Peter, b. 29 Aug. 1913, Vienna, Austria. Violinist; Music Professor. m. Marcelle Daeppen, 3 Apr. 1952. *Education:* Conservatoire of Prague; Studied with Carl Flesch in Paris and London. *Career:* Toured Europe as Soloist, 1934-38; Concertmaster Winterthur Symphony Orchestra; Teacher, Conservatoire of Winterthur and Leader, Winterthur Quartet, 1938-66; First Concertmaster, Orchestra Suisse Romand; Professor, Masterclass, Conservatoire Geneva, 1971-80; Many appearances as Soloist at Festivals in Salzburg, Montreux, Konstanz, Schaffhausen, Lucerne, Prague; Recital appearances with wife (pianist); Lecturer in Switzerland and abroad; Judge at International Competitions. *Recordings:* Numerous Recordings for Concert Hall Society, Westminster Recording Society, Philips, Chant du Monde. *Honours:* Art Prize, Ernst Foundation; Honorary Prize, Town of Winterthur. *Address:* Via Stazione 57, CH 6987 Caslano, Switzerland.

RYCROFT Eric Brian, b. 18 Nov. 1948, Stellenbosch, South Africa; Senior Lecturer; Viola Soloist; Chamber Music Player. m. Maryke Lintvelt, 10 Dec. 1982, 2 sons. *Education:* LRSM, Cape Town, 1968; ARCM, Honours, LTCL, London, 1971; FTCL Stellenbosch, South Africa, 1982. *Debut:* Wigmore Hall, London, England, 22 June 1971. *Career:* Sub-Principal Violist, 1972, Principal Viola, 1974, Capab Orchestra, Cape Town; Lecturer, 1978, Senior Lecturer, 1979-, Conservatoire, University of Stellenbosch, South Africa; performed as Soloist, number of occasions with professional orchestras in South Africa; performs regularly in Recital and Chamber Music Concerts; records regularly for SABC Radio and TV; Conductor, Organiser, Manager, University of Stellenbosch String Ensemble, 1977-; Conductor, Organiser, Manager, University of Stellenbosch Symphony Orchestra, 1981-; European Concert Tour with US String Ensemble, 1985, Principal Viola, Capab Orchestra, 1986-. *Compositions:* Composed and played music for film, Kirstenbosch Dream, 1972. *Recordings:* Musiek uit Stellenbosch, 1979. *Honours:* Ernest Tomlinson Prize, Royal College of Music, London, 1970; SABC Prize, Johannesburg, 1973. *Membership:* SASMT; Founder Member, Co-Director, Chamber Music Society. *Hobby:* Superbike Enthusiast. *Address:* 8 Erica Avenue, Westridge, Somerset West, Republic of South Africa, 7130.

RYDL Kurt, b. 8 Oct. 1947, Vienna, Austria. Singer (Bass). *Education:* Studied in Vienna and Moscow. *Debut:* Stuttgart 1973, as Daland in Der fliegende Holländer; Guest appearances in Barcelona, Venice and Lisbon; Bayreuth Festival 1975; Vienna Staatsoper from 1976, as Rocco in Fidelio, Zaccaria (Nabucco), Procida (Vêpres Siciliennes), Mephistopheles (Faust), King Philip (Don Carlos), Kecal (The Bartered Bride), the Landgrave (Tannhäuser) and Marke (Tristan und Isolde); Salzburg Festival 1985, in Il Ritorno d'Ulisse by Henze/Monteverdi; 1986 tour of Japan with Vienna Staatsoper company; Baron Ochs in Turin; sang Ochs at Monte Carlo and Florence, 1987 and 1989; Salzburg Festival 1987-89, as Mozart's Osmin; La Scala Milan 1990, as Rocco; Pimen at Barcelona, Rocco at the 1990 Salzburg Festival; Season 1991/92 as Titurel at La Scala, Verdi's Zaccaria at the Vienna Volksoper, Ramfis in Aida at Tel Aviv, Padre Guardiano at Florence and the Grand Inquisitor at the Verona Arena. *Recordings include:* Salome; Opera scenes by Schubert; Alceste; Manon Lescaut (Deutsche Grammophon). *Address:* c/o Staatsoper, Opernring 2, A-1010 Vienna, Austria.

RYHANEN Jaako, b. 2 Dec 1946, Tampere, Finland. Singer. *Education:* Studied in Helsinki. *Career:* Member of the Finnish National Opera at Helsinki from 1974; Appearances at the Savonlinna Festival and in Moscow and New York with the Helsinki Company; Further Engagements in Madrid, Hamberg, Berlin, Munich, Zurich and Stuttgart; Paris Opera, 1987, as Daland, Monte Carlo, 1988; Season 1991 as Daland at Munich, Titurel in Parsifal at Tampere and Mozart Bartolo at Helsinki; Sang Daland at Santiago, 1992, Sarastro at the Savonlinna Festival; Concerts with the Israel Philharmonic and Throughout Scandinavia. *Address:* Finnish National Opera, Bulevardi 23-27, SF-00180 Helsinki 18, Finland.

RYHMING Gudrun Kristina, b. 4 May 1934, Sweden. Singer. m. Inge Ryhming, 21 June 1958. *Education:* Studied at the University of Washington, Los Angeles Conservatory, the University of Stockholm. *Debut:* Liederabend Haag, 1967. *Career:* Concerts in Form of Liederabends Church Concerts; Concerts with Baroque Music and Contemporary Music; Dozens of

Appearances in Radio and TV. *Compositions include:* Lamento. *Recordings include:* Love Amour Amour; From Stockholm to Rome; Johan Helmich Roman, psalms and sacred songs. *Publications:* Several. *Honour:* Ristori Prize. *Memberships include:* Society Suisse de Musicologie; Association des Musiciens Suisses. *Hobbies:* Painting; Writing; Cooking. *Address:* 16 Rte du Grenet, 1074 Mollie-Margot, Switzerland.

RYKER Harrison Clinton, b. 11 Feb 1938, Oakland, California, USA. Musicologist; Conductor; Violinist. m. Ana Atanasijevic, 2 July 1987, 2 daughters. *Education:* BA, History, University of California, Berkeley, 1959; MM, Conducting, PhD, Musicology, University of Washington, 1962-71; Diplomas, Berkshire Music Center, Tanglewood, 1963, 1965. *Career:* Conductor and Violinst, Faculty, Hope College, 1968-72; Faculty, University of Wisconsin, 1972-74; Faculty, 1974-, Director of Graduate Studies, 1983-90, Chinese University of Hong Kong. *Publications:* Symphonic Music of Willem Pijper, 1971; Asian Composers' League Proceedings, 1983; New Music in the Orient, 1991. *Contributions to:* Articles on 19th and 20th century music in several journals; Concert and record-jacket notes for events in Hong Kong and Netherlands. *Address:* Res 14, 3-B The Chinese University of Hong Kong, Shatin, New Territories, Hong Kong.

RYPDAL Terje, b. 23 Aug 1947, Oslo. Composer; Musician. m. Elin Kristin Rypdal, 15 June 1988, 3 son, 1 daughter. *Education:* Grunnfag in Music at University of Oslo; Studied Composition with Finn Mortensen. *Career:* Piano from Age of 6 to 12; Electric Guitar with The Vanguards, 1962-67; The Dream, 1967-69; Jan Garbarch Quartet, 1969-71; Since 1971 Leader of Own Groups. *Compositions:* 5 Symphonies; 2 Operas. *Recordings include:* (due to interest in Classic CD): Q.E.D, Undisonus; Several Records on ECM. *Honours:* Deutscher Scallplattenpreis. *Membership:* Norwegian Composers Guild. *Hobby:* Icelandic Horses. *Address:* 6380 Tresfjord, Norway.

RYSANEK Leonie, b. 14 Nov. 1926, Vienna, Austria. Singer (Soprano). m. (1) Richard Grossmann (2) E.L. Gaussmann. *Education:* Vienna Conservatory with Alfred Jerger and Richard Grossmann. *Debut:* Innsbruck 1949, as Agathe in Der Freischütz. *Career:* Saarbrucken 1950-52; Bayreuth Festival 1951-68, as Sieglinde, Elsa, Senta and Elisabeth; Bavarian State Opera from 1952; Covent Garden debut 1953, as Danae in the first British production of Strauss's Die Liebe der Danae: returned to London until 1963; Guest appearances in Paris, Berlin and Salzburg; US debut San Francisco 1956, as Senta: returned as Lady Macbeth, Turandot and the Empress in Die Frau ohne Schatten; Metropolitan Opera from 1959, as Lady Macbeth, Chrysothemis in Elektra, the Marschallin, Tosca, Fidelio, Salome, Aida, Elisabeth de Valois and Abigaille in Nabucco; Gala concert at the Met 1984; Paris Opéra 1972, as the Empress; Orange Festival 1974, as Salome; Bayreuth 1982, as Kundry in Parsifal; Tour of Japan 1984, with the Hamburg Staatsoper; Metropolitan Opera 1986, as Ortrud in Lohengrin; Other roles include the Kostelnička in Jenůfa, Cherubini's Médée and the title role in Die Aegyptische Helena by Strauss; Video of Elektra (title role); Paris Opera and Metropolitan, New York 1988, 1991 as the Kostelnička; Sang in Elektra at Geneva 1990, Metropolitan 1992; Herodias in Salome at the Deutsche Oper Berlin, 1990; Season 1992 as Clytemnestra at the Met and the Countess in The Queen of Spades at Barcelona. *Recordings:* Der fliegende Holländer; Ariadne auf Naxos; Elektra; Lohengrin; Otello; Die Walküre; Fidelio; Die Frau ohne Schatten; Labels include Columbia, RCA, Deutsche Grammophon, Philips and Melodram. *Address:* c/o Deutsche Oper Berlin, Richard Wagnerstrasse 10, D-100 Berlin 1, Germany

RYSANEK Lotte, b. 18 March 1928, Vienna, Austria. Singer (Soprano). *Education:* Vienna Conservatory with Richard Grossmann. *Debut:* Klagenfurt 1950, as Massnet's Manon; Member of the Viena Staatsoper as Marzelline in Fidelio, Marguerite in Faust, Pamina,

Fiordiligi, Marenka in The Bartered Bride and Donna Elvira, and parts in operas by Wagner and Verdi; Guest appearances at the Vienna Volksoper, in Graz, Berlin, Dusseldorf and Hamburg; Bayreuth 1958; Well known in operetta and as a concert singer. *Recordings include:* Roles in operetta for HMV and Philips. *Address:* c/o Staatsoper, Opernring 2, A-1010 Vienna, Austria.

RYSSOV Michail, b. 25 Aug. 1955, Crimea, USSR. Singer (Bass). *Career:* Principal bass at the Opera in Minsk 1983-87, in Don Giovanni, Don Carlos, Aida, La Forza del Destino, Macbeth, Nabucco, I Vespri Siciliani, Faust, Eugene Onegin, Boris Godunov and Mefistofele; Treviso 1989, as the Commendatore in Don Giovanni; Has recently sung Ramfis at the Deutsche Oper Berlin and at the Verona Arena; Philip II at the Deutsche Oper am Rhein, Dusseldorf; Prince Gremin and the Inquisitor (Don Carlos) at La Fenice, Venice. *Honours include:* Winner, Glinka Competition, 1984; International Verviers competition, Belgium 1987; International Ettore Bastianini competition, Siena, 1988; International New Voice Competition in Pavia and the Toti dal Monte competition in Treviso, 1989. *Address:* c/o Athole Still Ltd., Greystoke House, 80-86 Westow Street, London SE19 3AF, England.

RZEWSKI Frederic Anthony, b. 13 April 1938, Westfield, Massachesutts, USA. Composer; Pianist. m. Nicole Abbeloss, 3 children. *Education:* BA Harvard University 1958 (study with Thompson and Piston); MFA Princeton University 1960, with Sessions and Babbitt; Italy 1960-61, with Dallapiccola. *Career:* Pianist and teacher in Europe from 1962; Played in premieres of Stockhausen's Klavierstuck X and Plus Minus; Co-founded electronic ensemble Musica Electronica Viva, Rome 1966; Returned to New York 1971; Professor of Composition at the Royal Conservatory, Liege, from 1977; Visiting Professor of Composition at Yale University 1984. *Compositions:* For Violin 1962; Nature Morte for instruments and percussion 1965; Composition for 2 1964; Zoologischer Garten 1965; Spacecraft 1967; Impersonation, audiodrama 1967; Requiem 1968; Symphony for Several Performers 1968; Last Judgement for trombone 1969; Falling Music for piano and tape 1971; Coming Together for speaker and instruments 1972; Piano Variations on the song No Place to go but Around 1974; The People United will Never be Defeated, 36 variations for piano 1975; 4 Piano Pieces 1977; Satyrica for jazz band 1983; Una breve storia d'estate for 3 flutes and small orchestra; A Machine for 2 pianos 1984; The Invincible Persian Army for low voice and prepared piano 1984. *Recordings:* As pianist, numerous items of contemporary music. *Address:* c/o ASCAP, ASCAP Building, One Lincoln Plaza, New York, NY 10023, USA.

S

SAARI Jouko Erik Sakari, b. 23 Nov 1944, Stockholm, Sweden. Conductor; Musical Director. m. Raija Syvänen, 1 son, 1 daughter. *Education:* Sibelius Academy, 1962-68; Music Science, Helsinki University, 1965-67; Conducting, Indiana University, USA, 1969-70; Praecentor Organist degree, 1966; School Music Division degree, 1966; Conservatory (trumpet) degree, 1966; Music Director degree, 1966; Church Music Division degree 1968; Conducting Diploma, 1968. *Career:* Musical Director, Helsinki Opera Society, 1973-74; Conductor, Tampere City Orchestra, 1973-74; Chorus Master, 1974-75, Conductor and Coach, 1976-78, National Opera Finland; Musical Director, Lahti City Orchestra, 1978-84; Conductor, Gothenburg Opera House, Stora Teatern, 1984-, Guest Conductor, 1985-; Broadcast recordings with Finnish Radio Symphony Orchestra, 1971 and 1973-75 and with Swedish Radio Symphony Orchestra, 1974 and 1976-77; Concerts in USA, Canada, BRD, Hungary, Denmark, Sweden and Finland; Currently Guest Conductor, Hämeenlinna Symphony Orchestra; Appearances on Swedish radio and on Finnish Radio and Television. *Compositions:* For Brass Band, recorded with Töölö Brass Band. *Membership:* American Symphonic Orchestra League. *Hobbies:* Hunting; Motor sport. *Address:* Etelätie 1 D, 15610 Lahti, Finland.

SAARI Seppo Ilari, b. 28 Mar 1948, Helsinki, Finland. Assistant Music Director. m. 11 July 1983, 1 son, 1 daughter. *Education:* BBA, Helsinki School of Economics & Business Administration; Diploma, Music Theory & Teaching, Sibelius Academy; MMus, Musicology, University of Illinois, USA, 1987; PhilLic (Musicology), 1991. *Career includes:* Assistant Conductor, Sibelius Academy Cantemus Chamber Choir; Research Fellow, University of Utrecht, Holland, 1979-80; General Manager of Turku Philharmonic Orchestra, 1980-81; Member of the Executive Board of Finland Festivals and Turku Chamber Music Week, Finland, 1980-81; Assistant Director of Kokkola Conservatory, Finland, 1984-1992; Teaching Assistant, University of Illinois, 1986-88. *Compositions:* Choral arrangements. *Recordings:* (As composer, conductor & keyboard player): Several tapes, harpsichord, Finnish Broadcasting Company; Appearances on 3 LP recordings, several TV programmes. *Publications:* Articles, musicology, journals including, Mozart Jahrbuch, Musiikki, Musiikkimuseo. *Address:* Fransuntie 16 C, 62200 Kauhava, Finland.

SAARIAHO Kaija, b.14 Oct 1952, Helsinki, Finland. Composer. *Education:* Studied at the Sibelius Academy in Helsinki and with Brian Ferneyhough and Klaus Huber at the Freiburg Hochschule für Musik. *Career:* Freelance Composer of Orchestral music and instrumental music with live Electronics and computers. Works include: Du cristal... á la fumée, for orchestra, Maa, a ballet music in seven scenes, Nymphea for string quartet. *Honours include:* Finnish Government Awards; Kranichstein Prize; Prix Italia; Priz aix Electronica. *Address:* Chester Music, 8/9 Frith Street, London W1V 5T2, England.

SAARMAN Risto, b. 25 Jan 1956, Jyvaskyla, Finland. Singer (Tenor). *Education:* Studied at the Sibelius Academy in Helsinki, graduated 1983. *Career:* Finnish National Opera from 1984, at first as M Triquet (Eugene Onegin), Beppe, Borsa (Rigoletto) and Don Curzio; Later sang Tamino, Don Ottavio, Ferrando, Belmonte, Almaviva, Lensky and Albert Herring; Savonlinna Festival and Opéra de Lyon 1987, as Tamino and Belmonte; Aix-en-Provence 1990, as Belmonte and Almaviva; Sang Jacquino at the 1992 Savonlinna Festival; Concert engagements in the St John and St Matthew Passions; Masses by Haydn, Handel, Mozart and Beethoven; L'Enfance du Christ by Berlioz and Mendelssohn's Second Symphony; Lieder repertoire includes Dichterliebe and Die schöne Müllerin; Songs by Strauss. *Address:* c/o Athole Still Ltd, Greystoke House, 80-86 Westow Street, London SE19 3AF, England.

SABBAGH Peter, b. 28 Dec 1965, Hamburg, Germany. Composer. *Education:* Studied at Hochschule fur Musik, Hamburg. *Career:* Lecturer in Theory at the Hochschule für Musik, Hamburg, 1988-89, 1992-93; Since 1992 Teaching at the Hochschule für Musik in Detmold. *Compositions include:* Works for Ensembles and Orchestras. *Address:* Gustav-Weihrauch-Weg 24, 22359 Hamburg, Germany.

SABBATINI Giuseppe, b. 11 May 1957, Rome, Italy. Singer (Tenor). *Education:* Studied Double Bass at the Conservatory Santa Cecilia, Rome, and singing privately. *Career:* Played double bass in various Italian orchestras. *Debut:* Opera debut: Edgardo in Lucia di Lammermoor at Spoleto, 1987; Further debuted titles: Faust, La Bohème, Werther, Massenet's Manon, Linda di Chamounix, Der Rosenkavalier, La Traviata, Rigoletto, I puritani, L'elisir d'amore, Frà Diavolo, Les pêcheurs de perles, Evgenij Onegin. Performed at main theatres including: Teatro alla Scala of Milan, Covent Garden, London, Staatsoper of Vienna, Opéra-Bastille of Paris, Lyric Opera of Chicago, Suntory Hall of Tokyo, Carnegie Hall of New York, Staatsoper of Hamburg; Concert repertoire includes: Donizetti's Requiem (Cologne 1988, Stuttgart 1993), Rossini's Stabat Mater (Roma 1991, Bologna 1992). *Recordings include:* La maga Circe (Bongiovanni); Gala Opera Concert - L'arte del belcanto, Mozart Gala - Suntory Hall Tokyo - Simon Boccanegra (Capriccio); Le maschere (Ricordi-Fonit Cetra); La Bohème (EMI Ricordi); Don Giovanni (Chandos Chan); Canzone sacre (Koch-Schwann). *Address:* c/o Stage Door Opera Management, Via Giardini 941/2, 41100 Modena, Italy.

SACCA Roberto, b. 12 Sept 1961, Sendehorst, Westfalen, Germany. Singer (Tenor). *Education:* Studied at the Musikhochschule of Stuttgart and Karlsruhe. *Career:* Sang in Germany from 1985, overseas engagements in Israel, Switzerland, France and England; Concert tour of Brazil 1987, with appearances at the Teatro Municipal Rio de Janeiro; Stadttheater Wurzburg, 1987-88, Wiesbaden from 1988; Sang at the Fermo Festival, Italy, as Leandro in a 1990 revival of Paisiello's Le Due Contese; Other roles include Mozart's Don Ottavio, Ferrando and Tamino; Belfiore and Ramiro in La Finta Giardiniera; Count Almaviva, Nemorino, Jacquino, Rinuccio (Gianni Schicchi), Abu Hassan, the Steersman in Der fliegende Holländer and Albert Herring; Concert repertoire includes sacred music by Monteverdi, Bach, Rossini, Mendelssohn and Britten. Debut: At Scala of Milan with Hans Werner Henze's Das Verratene, 1990; Brussels and Salzburg Festival, Ulisse/Dallapiccola), 1993; Vienna, Musikvereinsaal, 1993; From 1994 for three years, six member of Zurich Opera. *Recordings:* Messiah, Handel; Solo recital Album. *Contributions to:* Openwelt; Orpheus. *Honours:* Winner, Opera Prize in Geneva, Switzerland, 1989. *Current Management:* Seitter, (Austria). *Address:* c/o Hessisches Staatstheater, Postfach 3247, D-6200 Wiesbaden, Germany.

SACCO P Peter, b. 25 Oct 1928, Albion, NY, USA. Composer; Tenor. *Education:* Pupil of Vivian Major and Wiliam Willett at Fredonia State University; Eastman School of Music 1953-58 with Barlow, Rogers and Hanson; MM 1954, DMus 1958. *Career:* Pianist for 4th Divisioin General; studied composition with Wolfgang Niederste-Schee in Frankfurt 1950-52; Clarinettist with 4th Division Infantry Band; Music Faculty of San Francisco State University 1959-80; Visiting Professor at University of Hawaii 1970-71; Concert Tenor. *Compositions:* Dramatic: Jesu, Oratorio 1956; Midsummer Night's Dream Night, Oratorio 1961; Mr Vinegar, chamber opera 1967; Solomon, Oratorio 1976; Orchestral: 3 Symphonies: No 1 1955; No 2 The Symphony of Thanksgiving, 1965-76; No 3 The Convocation Symphony, 1968; Piano Concerto, 1964; Four Sketches on Emerson Essays, 1963; 2 Piano Sonatas, 1951, 1965; Moab Illuminations, 1972 solo piano; Violin Concerto, 1969-74; 5 Songs for mezzo-soprano and strings; Chamber: Clarinet Quintet, 1956; String Quartet, 1966; Variations on Schubert's An die

Musik for piano 4 hands, 1981; 60 solo songs; 25 Chouses; 4 Cantatas; 11 Anthems.

SACCOMANI Lorenzo, b. 9 June 1938, Milan, Italy. Singer (Baritone). *Education:* Studied in Milan with Vladimiro Badiali and Alfonso Siliotti. *Debut:* Avignon 1964, as Silvio in Pagliacci. *Career:* Sang the Herald in Lohengrin at Venice then appeared in many Italian houses, notably La Scala Milan in operas by Puccini, Gounod, Massenet and Verdi; London 1972, in a concert performance of Caterina Cornaro by Donizetti; US debut Dallas 1972, as Henry Ashton in Lucia di Lammermoor; Verona Arena 1983; Geneva 1985 as Guy de Montfort in Les vêpres siciliennes; Further appearances in Frankfurt, New York, Chicago and Buenos Aires; Other roles include Escamillo, Zurga (Les pêcheurs de Perles) and Verdi's Nabucco, Germont, Ezio (Attila), Amonasro, Rigoletto, Luna and Francesco (I masnadieri). *Recordings include:* Caterina Cornaro (MRF); Pagliacci (Decca).

SACHER Paul, b. 28 April 1906, Basle, Switzerland. Conductor; Music Educator. *Education:* Studied conducting wuth Weingartner at the Basle Conservatory; musicology with Karl Nef at Basle University. *Career:* Founded Basle Chamber Orchestra 1926; commissioned many composers to write for him: Bartók (Divertimento, Music for Strings, Percussion and Celesta), Hindemith (Symphony, Die Harmonie der Welt), Honegger (Symphonies Nos 2 and 4), Martin (Petite Symphonie Concertante), Strauss (Metamorphosen), Stravinsky (Concerto in D, A Sermon, a Narrative and a Prayer), Tippett, Britten, Henze, Birtwistle (Endless Parade) and Carter (Oboe Concerto); Founded Schola Cantorum Basiliensis 1931, for research into early music; Conducted Collegium Musicum of Zurich from 1941; regular appearances at Lucerne, Aix-en-Provence and Edinburgh Festivals; Glyndebourne 1954-63, The Rake's Progress, Die Entführung and Die Zauberflöte; Formed Musikakademie der Stadt Basel 1954 and was Principal until 1969. *Recordings include:* Brandenburg Concertos, Bach concerto for violin and oboe and A minor violin concerto; Mozart Cassations and piano concertos (Haskil); Henze Double Concerto (Holligers) and sonata for strings; More recent D.C's: Morat: Double concerto for violin, cello and orchestra; concerto for cello (Rostropovitch); Hymnes de Silence. Stravinsky: Concerto in D for violin and orchestra (Mutter). Honegger: symphony No 3, Chant de Joie; Horace Victorieux. *Memberships:* Managing Committee of the Association of Swiss Composers, 1931: director 1946-55, then honorary president; President of the Swiss section of the International Society for the Promotion of Contemporary Music, 1935-46. *Honours include:* Silver Medal of the Karls University (Prague Dr b.c. in Medicine and Surgery of the University of Genoe; Dr and Professor of the Budapest Franz Liszt-Hochschule für Musik, 1993; Crystal Crown award, Birmingham Festival of Arts (Alabama); the Grosse Verdienstkreuz mit Stern des Verdienstordens, Germany. *Address:* Schöenberg, CH 4133, Pratteln BL, Switzerland.

SACHS (Stewart) Harvey, b. 8 June 1946, Cleveland, Ohio, USA. Writer. m. Barbara Gogolick, 30 Sept 1967, 1 son. *Education:* Oberlin (Ohio) College Conservatory, 1964-65; Mannes College of Music, New York, 1965-66; Conductors' Workshop, University of Toronto, 1968-71. *Career:* Conductor, Peterborough (Canada) Symphony orchestra, 1972-75; Guest Conductor, Pomeriggi Musicali, Milan, Italy, 1977; Angelicum, Milan, 1977; Canadian Opera Touring Company, 1979; CBC Vancouver Chamber Orchestra, 1982, 1984; Orchestre Symphonique de Québec, 1984; Toronto Chamber Players, 1984, 1985; Full-Time Writer, Present. *Publications:* Toscanini (biography), 1978; Virtuoso, 1982; Music in Fascist Italy, 1987; Arturo Toscanini From 1915 to 1946: Art in the Shadow of Politics (exhibition catalogue), 1987; Reflections on Toscanini, 1991. *Contributions to:* The New Yorker; Times Literary Supplement, London; New York Times; Atlantic, USA; Corriere della Sera, Milan; La Stampa, Turin; Yale Review, USA; Grand Street, USA; Nouvel

Observateur, Paris; Le Monde de la Musique, Paris; Neue Zeitschrift für Musik, Germany; The New Republic, USA; Nuova Rivista Musicale Italiana; Opera, UK; Opera News, USA; many others. *Hobbies:* Reading; Hiking; Travelling. *Current Management:* Ned Leavitt Agency, 70 Wooster Street, New York, NY 10012, USA. *Address:* Via Ricasoli 5, 52024 Loro Ciuffenna (Arezzo), Italy.

SACHS Klaus-Jürgen, b. 29 Jan 1929, Kiel, Germany. University Professor. m. Eva-Marie Sachs, 2 daughters. *Education:* Staatsexamen Kirchenmusik, Hochschule für Musik, Leipzig, 1950; PhD, Hauptfach Musikwissenschaft, University of Freiburg, 1967; Dr phil habil, Musikwissenschaft, University of Erlangen-Nürnberg, 1978. *Career:* Professor für Historische Musikwissenschaft, University of Erlangen-Nürnberg. *Publications:* Mensura fistularum, Die Mensurierung der Orgelpfeifen im Mittelalter, 2 Bände, 1970, 1980; Der Contrapunctus im 14. und 15. Jahrhundert, 1974. *Contributions to:* Archiv für Musikwissenschaft; Riemann-Musiklexikon; Die Musik in Geschichte und Gegenwart; Handwörterbuch der musikalischen Terminologie; New Grove Dictionary of Music & Musicians; Geschichte der Musiktheorie; Miscellanea Mediaevalia; Schütz-Jahrbuch; Reger-Studien; Basler Jahrbuch für Historische Musikpraxis; Neues Handbuch der Musikwissenschaft; Lexikon des Mittelalters; Musiktheorie; Pirckheimer-Jahrbuch; Mozart-Jahrbuch; Warburg Institute Surveys and Texts. *Honours:* Otto-Seel-Preis, Universitätsbund Erlangen-Nürnberg, 1979. *Address:* Affalterbach Nr 14, D-91338 Igensdorf, Germany.

SACKMAN Nicholas, b. 1950, England. Composer. *Education:* Dulwich College; Nottingham University; Leeds University with Alexander Goehr. *Career:* Ensembles and Cadenzas performed 1973 at the International Gaudeamus Week and the BBC Young Composers' Forum; A Pair of Wings premiered at 1974 ISCM Festival; Leeds Festival 1976, with premiere of Ellipsis; Doubles and Flute Concerto commissioned by the BBC, and String Quartet by the Barber Institute of Fine Arts, Birmingham; Alap premiered by the BBC Philharmonic Orchestra, 1983; Hawthorn premiered at the 1993 London Proms. *Compositions:* Ensembles and Cadenzas, 1972; A Pair of Wings for 3 Sopranos and ensemble, 1970-73; Ellipsis for piano and ensemble, 1974-76; Doubles for two instrumental groups, 1977-78; String Quartet, 1978-79; Alap for orchestra, 1980-81; and the world- a wonder waking for mezzo-soprano and ensemble, 1981; SIMPLICIA, musical for schools, 1980; The Empress of Shoreditch, musical for schools, 1981; Holism for viola and cello, 1982; Time-Piece for brass quintet, 1982-83; Piano Sonata, 1983-84; Corronach for ensemble, 1985; Sonata for trombone and piano, 1986; Paraphrase for wind, 1987; Flute Concerto, 1988-89; String Quartet No 2, 1990-91; Hawthorn for Orchestra, 1993. *Address:* c/o Schott and Co, 48 Great Marlborough Street, London W1V 2BN, England.

SADAI Yizhak, b. 13 May 1935, Sofia, Bulgaria. Composer; Theorist. *Education:* Tel-Aviv Academy of Music with Haubenstock-Ramati and Boscovich, 1951-56. *Career:* Joined music staff of the University of Tel-Aviv, 1966; Professor of Music at Tel-Aviv University; As a composer influenced by the Second Viennese School, Haubenstock-Ramati, Pierre Schaeffer; Guest Professor, University of Pennsylvania, Universite de Sciences Humaines de Strasbourg, New York University, Johan-Wolfgang Goethe Universität, Frankfurt, Université de Paris Sorbonne, Hocschule für Musik und Darstellende Kunst, Frankfurt, F Liszt Academy of Music, Budapest, Conservatoire National Superieur de Musique de Paris. *Compositions:* Divertimento for flute, viola and piano, 1954; Ecclesiastes, chamber cantata, 1956; Ricercar symphonique, 1957, rev 1964; Psychoanalysis, cantata, 1959; Impressions d'un chorale for keyboard, 1960; Hazvi Israel, cantata, 1960; Interpolations variées for string quartet and keyboard, 1965; Nuances for chamber orchestra, 1965; Aria da capo for 6 instruments and tape, 1966; Prelude à Jerusalem for 3 reciters, chorus, orchestra and tape, 1968; Song into the Night for tape, 1971; From the Diary of a Percussionist for percussion and tape, 1972; Anagram for chamber orchestra and tape, 1973; 9 Pieces for piano, 1975; La prière interrompue for tape, 1975; Trial 19, for tape, 1979; Anamorphoses, for string quartet, 1983; Canti Fermi, for orchestra and Synclavier. *Publications:* Metodologia shel hateoria hamusikalit (A methodological approach to music theory), 1965; Harmony in its Systemic and Phemonemological Aspects, 1980; Analyses musicale: par l'oeil ou par l'oreille? in Analuse Musicale, 1, Paris, 1985; Les aspects systémiques et enigmatiques de la musique tonale, in International Review of the Aesthetics and Sociology of Music, 17/2, Zagreb, 1986; Le modéle syntagmatique-paradigmatique et son application à l'analyse des fonctions harmoniques, in Analyse Musicale, 2, Paris, 1986; Die Grundlagen einer systemischen Theorie der tonalen Musik, in Musiktheorie, 1990-92; articles. *Address:* c/o 83, Hayarden Street, Ramat-Gan 52 256, Israel.

SADIE Julie Anne, b. 26 Jan 1948, Eugene, Oregon, USA. Musician; Lecturer and writer on Baroque music. m. Stanley Sadie, 1978, 1 son, 1 daughter. *Education:* 1970 University of Oregon, BA, BMus; 1973 Cornell University, MA; PhD in Musicology, 1978; trained as a cellist and a viola da gambist, later took up Baroque Cello. *Career:* Taught at the Eastman School of Music, Rochester, NY, 1974-76; Freelance musician, lecturer and writer on Baroque music; Lecturer in Baroque Music King's College, University of London, 1982; Lecturer in Early Music, Royal College of Music, London, 1986-88. *Recordings:* As member of orchestra, with the Academy of Ancient Music in Mozart's Paris Symphony and with the English Bach Festival in Rameau's Castor et Pollux. *Publications:* The Bass Viol in French Baroque Chamber Music, 1980; Everyman Companion to Baroque Music, ed, 1991; The New Grove Dictionary of Women Composers, ed, with Rhian Samuel (London and New York, 1994). *Contributions to:* Gramophone, The Musical Times, Early Music, Chelys, Proceedings of the Royal Musical Association; The Times Literary Supplement. *Honours:* Ford Foundation Fellowship, 1970-74. *Memberships:* Royal Musical Association, American Musiclological Society, Viola da Gamba Society of Great Britain, American Viola da Gamba Society; Museums Association, Musicians' Union. *Hobby:* Yoga. *Address:* 12 Lyndhurst Road, Hampstead, London NW3 5NL, England.

SADIE Stanley, b. 30 Oct 1930, Wembley, Middlesex, England. Writer on Music. m. (1) Adèle Bloom, 10 Dec 1953, deceased 1978, 2 sons, 1 daughter; (2) Julie Anne McCornack, 18 July 1978, 1 son, 1 daughter. *Education:* St Paul's School, London, 1942-48; Gonville and Caius College, Cambridge University, 1950-56; BA, 1953; MusB, 1953; MA, 1957; PhD, 1958. *Career:* Professor, Trinity College of Music, 1957-65; Writer/Broadcaster, 1957-; Music Critic for The Times, 1964-81; Editor, Musical Times, 1967-87; Editor, The New Grove, 1970-; Musical Advisor, Man and Music (Granada TV), 1984-. *Publications:* Handel, 1962; Mozart, 1965; Pan Book of Opera, with A Jacobs, 1964, 1985; Beethoven (The Great Composers), 1967; Handel (The Great Composers), 1968; Handel Concertos, 1972; The New Grove Dictionary of Music and Musicians, Editor, 20 Volumes, 1980; Mozart, 1982; The New Grove Dictionary of Musical Instruments, Editor, 3 Volumes, 1984; The Cambridge Music Guide, with A Latham, 1985; The New Grove Dictionary of American Music, Editor, with H Wiley Hitchcock, 4 Volumes, 1986; Mozart Symphonies, 1986; Stanley Sadie's Brief Music Guide, 1987; Editor, The Grove Concise Dictionary of Music, 1988; Editor, History of Opera (New Grove Handbook), 1989; Editor, Man and Music (8-vol social history), 1989-; Performance Practice (New Grove Handbook), 2 Volumes, Editor, with Howard M Brown, 1990; Music Printing and Publishing (New Grove Handbook), Editor, with D W Krummel, 1990; Editor, New Grove Dictionary of Opera, 4 volumes, 1992. *Contributions to:* Many reviews, articles in Musical Times, Opera, Gramophone. *Honours:* Hon RAM, 1982; Hon LittD, 1982; CBE, 1982. *Memberships:* Royal Musical Association, President, 1989; Critics' Circle; American Musicological Society;

International Musicological Society. *Hobbies:* Watching Cricket; Drinking Wine and Coffee; Boats; Being with his family. *Address:* 12 Lyndhurst Road, London NW3 5NL, England.

SADLO Milos, b. 13 April 1912, Prague, Czechoslovakia. Cellist. *Education:* Self-taught in cello, then studied with K P Sadlo at the Prague Consevatory (1938-40) and with Casals (1955). *Career:* Member of the Prague Quartet, 1931-33; Czech Trio, 1940-56, 1973-; Suk Trio, 1957-60; Prague Trio, 1966-73; Soloist with the Czech Philharmonic Orchestra, 1949-; Teacher at the Prague Academy, 1950-; Has given the premieres of works by Khachaturian and Czeck composers; First modern performances of Dvořák's early A major Concerto and the C major Concerto of Haydn (discovered 1962). *Honour:* Artist of Merit 1962.

SAEDÉN Erik, b. 3 Sept 1924, Vanersborg, Sweden. Singer (Baritone). m. Elisabeth Murgard. *Education:* Studied at the Royal College of Music, Stockholm and at the Royal Opera School; Also Privately with Arne Sunnegarah, Martin Ohman and W Freund. *Career:* Royal Opera Stockholm from 1952 as Mozart's Figaro and Count, Wagner's Sachs, Beckmesser Pogner, Dutchman and Wolfram, Verdi's Jago, Renato, Macbeth, Germont, Ford and Nabucco; Berg's Wozzeck, Stravinsky's Nick Shadow, Tchaikovsky's Eugene Onegin, Busoni's Faust and the Title Role in Dallapiccola's Il Prigioniero; Created Leading Roles in Blomdahl's Aniara, Werle's Drommen om Therese, Berwald's Drottningen av Golconda, Dallapiccola's Ulisse, Rosenberg's Hus med Dubbel Ingang and Ligeti's Le Grand Macabre; Guest Appearances at Bayreuth, Edinburgh, Covent Garden, and Montreal; Also Savonlinna as Father Henrik in Singoalla; Recorded the Role in Complete Recording of Singoalla. *Recordings include:* The Speaker in Bergman Film Version of Die Zauberflöte; Swedish Romances, Schubert's Winterreise. *Memberships:* Stockholm Academy of Music. *Honours:* Swedish Court Singer; Order Litteris et Artibus. *Hobbies:* Sailing; Literature. *Address:* Hoglidsvagen 17 A, 182 46 Enebyberg, Sweden.

SAFFLE Michael Benton, b. 3 Dec 1946, Salt Lake City, Utah, USA. Professor. m. Sue Simmons, 21 March 1977. *Education:* Wasatch Academy, Mt Pleasant, Utah; BMus, BA, University of Utah; AM, Boston University; STM, Harvard Divinity School; PhD, Stanford University; Studies at several German Universities and Language Schools. *Career:* Instructor, Stanford University, 1977-78; Assistant Professor, Virginia Polytechnic Institute and State University, 1978-83; Associate Professor, 1983-93; Professor, 1993-; Virginia Polytechnic Institute and State University; Research Fellow, Alexander von Humboldt-Stiftung, Frankfurt a M and Heidelberg, West Germany, 1984-86; Senior Fulbright Research Fellow, Budapest, 1989-1990; Editor, Journal of the American Liszt Society, 1987-, and of the American Liszt Society Studies Series, 1989-; Co-Editor, Criticus Musicus, 1993-; Franz Liszt: A Guide to Research, (Garland 1991); Liszt in Germany, 1840-1845, Pendragon 1993. *Address:* Department of Music, Virginia Polytechnic Institute and State University, Blacksburg, VA 24061-0240, USA.

SAGAEV Dimiter, b. 27 Feb 1915, Plovdiv, Bulgaria. Composer. *Education:* Studied with Stoianov and Vladigerov at the Bulgarian State Conservatory, Sofia; graduated 1940. *Career:* Professor at the Bulgarian State Conservatory. *Compositions:* Operas: Under the Yoke, 1965; Samouil, 1975; ballet, The Madara Horseman, 1960; oratorio In the Name of Freedom, 1969; cantata poem The Shipka Epic, 1977; Youth Suite for orchestra, 1952; Sofia, symphonic poem, 1954; Three Bulgarian Symphonic Dances, 1956; 2 Violin Concertos, 1963, 1964; Viola Concerto, 1963; Oboe Concerto, 1964; Symphony for narrator, Singer, 2 Female choruses and orchestra, 1964; Bassoon Concerto, 1973; Flute Concerto, 1974; 7 String Quartets, 1945-68; 2 Wind Quintets, 1961, 1962; Trio for flute, violin, and piano, 1975; Quartet for flute, viola, harp and piano, 1975; songs; Symphony No. 2, 1977,

No. 3, 1979, No. 4, 1980, No. 5, 1981, No.6, 1982, and No. 7, 1987; Viloncello concerto, 1977; Ballet, Orpheus, 1978; Concerto, Wind orchestra, 1981; Clarinet concerto, 1983; Valdhorn concerto, 1986; Oboe concerto No. 2, 1991; Clarinet Sonata No. 3, 1989; Trumpet concerto, 1989; Piano concerto, 1992 and Oratorio in the name, The Artist, 1987. Incidental music. *Publications:* Textbook of Wind Orchestration, 1957; How to Work with Student Brass Bands, 1962; A Practical Course of Symphony and Orchestration, 1966. *Address:* KV. Istok, Bl. 25, et 6, App. 26, Sofia 1113, Bulgaria.

SAGEMULLER Dirk, b. 30 Nov 1950, Osnabruck, Germany. Singer (Baritone). *Education:* Studied in Hamburg with Gisela Litz. *Career:* Sang at the Hamburg Staatsoper From 1978, with Further Appearances at Munster, Kiel and Aachen, Teatro Verdi Trieste; Spoleto Festival as the Father in Hansel and Gretel; Other Roles have included Mozart's Count, Guglielmo, Don Giovanni and Papaageno, Rossini's Figaro and Dandini, Belcore, Valentin in Faust, Marcello, Demetrius and the Secretary in Henze's Junge Lord; Guest Engagements at Geneva, Dusseldorf, Mannheim, Wiesbaden and Charleston; Concert showings in works by Bach, Handel, Mozart and Orff. *Recordings include:* Count Ceprano in Rigoletto. *Address:* c/o Stadtheater, Theaterstrasse 1-3, 5100 Aachen, Germany.

SAHL Michael, b. 2 Sept 1934, Boston, Mass, USA. Composer. *Education:* Amherst College, BA 1955; Princeton University with Sessions and Babbitt, MFA 1957; Berkshire Music Center with Foss and Copland; With Dallapiccola in Florence 1957, on Fulbright Fellowship. *Career:* Creative Asssociate at SUNY, Buffalo, 1957; Worked at New York radio station WBAI-FM, music director 1972-73; Associated with Eric Salzman in several music-theatre productions. *Compositions:* Operas (collaborations with Salzman): The Conjuror, 1975; Stauf, 1976; Civilizations and its Discontents, 1977; Noah, 1978; The Passion of Simple Simon, 1979; Boxes, radio opera 1982; Instrumental: A Mitzah for the Dead for violin and tape, 1966; String Quartet, 1969; 5 Symphonies, 1972, 1973, 1978, 1982, 1983; Piano Sonata, 1972; Violin Concerto, 1974; Dances of Glass, 1980; Cocktail Wanderings for piano, 1982; The Exiles Cafe for chamber ensemble, 1984; In the Woods for clarinet, violin, piano and double bass, 1984; Vocal: Strangers in the Land of Beulah, hymn for soprano and piano, 1982; Reflections for 6 voices, string quartet and brass quintet; Film scores; Tape Pieces. *Publication:* Making Changes: a Practical Guide to Vernacular Harmony (with Salzman), 1977. *Honour:* Prix Italia 1980 for Civilizations and its Discontents. *Address:* c/o ASCAP, ASCAP Building, One Lincoln Plaza, New York, NY 10023, USA.

SAKS Gidon, b. 1960, Israel. Singer (Bass). *Education:* Studied at Royal Northern College of Music and at University of Toronto with Patricia Kern. *Debut:* Stratford Festival, Canada, as the Mikado. *Career:* Sang with Canadian Opera Company in Barbiere di Siviglia, Carmen, Les Contes d'Hoffmann, La Bohème and Anna Bolena; Gelsenkirchen Opera in Der Freischütz, Gianni Schicchi, Der Rosenkavalier, Die Zauberflöte and L'Italiana in Algeri; Member of the Bielefeld Opera, and sang Colline in La Bohème for New Israel Opera; Berlin debut in Les Beatitudes by Cesar Franck, with Dietrich Fischer-Dieskau; Season 1991-92 as Seneca in l'Incoronazione di Poppea at Madrid and Leporello with Scottish Opera; Season 1992/93 as Claggart in Billy Budd for Scottish Opera, followed by Achillas in a new production of Julius Caesar. *Recordings:* Zemlinsky's Der Kreidekreis; Schreker's Ferne Klang conducted by Gerd Albrecht. *Address:* Kaye Artists Management, Barratt House, 7 Chertsey Road, Woking GU21 5AB, England.

SALAFF Peter, b. 1942, USA. Violinist. *Career:* Member of the Cleveland Quartet 1968-; Regular tours of the United States, Canada, Europe, Japan, the Soviet Union, South America, Australia, New Zealand and the Middle East; On faculty of the Eastman School,

Rochester and in residence at the Aspen Music Festival, co-founding the Center for Advanced Quartet Studies; Tour of the Soviet Union and five European countries 1988; Season 1988-89 with appearances at the Metropolitan Museum and Alice Tully Hall, New York; Concerts in Paris, London, Bonn, Prague, Lisbon and Brussels; Festivals of Salzburg, Edinburgh and Lucerne; Many complete Beethoven cycles and annual appearances at Lincoln Center;s Mostly Mozart Festival; In addition to standard repertory, performances of works by Ives, John Harbison, Sergei Slonimsky, Samuel Adler, George Perle, Christopher Rouse and Toru Takemitsu. *Recordings:* Repertoire from Mozart to Ravel on CBS Masterworks, Pro Arte, Philips, RCA and Telarc labels; Collaborations with Alfred Brendel (Schubert Trout Quintet), Pinchas Zukerman and Bernard Greenhouse (Brahms Sextets), Emanuel Ax, Yo Yo Ma and Richard Stoltzman. *Address:* Eastman School of Music, 26 Gibbs Street, Rochester, NY 14604, USA.

SALLINEN Aulis, b. 9 Apr 1935, Salmi, Finland. Composer. *Education:* Studies with Aarre Merikanto and Joonas Kokkonen, Sibelius Academy, Helsinki, Finland. *Career:* Teaching post, Sibelius Academy, Helsinki, Finland; Administrator, Finnish radio Symphony Orchestra, 1960-70; secretary, Chairman, Finnish Composers Association; Board Member, Finnish National Opera; Chairman, Tedsto Professor of Arts, Life Appointment by the Finnish Government. *Compositions include:* Mauermusik, 1962; Elegy for Sebastian Knight, 1964; Cadenze, 1965; Notturno, 1966; Quattro per Quattro, 1965; Violin Concerto, 1968; String Quartet No 3, 1969; String Quartet No 4, 1971; Chaconne, 1970; Chorali, 1970; Symphony No 1, 1971; Symphony No 2, 1972; Opera: The Horseman, 1973; Symphony No 3, 1975; Symphony No 4, 1979; Chamber Music I, 1975; Chamber Music II, 1976; Sonata for Solo Cello, 1971; Cello Concerto, 1976; Suita Grammaticale, 1971; Songs for the Sea, 1974; Song Around a Song, 1980; Four Dream Songs, 1972; Opera: The Red Line, 1978; Dies Irae, 1978; The Iron Age; Shadows; Opera, The King goes forth to France, 1984; Symphony No 5, 1985; Opera: Kullervo 1988; Symphony No 6, 1989; Opera: The Palace, 1993. *Recordings:* The major works are recorded by BIS (Stockholm, Sweden) and Finlandia Records (Helsinki, Finland). *Honours:* Wihuri International Sibelius Prize, Member of the Royal Swedish Music Academy, 1983. *Address:* TEOSTO, Lauttasaarentie 1, 00200 Helsinki 20, Finland.

SALMINEN Matti, b. 7 July 1945, Turku, Finland. Singer (Bass). *Education:* Studied at the Sibelius Academy, Helsinki, and in Rome. *Debut:* Helsinki Opera 1969, as King Philip in Don Carlos. *Career:* Sang in Cologne, Zurich and Berlin 1972-76, in the principal bass parts; La Scala Milan 1973, as Fafner; Savonlinna Festival 1975 as The Horseman, Sarastro, Philip, in Don Carlos, Daland, Ramphis; Bayreuth 1978- as Daland, the Landgrave, Titurel, King Mark and in the Ring operas; Metropolitan Opera from 1981, as King Mark, Rocco, Osmin, Fasolt, Fafner, Hunding and Hagen; in Berlin, 1985 and Munich 1987, Fasolt, Hunding and Hagen; Prince Kchovansky 1984 in San Francisco and 1988 in Barcelona; Boris Godunow 1984 in Zurich and 1985 in Barcelona; in Zurich the Ponnelle productions of L'Incoroanzione di Poppea, Zauberflöte and Die Entführung and several principal bass parts in Vienna, Hamburg, Paris, Chicago, Tokyo; Sang Hunding in Die Walküre at the Metropolian 1990 (also televised); Rocco in Fidelio at the Los Angeles Music Center, Daland at the 1990 Savonlinna Festival; Season 1992/93 as Daland at the Met, Rocco at Zurich and Savonlinna, King Philip at the Deutsche Oper Berlin and Sarastro at the Savonlinna Festival. *Recordings:* St Matthew Passion, the Landgrave, and the Ring for Deutsche Grammophon; Sallinen's The Horseman for Finlandia; For Philips Daland and the Ring; For HMV Mozart's Requiem and the Ring; For Teldec, Osmin, Sarastro and the Ring. *Address:* c/o Ingpen and Williams Ltd, 14 Kensington Court, London W9 5DN, England.

SALMON Philip, b. 1960, England. Singer (Tenor). *Education:* Studied at the Royal College of Music. *Career:*

Debut Recital at the City of London festival, Folowed by the St Matthew Passion with the Rotterdam Philharmonic, Beethoven's Ninth with the Ulster Orchestra and the Netherlands Philharmonic, Mozart's Requiem with the Florida Philharmonic; Sang in Massenet's La Vierge at St Ettienne, 1991; Operatic repertoire includes Mozart's Tamino and Belmonte for Pavilion Opera and Debussy's Pelleas at Marseille and Strasbourg, 1990-91; Sang Belmonte in Die Entführung at the Buxton Festival, 1991, Albert Herring at St Albans. *Honours include:* Young Musicians Recordings Prize. *Address:* Anglo Swiss Limited, 3 Primrose Mews, 1a Sharpleshall Street, London NW1 8YW, England.

SALOMAA Petteri, b. 1961, Helsinki, Finland. Singer (Baritone). *Education:* Studied at the Sibelius Academy and with Hans Hotter and Kim Borg. *Debut:* Finnish National Opera, Helsinki, 1983 as Mozart's Figaro. *Career:* Appeared at the Ludwigsburg and Schwetzingen Festivals, 1984; Wexford Festival, 1985, as the King in Ariodante; Drottningholm from 1986, as Leporello and Nardo in La Finta Giardiniera; Geneva Opera, 1987, as Papageno and Amsterdam, 1988, as Masetto, conducted by Nikolaus Harnoncourt; North American debut 1988, with Messiah in San Francisco, followed by Figaro with Michigan Opera; Season 1989-90 at Freiburg Opera as Faninal, Ned Keene, the Father in Hansel and Gretel, and in Purcell's King Arthur; 1989-91 at Freiburg Opera as Billy Budd, Posa, Ned Keene and Belcore, 1991 at Frankfurt Opera as Papageno and Guglielmo, 1993 as Conte Robinson in Il matrimonio Segreto; Other roles include Oreste in Iphigénie en Tauride, Posa, Billy Budd and Albert in Werther. *Honours include:* First prize, National Singing Competition at Lappeenranta, 1981. *Recordings include:* Beethoven's Ninth Symphony (EMI); La Finta Giardiniera (World Video); The Fiery Angel by Prokofiev, and Peer Gynt with the Berlin Philharmonic, EMI; Le Nozze di Figaro (Decca); Mendelssohn Elias (Harmonia Mundi). *Address:* Festium Agency, Partiotic 34, 00370 Helsinki, Finland.

SALOMAN Ora Frishberg, b. 14 Nov 1938, Brooklyn, New York, USA. Musicologist; Professor of Music. m. Dr Edward Barry Saloman, 1 July 1968. *Education:* PhD, Musicology, MA, Musicology, AB, Music, Columbia University, New York; Studied violin with, Vladimir Graffman and Ivan Galamian; Chamber music with, Raphael Hillyer, Claus Adam and William Kroll. *Career:* Chairman, Department of Music, 1978-84, Professor of Music, Baruch College, City University of New York. *Publications:* Essays in Music and Civilisation: Essays in Honor of Paul Henry Lang, 1984; Music in America before 1825, in press; Essay in Music and the French Revolution, 1992. *Contributions to:* Acta Musicologica; Musical Quarterly; Music and Man; The Pennsylvania Magazine of History and Biography; Dallas Opera Magazine; American Music; The Journal of Musicology, (1992); International Review of the Aesthetics and Sociology of Music; The New Grove Dictionary of Opera, 1992; St James International Dictionary of Opera, 1993; American National Biography. *Address:* 14 Summit Street, Englewood, NJ 07632, USA.

SALONEN Esa-Pekka, b. 30 Jun 1958, Helsinki, Finland. Conductor. *Education:* Qualified French Horn player by age 19. *Career:* Composer, 1970-; Conducting Composer, 1980; Conducted performances of Mahler's 3rd Symphony, Philharmonia Orchestra, London, England, 1983; Music Director, Los Angeles Philharmonic Orchestra, 1992-; Chief Conductor, Swedish Radio Symphony Orchestra, 1985; Principal Guest Conductor, Philharmonia Orchestra, London, England; Oslo Philharmonic Orchestra; Led the first performance of Robert Saxton's The Circles of Light, 1986; Conducted Messiaen's St Francis d'Assise at the Salzburg Festival, 1992. *Recordings include:* Lutoslawski's Third Symphony, numerous works by Stravinsky, Sibelius' Symphony No 5, Messiaen's Turangalîla, Symphonie, Mahler's 4th Symphony; with various orchestras including the London Sinfonietta, the Philharmonia Orchestra and the Los Angeles Philharmonic Orchestra. *Compositions:* Horn Music 1, 1976; Cello Sonata; Nachtlieder, 1978; Goodbye, 1980;

Concerto for Saxophone and Orchestra; Auf der ersten Blick und ohne zu wissen; Giro; Baalal; Yta; Yta 1; 2; Meeting; Wind Quintet; Floof; Mimo II. *Address:* c/o Van Walsum Management, 26 Wadham Road, London, SW15 2LR.

SALTA Anita, b. 1 Sept 1937, NY, USA. Singer (Soprano). *Education:* Studied in New York. *Debut:* Jacksonville, 1959 as Aida. *Career:* Appearances at Such German Opera House Centres as Stuttgart, Wuppertal, Nuremberg, Dortmund, Cassel, Essen and Hanover; Other roles have included Gluck's Alceste, Mozart's Countess, Donna Elvira and Fiordiligi, Marquerite, the Trovatore and Forza Leonoras, Traviata, Desdemona, Helene and Elisabeth de Valois; Tatina, Antonida in A Life for the Tsar, Marenka, Mimi, Butterfly, Santuzza, Elsa, Eva, Chrysothemis, the Marschallin and Katerina Ismailova; Many concert appearances. *Address:* c/o Theatre, Rolandstrasse 10, 4300 Essen, Germany.

SALTER Lionel Paul, b. 8 Sept 1914, London, England. Musicologist; Critic; Broadcaster; Harpsichordist. m. Christine Fraser, 11 Oct 1939. 3 sons. *Education:* BA 1935, MusB 1936, MA 1938, St John's College, Cambridge; London Academy of Music, 1923-31; Royal College of Music, 1931-32 and 1935-36, LRAM, 1930. *Career:* Pianist/Arranger/Composer in films and TV, 1936-39; During Army Service, Guest Conductor Radio France, 1943-44; Assistant Conductor, BBC Theatre Orchestra 1945, Producer 1946, European Music Supervisor 1948, Artists Manager 1954, Head of Overseas Music 1955, Head of TV Music 1956, Head of Opera 1963, Assistant Controller (Music) 1967-74; Opera Coordinator & Chairman, Radio Music Group, European Broadcasting Union, 1972-75; Performances in 17 countries as Harpsichordist; Pianist; Conductor. *Compositions:* Music for radio plays; songs; Scottish Reel (for 2 pianos); Air & Scherzino (oboe); Performing editions of operas by Cavalli & Lully, numerous 18th century violin works; Editor, Associated Board examination music. *Recordings:* Concertos by Haydn & Bach; Harpsichord in numerous recordings. *Publications:* Going to a Concert, 1950; Going to the Opera, 1955; The Musician and his World, 1963; Music and the 20th Century Media, with J Bornoff, 1972; Gramophone Guide to Classical Composers, 1978; General Editor, BBC Music Guides, 1971-75; Translations of over 100 libretti. *Contributions to:* Gramophone, 1948-; Listener, Musical Times; New Grove Dictionary of Opera (Four Volumes), 1992. *Membership:* Vice-Chairman, British Federation of Music Festivals, 1985-88. *Address:* 26 Woodstock Road, London NW11 8ER, England.

SALTER Richard, b. 12 Nov 1943, Hindhead, Surrey, England. Singer (Baritone). *Education:* Studied at Royal College of Music, London, then at the Vienna Academy of Music with Christain Moeller, Ilse Rapf and Anton Dermota. *Career:* Sang with King's Singers and gave concert performances; opera debut Darmstadt 1973; sang further in Frankfurt and at Glyndebourne; Kiel Opera 1979, as Don Giovanni; Guest appearances in Berlin and Hanover; Hamburg Staatsoper 1979, as Lenz in the premiere of Wolfgang Rihm's Jakob Lenz; sang Beckmesser at the Paris Opéra 1988, Hamlet in Rihm's Die Hamletmaschine at Hamburg; Season 1992/93 as the Master in Höller's Meister und Margarita at Cologne and Cortez in the premiere of Rihm's Die Eroberung von Mexico at Hamburg. *Recording:* Jakob Lenz, on Harmonia Mundi. *Address:* c/o Hamburgische Staatsoper, Grosse Theaterstraase 34, D-2000 Hamburg 36, Germany.

SALTER Timothy, b. 15 Dec 1942, Mexborough, Yorkshire, England. Musician; Composer; Conductor; Pianist. *Education:* MA, St John's College, Cambridge University, 1960-64; MTC, London University, 1965, LRAM; ARCO. *Career:* Musical Director, The Ionian Singers; Pianist (Chamber Music) on tours in Great Britain and Internationally; Conductor and Pianist on recordings and broadcasts; Professor, Royal College of Music. *Compositions:* Instrumental works, chamber music, songs, choral works and orchestral works; Recordings include many choral works, piano works, 2 string quartets and other chamber music. *Recordings:* Selection of choral music; Fantasy on a Theme by J S Bach, Piano; String Quartets numbers 1 and 2; Abstractions (oboe trio); Variations, 1986; English Folk Song arrangements; Katharsios (chorus, piano, percussion); Perspectives (set two) (piano). *Publications:* Thomas Campion - Poet, Composer, Physician (co-author, Edward Lowbury and Alison Young), 1970. *Address:* 26 Caterham Road, London SE13 5AR, England.

SALVA Tadeas, b. 22 Oct 1937, Lucky Pri Ruzomberku, Slovakia. Composer. *Education:* Studied Composition with Alexander Moyzes and Jan Cikker in Slovakia, Szabelski and Lutoslawski in Poland. *Career:* Head of Music Broadcasting, Kosice Radio, 1965; Producer for Slovak TV in Bratislava, 1968; Dramaturg for the Slovak Folk art Group. *Compositions include:* Operas Margita and Besna; Tears; Mechurik Koscurik and His Friends; 4 String Quartets; Symphony of Love for Narrator; Concerto for Cello and Chamber Orchestra; Music in Memoriam Arthur Honegger for Organ, Bass Voice, Trumpet and Strings. *Address:* c/o SOZA (Slovakia), PRS Ltd, Member Registration, 29-33 Berners Street, London W1P 4AA, England.

SALVADORI Antonio, b. 1950, Venice, Italy. Singer (Baritone). *Education:* Studied at the Conservatorio Benedetto Marcello, Venice. *Career:* Sang first in Il Barbiere di Siviglia and Pagliacci; La Scala 1977 in Luisa Miller, with Caballe and Pavarotti; Verona Arena from 1978, notably as Amonasro (1988); Marcello and Belcore at La Scala 1987-88, tour with the company to Japan 1988; Has sung Rossini's William Tell in Milan, Linz, Nice, Zurich and New York (concert performance at Carnegie Hall); Vienna Staatsoper 1988, as Ezio in Attila; Sang Simon Boccanegra at Cremona, 1990; Other appearances at Chicago, Venice (Gerard in Andrea Chénier), Turin and Hamburg (Don Carlo in Ernani). *Address:* c/o Opernhaus Zurich, Falkenstrasse 1, CH-8008 Zurich, Switzerland.

SALVATORE Ramon, b. 25 Aug 1944, Oak Park, Illinois, USA. Concert Pianist; Educator. *Education:* BMus, Millikin University, Decatur, Illinois, 1967; MMus with honours, distinction in Piano Performance, New England Conservatory of Music, Boston, Massachusetts, 1969; Aspen School of Music, Colorado, 1970; Postgraduate study, Royal Academy of Music, London, England, 1974-77; Student of Gordon Green; Private study with William Masselos, New York City, 1985. *Debut:* Wigmore Hall, London, 1977; Carnegie Recital Hall, New York City, 1980; Orchestra Hall, Chicago, IL, 1990. *Career:* 2 broadcasts, Capitol Radio, 1975-76; 3 recitals, St Martin-in-the-Fields, London, 1976-78; Appearances, Purcell Room, 1979, Merkin Concert Hall, New York City, 1985; 2 appearances, American Music Festival at National Gallery of Art, Washington DC, live radio broadcasts, 1983, 1989; Numerous broadcasts, National Public Radio, USA, 1983-; Extensive performances on university campuses nationally, USA; Performances include commissions and rarely heard US works; Faculty positions: University of Kansas, 1969-70; St Cloud State University, Minnesota, 1970-74; Ithaca College, New York, 1977-86; Charterhouse School, England, 1975-76; Three-Concert Series, American Music in the Grand Tradition, performed concurrently at the Weill Recital Hall at Carnegie Hall, New York and at the Chicago Public Library Cultural Center, 1991; Faculty, Music Center of the North Shore, Winnetka, Illinois, 1991; Faculty, Merit Music Program, Chicago, Illinois, 1986-1992; Performances supported by the National Endowment for the Arts. *Current Management:* Chicago Concert Artists, 431 S Dearborn Street, Chicago, IL 60606 and 1752 Wilson Avenue, Arcadia, CA 91006, USA. *Address:* 5617 Capri Lane, Morton Grove, IL 60053, USA.

SALWAROWSKI Jerzy Hubert, b. 7 Sept 1946, Cracow, Poland. Conductor; Musical Director. m. Ewa Czarniecka, 19 Sept 1976, 2 sons, 2 daughters.

Education: II Liceum Ogolnoksztazcace im. 7 Sobieskiego, (Secondary School), 1965; Cracow Music High School, Conducting and Composition, Graduated, 1970. *Career:* Assistant Conductor, Cracow Philharmonic Choir, 1970-71; Second Conductor, Opole Philharmonic Orchestra, 1972-78; Second Conductor, Katowice-Silesian Philharmonic, 1978-81; Substitute Art Director, Silesian Philharmonic, 1982-84; Substitute Art Director, Polish Radio National Symphony Orchestra, 1985-; Guest Conductor, Lodz Great Opera House, tours in Europe. *Compositions:* Only elaboration and theatre music. *Recordings:* All Gershwin's Pieces for Piano and Orchestra (with A Ratusinski), 2 plates; All Symphonic Poems by M Karlowicz, 3 plates; J Sibelius: Saga and Violin Concerto (with V Brodski) for Musical Heritage Society, Amreco, USA, First Digital in Poland; H Wieniawski, Violin Concerto (with V Brodski) also for Amreco; Permanent Recording for Polish Radio and TV (about 250 minimum in year); TV Concerts, TV Cycles, Musical Drawing Room. *Publications:* New Elaborations of Karlowicz Scores in PWM Edition. *Contributions to:* Permanent Reviews. *Hobbies:* Yachting; Skiing; Cycling; Hunting. *Address:* 40-236 Katowice, VL Wietnamska 63B, Poland.

SALZEDO Leonard, b. 24 Sept 1921, London, England. Composer. *Education:* Royal College of Music, with Isolde Menges (violin) and Herbert Howells (composition) 1940-44. *Career:* Ballet: The Fugitive commissioned by Marie Rambert; Symphony premiered by Beecham 1956 at the Royal Festival Hall. *Compositions:* Ballets: The Fugitive, 1944; Mardi Gras, 1946; Witch Boy, 1956; The Travellers, 1963; Agriona, 1964; Realms of Choice, 1965; Hazard, 1967; Ballet Drei 1973, 1973; Orchestral: Gabble Retchit, symphonic poem, 1955; Symphony, 1956; Rendezvous, 1960; Concerto fervido, 1964; Paean to the Sun, 1966; Toccata, 1967; Percussion Concerto, 1969; 7 String Quartets; Songs; Divertimento for Brass, 1959; Capriccio for Brass, 1978. *Address:* 363 Bideford Green Leighton Buzzard, Bedford, LU7 7TX, England.

SALZMAN Eric, b. 8 Sept 1933, New York, USA. Composer; Writer on Music. *Education:* BA Columbia College, Columbia University, 1954; MFA Princeton University, 1956; teachers include Otto Luening, Ussachevsky, Jack Beeson, Roger Sessions and Milton Babbitt; continued studies in Europe with Petrassi in Rome and at Darmstadt. *Career:* Music critic for the New York Times, 1958-62; Music critic for New York Herald Tribune, 1963-66; taught at Queens College, New York, 1966-68; director, New Images of Sounds, series of concerts at Hunter College; 1970 founded Quog Music Theater, to explore novel ideas in the performing arts; editor, Musical Quarterly, 1984; Co-founder and Artistic Director, American Music Theater Festival, with Marjorie Samoff, Philadelphia, 1983-. *Compositions:* String Quartet, 1955; Flute Sonata, 1956; Inventions for orchestra, 1959; The Owl and the Cuckoo for soprano, guitar and chamber ensemble, 1963; Verses and Cantos for 4 voices, instruments and electronics, 1967; Larynx Music, dance piece with tape, 1968; The Nude Paper Sermon for actor, Renaissance consort, chorus and electronics, 1969; The Conjurer, multi-media spectacle, 1975; Civilization and its Discontents, opera buffa for radio, 1977; Noah, spectacle, 1978; The Passion of Simple Simon, for performance at the Electric Circus in Greenwich Village; Variations on a Sacred Harp Tune for harpsichord, 1982; Boxes, radio opera with Michael Sahl, 1983; Big Jim and the Small-Time Investors, music theater, 1985; adaptation of Gershwin's Strike up the Band, 1984. *Publications include:* 20th Century Music: an Introduction, 1967; new edition, 1987; Civilization and its Discontents and Making Changes, a handbook of vernacular harmony, both with Michael Sahl. *Address:* American Music Thater Festival, 1 Franklin Plaza, Philadelphia, PA 19103, USA.

SAMARITANI Pier Luigi, b. 29 Sept 1942, Novare, Italy. Opera Set and Costumes Designer; Director. *Education:* Accademia de Brera, Milan, Italy; Centre d'Art Dramatique, Paris. *Debut:* As Director, Werther,

Florence, 1978. *Career:* Assisted Stage Designer, Lila de Nobili, Paris; Set Designer: Théâtre du Gymnase, Paris, 1962, Teatre dell'Opera, Rome, 1964; Dance Design for American Ballet Theatre, 1980; Stage Designer for many companies in USA and Europe. Exhibited Stage Designs Spoleto Festival, 1972; Ernani Met/Eugene Onegin Lyric Opera of Chicago/Werther Vienna, Paris, Florence, Butterfly Berlin (1987); Season 1992 with Andrea Chenier at Florence and Turin and Die Meistersinger at Spoleto. *Current Management:* Herbert H Breslin Incorporated, New York City, USA. *Address:* c/o Herbert H Breslin Incorporated, 119 W 57th Street, New York, NY 10019, USA.

SAMKOPF Kjell, b. 6 Apr 1952, Baerum, Norway. Composer. *Education:* Studied at the Norwegian State Academy of Music and at the Institute for Sonology, Utrecht. *Career:* Percussionist in Trondheim Symphony Orchestra; Festival Composer at the North Norway Music Festival, 1985; JSCM Festival, Århus, 1982. *Compositions include:* Associations for Large Orchestra; Aqua; Tide. *Recordings:* Aqua; Contemporary Music for Big Band; Solo Percussion with Electronics. *Publications include:* Praktisk Trommeskole. *Honour:* Baerum Kommunes Kulturpris. *Hobby:* Chess. *Address:* Presteveien 38 A, N-1300 Sandvika, Norway.

SAMS Eric, b. 3 May 1926, London, England. Civil Servant (retired); Writer on Music. m. Enid Tidmarsh, 30 June 1952, 2 sons. *Education:* Westcliff, 1937-44; Corpus Christi, Cambridge, 1947-50; BA (1st class hons), 1950; PhD, 1972. *Career:* Army Cryptanalysis, 1947-50; Civil Service, 1950-78; Visiting Professor, McMaster University, Hamilton, Ontario, Canada, 1976-77; TV film on Code and Cipher in Music, 1989. *Publications:* The Songs of Hugo Wolf, 1961, 2/1983, 3/1993; The Songs of Robert Schumann, 1969, 2/1975, 3/1993; Brahms Songs, 1971, French translation, 1989. *Contributions to:* New Grove Dictionary of Music and Musicians: Ballad, Cryptography, Hanslick, Lied IV, Mörike, Wolf, Schubert (work list and bibliography), Schumann (work list and bibliography); Reviews and articles in Musical Times, 1965-89; TLS, 1974-93. *Honour:* Honorary Member of Guildhall School of Music and Drama, 1983. *Hobbies:* Shakespeare studies: Historical cipher and shorthand; chess. *Address:* 32 Arundel Avenue, Sanderstead, Surrey CR2 8BB, England.

SAMSON Thomas James, b. 6 July 1946, Northern Ireland. University Teacher. *Education:* Annadale Grammar School, Belfast, 1958-65; B Mus, First Class Hons, Queen's University, Belfast, 1965-69; M Mus, PhD, LTCL, University College, Cardiff, 1969-72. *Career:* Research Fellow in Humanities, University of Leicester, 1972-73; Lecturer in Music, University of Exeter, 1973-1986; Reader in Musicology, University of Exeter, 1986-1991; Professor of Musicology University of Exeter, 1991. *Publications:* Music in Transition, 1977; The Music of Szymanowski, 1980; The Music of Chopin, 1985; Chopin Studies, 1988; Man and Music vol 7 The Late Romantic Era, 1991; The Cambridge Companion to Chopin, 1992; Chopin: The Four Ballades, 1992. *Contributions to:* Rocznik Chopinowski, Journal of the American Musicological Society, Nineteenth-century Music, Tempo, Journal of Musicology, Music Analysis, Music and Letters, Musical Times. *Honours:* Szymanowski Centennial Medal 1982; Order of Merit of the Polish Ministry of Culture, 1990. *Membership:* Council member, Royal Musical Association. *Hobbies:* Walking; Reading. *Address:* University of Exeter, Music Department, Knightley, Streatham Drive, Exeter EX4 4PD, England.

SAMUEL Gerhard, b. 20 Apr 1924, Germany. Conductor; Composer; Professor of Music. *Education:* BM, Eastman School of Music; MM, Yale University. *Career:* Conductor, Ballet Ballads on Broadway, 1947-48; Attached to Cultural Attache, American Embassy, Paris, 1948-49; Associate Conductor and Violinist, Minneapolis Symphony, 1949-59; Director and Conductor, Collegium Musicum, Minneapolis Civic Opera, 1949-59; Director and conductor, San Francisco Composers Forum, 1959-71; Music Director/Conductor, San Francisco Ballet, 1960-70; Guest Conductor, San Francisco Opera; Music Director, Oakland Symphony Orchestra, 1959-71; Director and Conductor, Ojai Festival, 1971; Associate Conductor, Los Angeles Philharmonic Orchestra, 1970-73; Conductor of Orchestra and Opera and Director of Conducting Program, California Institute of the Arts, 1972-76; Director of Orchestral Activities, College-Conservatory of Music, University of Cincinnati, 1976-; Conductor, Music Director, Cincinnati Chamber Orchestra, 1983-; Guest conductor, USA, South America, Mexico, Canada, the Philippines, England, Belgium, France, Germany, Norway, Russia, Poland and Switzerland; Chief Guest Conductor, Oakland Ballet Company, 1983-. *Compositions include:* Requiem for Survivors, 1973; Looking at Orphans Looking, 1971 (2 string quartets); Chamber Concerto for Flute in the Shape of a Summer, 1981; Emperor and the Nightingale, 1980; Fanfare for a Pleasant Occasion, 1981; For Sandy on His Birthday, 1981; Harlequin's Caprice, 1980; On the Beach at Night Alone, 1980; The Naumburg Cadenza, 1985; Nocturne on an Impossible Dream, 1986; Nicholas and Concepcion, 1987; As Imperceptibly as Grief, 1988; Christ, what are patterns for?, 1988; Henry's Cadenza, 1989; Apollo and Hyocinth, 1989; His Cincinnati Philharmonia Orchestra participated in the 1989 Mahler Cyle, Châtelet Theatre, Paris. *Recordings:* Numerous. *Honours:* Recipient of several NEA grants; New York Composers Showcase awards; Meet the Composer grants. *Address:* 412 Liberty Hill 2C, Cincinnati, Ohio 45210, USA.

SAMUEL Harold E, b. 12 Apr 1924, Hudson, Wisconsin, USA. Music Librarian; Musicologist. m. Hella Deffner, 2 sons, 1 daughter. *Education:* BA, 1949, MA, 1955, University of Minnesota; Studied Musicology with A Cherbuliez, University of Zurich, 1950-51, with Hans Heinrich Eggebrecht at the University of Erlangen, 1955-57 and with Donald J Grout at Cornell University; PhD, Cornell University, 1963. *Career:* Music Librarian and Associate Professor of Music, Cornell University, 1957-71; (Chairman, Department of Music, 1970-71); Music Librarian and Professor of Music, Yale University, 1971-; Editor-in-Chief of Notes, the Quarterly Journal of the Music Library Association, 1965-70. *Publications:* The Cantata in Nuremberg during the Seventeenth Century, 1982. *Contributions to:* music encyclopedias and journals. *Address:* School of Music, 96 Wall Street, Yale University, New Haven, CT 06520, USA.

SAMUELSON Mikael, b. 9 Mar 1951, Stockholm, Sweden. Singer (Baritone). *Education:* Studied with Birgit Stenberg and Erik Werba. *Career:* Has sung in Sweden from 1968 in opera, oratorio, music theatre and films; Royal Opera Stockholm as Rossini's Figaro; Drottningholm Theatre 1987 and 1989, as Mozart's Figaro and Papageno; Sang in Die Schöpfung 1988; Appearances with the Stockholm Music Drama Ensemble in Pagliacci, Mahagonny and Death in Venice; Television engagements in Drömmen om Thérèse by Werle and Kronbruden by Rangström; Has appeared as cabaret artist in Sweden and Finland. *Address:* c/o Drottningholms Slottsteater, PO Box 27050, S-102 51 Stockholm, Sweden.

SAND Annemarie, b. 26 Nov 1958, Copenhagen, Denmark. Singer (Mezzo-soprano). *Education:* Studied at the Royal Academy of Music, and the National Opera Studio. *Career:* Appeared with English National Opera from 1987, as the Page in Salome, Linetta in The Love of Three Oranges and Dryad in Ariadne auf Naxos; Welsh National Opera 1989, as the Composer in Ariadne, conducted by Charles Mackerras; Other roles include Mother Goose in The Rake's Progress, Nancy in Albert Herring, Charlotte, Octavian, Hansel and the Mother in Amahl and the Night Visitors; Many concert appearances, including Mozart's Requiem at the Teatro San Carlo, Naples and 12 concerts in Denmark, 1989; Season 1992 as Kate Pinkerton for ENO and in Oliver's Mario and the Magician at the Almeida Theatre. *Honours include:* Elena Gerhardt Lieder Prize; Minnie Hauk Prize; Clifton Prize for best recital. *Address:* c/

o Athole Still Ltd, Greystoke House, 80-86 Westow Street, London SE19 3AF, England.

SAND Malmfrid, b. 1955, Oslo, Norway. Singer (Soprano). *Education:* Studied in Oslo and London. *Debut:* Sang Pamina in Die Zauberflöte at Oslo. *Career:* Appearances as Fiodiligi in Brussels, London and at the Bath Festival; Irene in Tamerlano for Orpheus Opera and Isaura in Jerusalem by Verdi for BBC Radio 3; Wexford Festival 1983, as the Queen in Marschner's Hans Heiling, returning as Donna Anna in Gazzaniga's Don Giovanni and in Busoni's Turandot; Recent Engagements as Electra in Idomeneo for the English Bach festival and Manon for Dorset Opera, 1991; Concert Repertoire includes Vivaldi Gloria, Messiah, Dvořáks Requiem; Concerts and Recitals in Scandinavia, the USA and Europe, notably with the Stavanger Symphony, the Oslo NRK Symphony and the Harmonien Symphony Orchestra of Bergen. *Address:* c/o English National Opera, St Martin's Lane, London WC2, England.

SANDERLING Kurt, b. 19 Sept 1912, Arys, Germany. Conductor. *Education:* Studied privately, while working as repetiteur with the Berlin Städtische Oper 1931. *Career:* Left Germany 1936 and was conductor of the Moscow Radio Symphony Orchestra, 1936-41; Leningrad Philharmonic Orchestra, 1941-60 (Chief professor of conducting and orchestral classes at the Leningrad Conservatory); Berlin Symphony Orchestra, 1960-77; Dresden State Orchestra, 1964-67; Guest apearances at the Prague, Warsaw, Salzburg and Vienna Festivals; British debut 1970, with the Leipzig Gewandhaus Orchestra; New Philharmonia Orchestra, 1972-; Recent visits to Japan, USA, Canada, Australia and New Zealand; Conducted the Los Angeles Philharmonic at Symphony Hall, Birmingham, 1991; Haydn's 39th Symphony and Shostakovich No 8. *Recordings:* All Beethoven's Symphonies with the Philharmonia Orchestra, 1981; Beethoven's Piano Concertos (Gilels); Complete Symphonies of Brahms and Sibelius; Prokofiev Sinfonia Concertante (Rostropovitch); Mozart Divertimento K334, Concertos K216 (Kogan) and K466 (Richter); Haydn Symphonies, 88, 45, 104, 82-87; Bruckner's 3rd Symphony and Shostakovich nos 8, 10 and 15. *Honours:* Soviet award of Honoured Artist; National Prize of the German Democratic Republic 1962, 1974. *Address:* c/o Norman McCann International Artists Limited, The Coach House, 56 Lawrie Park Gardens, London, SE26 6XJ, England.

SANDERLING Thomas, b. 2 Nov 1942, Nowosibirsk, USSR. Conductor. *Education:* School of the Leningrad Conservatory; German High School of Music, East Berlin. *Debut:* Conducted Berlin Symphony Orchestra, 1962. *Career:* Chief Conductor, Reichenbach, 1964; Music Director, Opera and Concerts, Halle, Democratic Republic of Germany, 1966; Permanent Guest Conductor, German State Opera, East Berlin, 1978-; Lived in West Germany since 1983; Has conducted at most major centres in East and West Germany and throughout Europe, including Stockholm, Oslo, Helsinki, Milan, Rome, London, Salzburg and Amsterdam; Gave the German premiere of Shostakovich's Symphonies 13 and 14 with Berlin Radio Symphony Orchestra, 1969 and A Petterson's 8th Symphony in 1979; Outstanding success with productions of Magic Flute and Marriage of Figaro at Vienna State Opera, 1979; Has worked with Rotterdam Philharmonic, Bournemouth Symphony Orchestra, Philharmonia (London), Vienna Symphony Orchestra and Nice, Vancouver, Rochester, New Zealand, Japan, Israel and Australia, with recent productions of Figaro (Nice) and Don Giovanni (Austria and Helsinki). *Recordings:* Shostakovich Michelangelo cycle (recording premiere) and Symphonies 2 and 4; Handel: Alexander's Feast and Italian Cantatas; Wolfgang Strauss: Symphony No 1; Udo Zimmermann: Ein Zeuge der liebe. *Honour:* Berlin Critics' Award, 1970. *Current Management:* Anglo-Swiss Artists' Management, London, England. *Hobby:* Chess. *Address:* c/o Anglo-Swiss Artists Management, 4 & 5 Primrose Mews, Regents Park Road, London NW8 8YL.

SANDERS Ernest H, b. 4 Dec 1918, Hamburg, Germany. Musicologist. m. Marion Hollander, 2 Nov 1954, 1 son, 1 daughter. *Education:* MA, Music-Historical Musicology, 1952, PhD, in the same, Columbia University, 1963. *Career:* Department of Music, Columbia University, Lecturer, 1954-58, Instructor, 1958-61 and 1962-63, Assistant Professor, 1963-65 and 1966-67, Associate Professor, 1967-72, Professor, 1972-86, Chairman, Department of Music, 1978-85. *Publications:* English Polyphony of the Thirteenth and Early 14th Centuries (Polyphonic Music of the Fourteenth Century Vol XIV, 1979); Vols XVI and XVII, co-editor. *Contributions to:* Numerous articles dealing with aspects of mediaeval polyphony in Journal of the American Musicological Society; The Musical Quarterly; Acta Musicologica; Archiv fur Musikwissenschaft; Music & Letters; Musica Disciplina; The New Grove Dictionary; Various Festschriften. *Hobbies:* Swimming; Hiking; Biking; Chamber music. *Address:* 885 West End Avenue, New York, NY 10025, USA.

SANDERS John Derek, b. 26 Nov 1933. Organist and Master of Choristers, Gloucester Cathedral. m. Janet Ann Dawson, 1967, 1 son, 1 daughter. *Education:* Felsted School, Essex; Royal College of Music; Gonville and Caius College, Cambridge; ARCM, 1952; FRCO, 1955; MusB, 1956; MA, 1958. *Career:* Director of Music, King's School, Gloucester and Assistant Organist Gloucester Cathedral, 1958-63; Organist and Master of Choristers, Chester Cathedral, 1964-67; Organist and Master of the Choristers, Gloucester Cathedral, 1967-; Director of Music, Cheltenham Ladies' College, 1968-; Conductor: Gloucestershire Symphony Orchestra, 1967-; Gloucester Choral Society, 1967-; Conductor of Three Choirs Festival, 1968, 1971, 1974, 1977, 1980, 1983, 1986, 1989, 1992. *Publications:* Festival Te Deum, 1962; Soliloquy for Organ, 1977; Toccata for Organ, 1979; Te Deum Laudamus, 1985; Day By Day, 1989; The Prayer of Saint Francis, 1989. *Honours:* DMus Lambeth, 1990. *Memberships:* President, Cathedral Prganists Association, 19990-92; Memer Council Royal College of Organists, 1979; Liveryman, Musicians Company, 1987; Freeman, City of London, 1986. *Hobbies:* Gastronomy; Travelling. *Address:* 7 Miller's Green, Gloucester GL1 2BN, England.

SANDISON Gordon, b. 1950, Aberdeen, Scotland. Singer (Baritone). *Education:* Studied at the Royal Scottish Academy. *Career:* Has sung with Scottish Opera from 1973 as Ppageno, the Figaros of Rossini and Mozart, Malatesta, Don Giovanni, Belcore, Don Alfonso, Falstaff, Marcello; Covent Garden Debut 1984, as Fieville in Andrea Chenier, followed by Mandarin, Morales, Starveling, Montano, Masetto and the Doctor and Shepherd in Pélleas et Mélisande; Further Appearances with English Nationl Opera, Théâtre du Châtelet Paris, Opera Northern Ireland and the Glyndebourne, Wexford and Edinburgh Festivals; Sang in Carmen at Earls Court, London and on Tour to Japan. *Address:* c/o Scottish Opera, 39 Elmbank Crescent, Glasgow G2 4PT, Scotland.

SANDON Nicholas John, b. 16 Feb 1948, Faversham, Kent, England. Musicologist. m. Edith Virginia Edwards, 1 July 1975, 1 step-son, 2 step-daughters. *Education:* Kent College, Canterbury, 1959-66; BMus, 1970, University of Birmingham, 1967-71; PhD, University of Exeter, 1983. *Career:* Lecturer in Music, 1971-86; Head of Music Department, 1983-86; Exeter University; Professor of Music and Head of Music Department, University College, Cork, 1986-1993; Professor of Music, University of Exeter, 1993-. *Publications:* John Shepard's Masses, 1976; Oxford Anthology of Medieval Music, 1977; The Use of Sailsbury, 1986-; Many other editions of English church music; General Editor of Antico Edition. *Contributions to:* Early Music; Music and Letters; Musica Disciplina; Proceedings of the Royal Musical Association; Royal Musical Association Research Chronicle; Musical Times; Music Review; The Consort; British Broadcasting Corporation Radio 3; Journal of Theological Studies.

Honour: University Scholar at Birmingham, 1967-70. *Memberships:* Royal Musical Association; Plainsong and Medieval Society (Member of Council); Henry Bradshaw Society. *Hobbies:* Liturgy; Cricket. *Address:* Department of Music, University of Exeter, Exeter EX4 4PD, Devon, England.

SANDOR György, b. 21 Sept 1912, Budapest, Hungary. Pianist; Conductor. *Education:* Piano student, Liszt Academy, Budapest, Hungary; Piano student of Bartók; Composition student of Kodály. *Career:* Appearances with the orchestras of Vienna, Baden-Baden, New York Philharmonic Orchestra and The Philadelphia Orchestra; Has performed at numerous music festivals worldwide; Concert tours, Mozarteum, Salzburg and the Assisi Festival; Gave the first performance of Bartók's 3rd Piano Concerto, Philadelphia, 1946; Judges International Piano Competitions; Holds master classes. *Recordings:* Has made numerous recordings including: Bartók and the Baroque. *Publication:* On Piano Playing, 1981. *Honour:* Grand Prix du Disque.

SANDSTRÖM Sven-Erik, b. 30 Oct 1942, Motala, Sweden. Composer. m. Gudrun Sandström. *Education:* Stockholm University, 1963-67; State College of Music, 1968-72 with Lidholm; Further study with Ligeti and Norgard. *Career:* Joined faculty of State College of Music Stockholm, 1980. *Compositions:* Stage: Strong like Death, Church opera, 1978; Hasta O Beloved Bride, chamber opera, 1978; Emperor Jones, music drama, 1980; incidental music for Strindberg's Dream Play, 1980; Ballet Den elfte gryningen, 1988; Orchestral: Pictures, 1969; Intrada, 1969; In the Meantime, 1970; Around a Line, 1971; Through and Through, 1972; Con tutta Forza, 1976; Culmination, 1977; Agitato, 1978; The Rest is Dross, 1980; Guitar Concerto, 1983; Invignings fanfar, 1988; Chamber: String Quartet, 1969; Mosaic for string trio, 1970; 6 Character Pieces, 1973; Metal, Metal for 4 percussionists, 1974; Utmost, premiered by Pierre Boulez London, 1975; Within for 8 trombones and percussion, 1979; Drums for timpani and 4 percussionists, 1980; Vocal: Inventions for 16 voices, 1969; Lamento, 1971; Birgitta-Music I, 1973; Expression, 1976; A Cradle Song/The Tiger, after Blake, 1978; Requiem, for the child victims of war and racism, 1979; Agnus Dei, 1980; Piano and organ music.

SANGER David John, b. 17 Apr 1947, London, England. Organist. *Education:* Studied at Eltham College, 1957-63 and Royal Academy of Music, 1963-66. *Career:* International Tours as Recitalist; International Jury Member for Competitions; Teacher in Many Countries. *Compositions:* Missa Brevis. *Recordings:* Complete Organ Symphonies of Louis, Vierne Meridian. *Publications:* Play the Organ 1 and 11. *Contributions to:* Various Articles for Organists Review. *Honours:* 1st Prize at St Albans International Organ Festival; 1st Prize at Kiel N Germany International Organ Festival. *Memberships:* Royal College of Organists; British Institute of Organ Studies. *Hobbies:* Fell walking; Swimming; Badminton. *Address:* Old Wesleyan Chapel, Embleton, Cockermouth, Cumbria CA13 9YA, England.

SANSOM Gilliam Rosemary, b. 30 Apr 1935, Belfast, Northern Ireland. Concert Violinist; Violin Teacher. m. Bella de Csillery, 2 June 1965, 2 s. *Education:* Studied with Gioconda de Vito, Accademia di Santa Cecilia, Rome, Italy. *Career:* Numerous Concerts, Great Britain, France, Netherlands, Italy, Switzerland; Appeared as Soloist with London Mozart Players, Royal Philharmonic Orchestra, Scarlatti Orchestra in Naples for Italian Radio, at Last Night of Henry Wood Promenade Concerts; Recitals with Roger Vignoles for BBC and Music Societies; Played Bach's Sonates and Partitas for Solo Violin at Several Haslemere Festivals; Violin Teacher, 1965-86; Head of Strings, 1985-86, Kent Junior Music School, Maidstone; Violin Tutor, Chethams School of Music, Manchester, 1984-. *Memberships:* Incorporated Society of Musicians; European String Teachers Association.

Hobbies: Gardening; Travel; Hill Walking. *Address:* 20 Faraday Road, Maidstone, Kent ME14 2DB, England.

SANTE Sophia (Maria Christina) van, b. 11 Aug 1925, Zaandam, Holland. Singer (Mezzo-Soprano). *Education:* Studied at the Amsterdam Muzieklyceum with van der Sluys and Ruth Horna; Further studies with Marietta Amstad in Italy; Many appearances from 1960 with the Amsterdam Opera as the Woman in Schoenberg's Erwartung, Marie in Wozzeck and Judith in Duke Bluebeard's Castle; Also sang in the Dutch premieres of Henze's Der Junge Lord and Dallapiccola's Il Prigioniero. *Recordings include:* Der Rosenkavalier (Philips).

SANTI Nello, b. 22 Sept 1931, Adria, Rovigo, Italy. Conductor. *Education:* Studied at the Liceo Musicale in Padua and with Coltro and Pedrollo. *Debut:* Teatro Verdi, Padua, 1951, Rigoletto. *Career:* Conductor of the Zurich Opera from 1958; Covent Garden debut 1960, with La Traviata; Vienna Staatsoper and Salzburg Festival debuts 1960; Metropolitan Opera 1962, Un Ballo in Maschera: regular appearances from 1976; La Scala Milan 1972; Paris Opera 1974; Guest engagements in Berlin, Munich, Florence, Geneva, Lisbon and Madrid, in the operas of Rossini, Bellini, Donizetti, Verdi, Puccini and Mascagni; Orchestral concerts with L'Orchestre National, Paris; RIAS, West Berlin, and the Munich Philharmonic; New Philharmonia Orchestra and the London Symphony; Returned to Covent Garden 1982, La Fanciulla del West; Conducted Aida in a new production by Vittorio Rossi, Zurich Opera 1987; Zurich 1990, Il Trovatore and Tosca; Aida at the Verona Arena 1990, La Forza del Destino at Naples; Season 1992 with Rgoletto at the Met, Semiramide at Zurich (followed by La Forza del Destino) and Aida at Verona. *Recordings:*Pagliacci; L'Amore dei Tre Re; Complete Verdi tenor arias, with Carlo Bergonzi; Aria recitals with Placido Domingo; Videos of Otello, La Bohème, Nabucco, Rigoletto, Andrea Chénier, Falstaff and the Verdi Requiem. *Honours:* Medallion de la Cité de Zurich; Commendatore of the Republic of Italy. *Address:* c/o Marks Management Ltd, 14 New Burlington Street, London W1X 1FF, England.

SANTUNIONE Orianna, b. 1 Sept 1934, Sassolo, Modena, Italy. Singer (Soprano). *Education:* Studied in Milan with Carmen Melis and Renato Pastorino. *Career:* After debut as Giordano's Fedora sang in Rome, Genoa, Bologna, Trieste, Naples, Parma and Palermo; Covent Garden, London, 1965 as Amelia in Un Ballo in Maschera and Elisabeth de Valois; Further appearances in Nice, Rouen, Turin, Venice, Munich, Hamburg, Amsterdam, Dallas, Philadelphia and Cincinnati; Verona Arena 1967-1977; Other roles include Desdemona, Elsa, Medea, Santuzza, Nedda, both Leonoras of Verdi, Mathilde in Guillaume Tell, Francesca da Rimini, Tosca, Madama Butterfly and Aida. *Recordings include:* Madame Sans-Gêne by Giordano; Pigmalione by Donizetti; Otello and Lohengrin for Italian TV. *Address:* c/o Arena di Verona, Piazza Brà 28, 1-37121 Verona.

SAPAROVA-FISCHEROVA Jitka, b. 7 Apr 1964, Brno, Czechoslovakia. Opera Singer (Soprano). m. Miroslav Fischer, 19 Oct 1991, 1 d. *Education:* High School of Musical Art. *Debut:* Mozart's Zauberflöte. *Career:* Soloist of Chamber Orchestre, Baroque and Renaissance Music, Musica Aeterna, 1985-86; Soloist of Slowak National Theatres Opera from 1986. *Operas include:* Faust; La Nozze di Figaro; Rigoletto; Suor Angelica; Carmen. *Recordings:* Rigoletto; La Sonnambula. *Honours:* 1st Prize 1985 Competition of M Schneider Trnausee; Laureate of Singing Competition of Antonin Dvořák. *Membership:* Association of Slovak Theatres. *Hobbies:* Tourism; Folklore. *Address:* Dankovskeho 14, 811 03 Bratislava, Slovakia.

SAPIEYEVSKI Jerzy, b. 20 Mar 1945, Poland. Composer; Conductor; Synthesizer Performer. *Education:* State Advanced School of Music, Gdansk, Poland, Theory and Conducting; Diploma with honours for conducting, 1964; Composition, Conservatory of

Music, Gdansk, 1964-67; Special Student in Composition and Conducting, Berklee School of Music, Boston, Massachusetts, USA, 1967-68; Master's Degree, Composition, The Catholic University of America, Washington DC, 1971; Composition, Berkshire Music Center, Tanglewood, summer, 1968; Temple University Conducting Institute, Ambler, Pennsylvania, 1970. *Career:* Composer/Conductor for Polish Radio, 1965-67; Teaching Fellow, Catholic University, Washington DC, USA, 1971-72; Part-time Faculty: Conducting, Catholic University, 1971-72; Orchestration, American University, 1971-72; Full-time Faculty: Visiting Lecturer, University of Maryland, 1972-74, American University, 1975-; Composer, Synthesizer Performer, Theatre Scores for Richard III, The Diary of Anne Frank, The Glass Menagerie; Artistic Director, Dumbarton Concerts in Washington DC: Active as composer and conductor. *Compositions:* String Quartet: Mazurka; Ensemble: Songs of the Rose; (Published) Orchestra: Concertos; Love Songs; Summer Overture; Wind Ensembles: Games; Morpheus; Scherzo di Concerto; Chamber Music: Aesop Suite; Aria; Trio for an Italian Journey; Solos with Piano: Aria; Concerto for Viola; Voice and Piano: Love Songs; Dance of the Planets, 1990, Band and Synthesizer; Synthesis, 1990, works for Synthesizers; Also orchestrations. *Publications:* Arioso for Trumpet and Woodwind. *Current Management:* Theodore Presser Company. *Address:* 3901 Cathedral Avenue NW, Washington DC 20016, USA.

SAPP Gary James Kehaulani, b. 11 May 1944, USA. Conductor; Composer. 1 son. *Education:* Studied at the DMA Catholic University of America, MM, BM, University of North Texas. *Career:* Conducted Over 1800 Wind Ensemble and Chamber Music Concerts internationally; Appearances at the Opera House, Trieste; Europahalle, Trier; Hall of Deputies, Moscow; Tivoli, Copenhagen; Alte Oper, Frankfurt; Bunka Kaikan, Toyko; Hollywood Bowl, Los Angeles; TV And Radio Appearances; Directed the Worldwide United States Air Force Band and Music Program; Assistant to the Conductor, Arlington Symphony Orchestra; Conductor, University of North Texas Brass Choir and Woodwind Ensemble; Composer in Residencies, Dallas Independent School District; United Sttes Armed Forces Bicentennial Band and Chorus; Music Curriculum Consultant, National Comprehensive Musicianship Project; Conducted Over 299 Music Clinics, Master Classes. *Compositions include:* Utoh; A Comedy of Errors; Sonata fur Klavier; Kwaidan; Shimo. *Recordings:* Declamation for Trumpet. *Publications:* Student Learning Plan, Teacher Implementation Plan, Evaluation Instruments. *Honours include:* Awards and Letters of Recognition from Presidents Ford, Nixon and Reagan. *Memberships:* American String Teachers Association; American Symphony Orchestra League; College Band Directors National Association; World Association of Symphonic Bands & Wind Ensembles. *Hobbies:* Aquatic Activities; Painting. *Address:* Landolfstrasse 18, 67661 Kaiserslautern, Germany.

SÁRAI Tibor, b. 10 May 1919, Budapest, Hungary. Composer; Professor of Music (retired). m. Ibolya Schwoelbl, 19 Dec 1947, 1 son. *Education:* Academy of Music, Budapest, 1942. *Career:* Head of Music Department, Ministry of Culture, 1949-50; Leader of Musical Section of Hungarian Radio, 1950-53; Professor of the Béla Bartók Conservatory, Budapest, 1953-59; Professor, Franz Liszt Academy of Music, Budapest, 1959-80. *Compositions:* Serenade for String Orchestra, 1946; Spring Concerto, 1955; Autumn Concerto, 1984; 3 String Quartets, 1958, 71, 82; 3 Symphonies, 1967, 1973, 1987; Musica per 45 Corde, 1971; Quartet for Flute, Violin, Viola and Cello, 1962; Dramma per Fiati for Wind Quintet, 1978; 2 Oratorios; 2 Cantatas; other Orchestral, Instrumental, Choral and Chamber Music. *Recordings:* Spring Concerto; Serenade for String Orchestra; Symphony No 1 and No 2; Diagnosis 69 for Tenor Solo and Orchestra; String Quartets No 1 and No 2; Musica per 45 Corde. *Publication:* The History of Czech Music, 1959. *Honours:* Erkel Prize, 1959; Kossuth Prize, 1975; Merited Artist of the Hungarian People's Republic, 1988. *Memberships:* Executive

Committe, International Music Council, 1972-78, Vice-President, 1976-78, re-elected, 1980-85, Secretary-General, 1980-82; Individual Member, Executive Committee, International Music Council, 1985. *Address:* Maros u. 36, Budapest H-1122, Hungary.

SARASTE Jukka-Pekka, b. 22 April 1956, Heinola, Finland. Conductor. *Education:* Studied violin and conducting at the Sibelius Academy, Helsinki. *Career:* Debut 1980 with the Helsinki Philharmonic and conducted them jointly with Okku Kamu on 1983 tour of USA; 1985 appointed Principal Guest Conductor of the Finnish Radio Symphony Orchestra; Principal Conductor from 1987; Principal Conductor Scottish Chamber Orchestra 1987-1991; Music Director of the Toronto Symphony from 1994; Tours to France, Finland and the Far East; Guest conductor with orchestras in Minnesota, Vienna, Rotterdam, Munich and Toronto; Conducted the Finnish Radio SO at the 1991 and the Scottish Chamber Orchestra at the 1992 Promenade Concerts, London. *Recordings:* Mozart Symphonies Nos. 32, 35, 36 with the Scottish Chamber Orchestra (Virgin); Sibelius Symphonies (RCA); Debussy La Mer and Images with the Rotterdam Philharmonic; Mahler 5th Symphony with the Finnish Radio Symphony Orchetra. *Address:* c/o Van Walsum Management Ltd, 26 Wadham Road, London SW15 2LR, England.

SARBU Eugene, b. 1950, Bucharest, Rumania. Violinist.*Education:* Following studies in Bucharest and Paris joined Curtis Institute, Philadelphia, for further study with Ivan Galamian; later at Juilliard, New York, and with Nathan Milstein in Zurich. *Career:* Made first solo appearance aged 6; won National Festival of Music Award in Bucharest, 1958; regular solo recials and concerts in Britain; Promenade Concert debut 1982; performances in United States, Europe, Australia and South America; Far East tour 1987/88 , with the New Japan Philharmonic in Tokyo and the Seoul Philharmonic in Tokyo; plays a Cremonese violin by Tomasso Balestieri made in 1756. *Recordings:* Sibelius Concerto for EMI with the Hallé Orchestra, 1980; Vivaldi's Four Seasons and Mozart Concertos with the European Master Orchestra, 1988. *Address:* c/o Anglo-Swiss Ltd, 4/5 Primrose Mews, 1a Sharpleshall Street, London NW1 8YW, England.

SARDI Ivan, b. 7 July 1930, Budapest, Hungary. Singer (Bass). *Education:* Studied with Antonio Mekandri at the Martini Conservatory Bologna. *Debut:* Brescia 1951, as Padre Guardiano in La Forza del Destino. *Career:* Sang in Naples, Bologna, Genoa, Trieste and Catania, as Mozart's Masetto and Bartolo and in Operas by Verdi; Glyndebourne 1956,as Don Alfonso; Further appearances in Florence, Milan and Lisbon; Staatsoper Munich 1956-61; Member of the Deutsche Oper Berlin from 1961; Concerts in Munich, Hamburg, Vienna and elsewhere in Europe; Sang Schigolch in Lulu at Dresden, 1992. *Recordings:* Don Giovanni, Le Nozze di Figaro, Verdi Requiem, Der junge Lord by Henze (Deutsche Grammophon); Sparafucile in Rigoletto (Philips); Guillaume Tell. *Address:* c/o Deutsche Oper Berlin, Richard Wagnerstrasse 10, D-100 Berlin 1, Germany.

SARDINERO Vincenzo, b. 12 Jan 1937, Barcelona, Spain. Singer (Baritone). *Education:* Studied at the Liceo Conservatory in Barcelona. *Career:* Sang first in operettas and Spanish zarzuelas; Opera debut Barcelona 1964, as Escamillo; In 1967 sang Germont in La Traviata at Barcelona and in Lucia di Lammermoor at La Scala, Milan; New York City Opera 1970, as Tonio in Pagliacci; Covent Garden debut 1976, as Marcello in La Bohème; Further appearances Lisbon, Rome, Vienna, Madrid, Lyons, Paris, Munich, Hamburg, Basle, Budapest and the Aix-en-Provence festival; Season 1991-92 as Marcello at Barcelona and Rigoletto at Palma; Other roles include Nottingham in Roberto Devereux, Valentin (Faust), Alphonse XI (La Favorite) and Verdi's Renato, Posa and Luna. *Recordings include:* L'Amico Fritz, L'Atlantida, Turandot and Manon Lescaut (HMV); Lucia di Lammermoor and Un Giorno di Regno (Philips); La

Navarraise by Massenet and Edgar by Puccini (CBS); La Straniera by Bellini (MRF).

SARFATY Regina, b. 1932, Rochester, New York, USA. Singer (Mezzo-Soprano). *Education:* Studied at the Juilliard School, New York. *Career:* Sang with New Mexico Opera from 1948; Santa Fe Opera from 1957, notably in the 1968 US premiere of The Bassarids by Henze; New York City Opera from 1958, as Cenerentola, Maria Golovin in the opera by Menotti, Jocasta (Oedipus Rex) and Dorabella; Frankfurt Opera from 1963, as Carmen and Octavian; Sang Octavian at Glyndebourne 1960, and returned 1984, as Adelaide in Arabella; sang Mme de Croissy in Dialogues des Carmélites at Baltimore, 1984; Member of the Zurich Opera; Notably as the Countess Geschwitz in Lulu and in the premiere of Die Erretung Thebens by Kelterborn, 1963. *Recordings:* Excerpts from Die Walküre, conducted by Stokowski (RCA); The Rake's Progress, conducted by Stravinsky, and the Choral Symphony conducted by Bernstein (CBS). *Address:* c/o Baltimore Opera Company Inc., 527 North Charles Street, Baltimore, MD 21201, USA.

SARGON Simon A, b. 6 Apr 1938, Bombay, India. Composer; Pianist; Music Director. m. Bonnie Glasgow, 17 Nov 1961, 1 daughter. *Education:* BA, Brandeis University, 1959; MS, Juilliard School, 1962. *Debut:* Carnegie Hall, with Jennie Tourel, 1963. *Career:* Musical Staff, New York City Opera, 1960; Associate Conductor, Concert Opera, 1962-68; Pianist for Concerts, J. Tourel, 1963-71; Faculty Member, Juilliard School, 1967-69; Chairman, Voice, Rubin Academy, Jerusalem, 1971-74; Faculty, Hebrew University, 1973-74; Director, Music, Temple Emanu-El, 1974-; Faculty, SMU, 1983-. *Compositions:* Patterns in Blue, 1976; Elul: Midnight, 1980; Praise Ye the Lord, 1980; Sing His Praise, 1981; The Queen's Consort, 1982; Lord Make Me to Know My End, 1985; Commission: Voices of Change, 1988; Symphony No.1, Holocaust, premiere Dallas Symphony, 1991; Jump Back, Southern Music; Before the Ark, Southern Music. *Recordings:* Music for French Horn and Piano; Huntsman, What Quarry, Crystal Records; Deep Ellum Nights, Onagaku Records. *Contributions to:* Dallas Opera Magazine, 1980-84. *Address:* 3308 Dartmouth Ave, Dallas, TX 75205, USA.

SAROSI Balint, b. 1 Jan 1925, Csikrakos, Hungary. Ethnomusicologist. m. Iolantha Benko, 18 Oct 1952. 2 daughters. *Education:* Diploma, Musicology and Composition, Academy of Music, Budapest, 1956; PhD, Pazmany Peter University, Budapest, 1948. *Career:* Research Fellow, 1958-74, Director, Ethnomusicological Section, 1974-88 retired, Institute for Musicology, Budapest; Dr of Science, 1990; Titular University Professor, 1991. *Recordings:* Editor of Scientific recordings: Hungarian Instrumental Folk Music; Hungarian Folk Music Collected by Bela Bartók, Phonograph Cylinders; Anthology of Hungarian Folk Music, V and VI. *Publications:* Die Volksmusikinstrumente Ungarns, first Volume of the Handbuch der europaischen Volksmusikinstrumente, 1967; Gypsy Music, 1978; Folk Music, 1986; Volksmusik, Das ungarische Erbe, 1990; Series of articles on the Hungarian Instrumental Melodie in: Magyar Zene, 1987-1992. *Address:* Aldas u.11, H-1025 Budapest, Hungary.

SARROCA Suzanne, b. 21 Apr 1927, Carcassonne, France. Singer (Soprano). *Education:* Studied at the Toulouse Conservatoire 1946-48. *Debut:* Carcassonne 1949, as Massenet's Charlotte. *Career:* Sang Carmen in Brussels 1951; Paris Opéra and Opéra-Comique from 1952 as Tosca, Rezia, Marina (Boris Godunov), Aida, Marguerite (La Damnation de Faust, Leonore and Octavian 1957, 1966; Also sang in Les Indes Galantes by Rameau; Guest appearances in Marseille 1961 (Donna Anna), Rome 1965 (Elisabeth de Valois) and in Buenos Aires, Geneva, New York, London, Lisbon, Strasbourg and Toulouse; Salzburg Festival 1968 in Cavalieri's La Rappresentazione di Anima e di Corpo; Further engagements in Rio de Janeiro, Hamburg and Vienna; Modern repertoire included La Voix Humaine

by Poulenc and Schoenberg's Erwartung; Director of the Centre d'art Lyrique at Strasbourg, 1983-85.

SARTORETTI Christine, b. 30 Aug 1943, Sion, Switzerland. Harpsichordist. m. Jean-Pierre Girardin, 10 Jan 1976, 1 son, 1 daughter. *Education:* Piano studies, Pierre Cerf, Lausanne, 1968; Harpsichord, Christiane Jaccottet; Diploma, Lausanne Conservatory; Master classes, Gustav Leonhardt, Kenneth Gilbert, Fernando Tagliavini. *Career:* Soloist & continuo player: Various concerts, Europe; Wurttembergische Kammerorchester, 1978- 81; Los Angeles Chamber Orchestra, 1980; Zurich Chamber Orchestra, 1985; Serenata Ensemble, Geneva, 1985. Teacher, harpsichord & continuo, Lausanne Conservatory, current; Several performances, Swiss Radio (Lausanne, Basle, Lugano); Swedish Radio, Stockhol. *Recording:* Bach, Concerti for several harpsichords (Vox). *Honour:* 1st prize, Lausanne Conservatory. *Memberships:* Association des Musiciens Suisses; Societé Suisse de Pedagogie Musicale. *Hobbies:* Playing organ; Walking in mountains. *Address:* 4 Chemin de Broye, CH-1020 Renens, Switzerland.

SASAKI Ken, b. 14 Sept 1943, Sendai, Miyagi, Japan. Concert Pianist. *Education:* Studied at University of Arts, Tokyo and at Warsaw Conservatoire; Attendeed master classes of Vlado Periemuter in Paris and Danuta Lewandowska in Warsaw. *Career:* Given many concerts in France, Poland, Holland, Switzerland, Austria, Germany, Japan; British debut 1972 at the Wigmore Hall; Coast to coast tour of the USA, 1979; Queen Elizabeth Hall, London, 1986 playing Bach's 1st Partita, Gaspard de la Nuit and Chopin's 2nd Sonata; Further appearances with the Warsaw Chamber Orchestra and the Berlin Octet. Other repertory includes Concertos by Bach (D minor) and Beethoven (C minor and G major); Mozart K449 and K466; Chopin No 1 and Schumann; Ravel in G; Rachmaninov Nos 1 and 3; Prokofiev No 3; Beethoven's Sonatas Op 57 and Op 111; Mozart K310, K311; Chopin Sonatas, Etudes Ballades, Nocturnes, Preludes and Polonaise; Schumann Fantasie Op 17, Fantasiestücke, Etudes Symphoniques and Kreisleriana; Ravel Miroirs and Le Tombeau de Couperin; Debussy Images; Suite Bergamasque and Images Book 1; Prokofiev 3rd and 7th Sonatas and Scriabin Etudes; Scarlatti Sonatas. *Recordings include:* Chopin Etudes (Nimbus). *Honours include:* Stefanie Niekrasz Prize 1984.

SASS Sylvia, b. 21 July 1951, Budapest, Hungary. Singer (Soprano). *Education:* Studied at the Liszt Academy Budapest with Ferenc Revhegyi. *Debut:* Budapest State Opera 1971, as Frasquita in Carmen. *Career:* First major role as Gutrune, 1972; Sang Giselda in I Lombardi 1973, and repeated the role at Covent Garden 1976; Sofia 1972, Violetta (also at Aix-en-Provence, 1976); Scottish Opera debut 1975, Desdemona; At the Budapest Opera 1977 sang in the premiere of Mozes by Zsolt Durko; Metropolitan Opera 1977, Tosca; Guest engagements at the State Operas of Hamburg and Munich and at the Paris Opéra and La Scala Milan; Other roles include Norma, Penelope (Il Ritorno d'Ulisse), Tatiana, Elvira (Ernani), Alceste, Odabella (Attila), Medea, Santuzza, Elisabeth de Valois, Lady Macbeth, Donna Elvira and Donna Anna, Countess Almaviva, Mimi, Manon Lescaut, Turandot, Adriana Lecouvreur, Nedda (Pagliacci), Juliette and Marguerite by Gounod, and Salome (Budapest 1989); Has sung Bartók's Judith on BBC television and in Montpellier and Metz, 1989; Many concert performances in music by Strauss and Wagner; modern repertoire includes Sogno di un Tramonto d'Autumno by Malipiero; Wigmore Hall debut 1979, in songs by Strauss and Liszt: invited to return for Andras Schiff's Beethoven-Bartók series, September 1990; Season 1993 as Adriana Lecouvreur at Budapest. *Recordings include:* Don Giovanni, Arias by Puccini and Verdi, Liszt and Bartók songs (Decca); Verdi Stiffelio, Il Trittico, Duke Bluebeard's Castle by Bartók (Philips); Wagner Wesendonck Lieder, Vier Letzte Lieder by Strauss, Medea, Ernani, I Lombardi, Macbeth, Attila, Faust, Mozes by Durko, Erkel's Hunyadi Laszlo (Hungaroton).

Address: c/o Ron Gonsalves, 10 Dagnan Road, London SW12 9LQ, England.

SASSON Deborah, b. 1955, Boston, Massachusetts, USA. Singer (Soprano). m. Peter Hofmann 1983 (divorced 1990). *Education:* Studied at Oberlin Colllge with Ellen Repp and Helen Hodam; New Engalnd Conservatory, Boston, with Gladys Miller. *Debut:* Hamburg Staatsoper 1979, as Maria in West Side Story. *Career:* Sang at the Stadttheater Aachen 1979-81; Guest appearances in Hamburg, Berlin, Venice and San Francisco; Has sung at the Bayreuth Festival from 1982; Other roles include Norina, Adina, Gilda, Rosina, Despina and Zerlina. *Recordings include:* Arias and Duets with Peter Hofmann (CBS); Mahler's 8th Symphony, from Tanglewood (Philips). *Address:* c/o PO Box Bayreuther Festspiele, 8580 Bayreth 1, Germany.

SATANOWSKI Robert Zdzislaw, b. 20 June 1918, Lodz, Poland. Conductor; Music Director. m. 2 sons. *Education:* Technical University, Warsaw, 1935-39; Theory of Music and Conducting, Academy of Music, Lodz, Poland, Graduated, 1951. *Debut:* Lodz State Philharmonic, 1951. *Career:* Conductor, Lublin State Philharmonic, 1951-54; Artistic Director, Principal Conductor, Bydgoszcz State Philharmonic, 1954-58; General Music Director, Staedtische Oper Karl Marx Stadt/former and later Chemitz, 1960-62; General and Artistic Director, State Opera Poznan, 1962-69; Founder and Artistic Director, Poznan Chamber Orchestra, 1963-69; General Music Director, Staedtische Buehnen Krefeld-Moenchengladbach, 1969-76, State Opera House, Cracow, 1975-77, State Opera House, Wroclaw, 1977-82, Grand Theatre Warsaw/National Opera, 1981-91; Guest Conductor, Operatic works, Staatsoper Vienna, Dresden, Berlin, Bolshoi Moscow, State Opera Bucharest, Operhaus Dresden, Oslo Opera House, Opera House Seattle, USA, National Opera House Genoa, Royal Opera Liege, Zagreb Opera House, Istanbul Festival, etc; Symphony Concerts, Paris, London, Moscow, Berlin, Dresden, Leipzig, Bucharest, Genoa, Stockholm, Goeteborg, Leningrad, Teheran, Ankara, Madrid, Vienna, Dusseldorf, Warsaw. *Compositions:* Symphony, Chamber and Vocal works composed until 1958. *Recordings:* With National Philharmonic, Warsaw, Warsaw Grand Theatre Orchestra, State Symphony Orchestra, Poznan, Poznan Chamber Orchestra, mainly Polish, classical and contemporary, symphony and operatic works. *Address:* Teatr Wielki, ul Moliera 3/5, 00-950 Warsaw, Poland.

SATUKANGAS Arto Untamo, b. 6 Sept 1962, Espoo, Finland. Pianist. *Education:* Studied at the Sibelius Academy of Music, Helsinki; St Petersburg Conservatory; Studies with Professor Vladimir Nilsen in St Petersburg Conservatory and Private Lessons with Nikita Magaloff in Switzerland. *Debut:* 1987 Paris Promoted by the Herbert Von Karajan Foundation. *Career:* Concerts in Finland, Sweden, Iceland, Germany, England , France, Italy, Israel, Japan and China. *Recordings:* Alexander von Zemlinsky; Max Bruch; George Enescu. *Contributions to:* Many Reviews in the Major Finnish Newspapers. *Honour;* 1st Prize in the National Maj Lind Competition. *Memberships:* Staatliche Hochschule für Musik, Karlsruhe. *Hobbies:* Reading; Literature; Languages; Psychology; Philosophy; Outdoor; Recreation. *Address:* Tullastraße 76, 76131 Karlsruhe, Germany.

SAULESCO Mircea Petre, b. 14 Sept 1926, Bucharest, Romania. Violinist. m. (1) 3 children, (2) Gunilla Sandberg-Saulesco, 1 child. *Education:* Bucharest Conservatory; Diploma, Bucharest Musical Academy, 1944; Studied with various masters including Iosif Dailis, Garbis Avachian, Georges Enesco and Jacques Thibaud; Studied Piano and Composition with vari masters. *Debut:* Bucharest, 1941. *Career:* Member, Bucharest Radio Symphony Orchestra, 1938-50; Founder, Saulesco String Quartet, 1945; Member, 1950-58, Leader, 1957-58, Bucharest State Philharmonic Orchestra Georges Enesco; Numerous chamber music and solo concerts in Eastern Europe until 1958; Member and one of leaders, Symphony

Orchestra, Swedish Broadcasting Corporation, 1958-; Founder, Swedish Saulesco Quartet, 1962; Co-founder, Leygraf (piano) Quartet, 1965; Numerous TV and Radio appearances; Various foreign concert tours. *Recordings Include:* Alfven Violin Sonata; Mozart Piano Quartets No 1 G minor and No 2 E flat major; Atterberg String Quartet op 11; Verdi, String Quartet E Minor. *Honours:* Swedish Record Prize, Grammis, 1970, 1972; Austrian Mozart Prize, 1974. *Membership:* Mazer Society for Chamber Music. *Hobbies:* Art books; Chess; Model Railways. *Address:* Pepparkaksgrand 26, S-128 66 Sköndal, Sweden.

SAUNDERS Antony Jefferis, b. 3 Sept 1935. Winchester, England. Piano Accompanist. m. Jennifer Faddy, 19 Aug 1961. 2 daughters. *Education:* Royal Academy of Music, London; ARAM; LRAM; ARCM; ARCO. *Debut:* Wigmore Hall, 1965. *Career:* Extensive London work includes: South Bank (all 3 halls), Royal Albert Hall, Barbican, St John's Smith Square, Wigmore; All major centres nationally and in Belgium, France, Germany, Holland, Austria, Italy, Greece, Norway, Portugal, Switzerland, Ireland, USA and Canada; Extensive work for BBC TV and Radio, Broadcasts in Canada, Belgium, France, Portugal, Norway, Ireland and New Zealand; Choral Conductor, Bruckner-Mahler Choir, 1973-74; London Chamber Singers, 1974-77; Zemel Choir, 1978-83; Yeovil Chamber Choir, 1992- ; On staff of Birmingham Conservatoire, 1989-, Welsh College of Music & Drama, 1990-; Royal Academy of Music, London, 1993-. *Compositions:* Choral Arrangement - Six English Lyrics by Malcolm Williamson arr for SATB, 1981, Pub. Weinberger. *Hobbies:* Cooking; Walking; Reading. *Address:* 'Lansdown', 146 Hendford Hill, Yeovil, Somerset, BA20 2RG, England.

SAUNDERS Arlene, b. 5 Oct 1935, Cleveland, Ohio, USA. Soprano; Teacher. *Education:* Baldwin-Wallace College, & New York. *Debuts:* Operatic, as Rosalinde with National Opera Company, 1958; New York City Opera debut as Giorgetta, in Il Tabarro, 1961; European debut as Mimi, Teatro Nuovo, Milan, 1961. *Career:* Joined Hamburg State Opera, 1964; Also sang Pamina, Glyndebourne Festival, UK 1966, as Pamina, Louise, San Francisco Opera 1967, Beatrix Cenci (world premiere), with the Washington DC Opera Society 1971, Eva, Metropolitan Opera 1976, Minnie, Royal Opera Covent Garden, London 1980; Farewell operatic appearance as the Marschallin, Teatro Colón, Buenos Aires, 1985; Other roles were Natasha (War and Peace), Nadia in The Ice Break (US premiere, Boston 1979), Mozart Donna Elvira and Fiordiligi, Wagner's Sieglinde, Elsa, Senta and Elisabeth, Tosca, Manon, Arabella and the Countess in Capricco; Teacher, Rutgers University, New Jersey, & Abraham Goodman School, New York, 1987-. *Recordings:* Several discs. *Honours:* Gold Medal, Vercelli Vocal Competition; Kammersängerin, Hamburg State Opera, 1967.

SAUTER Lily, b. 16 Nov 1934, Zurich, Switzerland. Singer. *Education:* Studied in Milan and Zurich. *Career:* Sang at the Deutsche Oper am Rhein Dusseldorf, 1961-64; Zurich Opera, 1965-66, Stuttgart Staatsoper, 1964-83; Guest Appearances at the State Operas of Hamberg and Munich, Berlin, Frankfurt, Barcelona, Venice, Milan, Genoa and Edinburgh; Roles have Included Mozarts Susanna, Blondchen and Despina, Rosina, Matha, Norina, Adina, Marzelline, Lortzings Gretchen and Marie, Musetta, Nannetta, Sophia in Der Rosenkavalier, Aennchen and Regina in Mathis der Maler; TV Appearances in Germany and Switzerland. *Address:* c/o Staatsoper Stuttgart, Oberer Schlossgarten 6, 7000 Stuttgart, Germany.

SAVAGE Stephen Leon, b. 26 Apr 1942, Hertford, England. Concert Pianist; Conductor; Teacher. m. Valerie Dickson, 2 sons. *Education:* Vienna Akademie with Bruno Seidlhofer; Royal College of Music with Cyril Smith. *Debut:* Wigmore Hall, London, 1966. *Career:* Concerts, Radio, Television, Recordings in Great Britain, Canada, Australia, Japan; Concertos with Boult, A. Davis, Zollman and others including 1st Australasian performance, Lutoslawski Concerto 1989; Director, Brisbane Tippett Festival, 1990; Dedicatee of major works by Justin Connolly and Roger Smalley; Professor of Piano and Co-Director, 20th Century Ensemble, Royal College of Music, 1967-81, Artistic Director/Conductor, Griffith University Ensemble, Brisbane, Australia; Frequent Residencies include, Universities of Adelaide, Toronto, Hong Kong, Guildhall School of Music etc; Noted for performances of classical repertoire and 20th Century Music including important first performances. *Recordings:* Roger Smalley, Accord for 2 Pianos with the Composer; Tippett, Sonatas 1 and 3. *Honours:* Dannreuther Prize, 1964; Hopkinson Medal, Worshipful Company of Musicians, Medal, 1965; Recommendation of Tippett Sonatas 1 and 3 by Gramophone, 1986. *Address:* c/o Queensland Conservatorium of Music, Griffith University, PO Box 28, Brisbane, Albert Street 4002, Brisbane, Australia.

SAVARY Jerome, b. 27 June 1942, Buenos Aires, Argentina. Stage Director. *Education:* Studied in Paris. *Career:* Stagings of Operettas by Offenbach and Johann Strauss at the Geneva Opera, 1982-91; La Scala Milan, 1983-92, with a Revival of Cherubini's Anacreon, the Premiere of Corghi's Blimunday, and Attila; Don Giovanni at Rome, 1984, Die Zauberflöte at Bregenz, 1985, Followed by Les Contes d'Hoffmann and Carmen; Directed Le Comte Ory for the Opera de Lyons 1988 and War and Peace for San Francisco Opera 1991. *Address:* c/o Teatro Alla Scala, Via Filodrammatici 2, Milan, Italy.

SAVASKAN Sinan Carter, b. 11 Aug 1954, England. Composer; Conductor; Educator. m. Sarah Katherine Carter, 23 Sept 1981, 2 sons, 2 daughters. *Education:* BA (hons) Performance Arts, Music major,; MMus, Composition, University of Surrey, 1981; Studied with Robin Maconie, Reginald Smith Brindle, Cornelius Cardew; Registered PhD work in Composition, University of York. *Career:* Composer of concert music, modern ballet, performance art shows; Improvisor on flutes, exotic instruments, electronics; Freelance Lecturer and in charge of Composition and Creative Music, Westminister School, London; Recent lecture-concert visits, Rumania, USSR, Netherlands, Germany; Commissions: ICA; Lontano Ensemble; Balanescu Quartet; Trio Basso/Cologne, John Harle, Myrha Sax, Quartet, Tim Brady. *Compositions:* Speed, 1969; Many Stares Through..., 1981; Anthedonia Endlessly, 1982; Trio No 2, Op 18, 1984; The Street; Past and Future Now, ballet music; Partage Midi, video music drama; Tango: Impressions-Tears, 1986; Panic in Needle Park, 1988; Collected Fantasies, piano; Anthems for the Sun No 2, 1990; Ovosomnes, 1992. *Recordings:* International Communication Disaster 1877, LMC2.Mayday. *Contributions to:* The Times Supplements; Time Out; Others. *Current Management:* Society of New Musics, 13 Langley Crecent, London E11, England. *Address:* c/o Association of Professional Composers, 34 Hanway Street, London, W1P 9DE, England.

SAVOIE Robert, b. 21 Apr 1927, Montreal, Canada. Singer (Baritone). *Education:* Studied with Pauline Donalda in Montreal and with Antonio Narducci in Milan. *Debut:* Teatro Nuovo Milan 1952, as Scarpia. *Career:* Sang with many seasons for L'Opéra de Montreal and made guest appearance with the Paris Opéra and the Opéra du Rhin Strasbourg; Opera houses in Nice, Toulouse, Lyon, Marseille, Dallas, Washington, Pittsburgh and London; Other roles have been Mozart's Leporello, Don Giovanni, Count and Guglielmo, Escamillo; Verdi's Iago, Amonasro and Ford; Puccini's Gianni Schicchi and Sharpless; Golaud in Pelléas et Mélisande, Albert in Werther and Ramiro in L'Heure Espagnole; Currently, Artistic Director, City of Lachine, Quebec, Canada; The Lachine Music Festival.*Recordings include:* Posa in the French version of Don Carlos (Voce). *Honours:* Doctorat Honoris Causa, in Music, University of Moncton, Canada. *Memberships:* President, Founder of L'Orchestra Metropolitan of Montreal. *Address:* 2100 Du Calvados, St Bruno, Quebec, Canada J3V 3K2

SAVOLAINEN Jarmo Tapio, b. 24 May 1961, Finland. Musician; Composer. *Education:* Classical Training in Conservatories in Finland; Studied in Berklee College in Boston and Private Studies in New York. *Career:* Performed in Major Jazz Festivals, Finland, Holland, France, Italy and USA. *Compositions include:* Solo Piano; Jazz Quartet. *Recordings:* Phases; Songs for Solo Piano; First Sight. *Honour:* Jazz Musician of the Year. *Memberships:* Teosto Elvis. *Hobbies:* Food; Cooking; Languages. *Address:* Helsinginkatu 23 B 40, 00510 Helsinki, Finland.

SAVOVA Galina, b. 1945, Sofia, Bulgaria. Singer (Soprano). *Career:* Sang first at the Sofia Opera before an international career at the opera houses of Rome, Naples, Karlsruhe and Bologna; Metropolitan Opera debut 1982, as Amelia in Un ballo in maschera; Other roles include Chrysothemis (Elektra), Puccini's Minnie, Turandot and Tosca, Amelia (Simon Boccanegra), Yaroslavna in Prince Igor and Leonore; In 1989 sang Aida at the Teatro Sao Carlos, Lisbon; Chicago Lyric Opera, 1992 as Turandot. *Address:* c/o Teatro Sao Carlos, Rua Serpa Pinto 9, 1200 Lisbon, Portugal.

SAWA Victor Norman, b. 22 May 1950, Canada. Musician; Conductor. 1 son. *Education:* New England Conservatory, Boston; McGill University. *Career:* Numerous appearances with CBC Radio and TV, European TV and Radio, American TV and Radio. *Recordings include:* Scott Joplin; Bartók Contrasts; Music for Berlin. *Honours:* Grammy Award; NY Times Top 10 Award; Top Musician Award, Tanglewood. *Membership:* Mensa. *Hobbies:* Golf; Travel; Baseball; Biblioholic. *Address:* 91 Stirling Avenue North, Kitchener, Ontario, Canada N2H 3G6.

SAWALLISCH Wolfgang, b. 26 Aug 1923, Munich, Germany. Conductor; Pianist. *Education:* Studied at the Munich Academy. *Career:* Repetiteur at Augsburg; conducted Hansel and Gretel on 1947 debut; Joint winner of prize for duos at 1949 Geneva International Competition; General Music Director at Aachen 1953-58; Wiesbaden 1959-60; Cologne 1960-63; Bayreuth debut 1957, Tristan und Isolde; later conducted Tannhäuser and Der fliegende Holländer there; London 1957, with Schwarzkopf in a Lieder programme and conducting the Philharmonia Orchestra; 1961- Principal Conductor Vienna Symphony Orchestra and Hamburg Philharmonic Orchestra; US debut 1964; General Music Director Bavarian State Opera Munich 1971-92; Philadelphia Symphony Orchestra, 1993; Covent Garden debut with the Munich company 1972, conducting operas by Strauss; Lieder programmes with Dietrich Fischer-Dieskau and Hermann Prey; Solo performances as pianist in works by Mozart and Beethoven; Conducted a new production of Strauss's Friedenstag at the Munich Festival, 1988; Mathis der Maler and Dantons Tod 1990; Arabella at La Scala 1992; Last new production as Chief Conductor of the Bavarian State Opera, Henze's Der Prinz Von Homburg, 1992. *Recordings:* Operas by Strauss, Mozart and Wagner; Orchestral music by Schubert, Mendelssohn and Beethoven; Video of The Ring, from Munich, 1989. *Address:* c/o Bayerische Staatsoper, Postfach 745, D-8000 Munich 1, Germany.

SAWER David, b. 14 Sept. 1961, Stockport, England. Composer. *Education:* University of York: DPhil studies with Richard Orton; Further study with Mauricio Kagel in Cologne. *Career:* Music performed by the London Sinfonietta and Music Projects/London; Commissions from MusICA 1986, the Kirklees Metropolitan Council, the 1988 Almeida Festival, King's Lynn Festival, BBC Singers, 1990, and BBC Symphony Orchestra for 1992 Proms; Directed in premiere productions of Kagel's Pas de Cinq and Kantrimusik (Huddersfield Festival 1983, 1984) and as soloist in Kagel's Phonophonie at the 1987 Summerscope season on South Bank; Music for radio and for theatre productions. *Compositions:* Solo Piano 1983; Etudes for two to six actor/musicians and ensemble 1984; Cat's-Eye for ensemble 1986; Take Off for ensemble 1987; Food of Love for actress and piano 1988; Good Night for ensemble 1989; Swansong, for radio, 1989; Songs of Love and War, 1990 for choir SATB, 2 harp, 2 percussion; The Panic, a chamber opera, 4 singers and 6 instruments, 1990-91; Byrnan Wood, 1992 for large orchestra; The Melancholy of Departure, 1990 for piano. *Contributions to:* Grove Dictionary of Opera, entry on Kagel. *Honours:* Sony Radio Award, for Swansong, 1990; DAAD Scholarship, 1984-85; Fulbright-Chester-Schirmer Fellowship in composition, 1992/93. *Current Management:* Universal Edition (London), Ltd. *Address:* c/o Universal Edition, Warwick House, 9 Warwick Street, London W1R 5FA, England.

SAWYER Philip John, b. 3 Feb. 1948, Birmingham, England. Lecturer; Organist and Continuo Player. m. Judith Susan Timbury, 9 Jan. 1981. *Education:* Royal College of Music 1966-68; ARCM 1966; ARCO 1967; Peterhouse, Cambridge 1968-71; BA Hons. 1971; MA 1975; Organ Study in Amsterdam with Piet Kee 1970; MMus, 1986. *Career:* Assistant Director of Music, Trent College, 1971-73; Lecturer, Napier Polytechnic of Edinburgh, 1975-89, Senior Lecturer, 1989-; Organist and Choirmaster: St Cuthbert's Parish Church, Edinburgh, 1975-78; Nicolson Square Methodist Church, Edinburgh, 1978-83; Director of Music, St Andrew's and St George's Parish Church, Edinburgh, 1983-86; Organ Recitals in: Westminster Abbey; Notre Dame, Paris, Nice Cathedral, Monaco Cathedral; St Laurens, Alkmaar; St Bavo's RC Cathedral, Haarlem; Hillsborough Parish Church, N Ireland; Universities of St Andrews, Edinburgh, Glasgow, Aberdeen; Cathedrals of Edinburgh, Glasgow, Dundee; Founder and Director of the Edinburgh Organ Week; First Performances of newly-commissioned organ works by Alan Ridout, and others; 1st performance of The Seven Sacraments of Poussin by John McLeod in Edinburgh, Glasgow and London, 1992; Appearances as Harpsichord Continuo Player with Scottish Chamber Orchestra and Scottish Baroque Ensemble; Head Music, Napier University, 1990. *Recordings:* Solo Organ Recitals for BBC Radio 3 and Radio Scotland; Harpsichord Continuo with Scottish Chamber Orchestra (Conductor, Gibson), on a record of Music by Handel (Academy Records); BBC Radio Scotland, recording of the 1st performance of The Seven Sacraments of Poussin, Edinburgh, 1992. *Contributions to:* Various contributions to Journals of the British Institute of Organ Studies. *Address:* Dept of Music, Napier University, Sighthill Court, Edinburgh EH11 4BN, Scotland.

SAXBY Joseph Anthony, b. 3 Jan. 1910, London, England. Musician; Harpsichord & Piano Player. *Education:* Studied harpsichord with Arnold Dolmetsch, piano with Herbert Fryer, composition with Herbert Howells; Royal College of Music. *Debut:* Accompanist to Michael Zacharewitsch, Russian violinist, USA tour, 1925. *Career:* Farewell tour of John McCormack, Ireland; 49 overseas tours with Carl Dolmetsch - Europe, USA, Australia, New Zealand, Japan, Italy, UK; Numerous radio & television appearances with Carl Dolmetsch. *Compositions:* Various accompaniments, from Figured Bass for Recorder Works. *Recordings:* Decca, EMI; Records of harpsichord recitals with Carl Dolmetsch. *Contributions to:* Various magazines & radio interviews. *Honours:* Honorary Fellow, London College of Music; Dedications in pieces for harpsichord, various artists including Arnold Cooke, Colin Hand, John Gardner. *Memberships:* President, Haslemere & Grayshott Recorded Music Society; Incorporated Society of Musicians; Royal College of Music Union; Governor, Dolmetsch Foundation. *Hobbies:* Reading; Television. *Address:* Red Cot, Three Gates Lane, Haslemere, Surrey, England.

SAXTON Beryl, b. 11 Dec 1934, Sutton In Ashfield, Notts, England. Private Teacher of Music. *Education:* Private Studies with Fred Garnett. *Career:* Private Teacher Since, 1961. *Memberships:* Incorporated Society of Musicians; British Voice Association; Friends of Trinity College, London. *Hobbies:* Gardening; Woodwork; Photography. *Address:* 'Overstones', 41 Dales Avenue, Sutton-in-Ashfield, Notts NG17 4BY, England.

SAXTON Robert, b. 8 Oct 1953, London, England. Composer. *Education:* Studied privately with Elisabeth Lutyens and Luciano Berio; 1972-75 Cambridge University, with Robin Holloway; 1975-76 Oxford University, with Robert Sherlaw Johnson. *Career:* Bristol University 1984-; Currently: Head of Composition, Guildhall School of Music and Drama. *Compositions:* Orchestral: Chorus to Apollo, 1980; Traumstadt, 1980; Ring of Eternity, 1982-83; Concerto for Orchestra, 1984; Viola Concerto, 1986; In The Beginning, 1987; Elijah's Violin, 1988; Violin Concerto, 1989; Music to Celebrate the Resurrection of Christ, 1988; Ensemble: Reflections of Narziss and Goldmund, 1975; Canzona, 1978; Processions and Dances, 1981; Piccola Musica per Luigi Dallapiccola, 1981; Vocal: La Promenade d'Automne for soprano and ensemble, 1972; Where are You going my Pretty Maid? for soprano and sextet, 1973; What does the Song hope for ? for soprano and ensemble, 1974; Brise Marine for soprano, piano and tape, 1976; Cantata on Poems of Hölderlin for tenor, countertenor and piano, 1979; Canatata No.2 for tenor, oboe and piano, 1980; Cantata No.3 for 2 sopranos and tape, 1981; Eloge for soprano and ensemble, 1981; Chaconne for double chorus, 1981; Caritas, opera, 1991; Chamber: Ritornelli and Intermezzi for piano, 1972; Krystallen for flute and piano, 1973; Echoes of the Glass Bead Game for wind quintet, 1975; 2 Pieces for piano, 1976; Poems for Melisande for flute and piano, 1977; Arias for oboe and piano, 1977; Study for a Sonata for flute, oboe, cello and harpsichord, 1977; Sonatas for 2 Pianos, 1977; Toccata for cello, 1978; Chiaroscuro for percussion, 1981; Piano Sonata, 1981; Fantasiestuck for accordion, 1982; The Sentinel of the Rainbow for sextet, 1984; Choral: I Will Awake The Dawn, 1987; Paraphrase on Mozart's Idomeneo, 1991; Celo concerto, 1992; Caritas, opera, 1990-91; Psalm, a song of ascents, 1992; At the Round Earth's Imagined Corners, 1992. *Reecordings:* Concerto for orchestra; Sentinel of the Rainbow; Circles of Light; Ring of Eternity (all on EMI); Violin concerto: In the Beginning; I Will Awake the Daw, (Collins Classics); Paraphrase on Mozart's Idomaneo, (EMI); Cantas, opera, (Collins Classics); At the Round Earth's Imagined Corners, (Hyperion); Night Dance, (Bridge Records); Muisc to Celebrate the Resurrection of Christ, (Collins Classics).*Publications:* All scores published by Chester Music. *Honours:* 1st Prize International Gaudeamus Music Week, Holland, 1975; Fulbright Arts Award, Visiting Fellow, Princeton University, USA, 1986; D.Mus Oxon, 1992. *Memberships:* Council SPNM, 1978-90; Music Advisory Panel, Arts Council, 1989-93. *Current Management:* Chester Music. *Address:*c/o Chester Music, 8/9 Frith Street, London, W1V 5TZ, England.

SAYERS Gavin, b. 7 Jan 1962, England. Singer (Tenor). *Education:* Studied at the Guildhall School of Music with Johanna Peters and Maureen Morelle. *Career:* Sang Arturo in a concert performance of Lucia di Lammermoor, 1986; British premiere of Nino Rota's La Notte di un nevrastenico at Morley College, 1990; Concert repertoire includes Puccini's Messa di Gloria; Hiawatha's Wedding Feast by Coleridge-Taylor; Haydn's Nelson Mass and Maria Theresa Mass; Messiah and Mozart's Mass in C; Hymn of Praise by Mendelssohn (2nd Symphony); Elijah (Harrow Choral Society, 1990); Britten's Serenade (East Surrey Orchestra, 1991); Has performed in a variety of amateur operatic performances. *Address:* c/o Korman International Management, Crunnells Green Cottage, Preston, Herts SG4 7UQ, England.

SAYLOR Bruce, b. 24 Apr 1946, Philadelphia, USA. Composer. *Education:* Studied with Hugo Weisgall and Roger Sessions; Accademia di Sanata Cecilia in Rome with Petrassi and Evangelisti, CUNY Graduate School with Weisgall and George Perle. *Career:* Lecturer, Queens College, 1970-76, NY University, 1976-79; Associate Professor t Queens College, 1979-, Composer-in-Residence, Chicago Lyric Opera, 1992-94. *Compositions include:* Ballets Cycle; Inner World Out; Wildfire; Notturno for Piano and Orchestra; Woodwind Quartet; Symphony in Two Parts, Turns and Mordents for flute and orchestra; Duo for Violin and Viola; St Elmos Fire for Flute and Harp; Lyrics for Soprano and Violin;

Love Play for Mezzo and Ensemble; Song from Water Street for Mezzo; See You in the Morning, meno and ensemble; Orpheus Descending (Opera in two acts); My Kinsman, Major Molineux (Opera in one act). *Publications include:* The Writings of Henry Cowell. *Address:* 318 W 85 Street, New York, NY 10024, USA.

SCALCHI Gloria, b. 1960, Trieste, Italy. Singer (Mezzo-soprano). *Education:* Studied with Iris Adami Corradetti and with Joseph Metternich in Munich; Seminars at the Rossini-Academy in Pesaro. *Career:* Sang Angelina in La Cenerentola at Catania in 1988; Further appearances at the Rome Opera (Emma in Zelmira, conducted by Philip Gossett and Andromaca in Rossini's Ermione); Concertgebouw Amsterdam (Maffio Orsini in Lucrezia Borgia); Verona (Rosina and Angelina), Bologna (Sinaide in Mosè); Carnegie Hall (Ermione); San Francisco (Zelmira); Monte Carlo (Roberto Devereux); Paris (Rossini's Petite Messe Solonnelle and Vivaldi's Juditha Triumphans); Musikverien Vienna (Cherubini's D minor Requiem); Rossini Festival Pesaro 1990, as Somira in Ricciardo e Zoraide. *Recordings include:* Juditha Triumphans. *Address:* c/o Athole Still Ltd, Greystoke House, 80-86 Westow Street, London SE19 3AF, England.

SCANDIUZZI Roberto, b. 1955, Treviso, Italy, Singer (Bass). *Debut:* Sang Bartolo in Mozart's Figaro under Riccardo Muti at La Scala, 1982. *Career:* Appearances in Opera at Paris, Munich, Hanburg, Amsterdam, Venice, Rome. US Debut in Verdi's Requiem, 1991; Sang Fiesco in a New Production of Simon Boccanegra at Covent Garden, 1991; Other conductors have included Patane, Giulini, Colin Davis; Festival Engagements 1992 at Florence as Padre Guardiano in La Forza del Destino, Ramfis at Caracalla and Philip II and Zaccaria at Verona; Other roles include Silva, Attila, Mefistofele and Don Giovanni. *Recordings include:* Aide conducted by Mehta, I Puritani, Turandot and Simon Bocanegra.

SCANO Guido, b. 12 Apr 1961, Cagliari, Italy. Pianist. m. Claudia Mattiotto, 1 Aug 1985, 1 son. *Education:* Science subjects, High School; Piano Diploma, Martini High Conservatory, Bologna and Ecole Internationale de Piano, Lausanne, Switzerland; Arts Academy, Arezzo. *Debut:* With Orchestra, 1978; As Soloist, 1979; Piano Duo, 1985. *Career:* Concerts throughout Europe and Asia; Performed in duo with wife, Radio Auditorium, Rome, Teatro Comunale, Trieste, Teatro Verdi, Venice, Florence, Turin, Naples, Milan, Perugia, Terni, Reggio Calabria, Gorizia, Alessandria, Cagliari, Pomposa Summer Festival, other festivals at Reggio Emilia, Olbia, Carloforte, Sarteano, Tolmezzo, Paularo, Arezzo, Marsala, Sassari; Duo performances abroad include Marseille, Athens, Thessaloniki, Innsbruck, Bucharest, Lausanne, also in Bombay, Calcutta, New Delhi as 1st Italian Piano Duo to play in India; Professor, masterclasses, Bavaria; Also plays with New Europe Quintet; Frequent Member of Jury, competitions in Italy and France; Italian, French and Rumanian broadcasting appearances. *Recordings:* 4 Steps in 4 Hands, 15 part programme for Radiokoper, Slovenia; For Montecarlo Broadcasting; RAI TV. *Contribution to:* Articles to Musica e Scuola magazine. *Honours:* 1st Prize, Lecce (contemporary music); Bardolino and Barcelona PG Competitions. *Membership:* National Syndicate of Musicians. *Hobbies:* Psychosomatics; Geography. *Address:* Via Bonomea 217, 34136 Trieste, Italy.

SCARABELLI Adelina, b. 1950, Milan. Singer (Soprano). *Education:* Studied in Brescia. *Career:* Sang at the Piccola Scala, Milan, from 1977; La Scala Milan from 1981, debut as Barbarina in Le nozze di Figaro; Salzburg Festival, 1984-85, as Despina and the Italian Singer in Capriccio; Florence 1988, as Lauretta in Gianni Schicchi; Rome Opera 1989, as Aminta in Mozart's Il re Pastore and as Susanna; She sang Zerlina in Don Giovanni at Parma in 1989; Other roles include Mozart's Servilia (La clemenza di Tito) and Ismene (Mitridate), Verdi's Oscar and Nannetta, Puccini's Musetta and Liu, and Micaela in Carmen. *Address:* c/o Teatro Dell'Opera, Piazza Beniamino Gigli 8, I-00184 Rome, Italy.

SCAUNAS Simona, b. 12 Nov. 1965, Rimnicu-Vilcea, Romania. Pianist. *Education:* Bacalaureat Diploma, High School of Art, George Enescu, Bucharest, 1984; Conservator of Arts and Music, George Enescu, Iasi. *Career:* Recitals at Romanian Athene, Bucharest 1989, also in other cities of Romania: Iasi, Cluj, Rimmiou-Vilcea, Ploiesti, Botosani, Participant in Young Talents Piatra-Neamt; Museum of Republic, 1987-88; Concerts with: Bacau Symphony Orchestra, 1987; Craiova Oltenia Philharmonic Orchestra, 1988; Radio appearances in musical programmes and with recitals, 1987, 1988; Television, 1987; Participant in Young Talents Festival, 1984, 1986, 1987, 1988; Piano recitals and chamber music colaboration in cities of Germany: Nordhausen, Gotha, Heidelberg and Darmstadt, 1991, 1992 and 1993. *Recordings:* Radio appearances, 1989, 1990. *Honours:* 2nd Prize, International Concours of Catanzaro, Italy; 1st Prize, Festival of Student Art and Creation, Cluj, 1989; Prize for chamber music colaboration, Cluj Gheorghe Dima Concours, 1988; 3rd Prize at Gheorghe Dima, Piano Competition, Cluj, 1989. *Membership:* Friends of Music and Theatre Society, 1984-. *Address:* Strada Muncii NR4, Rimnicu-Vilcea 1000, Romania.

SCHAAF Johannes, b. 7 Apr 1933, Bad Cannstatt, Germany. Stage Director. *Education:* Studied medicine. *Career:* Worked at the Stuttgart Schauspielhaus, then directed plays in Ulm and Bremen; Further theatre work at Munich (Twelfth Night), Vienna and Salzburg (Beaumarchais, Buchner and Lessing); Director of award winning films from 1967 (with some acting) and television programmes featuring Sviatoslav Richter, Edith Mathis, Peter Schreier and Dietrich Fischer-Dieskau; Opera productions have included Les Contes d'Hoffmann (Vienna Volksoper), Idomeneo (Vienna Staatsoper), Eugene Onegin (Geneva and Bremen) and Capriccio and Die Entführung (Salzburg); Produced Le Nozze di Figaro at Covent Garden 1987 and was invited to return for Così fan Tutte and Idomeneo (1989), Don Giovanni 1992; Also engaged for Fidelio (1989) and Die Frau ohne Schatten (1992) at Geneva Opera, The Nose by Shostakovich at Frankfurt (1990) and Schreker's Der Ferne Klang at Brussels; engaged to produce Boris Godunov to open the New Israel Opera House, 1994. *Contributions to:* Geo, on subjects including Chinese Opera. *Address:* c/o Harrison/Parrott Ltd, 12 Penzance Place, London W11 4PA, England.

SCHACHTSCHNEIDER Herbert, b. 5 Feb 1919, Allenstein, Germany. Singer (Tenor). *Education:* Studied at the Musikhochschule Berlin. *Career:* Sang at the Stadttheater Flensburg from 1953; Further engagements at Mainz and Essen; Holland Festival 1958; Cologne Opera 1959-72; Sang at the Festival Hall London 1963, in the British premiere (concert) of Schoenberg's Von Heute auf Morgen; Roles include Florestan, Walther, Tannhäuser, Lohengrin, Parsifal, Radames, Don Carlos, Cavaradossi and Don Jose; Guest appearances in Germany and elsewhere in Europe; Professor at the Musikhochschule Saarbrücken from 1975. *Address:* Musikhochschule des Saarlandes, Bismarckstrasse 1, 66 Saarlrücken, Germany.

SCHADE Michael, b. 1965, Geneva, Switzerland. Singer (Tenor). *Education:* Curtis Institute. *Career:* Early Experience as Ernesto in Belgium and Rameau's Pygmalion with Opera Atelier in Toronto; professional Debut 1990 as Jacquino, with the Pacific Opera of British Columbia; Sang Tamino at Bologna 1991; Appeared as Iago in Rossini's Otello at Pesaro; Vienna Staatsoper debut 1991, as Almaviva; Season 1991/92 as Alfred in Fledermaus at Geneva; Almaviva with Edmonton and Canadian Operas; Ernesto with Vancouver Opera and Elvino in La Sonnambula at Macerata; Season 1992/93 as Jacquino in San Francisco and the Chevalier in Dialogues des Carmelites at Geneva; Engaged by the Vienna Staatsoper as Ferrando, Almaviva, Nemorino, Tamino and Nicolai's Fenton; Salzburg Festival 1994 in a staged version of Mozart Arias; Cologne Opera as Telemaco in Monteverdi's Ulisse and Elvino at Trieste; Concert Repertoire include Beethoven's Missa Solemnis; The

Creation; The Seasons and Bach's St Matthew Passion; Mozart's Requiem; Carmina Burana; Schumann's Paradies und Die Peri Under John Eliot Gardiner and Elijah with the Cleveland Orchestra. *Recordings include:* Haydn's Maria Theresa Mass Conducted by Trevor Pinnock, The Creation and the Seasons, St Matthew Passion conducted by Rilling; Vogelgesang in Die Meistersinger, under Sawallisch. *Address:* c/o IMG Artists, Media House, 3 Burlington Lane, London W4 2TH, England

SCHAEFFER Boguslaw Julien, b. 6 June 1929, Lwow, Poland. Composer. *Education:* Studied composition with Arthur Malawski in Cracow and musicology with Jachimecki at the Jagiello University in Cracow, 1940-53; Studied further with Luigi Nono, 1959. *Career:* Director of the record library of Polish Radio in Cracow, 1952; Music Critic 1953-59; Professor for Composition at the Academy of Music in Cracow from 1963; at the Hochschule für Musik und dorstellende Kunst Mozarteum, from 1985, (1989 OH Prof); Experimental Studio of Polish radio in Warsaw, 1965-68; *Compositions include:* Concerto for 2 Pianos 1951; Music for string quartet 1954; Sonata for solo violin 1955; Permutations for 10 instruments 1956; 6 Models for piano 1954-93; Extremes for 10 instruments 1957; 4 String Quartets, 1957, 1964, 1971, 1973, 1986, 1993; 6 Movimenti for piano and orchestra 1957; 8 Pieces for piano 1954-58; Monosonata for 6 string quartets 1959; Equivalenze sonore for percussion and chamber orchestra 1959; Concerto Breve for cello and orchestra 1959; Concerto for string quartet 1959; Topofonica for 40 instruments 1960; Non-Stop for piano (8 hours playing time at premiere, 1964); Musica for harpsichord and orchestra 1961; 4 Pieces for string trio 1962; Musica Ipsa 1962; Expressive Aspects for soprano and flute 1963; Collage and Form for 8 jazz musicians and orchestra 1963; Audiences I-V for various performers 1964; Collage for chamber orchestra 1964; Howl, monodrama after poem by Allen Ginsburg 1966; Decet for harp and 9 instruments 1966; Piano Concerto 1967; Media for voices and instruments 1967; Jazz Concerto 1969; Synectics for 3 performers 1970; Algorithms for 7 performers 1970; Thema for tape 1970; Texts for orchestra 1971; 15 Elements for 2 pianos 1971; Variants for wind quintet 1971; Confrontations 1972; Conceptual Music 1972; Concerto for 3 Pianos 1972; Bergsoniana or soprano and ensemble 1972; Neues for 3 violins 1972; Symphony in 9 movements 1973; Tentative Music for 159 instruments 1973; Synhistory for tape 1973; Antiphona for tape 1975; Missa elettronica 1975; Iranian Set 1976; Spinoziana, action music 1977; Gravesono for wind instruments and percussion 1977; Self-Expression for cello 1977; Matan for 3 percussionists 1978; Kesukaan for 13 strings 1978; Miserere for soprano, choir, orchestra, organ and tape 1978; Jangwa for double bas and orchestra 1979; Te Deum for voices and orchestra 1979; Maah for orchestra and tape 1979; Berlin '80 for piano and tape 1980; Cantata 1980; Autogenic Composition 1980; Introductions and an Epilogue for small orchestra 1981; Duodrama for alto saxophone and percussion 1981; Euphony for double bass 1981; Stabat mater for Soprano Alto, Descant Choir, Strings and Organ, 1983; Organ Concerto, 1984; Miniopera, 1988; Liebesblicke, Opera, 1989; Kwaiwa for violin and computer, 1986; Missa Sinfonica, 1986; Piano Concerto, 1990, four Sonatas for organ solo (Vier Jahreszaiten), 1985-86, Lieder for voice and orchestra 1986, Saxophone Concerto 1986, Missa Brevis for choir 1988, Doppelhonsert for 2 violins and orchestra, Concert for percussion, piano and orchestra 1988, Kammersymphonie 1988, Concerto for soprano and or orchestra 1988, Sinfonia 1993; Violin Concerto, 1988. *Publications include:* Classics of Dodecaphonic Music 1961, 1964; Lexicon of 20th Century Composers 1963, 1965; Music of the 20th Century 1975; History of Music, Styles, and Authors 1979; Introduction to Composition (In English), 1975. *Address:* A-5020, Salzburg, Plainstr 85 Top 7, Poland.

SCHAEFFER Pierre Henri Marie, b. 14 Aug 1910, Nancy, France. Author; Composer. m. (1) Elisabeth Schmitt, 1935 (deceased 1941), 1 daughter, (2) Jacqueline de Lisle, 31 Oct. 1962, 1 son. *Education:* Ecole Polytechnique, Paris, 1929-31; Ecole superieure d'electricite, Paris, 1932-33; Ecole superieure des telecommunications, Paris, 1933-34. *Career:* Founder, Studio d'Essai, Radiodiffusion Francaise, 1942-45; Founder, Radio D'Outremer, France, 1950-55; Founder, Director, Serviee de la Recherche, ORTF, France, 1960-75; Founder, Groupe de Recherche Musique Electroacoustique, France; Professor, Copnservatoire National de Musique, Paris, 1968-76; Member, Haut Conseil de l'Audiovisuel, France, 1970-75; Leader of movement to form musique concrete, France, 1948. *Compositions:* Etudes de Bruit 1948; Symphonie pour un Homme Seul, 1950; Orphee, 1953; Etudes aux Objets, 1960; Triedre Fertile, 1975. *Publications:* Author of books and essays: Clotaire Nicole, 1935; Les enfants de coeur, 1948; Traite des Objets Musicaus, 1966; L'Avenir à reculons, 1967; Le gardien de volcan (prix Sainte Beuve, 1969), 1969; Machines à communiquer, Vol. 1 Genese des simulacres, 1970, Vol. 2 Pouvoir et Communications, 1972; La Musique et les Ordinateures, 1970; de l'experience musicale a l'experience humaine, 1971; De la Musique concrete a la Musique meme, 1977; Les antennas de Jericho, 1978; Excusez moi je Meurs, 1981; Psychanalyse et Musique, 1982; Prelude Choral et Fugure, 1983. *Honours:* Chevalier des Palmes Academiques; Officier Legion d'Honneur; Grand Officier Ordre National du Merite, Commander, des Arts et des Lettres.

SCHAFER Markus. b. 13 June 1961, Andernach am Rhein, Germany. Singer (Tenor). *Education:* Studied in Koblenz, Karlsruhe. *Career:* Sang at the Zurich Opera form 1985; Hamburg, 1986; Deutsche Oper am Rhein Dusseldorf From 1987; Sang Fenton in Die Lustige Weiber von Windsor at Duisburg, 1991; Damon in Acis and Galatea at the Elizabeth Hall; Other concerts include the Evangelist in Bach's Passions; Messiah, Elijah, St Paul, Die Schopfung and Rossini's Stabat Mater; Opera roles include Paisiello's Almaviva, Pedrillo, Ramiro and Caramelo in Eine Nacht in Venedig. *Recordings include:* St Paul, Mendelssohn's Christus, Beethoven's Mass in C; Haydn's L'Infedelta Delusa; Mozart's Mass K139. *Address:* c/o Deutsche Oper am Rhein, Heinrich Heine Allee 16, 4000 Dusseldorf, Germany.

SCHAFER Raymond Murray, b. 18 July 1933, Sarnia, Ontario, Canada. Composer; Writer on Music; Educationist. *Education:* Studied at the Toronto Conservatory with Guerrero (piano) and Weinzweg (composition). *Career:* Worked freelance for the BBC in Europe 1956-61; Founded Ten Centuries Concerts 1961, Toronto; Artist-in-residence at Memorial University, Newfoundland 1963-65; Simon Fraser University British Columbia 1965; Research into acoustic ecology from 1971. *Compositions:* Concerto for harpsichord and 8 instruments 1954; Minnelieder for mezzo and wind quintet 1956; Sonatina for flute and keyboard 1958; In Memoriam: Iberto Guerrero for strings 1959; Protest and Incarceration for mezzo and orchestra 1960; Brebeuf for baritone and orchestra 1961; Canzoni for Prisoners, orcestra 1962; Untitled Composition for Orchestra 1963; Loving/Toi, music theatre 1963-66; Requeims for the Party Girl 1966; Threnody 1966; Kaleidoscope for multi-track tape 1067; Son of Heldenleben for orchestra and tape 1968; From the Tibetan Book of the Dead for soprano, chorus and ensemble 1968; Yeow and Pax for chorus, organ and tape 1969; No Longer than Ten Minutes for orchestra 1070; sappho for mezzo and ensemble 1970; String Quartet 1970; Okeanos for 4-track tape 1971; In Search of Zoroaster for male voice, chorus, percussion and organ 1971; Music for the Morning of the World 1970; Beyond the Great Gate of Light 1972; Arcana for low voice and ensemble 1972; East for chamber orchestra 1972; Paria I and II music theatre 1969-72; North White for orchestra 1972; String Quartet No. 2, Waves, 1976; Adieu Robert Schumann for alto and orchestra 1976; Hymn to the Night for soprano and orchestra 1976; Cortège for orchestra 1977; Apocolypsis, music-theatre 1980; RA, multi-media piece based on the Egyptian God 1983; Flute Concerto, 1985; String Quartet no.4, 1989. *Publications include:* Edition of Ezra Pound's opera Le testament de François Villon, 1960; British Composers in Interview 1963; Ezra Pound and Music 1977; The Thinking Ear, 1986. *Honours:* Canada Council Grants 1961, 1963; From Foundation Award 1968; Canadian Music Council Medal 1972; Donner Foundation Grant 1972; Guggenheim Fellowship 1974.

SCHAFF Gabriel Jacob Gideon Polin, b. 9 Nov 1959, Philadelphia, Pennsylvania, USA. Violinist. m. Nancy McDill, 18 Dec 1988. 1 daughter. *Education:* BMus, 1981, Assistant teaching for Erick Friedman, 1979-81, Manhattan School of Music, New York City, 1981; Additional studies, New School of Music and Temple University, Philadelphia, also with Norman Carol, Philadelphia Orchestra. *Career:* Extensive symphonic, opera, ballet and chamber music performances at all 4 concert halls of Lincoln Center and Carnegie Hall, New York; Violin Soloist in Soviet-American Exchange Concerts organised by Claire Polin with performances in Philadelphia, New York, Moscow, Leningrad and Helsinki, 1979-88; Several commissions and premieres of works by US and Soviet composers; Personnel Manager, Metropolitan Opera Presentation Orchestra. *Recordings:* Recording on Bis, Essay and Music Masters Labels. *Contributions to:* Reviews in Music Journal Magazine, 1983-85, including 1984 International Festival of Contemporary Music, Moscow. *Honours:* Artist to Watch, Music Journal Magazine, 1983; Artist Ambassador Nominee, US Information Agency, 1986; Outstanding Young Men in America, 1987. *Membership:* Founder, Englewood Chamber Players, (community based, Professional Ensemble). *Hobbies:* Historical research of violins and bows with focus on the early Brescian makers and bowmakers of the Vuillaume shop and their contemporaries. *Address:* 136 Pleasant Avenue, Englewood, NJ 07631, USA.

SCHARINGER Anton, b. 5 Mar 1959, Austria. Singer (Baritone). *Education:* Studied at Vienna Conservatory. *Career:* Sang with the Salzburg Landestheater, 1981-83; Vienna Volksoper, from 1987; Sang Dr Falke in Fledermaus at Amsterdam, 1987; Mozart's Figaro at Ludwigsburg, 1989; Salzburg Festival, 1991; Guest Appearances at Cologne, Zurich; Other roles include, Masetto and Guglielmo; Many concert engagements, notably in sacred works by Bach; Television appearances include Bass Solos in the St Matthew Passion, with the Neubeuern Choral Society and the Munich Bach Collegium. *Recordings include:* Die Zauberflöte; Masetto in Don Giovanni; Mozart's L'Oca del Cairo. *Address:* c/o Zurich Opera, Falkenstrasse 1, CH-8008 Zurich, Switzerland.

SCHARLEY Denise, b. 1923, France. Singer (Mezzo-Soprano). *Education:* Studied at the Paris Conservatoire. *Debut:* Paris Opera Comique, 1942, as Genevieve in Pelléas et Mélisande. *Career:* Appeared at the Opera Comique until 1947, as Carmen, Dulcinee, Charlotte and Mignon; Sang at the Theatre de la Monnaie Brussels, 1947-48; Sang in Rome as Carmen; Paris Opera from 1951, as Maddalena in Rigoletto, Dalila, Amneris, Wagner's Erda, Fricka and Mary; Puck in Oberon, Bellone in Les Indes Galantes and Madame de Croissy in the local premiere of Les Dialogues des Carmelites; Guest appearances in Geneva, Lyons and Barcelona; Marseilles, 1961 as the Countess in the Queen of Spades. *Recordings include:* Werther and Carmen; Carmelites; L'Enfant et les Sortilèges. *Address:* c/o Théâtre National, 8 Rue Scribe, 75009 Paris, France.

SCHÄRTEL Elisabeth, b. 6 Oct 1919, Weiden, Oberpfalz, Germany. Singer (Contralto). *Education:* Studied with Helma Rodgier and Wilma Kaiser and with Anna Bahr-Mildenburg in Munich; Further study with Henny Wolff in Hamburg. *Career:* Sang first at Regensburg, then at Freiburg; Brunswick 1951-57; Bayreuth Festival from 1954, as Mary in Der fliegende Holländer, Erda, Magdalene and Waltraute; Cologne Opera from 1960 (sang in the premiere of Zimmermann's Die Soldaten, 1965); Appearances in Florence, Lisbon and Vienna as Adelaide in Araballa, Magdalene and Brangaene; Deutsche Oper Berlin as Kundry, Brangaene and the Kostelnička in Jenůfa;

Concert recitals, 1973. *Recordings:* Der fliegende Holländer (Philips); Die Zigeunerbaron (Eurodisc).

SCHATZBERGER Lesley Ann, b. 10 Mar 1953, Manchester, England. Clarinettist. m. Alan Norman George, 17 July 1976, 2 daughters. *Education:* Junior Exhibitioner, Royal Manchester College of Music; BA, Honours, University of York, 1974; ARCM, Royal Academy of Music, 1975. *Career:* Member of Northern Music Theatre; Classical Orchestra; Music Party; Yorkshire Baroque Soloists; English Concert; Lumina, Kaisers Harmonie, Finchcocks Collection; Harmonie Band; Formed Meridian Ensemble, 1976; Concerts with Fitzwilliam, Hagen, Guadagnini String Quartets, Hanover Band, Handel & Haydn Society of Boston; Karlheinz Stockhausen; Aulos Ensemble; Matrix; Gemini; Concert tours to USA, Finland, the Netherlands, Switzerland, Belgium, Germany, Spain, Greece, Japan, Hungary, Czech Republic; Italy, Portugal, France, USSR; Principal Clarinet, London Classical Players, English Baroque Soloists, Orchestra of the Age of Enlightenment, English Bach Festival; Academy of Ancient Music; Orchestre Revolutionnaire et Romatique. *Recordings:* With Academy of Ancient Music; For Amon Ra with Solomon String Quartet and Music Party; London Classical Players and Lumina; West German Radio with Capella Coloniensis. *Contributions to:* CASS Magazine. *Hobbies:* Cookery; Needlework; Motherhood. *Address:* 10 Bootham Terrace, York YO3 7DH, England.

SCHAUERTE-MAUBOUET Helga Elisabeth, b. 8 Mar 1957, Lennestadt, Germany. Organist. m. Philippe Maubouet, 22 July 1988, 1 daughter. *Education:* BA (Abitur), St Franziskusschule, Olpe, 1976; State examinations: Philosophy & Pedagogy, University of Cologne, 1982, Music & Artistic Maturity 1982, Organ Playing 1985, Musikhochschule, Cologne; Conservatory of Rueil-Malmaison, France, 1983. *Debut:* Public appearance as organist, aged 10; Chief organist, local parish church, aged 13. *Career:* Organist, German Church, Paris, 1982-, organ teacher at Conservatory Paris, 9th arrondissiment and in Andrisy; Recitals, lectures, master classes, Europe & USA, including Royal Academy of Music (London), University of Michigan (USA); Radio performances, West Germany & France. Concerts include: Performance, integral of Jehan Alain's organ works, Paris, 1986; 1st performance, Jean Langlais' organ works, BACH, & Miniature II and Mort et Resurrection. *Recordings:* Integral of Jehan Alain'a Organ Works; Poulenc Organ Concerto; Works of Langlais, Vierne, Dupré, J S Bach, Homilius, Walther, Kittel, Kellner, Buttstett, Armsdorff, Muthel. *Publications:* Jehan Alain: Das Orgelwerk, Eine monographische Studie, 1983; Jehan Alain: L'Homme et l'Oeuvre, 1985; Contributions, Ars Organi, Organists Review, The American Organist L'Orgue; Jehan Alain, Mourir A Trente Ans, Paris, in preparation, 1993; Rediscovered about 40 musical manuscripts as well as letters and photographs of Jehan Alain. *Honours:* Cultural Prize of Olpe (Germany), 1988. *Hobbies:* Mountain walking; Reading; Swimming. *Address:* 25 rue Blanche, 75009 Paris, France.

SCHAVERNOCH Hans, b. 1955, Australia. Stage Designer. *Education:* Studied at the Vienna Akademie. *Career:* Has designed productions of Erwartung, Iphigenie en Aulide, Elektra and La Clemenza di Tito in Vienna; Tanhhäuser and Werther at Hamburg, Orfeo and Die Zauberflöte at the Komische Oper Berlin; Collaborations with Producer Harry Kupfer in Berlin, at Salzburg for the premiere of Penderecki's Die Schwarze Maske, and the 1988 Ring des Nibelungen at Bayreuth; Metropolitan Opera with Der Fliegende Hollander, Erwartung and Bluebeard's Castle; Paris Opera with Der Rosenkavalier, Il Trittico, and Katya Kabanova; Royal Opera Covent Garden designs include Ariadne auf Naxos; Followed by Così fan Tutte, Idomeneo Elektra and La Damnation de Faust; Other designs include Alceste at Versailles, Pelleas et Mélisande at Cologne, Liszt St Elisabeth in Vienna, Parsifal and the Ring at the Berlin Staatsoper and Khovanshchina in Hamburg.

SCHECHTER John Mendell, b. 29 Apr 1946, Rockville Centre, New York, USA. Ethnomusicologist. m. Janis O'Driscoll, 25 June 1972, 1 daughter. *Education:* AB Music, Hamilton College, 1967; MMus Choral Conducting, Indiana University School of Music, 1970; PhD Ethnomusicology, University of Texas at Austin, 1982. *Career:* Associate Conductor of Choruses, New England Conservatory of Music, 1973-75; Postdoctoral Fellow in Music History, 1982-83; Assistant Professor of Music History, 1983-84, Syracuse University; Visiting Assistant Professor, 1985-86, Assistant Professor, 1986-91, (Ethnomusicology & Music Theory), University of California, Santa Cruz; Associate Professor (Ethnomusicology & Music Theory), University of California, Santa Cruz, 1991-. *Publications:* Music in a Northern Ecuadorian Highland Locus: Diatonic Harp, Genres, Harpists, and Their Ritual Junction in the Quechua Child's Wake, 3 vols, 1982; Book: The Indispensable Harp: Historical Development, Modern Roles, Configurations and Performance Practice in Ecuador and Latin America, Kent State University, 1992. Contributed to many articles on Latin American and Iberian musical instruments, The New Grove Dictionary of Musical Instruments, 1984. Latin America/Ecuador, Chapter for Worlds of Music, 2nd Edition, Schirmer Books, 1992-, The Current State of Bibliographic Research in Latin American Ethnomusicology, in D C Hazen, Ed., Latin American Masses and Minorities: Their Images and Realities (Madison, Wisconsin: Salalm Secretariat, 1987, pp. 334-345; 664-682). *Contributions to:* The New Grove Dictionary of Music and Musicians. *Address:* 101 Alamo Avenue, Santa Cruz, CA 95060, USA.

SCHECHTMAN Saul, b. 1924, USA. Conductor; Composer. *Education:* Studied conducting under Jean Morel and Dean Dixon, Juilliard School of Music, New York, 1947-51; Conducting under Leonard Bernstein, Tanglewood, 1948; Composition under Peter Mennin and Hall Overton. *Career:* Conductor, Juilliard Training Orchestra; Associate Conductor, Juilliard Opera Theater; Conductor, Ditson Festival, New York and Toronto Festival of Contemporary Music; Music Director, Bronx Symphony Orchestra, 4 years, then Bergen Philharmonic, New Jersey, 4 years; Music Advisor, Conductor, TV programme Omnibus, CBS network, 1954-58; Composed music for New York theatre production of Auntie Mame, 1956; Guest Conductor, various European cities including Oslo, Copenhagen, Reykjavik, Moscow, The Hague, Paris, 1958-74; Guest Conductor, Philadelphia Orchestra and Baltimore Symphony Orchestra, Norddeutscher Rundfunk; Conductor, several Broadway musicals, 1960-70; Music Director, Orchestra Piccola, Chamber Orchestra of Baltimore, 1976; Appointed Conductor, Oberhausen Opera House, Federal Republic of Germany, 1981. *Compositions:* Works published by MCA, Galaxy and Boston Music. *Honour:* Fellowship in Orchestral Conducting, Juilliard School of Music. *Address:* 1 Chemin de la Noue, F-57130 Vaux, France.

SCHECK Marianne, b. 18 Jan 1914, Geitbau, Germany. Singer (Soprano). *Education:* Studied in Munich. *Debut:* Koblenz 1937, as Martha in Tiefland. *Career:* Sang at Munster, Munich, Dusseldorf and Dresden 1937-51; Member of the Bayerische Staatsoper Munich 1945-70; Covent Garden 1955, as Venus in Tannhäuser; Paris Opéra 1957, 1960; San Francisco Opera 1959, as the Dyer's Wife in the US premiere of Die Frau ohne Schatten; Further appearances in Lisbon, Barcelona, Rio de Janeiro, Brussels, Hamburg, Stuttgart, New York and Vienna; Other roles include the Marschallin, Elsa, Senta, Chrysothemis, Pamina, and Sieglinde. *Recordings:* Der Rosenkavalier, Elektra, Hänsel und Gretel, Don Giovanni, Die Zauberflöte (Deutsche Grammophon); Der fliegende Holländer (HMV); Tannhäuser and Der fliegende Holländer, conducted by Konwitschny.

SCHEIBNER Andreas, b. 18 Jan 1851, Dresden, Germany. Singer. *Education:* Studied in Dresden with Gunther Leib. *Debut:* Gorlitz, 1972 as Dr Caius in Die Lustige Weiber Von Windsor. *Career:* Sang at Butzen,

1974, Stralsund, 1976-79, Potsdam, 1979-83; Engaged at the Dresden Staatsoper from 1983; Roles have included Mozarts Don Giovanni, Guglielmo, Papageno, Belcore, Eugene Onegin, Count Luna, Silvio, Marcello, Lortzings Zar Kilian in Der Freischutz; Concert Appearances in Austria, Holland, Poland and Throughout Germany. *Recordings include:* Der Freischutz, Conducted by C Davis; Bach Cantatas. *Address:* c/o Semper-Oper, 8012 Dresden, Germany.

SCHEIDEGGER Hans Peter, b. 23 Feb 1953, La Bottiere, Jura, Switzerland. Singer (Bass). *Education:* Studied at Berne University and in Essen with Jakob Stampfli and Paul Lohmann. *Debut:* Geneva Opera 1983, as Curio in Giulio Cesare, conducted by Charles Mackerras. *Career:* Has appeared at Lucerne and elsewhere in Switzerland as Fiesco (Simon Boccanegra), Britten's Theseus and Collatinus, Bartók's Buke Bluebeard, Zuniga, Leporello, Walter (Luisa Miller), Trulove (The Rake's Progress) and Rocco; Has sung at Karlsruhe from 1986 as King Henry (Lohengrin), Gremin, the Commendatore, Sarastro, Pogner, and the Doctor in Wozzeck; Other roles include Zoroastro in Handel's Orlando, Publio, La Clemenza di Tito, and Ferrando, Il Trovatore; Sang Rocco and King Marke at Basle, 1990; Concert repertoire includes Bach Cantatas, B minor Mass, St John Passion and Christmas Oratorio; Beethoven Missa Solemnis; Dvořák Requiem, Te Deum and Mass in D; Haydn Schöpfung, Jahreszeiten, Harmonie and Nicholas Masses, Salve Regina; Handel Messiah, Saul and Hercules; Mozart Requiem and other Masses; Schubert Mass in A flat and G; Graun Der Tod Jesu; Keiser Markus Passion; Telemann Matthew and Luke Passions; Conductors have included Armin Jordan, Horst Stein, Jeffrey Tate, Roderick Brydon, Kurt Sanderling, Charles Farncombe, Wolfgang Gönnenwein and David Lloyd-Jones. *Address:* Badisches Staatstheater, Baumeisterstrasse 11, D-7500 Karlsruhe, Germany.

SCHEJA Steffan, b. 1950, Sweden. Concert Pianist. *Education:* Studied at the Stockholm Coll of Music, Juilliard Sch, New York. *Debut:* Concert with Swedish Radio Symphony Orchestra, 1962. *Career:* New York Debut, 1972, Followed by Concerts With The French Radio Symphony Orchestra, Philharmonia Hungarica, Munich Philharmonic, English Chamber Orchestra, NHK Symphony Toyko and the Major Scandinavian Orchestras; Solo Recitals and Lieder Accompanist to Haken Hagegard, Barbara Bonney and Barbara Hendricks; Director of Chamber Music Festival at Gotland, Sweden, from 1986; Broadcasting Engagements, Tours of Europe, the USA and Asia, Recital Programmes with Violinst Young Uck Kim. *Recordings include:* Albums as Concert Soloist and as Recitalist. *Address:* c/o Nordic Artists Management, Sveavagen 76, S-11359 Stockholm, Sweden.

SCHELLE Michael, b. 22 Jan 1950, Philadelphia, Pennsylvania, USA. Composer; Music Educator. m. Joyce Tucciarone, 15 Jan 1972. 1 son, 1 daughter. *Education:* BA, Villanova University, 1972; BM, Butler University, 1974; MM, Hartt School of Music, University of Hartford, 1976; PhD, University of Minnesota, 1980; Private study with Aaron Copland, 1976-77. *Career:* Teaching Assistant, Hartt School of Music, University of Hartford, 1974-77; Instructor-Teaching Associate, University of Minnesota School of Music, 1977-79; Instructor, Carleton College, 1979; Instructor of Music 1979-81, Assistant Professor 1981-87, Associate Professor 1987-, of music, Composer in Residence 1981-, Director, New Music Ensemble 1981-, Jordan College of Fine Arts, Butler University; Guest composer, Lecturer, various universities and colleges, with orchestras and at festivals. *Compositions:* Stage: The Great Soap Opera, chamber opera, 1988; Orchestral: Lancaster Variations, 1976; Masque-A Story of Puppets, Poets, Kings and Clowns, 1977; El Medico, 1977; Pygmies for Youth Orchestra and Tape, 1982; Pygmies II for Youth Orchestra and Speaker, 1983; Golden Bells for Orchestra and Chorus, 1983, completion of an unfinished score by N Dinerstein; Oboe Concerto, 1983; Swashbuckler! 1984; Concerto for 2 Pianos and

Orchestra, 1986; Kidspeace for Orchestra and Voices, 1987; (restless dreams before) The Big Night, 1989; Symphonic Band: King Ubu, 1980; Cliff Hanger March, 1984; Seven Steps from Hell, 1985; Chamber Music; Piano Pieces; Vocal music includes: Swanwhite-Letters to Strindberg from Harriet Bosse, cycle for Soprano and Piano, 1980. *Honours:* Many composition awards and prizes, various commissions including: Indianapolis Symphony Orchestra; Buffalo Philharmonic Orchestra; Kansas City Symphony. *Address:* 5939 N Rosslyn Ave, Indianapolis, IN 46220, USA.

SCHELLEN Nando, b. 11 Oct 1934, The Hague, Netherlands. *Career:* Managing Director, Nederlandse Operastichting, Amsterdam, 1969-79; Associate General Director, 1979-87; Stage Director as of 1982; Debut Holland Festival 1982 with The Magic Flute; Debut on American Continent, 1983 with Lohengrin Toronto and Edmonton at the Occasion of the Centennial of Richard Wagner's Death; General Artistic Director of Sweelinck Conservatory of Music, 1991-93; General Artistic Director of Indianapolis Opera as of February 1993; Background Managerial Musical & Theatrical; 14 World Premieres during his engagement at Netherlands Opera; Initiated Major Policy Changes at Netherlands Opera including Expansion of Season from 90 to 165 Performances. *Address:* 250 E 38th Street, Indianapolis, IN 46205, USA.

SCHELLENBERGER Dagmar, b. 8 June 1958, Oschatz, Germany. Singer. *Education:* Studied at the Musikhochschule Dresden. *Career:* Has Sung at the Komische Oper Berlin from 1984; Guest Appearances at Dresden as Weber's Aennchen and Laura, Leipzig, and Hamburg; Anne in Hans Heiling at Utrecht and the Countess at the Berlin Staatsoper; US Debut on Tour with the Komische Oper as Euryduce, Elena in La Donna del Lago at New York City Hall; Further engagements as the Four Heroines in Les Contes D'Hoffmann in Berlin, Monteverdi's Poppea at Marseille and Beethoven's Ninth at Bordeau; Concert appearances at the Amsterdam Concertgebouw, The Salle Pleyel, Leipzig Gewandhaus, Philharmonie Berlin and the Alte Oper Frankfurt; Conductors include Masur, Marriner, Haennchen, Montgomery, Schreier, Jiri Kout, Klee and Hager. *Honours include:* Winner, Dvorak International Voice Competition; Kammersangerin, Komische Oper, 1988. *Recordings include:* Gluck's Orfeo, Bastien und Bastienne and Hasse Mass; Handel L'Allegro, Il Penseroso Ed il Monderato; Mozart Kleine Kirchenwerke; Ravel Sherherazade. *Address:* Atholl Still Limited, Greystoke House, 80-86 Westrow Street, London SE19 3AF, England.

SCHEMTSCHUK Ludmilla, b. 1948, Donezk, Ukraine, USSR. Singer (Mezzo-soprano). *Education:* Studied at the Odessa Conservatory. *Career:* Sang at the Minsk Opera from 1970; Bolshoi Theatre Moscow from 1978, as Pauline (The Queen of Spades), Azucena, Amneris, Eboli, Dorabella, Ortrud, Fricka, Carmen and Charlotte (Werther); Has sung at the Vienna Staatsoper from 1985 as Laura in La Gioconda, Marina (Boris Godunov), Ulrica and Marfa in Khovanshchina; Guest appearances at the Verona Arena (Azuceba 1985), Munich, Hamburg, Caracalla Festival, Rome and Stuttgart (Santuzaa 1987); Concert tours of Finland, Bulgaria and Hungary. *Address:* c/o Staatsoper, Opernring 2, A-1010 Vienna, Austria.

SCHENK Manfred, b. 23 Jan 1930, Stuttgart, Germany. Singer (Bass). *Education:* Studied at the Musikhochschule Stuttgart with Jarius. *Career:* Sang with the South German Radio Choir, then solo engagements with the Frankfurt Opera from 1967; Guest appearances at Vienna and Munich in the Wagner repertory; Glyndebourne 1973, as Sarastro; Bayreuth Festival 1981-86, as Pogner and Fasolt; Salzburg 1985, as Nettuno in the Henze version of Monteverdi's Il Ritorno d'Ulisse; Engagements at Covent Garden, the Metropolitan Opera, Teatro Liceo Barcelona, San Francisco Opera, and in Bregenz and Rome; Other roles include Daland, Hans Sachs, Gurnemanz, Wotan, Fafner, King Marke, the Landgrave, Ramphis, Padre

Guardiano, the Grand Inquisitor, Rocco and Kecal in The Bartered Bride; Bayreuth 1989, as King Heinrich, and the Landgrave in Tannhäuser; sang Fafner in Das Rheingold at Bonn, 1990; Sang Gurnemanz at the 1992 Bayreuth Festival. *Recordings include:* Feuersnot by Strauss (Acanta); Lulu (Decca); Bass Solo in the Choral Symphony (Denon). *Address:* c/o Allied Artists Agency, 42 Montpelier Square, London SW7 1JZ.

SCHENK Otto, b. 12 June 1930, Vienna, Austria. Opera Producer. *Education:* Studied acting with Max Reinhardt and production at the University of Vienna. *Debut:* First opera production Die Zauberflöte, Salzburg Landestheater 1957. *Career:* Don Pasquale at the Vienna Volksoper, 1961; Vienna Festival 1963, Dantons Tod and Lulu; Salzburg Festival 1963, Die Zauberflöte and Der Rosenkavalier; Jenůfa at the Vienna Staatsoper 1964: chief stage director form 1965; further productions include Macbeth and Der Freischütz; Opera productions in Frankfurt, Berlin, Munich (Der Rosenkavalier 1975) and Stuttgart; Metropolitan Opera from 1970: Tosca, Fidelio, Tannhäuser, Les Contes d'Hoffmann, Arabella and Der Ring des Nibelungen (1986-88); La Scala Milan 1974, Le Nozze di Figaro; Covent Garden 1975, Un Ballo in Maschera; Savonlinna Festival 1991, The Bartered Bride; Elektra and Die Meistersinger at the Metropolitan, 1992/93. *Recordings include:* Video of Der Ring des Nibelungen, from the Metropolitan. *Address:* c/o Bayerische Staatsoper, Postfach 745, D-8000 Munich 1, Germany.

SCHERLER Barbara, b. 10 Jan 1938, Leipzig, Germany. Singer (Contralto). *Education:* Studied at the Berlin Musikhochschule and with Margarete Barwinkel. *Career:* Sang at Frankfurt 1959-64; Cologne Opera 1964-68; Deutsche Oper Berlin from 1968, notably in the 1984 premiere of Gespensteronate by Reimann; Guest appearances in London, Brussels, Lisbon, Mexico City, Zurich and Venice; Noted concert artist, particularly in works by Bach. *Recordings:* Bach Cantatas (Erato); Masses by Mozart (Electrola); Penthesilea by Schoeck (BASF).

SCHERMERHORN Kenneth DeWitt, b. 20 Nov 1929, New York, USA. Conductor; Composer. m. (1) Lupe Servano, 1957, 2 daughters, (2) Carol Neblett, 1975, 1 son. *Education:* Artists Diploma; Highest Honours, New England Conservatory of Music. *Career:* Assistant Conductor, New York Philharmonic, 1959; Music Director, American Ballet Theatre, 1957-70; Music Director, New Jersey Symphony, 1963-68; Music Director, Milwaukee Symphony, 1968-80; Music Director, Nashville Symphony, 1984-; Music Director, Hong Kong Philharmonic, 1985-; Guest, San Francisco Opera; Boston, Cleveland, San Francisco, Philadelphia, New York Symphonies, et al. *Honours:* S. Koussevitsky Memorial Award; Honorary Doctorate, Ripon College. *Address:* 208 23rd Avenue North, Nashville, TN 37203, USA.

SCHEXNAYDER Brian, b. 18 Sept 1953, Port Arthur, Texas, USA. Singer (Baritone). *Education:* Studied at the Juilliard School New York. *Career:* sang in operas by Verdi and Puccini while at Juilliard; Metropolitan Opera from 1980 as Ashton (Lucia di Lammermoor), Marcello (La Bohème), Guglielmo and Lescaut in Manon Lescaut; Paris Opéra 1982-83, as Marcello; sang Marcello at the Metropolitan 1989, Valentin in Faust 1990. *Address:* c/o Metropolitan Opera, Lincoln Center, New York, NY 10023, USA.

SCHEYRER Gerda, b. 18 July 1925, Vienna, Austria. Singer (Soprano). *Education:* Studied at the Vienna Academy of Music. *Career:* Sang first at the Stadttheater Steyr, then at the Vienna Volksoper; Salzburg Festival 1955-56, in Die Zauberflöte and Ariadne auf Naxos and as Ilia in Idomeneo; Member of the Vienna Staatsoper from 1959-81; Glyndebourne Festival 1961, Donna Anna; Guest appearances in Dusseldorf, Stuttgart and other German opera houses; Also heard in Oratorios. *Recordings include:* Die Fledermaus and Zigeunerbaron by Johann Strauss; Der Ring des Nibelungen (Electrola).

Address: c/o Staatsoper, Opernring 2, A-1010 Vienna, Austria.

SCHIAVI Felice, b. 4 July 1931, Vimercate, Italy. Singer (Baritone). *Education:* Studied with Riccardo Malipiero in Monza and with Carlo Tagliabue, Carlo Alfieri and Enrico Pessina in Milan. *Career:* Has sung widely in Italy from 1955, notably at Rome, Parma, Bologna, Trieste, Naples, Milan and Venice; Verona Arena 1977; Vienna Staatsoper 1984, as Paolo in Simon Boccanegra; Further appearances in Nice, Marseille, Edinburgh, Prague, Barcelona, Moscow, Munich, Glasgow, Cardiff and Warsaw; Other roles include Amonasro, Renato, Luna, Iago, Posa, Don Carlos (La Forza del Destino), Simon Boccanegra, Scarpia, Gerard, Barnaba and Escamillo. *Address:* c/o Vienna Staatsoper, Opernring 2, A-1010 Vienna, Austria.

SCHICKELE Peter, b. 17 July 1935, Ames, Iowa, USA. Musician. m. Susan Sindall, 1962, 1 son, 1 daughter. *Education:* BA, Swarthmore College, 1967; Honorary Doctorate 1981; MS Juilliard School of Music 1960. *Career:* Composer of serious music as well as sole discoverer of works of highly figmental P.D.Q. Bach; public concerts of latter's music began April 1965-. *Compositions include:* Pentangle, 5 songs for horn and orchestra 1976; Chorus: After Spring Sunset 1961; Chamber Music: Elegies 1974; Hansel and Gretel and Ted and Alice; Howdy Symphony; Iphigenia In Brooklyn; The Abduction of Figaro; Bestiary 1982; Hornsmoke 1975; Quartet 1982; String Quartet No. 1, 1983; String Quartet No.2, In Memoriam, 1987; String Quartet No.2, The Four Seasons, 1988; Concerto for Flute and Orchestra, 1990. *Recordings include:* An Evening with P.D.Q. Bach; An Hysteric Return: P.D.Q. Bach At Carnegie Hall; Report From Hoople: P.D.Q. Bach On The Air; P.D.Q. Bach's Half-Act Opera, The Stoned Guest; The Wurst of P.D.Q. Bach; The Intimate P.D.Q. Bach; Portrait of P.D.Q. Bach; Black Forest Bluegrass, Liebeslieder Polkas; Music You Can't Get Out Of Your Head; A Little Nightmare Music; Good Time Ticket; The Lowest Trees Have Tops; Silent Running; Oh! Calcutta!; The Open Window; Three Views From The Open Window; Music of Peter Schickele; Bestiary and Quartet; Pentangle; 1712 Overture and Other Musical Assaults; Video: Oedipus Tex & Other Choral Calamities; The Abduction of Figaro. *Publication:* The Definitive Biography of P.D.Q. Bach, Random House 1976. *Hobbies:* Solving and Making Crossword Puzzles; Movies; Tennis. *Current Management:* Harold Shaw, Shaw Concerts, Inc. *Address:* c/o Shaw Concerts, Inc., 1990 Broadway, New York, NY 10023, USA.

SCHIFF András, b. 21 Dec 1953, Budapest, Hungary. Pianist. m. Yuuko Shiokawa, Sep. 1987. *Education:* Franz Liszt Academy of Music, Budapest, with Professor Paul Kadosa and Ferenc Rados, 1975; Private Tuition, George Malcolm, London, England. *Career:* Regular Orchestral Engagements: New York Philharmonic, Chicago Symphony, Vienna Philharmonic, Concertgebouw, Orchestre De Paris, London Philharmonic, London Symphony, Royal Philharmonic, Israel Philaharmonic, Berlin Philharmonic, Cleveland Orchestra; Artisic Director of Annual Mondsee Festival, Austria, 1989; Organised and took part in Haydn series at the Wigmore Hall, London, 1989; Bartók and Beethoven, 1990. *Recordings:* Bach Goldberg Variations, Well-Tempered Clavier Complete, English Suites, Mendelssohn Concertos, Schumann Concerto, Chopin 2, Tchaikovsky Concerto; All Mozart Concertos and Sonatas; Brahms 1; Lieder with Peter Schreier and Robert Holl; Won a Grammy in 1990 for the Bach English Suites. *Honours:* Prizewinner, Tchaikovsky International Piano Competition, Moscow, USSR, 1974; Leeds International Piano Competition, 1975; Liszt Prize laureate; 1st Prize, Hungarian television Talent Scouting Competition, 1968; Won RPS/Charles Heidsieck Award for best concert series of 1988-89; Instrumentalist of the Year in the First International Classical Music Awards, in 1991 was awarded the Bartók prize, in 1989 was awarded the Wiener Flötenuhr. *Hobbies:* Literature; Languages; Soccer. *Current Management:* Terry Harrison Artists Management. *Address:* 3 Clarendon Court, Park Street, Charlbury, Oxon OX7 3PS, England.

SCHIFF Heinrich, b. 18 Nov 1951, Gmunden, Austria. Concert Cellist; Conductor. *Education:* First studied piano, then cello with Tobias Kuhne in Vienna and André Navarra in Detmold. *Career:* Prize winner at competitions in Vienna, Geneva and Warsaw; Soloist with Vienna Philharmonic, Concertgebouw, Stockholm Philharmonic, BBC Symphony and Royal Philharmonic Orchestra; Season 1988-89 with Berlin Philharmonic, Israel Philharmonic and Los Angeles Philharmonic; Conductors include Haitink, Chailly, Masur and Previn; Recent British engagements with the London Philharmonic and Academy of St Martin in the Fields at the Festival Hall; Tokyo Metropolitan Orchestra in Manchester and London playing the Elgar Concerto; Schumann Concerto with the Philharmonia Orchestra and Sinopoli; Northern Sinfonia and City of London Sinfonia as soloist and conductor; Lutoslawski Concerto with the composer conducting the Philharmonia; Artistic Director of the Northern Sinfonia, 1990; Has also conducted (from 1984) the Vienna Symphony Orchestra and the Stockholm and Scottish Chamber Orchestras. *Recordings:* Deutsche Schallplatenpreis 1978 as Artist of the Year; Bach's Solo Suites (EMI); Philips contract from 1986: Schumann's Concerto with the Berlin Philharmonic and Haitink; Prokofiev's Sinfonia Concertante with the Los Angeles Philharmonic and Previn; Concertos by Vivaldi, Haydn, Dvořák and Lutoslawski. *Address:* c/o Van Walsum Management Ltd., 40 St Peter's Road, London W6 9BH, England.

SCHILDKNECHT Gregor, b. 18 Oct 1936, Biel, Switzerland. Singer (Baritone). *Education:* Studied in Vienna with Willi Domgraf Fassbaender in Nuremberg and at Dusseldorf. *Career:* Sang at the Oldenburg Opera 1965- 67, Coburg 1968-73, Detmold 1973-74, Krefeld 1974-77 and Bielefeld 1977-80; Guest Engagements from 1980 at the Berlin Staatsoper, Hamburg, Dusseldorf, Karlsruhe, Geneva, Amsterdam, Brussels and Prague; Roles have Included parts in Operas by Mozart, Donizetti, Rossini; Verdi's Luna, Rigoletto, Germont, Machbeth, Possa, Amonasro and Carlo in La Forza del Destino; Wolfram, Scarpia, the villians in Hoffman and Mandryka in Arabella; Concert Engagements in Germany, Holland and Switzerland. *Address:* c/o Deutsche Oper Am Rhein, Heinrich Heine Allee 16, 4000 Dusseldorf, Germany.

SCHILLER Allan, b. 18 Mar 1943, Leeds, Yorkshire, England. Concert Pianist. *Education:* Associate, Royal College of Music, Performance and Diploma, 1959; Moscow Conservatoire. *Debut:* Hallé Orchestra with Sir John Barbirolli, Leeds Town Hall, 1954. *Career:* Edinburgh Festival, Scotland, 1954; Promenade Concert, London, England, 1957; Subject of Philpott File, television documentary; Toured in Canada, Europe and USSR; Professor, Guildhall School of Music. *Recordings:* Recital for Pye, 1958; Chopin and Mozart on Classics for Pleasure; Bridge and Elgar Quintets with Coull Quartet. *Honour:* Harriet Cohen Medal, 1966. *Membership:* Incorporated Society of Musicians; Bristol Savages. *Hobby:* Walking. *Address:* 14 Lilymead Avenue, Knowle, Bristol 4, Avon, England.

SCHILLER Christoph, b. 17 May 1951, Zurich, Switzerland. Concert Violist, Solo and Chamber Music. m. Louise Pellerin, 29 Dec 1981, 1 son. *Education:* Realgymnasium Zurichberg; Matura 1970; University of Zurich; North Carolina School of Arts, 1972-73; Accademia Chigiana, Siena, Italy; Nordwestdeutsche Musikakademie, Detmold, Germany. *Career:* Violist of New Zurich String Quartet, 1973-88, tours in Europe, Israel, Scandinavia, North and South America; Viola soloist with orchestras throughout Europe; Professor at the Zurich and Basle Conservatories; Founder and artistic director of Ensemble Mobile, 1989-. *Recordings:* Charles Koechlin, Viola Sonata; Willy Burkhard, works for viola; Giacinto Scelsi, Solo and Chamber Music; String Quartets by Brahms, Mendelssohn, Debussy, Ravel, Dvořák, Grieg, Haydn; Chamber works by various Swiss Composers. *Honour:* Soloists Prize of Swiss

Musicians' Association, 1976. *Hobbies:* Family; Hiking; Reading. *Current Management:* Pro Musicis, Silvia Ackermann, Rütistrasse 38, CH-8032, Zürich.*Address:* Bombachstr 21, CH-8049 Zurich, Switzerland.

SCHIML Marga, b. 29 Nov 1945, Weiden, Germany. Singer (Mezzo-Soprano). m. Horst Laubenthal. *Education:* Studied with Hanno Blaschke in Munich and with Hartmann-Dressler in Berlin. *Debut:* Basle Opera 1967, in Tigrane by Hasse. *Career:* Has sung in Viena, Munich, Graz, Basle and Zurich; Appearances at the Orange and Salzburg Festivals; Bayreuth Festival 1981, 1986, as Magdalene in Die Meistersinger and in Parsifal and Der Ring des Nibelungen; sang at Turin 1986, as Fricka in Das Rheingold; Maggio Musicale Florence 1989, Annina in Der Rosenkavalier. *Recordings:* Puck in Oberon, La Clemenza di Tito (Deutsche Grammophon); Mozart Masses, Der Ring des Nibelungen (Philips); Choral Symphony (RCA); Masses by Weber (EMI). *Address:* c/o Festpielhaus, 8580 Bayreuth, Germany.

SCHIPIZKY Frederick Alexander, b. 20 Dec 1952, Calgary, Alberta, Canada. Composer; Conductor; Bassist; Teacher. m. Ruth Fagerburg (Violinist), 4 Aug 1984. *Education:* BMus. Composition, University of British Columbia 1974; Study with Elliot Weisgarber and Jean Coulthard; Private Study with Harry Freedman and Sophie Eckhardt-Gramatte, Courtenay 1974, and with Murray Adaskin, Victoria Conservatory 1975-76; MMus. Composition and Double Bass, Juilliard School, New York 1976-78, with Roger Sessions, David Diamond and David Walter. *Career:* Appearances on CBC Radio and TV with Vancouver Symphony Orchestra, and as Composer, Conductor and Bassist; Bassist, Vancouver Symphony Orchestra; Teacher of Theory and Composition, Vancouver Academy of Music; Faculty, Courtenay Youth Music Centre 1986; Performed with Montreal Symphony Orchestra; Faculty member Douglas College since 1989, performed with Esprit Orchestra and Arraymusic. *Compositions:* Symphonic Sketches 1977; Fanfare for the Royal Visit 1983; Divertimento for String Orchestra 1983; Symphony No. 1 1985 (Commissioned by Vancouver Symphony Orchestra for Japan Tour 1985). *Address:* 5390 Larch Street, Vancouver, British Columbia V6M 4C8, Canada.

SCHIRMER Astrid, b. 8 Nov 1942, Berlin, Germany. Singer (Soprano). *Education:* Studied at the Berlin Musikhochschule with Johanna Rakow and Elisabeth Grümmer. *Debut:* Coburg 1967, as Senta in Der fliegende Holländer. *Career:* Has sung at the Hanover Opera and widely in Germany, notably in Cologne, Mannheim, Berlin, Stuttgart and Nuremberg; Guest appearances in Barcelona and Zurich; Other roles include Santuzza, Leonore, Brünnhilde, Aida, Amelia (Un Ballo in Maschera), Sieglinde, Ariadne, Arabella, Tosca, Turandot and Lady Billows in Albert Herring; Many concert appearances. *Address:* Landesbühne Hanover, Bultstraase 7-9, D-3000 Hannover, Germany.

SCHLAEPFER Jean-Claude. b. 11 Jan 1961, Geneva, Switzerland. Composer; Teacher. *Education:* Academy of Music, Geneva; Academy of Music, Paris with Mrs Betsy Jolas, Diplomas in Musical Education and Musical Culture. *Career:* Composer; Professor, Department of Harmony and Analysis at the Conservatoire Superieur de Musique; Professor, Department of Musical Languages, University of Geneva. *Compositions include:* 3 Caprices, for violin in memory of N Paganini, 1988; 5 Pieces for Orchestra, in hommage of Anton Webern, 1988; Impressions, 1988, debut by L'Ensemble Orchestral de Genève, under the direction of Laurent Gay, Jan 1989; Dialogues, for Violoncello, debut by Christian Secretan, Istanbul, March 1989; Stabat Mater for Soprano, Choir and Orchestra, 1990, performed by L'Orchestre de la Suisse Romande and Le Choeur de La Psalette de Genève, soloist: Naoko Okada, in Geneva in March 1991; 7 Preludes for two pianos, debut at Lausanne in May 1991 by Denise Duport and Gui-Michel Caillat; Motets for soprano, harp and violin, de gambe, 1992; Three Dreams on poems by Georg Trakl for narrator, soprano, alto,

quintet for wind instruments, quatuars for string, piano, 1992; Instannes II for solo harp for the International Competition of Music in Geneva, 1993. *Recordings:* Impressions; Stabat Mater and 7 Preludes for two pianos, Radio Suisse Romande. *Honours:* Prix du Conseil d'Etat de Genève, 1986; Laureat du Concours de Composition de Swiss Musiciens Association, 1988; Prix de Composition du Conservatoire Superieur de Musique de Genève, 1988; Bourse de Composition de la ville de Genève, 1991. *Memberships:* SUISA; Swiss Musicians Association. *Hobbies:* Football; Tennis. *Address:* 1. Chemin de la Commanderie, 1228 Plan Les Ouates, Geneva, Switzerland.

SCHLEE Thomas Daniel, b. 26 Oct 1957, Vienna, Austria. Composer; Organist. m. Claire Aniotz, 24 May 1986. 1 daughter.*Education:* Theresianische Akademie Wien, Hochschule fur Musik, Vienna; Composition & Organ, Conservatoire National Supérieur, Paris, France; Musicology, History of Arts, Dr phil 1985, Theresianische Akademie Wien, University of Vienna. *Career:* Many organ concerts, Europe, USA, formerly, USSR; Participant, various international festivals; Musikdramaturg, Salzburger Landestheater, 1986-89; Teacher, Wiener Musikhochschule, 1988-90; Nominated Musikdirektor of the Brucknerhaus Linz (Upper Austria), 1990. *Compositions:* Organ, vocal, instrumental, orchestral music; Edited by Universal edition, Bärenreiter, Leduc, Lemoine, Choudens, Combre, Schola Cantorum Doblinger. *Recordings:* Radio & TV recordings, various European countries. *Contributions to:* Books: Ecrivains Français et l'Opera (Legende de Tristan, de Ch. Tournemire) 1986; Studien zur Wertungsforschung 20 (Die 'Cinq Rechants' von O. Messiaen) 1988; In: Meilensteine der Musik (1991), Neue MGG; Numerous music journals. Editor, Universal Organ series. *Honours:* Chevalier des Arts et Lettres, 1991. *Address:* Prinz Eugenstrasse 44/6, A-1040 Vienna, Austria.

SCHLEGEL Rudolf, b. 1950, New York, USA, Music Director. *Education:* State University of New York; Mannes College of Music; Manhattan School of Music. *Career:* Executive Director, Great Woods Educational Forum/Great Woods Center for the Performing Arts, Boston, 1987; Guest Conductor, The Chattanooga Symphony Orchestra, Riverbend Festival, 1985; Vermont Symphony Orchestra, 1984; Appearances with: The Rochester Philharmonic Orchestra, The Pittsburgh Symphony Orchestra, Orchestras and chorus of the State University of New York, the New York Youth Symphony Orchestra; Music Director, New Bedford Symphony Orchestra, 1978-81; Numerous appearances on radio and pre-concert talks about music and musicians; Has initiated numerous youth, family orientated and outreach programmes by the Philharmonic including In-School Performance Series, scholarships and competitions and visits by touring youth orchestras, Massachusetts; Conductor, Music Director, Plymouth Philharmonic Orchestra, 1976-. *Address:* Plymouth Philharmonic Orchestra, Plymouth, MA 02360, USA.

SCHLEMM Anny, b. 22 Feb 1929, Neu-Isenburg, Frankfurt, Germany. Singer (Mezzo-Soprano). *Education:* Studied with Erna Westenberger in Berlin. *Career:* Sang at the Berlin Staatsoper and the Berlin Komische Oper from 1949; Cologne Opera 1950-51; Has sung at Frankfurt Opera from 1951; Guest appearances in Hamburg, Munich and Berlin; Glyndebourne 1954, as Zerlina; Bayreuth Festival 1978-86, as Mary in Der fliegende Holländer; Netherlands Opera Amsterdam 1978, Herodias and Clytemnestra; Cologne 1981, as the Kostelnička in Jenůfa; Covent Garden debut 1984, Madelon in a new production of Andrea Chénier; Other roles include Susanna, Desdemona, the Marschallin, Octavian and Marenka in The Bartered Bride; Sang Clytemnestra in Elektra at Stuttgart, 1989; Modern repertoire has included Miranda in Martin's The Tempest, Europera I and II by Cage (premiere at Frankfurt 1987), Mumie in Riemann's Gespenstersonate and Mother in Cerha's Baal (Vienna 1992). Recordings: Madama Butterfly, Pagliacci

(Deutsche Grammophon); Hänsel und Gretel; Der fliegende Holländer, from Bayreuth (Philips); Video of Andrea Chénier. *Address:* 6078 Neeu-Isenburg, Graf-Folke-Bernasotte, Str 12, Germany.

SCHLESINGER John, b. 16 Feb 1926, London, England. Stage Director. *Education:* Studied At Oxford. *Career:* Film Actor then Director; Associate Director of the National Theatre London; Debut as Opera Producer Les Contes d'Hoffmann at Covent Garden, 1980; Staged Der Rosenkavalier at Covent Garden, 1984; Un Ballo in Maschera at the 1989 Salzburg Festival.

SCHLICK Barbara, b. 21 July 1943, Wurzburg, Germany. Singer (Soprano). *Education:* Musikhochschule Wurzburg; Paul Lohmann in Wiesbaden; Further study in Essen. *Career:* Engaged by Adolf Scherbaum for his Baroque Ensemble in 1966; Concert engagements in Munich, Hamburg, Rome, Geneva, Paris, Prague, Leningrad and New York; Russian tour 1971 and tour of the USA and Canada with the Chamber Orchestra of Paul Kuentz in 1972; Tour of Israel and USA 1975-76 with the Monteverdi Choir under Jürgen Juŕgens; Festival appearances in Aix, Paris, Berlin, Kassel and Herrenhausen; Sang at the Göttingen Handel Festival 1980, York Early Music Festival 1988, CPE Bach's Die Letzten Leiden; further appearances at the Haydn series on South Bank with the Orchestra of the Age of Enlightenment and in Mozart's Requiem with the Amsterdam Baroque Orchestra; Repertoire includes Carissimi's Jephte; Vivaldi's Gloria; Passions and Cantatas by Bach; Handel's Messiah, Acis and Galatea and Caecilia Ode; Haydn's Creation and Last Seven Words, Mozart's Requiem and Stravinsky's Cantata; Songs by Dowland, Purcell, Handel, Scarlatti and Haydn. *Recordings include:* Gagliano's La Dafne (Deutsche Grammophon); Bach's St Matthew Passion (HMV); Jephtha by Reinthaler; Hasse's Piramo e Tisbe. *Address:* D-8700 Wurzburg, Greingstrasse 9, Germany.

SCHLOIFER Eckart, b. 4 Apr 1941, Delmenhorst, Germany. Soloist; Chamber Musician; Teacher; Conductor. m. Inge Kellermann, 1965, 1 son, 1 daughter. *Career:* Teacher, viola classes, international masterclasses and courses, Hochschule fur Musik und Darstellende Kunst, Frankfurt/Main; Performed music by Paul Hindemith in Hans Emmerling's film Die junge Magd, 1986; Appeared on TV in Mozart Symphony concertante live concert, SWF, 1987; Principal solo-violist with Radio Symphony Saarbrücken since 1966; Founder and member of the Contra-Trio (viola, cello, double bass) and eSße, string quartet. *Compositions:* Wagnis, 1990-91. *Recordings:* 1 CD, works by Florent Schmitt, Cybelia, 1987; 1 CD with Saarbrücken String quartet, works by Y Höller, Wergo,, 1993; 1 CD with Contra-Trio Dabringhaus/Grimm, works by Brandmüller, 1994. *Publications:* Specific viola literature: Studies for Playing Contemporary Music, Breitkopf & Härtel, 1991; Orchestral Studies for Auditions, Schott, 1992; Orchestral Studies for solo-violists, Zimmermann, Verlag Franfurt, 1994. *Hobby:* Reading; Travelling; Hiking. *Address:* Ueberhofer Strasse 58a, D-66292 Riegelsberg, Germany.

SCHMALFUSS Peter, b. 13 Jan 1937, Berlin, Germany. Pianist; Professor of Piano. m. Sylvia Heckendorn, 7 Mar 1966. *Education:* Staatliche Hochschule für Musik, Saarbrücken, with Walter Gieseking, Alexander Sellier, Adrian Aeschbacher; Studied with Wilhelm Kempff, Beethoven Seminary, Positano, Italy. *Career:* Appearances as soloist and with orchestras in over 40 countries, since 1960-; Premieres of contemporary works; many concert trips to Asia and North Africa; Concerts and participation on many Music-Festivals up to now in 4 continents, China, 1989, South America, 1990, Canada and USA, 1992, Japan, 1993. *Recordings:* Works of R. Schumann, Edvard Grieg, Frederic Chopin, Friedrich Smetana, Karol Szymanowski; W A Mozart, Beethoven, Claude Debussy. *Publications:* Editor of educational literature for piano. *Memberships:* Chopin Society. *Hobbies:* Art; Nature;

Travel. *Address:* Im Harras 38, D-64293 Darmstadt, Germany.

SCHMID Erich, b. 1 Jan 1907, Balsthal, Switzerland. Conductor. m. Martha Stiefel, 2 sons, 1 daughter. *Education:* Dr Hoch's Conservatory, Frankfurt am Main, Germany, 1927-30; Master's Class, Arnold Schoenberg, Arts Academy, Berlin, 1930-31. *Career:* Music Director, Glarus, Switzerland, 1934-49; Chief Conductor, Tonhalle Orchestra, Zürich, 1949-57; Radio Orchestra, Beromünster, Zurich 1957-72; Leader, Gemischter Choir, Zürich, 1949-75, Conductor's Class, Music Academy, Basle; 1960-70, Guest Conductor in many European Countries, especially England; all BBC Orchestras of the UK, 1978-82; Principal Guest Conductor CBSO Birmingham, Aldeburgh, Cambridge, Israel, Australa (Adelaide Festival), California (San Diego Brahms-Festival). *Compositions include:* String Quartet 1930; Widmungen for piano 1935; Kleines Haus konsert, as Guest Conductor, 1937-40; Trio for flute, viola and cello 1955. *Recordings:* Armin Schibler, Passacaglia op. 24; Conrad Beck, Aeneas Silvius Symphony; Klaus Huber, Des Engels Anredüng; Rudolf Kelterborn, Elegie; Hermann Goetz, Klavierkonzert op. 18; Xavier Schnyder von Wartensee, Concerto für 2 Klarinetten und Orchester, CD grammont 33-2, Erich Schmid and various others. *Honours:* Mozart Prize, Frankfurt, 1928; Arts Prize, Canton Solothurn, 1973; Honoured by the town of Zürich with the Hans Georg Nägeli-Medaille. *Memberships:* Swiss Artists Guild; Pro Musica Zürich (IGNM). *Address:* Baumgarten 2, CH 8905 Arni, Switzerland.

SCHMID Hans, b. 31 May 1920, Munich, Germany. Music Historian. m. Hanna Auerbach, 2 Oct 1965. *Education:* Studies of Music History with R Von Ficker; PhD, music studies with H W Von Waltershausen. *Career:* Research Assistant, Music History Seminar, 1952-57; Assistant Professor, 1953-85, University of Munich; Research Co-worker, Music History Commission, Bavarian Academy of Sciences, 1960-84. *Publications:* Musica et Scolica Enchiriadis, editor, 1981. *Contributions to:* Lexikon des Mittelalters, 1978; Professional journals and anthologies; Editor of historical documents. *Memberships:* International Society for Musicology, Basle; Society for Music Research, Kassel; Society for Bavarian Music History, Munich, Secretary, 1958-84, Editor, Bavarian Musical Monuments, 1962-84. *Address:* Hauptstrasse 23, D-82275 Emmering, Germany.

SCHMID Patric James, b. 12 Apr 1944, Eagle Pass, TX, USA. Artistic Director. *Education:* San Francisco state College. *Career:* Founded Opera Rara 1970 and has given British Premieres in Stage & Concert Performances, including Donizetti's Maria di Rudenz, Maria Padilla, Rosmonda D'Inghilterra, Le Convenieze Teatrali, Francesca Foix and La Romanziera; Mercadante Orazi e Curiazi and Virginia, Offenbach's Robinson Crusoe, Pacini's Maria Tudor; Premiere of Donizetti's Gabriella di Vergy in its Revised Version, Belfast 1978 and Offenbach Pasticcio Christopher Columbus, Belfast 1976. *Recordings:* Donizetti Ugo, Conte di Parigi, Maria Padilla, Emilia di Liverpool, L'Assedio di Calais; Meyerbeer Dinorah and Il Crociato in Egitto; Offenbach Robinson Crusoe and Christopher Columbus; 100 Years of Italian Opera, Anthology. *Contributions to:* Opera Magazine. *Honours:* MRA Award; Best Opera Recording; Best Recording of the Year. *Hobbies:* Travel; Cooking. *Address:* 25 Compton Terrace, London N1 2NN, England.

SCHMIDT Andreas, b. 1960, Dusseldorf, Germany. Singer (Baritone). *Education:* Studied in Dusseldorf with Ingeborg Reichelt and in Berlin with Dietrich Fischer-Dieskau. *Debut:* Deutsche Oper Berlin 1984, as Malatesta in Don Pasquale. *Career:* Has sung in Berlin as Guglielmo, Lortzing's Zar, Wolfram in Tannhäuser and the title role in the premiere of Oedipus by Wolfgang Rihm, 1987; Sang in the premiere of Henze's Das verratene Meer, May 1990; Covent Garden London from 1986 as Valentin and Guglielmo. Further appearances in Munich, Vienna and Hamburg; Concert appearances in Israel, Europe and North and South America, under Colin Davis, Carlo Maria Giulini, Wolfgang Sawallisch, Leonard Bernstein and Giuseppe Sinopoli; Season 1989-90 sang Mephistopheles in La Damnation de Faust at the Barbican Hall; Wolfram in Hamburg and the Herald in Lohengrin at Berlin; Papageno in concert with the London Classical Players at the Proms; Olivier in Capriccio at the Salzburg Festival; Other roles include Posa, Marcello, Mozart's Count, Hindemith's Mathis, Amfortas and Don Giovanni (all in Berlin). *Recordings include:* Brahms and Fauré Requiems, Des Knaben Wunderhorn by Mahler, St Matthew Passion, Tannhäuser (Deutsche Grammophon); Faust (Philips); Die Frau ohne Schatten, Das Rheingold (EMI); Così fan Tutte (Harmonia Mundi); Bach B minor Mass (Intercord); St Matthew Passion by CPE Bach; Hansel and Gretel; Die Zauberflöte (EMI). *Address:* Askonas Ltd, 186 Drury Lane, London WC2B 5RY, England.

SCHMIDT Annerose, b. 5 Oct 1936, Wittenberg, Germany. Pianist; Professor. *Education:* Diploma, Melanchthon-Gymnasium, Wittenberg, 1954; Studied with Hugo Steurer, Hochschule für Musik, Leipzig, 1953-58. *Debut:* Wittenberg, 1945. *Career:* Numerous engagements as soloist with major orchestras including: Gewandhaus Orchestra, Leipzig; Dresden State Orchestra; Royal Philharmonic Orchestra, London; New Philharmonia Orchestra, London; Cleveland Orchestra; Chicago Symphony Orchestra; Tonhalle Orchestra, Zurich; Danish Radio Symphony Orchestra, Copenhagen; Concertgebouw Orchestra, Amsterdam; Residentie Orchestra, The Hague; NHK (Japan Broadcasting Corporation) Symphony Orchestra, Tokyo; Many festival appearances including: Salzburg; Holland; Prague Spring; Berlin; Dresden; Warsaw Autumn; Professor, Hochschule für Musik Berlin, 1986-. *Recordings:* Many recordings both as soloist with orchestra and recitalist. *Honours:* Diploma, International Chopin Competition, Warsaw, 1954; First prize, International Robert Schumann Competition, Zwickau, 1956; Artist's Prize, 1961; National prize, 1965; Meritorius order of the Fatherland, 1971, German Democratic Republic; Gold Bartók Medal, Hungarian People's Republic, 1974. *Memberships:* Rector of the Hochschule für Musik, Hanns Eisler, Berlin, since 1990. *Address:* Friedrich-Engels-Damm 131, Bad Saarow 75521, Germany.

SCHMIDT Carl Brandon, b. 20 Oct 1941, Nashville, Tennessee, USA. Professor of Music; Director of Graduate Studies. m. Elizabeth Jane Kady, 25 June 1967, 2 sons, 1 daughter. *Education:* AB, Stanford University, 1963; AM, 1967, PhD, 1973, Harvard University; Diploma, Fontainebleau School of Music, 1961, conducting with Boulanger, Solfège-Dieudonné. *Debut:* Conducting, Stanford, California, 1963, London, 1971. *Career:* Assistant Professor, Wabash College, 1970-73, Bryn Mawr College, 1973-79; Professor, The University of the Arts, 1978-. *Publications:* Antonio Cesti: Il Pomo d'oro (Music for Acts III and V from Modena, Biblioteca Estense, Ms Mus. E. 120), Recent Researches in the Music of The Baroque Era, Volume 42, 1982; A Catalogue raisonné of the Literary Sources for the Tragédies Lyriques of Jean-Baptiste Lully, forthcoming. *Contributions to:* Journal of the American Musicological Society; Harvard Library Bulletin; Rivista Italiana di Musicologia; Current Musicology; Recherches sur la Musique française classique; Dix-septieme siecle; Jean-Baptiste Lully and the Music of the French Baroque (Cambridge University Press); General Editor, Jean-Baptiste Lully: The Collected Works (The Broude Trust, forthcoming) The Music of Francis Poulene (1899-1963): A Catalogue (Oxford University Press, forthcoming); Jean-Baptiste Lully: Actes du colloque/ Kongressbericht; The New Grove Dictionary of Opera, 1992; Journal of Musicology. *Address:* 250 South Broad Street, Philadelphia, PA 19102, USA.

SCHMIDT Erika, b. 12 Jan 1913, Quirnheim, Germany. Singer (Soprano). *Education:* Studied in Frankfurt. *Career:* Sang at Frankfurt 1935-67 in operas by Mozart, Weber, Verdi, Strauss and Wagner; Guest appearances throughout Germany; Paris Opéra 1941;

Holland Festival 1958, Von Heute auf Morgen by Schoenberg, conducted by Hans Rosbaud; Glyndebourne Festival 1965, as the Marschallin; Lieder recitals; Oratorio performances. *Address:* Staatliche Hochschule für Musik, Escherheimer Landstrasse 33, Postfach 2326, Frankfurt, Germany.

SCHMIDT Manfred, b. 27 June 1928, Berlin, Germany. Singer (Tenor). *Education:* Studied with Jean Nadolovitch and with Herbert Brauer in Berlin. *Career:* Concert singer from 1956; many radio concerts; From the Bielefeld Opera moved to Cologne 1965, singing Ernesto, Ottavio, Tamino, Almaviva and other lyric roles; Sang at the Festivals of Salzburg, Holland, Perugia, Flanders and Prague; Guest appearances in London, Paris and Milan. *Recordings include:* Opera excerpts with Eurodisc, Deutsche Grammophon, Columbia, CBS and Electrola labels. *Address:* c/o Oper der Stadt Köln, Offenbachplatz, D-5000 Cologne, Germany.

SCHMIDT Ole, b. 14 July 1928, Copenhagen, Denmark. Conductor; Composer. *Education:* Royal Academy of Music Copenhagen; Studied conducting abroad with Albert Wolff, Sergiu Celibidache and Rafael Kubelik. *Career:* Played jazz piano on leaving school; First compositions performed while at University, notably the ballet Behind the Curtain for the Royal Theatre Copenhagen; Conductor Royal Danish Opera and Ballet 1959-65; Principal Conductor Danish Radio Orchestra 1971-; Artistic Director and Principal Conductor Aarhus Symphony Orchestra 1979-85; Guest engagements with major European orchestras; Often heard with the London Symphony, notably in Brian's Gothic Symphony 1980; Prom appearance with the Philharmonia Orchestra; Debut with BBC Symphony 1977; has since conducted all the regional BBC orchestras; Debuts with the Royal Liverpool Philharmonic and Hallé Orchestras 1978; US debut 1980, Oakland Symphony; Many performances of modern Danish music in Europe; Chief Guest Conductor at the Royal Northern College of Music, 1986-89; Appointed as Interim Chief Conductor and Musical Adviser for the Toledo Symphony, Ohio, USA, 1989-. In March 1989 conducted the first Czech language production of Janáček's From the House of the Dead in England (RNCM, Manchester). *Compositions:* Ballets: Fever, Behind the Curtain and Ballet in D; Opera Exhibition; 2 Symphonies 1955, 1958; Concertos for Horn, Trumpet, Trombone, Flute, Piano, Accordion, Violin, Tuba and Guitar; 5 String Quartets 1966-72. *Recordings:* The complete symphonies of Nielsen, with the London Symphony Orchestra; Bentzon Symphonies Nos. 3, 4, 5, 7, Concerto for piano No.4, Concerto for flute No.2, 5 Mobiles for orchestra; Chronicle on René Descartes; Colding Jorgensen To Love Music; Koppel Concerto for Cello and Orchestra; Gunnar Berg Essai Accoustique, Mutationen; Lovenskjold La Sylphide, complete ballet music (HMV 3); Sibelius Finlandia, Karelia Suite and Violin Concerto, with the Hallé Orchestra (EMI); Langgard Symphony No.10, Symphony No. 6 and Antichrist (EMI CD); Schmidt Concerto for brass instruments, Symphonic Fantasy and Allegro Op.20 for accordion and chamber orchestra. *Address:* Royal Northern College of Music, 124 Oxford Road, Manchester M13 9RD, England.

SCHMIDT Peter-Jurgen, b. 25 Jan 1941, Meiningen, Germany. Singer (Tenor). *Education:* Studied in Weimar. *Debut:* Weimar 1968, as Oberto in Alcina. *Career:* Sang at weimar until 1980, Staatsoper Berlin from 1981, Notably in 1989 Premiere of Graf Mirabeau by Siegfried Matthus; Guest Appearances in Concert and Opera at London, Oslo, Linz, Salzburg, Graz and Germany, Japan and Korea; Schwetzinger Festival 1989, as Bacchus in Ariadne auf Naxos; Other Roles Include Don Jose, Hoffmann, Radames, Walther Von Stolzing, Lohengrin and Laca in Jenůfa. *Recordings include:* Levins Muhle by Udo Zimmermann and Graf Mirabeau. *Address:* c/o Staatsoper Berlin, Unter Den Linden 7, 1086 Berlin, Germany.

SCHMIDT Trudeliese, b. 7 Nov 1943, Saarbrücken, Germany. Singer (Mezzo-soprano). *Education:* Studied in Saarbrücken with Hannes Richrath and in Rome. *Debut:* Saarbrücken 1965, as Hansel in Humperdinck's opera. *Career:* Sang at the Deutsche Oper am Rhein, Dusseldorf, from 1969 and appeared widely in Germany from 1971; Holland Festival 1972, 1974; Tour of Japan with the Munich Opera 1974; Glyndebourne Festival 1976, as Dorabella in Così fan Tutte; many engagements in Italy and at the Salzburg Festival; sang in Mozart's Coronation Mass in the 1985 concert at St Peter's Rome for the Pope (Karajan conducting); her best roles include Cherubino in Le Nozze di Figaro, the Composer in Ariadne auf Naxos, Isabella in Rossini's L'Italiana in Algeri and Octavian in Der Rosenkavalier; Sang at the Opéra-Comique Paris 1987, in Idomeneo and La Clemenza di Tito; Dusseldorf 1987, as Carlotta in Die Gezeichneten; La Scala 1989, as Fatima in Oberon; sang Jeanne in The Devils of Loudun at Dusseldorf 1989, the composer in Aridane at Barcelona 1990. *Recordings:* Roles in Der Barbier von Bagdad (Cornelius), Madame Butterfly, Egisto (Cavalli), Iphigenia in Aulis (Gluck), Die Lustigen Weiber von Windor (Nicolai), Mathis der Maler (Hindemith), Idomeneo, Dido and Aeneas and Monteverdi's L'Incoronazione di Poppea and Il ritorno di Ulisse; The Cunning Little Vixen. *Address:* c/o Lies Askonas Ltd, 186 Drury Lane, London WC2 5QD, England.

SCHMIDT Werner Albert, b. 29 July 1925, Bad Kissingen, Germany. Composer; Educator. *Education:* Studied philosophy with Ernesto Grassi; Musicology and old German language and literature, University of Munich, graduated 1969; conducting and composition under Hans Rosbaud, Joseph Haas and Karl Höller, Academy of Music, Munich, 1946-50; Master Class Diploma in composition, 1950; Pedagogic State Examination, State Academy of Music, Munich, 1972; Further studies with Carl Orff, Karl A. Hartmann (composition) and Kurt Eichhorn (conducting); PhD. *Career:* Freelance composer in Munich (Musica Viva, Munich, 1954); Worked as pianist with symphony and jazz orchestras; Music teacher, Grammar School and Junior Music School in Wangen/Allgau; Head of City Orchestra; Teacher of Music Theory at State Academy of Music, Mannheim, 1975-91; Professor, 1980-. *Compositions include:* Kassation (for strings), 1947; Partita (for piano), 1948; Sonata per il pianoforte, 1949; Sonate, Das Ballett, (for violin and piano), 1950; Tollhausballade (for speaker and chamber orchestra), 1952, new edition without speaker, 1956; Tre Pezzi drammatici per archi, 1953-54; Symphony, Aufsland der Massen, (Praeludium und Toccata) for large orchestra, 1953-55; Concerto grosso (for jazz combo and wind ensemble), 1955-56; Music for Helmuth Brandt (for jazz combo), 1956; Hieroglyphik (for large orchestra), 1956-57; Faszination, music for a filmic ballet (for 2 percussionists), 1957; Positiv-Negativ-Synthesis (for 4 instrumental respect vocal groups), 1958; Apokalypsis (for large orchestra, speaker and 6 vocalists), 1982-86. *Publication:* Theorie der Induktion, 1974. *Honours:* Achievement Awards, Bavarian Academy of Fine Arts, Munich; Composition Prize, Competition of German Composers Association. *Memberships include:* Several professional organizations; Deutsche Joly-Straüß, Gosellschaft. *Address:* Herzogstr 20, 68723 Schwetzingen, Germany.

SCHMIDT Wolfgang, b. 1955, Kassel, Germany. Singer (Tenor). *Education:* Studied at the Frankfurt Musikochschule. *Career:* Sang First with the Pocket Oper Nuremburg, then at the Court Theatre Bayreuth 1982-84; Keil 1984-86; Dortmund from 1986- Notably as Otello and as Seigfried in Wagner's Opera; Apperances at the Eutin Festival 1983-87 as Tamino, Max and Huon in Oberon; Bregenz Festival 1989 as Erik in Fliegende Hollander; Bayreuth 1992 as Tannhäuser; Further Engagements at Essen, Karlsruhe, Hanover, Stuttgart; Sang First Armed Man in Die Zauberflöte at the 1991 Salzburg Festival; Concert Repertoire Includes the Missa Solemnis with appearances in Mexico City, Parma, Prague. *Recordings include:* Die Zauberflote; Weills Linderberghflug. *Address:* c/o Opernhaus Kuhstrasse 12, 4600 Dortmund, Germany.

SCHMIEGE Marilyn, b. 1955, Milwaukee, Wisconsin, USA. Singer (Mezzo-Soprano). *Education:* Studied at at Valparaiso University (B Mus), and M Mus, Boston University; Further study at the Zurich Opera Studio. *Debut:* Wuppertal, as Dorabella, 1978. *Career:* Theater am Gärtnerplatz, Munich as Cherubino, Rosina, Hänsel, Orlovsky, 1978-82; Teatro La Fenice Venice, 1981; Aix-en-Provence as Zaide in Il Turco in Italia, 1982; Munich Radio 1982, in Dido by Jan Novák, conducted by Kubelik, 1982; Düsseldorf, Cherubino, 1983; La Scala title role in Orfeo by Rossi, 1983; Vienna Staatsoper debut as Rosina, later also Octavian, Komponist, 1885; Stuttgart Charlotte in Werther, later also Lady Macbeth von Mzensk, Marguerite in Berlioz Damnation de Faust, 1985; Aldeburgh Festival, in Das Lied von der Erde, 1985; Hamburg Staatsoper, as Komponist and Rosina, 1985; later also Venus in Tannhäuser; Dresden Staatsoper as Komponist, Octavian, 1986; later also as Kundry;New York Philharmonic with Novák Dido, 1986; Cologne, Lady Macbeth von Mzensk (Kupfer), 1988; Munich Staatsoper Octavian, 1988, later also Cherubino, Jeanne d'Arc, Silla (Palestrina), Dorabella, Venus, 1991; Carmen at Berlin Komische Oper (Kupfer), 1991; Judith (Bartók) in Berlin Schauspielhaus, 1993; Amsterdam Marie (Wozzeck), Châtelet Waltraute in Götterdämmerung, 1994. *Recordings include:* Vivaldi's Catone in Utica, Galuppi's La Caduta d'Adamo (Erato); Haydn Cantatas (Capriccio); Haydn Orfeo ed Euridice (Harmonia Mundi); Cherubino in Mozart's Figaro, dir. Colin Davis (BMG); Dido by Novák, dir. Kubelik; Schreker Die Gezeichneten (Marco Polo); Mélodies of Gabriel Fauré (Orfeo), 1994. *Address:* c/o Baaderstrasse 1a, D-8000 Munich 5, Germany.

SCHNABEL Karl Ulrich, b. 6 Aug 1909, Berlin, Germany. Concert Pianist; Piano Teacher. m. Helen Fogel, deceased 1974, 1 daughter. *Education:* Studied with Leonid Kreutzer, State Academy of Music, Berlin, 1922-26; Studied composition & conducting, State Academy of Music, 1922-28. *Debut:* Berlin, 1926. *Career:* Concert tours in USA, Canada, Great Britain (83 towns), Germany, Austria, Italy, Switzerland, France, Holland, Russia, Poland, Denmark, Sweden, Norway, Brazil, Argentina, Uruguay, Chile, Australia and New Zealand. Master Classes at more than 60 Universities, Colleges, Conservatories and Music Festivals in North and South America, Europe, Japan, Israel, Australia and New Zealand; Original compositions for one piano four hands; partners: Artur Schnabel (father) 1935-40, Helen Schnabel (wife) 1940-74, Joan Rowland since 1980. *Recordings:* Works for piano solo, 1 and 2 pianos four hands, pianos with orchestra and chamber music by Bach, Beethoven, Mozart, Schubert, Schumann, von Weber, Chopin, Mendelssohn, Brahms, Liszt, Dvořák, Bizet and Debussy. *Publications:* Modern Technique of the Pedal, published in USA, Canada, England, Italy, Germany and Japan. *Hobbies:* Photography; Mountain-climbing. *Address:* 305 West End Avenue, New York, NY 10023, USA.

SCHNAPKA Georg, b. 27 May 1932, Schlesisch Ostrau, Czechoslovakia. m. Elisabeth Schwarzenberg. Singer (Bass). *Education:* Studied at the Bruckner Conservatory Linz with Andreas Sotzkov. *Debut:* Heidelberg 1954, as Repela in Wolf's Der Corregidor. *Career:* Sang 1964-85 at the Vienna Volksoper in the buffo repertory, also appeared with the Vienna Staatsoper; Guest appearances in hamburg, Munich, Stuttgart, Saarbrucken, Desseldorf, Wuppertal, Cologne and Frankfurt; Further engagements in Florence (Maggio Musicale), Venice, Amsterdam, Strasbourg, Lisbon, Bucharest and Zurich; American centres include New York City Opera, Baltimore and Washington DC; Main roles have included Philip II in Don Carlos, Daland, Fafner, Hunding, Sarastro, Pimen, Osmin, Leporello, Nicolai's Falstaff, Baron Ochs and Rossini's Bartolo; Many concert engagements. *Address:* Opernhaus, Kuhstrasse 12, D-4600 Dortmund, Germany.

SCHNAUT Gabriele, b. 1951, Mannheim, Germany. Singer (Mezzo-Soprano; Soprano). *Education:* Studied in Frankfurt with Elsa Cavelti, in Darmsradt with Aga

Zeh-Landzettel and in Berlin with Hanne-Lore Kuhse. *Career:* Sang at Stuttgart from 1976; Darmstdat 1978-80; Member of the Mannheim Opera from 1980; Bayreuth Festival from 1977, as Waltraute, Venus and Sieglinde; Chicago 1983, as Fricka in a concert performance of Die Walküre; Dortmund 1985, as Isolde; Has sung at Stuttgart, Frankfurt, Hamburg, Barcelona, Rome and Warsaw; Covent Garden debut 1989, as Sieglinde in a new production of Die Walküre conducted by Bernard Haitink; sang in Dusseldorf and Hamburg 1989, as Lady Macbeth and Els in Schreker's Der Schatzgräber; Brünnhilde in Die Walküre at Cologne, 1990; Bayreuth 1987-89, as Ortrud in Lohengrin; Sang Isolde at San Francisco, 1991, Elektra at the Opéra Bastille, Paris 1992; Other roles include Octavian, Sextus (La Clemenza di Tito), Dorabella, Carmen, Brangaene, Kundry and Marie in Wozzeck. *Recordings include:* St Matthew Passion by Bach (CBS); Sancta Susanna and Lieder by Hindemith. *Address:* c/o Oper der Stadt Köln, Offenbachplatz, D-5000 Cologne, Germany.

SCHNEBEL Dieter, b. 14 Mar 1930, Lahr, Germany. Composer. *Education:* Studied at the Freiburg Hochschule fur Musik, at Darmstadt and the University of Thubingen (1952-56). *Career:* Active in the Lutheran Church, from 1976 Professor of experimental music and musicology at the Berlin Hochschule für Musik; Work with the experimental theatre group Die Maulwerker, from 1978; Collabortions with director Achim Freyer on Maul-werke and Cage-up. *Compositions include:* Music Theatre Maulwerke, 1968-74, Laut-Gesten-Laute, Zeichen-Sprache and Chili (Music and pictures on Kleist, 1989-91); Orchestral: Compositio, 1956, revised 1964; Webern Variationen, 1972; Canones, 1975; In motu proprio, 1975; Diaspason, 1977; Orchestra, 1977; Shubert-Phantasie, 1978; Wagner-Idyll, 1980; Thanatos-Eros, 1982; Sinfonie-Stucke, 1985; Beethoven-Sinfonie, 1985; Mahler Moment for Strings, 1985; Raumklang X, 1988; Chamber: reactions, 1961; Visable Music I, 1961; Nostalgie for Conductor, 1962; Espressivo, music drama for piano, 1963; Concert sans orchestre for piano and audience, 1964; Ansclage-auschlage, 1966; Beethoven-Sonate for Percussion, 1970; Quintet, 1977; Pan for flute, 1978; Monotonien for piano and electronics, 1989; Vocal: Fur Stimmen (.... missa est) for chorus, 1961; Glossolalie 61, 1961; Bach-Contrapuncti for chorus, 1976; Jowaeglili for 2 speakers, voices and chamber ensemble, 1983; Lieder Ohne Worte, 1980-86; Missa: Dahlemer Messe, 1984-87; Produktionprozesses series, 1968-75; Graphic works including mo-no: Musik Zum Lesen, 1969. *Publications include:* Study of Stockhausen's early works; Mauricio Kagel, Cologne, 1970; Denkbare Musik: Schriften 1952-72, Cologne 1972. *Address:* GEMA (Germany), c/o PRS Ltd, Member Registration, 29/33 Berners Street, London W1P 4AA, England.

SCHNEIDER Gary M, b. 1950, USA. Conductor; Composer. *Career:* Founder, Music Director and Principal Conductor of the Hoboken Chamber Orchestra; Debut in Europe at the International Zelt Musik Festival in Freiburg; New York debut with the American Composers Orchestra performing his Concerto for Jazz Clarinet and Orchestra; Has also conducted the Chamber Symphony of Princeton, and the New York Festival Orchestra; Artist-in- residence at Denison University in Ohio and composer-in-residence at the Rockport (Massachusetts) Chamber Music Festival. *Compositions include:* Sonata for solo cello 1976; String Quartet 1977; Study for a Ballet for piano, 1981; Piano Sonata 1989; Nocturne for bassoon and strings 1988; The Bremen Town Musicians 1989; The Tell-Tale Heart and The Voice of Eternity for soloists and ensemble. *Publications:* Compositions have been published by Peter Southern Organization, Berben edizioni musicali and American Composers Editions.

SCHNEIDER Peter, b. 26 Mar 1939, Vienna, Austria. Conductor. *Education:* Studied at the Academy for Music and Dramatic Art in Vienna (conducting with Hans Swarowsky). *Career:* Sang with the Wiener Sängerknaben as a boy; Head of studies at the Landestheater Salzburg from 1959 (conducting debut with Handel's Giulio Cesare); Principal conductor in Heidleberg 1961, Deutsche Oper am Rhein Dusseldorf from 1968: performances of operas by Janáček, Berg, Wagner, Mozart, Verdi and Dallapiccola; Guest conductor in Warsaw, Florence and Edinburgh; Music Director in Bremen 1978-85, Mannheim 1985-87; Bayreuth Festioval from 1981: Der fliegende Holländer, Der Ring des Nibelungen and Lohengrin; Conducted the Vienna Opera in Der Rosenkavalier on its 1986 tour of Japan, and the Vienna Philharmonic at the Salzburg Festival; Further appearances as a conductor of opera in Vienna, Berlin, London, Bologna, Barcelona and Madrid; Concerts in San Francisco; Die Soldaten by Zimmermann at the Vienna Staatsoper, 1990; Conducted Tristan und Isolde in Japan, 1990 and San Francisco, 1991; Music Director of the Bavarian State Opera, Munich, 1993. *Address:* c/o Ingpen & Williams Ltd., 14 Kensington Court, London W8 5DN, England.

SCHNEIDER Urs, b. 16 May 1939, St Gallen, Switzerland. Conductor; Music Director. *Education:* Violin Diploma, Zurich Conservatory; Conducting with Rafael Kubelik, Igor Markevitch, Otto Klemperer. *Debut:* With Own Orchestras at Age of 15 Years. *Career:* Founder, Conductor, Artistic Director, Ostchweizer Kammerochester, Camerata Helvetica; Guest Conductor, USA; Musical Director, Camerata Stuttgart; Musical Director, Camerata Academica Salzburg; Chief Conductor, Music Director, Haifa Symphony Orchestra; Concerts, Operas, Radio & TV; Guest Conductor, Numerous Major Orchestras all over the five continents; Member of the Jury of the Concours des Jeunes Chefs Orchestre of the Festival International de Besancon; Prinicpal Conductor, Artistic Director, National Taiwan Philharmonic Orchestra; First Guest Conductor of Prague Chamber Soloists. *Recordings:* 50 Records. *Honours:* Cultural Prize of City of St Gallen. *Memberships:* Swiss Musicians Association; Schweiz Berufsdirigenten Verband. *Hobbies:* Sports; Keeping Fit; History; Reading; Art. *Address:* Gattestr 1B, CH-9010 St Gallen, Switzerland.

SCHNEIDER Victoria, b. 28 Oct 1952, Reading, Pennsylvania, USA. Soprano (Opera and Concert). m. Riccardo Malipiero, 21 Dec 1988. *Education:* BM, MM, Performers Certificate, Eastman School of Music, Rochester, New York. *Debut:* Staatsoper Stuttgart, Germany, 1981. *Career:* Regular collaboration with Staatsoper Stuttgart and many concert appearances throughout Germany, 1981-85; Increased activity, Italy, 1984-: Teatro alla Scala, Milan; Teatro Comunale do Bologna; Teatro dellOpera di Roma; Teatro dellOpera di Genova; Many concerts with major Italian Orchestras: Santa Cecilia, Rome; Radio Orchestras (RAI) of Milan, Turin, Naples, others; Vast concert repertoire ranging from baroque to contemporary: Handel's Messiah; Beethoven's Mass in C Major and Missa Solemnis; Mozart's Requiem and Exultate Jubilate; Mahler's Kindertotenlieder; Many Strauss Orchesterlieder; Wagner's Wesendoncklieder; Berg's Sieben Frühe Lieder; Shostakovich's Seven Lyrics of Alexander Blok; Dallapiccola's An Mathilde and Commiato; Many world premieres with works by R Malipiero, S Sciarrino, Donatoni, Gentilucci, Guarnieri, others; Many concerts, Schoenberg's op 10 with Arditti String Quartet, 1989-. *Recordings:* Numerous radio recordings: Vara Radio, Netherlands; Suddeutsche Rundfunk, Stuttgart; Bayerische Rundfunk, Munich; Radio Bremen; RSI, Lugano; Frequent recordings, Italian National Radio RAI. *Hobbies:* Water-Skiing; Swimming. *Address:* Via Stradella 1, 20129 Milan, Italy.

SCHNEIDER-SIEMSSEN Gunther, b. 7 June 1926, Augsburg, Germany. Stage and Set Designer. m. Eva Mazar, 10 Mar 1969, 4 children. *Education:* Diploma, Akademie für Kunst, Munich, 1946. *Career:* Film Designer, 1946-51; Head Designer, Landestheater, Salzburg, 1951-54; Head Designer, Marionetten Theater, Salzburg, 1951-; State Theater, Bremen, 1954-59; Head Designer, Vienna State Opera, 1960-; Designed Der Ring des Nibelungen at Covent Garden,

1962-64; Guest Designer numerous opera houses; Professor, Stage Design, International Summer Academy Fine Arts, Salzburg, 1968-87; Designer, Salzburg Festival, 1965-89; Designer, Easter Festival, 1967-89; Notable productions include Boris Godunov, Tristan und Isolde, Die Frau ohne Schatten and Berio's Un Re in Ascolto; Designer Met. Opera New York and cities in USA, including the Ring in New York (also televised and recorded, 1990). *Honours:* Fellow M.I.T. USA, 1980-85. *Contributions to:* Professional Journals. *Memberships:* President, Society of the Stage of the Future; Rotary. *Address:* 4 Schlickgasse, Vienna, Austria.

SCHNEIDERHAN Wolfgang, b. 28 May 1915, Vienna, Austria. Violinist; Conductor. m. Irmgaard Seefried 1948 (died 1988). *Education:* Studied with Sevcik in Pisek and Julius Winkler in Vienna. *Career:* Made public debut in 1920; Played Mendelssohn's Concerto in Copenhagen 1926; Leader of the Vienna Symphony Orchestra 1933-37, Vienna Philharmonic 1937-51; Led Schneiderhan Quartet 1937-51; Teacher at the Salzburg Mozarteum 1938-56 appointed Professor in 1937 and at the Vienna Academy of Music (1939-50); Played in Trio with Edwin Fischer and Enrico Mainardi 1949-60; Taught violin at the Lucerne Conservatory from 1949 and with Rudolf Baumgartner formed the Lucerne Festival Strings 1956; Mozart, Schubert and Beethoven have been at the centre of his repertory, also performs modern works: with Irmgaard Seefried premiered Henze's Ariosi at the 1963 Edinburgh Festival; Conducted Franz Schmidt's Notre Dame at the Vienna Volksoper in 1975. *Address:* c/o Harold Holt Ltd., 31 Sinclair Road, London W14 ONS, England.

SCHNITTKE Alfred, b. 24 Nov 1934, Engels, USSR. Composer. *Education:* Studied piano with Charlotte Ruber in Vienna, 1946-48; Moscow Conservatory 1953-58, with Golubev and Rakov; further study with Philipp Herschkowitz. *Career:* Began composition while in Vienna; instrumental teacher at Moscow Conservatory 1962-72; tours throughout Europe from 1967; guest teacher at Vienna Hochschule für Musik 1980. *Compositions:* Dramatic: Labyrinths, ballet, 1971; Der Gelbe Klang, pantomime after Kandinsky, 1974; A Streetcar Named Desire, ballet 1983; Othello, ballet 1985; Sketches, ballet after Gogol, 1985; Peer Gynt, ballet 1986; Life with an Idiot, opera for Netherlands Opera 1992; Faust, opera for Frankfurt, 1995; Orchestral: Violin Concerto No.1, 1957, rev. 1962; Piano Concerto, 1960; Music for piano and chamber orchestra, 1964; Violin Concerto No.2, 1966; Pianissimo, 1968; Sonata for violin and chamber orchestra, 1968; Symphony No.1, 1969-72; Double Concerto for oboe, harp and strings, 1971; In Memoriam orchestral version of Piano Quintet, 1972-78; Requiem, after Schiller's Don Carlos, 1975; Concerto Grosso No.1, 1977; Violin Concerto No.3, 1978; Symphony No.2 St Florian for chamber chorus and orchestra, 1979; Passacaglia, 1980; Gogol Suite, after Dead Souls, 1980; Symphony No.3, 1981; Concerto Grosso No.2, 1982; "Seid Nuchtern und Wachet...."cantata after the Faust legend, 1983; Violin Concerto No.4, 1984; Symphony No.4, 1984; Ritual, 1985; Concerto Grosso No.3, 1985; Viola Concerto, 1985; Cello Concerto, 1986; Epilogue from Peer Gynt, 1987; Trio Sonata, after the String Trio, 1987; Four Aphorisms 1988; Concerto Grosso No.4, Symphony no.5 1988; Monologue for viola and strings 1989; Concerto for piano, 4 hands, 1990; Cello Concerto No.2 1990; Sutartines for percussion, organ and strings 1991; Concerto Grosso No.5 1991; Vocal: Three Madrigals for soprano and ensemble, 1980; Three Scenes for soprano and ensemble, 1980; Minnesang for 52 voices, 1981; Concerto for mixed chorus, 1985; Chamber: Violin Sonata No.1, 1963; Dialogue for cello and 7 instruments, 1965; String Quartet No.1, 1966; Violin Sonata No.2, 1968; Serenade for ensemble, 1968; Suite in Old Style for violin and piano, 1972; Piano Quintet, 1972-76; Hymns for cello and ensemble, 1974-79; Moz-art for 2 violins, 1976; Cello Sonata, 1978; String Quartet No.2, 1980; Septet, 1982; A Paganini for solo violin, 1982; String Quartet No.3, 1983; String Trio, 1985; Piano Sonata 1988; Piano Quartet 1988;

String Quaret No.4 1989; Five Aphorisms for piano 1990; Piano Sonata No.2 1991; incidental music to 60 films. *Publications include:* Essays on Shostakovich, Stravinsky, Bartók, Berio, Webern and Ligeti. *Memberships:* Federation of Russian Composers, 1961-; Federation of Cinematographers in the CIS, 1970-; Akademie der Kunste of the Former German Democratic Republic, 1981-; Bayerische Akademie der Schönen Kunste, Munich, 1981-. *Address:* c/o Boosey & Hawkes Ltd., 295 Regent Street, London W1 8JH, England.

SCHNITZLER Michael, b. 1940, Vienna, Austria. Violinist. *Education:* Studied in Vienna. *Career:* Performances of Hadyn and Other Composers in Vienna and Elsewhere, From 1968; Co Founder The Haydn Trio of Vienna, 1968 and has Performed in Brussels, Munich, Berlin, Zurich, London, Rome, Paris; New York Debut 1979 and has Made Frequent North American Appearances with Concerts in 25 States; Debut Tour of Japan, 1984 with Further Travels to the Near East, Russia, Africa, Central and South America; Series at the Vienna Konzerthaus Society from 1976, with Performances of more than 100 Works; Summer Festivals at Vienna, Salzbourg, Aixen Province, Flanders and Montreua; Master Classes at the Royal College and Royal Academy of London, Stockholm, Bloomington, Toyko and the Salzburg Mozarteum. *Recordings:* Complete Piano Trios of Beethoven and Schubert, Mendelssohn D Minor, Brahams B Major, Tchaikovsky A Minor, Schubert Trout Quintet; Albums of Works by Haydn, Schumann, Dvořák and Smetana. *Address:* c/o Sue Lubbock Concert Management, 25 Courthorpe Road, London NW3 2LE, England.

SCHNYDER Daniel, b. 12 Mar 1961, Zurich, Switzerland. Composer; Flautist; Saxophonist. m. Barbara Klap, 15 Aug 1992. *Education:* Studied at Berklee College of Music, Boston nd Conservatory Winterthur Switzerland. *Career:* TV Appearances at Several Major Festivals; Many Radio Interviews and Broadcasts all Over Europe. *Compositions include:* Inside The Dome, 2nd String Quartet; Concerto for Flute and Percussion. *Recordings:* The City; Decoding the Message; Mythology; Winds; Mythen; Secret Cosmos. *Publications:* Secret Cosmos; Trumpet Sonata. *Honour:* Conrad Fesdinanel Meyes Prize. *Address:* Schubertstr 21, 8037 Zurich, Switzerland.

SCHOLLUM Benno, b. 1953, Klagenfurt, Austria. Singer (Baritone). *Education:* Studied at the Vienna Musikhochschule with Josef Greindl and with his father, Robert Schollum; Master Classes in New York and Vienna with Sena Jurinac and others. *Career:* Has performed in Austria and elsewhere in Operettas by Lehar, Johann Strauss, Milloecker and Offenbach; Operas by Mozart, Britten, Lortzing, Mascagni; Lieder by Loewe, Schubert and Brahms; Oratorios include Schmidt's Das Buch mit Sieben Siegeln, the Brahms Requiem and Cantatas and Masses by Bach and Mozart; festival appearances at Bayreuth, Vienna, Antibes, Carinthia Summer and Gstaad; Guest Engagements in France, Yugoslavia, Italy, USA, Germany, Holland and Luxembourg; Berlin Philharmonic Debut in Herbst by Antal Dorati; British Debut 1991, with the English Symphony Orchestra in Arias by Mozart (Stage roles include Papageno); Teacher at the Vienna Musikhochschule from 1983. *Address:* c/o IMG Artists Europe, Media House, 3 Burlington Lane, London W4 2TH, England.

SCHOLZ Gottfried, b. 11 Sept 1936, Vienna, Austria. Professor of Music Theory (Analysis). *Education:* Teacher's Diploma, Academy of Music, Vienna, 1960; PhD, University of Vienna, 1962. *Career:* Professor, 1969-; Guest Professor, various Universities in USA and Asia, 1969, 1970-71, 1980, 1989; Deputy Rector, 1974-84, Rector, Vienna Hochschule für Musik, 1984-88. *Publications:* Instrumental Musik der Klassik und Romantik, 1972; Music in Austria, 1981; Tradition and Innovations in the Austrian Music, 1982; Instrumental - Gesangs lehrerbildung in Europe, 1970; The European Music Committees, 1980; Michael Haydn: Deutsches Hochamt in B-dur, 1979; Formen in der Musik, 1988;

Austrian Contemporary Music, 1993. *Memberships:* Past President, International Music Council, UNESCO; Past President, Austrian Music Council. *Address:* Hochschule für Musik, Lothringer Str. 18, A 1030 Vienna, Austria.

SCHOLZ Rudolf Franz Joseph, b. 26 Sept 1933, Vienna, Austria. Organist; Musicologist. m. Helga Margarethe Michelitsch, 29 Apr 1966. *Education:* DPhil, Vienna University, 1963; Diploma, Vienna Academy of Music and Dramatic Art, 1964. *Career:* Lecturer, methods of organ playing, improvisation, organ and thorough bass Vienna Academy of Music and Dramatic Art, 1964-69; Assistant for Organ, 1969-74; Professor for organ, Hochschule für Musik und darstellende Kunst in Wien, 1974-; Head, department of Keyboard Instruments, 1981-; Head, Institute of Organ Research and Documentation, 1975-; Head and Professor, International Organ Courses; Juror, International Organ competitions; Organist, Wiener Musikverein, Salzburg Summer Festivals, Salzburg Easter and Whitsun Festivals, Vienna and Berlin Festwochen, Festival of Luzerne, Internationale Hochschulwochen Alpbach; Radio recordings in Vienna, Salzburg and Munich; Numerous organ concerts in Austria and abroad. *Contributions to:* Articles to musical journals; Editor, Organa Austriaca, 1976-; Old and modern music. *Honour:* Recipient, Diploma, International Organ Competition, Graz-Seckau, 1960. *Memberships:* Gesellschaft zur Heraugabe von Denkmaelern der Tonkunst in Oesterreich, Franz-Schmidt- Gesellschaft (Vienna); Bach-Gemeinde Wien; Gesellschaft der Orgelfreunde; International Schoenberg-Gesellschaft; Oesterreische Gesellschaft für Musikwissenschaft; Oesterreiches Orgelforum. *Address:* 71 Ungargasse, A-1030, Vienna, Austria.

SCHOLZE Rainer, b. 13 May 1940, Sudetenland. Singer (Bass). *Education:* Studied at the Cologne Musikhochschule. *Career:* Sang in the Choru of the Lubeck Stadt Theatre, 1962-66; Discovered by Gerd Albrecht and Sang Small Roles; Studies Further and Sang Solo at Lubeck from 1966-70; Engaged at Brunswick, 1970-71; Kassel, 1971-81; Appeared at Kiel 1981-83; and Made Guest Outings to Munich, Dresden, Hamburg; Has often appeared in Operas by Mozart, Rossini, Lortzing and Notably as Baron Ochs. *Recordings include:* Masetto in Don Giovanni; Reinmar in Tannhäuser; Larkens in Fanciulla del West. *Address:* c/o Staatstheater am Gärtnerplatz, Gärtnerplatz 3, 8000 Munich, Germany.

SCHOMBERG Martin, b. 7 Nov 1944, Hoxter, Westfalen, Germany. Singer (Tenor). *Education:* Studied at the Hamburg Musikhochschule with Jakob Stampfli. *Debut:* Mainz 1972, as Lenski in Eugene Onegin. *Career:* Many appearances at the Opera houses of Cologne, Bsle, Hamberg, Duesseldorf; Zurich Opera in Lyric Roles and in the 1974 Premiere of Ein Whrer Held by Klebe; Concert Engagements at the Salzburg Festival and Elsewhere; Roles have Included Mozart's Belmonte, Ottavio and Tamino, Nencio in Haydn's L'Infedelta Delusa, Florindo in Le Donne Curiose by Wolf-Ferrari, the Italian Tenor in Rosenkavalier and Alfred in Fledermaus. *Address:* Opernhaus Zurich, Falkenstrasse 1, CH-8008 Zurich, Switzerland.

SCHONBACH Dieter, b. 18 Feb 1931, Stolp, Pomerania, Germany. *Education:* Studied in Detmold and Freiburg with Gunter Bialas and Wolfgang Fortner. *Career:* Music Director of the Bochum Schauspielhaus, 1959-73; Has Also worked at theatres in Munster and Basle. *Compositions include:* Die Geschichte von einem Feuer, mixed-media opera, Kiel, 1968; Canzona da sonar 6, mixed-media show with puppet, 1970; Bedrohung Und Uberleben, multi-media opera, Cologne, 1971; Hysteria-Paradies schwarz, mixed-media opera, Cologne, 1971; Der Sturm, mixed media show after The Tempest, Wiesbaden, 1971; Hymnus II-Morgen nach dem Feuer, mixed media show, Munich 1972; Come S Francesco, Munster, 1979; Farben und Klange, in memory of Kandinsky for orchestra, 1958; Piano Concerto 1958; Canticum Psalmi Resurrectionis, 1959;

Kammermusik for 14 instruments, 1964; Hoquetus for 8 wind instruments, 1964. *Honours include:* Joint Winner, Stamitz Prize of Stuttgart, 1972. *Address:* GEMA (Germany), c/o PRS Ltd, Member Registration, 29/33 Berners St, London W1P 4AA, England.

SCHONBERG Harold Charles, b. 29 Nov 1915, New York City, USA. Music Critic; Editor; Writer on Music. m. (1) Rosalyn Krokover, 28 Nov 1942, (2) Helene Cornell, 10 May 1975. *Education:* BA, Brooklyn College, 1937; MA, New York University, 1938. *Career:* Associate Editor, American Music Lover, 1939-41; Contributing editor, Music Digest, 1946-48; Music critic, New York Sun, 1946-50; Contributing editor, record reviewer, Musical Courier, 1948-52; Columnist, Gramophone, 1948-60; Music critic, record reviewer 1950-60, senior music critic 1960-80, cultural correspondent 1980-85, New York Times. *Publications:* Chamber & Solo Instrument Music, 1955; Collector's Chopin & Schumann, 1959; Great Pianists, 1963, revised 1987; Great Conductors, 1967; Lives of Great Composers, 1970, 1981; Facing the Music, 1981; Glorious Ones: Classical Music's Legendary Performers, 1985; Horowitz. His Life and Music, 1992. Also numerous articles, various publications. *Honours:* 1st music critic to win Pulitzer Prize in criticism, 1971. *Hobbies:* Drawing; Chess. *Address:* 160 Riverside Drive, New York, NY 10024, USA.

SCHÖNE Wolfgang, b. 9 Feb 1941, Bad Gandersheim, Germany. Singer (Bass-Baritone). *Education:* Studied with Naan Pold in Hanover and Hamburg, Diploma 1969. *Career:* Winner of awards from 1966 at Bordeaux, Berlin, Stuttgart and s' Hertogenbosch; Concert tours and Lieder recitals in Belgium, Holland, France, Denmark, USA, Mexico, Argentina and England; Appeared in film The Chronicle of Anna Magdalena Bach; Opera career from 1970 at the State Operas of Stuttgart, Vienna and Hamburg, notably as Guglielmo, Wolfram and Count Eberbach in Der Wildschütz by Lortzing; Schwetzingen Festival 1983, as Tom in the premiere of The English Cat by Henze; Komische Oper Berlin 1984, as Golaud in Pelléas et Mélisande; Sang at the 1984 reopening of the Stuttgart Opera, as Don Giovanni; Season 1988-89 sang Gunther ar Turin, Alidoro (Cenerentola) at Salzburg and Barak at Cologne; Hamburg 1990, as Wolfram; Sang Orestes and Pentheus (The Bassarids) at Stuttgart 1989; The Count in Capriccio at the 1990 Salzburg Festival; Dr Schön, in Lulu at the Paris Châtelet, 1992. *Recordings:* Bach Cantatas; St Matthew Passion by Schütz; Theresienmesse by Haydn (BASF); Bach B Minor Mass (CBS); Doktor und Apotheker by Dittersdorf; Giulio Cesare by Handel (Deutsche Grammophon); Lulu (EMI), Video of Der Freischütz (Thorn-EMI). *Address:* Wilhelm-Röntenstrasse 32, D-7302 Ostfildern 1, Germany.

SCHØNWANDT Michael, b. 10 Sept 1953, Copenhagen, Denmark. Conductor. m. Amalie Malling, 23 Mar 1991. *Education:* B.Mus., Musicology, Copenhagen University, 1975; Conducting & Composition, Royal Academy of Music, London, England, 1975-77. *Debut:* Copenhagen, 1977. *Career:* Concerts throughout Europe, Debut Royal Danish Opera, 1979; Guest Conductor: Covent Garden, London, Paris Opéra, Stuttgart Opera; Principal Guest Conductor, Théâtre Royal de la Monnaie, Brussels, 1984-87; Principal Conductor, Collegium Musicum, Copenhagen, 1981-; Principal Guest Conductor, Nice Opera, 1987-91; Danish Radio Symphony Orchestra, 1989-; Principal Conductor, Berliner Sinfonie Orchestra, 1992; Permanent Conductor, Vienna State Opera, 1990. *Recordings:* Mozart Piano Concertos and Violin Concertos; Beethoven Piano Concertos; Niels W. Gade Complete Symphonies; Kuhlau: Lulu, Complete Opera; Schoenberg/Sibelius Pelleas and Melisande, Berlioz: Requiem. *Honours:* Numerous musical prizes, Denmark. *Current Management:* Ingpen & Williams Ltd., 14 Kensington Court, London W8, England. Ltd., 14 Kensington Court, London W8, England. *Address:* Svalevej 24, DK 2900, Hellerup, Denmark.

SCHÖNZELER Hans-Hubert, b. 22 June 1925,

Leipzig, Germany. Conductor; Musicologist. m. (1) Margaret Gillian Wingate (divorced), 1 son. (2) Helmi, 21 May 1982. *Education:* New South Wales State Conservatorium, Sydney, Australia; Conductor's Diploma, Conservatoire Nationale de Musique, Paris, France, 1954. *Career:* Conductor, 20th Century Ensemble, London, England, 1957-61; Acting Resident Conductor, West Australian Symphony Orchestra, Perth, 1967; Guest Conductor, radio and TV performances in UK, Belgium, France, Germany, Holland, Australia, Canada and New Zealand. *Compositions:* Viola Sonata, Op. 5; Song Cycle, Tristesse, Op. 6. *Recordings:* Unicorn; RCA; Classics for Pleasure; Vox; Chandos; Virgin Classics, including Beethoven's, Ruins of Athens, King Stephan and Prometheus; Bruckner Requiem and Four Orchestral Pieces (LPO); Weber Symphonies (LSO); Sitsky's Fall of the House of Usher; Haydn Symphonies 96 and 102 (Royal Philharmonic); Janáček Idyll. *Publications include:* Bruckner, 1970; Editor, Of German Music, 1976; Dvořák, 1984; Furtwängler, 1990. *Honours:* Medal of Honor, Bruckner Society of America, 1971; Honorary Professorship, Austrian Government, 1976; Medal of International Bruckner Society, Vienna, 1978. *Memberships:* International Bruckner Society, Vienna; Honorary Member, Dvořák Society, Prague. *Hobby:* Reading. *Address:* Savage Club, 1 Whitehall Place, London, SW1A 2HD, England.

SCHOPPER Michael, b. 1942, Passau, Germany. Singer (Bass-Baritone). *Education:* Studied at the Musikhochschule Munich with Hanno Blaschke. *Debut:* Sang in the Christmas Oratorio by Bach with the Munich Bach Choir conducted by Karl Richter, 1968. *Career:* Has sung in concert in North and South America and Europe; Founded the ensemble Musica Poetica 1974, for the performance of Renaissance and Baroque music; Opera appearances at the Herrenhausen Festival, in Giulio Cesare by Handel and La Clemenza di Tito by Mozart. *Recordings include:* Giulio Cesare and Bach Cantatas (Deutsche Grammophon); St Matthew Passion by Bach (Telefunken); Masses by Mozart, Bach Cantatas (Harmonia Mundi).

SCHOTT Howard Mansfield, b. 17 June 1923, New York City, New York, USA. Musicologist; Harpsichordist. *Education:* BA, 1943, JD, 1948, Yale University; DPhil (Oxon), 1978; Studied Applied Music, Mannes College, New York; Musicology with Barry Brook, Emanuel Winternitz, H.C.Robbins Landon, City University of New York, Leo Schrade, Yale, Joseph Kerman and John Caldwell, Oxford; Keyboard with Ralph Kirkpatrick, Yale, and Hans Neumann, Mannes College; Composition with Richard Donovan and Luther Noss, Yale. *Career:* Lecturer, New England Conservatory, Boston, Massachusetts, 1988-; Lectures at Oxford, Kings College (London), Harvard, Yale (Sanford Fellowship, 1979), Cornell, Paris, City University of New York, Consultant to Boston Early Music Festival, East Nakamichi Festival, also Victoria and Albert Museum, Metropolitan Museum of Art. *Publications:* Playing the Harpsichord, 1971, 3rd edition, 1979, Italian edition, 1982, German edition, 1983; Oeuvres completes de J.J.Froberger, 1980-; Catalogue of the Musical Instruments in the Victoria and Albert Museum, I: Keyboard Instruments, 1985; The Historical Harpsichord series (editor), 1984-; Many articles in The New Grove Dictionary and New Harvard Dictionary of Music. *Contributions to:* Regularly to The Musical Times, and also to Early Music, including The Harpsichord Revival, and From Harpsichord to Pianoforte. *Address:* Suite 402, Brook House, 44 Washington Street, Brookline, MA 02146, USA.

SCHRADER David Dillon, b. 15 Sept 1952, Chicago, Illinois, USA. Musician (Organ, Harpsichord, Fortepiano). *Education:* BMus, Special Honours, University of Colorado, 1974; Performers Certificate 1975, MMus, High Distinction 1976, DMus, Distinction 1987, Indiana University. *Career:* Soloist: Symphony Orchestras, Chicago (with Solti, Abbado, Barenboim, Leinsdorf), Milwaukee, San Francisco (with Järvi), El Paso; City Musick; Music of Baroque; Numerous live

& recorded radio broadcasts, nationally distributed. Current appointments: Organist, Church of Ascension; Keyboardist, City Musick (period instrument orchestra); Professor of Organ & Harpsichord, Chicago Musical College. *Recordings:* Intercord Tongesellschaft, London (with Chicago Symphony; Centaur; Enharmonic. *Publications:* Articles: Continuo; Indiana Theory Review; Cantate Domino. *Hobbies:* Cooking; Physical Culture; Music. *Current Management:* Artra Artist Management, 410 South Michigan Avenue, Chicago, Illinois 60605, USA. *Address:* Church of the Ascension, 1133 North Lasalle Drive, Chicago, Illinois 60610, USA.

SCHRANZ Karoly, b. 1950, Hungary. Violinist. *Education:* Studied with András Mihaly at the Franz Liszt Academy Budapest, with members of the Amadeus Quartet and Zoltán Szekely. *Career:* Founder member of the Takacs Quartet, 1975; Many concert appearances in all major centres of Europe and the USA; Tours of Australia, New Zealand, Japan, South America, England, Norway, Sweden, Greece, Belgium and Ireland; Bartók Cycle for the Bartók-Solti Festival at South Bank, 1990; Great Performers Series at Lincoln Center and Mostly Mozart Festival at Alice Tully Hall, New York; Visits to Japan 1989 and 1992; Mozart Festivals at South Bank, Wigmore Hall and Barbican Centre 1991; Bartók Cycle at the Théâtre des Champs Elysées, 1991; Beethoven Cycles at the Zurich Tonhalle, in Dublin, at the Wigmore Hall and in Paris, 1991-92; Resident at the University of Colorado, Resident at the London Barbican 1988-91, with master classes at the Guildhall School of Music; Plays Amati instrument made for the French Royal Family and loaned by the Corcoran Gallery, Gallery of Art, Washington DC. *Recordings:* Schumann Quartets Op 41, Mozart String Quintets (with Denes Koromzay), Bartók 6 Quartets, Schubert Trout Quintet (with Zoltán Kocsis) Hungaroton; Haydn Op 76, Brahms Op 51 nos 1 and 2, Chausson Concerto (with Joshua Bell and Jean-Yves Thibaudet); Works by Schubert, Mozart, Dvořák and Bartók (Decca). *Honours:* Winner, International Quartet Competition, Evian 1977; Winner, Portsmouth International Quartet Competition, 1979. *Address:* Lies Askonas Ltd, 6 Henrietta Street, Covent Garden, London WC2, England.

SCHREIBMAYER Kurt, b. 1953, Klagenfurt, Germany. Singer (Tenor). *Education:* Studied at the Graz Musikhochschule. *Career:* Sang at Graz 1976-78, then at the Vienna Volksoper; Further appearances at the Theater am Gartnerplatz Munich (1987-88), Deutsche Oper am Rhein Dusseldorf (from 1987), Hamburg Staatsoper and the Zurich Opera; Théâtre Royal de la Monnaie, Brussels, from 1987 as Steva in Jenůfa and Luka in From the House of the Dead (1990); Bayreuth Festival engagements 1986-90, as Froh, Walter von der Vogelweide and Parsifal; Returned to the Vienna Volksoper 1988, as Max in Der Freischütz; Has sung at Liège as Lohengrin (1988-89); Other roles include Fra Diavalo, Babinsky in Shvanda the Bagpiper, Pedro in Tiefland, Gomez (Die drei Pintos), Wenzel (Zemlinsky's Kleider machen Leute) and parts in operettas. *Address:* c/o Théâtre Royal de la Monnaie, 4 Leopolstrasse, B-1000 Brussels, Belgium.

SCHREIER Peter, b. 29 July 1935, Gauernitz, near Meissen, Germany. Singer (Tenor); Conductor. *Education:* Sang in Dresden Kreuzchor as a child then studied with Polster in Leipzig and with Winkler at the Dresden Musikhochschule, 1956-59. *Debut:* Dresden Staatsoper 1961, as First Prisoner in Fidelio. *Career:* Lyric tenor at the Staatsoper Berlin and in Hamburg, Vienna, London and Munich in operas by Mozart, Rossini, Weber, Wagner and Lortzing; Mozart's Ferrando at Sadler's Wells theatre, London, 1966 and Tamino at the New York Metropolitan 1968; also celebrated as Mozart's Belmonte and Ottavio, Verdi's Fenton, Tchaikovsky's Lensky, Wagner's David and Loge and Strauss's Leukippos; sang in the premieres of Orff's De Temporum fine comoedia (1973) and Dessau's Einstein (1974); Salzburg Festival from 1967; Well known as the Evangelist in Bach's Passions and in concert works by Handel, Haydn, Beethoven, Berlioz and Mendelssohn; many Lieder recitals, notably in song cycles by Schubert and Schumann; debut as conductor with the Berlin Staatskapelle, 1970; First recital at Wigmore Hall, London, 1989; Conducted Mozart's Mitridate at the Cuvilliés Theater, Munich 1990. *Recordings:* Il Barbiere di Siviglia, St. Matthew Passion and Haydn's Die Jahreszeiten for Eurodisc; CPE Bach Mark Passion (CBS); Das Buch mit sieben siegeln (Orfeo); Das Lied von der Erde (Denon); Die Zauberflöte, Così fan Tutte, Johannespassion by Schütz and Das Rheingold for Deutsche Grammophon; Der Freischütz, Capriccio, Lortzing's Der Wildschütz and the Berlioz Requiem for Electrola; Mendelssohn's Elijah and Mozart's Requiem (as conductor) for Philips; Many Lieder recordings. *Address:* c/o Norman McCann Ltd, The Coach House, 56 Lawrie Park Gardens, London, SE26 6XJ, England.

SCHREINER Elisabeth, b. 1924, Germany. Singer (Soprano). *Career:* Sang in Opera at Kaiserslautern, 1949-52; Coburg, 1952-55; Krefeld, 1955- 59; Mainz, 1959-65; Many appearances in Operas by Wagner at Mannheim, 1966-82, And quest Engagements in Germany and abroad; Vienna Staatsoper from 1970, notably as Senta and Brünnhilde, Bordeaux 1967, Munich 1971, Barcelona and Turin, 1972; Paris Opera and Covent Garden 1972, Brünnhilde and Senta; Further Appearnces at Graz, Cologne, Nice and Vichy; Other roles include Elisabeth, Ortrud, Sieglinde, Gutrune, The Marschallin, Isolde, Ariadne, Lady Macbeth, The Countess in Capriccio, Amelia Grimaldi, Turandot, Elisabeth de Valois, Tosca and Aida; Noted Concert Artist. *Address:* c/o Staatsoper, Opernring 2, A-1010 Vienna, Austria.

SCHRODER Jaap, b. 31 Dec. 1925, Amsterdam, Holland. Violinist. m. Agnes Jeanne François Lefèvre, 3 daughters. *Education:* Diploma, Amsterdam Conservatory; First Prize, Ecole Jacques Thibaud, Paris, 1948. *Debut:* Holland 1949. *Career:* Leader, Radio Chamber Orchestra, 1950-63; Member, Netherlands String Quartet 1952-69; Founder, chamber music ensembles Quadro Amsterdam, and Concerto Amsterdam, 1962, Quartetto Esterhazy 1973-1981; Smithson String Quartet, 1983; Professsor of violin, Yale School of Music. *Hobby:* French Literature. *Address:* Gerard Brandtstraat 18, Amsterdam, Holland.

SCHRÖDER-FEINEN Ursula, b. 21 July 1935, Gelsenkirchen, Germany. Singer (Soprano). *Education:* Studied with Maria Helm in Gelsenkirchen, then at the Folkwang School, Essen. *Career:* Gelsenkirchen 1961-68, debut as Aida and sang Gershwin's Bess, Handel's Cleopatra, Beethoven's Leonore and Verdi's Oscar; Deutsche Oper am Rhein, Dusseldorf, 1968-72; New York Metropolitan debut 1970, as Chrysothemis in Elektra; Bayreuth 1971-, as Senta, Ortrud, Kundry and Brünnhilde; Wagner's Ortrud and Strauss's Dyer's Wife at Salzburg; British debut at the 1975 Edinburgh Festival, as Salome; Other roles include Puccini's Tosca and Turandot, Wagner's Isolde, Janáček's Jenůfa, Gluck's Alceste and Strauss's Elektra. *Recordings include:* Roles in Korngold's Violanta and Marschner's Hans Heiling.

SCHRÖTER Gisela, b. 19 Aug 1933, Sardehnen, East Prussia, Germany. Singer (Mezzo-soprano). *Education:* Studied at the Berlin State Conservatory and with Rudolf Dittrich at the Studio of the Dresden Staatsoper. *Debut:* Dresden 1957, as a page in Lohengrin. *Career:* Sang at the Dresden Staatsoper until 1964 in the mezzo and dramatic soprano repertory, notably as the Dyer's Wife in Die Frau ohne Schatten; Bayreuth Festival 1959, as a Flowermaiden in Parsifal; Berlin Staatsoper from 1964, as Carmen, Octavian and the Composer in Ariadne; Guest appearances in Barcelona, Lausanne, Bratislava, Vienna, Hamburg, Prague, Budapest, United States and Soviet Union; Guested with the Staatsoper in North America as Sieglinde, Kundry, the Composer and Marie in Wozzeck; Sang Herodias (Salome) in Berlin 1987; Many concert appearances. *Recordings include:* Hansel and Gretel, Der Wildschütz (Telefunken); Wozzeck (Eterna); Schumann's Genoveva (HMV). *Address:* c/o Deutsche

Staatsoper, Unter den Linden 7, D-1086 Berlin, Germany.

SCHRYER Claude, b. 3 Dec 1959, Ottawa, ON, Canada. Composer; Producer. *Education:* Self Guided Education in the Field of Acoustic Ecology and Radio Art; Wilfrid Laurier University; McGill University. *Career:* Artistic Director, Inter Arts Program, Banff Centre for the Arts, 1988-90; Artistic Director, Printemps Electro acoustique of ACREQ, 1990- 92; Numerous Radio And Concert Performances Throughout North America and Europe. *Compositions:* Marche Sonore 1; A Kindred Spirit; Revisiting the World Soundscape Project. *Recordings:* Sound Letter; Electro Clips; Gems. *Contributions include:* Musicorks 55, Soundscape Newsletter, Contact!. *Honours:* 2nd Prize 16 th Bourges International Electroacoustic Music Composition. *Memberships:* Canadian Electroacoustic Community; Canadian League of Composers. *Hobby:* Acoustic Ecology. *Address:* 4001, Berri No 202, Montreal, Quebec H2L 4H2, Canada.

SCHUBACK Thomas, b. 1943, Sweden, Conductor; Pianist. *Education:* Studied at the Stockholm College of Music. *Career:* Conductor, Royal Opera Stockholm from 1971; Productions at the Drottningholm Theatre include L'Incoronazione di Poppea, L'Arbore di Diana by Martin y Soler, Vogler's Gustaf Adolf och Ebba Brahe and Gluck's Paride ed Elena; Musical Director of Lyric Opera of Queensland from 1982; Guest Appearances with San Diego Opera and at Sydney and Copenhagen; Season 1992-93 included Performances with the Drottningholm Theatre at the Barbican Centre, London; Concerts with Major Swedish Orchestras and elsewhere in Scandinavia, USA and Australia; Lieder Accompanist to Haken Hagegard, Barbara Bonney and others; Professor of Vocal Coaching at the State Oper School in Stockholm. *Recordings include:* Electra by Haeffner. *Address:* c/o Ulf Torngrist, Artists Management, St Eriksgatau 100, S-113 31 Stockholm, Sweden.

SCHULER Gerhard, b. 27 Oct. 1922, Vienna, Austria. Teacher; Recording Supervisor. m. Rita Kohlert, 5 Mar. 1954, 1 daughter. *Education:* German, University of Vienna, 1948-52; Academy of Music, Vienna 1948-52; Magister Artium, Music and German 1982. *Career:* Vienna Studio, Westminster Records, New York 1952-57; Vienna Studio, Vanguard Records, New York 1958-65; Polyhymnia Vienna Recording Studios 1966-70; Teacher of Piano, Member of Institut für Musikanalytik, Care and Control of Recording Studios, Vienna High School of Music 1971-87; Supervisor of more than 800 long playing records; Retired 1988 from business but still working in music recording section. *Contributions to:* Newspapers (articles on Teaching Music and/or Education). *Honour:* Title of Professor conferred by the President of Austria 1978. *Hobbies:* Music; Nature; Books; Trips; Technic (especially cars and railways). *Address:* Linke Wasserzeile 17, 1238 Vienna, Austria.

SCHULLER Gunther, b. 22 Nov. 1925, New York City, New York, USA. Composer, Conductor. m. Marjorie Black, 8 June 1948, 2 sons. *Education:* St Thomas Choir School, New York City; Manhattan School of Music; MusDD, Northeastern University, 1967; MusD, University of Illinois, 1968; Colby College, 1969; Williams College, 1974. *Career:* Appeared as boy soprano, St Thomas Choir, at age 12; Teacher, Manhattan School of Music, 1950-63; Head, Composition Department, Tanglewood, 1964-84; President, New England Conservatory of Music, 1967-77; Artistic Director: Berkshire Music Center, Tanglewood, 1969-84; Festival at Sandpoint, Idaho, 1985; Founder, President: Margun Music Inc, 1975; GM Records, 1980; French Hornist, Ballet Theater, then 1st Hornist, Cincinnati Symphony Orchestra, Principal Hornist, Metropolitan Opera Orchestra, 1945-59. *Compositions:* Concertos: Nos 1, 2 for Horn, 1945, 1976; Concertos 1, 2, 3 (Farbenspiel) for Orchestra, 1966, 1976, 1985; Violin, 1976; Contrabassoon, 1978; Trumpet, 1979; Concerto Quaternio, 1983; Other works: Quartet for Double Bass, 1947; Fantasy for

Unaccompanied Cello, 1951; Recitative and Rondo for Violin and Piano, 1953; Music for Violin, Piano and Percussion, 1957; Contours, 1958; Woodwind Quintet, 1958; 7 Studies on Themes of Paul Klee, 1959; 6 Renaissance Lyrics, 1962; String Quartets Nos 1, 2, 3, 1957, 1965, 1984; Symphony, 1965; 2 Operas: The Visitation, 1966; Fisherman and His Wife, 1970; Capriccio Stravagante, 1972; The Power Within Us, 1972; 3 Invenzioni, 1972; Three Nocturnes, 1973; 4 Soundscapes, 1974; Triplum I, 1967, Triplum II, 1975; Diptych, organ, 1976; Sonata Serenata, 1978; Deai, 3 orchestras, 1978; Octet, 1979; Eine Kleine Posaunenmusik, 1980; In Praise of Winds, symphony for large wind orchestra, 1981; Symphony for Organ, 1982; On Light Wings, piano quartet, 1984; Concerto for string quartet and orchestra, 1988; Flute Concerto, 1988; Chamber Symphony, 1989; Concerto for piano 3 hands and orchestra, 1990; Impromptus & Cadenzer, 1990, 2 violin contero, 1991, Concertos 1 & 2 for piano, 1962, 1981. *Recordings:* Mozart Frau Partita, K.361; Stravinsky Octet, Sacre du Printemps, Berg Chamber Concerto, (as conductor); Schuller Octet, Impromptus and Cadenzes, string quartet No. 3, Troplum I (Bernstein, NY Phil), 7 studies on Themes of Paul Klee (as conductor). *Publications include:* Early Jazz: Its Roots and Development, 1968; Musings: The Musical World of Gunther Schuller, 1985; The Swing Era: The Development of Jazz - 1930-1945, 1989. *Honours:* Branders Creative Arts Award, 1960; Guggenheim Grantee, 1962, 1963; Deems Taylor Award, ASCAP, 1970; Alice M.Ditson Conducting Award, 1970; Rodgers and Hammerstein Award, 1971; William Schuman Award, Columbia University, 1989; MacArthur Foundation Fellowship, 1991. *Memberships:* National Institute of Arts and Letters; American Academy of Arts and Sciences. *Current Management:* John Gingrich Management. *Address:* Margun Music Inc, 167 Dudley Road, Newton Centre, MA 02159, USA.

SCHULTE Eike Wilm, b. 13 Oct. 1939, Plettenberg, Germany. Singer (Baritone). *Education:* Studied at the Cologne Musikhochschule with Joseph Metternich and at the Salzburg Mozarteum. *Career:* Member of the Deutsche Oper am Rhein Dusseldorf 1956-69; Bielefeld Opera 1969-73; Hessisches Staatstheater Wiesbaden 1973-88; Sang the Herald in Lohengrin at Bayreuth, 1988, and toured Japan with the Bayreuth Festival company, 1989; Munich Staatsoper from 1989, as Faraone in Mosè by Rossini, the Father in Hansel and Gretel and Schtschelkalov in Boris Bodunov; Baritone role in staged performances of Carmina Burana, 1990; Performances of Beckmesser in Die Meistersinger at the Paris Opéra and in Munich; Guest engagements in Vienna, Hamburg, Cologne, Bonn, Trieste, Rome and Brussels, notably as Rossini's Figaro and as Rigoletto; Sang Kurwenal in Japan 1990, conducted by Peter Schneider; Mahler's 8th Symphony with the London Philharmonic, conducted by Klaus Tennstedt, 1991; Also engaged for 1991-92 season: Deutsche Oper am Rhein; Lohengrin, Taormina; Lohengrin, Vienna State Opera; Die Zauberflöte, Metropolitan Opera New York; Zemlinsky, VARA Holland; Der Rosenkvalier, Cologne Opera; Der Rosenkavalier, Hamburg Opera; Brahms Requiem, Hamburg Philharmonic; Father, Hamburg Opera (Hansel und Gretel); 1991 - Götterdämmerung, RAI Rome (Sinopoli), Carmina Burana, Bayerischer Rundfunk, (Colin Davis). *Recordings include:* Die Meistersinger conducted by Sawallisch (EMI); Video of Mahler's 8th Symphony. *Address:* c/o Haydn Rawstron Management, PO Box 654, London SE26 4DZ, England.

SCHULTE Rolf, b. 4 Oct 1949. Koln, Germany, Musician. m. Elizabeth M Karrick, 1973, Divorced, 1 d. *Education:* Humboldt Gymnasium, Koln; Robert Schumann Institute, Düsseldorf; Curtis Institute of Music, Philadelphia. *Debut:* Mendelssohn Concerto with Philharmonica Hungarica in Koln, 1964. *Career:* Appeared with Berlin & Münchner Philharmonics, Museumsorchester, Frankfurt, Staatskappelle Stuttgart; Radio Orchestra of the USSR; Orchestra Del Teatro La Venice, Seattle Symphony, The radio Orchestras of Berlin, Köln, Stuttgart; Twice at Berliner Festwochen in Recital. *Recordings include:* R Schumann Fantasiestucke; Romanzen; Märchenbilder; Stucke im

Volkston Centaur Records; Milton Babbitt Sextets, New World Records; Elliott Carter Duo; Riconoscenza, Bridge Records; Mario Davidovsky Synchronisms No 9 (Wergo Records). *Honours:* Top Prize 1968 Munchen ARD Competition; Förderungspreis des Landes NRW, 1974. *Hobby:* The Arts. *Address:* 128 W 72nd Street, New York, NY 10023, USA.

SCHULTZ Andrew, b. 1960, Adelaide, South Australia, 1960. Composer; University Lecturer. *Education:* Composition studies with Colin Brumby, BMus 1st Class Hons, Queensland University; Composition studies with George Crumb, Conducting with Richard Wernick, University of Pennsylvania, USA, 1983; Composition with David Lumsdaine, MMus, King's College, London, England; PhD, Queensland University. *Career:* Currently Associate Professor Faculty of Creative Arts, University of Wollongong, New South Wales; Compositions performed and broadcast widely, Australia, USA, Europe; Commissions, University of Melbourne, Perihelion, Seymour Group, Elision, Flederman, Queensland Theatre Orchestra, 4MBS-FM, Duo Contemporain, Musica Nova; Discography includes: Garotte, 1981, on Tropic of Capricorn, Qld Symphony Orchestra, 02M 1002 (CD Cassette); Barron Grounds on Tapestry, Perihelion, Lion 192 (CD); Ekstasis on Avstraian Vocal Music, Vox Astralis, 1992 (CD). *Compositions include:* Spherics, flute, trombone (or bass clarinet), 1 percussion, synthesizer, cello, 1985; Stick Dance, clarinet, marimba, piano, 1987; Sea-Change, piano, 1987; Black River, opera, 1988; Barren Grounds, clarinet, viola, cello, piano, 1988; Mephisto, flute clarinet, violin, viola, double bass, guitar, 1990; Orchestral, choral and vocal works; Ekstasis, 1990, 6 solo voices; Calling Music, 1991, chamber orchestra; The Devil's Music, 1992, large orchestra. *Honours include:* Composer Fellowship, Australia Council Music Board, 1982; Fulbright/Music Board Grant, 1983; Commonwealth Scholarship and Fellowship Plan Award for study at King's College; 2 Composer Fellowships to Young Composer Summer Schools; Australian National Composers Opera Award; Dalley-Scarlett Award; Queensland University Medal; Commonwealth Postgraduate Research Award; Albert H Maggs Composition Award; Hilda Margaret Watts Prize, Kings College, London; Composer Fellowship, Australia Council, 1990; Commissions from The Hunter Orchestra and the Sydney Symphony Orchestra. *Address:* Faculty of Creative Arts, University of Wollongong, Northfields Avenue, Wollongong, New South Wales 2522, Australia.

SCHULZ Gerhard, b. 23 Sept 1951, Austria. Violinist. *Education:* Studied in Vienna, Dusseldorf and USA. Career: 2nd violin of the Alban Berg Quartet from 1978; Many concert engagements, including complete cycles of the Beethoven Quartets in 15 European cities 1987-88, 1988-89 seasons; Bartók/Mozart cycle in London, Vienna, Paris, Frankfurt, Munich, Geneva and Turin 1990-91; Annual concert series at the Vienna Konzerthaus and festival engagements worldwide; Associate Artist at the South Bank Centre, London; US appearances in Washington DC, San Francisco, New York (Carnegie Hall). *Recordings include:* Complete quartets of Beethoven, Brahms, Berg, Webern and Bartók; Late quartets of Mozart, Schubert, Haydn and Dvořák; Ravel and Debussy quartets; Live recordings from Carnegie Hall (Mozart, Schumann); Konzerthaus in Vienna (Brahms); Opéra- Comique Paris (Brahms). *Honours include:* Grand Prix du Disque; Deutsche Schallplatenpreis; Edison Prize; Japan Grand Prix; Gramophone Magazine Award. *Address:* Intermusica Artists' Management, 16 Duncan Terrace, London N1 8BZ, England.

SCHULZ Walther, b. 1940, Vienna, Austria. Cellist. *Education:* Studied in Vienna. *Career:* Performances of Haydn and Other Composers in Vienna and Elsewhere from 1968; Co Founder of the Haydn Trio of Vienna, 1968 and has Performed in Brussels, Munich, Berlin, Zurich, London, Paris and Rome; New York Debut 1979 and has made frequent North American appearances with Concerts in 25 States; Debut Tour of Japan 1984, with Further Travels to the Near East, Russia, Africa, Central and South America; Series at the Vienna Konzerthaus Society from 1976 with Performances of more that 100 Works; Summer Festivals at Vienna, Salzburg, Aix en Provence, Flanders and Montreux; Master Classes at the Royal College and Royal Academy in London, Stockholm, Bloomington, Toyko and the Salzburg Mozarteum. *Recordings include:* Complete Piano Trios of Beethoven and Schubert, Mendelssohn D Minor, Brahms B major, Tchaikovsky A Minor, Schbert Trout Quintet; Albums of Works by Haydn, Schumann, Dvořák, Smetana. *Address:* c/o Sue Lubbock Concert Management, 25 Courthorpe Road, London NW3 2LE, England.

SCHULZE-KURZ Ekkehard Burkhard, b. 4 Mar 1957, Brandenburg, Germany. Music Teacher. m. Renate Kurz, 22 Oct 1988. *Education:* Gymnasium Esslinger; Universitat Tubingen; PhD, 1989, Jugendmusihschule Esslingen; Private Education with Rolf Hempel. *Career:* Teacher at a Secondary School, 1976-79; Music Teacher, Private School, 1980-; Member of the Ensemble for Old Music, (Les Bouffons) from 1988. *Publications:* Die Laute and Ihre Stimmnager in der Ersten Halfte des 17 Juhrhunderts. *Memberships:* Lute Society of England; Lute Society of USA. *Hobbies:* Making Musical Instruments; Hiking. *Address:* Kirchstr 51, 70771 Leinfelden, Germany.

SCHUMAN Patricia, b. 4 Feb 1954, Los Angeles, USA. Singer (Soprano). *Education:* Studied at Santa Cruz University, California. *Career:* Sang minor roles with San Francisco Opera then appeared with the Houston Opera and in a touring company; Engagements at the New York City Opera, the Paris Opéra, Teatro La Fenice Venice and in Washington DC; Sang on tour with Peter Brook's version of Carmen; Théâtre de la Monnaie Brussels from 1983 as Dorabella, Zerlina, and as Angelina in La Cenerentola; St Louis 1986 in the US premiere of Il Viaggio a Reims by Rossini; Théâtre du Châtelet, Paris 1989, in the title role of L'Incoronazione di Poppea; Miami Opera and Long Beach Opera 1989, as Antonia in Les Contes d'Hoffmann and as Mozart's Countess; Seattle Opera 1990, as Blanche in Les Dialogues des Carmélites; Has also sung at the Vienna Staatsoper and in the concert hall; Metropolitan Opera debut, Donna Elvira, 1990; Covent Garden debut 1992, as Donna Elvira. *Recordings include:* Roggiero in Rossini's Tancredi (CBS); Messiah, Handel (Europa). *Address:* c/o Long Beach Opera, 6372 Pacific Coast Highway, Long Beach, CA 90801, USA.

SCHUNCKE Gottfried Michael, b. 8 May 1929, Dresden, Germany. Teacher; Consultant; Author. m. Dorothea Czibulinski-Dressler, 22 Dec. 1956. 2 daughters. *Education:* 4 years Theory of music/fugue/harmony with Professor Otto Schaefer, Baden-Baden. *Career:* Author; Teacher, 1966-1991; Writing consultant; Founder and Organizator, with spouse, of the series, Kleine Lichtentaler Kirchenkonzerte with young talents and professional musicians, since 1989; Founder of the private Schuncke-Archiv (more than 3,000 numbers of programs, music notes, letters, documents of family and friends) since beginning 19th Century till now, for musicologist's researching. *Compositions:* Creative Works: A New Article with unknown facts: Rachmaninoff in Dresden, with Keith Fagan, in New Letter, 1992, News Letter of The Rachmaninoff Society. *Publications:* Author: Sprecht die Sprache der Adressaten, 1982; Schlusselworte erfolgreicher Anzeigen, 1986; Praktische Werbehilfe fur den fortschrittlichen Handwerker, 1987; Catalog for the exhibition, Ludwig Schuncke und die Musikerfamilie Schuncke, 1984; Concept and edition of exhibition with Dr Joachim Draheim. *Contributions to:* Many articles in professional journals and magazines for example Finding a hand-drawing of F. Mendelssohn Bartholdy (Lyser), Publications 1957-58; Sammelbände I & II Robert-Schumann-Gesellschaft 1961 & 1966. *Memberships:* Robert-Schumann-Gesellschaft; Mendelssohn-Gesellschaft. *Hobbies:* History of musicians; Organ; Research the literature work of the

musical poet Dr Ludwig Finckh. *Address:* Heschmattweg 11, D-7570 Baden-Baden, Germany.

SCHUNEMAN Robert A., b. 22 Feb. 1934, Pittsburgh, Pennsylvania, USA. Music Publisher. m. Cynthia Ferguson, 1965, 1 son, 1 daughter. *Education:* Student, State Conservatory of Music & University, Freiburg, West Germany; MusB, Valparaiso University, USA, 1956; MA, Musicology, Stanford University, 1958. *Career:* Teacher: Westminster Choir College 1976-77, New England Conservatory of Music 1976-79; Editor, The Diapason magazine, 1970-76; Editor 1976-85, President & Principal owner 1985-, E. C. Schirmer Music Company, Boston. *Publications include:* Numerous reviews & articles in: Diapason; Music (AGO/RCCO magazine). *Honour:* Study grant, research in 19th century organology, West German Government, 1969-70. *Memberships:* Executive Board, Music Publishers Association; American Guild of Organists; American Musicological Society; Music Educators National Conference; College Music Society; Organ Historical Society. *Hobbies:* Player/Member, Newton (Massachusetts) United Soccer Club; Coach, Newton Youth Hockey. *Address:* E. C. Schirmer Music Company Inc, 138 Ipswich Street, Boston, MA 02215, USA.

SCHUNK Robert, b. 1948, Neu-Isenburg, Frankfurt, Germany. Singer (Tenor). *Education:* Studied with Martin Grundler at the Frankfurt Musikhochschule. *Career:* Sang at Karlsruhe 1973-75; Bonn Opera 1975-77; Dortmund 1977-79; Bayreuth Festival from 1977, as Siegmund, Erik and Melot; Hamburg Staatsoper 1981, as the Emperor in Die Frau ohne Schatten; Bregenz Festival 1983, Max in Der Freischütz; Engagements in Munich, Vienna, Frankfurt, London, Cologne and Berlin; Tour of Japan with the Hamburg Staatsoper 1984; Sang Florestan at the Met and Naples, 1986-87; Siegmund in New York and Munich, 1987, 1989; Emperor in Die Frau ohne Schatten and Vladimir in Prince Igor at Munich, 1989; Sang Wagner's Erik at Naples, 1992. *Recordings include:* Erik in Der fliegende Holländer, from Bayreuth (Philips). *Address:* Ingpen & Williams Ltd., 14 Kensington Court, London W8 5DN, England.

SCHURMANN Gerard, b. 19 Jan. 1924, Kertosono, Java, former Dutch East Indies. Composer; Conductor. m. Carolyn Nott, 26 May 1973, 1 daughter. *Education:* Studied Composition with Alan Rawsthorne; Piano with Kathleen Long; Conducting with Franco Ferrara. *Career:* Aircrew, 320 Squadron, RAF 1941-45; Acting Netherlands Cultural Attaché, London 1945-47; Resident Orchestral Conductor, Dutch Radio Hilversum 1947-49; Freelance Composer/Conductor 1949-; Guest Conductor: France, Italy, Spain, Switzerland, Czechoslovakia, Germany, Holland, Scandinavian Countries, Ireland, USA. *Compositions:* Orchestral: Six Studies of Francis Bacon 1968; Variants 1970; Attack and Celebration 1971; Piano Concerto 1972-73; Violin Concerto 1975-78; Chamber and Instrumental: Bagatelles 1945; Fantasia (previously entitled Dialogue) 1967; Sonatina 1968; Serenade 1971; Contrasts 1973; Leotaurus 1975; Wind Quintet for flute, oboe, clarinet, horn and bassoon 1976; Two Ballades for piano (1) Hukvaldy (2) Brno, 1981; Duo for violin and piano 1984; Quartet for Piano and Strings (Violin, Viola, Cello, Piano) 1986; Vocal and Choral Chuench'i, for high voice and piano 1966; Chuench'i for high voice and orchestra 1967; Summer Is Coming, madrigal for SATB unaccompanied 1970; The Double Heart, cantata for SATB unaccompanied 1976; Piers Plowman, opera-cantata in 2 acts 1979-80, Nine Slovak folk songs for high voice and piano or orchestra, 1988; The Garden of Exile, Concerto for cello and orchestra, 1989-90. *Recordings:* Six Studies of Francis Bacon, Variants, Chuench'i, The Double Heart, Claretta, Piers Plowman, Piano Concerto, Violin Concerto, Duo for Violin and Piano; Attack and Celebration; The Film Music of Gerard Schurmann. *Contributions to:* Introductory Essay to 3 Volumes' work on Alan Rawsthorne, published 1984. *Memberships:* PRS; ASCAP; MCPS; APC; Composers' Guild of Great Britain; Phyllis Court Club. *Current Management:* Helen Sykes Management. *Address:*

3700 Multiview Drive, Hollywood Hills, Los Angeles, CA 90068, USA.

SCHWAGER Myron August, b. 16 Mar. 1937, Pittsfield, Massachusetts, USA. Professor of Music History and Literature. m. (1) Katharine Lake, Sept. 1961, 1 son, 1 daughter, (2) Laurie Beth Lewis, June 1982. *Education:* Massachusetts Institute of Technology, 1955-56; BMus, Boston University, 1958; MMus, New England Conservatory of Music, 1961; MA, PhD, Harvard University, 1970. *Career:* Former Faculty Member, Holy Cross College; Worcester Community School of the Performing Arts; Jesuit Artists Institute, Italy; Chair, Department of Music, Hartt School of Music, University of Hartford, Connecticut, 1974-; Former Principal Cellist, Springfield Symphony Orchestra; Appearances with Cambridge Society for Early Music, Boston Chamber Players, Consortium Musicale, Hawthorne Trio, Hartford Chamber Orchestra, and Karas String Quartet; Revived and reconstructed Francesco Cavalli's La Virtu de' strali d'Amore (Venice, 1642), at the Wadsworth Atheneum, Hartford, 31 July-1 Aug. 1987. *Contributions to:* The Creative World of Beethoven, 1971; Current Musicology; Music and Letters; Early Music; Musical Quarterly; Studi Musicali; The American Music Teacher; Clavier; Boston Sunday Herald. *Honour:* Vincent Coffin Grant, 1987. *Memberships:* American Musicological Society; American Federation of Musicians. *Address:* 30 Hoskins Road, Bloomfield, CT 06002, USA.

SCHWANBECK Bodo, b. 20 July 1935, Schwerin, Germany. Singer (Bass-Baritone). *Education:* Studied with Franz-Theo Reuter in Munich and with KH Jarius in Stuttgart. *Debut:* Detmold 1959, as Varlaam in Boris Godunov. *Career:* Has sung in Frankfurt, Hamburg, Munich, Manheim, Dusseldorf, and Lisbon and at the New York City Opera; Zurich Opera 1967, in the premiere of Madame Bovary by Sutermeister; French TV as Mustafà in L'Italiana in Algeri; Théâtre de la Monnaie Brussels 1986; Sang at Madrid 1988, in Lulu; Brussels 1990, in From the House of the Dead; Covent Garden 1990, as Waldner in Arabella; Sang Antonio in Figaro with the Royal Opera on tour to Japan, 1992. Other roles include Baron Ochs, Osmin, Alfonso, Pizarro, Leporello, Mephistopheles, Nicolai's Falstaff, Don Pasquale, Dulcamara, Golaud, Don Magnifico and Wozzeck; Frequent concert appearances. *Address:*c/o Théâtre Royal de le Monnaie, 4 Léopoldstrasse, B-1000 Brussels, Belgium.

SCHWANN William, b. 13 May 1913, Salem, Illinois, USA. Musician. m. Aire-Maija Kutvonen, 1 June 1959. *Education:* AB, University of Louisville School of Music, 1935; Graduate studies, Boston University School of Music, 1935-36; Graduate School, Harvard Music Department, 1937-39; Organ performance with E Power Biggs, 1936-38. *Career:* Organist, Choir Director, Louisville churches, Kentucky, 1930-35; Organ concerts and broadcasts, 1930-42; Organ and Piano Teacher, Organist and Choir Director, Boston area, Massachusetts, 1935-50; Owner, The Record Shop, Cambridge, 1939-53; Compiler, Publisher, 1st Long Playing Record Catalogue (now Schwann Record and Tape Guide), 1949; Compiler, Publisher, Artists Listing LP Catalogs; Schwann Children's LP Record Catalog; Basic Record Library, Basic Jazz Record Library, 1953-; Compiler, Publisher, White House Record Library Catalogs, 1973, 1980; President, Treasurer, W Schwann Incorporated, 1949-77; President, Publisher, ABC Schwann Publications, 1976-. *Honours:* Honorary DMus, University of Louisville 1969, New England Conservatory 1982; Distinguished Alumni Award, University of Louisville 1980, Distinguished Services Citation, Music Library Association, 1983; George Peabody Medal, Peabody Conservatory of Music of the Johns Hopkins University, 1984; Honorary Commission, Kentucky Colonel, Governor Collins, Commonwealth of Kentucky, 1984; Honorary Gold Record for 35 years of service to the Music Industry and the public, Recording Industry Association of America, 1984; Distinguished Alumnus Silver Medal, Boston University, 1985.

Address: 26 Old Winter Street, Lincoln, MA 01773, USA.

SCHWARTNER Dieter, b. 6 Feb 1938, Plauen, Germany. Singer (Tenor). *Education:* Studied in Dresden. *Debut:* Plauen 1969 as the Baron in Der Wildschutz. *Career:* Sang at Plauen until 1972; Dresden, 1972-78; Dessau, 1978-79; Member of the Leipzig Opera from 1979 (Ligeti's Le Grand Macabre and the Duke of Parma in Busoni's Doktor Faust, 1991); Guest appearances in Dresden and at the Berlin Staatsoper; Other Roles have included Tamino, Faust, Max, Lionel in Martha, Florestan, Don Jose, Alvaro in La Forza del Destino and Walther Von Stolzing; Many Concert Engagements. *Address:* c/o Stadtische Theatre, 7010 Leipzig, Germany.

SCHWARTZ Elliott S, b. 19 Jan 1936, Brooklyn, NY, USA. Composer; Author; Professor. m. Dorothy Feldman, 26 June 1960, 1 s, 1 d. Education: Studied at Columbia University, New York; Bennington Composers Conference. *Career:* Professor of Music and Deptarment Chair, Bowdoin College, Brunswick, Maine, 1964-; Professor of Compositions, Ohio State University, 1985-88, 1988-; Visiting Appointments at Trinity College of Music, London, 1967-; University of california, 1973-; University of California, San Diego, 1978-79; Robinson College, Cambridge (UK), 1993-94. *Compositions:* Over 100 Compositions Published. *Recordings:* Grand Concerto; Extended Piano; Mirrors; Texture for Chamber Orchestras; Concert Piece for Ten Players; Chamber Concerto; Cycles and Gongs; Extended Clarinet; Dream Music with Variations. *Publications:* The Symphonies of Ralph Vaughan Williams; Contemporay Composers in Contemporary Music; Electronic Music, A Listeners Guide; Music Ways of Listening, Music since 1945. *Hobbies:* Travel; baseball; Basketball; Theatre; Cooking. *Address:* PO Box 451, South Freeport, ME 04078, USA.

SCHWARTZ Sergiu, b. 1963, Israel. Concert Violinist. *Education:* Studied with Ramy Shevelov, Rubin Academy, Tel-Aviv and with Sandor Vegh and Felix Galimir; Further study at the Juilliard School with Dorothy DeLay. *Debut:* London debut at the Wigmore Hall in the Outstanding Israeli Artists series; North American debut at the Museum of Fine Arts, Montreal. *Career:* Played with the Chicago Symphony at the Grant Park Festival, followed by appearances with leading orchestras in Germany, England, France, Italy and elsewhere in the United States; Carnegie Recital Hall debut 1982 and appearances at Lincoln Center, New York Town Hall and 92nd Street Y concerts; Kennedy Center and Library of Congress, Washington; Royce Hall and Ambassador Auditorium Los Angeles; Elizabeth Hall and Barbican Hall with the London Symphony; Broadcast recitals in Jerusalem, New York, Washington, Los Angeles, Boston, Chicago and London (premiere of the Concerto by Samuel Coleridge-Taylor). *Recordings include:* Works by Sibelius, Svendsen and Grieg with the London Symphony Orchestra. *Honours:* Scholarships from the America-Israel Cultural Fund and the Juilliard School; Winner, Arts International Competition, New York, 1982. *Address:* c/o Norman McCann International Artists Ltd, The Coach House, 56 Lawrie Park Gardens, London SE26 6XJ, England.

SCHWARZ Gerard (Ralph), b. 19 Aug. 1947, Weehawken, New Jersey, USA. Conductor. m. Jody Greitzer, 23 June 1984. 2 sons, 2 daughters. *Education:* Trumpet lessons, age 8; Summers 1958-60, National Music Camp, Interlochen, Michigan; Studied trumpet with William Vacchiano, 1962-68; BS, Juilliard School, 1972. *Career:* Trumpeter, American Brass Quintet, 1965-73; American Symphony Orchestra, NY, 1966-72; Co-principal Trumpet, New York Philharmonic Orchestra, 1972-75; Music Director 1975-85, Principal Conductor 1986-, Waterloo Festival, Stanhope, NJ; Honorary Doctorate, Fairleigh Dickinson University Music School, 1975-; Seattle, University of Puget Sound; Music Director, New York Chamber Symphony, New York, 1977-; Los Angeles Chamber Orchestra, 1978-86; Music Adviser 1982-84, Music Director 1984-

, Mostly Mozart Festival, NY; Music Adviser 1983-85; Principal Conductor 1985-86, Music Director 1986-, Seattle Symphony; Conducted Fidelio at Seattle, 1991. *Recordings:* For Angel-EMI; CBS; Composers Recordings Inc; Delos; Folkways; Laurel; Nonesuch, including Hanson's symphonies Nos. 1 and 2 (Seattle symphony); Clarinet Concertos by Weber, Spohr and Crusell (Emma Johnson, English Chamber Orchestra); Bach B minor Suite and Brandenburg Concertos; Schoenberg Op. 16 and Op. 9; Janáček's Mládi and Idyll; Mozart Symphonies K550, K551 (Los Angeles Chamber Orchestra). *Address:* c/o Seattle Symphony, 305 Harrison Street, Seattle, WA 98109, USA.

SCHWARZ Hanna, b. 15 Aug. 1943, Hamburg, Germany. Singer (Mezzo- Soprano). *Education:* Studied in Hamburg, Hanover and Essen. *Debut:* Hanover 1970, as Maddalena in Rigoletto. *Career:* Eutin 1972, as Carmen; Member of the Hamburg Staatsoper from 1973; Guest appearances in Zurich (1975-), San Francisco (1977-), Vienna, Paris (Preziosilla 1977), Deutsche Oper Berlin (Cherubino 1978); Munich Staatsoper 1974, 1980, 1984; Bayreuth Festival 1976-85, as Fricka and Erda; Sang in he first complete performance of Berg's Lulu, Paris Opéra 1979; Hollland Festival 1985, as Brangaene in Tristan und Isolde; Paris 1987, as Cornelia in Giulio Cesare; Sang Fricka in Das Rheingold at Bonn and Cologne, 1990; Season 1992 as Orpheus and Fricka at Bonn. *Recordings include:* Die Zauberflöte, The Queen of Spades, Lulu, Mahler's Rückert Lieder, Apollo et Hyacinthus by Mozart, Die Lustige Witwe (Deutsche Grammophon); Les Contes d' Hoffmann, Humperdinck's Königskinder, Die Heimkehr aus der Fremde by Mendelssohn (EMI); Rhinedaughter in The Ring (Eurodisc); Fricka in the Bayreuth Ring (Philips); Martha in Schubert's Oratorio Lazarus; Mother in Hänsel und Gretel (EMI). *Address:* c/o Oper der Stadt Köln, Offenbachplatz, D-5000, Cologne, Germany.

SCHWARZENBERG Elisabeth, b. 23 Sept. 1933, Vienna, Austria. Singer (Soprano). m. Georg Schnapka. *Education:* Studied in Vienna. *Debut:* Deutsche Oper am Rhein Dusseldorf 1956, as Eva in Die Meistersinger. *Career:* Sang in Munich, Paris, Brussels, Nice, Turin, Dublin, Geneva and Zurich; Many appearances at the Vienna Volksoper; Dusseldorf 1957, in the premiere of Die Räuber by Klebe; Salzburg Festival 1961, in the premiere of Das Bergwerk zu Falun by Wagner-Régeny; Bayreuth 1962-72; Teatro San Carlos Lisbon 1967; Other roles included the Marschallin and Donna Elvira. *Address:* c/o Volksoper, Währingerstrasse 78, A-1090 Vienna, Austria.

SCHWARZKOPF Elisabeth (Dame), b. 9 Dec. 1915, Jarotschin, Poland. Singer (Soprano). m. Walter Legge 1953 (deceased 1979). *Education:* Studied at the Berlin Hochschule für Musik 1934; later with Maria Ivogün. *Debut:* Berlin Städtische Oper 1938 as a Flowermaiden in Parsifal; recital debut Berlin 1942; joined the Vienna Staatsoper 1944 and visited Covent Garden 1947: until 1959 sang Mozart's Pamina and Susanna, Wagner's Eva, Puccini's Mimi and Butterfly, Strauss's Sophie and Marschallin and Massenet's Manon in London; Salzburg Festival 1947-64, debut as Mozart's Susanna; Created Ann Trulove in The Rake's Progress at Venice in 1951 and sang in the premiere of Orff's Trionfi at La Scala Milan 1953; US debut San Francisco 1955, as Marenka in The Bartered Bride; appeared in operas by Mozart at the Chicago Lyric Opera in 1959; Metropolitan Opera debut 1964, as the Marschallin; other opera roles included Debussy's Mélisande, Mozart's Donna Elvira and Fiordiligi, Wagner's Elisabeth and Elsa, Gounod's Marguerite and Verdi's Gilda; concert repertoire included Bach's Passions, oratorios by Handel and Haydn, the Requiems of Verdi and Brahms, Tippett's A Child of our Time and the Four Last Songs of Strauss; she was particularly noted as a singer of Lieder; retired from opera 1972 and from concerts in 1975; gave master classes in Europe and America. *Recordings:* Many operatic roles on Columbia; also recorded for Telefunken, Electrola, Olympic, Urania and Cetra including Don Giovanni; Figaro, Così fan Tutte, Rosenkavalier, Capriccio, Falstaff, Turandot (as Liù); Die

Meistersinger (Bayreuth 1951), St Matthew Passion (Klemperer); Les Contes d'Hoffmann (as Giulietta); Die Zauberflöte (First Lady); Die Fledermaus; Lieder recitals for EMI under the direction of Walter Legge. *Honours include:* Cambridge MUsD, National Socialist Party 1940, No 7548960; Grosses Verdienst-Kreuz der Bundesrepublik Deutschland; DBE, 1992.

SCHWEEN Astrid, b. 1960, NY, USA. Cellist. *Education:* Studied at the Juilliard School. *Career:* Soloist with the New York Philharmonic; Co Founder of the Lark String Quartet; Recent Concert Tours to Australia, Taiwan, Hong Kong, China, Germany and Holland; US appearances at the Lincoln Center New York, Kennedy Center Washington and in Boston, Los Angeles, Philadelphia, St Louis and San Francisco; Repertoire includes Quartets by Haydn, Mozart, Beethoven, Schubert, Dvořák, Brahms, Borodin, Bartók, Debussy and Shostakovich. *Honours include:* Gold Medals at the 1990 Naumberg, 1991 Shostakovich Competitions; Prizewinner at the 1991 London International String Quartet; 1191 Melbourne Chamber Music; 1990 Premio Paulio Borciani; 1990 Karl Klinger Competitions. *Address:* c/o Sonata (Lark Quartet), 11 Northpark Street, Glasgow G20 7AA, Scotland.

SCHWEIKART Dieter, b. 9 Jan. 1942, Iserlohn, Germany. Singer (Bass). *Education:* Studied in Wuppertal with Becker-Brill and with Thomas Lo Monaco in Rome. *Career:* Sang in Saarbrucken from 1964; Appearances at Dusseldorf, Krefeld and Bonn; Hanover from 1976; Has sung in Dortmund, Hamburg, Frankfurt, Helsinki, Florence, Copenhagen and Cologne; Bayreuth Festival 1983-86, as Hans Foltz in Die Meistersinger and as Fafner in Der Ring des Nibelungen; Sang Daland in Der fliegende Holländer at Naples, 1992. *Address:* c/o PO Box 100262, Bayreuther Festspiele, 8580 Bayreuth, Germany.

SCHWEIZER Alfred, b. 4 Nov 1941, Seveln, Switzerland. Composer. *Education:* University of Berne; Berne Conservatory; Music Academy of Basle; Swiss Centre for Computer Music. *Career:* Professor, Winterthur Conservatory, 1970-71; Professor, 1971-; Acting Director, 1979-80, Biel Conservatory; Manager, Classic 200, Concerts & CD's, 1982-. *Compositions include:* 3 Pieces for Orchestra; Canon for opera orchestra; Concertino Swiss Folk Instruments and Small Orchestra; Music for Piano No. 1 and No. 2; Music for Violin and Harpsichord; Music for Flute and Keyboard; Cosmos Nos. 1, 2 and 3 for instruments and computer; Music for Guitars. *Recordings:* Orchestral Pieces Nos. 1, 2, 3; Woodwind Quintet; Piano Concerto; Mantra Avec Violin Fou; Aton Quartet. *Honours:* 2nd Prize International Composers Competition; Recognition Prize Pro Arte Foundation Berne. *Memberships:* Schweizerischer Tonkunstlerverein; Schweizerischer Musikpadagogische Verband. *Address:* PO Box 17, CH-2513 Twann, Switzerland.

SCHWEIZER Daniel, b. 6 Nov 1953, Herisau, Switzerland. Conductor. m. Michiko Tsuda, 4 Oct 1980, 2 sons. *Education:* Zurich Konservatorium 1972-76; Cello, Musikhochschule Essen, 1976-77; Conducting, Musikhochschule Freiburg, 1979-81. *Debut:* With Zurich Symphony Orchestra, 23 Nov 1981. *Career:* Founder, Zurich Symphony Orchestra, 1981; Concerts at festivals in Spain and Estoril, Portugal; Guest conductor, Germany, Czechoslovakia, Italy, France, Austria, Singapore, Korea. *Recordings:* Grammont: Alfred Keller, Ossia; Classic 2000: Alfred Schweizer, orchestral works; Jecklin: Paul Muller, orchestral works; Jacklin: Paul Müller, orchestral works; Motette: Marcel Dupré, Symphony G. minor op.25; Classic 2000: Alfred Schweizer, orchestral works. *Contributions to:* Neue Zürcher Zeitung. *Membership:* Schweizerischer Tonkünstlerverein. *Hobbies:* Soccer; Hiking. *Current Management:* François Courvoisier, Bureau de Concerts, Chemin des Roses 6, CH-1202 Geneva, Switzerland. *Address:* Buecheneggstrasse 31, CH-8906, Bonstetten, Switzerland.

SCHWEIZER Verena, b. 9 May 1944, Solothurn, Switzerland. Singer (Soprano). *Education:* Studied at the Zurich Conservatory, in Frankfurt, Basle with Elsa Cavelti, in Aachen and Freiburg and in Mannheim with Anna Reynolds. *Career:* Sang at Aargau 1971-72, Mainz 1973-75, Dortmund 1975-83; Sang at Freiburg from 1985 and guested at Stuttgart (1986 as Jenůfa, 1990 as Marenka in The Bartered Bride); Ludwigsburg 1984-89, as Fiodriligi and Mozart's Countess; Further appearances in Leeds (with the Dortmund Opera), Geneva, Cologne, Dusseldorf and Wiesbaden; Other roles include Susanna, Zerlina, Marcelline, Adina, Gilda, Micaela, Nannetta, Mimi, Sophie in Der Rosenkavalier, Ann Trulove and Desdemona; Concert engagements in Paris, Rome, Buenos Aires and Copenhagen; St Gallen 1983, in the premiere of P Huber's Te Deum. *Recordings include:* Christmas Oratorio by Saint-Saëns; Magnificat and other sacred music by Vivaldi (Erato); Così fan Tutte (Harmonia Mundi); Hindemith's Cardillac (Wergo). *Address:* c/o Staatstheater Stuttgart, Oberer Schlossgarten 6, D-7000 Stuttgart, Germany.

SCHWERTSIK Kurt, b. 25 June 1935, Vienna, Austria. Composer; Orchestra Musician (French Horn). m. Christa, 2 children. *Education:* Academy of Music, Vienna, Reifeprufung. *Career:* Member, Nieder Osterreichesches Tonkunstler Orchester, 1955-59, 1962-68; Member, Wiener Symphoniker, 1968-; Founder with Friedrich Cerha, The Ensemble for Modern Music Die Reihe, 1959; Professor of Compositions at the Wiener Hochschule für Musik and Drammatische Kunst, 1989. *Compositions include:* Sonatine für Horn and Klavier, 1952-72; Trio for Violin, Horn and Piano, 1960; 5 Nocturnes for Piano, 1964; Blattause Schnecken Ohrenkreiser; Draculas Haus & Hofmusik, eine trassylvanische symphonie für Streicher, 1968; Musik vom Mutterland MU, fur 11 instruments, 1971; Entwurf for String Quartet, 1974; Der Lange Weg zur grossen Mauer, 1975; Macbeth for piano duo and percussion 1988; Concerto for tom-tom and orchestra 1988; Double bass Concerto 1989. *Recordings:* Kurt Schwertsik's Lichte Momente, Op. 21, BASF; Sterreichische Musik Der Gegenwart Kurt Schwertsik Classic Amadeo. *Membership:* Internationale Gesellschaft fur Neue Musik. *Hobbies:* English and American Science Fiction Books; Arts and Architecture. *Current Management:* Boosey and Hawkes, London. *Address:* Hockegasse 9, A-1180 Vienna, Austria.

SCIAMA Pierre, b. 1960, England. Singer (Countertenor). *Education:* Studied, Guildhall School with David Pollard and David Roblou, and at the GSM Early Music Course. *Career:* Sang Reason in Cavalieri's La Rappresentazione di Anima e di Corpo, Morley College, 1987; Purcell's Fairy Queen at the GSM conducted by William Christie; Sang in Rameau's Pygmalion at the Elizabeth Hall and in Gluck's Alceste at Covent Garden and in Monte Carlo; Acis and Galatea with Midsummer Opera in Tours and St John's Smith Square, London, 1989; Appeared in Dido and Aeneas with the Early English Opera Society and Apollo in Grabu's Albion and Albanus; Armindo in Handel's Partenope with Midsummer Opera. *Address:* c/o Norman McCann International Artists Ltd, The Coach House, 56 Lawrie Park Gardens, London SE26 6XJ, England.

SCIARRINO Salvatore, b. 4 Apr 1947, Palermo, Italy. Composer. *Education:* Studied with Tulio Belfiore, 1964 and attended electronic music sessions at the Accademia di Santa Cecilia in Rome, 1969. *Career:* Artistic Director of Teatro Comunale in Bologna; Teacher in Milan, Florence, and Citta del Castello; Milan Conservatory from 1974. *Creative works:* include: Instrumental pieces; Berceuse for orchestra 1967; Quartetto 1967; Da un divertimento 1970; Sonata du camera 1971; Arabesque for 2 organs 1971; Rondo for flute and orchestra 1972; Romanza for viola d'amore and orchestra 1973; Variazioni for cello and orchestra 1974; 2 Piano Trios, 1974, 1986; 2 Quintetes, 1976, 1977; Clair de Lune for piano and orchestra 1976; Kindertotenlied for soptano,, tenor and chamber orchestra 1978; Flos Forum for chorus and orchestra 1981; Nox apud Orpheum for 2 organs and instruments 1982; String Trio 1983; 3 Piano Sonatas 1976, 1983, 1986; Violin Concerto, Allegoria nella notte 1985; Morte di Borromini for narrator and orchestra 1989; Stage works: Amore e Psiche, Milan, 1973; Aspern, Florence, 1978; Lohengrin, 'azione invisible', Milan 1983; Perseo e Andromeda, Stuttgart 1991. *Address:* c/o Staatstheater Stuttgart, Oberer Schlossgarten 6, 7000 Stuttgart, Germany.

SCIMONE Claudio, b. 23 Dec. 1934, Padua, Italy. Conductor; Musicologist. *Career:* Studied with Franco Ferrara, Dmitri Mitropoulos and Carlo Zecchi. *Career:* Founded the chamber ensemble I Solisti Veneti 1959; performances of 18th and 19th century Italian music, Mozart, Schoenberg and modern works (Donatoni, Bussotti, Malipiero and others); Tours of USA, Europe and Japan; wrote for La gazzetta del Veneto, 1952-57; taught at Venice Conservatory, 1961-67; Chamber Music at Verona Conservatory, 1967-74; since then Director of Padua State Conservatory of Music; Permanent Conductor and Artistic Director of the chamber orchestra, Conducted Il Barbiere di Siviglia at Caracalla, 1992. *Recordings:* More that 200 LP and CD records with I Solisti Veneti and other orchestras (London Philarmonia, Royal Philharmonic, English Chamber Orchestra, Bamberger Symphoniker, others), including L'Elisir d'Amore (Ricciarelli, Carreras); Vivaldi flute concertos and Orlando Furioso; Concerti Grossi by Albinoni, Corelli and Geminiani; Marcello La Cetra; Italian flute and oboe concertos; Rossini string sonatas and Mozart's Salzburg Divertimenti; Operas by Rossini, including Zelmira, 1990. *Publications:* Editions of concertos by Tartini; Complete edition of Rossini; Segno, Significato, Interpretazione 1974; Numerous articles in music journals. *Honours include:* Elizabeth Sprague Coolidge Memorial Medal 1969; Grammy record award (Los Angeles); several Grand Prix du Disque de l'Academie Charles Cros, Academie du Disque Lyrique and others. *Address:* c/o Conservatory of Music, Padua, Italy.

SCIUTTI Graziella, b. 17 April 1927, Turin, Italy. Singer (Soprano); Opera Producer. *Education:* Accademia di Santa Cecilia, Rome. *Debut:* Aix-en-Provence 1951, as Lucy in Menotti's The Telephone; returned to Aix as Mozart's Susanna and Zerlina, and in the premiere of Sauguet's Les caprices de Marianne; Glyndebourne debut 1954, as Rosina in Il Barbiere di Siviglia; Milan, Piccola Scala, 1955 as Carolina in Il Matrimonio Segreto; Other roles in operas by Piccinni, Donizetti and Paisiello; Covent Garden debut 1956, as Oscar in Un Ballo in Maschera; returned to London as Mozart's Despina and Susanna and as Nannetta in Falstaff; US debut San Francisco 1961, as Susanna; Salzburg Festival 1957-66, in Mozart roles and in concert; Holland Festival 1957, as Anne Trulove in The Rake's Progress; Returned to Glyndebourne 1970 for Rossini's Il Turco in Italia and in 1977 produced Poulenc's La Voix Humaine; Other opera productions in New York, Chicago, Koblenz (Die Zauberflöte) and at Covent Garden (L'Elisir d'Amore). *Recordings:* Roles in: Don Giovanni, Così fan Tutte (Philips); Guillaume Tell, Le Nozze di Figaro (Cetra); Fidelio, Alcina (Decca); La Scala di Seta, La Rondine, Orlando (RCA); Donizetti's Rita, Paisiello's Barbiere di Siviglia, Pelléas et Mélisande, Il Matrimonio Segreto, L'Italiana in Algeri and Falstaff on other labels. *Address:* c/o Royal Opera House, Covent Garden, London WC2.

SCOGNA Flavio Emilio, b. 16 Aug. 1956, Savona, Italy. Composer; Conductor. m. Fiorenza Iademarco, 1993. *Education:* N. Paganini Conservatory, Genoa; Graduated in Music, University of Bologna, 1980; Studied conducting with Franco Ferrara, Rome. *Career:* His works performed in major international venues including Italian Radio of Rome and Naples, Centre Pompidou, Paris, Vienna Konzerthaus, also broadcast on RAI, BBC, Radio France, ORF and BRT; Numerous commissions, Italian Radio, Vienna Konzerthaus, Pomeriggi Musicali of Milan; Conductor, various musical groups and orchestras, appearing on Italian Radio, Teatro Massimo, Palermo; Teatro Opera Roma, Teatro

Communale Fireuze; Teaching, several Italian conservatories including S. Pietro a Maiella, Naples, and G.Rossini, Pesaro; Composer (Auditorium S Cecilia, Rome, Alicante, Spain); as Conductor: various international orchestras (Rai; Radiobroadcasting of Spain, Hungarian State symphony orchestra); Rifrazioni, for soprano and orchestra, 1989; Alternanze, for piano and strings, 1989; Musica Reservata, for strings and orchestra, 1990. *Compositions:* All Interlude dialoganti, 2 guitars, 1981; 2 studi, guitar, 1981; Salmo XII for violas and orchestra, 1990; Planc, chamber ensemble, 1982; Musica per tre, oboe, clarinet, fg, 1982; Epigrammi, 5 instruments, 1982; Mosaico, wind quintet, 1983; I profumi della notte, flute, guitar, piano, percussion, 1983; Quadri, orchestra, 1983; Arioso per Guillermo, 1984; Serenata, ensemble, 1984, new version, 1988; Anton, 1-act opera, 1984, new version, 1988; La Memoria Perduta, 2 acts, opera 1991-93; Incanto, string trio, 1985; Sonatina, trombone, 1985; Come un'onda di luce, oboe, clarinet, violin, viola, cello, 1985; Canto del mare, flute, violin, cello, 1985; Cadenza seconda, piano, 1986; Sinfonia concertante, orchestra, 1986-87; Frammento, after Mario Luzi's poem, soprano, piano, 1987; La mar, marimba, 1987; Concertino, 10 instruments, 1987; Tre invenzioni, piano, 1988; Risonanze, string quartet, 1988; Fluxus, orchestra, 1988; Verso, 3 wind, 3 strings, 1988; Relazioni ensemble, 1991; Diapphonia, for viola and orchestra, 1992; Trame, for trumpet, 1993; Avlos, for oboe, 1993. *Recordings:* As Conductor, for RCA, Edi-Pan: Planc; Serenata; Incanto; Anton; Alternanze, BMG/Ariola. *Address:* P.le Ionio 13, 00141, Rome, Italy.

SCOTT John Gavin, b. 18 June 1956, Wakefield, England. Organist and Conductor. m. Carolyn Jane Lumsden, 29 July 1979, 1 daughter, 1 son. *Education:* BA (Cantab), 1977; Mus.B., (Cantab), 1978; MA (Cantab), 1981; St John's College, Cambridge; Private study with Dr P. G. Saunders; Jonathan Bielby; Ralph Downes and Gillian Weir. *Debut:* Henry Wood Promenade Concert, Royal Albert Hall, 1977. *Career:* Solo organ recitals and broadcasts in United Kingdom, Europe, USA, Australia and Far East; Sub-Organist and Assistant Director of Music, St Paul's Cathedral, 1985-90; Organist and Assistant Conductor, The Bach Choir, 1979-92; Professor of Organ, Royal Academy of Music, 1988-91; Organist and Director of Music, St Paul's Cathedral, 1990-. *Recordings:* As accompanist to St John's College Choir, Cambridge and Conductor of St Paul's Cathedral Choir; Solo: Reubke - Sonata on 94th Psalm (Abbey); Liszt - Fantasia and Fugue: Ad nos ad Salutarem Undam (Guild); Organ Music by Marcel Dupré (Hyperion); Organ Spetacular (Cirrus); Organ Music by Maurice Duruflé (Hyperion); Janáček Glagolitic Mass (LSO); Organ Music by Mendessohn (Hyperion, 2 Vols.); Orrgan music by William Mathias (Nimbus). *Honours:* ARCO, Limpus Prize, 1971; FRCO, Limpus Prize, 1973; Dr F. J. Read Prize, 1974; John Stewart of Rannoch Scholarship in Sacred Music, University of Cambridge, 1975; 1st Prize, Manchester International Organ Festival, 1978; 1st Prize, Leipzig International J. S. Bach Competition, 1984; Hon. RAM, 1990. *Hobbies:* Reading; Travel; Ecclesiastical Architecture. *Current Management:* Magenta Music International Ltd. *Address:* 5 Amen Court, London EC4M 7BU, England.

SCOTT Vanessa, b. 11 Apr. 1955, Ely, Cambridgeshire, England. Singer. *Education:* Royal Academy of Music, 1973-79; Internal Student, London University; BMus (Hons.); FTCL; LRAM; Diploma, Royal Academy of Music; Music Teachers Certificate of Education; Studied with Gerard Souzay, France, 1979. *Debut:* Purcell Room, 1982. *Career:* Concert performances include Oratorio and recital, on the South Bank, all over the country and abroad; Les Illuminations, with the late Boyd Neel, Edinburgh, 1979; Oratorio for radio; Recital work for BBC Radio 3; Television; Glyndebourne Festival Opera, 1982-84; Glyndebourne Solo Debut, 1984; Glyndebourne Touring Opera, 1982-84; Examiner for the Associated Board of the Royal Schools of Music. *Hobbies:* Cooking; Reading; Tennis. *Address:* 4 Bakers Way, Perry, Huntingdon, Cambridgeshire PE18 0B5, England.

SCOTTO Renata, b. 24 Feb. 1933, Savona, Italy. Singer (Soprano). m. Lorenzo Anselmi. *Education:* Studied at the Giuseppe Verdi Conservatory, Milan, with Emilio Ghiriardini. *Debut:* Teatro Nuovo Milan 1953, as Violetta; Sang at La Scala from 1954 as Donizetti's Amina, Lucia and Adina and as Helena in I Vespri Siciliani; London debut Stoll Theatre 1957, as Adina, Mimi, Violetta and Donna Elvira; Edinburgh Festival 1957, as Amina in La Sonnambula; US debut Chicago 1960, Miami; Covent Garden debut 1962, as Butterfly; Metropolitan Opera from 1965, as Lucia, Verdi's Gilda, Helena, Luisa Miller, Desdemona, Elisabeth de Valois and Lady Macbeth, Norma, Adriana Lecouvreur and in Puccini's Trittico; Directed Butterfly at the Metropolitan 1986 and sang there for the last time in 1987; Returned to Edinburgh 1972, with the Palermo company in Bellini's La Straniera; Guest appearances as Anna Bolena in Dallas and in Verdi's Requiem at the Verona arena. *Publication:* More than a Diva, autobiography, 1984. *Recordings:* Roles in: Pagliacci, Cavalleria Rusticana, Lucia di Lammermoor, La Traviata, La Bohème, Edgar, Adriana Lecouvreur, Andrea Chénier, Robert le Diable, La Straniera, I Lombardi, I Capuleti e i Montecchi, La Sonnambula: Companies include Cetra, Columbia, Ricordi and HMV. 21. *Address:* c/o Metropolitan Opera, Lincoln Center, New York, NY 10023, USA.

SCOVOTTI Jeanette, b. 5 Dec. 1933, New York City, USA. Singer (Soprano). *Education:* Studied at the Juilliard School, New York. *Debut:* Metropolitan Opera 1962, as Adele in Die Fledermaus. *Career:* Teatro Colon Buenos Aires 1963-65; Munich Staatsoper 1965; Sang at the Hamburg Staatsoper 1966-77, as Mozart's Zerlina and Despina, Aminta in Die schweigsame Frau, Donizetti's Lucia and Norina, and in the premiere of Krenek's Sardakai; Many engagements at opera houses elsewhere in Europe; Other roles include Olympia, Gilda, the Queen of Night, Zerlina, Aminta in Die schweigsame Frau, Zerbinetta, Constanze and Carolina in Il Matrimonio Segreto; Boston Opera 1977, in the US premiere of Ruslan and Ludmila by Glinka; Sang Costanza in a Concert performance of Vivaldi's Griselda, London, 1978. *Recordings:* Les Contes d'Hoffmann (Electrola); Castor et Pollux by Rameau (Telefunken); Eine Nacht in Venedig (Hungaroton); Les Huguenots; Rinaldo by Handel (CBS); Die drei Pintos by Weber/Mahler (RCA); Die schweigsame Frau (EMI). c/o Hamburgische Staatsoper, Grosse Theaterstrasse 34, D-2000 Hamburg 36, Germany.

SCUDERI Vincenzo, b. 1961, NY, USA. Singer (Tenor). *Education:* Studied in New York and with Franco Corelli. *Career:* Long Island Opera, Pinkerton, Turiddu, Rodolfo; Appearances at Plovdiv and Zurich as Ishmaele in Nabucco and as Radames, 1987-89; Sang the Duke of Mantua on tour throughout France, 1989; Sang arias from Chenier and Fanciulla del West in Tribute Concert to Franco Corelli, Purchase, New York, 1991; Radames at the Baths of Caracalla, 1991. *Address:* Opera de Marseille, 2 Rue Molière, F-1321 Marseille Cedex 01, France.

SCULTHORPE Peter Joshua, b. 29 April 1929, Launceston, Tasmania. Composer. *Education:* Melbourne University Conservatory of Music; Wadham College Oxford, with Egon Wellesz and Edmund Rubbra. *Career:* Teacher at Sydney University from 1963; Composer in Residence Yale University 1966; Visiting Professor, Sussex University 1972-73. *Compositions:* Stage: Sun Music, ballet 1968; Rites of Passage, opera 1973; Quiros, television opera 1982; Tatea, music theatre piece 1988; Orchestral: Irkanda IV for violin and strings 1961; Small Town 1963-76; Sun Music I-IV 1965-67; Music for Japan 1970; Rain 1970; Lament for strings 1976; Port Essington for string trio and strings 1977; Mangrove 1979; Guitar Concerto 1980; Piano Concerto 1983; Little Suite for strings 1983; Sonata for strings 1983; Earth Cry 1986; Second Sonata for Strings 1988; At the Grave of Isaac Nathan 1988; Instrumental: The Loneliness of Bunjil for string trio 1954; 12 String Quartets 1947-88; Sonata for viola and percussion 1960; Tabuh Tabuhan for wind quintet and percussion 1968; How the Stars were Made for percussion ensemble 1971; Landscape for piano quartet 1979; Requiem for solo cello 1979; Cantares for guitars and string quartet 1980; Songs of Sea and Sky for clarinet and piano 1987; Vocal: Sun Music for Voices and Percussion 1966; Love 200 for rock band 1970; Ketjak for six male voices with tape echo 1972; The Songs of Tailitnama for high voice, 6 cellos and percussion 1974; Child of Australia for chorus, soprano, narrator and orchestra 1987; Piano Music; Music for the film Burke and Wills 1985. *Honours include:* Order of the British Empire 1977; Doctor of Letters, University of Tasmania. 1980; 1985 APRA Award for his Piano Concerto. *Address:* c/o Faber Music Ltd., 3 Queen Square, London WC1N 3AU, England.

SEAMAN Christopher, b. 7 Mar. 1942, Faversham, Kent, England. Conductor. *Education:* Canterbury Cathedral Choir School, 1950-55; The King's School Canterbury, 1955-60; ARCO, ARCM, Kings College, Cambridge, 1960; MA, 1963. *Career:* Principal Timpanist, London Philharmonic Orchestra, 1964-68; Assistant Conductor, BBC Scottish Symphony Orchestra, 1968-70; Principal Conductor, BBC Scottish Symphony Orchestra, 1971-77; Principal Conductor, Northern Sinfonia, 1973-79; Chief Guest Conductor, Utrecht Symphony Orchestra, 1979-83; Conductor-in-Residence, Baltimore Symphony Orchestra since 1987. *Honour:* FGSM 1972. *Hobbies:* People; Reading; Walking; Theology. *Address:* Harrison/Parrott Ltd., 12 Penzance Place, London W11 4PA, England.

SEAMARKS Colin Peter, b. 13 June 1943, Finedon, Northants, England. Music Organiser. m. Elizabeth Maralyn Povah, 24 May 1970, 1 s, 1 d. *Education:* Kimbolton School and London University. *Career:* Used to Compose and has One Composition Which Recieves World Wide Performances; Music Organizer and Concert Promoter, Barnet College, from 1978; Promoted Much C20 British Music; Formerly Extra Mural Lecturer for London and Surrey Universities. *Compositions:* Six Mehitabel Magpies. *Honours:* Distinction London Musical Competition. *Memberships:* Composers Guild; PRS; BASCA; RMA. *Hobbies:* Family; Eating Out; Music; Cinema; Watching Cricket; Snooker; Sumo Wrestling; Underground Train Systems. *Address:* 4 Merlin Gardens, Chase Cross, Romford, Essex RM5 3YD, England.

SEARS Nicholas, b. 1965, England. Singer (Baritone). *Education:* Studied at Trinity College, Cambridge and the Guildhall School, London. *Career:* Concert Engagements With The Songmakers' Almanac and Songscape, with regular appearances at the Aldeburgh Festival and under such conductors as Simon Rattle, David Atherton and Philippe Herreweghe; With Welsh National Opera has Sung Marullo in Rigoletto, Mozart's Count and Gorjanchikov in From the House of the Dead; Sang Choregos in Birtwistle's Punch and Judy at Aldeburgh, Berlin, Vienna, Malatesta for Opera 80 and Gluck's Oreste for Welsh National Opera; Appearances as Billy Budd for Opera North and in the Premiere of Jonathan Harvey's Inquest of Love for English National Opera. *Address:* c/o John Coast Ltd, 31 Sinclair Road, London W14 0NS, England.

SEBESTYEN András, b. 6 Feb. 1917, Debrecen, Hungary. Conductor; Composer; Deputy Director of Music. m. Magda Fontos, 14 July 1949. *Education:* Diploma, Composition with Zoltán Kodály, 1940; Cello with Adolph Schiffer, Jeno Kerpely, 1940; Ferenc Liszt Academy of Music, Hungary. *Career:* Conductor, Csokonai Theatre, State Youth Theatre, National Theatre, Home Affairs Symphony Orchestra, Gardonyi Theatre; Conductor of Film, TV and Radio Music, Musical Comedies, Operettas; Conducted concerts in Italy and Yugoslavia. *Compositions:* Orchestra Chamber Music; Songs; Choral; Wind Instrument Works; Stage, TV, Radio incidental music. *Recordings:* Conducted many records of own compositions; classical and contemporary operettas. *Honours:* Labour Awards, Bronze, 1967, Gold, 1978, 1983. *Memberships:* Hungarian Composers Union; Ferenc Liszt Society; Musicians Organisation.

Current Management: Inter Koncert, 1051 Budapest, Hungary. *Address:* SzoloKoz 5, H-1032 Budapest, Hungary.

SEBESTYEN Janos, b. 2 Mar. 1931, Budapest, Hungary. Organist; Harpsichordist. *Education:* Diploma, Ferenc Liszt Academy, Budapest. *Career:* Recitals, radio, TV in Hungary; Tours with organ and harpsichord recitals, all Eastern and Western European countries, UA, Japan, Philippines; Radio recordings; Founder and Professor of Harpsichord Faculty, Academy of Music, Budapest, 1970-; Producer-in-Chief, musical feature programme series, Radio Budapest; President of Jury, International Liszt Organ Competition, Budapest 1983, 1988 and 1993. *Recordings:* Over 80 records for Hungaroton, Vox-Turnabout, Vox-Candide, Price-less, Fonit-Cetra, Ars Nova, including complete organ works of Liszt on Vox-Box; Recently Naxos. *Publication:* Musical conversations with Miklos Rózsa, 1979. *Current Management:* Interkoncert Arts Rt, Budapest; Pere Porta, Barcelona. *Address:* Filler u 48, 1022 Budapest, Hungary.

SECUNDE Nadine, b. 1954, Independence, Ohio, USA. Singer (Soprano). *Education:* Studied at Oberlin Conservatory and at Indiana University School of Music with Margaret Harshaw; Further study in Germany on a Fulbright Scholarship. *Career:* Engaged first at the Hessisches Staatstheater Wiesbaden; Currently a member of the Cologne Opera, where her roles have been Katya Kabanova, Elsa, Agathe, Elisabeth, Chrysothemis and Ariadne; Vienna Staatsoper debut as Sieglinde, Hamburg Staatsoper as Katya; Bayreuth Festival debut 1987, as Elsa in a Werner Herzog production of Lohengrin: returned 1988, as Sieglinde in the Harry Kupfer production of Der Ring des Nibelungen; Covent Garden and Chicago 1988, as Elsa and Elisabeth; returned to London 1990, as Chrysothemis; Cologne 1990 as Sieglinde; Sang Elsa at La Fenice, Venice, 1990, Sieglinde at Bayreuth; Chrysothemis at Athens, 1992; Concert engagements include the Choral Symphony with the Los Angeles Philharmonic, conducted by Previn, and with the Orchestre de Paris under Barenboim; Penderecki's Dies Irae with the Warsaw Philharmonic. *Address:* c/o Ingpen & Williams Ltd., 14 Kensington Court, London W8 5DN, England.

SEDIVKA Jan Boleslav, b. 8 Sept. 1917, Prague, Czechoslovakia. Violin Teacher. m. Beryl Thomas, 1961. *Education:* Violin studies, Professor O. Sevcik; Master Diploma, Honours, Prague Conservatory (Professor J. Kocian); Ecole Normale de Musique, Paris, France (J. Thibaud), 1938-40; Professor Max Rostal, London, UK, 1942-45. *Career includes:* Head, Instrumental Department, Surrey College of Music, UK; Director, Chamber Music, Goldsmiths' College, University of London; Violin Professor, Trinity College, London; Principal Violin Lecturer, Queensland Conservatorium of Music, Brisbane, Australia; Director, currently Master Musician-in-Residence, Tasmanian Conservatorium, Hobart; Visiting Lecturer, string playing, pedagogy, numerous universities & conservatoria. Leader: London Czech Trio, London International Trio, Tasmanian Conservatorium Trio; Soloist, British & Australian orchestras; 1st performances, numerous contemporary works. *Recordings include:* Sedivka Plays Sitsky, Concerto, Violin, Orchestra & Female Voices; Sonata for Unaccompanied Violin Op. 1, with Tasmanian Symphony Orchestra, Opera Chorus & Lyric Singers; Gurdjieff: Violin Concerto No. 2 by Larry Sitsky with the Tasmanian Symphony Orchestra, conducted by Omri Hadari - Compact Disc Move Records, 1989. *Address:* 25 Browns Road, Kingston, Tasmania 7050, Australia.

SEEBASS Tilman, b. 8 Sept. 1939, Basel, Switzerland. Musicologist. m. Elisabeth Mischler, 23 Mar. 1968, 1 son, 1 daughter. *Education:* Swiss Maturitat type A (Classical Languages); Universities of Basel and Heidelberg; PhD, 1970. *Career:* Research Fellow, Swiss National Funds, 1970-75; Field work, Indonesia, 1972-73, 1983; Managing Director, Haus der

Bücher (new and rare books) Basel; Assistant Professor of Musicology, 1977-79, Professor of Musicology, 1989-, Duke University, Durham, North Carolina, USA; Director of the Institute for Musicology, University of Innsbruck, 1993-. *Recordings:* Ethnological recordings with commentary: Panji in Lombok I. A Cross Section of the Instrumental Music, 1977; Panji in Lombok II. The orchestras rebana, tawa'-tawa' and kelenang..., 1978; Panji in Bali I. Gamelan Semar Pegulingan, 1978; Ethnomusicological films with textbooks: Bali, District Karangasem: Caruk/Saron Ensemble of the Village Abiantihing (with D.Schaareman), 1981; Compressed Version of gambuh (Dance Drama) in Batuan (Gianyar District), Bali (with G.Van der Weijden), 1981. *Publications:* Musikdarstellung und Psalterillustration im früheren Mittelalter, 1973; Musikhandschriften in Basel. Exhibition catalogue, 1975; Die Allgemeine Musikgesellschaft Basel 1987-1976. Festschrift, 1976; The Music of Lombok: a first survey (with I.G.B.N.Panji, I.Nyoman Rembang, I.Poedijono), 1977; Musikhandschriften aus der Sammlung Paul Sacher: Festschrift zur Paul Sachers 70 Geburtstag, 1976; Bibliotheca Bodmeriana. Catalogue of the musical authographs 1600-1950, 1986; Editor, Imago Musicae, International Yearbook of Musical Iconography, 1984-. *Contributions to:* Mitteilungen der deutschen Gesellschaft fur Musik des Orients; Rivista Italiana di Musicologia. *Address:* Musikwissenschaftliches Institut der Universität, Karl-Schönherr Str. 3, 6020 Innsbruck, Austria.

SEEFEHLNER Egon Hugo, b. 3 June 1912, Vienna, Austria. Opera Director. *Education:* Theresianum; University of Vienna; Konsularakademie. *Career:* Co-founder, General Secretary, Austrian Cultural Association, 1945; Chief Editor, Der Turm (cultural) magazine, 1945; General Secretary, Wiener Konserthausgesellschaft, 1946-61; Deputy Director, Vienna State Opera, 1954-61; Deputy General Manager, Deutsche Oper, W. Berlin, 1961-72; Director General, 1972-76; Director, State Opera, Vienna, 1976-82, 1984-86. *Honours:* Decorated Commander's Cross, Papal Order of Silvester; Officer, Ordre des Arts et Lettres; Goldenes Ehrenzeichen fur Verdianste umidas Land Wien; Osterreichische Ehrenkreuz fur Wissenschaft und Kunst, 1st class; Clemens Krauss Silver Medal; Gold Cross of Republic of Austria. *Memberships:* Roman Catholic Church. *Address:* c/o Staatsoper, Opernring 2, Vienna, Austria.

SEEGER Horst, b. 6 Nov. 1926, Erkner, Germany. Musicologist. Critic; Director of Opera. *Education:* Studied musicology at the Humboldt University and the Berlin Musikhochschule with Ernst H. Meyer, 1950-55. *Career:* Teacher 1946-50; Music critic from 1954; Established Institute of Music Education at Greifswald University 1958-59; Editor-in-chief Musik und Gesellschaft 1959-60; Chief Dramaturg of the Berlin Komische Oper 1960-73; Intendant of the Dresden Staatsoper 1973-84: responsible for the first East European production of Schoenberg's Moses und Aron. *Publications:* Wolfgang Amadeus Mozart 1956; Joseph Haydn 1961; Musiklexikon 1966; Opern-Lexikon 1978-1986; Libretto for Siegfried Matthus's opera Spanische Tugenden 1964; Translations of opera libretti include works by Verdi, Weber and Tchaikovsky. *Address:* Spreeufer 1, Berlin O-10178, Germany.

SEERS Mary, b. 1958, England. Singer (Soprano). *Education:* Studied at Girton College, Cambridge (choral exhibitioner) and in Rome and London. *Career:* Appearances with the Landini Consort, the Consort of Musique, The Scholars and the Hilliard Ensemble; Festival engagements at Aix- en-Provence, Schleswig-Holstein and Greenwich; Tour of Britain and Italy 1988 with Pärt's St John Passion; Concerts in Sydney and Tokyo 1989 with John Eliot Gardiner and the Monteverdi Choir; Concerts: Bach B minor Mass, Wroclaw (Poland) with City of London Sinfonia; Other repertoire includes Mozart's C minor Mass, the Monteverdi Vespers (Bruges Festival), Messiah (St Martin in the Fields) and music by Finzi and Purcell; Further appearances at the Almeida, Cheltenham and Orkney Festivals and concerts with the Scottish Chamber Orchestra and the East of England Orchestra; US concerts in Chicago and New York, Pärt's St John Passion; Opera: with Music Theatre Wales, role of Madeleine in Philip Glass, The Fall of The House of Usher; Festivals: Warsaw Contemporary Music Festival, (Pärt Passio), 1992; Television: Took part in BBC 2 documentary on Eric Satie, 1992. *Recordings:* Fauré Requiem with English Chamber Orchestra and Corydon Singers (Hyperion); Monteverdi Vespers with The Sixteen (Hyperion). *Address:* Magenta Music International, 64 Highgate High Street, London N6 5HX, England.

SEGAL Uriel, b. 7 Mar 1944, Jerusalem, Israel. Conductor. m. Illana Finkelstein, 1 son, 3 daughters. *Education:* Studied violin from age of 7; Rubin Academy of Music, Israel; Conducting with Mendi Rodan at the Guildhall School of Music, London. *Debut:* With Seajillands Symphony Orchestra, Copenhagen, 1969. *Career:* Assistant conductor, working with George Szell and Leonard Bernstein New York, Philharmonic Orchestra, 1969-70; Chief Conductor, Philharmonica Hungarica, 1981-85; Principal Conductor, Bournemouth Symphony, 1980-83; Guest appearances with the Hamburg and Israel Philharmonics, Chicago Symphony, Spanish National Orchestra, London Symphony and Philharmonic, Philharmonia, French Radio Philharmonic, Montreal and New Zealand Symphony, Suttgart Radio Symphony, RAI Rome, Hallé Orchestra, Scottish National; Chief Conductor of the Israel Chamber Orchestra from 1982; Currently Music Director of the Chautauqua Festival (New York State) and Chief Conductor of the Osaka Century Orchestra, Japan; Opera experience includes Der fliegende Holländer at Santa Fe, 1973 and Il re Pastore, Opéra de Nice. *Recordings include:* Stravinsky's Firebird Suite and Symphony in C, with the Suisse Romande Orchestra; Mozart Piano Concertos with Radu Lupu and the English Chamber Orchestra; Schumann's Piano Concerto with Ashkenazy and the London Symphony; Beethoven Piano Concertos with Rudolf Firkusny and the Philharmonia. *Honours:* 1st Prize, Mitropoulos Conducting Competition, New York, 1969. *Hobby:* Reading. *Address:* c/o Terry Harrison Management, 3 Clarendon Court, Park Street, Charlbury, Oxon OX7 3PS, England.

SEGERSTAM Leif, b. 2 Mar 1944, Vasa, Finland. Conductor; Composer. *Education:* Violin, piano, conducting, composition, Sibelius Academy, Helsinki, until 1963; Conducting diploma, Juilliard School of Music, New York, USA, 1964; Postgraduate Diploma 1965. *Debut:* Violin soloist Helsinki, 1963. *Career:* Conductor, Finnish National Opera, 1965-68; Conductor, Royal Opera Stockholm, 1968-72 and Musical Director, 1971-72; 1st Conductor, Deutsche Oper Berlin, 1972-73; General Manager Finnish National Opera 1973-74; Chief Conductor ORF (Austrian Radio) Vienna 1975-82; Musical Director, Finnish Radio Symphony Orchestra, Helsinki, 1977-87; Principal Guest Conudctor from 1987; General Music Director, Staatsphilharmonie Rhenland-Pfalz 1983-89; Honorary Conductor, 1989; Conductor of the Danish Radio Symphony Orchestra from 1988. *Compositions include:* Divertimento for strings 1963; 6 Cello Concertos; 3 Piano Concertos; 18 Symphonies 1977-83; 8 Violin Concertos; 6 Double Concertos; Many works for orchestra under title Composed orchestral works called Thoughts, the most famous being, Monumental Thoughts, Martti Tavela in memorium; Orchestral Diary Sheets, 5 Songs of Experience after Blake and Auden for soprano and orchestra 1971; 27 String Quartets; 2 Piano Trios; 4 String Trios; Episodes for various instrumental combinations. *Recordings:* Works by Mahler, Sibelius, Brahms, Scriabin, Petterson, Schnittke, Rott, Ruders, Koechlin, Schmitt, Roussell, Caplet, Roger-Ducasse and own compositions. *Honours:* Grand Prix du Diogue, Academie Charles Cros, 1986; Second Prize with Symphony IV, Sibelius, 1991; Record of the Year, Sibelius III symphony (Chandos), 1992. *Memberships:* Royal Academy of Music, Sweden. *Address:* c/o Danish Radio Symphony Orchestra, Rosenornsallé 22, DK-1999 Frederiksberg, Copenhagen, Denmark.

SEIDEL Jan, b. 25 Dec. 1908, Nymburk, Czechoslovakia. Composer. *Education:* Prague Conservatory 1936-40, with Alois Haba; Further study with J.B. Foerster. *Career:* E.F. Burian's Theatre 1930-45, as composer, conductor and pianist; Artistic Adviser to the Gramophone Corporation 1945-53; Chief of the National Theatre Opera 1958-64. *Compositions:* Opera Tonka Sibenice 1964; Symphonic Prologue 1942; Symphony No.1 1943; Oboe Concerto 1955; Hunting Sinfonietta for horn and chamber orchestra 1966; Concerto for flute, strings and piano 1966; Giocosa for chamber orchestra 1972; Vocal: Cantatas Call to Battle 1946; May Prelude 1952; Message to the Living 1953; 4000 Folksong arrangements; Chamber: 4 String Quartets 1930-44; 2 Wind Quintets; Violin Sonata 1950. *Honours include:* National Artist 1976. *Address:* SOZA, Kollarova nam 20, 813 27 Bratislava, Slovakia.

SEIFERT Gerd-Heinrich, b. 17 Oct. 1931, Hamburg, Germany. Musician. m. 29 June 1957, 3 sons, 1 daughter. *Education:* Music High School, Hamburg, 1944-49; Studied horn with Albert Doscher. *Debut:* Soloist, Horn Concerto (Strauss), 1948. *Career:* Substitute, Hamburg Philharmonic Orchestra, 1947-49; Solo Horn, Düsseldorfer Symphoniker, 1949-64; Solo Horn, Bayreuth Festival, 1961; Solo Horn, Berlin Philharmonic Orchestra, 1964-; Performed with Düsseldorfer Waldhorn Quartett, also 13 Bläser Philharmonic Orchestra and Philharmonic Octet, Berlin; Teacher of Horn, Music High School, Düsseldorf, 1954-64; Teacher of Horn, Music High School, Berlin, 1970-. *Recordings:* With Berlin Philharmonic Orchestra/Octet: 4 horn concertos (Mozart); Trio (Brahms); Horn Quintet (Mozart); Octet (Schubert); Septet (Beethoven); Octet (Hindemith); Octet, Nonet (Spohr); Serenade for 13 Wind instruments by Mozart, and other Chamber music; Concert Piece for 4 horns (Schumann). *Contributions to:* Brass Bulletin. *Honours:* 1st Prize, ARD Competition, Munich, 1956; 125 Siegfried Calls at Bayreuth Festival since 1961; Grand Prix du Disque. *Hobby:* Photography. *Address:* Xantenerstrasse 1, 1000 Berlin 15, Germany.

SEIFERT Ingrid, b. 1952, Austria. Violinist. *Education:* Studied violin in Salzburg and Vienna. *Career:* Played with the Concentus Musicus, Vienna and studied further in Holland; With Charles Medlam co-founded London Baroque 1978; Teaches at summer courses, notably the Innsbruck Summer Academy for Baroque Music; With London Baroque led the first performance of Scarlatti's Una villa di Tuscolo and a revival of Gli Equivoci Sembiante, for the BBC; Season 1990/91 included Dido and Aeneas at the Paris Opéra, Blow and Lully at the Opéra-Comique, Aci, Galatea e Polifemo in Spain, Holland and England, and cantatas by Handel and Rameau in Austria, Sweden and Germany, with Emma Kirkby; Other recent repertoire includes Charpentier Messe de Minuit; 4 violin music by Telemann, Vivaldi and Wassenaar; Bach Brandenburg Concertos; Monteverdi Tancredi and Clorinda; Salzburg Festival debut 1991, with music by Mozart; Further festival engagements at Bath, Beaune, Versailles, Ansbach, Innsbruck and Utrecht. *Recordings:* Marais La Gamme, Theile Matthew Passion, Bach Trio Sonatas, Charpentier Theatre Music, Handel Aci, Galatea e Polifemo; Venus and Adonis, Purcell Chamber Music (Harmonia Mundi); Purcell Fantasias, Bach Violin Sonatas, Monteverdi Orfeo, Handel German Arias (EMI); A Vauxhall Gardens Entertainment; English Music of the 18th Century; François Couperin Chamber Music; Complete trios of Handel, Purcell, chamber music by Lawes. *Address:* Brick Kiln Cottage, Hollington, nr Newbury, Berks. RG15 9XX, England.

SEIFFERT Peter, b. 4 Jan 1954, Dusseldorf. Singer (Tenor). m. Lucia Popp, 1986, (dec 1993). *Education:* Studied at the Robert Schumann Musikhochschule Dusseldorf. *Career:* Sang first with with the Deutsche Oper am Rhein Dusseldorf in Der Wildschütz and Fra Diavolo; Member of the Deutsche Oper Berlin from 1982, notably as Lensky, Jenik in The Bartered Bride, Huon (Oberon) and Faust; Bayerische Staatsoper Munich 1983, as Fenton in Die Lustigen Weiber von Windsor; has returned in Dar Barber von Bagdad by Cornelius and as Narraboth and Lohengrin; Vienna Staastoper and La Scala Milan debuts 1984; Covent Garden debut 1988, as Parsifal in a new production of Wagner's opera conducted by Bernard Haitink; Season 1988/89 sang Faust at the Deutsche Oper Berlin and Lohengrin in Munich (repeated 1990); Sang at Salzburg 1992, as Narraboth; Concert engagements include Mozart's Requiem with Giulini in London, and the Choral Symphony with Muti in Philadelphia. *Recordings:* Elijah; Zar und Zimmerman; Matteo in Arabella, conducted by Jeffrey Tate; Die Fledermaus, conducted by Domingo; Gianni Schicchi (Patanè); Erik in fliegende Holländer, conducted by Pinchas Steinberg; the Choral Symphony (Muti) and Mozart's Mass in C Minor (Levine); Mendelssohn's Lobgesong and Beethoven's Symphony No. 9 (Sawallisch); Solo Records of Operetta, EMI; Solo Record of Opera, EMI. *Honours:* Kammersänger of the Bavarian State Opera. *Address:* c/o Hilbert Agentur, Maximilianstrasse 22, 8000 Munich 22, Germany.

SEISS Werner, b. 21 Mar 1944, Dortmund, Germany. Conductor; Lecturer. m. Kathrin, 5 Jan 1982, 2 s, 1 d. *Education:* Studied at the Academy of Music of Vienna, Also Studied Science of Music at the Universities of Cologne and Vienna. *Dbut:* Salzburg, 1967. *Career:* Appearances in the Konzerthaus of Vienna, The Opera House of Milano, Bologna, Sydney; Concerts in Nearly all Countries of Europe and Several Concert Tours to Asia ans USA; Appearances at Important Festivals. *Recordings:* phonothek; CBSFonit Cetra Milano; Brodcast Products with WDR ORF, RAI and DF. *Honours;* 1980 Music Prize; 1988 Appointment to Professor. *Hobbies:* Literature; Sport. *Address:* Graf-Ezzo-Weg 22, 58730 Frondenberg-Bausenhagen, Germany.

SEIVEWRIGHT Robert Peter, b. 11 July 1954, Skipton, England. Concert Pianist; Lecturer in Music. *Education:* BA, 1975, MA, 1981, Worcester College, Oxford; Royal Northern College of Music with Ryszard Bakst, 1976-79; FRCO Diploma, 1975. *Career:* Tutor, University of Keele, 1979-83; Instructor in Music, University of Leicester, 1980-84; Lecturer in Music, Royal Scottish Academy of Music and Drama, 1984-; University Pianist, University of Strathclyde, 1990-93; Concert career throughout UK and Europe including recitals, Huddersfield Contemporary Music Festival 1983, 1984; Tivoli Concert Hall, Copenhagen, Denmark, 1986; Aarhus Festival, Denmark, 1986; Munch-Museum, Oslo, 1986; Danish recital tours, 1986, 1989, 1990, 1991; Performances of complete Messiaen 20 Regards sur l'enfant Jésus, Dublin, Cork and Glasgow, 1988; Concertos with Hallé Orchestra, Glasgow Philharmonic Pops Orchestra, Northern Chamber Orchestra, Bradford Chamber Orchestra, Paragon Ensemble, Scottish Sinfonietta, Strathclyde Sinfonia; Opening recital, Heilbronn International Piano Forum, Heilbronn, Germany, 1993; Recordings for BBC Radio Manchester, BBC Radio Scotland, BBC Radio 3, Radio Denmark; Chamber music with the violinist Peter Manning, and with the Edinburgh String Quartet. *Compositions:* Jazz Intermezzo, for piano and brass band, 1973; numerous arrangements of Christmas music for choir and orchestra for RSAMD Carol Concerts, 1986-89; String Quartet 1989; Trio for flute, oboe and clarinet 1989. *Recordings:* Kemp's Nine Daies Wonder; Tintinnalogia; Piano Sonata; Contemporary British Piano Music, East Midlands Arts Association, 1987, (works by Trevor Hold, Nigel Osborne and Andrew Wilson-Dickson); Soloist Lambert, The Rio Grande with Scottish Sinfonietta Linn Records, 1987; Contemporary Scottish piano music, Merlin Records, 1990, (works by Thomas Wilson, John McLeod, Rory Boyle and Judith Weir). *Current Management:* c/o Tom Kristensen, Tivoli Festival Agency, 20 H C Andersens Boulevard, Copenhagen V, Denmark. *Address:* The Old Joinery, Lintfieldbank, Coalburn, Lanarkshire, Scotland, ML11 0NJ.

SELBY Kathryn Shauna, b. 20 Sep. 1962, Sydney, Australia. Concert Pianist. *Education:* Sydney

Conservatorium of Music, 1975-77; Bachelor degree, Bryn Mawr College, Pennsylvania, 1979-83; High School Diploma and Bachelors degree, Curtis Institute of Music, 1977-79 and 1983-85; MM, Juilliard School of Music, 1985-86. *Debut:* YMCA, 92nd Street, New York, 1981; Wigmore Hall, London, 1987. *Career:* Appearances with Sydney Symphony Orchestra, Philadelphia Orchestra, Pittsburg Symphony, St Louis Symphony, Cincinnati Symphony, Calgary and Erie Philharmonic, Indianapolis symphony Orchestra, Shreveport Symphony Orchestra, etc; As Chamber Musician, Spoleto Festival, Australia, 1986; Marlboro Music Festival, Caramoor Festival, Concerto Soloists of Philadelphia, Hartford Chamber Orchestra, Kennedy Center Washington; Founding Member, Selby, Pini, Pereira Trio (Australia), appearances, tours Musica Viva, Australia, 1985, 1987; ABC Film, Mozart in Delphi, with Australian Chamber Orchestra for ABC Australia; Recitals, New York, Washington DC, Seattle, Portland, Pittsburgh, Philadelphia; Sydney Australia; London UK; Munich Germany. *Hobbies:* Reading; Swimming; Tennis; Embroidery. *Current Management:* Shaw Concerts Inc. *Address:* 1900 Broadway, New York, NY 10023, USA.

SELEZNEV Georgi, b. 21 Oct 1938, Tbilisi, Georgia. Singer (Bass). *Education:* Studied at Toilisi and the Leningrad Conservatory. *Career:* Bass Soloist at the Maly Opera Leningrad, 1972-78; Appearances with the Bolshoi Opera Russia from 1978, notably on Tour to Western Europe and the USA; Solo Debut in the West as Kontchak and Galitzky in Prince Igor at Trieste, 1985; Returned as Dosifei in Khovanschina; Sang title role in Salambo for RAI in Rome; Appeared in all the international tours of the Bolshoi Company in recent years, engagements such as the Verdi Requiem under Chailly with the Royal Concertgebouw Orchestra in Amsterdam, Oroveso (with Joan Sutherland as Norma) at the Opera Pacific and with Michigan Opera, as Boris at the Wiesbaden Festival and as Pimen at the Opera du Rhin, Strasbourg, repeated at Bordeaux, 1993; Return to Bordeaus as Timur in production of Turandot, director Alain Lombard, 1994. *Recordings include:* Salambo for RCA; Oroveso in Norma for Olympia Records. *Honours include:* Lenin Prize. *Address;* c/o Athole Still Ltd, 80-86 Westow Street, London SE19 3AF, England.

SELF Susannah Jane, b. 2 Aug 1957, London, England. Opera Singer (Mezzo Soprano). m. Michael Christie, 20 Nov 1982. *Education:* Royal College of Music; ARCM; The Banff Centre, Canada; Studied Voice and Composition. *Debut:* Wigmore Hall, 1986. *Career:* 1st Priestess Iphigenias, Opera Factory, Queen Elizabeth Hall, 1987; Small parts and understudy, Royal Opera, Covent Garden, 1987-88; Drummer, Emperor of Atlantis, Mecklenburgh Opera, London International Opera Festival, 1988; Christoph in The Standard Bearer, Herodias in Salome, Royal Opera House, Garden Venture, 1989; Dorabella, Così fan tutte, Surrey Opera, 1990-91; Mallika, Lakmé, University College Opera, 1991; Idamante, Idomoneo, St Albans Opera, 1991; 4 Note Opera, Music Theatre, Wales, 1991; Glyndebourne Summer Season, 1991; Azucena in Trovatore, European Chamber Opera, 1992; Carmen, Covent Garden Festival, 1993; The Bacchae, Opera Factory, 1993; Baba the Turk, The Rake's Progress, Opera Factory, 1994; Founded selfmade music theatre, 1992; Many recitals including Wigmore Hall and Purcell Room. *Hobbies:* Painting; Walking; Cooking. *Current Management:* Simply Singers. *Address:* Basement Flat, 16d Hampstead Hill Gardens, London NW3 2PL, England.

SELIG Franz-Josef, b. 11 July 1962, Germany. Singer (Bass). *Education:* Studied at the Cologne Musikhochschule with Claudio Nicolai. *Career:* Concert Tours of Italy, Germany, France, Switzerland, Holland and Turkey; Engaged at the Essen Opera from 1989, as the King in Aida, Herr Reich in Die Lustige Weiber von Windsor and Sarastro in Die Zauberflöte; Sang Mozart's Speaker at Frankfurt, 1991 and Fafner in Das Rheingold at Covent Garden. *Recordings include:* Die

Zauberflöte; Sacred Music by Mozart. *Address:* Theatre, Rolandstrasse 10, 4300 Essen, Germany.

SELLARS James Edward, b. USA. Composer; Teacher; Musician. *Education:* BM, Manhattan School of Music, 1968; MM, Highest Honours, Southern Methodist University, 1970; PhD, North Texas State University, 1977. *Career:* Conductor, Music Director, Brooklyn Heights Chorale, 1966-67; Harpsichordist with Camerata Ensemble, New York City, 1966-69; Teaching associate, composition & theory, Hartt College of Music, 1976-78; Music critic, Hartford Courant, 1976-81; Conductor, Hartt Contemporary Players, 1977-82; Assistant/associate professor, composition & theory, Hartt School of Music, University of Hartford, 1978-; Chairman, Composition Department, ibid, 1984-. Freelance conductor; Pianist, keyboard player. *Compositions:* Commissions from 1st Chamber Dance Company, New York, 1972; American Society for Commissioning New Music, 1975; Hartford Chamber Orchestra, 1980; London Spectrum, 1986. Published by Carl Fischer, Quadrivium Music Press, Hog River Music; Music video Haplomatics with artist David Hockney. *Recordings:* Spectrum Records. *Address:* 1800 Albany Avenue, Hartford, CT 06105, USA.

SELLARS Peter, b. 27 Sept 1957, Pittsburgh, Pennsylvania, USA. Opera Producer. *Education:* Harvard University. *Career:* Directed opera theatre while at Harvard; Don Giovanni for New Hampshire Symphony 1980 and Haydn's Armida; At Cambridge, Mass., directed Handel's Saul and Orlando, 1981 and at the Chicago Lyric Opera The Mikado, 1983; For the Boston Shakespeare Company produced the US premiere of The Lighthouse by Peter Maxwell Davies, 1983; British debut, Glyndebourne, 1987, with the world premiere of Nigel Osborne's The Electrification of the Soviet Union; Houston Opera 1987, with the premiere of Nixon in China by John Adams (seen at the 1988 Edinburgh Festival); Other productions include the Da Ponte operas of Mozart for the Pepsico Summerfare, New York, and Tannhäuser for the Chicago Lyric Opera, 1988. Artistic Adviser of the Boston Opera Theatre 1990; produced Die Zauberflöte at the 1990 Glyndebourne Festival; Premiere of The Death of Klinghoffer at Brussels 1991; Staged Messiaen's St François d'Assise, Salzburg 1992. *Recordings include:* Videos of Mozart's Da Ponte Operas (Decca). *Address:* c/o Harrison/Parrott Ltd, 12 Penzance Place, London W11 4PA, England.

SELLHEIM Eckart, b. 29 Oct 1939, Danzig. Pianist; Fortepianist; Accompanist. *Education:* Hamburg Conservatory; Piano, Accompanying, Musikhochschule, Cologne; Concert Diploma, 1963; Musicology, Music History, History of Art, Theatre, Cologne University. *Career:* Lecturer, Rheinische Musikschule, Cologne, 1963-69; Professor: Piano, Musikhochschule, Cologne, 1969-83; Piano, Piano Chamber Music, University of Michigan, Ann Arbor, USA, 1983-89; Piano Accompanying, Director of Accompanying, Arizona State University, Tempe, 1989-; Concert tours: Germany, Austria, England, France, Spain, Italy, Poland, Netherlands, USA, Latin America, Middle East; Duo with Friedrich-Juergen Sellheim, cello, 1965-; Several 100 radio recordings, Germany, Europe, USA. *Recordings include:* With Fr-J Sellheim, cello, CBS: Mendelssohn, 2 Cello sonatas, 2 Variations concertantes, Lied ohne Worte, 1976, Brahms, 2 Cello sonatas, 1977, Schumann, Fantasiestücke, Adagio und Allegro, Stücke im Volkston, 1978, Schubert, Arpeggione-Sonata, Brahms, Sonata, 1979, Chopin, Cello sonata, Polonaise brillante, Grand Duo concertant, 1980; Julius Weismann, Preludes and Fugues (Der Fugenbaum), Etudes, Christophorus, 1979; Liszt, Tausig, Wolf, Busoni, von Bülow, Wagner, RBM Digital, 1983; Boccherini, Piano concerto in Eb, Schobert, Piano concerto in G, Field, Rondeau in Ab, Harmonia Mundi, 1985; Debussy, Piano trio en sol, Cello sonata'; Intermezzo for cello & piano; Ravel, Violin sonata, Musicmasters, 1985; Brahms, transcriptions of Chopin, Bach, Weber, Gluck, Schumann, Schubert, Rakoczi March, also Brahms transcriptions by Max Reger & Theodor Kirchner, RBM Digital, 1990. *Publications:*

Editor, Spielbuch fuer Klavier. *Contributions to:* Friedrich Gruetzmacher, 1966; Oskar von Pander, 1968; Instrumentale Ausbildung-Klavier, 1980; Die Klavierwerke W Fr Bachs, Concerto, 1984. *Hobbies:* Museums; Libraries; Bird-watching. *Address:* 2416 West Nopal Avenue, Mesa, AZ 85202, USA.

SELLHEIM Friedrich-Juergen, b. 23 Aug 1948, Rehren, Germany. Cellist; Professor of Violoncello Performance. m. Doris M Ammann, 28 Dec 1973, 2 sons, 1 daughter. *Education:* NWD Musikakademie Detmold with Andre Navarra, 1967-73; Studied with Pierre Fournier in Geneva 1971-72; Kuenstlerische Reifepruefung 1971; Konzertexamen, 1973. *Career:* As Soloist since 1971; duo-Partner of his brother pianist, Eckart Sellheim, and chamber musician concerts in most European and many other countries; Founder and artistic director of International Master Classes Porto Carras, Greece; Radio recordings for all German radio stations and many others; Professor for violoncello at the Hochschule fuer Musik Hannover; Masterclasses in many countries. *Recordings:* Mendelssohn - complete music for cello and piano (CBS); Brahms - complete music for cello and piano (CBS); Schumann - complete music for cello and piano (CBS); Schubert - Sonata a minor, Arpeggione (CBS); Chopin - complete music for cello and piano (CBS), all recordings together with his brother, pianist Eckart Sellheim. *Current Management:* Konzertdirektion Drissen, Mainz. *Address:* Eichkatzweg 25, D-29313 Hambuehren, Germany.

SELLICK Phyllis Doreen, b. 16 June 1911, Newbury Park, Essex. m. Cyril Smith 1937 (deceased), 1 son, 1 daughter. *Education:* Royal Academy of Music 1925-27. *Debut:* Harrogate 1933, with the Grieg Concerto. *Career:* Tours with husband to Portugal, Belgium, France, Middle East, India, Germany, Russia, New Zealand; TV appearances with husband This is Your Life and No Turning Back; 3 Royal Concerts. *Recordings:* Walton's Sinfonia Concertante, with the composer conducting; Tippett's First Sonata; 2 Piano Works and duets with husband. *Honours:* ARAM 1942; FRAM 1950; RCM 1960; Order of the British Empire 1971. *Hobbies:* Reading; Yoga.

SELTZER Dov, b. 26 Jan. 1932, Iasi, Rumania. Composer; Conductor; Orchestrator; Musician. m. Graziella Fontana, 15 May 1968, 1 stepson. *Education:* Studied piano and Theory privately, 1944-47; Piano and General Music, Haifa and Tel-Aviv Conservatory, Israel, 1949-50; Composition with Mordecai Setter, 1950-53, with Herbert Bruen, 1952-54; Diploma in Composition, The Mannes College of Music, New York City, USA, 1958; BS Music, State University of New York, 1960. *Career:* Music Director, Composer, Israel Army Nachal Theatrical Group, 1950-53; Music Teacher, Afek School, Haifa; Arranger, Music Director, Oranim Zabar Folk Singers and Theodore Bikel for Elektra, Columbia Record Company, USA, 1956-58; Music Teacher, The Mannes College of Music, 1958-60; Freelance Composer, Conductor for theatre, musicals, films, records, Israel, USA, France, Italy, England, Germany, etc. Appeared as conductor with the Israel Philharmonic Orchestra, concert of his music, 1987. *Compositions:* Stempeniu, symphonic poem, 1985; This Scroll, cantata for Ben Gurion centenary, 1986; 15 musicals including; The Megillah, original, 1966, Broadway, 1968, TV, 1981; Kazablan, original, 1967, film version, 1974; I Like Mike, 1968; To Live Another Summer, 1971; Comme la neige en été, 1974; Film, TV, theatre and show scores; Concert of Israel Philharmonic conducted by composer, dedicated to his music, 1987; Music for T.V. series Thieves In The Night for German T.V., 1988; Music Director & Conductor of film version, Three Penny Operas, 1988; The Assissi Underground; Others; Numerous songs. *Recording:* Tradition, as conductor with Itzhak Perlman and The Israel Philharmonic Orchestra, 1986. *Hobbies:* Photography; Skiing; Visual arts. *Address:* 19 Netiv Hamazalot, Jaffa, Israel.

SELWYN David Morton, b. 21 Nov. 1951, Bristol, England. Composer; Teacher; Librettist; Conductor. *Education:* BA 1973, MMus 1979, University of Bristol.

Career: Lecturer in History and Composition, Extra-Mural Department, Bristol University, 1974-; Teacher of Music and English, Bristol Grammar School, 1975-; Conductor/MD, Bristol Opera Company, 1977-90. *Compositions:* Operas: Conversations with Miss Brown, 1975; The Little Marchioness, 1976; The Rocking Stone, 1980; Beauty and the Beast, 1984; The Retirement of Theophrastus, 1986; Islanders, 1990; The Visitation, 1991. Cantatas: The Legend of St Julian; Mount Nebo; Five Songs for St Francis; Susanna and the Elders; Saint Edward; King John and the Abbot of Canterbury; The Colours of Mary (published 1983); Harvest Work Song (published 1984); Also songs, instrumental pieces, and others; Libretti include: Rumpelstiltskin (Derek Bourgeois); St Patrick (Raymond Warren); Coffee Cantata (Bach). *Recordings:* BBC commissions: Incidental music to The Idiot Lady, 1980; The Beatitudes, 1981. *Contributions to:* Numerous reviews, articles on music, and others. *Hobbies:* Literature; Art; Travel. *Address:* 8 Barrow Court, Barrow Gurney, Bristol, England.

SEMKOV Jerzy (Georg) b. 12 Oct 1928, Radomsko, Poland. Conductor. *Education:* 1948-51 State High School Krakow with Arthur Malawski; 1951-53 Leningrad Conservatory with Boris Khaikin; Further studies with Erich Kleiber, Bruno Walter, Tullio Serafin. *Career:* Assistant to Mravinsky at the Leningrad Philharmonic 1954-56; Bolshoy Theatre 1956-58; 1959-62 Artistic Director and Principal Conductor of the Warsaw National Opera; 1966-76 Principal Conductor of the Danish Royal Opera, Copenhagen; US debut 1968, with the Boston Symphony Orchestra; Guest appearances with the Chicago Symphony, New York Philharmonic, Cleveland Orchestra; UK debut 1968, with the London Philharmonic; Covent Garden 1970, Don Giovanni; Music Director St Louis Symphony 1976-79; Artistic Director RAI Rome 1979-. *Recordings:* Late Romantic music and contemporary Danish works. Nielsen's Helios overture and Violin Concerto (Tibor Varga); Chopin 1st Piano Concerto (Vasary); Boris Godunov and Prince Igor (EMI); Schumann Symphonies and Manfred overture (Vox); Scriabin 2nd symphony (London Philharmonic), Mozart's Symphonies Nos. 33 and 36. *Hobbies:* Reading; Yachting. *Address:* U1. Dynasy 6/1, Warsaw, Poland.

SENATOR Ronald, b. 17 Apr. 1926, London, England. Teacher; Composer. m. Miriam Brickman, 1986. *Education:* Hertford College, Oxford University; London University; Trinity College of Music. PhD, BMus, FTCL. *Career includes:* Professor, Guildhall School of Music, & London University Institute of Education; Visiting Professor, Universities of Queensland & Melbourne (Australia), City University of New York, & Massachusetts Institute of Technology (USA), Toronto & McGill Universities (Canada), Tel-Aviv University (Israel). *Compositions include:* Insect Play (libretto, Ursula Vaughan Williams; Echoes, Pageant of London; Trotsky (book, Anthony Burgess); Kaddish for Terezin; Basket of Eggs; Streets of London; Francis & the Wolf (libretto, Peter Porter); Mobiles; Spring Changes; My Animals; Sun's in the East. *Recordings:* (Counterpoint and Musica Nova label) Francis & the Wolf; Spring Changes; Mobiles; Shakespeare Sonnets; Poet to his Beloved; Delos label, Holocaust Requiem, Moscow Philharmonic. *Publications:* General Grammar of Music, 1975; Musicolour, 1975; Editor, review, Counterpoint, 1947-50. *Address:* 20 Denbigh Gardens, Richmond, Surrey TW10 6EN, England.

SENN Marta, b. 1958, Switzerland. Singer (Mezzo-soprano). *Education:* Legal training in Colombia, musical study in the USA. *Career:* Sang Carmen for the Washington Opera in 1982; Further appearances with the New York City Opera, Houston Grand Opera, Philadelphia Opera and the Lyric Opera of Chicago; La Scala Milan 1984, as Rosina and in the title role of Rossi's Orfeo; Has sung Charlotte in Stuttgart, Paris, Hamburg and Nantes; Giulietta (Les Contes d'Hoffmann) in Madrid; Isabella in Rome; Massenet's Dulcinée at the Liceo, Barcelona in a production by Piero Faggioni; US tour with Placido Domingo in programmes of zarzuelas; Salzburg Festival 1988 as Annius in La Clemenza di Tito and Rossini's Angelina; Season 1988-89 as Sara in Roberto Deveruex at Naples and Meg in a new production of Falstaff at Bologna; Fenena in Nabucco and Verdi's Preziosilla at the Verona Arena; Munich State Theatre role of Carmen (Sinopoli conducting); Stuttgart State Theatre, role of Carmen (new production, Garcia Navarro conducting); Liceo, Barcelona (Olympics Arts Festival) role of Charlotte in Werther; Concerts and recording role of Salud in La Vida Breve (Venezuela and Minnesota Orchestra, Mata conducting), 1993; Paris Opera, Bastille role of Carmen (debut), 1994. *Recordings include:* Maddalena in Rigoletto, from La Scala, conducted by Riccardo Muti; role of Musetta in La Bohème Leoncavallo (Nuovo Era) in Venice; Role of Lola Cavalleria Rusticana (Philips); Salud La Vida Breve, (Mata conducting), 1993; El Amor Brujo (original version) (Nuovo Era); Charlotte in Lisbon and Rome; Dorabella in Toulon and Fidalma (Il Matrimonio Segreto, in Bologna). *Honours include:* Concours International de Paris 1982 (winner); First prize, Baltimore Opera National Auditions, 1982. *Current Management:* Fedeli Opera International, via Montegrappa 3, 40121 Bologna, Italy; Musicaglotz, SARL, 11 Rue La Verrier, 75006 Paris, France; Robert Lombardo Associates, 61 West 62nd Street, Suite 6F, New York, NY 10023, USA. *Address:* c/o Athole Still Ltd., Greystoke House, 80-86 Westow Street, London SE19 3AF, England.

SEOW Yitkin, b. 28 Mar. 1955, Singapore. Pianist. *Education:* Yehudi Mehuhin School, 1967-72; LRSM, 1967; Royal College of Music, 1972-75. *Debut:* Wigmore Hall, 1968. *Career:* Televised, 1975-; Royal Festival Hall, Philharmonia, 1975; Berlin Radio Symphony Orchestra, Hong Kong Arts Fesitval, 1977; Royal Philharmonic Orchestra, London Promenade Concert, 1982; TV, BBC Scottish Orchestra, 1985; Russia Tour, BBC Welsh orchestra, 1988. *Recordings:* Satie Piano Works; Janacek Piano Works; Debussy; Rachmaninov Cello Sonata; Yellow River Concerto (Gold Disc); Bartók Quartet as Violist, 1972 (with Nigel Kennedy). *Honours:* Winner, BBC Piano Competititon, 1974; Rubinstein Prize, Tel Aviv, 1977. *Membership:* ISM. *Hobbies:* Reading; Gardening. *Address:* 8 North Terrace, London SW3 2BA, England.

SEQUI Sandro, b. 10 Nov 1933, Rome, Italy. Stage Director. *Education:* Studied Literture and Philosophy at Rome University. *Career:* Directed La Sonnambula at the Teatro La Fenice Venice, 1961; Staging of I Puritani seen at Florence 1971, Metropolitan 1976, Rome 1990; Guillaume Tell at Florence 1972, Les Contes d'Hoffmann at Dallas 1975; Staged the premiere production of Mannino's Il Principe Felice at La Scala 1987, Rigoletto at the Chicago Lyric Opera, 1991. *Address:* Lungotevere Sanzio 1, 00153 Rome, Italy.

SERBAN Andrei, b. 21 June 1943, Bucharest, Rumania. Opera Producer. *Education:* Theatre Institute, Bucharest. *Career:* Worked on theatre productions with Peter Brook in New York and Paris; Opera debut with Welsh National Opera, Eugene Onegin; returned for I Puritani, Rodelinda, and Norma; Produced Die Zauberflöte in Nancy, 1979; Alcina at the New York City Opera; Staging of Turandot for the Royal Opera was seen in Los Angeles and London in 1984; Premiere of The Juniper-Tree by Philip Glass for Baltimore Opera, 1985; Fidelio at Covent Garden and Prokofiev's Fiery Angel for Geneva and Los Angeles; Don Carlos in Geneva and Bologna; Permanent post with the Boston Repertory Theatre; produced Prince Igor at Covent Garden 1990; The Fiery Angel seen at the Holland Festival 1990; I Puritani in London, 1992. *Address:* c/o Lies Askonas Ltd., 186 Drury Lane, London WC2B 5RY, England.

SERBO Rico, b. 9 May 1940, Stockton, CA, USA. Singer (Tenor). *Education:* Studied in San Francisco. *Debut:* San francisco 1965 as Ramiro in Cenerentola. *Career:* Sang in Opera at Seattle, Santa Fe and San Francisco, Europe from 1970; Notably with Netherlands Opera and at Koblenz, Essen and the Theater am

Gärtnerplatz Munich; Further Engagements at San Diego, New York City Opera, Houston, Toronto and Vancouver; New Orleans, as Arvino in the US premiere of I Lombardi; Deutsche Oper and Theater des Westens Berlin, Belfast; Other Roles have included Mozart's Ferrando and Tamino, Almaviva, Ernesto, Fenton, Alfredo, Tom Rakewell, Rodolfo, Boito's Faust, Lord Barrat in Der Junge Lord and Tony in Elegy for Young Lovers. *Recordings include:* Donizetti's L'Assedio di Calais.

SEREBRIER José, b. 3 Dec. 1938, Montevideo, Uruguay. Musician; Conductor. m. Carole Farley, 29 Mar. 1969, 1 daughter. *Education:* Diploma, National Conservatory, Montevideo, 1956; Curtis Institute of Music, USA, 1958; BA, University of Minnesota, 1960; Studied with Aaron Copland, Antal Dorati, Pierre Monteux. *Career:* Apprentice Conductor, Minnesota Orchestra, 1958-60; Associate Conductor, American Symphony Orchestra, New York City, 1962-66; Music Director, American Shakespeare Festival, 1966; Composer-in-Residence, Cleveland Orchestra, 1968-71; Artistic Director, International Festival of Americas, Miami, 1964-; Guest Conductor, numerous orchestras including London Symphony, London Philharmonic, Paris Radio, Cleveland, Philadelphia, Pittsburgh Symphony Orchestras; Royal Philharmonic; Scottish Chamber Orchestra; Royal Scottish National Orchestra. *Compositions:* Over 100 works including: Variations on a Theme from Childhood, for orchestra; Symphony for Percussion, for chamber; Violin Concerto, 1992; also works for chorus, voice, keyboard. *Recordings:* Conductor for many recordings including Ives 4th Symphony (London Philharmonic); Menotti Sebastian (LSO); Barber Souvenirs; Violin Concerto (ASV), 1993; RPO Tchaikowsky Works, IMG Classics, 1993. *Publication:* Violin Concerto, (Kalmus Music Publishers), 1993. *Contributions to:* Over 50 periodicals. *Honours:* Ford Foundation Conductors' Award; Alice M Ditson Award, 1976; Commission Award, National Endowment for the Arts, 1978; Guggenheim Fellow, 1958-60; Rockefeller Foundation Grantee, 1968-70. *Membership:* American Symphony Orchestra League. *Hobbies:* Swimming; Walking; Writing Novels. *Current Management:* Gershunoff Inc., New York City, USA. *Address:* 270 Riverside Drive, New York, NY 10025, USA.

SEREMBE Gilberto, b. 17 Dec 1955, Milan, Italy. Conductor; Professor of Orchestral Conducting. *Education:* Diploma in composition, Conservatorio G Verdi, Milan with Bruno Bettinelli, 1979; Studied conducting with Mario Gusella, Superior Courses, Conservatorio G. Verdi, Milan, 1977-78-79; Diploma cum laude, Orchestral Conducting, Accademia Chigiana, Siena, with Franco Ferrara, 1981. *Career:* Assistant, Teatro alla Scala, Milan, 1980; Professor of Composition, Conservatorio of Brescia, 1979-81; Professor of Orchestral Rehearsing: Conservatorio of Mantova, 1982-83, Conservatorio G. Verdi, Milan, 1984-86, Conservatorio of Brescia, 1986-88, Conservatorio of Genoa, 1989-; Professor of Orchestral Conducting, International Superior Courses, Accademia Musicale Pescarese, 1988-; Guest conductor: Pomeriggi Musicali Orchestra, Milan, 1976-77,1980-83, 1987, 1990, 1992; AIDEM Orchestra, Firenze, 1979; Angelicum Chamber Orchestra, Milan, 1980-83; San Remo Symphony Orchestra, 1980-87; Bari Symphony Orchestra, 1982-84; RAI Radio Television Symphony Orchestra, Turin, 1984, 1993; Principal Guest Conductor, International Symphony Orchestra, Jeunesses Musicales, Italian Tournee, 1983; International Youth Symphony Orchestra, 1984-87; Haydn Symphony Orchestra, Bozen, 1985, 1987, 1989; Teatro Massimo Symphony Orchestra, Palermo, 1986-88; ORT, Orchestra Regionale della Toscana, Florence, 1986-88; Stradivari Orchestra, Milan, 1991-92 and Hungarian tournee, 1991; Teatro Regio Symphony Orchestra, Turin, 1991; Toscanini Symphony Orchestra, Parma, 1993; Gothenburg Symphonic Orchestra, Sweden, 1989; BRT Radio Television Symphony Orchestra, Brussels, 1991; Turku Philharmonic, Finland, 1991; Tirana Radio and Television Symphony Orchestra,

Albania, 1993. *Current Management:* Via Zanella 43/
1, 20133 Milano, Italy.

SERENI Mario, b. 25 March 1928, Perugia, Italy.
Singer (Baritone). *Education:* Studied at the Accademia
di Santa Cecilia in Rome and at the Accademia Chigiana,
Siena. *Debut:* Florence 1953, in Lualdi's Il Diavolo nel
Campanile. *Career:* Sang in The Stone Guest by
Dargomyzhsky, Florence 1954; Palermo 1955, as
Wolfram in Tannhäuser; Metropolitan Opera from 1957:
almost 400 performances in 26 roles, including Gerard,
Sharpless, Germont, Amonasro, Belcore and Marcello;
Vienna 1965, Verona Arena 1965-74; Further
engagements in London, Chicago, Dallas, Houston,
London, Milan and Buenos Aires. *Recordings:* Madama
Butterfly, Andrea Chénier, La Bohème, Cavalleria
Rusticana, Elisir d'Amore, Aida, La Traviata (EMI);
Ernani, Turandot, Lucia di Lammermoor (RCA). *Address:*
c/o Arena di Verona, Piazza Brà 28, 1-37121 Verona,
Italy.

SERKIN Peter, b. 24 July 1947, New York, USA.
Pianist. *Education:* Lessons in music and piano with
Blanche Moyse and Luis Battle; Curtis Institute for six
years studying with Lee Luvisi, Mieczyslaw Horszowski
and his father, Rudolf Serkin. Further lessons and
studies with Ernst Oster, Marcel Moyse and Karl Ulrich
Schnabel. *Career:* Public concerts from the age of
twelve; Mozart Concertos at the Malboro Festival and
concerts with Alexander Schneider; Premiered Peter
Lieberson's Piano Concerto commissioned by the Boston
Symphony, 1985; Seiji Ozawa, 1985; Also premiered
works by Hans Werner Henze, Oliver Knussen, Toru
Takemitsu, Alexander Goehr, Luciano Berio and others;
Performed several pieces (music) including Classics and
plays music by Bach, Mozart, Beethoven, Brahms,
Schoenberg and Stravinsky; Teaches at the Tanglewood
Music Center annually. *Honour:* Prize for outstanding
artistic achievement from the Premier Internazionale
Accademia Musicale Chigiana. *Memberships:* Faculty
Member of the Juilliard School of Music and the Curtis
Institute of Music. *Address:* Shirley Kirshbaum &
Associates, 711 West End Avenue, Suite 5KN, New
York, NY 10025.

SERMILÄ Jarmo Kalevi, b. 16 Aug 1939,
Hämeenlinna, Finland. Composer. m. Ritva Vuorinen,
10 Nov 1962. *Education:* MA, Helsinki University, 1975;
Composition Diploma, Sibelius Academy, 1975. *Career:*
After beginning his career as a Jazz Musician he studied
further and became a composer; Has worked for Finnish
Radio's Experimental Music Studio as Artistic Director,
1973-79; President, Finnish Section ISCM, 1975-79;
Composer-in-Residence, Hämeenlinna, 1977-82;
Freelance Composer, 1982-, and Vice-President,
Society of Finnish Composers, 1981-; Artistic Leader
of the Time of Music contemporary music festival
(Viitasaari, Finland), 1988-.*Compositions:* Two ballets:
Wolf Bride; Merlin's Mascarade; pieces for orchestra:
Mimesis 2; Manifesto; Labor! Quattro rilievi; works for
instrumental solos with orchestral accompaniment:
Pentagram; A Circle of the Moon; La Place Revisitée;
On the Road; numerous chamber music and electro-
acoustic music pieces. *Recordings:* for Love, MGE,
Tactus, Jase and Ondine labels by artists like James
McDonald, Horn, Russ Hartenberger, Percussion, The
Finnish Radio Symphony conducted by Jukka-Pekka
Saraste, Avanti! Ensemble conducted by Olli Pohjola,
Jouko Harjanne, Trumpet, Puhallus Brass Trio,
Brassologia Quintet. *Honour:* Hameenlinna Music Prize,
1981; Art reward of the provincial art committee of
Häme, 1988; The long term state grant, 1989.
Membership: Society of Finnish Composers. *Address:*
Niittykatu 7 A 7, 13100 Hämeenlinna, Finland.

SEROV Edward, b. 9 Sept 1937, Moscow, USSR.
Symphony Orchestra Conductor. m. Guenrietta Serova,
29 June 1961, 2 sons. *Education:* Gnessin Institute,
Moscow, 1954-59; Tschaikovsky Conservatoire, Kiev,
1958-61; Rimsky-Korsakov Conservatoire, Leningrad,
1961-64. *Debut:* Kiev Opera, 1960. *Career:* Conductor,
Leningrad Philharmonic Orchestra, 1961-68, 1985-90;
Founder, Chief Conductor, Uljanovsk Philharmonic,

1968-77; Founder, Chief Conductor, Leningrad
Chamber Orchestra, 1974-85; Founder, Chief
Conductor, Wolgograd Philharmonic Orchhestra, 1987-
; Professor, Leningrad (now St Petersburg)
Conservatoire, 1987-; Chief Conductor, Odense
Symphony Orchestra, Denmark, 1991-; Foreign tours:
Japan, USA, France, Germany, Austria, Spain, Sweden,
Norway, Finland, Denmark, Czechoslovakaia, Hungary,
Yugoslavia, others. *Recordings:* Over 50 discs, mostly
for Melodiya, including works of Webern, Tishchenko,
Arensky, Mozart, Rubinstein, Tchaikovsky, Prokofiev,
Sviridov, Purcell, Tartini, Bartók, Slonimski, Petrov,
Hindemith, Mendelssohn, Bach, Nielsen, Rossini,
Ginastera, Shostakovich, Rodrigo, Elgar, Suk,
Schumann, Spohr, and Schubert. *Contributions to:* The
Exploit of Service to Music, The Soviet Music Magazine,
1980; About Conductor's Art, The Soviet Music, 1980;
The original Symphonic Narration, The Music Life
magazine, 1984; Meditation about G Sviridov to book
on Sviridov; Others. *Honours:* People's Artist of Russia
honorary of title, President of Russia, 1990. *Hobbies:*
Basketball; Mountain climbing. *Address:*
Warschawskaja str 124 kw 95, St Petersburg 196 240,
Russia.

SERRA Enric, b. 1943, Barcelona, Spain. Singer
(Baritone). *Education:* Studied in Barcelona. *Debut:*
Teatro del Liceo Barcelona, 1986, as Morales in Carmen.
Career: Has sung in Spain (Madrid, Valencia, Bilbao and
Barcelona) from 1969, notably as Falstaff, Scarpia,
Escamillo, Enrico, Belcore and Alcandro in Pacini's
Saffo, 1987: Guest engagements in Zurich, Cologne,
Nice, Tours, Naples, Venice, Bogota and Caracas, as
Don Pasquale, Rossini's Figaro, Alfonso (La Favorita)
and Don Carlos in La Forza del Destino; Schwetzingen
Festival, 1987, as Taddeo in L'Italiana in Algeri; Sang
Lescaut in Manon Lescaut at Barcelona, 1990; Concert
repertoire includes Falla's L'Atlantida (Madrid 1977).
Recordings include: Madame Butterfly, with Caballé
(Decca). *Address:* Gran Teatro del Liceo, Sant Pau I bis,
08001 Barcelona, Spain.

SERRA Luciana, b. 4 Nov 1946, Genoa, Italy. Singer
(Soprano). *Education:* Genoa Conservatoire and with
Michele Casato. *Debut:* Budapest Opera 1966, in
Cimarosa's Il Convito. *Career:* Member of Teheran Opera
1969-76; Sang Gilda in Rigoletto at Genoa, 1974;
Bologna 1979, in La Sonnambula; Covent Garden 1980,
as Olympia in Les Contes d'Hoffmann; Rossini's
Aureliano in Palmira at Genoa 1980; Hamburg 1982
and La Scala Milan 1983, as Lucia; US debut at
Charleston as Violetta; Chicago Lyric Opera 1983 as
Lakmé; Parma 1986 as Lucia; Rossini Opera Festival
Pessaro 1987 in L'Occasione fa il ladro (Rossini); Vienna
1988 as the Queen of the Night; Maggio Musicale
Florence 1989, as Elvira in I Puritani; Sang Gilda at
Turin 1989, Hanna Glawari at Trieste 1990; Santiago
1990, as Donizetti's Marie; Schwetzingen Festival 1990,
as Giulia in La Scala di Seta; Season 1992 as Zerlina
in Fra Diavolo at La Scala and Pamira in Le Siège de
Corinthe at Genoa; Other roles include Rosina, Fiorilla;
Ophelia, Philine; Bellini's Giulietta; Norina; Adina; Linda
di Chamounix and Marie in La Fille du Régiment; Concert
appearances in pre-classical works and music by Vivaldi,
Mozart, Rossini and Rimsky-Korsakov. *Recordings:*
Zerline in Fra Diavolo (Cetra); Torquato Tasso by
Donizetti; Die Zauberflöte (Philips); Les Contes
d'Hoffmann (EMI); Don Pasquale, Barbiere di Siviglia,
Gianni di Parigi (Donizetti); Fille du régiment (Nuovo Era);
La Scala di Seta and l'Occasione fa il Ladro (Ricordi).
Address: c/o Teatro alla Scala, Via Filodrammatici 2,
1-20121 Milan, Italy.

SERVADEI Annette Elizabeth, b. 16 Oct 1945,
Durban, Natal. Italian Pianist. m. 1972-1981, 1 son,
1 daughter. *Education:* Began studies with concert
pianist mother, 1949; Further studies, Milan, Detmold,
Salzburg, London, with Deckers, Schilde, Kabos, Zecchi,
W. Kempff; Also violin & organ studies, diploma level.
LTCL(T), 1964; LRSM(P), 1965; FTCL, 1970; BMus,
1979. *Debut:* Wigmore Hall, London, 1972. *Career:*
Started broadcasting aged 10; Concerto debut with
major orchestra, age 12; Recitals & concertos, very wide

repertoire, UK, West Europe, Africa, USA; Frequent radio & TV broadcats; University Senior Piano Tutor; Lecture recitals, master classes; Eisteddfod adjudicator; Outstanding performer of Liszt, Ravel, & 20th century American music; Considered by Wilhelm Kempff, one of best Beethoven students; Played world premiere, Tavener's Palintropos, London. *Recordings:* Britten & Khachaturian Piano Concertos, with London Philharmonic Orchestra (Hyperion); Recital Disc of Piano pieces, Mendelssohn, Schumann and Brahms (Pickwick); Complete Piano Music of Sibelius (5 CDs); Complete Piano Music of Dohnanyi, 1994-. *Honours:* Scholarships, Oppenheimer Trust, & AB, 1963-70. *Memberships:* Incorporated Society of Musicians; European Piano Teachers Association. *Hobbies:* Dress design; Reading; Italian cooking. *Address:* 3 Bournemouth Drive, Herne Bay, Kent CT6 8HH, England.

SESTAK Zdenek, b. 10 Dec 1925, Citoliby, Czechoslovakia. Composer. m. Marie Zatecka, 2 Sept 1950, 1 son, 1 daughter. *Education:* Gymnasium, Louny, 1936-44; Conservatorium de la Musique, Prague, 1945-50; Charles University, Faculty of Philosophy, 1945-50 (PhDr). *Career:* Professor of Music, 1952-57; Freelance Composer, 1957-; Dramaturge, Centre for Symphonic Music, Radio Czechoslovakia, Prague, 1968-70. *Compositions:* Symphonie II 1970, III 1971, IV 1979, V Chronos 1978, VI L'Inquietude Eternelle du Coeur, 1979; Sonata Symphonica, 1976; Variations Symphoniques, 1980; I Concert for Violin (Sursum Corda) 1981; II Concert for Violin (Jean, Le Violinist) 1985; Concert for Viola (Meditations de Socrates) 1982; Memoria (La Fresque Symphonique de Variation), 1983; Fatum (Vocale - Symphonique Fragment d'Apres Sophocles) 1983; Queen Dagmar (Oratorium d'Apres Libreto Dagmar Ledecova, 1989; String Quartet III (Akroasis 1975), IV (La Voix Connue) 1976, V (Labyrint de L'Ame) 1976; String Quintet (Concentus musicus) 1975; Sonata da Camera, 1978; Euterpe (Auletika pour Houtbois et Piano) 1977; Hommage a Apolinaire (poem for mixed choir) 1972; Portrait du Poete Konstantin Biebl (chorus cycle) 1974; Vigilie du Pushkin (choral work) 1978; Les Cycles des Chants sur Vers de Villon, Michelangelo Buonarotti, Hora, Macha, Jelen, Sefl, King Salamon, Le testament Ancien (Book of Ecclesiasticas). *Publications:* La Musique de Maîtres de Citoliby de 18 Siècle, 1968, 1985. *Membership:* Association of Music Artist Tcheques. *Hobby:* Cycling. *Address:* Pracska 2594/87. 10600 Prague 10, Republique Tcheque.

SESTAKOVA Marie Langerova, b. 30 Aug 1951, Louny, Czechoslovakia. Concert Organist. m. Langer Milan, 30 June 1979. 2 daughters. *Education:* Conservatoire, Prague, 1973; Academy of Music, Prague, 1977; Postgraduate Study, Hochschule für Musik, Franz Liszt, Weimar, German Democratic Republic, 1979. *Career:* Teacher of Music, 1979-80; Freelance Organist, 1980-; Solo Concerts in Czechoslovakia, Russia, Finland, German Democratic Republic; Collaboration with Prague Chamber Orchestra, Prague Radio Orchestra and Virtuosi di Praga; Member, Pachta Chamber Harmony, Harpsichord; TV and Radio Appearances. *Recordings:* L Sluka, Ways for Organ, Way of a Shadow, Way of Silence, Way of a Recovery; Czech Masters of the 18th Century; Radio recordings. *Membership:* Union of Czech Composers and Concert Artists. *Current Management:* Pragokoncert, Praha. *Address:* Hajo Kropackova 559, 149 00 Prague 4, Czech Republic.

SETER Mordecai, b. 26 Feb 1916, Novorosysk, Russia. Composer. m. Dina Pevsner, 31 Aug 1939, 1 son, 1 daughter. *Education:* The Hertzelia Gymnasium, Tel-Aviv; Ecole Normale de Musique, Paris 1934-37; Studies with Paul Dukas, Nadia Boulenger, Lazare Levy; BA Piano; MA Harmony; MA Counterpoint; BA Composition. *Debut:* Préludes, V1. Perlemuter (Piano), Société Nationale de Musique, Paris 1934. *Career:* 4 hebdomadary Radio interviews at occasion of his 70th anniversary, Jerusalem, Kol Israel, (The Voice of Israel) October 1986. *Compositions:* Choral Music: Sabbath Cantata, Choir and Strings 1940; 3 Motets a capella 1940; Festive Songs a capella 1946; Midnight Vigil,

Oratorio, Choirs and Orchestra 1961; Jerusalem, Choral Symphony 1966; Hallel, c capella 1966; etc. Chamber Music: Sonata for 2 violins 1952; Sonata for Solo Violin 1954; Ricercar for Strings 1953; Chamber Music 6 works 1970; 4 String Quartets 1975-77; 2 Piano Trios; 2 Piano Quartets; 2 Quintets; Numerous Piano Works. Symphonic Music: Meditation 1966; Variations 1959; Sinfonietta 1960; Jephthah's Daughter, 1965. *Recordings:* Ricercar for String Quartet; Yemenite Suite for Voice and Orchestra; Sine Nomine for Piano Solo; Midnight Vigil, Radiophonic Version; Jephthah's Daughter, Orchestra; String Quartet No. 2 (to be released); Midnight Vigil, concert version (to be released). *Honours:* Professor Emeritus, University of Tel-Aviv Academy of Music 1984; Tel-Aviv Municipality Prize 1945, 1954; Société des Auteurs et des Compositeurs: 1956, 1957, 1981; Premio d'Italia, Verona 1962; Israel State Prize 1965; The Ricercar for Strings was chosen as one of the five best works presented at the International Competition of The Rostrum, Paris 1961. *Hobby:* Cycling. *Address:* 1 Karny Street, Tel- Aviv 69025, Israel.

SETTARI Olga, b. 22 Nov 1941, Czech Republic. Professor of Music; Interpreter. 1 daughter. *Education:* Studied at School of Foreign Language, Brno Masaryk University. *Debut:* Graduation Piano Recital, 1963. *Career:* Since 1963 Soloist, Pianist, Harpsichordist, Chamber Player; Regular Radio Appearances in Brno and Prague, TV Appearances, Over 250 Public Concerts; Artistic Leader of the Musical Ensemble Collegium Musicum of the University Brno; Professor of Piano Performance at the Janáček Academy of Music and the Faculty of Arts Masaryk University. *Recordings include:* J A Benda Concerto for Harpsichord and Strings; Bach, Händel, Telemann, Paradisi, Galuppi; Contemporary Music by Moravian Composers Miloslav Ištvan. *Publications:* Olga Settari; The Edition of the Sacred Songs of John Amos Comenius; Adolf Cmiral, The Monograph About the Czech Music Composer. *Contributions to:* Music Tradition in Moravia; Comenius and Music. *Honours:* 3 Honours for Research About J A Comenius. *Memberships:* International Musicological Society; The Czech Society of Music Performers; Czech Music Society; The Association of Music Artists. *Hobby:* Planting Flowers. *Current Management:* Masaryk University Brno. *Address:* Talichova 48, 623 00 Brno 23, Czech Republic.

SHACKLOCK Constance, b. 16 Apr 1913, Sherwood, Nottingham, England. Singer (Mezzo-soprano). *Education:* Studied at the Royal Academy of Music with Frederick Austin. *Career:* Sang first in Concert then joined the Covent Garden Opera Company, singing in its First Production, Purcell's Fairy Queen, 1946; Guest Artist at Berlin State Opera, 1952; Remained at Covent Garden until 1956 her repertory including Carmen, Marina in Boris Godunov, Magdalene in Die Meistersinger von Nürnberg, Mrs Sedley in Peter Grimes, Brangäne in Tristan und Isolde, Azucena in Il trovatore, Amneris in Aida, Octavian in Der Rosenkavalier, Fricka in the Ring, Herodias in Salome, Ortrud in Lohengrin and Erda in Siegfried; Has also sung in Ireland, the Netherlands, Russia and at the Teatro Colón, Buenos Aires and given many recitals, broadcasts and concerts. *Recordings include:* Tristan Act II duet with Flagstad and Svanholm; Messiah. *Honour:* OBE, 1971. *Address:* c/o Royal Opera House, Covent Garden, London WC2, England.

SHADE Ellen, b. 17 Feb 1944, New York, USA. Singer (Soprano). *Education:* Studied at the Juilliard Opera Center and with Cornelius Reid; Further study at the Santa Fe Opera, 1969-69. *Debut:* Frankfurt 1972, as Liu in Turandot. *Career:* Sang Micaela at Pittsburgh 1972 (US debut); Further engagements in Cincinnati, Milwaukee, Dallas and New Orleans; Chicago 1976, as Emma in Khovanshchina, returning as Eve in the premiere of Penderecki's Paradise Lost, 1978; Metropolitan Opera debut 1976, as Eva in Die Meistersinger; New York City Opera 1981, Donna Elvira; Sang in Paradise Lost at La Scala in 1979 and has made further European appearances at Hamburg,

Brussels, Vienna (Florinda in Schubert's Fierabras, conducted by Abbado), and Geneva (Katya Kabanova, 1988); Returned to the Metropolitan as Sieglinde in Die Walküre, conducted by James Levine; Season 1992 as the Empress in Die Frau ohne Schatten, at Amsterdam and Salzburg; Other roles include Verdi's Alice Ford, Wagner's Elsa and Freia, Climene in Cavalli's Egisto and Agathe in Der Freischütz. *Address:* c/o Metropolitan Opera, Lincoln Center, New York, NY 10023, USA.

SHADE Frederick Albert, b. 16 Oct 1944, Melbourne, Australia. Flautist. m. Elizabeth Grierson, 19 Feb 1966, 1 son, 2 daughters. *Education:* Performer's Diploma, AMusA, flute, 1963; BA, Music & Philosophy, Melbourne, 1971; Diploma, Religious Studies, LCIS, 1985. *Debut:* Flute concerto with orchestra, aged 12. *Career:* Freelance flautist, principal flute, various orchestras including: Astra Chamber, Elizabethan Trust, Melbourne Symphony, Melbourne Philharmonic & Philharmonia, 1960's-70's; Principal piccolo, Melbourne Symphony Orchestra, 1975-; Founder, Praetorius Wind Quartet, 1977-. Teaching includes: Specialist, Victoria Education Department, 1975-77; Melbourne College of Advancd Education, 1975-86; Victoria College of Arts, 1975-81; Chief Study Tutor, Faculty of Music, University of Melbourne, 1976-. Examiner, various bodies. *Recordings:* Numerous broadcasts, recordings, Australian Broadcasting Corporation, including 1st performances, commissioned works by Australian composers; J. S. Bach Sonatas, 1986; Mozart Sonatas, 1987; Romantic Flute, 1988; Handel, 1990. *Publications:* Editor, Flute Studies 1987, Mozart Sonatas 1988. *Address:* 20 Thomson Drive, Rosanna, Victoria 3084, Australia.

SHADE Nancy Elizabeth, b. 31 May 1949, Rockford, Illinois, USA. Opera and Concert Singer (Soprano). *Education:* De Pauw University; Indiana University; Principal Voice Teacher, Vera Scammon. *Debut:* Kentucky Opera Theatre, 1968, as Leonora in Il Trovatore. *Career:* Lulu, Frankfurt Opera; Countess in Figaro, Hamburg State Opera; Manon Lescaut, Munich State Opera; Marguerite in Faust, San Francisco Opera; Madame Butterfly, New York City Opera; Marie in Die Soldaten, Lyons; Sante Fe 1984, in the US premiere of Henze's We Come to the River; Stuttgart 1988, as Marie in Die Soldaten (repeated Vienna 1990). *Honours:* 1st prize, National Metropolitan Auditions, 1968. *Hobbies:* Studying in classes with inner-development author, Vernon Howard, Boulder City, Nevada. *Current Management:* Thea Dispeker, New York City, USA. *Address:* c/o Thea Dispeker, 59 East 54th Street, New York, NY 10022, USA.

SHAFF Stanley M., b. 14 Feb 1929, San Francisco, California, USA. Composer; Teacher. m. Anna Gordon, 15 Dec 1967, 1 son. *Education:* BA, Music and Education, San Francisco State College, 1946-50; MA, Music, 1950-52. *Career:* Professional Trumpet Player, 1945-63; Compositional, 1960-64; Concerts of electronic compositions at University of California, 1960; San Francisco State College, 1962; San Franciso Museum of Art, 1963, 1964; Creation and development of Audium, the first sound theatre for the spatial performance of electronic music, 1965-70; Re-establishment of Audium within a building designed from floor to ceiling for the special needs of spatial composition and performance, 1973-75; Weekly public performances, 1975-. *Compositions:* 9 music concrete works (untitled) performed at above listed institutions, 1960-64; 6 major music concrete works (untitled), various minor works composed for spatial performance at the Sound Theatre Audium, 1965-. *Contributions to:* Music Journal, Jan 1977. *Honours:* National Endowment for the Arts Grant, 1972; Six National Endowment for the Arts Grants for performance seminars series for colleges and for the creation of new compositions, 1975-81. *Membership:* Musicians Union. *Hobby:* Visual Arts. *Address:* c/o Audium, 1616 Bush Street, San Francisco, CA 94109, USA.

SHAGUCH Marina, b. 1964, Krasnodar, Russia. Singer (Soprano). *Education:* Studied at the Arts School

in Maikop and at the St Petersburg State Conservatoire. *Career:* Sang at the Kirov Opera Theatre in season 1991-92, Notably in Mussorgsky's Sorochinsky Fair and Il Trovatore; Concert Debuts at the Grand Hall of the Moscow Conservatoire and in the Glinka Capella in St Petersburg; Further Appearances elsewhere in Russia, USA, Germany, Wales; Concert reportoire has included works by Handel, Mozart, Rimsky, Schumann, Schubert, Wolf, Dvořák, Brahms. *Honours include:* Winner of the Mussorgsky All Russia and Glinka National Singing Competitions; Second Prize Tchaikovsky International Competition. *Address:* c/o Sonata, 11 Northpark Street, Glasgow G20 7AA, Scotland.

SHAHAM Gil, b. 1971, Ilinois, USA. Concert Violinist. *Education:* Studied at the Rubin Academy in Jerusalem, in Aspen and at Juilliard with Dorothy De Lay. *Debut:* Concert with the Jerusalem Symphony Conducted by Alexander Schneider. *Career:* Appeared with the Israel Philharmonic Under Zubin Mehta, 1982; Engagements with the New York Philharmonic, London Symphony and La Scala Philharmonic; Season, 1987-88 with the LSO at the Barbican, Bavarian Radio Orchestra in Munich, the RAI Turin and Recitals at La Scala and in Munich; Debut with the Philadelphia Orchestra and Tour of South America, 1988; Season, 1988-89 with the Berlin Philharmonic, Orchestre de Paris, Frankfurt Symphony and the Philharmonic under Sinopoli; Bruch and Sibelius Concertos with the LSO, 1989; Recital Debut at the Wigmore Hall, Lodnon, 1990. *Honours include:* First Prize, 1982 Claremont Competition, Israel. *Address:* c/o Anglo Swiss Ltd, 3 Primrose Mews, 1a Sharpleshall Street, London NW1 8YW, England.

SHAMIR Michal, b. 1960, Tel Aviv, Israel. Singer (Soprano). *Education:* Studied at the Rubin Academy of Music, Tel Aviv, and in London. *Career:* operatic Debut as Gluck's Euridice, Followed by Cherubino and Elvira in L'Italiana in Algeri; European Debut at Hamburg as Susanna, Followed by Pamina, Gretel and Frasquita; Geneva opera 1987, as Larissa in the Premiere of La Foret by Liebermann; Appearances with Frankfurt Oper as Susanna, Despina, Gilda, Marzelline & Jenny in Mahagonny; Has returned to Tel Aviv for Violetta, Nedda and Marquerite; Basle Opera in Zemlinsky's Der Zwerg, Currently Member of the Deutsche Oper Berlin; concert repertoire includes Lutoslawski's Chantefleurs et Chantefables, Performed with the Composer in San Francisco and Helsinki; British Debut as Violetta in La Traviata with Opera North, 1994; First Tatiana in Eugene Onegin in Lausanne, Switzerland, 1994. *Address:* c/o IMG Artists, Media House, 3 Burlington Lane, London W4 2TH, England.

SHANE Rita Frances, b. 1940, New York City, USA. Opera/Concert Singer. m. Daniel F Tritter, 1 son. *Education:* BA, Barnard College; Private Study: Beverly Peck Johnson, Elisabeth Schwarzkopf; Santa Fe Opera Apprentice Program; Hunter College Opera Workshop. *Career:* Appearances with: Metropolitan Opera, Chicago Lyric, San Francisco, New York City Opera, most American companies; La Scala, Vienna Staatsoper, Bavarian State Opera, Turin, Strasbourg, Scottish, other opera houses in Europe, South America; Orchestras of Philadelphia, Cleveland, Cincinnati, in USA, Santa Cecilia, Vienna. in Europe, Israel Philharmonic; Festivals: Salzburg, Vienna, Munich, Glyndebourne, Perugia, Aspen; Mostly Mozart, Canada; Roles at Met. Opera New York include the Queen of Night, Lucia, Berthe in Le Prophète, Pamira in The Siege of Corinth, Verdi's Gilda, Oscar and Violetta; Recitals; TV: CBC Canada, Bayerische Rundfunk, Germany; Sang title role in the premiere of Argento's Miss Havisham's Fire, New York City Opera, 1979. *Recordings:* Highlights from Handel's Athalia; Highlights from Handel's Rinaldo; Complete works of Schoenberg, volume 2; R. Strauss, Brentano Songs, Op. 68 with orchestra (Louisville Premiere); Various private recordings including: Les Huguenots, Die Zauberflöte, etc; Professor of Voice, Eastman School of Music, Rochester, New York. *Hobbies:* Purebred Dachshunds; Floral Arrangement. *Address:* c/o Daniel F. Tritter, 545 Fifth Avenue, New York, NY 10017, USA. 2. 5.

SHANKAR Ravi, b. 7 Apr 1920, Varanasi, India. Musician (Sitar Player). m. Sukanya Rajan, 23 Jan 1989. *Education:* Studied under Ustad Allaudin Khan of Maihar. *Debut:* 1939. *Career:* International career as solo sitarist; Former director of music, All-India Radio; Founded National Orchestra of All-India Radio; Founder/Director Kinnara School of Music, Bombay, 1962 and Los Angeles, 1967; Stage work Ghanashyam (A Broken Branch) premiered by the City of Birmingham Touring Opera, 1989. *Compositions:* 2 Concertos for Sitar and Orchestra, 1971, 1981; Film scores for Pather Panchali, Charlie, Chappaqua, Gandhi; Music for TV production of Alice in Wonderland; Opera-ballet Ghanashyam, 1989. *Recordings:* Concertos Nos. 1 and 2; Raga Jageshwari 1981; Homage to Mahatma Gandhi 1981 West meets East, with Yehudi Menuhin, and many others. *Publication:* My Music, My Life 1968. *Honours:* Fellow, Sangeet Natak Academy 1976; Padma Vibhushan 1981; Elected to Rajya Sabha (Indian Upper House) 1986. *Address:* Christopher Tennant Artists Magament, Unit 10, 39 Tadema Road, London SW10 OPY, England.

SHANKS Don, b. 5 July 1940, Brisbane, Australia. Singer (Bass- baritone). *Career:* Sang first in operettas by Gilbert and Sullivan, then toured Australia with the Williamson-Sutherland Opera Company; From 1964 has sung with the Australian Opera, Sydney, as Don Pasquale, Verdi's Zaccaria (Nabucco), Philip II, Fiesco and Grand Inquisitor, Rossini's Don Basilio and Dulcamara; Covent Garden 1974 as Fafner in Das Rheingold, repeated at the Paris Opéra under Solti; Sang the King in Aida at Sydney in 1988 and Osmin in Die Entführung aus dem Serail for the Lyric Opera of Queensland at Brisbane, 1989; Season 1991-92 as Baron Ochs and Mozart's Bartolo, at Sydney. *Address:* c/o Lyric Opera of Queensland, PO Box 677, South Brisbane, QLD 4101, Australia.

SHANKS Donald DeWitt, b. 10 Dec 1923, San Diego, California, USA. Organist. m. Sibyl Shipley, 3 Sept 1949, 3 sons. *Education:* BMus 1948, MMus 1949, Columbia University, New York; PhD, Wadham College, Oxford University, UK, 1958. *Career:* Organist & Choirmaster, St Joseph's Cathedral, San Diego, California; Organ recitals, Europe & USA. *Publication:* Dissertation (Oxford): Evolution of Organ & Development of use as an Instrument for Accompaniment of Choral Music in Major Cathedral & Collegiate Churches of Spain, 16th Century to Present, 1956. *Memberships:* Hymn Society of America; Past Dean, San Diego Chapter, American Guild of Organists; Oxford & Cambridge University Club, London, UK. *Hobbies:* International travel. *Address:* 2037 Torrey Pines Road, La Jolla, California 92037, USA.

SHANKS Lois, b. 13 Oct 1931, Wellston, OH, USA. Musician. m. William Shanks, 11 Sept 1955, 1 son, 1 daughter. *Education:* Studied at Ohio University, then Jacksonville University. *Debut:* Jacksonville, Florida, 1970. *Career:* Organist, Director of Music at St Lukes Episcopal Church, Orange Presbyterian Church; Director of the Culpeper, Piedmont Choral Society; Conduct 5 or 6 Yearly Concerts. *Honours:* Highest Grade Point Average During Graduating Year at Jacksonville University; Masters Degree, Catholic University of America. *Memberships:* American Choral Director Association; Mu Phi Epsilon at American University. *Hobbies:* Interior Decorating; Travel; Reading; Grandchildren. *Address:* 105 Jackson Court, Rt4, Warrenton, VA 22186, USA.

SHANNON Randall Phillip, b. 19 Feb 1953, Holywood, Northern Ireland. Musician; Administrator. m. Jae Lindsay Mussett, 13 Aug 1983. *Education:* Ulster College of Music, 1968-71; BMus, University of Surrey, England, 1971-74. *Career:* Freelance Musician, 1974-84; Orchestra Manager, Opera 80, 1979-84; Manager, Irish Chamber Orchestra, 1984-87; Founder and Administrator, Opera Theatre Company, 1986-88; Appointed General Manager, Opera Northern Ireland, 1 Jan. 1988. *Memberships:* International Society of Performing Arts Administrators (ISPAA). *Address:* 53 Belvedere Park, Belfast, BT9 5GT, Northern Ireland.

SHAO En, b. 1954, Tianjin, China. Conductor. *Education:* Piano Studies from age of four, Violin From five; Peking Centre Music Conservatory and Royal Northern College of Music. *Career:* Deputy Principal Conductor of the Chinese Broadcasting Symphony Orchestra and Principal Guest Conductor of the Central Philharmonic Orchestra of Ogina and the National Youth Orchestra; Engagements in Europe from 1988; Associate Conductor of the BBC Philharmonic Orchestra, 1990; Principal conductor and Artistic Advisor of the Ulster Orchestra, 1993; Guest Appearances with the Bournemouth Symphony, Northern Sinfonia, Royal Liverpool Philharmonic and Other BBC Orchestras; London Debut, 1992 with the LSO; European engagements with the Oslo Philharmonic the Berlin Symphony and the Czech Philharmonic; Prague Autumn Festival 1993; Concerts with the ABC Orchestras in Australia and the Hong Kong Philharmonic; North American showings with the Toronto Symphony and the Colorado and Vancouver Symphonies. *Honours:* Lord Rhodes Scholarship; First Edward Van Beinum Scholarship; Winner, Sixth Hungarian TV Conductors Competition. *Hobbies:* Chinese Cooking; Interior Design; Ballet; Jazz. *Address:* c/o IMG Artists, Media House, 3 Burlington Lane, London W4 2TH, England.

SHAPERO Harold (Samuel), b. 29 Apr 1920, Lynn, Massachusetts, USA. Pianist; Teacher; Composer. *Education:* Studied piano with Eleanor Kerr; Composition with Nicolas Slonimsky, Malkin Conservatory, Boston 1936-37; with Ernst Krenek, 1937, with Walter Piston, Harvard University, 1938-41; With Paul Hindemith, Berkshire Music Center, Tanglewood, summers, 1940, 1941; Nadia Boulanger, Longy School of Music, 1942-43. *Career:* Pianist; Teacher 1952-, Founder-director, electronic music studio, Brandeis University. *Compositions:* Orchestral: 9-Minute Overture, 1940; Serenade, 1945; Symphony for Classical Orchestra, 1947; Sinfonia: The Travelers Overture, 1948; Concerto, 1950; Credo, 1955; Lyric Dances, 1955; On Green Mountain for Jazz Ensemble, 1957; for orchestra, 1981; Partita for Piano and Small Orchestra, 1960; Chamber: String Trio, 1938; 3 Pieces for Flute, Clarinet and Bassoon, 1939; Trumpet Sonata, 1940, String Quartet, 1941; Violin Sonata, 1942; 3 Improvisations for Piano and Synthesizer, 1968; 3 Studies for Piano and Synthesizer, 1969; 4 Pieces for Piano and Synthesizer, 1970; Piano: Sonata for 4-hands, 1941; 3 sonatas, all 1944; Variations, 1947; Sonata, 1948; American Variations, 1950; Vocal: 4 Baritone Songs, 1942; 2 Psalms for Chorus, 1952; Hebrew Cantata for Soprano, Alto, Tenor, Baritone, Chorus and 5 Instruments, 1954; 2 Hebrew Songs for Tenor and Piano, 1970, also for Tenor, Piano and String Orchestra, 1980. *Recordings:* Several compositions recorded. *Honours:* American Prix de Rome, 1941; Naumburg Fellowship, 1942; Guggenheim Fellowships, 1947, 1948; Fulbright Fellowship, 1948. *Address:* c/o Music Department, Brandeis University, Waltham, MA 02254, USA.

SHAPEY Ralph, b. 12 Mar 1921, Philadelphia, Pennsylvania, USA. Composer; Conductor; Professor. m. (1) Vera Shapiro, 28 Oct 1957, 1 son. (2) Elsa Charlaton, 12 Oct 1985. *Education:* Studied violin with Emanuel Zeitlin; Composition with Stefan Wolpe. *Career:* Assistant Conductor, Philadelphia National Youth Administration Symphony Orchestra, 1938-47; Founder-Music Director, Contemporary Chamber Players, Chicago, 1954-; Teacher, University of Pennsylvania, 1963-64; Professor of Music, University of Chicago, 1964-85, 1986-; Distinguished Professor of Music, Aaron Copland School of Music, Queens College of the City University of New York, 1985-86. *Compositions:* Orchestral: Fantasy for Symphony orchestra, 1951; Symphony No 1, 1952; Concerto for Clarinet and Chamber Ensemble, 1954; Challenge-The Family of Man, 1955; Ontogeny, 1958; Invocation, violin concerto, 1958; Rituals, 1959; Double Concerto for

Violin, Cello and Orchestra, 1983; Groton: 3 Movements for Youth Orchestra, 1984; Symphonie Concertante, 1985; Concerto for Piano, Cello and Strings, 1986; Chamber: 7 string quartets: 1946, 1949, 1950-51, 1953, 1957-58, 1963, 1972; Piano Quintet, 1946-47; Violin Sonata, 1949-50; Oboe Sonata, 1951-52; Cello Sonata, 1953; Piano Trio, 1953-55; Evocation for Violin, Piano and Percussion, 1959; Chamber Symphony for 10 Instruments, 1962; Convocation for Chamber Group, 1962; Brass Quintet, 1963; String Trio, 1965; Evocation II for Cello, Piano and Percussion, 1979; III for Viola and Piano, 1981; Krosnick Soli for Cello, 1983; Mann Duo for Violin and Piano, 1983; Concertante for Trumpet and 10 Players, 1984; Kroslish Sonate for Cello and Piano, 1985; Concertante II for Alto Saxophone and 14 Players, 1987; Soli for Solo Percussion, 1985; Intermezzo for Dulceme & Piano/Celesta, 1990; Duo for 6 Winds, two players, 1991; Centeenial Celebration for Soprano, Mezzo Soprano, Tenor, Baritone & 12 players, 1991; Movement of Varied Movements for Two, Flute and Vibraphone, 1991; Trio 1992 for Violin, Cello, Piano, 1992; Trio Concertant for Violin, Piano & Percussion, 1992; Dinosaur Annex for Violin, Vibraphon & Marimba/Block, 1993; Constellations for Bang on Can All-stars, 1993. Piano pieces; Various vocal works. *Recordings:* Several works recorded. *Address:* 5532 South Shore Drive No 18D, Chicago, IL 60637, USA.

SHAPIRO Joel, b. 28 Nov 1934, Cleveland, Ohio, USA. Concert Pianist; Teacher. *Education:* AB, Columbia College, New York City; Private Study with Beryl Rubinstein and Frank Sheridan; Brussels Royal Conservatory with Stefan Askenase; Premier Prix avec Distinction, 1959. *Debut:* New York City, 1963; As a soloist with Royal Philharmonic Orchestra, 1968. *Career:* Extensive annual concert tours including piano recitals, concertos and chamber music in the World's leading music centres; Numerous radio and TV broadcasts; Professor of Piano, University of Illinois, 1970-1993; Professor of Piano, Staatliche Hochschule für Musik, Leipzig, 1994-. *Honours:* Winner, Young Concert Artists International Auditions, New York City, 1961; 1st Prize, Darche Competition, Brussels, 1962; Harriet Cohen International Bach Award, London, 1963; Awards from International Institute, 1964 and Rockefeller Foundation, 1965. *Address:* School of Music, University of Illinois, Urbana, IL 61801, USA.

SHAPIRO Michael Jeffrey, b. 1 Feb 1951, Brooklyn, New York, USA. Composer; Pianist. m. Theresa Vorgia, 14 Aug 1975, 2 sons. *Education:* BA, Columbia College, New York City; MM, Juilliard School, New York City. *Career:* Musical Assistant, International Opera Center, Zurich Opera, 1973-74; Many appearances on New York radio stations WQXR and WNYC and CBC Vancouver, KUHF Houston and National Public Radio Stations. *Compositions:* Orchestral: Concerto for guitar and strings; Lamentations; A Declaration of Independence, July 4, 1776 for narrator and orchestra; Sinfonia Concertante for violin, cello and strings; Symphony - Pomes Penyeach; Lyric Variations; Concerto for piano and orchestra. Opera: The Love of Don Perlimplin and Belisa in the Garden (Federico Garcia Lorca). Chamber Music: Sonata for violin and piano; Sonata for clarinet and piano; Kaddish for solo flute. Shir for flute and piano. Piano Music: Five Dance Preludes; Mysteries; Songs of the Jewish Ghetto; First Sonata; Second Sonata. Vocal Music: Three Early Songs; Canciones; Songs for American Poets; Dublin Songs; Erotic Songs; Child's Garden; Wordsworth Songs; Choral Music: Three Shakespeare Madrigals (SATB); Three Psalms (SSAA); There is That in Me (SATB); Psalm 137 (SATB, organ); Eight Medieval Lyrics (SSATB); Variations for solo Cello. *Contributions to:* An Everlasting Covenant, The 100 Most Influential Jews of All Time, Birch Lane Press (Carol Publishing Group, New York). *Hobbies:* Home renovation; Summer sports. *Address:* 974 Hardscrabble Road, Chappaqua, NY 10514, USA.

SHAPIRRA Elyakum b. 1926, Tel-Aviv, Israel. Conductor. *Education:* Studied with Bernstein and Koussevitzky at Tanglewood and the Juilliard School. *Career:* Assistant with the San Francisco Symphony Orchestra; Conducted the New York Philharmonic on tours to Canada and Japan, 1960-61; Associate Conductor of the Boston Symphony Orchestra 1962-67; Guest conductor with leading orchestras in England (1968) and the United States; Chief Conductor of the Malmo Symphony Orchestra, Sweden, 1969-74; Chief Conductor of the South Australian Symphony Orchestra at Adelaide, 1975; Has conducted opera in Scandinavia. *Recordings include:* Bruckner's F minor Symphony and G minor Overture with the London Symphony Orchestra (EMI).

SHARP Norma, b. 1945, Shawnee, OK, USA. Opera Singer (Soprano). m. Jens H Niggemeyer, 1 son. *Education:* Kansas University, USA; Hochschule für Musik, Hamburg, Cologne. *Career:* 1970-77 Permanent Member of the Opera Houses of Regensburg, Augsburg, Karlsruhe as Lyric Soprano; Since 1978 Free Lanced Opera Singer, Regular Guest at Berlin, Hamburg, Munich, Frankfurt, Cologne, Düsseldorf, Vienna; Further Guest Appearances at Dresden, Hannover, Stuttgart, Amsterdam, Antwerpen, Gent, Zurich, Basel, Bern, Geneva, Milan, Rome, Naples, Madrid, London, Glasgow, Prague, Budapest; Festivals: Bayreuth 1977-81, Glyndebourne, Vienna; Concerts throughout Europe with conductors Including Pierre Boulez, Carlo Maria Giulini, Marek Janowski, Neville Marriner, Wolfgang Sawallisch, Giuseppe Sinopoli, Horst Stein; Professor of Voice, Hochschule für Musik, Hanns Eisler, Berlin, 1992-. *Recordings:* Tales of Hoffmann; Peer Gynt; Ring of the Nibelung; Tannhäuser. *Current Management.* Marguerite Kollo, Berlin. *Address:* Seestr 119, D-13353 Berlin, Germany.

SHARVITT Uri, b. 24 Oct 1939. Ethnomusicologist; Composer. m. Shulamit, 16 Aug 1962, 1 son, 3 daughters. *Education:* BA, Hebrew University of Israel, 1968; Diploma in Composition, Conducting, Rubin Academy of Music, Israel, 1965; MA, Composition, 1972, MPhil, Ethnomusicology, 1975, PhD, Ethnomusicology, 1977, Columbia University of New York. *Career:* Professor of Ethnomusicology, Bar-Ilan University, Israel, 1977-; Chairman, Department of Musicology, Bar-Ilam University, Israel, 1988-; Visiting Professor, The University of Leeds, England, 1993; Professor of Musicology and Ethnomusicology, Bar-Ilan University, Israel. *Compositions:* Heterophonic Study for piano; andante Scherzando, viola and cello; Divertissement, voice and piano, drum, bassoon and flute; Psalms 30, mixed choir and clarinet and drum; Passacaglia for orchestra; Tehila - Psalm Verses for Bariton Solo and Mixed Choir. *Recordings:* The First Three Works, on CBC Records, CP34. *Publication:* A Treasury of Jewish Yemenite Chants, Renanot Publications, Israel, 1981. *Contributions to:* Enthnomusicology, 1979; Yearbook for Traditional Music, 1986; Asian Music, 1986; Yearbook for Traditional Music, 1993. *Honour:* 1st Acum Prize for Passacaglia, 1972; 1st Acum Prize for Tehila, 1987. *Memberships:* The Israel Musicological Society; International Council for Traditional Music; Board, Israel Chamber Orchestra. *Address:* 6 Mann Street, Jerusalem, Israel.

SHAVE Jacqueline, b. 1960, England. Violinst. *Career:* Co-Founded the Brindisi String Quartet at Aldeburgh, 1984; Wigmore Hall Debut 1984, with Peter Pears; Concerts in a wide repertory throughout Britain and in France, Germany, Spain, Italy and SwitzerInd; Festival Engagements at Aldeburgh, Arundel, Bath, Brighton, Huddersfiel, Norwich and Warwick; First London Performance of Colin Matthews 2nd Quartet, 1990; Quartet by Mark Anthony Turnage, 1992; Many BBC Recitals and Resident Artist with the University of Ulster. *Recordings include;* Quartets by Britten, Bridge and Imogen Holst; Works by Pierné and Lekeu. *Honours include:* Prize Winner at the Third Banff International String Quartet Competition. *Address:* c/o Owen/White Management, 14 Nightingale Lane, London N8 7QU, England.

SHAW John, b. 12 Oct 1924, Newcastle, New South Wales, Australia. Singer (Baritone). *Education:* Studied with Henri Portnoy in Melbourne. *Career:* Member of the (National Theatre Movement of Victoria) Opera Company, 1951-54; Sang 15 roles with the Italian Grand Opera Company on tour of Australia 1955; Appearances with National Theatre Movement of Victoria and the Elizabethan Opera, 1956-57; Covent Garden Opera (London), 1958-74, as Rigoletto, Scarpia, Amonasro, Macbeth, Di Luna, Posa, Ford, Gunther, Telramund, Marcello, Amfortas, Ramiro in L'Heure Espagnole and Tonio in Pagliacci; Guest appearances with Welsh National Opera, Netherlands Opera, (1959, Gerard), Vienna Staatsoper, (1961, Tonio) and at the Holland Festival (1962, Don Carlo in La Forza del Destino); Australian television 1963 as Simon Boccanegra (also in London); Sang Amonasro and Scarpia at San Francisco Los Angeles and guested further at the Edinburgh Festival, Philadelphia, Toulouse, Marseille, Bordeaux, Deutsche Oper Berlin (1968), Munich, Mannheim, Scottish Opera (1966-77), Das Rheingold, Wotan, Naples, 1978; Amfortas, Parsifal, 1988; Montreal, Brussels, Geneva and Santa Fe; Aldeburgh Festival, in the premiere of The Bear, by Walton; Sang Ruprecht in the 1965 London premiere of Prokofiev's The Fiery Angel (New Opera Company) and appeared at the opening of the Sydney Opera House, 1973, in War and Peace; Sang with Australian Opera until 1989 (last role as Jack Rance); Gave 355th performance as Scarpia at Opera-in-the-Park, Adelaide, 1990. *Recordings include:* The Bear, and Patience (HMV). *Honour:* OBE, 1977, AO, 1986, Joan Hammond Opera Award, 1990. *Address:* c/o Sydney Opera House, Sydney, New South Wales, Australia.

SHAW Robert (Lawson), b. 30 Apr 1916, Red Bluff, CA, USA. Conductor. *Education:* Studied at Pomona College, Claremont, California, 1934-38. *Career:* Conducted Fred Waring Glee Club, 1938-45; Founded and Conducted the Collegiate Chorale in New York, 1941-54, Commissioning and Premiering Hindemith's Walt Whitman Requiem, 1946; Debut as Symphonic Conductor with the Naumburg Orchestra New York, 1946; Prepared the Chorus for Toscanini's NBC concerts and directed the Choral Departments of the Juilliard School and the Berkshire Music Center, 1946-48; Founded and Conducted the Robert Shaw Chorale, 1948-67; Conducted the San Diego Symphony 1953-58 and was Associate Conductor to Szell at the Cleveland Orchestra, 1956-57; Music Director of the Atlanta Symphony, 1967-88; Music Director Emeritus and Conductor Laureate of the Atlanta SO, 1988. *Recordings:* Many Albums with the Robert Shaw Chorale. *Address:* c/o Atlanta Symphony Orchestra, 1293 Peachtree Street North East, Suite 300, Atlanta, GA 30309, USA.

SHAW Teresa, b. 1965, England. Singer (Mezzo-soprano), *Education:* Studied at the Royal Academy of Music. *Career:* Concert appearances in Debussy's Le Martyre de Saint Sebastien with the London Philharmonic under Kurt Masur; Vivaldi's Gloria with Richard Hickox; Handel's Dixit Dominus and Haydn's Nelson Mass conducted by David Willcocks; The Dream of Gerontius at the York and Ripon Festival, 1991; The Apostles and the Glagolitic Mass at Canterbury; Operatic roles include Octavian, Third Lady in Die Zauberflöte, Dorabella (Opera Factory) and Female Chorus in Goehr's Triptych; Season 1991 included Purcell Room, Conway Hall and Wigmore Hall recitals; Premiere production of The Death of Klinghoffer by John Adams in Lyon and Vienna; Season 1992 in title role of Oliver's Beauty and the Beast, at Portsmouth. *Recordings include:* Sorceress in Dido and Aeneas and Brahms Liebesliederwalzer, conducted by John Eliot Gardiner. *Honours:* Winner, Great Grimsby International Singing Competition, 1989. *Address:* c/o Opera Factory, 8a The Leather Market, Weston Street, London SE1 3ER, England.

SHAWE-TAYLOR Desmond (Christopher), b. 29 May 1907, Dublin, Ireland. Music Critic. *Education:* Shrewsbury School; Oriel College, Oxford. *Career:* Literary and occasional criticism, New Statesman; until 1939; Served War of 1939-45 with Royal Artillery;

Music Critic, New Statesman, 1945-58; Music Critic, The Sunday Times, 1958-83, thereafter, frequent contributiuons on musical subjects, especially gramophone record reviews; Guest Music Critic, New Yorker, 1973-74. *Publications:* Covent Garden, 1948; (with Edward Sackville-West, later Lord Sackville), The Record Guide (with supplements and revisions), 1951-56. *Honour:* CBE, 1965. *Membership:* Brooks's. *Hobbies:* Travel; Croquet; Gramophone. *Address:* Long Crichel House, Wimborne, Dorset, England.

SHEBANOVA Tatiana, b. 12 Jan 1953, Moscow, USSR. Musician (Pianist). m. 18 Sept 1986, 1 son. *Education:* Undergraduate and Postgraduate studies, Main Music School, Moscow Conservatory. *Career:* Represented Moscow Conservatory, various International competitions and meetings; Live concert performances include appearances in Czechoslovakia, Belgium, France, Germany, Switzerland, Italy, Netherlands, Greece, Portugal, Austria and many tours: Japan, Philippines, Yugoslavia, Poland, Spain; Repertoire includes about 30 recitals, about 30 piano concertos; 1st interpretation of Bach's 12 choral preludes in Feinberg's transcription, Moscow Conservatory; Currently teaching, Warsaw and Bygdoszoz Academies of Music, Poland. *Recordings:* Works by Tchaikovsky, Chopin (many), Szymanowski, Rachmaninov, Bach, Debussy, Brahms, on LPs and CDs for Panton, Victor, CBS-Sony, Pony Canyon, Muza PN, Melodia. *Current Management:* Artistic Elite, Poland. *Address:* Artistic Agency Elite, Aleja Ossolinskich 11, 85-903 Bydgoszcz, Poland.

SHEFFER Jonathan, b. 19 Oct 1953, NY, USA. Composer; Conductor. *Education:* Harvard. *Debut:* Conducting, San Diego Symphony, 1991. *Career:* Appearances, San Diego Symphony, Oregon Symphony, Seattle Symphony, Minneapolis Chamber Symphony, London Pro Arte Orchestra. *Compositions:* Film Music; TV; Opera. *Recordings:* Omen 4, Pure Luck. *Address:* 39 W.10 Street, New York, NY 10011, USA.

SHEFFIELD Philip, b. 1960, Kenya. Singer (Tenor). *Education:* Studied at Cambridge University, Guildhall School and Royal College of Music; Further Study with Philip Langridge and Malcolm King. *Career:* Season 1989-90 in L'Incoronazione di Popea at Brussel, Hans Jurgen von Bose's 63; Dream Palace at Munich and Capriccio at Glyndebourne; Cavalli's Egisto for the Berlin Kammeroper, Scaramuccio at Antwerp and the Count in Die Tote Stadt in Holland; Other Repertoire Encludes Mozart's Ferrando and Tamino, and Agenore in Il Re Pastore; Lensky, Tamino and Belmonte for Lucerne Opera; Recent Concert performances include Britten's Serenade for Tenor, Horn and Strings; Britten's Nocturne with the Berlin Symphony Orchestra in the Philharmonie, and again in Montepulciano, Haydn's L'isola disabitata in the Vienna Konzerthaus with Heinz Holliger, Alexander Goehr's Eve Dreams in Paradise with the BBC Philharmonic, Henze's Kammermusik 1958 in Amsterdam at the IJsbreker theatre, Schreker's Der Schatzgraeber for the Dutch Radio Philharmonic Orchestra in the Amsterdam Concertgebouw, Stravinsky's Renard with the Ensemble Modern in Frankfurt, Berlin and Vienna, Bach's St John Passion (Evangelist) with the North Netherlands Orchestra, Berio's Sinfonia in Leningrad and The Messiah in Antwerp with the Royal Flanders Philharmonic; Also many appearances throughout the UK including Monteverdi's Orfeo at the Proms, Poppea in the QEH and Bach's B Minor Mass in Canterbury, all with Roger Norrington. Sang at the Proms again in The Seven Deadly Sins with the London Sinfonietta conducted by Lothar Zagrosek, since repeated at the Barbican Centre with the LSO and the Queen Elizabeth Hall with the Philharmonia; Recent Operatic performances include Ferrando in Così fan tutte; Shere Khan and Harry in Baa Baa Black Sheep; Chevalier in Der Ferne Klang; Belmonte in Die Entführung; Tamino in Die Zauberflöte; Lensky in Eugene Onegin; Leading role in 63 Dream Palace; Bardolfo in Falstaff; Scaramuccio in Ariadne auf Naxos; Albert in Albert Herring and Male Chorus in The Rape of Lucretia. *Recordings include:* Berio's Sinfonia with Pierre Boulez; Baa Baa Black Sheep for BBC and Radio with CD to follow; Tippett's Midsummer Marriage for Thames TV and 63 Dream Palace for Bayerischer Rundfunk. *Current Management:* Andrew Rosner, Allied Artists. *Address:* c/o Anglo Swiss Ltd, 3 Primrose Mews, 1a Sharpleshall Street, London NW1 8YW, England.

SHELLEY Howard, b. 9 Mar 1950, London. Concert Pianist; Conductor. m. Hilary Macnamara 1975, 1 son, 1 stepson. *Education:* Highgate School Music Scholar; Royal College of Music Foundation Scholar with Harold Craxton, Kendall Taylor, Lamar Crowson and Ilona Kabos; ARCM (Hons) 1966, ARCO 1967.*Career:* First TV appearance at age of 10 playing Bach and Chopin; Adult debut Wigmore Hall, London, 1971; Televised Henry Wood Prom debut 1972; International solo career as pianist; Conducting debut 1985, with London Symphony Orchestra at the Barbican Hall, London; Performed world's first cycle of the complete solo piano works of Rachmaninov, Wigmore Hall 1983; Edward Cowie, Brian Chapple and Peter Dickinson have written concertos for him; 2 piano partnership with Hilary Macnamara 1976-; Principal Guest Conductor of The London Mozart Players, 1992-. *Recordings:* Complete solo piano works of Rachmaninov (Hyperion); Mozart Piano Concertos 21 and 24 (also conducting) and Chopin recital (Pickwick); Concertos by Howard Ferguson, Peter Dickinson (EMI); Schubert Sonatas (Amon Ra); Complete Concertos of Rachmaninov (Chandos), 2 piano works of Rachmaninov (Hyperion), Schumann recital (Chandos); Gershwin Piano Concerto, Rhapsody in Blue, Second Rhapsody, Hindemith Four Temperaments; Alwyn Piano Concerto Nos. 1 & 2; Mendelssohn Piano Concertos; Mozart Piano Concerto Cycle: Vol 1. K466/K488, Vol 2. K271/K453, Vol 3. K449/K595, Vol.4, K414/K459; Chopin Scherzi, Vaughan Williams Piano Concerto. *Honours:* Chappell Gold Medal and Peter Morrison Prize 1968; Dannreuther Concerto Prize 1971; Silver Medal of Worshipful Company of Musicians 1971. *Current Management:* Intermusica, 16 Duncan Terrace, London N1 8BZ. *Address:* 38 Cholmeley Park, London N6 5ER, England.

SHELTON Lucy, b. 1955, California, USA. Singer (Soprano). *Education:* Studied at Pomona College and the New England Conservatory. *Career:* Has performed as recitalist, soloist with orchestra and performer in opera from 1980; Sang Jenifer in Thames TV's production of Tippett's Midsummer Marriage, Jan. 1989; Other operatic roles have been Euridice in Gluck's Orfeo, Salud in La Vida Breve and appearances in Dallapiccola's Il Prigioniero, Mozart's Zaide, Milhaud's Médée and John Corigliano's The Ghost of Versailles; Concert appearances throughout the US and Europe; Repertoire includes music of all periods, from Monteverdi and Bach to Boulez, Goehr, Schoenberg (Erwartung) and many first performances of works written specially for her by such composers as Albert, Knussen, Maw and Schwantner. Has taught at the Eastman School of Music and the Cleveland Institute of Music. *Honours include:* Walter W Naumburg Competition (as member of the Jubal Trio) and in 1980 as winner of the International Solo Vocal Competition; National Endowment for the Arts award. *Address:* c/o Ingpen and Williams Ltd., 14 Kensington Court, London W11 4PA, England.

SHEN Sinyan, b. 12 Nov 1949, Singapore. Music Director; Composer; Author; Erhu Recitalist. m. Yuan-Yuan Lee, 4 Aug 1973, 2 sons. *Education:* BS, University of Singapore, 1969; MA, 1970, PhD, 1973, Ohio State University, USA. *Debut:* Erhu Solo, By the Qiantang River, Singapore, 1963. *Career:* Erhu Concert Recitalist, 1963-; Conductor, Ohio State University Chinese Choir, 1971-75; Music Director, Orchestra of the Chinese Music Society of North America, 1976-; Editor-in-Chief, Chinese Music International quarterly, 1978-; Erhu Soloist, TV, USA, 1981; Lecturer, Radio, USA, 1981, 1982, 1984, 1985, 1986, 1987; Film, Music of China - Thirty Years of Change 1982; Banhu Soloist, TV, USA, 1985, 1986; Lecturer, BBC, 1989; Music Director, Silk and Bamboo Ensemble, 1982-; Professor, Harvard University, 1989-; Music Director, Chinese Classical

Orchestra, 1989-. *Compositions:* The Stream, 1976; Bow Dance, 1976; The Dance of Yao, 1976; Blossoming of the Sweet Pea Flower; Lily Blossoms Crimson and Bright, 1978; Melody of Southern Anhui, 1978; Spring to a Hundred Households, 1983. *Recordings:* The Moon Mirrored in Erquan; Spring to a Hundred Households; Song of Joy; The Joy of Spring; Moderately Embellished Six Measure; Moon Over the Mountain Pass; Autumn Moon Over the Lake. *Publications:* Foundations of the Chinese Orchestra, 1980; Superfluidity, 1982; Acoustics of Ancient Chinese Bells, 1987; Chinese Music and Orchestration: A Primer on Principles and Practice, 1991. *Address:* Chinese Music Society of North America, National Headquarters, 2329 Charmingfare, One Heritage Plaze, Woodridge, IL 60517, USA.

SHEPARD John deBerard Jr, b. 16 May 1949, Greenville, South Carolina, USA. Music Librarian. *Education:* BMus, Theory, Composition, University of North Carolina at Greensboro, 1971; MS, Library Service, Columbia University, New York City, 1981. *Career:* Reference Librarian, 1974-86, Head, Rare Books and Manuscripts, 1986-, Music Division, New York Public Library. *Publications:* Bibliography and discography for The Music of Elliott Carter (David Schiff), 1983; 18 articles for The New Grove Dictionary of American Music, 1986. *Contributions to:* The Stravinsky Nachlass, in Notes, 1984; Book reviews for Notes and The Strad; Music score reviews for Notes. *Address:* 410 West 24th Street, Apt 6L, New York, NY 10011, USA.

SHEPHERD Frances Ann, b. 4 Apr 1946, Georgetown, British Guiana. Ethnomusicologist. *Education:* Dartington College of Arts; PhD, Ethnomusicology, Wesleyan University, USA; ARCM, 1970; PhD, 1976; BMus, 1985; MMus, 1987. *Career:* Secretary, Pandit Ram Sahai Music & Dance Academy, Varanasi, India, 1976-79; Music officer, National Association of Asian Youth, Southall, Middlesex, England, 1980-81; Lecturer in Music & Head of Indian Music Studies, Dartington College of Arts, Totnes, Devon, 1982-1991; Dancer/Musician, Dance Alliance Co, 1986-; Tabla player both within the traditional Indian and fusion music contexts, 1982-. *Publications:* Tabla and the Benares Gharana, 1976. *Honour:* Winston Churchill Research Fellow, 1980. *Memberships:* Administrator/Founder, Pt Ram Sahai Sangit Vidhyalaya, a trust for the promotion of Indian Music and Dance, education, examinations and publications. *Address:* 20 Brunel Close, Northolt, Middlesex, England.

SHEPPARD C. James, b. 23 Nov 1943, Aurora, Nebraska, USA. Composer; Electronic Music Performer, Teacher. m. Linda Lee Moore, 1 son, 1 daughter. *Education:* North High School, Omaha, Nebraska, 1962; BFA, University of Omaha, 1967; MM, University of Massachusetts, Amherst, 1968; PhD, University of Iowa, Iowa City, 1975. *Career:* Assistant Professor, Music, West Virginia University, 1976-78; Director, Electronic Music Studio, Professor of Composition, Miami University, Ohio, 1978-; Soloist, Electronic Valve Instrument, Second International Brass Congress, 1984; 11th International Computer Music Conference, 1985; Festival of Electronic Instruments, 1987; Res. Musica International Electroacoustic Music Festival, 1988. *Compositions:* Cat Dreams of Flying, 1980; Luminaria, 1980; Echo, In Amber, 1983; Cool Zephyrs, 1985; Snowfall, 1988; The Cloudtree, 1989. *Recordings:* Conductor, Miami University Ensemble for New Music, Echo in Amber, Luninaria, Opus One No. 126; Cat Dreams of Flying, Opus One, No. 85. *Honours:* Individual Artist Fellowships, Ohio Art Council, 1983 and 1988. *Address:* Electric Wind Performance, C James Sheppard, 7591 Brookville Road, Oxford, OH 45056, USA.

SHEPPARD Craig, b. 26 Nov 1947, Philadelphia, USA. Concert Pianist. *Education:* Studied at the Curtis Institute of Music and the Juilliard School of Music. *Career:* Artist-in-Residence, University of Washington, Seattle; Teacher, Yehudi Menuhin School, Surrey, 1978-88, Guildhall School of Music & Drama, 1981-86, University of Lancaster, 1979-81; Concert

Experience as Soloist in American Orchestras, British Orchestras, German and Italian Orchestras; Conductors have included Georg Solti, John Pritchard, Neeme Järvi and Charles Mackerras; TV Appearances on PBS America and BBC England. *Recordings:* EMI, Liszt and Rachmaninoff; Polygram, Rossini; Sony, Jolivet; Cirrus, Chopin. *Honours:* Arthur Rubinstein Prize; Silver Medal Leeds Internationl Pianoforte Competition; Dealey Award; Young Musicians Foundation of Los Angeles 1st Prize. *Address:* c/o School of Music, University of Washington, Seattle, WA 98195, USA.

SHEPPARD Honor, b. 1931, Leeds, Yorkshire, England. Singer (Soprano). m. Robert Elliott, 1 son, 1 daughter. *Education:* Studied with Elsie Thurston and others at the Royal Manchester College of Music; FRMCM. *Career:* Recitalist and Oratorio singer; Appearances at major British and European festivals; First Soprano with the Deller Consort, specialising in 17th and 18th Century music; Extensive tours of North and South America, Canada and Europe from 1961; Many broadcasts; Tutor in Vocal Studies at The Royal Manchester College of Music, since 1987. *Recordings include:* Belinda in Dido and Aeneas, conducted by Alfred Deller (Vanguard); The Fairy Queen, The Indian Queen and King Arthur (Harmonia Mundi); Handel's Acis and Galatea (HMV). *Honours include:* Curtis Gold Medal, RMCM. *Hobby:* Gardening. *Address:* The Firs, 27 The Firs, Bowdon, Cheshire WA14 2TF, England.

SHER Daniel, b. 25 Feb 1943, New York City, New York, USA. Dean, School of Music; Pianist; Piano Educator. m. Boyce Reid, 16 Aug 1969, 2 sons. *Education:* BM, Piano Performance, Oberlin College Conservatory of Music, Oberlin, Ohio, 1964; MS, Piano Performance, Juilliard School of Music, New York, 1967; EdD, Piano Pedagogy, Columbia University Teachers College, New York, 1980. *Debut:* Duo piano recital with Boyce Reid Sher, Alice Tully Hall, New York, 1974. *Career:* Joined Music Faculty, 1969, Acting Dean, 1984-85, Dean, 1985-1992, Louisiana State University, Baton Rouge; Currently serving as Dean, College of Music, University of Colorado; Active as soloist, chamber musician and collaborative pianist; Toured with Louisiana State University Festival Arts Trio, throughout USA; Performances as solo pianist throughout Southeast USA; Served as adjudicator; Taught workshops and master classes; Founder of Louisiana State University Bach Contest for Pianists. *Address:* College of Music, Box 301, University of Colorado, Boulder 80309, USA.

SHERBOURNE Janet Lynne, b. 28 Sept 1952, Southampton, England. Pianist; Singer; Composer. m. 7 Sept 1974, 2 sons. *Education:* Itchen College, Southampton; BA, Hons, Music, University of York, 1975; MA, Social Anthropology (Ethnomusicology) Queens University, Belfast, 1978. *Career:* IDA (Contemporary Chamber Music 1977-81; English Gamelan Orchestra 1979-83 (Contemporary Music Network Tour 1983); The Copy, 1982-85; Duo with Pianist Mark Lockett 1983-, American/Canadian tours in 1984 and 1986; 212!/Duo with Jan Steele (Saxophone) 1978-, Zürich Minimal Festival, 1985; Vienna, Töne-Gegentöne Festival, 1985; Bari, Times Zones Festival, 198; West German Tour, 1987; Metalworks Gamelan, 1988-; Radio Broadcasts include: BBC Radio 3 (as part of English Gamelan Orchestra); Radio Tirana (Albania); Holland, Switzerland, Belgium, Greece and USA, also local BBC Radio Stations; TV appearances include: BBC 2; Italia Sud. *Compositions:* Available on Record: Janet Sherbourne: Nobody But You; Mark Lockett/Janet Sherbourne: Slower Than Molasses; Walks Abroad, 1987; Desert Island Dusks (Les Disques du Soleil et de l'Acier); Other works for solo/ duo piano; Channel 4 film score Property Rites; Several collaborations with choreographer Tricia Durdey, 1989- . *Address:* 13 Salegate Lane, Temple Cowley, Oxford OX4 2HQ, England.

SHERE Charles, b. 20 Aug 1935, Berkeley, CA, USA. Composer; Writer on Music. m. Lindsay Remolif Shere. *Education:* Graduated University of California at Berkeley, 1960 and studied music at the San Francisco Conservatory. *Career:* Music Director at California radio stations 1964-73, instructor at Mills College, Oakland, 1973-84 and critic for the Oakland Tribune, 1972-88. *Compositions include:* Fratture for 7 instruments, 1962; Small Concerto for piano and orchestra, 1964; Ces desirs du vent des Greegoriens for tape, 1967; Nightmusic for diminished orchestra, 1967; Handler of Gravity for organ and optional chimes, 1971; Music for Orchestra (Symphony), 1976; Tongues for poet, chamber orchestra and tape, 1978; String Quartet No.1, 1980; The Bride Stripped Bare by Her Bachelors, Even, opera, 1981 and 1984; Certain Phenomena of Sound for soprano and violin, 1983; Concerto for Violin with Harp, Percussion and Small Orchestra, 1985; Requiem with Oboe, 1985; Ladies Voice, chamber opera, 1987; Symphony in 3 Movements, 1988; I Like it to be a Play for tenor baritone, bass and string quartet, 1989; Sonata: Bachelor Machine for piano, 1989; What Happened, chamber opera after Gertrude Stein (trilogy with Ladies Voices and I Like it to be a Play). *Contributions to:* EAR (monthly new-music magazine), which he co-founded and published. *Address:* c/o ASCAP, ASCAP Building, One Lincoln Plaza, New York, NY 10023, USA.

SHERLAW-JOHNSON Robert, b. 21 May 1932, Sunderland, County Durham, England. Musician. m. Rachael Maria Clarke, 28 July 1959, 3 sons, 2 daughters. *Education:* Associate (piano performance), Royal College of Music, 1950; Licentiate (piano teaching) 1952, Honorary Fellow 1984, Royal Academy of Music; BA honours Music 1953, BMus 1959, King's College, University of Durham; MA (Oxon), 1971; DMus (Leeds), D.Mus (Oxon), 1957-58; Studied with Nadia Boulanger, Olivier Messiaen and Jacques Février, Paris, France; DMus, (Oxon), 1990. *Career:* Assistant Lecturer in Music, University of Leeds, England, 1961-63; Director of Music, Bradford Girls Grammar School, 1963-65; Lecturer in Music, University of York, 1965-70; University Lecturer in Music and Fellow, Worcester College, Oxford University, 1970-. *Compositions include:* 3 Sonatas for Piano; 2 String Quartets; Quintet; Seven Short Pieces (piano); Astero genesis (piano); Piano Concerto; Clarinet Concerto; Carmina Vernalia (soprano and chamber orchestra); Triptych (chamber ensemble); Sonata for Flute and Cello; Anglorum Feriae (choir and chamber orchestra); The Lambton Worm (opera); Projections (chamber ensemble); Sinfonietta Concertante; Solo Contata: Hymn to the Seasons; Encounters for Sextet, 1988; Nocturn for 2 pianos, 1992; Various choral works and song cycles and pieces for voice and tape. *Recordings:* All 3 Piano Sonatas; String Quartet No 2; Incarnatio for unaccompanied Choir; Piano Music by Liszt. *Publications:* Messiaen, 1974 and 1989; The European Tradition, in How Music Works (editors: Spence and Swayne); Chapter on Analysis & the Composer, for Companion to Contemporary Musical Thought (ed. Paynter and others), 1992; Chapter on Messiaen's Birdsong, The Messiaen Companion, forthcoming. *Honours:* Charles W Black Award, 1957; Radcliffe Award for Composition, 1969. *Memberships:* Vice-Chairman, 1979-81, Composers Guild of Great Britain; Association of University Teachers. *Hobbies:* Croquet; Collecting playing cards; Wine Making. *Address:* Malton Croft, Woodlands Rise, Stonesfield, Oxon OX8 8PL, England.

SHERR Richard Jonathan, b. 25 Mar 1947, New York City, USA. Music Historian; Professor. *Education:* BA, Columbia University, 1969; MFA, 1972, PhD, 1975, Princeton University. *Career:* Lecturer, University of California at Los Angeles, 1973-74; Visiting Lecturer, University of Wisconsin, Madison, 1974-75; Assistant Professor, 1975-80, Associate Professor, 1980-86, Professor, 1986-, Smith College, Northampton, USA. *Publications:* Bertrandi Vaqueras: Opera Omnia, 1979; Sixteenth-Century Motet, Vols: 22. 1987, 19-20. 1988, 6-7. 1989, 23. 1989, 28. 1990, 1-4. 1991, 5. 1992, 27. 1993. *Contributions to:* The New Grove; The New Harvard Dictionary of Music; Journal of the American Musicological Society; The Musical Quarterly; Early Music; Analecta Musicologica; Studi Musicali; The Musical Times; The Burlington Magazine and others. *Honours:* Palestrina Prize awarded by the Lions Club,

Palestrina, Italy, 1992. *Memberships:* American Musicological Society, Member of the Council, 1981-83; Renaissance Society of America; International Musicological Society. *Address:* Department of Music, Smith College, Northampton, MA 01063, USA.

SHICOFF Neil, b. 2 June 1949, New York, USA. Singer (Tenor). m. Judith Haddon. *Education:* Studied with his father at a NY synagogue; Juilliard School with Jennie Tourel. *Debut:* 1975 Kennedy Center Washington as Narraboth in Salome; Metropolitan Opera 1976- as Rinuccio in Gianni Schicchi, Verdi's Duke of Mantua, Tchaikovsky's Lensky, Massenet's Werther, Offenbach's Hoffmann and Massenet's Des Grieux; European career from 1976: Don Carlos in Amsterdam, Alfredo and Cilea's Maurizio at the Munich Opera; Macduff in a BBC version of Macbeth and the Duke of Mantua at Covent Garden 1988; At La Scala he has sung Lensky and at the Paris Opéra Don Carlos; Gounod's Romeo for French TV; Chicago Lyric Opera debut 1979, San Francisco 1981; Sang Cavaradossi at Stuttgart, 1990; debut at Barcelona as Hoffmann, 1990; Returned to Covent Garden, 1993, as Pinkerton. *Recordings:* Macduff and the Duke of Mantua for Philips; Foresto in Attila, conducted by Muti (EMI). *Address:* c/o Harrison/Parrott Ltd., 12 Penzance Place, London W11 4PA, England.

SHILLING Eric, b. 12 Oct 1920, London, England. Singer. m. Erica Johns, 2 Children. *Education:* Guildhall School of Music; Royal College of Music; Further Study with Frank Titterton in London. *Debut:* Sadler's Wells, 1945 as Marullo in Rigoletto. *Career:* In Operas by Smetana, Wagner, Mozart, Donizetti, Rossini and Janacek; TV Appearances in Die Fledermaus, Orpheus in the Underworld, The Visitation, Trial by Jury and A Tale of Two Cities; Sang in the British Stage Premiere of Prokofiev's War and peace, London Coliseum, 1972; Further Appearances in Operas by Wagner, Mozart, Donizetti, Rossini, Puccini, Strauss, Prokoviev, Penderecki and Reimann; Premieres, Story of Vasco, Crosse, Clarissa, Holloway; Somarone in a New Production of Beatrice and Benedict. *Recordings:* Has Recorded for Argo, Saga, L'Oisea, Lyre, HMV, Pye, Supraphon and Charisma Labels. *Memberships:* ISM; Council Equity. *Honour:* Opera Prize, Royal College of Music. *Hobby:* Motoring. *Address:* 49 Belgrave Road, Wanstead, London E11 3QP, England.

SHIMELL William, b. 23 Sept 1952, Ilford, Essex, England. Singer (Baritone). *Education:* Guildhall School of Music with Ellis Keeler; National Opera Studio until 1979. *Debut:* English National Opera 1980, as Masetto: later sang Schaunard in La Bohème, Mercutio in Romeo and Juliet, Papageno and Don Giovanni; Opera North in Le Nozze di Figaro, The Cunning Little Vixen and The Rake's Progress; Scottish Opera in Cavalli's L'Egisto; Kent Opera as Guglielmo in Così fan Tutte ; Glyndebourne from 1983, in Cenerentola and Figaro; Welsh National Opera debut 1984, as Don Giovanni; Geneva, Vienna Staatsoper and La Scala Milan as Figaro; Paris Opera in La Gazza Ladra; San Francisco Opera as Nick Shadow; Covent Garden debut as Guglielmo, 1988; Concert appearances on South Bank and elsewhere in Britain; London Promenade Concerts 1989, as Figaro; Sang Malatesta in Don Pasquale at Amsterdam and Covent Garden, 1990; Capriccio San Francisco, 1990; Capriccio, Covent Garden, 1991; Lodoïska, La Scala, 1991; Ravenna Festival, Lodoïska, La Muette di Portici (Auber), 1991; Così, Covent Garden and on tour to Japan, 1992; Raimbaud in Le Comte Ory for Netherlands Opera, Marcello in London; TV engagements in L'Enfance du Christ and Mozart series with Jane Glover; Title role, Don Giovanni, Zurich Opera, 1992 and 1993. *Recordings include:* Cherubini's Lodoïska, conducted by Muti; Title role: Don Giovanni, (EMI); Cond. Riccardo Muti, Vienna Philharmonic, Bach B minor Mass, Solti, Chicago Symphony. *Current Management:* IMG Artists, Europe. *Address:* c/o IMG Artists, Europe, Media House, 3 Burlington Lane, Chiswick W4 2TH, England.

SHIMIZU Takashi, b. 13 Jan 1953, Yokosuka, Japan.

Violinist. m. Harue Shimizu, 18 Aug 1973, 1 son. *Education:* Yokosuka High School; University of Southern California, USA; Guildhall School of Music, London, England. *Debut:* Tokyo. *Career:* Performed with the Royal Philharmonic Orchestra, BBC Philharmonic Orchestra, London Mozart Players, City of Birmingham Symphony Orchestra, The Hague Philharmonic; Many TV appearances in France, Belgium, Spain, USSR and Japan. *Recordings:* For Adams, Japan; Polydor, Belgium; Fontec. *Honours:* Bronze Medal, Queen Elizabeth Competition; 2nd Prize and Beethoven Sonata Prize, Carl Flesch Competition; 1st Prize, Granada International Competition. *Current Management:* John Wright. *Hobby:* Collecting Austrian Jugendstil. *Address:* 18 Alyth Garden, London NW11, England.

SHIRAI Mitsuko, b. 1952, Japan. Singer (Contralto). *Education:* Studied in Stuttgart. *Career:* Appearances in Europe, Israel, Japan and USA; Recitals with piano accompanist Hartmut Holl and concerts with the Berlin Philharmonic, New Japan Philharmonic, Atlanta Symphony, Nouvel Orchestre Philharmonique de Paris and the Vienna Symphony; Conductors include Chailly, Inbal, Ahronovitch, Ferenczik and Sawallisch; Repertoire includes Mahler Symphony No 8, Berlioz Les Nuits d'Été, Berg 7 Early Songs, Hindemith Das Marienleben, Complete vocal works of Webern, Schubert Winterreise and Lieder by Brahms, Wolf and Schumann; Concert performances of Mozart's Lucio Silla, Wagner's Das Liebesverbot and Ariane et Barbe-Bleue; Opened Suntory Hall Tokyo with Alexander Nevsky by Prokofiev; Stage debut Frankfurt 1987, as Despina in Così fan Tutte; Master Classes with Hartmut Holl at the Savonlinna Festival, Schleswig-Holstein Festival, Aldeburgh Festival, in Switzerland and USA and at Isaac Stern's Music Centre in Jerusalem. *Recordings:* Mozart, Schumann and Brahms Lieder (Capriccio); Bach, Mozart and Spohr Lieder (Eurodisc); Sacred music by Mozart (Philips); Frauenliebe und-leben by Schumann; Lieder by Mendelssohn and Schumann (EMI). *Honours:* Winner of Competitions in Vienna, s'-Hertogenbosch, Athens and Munich; Winner, Robert Schumann Prize, Zwickau, 1982. *Address:* c/o Städtische Bühnen, Untermainanalage 11, D-6000 Frankfurt am Main, Germany.

SHIRLEY George Irving, b. 18 Apr 1934, Indianapolis, IN, USA. Opera Singer (Tenor). m. Gladys Ishop, 24 June 1956, 1 son, 1 daughter. *Education:* Studied at the Wayne State University and had Private Vocal Study with Amos Ebersole, Edward Boatner, Themy Georgi, Cornelius Reid and Others. *Debut:* As Eisenstein in Die Fledermaus at Woodstock, NY and Rodolfo in La Bohème at Milan. *Career:* Metropolitan Opera, Royal Opera, Covent Garden, La Scala, Deutsche Oper, San Francisco Opera, Chicago Opera, Teatro Colon, Scottish Opera, NY City Opera, Santa Fe Opera, Michigan Opera Theatre, Spoleto Opera; TV Appearances Include, Tamino in CBC Production of Magic Flute; Madwoman in CBC Production of Curlew River. *Recordings include:* Cosi Fan Tutte; Pelléas et Mélisande; Oedipus Rex; Friedenstag; Mozart Requiem; The Bells; Missa Solemnis. *Contributions to:* Opera, & Opera News. *Honours:* Honorary Degrees from Wilberforce University, Montclair State College, Lake Forest College; Emmy Award; Named Joseph Edgar Maddy Distinguished University Professor of Music at University of Michigan. *Memberships:* American Academy of Teachers of Singing; American Guild of Musical Artists; National Association of Teachers of Singing. *Hobbies:* Drawing Cartoons; Tennis. *Address:* c/o Ann Summers International, Box 188, Sta A, Toronto, M5W 1B2, Ontario, Canada.

SHIRLEY-QUIRK John, b. 28 Aug 1931, Liverpool, England. Concert and Opera Singer. m. Sara Van Horn Watkins, 29 Dec 1981, 2 sons, 2 daughters. *Education:* BSc, Diploma in Education, Liverpool University; Studied singing with Austen Carnegie and Roy Henderson. *Career:* Created roles in all Britten operas since Curlew River, notable Mr Coyle, Owen Wingrave and Traveller, Death in Venice (TV and Covent Garden, Metropolitan Opera, New York, USA); Performances with Scottish

Opera and all major orchestras throughout Europe and America; Created role of Lev in the Ice Break by Tippett; Sang Folk songs by Britten at the 1991 Aldeburgh Festival. *Recordings:* Numerous recordings especially of Britten's works for Decca; Messiah, A Child of Our Time, Die Jahreszeiten, Bach B minor Mass, Dido and Aeneas (Philips); A Village Romeo and Juliet, The Kingdom, The Pilgrim's Progress, Beethoven's Ninth (EMI). *Membership:* ISM. *Honours:* Hon RAM, 1973; CBE, 1975; Mus Doc (H.C.), Liverpool, 1976; D.Univ., Brunel, 1981. *Hobbies:* Canals; Clocks; Pottering. *Current Management:* Harrison/Parrott Ltd, 12 Penzance Place, London W11 4PA, England. *Address:* 4246 South 35th Street, Arlington, VA 22206, USA.

SHMITOV Alexei, b. 1957, Moscow, Russia. Concert Organist; Pianist. *Education:* Studied at the Moscow Conservatoire, with Roisman and Nikolayeva. *Career:* Many Concerts in the former Soviet Union as Organist and Pianist; Piano Concertos by Bach in Vilnius, Lithuania, and the Sonatas for Violin and Harpsichord and Violin with Viktor Pikaisen, Organ Recitals in Lithuania, Estonia and Latvia and at the Bach Festival in West Berlin; Recitals with the tenor Alexei Martynov in music by Bach, Handel, Scheidt, Schutz, Mendelssohn, Schumann and Verdi; Recitals at the Prokofiev Centenary Festival in Scotland, 1991; Organ Repertoire Includes Works by Bach, Widor, Taneyev, Liszt and Shostakovich. *Honours Include:* 2nd Prize at Organ Competition in Dom Zu Speyer, Germany. *Address:* c/o Sonata, 11 Northpark St, Glasgow G20 7AA, Scotland.

SHOKOV Vladimir, b. 1950, Crimea, Russia. Cellist. *Career:* Co-Founded the Rachmaninov Quartet, 1974, Under the Auspices of the Sochi State Philharmonic Society, Crimea; Many concerts in the Former Soviet Union and from season, 1975-76 Tours to Switzerland, Austria, Bulgaria, Norway and Germany; Participation in the 1976 Shostakovich Chamber Music Festival at Vilnius, and in Festivals in Moscow and St Petersburg; Repertoire has included Works by Haydn, Mozart, Beethoven, Bartok, Brahms, Schnittke, Shostakovich, Boris Tchaikovsky, Chalayev and Meyerovich. *Honours include:* Prizewinner at the 1st All Union Borodin String Quartet Competition. *Address:* c/o Sonata, 11 Northgate St, Glasgow G20 7AA, Scotland.

SHOOKHOFF William S., b. 9 May 1948, Brooklyn, New York, USA. Conductor; Composer; Pianist. m. Johanna Quartel, 17 May 1985, 1 daughter. *Education:* BMus, Distinction, Eastman School of Music, 1970. *Career:* Coach, University of Toronto Opera School, 1970-72; Assistant Conductor, Portland Opera Association, Oregon, USA, 1973-75; Associate Conductor, Canadian Opera Touring Company, 1975-77; Music staff, Netherlands Opera, 1977-79; Music Director, Edmonton Opera (Canada) 1981-83, Grant McEwan Theatre Arts, Edmonton 1983-, Workshop West Theatre; Artistic Director, Opera Theatre of Alberta, Composers & Performers Festival Association of Alberta; Director, Opera Workshop, University of Alberta. *Compositions:* Numerous songs, incidental music, dances for stage works including: Euripedes' Bacchae, 1980; Aeschylus' Oresteia, 1984; Shakespeare's Midsummer Night's Dream, 1985; Aristophanes' Birds, 1986; Original stage works: The Rich Man; Sliding for Home; Learning to Live with Personal Growth; Art of War. *Recording:* Monster Concert, live from Carnegie Hall. *Contributions to:* Music Magazine. *Membership:* Pi Kappa Lambda. *Hobby:* Swimming. *Address:* 11051 81st Avenue, Edmonton, Alberta, Canada T6G 0S3.

SHORE Andrew, b. 30 Sept 1952, Oldham, Lancashire, England. Singer (Bass-baritone). *Education:* Studied at Bristol University and the London Opera Centre. *Career:* Sang first with Opera for All and Kent Opera, as Mozart's Figaro and Papageno, and Dr Bartolo; Appearances with Opera North as King Dodon (The Golden Cockerel), Leandro (The Love for Three Oranges) and Varlaam in Boris Godunov; Roles with English National Opera include Falstaff and Don Alfonso; Doeg

in The Making of the Representative for Planet 8 by Philip Glass; Papageno, and Frank in a new production of Die Fledermaus; Buxton Festival as Don Polidoro in Cimarosa's L'Italiana in Londra; Season 1989-90 as Dr Bartolo on the Glyndebourne Tour and Falstaff and Mr Gedge (Albert Herring) at the Festival; Title roles in Opera North's new productions of Don Pasquale, Gianni Schicchi and King Priam; Vancouver and Ottawa 1991, as Dr Bartolo in Il Barbiere di Siviglia; Sang Don Jerome in the British premiere of Gerhard's The Duenna, Opera North, 1992. *Address:* c/o Athole Still Ltd., Greystoke House, 80-86 Westrow Street, London, SE19 3AF.

SHORE Clare, b. 18 Dec 1954, Winston-Salem, North Carolina, USA. Composer. *Education:* BA cum laude with honours, Music, Wake Forest University, 1976; MMus, University of Colorado, 1977; DMA, Juilliard School of Music, 1984; Studied with Annette LeSiege, Wake Forest University, Charles Eakin and Cecil Effinger, University of Colorado, David Diamond, Vincent Persichetti and Roger Sessions, Juilliard School. *Career:* Teaching: Fordham University, Manhattan School of Music, University of Virginia, and George Mason University, 1981-; Numerous commissions; Works performed in Carnegie Recital Hall, Alice Tully Hall, Lincoln Center, Merkin Concert Hall, Spoleto Festival, Charleston, The Barns of WolfTrap, National Gallery of Art, throughout USA and abroad. *Compositions:* Early works published by Arsis Press, Plucked String, and Seesaw Music; All subsequent works published by E.C.Schirmer Music Co. *Recordings include:* July Remembrances, Owl Recordings CD-34; Nightwatch, Opus One 132; Oatlands Sketches, CRS 8842. Contemporary Records Society Grant, 1988. *Hobbies:* Swimming; Gardening. *Current Management:* E.C.Schirmer Music Company Inc. *Address:* 12329 Cliveden Street, Herndon, VA 22070, USA.

SHORT Michael, b. 27 Feb 1937, Bermuda. Composer. m. Elaine Braithwaite, 28 July 1975. *Education:* Gillingham, England, Grammar School, 1949-55; BSc, Bristol University, 1955-58; London University and Morley College, 1959-63; Accademia Chigiana, Siena, 1966. *Career:* Music Librarian, 1961-74; Catalogue Editor, BBC Music Division, 1975-77; Freelance Composer and Lecturer, 1977-81; Principal Lecturer, Bath College of Higher Education, 1981-87; Academic Professor, Army Junior School of Music, 1989-91; Professor of Music History, Royal Military School of Music, 1991-. *Compositions:* String Quartets; Wind Ensembles; Choral, Orchestral and Vocal Music; Commercial Music for Radio; Symphonic Wind Band. *Recordings:* BBC Recordings for transmitted programmes; Polyphonic Records. *Publications:* Gustav Holst: A Centenary Documentation, 1974; Gustav Holst: Letters to W G Whittaker (Edited), 1974; Your Book of Music, 1982; Gustav Holst: The Man and His Music, 1990. *Honour:* Mendelssohn Scholarship, 1966; FTCL, 1989. *Memberships:* Composers Guild of Great Britain; Scottish Society of Composers; Performing Rights Society. *Hobbies:* Cycling; Swimming; Molinology. *Current Management:* Studio Music, London. *Address:* 24 Woodland Gardens, Isleworth, Middlesex, TW7 6LL.

SHOSTAKOVICH Maxim, b. 10 May 1938, Leningrad, USSR. Conductor. *Education:* Leningrad Conservatory, 1961-62; Moscow Conservatory. *Debut:* London Philharmonic Orchestra, 1968. *Career:* Assistant Conductor, Moscow Symphony Orchestra, 1964; Moscow State Symphony Orchestra, 1966; Principal Conductor, Moscow Radio Symphony Orchestra; Toured Canada with USSR State Symphony Orchestra, 1969; Guest Conductor, Europe, North America, Japan and Australia; Pianist, including Piano Concerto No. 2 by Shostakovich; Conducted New Orleans Symphony until 1991; Led Lady Macbeth of Mtsensk at Hamburg, 1990. *Recordings:* Father's ballet compositions, including Bolt, The Age of Gold, suites, music for films Zoya, Pirogov with Bolshoi Theatre Orchestra; Recordings EMI, Philips, including Shostakovich's Violin Concerto No. 1, Shostakovich's Symphony No. 5, Suite on Verses of Michelangelo, 1971, recording with Philips of Shostakovich's Cello

Concerti, 1984. *Address:* c/o Hamburgische Staatsoper, Grosse Theaterstrasse 34, D-2000 Hamburg 36, Germany.

SHRAPNEL Hugh Michael, b. 18 Feb 1947, Birmingham, England. Composer. *Education:* Eltham College, 1960-65; Royal Academy of Music, 1966-69; Goldsmiths' College, London, 1984-88; BMus. *Career:* Member: Scratch Orchestra, 1969-72, Promenade Theatre Orchestra, 1970-72, People's Liberation Music, 1975-79; Co-founder of Redlands Consort 1992 specialising in new music. Compositions widely performed in London, provinces and abroad including: Wigmore Hall, 1968, Purcell Room, 1970, San Diego, 1974, Conway Hall, 1986 and 1993; University of Redlands, Texas, 1986 and 1989, Leighton House, 1989, 1990, 1991, Slaughterhouse Gallery, 1991. *Compositions:* Steps (tuned percussion); 2 pieces for clarinet and piano; 4 Preludes for piano; many other works for solo piano, piano duet, songs, solo instrumental and ensemble pieces. Publisher Forward Music Ltd. *Hobbies:* Writing; Photography; Cooking; Cycling; Walking. *Current Management:* STR Music Marketing & Management. *Address:* 27A Shooters Hill Road, Blackheath, London SE3 7AS, England.

SHTOKOLOV Boris Timofeyevich, b. 19 Mar 1930, Kuznetsk, Russia. Singer (Bass). *Education:* Studied at the Sverdlovsk Conservatory. *Career:* Joined Sverdlovsky Opera, 1951, remaining until 1959; Appearances with the Khirov Opera from 1959, as the Miller in Dargomizhsky's Russalka, Glinka's Ruslan, Dosiphey in Khovanshchina, Gremin, Rossini's Basilio and Boris Godunov; Sang Andrei Sokolov in the Premiere of Dzerzhinsky's Destiny of a Man, Moscow, 1961; Mephisto in Gounod's Faust, Galitsky in Borodin's Prince Igor, Ivan Sussanin in Glinka's Life for Tsar. *Recordings include:* Boris Godunov and Ruslan and Ludmilla, from the Khirov; Highlights from Destiny of a Man; Burn My Star, Russian Songs and Romances (two discs album, 1984). *Honours include:* Peoples Artist of the USSR; Glinka Prize; State Prize of the USSR. *Address:* c/o Khirov Oper and Ballet Theatre, St Petersburg, Russia.

SHULMAN Andrew, b. 1960, London, England. Cellist. *Education:* Studies at the RAM and the RCM (Joan Dickson and William Pleeth). *Career:* Principal cellist of the Philharmonia (5 years) followed by solo career; repertoire includes concertos by Dvořák, Elgar, Beethoven (Triple), Vivaldi and Haydn; Strauss's Don Quixote and Bloch's Schelomo; Founder member of the Britten Quartet, debut concert at the Wigmore Hall 1987; Quartet in Residence at the Dartington Summer School, 1987, with quartets by Schnittke; Season 1988-89 in the Genius of Prokofiev series at Blackheath and BBC Lunchtime Series at St John's Smith Square; South Bank appearances with the Schoenberg/Handel Quartet Concerto conducted by Neville Marriner, concerts with the Hermann Prey Schubertiade and collaborations with the Alban Berg Quartet in the Beethoven Plus series; Tour of South America 1988, followed by Scandinavian debut; Season 1989-90 with debut tours of Holland, Germany, Spain, Austria, Finland; Tours from 1990 to the Far East, Malta, Sweden, Norway; Schoenberg/Handel Concerto with the Gothenburg Symphony; Festival appearances at Brighton, the City of London, Greenwich, Canterbury, Harrogate, Chester, Spitalfields and Aldeburgh; Collaborations with John Ogdon, Imogen Cooper, Thea King and Lynn Harrell; Formerly resident quartet at Liverpool University; teaching role at Lake District Summer Music 1989; Universities of Bristol, Hong Kong 1990. *Recordings:* Beethoven Op 130 and Schnittke Quartet no 3 (LDR); Vaughan Williams On Wenlock Edge and Ravel Quartet (EMI); Britten, Prokofiev, Tippett, Elgar and Walton Quartets (Collins Classics); Exclusive contract with EMI from 1991. *Honours:* Piatigorsky Artist Award in Boston, USA, 1989-90. *Address:* c/o Melanie Turner Management, 14 Kensington Court, London W8 5DN, England.

SHUMILOV Ivan, b. 12 July 1938, St Petersburg.

m. 1951, 2 daughter. *Education:* Conservatory in St Petersburg. *Debut:* The First Appearance is Connected with Jazz, Saxophone in Jazz Orchestras, 1957-70, Appearance with Philharmonic Orchestra, 1973. *Career:* in Ensembles Conducted by Fedotov Volkonskij, 1973-75; 1973 the Concert Performance, The King Arthur by Henry Percell; Play About Robin and Marion, 1973; Teacher at the Peterburg University; Recorders and Ensembles, Playing in the Ensemble Madrigal Conductor Volkonskij in the Moscow ensemble, Baroque, 1975-85; Own ensemble, Musica Practica conducted by I Shumilov with 50 different programmes, 1976-1989, Musici Segreti, A Facsimile of the original edition, 1991, Gustavsberg; STIM (Svenska Jonsättares Internationella Musikbyrå), 1993. *Compositions include:* Guide by Vivaldi, Guide by Mozart, Old Music for recorder, G Ph Telemann, Onata and Trios Rec; S Slonimskij, The Trubadurs Songs; Music Makes the Snow Melt Down; About 20 Films. *Recordings include:* G Ph Telemann Sonats and Trios; Music by Telemann, Fuchs, A Scarlatti, Pec, Haydn, Concerts by J S Bach, Telemann, Pepusch. *Memberships:* The Trade Union of Swedish Musicians. *Hobby:* Music. *Address:* Skyttevagen 1, 13437 Gustavsberg, Sweden.

SHUMSKY Oscar, b. 23 Mar 1917, Philadelphia, Pennsylvania, USA. Violinist; Conductor. *Education:* Studied with Leopold Auer from 1925, Curtis Institute, 1928-36; Private study with Efrem Zimbalist until 1938. *Career:* Played in the NBC Symphony under Toscanini from 1939; Leader of the Primrose Quartet; Appeared as soloist with leading US orchestras, and on radio and TV; Debut as conductor 1959, with the Canadian National Festival Orchestra; Musical Director of the Candian Stratford Festival 1959-67; Conducted the Westchester Symphony and the Empire Sinfonietta in New York; Further conducting posts with the San Francisco Symphony, the Lincoln Center Mostly Mozart Festival and the Canadian Broadcasting Symphony; Teaching posts at the Peabody Conservatory, Curtis Institute, the Juilliard School and Yale University; Ceased teaching activities 1981 and resumed career as violin soloist: engagements with the Philharmonia, London Symphony, English Chamber and City of Birmingham Orchestras, Chamber Orchestra of Europe and the Rotterdam Philharmonic; Recitals in London, Stuttgart, Berlin and at the Naples Festival; Concerts with the Vancouver Symphony as conductor. *Recordings include:* Mozart's Violin Sonatas with Artur Balsam (ASV); Beethoven Concerto with the Philharmonia and Andrew Davis; Concertos by Bach and Mozart with the Scottish Chamber Orchestra (Nimbus); Unaccompanied Sonatas by Ysaÿe; Mozart Concerto K216 and Sinfonia Concertante K364, with son Eric on viola (EMI). *Address:* ASV, Martin House, 179-181 North End Road, London, W14 9NL, England.

SHUTTLEWORTH Anna Lee, b. 2 May 1927, Bournemouth, England. Cellist. m. David Sellen, Sept 1973. *Education:* BA, Honours, Open University, 1977; Scholar, Royal College of Music, 1943-47; ARCM (Performers), 1947; Teachers Training Certificate, London University, 1958. *Career:* Cellist, Vivien Hind Quartet, Georgian Quartet, London Harpsichord Ensemble, Leonardo Piano Trio, Glickman String Trio; Leeds Piano Trio; Principal cellist, Kalmar, Harvey Philips, Sadler's Wells Opera, Tilford Bach Festival Orchestras, Midland & English Sinfonia & Philomusica; Solo recitals, London & provinces; BBC broadcasts; Examiner, Associated Board; Professor, Royal College of Music; Cello teacher, Marlborough College, Dauntseys School, Cranborne Chase & Downe House, Hull University; Currently teaches at Leeds University, Bretton Hall, Leeds Girls High School. *Publications:* Playing the Cello, Novellos-Cole & Shuttleworth, 1971. *Honours:* Lesley Alexander Prize, RCM, 1947; Boise Scholarship, 1957. *Memberships:* ESTA; ISM; MU; ISME; NATFHE. *Hobbies:* Walking; Languages; Alexander Technique Painting; Swimming. *Address:* 1 Buckingham Road, Leeds LS6 1BP, England.

SIDDONS James DeWitt, b. 1 Nov 1948, Narsarssauq, Greenland. Composer; Musicologist. m.

Joyce Lorraine Garbee, 2 July 1977. *Education:* BMus, PhD, University of North Texas; MMus, King's College, University of London, UK; Researach scholar Tokyo University of Arts, Japan, 1973-74. *Publications:* Japan Section, Directory of Music Research Libraries, 1979; Anthony Milner: Biobibliography in Music, 1989; Dictionary of Contemporary Japanese Music, in preparation. *Contributions to:* Various musical periodicals & reference works including: New Grove Dictionary of Music & Musicians (Libraries, Japan); Perspectives of New Music, 1984; Fontes Artis Musicae, 1977, 1986; Musica Judaica, 1988; MGG 2nd Ed; Asian Culture Quarterly, 1990. *Honours:* Pi Kappa Lambda, 1970; Mombusho research scholarship, Japan, 1972-74; Fulbright Senior Research Scholar, Tokyo University of Arts, 1989-90. *Hobby:* Gardening. *Address:* 106 Connecticut Avenue, Lynchburg, Virginia 24502, USA.

SIDOTI Raymond, b. 21 Aug 1929, Cleveland, Ohio, USA. Concert Violinist; Educator. m. Mary Sue Lawrence, 14 June 1971. *Education:* BM, 1951, MM, 1954, violin study with Joseph Knitzer, Cleveland Institute of Music; Post-graduate work, Santa Cecilia, Rome, Italy, violin study with Pina Carmirelli; DMA, Ohio State University, violin study with Robert Gerle. *Debut:* Cleveland, Ohio, USA. *Career:* Concert Soloist, Chamber Music, USA and Europe, 1958-; Recitals for Italian and Netherlands Radio and TV; WQXR radio network broadcasts, USA, Orient and Europe; Faculty; Soloist, Concertmaster, Rome Festival Orchestra, 1973, 1976, 1977; 1st Violin, Shiras String Quartet, 1973-75; Capital University String Quartet, 1979-82, Sidoti Trio, 1981-, Augustana Academy String Quartet, 1985-; Faculty, Baylor University, 1972-73, North Michigan University, 1973-75, Stephens College, 1975-79, Capital University, 1979-82, Augustana College, 1982-. *Recordings:* Pierrot Lunaire, A. Schoenberg (violin and viola) Robert Gerle Conductor, 1971. *Publications:* The Violin Sonatas of Bela Bartók: An Epitome of the Composer's Development, 1972; Abstract of the above in RILM. *Hobby:* Photography. *Address:* 218 Newburg Avenue, Baltimore, MD 21228, USA.

SIEBER Gudrun, b. 1953, Germany. Singer (Soprano). *Education:* Studied at the Dusseldorf Opera Studio. *Career:* Member of the Deutsche Oper am Rhein Dusseldorf 1974-83; Deutsche Oper Berlin from 1977, notably in the 1984 premiere of Reimann's Gespenstersonate; Sang at the Bayerische Staatsoper Munich, 1978-84, in operas by Gluck, Mozart and Lortzing; Schwetzingen Festival 1980 and 1982, Salzburg Festival, 1981, 1984 and 1986 as Papagena in Die Zauberflöte; Also sang Papagena at the Théâtre des Champs-Elysées, Paris, 1987; Sang in a double bill of Il Maestro di Capella (Cimarosa) and La Serva di Padrona at the Deutsche Oper foyer, 1990; Other roles include Marie in Zar und Zimmermann; Amour in Hippolyte et Aricie and Kristin in Miss Julie by Bibalo; Many concert appearances. *Recordings include:* Schumann's Manfred (Schwann). *Address:* c/o Deutsche Oper Berlin, Richard Wagnerstrasse 10, D-1000 Berlin, Germany.

SIEBERT Isolde, b. 1960, Hunfeld, Hesse, Germany. Singer (Soprano). *Education:* Studied at Fribourg from 1979. *Career:* Member of the Basle Opera, 1982-85; Sang at Darmstadt, 1985-87, debut as Zerbinetta; Hanover Opera from 1987, as Blondchen, Susanna, Gretel, Tytania in A Midsummer Night's Dream and Papagena; Bregenz Festival and Liège, 1986, 1988 as the Queen of Night in Die Zauberflöte; Sang in the 300th anniversary performance of Steffani's Enrico Leone at Hanover, 1989; Many concerts and recital appearances. *Recordings include:* Biblical Songs by Dvořák. *Address:* Niedersachsiche Staatstheater, Opernplatz 1, D-3000 Hannover, Germany.

SIEDEN Cyndia, b. 1960, CA, USA. Singer (Soprano). *Education:* Studied at Olympia, Washington, and with Elisabeth Schwarzkopf. *Career:* Sang Cunegonde in Candide for New York City Opera, 1989; Sang Sifare in Mozart's Mitridate at the 1989 Wexford Festival, the Queen of Night in Toulon, Adele in Fledermaus for

Scottish Opera and Offenbach's Olympia at Seattle; Salzburg Festival debut as Amor in Orfeo ed Euridice, conducted by John Eliot Gardiner; Appearances with the Bayerische Staatsoper Munich as Rosina, Helena in the Premiere of Reimann's Troades, 1986, Zerbinetta and Fiaker milli in Arabella; Further engagements at Nice as Blondchen and Aminta in Die schweigsame Frau at Palermo; Sang Xenia in a concert performance of Boris Godunov conducted by Abbado, 1984, Verdi's Oscar for Washington Opera, Donizetti's Marie with Florida Opera West, Nannetta at Omaha and Fido in the US Professional premiere of Britten's Paul Bunyan, at St Louis; Season 1990/91 as Blondchen at the Theatre de Chatelet Paris and on tour to Amsterdam, London, Lisbon and Stuttgart; Recent appearances as the Queen of Night at the Opéra Bastille Paris and Lucia di Lammermoor at Seattle; Zerbinetta for English National Opera and at the Vienna Staatsoper, season 1992/93 with Sophie in Der Rosenkavalier at the Châtelet; Concert repertoire includes Mozart's C minor Mass (Cleveland Orchestra), Carmina Burana, Bach's St John Passion at the Concertgebouw under Frans Brüggen, and Candide a the Barbican Centre, London. *Recordings include:* Guardian of the Threshold in Die Frau ohne Schatten, conducted by Sawallisch (EMI); Orfeo ed Euridice (Philips); Die Entfuhrung aus dem Serail. *Address:* c/o IMG Artists, Media House, Burlington Lane, London, W4 2TH, England.

SIEGEL Jeffrey, b. 18 Nov 1942, Chicago, USA. Concert Pianist. m. Laura Mizel, 20 May 1973, 1 daughter, 1 son. *Education:* DMA, Juilliard School of Music, 1971; Studies with Rudolph Ganz, Rosina Lhevinne, Franz Reizenstein, Ilona Kabos. *Debut:* Soloist, Chicago Symphony, 1958. *Career:* Soloist with orchestras of New York, Philadelphia, Boston, Cleveland, Los Angeles, London Symphony, London Philharmonic, Royal Philharmonic, Philharmonia, BBC Orchestras; NHK Orchestra of Japan; Nacionale Orchestra of Buenos Aires, Teatro Colón; Berlin Philharmonic; Recitals in Carnegie Hall, Festival Hall, Concertegebouw, Brussels, Berlin, Munich, Zurich, Tokyo, Tel Aviv, Oslo, Stockholm; TV Appearances; Frequent Radio Appearances. *Compositions:* Cadenza for Mozart C Minor Concerto. *Recordings:* Dutilleux Sonata and Hindemith Third Sonata; Gershwin Complete works for Piano and Orchestra with St Louis Symphony, 1974; Solo Works of Rachmaninov. *Honours:* Silver Medal, Queen Elizabeth Competition, Brussels, 1968; Honorary Doctorate, National College of Education, Evanston, Illinois, 1976. *Hobbies:* Cinema; Theatre; Cuisine. *Current Management:* ICM Artists Management. *Address:* c/o ICM Artists Management, 40 West 57th Street, New York City, NY 10019, USA.

SIEGEL Laurence Gordon, b. 23 July 1931, New York City, New York, USA. Conductor. m. 15 Oct 1959, 1 daughter. *Education:* BA, City College of New York, 1953; Studied under Boris Goldovsky and Leonard Bernstein, Berkshire Music Center, Tanglewood, 1953, 1955; MM, New England Conservatory of Music, 1955. *Career:* Conductor, NBC Symphony, Carnegie Hall concerts including tribute concert to Fritz Kreisler; Appearances with Honolulu Orchestra, Shreveport Festival Orchestra, Alexandria Symphony, Jacksonville Symphony and Opera Company, Connecticut Grand Opera Company; Director, Miami International Music Competition, Theater of Performing Arts, Miami Beach, 7 seasons; Worldwide conducting includes Orquesta Sinfonica del Salvador, Central America, Orquesta Sinfonica de Las Palmas, Spain, Manila Metropolitan Philharmonic Orchestra and Opera Association, Teatro Sperimentale di Spoleto Orchestra, Belgrade Symphony, Yugoslavia, Filharmonica de Stat Oradea-Romania; Regularly conducts RAI Milan Orchestra; Appointed Music Director and Conductor, Puccini Festival Orchestra, Italy, 1984; Currently Music Director, North Miami Beach Orchestra and Broward-Fort Lauderdale Symphony Orchestra; Has conducted numerous operas including The Impresario, Così Fan Tutte, La Périchole, Don Pasquale, Faust, Pagliacci, Samson and Dalila, Madame Butterfly, Tosca, La Bohème, Elisir d'Amore, Hansel and Gretel, La Traviata, Die Fledermaus, Otello, Ernani; Music Director and Conductor, Festival of the

Continents, Key West, FLA; Guest Conductor, Kensington Symphony, California, Sao Paulo Symphony, Brazil; Chief Conductor, Sakai City, Osaka Opera, Japan; Music Director, Pam-American Sinfonia. *Recordings:* Tchaikovsky Album with New Philharmonic Orchestra, London; Other recordings with London Symphony Orchestra, London Philharmonic Orchestra, Royal Philharmonic Orchestra, Philharmonia Orchestra of London. *Honours include:* Numerous citations and medals of honour; Doctor of Music, 1993. *Current Management:* International Artists Alliance. *Address:* 5225 La Gorce Drive, Miami Beach, FL 33140, USA.

SIEGEL Wayne, b. 14 Feb 1953, Los Angeles, USA. Composer. m. 22 Mar 1980, 1 son. *Education:* BA, Music Composition, University of California, Santa Barbara, 1975; Diplomeksamen, Composition, Royal Danish Academy of Music, Aarhus. *Career:* Active as Composer and Performer, Europe and USA, including many radio and TV broadcasts and numerous commissions; Major performances include: Danish Radio Festival, Copenhagen, 1980; Nordic Music Days, Helsinki, 1980; German Radio, 1981; New Music America, Chicago, 1982; Warsaw Autumn, 1984; Nordic Music Days, 1984; Rostrum, Stockholm, 1988. *Compositions:* String Quartet, 1975-79; East LA for 4 Marimbas or 2 guitars, 1975; Narcissus ad fontem, 1976; Mosaic, 1978; Autumn Resonance, 1979; Domino Figures, 1979; Music for 21 Clarinets, 1980; Watercolor, Acrylic, Watercolor, 1981; Polyphonic Music, 1983; 42nd Street Rondo, 1984; Devil's Golf Course, 1985; Last Request, 1986; Cobra, 1988. *Recordings:* String Quartet & Watercolor, Acrylic, Watercolor; Autumn Resonance & Domino Figures; East LA Phase. *Contributions to:* Danish Music Periodical, Nutida Musik, Contemporary Music Review. *Honours:* Danish Art Council 3-Year Grant for Composition, 1978-81. *Memberships:* Administrative Director, West Jutland Symphony and Chamber Ensemble, 1984-86; Director, Danish Institute of Electroacoustic Music, 1986-. *Address:* DIEM, The Concert Hall Aarhus, DK 8000 Aarhus, Denmark.

SIEGELE Ulrich, b. 1 Nov 1930, Stuttgart, Germany. Musicologist. m. Dr Leonore Siegele-Wenschkewitz. *Education:* D Phil, Tuebingen University, 1957. *Career:* Lecturer in Musicology, 1965-71, Professor of Musicology 1971-, Tuebingen University. *Publications:* Die Musiksammlung der Stadt Heilbronn, 1967; Kompositionsweise und Bearbeitungstechnik in der Instrumentalmusik Johann Sebastian Bachs, 1975; Bachs theologischer Formbegriff und das Duett F-Dur, 1978; Zwei Kommentare zum Marteau sans maître von Pierre Boulez, 1979; Beethoven/Formale Strategien der späten Quartette, 1990; Die Orgeln des Musikwissenschaftlichen Instituts im Pfleghof zu Tuebingen, 1992. *Contributions to:* Articles in periodicals, collections by several authors, musical encyclopaedias. *Address:* Am Hasenborn, 61389 Schmitten, Germany.

SIEPI Cesare, b. 10 June 1923, Milan, Italy. Singer (Bass/Baritone). *Education:* Studied privately and at the Milan Conservatory. *Debut:* 1941, as Sparafucile in Rigoletto at Schio. *Career:* La Fenice Venice 1946 as Silva in Ernani; La Scala Milan 1946-58, notably as Donizetti's Raimondo, Verdi's Grand Inquisitor, Wagner's Pogner and as Mefistofele and Simon Mago in the 1948 Boito celebrations conducted by Toscanini; New York Metropolitan, 1950-74, principally as Mozart's Don Giovanni and Figaro; Also sang Philip II in Don Carlos, Gounod's Mephistopheles, Verdi's Padre Guardiano, Ramfis, Silva, Zacccaria and Fiesco; First Wagner role in German was Gurnemanz, 1970; Sang Don Giovanni at Salzburg in the 1950s (also filmed) and on his Covent Garden debut, 1962; Appeared as Roger in Verdi's Jerusalem at Parma in 1985. *Recordings:* Don Giovanni, Mefistofele and L'Amore dei tre Re (RCA); Le Nozze di Figaro, Don Giovanni, La Gioconda, Rigoletto, La Forza del Destino, La Bohème, Il Barbiere di Siviglia, Lucia di Lammermoor (Decca); Faust (CBS); Boris Godunov, La Juive, Don Carlos, La Favorita, Ernani and Norma on various other labels; Five complete recordings of Don Giovanni. *Address:* c/o S.A.

Gorlinsky Ltd., 33 Dover Street, London W1X 4NJ, England.

SIERRA Roberto, b. 9 Oct 1953, Vega Baja, Puerto Rico. Composer; Music Educator. *Education:* Puerto Rico Conservatory of Music; Graduated, University of Puerto Rico, 1976; Royal College of Music, London; University of London, 1976-78; Institute of Sonology, Utrecht, 1978; Studied with Gyorgy Ligeti, Hamburg Hochschule fur Musik, 1979-82. *Career:* Assistant Director, 1983-85, Director, 1985-86, Cultural Activities Department, Unviersity of Puerto Rico; Dean of Studies, 1986-87, Chancellor, 1987-, Puerto Rico Conservatory of Music. *Compositions:* Salsa on the C String for Cello and Piano, 1981; Seis piezas faciles for 2 Violins, 1982; Bongo-O for Percussion, 1982; Conjuros for Voice and Piano, 1983; Salsa for Wind Quintet, 1983; Cantos Populares for Chorus, 1983; Cinco bocetos for Clarinet, 1984; El Mensajero de Plata, chamber opera, 1984; Concierto Nocturnal for Harpsichord, Flute, Clarinet, Oboe, Violin and Cello, 1985; Jubilo for Orchestra, 1985; Memorias Tropicales for String Quartet, 1985; Dona Rosita for Mezzo-soprano and Wind Quintet, 1985; El sueno de Antonia for Clarinet and Percussion, 1985; Invocaciones for Voice and Percussion, 1986; Cuatro ensayos orquestales for Orchestra, 1986; Glosa a la sombra..for Mezzo- soprano, Viola, Clarinet and Piano, 1987; Essays for Wind Quintet, 1987; Mano a mano for 2 Percussionists, 1987; El Contemplado, ballet, 1987; Glosas for Piano and Orchestra, 1987; Introduccion y Descarga for Piano, Brass Quintet and Percussion, 1988; Deascarga for Chamber Ensemble or Orchestra, 1988; entre terceras for 2 Synthesizers and Computer, 1988; Tributo for Harp, Flute, Clarinet and String Quartet, 1988; Piano pieces; Harpsichord pieces. *Recordings:* Number of works recorded. *Honours:* Several commissions; Many works performed in USA and Europe. *Address:* c/o Conservatorio de Musica de Puerto Rico, Apartado 41227, Minillas Station, Santurce, Puerto Rico 00940, USA.

SIGMUND Oskar Karl Friedrich (Dr), b. 13 Aug 1919, Karlsbad, Czechoslovakia. Pianist; Composer. *Education:* PhD, German University, Prague, 1942; Studied with Dr Eduard von Chiari, Professor Vilem Kurz, Professor Gustav Becking. *Debut:* Radio Munich, 1946. *Career:* Composer, various works for Organ and Piano, Chamber Music, Radio Bavaria, Austria, Yugoslavia, Stuttgart, Berlin; Compositions performed in Germany, Belgium, Switzerland, Yugoslvaia; Emerited, 1983. *Compositions include:* Published: Missa Christo Canamus Principi; La Folia, for 4 violins; Recorded: 5 Pieces for 3 Trumpets, 2 Trombones, Tuba and Organ; Toccata Super BACH for Organ. *Honours:* Kulturpreis des Obag, 1965; Anerkennungspreis für Musik der Sudetendeutsch Landsmannschaft, 1965; Bundesverdienstkreuz der Bundesrepublik Deutschland, 1991. *Current Management:* Docent and Stellvertretender Direktor of Fachakademie fur Kath. Kirchenmusik und Musikernichung, Regensburg. *Address:* Roter Brachweg 81, 93049 Regensburg, Germany.

SIGMUNDSSON Kristinn, b. 1 May 1951, Reykjavik, Iceland. Singer (Bass-baritone). *Education:* Studied at the Academy of Music in Vienna and in Washington DC. *Career:* Member of Wiesbaden Opera from 1989, as Don Giovanni, the Speaker in Die Zauberflöte and Eugene Onegin; Royal Court Theatre Drottningholm 1989-90, as Agamemnon and Thoas in Gluck's Iphigénie operas; Season 1990-91 as Geisterbote in Die Frau ohne Schatten at the Concertgebouw, Beethoven's 9th with the Essen Philharmonie, Eugene Onegin with the Deutsche Oper am Rhein and Bach's St John Passion in The Hague; Recital at the Stratford-upon-Avon Scandinavian Festival; Malcolm in La Donna del Lago for Vara Radio, Holland, 1992; Recent engagements as Don Giovanni at the Stuttgart Opera, Rossini's Basilio in Geneva and Escamillo at the Liceo in Barcelona; Concert appearances with the Dutch Radio Orchestra, the Rotterdam Philharmonic and the NDR Symphony Orchestra, Hamburg; Season 1991/92 includes Don Giovanni, Stuttgart Opera; Mozart

Requiem, Drottningholm, Sweden; Don Giovanni, Dusseldorf Opera; Mathis der Maler, KRO; Barber of Seville, Geneva; Rotterdam Philharmonic; Tannhäuser, Hamburg Opera; Iceland Symphony Orchestra; Tannhäuser, Hamburg Opera-Barcelona; Nozze di Figaro, Geneva Opera, June 1992. *Recordings include:* Commendatore in Don Giovanni, conducted by Arnold Östmann (Decca Florilegeum).*Honours include:* Prizewinner, Belvedere Singing Competition in Vienna, 1983; Winner, Philadelphia Opera competition, 1983. *Address:* c/o Haydn Rawstron Limited, PO Box 654, London SE26 4DZ, England.

SIGURBJORNSSON Thorkell, b. 1938, Iceland. Composer. *Education:*Reykjavik College of Music; Continuing Studies in USA. *Career:* Creative Associate, State University of New York, USA, 1973; Research Musician, Centre for Music Experiment, University of California, San Diego, 1975; Head of Theory and Composition, Reykjavik College of Music, Iceland, 1968-. *Compositions include:* Orchestral: Mist, 1972; Nidur, 1974; Bukolla, 1974; Wiblo, 1976; Cadensa and Dance; Seascape; Albumblatt, 1975; The Bull Man, ballet music; Caprice, 1986; Chamber Music: Differing Opinions; Intrada, 1971; For Renee, 1973; A Short Passion Story; Hasselby Icelandic Folk Sosngs, 1976; Ballade, 1960; Happy Music, 1971; Kissum, 1970; Copenhagen Quartet; For Better or Worse, 1975; Solstice, 1976; Auf Meinen Lieben Gott, 1981; Three Faces of Pantomine, 1982; Choir Music: Ode, 1975; Five Laudi, 1973; Beginning, 1978; Hosanna Son of David; Palm Sunday, 1978; The Artificial Flower; Seven Christmas Songs; David 121, 1984; Evening Prayers, 1983; Children's Music: Seven Songs from Apaspil; Apaspil, opera, 1966; Velferd; Four Icelandic Folk Songs; Three Songs; Gigjuleikur; The Ugly Duckling, 1981; The Last Flower, 1983; Electronic Music: La Jolla Good Friday I, 1975; La Jolla Good Friday II, 1975; fipur, 1971; Race Track, 1975. *Memberships:* President, Icelandic League of Composers.

SIKI Bela, b. 21 Feb 1923, Budapest, Hungary. Pianist. m. Yolande Oltramare, 18 Sept 1952, 1 son, 1 daughter. *Education:* University of Budapest; Academy Franz Liszt, Budapest; Conservatoire de Geneve, Switzerland. *Career:* Numerous concert tours worldwide; Appearances with major orchestras around the world; Extensive concert tours and master classes in Japan, Australia, USA and Canada, 1988. *Recordings:* Has made numerous recordings including music by Bach, Ravel, Liszt (B minor sonata), Beethoven (late sonatas) and Bartók. *Publications:* Piano Literature, 1982. *Honours:* Liszt Competition, Budapest, 1942, 1943; Concours International d'Executions Musicales, Geneva, 1948. *Address:* School of Music, University of Washington, Seattle, WA 98195, USA.

SIKORA Elizabeth, b. 1950, Edinburgh, Scotland. Singer (Soprano). *Education:* Studied at the Royal Scottish Academy and at Elsa Mayer Lismanns Opera Workshop. *Career:* Appearances with the Royal Opera Covent Garden in London and on Tour to Los Angeles, La Scala Milan, Japan, Korea and Greece; Solo Roles in Die Meistersinger, Butterfly, Die Frau ohne Schatten, Manon Lescaut, Parsifal, Rigoletto and Simon Boccanegra; Sang in the Britih Premieres of Henze's Pollicino and Menotti's the Boy Who Grew too Fast; Covent Garden, 1993, as the Maid in Jenůfa; Appearances as Carmen in Oundle and Germany with Royal Opera Education. *Address:* Royal Opera House, Covent Garden, London WC2, England.

SILJA Anja, b. 17 Apr 1935, Berlin, Germany. Singer (Soprano). Director. m. Christoph von Dohnányi. *Education:* Studied with Egon van Rijn. *Career:* Gave concert at the Berlin Titania Palace aged 15; Stage debut Brunswick 1956, as Rosina; Stuttgart from 1958, Frankfurt from 1959; Sang the Queen of Night at Aix, 1959; Bayreuth Festival, 1960-66, as Senta, Elsa, Eva, Elisabeth, Venus and Isolde; London debut at Sadler's Wells Theatre, 1963, as Leonore; Member of the Stuttgart Staatsoper from 1965; Covent Garden debut 1969, as Leonore: returned as Cassandre in Les Troyens,

Senta, and Marie in Wozzeck; Metropolitan Opera debut 1972: returned as Salome and Marie; Member of Hamburg Staatsoper from 1975; Vienna Staatsoper 1976, in the premiere of Von Einem's Kabale und Liebe; Paris Opéra 1985, as Marie; Glyndebourne Opera debut 1989, as the Kostelnička in Jenůfa; Produced the Nurse in Die Frau ohne Schatten at San Francisco, 1989; debut as Elektra at Leipzig, 1991; debut as opera producer at Brussels, 1990; Covent Garden, 1993, in Jenůfa. *Recordings:* Der fliegende Holländer, Tannhäuser, Lohengrin and Parsifal from Bayreuth (Philips); Schoenberg's Erwartung, Berg's Lulu and Wozzeck (Decca). *Address:* c/o Christoph von Dohnányi, Cleveland Orchestra, Severance Hall, 1101 Euclid Avenue, Cleveland OH 44106, USA.

SILLA Frederick, b. 1948, Vienna, Australia. Singer (Tenor); Composer. *Education:* Studied at the Vienna Musikhochschule with Friedrich Cerha and Anton Dermota. *Career:* Sang First at the Stadttheater Krefeld, Then Appeared at Opera Houses in Ulm, Kiel, Munster and Gelsenkirchen; Opera Jagdszenen aus Niederbayern Premiered at Karlsruhe 1979; Member of the Staatstheater am Gärtnerplatz Munich from 1985; Roles have Included Mozart's Ottavio, Tamino, Ferrando and Belmonte, Nemorino and Hoffmann; Modern Repertoire includes parts in the Lighthouse by Maxwell Davies, Jakob Lenz by Wolfgang Rihm and Die Veruteilung des Lukullus by Dessau; Guest Engagements in Pisa, Venice and Madrid, Concert appearances in Germany and elsewhere. *Address:* c/o Staatstheater am, Gärtnerplatz, Gartnerplatz 3, 8000 Munich, Germany.

SILLS Beverly, b. 25 May 1929, Brooklyn, New York, USA. Singer (Soprano); Opera Director. *Education:* Studied with Estelle Liebing from age 7. *Career:* Often sang on radio commercials as a child, with name Bubbles; Opera debut as Frasquita in Carmen, Philadelphia Civic Opera 1946; San Francisco Opera 1953, as Elena in Mefistofele; New York City Opera 1955-79 as Charpentier's Louise, Mozart's Donna Anna, Gounod's Marguerite, the heroines in Les Contes d'Hoffmann, Massenet's Manon, Donizetti's Tudor Queens and Bellini's Elvira; Success as Cleopatra in a version of Handel's Giulio Cesare led to engagements in Vienna (Mozart's Queen of Night 1967), La Scala (Pamira in Rossini's L'Assedio di Corinto 1969), and Covent Garden (Donizetti's Lucia 1970); Opera Company of Boston 1971-; Metropolitan Opera debut 1975, as Pamira; also sang Massenet's Thaïs, Donizetti's Norina and Violetta at the Met; Retired from opera 1979, in Menotti's La Loca; 1979-87 Director, New York City Opera. *Recordings:* Giulio Cesare, Lucia di Lammermoor and La Traviata (RCA), Les Contes d'Hoffmann, Manon, Thaïs, Maria, Stuarda, Don Pasquale, Roberto Devereux, L'Assedio di Corinto, Rigoletto, I Capuleti e i Montecchi and Norma (HMV). *Publication:* Beverly: an Autobiography, (New York, 1988).*Address:* c/o New York City Opera, Lincoln Center, New York NY 10023, USA.

SILVA Stella, b. 6 Jan 1948, Buenos Aires, Argentina. Singer (Mezzo-soprano). *Education:* Studied in Buenos Aires and at Vercelli, Italy. *Debut:* Bordeaux 1969, as Preziosilla in La Forza del Destino. *Career:* Many Appearances in Opera Houses at Parma, Lyon, Nice, Strasbourg, Hamburg, Vienna, Berlin, Barcelona and Buenos Aires; Verona Arena, 1973-74, as Amneris; Other roles have included Carmen, Ulrica, Eboli, Azucena, Adalgisa, Charlotte, Dalila and Ortrud; Laura in La Goconda, Leonora, Glucks Orpheus and Olofernes in Vivaldi's Juditha Triumphans; Frequent Concert Appearances. *Address:* c/o Teatro Colon, Cerrito 618, 1010 Buenos Aires, Argentina.

SILVASTI Jorma, b. 9 Mar 1959, Leppavirta, Finland. Singer (Tenor). *Education:* Studied at Savonlinna from 1975, Sibelius Academy Helsinki, 1978-81, Frankfurt, 1981-83. *Career:* Appearances with the Finnish National Opera at Helsinki from 1980; Frankfurt, 1981-82, Krefeld, 1982-85; Karlsruhe, 1985-88; Savonlinna Festival from 1983 as Jenik (Verkaufte Braut), the

Steersman in Fliegende Hollander and Tamino; Premiere of Veitsi by Paavo Heikinen, 1989; Sang Ottavio at the Vienna Volksoper, 1988, Henry Morosus in Schweigsame Frau at Dresden, 1989; Further Engagements at Essen, Karlsruhe and Bremen; Created Kimmo in Sallinen's Kullervo with the Company of Finnish National Opera At The Dorothy Chandler Pavilion, Los Angeles, 1992; Other Roles Include Ferrando, Fenton, Gluck's Pylades, Almaviva, Steva in Jenufa, Lensky, Belmonte, Vienna State Opera, 1993, Nemorino, Alfredo; Noted Concert and Oratorio Performer; Gregor in premiere of Sansibar by E Meyer in Schwetzingen with Bavarian State Opera Munich, 1994; Faust at the Dorothy Chandler Pavilion, Los Angeles; Further Engagements: Stuttgart, Düsseldorf, Frankfurt, Hannover, Hamburg, Munich, Vienna State Opera. *Address:* Finnish National Opera, Bulevardi 23-27, SF-00180 Helsinki, Finland.

SILVER Phillip Alan, b. 15 Apr 1946, Brooklyn, NY, USA. Pianist; Researcher; Educator. m. 17 Feb 1979, 1 daughter. *Education:* Studied at the New England Conservatory and the University of Washington. *Career:* Queen Elizabeth Hall, London; Israel Museum, Jerusalem; Alte Oper, Frankfurt; Royal Concert Hall, Glasgow; Radio Recordings Include, BBC3, Israel Broadcasting Authority, Swedish National Radio. *Recordings include:* Sonatas and Charactor pieces by Mendelssohn and Moscheles; 19th Century Music for Violoncello and Piano, W Noreen Silver. *Publications:* Ignaz Moscheles: A Reappraisal of His Life and Musical Influence. *Honours:* Doctor of Musical Arts, University of Washington. *Memberships:* Music Educators National Conference; The Spohr Society of Great Britain. *Hobbies:* Macintosh Computer Applications; Hiking; Travel. *Address:* 4 May Terrace, Glasgow G42 9XF, Scotland.

SILVERI Paolo, b. 28 Dec 1913, Ofena, Italy. Singer (Baritone). *Education:* Studied with Perugini in Milan and at the Accademia di Santa Cecilia in Rome with Riccardo Stracciari. *Debut:* Hans Schwarz in Die Meistersinger, Rome 1939. *Career:* Sang Germont in La Traviata at Rome, 1944; Visited Covent Garden with the company of the Naples Opera 1946, as Marcello, Scarpia and Figaro in Il Barbiere di Siviglia: returned to Covent Garden until 1952 with the resident company, and with La Scala, as Rigoletto, Count Luna, Amonasro and Iago; Edinburgh Festival with the Glyndebourne company, 1948-49, as Don Giovanni and Renato; La Scala, 1949-55; Metropolitan Opera, 1950-53, as Don Giovanni, Germont, Amonasro, Iago, Count Luna, Escamillo, Rossini's Figaro, Scarpia, Posa and Rigoletto; Appearances in Florence, Verona, 1950-51 and Turin; Sang Otello at Dublin, 1959, then reverted to baritone roles, making last engagement as Israele in Donizetti's Marino Faliero at the 1967 Camden Festival; Teacher in Rome from 1970. *Recordings:* Simon Boccanegra, La Gioconda, Tosca, Il Barbiere di Siviglia, Don Carlos, L'Arlesiana, Nabucco (Cetra); Il Trovatore; Alceste by Gluck. *Address:* c/o Conservatorio di Musica Santa Cecilia, Via Dei Greci 18, Rome, Italy.

SILVERMAN Faye-Ellen, b. 2 Oct 1947, New York City, New York, USA. Composer; Pianist; Author; Educator. *Education:* Mannes College of Music, 1966-67; BA cum laude, honours in Music, Barnard College, 1968; MA, Harvard University, 1971; DMA, Columbia University, 1974. *Career:* Works performed Europe (radio, live), South America (live), Asia (live), USA (radio, live, television); Formerly Adjunct Assistant Professor, City University of New York; Formerly Assistant Professor, Goucher College; Former Graduate Faculty, Department of Music History and Literature, Peabody Institute, Johns Hopkins University; Faculty, Center for Compositional Studies, Aspen Music Festival, 1986; Currently Graduate Faculty, Mannes College of Music; Currently freelance composer; Radio programme of own works, WNYC public radio, New York City, 1972, 1976, KUER public radio, Salt Lake City, Utah, 1982, KPFK, Los Angeles, 1986, 1988 and 1992. *Compositions include:* Kalends, brass quintet, 1981; Speaking together, violin, piano, 1981; Winds and Sines, orchestra, 1981; Trysts, 2 trumpets, 1982; Layered

Lament, English horn, tape, 1983; On Four, electronic valve instrument, oboe, English horn, piano 4 hands, 1983; Volcanic Songs, harp, 1983; Gliffs, piano, 1985; Passing Fancies, chamber ensemble, 1985; Restless Winds, woodwind quintet, 1986; Bridges in Time, trumpet, percussion, 9 strings, 1986; Adhesions, symphony orchestra, 1987; Zigzags, tuba, 1988; Candlelight, piano, orchestra, 1988; A Free Pen, for narrator, 4 soloists, chorus and large chamber ensemble, 1990; Journey Towards Oblivion, soprano, tenor, and chamber ensemble, 1991; Pas de Deux, Marimba, 1991; Xenium, flute and piano, 1992. *Publications:* Author of the 20th Century Section of the Schirmer History of Music. *Memberships:* American Music Center; ASCAP; College Music Society. *Hobbies:* Travel; Films; Tennis; Reading. *Address:* 330 W 28th Street 7G, New York, NY 10001, USA.

SILVERMAN Stanley J(oel), b. 5 July 1938, NY USA. Composer. *Education:* Studied at Mills College; Columbia University, 1958-59 and Berkshire Music Centre, 1961. *Career:* Writer of Incidental Music for Plays, Composer of Operas. *Compositions include:* Operas and Musical Plays, Elephant Steps, Tanglewood, 1968; Dr Selavy's Magic Theatre, Stockbridge, 1972; Hotel for Criminals, Stockbridge, 1974; Madame Adare, New York Opera, 1980; The Columbine String Quartet Tonight, Stockbridge, 1981; Up From Paradise, New York, 1983; The Golem, 1984; Africanaus Instructus, New York, 1986; A Good Life, Washington, 1986; Black Sea Follies, Stockbridge, 1986; Love and Science, 1990. *Address:* c/o ASCAP, ASCAP Building, One Lincoln Plaza, New York, NY 10023, USA.

SILVERSTEIN Joseph, b. 21 Mar 1932, Detroit, Michigan, USA. Violinist; Conductor. *Education:* Studied with Reynolds and Zimbalist, Curtis Institute of Music, Philadelphia, 1945-50; with Gingold and Mischakoff. *Career:* Houston Symphony Orchestra; Denver Symphony Orchestra; Philadelphia Orchestra; Member, 1955-62, Concertmaster, 1962-83, Assistant Conductor, 1971-83, Boston Symphony Orchestra; Faculty Member, Berkshire Music Center, Tanglewood; Boston University; Interim Music Director, Toledo (Ohio) Symphony Orchestra, 1979-80; Principal Guest Conductor, Baltimore Symphony Orchestra, 1981-83; Music Director, Utah Symphony Orchestra, Salt Lake City, 1983-; Chautauqua (NY) Symphony Orchestra, 1987-; Guest conductor with various orchestras. *Recordings:* Many discs as violinst and conductor. *Honours:* Winner, Queen Elisabeth of Belgium competition, 1959; Naumburg Foundation Award, 1960. *Address:* c/o Utah Symphony Orchestra, 123 West South Temple, Salt Lake City, UT 84101, USA.

SIMA Gabriele, b. 1955, Salzburg, Austria. Singer (Mezzo-soprano). *Education:* Studied at the Salzburg Mozarteum and the Vienna Musikhochschule. *Career:* Sang in the Baroque repertoire with the Viennese ensemble Spectaculum and studied with Nikolaus Harnoncourt from 1979; Opera Studio of the Vienna Opera, 1979-82; Has sung at the Vienna Staatsoper from 1982, Tebaldo in Don Carlos, 1989; Salzburg Festival from 1980, notably as Johanna in the premiere of Cerha's Baal, 1981 and in the 1984 premiere of Berio's Un Re in Ascolto; Guest appearances at the Hamburg Staatsoper and at Zurich, Berlin from 1988; Opera and Concert tour of Japan, 1989; Other roles include Rosina, Cherubino, Octavian, Siebel, Annio (Titus), Idamante in Idomeneo Feodor (Boris), Dorabella (Cosi), Zerlina. *Recordings:* Handel's Jephtha (Telefunken); Tannhaüser, as Shepherd Boy (EMI); Baal (Amadeo); Schoeck's Penthesilea (Schwann). *Address:* Staatsoper, Opernring 2, A-1010 Vienna, Austria.

SIMANDY Joszef, b. 18 Sept. 1918, Budapest, Hungary. Singer (Tenor). *Education:* Studied with Emilia Posszert in Budapest. *Debut:* Szeged National Theatre 1946, as Don José. *Career:* Sang at the Budapest Opera 1947-73, notably in the lyric tenor repertory and as Verdi's Otello and Radmaes and Wagner's Lohengrin and Walther; Sang as guest in Vienna and in Munich (1956-60). *Recordings include:* Liszt's Coronation Mass

(Deutsche Grammophon); Erkel's Laszlo Hunyadi, Pagliacci, Die Meistersinger, Lohengrin (Hungaroton). *Address:* Magyar Allami Operahaz, Nepoztarsasag utja 22, 1061 Budapest, Hungary.

SIMCOCK Iain Hamilton, b. 13 Mar 1965, Hemel Hempstead, England. International Concert Organist. *Education:* Studied at Solihull School, Christ Church Oxford and St Georges Chapel, Windsor Castle. *Debut:* Recitals for Major Venues all Over the UK and Europe. *Career:* Sub-organist of Westminster Abbey and Assistant Master of Music, Westminster Cathedral; Frequent Broadcaster for BBC Radio 3; Recitals at Notre Dame de Paris, Strasbourg Cathedral, Proms Royal Alberts Hall; Frequent Tours of Scandinavia, Germany and france. *Recordings:* Double DC Release of Christus; CD of Vierne Symphonies. *Contributions to:* Music of Louis Vierne for the Musical Times. Honours: FRCO Top Prizes for Performance & Improvisation; Second Grand Prix, Chartres International Organ Competition. *Membership:* Royal College of Organists. *Hobbies:* Cooking; Cycling. *Address:* 12 Vincent Square Mansions, Walcott St, London SW1P 2NT, England.

SIMIC Goran, b. 14 Oct 1953, Belgrade, Yugoslavia. Singer (Bass). *Education:* Studied at the Music High Schools of Belgrade and Sarajevo. *Career:* Sang in opera at Sarajevo 1978-84; Member of the Vienna Staatsoper from 1984, notably as Wurm (Luisa Miller), Timur, Sparafucile, the Commendatore, Colline, Pimen, Titurel and Rossini's Basilio; Guest appearances in Russia, Japan, Yugoslavia and the USA; Salzburg Festival from 1986, notably as Horn in Un Ballo in Maschera, conducted by Karajan and by Solti (1990); Other roles include Padre Guardiano, Ramphis, the Grand Inquisitor, Ferrando, Kecal in The Bartered Bride, Raimondo (Lucia di Lammermoor) and Konchak in Prince Igor. *Recordings include:* Un Ballo in Maschera (Deutsche Grammophon); Khovanshchina conducted by Abbado. *Honours:* Prize winner in competitions at Busseto (1981), Moscow (1982) and Philadelphia (1985). *Address:* Staatsoper, Opernring 2, A-1010 Vienna, Austria.

SIMIONATO Giulietta, b. 12 May 1912, Forli, Italy. Singer (Mezzo- soprano). *Education:* Rovigo with Ettore Locatello and Padua with Guido Palumbo. *Debut:* As Lola in Cavalleria Rusticana, Montagana 1928. *Career:* Sang in premiere of Pizzetti's Orsèolo 1933; La Scala Milan 1936-66, notably as Thomas' Mignon, Massenet's Charlotte, Rossini's Isabella, Rosina and Cenerentola, Donizetti's Giovanna Seymour and as Valentine in Meyerbeer's Les Huguenots; Sang in premiere of Falla's L'Atlantida 1962; UK debut 1947, as Mozart's Cherubino at Edinburgh; Royal Opera house Covent Garden 1953 as Bellini's Adalgisa and Verdi's Amneris and Azucena, opposite Callas; US debut San Francisco 1953; Chicago 1954-61; Metropolitan Opera debut 1959, as Azucena; Last appearance as Servilia in La Clemenza di Tito, Piccola Scala 1966. *Recordings:* Il Matrimonio Segreto, Cavalleria Rusticana, La Cenerentola, Il Barbiere di Siviglia (Cetra); L'Italiana in Algeri (HMV); Il Trovatore, La Favorita, Rigoletto, La Gioconda, La Cenerentola, Falstaff, Aida, Un Ballo in Maschera (Decca); As Carmen, Gluck's Orpheus, Meyerbeer's Valentine and in partnership with Maria Callas on various minor labels. *Address:* 29/C Via di Villa Grazioli, Rome, Italy.

SIMIONESCU Elena, b. 23 Apr. 1937, Bucharest, Romania. Singer (Soprano). *Education:* Graduate: George Lazar College, Bucharest, 1958; Ciprian Porumbescu Music Academy, 1963. *Debut:* Lyric Theatre, Constanta, 1963. *Career:* Lyrical artist, Constanta Lyric Theatre 1963- 68, Romanian Opera, Bucharest 1968-; Appearances, radio & television broadcasts, films. *Recordings:* Opera, operetta, lieder, songs, various radio & TV recordings; Die Fledermaus, Johann Strauss. *Honour:* Laureate, George Enescu International Competition, 1961. *Membership:* Romanian Theatre & Musical Artists Association. *Hobbies:* Knitting; Cooking; Reading. *Current Management:* Romanian Opera. *Address:* Aleea Vlsiei

Nr. 4, Bloc M2, Sc. B, Ap. 86, 77466 Bucharest, Romania.

SIMMONS Walter G, b. 19 Nov 1946, NY, USA. Musicologist; Critic. *Education:* Studied at the Manhattan School of Music, 1974 and the City College of New York. *Career:* Lecturer, Brooklyn College, 1973-75; Music Director, Educational Audio Visual Inc, 1975-85; Lecturer, T J Watson Research Centre, (IBM), 1983-86. *Publications include:* New Grove Dictionary of Music; NGD of American Music; Musik in Geschichte und Gegenwart; American Nationl Biography. *Contributions to:* American Record Guide; Fanfare. *Honours:* National Educational Film Festival Award; ASCAP Deems Taylor Award; Phi Beta Kappa. *Memberships:* ASCAP; Sonneck Society. *Address:* PO Box 21, 36 Maple Row, Crompond, New York, NY 10517, USA.

SIMON Abbey, b. 8 Jan. 1922, New York City, New York, USA. Concert Pianist. m. Dina Levinson Simon, 28 July 1942, 1 son. *Education:* Graduate, Curtis Institute of Music, Philadelphia, Pennsylvania. *Debut:* Town Hall, New York, as winner of Walter W.Naumberg Award, 1940. *Career:* Concert tours in recital and with orchestra on six continents, 1940-; Professor of Piano, Juilliard School of Music, New York City; Cullen Chair for Distinguished Professor, University of Houston, Texas, *Recordings:* Complete Chopin repertoire for solo piano and orchestra; Complete Ravel repertoire for solo piano and orchestra; Rachmaninov Concerto No 2 and preludes; Many other recordings including The Piano Virtuoso and works by Schumann, Brahms and Liszt. *Honours:* First Prize, Walter W.Naumberg Piano Competition; Best Recital of the Year, Federation of Music Clubs, New York; Elizabeth Sprague Coolidge Medal, London; Harriet Cohen Foundation, London. *Current Management:* Gutman & Murtha Associates Inc, New York City. *Hobby:* Tennis. *Address:* 45 Chemin Moise Duboule, 1209 Geneva, Switzerland.

SIMON Geoffrey, b. 3 July 1946, Adelaide, Australia. Conductor. *Education:* Studied at Melbourne University, the Juilliard School and Indiana University. *Career:* Guest appearances with leading orchestras 1974-; Music Director, Australian Sinfonia, London; Music Director, Albany Symphony Orchestra, New York, 1987-89; Music Director, Cala Records, 1991-; Artistic Advisor, Sacramento Symphony, California, 1993-; Regular concerts with The London Philharmonic and English Chamber Orchestras; Other engagements with the Munich, Israel and New Japan Philharmonic Orchestras, the American, City of Birmingham, Sapporo and Tokyo Metropolitan Symphonies, the orchestras of the Australian Broadcasting Corporation and the Australian Opera; Conducted the RPO in the premiere of Paul Patterson's 1st Symphony at the Cheltenham Festival; Vice-President, Stokowski Society, 1993-. *Recordings:* 1978: Music by French composers of the 1920's and the rare music by Respighi and Tchaikovsky (Chandos); Patterson's Mass of the Sea (RPO Records); The Warriors and other works of Percy Grainger (Koch International); Music by Debussy, Ravel, Respighi, Brahms, Borodin, Mussorgsky, Saint-Saens and Barry Conyngham (Cala Records); The London Cello Sound - the 40 cellos of The London Philharmonic, Royal Philharmonic Orchestra, BBC Symphony Orchestra and the Philharmonia Orchestra (Cala). *Honours:* Prize winner, John Player International Conductors Award, 1974; Prix de la Ville de Paris of the Academie du Disque Francais, 1985; Gramophone Award for Respighi recordings. *Address:* c/o Cala Records, 17 Shakespeare Gardens, London N2 9LJ, England.

SIMON Laszlo, b. 16 Jul 1948, Miskolc, Hungary. Pianist; Professor. 1978. Sabine Simon, 2 daughters. *Education:* Musica; education in Stockholm, Hannover, New York. Teachers: Hans Leygraf, Ilona Kabos, Claudio Arrau. *Debut:* 1966. *Career:* Appearances in Hamburg, Rome, Stockholm, Helsinki, Oslo, Berlin, Tokyo, Seoul, London, Porto, Professor, Karlsruhe State Academy, 1977-; Professor, Hochschule der Kunste, Berlin, 1981-; Stockholm 1988-; Master Classes at Murashino

Academy in Tokyo, 1988-. *Recordings:* BIS: Liszt, Clementi, Kodály; Caprice: Schubert, de Frumerie, Velte, Liszt etc. *Honours:* III Prize Busoni Competition, I Prize Casagrande Competition. *Hobby:* Cooking. *Current Management:* Konsertbolaget, Stockholm. *Address:* Hochschule der Kunste Berlin, Fasanenstr 1, D-1000 Berlin, Germany.

SIMONEAU Leopold, b. 3 May 1918, Quebec, Canada. Singer (Tenor). m. Pierette Alarie 1946. *Education:* Studied in Montreal with Salvator Issaurel and with Paul Althouse in New York. *Debut:* Montreal, Varietées Lyriques, 1941 as Hadji in Lakmé. *Career:* Sang in Montreal as Wilhelm Meister, Tamino and Ferrando; Sang in Central City Colorado, Philadelphia and New Orleans; Paris, Opéra-Comique, 1949 in Mireille by Gounod; Aix-en-Provence 1950 in Iphigénie en Tauride; Glyndebourne Festival 1951-54 as Don Ottavio and Idamante; Paris 1953, as Tom Rakewell in the French premiere of The Rake's Progress; La Scala debut 1953, Vienna Staatsoper 1954: visited London's Festival Hall with the Vienna company 1954; Salzburg Festival 1956-95, as Don Ottavio and Tamino; Chicago Lyric Opera 1959, as Alfredo; taught in Montreal after retirememt from stage; Director of the Opéra de Quebec from 1971. *Recordings:* Die Zauberflöte (Decca); Die Entführung, Così fan Tutte (Columbia); Don Giovanni, Orphée et Eurydice, Idomeneo (Philips); Iphigénie en Tauride; Berlioz Requiem. *Address:* c/o San Francisco Conservatory of Music, 1201 Ortega Street, CA 94122, USA.

SIMONINI-FONTANESI Simona, b. 3 Aug. 1943, Bologna, Italy. Educator; Composer. m. Gianni Fontanesi, 11 Feb. 1968. *Education:* Honours degrees: Pedagogy 1968, Doctrines of Arts, Music & Spectacles 1981, University of Bologna. *Musical:* Diploma, Piano, Parma Conservatory, 1977; Diplomas, Music Analysis 1984, History of Music (Honours) 1987, Diploma studies, Musical Composition, current, Milan Conservatory. *Career:* Liceo Professor (secondary school), History & Philosophy, 1968-; Seminars, History of Music, University of Bologna, 1981, 1982. *Compositions:* Avatar, 3 female voices & 4 instruments; Scorrendo, soprano & 4 instruments. *Publications:* Books: Art, Music, Language in the Thought of F. Nietzsche, 1983-84; Art & Utopia in the Thought of E. Bloch, 1988. Contributions, various journals including: Musica Domani; Prospettive Musicali; Quaderni di Musica e Realta. *Honours:* Scholarship (techniques of vocal & corporal expression), Council of Europe, 1986; Honourable mention for book, Accademia Nazionale dei Lincei, 1987. *Membership:* International League of Women Composers. *Address:* Via Don Franzoni no 12, 42100 Regio Emilia, Italy.

SIMONIS Christian, b. 4 July 1956, Vienna, Austria. Musician (Conductor). *Education:* Hochschule für Musik, Vienna; Konservatorium der Stadt Wien; Studied Bassoon, Theory, Singing, also Conducting with Professor Hans Swarowsky. *Career:* Choir Boy, Vienna, 1965-70; Founder, Leader, Jeunesse Chamber Orchestra, 1973-80; Chief Conductor, Philharmonic Orchestra, Bad Reichenhall, Germany, 1985-90; Chief Conductor, Göttinger Symphony Orchestra, Germany, 1990-. *Recordings:* With Jeunesse Chamber Orchestra and with Philharmonic Orchestra, Bad Reichenhall; 1st music-cassette with compositions by Joseph Gung'l, 1990. *Honours:* Mozart Interpretation Prize, Austrian Minister of Culture, 1979; Gold Pin of Honour, City of Bad Reichenhall, 1990. *Memberships:* President, Joseph Haydn Society, Vienna, 1974-87. *Address:* Mengershauser Weg 18, D-3405 Rosdorf, Germany.

SIMONOV Yuri Ivanovich, b. 4 March 1941, Saratov, USSR. Conductor. *Education:* Studied at the Leningrad Conservatory with Kramarov (viola) and Rabinovich (conducting). *Career:* Debut 1953, conducting school orchestra; Led several opera productions while a student; Principal Conductor of the Kislovodsk Philharmonic 1967-69; Assistant Conductor of the Leningrad Philharmonic 1968-69; Principal Conductor of the Bolshoi Theatre, Moscow, from 1970: toured with War and Peace to the Metropolitan Opera 1975; Premieres include Shchedrin's ballet Anna Karenina, 1972; Teacher at the Moscow Conservatory from 1975; Frequent Guest Conductor with British orchestras. *Recordings include:* Anna Karenina and Prokofiev's 5th Symphony (Melodiya); Tchaikovsky's 1st Piano Concerto, with Vladimir Ovchinikov and the London Philharmonic. *Honours:* Winner, Accademia di Santa Cecilia Competition, Rome, 1969; Artist of Merit of the RSFSR 1971. *Address:* Allied Artists Agency, 42 Montpelier Square, London SW7 1JZ, England.

SIMONSEN Anker Fjeld, b. 15 May 1944, Farum, Denmark. Composer; Musician. *Education:* Studied at the Royal Academy of Music, Copenhagen. *Debut:* Appeared in Stockholm 1967 as a Carl Nielsenplayer. *Career:* worked as an Accompanisher and Soloist Everywhere; Teacher Chamber Ensembles, Etoetera, Baltic Electronic Exhibition for Peace at the Island Bornholm, 1990; Reappearance at Musiana at Louisiana, 1993 with Like A Samurai. *Compositions:* Greek Alphabet; Mimesis Tragedy; A Pen Story; Like A Samurai. *Recordings:* Anthology of Danish Music; Greek Alphabet; Wnaturze Náròw. *Publication:* Saadan er nu Jeg, A Song Book for Children. *Contributions:* DMT. *Honours:* Small Grants from Statens Kunst Food. *Memberships:* DKF; DICEM. *Hobbies:* Philosophy; Cycling. *Address:* Dorthesvej 10, 3520 Farum, Denmark.

SIMOS Ioannis (John), b. 10 Aug 1956, Mytilene, Greece. Musician; Professor. m. 13 Jul 1980, 3 sons, 1 daughter. *Education:* Maraslios Pedogagical Academy, Theology Academy, studied harmony, counterpoint, fugue, classical music composition. *Career includes:* Tenor in rhapsody: Cosmas the Aetolos and in the folklore oratorium, Revolution of St Bernard at Lyvabetus in August 1979 and other cities in Greece; Administrator: Byzantine Dance of the Rizarios School; Mixed Quartet Choir Evagelistria Church of Piraeus; Children's Choir and Orchestra of Metamorphosis Piraeus; Trio Girls Choir of St Dimitri, Ambelokipi; Mixed Students Quartet Choir of Mitropolis, Piraeus; Founder (1986) Choir and Orchestra of Orphean Lyra; Annual participation in Choir Festival organized by the Church of Piraeus in Veakio; Conducting choirs in various festivals in Kilkis, 1981-; Twice-yearly presentation of festival programmes at the Police Academy, Mesogion 1984-88; Participation in festival for the 150 anniversary of the death of Eleftherios Venizelos, Dec 1980; Tutuor and principal of the Rapsody Cosmas the Aetolos; Co-operation with educational television. *Compositions include:* Oratorium of Christmas for a quartet choir; Quartet Choir for Holy Mass; Hymn, Peace on Earth; Quartet Choir and Orchestra for the work Fellowship of the World. *Recordings:* Participation in three records of Byzantine music; Soloist in disk with the Rapsody Cosmas the Aetolos; Cassette of nine compositions entitled Rainbow. *Publications:* Musical Anthology, for teaching music in secondary education; Author of book on Harmony, 1988 *Contributions to:* Various publications in newspapers and magazines. *Honours:* Festival and competition honours. *Memberships include:* Panhellenic Union of Music Teachers in Public Education; Universal Union of Music Companies; Federation of Chanters of Greece.*Address:* Conservatory Romanos the Methodist, Grigoriou Marasli 3, 187-57 Amfiali- Piraeus, Greece.

SIMPSON Dudley George, b. 4 Oct. 1922, Melbourne, Victoria, Australia. Composer; Conductor; Pianist. m. Jill Yvonne Bathurst, 8 Oct. 1960, 1 son, 2 daughters. *Education:* Studied Piano with Vera Porter, Victor Stephenson, Melbourne University; Orchestration with Elford Mack, Melbourne, Dr Gordon Jacob, England; Composition with John Ingram, Australia. *Debut:* 1st and 2nd M.D.Borovansky Ballet, Royal Ballet, Covent Garden. *Career:* Guest Conductor, Royal Ballet, Covent Garden, 1960-62; Principal Conductor at Great Britain and European major festivals including Monte Carlo, Nice, Athens and Middle East, 1961-63; 2 World Tours with Dame Margot Fonteyn and Rudolph Nureyev, 1962-64; Conducted Tokyo Philharmonic Orchestra, Ballet Festival, 1985;

Conducted premiere of own work, Class/Ballet, Covent Garden, 1986. *Compositions:* The Winter Play, ballet, Sadler's Wells Royal Ballet; Here We Come, ballet, transcription for Orchestra, Canadian National Ballet; Ballet/Class, Royal Ballet School; Margeurite and Armand for Fonteyn/Nureyev, transcription for orchestra; The Pastoral Symphony; Numerous TV themes and incidental music including Shakespeare Canon (BBC); A Trilogy of Psalms for Choir. *Honour:* Diploma of Music (Hons). *Hobbies:* Gardening; Photography. *Address:* 14 Marina Crescent, Gymea Bay, New South Wales 2227, Australia.

SIMPSON Robert, b. 2 March 1921, Leamington, Warwickshire, England. Composer. m. Angela Musgrave 1982. *Education:* Westminster City School; Studied with Herbert Howells 1942-46; DMus 1952. *Career:* BBC Music Producer 1951-80. *Compositions:* Orchestral: 11 Symphonies: 1951, 1956, 1962, 1972, 1972, 1977, 1977, 1981, 1986, 1988, 1990; Piano Concerto 1967; Flute Concerto 1989; Variations on a Theme of Carl Nielsen 1983; Variations and fugue on a theme of Bach, string orchestra, 1991; Chamber: 15 String Quartets: 1952-54, 1973-75, 1977, 1979, 1982 (Variations on a Theme of Haydn), 1983-84, 1987; String Trio, 1987; Variations and Fugue for recorder and string quartet 1959; Trio for clarinet, cello and piano 1967; Quintet for clarinet and string quartet 1968; Quartet for horn, violin, cello and piano 1975; Quintet for clarinet, bass clarinet, and string trio 1981; Trio for horn, violin and piano 1984; Sonata for violin and piano 1984; String Trio 1987; String Quintet 1987; Trio for violin, cello and piano 1988-89; Piano: Sonata 1946; Variations and Fugue on a Theme of Haydn 1948; Variations and Finale on a Theme of Beethoven, 1990; Sonata for 2 Pianos 1979; Organ: Eppur si muove (Ricercar e Passacaglia) 1985; Incidental and Choral music; Music for brass band; Cello Concerto, 1991; Canzona for brass, 1958; Allegro Deciso for strings, 1954. *Recordings:* First 12 string quartets, string quintet, Symphonies 1-4, 6, 7, 9, 10, all brass band music, string trio. *Publications:* Carl Nielsen, Symphonist 1952, 1979; The Essence of Bruckner 1966, 1978, revised edition 1992; Bruckner and the Symphony 1960; Sibelius and Nielsen 1965; The Beethoven Symphonies 1970; The Symphony, ed., 1966, 1972; The Proms and Natural Justice 1981. *Contributions to:* Numerous articles in musical journals. *Honours:* Carl Nielsen Gold Medal (Denmark) 1956; Kilenyi Medal of Honor, Bruckner Society of America 1962. *Memberships:* ISM; Composers' Guild of Great Britain; Association of Professional Composers; Fellow of the Royal Astronomical Society; British Astronomical Association. *Hobby:* Astronomy. *Address:* Síocháin, Killelton, Near Camp, Tralee, Co. Kerry, Eire.

SIMS Ezra, b. 16 Jan. 1928, Birmingham, Alabama, USA. Composer. *Education:* BA, Birmingham Southern College, 1947; BMus, Yale University School of Music, 1952; US Army Language School, 1953; MA, Mills College, 1956. *Career:* School Teacher, Choir Director, Mail Clerk, Display Designer; Steel Worker; Programmer, Cataloguer, Harvard University Music Library, 1958-62, 1965-74; Music Director, New England Dinosaur Dance Theatre, 1968-74; Member, Theory Faculty, New England Conservatory, 1976-78; President, Dinosaur Annex Music Ensemble, 1977-81; Composer; Lecturer, Mozarteum, 1992-93. *Compositions include:* Come Away, 1978; Twenty Years After, 1978; Quintet; Night Piece; Flight, Solo in Four Movements; Concert Piece, CRI CD 643; All Done from Memory, 1980; Ruminations, 1980; Two for One, 1980; Song, 1980; Phenomena, 1981; Sextet, 1981; Solo After Sextet, 1981; Quartet, 1982; Pictures for an Institution, 1983; Brief Elegies, 1983; String Quartet No 4, 1984; Night unto Night, 1984; The Conversions, 1985; Solo in Four Movements, 1987; Chase, 1987; Quintet, 1987; Night Piece, 1989; Concert Piece, 1990; Numerous others. *Recordings:* All Done from Memory, Sextet, et al., Northwestern NR224; String Quartet No 2 (1962), 1974; Elegie - nach Rilke, CRI 377; third Quartet, CRI 223; Chamber Cantato On Chinese Poems, CR 186. *Contributions to:* Professional journals. *Honours include:* Guggenheim Foundation Fellowship, 1962; NEA Fellowships, 1976, 1978; Artists Foundation

Fellowship, 1979; Koussevitzky Foundation Commission, 1983; American Academy of Arts and Letters Award, 1985; Recipient of numerous other honours and awards. *Memberships:* American Composers Alliance; Broadcast Music Inc. *Current Management:* Rosalie Calabrese, 170 W 74th Street, New York. *Address:* 1168 Massachusetts Avenue, Cambridge, MA 02138, USA.

SIMSON Julie, b. 13 Feb 1956, Milwaukee, Wisconsin, USA. Mezzo-Soprano; Artist Performer; Assistant Professor. *Education:* BMusFd, Western Michigan University; MMus, University of Illinois. *Career:* New York Recital debut, Weill Recital Hall, Carnegie Hall, 1989; Radio appearance, The Listening Room, New York Times Radio, 1989; Lyric Opera Cleveland debut, Minerva in The Return of Ulysses, 1991; Opera Colorado debut, Emilia in Otello, 1991; Other opera appearances with Santa Fe Opera, Dallas Civic Opera, Opera Colorado, Houston Opera Association; Appeared as Soloist with symphonies, Milwaukee, Des Moines, Missoula, Denver, Cheyenne; Currently Assistant Professor of Voice, University of Colorado. *Honours:* Mozart Prize, International Belevedere Competition, Vienna, 1985; Winner, East and West Artists International Competition for Carnegie Hall Debut; National 2nd Place Winner, NATS Artist Award. *Hobby:* Swimming. *Address:* University of Colorado-Boulder, College of Music, Campus Box 301, Boulder, CO 80309-0301, USA.

SINCLAIR James Brimmer, b. 28 May 1947, Washington, District of Columbia, USA. Orchestra Conductor; Music Educator. *Education:* Woodrow Wilson High School, 1962-65; Indiana University, 1965-70; University of Hawaii, 1970-72. *Career:* Conductor, Yale Theatre Orchestra, 1974; Visiting Lecturer, Yale University, 1973-77; Music Director, Chamber Orchestra of New England, 1975-84; Orchestra New England, 1985-; Executive Editor, Charles Ives Society, 1984-. *Recordings:* Charles Ives, Music for Theater Orchestra; The Orchestral Music of Charles Ives. *Publications:* Numerous Orchestra and Ensemble Works of Charles Ives in Critical Editions Including his Three Places in New England, 2nd Orchestral Set and 4th Symphony. *Honour:* Fellow, Berkeley College, Yale University. *Memberships:* Charles Ives Society; Sonneck Society; BMI. *Hobby:* Swimming. *Address:* 123 Yale Station, New Haven, CT 06520-0123, USA.

SINCLAIR John V, b. 8 Aug 1954, Kansas City, MI, USA. Professor of Music; Conductor. m. Gail Duve, 27 May 1977, 1 s, 1 d. *Education:* Studied at William Jewell College and the Conservatory of Music, University of Missouri. *Career:* Rollins College, Professor of Music, 1985-; Music Director, Conductor, Bach festival Society; Conductor, Messiah Choral Society, Orlando; Director of Music, First Congregational Church, Florida; Editor; Arranger; Composer. *Publications:* Cachez, Reaux Yeux; Que Je Plains Tous; Quand La Mer Rouge; Dont Marry A Man If He Drinks. Contributions to: Many Reviews for Choral Journal. *Honour:* McKean Teaching Award. *Memberships:* Conductor Guild; American Choral Directors Association; Sonneck Society; Phi Kappa Lambda; Phi Mu Alpha; American Federation of Musicians. *Hobbies:* Gardening; Sports; Travel. *Address:* Rollins College, Winter Park, FL 32789, USA.

SINGER Jeanne Walsh, b. 4 Aug. 1924, New York City, New York, USA. Composer; Concert Pianist; Teacher; Lecturer. m. Richard G. Singer, 1945, deceased 1972, 1 son. *Education:* BA magna cum laude, Barnard College, Columbia University 1944; 15 years study, piano, Nadia Reisenberg; Artist Diploma, National Guild of Piano Teachers. *Career:* Pianist, solo, with ensembles, 30 years; Radio and TV appearances including many public performances of own compositions; Lecturer; Private Teacher; Freelance Composer, many commissions; All-Singer Concert, Boston, Massachusetts, 1979; Bogota, Colombia, South America, 1980; Performances of own compositions throughout USA, 1978-94, including Kennedy Center, Washington DC, 1988, also in Toronto, Canada, 1982,

Rome, Italy, 1983, Toulouse, France, 1984, Vancouver, Canada, 1984, Budapest, Hungary, 1985, Belgium. Netherlands, 1986; recorded CD Album of own vocal music with various artists for Cambria Records, 1989. *Compositions include:* Suite in Harpsichord Style; A Cycle of Love; Nocturne for Clarinet; From the Green Mountains (trio); Selected Songs; Suite for Horn and Harp; Songs From Later Years; Songs of Reverence (song cycle); Composers' Prayer (choral); Mary's Boy (choral); Come Greet the Spring (choral); Five Wry Rimes (voice and clarinet); Recollections of City Island (trio); The Lost Garden (tenor, cello, piano), 1988; To Be Brave Is All, Orchestra and voice, 1993. *Address:* 64 Stuart Place, Manhasset, Long Island, NY 11030, USA.

SINGER Malcolm John, b. 13 July 1953, London, England. Composer/Conductor. m. Sara Catherine Nathan, 15 July 1984. *Education:* University College School, Hampstead; Magdalene College, Cambridge; Studied with Nadia Boulanger, Paris, Gyorgy Ligeti, Hamburg. *Career:* Teacher, Yehudi Menuhin School; Department of PCS at Guildhall School of Music and Drama. *Compositions:* Time Must Have A Stop, orchestra and piano solo, 1976; The Icarus Toccata, piano duet, 1979; A Singer's Complaint, 1979; Making Music, narrator and orchestra, 1983; Nonet for Strings, 1984; Sonata for Piano, 1986; Yetziah, Music for Dance, 1987; Piano Quartet, 1989; York, a cantata, 1990; Kaddish for a cappella choir, 1991. *Contributions to:* Composer. *Address:* 29 Goldsmith Avenue, London W3 6HR, England.

SINIMBERGHI Gino, b. 26 Aug 1913, Rome, Itly. Singer (Tenor). *Education:* Studied at the Academia di Sant Cecilia, Rome. *Career:* Sang at the Berlin Staatsoper, 1937-44; Italy, 1944-68 Notably as Ismaele in Nabucco; Sang in the Italin premiere of Hindemith's Long Christmas Dinner and Appeared in Milan, Venice and at the Caracalla Festival; Frankfurt 1960 in Monteverdi's Orfeo, RAI Italian Radio 1970, in Rossini's La Donna del Lago. *Recordings include:* Massenet's Therese; La Donna Del Lago, Donizetti Requiem; Nabucco. *Address:* c/o Teatro alla Scala, Via Filodrammatici 2, Milan, Italy.

SINOPOLI Giuseppe, b. 2 Nov. 1946, Venice, Italy. Conductor; Composer. *Education:* Benedetto Marcello Conservatory, Venice; Medical School at the University of Padua; Diploma in Medicine 1971; 1968- attended courses of Maderna and Stockhausen at Darmstadt; Conducting with Hans Swarowsky in Vienna. *Career:* Practised as a surgeon and psychiatrist; Faculty of Venice Conservatory 1972-; founded and conducted the Bruno Maderna Ensemble, for performances of contemporary music 1975; Opera debut Venice 1978, Aida; Concerts with the Berlin Philharmonic 1979; US debut 20 Jan. 1983, with the New York Philharmonic; Covent Garden debut 1983, Manon Lescaut; Principal Conductor Philharmonia Orchestra London, 1984-; Metropolitan Opera debut 1985, Tosca; Bayreuth Festival debut 1985, Tannhäuser; Conducted Der Rosenkavalier at Berlin, 1989, Salome 1990; Music Director of the Dresden Staatskapelle from 1991; Bayreuth 1990, Der fliegende Holländer; Conducted Carmen at Munich, 1992. *Compositions:* 25 Studi su tre Parametri 1969; Musica per calcolatori analogici 1969; Numquid et unum for harpsichord and flute 1970; Opus Ghimal for orchestra 1971; Symphonie Imaginaire for choruses, 10 children's voices and 3 orchestras 1972-73; Requiem Hashshirim for unaccompanied voices 1976; String Quartet 1977; Lou Salomé, opera 1981. *Recordings include:* Madama Butterfly 1988; Aida, Salome, Tannhäuser (Deutsche Grammophon); Verdi and Puccini arias, with Mirella Freni; Schubert's 8th Symphony (Philharmonica), Scriabin's 3rd (New York PO). *Address:* c/o Philharmonia Orchestra, 76 Great Portland Street, London W1N 5AL, England.

SIRKIA Raimo, b. 7 Feb 1951, Helsinki, Finland. Singer (Tenor). *Education:* Studied at the Sibelius Academy in Helsinki, 1977-80, and in Rome and London. *Career:* Has sung at the Savonnila Festival from 1982, Kiel Opera from 1983, as Tamino, Lionel in

Martha, Pollione and Cavaradossi; Sang dramatic roles at Dortmund Opera from 1985, Riccardo, Manrico, Otello, Alvaro, Walther, Parsifal, Don José, Bacchus, Huon (Oberon), Narraboth, and Vladimir in Prince Igor; Guest appearances at the Deutsche Oper am Rhein, Dresden, Stuttgart, Brunswick, Karlsruhe, Basle, Bordeaux and the Deutsche Oper Berlin (1989, Manrico); Member of the Finnish National Opera at Helsinki from 1989: sang Edgardo there and at Tallinn, 1990; Savonlinna 1990, as Radames and as Erik in Der fliegende Holländer; Sang Idomeneo at the Finlandia Hall, Helsinki, 1991; Frequent concert appearances. *Address:* Finnish National Opera, Bulevardi 23-27, SF-00180 Helsinki 18, Finland.

SISMAN Elaine Rochelle, b. 20 Jan. 1952, New York City, New York, USA. Musicologist. m. Martin Fridson, 14 June 1981, 1 son, 1 daughter. *Education:* AB, Cornell University, 1972; MFA, 1974, PhD, 1978, Princeton University. *Career:* Instructor, 1976-79, Assistant Professor, 1979-81, University of Michigan; National Endowment for the Humanities Fellowship, 1981-82; Assistant Professor, Columbia University, New York, 1982-90, Associate Professor, 1990-. *Publications:* Haydn and the Classical Variation, forthcoming; Brahms Studies, 1990; Keyboard Music of the 18th Century (forthcoming). *Contributions to:* Haydn Studies, 1981; Small and Expanded Forms: Koch's Model and Haydn's Music, in Musical Quarterly, 1982; Haydn Kongress, Wien 1982, 1986; The Orchestra: Origins and Transformations, 1986; The New Harvard Dictionary of Music, 1986; Haydn's Theater Symphonies, Journal of the American Musicological Society, 1990; Brahms and the Variation Canon, 19th Century Music, 1990; Tradition and Transformation in The Alternating Variations of Haydn and Beethoven, Acta Musicologica, 1990. *Address:* Columbia University, Department of Music, 703 Dodge Hall, New York, NY 10027, USA.

SITKOVETSKY Dmitry, b. 27 Sep. 1954, Baku, Ukraine. Violinist. m. Susan Roberts, 26 July 1983. *Education:* Moscow Central Music School, 1961-72; Moscow Conservatory, 1972-77; Artistic Diploma, Juilliard School of Music, USA, 1977-79. *Debut:* Berlin Philharmonic, 1980; Chicago Symphony, 1983; London Proms, 1986; New York Philharmonic, 1988. *Career:* Music Director, Korsholm Music Festival, Vaasa, Finland, 1984; Guest Soloist, Salzburg, Edinburgh, Berlin, Vienna, Ansbach, Helsinki, Istanbul, Newport, Spoleto and Mostly Mozart Festivals; Berlin, Munich, Royal, London, Rotterdam and Philharmonics; Chicago, Cincinnati, Detroit, Toronto, Montreal, London, Vienna, Munich Radio, BBC, NHK and Tokyo Symphonies; Cleveland Orchestra, Orchestre de Paris and Orchestre de la Suisse Romande; Promenade Concerts, London, 1989, Concertos by Beethoven and Tchaikovsky; Played the Elgar Concerto at the 1990 Proms, Brahms 1991. *Compositions:* Transcription of Bach, Goldberg Variations for string trio, 1984. *Recordings:* Grieg, all sonatas for violin and piano with Bella Davidovich, Orfeo 1983; Ravel, Orfeo 1984; Bach, Sonatas and Partitas for violin solo, Orfeo, 1985; Bach Goldberg Variations for string trio, Orfeo 1985; Mozart, Violin concerti with English Chamber Orchestra, Novalis 1986; Schubert, Complete Piano Trios with G.Oppitz and D.Geringas, Novalis 1986; Bach Violin Concerti with English Chamber Orchestra, Novalis 1987; Brahms Complete Sonatas for violin and piano, Novalis 1987; Prokofiev Violin Concerti Nos 1 and 2 with London Symphony Orchestra under Colin Davis, Virgin Classics, 1988. *Honours:* 1st Prize, Concertino Praha, 1966; 1st Prize, International Fritz Kreisler Competition, Vienna, 1979; Avery Fisher Career Grant, New York City, 1983. *Membership:* American Society of Authors, Composers and Publishers, 1986-. *Current Management:* Columbia Artists, USA; Harold Holt Limited, Europe. *Address:* c/o Susan Brunnert, Augustastrasse 1, D-5300 Bonn 2, Germany.

SITSKY Larry, b. 19 Sept. 1934, Tientsin, China. Composer; Pianist; Musicologist; Broadcaster. m. 8 Feb. 1961, 1 son, 1 daughter. *Education:* Graduated, 1956, Postgraduate studies, 1956-58, New South Wales State

Conservatorium, Sydney; Studied with Egon Petri, San Francisco Conservatory of Music, 1959-61. *Career:* 1st recital, age 11; Lived Australia, 1951-; Many recitals including contemporary Australian music, USA, 1959-61; Numerous commissions; Piano Teacher, Queensland State Conservatorium of Music, Guest Lecturer, Queensland University, 1961-65; Head, Keyboard Studies, 1966-78, Department Head, Composition, Electronic Music, 1978-81, Department Head, Composition, Musicology, 1981-, Canberra School of Music, ACT; External Examiner, Composition, Piano Performance, Australian Universities/Colleges of Advanced Education; Artistic Director, Bi-Centennial Recording Project; Director, Australian Contemporary Music Ensemble; Composer in Residence, University of Cincinnati, 1989-90. *Compositions:* Recorded and/or published include Orchestral: Apparitions, 1966; Prelude, 1968; A Song of Love, 1974; Songs and Dances, from The Golem, 1984; Solo instrument, ensemble, orchestra/ensemble: Narayana, piano trio, 1969; Concerto No 1, 1971; Concerto for Woodwind Quintet and Orchestra, 1971; Gurdjieff, Concerto No 2, 1983; Concerto for Guitar and Orchestra, 1984; Concerto for Piano and Orchestra, 1991; Instrumental Works: Sonata for Solo Violin, 1959; Sonata Nos 1, 2 for Solo Flute, 1959, 1979; Sonata for Solo Guitar, 1974; Armenia: Suite for Solo Saxophone, 1984; Khavar, Solo Trombone, 1984; Dagh, Solo Trumpet, 1984; Sayat-Nova, Solo Oboe, 1984; Tetragrammation, violin, piano, 1987; Necronomicone for clarinet and piano, 1989; The Phantom Drummer of Tedworth for solo percussionist, 1990; Keyboard: Fantasia No 1, piano, 1962; Dimensions for Piano and 2 Tape Recorders, 1964; Concerto, 2 Solo Pianos, 1967; Petra, piano, 1971; Nuctemeron of Appollonius of Tyana, piano, 1973; 7 Meditations on Symbolist Art, organ, 1975; Arch, piano, 1980; Choral: 5 Improvisations, 1961; The Ten Sephiroth of the Kabbalah, 1974; Music in Mirabell Garden, soprano, instruments, 1977; Opera: Fall of the House of Usher, 1965; De Profundis, 1982; In Pace Requiescat after Poe, for soprano & strings, 1989; Concerto for cello and orchestra, 1993; Trio No. 6, for flute, clarinet, piano, 1993; String Quartet, No. 3, 1993; Fantasia No. 9, on A-B-C, for solo cello, 1992; Fantasia No. 10, for double-keyboard piano, 1992; Opera, The Golem, 1993. *Recordings:* Numerous for ABC, EMI, MOVE, etc; Works in Anthology of Australian Music, Canberra School of Music; Complete Sonatas of Roy Agnew, 2MBS CD; Works of Schumann for oboe/piano, including transcriptions of the Schumann Canons for Pedal-Piano (Tall Poppies CD). *Publications:* Busoni and the Piano: The Music, the Writings, the Recordings: A Complete Survey, 1986; The Reproducing Piano Roll: A Treasure Trove of 19th Century Practice, 1982; Companion to Music in Australia (contributor), 1988; Index of the Classical Reproducing Piano Roll, 1989; A book, the Repressed Russian Avant-Garde 1900-1929. Greenwood Press, Conn. USA. *Contributions to:* Perspectives of New Music, Quadrant, International Journal of Music Education, The Piano Quarterly, Neue Zurcher Zeitung, Sovietskaya Muzika, The Music Review; Australian Dictionary of Biography, ANU Press; An Encyclopedic Dictionary of Russian and Soviet Music (Garland Press). *Address:* 29 Threlfall Street, Chifley, ACT 2606, Australia.

SIUKOLA Heikki, b. 20 Mar 1943, Finland. Singer (Tenor). *Education:* Studied at the Sibelius Academy Helsinki. *Career:* Sang in Opera at Tempere and Helsinki; Engaged at Wuppertal 1972-79, Krefeld 1980-83; Season 1989 as Erik at oslo, Siegmund in Naples and Tristan at Basle and Nancy; Sang Tristan at Lyon 1990, Tannhäuser at Montpellier 1991; Other Roles Include Andrea Chenier, Alfredo, Cavaradossi, Don Carlos, Pinkerton, Dick Johnson, and Hoffmann; Florestan in Fidelio, Lohengrin, Parsifal and Bacchus. *Recordings include:* Konrad in Marschner's Hans Heiling. *Address:* c/o Opera de Montpellier, 11 Boulevard Victor Hugo, F-34000 Montpellier, France.

SIWEK Roman, b. 5 Mar 1941, Rychwaldek, Poland. Musician. *Education:* MA, Diploma with distinction, under Professor Kwiatowski, Trombone class, State Higher School of Music, Katowice, 1963. *Career:* Solo Trombone, Radio and Television Orchestra, 1963; Trombone and Tuba Teacher, Music Academy, Katowice, 1973-80; Solo Trombone, National Philharmonic Orchestra, Warsaw, 1980-; Professor of Trombone and Tuba, Frederic Chopin Music Academy, Warsaw, 1980-; Currently Chief, Interdepartmental chair of Chamber Music, Frederic chopin Music Academy; Recitals; Solo performances in symphony concerts. *Recordings:* Concerto for trombone solo and orchestra, R Parris, TCI, 1967; Concertos for trombone and orchestra, K Serocki, M Spisak, H Tomasi, G Ch Wagenseil, Albrechtsberger, with Polish National Symphony Orchestra, Polish Radio; Trombone music with piano, Nowakoski, Serocki, Vivaldi, Hindemith; Concerto for trombones, G F Haendel, G Wagenseil. *Honours:* 2nd Prize, Prague Competition, 1962; 1st Prize, Geneva Competition, 1966. *Membership:* International Trombone Association. *Address:* ul Koncertowa 3 m 72, 00-368 Warsaw, Poland.

SIXTA Jozef, b. 12 May 1940, Jicin, Czechoslovakia. Composer. *Education:* Conservatory in Bratislava 1955-60, High School of Music, Bratislava, 1960-64; Postgraduate studies, Paris, 1971. *Career:* Lecturer, University of Music and Drama, Bratislava. *Compositions:* Asynchronie, 1968; Noneto, 1970; Flutes Quartet, 1972; Solo for Piano, 1973; Recitativo for violin solo, 1974; Octeto, 1977; Piano-Sonata, 1985. *Recordings:* Variations for 13 instruments, 1967; Asynchronie, 1968; Noneto, 1970; Punctum contra punctum, 1971; Flutes Quartet, 1972; Solo for Piano, 1973; Octeto, 1977; Piano-Sonata, 1985. *Membership:* Slovak Music Union. *Honours:* Prague Spring Festival Composition Competition, 1966; Radio Tribune UNESCO, Paris, 1970; Haydn Festival Competition, 1987 (Eisenstadt, Austria); Jan Leveslav Bella prize, 1987 and 1990. *Hobby:* Travelling. *Address:* Riazanska 68, 83102 Bratislava, Slovakia.

SKARECKY Jana Milena, b. 11 Nov. 1957, Prague, Czechoslovakia. Composer; Teacher. m. David Colwell, 6 Aug. 1983. *Education:* BMus, Honours Composition, Wilfrid Laurier University, Ontario, Canada, 1980; ARCT, Piano Performance, Royal Conservatory of Music, Toronto, 1984; MMus, Composition, University of Sydney, Australia, 1987. *Career:* Composer; Teacher, piano and theory, Canada, USA, Australia, 1977-; Faculty, Piano, Royal Conservatory of Music, Toronto, Canada; Co-founder, Runningbrook Music (publishing), Mississauga, Ontario; Compositions performed in North America, Europe, Australia and Japan. *Compositions include:* Sea Window, brass quintet, 1983; 3 Movements on Bach Themes, trumpet and strings/ trumpet and organ, 1984; Oresteia, solo double bass, 1985; Rose of Sharon, solo harp, 1985; Night Songs, 4 percussionists, 1986; The Sign of the Four, solo tenor recorder, 1986; Aquamarine, orchestra, 1986; Dayspring, mezzo-soprano, piano, 1987; Lullabies, voice, 1988; Flame of Roses, flute/cello/piano, 1989; The Living Wind, mezzo/flute/cello/harp, 1990; Consort Royal, recorder quartet, 1990; Numerous choral works; Sonata for Viola and Piano, 1992. *Publication:* Translator, The Foundations of Modern Harmony, by Karel Janéček On Her Wings, 1993, solo organ. *Memberships:* Executive of the Canadian League of Composers and the Association of Canadian Women Composers; Member of the Canadian Music Centre. *Address:* 2460 Brookhurst Road, Mississauga, Ontario, Canada L5J 1R3.

SKINNER John York, b. 5 Mar. 1949, York, England. Singer (Counter-Tenor). m. (1)Juanesse Adele Reeve, 15 Aug. 1970, (2)Janet Lesley Budden, 16 Jan. 1976, 2 daughters. *Education:* York Minster Song School; Colchester Institute; Royal Academy of Music, London; BMus(London); LRAM. *Debut:* Kassel Opera, West Germany. *Career:* Broadcasts on BBC, WDR, NDR, ORTF, Italian Radio; Opera appearances: Royal Opera, Covent Garden; La Scala, Milan; Scottish Opera; Festival Ottawa; English Music Theatre. *Recordings:* Works of John Dowland with Consort of Musicke, Decca; Handel's Partenope, Harmonia Mundi; Other Medieaval, Renaissance and Baroque music for Florilegium, CBS and Erato. *Honours:* Honorary Member, Royal College of Music, 1982; Associate of Royal Academy of Music, 1984. *Address:* Denstone College, Uttoxeter, Staffordshire ST14 5HN, England.

SKLENKA Peter, b. 16 Jan 1964, Kosice, Slovac Republic. Violinst. m. 18 Jan 1992, 1 d. *Education:* Studied at Conservatory in Kosice from 1978 to 1982 then at the Academy of Arts and Music, Prague from 1982 to 1988. *Debut:* Dvoraks Hall in Prague, 1988. *Career:* From 1983 I Have Always Played with Pianist Jane Klecatska Duo; I Was Primarius Cassoviae Quartet from 1986 to 1989 and from 1991 Concert Master in State Philharmony in Kosice. *Recordings include:* P Locatelli, F Minor; A Dvorak, F Major; B Martinu; Records for Violin Solo G P Telemann; Records for String Quartet. *Honours include:* 3rd Prize, Beethoven Competition in Czecho Slovakia; 1st Prize Competition of Chamber Music Czecho Slovaks High Schools. *Memberships:* Society of B Martinu; Slovak Music Society. *Address:* Kosice, Moyzesova ulica, Dom Umenia, Slovakia.

SKOBELEV Anatoly, b. 16 Apr 1946, Leningrad, USSR. Musician (trombonist), m. Natalia Anuzova, 1 Nov 1982, 1 daughter. *Education:* Graduated, Leningrad Conservatory, 1973. *Career:* Principal Trombonist of the Bolshoi Theatre Orchestra 1973-90; Principal Trombonist of the Russian National Symphony Orchestra 1990-, Moscow Conservatory 1989-. *Recordings:* Leningrad Philharmonic Trombone Quartet, 1972, Melodia; Soloists Ensemble of the Bolshoi - 16 records 1980-88, Melodia, EMI and others; A Shnitke, Sound and Echo, 1989, Melodia and others. *Publications:* Professional training of personnel for a conservatoire, 1991, ed Music, Moscow; On the Trombone Technique of D Wick, 1991, Music and others. *Contributions to:* Magazines - ITA Journal, Russian Brass. *Honour:* First Prize Winner, Geneva Competition, 1973. *Membership:* International Trombone Association. *Address:* Moscow Conservatory of Music, Gertsen St 13, Moscow, Russia.

SKOCZYNSKI Stanislaw, b. 20 May 1953, Warsaw, Poland. Musician (Percussionist). m. Barbara Skoczynska, 15 Jan. 1977. *Education:* Musical studies at Chopin Academy of Music, Warsaw; Master's degree in Percussion, 1976; Various courses in new music with percussionist Sylvio Gualda, France, 1981-. *Career:* Instructor, Chopin Academy of Music, Warsaw, 1977-; Tympani Soloist, Polish Radio and TV Symphony Orchestra; Founder, Warsaw Percussion Group; Soloist, many concerts of contemporary music including Polish and world premiere performances; Organiser, Bydgoszcz International Percussion Workshop with percussionists such as John Beck and Steven Schick (USA). *Recordings:* For record companies Polskie Nagrania, Arston Poland, Edition Still (Paris), Pro Viva (Germany) and for Polish, French, Hungarian and West German Radio. *Honours:* French Government Scholarship for studies with Sylvio Gualda, 1984-85; Wyspianski Prize for Young Polish Artists, 1986. *Memberships:* President, Polish Percussive Art Society, Polish Chapter; General Secretary of Jeunesses Musicales, Polish Section; Societé Internationale de Musique Contemporaine. *Current Management:* For Poland: Art Center Studio, 00-901 Warsaw, Poland; For Western Europe: Anne Bador-Neunert, Feldbergstr 55, D-6370 Oberursel, Germany.*Address:* ul Skalbmierska 2/34, 01-844 Warsaw, Poland.

SKOGLUND Annika, b. 5 Nov 1960, Vanersborg, Alvsborg, Sweden. Singer (Mezzo-soprano). *Education:* Studied at the Royal academy of Music, Gothenburg and London. *Career:* Sang Cherubino at Drottningholm, 1988, followed by Suzuki at the Royal Opera in Stockholm; Returned to Drottningholm as Ramiro in La Finta Giardiniera and made Italian Debut at Venice as Isolier in Le Comte Ory; Further engagements as Cherubino at Oslo, Suzuki in Stockholm and the Countess in Maw's The Rising of the Moon at the 1990 Wexford Festival; Concert Repertoire includes the Lieder eines Fahrenden Gesellen with Oregon Symphony; Songs of the Auvergne and Kindertotenlider and Das

Lied Von Der Erde. *Recordings include:* Video of La Finta Giardiniera. *Address:* Athole Still Ltd, 80-86 Westrow St, London SE19 3AF, England.

SKOLOVSKY Zadel, b. 17 July 1926, Vancouver, Canada. Concert Pianist. m. Alice Glass, 29 July 1947 (div. 1953). *Education:* Piano, conducting, violin, various teachers including last (& youngest) student, Leopold Godowsky; Graduate Diploma, Curtis Institute of Music, Philadelphia, USA. *Debut:* Solo recital as winner, Naumburg Award, New York Town Hall; Orchestral, with New York Philharmonic, Carnegie Hall. *Career:* Solo appearances, most great orchestras worldwide including NY Philharmonic, Philadelphia, Chicago, San Francisco, Toronto, London Philharmonic, Royal Philharmonic, BBC Symphony, French National Orchestra, Lamoureux, Israel Phiharmonic, under conductors including Monteux, Munch, Bernstein, Maazel, Leinsdorf, Kubelik, Kletzki. Appearances: Mexico, South America, many world capitals; Allied Arts Piano Series, Chicago; Aaron Richmond Celebrity Series, Boston; Eaton Series, Toronto; Stage & TV. Teaching: Professor of Music 1975-87, Professor Emeritus 1987-, Indiana University. *Recordings:* Various performances, Columbia Masterworks Records, also EMI, Philips. *Current Management:* Self. *Address:* 240 East 79th Street, Apt. 10-A, New York, NY 10021, USA.

SKOPAL Jiri, b. 15 Aug 1947, Velke Losiny. Choral Conductor; University Level Teacher. m. Kveta 28 Aug 1970, 1 s, 1 d. *Education:* Studied t Palacky University in Olomouc and Charles University Prague. *Debut:* Conductor of Palacky University Choir. *Career:* 9 Mixed Choir of Blacky University; 81 Mohelnice Choir; JITRO Choir, Hradec Kralove; Boni Pueri Boys Choir; NYC Merkin Conc Hall; Toyko Nissay Theatre. *Recordings:* JITRO Supraphon; Czech Carols; Czech Childrens Chorus JITRO; Vanoce Malych Zpevacku; Ceske Zpevy Vanocni; Boni Pueri Bohemia Music. *Publications:* Some Problems of Musical Apreception; Children Choir. *Honours:* Kladno 1st Prize; Llangollen 1st Prize; Olomouc Absolute Winner; Nantes Grand Prix. *Hobby:* Gardening. *Address:* Pod zameckem 381, 500 06 Hradec Kralove, Czech Republic.

SKRAM Knut, b. 18 Dec. 1937, Saebo, Norway. Singer (Baritone). *Education:* Montana University, voice with George Buckbee; European studies with Paul Lohmann in Wiesbaden, Luige Ricci in Rome and Kristian Riis in Copenhagen. *Career:* Oslo Opera from 1964, debut as Amonasro in Aida; 1967 won first prize in Munich Radio International Competition; Glyndebourne Festival 1969-76, as Mozart's Guglielmo, Papageno and Figaro; Così fan Tutte on French TV 1977; Aix-en-Provence, 1977-, in operas by Mozart; Spoleto Festival, Italy, 1978-; Concert appearances in Europe and America; Regular broadcasts on TV and radio in Scandinavia; Lyons 1984, as Tchaikovsky's Eugene Onegin; Sang Jochanaan in Salome with the Berlin Staatsoper on tour to Japan, 1987; Amfortas, Amonasro and Kurwenal in Berlin, 1988-89; appeared as Pizarro in Tel Aviv and Buenos Aires, 1988; Bolshoi Opera debut 1988, as Scarpia; Season 1989/90 in The Makropoulos Case at the Deutsche Oper Berlin; Amfortas at the Spoleto Festival, Charleston, and Don Giovanni at Trieste; Sang Hans Sachs at Nice, 1992. *Recordings include:* Video of Glyndebourne Festival Le Nozze di Figaro 1973 (Southern Television); Many recitals of Norwegian songs. *Address:* Haakon Tvetersvie, 29 N-0682 Oslo 6, Norway.

SKROWACZEWSKI Stanislaw, b. 3 Oct. 1923, Lwow, Poland (USA, 1960-). Conductor; Composer. m. Krystyna Jarosz, 6 Sept. 1956, 2 sons, 1 daughter. *Education:* Diploma, Philosophy, University of Lwow, 1945; Diplomas, Composition, Conducting, Lwow Academy of Music 1945, Krakow Academy 1946; LHD, Hamline University 1963, Macalester College 1972, USA. *Career:* Pianist 1928-, composer 1931-, violinist 1934-, conductor 1939-, guest conductor, Europe, South Africa, USA, 1947-. Permanent conductor, Music Director: Wroclaw Philharmonic 1946-47, Katowice National Philharmonic 1949- 54, Krakow Philharmonic

1955-56, Warsaw National Philharmonic 1957-59; Minnesota Orchestra 1960-79; Principal conductor, musical adviser, Hallé Orchestra, Manchester, UK, 1984-92; Musical adviser, St Paul Chamber Orchestra, 1986-87. *Compositions include:* 1st symphony & overture written & played (Lwow Philharmonic), aged 8; 4 symphonies, prelude & fugue for orchestra, 1948; Overture, 1947; Cantiques des Cantiques, 1951; String Quartet, 1953; Suite Symphonique, 1954; Music at Night, 1954; Ricercari Notturni, 1978; Concerti for clarinet & orchestra, 1980; Violin Concerto, 1985; Concerto for Orchestra, 1985; Fanfare for Orchestra, 1987; Also music for films, theatre, songs. *Recordings:* Numerous including Schubert 5, 8 and 9 symphonies; Chopin music for piano and orchestra (Weissenberg, EMI); Lalo and Schumann cello concertos (Starker); Beethoven 5th and Brahms 2nd piano concertos (Bachauer); Ravel orchestral works (Minnesota Orchestra); Brahms, 4 Symphonies; Bruckner, 6,7 and 8 Symphonies; Shostakovich, No. 5 No. 10 Symphonies; Stravensky and Prokofiev, all ballets; Mahler, No. 6 Symphony; Berlioz, Fantastique; Beethoven overtures, Inc. Recital Music. *Honours include:* National prize, artistic achievement, Poland, 1953; 1st prize, St Cecilia International Concours for Conductors, Rome, 1956; Numerous awards, compositions, Poland, Belgium, USSR, USA; Honorary LHD, University of Minnesota. *Memberships include:* Polish & American professional associations. *Address:* PO Box 700, Wayzata, Minnesota 55391, USA.

SLABBERT Wicus, b. 1941, Kroonstad, South Africa. Singer (Baritone). *Education:* Studied at the University of Pretoria, BA Fine Arts; with Josef Metternich in Germany. *Career:* Sang in German Repertory at Dusseldorf from 1968, Italian from 1973; Appearances at Essen, 1974-79, As Germont, Don Carlo, Rigoletto, Don Giovanni, Count Almaviva in Figaro, Scapia, Jochanaan, Mandryka and Hans Bechmesser; Staatsoper Kassel from 1979, Notably as Macbeth, Iago, The Villians in Hoffman, Dr Schön; Member of the Vienna State since 1991, with Performances as Boris in Lady Macbeth of the Mtsensk District and as Nabucco, 1992; Guest Engagements at the Breegenz Festival from 1988, in Les Contes d' Hoffmann and Der Fliegende Holländer, Dusseldorf, Stuttgart, Theater am Gartnerplatz Munich and Pretoria; Festival Engagements at Edinburgh, Florence, Stockholm and Warsaw; Teatro Colon Buenos Aires, 1992, as Wagners Dutchman; Alberich in the New Ring, Tosca, Salome, Dutchman. *Recordings include:* Bohni in Zemlinsky's Kleider Machen Leute. *Address:* c/o Staatsoper, A 1010 Vienna, Austria.

SLADE Julian Penkivil, 28 May 1930. Author; Composer. *Education:* Eton College; BA, Trinity College, Cambridge; Bristol Old Vic Theatre School, 1951. *Career:* Wrote incidental music for Bristol Old Vic production of Two Gentlemen of Verona, 1952; Joined Bristol Old Vic Company as Musical Director, 1952; Wrote and Composed Christmas in King Street (with Dorothy Reynolds and James Cairncross), Bristol, 1952; Composed Music for Sheriden's The Duenna, Bristol, 1953; Transferred to Westminster Theatre, London, 1954; Wrote and composed The Merry Gentlemen (with Dorothy Reynolds), Bristol, 1953; Composed incidental music for The Merchant of Venice, 1953 Stratford season; Wrote musical version of The Comedy of Errors for TV, 1954 and for Arts Theatre, London, 1956; Wrote (with Dorothy Reynolds) Salad Days, Bristol, 1965; Vaudeville, London, 1954; Duke of York's 1976; Free As Air, Savoy, London, 1957; Hooray for Daisy!, Bristol, 1959; Lyric, Hammersmith, 1960; Follow that Girl, Vaudeville, London, 1960; Wildest Dreams, 1960; Vanity Fair (with Alan Pryce-Jones and Robin Miller), Queens Theatre, London, 1962; Nutmeg and Ginger, Cheltenham, 1963; Sixty Thousand Nights (with George Rowell), Bristol, 1966; The Pursuit of Love, Bristol, 1967; Composed music for songs in: As You Like It, Bristol, 1970; A Midsummer Nights Dream and Much Ado About Nothing, Regents Park, 1970; Adapted A.A. Milne's Winnie The Pooh, Phoenix Theatre, 1970, 75; (music and lyrics) Trelawny, Bristol, then London West End, 1972; Out of Bounds (book, music and lyrics based

on Pinero's The Schoolmistress), 1973; Wrote (with Gyles Brandbreth) Now We Are Sixty, play with music, based on life and works of A.A. Milne, Arts Theatre, Cambridge, 1986-; Revival, Nutmeg and Ginger, New Orange Tree Theatre, Richmond, 1991. *Honours:* BASCA, Gold Badge of Merit, 1987. *Hobbies:* Drawing; Going to theatres and cinemas; Listening to music. *Address:* 86 Beaufort Street, London SW3 6BU, England.

SLATFORD Rodney Gerald Yorke, b. 18 July 1944, Cuffley, Herts., England. Musician; Publisher. *Education:* Royal College of Music, with Adrian Beers. *Career:* Principal bass with the Midland Sinfonia, the Academy of St Martin in the Fields; Principal bass, English Chamber Orchestra until 1981; Edited and published 100 works for his own Yorke edition, devoted to double bass literature; Founder member of the Nash Ensemble and guest appearances with leading string quartets; Tours to Australia, New Zealand and the Far East: first double bass recital at the Sydney Opera House; Lectures in the USA; Professor in residence at the Kusatsu International Summer Academy in Japan, 1984; Teaching at the Toho Academy in Tokyo and at the Conservatoire in Peking; 1974-84 Professor at the Royal College of Music; From 1984 Head of School of Strings at the Royal Northern College of Music, Manchester: Fellow RNCM 1987; Established teaching method for double bass 1978; Founder of The Yorke Trust, to promote the training of young bassists; Director and founder, RNCM Junior Strings project, 1991; Chairman, European String TEachers Association, 1992; Regular presenter of Radio 3, 1993. *Recordings include:* Rossini Duetto, in solo record with the Academy of St Martin in the Fields (EMI). *Publication:* The Bottom Line 1985. *Contributions to:* Woman's Hour; A Word in Edgeways; One Pair of Ears; Mainly for Pleasure, Radio 3; The Strad magazine; New Grove Dictionary of Music and Musicians 1980. *Hobby:* Gardening. *Address:* 31 Thornhill Square, London N1 1BQ, England.

SLATINARU Maria, b. 25 May 1938, Jassy, Rumania. Singer (Soprano). *Education:* Studied at the Bucharest Conservatory with Arta Florescu and Aurel Alexandrescu. *Debut:* Bucharest 1969, as Elisabeth de Valois. *Career:* Appearances as guest at Mannheim, Stuttgart, Zurich, Wiesbaden and Dusseldorf; Basle and Florence 1983, as Giorgetta in Il Tabarro; Strasbourg 1984, as Elisabeth in Tannhäuser; She has sung Tosca in San Francisco, Dallas (1988) and elsewhere; Other roles include Verdi's Abigaille and Amelia (Simon Boccanegra), Leonore in Fidelio, Wagner's Sieglinde, Senta and Elsa, Santuzza and Puccini's Turandot, Minnie and Manon Lescaut.

SLATKIN Leonard Edward, b. 1 Sept. 1944, Los Angeles, California, USA. Conductor; Music Director; Pianist. m. Linda Hohenfeld, 29 Mar. 1986. *Education:* Los Angeles City College; Juilliard School of Music with Jean Morel; University of Indiana School of Music; Aspen Music Festival with Walter Susskind; Conducting: Felix Slatkin, Amerigo Marino, Ingolf Dahl; Piano: Victor Aller, Selma Cramer; Composition: Mario Castelnuovo-Tedesco; Viola: Sol Schoenbach. *Debut:* Carnegie Hall, 1966. *Career includes:* Guest Conductor: Boston, Chicago, New York, Philadelphia, Pittsburgh, Cleveland, Los Angeles, San Francisco, Detroit, Atlanta, Dallas, Cincinnati, Washington DC, Denver, Houston, Montreal, Toronto, Vienna, London Symphony, London Philharmonia, London Royal Philharmonic, Concertgebouw, Royal Danish, Tivoli, English Chamber Orchestra, BBC Philharmonic, Orchestre National de Paris, Stockholm, Oslo, Gothenburg, Scottish National Orchestra, NHK Tokyo, Israel, Berlin. Opera: Vienna State Opera, Lyric Opera of Chicago, Stuttgart Opera, Opera Theatre of St Louis, Metropolitan Opera debut October 1991; Music Festivals: Tanglewood, Hollywood Bowl, Blossom, New York Philharmonic Horizons, Mann Music Center, Grant Park, Mostly Mozart, Saratoga; Music Director and Conductor, 1979-, European Tour 1985, Far East 1986, Saint Louis Symphony Orchestra; Artistic Director and Conductor, Minnesota Orchestra Sommerfest, 1979-89; Festival Director, Cleveland

Orchestra Blossom Festival, 1991-. *Compositions:* The Raven; Dialogue for Two Cellos and Orchestra; 4 String Quartets; Extensions 1, 2, 3 and 4. *Recordings:* Numerous, for RCA, Angel/EMI, Vox, Telarc, Philips, Virgin, Nonesuch, New World, Warner Brothers, MCA including a 3-disc set of Gershwin. *Honours include:* 5 Honorary Doctorates; 2 Grammy Awards for RCA recording of Prokofiev Symphony No. 5 with Saint Louis Symphony Orchestra, 1985; Austrian Government Declaration of Honour in Silver, 1986. *Membership:* Board of Governors, Chicago Chapter, National Academy of Recording Arts and Sciences. *Current Management:* ICM Artists, Limited; Harold Holt, Limited. *Address:* Saint Louis Symphony Orchestra, 718 North Grand Boulevard, St Louis, MO 63103, USA.

SLAVICKY Milan, b. 7 May 1947, Prague, Czech Republic. Composer; Producer; Music Writer; Lecturer. m. Eva Hachova, 7 July 1972, 2 sons. *Education:* Studied at Charles University, Prague and at the Janáček Academy of Music Arts, Brno. *Career:* Senior Music Producer of Classics, Supraphon, 1973-81; Producer of Electroacoustic Music, Radio Prague, 1981-82; Lectures in Boston, Luzern, London, Cardiff, Leipzig; Compositions Played at International Rostrum of Composers, UNESCO in Paris, 1979, at Music Festivals in Dresden, Ludwigsburg, Prague, Brno, Bratislava, Berlin, Salzburg, Lisbon, Bourges and Broadcast by BBC, BRT3, Radio Hilversum, Bayerische Rundfunk 4; Freelance Composer, 1982- 90; Assistant Professor at the Department of Musicology, Charles University, 1990-. *Compositions include:* Orchestral; Concerto; Chamber Music; Vocal; Electroacoustic. *Recordings Include:* As Musical Producer Produced Over 300 Records for Supraphon, Panton, Opus, and in Co Productions for EMI, Denon, DG, Orfeo, CBS. *Contributions to:* Studies; Interviews; Record and Book Reviews; Radio Programs; Critisms; Articles on Music Festivals. *Hobbies:* Travel; Family Life. *Address:* Lukesova 39, 142 00 Praha 4, Czech Republic.

SLAVIKOVA Jitka, b. 14 Mar 1954, Prague, Czech Republic. Musicologist; Music Journalist. *Education:* Studied at the Charles University, Prague. *Career:* Research Worker in Antonin Dvořák Museum in Prague, 1978-86; Since 1986 Journalist in the Musical Revue Hudebni Rozhledy. *Publications include:* Dvořák and France; Dvořák in England; Dvořák Man and Craftsman. *Contributions to:* A Large Number of Articles, Reviews in Newspapers and Journals. *Honours:* Honor Member of Dvořák Society; London Honor Citizenship of New Orleans. *Memberships:* Association of Music Artists and Scientists; Dvořák Societie in Prague and London. *Hobbies:* Singing; Travel. *Address:* 130 00 Praha 3, Cajkovskeho 7, Czech Republic.

SLAWSON A. Wayne, b. 29 Dec. 1932, Detroit, Michigan, USA. Composer; Professor of Music. *Education:* BA Mathematics, 1955, MA Music Composition, 1959, University of Michigan; PhD Psychology, Harvard University, 1965. *Career:* Assistant Professor of Theory of Music, Yale School of Music, Connecticut, 1967-72; Associate Professor, 1972-84, Chair, Department of Music, 1972-78, Professor of Music, 1984-86, University of Pittsburgh, Pennsylvania; Professor of Music, University of California, Davis, 1986-. *Compositions:* Electronic music works: Wishful thinking about Winter, 1966; Colors, 1981; Greetings, 1985; Quatrains Miniature, 1986; Variations for two violins, 1977; Interpolation of Dance for String Quartet, 1992; Grave Trunles for computer music and video tape (with Harvey Himelfarb), 1992; Warm Shades, an Octet for singers and woodwinds, 1993; If These Two Tolled, computer music, 1990. *Publication:* Sound Color, 1985. *Contributions to:* Book Reviewer for Journal of Music Theory, 1986. *Honours:* Fellow, American Council of Learned Societies, 1978-79; Outstanding Publication Award, Society for Music Theory. *Address:* c/o Music Department, University of California, Davis, CA 95616, USA.

SLIMACEK Jan, b. 31 July 1939, Kelc, Czechoslovakia. Composer. m. Marie Chvatikova, 19 Dec

1964, 2 d. *Eduction:* Studied at Prague Conservatory. *Debut:* Symfonietta for Strings Tape Recording Czechoslovak Radio. *Career:* Sonatina for Strings, Northern Music Festival, Ontario, 1988, Vassa 1992; Divertimento for Flute and Piano Inter Music Festival, Brno, 1983, Graz Wien, 1993; Quattro Intermezzi per Orchestra Gera, 1983, Musical Festival Rostow Don 1988; Concertino for Accordion, Electravox and Orchestra Gera, 1976, Nurmberg 1982, Bern 1983; Dramatic Picture Szczecin, Weimar, 1979; Piano Quartet, Warszawa 1977 Three Etudes for Piano, Bristol 1981. *Compositions include:* Piano Quartet; Sonatina for Strings; Three Etudes for Piano; Dramatic Picture; Songs for Childrens Choir and Piano; Variations for Strings and Harpsichord. *Recordings include:* Quattro Intermezzi per Orchestra; The Victory Overture for Orchestra; Musica per Orchestra; Three Minatures for Chamber Orchestra; Music per Ottoni. *Honours:* Audience Prize at Jihlava; Festival of Vocal Creation; Three 1st Prizes in Olomouc Song Festival. *Membership:* Association of Musicians and Musicologists. *Hobbies:* Travel; Hiking. *Address:* Mohylova 109, Plzen 312 06, Czech Republic.

SLIMACEK Milan, b. 20 Sept 1936, Brno, Czechoslovakia. Composer. m. Jane Nevrklova, 19 Apr 1969, 3 daughters. *Education:* Studied at Conservatoire in Brno and at the College of Performing Arts in Bratislava. *Debut:* Conservatoire in Brno. *Career:* Music for TV Films and Theatre Performances. *Compositions:* The Quintet for the Clarinet, Two Violins, The Viola and the Violoncello; The String Quartet No.1, No.2, No.3; Tre Preludes for the Flute and the Guitar; The Episodi for the Flute, Oboe, Violoncello and the Piano. *Recordings:* Fresque for the Orchestra; The Small Notes; Four Children Choirs. *Contributions to:* Confession OpusMusicum. *Honours:* First Prize for String Quartet no. 3. *Memberships:* Czech Musical Fund; Leos Janáček's Fund. *Hobbies:* Literature; Sports; Tennis. *Address:* 602 00 Brno, Rezkova 12, Czech Republic.

SLONIMSKY Nicolas, b. 27 April 1894, St.Petersburg, Russia. Lexicographer; Writer on Music; Conductor.m. 30 July 1931, 1 daughter. *Education:* St.Petersburg Conservatory. *Career:* Debut as conductor, Boston,1927; other appearances during 1930s in New York, San Francisco, Havana, Paris, Berlin, Budapest, Hollywood and Denver, giving early performances of music by Cowell, Ives, Ruggles and Schoenberg; Television appearance, The Mind, 1988; Personal appearance at Almeida Festival, London, 1988; 100th Birthday celebrations, 1994. *Compositions:* Studies in black and white for piano, 1928; My Toy Balloon for piano, 1942; Suite for cello and piano, 1951; Yellowstone Park Suite for piano, 1952; Gravestones for voice and piano, 1949; Piccolo Divertimento for chamber group, 1986. *Recordings:* Piano pieces and songs, Orion, 1968; History Making Premieres, conducting works of Ives, Varèse and Ruggles, Orion, 1970. *Publications:* Music Since 1900, 1937; 4th ed. 1971; Supplement, 1985; Music of Latin America, 1945; 2nd. ed., 1972; The Road to Music, 1947; Thesaurus of Scales and Melodic Patterns, 1948; Baker's Biographical Dictionary of Musicians, eds 5, 6, 7 and 8, 1958-78, 1984, 1992 (nos 7 and 8 with Dennis K McIntire); Lectionary of Music, 1989; Perfect Pitch, an autobiography, 1988. *Contributions to:* The Musical Quarterly, Musical America. *Honours:* Guggenheim Foundation, 1987. *Membership:* ASCAP, from 1952. *Hobbies:* Linguistics; Chess; Travel. *Address:* 2630 Midvale Avenue, Los Angeles, CA 90064, USA.

SLONIMSKY Sergey, b. 12 Aug. 1932, Leningrad, USSR. Composer; Teacher. m. 1973, 1 son. *Education:* Graduted, Composition 1955 (Professor O. Evlakhov), Piano 1956 (Professor V. Nilsen), postgraduate 1957-58, Leningrad (now St Petersburg) Conservatoire. *Career:* Teaching faculty (music theory & composition) 1959-, Professor 1976-, Leningrad Conservatoire. *Compositions:* Wide variety of musical forms & genres including: 9 symphonies, 1958-89, orchestral & vocal; Chamber works; Opera, ballet; Songs & choral pieces Titles include: Carnival Overture, 1957; Concerto Buffa (chamber orchestra, 1966; Antiphones (string quartet) 1969; Virinea, opera, 1969; Icarus, ballet in 3 acts, 1973; Master & Margarita, chamber opera, 3 acts, 1970-85; Merry Songs (piccolo, flute & tuba), 1971; Sonata for Violoncello & Piano, 1986. Works performed widely; Opera Mary Stuart performed at 1986 Edinburgh Festival, USSR & abroad; Hamlet, opera (drama for music), 1991; X Symphony, Cezch: dell' Inferno, secondo Dante, 1992; 24 Preludes and Figues for piano, 1993. *Recordings:* Numerous (Melodia label). *Publications:* Thesis (book), Symphonies of S. Prokofiev; Many works published, USSR & abroad. *Honours include:* Winner, M. I. Glinka State Prize, 1983; People's Artist of USSR, 1987. *Memberships:* Board, CIS Composers Union; Board, St Petersburg branch, CIS Composers Union. *Address:* St Petersburg Conservatoire of Music, Teatralnaya Ploshchad, St Petersburg, Russia.

SLORACH Marie, b. 8 May 1951, Glasgow, Scotland. Singer (Soprano). *Education:* Royal Scottish Academy of Music and Drama. *Career:* Member of Scottish Opera 1974-81: roles included Marzelline (Fidelio), Marenka (Bartered Bride), Zerlina (Don Giovanni), Eva (Die Meistersinger), Tatiana (Eugene Onegin), Fiordiligi (Così fan Tutte) and Jenifer (The Midsummer Marriage); Wexford Festival in Wolf-Ferrari's I Gioelli della Madonna and Smetana's The Kiss; English National Opera as Lisa in The Queen of Spades and Donna Elvira in Don Giovanni; Glyndebourne Touring Opera as Mozart's Donna Anna and Electra and Amelia in Simon Boccanegra; Opera North in Carmen, Die Meistersinger, Katya Kabanova and Così fan Tutte; Gabriella di Vergy and Giovanna d'Arco for Dorset Opera; Amelia for Australian Opera in Sydney; Sang Ellen Orford in a new production of Peter Grimes, Opera North, 1989; Concert engagements with the Hallé, Liverpool Philharmonic and Scottish National Orchestras, London Mozart Players and London Sinfonietta. *Address:* c/o Music International, 13 Ardilaun Road, Highbury, London N5 2QR, England.

SLOVAK Ladislav, b. 10 Sept 1919, Bratislava, Czechoslovakia. Conductor. *Education:* Studied at the Bratislava Conservatory, then the Academy of Music with Vaclav Talich 1949-53; Leningrad with Yevgeni Mravinsky, 1954-55. *Career:* Music producer of the Czech Broadcasting Company at Bratislava, 1946-61; Conducted the Symphony Orchestra of Radio Bratislava 1955-61; Slovak Philharmonic Orchestra, 1961-81; Tours of Italy, West Germany, Britain and France; Chief Conductor of the Prague Symphony Orchestra 1972-75; Conductor of the South Australia Symphony Orchestra at Adelaide 1966 and 1972-73; Tours with the Czech Philharmonic Orchestra to China, India, Japan, New Zealand and Russia in 1959 and the USA 1967; Conducted the premieres of works by Alexander Moyzes, Eugen Suchon, Dezider Kardoš and other Slovak composers; Conductor, Professor of the Academy of Muisc Bratislava. *Recordings include:* Tchaikovsky Symphonies with the Czech and Slovak Philharmonics; Shostakovich Symphonies nos. 2 and 9; Bartók Music for Strings, Percussion and Celesta; Prokofiev 5th Symphony; Music by Kubik, Ryba, Suchon, Loudova, Babusek, Cikker and Kardos; Shostakovich complete symphonies with the Symphony Orchestra of Radio Bratislava. *Address:* Banicka 3, 81104 Bratislava, Slovakia.

SLUYS Jozef, b. 22 Oct. 1936, Gaasbeek, Belgium. Organist. 2 sons, 1 daughter. *Education:* Lemmens Institute, Malines; Royal Conservatory of Music, Brussels. *Career:* Organist, Cathedrale St Michel, Brussels; Director, Rijksmuziekacademie, Schaarbeek, Brussels; Professor of Organ, Lemmens Institute, Louvain to 1987; Radio and TV performances, Belgium and abroad; Concerts, Belgium, France, Spain, Netherlands, Sweden, Germany, UK, Austria, Poland, Czechoslovakia, USSR, USA, New Zealand, Zaire; Founder, Chairman, Historical Concerts in Church of Onze-Lieve-Vrouw-Lombeek; Artistic Director, various festivals including Brussels Cathedral Concerts and International Organ Festival of Brussels; Founder, Jozef Sluys Trio; Regular performances with soprano Greta De Reyghere. *Recordings:* For BRT, Alpha, Phonic, EMI, Zephyr (including works by J.N. Lemmens, ZO4); Prezioso (Dupré, De Boeck August, Tinel Edgar, Peeters Flor Brcobalemo (Mendelssohn - Bartholdy); Reme Gailly International Productions: Bach - Johann Sebastian. *Honours:* Mailly Prize for Organists; Arnold Prize for Organists; Prizewinner, International J.S.Bach Contest, 1963; Pro Musica Medal, Belgian Ministry of National Education and Culture, 1963; Rene Snepvangers Prize for recording, Belgian Music Press, 1978; Caecilia Prize, 1979; Several other prizes. *Membership:* Commission for Music Education. *Address:* Domstraat 8, 1602 Vlezenbeek, Belgium.

SMALDONE Edward M., b. 19 Nov. 1956, Rockville Center, New York, USA. Composer. m. Karen Ajamian, 4 Aug. 1979. *Education:* BA, 1978, MA, Composition, 1980, Queens College, City University of New York; PhD, Composition and Theory, Graduate Center, City University of New York, 1986; Studied composition with Henry Weinberg, George Perle, Hugo Weisgall and Ralph Shapey. *Career:* Artistic Director, new music chamber series Sounds from the Left Bank, sponsored by Queens Symphony Orchestra, at Project Studios One, Long Island City, New York; Assistant Professor, Aaron Copland School of Music, Queens College, City University of New York. *Compositions:* String Quartet No 2; Wind Quintet; Diptych, for guitar; Trio: dance and nocturne for violin, clarinet and violoncello; Solo Sonata for clarinet; Icons, for oboe, clarinet and piano; Double Duo, for flute, clarinet, violin, violoncello; Dialogue, for orchestra; Django's Dance, orchestra; Two Sides of the Same Coin, clarinet and piano; Transformational Etudes, piano solo. *Recordings:* Double Duo, recorded by the Thira Ensemble, New Music Manitoba Label. *Publications:* Godanginuta, by Mitsuzaki Kengyo: a Structural Analysis, in Hogaku 1/2, 1983; Japanese and western Confluences in Large-Scale Pitch Organization of Tóru Takemitsu's November Steps and Autumn; Prespectives of New Music, Summer 1989. *Contributions to:* Composer and Audience in Attenzione, 1984; The Music of Luigi Dallapiccola in Attenzione, 1985. *Address:* 147-41 24th Avenue, Whitestone, NY 11357, USA.

SMALLEY Denis Arthur, b. 16 May 1946, Nelson, New Zealand. Composer. Divorced, 1 son. *Education:* MusB, Dip.Mus, University of Canterbury, 1967; BMus Honours, Victoria University of Wellington, 1969; Dip. de Musique Electro-Acoustique et de Recherche Musicale, Paris Conservatoire, 1972; DPhil, University of York, England. *Appointments:* Head of Music, Wellington College, New Zealand, 1969-71; Northern Music Critic, The Guardian, 1972-75; Composition Fellow, 1975-65, Senior Lecturer, Music, 1976-94, University of East Anglia, Norwich, England; Professor of Music, City University, London, 1994. *Compositions:* Gradual, 1974; Pentes, 1974; Ouroboros, 1975; Pneuma, 1976; Darkness After Time's Colours, 1976; Chanson De Geste, 1978; The Pulses of Time, 1979; Word Within, 1981; Vortex, 1982; Tides, 1984; Clarinet Threads, 1985; O Vos Omnes, 1986; Wind Chimes, 1987; Piano Nets, 1990; Valley Flow, 1992; Névé, 1994. *Recordings:* Gradual; Pentes; Chanson De Geste; The Pulses of Time; Pneuma; Vortex Tides; Clarinet Threads; Wind Chimes; Piano Nets, Valley Flow. *Publications:* Spectro-morphology and Structuring Processes, The Language of Electro-Acoustic Music, 1986; The Listening Imagination: Listening in the Electrocoustic Era, 1992. *Contributions to:* Does Acousmatic Music Exist? (Musiques et Recherches), 1991; Spatial Experience in Electroacoustic Music, (Musiques et Recherdes), 1991; Defining Transformations (Interface), 1993. *Honours:* Fylkingen Prize, 1975; 1st Prize, Bourges Electroacoustic Awards, 1983; Special Prize, International Confederation of Electroacoustic Music, 1983; Prix Ars Electronica, 1988. *Address:* Music Department, City University, Northampton Square, London EC1V 0HB, England.

SMALLEY Roger, b. 26 July 1943, Swinton, Manchester, England. Composer; Pianist. *Education:* Studied at Royal College of Music with Fricker and

White; later study with Walter Goehr at Morley College and with Stockhausen in Cologne. *Career:* Composer-in-residence King's College Cambridge 1967; co-founded and directed four-man group Intermodulation 1970; disbanded 1976; Has specialized as pianist in the music of Stockhausen; Appointed to University of Western Australia 1976, as teacher, composer and performer. *Compositions:* Piano Pieces I-V, 1962-5; Septet for tenor, soprano and ensemble, 1963; String Sextet, 1964; Variations for strings, 1964; Gloria tibi Trinitas I for orchestra, 1965; Gloria tibi Trinitas II for voices, chorus and orchestra, 1966; Missa Brevis, 1967; Missa parodia I for piano 1967; Missa parodia II for ensemble, 1967; The Song of the Highest Tower for solo voices, chorus and orchestra, 1968; Transformation I for piano and ring modulator, 1969; Pulses for 5 x 4 players, 1969; Melody Study I for 4 or more players, 1970; Melody Study II for 4-12 players, 1970; Beat Music for 4 electronic instruments and orchestra; Monody for piano and ring modulator; 1972; Zeitenbenen for ensemble and 4-track tape, 1973; Dijeridu for 4-track tape, 1974; Accord for 2 pianos, 1974-75; 6 Modular Pieces for 4 flutes, 1977; William Derrincourt, entertainment for baritone, male chorus and ensemble, 1977 ; String Quartet, 1979; Echo III for trumpet and tape, 1979; Konzertstuck for violin and orchestra, 1980; Symphony, 1980-81; Movement for flute and piano, 1980; Piano Concerto, 1985; Strung Out, for 13 Solo Strings, 1988; Ceremony I for Percussion Quartet, 1987. *Publications include:* Essays on Stockhausen, Debussy, Messiaen, and Peter Maxwell Davies for Musical Times and Tempo. *Address:* c/o Music Department, University of Western Australia, Perth, Western Australia, Australia.

SMALLWOOD Robert, b. 22 July 1958, Melbourne, Victoria, Australia. Composer; Conductor. *Education:* BMus, Melbourne University, 1979. *Career:* Founder-Director, New Audience Ensemble, 1979-84; Musical Director, Astra Chamber Music Society, 1983-84; Australia Council International Study Grant, 1985; Musician-in-Residence, Orange, New South Wales, 1987-90; Founder-Director, Orange Music Festival, 1989-90; Musical Director for many stage and music-theatre productions, in addition to concert work. *Compositions:* Discovery, 1979; Kyrie, 1984; Elements, 1985; Wake Up My Soul, 1987; Living Land, 1988; Psalm 150, 1991; Red Dirt, musical, 1991; Reminiscences, 1982. *Hobbies:* Golf; Cricket; Australian Rules football; Photography. *Address:* c/o 23 Stanley Road, Vermont South, Victoria 3133, Australia.

SMENDZIANKA Regina, b. 9 Oct. 1924, Torun, Poland. Pianist; Teacher. *Education:* Diploma with highest distinction, State College of Music, Cracow; MA, 1948. *Debut:* Soloist with Cracow Philharmonic Orchestra, 1947. *Career:* Numerous concert tours as recitalist and soloist with orchestras, Poland and abroad, 33 European countries, Asia, America; Teaching: 1964; Assistant Professor, 1966; Professor, 1977 at F Chopin Academy of Music in Warsaw; Rector of F Chopin Academy in Warsaw, 1972, 1973-; Courses in piano interpretation, lectures, Poland, Tokyo, Mexico, Weimar, Caracas, Tampere, Odense; Copenhagen, Berlin, Warsaw. *Recordings include:* Works of Chopin, Bach, Mozart, Franck, Bacewicz, Schubert, Malawski, Moniuszko, Paderewski for Polish, German, Dutch, Italian and Japanese producers; Polish pieromantic music recording in Poland and abroad. *Current Management:* Polish Artistic Agency, PAGART, Pl. Zwyciestwa 9, Warsaw. *Address:* 02-529 Warsaw, ul. Narbutta 76/10, Poland .

SMETANA Josef, b. 8 Dec 1915, Vienna, Austria. Professor; Conductor. m. Eva Depoltova, 6 Oct 1943, 2 sons. *Education:* Music Science, Charles University, Prague, 1935-46; Conducting, Prague Conservatoire. *Debut:* 1933. *Career:* Professor, State Conservatoire, Prague, 1950-90; Chief, Prague Town Theatre Orchestra, 1950-78. *Composition:* 120 stage music works. *Recordings:* Ultraphon; Supraphon. *Publications:* School for Accordeon, 1965; 175th Anniversary of State Conservatoire of Prague, 1986. *Contributions to:* Music

Lists, 1950-60. *Honours:* 1st Prize, FIS International Music Competition, 1935. *Membership:* Society of Czech Composers. *Hobbies:* Swimming; Gardening. *Current Management:* DICIA, OSA (International Authors Rights). *Address:* Haskova 8, 170 00 Prague, Czech Republic.

SMETANIN Michael, b. 1958, Sydney, Australia. Composer. *Education:* BM, composition, New South Wales State Conservatorium of Music, 1981; Australian Broadcasting Corporation's orchestral summer schools, 1981 and 1982; Composition study with Louis Andriessen, Royal Conservatorium, The Hague. *Career:* Composer in Residence, Musica Viva, 1988. *Compositions:* Ensemble works: Bellevue II, 1987; Ladder of Escape, 1984; Lichtpunt, 1983; Per Canonem, 1982, revised 1984; The Speed of Sound, 1983; Track, 1985; Undertones, 1981; Vault, 1986; Fylgjir, 1989; Spray, 1990; Strange Attractions, 1991. Orchestral Works: After the First Circle, 1982; Black Snow, 1987; Zyerkala; Blitz, 1989. Vocal Works: 3 Songs, 1981; The Skinless Kiss of Angels, 1991; Children's Music: Music for Children and Dancers, 1988; Instrumental and Keyboard Works: Afstand, 1983; Sting, 1987; Stroke, 1988. *Recordings:* Works on CD; Ladder of Escape (Attacca); Spray (Attacca); Sting (Eversound). *Address:* c/o Australian Music Centre, PO Box N690, Grosvenor Street, Sydney 2000, Australia.

SMILLIE Thomson John, b. 29 Sept 1942, Glasgow, Scotland. Opera Director. m. Anne Pringle, 15 July 1965, 2 s. *Education:* Hilhead High School, 1947-60; Glasgow University, 1960-63. *Career:* Director of PR Scottish Opera, 1966-78; Artistic Director, Wexford Festival, Ireland, 1973- 78; General Manager, Opera Company of Boston, 1978-80; General Director, Kentucky Opera, 1981-. *Contributions to:* Numerous Magazines. *Memberships:* Opera America. *Hobbies:* Reading; Cooking; Antique Collecting. *Address:* 4701 Kitty Hawk Way, Louisville, KY 40207, USA.

SMIRAGLIA Richard Paul, b. 18 Mar. 1952, New York, New York, USA. *Education:* BA, Music. Lewis & Clark College, Portland, Oregon, 1973; MLS, Indiana University, Bloomington, Indiana, 1974. *Career:* Music Catalogue Librarian, University of Illinois at Urbana-Champaign, 1974-86; School of Library Service, Columbia University, New York, 1987-; PhD. University of Chicago, 1992; Current position: Associate Professor of Library and Information Science. *Publications:* Shelflisting Music, 1981; Cataloging Music, 1983, 2nd Edition, 1986; Danish emigrant ballads, 1983; Music Cataloging, 1989; Origins, Content and Future of AACR2, 1992; Describing Archival Materials, 1991. *Contributions to:* Music in the OCLC Online Union Catalogue, 1981; Author, Theoretical Considerations in the Bibliographic Control of Music Materials in Libraries, in Cataloging and Classification Quarterly, 1985. *Memberships:* Music Library Association, 1973-, Member at Large, Board of Directors, 1986-88, Chair, Bibliographic Control Committee, 1981-86; International Association of Music Libraries, 1973-; Association for Recorded Sound Collections, 1981-; American Library Association, 1981-; Music Library Association, Editor, Technical Reports, 1988-; American Library Association, Editor, Library Resources and Technical Services, 1989. *Hobbies:* Carpentry; Cooking; Running. *Address:* Palmer School of Library and Information Science, Long Island University, Brookville, NY 11548, USA.

SMIRNOV Dmitri, b. 2 Nov 1948, Minsk, USSR. Composer. m. Elena Firsova, 2 children. *Education:* Studied with Edison Denisov at the Moscow Conservatoire, 1967-72. *Career:* Editor in publishing house Sovetsky Kompozitor 1973-80; Freelance composer from 1980; Operas Tiriel and The Lamentations of Thel performed in Freiburg and at the Almeida Theatre, London, 1989; Symphony No.1 The Seasons performed at Tanglewood 1989; Professor at Keele University, 1993. *Compositions:* 3 Piano Sonatas, 1967, 1980, 1992; 2 Violin Sonatas 1969, 1979; 2 Piano Concertos 1971, 1978; String Trio 1970; Six Poems by Alexander Blok for voice and orchestra 1972; 4 String Quartets 1973, 1985, (2) in 1993; Clarinet Concerto, 1974; Pastorale for orchestra 1975; The Sorrows of Past Days for voice and ensemble 1976; 2 Piano Trios, 1977, 1992; Sonata for cello and piano 1978; The Seasons for voice and ensemble 1979; Nine Pieces for piano 1979; 2 Symphonies 1980, 1982; Six Poems by William Blake for voice and organ 1981; Capriccio on Departure ..... for ensemble 1982; The Night Rhymes for voice and orchestra, 1982; Tiriel, opera 1985; Partita for solo violin, 1985; The Lamentations of Thel, chamber opera, 1986; Mozart-Variations for orchestra, 1987; The Visions of Coleridge for voice and ensemble, 1987; Songs of Love and Madness for voice and ensemble, 1988; The Seven Angels of William Blake for piano, 1988; The Moonlight Story for ensemble 1988; Eight-Line Poems for voice and ensemble 1989; Concerto for violin and 13 strings 1990; From Evening to Morning for mixed chorus 1990; Jacob's Ladder for ensemble 1990; A Song of Liberty, an oratorio, 1991; Abel for ensemble, 1991; The River of Life for ensemble, 1992; Quintet, 1992; Cello Concerto, 1992; Ariel Songs for voice and ensemble, 1993. *Address:* 32 Larchwood, Keele, Newcastle, Staffordshire ST5 5BB, England.

SMIRNOV Oleg, b. 1950, Moscow, Russia. Cellist. *Education:* Studied at the Moscow Conservatoire with Professor Kosolapova. *Career:* Co Founded the Amisted Quartet, 1973; Many concerts in the Former Soviet Union and Russia, with a repertoire including Works by Hadyn, Mozart, Beethoven, Schubert, Brahms, Tchaikovsky, Borodin, Prokofiev, Shostakovich, Bartók, Barber, Bucchi, Golovin and Tikhomirov; Recent Concert Tours to Mexico, Italy and Germany. *Recordings include:* Recitals for the US Russian Company Arts and Electronics. *Honours include:* Prizewinner at the Bela Bartok festival and the Bucchi Competition. *Address:* c/o Sonata (Amistad Quartet), 11 Northgate Street, Glasgow, G20 7AA, Scotland.

SMIT Leo, b. 12 Jan 1921, Philadelphia, USA. Composer; Pianist. *Education:* Studied Piano at the Curtis Institute, 1930-32, Composition with Nicolas Nabokov, 1935. *Debut:* Concert as Pianist at Carnegie Hall American Ballet Company, 1936-39. *Career:* Pianist with Balanchine's; Teacher at Sarah Lawrence College, 1947-49; University of California at Los Angeles, 1957-63, SUNY at Buffalo, 1962-84; Director of Monday Evening Concerts at Los Angeles, 1957-63; Composer in Residence at the American Academy in Rome, 1972-73 and at Brevard Music Center, 1980. *Compositions include:* Operas The Alchemy of Love 1969 and Magic Water, 1978; Melodrama A Mountain Eulogy, 1975; Ballets Yerma, 1946, Virginia Sampler, 1947; Orchestra: 3 Symphonies, 1956, 1965, 1981; Capriccio for Strings, 1958; Piano Concerto, 1968; Symphony of Dances and Songs, 1981; Variations for piano and orchestra, 1981; Chamber: Sextet for clarinet, bassoon and strings, 1940; Invention for clarinet and piano, 1943; In Woods for oboe, harp and percussion, 1978; Sonata for solo cello, 1982; Flute of Wonder, 1983; Instruments, 1984; String Quartet, 1984; Exuquy for string trio, 1985; Piano pieces, choruses, songs and Academic Graffiti for voice and ensemble to text by W H Auden, 1959. *Address:* c/o ASCAP, ASCAP Building, One Lincoln Plaza, New York, NY 10023, USA.

SMITH Barbara Barnard, b. 10 June 1920, Ventura, CA, USA. Ethnomusicologist. *Education:* Studied at University of Rochester. *Career:* Faculty, Eastman School of Music; University of Hawaii, Assistant, Associate, Professor, Professor Emeritus; Senior Fellow East West Center; Field Research in Asia and Pacific. *Publications:* Articles, MGG and New Grove. *Contributions to:* Ethnomusicology, Music Educators Journl; College Music Symposium; Journal of International Folk Music. *Honours:* Rockefeller Foundation Grants; Hawaii Governor's Award. *Memberships:* Society for Ethnomusicology; International Council for Traditional Music; International American Musicological Society; Pacific Science Association. *Hobby:* Travel. *Address:* 581 Kamoku, No 2004, Honolulu, HI 96826, USA.

SMITH Catriona, b. 1963, Scotland. Singer (Soprano). *Education:* Studied at the Royal Scottish Academy and the University of Toronto (Opera Division). *Career:* Sang Britten's Lucia and Miss Wordsworth at the Banff Summer arts Festival, 1988; Cathleen in Riders to the Sea at Toronto and Pamina for British Youth opera; Wigmore Hall Recital Debut 1988; Kent Opera as Juno in the Return of Ulysses; festival engagements include Aldeburgh in Goehr's Triptych and English Bach in Idomeneo; Sang Clorinda in La Cenerentola at Covent Garden 1991 and engaged at the Stuttgart Staatsoper 1991-95; Other roles include Mozarts Countess, Rossini's Berta, Dido, Frasquita, and Susanna and Barbarina in Le Nozza di Figaro; Roles in Stuttgart include: Pamina, Gilda, Nyade, Sophie (Der Rosenkavalier), Erénoira (world premiere) and Zerlina. *Honours include:* Winner, 1987 Maggie Teyte Competition. *Address:* c/o Stuttgart Staatsoper, Oberer Schlossgarten 6, 7000 Stuttgart, Germany.

SMITH Daniel (W.), b. 11 Sept. 1939, New York, New York, USA. Bassoon Soloist. m. Judith Smith, 18 June 1961, 1 son, 1 daughter. *Education:* BM, Manhattan School of Music, 1961; MA, 1962, Professional Diploma, 1969, Columbia University; Doctorate studies, Mannes College of Music, 1970-73. *Debut:* Carnegie Recital Hall, NY; Europe: Wigmore Hall, London. *Career:* Soloist on recordings and in concert with English Chamber Orchestra, I Solisti di Zagreb, Royal Philharmonic Orchestra, Orchestra Da Camera di Santa Cecilia, NY Virtuosi Chamber Symphony, Santa Cruz Symphony, Rome Festival Orchestra, Florida Chamber Symphony, NY String Ensemble, AIH Roma Orchestra; Recitals: BBC Concert Hall, London; Carnegie Recital Hall, NY; Wigmore Hall, London; Merkin Concert Hall, NY; Bruno Walter Auditorium, NY; Diligentia Hall, The Hague; Atalier, Belgium; Distinguished Artists Series, Long Island, NY; B'nai Brith Festival, Purcell Room, London; Premiered Contrabassoon Concerto of Gunther Schuller with Santa Cruz Symphony. *Recordings:* Volumes 1-6 (37 concerti) Antonio Vivaldi with English Chamber Orchestra and I Solisti di Zagreb, ASV; 3 Bassoon Concertos with English Chamber Orchestra, ASV and MHS; Bassoon Bon-Bons with Royal Philharmonic Orchestra; English Music for Bassoon and Piano with pianist Roger Vignoles, ASV; Volumes 1 and 2, 18th Century Bassoon Concerti with Ravina Chamber Ensemble; Vivaldi Concerti with Ravina Chamber Ensemble; Music for Bassoon and String Quartet with Coull String Quartet, ASV; 5 Bassoon Concertos with English Chamber Orchestra, ASV. *Hobbies:* Literature; Travel. *Address:* 3 Gateway Drive, Syosset, NY 11791, USA.

SMITH David Hector, b. 16 Aug 1939, Wallasey, Cheshire, England. Pianist/Piano Teacher. m. Mary Margaret Pugh, 3 Jan 1964, 1 daughter. *Education:* Cheshire School, England; Studied under Kendall Taylor at The Northern School of Music, Manchester, 1958-63; Awarded Diplomas in Piano Teaching and Performing and The Frederick Moore Piano Prize, 1962. *Career:* Debut as Concerto Soloist, 1963, with the late Maurice Handford; Further Concerto Appearances and numerous recitals and lecture recitals throughout England; Appointed to Piano Department, The Royal Northern College of Music, Manchester, 1969, subsequently promoted to Senior Lecturer in piano and assistant to the Head of Keyboard Studies; Appointed as Examiner to The Associated Board of The Royal Schools of Music, 1976, with extensive tours in UK, Malaysia and New Zealand. *Memberships:* The European Piano Teachers Association. *Hobbies:* Foreign Travel; Reading. *Address:* 61 Denison Road, Hazel Grove, Stockport SK7 6HR, England.

SMITH Donald, b. 1922, Bundaberg, Queensland, Australia. Singer (Tenor). *Education:* Studied in Brisbane. *Debut:* Brisbane 1948, as Faust. *Career:* Sang with the Touring Elizabethan Opera Company's Tamino, Almaviva and Pinkerton; Guest Appearances with the Italian Grand Opera Company throughtout Australia; Sang with the Sadler's Wells Company from 1961, as Don José, the Duke of Mantua, Ramirez, Jenik, Ernani,

Riccardo, Foresto in Attila and Don Alvaro; Covent Garden Debut 1965 as Calaf; Sang Corrado in Il Corsaro at the Camden Festival, 1966 and returned to Sydney, 1968 singing there as Manrico, Cavaradossi, Florestan, Radames, Canio, Luigi and Carlo in I Masnadieri; sang Erik in Fliegende Holländer at Melbourne, 1978 and retired 1982. *Recordings include:* Highlights from Rigoletto, Carmen, The Bartered Bride all Sadler's Wells Productions. *Honours:* Many accolades and honours including being the first singer to perform at the Sydney Opera house; OBE for services to music and his profession, 1973; Henry Lawson Festival Award, 1975; In honour of contributions to opera, the Lyric Opera of Queensland presented a Gala Concert, 1989; Advance Australia Award, 1990; Degree of Doctor of the University, Griffith University Queensland, 1992. *Address:* c/o Australian Opera, PO Box 291, Strawberry Hills, NSW 2012, Australia.

SMITH Douglas William, b. 6 Aug 1949, Winona, MI, USA. Music School Director. m. Elaine M Ruppel, 20 Mar 1971, 2 sons. *Education:* Studied at Winona State University and University of Minnesota. *Career:* Co Founder and Educational Director of Music Tech; Specialist in Guitar Pedegogy for Children; Lecturer Throughout USA and in germany. *Compositions:* Young Classical Guitarist; Guitar Etude. *Recordings:* The Young Classical Guitarist. *Publications:* Classical Guitar for Young Children. *Honours:* Inc 500 Award. *Memberships:* American String Teachers Association. *Hobbies:* Fishing; Reading; Theology. *Address:* 304 Washington Ave North, Minneapolis, MN 55401, USA.

SMITH James Gordon, b. 28 Aug 1935, Raleigh, North Carolina, USA. Conductor; Musicologist. m. (1) Victori Cox, 1955, 1 son, 1 daughter, (2) Beverly Burt, 1967, (3) Carolyn Dill, 1986. *Education:* BMus 1960, MMus 1961, Peabody Conservatory of Music, Johns Hopkins University; DMA, University of Illinois, 1973. *Career:* Conductor: University of Illinois Chamber Choir, 1973-77; Eastman Chorus & Eastman Chorale, 1977-80; George Mason University Chorale, Symphonic Chorus, & Gloriana Singers, 1980-; Cantata Chamber Orchestra, 1985-. Guest Conductor: University of Illinois Symphony Orchestra; Eastman Philharmonia Orchestra; Eastman Wind Ensemble; George Mason University Chamber Orchestra; Numerous choral festivals & clinics. *Publications:* Editor, New Liberty Bell: Anthology of American Choral Music, & numerous octavos, published Mark Foster Music Company. *Contributions to:* New Grove Dictionary of Music and Musicians; New Grove Dictionary of American Music. *Address:* 4124 Roberts Road, Fairfax, Virginia 22032, USA.

SMITH Jennifer, b. 13 July 1945, Lisbon, Portugal. *Career:* Sang in Europe before moving to Britain, 1971; Operatic roles have included Countess Almaviva for Welsh National, Scottish and Kent Operas; Gluck's Orfeo at the Wexford Festival; Rameau's Les Boréades and Hippolyte et Aricie at Aix-en-Provence; L'Incoronazione di Poppea conducted by Leonhardt; Aminta in Il Re Pastore, Lisbon; Cybelle in Lully's Atys at the Opéra-Comique Paris and in New York; Concert repertoire includes works by Bach, Handel, Poulenc, Purcell, Britten and Berlioz (Les Nuits d'Eté); Appearances with the English Chamber Orchestra, London Bach Orchestra, the English Concert, Steinitz Bach Players and the Orchestra of the Age of Enlightenment; Conductors include Rattle, Willcocks, Leppard, Pinnock, Gardiner, Boulez, Mackerras and Kempe; Tour of Europe with the B Minor Mass, conducted by Frans Brueggen; Song recitals in Portugal, France, Germany, Switzerland, Belgium and Britain; TV appearances include Scarlatti's Salve Regina with George Malcolm, Handel's Judas Maccabeus conducted by Norrington and Purcell's Come, Ye Sons of Art Away; Sang the Queen of Night (Mozart Experience, London) conducted by Norrington, QEH 1989; Rameau at Versailles (Flore and Nais) with the English Bach Festival, 1989; Season 1992 as Music in Monteverdi's Orfeo at ENO, Iphigénie en Tauride with the English Bach Festival at Covent Garden, and in Conti's Don

Chisciotte at Innsbruck. *Recordings:* Bach Mass in B Minor, Magnificat/Corboz (Erato), Cantata 208 (Hyperion); Carissimi Jephte (Erato); Falla Retablo de Maese Pedro and Psyche/Rattle; Gabrieli Sacrae Symphoniae; Handel Hercules and L'Allegro/Gardiner (Archiv), Il Trionfo del Tempo (Erato), Silete Venti/ Pinnock (Archiv), Messiah, Amadigi (Erato); Haydn Mariazeller Mass and Little Organ Mass/Guest (Argo); Lully Dies Irae, Miserere and Te Deum/Paillard; Rameau's Nais/McGegan, Castor et Pollux/Farncombe and Les Boréades/Gardiner; Purcell King Arthur, Indian Queen and Fairy Queen/Gardiner, Come Ye Sons of Art/Pinnock; Vivaldi Gloria and Kyrie/Corboz, Beatus Vir and Dixit Dominus/Cleobury (Argo); Schubert Lieder (HMV Lisbon); Platée (Rameau), Titon et l'Aurore (Mondonville) Alcyone (Marais) Il Trionfo del Tempo (Handel), all with Marc Minkowski; Ottone (Handel) with Robert King (Hyperion). *Address:* 3 Gumleigh Road, London W5 4UX, England.

SMITH Lawrence Leighton, b. 8 Apr 1936, Portland, Oregon, USA. Conductor; Pianist. m. (1) 2 sons, (2) Kathleen Dale, 4 June 1976. 1 daughter. 1 stepson, 1 stepdaughter. *Education:* BM, Music, Mannes College of Music, New York, 1959; Studied piano with Ariel Rubstein, Portland; Leonard Shure, New York. *Career:* Teacher, Mannes College of Music, 1959-62; University of Texas, 1962-63; Boston University, 1963-64; Curtis Institute of Music, 1968-69; California Institute of the Arts, 1970-72; Professional debut as Pianist, 1962; Assistant to Erich Leinsdorf, Berkshire Music Center, Tangelwood, Massachusetts, 1962- 64; Assistant Conductor, Metropolitan Opera, New York, 1964-67; Music Director, Westchester (NY) Symphony Orchestra, 1967-69; Principal Guest Conductor, Phoenix (Arizona) Symphony Orchestra, 1971-73; Music Director, Austin (Tex) Symphony Orchestra, 1972-73; Oregon Symphony Orchestra, Portland, 1973- 80; Artistic Adviser, Principal Guest Conductor, North Carolina Symphony Orchestra, Raleigh, 1980-81; Music Director, San Antonio Symphony Orchestra, 1980-85; Louisville Orchestra, 1983-; Music Academy of the West, Santa Barbara, California, 1985-; Guest conductor with various orchestras in the USA and overseas. *Recordings:* For Louisville and Sheffield Lab. *Honour:* 1st prize, Dimitri Mitropoulos International Conducting Competition, New York, 1964. *Membership:* American Federation of Musicians. *Address:* c/o Louisville Orchestra, 609 West Main Street, Louisville, KY 40202, USA.

SMITH Malcolm Sommerville, b. 22 June 1933, Rockville Centre, New York, USA. Opera and Concert Singer (Bass). m. Margaret Yauger, 4 Oct 1975. *Education:* BA Music Education, 1957, BA Singing, 1960, Oberlin Conservatory of Music, Oberlin, Ohio, USA; MA Educational Administration, Teachers College, Columbia University, New York, USA, 1958; Opera School, Indiana University School of Music, 1960-62. *Debut:* New York City Opera, 1965. *Career:* Leading Bass, New York City Opera, 1965-70; Leading Bass, Deutsche Oper am Rhein, Düsseldorf, Germany, 1971-; Metropolitan Opera debut, 1975; Has sung with opera companies: Vienna Staatsoper; Salzburg Festival; Bielefeld; Cologne; Hamburg; Krefeld; Mannheim; Stuttgart; East and West Berlin; Spoleto Festival; La Scala, Rome, Trieste, Turin, Chicago, Cincinnati, Miami, San Francisco, Dresden, Houston; Concerts with: Chicago Symphony, Hollywood Bowl; Los Angeles Philharmonic; Cincinnati Symphony; Tulsa Philharmonic; Washington National Symphony; Baltimore Symphony; Minnesota Symphony; Düsseldorf, Duisburg, Munich and Krakow Philharmonics; Radio orchestras of Milan, Rome, Madrid, Paris, Cologne. *Recordings:* Mahler 8th; Samson, Handel; Oedipus Rex; Requiem, Penderecki; War and Peace, Prokofiev. *Hobby:* Restoration of old automobiles. *Current Management:* Thea Dispeker, New York, USA. *Address:* Markgrafenstrasse 10, 4 Düsseldorf 11, Germany.

SMITH Maureen Felicity, b. 1935, Leeds, England, Violinist. m. Geoffrey Rivlin, 27 Aug 1974, 2 daughters. *Education:* Royal Manchester College of Music; Indiana

University, USA. *Debut:* Royal Festival Hall, 1961. *Career:* Soloist with most leading British orchestras; Debut at London Promenade Concerts, 1965; Regular broadcasts for Radio 3; Numerous television appearances; Appearances at major festivals including Aldeburgh and Leeds, Brighton, Cheltenham, English Bach and Three Choirs. *Recordings:* Mendelssohn Violin Concerto; Milhaud Duos; Brahms & Mahler Piano Quartets. *Honours:* BBC Violin Competition, 1965; Gulbenkian Foundation Fellowship, 1966; Leverhulme Fellowship, 1966. *Memberships:* European String Teachers Association. *Current Management:* Maureen Lunn Management, Top Farm, Parish Lane, Hedgerley, Bucks SL2 3JH, England. *Address:* 8 Heath Close, London NW11 7DX, England.

SMITH Michael John, b. 7 June 1937, London, England. Cathedral Organist; Teacher; Examiner. m. Marian Lesley Cooper, 16 Apr 1968, 1 son, 2 daughters. *Education:* MA, BMus, Oxon; DMus, Edinburgh, 1973; FRCO(CHM); ADCM; LRAM; LTCL; Postgraduate Certificate in Education, London. *Career:* Organist, Pontefract Parish Church, Head of Music, The King's School, 1960-64; Organist, Louth Parish Church and Director of Music, King Edward VI Grammar School, 1965-66; Assistant Choirmaster and Organist, Salisbury Cathedral, Deputy Conductor, Salisbury Musical Society, 1967-74; Organist, Master of the Choristers, Llandaff Cathedral, 1974-; Conductor, Llandaff Cathedral Choral Society, Llandaff, Wales, 1974-91; Director, Cardiff Tallis Singers, 1987-92; Examiner, Royal Schools of Music, 1969-, including tours to Singapore, Malaysia, Hong Kong, South Africa, Mauritius and New Zealand; Tutor, University College, Cardiff, 1974-77; St Michael's College, Cardiff, 1982-86; The Cathedral School, Llandaff, 1982-; Welsh College of Music and Drama, 1983-; Organ Recitalist throughout Britain. *Recordings:* With Salisbury Cathedral Choir, 1974, Llandaff Cathedral Choir, 1980, 1984, 1986, 1989; The Falkland Suite (John Cale), Llandaff Choristers, 1989. *Publications:* Editor, 2 Anthems by Michael Wise. *Membership:* Council, Royal College of Organists, 1983-. *Hobbies:* Travel; Camping; Looking at paintings. *Address:* 1 St Mary's, The Cathedral Green, Llandaff, Cardiff CF5 2EB, Wales.

SMITH Philip Richard, b. 6 Jan 1958, Colchester, Essex, England. Pianist. *Education:* LRAM, Recital Diploma, ARAM, Royal Academy of Music. *Debut:* Purcell Room, London, 1979. *Career:* Performances with RPO, ECO, BBC SSO, Recitals and broadcasts in 25 countries. *Recordings:* Numerous Radio and TV Broadcasts. CD/Cassette of Liszt's Soirées de Vienne, released 1993. *Honours:* Prizewinner of international competitions: Leeds 1978; Beethoven Competition, Vienna, 1985; Palm Beach Invitational, 1988; Franz Liszt Competition, Utrecht, 1989. *Membership:* Incorporated Society of Musicians. *Hobbies:* Tai Ch'i Chu'an; Alexander technique. *Address:* 43 St Francis Road, London SE22 8DE, England.

SMITH Richard Langham, b. 10 Sept 1947, London, England. Reader in Music. *Education:* BA Honours, Music, University of York; Private music study, Edward Lockspeiser. *Career:* Harpsichordist; Musicologist, specialising French Music; Lecturer, University of Lancaster until 1979, City University, London 1979-. *Composition:* Reconstruction, Debussy's unpublished opera, Rodrigue et Chimène premiered opéra de Lyon, 1993. *Publication:* Translator & Editor: Debussy on Music, 1977; Debussy, by Edward Lockspeiser, 5th edition with co-author R. Nichols Debussy: Pelléas et Mélisande, Cambridge Opera Handbook, 1989. *Contributions:* Numerous articles & reviews on Debussy, journals including: Music & Letters; Times Literary Supplement; 19th Century Music; Cahiers Debussy; Musical Times; The Listener; Early Music; The Strad Frequent broadcaster. *Hobbies:* Gardening; Wine. *Address:* 16 The Crescent, Barnes, London SW13 ONN, England.

SMITH Rodney Leon, b. 10 Dec 1944, Maidstone, Kent, England. Concert Pianist; Lecturer in Piano

Pedagogy. m. Janet Gare, 27 Oct 1973, 1 son, 3 daughters. *Education:* Royal Academy of Music, London; Studied with Vivian Langrish and Margaret Kitchin; Dip RAM; FRCO; LRAM; ARCM; LCSM; MIMT; MACE. *Career:* Piano Professor, Royal Academy of Music, 1972-78; Piano Adviser, Inner London Education Authority, 1972-78; Chairman, Keyboard Faculty, Adelaide Institute of Education School of Music, South Australia, 1978-; Visiting Professor of Music, University of Illinois, USA, 1986-87; Numerous piano recitals and pedagogy workshops in UK, Europe, USA and Australia. *Honours:* MacFarren Medal, Royal Academy of Music, 1967; Yvonne Loriod Prize, Messiaen Competition, 1969. *Memberships:* Chairman, South Australian Music Teachers Council, 1982-; Deputy Chairman, Australian Institute of Music Teachers, 1982-88; Chairman, Australian National Piano Pedagogy Conference, 1993. *Hobbies:* Architecture; Richard III. *Address:* Overton, 8 Cygnet Terrace, Kingston Park, South Australia 5049, Australia.

SMITH Ronald, b. 3 Jan 1922, London, England. Concert Pianist. m. Anne Norman, 6 Sept 1969, 1 daughter. *Education:* Royal Academy of Music, London; Private studies, Paris. *Debut:* London Promenade Concert, 1948. *Career:* Sir Michael Costa Scholarship for composition to Royal Academy of Music; Continental debut with Ansermet & Swiss Romande, Geneva, 1951; Concertos with major orchestras; Records for EMI and Nimbus; Specialises in works of Alkan; Tours USA and Canada, 1982, 1983, 1987, Russia, 1985, Australia, 1975, 1977, 1981, 1983, Far East, 1977; Alkan centenary concert at the Wigmore Hall, London, 1988. *Compositions:* Violin Concerto; Comedy Overture. *Recordings include:* Boxed sets of Alkan & Chopin; Recordings of Beethoven, Schubert, Russian composers, Liszt and others. *Publications:* Alkan, The Enigma, Volume I; Alkan, The Works, Volume II, 1987. *Contributions to:* Articles in Musical Times, Listener, Keyboard. *Honours:* FRAM, BMus (Dunelm), 1946. *Memberships:* President, Alkan Society, London; President, East Surrey Symphony Orchestra; Vice-President, Robert Simpson Society. *Hobbies:* Vegetable gardening; Herb growing. *Current Management:* Anthony Purkiss, Concert Management, 35 Fonthill Road, Hove, East Sussex BN3 6HB, England. *Address:* Tanners House, School Road, Saltwood, Hythe, Kent CT21 4PP, England.

SMITH Sidney Bertram, b. 12 Sept 1929, Corry, PA, USA. Administrator; Writer; Teacher. m. (2) Beverely, 1 Nov 1981, 1 s, 1 d. *Education:* Two Years at Baldwin Wallace College Conservatory; Three Years at Longy School of Music, Cambridge; BME, MME degrees, Boston University. *Career:* music Master at Fessenden School and Rivers Country Day School, MA; Head of Music, Endicott Junior College; Chairman of Music Dept, Holyoke Community Coll; Founder, Conductor, Holyoke College Civic Orchestra; Conductor, Plymouth Philharmonic, Holyoke Community College Chorale & Special Vocal Group, Endicott Junior College Chorus and Numerous Choral Festivals; Toured as Pino Accompanist; Retired 1985. *Publications:* Frequent Annotator for Music Recital Programs. *Honours:* Distinguished Service Award. *Memberships:* Chamber Music America. *Hobbies:* Art Galleries; Museums. *Address:* 1370 A Mount Vernon Avenue, Williamsburg, VA 23185, USA.

SMITH Trefor Leslie, b. 4 July 1948, Aberdeen, Scotland. Pianist. *Education:* MA Honours Music, Aberdeen University, 1970; BMus, Liverpool University, 1971; Associate (Performance), Royal Manchester College of Music, 1973; Concert Examination, State College of Music, Hamburg, Federal Republic of Germany, 1979; Studied with George Hadjinikos, Eliza Hansen, Wilhelm Kempff, Vlado Perlemuter, Paul Badura-Skoda, and Hans Leygraf. *Career:* Numerous appearances in Germany, Great Britain, France, Italy, Spain, Norway, Republic of Ireland, Austria and USA; Various radio recordings; Currently Staff, Musikhochschule, Hamburg. *Recordings:* Two Records of Piano Music by Theodore Kirchner (1823-1903);

Radio recordings for North German Radio, RTE, Dublin, Republic of Ireland, and NRK, Oslo, Norway. *Memberships:* Incorporated Society of Musicians; Verband Deutscher Musikierzieher und Konzertierender Kunstler. *Hobbies:* Foreign languages; Reading; Chess. *Address:* Wartenau 13, D-2000 Hamburg 76, Germany.

SMITH Wilma, b. 1960, New Zealand. Violinist. *Education:* Studied at the New England Conservatory. *Career:* Leader of the Boston Based Lydia Quartet; Co-Founded the New Zealand String Quartet, Under the Auspices of the Music Federation of New Zealand; Devut Concert in Wellington, 1988; Concerts at the Tanglewood School in the USA, the Banff International Competition in Canada and Performances with the Lindsay Quartet at the 1990 international Festival of the Arts; Solist with the New Zealand Cymphony Orchestra and Artist in Residence at Victoria University; Tour to Australia 1990 for Music Viva Australia; Tours of New Zealand 1992 and Concerts in New York, 1993. *Recordings include:* Albums for Kick International Classics. *Address:* c/o (New Zealand Quartet) Ingpen & Williams Ltd, 14 Kensington Court, London W5 5DN, England.

SMITH BRINDLE Reginald, b. 5 Jan 1917, Bamber Bridge, Lancs., England. Composer; Teacher. *Eduction:* Studied first as an architect then joined University College of North Wales as a music student; composition with Pizzetti and Dallapiccola in Italy. *Career:* Worked for Italian Radio 1956-61; Taught at University College, Bangor, 1957-70; Professor of Music, University of Surrey, 1970-85. *Compositions:* Opera Antigone, 1969; Orchestral: Symphony, 1954; Variations on a theme of Dallapiccola, 1955; Epitaph for Alban Berg for strings, 1955; Symphonic Variations, 1957; Cosmos, 1959; Homage to H.G.Wells, 1960; Clarinet Concerto, 1960; Creation Epic, 1964; Apocalypse, 1970; Interface, 1972; Fons bonitatis II, 1973; Vocal: Grafico de la Peternera for chorus and orchestra, 1956; Extremum Carmen for chorus and orchestra, 1961; Genesis Dream for voice and ensemble, 1962; Japanese Lyrics for voice and ensemble, 1966; Vivo sin Vivir for chorus, 1968; Amalgam for voice and ensemble, 1968; Discoveries and Windhover for chorus, 1970-71; Worlds without End for speaker, voices, orchestra and tapes, 1973. Chamber: String Quartet Music, 1958; Concerto for 5 instruments and percussion, 1960; Tre dimensione for harp, vibraphone and harpsichord, 1965; Segments and Variants for wind quintet, 1965; Tubal Cain's Legacy for trombone and piano, 1973; The Walls of Jericho for tuba and tape, 1975; Concerto on Cum Jubilo for brass quintet, 1975; Music for guitar; Electronic Music; Journey Towards Infinity, 1987; Symphony II - Veni Creator, 1990. Guitar orchestra and percussion: La Chante du Monde, 1984; Grande Chaconne, 1993. *Publications:* Serial Composition, 1966; Contemporary Percussion, 1970; The New Music, 1975; Musical Composition (OUP), 1980. *Address:* Fiorenza, 219 Farleigh Road, Warlingham, Surrey CR6 9EL, England.

SMITHERS Don Le Roy, b. 17 Feb 1933, New York, USA. Music Historian. m. 2. 1 Sept 1967, 1 daughter; 1 son and 1 daughter from previous marriage. *Education:* BS, Music/Physics and Philosophy, Hofstra University, 1957; Seminars in Musicology, New York University, 1957-58; Studied Renaissance and Reformation History, Columbia University, New York, 1958; PhD, History of Music, University of Oxford, England. *Career:* Teaching Career: Associate Professor, Department of Fine Arts and School of Music, Syracuse University, 1966-75; Docent for the History of Music and Musical Performance, and Director of the Collegium Musicum, Koninklijk Conservatorium voor Muziek, Den Haag, The Netherlands; Lectures and papers on Baroque ornament, Festival Books, the history of music and musical instruments and the history of musical performance for various groups, colleges and universities; Solo concert performances on Baroque trumpet, cornetto, various Renaissance wind instruments; Co-founder, first musical director and sometime conductor of Oxford Pro Musica, Oxford, 1965-. *Recordings:* About 50 solo and ensemble

recordings with various European and American groups, including New York Pro Musica; The Leonhardt Consort, Concentus Musicus Wien and Early Music Consort of London. *Publications include:* The Music and History of the Baroque Trumpet before 1721, Dent, London, 1973. *Contributions to:* Many articles contributed to professionaljournals and book chapters. *Honours include:* Research Fellow and study with the late Professor Arthur Mendel, Princeton University, 1978; The Japan Foundation, Grant for travel, lecturing and research in Tokyo, Kyoto, Nara and Nagasaki, Japan, 1982; ASECS/Folger Institute Fellowship for research at the Folger Shakespeare Library, Wasgington DC 1984. *Address:* 55 Van Houten Fields, West Nyack, NY 10994, USA.

SMITKOVA Jana, b. 26 Dec 1942, Prague, Czechoslovakia. Singer (Soprano). *Education:* Studied at the Prague Conservatory and Music Academy. *Debut:* Liberec 1967, as Nancy in Martha by Flotow. *Career:* Sang with the Brno Opera 1968-70, Ceske Budejovice 1970-73; Member of the Komische Oper Berlin from 1973, debut as Katya Kabanova; Frequent guest appearances in Dresden, notably as Agathe in Der Freischütz at the 1985 reopening of the Semper Opera House; Has also sung at the National Theatre Prague and in other East European centres; Sang Ludmila in Harry Kupfer's production of The Bartered Bride at Covent Garden (1989) on visit with the company of the Komische Opera; Other roles include Pamina, Smetana's Marenka and the leading role in Die Kluge by Orff. *Recordings include:* Opera sets for Supraphon and Eterna; Der Freischütz and Beethoven's Ninth (Denon). *Address:* Semper-Oper Dresden, D-8012 Dresden, Germany.

SMUTNY Jiri, b. 1 Apr 1932, Prague, Czech Republic. Composer; Conductor. m. 27 Jan 1959, 1 daughter. *Education:* Studied at the Academy of Music, Prague. *Debut:* Prague Symphony Orchestra, 1955; Opera of Theatre National Prague, 1955. *Career:* National Theatre Opera, 1959- 80; Repetiteur and Conductor; Teacher, School of Music, Prague. *Compositions include:* Opera, Clementine; The Double; Sonata de Requeim; Piano Solo et Orch. *Honours:* 1st Prize in a Czech Comp; 1st Prize Comp Radio. *Membership:* Association of Czech Composers. *Hobby:* Gardening. *Address:* Prague 5, Sterkova 820/2, 153 00 Czech Republic.

SMYTHE Russell, b. 19 Dec 1949, Dublin. Singer (Baritone). *Education:* Studied at the Guildhall School of Music and at the London Opera Centre. *Career:* Welsh National Opera from 1977, as Billy Budd, Eugene Onegin, Papageno, Count Almaviva, and Rossini's Figaro; Covent Garden from 1983, as Malatesta (Don Pasquale), Falke (Fledermaus) and Guglielmo; With English National Opera has sung Pelléas, Papageno, Figaro, and Tarquin in The Rape of Lucretia; Hamburg Staatsoper from 1980, Guglielmo, Figaro, Harlequin in Ariadne and Pelléas; Vienna from 1982, as The Count in Der Wildschütz, Harlequin and Falke; Paris Opera: Harlequin, Apollon (Alceste/Gluck), Brother (Dr.Faust), 1985; North American debut 1986, as Papageno in Vancouver; Has sung in Oberon at Lyon and in La Finta Giardiniera at Amsterdam, Berlin and Brussels; Buxton Festival 1988, as Donizetti's Torquato Tasso; Sang Rossini's Figaro for Opera North (1989), Don Giovanni in Dublin, 1990; Frankfurt: Finta, 1990; Basel: Orestes (Iphigenie en Tauride, Gluck), Germont (Traviata), Belcore (L'Elisir D'Amore), 1991; Catania: Papageno; Madrid: Ned Keene (Peter Grimes); ENO: Albert (Werther); Season 1992 as Eugene Onegin at Tel Aviv and Orestes in Iphigénie en Tauride with the English Bach Festival at Covent Garden; Concert engagements include the Berlioz L'Enfance du Christ with the Hallé Orchestra and Messiah in Valencia. *Recordings:* CD Edoardo III (L'Assedio di Calais/Donizetti), Opera Rara; Nardo (Finta/Mozart), Brussels Opera. *Current Management:* Athole Still. *Address:* c/o Athole Still, Greystoke House, 80-86 Westow Street, London SE19 3AF, England.

SNOW Ursula Mary, b. 8 Dec 1927, London, England.

Violinist. m. (1) W A Beamish, 1954, (dissolved), 2 sons, 1 daughter, (2) K F Henning, 1982, dissolved. *Education:* Scholar, Pupil of Isolde Menges, Royal College of Music, London; Later studied privately with Sascha Lasserson. *Debut:* Wigmore Hall, London, 1960. *Career:* Freelance Orchestral Player; Chamber Music Player and Coach; Duo with pianist Ruth Harte, gave many radio performances; Violin Teacher. *Honours:* Associate, Royal College of Music, Piano, 1947, Violin, 1948. *Memberships:* Musicians Union; Incorporated Society of Musicians; Royal Society of Musicians. *Hobbies:* Theatre; Chess. *Address:* Poates Cottage, The Square, Westbourne, Nr Emsworth, Hants PO 10 8UE, England.

SNOWMAN Nicholas, b. 18 Mar 1944, London, England. Music Administrator. m. Margo Michelle Rouard, 1983, 1 son. *Education:* Magdalene College, Cambridge. *Career:* Founder and Adminstrator, Cambridge University Opera Society 1965-67; Assistant to Head of Music Staff, Glyndebourne Festival Opera, 1967-69; Co-founder and General Manager, London Sinfonietta, 1967-72; Director, Department Artistique, Institut de Recherche et de Co-ordination Acoustique-Musique (IRCAM), Paris, France 1972-86; Conseiller Artistique Ensemble Inter-Contemporain, Paris, 1976-92; Member, Music Committee, Venice Biennale, 1979-86; Artistic Director, Projects in 1980, 1981, 1983, Festival d'Automne de Paris; Initiator and Member Steering Committee, National Studio for Electronic Music at South Bank, 1986-92. General Director (Arts) South Bank Centre, London: Responsible for 1988-89 series The Reluctant Revolutionary: Arnold Schoenberg His Work and His World. *Publications:* Co-editor The Best of Granta 1967; The Contemporary Composers 1982-; Introductions and articles in Orchestre de Paris, Centre Pompidou, Festival d'Automne programme books. *Honour:* Chevalier, l'Ordre des Arts et des Lettres, 1985. *Hobbies:* Films; Eating; Spy Novels. *Address:* South Bank Centre, Royal Festival Hall, London SE1 8XX, England.

SNYDER Barry, b. 6 Mar 1944, Allentown, Pennsylvania, US. Concert Pianist; Teacher. *Education:* BM, Master's degree, Performance and Literature, Artist Diploma in Piano, Eastman School of Music, University of Rochester. *Debut:* Soloist with Allentown Symphony Orchestra. *Career:* Has performed throughout USA, Canada, Europe, Poland, South America, Asia; Appearances with orchestras of Montreal, Atlanta, Houston, Baltimore, National, Detroit and Cracow, Poland, with such conductors as Sixten Ehrling, David Zinman, Charles Dutoit, Robert Shaw, Leopold Stokowski; Chamber music with Jan DeGaetani, Dong-Suk Kang, Zvi Zeitlin, Ani Kavafian, Bonita Boyd, Cleveland Quartet, Composers Quartet, Eastman Brass Quintet, New York Brass Quintet; Founding Member, Eastman Trio, touring Europe, South America, USA; Professor of Piano, Eastman School of Music, 1970-; Has given masterclasses with solo recitals. *Recordings:* Dohnanyi, solo CD; Dohnanyi chamber works with Cleveland Quartet; CD of complete cello music of Faure with Steven Doone, cellist; Stephen Jaffe's Two Piano Sonata with Anton Nel. *Honours:* Silver (2nd place), Van Cliburn International Piano Competition, 1966; Chamber Music Award; Pan American Union Award; Edward Peck Curtis Award for excellence in undergraduate teaching, University of Rochester, 1975. *Memberships:* Music Teacher National Association; American Liszt Society; College Music Society. *Hobbies:* Weather observation; Gardening; Socialising. *Address:* 166 Orchard Drive, Rochester, NY 14618-2344, USA.

SOBOLEVA Galina, b. 1960, Moscow, Russia. Cellist. *Education:* Studied at Moscow Conservatoire with Valentin Berlinsky. *Career:* Member of the Prokofiev Quartet (founded at Moscow Festival of World Youth and the International Quartet Competition, Budapest); Many concerts in former Soviet Union and on tour to Czechoslovakia, Germany, Austria, USA, Canada, Spain, Japan and Italy; Repertoire includes works by Haydn, Mozart, Beethoven, Schubert, Debussy, Ravel, Tchaikovsky, Brtok and Shostakovich. *Address:*

c/o Sonata (Prokofiev Quartet), 11 Northgate Street, Glasgow G20 7AA, Scotland.

SOCCI Gianni, b. 19 Mar 1939, Rome, Italy. Singer (Bass). *Education:* Studied at the Accademia di Santa Cecilia Rome and with Franco Cavara. *Debut:* Piccolo Teatro Comico Rome 1965, as Achmed in Paisiello's Il Re Teodoro in Venezia. *Career:* Sang in the buffo repertory at opera houses in Milan, Rome, Naples, Florence, Turin, Venice, Genoa and Trieste; Guest appearances in Brussels, Copenhagen, Toulouse, Strasbourg, Paris, Cologne, Frankfurt, Philadelphia, Montreal, Quebec, Monte Carlo and Barcelona; Many performances in operas by Mozart, Cimarosa, Rossini and Donizetti; Teatro Lirico Milan 1975, in the premiere of Al gran sole carico d'amore by Luigi Nono; Concert engagements in Italy and elsewhere. *Address:* c/o Teatro alla Scala, Via Filodrammatici, I-20121 Milan, Italy.

SÖDERSTRÖM Elisabeth Anna, b. 7 May 1927, Sweden. Soprano Opera Singer; Administrator. m. Sverker Olow, 1950, 3 sons. *Education:* Singing studies, Andrejewa de Skilonz, & Stockholm Opera School. *Career includes:* Royal Opera, Stockholm, 1950-; Appearances: Salzburg 1955, Glyndebourne 1957, 59, 61, 63, 64, 79 as the Composer (Ariadne), Octavian and Leonore (Fidelio); Metropolitan Opera, New York, 1959, 60, 62, 63, 83, 84, 86, 87; Frequent concert & TV appearances, Europe & USA; Tour, USSR, 1966. Roles include: Fiordiligi (Così Fan Tutte); Countess & Susanna (Figaro); Countess (Capriccio); Christine (Intermezzo); 3 leading roles, Der Rosenkavalier, 1959; Janáček's Emilia Marty and Jenůfa; Mélisande; Sang at Dallas 1988, in the premiere of The Aspern Papers by Argento; Artistic Director of the Drottningholm Court Theatre from 1993; Member of judging panel, Cardiff Singer of the World, 1991; Presented the Drottningholm Theatre Saga at the Barbican Hall, London, 1992. *Publications:* I Min Tonart, 1978; Sjung ut Elisabeth, 1986. *Honours:* Honorary Academician, Royal Academy of Music; Court Singer, Sweden, 1959; Order of Vasa; Stelle della Solidarieta, Italy; Prize, best acting, Royal Swedish Academy, 1965; Literis et Artibus Award, 1969; Commander, Order of Vasa, 1973; Commandeur des Arts et des Lettres, 1986; Commander, Order of British Empire. *Hobbies:* Sailing; Literature; Embroidery. *Address:* c/o Royal Opera House, PO Box 16094Stockholm, Sweden.

SOFFEL Doris, b. 12 May 1948, Hechingen, Germany. Singer (Mezzo-Soprano). *Education:* Early studies as violinist, then voice with Marianne Schech in Munich 1968-73. *Career:* Bayreuth Youth Festival 1972, in Das Liebesverbot; Stuttgart State Opera 1973-; 1976 sang Waltraute at Bayreuth and began career as a concert artist: noted in Bach and other Baroque music; 1977 Bregenz Festival as Puck in Oberon; 1983 sang Monteverdi's Poppea in Toronto and took part in the Hamburg premiere of J.C. Bach's Amadis de Gaule; Covent Garden 1983 as Sextus in La Clemenza di Tito and Orlovsky in Die Fledermaus; sang in the world premiere of Reimann's Troades in Munich 1986; Octavian in a production of Der Rosenkavalier at the renovated Brussels Opera House; Sang Angelina in Cenerentola at the Berlin Staatsoper, 1987; TV appearances include Das Lied von der Erde, 1988; Sang in the premiere of Penderecki's Ubu Rex, Munich 1991; Season 1992 as Cassandra in Reimann's Troades at Frankfurt and Elizabeth in Donizetti's Maria Stuarda at Amsterdam; engaged to sing Verdi's Preziosilla at Munich, 1994. *Recordings:* Bach Cantatas and Magnificat; Flotow's Martha; Lortzing's Der Wildschütz; Haydn's St Cecilia Mass; Das Liebesverbot; Schumann's Requiem; Zemlinsky's Eine Florentinische Tragödie; Troades (Electrola); Parsifal (Deutsche Grammophon); Mahler 2, Beethoven Missa Solemons (EMI); Wolff's Der Corregidor (Schwann). *Address:* c/o Ingpen and Williams Ltd., 14 Kensington Court, London W8 5DN, England.

SOHAL Naresh, b. 18 Sept 1939, Harsipind, Punjab, India. Composer. *Education:* University of Punjab, India;

London College of Music; Leeds University. *Career includes:* Asht Prahar performed by London Philharmonic Orchestra, conducted by Norman del Mar, at Royal Festival Hall, 17 Jan. 1970; BBC have commissioned four major works including The Wanderer first performed during the 1982 Promenade Concert, conducted by Andrew Davis; From Gitanjali commissioned by Philharmonic Society of New York, first performed by New York Philharmonic Orchestra, conducted by Zubin Mehta, Sept. 1985; Represented the West in two East-West Encounters one in the Netherlands and the other in Bombay in 1983; TV credits include: music score for Sir William in Search of Xanadu Scottish TV and three episodes of Granada TV's series End of Empire, 1985; Currently member of BBC Central Music Advisory Committee and the equivalent committee in Scotland. *Compositions include:* Orchestral: Indra-Dhanush 1973; Dhyan I, 1974; Tandava Nritya, 1984; Chamber and instrumental: Shades I 1974; Shades 117 1975; Shades III 1978; Chakra 1979; Shades IV 1983; Brass Quintet No 2 1983; Vocal and Choral: Inscape 1979; The Wanderer 1981; From Gitanjali 1985. *Contributions to:* Tempo magazine. *Membership:* Society for the Promotion of New Music. *Hobbies:* Photography; Chess; Badminton; Cricket; Films. *Address:* 50 Spottiswoode Street, Edinburgh EH9 1DG, Scotland.

SOHN Sung-Rai, b. 23 Sept 1950, Seoul, Korea. Violinist; Conductor. m. Patricia Esposito, 6 June 1980, 1 son, 3 stepdaughters. *Education:* USA; BM, Peabody Conservatory of Music (full scholarship student of Berl Senofsky), Baltimore, Maryland: MFA, Sarah Lawrence College (scholarship student of Dorothy DeLay); Quartet Seminar Julliard School of Music. *Debut:* As a winner of Artists International Competition, Carnegie Recital Hall, New York City, 1980. *Career:* Founder and the first violinist of the Laurentian String Quartet, Founder and Music Director/Conductor of Philharmonia Lawrencia Chamber Orchestra; Appeared: Korean National TV (KBS Radio); WNYC, New York, in Rising Star, Live, and Bosendorfer Concert Series; The Listening Room, WQXR, New York; NPR (USA); Maine TV Network; Kansas TV Network; (Japan) Sendai TV Network; Tours to Canada, USA, Europe, Africa, Asia. *Recordings:* Barber String Quartet op 11; Rochberg String Quartet No 3; Anthony Newman String Quartet No 1; Anthony Newman Piano Quintet; Meyer Kupferman Piano Quintet; CPE Bach Concerto in A Major; Ginastera Piano Quintet. *Publication:* Careers in Music. *Honours:* Grand Prize Winner, Korean National Competition in Violin, 1967; Grand Prize Winner, Korean National Competition in Chamber Music, 1968; Theodore Martin Violin Award, 1975; Winner, Jack Kahn Music Award, Artists International, 1978; Honoured Diplomat, Algiers 4th International Music Festival, 1987, teaches Violin at Sarah Lawrence College since 1986. *Current Management:* Jonathan Wentworth Associate; Korea Musica. *Address:* 69 Mile Rd, Suffern, NY 10901, USA.

ŠOJAT Tiziana, b. 28 Apr 1955, Rome, Italy. Singer (Soprano). *Education:* Studied with her mother, Alda Noni, and Elisabeth Schwarzkopf. *Debut:* Dublin, as Elsa in Lohengrin, 1984. *Career:* Sang Mimi at Ljubljana, 1984; Concert performances of Dido and Aeneas and Gianni Schicchi at Lausanne, 1985; Sang with the company of San Carlo Naples in Pergolesi's Stabat Mater at New York; Croatian National Opera, Zagreb, 1988, as Sieglinde in Die Walküre; Marseilles, 1989, as Elena in Mefistofele; Engaged at Karlruhe Opera, 1989-, notably as Butterfly and Arabella; Concert performances at Turin, Dubrovnik, Rome and Milan. *Recordings include:* Lieder by Wolf, Schumann, Liszt and Mahler. *Address:* Badisches Staatstheater, Baumeisterstrasse 11, 7500 Karlsruhe, Germany.

SOJER Hans, b. 20 Mar 1943, Innsbruck, Austria. Singer (Tenor). *Education:* Studied with Franziska Lohmann. *Debut:* Innsbruck, as David in Meistersinger, 1967. *Career:* Sang at Innsbruck until 1971, Bonn, 1971-73, Wiesbaden, 1973-81, Hanover, 1981-; Roles in operas by Rossini, Donizetti, Mozart, Wagner and Strauss at Graz, Cologne, Mannheim, Dusseldorf, Frankfurt, Berlin, Lisbon and Karlsruhe; Bregenz and Schwetzingen Festivals; Sang the Steersman and Narraboth at Barcelona, 1988, Ernesto at Kiel and Count Riccardo in Wolf-Ferrari's Quattro Rusteghi at Hanover, 1991; Concert repertoire includes Beethoven's Ninth and cantatas and Passions by Bach. *Recordings include:* Brighella in Ariadne auf Naxos. *Address:* c/o Niedersachsische Staatstheater, Opernplatz 1, 3000 Hanover, Germany.

SOKOL Ivan, b. 15 June 1937, Bratislava, Slovakia. Organist. *Education:* Hochschule fur Musik, Prag Studium; Laureat Prager Frühling; Leipzig Bachwettberwerb Preisträger. *Debut:* Praha. *Career:* Concerts in Europe, Asia, America, USA and Mexico; Television and radio appearances; Director for International Orgelfestival Košice, Slovakia. *Recordings include:* Complete works of Bach, Handel, Mendelssohn, Mozart, Brixi, Brahms, Reger-Orgelwerke, Hindemith, 1, 2, 1, Sonate, Slovakische Musik, Poulenc-Concerto for Organ and orchestra, Saint Saens, 3. Symphony, Janaček, Glagolitic Mass; Czech Music. *Honours:* 2 prizes d Stadt Kosice; National Prize, Verdienter Kunstler. *Hobbies:* Literature; Art; Sport. *Address:* Trenčianska 5, 82109 Bratislava, Slovakia.

SOKOLOV Grigory, b. 1950, St Petersburg, Russia. Pianist. *Education:* Specialist music school; Entered St Petersburg Conservatory, 1960. *Career:* First important public appearance at age 12; Toured with Moscow Philharmonic Orchestra, Italy, Portugal and Germany, then regular performances throughout Europe, North America and Far East; Worked with Philharmonia, UK, and Ulster Orchestra under Yan-Pascal Tortelier; Appeared with Orchestra of the Bolshoi under Alexander Lazarev at Edinburgh Festival; Has played with many foreign orchestras including Leipzig Gewandhaus, Dresden Philharmonic, Munich Philharmonic, Bamberg Symphony, Warsaw Philharmonic, Zurich Tonhalle, Norddeutscher Rundfunk, Helsinki Radio Symphony, Santa Cecilia and Philharmonic Orchestra of La Scala, Milan, with conductors such as Inbal, Flor, Järvi, Stein, Saraste, Groves, Rozhdestvensky, Rowicki, Kondrashin, Svetlanov, Lombard, Barshai, Weller, Blomstedt and Kitaenko; Recitals in Paris, Vienna (Musikverein), Munich, Berlin, Frankfurt, Salzburg, Helsinki, Copenhagen, Milan, Rome, New York (Carnegie Hall) and Tokyo; Repertoire ranges from Bach to Schoenberg, including Beethoven, Brahms, Chopin, Schubert and the Russian masters. *Recordings include:* Beethoven Sonatas (Op 90, Op 110) and the Diabelli Variations, Chopin Preludes, Bach's The Art of Fugue and Sonatas by Prokofiev, Rachmaninov and Scriabin. *Honours:* Winner, 1st Prize, 3rd International Tchaikovsky Piano Competition, at age 16, 1966. *Address:* c/o Christopher Tennant, Unit 2, 39 Tadema Road, London SW10 0PY, England.

SOKOLOV Ivan Glebovitch, b. 29 Aug 1960, Russia, USSR. Composer; Solo Concert Pianist; High School Lecturer. *Education:* Gnesin Musical College, 1977-78; Composition, Nik Sidelnikov, Piano, Lev Naumov, 1978-83, Assistant Probationer under Nik Sidelnikov, 1984-86, Moscow Conservatoire. *Career:* Concerts, solo, with other, Moscow, Leningrad, Sverdlovsk, Kharkov, Briansk, Serpukhov, Volgograd, Tashkent, Alma-Ata, Kazan, Erevan, Lvov, Tallinn, others, 1985-; Appears, artist's shows & author's concerts; Repertoire includes Stockhausen, J Cage, G Crumb, Skriabin, Shostakovich, Prokofiev, Debussy, Brahms; Participant, many musical festivals including: Moscow Autumn, 1987-90, Alternative, 1988-90; Festival of Music in USSR, Germany, 1990; Begegnungen mit Moscow, Bochum, Germany, 1990; Schleswig-Holstein Musical Festival, Hamburg, 1991; Solo concert, Chopin, 1991; Has met Cage, Stockhausen, Boulez, J Adams; Teacher, Composition, Musical College, 1986-; Leader, classes, Instrumentation & Musical Score-Reading, Moscow Conservatoire, 1988-. *Compositions:* 10 pieces, flute, piano, 1983; 5 visions, piano, 1983; The Night, cantata, 1983; Rus pevutchaya, cantata, 1985; Blazhenstvo i Beznadezhnos, vocal cycle, 1986; Skazotchnye Zvony, suite, 1987; Volokos, piano, 1988; Sonata, flute, piano, 1988; 13 pieces, piano, 1988; Since (from) 10 to 30 of September 1988, piano, other instruments, 1988; Eshtche 7 pieces, piano, 1989; Nepi(yes)'a, piano, violin, cello, percussion, 1989; Knigy na stole, piano, 1989; Zvezda, soprano, piano, 1990; Tchto nasha Igra; Zhizn, percussion ensemble, 1990; O, flute solo, 1990; Korably v more, 2 pianos, 1990; A little harmonious cosmogramme, percussion, 1991; Igra bez natchala i konza, percussion, 1991; Mysli o Rachmaninove, piano, 1991. *Address:* uliza Staryi Gaiy, dom 1, korpus 1, kvartira 116, 111539 Moscow, Russia.

SOKOLOV Vladimir, b. 21 Feb 1936, Komi, USSR. Clarinetist. m. Nadezda Seleznjova, 8 Apr 1962, 1 daughter. *Education:* City of Siktivkav Music School, Komi, ASSR 1950-54; Orchestra Faculty, Moscow Conservatory, 1954-59. *Debut:* With Moscow Radio Orchestra, 1959. *Career:* Professor of the Moscow Conservatory and Senior Music School; Clarinettist with The Radio and Television Symphony Orchestra, 1959-64; Clarinetist with The State Symphony Orchestra of the USSR, 1964-. *Recordings:* Concertos by Mozart and by Krommer and Weber; Quintets by Mozart, Brahms; Sonatas by Brahms, Glinka. *Honours:* Silver Medal, Vienna, July 1959; First Prize, Leningrad, Jan 1964. *Memberships:* Jury Member: Geneva, Sept 1986, Geneva, Sept 1990, Toulon, June 1991. *Hobbies:* Fishing; Swimming; Hunting. *Address:* Shosse Entusiastov, h 96, B 4, Apt 635, 141531 MoscowMoscow, Russia.

SOLBU Einar, b. 3 Feb 1942, Eidskog, Norway. Dean of Studies; Organist. m. Tove Dahl, 2 July 1966, 3 daughters. *Education:* American High School, Southampton, New York, 1960; Norwegian Baccalaureate, Trondheim, 1962; Higher Degree in Church Music, Oslo Conservatory of Music, 1965. *Career:* Lecturer, 1964-69, Dean, 1969-73, Music Conservatory, Oslo; Lecturer, 1973-76, Dean of Studies, 1977-, Norwegian State Academy of Music, Oslo; Visiting Scholar, Eastman School of Music, Rochester, New York, USA, 1988-89; Organist and Choir Conductor, 1966-73, 1982-; President, The Lindeman Foundation. *Publications:* The Music Conservatory of Oslo 1883-1973 (with Trygve Lindeman); The Theory of Music in the Professional Education of Musicians (editor), 1982; A Living Tradition (edited with Harald Jorgensen), 1983. *Contributions to:* Several Norwegian periodicals, International Journal of Music Education, and Cappelen Musikkleksikon, Oslo, 1980. *Memberships:* Board Member, International Society for Music Education; International Council for Fine Arts Deans. *Address:* Kalkfjellet 29, N-1370 Asker, Norway.

SOLDH Anita, b. 26 Sept 1949, Stockholm, Sweden. Singer (Soprano). *Education:* Studied at Stockholm University and with Erik Saéden (from 1969); Further study at the Stockholm and Vienna Music Academies (1971-75) and with Luigi Ricci in Rome. *Career:* Sang with Norrlands Opera 1975-77, notably as Britten's Lucretia and Mozart's Countess; Royal Opera Stockholm from 1977, debut as Eva in Die Meistersinger; and returned as Senta, Elizabeth, Arabella, Octavian, Chrysothemis, Mozart's Countess Elvira, Vitellia and Pamina, Tchaikovsky's Tatiana and Maid of Orleans; Concert tours of the USA, Brussels and Europe, 1984, as Cherubino; Bayreuth Festival 1983-84 as Freia in Das Rheingold; Sang Elsa in Lohengrin at Stockholm 1989 and First Lady in Die Zauberflöte at the Drottningholm Court Theatre; the Queen in Vogler's Gustaf Adolf och Ebba Brahe, 1990; Season 1991/92 as Agave in the premiere of Backanterna by Daniel Börtz, production by Ingmar Bergman, and at Drottningholm in Haeffner's Electra and as Gluck's Eurydice; Concert repertoire includes Schoenberg's Erwartung, Berg's Frühe Lieder and Haydn's Schöpfung. *Recordings:* Video of Idomeneo from Drottningholm as Elettra (Virgin Classics). *Address:* c/o Kungliga Teatern, P O Box 16094, S-10322 Stockholm, Sweden.

SOLERA Mario, b. 12 June 1960, San Jose, Costa Rica. Guitarist. m. Katia Guevara, 17 Dec 1983, 1 son, 1 daughter. *Education:* Anthropology, Physics, University of Costa Rica; Licentiate in Music, University of Costa Rica; Further musical studies, Spain, USA. *Debut:* Concierto de Aranjuez, National Theatre, 1982. *Career:* Recitals: Washington DC; Portland, Oregon; Guadalajara, Mexico; San Jose, Costa Rica; Panama City, Panama. *Publications:* Analysis of Costa Rican Music, 1994; The music in Costa Rica, 1994; Tales from Costa Rican musicians, 1994. *Contributions to:* Clasical review. *Honours:* Young Soloist, 1975. *Hobbies:* Photography; Scuba diving. *Current Management:* School of Music, University of Costa Rica. *Address:* Calle 18, Avenida 3 y 5, Casa 393, San Jose, Costa Rica.

SOLODCHIN Galina, b. 29 Apr 1944, Tientsin, China. Violinist. *Education:* Studied at the New South Wales Conservatorium. *Career:* Freelance musician, including member of Delmé Quartet from 1967; Many performances in Britain and Europe in the classical and modern repertory; Concerts at the Salzburg Festival and the Brahms Saal of the Musikverein Vienna; Season 1990 included Haydn's Last Seven Words in Italy and elsewhere, three Brahms programmes at St John's Smith Square with Iain Burnside, piano; Concerts at St David's Hall, Cardiff with quartets by Tchaikovsky and Robert Simpson (premiere of 13th quartet); Appearances in Bremen, Hamburg and Trieste, followed by festival engagements, 1991; Other repertory includes works by Paul Patterson, Daniel Jones, Wilfred Josephs, Iain Hamilton and Bernard Stevens. *Recordings include:* Haydn Last Seven Words; Vaughan Williams On Wenlock Edge and Gurney's Ludlow and Tame; Simpson quartets 1-9 and String Trio (Hyperion); Daniel Jones 3 quartets and Bridge No 2 (Chandos); Bliss Nos 1 and 2; Josef Holbrooke Piano Quartet and Clarinet Quintet (Blenheim); Brahms Clarinet Quintet and Dvořák F major Quartet (Pickwick); Verdi Quartet and Strauss A major Op 2 (Hyperion); Hummel, Nos 1, 2 and 3 on Hyperion and Bernard Stevens, Theme and Variations and Quartet No. 2 and Lyric Suite for string trio on Unicorn Kanchana, also Beethoven Op. 74 and Op. 95 on Helios and Favourite Encores on Helios. *Address:* c/o 33 Whittingstall Road, Fulham SW6, England.

SOLOMON Maynard Elliott, b. 5 Jan 1930, New York City, USA. Music Historian. m. Eva Georgiana Tevan, 22 Jan 1951, 2 sons, 1 daughter. *Education:* High School of Music and Art, New York; BA, Brooklyn College, 1950; Postgraduate studies, Columbia University, 1950-51. *Career:* Co-founder and Co-owner, Vanguard Recording Society, Inc, New York, 1950-86; Teacher, City University of New York, 1979-81; Visiting Professor, State University of New York, Stony Brook, 1988-; Associate Editor, American Imago; Visiting Professor, Columbia University, 1989-90; Visiting Professor, Harvard University, 1991-92. *Publications:* Marxism and Art, 1973; Beethoven, 1977; Myth, Creativity and Psychoanalysis, 1978; Beethoven Essays, 1988; Mozart: A Life, 1994. *Contributions to:* Articles in Beethoven Jahrbuch; Music & Letters; Musical Quarterly; 19th Century Music; Journal of the American Musicological Society; Beethoven's Tagebuch (Bonn & Mainz), 1990. *Memberships:* American Musicological Society; PEN; Phi Beta Kappa; Kinkeldey Award of American Musicological Society, 1989; Deems Taylor Award, ASCAP: 1978, 1989; New York University Society of Fellows; New York Institute for the Humanities. *Address:* 1 West 72nd Street, New York, NY 10023, USA.

SOLOMON Seymour Joseph, b. 23 May 1922, New York, USA. Owner, Producer, Gramophone Record Company. m. Pearl Canick, May 1973, 3 daughters. *Education:* Violin studies, Juilliard School of Music, 1940-43, 1947; BA, New York University, 1943; Graduate work, musicology, New York University, 1947. *Career:* Founded Vanguard Recording Society Inc, New York, 1950; Produced over 2000 long-playing records, mainly classical, some jazz & folk music, 36 years; Founded Omega Record Classics, 1986. Artists included: Misha Elman, Sir Adrian Boult, Paul Robeson,

Alfred Deller, Alfred Brendel, Leopold Stokowsky, Maurice Abravanel, Beverly Sills, Margaret Price, José Carreras, Heather Harper, John Shirley-Quirk; Many major orchestras. *Publications:* Reviews: Musical America, Musical Leaders, Music Forum & Digest; Articles on recording, High Fidelity magazine. *Honours:* President, Mu Sigma, 1943; Numerous awards for productions, Stereo Review. *Hobbies:* Playing chamber music, violin & piano. *Address:* 15 West 72nd Street, New York, NY 10023, USA.

SOLOMON Yonty, b. 6 May 1938, Cape Town, South Africa. Pianist. *Education:* Cape Town University, BMus 1958; Studied with Myra Hess in London and with Charles Rosen in USA. *Debut:* London 1963. *Career:* Concert appearances with leading orchestras in Europe, the USA, Canada, South Africa, Israel and Rumania; First performances of works by Bennett, Joseph, Merilaainen and Sorabji; Repertoire also includes works by Bach (Goldberg Variations), Schoenberg, Albeniz, Janáček, Ives, Granados, Debussy and Shostakovich; Duos with Sylvia Rosenberg (Violin) and Radu Aldulescu (Cello); Appearance on ITV programme in honour of Sorabji; Professor at the Royal College of Music; Master Classes at Prussia Cove, Cornwall, and at Nottingham University. *Recordings include:* Music by Sorabji (Altarus); Wilfred Josephs, 14 studies (Novello); Sonatas for cello and piano by Prokofiev and Fauré with Timothy Hugh for the BBC, 1991. *Honours include:* Beethoven International Award, 1963. *Address:* c/o Basil Douglas Artists' Management, 8 St George's Terrace, London NW1 8XJ, England.

SOLTESZ Stefan, b. 6 Jan 1949, Nyiregyhaza, Hungary. Conductor. *Education:* Studied at the Vienna Academy of Music with Dieter Weber, Hans Swarowsky, Reinhold Schmidt and Friedrich Cerha (1963-72). *Career:* Conductor at the Theater an der Wien, Vienna, 1971-73; Coach and conductor at Vienna Staatsoper, 1973-83; Salzburg Festivals 1978, 1979, 1983: assistant to Karl Böhm, Christoph von Dohnányi and Herbert von Karajan; Guest conductor of the Graz Opera 1979-81; Permanent conductor of the Hamburg Staatsoper 1983- 85; Permanent conductor of the Deutsche Oper Berlin, since 1985; Generalmusikdirektor of the State Theatre at Brunswick from 1988-93; Guest conductor with the Opera Royale de Wallonie (Liège), the Bavarian State Opera in Munich, Opera of Bonn, Vlaamse Opera Antwerp, State Theater of Stuttgart, Nederlandes Oper (Amsterdam), Festival de Radio France (Montpellier), Aix-en-Provence and the Paris Opéra, Vienna State Opera; Concerts in Bologna, Hamburg, Mexico City, Naples, Paris, Salzburg, Turin, Vienna Munich, Essen, Berlin, Hanover and Zagreb; Toured Japan with the German State Opera, Unter den Linden, 1990; Season 1992/93, Music Director of the Flanders Opera of Antwerp/Gent, Belgium; Principal Guest Conductor of the Opera of Leipzig 1992/93 season; Guest Conductor, Opera of Frankfurt, Hamburg Opera; US debut 1992 at Washington Opera, Kennedy Center, with Otello. *Recordings include:* Swan Lake excerpts with the Vienna Symphony (Denon); La Bohème with Lucia Popp and Francisco Araiza, Opera arias with Lucia Popp (EMI); Opera Arias, with Grace Bumbry (Orfeo); Don Giovanni, by Giuseppe Gazzaniga (Munich Radio Orchestra, Orfeo); The Chalk Circle, by Alexander Zemlinsky; Orchestral Songs by Hugo Wolf with Dietricu Fischer-Dieskan (Orfeo). *Address:* De Vlaamse Opera, Van Ertburnstraat 8, B-2000 Antwerp, Belgium.

SOLTI Georg (Sir), b. 21 Oct 1912, Budapest, Hungary. (Naturalised British subject, 1971-). Conductor; Pinist. m. (1) Hedi Oechsli, 29 Oct 1946, (2) Anne Valerie Pitts, 11 Nov 1967, 2 daughters. *Education:* Budapest Music High School; Piano and composition with Bartok, Kodaly, Dohnanyi and Leo Weiner. *Debut:* Concert debut as pianist. *Career:* Repetiteur, Budapest Opera, 1930-33; Conductor, 1934-39, debut with Le Nozze di Figaro, 1938; Assistant to Toscanini, Salzburg Festival, 1936-37; Pianist, Switzerland, 1939-45; General Music Director: Bayerische Staatsoper, Munich, 1946-52, Frankfurter

Oper, 1952-60; London concert debut with London Philharmonic Orchestra, 1949; US debut, 1953, with San Francisco Opera; Debut, Glyndebourne, 1954; Conducted Der Rosenkavalier at Covent Garden, 1959, then Music Director, 1961-71, leading notable productions of Don Giovanni, Le Nozze di Figaro, Die Frau ohne Schatten, Moses and Aaron, Der Ring des Nibelungen, Arabella, Tristan und Isolde; Music Director, Chicago Symphony Orchestra, 1969-91, with 7 European tours, Japan tour, and Bicentennial Tour, Australia, 1988; Principal Conductor, Artistic Director, later Conductor Emeritus, London Philharmonic Orchestra, 1979-91; Guest Conductor, Salzburg and Edinburgh Festivals, Vienna State and Paris Operas, Vienna, Berlin, New York and Los Angeles Philharmonics, London Symphony and Concertgebouw Orchestras; Conducted Der Ring des Nibelungen, Bayreuth, 1983; Played, conducted, Jacqueline du Pré Memorial Concert, Festival Hall, 1989; New productions, Salzburg Festival: Un Ballo in Maschera, 1989, 1990, Die Zauberflöte, 1991; Recent Covent Garden productions include Elektra, 1990, Simon Boccanegra, 1991, Otello, 1992; Otello in concert, Chicago, New York, 1991; Appointed Music Director Laureate, Royal Opera, 1992; Artistic Director, Easter Festival, Whitsun Concerts, Salzburg, 1992, conducting new production of Die Frau ohne Schatten; New production of Falstaff, Salzburg Easter and Summer Festivals, 1993. *Recordings:* 1st complete cycle of Wagner's major operas; Symphonies of Mahler (nine), Beethoven, Brahms, Schubert; Noted conductor of Mozart, Strauss, Bruckner; Moses and Aaron; St Matthew Passion; Bartok Concerto for Orchestra; Beethoven Piano Concertos (Ashkenazy); Verdi; Don Carlo; Un Ballo in Maschera; Falstaff; Aida; Simon Boccanegra; Otello; Die Frau ohne Schatten, Strauss; Sacre du Printemps, Stravinsky; Bruckner's 8th Symphony; Complete Haydn London Symphonies; Many others; Video films include: Mozart Rquiem Mass; Frau ohne Schatten. *Honours include:* CBE, 1868; KBE, 1971; Commander, Legion d'Honneur, 1974; 15 Grand Prix du Disque; 31 Grammy Awards. *Address:* c/o Secretariat Charles Kaye, 51 Elsworthy Road, London NW3 3BS, England.

SOLUM John Henry, b. 11 May 1935, New Richmond, Wisconsin, USA. Concert Flautist; Writer; Educator. m. Millicent Hunt, 30 July 1960, 2 sons. *Education:* BA, Princeton University, 1957; Private studies in flute with William Kincaid, Philadelphia, 1953-58; Flute, harmony, counterpoint, composition, musicology, various teachers. *Debut:* Solo, 1953; Soloist, Philadelphia Orchestra, 1957; New York debut recital, 1959. *Career:* Soloist, Chamber Music Player, 37 countries on 5 continents, including Asia, 1968, 1969, 1976, Latin America, 1978, 1979, 1980. USSR, 1983, and 13 New York recitals; Guest appearances with orchestras in over 50 cities; Many radio broadcasts; Festivals, Europe, North America; Teacher: Vassar College, 1969-71, 1977-; Indiana University, 1973; Oberlin Conservatory, 1976; Co- Director: Bath (England) Summer School of Baroque Music, 1979-89; Connecticut Early Music Festival, 1982-. *Compositions:* Cadenzas, Mozart's flute concertos. *Recordings:* Ibert, Jolivet, Honegger Flute Concertos, 1975; 2 Malcolm Arnold Flute Concertos, 1977; Romantic Music for Flute and Orchestra, 1978; Mozart Flute Concertos, 1980; Telemann Duets, 1981; Bach Flute Sonatas, 1988; Vivaldi Bullfinch Concerto, 1992; Bach, Handel, Telemann Trio Sonatas, 1992. *Publications:* Massenet and Delibes, 3 Original Pieces, 1978; Wilhelm Popp, Bagatelle, 1980; Wilhelm Popp, 30 Easy Studies, Op 520, 1981; J Andersen, 5 Songs Without Words, 1982; Boccherini Sextet, Op 15/6, 1990, de la Barre, Two Duets for Two Flutes, 1990; Arthur Foote, At Dusk, 1991; The Early Flute, 1992. *Contributions to:* New Grove Dictionary of Musical Instruments; Notes (Journal, Music Library Association); Flutist Quarterly; Consort; Historical Performance; Pan (Journal, British Flute Society); Musical America. *Hobby:* Swimming. *Address:* 10 Bobwhite Drive, Westport, CT 06880, USA.

SOLYOM Janos, b. 26 Oct 1938, Budapest, Hungary. Pianist; Conductor. *Education:* Piano, Conducting and Composition studies at Béla Bartók Conservatory, Franz

Liszt Academy of Music, Budapest; Further studies with Ilona Kabos, London, and Nadia Boulanger, Paris. *Debut:* Stockholm, 1958. *Career:* International. *Recordings:* Swedish EMI, CBS, Caprice, BIS, Artemis. *Contributions to:* Manads-Journalen. *Honour:* Litteris et Artibus (Royal Swedish Medal of Honour for Outstanding Achievements in the Arts), 1986. *Address:* Norr Malarstrand 54, S-112 20, Stockholm, Sweden.

SOLYOM-NAGY Sandor, b. 21 Dec. 1934, Siklos, Hungary. Baritone. *Education:* Ferenc Liszt Academy of Music, Budapest, 1960. *Career:* Budapest State Opera, 1964-; Numerous Guest Performances in Berlin, Brussels, Bratislava, Prague, Cologne, Barcelona, Moscow, Leningrad, Genoa, Rome, The Hague, Rotterdam, Paris, Rio de Janeiro, Sao Paulo, Sofia, Varna and Vienna; Frequent Guest Appearances, Bavarian State Opera, Munich, Federal Republic of Germany; Vienna State Opera, Austria; Japan; Regular Guest Artist, Bayreuth Festival, 1981-; (Grail Knight in Parsifal, 1992). *Recordings:* Has made numerous records including: Liszt: Christus oratorio; The Legend of Elisabeth; Via Crucis; The Queen of Sheba; Agamemnon in Gluck's Iphigénie en Aulide; Title role in Kodály's Háry János and in Strauss's Guntram and Respighi's La Fiamma; Sang Palatine Gara in Erkel's Hunyadi László at Budapest, 1989. *Honours:* Liszt Prize, 1972; Merited Artist of the Hungarian People's Republic, 1977; Hector Berlioz Prize, French Record Academy; Grand Prix, French Record Academy; Charles Cros Prize, French Record Academy; Golden Orpheus Prize, French Record Academy. *Address:* c/o Budapest State Opera, Budapest, Hungary.

SOMACH Beverly, b. 17 Jan 1935, New York City, New York, USA. Violinist. m. S. George Silverstein, 30 Aug 1959, 2 sons, 2 daughters. *Education:* BS, Columbia University, 1956; Certificate of Completion of Studies with Jascha Heifetz, University of California, Los Angeles, 1959. *Career:* Recitals, Town Hall, Carnegie Hall, Lincoln Center, Alice Tully Hall, New York City; Recitals in London (Wigmore Hall, Purcell Room), Edinburgh, Glasgow, Stockholm, Copenhagen, Zurich, Paris, Tokyo, Hong Kong, Montreal; Soloist with Orchestra: New York Philharmonic, Chicago Symphony, Los Angeles Symphony, American Synphony, Orchestra Luxembourg. *Recordings:* For Newport Classic, Heritage Society, Radio Free Europe, Voice of America. *Contributions to:* New York Times; Musical America. *Current Management:* Seymour F. Malkin Management. *Address:* 280 Greenridge Road, Franklin Lakes, NJ 07417, USA.

SOMARY Johannes Felix, b. 7 Apr 1935, Zurich, Switzerland. Musician. m. Anne Van Zandt, 20 July 1963, 2 sons, 1 daughter. *Education:* BA, Yale University, 1957; MMus, Yale School of Music, 1959. *Debut:* Conducting debut with Washington Square Music Festival, New York, Aug 1960. *Career:* Founder, Music Director, Conductor of Amor Artis, New York City, 1962-; Chairman, Arts and Music Department, Horace Mann School, New York City, 1971-; Conductor: Fairfield County Chorale, 1975-, Great Neck Choral Society, 1982-, Taghkanic Chorale, 1992-; Conductor, recordings with English Chamber Orchestra, London, 1968-79; Visiting Professor of Music, Yale School of Music, 1983-84; Choral Director, Madeira Bach Festival, 1984-86; Guest Conductor: Dubrovnik Music Festival, Yugoslavia, 1986, Sion Music Festival, Switzerland, 1990, Polish Radio and TV Orchestra, 1990, New Orleans Philharmonic, Royal Philharmonic (London), Brno State Philharmonic, others; Artist-in-residence, St Jean Baptiste Church, New York City; Commissioned by Jefferson Music Festival to write an oratorio for 1994. *Compositions:* Ballad of God and His People (recorded); The Ultimate Quest, oratorio for Great Neck Choral Society. *Recordings:* Conductor of 55 including Handel's Messiah; Bach's St Matthew Passion; Works by Haydn, Tschaikowsky, Prokofiev and Kurt Weill; Acis and Galatea by Handel; Vivaldi's Four Seasons; Bach cantatas and motets. *Honours:* Certificates of Merit, Yale School of Music Alumni Association and University of Chicago; Choirmaster Certificate, American Guild of

Organists; Record of the Year, Stereo Review, 1969, 1970, 1975, 1978. *Memberships:* Yale Club; Riverdale Yacht Club; Board of Directors, Friendship Ambassadors; Former Member, Archdiocesan Music Commission. *Hobbies:* Walking; Hiking; Gardening; Cycling; Reading. *Address:* 620 West 254 Street, Bronx, NY 10471, USA.

SOMFAI László, b. 15 Aug 1934, Jászladány, Hungary. Musicologist. m. Dorrit Révész-Somfai, 1 son, 1 daughter. *Education:* Diploma of Musicology, Ferenc Liszt Academy of Music, Budapest, 1958; Doctor of Musicology, Hungarian Academy of Sciences, Budapest, 1982. *Career:* Music Librarian, National Széchényi Library, Budapest, until 1962; Musicologist, Head of Budapest Bartók Archives, Institute for Musicology, Hungarian Academy of Sciences, 1972-; Professor of Musicology, Ferenc Liszt Academy of Music, 1980-. *Publications:* Co-author, Haydn als Opernkapellmeister, 1960; Joseph Haydn: Sein Leben in zeitgenössischen Bildern, 1966, English edition, 1969; Anton Webern, 1968; J.Haydn's Piano Sonatas, 1979; 18 Bartók Studies, 1981; Studies on J.Haydn, Liszt, Stravinsky, Webern, Bartók; Urtexteditions in Mozart Neue Ausgabe, Gluck Neue Ausgabe, Musica Rinata; Editor, Documenta Bartókiana. *Memberships:* Presidium, Zentralinstitut der Mozartforschung, Salzburg; Joseph Haydn-Institut, Köln; Board of Directors, International Musicological Society. *Address:* Falk Miksa u.12, V.4 Budapest, H-1055 Hungary.

SOMMER Raphael, b. 21 June 1937, Prague, Czechoslovakia. Cellist; Conductor. m. Geneviève Teulière, 25 Oct 1986, 2 sons. *Education:* Graduate, Rubin Academy of Music, Jerusalem, Israel; National Conservatory of Music, Paris, France. *Career:* Professor, Royal Northern College of Music, Manchester, England, 1967-; Director of 1st Chamber Orchestra, Royal College of Music, London, 1974-79; Professor, Guildhall School of Music, London, 1980-. *Publication:* English translation of Paul Tortelier's cello method: How I Play, How I Teach. *Honours:* Winner of 3 international cello competitions, 1961, 1962, 1963; 1st prize, National Conservatory of Music, Paris. *Membership:* Honorary Member, Accademia Filharmonica di Musica, Bologna, Italy. *Hobby:* Theatre. *Address:* 20 Elliott Square, London NW3, England.

SOMMER Vladimir, b. 28 Feb 1921, Dolni Jiretin, Czechoslovakia. Composer. m. 12 Feb 1983, 1 son, 1 daughter. *Education:* BA, 1940; School of Music, Prague, 1940-46; Graduate School of Art and Music, Prague, 1946-50. *Career:* Postgradual studies, 1950-52; Radio Assistant, 1952- 53; Secretary of Czechoslovak Union of Musical Composers 1953-56; Assistant Professor at Graduate School of Art and Music, Prague, 1956-60; Professor of Charles University, Prague, Department of the Theory of Music, 1960-87. *Compositions:* Concerto for a Violin and Orchestra - Score, Violin and Piano, Record: Czech Philharmonic Orchestra, L Jásek, V Jiráček, 1956; Concerto for Violoncello and Orchestra - Score, Record: Prague Philharmonic Orchestra, D Veis, J Bělohlávek, 1988; Overture to the Sophocles' Tragedy Antigone, Score a) Prague Philharmonic Orchestra, V Smetáček, 1960, Record; b) Czech Philharmonic Orchestra, Al Rahbari, 1987, Record; Vocal - Symphony No 1 for Mezzosoprano - Solo, Speaker, Chorus and Orchestra, Score 1965, a) Czech Philharmonic Orchestra, V Soukupová, O Brousek, Czech Chorus and V Neumann, 1964; London Symphony Orchestra, N Williams, P Ustinov, The Ambro sian singers, J Buketoff, String Quartet No 1 - Score, 1960 a) Smetana Quartet, 1959, Record; b)Škvor Quartet, 1978, record; c) Panocha Quartet, 1987 record; String Quartet No 2, Score 1989; Seven Songs for Mezzosoprano and Piano, 1988, H Beranova, L Čermaková, 1988, record. *Address:* Knezeveska 6, 16100 Prague 6 Ruzyne, Czech Republic.

SONDEREGGER Peter, b. 2 Oct 1960, St Gallen, Switzerland. Composer. *Education:* Konservatorium Basel, with Jacques Wildberger, 1980-85; Musikhochschule Karlsruhe, Germany, with Wolfgang Rihm, 1987-89. *Compositions:* Delirien I-III, chamber ensembles & live electronics, 1981-83; Piano Concerto No. 1, 1985; Tombeau per tre Clarinetti, 1985; Eclairs Errants, piano & orchestra, 1986-87; Webern, Variations to Symphony op. 21 for Orchestra, 1987; Zeit, Verjungendes Licht, clarinet, viola & guitar, 1987-88; 73 Pezzi Degli Scrovegni, pno, 1989-90; Missa Incontri, Piano trio, 1990-91; Auslöschung, for panflute and double-stringquartet, 1991; Various other compositions for chamber ensembles, piano solo, guitar solo. *Recordings:* Tombeau per tre Clarinetti; Zeit, Verjungendes Licht. *Honours:* Scholarships: Heinrich Strobel-Stiftung des Südwestfunks 1986, Schweizerischer Tonkünstlerverein 1987. *Hobbies:* Improvisation. *Address:* Rue de la Gare 30, CH-2613 Villeret, Switzerland.

SONDHEIM Stephen Joshua, b. 22 Mar 1930, New York City, USA. Composer; Lyricist. *Education:* BA, Williams College, 1950. *Compositions:* (incidental music) Girls of Summer, 1956, Invitation to a March, 1961; (lyrics) West Side Story, 1957, Gypsy, 1959; (lyrics) Do I Hear a Waltz?, 1965; (music and lyrics) A Funny Thing Happened on the Way to the Forum, 1962, Anyone Can Whistle, 1964; Evening Primrose, 1966; Company, 1970, Follies, 1971, A Little Night Music, 1973; The Frogs, 1974; (film score) Stavisky, 1974; (music and lyrics) Pacific Overtures, 1976, Sweeney Todd, 1979; (film score) Reds, 1981; Merrily We Roll Along, 1981; Sunday in the Park with George, 1984; Into the Woods, 1987; Assassins, 1990, (songs for film); (analogies) Side By Side By Sondheim, 1977, Marry Me a Little, 1980; You're Gonna Love Tomorrow, 1983; Putting It Together, 1992 (songs for film) Dick Tracy, 1991. *Memberships:* Dramatists Guild, President, 1973-81; American Academy and Institute of Arts and Letters. *Address:* c/o Flora Roberts Inc., 157 West 57th Street, New York, NY 10019, USA.

SONNTAG Ulrike, b. 1959, Esslingen, Germany. Singer (Soprano). *Education:* Studied with Eva Sava and Dietrich Fischer- Dieskau; Hartmann-Dressler. *Debut:* Sang Oriane in Amadis de Gaul by J C Bach as guest with the Hamburg Staatsoper, 1983. *Career:* Sang at the Stadttheater Heidelberg 1984-86; Nationaltheater Mannheim 1986-88; Has appeared in concerts all over Europe including: USA - Los Angeles, China, Brazil; Berlin as concert singer; Member of the Stuttgart Opera from 1988, as Euridice, Susanna, Donna Elvira, Marzelline, Frau Fluth, Gretel, Sophie in Der Rosenkavalier and Helena (A Midsummer Night's Dream); Sang Aennchen in Der Freischütz at the 1989 Ludwigsburg Festival; Pamina, 1992; Freischütz production, Trieste, 1994; Wildschütz production, Cologne, 1994; Lieder Tour Moscow/St Petersburg, 1994. *Recordings include:* Bach cantatas. *Address:* Staatstheater Stuttgart, Oberer Schlossgarten 6, D-7000 Stuttgart 1, Germany.

SOOTER Edward, b. 8 Dec 1934, Salina, Kansas, USA. Singer (Tenor). *Education:* Studied at the Friends University in Wichita with Elsa Haury, Kansas University with Joseph Wilkins and the Hamburg Musikhochschule with Helmut Melchert. *Debut:* Bremerhaven 1966, as Florestan. *Career:* Sang in Kiel, Karlsruhe, Wiesbaden, Bielefeld, Essen and Cologne; Metropolitan Opera from 1980 as Florestan, Tannhäuser, Otello, Aeneas in Les Troyens, Walther, Tristan and Lohengrin; Sang Siegmund in Ring cycles at Seattle; New Orleans Opera, 1992 as Florestan; Other roles include Parsifal, Don José, Otello, Canio, Aegisthus, Manrico, Ernani, Samson, and Babinsky in Schvanda the Bagpiper. *Address:* c/o Metropolitan Opera, Lincoln Center, New York, NY 10023, USA.

SORDELLO Enzo, b. 20 Apr 1927, Pievebovigliano, Macerata, Italy. Singer (Baritone). *Education:* Studied at the Milan Conservatory. *Debut:* Teatro Toselli in Cuneo as Enrico in Lucia di Lammermoor, 1952. *Career:* La Scala 1954-75, as Cinna in La Vestale, opposite Callas: later appeared in Milan as Belcore, Albert in Werther, Gerard in Andrea Chénier 1955, and Tonio; Metropolitan Opera 1956, Marcello; Vienna Staatsoper 1959, Stoll Theatre London 1960; Glyndebourne

Festival 1961-62, as Belcore; Frequent broadcasts on RAI. *Recordings include:* La Fanciulla del West (Columbia); La Vestale, Pagliacci (Cetra); Madama Butterfly (Decca); Lucia di Lammermoor. *Address:* 12018 Roccavione, (Cueno) Italy.

SORENSON VON GERTTEN Iwa Cecilia, b. 5 Sept 1946, Gothenburg, Sweden. Opera Singer (Soprano). m. Gustf von Gertten, 5 July 1980, 2 sons. *Education:* Music Conservatory, Gothenburg, 1966-74; Staatliche Hochschule fur Musik, Cologne, 1970-71; Trained as Singer, Singing Teacher and Organist, School of Theatre and Opera, Gothenburg, 1974-75, 1976-77. *Debut:* Malmo, Sweden, as Norina in Donizetti's Don Pasquale, 1978. *Career:* Opera soloist, Malmo Stadsteater, 1978-79; Opera soloist, Royal Opera of Stockholm, 1979-; Major roles: Rosina in The Barber of Seville, Musetta in La Boheme, Sophie in Der Rosenkavalier, Zdenka in Arabella, Fiordiligi in Cosi fan tutte, Susanna in The Marriage of Figaro, Blonde in The Abduction from the Seraglio, Aminta in Il Re Pastore, Violetta in La Traviata, Marguerite in Faust, Olympia in Tales of Hoffmann; Roles in operettas: Adele in Die Fledermaus by Strauss, Laura in Der Bettelstudent by Millocker, Jos ephine in HMS Pinafore, Fiametta in Boccaccio by von Suppé; Concert repertoire: Handel's Messiah and Judas Maccabaeus, Haydn's Creation, Mendelssohn's Elijah, Mozart's Requiem and Mass in C minor; Recitals with piano of German lieder, French art songs, Swedish repertoire, and contemporary music. *Recordings:* Mostly 19th and 20th century Swedish music. *Honours:* 3 gramophone prizes, 1983, 1984, 1985. *Address:* Hogbergsgatan 26 B, S-11620 Stockholm, Sweden.

SOROKINA Elena, b. 6 Apr 1940, Moscow, USSR. Pianist; Music Historian. m. Alexander Bakhchiev, 28 Nov 1962, 1 daughter. *Education:* Graduated, Central School of Music, 1958; MA, Performance, MA, History of Music, 1963, PhD, 1965, Moscow State Conservatory. *Debut:* Duet concert with A Bakhchiev, Mozart, Schubert, Central Arts House, Moscow. *Career:* Professor, Russian Music History, Moscow State Conservatory, 1965-; Regular duet performances, Beethoven, Mozart, Weber, Schumann, Schubert, Brahms, Glinka, Borodin, Rachmaninov, other Russian composers, 1968-; Regular radio appearances, duets with own comments, series of radio lectures on Russian composers, music genres, history of Moscow Conservatory, 1969-; Series of TV programmes, Chamber Music Concerts, 1970s; Tours with lectures on Russian music, France, Austria, Latin America; Participated with A Bakhchiev, international/national festivals of music, Moscow, Leningrad; The International Festival dedicated to Mozart in Tokyo, 1991; Works dedicated to Sorokina-Bakhchiev by A Boyarsky, L Lubovsky, G Fried, I Manukyan (USSR), T Moore (England); Tour, England (Cambridge, London), Soviet and British modern music piano duets; Holder of the Chair of Russian Music History, 1992; Moscow State Conservatory; Concerts in Israel, Italy, Germany, USA with A Bakhchiev (duets), 1992-93. *Recordings include:* Duets with A Bakhchiev: Mozart (3 discs); Schubert (2 discs); Music of France; Weber, Schumann, Mendelssohn; V Persichetti; Bartók, Lutoslawski; Enescu; Albums: Music of Old Vienna; J S Bach, his family and pupils; Music for 6 and 8 hands (with G Rozhdestvensky, V Postnikova). *Honours:* Honoured Artist of Russia, 1993. *Memberships:* Co-President, Association of Piano Duets, USSR; Union of CIS Composers; Russian Mozart-Society, 1991. *Hobby:* Antiques. *Current Management:* Soyuzconcert; Mosconcert. *Address:* 2 Sorokina, 4-32 Koshkin Str, Moscow 115409, Russia.

SOTIN Hans, b. 10 Sept 1939, Dortmund, Germany. Singer (Bass). *Education:* Studied privately with F.W. Hetzel; Dortmund Musikhochschule with Dieter Jacob. *Debut:* Essen 1962 in Der Rosenkavalier. *Career:* Hamburg Staatsoper 1964- in the standard bass repertory and in the premieres of operas by Penderecki, Klebe, Blacher, Von Einem and Kelemen; Visits with Hamburg Company to New York, Montreal, Rome, Stockholm and Edinburgh; 1970 sang in Beethoven's

Choral Symphony at the United Nations; Glyndebourne debut 1970, Sarastro in Die Zauberflöte; Bayreuth Festival 1972- as the Landgrave, Pogner, Titurel and Gurnemanz; New York Metropolitan 1972- as Sarastro and as Hunding and Wotan in Die Walküre; Covent Garden debut 1974, Hunding; La Scala Milan 1976, as Baron Ochs in Der Rosenkavalier; Sang Ochs at Covent Garden, 1986, Lodovico in Otello at the Met, 1988; Landgrave in Tannhäuser at Hamburg, 1990; Bayreuth 1989-90, as Gurnemanz and Daland; Season 1992 as the Landgrave at Berlin and Barcelona, Gurnemanz and Daland at Bayreuth; Often heard as concert singer, notably in music by Bach. *Recordings:* Die Zauberflöte, Tannhäuser, Aida, Fidelio (Decca); Salome, Doktor Faust, Der Wildschütz (Deutsche Grammophon); Cosi fan Tutte, Die Walküre, St Matthew Passion and Beethoven's Christ at the Mount of Olives (HMV); The Devils of Loudun, Mahler's 8th Symphony, Die Meistersinger, Tristan und Isolde (Philips); Flying Dutchman (DGG); Parsifal (Philips); Pauken Messe Haydn (DGG); Seasons Haydn (EMI). *Honours:* Forderpreis des Landes NRW; Friedrich Oberdörfer Preis, Hamburg; Kammersänger, Hamburg. *Address:* c/o Lies Askonas Ltd., 186 Drury Lane, London WC2B 5QD. England.

SOUDANT Hubert, b. 16 Mar 1946, Maastricht, Holland. Conductor. *Education:* Studied at the Maastricht Conservatory, with Franco Ferrara in Italy and at Netherlands Radio Course in Hilversum. *Career:* Assistant Conductor with the Hilversum Radio Orchestra 1967-70; Has conducted the Orchestra of Radio France and the Nouvel Orchestra Philharmonique, with which he gave the French premiere of Mahler's 10th Symphony (Strasbourg 1979); Conductor of Symphony Orchestra of Utrecht 1982; Musical Director, Orchestra Sinfonica dell'Emilia Romagna Arturo Toscanini (Parma) 1988; In 1980 conducted premieres of Rene Koering's opera Elseneur and the Nana-Symphonie by Marius Constant; Guest conductor in England, Germany, Belgium, Italy, Scandinavia, South Africa and Japan; Conducted Ernani at Parma, 1990; Berlioz Faust at Turin, 1992. *Recordings:* Tchaikovsky 4th and 6th Symphonies and Romeo and Juliet with the London Philharmonic (Pye); Liszt Piano Concertos, with the LPO. *Honours:* Winner, International Competituion for Young Conductors, Besançon 1971; 2nd Prize, Herbert von Karajan International Conducting Competition, 1973; First Prize, Guido Cantelli International Conducting Competition, Milan, 1975. *Address:* Orchestra Sinfonica dell'Emilia Romagna, Piazzale Cesare Battisti 15, I-43100 Parma, Italy.

SOUKUPOVA Vera, b. 12 Apr 1932, Prague, Czechoslovakia. Singer (Contralto). *Education:* Studied in Prague with L. Kaderabek and A. Mustanova-Linkova. *Career:* Has sung in concert from 1955; Stage debut 1957, Pilsen; Member of the Prague National Opera from 1960; Tour of Russia 1961, and sang Dalila in Bordeaux; Guest appearances in Vienna, France and Switzerland; State Operas of Hamburg and Berlin 1969-71; Prague National Opera 1983, as Radmila in Smetana's Libuse. *Recordings:* Erda in The Ring (Philips); Dvořák Stabat Mater (Deutsche Grammophon); Lieder by Mahler (Eurodisc); Choral Symphony (Denon); Libuse, The Brandenburgers in Bohemia, The Bride of Messina by Fibich, Oedpius Rex and Janáček Glagolitic Mass (Supraphon). *Address:* c/o National Theatre, PO Box 865, 112 30 Prague 1, Czech.

SOULIOTIS Elena, b. 28 May 1943, Athens, Greece. Opera Singer (Soprano and Mezzo-soprano). *Education:* Studied in Buenos Aires with Alfedo Bonta, Jascha Galperin and Bianca Lietti; Milan with Mercedes Llopart. *Debut:* Teatro San Carlo Naples as Santuzza, 1964; Sang in Italy and Spain from 1965; US debut 1965, as Elena in Mefistofele at the Lyric Opera Chicago; 1966 as Anna Bolena in a concert performance of Donizetti's opera at Carnegie Hall, New York; La Scala Milan as Abigail in Nabucco; Metropolitan Opera 1969, as Lady Macbeth; Guest appearances in Portugal, Greece, South America and Vienna; Covent Garden 1969-73, as Santuzza, Abigail and Lady Macbeth; Other roles included Manon

Lescaut, La Gioconda, Desdemona, Norma, Aida and Leonora in Il Trovatore; Sang at Florence 1986-88, in The Gambler by Prokofiev and as the Princess in Suor Angelica; appeared as the nurse in Mascagni's Guglielmo Ratcliff at Catania, 1990. *Recordings:* Verdi's Macbeth and Nabucco; Anna Bolena and Norma (Decca). *Hobbies:* Country Life; Animals. *Address:* Villa il Poderino, Via Incontri 38, Florence, Italy.

SOUSTER Tim(othy) Andrew James, b. 29 Jan 1943, Bletchley, England. Composer. *Education:* 1961-65 Oxford University, with David Lumsden and Egon Wellesz; 1964 Darmstadt; privately with Richard Rodney Bennett. *Career:* 1965-67 BBC producer; 1969-71 Composer-in-residence, King's College Cambridge; 1971-73 assistant to Stockhausen at the Cologne Musikhochschule; 1975-79 Research Fellow at Keele University; Co-founder with Roger Smalley of group Intermodulation, to explore electronic and improvisatory techniques; Chairman, Association of Professional Composers, 1988-89. *Compositions:* Songs of Three Seasons for soprano and viola 1965; Metropolitan Games for piano duet, 1969; Works with Electronics: Waste Land Music, with quartet, 1970; Spectral, with viola, 1972; World Music, with Octet, 1974; Afghan Amplitudes, with trio, 1976; Song, for instruments and four-track tape, 1977; Arcane Artefact, with trio, 1977; Arboreal Antecedents, with trio, 1977-78; Equalisation, for brass quintet, 1980; The Transistor Radio of St Narcissus, with flugelhorn, 1983; Hambledon Hill, for amplified string quartet and tape, 1985; Concerto for trumpet, live-electronics and orchestra, 1988; Triple Music II for 3 orchestras, 1970; Song of an Average City for small orchestra and tape, 1974; Zorna for soprano saxophone, tape and drums, 1974; The Music Room for trombone and tape, 1976; Driftwood Cortege for tape, 1978; Sonata for cello and ensemble, 1979; Mareas for 4 amplified voices and tape, 1981; Curtain of Light for percussion and tape, 1984; Le Souvenir de Maurice Ravel for septet, 1984; Paws 3D for orchestra, 1984; Rabbit Heaven, for brass quintet, 1986; Echoes, for brass band, live-electronics, 1990; La Marche, for bras quintet, 1993; TV scores: Africa, The Heart of the Dragon, The Midas Touch, Traffik, Calling the Shots, Circle of Deceit, South Bank Show on Elisabeth Frink. *Recordings:* Spectral, Afghan Amplitudes, Arcane Artefact on Transatlantic; Sonata, Equalisation on Nimbus, CD, NI 5317; The Transistor Radio of St Narcisus on UEA Recordings. *Honours:* BAFTA award for best TV Music of 1990, The Green Man, 1991. *Current Management:* Air-Edel Associates, 18 Rodmarton Street, London W1H 3FW. *Address:* 37 Windsor Road, Cambridge CB4 3JJ, England.

SOUSTROT Marc, b. 15 Apr 1949, Lyon, France. Conductor. *Education:* Studied trombone at the Lyon Conservatoire, 1962-69 and conducting with Manuel Rosenthal at the Paris Conservatoire, 1969-76. *Career:* Assistant to André Previn at the London Symphony Orchestra 1974-76; Deputy conductor, 1976, then musical director of the Orchestre Philharmonique of the Loire; Artistic Director of the Nantes Opera 1986-90; Conducted the premieres of Claude Baliff's Fantasio grandioso 1977, 1st Piano Concerto by Maurice Ohana 1981 and Concerto for Orchestra by Alain Louvier, 1987; Conducted Tristan and Isolde at Nantes, 1989, Manon Lescaut 1990; Les Contes d'Hoffmann at Geneva 1990; Conducted Carmen at the Bregenz Festival, Austria. *Recordings:* Trumpet Concertos, with Maurice André; Music by Franceschini, A Scarlatti, Vivaldi, Tartini and Telemann, with the Monte Carlo National Opera Orchestra (Erato). *Honours:* Winner, Rupert Foundation Competition for Young Conductors, London 1974; International Competition, Besançon, 1975. *Address:* Opera de Nantes, 1 Rue Moliere, F-44000 Nantes, France.

SOUTHERN Eileen, b. 19 Feb 1920, Minneapolis, MN, USA. University Professor. *Education:* University of Chicago, BA 1940, MA 1941; New York University, PhD 1961; Piano study at Chicago Music College, Juilliard School, N.Y., and Boston University. *Career:* Prairie View University, 1941-42; Southern University,

1943-45, 1949-51; City University of New York, 1960-75; Harvard University, 1975-86; now Professor Emerita of Music and Afro-American Studies at Harvard University. *Publications:* The Buxheim Organ Book, 1963; The Music of Black Americans: A History, 1971, rev. ed. 1983; Readings in Black American Music, 1971, 1983; Biographical Dictionary of Afro-American and African Musicians, 1982; Afro-American Traditions in Song: An Annotated Bibliography, 1990. *Contributions to:* Journal of AMS, Acta Musicologica;American Music; Musica Disciplina; Co-founder/ co-editor of The Black Perspective in Music, 1973-; articles in The New Grove Dictionary, 1980. *Memberships:* AMS, Board of Directors, 1974-76; Sonneck Society, Board of Directors, 1985-87. *Hobbies:* Travel; Gardening. *Address:* 115-05 179 Street, St.Albans, NY 11434, USA.

SOUTHGATE William, b. 4 Aug 1941, Waipukarau, New Zealand. Conductor; Composer. *Education:* Studied at Otago University and the Guildhall School of Music, 1967-71. *Career:* Freelance composer in London and guest musical director of the Royal Shakespeare Company; Conductor and arranger for the Phoenix Opera Company; Musical Director of the Wellington Youth Orchestra from 1977; Musical Director of the Christchurch Symphony Orchestra from 1984; Has conducted operas by Rossini, Verdi and Johann Strauss for the Wellington and Canterbury Opera Companies; Presenter of music programmes on New Zealand radio and TV; Toured Finland as conductor 1986, Sweden and Finland 1989; Debut with Honolulu Symphony 1989; Tour of New Zealand with the Royal New Zealand Ballet Company, 1989; Premieres of children's opera a Faery Tale and Cello Concerto in New Zealand, 1990; also engaged for the Dunedin Sinfonia, New Zealand, 1991; St Matthews Chamber Orchestra, New Zealand, 1991; SWF Sinfonia Orchestra, Spohr Competition, Baden-Baden, 1991; Christchurch Symphony Orchestra, New Zealand, 1991; New Zealand Symphony Orchestra, 1992. *Recordings include:* Second Symphony. *Honours include:* Guildhall School conducting prize; Second Prize, Besançon Conducting Competition.

SOUZAY Gerard, b. 8 Dec 1918, Angers, France. Baritone. *Education:* First Prize for Singing, First Prize for Vocalising, Paris Conservatoire. *Debut:* Faure's Requiem under direction of Charles Munch, Royal Albert Hall, London, 1945. *Career:* Operatic repertoire includes roles of Don Giovanni (title role); Marriage of Figaro (Almaviva); Pelléas et Mélisande (Golaud); Damnation of Faust (Mephisto); Manon (Lescaut); Orpheus in Monteverdi and Gluck; Has appeared at the Paris Opéra and Opéra-Comique, Grand Théâtre in Geneva, Rome Opera, Munich Opera, Vienna State Opera, Glyndebourne Festival, Metropolitan Opera; Made French songs famous worldwide and sings songs of foreign composers in many languages; Appeared at many major festivals: Salzburg, Edinburgh, Prades, Puerto Rico, Vienna, Berlin, Aix-en-Provence, Besançon, Bordeaux, Tanglewood, USA. etc; Sang under direction of such names as: Karajan, Munch, Ansermet, Maazel, Bernstein, Szell, Cluytens; Sang solo under direction of Stravinsky at San Marco Cathedral, Venice for first performance of Canticum Sacrum, 1956; As professor takes classes in Holland, England, St Jean de Luz (Academie Ravell), America (Juilliard and many American universities), Paris, Japan. *Recordings:* Has made many records and gained Grand Prix for Records in France, Germany, Italy, America and Japan. *Honours:* Chevalier of French Legion d'Honneur; Commander of the Order of Merit of FRG; Officer of the French National Order of Merit. *Address:* 26 Rue Freycinet, Paris 75116, USA.

SOVIERO Diana, b. 1952, USA. Singer (Soprano). *Career:* Sang first at St Paul (1974), appearing as Lauretta in Gianni Schicchi and as Massenet's Manon; Joined the New York City Opera 1976 and sang further at Miami, San Francisco and Chicago; Metropolitan Opera debut 1986, as Juliet in Roméo et Juliette; European engagements at Paris, Rome, Florence, Milan, Vienna and Hamburg; Geneva 1988, as Gretchen in Doktor Faust by Busoni; Philadelphia and San Diego 1988, as Margherita in Mefistofele and Marguerite in Faust; Sang Juliet and Manon at Montreal in 1989; Covent Garden debut 1989, as Nedda; Season 1992 as Tosca with Opera Pacific at Costa Mesa, Puccini's Trittico heroines at Dallas, Manon Lescaut at Miami and Adriana Lecouvreur at Sydney; Other roles include Puccini's Butterfly, and Mimi, Leila in Les pêcheurs de Perles and Norina in Don Pasquale.*Address:* c/o Royal Opera House, (Contracts), Covent Garden, London WC2, England.

SOYER David, b. 24 Feb 1924, Philadelphia, Pennsylvania, USA. Cellist. *Education:* Studied with Emanuel Feurmann, Palbo Casals. *Career:* Played with Bach Aria Group, Guilet Quartet, New Music Quartet and Marlboro Trio; Performed in chamber music with Rudolf Serkin at Marlboro Festival and prompted by Alexander Schneider to co-found the Guarneri String Quartet, 1964; Many tours of America and Europe, notably appearances at the Spoleto Festival, 1965, to Paris with Arthur Rubinstein and London 1970, in the complete quartets of Beethoven; Noted for performances of the Viennese classics, and works by Walton, Bartók and Stravinsky; Season 1987-88 included tour of Japan, concerts at St John's Smith Square, the Elizabeth Hall, London; On faculty of the Curtis Institute, Philadelphia, and the University of Maryland. *Recordings include:* Mozart's quartets dedicated to Haydn; Complete quartet of Beethoven; With Arthur Rubinstein Piano Quintets of Schumann, Dvořák and Brahms; Piano Quartets by Fauré and Brahms. *Honours include:* Edison Award for Beethoven recordings, 1971; Honorary Doctorates at University of S Florida and State University of New York. *Address:* c/o Curtis Institute of Music, 1726 Locust Street, Rittenhouse Square, Philadelphoa, PA 19013, USA.

SOYER Roger, b. 1 Sept. 1939, Thiais, France. Singer (Bass). *Education:* Studied at the Paris Conservatoire with Georges Daum and Georges Jouatte. *Career:* Sang at the Paris Opéra from 1963; La Scala Milan 1963, as Tiresias in Les mamelles de Tiresias by Poulenc; Aix-en-Provence Festival from 1965, as Pluto in Monteverdi's Orfeo, Don Giovanni, Don Basilio and Arkel; Paris 1965 in Rameau's Hippolyte et Aricie; Wexford Festival 1968, in La Jolie Fille de Perth by Bizet; US debut Miami 1973, as Frère Laurent in Roméo et Juliette by Gounod; Paris Opéra from 1972, in the premiere of Sud by Stanton Coe, and as Don Giovanni, Procida (Les Vêpres Siciliennes), Ferrando, Colline and Mephistopheles; Metropolitan Opera 1972; Edinburgh Festival 1973, as Don Giovanni in a new production of Mozart's opera conducted by Daniel Barenboim; Guest appearances in Cologne, Brussels, Geneva, Chicago, Lisbon, Prague, San Antonio and Salzburg; Sang Rodolfo in La sonnambula at Geneva 1982, Sulpice in La fille du régiment at Dallas, 1983; Sang in L'Heure Espagnole at Turin, 1992. *Recordings:* Les Troyens and Benvenuto Cellini, conducted by Colin Davis, Les pêcheurs de Perles (Philips); L'Enfance du Christ, Mozart Requiem, Lakmé, Werther (EMI); Maria Stuarda by Donizetti (Decca); Pelléas et Mélisande (Eurodisc); Dardanus by Rameau and David et Jonatas by Charpentier (Erato). *Address:* c/o Grand Théâtre de Genèva, 11 Boulevard du Théâtre, CH-1211 Geneva 11, Switzerland.

SPACAGNA Maria, b. 1951, Rhode Island, USA. Singer (Soprano). *Education:* Studied at the New England Conservatory. *Career:* Sang with Dallas Opera from 1977, New York City Opera 1978, St Louis Opera 1982, Detroit 1986; Sang Puccini's Liu at Toronto 1983 and appeared in Santa Fe, New Orleans and Trieste 1987; Debut at La Scala Milan 1988, as Butterfly; Spoleto Festival 1988, as Ismene in Traetta's Antigone; Sang Mimi for New Orleans Opera 1989, Liu and Butterfly at Costa Mesa California and Greater Mimai Opera, 1990; Appearances at Memphis, the Cologne Opera and elsewhere as Violetta, Susanna, Zerlina, Norina, Gilda, Marguerite, Rusalka, Micaela, Lauretta and Mascagni's Lodoletta; Active concert career.

Address: c/o Greater Miami Opera Association, 1200 Coral Way, Miami, FL 33145, USA.

SPALDING Daniel, b. 20 Feb 1952, Wichita, Kansas, USA. Conductor. m. Gabriela Imreh, 31 Mar 1986. *Education:* BME, MM, Northwestern University; Salzburg Mozarteum; University of Illinois; Private study with Mircea Cristescu and John Shenant. *Career:* Assistant Conductor, Houston Symphony, 1986-87; Music Director, Trenton State College Symphony Orchestra, 1988-93; Founder and Music Director, Philadelphia Virtuosi, 1991-; Music Director, Friends of the Russian All Star Ballet, 1992-; Principal Guest Conductor, Transylvanian State Philharmonic, 1986-; Guest Conductor in Europe and USA including: Belgrade Philharmonic, Rome Festival Orchestra, Kolozsvar Hungarian State Opera, Opera Romana, New Jersey State Opera Festival, Paris Chamber Orchestra Jean-Louis Petit, Philadelphia Orchestra Society, Greater Trenton Symphony, Chattanooga Symphony, others. *Contributions to:* Instrumentalist; Percussionist. *Memberships:* Phi Mu Alpha; Conductors Guild; Percussive Arts Society. *Current Management:* Albert Kay Associates Inc. *Address:* 8 Cambridge Drive, W Trenton, NJ 08628, USA.

SPARNAAY Harry Willem, b. 14 Apr 1944, Amsterdam, Holland. Bass Clarinettist. m. Roswitha Sparnaay-Mol. *Education:* Amsterdam Conservatory. *Debut:* Amsterdam 1969. *Career:* Performances with many leading orchestras, including BBC Symphony, Rotterdam Philharmonic, ORTF, Concertgebouw and Radio Chamber Orchestra Hilversum; Soloist, music festivals of Warsaw, Zagreb, Graz, Madrid, Poitiers, Witten, Como, Paris, Naples and The ISCM World Music Days (Boston, Athens and Bonn); Concerts in Europe and America; Professor of Bass Clarinet and Contemporary Music, Sweelinck Conservatory, Amsterdam- Rotterdam Conservatory and Royal Conservatory, The Hague; Composers who have written for him include: Donatoni, Ferneyhough, Bussotti, Isang Yun and Barry Anderson (premiere of ARC), 1987; Huddersfield Festival, 1987, with Time and Motion Studies by Ferneyhough; tour of Britain 1989 on the Contemporary Music Network, playing Echange by Xenakis. *Recordings:* Bass Clarinet Identity; Harry Sparnaay/Lucien Goethals; Composers' Voice; Music by Thon Tbuynel; Music by Earle Brown; Bass Clarinet Identity 2; The Garden of Delight. *Honours include:* First prize, bass clarinet soloist, International Gaudeamus Competition, 1972. *Address:* Z. Buiten Sparne. 120, 2012 AD Haarlem, The Netherlands.

SPASOV Ivan, b. 17 Jan 1934, Sofia, Bulgaria. Composer. *Education:* Graduated, Sofia Conservatory (Composition with Vladigerov), 1956, and studied further with Vladigerov at Warsaw Conservatory. *Compositions include:* Orchestra: Sonata Concertante, 1959; 3 Symphonies, 1960, 1975, 1978; Micro-Suite for chamber orchestra, 1963; Dances, 1964; Competition for 22 winds, 1969; Cello Concerto, 1974; Piano Concerto, 1976; Firework, 1980; Violin Concerto, 1980; Vocal: Plakat, oratorio, 1958; Monodrama for soprano and ensemble, 1976; Canti lamentosi for 2 sopranos and chamber orchestra, 1979; Chamber: Clarinet Sonata, 1959; Viola Sonata, 1960; Episodes, 1965; Movements I and II for strings, 1966-68; 10 Groups for hunting horn and piano, 1965; String Quartet, 1973; Cello Sonata, 1980; Piano Trio, 1981; Piano music. *Address:* JUSAUTOR (Bulgaria), c/o PRS Ltd Member Registration, 29-33 Berners Street, London W1P 4AA, England.

SPECTOR Johanna, b. 1915, Liepaja, Latvia. Ethnomusicologist; Pianist; Film maker. m. Robert Spektor, 1939, deceased 1941. *Education:* DHS, Hebrew Union College, 1950; MA, Columbia University, 1960. *Career:* Research Fellow, Hebrew University, Jerusalem, 1951-53; Faculty, Jewish Theological Seminary Am, 1954-; Dir Founder Dept Ethnomusicology, 1962-; Associate Profesor of Musicology 1966-70, Professor, 1971-85; Professor Emeritus, 1985-. *Compositions:* Field recordings of Jewish, Middle Eastern, Indian, Arabic, Armenian, Samaritan music, liturgical and secular; about 10,000 original field recordings, 3000 deposited, Hebrew University, Jerusalem; 7000 part of private collection of author. *Publications:* Ghetto-und KZ Lieder, 1947; Samaritan Chant, 1965; Musical Tradition and Innovation in Central Asia, 1966; Bridal Songs from San'a, Yemen, 1960. *Contributions to:* Many articles to numerous journals, encyclopaedias and magazines; Documentary films: The Samaritans 1971 (Chicago Cert. of Merit); Middle Eastern Music, 1973; About the Jews of India: Cochin 1976 (CINE Golden Eagle 1979); The Shanwar Telis or Bene Israel of India 1978 (CINE Golden Eagle 1979); About the Jews of Yemen, A Vanishing Culture, 1986 (CINE Golden Eagle 1986 and Blue Ribbon 1986); 2000 Years of Freedom and Honor, The Cochin Jews of India, 1992. *Honour:* Award Columbus International Film Festival, (2000 Years of Freedom and Honor), 1992. *Address:* 400 West 119th Street, New York, NY 10027, USA.

SPEDDING Frank Donald, b. 21 Aug 1929, Liverpool, England. Composer; Arranger. *Education:* Royal College of Musc; DMus (London). *Career:* Staff, Royal Scottish Academy of Music and Drama, 1957-86. *Compositions:* Orchestral and chamber works; Choral and vocal music; Music for films, theatre and television. *Honours:* Royal Philharmonic Society Prizeman, 1951, 1953; Fellowship, Royal Scottish Academy of Music and Drama, 1977. *Memberships:* Incorporated Society of Musicians; Musicians Union; Composers Guild of Great Britain. *Hobbies:* Books; Travel. *Address:* 17 Digby Avenue, Mapperley, Nottingham NG3 6DS, England.

SPEIDEL Sontraud, b. 30 Mar 1944, Karlsruhe, Germany. Concert Pianist; Professor of Piano. *Education:* Staatliche Hochschule fur Musik, Karlsruhe; Staatliche Hochschule für Musik, Frankfurt, Scholarship by German Academic Exchange Service for Brussels. *Career:* Concert performances, radio and television performances and recordings in many European countries as well as the Soviet Union, USA and Canada; Conducted Master Classes in the USA, Canada, Germany and Austria; Conducts piano master course within the Vienna Music Seminar each summer since 1983; Distinguished Visiting Professor at California State University, Chico; Has played world premieres of works by Kurt Hessenberg in the Schumann house in Bonn, Germany as well as by the Greek composer Yannis Papaioannou in Heidelberg, Germany. Currently: Professor of Music at the Music University of Karlsruhe, Germany. *Recordings:* Piano Works by Richard Wagner (LP); Piano Works by Dussek and Hummel (LP); The Six Partitas by Bach (LP Album); Piano Works by Fanny Hensel, Born Mendelssohn Bartholdy (LP and CD); Piano Works by Kirchner and Reinecke (CD); Works for Violin and Piano by Dvořák; Mendelssohn - Bartholdy; Grieg, Richard Strauss (with violinist Alfred Csammer). *Hobbies:* Music; Photography; Animals; Literature. *Current Management:* Franz Günther Buscher Heidelberg, Germany.

SPEISER Elisabeth, b. 15 Oct 1940, Zurich, Switzerland. Soprano. m. Hans Jecklin, 2 children. *Education:* Academy of Music, Winterthur. *Debut:* Zurich. *Career includes:* Concerts in all European countries, North and South America; Guest at many festivals; Many concerts with Karl Richter; Opera debut as Pamina, Zauberflöte; Pamina, Ludwigsburger Schloss-Festspiele, 1972-73; Glyndebourne Festival, 1973; Mélisande, St Gallen, 1974; Euridice, Ludwigsburger Schloss-Festspiele, 1975; Many Lied-Recitals with Irwin Gage; Television and radio appearances, Germany, Italy, Switzerland; Glyndebourne Festival, 1982, Euridice, Gluck Orfeo. *Recordings include:* Secular Cantatas & Geistliche Lieder (J.S.Bach); Caecilien - Mass (Haydn); Carissimi Cantatas; Berg/Schoenberg Lieder; Gluck Orfeo ed Euridice; Schubert - Lieder, 1984 and 1989; Brahms - Lieder, 1985; Haydn: Arianna a Naxos and English songs 1987 (CD). *Membership:* Swiss

Tonkunstlerverband. *Address:* Luegete 31, 8053 Zurich, Switzerland.

SPENCE Patricia, b. 12 Jan 1961, Salem, Oregon, USA. Singer (Mezzo-soprano). *Education:* Studied in San Francisco. *Debut:* San Francisco Opera as Anna in L'Africaine. *Career:* Has performed The Princess in Suor Angelica, Mother Goose in The Rake's Progress and Meg Page in Falstaff at San Francisco; New York City debut, 1988, as Rosina; Opera Colorado, 1989, as Mistress Quickly; European debut as Edwige in Guillaume Tell at Verona, followed by Mozart's Requiem at St Petersburg, Malcolm in La Donna del Lago at La Scala, 1992, and Cenerentola with Phoenix Opera, Arizona; Further engagements as Farnace in Mitridate at St Louis, Tsaura in Tancredi at La Scala, Lola at the Arena di Verona, Cenerentola at Covent Garden (UK debut, 1993) and Ramiro in La Finta Giardinera for Welsh National Opera; Recitals at Gottingen and Hesse Handel Festivals, further Handel performances with Nicholas McGegean and appearances with San Francisco, Detroit, St Louis and Sacramento Symphonies, and Fresno and Mexico City Philharmonics. *Recordings include:* Flora in La Traviata; Handel's La Resurrezione, Messiah and Ottone, conducted by McGegean. *Honours include:* Il Cenacolo Award in the 1987 Merola Opera Programme at San Francisco Opera Center. *Address:* c/o Atholl Still Ltd, 80-86 Westrow Street, London SE19 3AF, England.

SPENCER Robert, b. 9 May 1932, Ilford, Essex, England. Lutenist; Guitarist; Singer. m. Jill Nott-Bower. *Education:* Guildhall School of Music; Dartington School of Music; LRAM. *Career:* Professor of Lute, Royal Academy of Music; Member, Bream Consort, 1960-; Member, Deller Consort, 1974-; Tours of USA and Europe; Duo with Jill Nott-Bower. *Recordings:* For RCA Victor, Philips, EMI and Argo labels. *Publications:* Elizabethan duets for two Guitars 1973; Introduction to Facsimile Lute Manuscripts 1974. *Contributions to:* New Grove Dictionary of Music and Musicians 1980; Musical Times; Early Times. *Memberships:* ISM; Lute Society.

SPERSKI Krzysztof, b. 11 June 1942, Krakow, Poland. Musician (Violoncellist), Teacher. m. Janina Duda, 24 June, 1967, divorced 1986, 1 son. *Education:* Master of Arts (cello class of Professor R Suchecki), Academy of Music, Gdansk, 1969; Doctorate (Adjunct qualification), Academy of Music, Poznan, 1978; Habilitation (Docent qualification), Academy of Music, Lodz, 1985. *Debut:* Debut recital by Association of Polish Artists Musicians, Gdansk, 1964. *Career:* Soloist of symphony concerts, recitals, chamber concerts in Poland and foreign concert tours: Finland, UK, Sweden, Germany, Romania, Bulgaria, Iceland, Czechoslovakia, Austria, Greece, Italy, Switzerland; Professor of Cello, Academy of Music, Gdansk; Guest Professor: Music Master Classes, Mynamaki, Finland, 1976; Music Seminar, Kozani, Greece, 1990, 1991; 1992. *Recordings:* Radio and Television recordings. *Publications:* About faults of position, left and right hand of young cellists, 1979; Characteristics of Musical Utterance, 1981; Remarks of Performing Violoncello Baroque Music in the Light of Traditions and Contemporary Requirements, 1988; Polish Violoncello Pedagogic Literature, 1988. *Memberships:* Association of Polish Artists Musicians. *Honours:* Award for Polish Culture, 1979; Distinction of Merit for Town of Gdansk, 1981; Gold Cross of Merit, 1985. *Hobbies:* Photography; Folklore. *Address:* ul Goralska 55/A/9, 80-292 Gdansk, Poland.

SPIEGL Fritz, b. 27 Jan 1926. Musician; Writer; Broadcaster. m. (1) 1952, Bridget Katharine Fry (marriage dissolved 1970), 3 daughters, (2) Ingrid Frances Romnes, 1976. *Education:* Magdalen College School; Royal Academy of Music (FRAM, 1986). *Career:* Designer, Typographer, Colman Prentis & Varley, 1941-46; Principal Flautist, Royal Liverpool Philharmonic, 1948-63; Occasional spare flautist: RPO; CBSO; Hallé; BBC NSO; Founder-Conductor, Liverpool Music Group, Liverpool Wind Ensemble, 1949-; Director, The Spieglers, 1975-; Columnist: Liverpool Daily Post, 1970-; Classical Music, 1979-81; The Listener: broadcasts in various capacities. *Publications:* Various editions of music. *Contributions to:* Grove's Dictionary of Music. *Hobbies:* Printing; Cooking; Inventing and several deady sins. *Address:* 4 Windermere Terrace, Liverpool L8 3SB, England.

SPIESS Ludovico, b. 13 May 1938, Cluj, Rumania. Singer (Tenor). *Education:* Studied at the Budapest Music Academy and in Milan with Antonio Narducci. *Debut:* Galati 1962, as the Duke of Mantua. *Career:* Sang operetta at the Bucharest Operetta Theatre 1962-64; Bucharest Opera from 1964, debut as Cavaradossi; Salzburg Festival 1967, as Dmitri in Boris Godunov, conducted by Karajan; Vienna Staatsoper from 1968, debut as Smetana's Dalibor; Verona Arena 1969, as Calaf in Turandot; Covent Garden debut 1973, Radames; Bregenz Festival 1974, as Don José; Appearances at the Metropolitan Opera and in Hamburg, Houston, Buenos Aires, San Francisco, Naples and Berlin; Other roles include Florestan, Rodolfo, Lohengrin and Otello. *Recordings:* Boris Godunov (Decca); Iphigénie en Aulide (Eurodisc); Khovanshchina. 21. *Address:* c/o Staatsoper, Operning 2, A-1010 Vienna, Austria.

SPINK Ian, b. 29 Mar 1932, London, England. University Professor. m. 7 children. *Education:* BMus (London 1952); MA (Birmingham 1958). *Career:* Lecturer, Senior Lecturer, University of Sydney, New South Wales, 1962-68; Senior Lecturer, Reader, Professor, London University (RHBNC) 1969-; Dean Faculty of Arts, ibid., 1973-75 and 1983-85; Dean Faculty of Music, University of London, 1974-78; Member of Senate, ibid., 1975-81. *Publications:* Principal Publications: Ed., The English Lute-Songs vol. 17, 1961, 2nd. ed 1974, vol. 18 1963, vol. 19 1966; An Historical Approach to Musical Form 1967; Ed. English Songs 1625-1660, Musica Britannica, vol. 33, 1971; English Song, Dowland to Purcell, 1974, rev. 1986; Ed. Arne, The Judgment of Paris, Musica Britannica vol. 42, 1979; Purcell, A Song for the Duke of Gloucester's Birthday, 1695 (Purcell Society Edition, Vol. 4) 1990; The Seventeenth Century (Blackwell History of Music in Britain, Vol. 3), 1992. *Address:* Royal Holloway (University of London), Egham, Surrey, TW20 OEX, England.

SPINNLER Burkard, b. 17 July 1954, Goldbach, Federal Republic of Germany. Pianist. m. Claudine Orloff, 1 Oct 1983, 2 sons. *Education:* Staatsexamen, Musikhochschule Wurzburg, with J von Karolyi, 1978; Diplome Superieur, Brussels Royal Conservatory, with J Cl Vanden Eynden, 1982; Ecole de Maitrise Pianistique, 1981-84; Private studies with Eduardo del Pueyo, Brussels. *Debut:* With University Orchestra, Wurzburg, 1978. *Career:* Recording for Bavarian Radio, 1979, for Belgian Radio RTB, 1984; Appearances as Soloist and in chamber music, Germany, Belgium, France; Special L Godowsky commemorative programme, 1989; Regular concerts on 2 pianos with Claudine Orloff, including Musique en Sorbonne, Paris, 1991; Radio engagement, Hommage a Milhaud, RTB Brussels live, 1992; Private research of Liszt unpublished works, numerological problems in Bach's music, 136 unedited letters of Francis Poulenc; Taught, Brussels Conservatory, 1985-90. *Publication:* Zur Angemessenheit traditionelles Formbegriffe in der Analyse Mahlerscher Symphonik, in Form und Idée in G Mahlers Instrumentalmusik, 1980. *Hobby:* Photography. *Current Management:* F E de Wasseige Music Management. *Address:* 82 rue des Garennes, 1170 Brussels, Belgium.

SPITKOVA Jela, b. 1947, Czechoslovakia. Violinist. *Education:* Studied at the Bratislava Conservatory and in Vienna with Riccardo Odnoposoff; Graduate, Prague College of Music; Tchaikovsky Conservatory Moscow with David and Igor Oistrakh. *Career:* Has performed with leading Czech orchestras and in 40 other countries, including those in South and North America and Africa; Recitals in Paris, Rome, Moscow, Berlin, Prague, Amsterdam and Vienna; Television and radio recordings in Spain, Norway, Denmark, Austria, France, Finland and the USSR; Leader of the Mozarteum Orchestra 1980; Teacher at the Music Academy Vienna; Soloist with the Slovak Philharmonic in Bratislava; Repertoire includes Concertos by Tchaikovsky, Brahms, Beethoven, Sibelius, Mendelssohn, Mozart, Bach and Haydn; Lalo Symphonie Espagnole; Sonatas by Brahms, Beethoven, Franck, Schumann, Prokofiev, Mozart, Handel, Debussy and Dvořák. *Recordings:* Concertos by Haydn, Sibelius, Mendelssohn and Dittersdorf; Brahms D minor sonata (Opus). *Address:* c/o Mozarteum Orchester, Schwarzstrasse 4, A-5020 Salzburg, Austria.

SPIVAKOV Vladimir, b. 12 Sept 1944, Oufa, USSR. Violinist; Conductor. *Education:* Studied at the Leningrad Conservatory with Sigal and at the Tchaikovsky Conservatory Moscow with Jankelevitch. *Career:* Concerts in Russia and Eastern Europe followed by tour of USA 1975; Played the Tchaikovsky Concerto in London 1977; Founder, leader and conductor of the Moscow Virtuosi Orchestra, played in London and elsewhere in Europe (Promenade Concert at the Albert Hall 1990, with Mozart's Symphony K201, Shostakovich Chamber Symphony, arranged by Barschai, and the Four Seasons); Artistic Director of Colmar International Festival, France; One of the founders, Sakharov Foundation for Human Rights, (Strasbourg). *Recordings:* Albums for EMI and Melodya; BUG Classics, 16 CD's. *Honours:* 3rd Prize, Long-Thibaud Competition 1965; Interpretation Prize at Montreal 1968; 2nd Prize Tchaikovsky International at Moscow 1970. *Address:* Productions Internationals Albert Sarfati, 21 Rue du Pelletier, 75009 Paris, France.

SPIVAKOVSKY Tossy, b. 4 Feb 1907, Odessa, Russia. Violinist. m. Erika Lipsker, 21 Nov 1934, 1 daughter. *Education:* Berlin Hochschule fur Musik, studied with Professor Willy Hess and Professor Arrigo Serato. *Debut:* Berlin, Germany, aged 10 years. *Career:* Recitals and orchestra appearances in Europe, Australia, New Zealand, Canada, South America and with every major orchestra in USA, including New York Philharmonic, Boston Symphony, Philadelphia, Cleveland, Chicago, Los Angeles Philharmonic, and San Francisco Symphony; Teacher, Melbourne University Conservatorium, 1933-39; Faculty, Juilliard School, New York, 1974-. *Compositions:* Cadenzas to Beethoven's Violin Concerto, and to Mozart's Violin Concertos. *Recordings:* Recordings for various recording companies. *Contributions to:* The Music Review. *Honours:* Honorary D.Litt, Fairfield University, USA, 1970; Honorary DMus, Cleveland Institute of Music, 1975. *Membership:* American Musicological Society. *Address:* 29 Burnham Hill, Westport, CT 06880, USA.

SPOORENBERG Erna, b. 11 Apr 1926, Yogyakarta, Java. Singer (Soprano). *Education:* Studied in the Netherlands with Juius Rontgen and Aaltje Noordewier-Reddingius. *Debut:* Hilversum concert 1947, with Mozart's Motet Exsultate Jubilate. *Career:* Opera debut at the Vienna Staatsoper 1949; Sang in Vienna, Hamburg (1962), Dusseldorf and Amsterdam in operas by Mozart and as Debussy's Mélisande; Bordeaux 1964, in La Dame Blanche by Boildieu; Concert tours of Germany, South Africa, the USSR, Austria and Scandinavia; US debut at Lincoln Center, New York, 1967; Recital partnership with the pianist Geza Frid. *Recordings:* Pelléas et Mélisande conducted by Ansermet, Die Schöpfung (Decca); Mahler's 8th Symphony (Deutsche Grammophon); Bach Cantatas, Masses by Haydn (Telefunken).

SPRATT Geoffrey Kenneth, b. 16 Sept 1950, London, England. University Lecturer; Conductor. m. Frances Vivien Squire, 20 July 1974, 2 sons. *Education:* BA Honours 1973, PhD 1980, University of Bristol. *Career:* Part-time Tutor, Open University 1973-76, Bristol University 1974-76; Lecturer, Music, University College, Cork, Ireland, 1976-. Conductor, University College Choir & Orchestra, Madrigal '75, Galway Baroque Singers & Orchestra; Founder-Conductor, Irish Youth Choir; Guest Conductor, Radio Telefis Eireann Symphony Orchestra, Concert Orchestra, Chorus &

Chamber Choir, & Irish Chamber Orchestra; Former professional flute & viola player, Cyprus Broadcasting Company Orchestra & freelance, various English orchestras; Director, Cork International Choral Festival, 1987-. *Recordings:* Choral Music of S. de Barra, Irish Youth Choir & Madrigal 1975. *Publictions:* Catalogue des Oeuvres de Arthur Honegger 1986, Co- author with M. Delannoy, Honegger, 1986 (Geneva & Paris); Music of Arthur Honegger (Cork), 1987. Contributions to: Music Review; Revue Musicale Suisse; Musical Opinion; Brio; Counterpoint; Music Ireland. *Honour:* Napier Miles Prize, Bristol University, 1972. *Memberships:* Chairman, Association of Irish Choirs Music Association of Ireland; International Society for Music Education; Incorporated Society of Musicians, Council. *Hobby:* Campanology. *Address:* Music Department, University College, Cork, Ireland.

SPRECHER William Gunther (Baron), b. 20 Jan 1924, Saarbrucken, Germany. Pianist; Composer; Conductor; Diplomat. m. Blossom Tag, 6 Aug 1952. *Education:* Studied piano with Professor Wittels, Tel Aviv and Madame Vengerova, New York City; Composition with Paul Ben-Haim, Tel Aviv; Conducting with Georg Singer. *Career:* Choral Repetiteur, Israel Folk Opera, Tel-Aviv, 1940-43; Piano Soloist, Israel Philharmonic Orchestra, Tel-Aviv, 1946- 48; Music Director, Station WEVD, New York City, 1969-85; President, Music Director, Bronx Philharmonic, New York City, 1971-83; Piano Soloist, 1st performance of Gershwin's Concerto in F in Israel; Assistant Pianist accompanying Lotte Lenya, Richard Tucker, Jan Peerce, Itzhak Perlman, Jan Kiepura, Ilona Massey. *Compositions:* Yinglish, song book; Piano Sonata, 1945; Jerusalem Concerto for Piano and Orchestra, 1967; Great is Thy Faith, 1970. *Recordings:* Pianist-conductor, 24 albums; Member, The First Piano Quartet. *Honours:* DFA, DHum, London Institute for Applied Research, 1993; DDiv, 1993; Knight, Order of Knight Templars of Jerusalem, 1991; Knight Commander, Lofsensic Ursinius Order, 1991; Baron, Order of Bohemian Crown, 1992; Baron of Montsalvat, 1992; Gold Cross of Honour, Austrian Albert Schweitzer Society, 1992; Knight of the Holy Grail, 1993; Count of San Ciriaco, 1993; Albert Einstein Medal, Germany, 1993; Many others. *Memberships include:* American Society of Composers, Authors and Publishers; Founder, President, Bronx Philharmonic Symphony Society Inc; American Federation of Musicians; Robert Stolz Society, UK. *Hobbies:* Walking; Jogging; Cat lover; Collecting rare musical books and recordings. *Address:* Res Montsalvat, 1D 2235 Cruger Ave, New York, NY 10467, USA.

SRABRAWA Daniel, b. 1948, Cracow, Poland. Violinist. *Education:* Studied with Z Slezer in Cracow. *Career:* Leader of Cracow Radio Symphony Orchestra, 1979; Joined Berlin Philharmonic Orchestra, 1983, and became leader, 1983; Co-founder of the Philharmonic Quartet Berlin, giving concerts throughout Europe, USA and Japan; UK debut, 1987, playing Haydn, Szymanowski and Beethoven at Wigmore Hall; Bath Festival, 1987, playing Mozart, Schumann and Beethoven (Op 127); Other repertoire includes quartets by Bartok, Mendelssohn, Nicolai, Ravel and Schubert; Quintets by Brahms, Weber, Reger and Schumann. *Address:* Anglo-Swiss Ltd, 3 Primrose Mews, 1a Sharpleshall Street, London NW1 8YW, England.

SRAMEK Alfred, b. 5 Apr 1951, Nichtelbach, Vienna, Austria. Singer (Bass). *Education:* Studied with Ludwig Weber and Hilde Zadek. *Career:* Has sung with the Vienna Staatsoper from 1975, in Palestrina, and as Don Pasquale, Dulcamara, Beckmesser, Masetto, Leporello and Figaro; Salzburg Festival from 1976, Bregenz Festival 1982; Many concert appearances. *Recordings:* Lohengrin, Wozzeck, Don Giovanni, Ariadne auf Naxos, Die Lustigen Weiber von Windsor (Decca); Karl V by Krenek (Philips); Video of Wozzeck as First Workman, conducted by Abbado (Virgin). *Address:* c/o Staatsoper, Operning 2, A-1010 Vienna, Austria.

ST HILL Krister, b. Sweden. Singer (Baritone). *Debut:* Sang Escamillo, 1982. *Career:* Roles in Sweden have included Sancho Panza in Massenet's Don Quixote, Belcore, and Nick Shadow in The Rake's Progress (Malmo City Theatre), Lord Sidney Rossini, Il Viaggio a Reims, Bohéme, Ned Keene, Peter Grimes, Valentin, Faust and Wolfram in Tannhäuser; Garsington Opera, Oxford, as Ernesto in Haydn's Il mondo della luna; Houston, returning as Donny in premiere of New Year by Tippett, 1989; Glyndebourne Opera, 1990, in UK premiere of New Year; Lieder recitals in Scandinavia and abroad include Wigmore Hall recitals with Elisabeth Söderström. *Recordings include:* 3 solo albums; Title role in Jonny Spielt Auf by Krenek; Hindemith, Requiem. *Address:* Nordic Artists Management, Sveavagen 76, S-11359 Stockholm Sweden.

STAAHLEN Torhild, b. 25 Sept 1947, Skien, Norway. Opera Singer (Mezzo-soprano). m. Neil Dodd, 23 June 1975. *Education:* Studied with Aase Nordmo Lovberg and Marit Isene in Oslo, Clemens Kaiser-Breme in Essen and Bayreuth, Audrey Langford in London, Hannah Ludwig in Salzburg, Ingalill Linden in Gothenburg, Ellen Sundbye in Oslo, and dramatic soprano Ingrid Bjoner. *Debut:* Suzuki in Madam Butterfly, Oslo, 1971. *Career:* Wide range of mezzo-alto repertoire including: Title role in Carmen, Valencienne in The Merry Widow, Octavian in Der Rosenkavalier, Prince Orlovsky in Die Fledermaus, Olga in Eugene Onegin, Azucena in Il Trovatore, Ulrica in Un Ballo in Maschera, Amneris in Aida, Erda in Rheingold, Waltraute in Gotterdammerung; Frequently sings in oratorio, especially with all Bach Passions and Handel's Messiah; Concert repertoire includes Brahms' Alto Rhapsody, Wagner's Wesendonck Lieder, Beethoven's 9th Symphony, Mahler's 2nd and 4th Symphonies, Elgar's Sea Pictures, P Heise's Bergljot, Handel's Samson, Pergolesi's Stabat Mater; Has sung under such conductors as Heinrich Hollreiser, Paavo Berglund, Martin Turnovsky, Miltiades Caridis, Jiri Starek and Maurice Handford; Frequent radio and TV appearances. *Recording:* Expression, 1991. *Honours:* Numerous awards including: State Artist's Stipendium; Fund for Performing Artists; Rettspresident Klaestads Stipendium; Prize of Honour, Friends of Music in Telemark, 1981. *Membership:* Norsk Tonekunstner Samfund. *Hobbies:* Antiques; Dolls. *Address:* Munkerudveien 59c, 1165 Oslo, Norway.

STABELL Carsten, b. 5 Sept 1960, Trondheim, Norway. Singer (Bass). *Education:* Studied at the Norwegian Opera School, Oslo. *Debut:* Oslo 1984, as the King in Aida; Stuttgart Opera from 1986, as Osmin, Sarastro, the Commendatore, Pietro in Simon Boccanegra and the Hermit in Der Freischütz; Sang Rustomji in Satyagraha by Philip Glass, 1990; Concert repertoire includes Bach's Magnificat and St John Passion, Messiah, Judas Maccabeus, Acis and Galatea (Polyphemus), Die Schöpfung, the Requiems of Mozart and Verdi and Liszt's Christus; Engaged as The Commendatore, Opera Geneva, and Sarastro at the Opéra de Paris Bastille 1991, and in Perseo e Andromeda, La Scala Milano, 1992. *Address:* C30 Staatstheater Stuttgart, Oberer Schlossgarten 6, D-7000 Stuttgart 1, Germany.

STABRAWA Daniel, b. 1950, Krakow, Poland. Violinist. *Education:* Studied at the Krakow High School. *Career:* Leader, Krakow Symphony Orchestra, 1979; Member, Berlin Philharmonic, 1983, leader from 1986; Co-founder and leader, Philharmonia Quartet Berlin 1980; Many concerts in Europe, notably at the Salzburg Festivals, Bath Festival (1990), Wigmore Hall, London and the Berlin Festival 1991, with works by Mozart; Annual visits to Japan from 1986; International career as solo violinist. *Recordings include:* CD of quartets by Beethoven (Camerata/Tokyo). *Address:* c/o Anglo-Swiss Management, 4-5 Primrose Mews, Sharpeshall Street, London NW1 8YW, England.

STACEY Brian James, b. 3 Dec 1946, Sydney, New South Wales, Australia. Musician (Conductor, Coach). div., 2 daughters. *Education:* Dip Mus (Ed), Sydney Conservatorium of Music; BMus, 1968, 1st class hons, 1976, MMus, 1980, University of Queensland; Studied piano with Annie Brigden, Ramsay Pennicuick and Frank Hutchens; Studied with and was assistant to Sir Charles Mackerras, London, 1981-83. *Career:* Music Director, Queensland Ballet Co, 1976-80; Head of Music, Lyric Opera of Queensland, 1980-82; Music Director, The Australian Ballet, 1983-84; Head of Music, Victoria State Opera, 1985-88; Music Director, Australian production of The Phantom of the Opera, 1990-92; Freelance Conductor, 1993-. *Recordings:* Centre Stage, Anthony Warlow with Melbourne Symphony Orchestra, 1991; Leading Lady, Marina Prior with Melbourne Symphony Orchestra, 1991; On the Boards, Anthony Warlow with Melbourne Symphony Orchestra, 1992; Aspects of Andrew Lloyd Webber, Marina Prior and Melbourne Symphony Orchestra, 1992; An Evening of Classics with the State Orchestra of Victoria. *Publication:* Music with Hearing Impaired (with Hilary Mackerras), Journal of Hearing, 1979. *Honours:* Commonwealth Post-Graduate Fellowship, 1978. *Membership:* Australian National Association of Teachers of Singing. *Hobbies:* Cooking; Motor-cycle riding. *Current Management:* Performers' Management. *Address:* 377 Clarke St, Northcote, Victoria 3070, Australia.

STADELMANN Christian, b. 1958, Berlin, Germany. Violinist. *Education:* Studied with Charlotte Hampe and in Berlin. *Career:* Former member of the Junge Deutsche Philharmonie and its Chamber Orchestra; Member of the Berlin Philharmonic from 1985, leader of the 2nd violins 1987; Co-founder and second violinist of the Philharmonia Quartet Berlin 1980; Many concerts in Europe, notably at the Salzburg Festivals, Bath Festival (1990), Wigmore Hall, London and the Berlin Festival 1991, with works by Mozart; Annual visits to Japan from 1986; International career as solo violinist. *Recordings include:* CD of quartets by Beethoven (Camerata/Tokyo). *Address:* c/o Anglo-Swiss Management, 4-5 Primrose Mews, Sharpeshall Street, London NW1 8YW, England.

STADLEN Peter, b. 14 July 1910, Vienna, Austria. Writer on Music; Lecturer; Pianist. m. Hedi Simon, 2 sons. *Education:* Vienna Hochschule für Musik with Paul Weingarten (piano) and Joseph Marx (composition); 1929-33 Berlin Hochschule für Musik. *Career:* Concert pianist from 1934, giving the world premieres of Webern's Variations, 1937 and Krenek's Bagatelles, 1936 and local premieres of Schoenberg's Piano Concerto and Hindemith's Four Temperaments; Settled in England 1939; Master classes at Darmstadt 1947-51; Series of Lectures The Rise and Decline of Serialism, London 1960; Music Critic with Daily Telegraph from 1960 (chief music critic 1977-86); Lecturer in music at Reading University 1965-69; Visiting Fellow of All Souls Oxford 1967-68. *Publications:* Articles in Score, Musical Times, Music and Letters, Soundings, Oesterr. Musikgeltschrift, Congress Reports and other journals: Serialism Reconsidered, The Webern Legend, The Aesthetics of Popular Music, Beethoven and the Metronome, Schoenberg and Sprechgesang, Schindler's Beethoven Forgeries; Berg's Cryptography, Edition of Webern's Piano Variations with facsimiles of the composer's instructions, Exiled Austrian Musicians in Great Britain. *Honours:* Schoenberg Medal, Austrian Section of ISCM, 1952. *Memberships:* Royal Musical Association; Royal Philharmonic Society; Gesellschaft für Musikforschung; Schoenberg Gesellschaft; Critics' Circle; ISM.*Address:* 49 Downshire Hill, London NW3, England.

STADLER Irmgard, b. 28 Mar 1937, Michaelbeuren, Salzburg, Austria. Singer (Soprano). *Education:* Studied at the Salzburg Mozarteum and at the Vienna Academy of Music. *Debut:* Stuttgart 1962, as Micaela. *Career:* Salzburg Festival 1961-62, in Idomeneo, Mozart's Requiem 1962-63; Glyndebourne Festival 1967-72, as Sicle in L'Ormindo, Donna Elvira, Juno in La Calisto and the Composer (Ariadne auf Naxos); Stuttgart 1983, as Marie in Wozzeck; Guest appearances in Vienna, Munich, Berlin, Lisbon, Venice and Roma; Other roles include Eva, Gutrune, Jenůfa, Marenka in The Bartered Bride, Rusalka, Katya Kabonova, Lisa (The Queen of

Spades), Tatiana, Fiordiligi, Alice, Marina, Octavian and the Marschallin; Sang in Satyagraha by Philip Glass at Stuttgart, 1990; Concert appearances in sacred music by Bach and Mozart. *Address:* c/o Staatstheater Stuttgart, Oberer Schlossgarten 6, D-7000 Stuttgart 1, Germany.

STADLMAIR Hans, b. 3 May 1929, Neuhofen, Austria. Conductor. *Education:* Studied at the Vienna Academy of Music, 1946-52 with Clemens Krauss and Alfred Uhl and in Stuttgart 1952-56 with and Johann Nepomuk David. *Career:* Conducted the Stuttgart Chorus and became conductor of Munich Chamber Orchestra 1956: tours of Europe, North and South America, Asia, Africa, Canada and India; Has conducted own realisation of the Adagio from Mahler's 10th Symphony; Composed Concerto Profano for violin, cello and orchestra; Concerto capriccioso for two flutes and orchestra (composed for A Nicolet and J Pierre Rampal); Adagietto for strings, Ecce Homo, 5 Novelletten for strings. *Recordings:* W A Mozart, Piano Concertos Nr 8 KV 246, Lützow and Nr 9 KV 271, Jeunehomme; F Danzi: Phantasie on La ci darem la mano from Don Giovanni, C Stamitz; concerto for clarinet Nr 3 B-flat (E Brunner - clarinet); Haydn's Last Seven Words; Scarlatti Il Giardino di Amore; Mozart Bassoon Concerto, Clarinet Concerto and Violin Concerto K219; Vivaldi Four Seasons. *Address:* Münchener Kammerorchester EV, Wittelsbacherpl 2, D-80333 Munich, Germany.

STADLMAIR Vincent, b. 1959, Vienna, Austria. Cellist. *Education:* Studied at the Vienna Academy of Music. *Career:* Member of the Franz Schubert Quartet, Vienna, from 1983; Many concert engagements in Europe, the USA, Australia, including appearances at the Amsterdam Concertgebouw, the Vienna Musikverein and Konzerthaus, the Salle Gaveau Paris and the Sydney Opera House; Visits to Zurich, Geneva, Basle, Berlin, Hamburg, Rome, Rotterdam, Madrid and Copenhagen; Festival engagements include Salzburg, Wiener Festwochen, Prague, Spring Schubertiade at Hohenems, the Schubert Festival at Washington DC and the Belfast and Istanbul Festivals; Tours of Australasia, the USSR, USA; Frequent concert tours of Great Britain; Featured in the Concerto by Spohr with the Liverpool Philharmonic in Liverpool, the Festival Hall; Many appearances at the Wigmore Hall and Cheltenham Festival; Teacher at the Vienna Conservatory and Graz Musikhochschule; Masterclasses at the Royal Northern College of Music, Lake District Summer Music. *Recordings include:* Schubert's Quartet in G, D887; Complete quartets of Dittersdorf; Mozart: String Quartet in D, K575, String Quartet in B Flat, K589. *Address:* c/o Unit 2, 39 Tadema Road, London SW10 0PY, England.

STAEHELIN Martin, b. 25 Sept 1937, Basel, Switzerland. Musicologist. m. Elisabeth Schenker. *Education:* Diploma, Teacher Querflöte, 1962, School Music Diploma, 1963, Music Academy, Basel; PhD, University of Basel, 1967. *Career:* Teacher, Latin, Greek, Music, Basel, 1963; Musicology Teacher, University of Zurich, 1971-76; Head, Beethoven Archives, Bonn, Federal Republic of Germany, 1976-84; Teacher, 1976-77, Professor, 1977-83, University of Bonn; Professor, University of Gottingen, 1983-; Hon. Director of J S Bach-Institut, Göttingen, 1992. *Publications:* Editor, H.Isaac, Messen, 1970, 1973; Der Grüne Codex der Viadrina, 1971; Die Messen Heinrich Isaacs, 3 volumes, 1977. *Contributions to:* Archiv für Musikwissenschaft; Die Musikforschung; Fontes Artis Musicae; Schweizerische Beitrage zur Musikwissenschaft; Tijdschrift van de Vereniging voor Nederlandse Muziekgeschiedenis; Schweizerisches Archiv für Volkskunde. *Memberships:* Musicological Commission, Academy of the Sciences, Mainz; Akademie der Wissenschaften, Göttingen; Academia Europaea, London. *Honour:* Dent Medal, Royal Musical Association, 1975. *Address:* Musicology Seminar of Georg August University, 1, D-37073 Göttingen, Germany.

STAFFORD Ashley George, b. 3 Mar 1954, Holland,

Near Oxted, Surrey, England. Singer (Counter-Tenor). m. Shauni Lee McGregor, 4 June 1977, 2 sons. *Education:* Westminster Abbey Choir School, 1963-68; Trinity School, Croydon, 1968-72; Christchurch, Oxford, Choral Award, Academical Clerkship, 1972-75; BA Hons, 1975, MA, 1978; Certificate of Education, London, 1976; Musical Education: Choir School: Tutelage of Douglas Guest, Oxford under Simon Preston; Vocal Training: Hervey Alan, 1968-72, Paul Esswood, 1972-76, Helga Mott, 1976-80, Jessica Cash, 1980-93. *Debut:* Purcell Room, London, Dec. 1975. *Career:* Opera: Aix-en-Provence, Lyon, Oxford, London; Concerts: Major Festivals in every European country, Australia (Sydney & Melbourne 1989), Japan 1987 & 1989, Taiwan 1989, USA and Canada, including Bath, Edinburgh, Three Choirs, Aix-en-Provence, Seine Maritime, Göttingen, Berlin, Wroclaw, Rome, Venice, Perugia, Pompaeii, Provence, Madrid, Barcelona, Lisbon, Minneapolis, New York, Washington, Boston, Toronto, Ottawa, 1980-86; Sang in Judith Weir's A Night at the Chinese Opera for Kent Opera; BBC, Dutch, French, WDR, NDR, SDR radio stations; TV: Messiah in France; Visiting Professor (Voice) Royal College of Music, London, 1989. *Recordings:* Purcell; Ode to St Cecilia, King Arthur, From the Nativity of Time (Songs Sacred and Secular); Handel: Israel in Egypt; Dettingen Te Deum; F Valls, Mass Scala Aretina; Motets by Power, Dunstable and Josquin; Haydn: Nelson Mass; Bach: Motets; Scarlatti: Stabat Mater, Further recordings for DGG and Philips including: Schütz: Muzikalisches Exequien; Handel: Alexander's Feast. *Honour:* Young Musician, Greater London Arts Association. *Memberships:* Incorporated Society of Musicians; Equity, Committee Member; Royal Society of Musicians. *Hobbies:* Gardening; Squash; Table tennis; Computing; Cycling. *Address:* Fenton House, Banbury Road, Chipping Norton, Oxon OX7 5AW, England.

STAHL David, b. 4 Nov 1949, New York, NY, USA. Conductor. m. Karen Doss Stahl, 1989, 1 son, 1 daughter. *Education:* Queens College of the City University of New York, B.A., 1972, M.A., M.M., 1974. *Career:* Debut, Carnegie Hall, N.Y., 8 Dec 1973; assistant conductor, New York Philharmonic, 1976, and Cincinnati Symphony Orchestra, 1976-79; music director, St. Louis Philharmonic, 1976-81; Broadway and international tour of West Side Story, 1980-82; Charleston (SC) Symphony Orchestra, 1984-; guest conductor, Pittsburgh, Atlanta, Dallas, Indianapolis, St. Louis, Buffalo, Baltimore, Long Beach, Edmonton, Winnipeg, and Louisville symphonies; New York City Opera, Spoleto Festival, Lake George Opera, Dayton, Detroit, Hawaii and Tulsa opera companies; overseas: RAI orchestra, Rome, Teatro Massimo, Palermo, Teatro Comunale, Genoa, Festival of two worlds, Spoleto, Orchestre Colonne, Paris, Orchestra del Sodre, Montevideo and Seoul (South Korea) Philharmonic, Toronto Symphony Orchestra, Montreal Opera, Washington Opera; Stadtheater National Mannheim, Concertgebouw Amsterdam. *Recordings:* Proto concertos for double bass. *Current Management:* Colbert Artists Management, Inc., 111 West 57th Street, New York, NY 10019, USA. *Address:* 14 George Street, Charleston, SC 29401, USA.

STAHLAMMER Semmy, b. 5 Mar 1954, Eskilstuna, Sweden. Musician; Violinist. *Education:* Soloist Diploma, Royal Music College, Stockholm, 1972; Juilliard School of Music, USA, 1972-74; BMus, Curtis Institute of Music, 1975-79; Teachers: Jaime Laredo, Ivan Galamian, Felx Galimir, Isidore Cohen, Szymon Goldberg, Paul Makanowitsky, Josef Silverstein, Josef Gingold; Nathan Milstein, Isaac Stern and Henryk Szeryng. *Debut:* With Stockholm Philharmonic Orchestra, 1964. *Career:* 1st Concertmaster, Stockholm Royal Opera, 1979-83; Artistic Director, Chamber Music in the Mirror Hall, 1982-; Artistic Director, Chamber Music in the Parks, 1986-; Teacher, Stockholm Royal Music College, 1987-. *Recordings:* Collections of Swedish 20th Century music; Alfred Schnittke: Labyrinths; J S Bach: Sonatas and partitas for solo violin. *Honours:* Winner, J S Bach International Violin Competition, Washington, DC, 1985. *Hobbies:* Violin maker and restorer; Sports. *Address:* Norr Mälarstrand 24, 112 20 Stockholm, Sweden.

STAHLMAN Sylvia, b. 5 Mar 1929, Nashville, Tennessee, USA. Singer (Soprano). *Education:* Studied at the Juilliard School, New York. *Career:* Sang first on Broadway; Théâtre de la Monnaie Brussels 1951-54, debut as Elvira in I Puritani; Brussels and Amsterdam as Lucia di Lammermoor and Meyerbeer's Dinorah; Engaged at the Frankfurt Opera 1954-72; New York City Opera 1956, as Blondchen; Glyndebourne Festival 1959, as Ilia in Idomeneo; Chicago 1960, Metropolitan Opera 1961; Santa Fe 1964, in the US premiere of Daphne by Strauss; Sang at Aix-en-Provence, 1967; Frankfurt-am-Main, 1959-70. *Recordings:* Un Ballo in Maschera, La Sonnambula, Mahler's 4th Symphony, Haydn Lord Nelson Mass (Decca); Belshazzar by Handel (Vox).

STAICU Paul, b. 7 June 1937, Bucharest, Rumania. Conductor; Professor; Horn-Player (solo). m. Irina Botez, 6 July 1963, 1 son. *Education:* Graduate Diploma, Horn, Prague Academy of Music, 1961; Graduate Diploma, Vienna Academy of Music, studied with conductor Hans Swarowsky. *Debut:* As Horn Soloist, 1954, as Conductor, 1963, Bucharest Radio and Philharmonic Orchestra. *Career:* Horn Soloist, 1954-79; Solo Horn, Bucharest Philharmonic, 1961-69; Chief Conductor of Chamber Orchestra, 1966; Professor of Chamber Music, 1966-; Camerate, 1978; H. von Karajan Foundation, Medal with Camerata, orchestra 1974; Professor of Horn, 1969-89, Chief Conductor of Symphony Orchestra, 1975-78, Bucharest Music Academy; Chief Conductor, Symphony and Chamber Orchestra, Constanta Rumania, 1978-89; Professor, Conservatoire of Music, Montbeliard, France, 1990; Director, School of Music, Exincourt, France, 1990; Chief Conductor, Ensemble Orchestral Montbeliard, France, 1992; TV and radio performances in Rumania and abroad; Summer classes, Bayreuth, Gourdon, Europe, USA and Canada tours; Membership, Munich and Prague International Music Competitions. *Recordings:* Electrorecord, Romania, Nr 3, Beethoven Horn Sonata; Mozart, Beethoven, Quintets; Mozart Horn Concertos, Soloist and Conductor; Haydn Concertos, Conductor; Haydn Symphonies 100-103, Conductor; Radio: Beethoven Symphony No 14, Schoenberg Verkärte nacht, Shostakovitch Symphony No 4. *Publications:* Studiu introductiv si exercitii zilnice pentru corn (Introductory studies and daily exercises for horn). *Address:* 43, rue du Croissant, 25400 Exincourt, France.

STAIER Andreas, b. 13 Sept 1955, Göttingen, Germany. Harpsichordist; Pianist. *Education:* Baccalaureat In Göttingen; Studies in piano, harpsichord, chamber music in Hanover and Amsterdam. *Career:* Harpsichordist in Musica Antiqua, Köln, 1983-86; Professor, Schola Cantorum, Basle, Switzerland, 1987; Concerts in USA, Europe and Australia. *Recordings:* Haydn piano Sonatas; J S Bach harpsichord works; CPE Bach harpsichord works; Chamber music; Lieder. *Current Management:* Jean Michel Forest, Claudia Nitoche. *Address:* Rolandstr 65, D-50677 Köln 1, Germany.

STAJNC Jaroslav, b. 7 May 1943, Prague, Czechoslovakia. Singer (Bass-baritone). *Education:* Studied at Prague Conservatoire and Vienna Music Academy. *Debut:* Vienna Volksoper 1968, as the Hermit in Der Freischutz. *Career:* Vienna 1968, in the premiere of Der Zerrissene by Gottfried von Einem; Member of the Deutsche Oper am Rhein Dusseldorf and made guest appearances in Graz, Brno, Florence, Athens and Vancouver; Bregenz Festival 1983, as Kaspar in Der Freischütz; Other roles have included Kecal (The Bartered Bride), Orestes in Elektra, Dulcamara, Dikoy (Katya Kabanova), Rossini's Basilio, Mustafà (L'Italiana in Algeri) and Tiresias in Oedipus Rex; Wagner repertoire includes Fasolt, Fafner and Hunding, in Der Ring des Nibelungen; Many concert appearances. *Recordings:* Albums of operas by Smetana and other Czech composers for Supraphon; Il Lutto dell' universo, by Emperor Leopold I of Austria. *Address:* c/o Deutsche Oper am Rhein, Heinrich-Heine Allee 16, D-4000 Dusseldorf, Germany.

STALDER Hans Rudolf, b. 9 July 1930, Zurich, Switzerland. Clarinettist; Musician. m. Ursula Burkhard, 11 Apr 1957. *Education:* Konservatorium, Zurich; Bayerisches Staatskonservatorium, Wurzburg, Germany; Private studies with Louis Cahuzac, Paris. *Career:* International Soloist on Clarinet, Bassenthorn and Chalumeau, also with Chamber Music Groups including Stalder-Quintet, Zurich Chamber Ensemble, Zurich Clarinet Trio; Teacher at Musik-Akademie, Basle and Schola Cantorum Basiliensis. *Recordings:* First recording of Mozart Clarinet Concerto in original version with Bassetclarinet, 1968 (Schwann); Bassethorn Concerto from A.Rolla (Schwann); Das Chalumeau-ein Portrait, Harmonia Mundi; Various recordings on Disco, Philips, Musicaphon, Ex Libris, Electrola and EMI. *Memberships:* Schweizerischer Tonkunstlerverein. *Address:* Wengi 2, CH-8126 Zumikon, Switzerland.

STALHEIM Jostein, b. 23 July 1960, Voss, Norway. Composer; Accordionist. m. Ingvei Eikaas, 31 July 1982, 2 daughters. *Education:* Royal Danish Conservatory of Music, 1979-87; Norwegian Music High School, 1987-79; Exam in Composition, Oslo, 1989. *Debut:* Accordionist, Oslo and Copenhagen, 1987; Composition, 1989. *Career:* Appearances: NRK-TV, BBC-TV, SR-TV; Ung Nordisk Solist, 1984; MIDEM festival in Cannes, 1985; Soloist with orchestra, Oslo, Copenhagen, Gothenburg, Gdansk, Karlstad, Trondheim; His opera Dr Warrant's Progress performed in Bergen, 1993; Teacher, North Norwegian Conservatory of Music. *Compositions:* To-tve-tvil, string quartet, 1993; Allusion, piano solo, 1993; Tanchoreiaredas for orchestra and 3 soloists, 1993; Dr Warrants Progress, chamber opera, 1993; Indisium, composer's evening, 1993. *Recording:* In real time, with Inside, Norway. *Honours:* State Grant, 1993; Travel Grant, Norsk Komponistforening. *Memberships:* Musikerforbund; Norsk Komponistforening. *Hobby:* House building. *Address:* Ibsensgt 127, N-5037 Solheimsviken, Norway.

STALLMAN Robert Wooster, Jr, b. 12 June 1946, Boston, Massachusetts, USA. Flautist. m. Hannah Woods, 26 Sept 1981. *Education:* BMus 1968, MMus 1971, New England Conservatory of Music; Paris Conservatoire, France, 1968-69. *Debut:* Merkin Concert Hall, New York City, 1980. *Career:* Major solo appearances include: Library of Congress; Carnegie Hall; Weill Hall at Carnegie Recital Hall; Alice Tully Hall; Avery Fisher Hall; Symphony Hall, Boston; Salle Pleyel, Paris; Suntory Hall, Tokyo; St John's, Smith Square, London; Radio: Boston, New York, Nationwide USA, Canada. Guest artist appearances include: American Symphony, Mostly Mozart Festival, Netherlands Chamber Orchestras; Lincoln Center Chamber Music Society; Concerto Soloists of Philadelphia; Speculum Musicae; Muir, Mendelssohn and Orion String Quartets. Festivals: Canada, Finland, France, Holland, Japan, USA, Académie Internationale d'Eté, Nice, France, 1985; Boston Conservatory, 1986-90; Aaron Copland School of Music, Queens College, New York, 1980-. Master Classes, USA, Canada, Mexico, England, France, Japan. Founder, Artistic Director, Cambridge Chamber Players and Marblehead Music Festival, 1976-. Flute concertos written for him by (1986). *Recordings:* Dodgson Concerto with the Northern Sinfonia (Biddulph Records); McKinley Concerto with the Prism Orchestra (Owl Records). ASV releases include: The American Flute (20th c. works); Schubert Sonatas; Vivaldi Concerti. *Current Management:* Randall Fostvedt, 240 West End Ave. Suite 7C, New York, NY 10023, USA. *Address:* 408 W. 20th Street, New York, NY 10011, USA.

STALMAN Roger Claude, b. 30 July 1927, Uxbridge, England. Singer (Bass); Singing Teacher; Adjudicator. m. Jean Dorothy Kew, 1 son. *Education:* London University; Music studies wirth Eric Greene and Frederic Jackson. *Debut:* 1952. *Career:* Concerts, Opera, Recitals throughout UK and Western Europe, also in Israel and Canada; 250 performances of Handel's Messiah, including TV appearances; Berlin Festival 1967; Papal Concert, and tour of Israel in Stravinsky's Oedipus Rex, 1968. *Recordings:* Performances of Messiah conducted by Walter Susskind and by Frederick Jackson; Cathedral Music from Salisbury; Purcell Odes; Panufnik's Universal Prayer. *Honour:* ABSM 1970. *Address:* Came House, Monument Lane, Chalfont St Peter, Bucks., SL9 OHY, England.

STALMANN Joachim, b. 2 July 1931, Gottingen, Germany. Musician; Theologian. m. 19 July 1962, 1 son, 3 daughters. *Education:* Studied Theology, Philosophy, Musicology and Church Music at Gottingen, Tubingen, Munich and Basel, 1951-56; PhD, Musicology, Tubingen, 1960; Ordained Lutheran Minister, 1962. *Career:* Priest in Bremke, near Gottingen; Positions in Divine Service and in Church Music, Hanover, 1972-; Lecturer, College of Music, Dettmold, 1984-. *Publications:* Johann Walter, Samtliche Werke, vol VI, 1970; Georg Rhau, Neue deutsche geistliche Gesange, 1992; Handbuch zum Evangelischen Kirchengesangbuch (ed Georg Rhau). *Contributions to:* Die Musikforschung; Der Kirchenmusiker; Musik und Kirche; Musik en Geschichte und Gegenwart; Zied; Theological articles. *Honours:* Honorary Professor. *Memberships:* Gesellschaft fur Musikforschung; Chairman, Gesellschaft zur wissenschaftlichen Edition des deutschen Kirchenlieds. *Address:* Gorlitzer Strasse 16, D-31311 Uetze, Germany.

STAM Hendrikus Gerardus (Henk), b. 26 Sept 1922, Utrecht, Netherlands. Composer; Author; Lecturer; Pianist. m. Ienske Sterk, 1 child (3 by previous marriage). *Education:* Utrecht Conservatory; Utrecht State University; Study of composition and music reviewing, Germany. *Career:* Music Critic, Nieuw Utrechts Dagblad; Teacher, Municipal School of Music, Deventer; Principal, Zealand School of Music, 1954-62; Conductor, Society for Instrumental Music, Middleburg, 1954-60; Principal, Rotterdam School of Music, 1962-72; Lecturer, AVRO (Dutch Broadcasting Association). *Compositions:* 5 sonatinas for piano; Overture de Ruyter, orchestra; Hommage à Valéry, accordion band; Cassation, ballet, mime;Chamber music including: Sonatas for flute, violin, cello, piano; Suite, violin and piano; Sonata, unaccompanied violin; Serenade, unaccompanied cello; 3 string quartets. *Recording:* 3rd String Quartet. *Publications:* Robert Schumann, biography, 1948; Introduction to Contemporary Music, 1953; Programme Music, 1959. *Honour:* Ruytermedal, 1957. *Membership:* Honorary Member, KNTV (Royal Dutch Society of Musicians). *Hobbies:* Model trains; Collecting old guide books; Theology. *Address:* Noorderend 30, NL 9265 LN Suwâld, Netherlands.

STAMENOVA Galina, b. 5 Oct 1958, Sofia, Bulgaria. Violinist. *Education:* Musical studies from age 5 with her mother; Studies with Dorothy Delay, Juilliard School of Music, New York, USA. *Debut:* With André Previn and London Symphony Orchestra, Royal Festival Hall, London; American debut with Dallas Symphony, 1984. *Career:* Performances with most leading British orchestras, Antwerp Philharmonic and orchestras in Bulgaria; Radio and television appearances in Bulgaria, Netherlands, UK and Belgium; Accomplished recitalist having appeared at Harrogate and Aspen music festivals, live on BBC and Radio VARA in Netherlands and several other European countries. *Recordings:* Saint-Saëns No 3, Chausson-Poème, Sofia Radio Orchestra, Vassil Stefanov conducting. *Honours include:* Several 1st prizes for young violinists. *Hobbies:* Theatre; Arts; Ballet. *Address:* 33 Greinstraat, 2060 Antwerp, Belgium.

STAMM Harald, b. 29 Apr 1938, Frankfurt am Main, Germany. Singer (Bass). *Education:* Studied with Franz Fehringer. *Debut:* Gelsenkirchen 1968. *Career:* Sang at Cologne and Frankfurt; Hamburg Staatsoper 1975, in the premiere of Der Gestiefelte Kater by Bialas; Many appearances in German opera houses and in Budapest, Venice, Rome and Nice; Metropolitan Opera from 1979; Salzburg Festival 1985, in the Henze version of Monteverdi's Ulisse; Bregenz Festival 1986, as Sarastro in Die Zauberflöte; Other roles include Mozart's Commendatore, Beethoven's Rocco, Verdi's Grand Inquisitor and Zaccaria, Wagner's Daland, Marke, Fasolt and Hunding and Massenet's Don Quixote; Covent Garden debut 1987, as Raimondo in Lucia di Lammermoor; Sang the King in Schreker's Der Schatzgräber at Hamburg (1989), King Henry in Lohengrin at Brussels and Lisbon, 1990; Season 1992 as Gurnemanz at Essen; Also heard in recital and concert.*Honours:* nominated Kammersänger by the Hamburg Opera, 1989; Nominated Professor at the Hochschule der Künste Berlin, 1993. *Recordings:* Lieder by Liszt and Franz; Vier Ernste Gesänge by Brahms; Dittersdorf's Doktor und Apotheker; Schumann's Manfred; Massimila Doni by Schoeck. *Address:* c/o Hamburgische Staatsoper, Grosse-Theaterstrasse 34, D-20354 Hamburg, Germany.

STÄMPFLI Jakob, b. 26 Oct 1934, Berne, Switzerland. Singer (Bass). *Education:* Studied at the Berne Conservatory and in Frankfurt with Paul Lohmann. *Career:* Gave concerts in Germany while still a student; Sang with the Chorus of St Thomas' Leipzig. conducted by Gunter Ramin; Many performances of sacred music by Bach in Europe, the USA and Japan; Sang also with the Schola Cantorum Basiliensis; Lieder recitals with music by Brahms, Schubert and Schumann; Professor at the Saarbrücken Muiskhochschule from 1960, then at the Hamburg Musikhochschule. *Recordings:* Cantatas by Buxtehude (Deutsche Grammophon); Bach Cantatas, Monteverdi Orfeo (Columbia); Christmas Oratorio, St Matthew Passion and Magnificat by Bach; Plutone in L'Orfeo, conducted by Michel Corboz (Erato). *Address:* c/o Hochschule für Musik, Harvestehuderweg 12, 2000 Hamburg 13, Germany.

STANCZYK Anna Maria, b. 12 Sept 1948, Opoczno, Poland, Concert Pianist. 1 daughter. *Education:* MA, Chopin Academy of Music, Warsaw, 1975; Postgraduate studies with Louis Kentner, 1976-86. *Debuts:* Slupsk Pianists Festival, Poland, 1975; Wigmore Hall, London, 1976. *Career:* 800 concerts, radio and TV performances have been performed in Europe, USA, Canada, Cuba, Far East, USSR. *Recordings:* Polish Romance, White Tower Records (cassette), Pronit (disc); Szymanowski Piano Music, Libra (cassette); Polskie Nagrania (disc, cassette); Liszt Piano Music, (disc & cassette); Arston, Maria Szymanowska, (disc & cassette). *Honours:* Slupsk Pianists Festival Prize, 1975; Hungarian Government Scholarship, 1976; Liszt Medal, Hungarian Ministry of Culture, 1986. *Current Management:* Douglas Reed, Artists Management, 30 Beresford Road, Kingston Upon Thames, Surrey KT2 6LR, England. *Memberships:* Polish Association of Musicians; Incorporated Society of Musicians, England. *Hobbies:* Literature; Poetry; Art; Florestry; Sport; Dancing; Travel. *Address:* Secretariat, Dennis Carr, 61 Reedway, Spinney Hill, Northampton NN3 1BT, England.

STANDAGE Simon, b. 8 Nov 1941, High Wycombe, Buckinghamshire, England. Violinist. *Education:* Studied at Bryanston School and Cambridge; Violin studies with Ivan Galamian in New York, 1967-69. *Career:* Associate member of the London Symphony Orchestra and deputy leader of the English Chamber Orchestra; Appointed Leader of the English Concert, 1973; Leader of the Richard Hickox Orchestra and the City of London Sinfonia; Founded the Salomon Quartet 1981; performances of the 18th Century repertoire with original instruments; Teacher of Baroque violin at the Royal Academy of Music from 1983; Founded Collegium Musicum 90, 1990; Appointed Associate Director, Academy of Ancient Music, 1991; With Maggie Cole, played Beethoven's violin sonatas op. 24 and op. 30 No. 2, BBC, 1992. *Recordings:* Haydn Quartets op.71, op.74 and op.77; Mozart mature string quartets, string quintets, piano quartets and clarinet quintet; Beethoven op.18; Haydn 100 and 104 symphonies (arranged by Salomon). *Address:* 106 Hervey Road, London SE3, England.

STANDFORD Patric, b. 5 Feb 1939, Barnsley, Yorkshire, England. Composer. m. Sarah Blyth Hilton, 2 sons, 1 daughter. *Education:* GGSM, London, 1963;

992 INTERNATIONAL WHO'S WHO IN MUSIC

FGSM, London, 1973; MMus, London, 1979; Studied with Rubbra, Mendelssohn Scholarship, extended studies, Malipiero in Italy: Lutoslawski in Poland; Stanley Glasser at London University. *Career:* Professor of Composition, Guildhall School of Music, London, 1969-80; Head of Music School, Bretton Hall College, Yorkshire, 1980-1993. *Compositions include:* 5 symphonies (1971-85); Cello Concerto; Violin Concerto; Oratorio Christus Requiem; Messiah Reborn, 1993; 3 string quartets; Choral and instrumental works; Opera Villon; Film and Video Music. *Recordings:* Autumn Grass; Ancient Verses; String Music. *Contributions to:* Musical Times; Composer; Musical Opinion; Set to Music; Yorkshire Post. *Honours:* Premio, Citta di Trieste, 1972; Oscar Espla, 1973; Solidarity Award, Skopje, Yugoslavia, 1974; Clements Memorial Prize, 1975; Ernest Ansermet Award, City of Geneva, 1983. *Memberships:* Composers Guild of Great Britain, Chairman 1977-80, Council 1984-; Musicians Benevolent Fund, Council; British Music Information Centre; Council, Trustee 1987; Huddersfield Contemporary Music Festival, Management Committee. *Current Management:* RST Partnership. *Address:* c/o 17 Bradford Road, Wakefield, West Yorkshire, WF1 2RF, England.

STANFIELD Laura Danae, b. 27 Aug 1968, Illinois, USA. Musicologist; Music Librarian; Singer (Soprano). *Education:* BA cum laude, Music, Russian, Yale University, 1990; MM, Choral Music, 1991, MLS, 1994, currently PhD candidate, Musicology, University of Illinois, Urbana- Champaign; University of Chicago, 1993; Studied conducting and church music with Fenno Heath, Thomas Murray, Marguerite Brooks, Ann Howard Jones and Robert Shaw; Vocal master classes with Meredith Monk, Electric Phoenix, and Tito Capobianco. *Career:* Soprano, active in performance of contemporary music; Member of Joffrey II Ballet, 1986; Taught ballet technique and repertory, New Haven Ballet Company, 1988-89; Conductor, Founder, several choral groups, Yale University and University of Illinois; Teacher of Music History, University of Illinois, 1991-; Main areas of interest: American music, history of dance, American Indian music, musical instruments. *Recordings:* With Robert Shaw Festival Singers: Rachmaninoff Vespers and Poulenc Motets. *Honours:* Newberry Library Fellow, 1993; Visiting Scholar, University of Chicago, 1993. *Memberships:* Music Library Association; American Musicological Society; Sonneck Society for American Music; American Musical Instrument Society. *Hobbies:* Commissioning new music; Organising concerts; Driving fast cars. *Address:* Music Library, 1114 W Nevada St, Urbana, IL 61801, USA.

STANKOV Angel Mirchov, b. 28 Apr 1948, Sofia, Bulgaria. Solo Concert Violinist; Violin Duo Chamber Player (with Josif Radionov). m. Meglana Stankova, 15 July 1974, 1 daughter. *Education:* State High School; Bulgarian State Music Academy, Sofia; Specialised in London with Professor Parikian of the Royal Academy of Music. *Debut:* Pleven Philharmonic Orchestra, Beethoven Concerto, 1970. *Career:* Regular appearances with Sofia Philharmonic Orchestra and provincial orchestras; Appearances on Bulgarian radio and television; Live recital, Hague Radio, 1991; North France and Soviet TV appearances, 1991; Foreign tours to almost all European countries and Cuba; International Music Festivals, Llandaff, UK, 1975; Brno, Czechoslovakia, 1989; Warsaw, Bydgoscz and Crete, Greece, 1983; Currently Associate Professor of Violin and Chamber Music, Sofia State Music Academy; Performer as soloist and as member of violin duo with Josif Radionov. *Recordings:* Bulgarian Radio and TV; BBC London; BBC Oxford; Hague Radio; Prague Radio; Discs and cassettes; Some concertos specially dedicated to the Violin Duo by outstanding Bulgarian composers, also individual pieces. *Honours:* Golden Lyre, Union of Bulgarian Musicians; Diploma at 12th World Youth Festival, Moscow; B Bartok Prize in connection with composer's 100th anniversary, 1981; 1st Prize for Soloists, VIIth Competition of Symphony Orchestras in Bulgaria; Winner (with Violin Duo A Stankov-Josif Radionov and their pianist Theodora Nestorova), 1st Prize and Gold Medal at 1st International Chamber

Music Festa, Osaka, Japan, Apr 1993; Winner, other medals at festivals. *Membership:* Union of Bulgarian Musicians. *Hobbies:* Painting; Swimming; Antique books; Musical autographs. *Address:* 33 Hristo Botev Blvd, 1606 Sofia, Bulgaria.

STANZELEIT Susanne, b. 1968, Germany. Violinist. *Education:* Studied with Leonid Kogan and at Folkwang Hochschule in Essen (diploma, 1989) and with Yfrah Neaman at the Guildhall School of Music; Masterclasses with Nathan Milstein, Sandor Vegh and Gyorgy Kurtag at Prussia Cove. *Career:* Recitals throughout Germany, Italy, Hungary, Netherlands, Canada, USA and UK; Concerto appearances with leading orchestras, leader of Werethina Quartet (Haydn, Mendelssohn and Bartok at Purcell Room, 1993) and Prometheus and Ondine Ensembles; Purcell Room recital, 1993, with Julian Jacobson, playing Strauss, Schubert's C major Fantasy and Beethoven, Op 96; Broadcasts with BBC Radio 3, teaching and performing with the Paxos Festival in Greece, Dartington Summer School (1993) and International Bartok Festival in Hungary. *Recordings:* Bartok's music for solo violin and for violin and piano; Dvořák's music for violin and piano, Delius sonatas for violin and piano, Stanford, Bantock, Dunhill. *Address:* c/o Encord Concerts, Caversham Grange, The Warren, Mapledurham, Berks RG4 7TQ, England.

STAPP Olivia, b. 30 May 1940, New York, USA. Singer (Mezzo-Soprano). *Education:* Studied with Oren Brown in New York and with Ettore Campogalliani and Rodolfo Ricci in Italy. *Debut:* Spoleto Festival 1960, in L'Amico Fritz. *Career:* Sang in Vienna, Berlin, Wuppertal, Turin and Basle; Indiana University Bloomington in the 1971 premiere of Eaton's Heracles; New York City Opera from 1972, notably as Carmen and Norma; Metropolitan Opera from 1982, as Lady Macbeth and Tosca; Paris Opéra 1982; La Scala Milan 1983-84, as Turandot and Electra in Idomeneo; Geneva 1985, as Elena in Les Vêpres Siciliennes; Other roles include Verdi's Ulrica and Mistress Quickly, Santuzza, Dorabella, Isabella, Rosina, Idalma in Il Matrimonio Segreto and Jocasta in Oedipus Rex; sang Lady Macbeth at Geneva and Venice 1986; Frankfurt and Zurich 1988-89, as Elektra and Abigaille; Paris 1989, in La Noche Triste by Prodomide; sang Shostakovich's Katherina at Hamburg, 1990. *Recordings include:* Cyrano de Bergerac by Alfano. *Address:* c/o S.A. Gorlinsly Ltd., 33 Dover Street, London W1X 4NJ, England.

STAREK Jiri, b. 25 Mar 1928, Mocovice, Czechoslovakia. Conductor. m. Eva Iltis, 18 Feb 1964. 1 son. *Education:* Studies, State Conservatory of Music, 1939-40; Private music studies, 1940-45; Academy of Music Arts, Prague, graduation, 1950. *Career:* Conductor, chief conductor, Czechoslovakian Radio, Prague, 1953-68; Chief conductor, Music Theatre Prague, 1961-62; Artistic Leader, The Choir of Czechoslovakian Radio, Prague, 1963-64; Chief conductor/music director, Chamber Orchestra Collegium Musicum Pragense, 1963-68; Guest conductor, Radio Symphony Orchestra of Berlin, Stuttgart, Munich, Frankfurt, Munich Philharmonic, Bamberg Symphonic, Filharmony Oslo, Nuovel Philharmonique Orchestre-Radio France, Paris, Tonkunstler-orchester-Vienna, BBC Scottish Symphony Orchestra, BBC Langham Chamber Orchestra (London), San Francisco Chamber Orchestra, ABC Radio Symphony Orchestra Sydney, Melbourne, Perth (Australia), City of London Sinfonietta; Auckland Philharmonia Orchestra, New Zealand; Artistic leader, Sinfonietta RIAS-Berlin, 1976-80; Artistic leader/chief conductor, Trondheim Symphony Orchestra, Norway, 1981-84; Professor, Head of Conductor's Class/chief conductor, Music Academy Symphony Orchestra, Frankfurt Music Academy, Germany, 1975-; Dean of Artistic Department, 1980-1990; Seminars for Young Conductors, Norway, 1983, 1984; Principal Guest Conductor, ABC West Australian Symphony Orchestra, 1988-; General Musikdirector, Pfalztheater, West Germany, 1989-1992; Conducted in Czechoslovakia for the first time in 22 years, Smetana Hall, Prague, 1990; International Music Festival, Prague, concert to the

100th anniversary of the first performance of the Symphony No.9, From the New World, 1993. *Recordings:* With Prague Symphony Orchestra; FOK, soloists of Prague National Theatre; Choir, Czechoslovakia Radio, Prague; Sinfonietta RIAS, Berlin; Trondheim Symphony Orchestra, Norway; Radio Symphony Orchestra Berlin. *Honours:* OIRT Award, Vocal Symphony, 1964; Czech Radio awards for operas: Columbus, The Nose, The Prisoner, 1966-67. *Memberships:* Czechoslovak Society of Arts and Sciences; The Dvořák Society, London. *Hobbies:* Books; Dogs. *Address:* Brunnenweg 18, 61352 Bad Homburg vdH, Germany.

STARER Robert, b. 8 Jan 1924, Vienna, Austria. Composer. *Education:* Vienna State Academy 1937; Jerusalem Conservatory 1938-43 with Joseph Tal and Oedeon Partos; Juilliard School 1947; Studies with Copland at the Berkshire Music Center 1948. *Career:* Served as pianist with Royal Air Force 1943-46; Juilliard School faculty 1949-74; Professor of music at Brooklyn College 1963; CBS TV commissions 1960, 1973; Journals of a Songmaker commissioned by William Steinberg for the Pittsburgh Symphony; Violin Concerto written for Itzhak Perlman; Other music performed by Mitropoulos, Bernstein and Leinsdorf; Ballets for the Martha Graham Company. *Compositions:* Operas: The Intruder 1956; Pantagleize 1967; Apollonia 1978; The Last Lover 1974; Ballets: The Story of Esther 1960; The Dybbuk 1960; Samson Agonistes 1961; Phaedra 1962; The Sense of Touch 1967; The Lady of the House of Sleep 1968; Holy Jungle 1974; Orchestral: 3 Piano Concertos, 1947, 1953, 1972; 3 Symphonies, 1950, 1951, 1969; Mutabili 1965; Concerto for violin, cello and orchestra 1967; Journals of a Songmaker for soprano, baritone and orchstra 1975; Violin Concerto 1980; Serenade for trombone, vibraphone and strings 1984; Vocal music including settings of the Bible for various forces; Voices of Brooklyn, in 7 parts for solo voices, chorus and band 1980-84; Chamber music: String Quartet 1947; Woodwind Quintet 1970; Annapolis Suite for harp and brass quintet 1982; 6 Preludes for guitar 1984; The Ideal Self for piano 1985; Piano Trio 1985; Duo for Violin and Piano 1988; Cello Concerto 1988. *Address:* c/o ASCAP, ASCAP Building, Lincoln Center, New York, NY 10023, USA.

STARK Phil, b. 30 Dec 1929, Darmstadt, Germany. Singer (Tenor). *Education:* Studied in Darmstadt. *Debut:* Heidelberg, as Rossini's Almaviva, 1953. *Career:* Sang in opera at Solothurn-Biel, 1954-55, Dortmund, 1955-58; Appearances with Canadian Opera at Toronto, 1969- 87, as Jacquino, Don Ottavio, Ferrando, Ernesto, Jenik, Rodolfo, Tom Rakewell and Turiddu; Latterly in such character roles as Monostatos, Basilio, Valzacchi in Rosenkavalier, the Captain in Wozzeck and Pang in Turandot; Guest engagements at Seattle (1970), New Orleans and Washington; Metropolitan Opera, 1973-75, as Herod, Mime and Aegisthus; European performances at Zurich, Dusseldorf, Mannheim, Karlsruhe and Cologne. *Address:* c/o Canadian Opera Company, 227 Front Street East, Toronto, Ontario, Canada M5A 1E8.

STARKER Janos, b. 5 July 1924, Budapest, Hungary. Educator; Cellist. m. Rae Busch Starker, 3 daughters. *Education:* Franz Liszt Academy, Hungary; Hon. Dr. Music, Chicago Convs., 1961; Cornell College, 1978; East-West University, 1982; Williams College, 1983. *Career:* Solo Cellist with: Budapest Opera Philharmonic, 1945-46; Dallas Symphony, 1948-49; Metropolitan Opera, 1949-53; Chicago Symphony, 1953-58; Concert tours on all continents in recitals and as soloist with orchestras; Distinguished Professor of Cello, Music Department, Indiana University, Bloomington, Indiana. *Creative Works:* Invention of The Starker Bridge. *Recordings:* Over 85 LP's on Angel, Phillips, Mecury, Decca, Deutsche-Grammophon, Victor Japan, Japan Columbia, Star Records, Louisville Series; Over 115 LPs & CDs also on RCA. *Publications:* Author of many articles and essays including: An Organized Method of String Playing; Bach Suites; Concerto Cadenzas; Schubert-Starker Sonatina; Bottermund-Starker Variations;

Beethoven Sonatas; Beethoven Variations; Dvořák Concerto; Record Jacket Cover Notes. *Honours:* George Washington Award, Washingotn DC, 1972; Sanford Fellow, Yale University, 1974; Herzl Award, Israel, 1978; Ed Press Award, 1983; Kodály Commemorative Medallion, New York, 1983; Arturo Toscanini Award, 1986; Indiana University Tracy Sonneborn Award, 1986; Hon Doctorate, Lawrence University. *Current Management:* Columbia Artists, 165 W 57th, New York, NY 10019, USA. *Memberships:* Hon. Member, Royal Academy, London, England, 1981; American Federation of Musicians. *Hobbies:* Writing; Swimming. *Address:* Music Department, Indiana University, Bloomington, IN 47401, USA.

STAROBIN David Nathan, b. 27 Sept 1951, New York City, USA. Classical Guitarist. m. Rebecca Patience Askew, 22 June 1975, 1 son, 1 daughter. *Education:* BM, Peabody Conservatory, 1973; Guitar studies with Manuel Gayol, 1959-62, Abert Valdes Blain, 1963-67 and Aaren Shearer, 1967-73. *Debut:* American: Carnegie Recital Hall, New York, 1978; European: Wigmore Hall, London, 1979. *Career:* Played the premiere performances of more than 200 new compositions written for him including solo works, concerti and chamber music; Composers who have written for him include: Elliott Carter, Charles Wuorinen, Barbara Kolb, David Del Tredici, William K Bland, Tod Machover, Milton Babbitt, Roger Reynolds, Robert Saxton, Mel Powell, Elisabeth Lutyens, Lukas Foss, Poul Ruders, George Crumb, Mario Davidovsky; Member, Speculum Misicae. *Recordings:* New Music with Guitar, Volume 1, Volume 2, Volume 3; A Song from the East, Music from Russia and Hungary; Twentieth Century Music for Voice and Guitar; New Music with Guitar, Volume 4. *Publications:* Editor: Looking for Claudio, 1978; Three Lullabies, 1980; Changes, 1984; Acrostic Song, 1983. *Current Management:* Bridge Records Inc. *Address:* c/o Bridge Records Inc, GPO Box 1864, New York, NY 10116, USA.

STARYK Steven S, b. 28 Apr 1932, Toronto, Canada. Professor; Concert Violinist; Concert Master. m. 17 May 1983. 1 daughter. *Education:* Royal Conservatory of Music, Toronto; Private Studies, New York. *Debut:* Toronto. *Career:* Concert Master, Royal Philharmonic, London, Concertgebouw Amsterdam, Chicago Symphony, Toronto Symphony; Professor, Violin, Amsterdam Conservatory, Oberlin Conservatory, Northwestern University, University of Victoria, Academy of Music, Vancouver; Visiting Professor, University of Ottawa; University of Western Ontario; Professor, Royal Conservatory of Music, Toronto; Faculty of Music, University of Toronto; Professor and Head String Division, University of Washington, Seattle, USA, 1987-; Organiser, Quartet Canada; extensive Concert Tours, Radio & TV appearances, North America, Europe, Far East. *Recordings:* 190 compositions on 45 albums. *Honours:* Canada Council Arts Awards, 1967, 1975; Queen Elizabeth Centennial Award, 1978; Honorary Litt D, York University, Toronto, 1980; Shevchenko Medal, 1974. *Current Management:* Improsario. *Address:* 5244 17th Ave NE, Seattle, WA 98105, USA.

STAUFFER George Boyer, b. 18 Feb 1947, Hershey, Pennsylvania, USA. Musicologist; Organist. m. Marie Caruso, 26 May 1985, 1 son. *Education:* BA, Dartmouth College, 1969; PhD, Columbia University, 1978; Organ study, John Weaver & Vernon de Tar. *Career:* Director of Chapel Music & Organist, Columbia University 1977-; Adjunct Assistant Professor of Music, Yeshiva University, 1978-79; Assistant, Associate & Professor of Music, Hunter College & Graduate Centre, City University of New York, 1979-. *Publications:* Author, Organ Preludes of J. S. Bach, 1980; Co-editor, J. S. Bach as Organist, 1986; Editor, The Forkel - Hoffmeister & Kuhnel Correspondence, 1990; Co-author, Organ Technique: Modern & Early, 1992; General editor, Monuments of Western Music, Series; J S Bach: Mass in B minor, 1994. *Contributions to:* Early Music; Musical Quarterly; Bach-Jahrbuch. *Hobbies:* Canoeing; Harpsichord building. *Address:* 511 West 113th Street, New York, NY 10025, USA.

STEADMAN Robert Frederick, b. 1 Apr 1965, Chiswick, London, England. Composer; Conductor; Teacher; Musical Director; Administrator; Arranger. *Education:* ARCM, 1984; BA Hons, Keble College, Oxford, 1986. *Career:* Administrator, Hampshire Youth Brass Ensemble, 1983-86; Producer, Music Director, Oxford Revue Company, 1984-86; Music Director: University Drama Society, 1985-86, Hampshire Youth Theatre, 1987-88, Buttonhoe Theatre, 1992, Love Loyalty Community Festival, 1992; Conductor: Oxford Classical Orchestra, University Wind Orchestra, Keble College Music Society's Messiah, Handel Tercentenary, 1985, Stonesfield Choral Society, Choir of St James the Great, Stonesfield, Oxon, 1985-88, North Hampshire Area Schools Orchestra, 1987-90, Oxford Youth Band, 1990-92; Arranger, Holst's Planets Suite, brass, percussion, premiered Winchester Cathedral, 1985, brass band and wind ensemble arrangements; Freelance composer, arranger, conductor, 1986-; Composer-in-Residence, City of London Freemen's School, 1990-; Featured, TV series Music Makers, 1988. *Compositions:* Many orchestral, chamber, choral, brass band, education and wind band works. *Memberships:* Society for Promotion of New Music; Performing Right Society; British Academy of Songwriters, Composers & Authors. *Hobbies:* Cooking; Watching sport; Pub games. *Address:* c/o Vanderbeek & Imrie Ltd, 15 Marvig, Lochs, Isle of Lewis, Scotland PA86 9QP.

STEANE J(ohn) B(arry), b. 12 Apr 1928, Coventry, England. Critic and Writer on Music. *Education:* Studied English at Cambridge University. *Career:* Teacher of English, 1952-88; Reviewer of vocal music and opera for The Gramophone from 1972; Reviews and articles in Opera magazine and Opera Now, 1989- (Singers of the Century series). *Publications:* The Grand Tradition: Seventy Years of Singing on Record, 1974, revised 1993; Voices, Singers and Critics, 1992. *Contributions to:* New Grove Dictionary of Music, 1980, and New Grove Dictionary of Opera, 1992. *Address:* c/o Opera Now, Rhinegold Publishing, 241 Shaftesbury Avenue, London WC2H 8EH, England.

STEBLIANKO Alexei, b. 1950, USSR. Singer (Tenor). *Education:* Studied at the Leningrad Conservatory. *Career:* Has sung at the Kirov Theatre Leningrad as Lensky (debut), Radames, Manrico, Don José, Des Grieux, Andrei (Mazeppa), Hermann (The Queen of Spades), Andrei Khovansky, Dmitri (Boris Godunov), Cavaradossi, Lohengrin, Canio and Pierre Bezukhov in War and Peace; Tours of Europe with Kirov Theatre (Covent Garden debut 1987, as Hermann); La Scala 1982 as Aeneas in Les Troyens; Covent Garden 1989-90 as Jason in Médée, Vladimir in Prince Igor (both new productions) and Manrico; Season 1992 as Otello at Reggio Emilia; Television appearances include Prince Igor (also on video). *Address:* Allied Artists, 42 Montpelier Square, London SW7 1JZ, England.

STEDRON Milos, b. 9 Feb 1942, Brno, Czechoslovakia. Composer. *Education:* Musicology and Czech at Brno University, doctorate, 1967; Composition and music theory at Brno Academy, 1965-70. *Career:* Researched Janaček's music and worked in administration at the Moravian Museum in Brno, 1963-72; Teacher of theory at University of Brno from 1972. *Compositions include:* Operas: The Apparatus, after Kafka, 1967; Culinary Cares, Brno, 1979; The Chameleon, or Josef Fouche, Brno, 1984; Ballets: Justina, 1969; Ballet Macabre, 1986; Orchestra: Concerto for double bass and strings, 1971; Diagram for piano and jazz orchestra, 1971; Music for Ballet, 1972; Wheel, Symphony, 1972; Cello concerto, 1975; Sette Villanelle for cello and strings, 1981; Musica concertante for bassoon and strings, 1986; Lammento for viola and orchestra, 1987; Chamber: Musica Ficta for wind quintet, 1968; String quartet, 1970; Trium Vocum for flute, cello and drums, 1984; Danze, canti and lamenti for string quartet, 1986; Vocal: Mourning Ceremony, cantata, 1969; Vocal Symphony for soprano, baritone and orchestra, 1969; Attendite, populi, cantata for chorus and drums, 1982; Dolorosa gioia. Ommaggio á Gesualdo. Madrigal-cantata, 1978: Death of

Dobrovsky, cantata-oratorio, 1988; Solo instrumental music; Piano pieces. *Address:* c/o OSA (Czech Republic), PRS Ltd Member Registration, 29-33 Berners Street, London W1P 4AA, England.

STEED Graham (Percy), b. 1 Mar 1913, Newcastle-upon-Tyne, England. Organist; Choral Conductor. m. Rita Gellatly Ritchie, 12 Nov 1966. 1 son, 2 daughters by previous marriage. *Education:* BMus, Dunelm; Fellow, Royal College of Organists. *Debut:* BBC recital, Newcastle-upon-Tyne City hall, 1935. *Career:* Cathedral & church appointments, UK, Canada, USA; Recital tours, UK, Canada, USA, Austria, Australia, Belgium, France, Germany, Holland, Iceland, India, Italy, New Zealand, Switzerland. Currently: Organist Emeritus, St Mary's Cathedral Basilica, Halifax, Nova Scotia, Canada; Conductor Emeritus, Victoria Choral Society, British Columbia, Canada. *Compositions:* Variations on hymn tune, Durham (Ricordi), recorded Vista; Le Tombeau de Dupre, recorded ABC, Sydney. *Recordings include:* Organ works of Marcel Dupré, 3 discs, RCA Victrola; Symphony No 5 in F, CM Widor, RCA Red Seal; 3 Cathedral Organs, Vista; organ Works of Cesar Franck, 3-record album, L'Oiseau Lyre. *Contributions to:* Numerous articles, Musical Times, Musical Opinion, Organists Review, American Organist, Victorian Organ Journal, Sydney Organ Journal. *Hobbies:* Philately; Photography; Travel; Reading. *Address:* 9-4096 Torquay Drive, Victoria, BC, Canada V8N 3K7.

STEELE (Christopher) Michael, b. 28 May 1951, Port-of-Spain, Trinidad, West Indies. Conductor. *Education:* BMusEd 1975, MMus 1991, Temple University, Philadelphia, USA; Bachakademie, Oregon, USA, 1983; International Bachakademie, Stuttgart, West Germany, 1984. *Career:* Conductor: Southern Light Orchestra, Trinidad, 1976-78; Collegium Musicum, Trinidad, 1979-; Opera Ebony, Philadelphia, USA, 1984; International Bachakadamie, Stutttgart, Federal Republic of Germany, 1984; Szombathely Symphony Orchestra, Hungary also Hungarian Radio and TV Symphony Orchestra, 1986; Music Associate 1983-85, Assistant Music Director 1985-86, Temple Opera, Philadelphia, USA; Specialist Music Teacher, School District of Philadelphia, 1986-; Solingen Stadtisches Orchestra, Germany, 1988; Europäisches Musikfest, Stuttgart, 1991; Bohuslav Martinů Philharmonic, Czech Republic, 1992. *Honours:* Sonderpreis im Wettewerb, Vienna, 1980; May Johnstone Commemoration Trophy, Trinidad, 1982; Beryl McBurnie Award, Trinidad, 1983; American Biographical Insitute Medal of Honor, Gold, 1987. *Membership:* Conductors' Guild. *Hobbies:* Gourmet cooking; Dance; Theatre; Weights; Walking; Interior decorating; Tennis; Oil Painting. *Address:* 4503 Chester Avenue, 2nd Floor, Philadelphia, PA 19143, USA.

STEELE-PERKINS Crispian, b. 1944, England. Trumpeter. *Career:* Many appearances in the Baroque repertoire at the Barbican and Royal Festival Halls with the City of London Sinfonia and the English Chamber Orchestra; Haydn's Trumpet Concerto at the 1982 Edinburgh Festival; Performances on the Natural Trumpet with The King's Consort, The English Baroque Soloists, The Taverner Players and The Parley of Instruments; Professor of Trumpet, Guildhall School of Music, 1980; Workshops and masterclasses as preludes to concert presentations; Season 1989-90 in Boston, Tokyo, Lisbon, Stuttgart and Gstaad; British festival engagements at Edinburgh, the Proms, City of London, Cambridge, Chester, Dartington, Leeds and Glasgow; US tour 1988, Japan 1990. *Recordings:* Participation in more than 700 recordings, including 13 solo albums; Mr Purcell's Trumpeter with the City of London Sinfonia under Richard Hickox (EMI); Messiah featuring English trumpet of Handel's time (EMI); 80 film soundtracks. *Address:* Anglo-Swiss Management, 4-5 Primrose Mews, Sharpeshall Street, London NW1 8YW, England.

STEEN Kenneth William, b. 5 June 1958, Queens, New York, USA. Composer. m. Lyn Harper, 21 Sept 1985, 1 son. *Education:* BMus, Composition, Hartt School of Music, 1982; MFA, Music Composition, Bard

College, 1991. *Career:* Works performed throughout USA, with additional performances, Canada, Japan. *Compositions:* Metastasis for orchestra; Shadows and Light for solo electric violoncello; Looming for String Quartet; heal the wounds of war for clarinet in A or cello and videotape; Fragmentary Slate Jackal for electronic clarinet; While Conscience Slept for flute, clarinet, violoncello and keyboard synthesizer; Septet for Strings. *Hobbies:* Gardening; Cooking; Reading, in particular psychology, mythology and theology. *Address:* 3 Kelley Avenue, Wethersfield, CT 06109-1815, USA.

STEENLAND Thomas, b. 11 May 1950, Englewood, New Jersey, USA. Record Producer. *Education:* BA, Physics, 1972, Johns Hopkins University, 1968-72; Music, Goucher College, 1972-73; Composition and recording, University of Colorado, 1974-78. *Career:* Executive Director, Owl Recording Inc, 1979-, President, Starkland, 1992-, producing 14 recordings which have presented mostly premiere recordings of 48 works by 27 composers who include: Charles Amirkhanian, Tod Dockstader, Paul Dresher, Vincent Persichetti, Morton Subotnick, and Iannis Xenakis. *Membership:* American Music Center. *Address:* President Starkland, PO Box 2190, Boulder, CO 80306, USA.

STEER Mike, b. 22 Nov 1946, Limpsfield, England. Composer; Writer. m. Deirdre Clancy, 30 June 1975, 1 son, 2 daughters. *Education:* Cathedral Choir School, Canterbury, 1955-60; The King's School, Canterbury, 1960-63; Organ studies with Allan Wicks, Alan Harverson; Harpsichord with Jane Clark; Conducting with Sergiu Celibidache and Nicholas Conran. *Posts:* Head of Music, Camden Institute, 1973; Producer, BBC Radio 3, 1979; Associate Director of Music (London), Royal Shakespeare Co, 1980; Head of 20th Century Studies, Royal College of Music Junior Department, 1987. Productions as composer: Trinity Tales, BBC TV, 1975; Julius Caesar, BBC TV, 1978; Bognor, Thames TV, 1980-81; Many productions for BBC Radio inc. Mr V. (1989 Prix Italia nomination). Original BBC Radio programs as Writer, The Composer's Voice, 1985; Escape from the Harem, 1986; The Original American in Paris, 1988; Notes from Janáček's Diary (1991); Count Omega, 1987; Theatre Credits include: Composer, The Glass Tower, (one act electroacoustic opera commissioned by Arts Council), 1986; Writer, A Tormented God, (National Theatre Commission), 1984; Conductor, World Premiere, Nicholas Nickleby 1980; Music in Camera Films, Writer, A Concert for Mary Rose, BBC 2, 1987. Assistant Director, Love Elgin and some stories of no value, C4 1985. *Compositions:* Stones emerging through consciousness, 1986; Fron The Asylum, 1987; 3 Poems of Alan Brownjohn, 1987; Elegy (SPNM Premiere), 1991. *Address:* 116 Peckham Park Road, London SE15 6UZ, England.

STEFANESCU-BARNEA Georgeta, b. 25 Apr 1934, Satu-Mare, Romania. Piano Soloist; Performer; University Lecturer; Diplomat in Art. m. Jean Barnea, 3 Oct 1958. 2 sons. *Education:* Lyceum, Cluj, 1950-52; Academy of Music, GH Dima, Cluj, 1952-55; Academy of Music, C Porumbescu, Bucharest, 1955-57; Improvement, Weimar, GDR, 1968, 1969, 1979; Switzerland, 1970, 1972; France, 1971. *Career:* Piano Teacher, Music Lyceum, G Enescu, 1957-60; University Lecturer, Academy of Music, C. Porumbescu, Bucharest, 1960-91; Numerous concerts, piano recitals in Romania, GDR, Switzerland, Czechoslovakia, England, 1988; Appearances on Romania Radio and Television, Radio Weimar, Suisse Romande Radio, Geneva; University Reader from 1991-. *Recordings:* Concert for piano and orchestra On Tops of Charpathians by Stan Golestan with Radio Orchestra, 1971; Piano pieces Carol Miculi, 1971; Sabin Dragoi miniatures, 1982. *Contributions:* Edited: Romanian Pieces for Piano of the XIXth Century, two volumes, 1975; Romanian Sonatines for Piano, 1985; Lieds of Romanian Contemporary Creation, 2 vols 1987; Little Pieces for piano four hands, 1989, 3 vols. *Address:* Str Compozitorilor Nr 32, Bl F8 Ap 24 cod 77353, Bucharest, Romania.

STEFFEK Hanny, b. 12 Dec 1927, Biala, Poland.

Singer (Soprano). *Education:* Studied at the Vienna Music Academy and at the Salzburg Mozarteum. *Career:* Sang in concert from 1949, opera debut 1951; Sang at the Graz Opera from 1953, then the Frankfurt Opera; Munich Staatsoper from 1957-72; Salzburg Festival 1950-55, as Papagena, Ilia and Blondchen; Covent Garden 1959, as Sophie in Der Rosenkavalier; Aix-en-Provence 1960, Teatro Fenice Venice 1962; Sang Christine in the British premiere of Intermezzo by Strauss, Edinburgh 1965; Sang at the Vienna Staatsoper 1964-73. *Recordings include:* Despina in Così fan Tutte (Columbia); Das Buch mit Sieben Siegeln by Franz Schmidt (Vanguard). *Address:* c/o Bayerische Staatsoper, Postfach 745, D-8000 Munich 1, Germany.

STEFFENS Walter, b. 31 Oct 1934, Aachen, Germany. Professor; Composer. *Education:* Basic Music education with Toni and Max Spindler; Conducting with Rolf Agap; Music Theory and Composition with Klussmann, Maler and Philipp Jarnach at Musikhochschule Hamburg; Musicology, Phonetics, Theology, Arts and General History at University of Hamburg. *Appointments:* Dozent (Lecturer) in Composition and Music Theory at Hamburg Conservatorium, 1962-69; Professor of Composition and Music Theory, masterclasses, Hochschule für Musik, Detmold, 1969-. *Compositions:* Operas: Eli, librettos by composer, after Mystery of the Sorrow of Israel by Nelly Sachs, Dortmund, 1967; Under Milk Wood (English and German versions), libretto by composer, after Dylan Thomas, Hamburg State Opera, 1973, 1977 Staatsheater Kassel opening; Grabbes Leben, librettos by Peter Schütze, Landetheater Detmold, 1986, Hamburg State Opera; Der Philosoph, librettos by Schütze, Landesheater Detmold, 1990; Die Judenbuche, libretto by Schütze, after Annette von Droste-Hülshoff, Dortmund, 1993, Gelsenkirchen during the New Music Theatre Days; Bildvertonugen, over 50 individual musical settings after paintings by Bosch, Marc, Rubens, Chagall, Klee, Picasso, Aubertin, Harosch, Holzhäuser/Jäger, Soto, others, Kassel, 1977 and 1992; Chamber music, Lieder, concertos, symphonies, ballet music, oratorio. *Address:* Rosenstr 15, D-32756 Detmold, Germany.

STEGER Ingrid, b. 27 Feb 1927, Roding, Germany. Singer (Soprano and Mezzo-soprano). *Education:* Studied in Munich, at the Musikhochschule. *Debut:* Passau, as Azucena, 1951. *Career:* Sang in opera at Augsburg, 1952-54, Kassel, 1954-59, Trier, 1958-60, and Oberhausen from 1960; Further engagements at Berlin Staatsoper, 1965-68, Parma and Venice, 1965 and 1968, Salzburg Easter Festival, 1967, Graz, 1974-75, and Karlsruhe, 1975-77; Sang Elektra at San Francisco, 1973, and appeared further at State Operas of Vienna, Hamburg and Stuttgart; Sang until 1986 in such roles as Rodelinda, Leonore, Senta, Elsa, Ortrud, Elisabeth, Isolde, Kundry, the Composer in Ariadne, Lady Macbeth, Amneris, Amelia in Ballo in Maschera, Santuzza, Turandot, Judith in Bluebeard's Castle and Schoeck's Penthesilea. *Recordings include:* Die Walküre, conducted by Karajan. *Address:* c/o Stuttgart Staatsoper, Oberer Schlossgarten 6, 7000 Stuttgart, Germany.

STEIGER Anna, b. 13 Feb 1960, Los Angeles, USA. Singer (Soprano). *Education:* Guildhall School of Music, London; Further study with Vera Rozsa and Irmgard Seefried. *Career:* Associated with Glyndebourne Opera from 1983: sang Micaela on Tour in 1985, Poppea at the 1986 Festival and in the 1987 premiere production of Osborne's The Electrification of the Soviet Union; Lausanne Opera 1985, in Cenerentola; Opera North 1986, as Musetta; Covent Garden Opera from 1987, in Parsifal and Jenůfa; English National Opera in The Makropoulos Case; Geneva Opera as Concepcion in L'Heure Espagnole; Sang Despina in Così fan Tutte for Netherlands Opera, 1990; Eurydice in Milhaud's Les Malheurs d'Orphée at the Elizabeth Hall, 1990; Season 1991/92 as Despina at Stuttgart, A Hooded Figure in the premiere of Osborne's Terrible Mouth at the Almeida Theatre, and Zerlina for Netherlands Opera; Concert engagements include BBC recitals, Clarissa's Mad

Scene by Holloway with the London Symphony, Les Illuminations with the Bournemouth Sinfonietta and Fauré's Requiem with the Scottish National Orchestra. *Recording:* Poème de l'Amour et de la Mer by Chausson, with the BBC Scottish Symphony Orchestra. *Honours:* Sir Peter Pears Award 1982; Richard Tauber Award 1984; John Christie Award 1985. *Address:* c/o Harrison/Parrott Ltd, 12 Penzance Place, London W11 4PA, England.

STEIN Horst, b. 2 May 1928, Elberfeld, Germany. Conductor. *Education:* Studied at the Cologne Musikhochschule. *Career:* Conducted first at Wuppertal, then at the Hamburg Staatsoper (1951-); Berlin Staatsoper 1955-61; Opera Director in Mannheim 1963-70; Conducted the South American premiere of Schoenberg's Gurrelieder at Buenos Aires 1964; Bayreuth Festival from 1969, Parsifal and Der Ring des Nibelungen; Principal Conductor at the Vienna Staatsoper 1970-72; Music Director at the Hamburg Staatsoper 1972-79; Director of the Hamburg Philharmonic 1973-76; Has conducted Tristan und Isolde in Buenos Aires, Der fliegende Holländer in Sofia and Parsifal at the Paris Opéra; Conductor of the Orchestre de la Suisse Romande 1980-85; Director of the Bamberg Symphony from 1985, Basle Symphony from 1987; Conducted Fidelio at the 1990 Salzburg Festival; Often heard in the symphonies of Bruckner. *Address:* c/o Bamberger Symphoniker, Altes Rathaus, Postfach 110 146, D-8600 Bamberg, Germany.

STEIN Leon, b. 18 Sept 1910, Chicago, Illinois, USA. Musician; Educator. m. Anne Helman, 30 Oct 1937, 2 sons. *Education:* MusB, 1931, MusM, 1935, PhD, 1949, DePaul University. *Career:* Faculty, 1931-, Dean, 1966-76, Professor of Music, 1966-, Dean Emeritus, 1978-, School of Music, DePaul University, Chicago; Director, DePaul University Symphony Orchestra, 1965-; Chairman, College of Jewish Studies, Institute of Music, 1951-57; Member, Conducting class, Chicago Civic Orchestra, 1937-40; Conductor, Community Symphony Orchestra, Amalgamated Chorus, Skokie Valley Symphony Orchestra, 1962-66, City Symphony, Chicago, 1963-84; Founder, Conductor, DePaul University Chamber Orchestra; Guest Conductor, Illinois Symphony, Kenosha (Wisconsin) Symphony; Composer-in-residence, Ernest Bloch Composers Symposium, Newport, Oregon, 1-10 July 1993. *Compositions:* 4 symphonies; Sonatine for Two Violins, 1946; Three Hassidic Dances, 1947; Operas: The Fisherman's Wife, 1953-54; Deirdre, 1955-56; Trio for Trumpets; Quintet for Saxophone and Strings; Sextet for Saxophone and Winds, Quintets for Harp and String Quartet, 1977; Concerto for Violincello and Orchestra, 1977; Nonet for Winds and Strings, 1982; Compositions for violin, cello, piano and string quartets; Concerto for Clarinet and Percussion, 1979; Suite for String Trio, 1980; Anthology of Musical Forms, Kaddish for tenor and string orchestra, 1984; Concerto for Oboe and String Orchestra, 1986; Duo Concertante for Marimba and Bassoon, 1993; Trio Concertante for Violin, Cello and Piano, 1993; Quintet for Clarinet and String Quartet, 1993. *Recordings:* Numerous. *Publications:* Racial Thinking of Richard Wagner, 1959; Structure and Style (The Study and Analysis of Musical Forms), 1962, expanded edition, 1979. *Contributions:* Articles to music publications. *Honours:* Award for Triptych on Three Poems of Walt Whitman, American Composers Commission, 1950; Symphonic Movement for Orchestra Award, Midland Music Foundation Composition Prize, 1955; Symphony No 4 named Winner, International Competition, Elkhart (Indiana) Orchestral Association, 1977-78; Named to City of Chicago Hall of Fame, 1982; Winner, South Coast Symphony Performance Award, 1987. *Address:* 3405-B Calle Azul, Laguna Hills, CA 92653, USA.

STEIN Leonard, b. 1 Dec 1916, Los Angeles, California, USA. Musicologist; Pianist. *Education:* Studied at the University of Southern California 1935-36; DMA 1965; Teaching assistant to Schoenberg at UCLA 1939-42; BA 1939, MM 1941. *Career:* Taught at Los Angeles City College 1948-60; Pomona College 1960-62; UCLA 1962-64; Claremont Graduate School

1963-67; California State College at Dominguez Hills 1967-70; Member of the music faculty of the California Institute of the Arts 1970; Adjunct Professor in the School of Music at the University of Southern California 1975; Director of the Arnold Schoenberg Institute, University of Southern California, 1975-91, Director Emeritus, retired, 1991; Freelancing performer (pianist and conductor), lecturer, Writing and teaching privately; Tours of the USA and Europe as conductor and pianist: took part in the 1950 premiere of Schoenberg's Three Songs Op. 48, 1950; Member of the editorial board, A. Schoenberg Sämtliche Werke (1966-); Piano recitals in Mödling, Austria, 1992; Mannheim and Heidelberg, Germany, 1993; Monday Evening Concerts, Los Angeles, with Marni Nixon, soprano, 1993. *Publications:* Has edited and completed pedagogical works by Schoenberg: Preliminary Exercises in Counterpoint 1963; Structural Functions of Harmony 1969; Models for Beginners in Composition 1972; Style and Idea: Selected Writings of Arnold Schoenberg 1975; Editions of Schoenberg's Piano Concerto, Nachtwandler, Ode to Napoleon and Brettl Lieder; Reflections on Performing Schoeberg in Austrian Musical Journal, 1993. *Honours include:* Guggenheim Fellowship 1965-66; ASCAP Award 1976, for Style and Idea. *Address:* 2635 Carman Crest Drive, Los Angeles, CA 90068, USA.

STEIN Peter, b. 1 Oct 1937, Berlin, Germany. Stage Director. *Career:* Worked with Munich Kammerspiele from 1964, directing Saved by Edward Bond, 1967; Directed plays by Brecht in Munich, Goethe and Schiller in Bremen; Co-founded the Berlin Schaubuhne Company, 1970, artistic director until 1985; Debut as opera director with Das Rheingold in Paris, 1976; For Welsh National Opera has directed Otello, 1986, Falstaff, 1988, and Pelléas et Mélisande, 1992; Director of drama at Salzburg Festival, 1992-. *Recordings include:* Videos of Welsh National Opera productions (as director for television). *Address:* c/o Welsh National Opera, John Street, Cardiff CF1 4SP, Wales.

STEINAUER Mathias, b. 20 Apr 1959, Basel, Switzerland. Composer. m. Elena Gianini, 3 June 1991. *Education:* Teaching Diploma, Piano, with P Efler, Teaching Diploma, Composition, Theory, with R Moser, R Stuter, J Wildberger, Musik-Academie, Basel, 1978-86; Private study with G Kurtag, Budapest. *Career:* Began playing rock keyboard with Ephesus, The Wondergirls, others, 1972; Various Concerts of own music, radio productions, film music, 1982-; Founder, Komponisten forum, 1982; Teacher of Music Theory, Winterthur Konservatorium, 1986; Commissions, Cities of Basel and Zurich, Winterthur Konservatorium, Lausanne Chamber Orchestra. *Compositions include:* Works for piano, chamber works, lieder, rock music, 1968-82; Ballade sur le nom de K for piano, 1982; Divertissement for 3 pianos and 6 keyboard instruments, 1982; Erstes Streichquartett, 1983; Music for xylophone, marimba and 2 musical boxes, 1984; Musik in fünf Teilen for 3 cellists and 2 percussionists, 1985; Andante for percussion trio, 1985; Vier Klangbilder for baritone, large orchestra, female choir, 18 recorders, words by H Erni, 1966; Visions for 12 wind instruments, 2 percussionists, piano, 1987; Drei Skizzen for string quartet, 1987; Duat, 13 pieces for chamber orchestra, 1988; ...wie Risse im Schatten..., concerto for flute and orchestra, 1988-89; Blutenlese for 2 choirs, soprano, children's voices, ensemble, words by 12 authors, 1990-91; Undici Duettini for violin and viola, 1991; Orchesterstuck, 1991. *Recordings:* For various radio stations, Switzerland. *Honours:* 2nd Prize for Vier Klangbilder, Symphony Section, Ostschweizer Stiftung fur Musik und Theater, 1990; 1st Prizes for Ephesus group, national festivals. *Address:* c/o Konservatorium Winterthur, Tossertobelstrasse 1, CH 8400 Winterthur, Switzerland.

STEINBACH Heribert, b. 17 May 1937, Duisburg, Germany. Singer (Tenor). *Education:* Studied in Dusseldorf, and in Cologne with Clemens Glettenberg. *Career:* Sang st the Cologne Opera 1964-66; Staatstheater Karlsruhe 1966-68; Member of the Deutsche Oper am Rhein Dusseldorf 1968-76, Munich

Staatsoper 1977-80; Sang at the Bayreuth Festival 1971-76 as Froh and Melot; Guest engagements at the Paris Opera 1976 and 1978, Lisbon and Barcelona 1978; Loge in Das Rheingold at the 1979 Maggio Musicale, Florence (repeated at the Teatro Colon Buenos Aires 1982); Sang Tristan at Lausanne 1983, Walther von Stolzing at the Metropolitan 1985 followed by Siegfried at Kassel; Teatro Reggio Turin 1987-88 as Siegmund in Die Walküre; At the first season of the new Musiektheater Rotterdam (1988) sang Siegfried in Der Ring des Nibelungen; Lyric Opera of Queensland 1989, as Herod in Salome. *Recordings:* Pfitzner's Palestrina (Deutsche Grammophon); Tristan und Isolde conducted by Bernstein (Philips); Die Soldaten by Zimmermann. *Address:* c/o Lyric Opera of Queensland, P O Box 677, South Brisbane, Queensland 4101, Australia.

STEINBECK Hans David, b. 25 Mar 1925, Rupperswil, AG, Switzerland. Quintet Leader; Archivist. m. Betty Salter. 3 children. *Education:* Zurich University; Sorbonne, Paris, France; Diploma, Oboe Playing, Zurich Conservatory. *Career:* Member, Winterthur City Orchestra, 1953-62; Founder and Leader, Winterthur Baroque Quintet, 1958-78; Director, Swiss Music Archives, Zurich, 1962-89. *Publications:* Schweizer Komponisten unserer Zeit, 1975, re-edited, 1983; Editor, Swiss Music Handbook, published biennally, 1979-; Editor, many baroque and early classical chamber works. *Memberships:* Swiss Musicological Society; International Association Music Libraries. *Hobbies:* Chamber Music; Editing old music; Gardening. *Address:* Baumschulstrasse 5, CH-8542 Wiesendangen, Switzerland.

STEINBERG Pinchas, b. 12 Feb 1945, New York, USA. Conductor. *Education:* Studied in New York and at Tanglewood; Composition studies with Boris Blacher in Berlin. *Career:* Took part in the 1964 Tanglewood Festival and became professor/assistant at the University of Indiana; Associate conductor at the Lyric Opera Chicago from 1967, making his debut with Don Giovanni; Conducted leading orchestras in Europe from 1972; Conducted at the Frankfurt Opera from 1979 and has led performances in Stuttgart, Hamburg and Berlin and at Covent Garden, the Paris Opera and the San Francisco Opera; Musical Director at Bremen 1985-89; Chief Conductor at the Verona Arena 1989, and conductor of the Austrian Radio Symphony Orchestra (Janáček's Everlasting Gospel and Dvořák's Te Deum, 1990); Bregenz Festival 1990, Catalani's La Wally; Conducted Rossini's Tancredi at the 1992 Salzburg Festival. *Honours include:* Winner, Florence International Conductors' Competition, 1972. *Address:* c/o Austrian Radio SO, Argentinerrstrasse 30, A-1040 Vienna, Austria.

STEINER Elisabeth, b. 17 Mar 1935, Berlin, Germany. Singer (Mezzo-soprano). *Education:* Studied in Berlin with Frida Leider. *Career:* Sang at the Städtischen Oper Berlin from 1961, debut in Blacher's Rosamunde Floris; discovered by Rolf Liebermann and engaged for the Staatsoper Hamburg: sang in many premieres there, including Penderecki's The Devils of Loudun, 1969, Von Einem's Der Zerrissene, 1964, Kelemen's Der Belagerungszustand, 1970 and Stefens' Under Milk Wood, 1973; Appeared often at Bayreuth; Salzburg Festival 1962, as Artemis in Gluck's Iphigenia in Aulis; Guest engagements at the Maggio Musicale Florence, Metropolitan Opera New York and La Scala Milan; Vienna Staatsoper 1980, in the premiere of Jesu Hochzeit by Gottfried von Einem. *Recordings:* Roles in Tiefland, Die Fledermaus, The Devils of Loudun, Rienzi and Eine Nacht in Venedig. *Address:* c/o Staatsoper, Opernring 2, A-1010 Vienna, Austria.

STEINER Frederick (Fred), b. 24 Feb 1923, New York City, New York, USA. Composer; Conductor; Musicologist. m. Shirley Laura Steiner, 2 daughters. *Education:* Institute of Musical Art, New York City; BM, Oberlin Conservatory of Music, Ohio, 1943; PhD, Musicology, University of Southern California, 1981. *Career:* Composer, Conductor, Musicologist, Radio in New York City, 1943; Music Director, Radio Programme, This Is Your FBI; To Los Angeles, 1947; Many other radio programmes, 1st TV work, Columbia Broadcasting System, 1950; 1st film work, 1950; Major TV credits include: Andy Griffith; Danny Thomas; Gunsmoke; Have Gun Will Travel; Hogan's Heroes; Rocky & Bullwinkle Show; Movie of the Week; Rawhide; Star Trek; Twilight Zone; Hawaii Five-O; Dynasty; Amazing Stories; Tinytoons; Major film credits: Della; First to Fight; Hercules; The Man from Del Rio; Run for the Sun; St Valentine's Day Massacre; Time Limit; Shipwreck; The Color Purple; Lecturer, History & Art of Film Music: University of Southern California, 1984-89; College of Santa Fe, 1990-. *Compositions:* Perry Mason Theme; Navy Log March; Dudley Doright Theme; Transcriptions & pieces for TV & film. *Recordings:* King Kong (Conductor), Motion Picture Score by Max Steiner; Great Americana Film Scores; Music from the Paramount TV Series Star Trek. *Publications:* Fred Steiner on Film Music, in Film Score (Tony Thomas), 1991; Foreword, in Music on Demand (R R Faulkner), 1983; Music for Star Trek, in Wonderful Inventions (Iris Newsom), 1985; Interlude, in Hollywood Holyland, 1992. *Contributions to:* Journal of the Arnold Schoenberg Institute; Film Music Notebook; Quarterly Journal of the Library of Congress; New Grove Dictionary of American Music; Dictionary of American Biography; Record Album Notes. *Honours include:* Academy Award Nomination, 1986; City of Los Angeles Special Recognition Certificate; Award of Merit, Society for the Preservation of Film Music. *Memberships include:* American Musicological Society; American Federation of Musicians; Academy of Motion Picture Arts & Sciences; ASCAP; Board of Advisors, Society for the Preservation of Film Music. *Hobbies:* Viola da gamba; Music philately. *Address:* 1086 Mansion Ridge Road, Santa Fe, NM 87501, USA.

STEINER Gitta Hana, b. 17 Apr 1932, Prague, Czechoslovakia. Composer. *Education:* BM 1967, MS 1969, Juilliard School of Music. *Career:* Private teacher, piano, 1960-; Faculty, Brooklyn Conservatory Music, 1963-65; Prof composition, 1983-; Co-director Composer's Group for International Performance, 1968; Performed orchestral, chamber music throughout USA and abroad. *Compositions include:* Suite for Flute, Clarinet and Bassoon, 1958; Suite for Orchestra, 1958; Three Songs for Medium Voice, 1960; Three Pieces for Piano, 1961; Concerto for Violin and Orchestra, 1963; String Trio, 1964; Pages From a Summer Jour, 1963; Piano Sonata, 1964; Settings for Chorus, 1970; Duo for Cello and Percussion, 1971; Percussion Music for Two, 1971; Trio for Voice, Piano and Percussion, 1971; Four Choruses, 1972; Four Settings for A Capella Chorus, 1973; New Poems for Voice and Vibes, 1974; Dream Dialogues for Voice and Percussion, 1974; Cantos, 1975; Dialogue for Two Percussionists, 1975; Music for Four Players, 1976; 8 Miniatures for Vibraphone, Fantasy for Solo Percussion, Night Music for Marimba Solo, 1977; Duo for Vibe and Marimba, Duo for Trombone and Percussion, 1980; Five Pieces for Vibe and Marimba, Ten Solos for Vibe and Marimba, 1981; String Quartet, 1984; Piano Trio, 1985; Sonata for Solo Vibraphone, 1985; String Quartet, 1986; Piano Sonata, 1987; Chamber Concerto, 1988; 5 Movements for Marimba, 1988.

STEINHARDT Arnold, b. 1 Apr 1937, Los Angeles, California, USA. Violinist. *Education:* Studied at the Curtis Institute, Philadelphia, with Ivan Galamian. *Debut:* With Los Angeles Philharmonic, 1951. *Career:* Assistant Concertmaster, Cleveland Orchestra under George Szell; Performed in chamber music with Rudolf Serkin at the Marlboro Festival and prompted by Alexander Schneider to co-found the Guarneri String Quartet, 1964; Many tours in America and Europe, notably appearances at the Spoleto Festival, 1965, to Paris with Arthur Rubinstein and London 1970, in the complete quartets of Beethoven; Noted for performances of Viennese classics, works by Walton, Bartók and Stravinsky; Season 1987-88 included opening concert in New Concert Hall at Shufmotomo Festival, Japan and British appearances at St John's Smith Square and Elizabeth Hall; On faculty of Curtis Institute at University of Maryland. *Recordings include:* Mozart's quartets dedicated to Haydn; Complete quartets of Beethoven; With Arthur Rubinstein Piano Quintets of Schumann, Dvořák and Brahms; Piano Quartets by Fauré and Brahms. *Honours include:* Edison Award for Beethoven recordings, 1971.

STEINHARDT Milton Jacob, b. 13 Nov 1909, Miami, Oklahoma, USA. Musicologist. m. Ilse Boral, 1 son. *Education:* University of Kansas, 1926-28; BMus 1936, MMus 1937, Eastman School of Music, University of Rochester, 1950; PhD New York University; Violin studies New York, Munich, Paris and Berlin, 1929-33. *Career:* Assistant Professor, Central Washington College of Education, 1938-42; Instructor, Michigan State University, 1948-50; Associate Professor, Ohio University, 1950-51; Currently Professor Emeritus, Music History, University of Kansas. *Publications:* Jacobus Vaet and his Motets, 1950; Editor, Complete Works, Jacobus Vaet, 7 volumes, 1961-68; Alard du Gauquier, 1971; Philipe de Monte, The Motets, Volumes 1-7, 1975-86. *Contributions to:* Professional publications. *Honours:* Recipient of academic grants and fellowships. *Memberships include:* American Musicological Society. *Address:* 1331 Strong Avenue, Lawrence, KS 66044, USA.

STEINSKY Ulrike, b. 21 Sept 1960, Vienna, Austria. Singer (Soprano). *Education:* Studied with Margaret Zimmermann, Hilde Zadek and Waldema Kmentt in Vienna. *Career:* Many performances as Constanze in Die Entführung while a student; Debut at the Vienna Staatsoper 1983, as the Queen of Night; Has also sung in Die Zauberflöte with the Cologne Opera in Tel Aviv, Covent Garden in Los Angeles (1984) and at the 1985 Bregenz Festival; Appeared with the Bayerische Staatsoper Munich 1984-90 and at Zurich from 1985 (Zerline in Fra Diavolo in season 1989-90); Further guest engagements at Cologne (1984), Dortmund (1989), Barcelona (Fiakermilli in Arabella, 1989) and at Hamburg (1990); Season 1992 as the Fiakermilli in Arabella at La Scala; Other roles include Adele in Die Fledermaus, Musetta, Zerlina, Pamina, Despina, Aennchen and Papagena; has also sung in operettas by Oscar Straus, Lehar and Millöcker; Concert performances of Così fan Tutte, Don Giovanni and Mozart's La Finta Giardiniera. *Recording:* Die Fledermaus (EMI). *Address:* c/o Wiener Staatsoper, 1010 Vienna.

STEJSKAL Margot, b. 9 Feb 1947, Engelsdorf, Leipzig, Germany. Singer (Soprano). *Education:* Studied in Weimar and at Leipzig Musikhochschule with Hannelore Kuhse. *Debut:* Cottbus, as Musetta, 1975. *Career:* Sang in opera at Cottbus until 1977, Staatsoper Dresden, 1977-80, Chemnitz, 1980-84; Sang Sophie in Der Rosenkavalier at opening of Semper Oper Dresden, 1985; Guest appearances at Berlin Staatsoper and elsewhere in Germany; Other roles have included Blondchen, Susanna, Nannetta and Adele in Fledermaus; Many concert appearances. *Recordings include:* Der Rosenkavalier. *Address:* c/o Semper Oper Dresden, 8012 Dresden, Germany.

STELLA Antonietta, b. 15 Mar 1929, Perugia, Italy. Singer (Soprano). *Education:* Studied at the Accademia di Santa Cecilia, Rome. *Debut:* Leonora in Il Trovatore, Spoleto 1950; Rome debut 1951, as Leonora in La Forza del Destino; Germany from 1951, in Stuttgart, Wiesbaden and Munich; Sang as guest all over Italy: Verona Arena and La Scala debuts 1953; at the New York Metropolitan (debut 1956) she sang Aida, Butterfly, Tosca, Elisabeth de Valois (Don Carlos), Violetta and Amelia (Un Ballo in Maschera); At Naples in 1974 sang in the premiere of Maria Stuarda by de Bellis. *Recordings:* Roles in Verdi's Simon Boccanegra, Un Ballo in Maschera, Don Carlos, Il Trovatore, Aida and Il Battaglia di Legnano; Donizetti's Linda di Chamounix; Puccini's La Bohème and Tosca; Giordano's Andrea Chénier. *Address:* c/o Teatro San Carlo, Via San Carlo 98F, 1-80132 Naples, Italy.

STENZL Jurg Thomas, b. 23 Aug 1942, Basle,

Switzerland. Musicologist; Music Critic. *Education:* Universities of Berne and the Sorbonne, Paris, France; PhD, 1968. *Career:* Assistant to Professor L F Tagliavini 1969-75, Private Dozent and Chef de Travaux 1974-80, Fribourg University; Professor Titular, 1980-1992; Artistic Director, Universal Edition, Vienna, 1992-93; Editor, Schweiz Musikzeitung Revue musicale Suisse, 1975-83; Guest Professor, Universities of Berlin-TU, Geneva, Neuchatel, Basle, Zurich, Cremona and Berne; Numerous broadcasts for Swiss and German Radio & TV. *Publications:* Die vierzig Clausulae der Hs Paris, 1970; Repertorium der liturg. Musikhandschriften der Diozesen Sitten, Lausanne and Genf, 1972-; Von Giacomo Puccini zu Luigi Nono, Buren, 1990; Editor, L Nono, Texte/Studien zu seiner Musik, 1975; Art Nouveau, Jugendstil und Musik, 1980; A Corelli, Triosonatas op 2 and 4, 1986; Music Critic, Frankfurter Allgemeine Zeitung, Suddeutsche Zeitung, Tagesanzeiger and periodicals. *Honour:* Liszt Medal, Hungarian Cultural Ministry, 1986. *Memberships include:* Swiss Musicological Society; American Musicological Sopciety; Societe de Musicologie. *Address:* c/o Walfischgasse 12/7a, A-1010 Wien, Vienna, Austria.

STEPHAN Erwin, b. 23 June 1949, Worms, Germany. Singer (Tenor). *Education:* Studied in Frankfurt, Osnabruck and Karlsruhe; Further study with James King. *Debut:* Flensburg, 1978. *Career:* Sang in opera at Luneburg, Coburga and Giessen; Saarbrucken, 1984-86, debut as Florestan; Sang Tannhauser from 1985, notably at Dortmund, Bremen, Geneva and the 1986 Orange Festival; Freiburg, 1987, as Otello, Huon in Oberon at Catania and Max in Der Frieschütz at Cologne; US debut, 1989, as Walther von Stolzing at Seattle; Other roles have included Don José and Ismaele in Nabucco; Opera performances at Semper Oper Dresden and concert showings in France, Austria, Switzerland, Japan and South America. *Address:* c/o Semper Oper Dresden, 8012 Dresden, Germany.

STEPHENSON Donald James, b. 15 Feb 1947, Leeds, Yorkshire, England. Opera Singer (Tenor). m. 1 son, 1 daughter. *Education:* Royal Manchester College of Music, 1969-71; Diploma, ARCM with Honours (singing teaching), 1972; National Opera Studio, 1982-83. *Debut:* English National Opera, 1972; Royal Opera House, Covent Garden, 1978. *Career includes:* English National Opera, 1972-75; English Opera Group, 1975; English Music Theatre, 1976-79; Freelance opera singer, 1980-; Festival appearances, UK & Europe; Film, Death in Venice (Benjamin Britten), English Music Theatre; Regular TV & Radio appearances; Principal tenor, Welsh National Opera, roles include: Radames/Aida, Don José/Carmen, Siegmund/Die Walküre, Title role in Parsifal, Max/Der Freischütz; Glyndebourne Festival; Aldeburgh Festival; Numerous British premieres. World premieres include: No 11 Bus/Peter Maxwell Davies, London, Rome & New York, 1985; Other appearances include Freiburg Opera, roles of Tichon/Katya Kabanova, Alwa/Lulu, 1986; Erik/Fliegende Holländer, 1988; Scottish Opera, Florestan/Fidelio, 1984, Red Whiskers/Billy Budd, 1987; Opera North, Mark/Midsummer Marriage (Tippett), 1985, Wiesbaden, 1986; Regensburg Opera and Kaiserslautern Opera, Florestan/Fidelio, 1987-88; Edinburgh Festival, Herod/Salome, 1989; Hoffmann/Tales of Hoffmann, Stockholm 1990; Bob Boles/Peter Grimes, ENO 1991; First Jew/Salome, ENO 1991; Hague Philharmonic Orchestra Tour, Beethoven Ninth and Royal Philharmonic Orchestra, Missa Solemnis, RAH, 1992. *Honours:* ARCM with Honours, 1972; Arts Council scholarship to study with Otakar Kraus, 1974. *Memberships:* Equity; International Therapy Education Council. *Hobbies:* Mountain walking; Golf; Watercolour painting. *Current Management:* Helen Sykes Artists' Management, 4F Parkway House, Sheen Lane, London, SW14 8LS, England. *Address:* 65 Chatsworth Gardens, London W3 9LP, England.

STEPHINGER Christoph, b. 4 June 1954, Herrshing, Germany. Singer (Bass). *Education:* Studied at Munich Hochschule and the Opera Studio of Bayerisches

Staatsoper; Further study with Kurt Moll. *Career:* Sang at Bielefeld Stadttheater, 1982-86, Staatstheater Hannover from 1986; Guest appearances, Dusseldorf, Dortmund, Karlsruhe, Hamburg/Berlin, Nice and Spoleto; Roles have included Wagner's Gurnemanz, King Henry, Pogner and Daland, Mozart's Commendatore, Osmin, Sarastro and Alfonso, Kecal in Bartered Bride and Jim in Maschinist Hopkins by Max Brand (at Bielefeld); Sang Fasolt and Hunding in a new production of Rheingold/Walküre at Hanover, 1992; Concert repertoire includes Herod in L'Enfance du Christ by Berlioz, with the Gächinger Kantorei under Helmuth Rilling, 1989. *Address:* c/o Niedersachsische Staatstheater, Opernplatz 1, 30159 Hannover, Germany.

STEPTOE Roger Guy, b. 25 Jan 1953, Winchester, Hampshire, England. Composer; Pianist; Lecturer. *Education:* BA (Hons) Music, University of Reading, 1971-74; Royal Academy of Music, 1974-77. *Debut:* As composer, Purcell Room, 1977; As pianist, Wigmore Hall, 1982. *Career:* Composer-in-Residence, Charterhouse, 1976-79; Professor of Composition, Royal Academy of Music, 1980-1991; Administrator of Contemporary Music Projects, Royal Academy of Music, 1989-1991; Administrator: International Composer Festivals, Royal Academy of Music, 1991-1993. *Compositions:* Orchestral: Two Miniatures for strings, 1977; Cheers! (In memory of Allen Percival) for chamber orchestra, 1993; Concertos: Oboe Concerto, 1982; Tuba Concerto, 1986; Clarinet Concerto, 1989; Cello Concerto, 1991; Choral Works: Two Madrigals, 1976; Two Introits, 1977 & 1985; In Winter's Cold Embraces Dye (Cantata for soprano, tenor, chrous and chamber orchestra), 1985; Life's Unquiet Dream (for baritone, chrous and chamber orchestra), 1991; Chamber Works: String Quartet No 1, 1976; Clarinet Quintet, 1980; Brass Quintet No 2 (The Knight of the Sun), 1982; Four Sonnets for brass quintet, 1984; String Quartet No 2, 1985; String Quartet, 1988; Piano Trio, 1993; Vocal works: Aspects for high voice and piano, 1978; The Looking Glass for soprano, oboe & piano, 1980; A Little Music for baritone and piano, 1981; Chinese Lyrics Set 1 for soprano and piano, 1982; The Bond of the Sea for bass-baritone and piano, 1983; Chinese Lyrics Set 2 for contralto or counter-tenor and piano, 1983; Two Folksongs for baritone and violin, 1986; Elegy on the Death and Burial of Cock Robin for countertenor and strings, 1988; Five Rondos for soprano, baritone and piano, 1989; Sonnets to Delia for baritone and piano, 1993; Instrumental Works: Three Preludes for piano, 1976; Two Impromptus for solo clarinet, 1978; Equinox for solo piano, 1981; Three Pieces for viola and piano, 1982; Violin Sonata No 1, 1983; Two Studies for bassoon and piano, 1983; Violin Sonata No 2, 1986; Piano Sonata No 2, 1988; In the White and the Walk of the Morning (Five Poems for two guitars) 1989; Duo for oboe and harp, 1991. *Honours:* All prizes for composition, Royal Academy of Music; ARAM, 1984. *Memberships:* Royal Philharmonic Society; Incorporated Society of Musicians; Composers' Guild of Great Britain. *Hobbies:* Theatre; Travel; Cinema; Gardening; Seeing friends. *Current Management:* International Arts Promotion, 7 Jeffrey's Street, London NW1 9PS, England. *Address:* c/o 7 Jeffrey's Street, London, NW1 9PS, England.

STERN Isaac, b. 21 July 1920, Kremenets, USSR. Violinist. m. Vera Lindenblit Stern, 2 sons, 1 daughter. *Education:* 1928-31 San Francisco Conservatory of Music; Also studied with Louis Persinger and with Naoum Binder, 1932-37. *Debut:* 1931, with San Francisco Symphony Orchestra. *Career:* Los Angeles Symphony 1935, with Klemperer; Chicago Symphony 1937, with Friedrich Stock; New York debut 11 Oct. 1937; Toured Australia 1947; Appearances in Europe from 1948 (Lucerne Festival with Charles Munch); Premiered William Schuman's Concerto with Boston Symphony 1950 and Bernstein's Serenade at Venice Festival 1954; Played at Casals Festival Prades 1950; Edinburgh Festival 1953; Toured USSR 1956; Gave Mendelssohn's Concerto on Mt Scopus, Israel, following 1967 Six-day War, conducted by Bernstein; Member of Stern-Rose-Istomin Trio, 1960-84; 1960 formed group to save Carnegie Hall from demolition; Co-founded National Endowment for the Arts, 1964; Played on soundtrack of Fiddler on the Roof, 1971; 1985 premiered Henri Dutilleux's Violin Concerto L'Arbre des Songes in Paris; 1986 premiered the Violin Concerto of Peter Maxwell Davies, in Orkney. *Recordings:* All the great concertos from Bach to Bartók; Sibelius Concerto conducted by Ormandy; Dutilleux and Maxwell Davies Concertos (Maazel, Previn); Numerous chamber music recitals, including the complete Trios of Beethoven, Brahms and Schubert.*Honours:* Grammy Awards 1971, 1973; Commander, Ordre de la Couronne 1974; Numerous honorary doctorates.*Memberships:* President, Carnegie Hall Corporation; Board Chairman, American-Israel Cultural Foundation; Director, Jerusalem Music Center. *Address:* Harold Holt Ltd., 31 Sinclair Road, London W14 ONS, England.

STERNBERG Jonathan, b. 27 July 1919, New York City, USA. Conductor. m. Ursula Hertz, 15 Oct 1957, 1 son, 1 daughter. *Education:* AB, Washington Square College, 1939; New York University Graduate School, 1940; Harvard Summer School, 1940; Juilliard School; Manhatten School of Music; Private Studies. *Debut:* Vienna Symphony Orchestra, 1947. *Career:* Guest Conductor, major orchestras & operas, Vienna, Salzburg, Berlin, Munich, Zurich, Geneva, Paris, Brussels, Warsaw, Prague, Oslo, Buenos Aires, Shanghai, New York, Philadelphia, Montreal, 1947-; Musical Director, Royal Flemish Opera, 1962-66; Musical Director, Harkness Ballet, 1966-69; Visiting Professor, Conducting, Eastman School of Music, 1969-71; Professor, Temple University College of Music, 1971-89 (Professor Emeritus); Lecturer Chestnut Hill College 1989-; Conducted premiere performances in Europe and USA of music by Bloch, Ives, Rorem, Blackwood, Persichetti, Prokofiev, Messiaen. *Recordings:* 60 LP recordings for Haydn Society, Bach Guild, Oceanic; including, several Bach Cantatas and Haydn Symphonies, Haydn Lord Nelson Mass with della Casa, Hoengen and London, Mozart Concertos K449 and K482 (Badura-Skoda) and Posthorn Serenade, Rossini's Stabat Mater (Dermota and Schoeffler), Telemann's Pimpinone and Prokofiev's 5th Piano Concerto, (Brendel). *Contributions to:* A Bibliography of Periodical Literature in Musicolgy and Allied Fields, 1940; Musical Questions and Quizzes, 1942; Author, 200 Scripts for weekly Music Quiz Programme, Symphonic Varieties, WNYC, later known as So You Think You Know Music, NBC and CBS 1937-42; Editor, Conductors Guild Newsletter, 1984-. *Hobbies:* Tennis; Books; Travel; Visual Arts; Architecture. *Address:* 5 West Chestnut Hill Avenue, Philadelphia, PA 19118, USA.

STERNDALE-BENNETT Barry Monkhouse, b. 9 Mar 1939, London, England. Lecturer; Administrator; Baritone Soloist. m. Jane Fitch, 1 son, 2 daughter. *Education:* Sherborne School, Dorset and LaSalle Chicago University, BA (1965), FInst AM, FRSA; London College of Music, ALCM (1968) and Privately with Professor Roy Hickman. *Career:* Appearances at Leading Festivals in UK, Europe and Canada; Member of Philharmonia Chorus of London, 1962-; Waynflete Singers, 1979-90; Lecturer in Business and Music at 5 UK Univerisities, Director and Management Consultant; Custodian of the Sir William Sterndale-Bennett Music Library containing important 19th Century material. *Publications:* For the RAM and BMS Journals. *Honours:* Hon Dimploma in Music, Leipzig Conservatoire for Musicological Research. *Memberships:* Incorporated Society of Musicians; British Music Society; International Mendelssohn Foundation; Royal Naval Reserve Officer. *Hobbies:* Photography; Stamps; Travel. *Address:* White Windows, Longparish, Hants SP11 6PB, England.

STERNFIELD Frederick William, b. 25 Sept 1914, Vienna, Austria. Educator. m. Sophia Jung. *Education:* Candidate Phil, Vienna University, Austria, 1937; PhD, Yale University, USA, 1943; MA, Oxford University, England, 1956. *Career:* Reader, History of Music. *Publications:* Goethe and Music, 1954; Music in Shakespearean Tragedy, 1963; Editor: English Madrigal

Verse (with Fellowes and Greer), 1967; Editor: New Oxford History of Music, Vol VII (with Wellesz), 1973; Editor: Music from the Middle Ages to the Renaissance, 1973. *Contributions:* Musical Quarterly; Music and Letters; Shakespeare Quarterly; Annales Musicologiques. *Memberships:* Vice President, Royal Musical Association; Athenaeum. *Hobbies:* Swimming; Walking. *Address:* Sotwell Hill House, Brightwell-cum-Sotwell, nr Wallingford OX10 0PS, Oxford, England.

STERNKLAR Avraham, b. 21 Oct 1930, Trieste, Italy. Pianist; Composer; Educator. m. Evelyn Katz, 10 July 1953, 1 son. *Education:* Piano with L Kestenberg and Composition with P Ben Haim, Israel; Juilliard School of Music, New York, USA, 1949-54; Piano with J Friskin and E Steuermann; Composition, V Giannini; Graduate work, Chamber Music. *Debut:* Tel Aviv, Israel. *Career:* Recitals, Broadcasts and Performances, Israel Philharmonic, Jerusalem Symphony; Music Correspondent, Israel Broadcasting Service, 1949-52; Film; Siena Pianoforte, hundreds of concerts throughout USA, Canada, Europe, solo, chamber music and as soloist with orchestras; Guest Performer at Festivals, Lecturer at Seminars and Workshops; Specialist in Contemporary Music, premiered dozens of works several of which are now recorded; Faculty member, Chamber Music Workshop, sponsored by Training Orchestra, Long Island and New York University; Appeared in concerts with Misha Elman, Ruggiero Ricci, Oscar Shumsky, Zvi Zeitlin, Tossy Spivakovsky, Jascha Horenstein, The Hofstra String Quaret and the Bayview Chamber Players; Associate Professor of Piano Performance at the Aaron Copland School of Music, Queens College, 1992. *Compositions:* Educational Music, Piano Sonatinas, Violin and Piano Sonata, Cello and Piano Sonata, Clarinet and Piano Sonata, Piano Sonata, Duo Piano Works, Songs, Chamber Music, Choral Works, Recorder Collections, 12 Duets for 2 violins. *Hobbies:* Chess; Gardening; Philately; Travel. *Current Management:* E Florence. *Address:* 14 Jerold Street, Plainview, NY 11803, USA. 94.

STESZEWSKI Jan Maria, b. 20 Apr 1929, Kozmin, Poland. Musicologist. m. Barbara Zwolska, 1976. 3 sons. *Education:* Master of Philos, Poznan University; Dr of Liberal Arts, Institut of Arts, Polish Academy of Sciences; Piano Study, HS of Music, Poznan. *Career:* Collaborator, Inst of Arts, Warsaw, 1952-72; President of the Polish Composers Union 1973-79; Head, Musicological Dept, Poznan University, 1975-; President of the Polish Music Council 1979-; Vice-President of the International Music Council (UNESCO) 1981-1984; Guest Professor, George-August University, Göttingen 1987-88 and Freie University, Berlin West, 1978-79. *Publications:* Collections of folk songs and music from different regions: Kurpie, 1955; Lubelskie, 1955; Bielorussia, 1958-69; East Carpathians, 1965; Historical sources of the 17th Century, 1960, 1970; Polish religious songs in oral tradition (1990); Theory; Methodology. *Contributions to:* Muzyka; Jahrbuch fur Volksliedforschung; Studia Musicologica; Rocznik Historii Sztuki; Co-editor, Rocznik Chopinowski; Chopin Studies; Res Facta; Polish Musicological Studies; Editor in Chief, Polish Music Encyclopedia (Sachteil) in preparation. *Address:* Pecicka 38, PL 01-688 Warszawa, Warsaw, Poland.

STEUERMAN Jean Louis, b. 16 Mar 1949, Rio de Janeiro, Brazil. Concert Pianist. m. Monica Laport, 14 Aug 1981, 2 sons. *Debut:* Rio de Janeiro, 15 Sept 1963. *Career:* Appearances worldwide with major orchestras, UK debut, 1976; Recent engagements with Royal Philharmonic under Menuhin, Britten's Concerto at Athens Festival, with London Symphony Orchestra under Abbado and Liverpool Philharmonic and Gewandhaus Orchestra under Kurt Masur; Bach's D minor Concerto at the 1985 Promenade Concerts, London; Tour of Japan, 1989, with Stuttgart Chamber Orchestra, Schumann's Concerto with the Halle Orchestra; 1989-90 season included recital at Salle Gaveau in Paris, Mendelssohn's G minor Concerto with Philharmonic Orchestra of Florida and Tippett's Concerto with Helsinki Philharmonic; Further tours of

Switzerland, with EC Youth Orchestra conducted by James Judd, Italy and Japan, with the Gustav Mahler Youth Orchestra of Vienna, Czechoslovakia and Ireland; Recitals in San Francisco and Scotland; Chamber music concerts with leading instrumentalists, notably at the Menuhin Festival in Gstaad and Kuhmo Chamber Music Festival. *Recordings include:* Bach Partitas, Italian Concerto, French Overtures, Chromatic Fantasia and Fugue, Capriccio, Preludes and Fugues, Concerti; Scriabin Sonatas 3, 4 and 5. *Honours include:* 2nd Prize, Leipzig Bach Competition, 1972. *Hobbies:* Bridge; Poker. *Address:* c/o Anglo Swiss Ltd, 3 Primrose Mews, 1a Sharpleshall St, London NW1 8YW, England.

STEVENS Denis William, b. 2 Mar 1922, High Wycombe, Bucks., England. Musicologist; Conductor. m. (1) Sheila Elizabeth Holloway, 2 sons, 1 daughter (2) Leocadia Kwasny. *Education:* 1940-42, 1946-49 Jesus College Oxford, with R.O. Morris and Egon Wellesz; MA 1947. *Career:* 1946-49 played violin and viola in Philharmonia Orchestra and various chamber music groups; 1949-54 BBC Music Department as programme planner and producer: responsible for many performances of music by Machaut, Dufay, Dunstable, Mionteverdi, Tallis and other early composers; Opera productions of Monteverdi's Orfeo and Charpentier's Médée; Visiting professor of music at Cornell University 1955 and Columbia University NY 1956; 1956-61 Royal Academy of Music, London, and completed the supplement to the 5th edition of Grove's Dictionary; Visiting Professor at University of California at Berkeley 1962 and Pennsylvania State University 1963-64; Professor of musicology at Columbia University 1965; 1976-77 Brechemin Distinguished Chair of Music History at the University of Washington at Seattle; As a conductor was co-founder of the Ambrosian Singers and artistic director of the Accademia Monteverdiana; Tours of Europe and the USA, making more than 50 recordings. *Publications:* The Mulliner Book: a Commentary 1952; Tudor Church Music 1955, rev. 1973; Thomas Tomkins 1572-1656 1957 rev. 1967; Plainsong Hymns and Sequences 1965; Claudio Monteverdi: Sacred, Secular and Occasional Music 1977; Many articles on 16th and 17th Century music; Editions of Tallis, Carver, Monteverdi, Fayrfax, Early Tudor Organ Music and Venetian Ceremonial Motets. *Memberships:* Fellow of the Society of Antiquaries; Honorary member of the Royal Academy of Music 1961; Worshipful Company of Musicians 1961. *Honours:* Honorary degree Fairfield University Connecticut 1967; Commander of the British Empire 1984. *Hobbies:* Travel; Photography. *Address:* 3 The Quadrangle, Morden College, London, SE3 0PW.

STEVENS Elizabeth, b. 1965, Wales. Singer (Mezzo-soprano). *Education:* Studied at Welsh College of Music and Drama in Cardiff; Master classes with Brigitte Fassbaender. *Career:* Oratorio performances in works by Bach, Handel, Mozart and Vivaldi; Mahler's 3rd Symphony and Elgar's Sea Pictures at Llandaff and Stuttgart. *Honours include:* John MacIntyre Memorial Prize, 1991; Prizes at the National Mozart Competition and British Music Society Voice Awards; W Towyn Scholarship at the 1992 Royal National Eisteddfod.

STEVENS Risë, b. 1 June 1913, New York, USA. Singer (Mezzo-Soprano). *Education:* Juilliard School with Anna Schoen-Rene; Study in Europe with Marie Gutheil-Schoder and Herbert Graf. *Career:* 1936 Prague Opera as Mignon in the opera by Thomas; 1938 as Strauss's Octavian at the Vienna Staatsoper and at the Teatro Colon Buenos Aires; Glyndebourne Festival, 1939, as Dorabella and Cherubino; Metropolitan Opera 1938-61, as Mignon, Carmen, Dalila, Orfeo, Ponchielli's Laura and Mussorgsky's Marina: 337 performances in New York and on tour; 1940 sang in Chicago and San Francisco; Paris Opéra 1949, as Octavian; Glyndebourne 1955, as Cherubino; Retired from stage 1965 and became director of the Met National Company (until 1967) and president of the Mannes College of Music, 1975-78; Currently adviser to the Met's young artists development programme. *Recordings:* Carmen, Le Nozze di Figaro, Orpheus and Euridice and Die

Fledermaus for Columbia and RCA. *Address:* c/o Metropolitan Opera, Lincoln Center, New York, NY 10023, USA.

STEVENSON Robert Murrell, b. 3 July 1916, Melrose, New Mexico, USA. Professor of Music. *Education:* AB, University of Texas, 1936; Piano, Juilliard School of Music, New York; Composition & musicology, Yale University; Private lessons, composition, Stravinsky, 1939; Piano, Artur Schnabel, 1940; PhD, Eastman School of Music, Rochester, New York, 1942; Theology degrees, Harvard & Princeton; BLitt, Musicology, Oxford University, UK, 1954. *Career includes:* Instructor, University of Texas, 1941-43, 1949; US Army Chaplain, 1942-46; Recitals as concert pianist, USA & UK, 1942- 47; Lecturer, Church Music, Westminister Choir College, New Jersey, 1946-49; Music faculty 1949-, Professor of Music 1961-, Faculty Research Lecturer 1981-, University of California, Los Angeles; Visiting Professor, various universities. *Compositions include:* Orchestral works; Pieces for piano, clarinet & piano, organ, mixed chorus. *Publications:* Prolific writings, especially Latin American, Spanish & Portuguese music, Italian Renaissance, Baroque. (Mission, To rescue musical past of the Americas.); Titles include: Music in Mexico, Historical Survey, 1952; Patterns of Protestant Church Music, 1953; Cathedral Music in Colonial Peru, 1959; Spanish Cathedral Music in the Golden Age, 1961; Renaissance & Baroque Musical Sources in the Americas, 1970; Guide to Caribbean Music History, 1975; Antologia de la Musica Portuguesa 1490-1680, Lisbon 1984; La Musica en las Catedrales de Espana durante el siglo do oro, 1992; Over 400 articles, New Grove Dictionary; Numerous contributions, prestigious journals & books. *Honours include:* Research & teaching awards, fellowships; Honorary degrees: D.Mus, Catholic University of America, 1991; LHD (doctor of humane letters), Illinois Wesleyan University, 1992; Litt.D Universidade Nova, Lisbon, 1993. *Address:* Department of Music, University of California, 405 Hilgard Avenue, Los Angeles, California 90024, USA.

STEVENSON Ronald, b. 6 Mar 1928, Blackburn, Lancs., England. Composer; Pianist; Writer on Music. m. Majorie Spedding, 1 son, 2 daughters. *Education:* Royal Manchester College of Music, 1945-48; Accademia di Santa Cecilia Rome, 1955. *Career:* Resident in Scotland from 1952; Lecturer in composition at the University of Cape Town 1963-65; Promenade concert debut in own 2nd Piano Concerto 1972; 12 Busoni programmes on Radio 3 1973; Busoni documentary programme on BBC TV 1974. *Compositions:* Prelude, Fugue and Fantasy on Busoni's Faust for piano 1949-59; Passacaglia on DSCH for piano 1961-62; Jamboree for Grainger for orchestra 1961; Harpsichord Sonata 1968; Piano Concerto No. 1 (Faust Triptych) 1960, No.2 (The Contients) 1972; Peter Grimes Fantasy for piano 1970; Border Boyhood song cycle commissioned by Peter Pears for the 1971 Aldeburgh Festival; 9 Haiku for soprano, tenor and piano 1971; Ben Dorain, Choral Symphony, in progress; Violin Concerto (The Gypsy) 1979, commissioned by Menuhin; Corroboree for Grainger for piano and wind band, Napier College Commission premiere: Edinburgh, 1987; St Mary's May Songs, Song Cycle, poems: Chaucer, Tennyson, Rossetti, Joyce, for soprano and string orchestra; premiere: Edinburgh, 1988; String Quartet: Voces Vagabundae, premiere: Edinburgh String Quartet, Edinburgh 1990; Many settings for voice and piano and for chorus of Scottish folk songs; Transcriptions of works by Purcell, Bach, Chopin, Berlioz, Delius, Britten, Berg and Grainger. *Recordings:* Grainger's Salute to Scotland (Altarus); 20th Century Operatic Fantasies (Altarus); Passacaglia on DSCH. *Publications:* Ed., The Young Pianists' Grainger 1966; Western Music 1971; Beltane Bonfire (Test piece for Scottish International piano competition, Glasgow, 1990); Boosey, Novello, Robertson, Schott, VMP. *Contributions to:* The Listener, The Musical Times, Music and Musicians, Score. *Honour:* Harriet Cohen International Music Award for 1966 Busoni centenary radio progamme. *Memberships:* Scottish Arts Club, Edinburgh, Savile Club, London. *Hobbies:* Hillwalking; Reading. *Current Management:*

Camerata Artists Ltd, Birmingham. *Address:* Townfoot House, Main Street, West Linton, Peeblesshire, Scotland EHA6 7EE.

STEWART Donald George, b. 8 Jan 1935, Sterling, Illinois, USA. Musician (Clarinettist); Composer. 1 daughter. *Education:* BM, Indiana University, 1960; Manhattan School of Music, 1961-62; School of Jazz, 1959; Studied with Roy Harris, Bernhard Heiden, Gunther Schuller; Clarinet with Russianoff, Cioffi, Moyse. *Debut:* Boehm Quintette, Carnegie Recital Hall, 1972. *Career:* Over 1000 concerts of chamber music with Boehm Quintette and many other groups, 1955- ; Tanglewood, Newport Festival, Marlboro; Composer; Copyist; Administrator; Staff member, New York State Council on Arts, 1970-74; Founder, Chamber Music America, 1978; Board Member and Treasurer, 1982; President, Opera North, 1987-89; Founder, Trillenium Music Co. 1988; Board Member, Vermont Symphony Orchestra, 1989-1993. *Compositions:* 2 String Quartets; Sax Quartet; Wind Quintet; Brass Quintet; Duet for Flute and Bass Clarinet; Violin Sonata; 200 Bar Passacaglia; August Lions for Youth Orchestra; 1st Blue Symphony; Book of Sliding Things, for Trombones; Opera: Green Mountain Christmas Card, 1993; Numerous other compositions. *Recordings:* 3 records with Boehm Quintette, Music of Arthur Berger on New World Records and numerous others. *Memberships:* ASCAP, 1974; AFM, 1951. *Hobbies:* Swimming; Tennis. *Address:* Box 65, Tunbridge, VT 05077, USA.

STEWART John, b. 31 Mar 1940, Cleveland, Ohio, USA. Singer (Tenor). *Education:* Studied at Yale and Borwn Universities and with Cornelius Reid and Frederick Jagel. *Debut:* Santa Fe 1968, as Pinkerton. *Career:* Many appearances at the opera houses of Cincinnati, Milwaukee, Pittsburgh, San Diego, San Antonio, Washington DC, Fort Worth and Philadelphia; New York engagements at the City Opera and the Metropolitan (1974); Has sung in Europe at Amsterdam and Geneva; Ten year membership of the Frankfurt Opera; Roles have included Mozart's Don Ottavio, Ferrando and Tamino; Puccini's Rodolfo and Cavaradossi; Donizetti's Ernesto, Nemorino and Leicester (Maria Stuarda); Gounod's Romeo, and Vladimir in Prince Igor; Many appearances in concerts and oratorios. *Address:* c/o Städtische Buhnen, Untermainanalge 11, D-6000 Frankfurt am Main, Germany.

STEWART Thomas, b. 29 Aug 1926, San Saba, Texas, USA. Singer (Baritone). m. Evelyn Lear 1955. *Education:* Juilliard School of Music NY, with Mack Harrell. *Debut:* 1954 as La Roche in the first US performance of Strauss's Capriccio, at Juilliard. *Career:* New York City Opera 1954, as the Commendatore in Don Giovanni; European career from 1956: Berlin Städtische Oper 1957-64; Bayreuth 1960-72, as Amfortas, Donner, Gunther, the Dutchman and Wotan in The Ring; Covent Garden 1960-78, as Escamillo in Carmen, Gunther, Don Giovanni and the Flying Dutchman; Metropolitan Opera 1966- as Ford in Falstaff, Wagner's Wotan, Kurvenal and Sachs, Debussy's Golaud, Verdi's Iago, Britten's Balstrode, Mozart's Almaviva and as the villains in Les Contes d'Hoffmann; Santa Fe Opera 1967 as Cardillac in the first US performance of Hindemith's opera; 1972 Washington in A Village Romeo and Juliet, and in Donizetti's Maria Stuarda at the New York City Center; Many appearances with his wife, notably at San Francisco (Eugene Onegin 1971, Reimann's Lear 1981); Maggio Musicale Florence 1988, as Balstrode in Peter Grimes; Sang Falstaff at Louisville Kentucky 1988, San Francisco 1989; Boston Opera 1990, as the Speaker in Die Zauberflöte. *Recordings:* Die Walküre, Lohengrin, Der fliegende Holländer and Parsifal (Deutsche Grammophon); Götterdämmerung (Philips); Die Kluge, Iphigénie en Aulide, Johnny spielt auf and Das Rheingold on various other labels. *Address:* c/o Ingpen and Williams Ltd., 14 Kensington Court, London W8 5DN, England.

STICH-RANDALL Teresa, b. 24 Dec 1927, West

Hartford, Conn, USA. Singer (Soprano).*Education:* Hartford School of Music; Columbia University, New York. *Career:* While at college in NY created Gertrude Stein in Thomson's The Mother of us All (1947) and the title role in Luening's Evangeline (1948); 1949/50 Priestess (Aida) and Nannetta (Falstaff) conducted by Toscanini; European debut Florence 1951, as the Mermaid in Oberon; 1952 Salzburg Festival concert with arias by Mozart; Vienna Staatsoper 1952-; Aix-en-Provence Festival 1953-71, as Mozart's Pamina, Constanze, Countess, Donna Anna and Fiordiligi; Chicago Lyric Opera debut 1955, as Gilda; Metropolitan Opera 1961-65 as Fiordiligi and Donna Anna; Concert performances of works by Bach and Handel, retired 1971. *Recordings:* Così fan Tutte (Philips); A Life for the Tsar (HMV); Falstaff, Aida, Hercules (RCA); Orpheus and Euridice (Vanguard); Rodelinda (Westminster); Le Nozze di Figaro and Don Giovanni (Deutsche Grammophon); Beethoven's 9th Symphony, Brahms Requiem and Mozart's Coronation Mass on various labels. *Honour:* 1962 Austrian Kammersängerin (first American to be so honoured).

STILES Frank, b. 2 Apr 1924, Chiswick, London, England. Composer; Conductor; Violist. m. (1) 23 Dec 1969, (2) Elizabeth Horwood, 1 Sept. 1988. *Education:* BSc, Imperial College; BMus, Durham University; LGSM; AGSM; Post-grad, Paris Conservatoire. *Career:* Composer; Principal Conductor, Priory Concertante of London. *Compositions:* Dramatic Cantata, Masada; Song Cycle Mans's Four Seasons, Triple Concerto; 4 Symphonies; 4 String Quartets; Trios, Duos and Solo Works; Other Orchestral Works; Works for String Orchestra; 7 Concertos; Choral, Vocal Works and Various other Chamber Works. *Recordings:* Guitar Sonata; String Quartet No 3; Keyboard Sonata; Concerto For Five; First Piano Concerto; Equinox for Solo Piano. *Contributions to:* Composer; Musician. *Honours:* City of London Prize for Composition, 1955. *Memberships:* Composers' Guild of Great Britain; Incorporated Society of Musicians; Royal Society of Musicians; Chairman, Association for British Music. *Hobbies:* History; Reading. *Address:* 43 Beech Road, Branston, Lincoln LN4 1PP, England.

STILLER Andrew Philip, b. 6 Dec 1946, Washington DC, USA. Composer. m. Ernestine Steiner, 25 May 1975. *Education:* BA, Zoology, University of Wisconsin, 1968; MA 1972, PhD 1976, Composition, University of New York. *Career:* Center of Creative & Performing Arts, 1971-73; Decapod Wind Quintet, 1975; Age of Reason Ensemble, 1981; Buffalo New Music Ensemble, 1984-85; Network for New Music, 1986-89; Solo shows, Buffalo, 1970, 72, 73, 76; Works also heard, 2nd & 3rd North American New Music Festivals, 1984, 85; Editorial Consultant, New Grove Dictionary of Opera, 1990; Founder and Director, Kallisti Music Press, 1991-. *Compositions:* Orchestral: Periodic Table of Elements; Foster Song; Magnification; Orrery, 1990. Chamber music: Numerous works including Sonata, Chamber symphony. Also various pieces, keyboard & vocal. *Publications:* Handbook of Instrumentation, 1985; Buffalo Philharmonic Orchestra, 1985; Compositions available through Kallisti Music Press. *Contributions to:* Opus; Philadelphia Inquirer; Buffalo News; New Grove Dictionary of Opera; Musical Quarterly; Musical America. *Memberships:* American Society of Composers, Authors & Publishers; Pennsylvania Composers Forum. *Address:* 810 South Saint Bernard Street, Philadelphia, Pennsylvania 19143, USA.

STILWELL Richard (Dale), b. 6 May 1942, St Louis, Missouri, USA. Baritone. m. (1) Elizabeth Louise Jencks, 21 Mar 1967. (2) Kerry M McCarthy, 22 Oct 1983. *Education:* Anderson (Ind) College; BA, Indiana University School of Music, Bloomington, 1966; Studied voice with F St Leger, P Mathen and D Ferro. *Debut:* As Silvio, Pagliacci, St Louis Grand Opera, 1962. *Career:* First appearance as Pelleas, New York City Opera, 1970; British debut as Ulysses in Il Ritorno d'Ulisse in Patria, Glyndebourne Festival, 1973; Metropolitan Opera debut, New York as Guglielmo, 1975; Guest artists, Houston Grand Opera; Paris Opéra; Netherlands Opera;

Chicago Lyric Opera; Washington (DC) Opera Society; Berlin Deutsche Oper; Appearances as soloist with leading USA orchestras; Operatic repertory includes Don Giovanni, Papageno, Don Pasquale and Eugene Onegin; Created roles in Pasatieri's The Seagull and Ines de Castro; Argento's The Aspern Papers, (Dallas 1988); sang Malatesta in Don Pasquale at Dallas 1989; Sharpless in Madame Butterfly at Lyons, 1990 (repeated at Chicago 1992); Season 1992 as Mozart's Count at Dallas, Don Alfonso at Seattle and Sharpless with Opéra de Lyon at Symphony Hall, Birmingham. *Recordings:* For CBS; Telarc. *Honours:* National Society of Arts and Letters Award, 1963; Young Artists Award, St Louis, 1963; Fisher Foundation Award, Metropolitan Opera Auditions, 1965; Honorary MusD, Knox College, 1980. *Membership:* American Guild of Musical Artists. *Address:* c/o Columbia Artists Management Inc, 165 West 57th Street, New York, NY 10019, USA.

STOCK David Frederick, b. 3 June 1939, Pittsburgh, Pennsylvania, USA. Composer; Conductor. m. Celia Frankel Stock, 19 Oct 1963, 1 son, 2 daughters. *Education:* BFA, 1962, BFA, 1962, MFA, 1963, Carnegie Mellon University; MFA, Brandeis University, 1973; studied at Ecole Normale de Musique, Paris and Berkshire Music Centre, Tanglewood. *Career:* Conductor, Antioch Chamber Orchestra, 1970-74; Conductor, Carnegie Symphony, 1976-82; Conductor, Pittsburgh New Music Ensemble, 1975-; Associate Professor of Music, Duquesne University, 1990-; Guest Conductor: Monday Evening Concerts, Res Musica Baltimore, Los Angeles Philharmonic New Music Group, Minnesota Composers Forum, American Dance Festival, American Wind Symphony, Pittsburgh Symphony, Baltimore Symphony, Chautauque Symphony. *Compositions include:* A Joyful Noise; American Accents; Zohar; Inner Space; Nova; The Body Electric; The Philosopher's Stone; Tekiah, Yerusha, Night Vision, Rockin Ronde, On the Shoulders of Giants, Quick Opeaer, Fast Break, No Man's Lane; SCAT; Triple Play; Speaking Extravagantly; numerous other compositions including: Film, Theatre and TV Music; Three Miniatures for Solo Clarinet, 1983 In G, 1980; Starlight, Clarinet, Percussion; October Mountain, solo trumpet; Wild Card, solo trombone; Shadow Music, five percussion, harp. *Recordings:* Quintet for Clarinet and Strings; Inner Space; SCAT; Triple Play; The Philosopher's Stone; Serenade for Five Instruments. *Contributions to:* Perspectives of New Music; Music Critic, Boston Globe, 1966-68. *Hobbies:* Cooking; Reading. *Address:* 6538 Darlington Road, Pittsburgh, PA 15217, USA.

STOCKER Markus, b. 2 Apr 1945, Basel, Switzerland. Violoncellist. m. Mei-Lee Ong, 21 Mar 1975. 2 daughters. *Education:* University of Basel; Teachers and Soloists Diplomas under August Wenzinger, Academy of Music, Basel. *Debut:* London; Paris; Vienna; Berlin; New York; Tokyo; Beijing. *Career:* Concerts throughout Europe, USA, Far East, Israel, USSR; Performed at Lucerne, Salzburg and Menuhin Festivals, Marlboro and Lockenhaus; Appearances with Rudolf Serkin, Martha Argerich, Sandor Vegh, Gidon Kremer; Professor, Winterthur and Zurich Conservatories; Piano trio with violinist Wanda Wilkomirska and pianist Werner Genuit, 1985. *Recordings:* Live recording of Bach Suites; Mendelssohn, Complete works for cello and piano; Swiss Composers: Martin, Honegger. *Honours:* 1st Prize, Bloomington, Indiana, USA, 1972; Grand Prix, Maurice Marechal International cello competition, paris, 1972; Soloists Prize, Association of Swiss Musicians, 1973. *Memberships:* Association of Swiss Musicians; International Lions Club. *Hobbies:* Sport; Reading. *Address:* St Gallerstr 49, 8400 Winterthur, Switzerland.

STOCKHAUSEN Karlheinz, b. 22 Aug 1928, Modrath, nr. Cologne, West Germany. Composer; Teacher. *Education:* Studied at Cologne Musikhochschule, 1947-51, piano and theory; Cologne University from 1950; composition with Frank Martin 1950; studied with Messiaen in Paris, 1952-53. *Career:* Assistant to Herbert Eimert at electronic music studio of West German Radio, Cologne, 1953; edited magazine for serial music Die Riehe, from 1954; head of composition courses at Darmstadt, 1957-; lecture concerts in USA and Britain, 1958-; visiting professor at several US universities; founded Cologne Course for New Music, 1963, teaching composition until 1968; professor of composition, Cologne Musikhochschule, 1971-; Dienstag aus Licht premiered at Lisbon, 1992. *Compositions include:* Kreuzspiel for oboe, clarinet, piano and 3 percussion, 1951; Formel for 29 instruments, 1951; Punkte for orchestra, 1952; Kontrapunkte for ensemble, 1952; Klavierstücke I-XI, 1952-56; Zeitmasze for wind quintet, 1956; Gruppen for 3 orchestras, 1957; Gesang der Jünglinge for voice and tapes, 1956; Zyklus for percussion, 1959; Carré for 4 choruses and 4 orchestras, 1960; Refrain for ensemble, 1959; Kontakte for piano, percussion,and 4-track tape, 1960; Momente for soprano, 4 choruses and ensemble, 1961-4; Mikrophonie I and II for electronics, 1964-65; Mixtur for 5 orchestras, sine-wave generators and 4 ring modulators, 1964-67; Stop for instrumental ensemble, 1969-73; Telemusik for 4-track tape, 1966; Hymnen for 4-track tape, 1967; Stimung for voices and ensemble, 1968; Kurzwellen for electronics and 4 short-waves radios, 1968; Aus den sieben Tagen, 15 pieces for various instrumental groups, 1968; Spiral for soloist and short-wave receiver, 1969; Mantra for 2 pianos, woodblock and 2 ring modulators, 1970; Sternklang, parkmusic for 5 groups, 1971; Trans for orchestra and tape, 1971; Am Himmel wandre ich...for soprano and baritone, 1972; Intevall for piano duo, 1972; Inori for 1/2 soloists and orchestra, 1974; atmen gibt das Leben for chorus, 1974; Herbstmusik for 4 players, 1974; Musik im Bauch for 6 percussion, 1975; Sirius for soprano, baritone and ensemble, 1977; Jubiläum for orchestra, 1977; Operas Donnerstag aus Licht, 1981; Samstag aus Licht, 1984, and Montag aus Licht, 1987; Dienstag, 1992. *Publications:* Texte zur elektronischen und instrumentalen Musik, 1963; Texte zu eigenen Werken, zur Kunst Anderer, Aktuelles, 1963; Ein Schlüssel fur Momente, 1971; Texte zur Musik 1963-1970, 1971; Texte zur Musik 1970-77, 1978; Texte zur Musik, Komposition, 1977-84, 1988; Texte zur Musik 1977-84, Interpretation, 1988. *Address:* c/o Musikhochschule, Cologne, Germany.

STODLE Tori, b. 1 July 1942, Oslo, Norway. Pianist. m. Hakon Stodle, 6 Oct 1975, 1 son, 1 daughter. *Education:* Studied with Robert Riefling in Oslo, Jurgen Uhde in Stuttgart, and Adele Marcus in New York. *Debut:* Oslo, 1970; New York, 1990. *Career:* Recitals: Norway, UK, Germany, Russia, Italy, Netherlands, Denmark, US; Several TV and radio programmes for Norwegian Broadcasting; Guest Artist, major music festivals including Chamber Music Festival in Tromso, Bergen Festival and North Norwegian Festival; Piano Soloist for world premieres of Ketil Vea's Piano Concertos Nos 1 and 3; Music from the Top of the World, recital of music by 19th and 20th century Norwegian composers sponsored by various Norwegian organisations; Weill Recital Hall, Carnegie Hall, New York City, 1990; The Dream of a Sound, TV portrait, 1991; Promotes new music; Works dedicated to her by several Norwegian composers; Currently Associate Professor of Piano, North Norwegian Music Conservatory, Tromso. *Recordings:* Music from the North, LP; Music from the Top of the World, CD. *Honours:* Northern Light Prize, 1991. *Memberships:* 2 Norwegian Music Associations; European Piano Teachers Association. *Address:* Fogd Dreyersgt 21, 9008 Tromso, Norway.

STODT Francine Chloe, b. 2 Dec 1951, Burlington, Iowa, USA. Pianist; Organist; Music Instructor; Choral Conductor; Liturgist. *Education:* BA, Music Education, Piano, Ambrose, Davenport, Iowa, 1974; MM, Piano Performance, University of Colorado, Boulder, 1976; MA, Theology (Liturgical Studies), University of Notre Dame, Indiana, 1978; DMA in progress, Piano Performance, Pedagogy, University of Iowa, Iowa City; Studied Piano with Carole Thomas, Arthur Rowe, Paul Parmelee, Lewis Hoy; Organ with Delbert Disselhorst, Robert Triplett, Rodney Giles, Jan Overduin. *Career:* Piano Instructor: Division of Continuing Education, University of Colorado, 1975-77; Preparatory Department, University of Notre Dame, 1977-78;

Minister of Music, St Joseph's Church, Stratford, Ontario, Canada, 1978-80; Adjunct Instructor of Music, Avila College, Kansas City, Missouri, USA, 1980-82; Director of Music and Liturgy, St Patrick's Parish, Kansas City, Missouri, USA, 1980-84; Adjunct Associate Professor of Music, Black Hawk College, Moline, Illinois, 1986-88; Announcer, WVIK-FM Radio, 1987-89, Director of Community Music and Instructor of Piano, 1988-93, Augustana College, Rock Island, Illinois. *Honours:* Full Tuition Scholarship, St Ambrose College, 1970-74; Piano Accompanying Assistantship, University of Colorado, 1975-76; Language Scholarship, University of Iowa, summer 1992. *Memberships:* American Guild of Organists, Past Member Greater Kansas City Chapter Professional Concerns Committee, Past Member Blackhawk Chapter Professional Concern Committee, Past Member Blackhawk Chapter Executive Board; Faculty Member, National Guild of Piano Teachers; Associate, Notre Dame Center for Pastoral Liturgy; Patroness Member, Delta Tau Chapter, Sigma Alpha Iota; Xi Chapter, Pi Kappa Lambda; Alpha Tau Chapter, Delta Epsilon Sigma. *Hobbies:* Reading; Sewing; Swimming; Gardening; Mushroom hunting (morels). *Address:* Davenport, IA 52803, USA.

STOIANOV Carmen Antoaneta, b. 2 Dec 1950, Bucharest, Romania. Musicologist; Critic; Piano Teacher. m. Petru Stoianov, 25 Dec 1969, 1 daughter. *Education:* Bucharest Musical High School with Florino Delatolla, Piano and Canto, Lucia Anghel, Piano, Dan Mizrahi; Bucharest Conservatoire (Musicology, Composition, orchestration, Conducting). *Debut:* Radio Bucharest, 1973. *Career:* Musical Assistant, Radio Bucharest, 1973-; Musical Assistant, Bucharest TV, 1978-; Participation in Scientific Sessions, Musical Circles, Converences, Jury Member for Musical Performances; Piano Teacher, Bucahrest School 49, 1973-; Scientific Coordinator, Musicology Studies, Vol XIV Bucharest, 1979; Joint Author of The Dictionary of Musical Terms, Bucharest, 1985. *Publications:* Ioan Scarlatescu, 1976; George Stepheanescu, 1981; the History of the Romanian Opera of Bucharest, 1985; The Typology of Structure in the Contemporary Romanian Oratorios, 1986; The Dacian Myth of Zamolye in Liviu Goldeanu's Dramaturgical Conception, 1987; Filip Lazar's Concertos. *Contributions:* Professional publications of articles, essays, chronicles. *Address:* Calea Vacaresti No 276 BL 63 sc 1 et 2 ap 7, Sect 4, Bucharest 75176, Romania.

STOIANOV Konstantin, b. 1950, USSR. Violinist. *Education:* Studied at the Antwerp Conservatory from age 9 and in Berlin and Wirzburg. *Career:* Numerous solo appearances with leading orchestras; Radio broadcasts in Belgium, France and Italy; Leader of the Royal Philharmonic Orchestra of Flanders, Co-leader of the London Philharmonic from 1990; Professor at the International Menuhin Academy at Gstaad. *Hobbies:* Cooking; Swimming; Walking in the countryside. *Address:* c/o London Philharmonic Orchestra, 35 Doughty Street, London WC1N 2AA, England.

STOJANOVIC Milka, b. 13 Jan 1937, Belgrade, Yugoslavia. Singer (Soprano). *Education:* Studied at the opera school of La Scala, Milan, and with Zinka Milanov. *Career:* Sang with Belgrade National Opera from 1960, notably at Edinburgh Festival, 1962, and at Oslo and Lausanne (1968, 1971); Further appearances at the Metropolitan, New York, 1967-68, Graz, 1962, Vienna, Bari, Munich, Cologne and Barcelona, 1970-71; Opera and concert engagements in Denmark, England, Hungary, Finland, former Soviet Union, Egypt and Czechoslovakia; Roles have included Verdi's Aida, Desdemona and Amelia (Ballo in Maschera), Leonore, Mimi, Liu, Mozart's Countess, La Gioconda, Marenka, Santuzza and Tatiana. *Recordings include:* Several albums. *Address:* c/o Narodno Pozoriste, Francuska 3, 11000 Belgrade, Republic of Serbia.

STOKER Richard, b. 8 Nov 1938, Castleford, Yorkshire, England. Composer; Author. m. (1) Jacqueline Margaret Trelfer 1962, (2) Gillian Patricia Watson 1986. *Education:* Royal Academy of Music, with Lennox

Berkeley 1958-62; Nadia Boulanger 1962-63. *Career:* Debut with BBC Home Service 1953; Concerts as pianist at Purcell Room, Leighton House, BBC Radio 3, BBC TV, Channel 4, BBC Radio 4; Professor of Composition at Royal Academy of Music from 1963: pupils have included Paul Patterson, Malcolm Singer, Keith Clarke, Joe Jackson, Paul Parkinson, Irvine Arditti. *Compositions:* Operas: Johnson Preserv'd, Thérèse Raquin; Piano Concerto; Overtures Antic Hay, Feast of Fools; Passacagalia, Serenade, Petite Suite; 3 String Quartets; Wind Quintet; Sextet; Nocturnal; 3 Violin Sonatas; Piano Sonata; Partita for clarinet and piano; 3 Piano Trios; Festival Suite; Various choral works- Ecce Homo, Proverbs; Song Cycles- Music that Brings Sweet Sleep, Aspects of Flight, Aspects 1 in 3; Organ works- Partita, Little Organ Book, 3 Improvisations, Symphony; Music for guitar; Chinese Canticle, The Scholars (Yeats), Piano Sonata No 2, for Eric Parkin. *Recordings:* Sonatina for Clarinet & Piano: (Chandos, CD), 1992; 3 String Quartets, Gaudeamas, Sonata for Guitar Duo. *Publications:* Open Window-Open Door, autobiography; Words without Music (outposts); Portrait of a Town; Tanglewood (Merlin). *Contributions to:* Records and Recording; Books and Bookmen; Editor, Composer 1969-80. *Honours:* Mendelssohn Scholarship 1962; Dove Prize RAM 1962; Associate Royal College of Music RCM, 1962; Fellow of RAM 1971. *Memberships:* Executive Committee Composers' Guild 1969-74, 1974-80; Association of Professional Composers; BASCA (Professional Member); Royal Society; PRS; MCPS; RAM Guild; Founder Member, The Atlantic Council of the UK. *Hobbies:* Squash; Tennis; Swimming; Painting. *Address:* c/o Ricordi & Co. Ltd., The Bury, Church Street, Chesham, Bucks, England.

STOKES Eric (Norman), b. 14 July 1930, Hasdon Heights, New Jersey, USA. Composer. *Education:* Studied at Lawrence College, New England Conservatory, and with Dominick Argento at University of Minnesota (PhD, 1964). *Career:* Teacher at University of Minnesota, 1961-88, founding an electronic music programme and Minnesota Moving and Storage Warehouse Band, 1971. *Compositions include:* Operas: Horspfal, Minneapolis, 1969; HAPP, or Orpheus in Clover, Minneapolis, 1977; The Jealous Cellist and Other Acts of Misconduct, Minneapolis, 1979; Itaru the Stonecutter (for children), 1982; Apollonia's Circus, 1985; We're not Robots You Know (puppet opera), Chicago, 1986; The Further Voyages of the Santa Maria, 1990; Orchestra: A Center Harbour Holiday, 1963; On the Badlands-Parables, 1972; The Continental Harp and Band Report, 1975; The Spirit of Place among the People, 1977; Captains on the War against Earth, 1980; Prairie Drum, 1981; Concert Music for piano and orchestra, 1982; The Greenhouse Effect, 1983; Stages, 1988; Chamber: Trio for clarinet, cello and piano, 1955; Expositions for ensemble, 1970; Circles in a Ropund for piano and tape, 1972; Wind Quintete, 1981; Brazen Cartographies for brass quintet, 1988; The Lyrical Pickpocket for ensemble, 1990; Vocal: Smoke and Steel for tenor, men's chorus and orchestra, 1958, revised, 1989; The River's Minute by the Far Brook's Year for narrator, chorus and orchestra, 1981; Peppercorn Songs for chorus, piano and ensemble, 1984; Firecho for voices and percussion, 1987; Solo songs. *Address:* c/o ASCAP, ASCAP Building, One Lincoln Plaza, New York, NY 10023, USA.

STOLBA K Marie, b. 22 Apr 1919, Burlington, Iowa, USA. Musicologist; Professor and Coordinator of Music History, Music Literature and Musicologist; Violinist; Composer. *Education:* AA, Burlington Junior College, Iowa; BA and , Monmouth College, Illinois ; MA, University of Northern Colorado, Greeley; PhD, University of Iowa; Post-doctorate studies in Russian, Fort Hays State College, Kansas; Post-doctoral studies in violin with Robert Slaughter. *Career:* Professor and Coordinator of Music History, Music Literature, Musicology and Strings, Indiana University-Purdue University, Fort Wayne, Indiana. *Compositions:* And Jesus Came....for voice and piano; Christmas Story, for voice and piano; Homage, Choral Anthem with violin and organ. *Recordings:* Edited: 2 boxed sets of recordings to accompany The Development of Western

Music: An Anthology, records published by CBS Records, 1990. *Publications:* A History of the Violin Etude to about 1800, 2 volumes, 1968, revised 1979; Translator JS Bach: Sonaten und Partiten fur Violine Allein, 1982; Editor, A B Bruni: Caprices and Airs varies, Cinquante Etudes, 1982; The Development of Western Music: A History, 1989; The Development of Western Music: An Anthology, 3 volumes, published by Wm. C. Brown Co. Dubuque, IA, 1990. *Contributions to:* Journal of the American Musicological Society. *Honour:* Doctor of Humane Letters, honoris causa, from Monmouth College, 1990. *Address:* 5621 Joyce Avenue RR12, Fort Wayne, IN 46818, USA.

STOLTZMAN Richard Leslie, b. 12 July 1942, Omaha, Nebraska, USA. Clarinettist. m. Lucy Chapman. *Education:* Ohio State University (BA 1964); Yale University (MM 1967); Teachers included Robert McGinnis, Kalman Opperman and Keith Wilson. *Debut:* Metropolitan Museum, New York. *Career:* Recitals with David Ensemble, London, 1970-72; Program Director of the western region of Young Audiences, 1971-74; Taught at the California Institute of the Arts, Valencia, 1970-75; Guest Artist at the Marlboro Music Festival; With Peter Serkin co-founded chamber group Tashi 1973; Mozart concert debut Carnegie Hall, 1976; Performed with Amadeus Quartet at the Aldeburgh Festival, 1978; New York Philharmonic with James Levine, 1979; Performances with the Cleveland, Guarneri, Tokyo and Vermeer Quartets; Concert programmes with transcriptions and commissioned pieces; Debut at the Promenade Concerts, London with Mozart's Concerto, 1989. *Composition:* Edition of Schubert's Arpeggione Sonata. *Recordings:* Brahms, Clarinet Sonatas, Op 120, with Richard Goode; Corigliano, Clarinet Concerto, with Lawrence Leighton Smith and London Symphony; Copland, Clarinet Concerto; Bernstein, Prelude, Fugue & Riffs; Stavinsky, Ebony Concerto, with Woody Herman's Thundering Herd; Mozart, Clarinet Concerto, with English Chamber Orchestra; Mozart, Clarinet Quintet, with the Tokyo Quartet; Brahms, Clarinet Quintet, with the Cleveland Quartet; Beethoven, Quintet for Piano and Winds, with Rudolf Serkin, piano; Beethoven, Octet for Winds; Clarinet Trio with Rudolf Serkin, piano and Alain Meunier, cello; Mozart, Serenade No 10 in B-Flat, Marcel Moyse, conductor; Mozart, Serenade No 11 in E-Flat for Winds; Gounod, Petite Symphony. *Honours:* Avery Fisher Prize 1977; Yale University Order of Merit; Grammy Award, 1983. *Hobbies:* Pastry Chef; Tennis. *Address:* c/o Frank Salomon Associates, 201 West 54th Street 4C, New York, USA.

STONE Jeffrey, b. 11 June 1946, Texarkana, Arkansas, USA. Composer; Pianist; Conductor; Teacher. *Education:* BMus, University of Houston, 1968; MMus, University of Indiana, 1970. Piano studies, Harry Datyner; Composition, Bernhard Heiden; Conducting, Wolfgang Vacano, Sir John Barbirolli. *Career:* Conductor, state theatres, Hagen, Krefeld (Germany), Lucerne (Switzerland), & Schweizer Gastspiel Oper; Recitalist, accompanist; Concerts, Germany, Switzerland, Italy. Freelance composer, arranger (theatre, teaching), pianist, teacher, 1980-. *Compositions:* 5 Easy Pieces for Horn & Piano; Three for Two; Concert Etudes for Brass; Arrangements for the Philharmonic Brass Sechzylinder; Various piano pieces. *Publications:* Book, Das Kind am Klavier, 1988; Editor & contributor, Ars Nova publishing company. *Membership:* European Piano Teachers' Association. *Recreation:* Computers. *Address:* Rathausstrasse 4a, 6032 Emmen, Switzerland.

STONE William, b. 1944, Goldsboro, North Carolina, USA. Singer (Baritone). *Education:* Studied at Duke University and the University of Illinois. *Career:* Sang at first in concert and oratorios; Opera debut in La Traviata (Germont) in 1975 at Youngstown, Ohio; New York City Opera debut, 1981; European debut 1977, Spoleto Festival, Napoli Milionaria by Nino Rota; Lyric Opera Chicago 1978, as Adam in the premiere of Penderecki's Paradise Lost (repeated at La Scala 1979); Sang at the Maggio Musicale Florence 1979 as

Wozzeck, 1981 as Orestes in Gluck's Iphigénie en Tauride; Opéra-Comique Paris 1984 as Purcell's Aeneas, Aix en Provence 1987, as Ford in Falstaff; Further guest engagements at Trieste, Rome, Naples and Brussels (Germont 1987, Paolo and Simone in Simon Boccanegra 1990); Many appearances at the New York City Opera (Mozart's Count 1990) and sang at Santa Fe 1980 in the US premiere of Schoenberg's Von Heute auf Morgen; Wexford Festival 1989 as the Templar in Marschner's Der Templer und die Jüdin; Other roles include Rossini's Figaro, Enrico, Malatesta, Verdi's Ezio and Posa, Zurga, Albert in Werther, Golaud, Alfio and Eugene Onegin; Sang the title role in the US stage premiere of Busoni's Doktor Faust, New York City Opera, 1992; Concert repertoire includes the St Matthew Passion, Messiah, the Missa Solemnis, Beethoven's Ninth and Ein Deutsches Requiem. *Recordings:* Salammbo by Mussorgsky (CBS); Hindemith Requiem (Telarc); Walton, Belshazzar's Feast (Telarc); Robert Ward, Arias and Songs (Bay Cities); Bach B Minor Mass (Telarc); Mahler Symphony No.8 (Telarc); Schubert Mass in G (Telarc); Bach Magnificat (Telarc); Mozart C Minor Mass (Telarc); Handel, Mesiah (Video with Robert Shaw). *Address:* c/o Columbia Artists Management Inc, Arbib-Treuhaft Dn, 165 W 57th Street, New York, NY 10019, USA.

STORJOHANN Helmut, b. 8 Apr 1920, Hamburg, Germany. Artists and Repertoire Manager and Music Producer. m. Gisela Schunk-Storjohann. *Education:* Dr Phil (Musicology and Philosophy), University of Hamburg, 1953; Studied Piano, Harpsichord, Conducting and Composition. *Debut:* As Conductor, Collegium Musicum, Unviersity of Hamburg, 1948. *Career:* Permanent Conductor, Collegium Musicum, Hamburg University, 1948-53; Artist and Repertoire Manager, Pop and Classic Producer, Classic, Philips, Hamburg, 1955-63; Director of Classical Artist Department and Producer, EMI Electrola, Cologne, 1964-81; Freelance Producer. *Recordings:* Many Operas, Operettas, Oratorios, orchestral Works, Chamber Works, Lieder, mainly by German Composers. *Honours:* Recipient of many recording awards. *Membership:* International Music Centre, Vienna, Austria. *Hobbies:* Football; Travel. *Address:* Birkenallee 1, D-50858 Cologne 40, Germany.

STOROJEV Nikita, b. 9 Nov 1950, Harbin, China. Singer (Bass). *Education:* Studied at Tchaikovsky Conservatoire, Moscow. *Career:* Bolshoi Theatre, Moscow, from 1978, as Pimen, Prince Igor, Gremin, Basilio and Fafner; Appearances, 1983-, at Vienna, Paris, Rome, Florence, Berlin, London, New York, San Francisco and Toronto; Repertoire has included Verdi's Zaccaria, Ramphis and Grand Inquisitor, Sarastro, Mephistopheles, Boris Godunov and Ivan Khovansky; Sang in Prokofiev's War and Peace at San Francisco, Rimsky's Mozart and Salieri at the Komische Oper Berlin and Montreal, 1992; Rimsky's Ivan the Terrible at the Rome Opera, 1993, followed by Verdi Requiem at the Festival Deauville and Tchaikovsky's Iolanthe at Dresden Festival; Song recitals with David Ashkenazy and concert features with the Songs and Dances of Death at Festival Hall, 1991, Gorecki's Beatus Vir at New York and the Verdi Requiem at the Festival of Deauville, 1993. *Recordings include:* Shostakovich 13th and 14th Symphonies; War and Peace; Gorecki's Beatus Vir and Songs of the Forest by Shostakovich; Mozart and Salieri. *Honours include:* Diasposon d'Or and Choc de la Musique. *Address:* c/o Athole Still Ltd, 80-86 Westow Street, London SE19 3AF, England.

STOTT Kathryn Linda, b. 10 Dec 1958, Nelson, Lancashire, England. Concert Pianist. m. Michael Ardon. *Education:* Yehudi Menuhin School; Royal College of Music. *Debut:* Purcell Room, London, 1978. *Career:* Performances at the Elizabeth Hall, Wigmore Hall and Windsor and Gstaad Festivals; Piano Recital for Thames TV; Recordings for Dutch, German and BBC radio; CD of Fauré's Piano Works (Conifer). *Honours:* Martin Scholarship 1976; Churchill Scholarship 1979; Croydon Symphony Award; Chappell Medal; Royal Amateur Orchestral Society Silver Medal 1979. *Hobbies:* Films;

Horse Riding. *Address:* c/o AMS Concert Artists, 56 Westbourne Terrace, London W2 3UJ, England.

STOUT Alan (Burrage), b. 26 Nov 1932, Baltimore, Maryland, USA. Composer; Professor. *Education:* BS, Johns Hopkins University, 1954; Postgraduate studies, University of Copenhagen, 1954-55; MA, music and Swedish language, University of Washington, 1959; Studied composition with Henry Cowell, Peabody Conservatory. *Career:* Teacher 1963-76, Professor 1976- , Northwestern University School of Music; Visiting Lecturer, Johns Hopkins University, 1968-69; Royal Academy of Music, Stockholm, 1973; Berkshire Music Center, 1974. *Compositions:* Orchestral: 4 Symphonies: 1959, 1951-66, 1959-62, 1961-71; Intermezzo for English Horn, Percussion and Strings, 1954; Pieta for Strings, 1957; Serenity for Solo Cello or Bassoon, Percussion and Strings, 1959; Movements for Violin and Orchestra, 1962; Fanfare for Charles Seeger, 1972; Nimbus for 18 Strings, 1979; Pilvia, 1983; Chamber: 10 string quartets, 1952-62; Quintet for Clarinet and String Quartet, 1958; Toccata for Saxophone and Percussion, 1965; Cello Sonata, 1966; Recitative, Capriccio and Aria for Oboe, Harp and Percussion, 1970; Suite for Saxophone and Organ, 1973; Concertino for Clarinet and Chamber Group, 1978; Meditation for Tenor Saxophone and Organ, 1982; Brass Quintet, 1984; Piano pieces; Vocal music. *Memberships:* American Composers Alliance; Arnold Schoenberg Institute; International Webern Society; Alban Berg Society; College Music Society; Sonneck Society. *Address:* 2309 Grey Avenue, Evanston, IL 60201, USA.

STRAESSER Joep, b. 11 Mar 1934, Amsterdam, Netherlands. Composer. *Education:* Studied musicology at Amsterdam University, 1952-55, and with Ton de Leeuw at Amsterdam Conservatory. *Career:* Lecturer at Utrecht Conservatory, 1962-89. *Compositions include:* Opera, Uber Erich M: ein komi-tragisches Singspiel, performed in concert at the Royal Conservatory in The Hague, 1987; 22 Pages after John Cage, for ensemble and voices, 1965; Summer Concerto for oboe and chamber orchestra, 1967; Missa for chorus and wind instruments, 1969; Intersections I-V for various instrumental groups, 1969-71; Enclosures for wind and percussion, 1970; Spring Quartet (Sightseeing V), for string quartet, 1971; Intersections V-2, for bass clarinet and piano, 1975; Intervals I-III for chorus and instruments, 1975-81; Fusian a six, symphonic music, 1980; Signals and Echoes for bass clarinet and orchestra, 1982; Verzauberte Lieder for chorus and orchestra, 1986; Triplum for string trio, 1986; Faites vos Jeuz for organ, 1986; Motetus for chorus, 1987; Chamber Concerto I, for violoncello, wind ensemble, harp and percussion, 1991; Symphony III for orchestra, 1992; Gedanken der Nacht (R M Rilke) for mezzo soprano, 1992; Chamber concerto No. 2, for harp and chamber orchestra, 1993; To the point, music for 2 marimbas, 1993; Chamber concerto No. 3 for flute and chamber orchestra, 1993. *Publications:* Number of Essays on musical subjects, among which his analyses of works of Anton Webern are prominent; Article about composer Jacques Bank, 1988/89. *Honours include:* Matthijs Vermeulen Prize for Uber Erich M, 1988. *Address:* BUMA (Netherlands), c/o PRS Ltd Member Registration, 29-33 Berners Street, London W1P 4AA, England.

STRAKA Peter, b. 22 Feb 1950, Zlin, Czechoslovakia. Singer (Tenor). *Education:* Studied in Dusseldorf, Cologne and Munich. *Career:* Sang at St Gallen, 1978-79, Zurich Opera from 1979; Guest appearances at Basle, Berne, Staatsoper Berlin, Hanover, Marseilles, Volksoper Vienna, Opera-Comique Paris, Palermo and Orange; Visits to Dresden and Lausanne and Schwetzingen Festivals with the Zurich Company; Sang in the Nikolaus Harnoncourt-John Pierre Ponnelle Monteverdi cycle at Zurich and has appeared there and elsewhere as Mozart's Idamante and Tamino, Nemorino, Wagner's Froh and Steuermann, Rodolfo and Narraboth in Salome; Sang Jacquino in a concert performance of Fidelio at the Festival Hall, 1990, Alma in Lulu at

Théâtre du Châtelet, Paris, 1991; Metropolitan debut, 1991, in Katya Kabanova. *Recordings include:* Marzio in video of Mozart's Mitridate, conducted by Harnoncourt. *Address:* c/o Opernhaus Zurich, Falkenstrasse 1, CH-8008 Zurich, Switzerland.

STRATAS Teresa (Anastasia Strataki), b. 26 May 1938, Toronto, Ontario, Canada. Opera Singer. m. Tony Harrison.*Education:* Student of Irene Jessner, 1956-59; Graduate, Music Faculty, University of Toronto, 1959. *Career:* Winner, Metropolitan Opera auditions, 1959; Major roles in opera houses throughout the world including: Mimi in La Bohème; Tatiana in Eugene Onegin; Susanna in The Marriage of Figaro; Nedda in Pagliacci; Marenka in The Bartered Bride; Violetta in La Traviata; Title role in Rusalka; Jennie in Mahoganny; Created title role in completed version of Alban Berg's Lulu, Paris Grand Opera, 1979; Rectial artist; Film appearances; Salome, Lulu, Paganini, Zarewitsch, Eugene Onegin, Kaiser von Atlantis, La Traviata, 1983; sang Lulu at Brussels 1988, Mimi at Boston 1989; Suor Angelica, Lauretta and Giorgetta in Il Trittice at the Metropolitan, 1989; Sang Marie Antoinette in the premiere of Corigliano's The Ghosts of Versailles, Metropolitan Opera, 1991; Mélisande at Chicago, 1992. *Honours:* Decorated Order of Canada; named Performer of the Year, Canadian Music Council, 1979; 3 Grammy Awards-Total 7 Grammy Nominations; Winner of Drama Desk Award for Leading Broadway Musical Actress, 1986; Tony Nomination for 1986. *Address:* c/o Metropolitan Opera Company, Lincoln Center Plaza, New York, NY 10023, USA.

STRAUCH Jacek, b. 1953, London, England. Singer (Baritone). *Education:* Studied at Royal College of Music and National Opera Studio, London. *Debut:* Kent Opera, as Rigoletto, 1978. *Career:* Sang in opera at Wurzburg, 1980-82, Saarbrucken, 1982-85; Guest appearances in Modena and Pretoria, South Africa, 1985; Berne Opera, 1987, as Wozzeck, English National Opera, 1988, as Alfio and as Jaroslav Prus in The Makropoulos Case; Season 1988-90 as Amfortas, Iago and the Hoffmann villains at Brunswick, Kurwenal at Saarbrucken and Gunther in Götterdämmerung; Other roles include Mozart's Count; Broadcast engagements in Germany, England and Norway. *Honours include:* Winner, Kathleen Ferrier Competition, 1978; Prizewinner, Belvedere International at Vienna, 1984. *Address:* c/o English National Opera, St Martin's Lane, London WC2, England.

STRAUS Volker, b. 5 July 1936, Speyer, Germany. Producer and Sound Engineer (Classical Music). m. Janny van Donseldaar, 22 May 1964. *Education:* Studied Piano, Harmony, Counterpoint, History, Musicology, many more, Musikhochschule and University, Freiburg, 1954-57; Tonmeister Education, Music, Mathematics, Acoustics, others, Musikhochschule, Detmold, 1957-60. *Career:* Recording Producer and Sound Engineer, Philips Classics, Baarn, Netherlands, 1960-; 1st project was sonatas and partitas for violin (Bach-Grumiaux); Has made between 800 and 900 recordings with great artists such as Arrau, Brendel, Haebler, Grumiaux, Szeryng, Souzay, Fischer- Dieskau, Norman, Nilsson, Haitink, Jochum, Muti, Krips, Abbado, Dorati, Davis, Marriner, Leppard, many others; Teacher, Tonmeister Education, Musikhochschule, Detmold; Co-Founder, Tonmeister Education, Hague Conservatory, Netherlands. *Recordings:* Wagner Parsifal, Bayreuth Knappertsbusch; Concertgebouw Orchestra: works of Debussy, Ravel, Tchaikovsky and Brahms, with Haitink; Mozart, with Krips; Tosca and Pagliacci in Philadelphia, with Muti and Pavarotti; Forthcoming: Mozart, Vienna Philharmonic with Muti; Mahler, Berlin Philharmonic with Haiti; Salome, Staatskapelle Dresden, with Ozawa and Norman; Chamber music, Holliger; Beethoven sonatas for violin and piano, Mozart sonatas for violin and piano; Trio des Beaux Arts, Brahms, Schubert, Ravel, Dvořák, others. *Honours:* Best Engineering Recording, 1981; Grand Prix du Disques, several times; Deutscher Schallplattenpreis; Prizes in Japan, USA, other countries. *Membership:* AES. *Hobbies:* Swimming;

Sailing; Walking in the mountains. *Address:* Bernard Zweerslaan 31, 37-41 HL Baarn, Netherlands.

STRAUSSOVA Eva, b. 7 June 1934, Cheb, Czechoslovakia. Singer (Soprano). *Education:* Studied with Elisa Stunzner and with Rudolf Dittrich at the Dresden Opera Studio (1956-59). *Debut:* Landestheater Dessau 1959, as Helmwige in Die Walküre. *Career:* Sang at Dessau until 1963, notably as Eva in Die Meistersinger, then joined the Staatsoper Berlin: major roles have included Wagner's Elisabeth and Gutrune, Amelia (Un Ballo in Maschera), Donna Anna, Turandot, Elektra, Fiordiligi, Leonore and Katerina Ismailova; Guest engagements in Zurich, Berne, West Germany, Russia and Austria; Sang Isolde at Aachen Opera. *Recordings:* Albums for Eterna.

STREATFIELD Simon, b. 3 May 1929, Windsor, Berkshire, England. Violist; Conductor. m. Elizabeth Winship, 2 daughters. *Education:* Eton College; Royal College of Music, London. *Career:* Principal Viola, Sadler's Wells Opera 1953-55; Principal Viola, London Symphony Orchestra, 1956-65; Principal Viola, Vancouver Symphony Orchestra, Canada, 1965; Assistant Conductor 1967: Associate Conductor, 1972-77; Music Director and Conductor of the Vancouver Bach Choir 1969-81; Season 1970-71 included concerts with the City of Birmingham Symphony, the Royal Choral Society, the BBC and with the Vancouver Bach Choir in Holland; Visiting Professor, Faculty of Music, University of West Ontario, 1977-81; Conductor, Regina Symphony Orchestra, Canada, 1981-84; Conductor, Manitoba Chamber Orchestra, 1982-; Conductor, Quebec Symphony Orchestra, 1984-; Has also conducted the National Arts Centre Orchestra in Ottawa, the Danish Radio Symphony, the Oslo Philharmonic and the Belgian Radio Symphony. *Recordings include:* Telemann Viola Concerto (Oiseau Lyre); Berlioz Harold en Italie (CBC). *Hobbies:* Squash; Cricket; Ornithology.

STREET Tison, b. 20 May 1943, Boston, Massachusetts, USA. Composer; Violinist. *Education:* Harvard University; Composition with Leon Kirchner and David Del Tredici; Violin with Einar Hansen. *Career:* Composer in Residence, Marlboro Music Festival, 1964-66, 1972; Rome Prize Fellowship, 1973; National Endowment Grant to work at Experimental Music Studio, Massachusetts Institute of Technology, 1978; Associate Professor, Harvard University, 1979-82. *Compositions:* Adagio in Eb, 1977; Monsalvat, 1980; String Quartets I and II; String Quintet; Chorals from the Northeast, Piano Solo; John Major's Medley, Guitar. *Recordings:* String Quartet, 1972; String Quintet, 1974 with Marcus Thompson. *Honours:* National Institute, American Academy of Arts and Letters Award, 1973; Brandeis Creative Arts Award, 1979. *Membership:* Society of Fellows, Harvard University. *Address:* 28 Lawrence Street, Boston, MA 02116, USA.

STREHLE Wilfried, b. 1940, Stuttgart, Germany. Violist. *Education:* Studied at Stuttgart and Detmold Hochschulen. *Career:* Violist with Sudfunk-Sinfonia-Orchester at Stuttgart; Soloist with Chamber Orchestra Tibor Varga until 1971, then Principal Violist with Berlin Philharmonic Orchestra; Co-founded Brandis String Quartet, 1976, with chamber concerts in Paris, Munich, Hamburg, Milan, Tokyo and London, and appearances with Wiener Singverein and Berlin Philharmonic; Festival engagements at Edinburgh, Tours, Bergen, Salzburg, Lucerne, Florecne and Vienna; Co-premiered the 3rd Quartets of Gottfried von Einem and Giselher Klebe, 1981, 1983, and the Clarinet Quintet of Helmut Eder, 1984. *Recordings include:* Albums in the standard repertory from 1978 with several labels; Recent releases of quartets by Beethoven, Schulhoff, Weill and Hindemoth and the Schubert String Quartet. *Address:* c/o Anglo Swiss Ltd, 3 Primrose Mews, 1a Sharpleshall Street, London NW1 8YW, England.

STREHLER Giorgio, b. 14 Aug 1921, Barcola, Trieste, Italy. Stage Director. *Education:* Studied at

Accademia di Filodrammatici, Milan. *Career:* Actor from 1940, directed first theatre production, 1943, co-founder of the Piccolo Teatro Lian, 1947; Opera debut at La Scala, 1947, La Traviata; Co-founded Piccola Scala and has produced there and at La Scala such operas as The Love of Three Oranges, Lulu and Mahagonny (Italian premieres), premiere of Castro's Proserpina y el extranjero, 1952, and Die Dreigroschenoper, 1956; Directed Die Entführung aus dem Serail at Salzburg, 1965, followed by Die Zauberflöte, 1974; Simon Boccanegra at La Scala, 1971 (seen at Covent Garden, 1976), Macbeth, 1975, and Don Giovanni, 1988; Le nozze di Figaro at Versailles, 1973, conducted by Solti; Recent work at the Théâtre de l'Europe at the Odeon, Paris. *Publications include:* Io, Strehler (conversations with U Ronfani), Milan, 1986. *Address:* c/o Teatro alla Scala, Via Filodrammatici 2, 20121 Milan, Italy.

STREIT Kurt, b. 1960, Itazuke, Japan. Singer (Tenor). *Education:* Studied at the University of New Mexico with Marilyn Tyler. *Career:* Member of apprentice programmes in San Francisco and Santa Fe, also at the Texas Opera Theater; Appearances with the Milwaukee Skylight Comic Opera and in Dallas; European career with the Hamburg Staatsoper singing in operas by Mozart, Donizetti and Rossini; Guest appearances at Schwetzingen (1987), Aix-en-Provence (1989), Salzburg (1989) and at Glyndebourne (as Tamino in the 1990 production of Die Zauberflöte by Peter Sellars); Has also sung at the opera houses of Vienna (Staatsoper), Munich, Brussels, Leipzig, Dusseldorf and San Francisco (1990); Covent Garden debut 1992, as Ferrando; Concert engagements with the London Symphony, the Orchestre National de France, Leningrad Philharmonic, Hamburg Staatsorchester and the English Chamber Orchestra; Promenade Concerts, London, in a 1990 concert performance of Die Zauberflöte. *Recordings include:* Gluck's Echo et Narcisse (Harmonia Mundi); Ferrando in Così fan Tutte (also at Glyndebourne, 1990) with Daniel Barenboim and the Berlin Philharmonic; Die Entführung aus dem Serail. *Address:* c/o Ingpen and Williams Ltd., 14 Kensington Court, London W11 4PA, England.

STRENGERS Hendrik, b. 2 Apr 1935, The Hague, Netherlands. Government Official. m. Antonia G M van der Kleij, 1 Aug 1963, 1 daughter. *Education:* LLB; Bookkeeper; Training course in Banking; Self-taught in Music. *Career:* Deputy Manager, 1962-72; Management Official, Ministry of Economic Affairs, Netherlands, 1972-92. *Contributions:* Das Mechanische Musikinstrument: Lyraphon-Spieldose, No 47, 1989; J C Eckardt, Christbaum-Ständer mit Musik, No 48, 1989, No 57, 1993; Bulletin of the Musical Box Society International, USA: Adler and Fortuna Musical Boxes, 1975; Kalliope Musical Boxes, 1976; Tannhäuser Musical Boxes, 1977; Homeric Automata, 1980; Piano Rolls, 1984; ANWB Carillon The Hague, 1984; Odeola Player Pianos, 1988; The Pianovo, 1988; New Step in Composing, 1992; Series of articles in Het Pierement, Bulletin of Netherlands Mechanical Organ Society, 1983-; Judgement of Solomon, A Dutch Automaton by J K Elzinga, in Music and Automata, 1986. *Honours:* David Bowers Literary Award for Outstanding Contributions to the Field of Automatic Music, 1987; Knight, Order of Orange-Nassau, 1992. *Memberships:* Board Member, Athanius Kircher Foundation (research on musical automata and campanology); Contributing Editor, Musical Box Society International, USA; Ständige Mitarbeiter, Gesellschaft für Selbstspielende Musikinstrumente, Germany. *Hobby:* Collecting documentation related to mechanical musical instruments and automata. *Address:* Grabijnhof 28, 2625 LM Delft, Netherlands.

STROHM Reinhard, b. 4 Aug 1942, Munich, Germany. Musicologist. *Education:* Studied musicology, Latin and Italian literature at University of Munich, Scuola Normale Superiore Pisa, Technical University Berlin with Carl Dahlhaus; PhD Berlin (TU) 1971. *Career:* Part-time work for Repertoire International des sources Musicales, 1964-70; Editor of the Richard-Wagner-Gesamtausgabe, Munich, 1970-81; Lecturer in Music,

King's College, University of London, 1975-83; Professor of Music History, Yale University, 1983-89; Reader then Professor of Historical Musicology, King's College, London, 1990; Director, Institute of Advanced Musical Studies, King's College, London, 1991-. *Publications include:* Italienische Opernarien des frühen Settecento, 1976; Die italienische Oper im 18. jahrhundert, 1979; Music in Late Medieval Bruges, Oxford 1985; Essays on Handel and Italian Opera, Cambridge 1985; The Rise of European Music 1380-1500, Cambridge 1993. *Honours include:* Dent Medal of the Royal Musical Association, 1977; FBA, 1993. *Address:* Institute of Advanced Musical Studies, King's College, Strand, London WC2R 2LS, England.

STROUD Peter Lewis Townsend, b. 5 Apr 1933, Poona, India. Music Copyrighter Administrator. m. Averil Winton, 29 Apr 1961, 1 son, 1 daughter. *Education:* Corpus Christi College, Cambridge; Honours degree in Music, Cambridge. *Career:* Stainer and Bell Ltd, Music Publishers, 1958-60; Performing Right Society Ltd, 1960-, currently Repertoire Consultant. *Recording:* A Musicall Banquet, R Dowland (1610) (edited Stroud). *Publication:* A Musicall Banquet (1610) (Robert Dowland/edited P Stroud), 1968. *Honours:* Gold Badge for services to British music, Songwriters Guild (now British Academy of Songwriters, Composers and Authors), 1981. *Hobbies:* Collecting records and stamps; Choral singing. *Address:* 51 Platt's Lane, London ,NW3 7NL, England.

STROUD Stephen Lorre, b. 11 Jan 1951, Modesto, California, USA. Music Educator; Conductor. m. Janet Cole, 20 Dec 1975, 1 daughter. *Education:* AA, Music, Modesto Junior College; BA, Music, Teaching Credential in Music, University of California, Los Angeles; MS and EdD in Music Education (specialisation in Conducting), University of Illinois, Champaign; Participant, Eastman School of Music Conducting Seminar, 1992. *Career:* Student Conductor and Trumpet Player with high school band, Modesto Junior College, University of California at Los Angeles and Illinois Bands; Trumpet Player with American Youth Symphony of Los Angeles; Music Teacher and Conductor: University of California, Los Angeles; Atascadero High School, San Jose, California; Junior College, Modesto, California; University of Illinois, Urbana. *Recordings:* With High School and College Wind Bands. *Publication:* An Examination of Five Active University Band Directors Selected As Exemplary Conductors, 1991. *Contributions to:* Lifelong Learning in Music (with Mary Hoffman), articles in Podium Magazine. *Honours:* California Teachers Scholarship, 1986; Excellence in Teaching Award for US Community Colleges, 1989; Begian Conducting Award, 1987; Selected to participate in Conductors Guild Symposium, 1992. *Memberships:* Conductors Guild; Music Educators National Conference; College Band Directors National Association; World Association for Symphonies, Bands and Ensembles. *Hobbies:* Sourdough breads; Antique restoration. *Address:* 312 Harrow Court, Modesto, CA 95350-1425, USA.

STROW-PICCOLO Lynne, b. 17 June 1947, Waterbury, Connecticut, USA. Opera Singer; Dramatic Soprano. m. Tommaso Piccolo, 24 Jan 1975. *Education:* BMusEd, Hartt College of Music, University of Hartford, Connecticut, USA; Vocal Studies with Cantor Arthur Koret, Hartford and Carlo Alfieri, Parma, Italy. *Debut:* Siena, Italy, 1975. *Career:* Performances in major opera houses in England (Covent Garden); Germany (Hamburg, Berlin, Munich); Italy (La Scala); Austria (Vienna Staatsoper); France, Spain, Norway, Hungary, Yugoslavia, Roumania, Poland, Chile, Canada, South Africa and USA; Television appearances in Canada, Spain, USA and Italy; Radio concerts in Germany, Holland, Italy, France, Spain, USA and Canada. *Recordings:* Zazà by Leoncavallo; Nerone by Mascagni. *Honours:* 1st prize, F Neglia Opera Contest, Sicily, 1973; 1st prize, Busseto Verdi Voices Contest, Italy, 1974; Absolute Winner, Italian RAI-TV Opera Voices Contest, 1974. *Hobby:* Astrology. *Address:* Musicart Raphael, Glaubergstrasse 95, 6000 Frankfurt 1, Germany.

STRUMMER Peter, b. 8 Sept 1948, Vienna, Austria. Singer (Bass- baritone). m. Linda Roark. *Studied at Cleveland Institute of Music. Debut:* Atlanta City, as Mozart's Antonio, 1972. *Career:* Opera engagements with Minnesota Opera Company and at Santa Fe and San Francisco; Sang at Heidelberg and Linz, 1978-85; Metropolitan Opera debut, 1985, as Beckmesser; US and European appearances as Don Alfonso (at Miami), Mozart's Bartolo, Dulcamara, Don Magnifico (at Baltimore) and Bartolo in Il Barbiere di Siviglia (Toronto, 1992); Season 1989-90 as Baron Zeta in Die lustige Witwe, Fabrizio in La Gazza Ladra at Philadelphia, the Music Master at Milwaukee and Faninal at Montreal; New Orleans, 1991, as Melitone in La Forza del Destino. *Address:* c/o Canadian Opera Company, 227 Front Street East, Toronto, Ontario, Canada M5A 1E8.

STUBBS Stephen, b. 1951, Seattle, Washington, USA. Chitarrone and Archlute player; Director. *Career:* Director of Tragicomedia, ensemble performing in the Renaissance and Baroque repertory; Concerts in Britain and at leading European early music festivals; Gave Stefano Landi's La Morte d'Orfeo at the 1987 Flanders Festival; Francesca Caccini's La liberazione di Ruggiero dall'isola d'Alcina at the 1989 Swedish Baroque Festival, Malmo; Conducted Monteverdi's L'Incoronazione di Poppea, for Norrlands Opera in Umea, Sweden, 1993. *Recordings include:* Solo lute recordings - David Kellner's XVI. Auserlesene Lauten-Stucke (CPO), J S Bach and S L Weiss Lute Suites (EMI Classics); with Tragicomedia - Proensa (Troubador songs on ECM), My Mind to me a Kingdom is (Elizabethan ballads on Hyperion) A Musicall Dreame (duet's from Robert Jones 1609 collection), Orpheus I am (masque and theatre music by Robert Johnson and William Lawes on EMI), Sprezzatura (Italian instrumental music on EMI), Il Ballo dell'Ingrate (this and other theatrical music by Monteverdi on Teldec), The Notebook of Anna Magdalena Bach (Teldec) Le Canterine Romane (music for three sopranos by Luigi Rossi on Teldec); Concert programmes include all of the recorded repertoire and other music of the 17th and 18th centuries including Orpheus Britannicus (the best of Purcell's secular music for up to 5 singers, violins and oboes). *Current Management:* Robert White Artist Management, England. *Address:* Robert White Artist Management, 182 Moselle Avenue, London N22 6EX, England.

STUCKY Rodney D, b. 9 Sept 1944, Halstead, Kansas, USA. Classical and Baroque Guitarist; Lutenist; Teacher. m. May Henderson, 20 June 1992. *Education:* BM, Bethany College, Lindsborg, Kansas; MM, Southern Methodist University, Dallas, Texas; Early Music coaching with Nicholas McGegan, Paul O'Dette, Trevor Pinnock and James Tyler; Guitar study with Aaron Shearer at Peabody Conservatory, Baltimore, Maryland. *Career:* Head, Guitar Department and Early Music Ensemble, University of South Carolina, 1973-77; Head, Guitar Department and Co-Director, Early Music Ensemble, St Louis Conservatory of Music, 1977-90; Taught at National Music Camp, Interlochen, Michigan, 1977-82; Guest Lecturer at 1st and 2nd American Classical Guitar Congress, 1986, 1989; Guest Artist with Synchronia, new music ensemble of St Louis, 1988-91; Performances with members of St Louis Symphony on the Discovery Series, 1993; Performances with wife, mezzosoprano Mary Henderson, throughout Mid-West and Central Eastern USA and at Ecole Normale, Alfred Cortot Hall, Paris, France. *Publication:* Guitar for the Young, a method for teaching young children Classical Guitar, to be published. *Hobbies:* Science; Hiking. *Address:* 7066 Sweetwater Dr, Florence, KY 41042, USA.

STUDER Cheryl, b. 24 Oct 1955, Midland, Michigan, USA. Singer (Soprano). *Education:* Studied in USA and with Hans Hotter in Vienna. *Career:* Concert engagements in US then sang with the Munich Staatsoper from 1980, notably as Marenka in The Bartered Bride; Darmstadt 1983-85, in Mozart roles and as Bizet's Micaela, Strauss's Chrysothemis and Wagner's Irene and Eva; Berlin Deutsche Opernhaus from 1985; Bayreuth debut 1985, as Elisabeth in Tannhäuser: returned 1988 as Elsa in Lohengrin; Paris Opera 1986, as Pamina in Die Zauberflöte; Covent Garden 1987-88, as Elisabeth and Elsa; sang Sieglinde and the Empress in Die Frau ohne Schatten at La Scala 1987; Metropolitan debut 1988, Micaela; Season 1989 sang Chrysothemis at Salzburg and Vienna, Lucia at Philadelphia; Opening night of season, La Scala 1989, as Hélène in I vespri siciliani; Elsa at Vienna 1990 (opposite Domingo); Deutsche Oper Berlin 1990, as Salome; Sang Mozart's Elettra at the 1990 Salzburg Festival, Donna Anna at Vienna; Season 1992/93 as Lehar's Giuditta at the Vienna Volksoper, the Empress in Die Frau ohne Schatten and Mdme Cortesa in Il Viaggio a Reims at Salzburg; Covent Garden 1994, as Aida. *Recordings:* Zemlinsky's Der Zweg; Sieglinde in the Haitink recording of Die Walküre (EMI); Aida and Tannhäuser (Sinopoli); Salome (Sinopoli); Guillaume Tell; I Vespri siciliani and Attila (Muti); La traviata (Levine); Die Zauberflöte (Marriner); Lohengrin (Abbado); Lucia d Lammermoor. *Address:* c/o Deutsche Oper Berlin, Richard Wagnerstrasse 10, D-1000 Berlin 1, Germany.

STUDER Ulrich, b. 27 Aug 1945, Berne, Switzerland, Singer (Baritone). *Education:* Studied at Berne Conservatory and Musikhochschule Munich. *Career:* Many appearances at opera houses in Italy, Netherlands (The Hague), Austria (Innsbruck), Australia and Czechoslovakia; Concert and broadcast engagements in Switzerland, Germany and France, notably in Bach's sacred music and contemporary works by Burkhard, Milhaud and Huber; Recitals featuring German Lieder and French Chansons; Opera performances at Berne, 1979-83, and at Basle, Lausanne and Munich; Roles have included Morales in Carmen, Belcore, Malatesta, Valentin, Creonte in Haydn's Orfeo, Masetto, Suppé's Boccaccio and Monteverdi's Orfeo. *Recordings include:* Cantatas by Bach and Charpentier; Messe des Morts by Gilles; Cantatas by Vivaldi; Elviro in Handel's Serse; Lully's Armide; Erode in Stradella's San Giovanni Battista. *Address:* c/o Stadttheater Bern, Nageligasse 1, CH-3011 Bern, Switzerland.

STUDNICKA Vladimir, b. 24 Aug 1935. Composer; Music Director. 2 daughters. *Education:* Completed Composition studies, 1957, completed Classical Guitar Performance, 1966, Conservatory of Music. *Debut:* Suite for Orchestra performed by Janaček Philharmonic Orchestra, 1957. *Career:* Teacher at Music School, 1961-75; Music Director, Radio Ostrava, 1975-; Works as a Conductor; Established and conducts Beskydska muzika harmonic folk orchestra. *Compositions:* All kinds, especially concert pieces for harmonic orchestras; adaptations of folk songs of the Janacek region; Chamber and symphony compositions; Works include: Suite for Orchestra, 1957; The May Dance, recorded, Prague Radio, 1973; The Beskydy Nocturno, Radio Ostrava, 1984; The Ondra's Dance, Radio Ostrava, 1985; Salut J V Stich-Punto, for 12 horns, Radio Ostrava, 1986. *Recordings include:* Radio recordings; Many smaller pieces. *Publications:* The Round, 1985; The Song of the Rising Sun by Wilhelm Halter, 1990; Slazsky dance Musikvarlag Rundal, 1993. *Hobbies:* Tourism; Nature; Picking mushrooms. *Address:* ul prof Jana Soupala 1607, 70800 Ostrava-Poruba, Czech Republic.

STULBERG Neal (Howard), b. 12 Apr 1954, Detroit, Michigan, USA. Conductor; Pianist. m. Leah Shahmoon, 12 July 1987. *Education:* BA, Harvard College, 1976; MMus, University of Michigan, 1978; Postgraduate studies, Juilliard School, 1979-80. *Career:* Conductor, Massachusetts Institute of Technology Symphony Orchestra, 1980-82; Young Musicians' Foundation Debut Orchestra, Los Angeles, 1981-84; Exxon Arts Endowment Assistant Conductor, Los Angeles Philharmonic Orchestra, 1983-85; Music Director, New Mexico Symphony Orchestra, Albuquerque, 1985-1993. *Honours:* Seaver/National Endowment for the Arts Conductors Award, 1988. *Current Management:* Shaw Concerts, Inc, 1 Lincoln Plaza, 1900 Broadway, 2nd Floor, New York, NY 10023, USA. *Address:* 201

Ocean Avenue No 1208P, Santa Monica, CA 90402, USA.

STURROCK Kathron, b. 17 July 1948, Bournemouth, England. Pianist. *Education:* Studied at the Royal College of Music and with Alfred Brendel in Vienna; Further study with Mstislav Rostropovitch in Moscow. *Career:* Concert and television appearances throughout Europe and in North America, India and Australia; Regular performances for the BBC and concerts in the major London halls; Founded the Chamber Music ensemble, The Fibonacci Sequence; Has taught at Morley College, the Royal College of Music, Royal Academy of Music and the Birmingham School of Music; Artist in residence at the Brisbane Conservatoire 1987; British Council tour of Oman 1989; BBC recitals include Schubert's Wanderer Fantasy, Beethoven op. 109. Rawsthorne Ballade. Prom debut in 1994 Rawsthorne 2 piano concerto with Piers Lane. *Recordings include:* Bliss Viola Sonata, with Emanuel Vardi (Chandos); Beethoven Spring Sonata, (Sain records), Brahms Violin and Viola Sonatas, Cello Sonatas by Beethoven, Schnittke, Shostakovich and Kabalevsky, Songs by Rebecca Clarke with Patricia Wright. *Honours:* Sofia International Opera Competition (as accompanist); Martin Musical Scholarship Fund and the Countess of Munster Award, RCM. *Address:* 81 Lacy Road, London SW15 1NR, England.

SUART Richard Martin, b. 5 Sept 1951, Blackpool, England. Singer (Baritone). m. Susan Cook, 1981, 2 sons, 1 daughter. *Education:* Sang in choir of St John's College, Cambridge and studied at the Royal Academy of Music. *Career:* Has sung with English Music Theatre, notably in Henze's La Cubana, and toured with the Singer's Company; Appearances with Opera Factory in Punch and Judy and Yan Tan Tethera (Birtwistle), Eight Songs for a Mad King and Osborne's Hells Angels; With English National Opera in Orfeo, War and Peace, Don Carlos and The Mask of Orpheus; Has also sung with D'Oyly Carte (Gilbert and Sullivan), Kent Opera (Swallow in Peter Grimes) and Opera North (Schaunard in La Bohème); Sang in the premiere production of Greek by Mark Anthony Turnage at Munich and Edinburgh (1988); Eight songs for a Mad King at Gelsenkirchen, Milan, and Helsinki; Further engagements with the Winnipeg Symphony in Canada and at the Almeida, Cheltenham and Orkney Festival in The Fall of the House of Usher by Glass; A Midsummer Night's Dream for Opera London at Sadler's Wells; Season 1992 as Gianni Schicchi at Cambridge, Guttil in Broken Strings by Param Vir at Amsterdam and Taddeo in The Italian Girl in Algiers at Buxton. *Recordings include:* Video of Greek; Elgar's Caractacus with Charles Groves; Holst's At the Boar's Head conducted by David Atherton; Bernstein's Candide under the composer; A Midsummer Night's Dream (Virgin Classics); The Fairy Queen with The Sixteen (Collins Classics). *Hobbies:* DIY; Gardening; Home brewing. *Current Management:* Magenta Music International, 64 Highgate High Street, London N6 5HX, England. *Address:* 23 Dry Hill Park Road, Tonbridge, Kent TN10 3BL, England.

SUBEN Joel Eric, b. 16 May 1946, New York City, USA. Symphony Conductor; Composer; Professor. m. (1) Judith Ann Gundersheimer, 21 Oct 1979, divorced 1985, (2) Linda Rodgers, 20 July 1993. *Education:* BMus, Distinction, Eastman School of Music, 1969; MFA, 1974, PhD, 1980, Brandeis University; Hochschule Mozarteum, Salzburg, Austria; Certificate, Orchestral Conducting; Private Study, Conducting with Jacques- Louis Monod, 1973-77. *Career:* Music Director, Permanent Conductor, Peninsula Symphony of Virginia, 1982-87; Guest Conductor, Silesian Philharmonic Orchestra, Poland, 1986; Artistic Director, Brooklyn Heights Music Festival, 1986; Principal Conductor, Center Orchestra, New Jersey, 1987-88; Guest Conductor, New Jersey Composers Orchestra, 1987-; Principal Guest Conductor, Cygnus Ensemble, 1989-; Guest Lecturer, New York Philharmonic Pre-Concert Lecture Series, 1989-; Guest Conductor, Czestochowa Philharmonic Orchestra, Poland 1992, 1993; Guest Conductor, Bialystok Philharmonic Orchestra, Poland 1992; Director of Orchestras, College of William and Mary (Virginia), 1983-92; Guest Conductor, Polish Radio National Symphony Orchestra, 1993; Music Director, Composers Chorus, 1992-; Music Advisor, Wellesley Philharmonic (Massachusetts), 1993-. *Compositions include:* Gesualdo Triptych, 1984, string orchestra; Idyls, 1984, 2 pianos; Symphony in Old Style, 1987, orchestra; Winter Love, 1987, chorus and orchestra; Concerto Classico, 1991, for flute and small orchestra; The Silver Swan for soprano and five instruments, 1992; Breve Sogno, 1993, for large orchestra. *Recordings:* CGNJ label, CD released 1993; MMC label, CD released 1994; New World Records, CD released 1994; Opus One Records, CD released 1994; as composer, MMC label, CD released 1994. *Publication:* Debussy and Octatonic Pitch Structure, University Microfilms, 1980. *Current Management:* Linda Rodgers Associates, USA. *Address:* c/o Linda Rodgers Associates, 628 Bloomfield Street, Hoboken, NJ 07030, USA.

SUBLET Pierre Rene Joseph, b. 26 Aug 1954, Vevey, Switzerland. Pianist. *Education:* Prix de virtuosite at the Geneva Conservatoire. Studies with Cl. Helffer, Paris. *Career:* Regular performances in concerts and on radio and television throughout Europe (on the piano and fortepiano); 1985 debut in New York at the Theatre La Mama ETC; Tour of Brazil 1989; Tour of Japan 92; Member of the Directorate of the Conservatoire de Bienne, Switzerland, 1985-. *Recordings:* Tetraclacier, Stockhausen and Swiss Composers; Piano Music from Christian Giger (Gallo 30-417); Mauro Giuliani: Musiche de Camera, with fortepiano (Jecklin Disco 624-2). *Membership:* Association of Swiss Musicians. *Honours:* Several prizes at home and abroad for piano solos and chamber music, including 1981, First Prize in 2nd Competition of Contemporary Music Interpretation in Lausanne. *Hobbies:* Cooking; Literature; Mountain hiking. *Address:* rue de Stand, 2502 Bienne, Switzerland.

SUBOTNICK Morton, b. 14 Apr 1933, Los Angeles, California, USA. Composer; Clarinettist; Conductor; Teacher. m. Joan La Barbara, 18 Dec 1979.1 son. *Education:* BA, composition, University of Denver, 1958; MA, Mills College, 1960. *Career:* Various appearances as Clarinettist and Conductor; Co-founder and Director, San Francisco Tape Music Center, 1961-65; Music Director, Ann Halprin Dance Company, 1961-67; Lincoln Center Repertory Theater, 1967-68; Teacher, Mills College, 1959-66; New York University, 1966-69; Co-director, Composition Program and the Center for Experiments in Art, Information and Technology (CEAIT) at California Institute of Arts; California Institute of the Arts, Valencia, 1969-; Composer-in-Residence, Deutscher Akademischer Austauschdienst, West Berlin, 1979-80; Various visiting professorships. *Compositions:* Orchestral: Lamination for Orchestra and Tape, 1968; Lamination II for Chamber Ensemble and Electronics, 1969; Before the Butterfly, 1975; 2 Butterflies for Amplified Orchestra, 1975; Place, 1978; Axolotl for Cello, Chamber Orchestra asnd Electronics, 1982; Liquid Strata for Piano, orchestra and Electronics, 1982; The key to Songs for Chamber Orchestra and Synthesizer, 1985; In Two Worlds, concerto for Saxophone, Electronic Wind Controller and Orchestra, 1987-88; And The Butterflies Begin to Sing, for string quintet, piano and computer, 1989; All my Hummingbrids have Alibis, 1991, for flute, cello, midi piano, midi mallets and computer, CD-ROM on the Voyager label; first piece of music composed specifically for CD-ROM; music intergrated with Max Ernst's visual imagery and text; Jacob's Room, chamber opera, was premiered at the American Music Theater Festival, Philadelphia, 1993; Various mixed-media scores; Tape pieces; Chamber music; Vocal scores; Instrumental works with electronics; Incidental music. *Recordings:* Several compositions recorded. *Honours:* Fellow, Institute for Advanced Musical Studies, Princeton University, 1959, 1960; National Endowment for the Arts grant, 1975; American Academy and Institute of Arts and Letters award, 1979; Brandeis University Creative Arts award, 1983; Many commissions.

Address: 121 Coronado Lane, Santa Fe, NM 87501, USA.

SUHONEN Antti, b. 5 Nov 1956, Nurmes, Finland. Singer (Bass). *Education:* Studied at Sibelius Academy and at the National Opera studio, Helsinki and at the International Opera Studio, Zürich; Masterclasses with Charles Farncombe. *Career:* Sang minor roles at Zurich from 1987, engaged at Karlsruhe, 1987-91 and at Helsinki from 1991-; Made guest appearances at Dresden, Wiesbaden, Hanover and Mannheim and Munich State Opera and Berlin State Opera; Karlsruhe, 1989, in shared premiere of Graf Mirabeau by Siegfried Matthus; Appearances at Helsinki and elsewhere as Mozart's Leporello, Masetto, Figaro, and Alfonso, Sparafucile, Dulcamara, Paisiello's Basilio and Varlaam in Boris Godunov, Méphistophélès in Gounod's Faust; Sang Klaus in premiere of Linkola's Elina, Helsinki, 1992; Savonlinna Festival, 1992, as Don Fernando in Fidelio; Bluebeard in Bartók's Bluebeard Castle, 1994. *Address:* c/o Finnish National Opera, Helsinginkatu 58, SF 00260 Helsinki 18, Finland.

SUITNER Otmar, b. 16 May 1922, Innsbruck, Austria. Conductor; Musical Director. m. Marita Wilckens. *Education:* Innsbruck Conservatory; Salzburg Mozarteum 1940-42 under Ledwinka; Studied conducting with Clemens Krauss. *Debut:* Landestheater, Innsbruck, 1942. *Career:* Musical Director Remschied, Germany, 1952-57; Musical Director of the Pfalz Orchestra Luwigshafen 1957; Guest appearances in Vienna, Munich, Hamburg and Berlin; Chief Conductor of the Dresden Staatsoper and Staatskapelle 1960; Musical Director of the Deutsche Oper, East Berlin, 1964: conducted the premieres of Dessau's Puntilla (1966), Einstein (1974) and Leonce und Lena (1979); Tours with the Berlin company to Paris, Warsaw, Cairo and Lausanne; Bayreuth Festival 964-69, Der fliegende Holländer, Tannhäuser and Der Ring des Nibelungen; Conducted Der Freischütz at the 1990 Munich Festival; Engagements at the San Francisco Opera from 1969; Honorary Conductor of the Tokyo NHK Symphony Orchestra 1973; Professor Hochschule für Musik Vienna (Austria), 1977-. *Recordings:* For EMI, Teldec, Deutsche Grammophon Denon and Eterna labels, including Figaro, Così Fan Tutte, Salome, Die Entführung, Il Barbiere di Siviglia. *Honours:* Commendatore Gregorius Order, 1973; Austrian Ehrenkreuz für Wissenschaft & Kunst, 1982. *Address:* c/o A-1090/Vienna, Widerhofer Platz, 4/48.

SUK Josef, b. 8 Aug 1929, Prague, Czechoslovakia. Violinist. m. Marie Polakova. *Education:* Conservatory of Music in Prague; Prague Academy 1951-53. *Debut:* 1940. *Career:* Western European engagements from 1948 (Paris and Brussels); Leader of Prague Quartet 1951-52; Joined Suk Trio 1952; Leader of orchestra at Prague National Theatre 1953-55; Soloist with Czech Philharmonic Orchestra, US debut 23 Jan. 1964, with the Cleveland Orchestra; British debut 1964 at the Promenade Concerts, playing Mozart and Dvořák; Formed duo with Zuzana Ruzickova in 1963 and a trio with Janos Starker and Julius Katchen 1967-69; Duos with Jan Panenka, piano; Founded Suk Chamber Orchestra 1974, played at the Bath Festival 1991: Janáček's Sonata, Brahms op.108, Beethoven op.96. *Honours:* Grand Prix du Disque 1960, 1966, 1968, 1974; State Prize 1964; Artist of Merit 1970; Edison Prize 1972; Wiener Floteuhr 1974; National Prize 1977; President of the Antonin Dvořák Foundation; President of ther Prague Spring Foundation. *Address:* Karlovo Namesti 5, 120 00 Prague 2.

SULLIVAN Timothy, b. 16 Dec 1954, Ottawa, Canada. Composer. *Education:* Studied music at Harper College, Illinois, 1972-74, composition at Toronto Conservtory, 1974-78; Toronto University from 1977, with John Beckwith. *Career:* Teacher of theory and composition at Toronto Conservatory, 1979, head of composition department, 1985-89; Teacher of Composition at University of Victoria, 1989-90; Composer-in-residence for Canadina Opera Company, 1987-88. *Compositions include:* Tomorrow and

Tomorrow, monodrama, New York, 1987; Dream Play, opera in 1 act after Strindberg, Toronto, 1988; The Imaginary Couple, opera after Moliere, 1990; Florence, opera, 1990. *Address:* c/o SOCAN (Canada), PRS Ltd Member Registration, 29-33 Berners Street, London W1P 4AA, England.

SUMMERS Hilary, b. 1965, Newport, Gwent, Wales. Singer (Contralto). *Education:* Studied at Reading University, Royal Academy of Music and the National Opera Studio. *Career:* Concert appearances at Festival Hall, Barbican Centre, Purcell Room and St John's, Smith Square; The Dream of Gerontius with Liverpool Philharmonic and Henze's Novae de Infinito Laudes with London Sinfonietta; Other modern repertory includes Schoenberg's Pierrot Lunaire and works by Berio, Stravinsky, Webern, Berg, Rihm and Jonathan Harvey; Opera debut as a Valkyrie in Die Walkure for Scottish Opera, 1992; Has also sung in Die Königskinder for English National Opera and appeared as Britten's Lucretia, Ursule in Beatrice et Benedict, Cornelia in Giulo Cesare, Merecedes in Carmen, Gaea in Daphne, Martha in Mefistofele and Anna in Les Troyens. *Honours include:* The Worshipful Company of Musicians Silver Medal; Shinn Fellowship, Royal Academy of Music; Recital Diploma, Royal Academy of Music. *Recordings include:* Messiah, with Kings College Choir. *Address:* c/o Ingpen and Williams Ltd, 14 Kensington Court, London W8 5DN, England.

SUMMERS Jonathan, b. 2 Oct 1946, Melbourne, Australia. Singer (Baritone). *Education:* Studies with Bettine McCaughan in Melbourne and with Otakar Kraus in London. *Debut:* Kent Opera 1975, as Rigoletto. *Career:* has sung with Royal Opera Covent Garden from 1976, as Malatesta (Don Pasquale), Papageno, Albert (Werther), the High Priest in Samson et Dalila, Balstrode (Peter Grimes), Hercules (Alceste), Mozart's Figaro, Marcello, Ford (Falstaff) and Sharpless (Madama Butterfly); With English National Opera has sung Posa, Renato, Rigoletto, Macbeth, Balstrode, Simon Boccanegra and Eugene Onegin; Apperances with Scottish Opera as Count Almaviva and Don Giovanni, Opera North as the High Priest, Nabucco and Onegin, and at Glyndebourne as Ford; Australian Opera, debut 1981, as Germont Père: has returned as Count Luna and Renato, and in Les Contes d'Hoffmann; Victorian State Opera in Le Nozze di Figaro and Andrea Chénier; European engagements in Hamburg (as Posa), Frankfurt (Rigoletto), Munich (Le Nozze di Figaro), Florence (Marcello and Sharpless), La Scala Milan (Marcello), Avignon (Renato), Paris Opéra (Traviata and Lohengrin), and Geneva (Alceste and Das Rheingold); Metropolitan Opera as Marcello in La Bohème, conducted by Carlos Kleiber; San Diego Opera in Il Trovatore; debut at the Lyric Opera Chicago 1990, as Enrico in Lucia di Lammermoor; Season 1992 as Rodrigo in Don Carlos for ENO, High Priest in Samson et Dalila at Covent Garden, and Don Carlo in The Force of Destiny at the London Coliseum. *Recordings include:* Peter Grimes; Samson et Dalila, with Baltsa and Carreras; Carmina Burana; Vaughan Williams Sea Symphony, with the London Philharmonic, conducted by Haitink; Videos of Samson et Dalila (Royal Opera) and Il Trovatore (Australian Opera, with Sutherland); Der Rosenkavalier with Royal Opera under Solti; Count Arnheim in The Bohemian Girl (Argo). *Address:* c/o Patricia Greenan, 19b Belsize Park, London NW3 4DU, England.

SUMMERS William John, b. 8 Feb 1945, Sonora, California, USA. Historical Musicologist; University Professor. m. Edith Kimber, 2 May 1970, 1 daughter. *Education:* BA, San Luis Rey College, 1969; MA, California State University, 1973; PhD, University of California, Santa Barbara, 1978. *Career:* Fellow, Music, University of California, 1975-77; Visiting Scholar, Kings College, University of London, England; Associate Professor, Music, Chairman, Fine Arts, Seattle University, 1982-84; Associate Professor, Music, Chairman, Music, Dartmouth College, Hanover, 1984-87. *Publications:* English Fourteenth Century Polyphony; Facsimile Edition of Sources Notated in Score, 1983; The Journal of Musicology, VIII (1990); XIV Congress

Report of the International Musicological Society, Bologna, 1987 (1990). *Contributions to:* Music Magazine; New Grove Dictionary of Music and Musicians; New Grove Dictionary of American Music; Soundings/Santa Barbara; Revista Musical Chilena; Music and Letters; Early Music History IV; Reports of the Twelfth and Thirteenth Congresses of the International Musicological Society, Berkeley, 1979, Strasbourg, 1982; Congress Report of the Gesellschaft fur Musik Forschung, Stuttgart, 1985; The Journal of Musicology, VIII, no.1 and no.2, 1990; Inter-American Music Review, XI, 1991; Plainsong and Medieval Music, I, 1992; Music and Letters, 75, 1984. *Hobbies:* Tennis; Walking; Swimming. *Address:* PO Box 632, 6 Grant Road, Hanover, NH 03755, USA.

SUMSION Herbert Whitton, b. 19 Jan 1899, Gloucester, England. Organist; Director of Music; Composer. m. 1927, Alice Hartley Garlich, 3 sons. *Education:* MusB, Durham University, 1920; DMus, Lambeth, 1947; FRCM. *Career:* Organist, Gloucester Cathedral, 1928-67; Director of Music, Ladies College, Cheltenham, 1935-68; Organist and Choirmaster, Christ Church, Lancaster Gate; Director of Music, Bishops Stortford College; Assistant Instructor in Music, Morley College, London; Teacher of Harmony and Counterpoint, Curtis Institute, Philadelphia, Pennsylvania, USA, 1926-28; Conductor, Three Choirs Festival, 1928, 1931, 1934, 1937, 1947, 1950, 1953, 1956, 1959, 1962, 1965. *Compositions:* Introduction and Theme for Organ, 1935; Morning and Evening Service in G, 1935; Two Pieces for cello and piano, 1939 (No 1 arranged for String Orchestra): Magnificat and Nunc Dimittis in G for Boys' Voices, 1953, for Men's Voices, 1953, for Boy's Voices in D, 1973; Cradle Song for Organ, 1953; Benedicite in B flat, 1955; Four Carol Preludes for Organ, 1956; Festival Bendicite in D, 1971; They That Go Down to the Sea in Ships (anthem) 1979; Transposition Exercises, 1980; Piano Technique, a Book of Exercises, 1980; There is a Green Hill Far Away (anthem), 1981; Two Anthems for Holy Communion, 1981; In Exile (By the Waters of Babylon) (anthem), 1981. *Honours:* CBE, 1961; Honorary RAM, FRCO, FRSCM. *Address:* Church End House, Frampton-On-Severn, Glos., GL2 7EH, England.

SUNDBERG Johan E F, b. 25 Mar 1936, Stockholm, Sweden. University Professor. m. Ulla, 3 Dec 1983, 2 sons. *Education:* Studied at the Uppsala University and Singing with Dagmar Gustafson, Stockholm. *Debut:* Stockholm, 1986. *Publications:* The Science of the Singing Voice; The Science of Musical Sounds; Editor, Harmony and Tonality; Gluing Tones and others, about 200 articles in different scientific journals and books such as: Acoustics of the Singing Voice; Generative Theories in Language and Music. *Honour:* Gould Award. *Memberships:* Royal Swedish Academy of Music; Acoustic Society of America. *Hobby:* Singing. *Address:* Music Acoustics, KTH, Box-70014, S-10044, Stockholm, Sweden.

SUNDIN Nils-Göran, b. 18 May 1951, Växjö, Sweden. Music Director; Composer; Author. *Education:* Diploma as Choirmaster and Organist, Lund, 1968; Piano master-classes with Hans Leygraf, Mozarteum, Salzburg, 1969, 1970; Master's degree, Musical Theory, Pedagogy of Musical Theory, Stockholm State School of Music; PhilCand, Musicology, History of Literature and Fine Arts, Stockholm University; PhD in Philosophy of Music, USA, 1988; Studied composition with György Ligeti and Ingvar Lidholm, Stockholm College of Music, 1972-74, Analysis and composition with Olivier Messiaen, Paris, 1975, orchestral conducting and theory in Sergiu Celibidache's master-classes; Med Cand, Lund University. *Career:* Lecturer in Music Theory and Interpretation, Stockholm State College of Music and Edsberg College of Music, Sollentuna, 1975-85; Lecturer in Music History, Stockholm University, 1976; Music Critic, Svenska Dagbladet, 1977-81; Executive Music Chief, Kronoberg Music Foundation, Växjö, 1987. *Compositions:* Numerous works for piano, chamber music, voice, choir, orchestra, including: Symphony for Peace, for orchestra and choir with poems by Dag

Hammarskjöld (commissioned for The Great Peace Journey), Invitazione, Emmanuel Swedenborg in memorium, 1988; Concerto St George for piano and orchestra, 1990; Violin concerto, 1994. *Publications:* Books include: Musical Interpretation in Performance, 1983; Bilder ur Musikens Historia, 1984; Musical Interpretation Research, 1984, MIR Vols. I-II, 1984; Aesthetic Criteria of Musical Interpretation in Contemporary Performance, 1994. *Contributions to:* About 300 articles and reviews in numerous publications including Nutida Musik, Bonniers musiklexikon, Sohlmans musiklexikon. *Memberships:* STIM; Sveriges Författarförbund; New York Academy of Sciences; International Musicological Society. *Address:* c/o Lorovic, Innere Ringstrasse 12, CH-3600 Thun, Switzerland.

SUNDINE Stephanie, b. 1954, Illinois, USA. Singer (Soprano). *Education:* Studied in Illinois and New York. *Career:* Sang with the New York City Opera 1981-84 as Ariadne, Santuzza and Margherita in Boito's Mefistofeles; Sang the title roles in the US premieres of Prokofiev's Maddalena (St Louis 1982) and Judith by Siegfried Matthus (Santa Fe 1990); best known as Strauss's Salome (Covent Garden and Metropolitan Opera debuts, 1988 and 1990, Welsh National Opera 1991); Sang Isolde at Nantes in 1989 and Fusako in the premiere production of Henze's Das verratene Meer at the Deutsche Oper Berlin, 1990; Other roles include Janáček's Emilia Marty, Tosca, La Gioconda and Elsa.

SUNDMAN Ulf Johan, b. 27 Feb 1929, Stockholm, Sweden. Organist; Musical Director. m. Anna-Greta Persson, 10 July 1954, 1 daughter. *Education:* Hogre organistexamen, 1949; Högre Kantorsexamen, Musiklaarexamen, 1951; Diplom Organ Playing, 1974; Royal Academy of Music, Stockholm; International Academy for Organ, Haarlem, Holland, 1967. *Career:* Organist, Skelleftea St Olovs Church, 1954-81; Organist, Gavle Heliga Trefaldighets Church, 1981-; Organ concerts in Sweden, Finland, Norway, West Germany, Austria, Netherlands, Switzerland, France, Italy, Spain, East Germany, Czechoslovakia, Poland, USSR, 1974, 1976, 1979, Denmark and Belgium; Organ Music Festivals, Gottingen, West Germany, 1972, Vilinius, USSR, 1974, Madrid, 1982, Naples, Toulon, 1983, Ratzeburg, 1985, Verona and Asola, 1986, Büren 1987, Göttingen 1987, Zug 1988, Biella 1988; Concerts on Radio Sweden and Radio Netherlands. *Recordings:* Soviet (Melodia) Sweden (Proprius), (Opus 3). *Honours:* PA Berg Medal, Royal Academy of Music, Stockholm; Culture Prize of the Town of Skelleftea, 1972, and Province of Vasterbotten, 1973. *Address:* N Köpmangatan 22A, S-803 21 Gävle, Sweden.

SUNNEGARDH Thomas, b. 11 July 1949, Stockholm, Sweden. Singer (Tenor). *Education:* Studied at the Royal School of Music in Stockholm. *Career:* Sang at the Vadstena Academy 1978-79; Appeared in Die Fledermaus and Der Vogelhändler with the National Touring Company; Royal Opera Stockholm from 1982, as Albert Herring, Walther von der Vogelweide, Taverner, Ferrando, Riccardo, Fra Diavolo, Tamino and Steuermann in Der fliegende Holländer; Has sung Lohengrin in Stockholm, Moscow (Bolshoi), Wiesbaden, and Stuttgart (conducted by Silvio Varviso, 1990); Macduff at the Bergen Festival, 1988; Other roles include Florestan, Erik, Parsifal (in Denmark and Antwerp) and parts in Iphigénie en Aulide and Genoveva (Deutsche Oper am Rhein) and Die Meistersinger (Nice, 1992); Also engaged for season 1991/92, Lohengrin, Barcelona; Parsifal, Aarhus; Die Meistersinger, Nice Opera; Der fliegende Holländer, Royal Opera Covent Garden; Das Lied von der Erde, London Philharmonic Orchestra; Season 1992/93 with Meistersinger in Brussels, Berlin (Deutsche Oper), Munich, Tokyo, Stuttgart (new production); Dutchman/Erik in Munich, Parsifal in Essen & Deutsche Oper Düsseldorf, Lohengrin in Frankfurt, Berlin and Tokyo and Toulouse. *Address:* c/o Haydn Rawstron Ltd, PO Box 654, London SE26 4DZ, England.

SUNSHINE Adrian, b. 1930, New York City, USA.

Conductor. m. Sheila A. Genden, 1 son, 1 daughter. *Education:* San Francisco State University; University of California, Berkeley; Private Studies with: Janet Hale, Georg Gruenberg, Ludwig Altman, Gabriel Sunshine (Father), Herman Reinberg. *Career:* Appearances with: Philharmonia (London), Leningrad, Berlin, BBC, Bucharest, Cleveland, Suisse Romande, Lausanne, Holland, Denmark, Sweden, Poland, Athens, Miami, San Francisco, Rio de Janeiro, Mexico City, Buenos Aires, Caracas, Lugano, Manchester, Bournemouth, Israel, Paris, Lille, Amsterdam, Concertgebouw, Rotterdam, BBC Opera, Barcelona, Bilbao, Luxembourg, Madrid, San Sebastian Bach Festival, Maubeuge Festival (France) and others. Festivals include: Blossom, Athens, Sao Paulo, Montreux-Vevey, Ascona, Cheltenham, Gulbenkian(Lisbon), Reims,, Seville, Cluj(Romania), Lille, Chamonix, etc. Founder-conductor, San Francisco Chamber Orchestra; Chief Conductor, Gulbenkian Orchestra, Lisbon; Principal Guest Conductor, Romania; Music Director, London Chamber Players, 1979-; Principal Guest Conductor, Athens; Guest Professor, Bowling Green State University, Ohio; Guest Lecturer, University of London Institute of Education. *Publications:* Various articles on music, music criticism. *Honours:* Newhouse Foundation Scholarship. *Memberships:* College Music Society; Conductor's Guild. *Current Management:* Bureau de Concerts Camille Kiesgen, 252 Faubourg St. Honore, 75008 Paris, France. *Address:* PO Box 84, London, NW11 8AL, England.

SUPPAN Wolfgang, b. 5 Aug 1933, Irdning, Austria. Musicologist; University Professor. m. Elfriede Vass, 24 Nov 1957, 1 son. *Education:* Dr.phil, Musicology, University of Graz, 1959; Habilitation, Musicology, University of Mainz, Federal Republic of Germany, 1971; Clarinet, Piano and Violin, Conservatory for Music, Graz. *Career:* German Folksong Archives, Freiburg, Federal Republic of Germany, 1961; Professor of Musicology, University of Mainz, 1971; Professor for Ethnomusicology, University of Graz, Austria, 1974-. *Publications:* About 25 books. *Contributions to:* Over 240 articles in journals, festschriften, yearbooks. *Honour:* Grosses Goldenes Ehrenzeichen, Styria, 1993; Bundesverdientkreuz i Klosse, Germany, 1993. *Memberships:* President, International Society for the Promotion and Investigation of Band Music; President elect of World Association for Symphonic Bands and Ensembles; Many international societies. *Hobbies:* Skiing; Swimming. *Address:* Institute für Musikethnologie, Hochschule für Musik und darstellende Kunst, 8010 Graz, Leonhardstraße 15, Austria.

SUSA Conrad, b. 26 Apr 1935, Springfield, Pennsylvania, USA. Composer. *Education:* Studied at Carnegie Institute of Technology at Pittsburgh (BFA, 1957); Juilliard School, New York, with William Bergsma and Vincent Persichetti. *Career:* Composer in residence at the Old Globe Theatre, San Diego, 1959-60; Music Director of APA-Phoenix Repertory Company in New York, 1961-68, and the American Shakespeare Festival in Stratford, Connecticut, 1969-71; Dramaturg of the Eugene O'Neill Center in Connecticut, 1986-. *Compositions include:* Operas: Transformations, Minneapolis, 1973; Black River: a Wisconsin Idyll, St Paul, 1975; The Love of Don Perlimplin, Purchase, New York, 1984; A Sonnet Voyage, Symphony, 1963; Chamber music: Choral works: Dawn Greeting, 1976, The Chanticleer's Carol, 1982, and Earth Song, 1988; Piano pieces. *Address:* c/o ASCAP, ASCAP Building, One Lincoln Plaza, New York, NY 10023, USA.

SUSS Reiner, b. 2 Feb 1930, Chemnitz, Germany. Singer (Bass). *Education:* Member of the Thomas Choir, Leipzig, 1939-48; Hochschule für Musik Lepizig 1948-53. *Career:* Sang with Radio Leipzig 1953-56; Sang with the opera company at Bernburg an der Saale 1956-57, debut in Tiefland by d'Albert; Theater der Stadt Halle 1957-59, notably as Ochs in Der Rosenkavalier; Member of the Staatsoper Berlin from 1959, as Leporello, Beckmesser, Falstaff (Nicolai), Kecal (The Bartered Bride), Varlaam and Baculus in Der Wildschütz, Dr. Bartolo (Barbiere), Kowaljoff (The Nose by

Shostakovich), Don Pasqnale, Osmin (Entführung); Guest engagements at the Vienna Staatsoper and in Budapest, Helsinki, Lyon, Lausanne, Florence, Moscow, Prague, Warsaw and Tokyo. *Recordings include:* Tannhäuser conducted by Franz Konwitschny, Tosca and Der Wildschütz (Deutsche Grammophon); La Serva Padrona (Telefunken); Mozart's Zaide and Die Kluge by Orff (Phillips); Der Mond by Orff (Eterna); Don Pasquale (Phillips). *Address:* c/o Deutsche Staatsoper, Unter den Linden 7, D-1086 Berlin, Germany.

SUTCLIFFE Sidney Clement, b. 6 Oct 1918, Edinburgh, Scotland. Musician; Oboe Player; Teacher; Conductor. m. Marion Roberts, 3 daughters. *Education:* George Watson's College; Royal Collge of Music with Leon Goossens and John Snowden. *Debut:* Sadler's Wells Orchestra 1938. *Career:* Member, Philharmonia Orchestra and BBC Symphony Orchestra; Professor, Royal College of Music; Woodwind coach; Various conducting engagements. *Recordings:* With Philharmonia Orchestra 1949-62, notably Mozart's Sinfonia Concertante K297b conducted by Karajan; Quintets by Mozart and Beethoven with Walter Gieseking, B Walton, C James, Dennis Brain. *Honours:* Honorary ARCM. *Hobbies:* Music; Golf; Swimming; Photography. *Address:* 94 Woodfield Lane, Ashtead, Surrey, KT21 2DP, England.

SUTERMEISTER Heinrich, b. 12 Aug 1910, Feuerthalen, Switzerland. Composer; Music Educator. m. Vrena-Maria Renker 1948, 1 daughter. *Education:* Academy of Music, Munich; Studied philosophy at the Sorbonne, Paris; Academy of Music, Munich, 1931-34 with Carl Orff and Walter Courvoisier. *Career:* Freelance composer; Taught at the Hochschule für Musik Hanover 1963-75. *Compositions:* Operas: Die schwarze Spinne 1935; Romeo und Julia 1940; Die Zauberinsel 1942; Raskolnikoff 1948; Der rote Stiefel 1951; Titus Feuerfuchs 1958; Seraphine 1959; Madame Bovary 1967; La Crosade des Enfants 1969; Der Flaschenteufel 1970; Le Roi Bérenger. 1985; 8 Cantatas: No.1 Andreas Gryphius 1936; No.2 1944; No.3 Dem Allgegenwartigen 1958; No.4 Das Hohelied 1960; No.5 Der Papagei aus Kuba 1961; No.6 Erkennen und Schaffen 1963; No.7 Sonnenhymne des Echnaton 1965; No.8 Omnia ad Unum 1966; Missa da Requiem 1952; Ecclesia 1973; Te Deum 1974; 2 Divertimenti 1936, 1960; 3 Piano Concertos 1943, 1953, 1962; 2 Cello Concertos 1955, 1971; Serenade pour Montreux 1970; Clarinet Concerto 1974; Chamber music. *Memberships:* President, Schweizerische Mechanlizenz; Bayerische Akademie der Schönen Kunste. *Honours:* Salzburg Opera Prize 1965; Association of Swiss Composers Prize 1967. *Hobby:* Breeding Belgian shepherd dogs.

SUTHERLAND Bruce, b. 1940, Florida, USA. Composer; Pianist. *Education:* BMus, University of Southern California; MMus ibid; Studied Composition with Halsey Stevens and Ellis Kohs, Piano with Ethel Leginska and Amparo Iturbi. *Debut:* With KFI Symphony, James Sample Conducting. *Career:* Director, Bach Festivals for California Music Teachers Association; Harpsichord Soloist with Telemann Trio; Church Organist; Piano Teacher; Piano Faculty, California State University at Northridge; Teacher, Masterclass for Pianists; University of Texas, Austin; Adjudicator, NGPT, Austin, Texas, California Music Teachers Association, National Arts & Letters Society; Director, Brentwood-Westwood Symphony Annual Competition for Young Artists. *Compositions:* Allegro Fanfara for Orchestra, world premiere conducted by José Iturbi with Bridgeport Symphony Orchestra; Saxophone Quartet; Quintet for Flute, Violin, Viola (Clarinet), Cello and Piano; Notturno for Flute and Guitar; String Trio; Piano and Vocal works. *Contributions to:* Music articles published in Christian Science Monitor. *Honours:* Grand Prize, International Competition Louis Moreau Gottschalk, 1970; Stairway of the Stars Award, Music Arts Society, Santa Monica, 1973; Named one of Los Angeles finest Piano Teachers, New West (California) Magazine, 1977; Honoured at the White House, as the Distinguished Teacher of a 1991, Presidential Scholar in the Arts, Anders Martinson, who performed as piano soloist at the Kennedy Center during a week of ceremonies in Washington DC. *Memberships:* Pi Kappa Lambda; National Association of American Composers and Conductors; American Music Center, New York. *Address:* 2336 Pier Avenue, Santa Monica, CA 90405, USA.

SUTHERLAND Joan (Dame), b. 7 Nov 1926, Sydney, Australia. Singer (Soprano). m. Richard Bonynge, 1954. *Career:* Came to London 1951, to study at the Royal College of Music, Richard Bonynge became her accompanist and musical adviser; Engaged as member of Covent Garden Opera Company, first role was First Lady in The Magic Flute 1952; During early years sang Amelia in A Masked Ball; Aida; Eva in The Mastersingers; Gilda in Rigoletto, Desdemona in Othello, Agathe in Der Freschütz; Olympia, Giulietta, Antonia, and Stella in The Tales of Hoffmann; Became an international star with her Covent Garden performance of Lucia di Lammermoor, 1959; sang at Covent Garden in operas which included: I Puritani; Dialogues of the Carmelites; Lucia di Lammermoor; Norma; Sang in world's major opera houses including; Paris, Vienna, La Scala, Hamburg, Buenos Aires, Metropolitan in New York, Chicago Lyric, San Francisco, Australian Opera in Sydney, Glyndebourne, and in Edinburgh, Leeds and Florence Festivals; Specialized not only in bel canto operas, particularly those of Rossini, Donizetti, and Bellini and in operas of Handel, but also in French repertoire of 19th Century; Both she and her husband were responsible for bringing back into standard repertoire some of previously more obscure works such as Esclarmonde, Le Roi de Lahore, Semiramide, Les Huguenots etc. of French and Italian composers; Retired, 1990; Last Operatic role Marguerite de Valois in Les Huguenots for Australian Opera, 1990; sang as guest in Die Fledermaus at Covent Garden. *Recordings:* Lucia di Lammermoor, Alcina, La Sonnambula, Semiramide, Faust, I Puritani, Les Huguenots, Turandot, La Traviata, Les Contes d'Hoffmann, Don Giovanni, Don Pasquale, Adriana Lecouvreur, Le Roi de Lahore, Rodelinda, Athalia, Norma, Anna Bolena, La Fille du régiment (Decca). *Honours:* Commander of The Order of Australia 1975; Named Dame of British Empire by HM Queen Elizabeth II, 1979. *Address:* c/o Ingpen and Williams, 14 Kensington Court, London W8, England.

SUTHERLAND Rosalind, b. 1963, Glasgow, Scotland. Singer (Soprano). *Education:* Studied at London College of Music and with Joseph Ward at Royal Northern College of Music. *Career:* Appearances with Royal Northern College of Music in Suor Angelica, L'Elisir d'Amore and Madama Butterfly; Sang Pamina with Liverpool Mozart Orchestra, Bournmouth Sinfonietta and Scottish National Orchestra; Recent engagements with Welsh National Opera as Madama Butterfly, Tatyana and Liu; Mimi for New Israeli Opera; English National Opera debut season, 1993-94, as Mimi. *Honours include:* Peter Moores scholarship and winner of the Anne Ziegler Prize for a singer showing outstanding promise. *Address:* c/o John Coast Ltd, 31 Sinclair Road, London W14 0NS, England.

SUTTER Ursula, b. 26 Mar 1938, Berne, Switzerland. Singer (Mezzo- soprano). *Education:* Studied in Berne and Stuttgart. *Career:* Sang at Biel-Solothurn, 1961-63, Trier, 1963-64, Essen, 1964-66; Engaged at Stuttgart Staatsoper, 1966-85, notably in premiere of Orff's Prometheus, 1968; Guest appearances at State Operas of Vienna, Munich and Hamburg, Cologne, Nuremburg and Dusseldorf; Further engagements at Bucharest, Lisbon, Monte Carlo, Essen and Schwetzingen Festival (premiere of The English Cat by Henze, 1983); Roles have included Dorabella, Cherubino, Rosina, Isabella, Maddalena, Preziosilla, Magdalene in Meistersinger, the Composer in Ariadne and Britten's Lucretia. *Address:* c/o Stuttgart Staatsoper, Oberer Schlossgarten 6, 7000 Stuttgart, Germany.

SUTTON R(ichard) Anderson, b. 16 Nov 1949, Bryn Mawr, Pennsylvania, USA. Ethnomusicologist. m. Peggy Choy, 22 June 1978, 1 son, 1 daughter. *Education:* BA,

Music, Wesleyan University, Middletown, Connecticut, 1971; MA, University of Hawaii, 1975; PhD, Musicology, University of Michigan, 1982. *Career:* Lecturer in Music, University of Hawaii, 1975-76, summers 1977, 78, 80; Visiting Lecturer 1982, Assistant Professor 1982-88, Associate Professor of Music, University of Wisconsin-Madison, 1988-; Also: Director, Javanese Gamelan Ensembles, Universities of Hawaii 1977, Michigan 1978, Wisconsin-Madison 1982-; Director for Southeast Asian Studies, University of Winconsin-Madison, 1991-. *Publications:* Variation in Central Javanese Gamelan Music, 1993; Traditions of gamelan music in Java: musical pluralism and regional identity (published by Cambridge University Press, 1991). *Contributions to:* Books: Aesthetic Tradition & Cultural Transition in Java & Bali, 1984; Women & Music in Cross-Cultural Perspective, 1987; Asia/Indonesia in Worlds of Music, 1992. *Address:* School of Music, University of Wisconsin-Madison, 455 North Park Street, Madison, WI 53706, USA.

SUZUKI Hidetaro, b. 1 June 1937, Tokyo, Japan. Violinist; Conductor. m. Zeyda Ruga, 16 May 1962, 2 sons, 1 daughter. *Education:* Toho School of Music, Tokyo, 1953-56; Curtis Institute of Music, Philadelphia, Pennsylvania, USA, 1956-63; Studied with Efrem Zimbalist. *Debut:* Tokyo, 1951. *Career:* Concertmaster, Quebec Symphony, Canada, 1963-78; Professor, Conservatory of Province of Quebec, 1963-79; Professor, Laval University, 1970-79; Concertmaster, Indianapolis Symphony, Indiana, USA, 1978-; Concert appearances as soloist, recitalist, conductor, Great Britain, Western Europe, Soviet Union, Central America, USA, Canada, Japan, South East Asia. *Recordings:* Beethoven Sonatas, Toshiba-EMI; Hidetaro Suzuki Encore Album, Toshiba-EMI; Franck, Ravel Sonatas, Select Canada; Beethoven Piano Trios, Marlboro Festival. *Honours:* Laureat, Tchaikovsky International Competition, 1962; Laureat, Queen Elizabeth International Competition, 1963, 1967; Laureat, Montreal International Competition. 1966. *Address:* 430 West 93rd Street, Indianapolis, IN 46260, USA.

SVECENY Jaroslav, b. 8 Dec 1960, Hradec Kralove, Czechoslovakia. m. Monika Svecena. Concert Violinist. *Education:* Studied at the Prague Conservatoire and the Prague Academy of Arts with Vaclav Snitil; Master Classes with Nathan Milstein, Zurich and Gidon Kremer, Kuhmo. *Career:* Concert appearances in Germany, Spain, France, Italy, Britain, Finland, Denmark, USA, Soviet Union, Poland, Hungary and Rumania; Participated in festivals in Berlin, Constance, Helsinki, Bilbao, Madrid, Granada, Havana, Prague, Leipzig and Palermo; Repertoire includes Concertos by Dvořák, Beethoven, Brahms, Mozart, Bach, Vivaldi, Haydn, Reicha and Martinů; Reicha complete works for violin and piano and Benda 24 Capriccios (only artist with this repertoire); Sonatas by Brahms, Beethoven, Dvořák, Benda, Handel and Ysaÿe. *Recordings include:* Reicha 4 Sonatas, Grand Duo Concertante and Rondo (Panton); Sonatas by Benda, Stamitz, Corelli, Handel and Tartini; Vivaldi Four Seasons (Panton). *Honour:* Winner, Pablo de Sarsate International Violin Competition. *Address:* Trojanova 18, 120 00 Prague 2, Czech Republic.

SVENDEN Birgitta, b. 20 Mar 1952, Porjus, Sweden. Singer (Mezzo- soprano). *Education:* Studied at the Stockholm Opera School. *Career:* Has sung at the Royal Opera in Stockholm as Cherubino, Dorabella, Orga and Erda; Sang a Rhinemaiden in the Ring production conducted by Solti at Bayreuth, 1983; Nice Opera from 1985, in Carmen and as Meg Page and Anna (Les Troyens); Created Queen Christina in the opera by Hans Gefors, 1988; Metropolitan Opera from 1988, as Erda in Rheingold and Siegfried and Maddalena in Rigoletto; Seattle Opera 1989, as Magdalena in Die Meistersinger; Ravinia Festival Chicago in Mahler's 3rd Symphony, conducted by James Levine; Sang at La Scala, Munich and San Francisco 1990, as Magdalena, Erda and First Norn; Covent Garden debut 1990, in a new production of Siegfried, conducted by Bernard Haitink. Théâtre du Châtelet, Paris, as Margret in a production of Wozzeck by Patrice Chéreau, conducted by Daniel Barenboim;

Also engaged for: BBC Philharmonic, Verdi Requiem (Edward Downes) 1991; Gürzenich Orchestra, Mahler III (James Conlon) 1992; Los Angeles Philharmonic, Mahler III, 1992; Eugene Onegin, Die Meistersinger, Metropolitan, New York, 1993; Season 1993 with mahler 3 at Boston and NY Carnegie Hall/Ozawa, Mahler 3 and 8 at Rome and Rotterdam/ with Conlon, Missa Solemnis Paris/Solti, Octavian/Rosenkavalier Paris Châtelet; Season 1994 with new Ring production at Bayreuth, Covent Garden and Cologne. *Recordings:* Rheingold, Siegfried/DGG, Mahler, Elgar, Zemlinsky/ Forlane. *Address:* Artistsekretariat Ulf Törnqvist, Sankt Eriksgatan 100, 2tr, S-113 31, Stockholm.

SVETE Tomaz, b. 29 Jan 1956, Ljubljana, Yugoslavia. Composer; Conductor. *Education:* Graduated in Composition, 1980, Conducting, 1981, Academy of Music, Ljubljana; Studied with Professor F. Cerha, Hochschule für Musik und Darstellende Kunst, Vienna, Dimploma with Distinction 1986; Studies in conducting with Otmar Suitner, Diploma 1988 and electroacoustic music with Dieter Kaufmann, Vienna; Magister Artis on the Hochschule für Musik und Darstellende Kunst, Vienna, 1989. *Debut:* 1st composition performance, Ljubljana, 1978. *Career:* Works performed in Ljubljana, Skopje, Opatija, Zagreb/Music biennale/, Vienna/ Konzerthaus-Wien/, Trieste, Klagenfurt; Spittal/Drau Salzburg, Prague, Tivana; Appeared as conductor, Slovene Philharmonic Orchestra, Ljubljana; Pro Arte Orchestra, Vienna and now as conductor of Singkreis Währing, Vienna. Professor for composition at the Karl Prayner conservatory, Vienna; Concert of own works in Brahmssaal, Musikvereln (Vienna), works also performed in Amsterdam and Middleburgh (Holland); Conducting with Radio Symphony Orchestra, BRNO (ČSFR). *Compositions:* King Malhus (TV opera-recorded Yugoslav Radio and TV); L'Amor Sul Mar for orchestra; Hefaistos for violin and piano; (First performance in the famous Arnold Schöenberg House in Mödling by Vienna, and at the Internationale Music Biennale, Zagreb); Orgelstück (performed in Taborkirche, Vienna); Curriculum for two pianos, clarinet, double bass and percussion (Musikverein, Vienna); Objet trouvé-perdue for guitar, mandoline and harp, performed at the festival of Mediteranian Music in Middleburgh, Holand 1990; Requiem for Soli, 2 Chrouses, 2 Ensembles, Narrator and Great Orchestra, First Performance, Prague 1991; Ein Komplizierter Engel for Soprano, String Quartet and Harp, Salzburg, 1991; Quartet, INO, D'Arch, Salzburg, 1991; Divertimento, for orchestra, recorded from Slovene Radio, 1993; Jsomerisms for chamber ensemble, first performance Spittal/Drau, Expan, 1993 Opera: Die Entführung von Laudachsee, first performance in Ljubljana (3 soloists, chamber orchestra, 1993. *Address:* Hudovernikova 4, 61000 Ljubljana, Slovenia.

SVETLANOV Evgeny Fyodorovich, b. 6 Sept 1928, Moscow, USSR. Conductor; Composer; Pianist. *Education:* Graduated Gnesin Institute 1951; Moscow Conservatory 1951-55, with Shaporin (composition) and Gauk (conducting). *Career:* Conducted All-Union Radio orchestra 1953; Bolshoy Theatre Moscow from 1955 (Principal Conductor 1962-64); Performances of operas by Tchaikovsky, Borodin, Rimsky-Korsakov and Dargomizhsky, Bartók's Bluebeard's Castle and works by Soviet composers; Principal Conductor of the USSR State Symphony Orchestra from 1965, notably in symphonies by Myaskovsky, Tchaikovsky, Prokofiev and Shostakovich; Tours to Europe, Britain, USA and Japan; Principal Guest Conductor of the London Symphony Orchestra 1979. *Compositions:* Symphony; Tone Poem Festival 1950; Daugava 1953; Siberian Fantasy 1953; Rhapsody 1954; Cantata, Home Fields 1949; Concerto 1951; 5 Sonatinas; 5 Sonatas; 50 Romances and Songs. *Recordings:* Tchaikovsky and Rachmaninov complete symphonies; Alexander Nevsky; Le Sacre du Printemps; Borodin 2nd Symphony; Rimsky-Korsakov Overtures. *Honours:* People's Artist of the USSR 1968; Lenin Prize 1972; Glinka Prize 1975. *Address:* c/o Russian State Symphony Orchestra, 31 Ulitsa Gorkogo, Moscow, Russia.

SVETLEV Michail, b. 6 Mar 1943, Sofia, Bulgaria. Singer (Tenor). *Education:* Studied at the Sofia Conservatoire. *Debut:* Passau 1971, as Manrico. *Career:* Appearances in Munich, Hamburg, Berlin and Vienna; La Scala Milan 1979; US Debut as Riccardo in Un Ballo in Maschera, Washington DC 1980; Further US appearances at Houston (1980), San Francisco (1980, 1983), Philadelphia (1982); Sang Dimitri (Boris Godunov) at Covent Garden 1983 and has appeared elsewhere as Verdi's Radames and Gabriele Adorno, Andrea Chénier and Cavaradossi; Season 1985-86 as Hermann (The Queen of Spades) at Marseilles and Lykov in Rimsky's The Tsar's Bride at Monte Carlo; Other roles include the Duke of Mantua, Don Carlos, Bacchus, Lensky, Edgardo and the Prince in Rusalka. *Address:* c/o Opéra de Monte Carlo, Place du Casino, Monte Carlo.

SVOBODA Josef, b. 10 May 1920, Caslav, Czechoslovakia. Stage Designer. *Education:* Trained as a cabinet maker; Architectural studies 1941-43, then at Prague Art College 1945-50. *Career:* Worked for an amateur theatre group in Caslav then designed for the New Group in Prague, 1943-45; Worked at the Smetana Theatre 1945-48; From 1951 Chief Designer and Technical Director of the National Theatre Prague; Techniques of collage, mirrors, lenses and film projection seen at the premiere production of Nono's Intolleranza (Venice 1961); Other designs for Il Trovatore (Berlin 1966); Die Frau ohne Schatten, Pelléas et Mélisande, Nabucco and The Ring (Covent Garden 1967-76); Oberon, Die Soldaten and Die Zauberflöte (Munich 1968-70); Les vepres Siciliennes (Hamburg 1969); Wozzeck (La Scala 1971); Carmen and The Bartered Bride (Metropolitan Opera 1972, 1978); Czech premiere of Martinů's Ariadne at Prague, 1987; Designs for The Bartered Bride at Stuttgart, 1990, Luisa Miller at Trieste; Salome at the Deutsche Oper Berlin, 1990; Macerata Festival, 1992, with production and designs for La Sonnambula, designs for La Traviata. *Publications include:* Designing for the Stage, Opera Magazine 1967. *Address:* c/o Deutsche Oper Berlin, Richard Wagnerstrasse 10, D-1000 Berlin 1, Germany.

SVOBODA Tomas, b. 6 Dec 1939, Paris, France. Composer; Pianist; Conductor; Professor of Music. m. Jana Demartini, 9 Oct 1965, 1 son, 1 daughter. *Education:* Degree in Percussion, 1956, Composition, 1958, Conducting, 1962, Conservatory of Music, Prague, Czechoslovakia; Composition Degree, University of Southern California, USA, 1969. *Debut:* FOK Prague Symphony Orchestra, Symphony No. 1 June 20, 1957. *Compositions:* Symphonies, 1 to 6; Overture of the Season, Op 89; Eugene Overture (Festive) Op 103; Nocturne for Orchestra Op 100; Serenade for Orchestra Op 115; Sinfonietta (à la Renaissance) Op 60; Reflections for Orchestra Op 53; Concerto for Piano and Orchestra Op 71; Concerto for Violin and Orchestra Op 77; Ex Libris Op 113; Child's Dream, for children's choir and orchestra, Op 66; 72 chamber pieces and 42 keyboard compositions; Concerto for chamber orchestra, Op. 125; Journey, Cantata for Mezzosoprano, Baritone, Choir & Orchestra, Op. 127; Dance Suite, for orchestra, Op. 128; Concerto No. 2, for piano & orchestra, Op. 134. *Recordings:* Symphony No. 4 (Apocalyptic) Op 69; Ex Libris Op 113 for orchestra; CD Recording (Mirecourt Trio), Passacaglis & Fugue for piano trio, Op.87. *Honours:* Meet the Composer Award, ASCAP Foundation, 1985; Featured on front cover of The Piano Quarterly (Summer 1981); Governor's Award for the Arts for his Musical Achievement, 1992. *Current Management:* Thomas C Stangland Co, PO Box 19263, Portland, OR 97219, USA. *Hobbies:* Chess; Photography; Meteorology. *Address:* c/o Thomas Stangland Co., PO Box 19263, Portland, OR 97219, USA.

SVORC Antonin, b. 12 Feb 1934, Jaromer, Czechoslovakia. Singer (Bass-baritone). *Education:* Studied with Jan Berlik in Prague. *Debut:* State Theatre of Liberet as Pizarro in Fidelio, 1955. *Career:* Member of the National Theatre Prague from 1958: visited Edinburgh with the company 1964, in the British premiere of From the House of the Dead by Janáček;

Guest appearances at the Berlin Staatsoper and in Vienna, Paris, Dresden, Cologne, Dusseldorf, Kassel, Zurich, Trieste, Venice and Barcelona; Sang in Prague 1974 in the premiere of Cikker's Coriolanus and as Chrudos in Libuse at the 1983 re-opening of the National Opera; Sang as guest at the Paris Opera 1988, in Janáček's From the House of the Dead. *Recordings:* Operas by Smetana, including Dalibor and Libuse (Supraphon). *Honours include:* National Artists of Czechoslovakia 1985. *Address:* c/o National Theatre, P O Box 865, 112 30 Prague 1, Czech Republic.

SWAFFORD Jan Johnson, b. 10 Sept 1946, Chattanooga, Tennessee, USA. Composer. *Education:* Harvard College; Yale School of Music; Tanglewood. *Career:* Teacher at: Boston University, Goddard College, Hampshire College, Amherst College, Tufts University. *Compositions:* Midsummer Variations, 1985; Music Like Steel and Like Fire, 1983; Shore Lines, 1982; In Time of Fear, 1984; After Spring Rain, 1982; Labyrinths, 1983; Landscape with Traveler, 1981; Passage, 1975; Peal, 1976; Chamber Sinfonietta, 1988; They Who Hunger, 1989; Requiem in Winter, 1991; Iphigenia Choruses, 1993. *Recordings:* Midsummer Variations, They Who Hunger, CRI, 1993 *Publications:* A Life of Charles Ives (in progress for W W Norton & Co.); The Vintage Guide to Classical Music, Vintage 1992, A Life of Brahms, in progress for Knopf. *Contributions to:* of articles and reviews to Symphony; New England Monthly; Musical America; Yankee. *Hobbies:* Reading; Cooking; Hiking; Skiing. *Address:* 37 Magnolia Ave. 1, Cambridge, MA, USA.

SWANSTON Roderick Brian, b. 28 Aug 1948, Gosport, England, Professor of Music Theory, Royal College of Music. *Education:* Music Scholar, Stowe School, 1961-66; Royal College of Music, 1966-69; Organ Scholar, Pembroke College, Cambridge, 1969-71; MA; Mus. Bac.; Graduate, Royal Schools of Music; Fellow, Royal College of Organists; Licentiate of Royal Academy; Associate of Royal College of Music. *Career:* Organist, Christ Church, Lancaster Gate, 1972-77; Organist, St James, Sussex Gardens, 1977-80; Conductor, Christ Church Choral Society, 1972-80; Part-time Tutor, University of London, Department of Extra Mural Studies, 1972-;Academic Adviser in Music to Birkbeck College, University of London, Centre for Extra-Mural Studies, 1987-; Visiting Lecturer for many organizations including: English National Opera, Royal Opera House Covent Garden, BBC, Oxford University, Goldsmiths' College. *Compositions:* A Time There Was, for tenor, choir and strings; Let Us Gather Hand in Hand, for choir and brass à 5 (recorded by BBC). *Recording:* Organ recital from Framlingham Parish Church. *Publications:* Concise History of Music; Contributions to The British Composer Today. *Contributions to:* Times Educational Supplement; Tempo; RCM Magazine; Tempo South East. *Honour:* Sawyer Prize, Royal College of Organists, 1969. *Memberships:* Incorporated Society of Musicians; President of London Music Diploma Society; Honorary Chairman, Bernard Stevens Memorial Trust. *Hobbies:* Reading; Arguing. *Address:* Royal College of Music, Prince Consort Road, London, SW7, England.

SWARTZ Samuel John, b. 23 Nov 1947, Waterloo, Iowa, USA. Organist. *Education:* Akademie fur Musik und darstellende Kunst, Vienna, 1968; BA cum laude,. 1969, MA, 1970, DMA, 1973, Stanford University; Concert Diploma, Musikhochschule, Cologne, 1971. *Debut:* Stephansdom, Vienna, 1971. *Career:* Solo and orchestral performances through USA, England, Ireland, France, Germany, Switzerland, Austria, Italy and Hungary, 1971-; Over 1000 recitals and concerts in 23 years. *Compositions:* Song of the Gypsy Princess, 1979; Organ Sonata: organ solo, 1991. *Recordings:* Amerikanische Orgelmusik; Samuel John Swartz; J S Bach Recital; Gilbert and Sullivan; Inspirational Music: Cho's Shell Group, Korean. *Honours:* Collegiate Division, BMI Composition (Operetta), 1968; Ohio State and Peabody Awards, 1976. *Memberships:* Pi Kappa Lambda; Phi Mu Alpha Sinfonia. *Hobby:* Swimming. *Current Management:* Artist Recitals, Los Angeles,

California, USA. *Address:* 1518 E Brockton, Redlands, CA 92374, USA.

SWAYNE Giles, b. 30 June 1946, Hitchin, Herts., England. Composer. m. Camilla Brett, 1 son, 3 stepchildren. *Education:* Trinity College Cambridge; Royal Academy of Music; Studies with Nicholas Maw and Messiaen; Conducting course at Siena 1968. *Career:* Performances at Aldeburgh and Bromsgrove Festivals; Purcell Room London; Opera repetitour at Wexford Festival 1972-73 and Glyndebourne 1973-74; Teaching staff at Bryanston School 1974-76; Visited West Africa 1980 to study the music of the Jola people of Sengal and The Gambia. *Compositions:* 4 Lyrical Pieces for cello and piano 1970; 2 String Quartets 1971, 1977; The Good Morrow, settings for mezzo and piano of John Donne 1971; Paraphrase on a theme of Tallis for organ 1971; Canto for guitar 1972; Canto for piano 1973; Canto for violin 1973; Synthesis for 2 pianos 1974; Orlando's Music for orchestra 1974; Canto for clarinet 1975; Duo for violin and piano 1976; Suite for guitar 1976; Pentecost-Music for orchestra 1976; Cry for 28 amplified voices, depicting the creation of the world, 1979; A World Within, ballet with tape on the Bronte sisters 1978; Freewheeling for viola, baryton and cello 1980; Count-Down for chorus and 2 percussionists 1981; Song for Haddi for drums and instrumentalists; Le Nozze di Cherubino, opera 1984; Riff-Raff for organ 1983; Missa Tiburtina 1985; god-song for mezzo and 4 players 1985-86; solo for guitar 1986; into the light for 7 players 1986; Symphony for small orchestra 1984; Naaotwa Lala for orchestra 1984; Tonos for 5 players 1987; Veni Creator 1 and 2 for chorus and organ 1987; Songlines for flute and guitar 1987; Harmonies of Hell, melodrama for 13 musicians 1988; The Song of Leviathan for chamber orchestra 1988; A Memory of Sky for brass quintet 1989; No Quiet Place for children's voices, string trio and xylophones 1989; No Man's Land for chorus and ensemble 1990; Circle of Silence, for six voices, 1991; Zebra Music, piano pieces for children, 1991; The Song of the Tortoise, for narrator children's voices, recorders, choir and orechestra, 1992; The Owl and the Pussycat, for narrator and seven instruments, 1993; String Quartet No. 3, 1993. *Memberships:* PRS; APC; MCPS. *Address:* c/o Performing Arts, 6 Windmill Street, London W1P 1HF, Engalnd.

SWEENEY Peter Alan, b. 7 Apr 1950, Dublin, Ireland. Musician; Organist. 1 son, 1 daughter. *Education:* Trinity College, Dublin; College of Music, Dublin; Conservatoire de Musique, Geneva, Switzerland. *Debut:* Organ recital, Dublin's Pro-Cathedral. *Career:* Organ recitalist, North America, Europe, Scandinavia; Senior Organ teacher, College of Music, Dublin; Performances for: BBC Invitation Concert, Belfast; RTE Television broadcasts; BBC Radio 3 & RTE Radio recordings. *Recordings:* Buxtehude & Bach; Buxtehude, Bach, Reger, etc; Home Ground, Christ Church Cathedral; Choral Evensong, Choir of Christ Church Cathedral. *Membership:* Hibernian Catch Club, Dublin, music director. *Hobbies:* Tennis; Swimming; Interior design. *Current Management:* Helen Roycroft, 4 Orwell Park, Rathgar, Dublin 6. *Address:* 4 Orwell Park, Dublin 6, Eire.

SWEET Sharon, b. 16 Aug 1951, New York, USA. Singer (Soprano). *Education:* Studied with Margaret Harshaw at the Curtis Institute, Philadelphia and with Marinka Gurewich in New York. *Career:* Sang in private recitals at Philadelphia, then appeared in the title role in concert performance of Aida at Munich, 1985; Dortmund Opera 1986-88, debut as Elisabeth in Tannhäuser; Deutsche Oper Berlin from 1987, notably as guest in Zurich and Japan (Elisabeth, and in the Ring); Paris Opera and Hamburg 1987, as Elisabeth de Valois; Season 1987-88 as Desdemona in Brunswick, Dvořák's Stabat Mater at the Salzburg Festival, Gurrelieder in Munich, under Zubin Mehta and Wagner's Elisabeth at the Vienna Staatsoper; Norma in a concert performance of Bellini's opera at Brussels, 1988; US debut as Aida at San Francisco 1989; Season 1992 as Aida at Dallas and the Trovatore Leonora at Orange; Sang in the house premiere of Verdi's Stiffelio at the Metropolitan Season 1993-94. *Recordings include:*

Verdi Requiem (Deutsche Grammophon). *Address:* c/o Deutsche Oper Berlin, Richard Wagnerstrasse 10, D-1000 Berlin, Germany.

SWENSEN Joseph, b. 4 Aug 1960, New York, USA. Conductor; Violinist. *Education:* Studied violin at the Juilliard School with Dorothy DeLay, Conducting studies with Paavo Berglund, Jorge Mester, Otto-Werner Mueller and Lawrence Foster. *Career:* Studied piano with Christian Sager and Thomas Schumacher; Guest conductor with the Jerusalem Symphony, Bournemouth Symphony Orchestra, Colorado Symphony, Aalborg Symphony (Denmark), Helsinki Chamber Orchestra, Stockholm Chamber Orchestra, Israel Chamber Orchestra, Saarbrucken Radio Orchestra, Bergen Philharmonic, Spoleto Festival Orchestra, New World Symphony, Kansas City Philharmonic, Tucson Symphony; Engagements as violin soloist with the Cleveland Orchestra, Los Angeles Philharmonic, the Bavarian Radio Symphony, Leipzig Gewandhaus, Stuttgart Philharmonic, Royal Philharmonic, Philharmonia Orchestra, Pittsburgh Symphony, Bournemouth Symphony, and Finnish Radio Symphony Orchestras. *Recordings include:* Beethoven's Violin Concerto, with the Royal Philharmonic under André Previn; Complete works of Schubert for violin and piano, with Jeffrey Kahane; Sibelius Violin Concerto and Humoresques, Jukka-Pekka Saraste and the Finnish Radio Symphony; Chamber works with James Galway and Kazuhito Yamashita; Complete works for violin and Harpsichord, J. S. Bach with John Gibbons, Harpsichord and Elizabeth Anderson, Cellist (all for RCA Victor Red Seal). *Address:* c/o Victoria Rowsell, Van Walsum Management Ltd., 26 Wadham Road, London SW15 2LR, England.

SWENSSON Evelyn Dickenson, b. 18 Sept 1928, Woodstock, Virginia, USA. Conductor. m. Sigurd Simcox Swensson, 9 June 1949, 2 sons, 2 daughters. *Education:* MusM, West Chester University, 1972. *Career:* Conductor: Aldersgate Methodist Church, Wilmington, Delaware, 1969-; Brandywiners Ltd, Kennett Square, Pennsylvania, 1973-; Conductor and Director of Education, Opera Delaware, Wilmington, 1974-; Conductor: Bi-Centennial Chorus, Wilmington, 1976; Northern Delaware Choral Society, Wilmington, 1977; Guest Conductor, Delaware Symphony Orchestra, Wilmington, 1977; Conductor: Ardensingers, Wilmington, 1978-80; Methodist Bi-Centennial in America, 1984; First State Chorus, Wilmington, 1987; Vice-President, Opera for Youth Inc, Tampa; Conductor, 50 operas including US premieres of Sleeping Beauty (Respighi), 1977, The Zoo (Sullivan and Rowe), 1979, 1980, World Premieres of The Lion, the Witch and the Wardrobe (McCabe) 1990; The Boy Who Grew Too Fast (Menotti), 1982, Charlotte's Web (Strouse), 1989. Conductor of inaugural concert for Governor P.S.duPont IV, Wilmington, 1977, Black History Celebrations, Wilmington, 1985, 1987; Conducted World premiere of A Wrinkle in Time, Libby Larsen, 1992; World premiere of The Enormous Egg by Evelyn Swensson, 1993. *Honours:* Distinguished Music Alumna Award, West Chester University, 1992. *Address:* Heyburn Road, Box 58A, Chadds Ford, PA 19317, USA.

SWIERCZEWSKI Michel, b. 1960, France. Conductor. *Education:* Studied with Jean-Claude Hartemann in Paris and Charles Mackerras at the Vienna Hochschule. *Career:* Made debut in 1976, was then Assistant conductor to Pierre Boulez and Peter Eötvös at the Ensemble Intercontempoain, 1983-85; Claudio Abbado at La Scala, including the premiere of Nono's Prometeo, 1985-86; Paris Opera 1986, with Georges Prêtre; Has conducted such contemporary music ensembles as Itineraire, Musique Oblique, Antidogma and New Music Ensemble, giving many premieres; Guest engagements in France, Germany, Italy, Spain, Portugal and Australia. *Recordings:* La Conference des Oiseaux by Michael Levinas (Ades); Works by Roussel with the Gulbenkian Foundation Orchestra; Complete symphonies of Méhul (Nimbus). *Honours:* Finalist, 1984 Tanglewood International Conducting Competition; Prize Villa Medicis hors les murs. *Address:* Anglo-Swiss Management, 4-5 Primrose Mews, Sharpleshall Street, London NW1 8YW, England.

SWINGLE Ward Lamar, b. 21 Sept 1927, Mobile, Alabama, USA. Choral Conductor; Composer; Arranger; Clinician. m. Françoise Demorest, 23 Sept 1952, 3 daughters. *Education:* BM, MM, Piano Major, Cincinnati Conservatory of Music, 1947-51; Master classes with Walter Gieseking, Saarbrücken, Federal Republic of Germany, 1951-53. *Career:* Solo piano recitals and Accompanist, 1953-55; Conductor, Ballets de Paris, Paris, France, 1955-59; Founded Swingle Singers, worldwide concert touring group, 1963; Numerous radio and TV appearances with Swingle Singers in most major capitals and approximately 2000 concerts around the world, 1963-91. *Compositions:* Over 100 arrangements and compositions for the Swingle Singers. *Recordings:* About 30 with the Swingle Singers including: Bach's Greatest Hits; Going Baroque; Luciano Berio's Sinfonia. *Contributions to:* Article in ACDA Choral Journal, 1986. *Honours:* 5 Grammy Awards, 1964, 1965, 1966, 1970; Grand Prix du Disque, 1964; Edison Award, 1970. *Memberships:* La Societé des Auteurs, Compositeurs et Editeurs de Musique, 1963-86; Phi Mu Epsilon, 1947-51; American Choral Directors Association, 1984-89. *Hobbies:* Gardening; Tennis. *Current Management:* Piers Schmidt, 45a Chalcot Road, London, NW1 8LS. *Address:* 4 Thomas Road, Glen Gardner, NJ 08826, USA.

SWINNEN Hans Rosa Frans, b. 20 July 1941, Lier, Belgium. Composer; Arranger. m. Maria Gijbels, 24 July 1963, 1 son, 2 daughters. *Education:* St Gummarus College, Lier; Antwerp Conservatorium; Brussels Conservatorium. *Career:* Founder, Director, Herentals Music School; Sound Engineer, Opera Antwerp. *Compositions include:* Missa in hon Sta Lutgardis, 1962; Synfonietta, 1964; Cantatas for Flemish Holy Days, 1965, 1966; Art in Brass Quintet, 1971; Trio Lyrica, legni, 1972; Elegie, for viola and piano, 1974; Concerto per Violino ed Orchestra, 1982; Grave ed Allegro, Flicorno & Piano, 1982, Pezzeto Capriccioso, Viola & Orchestra, 1982; Romanza, Viola & Orchestra da Camera, 1982; Grave e Mestoso, clarinet and piano, 1983; Rapsodia, Flauto & Orchestra, 1983; Serenata Civettata, Cello & Orchestra, 1983; Canto del Capobanda, Viola & Orchestra da Camera, 1984; Divertimento a 5, legni, 1984; Variazioni per Orchestra, 1984; Nieuws..., musical, 1988; Lieder and Pianowork, music for school and education; Landscapes, for Symphonic Band & Carillon, 1991. *Recordings:* Landscapes, RG International Recordings. *Honours:* Rotary International Prize, 1963; Grand Prix de Rome for Composition, 1971. *Memberships:* Union of Belgian Composers; SABAM. *Hobbies:* Computers; Travel. *Address:* Gerhees 53, 3945 Ham, Belgium.

SWITTEN Margaret, b. 14 Apr 1926, Chicago, Illinois, USA. Professor of French. m. Henry Switten, 6 June 1950, dec. *Education:* BMus, Voice, Violin, Piano, Westminster Choir College, Princeton, 1947; BA magna cum laude, distinction in French, 1948; MA, French, Philosophy, 1949, PhD, French, 1952, Bryn Mawr College. *Career:* Professor of French and Music, Hampton University, Virginia, 1952-63; Professor of French, Mount Holyoke College, Massachusetts, 1963-. *Publications:* The Cansos of Raimon de Mivaval, 1985; The Medieval Lyric (with Howell Chickering), 4 anthologies, 5 cassettes, 1988; Music and Poetry in the Middle Ages: A Guide to Research on French and Occitanian Song, in progress. *Contributions to:* Articles to Romania, PMLA, Cahiers de l'Association Internationale d'Etudes Francaises, Meleanges de langue et de litterature occitanes en hommage a Pierre Bec, Acta VII Words and Music, Contacts de langues, de civilisations et intertextualite; Reviews to Speculum, Journal of the American Musicological Society. *Honours:* Order of the Academic Palm for Service to French Culture (for Mediaeval Lyric), 1992. *Memberships:* American Musicological Society; Medieval Academy of America. *Address:* 16 N Sycamore Knolls, South Hadley, MA 01075, USA.

SYLVESTER Michael, b. 1955, Indiana, USA. Singer (Tenor). *Education:* Studied with Margaret Harshaw at Bloomington. *Career:* Sang Radames and Pinkerton at Stuttgart, 1987; Cincinnati Opera from 1987 as Pinkerton and Sam in Floyd's Susannah; New York City Opera debut, 1987, as Rodolfo in La Bohème; Further engagements at La Scala and Santiago as Pinkerton, 1990, Paris Opera (Pollione in Norma), Hamburg Staatsoper (Rodolfo and Don José) and Vienna Staatsoper (Cavaradossi); Covent Garden debut, 1990, as Samson, followed by Gabriel Adorno in new production of Simon Boccanegra, 1991; Bregenz Festival, 1990, as Hagenbach in La Wally; Metropolitan Opera debut, 1991, as Rodolfo in Luisa Miller, followed by Don Carlos, 1992; Appearances as Radames at Deutsche Oper Berlin, Chicago, Orange Festival and Seattle, 1992; Further engagements at Bonn (Bacchus, 1990), San Francisco (Calaf), Venice (Don Carlos) and Geneva (Foresto in Attila). *Recordings include:* Title role in Oberon; Don Carlos conducted by James Levine.

SYNOWIEC Ewa Krystyna, b. 12 Apr 1942, Cracow, Poland. Composer; Pianist; Teacher. *Education:* Diploma with honours, 1967; Studied piano with Ludwik Stefanski, Cracow Music Academy; Suzanne Roche and Vlado Perle- muter, Paris, 1967, 1968; Composition with Boguslaw Schaeffer, 1973; Adjunct Professor Composition, 1976; Docent, 1985. *Career:* Pianist, recitals and concerts at home and abroad, 1948-78; Exhibitions and performances in Dublin, Katowice, Cracow, London, Paris, Salzburg, Zurich (Switzerland). *Compositions:* Over 100 works (orchestral, choral and chamber music); Over 100 musical graphics. *Publication:* Instrumental Theatre of Boguslaw Schaeffer, 1983. *Hobbies:* Painting; Poetry. *Address:* Malczewskiego 78/92, 80-107 Gdansk, Poland.

SZABÓ Helga, b. 21 July 1933, Nyiregyháza, Hungary. Teacher. m. 4 Aug 1956, 1 son, 1 daughter. *Education:* Faculty of Secondary School Music Teachers and Choir Conductors, Franz Liszt Academy, 1956; PHD of Musicology, Professor of Music, Eötvös University, Music Department, Budapest. *Career:* Var. Progs., Hungarian Radio 1960, School Radio Programmes; Competitions about music for young people; Teaching Programmes about music styles for children etc; Various films about the Kodály Concept; TV in Hungary, Germany, Finland; Lectures in the USA, Canada, Japan, Australia, Switzerland, Finland, France, Norway, Holland, England. *Recordings:* The Kodály Concept of Music Education (3 records), Boosey and Hawkes; Hungarian folksongs with chamber chorus. *Publications:* Schoolbooks for classes 1-8 in special music schools, 1961-88; The Kodály Concept of Music Education, 1969; Te is tudsz énekelni, You also can sing, eng/Du Kan oksa synge/dan/Musikbog, 1973, 1979, 1986; Singing Improvisation in the School I-IV; Vocal Improvisation in the School IV: Canon, Imitation and Fugue, eng/, 1976-86, Italian 1991-; A Magyar énektanitás története, History of Hungarian Music Education, 1989; Pentatonic World, 1991; Modal World, 1993. *Honour:* Excellent Teacher, 1972; Kodály Prize, 1982. *Memberships:* International Kodály Society; International Society of Music Educators. *Hobbies:* Hiking; Nature. *Address:* Gépmadár II, Budapest 1106, Hungary.

SZALONEK Witold Jozef, b. 2 Mar 1927, Czechowice, Poland. Composer. m. Beata Zygmunt, 23 Apr 1963, 2 sons. *Education:* Diploma of Music, Lyceum Katowice, 1949; Diploma (with distinction), MA, Composition, High School of Music, Katowice, 1956; Studied with Nadia Boulanger, Paris, 1962-63. *Debut:* Katowice, 1954. *Career:* Assistant, High School of Music, Katowice, Poland, 1956-61; Adjunct Professor, 1961-67; Professor of Composition, 1967-75; Rector, 1972-73; Full Professor of Composition and Theory, High School of Arts, Berlin West, 1973-; Lecturer, Universities and High Schools of Music, Munster, Osnabruck, Heidelberg, Mannheim, Aarhus, Helsinki, Graz, Cracow, Warsaw, Jyväskylä, Turku; Lecturer, Viitasaari. *Compositions:* Pastorale for Oboe and Orchestra; Toccata Polyphonica, String Orchestra; Symphonic Satire; Concertino for Flute and Orchestra; Les Sons for Orchestra; Mutazioni for Orchestra; Musica Concertante for Double Bass and Orchestra; Little B-A-C-H Symphony for Orchestra; Confessions for Speaker, Choir and Orchestra; O, Pleasant Earth, Voice and Orchestra; Sonata for Cello and Piano; Quattro Monologhi for Oboe Solo; Proporzioni I for Flute, Viola and Harp; Mutanza for Piano; ++++ per 1-4 strumenti ad arco; Aarhus Music for Windquintet; Connections for Chamber Ensemble; Piernikiana for Tuba; DP's Five Ghoulish Dreams for Saxophone; Inside?-Outside? for Bass Clarinet and String Quartet, 1988; Alice's Unknown Adventures In The Fairy Land of Percussion; Take The Game for 6 percussionists; Nocturne for Baritone, Harp and String Orchestra; Dialogs for Four Hands and Four Feet for Piano; Elegy for Clarinet and Piano. *Recordings:* Mutanza for piano; Improvisations Sonoristiques for clarinet, trombone, cello and piano; Piernikiana for tuba solo; Concertino for flute, Les Sons; Mutazioni for orchestra; Musica Concertante for Double Bass and Orchestra; Little B-A-C-H Symphony for Orchestra; Connections; O Pleasant Earth, Cantata for Voice and Orchestra. *Address:* Hittorfstr. 12, D-1000 Berlin 33 West, Germany.

SZÁVA Babi (Amalia), b. 26 June 1934, Tirana, Albania. Music Teacher. m. Gábor Száva, 26 June 1955, 3 daughters. *Education:* Bartok Music Conservatory, Budapest, Hungary, 1952; Degree in Political Sciences, Budapest, 1955; Courses in Pedagogy, Concert Organising, others, in Norway and Sweden. *Career:* Teacher in Music, Skjeberg Folkehoyskole, Norway, 1969-; President, Musikkens Venner, Sarpsborg, 1982- ; Member, Board of Director, Rikskonsertene, concert organising State Institution of Norway, 1989-; President, Musikkens Venners Landsforbund, 1992-. *Membership:* Norwegian Teachers Association. *Hobbies:* Emrboidery; Sailing. *Address:* Nils Pedersens 5, N-1706 Sarpsborg, Norway.

SZEGEDI Erno, b. 29 Apr 1911, Szeged, Hungary. Pianist; Professor. m. (1) Magda Vasarhelyi, 18 Feb 1937, 1 son, 2 daughters, (2) Klara Gyulai, 9 Nov 1952. *Education:* Music Master's degree, 1936; Pianist's diploma, 1939. *Debut:* Music teacher, National Conservatoire, 1937; Pianist, Ferenc Liszt Acdemy of Music, 1939. *Career:* Several piano recitals, Budapest & Hungrian provinces; 1st foreign tour, (Warsaw, Riga, Tallin, Helsinki, Stockholm, Berlin, 1939; Romania, Transylvania, 1942, 1956; Italian tour, 1947-48; Paris appearance, French TV, 1957; Czechoslovakian-German tour (Pressburg, Prague, Hamburg), 1958; Director, 2 summer courses, Sibelius Academy of Music, Helsinki, Finland, 1978, 1979; Full University Professor (retired), Ferenc Liszt Academy of Music, Budapest. *Recordings:* Bela Bartók for Children; Franz Liszt's Christmas Tree & Late Piano Works; Ernest von Dohnányi's Quintet in E Flat Minor & Sextet in C Major; F. Liszt's Late Piano Music. *Publications:* Liszt: Rákóczi March for 2 Pianos; Mozart-Liszt: Reminiscences de Don Juan for 2 pianos. *Address:* 42A Keleti Karoly utca, 1024 Budapest, Hungary.

SZEGHY Iris, b. 5 Mar 1956, Presov, Czechoslovakia. Composer. *Education:* Studied Cmposition and Piano, Kosice Conservatory, 1971-76; Composition, Academy of Music and Drama, Bratislava, 1976-81; Postgraduate study of Composition, Bratislava Academy, 1986-89. *Career:* Composition Scholar, Slovak Music Fund, Bratislava, 1984-86; Teaching, Bratislava Academy, 1986-89; Freelance Composer, 1989-; Her works performed and broadcast in various European countries, America and Australia; 2 monthly study stays, 1989 in Budapest, 1991 in Warsaw; Scholarship of the Akademie Schloss Solitude in Stuttgart, 1992-93. *Compositions:* Symphonic, chamber and vocal works; Works for children. *Recordings:* Slovak Radio, Bratislava; SDR Stuttgart; Music Fund Bratislava; Canto Triste for Trombone and Piano, OPUS; Afforismi II for Woodwind trio, Akademie Schloß Solitude, Stuttgart. *Current management:* Music Fund, Medena 29, 81102, Bratislava, Slovakia. *Address:* Tematinska 4, 85101 Bratislava, Slovakia.

SZEKELY Erik, b. 2 Jan 1927, Lugano, Switzerland. Composer; Music Teacher. m. Humair Chantal, 25 Feb 1972. *Education:* Piano Diploma, Conservatoire de Lausanne, 1951; Studied Horn, Conservatoire de Geneve. *Career:* Music Teacher, Gymnase cantonal de Neuchatel, Switzerland, 1960-89; Composer. *Compositions:* Garrigues for piano, 1958; Rhodoraies for horn and piano, 1975, worked ordered as imposed piece for the concours international d'execution musicale de Geneve, 1976; Suite Symphonique, 1984; Transmutations for twelve string instruments, 1987; Polarisation for six trumpets, six trombones, Bass Tuba, piano, celesta and percussion, 1989; Crast' Aguzza for six horns, 1991. *Recordings:* A Enide - Les Desolences-Garrigues, Vancoff, Geneva, 1959; Rhodoraies, G M Newton, Massachusetts, USA, 1984. *Publications:* Published works: A Enide - Les Desolences, impr. Attinger, Neuchatel, 1959; Rhodoraies, ed. Henn, Geneva, 1976. *Honours:* Laureate of the following composition competitions: Societa del Quartetto Vercelli (Italy) 1951; International Academy of Music, Genova (Italy) 1952; Ville de Liège, Liège (Belgium) 1953. *Address:* La Corne-du-Bois, CH-2027 Montalchez, Switzerland.

SZIRMAY Marta, b. 1939, Kaposvar, Hungary. Singer (Mezzo- soprano). *Education:* Studied at the Budapest Conservatory. *Career:* Member of the Hungarian State Opera from 1964, singing the mezzo repertory in operas by Wagner and Verdi; Cologne Opera from 1976; Covent Garden debut 1977, as Clytemnestra in Elektra: later London appearances as Erda (Das Rheingold) and Mistress Quickly (Falstaff); Further appearances in Hamburg, Berlin, Vienna, Barcelona, Venice and Naples; Salzburg Festival 1985, as Ericles in Il ritorno di Ulisse by Monteverdi, arranged by Henze; Other roles include Gaea in Daphne, Gluck's Orpheus and Brangaene in Tristan and Isolde; Season 1992 in Corghi's Blimunda at Turin. *Address:* c/o Oper der Stadt Koln, Offenbachplatz, D-5000 Cologne, Germany.

SZMYTKA Elzbieta, b. 1956, Prochowice, Poland. Singer (Soprano). *Education:* Studied in Krakow 1975-82 with Helena Lazarska. *Career:* Sang at the Karkow Opera from 1978, then at Bytom and Wroclaw; Toured to West Germany and Luxembourg as Blondchen in Die Entfuhrung; Sang widely in Western Europe from 1983, notably at Ghent, Antwerp and Brussels (Despina, Blondchen and Serpina; Nanetta 1987-88); Aix-en-Provence Festival 1987-88, as Nannetta and as Servilia in La Clemenza di Tito; Holland Festival 1987, as Serpina in La Finta Giardiniera; Sang at the Vienna Staatsoper 1988 (Papagena) and in Amsterdam and Antwerp 1989 (Gilda and Zerbinetta); Glyndebourne Festival 1991 as Ilia in Idomeneo and Servilia in La Clemenza di Tito; Salzburg Summer Festival 1992, as Alyeya in From the House of the Dead and Mozartwoche 1993 as Cinna in Lucio Silla; Other roles include Susanna, Norina (Don Pasquale) and Aennchen (Der Freischütz). *Recordings include:* La Finta Giardiniera (Ricercar); Despina in Cosí fan Tutte and Mozart arias (Philips); Die Entführung (Song); Il Matrimonio Segreto; Music by Szymanowski, conducted by Simon Rattle. *Current Management:* John Coast Opera Management. *Address:* 31 Sinclair Road, London, W14 0NS, England.

SZOKA Marta, b. 24 June 1955, Lodz, Poland. Lecturer; Concert Organist. *Education:* MA, Theory of Music, 1979, Diploma, Organ Concert Class, 1982, Academy of Music, Lodz; International Course of Organ Playing, Bayreuth, 1982; Organ Masterclass of F Peeters, Mechelen, 1983; Doctorate of Musicology, Polish Organ Music 1945-1985, Institute of Art, Polish Academy of Sciences, Warsaw, 1988; Grant of Paul Sacher Stiftung in Basel (Switzerland) in 1991 and 1992; Fulbright Scholarship (University of North Carolina in Chapel Hill, USA), 1993/94. *Career:* Recitals, Federal Republic of Germany, 1983, 1985, Switzerland, 1992; Concerts during main organ festivals, Poland, including Frombork, Gdańsk-Oliwa, Koszalin, Legnica; Some 1st performances of contemporary Polish organ music, Dusseldorf, 1985; Theory of Music, Academy of Music, Lodz. *Recordings:* Live recording, Gestures of Soul by Tadeusz Wielecki, Warsaw Autumn, 1990. *Publications include:* Marcel Dupré and his Le Chemin de la Croix, 1981; Flor Peeters - universalism and perfection, 1984; Tradition and avant-garde - à propos Joachim Dorfmuller's book, 1986; Four glances at Oratorium of Augustyn Bloch 1986; The experiment of Legnica - music for organ and accordion, 1987; The inspirations of Olivier Messiaen in the Polish organ music, 1988; The cluster and its function in organ music, 1988; Polish organ music in 1945-1985, monograph, 1993; Uber die Traditionen der Polnischen Schule des Orgelspiels im 20 Jahrhundert, Ars Organi, 1992/93. *Memberships:* Polish Composer's Union, musicology section. *Hobbies:* Literature; Church architecture. *Address:* ul Burzliwa 23, 94-109 Lodz, Poland.

SZOKOLAY Sándor, b. 30 Mar 1931, Kunágota, Hungary. Composer. m. (1) Sari Szesztay 1952 (2) Maja Weltler 1970, 4 sons 1 daughter. *Education:* Studied with Szabo and Farkas at the Budapest Music Academy 1950-57; Composition department graduate in 1957. *Career:* 1952-55 music teacher, Budapest Conservatory; 1955-59 musical adviser and editor at Hungarian Radio; 1959-66 Composition Teacher, Budapest Music Academy; 1966- musical adviser Hungarian Television. *Compositions:* Dramatic: The Ballad of Horror, ballet, 1961; Blood Wedding, opera, 1964; Hamlet, opera, 1968; Sacrifice, ballet, 1973; Ecce Homo, passion-opera, 1987; Orchestral: Concert Rondo for piano and strings, 1955; Violin Concerto, 1956; Piano Concerto, 1958; Trumpet Concerto, 1969; oratorios The Fire of March, 1958, and Isthar's Descent into Hell, 1960; Negro Cantata, 1962; Deploration, Requiem in Memory of Poulenc, 1964; The Power of Music, choral fantasy with orchestra; Chamber: Sonata for Solo Violin, 1956; String Quartet, 1973. *Honours:* Erkel Prize 1960, 1965; 1966 Kossuth Prize; 1967 Paris International Dance Festival Golden Star Prize for best composition; 1976 Merited Artist; 1986 Honoured Artist; 1987 Bartók-Pasztory Prize. *Membership:* Chairman of Hungarian Kodály Society. *Hobbies:* Motoring; Hiking. *Current Management:* Martin Perdoux, 5014 Chaparral Way, San Diego, CA 92115, USA. *Address:* 1112 Budapest, Hegyalja ut 70, Hungary.

SZÖLLÖSY Andras, b. 27 Feb 1921, Szaszvaros, Transylvania. Composer; Music Historian. m. Eva Kemenyfy. *Education:* 1939-44 Academy of Music, Budapest, with Kodály; 1947-48 Accademia di Santa Cecilia, Rome, with Petrassi; PhD, University of Budapest. *Career:* Academy of Music Budapest from 1950. *Compositions:* Ballets: Improvisations on the Fear 1963, Pantomime 1965 and Sons of Fire 1977; Orchestral: Concerto for piano, brass, percussion and strings 1957; Concerto for Strings 1968; Trasfigurazioni 1972; Musica concertante, 1973; Musica per orchestra 1973; Sonorità 1974; Concerto for harpsichord and strings 1978; Tristia (Maros Siratò) for Strings 1983; Concerto No V (Lehellet) 1975; Chamber music: Pro Somno Igoris Stravinsky Quieto for small ensemble, 1978; Fragmenti for Mezzosoprano flute and viola; Suoni di tromba for trumpet and piano, 1983; Musiche per ottoni for brass instruments, 1975; Quartetto di tromboni, 1986; Quartetto per archi, 1988; Elegy (dixtuor), 1992; Choral Works: Fabula Phaedri, 1982; In Phariaeos, 1981); Plactus Mariae, 1982; Miserere, 1984. *Publications:* Arthur Honegger 1960, 1980; Editor of various writings by Bartók and Kodály; Critical edition of Bartók's writings 1967. *Honours include:* First Prize, UNESCO International Rostrum of Composers, Paris, 1970; Kossuth Prize, 1985; Bartók-Pásztory Prix, 1986; Commendeur de l'Ordre des Arts et Lettres, 1987. *Address:* Somloi ut 12, 1118 Budapest, Hungary.

SZOMJAS-SCHIFFERT György, b. 25 Apr 1910, Dunakeszi, Hungary. Ethnomusicologist; Composer. m. Magda Imrik, 22 Dec 1953. *Education:* Composition and Singing, Szeged Conservatory, 1930-35; Dr. LLD, University of Szeged 1928-34; Librarian Diploma, Budapest, 1940; Candidate of Musical Science, Budapest, 1969. *Debut:* Songs in Radio Paris-Inter, 23 May 1960; Osaka, Japan, Mellag, 1990. *Career:*

Librarian, Central Office of Statistics 1936-40; Musical Columnist, Korunk Szava 1936-42;Assistant, finally Ministerial Secretary, Ministry of Education, Budapest 1940-49; Scientific Contributor, then Principal Contributor, Institute of Musical Science, Hungarian Academy of Science, 1948, 1954-76; Concert tour in North Europe and USA with University Choir of Budapest as singer, 1936-37; Composer with Songs in Radio Paris-Inter, 1960; Lecturer at Musical Congresses at Prague 1958, Budapest 1960, 1975, Helsinki 1965, Tallinn/Estonia 1970, Bayonne, France, 1973, Turku, Finland 1980, Brno, Czechoslovakia 1983, 1984; Schladming, Austria, 1989, Debrecen, Hungary, 1990. *Compositions:* Two masses for mixed choir; violin concerto; violin serenade; Two siunging duets; songs; arranging of folksongs; collected over 6,000 folksongs in Hungary, Czechoslovakia and Lapland. *Address:* Solymár-u 8, 1032 Budapest, Hungary.

SZONYI Erzsebet, b. 25 Apr 1924, Budapest, Hungary. Composer; Music Educator. *Education:* Budapest Music Academy, 1942-47; Paris Conservatory, 1948, with Aubin, Messiaen and Nadia Boulanger. *Career:* Teacher of Music Education at Budapest Music Academy, 1948-81 (promoted the Kodaly Method in Hungary and elsewhere). *Compositions include:* Operas: Dalma, 1953; The Florentine Tragedy, Meiningen, 1960; Le Malade Imaginaire, Budapest, 1961; Joyful Lament, Budapest, 1980; Break in Transmission, Szeged, 1982; Elfrida, 1985; 2 Divertimentos, 1948, 1951; Organ Concerto, 1958; Musica Festiva for orchestra, 1964; 3 Ideas in 4 Movements for piano and orchestra, 1980; Trio for oboe, clarinet and bassoon, 1958; Sonata for piano trio, 1965; Sonata for double bass and piano, 1982; Evocatio for piano and organ, 1985; 2 piano sonatinas, 1944, 1946; Piano Sonata, 1953; Choral works. *Publications include:* Methods of Musical Reading and Writing, 4 volumes, Budapest, 1953-65, English translation, 1972; Study of Kodaly's teaching methods, Budapest, 1973. *Honours include:* Liszt Prize, 1947; Erkel Prize, 1959. *Address:* ARTISJUS (Hungary), c/o PRS Ltd Member Registration, 29-33 Berners Street, London W1P 4AA, England.

SZÖRENYI Suzana, b. 23 Oct 1929, Bucharest, Romania. Pianist; Lecturer. m. Corneliu Radulescu, 26 Sept 1968. *Education:* Diploma, C Porumbescu Music Academy of Bucharest 1954; Piano Studies with Dusi Mura and Music Forms with Tudor Ciortea. *Debut:* Recital, Romanian Atheneum, Bucharest 1946. *Career:* Currently, Professor by the Music Academy (Bucharest); Soloist, Symphony Concertos, Piano Solo Recitals, Piano Duets, Lieder, Chamber Music, Tours abroad; Recordings for Romanian Broadcasting, from Romanian and universal repertoire; Premieres of recorded and stage performances of Romanian music by George Enescu, Constantin Silvestri, Hilda Jerea, Dan Constantinescu and others; Premieres of works by Beethoven, Brahms, Schumann and Mendelssohn in Romania; Television films with famous pages of the pianistic literature; Participation in George Enescu International Festival Bucharest - 11th Edition - Sept. 1988; Tour abroad: Germany, Suisse, with Cornelia Bvonzetti (violin), 1991; Participation in the Gala, first EPTA Congress in Romania, Constanto, 1992; Symphonic Conontante for Two Pianos and String Orchestra by Dina Lipatti. *Recordings:* Lieder by Brahms with Marta Kessler; Romanian Lieder with Emilia Petrecu; Romanian Dances for two pianos by Dinu Lipatti with Hilda Jerea; Beethoven's complete works for piano - four hands; Symphony Concertante for Two Pianos and String Orchestra by Dinu Lipatti, and George Enescu's works for piano - four hands with Corneliu Radulescu; Original four-hands works by Brahms, Schumann, Mendelssohn-Bartholdy and Max Reger (with Corneliu Radulescu). *Contributions to:* Musica Revue; Elore, newspaper. *Current Management:* Academia de Muzica Bucuresti, Str Stirbei Voda 33, Romania. *Hobbies:* Ballet; House Plants; Domestic Animals; Swimming; Badminton. *Address:* Colentina 37-VI/26, 72.245 Bucharest 10, Romania.

SZOSTTEK-RADKOVA Krystina, b. 14 Mar 1933, Katowice, Poland. Singer (Mezzo-soprano). *Education:* Studied at the Katowice Conservatory with Faryaszevska and Lenczevska. *Debut:* Katowice 1960 as Azucena in Il Tranatore. *Career:* National Opera Warsaw from 1962, as Eboli, Amneris, Ortrud, Kundry and other roles in the dramatic mezzo repertory; Guest engagements in Vienna, Hamburg, Berlin, Prague, Sofia, Belgrade, Moscow and Leningrad; Paris Opera 1981, as Ulrica in UI Ballo in Maschera; Grand Théâtre, Geneva, 1983, Herodias in Salome; Appeared at the Théâtre de la Monnaie Brussels and the Opera de Lyon in operas by Verdi and Wagner; Sang Fricka in the Ring at Warsaw, 1988; Concert tours of France and South America. *Recordings:* Many opera albums for the Muza label, and works by Penderecki and Tadeusz Baird. *Address:* Teatr Wiekli, Plac Teatrainy, 00-076 Warsaw, Poland.

SZUCS Marta, b. 1964, Hungary. Singer (Soprano). *Education:* Studied violin at first, then singing, in Budapest. *Career:* Sang in concert in Hungary and abroad, 1976-78; Guest appearances at Hamburg Staatsoper and Frankfurt from 1979; Member of Hungarian National Opera from 1981, debut as Gilda; Further engagements at Vienna Staatsoper, 1985-87, Scottish Opera (as Gilda, 1984, Anna in Anna Bolena, 1989); Liège, 1986-87, as Lucia di Lammermoor, Monte Carlo, 1988, in Cimarosa's Il Pittore Parigino; Sang Anaide in Moise et Pharaon by Rossini at Budapest, 1992. *Address:* c/o Hungarian State Opera House, Nepoztarsasag utja 22, 1061 Budapest, Hungary.

SZWAJGIER Olga, b. 15 Jan 1944, Siowikowa, Poland. Singer. m. Krzysztof Szwajgier, 4 Sept 1969, 2 daughters. *Education:* Studied Biology and Chemistry, Teachers College, 1962-64; Vocal studies with Leokadia Kukawska and Stanislawa Hoffman, Academy of Music, Cracow, 1965-70; MA diploma, 1970. *Career:* Soloist, Baltic Opera, Gdansk; Appearances, opera theatres, philharmonic orchestras and chamber ensembles, Poland, 1972-; Participated at festivals: Warsaw Autumn Festival; Incontroazione, Palermo, Sicily; Foro Internazionale de Musica Nueva, Mexico; Aterforum, Ferrera; Others; Specialist in contemporary music, 1971-; Has premiered numerous new works composed for her special abilities to widen voice range to 5 octaves. *Hobby:* Science fiction. *Address:* U1 Chrobrego 29/6, 31-428 Cracow, Poland.

T

T'HEZAN Helia, b. 23 Aug 1934, Rieumes, France. Singer (Soprano). *Education:* Studied at the Toulouse Conservatory and the Musikhochschule, Berlin. *Debut:* Bordeaux 1958, in Armide by Lully. *Career:* Sang at the Paris Opéra and the Opéra-Comique from 1959; Covent Garden 1965, in the title role of Gluck's iphigénie en Tauride; Glyndebourne 1966, as Charlotte in Werther; Monte Carlo 1973, in the premiere of La Reine Morte by Rossellini; Has sung at Lyon, Marseille, Geneva, Rome, Trieste, Turin, Lisbon and Philadelphia; Sang at the Paris Opéra 1988, as Iuno in Orphée aux Enfers. *Recordings include:* Manon by Massenet (EMI). *Address:* Theatre National, 8 Rue Scribe, F-75009 Paris, France.

TABACHNIK Michel, b. 10 Nov 1942, Geneva, Switzerland. Conductor; Composer. m. Sabine Tabachnik, 24 June 1981, 2 sons, 1 daughter. *Education:* Piano, Conducting, Writing, Composition; Assistant of Markevitch and Boulez. *Debut:* BBC, London, 1966; National Orchestra, Paris, 1971; Berlin Philharmonic, 1972. *Career:* Conducting all major orchestras including: NHK Tokyo; Orchestra de Paris; Israel Philharmonic; Berlin Philharmonic; Philharmonic, London; St Cecilia, Rome; Suisse Romande, Geneva; Concertgebouw, Amsterdam. *Compositions:* Cosmogonie for orchestra; Haisha for choir and orchestra; Le Pacte des Onze for choir and orchestra; L'Arch for soprano and orchestra; Concerto for Piano; Quatuor; Les Perseïdes for orchestra. *Recordings:* Schumann, Grieg, Lalo, St Saens; Pacte des Onze and Cosmogonie. *Hobbies:* Mountaineering; Reading. *Address:* CH-1985 Villaz-La Sage, Switzerland.

TABAKOV Emil, b. 1947, Bulgaria. Conductor; Composer. *Education:* Bulgarian State Conservatoire, degree in Conducting, Composition and Double Bass. *Career:* Founded and conducted the Bulgarian State Conservatoire Chamber Orchestra of Sofia, 1977; Director of the Sofia Soloists Chamber Orchestra 1979-, touring Bulgaria, Europe, Asia, Latin America, Australia and the USA; Principal Conductor of the Sofia Philharmonic Orchestra 1985, tours of the USA, Japan, Hong Kong, South America and the UK; Guest conductor in Denmark, Sweden, Germany, Poland, Brazil, Romania, Greece and France. *Compositions:* Concerto for Double Bass and Orchestra; Turnovgrad Velki; 1393 Cantata; Concerto for Percussion Instruments; Three Symphonies. *Recordings:* Mozart, the Complete Church Sonatas; Works by J S Bach, Handel, Haydn, Mendelssohn, Shostakovich, Britten and Schoenberg (with the Sofia Soloists); Complete Symphonies of Mahler, Rachmaninov and Bruckner (with the Sofia Philharmonic Orchestra). *Honours:* Prize Winner, Nikolai Malko International Competition for Young Conductors, Copenhagen, 1977. *Address:* c/o Norman McCann International Artists Ltd, The Coach House, 56 Lawrie Park Gardens, London SE26 6XJ, England.

TACHEZI Herbert, b. 12 Feb 1930, Wiener Neustadt, Austria. Organist. *Education:* Studied piano, composition and organ at the Vienna Conservatoire; Harpsichord studies with Fritz Neumeyer at Fribourg. *Career:* Many concert performances with Nikolaus Harnoncourt and the Concentus Musicus, Vienna: continuo, harpsichord and organ; Solo performer in music by Bach (JS and CPE), Handel and music of the Renaissance; Professor of organ, theory and improvisation at the Vienna Conservatoire; Has composed works for organ, piano and chamber ensemble. *Recordings include:* Organ Concertos by Handel. *Honours:* Prize winner at international competitions of Geneva (1955), Innsbruck (1958) and Vienna (1965). *Address:* c/o Konservatorium für Musik, Muhlgasse 28-30, A-1040 Vienna, Austria.

TACUCHIAN Ricardo, b. 18 Nov 1939, Rio de Janeiro, Brazil. Professor; Composer; Conductor. m. (1) Div, 2 sons, (2) Maria de Fátima Granja Tacuchian. *Education:* Colégio Pedro II (High School); Graduated Piano 1961, Composition and Conducting, 1965; Postgraduate Conducting 1967, Composition and Orchestration 1968. *Debut:* Imagem Carioca for Orchestra 1963. *Career:* Has conducted own works in the main Brazilian orchestras; Creator of the Ensemble Arts Contemporanea, specialising in contemporary music; Has twice travelled to Europe to participate in Music Festivals, and his music is performed in Europe, North and Latin America; Doctor of Musical Arts (Composition), University of Southern California, 1990; Presently Head of the Post Graduate Music Department, UFRJ and President of the Academia Brasileira de Música. *Compositions:* For orchestra: Estruturas Sinfonicas, Imagem Carioca, Nucleos, Dia de Chuva, Hayastan, (ballet), 1990; Cantatas: O Canto do Poeta, Cantata dos Mortos, Cantata de Natal, Ciclo Lorca; Concertos: for Piano, Flute, 2 String Quartets, Wind Quintet; Chamber music, Light and Shadows, 1988; Rio/LA, 1988; Choir music; Piano pieces. *Recordings include:* O Canto do Poeta; Cantata dos Mortos; Estruturas Verdes; Estruturas Divergentes; Ritos; 2 Sonatas for Piano. *Publications:* A Música na Educação como Processo (2nd edition 1982); Bandas Anacrônicas ou Atuais?, 1982; Definiçoes Estéticas e Comuniçacao Artística, 1984. *Address:* Rua Sao Salvador 31 Apt 501, Flamengo 22231-130, Rio de Janeiro, RJ, Brazil.

TADDEI Giuseppe, b. 26 June 1916, Genoa, Italy. Singer (Baritone). *Education:* Studied in Rome. *Debut:* Rome 1936, as the Herald in Lohengrin. *Career:* Sang in Rome until 1942, as Alberich and Germont and in Dallapiccola's Volo di Notte; Vienna Staatsoper 1946-48, as Amonasro, Rigoletto and the Figaros of Mozart and Rossini; Cambridge Theatre London 1947, as Scarpia and Rigoletto; Salzburg Festival 1948, Mozart's Figaro; La Scala 1948-61, as Malatesta, the villains in Les Contes d'Hoffmann and Pizarro; Sang Wagner's Dutchman, Gunther and Wolfram elsewhere in Italy, and Mozart's Papageno and Leporello; US debut San Francisco 1957, Macbeth; Chicago 1959, Barnaba; Teatro Masimo Palermo 1959, in Beatrice di Tenda by Bellini; Covent Garden 1960-67, Macbeth, Rigoletto, Iago and Scarpia; Bregenz Festival 1968-71, as Falstaff, Dulcamara and Suplice in La Fille du Régiment; Vienna Staatsoper 1980, in Il Tabarro; Metropolitan Opera debut 1985, as Falstaff; Vienna Staatsoper 1986, as Scarpia (to celebrate 70th birthday); Sang Gianni Schicchi at Torre del Lago 1987; Stuttgart Staatsoper 1990, as Falstaff. *Recordings:* La Bohème, Ernani, Un Ballo in Maschera, Guillaume Tell, Rigoletto, Falstaff, Don Giovanni, Il Maestro di Capella (Cetra); Andrea Chénier (HMV); Le Nozze di Figaro, Così fan Tutte, Don Giovanni, L'Elisir d'Amore (Columbia); Mosè in Egitto, Linda di Chamounix, Falstaff, Tosca (Philips); Macbeth (Decca). *Address:* c/o Staatstheater Stuttgart, Oberer Schlossgarten 6, D-7000 Stuttgart 1, Germany.

TADDEI Ottavio, b. 15 July 1926, San Miniato, Tuscany, Italy. Singer (Tenor). *Education:* Studied in Siena. *Debut:* Siena, as Rodolfo in La Boheme, 1953. *Career:* Sang the Duke of Mantua and Edgardo at Rome, 1954; Appearances at Milan, Florence, Modena and San Jose in Costa Rica; Teatro San Carlo, Naples, 1959, as Mateo in Conchita by Zandonai; Sang at Teatro Comunale, Florence, from 1960, and made tours of Netherlands, Turkey and England; Hamburg, Nuremberg and Frankfurt from 1966, notably as Pinkerton; Sang in Monteverdi's Poppea at Rome, 1966; Many opera broadcasts for Italian Radio RAI, including the Queen of Spades, 1963. *Address:* Teatro Comunale di firenze, Via Solferino 15, 50123 Florence, Italy.

TADEO Giorgio, b. 2 Oct 1929, Verona, Italy. Singer (Bass). *Education:* Studied in Parma with Ettore Campogalliani and at the Opera School of La Scala, Milan. *Debut:* Palermo 1953, as Mephistopheles in Faust. *Career:* Sang at Turin, Rome, Florence and Trieste, as well as La Scala; Verona Arena 1955 and 1973-74; Covent Garden debut 1974, Don Pasquale; Further engagements at Buenos Aires, Mexico City, Dallas, Chicago, Paris and Salzburg. *Recordings include:* Tosca (HMV); Andrea Chénier conducted by Chailly; Leonore by Paer and Antonio in Le nozze di Figaro (Decca); Manon Lescaut.

TAGLIAVINI Ferruccio, b. 14 Aug 1913, Barco, Reggio Emilia, Italy. Singer (Tenor). m. Pia Tassinari 1941. *Education:* Studied with Brancucci at the Parma Conservatory and with Amadeo Bassi in Florence. *Debut:* Florence 1938, as Rodolfo in La Bohème. *Career:* Maggio Musicale 1940, in Semiramide by Rossini; La Scala Milan, 1942-53, as Elvino, Werther and Fritz in L'Amico Fritz by Mascagni; Toured South America, 1946; Chicago Lyric Opera debut 1946, Rodolfo; Metropolitan Opera, 1947-62, as Nemorino, Almaviva, Edgardo, the Duke of Mantua, Alfredo and Cavaradossi; San Francisco Opera, 1948-52, notably as Boito's Faust; Covent Garden, 1950, 1955-56 as Nemorino, Cavaradossi and Nadir in Les pêcheurs de Perles; Further appearances in Buenos Aires, Brussels, Paris and Verona; Last stage appearance 1965 as Werther at the Teatro La Fenice, Venice. *Recordings include:* La Sonnambula, Martha, La Bohème, L'Arlesiana, Tosca, Rigoletto, Un Ballo in Maschera, Madama Butterfly, Werther, Mefistofele (Cetra); L'Amico Fritz (Parlophone); Lucia di Lammermoor (RCA).

TAGLIAVINI Franco, b. 29 Oct 1934, Novellara, Reggio Emilia, Italy. Singer (Tenor). *Education:* Studied at Liceo Musicale Vercelli and with Zita Fumagalli-Riva. *Debut:* Teatro Nuovo Milan 1961, as Canio in Pagliacci. *Career:* Bologna 1962, as Pinkerton; Edgardo in Lucia di Lammermoor, in Tunisia; Rome Opera as Dmitri (Boris Godunov), Cavaradossi and Lensky; US debut 1964, as Ismaele in Nabucco and Calaf (Turandot) at San Francisco; Sang Alfredo for Dallas Opera, 1965; La Scala Debut 1965, in Mosè by Rossini; Royal Opera House Covent Garden, 1967-76, as Pollione, Cavaradossi, the Duke of Mantua and Macduff; Chicago Lyric Opera, 1959-73, as Turiddu, Calaf, Pinkerton, Alfredo and Riccardo (Un Ballo in Maschera) and I Due Foscari and Maria Stuarda; Appearances at the Metropolitan Opera New York in Norma, Un Ballo in Maschera, Tosca, Vespri Siciliani and Macbeth; Guest appearances in Munich, Paris, Berlin, Vienna, Parma, Geneva, Zurich, Verona and Brussels; Other roles include Enzo (La Gioconda), Don Carlos, Don José, Des Grieux (Manon Lescaut), Paolo (Francesca da Rimini), Maurizio (Adriana Lecouvreur) and Don José; Sang Rodolfo in Luisa Miller at Brussels, 1982; Retired 1989. *Recordings include:* Te Deum by Berlioz (Philips); Madame Sans-Gêne by Giordano; Olympia by Spontini (RIAS/Orfeo); Adriana Lecouvreur and Francesca da Rimini for Italian TV. *Address:* c/o SA Gorlinsky Ltd., 33 Dover Street, London W1X 4NJ, England.

TAGLIAVINI Luigi Ferdinando, b. 7 Oct 1929, Bologna, Italy. Organist; Harpsichordist; Musicologist. *Education:* Studied at the Conservatories of Bologna and Paris with Marcel Dupré (organ) and Riccardo Nielsen (composition); University of Padua, PhD 1951. *Career:* Teacher of organ at the Martini Conservatory Bologna 1952-54, librarian 1953-60; Organ Professor at the Monteverdi Conservatory Bolzano 1954-64; Founder and co-editor from 1960 of L'organo; Many concert appearances in Europe and North America, playing the harpsichord and organ; Visiting Professor at Cornell University 1963; SUNY, Buffalo 1969; Director of the Institute of musicology at Fribourg University 1965, Professor from 1971; Editor of Monumenti di Musica Italiana. *Recordings include:* Two-organ works with Marie Claire Alain. *Contributions to:* Neue Mozart-Ausgabe (3 volumes: Ascanio in Alba, Betulia Liberata, Mitridate re di Ponto); Articles in L'organo, Musik in Gesicht und Gegenwart, Ricordi, La Musica, Larousse de la musique.

TAHOURDIN Peter, b. 1928, England. Composer. *Education:* Studied composition with Richard Arnell, Trinity College of Music, London, graduated 1952; Studied, Toronto University, Canada, 1966-67. *Career:* Visiting Composer, University of Adelaide, 1965; Staff, Faculty of Music, University of Melbourne, 1973-88; Chairman, Composers Guild of Australia, 1978-79. *Compositions:* Works for Orchestra: Symphony No 1, 1960; No 2 1968-69; No 3, 1979; No 4, 1987; Sinfonietta No 1, 1952; No 2, 1959; Diversions for Orchestra, 1958-59; Fanfares and Variations-A Festival Overture, 1983.

Works for Solo Instrument and Orchestra: Sinfonia Concertante, 1966; Works for Ensemble: Three Pieces for Wind Quintet, 1959; Quartet for Oboe and Strings, 1963; Celebration, 1979; Quartet for Strings, 1982; Raga Music 3-Elision, 1988. Instrumental Works: Sonata for Clarinet and Piano, 1962; Dialogue No 1, 1971, No 2, 1976; No 3, 1978; No 4, 1984; Raga Music 4 - For Two, 1990. Works for Piano: Capriccio, 1963. Vocal Works: Raga Music 1-The Starlight Night, 1985; Choral Works: Seven Gnomic Verses, 1968; King Oswald's Victory, 1970. Music Theatre Works: Ern Malley-A Dramatic Testament, 1975-76. Works for the Stage: Inside Information-One Act Opera, 1955; Illyria-One Act Ballet, 1965; Works for Tape; Education Works. *Memberships:* Australian Performing Right Association, Fellowship of Australian Composers. *Address:* c/o Australian Music Centre, PO Box 49, Broadway 2007, Australia.

TAILLON Jocelyne, b. 19 May 1941, Doudeville, France. Singer (Mezzo-Soprano). *Education:* Studied with Suzanne Balguerie and Germaine Lubin at the Grenoble Conservatory. *Debut:* Nurse in Ariadne et Barbe-Bleue at Bordeaux, 1968. *Career:* Glyndebourne 1969, as Genevieve in Pelléas et Mélisande; Paris Opéra from 1973, in Pelléas, Il Trovatore, Faust, Dialogues des Carmélites and Falstaff; Geneva Opera in Macbeth by Bloch: returned for season 1983/84; Guest appearances in Madrid, Aix-en-Provence, Brussels, Nantes and Marseille; Metropolitan Opera from 1979, as La Cieca (La Gioconda), Geneviève, Anna (Les Troyens), Erda and Mistress Quickly; sang Arnalta in L'Incoronazione di Poppea at the Théâtre du Châtclet, Paris, 1989 (repeated Geneva); Martha in Faust at Orange, France, 1990. *Recordings include:* Edwige in Guillaume Tell, conducted by Gardelli; Merope in Oedipe by Enesco, conducted by Lawrence Foster. *Honour:* Officier, des Arts et Lettres, chevalier dans l'ordre du Mérite. *Address:* 16 Avenue Franklin Roosevelt, 75008 Paris, France.

TAKACS Klara, b. 24 Apr 1945, Hungary. Singer (Mezzo-soprano). *Education:* Studied at the Ferenc Liszt Academy Budapest. *Career:* Has sung at the Hungarian State Opera from 1973, notably as Orpheus, Adalgisa, Goldmark's Königin von Saba, Cenerentola and Cherubino; Guest appearances in Europe's leading opera houses and concert halls; Sang with the Vienna Staatsoper in tour of Japan 1986; Teatro Colón Buenos Aires 1987, as Charlotte and as Eudossia in La Fiamma by Respighi; Sang Mozart's Marcellina at the 1992 Salzburg Festival. *Recordings:* Médée by Cherubini, with Sylvia Sass; Die Königin von Saba; Boito's Nerone, Hunyadi Laszlo by Erkel, Haydn's Apothecary; Mozart Requiem, Liszt Legend of Saint Elizabeth, Missa Solemnis by Beethoven, Mahler Lieder eines fahrenden Gesellen, Kodály Háry János and sacred music by Haydn (Hungaroton). *Honours:* Prize winner, Erkel International Singing Competition, Budapest, 1975; Liszt Prize Laureate; Grand Prix de l'Academie du Disque, Paris, 3 times. *Address:* c/o Hungarian State Opera, Nepoztarsasag utja 22, 1061 Budapest, Hungary.

TAKACS Tamara, b. 1950, Hungary. Singer (Mezzo-soprano). *Education:* Studied with Joszef Reti at the Ferenc Liszt Academy Budapest until 1978. *Career:* Has sung at Hungarian State Opera House 1978-, as Vivaldi's Griselda, Orpheus, Mozart's 2nd Lady and Dorabella; Verdi's Azucena, Maddalena, Ulrica, Emilia, Mrs Quickly and Eboli; Wagner's Waltraute and Magdalena; Charlotte and Carmen; Sang Orzse in Kodály's Háry János 1988; Appeared as Judit in Duke Bluebeard's Castle at Covent Garden 1989, on visit with Hungarian State Opera; Season 1992 as Public Opinion in Orphée aux Enfers at Budapest; Concert repertoire include Purcell Ode for St Cecilia's Day; Vivaldi Stabat Mater, Gloria, Juditha Triumphans and Nisi Dominus; Donizetti and Verdi Requiems; Messiah and Rossini Stabat Mater. *Recordings:* Numerous albums for Hungaroton. *Address:* Hungarian State Opera, Nepoztarsasag utja 22, 1061 Budapest, Hungary.

TAKACS-NAGY Gabor, b. 17 Apr 1956, Budapest,

Hungary. Violinist. *Education:* Studied with András Mihaly at the Franz Liszt Academy, Budapest, with members of the Amadeus Quartet and Zoltan Szekely. *Career:* Founder member of the Takacs Quartet, 1975; Many concert appearances in all major centres of Europe and the USA; Tours of Australia, New Zealand, Japan, South America, England, Norway, Sweden, Greece, Belgium and Ireland; Bartók Cycle for the Bartók-Solti Festival at South Bank, 1990; Great Performers Series at Lincoln Center and Mostly Mozart Festival at Alice Tully Hall, New York; Visits to Japan 1989 and 1992; Mozart Festivals at South Bank, Wigmore Hall and Barbican Centre 1991; Bartók Cycle at the Théâtre des Champs Elysées 1991; Beethoven Cycles at the Zurich Tonhalle, in Dublin, at the Wigmore Hall and in Paris 1991-92; Resident at the University of Colorado, Resident at the London Barbican 1988-91, with master classes at the Guildhall School of Music; Plays Amati instrument made for the French Royal Family and loaned by the Corcoran Gallery, Gallery of Art, Washington DC. *Recordings:* Schumann Quartets Op 41, Mozart String Quintets (with Denes Koromzay), Bartók 6 Quartets, Schubert Trout Quintet (with Zoltan Kocsis) Hungaroton; Haydn Op 76, Brahms Op 51 nos 1 and 2, Chausson Concerto (with Joshua Bell and Jean-Yves Thibaucet); Works by Schubert, Mozart, Dvořák and Bartók (Decca). *Honours:* Winner, International Quartet Competition, Evian 1977; Winner, Portsmouth International Quartet Competition, 1979. *Address:* 22 Tower Street, London WC2H 9NS, England.

TAKAHASHI Yoriko, b. 27 June 1937, Kanazawa, Japan. Pianist. m. Gabriel Chodos (divorced), 1 son. *Education:* Diplomas in Piano, Toho Conservatory High School, 1957; BA, Tokyo University of Arts, 1961; University of California at Los Angeles, USA, 1964-65; Juilliard School of Music, USA, 1964; Akademie für musik und darstellende Kunst, Vienna, 1966; Piano studied with various teachers. *Career:* Concerts throughout Japan, USA and Europe; Official accompanist for NHK, Tokyo; Appearances with University of California at Los Angeles Symphony and with Eugene, Oregon, Symphony Orchestras, USA; Solo recitals, Oregon Educational Television Network and RIAS, Italy. *Recordings:* MacDowell Sonatas No. 2 and No. 3. *Current Management:* Takayanagi Music Management, 1 Samon Shinjuku-Ku, Tokyo, Japan 160. *Address:* 8-4-2 Kinuta Setagaya-ku, Tokyo 157, Japan.

TAKEMITSU Toru, b. 8 Oct 1930, Tokyo, Japan. Composer. *Education:* Studied privately and with Kiyose, 1948-50. *Career:* Co-founded an artists group Experimental Workshop in Tokyo, 1951; Artistic director of Space Theatre at Osaka Exposition, 1970; Featured composer at Aldeburgh Festival, 1986; To the Edge of Dream and Orion and Pleiades performed at 1989 Promenade Concerts, London; UK Premiere of Gemeaux at 1989 Edinburgh Festival, with Simon Rattle, Oliver Knussen, Heinz Hollinger and Vinko Globokar. *Compositions:* Requiem for strings, 1957; Music of Trees for orchestra, 1961; Textures for piano and orchestra, 1964; The Dorian Horizon for 17 strings, 1966; November Steps for biwa, shakuhachi and orchestra, 1967; Asterism for piano and orchestra, 1968; Cassiopeia for percussion and orchestra, 1971; Gitimalya for marimba and orchestra, 1975; A Flock Descends into the Pentagonal Garden for orchestra, 1977; Dreamtime for orchestra, 1981; Rain Coming for chamber orchestra, 1982; To the Edge of Dream for guitar and orchestra, 1983; Star-Isle for orchestra, 1984; Orion and Pleiades for cello and orchestra; Gemeaux for oboe, trombone and orchestra; I Hear the Water Dreaming for flute and orchestras, 1987; Twill by Twilight, 1988; Tree Line, 1988; A String Around Autumn for viola and orchestra, 1989; From Me Flows What You Call Time, 1990; Chamber music, including string quartet A Way Alone, 1981, and a series of works for instruments entitled Stanza; works for tape. *Address:* c/o Schott Japan Company Ltd, 2-9-3 Iidabashi, Chiyoda-ku, Tokyo 102, Japan.

TAL Josef, b. 18 Sept 1910, Pinne, now Poland. Composer. m. Jan 1940, 1 son. *Education:* Hochschule für Musik, Berlin, Germany. *Career:* Director, Jerusalem Academy of Music, Israel, 1948-52; Director, Israel Centre for Electronic Music, 1961; Head of Musicology Department, Incumbent Arthur Rubinstein Cathedra, Hebrew University, Jerusalem, 1965. *Compositions include:* 8 operas: Saul at Ein Dor, 1957; Ammon and Tamar, 1961; Ashmedai, 1971; Massada 967, 1973; Die Versuchung, 1976; Der Turm, 1987; Der Garten, 1988; Josef, 1993; 6 symphonies; 6 piano concertos; 5 concertos for different instruments; Requiem: The Death of Moses; Chamber music works; Vocal music; Cantatas; Psychodrama Die Hand. *Recordings:* CBS, RCA, Grenadilla and Folklore, USA; Eastronics and Nimbus, Israel; Else (Hommage), 3 Essays for Piano, Academy/edel Company. *Publication:* Autobiographie, 1984. *Honours:* 3 Engel Prizes, Tel Aviv Municipality; Unesco Fellowship, 1957; Israel State Prize, 1971; Art Prize of the City of Berlin, 1975; Wolf Prize, 1982; Verdienstkreuz 1 Klasse, BDR, 1984; Commandeur de l'ordre des Artes et des Lettres, France, 1985. *Memberships:* West Berlin Academy of Arts, 1975; Honorary member, American Academy and Institute of Arts and Letters, 1981. *Hobbies:* Photography; Theatre. *Address:* Kfar Etzion Str. 39, 93392 Arnona-Jerusalem, Israel.

TALARICO Rita, b. 30 May 1941, Rome, Italy. Singer (Soprano). *Education:* Studied in Rome with Gabriella Besanzoni and at the Accadmia di Santa Cecilia with Maria Teresa Pediconi. *Debut:* As Eleonora in Il Furioso all'Isola di San Domingo by Donizetti, at the 1967 Spoleto Festival. *Career:* Has sung at leading Italian opera houses and in Lyon, Rouen, Montreal, New York and Philadelphia; Other roles include: Elvira (I Puritani), Amina (La Sonnambula), Leila (Les pêcheurs de Perles), Mimi, Violetta, Medora (Il Corsaro), Elsa, Agathe, Donna Anna, Susanna, Countess Almaviva, Marguerite, Carolina (Il Matrimonio Segreto) and Margherita (Mefistofele); La Scala 1985, in Orfeo by Luigi Rossi. *Recordings include:* Il Furioso all'Isolo di San Domingo. *Address:* c/o Teatro alla Scala, Via Filodrammatici 2, Milan, Italy.

TALBOT Désirée Ruth, b. 24 Oct 1926. Singer; Teacher. *Education:* LUCT, Piano; LUCT, Singing; UPLM, singing. *Debut:* Suor Angelica-Puccini Cape Town, South Africa. *Career:* Teacher, piano, singing, aural, theory, schools and conservatories, 1954-60; Milan 1960-62; Lecturer in Singing, University of Stellenbosch, South Africa, 1962-67; Senior Lecturer 1967-, Professor 1979-, Deputy Dean 1984, University of Cape Town. Leading roles, over 500 performances of 28 operas; Sang Judith, First British performance, Duke Bluebeard's Castle, Bartók, 1957. *Recordings:* SABC, BBC Overseas Services. *Publications:* For the Love of Singing, 1978; I'd Do It Again, 1982. *Contributions to:* Various professional journals including: Masterclasses, Melbourne University, Sydney National Conservatorium of Music, Australia. *Hobby:* Dressmaking. *Address:* Faculty of Music, University of Cape Town, South Africa.

TALBOT John William, b. 28 Feb 1941, Sydney, New South Wales, Australia. Pianist; Teacher; Lecturer. *Education:* LMusA (Performance), 1961, BA (Hons), 1964, University of Queensland; Queensland Conservatorium of Music; MA, Music, University of Melbourne, 1966. *Career:* Lecturer in Music, Portsmouth Polytechnic, 1971-77; Lecturer in Music, Victorian College of the Arts, 1977-82; Now freelance pianist, accompanist, teacher; Artist-in-Residence, Bishopsgate Institute; Recitals with Brian Rayner-Cook, Yfrah Neaman. *Recording:* Moeran, Violin Sonata, with Donald Scotts, violin. *Honours:* Dalley-Scarlett Memorial Scholarship, 1963. *Memberships:* Incorporated Society of Musicians; European Piano Teachers' Association; MIMT, Australia; Vice-Chairman, Recordings Manager, British Music Society. *Hobbies:* Reading; Swimming. *Address:* 7 Rosehill Walk, Tunbridge Wells, Kent TN1 1HL, England.

TALBOT Michael Owen, b. 4 Jan 1943, Luton, England. Professor in Music. *Education:* BA Honours,

MusB, PhD, Clare College, Cambridge University; Royal College of Music. *Career:* Reader, now Professor (1986-) in Music, Liverpool University. *Compositions:* Many editions, baroque music. *Publications:* Vivaldi, 1978, 1979-93; Albinoni, Leben und Werk, 1980; Antonio Vivaldi: A Guide to Research, 1988; Tomaso Albinoni: The Venetian Composer and his World, 1990-94; Benedetto Vinaccesi: A Musician in Brescia and Venice in the Age of Carelli, 1994. *Contributions to:* Early Music; Music & Letters; Music Review; Musical Times; Soundings; The Consort; Note d'archivio; Informazioni e Studi Vivaldiani. *Honours:* Cavaliere, Italy, 1980; Oldman Prize, 1990. *Memberships:* Historical adviser, Vivaldi Society; Royal Musical Association; FBA, 1990. *Address:* Department of Music, The University, PO Box 147, Liverpool L69 3BX, England.

TALICH Jan, b. 30 Oct 1945, Plzen, Czechoslovakia. Violist. *Education:* Studied at the Prague Conservatory. *Career:* Co-founded the Talich Quartet 1961; After success in competitions at Kromeriz and Belgrade gained title of Laureate by the Association of International Music Festivals in Bayreuth; Moved from leader of Talich quartet to violist, 1972; Appearances in Europe and North America, Egypt, Iraq, Indonesia and Japan; Annual visits to France from 1976, including the complete Beethoven quartets; Engagements with festivals and music clubs in Britain; Wigmore Hall, London, 1991 with the quartets of Smetana, Beethoven's Op.74, Brahms A minor and Mozart D minor; Bath and Bournemouth Festivals June 1991; Queen Elizabeth Hall Nov. 1991; Janáček's 2nd Quartet for BBC2's The Late Show. *Recordings:* Albums for Collins Classics, Sarastro and Calliope. *Address:* c/o Clarion/Seven Muses, 64 Whitehall Park, London N19 3TN, England.

TALLEY-SCHMIDT Eugene, b. 10 Feb 1932, Rome, Georgia, USA. Tenor Singer; Professor of Voice & Chairman of Voice Department, Houston Baptist University. m. Jeanette Lombard Pecorello, 22 Nov 1960, 2 sons. *Education:* San Diego State College; Indiana University; Opera Arts, Atlanta, Georgia; Teatro dell'Opera, Rome, Italy; Diploma, Teatro Lirico, Spoleto, Italy; Voice study, Ethel Wilkerson, Rome, Georgia, John Walsh & Raoul Couyas, San Diego, California. *Debut:* USA: Hans/Bartered Bride, San Diego, California. Europe: Fritz/L'Amico Fritz, Spoleto, Italy. *Career includes:* Leading tenor, Deutsche Oper am Rhein, Düsseldorf, Staatsoper, Hamburg, Wuppertal & Münster Operas; Sang over 50 leading tenor roles, opera houses in USA & Europe; TV & radio performances, Europe & USA. Performed in international festivals, appeared with Atlanta, Birmingham, Mobile, Miami, Palm Beach, Indianapolis, Rome, San Diego Symphony Orchestras. *Recording:* Robert Schumann, complete duets for tenor & soprano, Cantabile Records. *Hobbies:* Philately; Lapidary; Golf. *Address:* 3506 Oyster Cove Drive, Missouri City, TX 77459, USA.

TALMI Yoav, b. 28 Apr 1943, Kibbutz Merhavia, Israel. Conductor; Composer. m. Er'ella Talmi, 2 Sept 1964, 1 son, 1 daughter. *Education:* Diploma, Rubin Academy of Music, Tel-Aviv, 1961-65; Postgraduate Diploma, Juilliard School of Music, New York, 1965-68; Summer study courses with W. Susskind, Aspen, 1966; B. Maderna, Salzburg, 1967; J. Fournet, Hilversum, 1968; E. Leinsdorf, Tanglewood, 1969. *Career:* Co-Conductor, Israel Chamber Orchestra, Tel-Aviv, 1970-72; Artistic Director and Conductor, Gelders Symphony Orchestra, Arnhem, 1974-80; Principal Guest Conductor, Munich Philharmonic Orchestra, 1979-80; Music Director and Principal Conductor, Israel Chamber Orchestra, 1984-88; Music Director, New Israeli Opera, 1985-89; Music Director, San Diego Symphony, USA, 1989; Guest Conducting: Berlin Philharmonic, Munich Philharmonic, London Symphony Philharmonia, London Philharmonic, Amsterdam's Concertgebouw, Israel, New Japan Philharmonics, Vienna Symphony, St. Petersburg and Oslo Philharmonics; Tonhalle Orchestra, Zurich, Detroit, Houston, Dallas and St Louis Symphonies; Los Angeles Chamber Orchestra, New York Chamber Symphony.

Compositions include: Dreams for choir a capella; Music for flute & strings; Overture on Mexican Themes (recorded by Louisville Orchestra); 3 monologues for flute solo (published). *Recordings include:* Bruckner: Symphony No 9 (Oslo Phil/Chandos); Glière: 3rd Symphony (San Diego/Pro Arte), Brahms: Sextet/4 Serious Songs/(San Diego Symphony/Pro Arte); Tchaikovsky/Schoenberg (Israel Chamber Orchestra/Teldec), Bloch/Barber/Puccini/Grieg/ (Israel Chamber Orchestra/Chandos). *Current Management:* Joy Mebus Artists Management, Waterstraat 43, 3770 Zussen, Belgium. *Address:* PO Box 1384, Kfar Saba 44113, Israel. Also c/o San Diego Symphony, 1245 7th Avenue, San Diego, CA 92101, USA.

TALVI Ilkka Ilari, b. 22 Oct 1948, Kuusankoski, Finland. Violinist; Concertmaster. m. Marjorie Kransberg, 29 Aug 1984, 3 daughters. *Education:* Diploma, studied with Arno Granroth, Sibelius Academy, Helsinki, 1960-66; Studied with: Jascha Heifetz, University of Southern California, USA; Ivan Galamian, Curtis Institute of Music; Ricardo Odnoposoff, Vienna; Gabriel Bouillon, Paris. *Debut:* With orchestra at age 10; Recital debut at age 15, Helsinki. *Career:* Performances as soloist and recitalist in Europe and USA; Lecturer, Sibelius Academy, Finland, 1969-75; Lecturer, Pori School of Music, 1970-76; Concertmaster, Malmo Symphony, Sweden, 1976-77; Working in motion picture business, Los Angeles, USA, 1977-85; Principal, Los Angeles Chamber Orchestra, 1979-85; Guest Concertmaster 1983-85, Concertmaster, Seattle Opera, 1985-; Concertmaster, Waterloo Festival, New Jersey, 1988-. *Recordings include:* Klami Violin Concerto; Albert Im Concordiam. *Honours:* Numerous honours and prizes in Finland. *Hobbies:* Dogs; Computers; Outdoors. *Current Management:* Festium, Helsinki, Finland. *Address:* 3456 10th Avenue West, Seattle, WA 98119, USA.

TAMASSY Eva, b. 19 Mar 1937, Budapest, Hungary. Singer (Contralto). *Education:* Studied with Geza Laszlo in Budapest and with Gerda Gleuer and Kurt Schneider in Germany. *Debut:* Hungarian State Opera 1961, as Maddalena in Rigoletto. *Career:* Sang at the Cologne Opera, the Deutsche Oper am Rhein and the State Operas of Hamburg, Vienna, Munich and Stuttgart; Further engagements in Hanover, Nuremberg, Paris, Nancy, Nice, Lisbon, Bucharest, Prague, Rome, Venice, Naples and Berne; Other roles have been Carmen, Dalila, Verdi's Azucena, Amneris, Ulrica and Eboli; Wagner's Erda, Fricka, Waltraute and Brangaene; Konschakovna in Prince Igor and Marina in Boris Godunov; Mary Louise in Háry János and the Queen in Szokolay's Hamlet; Clytemnestra in Elektra; Many concert appearances. *Address:* c/o Hungarian State Opera, Nepoztarsasag utja 22, 1061 Budapest, Hungary.

TAMAYO Arturo, b. 3 Aug 1946, Madrid, Spain. Conductor. *Education:* Studied at the Royal Conservatoire Madrid, with A Barrera (harmony), Francisco Cales and Gerardo Gombau (composition). *Career:* Gave concerts in Spain from 1967; Studied further with Pierre Boulez at Basle and at the Musikhochschule Fribourg-en-Brisgau; Studied conducting with Franc Travis, 1971-76, composition with Wolfgang Fortner and Klaus Huber; Assisted Huber at Fribourg from 1974 and directed concerts of contemporary music; Frequent appearances at the Deutsche Oper Berlin from 1982, notably with the 1983 premiere of Wolfgang Rihm's ballet Tutuguri; Conducted the premiere of Kelterborn's Ophelia at the 1984 Schwetzingen Festival, Maurice Ohana's La Celestine at the Paris Opéra 1988; Théâtre des Champs Elysées, Paris, 1990 with the local premiere of La Noche Triste by Jean Prodomide. *Address:* c/o Théâtre des Champs Elysées, 15 Avenue Montaigne, F-75012 Paris, France.

TAMBERG Eino, b. 27 May 1930, Tallinn, Estonia. Composer. *Education:* Studied with Eugen Kapp at Tallinn Conservatory (graduated 1953). *Career:* Music supervisor for Estonian Radio, then teacher at Estonian Conservatory, 1967-, Professor, 1983. *Compositions include:* Operas: The Iron House, 1965, Cyrano de

Bergerac, 1976, and Soaring, 1983 (all premiered in Tallinn); Ballets: Ballet Symphony, Schwerin, 1960, The Boy and the Butterfly, Tallinn, 1963, and Joanna Tentata, Tallinn, 1971; Orchestra: Concerto Grosso, 1956; Symphonic Dances, 1957; Toccata, 1967; Trumpet Concerto, 1972; 3 Symphonies, 1978, 1986, 1989; Concerto for mezzo-soprano and orchestra, 1986; Alto Saxophone Concerto, 1987; Chamber: String Quartet, 1958; 2 Wind Quintets, 1975, 1984; Vocal: Moonlight Oratorio, 1962; Fanfares of Victory, cantata, 1975; Amores, oratorio, 1981; Songs and piano pieces. *Honours:* People's Artist of the Estonian SSR, 1975. *Address:* Tallinn State Conservatory, Vabaduse Pst 130, 200015 Tallinn, Estonia.

TAN Melvyn, b. 13 Oct 1956, Singapore. Musician (Harpsichord and Fortepiano). *Education:* Studied at the Yehudi Menuhin School, Surrey, from 1968: teachers included Vlado Perlemuter and Nadia Boulnager; Royal College of Music from 1978, where he made a special study of performing practice. *Career:* International appearances in the keyboard works of Baroque, Classical and early Romantic composers; Played piano until 1980, then turned to harpsichord and fortepiano; Engagements with the Academy of Ancient Music, the English Chamber Orchestra, Royal Philharmonic and London Classical Players; Tour of USA 1985; Series of Beethoven concerts 1987, with Roger Norrington and the London Classical Players; Flanders Festival 1988, followed by South Bank Beethoven Plus series; Appearances during 1989 at the Bath Festival, Holland Festival, Midsummer Mozart Festival, San Francisco, and The Beethoven Experience with the London Classical Players in Purchase, New York; Season 1990 visits to France, Germany, Japan, Australia, San Francisco, Vancouver and New York, Carnegie Hall; Played the Schumann Concerto at the Elizabeth Hall, London, 1990; debut at the Paris Opéra 1991; debut concerts as director of The New Mozart Ensemble in Britain, France, Holland and Hong Kong; Repertoire includes Weber, Mendelssohn, Chopin and earlier music. *Recordings:* Beethoven's Waldstein and Appasionata Sonatas; Schubert Impromptus; Beethoven Concertos and Choral Fantasia conducted by Roger Norrington (EMI). *Address:* c/o Valerie Barber Management Ltd, Fifth Floor, 24 Chancery Lane, London WC2A 1LS, England.

TANG Muhai, b. 10 July 1949, Shanghai, China. Conductor. *Education:* Music Conservatory, Shanghai; Musik Hochschule, Munich, West Germany, Masterclass Diploma. *Career:* Conducted: Berlin Philharmonic, London Philharmonic, Orchestre de Paris, San Fransisco Symphony, Montreal Symphony, Santa Cecilia Orchestra, Rome, Tonhalle Orchestra Zurich, Helsinki Philharmonic, Hallé Orchestra, Scottish National Symphony Orchestra, National Symphony Orchestra, Spain, Mozarteum Orchestra Salzburg, Polish Chamber Orchestra, Oper Orchestra, Hamburg, Frankfurt, Munich, Bonn, Monte Carlo; Radio Symphony Orchestra Munich, Berlin, Hamburg, Cologne; Chief Conductor of Peking Central Philharmonic and Gulbenkian Orchestra, Lisbon. Classic Aid Television Gala Concert (UN Genéve), 1986. *Current Management:* Columbia Artists Management, NY and Harold Holt Ltd, London. *Address:* c/o Keils, Treibjagdweg 31, 1 Berlin 37, Germany.

TANYEL Seta, b. 1950, Armenia. Concert Pianist. *Education:* Studied at Vienna Hochschule fur Musik and with Louis Kentner in London. *Career:* First recital aged 6; Performed and broadcast works by Mozart and Grieg aged 12; Debut recitals in the USA in Philadelphia, Detroit and New York, 1978; London orchestral and recital debuts in the Elizabeth Hall, 1978; Played with Yehudi Menuhin and Igor Oistrakh at the Festival Hall, 1988; Beethoven's 5th Concerto in Paris with the London Symphony conducted by Frühbeck de Burgos, 1989; Season 1990 included appearances at the Barbican, the Festival Hall, Bury St Edmunds, Cambridge, Chichester, Reading and Henley festivals. *Recordings include:* Brahms and Beethoven recital; Beethoven Concertos 2 and 5 and the Grieg and

Schumann Concertos conducted by Fruhbeck de Burgos; Brahms 1 under Vaclav Neumann; Scharwenka Concerto with Yuri Simonov; Schubert Trout Quintet with the Alberni Quartet; Chopin recital (Collins Classics). *Honours:* Prizewinner at competitions, including the Busoni in Italy, International Beethoven Vienna, Queen Elisabeth of Belgium , first Arthur Rubinstein, Israel. *Address:* Collins Classics, 77-85 Fulham Palace Road, London W6 8JB, England.

TAPPY Eric, b. 19 May 1931, Lausanne, Switzerland. Singer (Tenor). *Education:* Studied with Fernando Carpi in Geneva, Ernst Reichert in Salzburg and Eva Liebenberg in Hilversum. *Debut:* Strasbourg 1959, as the Evangelist in the St Matthew Passion by Bach. *Career:* Concert performances of Milhaud's Les Malheurs d'Orphée and Martin's Le Mystère de la Nativité and Monsieur de Pourceaugnac; Sang in he premiere of Klaus Huber's Soliloquia, 1962; Stage debut Opéra-Comique Paris 1964, as Rameau's Zoroastre; Herrenhausen 1966, as Monteverdi's Orfeo; Geneva Opera 1966, in the premiere of Milhaud's La Mer Coupable; Hanover 1967, in L'Incoronazione di Poppea; Covent Garden debut 1974 in the title role of La Clemenza di Tito; US debut 1974, Don Ottavio at San Francisco: returned in Poppea and as Idomeneo 1977-78; Rome Opera 1980, as Titus; Appearances in Chicago, Drottningholm, Aix-en-Provence, Salzburg (as Tamino), Amsterdam, Lyon, Brussels and Lisbon; Other roles included Schoenberg's Aron, Pelléas, Lysander (A Midsummer Night's Dream), Don Ramiro, Lensky and Stravinsky's Oedipus; Concert repertoire included music by Handel, Haydn, Campra, Carissimi, Vivaldi, Bach, Berlioz and Schütz; retired 1982. *Recordings include:* Monteverdi's Orfeo and Poppea, Zoroastre, Pelléas and Mélisande (Erato); Die Jahreszeiten by Haydn, Die Zauberflöte (RCA); La clemeza di Tito (Deutsche Grammophon).

TARLING Judith, b. 1947, England. Violinist; Violist. *Career:* Member of The Parley of Instruments; Frequent tours in Britain and abroad, including the British Early Music Network; Performances in Spain, France, Germany, Holland, Poland and Czechoslovakia; US debut in New York, 1988; Many concerts with first modern performances of early music in new editions by Peter Holman; Numerous broadcasts on Radio 3 and elsewhere; Repertoire includes Renaissance Violin Consort Music (Christmas music by Michael Praetorius, Peter Philips, music for Prince Charles I by Orlando Gibbons and Thomas Lupo); Baroque Consort Music (by Monteverdi, Matthew Locke (anthems, motets and ceremonial music), Purcell (ayres for the theatre), Georg Muffat (Armonico Tributo sonatas 1682), Heinrich Biber (Sonate tam aris, quam aulis servientes, 1676), Vivaldi (sonatas and concertos for lute and mandolin, concertos for recorders) and J S Bach (Hunt cantata, No 208); English Eighteenth Century Music (Dr Arne at Vauxhall Gardens), William Boyce (Solomon) and John Stanley (6 concertos in seven parts, op. 2): with Chrispian Steele-Perkins, trumpet and Emma Kirkby, soprano, among others; Principal viola of Brandenburg Consort Director, Roy Goodman (recordings include Bach Brandenburg concertos and suites); Pricipal viola of the Hanover Band-numerous recordings include complete symphonies of Beethoven, Schubert and Haydn. *Recordings:* Many albums on the Hyperion label. *Address:* 3 North Street, Punnetts Town, Heathfield, E Sussex, England.

TARR Edward H(ankins), b. 15 June 1936, Norwich, Connecticut, USA. Trumpeter; Musicologist. *Education:* Studied trumpet with Roger Voisin in Boston, 1953 and with Adolph Herseth in Chicago (1958-59); Musicology with Leo Schrade in Basle, 1959-64; Dr.phil University of Hamburg, 1986. *Career:* Founded the Edward Tarr Brass Ensemble 1969, giving many performances of Renaissance and Baroque music in Europe and the United States; Early repertoire includes the trumpet concertos of Torelli; modern works include those by Kagel (Atem and Morceau de concours) and Stockhausen (Spiral, 1970); Has collaborated on the reconstruction of early instruments with the German firm Meinl & Lauber and the Swiss firm Adolf Egger

& Son; Teacher of trumpet, Rheinische Musikschule Cologne 1968-70; Cornett and natural trumpet at the Schola Cantorum Basiliensis 1972; Trumpet at the Basle Conservatory 1974; Director of the Trumpet Museum in Bad Säckingen, Germany, 1985. *Publications include:* Die Trompete, 1977; Performing editions of Baroque music. *Address:* c/o Trumpet museum, PO Box 1143, 79702 Bad Säckingen, Germany.

TARRES Enriqueta, b. 18 March 1934, Barcelona, Spain. Singer (Soprano). *Education:* Studied at the Barcelona Conservatory with Concepcion Callao di Sanchez Parra. *Debut:* Valencia 1956, as the Trovatore Leonora. *Career:* Sang in Spain, notably at the Teatro Liceo, Barcelona; Basle and Wuppertal Opera houses 1960-64; Glyndebourne 1962, l964 as Ariadne and Elettra in Idomeneo; Hamburg Staatsoper from 1964: visited Sadler's Wells 1966, as the Empress in the first British performance of Die Frau ohne Schatten by Strauss; Engaged with Dusseldorf, Cologne and Stuttgart Operas; Metropolitan Opera 1973, as Mimi; Lausanne 1983, the Marschallin; Verona 1984, Carmen; Frequent concert appearances; Sang the Mother in Luis de Pablo's El viajero indiscreto at the Teatro de la Zazuela at Madrid, 1990. *Recordings:* Atlantida by Falla (EMI); Trionfi by Orff (BASF); Les Huguenots; Idomeneo. *Address:* c/o Arena di Verona, Piazza Brà 28, 1-37121 Verona, Italy.

TARUSKIN Richard (Filler), b. 2 Apr 1945, New York City, New York, USA. Musicologist; Critic. *Education includes:* PhD, Columbia University, 1975. *Career:* Teacher at Columbia University, 1973-87; Professor at University of California, Berkeley, 1987; Music critic for Opus and the New York Times. *Publications include:* Opera and Drama in Russia, Ann Arbor, 1981; Study of Stravinsky and articles on the 15th century chanson, the Early Music movement and on Russian music. *Contributions to:* New Grove Dictionary of Opera, 4 volumes, 1992 (articles on Russian Composers and Operas). *Address:* University of California, Music Department, Berkeley, Morrison Hall, Berkeley, CA 94720, USA.

TASKOVA Slavka, b. 16 Nov. 1940, Sofia, Bulgaria. Singer (Soprano). *Education:* Studied at the Accademia di Santa Cecilia with Gina Cigne and in Milan with Lina Pagliughi. *Debut:* Milan 1966, as Rosina in Il Barbiere di Siviglia. *Career:* Has sung in Venice, Bologna, Berlin, Munich, Paris, Vienna, Sofia, Warsaw and Zagreb; Schwetzingen Festival 1971, in the premiere of Melusine by Reimann; Teatro Lirico Milan 1975, in the premiere of Nono's Al gran Sole carico d'amore; Genoa 1983, as Violetta. *Recordings include:* Anacréon by Cherubini. *Address:* c/o Teatro Carlo Felice, I-16100 Genoa, Italy.

TASOVAC Ivan, b. 21 June 1966, Belgrade, Yugoslavia. Pianist. *Education:* Mokranjac Music School, Belgrade, 1972-82; Secondary Music School attached to Tchaikovsky Conservatory, 1982-86; Pupil of Sergei Dorensky, Moscow State Conservatory Tchaikovsky, 1986-. *Debut:* With Belgrade and Zagreb Philharmonic Orchestras at age 12. *Career:* Concerts throughout Yugoslavia including with major orchestras, Soviet Union and Switzerland; Appearances in competitions, Republic of Ireland and Italy; Recordings for Irish TV and Yugoslav Radio and TV including with RTV Belgrade Symphony Orchestra. *Hobbies:* Films; Theatre; Studying various forms of Russian Avant-Garde Art (1920s- 30s). *Address:* c/o Mr Toma Tasovac, George Washington 28A, 11000 Belgrade, Serbia.

TATE Jeffrey, b. 28 April 1943, Salisbury, Wiltshire, England. Conductor. *Education:* Farnham Grammar School; Christ's College Cambridge; St Thomas' Hospital London; MA, MB, B CHIR, Cantab.; London Opera Centre. *Career:* Music Staff Covent Garden 1970-77; Assistant to Boulez at Bayreuth and Paris 1976-80; Assistant conductor Cologne Opera 1977-79; Opera debut Gothenburg 1978, Carmen; New York Metropolitan debut 1980, Lulu: returned for Der Rosenkavalier, Wozzeck and Lohengrin; Covent Garden debut 1982, La Clemenza di Tito: Ariadne auf Naxos 1985; Principal Condcutor 1986-; Conducted new production of Così fan Tutte 1989; Principal Guest Conductor Geneva Opera 1984-; Principal Conductor English Chamber Orchestra 1985; Conducted new production of Henze's realization of Monteverdi's Il ritorno di Ulisse, Salzburg Festival 1985; Conducted premiere of Liebermann's Le fôret at Geneva, 1987; Principal Guest Conductor Orchestre National de France 1989-; Principal Guest Conductor, Royal Opera House, 1991-; Works regularly with London Symphony Orchestra, Boston Symphony, Toronto Symphony, Rotterdam Philharmonic, Berlin Philharmonic, Bayerische Rundfunk Orchestra, Berlin Philharmonic, Los Angeles Philharmonic, Orchestre de la Suisse Romande, Lausanne Chamber Orchestra; From Sept 1991, Music Director, Rotterdam Philharmonic Orchestra; Season 1991/92 with Mozart's Zaide in Amsterdam and at the Barbican Hall, Le Nozze di Figaro, Les Contes d'Hoffmann and Fidelio at Covent Garden, Weill's Mahagonny at Geneva. *Recordings:* Exclusive orchestral music contract with EMI; Operatic recordings for Decca and Phonogram; Orchestras include English Chamber, London Symphony, Dresden Staatskapelle, Royal Opera House. *Honours:* SWET Opera Award 1984; Honorary Fellowship Christ's College, Cambridge 1988; CBE, 1990; Chevalier des Arts et des Lettres, 1990. *Hobbies:* Collecting early 18th Century Continental Porcelain; Gastronomy. *Current Management:* Columbia Artists Management Inc., 165 W. 57th Street, New York NY10019; Artists Management Zurich, CH-8044 Zurich Rutistrasse 52. *Address:* c/o Betty Scholar, Secretary, Royal Opera House, Covent Garden, London WC2, England.

TATLOW (Peter) Mark, b. 29 Dec. 1955, Wolverhampton, England. Pianist; Conductor. m. Ruth Mary Ballard, 21 July 1979. 1 son, 2 daughters. *Education:* BA 1976, MA 1980, Corpus Christi College, Cambridge; Royal Academy of Music, 1976-78; MMus, Goldsmiths College, University of London, 1980; National Opera Studio, London, 1980-81; Fellow, Trinity College, London, Associate, Royal Academy of Music; Licenciate Guildhall School of Music; Associate, Royal College of Music. *Debut:* Purcell Room, London, 1980. *Career:* Assistant principal, Bourne School of Music, Harpenden, 1978-80; Music staff, Opera Barga, Italy 1981-82, Glyndebourne Festival 1983; Professor, Royal Academy of Music, 1981-83; Staff 1981-86, Head, Music Preparation 1983-86, Kent Opera; Chief coach/chorus master, Drottningholm Theatre Festival, 1986-; Assistant conductor, Opéra de Nice, France, 1987-88; Music Staff, Opera School, Stockholm, 1989-. *Contributions to:* Various Kent Opera publications; Insight Into Opera; Music in Worship. *Honours:* Various prizes, including Thomas Jennings Exhibition, Royal Academy of Music. *Memberships:* Arts Center Group, Christien Impact. *Hobbies:* Reading; Walking. *Address:* 94 New Cavendish Street, London W1M 7FA, England.

TATRAI Vilmos, b. 7 Oct 1912, Kispest, Hungary. Violinist. *Education:* Studied in National Conservatory Budapest with Vilmos Kladivko, Lazlo Lajtha. *Career:* Played in various orchestras 1931-33; Municipal Orchestra Budapest 1933-36; Radio Orchestra of Buenos Aires 1936-37; Leader of the Hungarian State Symphony Orchestra 1940-78; Founded the Tatrai Quartet, 1946: has toured widely in Europe and Japan from 1955, with festival engagements at Salzburg, Vienna, Edinburgh, Prague, Florence and Dubrovnik; Repertory 360 compositions; 64 first performances of Hungarian composers and 54 first performances of foreign composers; Teacher of Violin and Chamber Music at the Béla Bartók Conservatoire, 1947-54; Founder-Leader, the Hungarian Chamber Orchestra 1957 and premiered Helmut Eder's 2nd violin concerto 1967; Professor at the Franz Liszt Academy, Budapest 1965. *Recordings include:* 130 recordings including: Complete cycles of the quartets of Haydn, Mozart Quintets, Bartók (Hungaroton) and Kodály, Hungaroton, Polskie Nagranie, Teldec, Vox. *Honours:* (with Tatrai Quartet): Winner, Bartók Competition 1948; Kossuth Prize 1958; Liszt Prize, 1952, 1972; Pro Urbe, 1979;

Bartók-Pasztori Grand Prize, 1985; Flag Order, 1987 and many other distinctions; Cross of Merit, 1992. *Memberships* Hon Member, F Liszt, 1992 and Kodaly Associations. *Address:* 1136 Budapest XIII, R. Wallenberg u.4, Hungary.

TATTERMUSCHOVA Helena, b. 28 Jan. 1933, Prague, Czechoslovakia. Singer (Soprano). *Education:* Studied at the Prague Conservatory with Vlasta Linhartova. *Debut:* Ostrava 1955, as Musetta. *Career:* National Theatre Prague from 1959: visited Edinburgh with the company 1964, 1970 in the British premieres of Janáček's From the House of the Dead and The Excursions of Mr Brouček; Guest appearances at opera houses in Barcelona, Brussels, Amsterdam, Warsaw, Naples, Venice and Sofia; Repertoire included works by Janáček, Smetana, Mozart, Puccini and Strauss; Also sang in concert. *Recordings:* Orfeo ed Euridice, Trionfi by Orff, The Makropoulos Case, From the House of the Dead, Glagolitic Mass (Supraphon); The Cunning Little Vixen (Eurodisc). *Address:* c/o National Theatre, PO Box 865, 112 30 Prague 1, Czech Republic.

TATUM Nancy, b. 25 Aug. 1934, Mempis, Tennessee. Singer (Soprano). m. Wiley Tatum. *Education:* Studied with Zelma Lee Thomas in Memphis and with Samuel Margolis and Wiley Tatum in New York. *Debut:* Saarbrucken 1962, as Santuzza. *Career:* Has sung in Paris, Geneva, Lyon, Minneapolis, Vancouver and Sofia; Member of the Deutsche Oper am Rhein Dusseldorf from 1964; Metropolitan Opera from 1973; Further appearances in Budapest, Bucharest, Zagreb, Brussels and Amsterdam; Repertoire includes major roles in operas by Wagner and Verdi. *Address:* c/o Metropolitan Opera, Lincoln Center, New York, NY 10023, USA.

TAUB Robert David, b. 25 Dec. 1955, New York, USA. Concert Pianist. m. Tracy Elizabeth Milner, 27 Aug. 1983. *Education:* AB, Princeton University, 1977; MMus, 1978, DMA, 1981, The Juilliard School. *Career:* Concert Pianist performing throughout the USA, Europe, Latin America and the Far East with a Solo and Concerto Repertoire which spans from the Baroque to music of the present time. *Recordings:* Harmonia Mundi-Schumann and Liszt; Babbitt; Beethoven; Scriabin (complete Sonatas); New World Records - Persichetti Piano Concerto with The Philadelphia Orchestra, Dutoit conductor. *Contributions to:* The Princeton Journal of the Arts and Sciences, 1977: The Autograph of Beethoven's Piano Trio Op 70 No. 1, First Movement. *Current Management:* Columbia Artists Management Inc, 165 West 57th Street, New York, NY 10019, USA. *Address:* 185 West End Avenue, 26E, New York, NY 10023, USA.

TAUSKY Vilem, b. 20 July 1910, Perov, Czechoslovakia. Director of Opera; Artistic Director; Conductor; Composer. m. Margaret Helen Powell, 1948. (deceased 1982), *Education:* University of Brno; Janáček Conservatoire, Brno; Meisterschule, Prague. *Career:* Military Service in France and England, 1939-45; National Opera House, Brno, Czechoslovakia, 1929-39; Musical Director, Carl Rosa Opera, 1945-49; Guest Conductor: Royal Opera House, Covent Garden, 1951-; Sadler's Wells Opera, 1953-; Director of Opera, Guildhall School of Music, 1966-; Artistic Director, Pheonix Opera Company, 1967-; BBC Conductor, 1950-; in 1972 conducted the first British performance of Janáček's Osud. *Compositions:* Czechoslovak Christmas Carols, 1942; Oboe Concerto, 1957; Concertina for harmonica and orchestra, 1963; Divertimento for strings, 1966; Soho: Scherzo for orchestra, 1966; Concert Overture for Brass Band, 1969; Cakes and Ale: Overture for Brass Band, 1971; Ballad for Cello and Piano; From Our Village: Orchestral suite, 1972; Sonata for Cello and Piano, 1976; Suite for Violin and Piano, 1979; String Quartet, 1981. *Publications:* Vilem Tausky Tells His Story, 1979; Leos Janáček, Leaves from His Life, 1982; Contributor to: Tension in the Performance of Music, 1979; The Spectator, 1979. *Honours:* Freeman, City of London, 1979; Czechoslovak Military Cross, 1944; Czechoslovak Order of Merit, 1945; CBE,

1981; Fellow of Guildhall School of Music, 1968. *Hobby:* Country Life. *Address:* 44 Haven Green Court, London W5, England.

TAUTU Cornelia, b. 10 Mar 1938, Odorhei, Rumania. Composer. m. Valentin Curocichin, 6 Aug 1976, 1 daughter. *Education:* Ciprian Porumbescu Conservatory, Bucharest; Postgraduate studies, Long Island University, New York, USA, Sept 1971-Mar 1972. *Compositions:* Film music: Tragic Holiday; The Woman of Ursa Major; The Apple Cart; The Scythe; The Riddle; Together Again; The Teacher (Five minutes before midnight...); I'm Staying with You; The Wall; The Passion; The Three-Seal Mace; Pyre & Flame; The Marvellous Grove; The Impossible Love; The Golden Train (Rumanian-Polish co-production); Morometii; The Riddle; The Staying (The village Staying); Forgotten by God, 1991; The Way of the Dogs, 1992; Stage music for: Prometheus (Aeschylus); La Locandiera (Goldoni); Medeea (Seneca); Cherry Orchard (Chekov); The Third Stake (M Sorescu); Cold Heart (W Hauff); Symphonic music: Counterpoint, string orchestra; Segments, string orchestra; Inventions for Piano & Orchestra; Dice, symphonic sketch; Palingenesia - Poem for 1907, orchestra; Engravings, orchestra; Sinfonietta; Symphony No 1 - 1907, 1987; Concerto for Piano & orchestra, 1989; Chamber music: Concerto for Twelve Instruments; Inventions for Piano; Collage, string quartet; Carol Echoes, quintet for flute, oboe, clarinet, bassoon, horn; Homage for Peace, string quintet; Piano Sonata; Trio for Flute, Piano & Harp; 8 progressive pieces for piano, 1988; Three lieder, rhymes by M Eminescu; Choral music: Triptych. *Address:* Sos Stefan cel Mare No 2 Bl 13 sc B ap 36 sect 1, Bucharest, Rumania.

TAVENER Alan, b. 22 Apr 1957, Weston-Super-Mare, Avon, England. Conductor; Organist; Manager. m. Rebecca Jane Gibson, 30 Aug 1980. *Education:* Organ Scholar, Brasenose College, Oxford, 1976-79, ARCO/ARCM 1978, graduated with BA, Hons, Music, 1979; Subsequently gained MA degree. *Career:* Director of Music, University of Strathclyde, 1980-; Founder Director, Cappella Nova, 1982-; Conducted several world premieres of new choral works, including John Tavener's Resurrection (Glasgow, 1990). *Recordings:* Robert Carver, The Complete Sacred Choral Music (3CDs, 1990); Scottish Medieval Plainchant, Columba, most Holy of Saints, 1992; Sacred Music for Mary Queen of Scots, 1993; (all ASV). *Hobbies:* Architecture; Exhibitions; Theatre; Food and Drink. *Address:* Director of Music, University of Strathclyde, Livingstone Tower, Richmond Street, Glasgow G1 1XH, Scotland.

TAVENER John, b. 28 Jan. 1944. Composer; Professor of Music. m. Victoria Marangopoulou, 1974. *Education:* Highgate School, England; Royal Academy of Music (LRAM). *Career:* Professor of Music, Trinity College of Music, 1969-. *Compositions:* Piano Concerto; Three Holy Sonnets (Donne); Cain and Abel (first prize Monaco); Chamber Concerto; The Cappemakers; Three Songs of T.S. Eliot; Grandma's Footsteps; In Memoriam Igor Stravinsky; Responsorium in memory of Annon Lee Silver; The Whale; Introit for March 27th; Three Surrealist Songs; In Alium; Akhmatova: Requiem; Ultimos Ritos, 1972; Thérèse (opera) 1972; A Gentle Spirit (opera) 1977; Kyklike Kinesis; Palin; Palintropos; Canticle of the Mother of God; Divine Liturgy of St John Chrysostom; The Immurement of Antigone; Lamentation, Last Prayer and Exaltation; Six Abbasid Songs; Greek Interlude; Sappho: Lyrical Fragments; Prayer for the World; The Great Canon of St Andrew of Crete; Trisagion; Risenl; Mandelion; The Lamb (Carol); Funeral Ikos, Doxa, Lord's Prayer; Mandoodles; Towards the Son; 16 Haiku of Seferis; Ikon of Light; Orthodox Vigil Service; Two Hymns to the Mother of God; Eis Thanaton; Nativity; Angels; Love Bade Me Welcome; Panikhida (Orthodox Funeral Service); Ikon of St Cuthbert; Magnificat and Nunc Dimittis (Collegium Regale); Akathist of Thanksgiving; Meditation on the Light; Wedding Prayer; Many Years; Acclamation; The Protecting Veil; Ikon of St Seraphim; God is With Us; Hymn to the Holy Spirit; The Tyger; Apolytikion for St Nicholas; The Call; Let Not the Prince be Silent;

Resurrection, 1989; The Hidden Treasure (string quartet), 1989; The Repentant Thief for clarinet and strings, 1990; Mary of Egypt, chamber opera, 1991 (premiere at the Aldeburgh Festival, 1992). *Honours:* Hon. FRAM; Hon. FTCL. *Membership:* Russian Orthodox Church. *Address:* c/o Chester Music, 8/9 Frith Street, London W1V 5TZ, England.

TAYLOR Jack Arthur, b. 28 Jan. 1935, Cheyenne, Wyoming, USA. Professor. m. 20 Sept. 1958, 2 sons. *Education:* AA, Sacramento City College; BA, University of California; MA, PhD, University of Washington. *Career:* Music instructor, San Lorenzo Valley Schools, California, 1960-67; Director & Professor, Center for Music Research, Florida State University, Tallahassee, 1970-. *Publications:* Involvement with Music: Programmed Approach to Creative Musicianship, with Alfred Balkin, 1978; Introduction to Computers & Computer-Based Instruction in Music, 1981. *Contributions to:* Numerous articles on music perception, music cognition, computers in music, to publications including: Journal of Research in Music Education; Music Educator's Journal; Journal of Computer-Based Instruction; Psychomusicology. Also: Past editor, Journal of Research in Music Education; Consulting Editor, Psychomusicology; Editorial Board (Music Yearbook), Journal of Computer-Based Instruction. *Honours:* Outstanding Educator of America, 1974; Honorary member, Phi Mu Alpha, 1981. *Hobbies:* Square dancing; Camping. *Address:* Center for Music Research, 214 KMU, Florida State University, Tallahassee, FL 32306, USA.

TAYLOR Paul Arden, b. 4 Jan 1954, Harpenden, Hertfordshire, England. Oboist; Early Wind Instrumentalist. *Education:* Royal Academy of Music, 1971-74; LRAM; ARCM; LTCL. *Career:* Principal Oboe: Sadlers Wells Royal Ballet, 1974-79, BBC Midland Radio orchestra, 1979-80; Much freelance orchestral, solo, chamber and recording work, 1980-; BBC Radio 3 recitals with James Walker (piano); Member: Praetorius Consort, 1971-, London Baroque Trio, 1979- Telemann Trio, 1983-; Director, English Wind Ensemble, 1986-; Principal Oboe, English Symphony Orchestra. *Compositions:* Carry On Bach, 3 Fugues for wind trio. *Recordings:* Vivaldi D minor Oboe Concerto with Vivaldi Chamber Ensemble, Meridian Records; Many CDs as Principal Oboe with English Symphony Orchestra, Nimbus Records; Various early music recordings, Praetorius Consort. *Honours:* Leila Bull Oboe Prize, Royal Academy of Music, 1974. *Hobbies:* Amateur radio; Digital audio recording; Tennis; Snooker; Organ recitals; Advanced driving. *Current Management:* Carol Holt Artists, The Spinney, 20 Geraldine Road, Malvern, Worcs WR14 3PA, England. *Address:* 11 Romsley Hill Grange, Farley Lane, Romsley, Nr Halesowen, West Midlands B62 0LN, England.

TAZZINI Rinaldo, b. 15 Feb. 1942, New York City, USA. Producer; Director; Artistic Director. m. Helen Neswald, 15 Sept. 1965, 1 son, 2 daughters. *Education:* High School of Music and Art, New York City; BA Music, Hunter College; Mannes School of Music with Paul Berl and Carl Bamberger; Conservatorio di Cherubini with Clelia Castelana-Zotti, Florence, Italy; Accademia di Chigiana with Gino Bechi; Accademia di Santa Cecilia with Tito Gobbi. *Career includes:* Fanny (Cesario), 1955; Huck Finn (Tom Sawyer), 1957; New York City Opera, 1971-72; Teatro dell'Opera, Rome, Italy, 1972-74; Teatro Massimo Bellini, Catania, 1974; Teatro Lonigo, 1974; Artistic Director and Director of Productions, Brooklyn Opera Society, USA, 1977-; Madame Butterfly, Japanese Garden, New York City, 1st opera for television shot on location in USA, 1980; Producer, Director, The George Gershwin Festival Tour, 1982; Creator, Director, Hot Rags musical, Lincoln Center, 1983. *Address:* c/o Bernard Lewis, Director of Communications, The Brooklyn Opera Society, Borough Hall, Brooklyn, NY 11201, USA.

TE KANAWA Kiri, (Dame), b. 6 Mar 1944, Gisborne, New Zealand. Soprano. m. Desmond Park, 1967, 2 children. *Education:* St. Mary's College, Auckland; London Opera Centre. *Debut:* Royal Opera, Covent Garden, London, 1970. *Career:* Sante Fe Opera, USA, 1971; Lyons Opera, France, 1972; Metropolitan Opera, New York City, USA, 1972, as Desdemona in Otello; Appeared at Australian Opera, Royal Opera House Covent Garden, Paris Opéra, 1976-77 season; Houston Opera, Texas, and Munich Opera, 1977; Debut at La Scala, Milan, 1978; Salzburg Festival, 1979; San Francisco Opera Company, 1980; Edinburgh Festival and Helsinki Festival, 1980; Operas include: Boris Godunov 1970-71, Parsifal 1971, The Marriage of Figaro 5 times 1971-79, Otello 3 times 1972-74, Simon Boccanegra 7 times 1973-80, Carmen 1973, Don Giovanni 5 times 1974-81 and film version 1979, Faust 1974, The Magic Flute 1975 and 1980, La Bohème 5 times 1975-80, Eugene Onegin 1975 and 1976, Così Fan Tutte 1976 and 1981, Arabella 1977, 1980 and 1981, Die Fledermaus 1978, La Traviata 1978 and 1980, Der Rosenkavalier 1981, Manon Lescaut 1983; Don Giovanni,1988; Sang at the wedding of the Prince of Wales, London, 1981; Sang the Countess in Capriccio at San Francisco 1990 and at Covent Garden; premiere of Paul McCartney's Liverpool Oratorio (written by Carl Davis) Liverpool Cathedral and London 1991; Amelia in a new production of Simon Boccanegra at Covent Garden, 1991; Season 1992 with Mozart's Countess at the Met and Desdemona at Covent Garden. *Recordings include:* Elvira in Don Giovanni; Fiordiligi in Così Fan Tutte, Otello; Micaela in Carmen; Mozart Vespers; Mozart C Minor Mass; Pamina in The Magic Flute; The Marriage of Figaro; Hansel and Gretel; Strauss Songs with Orchestra; Die Fledermaus; Woodbird in Siegfried (EMI); Recitals records. *Honour:* OBE, DBE; Honourary Degrees, Oxford, Nottingham, Dundee, Auckland, Durham, Post University (USA). *Address:* c/o Royal Opera House, Covent Garden, London, WC2, England.

TEAR Robert, b. 8 Mar. 1939. Barry, S. Wales. Tenor and conductor. *Education:* Studied at King's College, Cambridge. *Debut:* With English Opera Group, 1963; Later sang as Lensky in Eugene Onegin, Covent Garden from 1970 as Dov in The Knot Garden (premiere), Lensky, Paris (King Priam), Wagner's Froh and Loge, Tom Rakewell, Admetus in Alceste, Rimbaud in Tavener's Thérèse (premiere 1979), David, Jupiter in Semele. *Career:* The Director in the British premiere of Berio's Un re in Ascolto, 1979, Shuisky in Boris Godunov, 1991, and the Schoolmaster in The Cunning Little Vixen, 1990; Sang in the world premiere of Tippett's The Mask of Time with the Boston Symphony Orchestra; Regular guest of the great US Orchestras, including Boston, Chicago, Los Angeles and New York Philharmonic; 1985 conducting debut in Minneapolis, subsequently conducted many orchestra including the London Mozart Players, the Northern Sinfonia, English Chamber Orchestra, Philharmonia, BBC Welsh Symphony, Royal Liverpool Philharmonic and the Royal Scottish National Orchestra; Season 1994/95 as Janáček's Mr Brouček at Munich, Captain Vere in Billy Budd in Geneva and Figaro and The Rake's Progress at Glyndebourne; created roles in Britten's The Burning Fiery Furnace and Prodigal Son; Large repertoire in opera and lieder; well known Mime in Das Rheingold in London and Bayreuth; other roles include Peter Grimes, Matteo (Arabella); appeared in Europe at Paris Opéra (e.g. in premiere of three-act version of Berg's Lulu), La Scala, Milan and Salzburg; Salzburg Festival 1985, as Eumetus in the Henze/Monteverdi Ulisse; Season 1990-91 with the War Requiem in Detroit and The Mask of Time in London; The Turn of the Screw at Montpellier and Peter Grimes with Geneva Opera; Beethoven and Tippett in Florida and Los Angeles; title role in the premiere of Ubu Rex by Penderecki at Munich; Mephisto in the Covent Garden premiere of Prokofiev's Fiery Angel, 1992; Season 1994/95 as Janáček's Mr Brouček at Munich, Captain Vere in Billy Budd in Geneva and Figaro and The Rake's Progress at Glyndebourne. *Address:* c/o Harold Holt Ltd, 31 Sinclair Road, London W14 0NS, England.

TEBALDI Renata, b. 1 Feb. 1922, Pesaro, Italy. Singer (Soprano). *Education:* Studied at Arrigo Boito Conservatory, Parma and the Rossini Conservatory at

Pesaro; Further study with Carmen Melis and Giuseppe Pais. *Debut:* Elena in Mefistofele, Rovigo, 1944. *Career:* First sang at La Scala, Milan, at post-war reopening concert conducted by Toscanini; Stage appearances in Milan until 1955 as Marguerite (Boito and Gounod), Eva, Tatiana and Catalani's Wally; Naples from 1958, as Violetta, Elisabeth de Valois, Refice's Cecilia, Giovanna d'Arco and Amazily in Fernand Cortez by Spontini; Maggio Musicale Fiorentino 1948-53, as Elsa, Pamira (L'Assedio di Corinto), Mathilde in Guillaume Tell and Olympie in the opera by Spontini; Sang Desdemona at Covent Garden 1950, Aida; Metropolitan Opera from 1955 in more than 200 performances: Tosca, Mimi, La Gioconda, Desdemona, Adriana Lecouvreur, Manon Lescaut, Amelia Boccanegra, Minnie in La Fanciulla del West, Violetta, Butterfly, Leonora (La Forza del Destino) and Alice Ford; Further appearances at the Chicago Lyric Opera, Vienna Staatsoper, Paris Opera, Deutsche Oper Berlin and in Japan; Retired from opera 1973, concerts 1976. *Recordings include:* La Bohème; Tosca, Manon Lescaut, Il Trovatore, La Gioconda, Puccini's Trittico, Turandot, Otello, Un Ballo in Maschera, Don Carlos, Cavalleria Rusticana, Mefistofele, Adriana Lecouvreur, La Forza del Destino. *Address:* c/o S.A Gorlinsky Ltd, 33 Dover Street, London, W1, England.

TEBBETT Eric William, b. 8 Sept 1951, Hartlepool, England. Teacher. m. Dorothy Bagnall, 7 Sept 1985, 2 daughters. *Education:* National Youth Orchestra, 1968-70; DipMus Ed, Royal Scottish Academy of Music and Drama, 1970-73; PGCE, University of Newcastle-upon-Tyne, 1973-74. *Career:* Teaching: Head of Brass, Northamptonshire, 1984-90; Wellingborough School, 1990-; As singer (tenor) and trumpet player, several TV and radio appearances; Also toured Europe and USA; Conductor, Northamptonshire County Youth Orchestra, 1987-89; Currently conducts Kettering Symphony Orchestra and the Wellingborough Singers; Examiner for Trinity College, London, 1990-, also adjudicator and conductor; Toured New Zealand, 1993. *Honours:* Hugh S Roberton Prize for Vocal Ensemble, 1972. *Memberships:* British Federation of Festivals for Music, Dance and Speech; Rotary International. *Hobbies:* Rotarian; A 1970 MGB GT; Gardening; Travel. *Address:* 49 Chatsworth Drive, Meadow View, Wellingborough, Northants NN8 5FD, England.

TEDE Margery, b. 1940, USA, Singer (Mezzo-soprano). *Education:* Studied at San Francisco State College, the Madrid Conservatory and the Hochschule fur Musik in Berlin. *Career:* Sang with the San Francisco Opera as Fricka, Amneris, Azucena, Judith (Bluebeard's Castle), Jocasta and Herodias (Salome); Sang Countess Carolina in the local premiere of Henze's Elegy for Young Lovers, conducted by Christopher Keene; Lake Tahoe Summer Music Festival as Susan B Anthony in Virgil Thomson's The Mother of Us All; Concert appearances with the San Francisco Symphony under Seiji Ozawa and in Mozart's Coronation Mass in New York; Opera, concerts and recitals in Europe, Central America, Alaska and the South Pacific; Sang world premiere of Roger Nixon's Three Transcendental Songs in New York and songs by Charles Ives in Hamburg; Now retired as singer and active as teacher. *Honours include:* International Scholarship from the Federation of Music Clubs. *Address:* Steorra Enterprises, 243 West End Avenue, Suite 907, New York, NY 10023, USA.

TEITELBAUM Richard Lowe, b. 19 May 1939, New York City, USA. Composer; Performer; Teacher. *Education:* BA, Haverford College, 1960; MMus, Yale University School of Music, 1964; Mannes School, 1960-61; Accademia di S Cecilia, Rome, 1964-65; Composition: Luigi Nono, Venice, Italy, 1965-66; Wesleyan University World Music Program, 1970-71. *Career:* Founding Member, Musica Electronica Viva, Rome, 1966; Instructor, California Institute of the Arts, 1971-72; Founder and Director, Electronic Music Studio, Art Institute of Chicago, 1972-73; Co-Director and Visiting Professor, York University, Toronto, 1973-76; Soloist, Berlin Philharmonic Hall, Concertgebouw, Centre Pompidou, WDR Cologne, etc. 1984-86; Visiting

Professor, Bard & Vassar Colleges, 1988-89. *Compositions include:* In Tune for live electronics, 1966; Intersections for piano, 1964; Digital Piano Music, 1983; Concerto Grosso for Robotic Pianos, Winds Trombone and Synthesizers; Iro wa Nioedo for 20 Buddhist Monks. *Recordings include:* Hi Uchi Ishi, 1977; Time Zones, 1977; Concerto Grosso, 1987. *Memberships:* American Music Center; Composers Forum; College Music Society; International Computer Music Society. *Current Management:* Barbara Mayfield, New York City. *Address:* 250 Cold Brook Road, Bearsville, NY 12409, USA.

TELLEFSEN Arve, b. 1948, Trondehim, Norway. Violinist. *Education:* Studied with Arne Stoltenberg; with Professor Henry Holst; with Professor Ivan Galamian, New York, 1960. *Career:* Numerous recitals and concerts in Europe; Professor of the Academy of Music in Oslo from 1973; tour of Norway, 1985, with the RPO under Ashkenazy; Oslo Philharmonai concerts 1987, with Mariss Jansons, Neeme Järvi and Esa-Pekka Salonen; British engagements with David Zinman, Jerzy Maksymiuk, Marek Janowski, Okko Kamu, Vernon Handley and Kurt Sanderling; Festival concerts at Schleswig-Holstein, Lockenhaus and Montreux; Founded Oslo Chamber Music Festival 1989. *Recordings:* Numerous discs include concertos by Nielsen, Shostakovitch, Berwald, Aulin, Valen, Sinding, Svendsen, Sibelius and Beethoven and Grieg Sonatas for EMI, Philips and Virgin Classics. *Honours:* First Prize, Princess Astrid's competition for young Norwegian artists, 1956; Harriet Cohen International Award, 1962; Awarded the prize of Bergen Festival, 1964; Grieg Prize, 1973. *Address:* c/o Norman McCann Ltd, The Coach House, 56 Lawrie Park Gardens, London SE26 6XJ, England.

TEMESI Maria (Maria Toth), b. 1957, Szeged, Hungary. Singer (Soprano). *Education:* Studied at Franz Liszt Academy, Szeged, (Klaisër und Gesaug) and in Budapest; Masterclasses at Weimar Music Academy and at the Mozarteum, Salzburg. *Debut:* Budapest State Opera as Elsa in Wagner's Lohengrin, under G Patane, 1982. *Career:* Appearances: Staatsoper Hamburg, Oper der Stadt Koln, Semperoper Dresden, Staatsoper Berlin, Komische Oper Berlin, Opernhaus Zurich, Teatro Farnese Parma, Teatro de la Zarzuela Madrid, Opera de Nice, Theatre du Capitole Toulouse, Opera Company of Philadelphia, Smetana Theatre Prague, Herodes Atticus Amphitheatre Athens, Opernhaus Graz; Main roles: Donna Anna in Don Giovanni, Vitellia in La clemenza di Tito, Mozart, Adriana Lecouvreur, (Lamberto Gardelli), Tatiana, Lisa in Pique Dame, Amelia in Ballo in maschera, Leonore in Trovatore, Elisabeth de Valois, Elena in Vespri siciliani, Desdemona, Alice in Falstaff, Elsa in Lohengrin, Eva in Meistersinger, Elisabeth in Tannhauser; Estrella in Schuberts: Alfonso und Estrella; Sang in a concert performance of Guntram by Strauss for Manhattan Cable TV, New York, Gotterdammerung (Gutrune) conducted by Lovro von Matacic, Mahler's 2nd Symphony under Dorati, Handel's Messiah under Gonnenwein, La clemenza di Tito conducted by Sir John Pritchard at Cologne; Liederabenden at Budapest Music Academy, Lisbon Fundacao Calouste Gulbenkian, Cairo Academy of Arts. *Recordings:* Liszt: Missa choralis; Mahler: 8th Symphony. *Honours include:* Prizewinner in competitions in Athens, 1979, Toulouse, 1980; 1st Prize in Rio de Janeiro, 1981; Winner, Pavarotti Competition, Philadelphia, 1985. *Address:* Templom u 22, 1028 Budapest, Hungary.

TEMIRKANOV Yuri, b. 10 Dec 1938, Nalchik, Caucasus, USSR. Conductor. *Education:* Leningrad Conservatory for Talented Children, 1953-56; Leningrad Conservatory of Music, graduated as a violinist 1962, conductor 1965. *Career:* Conductor, Leningrad Opera, all major Soviet Orchestras, 1968-; Director, Leningrad Symphony Orchestra, 1969, touring extensively; Artistic Director, Kirov Opera, 1977. Has conducted Berlin Philharmonic, Vienna Philharmonic, Dresden State Orchestras, Orchestre de Paris. Following London debut with Royal Philharmonic Orchestra, 1977, worked with Philharmonia, City of Birmingham, Royal Liverpool

Philharmonic Orchestras; Principal guest conductor, RPO, 1979; Conducted BBC Symphony Orchestra, Italy, USSR, 1987; Conducted Philadelphia, Boston and New York Philharmonic Orchestras, USA; Artistic Director of the Leningrad (now St Petersburg) Philharmonic 1988; Conducted The Queen of Spades for RAI, Turin, 1990; Principal Conductor of the Royal Philharmonic Orchestra, from 1992; Season 1992/93 included Tchaikovsky Cycle with St Petersburg Philharmonic in Japan and Europe, tours of the USA and Germany with the Royal Philharmonic. *Honour:* 1st prize, National Conducting Competition, USR, 1968. *Current Management:* IMG Artists (Europe), Media House, 3 Burlington Lane, London W4 2TH, England.

TEMPERLEY Nicholas, b. 7 Aug. 1932, Beaconsfield, England (US citizen, 1977-). Musicologist. m. Mary Dorothea Sleator, 17 Sept. 1960, 1 son, 2 daughters. *Education:* ARCM, Royal College of Music, 1952; BA, BMus, MA, PhD, King's College, Cambridge University, 1952-59. *Career:* Assistant Lecturer, Music, Cambridge University & Fellow, Clare College, Cambridge, 1961-66; Assistant Professor, Musicology, Yale University, USA, 1966-67; Associate Professor 1967-72, Professor 1972-, Chairman Musicology Division 1972-75, 1992-, University of Illinois. *Publications include:* Critical editions, music: Raymond & Agnes, Edward J. Loder, performed Cambridge, 1966; Symphonie Fantastique, Berlioz, New Berlioz Edition, 1972; English Songs 1800-60, Musica Britannica Vol. 43, 1979; London Pianoforte School 1766-1860, 20 volumes, Garland, 1984-87; Haydn's Creation, with authentic English text, 1987. Also: Music of English Parish Church, 2 vols, 1979; Athlone History of Music in Britain, vol. 5, Romantic Age, 1981; Fuging Tunes in 18th Century, with C. G. Manns, 1983. *Contributions to:* Numerous musical journals; Over 100 entries, New Grove Dictionary. *Honours:* John Stewart of Rannoch scholarship, 1953; Award, American Musicological Society, 1980; University Senior Scholar, Illinois, 1986. *Memberships:* Past Editor-in-Chief, offices, American Musicological Society; Past office, Hymn Society of America; Midwest Victorian Studies Association. *Hobbies:* Piano playing; Chamber music; Bridge; 19th century novels. *Address:* 805 West Indiana Street, Urbana, Illinois 61801, USA.

TENNFJORD Oddbjørn, b. 1941, Oslo, Norway. Singer (Bass). *Education:* Studied at the Bergen and Oslo Conservatories, in Essen with Clemens Kaiser-Breme, in Rome with Luigi Ricci and in London with Roy Henderson. *Career:* Has sung with the Norske Opera Oslo from 1971, as Osmin, Don Pasquale, Basilio, Falstaff, Pogner, Boris Godunov, Sarastro, Wotan, King Marke, Gremin and Fiesco; Concert and opera engagements for Norwegian Radio and Television in Germany, Italy, Poland, Sweden, Denmark, Israel, Yugoslavia, France and the USA; Appearances with Scottish Opera as the Commendatore, Daland, Sarastro and Fafner; Bologna 1988 and Ravenna Festival, 1989, as the Grand Inquisitor in Don Carlos; Scottish Opera 1989, as the Fafner in Das Rheingold, and the Commendatore; Sang Daland at Oslo, 1989. *Address:* Unit 2, 39 Tadema Road, London SW10 0PY, England.

TENNSTEDT Klaus, b. 6 June 1926, Merseburg, Germany. Conductor. *Education:* Studied at the Leipzig Conservatory. *Career:* Leader of the orchestra at the Halle Municipal Theatre; Conducting appointments with Dresden Opera and the Schwerin Orchestra; Conducted at the Stora Theatre Gothenburg and with the Swedish Radio Orchestra from 1971; Music Director of Kiel Opera 1972; North American debut 1974, with the Toronto Symphony and the Boston Symphony; Chief Conductor of the Norddeutscher Rundfunk Orchestra 1979; Guest Conductor of the Minnesota Orchestra 1979-82; Musical Director of the London Philharmonic Orchestra 1983-87; Metropolitan Opera debut 1983, Fidelio; Conducted the LPO in Mahler's 8th Symphony at the Festival Hall, 1990; Conducted Glyndebourne Company in concert performances of Fidelio, 1993. *Recordings include:* Complete Symphonies of Mahler, including video of the 8th Symphony. *Address:* c/o London Philharmonic Orchestra, 35 Doughty Street, Bloomsbury, London WC1N 2AA, England.

TENZI Fausto, b. 1 Apr 1939, Lugano, Switzerland. Singer (Tenor). *Education:* Studied in Milan. *Career:* Sang at La Scala, Milan, Theatre des Champs Elysees, Paris, Teatro Comunale, Bologna and in Florence, Lucerne, Aachen and Perugia; Engaged at Buxton Festival, England, and made concert appearances in Rome, Paris, Berlin, Moscow, Leningrad and North America; Opera roles have included Don José, Edgardo, Manrico, Don Carlos, Pinkerton, Rodolfo, Turiddu and Ivan Khovansky in Khovanshchina. *Recordings include:* The Queen of Spades; Scriabin's 1st Symphony. *Address:* c/o Teatro alla Scala, Via Filodrammatici 2, 20121 Milan, Italy.

TÉREY-SMITH Mary, b. 1920, Budapest, Hungary. Musicologist; Opera Conductor; Vocal Coach. m. C.A.C.Smith. *Education:* BMus, Conducting & Composition, Liszt Academy of Music; MA, Music Literature, University of Vermont, USA; PhD, Musicology, Eastman School of Music, University of Rochester. *Debut:* Conductor, Tatabanya Symphony Orchestra, Budapest, 1951. *Career includes:* Vocal coach, then assistant conductor, Hungarian State Opera, 1950-56; Resident conductor, Tatabanya Symphony Orchestra, 1951-56; Vocal coach, Toronto Royal Conservatory Opera School, Canada, 1957-58; Assistant Professor, 1967-72, Associate Professor, 1972-85, Professor of Music History and Literature, 1985-, Western Washington University; Director, Opera Workshop, 1967-75, Director of the Collegium Musicum Ensemble, 1969-, Western Washington University. *Publication:* Selection of published articles and studies: Editor, French Baroque Orchestral Dances, by Jean-Philippe Rameau, Canada 1986; Orchestral Practice in the Paris Opera, (1690-1764), and the Spread of the French Influence in Europe, in Studia Musicologica, xxxi, 1989, pp 81-159; International Dictionary of Opera: Rameau: Les Boreades, essay, 1993. *Contributions to:* Two reviews for Music and Letters, P Brun: A History of the Double Bass, 1991; a Meyer: A Thematic Index of the Works by Johannes Sperger. *Honours:* Toured Hungary twice, 1990 and 1992 with the Collegium Musicum ensemble on the invitation of the Albert Schweitzer Chorus and Orchestra. *Memberships:* American Musicological Society; International Musicological Society; Early Music America. *Address:* 1809 Harris Avenue, Bellingham, WA 98225, USA.

TERFEL Bryn, b. 9 Nov 1965, Pwllheli, Gwynedd, Wales. Singer (Baritone). *Education:* Studied at Guildhall School of Music. *Debut:* Welsh National Opera, as Guglielmo, 1990. *Career:* Has sung Mozart's Figaro at Santa Fe, with the English National Opera, 1991, and at Hamburg; Covent Garden debut, 1992, as Masetto in Don Giovanni, repeated on tour to Japan; Salzburg Festival, 1992, as the Spirit Messenger in Die Frau ohne Schatten, conducted by Solti, and as Jochanaan in Salome; Salzburg, 1994, as Leporello in Patrice Chereau's production of Don Giovanni; Further appearances at Vienna Staatsoper as Mozart's Figaro and at Chicago as Donner in Das Rheingold; Sang in the Brahms Requiem under Colin Davis and at Salzburg Easter Festival, 1993, under Claudio Abbado (Herbert von Karajan In Memoriam); Concert repertoire also includes Schubert's Schwanengesang. *Recordings include:* Salome conducted by Sinopoli, Figaro in version of Le nozze di Figaro conducted by John Eliot Gardner; Schwanengesang. *Honours:* Gramophone Young Artist of the Year Award, 1992; Critics' Circle Music Section Award, 1992. *Address:* Harlequin Agency Ltd, 203 Fidlas Road, Cardiff CF4 5NA, Wales.

TERRACINI Lyndon, b. 1950, Australia. Singer (Baritone). *Education:* Studied in Australia. *Debut:* With Australian Opera at the Sydney Opera House as Sid in Albert Herring, 1976. *Career:* Sang in London 1983 as Ivan in Brian Howard's Inner Voices; Daniello in the local premiere of Krenek's Jonny Spielt Auf, 1984; US debut 1984 at the Cabrillo Music Festival in Australian Folksongs; German debut in the title role on Hans

Zender's Stephen Climax, at Frankfurt; Italian debut as Sancio Panza in world premiere of Henze/Paisiello Don Quischotte and Montepulciano Festival; Has sung with Opera Factory Zurich as Agamemnon and Orestes in the Iphigenias by Gluck; Der Alte in Reimann's Ghost Sonata and Landsknecht in Hartmann's Simplicius Simplicissimus; Appearances in Ullmann's posthumous The Emperor of Atlantis, and as Marcello (La Bohème) and Byron in the premiere of Richard Meale's La Mer de Glace, at Sydney; Don Giovanni in Adelaide, 1991 and appearances with Opera Factory London as Figaro in The Marriage of Figaro on stage and on film for Channel 4 television; Concert repertoire includes Syringa by Elliott Carter, with Collegium Musicum, Zurich, and El Cimarron by Hans Werner Henze. *Address:* Performing Arts, 6 Windmill Street, London W1 1HF, England.

TERRONI Raphael, b. 6 Nov. 1945, London, England. Pianist. m. 31 July 1971, 2 sons, 1 daughter. *Education:* St Ignatius College, 1956-62; Studied piano with John Vallier, London College of Music, 1965-68; Studied with Cyril Smith for 3 years; GLCM; ARCM (Performers). *Debut:* Wigmore Hall, London, 1974. *Career:* Performances, Festival Hall, Queen Elizabeth Hall, Purcell Room, music clubs and festivals throughout UK; Classical music cruises; BBC Pebble Mill; Head of Piano Faculty, London College of Music; Member of Terroni Piano Trio which has toured the Ukraine, 1991. *Recordings:* 2 recordings with Richard Baker as narrator, Unicorn-Kanchana; Berkeley's 80th Birthday Record of Piano Sonata, Pearl; Songs of Eric Coates with singer Brian Rayner Cook, ASV; Piano Quintets by Scott and Bridge for British Music Society. *Hobbies:* Golf; Watching Cricket. *Current Management:* Stephanie Williams Artists. *Address:* 4 Windsor Drive, Ramsey Forty Foot, Huntingdon, Cambs PE17 1XX, England.

TERZAKIS Zachos, b. 1953, Greece. Singer (Tenor). *Education:* Studied in Athens. *Career:* Sang at Athens Opera as Alfredo, Dimitri in Boris Godunov and Jim Mahoney in Mahagonny; Opera engagements at Kiel and Bielefeld from 1978, notably as Faust, the Duke of Mantua, Riccardo, Lensky, Rodolfo, the Prince in Rusalka and Guidon in The Tale of Tsar Saltan by Rimsky; Member of Nuremberg Opera from 1982, Bregenz Festival, 1987-88, as Hoffmann, Deutsche Oper Berlin and Berne Opera, 1988, as Alfredo and Werther; Vienna Staatsoper and Bielefeld, 1991, as Mozart's Tito, and Vasco da Gama in L'Africaine; Lieder recitals and concert appearances. *Address:* Städtisches Buhnen, Brunnenstrasse 3, 4800 Bielefeld 1, Germany.

TERZIAN Anita, b. 12 Oct 1947, Strasbourg, France. Singer (Mezzo- soprano). *Education:* Studied at the Juilliard School New York with Jennie Tourel. *Debut:* Brussels 1973, as Rosina. *Career:* Has appeared at many operatic centres in Europe and the USA: Opera du Rhin Strasbourg, Brussels, Liège and San Francisco Opera; Best known in such coloratura mezzo repertoire as Rossini's Isabella and Sinaide (Mosè), Elisetta in Il Matrimonio Segreto and Sesto in La Clemenza di Tito; Other roles include Carmen, Charlotte, Olga, Orlofsky and Konschakovna in Prince Igor; Many concert appearances. *Recordings include:* Title role in Handel's Serse (Schwann). *Address:* c/o Opéra du Rhin, 19 Place Broglie, F-67008 Strasbourg Cedex, France.

THALLAUG Edith, b. 16 June 1929, Oslo, Norway. Singer (Mezzo-soprano). *Education:* Studied with Giurgja Leppee and Joel Berglund in Stockholm. *Debut:* Stage debut as actress, 1952; Song recital in Oslo 1959. *Career:* Stage debut as Dorabella at Gothenburg, 1960; Royal Opera Stockholm from 1964, notably as Carmen, Cherubino, Rosina, Bradamante (Alcina), Maddalena (Rigoletto), Eboli, Azucena, Amneris, Venus, Fricka, Waltraute, Octavian, and the Composer in Ariadne, Judith in Bluebeard, Miss Julie, Ada (Berio); Frequent appearances at the Drottningholm Court Theatre from 1964; Glyndebourne Festival 1971, as Dorabella; Sang at Basle 1976 in Schoenberg's Gurrelieder; Swedish television as Carmen; Guest engagements in Oslo, Copenhagen, Moscow, USA, Japan, Korea, Germany,

Milan-Scala, Italy, Paris, Prague and Vienna. *Recordings include:* CD: Songs from De Falla, Montsalvatge, Ravel and many other recordings of Scandinavian songs; Opera arias; Songs by Grieg; Duets with Gösta Winbergh. *Honours:* Critic Prizes for Cenerentola, Oslo, 1972; Grieg Prize, 1978; Court Singer, 1976; Litteris et Artibus, 1982; Drottningholm Court Theater, Gold Medal, 1979. *Address:* c/o Kongliga Teatern, P O Box 16094, S-10322 Stockholm, Sweden.

THANE Amanda, b. 1960, Australia. Singer (Soprano). *Education:* New South Wales Conservatorium of Music, Sydney. *Career:* Roles with the Australian Opera since 1983 include Fiordiligi, Violetta, Marzelline, Constanze, Mimi, Norina, Pamina, Cintessa, Micaela, Lauretta, Antonia, Leila, Nedda, Liu, Valentine (in Joan Sutherland's farewell performance of Les Huguenots), Governess and Maria Stuarda; Additional roles sung with other Australian companies include: Gilda, Euridice, Marenka, Alice Ford, Rosalinde; Suor Angelica and Madama Butterfly; London performances include Suor Angelica, Adrianna, Lecouvreur and Liu; R.O.H. Covent Garden debut season 1991-92, as Valentine in a new production of Les Huguenots and Antonia in Les Contes d'Hoffman; European debut, 1993 as Lina in Stiffelio with Opera Forum, The Netherlands; 1993 season included new roles of Donna Elvira in Don Giovanni for Grand-Théâtre de Bordeaux, Eva in Die Meistersinger and Eurydice in Gluck's Orphée for the Australian Opera; Future engagements include roles as Nedda, Liu, Gilda and Fiordiligi. Many concert appearances throughout Australia, UK, Europe, USA, Japan and Korea. *Honours include:* Prizewinner, Metropolitan Opera Auditions; Winner of ABC Instrumental and Vocal Competition; Queen Elizabeth II Silver Jubilee for Young Australians; Australian Music Foundation Award (London), Churchill Fellowship 1990. *Recordings:* Videos: The Australian Opera video releases of Les Huguenots (Valentine), Turandot (Liu) and Mozart Bi-Centenary recording (Fiordiligi).*Address:* c/o Athole Still Ltd., Greystoke House, 80-86 Westow Street, London SE19 3AF, England.

THAW David, b. 19 June 1928, New York, USA. Singer (Tenor). m. Claire Watson (died 1986). *Education:* Studied at Columbia University, with Giovanni Martinelli in New York and Giuseppe Pais in Milan. *Debut:* Vichy 1950, as Vincent in Mireille. *Career:* Sang at the Theater am Gärtnerplatz Munich from 1955, debut as the Duke of Mantua; Frankfurt-am-Main Opera from 1958, debut as Lenski in Eugene Onegin (visited London with the company 1963, Fidelio, Salome and Die Entführung); Bayreuth Festival 1961, as Froh in Das Rheingold; Member of the Bayerische Staatsoper Munich from 1963; Guest appearances in Berlin (Deutsche Oper and Staatsoper), Hanover and elsewhere; Salzburg Festival 1964-68; Munich 1986 in the premiere of Belshazzar by V D Kirchner; Many appearances in musicals, notably as Professor Higgins in My Fair Lady. *Address:* c/o Bayerische Staatsoper, Postfach 745, D-8000 Munich 1, Germany.

THEBOM Blanche, b. 19 Sept. 1918, Monessen, Pennsylvania, USA. Singer (Mezzo-Soprano). *Education:* Studied with Margharete Matzenauer and Edyth Walker in New York. *Debut:* Sang in concert from 1941. *Career:* Stage debut 1944 Philadelphia 1944, with the Metropolitan Opera, as Brangaene; Sang in New York until 1966 as Marina, Eboli, Baba the Turk, Herodias, Orlofsky and in Wagner roles (Venus and Fricka); Chicago 1946, as Brangaene; San Francisco Opera 1947-59, debut as Amneris; Glyndebourne 1950, Dorabella; Covent Garden 1957, as Dido in the first British professional performance of Les Troyens; Tour of Russia 1958; Directed the Atlanta Opera Company 1967-68; Professor at the University of Arkansas. *Recordings:* Tristan und Isolde, conducted by Furtwängler (HMV); The Rake's Progress (Columbia).

THEISEN Kristin, b. 13 Jan 1955, Oslo, Norway. Opera Singer (Soprano). *Education:* Studied German, Oslo University, 1 year; Vocal pedagogic studies, Music

Conservatorium, Oslo, 4 years; Norwegian State Opera School, 3 years; Studied in Vienna, Salzburg and Bayreuth; Teachers: Erna Skaug, Ingrid Bjoner, Kim Borg, Anna Reynolds and Jean Cox. *Debut:* Recital, Oslo, 1979; As opera singer, Pagliacci's Nedda, Gelsenkirchen, 1982. *Career:* Has appeared in Hamburg, Frankfurt, Nuremberg, Catani, Strasbourg, Eutin, Basel, Lubeck; TV, radio and film in Norway, Austria and Poland; Important opera roles: Agathe in Freischutz, Rezia in Oberon, Susanna in Figaro, Giulietta in Hoffmann, Ellen Orford in Peter Grimes, Euridice in Orpheus and Euridice, Sieglinde in Walkure, Santa in Hollander. *Recordings:* Zigeunerlieder, with Audin Kayser, piano; Irmgard in Franz Schreker's opera Flammen, conducted by Frank Strobl. *Hobbies:* Tennis; Skiing. *Current Management:* Kollo, Berlin, and Heissler-Remy, Dusseldorf. *Address:* Sarbuvollveien 8A, N-1322 Hovik, Norway.

THEW Lisbet, b. 22 Apr. 1920, Freiburg, Germany. Music Librarian; Organist. m. Warren Thew, deceased, 16 Feb. 1952. *Education:* Diploma, Business High School, 1938; Diploma, Literary High School, 1939; B.Mus., Theory, 1945; MMus., Musicology, 1948; Organ, Eastman School of Music; Library Science, University of Michigan, Ann Arbor, 1949. *Career:* Head Cataloguer, Sibley Music Library, Rochester, 1949-51; Senior Music Cataloguer, Library of Congress, Washington DC 1952-56; Building Library for Musikschule und Konservatorium Winterthur, 1968-70; Member, Cataloging Project, Bayerische Staatsbibliothek, Munchen, 1970-73; Building and Directing Library, Konservatorium und Musikhochschule, Zurich, Switzerland, 1974-86; Editor, Creative Legacy of Warren Thew: Poetry, Cartoons, Music, 1986-. *Publications:* Grundlagen zur Sachbearbeitung der Musikalien u. der Musikliteratur, 1971; Katalog der Musikhandschriften der Benediktinerinnenabtei Frauenworth und der Pfarrkirchen Wasserburg am Inn, Co-author, 1975; Musikalische Form und Gattungsnamen: Schema einer Schlagwortliste, co-author, 1977. *Hobbies:* Languages and their Literature. *Address:* Schlimbergstrasse 24, CH 8802 Kilchberg/ZH, Switzerland.

THIBAUD Pierre, b. 22 June 1929, Proissans, France. Trumpeter. *Education:* Studied violin and trumpet at the Bordeaux Conservatoire; Premier prix for cornet playing at the Paris Conservatoire. *Career:* Principal trumpet with the orchestra of the Paris Opera, the Ensemble Ars Nova, Domaine Musicale, Musique Vivante, Musique Plus and the Chamber Orchestra Fernand Oubradous; Further experience with the Concerts Lamoureux, Concerts Colonne and Musique de la Garde Republicaine; Founded the Brass Quintet Ars Nova and collaborations with the Société des Concerts du Conservatoire and IRCAM (electronic music studios) Paris; Concert appearances with leading European orchestras in the standard classics; also plays music by Marius Constant, Xenakis, Messiaen, Varèse, Berio and Enesco; Professor of trumpet at the Paris Conservatoire 1975. *Recordings:* Brandenburg Concerto No. 2 (Archiv); Concertos by Haydn, Hummel and Telemann. *Address:* Conservatoire National Superieur de Musique de Paris, 209 Avenue Jean-Jaures, 75019 Paris, France.

THIBAUDET Jean-Yves, b. 7 Sept. 1961, Lyon, France. Concert Pianist. *Education:* Lycee Musical, Lyon; Lycee St Exupéry, Lyon; Conservatory of Music, Lyon; National Conservatory of Music, Paris. *Career:* Debuts and appearances throughout the world; Recitals in New York, Chicago, Washington DC, Los Angeles, San Francisco, London, Paris, Milan and Amsterdam; Appearances with Montreal, Saint-Louis National, Indianapolis, New World, The Boston Symphony, The Cleveland Orchestra, The Chicago Symphony, The Philadelphia Orchestra, The New York Philharmonic, and Toronto Symphonies, the Los Angeles Philharmonic, the Concertgebouw Orchestra, Orchestre de Paris, Ensemble Orchestral de Paris, Rotterdam Philharmonic and Stuttgart Radio Orchestra; Participated in Spoleto Festivals in USA, Italy and

Australia; Regular guest, Chamber Music Society, Lincoln Center; Debut appearances at Casals and Schleswig-Holstein festivals; Hollywood Bowl, 1989. *Recordings:* Numerous including music by Ravel, Liszt and Chopin; Violin sonatas by Debussy, Franck and Fauré, with Joshua Bell; Chausson Concerto for piano, violin and string quartet (Takacs); Ravel Trio (Bell, Isserlis); Liszt works for piano and orchestra (Montreal Symphony); Ravel: Complete solo piano works; Messiaen: Turangaĺila Symphony (Concertgebouw Orchestra). *Honours:* Lyon Conservatory of Music, Gold Medal, Piano, 1974; Paris National Conservatory of Music, 1st prize Piano & chamber music, 1977; Viotti, International-piano competition, Vercelli, Italy, 2nd prize, 1978; R Casadesus International Piano competition, Cleveland, USA, 2nd prize, 1979; Tokyo, International Piano Competition of Japan, winner, 1980; Young Concert Artists Auditions International, New York, winner, 1981; Grammy Award, nominee, 1992. *Hobbies:* Tennis; Swimming; Horseback riding; Water skiing; Museums; Movies; Racing cars. *Current Management:* IMG Artists. *Address:* c/o IMG Artists, 22 East 71st Street, New York, NY 10021, USA.

THIEME Helga, b. 27 Feb 1937, Oberlengsfeld, Germany. Singer (Soprano). *Education:* Studied in Frankfurt. *Career:* Sang in opera at Basle, 1962-65, Bielefeld, 1965-67, Wiesbaden, 1967-68; Hamburg, 1968-83, notably in premieres of The Devils of Loudon by Penderecki, 1969, and Josef Tal's Ashmedai, 1971; Sang at Bremen, 1974-76, St Gallen from 1980, and Zurich, 1984-85; Guest engagements at Berne, Berlin (Deutsche Oper), State Operas of Munich and Stuttgart, Dusseldorf, Vienna (Volksoper), Barcelona and Cologne; Roles have included Susanna, Zerlina, Despina and the Queen of Night; Norina and Adina, Lortzing's Gretchen and Marie, Gilda, Aennchen, Marenka, Sophie in Rosenkavalier, Isotta (Die schweigsame Frau) and Ida in Henze's Junge Lord. *Recordings include:* The Devils of Loudoun. *Address:* c/o Opernhaus Zurich, Falkenstrasse 1, CH-8008 Zurich, Switzerland.

THIEME Ulrich, b. 5 Aug. 1950, Hamm, Federal Republic of Germany. Professor of Recorder; Musicologist. *Education:* State Diploma, Music Teaching, 1973; Concert Diploma, Recorder, 1974; PhD, Musicology. *Career:* Recorder Teacher, Academy of Music, Cologne, 1973-78; Recorder Teacher, Academy of Music, Hannover, 1978-; TV appearances: Broadcasts for several German stations, 1969-; Concert tours throughout Europe, in Eastern Asia and South America; 50 concerts with recorder/lute-guitar duo, Germany. *Recordings:* Jürg Baur, Tre Studi per Quattro; Bach, Brandenburg Concertos; Baroque recorder music (Delalande, Bononcini, Mancini, etc). *Publications:* Studien zum Jugendwerk A. Schoenbergs, Bosse publishers, 1979; Affektenlehre im barocken Musikdenken, published Moeck, Celle, 1984. *Contributions to:* Editor of Baroque Recorder Music (Castello, Monteclair), published Moeck, Celle; Several contributions to TIBIA. *Honour:* 1st Prize, German Young Musicians Competition, 1967. *Memberships:* Vice-President, ERTA, European Recorder Teachers Association, German section. *Address:* c/o Staatliche Hochschule für Musik, D-3 Hannover, Germany.

THIJSSE Wilhelmus Hermanus, b. 2 Aug. 1916, Delft, The Netherlands. Musicologist; Organist; Composer. m. G J Schildt, 27 Dec. 1943, deceased 17 Feb. 1986, 1 son, 3 daughters. *Education:* State Diploma, Organ, 1942; Diploma in Music History, Royal Conservatoire, 1945. *Career:* Director, Municipal Music Library, 1950-60; Music Editor, Het Vaderland newspaper, 1960-72; Head of Department, Municipal Music School, 1974-81; Doctor Mus Sc, 1992-. *Compositions:* Sonata, recorder and harpsichord; Small Pieces for Small Fingers on the Small Harp; The Bells, Carillon; Divertimento Serioso, piano duet. *Publications:* Seven Centuries of Dutch Music, 1947; Haydn, 1948; About Melody, 1977; Music from Then till Now, 1978; The Other Switzerland, 1982; Rokoko, 1985; Music in the Netherlands, 1989. *Contributions to:* Mens en Melodie, 1947-. *Honour:* Ehrenurkunde Internationale

Robert Stolz Gesellschaft, 1982. *Memberships:* Society of Dutch Composers; Society for Dutch Music History. *Hobbies:* Filming; Gardening; Model trains. *Address:* Hyacintweg 44, 2565 R J Den Haag, The Netherlands.

THIOLLIER Francois-Joel, b. 12 Nov 1943, Paris, France. Concert Pianist. m. Beatrice Fitch, 9 June 1978, 1 son. *Education:* Studied in Paris with Robert Casadesus, 1951-53; the Juilliard Preparatory College, 1953- 63. *Career:* Many concerts in over 30 countries, including appearances with the Orchestre de Paris, Nouvel Orchestre Philharmonique; Moscow and Leningrad Philharmonic Orchestras; the Hague Residentie Orkest and RAI in Italy; Concert halls include the Amsterdam Concertgebouw, the Théâtre des Champs Elysées, th Teatro Real of Madrid, Accademia di Santa Cecilia, Rome, Victoria Hall Geneva, Tokyo, Berlin Philharmonics; Played the Busoni Concerto in Berlin. *Recordings:* Complete works of Rachmaninov and Gershwin; Beethoven Sonatas Op 27 no 2, Op 13 and Op 57; Liszt Sonata and complete songs for tenor and piano; Brahms Sonata Op 5 and Paganini Variations; Mozart Sonata K330 and Quintet K452. *Honours:* Prizewinner at International Piano Competitions: Viotti, Casella, Busoni, Pozzoli, Montreal, Tchaikovsky Moscow, Marguerite Long, Paris, Queen Elisabeth, Brussels. *Hobbies:* Fishing; Snorkeling; Tennis. *Address:* c/o Ms Patricia Garrasi, 31 via Manzoni, 20121 Milan, Italy.

THOMAS Caryl, b. 23 Oct. 1958, Aberystwyth, Dyfed, Wales. Harpist. m. Huw Williams, 22 Oct, 1985. *Education:* Welsh College of Music & Drama; MA, New York University, USA; Associate, Royal College of Music. *Debut:* Carnegie Hall, New York, Nov. 1981. *Career:* Freelance harpist, concentrating solo & concert work, great emphasis on BBC Radio 3 & Channel 4 ITV broadcasting. Appearances include: London debut, Wigmore Hall; Concerto soloist, BBC Welsh Symphony Orchestra 1982, Mozarteum Orchestra, Salzburg (Austria) 1984. *Recording:* Mozart Concerto for Flute & Harp, with London Philharmonic Orchestra, Jonathan Snowden (flute), Andrew Litton (conductor), Jan. 1987; French Impressions, Prometheus Ensemble. *Honours:* 1st British harpist to win prize, International Harp Contest, Jerusalem, Israel, 1976; Award, Concert Artists Guild, New York, 1981; ISM & Park Lane Young Musician, 1982. *Memberships:* Musicians Union; Incorporated Society of Musicians (ISM); UK Harpists Association. *Hobbies:* Cookery; Sport. *Current Management:* London Musicians and Harlequin, Cardiff. *Address:* 47 Belgrave Road, Wanstead, London E11 3QP, England.

THOMAS David, b. 26 Feb. 1943, Orpington, Kent. Singer (Bass/Baritone). *Education:* St Paul's Cathedral Choir School; King's College Canterbury; King's College Cambridge. *Career:* Many concerts with the world's leading orchestras; Sang Messiah with the Los Angeles Philharmonic at the Hollywood Bowl, 1984; Bach Passions and B Minor Mass at the 1985 International Bach Festival in Japan, conducted by Helmuth Rilling; Oratorio and concert repertory includes works by Walton, Tippett, Britten, Stravinsky and Schoenberg; US engagements in Messiah at Lincoln Center with the Academy of Ancient Music, Schubert's Winterresie at Duke University, Haydn's Creation at Boston Symphony Hall with Christopher Hogwood and Handel's Susanna with Nicholas McGegan in San Francisco; Appearances at the Tanglewood, Edinburgh, Salzburg and Lucerne Festivals and the London Promenade Concerts (Handel's Orlando 1990, conducted by Hogwood); Recital tours of the USA with Anthony Rooley and Emma Kirkby; Season 1990-91 tour of Switzerland with the Academy of Ancient Music, Winterresie and lectures at Tokyo University and Handel's Theodora in San Francisco; Season 1992-93 with Schubert's Winterreise at Cornell University, Handel's Susanna, Theodora and Judas Maccabaeus with Philharmonia Baroque/Nicholas McGegan; UK Engagements: TV Recording of Beethoven's 9th Symphony with London Classical Players/Roger Norrington, Creation, with Chamber Orchestra of Europe/Frans Bruggen; Dido and Aenees

at the Barbican. *Recordings include:* Handel's Messiah (twice), Semele, La Resurrezione, Alceste, Apollo e Dafne, Esther, Athalia and Acis, Galatea e Polifemeo; Bach's B minor Mass, Coffee Cantata and Ich habe Genug, cantata no 82; Mozart's Requiem and C minor Mass with Hogwood; Handel's Israel in Egypt (Taverner Players), Susanna (Philharmonic Baroque Orchestra) and Orlando (Academy of Ancient Music); Stravinsky's Pulcinella conducted by Hickox; Haydn's Creation with the CBSO conducted by Rattle; Bach's St John Passion conducted by Andrew Parrott and Cantatas with Gustav Leonhardt; Mozart's Requiem conducted by Roy Goodman. *Memberships:* Chairman of the artistic advisory committee and member of the board of Blackheath concert halls. *Current Management:* Allied Artists, 42 Montpelier Square, London SW7 1JZ, England. *Address:* 74 Hyde Vale, Greenwich, London SE10 8HP, England.

THOMAS John David, b. 30 Mar 1951, US. Musician; Composer; Photographer. m. Rosalie Faith Baldwin, 27 July 1974, 1 son, 1 daughter. *Education:* Electrical Engineering, Mathematics, Purdue University, 1969-71; Music Theory, Composition, 1971-74, BS, 1986, Ball State University. *Career:* Synthetist, Keyboardist, Lefthand Key Bassist: Jet Stream, Indianapolis (also Audio-visual Sound Technician), 1979-83, Pinnacle Peak Patio, Scottsdale, Arizona, 1984, Dee Dee Ryan, The Longhorn Saloon, Apache Junction, Arizona, 1984-86; Solo Pianist: Clarion Inn/ McCormick's Ranch Resort, Scottsdale, 1986, Boulders Resort, Carefree, Arizona, 1987, Wrigley Mansion, Phoenix, Arizona, 1988; Audio-visual Sound Technician, Valley Cathedral, Phoenix, 1987. *Compositions:* Over 200 advanced music compositions, songs, themes in all styles from classical, avant-garde and new music for tape to jazz-rock, top 40 rock, disco, Christian praise and worship music, movie theme music, love songs, others, including: Someday, 1969; Death of Rock and Roll, 1970; Untitled New Music for French Horn, Cello and Piano, 1973; Alabama D A, 1973; Love Theme In B Minor, 1978; Song of the Ocean, 1980; Olympic Brass, 1988; Praise Him, The King Liveth, 1989; Jubilee in F-for French Horn, Brass, Synthesizer and Pipe Organ, 1989; The Emancipation of the Cascade Bell Choir, 1989; The New Mozart Reincarnation Channel No 1- A, 1989; Fantasy in C, 1990; Etude for Virtuoso Cello, 1990; Love Flowers, 1990; Praise and Adoration, 1990. *Honours include:* Outstanding Musician Awards: T C Howe High School, Indianapolis, 1969, Purdue Symphonette, West Lafayette, 1970; Palmer Memorial Music Scholar, 1971-74. *Memberships include:* American Society of Composers, Authors and Publishers; Piano Technicians Guild; Former Member, Broadcast Music Inc. *Hobbies:* Music; Photography; Movies; TV; Reading; Bridge; Chess; Euchre; Sports; Computers (Atari); Travel; Church; Culinary cuisine; Poetry; Drama and plays. *Address:* 12730 43rd Avenue NE. Marysville, WA 98270-8702, USA.

THOMAS Judith, b. Rugby, Warwickshire, England. Musician. *Education:* LRAM, ARCM, Royal Academy of Music, London. *Career:* Performer, oboe, oboe d'amore, cor anglais; Currently Oboist, Cor Anglais Player with English National Opera; Freelance soloist, chamber music and orchestral player; Teacher. *Honours:* F Vivian Dunne Prize for Woodwind, Royal Academy of Music, 1960. *Membership:* Incorporated Society of Musicians. *Hobbies:* Reading; Travel; Photography. *Address:* 53 Station Road, Teddington, Middlesex TW11 9AA, England.

THOMAS Michael, b. 1960, England. Violinist. *Education:* Studied at the Royal Northern College of Music. *Career:* Founder member and leader of the Brodsky String Quartet (sister Jacky Thomas plays cello in the Quartet); Resident at Cambridge University for four years and later residencies at the Dartington International Summer School, Devon; Concert engagements include the Shostakovich quartets at the Elizabeth Hall, London and performances at the Ludwigsburg and Schleswig-Holstein Festivals; New York debut at the Metropolitan Museum; Scheduled tours of Italy, North America, Australia, Poland, Czechoslovakia and Istanbul; Complete quartets of Schoenberg for the BBC, 1992; French concerts include visit to the Théâtre du Châtelet, Paris; Founder and Director of Kreisler String Orchestra, 1980-90. *Recordings include:* Quartets of Elgar and Delius; Schubert A minor and Beethoven Op. 74 (Harp); Complete quartets of Shostakovich (Teldec). *Address:* c/o Harrison/Parrott Ltd, 12 Penzance Place, London W11 4PA, England.

THOMAS Michael Tilson, b. 21 Dec. 1944, Los Angeles, California, USA. Conductor; Pianist. *Education:* Studied at the University of Southern California with Ingolf Dahl, John Crown and Alice Ehlers. *Career:* Conducted the Young Musicians Foundation Debut Orchestra: pianist and conductor at the Monday Evening Concerts, with premieres of works by Copland, Stockhausen, Kraft, Stravinsky and Boulez; Conducted at the Ojai Festival 1968-69 and 1973; Has conducted the Boston Symphony Orchestra from 1969 (Principal Guest Conductor 1972-74); Pianist and conductor with the Boston Symphony Chamber Players; Music Director of the Buffalo Philharmonic 1971-79; Directed the young people's concerts of the New York Philharmonic 1971-76; US premiere of Berg's Lulu (3-act version) at Santa Fe, 1979; Regular conductor of the Chicago, Pittsburgh and Philadelphia Orchestras; Directed a new production of Der fliegende Holländer in France, Janáček's The Cunning Litle Vixen, New York 1980; Fidelio at Houston and Tosca at the Chicago Lyric Opera; Principal Guest Conductor of the Los Angeles Philharmonic 1981-85; Premiered Steve Reich's Desert Music, 1984; Engagements with the Berlin Philharmonic, Philharmonia, Royal Philharmonic, Vienna, Concertgebouw and Bavarian Radio Symphony Orchestras; Principal Conductor of the London Symphony Orchestra from 1988 (Gershwin festival 1987); Founder and Music Director the New World Symphony 1988, a national fellowship orchestra for young professionals; Conducted the LSO in Bernstein's On the Town at the Barbican Hall, London, 1992; Forthcoming: Music Director, Designate of the San Francisco Symphony. *Recordings include:* Beethoven, Tchaikovsky, Debusssy and Stravinsy (with Ralph Grierson, first recording of the 4-hand version of The Rite of Spring); Charles Ives (2nd Symphony with the Concertgebouw Orchestra), Carl Ruggles (Complete Works, with the Buffalo Philharmonic), John Cage, Steve Reich and George Gershwin (CBS). *Honours include:* Koussevitzky Conducting Prize at the Berkshire Music Center, 1968; Many Grammy nominations and international awards for his recordings. *Address:* c/o Columbia Atists Management Ltd, 28 Cheverton Road, London N19 3AY, England.

THOMAS Nova, b. 1960, North Carolina, USA. Singer (Soprano). *Education:* Studied at University of Bloomington with Eileen Farrell. *Career:* Appearances at opera houses in Cologne, Hamburg, Belfast (Opera Northern Ireland), St Louis, Seattle, San Diego, Detroit and New York (City Opera); Season 1991-92 in Cologne and Paris as Giulia in La Scala di Seta; Roles have included Violetta, the four heroines in Les contes d'Hoffmann, the Trovatore Leonora, and Anna Bolena; Further engagements as Mozart's Constanze for Cologne Opera, Norma with Seattle Opera and Hoffmann under Richard Bobynge. *Recordings include:* Title role in the Bohemian Girl, conducted by Bonynge. *Honours include:* Winner, Metropolitan Opera National Council Auditions of 1984. *Address:* c/o IMG Artists, Media House, 3 Burlington Lane, London W4 2TH, England.

THOMAS Paul Lindsley, b. 18 Mar 1929, New York, New York, USA. Music Director, Organist, Composer. m. Joyce Robertshaw, 3 Sept 1955, 1 son. *Education:* BA, Trinity College, Hartford, Connecticut, 1950; B Mus, 1957, M Mus, 1958 Yale University; DMA, North Texas University, 1979; AAGO, American Guild of Organists, 1953; Diploma, American Conservatoire, Fontainbleau, France, FAGO, 1958. *Debut:* First organ recital at the Cathedral of St John the Divine, New York City, June 1944. *Compositions:* Shout the Glad Tidings; The Strife is O'er; Variations on the Welsh Hymn Tune, Aberystwyth, published by the Oxford University Press; Fanfare and Alleluias; Come See the Place; 2 Preludes on Christmas Carols for Organ Duet published by Belwin-Mills; O Send Out They Light and Thy Truth and Hark the Glad Sound, by Concordia, St Louis and Hymn to the Trinity and A Christmas Diptych by Unicorn Press. *Honours:* First Prize in Scholarship, Yale, 1957; First Prizes in Organ and in Composition, Yale, 1958; Canon of Church Music, Episcopal Diocese of Dallas, 1980. *Memberships:* Dean of the Dallas Chapter, American Guild of Organists, 1967-69; Member of the National Council AGO, 1972-75; General Chairman, National Convention of the AGO in Dallas, 1972, Chairman and Member of Examination Committee, Dallas Chapter, 1965-. *Address:* Director of Music and Organist Saint Michael and All Angels Church, 8011 Douglas, Dallas, TX 75225, USA.

THOMAS Peter, b. 1944, South Wales. Violinist. *Education:* Studied in England, winning the Menuhin Prize at Bath Festival, 1958. *Career:* Second violinist of the Allegri Quartet, 1963-68; Co-founder of Orion Piano Trio, becoming resident ensemble at Southampton University; Leader of BBC Welsh Symphony Orchestra, 1972, then Philharmonia; Currently leader of City of Birmingham Symphony Orchestra and artistic director of Birmingham Ensemble; String Adviser to Gustav Mahler Youth Orchestra, Vienna; Purcell Room, London, recital, 1993, with works by Schubert, Berio (Sequenza VIII), Schoenberg and Busoni (2nd Sonata). *Honours include:* With Orion Piano Trio: BBC Prize for British and Commonwealth ensembles. *Address:* Camerata Artists, 4 Margaret Road, Birmingham B17 0EU, England.

THOMAS Steven Murray, b. 26 June 1946, Peterborough, Ontario, Canada. Opera, Stage & TV Producer. m. Irene Wronski, 6 July 1985. *Education:* BA, English, Psychology, University of Western Ontario; Diploma, Piano, Royal Conservatory of Toronto; Private Studies, Brass. *Debut:* With New Jersey State Opera, 1976. *Career:* Producer, Artistic Director, Actor, Dramatic Theatre, 1964-72; Producer, Stage Director, Opera (Freelance), 1972-78; Production Manager, Opera Festival, National Arts Centre, Ottawa, 1978-79; Artistic Director, Opera Hamilton, 1979-86; Producer, TV Opera, CHCH TV, Hamilton, 1979-86; Operas Produced for TV include: La Bohème; La Traviata; Madame Butterfly; Barber of Seville; Rigoletto; Aida; Manon Lescaut; Marriage of Figaro; La Traviata; Hansel & Gretel; Carmen. *Honours:* CANPRO Awards for Excellence in the Performing Arts, Canadian TV National Competition, for La Bohème, 1980, La Traviata, 1981, Barber of Seville, 1983, Aida, 1985; Canadian Music Council Award for TV, La Traviata, 1983; Iris Award, USA National Association of Broadcast Executives, 1st Runner Up, Madame Butterfly, 1985. *Address:* 226 Westmount Avenue, Toronto, Ontario M6E 3M8, Canada.

THOMASCHKE Thomas Michael, b. 2 Sept 1943, Pirna, Germany. Concert and Opera Singer. m. 1964, 1 son, 1 daughter. *Education:* Dresden Hochschule für Musik, awards in Lieder, opera and oratorio; 1967; Singing Teachers' Certificate, 1970. *Debut:* Freiberg German Democratic Republic, in Tosca, 1963. *Career:* Sang in Leipzig, Dresden and at the Komische Oper Berlin in the 1960s; La Scala, Bavarian State Opera, Glyndebourne, Covent Garden, Paris, Lisbon, Buenos Aires, Vienna, Edinburgh, Venice, Cape Town, Rome, Florence and Amsterdam; Has sung Figaro, Don Giovanni, Rocco (Fidelio), Sarastro (Magic Flute), Gurnemanz (Parsifal). *Recordings include:* For EMI, Philips, Teldec, Decca, Opus (CSSR), Eterna: Bach and Handel (conducted by Nikolaus Harnoncourt): Weber Frieschütz, Philips, Colin Davis, Beethoven 9th Symphony, Yehudi Menuhin. *Contributions to:* Opernwelt. *Honours:* Schumannpreis, 1966; Tschaikowskypreis, 1970; Preis Hertogenbosch (first prize), 1971. *Memberships:* Artistic Director of Festival

Mitte Europa. *Hobbies:* Cooking; Painting; Fine Arts. *Current Management:* SYM Music Company Limited, 110 Gloucester Avenue, London NW1 8JA, England. *Address:* Fliederweg 108, D-50859 Cologne, Germany.

THOME Diane, b. 25 Jan. 1942, Pearl River, NY, USA. Composer; Pianist; College Professor; Lecturer. *Education:* Studied Piano with Dorothy Taubman, New York; Composition with Robert Strassburg, Darius Milhaud, Aspen, Colorado; Roy Harris at Inter-American University, Puerto Rico; PhD, in Music, Princeton University, 1973. *Career:* Taught Music, Princeton University, New Jersey, 1973-74; Taught Theory and 20th Century Music, SUNY, Binghamton, 1974-77; Professor of Theory and Composition, University of Washington School of Music, Seattle. *Compositions include:* Chamber Works: 3 Pieces 1958; 3 Movements 1958; Sonatine 1960; Suite 1961; Quartet 1961; Constellations 1966; Electronic Music: Le Berceau de Miel 1968; Spectrophonie 1969; Polyvalence 1972; January Variations 1973; Los Nombres 1974; Alexander Boscovich Remembered 1975; Anais 1976; Sunflower Space 1978; Winter Infinities 1980; To Search the Spacious World 1986; The Ruins of the Heart for soprano, orchestra and tape, 1991; Angels for virtual reality artwork, 1992; The Palaces of Memory for large chamber ensemble and tape, 1993; Multimedia Compositions: In My Garden 1956; Caprice 1957; Night Passage 1973; Orchestral Works: 3 Movements 1962; S'Embarquement 1971; The Golden Messengers 1984; Lucent Flowers, 1988; Piano Works: Sonatine 1959; Pianismus; Sacred Works: 3 Psalms 1979; Vocal Works: Ash On An Old Man's Sleeve 1962; Spring and Fall: To A Young Child 1962; Cantata 1964; Songs On Chinese Verses 1964; The Yew Tree 1979; 3 Sonnets by Sri Aurobindo: Settings for Soprano and Orchestra 1984. *Address:* School of Music DN-10, University of Washington, Seattle, WA 98195, USA.

THOMPSON Adrian, b. 1954, London, England. Singer (Tenor). *Education:* Studied at the Guildhall School of Music and Drama, London. *Career:* Opera engagements with the Glyndebourne Festival, Scottish Opera, Handel Opera Society and the Buxton, Aldeburgh, Wexford, Lausanne and Göttingen Festivals; appearances include Ariodante (Ordonte), A Midsummer Night's Dream (Snout and Flute), Albert Herring, Mozart's La Finta Giardiniera (Podesta), Die Entführung (Pedrillo), Le Nozze di Figaro, Cosi fan Tutte, Falstaff (Bardolph), Conti's Don Quixote in Sierra Morena, Boris Godunov (Simpleton) and L'Incoronazione di Poppea (Nurse); Sang Alfred in Fledermaus at Belfast, 1990; Title role in Haydn's Orlando Paladino at Garsington Manor, Oxford; Britten's Flute at Sadler's Wells, 1990 (Snout at Glyndebourne, 1989); Concert performances throughout Europe and Britain in works by Purcell, Bach, Handel, Berlioz, Schoenberg and Tippett; Britten repertoire includes Les Illuminations, the Serenade, Nocturne, Canticles, and Song Cycles; Appearances with leading British orchestras, the Netherlands Chamber Orchestra, Nash ensemble and Stockholm Bach Choir; Frequent Promenade concerts and recitals at the Aldeburgh, Lichfield, Bath and Buxton Festivals; Has sung Schubert's Die schöne Müllerin at the Wigmore Hall and songs by Schubert and Schoenberg at South Bank; Recitals in Israel, Canada, Germany, France and Switzerland; Season 1992/93 with recitals in USA, Salome in Netherlands; Tamerlano (Handel) at Karlsruhe and Irus in Monteverdi's Ulisse at the Coliseum, London. *Recordings:* Die schöne Müllerin (Pickwick); Gurney's Ludlow and Teme, On Wenlock Edge by Vaughan Williams, with the Delmé Quartet (Hyperion); Hyperion, Schubert Recital with Graham Johnson; Hyperion, Beggar's Opera, Virgin, A Midsummer Night's Dream. *Address:* c/o Ron Gonsalves Management, 10 Dagnan Road, London SW12 9LQ, England.

THOMPSON Alton, b. 31 Jan 1959, Tampa, Florida, USA. Conductor. *Education:* BME, Florida State University; MM, Memphis State University; DMA in progress, Peabody Conservatory of Music; Conducting teachers include Tsung Yeh, Frederik Pravsnitz,

Jonathan Sternberg, Robert Griffith, Don Freund, Carl Bjerregaard. *Debut:* Cosi fan tutte, Memphis State University Opera, Memphis, 1986; State Philharmonia of Kielce, Poland, 1993. *Career:* Assistant Conductor, Memphis State University Opera and Orchestra; Music Director, Memphis Harmonie, Playhouse-on-the-Square; Music Director, Musica Humana chamber orchestra; Music Director, Arion Gesangverein; Guest Conductor, State Philharmonia of Kielce, Poland; Conducted premieres of Lynn Gillie Joyner's Medea, Mark Hijleh's On the Head of a Pin; Memphis premiere of Andre Previn's score, Every Good Boy Deserves Favour (Stoppard). *Address:* 612 Shipley Road, Baltimore, MD 21090, USA.

THOMPSON Arthur, b. 27 Dec 1942, New York City, New York, USA. Singer (Baritone). *Education:* Studied at Manhattan School of Music, Hartt College and Juilliard School. *Debut:* Chautauqua, as Papageno, 1964. *Career:* Performances with Metropolitan Opera Studio, 1966-71; More than 50 comprimario roles with Metropolitan New York from 1970, including Mandarin in Turandot, 1970; Many performances of Porgy and Bess in USA and abroad; Covent Garden, 1987, as Mel in The Knot Garden. *Recordings include:* Four Saints in Three Acts by Virgil Thomson; Jake in Porgy and Bess, conducted by Lorin Maazel. *Address:* c/o Royal Opera House, Covent Garden, London WC2, England.

THOMPSON Donald Prosser, b. 28 Feb. 1928, Columbus, Ohio, USA. University Professor; Conductor; Writer. m. Ana Christina Figueroa Laugier, 23 Jan. 1972, 2 sons, 1 daughter. *Education:* AB, University of Missouri, 1952; MA, University of Missouri, 1954; Akademie für Musik, Vienna, Austria; Eastman School of Music; PhD, University of Iowa, 1970. *Career:* Retired as Professor and Chair, Department of Music, University of Puerto Rico, 1956-85; Conductor, opera, music theatre, television, San Juan, Puerto Rico, 1956-; Music Critic San Juan Star, 1957-60, 1975-; Consultant in Arts Management, 1985-. *Publications:* Manual para monografías musicales, 1980; The New Grove Dictionary of Music, 1980; The New Grove Dictionary of American Music, 1986; Music Research in Puerto Rico, 1982; The Puerto Rico Symphony Orchestra, 1985; The New Grove Dictionary of Opera, 1992; El joven Tavárez; nuevos documentos y nuevas perspectivas, 1993; Diccionario de musica espanola e hispanoamericana, 1994. *Contributions to:* Revista musical chilena, 1984; African Music, 1975-76; Inter American Music Review, 1989; Revista musical de Venezuela, 1989; Bibliografia musicologica latinoamericana, 1992, 1993; Latin American Music Review, 1983, 1985, 1990, 1993. *Honour:* Phi Beta Kappa, 1952. *Memberships:* American Musicological Society; College Music Society, Member, Editorial Board, 1979-86; Puerto Rico Musical Society, President, 1973-77. *Hobbies:* Sailing; Tennis. *Address:* Calle Acadia N-64, Rio Piedras, Puerto Rico.

THOMPSON James Christopher, b. 7 Mar 1953, Savannah, Georgia, USA. Professor of Violin (University). m. Laura Ann Mobley, 20 Aug 1974, 1 daughter. *Education:* MMus, Violin Performance, University of Alabama, 1976; MMus, Violin Performance, Memphis State University, 1977; DMA, Violin Performance, Louisiana State University School of Music, 1986. *Debut:* Teatro dei Rozzi, Siena, Italy, 23 July 1992. *Career:* Critically acclaimed recitals and solo appearances in USA and Europe, including recital tours of Switzerland and Italy, 1992; Concertmaster, Jackson Symphony in Tennessee; Artist, Teacher of Violin: University of Mississippi; Murray State University; Currently Artist, Teacher of Violin, Chairman of String Division, Northeast Louisiana University School of Music, 1989-; His students successful in orchestra positions and critically acclaimed as soloists in USA, Europe and Far East. *Publications:* A Practice Manual for 24 Studies, Opus 37 of Jacob Dont, 1986; A Videotape Practice Manual: Jacob Dont's "24 Opus Studies" Opus 37, 1989. *Honours:* Winner, Young Artist Auditions, National Federated Music Clubs, 1983; Appointed to Artist/Faculty of Sessione Senese per la

Musica e l'Arte summer music institute, University of Siena, Italy, conducted masterclasses, 1992; Recipient, Fulbright Senior Scholar Award, lectureship in Taiwan to serve as visiting artist with Taipei Symphony, 1993. *Memberships:* American String Teachers Association; Music Teachers National Association. *Address:* 322 Holly Ridge Drive, Monroe, LA 71203, USA.

THOMPSON Robert Ian, b. 5 Apr 1943, Bradford, England. Singer (Tenor); Harpsichordist; Conductor. m. Judith Welch, 18 Apr 1970. *Education:* Organ Scholar, Queens' College, Cambridge, 1961-64; MA, Cambridge University; ARCM; ARCO; Singing tuition with Campogalliani, Italy. *Career:* BBC Chorus, 1966-67; Vicar Choral, St Paul's Cathedral; Opera and concert singer; Kent Opera, Opera North, debut, Royal Opera House, Covent Garden, 1993; Appearances, numerous European theatres including La Scala, Milan, and Teatro San Carlo, Naples, 1991; Broadcasts in most European Countries. *Recordings:* With Pro Cantione Antiqua, Early Music Consort, Societa Cameristica di Lugano, Capella Clementina. *Memberships:* Incorporated Society of Musicians; Royal College of Organists; The Alpine Club; Member of Amaryllis Consort;. *Hobbies:* Alpine mountaineering; Gardening; Cooking. *Current Management:* Athole Still International Management; Concert Directory International. *Address:* 4 Rylett Road, London W12 9NL, England.

THOMPSON Terence James, b. 19 Jan 1928, Staffordshire, England. Composer; Teacher; Clarinettist. *Education:* ABSM (Performer and Teacher), ABSM (TTD), Birmingham School of Music. *Career:* Music Master, West Bromwich High School, 1950-59; Clarinet and Saxophone Teacher, School of S Mary and S Anne, Abbots Bromley, 1957-; Head of Music, March End School, 1960-66; Lecturer, West Midlands College of Higher Education, 1965-90; Senior Teacher, Wolverhampton Music School, 1968-93. *Compositions:* Back to Bach; Romance in Sepia; Suite-City Scenes; Something Blue; Suite- Chalumeau Swing; Brother Anansi and the Peacock; Models in Blue; The Pied Piper of Hamelin; Two Syncopated Dances; Boogie and Blues; Suite-Georgian Swing; Nathan's Wedding; Sweet-Talk Blues; Boogie Bounce; Song and Dance, The Buffoon; Numerous arranged and edited works, mostly for saxophone quartet or various wind instruments. *Recordings:* Something Blue; When the Saints Go Marching In and others; London Saxophone Quartet in Digital; Various other works recorded for TV and radio. *Contributor to:* Winds; Clarinet and Saxophone; Media interviews. *Memberships:* Performing Right Society; Mechanical Copyright Protection Society; Composers Guild of Great Britain; National Association of Schoolmasters/Union of Women Teachers; Clarinet and Saxophone Society; Woodwind Teachers Association; British Association of Symphonic Bands and Wind Ensembles; Schools Music Association; Musicians Union; Wolverhampton Music Society. *Hobbies:* Motoring; The canal scene; Philately. *Address:* 58 Willenhall Road, Bilston, West Midlands WV14 6NW, England.

THOMSON Brian, b. 5 Jan 1946, Sydney, New South Wales, Australia. Stage Designer. *Education:* Studied architecture in Perth. *Career:* Designed production of rock-opera Tommy in Australia, Jesus Christ Superstar and The Rocky Horror Show in London, 1972-73; Britten's Death in Venice for the State Opera of South Australia, 1980; Janáček's The Makropoulos Case for Adelaide Festival of the Arts, 1982; Designs for Australian opera have included the 1986 premiere of Voss by Richard Meale, Death in Venice, 1989, and Tristan und Isolde, 1990. *Address:* c/o Australian Opera, PO Box 291, Strawberry Hills, NSW 2012, Australia.

THOMSON Heather, b. 7 Dec. 1940, Vancouver, Canada. Opera Singer, Soprano. m. Perry Price. *Education:* Studied at the Toronto Conservatory with Herman Geiger-Torel and Irene Jessner. *Debut:* Toronto 1962, in Hansel and Gretel. *Career:* Debut: with Sadler's Wells as Micaela, also sang Mimi, (La Bohème), Marguerite, (Faust), Anne Trulove, in (Rakes Progress).

Canadian Opera Company roles include: Manon, Rosalinda (Die Fledermaus) Donnna Anna and Donna Elvira (Don Giovanni) Ellen (Peter Grimes), and world premieres of Heloise and Abelard by Wilson and Mario and The Magician by Sommers. Has sung with Welsh National Opera and the USA. Roles with New York City Opera include Violetta, La Traviata, Nedda, Pagliacci, Donna Anna and Donna Elvira (Don Giovanni), Marguerite (Faust), Rosalinda (Die Fledermaus), Agathe (Der Freischütz) 1993-94 season; Lady MacBeth, (Macbeth) in Chemnitz, Germany, Violetta (La Traviata) in Toledo, Ohio, Hanna (Merry Widow), Victoria BC and Concerts in Germany and Canada. *Recordings:* Manon in Manon for CBC-TV; Lady Billows, Albert Herring for CBC-BBC Radio; Mother, Hansel and Gretel, CBC-Radio. *Contributions to:* America's Who's Who; Canadian Encyclopedia of Music. *Honours:* Winner CBC Talent Festival and Canadian Council Awards, 1961; Winner Metropolitan Opera Auditions, 1961; Winner San Francisco Opera Auditions, 1964. *Memberships:* AGMA; ACTRA. *Current Management:* Germany: Bühnen u. Konzert Agentur, Marianne Böttger, Dahlmannstr 9, 1000 Berlin 12. James Sardos Artists Management, 180 West End Ave, New York, NY 10023, USA. *Address:* c/o Canadian Opera Co, 227 Front Street East, Toronto, Ontario, Canada M5A 1E8.

THOMSON Neil, b. 1966, London, England. Conductor. *Education:* Studied, Royal Academy of Music with George Hurst and the Royal College with Norman del Mar and Christopher Adey. *Career:* Director, Manson Ensemble at RAM, gave many performances during Henze Festival, 1988 and Messiaen Festival, 1987; Conducted major orchestral and instrumental works of Paul Patterson at venues around Britain; Founded contemporary music group, Terre Nova, 1986 (debut: St John's Smith Square); Concerts at the Purcell Room, South Bank and the Huddersfield Contemporary Music Festival; Worked with soloists such as Christopher Bunting (Dvořák's Cello Concerto and the Brahms Double Concerto, with Emanuel Hurwitz), Philip Langridge (And Suddenly It's Evening by Elisabeth Lutyens) and Philip Gammon (Saint-Saëns 2nd Concerto); Concerts with Royal Tunbridge Wells Symphony Orchestra; Music Director, Sadler's Wells Youth Ballet Workshop; Concerts with the Bombay Chamber Orchestra in India. *Honours include:* Bursary for conductors, National Association of Youth Orchestras. *Address:* c/o Norman McCann International Artists Ltd, The Coach House, 56 Lawrie Park Gardens, London SE26 6XJ, England.

THORARINSSON Jon, b. 13 Sept 1917, Iceland. Composer; Teacher; Writer on Music. m. Sigurjona Jakobsdottir, 24 Dec 1963. *Education:* Graduated Akureyri College, 1937; Reykjavik College; MMus, Yale School of Music, New Haven, Connecticut, USA; Studied with Paul Hindemith. *Career:* Musical Advisor, Icelandic State Radio, 1947-56; Head, Department of Theory and Composition, Reykjavik College of Music, 1947-68; Active in founding Icelandic Symphony Orchestra, 1950, and Chairman of its 1st Board of Directors; Programme Director, Icelandic State TV, 1968-79; Presently engaged in writing a history of music in Iceland. *Compositions:* Many songs; Children's songs, including 25 folk songs; Music for Organ; Sonata for Clarinet and Piano; Of Love and Death, song cycle for baritone and orchestra, words by C G Rossetti. *Recordings:* On tape, Icelandic Radio: Voluspa, for choir and orchestra (City of Reykjavik commission for 1100th anniversary of settlement of Iceland), 1974; Ingolfs minni (City of Reykavik commission for its 200th anniversary), 1986; Many of his songs. *Publications:* Textbook in elementary music theory, 1963; Pall Isolfsson (prominent Icelandic organist and composer), 1963; Sveinbjorn Sveinbjornsson (first professional Icelandic composer), a biography, 1969; A History of Music in Iceland, in preparation. *Contributions to:* Several articles in periodicals; Numerous articles in newspapers, including periodical musical criticism. *Honours:* Knight, 1978, Commander, 1989, Order of the Icelandic Falcon. *Memberships:* Union of Icelandic Artists, President 1951-52, 1963-66; Icelandic Composers Society. *Address:* Blonduhlid 4, 105 Reykjavik, Iceland.

THORBURN Melissa Rachel, b. 9 July 1956, Monmouth, Illinois, USA. Opera and Concert Singer (Mezzo-Soprano). m. Timothy Richard Sobolewski, 13 Apr 1985, 1 son. *Education:* BMus, Piano, 1977, BMus, Voice, 1980, Louisiana State University; Private study with Yvonne Lefebure, Paris, 1977-79; MMus, Voice, New England Conservatory, 1982. *Career:* Handel's Messiah with Philadelphia Orchestra, 1987-91, annually; Berlioz's L'Enfance du Christ with Seattle (Washington) Symphony, 1987; Gounod's Faust (Siebel), Deutsche Oper, Berlin, 1988; Pergolesi's Stabat Mater with Puerto Rico Symphony, 1988; Mozart's Le Nozze di Figaro (Cherubino), Sarasota (Florida) Opera, 1988; Gilbert and Sullivan, The Yeomen of the Guard (Phoebe), Lyric Opera of Kansas City, 1990; Mozart's Requiem with Los Angeles Philharmonic conducted by Gerard Schwarz, 1991; Handel's Messiah with National Symphony, 1992. *Recordings:* Vaughan Williams, Serenade to Music, Moss Music Group, The New York Virtuosi Chamber Symphony conducted by Kenneth Klein. *Current Management:* Thea Dispeker Inc, Artists Representative, 59 East 54th Street, New York, NY 10022, USA. *Address:* 26 Silver Thorne Drive, Williamsville, NY 14221, USA.

THORKELSDOTTOR Mist Barbara, b. 2 Aug. 1960, Urbana, Illinois, USA. Composer. m. 29 June 1984. 1 son, 1 daughter. *Education:* BA, cum laude, Composition, Hamline University, St Paul, USA, 1982; Graduate work, State University of NY at Buffalo, 1983. *Career:* Taught piano, music history; Composer of theatre music, solo, chamber and orchestral music. *Compositions:* Solo: Dans (guitar); Lif i Tuskunni (viola); Run (flute). Chamber: Thronning (piano, clarinet, cello); Danslag (guitar, voice); Smalasongvar (piano, clarinet, voice); Strings Attached (3 violins, 1 viola); Mixed choir: Scissors; Lofsongur; Varir pu hja mer. orchestra: David 116 (small orchestra & baritone solo); Fantasea (full orchestra). *Hobbies:* Music; Travelling; Family; Fishing. *Current Management:* Icelandic Music Information Centre. *Address:* Melaheidi 5, 200 Kopavogur, Iceland.

THORN Penelope, b. 19 Sept 1957, Kent, England. Singer (Soprano). *Education:* Studied at Guildhall School of Music and with Tito Gobbi in Italy. *Career:* Sang with Karlsruhe Opera from 1980 as Adriana Lecouveur, Alice Ford, Amelia (Ballo in Maschera), Princess (Rusalka), Giorgetta (Il Tabarro), Greia, Giulietta and Armida in Handel's Rinaldo (also at Barcelona); Sang at Dusseldorf and Mannheim, then appeared at Hanover from 1985 as Tosca, Abigaille and Jenůfa; Freia and Gutrune in Der Ring des Nibelungen for Deutsche Oper am Rhein; Guest appearances at Giessen in Menotti's Mara Golovin, 1986, at Bielefeld as the Forza Leonora and Asteria in Boito's Nerone, at Zurich as Santuzza and Gutrune and at Nice as Minnie in La Fanciulla del West; Has sung Senta at Freiburg, Lyon and Mannheim, Strauss's Empress at Karlsruhe and Bremen and Third Norn in Götterdämmerung at Munich Staatsoper; Appearances at Saarbrucken as Aida, Salome, Leonore, Butterfly and Elsa. *Honours include:* Winner, Voci Verdiane at Bussetto, 1985. *Address:* c/o Atholl Still Ltd, 80-86 Westrow Street, London SE19 3AF, England.

THORNTON William James, b. 31 July 1919, Birmingham, Alabama, USA. Composer; Emeritus Professor of Music. m. (1) Vivian Dyer, 11 Nov. 1939, deceased, 1981, (2) Alice Marilyn Dutcher, 3 Mar. 1984, deceased 1993, (3) Katherine Cornell, 26 Nov 1993. *Education:* PhD, University of Southern California, 1953; Student of Halsey Stevens, Ingolf Dahl, Miklos Rosza, Roger Sessions. *Career:* Instructor of Music, University of Minnesota, 1955-56; Professor of Music, Head, Department of Music, Parsons College, 1956-60; Professor of Music, 1960-88; Chairman, Department of Music, Trinity University, 1960-80, Composer-in-Residence, 1980-88, Trinity University. *Compositions:* String Quartet No 1, 1949; Serenade for winds, percussion, double bass, 1950; Sonata for violincello, piano, 1950; Symphony No 1, 1953; Sonata for piano, 1955; Three Songs of H.L.Sotten, 1957; String Quartet No 2, 1959; Contrastes Mexicanos for 2 pianos, 1959; Aperite Mihi for choir, 1959; Festive Music for orchestra,

1961; Introduction and Dance for orchestra, 1963; Serenade for flute, clarinet, strings, 1966; Sonata for harpsichord, 1966; Ceremony of Psalms for choir, soloists, organ, percussion, 1969; Sinfonia Bejar, 1976; Sonata for piano 4 hands, 1982; Solomon Songs, 1984; Water Tower Music for electro- magnetic tape, 1984; Sonata for saxophone and piano, 1985; Sonata for harp, 1986; Homage for chamber orchestra, 1987; The Grasshopper for chorus, 1987; Happy Are They for voice, flute, harp, 1988; Then, In Thy Mercy for voice and organ, 1988; Woodwind Quintet, 1992. *Address:* 15927 Alsace, San Antonio, TX 78232, USA.

THORPE Marion (née Stein), b. 1926, Vienna, Austria. Pianist; Writer; Musical Administrator; Teacher. m. (1) The Earl of Harewood; (2) Rt Hon Jeremy Thorpe, 3 sons, 1 stepson. *Education:* Private study with Franz Osborn. *Career:* Lectures; talks and interviews; Programme notes. *Publications:* Editor, Form and Performance by Erwin Stein, 1962; Classical Songs for Children, 1964; Series of 19 volumes of Piano Lessons and Pieces, The Waterman/Harewood Series, 1967- . *Memberships:* Aldeburgh Foundation; Co-founder, Leeds International Pianoforte Competition; Corporation of TCM; Chairman/M, Britten Pears Foundation. *Hobbies:* Reading; Sightseeing; Swimming. *Address:* 2 Orme Square, London, W2 4RS, England.

THURLOW Alan John, b. 18 May 1947, Woodford Green, Essex, England. Cathedral Organist. m. Christina Mary Thurlow, 10 Aug 1974. *Education:* BA, Music, Sheffield University, 1968; Emmanuel College, Cambridge, 1968-71; Fellow, Royal College of Organists, Diploma in Choir Training. *Career:* Sub-organist, Durham Cathedral, 1973-80; Organist, Master of Choristers, Chichester Cathedral, Sussex, 1980-. *Honours:* University Organ Scholar, Sheffield Cathedral, 1967-68. *Hobbies:* Walking; Swimming. *Address:* 2 St Richard's Walk, Cathedral Close, Chichester, West Sussex PO19 1QA, England.

THURMER Harvey, b. 1950, Vienna, Austria. Violinist. *Education:* Studied at the Vienna Academy of Music. *Career:* Member of the Franz Schubert Quartet 1983-90; Many concert engagements in Europe, USA, Australia, including showings in the Amsterdam Concertgebouw, the Vienna Musikverein and Konzerthaus, the Salle Gaveau Paris and the Sydney Opera House; Visits to Zurich, Geneva, Basle, Berlin, Hamburg, Rome, Rotterdam, Madrid, Copenhagen; Festival engagements include Salzburg, Wiener Festwochen, Prague Spring Schubertiade at Hohenems, the Schubert Festival at Washington DC, Belfast, Istanbul Festivals; Tours of Australasia, the USSR USA; Frequent concert tours of Great Britain; Featured in the Concerto by Spohr with the Liverpool Philharmonic in Liverpool, the Festival Hall, Wigmore Hall series includes Master Concerts, Russian Series, Summer Nights, Coffee Concerts, Performance of Alun Hoddinott's Quartet at 1989 Cheltenham Festival featured on BBC Welsh TV; Teacher at the Vienna Conservatory and Graz Musikhochschule; Masterclasses at the Royal Northern College of Music and at Lake District Summer Music. *Recordings include:* Schubert's Quartet in G, D877; Complete quartets of Dittersdorf. *Address:* c/o Christopher Tennant Management, 11 Lawrence Street, London SW3 5NB, England.

THWAITES Penelope Mary, b. 18 Apr 1944, Chester, England. Pianist; Composer. m. Edward Jackson CBE, 5 Dec 1981, 1 son, 1 daughter. *Education:* BMus, 1st class hons, Melbourne University, 1965; Postgraduate study: Piano with Albert Ferber, Composition with William Reed. *Debut:* Wigmore Hall, London, 1974. *Career:* Regular concerts and broadcasts in London; Tours on 5 continents; Concertos with leading orchestras, Australia, UK, America; Lectures, lecture recitals, TV and video appearances. *Compositions:* Ride! Ride!, 1976; Dancing Pieces, 1989; A Lambeth Garland, 1990. *Recordings:* Australian Piano Music, 1981; Percy Grainger-complete original music for 4 hands, with John Lavender, Vol I, 1989, Vol I, 1991, Vol III, 1993; Percy Grainger: Chosen Gems for Piano, solo disc, 1992;

Peggy Glanville-Hicks: Etruscan Concerto, 1993; Her own songs recorded, 1985, 1991. *Honours:* Exhibitions, Melbourne University, 1963, 1965; Medallion, International Grainger Society, 1991. *Memberships:* Grainger Society; Incorporated Society of Musicians; Performing Rights Society; MCPS; The Royal Philharmonic Society. *Hobbies:* Reading; Theatre; Conversation. *Address:* 23 Lyndale Avenue, Child's Hill, London NW2 2QB, England.

THYM Jürgen, b. 2 July 1943, Bremervörde, Germany. Musicologist. m. Peggy Dettwiler, 6 June 1992. *Education:* Diploma in School Music, Hochschule für Musik, Berlin, 1967; PhD, Musicology, Case Western Reserve University, 1974; Studies Theory and Composition with Reinhard Schwarz-Schilling, Counterpoint with Ernst Pepping, 12-tone technique with Josef Rufer, Musicology with Reinhold Brinkmann, Rudolph Stephen, Jon G Suess. *Career:* Visiting Instructor, Oberlin College, USA, 1973; Instructor, Assistant professor, Associate Professor, Professor, 1973-, Chair of Musicology, 1982-, Eastman School of Music, Rochester, New York. *Publications:* The Solo Song Settings of Eichendorff's Poems by Schumann and Wolf 1974; Translations of Kirnberger's The Art of Strict Musical Composition, 1982 and Schenker's Counterpoint, 1987; 100 Years of Eichendorff Songs 1983; Schoenberg Collected Works Edition, Vol. XIII, 1993, Vol. XIV, 1988. *Contributions to:* Articles in: Journal of Music Theory; Notes; American Choral Review; Comparative Literature; Journal of Musicological Research, Fontes Artis Musicae; Musica Realtà, Aurora (Eichendorff Year Book), others; Essays on Mendelssohn and Schumann. *Honours:* Modern Language Association Award for best review, 1979; Modern Language Association Award for best article-length bibliography, 1980; Deems-Taylor Award, American Society for Composers, Authors and Publishers, 1983. *Memberships:* American Musicological Society; Lyrica. *Hobbies:* History; Travel; Chess.

TICHOTA Jiri, b. 18 apr 1937, Tocna, Czechoslovakia. Musicologist; Lutenist; Guitarist. m. Zdenka Tichotova, 11 Nov 1976, 1 son, 1 daughter. *Education:* Student, 1960-65, PhD, Musicology (Songs and Vocal Compositions in Prague Lute Tablatures ar 1600), 1968, Faculty of Philosophy, Charles University; Self-taught instrumentalist. *Career:* Director of Spiritual Quintet ensemble, 33 years; Lutenist, Guitarist, collaborating with many soloists and orchestras; Regular appearances with Prague Madrigal Singers; Assistant Professor of Musicology, Charles University, Prague, 23 years. *Recordings:* About 25 recordings of lute or guitar solos and continuo with many Czech chamber orchestras; 11 LP's and 5 CD of Spiritual Quintet. *Publications include:* Francisco Tarrega: Work I, II, 1959; Hudba ceskych loutnovych tabulatur, 1968, 1980; Claves musicae ad fides compositae manu Nicolai Smal de Lebendorf scriptai, 1969; Papers: Deutsche Lieder in Prager Lautentabulaturen des beginenden 17 Jahrhunderts, 1967; Die Aria tempore adventus producenda, 1970; Intabulationen und tschechischer Gemeinschaftgesang an der Wende des 16 Jahrhunderts, 1970; Francouzska loutnova hudba v Cechach, 1973; Ceskobudejovicky zlomek varhanni tabulatury, 1975; Problemes d'edition des tablatures de redaction defectueuse, 1984; Die Bohemica und das bohmische Repertoire in den Tabularisen fur die Renaissance-Laute, 1984. *Memberships:* Lute Society of America; Czech Lute Society; Czech Music Society; Society of Ancient Instruments. *Hobbies:* Lepidopterology; Photography of insects. *Address:* Vzdusna 773, 14200 Prague 4, Czech Republic.

TICHY Georg, b. 9 June 1944, Vienna, Austria. Singer (Baritone). *Education:* Studied with Hilde Zadek in Vienna. *Debut:* Vienna Staatsoper 1973, in Tristan und Isolde. *Career:* Sang in Vienna in operas by Verdi, Rossini, Mozart, Puccini, Britten and Wagner; Maggio Musicale Florence 1984, as Rigoletto; Bregenz Festival 1986, as Papageno; Sang in Schubert's Fierabras and Wagner's Lohengrin, Vienna 1990; Frequent concert appearances. *Recordings:* Ariadne auf Naxos (Decca); Parsifal (Deutsche Grammophon); Alfonso und Estrella by Schubert (Pan).

TIERNEY Vivian, b. 26 Nov 1957, London, England. Singer (Soprano). *Education:* Studied at Manchester Grammar School. *Career:* Sang as principal soprano with D'Oyly Carte Opera Company; Freelance, 1982-, at first with New Sadler's Wells Opera Company in Kalman's The Gypsy Princess and Lehar's The Count of Luxembourg; Edwige in Offenbach's Robinson Crusoe for Kent Opera; Hanna Glawari in Die Lustige Witwe for Opera North; English National Opera from 1987 as Frasquita, Euridice in Orpheus in the Underworld and Regan in the UK premiere of Reimann's Lear, 1989; Sang the title role in world premiere of Robin Holloway's Clarissa, 1990; Has sung with Freiburg Opera as Lady Macbeth of Mtsensk, Ellen Orford and Giulietta (Les Contes d'Hoffmann); Has appeared in Handel's Alceste at Versailles; Mimi in La Bohème at Montpelier Festival; Euridice in Milhaud's Les Malheurs d'Orphée at Frankfurt; Donna Anna for Flanders Opera; Sang in Sullivan's cantata The Golden Legend for Colorado Springs Orchestra; Appearance with Opera 80 as Donna Anna; Marie in Wozzeck (Almeida Festival, 1988); Other roles include the Marschallin Rosenkavalier Jenny (in Mahagonny) NY, Freiburg), Rosalinde (Die Fledermaus) and Malinka (The Adventures of Mr Broucek) Mimi La Bohème for English National Opera, 1992; Gypsy Princess (Los Angeles), Sang Ellen Orford in a new production of Peter Grimes at Glyndebourne, 1992, Renata (Fiery Angel) in Freiburg, 1993; Berg's Marie for Opera North, 1993. *Address:* c/o Athole Still Ltd, Greystoke House, 80/86 Westow Street, London SE19 3AF, England.

TIKKA Kari Juhani, b. 13 Apr 1946, Siilinjärvi, Finland. Conductor. m. Eeva Relander, 18 May 1979, 3 sons, 1 daughter. *Education:* Oboe Diploma, Conducting Diploma, Sibelius Academy, Helsinki; Private studies with Arvid Jansons and Luigi Ricci. *Debut:* Helsinki, 1968. *Career:* Conductor; Tampere Theatre, 1969-70; Finnish National Opera, Helsinki, 1970-72; 1979-; Finnish Radio Symphony Orchestra, 1972-76; Royal Swedish Opera, Stockholm, 1975-77; Symphony Orchestra, Vivo, Helsinki, 1986-; Guest Conductor, Scandinavian, West and East Europe, Israel. *Compositions:* Two Aphorisms; Due Pezzi; Many songs; Cantatas; The Prodigal Son, oratorio; Concerto for Cello; Music for choir; Chamber music. *Recordings:* Triplet; Jumala on Rakkaus; Armolaulu; Triplet, Jumala on rakkaus, Armolaulu, VIVO Finlandia. *Hobby:* Spectator sports. *Current Management:* Allegro, Artist Management, Espoo, Finland. *Address:* Mannerheimintie 38A4, 00100 Helsinki 10, Finland.

TILNEY Colin b. 31 Oct 1933, London, England. Harpsichordist. *Education:* Studied harpsichord with Mary Potts at Cambridge and with Gustav Leonhardt in Amsterdam. *Career:* Soloist and ensemble player in Britain and Europe from the early 1960s; US debut 1971; Repertoire has included music by Renaissance and Baroque composers; Has performed on various clavichords, harpsichords, virginals and early pianos, employing both historical instruments and modern copies. *Recordings include:* Parthenia (collection of pieces by Byrd, Bull and Gibbons, published 1611); Complete keyboard works of Matthew Locke and the suites of Purcell and Handel; CD of Bach's Toccatas on Dorian (Conifer) label issued 1990. *Publications include:* Edition of the harpsichord music of Antoine Forqueray. *Address:* c/o Conifer Records, Horton Road, West Drayton, Middlesex UB7 8JL, England.

TIMMERMANN Leni, b. 5 Mar 1901, Witten/Ruhr, Germany. Music Teacher; Pianist (retired). m. Franz Timmermann, 26 Feb 1931, 1 son, 1 daughter. *Education:* Conservatories of Recklinghausen and Essen, Westphalian Academy of Music, Muenster, 1919-27; Final examination as a music teacher. *Career:* Music teacher and Pianist in Marl-Huels, Westphalia; Songs are played numerous times a year on Radio programmes in Germany and other countries.

Compositions: Kleine Trommler; Erster Frühling; Frühlings Willkommen; Lüdenscheider Wanderlied; Lüdenscheider Heimatlied; Eine Oma ging spazieren; Gehst du der Sonne entgegen; Der Sommer achtundsiebzig; Wir gratulieren unsrer Düsseldadt; Herrlicher Rhein; Memories of Yesteryear; Denk daran-Schön ist die Welt; Fromm sich die Blümelein neigen; Verträumtes Dämmerstündchen; Das bunte Bällchen; Bübchen muss jetzt schlafen gehn; Nun geht die Sonne zur Ruh; Wiegenlied für Julia; Draussen am Fenster; Stolzer November; Weihnachtserwartung; Leise schwebend auf Engelshänden (See descending from realms of glory); The Christmas Tree Legend (Christbaum- Legende); Miracle in Bethlehem (Wunder von Bethlehem). *Recordings:* LPs; EP, Abend sinkt leis auf die Welt, 1974; Christian Brückner liest Weihnachtsegschichten 1977; Lieder aus dem Sauerland, 1980; Miracle in Bethlehem, 1983; Gehst du der Sonne entgegen, 1983; Das bunte Bällchen, 1983; Weihnachtserwartüng, 1984; CD: Schön ist die Welt, 1988; LP/MC Lieder für Mutter und Kind, 1989; Leni Timmermann - Worte und Weisen, 1990. *Publications:* Three German Carols, 1983; Lieder Album von Leni Timmermann, 1984; Leni Timmermann; Lieder 1979. *Memberships:* GEMA; Internationaler Arbeitskreis Frau und Musik. *Address:* c/o Dr Franz Hubert Timmermann, Gerckensplatz 17, D 22339 Hamburg 63, Germany.

TINNEY Hugh, b. 28 Nov 1958, Dublin, Ireland. Pianist. *Education:* Trinity College, Dublin, 1976-79; Private Piano studies with Mabel Swainson, Louis Kentner, Bryce Morrison, Maria Curcio; LRSM Diploma, 1974. *Debut:* Purcell Room, London, 1983. *Career:* Performed Concertos, recitals in 30 countries in 4 continents; Radio Broadcasts in 12 countries; 2 Recitals for Irish TV (RTE); Concerto Appearances on Irish, Italian & Spanish TV; Recitals at Queen Elizabeth Hall, London; Musikverein, Vienna; Kennedy Center, Washington; Festivals including: Newport, Rhode Island; Granada; Prague Spring; Performances with Gulbenkian, Lisbon, Spanish National, Spanish Radio, Brazil Symphony Orchestras; Proms debut 1989 with BBC Welsh S.O. Other performances with British Orchestras such as London Philharmonic, Philharmona, Royal Philharmonic, Royal Liverpool Philharmonic, City of Birmingham, Royal Scottish. *Recordings:* Liszt Recital - Dante Sonata, Benediction de Dieu dans La Solitude; Harmonies Poétiques et Religieuses (CD and tape, Meridan), Liszt, 1993. *Honours:* Voted Best Spanish Production, by Ritmo, Spanish Classical Music Magazine, 1985; RTE Musicians of the Future Winner, 1976; Ettore Pozzoli International Piano Competition, 1983; First Prize; Benson & Hedges Threshold Award, 1984; First Prize, Paloma O'Shea International Piano Competition, 1984; Finalist, Leeds International Piano Competition, 1987; (Irish) National Entertainment and Arts Award winner, 1990. *Hobbies:* Tennis - Nestlé Schoolboy Champion of Great Britain & Ireland, 1976; Reading; Films; Swimming. *Current Management:* Christopher Tennant Artists Management. *Address:* 258.B Camden Road, London NW1 9AB, England.

TINSLEY Pauline, b. 27 Mar 1928, Wigan, England. Singer (Soprano). *Education:* Northern School of Music, Manchester; Opera School, London; Further study with Eva Turner and Eduardo Asquez. *Career:* Professional engagements in Britain from 1961 include London debut as Desdemona, Rossini's Otello; leading roles in Verdi's I Masnadieri, Ernani, Il Corsaro and Bellini's Il Pirata; Welsh National Opera from 1962 as Susanna, Elsa, Lady Macbeth, Sinaide (Rossini's Moses), Abigaille, Aida, Tosca, Turandot, Kostelnička (Jenůfa), Elektra and Dyer's Wife (Frau Ohne Schatten) 1981; Sadler's Wells/ English National Opera from 1963 as Gilda, Elvira (Ernani), Fiordiligi, Queen of Night, Countess, Donna Elvira, Beethoven's Leonore and Fidelio, Leonora (Force of Destiny), Elizabeth (Mary Stuart), 1973, Mother/ Witch (Hansel and Gretel), 1987, Kabanicha (Katya Kabanova), 1989; Covent Garden from 1965 as Overseer (Elektra), Amelia (Ballo in Maschera), 1971, Helmwige and 3rd Norn (The Ring), Santuzza, 1976, Mêre Marie (Carmélites), 1983, Lady Billows (Albert Herring), 1989; various roles with Scottish Opera

including Kostelnička (Jenůfa) and Opera North (Fata Morgana in Love for 3 Oranges) and with Handel Opera Society; From 1966, performed abroad in Germany, Netherlands, Italy, USA, Canada, Switzerland, Czechoslovakia, Spain and Belgium; concerts, recitals, broadcasts and television operas; Wexford Festival as Lady Jowler in The Rising of the Moon, 1990. *Recordings include:* Electra in Idomeneo (Philips). *Address:* c/o Music International, 13 Ardilaun Road, Highbury, London N5 2QR, England.

TINTNER Georg Bernhard, b. 22 May 1917, Vienna, Austria. Conductor; Musical Director. m. (1) Rosa Muriel Norman, 1941, 3 sons, 4 daughters, (2) Cecilia Gretel Lawrence, 30 Oct 1965, (3) Tanya Ruth Buchdahl, 27 May 1978. *Education:* Vienna Boys' Choir; Graduate in Composition and Conducting, Vienna State Academy. *Career:* Resident Coach/Conductor, Wiener Volksoper, 1938; Conductor, Auckland String Players, New Zealand, 1945-54; Conductor, Elizabethan Theatre Trust (later Australian Opera), 1954-63; Music Director, New Zealand Opera, 1964; Music Director, Cape Town Municipal Orchestra, 1967-68; Sadler's Wells, 1968-70; Music Director, West Australian Opera Company, 1971-72; Resident Conductor, Australian Opera, 1973-76; Music Director, Queensland Theatre (Philharmonic), Orchestra, 1977-87; Music Director, Resident Conductor, Symphony Nova Scotia, Canada, 1987-; Regular appearances with all Canadian, Australian and New Zealand orchestras, including Montreal and Toronto Symphonies; Regular appearances with Canadian, Australian and New Zealand opera companies; 8 seasons with National Youth Orchestra of Canada, 1971-89; Appearances, Hong Kong Philharmonic, Singapore Symphony, Bournemouth Symphony, London Symphony Orchestra, London Mozart Players, Northern Sinfonia, many others. *Recordings:* Beethoven 5th Symphony and other works with Canadian Brass, principal brass of New York Philharmonic and Boston Symphony, Philips; 1st North American performance, Bruckner 8th Symphony (1887 version), National Youth Orchestra of Canada, Jubal Records; Mozart dance music, marches; Symphony Nova Scotia, CBC Records; Music of Australia, New Zealand, Canada, Symphony Nova Scotia, CBC Records; also for Festival Records, Australia, Australian Broadcasting Corp., CBC, Broadcasting Corp. *Contributions to:* Many broadcast talks & reviews Australian Broadcasting Corp.; CBC, Broadcasting Corp. of New Zealand. *Honours:* Grosses Ehrenzeichen (Officer's Cross of the Austrian Order of Merit), 1992; Commemorative Medal for the 125th Anniversary of Canadian Confederation, 1993; Doctor of Laws (honoris causa), Dalhousie University, 1989. *Hobbies:* Gardening; Cycling. *Address:* c/o Symphony Nova Scotia, 1646 Barrington Street, Suite 401, Halifax, Nova Scotia, Canada B3J 2A3.

TIPLER Brian Archer, b. 1 Jan 1933, Manchester, England. Schoolmaster (retired). m. Vivien Tipler, 2 Apr 1966, 2 sons, 1 daughter. *Education:* Didsbury Teachers' Training College; Music education self- taught apart from music course at Teacher Training College. *Career:* Theatre, choral society, orchestral and band conducting; Lecturer for Workers Educational Association; Professional teaching in state schools and Manchester Music Service. *Compositions:* Cantatas for School Use; 3 Dance Miniatures for orchestra; These Things Shall Be for choir and brass band or orchestra; Romance, a musical play; Dreamsong and Minimarch for clarinet choir; Hymn Tunes; Magnificat for choir and optional recorders; Carols arranged for orchestra or brass; Cymanfa Ganu for male voices and brass band with audience participation; Im Alten Tirol for balalaikas and recorders; An English Rhapsody for recorder and string orchestra; Tubarondo for tuba and concert band. *Contributions to:* Competition musical crosswords to Manamag. *Memberships:* Guild of Composers of Great Britain; National Association of Schoolmasters/Union of Women Teachers. *Hobbies:* Travel; Aircraft spotting; Rugby League; Listening to music; Collecting CD's; Hymnody; Languages. *Address:* 24 Catherine Road, Bredbury Green, Romiley, Stockport, Cheshire SK6 3DH, England.

TIPPETT Michael (Kemp), (Sir), b. 2 Jan. 1905, London, England. Composer. *Education:* Stamford Grammar School; Royal College of Music (Foley Scholar; FRCM, 1961). *Career:* Ran Choral and Orchestral Society, Oxted, Surrey and taught French at Hazelwood School till 1931; Adult Education work in Music, LCC and Royal Arsenal Cooperative Society Education Departments, 1932; Director of Music, Morley College, London, 1940-51; Artistic Director, Bath Festival, 1969-74; President, Kent Opera Company, 1979-; London College of Music, 1985-; Opera, New Year, premiered Houston, 1989; Byzantium for soprano and orchestra premiered at Chicago, 1991. *Compositions include:* 5 String Quartets, 1935, 1943, 1946, 1979, 1991; 4 Piano Sonatas, 1938, 1962, 1973, 1979; Symphony No.1, 1944; Concerto for Double String Orchestra, 1939; Fantasia on a Theme of Handel, 1939-40; A Child of Our Time, Oratorio, 1941; Song Cycle, The Heart's Assurance, 1951; Opera, The Midsummer Marriage, 1952; Fantasia Concertante on a Theme of Corelli, 1953; Concerto for piano and orchestra, 1956, commissioned by City of Birmingham Symphony Orchestra; Symphony No. 2, 1957, commissioned by BBC; Opera, King Priam, commissioned by Koussevitsky Foundation of America; Praeludium, 1962; Incidental Music to The Tempest, 1962; Concerto for Orchestra, 1962-3; Choral: The Vision of Saint Augustine, 1965; The Shires Suite, 1970; Opera, The Knot Garden, 1970; Symphony No. 3, 1970-72; Opera, The Ice Break, 1977; Symphony No. 4 1976-77; Concerto for String Trio and orchestra, 1979; The Mask of Time, 1983 (commissioned by Boston Symphony Orchestra); Festal Brass with Blues, 1983, commissioned by Hong Kong Festival; Triumph for Concert Band, 1992. *Publications:* Moving Into Aquarius, 1959, revised 1974; Music of the Angels, 1980; Autobiography, Those Twentieth Century Blues, 1991. *Honours:* Cobbett Medal for Chamber Music, 1948; CBE, 1959; Kt., 1966; CH, 1979; OM, 1983; Gold Medal, Royal Philharmonic Society, 1976; Honorary Degrees from Universities in England and USA; Prix de Composition Fondation Prince Pierre de Monaco, 1984; Commandeur de L'Ordre des Arts et des Lettres, 1988. *Memberships:* Hon. Member, American Academy of Arts and Letters; Extraordinary Member, Akademie der Kunste, Berlin. *Hobby:* Walking. *Address:* c/o Schott & Company, 48 Great Marlborough Street, London W1Y 2BN, England.

TIPTON Thomas, b. 18 Nov 1926, Wyandotte, Michigan, USA. Singer (Baritone). *Education:* Studied at Michigan State College with Herbert Swanson and at Ann Arbor with Chase Baromeo. *Debut:* New York City Opera 1954, as Bob in The Old Maid and the Thief by Menotti. *Career:* Sang two seasons in New York, then visited Europe; Mannheim Opera 1960-63, Stuttgart 1964-66; Bayerisches Staatsoper Munich from 1966; Guest appearances in Vienna, Berlin and Hamburg; Salzburg Festival 1964-65; Bayreuth Festival 1967, as Wolfram, and the Herald in Lohengrin; Covent Garden 1972-74, Rigoletto; Other roles included Nabucco and Macbeth; Concert appearances in North and South America.*Publications:* Thomas Tipton ein Leben in Bildern (Munich 1987). *Address:* c/o Bayerisches Staatsoper, Postfach 745, D-8000 Munich 1, Germany.

TIRIMO Martino, b. 19 Dec 1942, Larnaca, Cyprus. Concert Pianist; Conductor. m. Mione J Teakle l973, 1 son, l daughter. *Education:* Bedales School; Royal Academy of Music, London; Vienna State Academy. *Debut:* Cyprus 1949 (recital). *Career:* Conducted La Traviata at Cyprus Festival, 1955; London debut 1965; Concert performances and recitals, TV and radio appearances, in USA, Canada, Britain and Europe from 1965; Gave public premiere of complete Schubert Sonatas, London 1975, l985; Public premiere of the Beethoven Concertos, directing from the keyboard, Dresden and London, l985, l986; Gave Danish and East German premieres of the Tippett Concerto, 1986-87. *Recordings:* Chopin; Early Schubert Sonatas; Brahms Piano Concertos; Rachmaninov Paganini Rhapsody; Rachmaninov 2nd piano concerto; Complete Debussy Solo piano works. *Honours:* Liszt Scholarship, RAM; Fifth Prize, Beethoven Competition Vienna 1965;

Gulbenkian Foundation Scholarship 1967-69; Joint Winner, Munich International Competition 1971; Winner, Geneva International Competition 1972; Silver Disc, 1988. *Hobbies:* Chess; Reading; Philosophy; Theatre; Badminton. *Address:* c/o Vivace Artist Management, 2 Combemartin Road, London SW18 5PR, England.

TISHCHENKO Boris, b. 23 Mar 1939, Leningrad, USSR. Composer. m. Irene Donskaya 1977, 3 sons. *Education:* Leningrad with Salmanov, Voloshinov and Evlachov; with Logovinsky as a pianist; Later study with Shostakovich. *Career:* Freelance composer; Pianist; Teacher at Leningrad (later St Petersburg) Conservatory 1965, Assistant professor 1980, Full Professor at Leningrad Conservatory 1986.*Compositions:* Stage: The Twelve, ballet 1963; Fly-bee, ballet 1968; The Stolen Sun, opera 1968; A Cockroach, musical comedy 1968; The Eclipse, ballet 1974. Orchestral: 6 Symphonies 1961-1988; 1st Violin Concerto 1958; Piano Concerto 1962; 1st Cello Concerto 1963; Sinfonia Robusta 1970; Concerto for flute, piano and strings 1972; Harp Concerto 1977; 2nd Cello Concerto, 1969; 2nd Violin Concerto 1981; Concerto allamarcia for 16 soloists, 1989; Symphony The Siege Chronicle 1984; Vocal: Lenin is Alive, cantata 1959; Requiem to text by Akhmatova 1966; To my Brother for soprano, flute and harp 1986; The Will for soprano, harp and organ, 1986; Garden of Music, cantata in 2 parts 1987; Chamber music including 5 String Quartets 1957-84; Quintet for strings and piano 1985; 9 Piano sonatas, 1957-92; 2 sonatas for violin solo, 1957, 75; 2 sonatas for cello solo 1960, 1979; Dog Heart, novelettes for chamber ensemble, 1988; Incidental music for plays; Concerto for clarinet and piano trio, 1990; Vocal cycles, Music for films, Orchestral suites; Pieces for different instruments, songs, works for chorus a capella; 2 Piano Suites, 1957; The Chelom Wise Men, a vocal instrumental quartet for violin, soprano, bass and piano. Words by O Driz, 1991; Twelve Inventions for organ, 1964; Twelve portraits for organ, 1992; The French Symphony, 1958-1993; Orchestrations: K Monteverdi, Coronation of Poppea, 1967; D Shostakovich, Satires, words by S Chorny, 1980; Four Poems by Captain Lebjadkin, words by F Dostoevsky, 1986; Antiformalistic Little Paradise, 1989; E Grieg: four Romasces, 1991; G Mahler: 7 songs, 1993; S Prokofiev: 3 choruses, 1972. *Honours:* 1st prize, on the International Contest of Young Composers in Prague, 1966; State prize of Russian Federation named by Glinka, 1978; The title, People's Artist of Russia, 1987. *Hobbies:* Reading; Travelling; Walking; Nature. *Address:* Rimsky-Korsakov Avenue, 79-10, St Petersburg 190121, Russia.

TITTERINGTON David Michael, b. 10 Jan 1958, Oldham, England. Concert Organist. *Education:* BA (Hons), 1980, Organ Scholar, 1977-81, Pembroke College, Oxford; Conservatoire National de Rueil-Malmaison, Paris, 1982-85; Premier Prix d'Orgue, 1984; Prix Excellence, 1985. *Debut:* Royal Festival Hall, 1986. *Career:* Recitals in Cathedrals, Halls throughout UK; Concert Tours of Germany, Scandinavia, France, USA, Far East & Australia; Appearances at Major International Festivals (Hong Kong, Harrogate, Istanbul, Adelaide, Sydney, Brighton); Concert Halls (Wigmore Hall, Royal Festival Hall, Herkules Saal, Munich, Academy for Performing Arts, Hong Kong); TV appearances on BBC2 and Anglia TV; Professor of Organ, Royal Academy of Music, London, 1990-; Concertos with Orchestras, Berlin Symphony; BBCSSO; City of London Sinfonia; English Sinfonia. *Recordings:* Messiaen: La Nativité du Seigneur (Hyperion Records), also recordings for BBC Radio 3 and BBC Television, 1986, Danish Radio, Austrian Radio, German Radio, Australian Radio; Petr Eben's Job, for Multisonic; César Franck, complete works, BBC.. *Publications:* Edited Works of Petr Eben; Editor, Organ works published by United Music Publishers, London. *Honours:* Premier Prix d'Orgue, 1984; Prix d'Excellence, 1985, Conservatoire National de Rueil-Malmaison, Paris; Ian Fleming Music Award (joint winner), 1983; Craxton Memorial Award, 1983; British Council Scholarship, 1983-84; Arts Council of Great Britain Bursary, 1984; Honorary Fellow, Bolton Institute of Higher Education, 1992. *Hobbies:* Silence;

Reading; Going out to Dinner. *Address:* c/o Clarion/ Seven Muses, 47 Whitehall Park, London N19 3TW, England.

TITUS Alan, b. 28 Oct 1945, New York City. Singer (Baritone). *Education:* Studied with Askel Schiotz at the Colorado School of Music and with Hans Heinz at Juilliard. *Debut:* Washington DC 1969, in La Bohème. *Career:* Sang the Celebrant in the premiere of Bernstein's Mass at Washington DC, 1971; New York City Opera 1972, in Summer and Smoke; European debut Amsterdam 1973, Debussy's Pelléas; Metropolitan Opera I976, as Harlekin in Ariadne auf Naxos; Glyndebourne 1979, as Guglielmo; Deutsche Oper am Rhein Dusseldorf 1984, Don Giovanni; Santa Fe 1985 in Intermezzo by Strauss; Engagements in Aix-en-Provence, Hamburg and Frankfurt; Meggio Musicale Florence 1987, as Olivier in Capriccio; Sang Dandini at San Francisco 1987, Munich as Valentin (sang in Mathis der Maler 1989); Bologna 1990, as Storch in the Italian premiere of Intermezzo; Sang Kovalyov in The Nose by Shostakovich at Frankfurt, 1990; Season 1992/93 in Arabella at La Scala, title role in Donizetti's II Duca d'Alba at Spoleto, and Hans Sachs at Frankfurt. *Recordings include:* Haydn's La Fedeltà Premiata (Philips); La Bohème (Orfeo); L'Elisir d'Amore; Don Giovanni La Wally, Le Nozze di Figaro, Falstaff, Paradies und die Peri (RCA); La Bohème and Genoveva (Orfeo); Carmen (Naxos). *Address:* c/o L S Artists, Lydia Störle, Orlando strasse 8, 8000 München 2, Germany.

TITUS Graham, b. 15 Dec 1949, Newark, Nottinghsamshire, England. Singer (Baritone). *Education:* MA Clare College Cambridge University (Organ Scholar); FRCO; Cologne Musikhochschule. *Debut:* Purcell Room, London, 1974. *Career:* Appearances with New Opera Company, Handel Opera, English National Opera; Radio recitals from 1974; Dutch TV and radio; Concert tour of South America; Recital and Oratorio work throughout Britain, including the Aldeburgh Festival 1975; Glyndebourne Festival 1979, Guglielmo. *Honours:* Winner, Young Musicians 1974; Winner, s'Hertogenbosch Competition, 1977. *Hobbies:* Gardening; Psychic Phenomena. *Address:* c/o English National Opera, St Martin's Lane, London WC2.

TOCZYSKA Stefania, b. 19 Feb 1943, Gdansk, Poland. Singer (Mezzo-Soprano). *Education:* Gdansk Conservatory with Barbara Iglikovska. *Debut:* Danzig 1973, as Carmen. *Career:* Sang in Poland as Azucena, Leonora in La favorite and Dalila; Western debut 1977 as Amneris at Basle Opera; Vienna Staatsoper 1977 as Ulrica in Un Ballo in Maschera: returned as Carmen and as Verdi's Azucena, Eboli and Preziosilla; Munich and Hamburg 1979, as Eboli in Don Carlos; San Francisco Opera as Laura in La Gioconda, Amneris, and in Roberto Devereux; Royal Opera Covent Garden 1983-84, as Azucena and Amneris; Bregenz Festival and Chicago Lyric Opera 1986, as Giovanna Seymour in Anna Bolena; Houston Opera 1987, as Adalgisa and Amneris; Barcelona 1987 and Hamburg 1990, as Venus in Tannhäuser; Sang Laura in La Gioconda at the Metropolitan, 1989; Washington Opera and Houston 1990, as Amneris and Dalila; appeared in Aida at the Caracalla Festival, Rome, July 1990; Season 1992 as Azucena at Munich, Massenet's Dulcinée at Toulouse, Donizetti's Maria Stuarda at Barcelona and Carmen at the Munich Festival. *Address:* c/o Harrison/Parrott Ltd., 12 Penzance Place, London W11 4PA, England.

TODA Kunio, b. 11 Aug 1915, Tokyo, Japan. Composer. *Education:* Graduated, Tokyo University, 1938, studied composition with Saburo Moroi in Tokyo; Further study of 12-tone technique after the War. *Career:* Diplomat in Far East until 1964; Professor at Toho Gakuen School of Music, 1964-76, Senzoku Gakuen College, 1977-88. *Compositions include:* Operas: Akemi, Tokyo, 1956; St Paul, mystery play, Tokyo, 1973; The Story of Kyara City, Tokyo, 1973; Anna the Maid, monodrama, Tokyo, 1978; Kesa and Morito, Tokyo, 1980; Orchestra: Legend, symphonic fantasy, 1944; 2 Piano Concertos, 1944, 1955; Symphony in G, 1953; Concerto Grosso, 1968; Chamber: Piano Trio,

1947; Violin Sonata, 1957; Bassoon Sonata, 1966; Vocal: O'Shichi the Prisoner, mono-cantata, 1981; Song of Lute for soprano and piano, 1982; Song of River for mezzo-soprano, baritone and orchestra, 1989; Piano music, choruses and songs. *Address:* JASRAC (Japan), c/o PRS Ltd Member Registration, 29-33 Berners Street, London W1P 4AA, England.

TODISCO Nunzio, b. 1942, Italy. Singer (Tenor). *Career:* Has sung from 1970 in Italy and at Orange, Lisbon, Rome and Zurich; US debut San Francisco 1978, as Pollione in Norma; In 1989 sang Loris in Fedora at the Metropolitan Opera and in Naples; Verona Arena 1989, as Ismaele in Nabucco; Other roles include Verdi's Carlo (I masnadieri), Foresto (Attila), Arrigo (La battaglia di Legnano), Manrico, Ernani and Radames, Puccini's Dick Johnson, Luigi and Cavaradossi, and Licinius in La Vestale by Spontini; Sang Ismaele at Verona, 1992. *Address:* c/o Arena di Verona, Piazza Brà 28, 1-37121 Verona, Italy.

TODOROV Nedyalcho Geogiev, b. 27 Oct 1940, Plovdiv, Bulgaria. Professor. m. Todorova Veneta Assenova, 26 Nov 1967, 1 son, 1 daughter. *Education:* MA, State Academy of Music, Sofia, 1967; Gnessini State Music Paedogogy Institute, Moscow, 1973-74. *Career:* Violin Teacher, Secondary School of Music, Plovdiv, 1964-67; Violin Professor, 1967, Deputy-Rector, 1979-83, Rector, 1979-1983, Academy of Music, Plovdiv; First violinst, Plovdiv Chamber Orchestra, 1969-73; Director, Plovdiv Philharmony, 1970-72; First violinst: Plovdiv Philharmony Orchestra, 1976-79, Plovdiv String Quartet, 1978-; Director, Educational Department, Ministry of Culture, Sofia, 1983-91; Concert performer (recitals, concerts as soloist with orchestra, chamber music concerts) during all that time; Repertoire: Concertos (Bach, Mozart, Beethoven, Mendelssohn, Bruch, Hindemith, Shostakovich, V Stoyanov, others), sonatas (Händel, Bach, Mozart, Beethoven, Schubert, Brahms, Frank, Debussy, Ravel, Hindemith, Prokoviev, D Nenov, K Iliev, A Raychev, P Stoyanov, N Stoykov, N Stoykov, others), pieces (Mozart, Beethoven, Schubert, Paganini, Sarasate, Dvořák, Tchaikovsky, Kreisler, Prokofiev, Shostakovich, Messiaen, P Vladigerov, L Pipkov, V Kazandjiev, others), duos, trios, quartets (Boccherini, Haydn, Mozart, Beethoven, Schubert, Brahms, Bartok, Prokofiev, Shostokovich, M Goleminov, I Spassov, N Stoykov, others) *Publications:* 1st performances, recordings, editions (pieces for violin and piano, duos for 2 violins and chamber ensembles by modern Bulgarian composers, 6 vols, Sofia, 1977, 1979, 1980, 1984, 1986, 1988; Recordings, editions (collections of classical concertso for oboe and violin), Sofia, 1990; Editor, Guide (Catalogue), Bulgarian Violin Literature, Sofia, 1992. *Honours:* Order of Cyril and Methodius; The Golden Lyre of the Union of Bulgaria; Distinguished Service Order. *Memberships:* EMU; National Competition of Young Instrumentails and Singers; Union of Scientific Works in Bulgaria; Union of Bulgarian Musicians. *Hobbies:* Numismatics; Chess. *Address:* Computer Hippodrome, Block 139, Entyr A, Apt 33, 1612 Sofia, Bulgaria.

TOKODY Ilona, b. 27 Apr 1953, Szeged, Hungary. Singer (Soprano). *Career:* Has sung at the Hungarian National Opera from 1973; Engaged at Bratislava and the Vienna Staatsoper from 1978; Further appearances in Munich, Hamburg, Leningrad, Moscow, Prague, Naples, Barcelona and Cologne; Covent Garden debut 1986, as Mimi; San Diego 1986 as Desdemona, singing the same role in Los Angeles, 1989; Boston 1989, as Mimi; Other roles include Violetta, Tosca, Asteria in Boito's Nerone, Rachel in La Juive, Suor Angelica, Giselda (I Lombardi), Leonora in II Trovatore and La Forza del Destino and Puccini's Lauretta, Liu and Butterfly; Sang the Trovatore Leonora at Madrid, 1992. *Recordings include:* Suor Angelica, Nerone, La fedeltà premiata by Haydn, Strauss's Guntram, Hunyadi Laszlo by Erkel and La Fiamma by Respighi (Hungaroton); Mascagni's Iris (CBS). *Address:* c/o Allied Artists, 42 Montpelier Square, London SW7 1JZ, London, England.

TOLEDO Josefino Chino Javier, b. 6 Mar 1959,

Manila, Philippines. Conductor; Composer; Musical Director; Teacher. m. Ma. Immaculada Concepcion Ramos, 18 Oct 1986. 1 daughter. *Education:* BMus. in Composition, University of the Philippines, 1979; MMus. in Composition, Cleveland Institute of Music, 1986. *Career:* Faculty Member: University of the Philippines; Musical Director and Conductor: Siena-Letran Chorale, 1983; UP Percussion Ensemble, 1983; Manila Symphony Orchestra, 1985; Company Director, Score! Music Consultant Co., 1987; Chairman, Department of Theory and Composition, University of the Philippines, College of Music, 1990-. *Compositions:* UG-NAY for Orchestra, 1984; Tulâ-li for 2 Flutes; Zng Ug-Og, for wind and percussion ensemble, 1986; Aliw-iw for 8 Sopranos and 4 Percussions, 1985; For Edwin Thumboo and All of Us Who Suffer Through English In Asia, for Soprano, Oboe, Clarinet, Vibraphone, Cello, 1986; Kulambo: Isang Kayumangging, Puntod, for Chorus and Orchestra, 1986; Kah-non, for orchestra, 1987; Musika Para Sa..., for chamber ensemble, 1988: 1. Ako ang Daigdig (for chorus); At Maging Ang Kwerdas, violin solo, 1990; ABE..., music for dance, 1993; Komiks, 3 act ballet, 1993. *Honours:* UPIP, Professional Chair in Composition, University of the Philippines; Asian Cultural Council Grant in Composition; ASCAP-Raymund Hubbel Award in Composition; French Government Scholarship in Composition; Young Artists of the Philippines; several prizes from the League of Filipino Composers-Young Composers Competition. *Current Management:* Score Music Management, 83 Union Civica Street, Galas, Quezon City. *Address:* University of the Philippines, College of Music Diliman, Quezon City, Philippines.

TOLL John, b. 1947, England. Organist; Harpsichordist. *Career:* Keyboard player and repertoire researcher for the Bournemouth Symphony Orchestra and Bournemouth Sinfonietta; Founder-member of London Baroque, with whom he visited 20 countries; Regular appearances with the Taverner Players, London Classical Players and the Academy of Ancient Music; Director, Early Music Department, Royal Academy of Music; As member of Musica Secreta has performed at the Early Music Centre Festival, the Lufthansa Festival of Baroque Music and at the National Gallery; Early Music Network tour of Britain Nov 1991 with programme Filiae Jerusalem (sacred music for women's voices by Monteverdi, Carissimi, Cavalli, Viadana, Grandi and Marco de Gagliano); Other repertoire includes works by Marenzio, Wert, Luzzaschi, Luigi Rossi and the women composers Francesca Caccini and Barbara Strozzi; Participation in lecture-recitals and workshops on performance practice and ornamentation. *Recordings include:* 15 albums with London Baroque. *Address:* Robert White Management, 182 Moselle Avenue, London N22 6EX, England.

TOMASZEWSKI Rolf, b.18 Mar 1940, Deutzen, Leipzig, Germany. Singer (Bass). *Education:* Studied in Dresden with Johannes Kemter. *Debut:* Wittenberg 1959, as Baculus in Der Wildschütz by Lortzing. *Career:* Teacher until 1971, then sang in opera at Dresden-Radebeul 1971-75; Performances at the Dresden Staatsoper and elsewhere in Germany from 1975, as Sarastro, Osmin, the Commendatore, Don Alfonso, Kaspar in Der Freischütz, the Landgrave (Tannhäuser), King Henry in Lohengrin and buffo roles; Many concert appearances. *Address:* c/o Semper-Oper, Dresden 01067, Germany.

TOMLINSON John, b. 22 Sept 1946, Oswaldtwistle, Lancashire, England. Operatic Bass. m. Moya Joel, 1969, 1 son, 2 daughters. *Education:* BSc, Civil Engineering, Manchester University, England; Royal Manchester College of Music. *Career:* Since beginning career with Glyndebourne in 1970, has sung over 100 operatic bass roles with English National Opera and Royal Opera House, Covent Garden and in Geneva, Lisbon, Milan, Paris, Stuttgart, San Diego, Vancouver (Hagen and Hunding), San Francisco, Bordeaux, Aix-en-Provence, Avignon and Copenhagen; English National Opera from 1975 as Masetto, Wagner's Pogner, Fasolt and Mark, Bluebeard (Bartók), Moses

(Rossini), Mephistopheles, Padre Guardiano and Baron Ochs; Bayreuth Festival, 1988 as Wotan in Das Rheingold and Die Walküre; Sang the Wanderer in Siegfried 1989; Opera North 1991, as Attila; Covent Garden 1991, as Hagen and as the Green Knight in the premiere of Birtwistle's Gawain; Sang in the Reginald Goodall Memorial Concert, London 1991; Season 1992/93 as Boris Godunov for Opera North, Wotan and Wanderer at Bayreuth and Gurnemanz at the Berlin Staatsoper; Season 1993/94 as Hans Sachs at Covent Garden, Baron Ochs for ENO and Wotan in a new production of The Ring at Bayreuth. *Recordings:* Roles in Donizetti's Maria Stuarda, Handel's Hercules, Rameau's Naïs, Thomas'Hamlet, Martinů's Greek Passion and Verdi's Macbeth. *Address:* c/o Music International, 13 Ardilaun Road, Highbury N5 2QR, England.

TOMOWA-SINTOW Anna, b. 22 Sept 1943, Stara Zagora, Bulgaria. Singer (Soprano). *Education:* Studied at the Sofia Conservatory with Zlatew-Tscherkin. *Debut:* Stara Zagora as Tatiana in Eugene Onegin. *Career:* Leipzig 1967, as Abigaille in Nabucco; Berlin 1972, as Butterfly: member of the company 1972-76; Discovered by Karajan and sang in the premiere of De Temporum fine Comoedia by Orff (Salzburg 1973); Appearances in Milan, Brussels, Munich, San Francisco and London (Covent Garden debut 1975, Fiordiligi); Salzburg Easter and Summer Festivals 1976, as Elsa and Countess Almaviva; Vienna Staatsoper from 1977; Metropolitan Opera from 1978, as Donna Anna, Elsa, Aida, the Marschallin and Amelia Boccanegra; Salzburg 1983, as the Marschallin; Paris Opéra 1984, Elisabeth in Tannhäuser; Salzburg 1987-89, as Donna Anna and Tosca; Sang in Der Rosenkavalier at Florence 1989, Chicago 1990; appeared as Yaroslavna in a new production of Prince Igor at Covent Garden, 1990; Season 1992/93 as Tosca at Helsinki and Strauss's Helen in Athens. *Recordings:* Beethoven's 9th Symphony and Missa Solemnis, Verdi Requiem, Ein Deutsches Requiem; De Temporum fine Comoedia, Don Giovanni, Der Rosenkavalier (Deutsche Grammophon); Mozart's Requiem and Coronation Mass, Bruckner Te Deum, Lohengrin (EMI); Le Nozze di Figaro (Decca); Ariadne auf Naxos; Die Frau ohne Schatten, Covent Garden, 1992; Salzburg, Barcelona, Berlin and Vienna; Capriccio, 1985, 1986, 1990; Also recordings with H von Karajan 4 Last Songs and Capriccio/Strauss, (Deutsche Gramaphone; Most recent recordings with Decca: Korugold, Das Wunder der Heliane. *Honours:* Prize-winner, International Competition, Sofia, 1970; Winner, Rio de Janeiro Competition, 1971; Made Kammersangerin in Berlin. *Address:* c/o Royal Opera House, Covent Garden, London WC2.

TOOLEY John, (Sir) b. 1 June 1924, Rochester, Kent, England. Theatre Administrator. m. (1) Judith Craig Morris, 1951 (dissolved 1965) 3 daughters, (2) M. Patricia Janet Norah Bagshawe, 1968, 1 son. *Education:* Repton School; Magdalene College, Cambridge. *Career:* Served the Rifle Brigade, 1943-47; Secretary to Guildhall School of Music, 1952-55; Assistant to General Administrator, 1955-60, Assistant General Administrator, 1960-70, General Administrator, 1970-80, General Director, 1980-87, Royal Opera House, Covent Garden, London; Governor, The Royal Ballet and The Royal Ballet School, also Repton School; Director, Royal Opera House Trust. *Honours:* Commendatore, Italian Republic, 1976; Knighted by Her Majesty the Queen's Birthday Honours List, 1979; Honorary Fellow, Royal Academy of Music and Honorary Member, Guildhall School of Music and the Royal Northern College of Music. *Memberships:* Garrick Club; Arts. *Hobbies:* Walking; Theatre. *Address:* 2 Mart Street, London WC2, England.

TOOPS Gary Charles, b.15 Sept 1944, Oakland, California, USA. Educator; Concert Organist. m. Jennifer Fog, 27 Jan 1984. *Education:* BA, University of California, 1966; MMus, University of the Pacific, 1968; ChM, Amerigan Guild of Oragnists. Master classes with John Walker, Pierre, Cocherean, E Power Biggs and Virgil Fox. *Debut:* Piedmont, California, 1963. *Career:*

Professor of Music and College Organist, Mt San Antonio College, CA; Artistic Director, The Festival Singers; Concert Organ Recital Tours throughout California, New England, and South Korea. *Compositions:* Commissioned by Gary Toops from Daniel E Gauthrop, Rodomontade for organ, 1991; From William Thomas McKinley, Untitled, for organ and orchestra, 1994. *Memberships:* American Guild of Organists; American Theatre Organ Society; College Music Society. *Hobbies:* Photography. *Address:* 1010 Oxford Street, Claremont, CA 91711, USA.

TOOVEY Andrew, b. 1962, England. Composer. *Education:* Studied at the Universities of Surrey and Sussex with Jonathan Harvey and at Dartington with Morton Feldman. *Career:* Music has been performed by Alan Hacker, Michael Finnissy, the Mistry Quartet and the Endimion Ensemble; Director of Ixion (founded 1987) giving performances of works by Cage, Feldman, Ferneyhough, Finnissy, James Dillon and Xenakis. *Compositions:* Chamber and ensemble: Winter Solstice, 1984; String quartet 1985; Cantec for Viola and piano 1986; Ate 1986; Shining for violin and cello 1987; Shining Forth 1987; Shimmer Bright for string trio 1988; White Fire 1988; Snow Flowers 1988; Black Light 1989; An die Musik, 1989; Adam 1989; Solo instruments: Veiled Wave 1 and 2, for flute and for clarinet, 1985; Artaud for piano 1986; Fragments after Artaud 1988; Lament, Strathspey, Reel for violin, 1988; Out Jumps Jack Death and Down There by the Sea, for piano, 1989; UBU, Opera in two acts, (five scenes), 1990-92; The Juniper Tree, Opera in one act (4 scenes), 1993. *Recordings:* Albums on the Musica Nova label include Artaud and Out Jumps Jack Death. *Honours include:* Tippett Prize for Untitled String Quartet; Terra Nova Prize for Ate; Bernard Shore Composition Award for Cantec; Young Concert Artists Trust Associate composer, 1993-. *Address:* 57B Station Road, Willesden, London NW10 4UX, England.

TÖPPER Hertha, b. 19 Apr 1924, Graz, Austria. Singer (Mezzo-Soprano). *Education:* Studied at the Graz Conservatory. *Debut:* Graz 1945, as Ulrica in Un Ballo in Maschera. *Career:* Sang in Graz 1945-51; Munich Staatsoper from 1951, notably in the 1957 premiere of Hindemith's Die Harmonie der Welt; Bayreuth Festival from 1951 as Brangaena and Fricka; Visited Covent Garden with Munich Company 1953, as Clairon in Capriccio; San Francisco 1960 and Metropolitan Opera 1962, as Octavian in Der Rosenkavalier; Munich 1972, in the premiere of Isang Yun's Sim Tjong; Other roles included Verdi's Eboli and Amneris, Mozart's Dorabella, Magdalena in Die Meistersinger and Nancy in Martha; retired from stage, 1981; Often heard in sacred music by Bach; Professor at the Munich Musikhochschule from 1971. *Recordings:* Die Meistersinger; Blueabeard's Castle; Oedipus Rex; Schoenberg's Gurrelieder; Bach's B Minor Mass; Der Rosenkavalier. *Address:* c/o Bayerische Staatsoper, Postfach 745, D-8000 Munich 1, Germany.

TORKE Michael, b. 22 Sept 1961, Milwaukee, Wisconsin, USA. Composer; Pianist. *Education:* Graduated Eastman School of Music, Rochester, 1984. *Career:* Prix de Rome and Koussevitsky Foundation Award; Commissions from New York City Ballet and the Huddersfield Festival; European perfomances with the Danish Radio Symphony Orchestra, the Ensemble InterContemporain, London Sinfonietta and Lontano; As pianist has recorded on several labels. *Compositions:* Laetus for piano solo, 1982; Ceremony of Innocence for flute, clarinet, violin, cello and piano, 1983; Ecstatic Orange for ensemble, 1984; Vanada for keyboards, brass and percussion, 1984; The Yellow Pages, 1984; Bright Blue Music for ensemble, 1985; Verdant Music for ensemble, 1986; The Directions, 1-act opera based on The Yellow Pages, 1986; Adjustable Wrench for ensemble, 1987; Black and White for wind instruments, percussion and synthesizer, 1988; Copper for brass quintet and orchestra 1988; Ash for orchestra or Chamber orchestra 1989; Slate for concertante group and orchestra (ballet) 1989; Rust for piano and wind

instruments 1989. *Address:* c/o Boosey & Hawkes Ltd, 295 Regent Street, London W1R 8JH, England.

TORP Lisbet, b. 27 Jan 1949, Copenhagen, Denmark. Ethnomusicologist; Ethno-Choreologist. m. Kurt Larsen, 2 sons. *Education:* Royal Danish Academy of Music. *Career:* Lecturer, Royal Danish Academy of Educational Studies, 1972-87; Adjudicator for the International Festival for Traditional Music and Dance in Middlesborough, Cleveland, UK; Chairman, Danish National Committee, ICTM, 1986-; Co-chairman, Study group for Ethno-choreology under ICTM, 1986-; Member, Executive Board of I.C.T.M., 1987-; Freelance producer, Danish Radio, several programmes on traditional music of Balkan countries in general, & Greece in particular, 1979-87; A series of programmes for the Swiss and the German Radios, 1987-88; Research Fellowship, University of Copenhagen, project: An Urban Milieu and its Means of Expression - A Case Study of the Rebetika (Greece). *Publications:* Major work: Chain and Round Dance Patterns - A Method for Structural Analysis and its application to a European material. *Address:* Kaersangervej 23, 1.Th, DK-2400 Copenhagen, Denmark.

TORRES-SANTOS Raymond, b. 19 June 1958, Puerto Rico. Composer; Arranger; Keyboardist; Conductor; Music Educator. *Education:* BA, Puerto Rico University and Conservatory of Music, 1980; MA 1982, PhD 1986, University of California, Los Angeles; Ferienkurse fur Neue Musik, 1982; CCRMA, Stanford University, 1985; Centro di Sonologia Computazionale, 1988. *Career:* Arranger, Music Director, for best American singers & entertainers; Composer of film music, studio musician in Hollywood; Professor, California State University, San Bernardino, 1986-91; Chairman of Music Department, University of Puerto Rico, 1991-93; Chancellor, Puerto Rico Conservatory of Music, 1994-. *Compositions include:* Sinfonieta Concertante for orchestra, 1980; Summertime, clarinet consort, 1982; Exploraciones for string orchestra, 1982; Areytos: a Symphonic Picture, 1985; Enchanted Island, piano & tape, 1986; Monchin del Alma: Ballet, 1988; El Pais de los Cuatro Pisos: a Symphoonic Overture, 1988; Viaggio Senza Destinazione for tape, 1988; La Cancion de las Antillas: a Symphonic Poem, for Wind Quintet, 1992. Performed and/or commissioned by the Casals Festival, Inter-American University, Youth Symphony of the Americas, San Juan Ballet and Pops Orchestra; Symphony Orchestra from Puerto Rico, Virginia, Pacific, Northwestern University and UCLA. *Recordings:* 15, as arranger and/or conductor. *Address:* PO Box 361743, San Juan, Puerto Rico 00936-1743, USA.

TORTELIER Yan Pascal, b. 19 Apr 1947, Paris. Conductor. m. Sylvie Brunet-Moret, 1970, 2 sons. *Education:* Paris Conservatoire, general musical studies with Nadia Boulanger; conducting studies with Franco Ferrara. *Career:* Principal Conductor BBC Philharmonic, 1992-; Principal Conductor and Artist Director Ulster Orchestra, N.I. 1989-92; Leader and Associate Conductor Orchestre du Capitole in Toulouse, 1974-83. Has conducted all the major British orchestras and toured extensively in the USA, Canada, Japan, Australia, Scandinavia, Eastern and Western Europe. Opera debut 1978. *Recordings:* Numerous recordings including complete symphonic works of Debussy and Ravel with Ulster Orchestra and highly acclaimed series of Hindemith and Henri Dutilleux with BBC Philharmonic. Currently exclusive to Chandos Records. Earlier recordings for EMI, Virgin, and Philips. *Publications:* Première orchestration of Ravel's Piano Trio 1992 published by Durand. *Honours:* Honorary Doctorate of letters, University of Ulster, 1992. *Address:* c/o Intermusica Artists' Management, 16 Duncan Terrace, London N1 8BZ, England.

TORZEWSKI Marek, b. 1960, Poland. Singer (Tenor). *Education:* Studied at the Poznan Academy of Music. *Debut:* Lodz Opera 1984 as Edgardo in Lucia di Lammermoor. *Career:* Sang in Idomeneo at the Théâtre de la Monnaie Brussels, 1984; Appearances in La Finta

Giardiniera at Vienna, Salzburg, Amsterdam, Berlin and New York, 1985; Further engagements at Brussels and in Hamburg, Montpellier, Philadelphia and Lausanne; Season 1989-90 in L'Incoronazione di Poppea in Paris, Rosenkavalier, Cosi fan Tutte and Fierabras by Schubert in Brussels, Don Ottavio at Toulouse and Glyndebourne Festival debut as Fenton in Falstaff; Season 1991-92 as Tamino at Lausanne, Alfredo for Scottish Opera and the Mozart Requiem under Muti at Le Scala, Milan; Debut with the Berlin Philharmonic 1992, singing in Nono's Il Canto Sospeso, under Abbado; Opera National de Lisbon, Eugene Onegin - Lenski, Staatsoper Leipzig, Così fan tutte - Ferrando, 1993; Théâtre Municipal de Lausanne, Iphigénie en Tauride - Pylade, 1994. *Recordings include:* Il Canto Sospeso (Deutsche Grammophon). *Address:* c/o John Coast Ltd, 31 Sinclair Road, London W14 0NS, England.

TOTENBERG Roman, b. 1 Jan 1911, Lodz, Poland. Violinist; Conductor. m. 30 July 1941, 3 daughters. *Education:* Baccalaureat, Warsaw; Chopin School, Warsaw; Gold Medal (Mendelssohn Prize), College of Music, Berlin. *Debut:* 1922. *Career:* Soloist, most major orchestras, Europe, USA, S. America; BBC International Concert TV; Director, Radio, Ch.M., WQXK, New York; Director, Longy School of Music; Professor, Boston University; Director, Kneisel Hall Festival; Professor, Aspen and Salzburg Festivals. *Compositions:* UGR, Beethoven, Szymanowski Concertos, 1992. *Recordings:* Bach - all Sonatas and Partitas; Schumann Sonatas; German Baroque Concerti; Brahms & Lipinksi; Concertos; Bloch Concerto, Vangard, 1992. *Contributions to:* Various publications including Gustave Reese Compendium. *Honours:* Wieniawski Medal, 1976; Artist of the Year (American String Society), 1982; Ysaye Medal, 1966; Medal of Cultural Contribution to Poland (Polish Government, 1989). *Membership:* St Botolph Club (Boston). *Hobbies:* Photography; Sports; Chess. *Current Management:* Walter Pierce (Wang Centre), Boston, USA. *Address:* 329 Waverley Avenue, Newton, MA 02158, USA.

TOUCHIN Colin Michael, b. 3 Apr 1953, Liverpool, England. Composer; Conductor; Performer (clarinet & recorder); Teacher. *Education:* BA, Music, Keble College, Oxford, 1974; MA, 1980; Cert in Education, Manchester Univ Dept of Education, 1975; Recorder Performers Diploma, LTCL, 1969; Studied Clarinet with Graham Turner. *Career:* Staff Tutor, Stockport Recorder College, 1974-82; Staff Tutor, Stockport Youth Orchestra, 1976-79; Conductor, Trafford Youth Training Orchestra & Wind Band, 1978-82; Tutor 1982-, Head of Composition 1987-, Chetham's School of Music, Manchester; Musical Director, Gorton Philharmonic Society, 1982-; Conductor, King Edward Musical Society, Macclesfield, 1984-; Conductor, North Staffordshire Symphony Orchestra, 1987-; Member of Heriot Trio, 1985-. *Compositions:* Hilarion, oratorio-requiem, 1988; Topaz, 1987; Ode to St Cecilia, 1986; Bartholomew the Bass Makes Music, 1986; G-Max Fanfare, 1986; Contrafonia, 1985; Antifonia, 1985; Metamorphosis, for narrator, bassoon & piano, 1983; Sinfonia Aquilonia, 1982; Havelock, dance-drama, 1981; Sinfonietta No 2, 1981; Pale Cast of Thought, 1980; Stars in the Dark Clouds (Hale Barns Festival commission, 1980); Concertante, Op27, premiered Wigmore Hall, 1979. *Hobbies:* Cycling; Reading; Theatre; Photography. *Address:* 9 Albert Road, Sale, Cheshire M33 3EA, England.

TOWER Joan (Peabody), b. 6 Sept 1938, New Rochelle, New York, USA. Composer; Pianist; Teacher. *Education:* BA, Bennington College, 1961; MA 1964, DMA 1978, Columbia University. *Career:* Co-founder and Pianist, Da Capo Chamber Players, NY, 1969-84; Faculty Member, Bard College, Annadale-on-Hudson, 1972-; Composer-in-Residence, St Louis Symphony Orchestra, 1985-87. *Compositions:* Pillars for 2 Pianos and Percussion, 1961; Study for 2 Strings and 2 Winds, 1963; Percussion Quartet, 1963, revised 1969; Circles for Piano, 1964; Brimset for 2 Flutes and Percussion, 1965; Composition for Oboe, 1965; Fantasms for Piano, 1966; Opa eboni for Oboe and Piano, 1967; Composition for Orchestra, 1967; Movements for Flute and Piano,

1968; Prelude for 5 Players, 1970; 6 Variations for Cello, 1971; Hexacords for Flute, 1972; Breakfast Rhythms I and II for Clarinet and 5 Instruments, 1974-75; Black Topaz for Piano and 6 Instruments, 1976; Platinum Spirals for Violin, 1976; Amazon I for Flute, Clarinet, Viola, Cello and Piano, 1977, orchestrated as Amazon II, 1979; Red Garnet Waltz for Piano, 1977; Petroushskates for Flute, Clarinet, Violin, Cello and Piano, 1980; Wings for Clarinet, 1981; Sequoia for Orchestra, 1981; Amazon III for Chamber Orchestra, 1982; Noon Dance for Flute, Clarinet, Violin, Cello, Piano and Percussion, 1982; Fantasy for Clarinet and Piano, 1983; Snow Dreams for Flute and Guitar, 1983; Cello Concerto, 1984; Island Rhythms, overture, 1985; Piano Concerto: Homage to Beethoven, 1985; Silver Ladders for Orchestra, 1986; Island Prelude for Orchestra, 1989. *Recordings:* Several compositions recorded. *Honours:* Guggenheim Fellowship, 1976; National Endowment for the Arts Fellowships, 1974, 1975, 1980, 1984; Koussevitzky Foundation Grant, 1982; American Academy and Institute of Arts and Letters award, 1983. *Address:* c/o Music Department, Bard College, Annandale-on-Hudson, NY 12504, USA.

TOWNSEND Douglas, b. 8 Nov. 1921, New York City, USA. Composer; Writer; Musicologist. *Education:* High School of Music and Art, New York City; Composition Teachers: Stefan Wolpe; Tibor Serly; Aaron Copland, Tanglewood, 1947; Otto Luening, Summers, 1948, 1949. *Compositions include:* Ballet Suite, for 3 Clarinets; Duo for Violas; 4 Fantasies on American Folk Songs; 2 Chamber Symphonies; 2 String Symphonies; 4 Chamber Concertos; Rag for Piano 4 hands and orchestra; Tower Music, for brass quintet; (Recorded): Chamber Concertos 2 & 3; Suite No. 1 for Strings; Fantasy on Motives of Bacharach; Two Madrigals. *Publications:* Chamber Symphony No. 1, Chamber Concerto No. 2, 5 Madrigals, also many publications of music discovered and edited by Townsend; Hundreds of notes for record jackets including 50,000 words on Complete Piano Music of Schumann. *Honours:* Research Commission, New York State Bicentennial Revolution Committee, 1975; Research, New York State Council on the Arts, 1976; Composition, National Endowment on the Arts, 1981. *Address:* 72-28 153 St, Flushing, NY 11367, USA.

TOWSE David, b. 1956, Bridlington, England. Violinist. *Education:* Studied piano and violin from 1961; Royal College of Music from 1974, with Leonard Hirsch, Peter Element and Herbert Howells. *Career:* Leader of the East Riding County Youth Orchestra and British Youth Symphony Orchestra 1972; Leader of the London Youth String Ensemble while at the RCM; Freelance in and around London before joining the Royal Philharmonic Orchestra 1978 (Associate Leader, 1982); Performances of Piano Quintets and Quartets with the Forellen Ensemble (members of the RPO) at music clubs and festivals throughout Britain from 1978. *Address:* c/o Royal Philharmonic Orchestra, 16 Clerkenwell Green, London EC1R 0DP, England.

TOZZI Giorgio, b. 8 Jan 1923, Chicago, Illinois, USA. Singer (Bass). *Education:* Studied with Rosa Raisa, Giacomo Rimini, and John Daggert Howell. *Debut:* Tarquinus in The Rape of Lucretia, on Broadway, 1948. *Career:* Studied further in Italy and sang Rodolfo in La Sonnambula at the Teatro Nuovo Milan, 1950; La Scala 1953, in La Wally by Catalani; Metropolitan Opera from 1955, as Alvise (La Gioconda), Sparafucile, Pimen, Boris Godunov, Mozart's Figaro, Daland, Pogner, Sachs, Rocco and Philip II; Created the Doctor in Barber's Vanessa (1958); San Francisco from 1955, as Ramfis, Calkas in Troilus and Cressida and Archibaldo (L'Amore dei tre Re); Salzburg Festival 1958, 1961 in Vanessa and as Fiesco in Simon Boccanegra; Hollywood Bowl 1956, in the US premiere of David by Milhaud; La Scala 1962, in a revival of Les Huguenots; Appearances in Florence, Palermo, Hamburg, Frankfurt, Lisbon and Munich as Sarastro, Padre Guardiano, Don Giovanni, Gurnemanz, Arkel and Gremin; Boston Opera 1977, in the US premiere of Ruslan and Ludmilla by Glinka; Active in films, television and musical comedy.

Recordings: Rigoletto, Guillaume Tell (Cetra); Der fliegende Holländer, Vanessa, La Forza del Destino, Aida, La Bohème, Le Nozze di Figaro, Luisa Miller (RCA); Il Trovatore, La Fanciulla del West, Rigoletto (Decca). *Address:* c/o Opera Company of Boston, Inc. PO Box 50, Boston, MA 02112, USA.

TRACEY Edmund, b. 14 Nov 1927, Preston, England. Translator; Administrator; Librettist. *Career:* Music Critic for The Observer 1958- 65; Sadler's Wells (later English National Opera) Director from 1965, as dramaturg and repertory planner; Translated for ENO such texts as Les contes d'Hoffmann 1970, Aida, 1978 and Manon, 1979; La Finta Giardiniera by Mozart for English Music Theatre at Sadler's Wells, 1976; Librettist for Malcolm Williamson's Lucky-Peter's Journey (after Strindberg), Sadler's Wells 1969. *Address:* English National Opera, St. Martin's Lane, London WC2, England.

TRACK Gerhard, b. 17 Sept 1934, Vienna, Austria. Conductor; Composer. m. Micaela Maihart, 3 Aug 1958, 2 sons. *Education:* Music Theory, Conducting and Piano, Academy of Music and Performing Arts, Vienna, Austria; Teacher Training College, Vienna, Austria, 1953; Vienna Boys Choir, 1942-48. *Debut:* Conductor, Vienna Boys Choir, 1953. *Career:* Conductor, Vienna Boys Choir, 1953-58; Music Director, St John's Symphony Orchestra, Associate Professor, Music, St John's University, Mens Chorus, Minnesota, USA, 1958-69; Music Director, Pueblo Symphony Orchestra, Chorale and Founder, Annual Mozart Festival, Pueblo, Colorado, USA, Thatcher-Professor of Music University of Southern Colorado, Pueblo, Colorado; Music Director and Conductor of Choral- Society Jung-Wien (Young Vienna) and Orchestra Pro Musica International Vienna, Austria, 1986; Teacher: Conservatory of Music, Vienna; Hochschule (University) of Music and Performing Arts, Vienna; President of the Austrian Composer Society, 1988-, Osterreichischer Komponistenbund; International Guest Conductor: Europe, USA, Asia; President and Founder of PMI-Music Publication, Colorado. *Compositions:* Over 450 compositions, orchestral works, choral compositions and arrangements, chamber music, songs, 3 operas, 6 Masses, published in Europe and USA. *Recordings:* Euro-Disc Ariola, Germany; Columbia; Polyhymnia; Rubin; Superchord; GIA; PMI. *Contributions to:* Sacred Music; Oesterreichische Musikzeitschrift. *Hobbies:* Radio work (MC, Producer); Tennis; Swimming; Biking. *Current Management:* Conductors International Management CIM, New Jersey, USA. *Address:* Praterstrasse 76/8, A-1020 Vienna, Austria.

TRACK Micaela Maihart, b. 13 Aug 1937, Amstetten, Austria. Concert Pianist. m. Gerhard Track, 3 Aug 1958, 2 sons. *Education:* Concert Diploma in Piano, Academy of Music and Performing Arts, Vienna, Austria; Teachers, Walter Kerschbaumer and Viola Therm, Vienna, Austria. *Debut:* Bad Gastein, Austria, 1955. *Career:* International Concert Pianist, USA, Canada, South America, Europe, Asia; Master Classes in Canada, USA, Austria and Taiwan; Appearances on International Television and Radio Networks in USA and Europe. *Recordings:* Rubin, Polyhymnia, Austria; Austrian State Radio Network, ORF, Vienna, Austria. *Honour:* 1st Prize in piano, Bad Gasteiner, Musikpreis, 1955. *Hobbies:* Hiking; Swimming. *Address:* Praterstrasse 76/8, A-1020 Vienna, Austria.

TRAERUP SARK Einar, b. 27 Mar 1921, Kolding, Denmark. Composer; Organist. *Education:* The Royal Danish Academy of Music, Copenhagen, Denmark. *Debut:* Piano, 1947; Organ, 1949. *Career includes:* Solo performances, Radio Denmark and Radio France. *Compositions:* Organ works: Toccata primi toni; Dronning Dagmars Dod, stage music; The Death of Queen Dagmar, suite; Klokketaarnet i Barseback; Carillon; Toccata No 2; Bordone; Piano music: Toccata; 5 sonatinas; 3 suites; Tambutsak; Visages du Temps; La deesse du printemps; Cathedrale de verre, chaconne; La creole melancolique, nocturno; Old man goes to town; Various publications of shorter pieces; Music for 2 electric guitars: La clef inaccessible, suite; Dies irae;

Church music: Motets to Danish and Swedish texts; 3 Missae Breves; Other liturgical music; Orchestral works: Capriccio; Pablo, ballet suite; 2 Suites for Chamber Orchestra; Divertimento for Chamber Ensemble; Trombone and Piano: Inroduction and Carillon. *Recording:* Toccata primi toni, for organ. *Membership:* Danish Composers' Society. *Address:* Lyngbyvej 32 E 1.MF, DK-2100 Copenhagen O, Denmark.

TRAMA Ugo, b. 4 Aug 1932, Naples, Italy. Singer (Bass). *Education:* Studied with Emilia Gubitosi in Naples, at the Accademia Chigiana in Siena and at the Accademia di Santa Cecilia Rome. *Debut:* Spoleto Festival 1951, as Banquo in Macbeth. *Career:* Sang in Cairo and the Italian provinces; Holland Festival 1960, as Fiesco in Simon Bocanegra; Wexford festival 1961, as Silva in Ernani; Dallas Opera 1961; San Francisco Opera 1965; Appearances at the Maggio Musicale Florence, Teatro Liceo Barcelona and Strasbourg; Glyndebourne 1964-79, as Asdrubale in La Pietra del Paragone, Giove and Pane (Calisto), Antinoo and Tempo (Il Ritorno d'Ulisse), Bartolo (Le Nozze di Figaro), Pistol (Falstaff)and Farfallo (Die schweigsame Frau). *Recordings include:* Ramphis in Aida; La Cenerentola (Deutsche Grammophon); Il Ritorno d'Ulisse (CBS). *Address:* c/o Glyndebourne Festival Opera, Lewes, Sussex.

TRAMPLER Walter, b. 25 Aug 1925, Munich, Germany. Violist. m. (1) Margaret Stark, 1 son, 1 daughter (2) Karen Philips. *Education:* State Academy, Munich. *Debut:* As violinist, Munich 1933, with Beethoven's Concerto; As violist, Berlin 1935, in Mozart's Sinfonia Concertante. *Career:* Member Strub Quartet; Violist, German Radio Symphony Orchestra; Emigrated to USA 1939 (naturalised 1944); Entertained troops, playing violin and viola, World War II; Founding Member, New Music Quartet, 1947-56; Guest with Budapest Quartet 1955, Juilliard Quartet 1955; Also played with Guarneri and Emerson Quartets and Beaux Arts Trio; Gave premieres of works by Fortner (1937), Henze, Perle, Berio, Neikrug and Simon Bainbridge (1978); Appearances at Casals Festival 1958-60; Soloist, Aspen Music Festival, Colorado, 1953-56; Associate Professor, Rollins College Conservatory of Music, 1939-42; Professor, Juilliard School of Music, 1962-; Professor at Yale School of Music 1971; Boston University 1972. *Recordings:* Mozart and Brahms Quintets with the Budapest Quartet; Brahms Piano Quartets with the Beaux Arts Trio; Solo recordings of Reger's Suites, Stravinsky's Elegie, Hindemith's Sonatas; Harold in Italy by Berlioz with the London Symphony Orchestra; Chamber works by Berio with the Juilliard Quartet. *Address:* 33 Riverside Drive, New York, NY 10023, USA.

TRÂN Quang Hai, b. 13 May 1944, Vietnam. Ethnomusicologist; Education; Musician; Composer. m. Bach-Yen Quach, 17 June 1978, 1 child. *Education:* National Conservatorium of Music, Saigon, 1961; Sorbonne, 1963; Institut d'Ethnologie, 1964; Vietnamese Music, Centre of Studies for Oriental Music, 1969; Ministry of Culture, Paris. *Career:* Ethnomusicologist, Musee National des Arts et Traditions Populaires, 1968- 87, Musee de l'Homme, Paris, 1968-; Professor, Centre of Studies for Oriental Music, 1970-75; Lecturer, Universities of Paris, X and Nanterre, 1987; Over 2000 concerts in 45 countries, 1966-; Played at many international music festivals and in films. *Compositions:* 300 pop songs, 100 for zither, monochord, spoons, Jew's harp, split-tone singing; 3 electro-acoustic works, 1975-89. Film: Le Chant des Harmoniques, co-author, principal actor and composer of the film, 1989; Scientific Film Festival in France, 1990; Scientific Film Festival in Montreal, Canada, 1991; CG: Cithare Vietnamienne/Trân Quang Hai, edited by Playasound, PS 75103, 1993. *Recordings:* 15 Lps, Vietnamese Music; Music of Vietnam, South Australia Ministry of Education, 1989. *Publications:* Am Nhac Viet Nam, 1989; Musiques du Monde with Michel Asselineau and Eugène Bérel, edited by J-M Fuzeau, France, (320p and 3CD), 1993. Over 200 articles on

Asian music. *Honours:* Medaille d'Or de la Musique, Academic Culturelle Asiatique, Paris, 1986; Hon DMus, International University Foundation, USA, 1987; Hon PhD, 1989, Alfred Nobel Medal, 1991; Albert Einstein International Academy Foundation, USA: Ferens Institute Prize, University of London, 1991; Grand prize of the Interna: Film Festival in Estonia, 1990, Best Ethnomusicological Film by the Academy of Sciences in Estonia, 1990; Special Prize of Research of the 6th Internat; Grand Prize ofd the 2nd Internat. *Memberships:* Society for Ethnomusicology, USA: Asian Music, USA: Liaison Officer, International Council for Traditional Music; International Musicological Society; Founding member, Societe Francaise d'Ethnomusicologie. *Address:* Department d'ethnomusicologie, Music de l'Homme, 17 Place du Trocadero, 75116 Paris, France.

TRANCHELL Peter Andrew, b. 14 July 1922, Cuddalore, British India. University Lecturer; Composer; Critic; Conductor. *Education:* Dragon School, Oxford, England, 1930-36; Scholar in Classics, Clifton College, Bristol, 1936-41; Exhibitioner in Classics, King's College, Cambridge, 1941-42, 1946-49; MA, 1950; Scholar in Music, King's College, Cambridge, 1946-49; MusB, 1949. *Career:* Captain, Royal Signals (war service), 1942-46; University, 1946-49; Schoolmaster, Eastbourne College, 1949-50; Assistant University Lecturer, 1950-52, University Lecturer, 1952-89, Cambridge; Fellow, Caius College, Cambridge, 1960-; Precentor, Caius College, 1962-89. *Compositions:* Operas: Mayor of Casterbridge (after Thomas Hardy), Cambridge Arts Theatre, 1951; Twice a Kiss (Libretto Maurice Holt), Cambridge, 1955; Ballets: Images of Love (Choreographer: K. Macmillan), Covent Garden, 1964; Fate's Revenge (Ballet Rambert) Lyric, Hammersmith, 1951; Nine separate ballets for Theatre Royal, Windsor, 1952-61; Symphonic Works; Chamber Music; Church Music; Musical Comedies: Zuleika (after Max Beerbohm) 1954; Daisy Simpkins, 1955; Murder at the Towers, 1955; His First May Week, 1962; The Robot Emperor, 1964; The Mating Season, 1969; Latin Greek Plays: Seneca's Troades, 1957; Euripides Bacchae, 1956; Sophocles Antigone, 1959; Cantatas: This Sorry Scheme of Things, 1952; The Joyous Year, 1962; Saul's Successor, 1970. *Contributions to:* Music and Letters; Cambridge Review; Books of Today. *Memberships:* Composers Guild of Great Britain; Performing Right Society; International Society of Musicians. *Hobbies:* Archaeological, Classical, Anthropological, Etymological Studies; Drawing; Design; Travel. *Address:* Caius College, Cambridge CB2 1TA, England.

TRANTER John, b. 1948, Chesterfield, Derbyshire, England. Singer (Bass). *Education:* Studied singing with John Dethick in Sheffield; London Opera Centre.*Debut:* Forethcoming: Hobson in Peter Grimes, Chatalet Opera in Paris. *Career:* Opera for All; Kent Opera as the Commendatore in Don Giovanni and Seneca in L'Incoronazione di Poppea; English National Opera from 1976 as Sarastro, Colline, Monterone in Rigoletto, Verdi's Grand Inquisitor Opera North as Zaccaria in Nabucco, Rossini's Don Basilio, Daland in Der fliegende Holländer, Gremin in Eugene Onegin, Pogner in Die Meistersinger and Trulove in The Rake's Progress; Welsh National Opera as Wagner's Fasolt and Hagen and Grigoris in The Greek Passion; Other engagements in Nancy, Nîmes, Wellington and Lausanne; Other roles include Oroveso (Norma), Ramphis (Aida), Nourabad (Les pêcheurs de Perles), Henry VIII (Anna Bolena) and Tiresias (Oedipus Rex); Fafner at Covent Garden and Pope Leone in Attila at Covent Garden, 1990; Banquo in Metz, France, and engagements in Marseille. Debut in Pittsburgh as Varlaam (Boris), Oct 1991; Season 1992 as Melchtal in Guillaume Tell at Covent Garden and Monterone for Opera North; Has sung in concert at the Royal Albert Hall, Royal Festival Hall, Canterbury Cathedral, York Minster and Leeds Town Hall; Also sung with the Scottish Opera as Gremin, King Aida, Billy Budd, Pearl; Fishers. *Address:* c/o Music International, 13 Ardilaun Road, Highbury, London, N5 2QR, England.

TRAUTWEIN George, b. 5 Aug 1927, Chicago,

Illinois, USA. Conductor; Violinist; Educator. m. Barbara Wilson, 20 Jan 1956, 2 sons. *Education:* BMus, Oberlin College, 1951; MMus, Cleveland Institute of Music, 1955; PhD, Indiana University, 1961; Mozarteum, Salzburg, 1957-58. *Debut:* Salzburg, 1958. *Career:* Associate Conductor, Dallas Symphony, 1962-65, Minneapolis Symphony, 1965-73; Music Director: Savannah Symphony, 1973-75, Tucson Symphony, 1976-80, Piedmont Chamber Orchestra, 1980- 82, RIAS Ed Network, Berlin, 1977, International Congress of Strings, 1966-69; Director Instrumental Ens, Wake Forest University, 1982-; Director, Wake Forest University Artists Series, 1984-. *Honours:* ASCAP Award, 1977; Ministry of World Culture Award, 1975; Fulbright Grants, 1957-58, 1989-90. *Memberships:* American Federation of Musicians; Chamber Music America; Wilhelm Furtwaengler Society; Errich Wolfgang Korngold Society; Emil Von Reznicek Society. *Hobbies:* Art reproduction; Chamber Music; Nautilus training; Hindustani and Karnatic Ragas. *Address:* Box 7411 Reynolda Station, Winston-Salem, NC 27109, USA.

TRAVIS Francis Irving, b. 9 July 1921, Michigan, USA. Conductor. *Education:* BMus, 1943, Michigan State University; MMus, University of Michigan, 1948; PhD, Musicology, University of Zurich, 1955; Private study with Hermann Scherchen. *Career:* Freelance Conductor of concert, opera, radio, 1955; Professor for Orchestra Conducting, Staatliche Hochschule fur Musik, Freiburg, 1964-89, concurrently with Conductor, Swiss Radio in Lugano; Frequent engagemnts at Dutch National Opera and appearances at international festivals such as Berliner Festwochen, Holland, Copenhagen and Lucerne Festivals; Currently Professor for Conducting, Tokyo National, University of the Fine Arts and Music. *Memberships:* President, Swiss section, ISCM; Hon Member, Jan Sibelius Academi, Helsinki; Hon Member, Richard Strauss Society, Tokyo. *Hobbies:* Languages; Sailing; Swimming. *Address:* 6-5-12 Hon-Komagome, Bunkyo-ku, Tokyo 113, Japan.

TRAVIS Roy (Elihu), b. 24 June 1922, New York, USA. Composer. *Education:* Studied with Otto Luening at Columbia University, MA 1951, with Bernard Wagenaar at Juilliard, MS 1950 and with Darius Milhaud in Paris, 1951-52. *Career:* Teacher at Columbia University 1952-53, Mannes College of Music 1952-57 and the University of California at Los Angeles, from 1957, Professor 1968. *Compositions include:* Operas: The Passion of Oedipus, Los Angeles, 1968 and the Black Bacchants, 1982; Symphonic Allegro 1951; College for orchestra 1968; Piano Concerto 1969; String Quartet 1958; Duo Concertante for violin and piano 1967; Barma, Septet, 1968; Switched-On Ashanti for flute or piccolo and tape; Piano pieces and songs. *Honours:* Gershwin Award; Martha Baird Rockefeller Award 1968; Guggenheim Fellowship 1972-73; Ford Foundation Grant 1975; NEA Grants 1976, 1978. *Publications include:* Study of Britten's Death in Venice, 1978. *Address:* ASCAP, ASCAP Building, One Lincoln Plaza, New York, NY 10023, USA.

TREACHER Graham, b. 1932, England. Conductor; Composer; Lecturer. *Career:* Conducted the London New Music Singers 1958-63, with first performances of works by Davies and Bennett, British premieres of works by Penderecki and Schoenberg; Tours of Europe, Henry Wood Promenade Concerts; Conductor at Morley College, London, Holst Choir and Opera Group; Director of the Thaxted Festival, Essex until 1963; Assistant Chorus Master Royal Opera House, Covent Garden 1962-64 for the British premiere of Schoenberg's Moses und Aron; Associate conductor of the BBC Scottish Symphony Orchestra and Chorus, 1964-67; Director of the Purcell School, London 1968-70; Director of Music at the University of Warwick, 1969-70; Lecturer in Style, Interpretation and Conducting, University of York, 1972-85; Founder of the Amati Ensemble, baroque quartet, playing harpsichord and chamber organ, 1978- 85; Director and conductor, Northern Music Theatre 1980-84, with first performances of works by Vic Hoyland, Philip Grange and UK Premieres of Kagel and Henze;

Artistic Director of the John Loosemore Early Music Centre, Devon, 1988-92. *Compositions include:* Music for children, vocal and instrumental music including music for Strings, Percussion and Celestine, for the 1990 Orkney Summer Festival; Choral music with settings of Chaucer and Christmas music, *Publications include:* Editions of Gesualdo (Cantiones Sacrae 1603) and Pallavicino's three act Carnival opera Messalina, for performance at the Vadstena International Opera Festival, Sweden; Dixit Dominus by Pallavicino. *Address:* Warren Cottages, Hippenscombe, Nr Marlborough, Wilts SNB 3NN, England.

TREE Michael, b. 19 Feb 1934, Newark, New Jersey, USA. Concert Violinist; Violist. m. Johanna Kreck, 1 son, 1 daughter. *Education:* Diploma, Curtis Institute of Music, 1955. *Debut:* Carnegie Hall, 1954. *Career:* Soloist with major American orchestras; Solo & chamber music appearances at major festivals, including Israel, Athens, Spoleto, Casals, Marlboro; Founding member, Guarneri String Quartet; Faculty member, Curtis Institute of Music, University of Maryland, Rutgers University, Manhattan School of Music; Repeated appearances on the Today Show and first Telecast of Chamber Music Live from Lincoln Center. *Recordings:* Over 60 chamber music works on Columbia, Nonesuch, Philips and RCA labels. Complete Beethoven quartets, 10 works for piano & strings, with Artur Rubinstein; Collaborations with Emanuel Ax, Jaime Laredo, Leonard Rose, Alexander Schneider, Rudolf Serkin and Pinchas Zuckerman. *Honours:* New York City Seal of Recognition, 1982; Honorary degrees, Doctor of Fine Arts, University of South Florida, State University of New York at Binghampton. *Memberships:* President of the First American String Quartet Congress at University of Maryland and Smithsonian Institute, 1989. *Hobbies:* Tennis; Hiking. *Current Management:* Herbert Barrett Management. *Address:* 1776 Broadway, New York, NY 10019, USA.

TRÉFÁS György, b. 6 Oct 1931, Budapest, Hungary. Opera Singer; Soloist; Bassist. m. Szabó Katalin, 27 Dec 1972. *Education:* Private education: Dr Werner Alajos, Makai Mihály, Lendvay Andor, Hetényi Kálmán. *Debut:* Csokonai Theatre, Debrecen, Hungary. *Career:* Bass characters of operas: King Philip, Don Carlos; Attila; De Silva, Ernani; Rocco, Fidelio; Duke Bluebeard, Bartók: Duke Bluebeard's Castle - radio recording, Dresden, Antwerp, Zaccaria, Nabucco, Sofia; Magdeburg, Mephisto, Faust; Ibert: Angelica; King Nero TV Film; Sarastro, Zauberflöte; Osmin, Entführung. *Honours:* Franz Liszt Prize, 1968; Merited Artist of the Hungarian People's Republic, 1980. *Memberships:* Association of Hungarian Music Artists; International Theatre Institute; Foundation member, Hungarian Kodály Society. *Hobbies:* Reading; Tennis. *Current Management:* Interconcert, Budapest. *Address:* Darabos-u. 6, H-4026 Debrecen, Hungary.

TREKEL Roman, b. 1962, Pirna, Saxony, Germany. Singer (Baritone). *Education:* Studied at the Berlin Musikhochschule 1980-86 and with Siegfried Lorenz and Hans Hotter. *Career:* Sang with the Berlin Staatsoper from 1986, notably in Erwin and Elmire by Reichardt 1987 and Kaiser's Emperor of Atlantis 1989; Many roles in operas by Mozart in Berlin and elswhere; Season 1992 as Ulysses in Erendira by Violet Dinescu and as Tarquinius in the Rape of Lucretia with the Berlin Kammeroper; Concerts and Lieder recitals in Germany, Belgium, Austria, Czechoslovakia, Sweden and England. *Honours include:* Prize winner, Dvořák Competition, 1985; Karlovy Vary, 1987; DDR Competition Germany; 1989 International Lieder Competition Walter Gruner in London. *Address:* Stuttgart Staatsoper, Oberer Schlossgarten 6, 7000 Stuttgart 1, Germany.

TREKEL-BURCKHARDT Ute, b. 3 Nov 1939, Pirna, Saxony, Germany. Singer (Mezzo-soprano). *Education:* Studied in Berlin with Rita Meinl- Weise. *Debut:* Komische Oper Berlin 1963, as the Page in Salome. *Career:* Sang at the Komische Oper until 1978, then joined the Staatsoper Berlin; Guest appearances in Vienna, Cologne, Brussels, Madrid and Dresden;

Cologne 1984, as Renata in The Fiery Angel by Prokofiev; Nancy 1985, as The Woman in Schoenberg's Erwartung; Created Queen Marguerite in Sutermeister's Le roi Bérenger at Munich in 1985; Other roles include the Countess Geschwitz in Lulu, Mozart's Sextus and Cherubino, Verdi's Eboli, Amneris and Ulrica, Strauss's Nurse (Die Frau ohne Schatten), Composer and Octavian, and Wagner's Fricka, Kundry and Ortrud (Wiesbaden 1988); Sang Venus in Tannhäuser as guest with the Berlin Staatsoper at Las Palmas in 1986; Many concert appearances. *Address:* Deutsche Staatsoper, Unter den Linden 7, 1086 Berlin, Germany.

TRELEAVEN John, b. 1950, Cornwall, England. Singer (Tenor). *Education:* Studied in London and Naples. *Career:* With Welsh National Opera has sung Tamino, Alfredo (La Traviata), Pinkerton, Nadir (Les Pêcheurs de Perles and Mark (The Midsummer Marriage); At English National Opera his roles have included Don José, Cavaradossi, Faust (Berlioz), Erik in Der fliegende Holländer, the Prince in Rusalka, Hoffmann, Don Carlos and Wozzeck in a new production of Berg's Opera (1990); Royal Opera, Covent Garden, debut as Tamino, followed by Froh in Das Rheingold and Peter Grimes 1989; Appearances with Scottish Opera have included Florestan, Jenik (The Bartered Bride), Werther and Radames; Opera North as Dick Johnson (La Fanciulla del West), Cavaradossi, Radames and Peter Grimes; Recent engagements in The Damnation of Faust at the Adelaide Festival, Pylades (Iphigénie en Tauride) at the Paris Opéra, Verdi's Attila at the Concertgebouw, Amsterdam and Prince Golitisin (Khovanshchina) at the San Francisco Opera, 1990; Concert performances include a 1981 debut at the Festival Hall in Puccini's Messa di Gloria and Rossini's Stabat Mater; Verdi Requiem under Nello Santi at the 1984 Festival de la Mediterranée; Dream of Gerontius 1989, with the Scottish National Orchestra; Concert performance of Bernstein's Candide at the Barbican in London, 1989; Season 1992 as Erik at Buenos Aires, Essex in Gloriana at Mainz (Siegmund 1993) and Weill's Jimmy Mahoney in Karlsruhe. *Recordings include:* Solo parts: Le Prophète, Meyerbeer cond. Henry Lewis CBS; L'Assedio di Calais, Donizetti Opera Rara; Il Trovatore, Colin Davis with José Carreras, Philips; Il Tabarro, Maazel with Placido Domingo, CBS; Rachmaninov Vespers, Candide, Leonard Bernstein, DGG. Videos of Rusalka for English National Opera; Richard Dauntless in Ruddigore for Brent Walker Ltd; Candide (Deutsche Grammophon). *Address:* c/o Athole Still, International Management Ltd, 113 Church Road, London SE19 2PR, England.

TREMBLAY Gilles L, b. 6 Sept 1932, Arvida, Quebec, Canada. Composer. *Education:* Conservatoire de Montréal; Conservatoire de Paris. *Career:* Professor of Analysis and Composition, Conservatoire de Montréal; Participation in numerous concerts as pianist and conductor. *Compositions:* Champs I, II, III Le Sifflement des Vents Porteurs del' Amour; Soltices; Oralléluiants; Fleuves; Compostelle I, Envoi; Vêpres de la Vierge, Atadrone. *Recordings:* Anthology of Canadian Music; Les Vepres de la Vierge; Vers le soleil; Triojubilus. *Publications:* Champs I, II, III, 1969; Fleuves, 1976; Compostelle I, 1978; Triojubilus, 1984; Acoustique et forme chez Varese, 1983. *Honours include:* First prizes, Montreal and Paris Conservatories, 1953, and 1957 respectively; Medaille du Conseil Canadien de la Musique, 1991; Chevalier de l'ordre des Arts et des Lettres, 1992. *Memberships:* Canadian League of Composers; Societe francaise d'analyse musicale; Societe de musique contemporaine de Quebec; SOCAN. *Hobbies:* Hiking; Swimming; Gardening; Socialising. *Address:* 439 Ouest Blvd St Joseph, Montreal, Quebec H2V 2P7, Canada.

TRENKOVA Rossitza, b. 7 Oct 1935, Samokov, Bulgaria. Opera and Concert Singer (Soprano). m. 1 daughter. *Education:* Academy of Music and Opera School, Sofia, 1959; Specialist study with Maria Brand, Vienna, 1967-68; Weimar International Music Seminar with Professor Lore Fischer, Germany. *Debut:* Bourgas, opera, in Matrimonco Segreto, 1960. *Career:* Opera singing activity, Bourgas, Stara Zagora, 1963-70; Regular concert appearance, Sofia and elsewhere in Bulgaria, 1970-; Appeared in TV film, 1974; Repertoire includes: Lieder of Mozart, Beethoven, Schubert, Brahms, Mendelssohn, Hindemith, Britten, Debussy, Gounod, Rossini, Tchaikovsky, Rachmaninov, Villa-Lobos, many others; Cantatas and oratorios, Handel, Bach, Scarlatti; Susanna in Marriage of Figaro; Violetta in La Traviata; Gilda in Rigoletto; Mimi in La Bohème; Leila in Les pêcheurs de Perles; Iolanthe in Iolanthe; Title roles in Cinderella; State Artist, Directorate of Bulgarian Music; Performer in Society for contemporary music, 1992-93. *Recordings:* For Radio Sofia, 1960-90 and 1993; Bulgarian songs by Dimiter Nenov, Balkanton, 1991. *Publications:* A research work on works of D Nenov. *Hobbies:* Cooking; Contributing to magazine. *Address:* Khadji Dimitar 2, Sofia 1000, Bulgaria.

TREW Graham Donald, b. 18 July 1948, Epping, England. Singer (Baritone); Teacher; Adjudicator. *Education:* Guildhall School of Music and Drama, AGSM with distinction; M Mus, University of London. *Career:* Performed, English Opera Group, Nottingham Music Theatre, Cockpit Opera Workshop (20 productions plus title role in video of Marriage of Figaro); Recitals, Wigmore Hall, Purcell Room, Queen Elizabeth Hall, Barbican; Oratorio and concerts throughout UK, Europe, USA and Caribbean; English song recitals for Radio 3, Friday Night Is Music Night, Songs from the Shows, Melodies for You, for Radio 2; Gentleman of Her Majesty's Chapel Royal, St James's Palace, 1975-; Teaches privately; Guest Lecturer, Royal Academy of Music lieder class and Birmingham Conservatoire; Adjudicates throughout UK. *Recordings:* English song recordings for Meridian and Hyperion with Roger Vignoles; Recordings for Priory Records and the British Music Society with John Alley; Marcello-Cantatas; Rodolophe, Florence. *Honours:* Gold Medal, Guildhall School of Music, 1973; Vocal Record of the Year Award for A Shropshire Lad, Gramophone Magazine, 1980. *Memberships:* Equity; Royal Society of Musicians; Adjudicator, British Federation of Music Festivals. *Hobbies:* Squash; Theatre. *Current Management:* Music International. *Address:* 61 Sydner Road, Stoke Newington, London N16 7UF, England.

TRIER Stephen Luke, b. 13 Mar 1930, Woolton Hill, England. Musician, Clarinettist. m. Caroline Fraser Scott, 18 July 1953, 2 daughters. *Education:* Foundation scholar, Royal College of Music, 1947-50. *Career:* Bass clarinet, clarinets, saxophones, Royal Philharmonic Orchestra 1950-56, London Symphony Orchestra 1956-68, London Philharmonic Orchestra 1968-; Clarinet, Sadler's Wells, 1953-56. Freelance appearances, various groups. Professor, Saxophone & Bass Clarinet, Royal College of Music. *Recordings:* Many, with various orchestras & groups. *Publications:* Essential Clarinet Repertoire, editor with Alan Boustead, 1966; Playing the Saxophone, by Jean-Marie Londeix, English editor, 1974; 100 Classical Clarinet Studies, editor with Gunther Joppig, 1987. *Honour:* Honorary Associate, Royal College of Music. *Hobbies:* Wine & food; Tinkering with clarinets & basset horns. *Address:* 6 Carthew Villas, London W6 0BS, England.

TRIMARCHI Domenico, b. 21 Dec 1940, Naples, Italy. Singer (Bass- Baritone). *Education:* Studied at the Naples Conservatory and with Gino Campese. *Debut:* Teatro La Fenice Venice 1964, as Belcore in L'Elisir d'Amore. *Career:* Has sung widely in Italy (Verona Arena 1975-78), Edinburgh, London, Stuttgart, Frankfurt, Chicago and Dubrovnik; Teatro Regio Parma 1987, as Falstaff in the operas by Salieri and Verdi; Repertoire also includes Leporello, Alfonso, Papageno, Arbace and Count Almaviva (Mozart); Varlaam (Mussorgsky); Germont, Paolo and Fra Melitone (Verdi); Dulcamara, Belcore, Don Pasquale, Malatesta, Enrico and Alfonso (Donizetti); Dallapiccola's Job; Marcello, Sharpless, Gianni Schicchi and Bambaldo (Puccini); Sang Donizetti's Mamma Agata at Luga di Romagna, 1988; Marchese in Linda di Chamounix at Trieste, 1989, Leporello at Parma; Sang in Wolf-Ferrari's Quattro

Rusteghi at Geneva, 1992. *Recordings:* Haydn's La Vera Costanza, L'Incontro Improvviso and Il Mondo della Luna, Il Barbiere di Siviglia, Vivaldi's Tito Manlio, Tosca (Philips); Elisa e Claudio by Mercadante; La Straniera by Bellini; La Cenerentola (CBS); Pimpinone by Albinoni. *Address:* Athole Still Management, 113 Church Road, London SE19 2PR, England.

TRIPODI Joseph Francis, b. 26 Dec 1952, New York, USA. Violin making and restoration. *Education:* BA, Hobart College, NY, 1975; Kenneth Warren School of Violin Making, Chicago, 1976-77; International School of Violin Making, Italy, 1978-79. *Career:* Worked for established shops in New York City and Long Island area, 1980-84; Established own business in 1985, working with two apprentices. Currently working alone producing three violins and two violas yearly. Extensive restoration of instruments over the years, completing 28 violins and 8 violas to date. Instruments used by NY Philharmonic, Orpheus, and the San Francisco Symphony and will soon be heard in a complete Beethoven quartet recording by the Arnadi Quartet. *Hobbies:* Playing viola in an amateur string quartet; Sailing and restoration of wooden dinghys. *Address:* 175 Hempstead Avenue, Lynbrook, NY 11563, USA.

TRITT William, b. 1950, Canada. Concert Pianist. *Education:* Studied at the Ecole Vincent d'Indy in Montreal with Lucille Brassard and Yvonne Hubert; Further study with Yvonne Lefèbure in Paris and György Sebok at Indiana University. *Career:* First solo appearance aged 15 with the Little Orchestra Society at Avery Fisher Hall, New York; Further engagements with the Montreal Symphony and the CBS Orchestra in Quebec; Boston Pops Orchestra and the Chicago Symphony at the Ravinia Festival; Cincinnati and Houston Symphony Orchestras; Nationwide appearances in Canada, including Toronto, Edmonton, Winnipeg and Halifax; London recital debut 1981, Wigmore Hall. *Recordings include:* Bach D minor Concerto; Beethoven C major Concerto and Schumann A minor; Liszt Totentanz. *Honours:* Winner of all major competitions in Canada, 1966-71.

TROEGER Richard Walter, b. 1 Sept 1953, Santa Barbara, California, USA. Harpsichordist; Clavichordist; Fortepianist. m. Paulette Grundeen, 12 Apr 1982. *Education:* BM, 1977, MM, 1982, DMus, 1987, Indiana University, USA. *Debut:* New York City, 1981. *Career:* Performances throughout USA and Canada; Appearances on CBC radio; Lecturer, The King's College, Edmonton, Canada, 1986-89; Assistant Professor, University of Alberta, Edmonton, 1989-. *Publications:* Technique and Interpretation on the Harpsichord and Clavichord, 1987; Forthcoming: The French Unmeasured Harpsichord Prelude; Baroque and Classical Keyboard Articulation. *Contributions to:* Articles in Early Music; Diapason; Continuo; Garland Encyclopaedia of Keyboard Instruments; American String Teacher; Clavier; Early Keyboard Journal; Het Clavichord. *Memberships:* American Musicological Society; College Music Society; Nederlands Clavichord Genootschap; American Musical Instrument Society. *Hobbies:* Woodworking; Writing. *Address:* Department of Music, 3-82 Fine Arts Building, University of Alberta, Edmonton, Alberta, Canada T6G 2C9.

TROGE Thomas Alexander, b. 27 Sept 1950, Erlangen, Germany. Musician and Researcher. m. Dott Margherita Galetto Troge, 20 Aug 1980. *Education:* Studied with Alexander Furtwangler, Olga Rissin-Morenowa, and E W Velte. *Debut:* 1960. *Career:* Besides musical activities, Founder of the Centre for Musical Research, in the field of musicology; Consultant for the application of digital technologies in art and science; Chair for Music Informatics, Staatliche Hochschule für Musik Karlsruhe, 1990. *Compositions:* Piano Sonata, 1981; Electronic works, 1989-93. *Recordings:* Russian Piano Music, disks and radio broadcast series, 1980-83. *Publications:* Musikausbildung Zwischen Angebot und Nachfrage, 1979; Musikatlas Baden-Württermnberg, 1985; Gesangvereine-ohne Zukunft, 1988; Zwischen Gesangverein und Musikcomputer,

1993; Article, Concept for the Center for Arts and Media Technology Karlsruhe, 1988. *Membership:* VDMK, ASPM, IFM, IGEB a.o. *Address:* Königsberger Str 1, 76139 Karlsruhe, Germany.

TROTTER Thomas Andrew, b. 4 Apr 1957, Birkenhead, England. Concert Organist. *Education:* ARCM, Royal College of Music (RCM), London, 1976; MA, Cambridge University, 1979; Conservatoire Rueil-Malmaison, France, 1979-81. *Debut:* Royal Festival Hall, 1980. *Career includes:* Regular broadcasts, Radios 2 & 3; Performances, festivals throughout Europe; Proms debut, 1986; Concert tours, USA, Australia, Japan. Organist: St Margaret's Church, Westminster, London, 1982-; City of Birmingham, 1983-. *Recordings:* The Grand Organ of Birmingham Town Hall, Hyperion; Liszt Organ Works and Reubke Sonata, Decca/Argo; Jehan Alain Organ Works, Decca/Argo; Charles-Marie Widor, organ works; Antonio Soler Concertos for 2 organs; Olivier Messiaen, organ works. *Honours:* Scholar, RCM; Organ scholar, St George's Chapel, Windsor & King's College, Cambridge (John Stewart of Rannoch Scholarship in Sacred Music, 1979); Walford Davies Prize, RCM, 1976; 1st prize & Bach prize, St Albans International Organ Competition, 1979; Prix de Virtuosite, 1981. *Current Management:* Karen McFarlane Artists Inc, 12429 Cedar Road, Cleveland Heights, Ohio 44106, USA. *Address:* c/o Town Hall, Birmingham B3 3DQ, England.

TROUP Malcolm, b. 22 Feb 1930, Toronto, Canada. Concert Pianist; Professor of Music City University, London, UK; Former Director of Music, Guildhall School of Music & Drama. m. Carmen Lamarca Bello Subercaseaux, 1 daughter. *Education:* DPhilMus, University of York; Associate, Royal Conservatory of Music, Toronto; FGSM: LLD, Memorial University of Newfoundland. *Debut:* With CBC Symphony Orchestra, Toronto, age 17. *Career includes:* Recitals & concertos with leading orchestras, Europe, North & South America; Premieres, important modern works; Frequent broadcaster with BBC; External examiner, Universities of York, Keele, London, etc; Member of International Juries: Chopin Competition of Australia, CBC National Talent Competition, Young Musician of the Year. *Recordings:* RCA, CBC, Altarus, Continuum. *Publications:* Editor: The Piano Journal. *Contributions to:* Composer; Music & Musicians; Music Teacher; Times Educational Supplement; etc. *Honours:* Professor, University of Chile; Gold Medal, Canadian National Exhibition; Commonwealth Medal; International Music Award. *Memberships:* Chairman EPTA (European Council); Chairman, Beethoven Piano Society of Europe; Vice-President, National Power World Piano Competition; Governor, Music Therapy Charity; Director, London International String Quartet Competition; Executive Committee, Anglo-Chilean Society. *Address:* 86 Lexham Gardens, London W8 5JB, England.

TROWELL Brian Lewis, b. 21 Feb 1931, Wokingham, Berkshire, England. Professor of Music. m. Rhianon James, 1958, 2 daughters. *Education:* Christ's Hospital; MA, 1959, PhD, 1960, Gonville and Caius College, Cambridge. *Career:* Assistant Lecturer, later Lecturer in Music, Birmingham University, 1957-62; Freelance Scholar, Conductor, Opera Producer, Lecturer and Editor, 1962-67; Head of BBC Radio Opera, 1967-70; Regents' Professor, University of California at Berkeley, USA, 1970; Reader in Music, 1970, Professor of Music, 1973, KCL; Visiting Gresham Professor of Music, City University, 1971-74; King Edward Professor of Music, University of London at King's College, 1974-88; Chairman, Editorial Committee, Musica Britannica, 1983-93; Heather Prrofessor of Music, University of Oxford, 1988-. *Publications:* The Early Renaissance, Pelican History of Music, vol ii, 1963; Four Motets by John Plummer, 1968; Joint Editor, John Dunstable: Complete Works, Editor, M. F. Bukofzer, 2nd Revised edition, 1970; Editor, Invitation to Medieval Music, vol 3, 1976, vol. 4, 1978; Opera translations; Contributor to dictionaries of music and articles in books and learned journals, e.g. Libretto (ii), The New Grove Dictionary of Opera, London 1992, ii, 1191-1252; Acis, Galatea and Polyphemus: a sorenata a tre voci?, Music and Theatre: Essays in honour of Winton Dean, ed. N. Fortune, Cambridge 1987, 31-93; Elgar's Use of Literature, Edward Elgar Music and Literature, ed. R Monk, Aldershot, 1993, 182-326. *Honours:* Honorary RAM, 1972; Honorary FGSM, 1972; FRCM, 1977; FTCL, 1978. *Memberships:* President, Royal Musical Association, 1983-88; PMMS. *Hobbies:* Theatre; Reading; Gardening. *Address:* Faculty of Music, St Aldate's, Oxford OX1 1DB, England.

TRUEFITT Alison, b. 1958, England. Singer (Soprano). *Education:* Studied at London University and the Royal Academy of Music. *Debut:* Sang at the Purcell Room, London, 1979. *Career:* Has appeared in recital with the Songmakers' Almanac and with the BBC in songs by Britten, Bartók, Fauré, Holst, Milhaud, Poulenc, and Tippett; With orchestra or ensemble in works by Gerald Finzi, Stephen Dodgson and Frank Martin; Promenade Concerts debut in La Forza del Destino; Sang Gluck's Iphigenia with Opera Factory, 1985, and created Kathe in John Metcalf's The Crossing (tours of US, UK and Canada); Sang in the British stage premiere of Schubert's Fierabras, Oxford University 1986; English National Opera 1988, as Manassah in Salome; Sang Donizetti's Rita, Madame Herz in Mozart's Impresario and Musetta with London Chamber Opera 1988; Appearances as the Queen of Night with Birmingham Touring Opera, 1988-89; Other repertory includes Leila in Les pêcheurs de Perles, the Governess in The Turn of the Screw and Britten's Phaedra and Major Stone in Weill's Happy End; Translated Orfeo for Opera North 1990 and has provided several sets of surtitles for Covent Garden. *Address:* c/o Royal Opera House, Covent Garden, London WC2, England.

TRUSSEL Jacques, b. 7 Apr 1943, San Francisco, California, USA. Singer (Tenor). *Education:* Studied at Ball State University, Muncie, Indiana, and in New York. *Career:* Sang at first in concert then made opera debut at the Oberlin Festival 1970, as Pinkerton; Has appeared in Boston, Dallas, Houston, Santa Fe, New Orleans, Chicago (from 1976), Pittsburgh (1979), Washington (1981) and San Francisco (Loge in Das Rheingold 1990); Sang Don José at Cincinnati 1988 and has appeared as Rodolfo, Cavaradossi, Berg's Alwa, Araquil in La Navarraise by Massenet, Steva in Jenůfa, Max (Der Freischütz) and Nero in L'Incoronazione di Poppea (Geneva 1989); Sang at Houston in the title role of Hugh the Drover by Vaughan Williams (US premiere 1973) and in the 1974 world premiere of The Seagull by Pasatieri; European debut Spoleto Festival 1976, as Hermann in The Queen of Spades; Sang Alwa at Florence 1985 and at Chicago 1987; Covent Garden and Nancy 1989, as Peter Grimes and as Sergei in the French premiere of Lady Macbeth of Mtsensk by Shostakovich; Appeared with Greater Miami Opera 1990, as Pollione in Norma; London appearances 1991, as Don José; Season 1991/92 as Alexey in the US premiere of The Gambler, at Chicago; Sergei at the Opéra Bastille, Monteverdi's Nero in Florence, Don José in Birmingham and Roderick in The Fall of the House of Usher by Philip Glass at the Maggio Musicale. *Address:* c/o John Coast, 31 Sinclair Road, London W14 0NS, England.

TRYON Valerie, b. 1934, Portsmouth, England. Pianist. Associate Professor, McMaster University, Hamilton, Ontario. *Education:* Studied at the Royal Academy of Music and with Jacques Fevrier in Paris. *Debut:* Wigmore Hall, 1954. *Career:* Has appeared in the Cheltenham Festival and in all the major concert halls in Britain with leading conductors and orchestras; Recitals in Europe and Africa and in North America; Repertoire ranges from Bach to contemporary composers, with 50 concertos; Noted for playing of Chopin, Liszt and Rachmaninov; Frequent broadcasts for the BBC and other radio stations and regular chamber music concerts; Adjudicator and performer at many music festivals and competitions in Europe and North America; Fellow of the RAM; Associate Professor of Music at McMaster University, Hamilton, Ontario. *Recordings:* Albums for Pye (Virtuoso Series), BBC

Enterprises, Omnibus, Argo, Lyrita, Educo and the CBC; Dorian Records: Tchaikovsky CD's; Brahms (The Rembrandt Trio); Dvořák, Trio; Bloemendaal, Tryon, Kantarjian. *Honours include:* Harriet Cohen Award; Ferenc Liszt Medal of Honour. *Address:* Department of Music, McMaster University, 1280 Main Street West, Hamilton, Ontario, Canada.

TRYTHALL (Harry) Gil(bert), b. 28 Oct. 1930, Knoxville, Tennessee, USA. Composer; Teacher. m. 2 daughters. *Education:* BA, University of Tennessee, 1951; MMus, Northwestern University, 1952; DMA, Cornell University, 1960; Studied with David Van Vactor, Wallingford Riegger, Robert Palmer and Donald Grout. *Career:* Band and choral director, Loudon, Tennessee, public school system, 1950-51; Assistant Professor of Music, Knox College, Galesburg, Illinois, 1960-64; Professor of Music Theory and Composition 1964-75; Chairman, School of Music 1973-75, George Peabody College for Teachers, Nashville, Tennessee; Professor of Music 1975-, Dean, Creative Arts Center 1975-81, Virginia University, Morgantown, West Virginia; Guest lecturer at various universities and colleges. *Compositions:* Operas: The Music Lesson, 1960; The Terminal Opera, 1982, revised 1987. Orchestral: A Solemn Chant for Strings, 1955; Symphony No 1 1958, revised 1963; Harp Concerto, 1963; Dionysia, 1964; Chroma I, 1970; Cindy the Synthe (Minnie the Moog) for Synthesizer and Strings, 1975. Chamber: Flute Sonata, 1964; A Vacuum Soprano for Brass Quintet and Tape, 1966; Entropy for Brass, Harp, Celesta, Piano and Tape, 1967; Echospace for Brass and Tape, 1973; Choral music; Piano pieces; Organ music; Electronic scores; Mixed media pieces; Film music; Chamber Opera: The Pastimes of Lord Caitanya, 1992. *Publication:* Principles and Practice of Electronic Music, 1974; Eighteenth Century Counterpoint, William C Brown and Co. 1993. *Address:* 41 W Main, Morgantown, WV 26505, USA.

TSCHAIKOV Basil Nichols, b. 30 May 1925, London, England. Musician, (Clarinettist). m. Dorothy Gallon, June 1966, 2 daughters (by previous marriage). *Education:* St. Paul's School, London, England; Royal College of Music. *Career:* London Philharmonic Orchestra, 1943-47; Royal Philharmonic Orchestra, 1947-55; Philharmonia Orchestra, 1958-79; Visiting Lecturer, Middlesex Polytechnic, England, 1959-79; Professor, Royal College of Music, 1964-84; Director, National Centre for Orchestral Studies, London University, Goldsmiths' College, 1979-89; Artistic and Executive Director, Orchestra for Europe, 1989-90; Chairman, Music Performance Research Centre, 1987-; Editor-in-Chief, Musical Performance, Harwood Academic Publ. *Compositions:* First Tunes & Studies; Play the Clarinet. *Recordings:* various chamber ensembles. *Publications:* Play the Clarinet Teachers Handbook; How to be a Musician. *Honours:* Honorary RCM. *Memberships:* Fellow, Royal Society of Arts; Incorporated Society of Musicians; Musicians Union. *Address:* Hillside Cottage, Hillbrow, Liss, Hants GU33 7PS, England.

TSIOLAS Stelios, b. 28 Dec 1955, Kondea, Famagusta, Cyprus. Composer. *Education:* Diploma, American Academy, Larnaca, Cyprus, 1974; Diploma of Music, ACMM, Melba Memorial Conservatorium, 1978-81; BMus (Composition), University of Melbourne, 1981-83. *Debut:* Larnaca, Cyprus, 1976. *Career:* Orchestrator, Conductor, Greek Song Festival, Dallas Brooks Hall, 1983; Composer, Dollar Culture, New Audience Ensemble, Melba Hall, 1983; Composer/ Musician-in-Residence, Australia Council, Carringbush Library, 1984; Orchestrator, Greek Song Festival, Dallas brooks Hall, 1984; Composer, Musical Director, Victorian Arts Centre, 1985; Composer, Conductor, Greek Progressive Youth of Australia, 1986, 1987; Composer, Conductor, Greek Orthodox Community of South Australia, 1986; Founder, Australian-Greek Choir, 1987. *Compositions include:* Greek Kangaroo; Antigone; Metamorphosis; Freedom Tonight; At Dawn; A Rock Experience; Ilie, Ilie Vasilia (Sun, Sun my King); At Dawn; Musical Reflections of Composers of Diaspora;

numerous songs with traditional Greek-music elements; Song-cycle of 12 poems, Thoughts from Unconjuncted Colours, poetry by Anastasis Barkatsas, 1980; Song-cycle Confession, poetry by Doros Loizou, 1981; Twelve-Tone and Avant-Garde Compositions: Electronique Pieces and Musique Concrète; Short Compositions for Soloistic Use and Small Chamber Ensembles. *Recordings:* The Greek Kangaroo-Children's Songs; Freedom Tonight; Ilie, Ilie Vasilia (Sun, Sun my King). *Hobbies:* Travelling; Learning. *Address:* 7 Williamstown Road, W Foostcray, 3012 Melbourne, Victoria, Australia.

TSUTSUMI Tsuyoshi, b. 28 July 1942, Tokyo, Japan. Recording Artist; Concert Cellist; Professor of Music. m. Harue Saji, 14 May 1978, 1 son, 1 daughter. *Education:* Toho Gakuen High School of Music, Tokyo, 1961; Artist Diploma, Indiana University, USA, 1965. *Debut:* Tokyo, Japan, 1955. *Career:* Soloist (Iwaki), European Tour, NHK Symphony Orchestra of Tokyo, 1960; Soloist (Ozawa), Chicago Symphony, Ravinia Festival, Ravinia Park, Chicago, Illinois, USA, 1967; Soloist (Ozawa), American and European Tour, New Japan Philharmonic, 1974; Soloist (Akiyama), American Symphony, New York City, 1978; Soloist (Ceccato), Czech Philharmonic, Prague, Czechoslovakia, 1984; Professor of Music, School of Music, University of Illinois, Urbana, Illinois, USA; Currently, Professor of Music, School of Music, Indiana University, Bloomington, IN, USA. *Recordings:* CBS/Sony: Bach, Unaccompanied Suites, complete; Beethoven, Sonatas and Variations (Turini, piano); Dvořák Concerto, Czech Philharmonic (Kosler, conductor); Haydn, Concertos, English Chamber Orchestra. *Hobbies:* Reading; Trains; Stamp Collecting. *Address:* 2715 Bluff Court, Bloomington, IN 47401, USA.

TUCAPSKY Antonin, b. 27 Mar 1928, Opatovice, Czechoslovakia. Composer; Conductor; Professor. m. Beryl Musgrave, 13 Oct 1972. 1 son, 1 daughter. *Education:* Teachers' Training College, Phdr Masaryk University, Brno, Czechoslovakia. Music Education: Conducting, Choral singing, Composition, Janáček Academy of Music, Brno. *Debut:* Ostrava. *Career:* Conductor of various choirs, 1954-65; Children's Radio Choir, Ostrava, 1960-62; Chief Conductor, Moravian Teachers Choir, 1964-73; Appearances on Czech Radio, Supraphon Records, BBC Radio and Television, Belgian Radio. *Compositions:* In Honorem Vitae; Lands; 5 Lenten Motets (Choral cycles); The Time of Christmas; The Sacrifice (Cantatas); Four dialogues (clarinet & Piano); Pocket Music (wind quintet); Adieu; Moravian Polka (Orchestra); Missa Serena (Oratorio); Stabat Mater (Oratorio); The Undertaker (Opera); Triptychon, Symphony Orchestra, 1991; Concertino, for piano and string orchestra, 1992; Concerto, for violin and orchestra, 1993. *Recordings:* Choral Music; Comoedia (Cantata), Veni, Sancte Spiritus, BBC Recordings. *Publications:* Sightreading and Sightsinging, 1969; Janáček's Male Choruses and their Interpretation, 1971. *Hobbies:* Gardening; Swimming. *Address:* 50 Birchen Grove, Kingsbury, London NW9 8SA, England.

TUCCI Gabriella, b. 4 Aug 1929, Rome, Italy. Singer (Soprano). *Education:* Studied at the Accademia di Santa Cecilia and with Leonardi Filoni. *Debut:* Teatro Giglio Lucca 1951, as Violetta. *Career:* Spoleto Festival 1952, as Leonora in La Forza del Destino; Florence 1953, as Cherubini's Medee; Tour of Australia 1955; La Scala Milan from 1959, as Mimi and in the Italian premiere of A Midsummer Night's Dream; Verona Arena 1959-69; US debut San Francisco 1959, as Madeleine in Andrea Chénier; Metropolitan Opera, 1960-73 as Butterfly, Aida, Euridice, Leonora in Trovatore and La Forza del Destino, Violetta and Marguerite; Covent Garden 1960, as Tosca; Appearances at Buenos Aires, Sydney, Oslo, Johannesburg, Dallas, New Orleans and Philadelphia; Other roles include Desdemona, Anaide in Mosè by Rossini, Luisa Miller, Micaela and Elvira in I Puritani; Teacher at Indiana University from 1983. *Recordings:* Pagliacci (Decca); Il Trovatore (Columbia); Requiems by Bellini and Donizetti. *Address:* Music Faculty, Indiana University, Bloomington, IN 47405, USA.

TUCEK Rene, b. 8 Jan 1936, Pizen, Czechoslovakia. Singer (Baritone). *Education:* Studied in Pizen with M Gartnerova and in Vienna with F Schuch-Tovini. *Debut:* Brno 1960, as Count Luna in Il Trovatore. *Career:* Sang first in Brno, Pizen and Ceske Budejovice; Prague National Theatre from 1971, in the standard repertory and in operas Prokofiev, Martinů, Gershwin and Mysliviček; Guest appearances in Spain, Austria, Bulgaria, Luxembourg and Cuba; Has sung in concert and in song recitals; Teacher at the Prague Conservatory from 1973. *Recordings:* The Jacobin by Dvořák and operas by Smetana (Supraphon). *Address:* c/o National Theatre, P O Box 865, 112 30 Prague 1, Czech Republic.

TUCKER Mark, b. 10 Aug 1958, England. Singer (Tenor). *Education:* Studied at Cambridge and the Guildhall School of Music and Drama. *Career:* Active as concert singer throughout Europe under such conductors as Michel Corboz, John Eliot Gardiner, Ton Koopman, Roger Norrington and Sigiswald Kuijken; Appearances at the festivals of Aix-en- Provence, Beaune, Florence, Flanders and Utrecht; Sang the Evangelist in the St Matthew Passion at the Maltings, Snape, and in the St John Passion with the choir of King's College, Cambridge, under Stephen Cleobury; Monteverdi Vespers at St Mark's Venice, conducted by Gardiner, with the Monteverdi Choir; Other ensembles with whom he has worked include the Amsterdam Baroque Orchestra, The Sixteen, City of London Sinfonia, the Netherlands Bach Choir, the Northern Sinfonia and the Taverner Choir; Bruges Festival 1984, as Monteverdi's Orfeo; London recital debut 1984, at the Purcell Room; Festival Hall debut in Messiah, 1984; Contributed to European Music Year 1985 with Peri's Orfeo under Phillipe Herreweghe in Florence; BBC Radio 3 in Peter Schmoll by Weber and the premiere of Scarlatti's Una villa di Tuscolo; Appearances in Granada TV's Man and Music series; Recitals with Nigel North and David Mason; Season 1990-91 in Die Entführung at the Newbury and Spitalfields Festivals, and Bach's St Matthew Passion in Aarhus, Denmark, conducted by Richard Hickox; Further operatic roles include Cavalli's Egisto, Alcide in Rameau's Les Fêtes de Polymnie, Eurimaco in Monteverdi's Ulisse, (ENO 1992) and Mozart's Bastien, Belmonte and Tamino; Has sung in concert performances of Rameau's Pygmalion in Stuttgart, Rouen and Utrecht, conducted by Sigiswald Kuijken; Later repertory includes Nicolai's Fenton and Stravinsky's Oedipus. *Address:* c/o Harrison Parrott Ltd., 12 Penzance Place, London W11 4PA, England.

TUDORAN Ionel, b. 24 June 1913, Baragti de Vede, Rumania. Singer (Tenor); Teacher. *Education:* Studied at the Conservatory of Iasi. *Debut:* Iasi 1936, in the operetta Die Landstreicher by Ziehrer. *Career:* Sang at Cluj and Timisoara 1937-48; Principal tenor at Bucharest from 1948, notably as Otello, Faust and Cavaradossi; Guest appearances in Leipzig, Dresden, Prague, Brno, Sofia and Budapest; From 1957 sang in Russia at opera houses in Riga, Minsk, Leningrad and Moscow; Warsaw and Poznan 1958, Belgrade, Ljubljana and Zagreb 1959; Retired 1962 and taught at the Bucharest Conservatory until 1972.

TULACEK Thomas, b. 26 Apr 1955. Violinist. *Education:* Studied at the Prague Conservatory, the Prague Academy of Musical Arts and the Guildhall School of Music. *Career:* First Violin section, BBC Scottish Symphony Orchestra, 1985-89; Leader, New Chamber Orchestra, Oxford, 1990-; Associate Professor, Trinity College of Music, London, 1991. Recital work has taken him to countries such as Italy, Switzerland, France, Israel and the Czech Republic and has recorded for Czech Radio and Radio Vatican. Since 1990 has been performing regularly with the English pianist Steven Wray and they have formed a piano trio with Jaroslav Ondracek. Concerto performances have included works by Prokofiev, Bruch, Haydn, Mozart and most recently Neilsen, with the Teplice Symphony Orchestra, in the Czech Republic. *Address:* 1 Brookes Court, Longley Road, London SW17 9LF, England.

TUMA Jaroslav, b. 1956, Czechoslavakia. Organist.

Education: Studied at the Prague Academy of Arts with Milan Šleehta and with Zuzana Růžičková; with Hans Haselböck, Summer school at Haarlem, Holland, studying improvisation, and Bach interpretation with Piet Kee. *Career:* Laureate of organ competitions in Prague, Linz, Leipzig, Nuremberg and Haarlem; Festival appearances by Nuremberg, Linz, Prague and Mechelen; Engagements in Europe, Japan and the USA; Concerts with Czech Philharmonic Orchestra, Three years cycle of complete organ works by J S Bach in Prague; Repertoire includes works by Bach, Franck, Liszt, Reger, Hoffhaimer, Sweelinck, Isaac and Eben and Husa; Accompanies major soloists on the harpsichord. *Recordings:* L and H Hassler, Muffat; Handel; Series organs of Bohema I-IV, Czech compositions for harpsichord. *Current Management:* Bohemia-Concert, PO Box 5, Prague, 100 05, Czech Republic. *Address:* Bohemia Concert, PO Box 5, 100 05 Prague 105, Czech Republic.

TUMAGIAN Eduard, b. 1944, Bucharest, Rumania. Singer (Baritone). *Career:* Sang at Bucharest from 1968 as Papageno, ALfonso, Mozart's Count, and Wolfram in Tannhäuser; Opéra du Rhin Strasbourg from 1974, as Germont, Iago, Enrico in Lucia di Lammermoor, Scarpia, Marcello, Belcore, Escamillo and Eugene Onegin; Guest appearances at Lyon, Stuttgart, Karlsruhe and Orange; Sang Rigoletto at Basle 1981 and appeared further with Welsh and English National operas, Frankfurt (Renato 1983), Nice (in Puritani and Vespri Sicilliani), Amsterdam, Chent, Antwerp and Graz; Engagments at La Scala Milan from 1986, as Nabucco and in Vespri Sicilaini (Montfort), I Due Foscari and Riccardo III by Flavio Testi; Paris Opera 1985, as Germont; US debut 1986 at Pittsburgh as Don Carlo in La Forza del Destino; Carnegie Hall New York in concert performances of Béatrice at Bénédict and Nabucco; Recent appearances at the Deutsche Oper Berlin, Staatsoper Hamburg, Vienna Staatsoper (Scarpia in season 1988-89), Toulouse (La Franciulla del West) and Oviedo Festival (Simon Boccanegra and La Favorita); Season 1991 as Nabucco at Trieste and Buenos Aires, Rigoletto at Philadelphia; Concert repertoire includes music by Bach, Handel, Beethoven, Mussorgsky, Britten and Shostakovich (14th Symphony at the 1984 Salzburg Festival). *Recordings include:* Miller in video of Luisa Miller from Opera de Lyon (Pioneer); Napoleon in War and Peace; Turandot. *Address:* c/o Teatro alla Scala, Via Filodrammatici 2, 2012 Milan, Italy.

TUMANYAN Barseg, b. 1958, Jerevan, Armenia. Singer (Bass-Baritone). *Education:* Studied at the Komitas Conservatoire and at La Scala, Milan; Further study with Evgeny Nesterenko at the Moscow Conservatoire, 1985. *Career:* Sang with the Spenderian Opera (Armenia) from 1980; Performances of Basilio at the Teatro San Carlo Naples 1988; Appeared in Gala Concert for Armenia at Covent Garden 1989, and invited back to sing in La Bohème, Les Contes d'Hoffmann and Carmen; US debut with Boston Opera as Ramfis in Aida, 1989; Appearances in USA 1989 with the Armenian State Opera; Sang Colline in La Bohème at Covent Garden and Monte Carlo, 1990, King Philip in Don Carlos at Los Angeles; Wigmore Hall recital, June 1990. *Honours:* Prizewinner, Bussetto Competition 1983; 2nd Prize, Tchaikovsky Competition, Moscow, 1986; Joint First Prize, Rio de Janeiro Competition, 1987. *Address:* c/o Royal Opera House, Covent Garden, London WC2, England.

TUNLEY David Evatt, b. 3 May 1930, Sydney, Australia. Professor of Music. m. Paula Patricia Laurantus, 26 May 1959, 1 son, 2 daughters. *Education:* Diploma, New South Wales State Conservatorium of Music, 1949-51; BMus, University of Durham, England, 1957; MMus 1963, DLitt 1970, University of Western Australia. *Career:* Music master, Fort Street Boys High School, Sydney, 1952-57; University of Western Australia, 1958-. *Compositions:* Concerto for Clarinet & Strings, recorded. *Publications:* Monographs: The 18th Century French Cantata, London 1974; Couperin, London 1982; Harmony in Action, London 1984; The French Contata Facsimile, 17 Vols. New Yor, 1990-91.

Contributions to: New Grove Dictionary; New Oxford History of Music, volumes 6 & 9. *Honours:* Fellow, Australian Academy of the Humanities, 1980; Chevalier dans l'Ordre des Palmes Académiques, 1982; Order of Australia, 1987; Member of the Order of Australia, 1987. *Memberships:* Chairman, Music Board, Australia Council, 1984-85; Past President, Musicological Society of Australia. *Hobbies:* Reading; Theatre; Travel. *Address:* 100 Dalkeith Road, Nedlands, Western Australia 6009, Australia.

TUNNELL Jonathan, b. 1955, England. Cellist. *Debut:* Wigmore Hall, 1984, with Peter Pears. *Career* : Member of the Tunnell Trio; Co-founded the Brindisi String Quartet at Aldeburgh 1984; Concerts in a wide repertory throughout Britain and in France, Germany, Spain, Italy and Switzerland; Festival engagements at Aldeburgh (residency 1990), Arundel, Bath, Brighton, Huddersfield, Norwich and Warwick; First London performance of Colin Matthews' 2nd Quartet, 1990, premiere of David Matthews' 6th Quartet 1991; Quartet by Mark-Anthony Turnage 1992; Many BBC recitals and resident artist with the University of Ulster. *Recordings include:* Quartets by Britten, Bridge and Imogen Holst; Works by Pierné and Lekeu. *Honours include:* Prize winner, Third Banff International String Quartet Competition in Canada, 1989, with Brindisi Quartet. *Address:* c/o Owen-White Management, 14 Nightingale Lane, London N8 7QU, England.

TURCANO Lucia, b. 1913, Bucharest, Romania. Singer (Soprano). *Education:* Studied at the Bucharest Conservatory with Elena Saghin and Demetru Baxiliu. *Debut:* Bucharest 1939, as Marguerite in Faust. *Career:* Sang in Bucharest until 1946 as Rachel in La Juive, Leonora (Il Trovatore), Aida and Elsa in Lohengrin; Vienna Volksoper 1942-45; La Scala Milan from 1946, notably as Abigalle in Nabucco, Gioconda and Turandot; Guest appearances in Venice, Palermo, Naples, Bologna, Trieste, Rome and Cagliari; New York City Opera 1950-60, with further appearances in Philadelphia; Returned to Rumania in 1963, gave concerts and taught.

TURCHI Guido, b. 10 Nov 1916, Rome, Italy. Composer. *Education:* Studied at the Rome Conservatory and with Pizzetti at the Accademia di Santa Cecilia. *Career:* Taught at the Rome Conservatory, Director, Para and Florence Conservatories 1967-72; Artistic Director, Accademia Filormonica Romana 1963-66, and Teatro Comunale Bologna, 1968-70; Artistic Director, Accademia di santa Cecilia from 1970. *Compositions include:* Opera Il buon soldato Svejk, La Scala Milan 1962; Trio for flute, clarinet and viola 1945; Invettiva for small chorus and 2 pianos 1946; Concerto for string orchestra 1948; Piccolo concero notturno 1950; 3 Metamorfosi for orchestra 1970: Dedalo, ballet, Florence 1972; Dedica for flute 1972; Choruses, songs and incidental music. *Address:* c/o Accademia Nazionale di Santa Cecilia, Via Vittoria 6, 1-00187 Rome, Italy.

TURECK Rosalyn, b. 14 Dec. 1914, Chicago, Illinois, USA. Concert Artist (Pianist); Author; Editor; Professor. *Education:* Studied with Sophia Brilliant-Liven, Jan Chiapusso; Graduated Cum Laude, Juilliard School of Music, 1935, studied with Olga Samaroff; Studied Electronic Instruments with Theremin. *Career includes:* Concert Tours: Extensive US tours since 1937 annually; European Tours since 1947; Also tours of South Africa, South America, Middle East, Far East. Experience as Conductor Soloist with London Philharmonia, 1958, New York Philharmonic 1958, Tureck Bach Players (London) 1958, San Antonio Symphony, Oklahoma Symphony, 1962, Scottish National Symphony, Israel Philharmonic, Kol Israel Orchestra, 1963, International Bach Society Orchestra, 1967, 1969, 1970, Kansas City Philharmonic 1968, Washington National Symphony 1970, Madrid Chamber Orchestra, 1970, Tureck Bach Players (New York) 1981, 1984, 1985, St Louis Symphony Orchestra 1981. Repeated solo appearances at major British and European Bach Festivals; Numerous TV appearances in US and England 1963-; Numerous

academic appointments including Professor of Music, University of Maryland, 1982-84; Founder-Director, Tureck Bach Players (London) 1957; International Bach Society, Inc 1966; Institute for Bach Studies 1968; Tureck Bach Players (New York) 1981; Tureck Bach Institute, Inc 1981. *Recordings:* Numerous recordings on Decca, HMV, Brunswick, Odeon, Allegro, Capitol, Columbia including: Goldberg Variations, Aria and Ten Variations in the Italian Manner harpsichord; Italian Concerto, Chromatic Fantasia and Fugue; 4 duets (piano); Introduction to Bach, performance of compositions discussed in book Introduction to the Performance of Bach Columbia Masterworks; Video and recordings; Video Artists International, 1992-; Video Teatro Colon, 1992; CDs, 1992-. *Publications include:* Introduction to the Performances of Bach 3 Vols, 1959-60; Tureck Bach Urtext Series: Italian Conerto, 1983, Lute Suites, E minor and C minor, edited for Classical Guitar; Italian Concerto, 2nd edition, 1991. *Contributions to:* Royal Institution of Great Britain, London, University of Southampton, Oxford University, All Lectures, 1993; Numerous articles to musical journals. *Honours:* Numerous prizes and awards in the US and Europe. *Memberships:* Century Club, New York; Oxford and Cambridge, London. *Current Management:* Christa Phelps, Lies Askonas Ltd. *Address:* Christa Phelps, Lies Askonas Ltd, 6 Henrietta Street, London WC2 E8LA, England.

TURETZKY Bertram (Jay), b. 14 Feb 1933, Norwich, Connecticut, USA. Double Bass player; Composer. *Education:* Studied at the Hartt School of Music (graduated 1955), at New York University (musicology with Curt Sachs) and with David Walter; Further study at the University of Hartford, MM 1965. *Career:* Played double bass in various orchestras and ensembles; Solo debut at Judson Hall, New York, Oct 1964, with works by Donald Erb and Barney Childs; Novel performing techniques have been exploited by such composers as Donald Martino, Richard Felciano, Paul Chihara, Kenneth Gaburro, George Perle and Ben Johnston. *Compositions:* Collages I-IV 1976-81; Reflections on Ives and Whittier for double bass and tape 1979-81; In memoriam Charles Mingus 1979; Baku for tape 1980. *Publications include:* The Contemporary Contrabass 1974; Editions of double bass studies for the American String Teachers Association; Editor of series published by the University of California Press on contemporary performance techniques. *Address:* ASCAP, ASCAP Building, One Lincoln Plaza, New York, NY 10023, USA.

TURGEON Bernard Romeo, b. 20 Oct 1931, Edmonton, Alberta, Canada. Singer; Professor of Voice. m. 15 May 1978, 1 son, 2 daughters. *Education:* Royal Conservatory of Music, Toronto; Toronto Opera School, RCM. *Debut:* Canadian Opera Company, 1953. *Career:* Opera performances in Canada, US, Mexico and UK, 3 tours of the former USSR in roles such as Rigoletto, Amonasro, Tonio, and Germont. Created title role of the opera Louis Riel, commissioned for the Centennial of Canada, 1967, produced for TV 1969 and produced on record from a live performance at Lincoln Centre 1975 in celebration of the Bicentennial of the US. Appearances on CBC and Radio Canada as guest panelist in multi-nation Arts Festival round-table, 1983. Designed and developed Opera Training Programs for the University of Alberta, the University of Victoria, The Banff Centre, and McGill, University. Established the St Jude Scholarship in Voice at the University of Victoria, 1979. *Honours include:* Canada Council Fellowship, 1964, and Senior Arts Award, 1975; Government of Alberta Achievement Award, 1972; Instated in the National Music Museum, London, England, 1988. *Memberships include:* Adjudicator, Canada Council; BC Arts Board, Ministry of Culture; Founding Member, Johann Strauss Foundation of BC; Advisory Panel, Debut Concerts, Montreal. *Hobbies:* Sailing; Dog Breeding. *Current management:* Alison Pybus of Dean Artists Management, Toronto, Ontario. *Address:* 3450 rue Drummond 402A, Montreal, Quebec, Canada H3G 1Y2.

TURNAGE Mark Anthony, b. 10 June 1960, Grays,

Essex, England. Composer. *Education:* Royal College of Music, with Oliver Knussen and John Lambert; Tanglewood USA with Henze and Gunther Schuller. *Career:* Commissions from the London Sinfonietta, Bath Festival, the Feeney Trust, the BBC and the Munich Biennale; Featured composer at 1986 Bath Festival and 1987 Glasgow Musica Nova; Radcliffe Trust Composer-in-Association with the City of Birmingham Symphony Orchestra, 1989-93; Radcliffe Trust Composer-in-Association with the City of Birmingham Orchestra, 1989-93. *Compositions:* And still a Softer Morning for flute, vibraphone, harp and cello 1978/83; Night Dances for orchestra 1980-81; Kind of Blue for orchestra 1981-82; Entranced for piano 1982/86; Let us Sleep Now for chamber orchestra 1979/82; After Dark for wind quintet and string quintet; Lament for a Hanging Man for soprano and ensemble 1983; Ekaya for orchestra 1984; On all Fours for chamber ensemble 1985; One Hand in Brooklyn Heights for 16 mixed voices 1986; Beating about the Bush for mezzo-soprano and chamber ensemble 1987; Release for 8 players 1987; Greek, opera in 2 acts 1987-88; Greek Suite for mezzo-soprano, tenor and ensemble 1989; Three Screaming Popes for orchestra 1989; Kai for Cello and Ensemble, 1990; Momentum for orchestra, 1990-91; Are you sure? for string quartet, 1991; Leaving for Soloists, mixed chorus and large ensemble, 1992; Killing Time (television scena), 1991; Sleep on for cello and piano, 1992. *Recordings:* Three Screaming Popes (CBSO/Rattle), EMI CD. *Honours:* 1982 Guinness Prize for composition and Yorkshire Arts Young Composers' Competition; 1983 Benjamin Britten Young Composers' Prize; BMW Music Theatre Prize, 1988. *Address:* c/o Schott & Co. Ltd., 48 Great Marlborough Street, London W1V 2BN, England.

TURNBALL Pamela Margaret, b. 25 Aug 1969, Peterhead, England. Private Music Teacher. m. James McCabe Turnbull, 24 Aug 1991. *Education:* Peterhead Academy, 1981-87; Aberdeen College of Commerce; LTCL Clarinet Teacher. *Debut:* Clarinet Solo, 1984. *Career:* Played First Clarinet, Aberdeen University Orchestra, 1988; Northeast Wind Band, 1987-88; Musical Director, Petershead Pantomime Group, 1988-90; Woodwind Teacher, 1990- *Memberships:* Incorporated Society of Musicians. *Hobbies:* Hill walking. *Address:* 10B St Mary Street, Peterhead, Aberdeen AB42 6TB, Scotland.

TURNER Charles Lloyd, b. 10 July 1948, Houston, Texas, USA. Musicologist; Bibliographer; Performer. *Education:* BMus, 1970; MMus, 1976; MSLS, 1979, University of Texas; DMus, Indiana University, 1986. *Career:* Founding Director, La Primavera (Early Music Ensemble); Concert tours of Texas, California, Southwest USA; Tour of Mexico sponsored by US State Department; Musicologist, Director of Hartt Early Music Ensemble, Hartt School, University of Hartford. *Recordings:* Popular Elizabethan Music; The Greater Passion Play from Carmina Burana. *Publications:* Bibliographer, Medieval Music, 1986; The Isorhythmic Motet in Continental Europe, Proportion and Form, 1986; Articles in Journal of the Lute Society of America and Music Analysis; Reviews in Notes. *Honours:* Phi Beta Kappa; Crane Award in the Arts, 1979. *Memberships:* American Musicological Society; Lute Society of America; Early Music America. *Hobbies:* Chess; Photography; Early Jazz; Pet Greyhound. *Address:* University of Hartford, 200 Bloomfield Avenue, West Hartford, CT 06117, USA.

TURNER Claramae, b. 28 Oct 1920, Dinuba, California, USA. Singer (Contralto). *Education:* Studied with Nino Comel, Armando Angini and Giacomo Spadoni at San Francisco and with Dick Marzollo in New York. *Debut:* Sn Francisco 1942, in Les Contes d'Hoffmann. *Career:* Sang at the Metropolitan Opera 1946-50, notably as Amneris; Sang in the premieres of Menotti's The Medium (1946), The Tender Land by Copland (1954) and Bomarzo by Ginastera (1967); Teatro Liceo Barcelona 1957-58; Chicago Lyric Opera 1956, as Azucena; San Diego 1967, in the US premiere of Der junge Lord by Henze; Appearances in Buenos Aires,

Mexico City, Venice, Monte Carlo, Boston, Dallas, Houston, Baltimore, Philadelphia and Pittsburgh. *Recordings:* Un Ballo in Maschera, conducted by Toscanini (RCA); Bomarzo (CBS).

TURNER Jane, b. 1960, County Durham, England. Singer (Soprano). *Education:* Guildhall School of Music; Opera Studio, London. *Career:* West German debut 1984, as Wellgunde and Siegrune in the Ring at Bayreuth; 1987-90 as a Flower Maiden and Flosshilde; UK opera debut 1985, as Carmen with the Glyndebourne Tour; Flora in Peter Hall's production of Traviata at the Festival, 1987; Covent Garden debut 1987, as Ann Who Strips, in the Hytner production of The King Goes forth to France; returned as a Flower Maiden in Parsifal and as Flosshilde in Das Rheingold; English National Opera as Maddalena in Rigoletto and as Lola in Cavalleria Rusticana. *Address:* c/o Lies Askonas Ltd., 186 Drury Lane, London WC2B 5RY, England.

TURNER John Brierley, b. 1 Apr 1943, Stockport, England. Solo Recorder Player; Composer; Editor. m. Margaret Cordall Lister, 14 Apr 1988. *Education:* Fitzwilliam College, Cambridge; MA; LLM; Northern School of Music; LRAM; Solicitor (Hons). *Debut:* Aldeburgh Festival, 1968. *Career:* Regular concerts and recordings with Early Music Consort of London, 1969-76; Co-Founder, Legrand Ensemble, 1968-; Duo recitals with Neil Smith (guitar) and Peter Lawson (piano); 1st performances include: Leighton's Concerto, Alwyn's Seascapes, McCabe's Desert IV: Vista, Crosse's Watermusic, Burgon's Nearing the Upper Air, Pitfield's Concerto, Ball's Danserye, Fricker's Two Dreams. *Compositions:* Four Diversions, 1969; A Christmas Garland, 1981; Six Bagatelles, 1983. *Recordings:* Brandenburg Concerto No 4 with English Chamber Orchestra, Academy of St Martin-in-the-Fields, London Philharmonic Orchestra and Virtuosi of England; Telemann Concerto for recorder and flute with Academy of Ancient Music; Many recordings with Early Music Consort of London. *Publications:* Editor: A Birthday Album for Thomas Pitfield, 1983; Modern Wind Music, 6 vols, 1984-86; A Birthday Album for the Society of Recorder Players, 1987; Pieces for Solo Recorder, 3 vols, 1987-. *Address:* 40 Parsonage Road, Heaton Moor, Stockport, Cheshire SK4 4JR, England.

TURNER Margarita, b. 11 March 1943, Perth, Australia. Singer (Soprano). *Education:* Studied in London and West Germany. *Debut:* Krefeld 1969, as Micaela. *Career:* Appearances in opera at Cologne, Saarbrucken, Wiesbaden and Wuppertal; 15 year career at the Essen Opera as Fiordiligi, Pamina, Marguerite, Martha, Marenka, Violetta, Marzellime (Fidelio), Mélisande, Eva, Concepcion and Nedda; Sophie in Der Rosenkavalier, Mimi, Liu, Rosalinde and Luise in Der Junge Lord by Henze; Frequent concert engagements; Teacher at the Essen Musikhochschule. *Address:* c/o Theater, Rolandstrasse 10, 4300 Essen, Germany.

TURNOVSKY Martin, b. 29 Sept 1928, Prague, Czechoslovakia. Conductor. *Education:* Music Academy, Prague; Studied Conducting in Dedecek, Prague Academy of Music, 1948-52; Private Studies in Conducting with Szell 1956. *Career:* Conductor, Czech Army Symphony Orchestra 1955-60; State Philharmonic Orchestra, Brno 1960-63; Music Director, Pilsen Radio Orchestra 1963-66; Dresden State Opera and State Orchestra 1966-68; Guest Conductor with numerous well-known orchestras including Radio Orchestra, Berlin; Cleveland Orchestra; New York Philharmonic Orchestra; Detroit Symphony Orchestra; Toronto Symphony; Stockholm Philharmonic; Bournemouth Symphony; Liverpool Royal Philharmonic Orchestra; BBC Northern Orchestra, Manchester 1968; Music Director, Norwegian Opera, Oslo 1975-80; Music Director, Bonn Opera 1979-83; Opera engagements with the Deutsche Oper Berlin, Welsh National Opera, Staatsoper Stuttgart, Royal Opera Stockholm and the Savonlinna Festival, Finland; Season 1992/93 appointed as Music Director of the Prague Symphony Orchestra and Conducted Otello and Un Ballo in Maschera at the Prague State Opera. *Recordings:* Has made many recordings for Supraphon including 4th Symphony of Bohuslav Martinů, Grand Prix du Disque 1968. *Honours:* Recipient, 1st Prize, International Competition for Conductors, Besancon, France 1958. *Address:* A-1190 Wien, Grinzinger Allee 39, Austria.

TUROK Paul Harris, b. 3 Dec 1929, New York City, USA. Composer. m. Susan Kay Frucht, 24 Mar 1967. *Education:* BA, Queens College, 1950; MA, University of California, Berkeley, 1951; MS, Baruch College, 1986; Special Studies, Juilliard School of Music, 1951-53. *Career:* Music Director, Experimental TV, U.S. Army, Augusta, Georgia, 1954; Music Director, KPFA, Berkeley, 1955-56; Lecturer, City College New York, 1960-63; Visiting Professor, Williams College, 1964. *Compositions:* Operas: Richard III, A Secular Masque, Scene Domestic; Orchestral: American Variations, Chartres West, Ultima Thule, Great Scott!, Joplin Overture, Sousa Overture, Danza Viva, Concertos for Violin, English Horn, Trombone, Cello, Oboe, Symphony; Chamber Music: 4 String Quartets, English Horn Quintet, Sonatas for Flute, Bassoon, Horn, Trumpet, Viola, Cello, Harp, Harpsichord; Numerous other works; Organ: Toccata, Piano; Passacaglia; Transcendental Etudes; Brass: Elegy, Quintet; Vocal: Lanier Songs; Evocations; To Music; Three Popular Songs. *Address:* c/o G. Schirmer Incorporated, 24 East 22 Street, New York, NY 10010, USA.

TURSKA Joanna Lucja, b. 16 Oct 1958, Warsaw, Poland. Musician (Flautist). m. Roman Siczek, 28 June 1986, 1 daughter. *Education:* MMus, Flute Performance, Warsaw Academy of Music; Postgraduate studies: Royal Conservatory, The Hague, Netherlands; Conservatories in Creteil and Paris, France; Teachers include E.Gajewska, F.Vester, A.Marion (flute), S.T.Preston, P.Sechet (baroque flute). *Career:* Appearances at recitals, chamber music concerts and as soloist with orchestras in Europe and America including: Germany, France, Italy, Switzerland, Austria, Netherlands, Belgium, Luxembourg, Poland, Cuba, USA; Performances at such festivals as Paris, Youth Music Festival (Bayreuth, Germany), Warsaw Autumn, New Music Festival and Early Music Festival (Chicago, USA). *Recordings:* Solo, chamber music and orchestral performances recorded by Polish Radio and TV, Belgian Radio, French Radio, and US radio, TV classical and ethnic channels; Album for winners of Premio Ancona competitions. *Hobbies:* Skiing; Tennis; Travel. *Address:* 1426 Portsmouth, Westchester, IL 60153, USA.

TUSA Andrew, b. 1966, England, Singer (Tenor). *Education:* New College, Oxford, Studied at the Pears-Britten School. *Career* Sang in the Play of Daniel at the Elizabeth Hall 1989, followed by Asterion in Rameau's Nais for the English Bach Festival; Concert engagements include Messiah with the Leicester Bach Choir, St. John Passion in Krefeld, soloist with Gothic Voices in Milan and Second Shepherd in Monteverdi's Orfeo at the 1990 Salzburg Festival; Appearances with the Gabrieli and Taverner Consorts, Christmas Oratorio under Andrew Parrott in Oslo, Masses by Mozart in Barbican Hall, 1991, St. Matthew Passion with the Birmingham Bach Society and Messiah with the Stavanger Symphony in Norway. *Recordings include:* Mozart's Salzburg Masses with the Winchester College Choir and Monteverdi Madrigals with I Fagiolini. *Address:* Robert Gilder & Co. Enterprise House, 59/65 Upper Ground, London SE1 9PQ, England.

TUTINO Marco, b. 30 May 1954, Milan, Italy. Composer. *Education:* Studied at the Giuseppe Verdi Conservatory, Milan. *Career:* Works performed at the 1976 Gaudeamus Festival in Amsterdam; Operas produced in Genoa, Alessandria, Livorno and Modena. *Compositions:* A synthesis between 19th century procedures and more modern methods. *Compositions include:* Operas Pinnochio, Genoa 1985; Cirano, commedia lirica, Alessandria 1987; La lupa, Livorno 1990; Le vite immaginarie, chamber opera, Modena 1990. *Address:* c/o Teatro Comuale di Genova, Via I. Frugoni 15-6, 16121 Genoa, Italy.

TWARDOWSKI Romuald b. 17 June 1930, Wilno, Poland. Composer. m. Alice Stradczuk, 16 June 1981, 1 son. *Education:* Diplomas, Composition & Piano, Wilno Conservatory, 1957; Diploma, Composition, Higher School of Music, Warsaw; Postgraduate studies, Nadia Boulanger, Paris, 1963. *Career:* Professor, Academy of Music, Warsaw. *Compositions:* Operas including: Cyrano de Bergerac, 1963; Tragedy, 1969; Lord Jim, 1976; Story of St Catherine, 1985. Also numerous works for orchestra, choirs, theatre, cinema most recent include: Old Polish Concerto for Strings, Little Concerto for Vocal Orchestra, Michelangelo Sonnets for Baritone & Piano, Lithuanian Variations for Winds/Wind Quartet, all 1988. *Recordings include:* Gershwin, Variations for Symphony Orchestra, Polish Radio, Cracow; Spanish Fantasy for Cello & Orchestra, Polish Radio, Warsaw; Alleluia for mixed choir, 1990; Espressioni for violin and piano, 1990; Classic melodies for violin and piano or orchestra; Numerous recordings, own compositions. *Address:* ul. Miaczynska 54 m. 61, 02-637 Warsaw, Poland.

TYL Noel, b. 31 Dec 1936, West Chester, Pennsylvania, USA. Singer (Baritone). *Career:* Studied with Gibner King in New York. *Debut:* Teatro della Pergola Florence as Basilio in Il Barbiere di Siviglia. *Career:* Has sung in Boston, Houston, Cincinnati, New Orleans, San Diego and New York (City Opera); Further appearances at the Vienna Staatsoper and in Dusseldorf, Munich, Barcelona and Vancouver; Other roles include Massenet's Don Quichotte, Wotan, Amfortas, the Grand Inquisitor, Scarpia, King Dodon in The Golden Cockerel and Ramphis; Also sings in concert. *Address:* New York City Opera, Lincoln Center, New York, NY 10023. USA.

TYLER James Henry, b. 3 Aug 1940, Connecticut, USA. Lutenist; Music Director; Author; Professor. m. Joyce Geller, 7 May 1975. *Education:* University of Connecticut; Private study with Joseph Iadone, 1958-61. *Debut:* Library of Congress, Washington DC, 1962. *Career includes:* Member of the Early Music Consort of London, 1969-76, and Julian Bream Consort, 1975-; Founding Dirctor, London Early Music Group, 1976-; Tours of Australia, America, Japan, East and West Europe; Performances in festivals including those at Edinburgh, Sydney and Lucerne; Professor of Music, and Director, Early Music Performance Programme, University of Southern California, 1986-. Carnegie Hall recital, 1987. *Compositions:* Music for BBC TV productions of Romeo and Juliet, Measure for Measure, Henry VIII and Hamlet. *Recordings include:* Music of the Renaissane Virtuosi; Vivaldi: Double concertos, Alla Rustica; Italian Airs and Dances; La Mantovana; Elizabethan Social Music; Seventeenth-century Bel Canto; Songs in Shakespeares's Plays. *Publications:* The Early Guitar, 1980; A Brief Tutor for the Baroque Guitar, 1984; Gasparo Zanetti: Il Scolaro 1645, 1984; The Early Mandolin, 1989. *Hobbies:* Collecting early instruments and early lighting. *Current Management* Los Angeles Musica Viva, 2185 Las Lumas Street, Pasedena, CA 91107, USA. *Address:* University of Southern California, School of Music, Los Angeles, CA 90089-0851, USA.

TYLER Marilyn, b. 6 Dec 1928, New York City, USA. Singer (Soprano). *Education:* Studied with Friedrich Schorr in New York and with Toti dal Monte in Venice. *Career:* Sang first in operetta; Basle Opera 1948; Netherlands Opera 1955, as Violetta; Sang title role in Die Kluge by Orff, 1956; Rome 1959, as Constanze in Die Entführung; Bayreuth 1961, Brünnhilde in Die Walküre; Appearances in Italy, Germany, North America and Israel; Teacher at the Maastricht Conservatory, Holland. *Recordings include:* Die Zauberflöte; Die Entführung; Serse by Handel (Westminster); Stravinsky's Pulcinella (Decca). *Address:* c/o Conservatorium Voor Musik, Bonnerfantstraat 15, Maastricht, Holland.

TYNES Margaret, b. 11 Sept 1929, Saluda, Virginia, USA. Singer (Soprano). *Education:* Studied with Emil Cooper in New York and with Tullio Serafin in Italy. *Debut:* New York City Opera 1952, as Fata Morgana in The Love for Three Oranges. *Career:* Montreal 1959, as Lady Macbeth; Has sung in Spoleto (as Salome), Vienna, Budapest, Toronto, Milan, Prague, Naples and Bologna; Metropolitan Opera debut 1973, as Jenůfa; Other roles include Norma, Aida, Desdemona, Dido and Marie in Wozzeck; Many concert appearances.

TYREN Arne, b. 27 Feb 1928, Stockholm, Sweden. Singer (Bass-Baritone). *Education:* Studied with Ragnar Hulten at the Stockholm Opera School. *Debut:* Royal Opera Stockholm 1955, as Bartolo in Le Nozze di Figaro. *Career:* Has sung in Scandinavia as Leporello, Baron Ochs, the Grand Inquisitor, Sarastro and Wozzeck; Drottningholm Festival from 1955, as Bartolo in Paisiello's Il barbiere di Siviglia, Don Alfonso, Il Maestro di Capella, Buonafede in Haydn's Il Mondo della luna and Seneca in L'Incoronazione di Poppea; Sang at Stockholm in the premieres of Blomdahl's Aniara (1959) and Herr von Hancken (1965) and Tintomara by Werle (1973); Edinburgh Festival 1959, Wozzeck; Further engagements in Hamburg, Cologne, Turin, Lisbon and Tel Aviv; Director of the Stockholm Opera School from 1977. *Recordings include:* Aniara (Columbia). *Honour:* Swedish Court Singer 1978. *Address:* Opera School, Kungliga Teatern, PO Box 16094, S-10322, Stockholm, Sweden.

TYRRELL John, b. 17 Aug. 1942, Salisbury, Southern Rhodesia. Musicologist. *Education:* BMus, University of Cape Town, 1963; Oxford. *Career:* Former associate editor of the Musical Times; Editorial staff, New Grove Dictionary of Music, to 1980; Lecturer, Nottingham University 1976, Reader in Opera Studies 1989. *Contributions to:* Many learned journals, articles on Janáček and his operas in the New Grove Dictionary of Opera, 4 volumes, 1992. *Publications:* Leos Janáček: Kat'a Kabanova, Cambridge 1982; Czech Opera, Cambridge 1988; Janáček's Operas: A Documentary Account, London, 1992. *Address:* University of Nottingham, Department of Music, University Park, Nottingham NG7 2RD, England.

TYSON Alan, b. 27 Oct 1926, Glasgow, Scotland. Musicologist. *Career:* Fellow, 1952; Senior Research Fellow, 1971, All Souls College, Oxford University; Visiting Professor, Music, Columbia University, New York City, USA, 1969; Lyell Reader in Bibliography, Oxford University, 1973-74; Ernest Bloch Professor of Music, University of California, Berkeley, 1977-78; Member, Institute for Advanced Study, Princeton, 1983-84; Visiting Professor, Graduate Center, City University of New York, 1985. *Publications:* The Authentic English Editions of Beethoven, 1963; English Music Publishers' Plate Numbers (with O.W. Neighbour), 1965; Selected Letters of Beethoven (Editor), 1967; Thematic Catalogue of the Works of Muzio Clementi, 1967; Beethoven Studies (Editor) Volume 1, 1973, Volume 2, 1977, Volume 3, 1982; The Beethoven Sketchbooks : History, Reconstruction, Inventory, with Douglas Johnson, Editor, and Robert Winter, 1985; Mozart: Studies of the Autograph Scores, 1987; with A Rosenthal, Mozart's Thematic Catalogue: a facsimile, 1990; 2 Vols. Watermarks in Mozart's autographs, published in the Neue Mozart-Ausgabe, X/33/Abteilung 2, 1992. *Address:* 7 Southcote Road, London, N19 5BJ, England.

TZINCOCA Remus, b. 1920, Iassy, Rumania. Conductor; Composer. m. Anisia Campos. *Education:* Diploma, Iassy Conservatory of Music; Conservatoire National Superieur de Musique de Paris; Disciple and musical assistant of George Enescu. *Debut:* Led Colonne Orchestra with George Enescu as soloist, Paris. *Career:* Conducted major orchestras in Europe and North America including: London Philharmonia, Zurich Tonhalle, Lamoureux, Pasdeloup and Colonne in Paris, Radiotelevision Française, New York Philharmonic, Cleveland Orchestra, CBC Orchestra, Bucharest Philharmonic; Radio TV and Bucharest Opera; Founder, Musical Director, Newport Music Festival, Rhode Island, USA; Founder, Musical Director, New York Orchestra da Camera, with concerts at Metropolitan Museum, Carnegie Hall and Town Hall; Discovered with Anisia Campos, original version, in Rumanian, of Bartók's

Cantata Profana, in New York Bartók Archives and gave 1st world performance in Bucharest with the Philharmonic Orchestra, 1984. *Compositions:* Oratorios, symphonies, lieder, and a Byzantine Mass. *Honours:* 1st Prize in Conducting, Conservatoire National Superieur de Musique de Paris; Freedom Baton, Crusade for Freedom, USA, 1953; Doctor Honoris Causa, Music Academy of Cluj, Romania, 1994. *Hobbies:* Backgammon; Chess. *Address:* 632 Avenue Herve-Beaudry, Laval, Quebec, Canada.

U

UCHIDA Mitsuko, b. 20 Dec 1948, Tokyo, Japan. Pianist. *Education:* Studies at the Hochschule für Musik und Darstellende Kunst, Wien, with Professor R. Hauser, 1961-68; Diploma, 1968. *Debut:* Vienna, 1963. *Career:* Extensive world-wide engagements in recitals and concerto performances with all major London orchestras, Chicago Symphony, Boston Symphony, Berlin Philharmonic Orchestras; Played and directed the Mozart Piano Concerto Cycle (21 Concertos from K175 to K595), in London with English Chamber Orchestra in 1985-86 season. *Recordings:* Mozart Piano Sonatas, Piano Concertos with Jeffrey Tate and English Chamber Orchestra (Philips); Chopin piano sonatas; Debussy, 12 Etudes. *Honours:* 1st Prize, Beethoven Competition, Vienna, 1969; 2nd Prize Chopin Competition, Warsaw, 1970; 2nd Prize, Leeds Competition, 1975. *Hobbies:* Cycling. *Address:* c/o Van Walsum Management, 26 Wadham Road, London SW15 2LR, England.

UCHIDA Ruriko, b. 8 Aug 1920, Tokyo, Japan. Ethnomusicologist; Singer (Alto). *Education:* Graduate, Tokyo University of Fine Arts, 1947. Music education: Vienna University, Vienna Music Academy, 1959-62. *Career:* Performances include Concerts, Opera, Television and Radio in Japan; Performances in Concerts, Television and Radio in Austria, Hungary, Yugoslavia, Japan; Professor, Kunitachi College of Music, Tokyo, Japan. *Recordings:* Japanese Songs of Contemporary Composers; Japanese Folksongs Collection; Music of minorities in Nothern Thailand. *Publications:* Tauebayashi (Study of Rice Planting Music), 1978; Amami Minyo (Study of Folksong of Amami Islands), 1983. *Honours:* State prizes of Japanese Minister of Education, 1949, 1967; Academic prize, Society for Japanese Ballands and Songs, 1984. *Memberships:* International Musicological Society, ICTM; Society for Ethnomusicology; Society for Japanese Ballads and Songs. *Hobby:* Photography. *Current Management:* Shin-enshoka-Kyokai, Management Association. *Address:* 4-3-13-502 Kichijoji-Minamicho, Musashino-city, Tokyo, Japan.

UDAGAWA Hideko, b. 1960, Japan. Violinist. *Education:* Tokyo University of Arts; studied with Milstein, London, and Juilliard School of Music, New York. *Debut:* At age 15. *Career:* Television appearances and radio broadcasts, Europe; Concerts in USA, many European countries; Recitals, Queen Elizabeth Hall; Lincoln Center; Concerto performances with London Symphony Orchestra, the Philharmonia, the Royal Philharmonic, the London Philharmonic, the Royal Liverpool Philharmonic, the City of Birmingham Symphony, the English Chamber and the Polish Chamber Orchestras; Toured UK and Ireland with Berlin Symphony and the Bucherest Philharmonic Orchestra. *Recordings:* Virtuoso violin pieces for EMI Japan; Heitetz Transcriptions for ASV; Brahms and Bruch Concertos with Sir Charles Macherras and London Symphony for Chandos. *Address:* c/o Norman McCann Ltd, The Coach House, 56 Lawrie Park Gardens, London SE2 6XJ, England.

UGHI Uto, b. 21 Jan 1944, Busto Arsizio, Italy. Violinist. *Education:* Studied with George Enescu, 1954. *Debut:* Teatro Lirico Milan, 1951, Bach's Chaconne and Paganini Caprices). *Career:* Performed Mendelssonh's Violin Concerto, 1954; First European Tour, 1959; Organizer, Omaggio a Venezia Festival; Collaborated with major orchestras including: Concertgebouw Orchestra, Boston Symphony Orchestra; Philadelphia Orchestra; Washington Symphony Orchestra; Santa Cecilia with major conductors; Tours: USA, USSR, Japan, South Africa, South America, All Europe; Has appeared with such conductors as Barbirolli, Prêtre, Haitink, Cluytens, Sawallisch and Sinopoli. *Recordings:* Brahms Concerto; Beethoven; Mendelssohn; Bruch; Paganini; Viotti, Mozart Concertos; Beethoven Sonatas; Mozart Sonatas; Dvořák Concerto; Vivaldi, Le 4 Stagioni; Bach: Sonatas and Partitas; Schumann: Concerto. *Memberships:* Accademico of Santa Cecilia. *Current Management:* Eugenia Reato, 45030 S Martino Di Venezze, Italy. *Hobbies:* Football; Tennis; Swimming; Skiing; Reading. *Address:* Canareggio 4990/E, 30121 Venice, Italy.

UHL Fritz, b. 2 Apr. 1928, Vienna, Austria. Operatic Singer (Dramatic tenor). 1 son. *Education:* State Music Academy, Vienna 1947-52. *Debut:* Graz, 1952. *Career Includes:* With Munich State Opera, 1956; Bayreuth 1957-64, as Siegmund, Erik and Loge; Vienna State Opera, 1961-; Covent Garden 1962, as Walther in Die Meistersinger; Festival appearances throughout Europe and USA, Japan, Korea, Canada, Argentina; Salzburg Festival 1968 (Florestan), 1971 and 1972 (Drum Major in Wozzeck); Sang at Linz, 1976 in the premiere of Der Aufstand by Helmut Eder; Professor at the Vienna Conservatory from 1981. *Recordings include:* Tristan (Decca); Flying Dutchman (Philips); Elektra, Arabella and Antigonae (Deutsche Grammophon); Wozzeck (CBS). *Honour:* Bayerischer Kammersanger, 1962. *Membership:* Vienna Male Voice Choral Society, 1947. *Hobbies:* Books; Records; Astronomy. *Current Management:* Dr G Hilbert, Munich; Vladarski, Vienna. *Address:* Lindauerstr 9, D-81735 Munich, Germany.

ULFUNG Ragnar, b. 28 Feb 1927, Oslo, Norway. Singer (Tenor); Opera Producer. *Education:* Studied at the Oslo Conservatory and in Milan. *Debut:* Sang in concert from 1949; first stage role in Menotti's The Consul, Oslo 1952; Member of Royal Opera Stockholm from 1958; Sang Gustavus in Un Ballo in Maschera at Covent Garden 1960; returned in the premiere of Maxwell Davies's Taverner, 1972 and as Mime in the Götz Friedrich production of the Ring, 1974-6; Metropolitan Opera debut 1972, as Mime; later sang Strauss's Herod, Wagner's Loge, Berg's Captain and Weill's Fatty in New York; Other appearances include Strauss's Liebe der Danae and Penderecki's Die schwarze Maske in Santa Fe, as Kent in Reimann's Lear in San Francisco and Tom Rakewell in The Rake's Progress; Concert performances of Messiaen's St François d'Assise in London and Lyon; Sang Herod in Salome at San Francisco 1986; Paris Opéra and Geneva 1988, as Shuisky (Boris Godunov) and in The Fiery Angel; Alfred in Die Fledermaus at Oslo, 1988; Festival Hall London 1989, Aegisthus in Elektra; Herod at Los Angeles; Valzacchi in Der Rosenkavalier at Santa Fe 1989; Sang Goro in Butterfly at Lyons, 1990; Season 1992 as the Witch in Hansel and Gretal at Los Angeles, Fatty in Mahagonny at Geneva and Valzacchi in Rosenkavalier at the Santa Fe Festival; Debut as stage director Santa Fe 1973, with La Bohème; Other stagings include Lulu for Santa Fe, Otello in Stockholm and Der Ring des Nibelungen in Seattle. *Recordings include:* Monostatos in Ingmar Bergman's version of Die Zauberflöte. *Address:* c/o Lies Askonas Ltd., 186 Drury Lane, London WC2B 5RY, England.

ULRICH Jurgen Heino, b. 21 Nov 1939, Berlin, Germany. Lecturer. m. Uta Krackau, 2s, 1d. *Education:* Studied at the Musikhochschule, Detmold, 1959-63. *Career:* Piano Teacher, Youth Music School, Frankfurt; Education of Music Teachers, Teachers' Training College of State of Hessen, Jugenheim an der Bergstrasse, 1964-67; Teacher, Theory and Aural Training, Bergisches Conservatory, Wuppertal, 1967; Professor, Musikhochschule, Detmold. *Compositions:* Orchestral and chamber music; Spots for harpsichord and percussion, 1968; Verwehendes, 2 movements for chamber ensemble, 1968; Im kuehlen August, for piano, flute, and string trio, 1970; Nocturnal Fanfare for trumpet and piano, 1982; Various educational music, including High School Symphony, 1965. *Honours:* Stuttgart Prize for Young Composers, 1963, 1967; Kuhlau Competition of Uelzen, 1970; Prize of Musikgesellschaft Brunswick (chamber music), 1977; New Music for Music Schools, Hamm, 1976. *Address:* 33 Papenbergweg, D-32756, Germany.

UNDERWOOD John, b. 11 Oct 1932, Luton, Bedfordshire, England. Violist. *Education:* Studied with Frederick Riddle at the Royal College of Music. *Career:* Co-principal viola of the RPO under Beecham, 1962-62; Co-founder of the Delmé Quartet 1962; Many performances in Britain and Europe in the classical and modern repertory; Concerts at the Salzburg Festival and the Brahms Saal of the Musikverein Vienna; Season 1990 included Haydn's Last Seven Words in Italy and elsewhere, three Brahms programmes at St John's Smith Square with Iain Burnside, piano; Concerts at St David's Hall Cardiff with quartets by Tchaikovsky and Robert Simpson (premiere of 13th quartet); Appearances in Bremen, Hamburg and Trieste, followed by festival engagements, 1991; Other repertory includes works by Paul Patterson, Daniel Jones, Wilfred Josephs, Iain Hamilton and Bernard Stevens. *Recordings include:* Haydn Last Seven Words; Vaughan Williams On Wenlock Edge and Gurney's Ludlow and Teme; Simpson quartets 1-9 and String Trio (Hyperion); Daniel Jones 3 quartets and Bridge No 2 (Chandos); Bliss Nos 1 and 2; Josef Holbrooke Piano Quartet and Clarinet Quintet (Blenheim); Brahms Clarinet Quintet and Dvořák F major (Pickwick); Verdi Quartet and Strauss A major Op 2 (Hyperion). *Address:* c/o J Williams, 33 Whittingstall Road, Fulham, London SW6, England.

UNGER Gerhard, b. 26 Nov 1916, Bad Salzungen, Thuringia, Germany. Singer (Tenor). *Education:* Studied at Eisenach and the Berlin Musikhochachule. *Career:* Sang lyric roles at Weimar from 1947, Tamino, Pinkerton and Alfredo; Bayreuth Festival 1951-52 as David in Die Meistersinger; Guest appearances at the Dresden Opera as Tamino and Pinkerton; Engaged at the Berlin Staatsoper from 1952, Stuttgart from 1982; Member of the Hamburg Staatsoper 1962-73, appearing also in Vienna, Milan, Paris and the Metropolitan New York; Salzburg Festival 1961-64, as Pedrillo in Die Entführung and Brighella in Ariadne auf Naxos; Character roles later in career (Captain in Wozzeck, Mime and Shuratov in From the House of the Dead) in Europe and North and South America (Mime at Dallas 1984); Bregenz Festival 1980 as Pedrillo, Stuttgart 1987 as Mime (last major role). *Recordings include:* Der Waffenschmied, Steuermann in Fliegende Holländer, Die Meistersinger, Alwa in Lulu; Die Entführung, Die Meistersinger; Fidelio, Königskinder by Humperdinck, Die Zauberflöte, Carmina Burana, Elektra, Ariadne auf Naxos, Der Rosenkavalier, Tannhäuser (EMI); La Finta Giardiniera. *Address:* c/o Stuttgart Staatsoper, Oberer Schlossgarten 6, 7000 Stuttgart, Germany.

UNGVARY Tamas, b. 12 Nov 1936, Kalocsa, Hungary. Composer; Conductor; Double-Bass Player; Teacher. 1 daughter. *Education:* Philosophy, Budapest; Diploma, Conducting, Mozarteum, Salzburg; Béla Bartók Conservatory, Budapest (double-bass). *Career:* Hungarian State Philharmonic, 1957; Solo double-bass, Camerata Academica, Salzburg 1967-69; (as Composer) ISCM Festivals 1973, 1974, 1978, 1988; Warsaw, Autumn 1978; all major European radios; Lecturer, Computer Music; Artistic Manager, EMS, Stockholm, Sweden and Director of the Kineto-auditory Communication Research at the Royal Institute of Technology, Stockholm. *Compositions include:* Seul; Basic Barrier; Traum des Einsamen; Incrementum; Akonel No. 2 (flute and tape); Intereaction No. 2 (organ and tape); Sinus-Coitus (piano and tape); Ite missa est; L'aube des flammes, Gypsy children's giant dance with Ili Fourier; Dis-Tanz (ensemble and tape); Istehem, Uram! (tape). *Recordings:* Caprice; Fylkingen; Hungaroton; Phono Suecia. *Contributions to:* Melos; Nytida Musik; Muzsika; Leonardo. *Honours:* Prize, Swedish Competition for Conductors, 1970; Prize, Premio Firenze for Young Conductors, 1971; 1st Prize at the International NEWCOMP computer music competition in 1987; Honorary awards at the 7th and 15th international electro-acoustic music competition in Bourges, France. *Memberships:* Swedish Society for Composers; Fylkingen; Swedish Section of International Society of Contemporary Music; Composers Forum, USA; EMAS, Great Britain. *Address:* Hagalundsgatan 31, 17151 Solna, Sweden.

UNO Koji, b. 30 Aug 1925, Tokyo, Japan, Flautist; Professor of Showa Musical College, Atsugi, Japan. m. 25 Dec 1957, 1 son, 1 daughter. *Education:* Diploma, National Music School of Tokyo, 1951; Corso Straordinario, Conservatorio di Musica S Cecilia, Rome, Italy, 1962-63; Studied with Severiano Gazzelloni, Rome 1962-63. *Debut:* Brandenburg Concerto. No. 5, J. S. Bach, Sapporo Chamber Orchestra, Sapporo, 1950. *Career:* Principal Flautist, Konoe Symphony Orchestra, 1951-56; Principal Flutist, ABC Symphony Orchestra, 1956-58; Concerto in G, Mozart, Sapporo Symphony Orchestra, Obihiro, 1967; 20 recitals in Tokyo, 1962-91; Molnar Harp. Trio, 1959-71; Tokyo Baroque Quintet, 1964-70; Uno Quartet, 1978-89; Numerous broadcasts on radio in Japan. *Recordings:* Song of Londonderry, solo and chamber music, 4 track tape. *Publications:* Flute, Music Encyclopaedia, Heibon-sha, 1957, 1983; Knowledge for Flute, Wind Instruments Series, Ontomo-sha, 1969, 1983; 2 Flute Quartets of Mozart, Flute Club, 1965; 5 Movements by Japanese Folksongs, 1989. *Contributions to:* Japan Music Journal; Japan Flutists Association Journal; Showa College Bulletin. *Hobby:* Study of 1 Keyed Flute and 8 Keyed Flute. *Current Management:* Japan Concert Association, Yamanosoen 110, 3-10-6 Sendagaya, Japan. *Address:* 4-21-21 Nishi-Oi, Shinagawa-ku, Tokyo 140, Japan.

UNRUH Stan, b. 20 Nov 1938, Beaver, Oklahoma, USA. Singer (Tenor). *Education:* Studied at the Juilliard School New York. Debut: Geneva 1970, as Melot in Tristan. *Career:* Appearances at Paris, Orange, Rouen, Bordeaux (Lohengrin 1979 and Aeneas 1980) and Toulouse; Member of the Krefeld Opera 1977-85, notably in Der Ring des Nibelungen; New York City Opera 1976, as Erik in Der Fliegende Holländer, Strasbourg 1977, as Parsifal; Further guest appearances at Barcelona 1978, Brunswick and Innsbruck 1983, Buenos Aires 1985 (Siegfried in Götterdämmerung) and Freiburg 1986, in the premiere of Hunger und Durst by Violeta Dinescu; Sang at the Staatstheater Kassel 1989-90; Other roles include Wagner's Tristan, Siegmund, Loge and Walther von Stolzing, Florestan, Shuratov in From the House of the Dead, Max, Don José, Samson, Stravinsky's Oedipus and Bacchus. *Address:* Staatstheater, Friedrichplatz 15, 3500 Kassel, Germany.

UNWIN Nicholas, b. 1962, Cambridge, England, Concert Pianist. *Education:* Studied at the Royal College of Music and with Philip Fowke. *Career:* Played Bartok, Lambert and McCabe at the Purcell Room, London, 1986; Bartok's 2nd Concerto at John's Smith Square (also on Radio 3); Wigmore Hall recital 1987; BBC recital 1989, followed by Birmingham University and Leeds Town Hall; Artist-in-residence at the King's Lynn Festival 1989, with Nights in the Gardens of Spain and Ravel's G major Concerto; BBC Documentary on Michael Tippett 1990, playing the Second Sonata. *Honours include:* Chappell Gold Medal and Cyril Smith Recital Prize, RCM; Winner Lambeth Music Award; Hastings Concerto Festival, and the Brant Piano Competition; Schott Award 1990. *Address:* 95 Station Road, Impington, Cambridge CB4 4NP, England.

UPPMAN Theodor, b. 12 Jan 1920, San Jose, California, USA. Concert and Opera Singer. m. Jean Seward, 31 Jan 1943. 1 son, 1 daughter. *Education:* Curtis Institute of Music, 1939-41; Stanford University, Opera Department, 1941-42; University of Southern California, 1949-50. *Debut:* Pelléas with San Francisco Symphony, Monteux, 1947. *Career:* Billy, Billy Budd premiere, Royal Opera House, Covent Garden, London, 1951, and in USA premiere, NBC TV Opera, 1952; Leading Baritone, Metropolitan Opera, 1953-77 as Masetto, Papageno, Sharpless, Guglielmo, Pélleas, Paquillo (La Périchole), Taddeo (L'Italiana in Algeri), Harlekin (Ariadne auf Naxos), Kothner (Die Meistersinger), Eisenstein (Die Fledermaus); Appearances with opera companies throughout USA and Europe including Traveler (Death in Venice), Geneva Opera and Passion of Jonathan Wade at the New York City Opera, 1962; Recitals throughout USA and Canada; Sang in the premieres of Floyd's The Passion of Jonathan Wade 1962 and Yerma by Villa-Lobos 1971; Soloist with most major USA orchestras; Appearances on Radio and television; Faculty, Manhattan School of Music; Mannes College of Music; Britten-Pears School for Advanced Musical Studies; Sang in World Premiere of Bernstein's A Quiet Place at Houston 1983, La Scala 1984, Washington DC, Vienna 1986. *Recordings:* For Victor Records; Capitol; Internos; Deutsche Grammophon. *Honours:* Musical Prizes: Atwater Kent Auditions; Gainsborough Award; Honorary Director Britten-Pears School for Advanced Musical Studies. *Memberships:* Professional Committee, Regional Auditions Metropolitan Opera; National Association of Teachers of Singing. *Address:* 201 West 86th Street, New York, NY 10024, USA.

UPSHAW Dawn, b. 17 July 1960, Nashville, Tennessee, USA. Singer (Soprano). *Education:* Studied at the Manhattan School of Music and at the Metropolitan Opera School. *Career:* Sang in the 1983 US premiere of Hindemith's Sancta Susanna while at college; Metropolitan from 1985, as Countess Ceprano, Echo (Ariadne), Adina, Despina, Sophie (Werther), the Woodbird and Zerlina (1990); Salzburg Festival 1987 as Barbarina, Aix-en-Provence 1988-89, as Despina and Pamina; Sang Pamina in a concert performance at the 1990 Promenade Concerts, conducted by Roger Norrington; Other roles include Marzelline (Fidelio) and Constance in Les Dialogues des Carmélites; Season 1992 as Despina and Susanna at the Met, L'Ange in St François at Salzburg and Anne Trulove at Aix-en-Provence. *Recordings:* Ariadne auf Naxos (Deutsche Grammophon); Mass in G by Schubert (Telarc). *Address:* c/o Metropolitan Opera, Lincoln Center, New York, NY 10023, USA.

URHO Ellen Alli Marjatta, b. 22 Jan 1920, Pirkkala, Finland. Professor of Music Education. m. Valo Urho, 10 Aug 1945, 1s, 2d. *Education:* MA, Helsinki University, 1950; Sibelius Academy, Finland, 1944. *Debut:* Choir Conductor, 1964. *Career:* Lecturer, Teachers' Training College, Helsinki, 1959-70; Head, Music Department, Sibelius Academy, Finland, 1970-75, Vice Director, 1975-81, Professor of Music Education, 1980-87, Rector, 1981-87; Visiting Professor, and guest lecturer at universities in USA; Various TV and radio appearances in Finlnad; Organizer of the World Conference of the International Society for Music Education, Finland, 1990. *Publications:* Sanoin ja savelin, 1960; A Music Book Series for Comprehensive Schools, 1970-77; Musiikin didaktiikka, 1981, 1988; Lukion Musiikki, 1983-84, all co-authored; Preparation and Organization of a Conference, 1991. *Honours:* Knight of the Order of the White Rose of Finland, 1970; commander of the Order of the Lion of Finland, 1986; Hon Member, ISME, 1992. *Memberships:* Board, ISME, Member of the Board of Directors of International Society for Music Education, 1980-1992; Pres, 1986-88; Board, national Opera in Finland, 1984-; Ch, Association for the Symphony Orchestras of Finland, 1987-90. *Address:* Lauttasaarentie 16, 00200 Helsinki, Finland.

URROWS David Francis, b. 25 Oct. 1957, Honolulu, Hawaii, USA. Composer, Music Historian. *Education:* AB, Brandeis University 1978; MMus, University of Edinburgh 1980; DMA, Boston University, 1987. *Career:* Compositions performed, commissioned and broadcast in USA, Asia and Europe; Many publications on contemporary music history; Lecturer at several American universities. *Compositions:* String Quartet, 1978; Piano Sonata 1979, Quintet for winds, 1981; Three Vailima Episodes, soprano and string orchestra, 1984; A New England Almanack, baritone and piano 1985; Sonata for oboe and harp. 1985; An Advent Litany, organ, 1985; Sonata for violin and piano, 1991; Sonata, San Angelo, two violas, 1986; Ricordanza dell Umbria, piano, 1987; Winterreise, soprano and chamber orchestra, 1988; Opera: A Midsummer Nights Dream, 1980; Oratorio: Lycidas, 1987; Epiphany Cantata 1993, Many songs and anthems. *Publicationsinclude:* Sea Ballads and Songs in Whalsay, Shetland, 1983; The Choral Music of Christopher le Fleming, 1986; Randall Thompson: A Bio-Bibliography, 1991. *Honours:* Winner, National Association of Teachers of Singing Art Song Composition Contest 1987; ASCAP Special Awards 1987; Malloy Miller Prize, 1985; ASCAP Foundation Grant, 1981 Stratton Prize- Fellowship, 1980; Reiner Prize in Composition, 1987. *Memberships:* ASCAP; Pi Kappa Lambada; Sonneck Society for American Music; American Guild of Organists. *Address:* 1590 Mizzen Lane, Half Moon Bay, CA 94019-1536, USA.

USHER Julia, b. 21 July 1945, Oxford, England. Composer; Music Therapist; Publisher. m. Rodney Gordon Usher, 20 July 1968, 2 sons. *Education:* Newnham College, Cambridge, 1964-67; BA(Cantab), 1967; PGCE Diploma, University of York, 1968; Diploma in Music Therapy (NR), City University, London, 1986. *Career:* Compositions performed by Gemini, Nash Ensemble, Park Lane Group, St James Singers, Coull Quartet, Lambeth Orchestra, BBC Singers, Angela Malsbury, John Turner, Peter Lawson, Sarah Francis, Penelope Walmsley-Clarke, Michael Finnissy, and Sounds Positive; Many BBC broadcasts. *Compositions:* Self-published under name Primavera: Encounter; Byzantine Mosaics; Asolando; Ordnance Survey; Ra 1; Handbook; Season's End; Aquarelles; A Reed in the Wind; Subsequent Darkness; A Grain of Sand in Lambeth; The Orford Merman; Ode to the West Wind; The Angel Standing in the Sun; The Causeway; L'Isole della Laguna; Unfinished Business, 1990-91; Marak; Mental maps and Perceived Distance; Wellsprings; Hope's Perpetual Breath, 1993. *Recordings:* By BBC: L'Isole della Laguna; Encounter; Season's End; A Reed in the Wind; Byzantine Mosaics; Ordnance Survey; Asolando; Marak and Pentimento, Gabriel Keen, piano, 1993. *Publication:* Articles on 20th century music in Encyclopaedia Britannica, 1968. *Contributions to:* Composer Magazine. *Hobbies:* Sailing; Theatre; Reading; Travel. *Address:* 110 Wyatt Park Road, Streatham, London SW2 3TP, England.

USROLSKAYA Galina, b. 17 June 1919, Petrograd, Russia. Composer. m. Makuhin Konstantin, 23 Dec 1966. *Education:* Leningrad Conservatory, 1939-47; Postgraduate Courses in composition, Leningrad Conservatory, 1947-50. *Career:* Tutor, Composition, Leningrad Conservatory College, 1948-77. *Compositions include:* Doha Nobis Pacem, piccolo, tuba, piano, 1970-71; Dies Irae, 8 double basses, percussion and paino, 1972-73; Benedictus, Qui Venit, 4 flutes, bassoons and paino, 1974-75; Symphony No 2, orchestra and solo voice, 1979; Symphony No 3, orchestra and soloist, 1983; Symphony No 4, trumpet, tamtam, piano and contralto, 1985-87; Sonata No 5, piano, 1986; Sonata No 6, piano, 1988; Symphony No 5, oboe, trumpet, tuba, violin, percussion and soloist, 1989-90. *Recordings include:* 3 Sonatas 1947, 1952, 1957; Grand Duet for violoncello and paino, 1959. *Honours:* Heidelberger Kunstlevinnenpreis, 1992. *Memberships:* Russian Composer's Union. *Hobbies:* Solitude; Nature. *Address:* Gagarina Avenue 27-72, St Petersburg 196135, Russia.

UTEGALIEVA Saule Iskhakovna, b. 31 May 1958, Astrakhan. Ethnomusicologist. *Education:* Alma-ty State Conservatory; St Petersburg Institute of Theatre, Music and Cinematography. *Career:* Doctor, 1987, Assistant, 1988, Associate Professor, Department of Theory of Music, Alma-ty State Conservatory. *Publications:* Functional context of the Kazakh folk performers' musical thinking, 1987; Articles in: Problems of the USSR peoples' instrumental music, 1986; Folk music instruments and instrumental music, 1987; Materials of the VII and VIII ESEM, 1990, 1991. *Honours:* Musicology Degree, 1987. *Memberships:* Folklore commission, Kazakh Union of Composers. *Hobbies:* Collecting folk music recordings and instruments; Swimming. *Address:* ul Puschkina 80 fl 8, 480100 Alma ty, Kazakhstan.

UYTTENHOVE Yolande Irene M L, b. 25 July 1925, Leuze, Belgium. Head, Academy of Music; Pianist. m. Rene De Macq, 2s. *Education:* Royal Conservatory of Music, Brussels; Performance, RAM, London, 1953. *Debut:* 1929. *Career:* Concerts throughout Europe and the US. Radio and television performances in France and Belgium; Head, Hon Director, Academy of Music, Braine-L'Alleud, Belgium. *Compositions:* Sonatina for piano, 1962; Sonatina for flute and paino, 1964; Methode de Piano; Cancale & Retour, 1967; Diner a piano piece for 6 hands, 1962; Piece pour Cor, 1962; Piece Triste pour Trompette, 1962; Recueil de Dictees Atonales, 1966; Le Sire de Lisigny, piano, 1967; Berdikir, cello and paino, 1987); Siciliano, flute, violin, piano, 1987; Halloween, 5 flutes, 1988; Sonata for viola and piano, 1989; Cendrillon for piano and four hand; Trio for trumpet, 4 timbales and paino. *Honours:* Bronze medal of Arts Sciences and Literature, Paris, 1950; Diploma of Honour, International Concours of Pianists, Barcelona, 1954; Medalle d'or Concours International de Composition du Lutece; Prix fuga, 1987; Officier de L'Ordre de Leopold II. *Memberships:* ILWC: SABAM; Administrator, Union des Compositerus Belges; CEBEDEM. *Address:* 128 Rue des Confederes, 1040 Brussels, Belgium.

V

VACEK Milos, b. 20 June 1928, Horni Roven, Pardubice, Czechoslovakia. Composer. *Education:* Studied at the Prague Conservatory, 1942-47; Academy of Musical Arts 1947-51. *Career:* Freelance composer from 1954. *Compositions include:* Operas Jan Zelivsky, composed 1956-58, performed Lomouc 1984; Brother Zak, Ostrava 1982; Romance of the Bugle, Ceske Budejovice 1987; Mikes the Tomcat, Brno 1986; Ballets The Comedian's Fairytale, 1958, Wind in the Hair 1961, The Mistress of the Seven Robbers 1966, Meteor 1966 and Lucky Sevens 1966; Musicals The Night is my Day (on Bessie Smith) 1962, The Emperor's New Clothes 1962, Madame Sans Gene 1968 and Wind from Alabama 1970; Orchestral: Sinfonietta 1951; Spring Suite for wind instruments and strings 1963; Serenade for Srtings 1965; May Symphony 1974; Poem of Fallen Heroes for alto and orchestra 1974; Olympic Flame, symphonic poem 1975; A Solitary Seaman, symphonic Picture, 1978; World's Conscience in memory of Lidice 1981; Chamber and piano music, cantatas, songs, choruses and organ music. *Address:* OSA (Czech Republic), c/o PRS Ltd. Member Registration, 29/33 Berners Street, London W1P 4AA, England.

VACHHA Michel Rumy b. 20 Sept 1955, Bombay, India. Pianist. *Education:* BA, Honours, Jawahrlal Nehru University, 1976; LRSM, London, 1976; Diploma, Conservatorio di Musica Rome, 1980; Diploma, Musikhochschule, Zurich, 1984; Diploma, Conservatoire National de Paris, 1986. *Debut:* Rome, 1974. *Career:* Several performances, solo & with Orchestra in India, Italy, France, Austria, Yugoslavia, Switzerland, Tunisia, Kuwait, Germany; Recordings for Radio & TV in India, France, Italy; TV Documentaries. *Compositions:* Fantasia & Fugue, 1980; Allegro Furioso for piano & orchestra,1982; Sonate pour piano, 1984. *Publications:* Articles in: Music World; and other magazines. *Memberships:* Accademia di Musica, Palestrina, Rome. *Hobbies:* Water Sports; Animals; Mountaineering; Cinema; Theatre; Skiing. *Address:* Piazza Garibaldi, No 4, 00036 Palestrina, Rome, Italy.

VADUVA Leontina, b. 1964, Rumania. Singer (Soprano). *Education:* Studied with mother and at Bucharest Conservatory. *Debut:* Sang Manon at Toulouse 1987, conducted by Michel Plasson. *Career:* Appeared as Ninetta in La Gazza Ladra at the Théâtre des Champs Elysées, Paris, July 1988, followed by Manon at Covent Garden; Returned to London in a production of Rigoletto by Nuria Espert, and sang Drusilla at Théâtre du Châtelet, Paris and at the Grand Théâtre, Geneva; Engagements for season 1990-91 included appearances in Les Pêcheurs de Perles and L'Elisir d'Amore at Toulouse; Manon at Montpellier, Bordeaux, Avignon, Paris (Opéra Comique) and Vienna; Rigoletto at Bonn; Donizetti's Il Campanello di Notte at Monte Carlo; Les Contes d'Hoffmann in Paris (Théâtre du Châtelet) and London (Covent Garden); Ismene in Mitridate by Mozart at the Châtelet, conducted by Jeffrey Tate; Micaela in Carmen at Covent Garden. *Recordings include:* Mitridate; Le Nozze di Figaro, conducted by John Eliot Gardiner (release 1993). *Honours include:* Winner, Concours de Chant, Toulouse, 1986; Winner, s'Hertogenbosch Competition, Holland, 1987; Laurence Olivier Prize, London 1989. *Address:* Stafford Law Associates, 26 Mayfield Road, Weybridge, KT13 8XB, England.

VAGGIONE Horacio, b. 21 Jan 1943, Cordoba, Argentina. Composer. *Education:* Composition, Arts School, National University of Cordoba. *Career:* Co-Founder, Experimental Music Centre, University of Cordoba, 1964-69; Alea Electronic Music Group, Madrid, Spain, 1969-74; Computer Music Project, University of Madrid, 1970-73; Guest Composer, IRCAM/Centre Georges Pompidou, 1981-85; Groupe de Musique Experimentale de Bourges, France, 1983; Technische Universität, West Berlin, 1987-88; Director, Electroacoustic Music Studio, University of Paris VIII, 1985-. *Compositions:* 48 including symphonic, chamber and electronic music; Performances of works at Festivals

of Warsaw, Stockholm, Berlin, Kassel, Frankfurt, Amsterdam, Helsinki, Oslo, Paris, Venice, La Rochelle, Bourges, Geneva, Lausanne, Milan, Turin, Rome, Madrid, Athens, and at UNESCO's Rostrum of Composers, World Music Days, Los Angeles Olympic Arts Festival, ICMC (Rochester, Illinois, The Hague, Venice, Paris, Cologne), British Arts Council Contemporary Music Tours. EMAS and ICA of London, Berlin Kulturstadt Europas 88, Darmstadt Ferienkurse für Neue Musik. *Recordings:* On: Compact Disk ADDA, Paris; Le Chant du Monde, Paris; WERGO, Germany. *Address:* Editions Salabert, 22 Rue Chauchat, 75009 Paris, France.

VAIDA John Michael, b. 28 Mar 1951, Connecticut, USA. Conductor; Teacher; Singer. m. Deborah Karr, 9 July 1975, 1s, 1d. *Education:* Westminster Choir College, 1969-73; Marywood college, 1978-80. *Career:* Adj Professor, choral conducting, vocal pedagogy, Wilkes University, PA, 1985-89; Lecturer in Fine Arts, College Misericordia, Dallas, PA, 1990-; Consultant, American Council for International Studies, 1984-; Chairman, Fine Arts Department, Director, Buckingham Performing Arts Center, Conductor, Wyoming Seminary Chorale and Madrigal Singers, Wyoming Seminary College Prep School, Kingston, PA, 1975-. Music Director, Catholic Choral Society of Scranton, 1985-; Concert Lecturer for pre-concert Series, NE Pennsylvania Philharmonic League of Wilkes-bare and Scranton, 1988-. *Publications:* Article, What Music Educators and Families Should Know about International Travel, Foreign Student Exchanges and Concert Touring, 1989. *Honours:* Frances and Louis Maslow Award for Excellence in Teaching, 1989; John M Vaida Choral Music Endowment, Wyoming Seminary College Prep School, 1986; Outstanding Educator Award, 1984. *Memberships:* Music Educators National Conference; International Choral Network; American Choral Directors Association; American Federation of Musicians; International Federation for Choral Music; Chorus America. *Hobbies:* Skiing; Gardening. *Address:* Wyoming Seminary, Kingston, PA 18704, USA.

VAJDA Cecilia, b. 18 Mar 1923, Budapest, Hungary. Music Educator; Conductor. *Education:* Diploma in Education, Conducting, Composition, Liszt Academy of Music, Budapest, Hungary, 1946. *Debut:* 1946. *Career:* Professor, Education Department, Liszt Academy of Music, 1948- 66; Artistic Director and Chief Conductor, Hungarian Radio Chorus, 1956-66; Tutor at the Menuhin School, Stoke d'Abernon, 1967-69; Senior Lecturer, Welsh College of Music and Drama, Cardiff, 1973-89. *Recordings:* Bach: Jesu, meine Freude (Hungaroton); Bartok: Cantata Profana (Hungaroton); Opera Recordings (Hungaroton and Hungarian Radio); Bartok: Unaccompanied Partsongs and Village Scenes (piano); Kodály: Partsongs in English, FTD Audio, Cardiff. *Publications:* Textbooks for Teacher Training, Hungary 1954, 1955; Textbooks for the Liszt Academy of Music, 1965 EMB; Editing Monteverdi's Scherzi Musicali,1964 EMB; The Kodály Way to Music, Book 1, B&H 1974; The Kodaly Way to Music, Book 2, BKA, 1992. *Contributions to:* Education for Teaching; Music Teacher; Classical Music; Chorale; British Journal of Music Education. *Memberships:* Incorporated Society of Musicians, Music Education Section; President of the British Kodaly Academy (BKA). *Honours:* Liszt Medal, 1986 (Centenary); Zoltan Kodály Commemorative Medal, 1982; Order of Merit from the Republic of Hungary, 1992. *Address:* 105 Hallam Street, London W1N 5LT, England.

VAJDA Igor Joseph Milan, b. 16 Mar 1935, Banska Bystrica, Slovakia. Musicologist; Critic; Publisher. *Education:* MPh, Faculty of Philosophy, Comenius University, Bratislava, 1959. *Career:* Assistant, Slovak Academy of Sciences; Professor of Musical Theory, State Conservatory, Kosice; Dramaturgist, Opera Banska Bystrica; Editor, Slovak Music. TV broadcasts including: What Is Opera?; 50 Years of Slovak National Theatre; Andrej Ocenas; Eugen Suchon; Jesuit priest, 1984, in Pastorian, 1990, docent, 1991, editor in Pliester, Slovak Television, 1992-93. *Publications:*

Kantate Eugen Suchon's Zalm Zeme Podkarpatskej (monograph); Sergei Prokofiev, Popular Monographie, 1964; National Artist Eugen Suchon, co-author, 1978; Storocnica Ceskeho Divadla, co-author, 1983; Slovak Opera, 1988; Experiemtn about (music) symbol of Eugen Suchon, 1993; Subjecty (Motivic) work in Suchon Opera's, 1993. *Contributions to:* Musicologica Slovaca; Hudobny Zivot (Musical Life); Slovenska Hudba (Slovak Music); Slovenske Divadlo (Slovak Theatre). *Hobbies:* Travel; Theology. *Address:* Dubnicka 4, 851 02 Bratislava, Slovakia.

VAJNAR Frantisek, b. 15 Sept 1930, Strasice u Rokycan, Czechoslovakia. Conductor. *Education:* Studied violin and conducting at the Prague Conservatoire. *Career:* Played in the orchestra of the Prague National Theatre; 1950-53, conducted the ensemble of Czech Army, 1953- 55; Conducted at the State Theatre of Karlina 1955-60, Ostrava 1960-62; Director of the Nejedly Theatre Usti nad Labem 1962-73, with operas by Smetana (complete), Dvořák, Janáček, Wagner, Verdi, Puccini, Strauss, Prokofiev, Henze and Hartmann; Conductor at the National Theatre Prague 1973-79, Artistic Director from 1985; Chief Conductor of the Czech Radio Symphiony Orchestr 1979-85, Guest Conductor of the Czech Philharmonic; Director of the Collegium Musicum Pragense and guest conductor in Australia, Brazil, Germany, France, Greece, Italy, Japan, Poland, Scandinavia, USSR and Switzerland; Festival appearances at Salzburg, Vienna, Prague; Conducted Prokofiev's Betrothal in a Monastery at the 1979 Wexford Festival; Teacher at Prague Academy of Arts. *Recordings include:* Smetana The Kiss; Shostakovich 10th and 15th Symphonies (Czech Philharmonic); Beethoven Overtures; Brixi Organ Concertos; Mozart arranged Wendt Le Nozze di Figaro; Hunting of Old Czech Masters (Supraphon). *Address:* Pragokoncert, Maltezske nam 1, 118 13 Prague 1, Czech Republic.

VAKARELIS Janis, b. 1950, Greece. Concert Pianist. *Education:* Studied at the Vienna Music Academy with Nikita Magaloff and Bruno Leonardo Gelber. *Career:* Engagements from 1979 with the Gewandhaus Orchestra, Mozarteum Orchestra of Salzburg, Zurich Chamber, Monte Carlo Philharmonic, Berlin Symphony, Stuttgart Philharmonic, Staatskapelle Dresden and BBC Symphony; Conductors have included Rattie, Weller, Masur, Kurt Sanderling, Ashkenazy, Litton and Rowicki; Recitals at the Concertgebouw in Amsterdam and the Teatro Real Madrid; Festival appearances at Spoleto and Athens, BBC Prom Concerts 1986. *Recordings include:* Prokofiev's 3rd Concerto and works by Brahms and Liszt; Labels include RCA, ASV and RPO. *Honours include:* Winner, 1979 Queen Sofia Competition, Madrid; Pan-Hellenic Piano Competition and the Prix d'Academie d'Athenes. *Address:* c/o Anglo Swiss Ltd, 3 Primrose Mews, 1a Sharpleshall St, London NW1 8YW, England.

VALADE Pierre-Andre, b. 14 Oct 1959, Brive, France. Flautist; Conductor. m. 5 May 1990. *Education:* Michel Debost's private class, Paris, 1979-81; Occasional lessons from Marcel Moyse, Maxence Larrieu and Alain Marion. *Debut:* Paris, 1979. *Career:* Flautist, numerous stage including ensemble, chamber music and soloist appearances in repertoire from Mozart 1982-; Soloist: numerous world premieres including Eolia by Philippe Hurel, Paris, Radio-France, 1983; Jupiter by Philippe Manoury on Flute-4X, IRCAM, Paris, Apr 1987; ...explosante-fixe... by Pierre Boulez, for flute, computer and ensemble, conducted by composer, Paris, 1991; TV-recording for BBC programme Tomorrow's World, 1988; Guest Artist, concerts, masterclasses, conferences, 8th Australian Flute Convention, Perth, 1991; Concerts with ensembles: Ensemble Musique Oblique, 1983-; Co-Founder, Espace Musique contemporary music ensemble, 1984; Ensemble Inter-Contemporain, 1985-90, including London Proms, 1985, US tour with Pierre Boulez, 1986; ...explosante-fixe...flute concerto in New York, Carnegie Hall, with P Boulez, 1993; Co- Founder, Musical Director, Court-Circuit ensemble, Paris, 1991-; Director, Collection Pierre-Andre Valade, Editions Henry Lemoine, Paris, 1985-; In charge of Flute 4X

research project, 1986-90. *Recordings:* A Schoenberg: Pierrot Lunaire, Harmonia Mundi, 1992. *Publications:* La Flute dans le Repertoire du XXe Siècle pour Ensemble Instrumental, 1987; Flute et Creations, 1991. *Current Management:* Anne-Marie Reby, France. *Address:* c/o Anne-Marie Reby, 52 rue Pierre Louvrier, 92140 Clamart, France.

VALAVANIS Tasso George, b. 7 Jan 1928, Athens, Greece. Composer; Conductor; Pianist; Musicologist. *Education:* Diplomas, Economics and Political Science, Business Administration; Graduate, Nice-Aosta, Cincinnati, Strasbourg Universities; Diplomas in Piano, Literature, Theory of Music, Conducting; Pianist; Musicology; PhD, Strasbourg University. *Career:* Composer; Conductor; Pianist; Musicologist; Music and Drama Film Critic; Professor Athens Graduate School of Journalism, Director, Athens Graduate School of Musicology; Chairman, National Hellenic Committee, CUNY. *Publications:* The Future of the Music Drama; Politics and The Arts. *Contributions to:* Over 2,300 articles to magazines. *Honours:* Recipient of numerous awards including National Conservatory in Piano, 1961, in Musicology, Athens, World Affairs Organisation 1972; International Federation of Tourist Writers 1973. *Memberships:* International Musicological Society; League of Composers, Athens; International Press Institute; National Union of Writers; Fijet of Athens; Society of Publishers and International Affairs. *Hobbies:* Skiing; Golf. *Address:* Eclos Street, PB 3039, Athens 102-10, Greece.

VALCARCEL Edgar, b. 4 Dec. 1932, Puno, Peru. Musician (Pianist); Composer. m. Carmen Pollard, 1 Jan. 1958, 2 sons, 2 daughters. *Education:* Catholic University, Lima, Peru; National Conservatory of Music, Lima; Instituto Torcuato de Tella, Buenos Aires, Argentina; Columbia Princeton University, New York, USA. *Career:* As Pianist: Soloist, National Symphony Orchestras of Lima, Rio de Janeiro and La Habana; As Composer: Commissions, V Inter-American Festival, Washington DC, 1971, Rochester Festival, 1972, Maracaibo Festival, Venezuela, 1977; Works premiered at Panamerican Union Peer International Corporation, 1968, Tonos, Darmstadt, 1977, Veracruz University, Mexico, 1983; Currently Head of Music Department, Newton College, Lima. *Compositions:* Dichotomy III, for 12 instruments, 1968; Montaje 59, for chamber ensemble, 1977; Chegan IV, for choir, 1977; Karabotasat Cutintapata, for orchestra, 1977; 4 Children's Songs, 1983. *Recordings:* American Contemporary Music, EDS-030-Stereo; Edul, Organization of American States; Antologia Music Peruana Siglo XX, Vol III, Eubanco. *Honours:* Professor honoris causa, Puno University, Peru; National Award for Composition, Lima, 1956, 1965; Inocente Carreno Composition Award, Caracas, Venezuela, 1981. *Address:* Avenida Angamos (Oeste) 862- C, Miraflores, Lima 18, Peru.

VALDENGO Giuseppe, b. 24 May 1914, Turin, Italy. Singer (Baritone). *Education:* Studied in Turin with Michele Accoriuti. *Debut:* Parma 1936, as Rossini's Figaro. *Career:* Sang at La Scala 1941-43; New York City Opera 1946, debut as Sharpless in Madama Butterfly; San Francisco 1947, as Valentin in Faust; Metropolitan Opera from 1947, as Germont, Belcore, Mozart's Almaviva, Marcello and Germont; Sang Iago, Falstaff and Amonasro, with the NBC Symphony under Toscanini, 1947-50; Covent Garden and Glyndebourne 1955, Don Giovanni and Raimbaud in Le Comte Ory; Guest appearances in Buenos Aires, Paris, Vienna, Philadelphia, Cincinnati and Rio de Janeiro. *Recordings:* Falstaff, Aida and Otello, conducted by Toscanini (RCA); Pagliacci (CBS); Il Segreto di Susanna (Cetra); Don Pasquale (Philips). *Publication:* Ho cantato con Toscanini, 1962.

VÁLEK Vladimír, b. 1935, Czech Republic. Conductor. *Education:* Graduated, Prague Academy of Performing Arts, 1962. *Career:* Conductor, Czech Radio Studio Orchestra in Prague 1965-75; Founder and leader, Dvořák Chamber Orchestra; Conductor, Prague

Symphony Orchestra, 1977-88; Chief Conductor, Prague Radio Symphony Orchestra, since 1985; Guest performances with the Czech Philharmonic, USA, Russia, Japan, Britain, Germany, Austria, Holland, Switzerland, Korea, Taiwan; Festival engagements at Luzern, Interlaken, Montreaux, Berlin, Linz, Istanbul, Prague, Bratislava. *Recordings include:* Bartók's Concerto for Orchestra and Prokofiev's Romeo and Juliet Ballet Suites with the Czech Philharmonic, Dvořák's symphonies No 8, 9 and Slavonic Dances, Schubert's Mass in A flat, Sibelius' Symphony No 2. Saint-Saëns Symphony No. 3, Martinů's Symphony No. 6 with the Prague Radio Symphony Orchestra for Supraphon, Martinů's The Frescos, Stravinsky's Petrushka and Rite of Spring, Dvořák's symphonies No 5 and 7 and Suk's Symphony Asrael with the Prague Radio Symphony Orchestra for Chant du Monde (Paris). *Current Management:* Czech Artists Agency, Dr Bechyně, 100 00 Prague 10, Volšinách 114, Czech Republic. *Address:* Na vápenném 6, 147 00 Praha 4, Czech Republic.

VALENT Joseph Arthur, b. 8 July 1955, New York, USA. Conductor; Pianist; Organist; Composer. *Education:* BMus, New England Conservatory of Music, 1977; MMus, Ithaca College, 1984. *Career:* Former Conductor, Indiana Wesleyan University, and East Central Indiana Youth Symphony Orchestra; Was Conductor, of the new production for the Ball State University Opera Workshop; Former, Organist, High St Methodist Church; Director of Music, St Lawrence Church, Muncie, IN; Currently Assistant Conductor, Marion Philharmonic Orchestra. *Compositions:* Chicago, 2 pieces for orchestra; Fatima, for horn and piano; String Quartet; religious music, songs and works for clarinet. *Memberships:* American Orchestra League; Conductors' Guild; Association of Canadian Directors; Sonneck Society; American Music Centre; Opera America; National Pastoral Musicians; American Guild of Organists; Amerian Choral Directors Symphony. *Hobbies:* Tennis; baseball. *Address:* 2900 W State Road 28, Muncie, IN 47303-9337, USA.

VALENTE Benita, b. 19 Oct 1934, Delano, California, USA. Lyric Soprano. m. Anthony Phillip Checchia, 21 Nov. 1959, 1 son. *Education:* Graduated, Curtis Institute of Music, 1960; studied with Chester Hayden, Martial Singher, Lotte Lehmann, Margaret Harshaw. *Debut:* Freiburg Opera, 1962; Metropolitan Opera, 1973, as Pamina. *Career:* Leading roles, Orfeo, Rigoletto, Traviata, Idomeneo, Marriage of Figaro, Faust, La Bohème, Turandot, Magic Flute, Rinaldo; Appeared throughout USA & Europe in operas & symphonies; has sung in New York as Susanna, Ilia, Nannetta and Almirena in Rinaldo 1985; Santa Fe 1987, as Ginerva in Ariodante. *Recordings:* Records for Columbia, Desmar, RCA, Pantheon, CRI. *Honours:* Winner, Metropolitan Opera Council auditions, 1960. *Address:* c/o Anthony P. Checchia, 135 S.18th Street, Philadelphia, PA 19103, USA.

VALENTINI-TERRANI Lucia, b. 28 Aug. 1946, Padua, Italy. Singer (Mezzo-Soprano). *Education:* Studied in Padua. *Debut:* Padua 1969, in the title role of La Cenerentola by Rossini. *Career:* Sang Cenerentola, Isabella and Rosina at La Scala from 1973; Marina in Bois Godunov 1979; Metropolitan Opera 1974, as Isabella in L'Italiana in Algeri; Los Angeles 1979, in the Verdi Requiem conducted by Giulini; Guest appearances in Moscow, Paris, Vienna, Monte Carlo, Brussels, Nice, Dresden, Munich, Frankfurt and Chicago; Florence and Los Angeles 1982, as Mistress Quickly in Falstaff; Covent Garden 1987, as Rosina in Il Barbiere di Siviglia; Pesaro Festival and Vienna Staatsoper 1984 and 1988, in Il Viaggio a Reims; Pesaro 1986, in Maometto II; Naples 1988, as Gluck's Orpheus; sang Isabella n L'Italiana in Algeri at Monte Carlo, 1990 (repeated at Turin, 1992). *Recordings include:* La Fedeltà Premiata and Il Mondo della Luna by Haydn (Philips); Orlando Furioso by Vivaldi (RCA); L'Italiana in Algeri; Falstaff, Don Carlos, Pergolesi Stabat Mater and Il Viaggio a Reims by Rossini (Deutsche Grammophon); La Cenerentola and La Donna del Lago, by Rossini (CBS).

Address: c/o John Coast, 31 Sinclair Road, London W14 0NS, England.

VALJAKKA Taru, b. 16 Sept 1938, Helsinki, Finland. Singer (Soprano). *Education:* Studied with Antti Koskinen in Helsinki, with Gerald Moore in Stockholm and London, Erik Werba in Vienna and Conchita Badia in Santiago. *Debut:* Helsinki 1964, as Donna Anna in Don Giovanni. *Career:* Sang in Helsinski (premiere of Sallinen's The Red Line, 1978), Budapest, Oslo, Prague and Berlin; Kiel Opera 1980, in the German premiere of The Horseman by Sallinen; Metropolitan Opera 1983, in The Horseman with the Helsinki company; Savonlinna Festival Finland 1983, as Senta in Der fliegende Holländer; Other roles include the Trovatore Leonora, Aida, Countess Almaviva, Fiordiligi, Desdemona, Pamina and Mélisande; Teatro Colon Buenos Aires 1987, as Senta; Many recitals in the songs of Sibelius. *Recordings include:* Joonas Kokkonen, The Last Temptation; Lady Macbeth of Mtsensk (EMI); Juha by Merikanto; The Horseman. *Address:* Bulavardi 1942 00120, Helsinki, Finland.

VÄLKKI Anita, b. 25 Oct 1926, Saakmaki, Finland. Singer (Soprano). *Education:* Studied with Tynne Haase, Jorma Huttunen and Lea Piltti in Helsinki. *Career:* Performed first as an actress and sang in operettas at the theatre in Kokkola; Sang at the Helsinki National Opera from 1955; Royal Opera Stockholm from 1960, as Aida, Santuzza and Brünnhilde; Covent Garden 1961-64, as Brünnhilde; Metropolitan Opera 1962-65, Brünnhilde, Kundry; Bayreuth Festival 1963-64; Guest appearances in Mexico City, Palermo and Philadelphia; Savonlinna Festival Finland 1983, as Mary in Der fliegende Holländer; sang at Helsinki 1986, in Juha by Merikanto. *Recordings include:* Third Norn in Götterdämmerung, conducted by Solti (Decca); The Horseman by Sallinen. *Address:* c/o Finnish National Opera, Bulevardi 23-27, SF 00180 Helsinki 18, Finland.

VALLE Jose Nilo, b. 20 Feb 1946, Santa Catarina State, Brazil. Conductor; Composer; Teacher. *Education:* Paramá Music College; School of Music, Federal University of Rio de Janeiro; MMus, DMA, University of Washington School of Music, USA. *Debut:* Federal University of Rio de Janeiro, 1983. *Career includes:* Teacher, Music Theory, Parana Music College, Curitiba, Brazil; Assistant Conductor, FURJ, 1981-83; Assistant Conductor, University of Washington, 1989-91; Conductor and Founder, Proconart Ensemble for Contemporary Music, University of Washington, 1989-91; Conductor, Founder, Camerata Orchestra, 1989-91; Founder and Current Music Director and Conductor, St Catherine Symphony Orchestra, Florianópolis, St Catherine State, Brazil, 1993. *Recordings:* Sparrows by Joseph Sohwantner and The Yew Tree, by Diane Thome. *Publications include:* Series of six Travessuras (children's plays), 1978; Book: Language and Musical Structure, editions, 1978, 1982, 1986.. *Honours:* Best Musician, Parana Musical College, 1974. *Memberships:* Conductors' Guild Inc, USA. *Hobbies:* Languages; Poetry; Literature. *Address:* CP 1004, 88010-970 Florianopólis, SC, Brazil.

VALLER Rachel, b. 14 Sept 1929, Sydney, Australia. Pianist. m. Walter Travers, 28 Feb 1965. *Education:* BA, 1952; DipEd, 1960; LTCL, 1947; Conservatorium of Music, Sydney; University of Sydney; Pupil of Ignaz Friedman. *Debut:* Sydney, 1940. *Career:* Soloist, Associate Artist Chamber Ensembles, ABC Radio, TV; Appearances with Sydney, Melbourne and Queensland Symphony Orchestras; Toured with cellist André Navarra, with violinists Wanda Wilkomirska, Stoika Milanova, Zvi Zeitlin, Erick Friedman, Erich Gruenberg, Thomas Zehetmair and bassoonist George Zukerman. *Recordings:* For ABC and for World Record Club some of the lesser known piano works of Beethoven issued to mark Beethoven bicentenary, 1970; In Germany in 1978 for 150th anniversary death of Schubert she recorded on Intercord label that composer's sonatinas with violinist Susanne Lautenbacher. *Address:* 22 Allen's Parade, Bondi Junction, New South Wales 2022, Australia.

VALLETTI Cesare, b. 18 Dec 1921, Rome, Italy. Singer (Tenor). *Education:* Studied with Tito Schipa. *Debut:* Bari 1947, as Alfredo. *Career:*Sang in Rome, Palermo and Naples 1947-50, as Almaviva, Narciso in Il Turco in Italia and Elvino in La Sonnambula; Sang Fenton with La Scala company at Covent Garden, 1950; Milan from 1950, as Nemorino, Vladimir in Prince Igor and Lindoro; US debut San Francisco 1953, as Werther; Metropolitan Opera from 1953, as Don Ottavio, Almaviva, Massenet's Des Grieux, Ernesto, Ferrando and Tamino; Covent Garden 1953, as Alfredo, with Callas; Florence 1958-65, as Giacomo in La Donna del Lago, Idamante and Gianetto in La Gazza Ladra; Salzburg Festival 1960, Don Ottavio; Carramoor Festival New York 1968, as Nero in L'Incoronazione di Poppea. *Recordings:* Don Pasquale, L'Elisir d'Amore, La Fille du Régiment, La Cenerentola, Il Matrimonio Segreto (Cetra); La Traviata, L'Enfance du Christ, Madama Butterfly (RCA); Linda di Chamounix (Philips); Don Giovanni, conducted by Leinsdorf. *Address:* c/o Metropolitan Opera, Lincoln Center, New York, NY 10023, USA.

VAN ACKERE Jules-Emile, b. 8 Feb 1914, Heule, Belgium. University Professor. m. Mady Cattebeke, 2 sons. *Education:* University of Ghent; Royal Conservatory, Ghent. *Career:* Numerous public conferences, performances; Several hundred radio lectures (including complete works of Frederick Delius, P. Hindemith, A. Schoenberg); Professor (now Professor Emeritus), University of Antwerp. *Publications include:* Igor Stravinsky; Aspecten van het Melos by Ravel, 1950; Pelléas et Mélisande ou la rencontre miraculeuse d'une poésie et d'une musique, 1952; Muziek van onze eeuw 1900-50, 1954; Maurice Ravel, 1957; Eeuwige Muziek, 1960; Claude Debussy; Debussy's Images, 1962; Schubert en de Romantiek, 1963; Meesterwerken van het Klavier, 1966; L'Age d'Or de la Musique Francaise, 1966; De Kamermuziek en het lied, 1967; Bartók's Concertos; Frederick Delius, Musicien Méconnu, 1968; Arnold Schoenberg en Alban Berg, 1978; Frederick Delius of de Wellust van de Klank, 1983; Van Bach tot de Jong, 1985; Ravel en zÿn tÿd, 1987; De Liederen van Hugo Wolf, 1991; De Vocale Muziek van Brahms, 1992. *Contributions to:* Numerous professional journals. *Address:* 38 Avenue Jean de Bologne, 1020 Brussels, Belgium.

VAN ALLAN Richard, b. 28 May 1935, Clipstone, Nottinghamshire, England. Opera Singer. (Bass-Baritone). m. div, 2 sons, 1 daughter. *Education:* Dip Ed Science, Worcester College of Education; Birmingham School of Music. *Debut:* Glyndebourne Festival Opera, 1964; sang in 1970 premiere of Maw's The Rising of the Moon: other appearances as Osmano in L'Ormindo, Leporello, Osmin, Trulove, the Speaker in Die Zauberflöte and Melibeo in La Fedeltà Premiata. *Career:* Welsh National Opera; English National Opera; Royal Opera House, Covent Garden, London; Scottish Opera; Paris Opéra, France; Boston, San Diego, and Miami Operas, USA; Metropolitan Opera, New York; Brussels Opera, Belgium; Buenos Aires Opera, Brazil; Director, National Opera Studio, 1986; Sang Don Alfonso at the Metropolitan 1990, Pooh-Bah in The Mikado for ENO; Glyndebourne Festival 1990, as Budd in Albert Herring and Pistol in Falstaff; Season 1992 as Tiresias in the premiere of Buller's Bacchae at ENO and in Osborne's Terrible Mouth; Sang the Grand Inquisitor in Don Carlos for Opera North, 1993, Don Jerome in the world stage Premiere of Gerhard's The Duenna (Madrid, 1992). *Recordings include:* Phillips: Brander, La Damnation de Faust, conductor, Colin Davis; Don Alfonso, Così fan Tutte, conductor, Colin Davis; EMI: Leporello, Don Giovanni, conductor, Bernard Haitink. *Honours:* Grand Prix du Disque, La Damnation de Faust; Grammy Award, Così Fan Tutte; Grammy Nomination, Don Giovanni; Gloriana conducted by Charles Mackerras, Decca, 1992 . *Hobbies:* Shooting; Tennis. *Address:* c/o John Coast, 31 Sinclair Road, London, W14 0NS, England.

VAN APPLEDORN Mary Jeanne, b. 2 Oct 1927. Paul Whitfield Horn Professor of Music. *Education:* BM, 1948, MMus, 1950, PhD, 1966, Eastman School of Music. *Debut:* Carnegie Hall, 1956. *Career:* Lux Legend of Sankta Lucia for Band, 1982; Concerto for Trumpet, International Trumpet Guild, 1985; New York Ballet 40th Anniversary Festival, 1988; Terrestrial Music, 1992; *Compositions:* Catata: Rising Night After Night, 1979; Concerto for Trumpet and Band, 1977; Passacaglia and Chorale, for orchestra, 1974; Terrestrial Music, double concerto for violin, piano and string orchestra, 1992. *Recordings:* Rising Night After Night; Sonatine; Four Duos, Liquid Gold; Incantations, Patterns; Conceto for Trumpet and Band; Passacaglia and Chorale; A Liszt Fantasie. *Publications:* Concerto for Trumpet and band, 1992; Rising Night After Night, 1979; Set of Five (piano), 1978; A Liszt Fantasie, 1992; Article, In Quest of the Roman Numeral, 1970. *Honours:* ASCAP Standard panel Awards, 1980-92; Premiere Prix for 1993; Suite for Carillon, for World Carillon Federation, Dijon, 1980; Liquid Gold IX Premio Ancona, Italy, prize. *Memberships:* ASCAP: SCI. *Hobbies:* Reading; Travel. *Address:* PO Box 1583, Lubbock, TX 79408-1583, USA.

VAN BARTHOLD Kenneth, b. 10 Dec. 1927 Sourabaya, Java, Indonesia. Concert Pianist; Teacher. m. (1) Prudence C Mary: (2) Sarianne May Campbell, (3) Gillian Rose Knight, 2 sons, 2 daughters. *Education:* Music Scholar, Bryanston School; Paris National Conservatoire of Music (Laureat du Conservatoire National de Musique de Paris). LRAM. *Debut:* Bournemouth Municipal Orchestra 1944; Wigmore Hall, London 1956. *Career:* Concerts in UK. Eire, Canada Israel and France; Various Radio and TV Solo Performances; Professor, Trinity College of Music 1959-64; formed Music Department, City Lit Centre for Adult Studies in 1959; Edinburgh University Annual Master Classes during International Festival 1968-, Israel, 4 tours of Canada, Numerous other masterclasses, teaching, lecturing in UK, Eire, Canada, Israel; Wrote and presented first BBC TV studio music documentary 1964; Scriptwriting, presenting, linking, performing in over 25 programmes to date. *Publications:* The Story of The Piano 1975. *Address:* Arvensis, Stour Lane, Stour Row, Shaftsbury, Dorset SP7 OQJ, England.

VAN BLERK Gerardus J M, b. 14 May 1924, Tilburg, The Netherlands. Concert Pianist. m. A Van den Brekel. *Education:* Studied Piano with Professor W Andriessen, Amsterdam Conservatory; Piano-Soloist (Prix d'excellence); Studied with Yves Nat, Paris, France 1950-52. *Career:* Solo concerts with Concertgebouw Orchestra, Residentie Orchestra, The Hague, Rotterdam Philharmonic Orchestra with Haitink, Jochum, Fournet; Recitals, Chamber Music, Accompaniments (instrumental and singers); Professor of Piano, Royal Conservatory, The Hague. *Recordings:* Hindemith, Kammermusik Number 2 Klavierkonzert, op 36 Number 1; Chopin, Grand duo Concertant, Polonaise brillante op 3, Sonata in G minor op 65 with Anner Bylsma (violoncellist); Max Reger; Sonate for Cello and Piano, Caprice and Romance with Anner Bÿlsma; Brahms Lieder with Jard Van Nes (Alto); French violin sonatatas; works of M Ravel. *Hobbies:* Chess; Bridge. *Current Management:* Interartists, The Hague and Netherlands Impresariaat, Amsterdam. *Address:* Prinsengracht 1095, 1017 Amsterdam, The Netherlands.

VAN BOER Bertil Herman Jr, b. 2 Oct 1952, Florida, USA. Musicologist; Conductor. m. Margaret Fast, 12 Jne 1977. *Education:* PhD, Uppsala University, Sweden, 1983. *Career:* Musical Director, Opera Kansas, 1989- ; Assistant/Associate/Full Professor, Wichita State University, 1987-; Assistant Professor of Music, Brigham Young University, UT, 1983-87; Instructor, Shasta College, 1981-83. *Publications:* Dramatic Cohesion in the Works of Joseph Martin Kraus, 1989; Joseph Martin Kraus: Systemtisch-thematiches Werkverzeichnis, 1988; Josept Martin Kraus Der Tod Jesu, 1987; The Symphony: Richter, Sweden I & II, 1983-86; Articles in Fontes, Svensk tidskrift för Musikforskning, Journal of Musicology, Journal of Musicological Research. *Address:* 316 S Belmont, Wichita, KS 67218, USA.

VAN DAM José, b. 25 Aug 1940, Brussels, Belgium. Singer (Bass). *Education:* Brussels Conservatory with Frederic Anspach. *Debut:* Liège 1960, as Basilio. *Career:* Paris Opéra 1961-65, debut in Les Troyens; Geneva Opera 1965-67, taking part in the premiere of Milhaud's La mère coupable, 1966; Deutsche Oper Berlin from 1967, as Verdi's Attila, Mozart's Leporello and Don Alfonso and Paolo in Simon Boccanegra; Sang Escamillo at his US debut (Santa Fe 1967) and at Covent Garden in 1973; Salzburg from 1968, in La Rappresentazione di Anima e di Corpo by Cavalieri, as Jochanaan in Salome, the villains in Les Contes d'Hoffmann, Mozart's Figaro and Amfortas in Parsifal; Vienna Staatsoper debut 1970, as Leporello; Metropolitan Opera debut 1975, as Escamillo: returned to New York as Golaud in Pelléas et Mélisande, Berg's Wozzeck and Jochanaan; Other appearances in Venice, Stockholm, Lisbon and Munich; Salzburg Easter Festival 1982, as the Flying Dutchman; Paris Opéra 1983 as St Francis of Assisi, in the premiere of Messiaen's opera; Sang Hans Sachs in Paris, 1990, Jochanaan in Salome at Lyons; Simon Boccanegra at Brussels; Sang as Falstaff at the Salzburg Festival, 1993; Season 1992/93 as Figaro (Mozart) in Brussels, Dapertutto at the Opéra Bastille, Don Quichotte at Toulouse and Saint François at Salzburg; Concert appearances in Chicago, Boston, Tokyo, Los Angeles and London. *Recordings:* Roles in: Carmen, Fidelio, Salome, Pelléas et Mélisande, Così fan Tutte, Simon Boccanegra, Louise, Mireille and La jolie fille de Perth (HMV); Un Ballo in Maschera, La Damnation de Faust, Le Nozze di Figaro (Decca); Parsifal, Die Zauberflöte (Deutsche Grammophon); Don Giovanni (CBS); Pénélope, Dardanus (Erato); Also heard in the Requiems of Brahms and Verdi and Bach's B Minor Mass. *Address:* c/o Théâtre Royal de la Monnaie, 4 Léopoldstrasse, B-000 Brussels, Belgium.

VAN DE VATE Nancy Hayes, b. 30 Dec 1930, Plainfield, New Jersey, USA. Composer; Record Producer. m. (1) Dwight Van de Vate Jr, 9 June 1952, 1 son, 2 daughters, (2) Clyde Arnold Smith, 23 June 1979. *Education:* Eastman School of Music, University of Rochester, 1948-49; AB, Wellesley College, 1952; MM, University of Mississippi, 1958; DMus, Florida State University, 1968; Private piano student of Anton Rovinsky, New York City, Bruce Simonds, New Haven, Connecticut; Postdoctoral study, electronic music, Dartmouth and University of New Hampshire, 1972. *Career:* Orchestral premieres: Distant Worlds, Concerto for Percussion and Orchestra, Concertpiece for Cello and Small Orchestra all premiered by Polish Radio Symphony Orchestra of Cracow, Szymon Kawalla conductor, 1987-89; Premieres, Musica Viva Festival, Munich, Aspekte, Salzburg, Poznan Spring Festival, Poland; Vice-President and Artistic Director of Vienna Modern Masters. *Compositions:* The Saga of Cocaine Lil, 5 singers, percussion; Teufelstanz, percussion ensemble; A Night in the Royal Ontario Museum, soprano, tape; Pura Besakih for large orchestra; Nine Preludes for Piano; Twelve Pieces for Piano; Trio for Viola, Violoncello and Piano; Many choral, vocal, brass and solo string works; Viola Concerto; Four Somber Songs, for mezzo and orchestra; Premieres: Katyn, 1989, Polish Radio Symphony Orchestra and Chorus, S. Kawalla, Cond.; Concerto for Violin and Orchestra, 1992, Wiener Konzerthaus, Wiener Musiksommer. *Recordings:* Orchestral works, Polish Radio Symphony Orchestra of Cracow: Many solo and chamber works also commercially recorded. *Hobbies:* Travel; Photography; Languages. *Current Management:* Vienna Associates Inc. *Address:* Margaretenstrasse 125/15, A-1050 Vienna, Austria.

VAN DEN HOEK Martijn, b. 1955, Rotterdam, Holland. Concert Pianist. *Education:* Studied at the Rotterdam Conservatory, in Moscow with Valeri Kastelskii, in Budapest with Pal Kadosa and in Weimar with Ludwig Hofmann; New York with Joseff Raieff and Eugene List; Further study in Vienna with Paul Angerer. *Career:* Has performed as soloist with the Amsterdam Concertgebouw Orchestra, the Wiener String Quartet and the National Hungarian Post Orchestra; Performances in Belgium, France, Germany, Austria, Portugal, USA, Japan and Hong Kong; Recital with the

BBC, London; Repertoire includes concertos by Bach, Bartók, Beethoven, Chopin, Haydn, Hummel, Mozart and Schumann; Sonatas by Beethoven, Berg, Brahms, Chopin, Haydn, Mozart, Scarlatti, Schubert, Impromptus and Moments Musicaux, Schoenberg's Op 23; Schumann's Kreisleriana and Faschingsschwank aus Wien; Liszt Consolations, Sonata, Spanish Rhapsody, Valses oubliées and Opera transcriptions. *Honours:* Prix d'Excellence and Goethe Prize 1978; Public Prize of the City of Amsterdam 1981; First Prize, International Liszt Competition in Utrecht, 1986.

VAN DER ROOST Jan Frans Joseph, b. 1 Mar 1956, Duffel, Belgium. Composer. m. Bernadette Johnson, 16 May 1980. 2 sons, 2 daughters. *Education:* Lemmens Institute, Leuven; Royal Academy of Music, Antwerp and Ghent; Graduated in Music Theory, Harmony, Counterpoint, Fugue, Musical History, Trombone, Choral Conducting and Composition. *Compositions:* Sono Aeris for Brass Quintet, 1979; Herfst (Autumn), for mixed choir, 1981; Divertimento, for Piano, 1982; Canzona Gothica, for Trombone and Piano, 1982; Melopee e Danza, for 2 Guitars, 1982; Per Archi, for String Orchestra, 1983; 3 Bagatels, for Flute and Piano, 1984; Rikudim, for Band or orchestra, 1985; Van Maan en Aarde (Of the Moon and the Earth), for mixed choir, 1985; Mozaieken (Mosaics), for Orchestra, 1986; Concerto Grosso, for Cornet, Trombone and Brass Band, 1986; Jaargang (Turning of the Year), for Choir and Piano, 1986-87; Puszta, for Band, 1987; Excalibur, for Brass Band, 1987; Elckerlyc (Everyman), Oratorio for Soloists, Choir and Orchestra, 1987; Obsessions, for Brass Instrument and Piano, 1987-88; Arghulesques, for Clarinet Quartet, 1988; Spartacus, for band, 1988; Symphony, for Orchestra, 1988-89; Chemical Suite, 1990 for Trombone Quartet; Amazonia, 1990 for band; Met Annie in Toverland, 1990 for Children's Choir and Ensemble; Quattro Miniature for Woodwind Quintet, 1991; Olympica for Band, 1992; Stonehenge for Brass Band, 1992; A Year has Four Lives, for female choir and guitar, 1993. *Address:* Albrecht Rodenbachlaan 13, 2550 Kontich, Belgium.

VAN EETVELT François, b. 23 May 1946, Bornem, Belgium. Bass Baritone. m. Louizette Michiels, 4 July 1970, 1 son, 1 daughter. *Education:* Antwerp Conservatory; Graduate of Mastersinging class, Brussels Conservatory; Voice training in Italy and Germany. *Debut:* Flemish Opera House, Antwerp, Belgium. *Career:* Engagements in Antwerp, 1976; Amfortas, R. Wagner's Parsifal, Royal Flemish Opera, Antwerp, 1976; Guest appearances and concerts in Bratislava, Prague, Brussels, Mexico City, Amsterdam, Dresden, San Luis, Leipzig, Helsinki and Festival International Cervantino, Guanajuato; Regular guest, Festival of Flanders; Performances for BRT and RTB; Cast, Orfeo production during Rubensyear; Recital at Aldeburgh Festival, England; Das Schloss, F. Kafka, A. Laporte, Brussels Opera, Belgium; Repertoire: Apollo in Monteverdi's Orfeo; Mozart's Don Giovanni; Amfortas in Parsifal; Donner in Rheingold, Gunther in Götterdämmerung, Wolfram in Tannhäuser, Kurwenal in Tristan and Isolde; Sharpless in Butterfly; Jochanaan in Salome; Collatinus in Benjamin Britten's The Rape of Lucretia. *Honours:* Winner, International Opera Belcanto Concert, Ostend, 1978. *Hobbies:* Walking his dog; Playing tennis. *Address:* Puursesteenweg 263, 2680 Bornem, Belgium.

VAN EMMERIK Paul, b. 29 March 1957. Amsterdam, Netherlands. Musicologist. *Education:* studied musicology, American studies and library science, University of Amsterdam. *Career:* music critic, Het parool, Amsterdam, 1983-88; lecturer, Utrecht University 1989-; research fellowship, University of Amsterdam, 1990-. *Contributions to:* Archiv für Musikwissenschaft, Musik-Konzepte, Musiktexte, Muziek Wetenschap, Neuland. *Address:* PO Box 17448, 1001 JK Amsterdam, Netherlands.

VAN KERCKHOVEN Alain, b. 10 Oct 1964, Brussels, Belgium. Publisher; Writer on Music and Technology. *Education:* Catholic University of Leuven.

Career: Founder of the Belgian Association of Music Software, 1987-89; Administrator of ACME, 1989-; Journalist and writer 1988-; Publisher of the New Consonant Music, 1989-; President of Agence Graphique Musicale, 1990-. *Publications:* Lexique Anglais-Francais d'Informatique Musicale, 1990; The Computer Music Lexicon, 1991. *Contributions to:* Bordas, Les Cahiers de L'ACME, MENSA, and others. *Memberships:* Audio Engineering Society; SABAM. *Hobby:* Photography. *Address:* B P 28, B-1030 Brussels 3, Belgium.

VAN KEULEN Isabelle, b. 16 Dec. 1966, Mijdrecht, The Netherlands. Concert Violinist and Violist. *Education:* Studied at the Sweelinck Conservatoire in Amsterdam and with Sandor Vegh at the Salzburg Mozarteum; Masterclasses with Max Rostal and Vladimir Spivakov. *Debut:* Violist, Italy, Feb 1992; British concerts in 1993 at Birmingham and Cardiff. *Career:* Has appeared from 1983 with Berlin Philharmonic, Vienna, Montreal, Detroit, Minnesota and BBC Welsh Symphonies, NHK of Tokyo and the Concertgebouw; Conductors have included Baumgartner, Chailly, Colin Davis, Dutoit, Ehrling, Leitner, Leppard, Marriner, Neumann, de Waart and Zinman; Appearances at the Salzburg Festival and tours with the Bamberg Symphony and Gidon Kremer's Lockenhaus Soloists; BBC Proms debut 1990, in Mozart with the Rotterdam Philharmonic; Strauss's Concerto with the BBC Philharmonic and the Dutilleux Concerto with the Concertgebouw; Other repertoire includes concertos by Bach, Haydn, Henkemans, Schnittke, Spohr and Stravinsky, in addition to the standard items; also plays the Adelaide Concerto by Casadesus (attributed to Mozart); as violist has collaborated with the Hagen, Orlando and Borodin Quartets. *Recordings include:* Saint-Saëns and Vieuxtemps Concertos, London Symphony; Schubert's Octet; Shostakovich Sonatas for violin and viola (Fidelio). *Honours include:* Silver Medal, International Yehudi Menuhin Violin Competition, 1983; Winner, Eurovision Young Musician of the Year Competition, 1984. *Address:* c/o Georgina Ivor Associates, 66 Alderbrook Road, London SW12 8AB, England.

VAN POUCKE Peter Guy Camille, b. 6 Sept. 1960, Ghent. Musicologist; Singer (Basso). *Education:* Lic.Musicology, 1983, AggHSO, 1985, State University, Ghent; Studies at the Academie de Musique, Wetteren, Royal Conservatory of Music, Ghent. *Career:* Teacher, Musical Aesthetics, Ghent; Assistant, Musicology, University of Ghent; Assistant, Special Methodics, University of Ghent; Professor, Aesthetics and History of Music, Higher State Institute for Theater and Cultural Propagation, Brussels. *Publications:* Hildegard of Bingen Symphonie, 1991. *Contributions to:* various journals, Encyclopedias & magazines. *Memberships:* International & American Musicological Societies; Societé Belge de Musicology. *Address:* Adolf Samuelstraat 1, 9050 Gentbrugge, Belgium.

VAN SICE Robert William, b. 5 Sept 1961, Colorado Springs, USA. Solo Concert Marimbist. m. Cecile Le Juge de Segrais, 1 daughter. *Education:* B Mus, Cleveland Institute of Music, 1982; M Mus, University of Cape Town, 1984. *Debut:* Albequerque, New Mexico, 1976. *Career:* Over 400 recitals and appearances as soloist with orchestras throughout North America, Europe and the Far East, 1984-; Given Master Classes in over 20 countries, 1985-; Recordings for radio at NHK Tokyo, KBS Seoul, Suisse Romande Geneve, BRT Bruxelles, RTE Dublin, 1984-; First ever recital by a marimbist in Concertgebouw in Amsterdam, 1989; Professor of Percussion at the Brussels Royal Conservatory, 1987-; Founder of the only existing programme for solo marimbist in Rotterdam Conservatory, 1989; Visting lecturer at Geneva and Freiburg Conservatories, 1990. *Recordings:* Contemporary Music for Marimba (Claremont) 1984; Three Concertos for Marimba (Etc), 1989; Zodiak (Etc) 1991; Japanese Music for Marimba (Etc) 1991. *Honour:* Youngest Winner of Cleveland Institute Competition, 1979.

VANAUD Marcel, b. 1952, Brussels, Belgium. Singer (Baritone). *Education:* Studied at the Brussels Conservatoire and at Liège. *Career:* Sang at the Liège Opera 1975-83, notably as Papageno, Escamillo, Alfonso in La Favorita, Renato and Ourrais in Mireille; Guest appearances at Pittsburgh and New Orleans 1984; New York City Opera 1985 as Zurga in Les Pecheurs de Perles; Théâtre de la Monnaie Brussles as Raimaud in Comte Ory and Mozart's Figaro; Season 1987-88 as Lescaut at Montreal, Posa in Don Carlos at Tulsa, Figaro at Santa Fe and Raimbaud at Toulouse; La Scala Milan 1989 in the premiere of Doktor Faustus by Manzoni; Returned to Liege 1992 as Mephistopheles in La Damnation de Faust and sang Germont at Los Angeles; Festival de Radio France at Montpellier 1992, as Sacchini's Oedipus and in Chateau des Carpathes by Philippe Hersant. *Recordings include:* Les contes d'Hoffmann and Franck's Les Beatitudes; Karnac in Le Roi d'Ys

VANDENBURG Howard, b. 18 May 1918, Bufalo, New York, USA. Singer (Tenor). m. Anna Green. *Education:* Studied at the Curtis Institute Philadelphia. *Debut:* Philadelphia 1937, as Mozart's Almaviva. *Career:* Sang as tenor from 1951, in New York; Munich Staatsoper from 1952, as Don José, Radames, the Emperor in Die Frau ohne Schatten, Florestan, Laca (Jenufa) and Julien in Louise; Covent Garden 1953 with the Munich company as Midas in the British premiere of Die Liebe der Danae by Strauss; Zurich 1953, Naples and Florence 1954; Guest appearances in Vienna and Germany; Sang at Dortmund 1963-72, as a baritone. *Recordings:* Die Zauberflöte (Deutsche Grammophon); Euryanthe (Cetra). *Address:* c/o Opernhaus Kuhstrasse 12, D4600 Dortmund, Germany.

VANDOR Ivan, b. 13 Oct. 1932, Pecs, Hungary. Composer. *Education:* MA, Ethnomusicology, UCLA, 1970. *Career:* Member, Musica Elettronica Viva, 1966-68; Member, Nuova Consonanza Improvis Group, 1967-68; Research in Tibetan Budhist Music, 1970-71; Director, International Institute for comparative Music Studies, Berlin, 1977-83; Founder, Director, Scuola Interculturale di Musica, 1979-; Professor, Composition, Conservatory of Music, Bologna, 1979-. *Compositions:* Quartetto Perachi, 1962; Moti, 1963; Serenata, 1964; Dance Music, 1969; Winds, 1970; some short pieces for Harpsichord. *Publications:* La Musique du Bouddhisme Tibetain, 1976; Die Musik des Tibetischen Buddhismus, 1978; Editor, The World of Music, 1975-85. *Contributions to:* various journals. *Memberships:* Italian Society for Contemporary Music; Italian Society for Ethnomusicology; Nuova Consonanza. *Address:* Viale Parioli 73, 00197 Rome, Italy.

VANESS Carol, b. 27 July 1952, San Diego, California, USA. Singer (Soprano). *Education:* Studied in California with David Scott and in 1976 won the San Francisco Opera Auditions. *Career:* San Francisco 1977, as Vitellia in La Clemenza di Tito; New York City Opera from 1979, as Alcina, Antonia in Les Contes d'Hoffmann, Vitellia, Flotow's Frau Fluth, Mimi, and Leila in Les pêcheurs de Perles, Rigoleto (Gilda), Traviata (Violetta); Donna Anna; Glyndebourne Opera from 1982, as Donna Anna, Electra in Idomeneo, Fiordiligi and Amelia Boccanegra (1986); Covent Garden debut 1982, as Mimi: returned for Vitellia and Dalila in Handel's Samson; Countess Almaviva, 1989; Rosalinda in Der Fledermaus; Metropolitan Opera from 1984, as Armida in Rinaldo, Fiordiligi, Electra and the Countess in Figaro, Manon; Australian Opera 1985, Amelia in Un Ballo in Maschera; Seattle Opera 1986, as Massenet's Manon; Desdemona, 1986; Violetta, 1988; Trovatore, 1989; Concert appearances in the Choral Symphony in Paris, the Verdi Requiem in Philadelphia and at the Lincoln Center New York with Pavarotti; Sang in Beethoven's Missa solemnis at the Barbican Hall, London, 1989; Royal Opera, Vitellia in La Clemenza di Tito 1989; Trovatore 1990 at the Metropolitan Opera and Faust (Marguerite); Don Giovanni (Anna) at Covent Garden, 1992; Season 1992/93 as Iphigénie en Tauride at La Scala, Mathilde in Guillaume Tell at San Francisco, and Olympia at the Met; Engaged to sing Desdemona at the Metropolitan, 1994; Norma at Seattle, 1994, (Amelia, Ballo in Maschera, 1995). *Recordings include:* Donna Anna in the Glyndebourne production of Don Giovanni conducted by Bernard Haitink; Masses by Haydn; Glyndebourne, Haitink, Così fan Tutte; Beethoven's Ninth with Dohnányi and Cleveland Orchestra; Missa Solemnis with Tate and the ECO; Don Giovanni (Elvira), conducted by Muti, EMI; Tosca, Philips; Rossini, Stabat Mater, Philips (Bychkov). *Address:* c/o Herbert H Breslin, 119 West 57th Street, NY 10019, USA.

VÁNTUS István, b. 27 Oct 1935, Vaja, Hungary. Composer; Professor. m. Judit Gál, 30 Apr 1958, 1 son. *Education:* Baccalaureat, Reformed College of Debrecen, 1950-54; Composers Diploma, Academy of Music Ferenc Liszt, Budapest, 1960. *Debut:* 1960. *Career:* Performances on radio and television; Subject of a portrait film; Professor, Academy of Music, Szeged. *Compositions:* Operas, The Three Wanderers, The Golden Coffin; Orchestral works; Cantatas; Choral works and compositions for chamber orchestra; Numerous works have been recorded. *Publications:* Chess and Music, Connection between chess and music?, published in Hungary by Muzsika, 1991. *Honours:* Art Award, Szeged Town, 1967 and 1975; Erkel Prize, 1976. *Memberships:* Federation of Hungarian Musicians; Foundation of Art of the Hungarian People's Republic; Fészek Artist Club. *Hobby:* Re-arrangement of old pieces. *Address:* Kölcsey u 10, 6720 Szeged, Hungary.

VANZO Alain, b. 2 Apr 1928, Monaco. Singer (Tenor); Composer. *Education:* Studied with Rolande Darcouer in Paris. *Debut:* Paris Opera 1954, as the Pirate in Oberon. *Career:* Appearances in Paris as Edgardo, the Duke of Mantua, Don Otttavio, Des Grieux, Werther and Benvenuto Cellini; Covent Garden 1961-63; Appearances at the Wexford Festival, Barcelona, Lisbon, Vienna, Edinburgh, Aix-en-Provence, Montreal, San Francisco and New York (Metropolitan Opera with the company of the Paris Opéra); Sang the title role in Meyerbeer's Robert le Diable, Paris Opéra 1984; sang Faust at Philadelphia, 1984. *Compositions:* Operetta Le Pêcheur d'etoiles (performed Lille 1972) and opera Le Chouans (performed Avignon 1982). *Recordings:* Lakmé, with Joan Sutherland (Decca); Mignon by Thomas, La Navarraise by Massenet (CBS); Le pêcheurs de Perles (Philips); Mireille by Gounod (EMI); Fauré's Pénélope (Erato). *Address:* c/o Théâtre National, 8 Rue Scribe, F-75009 Paris, France.

VARADY Julia, b. 1 Sept 1941, Oradea, Rumania. Singer (Soprano). m. Dietrich Fischer-Dieskau 1977. *Education:* Studied in Cluj with Emilia Popp and in Bucharest with Arta Florescu. *Debut:* Cluj 1962, as Fiordiligi. *Career:* Guest appearances at the Budapest and Bucharest Operas; Moved to Frankfurt, West Germany 1972; Sang Violetta at Cologne, 1972; Munich from 1973, as Vitellia in La Clemenza di Tito, Lady Macbeth, Butterfly, Giorgetta (Il Tabarro), Elektra in Idomeneo, Santuzza, Liu, Leonora (La Forza del Destino), Elisabeth de Valois and Cordelia in the premiere of Lear by Reimann (1978); Scottish Opera 1974, as Gluck's Alceste; Metropolitan Opera 1978, Donna Elvira; Tours of Japan, Israel and the USA; Appearances at the Berlin, Edinburgh, Munich and Salzburg Festivals and at the Promenade Concerts London; La Scala Milan 1984, in Idomeneo; Other roles include Countess Almaviva, Judith (Bluebeard's Castle), Tatiana, Desdemona and Rosalinde; sang Wagner's Senta at Munich 1990, Covent Garden 1992; Vitella in La Clemenza di Tito at the Elizabeth Hall, 1990; appeared as Abigaille in Nabucco at the 1990 Munich Festival; Season 1992/93 as the Trovatore Leonora at Munich, in concert performances with the Glyndebourne Company of Fidelio and Elisabeth de Valois at the Deutsche Oper Berlin; Featured Artist (People, no 181), Opera Magazine, 1992; Concert repertoire includes arias by Mozart and Beethoven, Vier Letzte Lieder by Strauss, Britten's War Requiem, the Verdi Requiem, the Faust oratorios of Schumann and Berlioz; Requiem by Reimann (premiere, 1982). *Recordings include:* Lucio Silla by Mozart (BASF); Die Fledermaus, Il Matrimonio Segreto, Lear, Idomeneo, La Clemenza di Tito, Duke Bluebeard's Castle (Deutsche Grammophon); Gli Amori di Teolinda by Meyerbeer (Orfeo); Cavalleria Rusticana (Decca); Les Contes d'Hoffmann, Arabella (EMI); Don Giovanni (Eurodisc); Handel's Saul (Telefunken). *Address:* AMI, Artist Management International, 12/13 Richmond Buildings, London, W1V 5AE.

VARCOE (Christopher) Stephen, b. 19 May 1949, Lostwithiel, Cornwall, England. Singer (Bass-baritone). m. Melinda Davies, 22 April 1972, 3 sons (1 son deceased), 2 daughters. *Education:* Cathedral Choir School and King's School, Canterbury; MA, King's College, Cambridge; Guildhall School of Music, London. *Career:* Concerts in most of the major British and European Festivals; Specialist in Lieder, French Mélodies and English Song; Many appearances on British, French and German Radio; sang in Haydn's L'infedeltà delusa at Antwerp 1990; Sarastro in Die Zauberflöte at the Mozart Experience, London, 1989; Created Zossima in the premiere of Tavener's Mary of Egypt, Aldeburgh, 1992. *Recordings:* Purcell: Indian Queen; Fairy Queen; King Arthur; The Tempest; Handel: Partenope; L'Allegro; Triumph of Time and Truth; Alessandro; Israel in Egypt; Bach: B Minor Mass; Masses; Cantatas; Johannes Passion; Fauré: Requiem; Finzi: Songs of Thomas Hardy; Rameau: Motets; French Mélodies, La Procession; Britten Cantata Misericordium, Mary of Egypt, Schubert Lieder, and many others. *Honours:* Gulbenkian Foundation Fellowship, 1977. *Hobbies:* Painting; Carpentry; Gardening. *Current Management:* Ron Gonsalves, 10 Dagnan Road, London SW12 9LQ, England.

VARGA Balint Andras, b. 3 Nov 1941, Budapest, Hungary. Music Publisher; Music Interviewer. m. Katalin Zsoldos, 14 Jan 1977, 2 daughters. *Education:* Teacher's degree, English and Russian, University of Budapest, 1960-65; Hungarian Journalists' School, 1966-67; Studied piano privately for 13 years. *Career:* Regular radio programmes in Budapest, 1965-; Some foreign radio programmes; Occasional programmes on Hungarian Television; Head of Promotion, Editio Musica Budapest, 1971-; Deputy Director of the Hungarian Cultural Institute, Berlin, 1991-. *Publications:* Conversations with Lutoslawski, 1974; Conversations with Iannis Xenakis, 1980; Conversations with Luciano Berio, 1981; 4 other anthologies of musical interviews published in Hungarian 1972, 1974, 1979, 1986; Translated Aaron Copland's The New Music into Hungarian, 1973, also, two books published in English and one published in German. *Contributions:* Regular articles in Muzsika. *Honours:* Several minor prizes and decorations in Hungary. *Memberships:* Hungarian Journalists' Association; Hungarian Art Fund. *Hobbies:* Playing the Piano; Walking; Reading. *Address:* 1020 Berlin, Fischerinsel, 1.03.01, Germany.

VARGA Gilbert, b. 17 Jan. 1951, London, England. Conductor. m. Delia Bogatila 6 Dec. 1979. *Education:* Studied with Franco Ferrara, Sergiu Celibidache and Charles Bruck. *Career:* Principal Conductor, Hofer Symphoniker, 1980-85; Chief Conductor of the Philharmonia Hungarica 1985-90; Permanent Guest Conductor with the Stuttgart Kammer Orchester; Guest engagements include Orchestre de Paris, Rotterdam Philharmonic, City of Birmingham Symphony, BBC Philharmonic, RAI Rome, Radio-Sinfonie Orchester Basel, Scottish Chamber Orchestra, Indianapolis Symphony, Sydney Symphony Orchestra. *Recordings include:* Symphony No. 6 of Anton Rubinstein with Philharmonia Hungarica and solo cello contertos with BBC Philharmonic/Rolland. *Address:* c/o Intermusica Artists Management Ltd. 16 Duncan Terrace, London N1 8BZ, England.

VARGA Tibor b. 4 July 1921, Györ, Hungary. Violinist; Conductor. *Education:* Studied with Jeno Hubay and Carl Flesch at the Franz Liszt Academy Budapest, 1931-38. *Career:* Concerts worldwide 1933-, notably in the romantic repertory and with concertos by Berg, Bartok and Schoenberg; Professor of Violin at the Academy of Music Detmold 1949; Founded the Tibor

Varga Chamber Orchestra 1954 conducted it until 1988; Settled in Switzerland 1955, founded the Tibor Varga Festival in Sion 1964; Masterclasses at the Salzburg Mozarteum, Switzerland; Musical Director of the Orchestre des Pays de Savoie at Annency, 1989; Plays a Guarnerius of 1733; Repertoire has included Concertos by Bach, Beethoven, Blacher (Creation, 1950), Brahms, Bruch, Elgar, Mozart, Paganini, Sibelius, Stravinsky, Tchaikovsky; Solo sonatas by Bach, Bartók; Sonatas by Bach, Bartók, Beethoven, Brahms, Debussy, Franck, Mozart, Schubert. *Honours include:* Bundesverdienstkreuz 1969. *Address:* c/o Kammerorchester Tibor Varga, Box 528, D-4930 Detmold, Germany.

VARGAS Milagro, b. 1958, USA. Singer (Mezzo-soprano). *Education:* Studied at Oberlin College and the Eastman School of Music with Jan DeGaetani. *Career:* Member of the Stuttgart Staatsoper 1983- 88, notably in the premiere of Akhnaten by Philip Glass (1984) and as Cherubino, Nancy in Albert Herring, Orlofsky, and Lybia in Jommelli's Fetonte; Komische Oper Berlin as Cherubino, Heidelberg Festival as Ramiro in La Finta Giardiniera; Sang Charlotte in Zimmermann's Die Soldaten at Strasbourg and Stuttgart, 1988; Sang Ravel's Sheherazade at the Cabrillo Festival 1986 and has appeared elswhere in concert at the Aspen and Marlboro Festivals, with the Philadelphia Orchestra and the Rochester Philharmonic. *Recordings include:* Akhnaten; Die Soldaten. *Address:* c/o Staatsoper Stuttgart, Oberer Schlossgarten 6, 7000 Stuttgart 1 Germany.

VARGAS Ramon, b. 1959, Mexico City, Mexico. Singer (Tenor). *Career:* Has sung in opera a Mexico City as Fenton in Falstaff, Nemorino, Don Ottavio and Count Almaviva; Sang Gelsomino in I1 Viaggio a Reims at the Vienna Staatsoper, 1987; Pesaro and Salzburg Festivals 1987, Mexico City 1988 as Tamino: Further appearances at Lucerne 1989, Zurich 1990 as Lorenzo in Fra Diavalo and Enschede Holland, as Fenton; Season 1991-92 as Leicester in Rossini's Elisabetta at Naples, Almaviva at Rome, Rodrigo in a concert performance of La Donna del Lago at Amsterdam and Paolino in I1 Matrimonio Segreto at Martina Franca. *Address:* c/o Pernhaus Zurich, Falkenstrasse 1, CH-8008 Zurich, Switzerland.

VARGYAS Lajos Karoly, b. 1 Feb. 1914, Budapest, Hungary. Musical Folklorist; Ethnographer. m. 17 Dec. 1949. *Education:* Pupil of Kodály in Musical Folklore, Budapest University; Church Music, Budapest Music Academy, 1936-37; Doctor of Ethnography, Linguistics, Hungarian Literature, 1941; Academic DMus, 1963. *Career:* Assistant Professor, Budapest University, 1952-54; Director, Folk Music Research Group, Hungarian Academy, 1970-73. *Recordings:* Mongolian Folk Music, UNESCO-Hungaroton, 1971. *Publications:* Aj falu zenei elete (The musical life of the village Aj), 1941; Kodály: A magyar nepzene, A peldatart szerkesztette Vargyas Lajos (The Hungarian Folk Music. Collection of tune-examples) (Compiler), 1952; A magyar vers ritmusa (The rhythm of the Hungarian verse), 1952; Regi nepdalok Kikunhalasrol (Old folksongs from Kiskunhalas), 1954; Studia Memoriae Belae Bartok Sacra (editor, author), 1956, 1957, 1959; Aj falu zenei anyaga (The tune-material of the village Aj), 1960, 1961, 1963; Magyar vers - magyar nyelv (Hungarian verse - Hungarian language), 1966; Zoltan Kodály: Folk Music of Hungary, 2nd edition revised and enlarged, 1971; Balladaskonyv (Book of ballads with their tunes), 1979; A magyarsag nepzneje (The folk music of the Hungarians), 1981; Hungarian Ballads and the European Ballad Tradition (in Hungarian, 1976), 1983; Keleti hagyomany - nyugati kultura. Tanulmanyok (Eastern traditions - Western culture, Essays), 1984; Magyar Néprajz V. Népköltészet (Hungarian Ethnography Folkpoetry) 1988; Kodály hatrahagyott foljegyzesei I (Kodály's records left behind) (editor), 1989; Editor, Author, VI, Folkmusic, Dance Childrens Games, 1990; Researches into The Mediaeval History of Folk Ballad 1967; Corpus Musicale Popularis Hungaricae VIII/A-B, Editor, 1993. *Contributions to:* 151 contributions on musical themes. *Honours:* Erkel Prize,

1980; Széchényi Prize, 1991. *Memberships:* President, Committee for Scientific Classification in Musicology and Ethnography, Hungarian Academy; Music Committee, Hungarian Academy. *Address:* Lajos Vargyas, 1022 Budapest, Szemlöhegy Str 41B, Hungary.

VARNAY Astrid, b. 25 April 1918, Stockholm, Sweden. Singer (Soprano/Mezzo-Soprano). *Education:* Studied with Paul Altouse and Hermann Weigert in New York. *Debut:* Metropolitan Opera 1941, as Sieglinde. *Career:* Sang at the Metropolitan until 1956, as Brünnhilde, Isolde, Senta, Elsa, Elisabeth, Kundry, Venus, Ortrud, the Marschallin, Amelia Boccanegra, Santuzza and Salome; Sang in the premiere of Menotti's The Island God, 1942; Chicago Opera debut 1944, Sieglinde; San Francisco Opera 1946-51, notably as Gioconda and Leonore; Mexico City 1948, as Tosca, Aida and Santuzza; Covent Garden debut 1948, as Brünnhilde in Siegfried: returned to London 1951, 1958-59 and 1968 (Kostelnička in Jenůfa); Bayreuth Festival 1951-67, as Brünnhilde, Isolde, Ortrud, Kundry and Senta; Paris Opéra and La Scala Milan as Isolde, 1956, 1957; Stuttgart 1959, as Jocasta in the premiere of Oedipus der Tyrann by Orff; Mezzo roles from 1962: Clytemnestra, Herodias and the title role in Einem's Der Besuch der Alten Dame; Salzburg Festival 1964-65, as Elektra; Professor at the Dusseldorf Musikhochschule from 1970; Returned to the Metropolitan 1974, as the Kostelnička, then sang Herodias, Clytemnestra and Begbick in Mahagonny. *Recordings:* Der fliegende Holländer, Lohengrin (Decca); Oedipus der Tyrann (Deutsche Grammophon); Cavalleria Rusticana (HMV); Private recordings from Bayreuth and the Metropolitan; Der Ring des Nibelungen conducted by Clemens Krauss, Bayreuth 1953; Sang in recordings released 1984-85 by Decca: Andrea Chénier and The Rake's Progress. *Address:* c/o Metropolitan Opera, Lincoln Center, New York, NY 10023, USA.

VARONA Jose Luciano, b. 14 Aug. 1930, Mendoza, Argentina. Stage and Costume Designer. *Education:* Studied at the Escuela Superior de Bellas Artes in Buenos Aires. *Debut:* Teatro Colon Buenos Aires 1959, Prokofiev's The Love for Three Oranges. *Career:* Collaborated with Tito Capobianco at the New York City 1966-73, with Giulio Cesare, The Golden Cockerel, Manon, Lucia di Lammermoor and Donzetti's Tudor trilogy; Handel's Ariodante for the opening of the Kennedy Center at Washington DC, 1971; San Francisco and Vancouver Opera 1972-73, with Norma and Lucrezia Borgia; Further association with Capobiano at the Deutsche Oper Berlin and the Netherlands Opera 1971-74, Attila, Aida, Rodelinda and La Traviata; Returned to the Teatro Colon 1981-88, with designs for Romeo et Juliette, Die Zauberflöte, Carmen and Die Entführung. *Address:* c/o Teatro Colon, Cerrito 618, 1010 Buenos Aires, Argentina.

VARVISO Silvio, b. 26 Feb 1924, Zurich, Switzerland. Conductor. *Education:* Studied at the Zurich Conservatory and in Vienna with Clemens Krauss. *Debut:* St Gallen 1944, Die Zauberflöte. *Career:* Assistant, then Principal Conductor of Basle Opera, 1950-62; Conducted opera in Berlin and Paris, 1958; San Francisco Opera from 1959 (US premiere of A Midsummer Night's Dream, 1960); Metropolitan Opera from 1961, Lucia di Lammermoor, Die Walküre, Die Fledermaus, Die Meistersinger, and Italian repertory; Glyndebourne and Covent Garden 1962, Le Nozze di Figaro and Der Rosenkavalier; Principal Conductor of the Royal Opera, Stockholn 1965-71; Bayreuth Festival 1969-74, Die Meistersinger, Der fliegende Holländer and Lohengrin; Conducted new production of La Bohème at Covent Garden, 1974; Musical Director at Stuttgart 1972-80: has led performances of Rossini, Donizetti, Bellini, Strauss, Mozart and Wagner; Musical Director of the Paris Opéra 1980-85; Conducted Lohengrin at Stuttgart 1990, Manon Lescaut at Barcelona; Season 1992/93 with Tosca at Antwerp and Die Frau ohne Schatten in Florence. *Address:* c/o Staatsheater Stuttgart, Oberer Schlossgarten 6, D-7000 Stuttgart 1, Germany.

VÁSÁRY Tamás, b. 11 Aug 1933, Debrecen, Hungary. Pianist; Conductor. m. Ildiko Kovacs, 15 Mar 1967. *Education:* Franz Liszt Music Academy, Budapest, 1951. *Debut:* First Concert, aged 8. *Career:* Performed in major music centres, worldwide; Festivals include: Salzburg, Edinburgh, Berlin; Conducting Debut in 1970; conducted over 70 orchestras; Music Director, Northern Sinfonia, 1979-83; Principal Conductor, Music Director, Bournemouth Sinfonietta, 1989-; Musical Director of Hungarian Radio Orchestra, 1993. *Recordings:* Chopin; Liszt; Debussy; Brahms; Mozart; Rachmaninov. *Honours:* Paris, Marguerite Long, 1950; Queen Elisabeth of Belgium, 1956; Rio de Janeiro International Competition, 1956; Bach and Paderewski medals, 1960. *Hobbies:* Yoga; Writing. *Address:* 9 Village Road, London N3 1TL, England.

VASILYEVA Alla, b. 1933, Moscow, Russia. Concert Cellist. *Education:* Studied at the Central Music School and at the Moscow State Conservatoire, with Rostropovitch. *Career:* Joined the Moscow Chamber Orchestra under Rudolf Barshai 1958 and remains as principal cellist; many tours with the Moscow Chamber Orchestra and as solo recitalist, notably in modern Russian works; plays her own arrangements of works by Resphighi and Vivaldi. *Recordings:* Works by Bach, Geminiani, Vivaldi, Moshei Wainberg, Boris Tchaikovsky, Khrennikov and Shostakovich (Melodiya). *Address:* c/o Sonata, 11 Northpark Street, Glasgow G20 7AA, Scotland.

VASSAR Frédéric, b. 1948, France. Singer (Baritone). *Education:* Studied at the Opera Studio of the Théâtre de la Monnaie Brussels. *Career:* Sang first as bass in Opera at Brussels from 1973 (Alberich), then at Ghent (Wotan, Hoffmann, Boccanegra) and for French Radio; Sang Mephistopheles in Faust at Marseilles 1977, followed by visits to Strasbourg, Avignon, Dublin and Orange; Engagements at Liège 1985-86 as (Escamillo, Oubbias in Mireille), Angers, Metz (Golaud), Don Giovanni and the Villains in Hoffman; Season 1989-90 as Mephistopheles at Avignon, Lescaut at Nantes and Telramund at Limoges and Scarpia for Opera Northern Ireland in Belfast. *Honours:* Winner, 1976 Voix d'or Enrico Caruso and Henri Duparc, France; Winner Toti dal Monte. *Address:* c/o Opera Northern Ireland, 181a Stranmillis Road, Belfast, Northern Ireland BT9 5DU.

VAUGHAN Denis Edward, b. 6 June 1926, Melbourne, Australia. Orchestral Conductor. *Education Includes:* MusB, University of Melbourne, 1947; Royal College of Music, London, England, 1947-50. *Debut:* As Conductor, Royal Festival Hall, London, 1953. *Career Includes:* Annual harpsichord concerts, Royal Festival Hall, 1948-58; Concert to honour Toscanini, with Bernstein, Klemperer, Celibidache and Maazel, Parma, 1959; Adviser to UNESCO and Berne Union on musical aspects of copyright matters, 1962-67; Music Director, Australian Elizabethan Theatre Trust, 1966; Orchestral concerts, operas in Europe, Australia, USA, Canada etc, 1970-89; Munich State Opera House, 1972-80; Musical Director, State Opera of South Australia, 1981-84. *Recordings include:* 23 with Orchestra of Naples, including complete Schubert symphonies, 12 Haydn, 11 Mozart, Re Pastore etc, RCA Victor. *Publications:* Le Discrepanze Nei Manoscritti Verdiani, La Scala, 1959; Preface on organ articulation and phrasing, Stanley Voluntaries, 1959; Puccini's Orchestration, Royal Musical Association, 1961. *Contributions to:* Opera News; High Fidelity; Journal of Sound and Vibration; Das Orchester; Musical Times; Opernwelt Jahrbuch; Studio Sound; Symphony, USA; Gramophone. *Honours:* Tagore Gold Medal, Royal College of Music, 1949; Silver Medal, Worshipful Company of Musicians, 1951. *Hobbies:* Running; Walking; Aerobic training; Theatre; Film; EAV diagnostic system; New spiritual paths; Complementary medicine; Promotion National Arts/ Sports/Environment Lottery; Promotion Performing Arts Centre in Covent Garden, incorporating Opera House, Drury Lane, Coliseum and Lyceum Theatre. *Current Management:* Marvin Schofer (USA), Germinal

Hilbert (Europe). *Address:* 41 Floral Street, London WC2E 9DG, England.

VAUGHAN Elizabeth, b. 12 March 1937, Llanfyllin, Montgomeryshire, Wales. Singer (Soprano). *Education:* FRAM, Hon. D. Mus. *Debut:* Welsh National Opera 1960, as Abigaile in Nabucco. *Career:* Covent Garden from 1961, as Mimi, Liu (Turandot), Teresa (Benvenuto Cellini), Gayle (The Ice Break, world premiere), Andromache and Hecuba (King Priam), Mozart's Elvira and Electra, Madame Butterfly, and Verdi's Amelia, Abigaille, Alice, (Boccanegra), Leonora (Trovatore), Gilda and Violetta; Opera North as Tosca, Lady Macbeth and Abigaille; Welsh National Opera as Tosca, Leonora (La Forza del Destino) and Maddalena in Andrea Chénier; English National Opera as Aida, Penelope Rich (Gloriana) and Beethoven's Leonore; Metropolitan Opera debut 1972, as Donna Elvira; Guest engagements in Vienna, Berlin, Paris, Hamburg, Munich and Prague; appearances in Australia, Canada, S America, Japan; Toured USA with English National Opera 1984; Chelsea Opera Group 1988, as Laura in La Gioconda; Professor of Singing, GSMD and WCMD; sang the Overseer in Elektra at Covent Garden 1990, Herodias in Salome for Scottish Opera. *Address:* c/o Music International, 13 Ardilaun Road, Highbury, London N5 2QR, England.

VAUGHAN WILLIAMS (Joan) Ursula (Penton), b. 15 Mar 1911, Valletta, Malta. Writer. m. (1) Michael Forrester Wood, 24 May 1933; (2) Ralph Vaughan Williams, 6 Feb 1953. *Career:* Writer of songs, song cycles, and lebretti for cantatas and opera libretti. *Publications:* A biography of Ralph Vaughn Williams, OM, 1964; also 6 books of poems and 3 novels. *Honours:* FRCM; Hon FRAM; MRNCM. *Memberships:* Committee, RVW Trust and of BMIC. *Hobbies:* Reading; Theatre; Films; Travel; Gardening. *Address:* 66 Gloucester Crescent, London NW1 7EG, England.

VAVRINECZ Béla, b. 18 Nov 1925, Budapest, Hungary. Composer; Conductor. m. Amalia Endrey, 1950, 1 son, 6 daughters. *Education:* Diploma in Composition, 1950, Diploma in Conducting, 1952, Budapest Academy of Music. *Debut:* Budapest Academy of Music, 1949. *Career:* 1st Conductor, Philharmonic Orchestra, Györy, 1957-58; Chief Conductor, Ministry of Home Affairs Symphony Orchestra, Budapest, 1961-73; Artistic Director, Dance Ensemble Budapest 1974-83; Artistic Director, Ensemble Duna Budapest, 1983-85; Works frequently performed on radio and television. *Compositions:* 1 opera, 2 ballets, 112 music pieces for dance theatre, 12 incidental works, 2 oratorium, 5 cantata, 17 works for choir & orchestra, 20 works for symphony orchestra, 5 works for chamber orchestra, 6 concerts, 36 chamber music, solo pieces, 23 choral works, songs, arrangements, music for windbands. *Recordings:* Numerous. *Publication:* Kodály Memorial Book, Budapest, 1953. *Contributions to:* Articles in different Hungarian periodicals. *Honours:* 2 prizes, World Youth Festival, 1957. *Memberships:* Hungarian Composers Association; Hungarian Dancers Association; Franz Liszt Society Hungarian Kodàly Society. *Hobbies:* Tennis; Skiing; Swimming. *Address:* Cinkotai út 39, H-1141 Budapest, Hungary.

VEA Ketil, b. 5 Feb 1932, Bø, Vesteralen, Norway. Teacher; Composer. m. Heid Refshal, 5 Feb 1988, 1 son, 1 daughter. *Education:* Teacher Examination, 1954; Music Teacher, 1957; Orchestral Conducting, Oslo Conservatory, 1962; Private studies in Composition. *Career:* Music Teacher, Teacher Training School, Nesna; Music Teacher, North Norwegian Music Conservatory, Tromsø; Rector, North Norwegian Music Conservatory, Tromsø; Currently Lecturer, Toneheim Music Gymnasium, Hamar. *Compositions:* Violin Concerto; 3 Piano Concertos; Concerto for trumpet, horn and orchestra; Concerto for tuba and orchestra; Several works for orchestra, for choirs, and for choir and orchestra; Songs, chamber music. *Recordings:* Jieuna for Symphony Orchestra with Soprano; Suite for clarinet and piano; Stallogargo for piano; Angry Cockerl for piano; Lyrical Suite for piano; Psalm 42 for mixed choir. *Publications:* Spilleboken, 1962, 1979; Metodisk Improvisasjon, 1964; Temaboka, 1969; Musikkpedagogisk grunnbok (co-author), 1972; Vi gjør musikk (co-author), 1977; I musikk, 1990; Inn i musikken, 1991. *Contributions to:* Several articles etc in pedagogical and music magazines. *Honours:* Nordland Fylkes Kulturpris, 1983; Lindeman Prize, 1983; Petter Dass Prize, 1983. *Memberships:* Norwegian Composers Society. *Address:* Marcus Thranes gt 18, 2800 Gjovik, Norway.

VEALE John, b. 15 June 1922, Shortlands, Kent, England. Composer. m. Diana Taylor, 26 Aug 1944, div 1971, 1 son, 2 daughters (1 dec). *Education:* Repton School; MA, Oxford University; Mainly self-taught musical education but some study with Thomas Armstrong, Egon Wellesz, Roger Sessions, Roy Harris. *Career:* Commonwealth Fellowship, USA, 1949-51; Research Fellowship, Corpus Christi College, Oxford, 1952-54; Film Correspondent, Oxford Mail, 1964-80; Copy Editor, Oxford University Press, 1968-87. *Compositions:* Symphonies 1 & 2; Clarinet Concerto; Violin Concerto; Panorama for Orchestra; Metropolis, Concert-Overture for Orchestra; Elegy for Flute, Harp and Strings; String Quartet; Kubla Khan for Baritone Solo, Mixed Chorus and Orchestra; Song of Radha for Soprano and Orchestra; Demos Variations for Orchestra; Apocalypse for Chorus and Orchestra; Triune, for Oboe/Cor Anglais and Orchestra; Film scores for The Purple Plain, The Spanish Gardener, Portrait of Alison, High Tide at Noon, Emergency, Film no 12 of BBC War in the Air Series. *Contributions to:* Various publications, with articles and reviews. *Memberships:* Performing Right Society Ltd; Composers' Guild of Great Britain; International Music Association; Royal Philharmonic Society. *Hobbies:* Reading; Walking; Ornithology; Astronomy. *Address:* 7 Nourse Close, Woodeaton, Oxford OX3 9TJ, England.

VEASEY Josephine, b. 10 July 1930, London, England. Opera Singer (mezzo soprano) (retired); Private Teacher; Teacher of Voice Production and Interpretation. m. dissolved, 1 son, 1 daughter. *Career:* Joined chorus of Royal Opera House, Covent Garden, 1949; a Principal there, 1955-83 (interval on tour in opera for Arts Council); Singer, Royal Opera House, Glyndebourne, Metropolitan (New York), La Scala and in France, Germany, Spain, Switzerland, South America; Operatic roles include: Octavian in Der Rosenkavalier; Cherubino in Figaro; name role in Iphigenia; Dorabella in Così fan Tutte; Amneris in Aida; Fricka in Die Walküre; Fricka in Das Rheingold; name role in Carmen; Dido and Cassandra in the Trojans; Marguerite in The Damnation of Faust; Charlotte in Werther; Eboli, Don Carlos; name role, Orfeo; Adalgisa in Norma; Rosina in The Barber of Seville; Kundry in Parsifal; Gertrude in Hamlet, 1980; Concerts, 1960-70; Aix Festival, 1967; Various works of Mahler; Two tours of Israel (Solti); Sang in Los Angeles (Mehta); Handel's Messiah, England, Munich, Oporto, Lisbon; Berlioz Romeo and Juliette, London and Bergen Festival; Emperor in 1st performance, Henze's We Come to the River, Covent Garden, 1976; Private teacher, 1982-; Teacher of Voice Production and Interpretation, Royal Academy of Music, 1983-; Voice Consultant to English National Opera, 1985-; Final appearance at Covent Garden 1982, as Herodias. *Recordings:* Numerous. *Contributions to:* Time Well Spent (Profile) Opera Magazine, July 1990. *Honours:* CBE, 1970; Hon. RAM, 1972. *Hobbies:* Reading; Gardening. *Address:* 2 Pound Cottage, St Mary Bourne, Andover, Hampshire, England.

VEDERNIKOV Alexander (Filoppovich), b. 23 Dec 1927, Mokino, nr, Kirov, USSR. Singer (Bass). *Eucation:* Studied in Moscow with Alpert-Khasina. *Debut:* Bolshoy Theatre Moscow 1957, as Ivan Susanin in Glinka's A Life for the Tsar. *Career:* Appearances in Moscow, Leningrad, Tiblisi and Kiev as Boris and Varlaam in Boris Godunov, Dosifey (Khovanshchina) and Konchak in Prince Igor; Engagements with the company of the Bolshoy at Paris, New York and Milan as Philip II and the Grand Inquisitor in Don Carlos and Massimilione in Verdi's I Masnadieri; Toured West Germany with the Bolshoy 1987; Other roles include Daland in Der fliegende Holländer, Prince Gremin (Eugene Onegin), Kutuzov in War and Peace and Mephistopheles (Faust).

Recordings include: The Stone Guest by Dargomizhsky; Rimsky-Korsakov's The Snow Maiden, Pimen in a video of Boris Godunov from the Boshoy (National Video Corporation). *Address:* c/o Bolshoy Theatre, Pr Marxa 8/2, 103009 Moscow, Russia.

VEDERNIKOV Alexander, b. 1964, Moscow, Russia. Conductor. *Education:* Studied at Central Music School Moscow and at the Tchaikovsky Conservatoire with Mark Ermler. *Career:* Moscow Musical Theatre from 1989, conducting La Finta Glardiniera, Le Nozze di Figaro, Cav and Pag, I1 Barbiere di Siviglia, La Traviata, Eugene Onegin, The Queen of Spades, Boris Godunov and ballets by Tchaikovsky; Assistant Conductor at the Moscow Radio Symphony Orchestra 1990; conducted the Junge Deutsche Philharmonie 1990, contract with the Rome Opera, 1991, debut with The Nutcracker; led the Moscow Radio Symphony at the Athens and Ankara Festivals 1992 and in Scotland, featuring music by Frank Martin, Glinka, Shostakovich and Vaughan Williams; tours to the United States and Japan in season 1992-93; Guest engagements with orchestras in the UK. *Address:* c/o Sonata, 11 Northpark Street, Glasgow G20, 7AA Scotland.

VEENEMAN Curt H, b. 4 Aug 1953, Grand Rapids, Michigan, USA. Composer; Theorist; Educator. m. Colleen Faye Minhinnick, 12 Jan 1980, 2 sons, 1 daughter. *Education:* BA, Grand Valley State University, Michigan, 1981; MA, University of Iowa, 1985; PhD, University of California, Berkeley, 1989. *Career:* Founder, Director, Sonor Borealis new music group, Edmonton, Canada, 1989-90; Faculty, University of Alberta, Canada, 1989-90; Assistant Professor, University of the Pacific, Stockton, California, 1990-; Founder and Director, Pacific Market: Fresh Music from Around The World, Stockton, 1991-. *Compositions:* Symphony No 1: Phtongitates Malleorum; Symphony No 2: Alcuin's Riddle; Orbits for String Quartet; Cymbolic for percussion; Essai pour les triangles, 2 track tape; River (Ordeal by Water), 4 track tape; The Wiry Concord for mixed ensemble. *Honours:* Hubbell Award for Composition, ASCAP, 1984; Nicola DeLorenzo Prize in Composition, 1989. *Memberships:* Society of Composers Inc; Society for Electro-Acoustic Music in the US; American Composers Alliance; BMI; National Association of Composers, USA. *Hobbies:* Photography; Pottery; Reading; Mountain hiking; Biking. *Address:* 14 East Wyandotte Street, Stockton, CA 95204, USA.

VEGH Sandor, b. 17 May 1905, Koloszvar, Hungary. Violinist; Conductor. *Education:* Studied violin with Jeno Hubay and composition with Kodaly in Budapest. *Career:* Played in a Strauss concert conducted by the composer 1927; Member of the Hungarian Trio 1931-33; Leader, then second violin in the Hungarian Quartet 1935-40, taking part in the European premiere of Bartok's 5th quartet, Barcelona 1936; Founder and leader of the Vegh Quartet 1940-80, touring to Europe, North and South America, Asia; Complete cycles of the quartets of Bartok and Beethoven; Professor at the Academy of Music in Budapest 1941-46, emigrated to Switzerland 1946; Teacher of the summer course at Zermatt 1952-62; Conservatories of Basle 1953-63, Fribourg 1954-62, Duseldorf 1962-79; Salzburg Mozarteum from 1971; Founded Festival of Chamber Music at Cervo, Italy 1962, International Seminar at Prussia Cove, Cornwall 1972; Collaborations with Casals at the Prades Festival 1953-69, with Erno Dohnanyi, Willem Mengelberg, Ferenc Fricsay, Krips, Kertesz, Wilhelm Kempff and Rudolf Serkin; Directed the Sandor Vegh Chamber Orchestra 1968-71, Orchestra of the Marlboro Festival 1974-77, the Camerata of the Salzburg Mozarteum from 1979; With Vegh Quartet premiered the first two quartets of Hartmann, 1936, 1949, 2nd Quartet of Pierre Wismer, 1949, the Quartet Concerto of Sandor Veress, 1962; In 1978 the Quartet's recording of Beethoven's Op 130 was launched by NASA on Voyager's extra-solar trajectory; Conducted the Chamber Orchestra of Europe at the Barbican, London 1990. *Recordings:* Many albums of the Viennese Classics for Decca, Capriccio, Philips, Hungaroton: Mozart Divertimenti and Serenades, Piano Concertos (Andra's Schiff and the

Camerata Academica). *Honours include:* CBE 1989; Grand Prix du Disque, 1989 (for Mozart Divertimenti and Serenades); Chevalier of Legion d'honneur, Arts et Literature. *Address:* c/o Chamber Orchestra of Europe, 64 Lincoln Inn Fields, London WC2A 3JX, England.

VEIRA Jonathan, b. 1960, England. Singer (Bass). *Education:* Studied at Trinity College of Music, London, and at the National Opera Studio. *Career:* Sang Dipsicus in The Poisoned Kiss and Falstaff in The Merry Wives of Windsor at the Bloomsbury Theatre; Königskinder by Humperdinck at the Wexford Festival; At Glyndebourne appeared as Lemokh in the premiere of The Electrification of the Soviet Union and in Die Entführung and Capriccio; Other engagements have included a tour with Opera 80, Antonio in Le Nozze di Figaro at the Prom concerts, Don Carlos at Covent Garden, Salome for Scottish Opera and Tippett's New Year for the Glyndebourne Tour; Broadcasts of Mahagonny and Rossini's Tancredi for the BBC; Television appearances in La Traviata, The Electrification of the Soviet Union and Death in Venice; Engagements with Opera Factory, London. *Address:* Lies Askonas Ltd, 186 Drury Lane, London WC2B 5RY, England.

VEJZOVIC Dunja, b. 20 Oct 1943, Zagreb, Yugoslavia. Singer (Soprano). *Education:* Studied in Zagreb, Stuttgart, Weimar and Salzburg. *Career:* Sang first at Zagreb, then in Frankfurt, Dusseldorf, Vienna, Hamburg and Stuttgart; Bayreuth Festival 1978-80, as Kundry in Parsifal: also sang the role at the Salzburg Easter Festival; Metropolitan Opera 1978-79, as Venus in Tannhäuser; Paris Opéra 1982, Ortrud; Teatro Liceo Barcelona 1983 in the title role of Herodiade by Massenet; La Scala Milan 1984, as Venus; Théâtre de la Monnaie, Brussels 1984, Senta in Der fliegende Holländer; Also sings Chimène in Le Cid by Massenet; sang Ortrud at the Vienna Staatsoper, 1990; Season 1992 as Kundry in Robert Wilson's production of Parsifal at Houston. *Recordings:* Parsifal, conducted by Karajan (Deutsche Grammophon); Christus by Liszt; Lohengrin and Der fliegende Holländer (EMI). *Address:* c/o Allied Artists Agency, 42 Montpelier Square, London SW7 1JZ, England.

VELAZCO Jorge, b. 12 Jan 1942, Mexico City, Mexico. Conductor; Music Director. m. Marcia Elizabeth Yount, 25 May 1983, 2 sons. *Education:* General: Degree in Law, National University of Mexico; Lower Certificate in English, Cambridge University; Musical: Student of Conrado Tovar (piano), Antonio Gomezanda (piano, music theory), Rodolfo Halffter(composition, music analysis), Lukas Foss (conducting), Franco Ferrara (conducting at the Accademia Musicale Chigiana, Siena, Italy) and Herbert von Karajan (conducting). *Career:* Professor at the National Conservatory (Mexico City) 1973-84; Researcher in Music at the National University of Mexico 1974-; Visiting Professor: Wyoming State University, Michigan State University, Phoenix College 1975-76; Assistant Chairman of Mexico's Federal Government Music Department 1972-73; Chairman of National University of Mexico's Music Department 1973-74; Vice-President for Cultural Affairs of National University of Mexico 1974-76; Associate Conductor of the UNAM Philharmonic 1977-81; Assistant to Herbert von Karajan at Salzburg's Easter Festival, 1977; Founder and Music Director of the Mineria Symphony Orchestra, 1978-84; Music Director of the UNAM Philharmonic, 1985-89; Principal Guest Conductor, Florence Chamber Orchestra (Italy), 1990-; Director of International Studies, Texas Music Festival, Houston, USA, 1992-; Guest Conductor: Interamerican Music Festival Orchestra in Washington, DC; Brooklyn Philharmonic; Atlanta, Baltimore, Milwaukee, Louisville, San Antonio, ROW (Poland), Reutlingen, Zarajevo, Sacramento, Houston, and Berlin Symphonies; Sinfonietta RIAS and Berlin Radio Symphony Orchestra (RSOB). *Recordings:* Several recordings with the Berlin Radio Symphony Orchestra, Berlin Symphony and Sinfonietta RIAS, issued by Schwann in Germany. *Honours:* Guggenheim Fellowship, 1987; Wortha, Chair in the Performing Arts,

University of Houston, 1991. *Memberships:* Member, Sociedad Espanola de Musicologia, Madrid, Spain, 1990-; International Musicological Society, Basel, Switzerland, 1991-, Royal Musical Association, London, England, 1992-. *Address:* Anahuac 33 esq. Tehuantepec, Col. Roma Sur, Mexico, DF 06760.

VELIS Andrea, b. 7 June 1932, New Kensington, Pennsylvania, USA. Singer (Tenor). *Education:* Studied with Louise Taylor in Pittsburgh, at the Royal College of Music, London, and at the Accademia di Santa Cecilia, Rome. *Debut:* Pittsburgh 1954, as Goro in Madame Butterfly. *Career:* Appearances in Chicago, Cincinnati, Philadelphia and San Francisco; Metropolitan Opera from 1961 in 1600 performances of 50 operas, including La Fanciulla del West, Death in Venice, Hansel and Gretel, Eugene Onegin, The Ring (Mime), Les Contes d'Hoffmann, Otello, Der Rosenkavalier, Tosca and Boris Godunov; Sang Mardian in the premiere of Barber's Antony and Cleopatra, 1966. *Recordings include:* Tosca (HMV). *Address:* c/o Metropolitan Opera, Lincoln Center, New York, NY 10023, USA.

VELTRI Michelangelo, b. 18 Aug 1940, Buenos Aires, Argentina. Conductor. *Education:* Studied in Argentina. *Career:* Conducted in Argentina, Chile, Venezuela and Brazil; Moved to Europe 1970 and worked at the Stuttgart Opera, then in Milan; Appointments include Artistic Director at the Teatro Liceu Barcelona, and Artistic and Music Director with the Opera d'Avignon; Guest conductor at the Vienna Staatsoper, La Scala Milan, Covent Garden, (Lucia di Lammermoor 1986), Paris Opéra, Rome, Verona, Marseille and Toulouse, notably in operas by Verdi; Regular engagements in the USA include San Francisco and the Metropolitan Opera (La Traviata in season 1989-90); Verdi repertoire includes Giovanna d'Arco (Parma 1980), Macbeth and Un ballo in Maschera (Avignon 1980-81) Don Carlos (Marseille 1984), Aida (Orange 1983), Otello and La Forza del Destino (Buenos Aires), I due foscari and La Traviata (Santago); conducted Il Trovatore at Buenos Airea 1990, Adriana Lecouvreur for L'Opéra de Montréal. *Recordings include:* Live concert with Alfredo Kraus and June Anderson (EMI); Albums of arias by Rossini, Bellini and Donizetti, with Raul Gimenez and the Scottish Chamber Orchestra (Nimbus). *Address:* c/o Patricia Greenan, 19b Belsize Park, London NW3 4DU, England.

VENDICE William, b. 24 Nov 1948, San Francisco, California, USA. Pianist; Conductor. *Education:* BA Piano & Conducting, California State University, San Francisco. *Debut:* Metropolitan Opera, New York, 1984. *Career:* Conductor or Assistant Conductor at Western Opera Theatre, Santa Fe Opera, Opera Company of Boston, Metropolitan Opera, New York, San Francisco Opera, Hamburg Opera, Chautaugva Opera; Artistic Director, Artscope Festival, Palm Springs, California; Musical Director, Opera Music Theater of New Jersey; European Debut: Porgy & Bess, Theater des Westens, Berlin 1988. *Recordings:* Thompson, Mother of Us All; Stravinsky, Les Noces. *Current Management:* SAFIMM, 250 West 57th Street, NY 10107, USA. *Address:* 344 W 72 Street, New York, NY 10023, USA.

VENGEROV Maxim, b. 15 Aug 1974, Novosibirsk, Siberia. Concert Violinist. *Education:* Studied with Zakhar Bron. *Debut:* Moscow 1985, playing Schubert's Rondo Brillant. *Career:* Many recitals and concerts in Moscow and Leningrad. Solo debuts with the Concertgebouw Orchestra, the BBC Philharmonic at the Lichfield Festival, England, and with the USSR State Symphony under Simonov on tour to Italy; Recital debuts at the Wigmore Hall, Suntory Hall Tokyo and the Mozarteum, Salzburg; Season 1990-91 with US debut in concert with the New York Philharmonic, Israel Philharmonic at Tel-Aviv and on tour to USA under Zubin Mehta; Season 1991-92 included concerts with the Berlin Philharmonic under Abbado, the LPO under Mehta, St Petersburg Philharmonic at the London Proms (Sibelius Concerto) and the Salzburg Festival with the

Mozarteum Orchestra and Trevor Pinnock; Season 1992-93 with the Rotterdam Philharmonic, the Chicago Symphony under Barenboim, Los Angeles Philharmonic and Mehta; Prom Concerts 1993 with the BBC SO, Brahms Concerto with the Berlin Philharmonic and Abbado, Vienna Philharmonic under Yehudi Menuhin. *Recordings include:* Albums for Melodiya; Sonatas by Beethoven and Brahms, Paganini 1st Concerto. *Honours:* Winner, Junior Wieniawski Competition, Poland, 1984; Winner, 1990 Carl Flesch International Violin Competition, London. *Address:* c/o AMI Ltd. 22 Tower Street, London WC2H 9NS, England.

VENTRIGLIA Franco, b. 20 Oct 1927, Fairfield, Connecticut, USA. Opera Singer (Bass). m. 12 Feb 1945. *Education:* American Theatre Wing, Toti Dal Monte International School of Bel Canto in Rome and Venice. *Debut:* Teatro Massimo Palermo, Italy, Meistersinger, Tullio Serafin, Conductor. *Career:* Appearances in various operas, Academia Di S Cecilia, Rome; La Scala, Vienna Staatsoper, Berlin Staatsoper; San Carlo; Reggio di Parma; Reggio di Torino; Comunale di Firenze; King's Theatre, Edinburgh; Chicago Lyric; Dallas Opera; Wexford Festival; La Fenice Venezia; Arena di Verona; Teatro de L'Opera Roma; Milwaukee; Concertgebouw, Amsterdam; Dutch Radio; Roles have included Rossini's Basilio, Raimondo, Elmiro (Otello by Rossini), Walter and Wurm in Luisa Miller, Loredano (I due Foscari), the Grand Inquistor, Alvise, Colline and Sparafucile (Rigoletto). *Recordings:* La Traviata, RCA; Manon Lescaut, EMI; Angelieum, Vedette Records. *Contributions to:* Opera News. *Membership:* AGMA. *Hobby:* Musical Box Collecting. *Current Management:* Robert Lombardo Associates. *Address:* 515 Brookside Drive, Fairfield, CT 06430, USA.

VENTRIS Christopher, b. 1960, London. Singer (Tenor). *Education:* Studied at the Royal Academy of Music. *Career:* Joined Glyndebourne Festival Chorus 1987; Touring Opera debut 1988, as Vanya in Katya Kabanova; Later appearances (as Tom Rakewell, Glyndebourne Festival Opera, and the Porter in Death in Venice, Glyndebourne Touring Opera, Jacquino, Fidelio); Concert engagements include Messiah, Mozart's Requiem in Madrid, Beethoven's Mass in C, Mendelssohn's Lobgesang (Second Symphony) and Elijah and Tippett's A Child of our Time; South Bank debut at the Purcell Room and at the Festival Hall sang in one of the last concerts conducted by Antal Dorati, in the Liebesliederwalzer by Brahms; Covent Garden debut 1989, in Der Rosenkavalier; Opera North from 1990 in Jerusalem, Attila and King Priam; Robert Lonle in the premiere of Caritas by Robert Saxton, 1991; Engagements in 1992 include, ENO, Antwerp and Leipzig Operas; Sang Paris in King Priam at Antwerp, 1992; Season 1993/94 at Geneva, Antwerp and Leipzig; ROH, Covent Garden, 1993-94. *Honours include:* 1988-89 Esso GTFO Singers Award; John Christie Award, Glyndebourne. *Address:* IMG Artists Europe, Media House, 3 Burlington Lane, London, W4 2TH, England.

VENZAGO Mario, b. 1 July 1948, Zurich, Switzerland. Conductor. *Education:* University of Zurich; Conservatories of Zurich & Vienna. *Career:* Conductor: Swiss Radio Lugano, Swiss Romande, Geneva, Musikkollegium, Winterthur; General Music Director, Heidelberg. *Recordings:* Extensive catalogue of Schumann, Janáček. *Honours:* Prix Edison, Grand Prix du Disque. *Address:* Balmer und Dixon Management, Granitweg 2, CH-8002, Zurich, Switzerland.

VERA-RIVERA Santiago Oscar, b. 2 Nov 1950, Santiago, Chile. Professor; Composer. m. Maria Angelica Bustamante, 25 May 1974, 2s, 1d. *Education:* University of Chile; Doctorate in Musicology, University of Oviedo, Spain, 1991. *Career:* Professor, University of Chile, 1974-81, University of Tarapaca, 1984; Acad Pedag. Santiago, 1981-85; University Metropolitana, 1986; Escuela Moderna de Musicas, 1976-87; Intem/ODE, 1984. *Compositions:* Choral, piano, electronic, persussion, guitar and orchestral pieces. *Recordings include:* Tres Tempo varias, 1987; Tres aquareskas,

1989; Chiloe, Tierre de Ajva, 1989; Cirrus, 1987. *Publications:* Harmony for two voices, 1990; Contributor to Dictionary of Music, Hispano Americane and Espanola, 1989-92; Informusicz, Spain, 1992. *Hobbies:* Producing TV and radio music programmes. *Address:* La Fetra 185-D, Santiago, Chile.

VERBRAEKEN Carl Gustav, b. 18 Sept 1950, Antwerpen, Belgium. Composer; Pianist; Academy Director. *Education:* PhD Applied Sciences, Microelectronics, Leuven, 1976; Diplomas, Music History 1976, Pianist-Accompanist, 1979, Fugue 1982, Higher Diploma Piano 1981, Royal Conservatory, Brussels. *Career:* Microelectronics Research Engineer, Leuven University, 1972; Piano Teacher and Accompanist, 1977; Assistant Professor in keyboard harmony 1979-, Professor of keyboard harmony and piano accompaniment 1985, Royal Conservatory, Brussels; Accredited Composer, SABAM, 1979; Accompanist, International Queen Elisabeth Competition, 1985; Conductor, Flanders Engineers Orchestra, 1986-; Director, Academy of Music, SPW Brussels, 1987; Concert appearances as a pianist, Europe, USA and Far East. *Compositions include:* Symphonic orchestra: Elementen, op 17; Phainomena, op 21; 5-inch Symphonie, op 31; Opera/Ballet: Prinsje Sneeuwwit en de Zeven Elfjes, op 6; Solo with orchestra: Liederen van de Hoop (recorded), op 12; Mystic Concerto, piano, op 30; 3 cantatas. *Recordings include:* Poëma, violin and piano. *Publication:* Beknopt Overzicht Van Compositorische Technieken en Begrippen, 1986. *Address:* Moorkensplein 23, B 2140 Antwerpen, Belgium.

VERBRUGGEN Marion, b. 2 Aug 1950, Amsterdam, Netherlands. Recorder Player; Teacher. *Education:* Study with Kees Otten, Amsterdam Conservatory, 1966; With Frans Bruggen, Muziek Lyceum, Amsterdam, and Royal Conservatory, The Hague, 1967; B Diploma, 1971; Solo degree cum laude, Royal Conservatory, The Hague, 1973. *Career:* Performances with various ensembles and solo concerts, Netherlands, USA, Canada, Japan, most European countries; Regular guest, Gustav Leonhardt, Amsterdam Baroque Orchestra, Musica Antiqua, Cologne, Tafelmusik Toronto, many others; Plays at Holland Festival of Early Music; Radio appearances, Netherlands, Belgium, Germany, Canada, Italy, Norway, USA, Hungary, TV appearances, Netherlands, Norway, Belgium, Italy, Federal Republic of Germany, USA; Teacher: Royal Conservatory, The Hague; Utrecht Conservatory; Guest Teacher, Malmo Conservatory, Sweden; Masterclasses and workshops, Stanford University, Toronto, Montreal, New York, Philadelphia, Malmo, Trondheim, Copenhagen, Jerusalem. *Recordings:* For EMI, Philips/Seon, Titanic, Hungaroton, ASV London, L'Oiseau Lyre, Monumenta Belgicae Musicae; Archiv, Harmonica Mundi. *Address:* Vondelstraat 99, 1054 GM Amsterdam, Netherlands.

VERGARA Victoria, b. 1948, Santiago, Chile. Singer (Mezzo-soprano). *Education:* Studied in Santiago and in New York with Nicola Moscona, and Anton Guadagno, and at the Juilliard School with Daniel Ferro and Rose Bampton. *Career:* Sang minor roles in the USA, before New York City Opera debut, 1977; Sang at Detroit from 1977, Santiago 1978; Houston Grand Opera from 1980; Has sung Carmen at San Francisco, Cincinnati, Zurich, Lisbon, Vancouver, Philadelphia, Seattle, New Orleans and Berlin; Chicago Lyric Opera 1982, Vienna Staatsoper 1984, as Amneris; Washington Opera 1987, as the Duchess of Alba in the premiere of Menotti's Goya, opposite Placido Domingo; Metropolitan Opera dubut 1988, as Carmen; Teatro Liceo Barcelona 1989, in the premiere of Cristobal Colon by Leonardo Balada, with Caballé and Carreras; Season 1990 sang Herodias (Salome) at Santiago and at the Zarzuela Theatre Madrid in El viajero indiscreto, as Dona; Other roles include Donna Elvira, Cherubino, Frederica in Luisa Miller, Maddalena, Rosina, Dalila, Nicklausse, Charlotte and Massenet's Dulcinée. *Recordings include:* Maddalena in Rigoletto (Decca). *Address:* c/o IM Röhrich 55, 6702 Bad Dürkheim 2, Germany.

VERMEERSCH Jef, b. 7 Feb. 1928, Bruges, Belgium. Singer (Baritone). *Education:* Studied in Bruges, Ghent and Antwerp. *Career:* Concert singer from 1952; Stage debut Antwerp 1960, as Wotan in Das Rheingold; Sang at Gelsenkirchen from 1966; Member of the Deutsche Oper Berlin from 1973; Guest appearances in Germany and in Brussels, Amsterdam, Lyon, Venice, Lisbon, Prague, Geneva, San Francisco, Barcelona and Stockholm; Salzburg Easter Festival 1973, as Kurwenal in Tristan und Isolde, conducted by Karajan; Bayreuth Festival 1981-83, Kothner in Die Meistersinger; Other roles include Hans Sachs, Amfortas, the Dutchman, Boris Godunov, Golaud, Pizarro, Kaspar, the title role in Giulio Cesare by Handel, Leporello, Jochanaaan, Kepler in Die Harmonie der Welt, Falstaff, Amonasro and St Just in Dantons Tod; sang Kothner at Bayreuth 1988; Kurwenal at Wuppertal 1989. *Address:* Wuppertaler Bühnen, Spinnstrasse 4, D-5600, Wuppertal.

VERMILLION Iris, b. 1960, Bielefeld, Germany. Singer (Soprano). *Education:* Studied flute at first, then voice with Mechthild Bohme and Judith Beckmann. *Debut:* Brunswick 1986, as Zulma in L'Italiana in Algeri and as Barbara in Eine Nacht in Vendig. *Career:* Sang Dorabella and Octavian in Brunswick; Deutsche Oper Berlin from 1988, as a Rhinemaiden, Hansel and Cherubino; Darmstadt 1988, as Judith in Duke Bluebeard's Castle; Sang Dorabella with Netherlands Opera in Amsterdam, 1990; Salzburg Festival 1990, as Clairon in Capriccio; Other roles include Werther (Charlotte) and Mozart's Sextus; Also sings in the St Matthew Passion and Mozart's Davidde Penitente. *Recordings include:* Second Lady in Die Zauberflöte, conducted by Neville Marriner (Philips).*Honours include:* Prize winner at Cardiff Singer of the World Competition. *Address:* c/o Deutsche Oper Berlin, Richard Wagnerstrasse 10, D-1000 Berlin, Germany.

VERNEY Myra, b.6 Nov 1905, London, England. *Education:* Hons Degree, Oxford, 1929. *Debut:* 1939. *Career:* Broadcasts with teh BBC Symphony Orchestra, debu tin 1940; French government concerts and performances at Wigmore Hall, London. *Recordings:* Broadcast recital of Spanish music to Spain for the BBC. *Honours:* Scholarship to study in France, 1935-39. *Memberships:* Incorporated Society of Musicians. *Hobbies:* Philately. *Address:* 14 Gurney Drive, London N2 0DG, England.

VERNON Richard, b. 1950, Memphis, Tennessee, USA. Singer (Bass). *Education:* Studied at Memphis State University. *Debut:* Memphis 1972, as Pimen in Boris Godunov. *Career:* Has sung with Houston Opera Studio from 1977, in operas by Verdi; Appearances with Washington Opera and Pittsburgh Opera; Metropolitan Opera from 1981, in L'Enfant et les Sortilèges, and as Titurel (Parsifal) and the Commendatore (Don Giovanni); Sang Foltz in a new Production of Die Meistersinger at the Metropolitan, 1993. *Address:* c/o Metropolitan Opera, Lincoln Center, New York, NY 10023, USA.

VERONELLI Ernesto, b. 1948, Milan, Italy. Singer (Tenor). *Education:* Studied at the Giuseppe Verdi Conservatory, Milan. *Career:* Has sung in operas by Verdi, Puccini, Massenet and Giordano at Paris, Zurich, Barlin, Barcelona, Vienna and Verona; Debut with the Royal Opera Covent Garden at Manchester as Cavaradossi (1983), later singing Chevalier Roland in Esclarmonde, opposite Joan Sutherland; Season 1985-86 sang Canio at the Metropolitan, Cavaradossi in Pretoria and Pinkerton at the Cologne Opera; Calaf in Detroit and Radames at Toronto; Other roles have been Verdi's Macduff, Carlo (Giovanna d'Arco), Don Carlos and Manrico.

VERRETT Shirley, b. 31 May 1931, New Orleans, Louisiana, USA. Soprano/Mezzo-Soprano. *Education:* Studied in Los Angeles with Anna Fitziu and Hall Johnson; Juilliard School with Mdme. Szekely-Freschl. *Debut:* Yellow Springs Ohio 1957, as Britten's Lucretia; New York City Opera 1958, as Irina in Lost in the Stars

by Weill; European debut Cologne 1959, in Rasputins Tod by Nabokov; First major success as Carmen, at Spoleto (1962), New York City Opera (1964) and La Scala (1966); Covent Garden from 1966, as Ulrica, Azucena, Amneris, Eboli, Carmen, Orpheus and Selika in L'Africaine; Metropolitan Opera from 1968, as Carmen, Eboli, Cassandra and Dido in Les Troyens, Judith (Bluebeard's Castle), Adalgisa, Norma, Neocle (L'Assedio di Corinto) and Leonore in La favorita; Florence 1969, as Elisabetta in Maria Stuarda; Paris Opéra 1983, in Moise by Rossini; Verona Arena 1984, Carmen; Appearances at Salzburg, Dallas Opera, Moscow, Kiev and San Francisco; Other roles include Lady Macbeth, Tosca, Dalila and Federica in Luisa Miller; Sang Dido in Les Troyens, opening production of the Bastille Opera, Paris, 1990; Season 1991/92 as Azucena at Genoa and Leonora in La Favorita at Madrid; Recital repertoire includes songs by Mahler, Brahms, Schubert and Milhaud. *Recordings:* Orpheus, Un Ballo in Maschera, La Forza del Destino, Luisa Miller, Lucrezia Borgia (RCA); Don Carlos (Electrola); L'Africaine; Macbeth (Deutsche Grammophon); Video of L'Africaine, San Francisco Opera (Virgin Classics). *Address:* c/o Opéra de la Bastille, 11 bis Avenue Daumesnil, F-75012 Paris, France.

VERROUST Denis, b. 21 Feb 1958, Vincennes, France. Flautist; Musicologist. m. Marguerite Sopinski, 27 Dec 1986. *Education:* Baccalaureat A, 1975; DEUG, Economics, 1979. Music Education: Graduate, Saint-Maur CNR; DE, flute teacher, 1988. *Career:* Appearances, St Malo Festival, Brittany, 1980-; Several tours in France, Germany, Holland with Cologne Chamber Orchestra, as soloist; Radio programme for Radio-France, 1982; Invited lecturer in several American Universities. *Publications:* 5 titles proposed and edited for the Billaudot Edition, Paris, 1980 and 1982; J S Bach: Sinfonia from Cantata BWV 209; 4 characteristic XIXth century pieces by W. Popp, F. Doppler and A. Fürstenberg; Principal editor and director of collections for the Stravaganza Edition, Paris; Mozart, Haydn, Rossini (Opera overtures for 2 flutes); A Hugot (Trios for 2 flutes and bass); Jean-Pierre Rampal, over 40 years of recordings 1946-1989; The flute in France from Devienne to Taffanel (150 years 1770-1920) in progress; Complete Catalogue of XIXth Century Flute Literature, in progress; The Romantic Flute, in progress; Exhaustive Researchers and Leading Authority on the Late Classical and Romantic Flute Repertoire. *Contributions to:* Numerous articles to professional journals. *Hobby:* Tennis. *Address:* 16 avenue Aubert, 94300 Vincennes, France.

VERSALLE Richard, b. 1933, Michigan, USA. Singer (Tenor). *Career:* Submariner, US Marines; Studied singing and appeared with a Baroque music group in Chicago; Sang minor roles at Metropolitan Opera; engaged as Otello at Saarbrucken; Deutsche Oper am Rhein Dusseldorf from 1984 as Verdi's Riccardo, Cavaradossi, Peter Grimes and in operas by Wagner; Guest appearances in Stuttgart and Frankfurt (Florestan, 1984); Has sung at Bayreuth from 1985, notably as Tannhäuser; Sang with Nikikai Opera in Tokyo as Tannhäuser, 1988: repeated at the Vienna Staatsoper and in Bonn; Madrid Opera 1989, as Tristan, opposite Montserrat Caballé; Salzburg Festival 1988 in a concert performance of Der Prozess, by Gottfried von Einem. *Address:* c/o Staatsoper, Opernring 2, A-1010 Vienna, Austria.

VERSCHRAEGEN Herman Elie Bertha, b. 4 Apr 1936, Ghent, Belgium. Organist; Director of Music Academy; Organ Master. m. Van Hove Genevieve, 2 July 1963, 1 son, 1 daughter. *Education:* Several First Prizes and Higher Diploma in Organ, 1960, Royal Conservatory of Music, Ghent; Virtuosity Prize, Organ,1965. *Debut:* Ghent, 1957. *Career:* Organist, St. Josef Church, Antwerp, 1962; Master of Music Theory and History, Music Academy of Wilrijk 1963-73; Organ Master, Music Academy of Aalst 1965-73 and Music Academy of Geel 1966-73; Director, Music Academy of Wilrijk-Antwerp 1974-; Organ Master, Royal Conservatory of Music, Brussels, 1976-; Over 700 organ concerts and recitals in Austria, Belgium, Czechoslovakia, Denmark, East and West Germany, France, Holland, Israel, Italy, Japan, Poland, South Africa, Sweden, Switzerland, United Kingdom, United States, Philippines; Several seminars about C. Franck and the Flemish Organ School and also masterclass in Japan. Member of Jury of International Organ Contests: Nurenberg 1970, Lokeren 1972; Recitals for International Broadcasting Corporations Belgium, Denmarks Radio, Suddeutscher Rundfunk, Hessischer Rundfunk, Bayerischer Rundfunk, Sender Freies Berlin, Sudwestfunk, Nordd Rundfunk, Czechoslovakia, Sweden, Radio Geneva, Bern, Zurich, Suisse Romande, USA, South Africa. *Composition:* Fantasy for Organ. *Recordings:* Handel, Bach, Couperin, Van den Gheyn (Polydor). *Hobby:* Travel. *Address:* 5 Schansweg, B-2610 Wilrijk-Antwerpen, Belgium.

VERSHININA Irina, b.24 Feb 1930, Moscow, Russia. Musicologist. div. 1s. *Education:* Gnesin's Musical Academy; Institue of Art Studies, Moscow. *Debut:* Sowjetunion Heute, 1953. *Career:* Tutor, Theory of Music, Moscow Musical School; Researcher, Russia Institue of Art Studies; Senior Editor, Sovetsky Kompositor Publications (Musical Folklore of USSR). *Publications:* Stravinsky's Early ballets, 1967; contributor, 20th Century Music 1890-1917, 1976; History of Music of Peoples of USSR, 1957-67, 1974; Russian Art culture 1907-1917, 1978; Ed, Igor Stravinsky, Vocal Music, 1988; Musorgsky and Stravinsky 1990. *Honours:* Dr of Art Studies, 1968. *Memberships:* Composer's Society of Russia. *Hobbies:* History of literature. *Address:* Acad Scriabin Str 26-1-84, Moscow 109378, Russia.

VIALA Jean-Luc, b. 5 Sept 1957, Paris, France. Singer (Tenor). *Education:* Studied in Paris with Michel Senechal. *Debut:* Paris Opera-Comique 1983, in Pomme d'Apis by Offenbach. *Career:* Sang at the Opera-Comique in Cesar Franck's Stradella and has made many appearances at provincial French opera houses; Glyndebourne Festival 1986, as the Italian Singer in Capriccio, Dublin 1987, Aix-en-Provence Festival 1989, as the Prince in the Love for Three Oranges; Recent engagements at the Opera de Lyon including Rodolfo 1990; Sang in Sacchini's Oedipe a Colone for the Festival de Radio France at de Montpellier, 1992; other roles include Paolino in I1 Matrimonio Segreto, Giannetto (La Gazza Ladra), Fenton, George Brown in La Dame Blanche and Iopas in Les Troyens. *Recordings include:* Guercoeur by Magnard and Les Brigands by Offenbach; Narraboth in the French version of Salome, Osmin in Gluck's La Rencontre Imprevue and Benedict in Beatrice at Benedict, all with the Lyon Opera; The Love for Three Oranges. *Address:* c/o Opera de Lyon, 9 Quai Jean Moulin, F-69001 Lyon, France.

VICK Graham, b. 30 Dec 1953, Liverpool, England. Opera Producer. *Career includes:* Productions for the ENO include Ariadne auf Naxos, the Rape of Lucretia, Madame Butterfly, Eugene Onegin, Timon of Athens by Stephen Oliver, (world premiere, 1991), and the Marriage of Figaro; for Opera North, Così fan Tutte, Die Zauberflöte and Katya Kabanova; For Glyndebourne Festival, Queen of Spades; Artistic Director, City of Birmingham Touring Opera; European engagements in Brussels, Bonn, Venice, Netherlands, Berlin, Paris, Italy, and St Petersburg. Covent Garden debut in 1989 with the British premiere of Un Re in Ascolto by Berio, returning for Mozart's Mitridate, 1991 and Die Meistersinger, 1993; (Television works) include Il Segreto di Susanna for Scottish TV, The Rape of Lucretia for Channel Four, a live BBC TV Broadcast of War and Peace from St Petersburg, and Queen of Spades from Glyndebourne. *Honours include:* Premi Abbiati award as Best Director for Mahagonny at the Teatro Communale in Florence and a SWET Oliver award for Mitridate at the Royal Opera, Covent Garden. *Address:* c/o Ingpen & Williams Ltd, 14 Kensington Court, London W8 5DN, England.

VICKERS Jon, b. 29 Oct 1926, Prince Albert, Saskatchewan, Canada. Tenor. m. Henrietta

Outerbridge, 1953, 3 sons, 2 daughters. *Career:* Concert and Opera Singer, Canada; Joined Royal Opera House, Covent Garden, London, 1957-84, as Riccardo, Don Carlos, Radames, Florestan, Giasone (Médée), Samson (Handel and Saint-Saëns), Aeneas, Siegmund and Tristan; Sang at Bayreuth Festival, Vienna State Opera, San Francisco, Chicago Lyric Opera, Metropolitan Opera, La Scala, Milan, Paris Opera, Boston, Buenos Aires, Athens, Ottawa, Houston, Dallas, Hamburg, Berlin, Munich, Athens Festival, Salzburg Festival, Festival, Festival of Orange, Tanglewood Festival, Rio de Janeiro. *Recordings:* Messiah; Otello; Aida; Die Walküre, Samson and Delilah; Fidelio; Italian arias; Verdi's Requiem; Peter Grimes; Das Lied von der Erde; Les Troyens; Tristan und Isolde; Films include: Carmen; Pagliacci; Norma; Otello; Peter Grimes. *Honours:* Honorary LLD, Saskatchewan; Honorary CLD, Bishop's University; Mus D, Brandon University, University of Western Ontario; LLD, University of Guelph; Civ LD, University of Laval; DMus, University of Illinois; Critics Award, London, 1978; Grammy Award, 1979. *Membership:* Royal Academy of Music, London. *Address:* c/o Metropolitan Opera, New York, NY 10029, USA.

VICTORY Gerard, b. 24 Dec 1921, Dublin, Ireland. Composer. m. 1948, 2 sons, 3 daughters. *Education:* Graduate, National University of Ireland (Celtic Studies, Modern Languages); DMus, Trinity College, Dublin. *Career:* Producer, Irish Radio and TV, RTE, 1952-62; Deputy Director Music, RTE, 1962-67; Director of Music, RTE, 1967-82. *Compositions:* Jonathan Swift; Symphonic Portrait; Voyelles for soprano and orchestra; Songs from Lyonnesse for chorus; Overture, Monte Cristo; March Bizarre. *Recordings:* Jonathan Swift; Prelude and Toccata for Piano; Miroirs for Orchestra; New Irish Recording Co. *Contributions to:* BBC Talks The Melodious Soothsayer (J.J Rousseau), Thomas Moore. *Honour:* Hamilton Harty Bursary 1981. *Membership:* President International Rostrum of Composers (Unesco-Paris) 1981-84). *Hobbies:* Swimming; Walking. *Address:* 29 Lawnswood Park, Stillorgan, Co. Dublin, Republic of Ireland.

VIDOVSZKY László, b. 25 Feb 1944, Békescsaba, Hungary. Composer. 1 daughter. *Education:* Budapest Music High School, 1962-67. *Career:* Founder, New Music Studio, 1970-; Lecturer, Budapest Music High School, 1972-84; Head of Music Department, Pécs University, 1984-88. *Compositions:* Double; Schroeder's Death; Narcissus and Echo, opera in one act; Autokoncert; Romantic Readings. *Recordings:* Double; Solo; Hommage à Kurtág; Schreder's Death; Three Part Inventions 1-IV; Twelve Duos. *Honours:* Kisz Prize, 1978; Kassák Prize, 1979; Erkel Prize, 1983. *Address:* H-1056 Budapest, Belgrad rkp. 17, Hungary.

VIERU Anatol, b. 8 June 1926, Iasi, Romania. Composer; Musicologist; Educator. m. Nina Shutikova, 29 July 1954, 1 son, 1 daughter. *Education:* Bucharest Conservatory; Moscow Conservatory, USSR. *Debut:* Enesco Composition Contest, 1946. *Career:* Conductor, National Theatre, Bucharest, Romania, 1947-50; Editor, Musica magazine, 1950-51; Composition Teacher, Bucharest Conservatory, 1955-86; Initiated concerts Parallel Music, Bucharest, 1970; Doctor of Music, Cluj, 1978; Lectures: Sarah Lawrence College, Juilliard School NY, USA; Rubin Academy of Music, Jerusalem, Israel; Darmstadt International Courses, 1992-93; Composer in Residence of the New York University, *Compositions include:* The Feast of the Cadgers, opera, 1978-81; Concertos: For Violin, 1964; For Clarinet, 1975; For Violin and Cello, 1980; Narration II for saxophone, 1985; On Records. Orchestra: Symphony 1 - Ode to Silence, 1967 on records; Symphony III - In the Memory of an Earthquake, 1976; Symphony V with choir, 1985; Chamber Music: Mosaics, 1972; String Quartet VI, 1986; Recorded: Nocturnal Scenes, choir acappella, 1964; Jonas, opera, 1972-76; Stone Country, tape music, 1972; Orchestra: Clepsydra I and II, 1969 and 1971; Ecran, 1970; Concertos: For Orchestra, 1955; For Flute, 1958; For Cello, 1962; Jeux for piano, 1963; Museum Music for harpsichord, 1968; Narration I for

Organ, 1975; Concerto for violin and cello, 1980; VII String quartet; From Modes Toward the Musical Time; 6 Symphonies, 1967-73, 77, 83, 85, 87, 88; String Quartets, 1955-56, 73, 80, 82, 86, 87, 91. *Address:* Str Stirbei-Voda 68 ap 3, Bucharest 70734, Romania.

VIGAY Denis, b. 14 May 1926, Brixton, London, England. Cellist. m. Greta Vigay, 24 July 1952, 1 son, 2 daughters. *Education:* Battersea Grammar School, London; Royal Academy of Music, London. *Debut:* BBC 1941. *Career:* Principal Cello, Royal Liverpool Philharmonic Orchestra; BBC Symphony Orchestra; Soloist, Promenade Concerts, Royal Albert Hall; Soloist & principal cello, Academy of St. Martin- in-the-Fields. *Recordings:* Complete chamber works of Handel; Schubert Octet; Beethoven Septet; Mendelssohn Octet; Complete Boccherini Guitar Quintets; Mozart Clarinet Quintet; Mozart Oboe Quartet; Mozart Horn Quintet; Fantasia on a Theme of Corelli, Michael Tippett. *Honour:* F.R.A.M., 1972. *Membership:* Incorporated Society of Musicians. *Hobbies:* Sailing; Gardening. *Address:* 12 Chesterfield Road, Finchley, London N3 1PR, England.

VIGNOLES Roger Hutton, b. 12 July 1945, England. Pianoforte Accompanist; Conductor. m. (1) Teresa Ann Elizabeth Henderson 1972, diss 1982, (2) Jessica Virginia Ford, 1982. *Education:* Canterbury Cathedral Choir School; Sedbergh School; BA, BMus, Magdalene College, Cambridge; Royal College of Music, London (ARCM). *Career:* Accompanist of national and international reputation, regularly appearing with the most distinguished international singers and instrumentalists, in London and provinces and at major music festivals including Aldeburgh, Cheltenham, Edinburgh, Brighton, Bath, Salzburg, Prague, etc; Broadcasting for BBC Radio 3 and TV; International tours include: USA, Canada, Australia, New Zealand, Hong Kong, Scandinavia; Recitals at Opera Houses of Cologne, 1982; Brussels, 1983; Frankfurt, 1984; Lincoln Center, New York, 1985; San Francisco, 1986; Tokyo, 1985 and 1987; Repetiteur: Royal Opera House, Covent Garden, 1969-71; English Opera Group, 1968-74; Australian Opera Company, 1976; Professor of Accompaniment, Royal College of Music, 1974-81; Conducted Handel's Agrippina at the 1992 Buxton Festival. *Recordings include:* English song, various, with Graham Trew, Baritone; Lieder by Schumann and Brahms/Dvořák; Cabaret Songs by Britten, Gershwin and Dankworth, with Sarah Walker, Mezzo; Premiere recording of The Voice of Love (Nicholas Maw); Franck and Grieg cello sonatas with Robert Cohen, Cello; The Sea, songs and duets with Sarah Walker and Thomas Allen, Baritone; Parry Violin Sonatas with Erich Gruenberg, Violin. *Honour:* Honorary RAM, 1984. *Hobbies:* Drawing; Painting; Looking at Pictures; Swimming; Sailing. *Address:* 1 Ascham Street, Kentish Town, London NW5 2PB, England.

VIKÁR László, b. 8 June 1929, Szombathely, Hungary. Ethnomusicologist. m. Katalin Forrai, 2 sons, 1 daughter. *Education:* PhD; Music Teacher and Choral Conducting Diploma; Ethnomusicology Diploma (Professor Z. Kodály). *Career:* Member, Institute of Musicology, Hungarian Academy of Sciences; Research: Hungary, Slovakia, Romania, China, Korea, Finland, Turkey, Bulgaria, Mongolia and especially among Finno-Ugrian and Turkic peoples, USSR. Professor, Liszt Academy of Music; Scientific Adviser, Institute of Musicology, Hungarian Academy of Sciences. *Publications:* Cseremisz Népdalok, 1967; Cheremis Folksongs, 1971; Editor: Finno-Ugrian Music (record), 1972; Editor, Béla Bartók's Folk Music Research in Turkey, 1976; Editor: Music of the Tatar People (record), 1978; Chuvash Folksongs, 1978; Editor: Folk Music of Finno-Ugrian and Turkich Peoples (3 records) 1984; Editor: International Kodály Conference Budapest 1982, 1985; Editor: Songs of the Forest (Finno-Ugrian Song Collection) 1985; Editor: Reflections on Kodály, 1985; Editor: Anthology of Hungarian Folk Music II (5 records) 1986; Collection of Finno-Ugrian and Turkich Folk Music in the Volga-Kama-Belaya Region 1958-1979, 1986; Votyak Folksongs, 1989; A Volga-Kémai finnugorok és förökök dallamai, 1993. *Contributions to:* Studia Musicologica, Hungarian Academy of Sciences; Journal of International Council of Traditional Music. *Membership:* President, Hungarian National Committee ICTM. *Honours:* Academic Prize, 1976; Erkel Art Prize, 1977; Order of Labour. *Address:* 1054 Budapest, Bajcsy 60, Hungary.

VILEN Asko Kalevi, b. 21 May 1946, Tyrvaa, Finland. Composer. 1s. *Compositions:* Aspects, Opusculum and Overture, for orchestra; Sampo Symphony, Sarcastic Dances No 1 and 2, Episodes, March-Fantasy and 10 pieces (series) with trumpet-solo (for wind orchestra), chamber music and songs. *Recordings:* Sarcastic Dances; Episodes; Sampo-Symphony, and Invention, for flute solo. *Memberships:* Society of Finnish Composers; Society of Finnish Light Music Composers. *Address:* Kylasepankatu 4 C, 33270 Tampere, Finland.

VILJAKAINEN Raili, b. 1954, Helsinki, Finland. Singer (Soprano). *Education:* Studied at the Sibelius Academy 1973-78; Further study with Luigi Ricci in Rome. *Career:* Has sung in Stuttgart from 1978, as Aennchen in Der Freischütz, Sophie, Pamina, Ilia, Micaela, Mimi, Liu, Eva, Freia in Das Rheingold and Marie in Die Soldaten; Guest appearances at the Savonlinna Festival, Salzburg and the Saratoga Springs Festival; Concert appearances in works by Bach, Mozart, Beethoven, Handel and Mahler; Has sung at Carnegie Hall New York and in Finland, East and West Germany, Austria and the USA; Sang Pamina at the Savonlinna Festival, 1989. *Recordings include:* Aennchen in Der Freischütz (Thorn-EMI Video). *Address:* c/o Finnish National Opera, Bulevardi 23-27, SF-00180, Helsnki 18, Finland.

VILLA Edoardo, b. 19 Oct 1953, Los Angeles, USA. Singer (Tenor). *Education:* Studied at the University of Southern California and with Martial Singher, Horst Gunter and Margaret Harshaw. *Career:* Many appearances in opera throughout the USA and abroad; Paris Opera 1986, as Don Carlos, Houston 1988 as Don José; sang at the Munich Staatsoper 1989 and has appeared widely in Canada; Sang Jacopo Foscari in I Due Foscari with the Opera Orchestra of New York, 1992; Other roles include Corrado in I1 Corsaro, Ruggero in La Rondine, Hoffmann, the Italian singer in Rosenkavalier, and Albert Herring. *Recordings include:* Le Roi d'ys by Lalo.

VINAY Ramon, b. 31 Aug 1912, Chillan, Chile. Singer (Tenor and Baritone). *Education:* Studied with Jose Pierson in Mexico City. *Debut:* Mexico City 1931, as Alfonso in La favorita. *Career:* Sang baritone roles of Luna, Rigoletto and Scarpia; First Tenor roles as Don José and Otello, Mexico City 1943-44; New York City Opera 1945, as Don José; Metropolitan Opera 1946-61, as Canio, Tristan, Samson, Herod and Otello; First Wagner role as Tristan, San Francisco 1950; Bayreuth 1952-57, Tristan, Parsifal, Siegmund and Tannhäuser; Sang Verdi's Otello at La Scala, Salzburg and Covent Garden, 1947, 1951, 1955; Resumed baritone roles 1962, singing Telramund at Bayreuth and Iago, Falstaff and Scarpia elsewhere; returned to the Metropolitan 1966, as Rossini's Bartolo; Last stage role as Otello at Santiago, 1969; Worked as opera producer until 1972. *Recordings:* Otello, conducted by Toscanini (RCA); Bayreuth recordings on Melodram, Cetra, Foyer and Philips (Lohengrin, 1962). *Address:* c/o Opera del Teatro Muncipal, Agustinas 794, PO Box 18, Santiago, Chile.

VINCO Ivo, b. 8 Nov 1927, Verona, Italy. Singer (Bass). m. Fiorenza Cossotto. *Education:* Studied at the Liceo Musicale Verona and at the La Scala Opera School with Ettore Campogalliani. *Debut:* Verona 1954, as Ramfis in Aida. *Career:* Appearances at La Scala and in Rome, Naples, Bologna, Venice, Turin and Florence; Has sung at the Verona Arena almost every year from 1954; Further appearances in Vienna, Hamburg, Berlin, Buenos Aires, Paris, Lisbon, Barcelona, Monte Carlo, Moscow, Chicago, Miami and Seattle; Metropolitan Opera debut 1969; Roles include Raimondo (Lucia di Lammermoor), Alvise (La Gioconda), the Grand

Inquisitor, Oroveso (Norma), Sparafucile (Rigoletto), Ferrando (Il Trovatore) and Bartolo (Le Nozze di Figaro); Sang Alvise in La Gioconda at Barcelona, 1988; Ramphis at Palma, 1992. *Recordings include:* Lucia di Lammermoor, Il Trovatore, Rigoletto, Don Carlos (Decca); La Gioconda, Le Nozze di Figaro (Columbia); Iris by Massenet; Norma. *Address:* c/o Arena di Verona, Piazza Brà 28, 1-37121 Verona, Italy.

VINE David, b. 1943, London, England. Conductor; Harpsichordist. *Education:* Royal College of Music, London, 1961-65; Studied piano with Cornelius Fischer, Bernard Roberts, Eric Harrison, piano accompaniment with Joan Trimble, harpsichord with Millicent Silver, baroque ensemble playing with Hubert Dawkes, conducting with Sir Adrian Boult; ARCM; MusB 1st class honours, Harpsichord Performance, Canterbury University. *Career:* Cellist, local youth orchestra, Northampton; Specialist Music Teacher, Inner London Education Authority; Tutored in Baroque Music, Guildhall School of Music and City Literary Institute; Founder, London Telemann Ensemble; Worked with Isobel Baillie, Janet Craxton, Paul Esswood, Kenneth Montgomery, Sarah Walker, Carl Davis, Settled in New Zealand, 1974; Conductor, New Zealand National Youth Orchestra, Wellington Polytechnic Orchestra, Dunedin Sinfonia and Schola Cantorum, Amici Chamber Orchestra, Christchurch Symphony Orchestra, Orpheus Choir, Cantoris; Musical Director, Gisborne Choral Society, Christchurch Operatic Society, Jubilate Singers, Perkel Opera, Academy Chamber Orchestra, Ensemble Divertimento; Orchestral Keyboard: New Zealand Symphony Orchestra; Recitalist, Presenter, Announcer with Radio NZ's Concert FM; Currently Musical Director, Academy Opera, conducting 6 major New Zealand premieres of Handel and Mozart operas; Lectures, Universities of Canterbury, Auckland and Waikato. *Publications:* Handel: Suite in C minor, reconstruction for 2 keyboards, 1992. *Honours:* 1st prize, 3 times, Northampton Eisteddfod Piano Section; Acknowledged 1 of New Zealand's finest harpsichordists and conductors. *Address:* PO Box 2815, Wellington, New Zealand.

VINTON John, b. 24 Jan 1937, Cleveland, Ohio, USA. Storyteller; Compiler; Writer on Music. *Education:* Ohio State University 1954-58; New York University, 1958-63; University of Southern California 1965-66. *Career:* Editorial and Research Assistant, Bela Bartók Archives, New York, 1962-65; General Manager, Dance Theatre Workshop, New York, 1971-73; Assistant Music Critic, Washington Star-News, 1966-67; Left music field and specialized in story telling in literature of Adirondack mountains. *Publications:* Dictionary of Contemporary Music, 1974: Published in England as Dictionary of 20th Century Music; Essays after a Dictionary 1977; A Treasury of Great Adriondack Stories, 1991. *Contributions to:* Music Quarterly; Music Review; Music and Letters; Journal of the American Musicological Society; Arte Musical; Studia Musicologica; Sohlmans Musiklexikon; Notes. *Honours:* Research on Béla Bartók won bronze medal from Hungarian Academy of Sciences, 1981. *Hobbies:* Mycol; Cooking; Conversation; Creative Writing; Contemporary History. *Address:* 167 Hicks Street, Brooklyn, NY 11201, USA.

VINZING Ute, b. 9 Sept 1936, Wuppertal, Germany. Singer (Soprano). *Education:* Studied with Martha Mödl. *Career:* Sang at Lubeck 1967-70, notably as Marenka in The Bartered Bride and Senta in Der fliegende Holländer; Wuppertal Opera 1971-76: sang Brünnhilde in Der Ring des Nibelungen; Has sung in Hamburg, Munich, Vienna, Buenos Aires, Geneva and Seattle (as Brünnhilde); Paris Opéra 1977, 1985 as Brünnhilde and Isolde; Teatro Liceo 1983; Metropolitan Opera from 1984, debut as Elektra; Other roles include Ortrud, Kundry, Leonore and the Dyer's Wife in Die Frau ohne Schatten; Teatro Colón, Buenos Aires 1987, as Elektra; sang Isolde at Florence 1988; Elektra at Marseilles 1989; Sang Ortrud at Buenos Aires, 1991. *Recordings include:* Elektra (Harmonia Mundi); Die Frau ohne Schatten, conducted by Sawallisch. *Address:* c/o Ingpen and Williams Ltd, 14 Kennsington Court, London, W8 5DN.

VIOTTI Marcello, b. 29 June 1954. Conductor. m. Marie-Laurence, 10 July 1982. 2 daughters. *Education:* Piano, Cello, Singing, Lausanne, Geneva. *Career:* Founder, Jeunesse Musicales d'Italie Orchestra, 1981; Regular Guest Director, Teatro Regio, Turin, 1985; Musical Director, Lucerne Opera, 1987-92; General Music Director in Bremen; Guest, various orchestras in Europe, Suisse Romande, South West German Radio, Hamburg Philharmonic; Bamberg Symphony Orchestra, Northern Sinfonia; English Chamber Orchestra; Conducted Andrea Chénier at Frankfurt 1989; Teatro Reggio Turin 1989, Tosca and the Verdi Requiem; Die Zauberflöte and La Sonnambula at Lucerne, 1989; Chief Conductor of the symphony orchestra of the Saarländische Rundfunk, Saarbrücken, 1991. *Recordings:* Frank Martin's Piano Concerto; Il Signor Bruschino; La Sonnambula, Bellini, Andrea Chénier (Capriccio); L'occasione fa il ladro and L' inganno felice, by Rossini (Claves); Franchetti's Christoforo Colombo (Koch Schwann). *Honours:* 1st Prize, Gino Marinuzzi International Competition, San Remo, 1981. *Hobby:* Sailing, Catamaran. *Current Management:* Riaskoff Concert Management, Amsterdam. *Address:* Rosenberg 22, 6017 Ruswil, Switzerland.

VIRKHAUS Taavo, b. 29 June 1934, Tartu, Estonia. Symphony Orchestra Conductor. m. Nancy Ellen Herman, 29 Mar 1969. *Education:* BM, 1955, University of Miami, Florida, 1951-55; MM 1957; DMA 1967; Eastman School of Music, Rochester, NY; Pierre Monteux Master Class 1960 and 1961; Fulbright Grant to Cologne, Germany 1963-64. *Debut:* Conducting the Miami Ballet Guild Orchestra 1956. *Career:* Director of Music, University of Rochester, 1966-77; Music Director and Conductor, Duluth-Superior Symphony Orchestra, Duluth, Minnesota 1977-; Guest Conductor with Rochester Philharmonic; Baltimore Symphony; Estonian SSR State Symphony; Minnesota Orchestra; Music Director and Conductor of Huntsville (AL) Symphony Orchestra, 1990-. *Compositions:* 4 Symphonies, Violin Concerto. *Honour:* Howard Hanson Prize 1966. *Current Management:* Joanne Rile Artists Management, Philadelphia, Pennsylvania, USA. *Address:* 111 Lake Shore Drive, Madison, AL 35758, USA.

VIRSALADZE Eliso, b. 14 Sept 1942, USSR. Concert pianist. *Education:* Studied with Anastasia Virsaladze, then at Tbilsi Conservatory. *Career:* Since winning prizes at competitions in Moscow and Leipzig (1962, 1966) she has played all over the world, including Japan, Germany, Italy, Austria, Poland and Bulgaria; tours of America and Europe with the Leningrad Philharmonic; British recital debut at the Elizabeth Hall 1981, followed by concerto debut with the Royal Philharmonic and Yuri Temirkanov; Season 1983-84 toured UK with the USSR Symphony Ochestra; returned 1987-89 with the Bournemouth Symphony, the Royal Philharmonic under Dorati, the Royal Liverpool Philharmonic, BBC Philharmonic, City of Birmingham Symphony and the Philharmonia under Kurt Sanderling; Season 1988-89 appearances at the Berlin Festival, Prague Spring Festival, and with the Cologne Radio Orchestra; tours of the USA and Japan. *Honours:* Winner, Soviet Competition of Performing Musicians, 1961; Bronze medal Tchaikovsky Competition Moscow, 1962; Prize Winner at 1966 Schumann Competition Leipzig. *Current Management:* Münchner Konzertdirektion Hörtnagel GmbH, Neufahrner Strasse 23, 8000 Müchen 80, Germany.

VISHNEVSKAYA Galina, b. 25 Oct 1926. Leningrad, USSR. Soprano. m. 1955, Mstislav Rostropovich, 2 daughters. *Education:* Studied with Vera Garina. *Career:* Toured with Leningrad Light Opera Company, 1944-48, with Leningrad Philharmonic Society, 1948-52; Joined Bolshoi Theatre, 1952; Concert appearances in Europe and USA, 1950-; has often sung in the 14th Symphony of Shostakovich, including first performance, 1969. First appeared at Metropolitan Opera, New York, USA, 1961; Roles included: Leonora in Fidelio; Tatiana in Eugene Onegin, Iolanta; Aida; Has sung in England at Festival Hall, Aldeburgh Festival, Edinburgh Festival,

Covent Garden, Rostropovich Festival, Snape; Made concert tours with husband; Member of Jury, Cardiff Singer of the World, 1991. *Recordings:* Numerous recordings. *Publications:* Galina (autobiography). *Address:* c/o Victor Hochhauser, 4 Holland Park Avenue, London W11 3QU, England.

VISSE Dominique, b. 30 Aug 1955, Lisieux, France. Singer (Counter-Tenor). m. Anges Mellon. *Education:* Chorister at Notre Dame in Paris, organ and flute studies at the Versailles Conservatory. *Debut:* Opera debut at Tourcoing 1982, in Monteverdi's Poppea; Sang Flora in the first modern performances of Vivaldi's L'Incoronazione di Dario at Grasse, 1984; Charpentier's Acteon at Edinburgh 1985, Nirenus in Nicholas Hytner's production of Giulio Cesare at the Paris Opera 1987 and Delfa in Cavilli's Giasone at the 1988 Innsbruck Early Music Festival; Created Geronimo in the premiere of Le Rouge et Noir by Claude Prey, Aix 1989; Sang Annio in Gluck's La Clemenza di Tito at Lausanne, 1991. *Career:* Instrumentalist in medieval and Renaissance music; further study with Alfred Deller, René Jacobs and Nigel Rogers, 1976-78; Founded the Ensemble Clement Janequin and sang with Les Arts Florissants under William Christie. *Recordings include:* L'Incoronazione di Dario by Vivaldi; Charpentier's Acteon, Les Arts Florissants and David et Jonathas; Cavalli's Xerse and Giasone; Octavia's Nurse in L'Incoronazione do Poppea; Rameau's Anacreon and Hasse's Cleofide: Labels include Erato and Harmonia Mundi. *Address:* c/o Opera de Lausanne, PO Box 3972, CH-1002 Lausanne, Switzerland.

VISSER Lieuwe, b. 23 Aug 1940, Diemen, Holland. Singer (Bass). *Education:* Studied with Jo van de Meent in Amsterdam and at the Accademia di Santa Cecilia Rome with Giorgio Favaretto. *Debut:* Netherlands Opera Amsterdam, as Don Basilio in Il Barbiere di Siviglia. *Career:* Has sung with Netherlands Opera in the 1974 premiere of The Picture of Dorian Gray by Kox and as Masetto (1984); Glyndebourne Festival 1981, in A Midsummer Night's Dream; Centre France Lyrique Paris 1983, in the stage premiere of Frankenstein by Gruber. *Recordings include:* Lucrezia Borgia by Donizetti (Decca).

VIVIER Guy Jean, b. 30 Jan 1942, Paris, France. Concert Performer; Teacher; Accordionist and Organist. *Education:* Teacher's Degree, 1965.*Career:* Founder, Chairman and MD, Conductor, Melomane-Club, 1973; Author of musical, Once upon a time love, 1979; President elect, Federal and Educational Center of Organ and Accordion, France, 1982; Festivals Switzerland, Belgium, Luxembourg, Holland, Japan, and UK; Participant, jubilee of American Accordionists Association, NY, 1988; Concert in Austria and Rcital in Singapore, 1989; Further performances in Austria, Kansas City, Honk Kong, Shanghai, Xi'an, and Bejing; Tour of Asia and the Antipodes, 1992; Numerous appearances on BBC television and radio at home and abroad. *Recordings include:* Two LPs, 1985. *Publications:* Two books and articles published in Accordion Gram, Red Block, Accordion Review, Artistes et Varietes, Accordion Monthly News; Bulletin Officiel; Harmonika International. *Honours:* Jurer, Accordion Examination Competition, China and Peking; Judge, Coupe de France, in ballet on Ice, 1992. *Memberships:* Society of Music Authors, Composers and Editors, 1967; American Accordonist's Association; Accordion Teacher's Guild; Academia de musica Juan Sebastian Bach; Accordion Society of Australia; Chinese Accordion Teachers Association. *Address:* 8 Esplanade Salvador Allende, F-95100 Argenteuil, France.

VLAD Marina Marta, b. 8 Mar 1949, Bucharest, Romania. Composer. m. Ulpiu Vlad, 15 Sept 1973, Bucharest, 1 son. *Education:* Music High School, Bucharest, 1960-65; High School, Il Caragiale, 1965-67; Graduate, Composition, The C. Porumbescu Academy of Music, 1973. *Career:* University Assistant at The C. Porumbescu Academy of Music, 1973-; Professor at the Academy of Music, Bucharest, 1991. *Compositions:* (recorded at the Romanian Radio): Sonata for Violin and Piano, 1978; Rondo for Piano, 1978;

Symphony Movement, 1979; Images for String Orchestra, 1980; Sonata for Piano, 1981; String Quartet No. 1, 1981; String Quartet No. 2, 1982; Legend and In Search of the Game, for Piano, 1983; String Trio No. 1, Inscriptions for Peace, 1984; String Trio No. 2, Dream of Peace, 1985; String Trio No. 3, 1986; This Country's Land, Cantata for a Solo Voice, Choir and Orchestra, a verse by Jon Brad, 1987; Light Rays, Trio for Flute, Oboe, Clarinet, 1988; Thoughts for the Future, quartet for flute, violin, viola and cello, 1989. *Recordings:* String Quartet No. 2 and Sonata for Piano, Electrecord, 1984. *Publications:* Rondo for Piano, 1983; Sonata for Violin and Piano, 1982; String Trio No. 1, Inscriptions for Peace, 1986; Dream of Peace, String Trio No. 2, Printed by Romanian Musical Publishing House, 1988; Light Rays, Trio for flute, oboe, clarinet 1989, printed by Romanian Musical Publishing House. *Honour:* Prize granted by the Conservatory of Music, C. Porumbescu for the Cantata Resonance, 1972. *Membership:* Union of Composers of Romania. *Address:* Str. Andrei Popovici No. 18, BL 8A, Sc.c, et IV, ap.39, 71254 Bucharest, Romania.

VLAD Roman, b. 29 Dec 1919, Cernauti, Rumania. Composer; Writer on Music. *Education:* Studied at the Cernauti Conservatory and in Rome with Casella. *Career:* Active as a pianist and lecturer from 1944; Artistic Director of the Accademia Filarmonica in Rome 1954-58 and 1966-69; Artistic Director of the Maggio Musicale Fiorentino 1964 and of the Teatro Comunale Florence 1968-72; Taught at Dartington Summer School 1954-55; Co-editor of the Enciclopedia dello spettacolo 1958-62 and the Nuova rivista musicale Italiana 1967-; President of the Italian section of the ISCM 1960-63; Professor of Composition at the Perugia Conservatory 1968; Supervisor of the Turin Radio Symphony Orchestra 1976-80; Artistic Adviser of the Turin Settembre Musica Festival from 1985; President of SIAE (Society of Italian Composers) from 1987. *Compositions:* Ballets: La Strada 1943; La Dama delle Camelie 1945; Fantasie 1948; Masques Ostendias 1959; Die Wiederkehr 1962; Il Gabbiano 1968; Il Sogno 1973; Operas: Storia di una Mamma 1951; Il Dottore di Vetro 1960; La Fantarca 1967; Orchestral: Sinfonietta 1941; Suite 1941; Sinfonia all'antica 1948; Variazioni concertanti su una serie di 12 note dal Don Giovanni di Mozart for piano and orchestra 1955; Musica per archi 1957; Musica Concertata for harp and orchestra 1958; Ode super Chrysae Phorminx for guitar and orchestra 1964; Divertimento sinfonico 1967; Vocal: 3 Cantatas 1940-53; Letture di Michelangelo for chorus 1964; Immer wieder for soprano and 8 instruments 1965; Piccolo divertimento corale 1968; Lettura di Lorenzo Magnifico for chorus 1974; La Vespa di Toti for boys' voices and instruments 1976; Chamber: Divertimento for 11 instruments 1948; String Quartet 1957; Serenata for 12 instruments; Il Magico Flauto di Severino for flute and piano 1971; Piano Music; Music for more than 100 Films. *Publications include:* Collected Essays 1955; Luigi Dallapiccola 1957; Storia della dodecafonia 1958; Stravinsky 1958, rev. 1973 and 1979; Essays on Busoni, Schoenberg and Stravinsky. *Address:* c/o SIAE, Viale della Letteratura n. 30, 00100 Roma (EUR), Italy.

VLAD Ulpiu, b. 27 Jan 1945, Zarnesti, Romania. Composer. m. Marina Marta Vlad, 15 Sept 1973, 1 son. *Education:* Music High School, Bucharest, 1958-64; Academy of Music C Porumbescu, Bucharest, 1964-71; Seminar in Composition organised for foreign students, Conservatory of Music, Santa Cecilia, Rome. *Debut:* Septet for Winds, Piano, 1970, Conservatory of Music C Porumbescu, Bucharest. *Career:* Researcher in Romanian Folk Music, Conservatory of Music C Porumbescu, Bucharest, 1971-77; Researcher in Romanian Folk Music, Institut de Cercetari Etnologice si Dialectologice, Bucharest, 1977-80; Editor, 1980-84; Manager 1984-92, Romanian Musical Publishing Company; Romanian TV and radio appearances; Music Department Director, Romanian Ministry of Culture, 1992-93; Professor at the Academy of Music, Bucharest, 1990-. *Compositions include:* Inscriptions in Hearts symphonic work, 1978; First Symphony Roads in the Light 1979; Dreams I work for string orchestra, 1972;

Dreams II concerto for string orchestra, 1982; Sinfonia Concertante How Hardly from the Depths 1983; Second Symphony From Our Hearts 1984; Trio No 1 The Spring 1984; Quintet for Winds Voices of Peace 1986; The Joy of Peace, Trio for Flute, Oboe, Clarinet, 1986; Portraits, Piece for Harp, 1987; Thoughts for Peace, theme with variations for Oboe and Pianoforte, 1987; Sources, Symphonic Poem, 1987; On this Sun-lit Earth, String Trio no. 3, 1988; The Joy of Achievement, Wedding Songs, Cantata, for choir a Cappella, 1988; August Remembrances, septet for winds, piano and percussion, 1989; The Joy of Dreams. Quintet for flute, string trio and percussion, 1990; Lights in the Sunset, symphonic work 1991; From the Joy of Dreams, concerto for string orchestra, 1991; The Joy of the Passage, string trio, 1991; The Secret of Dreams. Quintet for winds No 2, 1992; The Game of Dreams, Concerto for Chamber Orchestra, 1992. *Hobby:* Mountain climbing. *Address:* Av. Andrei Popovici 18, Bl.8A, Sc.C, Et.IV, Ap.39, 71254 Bucuresti, Romania.

VLASOV Sergei, b. 25 Jan 1952, Kiev, Ukraine. Conductor. *Education:* Studied in Kiew and at the Moscow Conservatoire with Yuri Simonov, until 1984. *Debut:* Bolshoi Theatre Moscow 1983, with II Trovatore. *Career:* Established the Ukrainian Chamber Orchestra while still a student; Assistant Conductor at the Solshol until 1985; Music Director of the Kislovodsk State Philharmonic Orchestra 1985, Chief Conductor of the Kiev State Radio Orchestra from 1990; British debut 1991 directing the National Youth Orchestra of Scotland in France, England and Scotland with music by Britten, Prokofiev and Vaughan Williams; further guest appearances with the St Petersburg Philharmonic and Moscow Radio Orchestras; repertoire includes 20th-century classics and contempory music. *Address:* c/o Sonata, 11 Northpark Street, Glasgow G20 7AA, Scotland.

VLATKOVIC Radovan, b. 1962, Zagreb, Yugoslavia. Horn Player. *Education:* Studied at the Zagreb Academy of Music and the Northwest German Music Academy at Detmold. *Career:* Principal of the Berlin Radio Symphony Orchestra, 1982; Solo engagements from 1983, notably at Salzburg (1984), the Vienna Konzerthaus, the Barbican, the Théâtre de la Ville in Paris, Pushkin Museum Moscow, Metropolitan Museum New York and Orchestra Hall Chicago; Soloist with leading orchestras and chamber music performer with Gidon Kremer, Heinz Holliger, András Schiff and Aurèle Nicolet. *Honours include:* Prizes at the Wind Instruments Competition in Ancona, 1979; Horn Competition in Liège, 1981; First Prize, International ARD Competition in Munich, 1983. *Recordings Include:* Mozart's Four Concertos, with the English Chamber Orchestra conducted by Jeffrey Tate. *Address:* c/o Ingpen and Williams, 14 Kensington Court, London W8 5DN, England.

VLIJMEN Jan van, b. 11 Oct. 1935, Rotterdam, Holland. Composer; Administrator. *Education:* Studied composition with Kees van Baaren. *Career:* Director of the Amersfoort Music School 1961-65, Lecturer in theory at the Ucrecht Conservatory 1965-67; Deputy Director of the Royal Conservatory, The Hague 1967, Director 1971; General Manager of Netherlands Opera 1985-88, Director of the Holland Festival 1991. *Compositions include:* Reconstructie, 'morality' in collaboration with Louis Andriessen, Reinbert de Leeuw, Mischa Mengelberg and Peter Schat, Holland Festival 1969; Axel, opera with de Leeuw, Holland Festival 1977; opera on Van Gogh's last years, Un Malheureux vetu de Noir, 1990; Morgensterlieder for mezzo and piano 1958; 2 Wind Quintets 1958, 1972; Construzione for 2 pianos 1959; Serie for 6 instruments 1960; Gruppi for 20 instruments in 4 groups 1962, revised 1980; Mythos for mezzo and 9 instruments 1962; Spostamenti for orchestra 1963; Serenata I and II 1965-67; Sonata for piano and 3 instrumental groups 1966; Dialogue for clarinet and piano 1966; Per diciasette for 17 winds 1967; interpolations for orchestra and electronics 1968, revised 1981; Omaggio a Gesualdo for violin and 5 instrumental groups 1971; 4 songs for mezzo and

orchestra 1975; Quaterni for orchestra 1979; Trimurti for string quartet 1981; Solo II for clarinet 1986. *Address:* Royal Conservatory of Music and Drama, Juliana van Stolberglaan 1, 2595 CA The Hague, Holland.

VODICKA Leo Marian, b. 1950, Brno, Czechoslovakia. Singer (Tenor). *Education:* Studied at the Janáček Academy of Arts with Josef Valek. *Career:* Has sung in most Czech opera houses, notably the Janáček Opera Brno and the Prague National Theatre; Guest engagements in Bologna, Rome, Milan, Geneva, Zurich, Berne, Graz, Salzburg, Cologne, Paris, Nice, Tokyo, Osaka and in Bulgaria, Hungary, the former Soviet Union and East Germany; Major roles have included Verdi's Rigoletto, Don Carlos, Manrico and Otello; Puccini's Cavaradossi, Des Grieux, Pinkerton and Rodolfo; Janáček's Laca and Boris; the Prince in Rusalka and Smetana's Jenik and Dalibor; Don José and Stravinsky's Oedipus; Concert repertoire includes Verdi Requiem; Dvořák Stabat Mater and Requiem; Janáček Amarus, Glagolitic Mass, Diary of One Who Disappeared and Everlasting Gospel; Martinů's Field Mass and Bartók's Cantata Profana; Staatsoper Vienna for role of Prince in Rusalka by Dvořák, 1990; Vienna, L Janáček-Glagolitic mass & Osud (Fate), 1990; Solo tour in Japan/ Tokyo, Koriyama, Kumamoto, Matsuyama with airs from Carmen, André Chénier, La Forza del destino, Othello, Tosca, Traviata, conducted by Shigeo Genda, 1992. *Recordings:* Smetana The Kiss, The Secret and Libuse; Dvočák The Cunning Peasant; Foerster Eva; Janáček Amarus conducted by Charles Mackerras (Supraphon); Antonín Dvořak - Dimitrij, tite role, conducted by Gerd Albrecht, Supraphon, 1989; London - BBC, Diary of One Who Disappeared, with Radoslav Kvapil-piano, 1993. *Current Management:* Pragokoncert, Maltézské nám.1, Prague 1, Czech Republic. *Address:* Zlichovska 6, Prague, Czech Republic.

VOGEL Beniamin, b. 5 May 1945, Biala Woda, USSR. Musicologist; Organologist. m. (1) Lubomira Swiczeniuk, 3 Apr 1971, 1 daughter, div 1990, (2) Aurelia Holcman, 1 Sept 1991. *Education:* Walbrzych Music High School, 1968; MA, Musicology, 1973, PhD, Musicology, 1977, Warsaw University. *Career:* Associate Professor, Musicology Institute Warsaw University, 1978-; Expert in Historical Music Instruments, Polish Ministry of Culture, 1978-; Custodian, Industrial History Museum in Opatowek n. Kalisz, Piano Division, 1986-; Head of Warsaw University Musicological Research Station in Bydgoszcz, 1981-89. *Publications:* Musical Instruments in Culture of the Polish Kingdom (In Polish), 1980; Old Pianos Collection of Pomeranian Philharmonic (2nd Edition in English), 1987; Piano making on the Polish soil till World War II (in Polish), Warsaw 1988. *Contributions to:* Pianos and Keyboard Idiophones in the Polish Kingdom during Chopin's Younger Years (in Polish), Rocznik Chopinowski Vol. 9, 1975; Der Einfluss des professionellen auf den nicht professionellen Instrumentenbau in Polen, Studia Instrumentorum Musicae Vol. 6, 1979; Musica Antiqua; Muzyka, etc; Piano as a Symbol of Burgher Culture in Nineteenth-Century Warsaw in: The Golpin Society Journal, vol XLVI, 1993. *Honours:* Gold award for preservation of ancient monuments; Collective award for preservation of historical music instruments in Poland. *Memberships:* Polish Composers Union; American Musical Instruments Society. *Hobbies:* Tinkering; Swimming; Skiing; Playing Bridge. *Address:* S:t Hans gränd 24 B, S-226 42 Lund, Sweden.

VOGEL Howard Levi, b. 21 Feb 1933, New York City, NY, USA. Recorder Player and Bassoonist. m. Susan Bradford Walker, 7 July 1984. *Education:* BM Bassoon 1955; MM Musicology 1960; Manhattan School of Music; Studied bassoon with Simon Kovar and Musicology with Joseph Braunstein; Studied Lute with Suzanne Bloch, Recorder with Frans Brüggen and Viol with Martha Blackman, 1958-69. *Career:* Bassoonist with Kansas City Philharmonic 1956-58; Robert Shaw Chorale, New York City Opera, Metropolitan Opera and New York City Ballet, 1959-75; Recorder Soloist, New York Baroque Ensemble 1961-81; Bassoonist and

Contrabassoonist, Little Orchestra Society, New York Philharmonic and Musica Sacra, 1982; Live TV Broadcasts teaching recorder master classes and performing with New York Baroque Ensemble; School Director and Teacher of Recorder, Village Music Workshop, New York, 1965-; Assistant Professor of Music, City University, New York, 1967-75; Artist in Residence, Somerset Co. College, New Jersey, 1976-79; Recorder recitals with harpsichord in Pennsylvania, New York and Massachusetts, summer 1986. *Publications:* On Making Baroque Music, 1975. *Contributions to:* Woodstock Times-music reviews and previews, regular columnist, 1989-. *Memberships:* Galpin Society; American Lute Society; American Musical Instrumental Society; American Recorder Society; Guild of American Luthiers. *Hobbies:* Research Into Baroque String Playing Technique Especially Bowing; Baroque Recorder Playing and Ornamentation. *Address:* Bonna Creek Hollow, Woodstock, Mt Tremper, NY 12457, USA.

VOGEL Matthias, b. 14 Aug 1920, Bern, Switzerland. Concert Singer. m. Dominique Anne-Louise Pauli, 1945. 5s. *Education:* Private studies with Helene Fahrni, Federic Anspach and Paul Lohmann. *Debut:* St Matthew's Passion, Liege, Belgium. *Career:* Oratorios and recitals on TV and radio; Recitals in concerthalls and festival concerts in most European countries; Professor, Conservatoire Europeen and Tours University. *Recordings:* Schumann: Dichterliebe; Beethoven: An dia ferne Geliebte; Brahms: Vier ernste Gesänge; Shubert: Melodies. *Memberships:* Swiss Music Association. *Hobbies:* Mountaineering; Gardening. *Address:* Rue du Theatre 103, F-75015 Paris, France.

VOGEL Siegfried, b. 6 March 1937, Chemnitz, Germany. Singer (Bass). *Education:* Studied in Dresden with H. Winkler and J. Kemter. *Debut:* Dresden Staaatsoper 1959, as Zizell in Si j'etais roi by Adam. *Career:* Sang Mozart roles in Dresden: Sarastro, Osmin and the Commendatore; Berlin Staatsoper from 1965 as Leporello, Alfonso, Hunding, Basilio, Count Almaviva, Escamillo, Kecal and Ochs; Guest appearances in Moscow, Paris, Lausanne (Hans Sachs and Baron Ochs 1983), Brussels and Vienna; Further engagements at La Scala and in Venice, Stockholm, Helsinki, Amsterdam and Cairo; Bayreuth Festival 1985-86, as Biterolf in Tannhäuser; Sang Kaspar, Rocco and the King Henry in Lohengrin, 1986 at the Berlin Staatsooper; Metropolitan debut 1986, as Hunding, sang Morosus in Die schweigsame Frau at Palermo, 1988, Bayreuth 1989, as Fasolt, Biterolf and Titurel; Toronto Opera 1990, as the Doctor in Wozzeck; Sang the Athlete in Lulu at the Semper Oper Dresen, 1992; Concert repertoire includes sacred music by Bach and Handel. *Recordings:* Der Freischütz; Ariadne auf Naxos, Die Meistersinger, Zar und Zimmermann, Genoveva, Rienzi (EMI); St Matthew Passion (Eurodisc); Karl V by Krenek (Philips). *Address:* c/o Berlin Staatsoper, Unter den Linden 7, D-1086 Berlin, Germany.

VOGLER Jan, b. 18 Feb 1964, Berlin, Germany. Cellist. *Education:* Hanns Eisler Hochschule für Musik, Berlin; Basle Music Academy, Switzerland. *Teachers:* Josef Schwab, Heinrich Schiff. *Career:* Concert Master, cello, Staatskapelle Dresden, 1985-; Concerts as soloist, orchestras including: Berlin Radio Orchestra 1986, 1987, 1989, Staatskapelle Dresden, Berlin Chamber Orchestra, Dresden Chamber Orchestra, Virtuosi Saxoniae; US debut, Chicago, 1987; Marlboro Festival, USA, 1988, 1989; Numerous radio broadcasts, live recordings; Recitals, many countries. *Current Management:* Kunstleragentur, Krausenstrasse 9/10, GDR-1080, Berlin. *Address:* Bahnhofstrasse 47, GDR-1123 Berlin, Germany.

VOGT Lars, b. 8 Sept 1970, Duren, Germany. Concert Pianist. m. Tatiana Komarova. *Education:* Hannover Conservatoire with Professor Kämmerling. *Career:* Concerto appearances in Germany, including Dresden, Nuremberg, Dusseldorf and Bremen; Recitals with the Trio Alani in Berlin and at the Alte Oper in Frankfurt;

Further invitations for Munich, Hannover, Bonn and Schleswig-Holstein; British engagements with the City of Birmingham Symphony under Simon Rattle and at the Albert Hall with the Staatsphilharmonie Rheinland-Pfalz; May 1991 with the Northern Sinfonia and Heinrich Schiff; Played with the Scottish Chamber and BBC Symphony Orchestras and at the South Bank International Piano Series, Feb 1992; US debut summer 1991, with Beethoven's 4th Concerto (Los Angeles Philharmonic conducted by Rattle); Tour with the Salzburg Mozarteum Orchestra, 1993; Season 1993/94 with debuts in Milan and Zurich; Concerts with the Cleveland Orchestra, Hong Kong Philharmonic, Royal Philharmonic, Ulster Orchestra and London Philharmonic; Beethoven concerts (cycle) with Santa Cecilia Orchestra in Rome and with the Rotterdam Philharmonic; Further engagements with the Leipzig Gewandhaus and Salzburg Mozarteum Orchestras; recitals in Britain and North America; Concerts with the Trio Nova Vita. *Recordings:* Exclusive contract with EMI (from 1991). *Honours:* Winner of competitions in Germany, Italy and Czechoslovakia as soloist and as member of Trio Alani; Second Prize, 1990 Leeds International Piano Competition, playing the Schumann Concerto. *Address:* Harold Holt Ltd, 31 Sinclair Road, London W14 0NS, England.

VOGT Matthias Theodor, b. 5 May 1959, Rome, Italy. Opera Director, Music Researcher. m. Tina Nelsson, 1 son. *Education:* Dr.Phil in Musicology, with Carl Dahlhaus, RES; Studied violoncello with Atis Teichmanis, composition with Digter Agricola. *Debut:* 1979. *Career:* Appearances at Salzburg Festival, Vienna State Opera, Biennale di Venezia, Teatro alla Scala di Milano; 1986-89 Chief Dramaturg and Head of Press Department at Richard Wagner Festival, Bayreuth; Productions include Rigoletto at Narodni Opera, Russe, Bulgaria, 1989; Alexander Knaiffel: Kentervilskoje Prividenje, Theater Forum, Moscow, Russe 1990; Organised and directed the International Gustav Mahler Congress Hamburg 1989; Lectures on Contemporary Music Tehatre throughout Europe and the Far East. *Publications:* Allan Petterson Jahrbuch (editor), 1986, 1987, 1988; Das Gustav Mahler Fest Hamburg 1989, Kassel 1991; Edition of Histoire du Soldât, Version 1918 (in prep). *Contributions to:* Frankfurter Allgemeine Zeitung, Neue Zeitschrift für Musik, Cambridge Opera Journal and others; Broadcasting in France, Germany, Austria. *Current Management:* Agency Matthias Vogt, Kaulbachstr. 64, 8000 München 22. *Address:* Zieglerstr. 4b, D-8162 Schliersee 2, Germany.

VOICULESCU Dan, b. 20 July 1940, Saschiz-Sighisoara, Rumania. Composer; Musicologist; Professor. *Education:* Diplomas, Composition (S. Todutza) & Piano (M. Kardos), Conservatory G. Dima, Cluj (Academy of Music), 1958-64; Classes with V. Mortari, Venice, Italy 1968, K. Stockhausen, Cologne, Germany 1971-72; Doctor of Musicology, 1983. *Career:* Professor of Counterpoint and Composition, Academy of Music, Cluj; Editor of the Lucrari de Muzicologie (Musicological Works), Cluj. *Compositions:* Sinfonia Ostinato, 1963; Visions Comiques, 1968; Music for Strings, 1971; Pieces for Orchestra, 1973; Fables, Dialogues, Sonata, Croquis, Sonantes, Spirals, 3 Toccatas, for piano solo; 5 Sonatas, flute solo; Sonata, clarinet solo; Fiorituri, violin & piano; Cantata, baritone, choir & orchestra, 1977; Homage to Blaga, mixed choir; 4 volumes choral music for children; Book Without End, 3 volumes piano pieces for children; The Bald Chanteuse, (Chamber Opera), 1993. *Publications:* Polyphony of Baroque in the Works of J. S. Bach, 1975; Polyphony of the 20th Century, 1983; Bachian Fugue, 1986; *Honours:* Prize, Union of Rumanian Composers, 1972, 1974, 1976, 1978; Prize, G Enescu of The Rumanian Academy, Bucarest, 1984. *Membership:* Union of Rumanian Composers. *Address:* Academy of Music, Str IC Bratianu 25, Cluj, Rumania.

VOIGHT Deborah, b. 1958, San Francisco, USA. Singer (Soprano). *Education:* Graduate of San Francisco Opera's Merola Program. *Debut:* Shostakovich's 14th Symphony, San Francisco Chamber Symphony. *Career:*

Concerts include Beethoven's Ninth in Honolulu, Verdi's Requiem at Carnegie Hall (1988) and Mahler's 8th with the Atlanta Symphony; Rossini's Stabat Mater at the Kennedy Centre, Washington, and Mozart's Requiem with the Boston Symphony; European engagements include Schubert's Fierabras at Brussels, Electra in Idomeneo for Finnish National Opera, 1991 and Elvira in Ernani for Chelsea Opera Group (1990); Other opera performances in concert include Das Rheingold with the Minnesota Orchestra, Weber's Agathe in New York, Die Walkure, La Wally and I1 Piccolo Marat for Dutch Radio; Season 1990- 91 with Amelia (Ballo in Maschera) at San Francisco and Strauss's Ariadne with the Boston Lyric Opera; Metropolitan Opera debut 1991, as Amelia. *Honours:* Prize winner, Metropolitan Opera Auditions and the Pavarotti International Competition at Philadelphia; Winner, 1989 Bussetto Verdi Competition and 1990 Tchaikovsky International at Moscow. *Address:* c/o Metropolitan Opera, Lincoln Center, New York, NY 10023, USA.

VOKETAITIS Arnold, b. 11 May 1931, New Haven, Connecticut, USA. Singer (Bass). *Education:* Studied in New York. *Debut:* New York City Opera 1958, as Vanuzzi in Die Schweigsame Frau. *Career:* Sang in New York as Britten's Theseus, Creon in Oedipus Rex and the Father in the local premiere of Douglas Moore's Carrie Nation (1968); Guest engagements at Houston, Miami, Pittsburgh, Mexico City, San Antonio, Montreal and Vancouver; Chicago 1968-73 in Le Rossignol, Madama Butterfly, Carmen, I Due Foscari, Werther and Billy Budd; Other roles have included Don Magnifico (Metropolitan Opera National touring company), Don Pasquale, Dulcamara, Basilio and John Hale in The Crucible by Robert Ward, Milwaukee 1976. *Recordings:* Le Cid by Massenet.

VOLDEN Torstein, b. 6 Nov 1934, Trondheim, Norway. Senior Lecturer. m. 2s. *Education:* Cand Philol., University of Oslo, 1967. *Career:* Concerts in Norway; Programmes on Norwegian Broadcasting company, radio, and TV as guitarist and lutenist. *Publications:* Studies in Edward Grieg's Haugtussen Songs, 1967; Contributor to Riemann Musiklexicon, Personenteil, I, II, 1972, 1975. *Address:* Skogstovn 40, N-4029 Stavanger, Norway.

VOLKERT Gudrun, b. 1942, Brno, Czeckoslovakia, Singer (Soprano). *Education:* Studied at the Linz Conservatory. *Career:* Sang dramatic roles at Klagenfurt 1966-67, Kiel 1967-74, Bielefield 1974-83; Guest appearances at Brunswick 1983-88, Kassel from 1984, Hamburg 1986 and Turin 1987; Performances as Brünnhilde in Der Ring des Nibelungen at Rotterdam (1988), Warsaw (1988-89), and Seattle (1991); Sang Cherubini's Médée at Wuppertal 1988, followed by Isolde 1989; Metropolitan Opera 1990, as Brunnhilde; Scottish Opera 1991, as Leonore in a new production of Fidelio; Other roles include Senta, Ortrud, Salome, the Marschallin, Gioconda, Tosca, Turandot and the Countess in Die Soldaten. *Address:* c/o Seattle Opera Association, PO Box 9248, WA 98109, USA.

VOLZ Manfred, b. 1949, Darmstadt, Germany. Singer (Bass- baritone). *Career:* Sang in concert from 1972; Stage debut as Mozart's Figaro at Trier, 1980; Further appearances as Melitone in La Forza del Destino and Papageno; Engaged at Aachen 1981-83, Kassel from 1985, as Alberich, Ford, Amonasro, Mozart's Count, and Faninal; Bad Gandersheim 1986, as the King in Der Kluge by Orff; Sang Alberich in Ring cycles at Rotterdam 1988 and Dortmund 1991; Concert repertoire includes Verdi's Requiem. *Address:* c/o Opernhaus, Kuhstrasse 12, 4600 Dortmund, Germany.

VON DASSANOWSKY Elfriede, b. 2 Feb 1924, Vienna, Austria. Opera and Concert Singer (Soprano/ Mezzo); Pianist; Educator. 1 son, 1 daughter. *Education:* Hochschule für Musik und darstellende Kunst, Vienna; Piano studies with Emil von Sauer and Eugenie Wild-Volek; Vocal studies with Paula Mark-Neusser. *Debut:* Susanna, Le nozze di Figaro. *Career:* Principal roles and concert appearances in Vienna, St Pölten, Munich, Flensburg, Hamburg, 1940's-1950's include: Agathe, Freischütz, Inez and Azucena, Trovatore; Mimi, La Bohème; Title roles: Hansel and Gretel; Hannerl and Heiderl; Das Dreimäderlhaus; Title role: Carmen; Baroness Adelaide, Der Vogelhandler; Lola, Cavalleria Rusticana; Komtesse Lizzi, Das Sperrsechserl; Prince Orlofsky, Fledermaus; Others: Numerous operetta performances and Lieder recitals, Austria and Germany; Concert and radio recitals as Pianist; Lecturer, Piano, Hochschule für Musik, Vienna; Broadcaster, Forces Broadcasting and BBC, Vienna, 1948-52; Co-Founder, Belvedere Film Production, Vienna; Private Vocal Coach, Piano Instructor. *Address:* 13052 Moorpark St 203, Studio City, CA 91604, USA.

VON STADE Frederica, b. 1 June 1945, Somerville, New Jersey, USA. Mezzo-soprano. m. Peter Elkus, 1973. 2 daughters. *Education:* Norton Academy; Studied with Sebastian Engelberg, Paul Berl and Otto Guth, Mannes College of Music. *Career:* Apprenticeship, Long Wharf Theater, New Haven, Connecticut; Metropolitan Opera debut, New York, 3rd Boy, Die Zauberflöte, 1970; Cherubino, Opera House, Versailles Palace, 1973; Covent Garden debut, London, England, as Rosina, 1975; Appearances with many of the world's major opera companies; Various festival engagements; Soloist with orchestras, recitalist; Member, Chamber Music Society of Lincoln Center, New York; Operatic roles included Mozart's Idamante and Dorabella; Bellini's Adalgisa; Massenet's Charlotte; Debussy's Mélisande; Strauss's Octavian; Created roles in several operas including: Nina in Pasatieri's The Seagull, 1974; Tina in Argento's The Aspern Papers, 1988; Sang Massenet's Charlotte at Milan (La Scala) and the Vienna Staatsoper, 1988; Cherubino at Los Angeles, 1990, Rosina at Chicago 1989 and at the Metropolitan, 1992; Season 1992/93 as Rosina at the Met and San Francisco, Cherubino at the Met and Mélisande at Covent Garden; Appearances in many operatic films; Crossover artist, Broadway musical recordings. *Recordings:* For Angel-EMI; CBI; Decca-London; Deutsche Grammophon; Erato; Pantheon; Philips; RCA. *Honour:* Honorary DMus, Yale University, 1985. *Address:* c/o Columbia Artists Management Inc, 165 West 57th Street, New York, NY 10019, USA.

VONK Hans, b. 18 June 1942, Amsterdam, Netherlands. Conductor. *Education:* Studied at the Amsterdam Conservatory. *Career:* Chief Conductor of the Netherlands Ballet, 1966; Associate Conductor of the Concertgebouw Orchestra, 1969-73, and Chief Conductor of the Netherlands Radio Philharmonic, 1970; US debut 1974, with the San Franciosco Symphony; UK debut 1974 with the Royal Philharmonic Orchestra; Chief Conductor of Netherlands Opera 1975-85; La Scala Milan debut 1980, The Rake's Progress; Music Director of the Residentie Orchestra in the Hague 1980-; Tours of USA (1982), Europe and Britain; Tour of UK with the Vienna Symphony Orchestra 1984; Guest appearances with the Munich Philharmonic, the Philadelphia Orchestra and at La Fenice, Venice; 1992 Principal Conductor and Artistic Director of the Dresden Staatskapelle and the Dresden State Opera; toured the UK, Europe, USSR and USA with the Staatskapelle; Repertoire includes music by Mozart, Tchaikovsky, Bruckner and Stravinsky; 1991-92 Season became Chief Conductor of the WDR Köln (West German Radio, Cologne); Regularly conducts in the USA with the Philadelphia Orchestra & has been a guest conductor with the National Symphony Orchestra (Washington DC), Pittsburgh Symphony Orchestra, Boston Symphony Orchestra, St Louis Symphony, Toronto Symphony Orchestra, Detroit Symphony Orchestra. *Recordings:* Extensive list of recordings with DECCA & EMI; Major series of recordings for EMI with the WDR Köln Orchestra (Schumann symphonies) *Address:* c/o Harold Holt Ltd., 31 Sinclair Road, London W14 ONS, England.

VOSS Friedrich, b. 12 Dec 1930, Halberstadt, Germany. Composer. m. Erna Lewann, 10 Dec 1965, 1 son. *Education:* Abitur, Gymnasium Halberstadt, 1949; Studied composition & piano, Hochschule für Musik,

West Berlin, 1949-54. *Career:* Performances with: Berlin Philharmonic Orchestra, under Karajan; Radio Symphony Orchestra, Berlin, under Maazel; Japan Philharmony Orchestra, under James Loughran; etc; in Germany, Western Europe, USA, Japan, Australia, Asia, South Africa, Latin America. Television performances in Madrid, Johannesburg, Adelaide (Australia). *Compositions include:* Over 70 works: 4 symphonies; 2 violin concertos; 1 cello concerto; 1 cello concertino; 4 string quartets; 1 saxophone quartet; concertino for organ, strings and timpani; 2 works for choir; Hamlet overture; Dithyrambus for Orchestra; Metamorphosis for Orchestra; ballet, Die Nachtigall und die Rose; opera, Leonce und Lena; Cantata of Psalms for soloists, choir and orchestra. *Recordings:* About 100 broadcasting recordings in Germany & Western Europe; CD: CTH 2069, THOROFON (4 works). *Address:* Eichertstrasse 3, D-75365 Calw/Schwarzwald, Germany.

VOSS Hermann, b. 9 July, 1934, Brunen, Germany. Violist. *Education:* Studied in Dusseldorf with Maier and in Freiburg with Vegh. *Career:* Former member of Karl Munchinger's Stuttgart Chamber Orchestra in Heibronn; Co-founded the Melos Quartet of Stuttgart 1965; First concert tours sponsored by the Deutsches Musikleben Foundation and represented West Germany at the Jeunesse Musicales in Paris, 1966; International concert tours from 1967; Bicentenary concerts in the Beethoven Hous at Bonn, 1970, and soon toured the USSR, Eastern Europe, Africa, North and South America, the Far East and Australia; British concerts and festival appearances from 1974; Cycle of Beethoven quartets at Edinbourgh Festival 1987: Wigmore Hall, St. John's Smith Square and Bath Festival 1990; Associations with Rostropovitch in the Schubert Quintet and the Cleveland Quartet in works by Spohr and Mendelssohn; Teacher at the Stuttgart Musikhochschule. *Recordings:* Complete quartets of Beethoven, Schubert, Mozart and Brahms; Quintets by Boccherini with Narciso Ypes and by Mozart with Franz Beyer.*Honours:* (with members of the Melos Quartet) Grand Prix de Disque and Prix Caecilia from the Academie du Disque in Brussels. *Address:* c/o Ingpen & Williams Ltd. 14 Kensington Court, London W8 5DN, England.

VRIEND Jan, b. 10 Nov 1938, Benningbroek, The Netherlands. Composer. *Education:* Conservatory of Amsterdam, 1960-67; Paris 1967-68, GRM/ORTF and Schola Cantorum; Institute of Sonology, Utrecht, 1965-66; Self-taught in mathematics.*Career:* Founder and first conductor of ASKO-Amsterdam, 1964; 1961-70 conductor of choirs and freelance conductor of orchestras and ensembles; lectured on many topics concerning composition, the use of mathematics in composition, philosophy of music; Conductor of the New Stroud Orchestra, 1989-94. *Compositions:* Paroesie for 10 instruments, 1963-67; Huantan for organ and winds, 1968; Bau for chamber orchestra, 1969-70; Ensembles for mixed choir, 1969-70; Elements of Logic for large wind orchestra, 1972; Kri, for mezzo soprano, mixed choir and ensemble, 1975; Heterostase for flute, bass clarinet and piano, 1980-81; Vectorial for 6 wind-instruments and piano, 1983-87; Gravity's Dance for piano, 1983-86; Jets d'Orgue I, II and III, 1984-91; Athena Keramitis for contrabass-flute and bass clarinet, 1985; Hallelujah I for bass clarinet and large orchestra, 1986-90; Wu Li for cello, 1986; Hallelujah II for large ensemble, 1987-88; 3 Songs for Soprano and Orchestra (Paul Celan), 1991; de Orígen Volcanico for Orchestra, 1992; Symbiosis for flute, bass clarinet, trombone and string quintet. *Publications:* Essays on the music of Xenakis and Varèse and on musical life in Holland, published in the Netherlands and France, 1977-88. *Honours:* 1966 Schnittger Organ Prize for Herfst; 1967 Prize for Composition, Amsterdam Conservatory; 1969 First Prize International Gaudeamus Festival for Huantan. *Address:* Benwell Coach House, Park Lane, South Woodchester, GL5 5HW, England.

VROOMAN Richard van, b. 29 July 1936, Kansas City, Missouri, USA. Singer (Tenor). *Education:* Studied at the Kansas City Conservatorium and with Max Lorenz

at the Salzburg Mozarteum. *Debut:* Bregenz Festival 1962, as Lorenzo in Fra Diavalo. *Career:* Many appearances in West Germany, Austria and Switzerland, notably at the Zurich Opera (1964-78); Guest engagements at Salzburg 1964-65, Aix-en-Provence, with the Deutsche Oper am Rhein and the Paris Opéra, and in Lisbon, Geneva, Frankfurt, Hamburg, Rome, Bordeaux and Marseille; Glyndebourne Festival 1968, as Belmonte in Die Entführung; Best known in operas by Mozart, Rossini and Donizetti and in the Baroque repertoire; Many concert appearances. *Recordings:* Wozzeck (CBS); Mozart Davidde Penitente and Handel Acis and Galatea (Schwann); Doktor und Apotheker by Dittersdorf; Cimarosa Requiem (Philips); Haydn Salve Regina (EMI). *Address:* c/o Opernhaus Zurich, Falkenstrasse 1, CH-8008, Zurich, Switzerland.

VYZINTAS Algirdas, b. 30 July 1929, Vyzuonos, Utena region, Lithuania. Conductor; Pedagogue. m. Lygija Vyzintiene, 5 Sept 1955, 2 sons. *Education:* Graduated, Department of Musical Instruments, Vilnius Conservatoire; Doctorate, 1983. *Debut:* Chorus Competition, 1955. *Career:* Conductor, all song festivals, Lithuania, 1960-; Participant, over 1000 concerts, Lithuania and abroad; Professor, Vilnius Conservatoire, 1983-; Director, Lituanian Postgraduate Studies Cultural Institute; Head, Department of Ethnic Culture; Head of National Musical Instruments Department of Lithuanian Academy of Music. *Compositions:* Published and recorded: Adaptions of folklore music for instrumental ensembles and orchestra. *Recordings:* For ITV and radio programmes. *Publications:* Manual for Lithuanian national instruments Birbynes, a type of clarinet, 1962; Research book about Skuduciai, 1975; research book about Jonas Svedas, composer and founder of State Song and Dance Ensemble, 1979; Doctoral thesis about archaic Lithuanian ensembles of traditional instruments Skuduciai (type of Pan Flute) and Trumpets; their ethnogenesis, 1983; Research book: Traditional Lithuanian Instrumental Ensembles - historical - structual - functional problems, 1991. Contributions to: 200 articles in magazines. Address: Zirmunu 34-26, 2051 Vilnius, Lithuania.

W

WÄCHTER Erich, b. 3 July 1945, Bielefeld. *Education:* Hochschule for Musik, Berlin. *Career:* Repetiteur at Kaiserslautern 1969-71, Kapellmeister der Opera, 1971-74; Kapellmeister at the Saarbrucken State Opera, 1974-77; Musical Director of the Saarbrucken City Choir; Musical Assistanta, Bayreuth, 1975, and Conducted Der Fliegende Holländer and Die Zauberflöte at Tbilisi; Conductor at the Baden Staet Opera in Karlsruhe, 1977- 85; Guest Conductor, Wiesbaden, leading Der Rosenkavalier, Carmen and La Forza del Destino; Lecturer in Music, State Music Academy, Karlsruhe, 1980; Kapellmeister at Darmstadt, 1985-87; Kapellmeister Nationaltheatre, Mannheim, 1987-90; Generalmusikdirektor Lübeck Opera, 1987-; Also engaged by the Stuttgart Opera, Vienna Volksoper, Oslo, Munich State Opera, Hamburg, Leipzig, Dresden, Stockholm, Antwerp; Regular conductor at the Zurich Opera. *Address:* Braunstr 13, 23552 Lubeck, Germany.

WADSWORTH Stephen, b. 3 Apr 1953, Mount Kisco, New York, USA. Stage Director; Translator; Librettist. *Career:* Artistic director and stage director of the Skylight Opera in Milwaukee: productions of Monteverdi's three principal operas, from 1982; wrote libretto for Bernstein's A Quiet Place 1983 and has directed productions of it at La Scala, Milan, and in Vienna; for Seattle Opera has directed Jenůfa, Fliegende Hollander, and Gluck's Orphee; Handel's Xerxes at Milwaukee 1985 and Partenope at Omaha, 1988; Fidelio and La Clemenza di Tito for Scottish Opera, 1991, Die Entfuhrung at San Francisco, 1990 other productions include Le nozze di Figaro and Alcina (St Louis) and Simon Boccanegra (Netherlands Opera); Head of the Opera Program at the Manhattan School of Music, 1991; translations of Monteverdi's Orfeo and Handel's Xerexes, Alcina and Partenope; Covent Garden debut 1992, Handel's Alcina.

WAGNER Sieglinde, b. 21 Apr 1921, Linz, Austria. Singer (Mezzo-Soprano). *Education:* Studied at the Linz Conservatory and with Luise Willer and Carl Hartmann in Munich. *Debut:* Linz 1942, as Erda in Das Rheingold. *Career:* Sang at the Vienna Volksoper 1947-52; Sang in Berlin from 1952; Appearances in Milan, Rome, Amsterdam, Madrid and Barcelona; Salzburg Festival from 1956, notably as Leda in the 1952 premiere of Der Liebe der Danae by Strauss, and in the premieres of Julietta by Erbse and Das Bergwerk zu Falun by Wagner-Régeny; Also sang at Salzburg in Romeo und Julia by Blacher, Elektra, Die Zauberflöte, Der Rosenkavalier and Le Nozze di Figaro; Bayreuth Festival from 1962 (Mary in Der fliegende Holländer, 1971); Sang at the Städtische Oper Berlin until 1986; Extensive concert repertoire includes sacred music by Bach. *Recordings:* Christmas Oratorio by Bach, Die Zauberflöte, Der fliegende Holländer (Deutsche Grammophon); Die Fledermaus (Decca); Solo in Beethoven's Missa Solemnis (Cetra). *Address:* c/o Deutsche Oper Berlin, Richard Wagnerstrasse 10, D-1000 Berlin 1, Germany.

WAGNER Wolfgang, b. 30 Aug 1919, Bayreuth, Federal Republic of Germany, Opera Director. m. (1) Ellen Drexel, 11 Apr 1943, 1 son, 1 daughter, (2) Gudrun Armann, 1 daughter. *Career:* Stage Manager, Bayreuth Festivial, 1940; Assistant, Preussischer Staatsoper, Berlin, 1940-44; Director, annual Wagner operatic festival, 1951-; Numerous guest appearances and international tours; Productions include: Andreasnacht, Belin, 1944; Das Rheingold, Naples, 1952; Die Walküre, Naples 1952 and 1953, Barcelona 1955, Venice 1957, Palermo 1962, Osaka 1967; Lohengrin, Bayreuth, 1953 and 1967; Siegfried, Naples 1953, Brussels 1954, Venice 1957, Bologna 1957; Der fliegende Holländer, Bayreuth, 1955; Dresden, 1988; Tristan und Isolde, Barcelona 1955, Bayreuth 1957, Venice 1958, Palermo 1960, Osaka 1967, Milan 1978; Parsifal, Barcelona 1955, Bayreuth 1975, 1989; Don Giovanni, Brunswick, 1955; Die Meistersinger von Nuremburg, Rome 1956, Bayreuth 1968 and 1981, Dresden, 1985, Der Ring des Nibelungen, Venice 1957, Bayreuth 1960 and 1970;

Götterdämmerung, Venice, 1957, Tannhäuser, Bayreuth, 1985. *Address:* PO Box 100262 Bayreuther Festspiele, 8580 Bayreuth 1, Germany.

WAHLGREN Per-Arne, b. 1953, Sweden. Singer (Baritone). *Education:* Studied at the opera school of the Royal Opera, Stockholm. *Debut:* Norrland Opera 1978, as Don Giovanni. *Career:* Sang at the Stora Teater Gothenburg from 1979 as Germont and Belcore; Guest appearance at the Theater an der Wien, Vienna 1980, in the premiere of Jesu Hochzeit by Gottfried von Einem; Royal Opera Stockholm from 1981, as Mozart's Count and Guglielmo, Marcello, Sharpless and Wolfram; Further engagements at Nice in Tannhäuser and The Queen of Spades, at Lausanne in Dido and Aeneas and in Madrid in Mendelssohn's Elijah; Stockholm 1986 in the premiere of Christina by Hans Gefors; Drottningholm Court Theatre 1991, as Orestes in a revival of Electra by J.C.F. Haeffner; Concert repertory includes Bach's Passions, Christmas Oratorio and Cantatas, the Brahms Requiem, Messiah, Utrecht Te Deum by Handel, the Fauré Requiem, Lieder eines fahrenden Gesellen and Carmina Burana. *Recordings include:* Dido and Aeneas. *Address:* Kungliga Teatern PO Box 16094, S-10322 Stockholm, Sweden.

WAKASUGI Hiroshi, b. 31 May 1935, Tokyo, Japan. Conductor. *Education:* Studied conducting with Hideo Sati and Nobori Kaneko. *Career:* Conducted the Kyoto Symphony Orchestra from 1975; Regular concerts with the Berlin Philharmonic, Vienna Symphony, Munich Philharmonic, Toronto Symphony, Montreal Symphony, Pittsburgh Symphony, NHK Symphony, Bavarian Radio Symphony and the Frankfurt Museum Society; Chief Conductor of the Cologne Radio Symphony 1977-83; US debut 1981, with the Boston Symphony Orchestra; Music Director of the Deutsche Oper am Rhein Dusseldorf 1981-86; Principal Guest Conductor of the Dresden State Opera and Dresden Staatskapelle 1982; Chief Conductor, Tokyo Metropolitan Orchestra; Chief Conductor and Artistic Director of the Tonhalle Orchestra Zurich, from 1987, 1987-91; Has conducted first Japanese performances of Schoenberg's Gurrelieder and Pelléas und Mélisande, Wagner's Parsifal, Der fliegende Holländer, Rheingold and Siegfried, Strauss's Capriccio and Ariadne auf Naxos, and many contemporary works. *Honours include:* Suntory Prize, 1987. *Address:* c/o Astrid Schoerke, Kunstler Secretariat, Mönckebergallee 41, D-3000 Hannover, Germany.

WAKEFIELD John, b. 21 June 1936, Yorkshire, England. Professor of Singing. m. Rilla Welborn, 1 son, 1 daughter. *Education:* Royal Academy of Music, FRAM; Hon FTCL. *Debut:* Welsh National Opera, 1960. *Career:* Macduff, Glyndebourne, 1964; Rinuccio Royal Opera House, 1965; Other roles include Fenton, Tamino, Paris Don Ottavio, Ferrando, Belmonte, Idamante, Rodolfo, Orfec, Ormindo, Essex and Saul. *Recordings:* La Traviata: Ormindo; Mikado; Messiah. *Honours:* Kathleen Ferrier Scholarship, 1958; Tenor Prize, S'Hertogenbusch, 1959. *Memberships:* Equity; NATFHE. *Hobbies:* Golf; ball games and sport. *Address:* 12 Avenue Gardens, Teddington, Middlesex TW11 0BH, England.

WALACINSKI Adam, b. 18 Sept 1928, Krakow, Poland. Composer. *Education:* Studied at the Krakow Conservatory 1947-52: Further study with Boguslaw Schaffer. *Career:* Violinist in the Krakow Radio Orchestra 1948-56; Teacher at the Krakow Conservatory 1972; Member of the Grupa Krakowska, for the promotion of the New music. *Compositions include:* Alfa for orchestra 1958; String Quartet 1959; Intrada for 7 players 1962; Canto Triodore for flute, violin and vibraphone 1962; Horizons for chamber orchestra 1962; A Lyric before Falling Asleep for soprano, flute and 2 pianos 1963; Concerto de Camera for violin and strings 1964; Fogli volanti for string trio 1985; Canzona for cello, piano and tape 1966; Epigrams for chamber ensemble 1967; Refrains and Reflections for orchestra 1969; Notturno 70 for 24 strings, 3 flutes and percussion; Torso for orchestra 1971; Divertimento interrotto for 13 players 1974; Mirophonies for soprano and ensemble 1974; Ballada for flute and piano 1986; Little LAutumn Music for flute and string trio 1986; Drama e Burla for orchestra 1988. *Address:* ZAIKS (Poland), c/o PRS Ltd. Member Registration, 29-33 Berners Street, London W1P 4AA, England.

WALBANK Jeremy Simon, b. 10 Jan 1958, Southport, England. Organist; Composer; Writer; Producer. *Education:* St. Mary's College, Liverpool; Bangor University; Durham University; Studied privately in Paris with Jean Langlais. *Career:* Performances in UK (including Edinburgh and City of London Festivals, QEH); France, Germany, Malta, USSR, Menorca, Romania; TV productions for BBC, ITV, Xandir Malta, Soviet TV,has also given premiere of works by Langlais, Camilleri, McGregor, Tjeknavorian; Director of Music, St. Katharine Cree Church, London; Director, Abingdon Little Arts Festival; Guest Conductor, Latvian State Opera; Visiting Teacher at Riga Conservatoire and Royal University of Malta. *Compositions:* Pulcinella Fantasy (organ); Seven Songs On Death; Party (Chamber Ensemble); Readings of Poetry; Legacy of Faritius, 1987; Tromb, 1987; Symphonic Poems, 1990; Gradualia, 1990; Recorder Music, 1991. *Recordings:* Pictures at An Exhibition on Phoenix Label; Pachelbel Fugues and Praetorius-Terpsichore, both on Linn Labels. *Current Management:* Choveaux Management; Artemis Arts Development and Tivoli Festival. *Address:* 35 East Saint Helen's Street, Abingdon, Oxon OX14 5EE, England.

WALDHANS Jiri, b. 17 Apr 1923, Brno, Czechoslovakia. Conductor. *Education:* Studied at the Brno Conservatory until 1948 and with Igor Markevitch in Salzburg. *Career:* Repetiteur and chorus master at the Ostrava Opera 1949-51; Conducted the Brno State Philharmonic 1951-54, Ostrava Symphony Orchestra 1955-62; Returned to the Brno State 1962-80; Janáček Academy at Brno from 1980; Guest conductor in Czechoslovakia and elsewhere in Europe. *Recordings include:* Dvořák Cello Concerto with the Czech Philharmonic (Supraphon); 15 Pages after Durer's Apocolypse by Liboš Fišer; Janáček's Lachian Dances, Jealousy (Jenůfa) Overture, The Fiddler's Child and The Ballad of Blanik Hill; Suites from Martinů's ballets Istar and Spalicek; Cello Concertos by Milhaud; Beethoven's piano arrangement of his Violin Concerto and early Concerto in E flat, 1784, with Felicia Blumenthal. *Address:* Slezské divadlo, Marketing Manager, Aleš Waldhans, Horní Namestí 13, 749 69 Opava, Czech Republic.

WALKER Alan, b. 6 Apr 1930, Scunthorpe, England. Writer; Teacher; Musicologist. *Education:* DMus, Durham University; Fellow, Royal Society of Canada; Fellow, Guildhall School of Music; Associate, Royal College of Music. *Career:* British Broadcasting Corporation Music Production, 1961-71; Professor, Chairman, Music Department, McMaster University, Hamilton, Ontario, Canada, 1971-. *Publications include:* A Study in Musical Analysis 1962; An Anatomy of Musical Criticism 1966; Editor, Frederic Chopin: Profiles of the Man and His Music 1970; Editor, Robert Schumann: The Man and His Music 1971; Franz Liszt: A Biography 1971; Franz Liszt: The Virtuoso Years (1811-47) (vol. 1 of biography), 1983; Franz Liszt: The Weimar Years (1848-61) (Vol. 2 of Biography), 1989; Liszt, Carolyne and the Vatican: The Story of a Thwarted Marriage, 1991. *Contributions to:* Encyclopedia Britannica; Times Literary Supplement; Times Educational Supplement; Music and Letters; Music Review; The Listener; Musical Times; Various others. *Honours:* Fellow, Royal Society of Canada, 1984; Liszt Medal, American Liszt Society, 1984; Liszt Medal, Hungarian Minister of Culture, 1986. *Hobby:* Collecting books. *Address:* Department of Music, McMaster University, Hamilton, Ontario, Canada L8S 4M2.

WALKER Arthur Dennis, b. 14 Sept 1932, Bradford, Yorkshire, England. Music Librarian; Musicologist; Honorary Special Lecturer In Music Bibliography, Manchester University. *Education:* Private study of music; MA, Manchester University, 1980. *Career:* Assistant, Bradford Public Libraries, 1951-57; Senior Assistant, Battersea Public Libraries, London, 1958-64; Music Librarian, Manchester University, 1964-. *Compositions:* Various works have been performed. *Publications:* Music Printing A Bibliography, 1963; Translator, Schoenberg, Gurrelieder, 1966; A Short History of Breitkopf and Härtel, 1969; Handel, Dettingen Te Deum, 1970; Bruckner, Overture in G Minor, 1972; GF Handel, The Newman Flower Collection in the Henry Watson Music Library: A Catalogue, 1972; Handel, Judas Maccabaeus, 1973; Wagner, Polonaise, 1973; Mozart Symphony K 338/Minuet K 409, 1976; Gustav Mahler: A Bibliographical Study of the Printed Scores (thesis), 1980; The Correspondence of the Brontë Family: A Guide, 1982. *Contributions to:* Music Teacher; Musical Times; Audio Record Review; Music and Letters; Records and Recording; Brio; Library Association Record; RMA Research Chronicle; Die Musik in Geschichte & Gegenwart; J Bennett, HF Redlich in New Grove Dictionary of Music, 1980. *Memberships:* Bibliographical Society; Brontë Society. *Hobbies:* Bruckner; Handel; Mahler; Brontë Family; Trams; Railway History. *Address:* 15 Maitland Avenue, Manchester M21 7ND, England.

WALKER David, b. 18 July 1934, Calcutta, India. Stage Designer. *Education:* Studied at the Central School of Arts and Crafts, London. 1952-56. *Career:* Designs for Joan Littlewood's Theatre from 1955; Opera designs for Werther and La Bohème at Glyndebourne, 1966-67; Royal Opera House designs (some in collaboration with producer John Copley) 1965-82, Suor Angelica, Così fan Tutte, Don Giovanni, and Semele; Costumes for Carmen at the Metropolitan 1972, Manon Lescaut at Palermao and Lucia di Lammermoor at La Fenice, Venice; Production designs for La Traviata and Der Rosenkavalier at English National Opera, 1973, 1975; Sets and Costumes for Donizetti's Roberto Devereux at the Teatro dell'Opera Rome, 1988; Collaborated with John Conkin on designs for Der Rosenkavalier at Santa Fe, 1989; ENO designs for La Traviata seen at Philadelphia, 1992.

WALKER Diana, b. 1958, Salt Lake City, Utah, USA. Singer (Soprano). *Career:* Has sung at the New York City Opera 1983- as Leila (Les Pêcheurs de Perles), Gilda, Adele, Micaela, Barbara (Argento's Casanova) and Ninetta (The Love of Three Oranges); Seattle Opera in the title roles of The Ballad of Baby Doe and Lucia di Lammermoor; Utah Opera as the Queen of Night; European debut as Blonchen in Die Entführung with Nice Opera; Modern repertory includes Laetitia in The Old Maid and the Thief with St Louis Opera, Abigail in The Crucible by Robert Ward and Ariel in Lee Hoiby's The Tempest (Kansas City); Performances of the ballet Alice, after Del Tredici's In Memory of a Summer Day, in Toronto, Chicago, Washington DC, Florida, California, New York (Met Opera) and London; Sang Lakmé for Chicago Opera Theatre, 1990; Premieres of Victoria Bond's Gulliver's Travels in Virginia; Concert repertory includes Messiah, Handel's Joshua and Rinaldo (at Kennedy Center) and Mahler's 4th Symphony; Further roles include Donizetti's Norina, Adina and Marie; Gluck's Iphigénie; Mozart's Mme. Silberklang, Blondchen and Susanna; Strauss's Sophie and Zerbinetta; Verdi's Nannetta and Ophelia in Hamlet by Thomas; Sang Carlotta/Mme Firmin in The Phantom of the Opera, Canadian National Tour, 1991-1993; Guest artist with Miami Chamber Symphony, Brooklyn Symphony, New York, Utah Symphony, Kansas City Philharmonic, Roanoke, Virginia Symphony, Aspen Symphony; Special Guest in Soap opera, Another World, as Oper Singer; Starring in: Look at Me, a National Endowment of the Arts Grant Film, 1994. *Honours:* 2nd Place International American Music Competition, Carnegie Hall; Alumnus of the Year, University of Missouri, Kansas City. *Current Management:* c/o Anthony George Management, 250 W 77th Street, No 304, New York City, NY 10024, USA. *Address:* 2-12 Seaman Avenue, No 2-M, New York, NY 10034, USA.

WALKER George Theophilus, b. 27 June 1922, Washington DC, USA. Composer; Pianist. m. Helen

Siemens, 2 sons. *Education:* MusB, Oberlin College, 1941; Artist Diploma, Curtis Institute of Music, 1945; DMA, University of Rochester, 1957. *Debut:* Town Hall, New York, 1945. *Career:* Numerous concerts, as pianist, managed by National Concert Artists; Professor Emeritus, Rutgers University, 1992. *Compositions include:* 4 piano sonatas; Concertos for cello, trombone, violin, piano; 2 string quartets; 2 sonatas, violin & piano; Address for Orchestra; 2 Sinfonias for Orchestra; Serenata for Chamber Orchestra; Sonata, cello & piano; Music for brass; Mass for Chorus and Orchestra. *Recordings:* Cantata for Soprano, Tenor, Boys Choir & Chamber Orchestra; Concertos, Piano & Orchestra, Trombone & Orchestra; Lyric for Strings; 4 Piano Sonatas; Poem for Soprano and Chamber Ensemble; Variations for Orchestra; Antifonys for Chamber Orchestra; CBS, Mercury, Desto, Timeless, Orion, CRI, Serenus, Centaur, BIS, Da Camera Magna, Mastersound. *Publications:* Make Room For Black Classical Music, New York Times, 1992. *Hobbies:* Tennis; Audio. *Address:* 323 Grove Street, Montclair, New Jersey 07042, USA.

WALKER Helen, b. 1952, Tunbridge Wells, England. Singer (Soprano). *Education:* Guildhall School, London, with Noelle Barker. *Career:* Sang Verdi's Giovanna d'Arco 1977; Glyndebourne Festival as Fiordiligi, Monteverdi's Poppea (1984) and Helena in A Midsummer Night's Dream; Glyndbourne Touring Opera as Pamina, Ann Trulove in The Rake's Progress, and Ninetta in L'Amour des Trois Oranges; Opera North as Pamina, and Fenena in Nabucco; Helena at Aldeburgh and Covent Garden; Handel roles include Polissena in Radamisto (Handel Opera Society) and Teseo, for the English Bach Festival at Sadler's Wells theatre; Foreign engagements in Hong Kong and Nancy (with Glyndebourne Touring Opera), Montpellier and La Fenice, Venice (as Ann Trulove); Sang a Maid in Elektra at Covent Garden, 1990; Freia, Sieglinde and Gutrune in the City of Birmingham Touring Opera version of the Ring; Premiered Leaving by Turnage, Symphony Hall & Radio 3, 1992. *Recordings:* Dido & Aeneas (1st Witch), Philips. *Honours include:* Winner, Susan Longfield Competition 1977; Ricordi Prize for Opera; Mozart Memorial Prize 1978; South East Arts Young Musicians Platform; Glyndebourne Touring Award; Christie Award, Glyndebourne. *Current Management:* Magenta Music International, 64 Highgate High Street, London N6 5HX.

WALKER John Edward, b. 19 Aug 1933, Bushnell, Indiana. Singer (Tenor). *Education:* Studied at the Universities of Denver, Urbana and Bloomington. *Debut:* Berne 1963, as Tamino. *Career:* Appearances in Europe at Zurich, Cologne, Frankfurt, Stuttgart and Brussels; US engagements at San Francisco, Dallas, Santa Fe, Chicago, Seattle, San Diego, Omaha and Portland; Other roles have included Mozzart's Belmonte, Don Ottavio and Ferrando, Nadir, Almaviva, Alfredo, Fenton, Ernesto, Nemorino, Werther, Lensky and Britten's Lysander; Has also sung Jenik in The Bartered Bride, Nureddin in The Barber of Bagdad, Albert Herring, and David in Die Meistersinger; Many concert and oratorio engagements. *Address:* c/o Staatsoper Stuttgart, Oberer Schlossgarten 6, 7000 Stuttgart 1, Germany.

WALKER Penelope, b. 12 Oct 1956, Manchester, England. Singer - Concert and Opera. m. Phillip Joll, 2 children. *Education:* GSMD, 1974-78 (AGSM and advanced studies); National Opera Studio, 1979-80. *Debut:* Royal Albert Hall, 1976; Prom Debut, Grimgerde in Die Walküre with Gwyneth Jones and The National Youth Orchestra, 1989; Canada with Regina Symphony Orchestra, 1993, singing Wesendonck Lieder, and Chausson's Poème de l'amour et de la mer; Royal Opera House, Covent Garden, Die Walküre Flosshilde, 1994. *Career:* BBC TV and Radio - including Elgar documentary with Simon Rattle and C.B.S.O.; Operatic debut in Paris, 1982 with Opéra-Comique; London debut at Camden Festival, Maria Tudor (Pacini) Opera Rara; ENO - Siegrune (Die Walküre), Kate Pinkerton (Madame Butterfly) and Madame Sosostris (Midsummer Marriage); Opera North, Madame Sosostris; Welsh National Opera, Fricka (Das Rheingold and Die Walküre),

Anna (The Trojans), Scottish Opera, Madame Sosostris and Erda (Das Rheingold); Has sung oratorio with all major British orchestras; Messiah with Berlin Philharmonic, Berlin, conducted by Zubin Mehta (Dec 1981); Has sung at major British Festivals including Edinburgh, Three Choirs, Llandaff, Fishguard, City of London, Cambridge, Camden, Ely, etc; Handel operas during tricentenary year, Sadler's Wells, Tirinto (Imeneo) Tangia (Poro) at Barber Institute, Birmingham; Arsace (Teseo) for English Bach Festival, Royal Opera House, Covent Garden; Herodes Atticus, Athens; Siena and Sadler's Wells Theatre, London; Sang in the premiere of Tornrak by John Metcalfe with the Welsh National Opera, 1989-90; Midsummer Night's Dream, Sadler's Wells, 1990; Die Zauberflöte, Monte Carlo, 1991; Debut in: Vienna at Konzerthaus, 1990, Milan for RAI, 1991, Florida, with the Philharmonic Orchestra of Florida, 1991; Joins (as Principal) Zürich Opera for 3 year contract; Dream of Gerontius Hallé at Musikverein, Vienna, 1992; Flora, La Traviata for Bath and Wessex Opera, 1993; Madame Larina, Eugene Onegin, WNO, 1993; Wesendoncklieder Noord Nederlands Orkest; Zurich Opera, 3rd Lady, Hedwig, William Tell, Maddalena, Grimgerde; Mozart Requiem for the Ballet; Genevieve in WNO Stein Production of Pelléas under Boulez also at Chatelêt, Paris; Jeffrey Tate, Die Walküre, 1994. *Recordings include:* Bach Cantata 53; Lennox Berkeley - Four Poems of St Teresa; Opera Rara - Mayr - Trio and Aria; Mathias - Lux Aeterna (Chandos) (Bach Choir, LSO David Willcocks); Midsummer Night's Dream, Sadler's Wells (Virgin Classics); Decca, Cleveland Orchestra, Dohnanyi, Schwertleite; Animated Opera, Cartoon of Rheingold, Flosshilde & Fricka. *Membership:* Equity. *Hobbies:* Squash; Cooking; Travel; Windsurfing. *Current Management:* Robert Gilder & Co. *Address:* Llwyni Cottage, Llandewi Rhydderch, Abergavenny, Gwent, NP7 9TP, Wales.

WALKER Robert Ernest, b. 18 Mar 1946, Northampton, England. Composer. *Education:* Chorister at St Matthew's Church, Northampton; Choral scholar, Organ scholar at Jesus College, Cambridge. *Career:* Organist and schoolmaster in Lincolnshire; Freelance composer from 1975; Featured composer at 1982 Greenwich Festival; Living Composer: Eastern Orchestral Board, 1990/91; Works performed by Royal Philharmonic Orchestra at Chichester and Exeter Festivals; Regular broadcasts on BBC Radio 3. *Compositions:* Orchestral: Pavan for violin and strings 1975; At Bignor Hill 1979; Chamber Symphony No.1 1981; Variations on a Theme of Elgar 1982; Charms and Exultations of Trumpets 1985; Symphony No.1 1987; Vocal: The Sun on the Celandines 1973; Psalm 150 1974; Requiem 1976; The Norwich Service 1977; Canticle of the Rose 1980; The Sun used to Shine for tenor, harp and strings 1983; Magnificat and Nunc Dimittis in D 1985; Missa Brevis 1985; Singer by the Yellow River for soprano, flute and harp 1985; Five Summer Madrigals 1985; Jubilate 1987; Englsh Parody Mass for choir and organ, 1988; Instrumental: String Quartet No.1 1982; Five Capriccios, 1 and 2 1982/1985; Piano Quintet 1984; Passacaglia for 2 pianos; Serenade for flute, harp, violin, viola and cello; Journey into Light, A Choral Symphony 1992 and Music for BBC1, BBC2 and Channel 4. *Address:* c/o Po Box 46, UBVD 80571, Bali, Indonesia.

WALKER Sandra, b. 1 Oct. 1948, Richmond, Virginia, USA. Singer (Mazzo-soprano). *Education:* Studied at the University of North Carolina and the Manhattan School of Music, New York *Debut:* San Francisco 1972, as Flosshilde in Das Rheingold. *Career:* Sang in opera at Philadelphia, Chicago and the New York City Opera; European engagements at Gelsenkirchen, 1985 and Wiesbaden, 1987; Sang the Nurse in Ariane at Barbe Bleu at Amsterdam 1989; San Francisco Opera 1989 and 1992, as Bradamante in Vivaldi's Orlando Furioso and Hedwige in Guillaume Tell; Lyric Opera Chicago 1990-91, as Olga in Eugene Onegin and Marta in Mefistofele; Other roles include Carmen, Suzuki, Lola, the Marquise in La Fille du Regiment and Frugola in Il Tabarro. *Address:* c/o San Francisco Opera, War Memorial Opera House, San Francisco, CA 94102, USA.

WALKER Thomas,b. 5 Nov 1936, Malden, Massachusetts, USA. Music Historian. m. Barbara Bland, 30 Jan 1965, 1 daughter. *Education:* AB, Harvard University, 1961; Fulbright Scholarship, Copenhagen, 1961-62; Graduate Study, University of California, Berkeley. *Career:* Assistant Professor, State University of New York, Buffalo, 1968-73; Lecturer, University of London King's College, 1973-80; Professore Ordinario di Storia della Musica, Università della Calabria, 1980-81; Università di Ferrara, 1981-. *Publications:* Edited to date (with Giovanni Morelli and Reinhard Strohm), 8 volumes of Drammaturgia Musicale Veneta, Milan, Ricordi, 1983-. *Contributions to:* Musica Disciplina, Journal of the A.M.S. Musica/Realtà, Rivista Italiana di Musicologia; Concert Criticism for The Times and other London newspapers, 1973-77. *Memberships:* Member of Consiglio Direttivo, Società Italiana di Musicologia; Responsible for Rivista Italiana di Musicologia. *Hobby:* Computer Science. *Address:* Piazza S Giorgia 40, 44100 Ferrara, Italy.

WALKER William, b. 29 Oct 1931, Waco, Texas, USA. Singer (Baritone). *Education:* Studied at the Texas Christian University in San Antonio. *Debut:* Fort Worth Opera 1955, as Schaunard in La Bohème. *Career:* Appearances at Opera houses in New Orleans, Santa Fe, Milwaukee, San Antonio, Vancouver, Washington and Fort Worth; Metropolitan Opera New York from 1962, as Mozart's Guglielmo and Papaganeo, Malatesta, Germont, Ford, Amonasro, Rigoletto, Valentin, Rossini's Figaro, Marcello, Alfio, Tonio and Escamillo; Noted concert artist. *Address:* c/o Metropolitan Opera, Lincoln Centre, New York NY 10023, USA.

WALKER-HILL Helen Siemens, b. 26 May 1936, Manitoba, Canada. Pianist; Lecturer; Professor. 2 sons. *Education:* BA University of Toledo; MM, Smith College; DMA, University of Colorado. *Career:* Assistant Professor: Piano, University of Colorado, 1984-90, Music History, Muhlenberg College, Pennsylvania, 1993-94. *Recordings:* Music by African American Women Composers, 1994. *Publications:* Piano Music by Black Women Composers: A Catalogue of Solo and Ensemble works, 1992; Black Women Composers: A Century of Piano Music, 1893-1990. Numerous articles in Black Music Research Journal, American Music Research Centre Journal, American Music Teacher. *Honours:* Fulbright Grant, 1957; Newberry Library Fellowship, 1989; NEA Grant, 1993. *Address:* 1624 Rainbow Avenue, Laramie, WY 82070, USA.

WALLACE Ian Bryce, b. 10 July 1919, London, England. Singer; Actor. m. Patricia Gordon Black, 26 June 1948, 1 son, 1 daughter. *Education:* MA, Law, Charterhouse, Trinity Hall, Cambridge. Private Study with Rodolfo Mele. *Debut:* Schaunard, La Bohème, Puccini, London, 1946. *Career:* Ten Glyndebourne Seasons, 1948-61; as Masetto in Don Giovanni, Bartolo in Le Nozze di Figaro, Don Magnifico in La Cenerentola and Matteo in Arlecchino; Cesar in Fanny, Theatre Royal Drury Lane, London, 1956; Berlin Festwoche, 1954; Teatro Reale, Rome 1955; Scottish Opera 1966-75 (3); Panellist, My Music, Radio & TV, 1966-; Porterhouse Blue Channel 4 TV, 1987. *Recordings:* Ian Wallace - My Music; Your Hundred Favourite Hymns. *Publications:* Promise Me You'll Sing Mud 1975; Nothing Quite Like It 2nd volume, 1982; Reflections on Scotland, 1988. *Honours:* OBE, 1983; Honorary Degree Doctor of Music, St Andrew's Univeristy, Scotland, 1991. *Memberships:* Honorary RAM; Honorary RCM; President, Incorporated Society of Musicians, 1979-80; Garrick Club; MCC; President, Council for Music in Hospitals, 1989-. *Hobbies:* Watching Sport; Walking; Bowls; Birdwatching; Elementary Boating. *Current Management:* Fraser & Dunlop Ltd., London. *Address:* Fraser & Dunlop Ltd., Fifth Floor, The Chambers, Chelsea Harbour, Lots Road, London SW10, England.

WALLACH Joelle, b. 29 June 1950, New York, USA. Composer. *Education:* DMA, Composition, Manhattan School of Music, 1984. *Career:* Composer Residencies with Billings Symphony, 1994; Lake Placid Symphonietta, 1992, Ragdale Foundaton, 1992, 1993,

Yaddo, 1991, Banff, Leighton Artist Colony, Alberta, 1989; Hudson Valley Philharmonic, NY, 1985, 1987; Lecturer, CUNY, 1974, 1978-81; Teaching Fellow, Manhattan School of Music, 1980-82; Assistantt Professor of Music, Fordham University, 1981-83; Teaching Artist, Lincoln Centre Institute, 19890-; Preconcert Lecturer, NY Philharmonic Orchestra, 1990-. *Compositions:* Numerous orchestral works, dramatic and stage works, chamber, vocal and choral works and works for solo instruents. *Recordings:* The Tigers Tail; Mourning Madrigals; Opus Works Choral Works; Organal Voices. *Address:* Gayle Ober, Delaware Avenue, St Paul, Minnesota, USA.

WALLAT Hans, b. 18 Oct 1929, Berlin, Germany. Conductor. *Education:* Studied at the Conservatory of Schwerin. *Career:* Conductor at Stendal 1950-51, Meiningen 1951-52, Schwerin Opera 1953-56 and Cottbus Opera 1956-58; Conductor at Leipzig Opera 1958-61, Stuttgart 1961-64, Deutsche Oper Berlin 1964-65; Music Director at Bremen 1965-70, Mannheim 1970-80; Regular appearances at the Vienna Staatsoper from 1968, Bayreuth from 1970; Metropolitan Opera debut 1971; Music Director at Dortmund 1979-85, Deutsche Oper am Rhein Dusseldorf from 1986 (conducted new production of Macbeth 1988 and led the company in Schreker's Die Gezeichneten at the 1989 Vienna Festival); Many engagements at the Hamburg Staatsoper. *Address:* c/o Deutsche Oper am Rhein, Heinrich-Heine Allee 16, D-4000 Dusseldorf, Germany.

WALLBERG Heinz, b. 16 Mar 1923, Herringen, Westphalia, Germany. Conductor. *Education:* Studied at the Dortmund Conservatory and the Hochschule fur Musik in Cologne. *Career:* Played the trumpet and violin in various orchestras; Conductor at Munster, Trier, Flensburg, Hagen and Wuppertal (1946-54); Music director at Augsburg and Bremen, 1955-60; Wiesbaden 1960-74; Niederosterreichisches Tonkunstlerorchester, Vienna, 1964-75; Conductor of 450 performances at the Vienna Staatsoper; Conducted the Bavarian Radio Symphony Orchestra 1975-82 and the Essen Philharmonic 1975-91; Guest appearances with the leading orchestras of Vienna, Berlin, Munich, Dresden and Leipzig; Festival engagements at Salzburg (premiere of Wagner-Regeny's Das Bergwerk zu Falun, 1961), Florence, Barcelona, Prague, Budapest and Montreux; Has conducted opera at Covent Garden, Munich, Dresden and Hamburg; Regular concerts at the Vienna Musikverein and from 1970 with the NHK Tokyo; US debut with the National Symphony Orchestra in Washington 1991, Also sprach Zarathustra; French debut 1992, Orchestre National de France; Concerts with the Helsinki, Oslo, BBC, Essen and Liverpool Philharmonic Orchestras, 1991-92; New Zealand, Malmo and Bournemouth Symphony Orchestras, 1991-92; Opened Australian Opera 1992 season with Fidelio; Engaged for: New Zealand Symphony Orchestra, Helsinki Philharmonic, Rheinische Philharmonic, Danish Radio S Orchestra, Malmo Symphony Orchestra, Oslo Philharmonic, Bergen Philharmonic, Cologne Opera, Rome Symphony Orchestra, Australian Opera, Suddeutscher Rundfunk Orchestra, Orchestre Nationale de France, Gesellschaft der Musikfreunde, and Tonkunstler Orchestra all for 1991-92 season. *Honours include:* Bruckner Medal from the International Bruckner Gesellschaft, Vienna; German Federal Service Cross, 1st Class; Austrian Verdienstkreuz 1st class; City of Vienna's Medal of Honour. *Recordings include:* Operas, Schubert's Die Vierjährige Posten, Die Königskinder by Humperdinck, Hansel and Gretel, Zar und Zimmermann, Shvanda the Bagpiper; Bruckner's Symphonies 4, 8 and 9 and Te Deum; Mahler's Kindertotenlieder, with Hilde Rössl-Majdan; Beethoven's Piano Concertos nos. 2, 3 and 4, with Alfred Brendel, Triple Concerto and Missa Solemnis; Bruch's G minor Concerto and Scottish Fantasia, with Arthur Grumiaux; Haydn's Symphony 101 and Mozart's K550, with the Bamberg Symphony. *Address:* c/o Haydn Rawstron Limited, PO Box 654, London SE26 4DZ, England.

WALLÉN Martti, b. 20 Nov 1948, Helsinki, Finland. Opera Singer (Bass). *Education:* Sibelius Academy, Helsinki. *Debut:* Helsinki, Finland. *Career:* Finnish National Opera, 1973-75; Principal Bass, Royal Opera, Stockholm, 1975-; Roles include: Colline (Bohème), Ferrando, Philip II (Don Carlos), Sparafucile (Rigoletto), Spirit Messenger (Die Frau ohne Schatten), Dikoy (Katya Kabanova), Baron Ochs, Marke, Landgraf, Daland, Orestes, Pimen, Falstaff and Finnish modern operas such as The Last Temptations (Paavo), The Horseman (Judge). *Current Management:* Kommanditbolag Bella Voces. *Address:* KB Bella Voces, Vintergatan 19 111, 17230 Sundbyberg, Sweden.

WALLER Adalbert, b. 1932, Danzig, Germany. Singer (Baritone). *Education:* Studied in Frankfurt. *Career:* Opera appearances at Bielefeld 1958-59, Passau 1962-65; Aachen 1968-74, as Rigoletto, Scarpia and Alfio (sang Telramund in Lohengrin, 1976-77, Sang Wozzeck in the Brasilian premiere of Berg's opera, at Sao Paulo, Cologne 1981 as the Dutchman, Brunswick 1985 as Reimann's Lear, Antwerp 1982 as Dr. Schön in Lulu; Further engagements as Alberich in Der Ring des Nibelungen at Buenos Aires 1982, as Kurwenal at Bologna, 1984 and at other centres as Hans Sachs, Wotan, Falstaff and Count Luna; Member of the Frankfurt Opera from 1981. *Address:* Städtische Buhnen, Untermainanlage 11, 6000 Frankfurt am Main, Germany.

WALLFISCH Elizabeth, b. 1948, England. Violinist. *Career:* Member of the London Fortepiano Trio from 1978; performances of the Viennese repertory on original instruments in Britain, Italy, Belgium, France, Germany and the Netherlands; Complete piano trios of Haydn in London 1982, to celebrate the 250th anniversary; Complete Beethoven piano trios at the Wigmore Hall 1987; Season 1991 with Mozart trios and quartets in London, tour on the Early Music Network and Mozart performances in Barcelona, Lisbon and Germany; Member of the Purcell Quartet, debut concert at St John's Smith Square, London 1984; Extensive tours and broadcasts in France, Belgium, Holland, Germany, Austria, Switzerland, Italy and Spain; Tours of the United States and Japan, 1991-92; British appearances include four Purcell concerts at the Wigmore Hall, 1987, later broadcast on Radio 3; Repertoire includes music on the La Folia theme by Vivaldi, Corelli, CPE Bach, Marais, A Scarlatti, Vitali and Geminiani; instrumental works and songs by Purcell, music by Matthew Locke, John Blow and Fantasias and Airs by William Lawes; 17th Century virtuoso Italian music by Marini, Buonamente, Gabrieli, Fontana, Stradella and Lonati; J S Bach and his forerunners - Biber, Scheidt, Schenk, Reincken and Buxtehude. *Recordings include:* Six record set on the La Folia theme; Piano trios by Beethoven, Haydn and Mozart (Hyperion); Purcell Sonatas for two violins, viola da gamba and continuo; Sonatas by Vivaldi and Corelli (Chandos). *Address:* c/o Robert White Management, 182 Moselle Avenue, London N22 6EX, England.

WALLFISCH Lory, b. 21 Apr 1922, Ploesti, Rumania. Pianist; Harpsichordist; Professor of Music. m. Ernst Wallfisch, 12 Nov 1944, 1 son. *Education:* Royal Academy of Music, Bucharest; Studied with Florica Muzicescu and M. Jora. *Debut:* Duo with Ernst Wallfisch, Bucharest, 1943. *Career:* Taught: Bucharest; Switzerland; Cleveland, USA; Detroit; Smith College, Northampton, Massachusetts, 1964-, currently Professor of Music; Masterclasses and lectures, USA and abroad; Pianist-Harpsichordist, Wallfisch Duo; Concerts, TV appearances, radio recordings, USA, Canada, Europe, North Africa, Israel; Occasional appearances as soloist and in chamber music; Participated in music festivals, Western Europe, UK; Member of Jury, International Piano festival and competition, University of Maryland, 1986. *Recordings:* Vox/Turnabout; Concert Hall Society; Musical Heritage; Advance; Da Camera; Odeon; Fonit. *Address:* Smith College Music Department, Sage Hall, Northampton, MA 01063, USA.

WALLFISCH Raphael, b. 15 June 1953, London, England. Concert Cellist. *Education:* Studied with Amarylis Fleming, Amadeo Baldavino in Rome, Derek Simpson at the Royal Academy and Gregor Piatigorsky in California. *Career:* Since winning the 1977 Gaspar Cassado International Cello Competition in Florence he has appeared widely in Europe, Australia and the USA (Indianapolis Symphony Orchestra 1988); Chamber music formerly with Heifetz in California and with the Amadeus Quartet; Recitals with his father, Peter Wallfisch, and with Solti on TV; Piano Trio concerts with Ronald Thomas and Anthony Goldstone; Performances with most major British orchestras, including Prokofiev's Sinfonia Concertante at the Festival Hall; Promenade Concerts, London, August 1989. *Recordings:* Tchaikovsky's Rococo Variations, Strauss's Don Quixote and Romanze, Britten's Cello Symphony, Prokofiev's Sinfonia Concertante, and concertos by Shostakovich, Barber, Kabalevsky, Khachaturian, Finzi, Bax, Moeran, Bliss, Dvořák, and Brahms (Chandos); Delius violin and cello concerto, with Tasmin Little, and cello concerto (EMI). *Address:* Clarion/Seven Muses, 64 Whitehall Park, London N19 3TN, England.

WALLIN Rolf, b. 7 Sept 1957, Oslo, Norway. Composer. *Education:* Norwegian State Academy of Music; University of California. *Compositions:* Ring for Oboe, and violin; Though What Made it has Gone, for Mezzo and piano; Stonewave, for 6 percussionists; Concerto for Timpani and Orchestra; Onda di Ghiaccio for 16 instruments; Solve et coagula, for flute, clarinet, percussion, piano, viola and vc. *Recordings:* Stonewave; Though what made it has gone; Onda di Ghiaccio; CD with chamber works by Rolf Waller. *Honours:* Best Work, World Music Day, 1992; Bang and Olufsen's Music Prize, 1989. *Memberships:* Norwegian Society of Composers. *Hobbies:* Theatre; Art; Cooking. *Address:* Steenstrupsgate 7, 0554 Oslo, Norway.

WALLIS Delia, b. 1944, Chelmsford, Essex, England. Singer (Mezzo-Soprano). *Education:* Studied at the Guildhall School of Music, London. *Debut:* Wexford Festival 1968, as Annius in La Clemenza di Tito. *Career:* Welsh National Opera from 1968, as Hansel and Cherubino, Covent Garden from 1970; Glyndebourne 1971-72, 1976, as Cathleen in The Rising of the Moon, the Composer in Ariadne auf Naxos and Cherubino; Has sung at the Hamburg Staatsoper from 1973. *Recordings include:* Italian Singer in Manon Lescaut (EMI). *Address:* c/o Harrison/Parrott Ltd., 12 Penzance Place, London W11 4PA, England.

WALMSLEY-CLARK Penelope, b. 1958, England. Soprano. *Career:* Sang the Queen of Night in Die Zauberflöte at Covent Garden: returned for the British premiere of Berio's Un Re in Ascolto, 1989; Glyndebourne Festival in The Electrification of the Soviet Union by Nigel Osborne; Has sung the Queen of Night for Geneva Opera and the English National Opera, 1989; Ligeti's Le Grand Macabre in Vienna; Concert engagements include the Brahms Requiem at the City of London Festival; Carmina Burana with the London Symphony Orchestra; Elijah in Liverpool with Marek Janowski; Shostakovich Symphony No.14, with the City of London Sinfonia; Concert performances of the operas Moses und Aron at the Festival Hall and Elegy for Young Lovers at La Fenice, Venice; Further appearances in Vienna, Berlin, Salzburg, Frankfurt, Czechoslovakia and Russia; Conductors include Birtwistle, Boulez, Colin Davis, Charles Groves, Haitink, Norrington and Leppard; Sang as Guinevere in the world premiere of Birtwistle's Gawain at Covent Garden, 1991. *Address:* c/o Allied Artists, 42 Montpelier Square, London SW7 1JZ, England.

WALSH Colin Stephen, b. 26 Jan 1955, Portsmouth, England. Organist. *Education:* Portsmouth Grammar School, 1966-73; Organ tuition: Nicholas Danby, Jean Langlais; Organ Scholarship, St George's Chapel, Windsor Castle 1973-74; Organ Scholarship, Christ Church, Oxford, 1974-78; FRCO 1976; ARCM 1972; MA (Hons) 1980. *Career:* Assistant Organist, Salisbury Cathedral 1978-85; Director of Music, Salisbury

Cathedral School, 1978-85; Assistant Conductor, Salisbury Musical Society, 1978-85; Conductor, Farrant Singers, 1982-85; Organist and Master of the Music, St Albans Cathedral, St Albans, 1985-88; Conductor, St Albans Bach Choir 1985-; Artistic Director, St Albans International Organ Festival, 1985-; Organist and Master of the choristers, Lincoln Cathedral, 1988-; Many organ recitals including Royal Festival Hall; tours abroad; USA, Sweden, Denmark, France, Czechoslovakia. *Recordings:* BBC Radio 3, regular solo organist; French Organ Music Vol I and Vol II from Salisbury Cathedral (Priory label); French Organ Music Vol III from St Albans Cathedral (Priory label); Great European Organs, Lincoln Cathedral; Vierne: 24 pieces on style libre and Triptyque. *Memberships:* Royal College of Organists, Fellow; Franco-British Society. *Hobbies:* Walking; Travel; Food and wine. *Address:* 12 Minster Yard, Lincoln, England.

WALT Deon van der, b. 28 July 1958, Cape Town, South Africa. Singer (Tenor). *Education:* Studied at the University of Stellenbosch. *Debut:* Sang Jacquino in Fidelio at the Nico Malan Opera House, Cape Town, 1981. *Career:* From 1982 has sung at Stuttgart, Munich, Gelsenkirchen and Hanover; Covent Garden from 1985, as Almaviva (Il barbiere di Siviglia), Hermes in King Priam and Belmonte in Die Entführung aus dem Serail; Sang in concert at Salzburg 1985, returning 1989 as Belmonte; Vienna Staatsoper and Zurich 1989, as Tamino and as Tonio (La fille du régiment). *Recordings include:* Ferrando in Così fan Tutte, from the Ludwigsburg Festival (Harmonia Mundi); Massimila Doni by Schoeck (Schwann).

WALTA Jaring Douwe, b. 12 May 1941, Leeuwarderadeel, Friesland, Netherlands. Violin Player. *Education:* Conservatory Diploma, solo violin player, 1962. *Debut:* Silver Circle of Friends, 1963. *Career:* 1st violin, Concertgebouw Orchestra, 1962, 1965; 1st Concertmaster, Overijssel Philharmonic, 1965, 1970; 1st Concertmaster Residentie, Orchestra; Teacher Royal Conservatory, The Hague, 1981; Numerous solo concerts, radio and television appearances; President, European String Teachers Association, 1977-81. *Recordings:* Heldenleben (Richard Strauss), 1985, Residentie Orchestra Conductor, Hans Vonk; Horn Trio (Johannes Brahms), with Vic Zarzo and Jan vander Meer. *Membership:* European String Teachers Association. *Address:* De Melkpotte 12, 2631 PV Nootdorp, The Netherlands.

WALTER David, b. 22 Mar 1913, Brooklyn, New York, USA. Musician; Teacher. Divorced, 1 son, 1 daughter. *Education:* BS, City College, New York, 1932; Diploma, Graduate Diploma, Juilliard School, 1937, 1938. *Debut:* Brooklyn, New York, 1925. *Career:* 15 years of performance with Toscanini and NBC Symphony; 17 years of performance with Pablo Casals and the Festival Casals, Puerto Rico; Principal Bass, Pittsburgh Symphony, Symphony of the Air, Festival Casals Orchestra; Faculty, Juilliard School, 1969-, Manhattan School of Music, 1957-; New England Conservatory; Seminars and Workshops throughout USA, Europe, China; Soloist; Recitalist. *Compositions:* The Elephant Gavotte; The Melodious Bass; Editions of many works for double bass. *Recordings:* David Walter in Recital, Volumes I and II; Musiminus One Double bass, Volumes I, II, III; many recordings with NBC Symphony of the Air. *Hobbies:* Bicycling; Films; Collecting Bass Player Miniatures. *Address:* The Juilliard School, New York, NY 10023, USA.

WALTER Horst, b. 5 Mar 1931, Hannover, Germany. Musicologist. m. Liesel Roth, 1959, 2 sons. *Education:* Musicology, German philology, philosophy, University of Cologne; DPh. *Career:* Scientific Cooperator, Joseph Haydn Institute, Cologne, 1962-92, Since 1992 Director of the Institute. *Publications include:* Music History of Lüneburg, from end 16th Century to early 18th Century, Tutzing, 1967; Editor, Complete Haydn Edition (J Haydn's Werke, München): Symphonies i/4, i/17 (1964, 1966), Baryton trios xiv/5 (1968), La Vera Costanza xxv/8 (1976), Keyboard Concertos xv/2

(1983), Accompanied Keyboard Divertimenti & Concertini xvi (1987), Wind-band Divertimenti & Scherzandi viii/2 (1991); G. van Swieten's manuscript notebooks of the Creation & the Seasons, Haydn Studies i/4 (1967); Haydn's Pianos, Haydn Studies, ii/4 (1970); The Biographical Relationship Between Haydn & Beethoven, Report of Bonn Conference, 1970 (1973); An Unknown Schütz Autograph in Wolfenbüttel, Festschrift K.G. Fellerer, (1973); The Posthorn Signal in the Works of Haydn & Other 18th Century Composers, Haydn Studies iv/1 (1976); Haydn's Pupils at the Esterhazy Court, Festschrift H. Hüschen (1980); Haydn Bibliography 1973-83, Haydn Studies v/4 (1985); Haydn Bibliography 1984-90, Haydn Studies VI/3, 1992; String Quartets dedicated to Haydn, Tradition and reception, Report of the Gesellschaft für Musikforschung Köln 1982 (1985). *Contributions to:* Music Past & Present, MGG; New Grove Dictionary; Proceedings, International Haydn Conference, Washington DC, USA, 1975 (1981), International Haydn Congress, Vienna 1982 (1986). *Address:* Herkenfelder Weg 146, 51467 Bergisch Gladbach, Germany.

WALTER Rudolf, b. Jan 1918, Gross Wierau, Silesia. University and College Professor. m. Marianne Marx, 30 Apr 1946, 1 son, 3 daughters. *Education:* Universities Breslau, Strasburg, Mainz; studies of Philosophy, Fine Arts, German Studies, School Music, Church Music, Musicology; Doctor of Philosophy, University of Mainz. *Career:* Founder and conductor of Kissinger Kantorei and Cappella Palatina Heidelberg; Radio broadcasts in Germany, Austria, Switzerland, Czechoslovakia, France; Professor of Musicology, University Mainz. *Recordings:* 12 Organ Records; 1 Choral Record (Monteverdi - Mass for 4 voices). *Publications:* Book: J C F Fischer, Frankfurt, 1990; Book Articles on Southern German Organ Music; Austrian Musicology; Organs of J A Silbermann; Organs of J Ph Seuffert; Sueddeutsche Orgelmeister; the Organ of O. Messiaen; Max Reger's Sacred Music; Silesian Musicology and others. *Contributions to:* Editor of Sueddeutsche Orgelmeister des Barock, 20 volumes; Orgelwerke von Schlick Tunder, Sweelinck, Reichardt, Merulo, Fasolo; Organum in missa cantata, 3 volumes; Sacred vocal works of German, English, French, Spanish and Italian Masters; J C F Fischer, Psalmi vespertini and J C Fischer, Litaniae Lauretanae both in Erbe Deutscher Musik; F X A Murschhauser, Vespertinus...cultus in Denkmäler der Tonkunst in Bayern; J J Fux, 8 Offertoria and 10 Offertoria (2 vols) in Gesamtausgabe der Werke. *Memberships:* Johann Gottfried Herder Research Council, Marburg; Schlesisches Kulturwerk, Würzburg; Mitglied der Hist Kommission für Schlesien; Allgemeiner Caecilienverband, Regensburg. *Hobbies:* West and East European languages. *Address:* Lessing-Strasse 3, D 69 214 HD-Eppelheim, Germany.

WALTON VERCOE Elizabeth, b. 23 Apr 1941, Washington, District of Columbia, USA. Composer. 1 son, 1 daughter. *Education:* BA, Music, Wellesley College, 1962; Master of Music Composition, University of Michigan, 1963; Doctor of Musical Arts in Composition, Boston University, 1978. *Career:* Instructor of Music Theory, Westminster Choir College, 1969-71; Assistant Professor of Music, Framingham State College, Massachusetts, 1973-74; Composer, Cite Internationale des Arts, Paris, France, 1983-85; Composer, Charles Ives Center for American Music, 1984 & 1992; Co-Director, Women's Music Festival/85, Boston; Macdowell Colony, 1992, St Peterburg, Russia, Spring Music Festival, 1993. *Compositions:* Arsis Press: Fantasy for Piano, Balance: Duo for Violin and Cello; Sonario for Cello; Three Studies for Piano; Irreveries from Sappho for SSA and piano or soprano and piano; Herstory II for soprano, piano and percussion; Herstory III; Persona for Piano; Rhapsody for Violin and Orchestra; Despite our differences No 1 for piano trio, No 2 for piano & orchestra, 1988; Plucked String Editions: A la fin - tout seul for mandolin and optional piano. *Recordings:* Northeastern Records, Herstory II: 13 Japanese Lyrics for soprano, piano and percussion; Coronet Records, Fantasy for Piano; Coronet Records, Irreveries from Sappho for voice and piano; Changes for Chamber Orchestra, 1991; A Dangerous Man for

Baritone & Piano, 1990; Four Humors for Cl & Pho, 1993; Herstory II reissued on Capstone CD, Herstory III on Owl CD. *Contributions to:* Music Critic, Concord Journal, 1979-82. *Address:* 74 Judy Farm Road, MA 01742, USA.

WAMSLEY Alice Mary (Bowes), b. 11 Apr 1922, Lawrence, Massachusetts, USA. Voice Teacher; Singer; Conductor. m. 19 Mar 1948, 3 sons, 4 daughters. *Education:* Voice Study with Maestro Arturo Papalardo and Myron C Whitney, Washington, District of Columbia, 1943-49; BS Music, Old Dominion University, Norfolk, Virginia, 1976; MM Voice Performance, Norfolk State University, 1981; Advanced Professional Certification, Voice Teacher, National and Virginia Music Teachers Association. *Career:* United States Navy, 1943-49; Concert Singer; Voice Teacher; Conductor, Music Director, Concerts, 1976-; Choir Director, 1978-; Founder, Director, Ocean View Civic Chorale, SATB, 1978-; Founder, Director/Conductor, Norfolk Musical Theater, 1983-. *Honours:* St George's Medal, 1970, Silver Beaver 1974, Boy Scouts of America; Sword of Honor, SAI, Gamma Zeta Chapter, 1976. *Memberships:* National Association of Teachers of Singing; Life member, Treasurer 1976, SAI; Local Record Secretary, National Federation of Music Clubs; American Women Composers; National Music Teachers Association; Virginia Music Teachers Association. *Hobbies:* Research in musicology; Sewing; Embroidery. *Address:* 143 Commodore Drive, Norfolk, VA 23503, USA.

WANAMI Takayoshi, b. 1945, Tokyo, Japan. Concert Violinist. m. Mineko Tsuchiya. *Education:* Studied with Kichinouske Tsuji, Saburo Sumi and Toshiya Eto. *Debut:* Played the Glazunov Concerto with the Japan Philharmonic, 1963. *Career:* Made European studies with Joseph Szigeti, David Oistrakh and Sandor Vegh; Toured the USA 1964, with Toho Conservatory String Orchestra; Numerous recitals and concerts in Japan 1965-; Berlin and London (Wigmore Hall) debuts 1969; Appearances with the Leipzig Gewandhaus Orchestra, Vienna Chamber, London Mozart Players, Bournemouth Symphony, Basle Symphony, Festival Strings Lucerne, Paillard Chamber; Conductors include: Rudolf Barshai, Harry Blech, Serge Baudo, Gary Bertini, George Hurst, Kurt Masur and Seiji Ozawa; Recorded Ysäye's Sonatas at the Japan Arts Festival 1971; Further tours of the US 1973, 1981, Soviet Union 1983; Season 1985-86 with Elizabeth Hall and Wigmore Hall recitals, concerts in France, Switzerland, Germany and Czechoslovakia; Highlights of season 1986-87 were concerts in Egypt, Morocco and Italy, Four concertos with the London Mozart Players and the Beethoven Concerto with the City of Birmingham Symphony; Brahms Concerto with the BBC Philharmonic; Concert tour of East Germany; 1988-89 featured 20th Century Music for solo violin and Beethoven Sonatas in Tokyo; Tours of the USSR, Hungary and the USA; Concerts with the BBC Welsh Symphony, the New Japan Philharmonic and the Slovak Chamber Orchestra; Founded the Takayoshi Wanami String Orchestra; Wigmore Hall recital March 1990, featuring Schubert, Bach (C Major solo sonata), Messiaen, Debussy and Ravel, with Mineko Tsuchiya; Other duo recitals in Japan, throughout Europe, the USA and the Middle East. *Recordings include:* Tchaikovsky, Bruch and Mendelssohn Concertos with the Philharmonia; Bach Concertos with the London Mozart Players; Brahms & Schumann Concertos with London Philharmonic; Bach Solo Sonatas & Partitas (Complete) Ysaye Six Solo Sonatas. *Honours:* Prize winner at the 1965 Long-Thibaud Competition and the Carl Flesch International, London 1970; Ysäye Medal 1970; Mobil Music Award, 1993. *Current Management:* Mark Bonello Artists Management. *Address:* 61 Woodhill Crescent, Kenton, Harrow HA3 0LU, England.

WAND Gunter, b. 7 Jan 1912, Elberfeld, Germany. Conductor. *Education:* Studied in Wuppertal and at Cologne University with Philip Jarnach (composition) and Paul Baumgartner (piano). *Career:* Worked at Wuppertal and Allenstein as repetiteur and conductor; Chief Conductor at Detmold; Conducted at the Cologne Opera 1939-44: Musical Director 1945-48; Director of the Gurzenich Concerts at Cologne from 1946, giving works by Ligeti, Varèse, Schoenberg and Zimmermann, in addition to the Viennese Classics; Professor of Conducting at the Cologne Musikhochschule from 1948; Tours of Europe, Japan and the USSR; British debut with the London Symphony at Covent Garden, 1951; Moved to Switzerland 1974 and conducted the Berne Symphony Orchestra; Principal Conductor of the NDR (North German Radio) Symphony, Hamburg, from 1982. *Recordings include:* Haydn Symphonies Nos. 82, 92 and 103; Mozart Serenades and late Symphonies; Beethoven, Missa Solemnis; Bartók's Divertimento and Music for Strings, Percussion and Celesta; Schoenberg's Five Pieces for Orchestra; Webern's Cantata No. 1; Schumann Piano Concerto, with Backhaus (Decca); Complete Symphonies of Schubert, Beethoven, Brahms and Bruckner (BMG Classics). *Address:* c/o Symphonie Orcheser des Norddeutschen Rundfunks, Rothenbaum, Chausee 132-134, D-2000 Hamburg, Germany.

WANG Ya-hui, b. 29 Feb 1968, Taiwan. Conductor. *Education:* MM, BM, Peabody Conservatory of Music, Baltimore; Curtis Institute of Music. *Career:* Music programmes in China Broadcasting Corporation of Taiwan and Singapore Braodcasting Corporation. *Honours:* South East Asian Electone Festival, Grand Prize, 1984, 1985; International Electone Festival, Hamburg, Silver Medal, 1985. *Memberships:* Phi Kappa Lambda. *Hobbies:* Collecting Stationery. *Address:* 4F No 312-1 Sec 2 Anho Road, Taipei 10663, Taiwan.

WANGENHEIM Volker, b. 1 July 1928, Berlin, Germany. Conductor; Composer; Professor. 1 daughter. *Education:* State Academy of Music, Berlin. *Career:* Founder/principal conductor, Berlin Mozart Orchestra, 1950-59; Conductor/director of studies, Mecklenburg State Opera, Schwerin, GDR, 1951-52; Conductor, orchestra, Berlin Musikfreunde, 1952-55; Conductor, Berlin Academic Orchestra, 1954-57; 1st concert with Berlin Philharmonic Orchestra, 1954; Guest conductor, Germany & worldwide, 1953-; Music Director, City of Bonn, 1957; Principal conductor, orchestras of Beethovenhalle & Philharmonic Choir, Bonn; Artistic director, Bonn Beethoven Festival; General music director, 1963-78; Professor, State Academy of Music, Cologne, 1972-; Co-founder, principal conductor, artistic director, German National Youth Orchestra, 1969-84. *Compositions include:* Sonatina for orchestra; Sinfonietta Concertante; Concerto; Sinfonia Notturna; Sinfonie, 1966; Klangspiel I & II; Mass, Stabat Mater; Psalms 70, 123, 130; Nicodemus Iesum nocte visitat; Passio secundum Ioannem; German & European folksongs for mixed choir a cappella; Hymnus Choralis. *Recordings:* Classical; Baroque; Chamber Orchestra; Symphonic and Choral. *Honours:* Berlin Arts Prize for Music, 1954; Federal Service Cross of Merit, 1972; Medal of Merit for Polish Arts, 1978. *Memberships:* German Music Council; German Heather Society. *Hobbies:* Heather gardening; Astronomy; Aquaristic. *Address:* 9 Gerhart-Harptmann-Strasse, 57610 Alten, Kirchen, Germany.

WAPP (WAHPECONIAH) Edward, b. 19 May 1943, Winfield, Kansas, USA. Ethnomusicologist. *Education:* BA Music, Utah State University; MA Ethnomusicology, PhD in progress, University of Washington. *Career:* Instructor/Lecturer, American Indian Music: Institute of American Indian Arts, 1970-73; University of New Mexico, 1972; University of Wisconsin, Milwaukee, 1973-74; University of Minnesota, 1975-77; University of Washington, 1977-; Professor of Music, Institute of American Indian Arts and Culture, 1990-; Professional performer of American Indian courting flute and vocal music; Revival of courting flute and its music. *Compositions:* Music for several documentaries on the American Indian. *Recordings:* American Indian Flute Melodies; Flute Music of Woodland Tribes. *Hobbies:* American Indian traditional arts and crafts (craftman); Ethnic arts and crafts and culinary arts. *Address:* 1521 Cochiti Street, Santa Fe, New Mexico, USA.

WARCHAL Bohdan, b. 27 Jan 1930, Orlova, CSSR.

Violin Soloist; Artistic leader, Slovak Chamber Orchestra, Bratislava. m. Eva Warchalova, 3 Aug 1957, 1 son. *Education:* Graduated, 1948; Masaryk's Music Institute, State Conservatory, Janáček University of Music Arts in Brno, 1957. *Career:* First Violinist, Slovak Philharmony, Bratislava, 1957; Teacher of violin, State Conservatory; Soloist of recitals and concerts; Founded, Slovak Chamber Orchestra, 1960-. *Recordings:* More than 80 records and CD for Opus; Supraphon. *Honours:* Special Award, Record Company Opus, 1989; National Artist, Czechoslovak Socialist Republic, 1983; Professor, University of Music Arts, Bratislava. *Membership:* Union of Slovak Composers. *Hobbies:* Collecting old fashioned cameras; Photography; Tourism. *Address:* c/o Slovkoncert, Michalska 10, 81536 Bratislava, Slovakia.

WARD David W.B., b. 28 Dec 1942, Sheffield, Yorkshire, England. Musician; Pianist; Conductor; Teacher; Lecturer. m. Elizabeth Gladstone, 1 Aug 1963, 1 son, 1 daughter. *Education:* Bryanston School, Dorset (Music Scholar), 1956-61; Music Exhibitioner, Caius College, Cambridge, 1962-63; Royal College of Music, London, 1963-67; Studied with Nadia Boulanger, Paris, 1968-69. *Debut:* Purcell Room, London, 1972. *Career:* Many Concerts as Soloist in London, elsewhere in UK, also in Ireland, Holland, France, Germany and in America and Australia. Conductor of La Spiritata Chamber Orchestra and others; Professor at Royal College of Music, 1969-; Well-known for interpretation of Mozart; Now playing harpsichord and more especially the fortepiano; Much recital work in UK and Holland. *Recordings:* Mozart Piano Music - 3 Records (1 Saga, 2 Meridian); Tapes of Duets with Susan Rennie and Solo Works; Also Radio Recordings, BBC, RTE, ORTF; Mozart piano and violin sonatas with Yossi Zivoni, CD and cassette; Haydn Trios and piano solos with Badinage, on fortepiano and original intruments; Duets and solos by J C and C P E Bach, Haydn and first recording of a new piece by David Stoll for two fortpianos, with Marejka Smit-Sibinga, Amsterdam; Mozart Keyboard Music on Fortepiano; David Stoll Chamber Music, including a Piano Sonata and a two Piano Sonata with Noel Skinner. *Hobbies:* Philosophy (Practical); Meditation; Tai Chi; Walking; Eating and Drinking; Singing. *Address:* 4 Patten Road, London SW18 3RH, England.

WARD John Owen, b. 20 Sept 1919, London, England. Music Publishing Executive; Writer. *Education:* Dulwich College, 1933-37; MA, Oxford University, 1956; London Violoncello School. *Career:* Principal Cellist, Oxford University Orchestra, 1950-56; Manager, Music Department, Oxford University Press, New York, USA, 1957-72; Director of Serious Music, Boosey Hawkes, New York, 1972-79. *Publications:* Editor: Oxford Companion to Music, 1957-77; Junior Companion to Music; Concise Oxford Dictionary of Music; Author, Careers in Music, 1968. *Contributions to:* New Grove Dictionary of Music; Musical America; Notes; Playboy. *Memberships:* Music Publishers Association, President 1974-76; International Musicological Association; American Musicological Association; Royal Musical Association; Music Library Association. *Hobby:* Chamber music. *Address:* 325 West 76th Street, New York, NY 10023, USA.

WARD Joseph, b. 22 May 1942, Preston, Lancashire, England. Singer (Tenor); Vocal Consultant. *Education:* Studied at the Royal Manchester College of Music; FRMCM; FRNCM. *Debut:* Royal Opera House Covent Garden 1962. *Career:* Many appearances in opera in the USA, London, Germany, Portugal, France and Austria; Formerly Head of vocal studies at the Royal Northern College of Music; Fomerly Principal Tenor, Royal Opera House, Covent Garden; Consultant in Opera and Vocal Studies, Hong Kong Academy for performing arts; Director of Opera (Freelance); Many BBC broadcasts. *Recordings include:* Norma, Beatrice di Tenda, Montezuma, Wuthering Heights, Pilgrim's Progress; Albert Herring. Many recordings for Decca, EMI, and Pye. *Honours:* OBE, 1991. *Hobbies:* Swimming; Horse Riding. *Address:* c/o Royal Northern College of

Music, 124 Oxford Road, Manchester M13 9RD, England.

WARD Paul Clarendon, b. 29 Aug 1918, Taunton, England. Cellist; Conductor. m. Susan Watmough, 25 July 1949, 1 son, 1 daughter. *Education:* St Paul's Cathedral Choir School, Haileybury College; Royal College of Music; ARCM, Cello Performance. *Career:* Founder, Conductor, Manchester Mozart Orchestra; Conductor, Northenden Choral Society, 1956-59, City of Chester Symphony Orchestra, 1966-76, Stockport Youth Orchestra, 1955-74; Member, Boyd Neel Orchestra, 1946-48; Sub-Principal Cellist, Hallé Orchestra, 1948-54; Cellist, Turner Quartet, 1948-53, 1957-63, Wissema Quartet, 1966-76; Brodsky Trio, 1979-81; Continuo Cellist; Teacher, Royal Manchester College of Music, 1948-72, Northern School of Music, 1953-72, Royal Northern College of Music, 1972-76; Various orchestral courses; Conductor, Cello Tutor; Festival Adjudicator; Examiner, Associated Board, Royal Schools of Music, 1978-87; Lecturer. *Contributions to:* Music Journal. *Memberships:* ISM; Musicians Union; Federations of Festivals; Galpin Society. *Hobbies:* Reading; Architecture. *Address:* 26 Drybridge Hill, Woodbridge, Suffolk IP12 4HB, England.

WARD Robert (Eugene), b. 13 Sept 1917, Cleveland, Ohio, USA. Composer; Teacher. m. Mary Raymond Benedict, 19 June 1944. 3 sons, 2 daughters. *Education:* BMus, Eastman School of Music, 1939; Certificate, Juilliard Graduate School, 1946; Studied composition with Rogers, Royce, Hanson, Jacobi and Copland; Conducting with Stoessel and Schenkman. *Career:* Teacher, Columbia University, 1946-48; Juilliard School of Music, 1946-56; Music Director, Third Street Music Settlement, New York, 1952-55; Vice-President and Managing Editor, Galaxy Music Corp, 1956-67; President 1967-74, Teacher of Composition 1967-79, North Carolina School of the Arts; Mary Duke Biddle Professor of Music, Duke University, 1979-87. *Compositions:* Operas: He Who Gets Slapped, 1955, revised 1973; The Crucible, 1961; The Lady from Colorado, 1964, revised and retitled, Lady Kate, 1981 (Operetta); Claudia Legare, 1973; Minutes till Midnight, 1982; Abelard and Heloise, 1981; 1 Act Opera, Roman Fever, Based on Short Story by Edith Wharton, 1993; Orchestral: 6 symphonies: 1941, 1947, 1950, 1958, 1989; Canticles of America, 1976; Jubilation Overture, 1946; Night Music for Small Orchestra, 1949; Fantasia for Brass and Timpani, 1953; Euphony, 1954; Divertimento, 1960; Invocation and Toccata, 1963; Piano Concerto, 1968; Sonic Structure, 1981; Dialogues for Violin, Cello and Orchestra, 1983; Saxophone Concerto, 1984; Byway of Memories, 1991; Chamber: Violin Sonata, 1950; String Quartet, 1966; Raleigh Divertimento for Wind Quintet, 1986; Appalachian Ditties and Dances, violin and piano, 1989; 2nd Sonato for violin and piano, 1990; Piano pieces; Ballet: The Scarlet Letter, 1990; Chorus: Images of God, 1989; Various vocal works; Cantatas: Earth Shall Be Fair, 1960; Sweet Freedom' Song, 1965; Songs for Ravenscroft, 1993; Concertos: Tenor Saxophone and Orchestra or Band, 1984, revised 1987. *Recordings:* Many works recorded. *Honours:* The Pulitzer Prize for Opera, The Crucible, 1962; 3 Guggenheim Fellowships; Honorary Doctorates from Peabody Conservatory, Duke Unviersity, The University of North Carloina, Greensboro. *Membership:* American Academy of Arts and Letters. *Address:* The Forest At Duke, 2701 Pickett Road No 4029, Durham, NC 27705, USA.

WARD JONES Peter Arthur, b. 30 Mar 1944, Chester, England. Music Librarian; Organist; Harpsichordist. m. Shirley Bailey, 20 May 1978, 1 son, 1 daughter. *Education:* FRCO, 1962; Balliol College, Oxford, 1963-69; Organ Scholar, 1963-66; MA(Oxon), 1970. *Career:* Part-time Professor, Royal College of Music, 1967-69; Music Librarian, Bodleian Library, Oxford, 1969-; Harpsichordist, City of Oxford Orchestra, 1968-; Conductor, Oxford Harmonic Society, 1971-80; Organist, St Giles' Church, Oxford, 1971-; Complete Bach organ works recital series, 1988-89. *Publications:* Catalogue of the Mendelssohn Papers in the Bodleian

Library, vol 3, 1989; revised edition of P Radcliffe's Mendelssohn, 1990. *Contributions to:* Music and Letters; Brio; New Oxford History of Music, vol 7; A History of Western Music, ed. Sternfeld, vol 1; Rudolf Elvers Festschrift. *Honour:* Read Prize for FRCO. *Memberships:* Royal Musical Association; Royal College of Organists; Mendelssohn-Gesellschaft. *Hobbies:* Mountain walking; Collecting Alpine books. *Address:* 25 Harbord Road, Oxford OX2 8LH, England.

WARD-STEINMAN David, b. 6 Nov 1936, Alexandria, Louisiana, USA. Composer. m. Susan Diana Lucas, 28 Dec 1956, 1 son, 1 daughter. *Education:* BMus, cum laude, Florida State University, 1957; MM, University of Illinois, 1958; DMA, University of Illinois, 1961; Postdoctoral Visiting Fellow, Princeton University, 1970; National Music Camp, Interlochen, summers, 1952-53; Aspen Music School, summer, 1956; Berkshire Music Center, Tanglewood, summer, 1957; Paris, 1958-59; Fulbright Senior Scholar in Music to Australia, 1989-90. *Career:* Composer-in-Residence, Brevard Music Centre, North Carolina; University Research Lecturer, San Diego State University, 1986-87; Faculty, California State Summer School for the Arts, Loyola Marymount Univ., Los Angeles, 1988; Numerous commissions; major orchestral performances of his work include those by Chicago Symphony, Japan Philharmonic, New Orleans Philharmonic, San Diego Symphony, Orchestra USA, Belgrade Radio Orchestra, Yugoslavia and the Seattle Symphony, Joffrey Ballet, California Ballet Co. *Compositions:* Major works for orchestra, ballet, band, chamber groups and vocal ensembles, over 30 in print, 20 in publishers rental catalogues. *Recordings:* Fragments from Sappho; Duo for cello and piano; Brancusi's Brass Beds; Childs Play; 3 Songs for Clarinet and Piano; Sonata for Piano; The Tracker; Scorpio; Western Orpheus, Concert Suite; Sonata for Piano Fortified, Moiré. *Address:* 9403 Broadmoor Place, La Mesa, CA 92042, USA.

WARFIELD Sandra, b. 6 Aug 1929, Kansas City, Missouri, USA. Singer (Mezzo-Soprano). m. James McCracken (died 1988). *Education:* Studied at the Kansas City Conservatory with Harold von Duze; Further study with Irra Petina, Elsa Seyfart and Joyce McClean. *Debut:* Metropolitan Opera 1953, in Le Nozze di Figaro. *Career:* Sang in New York until 1957, as Marcellina, Madelon in Andrea Chénier, La Cieca and Ulrica, then moved to Europe; Sang at the Zurich Opera from 1959, notably in the premiere of The Greek Passion by Martinů and as Fides, Azucena, Dalila, Amneris and Leonore in La Favorita; San Francisco Opera 1963, Dalila; Appearances in Berlin, Vienna, Perugia and elsewhere in Europe as Carmen and Fricka; Metropolitan Opera 1972, in Samson et Dalila, with James McCracken. *Recordings:* Les Contes d'Hoffmann, Le Nozze di Figaro (RCA).

WARFIELD William, b. 22 Jan 1920, West Helena, Alabama, USA. Singer (Bass). *Education:* Studied at the Eastman School and with Otto Herz and Rosa Ponselle (1958-65). *Debut:* Recital debut at New York Town Hall, 1950. *Career:* Concert tours to Australia, Africa, the Middle East, Europe, Asia, Cuba, Brazil and Greece; Sang in Mozart's Requiem conducted by Bruno Walter, New York 1956; Concerts at the Prades Festival Puerto Rico 1962-63; Sang in Showboat and Porgy and Bess at the Vienna Volksoper and in New York; Repertoire also includes Messiah, operatic arias and songs from the shows; Faculty of the University of Illinois from 1974; President of the National Association of Negro Musicians, 1984. *Recordings include:* Messiah (CBS). *Honour:* President of the National Association of Negro Musicians, 1984. *Address:* c/o Musci Building, University of Illinois at Urbana-Champaign, Urbana, IL 61801, USA.

WARING Kate, b. 22 Apr 1953, Alexandria, Louisiana, USA. Composer. m. 22 May 1981, 1 son, 1 daughter. *Education:* BMus., Flute performance, 1975, MMus., Composition, 1977, Louisiana State University; Doctorate Science Humaine, Sorbonne, Paris, France, 1984. *Career:* Solo Flute Recitals in Italy, France,

Germany, USA; Original Compositions performed in USA, Italy, France, Switzerland and Germany; Radio Performances of Compositions on Swiss, German and USA Radio; Founder of annual American Music Week in Germany concert series; Appearances on American PBS and Worldnet Television. *Compositions:* Over 60 works; Variations, flute and harpsichord, 1984; Assemblages, soprano, flute, trombone, percussion and piano, 1977; 3 Act Ballet, Acteon, for large orchestra, 1983; Chamber opera, Rapunzel, 1988; Remember the Earth Whose Skin You Are, an Oratorio, 1994. *Hobbies:* Modern Dance. *Address:* Hirschberg str 1e, D-53639 Konigswinter, Germany.

WARNER Keith, b. 6 Dec 1958, England. Stage Director. *Education:* Studied in London, at Bristol University and at Bayreuth. *Career:* Early work in fringe theatre; Staff Producer at English National Opera from 1981, Deputy Director of Productions from 1984, staging Rossini's Moise, Dargomizhsk's Stone Guest, Pacific Overtures and Werther; with David Poutney co-produced A Midsummer Marriage, The Flying Dutchman and The Queen of Spades; Associate Director of Scottish Opera, with Carmen, Tocsa, Werther, Die Zauberflöte and Iolanthe; Handel's Flavio at Florence and Batignano, Further productions of Trovatore at Dortmund, Norma in Bielefeld and Ballo in Maschera with the Canadina Opera Company; Madama Butterfly and Casken's Golem at Omaha, The Queen of Spades in Madrid, Tannhäuser for the Brighton Festival, La Bohème for Houston, Production of Janáček's, The Makropoulos Case in Oslo, 1992, Der Fliegende Hollander in Vancouver (transferring to Omaha and Tulsa) Figaro for Opera Pacific and Lohengrin at Brighton 1993; Head of Productions for Omaha Opera and the Omaha Festival from 1992 (Les contes d'Hoffmann, 1993). *Address:* c/o Atholl Still Ltd. Greystoke House, 80-86 Westrow Street, London SE19 3AF, England.

WARRACK John, b. 9 Feb 1928, London. Musicologist. m. (1) Elizabeth Cowley 1955, 2 sons (2) Lucy Beckett 1970, 2 sons. *Education:* Winchester College 1941-46; Royal College of Music 1948-52. *Career:* Freelance oboist 1951-54; Assistant music critic, Daily Telegraph 1954-61; Chief Music Critic, Sunday Telegraph 1961-72; Director, Leeds Musical Festival 1977-83; University Lecturer in Music and Fellow of St Hugh's College, Oxford, 1984-93; General Editor of series National Traditions of Opera (Cambridge); Advisory Editor, Cambridge Opera Journal. *Publications:* Concise Oxford Dictionary of Opera (with Harold Rosenthal) 1964, rev. 1979; Carl Maria von Weber 1968, rev. 1976; Tchaikovsky Symphonies and Concertos 1969, rev. 1974; Tchaikovsky 1973; Tchaikovsky Ballet Music 1979; Editor, Carl Maria von Weber, Writings on Music (trans. Martin Cooper) 1981; Oxford Dictionary of Opera (with Ewan West), 1992. *Contributions to:* Musical Times; Music and Letters; Opera; Gramophone; Opera translations; Articles in the New Grove Dictionary of Music and Musicians 1980. *Honours:* Colles Prize, Royal College of Music, 1951; ARCM 1952; MA (Oxon.) 1984; D.Litt (Oxon) 1989. *Membership:* Royal Musical Association. *Hobbies:* Gardening; Cooking. *Address:* Beck House, Rievaulx, Helmsley, Yorkshire, England.

WARREN Raymond (Henry Charles), b. 7 Dec 1928, Weston-super-Mare, England. composer. Professor of Music. *Education:* Studied at Corpus Christi College, Cambridge with robin Orr, 1949-52, then with Michael Tippett and Lennox Berkeley. *Career:* Teacher, Queens' University of Belfast from 1955, Professor of Composition, 1966; Professor of Music, Bristol University, 1972. *Compositions:* Incidental music for 11 plays by WB Yeats: The Lady of Ephesus, chamber opera, Belfast, 1959; Finn and the Black Hag, children's oepra, Belfast, 1959; Graduation Ode, opera in 3 acts, Belfast, 1963; Church operas, Let my People Go, Liverpool, 1972, St Patrick, Liverpool, 1979, and In the Beginning, Bristol, 1982; Principal compositions include: Oratorio, The Passion, 1962, Violin Concerto, 1961, Three String Quartets, 1965, 1975 and 1977, Oratorio Continuing Cities, 1989, Violin Sonata, 1993. *Address:* University of Bristol, Department of Music, Royal Fort House, Tyndall Avenue, Bristol BS8 1UJ, England.

WARREN-GREEN Christopher, b. 30 July 1955, Cheltenham, England. Musician; Educator. *Education:* Royal Academy of Music. *Debut:* Berlin. *Career includes:* Leader, BBC Welsh Symphony Orchestra 1977, Philharmonia Orchestra 1980, Academy of St Martin-in-the-Fields 1985; Music director, London Chamber Orchestra, 1987; Solo debut, Berlin, 1983; Tours as soloist, 1983-; London debut, 1984; Television presenter, BBC Music & Arts/Professor, Royal Academy of Music, 1985-. *Recordings:* Mozart Violin concerti (RCA), Vivaldi 4 Seasons (Phonogram), 4 records Haydn Concerti, Philharmonia (Nimbus), Mendelssohn Concerto (Sefel), Tchaikovsky (EMI), Exclusive to Virgin Classics 1987-, Berlin Chamber Akademie. *Honour:* Honorary ARAM, 1983. *Current Management:* Anglo-Swiss (UK); Columbia Artistes (Worldwide). *Address:* c/o Anglo-Swiss Artists' Management, PO Box 719, London N6 5UX, England.

WASHINGTON Daniel, b. 1955, Summerville, South Carolina, USA. Singer (Baritone). *Education:* BMus, Furman University; MMus, Northwestern University; International Opera Studio in Zurich. *Career:* Sang Marcello (La Boheme) and Crown in Porgy and Bess for Zurich Opera; Sang Tarquino in Respighi's Lucrezia with the Festa Musica Pro Summer Festival; Stadttheater Luzern 1982-87, as Don Giovanni, Simon Boccanegra, Renato, Germont, Escamillo and Guglielmo; Engagements at the International Music Festival Lucerne, the Spoleto Festival USA, Festa Musica Riva del Garda and the Hamburg and Essen Operas; Has appeared in Porgy and Bess at the Theater des Westens Berlin, at the Musikverein Vienna and with the Royal Liverpool Philharmonic; Sang with the Frankfurt Alte Oper and the Royal Opera Liège 1987-88; Bad Hersfeld Summer Festival as Jochanaan in Salome; Concerts with the Milwaukee Symphony Orchestra and on Austrian television. *Recordings include:* Respighi's Lucrezia. *Honours:* First Prize, 1986 International Voice Competition Toulouse; First Prize 1987 International Competition of Lyric Singing, Verviers. *Address:* c/o Norman McCann International Artists Ltd, The Coach House, 56 Lawrie Park Gardens, London SE26 6XJ, England.

WASHINGTON Paolo, b. 24 May 1932, Florence, Italy. Singer (Bass). *Education:* Studied in Florence with Flaminio Contini and Bruno Bartoletti. *Debut:* Florence 1958, as Douglas in La Donna del Lago. *Career:* Appearances in Parma, Palermo, Bologna, Milan, Rome and Naples; Verona Arena 1968-86; Further engagements in Athens, Budapest, Mexico City, Brussels, Geneva, Barcelona and Edinburgh; Repertoire includes roles in operas by Rossini, Cherubini, Bellini, Donizetti and Verdi; Sang Arkel in Pelléas et Mélisande at Florence, 1989. *Recordings:* Requiem by Donizetti (Decca); Lucia di Lammermoor (Eurodisc); Il Bravo by Mercadante; Zelmira and La Donna del Lago by Rossini; La Forza del Destino. *Address:* c/o Teatro Comunale di Firenze Teatro Comunale, Via Solferinois, I-50123 Florence, Italy.

WASSERTHAL Elfriede, b. 12 Mar 1911, Lubeck, Germany. Singer (Soprano). *Debut:* Stettin 1935, as Marzelline in Fidelio. *Career:* Sang in Essen and Dusseldorf then at the Deutsche Oper Berlin (Charlottenburg), debut as Fiordiligi; Sang at Dusseldorf 1941, in the premiere of Die Hexe von Passau by Gerster; Hamburg Staatsoper 1947-64, notably as Tosca, Desdemona, Jenufa and Magda Sorel in The Consul; Visited Edinburgh Festival with the Hamburg company 1952, for the British premiere of Mathis der Maler by Hindemith; Staatsoper Berlin 1951, as Selika in L'Africaine; Sang at Covent Garden as Eva, Sieglinde, Donna Elvira, Elsa and Marie in Wozzeck; Copenhagen 1960; Frequent concert appearances.

WASSON D DeWitt, b. 20 Feb 1921, Orangeburg, New York, USA. Conductor; Organist; Church Musician.

m. Josephine B Diener. *Education:* Diploma Music, Nyack College, 1943; B Sacred Music, Eastern Baptist College, 1944; M Sacred Music, 1947, D Sacred Music, 1957, Union Theological Seminary; New York State Permanent Teachers Certificate in Music; Choirmaster Diploma, AGO; Summer workshops, Ball State University, The Orff Institute of the Salzburg Mozarteum, New College, Oxford University. *Career:* Organ concert tours of Europe have included appearances at international organ festivals at Aurich, Bonn, Bremen, Essen, Karlsruhe, Meldorf, Norden, Tholey (Germany), Fredrikstad, Toonsberg (Norway), Ribe (Denmark), Goteborg (Sweden), Salzburg (Austria), Basel (Switzerland); Formerly Visiting Professor of Music, The King's College, New York; Formerly Organist and Musical Director of St. Matthew's Lutheran Church, White Plains; Music and Book Reviewer for the American Organist. *Publications:* Editor, Free Harmonizations of Hymn Tunes, Volumes 1 and 2. *Hobbies:* Travelling. *Address:* Laurel Place 110, PO Box 125, Cornell, PA 17016-0125, USA.

WASSON Jeffrey, b. 24 Aug 1948, Illinois, USA. Musicologist. *Education:* BMus 1970, MMus 1973, PhD Music History and Literature, 1987, Northwestern University. *Career:* Instructor, 1980-85, Visiting Association, 1990, 1993, Northwestern University; Associate Professor of Music, Barat Col Lake Forest, Illinois, 1985-; Director of Music, St Mary of the Angels Church, Chicago, 1992-; Lecturer at Universities of Yale, Michigan, Minnesota, Michigan State and Nebraska. *Recordings:* Jacket annotations for HNH Records and Vanguard Records. *Publications include:* Editor, Essays in Honour of John F Ohl: A Compendium of American Musicology; Self Study Modules for History of Music in the Middle Ages and Renaissance; First Mode Gradual Salvum fac Servum: Modal practice reflected in a chant that begins on B-flat. *Honours:* Phi Kappa Lambda; Grants from Barat College and Northwestern University. *Memberships:* American Musicological Association; Medieval Academy of America; New Music Chicago, President, 1988-92. *Hobbies:* Collector of Fine art and Lionel electric trains. *Address:* 1500 Oak Avenue, Evanston, IL 60201, USA.

WATANABE Yoko, b. 1956, Fukuoka, Japan. Singer (Soprano). m. Renato Grimaldi. *Education:* Studied at the University of Tokyo. *Debut:* Treviso 1978, as Nedda in Pagliacci. *Career:* has sung in Turin, Naples, Genoa, Madrid, London, Hamburg, Stuttgart, Berlin and Pittsburgh, notably as Madama Butterfly; Further appearances in Cologne, Frankfurt, Strasbourg and Florence, as Micaela, Donna Elvira, Mimi, Liu and Suor Angelica; Los Angeles 1985; La Scala Milan 1985; Sang Liu in Turandot at Pittsburgh 1987, Margherita in Mefistofele at Zurich, 1988; Covent Garden debut 1989, as Butterfly (also at Boston and Santiago, 1990); Concert repertoire includes the Choral Symphony, and the Stabat Mater by Rossini; Sang in Tokyo 1986. *Address:* c/o Stafford Law Asociates, 26 Mayfield Road, Weybridge, Surrey KT13 8XB, England.

WATERHOUSE William, b. 18 Feb 1931, London, England. Bassoonist. *Education:* Studied at the Royal College of Music with Archie Camden. *Career:* Played first with the Philharmonia Orchestra; Royal Opera House Orchestra 1953-55; First bassoon, Italian-Swiss Radio Orchestra in Lugano, 1955-58; First bassoon, London Symphony Orchestra 1958, BBC Symphony 1964-82; Member of the Melos Ensemble from 1959; Tutor in Bassoon, Royal Northern College of Music from 1966, Fellow 1991; Hon Archivist, Galpin Society; Chairman of British Double Reed Society; Visiting Faculty at Indiana University, 1972, Melbourne 1983, Sarasota 1985, Banff 1987, Victoria 1988; Competition Juror at Munich, 1965, 1975, 1984, 1990, Prague 1986, Eindhoven 1988, Markneukirchen 1990; Member of Arts Council of GB Music Advisory Panel, 1983-85; 2nd Vice President of International Double Reed Society, 1987-91; Host of 18th Annual IDRS Conference, Manchester 1989; Tours of Europe and the USA with the Melos Ensemble; Many solo appearances; Dedicatee of works by Gordon Jacob, Jean Françaix, Elliott

Schwartz and other composers; Faculty Artist, New College Music Festival, US-Sarasota 1985, College of the Arts Banff, Canada, 1987. *Recordings:* Numerous with Melos Ensemble and various orchestras. *Publications:* Numerous editions of wind music; Translations; Articles for Grove's Dictionary; Bibliography of bassoon music, 1962; Joint Editor of Universal Bassoon Edition; The New Langwill Index: Dictionary of Historical Wind Instrument Makers & Inventors, 1993. *Memberships:* RMA; Galpin Society, AMIS, GeFAM, ISM. *Hobbies:* Swimming; Skiing; Travel. *Address:* 86 Cromwell Avenue, London N6 5HQ, England.

WATERMAN David Allen Woodrow, b. 24 Mar 1950, Leeds, England. Musician; Cellist. *Education:* MA, PhD in Philosophy, Trinity College, Cambridge; Musical Studies with Martin Lovett, William Pleeth, Jane Cowan and with Sandor Vegh, International Musicians Seminar. *Career:* Cellist, Endellion Quartet (founded 1979); Appearances at Kennedy Centre, Washington, Ambassadors Auditorium, Los Angeles, many times at London, Bath Festival, Concertgebouw, Amsterdam, Lucerne and Gstaad Festivals, Switzerland, Spoleto and Fiesole Festivals; South Bank Festival; City of London Festival; Aldeburgh Festival. Tours of USA, Australia, New Zealand and most major European centres and radio stations. Award-winning recording of Quartetto Intimo, John Foulds. *Recordings:* Complete Britten Chamber Music on EMI Label; Haydn, Mozart, Dvořák, Smetana, Bartók, Martinů, Walton and Frank Bridge for Virgin Classics. *Contributions to:* European String Teachers Association Magazine. *Honours:* 2nd Prize, Audience Prize, Portsmouth International String Quartet Competition 1979; 1st Prize, British National String Quartet Competition 1979; Winner, Young Concert Artists Awards, NY, USA 1981. *Current Management:* Hazard Chase Ltd, 25 City Road, Cambridge CB11 DP, England. *Hobbies:* Films; Reading; Dining with friends. *Address:* 27 Lancaster Grove, London NW3 4EX, England.

WATERMAN Fanny, b. 22 Mar 1920, Leeds, England. Chairman, Leeds International Pianoforte Competition; Chairman of Jury. m. Dr Geoffrey de Keyser, 1944. 2 sons. *Education:* Royal College of Music, London with Tobias Matthay, Cyril Smith; FRCM, 1972. *Career:* Concert pianist; Teacher of international reputation; Vice-President, European Piano-Teachers Association, 1975-; Trustee, Edward Boyle Memorial Trust, 1981-; Governor, Harrogate Fest, 1983; Founded (with Marion Harewood), 1961; Chairman 1963-, Chairman of Jury 1981-, Leeds International Pianoforte Competition; Member of International Juries in Austria, Italy, Germany, USA, Israel, Bulgaria, Portugal, former Soviet Union, Taiwan, Japan and China; Piano Progress series on ITV Channel 4. *Publications:* (with Marion Harewood): series of Piano Tutors 1967-; With Paul de Keyser, Young Violinists Repertoire books, 1984; Fanny Waterman on Piano Playing and Performing, 1983; Music Lovers Diary, 1984-86; Merry Christmas Carols, 1986; Christmas Carol Time, 1986; Nursery Rhyme Time, 1987; Piano for Pleasure Books 1-2, 1988; Me and My Piano - duets, Books 1 and 2, 1988; Playtime Studies and Progress Studies. *Honours:* OBE 1971; Hon.D Mus, Honoris causa, University of Leeds, 1992. *Hobbies:* Travel; Reading; Voluntary work; Cooking. *Address:* Woodgarth, Oakwood Grove, Leeds LS8 2PA, England.

WATERMAN Ruth Anna, b. 14 Feb 1947, Harrogate, Yorkshire. Violinist. *Education:* Juilliard School, NY; Royal Manchester College of Music. *Career:* Recitals and concertos throughout Europe and USA, Radio and television; Festivals include Aldeburgh, Harrogate, Montreux, Lyon, Stuttgart (Complete Bach sonatas) Madeira and York; Soloist with such orchestras as London Symphony, Royal Philharmonic, BBC Symphony, BBC Scottish, English Chamber, Orpheus Chamber. Televised Prom concert, 1969; International Artists Recital at Carnegie Recital Hall, 1974; Professor, Queen's College, CUNY; Faculty member, New York University, Royal Academy of Music. *Recordings:* J S

Bach complete sonatas with keyboard; Granados; Bach Brandenburg Concertos. *Publications:* Master Classes on Bach, reviews in The Strad Magazine. *Memberships:* International Bach Society. *Hobbies:* Photography; Table Tennis. *Current Management:* Del Rosenfield, NY. *Address:* c/o 714 Ladd Road, New York, NY 10471, USA.

WATERS Susannah, b. 1965, England. Singer (Soprano). *Education:* Studied at the Guildhall School of Music and Drama, graduated 1989. *Debut:* Sang Belinda in Dido and Aeneas at Symphony Place, New York, 1986. *Career:* The Princess in L'Enfant et les Sortilèges at the 1989 Aldeburgh Festival and Louise in a German production of Henze's The English Cat, directed by the composer; Season 1990-91, Nannetta in Falstaff with Scottish Opera, Papagena at Glyndebourne, Philine in Thomas' Mignon at the Vienna Volksoper and Cherubino for Opera Factory, London; Many recital and oratorio appearances; Season 1991-92, Despina (Così fan Tutte) and Zerlina (Don Giovanni) with Opera Factory London; Martha in Martha (Flotow) with Sarasota Opera, USA; 1st Niece (Peter Grimes) with Glyndebourne Festival Opera; Dorlinda (Orlando) with Musica nel Chiostro, Italy; 1992-93 Season, Gilda (Rigoletto) with Opera Northern Ireland; Pamina, (The Magic Flute) with Scottish Opera; Susanna (The Marriage of Figaro), Opera Factory London; Cunegonde (Candide) with Musica nel Chiostro, Botisano, Italy; 1993-94 Season, Fairy Godmother (Cendrillon) with Welsh National Opera; Dalinda (Ariodante), Welsh National Opera; Blonde (Abduction from the Seraglio) with Santa Fe Opera. *Current Management:* IMG Artists Europe, Tom Graham. *Address:* c/o 4 Tremadoc Road, London SW4 7NE, England.

WATERS Willie Anthony, b. 1952, Miami, Florida, USA. Conductor. *Education:* Studied at the University of Miami. *Career:* Assistant Conductor of the Memphis Opera 1973-75; Music assistant to Kurt Herbert Adler at San Francisco Opera, 1975-79; Music Director of the San Antonio Festival 1983-84; Artistic Director of the Greater Miami Opera, for whom he has conducted La Gioconda, L'Italiana in Algeri, Madama Butterfly, Ernani, 1984-85; Of Mice and Men (Floyd), Rigoletto, Cav and Pag, 1985-86; Salome, La Traviata, Hamlet, Aida 1986-87; Bellini's Bianca e Falliero, Tosca, Otello, 1987-88; Le Nozze di Figaro, Die Walküre, La Forza del Destino, 1988- 89; I Vespri Siciliani, Idomeneo, Elektra, 1989-90; Così fan Tutte and Falstaff 1990-91; Has also worked with the Detroit Symphony Orchestra, Fort Worth Opera, Miami City Ballet, Florida Symphony Orchestra, Cincinatti, Chautaqua and Connecticut Opera Companies; Australian Opera Sydney; Cologne Opera, Sudwestfunk Orchestra and Essen Philharmonic (debuts 1990-91); Susannah by Carlisle Floyd; engaged for 1991-93: Aida, Connecticut Opera; Greater Miami Opera; SWF Sinfonieorchester, Baden-Baden; Florida Philharmonic Orchestra; Macbeth, Charlotte Opera.

WATHEY Andrew Brian, b. 19 July 1958, Plymouth, England. Musicologist. *Education:* BA, St Edmund Hall, Oxford University, 1979; MA, 1983; DPhil, 1987. *Career:* Harmsworth Senior Scholar 1981, Fellow of Merton (Junior Research Fellow) 1982-85, Oxford University; Research Fellow, Downing College, Cambridge University, 1985-88; Visiting Professor, Keio University, Tokyo, Japan, 1987; Lecturer in Music, University of Lancaster, 1988-89; Lecturer in Music, RHBNC, University of London, 1989-. *Recording:* Broadcast Radio talks for BBC Radio 3. *Publication:* Music in the Royal and Noble Households in Late Medieval England, 1989. *Contributions:* Articles in various musicological and historical journals. *Honours:* J A Westrup prize, 1986; Fellow, Royal Historical Society, 1986-; Fellow, Society of Antiquaries, London 1989. *Memberships:* Royal Musical Association; American Musicological Society. *Address:* Department of Music, Royal Holloway and Bedford New College, Egham Hill, Egham, Surrey, TW20 0EX, England.

WATKINS Glenn, b. 30 May 1927, McPherson, Kansas, USA. Musicologist. *Education:* BA, 1948,

MMus, 1949, University of Michigan; PhD, University of Rochester, 1953; Diploma, American Conservatory, Fontainbleau, 1956. *Publications:* Gesualdo, Complete Works (co-editor), 1959-66; Gesualdo: The Man and His Music, 1973, 2nd edition, 1991; S.D'India, Complete Works (co-editor), 1980-; Soundings Music in 20th Century, 1988; Pyramids at the Louvre, 1994. *Honours:* Fulbright (England), 1953-54; National Book Award Nominee, 1974; Senior Fellow, National Endowment for the Humanities, 1976-77. *Address:* 1336 Glendaloch Circle, Ann Arbor, MI 48104, USA.

WATKINS Michael Blake, b. 4 May 1948, Ilford, Essex, England. Composer. m. Tessa Marion Fryer, 8 Feb 1975, 2 daughters. *Education:* Sibford School, Oxfordshire, 1959-64; Studied privately, guitar and lute with Michael Jessett, 1964-67, Composition with Elisabeth Lutyens, 1966-70, and Richard Rodney Bennett, 1970-75. *Career:* Appointed Fellow in Television Composition with London Weekend Television, 1981-83. *Compositions:* Orchestral Works: Clouds and Eclipses for guitar and strings, 1973; Aubade for brass band, 1973; Horn Concerto, 1974; Violin Concerto, 1977; Etalage for symphony orchestra, 1979; Trumpet Concerto, 1988; Cello Concerto, 1992; Chamber Works: The Wings of Night for solo violin, 1975; String Quartet, 1979; The Magic Shadow Show for cello and ensemble, 1980; Clarinet Quintet, 1984; Solus for guitar solo, 1975; The Spirit of the Earth for guitar solo, 1978; Somnial for guitar solo, 1968; All That We Read In Their Smiles for tenor, horn and piano, 1977; The Spirit of the Universe for soprano and ensemble, 1978; Sinfonietta for 12 instruments, 1982. *Recordings:* Trumpet Concerto (Philips CD); Håkan Hardenberger, BBC Philharmonic Orchestra, conducted by Elgar Howarth. *Publications:* Trumpet Concerto; Violin Concerto; The Wings of Night for solo violin; String Quartet; Solus for guitar solo; The Spirit of the Earth for guitar solo. *Honours:* Menuhin Prize, 1975; Carl Flesch Composition Prize, 1976; Guinness Prize, 1978. *Membership:* Association of Professional Composers. *Hobbies:* Cinema; Cooking. *Current Management:* Novello & Co, Publishers. *Address:* Acacia House, Uxbridge Road, Hillingdon, Middlesex, UB10 0LF, England.

WATKINS Sara Van Horn, b. 12 Oct 1945, Chicago, Illinois, USA. Oboist; Conductor. m. John Shirley-Quirk, 29 Dec 1981, 1 son, 2 daughters. *Education:* BMus, Oberlin Conservatory of Music, 1967; Studied with Ray Still, Marc Lifschey, Marcel Moyse; Fellowship student at Tanglewood Music Festival, 1967. *Career:* Principal Oboist, American National Opera Company, 1967; Honolulu Symphony Orchestra, 1969-73; National Symphony Orchestra, 1973-81; Professor of Oboe, University of Hawaii, 1969-73; Catholic University, 1973-81; Oberlin Conservatory, 1984; In residence, Scottish Academy of Music, 1985; Oboe Soloist, Conductor, 1981-; Oboe Soloist at Aldeburgh, Sofia, Spoleto Festivals, Vienna, The Hague, Moscow, Leningrad, London, Sao Paulo, New York and other major U S Cities; Recent conducting appearances in Glasgow, Cambridge, London Queen Elizabeth Hall, Britten-Pears School, Snape Maltings, Paris, New York Glimmerglass Opera. *Recordings:* Britten Chamber Music with John Shirley-Quirk, Osian Ellis, Philip Ledger on Meridian Compact Disc; Handel Cantatas, Arias and Sonatas with Yvonne Kenny, John Shirley-Quirk, Martin Isepp on Meridian Compact Disc. *Memberships:* Musicians Union of Chicago and London; Conductors Guild, USA.*Hobbies:* Yoga; Tennis. *Current Management:* Columbia Artists Management. *Address:* 51 Wellesley Road, Twickenham, Middlesex TW2 5RX, England.

WATKINSON Carolyn, b. 19 Mar 1949, Preston, Lancashire, England. Singer (Mezzo-Soprano). *Education:* Royal Manchester College of Music; Muzieklyceum, The Hague, Holland. *Career:* Early specialization in Baroque music, and sang with Syntagama Musicum, the Grande Ecurie de la Chambre du Roi, with Jean-Claude Malgoire and the Gächinger Kantorei, under Helmuth Rilling; Sang Phèdre in

Hippolyte et Aricie at Covent Garden and Versailles 1978, English Bach Festival; Nero in L'Incoronazione di Poppea with Netherlands Opera 1979; 1980 sang as guest in Stuttgart as Rossini's Rosina and at Ludwigsburg as Mozart's Cherubino; 1981 as Handel's Ariodante at La Scala, Milan; 1982 Edinburgh Festival, Ariodante; Glyndebourne Festival debut 1984, as Cherubino: returned as Cenerentola; Aix-en-Provence debut 1985, as the Messenger in Monteverdi's Orfeo; Concerts include Mahler's 3rd and 8th Symphonies, conducted by Haitink, and appearances with the Royal Liverpool Philharmonic, BBC Symphony, Scottish Chamber and National Orchestras and the Philharmonia; Sang with the Boston Symphony at Tanglewood, 1985; Engagements in Paris, Vienna, San Francisco, Washington, Madrid and Barcelona; Toured Australia 1987 and appeared at the Sydney Opera House; Sang in Gloucester Cathedral performance of the St John Passion, shown by BBC TV on Good Friday 1989; Sang Nero in L'Incoronazione di Poppea at Montpellier, 1989; Purcell's Dido conducted by John Eliot Gardiner at Salerno Cathedral, 1990; Nero at the 1990 Innsbruck Festival. *Recordings:* Handel's Messiah (Hogwood), Rinaldo and Xerxes; Solomon (Gardiner); Mozart's Requiem; Bach's B Minor Mass (Schreier) and St Matthew Passion; Solo album recorded live at her debut Wigmore Hall recital in London. *Address:* c/o Lies Askonas Ltd., 186 Drury Lane, WC2B 5RY, England.

WATSON Elizabeth, b. 1933, Nottingham, England. Viola player; Teacher. *Education:* ARCM, studied with Frederick Riddle, Keith Cummings, Manoug Parikian, Sandor Vegh, Eduard Melkus. *Debut:* Wigmore Hall with Andrew Davis. *Career:* Freelance Viola, Viola D'Amore and baroque/classical player; Concetos, sonatas and chamber orchestras, often as principal; chamber music; String quartet Tutor, The City Lit, London; Teacher, Centre for Young Musicians (formerly Westminister School); Adjudicator and coach, Guildhall and Birmingham Schools of Music. *Recordings:* Many as member of Academy of St Martin in the Fields and Philharmonic Orchestra; Viola D'Amore soloist in Telemann Triple Concerto recording with London Harpsichord Ensemble. *Publications:* Chapter in Choose Your Instrument, 1979. *Honours:* RCM Viola Gradd V Prize, 1954; Lionel Tertis Open Competition, 1954. *Memberships:* ISM; ESTA; MU; Barnes and Castelnau Music Society (Hon Recitals Secretary, 1987-88); Viola D'Amore Society of America. *Address:* 3 Ormonde Road, London SW14 7BE, England.

WATSON Janice, b. 1964, England. Singer (Soprano). *Education:* Studied at the Guildhall School, further study with Johanna Peters. *Career:* Concert repertory has included the Four Last Songs of Strauss, Stravinsky's Pulcinella, Les Nuits d'été by Berlioz, Mahler's 4th Symphony and Berio's Sinfonia (Barbican Hall, London); Has sung the Brahms Requiem with Dulwich Choral Society, Haydn's Nelson Mass and Seasons at the Usher Hall, Edinburgh; Bach's Magnificat, Christmas Oratorio and St Mark Passion on South Bank; Britten's Les Illuminations at Salisbury Cathedral; Elgar's The Spirit of England with the Hallé Orchestra; Messiah in St Albans's Cathedral and Beethoven's Missa Solemnis with the Chichester Singers; Hummel's E flat Mass and Schubert's Stabat Mater at the Elizabeth Hall; Mendelssohn's Elijah with the Bristol Bach Choir; Further repertory includes Handel's Saul, Mendelssohn's Hymn of Praise (2nd Symphony), Vaughan Williams Pastoral Symphony and Beethoven's Mass in C (Barcelona Palace of Music); Recitals with the Songmakers' Almanac and in the crush bar at Covent Garden; Opera engagements at Glyndebourne, in Moneverdi's L'Incoronazione di Poppea at the City of London Festival and Musetta in La Bohème at Covent Garden (1990); with Welsh National Opera has sung Musetta, Fiordiligi, Micaela, Adèle in Le Comte Ory, Pamina and Rosalinde (Die Fledermaus); US and Canadian debuts in Messiah, conducted by Trevor Pinnock, 1990; Eugene Onegin for Welsh National Opera and recently Lucia de Lammermoor, Daphne for San Francisco Opera and Daphne in The London Promenade Concertos, Les illuminations by Benjamin Britten in The Proms,

Messiah at the Barbican with Richard Hickox. *Address:* c/o Ron Gonsalves Ltd., 10 Dagnam Road, London SW12 9LQ, England.

WATSON Lillian, b. 4 Dec 1947, London, England. Singer (Soprano). *Education:* Studied at the Guildhall School of Music and the London Opera Centre. *Career:* Sang first at the Wexford Festival, then with the Welsh National Opera; Glyndebourne from 1976, as Susanna, Despina, Sophie, Titania in A Midsummer Night's Dream and Blondchen (1988); Covent Garden debut 1981: appearances in Die Entführung, Der Rosenkavalier, and Arabella; Guest engagements with English National Opera and Scottish Opera and in Munich, Paris, Rouen, Marseilles and Bordeaux; Salzburg Festival 1982, as Marzelline in Fidelio; Vienna Staatsoper in Così fan Tutte and Le Nozze di Figaro; Sang Strauss's Sophie at the Théâtre des Champs-Eysées, 1989; Norina in Don Pasquale at Amsterdam; title role in The Cunning Little Vixen at Covent Garden, 1990; Sadler's Wells Theatre, 1990, as Britten's Tytania; TV engagements in Don Pasquale and Orpheus in the Underworld. *Recordings:* Carmen (HMV); Le Nozze di Figaro (Philips); Monteverdi Madrigals and Handel's Israel in Egypt (Argo); Die Entführung aus dem Serail (Telefunken); The Cunning Little Vixen, (EMI). *Address:* c/o Harrison/Parrott Ltd., 12 Penzance Place, London W11 4PA, England.

WATTS André, b. 20 June 1946, Nuremberg, Germany. Pianist. *Education:* Studied with Genia Robiner, Doris Bawden and Clement Petrillo, Philadelphia Musical Academy; Artist's Diploma, Peabody Conservatory of Music, Baltimore, 1972 and with Leon Fleisher. *Debut:* Soloist, Haydn's Concerto in D Major, Philadelphia Orchestra Children's Concert, 1955. *Career:* Soloist, Franck's Symphonic Variations, Philadelphia Orchestra, 1960; Soloist, Liszt's Concerto No 1, with Bernstein and New York Philharmonic Orchestra, 1963; European debut, London Symphony Orchestra, 1966; New York recital debut, 1966; World tour, 1967; First pianist to play a recital on live network television in USA, New York, 1976; Celebrated 25th anniversary of debut as soloist with New York Philharmonic Orchestra, Liszt Concerto No 1, The Beethoven Concerto No 2 and Rachmaninoff Concerto No 2 telecast live nationwide, 1988. *Recordings:* For Angel-EMI; CBS. *Honours:* Honorary Doctorates from: Yale University, 1973; Albright College, 1975; Film documentary of Career; Avery Fisher Prize, 1988. *Address:* c/o Columbia Artists Management Inc, 165 West 57th Street, New York, NY 10019, USA.

WATTS Helen, b. 9 Dec 1927, Milford Haven, Wales. Singer (Contralto). *Education:* Studied at the Royal Academy of Music with Caroline Hatchard and Frederick Jackson. *Career:* Sang in the BBC Chorus; Solo engagements from 1953, including Gluck's Orpheus; Promenade Concerts 1955, singing Bach Arias with Malcolm Sargent; sang with Handel Opera Society from 1958, as Didymus in Theodora, Ino and Juno in Semele and Rinaldo; Toured with the English Opera Group to Russia 1964, performing Britten's Lucretia under the composer; Covent Garden 1965-71, as First Norn in Götterdämmerung, Erda and Sosostris in The Midsummer Marriage; Welsh National Opera 1969, as Mistress Quickly; US debut New York Philharmonic Hall 1966, in A Mass of Life, by Delius; Carngie Hall 1970, in Kindertotenlieder by Mahler with the Chicago Symphony under Solti; Repertoire included music by Strauss, Schoenberg, Stravinsky, Mendelssohn, Elgar and Berlioz. *Recordings:* Handel's Sosarme and Semele (L'Oiseau Lyre); Bach B Minor Mass, First Norn in Götterdämmerung, A Midsummer Night's Dream, Béatrice et Bénédict (Decca); Messiah; St Matthew Passion; The Apostles by Elgar (EMI); Handel's Samson (Erato). *Honours include:* Commander of the British Empire 1978. *Address:* c/o Harold Holt Ltd., 31 Sinclair Road, London W14 ONS, England.

WAYENBERG Daniel (Ernest Joseph Carel), b. 11 Oct 1929, Paris, France. Pianist; Composer. *Education:* Studied with mother, and with Marguerite Long. *Career:* Played in private houses 1939-46; Public debut Paris 1949; Opening recital of the Chopin Centenary Festival, Florence 1949; Besançon Festival 1951; US debut Carnegie Hall 1953, conducted by Mitorpoulos; Numerous concerto appearances throughout the world (tours of USA and Indonesia 1955); repertoire centres on 19th century classics but also plays Haydn and Stockhausen; Teacher at Conservatory of Rotterdam. *Compositions:* Ballet Solstice 1955; Sonata for violin and piano; Concerto for 5 wind instruments and orchestra; Capella, symphony; Concerto for 3 pianos and orchestra 1975. *Recordings:* Numerous concertos including Brahms, Tchaikovsky, Beethoven, Gershwin and Rachmaninov. *Hobbies:* Computer Chess; Building miniature railways; Swimming. *Current Management:* Concert Director, Samama 8C, Netherlands. *Address:* 17 rue Thibault, 94520 Mandres-Les Roses, France.

WAYNE William Hayden, b. 2 Mar 1949, New York, USA. Composer; Librettist. m. Yitka Zajacova, 13 Sept 1989. *Education:* Studied piano, keyboard harmony, orchestration, vocal technique and clarinet with teachers including Philip Wayne, Tony Aless, Larry Wilcox, Hank Freeman and Dan Merriman. *Compositions:* The Symphony of Friends; Symphony No 2, Reggae; Symphony No 3, Heavy Metal; Symphony No 4, Funk; Symphony No 5, Africa; Fanfare: Winterfest; Capriccio; Fantasy; Adagio; Neon (a street opera); Cirgne de la Lune; Dracula (opera erotica); In Memoriam: a celebration, chorus and orchestra, (world premiere November 1993). *Recordings:* Symphony No 4 and No 5, State Philharmonic of Brno, The Czech Republic. *Honours:* First Prize, National Institute for Music Theatre, 1987; New York State Music Award, 1966. *Memberships:* Musician's Union; ASCAP; SAG; AFTRA. *Address:* 21 W 86 Street, Suite 807, New York, NY 10024, USA.

WEALE Malcolm Angus, b. 11 Mar 1947, London, England. Professor of Music. m. Janet Kerr Corbett, 27 Mar 1971, 2 daughters. *Education:* Graduate 1968, Licentiate (Trumpet), Royal Academy of Music; Licentiate (Trumpet), Guildhall School of Music; Associate (Pianoforte), London College of Music. *Debut:* London Symphony Orchestra, 1968. *Career:* Principal trumpet, Bolshoi & Kirov Ballet Companies UK tour 1969, Bournemouth Symphony & Sinfonietta Orchestras 1969-81; Appearances, British & German television (Music in Camera series), BBC Radio 3 (soloist & performer); Conductor, adjudicator, teacher, lecturer, Bournemouth & Poole College of Further Education & Crickland College, Andover; Professor of Music, Ministry of Defence, 1983-; Examiner, Associated Board, Royal Schools of Music. *Recordings:* Manfredini Double Trumpet Concerto, 1979; Bournemouth Symphony; Bournemouth Sinfonietta; London Symphony Orchestra, Scottish National Orchestra. *Contributions to:* Music Lover's Guide to Instruments of the Orchestra; British Musical Directory; Music & Musicians (biographies). *Membership:* Incorporated Society of Musicians. *Hobbies:* Travel; Sport; Reading. *Address:* 73 Beaufoys Avenue, Ferndown, Wimborne, Dorset BH22 9RN, England.

WEATHERS Felicia, b. 13 Aug 1937, St Louis, Missouri, USA. Singer (Soprano). *Education:* Studied at Lincoln University in Jefferson City; Indoana University with Frank St Leger; Further study with Charles Kullman and Dorothea Manski. *Career:* Sang in Kansas City, Chicago and Detroit; Kiel Opera, Germany, from 1961; Member of the Hamburg Staatsoper 1963-70; Metropolitan Opera debut 1965, as Lisa in The Queen of Spades; Lisbon 1968; Chicago Lyric Opera 1968, as Salome; Appearances in Sweden, Yugoslavia, Germany and North America; Other roles included Aida the Trovatore Leonora, Tosca and Adriana Lecouvreur; Often heard in Negro Spirituals. *Address:* c/o Hamburgische Staatsoper, Grosse Theaterstrasse 34, D-2000 Hamburg 36, Germany.

WEAVER James (Merle), b. 25 Sept 1937, Champaign, Illinois, USA. Harpsichordist; Pianist; Fortepianist; Teacher. *Education:* BA 1961, MM 1963, University of Illinois, Urbana-Champaign; Studied with

Gustav Leonhardt, Sweelinck Conservatory, Amsterdam, 1957-59. *Career:* Many appearances as keyboard artist; Curator of historic instruments, Smithsonian Institution, Washington, DC, 1967; Co-founder, Smithsonian Chamber Players, 1976; Teacher, Cornell University; American Unviersity; Various master classes in 18th-century performance practice. *Recordings:* For Cambridge; Nonesuch; Smithsonian Collection. *Address:* c/o Smithsonian Chamber Players, Smithsonian Institution, Washington, DC 20560, USA.

WEAVING John Weymouth, b. 23 Feb 1936, Melbourne, Australia. Singer (Tenor). *Education:* Studied with Browning Mummery in Melbourne; Audrey Langford in London; Ken Neate in Munich. *Debut:* Sadler's Wells 1960, as Eisenstein in Die Fledermaus. *Career:* Has sung in operas by Wagner with the English National Opera; Engagements at opera houses in Kiel, Essen, Hanover, Lyon, Wiesbaden and Munich; Other roles include Florestan, Huon (Oberon), Alvaro (La Forza del Destino), Otello, Don José, Bacchus, Herman (The Queen of Spades) and Sali (A Village Romeo and Juliet); Many concert appearances. *Address:* c/o English National Opera, St Martin's Lane, London WC2, England.

WEBER Margit, b. 24 Feb 1924, Ebnat-Kappel, St Gallen, Switzerland. Pianist. *Education:* Studied the organ with Heinrich Funk in Zurich and the piano with Max Egger and Walter Lang at the Zurich Conservatory. *Career:* Frequent concert tours of the USA and Europe; Festival appearances at Lucerne, Munich, Venice, Berlin and Vienna; Has given the premieres of Martinů's Fantasia Concertante, 1958, Stravinsky's Movements, 1960, Tcherepnin's Bagatelles and 5th Piano Concerto; Moeschinger's Piano Concerto, 1962; Schibler's Ballade for piano and strings, 1964; Fortner's Epigrams for piano, 1964; Vogel's Horformen for piano and strings, 1972; Concert class at the Zurich Musikhochschule from 1971. *Recordings include:* Mozart Concerto K414 conducted by Baumgartner; Nights in the Gardens of Spain, Franck Symphonic Variations, Weber's Konzertstück, Stravinsky's Movements with the Berlin Radio Symphony Orchestra conducted by Fricsay (Deutsche Grammophon). *Honour:* Hans Georg Nägeli Medal of Zurich, 1971.

WEBER Peter, b. 1955, Vienna, Austria. Singer (Baritone). *Education:* Diploma, Hochschule für Musik, Vienna. *Career:* Engaged by the Studio of the Vienna Staatsoper, 1976; Member of ensemble of the Vienna Staatsoper 1978; Engaged at the Nuremberg Opera 1980, Hanover Staatsoper 1982; Regular appearances at the Salzburg Festival and the Vienna Festwochen from 1977; Glyndebourne Festival 1985-89, as Mandryka (Arabella) and Olivier (Capriccio); Debut at the Teatro Colón Buenos Aires 1986, as Mozart's Count; Debuts at the Teatro Liceo Barcelona and the Teatro dell'Opera Rome 1988; Guest engagements in Hamburg, Dusseldorf, Geneva, Paris and Milan; Sang Mandryka at Covent Garden 1990; USA debut as Amonasro, Dallas Opera, 1991; contracted to Vienna State Opera, 1992; Other roles include Silvio, Sharpless, Malatesta, Falke and the Secretary in Der junge Lord by Henze, Don Giovanni, Don Alfonso, Telramund, Pizarro, Amfortas, Eisenstein, Onegin; Debuts as Wagner's Gunther and Strauss's Barak at Hanover, 1993; Concerts and recitals in Europe and the United States; Radio and television appearances. *Recordings:* Ariadne auf Naxos and Un Ballo in Maschera (Decca); Die Frau ohne Schatten (Deutsche Grammophon); Die Zauberflöte (RCA); Schoeck Penthesilea (Atlantis); Schubert Alfonso und Estrella and Haydn Die Feuerbrunst (Pan). *Honours:* Prize winner, Hugo Wolf Competition, Salzburg 1976; Interpretation Prize from the Mozartgemeinde Vienna 1976; International Schubert-Wolf Competition, Vienna 1978. *Address:* c/o Vienna State Opera, Ringstrasse, Vienna, Austria.

WEBSTER Beveridge, b. 30 May 1908, Pittsburgh, USA. Pianist. *Education:* Studied at the Pittsburgh Conservatory and with Isidor Philipp at the Paris Conservatoire; Graduated 1926; Further study with Artur Schnabel. *Career:* Many solo orchestral and recital engagements in USA and abroad; Associated with Ravel and performed Tzigane 1924; US debut 1934, in MacDowell's 2nd Concerto with the New York Philharmonic; Many appearances with Curtis, Juilliard, Kolisch, Fine Arts and Pro Arte String Quartets; Often heard in modern American music and works by Debussy and Ravel; Jury member for numerous important competitions and awards; Lecture-concerts, master classes, at leading colleges and universities throughout USA; Taught at New England Conservatory 1940-46; Professor of Piano at Juilliard School from 1946; Music Editing for International Music Co.; Gave recital at Juilliard 1978, to celebrate 70th Birthday. *Recordings:* For MGM, Dover, Columbia, Desto, Helidor. *Honours:* First Prize in Piano at the Paris Conservatoire; NAAAC Award for Outstanding Services to American Music; Honorary DMUs University of New Hampshire 1962. *Membership:* National Society of Literature and Arts, 1975-. *Address:* Juilliard School of Music, Piano Faculty, Lincoln Center Plaza, New York, NY 10023, USA.

WEBSTER Gerald Best, b. 6 Jan 1944, Antioch, California, USA. Professor; Professional Musician. 1 son. *Education:* BME, MM, Indiana University. Additional study at University of the Pacific; Private Trumpet Study with Herbert Mueller, Gordon Finlay, Raymond Crisara. *Career:* Member of New York Brass Sextet; Edward J Tarr Brass Ensemble; USMA Band at West Point; Hudson Valley Philharmonic; Spokane Symphony; Spokane Chamber Orchestra; Washington State Brass Sextet; Musical/Artistic Director for World's Fair, Expo 1974; Soloist with numerous orchestras; Recitals throughout United States and Europe. *Recordings:* East German Radio and Television; Southwest German Radio; Northwest German Radio. *Publications:* Method for Piccolo Trumpet, 1980, Volume II, 1987; Concert Duets for Piccolo Trumpet, submitted; English Translation of Methode pour la Trompette by Dauverne, submitted. *Contributions to:* Articles for Voice; Article for the Instrumentalist. *Honour:* Ford Foundation Grant. *Memberships:* ITG; MENC; Phi Kappa Lambda; The Musician's Union. *Hobby:* Windsurfing. *Address:* NW 340 Larry Street, Pullman, WA 99163, USA.

WEBSTER Gillian, b. 2 May 1964, Scotland. Singer (Soprano). *Education:* Studied at the Royal Northern College of Music (graduated 1987) and the National Opera Studio. *Career:* Appearances with the English Bach Festival, Scottish Opera, Glyndebourne Festival and English National Opera; Roles include Micaela, Pamina, Agilea (Handel's Teseo) and Ilia in Idomeneo; Sang Klin (debut) in The Making of the Representative from Planet 8 by Philip Glass, for ENO; Covent Garden from 1988 as Servilia in La Clemenza di Tito and in Rigoletto, Peter Grimes, Médée, Elektra and Prince Igor; Other Royal Opera roles include Micaela and Euridice; Sang Micaela with Welsh National Opera 1990; television appearances include Gluck's Euridice (Covent Garden). *Honours include:* John Noble Award from Scottish Opera, 1986. *Address:* c/o Athole Still Ltd., Greystoke House, 80-86 Westow Street, London SE19 3AF, England.

WECHSLER Bert, b. 18 Aug 1933, New York City, New York, USA. Editor; Critic; Writer. m. (1) Sally Sears Thayer, 17 May 1960, (2) Helle Janne Hansen, 7 Jan 1971. *Education:* BA, Queens College, New York City, 1954; Music, New York and Frankfurt/Main, Germany. *Debut:* Kennebunkport, Maine, 1952. *Career:* Actor; Singer; Producer: Co-Founder, Manhattan Festival Ballet; Center for Contemporary Opera; Dance Focus. *Publications:* Editor, Music Journal Magazine, 1979-87; Paganiniana Pub, 1983, Music and Dance Critic for over 40 US, European and Japanese publications. *Honours:* Honorary Life Member, New York Mahlerites. *Memberships:* The Bohemians (New York Music Club); Music Critics Assocation of North America; Outer Critics Circle; Foreign Press Association, Executive Committee; Four Performing Unions. *Hobby:* Travel. *Address:* 215 East 80 Street, New York, NY 10021, USA.

WEDDINGTON Maurice Henry, b. 16 May 1941, Chicago, Illinois, USA. Composer. m. Ute Pox, 28 Oct 1978 (div). *Education:* Studied at Woodrow Wilson City college and American Conservatory of Music. *Debut:* Copenhagen, Denmark, 1963. *Career:* Numerous performances world wide; Composition in honour of George Rickey, 1977; Het Rijnmond Saxofoon Kwartet, Holland, 1978; Het Nederlands Klarinetkwarte, 1979; Stockton Symphony Orchestra, California, 1982; Commission from the ity of Berlin, 1989; Composer-in- Residence, Djerassi Foundation, California, 1985; Radio broadcasts. *Compositions include:* Stardrive, orchestra; Seul, bass clarinet; Forever present, 16 woodwinds; Fire in the Lake II, saxophone quartet; Fire in the Lake I, concerto for bass clarinet and orchestra; Isola, clarinet quartet; Midnight, orchestra and Narrator; Fire in the Lake III, concerto for symphony orchestra; Nearness, flute, oboe, bass clarinet and orchestra; Deovolente, flute; Daybreak, orchestra. *Honours include:* International Gaudeamus Composer Competition, Holland, 1971-73; Grant, German Academic Exchange Service, 1975; Fellow, Salzburg Seminar on Contemporary American Music, 1976; Prize, 4th International Composers Seminar of the Boswil Foundation, Switzerland, 1976; Danish States Art Fund Grants, 1976-78. *Memberships:* Gesellschaft fur Musikalische Auffuhrungs aund Mechanische Vervielfaltigungsrechte, 1978-; International Society for Contemporary Music, German Section, 1979-. *Address:* Lorenzstrasse 9, D-12209 Berlin, Germany.

WEGELIN Arthur Willem, b. 5 Mar 1908, Nijmegen, Netherlands. Violin Teacher; Chamber Music Player; Orchestral Violinist; Composer; Theorist; Educator; Director of Conservatory of Music; Professor and Head of Music Department; Researcher. m. (1) Sophia Betsy Hiebendaal, (2) Wytske Johanna Zoetelief Tromp, 1 son, 1 daughter. *Education:* BMus, MMus UNISA, Pretoria; FTCL. *Career:* In Holland: Violinist, Utrechtsch Stedelijk Orchestra, various chamber orchestras and violin teacher; In RSA: Lecturer, Potchefstroom University; Director and Founder, Conservatoire and Department of Music, University Port Elizabeth; Senior Research Officer, Human Sciences Research Council, subject Musical Aptitude Tests; National President SA Society Music Teachers, 1969-71; Mentioned on five pages biography in SA Music Encyclopedia. *Compositions include:* Works for piano, for violin, for organ, for windwood, for choir unaccompanied and with orchestra, for voice and orchestra, for string orchestra and symphony orchestra, Violin Concerto, Harp Concerto, Lieder, Sonatas, Piano Trios, String Quartets, Wind Quartet and educational series; Old Man's Diary I, II, III; Numerous commissions. *Publications:* Gevorderde Harmonie, 1968; Junior and Senior Musical Aptitude Tests, 1977. *Contributions to:* Newspapers; Journals; Encyclopedia. *Memberships:* Number of professional organizations. *Hobby:* Poetry. *Address:* Zoetelief, Kruinsingel, Montagu 6720, South Africa.

WEGG S James, b. 3 June 1952, Toronto, Ontario, Canada. Conductor. m. Mary Alice Baerg, 2 Aug 1974, 1 son, 1 daughter. *Education:* BMus Clarinet and Composition, University of Ottawa, 1975; MFA Conducting, Carnegie-Mellon University, Pittsburgh, USA, 1980. *Debut:* Ottawa, Canada, 1974. *Career:* Music Director, Nepean Symphony, Nepean, Ontario, 1974-; Music Director, Deep River Symphony, 1974-78 and 1981-; Music Director, Deep River Festival, 1986-; Guest Conductor, Charlottetown, Fredericton, Peterborough, Pittsburgh; Music Director, Canadian Composers Forum, premiered over 40 new works, 1984-. *Honour:* 1st Prize, Heinz Unger Conducting Competition, 1982. *Membership:* Chairman Conductors Committee, Ontario Federation of Orchestras. *Address:* c/o Nepean Symphony Orchestra, 25 Esquimault Avenue, Nepean, Ontario K2H 6Z5, Canada.

WEHOFSCHITZ Kurt, b. 3 May 1923, Vienna, Austria. Singer (Tenor). *Education:* Studied at the Vienna Music Academy. *Debut:* Linz 1948, as Wilhelm Meister. *Career:* Sang at Kiel 1953-44, Munich 1956- 59, notably as Ulrich Greiner-Mars in the premiere of Hindemith's

Harmonie der Welt, 1957; Sang at Dusseldorf 1959-64, Frankfurt 1964-66, notably in The Photo of the Colonel by Humphrey Searle; Dusseldorf 1960, in the German premiere of Edipo Re by Enescu, as Creon; Guest appearances at Zurich, Lisbon, Rio de Janeiro and the Vienna Staatsoper; sang at the Vienna Volksoper until 1980; Other roles have included Mozart's Belmont and Basilio, Leandro in Haydn's Mondo della Luna, Strauss's Leukippos and Flamand, Alfredo Germont, Don Carlos, Riccardo and Tom Rakewell. *Recordings include:* Carmen. *Address:* c/o Volksoper, Wahringerstrasse 78, A-1090 Vienna, Austria.

WEICH-SHAHAK Susana, b. 5 June 1938, Buenos Aires, Argentina, Musicologist. m. (1) Henry Weich, 25 Jan 1958, 1 son, 2 daughters. (2) Yeheskel Shahak, 29 Sept 1976, (dec). *Education:* PhD, Musicology, Tel Aviv University, Israel. *Career:* Research on the Judeo-Spanish repertory, Jewish Music Research Centre, Hebrew University, Jerusalem, Israel, 1973-; Ethnomusicological fieldwork among Yagua, Campa, Mashco and Orejon tribes of Forest Aborigines, Peru; Radio programmes on Sephardic Heritage and South American Folklore; Inspector of Musical Education, Tel Aviv Area School System. *Recordings:* Sephardic Songs of the Balkans, in series of Anthology of Jewish Musical Traditions, Jerusalem, Music Research Centre, Hebrew University, 1982. *Publications:* Anthology of Judeo-Spanish Moroccan Songs for the Life Cycle; The Music of Four Indian Tribes of the Peruvian Forest: Yagua, Campa, Mashco and Orejon (thesis), 1986; Judeo-Spanish Moroccan Songs for the Life Cycle, 1989; Buquieto de romances y coplas, 1991; Cantares y romances tradicionales sefardíes de Marruecos, 1991; Musical y tradiciones sefardíes, 1992. *Contributions to:* Structural Phenomena in the Wedding Songs of the Bulgarian Sephardic Jews, in The Sephardic and Oriental Jewish Heritage, 1982; Towards a study of the Linguistic Features of the Judeo-Spanish Romances: A Preliminary Appraisal, in Judeo-Romance Languages, 1985; The Spanish and the Sephardic Romances: Musical Links (with J.Etzion), in Ethnomusicology. *Memberships:* International Musicological Society; International Society for Music Education. *Hobbies:* Modern dance; Spanish dance (flamenco). *Address:* Shalom Ash 10, Tel Aviv, Israel.

WEIDENAAR Reynold Henry, b. 25 Sept 1945, East Grand Rapids, Michigan, USA. Composer; Video Artist. *Education:* BMus, Composition, Cleveland Institute of Music, 1973; MA, 1980, PhD, 1989, Composition, 1989, New York University; Studied Composition with Donald Erb & Brian Fennelly. *Compositions:* Between the Motion & the Act Falls the Shadow: Love of Line, of Light & Shadow; The Brooklyn Bridge; The Stillness; Night Flame Ritual; The Thundering Scream of the Seraphim's Delight; Long River, 1993. *Recordings:* The Tinsel Chicken Coop, Crystal Records, 1978; The Tinsel Chicken Coop, Wiener, Advance Recordings, 1982; Twilight Flight, Harmony, Imprint: Footfalls to Return, Night Flame Ritual, Capstone Records, 1986. *Publication:* Magic Music from the Telharmonium: The Central Station for Electrical Music, 1893-1918, 1994. *Contributions to:* New Music America: A Moveable Fest, The Independent, 1984; Down Memory Lane: Forerunners of Music & the Moving Image, & So You Want to Compose for the Moving Image, Ear Magazine, 1985; Live Music & Moving Images: Composing & Producting the Concert Video, Perspectives of New Music, 1986; The Alternators of the Telharmonium, 1906, Proceedings of the International Computer Music Conference, 1991; Editor: Sci Online News, 1993. *Hobbies:* Jogging; Cooking. *Address:* William Paterson College, Department of Communication, Wayne, NJ 07470, USA.

WEIDINGER Christine, b. 31 Mar 1946, Springville, New York, USA. Opera Singer (Dramatic Coloratura). m. Kenneth Smith, 7 July 1976. *Education:* BA, Music, Grand Canyon College, Phoenix; Singing with Marlene Delavan, Phoenix, 1967-70; Adrian de Peyer, Wuppertal, BRD, Dean Verhines, Los Angeles. *Debut:* Musetta in Bohème, Metropolitan, 1972. *Career:*

Metropolitan Opera, 1972-76; Stuttgart and Bielefeld Operas, West Germany, 1981-; Guest artist, La Scala, State Opera, Vienna; Barcelona; Venice; Bologna; West Berlin and others. Regular guest in Marseille; Specialist for bel-canto roles of Bellini and Donizetti; Interpreter of Constanze (Abduction from the Seraglio). Repertoire: Norma; Donna Anna; Electra (Idomeneo); Queen Elizabeth (Roberto Devereux); Amina (Sonnambula); Beatrice di Tenda; Gilda; Leonora (Trovatore); Mimi; Liu; Butterfly; Sang Constanze at Monte Carlo 1988, Adèle in Le Comte Ory at Montreal 1989; Vitellia in La Clemenza di Tito at La Scala, 1990; Cincinnati Opera 1990, as Lucia di Lammermoor; Violetta for San Diego Opera, 1991. Recordings: Handel's Rinaldo, with Marilyn Horne; L'Africaine, with Caballé and Domingo; Die Freunde von Salamanka (Schubert); Medea with Caballé and Lima; Mitridate (Mozart). Honour: National First Prize, Metropolitan Opera Auditions, 1972. Hobbies: Yoga; Jogging; Electric trains. Current Management: Robert Lombardo Associates. Address: c/o Robert Lombardo, 1 Harkness Plaza, 61 W 62nd St Suite 6F, New York 10023, USA.

WEIGEL Wolfgang Friedrich Joschka, b. 27 Jan 1954, Saarbrucken, Germany. m. Brigitte, 1 son, 1 daughter. Education: Music Academies of Saarbrucken and Lubeck; Private studies with Karl Scheit in Vienna. Career: Solo recitals with orchestras and chamber music throughout Europe and the USA; Appearances in major festivals including Prague Spring, Zurich, Phonix, Bremen, and Paris. Recordings: Spanish contemporary music, 1991; Contemporari Spanish music for guitar and string orchestra, 1992; Contemporary music for two guitars, 1992; Concertos for guitar and orchestra, 1993. Honours: Stipendium from the German Music Council. Hobbies: Litearture; Film; Art; Travel; Wine and Cooking. Current Management: Euro Concert H&W Walschburger. Address: Boningweg 33, D-29614 Soltau, Germany.

WEIGLE Jorg-Peter, b. 1953, Greifswald, Germany. Conductor. Education: Studied at the Thomasschule, Leipzig 1963-71; Hochschule fur Musik East Berlin from 1973. Career: First kapellmeister at the State Symphony Orchestra of Neubrandenburg 1978-80; Conductor of the Leipzig Radio Chorus 1980; Currently Chief Conductor of the Dresden Philharmonic Orchestra; Repertoire has included Bach's Christmas Oratorio, St John Passion and B minor Mass; Symphonies by Beethoven, Haydn, Mozart, Shostakovich and Schubert; Janáček's Sinfonietta; Season 1990/91 included Mahler Das Klagende Lied; Haydn 92 Symphony; Mozart Requiem and Concertante K364; Sibelius Symphonies 2, 3 and 7; Brahms 2 Symphony and D minor Concerto; Berg Violin Concerto; Concert performance of Meyerbeer's Il Crociato in Egitto to celebrate the bicentenary of the composer's birth; Visited Wales and the West Country with the Dresden Philharmonic 1989, with works by Beethoven (7th Symphony), Brahms, Weber and Tchaikovsky; Hamburg and Spain 1989; Czechoslovakia 1990. Recordings: Albeniz Iberia Suite; Falla Three Cornered Hat; Mozart Horn Concertos, Arias and Duets; Ravel Rhapsodie Espagnole; Reger Böcklin Tone Pictures and Mozart Variations. Address: Dresden Philharmonic Orchestra, Kulturpalast am Altmarkt, D-8012 Dresden, Germany.

WEIKERT Ralf, b. 10 Nov 1940, St Florian, Linz, Austria. Conductor. Education: Studied at the Bruckner Conservatory Linz, the State Academy Vienna with Hans Swarowsky. Career: Coach, Conductor at the Landestheater Salzburg 1963; Concerts in Austria, Scandinavia from 1965; Conductor at the Bonn Opera 1966, music director 1968; Salzburg Festival (concert) 1971; Guest engagement at the Royal Opera Copenhagen, 1972, with works by Mozart, Verdi, Stravinsky; Hamburg Staatsoper from 1975, with Don Quichotte, works by Mozart, Puccini and Donizetti; Vienna Staatsoper debut 1974, Il Trovatore; Zurich Opera 1976-80, with Le Nozze di Figaro, Arabella, Fidelio, La Cenerantola and Il Barbiere di Siviglia; Deutsche Oper Berlin 1978-80, Figaro and Don Pasquale; US debut 1980, with the City Opera's Giulio Cesare in New York and Los Angeles;

Teatro La Fenice Venice 1981, Tancredi by Rossini; Further engagements in Barcelona, Munich, Vienna, 1986-88, Rosenkavalier, Carmen, Die Entführung and L'Elisir d'Amore; Metropolitan Opera 1987-90, Elisir, Barbiere and Bohème; Concert engagements with leading orchestras in Berlin, Vienna, Scandinavia, Paris, Hungary, West Germany, Britain (English Chamber Orchestra, Academy of St Martin's and Scottish Chamber Orchestra); Festival appearances at Salzburg (Mozart Matinées, Serenades and Cenerentola), Aix-en-Provence, Orange, Bregenz and Lucerne. Recordings: Rossini Tancredi (CBS Masterworks) Schoeck Lebendig Begraben; James Morris Recital (EMI); Love Duets Araiza-Lind (Philips); Video-tape and laser disc: Barbiere di Siviglia, Metropolitan Opera (Deutsche Grammophon). Address: Neubruchstrasse 5, CH-8127, Forch Zurich, Switzerland.

WEIKL Bernd, b. 29 July 1942, Vienna, Austria. Opera Singer (Baritone). Education: Hannover Musikhochschule. Career: Sang Ottokar in Der Freischütz, Hannover 1968; Deutsche Oper am Rhein, Dusseldorf, 1970-73; Bayreuth Festival from 1972, as Wolfram, Amfortas and Hans Sachs: more than 160 performances; Member of the Deutsche Oper Berlin from 1974, debut as Eugene Onegin; Covent Garden debut 1975, as Rossini's Figaro: later sang Giordano's Gerard and Strauss's Mandryka in London; 1976 at the Vienna Staatsoper, for the premiere of Von Einem's Kabale und Liebe; Metropolitan Opera debut 1977, as Wolfram: later New York appearances as Mandryka, Jokanaan in Salome, and Beethoven's Don Fernando; Guest engagements at La Scala Milan, the Bavarian State Opera, Hamburg State Opera and the Salzburg Festival; Further appearances as Hans Sachs under Sawallisch at La Scala and under Dohnányi at Covent Garden, 1990; Sang Iago at Stuttgart, 1990, Boccanegra at Hamburg, 1991; Dutchman at Bayreuth, 1990; Sang Sachs in a new production of Die Meistersinger at the Metropolitan, 1993; Also sings in Lieder and oratorio; Television appearances include Mendelssohn's Elijah, from Israel, 1983. Recordings: Opera sets include L'Elisir d'Amore, Tristan und Isolde, Palestrina, Der Freischütz, Tiefland, Samson et Dalila, Eugene Onegin, Don Giovanni, Alceste, Lohengrin; Solo in Ein Deutsches Requiem by Brahms. Address: c/o Lies Askonas Ltd., 186 Drury Lane, London WC2B 5RY, England.

WEIL Bruno, b. 1949, Hahnstatten, Germany. Conductor. Education: Studied with Franco Ferrara in Italy and with Hans Swarowsky in Vienna. Career: Conducted at the opera houses of Wiesbaden and Brunswick; Debut with the Berlin Radio Symphony Orchestra 1977; Concerts with the Berlin Philharmonic from 1979; Music Director of Augsburg Opera 1979-89; Debut at the Deutsche Opera Berlin 1980, Die Sieben Todsünden by Weill; Salzburg Festival from 1982 (Don Giovanni at the 1988 Festival); Conducted Fidelio for Radio France, Paris 1984, and led the Yomiuri Nippon Symphony Orchestra in Japan; In 1985 conducted Aida at the Vienna Staatsoper and Ariadne auf Naxos at Bordeaux; Trieste 1986, Le Nozze di Figaro; Initiated series of Mozart operas in joint production with the Vienna Volksoper and Austrian TV, 1987; Die Entführung aus dem Serail in Bonn and Die Zauberflöte in Karlsruhe, 1987; United States debut 1988 in a Schubertiade in New York; Concerts in Holland with the Residentie Orchestra and Rotterdam Philharmonic; Concerts with the Los Angeles Philharmonic and the BBC Scottish Symphony from season 1988-90; Tour of Germany with the English Chamber Orchestra; Season 1990-91 with the Orchestre National de France and the Montreal Symphony. Honours include: Second Prize, Herbert von Karajan Conductors' Competition, 1979. Recordings: Various albums with RCA/Ariola conducting the Deutsche Philharmonie. Address: c/o Ingpen and Williams Ltd., 14 Kensington Court, London W8 5DN, England.

WEIL Tibor V, b. 16 May 1942, Hungary. Baritone Singer; Pianist; Cellist; Impressario; Economist. Education: Economist, Mackenzie University, Sao Paulo, Brazil; Master's degree, New York University, USA;

Pianist and Cellist: Budapest Music High School, Salvador Music High School, Pro Arte Music High School. *Debut:* Piano and Cello, 1960. *Career:* Concerts, TV appearances, Sao Paulo, Rio de Janeiro, Salvador, 1958-; Regular chamber music activities; Frequent concerts as lieder and light opera singer, sacred music, requiems, 1989-. *Honours:* Viscua Konservatoire Scholarship, 1956; Pro Arte Scholarship, 1959. *Memberships:* Pro Arte, Sao Paulo; Managing Advisor, Centro de Musica Brasileira. *Hobbies:* Travel; Sports. *Current Management:* TAW Promotions SP. *Address:* Rua Angatuba 80, Bairro, Pacaembu, CEP 01247 Sao Paulo SP, Brazil.

WEILAND Frederik Christoffel, b. 14 Sept 1933, Bilthoven, Netherlands. Composer; Film Maker; Musicologist. *Education:* BA, Higher School for Radio Engineering, Hague, 1957; Physics of Architecture, Delft Technical University; Hilversum School of Music, 1957-59; MA, Royal Academy of Music, Hague, 1966. *Career:* Recording engineer, radiophonic experiments, Radio Nederland, 1957-59; Video editor, Nederlandse Televisie Stichting, 1959-61; Studio for Electronic Music 1961-67, Institute of Sonology 1967-86, University of Utrecht; Lecturer, researcher, Sonology Department, Royal Conservatory, Hague, 1986-; Guest Lecturer, Amsterdam Film & Television Academy; Musical Adviser, Stedelijk Museum (Amsterdam), Utrecht Music Centre. *Compositions include:* Etude 59, 1959; A City Awakes, 1959; Filmproject I, 1969; Play Without Words (music, Beckett TV production), 1970; Art of Flying, 1984; Music for Mesa, 1986; 4 American Pieces, 1982-83; Nevers Mon Amour, 1985. *Recordings:* Several. *Publications:* Books: International Electronic Music Discography, 1979; Stockhausen in The Hague, 1983. Co-Editor, Interface, journal of new music research. *Honours:* Composition grants, film subsidies, Dutch Ministry of Culture, Amsterdam Foundation for Arts. *Memberships:* Society of Dutch Composers; Confederation International de Musique Electroacoustique; Vereniging Producenten Elektronische Muziek. *Address:* Bruntenhof 14, NL-3512 KZ, Utrecht.

WEILERSTEIN Donald, b. 14 Mar 1940, Washington DC, USA. Violinist. *Education:* BS, MS, Julliard School of Music, 1966. *Debut:* New York, 1963. *Career:* Founding First Violinist, Cleveland Quartet, 1969-89; Professor of Violin and Chamber Music: Cleveland Institute of Music, 1967-71, 1989-, SUNY at Buffalo, 1971-76, Eastman School of Music, NY, 976-89. *Recordings:* Complete Brahms Quartets; Complete Beethoven Quartets; Schubert 2 cello Quintet; Schubert Trout Quintet; Mendelssohn and Schubert Octets; Complete Violin and Piano and Solo Violin works of Ernest Bloch; Sonatas of Dohnanyi, and Janáček. *Honours:* NEA Grant; Grammy nominations for recorded works; Prize winner, Munich Competition for violin and piano duo. *Memberships:* American String Teachers' Association. *Hobbies:* Reading; Swimming; Hiking; Basketball; Sport. *Current Management:* Deborah Fleischman. *Address:* 2645 Fairmount Blvd, Cleveland Heights, OH 44106, USA.

WEIN Ericka, b. 2 Sept. 1928, Vienna, Austria. Singer (Mezzo-soprano). *Education:* Studied at the Vienna Music Academy with Erik Werba. *Career:* Sang at the Vienna Volksoper 1952-53, Bremen 1953- 59, Dusseldorf 1959-64; Engagements at the Zurich Opera 1964-80, notably in the premieres of Sutermeister's Madame Bovary, 1967, and Kelterborn's Ein Engel Kommt nach Babylon, 1977; Guest appearances in Berlin, the State Operas of Munich, Hamburg Stuttgart, Frankfurt, Cologne, at the Holland Festival, Florence, Lyon, Buenos Aires, Paris, San Francisco and Turin; Roles included Carmen, Azucena, Amneris, Eboli, Ulrica, Ortrud, Fricka, Brangane, Venus, Orpheus, Marina (Boris Godunov). Clytemnestra and Berg's Marie; Concert Showings in works by Bach, Beethoven and Brahms; Lieder recitals and concerts in Germany, Switzerland, Spain and Austria. *Recordings include:* Highlights from Rigoletto and Nabucco. *Address:* c/o Opernhause Zurich, Falkenstrasse 1 CH-8008 Zurich, Switzerland.

WEINBAUM Wiktor, b. 14 Dec 1915, Poland. Musician. m. Bogna Halacz, 27 Apr 1966. *Education:* Graduated: University, 1939; Vilno Conservatory of Music, 1939. *Career:* Lecturer, piano playing, conservatories & music institutions, Vilno; Director, Chopin international piano competitions, Warsaw Chopin Society, until 1982; Music Department, Ministry of Culture & Art. Judge, numerous international music competitions including: Leeds, England; Lisbon, Portugal; Leipzig, Germany; Budapest, Hungary; Palma de Majorca & Santander, Spain; Sydney, Australia; Salt Lake City (Utah) & Washington, USA; Bolzano, Monza, Rome, Senigalia, Terni & Vercelli, Italy; Munich, Germany. *Publications:* Chopin Cult in the World; International Music Competitions; Promotion of Career & Artistic Growth of the Young Musician; Chopin & Contemporary Sensibility; The Jury in Musical Competitions, Some Reflections. *Honours:* Honorary member, Federation of International Music Competitions; Chopin Society, Austria; American Liszt Society; Academico Correspondente Real, Academy de Belles Artes de San Jorge, Barcelona, Spain; Knight, Polonia Restituta; Knight, National Order of Merit, France. *Membership:* Polish Music Council. *Hobbies:* Records; Aesthetics; Philosophy. *Address:* Piekarska 5 m 6, Warsaw, Poland.

WEINGARTNER Eliszbeth, b. 23 Jan 1938, Sissach, Switzerland. Singer (Mezzo-soprano). *Education:* Studied in Basle and with Res Fischer in Stuttgart. *Career:* Sang at the Basle Opera 1973-81 and made quest appearances at Nantes, Paris, Trier and Cannes; Roles have included Così fan tutte, Mozart; Carmen, Bizet; Isabella (L'Italiana in Algeri), Idamantes in Idomeneo, Genevieve (Pelléas), Annina and the Hostess in Boris Godunov; Strasbourg 1984, in the premiere of H H Ulysse by Prodromides; Concert and Lieder engagements in France and Switzerland and at Liege, Stuttgart and Vienna; Verdi Requiem, Paris, Orchestra Lamoureux; Dvořák Requiem, San Sebastian, Spain. *Recordings include:* H H Ulysee. *Address:* Opera du Rhin, 19 Place Brogile, F-67008 Strasbourg Cedex, France.

WEINSCHENK Hans-Jorg, b. 14 Nov 1955, Stuttgart, Germany. Singer (Tenor). *Career:* Sang in Opera at Heidelberg 1974-76, Wuppertal 1976- 80; Member of the Zurich Opera 1981-85, Theater am Gärtnerplatz Munich from 1984; Guest appearances at Lausanne 1985, Grand Opera Paris 1986; Sang in the premiere of Der Meister und Margarita by Kunad, Karlsruhne 1986; Roles have included such buffo and character repertory as Pedrillo, the witch in Hansel and Gretel, Monostatos, David in Die Meistersinger and the Steuermann in Fliegende Holländer; Frequent concert engagements.

WEIR Gillian Constance, b. 17 Jan 1941, New Zealand. Concert Organist. m. Lawrence I Phelps, 4 Aug 1972. *Education:* Royal College of Music, London. Further studies with Nadia Boulanger, Marie-Claire Alain and Anton Heiller. *Debut:* Royal Festival Hall, 1965. *Career:* Concerto appearances with leading British and foreign orchestras; Regular appearances at international festivals in Edinburgh, Aldeburgh, Proms, Europalia, performing at the Royal Festival and Albert Halls, Lincoln and Kennedy Centers, Palais des Beaux Arts and Sydney Opera House; Frequent radio and TV appearances worldwide, including BBC programme, The King of Instruments, as presenter and performer in 1989; Adjudicator at international competitions; Artist in residence at several universities, giving lectures and master-classes internationally; Consultant for new organ, Symphony Hall, Birmingham. *Recordings include:* Complete organ works for: Virgin, Classics and Chandos; Complete organ works of: Olivier Messiaen, (Collins Classics), 1994. *Honours include:* Hon FRCO, 1975; Hon FRCCO, Canada, 1983; CBE, 1989; Hon Mem, RAM; President Incorporated Assoc. Organists, 1982-84; President Incorporated Society of Musicians, 1992-93. *Memberships:* Incorporated Society of

Musicians; Royal College of Organists; Incorporated Association of Organists. *Hobbies:* Reading; Theatre. *Address and Current Management:* Karen McFarlane Artists Inc, Cleveland, USA.

WEIR Judith, b. 11 May 1954, Cambridge, England. Composer. *Education:* Studied composition with John Tavener; King's College, Cambridge 1973-76, with Robin Holloway; Tanglewood 1975, with Gunther Schuller. *Career:*Southern Arts Association's Composer-in-Residence 1976-79; Music Department Glasgow University 1979-82; Creative Arts Fellowship at Trinity College, Cambridge, 1983-85; Composer in Residence, Royal Scottish Academy of Musaic and Drama, 1988-91. *Compositions:* Stage: The Black Spider, opera in 3 acts 1984; The Consolations of Scholarship, music drama 1985; A Night at the Chinese Opera, opera in 3 acts 1986; The Vanishing Bridegroom, opera, 1990; Blond Eckbert, 1993. Orchestral: Music Untangled, 1991-92; Heroic Strokes of the Bow, 1992; Vocal: King Harald's Saga 1979; Missa del Cid, 1988; Heaven Ablaze in His Breast for voices, 2 pianos and 8 dancers, 1989. *Address:* c/o Chester Music, 8-9 Frith Street, London W1V 5TZ, England.

WEISBERG Arthur, b. 4 Apr 1931, New York City, USA. Bassoonist; Conductor; Teacher. *Education:* Studied bassoon with Simon Kovar; Conducting with Jean Morel, Juilliard School of Music, New York. *Career:* Bassoonist, Houston Symphony Orchestra; Baltimore Symphony Orchestra; Cleveland Orchestra; Member, New York Woodwind Quintet, 1956-70; Founder-Director, Contemporary Chamber Ensemble, New York, 1969-; Chief Conductor, Iceland Symphony Orchestra, Reykjavik, 1987-88; Guest conductor with various orchestras including New York Philharmonic Orchestra, 1983, 1984; Teacher, Juilliard School of Music, 1960-68; State University of New York, Stony Brook, 1971-89; Yale University, 1975-89. *Recordings:* Several discs. *Publicatons:* The Art of Wind Playing, 1973. *Address:* 12008 S 35th Ct, Phoenix, AZ 85044, USA.

WEISBROD Annette, b. 9 Dec 1937, Blackburn, Lancashire, England. Pianist. m. Charles Kirmess, 21 Jan 1967. *Education:* Teaching Diploma, Chamber Music Diploma, Zurich Conservatory; Soloist and Concert Diploma, Basle Conservatoire. *Debut:* Wigmore Hall, London, 1960. *Career:* Concert appearances around the world; Radio and TV appearances in: Switzerland, Germany, England, France, Yugoslavia, China; Professor, Berne Conservatoire. *Recordings:* Over 30 LPs and CDs including: Haydn Trios (Swiss Festival Trio); Complete works for piano and cello by Beethoven; Several piano concertos and many piano works. *Memberships:* Swiss Tonkunstler-Verein; Swiss Musikpädagogischer Verein; International Piano Teachers Association. *Hobbies:* Walking; Cooking. *Address:* Heuelstr 33, CH-8032 Zurich, Switzerland.

WEISEL-CAPSOUTO Robin, b. 1952, USA. Singer (Soprano). *Education:* Studied at Oberlin College, the University of Illinois, with Jenn Tourel in Jerusalem and with Heather Harper in London. *Debut:* Sang Vivald's Gloria with the Jerusalem Symphony Orchestra 1974. *Career:* Sang in Mahler's 4th with the Israel Philharmonic 1976; Opera engagements in the USA and Israel as Gluck's Amor, Lucy in The Beggar's Opera, and in La Voix Humaine, Le Roi David, Bacchus and Ariadne by Thomas Arne and Rameau's Les Fetes d'Hebe; New England Opera Company 1984, as Zerlina; Sang the Governess in The Turn of the Screw for New Israeli Opera, 1992; Concert repertoire includes Bach's B Minor Mass, Carissimi's Jephte, Solomon and other oratorios by Handel.

WEISGALL Hugo, b. 13 Oct 1912, Ivancice, Czechoslovakia. Composer. *Education:* Studied at the Peabody Conservatory 1927-32; Composition studies with Roger Sessions between 1932-41; Diplomas in composition and conducting at the Curtis Institute Philadelphia 1938, 1939; PhD from Johns Hopkins University 1940. *Career:* Cultural attache in Prague 1946-47; Guest conductor with leading European orchestras; Founded and conducted the Chamber Society of Baltimore 1948 and the Hilltop Opera Company 1952; Directed the Baltimore Institute of Musical Arts 1949-51; Teacher at Johns Hopkins 1951-57; Professor at Queen's College, City University of New York 1961; Teacher at Juilliard School 1975-70; Composer-in-residence at the American Academy in Rome 1966. *Compositions:* Operas: The Tenor 1948-50; The Stronger 1952; Six Characters in Search of an Author 1953-56; Purgatory 1958; The Garden of Adonis 1959, 1977-81; Athaliah 1960-63; Nine Rivers from Jordan 1964-68; Jennie, or The Hundred Nights 1975-76; Ballets: Quest 1938; Art Appreciation 1938; One Thing is Certain 1939; Outpost 1947; Vocal: Soldier Songs for baritone and orchestra 1944-46, 1965; A Garden Eastward, cantata, 1952; Two Madrigals 1955; The Golden Peacock 1960, 1976; Fancies and Inventions for baritone and ensemble 1970; Translations for mezzo and piano 1971-72; End of Summer 1973-74; Song of Celebration for soprano, tenor, chorus and orchestra 1975; Liebeslieder 1979; Lyrical Interval 1985; Instrumental music including 2 Piano Sonatas 1931 and 1982; Proclamations for orchestra 1960; Prospects for orchestra 1983; Tekiator for orchestra 1985. *Honours include:* Three Guggenheim fellowships; Elected to National Institute of Arts and Letters 1975; Distinguished Professor of Music, City University of New York, 1979. *Address:* c/o 81 Maple Drive, Great Deck, NY 11021, USA.

WEISGARBER Elliot, b. 5 Dec 1919, Pittsfield, Massachusetts, USA. Composer; Conductor; Researcher; Performer, Japanese Music. m. Bethiah Setter, 21 Dec 1943, 1 daughter. *Education:* BMus, MMus, Performer's Certificate, Eastman School of Music, University of Rochester; Studies, clarinet, chamber music, composition, Japanese music. *Career includes:* Instructor to Professor 1960-85, Emeritus Professor 1985-, University of British Columbia, Canada. *Compositions include:* Kyoto Landscapes, 1973; Lyrical Evolution for Orchestras and Night for Baritone, Chorus and String Quartet; Concerto, violin & orchestra, 1974; Pacific Trilogy, full orchestra; Fantasia a Tre, horn, violin & piano; Illusions of Immortality, song cycle soprano & piano, poems by Clive Simpson; Crown of Fire, film music; Music for Morning of World, wind & percussion; Quintet, flute, oboe, clarinet, horn, bassoon; Fantasia, Eclogue & Rondo, clarinet & piano, 1982; Epigrams, flute & piano; Songs of 1,000 Autumns, commissioned New Vancouver Music Society, 1984; 32 concert etudes, solo clarinet, 1985-86; Clarinet quintet, string quartet, 1988; Music in Memory of Andrei Sakharov, commissioned by Augustines Artists, Anchorage, Alaska, 1990; Sonata Piacevole for clarinet and piano, 1990; Adaptions for Clarinet & Piano: Claude Debussy Sonate Pour Violin & Piano, 1991; Claude Debussy Suite Bergamasque, 1993; Claude Debussy L'isle Joyeuse; Claude Debussy 12 Preludes under title Paysages Intimes, 1992. *Recordings:* Night, Vancouver Chamber Choir, Jon Washburn and Bruce Pullen, Baritone; Purcell String Quartet with Wilmur Fawcett, double bass, CMC-CD 3790. *Address:* 4042 West 33rd Avenue, Vancouver, British Columbia, Canada V6N 2J1.

WEISS Ferdinand, b. 6 June 1933, Vienna, Austria. Composer; Educator. m. Ingeborg Scheibenreiter, 16 Sept 1967, 2 sons. *Education:* Diplomas: Music 1958, Composition (prize) 1960, Conducting (prize) 1961, Flute, Viennese Academy of Music. *Debut:* (As composer) Eisenstadt, 1957. *Career:* Freelance composer, private teacher (music theory), conductor, orchestra musician, 1960-; Music Master, Vienna Conservatory & Baden Pedagogische Academie; Manager, Concert Chamber Ensemble, Lower Austria Composer's Society; President of Inoek. *Compositions:* Approx. 205 works including: Orchestral (3 symphonies); Concertos for flute, oboe, clarinet, trumpet, trombone; Chamber music; Lieder; Approx. 700 performances, concerts & radio, Austria, USA. Italy, Argentina, Germany, France, Netherlands, Hungary, Belgium, Portugal, Spain, Norway, Poland, England, Switzerland, Finland, Australia, Japan; Quattrofonia for Saxophone Quartet at Carnegie Hall; 5 Scences pour

Quatuor De Guitares in Paris. *Recordings:* Konzert-Stueck for Oboe & String Orchestra; Flute en Miniature, Die Fliege, Ragtime, Trio Infernale (CD Tuning Pro, Wien); Trio for Mandolin Guitar and Harp; Relazioni Variabili. *Publications:* Pedagogical works. *Contributions to:* Bildung und Kulturaktuell. *Hobbies:* Photography; Sports; Travel. *Address:* Christalnigg-Gasse 11, A-2500 Baden, Austria.

WEISS Howard A, b. Chicago, Illinois, USA. Violinist; Concertmaster; Conductor; Educator. *Education:* BM, 1960, and MM with honours, 1966, Chicago Musical College of Roosevelt University. *Career:* Music Director, Conductor, Rochester Philharmonic Youth Orchestra, 1970-89, with 12 tours including England, Scotland, 1984, Germany, Austria, Switzerland, 1986, Dominican Republic, 1987, Alaska, 1988, Jamaica, 1989, also appears on Voice of America; Member, Advisory Board; Young Audiences of Rochester, 1975-; Rochester Chamber Orchestra, 1981-; Professor, Violin: Eastman School of Music, Rochester, New York, 1981-; Nazareth College, Rochester, 1983-85; Concertmaster: Chicago Chamber Orchestra, 1962-70; San Francisco Ballet Orchestra, 1962; Virginia Symphony, 1964; Concertmaster, 1967-87, Concertmaster Emeritus, 1987-, Rochester Philharminc; Concertmaster, Rochester Oratorio Society, 1987-; Concertmaster, Eastern Music Festival, Greensboro, North Carolina, 1976-80; Concertmaster, Grand Teton Music Festival Seminar, Jackson Hole, Wyoming, 1983-86; Concertmaster, Bear Lake Music Festival, Utah, 1992, Ongoing, 1992-; 1st Violinist, Cleveland Orchestra,, 1965-67; Violin Soloist over 40 concerti with Cleveland Orchestra, Rochester and New Orleans Philharmonics, Chicago Grant Park Symphony and Cincinnati, Chicago and Rochester Chamber Orchestras; Soloist, complete concerti of J S Bach for violin and orchestra with Rochester Bach Festival (5) and Haydn for violin and orchestra with Rochester Chamber Orchestra (3); Leader, Hartwell String Quartet, 1975-78; Participant, Casals Festival, Puerto Rico, 1975-80; Chamber Music with Misha Dichter, leonard Rose, Lynn Harrell, Yo-Yo Ma, Elly Ameling, Jaime Laredo, Walter Trampler, Lillian Fuchs, James Buswell, Gary Karr, Alan Civil, Lukas Foss. *Recordings:* Amram Elegy for Violin and Orchestra, David Zinman, Rochester Philharmonic, on RCA Red Seal; 21 LPs as Music Director and Conductor, Rochester Philharmonic Youth Orchestra. *Honours:* Outstanding Graduate of 1966, Roosevelt University, 1973; Monroe County (NY) Medallion, 1986. *Address:* 228 Castlebar Road, Rochester, NY 14610, USA.

WEISS Susan Forscher, b. 22 July 1944, New York City, USA. Professor; Musicologist. m. James L Weiss, 23 July 1967. 1 son, 1 daughter. *Education:* BA, Goucher College, 1965; MA, Smith College, 1967; PhD, University of Maryland, 1985; Further studies at New York University 1967-68, University of Michigan 1968-70, Juilliard School of Music 1957-61, Aspen Music Festival 1960-61 and Écoles d'Art Américaines, 1962. *Career:* Chairman, Music Department, The Garrison Forest School, Garrison, Maryland, 1973-; Lecturer in Music, Goucher College, Towson, Maryland, 1985-87; Instructor in Music History, The Peabody Conservatory of the Johns Hopkins University, 1987-. *Publication:* Dissertation: The Manuscript Bologna Q18: A Bolognese Instrumental Collection of the Early Cinquecento, 1985; Bologna Q18: Some Reflection on Content and Context, The Journal of the American Musicological Society, 1988; Musical Patronage of The Bentivoglio Signoria, 1465-1512; Atti del XIV Congresso della Società Internazionale de Musicologia, Trasmissione e recezione delle forme di cultura musicale, Bologna, 1987 (1990) vol III, 703-15. *Contributions:* Journal of the American Musicological Society; Acta musicologica. *Address:* 8302 Tally Ho Road, Lutherville, MD 21093, USA.

WEISSENBERG Alexis, b. 26 July 1929, Sofia, Bulgaria. Pianist. *Education:* Studies, piano & composition, with: Pancho Viadiguerov, age 3; Olga Samarov, Juilliard School of Music, New York, USA, 1946. *Debut:* Concert, New York Philharmonic (George Szell), Carnegie Hall, New York. *Career:* 1st orchestral concert, Israel, 1944; Concert tour, South Africa, 1944; US coast-to-coast tour, & concerts, Paris, Vienna, Madrid, Milan, Philadelphia Orchestra (Eugene Ormandy), 1951; Soloist, Tchaikovsky's 1st Piano Concerto, Berlin Philharmonic Orchestra (Herbert von Karajan), 1966; Invited performer, numerous great conductors & orchestras worldwide (Abbado, Bernstein, Celibidache, Giulini, Karajan, Ormandy), 1967-; Royal Festival Hall, London, 1974; Various recent world tours, Maazel & New Philharmonic Orchestra. *Recordings:* Notably music by Beethoven, Chopin, Tchaikovsky, Rachmaninov, Bach and Schumann, various labels; Recordings for EMI and Deutsche Grammophon. *Address:* c/o Michal Schmidt/Thea Dispeker Inc, 59 East 54th Street, New York, NY 10022, USA.

WELITSCH Luba, b. 10 July 1913, Borisovo, Bulgaria. Singer (Soprano). *Eucation:* Studied with Gyorgy Zlatov in Sofia and with Theodor Lierhammer in Vienna. *Debut:* Sofia 1934, in Louise by Charpentier. *Career:* Sang at Graz from 1936; Hamburg Staatsoper 1940-43; Vienna Volksoper from 1942; Staatsoper Munich 1943-45; Vienna Staatsoper from 1944, as Salome, Butterfly, Nedda, Minnie, Elisabeth, Chrysothemis, Fiordiligi and Desdemona; Salzburg 1946, Donna Anna; Covent Garden 1947-52, as Salome, Donna Anna, Musetta, Lisa, Aida and Tosca; Sang with the Glyndebourne Company at Edinburgh 1948-49, as Donna Anna and Amelia in Un Ballo in Maschera; Metropolitan Opera 1949-52, as Salome, Donna Anna, Musetta, Tosca, Aida and Rosalinde; Sang at the Vienna Staatsoper until 1959, in Der Revisor by Egk; Returned to the Metropolitan 1972, in the speaking role of the Duchess of Crakentorp in La Fille du Régiment; Sang at the Vienna Volksoper until 1981. *Recordings:* For Columbia and Decca; Don Giovanni (Olympic); Elektra (Rococo). *Address:* c/o Staatsoper, Opernring 2, A-1010 Vienna, Austria.

WELKER Hartmut, b. 27 Oct 1941, Velbert, Rhineland, Germany. Opera Singer (Bass-baritone). m. Edeltraut, 2 July 1982, 1 son, 1 daughter. *Education:* Studied for technical career, took up singing, 1972. *Debut:* Opera, Aachen, 1974. UK debut, Edinburgh Festival with LSO/Abbado, 1983. *Career:* Aachen Opera, 1974-80. Since then, has had 3-year contract with Karlsruhe Opera; Sang at La Scala (Lohengrin with Abbado), Geneva, Paris (Khovanshchina). Sang Don Pizarro (Fidelio), Madrid and at Maggio Musicale, Florence, Italy, & for Scottish Opera, 1984. Appeared in Hamburg, Munich & Stuttgart; Boris Godunov in North America with Chicago Symphony Orchestra/Abbado; Paris Opera, Vienna State Opera, Berlin & Hamburg, in productions of Fidelio, Flying Dutchman, Salome, Lohengrin. Covent Garden debut, Fidelio, 1986; Sang also with Philharmonia Orchestra/Muti, also at Turin, Vienna, Madrid, Bologna, Naples, Tokyo, Chicago. Season 1988 included appearances in San Francisco, Berlin, Geneva, with further visits to La Scala, Covent Garden & Salzburg; Sang in London 1986-89 as Pizarro and Kaspar; Theater an der Wien and Turin, 1989, in Schubert's Fierabras and as Wozzeck; Telramund in Lohengrin at the Vienna Staatsoper and the Deutsche Opera Berlin, 1990; other roles include Kurwenal, Klingsor, Macbeth, Carlos in La Forza del destino; Amonasro, Barnaba and Scarpia; Sang Pizarro in Fidelio at the Metropolitan, 1991. *Recordings include:* Der Traumgörge as Kaspar/Hans; Notre Dame as Archidiakonus; Fierrabras, Brutamonte, 1992, Fidelio (Pizarro), Lohengrin (Telramund); Das Wunder der Heliane, Korngold, 1992. *Address:* Frühlingstrasse 10, D-76327 Pfintzal/Wöschbach, Germany.

WELLEJUS Henning, b. 23 Aug 1919, Roskilde, Denmark, Composer m. Inge Osterby, 2 children. *Education:* Studied with composer Svend Erik Tarp and conductor Giovanni Di Bella; University of Copenhagen. *Debut:* Copenhagen. *Compositions include:* 3 Symphonies; 4 Concerts for Violin and Orchestra, Oboe and orchestra, cello and orchestra, and piano and orchestra; Symphonic Fantasies: The History of the Year, Nina; Our Childhood's Friends and from Hans Christian

Anderson's picturebook, 2 suites from ballet, The Swan; Wind Quintet, Flute Serenade Just for Fun, for flute, violin, viola and cello; 2 String quartets; Several Songs; trio for clarinet, viola and piano; The Dream, ballet; Passacaglia for orchestra; A Freedom Overture; Copenhagen Rhapsody; A Danish Summer Pastorale; Grates Nune Omnes Reddamus Domini, for soprano, chorus and orchestra; A Danish Requiem for soprano, baritone and orchestra; A Trio for Piano, Violin and Oboe; 3 Symphonic Fantasies, Dionysia A Summer Morning in Hornbak and the distant Morningsong of the Stars; A Trio for Violin, Viola and Cello, Operas, The Changed Bridegroom and Barbara; Numerous other works. *Honours:* Lange-Müller Stipendiet, 1956. *Hobby:* Summer Cottage. *Address:* Godthaabsvej 99, 2000 Frederiksberg. Denmark.

WELLER Dieter, b. 25 May 1937, Essen, Germany. Singer (Bass-Baritone). m. Dorte Fischer. *Education:* Studied with Erwin Rottgen in Essen; Further study in Cologne. *Career:* Bremerhaven 1963-66, debut as Padre Guardiano in La Forza del Destino; Member of the Frankfurt Opera from 1966; San Francisco 1974, as Wurm in Luisa Miller; Appearances in Berlin, Dusseldorf, Hamburg, Brussels and Edinburgh; Teatro Regio Turin 1983, in Lulu by Berg; Metropolitan Opera 1985, as the Music Master in Ariadne auf Naxos; Many appearances in operas by Rossini, Lortzing, Weber, Rossini, Smetana, Wagner and Wolf-Ferrari; Frequent concert appearances. *Recordings:* Der Freischütz and Martha (Electrola); Der Zwerg by Zemlinsky (Schwann).

WELLER Walter, b. 30 Nov 1939, Vienna, Austria. Conductor; Violinist. m. Elisabeth Samohyl 1966, 1 son. *Education:* Studied violin, High School for Music and Dramatic Art, Vienna. *Career:* Member 1946-; Solist 1951-; Violinist, Concertmaster, 1956-69; Vienna Philharmonic Orchestra; Founder, Director, Weller Quartet and toured Europe, Asia and North America; Conductor, Vienna State Opera 1969-, touring USA, Scandinavia, Israel, Italy, Netherlands, Spain, Switzerland, Belgium, France, Principal conductor, artistic advisor, Royal Liverpool Philharmonic Orchestra 1977-80; Principal conductor, Royal Philharmonic Orchestra, London, 1980-85; President of the Rodewald Concert Society in England, 1984-, touring Japan, Germany, East-Germany, Scotland, Hong Kong, Russia. Chief Guest Conductor of Royal Philharmonic Orchestra, London, 1985-; Conductor Laureate of the Royal Philharmonic Orchestra, Liverpool, 1980-; Chief Guest Conductor National Orchestra of Spain, 1987-; Conducted Prince Igor at the Deutsche Staatsoper, Berlin, 1989; Principal Guest Conductor of the Royal Flanders Philharmonic Orchestra in Belgium, 1990; has conducted Fidelio and Der Rosenkavalier for Scottish Opera, Der fliegende Holländer and Ariadne auf Naxos for English National Opera; Der Freischütz at Bologna and Holländer at La Scala, Milan. *Recordings:* Numerous (Grand Prix du disque Charles Cros). *Honours:* Beethoven Gold Medal, Mozart Interpretation Prize; Medal of Arts and Science, Austria 1968. *Address:* Doblinger Hauptstrasse 40, 1190 Vienna, Austria.

WELLINGTON Christopher Ramsay, b. 5 Feb 1930, London, England. Viola & Viola d'Amore Player. m. (1) Joanna Donat, 30 Oct 1954, 1 son, 1 daughter, (2) Eileen Darlow, 1 July 1988. *Education:* MA, Oxford University, 1953; ARCM, Royal College of Music, 1954. *Career:* Sadler's Wells Opera Orchestra, 1954-58; Philharmonia Orchestra, 1958-65; Principal viola, London Bach Orchestra, Philomusica of London, Tilford Bach Orchestra; Now Principal Viola of London Festival Orchestra, English Baroque Orchestra; Viola player of Zorian String Quartet, Amici String Quartet, Nemet Piano Quartet, Music Group of London, Rasumovsky String Quartet; Frequent soloist at Queen Elizabeth Hall; Professor of Viola, Royal College of Music. *Recordings:* Elegiac Meditation, Robin Milford; Works by Haydn, Rubbra, Charles Ives, Shostakovich, with Amici Quartet; Works by Elgar, Vaughan Williams, Frank Bridge, Schubert, with Music Group of London. *Memberships:* Warden, Solo Performers Section 1986-87, Incorporated Society of Musicians. *Hobby:* Sailing.

Address: 13 Cambridge Road, New Malden, Surrey KT3 3QE, England.

WELSBY Norman, b. 7 Feb 1939, Warrington, Cheshire, England. Singer (Baritone). *Education:* Studied at the Royal College of Music in Manchester and with Gwilym Jones and Otakar Kraus in London. *Debut:* Sadler's Wells Opera London 1968, as Masetto. *Career:* Many appearances at Covent Garden and with English National Opera in the standard repertoire and in modern works; Sang Gunther in the Ring, conducted by Reginald Goodall, 1973-74; Sang in the premiere of The Magic Fountain by Delius, BBC 1977; Pentheus in the British premiere of The Bassarids (ENO 1974) and the General in the premiere of We Come to the River (Covent Garden 1976); Many concert appearances. *Recordings include:* The Ring of the Nibelung (EMI); The Magic Fountain (BBC Artium). *Address:* c/o English National Opera, London Coliseum, St Martin's Lane, London WC2, England.

WELSER-MÖST Franz, b. 16 Aug 1960, Linz, Austria. Conductor. *Education:* Completed music studies with Professor Balduin Sulzer. *Career:* Principal Conductor of the Austrian Youth Orchestra until 1985; Mahler's 1st Symphony and Bruckner's 5th Symphony in the Musikverein, Vienna; Salzburg Festival debut 1985; British debut 1986 with the London Philharmonic; European tour with the orchestra to Vienna, Berlin and Amsterdam; Guest engagements with the Zurich Tonhalle, Vienna Symphony, Bavarian Radio Symphony and several orchestras in Scandinavia; Opera debut in October 1987, with a new production of L'Italiana in Algeri at the Vienna State Opera; Così fan Tutte at the Deutsche Oper, Berlin; Covent Garden debut scheduled 1990; formerly Chief Conductor in Norrkoeping and Winterthur; Principal Conductor of the London Philharmonic Orchestra, 1990; Season 1991/92 with La Clemenza di Tito at the Deutsche Oper Berlin and Rosenkavalier at Zurich; Season 1993/94 with Tristan und Isolde at the Festival Hall, London and Peter Grimes at Glyndebourne. *Recordings include:* Mozart's C minor Mass and Carmina Burana with the London Philharmonic Orchestra (EMI); Mendelssohn Symphonies 3 and 4, Bruckner; Oedipus Rex, Miraculous Mandarin; Dvořák Violin Concerto with Frank Peter Zimmermann. *Current Management:* IMG Artists Europe. *Address:* c/o Media House, 3 Burlington Lane, Chiswick, London W4 2TH, England.

WELSH Moray, b. 1 Mar 1947, Haddington, Scotland. Cellist. m. Melissa Phelps, 13 Oct 1984. *Education:* York University; Moscow Conservatoire. *Debut:* Wigmore Hall, 1972. *Career:* Concertos with LSO, RPO, Philharmonia, BBC Symphony; Tours to Scandinavia, US, Russia, Europe. Principal Cellist, LSO, 1992-. *Recordings:* Concertos by Boccherini, Vivaldi, Hug Wood (Sunday Times Record of the Year), Alexander Goehr, as well as chamber music. *Honours:* British Council Awards, 1969; Gulbenkian Fellowship, 1972-74. *Hobbies:* Skiing; Walking; Gardening; Instrument making. *Address:* 28 Summerfield Avenue, Queens Park, London NW6 6JY, England.

WELTING Ruth, b. 11 May 1949, Memphis, Tennessee, USA. Singer (Soprano). m. Edo de Waart. *Education:* Studied with Daniel Ferro in New York, Luigi Ricci in Rome and Jeanne Reiss in Paris. *Debut:* New York City Opera 1970, as Blondchen in Die Entführung. *Career:* Has sung at opera houses in Dallas, Houston, San Antonio, Santa Fe and San Francisco; Covent Garden and Metropolitan Opera 1975-76, as Zerbinetta in Ariadne auf Naxos; Ottawa and Washington 1979-80, as the Fairy Godmother in Cendrillon by Massenet; Teatro Liceo Barcelona 1984, as Marie in La Fille du Régiment; Sang Lucia di Lammermoor at Cincinnati, 1985, Rosina, 1987; Teatro Regio Parma 1985, as Olympia in Les Contes d'Hoffmann; Chicago Lyric Opera 1990, as Ophelia in Hamlet; Olympia at Barcelona, June 1990; Other roles include Zerlina, the Princess in L'Enfant et les Sortilèges; Norina, Gilda and Adele in Die Fledermaus; Many Lieder recitals. *Recordings:* Sophie in Der Rosenkavalier, Der Schauspieldirektor

(Philips); Mignon by Thomas, Hansel and Gretel, Cendrillon (CBS). *Address:* c/o Lyric Opera of Chicago, 20 North Wacker Drive, Chicago, IL 60606, USA.

WENKEL Ortrun, b. 25 Oct 1942, Buttstadt, Thuringia, Germany. Singer (Mezzo-soprano and Alto). m. Dr. Peter Rothe, 7 June 1966. *Education:* Franz Liszt Hochschule Weimar, Hochschule für Musik, Frankfurt, Lohmann master class, operatic studies with Cavelti. *Debut:* Concert, as student, London, 1964; Opera Heidelberg, 1971. *Career:* Performed at opera houses throughout Europe including Milan Scala, Covent Garden, Bayerische Staatsoper, Hamburg, with appearances at the Salzburg Festival, Munich Opera Festival, Festivals of Schwetzingen, Edinburgh, Berlin and Vienna, one of the most notable performances being Penelope in the Zurich production of the Monteverdi cycle. Has given numerous lieder recitals and made guest appearances with symphony orchestras in New York, London, Berlin, Vienna, Paris, Bayreuth, Amterdam, Buenos Aires, and Rio de Janeiro, among others. *Recordings include:* Boulez Bayreuth Centenary Ring, The Ring with Dresdner Staatskapelle; Mahler's 3rd Symphony; Mahler's 8th; Mozart Requiem; The Magic Flute; Schönberg Jacob's Ladder; Dvořák Stabat Mater; Handel Xerxes; Solo recitals of Italian Baroque Music; St Matthew's Passion by Bach and several of his cantatas; Zemlinsky-Lieder, Schreker and Schostakovitch-Lieder; The Bassarids (Henze). *Honours:* GRAMMY for Wagner, Ring des Nibelungen, principal soloist, 1982; Deutscher Schallplattenpreis Mozart Requiem, 1983. *Hobbies:* Gardening; Birds. *Address:* Eichendorffstr 25, D-69493 Hirschberg/Bergstrasse, Germany.

WENKOFF Spas, b. 23 Sept 1928, Tirnovo, Bulgaria. Singer (Tenor). *Education:* Studied with J. Jossifov in Sofia, Mdme Saffiriva in Russe and with Johannes Kemter in Dresden. *Debut:* Tirnovo 1954, in Keto and Kote by Dolidse. *Career:* Sang in Russe (Bulgaria) 1962-65; Sang in East Germany from 1965: Dobben, Magdeburg, Halle and the Staatsoper Berlin; Sang Tristan at the Dresden Staatsoper 1975; Bayreuth Festival 1976-83, as Tristan and Tannhäuser; Has sung roles in operas by Verdi and Puccini as well as leading parts in operas by Wagner; Vienna Staatsoper 1982, as Tannhäuser; Further appearances at the Deutsche Oper Berlin (1984), Munich and Cologne; Sang Tannhäuser at Berne, 1987. *Address:* c/o SA Gorlinsky Ltd., 33 Dover Street, London W1X 4NJ, England.

WENNBERG Siv Anna Margareta, b. 18 Sept 1944, Timra, Sweden. Singer (Soprano). *Education:* Ingesunds Musikskola, Sweden; Musikaliska Akademien Stockholm; qualified organist and music director. *Debut:* Royal Opera House, Stockholm, 1972. *Career includes:* Opera performances from 1974 throughout Europe; Extensive concert appearances with roles such as Brünnhilde (Siegfried and Valkyrie); Empress (Woman Without a Shadow); Amelia (Ballo in Maschera); Alice (Falstaff); Pucinni's Tosca; Leonora (Fidelio); Mozart's Donna Elvira; Daisy Doody (Aniara); Maria Eleonora (Kristina); Euridice (Orpheus in the Underworld); and Beatrice in von Suppe's Boccaccio. TV and Radio appearances at home and throughout Europe and the USA; Permanent member of the Royal Opera Stockholm, Stuttgart Opera and Frankfurt Opera. *Recordings:* Scandinavian Songs with Geoffrey Parsons; Wagner's Rienzi, with Dresden Staatskapelle. *Honours:* First prizes, Jussi Bjorling Competition and Scandinavian Singing Contest, 1971; Swedish Opera Prize for Wagner's Isolde, 1988. *Hobbies:* Classical music. *Address:* Odengatan 32, S-11351 Stockholm, Sweden.

WENZINGER August, b. 14 Nov 1905, Basle, Switzerland. Cellist; Conductor; Educator. m. Ilse Hartmann. *Education:* Studied cello at the Basle Conservatory 1915-27; Studied in Cologne with Jarnach and Grummer 1927- 29. *Career:* First cellist of the Bremen Orchestra 1929-34, Basle Allgemeine Musikgesellschaft 1936-70; Cellist in the Basle String Quartet 1933-47; Co-founded the Schola Cantorum Basiliensis 1933: has taught viola da gamba, ensemble

and ornamentation there; Co-leader Kammermusikkreis Scheck-Wenzinger 1936-43; Lectured at Harvard University on performance practice and viola da gamba playing, 1953; Directed the Capella Coloniensis for West German radio in Cologne 1954-58; Directed performances of baroque operas at Herrenhausen, 1958-66; Founded the viola da gamba trio of the Schola Cantorum Basiliensis 1968; Musical Director of Baroque concerts at Oberlin, Ohio; Guest Professor for Viola da gamba at the Hochschule für Musik, Vienna, 1976-; Concert tours of Europe, Asia and the USA; Gave the premieres of Martin's Ballade for cello and Schoeck's Cello Concerto. *Publications include:* Bach Solo Suites for Cello; JCF Bach Sonata in A; Monteverdi Orfeo 1955. *Honours include:* Hon DMus, University of Basle, 1960; Fellow, Royal Swedish Academy of Music, 1965; Hon.D Mus Berlin College, 1981. *Address:* 3 Zehntenfreistrasse, CH-4103 Bottmingen, Switzerland.

WERLE Lars Johan, b. 23 June 1926, Gavle, Sweden. Composer. *Education:* Studied musicology with Moberg at Upsala University; Counterpoint with Sven-Erik Back. *Career:* Music Producer for Swedish Radio 1958; Teacher at the National School for Music and Drama in Stockholm; Opera Drömmen om Therese performed at the 1974 Edinburgh Festival and elsewhere; Resan commissioned by the Hamburg Staatsoper; Tintomara premiered for the bicentenary of the Stockholm Opera House. *Compositions:* Operas and Musicals, Drommen om Therese 1960-64; Resan 1969; Tintomara 1973; TV opera En saga om sinnen 1971; Medusan och djaavulen 1973; A Midsummer Night's Dream 1985; Lionardo 1988; Orchestral and instrumental: Pentagram for string quartet 1959-60; Sinfonia da camera 1961; Summer Music for strings and piano 1965; Attitudes for piano 1965; ballet Zodiak 1966; Varieté for string quartet 1971; Det himelska djuret for tape 1975; Vaggsang for jorden 1977; Film music for Bergman's Persona; Vocal: Canzone 126 di Francesco Petraca for chorus 1967; Sound of M4b; Nautical Preludes 1970; Now all the fingers of this tree (Cummings) for soprano and ensemble 1971; Chants for Dark Hours for mezzo, flute, guitar and percussion 1972; Night Hunt for mezzo and piano 1973; Turned Away Songs 1973; Fabel for 5 voices 1974; Flower Power for 6 or more voices and instruments 1974; En hog visa for baritone and piano 1975. *Address:* c/o STIM, Sandhamnsgatan 79, PO Box 27327, S-102 54 Stockholm, Sweden.

WERNER Regina, b. 9 April 1950, Zwickau, Germany. Singer (Soprano). *Education:* Studied at the Thomasschule and the Musikhochschule, Leipzig. *Career:* Sang in sacred concerts at Leipzig 1974-87; Engagements at the Komische Oper Berlin 1975-77 and 1989, Halle from 1979, Leipzig and Chemnitz Operas from 1986; Guest appearances throughout Eastern Europe, Korea, Holland, Belgium, Switzerland, Portugal, Japan, Germany and Austria; Roles have included Mozart's Susanna, Bastienne and the Queen of Night, Marzelline, Gilda, Adele in Fledermaus and Sophie; Concert repertoire includes music by Bach, Handel, Haydn, the Requiems of Brahms, Mozart and Dvočák, Mahler's Knaben Wunderhorn and Carmina Burana; Professor at the Leipzig Musikhochschule from 1987. *Address:* c/o Komische Oper Berlin, Behrenstrasse 55-57, 1086 Berlin, Germany.

WERNICKE Herbert, b. 24 March 1946, Auggen, Germany. Stage Director and Designer. *Education:* Studied at the Brunswick Musikhochschule and at the Munich Kunstakademie. *Career:* Designs for the theatre at Landshut and Wuppertal; Staged Handel's oratorios Belshazzar at Darmstadt, 1978, and Judas Maccabeus at the Bayerische Staatsoper; Rameau's Hippolyte et Aricie at the Deutsche Staatsoper Berlin and the 1980 Schwetzingen Festival; Other work includes Fliegende Holländer at Munich and Die Meistersinger at Hamburg; Completed a production of Der Ring des Nibelungen at the Théâtre de la Monnaie, Brussels, 1991; Engaged at Basle Opera for Simon Boccanegra, followed by Don Giovanni, Cosi fan Tutte and Die Fledermaus, 1991-92. *Address:* Theater Basel, Theaterstrasse 7, CH-4010 Basel, Switzerland.

WERRES Elizabeth, b. 1954, Bonn, Germany. Singer (Soprano). *Education:* Studied in Chicago and Cologne. *Career:* Sang small roles at the Cologne Opera for one season then engaged at the Staatstheater Karlsruhe 1978-80. Roles including Marguerite in Gounod's Faust, Frau Fluth, Adele, Rosina, Achilles in Händel's Deidamia, Sang also in the European premiere of Argento's Postcard from Morocco; Engaged at Dortmund 1980-82 as Nedda, Gilda, Susanna, Despina, Aminta, Martha, Adele, Musetta; From 1982 Guest Engagements at: Staatsoper, Hamburg, Staatsoper Munich, Essen, Duesseldorf, Cologne, Zürich, Mannheim, Theater des Westens Berlin, Vienna Volksoper and many more. Roles include: The Merry Widow, Rosalinde, Marie in The Bartered Bride, Elvira; Radio concerts and recordings followed with the Westecutscher Rundfunk, the Norddeutscher Rundfunk, the Oesterreichischer Rundfunk, the Sueddeutscher Rundfunk and the Sender Freies Berlin; Television appearances as well as concerts in Tokyo, Chicago, Barcelona, Vienna and Germany; Engaged at the Staatsoper Hannover from 1989, notably as Tatjana in Eugene Onegin, Giulietta in Tales of Hoffmann, Musetta, Freia in Das Rheingold, Rosalinde, The Merry Widow and most recently in the role of Frieda in Das Schloss by Aribert Reimann. *Recordings:* CD's first complete recordings of Hindemith's comic opera Neues vom Tage; Live recordings of the Offenbachiade for the opening of the Cologne Philharmonic Hall. *Address:* c/o Niedersächsische Staatstheater, Openplatz 1, 30159 Hannover, Germany.

WESLEY-SMITH Martin, b. 1945, Adelaide, Australia. Composer. *Education:* Studied composition University of Adelaide and York, England; DPhil. *Career:* Senior Lecturer, Composition and Electronic Music, New South Wales State Conservatorium of Music, Sydney; Established, First Computer Music Studio, Central Conservatory of Music, Peking, People's Republic of China, 1986. *Compositions:* Orchestral Works: Interval Piece, 1970; Hansard Music, 1970; Sh.., 1973. Ensemble Works: Snark-Hunting, 1984; White Knight, 1984. Instrumental Works: Improvisations, 1966; Piano Piece, 1968; Small Bitonal Study, 1968; Tiger, Tiger, 1970; Guitar Music I, 1973. Vocal Works: Gum Tears of an Arabian Tree, 1966; To Noddy-Man, 1969; Doublets 2(b), 1975. Choral Works: Three Shakespearean Songs, 1965-87; Who Killed Cock Robin, 1979; Lost in Space, 1982; Songs for Snark-Hunters (from Boojum!), 1985. Stage Works: The Wild West Show, 1971; Machine, 1972; Boojum!, 1985-86. Works for Tape: Vietnam Image, 1970; Media Music 1, 1971; 2, 1973; Kdadalak (For the Children of Timor), 1977; Japanese Pictures, 1981; Echoes and Star Tides, 1981; Electronic Study 37(b), 1982; Dah Dit Dah Dah (from Night Satellite), 1983; Wattamolla Red, 1983; Music Box Music, 1984; Venceremos!, 1984; Tango, 1984; Snark-Huntingdon 2 (from Boojum!), 1986. *Honours:* Recipient of numerous awards including Don Banks Composer Fellowship, Australia Council, 1987. *Address:* c/o Australian Music Centre, P O Box 49, Broadway 2007, Australia.

WESSELY Helene, b. 29 July 1924, Vienna, Austria. Musicologist. m. Othmar Wessely. *Education:* Teachers Training College, Vienna; Phd, University of Vienna, 1950. *Career:* Assistant, Commission for Musicology, Austrian Academy of Sciences, 1954-56; Musicological Studies, Italy, 1956-58. *Publications:* Henry Purcell als Instrumentalkomponist, 1955; Romanus Weichlein, 1958; Lelio Colista, 1961; Romanus Weichlein: Encaenia Musices, 1979-80; William Young, 1983; New Editions, 4 Trio Sonatas of Lelio Colista, 1952, 1960, 1978; Ergaenzungen zur Biographie von Lelio Colista, 1993. *Contributions to:* Various professional journals and encyclopedias. *Membership:* Austrian Musicological Society. *Hobbies:* Painting; Photography. *Address:* Waehringer Str. 55, A 1090 Vienna, Austria.

WESSELY Othmar, b. 31 Oct 1922, Linz, Upper Austria. Professor of Musicology. m. Helen Kropik, 19 Sept 1951. *Education:* Academy of Music and dramatic art, Vienna, 1940-42; PhD, University of Vienna, 1947.

Career: Archivist, State Opera, Vienna, 1948-49; Secretary, Publishing Society of Monuments of Music in Austria, 1949; Assistant, 1950-63, Lecturer, 1958-63, Musicology, University of Vienna; Professor, Musicology, University of Graz, 1963-71, University of Vienna, 1971-. *Books:* Musik in Oberoesterreich, 1951; Die Musikinstrumentensammlung des Oberoesterreichischen Landesmuseums, 1952; Johannes Brassicanus: Ausgewaehile Werke, 1954; Arnold von Bruck: Sämtliche lateinische Motetten, 1961; Die grossen Darstellungen de Musikgeschichte in Barock und Aufklaerung, 1964-; E.L. Gerbers Tonkuenstlerlexika, 1966-77; Fruehmeister des stile nuovo in Oesterreich, 1974; Musik, 1973; Philippus de Monte, Madrigals for five voices, 1977-82. *Contributions to:* Numerous national and international scientific journals. *Honour:* Honorary Member, Johann Joseph Fux- Society, Graz, 1978-. *Memberships:* President, Publishing Society for Monuments of Music in Austria, 1974-91; Ordinary Member, Academy of Sciences, Austria, 1982-; Head, Commission for Musicology, Austrian Academy of Sciences and Head for Commission for Science of Sound; Trustee for the Istituto Storico Austriaco, Rome, Italy. *Address:* Universitaetstrasse 7, A-1010 Vienna, Austria.

WEST Ewan Donald, b. 9 Aug 1960, Cheltenham, Gloucestershire, England. Writer; Teacher. *Education:* University of Oxford. *Career:* Lecturer, History of Music, Worcester College, Oxford, 1986-; Junior Research Fellow, Mansfield College, Oxford, 1988-92; Director of Studies in Music, Sommerville College, Oxford, 1989-. *Publications:* Oxford Dictionary of Opera, 1992 (with John Warrack). Articles in Music and Letters; Austrian Studies. *Honours:* James Ingham Halstead Scholar, University of Oxford, 1985-87. *Memberships:* American Musicological Society, Royal Musical Association. *Hobbies:* Composing; Fast Cars; Cooking; Wine. *Address:* 8 Drakes Place, Malvern Road, Cheltenham, Glos GL50 2JF, England.

WEST John, b. 25 Oct 1938, Cleveland, Ohio, USA. Singer (Bass). *Education:* Studied with Martial Singher at the Curtis Institute and with Beverley Johnson in New York. *Debut:* San Francisco 1963, as Sarastro. *Career:* Many appearances at such US opera centres as Houston, Philadelphia, Seattle, Santa Fe, Portland, San Francisco, Washington and Fort Worth; Guest engagements at Vancouver, Mexico City, Hanover and Spoleto; Other roles have included Don Alfonso, Oroveso in Norma, Basilio, Mephistopheles of Gounod and Berlioz, Boris Godunov, Ramphis, Arkel, Ochs, La Roche in Capriccio, Hunding and Tiresias; Frequent concert engagements. *Address:* c/o San Francisco Opera, War Memorial Opera House, San Francisco, CA 94102, USA.

WEST Kevin, b. 1960, England. Singer (Tenor). *Education:* Studied at the Guildhall School with Walter Gruner. *Career:* Sang first with the D'Oyly Carte Opera Company; Appearances with Opera 80 as Sellem in The Rake's Progress and Don Ottavio; Britten's Peter Quint for Music Theatre Wales; Engagements with Opera Restor'd in English Baroque music and throughout Britain; Monteverdi's Orfeo at the Prom Concerts London; English National Opera debut 1989, as David in the Mastersingers; Has also sung with English National Contemporary Opera Studio, Opera Factory (Trimalchio in Maderna's Satyricon, 1990) and the Montepulciano Festival (The English Cat, 1990); Opera Northern Ireland 1991, as Mozart's Don Basilio; Concert repertoire includes Bach's St. John Passion and Easter Oratorio, works by Handel, Mozart and Schubert and Tippett's A Child of our Time (South Bank, London). *Address:* c/o Anglo Swiss Ltd. 3 Primrose Mews, 1a Sharpleshall St. London NW1 8YW, England.

WESTENBURG Richard, b. 26 Apr 1932, Minneapolis, USA. Conductor. *Education:* Studied at Lawrence University and the University of Minnesota (MA 1956); Further study in Paris with Nadia Boulnager and Pierre Cochereau; Postgraduate study at Theological Seminary School of Sacred Music in New York, 1960-

66. *Career:* Taught at University of Montana 1956-60; Director of Music at the First Unitarian Church in Worcester, Masachusetts, 1960-62; Organist and Choirmaster of the Central Presbyterian Church, New York, 1964-74; Music Director of Musica Sacra from 1968, giving five concert winter season, and six concert Bach Festival, annually at Avery Fisher Hall; Frequent guest conductor of choruses and orchestras throughout the USA; Music Director, Collegiate Choral, 1973-79; Head of Choral Department at the Juilliard School of Music from 1977; Visiting Professor, Rutgers University, 1986-87. *Honours include:* Honorary Doctor of Fine Arts, Lawrence University, 1980. *Address:* c/o Juilliard School of Music, Lincoln Center Plaza, New York NY 10023, USA.

WESTENDORF Craig J., b. 22 Sept 1953, Waterloo, Iowa, USA. Choral Conductor; Musicologist. m. Sue Anne Vaughn, 22 June 1975, 1 son, 1 daughter. *Education:* BM, Eastman School of Music, 1975; MM, University of Notre Dame, 1977; Universitat Erlangen-Nurnberg, 1980-81; DMA, University of Illinois, Urbana-Champaign, 1987. *Career:* Assistant Professional Specialist, University of Notre Dame, Notre Dame, Indiana; Director of Liturgical Choir; Instructor in Church Music, Hymnody, Music and Liturgy, Music History; University of Illinois at Urbana, Champaign; Urbana, Illinois, Visiting Professor in Musicology, 1989-. *Publications:* Glareanus Dodecachordon in German Theory and Practice: An Expression of Confessionalism, in Current Musicology, 1984; Continuo Figuration as a Stylistic Problem in the Kleine geistliche Konzerte of Heinrich Schütz, 1989; The Works of Heinrich Schütz in their Devotional Tradition, 1989; Max Reger and the Lied in the 20th Century, 1991. *Honours:* Julius Herford Award for best dissertation in choral music, 1987; Numerous grants for study in German libraries. *Memberships:* American Choral Directors Association; American Musicological Association; Officer, International Heinrich Schutz Society, American Chapter. *Hobbies:* Camping and hiking. *Address:* 404 W. Nevada, Urbana, Illinois 61801, USA.

WESTERGAARD Peter, b. 28 May 1931, Champaign, Illinois, USA. Professor of Music. *Education:* AB, magna cum laude, Harvard College 1953; MFA, Princeton University 1956; Studied composition with Walter Piston, Darius Milhaud, Roger Sessions, and Wolfgang Fortner. *Career:* Assistant, Salzburg Seminar in American Studies, summer session 1953; Assistant in Instruction, Princeton University 1955-56; Assistant to Professor Wolfgang Fortner, Staatliche Hochschule für Musik, Freiburg, Germany 1957; Fulbright Guest Lecturer, Staatliche Hochschule für Musik, Freiburg, Germany 1958; Instructor in Music 1958-63, Assistant Professor 1963-66, Columbia College; Visiting Lecturer with rank of Associate Professor, Princeton University 1966-67; Associate Professor: Amherst College 1967-68; Princeton University 1968-71; Professor, Princeton University 1971-; Chairman, Department of Music, Princeton University 1974-78, 1983-86; Director, Princeton University Orchestra 1968-73; Board of Directors: American Music Centre 1969-72; International Society for Contemporary Music 1970-74; Director, Princeton University Opera Theatre 1970-; Executive Board 1977-81; Programme Committee 1983-84; Society for Music Theory, Publications Awards Committee, 1987-1991; Chairman, 1988-89; Director, June Opera Festival of New Jersey 1983-86; Visiting Professor, University of British Columbia, 1987; Lecturer, International Music Seminar, University of Bahia, Brazil, 1992; Interdepartmental Committee for the Program in Musical Performance, Princeton University, 1992-93. *Compositions Include:* 5 Movements for small orchestra 1959; Cantata II, 1959, III, 1966; Quartet for Violin, Vibraphone, Clarinet, and Violoncello 1961; Variations for 6 Players 1967; Mr. and Mrs. Discobbolos 1967; Divertimento on Discobbolic Fragments 1967; Noises, Sounds and Sweet Airs, 1968; Tuckets and Sennets 1969; Cantata I 1956; Ariel Music, 1987; Two Fanfares for the Installation of Harold Shapiro as President of Princeton University, 1988, Ode, 1989; The Tempest, opera in three acts after William Shakespeare, 1990; Singing Translations of following

operas: The Magic Flute, Don Giovanni, Der Freischütz, Fidelio (original version of 1805), Così fan tutte, The Marriage of Figaro and Cinderella. *Address:* 40 Pine Street, Princeton, NJ 08542, USA.

WESTERLINCK Wilfried A M, b. 3 Oct. 1945, Leuven, Belgium. Musician; Composer. *Education:* Royal Conservatory of Brussels and Antwerp. *Career:* Professor,Music Analyse. Compositions, Antwerp, 1971-83; BRT Producer, Belgian Radio, 1972. *Compositions:* Metamorfose for orchestra; String Quartet; Landscapes 1 to V; Sonate 1-3 for piano solo; Variations on theme of Paganini for Piano; Sinfonietta; Solo works for Guitar, cello, flute, harp, harpsichord; songs; etc. *Honours:* Tenuto Prize for Metamorfose, 1972; Composition Prize of Antwerp, 1977; E Baie Prize, total work, 1985; J. Van Hoof Prize, song Cycle, 1986; Composition Prize Town of Mechelen for Bells, 1986; Adam Opel prize for Symphonic work, 1987. *Memberships:* SABAM; Board, Belgian composers Society; Flemish Composers Rep, CeBeDeM. *Hobbies:* Walking; Swimming; Reading. *Address:* Potvlietlaan 1/ 106 app 15a, B-2600 Belgium.

WESTERN Hilary, b. 1948, Cardiff, Wales. Singer (Soprano). *Education:* Studied at the Royal Academy of Music and the London Opera Centre. *Career:* Sang at the Wexford and Glyndebourne Festivals and in Angers (Mimi) and Toulouse (Frasquita); Appearances as Fiordiligi in Grenoble, Anchorage and Britain; Mimi, Papagena and Diana for Opera North as Ariadne, Louise, Micaela, Christine (Blake's Toussaint), Musetta and Diana: Almeida Festival 1990, in the world premiere of Europeras III and IV by John Cage; Performances of Birtwistle's Punch and Judy, The Beggar's Opera and Orfeo with Opera Factory; Schoenberg's Pierrot Lunaire for Ballet Rambert; Has sung in musicals (Chess, A Little Night Music) in the West End and at the Chichester Festival (Born Again). *Honours include:* Arts Council award to study with Martin Isepp in New York. *Address:* c/o Korman International Management, Crunnells Green Cottage, Preston, Herts SG4 7UQ, England.

WESTI Kurt, b. 22 March 1939, Oro, Holbaek, Denmark. Singer (Tenor). *Education:* Studied at the Copenhagen Music Academy. *Debut:* Funen Opera at Odense, 1960. *Career:* Sang in opera at Kiel 1962-63, Hanover 1963-66 and Copenhagen 1966-79; Member of the Oslo Opera 1980-86, Nationaltheater Mannheim from 1986; Guest appearances in concert and opera at Leipzig, Stockholm, Bergen, Hamburg, Berlin, Stuttgart, Buenos Aires, Minneapolis, and with Scottish Opera at Glasgow, 1969; Roles have included Mozart's Don Ottavio and Ferrando, Rossini's Lindoro, Fenton, Albert Herring, Edgardo, Cavaradossi, Rodolfo, Alfredo Germont, Radames, Turiddu, Gluck's Pylades, Strauss's Narraboth and Matteo, and Dimitri in Boris Godunov. *Address:* c/o Nationaltheater, Am Goetheplatz, 6800 Mannheim, Germany.

WETHERELL Eric David, b. 30 Dec 1925, Tynemouth, Northumbria, England. Musician. *Education:* Carlisle Grammar School 1936-44; BA, MMus, The Queen's College Oxford 1945-47; Royal College of Music 1948-49. *Career:* Horn Player 1949-59; Repetiteur, Royal Opera House Covent Garden 1960-63; Assistant Music Director Welsh National Opera 1963-69 Chief Conductor BBC Northern Ireland Orchestra 1976-81. *Compositions:* Airs and Graces and Welsh Dresser for orchestra; Bristol Quay for string orchestra; Your Gift to Man, chorus; Music for TV plays and films; *Memberships:* Savage Club, ISM. *Hobbies:* Jazz and Films. *Address:* 24 The Crescent, Henleaze, Bristol BS9 4RW, England.

WETHERILL Linda, b. 1950, USA. Flautist. *Career:* Recital and Concerto soloist in major cities of Europe, Canada, USA; Principal flautist with the orchestras of Hessischer Rundfunk Frankfurt and of Pierre Boulez's IRCAM at Pompidou Centre, Paris, France; Repertoire includes Baroque, Classic, Romantic and Impressionist works; Performed and premiered the flute music of

Luciano Berio, Pierre Boulez, Elliott Carter, Olivier Messiaen, Goffredo Petrassi and Karl-Heinz Stockhausen; Taught master classes in English, French, German, Spanish and American Conservatories. *Recordings:* Numerous for DTR and Deutsche Grammophon. *Honours:* Won New York Young Artists debut, 1979; First American and first flautist to be featured artist, 35-year-running World Peace Festival, Llangollen, Wales, 1982; Selected by West German Broadcasting Association for a 10 country European concerto debut, 1975. *Address:* c/o Norman McCann Ltd, The Coach House, 56 Lawne Park Gardens, London SE26 6XJ, England.

WETTSTEIN Peter, b. 15 Sept. 1939, Zurich, Switzerland. Composer; Conductor; Violinist. m. Elisabeth Wille, 2 sons. *Education:* Violin Teacher's Diploma, Zurich Music Academy, 1969; Composer's Diploma 1964, Conductor's Exam 1965, Detmold Music Academy, Germany. *Career:* Theory teacher, Zurich Music Academy, 1965; Lehrauftrag (akustik, gehoerbildung), Zurich University, 1973; Vice-Director, Conservatory & Music High School, Zurich, 1976-. *Compositions:* Works for choir & orchestra; Chamber music. *Publication:* Akustik und Instrumentenkunde, 1976. *Memberships:* Schweizerischer Tonkunstlerverein; Schweizerischer Musikpadagogischer Verband; President, Schweizer Musikinstitut. *Address:* Seestrasse 146, CH-8700 Kusnacht, Switzerland.

WEWEL Gunter, b. 29 Nov 1934, Arnsberg, Sauerland, Germany. Singer (Bass). *Education:* Studied with Johannes Kobeck in Vienna, Rudolf Watzke in Dortmund, Emmi Muller in Krefeld. *Career:* Member of the Dortmund Opera from 1963; Guest appearances in Dusseldorf, Cologne, Karlsruhe, Hanover, Budapest, Paris, Zurich, Salzburg, Munich; Radio and television engagements in Germany, France; Roles include Wagner's Daland, Titurel, Fafner, King Mark, Landgrave and King Heinrich; Philip II in Don Carlos, Gremin in Eugene Onegin and Beethoven's Rocco; Mozart's Sarastro, Osmin and Commendatore; Nicolai's Falstaff and Rossini's Bartolo. *Recordings include:* Die Zauberflöte conducted by Sawallisch; Schumann's Paradies und die Peri under Henryk Czyz; Suppé's Boccaccio with Willi Boskovsky; Die Königskinder, Mendelssohn's Die Beiden Pädagogen, Les Contes d'Hoffmann and Millöcker's Gasparone, conducted by Heinz Wallberg; La Vie Parisienne, with Willy Mattes (EMI-Electrola).

WEYDAHL Hanna-Marie, b. 30 June 1922, Tjome, Norway; Pianist; Lecturer; Widow. 1 son, 2 daughters. *Education:* Ecole Normale de Musique, Paris, 1937; Conservatory Royal de Musique, Brussels, 1948; Studies with Elisabeth Onarheim and Reimar Riefling. *Debut:* Oslo, 1940. *Career:* Recitals in all Nordic countries, UK, Belgium, France, Austria, Czechoslovakia, Russia; Professor, Norwegian Academy of Music; TV appearances in norway and radio appearances in many European countries; Jury member and chairman at Norwegian and international piano competitions. *Recordings:* Fartein Valen, piano music epic; Geirr Tveitt, Harding Tonar; Finn Arnestao; Enstroken D for klaver. *Publications: Honours:* Harriet Cohen International Music Awards for Performance of Contemporary Music, 1966; Gold Medal of Merit, King Olav V, 1985. *Memberships:* Norsk Tonekunstnersamfund Norske Musikklereres Landsforbund, EPTA; *Hobbies:* Languages; Gardening; Swimming. *Address:* Bjerkelia 17, 1170 Oslo, Norway.

WHEATLEY Patrick, b. 1950, Hinckley, Leicestershire, England. Singer (Baritone). *Education:* Studied at London Opera Centre, 1973. *Career:* Appeared with English National Opera 1974-80 as Germont, Amonasro, Marcello, Sharpless, Donner, Gunther, De Bretigny (Manon), Albert (Werther), Schelkalov (Boris Godunov) and the King in Dalibor; Guest appearances as Escamillo, Kothner, Hans Sachs and Talbot and Cecil in Maria Stuarda; Other roles include Renato (Northern Ireland Opera Trust); Ezio in

Attila (University College Opera); Falstaff and Papageno (City of Birmingham Touring Opera); Zurga in Les Pêcheurs de Perles (Scottish Opera); Jochanaan, and Yeletsky in The Queen of Spades (Chelsea Opera Group); Nabucco (Opera West); Mercutio in Roméo et Juliette (Las Palmas); Don Pasquale (Neath Opera); Rigoletto (Welsh National Opera); Sang Wotan and the Wanderer in a version of Wagner's Ring for the City of Birmingham Touring Opera, 1990-91; Concert engagements in Italy, Belgium and Spain and at the Promenade Concerts, London. *Address:* Music International, 13 Ardilaun Road, London N5 2QR, England.

WHEELOCK Donald Franklin, b. 17 June 1940, Stamford, Connecticut, USA. Composer; College Teacher. 1 son, 2 daughters. *Education:* AB Union College, Schenectady, New York, 1962; MM, Yale School of Music, New Haven, 1964. *Career:* Works performed by Rochester & Hartford Symphonies; Boston Musica Viva, Lenox Quartet and others; Teacher, Colgate University, and Amherst College; Currently, Professor, Music, Smith College, Northampton. *Compositions:* 11 works for orchestra, including voices and orchestra; 4 string quartets; many ensemble pieces; works for piano solo, solo cello, solo flute; Many vocal and choral compositions using own texts; Ten Bagatelles for oboe and string quartet; Sonata for solo flute. *Recording:* Dreams Before a Sacrifice (dramatic monologue for mezzo soprano and orchestra). *Address:* Department of Music, Smith College, Northampton MA 01063, USA.

WHELAN Paul, b. 1966, New Zealand. Singer (Baritone). *Education:* Studied at the Wellington Conservatoire and the Royal Northern College of Music. *Career:* Concerts and recitals in New Zealand, the USA and Europe; Nielsen's 3rd Symphony under Simon Rattle, Messiah in Russia with Yehudi Menuhin and in London with the London Mozart Players; Vaughan Williams's Five Mystical Songs and Sea Symphony, Messiah at the Albert Hall under Charles Farncombe; Opera engagements include roles in Death in Venice for Glyndebourne Opera, Schaunard in La Bohème at Stuttgart, Masetto in Bordeaux (1993), Britten's Demetrius for Australian Opera and on tour in France and Guglielmo for Dublin Grand Opera; Welsh National and Scottish Opera debuts 1994, as Timur in Turandot and Mozart's Figaro; Messiah with Halle Orchestra, conductor Roger Vignoles; Verdi, Requiem, Budapesy Symphony Orchestra, conductor Paolo Olmi; Recitals Blackheath and Wigmore Halls, London; Demetrius, Edinburgh Festival, 1994; Forthcoming: Schaunard, Netherlands Opera. *Honours include:* Brigitte Fassbaender award for Lieder. *Address:* c/o IMG Artists, Media House, 3 Burlington Lane, London W4 2TH, England.

WHETTAM Graham Dudley, b. 7 Sept. 1927, Swindon, Wiltshire, England. Composer. m. (1) Rosemary B Atkinson, 20 Nov. 1948. (2) Janet Rosemary Lawrence, 31 Mar. 1959, 4 sons, 1 daughter. *Education:* Self-taught composer. *Concert Debut:* C.B.S.O., Birmingham, 1950; Radio Debut: BBC 3rd Programme, 1951. *Career:* Works in concert and broadcast in Britain and abroad; Has withdrawn recognition of works written mostly prior to 1959. *Compositions include:* Orchestra: Clarinet Concertos No 1, 1959, No 2, 1982; Introduction and Scherzo Impetuoso, 1960; Sinfonia Contra Timore, 1962; Cello Concerto, 1962; Sinfonia Intrepida, 1976; Sinfonia Drammatica, 1978; Hymnos for Strings, 1978; Symphonic Prelude, 1985; Ballade for Violin & Orchestra, 1988; Choral: The Wounded Surgeon Plies the Steel, 1960; Magnificat and Nunc Dimmitis, 1962; Do Not Go Gentle Into That Good Night, 1965; Consecration, 1982; A Mass for Canterbury, 1986; Chamber Music: 3 String Quartets, 1967, 1978, 1980; Sextet for Wind and Piano, 1970; Quintetto Concertato, Wind Quintet, 1979; Percussion Partita for six players, 1985; Quartet for Four Horns, 1986; Piano: Prelude, Scherzo and Elegy, 1964, revised 1986; Prelude and Scherzo Impetuoso, 1967; Night Music, 1969; Solo Violin Sonatas No 1, 1957, revised 1987, No 2, 1972; Solo Violin Sonata No 3, 1989; Suite for Timpani, 1982;

Solo Cello Sonata, 1990: Andromeda for Percussion Quartet, 1990; Concerto Ardente for horn and strings, 1992; Les Roseaux au Vent for two oboes, Cor Anglais and strings, 1993; Romanza for solo violin (also arr. for solo viola and solo cello), 1993. *Recordings:* Quartet for Four Horns, 1989. *Contributions to:* Listener; Times Educational Supplement; Guardian. *Honours:* Gregynog Arts Fellowship, Welsh Arts Council and University of Wales, 1978. *Memberships:* Chairman 1971 and 1983-86, Composers' Guild of Great Britain; Vice-Chairman 1972-85, 1987- British Copyright Council; Director, Mechanical Copyright Protection Society Limited, 1984-; Director, National Discography Limited, 1985-93; Director, The Performing Right Society Limited, 1988-; Royal Society of Musicians. *Address:* Meriden Music, Chapel House, 13 Market Place, Ingatestone, Essex CM4 0BY, England.

WHITE Andrew Nathaniel, b. 6 Sep. 1942, Washington, District of Columbia, USA. Musician; Recording Engineer; Composer-Arranger; Conductor; Musicologist; Lecturer; Publisher; Impresario. m. Jocelyne H J Uhl. *Education:* BMus Music Theory, Howard University, Washington, 1964. *Debut:* Solo, Carnegie Hall, 1974. *Career:* Jazz Saxophonist, JFK Quintet 1960-64, New Jazz Trio 1965-66; Oboist and English Horn Player, Center of Creative and Performing Arts, 1965-67; Principal Oboe and English Horn, American Ballet Theatre, 1968-70; Electric Bassist, Stevie Wonder 1968-70, Motown Record Company, 1968-70, Fifth Dimension 1970-76, The Jupiter Hair Company 1971-, Weather Report (recording) 1972-73; Jazz Saxophonist, Elvin Jones 1980-81, Beaver Harris, 1983-. *Compositions Include:* Concerto, 1963; Concertina, 1963; Shepherd Song, 1963; Andrew with Strings, 1987; A Jazz Concerto, in five versions, 1988. *Recordings:* 42 Self-produced among others. *Publications Include:* Saxophone Transcriptions: The Works of John Coltrane, 10 volumes; The Eric Dolphy Series Limited; The Charlie Parker Collection, 4 volumes; The Andrew White Transcription Series; Big Band Series; Small Band Series; Andy's Song Book; Chamber Music Series; Saxophone Recital Series; Saxophone Etudes; Saxophone Trios, Quartets, Quintets; 2 Symphonies for 8 Saxophones; 4 Jazz Duets; 4 Jazz Trio Sonatas; 12 Jazz Miniatures; Books on Improvisation, Professionalism, Practice, Transcription, Jazz Education, Coltrane's Music, Self-Production, Five Comedy Books and numerous articles in trade journals; Staff writer for Saxophone Journal. *Honours include:* Numerous study grants; Conductor, Dean Dixon Memorial Award, 1984; Washington Area Music Association Award, 1985. *Current Management:* Andrew's Musical Enterprises Incorporated. *Memberships include:* Pi Kappa Lambda; International Double Reed Society. *Address:* 4830 South Dakota Avenue NE, Washington, DC 20017, USA.

WHITE (Edwin) Chappell, b. 16 Sept 1920, Georgia, USA. Educator; Musicologist. m. Barbara Tyler, 22 Aug 1959, 1s, 2d. *Education:* BA, Emory University, 1940; BMus, Westminster Choir College, 1947; MFA, Princeton University, 1957. *Career:* Instructor, Agnes Scott College, 1950-52, Instructor and Associate Professor, Emory University, 1952-74; Professor, Kansas State University, 1974-91 (retired); Violist, Atlanta Symphony, 1950- 57; Music Critic, Atlanta Journal, 1959-72; Visiting Professor, Indiana University, 1972-73, University of Georgia, 1970-71; Brown Foundation Fellow, University of the South, 1993. *Publications:* From Vivaldi to Viotti: A History of the Classical Violin Concerto, 1992; G B Viotti: A Thematic Catalogue of his works, 1985; Intro to Life and Works of R Wagner, 1969; Ed, 4 concertos by G B Viotti, 1976; 15 articles, New Grove Dictionary, 1980; Contributor to the Journal of American Musicological Society, Fontes Artis Musiche and Musical Quarterly. *Honours:* Research Grant, NEH, 1982-83. *Memberships:* College Music Society (President, 1979-80); American Musicological Society. *Hobby:* Golf. *Address:* 150 Bobtown Circle, Sewanee, TN 37375, USA.

WHITE David Ashley, b. 11 Dec 1944, San Antonio,

Texas, USA. Composer; Professor. *Education:* BMus, MMus, University of Houston; DMA, University of Texas, 1978. *Career:* Professor of Composition and Theory, Dirctor of Graduate Studies, University of Houston School of Music. *Compositions:* Elegy and Exaltation, violin, cello, piano; Homages, mezzo-soprano, viola, piano; This Bitterly Beautiful Land, cantata for mixed chorus, soloists, and chamber ensemble; The Ruins of Missolonghi, orchestra; Evening Service, mixed chorus a cappella, manus. *Publications include:* Elegy and Exaltation, Homages, The Ruins of Missolonghi; The Lord Is King; The David Ashley White Hymnary, 1993; Hymns included in Worship Songs Ancient and Modern, 1992. *Honours:* Composer in Residence, Houston Chapter, American Guild of Organists, 1992-94. *Memberships:* Association of Anglican Musicians; Texas Composers Forum; American Guild of Organists. *Hobbies:* Walking; Cooking; Travelling. *Address:* School of Music, University of Houston, TX 77204-4893, USA.

WHITE Donald H, b. 28 Feb. 1921, Narberth, Pennsylvania, USA. Professor; Composer. m. L Rosalie Allison, 4 Sept. 1948, 3 daughters. *Education:* BS Music Education, Temple University, 1942; Philadelphia Conservatory, 1946; MM 1947, PhD 1952, Eastman School of Music. *Career:* Professor 1947-81, Director of School of Music 1974-79, DePauw University; Chairman, Music Department, Central Washington University, 1981-; Retired 1990, became Emeritus Professor of Music. *Compositions:* Miniature Set for Band (recorded); Dichotomy (recorded); Terpsimetrics; Concertino for Solo Timpani and Winds; Sonnet for Band; Introduction and Allegro; Ambrosian Hymn Variants; Divertissement for Blue Lake; Patterns; Recitals; Air and Dance; Marchisma; Trombone Sonata; Trumpet Sonata; Lyric Suite for Euphonium and Piano; Tetra Ergon for Bass Trombone and Piano (recorded); Sonata for Tuba and Piano; 3 for 5, woodwind quintet (recorded); Serenade for Brass Quartet; Diversions for Brass Sextet; Quintet for Brass; Divertissement for Strings; Andante for Oboe, Harp and Strings; Pslam. *Honours:* 19 successive awards from the Standard Awards Panel, ASCAP; Many commissions. *Hobbies:* Reading; Swimming; Walking; Golf; Philately. *Address:* 14501 N Rock Springs Ln, Tucson, AZ 85737, USA.

WHITE Emily, b. 15 Dec 1962, Rye, New York, USA. Concert Pianist. *Education:* BMus, Summa cum laude with High Honours in music, University of Maryland; MMus, The Juilliard School; Recital Diploma, First Class Honours, Royal Academy of Music; Doctor of Musical Arts in progress, Manhattan School of Music; Studies with Sascha Gorodnitzki, Christopher Elton, Nelita True, Solomon Mikowsky, Donn-Alexandre Feder; Teaching Fellowships at The Juilliard School and Royal Academy of Music; Coaching Fellowship at the Juilliard Opera Center. *Career:* New York debut in all-Chopin programme, Weill Recital Hall, Carnegie Hall, 1988; Recitals and concerts throughout the United States and Great Britain; Soloist with the Lambeth Orchestra of London, 1988; Soloist with the Bergen Philharmonic, New Jersey, 1991; Recitals in Switzerland, Belgium and Canada; One-hour feature on WNYC radio, 1993; *Recording:* MacDowell's, Woodland Sketches, 1993. *Honours include:* London Symphony Orchestra Foundation Grant, 1986; Chappell Gold Medal and Queen's Commendation for Excellence at the RAM; Tope Prizes in the International Young Concert Artists Competition of Royal Tunbridge Wells, Chopin Foundation Council of Greater New York National Auditions, International Mozart Competition at Salzburg, Concerts Atlantique Touring Artists Competition, Friends of the Bergen Philharmonic Competition, Sigma Alpha Iota National Awards. *Address:* 825 West 187th Street. Apt. 1C, New York, NY 10033, USA.

WHITE Harry, b. 4 July 1958, Dublin, Republic of Ireland. University Professor of Music. m. Eithne Graham, 11 June 1980. 1 son. *Education:* University College, Dublin; University of Toronto; Trinity College, Dublin. *Career:* Part Time Lectureship, St Patrick's College, 1984-85; Assistant Lectureship in Music, 1985-88; College Lectureship in Music, 1988-93,

University College Dublin, Professor of Music, 1993; Director, Irish Opera Theatre Co, 1987-. Publications: J J Fux, Il Trionfo della Fede; Irish Musical Studies I; Musicology in Ireland; Irish Musical Studies II: Music and The Church; Johann Joseph Fux and the Music of the Austro - Italian Baroque (ed). Contributions to: Acta Musicologica; Fontes Artes Musicae; Bach; Kirchenmusikalisches Jahrbuch; International Review of the Aesthetics and Sociology of Music; Journal of American Studies; Musik und Kirche; Hermathena; Modern Drama; Journal of Musicology. Honours: Open Fellowship; E J Pratt Medal for Poetry. Membership: Royal Musical Association; International Musicological Society; 18th Century Ireland Society. Hobbies: Canadiana; Walking. Address: Department of Music, University College, Belfield, Dublin 4, Republic of Ireland.

WHITE Jeremy, b. 1953, Liverpool, England. Singer (Bass- baritone). Education: Studied at Queen's College and Christ Church, Oxford; Singing studies with David Johnston, Elisabeth Fleming. Career: Many performances with early music ensembles in Britain and Europe; Acis and Galatea for Swiss television, debut at the Amsterdam Concertgebouw in Bach cantatas under Ton Koopman; Performances in Vienna, Budapest and Turku (Finland); Bach's St John Passion in England and Spain with The Sixteen; CPE Bach's oratorio Auferstehung und Himmelfahrt Jesu, in Munich; Bach's Magnificat and Christmas Oratorio in Oxford and London with the King's College Choir and English Chamber Orchestra; Handel/Mozart Messiah in Paris and Lucerne; Bach's Passions in English cathedrals; Modern concert repertoire includes Abraham and Isaac by Stravinsky, and music by Berio and Tavener; Has sung in The Lighthouse by Maxwell Davies, Walton's The Bear (title role), Pfitzner's Palestrina (Cardinal Morone), Les Troyens and Der Rosenkavalier (the Notary, Aix-en-Provence festival); Roles in operas by Mozart and Rossini; Recent engagements 1993: Tour of Verdi's Requiem, including Paris and the Flanders Festival; Series of performances of Arvo Pärt's Passio in Jerusalem, Seville and throughout Poland and Finland, Berio in Helsinki conducted by the composer and Beethoven's Ninth Symphony for Swiss Radio; Sang Don Prudenzio in Rossini's Il Viaggio a Reims, Covent Garden; Sang Webern's Second Cantata with Pierre Boulez in a broadcast from Birmingham Symphony Hall. Season 1993/94: Contemporary Music Network tour as Peter in Jonathan Harvey's Passion and Resurrection, followed by a return to the Royal Opera to sing Benoit in La Bohème; Visit to Brazil with the Scottish Chamber Orchestra; Return to Swiss Radio in Lugano; Concert appearances with The Sixteen and The Taverner Players in Beethoven and Schütz in Germany, Norway and Switzerland, and Handel's La Resurrezione in Paris and Bourges; Concerts in London and the provinces. Recordings include: John Tavener's Great Canon of St Andrew; Monteverdi's Vespers, with The Sixteen; Handel Israel in Egypt conducted by Andrew Parrott. Current Management: (Opera and Concerts): Magenta Music International; (Concerts only): Musicmakers, Little Easthall Farmhouse, St Paul's Walden, Nr Hitchin, Herts SG4 8DH. Address: Magenta Music International. 4 Highgate High Street, Highgate Village, London N6 5JL, England.

WHITE Jillian Mary, b. 29 Jan 1942, Leicestershire, England. Senior Music Producer. Education: RAM, London, 1960-64; Acad Music and Drama, Vienna, 1966-67; ARAM, 1988, Career: Opera and Lieder Singer, to 1970; Professor of Music, Vienna, Austria, 1967-78; BBC Gramophone Lib, England, 1970-71; Music Selector, BBC Sound Archive, 1971-75; Music Prod, BBC Pebble Mill, 1975-86; Director of Music of the National Youth Orchestra of Great Britain, 1993; Guest Artistic Director, Bournemouth International Festival of the Arts; LP/CD Prod for various record companies; Visiting Lecturer, Founder, Production Tech Course, Birmingham Conservatoire. Honours: Gramophone Award for Faure Requiem, 1985; Hon Member, Polish Composers Union, 1990; Hon Fellow, Birmingham Schools Music, 1990; Works dedicated to her by various composers; First woman Senior Music

Producer in the BBC regions. Memberships: Governor, Dartington College of Arts; VP, Friends of Exeter Festival; VP, Bristol Friends of Bournemouth Orchestras; Patron of Frome Choral Society; Trustee and Director, Gloucester Academy of Music and Performing Arts. Hobbies: Music; Painting; Life drawing; Cooking; Cats. Address: 11 Hampton Park, Bristol BS6 6LG, England.

WHITE John, b. 28 May 1938, Leeds, Yorkshire, England. Musician; Professor of Viola; Royal Academy of Music. m. Carol Susan Shaw, 29 Aug. 1964, 1 son, 1 daughter. Education: Charles Oldham Scholar, 1959-63, Royal Academy of Music; Associate, Royal College of Music; Huddersfield Technical College, Music Department, 1953-57. Career: Member, Alberni String Quartet, 1960-67, Stadler Trio, 1967-76; Senior Lecturer, Hockerill College of Education, 1970-78; Tutor, RNCM, 1974, BSM, Colchester Institute; Adjudicator, Music Festivals; Conductor and coach at various music courses; Professor, Junior Department, 1967-75, Viola, 1976-, Presently Professor of Viola, Royal Academy of Music; British Representative, Viola Society; Joint Organiser, International Viola Congress, London, 1978; Committee and professional staff, Lionel Tertis International Viola Competitions and workshops, 1980, 1984, 1988, 1991 and 1994; Viola Tutor to European Community Youth Orchestra, 1984-92; Viola Tutor to Gustav Mahler Youth Orchestra, Vienna, 1991; Master Classes in Greece, 1989 and 1990; 1991 in the Jury for the William Primrose International Viola Competition in the USA; Presented a Lecture at the 1991 International Viola Congress, USA; Artistic Director, Annual Viola Festival, Harlow; Professor of Viola and former Head of Instrumental Studies, Royal Academy of Music, 1984-90; Host Chairman for the 1994 International Viola Congress. Recordings: Haydn String Quartets; Rawsthorne String Quartets. Publications: Sonatina for Viola and Piano by Alan Bush; Editor, Three Miniature String Quartets by Richard Stoker; Ballade for Viola and Piano, Minna Keal viola, edited, John White; Scales and Arpeggius for viola players, Watson Forbes (ed John White), Corda Publications; In preparation: An Anthology of British Viola Players by John White. Hobby: Cricket. Address: 36 Seeleys, Harlow, Essex, CM17 0AD, England.

WHITE John, b. 5 Apr 1936, Berlin, Germany. Composer. Education: Studied with Elisabeth Lutyens at the Royal College of Music, 1954-57. Career: Music Director of the Western Theatre Ballet, 1959-60; Teacher of composition at the RCM 1961-66, tuba player with the London Gabrieli Brass Ensemble, 1971-72. Compositions include: 119 Piano Sonatas; 21 Symphonies; 30 Ballets; Music for films and television; Operas Stanley and the Monkey King, London 1975, and the Trial; Orpheus: Eurydice, London 1976; Music theatre Man-Machine Interface. Address: c/o PRS Ltd. Member Registration, 29-33 Berners Street, London W1P 4AA, England.

WHITE John David, b. 28 Nov 1931, Rochester, Minnesota, USA. Composer; Cellist. m. Marjorie Manuel, 27 Dec 1952, 2 sons, 1 daughter. Education: BA, University of Minnesota 1953; MA 1954; PhD 1960; Eastman School of Music, University of Rochester, 1960. Career: University of Wisconsin, Kent State University, Music Department, Chair, Whitman College 1978-80; Dean, School of Music, Ithaca College 1973-75; Professor and Head of Composition and Theory, University of Florida 1980-; Active Cellist in recital and chamber music; Soloist with Atlanta, Rochester, Madison and Akron Orchestras; Composer of 50 works, performances by Cleveland, Atlanta, Rochester, Madison and Akron Orchestras; Music published by G. Schirmer, Galaxy, Carl Fischer, Lawson- Gould; Author of Five Books; Taught at University of Michigan. Compositions: Symphony No. Two, 1960; Symphony No. 3; Legend of Sleepy Hollow, 1962; 3 Choruses from Goethe's Faust; 3 Madrigals for Chorus and Orchestra; Numerous choral works, 1960-87; Variations for Clarinet and Piano; Zodiac, Chorus and Piano; Music for Oriana, 1979 (for Violin, Cello and Piano); Pied Beauty, Chorus and Piano; Eiseleic Madrigals; Sonata for Cello and Piano, 1982; Music for Violin and Piano 1983; Concerto for Flute and Wind Ensemble, 1984; Symphony for Wind Band 1985; Dialogues for Trombone and Piano 1984; Symphony For A Saint 1987; Songs of the Shulamite, 1988; Mirrors for Piano and Orchestra, 1990. *Recordings:* Variations for Clarinet and Piano, Advent 5005. *Publications:* Understanding and Enjoying Music 1968; Music in Western Culture 1972; Guidelines for College Teaching of Music Theory 1981; The Analysis of Music, 2nd Edition, 1984. *Contributions to:* Journal of Music Theory; Journal for Musicological Research; Music and Man. *Hobbies:* Tennis; Skiing. *Address:* 5715 NW 62nd Court, Gainesville, FL 32606, USA.

WHITE Willard, b. 10 Oct 1946, St. Catherine, Jamaica. Singer (Bass). *Education:* Juilliard School of Music, New York, with Beverley Johnson, Giorgio Tozzi and Erik Thorendahl. *Debut:* New York City Opera 1974, as Colline in La Bohème: later sang Giorgio in I Puritani, Creon in Medéé and Osmin in Die Entführung; Washington Opera as Trulove in The Rake's Progress; Houston Opera in Scott Joplin's Treemonisha; European debut 1976 with Welsh National Opera, as Osmin; English National Opera 1976, as Seneca in L'Incoronazione di Poppea: Hunding in Die Walkure 1983; Glyndebourne 1978-, as The Speaker in Die Zauberflöte, the King in Love for Three Oranges, and Gershwin's Porgy, 1986; Guest appearances with Netherlands Opera (Oroveso in Norma), Bavarian State Opera (Munich) and in Florence; Covent Garden debut 1980, as Don Diego in L'Africaine: returned as Klingsor (Parsifal), Fafner (Das Rheingold) and the Grand Inquisitor (Don Carlos, 1989); Also heard in concert, notably in the 14th Symphony of Shostakovich; Sang Wotan in Act III of Die Walküre at the Festival Hall, 1990; Ferrando in Il Trovatore and Fafner in Siegfried at Covent Garden, 1990; Teatro de la Zarzuela, Madrid, 1990, in Il Turco in Italia; Sang Wotan for Scottish Opera 1991, Porgy at Covent Garden, 1992. *Recordings:* Porgy and Bess (Decca); Die Aegyptische Helena (Decca); Acis and Galatea (Deutsche Grammophon). *Address:* c/o Harrison/Parrott Ltd., 12 Penzance Place, London W11 4PA, England.

WHITEHEAD Gillian, b. 23 Apr 1941, Whangarei, New Zealand. Composer. *Education:* University of Auckland; BMus, University of Wellington; MMus, University of Sydney, New South Wales; Studied with Peter Maxwell Davies in Adelaide, then in Britain. *Career:* Lived in UK and Europe, 1967-81; Appointed 1st Composer-in-Residence, Northern Arts, Newcastle-upon-Tyne, England, 1978; Lecturer in Composition, Sydney Conservatorium of Music, New South Wales, Australia, 1981-; Various commissions funded by Music Board of Australia Council, Arts Council of Great Britain, New Zealand Arts Council. *Compositions:* Published and/or recorded: Missa brevis, SATB, 1963; Qui natus est, carol, SATB, 1966; Fantasia on Three Notes, piano solo, 1966; Whakatau-ki, chamber music with voice, 1970; La cadenza sia corta, piano solo, 1974; Tristan and Iseult, for 4 singers, mimes and puppets, instrumental ensemble, 1975; Voices of Tane, piano solo, 1976; At Night the Garden Was Full of Flowers, for 4 recorders, 1977; The Tinker's Curse, children's opera, 1979; Requiem, for male soprano and organ (dance score), 1981. *Honours:* Recipient of numerous grants including New Zealand Queen Elizabeth II Arts Council and Vaughan Williams Trust. *Current Management:* Helen Lewis. *Address:* c/o Helen Lewis, 10 John Street, Woollahra, New South Wales 2025, Australia.

WHITEHEAD William John, b. 30 June 1938, New Mexico, USA. Conductor; Organist. m. 29 Dec 1960, 1 daughter. *Education:* BMus, University of Oklahoma, 1959; Artists Diploma, Curtis Institute of Music, 1962; MA, Columbia University, 1970. *Career:* Director of Music, First Presb Church, Bethlehem, 1961-73; Dir of Music, Fifth Avenue Presb Church, NY, 1973-90; Professor, Organ, Westminster Choir College, 1966-71; Mannes College of Music, 1975-90; Organist in Residence, Union Theo Sem, NY, 1981-85. *Recordings:*

The Organ of the Philadelphia Academy of Music, VolI, 1962, Vol II, 1963; Mendelssohn's Bach Recital, Bethlehem Bach Festival Rec, 1970; Music of Leo Sowerby at Washington Cathedral, 1989. *Honours:* Young Artist Award, Philadelphia Orchestra, 1962. *Memberships:* American Guild of Organists; Presb Association of Musicians; Phi Mu Alpha Sinfonia; Hymn Society of America; American Choral Director's Association. *Current Management:* Roberta Bailey Artists International, PO Box 3665, Boston, MA 02101, USA. *Address:* 1340 West Long Lake Road, Bloomfield Hills, MI 48302, USA.

WHITELEY John Scott, b. 1 Jan. 1950, Leicester, England. Cathedral Organist. m. Hilary Elizabeth Holte Cox, 3 Aug. 1974, 2 sons. *Education:* BSc, London University, 1971; PhD Candidate, Leeds University; Associate, Royal College of Music; Fellow, Royal College of Organists. *Debut:* Royal Festival Hall, London, March, 1983. *Career:* Radio appearances on Choral Evensong, 1978, 1979, 1983-93. Record Review, 1979, Choirs of Britain, 1983-84, Sunday Half Hour, Songs of Praise; Sub-Organist, St Edmundsbury Cathedral, 1973-75; Assistant Organist, York Minster, 1975-; Organ Tutor, Hull University, 1978-; Formed York Piano Duo, 1982; 1st Concert Tour of North America, May and June 1985; Concert tour of Australia, 1988. *Compositions:* Anthem, Jesu Redemptor Omnium, 1983; Magnificat & Nunc Dimittis (York Service), 1984, published Banks; 2 Anthems, 1991; Complete Organ Works of Joseph Jongen (Vols I and II), 1990-92. *Recordings:* The Organ at York Minster, Volumes 1 and 2; several records with the Choir of York Minster; Great Romantic Organ Music (Hearne 1986); Cathedral Windows (The Organ of York Minster) (Priory 1987); Haarlem Grote Kerk, 1988; Hadersiev, DK 1989, Music of Prague and Vienna. *Publications:* Editor, For Manuals Only (8 pieces for organ), 1982; Jongen J Petit Prelude, 1973, Jongen J Four Pieces, 1983; Editor, Jongen: Mass Op. 130, 1990. *Contributions to:* Musical Times; Organists Review; Magazine of AGO, USA. *Honours:* Studies with Fernando Germani and Flor Peeters; Turpin Prize of Royal College of Organists; Studies with Ralph Downes. *Address:* 1 Chapter House, York, YO1 2JH, North Yorkshire, England.

WHITFIELD John Peter, b. 21 Mar 1957, Darlington, County Durham, England. Conductor; Musical Director; Bassoonist. *Education:* Chetham's School of Music, 1973-75; Keble College Oxford, 1975-78; National Youth Orchestra, 1973-77; European Community Youth Orchestra, 1978; International Youth Orchestra; Bassoon studies with Charles Cracknell, Martin Gatt and Mordechai Rechtmann, Tel Aviv. *Debut:* South Bank Conducting debut, 27 Mar. 1983. *Career:* Israel Chamber Orchestra; City of London Sinfonia; English Baroque Orchestra; London Sinfonietta; London Symphony Orchestra, also tours; LSO Israel Chamber Orchestra; Founder and Musical Director of Endymion Ensemble; many concerts in London and UK festivals as bassoonist, conductor, with soloists. Commissioned and conducted premieres of works by David Bedford, Dominic Muldowney, Nigel Osborne, Martin Stebbing, Michael Nyman, Giles Swayne, Anthony Payne; Assistant Conductor for Spitalfields Festival Production and EMI recording of Armide (Gluck) with Felicity Palmer in title role; Assistant to Richard Hickox; Stage Debut as conductor of Birtwistle's Down by the Greenwood Side Bath Festival, also broadcast by Radio 3. *Recordings:* Stravinsky record including Symphonies of Wind and Dumbarton Oaks and Britten Record with Gomez and Palmer on EMI. *Current Management:* Music & Musicians Artists Management, London. *Address:* 45 Chalcot Road, London, NW1 8LS, England.

WHITICKER Michael, b. 1954, Gundagai, New South Wales, Australia. Composer. *Education:* Degree, composition, NSW State Conservatorium of Music, 1982; Studied with Richard Troop; Postgraduate composition studies, West Germany with Isang Yun and Witold Szalonek. *Compositions:* Orchestral Works: Ad Marginem, 1986; Tartengk, 1985; Tya, 1984. Works for the Stage: The Bamboo Flute, 1982; Gesualdo, 1987.

Ensemble Works: Hunufcu, 1979; Korokon, 1983; Quidong, 1983; Kwa, 1986; Winamin, 1986; Orpheus and Persephone, 1987; Plangge, 1987; Venus Asleep, 1987; Min-amé, 1988; Ad Parnassum, 1989; Redror, 1989. Solo Instrumental Works: Vibitqi, 1980; Tulku, 1982; If Buifs, 1981; Kiah, 1986; The Hands, The Dream, 1987; In Prison Air, 1988; On Slanting Ground, 1988. Vocal Works: A Voice Alone, 1982; Night Swimming, 1984; Sheaf Tosser, 1984; As Water Bears Salt, 1989. Works for Students: Boinko the Billio, 1979; Hommage to Alban Berg, 1980; Liexliu, 1980; Introduction for Concert Band, 1985; Karobaan, 1985; Taldree, 1985; The Bankstown Pageant, 1985; The Hollow Crown, 1985; The Serpent Beguiles, 1985; Three Episodes, 1985. Works for Tape Alone: Cement Mounted Inlays, 1981; Model Sequence II, 1981; Slid PC, 1982; Ballets: Factor X, 1980; Passion, 1989; Film Scores: Atlantis, 1981; Conferenceville, 1982; The Bus Trip, 1982; Man, The Skin Cancer of the Earth, 1991 for three voices, sax, percussion and tape; Jellingroo, 1990 for didjeridoo, flute and cello; Encircled by Lillies, 1991, for soprano, tenor and piano. *Address:* c/o Australian Music Centre, P O Box 49, Broadway 2007, Australia.

WHITMORE Lee Evans Jr, b. 24 Dec 1964, New Jersey, USA. Educational Director; Instructor. *Education:* BS Music Education, 1987, MM Education, 1989, West Chester University. *Career:* Educational Director and Product Manager, Korg USA Inc, electronic music instrument manufacturer and distributor, 1989-; Instructor of Electronic Music, Columbia University Teacher's College, NY, 1992-. *Honours:* Phi Delta Kappa; Phi Mu Alpha Sinfonia; Phi Kappa Lambda. *Address:* Korg USA Inc, 98 Frost Street, Westbury, NY 11590-5007, USA.

WHITTLESEY Christine, b. 12 Jan 1950, New York City, USA. Singer (Soprano). *Education:* Studied in Boston. *Career:* Sang with opera companies in Boston, Washington and Santa Fe; Concerts with the New York Pro Musica Antique and other chamber ensembles; Resident in Europe from 1981: concert engagements with the Sudwestfunk and Austrian Radio, conducted by Boulez and Michael Gielen; Tours of Russia and South America with Ensemble Modern; Ensemble InterContemporain in Paris and Ensemble Kontrapunkte in Vienna; Debut with the BBC Symphony 1988, in Pli selon Pli under Boulez; Sang in Dallapiccola's Ulisse with the BBC SO under Andrew Davis and appeared at the Henze Festival at the Barbican Centre London, 1991, with the BBC Philharmonic and the Scottish Chamber Orchestra; Further concerts in Berlin, Salzburg, Strasbourg and Warsaw; Season 1992-93 with Dubussy's Damoiselle Elue in the Netherlands and Russian songs in Paris. *Recordings include:* Hommage to T S Eliot by Gubaidulina (Deutsche Grammophon) and albums for Harmonia Mundi, Bridge Records and Intercord. *Address:* c/o Ingpen & Williams Ltd. 14 Kensington Court, London W8 5DN, England.

WIBAUT Frank, b. 10 Nov 1945, London, England. Concert Pianist. m. Kay Alexander. *Education:* Studied at the Royal College of Music; ARCM. *Debut:* Wigmore Hall London 1969. *Career:* Concert performances in Holland, Belgium, Denmark, Germany, Ireland, Spain and Malta; Frequent broadcaster on radio and TV; Member, The Camirilla Ensemble. *Recordings:* The Romantic Chopin; Favourite Piano Classics; Elgar's From the Bavarian Highlands (in original form); Piano Quintets by Elgar, Suk and others. *Memberships:* Musicians Union; Incorporated Society of Musicians. *Honours:* Senior Foundation Scholarship, Leverhulme Scholarship and Countess of Munster Award, RCM; 1st Prize, Chopin Competition, London; Chappell Gold Medal; BBC Piano Competition, 1968. *Address:* Highfield Lodge, 68 Harborne Road, Edgbaston, Birmingham B15 3HE, England.

WICH Gunther, b. 23 May 1928, Bamberg, Germany. Conductor. *Education:* Studied in Freiburg, 1948-52. *Career:* Conduted at the Freiburg town theatre 1952-59; Opera director at Graz 1959-61; General Music Director at Hanover 1961-65: conducted the first production of Schoenberg's three one-act operas as a triple bil, 1963; General Music Director of the Deutsche Oper am Rhein, Dusseldorf/Duisburg 1965-87: took the company to Edinburgh 1972, for the British premiere of Zimmermann's Die Soldaten; Covent Garden debut 1968, Die Zauberflöte; Professor of Conducting at the Folkwang Hochschule, Essen, 1969-73; Guest conductor with major orchestras in Europe and the USA; Has led the Capella Colonsiensis on tours to North and South America. *Recordings include* Handel's Concerti Grossi Op.3 and Alexander's Feast; Haydn's Symphonies Nos. 82 and 85; Serenades by Dvorák, Mozart and Tchaikovsky; Early Mozart Piano Concertos, with Martin Galling; Pfitzner's Violin Concerto, with Susanne Lautenbacher. 21. *Address:* c/o Spitalrain 10, 97234 Reichenberg.

WICK Tilmann Eugen, b. 6 Oct 1959, Ludwigshafen, Germany. Solo Concert Cellist. *Education:* Architecture, University of Munich, 1980- 81; Concert Artist Diploma with distinction, Northwest German Music Academy, Detmold, 1987. *Debut:* Soloist with Osnabrück Symphony Orchestra, 1976. *Career:* Principal Cellist, Chamber Orchestra of Europe, conductors Claudio Abbado and Sir Georg Solti, 1981-84; Worldwide tours, 1985-; Highlights include: Debut at Carnegie Hall, New York, Tonhalle, Zurich, Alte Oper, Frankfurt, Montreal, Santiago, Melbourne, Seoul, Brussels, London, Boston, Washington DC and appearances at the Berlin Festival, 1986, St Moritz Musiktreffen, 1987, Ludwigsburg Festival, 1988, Salzburg Festival, 1989, with the Hallé Orchestra in Manchester, with the Bavarian State Orchestra under Wolfgang Sawallisch in Munich, 1990, at the Spanish Festival Quincena Musical, 1991, with the MDR Symphony Orchestra Leipzig, 1991, 1992; Many appearances on radio and television in over 20 countries; Performed in chamber music concerts with Shlomo Mintz and Rudolf Buchbinder; Conducted master classes in Canada, Italy, Seoul and Melbourne, 1986-. *Recordings:* MD&G and EMI/Electrola: Schubert, Mendelssohn, Schumann with Koko Sakoda, piano, 1984; Mozart piano quartets with Frank Peter Zimmermann, Tabea Zimmermann, Christian Zacharias, 1988; Miaskovsky, Carter, Poulenc with Heasook Rhee, piano, 1991. *Hobbies:* Writing; Chess; Cabinetmaking; Free climbing; Astrology. *Address:* c/o LS Artists Management, Orlandostrasse 8, D-8000 Munich 2, Germany.

WICKER Vernon Estil, b. 5 May 1937, Colorado Springs, USA. Baritone; Professor. m. Jutta Rott, 27 Dec 1965, 1 son, 3 daughters. *Education:* BM, Music Education & Religion, Biola University, Los Angeles, 1961; MM, Voice, Music History, Indiana University, 1964; DMA, Voice, Music History (Teaching Fellow), University of Oregon, 1979. *Career:* Soloist, Community Concerts Inc., Columbia Artists Management, 1964; Baritone-in-Residence, Concordia College, 1967-68; Resident Singer, Choral Conductor, Lecturer, Church Musical Subjects, central Europe, 1964-66, 1968-76; Musical Director, Kansan Raamattuseuran Säätio, Finnish Lutheran Church, Helsinki; Professor, Voice & Church Music, Seattle Pacific University, 1979-. *Compositions:* Editor, Six First Editions of Church Cantatas by Christoph Graupner 1683-1760, Hänssler Verlag, Stuttgart, 1979-87; English Singing Translations, together with wife, of 67 J.S. Bach Cantatas, and numerous motets and cantatas by Bach Family and contemporaries, 1981-87. *Publications:* Major section of Festschrift: Christoph Graupner in Darmstadt in series: Beiträge zur mittelrheinischen Musikgeschichte, 1983; etc. *Contributions to:* The Hymn; Der Kirchenchor. *Honours:* Recipient, various honours & awards. *Memberships:* Hymn Society of America; Internationale Arbeitsgemeinschaft für Hymnologie; National Association of Teachers of Singing. *Address:* 8125 Sportsman Club Road, Bainbridge Island, WA 98110, USA.

WICKS Camilla, b. 1925, USA. Concert violinist; Professor of Violin. m. 5 children. *Education:* Fellowship to Juilliard School aged 10. *Debut:* New York Town Hall aged 13. *Career:* Solo appearances with the Hollywood

Bowl Orchestra, the Loa Angeles and New York Philharmonic Orchestras and the Chicago Symphony; Many concerts with European orchestras from age 18; Played the Sibelius Concerto before the composer in Helsinki and has also featured the Bloch Concerto in addition to the standard repertory; Frequent engagements in Norway and elsewhere in Scandinavia; Teaching appointments 1960s -, notably faculties of North Texas State University, California State College at Fullerton, San Francisco Conservatory of Music, Banff Centre for the Performing Arts, University of Washington and University of Southern California; Professor and head of the string department, Royal Academy of Music, Oslo; Professor of Violin, University of Michigan School of Music, 1984, Shepherd School of Music at Rice University, Houston, Texas 1988-; Continuing performances in recital and as orchestral soloist and in chamber music concerts. *Recordings:* Albums for Capitol, Philips and HMV, including the Sibelius Concerto. *Address:* Shepherd School of Music, Rice University, Houston, Texas, USA.

WICKS Dennis, b. 6 Oct 1928, Ringmer, Sussex. Singer (Bass). *Education:* Studied with Jani Strasser and David Franklin. *Career:* Sang at Glyndebourne from 1950 as Antonio (le Nozze di Figaro), Alcade in La Forza del Destino, Doctor (Macbeth), Keeper of the Madhouse and Trulove (The Rake's Progress), Lictor (L'Incoronazione di Poppea), Truffaldino (Ariadne), Priest and Man in Armour (Die Zauberflote) and Voice of Neptune (Idomeneo); Sang in the British premiere of Rossini's La Pietra del Paragone, Camden Festival 1963; Sang the Police Commissioner in a new production of Der Rosenkavalier for Welsh National Opera, 1990; Sang with the English National Opera and in Cardiff and Glasgow; US appearances with the Chicago Opera; Many performances in operas by Verdi, Mozart, Beethoven, Smetana, Wagner and Strauss at the Royal Opera House, Covent Garden. *Address:* c/o Royal Opera House, Covent Garden, London WC2, England.

WIDDESS (David) Richard, b. 8 June 1951, Keswick, England. Lecturer. m. Margaret Jennifer Hall, 19 July 1974, 2 sons. *Education:* Lancaster Royal Grammar School 1961-69; BA, Mus.B., PhD, Gonville and Caius College, Cambridge 1969-73 and 1974-77; MA, School of Oriental and African Studies, London 1973-74. *Career:* Research Fellow in Music, Christ's College, Cambridge 1977-79; Director of Studies in Music, Christ's College, Cambridge 1978-82; Lecturer in Indian Music, School of Oriental and African Studies, University of London 1979-; Chairman, Centre of Music Studies, School of Oriental and African Studies, University of London 1982-86. *Publications:* Edited (with R.F. Wolpert): Music and Tradition: Essays on Asian and Other Musics presented to Laurence Picken, Cambridge University Press 1981; Edited: Musica Asiatica 5, 1988. *Contributions to:* Articles in: Musica Asiatica 2; Bulletin of The School of Oriental and African Studies; New Oxford Companion To Music. *Membership:* Member of European Seminar in Ethnomusicology; Member, Indian Musical Congress; Member, Royal Musical Association. *Hobbies:* Gardens; Computers; Indian Cookery. *Address:* School of Oriental and African Studies, University of London, Malet Street, London WC1E 7HP, England.

WIDDICOMBE Gillian, b. 11 June 1943, Aldham, Suffolk, England. Music Critic; Journalist. m. Jeremy Isaacs, 1988. *Education:* Studied at the Royal Academy of Music and Gloucester Cathedral. *Career:* Music Division, BBC, 1966; Glyndebourne Festival Opera 1969; Critic and journalist various publications including Financial Times 1970-76; The Observer 1977-1993; Sub-titles for TV opera productions; Opera consultant, Channel Four TV, 1983-88; Arts Editor, The Observer, 1988-1993; Currently, Feature Writer, the Independent. *Honours:* ARAM. *Address:* 80 New Concordia Wharf, Mill Street, Bermondsey, London, SE1 2BB, England.

WIDMER Oliver, b. 1965, Zurich, Switzerland. Singer (Baritone). *Education:* Studied at the Basle Music Academy with Kurt Widmer; Masterclasses with Fischer-Dieskau in Berlin, 1986 and 1989. *Career:*

Concert appearances at the Salzburg Festival, Festival de Musique de Strasbourg, the Vienna Musikverein, the San Francisco Symphony Hall and the Leipzig Gewendhaus; Recitals at the Schubertiade in Hohenems, the Wigmore Hall London, the Residenz in Munich, Alte Oper Frankfurt, Fetes Musicales de Touraine, Louvre de Paris, the Vienna Konzerthause and the 1992 Aldeburgh Festival; Zurich Opera from 1991 as Mozart's Papageno and Guglielmo, Olivier in Capriccio and Harlequin in Ariadne auf Nazos; Salzburg Festival 1993, conducted by Harnoncourt. *Recordings:* Die Zauberflote and Schreker's Die Gezeichneten. *Honours:* Prizewinner at ARD Competition Munich, Hugo Wolf International Competition Stuttgart and the Othmar Schoeck Competition in Lucerne. *Address:* c/o IMG Artists, Media House, 3 Burlington Lane, London W4 2TH, England.

WIEGOLD Peter John, b. 29 Aug 1949, Ilford, Essex, England. Composer; Conductor; Teacher. *Education:* University College of Wales, Aberystwyth (BMus, MMus); University of Durham, PhD. *Career:* Director of Gemini, regular tours of Britain including many broadcasts; Many residencies involving local participants in shared concerts; Artistic Director, Performance and Communication Skills Project, Guildhall School of Music; Has directed many workshops in music and music theatre including those with London Sinfonietta, Royal Opera House, English National Opera, Scottish Chamber Orchestra and City of London Sinfonia; Junge Deutsche Philharmonie in Greece, Canada, Spain and Sweden; London Symphony Orchestra. *Compositions:* Works published by Universal Edition include Gemini; Sing Lullaby; The Flowers Appear on the Earth; Preludes 1-V; The Dancing Day; Songs from Grimm; Half- hour opera commissioned by the Royal Opera House, performed 1989. *Honours:* Several Arts Council awards. *Membership:* Past member, Council and Executive Committee of SPNM. *Hobbies:* Bhuddism; Cycling; Football. *Address:* 82 Lordship Park, London N16 5UA, England.

WIENER Otto, b. 13 Feb 1913, Vienna, Austria. Singer (Baritone). *Education:* Studied in Vienna with Kuper and Hans Duhan. *Career:* Sang in concert from 1939; Stage debut Graz 1953, as Simon Boccanegra; Sang at the Salzburg Festival from 1952: in Pfitzner's Palestrina 1955 and in the stage premiere of La Mystère de la Nativité by Martin 1960; Deutsche Oper am Rhein Dusseldorf 1956-59; Bayreuth Festival from 1957, as Hans Sachs, Gunther and the Dutchman; Member of the Vienna Staatsoper from 1957, Munich Staatsoper 1960-70; Guest appearances in Paris, London, Rome and Brussels, often in operas by Wagner; Glyndebourne Festival 1964, as La Roche in Capriccio; Retired from stage 1976 and led an opera school at the Vienna Staatsoper. *Recordings include:* Missa solemnis, conducted by Klemperer (Vox); Faninal in Der Rosenkavalier (Decca); Lohengrin (Eurodisc); St Matthew Passion. *Address:* c/o Staatsoper, Opernring 2, A-1010 Vienna, Austria.

WIENS Edith, b. 1954, Canada. Singer (Soprano). *Career:* Concert engagements with orchestras in Berlin, London, Israel, Munich and New York (Philharmonic); Cleveland, Philadelphia, San Francisco, Montreal and London Symphony Orchestras; Bavarian Radio, Dresden Staatskapelle, Leipzig Gewandhaus Orchestras; Conductors include Barenboim, Georg Solti, Colin Davis, Haitink, Marriner and Tennstedt; Salzburg debut 1984, with the Boston Symphony under Ozawa with whom she has also sung Mozart's Ilia in Japan; Other operatic roles include Donna Anna (at Glyndebourne under Haitink, in Paris and at Amsterdam under Harnoncourt) & Mozart's Countess (Buenos Aires); St Matthew Passion in Paris and Salzburg under Masur with whom she also appeared in Mendelssohn's Elijah in New York; L'Enfant et les Sortilèges at Carnegie Hall; Mahler's 4th Symphony in Munich; Recitals in Paris, Vienna, Florence, Buenos Aires, New York and Montreal; Concertgebouw, Amsterdam, and the Pushkin Museum, Moscow. *Recordings include:* Schubert and Schumann Lieder, The title role in Schumann's Das Paradies und die Peri, which won a Grammy in 1990, and the Maurice Fleuret (Paris) Prize in 1991; Flowermaiden in Parsifal, conducted by Barenboim; Albums for Philips, Erato, Teldec and EMI (Mahler's 8th Symphony, conducted by Tennstedt), as well as Hadyn's Creation, Conducted by Neville Marriner. *Address:* Georg Schuster, Str. 10, 82152 Krailling, Germany.

WIESEHAHN Willem, b. 31 May 1914, Amsterdam, The Netherlands. Conductor; Composer. m. Helena Wiesahahn-Schipperijn, 2 sons. *Education:* Pupil of Fred. Roeske, Spaanderman, Stroomenbergh; Diploma, Royal Oratory Society. *Career:* Conductor, choirs at approximately 500 concerts in Holland, Belgium, Switzerland, Germany and England with Het Amsterdams Philharmonic Orchestra, The Radio Philharmonic Orchestra, LSO, Het Residentie Orchestra (The Hague), Het Utrechts Symphony Orchestra, Luzerner Festwochen Orchestra, etc.; Many radio appearances; Conductor, The Amsterdam Mixed Choir; the Oratory Society; etc. *Compositions include:* Orchestra Te Deum for mixed choir, Soprano; Te Deum for male choir and organ; A Christmas Cantata; Compositions for male voice choir and female voices; Requiem (in order of the Ministry for Culture) Missa pro Patria - both works for mixed choir - soloists - and orchestra, and edited by Donemus - Amsterdam; 8 songs for soprano and piano; Adagio for organ and Strings. *Recordings:* Mijne Moedertaal. *Contributions to:* Euphonia. *Honours:* The Gold Pin of the Town of Amsterdam. *Memberships:* Royal Musicians Society; The Dutch Conductors Society. *Address:* Sonneveld 43, 1082 EZ Amsterdam, The Netherlands.

WIGGLESWORTH Frank, b. 3 Mar 1918, Boston, Massachusetts, USA. Composer. *Education:* Studied at Columbia University with Otto Luening andHenry Cowell (BS 1940). *Career:* Teacher at Columbia 1941-88; Fellow of the American Academy at Rome 1951-54, Composer-in-residence 1969-70, Chairman of the music department at the New School for Social Research, New York, from 1965; Composer-in-residence at Bennington College's Chamber Music Conference, 1985. *Compositions include :* Ballet Young Goodman Brown 1951; Between the Atoms and lthe Stars, musical play 1959; Ballet for Esther Brooks 1961; The Willowdale Handcar, opera, 1969; Orchestral: New England Concerto for violin and strings 1941; Music for Strings 1946; Summer Scenes 1951; Concertino for piano and strings 1953; 3 Symphonies 1953, 1958, 1960; Concertino for viola and orchestra 1956; Music for Strings 1981; Aurora 1983; Sea Winds 1984; Isiah for chorus and orchestra 1942; Sleep Becalmed for chorus and orchestra 1950; Duets, song cycle for mezzo and clarinet 1978; Chamber: Brass Quintet no.1 1958; Viola Sonata 1965; String Trio 1972; Brass Quintet no.2 1980; Viola Sonata 1980; After Summer Music for flute, viola and guitar 1983; masses, anthems and solo songs; Opera The Police Log of the Chronicle, New York 1984. *Address:* c/o ASCAP, ASCAP Building, One Lincoln Plaza, New York, NY 10023, USA.

WIGGLESWORTH Mark, b. 19 July 1964, Sussex, England. Conductor. *Career:* Has conducted the Hague Residentie Orchestra, the Netherlands Wind Ensemble and the Dutch National Youth Orchestra; Berlin debut at the Philharmonie with the Radio Symphony Orchestra, Dec 1990; British appearances with the Bournemouth Symphony, BBC Symphony, BBC Welsh, London Philharmonic, English Chamber Orchestra, and the National Youth Orchestra; Conducted the BBC Symphony in 60th anniversary season at the Barbican March 1991, in Shostakovich's 10th Symphony, the world premiere of Muldowney's Three Pieces for Orchestra, and Mahler's 10th Symphony; Promenade Concert debut 1991, with the BBC SO; Music Director of Opera Factory for whom he has conducted Don Giovanni and Così fan tutte; The Marriage of Figaro with Scottish Opera, 1991; Associate Conductor of the BBC SO 1992; Opera Factory Production, conducted by Mark Wigglesworth, of Yan Tan Tethera by Harrison Birtwistle; 1992 included debuts with the Philadelphia Orchestra and the Dallas Symphony Orchestra; 1993,

Shostakovich 10 with the European Community Youth Orchestra at London's Royal Festival Hall and Messiaen Turangalîla Symphony with both the BBC Symphony and the Royal Scottish National Orchestra. *Honour:* First Prize, International Kondrashin Competition, Netherlands, 1989. *Hobby:* Cricket. *Address:* Harold Holt Ltd, 31 Sinclair Road, London W14 0NS, England.

WIGHTMAN Brian Robin, b. 8 Oct 1942, Ilford, Essex, England. Bassoonist. m. Joanna Mary Graham, 2 Dec 1972, 1 son, 1 daughter. *Education:* Wanstead County High School; Trinity College of Music, London. *Career:* Principal Bassoon, English National Opera, Nash Ensemble; Professor, Trinity College of Music, London; London College of Music. *Recordings:* Chamber music with the Nash Ensemble. *Memberships:* Incorporated Society of Musicians; Royal Society of Musicians. *Hobbies:* Boating; Flying; Chess; Ornithology; Real Ale. *Address:* 20 Park Avenue, Finchley Central, London, N3, England.

WILBRAHAM John, b. 15 Apr 1944, Bournemouth, England. Trumpet Player. m. Susan Drake. *Education:* Royal Academy of Music, London; LRAM; ARCM. *Career:* New Philharmonia Orchestra 1966-68; Royal Philharmonic Orchestra 1968-72; BBC Symphony Orchestra from 1972. *Recordings include:* Concertos by Haydn, Hummel, Mozart, Telemann and Torelli. *Memberships:* Savage Club; ISM. *Honour:* Silver Medal, Worshipful Company of Musicians, 1965. *Hobby:* Cooking. *Address:* 14b Elizabeth Mews, London NW3, England.

WILBRINK Hans, b. 1933, Holland. Singer (Baritone). *Education:* Studied in Utrecht and Amsterdam. *Debut:* Amsterdam 1956, in Beethoven's Ninth. *Career:* Amsterdam 1958, in the premiere of François Villon by Sam Dresden; Member of the Frankfurt Opera 1959-66, notably in the 1964 premiere of Wimberger's Dame Kobold; Sang at the Bayerische Staatsoper Munich 1966-86, including the premieres of Aucassin und Nicolette by Bialas, 1969, Der Versuchung by Josef Tal, 1976 and Belshazar by V D Kirchner, 1986; Guest appearances in Paris 1962, Glyndebourne 1963 (Pelléas), Cologne and Vienna; other roles have included Henze's Prinz van Homburg, Stolzius in Die Soldaten, Mozart's Figaro, Papageno and Guglielmo, Malatesta, Strauss's Olivier and Britten's Oberon. *Recordings include:* Masses by Mozart and Schubert, Reimann's Lear. *Address:* c/o Bayerische Staatsoper, Postfach 100148, 80539 Munich, Germany.

WILBY Philip, b. 1949, Pontefract. Composer. *Education:* Leeds Grammar School; with Herbert Howells and at Keble College, Oxford. *Career:* Violinist with the Covent Garden Orchestra and City of Birmingham Symphony Orchestra; Senior Lecturer at Leeds University from 1972. *Compositions:* Orchestral: Sunstudy; The Wings of Morning 1988; Vocal: Et surrexit Christus for 3 sopranos and ensemble 1979; Ten Songs of Paul Verliane for baritone and piano 1983; The Temptations of Christ for soprano and ensemble 1983; Winter Portrait in Grey and Gold for voice and ensemble 1977-85; Cantiones Sacrae: In Darkness Shine 1987; Magnificat and Nunc Dimittis 1988; Easter Wings for soprano and ensemble 1989; Chamber: Little Symphony for Brass 1985; The Night and all the Stars, horn quintet 1985; Sonata Sacra: In Darkness Shine for clarinet, viola and piano 1986; And I move around the Cross for double wind quintet 1985; Two Concert Studies for violin and piano 1986; Capricorn Suite for 4 trombones 1987; Parables for cello and piano 1988; Classic Images, partita for brass quintet 1988; Concertmusic for winds 1988; Green Man Dancing, wind quintet 1988; Breakdance for recorder and tape 1988; Wind Band: Firestar 1983; Symphonia Sacra: In Darkness Shine 1986; Catcher of Shadows 1988; Keyboard: Roses for the Queen of Heaven 1982; Two Preludes on English Tunes 1987; Lifescape-Mountains 1987; ....Aunque es de Noche 1989; Mozart reconstructions include Concerto for violin and piano K315f and Concerto for Violin, viola, cello and orchestra K320e, for the Philips Mozart edition; Commissions include Symphony for the

BBC Philharmonic. *Address:* c/o Chester Music, 8/9 Frith Street, London W1V 5TZ, England.

WILD Earl, b. 26 Nov 1915, Pittsburgh, Pennsylvania, USA. Pianist; Composer; Teacher. *Education:* Carnegie Technical College, 1930-34; Studied Piano with Egon Petri, Selmar Jansen, Paul Doguereau. *Debut:* New York City, 1934. *Appointments:* Pianist, KOKA Radio, Pittsburgh, 1930-35; Pianist, NBC Symphony Orchestra, under Toscanini, 1937-44; Soloist with Toscanini and NBC Symphony, 1942; Staff Pianist, Composer, Conductor, ABC TV, New York City, 1945-68; Teacher, Juilliard School of Music, 1977-; Teacher, Manhattan School of Music, 1981-83. *Compositions:* 14 Rachmaninoff Song Transcriptions; 7 Gershwin Song Transcriptions Porgy & Bess Fantasy; Dance of the Four Swans, Tchaikowsky's Swan Lake. *Recordings:* Liszt the Virtuoso, Transcriber & Poet; Beethoven Sonatas Op 22, Op 31 No 3; Rachmaninoff Concertos; Fauré Cello Sonatas Nos 1 & 2; Chopin Record. *Publications:* 2 Volumes of Liszt Piano Music for Schirmer Music, 1986. *Honours:* Performed for US Presidents: Hoover, Roosevelt, Truman, Eisenhower & Kennedy; Performed for Kennedy at his Inauguration, 1961. *Current Management:* Judd Concert Bureau, New York City. *Address:* c/o Michael Davis, Business Manager, Claridges, 101 West 55th St., Suite 5D, New York, NY 10019, USA.

WILD Stephen Aubrey, b. 17 Jan 1941, Fremantle, Western Australia, Australia. Ethnomusicologist. *Education:* BA(Hons), 1963; MA, 1967; PhD, 1975. *Career:* Lecturer, Monash University, Melbourne, Victoria, 1969-73; Assistant Professor, Brooklyn College, New York, USA, 1973- 78; Research Officer, Australian Institute of Aboriginal Studies, Canberra, Australian Capital Territory, 1978-89. *Recordings:* Co-editor, Djambidj, an Aboriginal song series from Northern Australia, 1982; Editor, Songs of Aboriginal Australia, 1987. *Publications:* Editor, Rom: An Aboriginal Ritual of Diplomacy; Co-editor, Songs of Aboriginal Australia, 1987. *Contributions to:* Ethnomusicology, 1967, 1982, 1984; The Encyclopedia of Religion, 1986; Theatrical Movement, 1986; Australians to 1788, 1987; The Australian People, 1988; Companion to Theatre in Australia. *Memberships:* Musicological Society of Australia, President 1986-88; Editor, Musicology Australia journal, 1985-89; Editor, Special Series, Society for Ethnomusicology, 1977-81. *Address:* 22/6 Wilkins Street, Mawson, ACT 2607, Australia.

WILDE David Clark, b. 25 Feb 1935, Manchester, England. Pianist; Composer; Conductor; Professor of Piano. m. (1) Jeanne Lukey, 23 May 1956, 1 son, 1 daughter. (2) Jane Heller, 14 June 1984. *Education:* Arnold Boys School, Blackpool; Private tuition Solomon/Reizenstein, 1945-47; Royal Manchester College of Music, Piano with Elinson, Composing with Hall, Conducting with Cohen, 1948-53; Nadia Boulanger, Privately and at the American Conservatoire, Fontainebleau; Caird Foundation Scholarship, 1963-64. *Career:* Concerts given in US, Canada, USA, Australia, New Zealand, India, Brazil, France, Belgium, Holland, Spain, Germany and Hungary; Recordings and concerts as International artist for BBC, 1961-; Soloist, Royal concert in the presence of HM the Queen, Royal Festival Hall, 1962; Soloist, Inaugural Concert of BBC TV2, Manchester, (Hallé Orchestra, Barbirolli), 1962; Performances at Edinburgh, Cheltenham, Three Choirs, Perth (Australia), Festivals; Performances at Henry Wood Promenade Concerts, 1961-; Has toured with all leading British Orchestras; Conductor, Worthing Symphony, season, 1967-68; Guest Conductor, Royal Philharmonic, 1975; Documentary programmes as writer, narrator and pianist for BBC TV, on Liszt and Bartók, 1972-73; Film, Liszt in Weimar, Granada TV, 1986. *Compositions:* Love, song for baritone and cello, 1981; Jens Heidi, und die Schneekönigen, 1984; Vocalise for mezzo soprano and guitar; Die Jahreszeiten, (The Seasons) song cycle, 1986; Mandala for solo viola, 1986; Piano trio, 1987-88; String Quartet, 1991; The Cellist of Sarafevo (solo cello), 1992; Cry Bosnia-

Herzegovina (violin and piano), Opus 14, 1993. *Recordings include:* Schumann Fantasie; Liszt Sonata - Saga 5460: Beethoven, Violin and Piano Sonatas, complete, with Gruenberg, violin - CRDD 1115/9; Many other recordings. *Publications:* Chapter, Transcriptions for piano, in Franz Liszt, The Man and His Music, 1970; Editor, Liszt's Consolations, (complete), 1978. *Honours:* 1st Prize, Liszt-Bartók Competition, Budapest, 1961; 2nd Prize; Rio di Janeiro Composition, 1962; Queen's Prize, London, 1962; Arts Council Award, 1967; Elected Life Professor, Hannover, West Germany, 1985. *Memberships:* The Composers Guild of Great Britain, Performing Rights Society. *Current Management and Address:* c/o J Audrey Ellison International Artists' Management, 135 Stevenage Road, Fulham, London SW6 6PB, England.

WILDMAN Mark, b. 2 Sept 1953, Huddersfield, Yorkshire, England. Singer (Bass). *Education:* Chorister, Gloucester Cathedral, 1963-67; Royal Academy of Music, 1972-78. *Debut:* Royal Festival Hall, 1980. *Career:* Chorister Gloucester Cathedral, 1963-67; Choral Scholar, St George's Chapel, Windsor Castle, 1976-80; BBC Singers, 1980-84; Concerts throughout Europe, Scandinavia, USA, including opera, oratorio and recitals; Professor of Singing, Head of Vocal Studies, Royal Academy of Music, 1991-; Joint Head of Vocal Studies, London Royal Schools Vocal Faculty, 1992-. *Recordings:* Cry, Giles Swayne, Bach's St Matthew Passion (Christus); BBC Radio Recordings include Liszt Requiem. *Honours:* Scholarship, RAM, 1973; Mario Prize, 1978; J W Pearce Prizew, 1978; Fisher Memorial Scholarship, 1978; GLAA Young Musician, 1982; ARAM, 1986. *Memberships:* RAM Club; Elgar Society; Warlock Society. *Hobbies:* Current Affairs; Reading; food; Politics; Swimming; Rowing; Climbing; Walking. *Current Management:* Stephanie Williams Artists. *Address:* The Royal Academy of Music, Marylebone Road, London NW1 5H7, England.

WILKE Elisabeth, b. 19 May 1952, Dresden, Germany. Singer (Mezzo-soprano). *Education:* Studied at the Musikhochschule Dresden. *Debut:* Dresden 1974, as Hansel. *Career:* Appearances with the Dresden Staatsoper-Semper Oper in Germany and on tour as Dorabella, Amastris in Handel's Serse, Olga (Eugene Onegin) and Tisbe in Cenerentola, 1992; Sang Veronika in the premiere of Der goldene Topf by E. Mayer 1989. *Recordings include:* Symphoniae Sacrae by Schutz (Capriccio). Saint-Saens Christmas Oratorio, Missa Brevis by C.P.E Bach; J.S. Bach's St. Matthew Passion. *Address:* c/o Semper Oper, 8012 Dresden, Germany.

WILKENS Anne, b. 1948, England. Singer (Mezzo-Soprano). *Education:* Guildhall School of Music; London Opera Centre; Further Study with Dame Eva Turner. *Career:* Sang in Verdi's Ernani at the Festival Hall, 1972; The Nose by Shostakovich for the New Opera Company 1973; Sang with English Opera Group in operas by Britten, in Aldeburgh, Venice and Brussels; Sang in world premieres of Death in Venice 1973, and Musgrave's The Voice of Ariadne 1974; Member of the Royal Opera Company, Covent Garden, 1974-78, as Olga in Eugene Onegin, Maddalena in Rigoletto, and in the world premiere of Henze's We Come to the River 1976; Appearances with Handel Opera Society: Handel roles include Julius Caesar, Dejanaira (Hercules) and Ezio; Welsh National Opera 1979, as Brangaene in Tristan und Isolde; Guest appearances in Frankfurt (Azucena), Marseille and Stuttgart (Brangaene); Bayreuth 1983, in the Solti/Hall production of The Ring; Karlsruhe from 1983, as Eboli in Don Carlos and as Wagner's Venus, Fricka, Ortrud, Fricka and Waltraute; Sang in the premiere of Der Meister und Margarita by Kunaud, Karlsruhe 1986; Concert engagements with the London Symphony Orchestra, Hallé Orchestra, Bournemouth Symphony and in Holland, Spain, Brussels and Stockholm. *Recordings include:* Tristan und Isolde, conducted by Reginald Goodall (Decca). *Address:* c/o Music International 13 Ardilaun Road, Highbury, London N5 2QR, England.

WILKINS Margaret Lucy, b. 13 Nov 1939, Kingston-upon-Thames, England. Composer; Music Educator. m. Nigel E Wilkins, 11 Aug 1962, div. 1977, 2 daughters. *Education:* Trinity College of Music, London, 1952-57; BMus, University of Nottingham, 1960; LRAM, 1960. *Debut:* BBC. *Career:* Works performed worldwide, South Bank & Wigmore Hall, London, England, Scotland, Canada, Germany, Italy, Switzerland, Holland, America, Spain and Poland; Commissions: BBC SSO, University of St Andrews, New Music Group of Scotland, William Byrd Singers, John Turner, Goldberg Ensemble; Festivals, Durham, Edinburgh, Huddersfield, Nottingham, Donne in Musica, Llangollen Eistedfodd, ISCM, World Music Days, Poland, Middelburg, Netherlands; Member Scottish Early Music Consort, 1970-76; Senior Lecturer, Music, University of Huddersfield, 1976-; Artistic Director, Polyphonia, 1989-. *Compositions:* Hymn to Creation, 1973; Struwwelpeter, 1973; Orpheus, 1973; Etude, 1974; Ave Maria, 1975; Music of the Spheres, 1975; Circus, 1975; Gitanjali, 1981; Aspects of Night, 1981; Study in Black & White, 1983; Epistola da San Marco, 1987; Réve, Réveil, Révélations, Réverbérations, 1988; Revelations of the 7 Angels, 1988; Symphony 1989; Kanal, 1990; Musica Angelorum, 1991; Stringsing, 1992. *Address:* 4 Church Street, Golcar, Huddersfield HD7 4AH, West Yorkshire, England.

WILKINSON Katie, b. 1960, England. Violist. *Debut:* Wigmore Hall debut 1984, with Peter Pears. *Career:* Co-founded the Brindisi String Quartet at Aldeburgh 1984; Concerts in a wide repertory throughout Britain and in France, Germany, Spain, Italy and Switzerland; Festival engagements at Aldeburgh (residency 1990), Arundel, Bath, Brighton, Huddersfield, Norwich and Warwick; First London Performance of Colin Matthews' 2nd Quartet 1990, premiere of David Matthews' 6th Quartet 1991; Quartet by Mark-Anthony Turnage 1992; Many BBC recitals and resident artist with the University of Ulster. *Recordings include:* Quartets by Britten, Bridge and Imogen Holst; Works by Pierné and Lekeu. *Honours include:* (with Brindisi Quartet) Prize winner at the Third Banff International String Quartet Competition in Canada, 1989. *Address:* c/o Owen-White Management, 14 Nightingale Lane, London N8 7QU, England.

WILKINSON Philip George, b. 28 Aug 1929, London, England. Music Educator. m. Margaret Matterson, 9 Sept 1957, 1 son, 1 daughter. *Education:* Royal College of Music; University of London. *Career:* Music Staff, Cranleigh School, 1953-59; Royal College of Music, Professor, 1959-; Examiner, Associated Board of Royal Schools of Music, 1959-; Board of Studies in Music, London University, 1963-. *Compositions:* Shakespearean Suite, Prelude and Scherzo, Miniature Symphony, all for orchestra. *Publications:* Contributor to Beethoven's Piano Sonata Op 106 and Symphony No 9 compared. *Honours:* Royal Philharmonic Society, 1952; Madrigal Society, 1955. *Memberships:* PRS; ISM; Royal Socety of Musicians of Great Britain. *Hobbies:* Carpentry; Hill Walking; The German language. *Address:* "Lyndhurst" Avenue Road, Cranleigh, Surrey GU6 7LE, England.

WILKOMIRSKI Jozef, b. 15 May 1926, Kalisz, Poland. Conductor; Composer; Broadcaster; Lecturer; Freelance Journalist. m. Margaret Zasinska, 16 Aug. 1980, 1 daughter. *Education:* Diploma, Warsaw Music High School; Master of Arts, 1950. *Debut:* Warsaw Philharmonic, June 1950. *Career:* Assistant Conductor, Cracow Philharmonic, 1950-51; Conductor, Poznan Philharmonic, 1954-57; Director and Chief Conductor of State Philharmonic at Szczecin, 1957-71; Chief Manager and Artist Director of Sudettic Philharmonic at Walbrzych, from 1978; Guest conductor, numerous countries in Europe, Asia & America. *Compositions:* 2 sinfoniettas; Symphonic poems; Symphonic suite, Royal Castle in Warsaw; Sonatas for: violin, cello, double-bass; Harp concerto; Concerto for violin & cello; Trio; Songs. *Recordings:* Various broadcasting companies, Poland, Ireland, Luxembourg. *Honours:* Pomeranian Gryphon Medal, 1960; Musical prize, 1961; Cavalry Cross 1963, Officer's Cross 1979, Order of Polonia Restituta; Medal, Cultural Merit, 1967; Prize, public cultivation of music,

1970; Order of Labour Flag, 1st class, 1986. *Hobbies:* Literature; History; Psychology. *Address:* Sudettic Philharmony, ul. Slowackiego 4, 58-300 Walbrzych, Poland.

WILKOMIRSKI Kazimierz, b. 1 Sept 1900, Moscow, USSR. Cellist; Conductor; Composer. m. (1) Maria Fryde, (2) Teresa Lisica-Sulkowska, 1 daughter. *Education:* Imperial Conservatory, Moscow; Diploma with honourable mention, National Conservatory, Warsaw, 1923. *Debut:* Wilkormirski Trio, Moscow, 1915. *Career:* Cellist, Member of Chamber Groups, 60 years; Conductor, Symphony and Opera, Poland, Russia, Czechoslovakia, Hungary, Romania, France, Bulgaria, Iran, Israel, Cuba, East and West Germanies, 50 years; Radio and TV appearances; Professor, Conservatories inLodz, Wroclaw, Gdansk and Warsaw; Director, Operas and Symphonies, Gdansk and Wroclaw. *Compositions:* String Quartet; Symphonie Concertante for cello and orchestra; 3 Cantatas for choir, soloists and orchestra; Air; 4 pieces and 12 Etudes for cello; Ballade for violin; Missa Solemnis for choir and organo. *Recordings include:* Beethoven - Trio B-Flat Op 11, 1951; C.P.E. Bach and Vivaldi Cello Concertos, 1967; Tchaikovsky trio; unaccompanied Bach suites, 1974. *Publications:* Cello Technique and Interpretation Problems; Reminiscences (autobiography). *Contributions to:* Ruch Muzyczny. *Honours:* Recipient of State and Festival Prizes; Honorary President, Union of Polish Artists Musicians. *Address:* Hoza 54 m 36, 00-682, Warsaw, Poland.

WILKOMIRSKA Wanda, b. 11 Jan 1929, Warsaw, Poland. Violinist. m. 2 sons. *Education:* Studied with Irena Dubiska, Lodz Conservatory, Studied with Ede Zathureczky, Budapest, Hungary; Studied with Henryk Szeryng, Paris, France. *Debut:* Age 7; With orchestra, Cracow, Poland, at age 15. *Career:* Appears frequently with most major orchestras throughout the world; Defected whilst on tour of Federal Republic of Germany, 1982. *Recordings:* Numerous. *Honours include:* Polish State Prize, 1952 and 1964; Several foreign prizes including Bach Competition Award, German Democratic Republic Radio; Officer's Cross of Polonia Restituta, 1958; Order of Banner of Labour 2nd Class 1959, 1st Class 1964; Minister of Culture and Arts Prize 1st Class, 1975; Orpheus Prize, Polish Musicians' Association, 1979. *Hobbies:* Theatre; Literature; Sports.

WILL Jacob, b. 8 June 1957, Hartsville, South Carolina, USA. Singer (Bass). *Education:* Studied at the Cincinnati Conservatory and at San Francisco opera studio. *Career:* Sang Masetto at San Francisco, followed by appearances with Long Beach and Anchorage Operas, as Basilio in Il Barbiere di Siviglia; Carmel Beach Festival as Mozart's Figaro; Appearances throughout the USA as Don Giovanni, Frank in Die Fledermaus, and Dulcamara; Sang in Europe from 1986, Zurich Opera from 1988 as Basilio and Melcthal in Guillaume Tell; St. Gallen as Sparafucile and Raimondo in Lucia di Lammermoor, Barnaba in Andrea Chenier 1989; Vancouver 1990, as Oroveso, Bregenz Festival 1992 as Zuniga in Carmen; Concert engagements include Rossini's Petite Messe Solonelle, Lincoln Center 1989. *Recordings include:* Zemlinsky's Kleider machen Leute. *Address:* c/o Opernhaus Zurich, Falkenstrasse 1, CH-8008 Zurich, Switzerland.

WILLCOCKS David Valentine (Sir), b. 30 Dec 1919, Newquay, Cornwall, England. Conductor. m; Rachel Blyth, 8 Nov 1947, 2 sons (deceased), 2 daughters. *Education:* Chorister, Westminster Abbey, King's College, Cambs; Royal College of Music. *Career:* Organist, Salisbury Cathedral, 1947-50; Organist, Worcester Cathedral, 1950-57; Conductor, City of Birmingham Choir, 1950-57; Fellow and Organist, Kings College, Cambs, 1957-73; University Lecturer, 1957-74, Organist, 1958-74, Cambs; Conductor, Cambs University Musical Society, 1958-73; Director, The Royal College of Music, 1974-84; Musical Director, The Bach Choir, 1960-. *Compositions:* Ceremony of Psalms; Carols for Choirs (4 vols) (joint Ed.). *Recordings:* Many with The Bach Choir, Royal College of Music Chamber

Choir, Choir of King's College Cambs and the principal London orchestras. *Honours:* MC, 1944; CBE, 1971; Knight Bachelor, 1977; Hon MA, Bradford, 1973; Hon DMus, Exeter, 1976, Leicester, 1977, Westminster Choir College, Princeton, 1980, Bristol, 1981, St Olaf College, 1991; Hon D Litt, Sussex, 1982, Hon Doctor of Sacred Letters, Trinity College, Univ of Toronto, 1985; Freeman, City of London, 1981. *Memberships:* Pres, RCO, 1966-68; Pres, ISM, 1978-79; Pres, NFMS, 1980-89; Pres, Association of British Choral Directors, 1993-. *Address:* 13 Grange Road, Cambridge CB3 9AS, England.

WILLIAM Louis Hagen, b. 1950, New Orleans, USA. Singer (Bass- baritone). *Education:* Studied at University of Los Angeles Opera Workshop and at Paris Conservatoire. *Career:* With Lyons Opera sang Sarastro, Daland and the Langrave in Tannhäuser, Paris Opera Company in Turandot and L'Heure Espagnole; Other roles include Mephistopheles, Nilakanta in Lakmé, Rossini's Bartolo and the villains in Les Contes d'Hoffmann; Has sung in various versions of Porgy and Bess with the Royal Liverpool Philharmonic, the Scottish Chamber Orchestra under Carl Davis, the Ulster Orchestra under Yan Pascal Tortelier, and the Hallé and Royal Philharmonic Orchestras; Has also sung in Handel's Judas Maccabeus and on French Radio and television. *Recordings include:* Negro Spirituals (Quantum) and Mozart Concert Arias. *Honours:* First prizes for opera and concert singing at the Paris Conservatoire. *Address:* c/o Norman McCann International Artists Ltd, 56 Lawrie Park Gardens, London SE26 6XJ, England.

WILLIAMS Adrian, b. 30 Apr. 1956, Watford, Hertfordshire, England. Composer; Pianist. *Education:* Royal College of Music, London. *Career:* Composer-in-Residence, Charterhouse, 1980-82; Founder Director, Presteigne International Festival, 1983-92. *Compositions:* Sonata for Solo Cello, 1977; String Quartet No 2, 1981; Tess, Orchestral poem, 1982; Cantata: September Sky, 1985; Mass, 1986; Chaconne for Guitar, 1986; Images of a Mind, Cello and piano, 1986; Cantata: Not Yet Born, 1986; Leaves from the Lost Book, 1987; Dies Irae, 1988; Music for the film Gernika, 1987; Cantata: The Ways of Going, 1990; String Quartet No. 3, 1991; The King of Britain's Daughter, 1993. *Honours:* Menuhin Prize, 1978; Guinness Prize, 1986. *Memberships:* Composers' Guild of G.B. *Hobbies:* Walking; Railways; Gardening; Cooking. *Current Management:* GBZ Management*Address:* 33 St Mark's Road, Old Hanwell, London W7 2NP, England.

WILLIAMS Camilla, b. 8 Oct 1922, Danville, Virginia, USA. Concert Singer, Professor of Voice, Indiana University. m. Charles T. Beavers, 28 Aug. 1950. *Education:* Honour Graduate, Virginia State College; Studied Music under Madame Marion Szekely-Freschl. *Career:* Sang role of Madame Butterfly as first black singer, New York City Centre, 1946; Created first Aida, New York City Centre, 1948; First NY Performance of Mozart's Odomeneo, Little Orchestra Society, 1950; First Tour of Alaska, 1950; First European Tour (London) 1954; First Viennese Performance of Menotti's Saint of Bleecker Street, 1955; American Festival, Belgium, 1955; First African Tour for US State Department (14 countries), 1958-59; First Tour of Israel, 1959; Guest of President Eisenhower, Concert for Crown Prince of Japan, 1960; Tour of Formosa, Australia, New Zealand, Korea, Japan, Philippines, Laos, South Vietnam, 1962; First NY Performance of Handel's Orlando, 1971; First Tour of Poland, 1974; Appearances with Orchestras: Royal Philharmonic; Vienna Symphony; Zurich; Berlin Philharmonic; NY Philharmonic; Chicago Symphony; Philadelphia Orchestra; BBC Orchestra; Stuttgart Orchestra; Geneva; Belgium and others. Professor of Voice, Brooklyn College, 1970-73; Professor of Voice, Bronx College, 1970-; Professor of Voice, Queens College, 1974-; First Black Professor of Voice, Indiana University, Bloomington, Indiana, 1977-. *Address:* Professor of Voice, School of Music-Studio MU104B, Indiana University, Bloomington, IN 47405, USA.

WILLIAMS David Russell, b. 21 Oct 1932, Indiana, USA. Professor of Music Theory. m. Elsa Buehlmann, 30 Jan 1960. *Education:* BA, MA, Columbia University, NYC; PhD, University of Rochester. *Compositions:* Five States of Mind (Carl Fischer); Recitation for 8-part trombone choir. *Recordings:* Producer, Highwater Records album 8201: John Stover, Classical Guitar, 1983. *Publications:* Music theory from Zarlino to Schenker: A bibliography and guide, with David Damschroder, 1990; Bibliography of the History of Music Theory, 1970, 1971; Conversations with Howard Hanson, 1988. *Honours:* Eastman School of Music publication award, 1970; Edward Benjamin Contest for Tranquil Music, winner, 1963. *Memberships:* College Music Society, Sec, 1973-83; National Association of Schools of Music, Ch, Region 8, 1989-92); National Academy of Recording Arts and Sci, Treas, local chapter, 1984-86. *Hobbies:* Word puzzles; Stock market study; Languages. *Address:* 273 Central Park West, 1, Memphis, TN 38111-4570, USA.

WILLIAMS Edgar Warren, b. 12 June 1949, Orlando, Florida, USA. Professor; Composer; Conductor. m. Christine Anderson, 19 June 1971, 1 son, 1 daughter. *Education:* BA, Duke University, 1971; MA, Columbia University, 1973; MFA 1977, PhD 1982, Princeton University. *Career:* Teaching Assistant, Columbia University, 1972-73; Assistant in Instruction, Princeton University, 1977-78; Visiting Lecturer in Music, University of California, Davis, 1978-79; Assistant Professor, The College of William and Mary, Williamsburg, Virginia, 1979-82; Associate Professor, 1982; Guest Conductor with orchestras including Bennington Composers Conference Ensemble, 1969-70 and Columbia Composers Ensemble, 1973; Conductor, William and Mary Orchestra, 1979-82. *Compositions:* Numerous published including: Three Songs, 1977; Across a Bridge of Dreams, 1979-80; Amoretti, 1980; Some Music for Merry Wives, 1982; Landscapes With Figure, 1983. *Contributions to:* In Theory Only; 19th Century Music. *Honour:* Prize winner for Amoretti, East and West Artists Sixth Annual Composition Contest. *Current Management:* Broadcast Music Incorporated; Mobart Music Publications, Hilsdale, New York. *Address:* Department of Music, College of William and Mary, Williamsburg, VA 23185, USA.

WILLIAMS Edgar, b. 11 Mar 1926, Porth, Rhondda, Wales. Principal Lecturer; Bassoonist. m. Patricia Ann Jones, 26 Mar 1965, 2 daughters. *Education:* Trinity College of Music, London; Hon. FTCL. *Career:* Principal Bassoonist, Bournemouth Symphony Orchestra, 1951-63; Freelance with major London Orchestras, 1963-70; Head of Wind Instrument Studies, Royal Scottish Academy of Music, Glasgow, 1970-91; Performances in Festivals in Aldeburgh, Edinburgh, Berlin, Moscow, Prague, Warsaw and USA. *Recordings:* Many recordings with London Symphony Orchestra; London Philharmonic Orchestra; English Chamber Orchestra and Melos Ensemble. *Honour:* Honorary FTCL, 1982; FRSAMD, 1989. *Hobbies:* Theatre; Reading. *Address:* 12 Westbourne Gardens, Glasgow G12 9XD, Scotland.

WILLIAMS Elwyn Gildas, b. 31 May 1946, Neath, West Glamorgan, Wales. Lecturer in Music; Welsh College of Music and Drama; Conductor. m. Elaine Maddox, 5 Feb 1977, 2 sons. *Education:* Royal Academy of Music, London, 1965-70; Academy of Music, S Cecilia, Rome, 1970-71; LRAM Diploma; University of Wales College of Cardiff, 1987-90; MA. *Debut:* Conductor, BBC Welsh Orchestra, 1972. *Career:* Television appearances as Conductor and Accompanist, 1972-79; Conductor, Cardiff Polyphonic Choir, 1975-76; Assistant Musical Director, HTV Wales, 1976-77; Tutor, Welsh College of Music and Drama, 1975-81; Lecturer in Music, 1981-; Musical Director of Opera, 1982-; Pianist on BBC Wales TV, 1963; Toured Western Slovakia with Glamorgan Youth Chamber Choir as Pianist and Accompanist, 1967-; Studied Conducting with Igor Markevitch and The Opera Orchestra of Monte Carlo, 1968; International Master Class for Young Conductors, Bologna, Director: Franco Ferrara,

Orchestra of the Teatro Communale, Bologna, 1974; Appearances in North America, Canada, Belgium and Italy as Conductor; Conducted The World Premiere of Mervyn Burtch's Opera, The Fountain, Bute Theatre, WCMD, Cardiff, 1982; Founder and Conductor of The New Chamber Orchestra, 1986-; Head, Opera Studies, WCMD, 1987-; Welsh College of Music and Drama: Lecturer in Music, 1981-91; Musical Director of Opera, 1982-1991; Head of Opera Studies, 1987-91. *Hobby:* Swimming. *Current Management:* Harlequin Agency, 203 Fidlas Road, Cardiff, CF4 5NA, Wales. *Address:* 41 St Benedict Crescent, Heath, Cardiff, Wales.

WILLIAMS Hermine Weigel, b. 4 Feb 1933, Sellersville, Pennsylvania, USA. Teacher; Writer and Editor; Musician. m. Jay Gomer Williams, 9 Sept 1956, 2 sons, 2 daughters. *Education:* PhD Musicology, Columbia University, 1964; Private study with Grete Sultan. *Career:* Teacher, Vassar College, 1954-56, Hamilton College, 1964-65, 1972-92; Assistant to General Editor of The Operas of Alessandro Scarlatti; Associate Editor, The Facts Behind the Songs; A Handbook of American Popular Music; Member of international editorial board for complete works edition of Giovanni Pergolesi; Professional accompanist; Organist and choral director in area churches; Organ soloist with Utica Symphony; Solo and ensemble recitals; Freelance writer, and opera consultant. *Compositions:* Piano vocal score of A Scarlatti's The Triumph of Honor 1718, 1984, and La Caduta Dei Decemviri 1697, 1980. *Publications:* The Operas of Alessandro Scarlatti, vol 6, 1980; The Symphony 1720-1840, 1983; A Short History of Opera, 1988; Giovanni Battista Pergolesi: A Guide to Research, 1989; Contribution include those to Current Musicology, New Grove Italian Baroque Opera, New Grove Dictionaries of Music and Musicians and of Opera; Studi Pergolesiani; Music and Civilization. *Honours:* Maarston Fellowship; Theodore Presser Award in Composition: Commission from San Francisco Opera, 1982; Fulbright Lecturer in Musicology, New Zealand, 1987. *Memberships:* American Musicological Society; American Handel Society. *Hobbies:* Swimming. *Address:* 300 College Hill Road, Clinton, NY 13323, USA.

WILLIAMS Howard, b. 25 Apr 1947, Hemel Hempstead, Hertfordshire, England. Conductor. m. Juliet Solomon, 24 Dec 1977, 1 son, 1 daughter. *Education:* King's School, Canterbury; BA, New College, Oxford; BMus, Liverpool University; Advanced conducting course, Guildhall School of Music and Drama. *Career:* Conducted over 40 opera productions with English National Opera and elsewhere, including Punch and Judy and The Knot Garden for Channel 4 TV; Other modern repertory includes the premieres of Holloway's Liederkreis and Concertino No. 1, Hamilton's Anna Karenina, and Cowie's Choral Symphony and Concerto for Orchestra; Many productions with Royal Ballet at Covent Garden and abroad; Regular Guest Conductor, BBC Symphony Orchestra, BBC Welsh Orchestra; Regular appearances with Royal Philharmonic, Scottish National, Bournemouth Symphony, Northern Sinfonia, English Chamber, London Sinfonietta, Royal Liverpool Philharmonic; Regular visitor overseas to orchestras in France, Belgium, Netherlands, Sweden and Hungary; Principal Conductor, Pecs Symphony Orchestra, Hungary, 1989- (1st British Conductor to hold appointment in Hungary). *Recordings include:* 3 discs of music by Frank Bridge including his opera The Christmas Rose; premiere pressing of Bizet's Ivan the Terrible. *Memberships:* Royal Philharmonic Society. *Current Management:* Christopher Tennant Artists. *Address:* c/o Christopher Tennant Artists, 11 Lawrence Street, London SW3 5NB, England.

WILLIAMS John, b. 24 April 1941, Melbourne, Australia. Guitarist. *Education:* Began playing the guitar aged four; moved to London 1952 and studied with Segovia; later study at the Accademia Musicale in Siena and the Royal College of Music, London. *Debut:* Wigmore Hall, London, 1958. *Career:* Toured Soviet Union 1962, Japan and USA 1963; regular tours of US, Australia, Far East, South America and Europe; frequent appearances on TV, bringing his music to widest possible audience; with four other musicians played in group SKY 1979-84, performing at Ronnie Scott's Jazz Club and other popular venues; many concerts with group John Williams and Friends, including a tour of Italy, 1987; has appeared with the Academy of St. Martin-in-the-Fields, City of Birmingham Symphony Orchestra, English Chamber Orchestra and London Symphony Orchestra; performed with the National Youth Jazz Orchestra at the 1988 Promenade Concerts; composers who have written for him include Takemitsu, Leo Brouwer, Stephen Dodgson and André Previn; Artistic Director of the South Bank Summer Music Festival for two years and Artistic Director of the Melbourne Arts Festival in 1987; Played Brouwer's 4th Concerto in Paris, Oct 1988; tour of US 1989, and recital at the South Bank Latin American Festival; premiered Sculthorpe's Second Concerto in Australia, 1989; Attacca tour of UK and Australia, 1992. *Compositions:* Concertos by Peter Sculthorpe and Nigel Westlake, written for John Williams; The latter's Antarctica was premiered by John Williams and the London Symphony in Autumn, 1992. *Recordings:* Most of the classical repertoire with Sony Classical and popular works with various other labels; Recordings made under John Williams' ongoing exclusive contract have recently included Vivaldi Concertos, Iberia, both bestsellers. *Address:* c/o Harold Holt Ltd, 31 Sinclair Road, London W14 ONS, England.

WILLIAMS John, b. 8 Feb 1932, New York, USA. Composer; Arranger; Conductor; Pianist. *Education:* Studied with Bobby Van Eps in Los Angeles with Rosina Lhevinne at the Juilliard School and Castelnuovo-Tedesco at UCLA. *Career:* Orchestrated for and conducted USAF bands; Wrote music for feature films and for television, including the Kraft Theatre Series; Pianist, arranger and conductor for Columbia Records, with collaborations with André Previn; Film music association with Steven Spielberg and other leading directors; Conductor of the Boston Pops Orchestra from 1980; Guest conductor with orchestras in London, Canada and most American cities. *Compositions:* Film scores include The Towering Inferno 1974, Jaws 1975, Close Encounters of the Third Kind 1977, Star Wars 1977, Superman 1978, Raiders of the Lost Ark, ET 1982, Indiana Jones and the Temple of Doom 1984; Symphony 1966; Essay for strings 1966; Violin Concerto 1974; Flute Concerto 1980; Pops on the March 1982; Olympic Fanfare and Themes 1984. *Address:* c/o ASCAP, ASCAP Building, One Lincoln Plaza, New York, NY 10023, USA.

WILLIAMS Julius Penson, b. 22 June 1954, Bronx, New York, USA. Composer; Conductor. m. Lenora B Williams, 7 Aug 1977, 1 son, 1 daughter. *Education:* Music Major, Andrew Jackson High School, 1972; BS, Herbert H Lehman, City University of New York, 1977; MM, Hartt School of Music, 1980; Aspen Music School, 1984; Professional Fellow, Aspen, 1985. *Debut:* Premiere of A Norman Overture, New York Philharmonic, Zubin Mehta, 1985. *Career:* Music Director, CPTV, 1984-85; Arts Award Guest Conductor, Connecticut Opera, 1983, Dallas Symphony, 1986, Savannah Symphony, 1987; Conductor/Composer in Residence, Nutmeg Ballet, Connecticut, 1986-88; Assistant Conductor, Aspen Music Festival, 1985; Guest Conductor, New Haven Symphony, May 1987; Guest Conductor, Amor Artist Chamber Orchestra, 1987; Artistic Director, New York State Summer School of the Arts (Choral Studies), 1988-; Principal Guest School of Orchestral Studies; Associate Professor University of Vermont, (Artist in Residence), Saratoga Arts Festival, Aug 1988; National T.V., C.B.S. Sunday Morning with Charles Kuralf, Sept 11, 1988. *Compositions:* A Norman Overture, Tocatina for Strings, published MMB; Incommendation of Music, The Spring, both published by Lawson-Gould pub.; Rise Up Shepherd and Follow, Augsburg Publishing House; Vermonts Escape, MMB Publishers; Alison's Dream, MMB Publishers; The Fall, Summers Good Ecelin, Published by Lawson Gould. *Contributions to:* American Choral Directors Journal Choral Review, 1982. *Current Management:* Euphonia

Artist Management. *Address:* Euphonia Artist Management, PO Box 809, Cambridge, MA 02238, USA.

WILLIAMS Laverne, b. 1935, San Francisco, California, USA. Professional Opera and Concert Singer. *Education:* Master's Degree, University of California; Alfred Hertz Memorial Scholarship and Rockefeller Foundation Scholarship for studies in Europe. *Career:* Concerts and opera appearances ranging from Baroque to contemporary; L'Incoronazione di Poppea, Salome, Idomeneo and Porgy and Bess, Switzerland; Appeared with Jessye Norman in Great Day in the Morning, Paris; Porgy and Bess, Glagolitic Mass and Jenůfa under Simon Rattle, UK; Appearances with most major orchestras in London and UK including London Symphony, Royal Philharmonic and the Royal Liverpool Philharmonic Orchestra; Directed and sung in an experimental evening of spirituals, Almeida Theatre; Performed Virgil Thomson's Four Saints in Three Acts, Almeida Theatre; European opera appearances include Zurich, Lyon and Brussels operas; Television and radio appearances include: Gershwin's Blue Monday in Switzerland; Hermann Prey Show for German television; Here Come The Classics and excerpts from Carmen Jones, BBC Television; Club Mix, Channel 4; Leading role, European premiere of Carmen Jones; Weber's Oberon, Edinburgh Festival, Tanglewood and Frankfurt, 1986. *Recordings:* Great Day in the Morning, with Jessye Norman. *Honours:* Competition successes in S'Hertogenbosch, Rio de Janeiro and Barcelona. *Hobbies:* Tennis; Squash; Art work of all kinds; Pottery. *Address:* Ingpen and Williams International Limited, 14 Kensington Court, London W8 5DN, England.

WILLIAMS Louise, b. 23 Sept 1955, England, Violinist and Violist. *Career:* Co-founder and second violinist Endellion Quartet, 1979-83; Violist of the Chilingirian Quartet, joined 1987-92; Resident Quartet of Royal College of Music; Resident Quartet of Royal College of Music, 1986-; Annual series of concerts at the Elizabeth Hall and the Wigmore Hall; Performances at the Edinburgh, Bath, Aldeburgh Festivals; Munich Herkulessaal, Amsterdam Concertgebouw, Zurich Tonhalle, Vienna Konzerthaus, Stockholm Konserthuset; New York debut 1976; Annual coast-to-coast tours of the USA and Canada; Represented Britain at the New York International Festival quartet series; Tours of Australia, New Zealand, South America, the Far East; Television and radio throughout Europe, National Public Radio in the USA, the BBC; Presently, Free-Lance Chamber Musician and Soloist, Violin and Viola. *Recordings:* Complete Quartets of Bartók and Dvořák; Bartók Piano Quintet; Mozart Flute Quartets; Beethoven Serenade; Labels include EMI, RCA, CRD, Nimbus and Chandos. *Address:* The Top, Exbury House, Exbury, Southampton SO4 1AF, England.

WILLIAMS Martyn John, b. 30 Mar 1953, Cardiff, Wales. Director of Examinations, London College of Music. m. Anthea Jefferson 1980. *Education:* Llandaff Cathedral School 1961-66; Ellesmere College 1966-71; Royal College of Music 1971-76; BMus (Hons.) GRSM, FRCO, FLCM, ARCM, MTC (London). *Career:* Professor of Theory and Composition, London College of Music 1976-82; Purcell School, Assistant music teacher 1981-82; From 1982 Academic Administrator and from 1988 Director of Studies, London College of Music; Editor, London College of Music Magazine, 1986-88; Director of Examinations, London College of Music, Thames Valley University from 1992. *Composition:* Mass of St Mark, for chorus and organ 1980. *Recording:* Orchestration of Meeting Place/Lloyd Webber 1980. *Contributions to:* Organ Critic; Musical Times 1983-86. *Honours:* Hon. LCM. *Memberships:* ISM; Royal College of Music; Royal College of Organists. *Hobbies:* Cooking; Good wine; Reading; Cycling. *Address:* The Vicarage, Rolvenden, Kent TN17 4ND, England.

WILLIAMS Peter Fredric, b. 14 May 1937, Wolverhampton, Staffs., England. University Professor, Organ and Harpsichord Recitalist. m. Rosemary Seymour, 10 June 1982, 3 sons, 1 daughter. *Education:*

Wolverhampton School; Birmingham Institute; St John's College, Cambridge, 1955-62. *Career:* Lecturer, 1962; Reader, 1972; Professor, 1982; Dean, 1984; University of Edinburgh, Scotland; Director, Russell College of Harpsichords, Edinburgh, 1969; Distinguished Professor and University Organist, Duke University, North Carolina, USA, 1985. *Recordings:* EMI; BBC Archives; SCH Label; Editions: Bach, Musical Offering and Art of Fugue (Eulenburg), Handel Op IV and VII (Eulenburg), Handel Organ Concertos (OUP), Handel Harpsichord Music, 3 vols (Schott), misc organ music (Stainer & Bell, Galaxy, OUP, Hinrichsen-Peters), projected Bach organ music, 15 vols (OUP). *Publications:* The European Organ, 1966; Figured Bass Accompaniment, Two Volumes, 1970; Bach Organ Music, 1972; New History of the Organ, 1980; The Organ Music of J. S. Bach, Three Volumes, 1980-84; The Organ: New Grove Instrument Series, 1988; Playing the Organ Music of Bach, 1986; Translated Vente/Peeters The Organ of the Netherlands, 1971; Edited Tercentenary Essays, 1985; Series editor: Cambridge Studies in Performance Practice (2 Vols. by 1993); The Organ in Western Culture, (CUP), 1993; The King of Instruments: How Do Churches Come to Have Organs? (SPCK), 1993. *Contributions to:* Essays in virtually all serious journals; Editor of The Organ Yearbook, Amsterdam, 1969-; Editor of series Biblioteca Organologica (80 vols), 1966-. *Address:* St Cecilia's Hall, University of Edinburgh, Scotland.

WILLIAMS Rodney John, b. 3 July 1941, Beckenham, Kent, England. Singer (Bass/Baritone); Lay Vicar; Conductor. *Education:* Chorister under Dr Boris Ord, King's College, Cambridge, 1952-55; Music Scholar, Cranleigh, Surrey, 1955-60; Royal College of Music (Associate 1962), 1960-63; Studied singing with Norman Allin and Hervey Alan, organ with Dr H K Andrews and Dr Sidney Campbell, piano with Edwin Benbow, harmony with Dr W Lloyd Webber and Michael Mullinar. *Career:* Opening Solo, Carol Service from King's College Chapel, Cambridge, 1954 (first television) and first long playing record of Carols, 1954; Member of Choir of Her Majesty's Chapel Royal at the Tower of London, 1969-72; Lay Vicar, Choir of Westminster Abbey, 1972-; Various broadcasts and television appearances with the Abbey Choir, British Broadcasting Corporation Singers and other choirs; Solo roles in oratorio and concert work; Member, Westminster Glee Singers; Solo singing classes; Director, Rodney Williams Singers. *Recordings:* Cantor on recording of Litany of the Saints, William Byrd; (Soloist) and on Compact Disc, Christmas Ancient and Modern for Accademia, 1992. *Address:* 175 Farnaby Road, Shortlands, Kent, BR2 0BA, England.

WILLIAMS Sioned, b. 1 July 1953, Mancot, Clwyd, North Wales, Harpist. m. Kim A. L. Sargeant, 6 Aug 1977. *Education:* Welsh College of Music and Drama, 1971-74, Recital Diploma, Royal Academy of Music. *Debut:* Purcell Room, Park Lane Group Young Artists/20th Century Music, 1977; Carnegie Hall, New York, USA (Concert Artists Guild Award), 1980. *Career:* Appearances worldwide with London Symphony Orchestra, Philharmonia, London Philharmonic Orchestra, RPO, BBC Symphony Orchestra, BBC Philharmonic, CBSO, Royal Ballet, London Sinfonietta, Royal Opera House, ENO, WNO, SNO, etc; Solo and concerto performances, premiering over 80 works; Chamber music with Uroboros, Gemini, Spectrum, Endymion, Divertimenti, Koenig, Grosvenor, Circle; Theatre, radio, TV and festival appearances; Professor of Harp, Royal College of Music Junior Department, 1976-85; Royal Academy of Music, 1983-84; London College of Music, 1985-86; Trinity College of Music, 1986-; Adjudicator at major Welsh Eisteddfods, 1981-. *Compositions:* Cyfres i'r Delyn, 1973 (special prize, 17th International Harp Week); Serenata e Danza, 1983. *Recordings:* Harp Music, John Thomas; Harp Music, John Parry; Spun Gold for Flute and Harpa; Ceremony of Carols, Britten; Nielsen with James Galway. *Publications:* Editor, John Parry: Four Sonatas, 1982; Four Sonatas, 1982; J.S. Bach: Suite BMV1006a, 1986. *Honours:* Numerous prizes, awards and scholarships including Bursary, Arts Council Advanced Training

Scheme, 1982. *Memberships:* Telynores Garmon in Bardic Circle; Incorporated Society of Musicians; United Kingdom Harpists Association; World Harp Congress; American Harp Society; Cymdeithas Cerdd Dant; Guild for the Promotion of Welsh Music. *Hobbies:* Embroidery; Reading. *Address:* 181 Gloucester Road, Cheltenham, GL51 8NQ, England.

WILLIAMS Wayne, b. 1960, Cleveland, Ohio, USA. Singer (Tenor). *Education:* Studied at the Cleveland Music Settlement, the Baldwin Wallace Conservatory and the University of Illinois; Further study with Gerard Souzay in Europe. *Career:* Has sung with most Swiss orchestras and the Orchestre Lamoureux, Nouvel Orchestre Philharmonique, Orchestre Symphonique du Rhin and Shanghai Symphony; Sang in Porgy and Bess with the Royal Liverpool Philharmonic in Leeds, Liverpool and Huddersfield; Dvořák's Requiem in Paris and Donizetti's Requiem with the Berlin Philharmonic; Sang in Martinů's The Three Wishes for Lyons Opera, 1990; Recital with Geoffrey Parsons for Swiss Radio, 1992. *Recordings include:* Poulenc's Gloria (Decca); Dvořak's Stabat Mater (BNL, France); Great Day in the Morning, with Jessye Norman (Philips). *Address:* c/o Norman McCann International Artists Ltd, The Coach House, 56 Lawrie Park Gardens, London SE26 6XJ, England.

WILLIAMS Wayne, b. 1950, Cleveland, Ohio, USA. Singer (Tenor). *Education:* Studied at the Cleveland Music Settlement and with Gerard Souzay in Geneva. *Career:* Concert appearances with the Suisse Romande, Chamber Orchestra of Lausanne, Berne Symphony, Tonhalle Zurich, YMSO (London), Orchestra Haydn (Italy) and the Shanghai Symphony (China); Conductors have included Armin Jordan, Peter Maag, Horst Stein, Lopez-Cobos, James Blair, Paul Angerer and Herbert Handt; Recitals throughout the USA and Europe with Dalton Baldwin; Appearances in Paris in Dvořák's Requiem and Stabat Mater, Switzerland in The Creation and St Matthew Passion; Opera repertoire includes Schubert's Fierabras, L'Elisir d'Amore, La Traviata and A Midsummer Night's Dream. *Recordings include:* Poulenc Gloria; Great Day in the morning, with Jessye Norman; Dvořak Stabat Mater. *Address:* c/o Anglo Swiss Ltd. 3 Primrose Mews, 1a Sharpleshall St. London NW1 8YW, England.

WILLIAMS-KING Anne, b. 1960, Wrexham, Wales. Singer (Soprano). *Education:* Studied at the Royal Northern College of Music and the National Opera Studio in London. *Career:* With the Welsh National Opera has sung Lenio in The Greek Passion by Martinů, Mimi, Gilda, Fiordiligi, Marzelline in Fidelio and Micaela; Covent Garden debut 1988, as Freia in Das Rheingold; Appearances with Opera North as Mimi and in Rebecca by Josephs and A Vilage Romeo and Juliet by Delius; Scottish Opera as Freia and as Violetta: invited to return as Jenůfa, Madama Butterfly, and Mimi; Foreign engagements include Anne Trulove in The Rake's Progress, at Berne; Frequent concert appearances with leading British orchestras and on television; Sang Butterfly with Scottish Opera at Edinburgh, 1990. *Address:* c/o Stafford Law Associates, 26 Mayfield Road, Weybridge, Surrey KT13 8XB, England.

WILLIAMSON Malcolm (Benjamin Graham Christopher), b. 21 Nov 1931, Sydney, New South Wales, Australia. Composer; Pianist; Organist. m. 9 Jan 1960, Dolores Irene Daniel, 1 son, 1 daughter. *Education:* Studied at the Sydney Conservatory with Eugene Goossens and in London with Elisabeth Lutyens and Erwin Stein. *Debut:* (Organ) London 1966. *Career:* Soloist with numerous orchestras including London Philharmonic, London Symphony, BBC Symphony, English Chamber Orchestra, Hallé, Danish Radio Orchestra, Ulster, Vienna, Lusaka, Haifa, Melbourne and Sydney Symphonies; Lecturer in Music, Central School of Speech and Drama, 1961-62; Composer-in-residence Westminster Choir College, Princeton, 1970-71; Florida State University, USA 1975; Visiting Professor at Strathclyde University 1983-86; Myth of the Cave premiered at the 1991 Promenade Concerts, London.

Compositions: Operas: Our Man in Havana 1963; English Eccentrics 1966; The Happy Prince 1965; Julius Caesar Jones 1966; The Violins of St Jacques 1966; Dunstan and the Devil 1967; The Growing Castle 1968; Lucky Peter's Journey 1969; The Red Sea 1972; Ballets The Display 1964; Sun into darkness 1966; BigfellaTootsSquoodge and Nora 1967; Orchestral: 7 Symphonies 1956-84; Sinfonia Concertante for 3 trumpets, piano and strings 1958-62; Sinfonietta 1967; Symphonic Variations 1965; Fiesta 1978; 3 Piano Concertos 1957-62; Organ Concerto 1961; Violin Concerto 1965; Concerto for 2 pianos and strings 1972; Myth of the Cave, 1991; Cassations; Works for solo voice and orchestra and for chorus and orchestra; Ode to Music 1972; Jubilee Hymn for chorus and orchestra; Mass of Christ the King for soloists, chorus and orchestra 1978; Works for chorus and organ or piano; Unaccompanied works for chorus; Chamber music; Brass Band music; 2 Piano Sonatas, Sonata for 2 Pianos; Organ Music; Now is the Singing Day, 1981; A Pilgrim Liturgy, 1984; The True Endeavour, 1988; The Dawn is at Hand, 1989; Our Church Lives, 1989; Mass of St Etheldreda, 1990; Requiem for a Tribe Brother, 1992. *Honours include:* Sir Arnold Bax Memorial Prize 1963; DMus Westminster Choir College, Princeton NJ, USA, 1971; Creative Arts Fellowship, Australian National University, Canberra, 1973; Master of the Queen's Music, 1975; CBE, 1976; AO, 1987. *Hobbies:* Literature. *Address:* c/o Campion Press, Sandon, Buntingford, Hertfordshire, SG9 0QW, England.

WILLIS Helen, b. 25 July 1959, Newport, Gwent, Wales. Singer (mezzo-soprano). m. Robert Venn, 17 Dec 1983. *Education:* Dip Ram, Royal Academy of Music, 1977-83. *Debut:* Wigmore Hall, London, 1983. *Career:* Glyndebourne Festival Chorus, 1983-85; Solo Operatic debut with Welsh National Opera, as Siegrune in Die Walküre, 1984; Concerts and recitals throughout UK and Abroad; Broadcasts include, Sea Pictures and Wesendonk Lieder with BBC Welsh Symphony Orchestra. *Honours:* Triennial Young Welsh Singer of the Year, 1982. *Hobbies:* Food and Cooking; Walking. *Address:* c/o Welsh National Opera, John Street, Cardiff, Wales, CF1 4SP.

WILLIS Nuala, b. 1950, England. Singer (Mezzo-soprano). *Career:* Worked as designer/costumier and as actress in England and North America; Sang with the Opera Studio in Brussels and small roles with the Glyndebourne Tour; Aldeburgh Festival in Eugene Onegin and A Midsummer Night's Dream; Guest appearances at Nancy, Metz, Marsailes, (Herodias in Salome), Geneva (Larina in Eugene Onegin), Marseilles (Jezibab in Rusalka) and Zurich (the Hostess in Boris Godunov); At Covent Garden has appeared in A Midsummer Night's Dream, Eugene Onegin and Faust (as Martha); In the Irish Republic has sung Widow Bebick (Mahagonny) at Wexford and Clytemnestra in Elektra conducted by Janos Fürst, in Dublin; Season 1989-90 included Herodias in the Swedish Folkopera's Salome at the Edinburgh Festival; Ulrica in Un Ballo in Maschera for Canadian Opera in Toronto; Royal National Theatre in Sondheim's Sunday in the Park with George; Engagements with the D'Oyly Carte Opera. *Address:* c/o Athole Still Ltd., Greystoke House, 80-86 Westow Street, London, SE19 3AF, England.

WILLISON David, b. 13 Feb 1936, Surrey, England. Musician. m. Pamela J Edwards, 3 Sept 1960, 3d. *Education:* Royal Academy of Music; Guildhall School of Music and Drama. *Debut:* Wigmore Hall. *Career:* Concert Acc/Chamber Music Pianist; Professor, Royal Academy of Music, Creative Director, Lengnick Music Publishers. *Recordings:* Selected pieces under various record labels.*Publications:* Piano Volumes, 1989, and continuing. *Honours:* ARAM, 1986. *Memberships:* Incorporated Society of Musicians. *Hobbies:* Cricket; Walking; Photography. *Address:* The Other House, West Street, Rye, East Sussex TN31 7ES.

WILLNER Channan, b. 25 Sept 1951, Zurich, Switzerland. Music Librarian; Critic; Theorist. *Education:* BM, Mannes College of Music, USA, 1977; MA, Music,

Queens College, 1980; MS, Library Service, Columbia University, 1985; M.Phil, City University of New York, 1990. *Career:* Music Librarian, Library and Museum of the Performing Arts, Lincoln Center, New York, USA; Acquisitions Librarian, Music Division, The New York Public Library, 1987-. *Publications:* Theory and Practice (editor), 1983-86; Handel's Borrowings from Telemann: An Analytical View, in Trends in Schenkerian Research, 1990; Chromaticism and the Mediant in Four Late Haydn Works, Theory and Practice, Vol. 13, 1988; Analysis and Interpretation in the Performance of Handel's Concerti Grossi Op. 6, Musical Times, Mar 1989; The Two-Length Bar Revisited: Handel and the Hemiola, in Göttinger Händel-Beiträge, Vol. 4, 1991. *Contributions to:* Book and music reviews in MLA Notes; Concert and recording reviews in The Strad and The Musical Times. *Honour:* Ida Rosen Prize in Music Librarianship, Columbia University, 1984. *Memberships:* American Musicological Society; American Handel Society; Music Library Association; Society for Music Theory; American Bach Society; International Association of Music Libraries. *Hobbies:* Hiking; Architectural sightseeing. *Address:* Music Division, The New York Public Library, 40 Lincoln Center Plaza, New York, NY 10023-7498, USA.

WILLS Arthur, b. 19 Sept. 1926, Coventry, England. Composer; Cathedral Organist. m. Mary Elizabeth Titterton, 14 Nov 1953, 1 son, 1 daughter. *Education:* St John's School, Coventry; St. Nicholas College, Canterbury. *Career:* Organist, Ely Cathedral, 1958-90; Professor, Royal Academy of Music, 1964-92; Organ recitals in Europe, USA, Australia and New Zealand. *Compositions:* Organ Concerto, 1970; An English Requiem, 1971; Guitar Sonata, 1974; Three Poems of EE Cummings for Tenor, Oboe and Piano, 1974; Love's Torment (Four Elizabethan Love Songs) for Alto and Piano, 1975; The Fenlands (Symphonic Suite for Brass Band and Organ), 1981; Overture: A Muse of Fire for Brass Band, 1983; Concerto Lirico for Guitar Quartet, 1987; When the Spirit Comes (Four Poems of Emily Brontë for Mezzo Soprano and Piano), 1985; Piano Sonata "1984"; The Dark Lady (Eight Sonnets of Shakespeare for Baritone and Piano), 1986; Sacrae Symphonia: Veni Creator Spiritus, 1987; Choral Concerto: The Gods of Music, 1992; Eternity's Sunrise, Three Poems by William Blake, 1992; A Toccata of Galuppi's, Scena for Countertenor and String Quartet), 1993. *Recordings:* Mussorgsky: Pictures at an Exhibition (Trans. Wills), Hyperion; Bach at Ely: Nine transcriptions (Wills), Hyperion; Christmas Eve at Ely (Priory); The Music of Arthur Wills (Priory); Symphonic Suite: The Fenlands for Organ and Brass Band, Hyperion. *Publication:* Organ, Menuhin Music Guide Series, 1984 and 1993. *Contributions to:* Musical Times. *Honour:* OBE, 1990. *Memberships:* Royal Academy of Music. *Hobby:* Reading. *Address:* Paradise House, 26 New Barns Road, Ely, Cambridgeshire, CB7 4PN, England.

WILSON Catherine, b. 1936, Glasgow, Scotland. Singer (Soprano). *Education:* Royal Manchester College of Music with Elsie Thurston; Further study with Ruth Packer in London and Maria Carpi in Geneva. *Debut:* Sadler's Wells London 1960 as Angelina in La Cenerentola. *Career:* Glyndebourne 1960, in Die Zauberflöte; Sadler's Wells 1965, in the premiere of Bennett's The Mines of Sulphur; Scottish Opera 1974, in the premiere of Hamilton's The Catiline Conspiracy; Guest appearances in Aldeburgh, Geneva, Houston, London (Covent Garden and English National Opera) and Santa Fe; Often heard in operas by Mozart, Rossini, Puccini, Strauss and Britten and as a concert singer; Currently Teaching at Royal Northern College of Music. *Recordings include:* Albert Herring by Britten (Decca); The Merry Widow; Dido and Aeneas. *Honour:* Fellow, Royal Manchester College of Music. *Hobbies:* Gardening; Cooking. *Address:* 18 St Mary's Grove, London N1, England.

WILSON Charles, b. 8 May 1931, Toronto, Canada. Composer. *Education:* Studied with Godfrey Ridout at the Toronto Conservatory, DMus Toronto University 1956; Further study with Lukas Foss and Carlos Chavez at the Berkshire Music Center. *Career:* Head of the music department at Guelph Collegiate Institute, 1962-70; Composer-in-residence at the Canadian Opera Company from 1972, and at the University of Guelph, Ontario. *Compositions include:* The Strolling Clerk from Paradise, chamber opera, 1952; Johnny Fibber, operetta, 1970; Phrases from Orpheus, multi-media opera, Guelph 1971; The Summoning of Everyman, Church opera, Dalhousie 1973; Heloise and Abelard, opera in 3 acts, Toronto 1973; The Selfish Giant, children's opera, Toronto 1973; Psycho Red, opera in 2 acts, Guelph 1978; Kamouraska, opera in 3 acts, Toronto 1979; 3 String Quartets 1950, 1968, 1975; Symphony in A 1954; Sonata de Chiesa For oboe land strings 1960; String Trio 1963; The Angels of the Earth, oratorio, 1966; En Guise d'Orphée for baritone and strings 1968; Concerto 5x4x3 for string quintet, woodwind quartet and brass trio 1970; Sinfonia for double orchestra 1973; Image out of Season for chorus and brass quintet 1973; Christo paremus canticum for chorus and orchestra 1973; Symphonic Perspectives: Kingsmere, for orchestra, 1974; Missa Brevis for chorus and organ 1975. *Address:* SOCAN (Canada), c/o PRS Ltd. Member Registration, 29-33 Berners Street, London W1P 4AA, England.

WILSON Christopher, b. 1951, England. Lutenist; Vihuela player. *Education:* Studied the lute at the Royal College of Music with Diana Poulton. *Career:* Has specialised in the performance of Renaissance music throughout Britain; Concert tours of Europe, Scandinavia, the USA, the Baltic States, Russia and Far East; As well as working with his own group Kithara, Interest in the lute song repertoire has led him to work with such song recitalists as countertenor Michael Chance and the tenor Rufus Müller. He also performs with Fretwork, Gothic Voices, The Consort of Musicke and the English Baroque Soloists; Concerts 93-94 include tours to Sweden, Hong Kong and Japan, Poland and Taiwan. *Recordings:* Has appeared on over 50 recordings on Hyperion, Florilegium, Philips, Telefunken, Harmonia Mundi, Chandos, ASV and Virgin Classics. Solo recordings on Virgin Classics and Naxos Records. *Address:* Magenta Music International, 64 Highgate High Street, London N6 5HX, England.

WILSON Fredric Woodbridge, b. 8 Sept 1947, Point Pleasant, New Jersey, USA. Musicologist. *Education:* BA, Music, Lehigh University, Bethlehem, Pennsylvania, 1969; MA, Musicology, New York, University, 1977. *Career:* Director, The Wall Choirs, New Jersey, 1969-81; Editor, Allaire Music Publications, 1980-; Curator, The Pierpont Morgan Library, 1981-; Musical and Textual Consultant to opera companies. *Compositions:* More than 50 musical editions published, including motets by Gallus, Charpentier, mass by Lotti. *Publications:* Introduction to the Gilbert and Sullivans Operas, 1989; Index to the Opus Musicum of Jacob Handl, 1992; General editor, The W S Gilbert Edition 1986-. *Contributions to:* New Grove Dictionary of Opera; Many papers and articles; Organised conferences in English Opera, New York, 1985, Gilbert and Sullivan, 1989; Organised exhibitions at Pierpont Morgan Library, 1985, 1989. *Memberships:* Society for Textual Scholarship; American Musicological Society; Theatre Library Association; Music Publishers Association. *Honours:* Music Publishers Association and American Choral Directors Association - Awards for Excellence in editing early music - 4 1st place awards, 1986, American Library Association, 1st place Award for excellence in exhibition catalogue, 1986. *Address:* Pierpont Morgan Library, 29E 36th Street, New York, NY 10016, USA.

WILSON James, b. 27 Sept 1922, London, England. Composer. *Education:* Studied at Trinity College of Music, London. *Career:* Resident in Ireland from 1948, freelance composer of music for the stage and other works. *Compositions:* The Hunting of the Snark, children's opera, 1965; The Pied Piper of Hamelin, masque, Wexford 1969; Twelfth Night, opera in 3 acts, Wexford 1969; The Tain, monodrama, Dublin 1972; Fand, monodrama, Kilkenny 1975; Letters to Theo, opera in 1 act, Dublin 1984; Grinning at the Devil, opera in 2 acts, Copenhagen 1989; The King of the Golden River, opera, 1990; Concertos and songs. *Address:* 10a Wyvern, Killiney Hill, Co Dublin, Ireland.

WILSON John, b. 31 Jan 1940, Manchester, England. Musician; Accompanist; Teacher; Composer. m. Pauline Janet Millin, 2 sons, 1 daughter. *Education:* LRAM; ARCM; FNSM, FRNCM, Northern School of Music, England, 1955-61. *Career:* Staff Accompanist, Northern School of Music, 1961-73; Head, Opera Music Staff, 1973-75, Senior Accompanist, 1975-, Royal Northern College of Music; many radio broadcasts & TV appearances. *Compositions:* 3 Westmorland Sketches for Oboe/Flute and Piano; Flight of the Bumble Bee for 2 pianos, 1992; Carmen Fantasia for 2 pianos, 1992. *Memberships:* Member, Incorporated Society of Musicians; Member, OSA, Royal Northern College of Music; Association of Friends, Royal Northern College of Music.*Honours:* FRNCM. *Hobbies:* Woodwork; Gardening; Boating. *Address:* Meadoway, Church Road, Mellor, Stockport SK6 5LY, England.

WILSON Neil, b. 4 June 1956, Lubbock, Texas, USA. Singer (Tenor). *Education:* Studied at Dallas and Oklahoma Universities and in New York. *Debut:* Wolf Trap Washington 1980, as Verdi's Fenton. *Career:* Sang with the Houston Opera and appeared with Stuttgart Opera from 1985, debut as werther; Further appearances in Munich, Vienna, Hamburg, Bologna, Los Angeles and Cologne (as the Duke of Mantua, 1987); Washington Opera 1987, as Gounod's Romeo, New York Metropolitan 1988, as Macduff; Sang Boito's Faust at the Zurich Opera 1989-90 Glyndebourne Festival 1986, as Monteverdi's Nero; Sang Rodolfo with Florentine Opera at the Performing Arts Center, Milwaukee, 1992; Other roles include: Alfredo, Giasone in Medee, Nemorino, Lensky, Don Ottavio, Tamino and Pelléas; Concert repertoire includes Verdi's Requiem (Israel 1986). *Address:* c/o Zurich Opera, Falkenstrasse 1, CH-8008 Zurich, Switzerland.

WILSON Paul, b. 1952, Gloucester, England. Singer (Tenor). *Education:* Studied at Jesus College Oxford and at the Royal College of Music. *Career:* British appearances with English National, Welsh National and Scottish Opera companies; Kent Opera, Glyndebourne Festival, Chelsea Opera and Opera North; Foreign engagements with the Opera Factory Zurich, Pocket Opera Nürnberg, and Nairobi Opera; Roles include Tom Rakewell, Andrea Chénier, Bacchus, Mark (The Wreckers), and Don Jose; Royal Opera Covent Garden in Handel's Samson, Ariadne auf Naxos, King Priam and Der Rosenkavalier; Welsh National Opera debut 1987, as Florestan, and English National Opera debut 1988 as Monostatos; Opera North from 1990, in Gianni Schicchi and L'Heure Espagnole; Sang Siegmund and Siegfried in Birmingham Touring Opera's truncated Ring performances in Britain, 1990-91; Has sung in the world premieres of Golem by John Casken and Cage's Europeras III and IV (Almeida Festival, 1989-90) and Oliver's Timon of Athens (ENO 1991); Concert repertory includes The Dream of Gerontius, the Glagolitic Mass, Verdi's Requiem and Beethoven's 9th Symphony, conducted by Roger Norrington; Performance of Stravinsky's Les Noces with the National Youth Orchestra of Spain; Aldeburgh Festival 1990, in Goehr's Triptych; Garsington Manor Opera, Ariadne Auf Naxos, 1993. *Recordings:* Golem, John Casken, Virgin Classics, 1991; Caritas, Robert Saxton, Collins Classics, 1992. *Honours include:* First Wagner Society Bayreuth Bursary, 1983; Arts Council Bursary. *Current Management:* Opera Concert Artists (Judith Newton). *Address:* 75 Aberdare Gardens, London NW6 3AN, England.

WILSON Richard E, b. 15 May 1941, Cleveland, Ohio, USA. Composer; Pianist; Professor of Music. m. Adene Stevenson Green, 15 May 1971, 1 son, 1 daughter. *Education:* AB, Harvard University, 1963; Studies Cello with Ernst Silberstein, Piano with Leonard Shure, Composition with Robert Moevs; Composer in Residence, American Symphony, 1992. *Career:* Works

performed in New York including Tully Hall, 1991, London, Tokyo, San Francisco, Los Angeles, Bogota, Stockholm, Aspen, Boston, Chicago, other venues; Assistant Professor, 1966, Associate Professor, 1970, Professor, 1976-, Vassar College, Poughkeepsie, New York. *Compositions:* Recorded: Quartet 3: Eclogue for piano; The Ballad of Longwood Glen; Concert Piece for violin and piano; Music solo for flute; Music for violin and cello. *Recordings:* Concerto for Piano and Orchestra; Concerto for Bassoon and Chamber Orchestra; Persuasions; Lord Chesterfield. *Publications:* Sour Flowers; Profound Utterances; A Dissolve; Light in Spring Poplars; Hone from the Range; Soaking; Fixations, 1991; Intercalations, 1991. *Address:* c/o Department of Music, Vassar College, Poughkeepsie, NY 12601, USA.

WILSON Robert, b. 4 Oct 1941, Waco, Texas, USA. Playwright; Stage Director; Designer. *Education:* University of Texas 1959-65; BFA in architecture, Pratt Institute, New York. *Career:* Produced plays from 1969, at first in New York then Europe (12-hour The Life and Times of Joseph Stalin, Copenhagen 1973); Collaboration with Philip Glass, Einstein on the Beach, premiered at Avignon 1976 and repeated at the Metropolitan Opera; Further music theatre work with Glass and Gavin Bryars on Civil Wars (1984); Directed Charpentier's Médée and Medea by Bryars at Lyons, 1984; Designed the opening concert of the Opera de Bastille, Paris, 13 July 1989; Premiere of Louis Andriessen's Die Materie at Amsterdam 1989; Produced and designed Gluck's Alceste for Chicago Lyric Opera, 1990, with Jessye Norman; Lohengrin for Zurich Opera, 1991; Palace of Arabian Nights, music by Philip Glass, produced at Lisbon and the Seville World Fair, 1992; Parsifal at Houston, 1992. *Address:* c/o Lyric Opera of Chicago, 20 North Wacker Drive, Chicago, IL 60606, USA.

WILSON Thomas Brendan, b. 10 Oct 1927, Trinidad, Colorado, USA. Composer; Professor. m. Margaret Rayner, 20 Sept 1952, 3 sons. *Education:* MA, 1951, BMus, 1954, University of Glasgow, Scotland; ARCM, RCM, 1954. *Compositions:* 4 symphonies, other orchestral music including: Piano concerto, orchesra and triple wind, 1985; Willow Branches, 1986; Chamber music including: Chamber Concerto, 1986; St Kentigern Suite, string orchestra, 1986; Much music for films, TV and radio including Splendid Silent Sun, Voyage of St Brendan and Music for Sunset Song, Cloud Howe, Grey Granite; Numerous commissions including One-Act Opera for BBC TV; 3 act opera, for Scottish Opera; Ballet, for Scottish ballet; Te Deum, Edinburgh International Festival; Passeleth Tapestry, for Scottish National Orchestra, 1989; Cantigas Para Semana Santa, 1991; Symphony No 3, 1978; Symphony No 4, 1988; Violin concerto, 1993; Also numerous vocal works, choral pieces, instrumental and brass band music; Freelance composer; 3 anthems under the overall title: Confitemini Domino, commissioned for their centenary by the Royal College of Organists and performed by St Paul's Cathedral choir, brass ensemble and organ, London, 1993. *Recordings:* Piano Concerto, Introit, David Wilde, Bryden Thomson, SNO; Chamber Symphony; Violin Concerto; Piano Sonata, St Kentigern Suite; CD, performance at the Albert Hall, 1993; Violin Concerto, commissioned by National Youth Orchestra of Scotland with Ernst Kovacie and Christopher Seaman, 1993. *Honours:* CBE, 1990; Hon DMus, Glasgow, 1991; FRSAMD, 1991. *Memberships:* Chairman, Composers Guild of GB; President, Scottish Society of Composers. *Hobbies:* Golf; Talking shop with like-minded friends. *Address:* 120 Dowanhill Street, Glasgow G12 9DN, Scotland.

WILSON Timothy, b. 18 July 1961, England. Singer (Counter-tenor). *Education:* Studied at the Royal Academy of Music. *Career:* Operatic engagements have included Handel's Orlando and Britten's Death in Venice for Scottish Opera, Dido and Aeneas in Frankfurt, Gluck's Orfeo in Kassel, L'Incoronazione di Poppea in Gelsenkirchen, The Fairy Queen in Florence, A Midsummer Night's Dream in Kentucky, the modern premiere of Cesti's I1 Pomo d'Oro (Vienna) and the world premieres of Maxwell Davies's Resurrection (Darmstadt) and Luis de Pablo's El Viajero Indiscreto (Madrid); Season 1990-91 with Vivaldi in Prague, Messiah in Valencia, Bach in the Phillipines and the title role in Handel's Xerxes at Innsbruck; Covent Garden debut 1992, as Oberon in A Midsummer Night's Dream; Agrippina at the Buxton Festival, Alcina at the Halle Festival and Giulio Ceasare at Ludwigshafen, 1992-93; Further concert appearances with Mackerras, Hickox, Pinnock, Herreweghe, Leonhardt, Norrington and Parrott; Venues include Holland, France, Germany, Austria, Spain, Italy and Britain (including the Promenade Concerts). *Recordings include:* Alcina, Purcell's Come ye Sons of Art Away and Handel's Israel in Egypt. *Address:* c/o Ingpen & Williams Ltd. 14 Kensington Court, London W8 5DN, England.

WILSON Todd Rodney, b. 3 Nov 1954, Toledo, Ohio, USA. Musician. m. Anne Carolyn Ferguson, 3 Mar 1979, 2 daughters. *Education:* BMus, 1976, MMus, 1978, College-Conservatory of Music, University of Cincinnati; Choirmaster Certificate, 1983, Fellowship Certificate, 1984, American Guild of Organists. *Compositions:* Published: Various choral anthems, 1986, 1991. *Recordings:* Organ Music of Charles Tournemire, Harmonia Mundi, 1980; 20th-Century Organ Music, Gothic Records, 1984; Complete Organ Works of Maurice Duruflé, DELOS DC, 1987. *Contributions to:* Occasional reviews for The Diapason. *Honours:* Winner, Fort Wayne National Organ Competition, 1977; Winner, Grand Prix de Chartres, France, 1978; S Lewis Elmer Prize, American Guild of Organists, 1982. *Memberships:* American Guild of Organists, Member of Natinal Examination Committee; Presbyterian Association of Musicians. *Hobbies:* Golf; Baseball. *Current Management:* Karen McFarlane Artists Inc, Cleveland, OH, USA. *Address:* Church of the Covenant, 11205 Euclid Avenue, Cleveland, OH 44118, USA.

WILSON-JOHNSON David, b. 16 Nov. 1950, Northampton, England. Singer (Baritone). *Education:* St Catharine's College, Cambridge; Royal Academy of Music, London. *Career:* Royal Opera House Covent Garden from 1976 in Le Rossignol, L'Enfant et les Sortilèges, Boris Godunov and Die Zauberflöte; also appearances with Welsh National Opera and Opera North, in operas by Delius, Rossini and Mozart; concerts with the Ensemble Intercontemporain, under Boulez; other conductors with whom he has worked include Harnoncourt (Vienna Musikverein) and Zubin Mehta; sang title part in the first British performance of Messiaen's St Francois d'Assise, Royal Festival Hall 1988, and took part in a televised production of Tippett's Midsummer Marriage, 1989; sang in Zemlinsky's Lyric Symphony at the 1988 Promenade Concerts, London ; tours of the UK with David Owen Norris in Schubert's Winterreise; Sang the Berlioz Mephistopheles at the Barbican Hall, 1989; Lev in the Ice Break at the 1990 Prom Concerts; Sang Choregos in Birtwistle's Punch and Judy for Netherlands Opera, 1993. *Recordings:* Mozart Masses, Winterreise, Tippett's King Priam, Birtwistle's Punch and Judy and Walton's Belshazzar's Feast for Hyperion, Erato, CBS, Decca and Deutsche Grammophon. *Address:* c/o Askonas Ltd, 186 Drury Lane, London WC2B 5RY, England.

WIMBERGER Peter, b. 14 May 1940, Vienna, Austria. Singer (Bass-Baritone). *Education:* Studied at the Vienna Music Academy with Paul Schoffler and Adolf Vogel. *Debut:* Dortmund 1963, as Pietro in Simon Boccanegra. *Career:* Appearances in the opera houses of Frankfurt, Karlsruhe, Kassel, Dusseldorf, Munich, Warsaw and Copenhagen; Member of the Vienna Staatsoper from 1968; Barcelona 1985, as the Wanderer in Siegfried; Festivals of Bregenz and Florence; Repertoire includes principal roles in operas by Mussorgsky, Mozart, Wagner, Rossini, Verdi and Strauss; Sang at Palermo and Naples 1988, as Amfortas; Rangoni at the Vienna, Staatsoper, 1988. *Recordings:* Haydn's Harmoniemesse; Spirit Messenger in Die Frau ohne Schatten by Strauss. *Address:* c/o Landestheater, Promenade 39, A 4010 Linz, Austria.

WINBERGH Gösta, b. 30 Dec. 1943, Stockholm, Sweden. Singer (Tenor). m. Elena Jungholm 1967, 1 son, 1 daughter. *Education:* Music Academy of Stockholm, vocal studies with Eric Saeden; Stockholm Opera School. *Debut:* Gothenburg 1971, as Rodolfo in La Bohème. *Career:* Principal tenor, Royal Opera, Stockholm, 1973-80; Joined Zurich Opera Company 1981; Guest appearances in Geneva, Berlin, Hamburg, Munich, Stuttgart, Amsterdam, Paris, Madrid, London and New York; Glyndebourne 1980, as Belmonte in Die Entführung; Salzburg Easter Festival and Vienna Staatsoper 1983; Drottningholm Opera 1984, as Ferrando in Così fan Tutte ; La Scala Milan 1985, as Tamino in Die Zauberflöte; Sang in Mozart's Coronation Mass at St Peter's Rome 1985; Other roles include Mozart's Mitridate and Don Ottavio, Lensky in Eugene Onegin, Gennaro in Lucrezia Borgia and Donizetti's Dom Sebastian, Gluck's Admetus and Narraboth in Salome; Sang Ottavio at Barcelona 1986; Salzburg Festival 1987-88, as Ottavio and Titus; Houston Opera 1988, Ferrando in Così fan Tutte; Grand Théâtre Geneva 1989, as Des Grieux in Manon; Tito at Chicago 1989, and La Scala, 1990; Covent Garden debut 1993, as Walther in a new production of Die Meistersinger; Appearances in numerous concerts. *Recordings:* Don Pasquale; Liszt's Faust Symphony; Laertes in Hamlet by Thomas; Le Roi Arthus by Chausson (Erato); Bruckner's Te Deum (Deutsche Grammophon). *Hobbies:* Golf; Sailing; Skiing. *Address:* c/o Balmer and Dixon Management Ltd., Klausstrasse 19, CH 8008 Zurich, Switzerland.

WINCKEL Fritz, b. 20 June 1907, Bregenz, Austria. Professor, Institute Director. *Education:* Dipl-Ing (telecommunications and Musical acoustics) Technical University, Berlin, 1932; Research on electronic music and audiovision, Heinrich-Hertz Institute and Academy of Music, Berlin; Dr-Ing, 1952; Studied piano and solo singing for purpose of research, 1948-53. *Career:* Worked with Physicist Walter Nernst, University of Berlin, to develop Neo-Bechstein-Flugel (1st electrified Grand Piano), 1932-34; Founder with composer Boris Blacher of Tonmeister School, Academy of Music, Berlin and Studio for Experimental Music, Technical University, Federal Republic of Germany; Director of Institute of Communication Sciences of Music and Speech and of Studio of Experimental Music; With Boris Blacher and Studio of Electronic Music has composed Incidents at a Forced Landing (opera) and numerous electronic works and 5 audiovisual films; Student and lecturer in medicine (Larynx and Ear) and Architecture; Consultant in Acoustics and Construction of Concert Halls; Lecturer, Information Theory and Cybernetics; Studies of Neuro-control of singers voices for electronic measuring device. *Recording:* Music by Boris Blacher. *Publications include:* Klangwelt unter der Lupe 1952; Klangstruktur der Musik (editor and Joint author) 1955; Experimentelle Musik (editor and joint author) 1970. *Contributions to:* Professional journals. *Honour:* Festschrift Tiefenstruktur der Musik to 75th birthday by Technical University of Berlin, 1982, 1987. *Memberships:* Professional societies. *Hobbies:* Research tours to old Egyptian cultures. *Hobbies:* Hoehmannstrasse 9, D-1000 Berlin 33, Germany.

WINDMULLER Yaron, b. 1956, Israel. Singer (Baritone). *Education:* Studied in Tel Aviv, in Munich with Ernst Haefliger and in Vicenza with Malcolm King. Further Study at the Opera Studio of the Bayerische Staatsoper. *Debut:* City of London Festival 1982, in Gluck's Armide. *Career:* Sang as soloist with the Israel Philharmonic, member of the Theater am Gärtnerplatz Munich from 1986 as Purcell's Aeneas, Mozart's Count, Guglielmo, Don Giovanni and Papageno, Wolfram, Marcello, Hans Jurgen von Bose's Werther and Kaspar in Der Zaubergeig by Werner Egk; Sang Trinity Moses in Weill's Mahogonny at Frankfurt, 1990; Many concert appearances and Lieder recitals. *Address:* c/o Staatstheater am Gartnerplatz, Gertnerplatz 3, 8000 Munich 1, Germany.

WINKLER Hermann, b. 3 Mar 1924, Duisburg, Germany. Singer (Tenor). *Education:* Studied at the Hanover Conservatory. *Career:* Has sung at the Bayreuth

Festival from 1957, notably as the Steersman in Der fliegende Holländer 1965 and Parsifal 1976-77; Member of the Zurich Opera from 1970; Frankfurt Opera 1970, as Lohengrin and Florestan; Munich 1972, as Mozart's Don Ottavio and Idomeneo; Salzburg Festival and Deutsche Oper Berlin 1976, 1981, Idomeneo; US debut 1980, as Don Ottavio; Sang Florestan in USA and Japan 1981; Convent Garden debut 1984, as the Captain in Wozzeck; Zurich Opera 1985, as the Emperor in Die Frau ohne Schatten; Guest appearances in Vienna and Hamburg; Sang Herod in Selome at La Scala (1987), Loge at Bologna; Season 1987-88 at the Teatro Real Madrid in Wozzeck and Lulu; Marseilles and Barcelona 1989, as Aegisthus in Elektra; Sang Peter Grimes at Zurich, 1989; Many appearances in the concert hall, often in Das Lied von der Erde by Mahler. Recordings: Arabella (Electrola); Mahler's 8th Symphony (CBS); Idomeneo (Deutsche Grammophon); Drum Major in Wozzeck (Decca). Address: c/o Allied Artists Agency, 42 Montpelier Square, London SW7 1JZ, England.

WINSLADE Glenn, b. 1958, Australia. Singer (Tenor). Education: Studied at the New South Wales Conservatorium and at the Vienna Conservatory. Career: Has sung with English National Opera as Ferrando; Victoria State Opera as Belmonte, Walter von der Vogelweide and Don Ottavio; Scottish Opera as Mozart's Titus and Australian Opera as Oronte in Alcina; Covent Garden debut 1990, as Vogelgesang in Die Meistersinger; Further appearances with Glyndebourne Festival and Touring Opera, New Sadler's Wells Opera (Merry Widow); Freiburg Oper, Semper Oper Dresden (Belmonte), Stuttgart Opera and the Netherlands Opera (Idomeneo); Other roles include Tamino, the Prince in The Love of Three Oranges, Stroh (Intermezzo), Elemer (Arabella), Amenophis (Moses), Ernesto and Nemorino; Fracasso in La Finta Semplce; Lindoro and Alfredo; Jacquino in Fidelio, Steuermann (Der fliegende Holländer) and Jason in Cherubini's Médée; Concert engagements with the Musica Antiqua Vienna, Duke University North Carolina, RAI Milan and the BBC. Recordings include: Messiah with the Scottish Chamber Orchestra; Merry Widow. Honours: Winner, Australian Opera Auditions, Esso/Glyndebourne Touring and John Christie Glyndebourne awards. Address: c/o Lies Askonas Ltd., 186 Drury Lane, London WC2B 5RY, England.

WINSLOW Walter K, b. 16 Sept 1947, Salem, Oregon, USA. Composer; Teacher. Education: AB Russian, BMus, Composition, Oberlin College and Conservatory of Music, 1965-70; MA, PhD, University of California, 1970-75. Career: Assistant Professor of Music, University of California, 1975-82; Visiting Assistant Professor of Music Theory, Oberlin Conservatory, 1983-84; Visiting Assistant Professor of Music, Reed College, 1985-86; Assistant Professor of Music, Columbia University, 1987-89; Instructor of Piano, The Lawrenceville School, 1990-. Compositions: String Quartet, 1978; Nineteen Madrigals for Five Voices, 1980; Canzone, 1981; Palinurus, 1982; Himene, 1985; The Piper of the Sacred Grove, 1990; Locus Amoenus, 1992. Recordings: Nahua Songs; The Piper at the Gates of Dawn; Nineteen Madrigals for Five Voices; Four Kauai Studies, Sette Bagatelle di Primavera. Honours: Rome Prize, American Academy in Rome, 1990; Guggenheim Fellowship, 1986; Goddard Lieberson Fellowship, American Academy and Institute of Arts and Lettres, 1983. Memberships: American Music Center, American Composers Alliance, Composers Guild of New Jersey, Society of Composers Inc. Hobbies: Hiking; Reading; Travel. Address: 54 Humbert Street, Princeton, NJ 08542, USA.

WINSTANLEY John Harold, b. 30 June 1922, Melbourne, Australia. Composer; Conductor; Educator. m. Margaret Seton Adey, 24 Aug 1948, 1s, 2d. Education: BMus, LRAM, ARCO, FLCM, University of Adelaide. Career: Director of Music: St Peter's College, Adelaide, 1946-60, Sydney C of E Grammar School, Sydney University Musical Society, 1961-66, Harrow School, 1967-76; head of Music, Claremont College, Senior Lecturer, Western Australia Conservatorium of

Music, 1976-87; Conductor, University of Western Australia Choral Society, 1979-86. Compositions: Regimental March, 1942; Overture for a Royal Occasion, 1953; Christmas Motet, choir and orchestra, 1959; Sonata in A minor for violin and piano, 1959; Music for School Operetta, 1964; Hodie, Sydney University, 1965; Divertimento for organ and orchestra, 1973; Odyssey for piano and prepared tape, 1975. Address: 22 Ryan Way, Lesmurdie, WA 6076, Australia.

WINSTANLEY Margaret Seton, b. 18 Oct 1926, Adelaide, Australia. Violinist. Educator. m. John Harold Winstanley, 28 Aug 1948, 1s, 2d. Education: Elder Conservatorium of Music, University of Adelaide; Advanced studies with David Martin, London, 1953-54; LRSM, 1946; ARCM, 1954. Career: Prof Violinist, Lecturer and Tutor, 1943-90; Concert performances with Adelaide, Sydney and Western Australia Symphony Orchestras, as well as broadcasts on ABC; Leader, St George's Cathedral Sinfonia, Perth, 1967-76; Principal String Teacher, Harrow School, Leader, Harrow Chamber Orchestra, England; Examiner for AMEB and Tutor for WA Youth Orchestra, 1978- 83; Adujdicator, city and country Eisteddfods and adviser to community music groups; Chamber music and sonata recitalist. Address: 22 Ryan Way, Lesmurdie, WA 6076, Australia.

WINSTEAD William Owen, b. 11 Dec. 1942, Hopkinsville, Kentucky, USA. Bassoonist; Composer. Education: BM, Bassoon, Curtis Institute of Music, 1964; MM, Composition, West Virginia University, 1965. Career: Principal Bassoon, Marlboro Festival Orchestra, 1965-71; Professor of Music, West Virginia University, 1965-78; Principal Bassoon, Fort Wayne, Indiana Philharmonic, 1977-78; Professor of Music, Florida State University, 1979-87; Principal Bassoon, Cincinnati Symphony Orchestra, 1986-; Professor of Bassoon, Oberlin College Conservatory, 1988-89; Professor of BSN, Cincinnati College Conservatory of Music, 1989-; Solo recitalist in USA and Europe; Faculty, Sarasota Music Festival, 1987-. Composition: The Moon Singer, for narrator and orchestra. Recordings: With Marlboro Festival Orchestra, Pablo Casals, Conductor for Columbia, Epic, Marlboro Recording Society, and Sony Classics Labels; with Cincinnati S.Orchestra for Telare label; Chamber Music for Columbia, Marlboro Recording Society, and Sony Classics Labels. Publications: Ten Vivaldi Concerti; co-edited, with Sol Schoenbach, published G Schirmer; Program Solos for the bassoon, co-edited with Sol Schoenbach, published Theo Presser. Address: 4663 Glenway Avenue, Cincinnati, OH 45238, USA.

WINTER Louise, b. 29 Nov. 1959, Preston, Lancashire. Singer (Mezzo-soprano). m. Gerald Finley. Education: Studied at Chethams School of Music and at the Royal College of Music with Frederick Cox. Career: With Glyndebourne Touring Opera has sung Tisbe in La Cenerentola, Dorabella in Cosi fan Tutte and Mercedes in Carmen; Sang Zerlina on Glyndebourne's tour to Hong Kong, Nancy in Albert Herring at the 1986 summer festival and in the Ravel double bill in 1987-88; Covent Garden debut 1988, as a Flowermaiden in Parsifal; Has sung Janáček's Varvara and Ravel's Concepcion for Opera North; Netherlands Opera as Rosina in Il barbiere di Siviglia and Second Lady in Die Zauberflöte; Appearances with the Canadian Opera Company in Eugene Onegin and as Dorabella in Cosi fan Tutte (1991); Glyndebourne Festival 1988-90, in Katya Kabanova, Il barbiere di Siviglia and the Ravel double bill; Concert engagements with the König Ensemble and in the Choral Symphony conducted by Simon Rattle. Address: c/o Harrison Parrott Ltd., 12 Penzance Place, London W11 4PA, England.

WINTER Quade, b. 1950, Oregon, USA. Singer (Tenor). Debut: Sang Max in Der Freischütz at San Francisco. Career: Has sung the Duke of Mantua for Eugene Opera, Canio at Anchorage, Don Ottavio at the Carmel Bach Festival and Ishmael in Nabucco for San Francisco Opera; Appeared in US premiere of The Excursions of Mr Broucek with the Berkeley Symphony;

Concerts have included Beethoven's Ninth with the Stockton Symphony and the Verdi Requiem at the San Francisco Festival of Masses, conducted by Robert Shaw; European debut as Hermann in The Queen of Spades with Graz Opera, 1982; La Scala Milan 1982, as Cherubini's Anacréon; Roles with the Stadtheater Wurzburg have included Don Carlos, Lensky, Herod, Rodolfo and Canio; Has sung Parsifal at Graz and Herod in Heidelberg and Seattle; Scottish Opera debut as Mark in The Midsummer Marriage, 1989. *Address:* Music International, 13 Ardilaun Road, London N5 2QR, England.

WION John Hamilton, b. 22 Jan. 1937, Rio de Janeiro, Brazil. Musician; Flautist; Teacher. m. Victoria Simon, 10 Feb. 1960, 2 sons. *Education:* University of Melbourne, Australia, 1955-58; Studied flute with Leslie Barklamb, Julius Baker, William Kincaid, Claude Monteux and Marcel Moyse. *Career:* First Flute, New York City Opera, 1965-; Founding Member, American Symphony, 1963-65; Member, Bronx Arts Ensemble, 1977-; Recitalist with Gilbert Kalish and Tokyo Quartet; Concert tours Australia and New Zealand, 1973, 1977, 1980, 1981, 1984, 1985, 1992; Professor of Flute, Director of Instrumental Studies, 1992-93, Hartt School of Music. *Recordings:* French Salon Music for Flute; Virtuoso Flute Concertos; Quintets of Molique and Romberg; Complete Wind Chamber Music of Nielsen; Nonets of Rheinberger and Farrenc; Serenade and Octet of H. Hofmann; John Wion, Solo Flute (MHS 513074), John Wion plays, French Flute Solos (HMP 2W91514). *Publications:* Opera Excerpts for Flute, Vol. 1, 1990, Vol. 2, 1992, Vol. 3, 1993, Vol. 4, 1993. *Contributions to:* The Instrumentalist, 1982, 1983; Flute Talk, 1990. *Membership:* National Flute Association, President, 1984-85. *Hobby:* Genealogy. *Address:* 180 Riverside Drive, New York, NY 10024, USA.

WIORA Walter, b. 30 Dec. 1906, Katowice, Poland. Professor Emeritus; Musicologist. m. Dr. Christa Wiora-von Hertzberg. *Education:* Hochschule für Musik and University, Berlin, with Blume, Gurlitt and Schering; PhD University of Freiburg 1937. *Career:* Archivist, Deutsches Volkslied Archiv, 1937- 57; Lecturer, University of Freiburg 1940; Full Professor, Universities of Kiel (1958-64), Saarbrücken (1964-73); Visiting Professor, Columbia University New York 1962-63. *Publications:* Das Deutsche Volkslied und der Osten 1940; Zur Frühgeschichte der Musik in den Alpenländern 1949; Das echte Volkslied 1950; Europäischer Volksgesang 1952; Biography of Bruckner 1952; Europäischer Volksmusik und abendländische Tonkunst 1957; Die Vier Weltalter der Musik 1961, 1988; Das deutsche Lied 1971; Ideen zur Geschichte der Musik 1980; Das musikalische Kunstwerk 1983. *Honours:* Honorary member, Deutscher Musikrat und Gesellschaft fur Musikforschung; Festschriften 1967, 1979, 1988. *Memberships:* Bayerische Akademie der Schönen Kunste; International Musicological Society; Gesellschaft fur Musikforschung; International Council for Traditional Music. *Address:* D-82327 Tutzing, Oberes Vocherlj, Germany.

WIRTZ Dorothea, b. 13 March 1953, Tuttlingen, Germany. Singer (Soprano). *Education:* Studied in Berlin with Hugo Diez and in Munich with Hanno Blaschke. *Career:* Sang at the Munich Staatsoper 1979-80, Kassel 1980-84; Member of the Zurich Opera from 1984; Guest appearances in Dusseldorf, Venice, Naples, Lisbon, Bologna, Berlin, Cologne, Wiesbaden, Florence and Strasbourg; Roles include Olympia in Les Contes d'Hoffmann, Blondchen, the Queen of Night, Zerlina, Despina, Ilia in Idomeneo, Rosina, Sophie in Der Rosenkavalier; Zerbinetta, Norina, Adina, Marzelline and the Woodbird in Siegfried; Sang Blondchen at Buenos Aires, 1987; Concert repertoire includes works by Handel, Mozart, Bach and Schumann (Paradies und die Peri). *Recordings include:* Daphne by Strauss (EMI). *Address:* c/o Operhaus Zurich, Falkerstrasse 1, CH-8008, Zurich, Switzerland.

WISE Patricia, b. 31 July 1944, Wichita, Kansas, USA. Singer (Soprano). *Education:* Studid at Kansas University, in Santa Fe and in New York with Margaret Harshaw. *Debut:* Susanna in Mozart's Marriage of Figaro, Kansas City, 1966. *Career:* Appearances at the Houston Opera, New York City Opera, New Orleans, Philadelphia, Chicago, San Francisco, Washington, Miami, Baltimore, San Antonio and Pittsburgh; Carnegie Hall New York 1971, in Ariodante by Handel, Covent Garden, London, 1971, Rosina in Rossini's Barber of Seville, New York City Opera; Glyndebourne 1972, as Zerbinetta in Ariadne auf Naxos; Vienna Staatsoper 1983, Pamina, Nannetta and Sophie; Sang at the 1984 Salzburg Festival in the premiere of Un re in Ascolto by Berio; Geneva 1985, 1st time as Lulu; repertoire includes roles in operas by Donizetti, Gounod, Gluck, Verdi (Gilda); Sang with the Vienna Staatsoper, 1976-1991 in 300 performances, many of which were Strauss or Mozart operas; Sang Lulu at Madrid 1987; Sophie in Der Rosenkavalier at Budapest, 1989; Gilda in Rigoletto at Madrid, 1989; Fiordiligi in Mozart's Così fan tutte, Violetta in Verdi's Traviata, 1990; Since 1985 has appeared in five other productions of Berg's 3-Act Lulu, from Berlin to Paris; Guest appearances in European opera houses including La Scala, Munich, Berlin, Hamburg, Barcelona, Geneva, Glyndebourne and the Salzburg Festival. *Address:* c/o John Coast, 31 Sinclair Road, London, W14 0NS.

WISEMAN Debbie, b. 10 May 1963, London, England. Composer. m. Tony J Wharmby, 21 Sept 1987. *Education:* Saturday Exhibitioner, Trinity College of Music, 1977-81; Kingsway-Princeton/Morley College, 1979-81; Guildhall School of Music and Drama; GGSM, 1984. *Career:* Composer and Conductor, music for film and TV productions including: Tom and Viv, feature film for Samuelson/IRS Media; The Good Guys, for Network ITV; The Upper Hand, for Network ITV; A Week in Politics, Channel 4; The Second Russian Revolution, for BBC TV; The Cuban Missile Crisis, for BBC TV (Winner Emmy Award 1993 for Outstanding Historical Documentary); Children's Hospital, for BBC TV; Special performance of original compositions with The Debbie Wiseman Collection, St John's Smith Square, London, 1989. *Honours:* David Taylor Memorial Prize, Trinity College of Music, 1981; TRIC Award for TV Theme Music of the Year 1993 for The Good Guys. *Memberships:* Association of Professional Composers; Performing Right Society; British Association of Film and Television Artists; Musicians Union. *Hobbies:* Snooker; Origami. *Address:* 25 Brim Hill, London N2 0HD, England.

WISHART Trevor, b. 11 Oct 1946, Leeds, England. Composer. m. Jacqueline Joan Everett, 2 daughters. *Education:* BA, Music, Oxford University; MA, Analysis of Contemporary Music, Nottingham University; DPhil, Composition, York University. *Career:* Foreign tours: Scandinavia, Australia, Japan, USA, Netherlands, Spain, Germany, IRCAM commission, Vox-5, 1986; Vox cycle performed at London Proms, 1988; Sound Designer, Jorvik Viking Centre Museum, York. *Compositions:* Red Bird; Anticredos; The Vox cycle; Pastorale - Walden 2; Beach Singularity. *Recordings:* Vox, Virgin Classics; Vox-5, Wergo Digital Music Series; Red Bird/Anticredos; October Music. *Publications:* Sounds Fun, educational musical games, 1974, also in Japanese; On Sonic Art, 1985; Sun, Creativity and Environment; Sun-2, A Creative Philosophy; Whose Music, A Sociology of Musical Language. *Contributions to:* Contact; Musics; Ear Magazine, New York; Interface, Utrecht; Computer Music Journal, USA; Musica Realta, Milan. *Honours:* Prizewinner: Bourges International Electro-Acoustic Music Festival, 1978; Gaudeamus International Festival, Netherlands, 1979; Linz Ars Electronica, 1985. *Memberships:* Chair, Sonic Arts Network, 1990-92; Founder, Composers Desktop Project. *Hobbies:* Philosophy of science; Mathematics; Fell-walking. *Address:* 83 Heslington Road, York YO1 5AX, England.

WISŁOCKI Leszek, b. 15 Dec 1931, Chorzow, Poland. Composer; Pianist. m. Renata Krumpholz, 9 July 1968, 2 sons. *Education:* Piano, 1955, Composition, 1957, Conducting, 1962, Academy of Music, Wroclaw. *Career:* Concerts as Pianist and Composer, Polish Radio and

TV. *Compositions:* Andante and Presto for Xylophone and piano; Two miniatures for violin and cello; Sonata for oboe and cello; Ostinato and Toccatina for piano solo; Polonaise for piano solo; Suita Lubuska for wind orchestra; Songa for choir a cappella (male and female). *Recordings:* Many tapes, Radio-Wroclaw; Andante and Presto for xylophone and piano, Polskie Nagrania. *Honours:* Prize, Ministers of Culture and Art, 1973; Prize, City of Wroclaw, 1977; Honorary Diploma, Ministers of Culture and Art. *Memberships:* Polish Composers Society; President, Lower Silesian Musical Society. *Hobbies:* Collecting old instruments and antiques. *Address:* ul Komandorska 48-8, 53-343 Wroclaw, Poland.

WISŁOCKI Stanislaw, b. 7 July 1921, Rzeszow, Poland. Conductor; Composer; Pianist. m. 31 Dec 1944. *Education:* Academy of Music, Timisoara, 1942. *Debut:* Pianist, 1941; Conductor, Composer, 1944. *Career:* Chief Conductor, Warsaw Chamber Orchestra, Philharmonic Orchestra, Poznan, Poland, 1947-58; Conductor, National Philharmonic Orchestra, Warsaw, 1961-66; Art Director, Chief Conductor, Polish Radio/ TV National Symphony Orchestra, Katowice, 1978-82; Musical Director, Philharmonic Orchestra Teatro Colon Buenos Aires, 1981; Concerts in Europe, Japan, USA, Latin America; Lecturer, Opera High School, Poznan, 1948, Conservatoire Poznan 1949-55; Junior Lecturer, Conservatoire Poznan, 1955-58, Conservatoire Warsaw 1955-65; Professor, Academy of Music, Warsaw, 1965-. *Compositions:* Symphony of Dance; Concerto for Piano & Orchestra; Overture; nocturne; Ballade for Orchestra; Chamber Music; Music for Film & Theatre, numerous. *Memberships:* Union of polish Composers, Vice President, 1958-60. *Address:* Ul Zdrojowa 55, 02 927 Warsaw, Poland.

WISSMER Pierre, b. 30 Oct 1915, Geneva, Switzerland. Composer. m. Laure-Anne Etienne, 6 Feb 1948. *Career:* Professor of Composition, Conservatoire, Geneva, Music Critic, La Suisse Journal, Music Department, Radio-Geneve, 1944-48; Director, Radio-Luxembourg, 1951-57; Director, Schola Cantorum, Paris, 1957-63; Director, l'Ecole nationale de Musique du Mans, 1969-81; Professor of Composition and Orchestration, Conservatoire, Geneva, 1973-86. *Compositions include:* 3 operas; 4 ballets; 9 symphonies, 3 oratorios, 12 concertos and numerous other compositions. *Recordings:* VI Symphonie: 2eme Quatuor a cordes; Sonatine Flute et guitare; Prestige de votre discotheque, trois silhouettes pour piano; Reflexions et Variations sur un Noel Imaginaire pour orgue; Partita pour guitare; Prestilagoyana pour 2 guitares; CD, concerto piano et Suite Syphonique que Alerte, Pirts 21. *Honours:* Grand Prix Suisse de la Radio, 1950; Prix Lyrique, Societe des Auteurs et compositeur Dramatiques, 1956; Grand Prix Paul Gilson, Communauté Radiophonique, 1965; Grand Prix Musical, Ville de Paris, 1967; Grand Prix Musical, Ville de Geneve, 1983; Chevalier, Ordre des Arts et des Lettres (France), 1988. *Memberships:* SACEM; SACD (France). *Hobby:* Skiing. *Address:* 9 square de Mondori, F-78150 Le Chesnay, France.

WIT Antoni, b. 7 Feb 1944, Cracow, Poland. Conductor. m. 12 Oct 1977. *Education:* Law, Jagiellonian University, 1969; Conducting, Academy of Music, Cracow, 1967. *Career:* Assistant, National Philharmonic, Warsaw, 1967-70; Conductor, State Philharmonic, Poznan, 1970-72; Dir artist, Pomeranian Philharmonic, Bydgoszcz, 1974-77; Director, Polish Radio & TV Choir & Orchestra, 1977-83; Director, Polish Radio National Orchestra (WOSPRi TV), 1983-. *Recordings include:* Mahler, Tchaikovsky's Symphonies, Szymanowski, Harnasie, Stabat Mater; Penderecki, Polish Requiem; EMI. *Honours:* 2nd Prize, Herbert von Karajan Competition, West Berlin, 1971; Fulbright Stipendium, Tanglewood, 1973. *Hobbies:* Cycling; Travel; Languages. *Address:* Klonowa 34A, 40 168 Katowice, Poland.

WITTE Erich, b. 19 Mar 1911, Graudenz, Bremen, Germany. Singer (Tenor); Producer. *Education:* Studied at the Bremen Conservatory with P. Kraus. *Debut:* Bremen 1930, as Nando in Tiefland. *Career:* Sang at Bremen until 1937, then at Wiesbaden and Breslau (1937-42); Metropolitan Opera 1938-39, as Froh, Mime and the Simpleton in Boris Godunov; Bayreuth Festival 1943-44, as David in Die Meistersinger; Sang at the Berlin Staatsoper from 1941; Städtische Oper Berlin 1947, in Peter Grimes; Bayreuth 1952-53, as Loge; sang Loge at Covent Garden in the 1950s; Walther in Die Meistersinger 1957; Chief opera producer at Frankfurt from 1961, Staatsoper Berlin from 1964; Lecturer at the Berlin Musikhochschule.

WITZENMANN Wolfgang, b. 26 Nov 1937, Munich, Germany. Musician. m. Renata Di Salvo, 5 Mar 1977, 1 son, 1 daughter. *Education:* Privatmusiklehrer Diplom, Musikhochschule Stuttgart, 1960; D Phil History of Music, Universität Tübingen, 1965. *Career:* As composer: Gaudeamus-Festival, Netherlands, 1967, 1968, 1970 and 1971; Internationale Ferienkurse für Neue Musik, Darmstadt, Federal Republic of Germany, 1969; Autunno Musicale, Como, Italy, 1975; Festival Internazionale Nuova Consonanza, Rome, 1985; Festival Internazionale Terenzio Gargiulo, Naples, 1986. *Compositions:* Choirs; Oden I-V for voice and piano; 6 cycles of Lieder; Eigenklänge, Natur, Opers Nivasio and Mary, Deutschland -Lieder for orchestra; Sinfonia 1 and 2 for orchestra; Violin Concerto; Antiphonales Konzert, for trumpet and orchestra; Piano and organ music, chamber music, and music for early instruments. *Recordings:* Monographic disc, EDI-PAN, Rome, 1989. *Publication:* Domenico Mazzocchi (1592-1665), Dokumente und Interpretationen, 1970. *Contributions to:* Analecta Musicologica; Acta Musicologica; Die Musikforschung; Rivista Italiana di Musicologia; Studi Musicali. *Hobbies:* Hiking; Swimming; Skiing. *Address:* Via Licinio Calvo 14, I-00136, Rome, Italy.

WIXELL Ingvar, b. 7 May 1931, Lulea, Sweden. Singer (Baritone). *Education:* Studied in Stockholm with Dagmar Gustavson. *Debut:* Sang at Gavle, 1952. *Career:* Stockholm 1955, as Papageno; Member of the Royal Opera Stockholm from 1956: appeared with the company in Alcina at Covent Garden, 1960; Glyndebourne Festival 1962, as Guglielmo in Cosi fan Tutte; US debut Chicago Lyric Opera 1967, as Belcore in L'Elisir d'Amore; Salzburg Festival 1966-69, as Count Almaviva and Pizarro; Hamburg Staatsoper 1970, as Rigoletto and Scarpia; Covent garden 1972-77, Simon Boccanegra, Scarpia, Belcore and Mandryka in Arabella; Metropolitan Opera from 1973, as Rigoletto, Germont, Amonasro, Marcello and Renato in Un Ballo in Maschera; Other roles include Don Carlo (La Forza del Destino), Count Luna, Posa, and Pentheus in The Bassarids by Henze; Sang Amonasro at Houston 1987; Covent Garden 1987-90 as Rigoletto and Belcore; Stuttgart Staatsoper 1990, as Scarpia; Sang in Tosca at Earl's Court, London 1991. *Recordings:* Le Nozze di Figaro, Don Giovanni, Zaide, La Bohème, Un ballo in Maschera, Tosca, Un Giorno di Regno (Philips); Il Trovatore (Decca); L'Elisir d'Amore (CBS); Video of Tosca. *Address:* c/o John Coast, 31 Sinclair Road, London W14 0NS, England.

WLADYCZKA Anna Dorota, b. 21 Mar 1964, Wroclaw, Poland. Musicologist. *Education:* Ballet dancing classes 1967-77; Private piano lessons 1973-77; Graduated, classical guitar studies, Primary School of Music, Wroclaw, 1981; Private vocal studies 1984-85 and still occasionally continued; Student, Institute of Musicology, Warsaw University, 1983-. *Career:* Active participant in the Scientific Circle of Students, Institute of Musicology; participant in the Student Scientific Research Programme in North Africa (Morroco, Algeria, Tunisia) 1985-86; participant in the 7th Summer Courses for Young Composers at Radziejowice, 1987; Organizing Secretary, Scientific Seminar, Hommage à Karol Szymanowski organised by Scientific Circle of Institute of Musicology in co-operation with Section of Musicologists at the Polish Composers' Union, Oct 1987; Elected secretary 1988 and Chairman 1990, Board of the Youth Circle of Polish

Compoers' Union, involved in organising concerts, festivals, seminars, publications; Elected Secretary General, ISCM Polish Section 1989-, taking part in the preparation of concerts, Summer Courses for Young Composers, The ISCM World Music Days, Warsaw, 1992. *Address:* Plac Solny 6/7a m 13, 50-061 Wroclaw, Poland.

WLASCHIHA Ekkerhard, b. 28 May 1938, Pirna, Germany. Singer (Baritone). *Education:* Studied at the Franz Liszt Musikhochschule in Leipzig and with Helene Jung. *Debut:* Gera 1961, as Don Fernando in Fidelio. *Career:* Sang in Dresden and Weimar 1964-70; Leipzig Opera from 1970, as Scarpia, Pizarro, Alfio, Tonio, Dr Coppelius, and Jochanaan in Salome; sang in the premieres of Greek Wedding by Hanell 1969 and The Shadow by Fritz Geissler 1975; Lausanne Opera and Staatsoper Berlin 1983, as Kurwenal and Telramund; Sang Kaspar in Der Freischütz at the reopening of the Semper Opera House, Dresden, 1985; Bayreuth Festival 1986, as Kurwenal; Appeared on Russian TV in Fidelio by Beethoven; Sang Telramund at the Berln Staatsoper, 1990; Alberich in a new production of Siegfried at Covent Garden, 1990. *Address:* c/o Allied Artists Agency, 42 Montpellier Square, London, SW7 1JZ.

WOHLERS Rudiger, b. 4 May 1943, Hamburg, Germany. Singer (Tenor). *Education:* Studied at the Hamburg Musikhochschule. *Career:* Sang at Darmstadt 1968-71; Sang Mozart roles at Zurich 1971-74, Belmonte, Ferrando, Tamino and Don Ottavio; Sang at Stuttgart from 1974, and has made guest appearances in Hamburg, Munich, Vienna and Frankfurt; Schwetzingen Fesival 1975, as Belmonte; Deutsche Oper Berlin from 1977; Sang Tamino at the 1981 Salzburg Festival; La Scala Milan 1983, as Ferrando in Così fan Tutte; Sang in Cavalli's L'Ormindo at the Hamburg Staatsoper 1984, and toured with the company to Japan; Stuttgart 1984 as Don Ottavio in the newly restored opera house; Other roles include Fenton in Die Lustigen Weiber von Windsor, Lionel (Martha), Nemorino, Lensky and Almaviva in Il Barbiere di Siviglia; Many concert engagements and Lieder recitals; Sang Idomeneo with the English Bach Festival at Covent Garden, 1990. *Recordings:* Jacquino in Fidelio (Eurodisc); Cantatas by Bach, Fux and Scarlatti (Schwann); Die Schöpfung by Haydn (Decca). *Address:* c/o Hamburgische Staatsoper, Grosse Theaterstrasse 34, D-2000 Hamburg 36, Germany.

WOHLHAUSER René Claude, b. 24 Mar 1954, Zürich, Switzerland. Composer. m. Eva Ruth Sieber, 29 Feb 1980, 2 sons, 2 daughters. *Education:* Basel Conservatory, 1975-79 (Diploma as Teacher of Music Theory); Composition courses with Kazimierz Serocki, Mauricio Kagel, Herbert Brün and Heinz Holliger; Study with Klaus Huber, Staatliche Musikhochschule, Freiburg, 1980-81; Composition with Brian Ferneyhough, 1982-87. *Career:* Works played by Arditti String Quartet, Basel Symphony Orchestra, Biel Symphony Orchestra, Luzern Symphony Orchestra, also at Schweizer Tonkünstlerfeste 1984, 1988, 1990, 1993, International Darmstädter Ferienkurse für Neue Musik, 1984, 1988, 1990, 1992, Notre Dame de Paris, Toronto New Castle, Baku; Portraits in radio programmes; Works performed on radio; Delivered lectures on musical and philosophical aspects of his works at Darmstadt, Winterthur, Basel; Founder, Komponistenforum. *Compositions:* Lemuria, for 2 flutes and tape, 1977; Nesut, for piano solo, 1977; Cemaltorz, for soprano and piano, 1977; Souvenirs de l'Occitanie for clarinet solo, 1978; Modulaltica for alto flute and synthesizer, 1978; Fragmente für Orchestra, 1979; Flautando, for 2 flutes, 1980-81; Musica Assoluta Determinata, for chmaber ensemble, 1981; Klavierquartett for 2 violins, viola, cello and piano, 1979, 1983-84, rev 1987; Schlagzeugtrio for percussion trio, 1984-85; CI-IC, for flute and viola, 1985; Duometrie, for flute and bass clarinet, 1985-86; Orgelstück, for organ solo, 1986; Drei Stücke für Klavier, for piano solo, 1986-87; Klarinettentrio for 3 clarinets, 1986-87; Adagio assai, for string quartet, 1982-88; Atemlinie, for horn solo (and tatam played by the same player), 1988; Lumières, for organ solo, 1989; in statu

mutandi, for orchestra, 1991-93. *Contributions to:* 'Von einfachen graphischen Notationen und Verbalpartituren zum Denken in Musik', in Schweizer musikpädagogische Blätter, 1989, in: schweizer Schule, 1990; 'Ueber kompositorische, ästhetische und philosophische Aspekte eigener Werke, in: MusikTexte, Köln, 1990; Transzendnetale Exerzitien', in: Neue Zürcher Zeitung, 1991. *Address:* Schillerstrasse 5, CH-4053 Basel, Switzerland.

WOLANSKY Raymond, b. 15 Feb 1926, Cleveland, Ohio. Singer (Baritone). *Education:* Studied in Cleveland. *Career:* Sang at the Stuttgart State Opera from 1952; Rio de Janeiro 1959, as Count Almaviva; Teatro San Carlos Lisbon 1961, in Iphigénie en Tauride; Sang at the Hamburg Staatsoper from 1960: visited Edinburgh with the company 1966; Glyndebourne Festival 1963-64, as Olivier in Capriccio; Sang at San Francisco 1972, in the US premiere of The Vist of the Old Lady by Von Einem; Covent Garden 1973, as Mandryka in Arabella; Sang at La Scala 1976, as Faninal in Der Rosenkavalier; Repertoire includes roles in operas by Wagner, Verdi, Puccini and Bizet; Many concert appearances. *Recordings:* Excerpts from Il Trovatore (Deutsche Grammophon); Carmina Burana (Electrola). *Address:* c/o Hamburgische Staatsoper, Grosse Theaterstrasse 34, D-2000 Hamburg 36, Germany.

WOLF Friedrich, b. 5 Apr 1935, Loosdorf, Austria. Conductor; Teacher. m. Maria Hahn, 26 Nov 1955, 4 sons. *Education:* Teacher Training College, Vienna; Studied Choral Direction, Voice, Composition, Academy of Music, Vienna; Diploma, Magister artium. *Career:* Conductor, Servitenkirche Choir, Vienna, 1957; Conductor, Choir of St Augustin, Vienna, 1969-; Teaching, Pedagogical Academy. *Compositions:* Lateinische Messe, motet (manuscript); Deutsche Messe (published). *Recordings:* For Philips, Austria: Schubert, Missa in C, G, A flat, E flat; Mozart, Krönungsmesse, Missa solemnis; Bruckner, Requiem; Haydn, Missa Cellensis. *Honours:* Prize, Choral Competition, Spittal a.d.Drau Joseph-Haydn Gesellschaft, Vienna, 1971; Honorary Member, Mozartgemeinde Wien, 1977; Honorary Member, Eques ordinis Sancti Silvestri Papae, 1980. *Address:* Raxstrasse 22/3/7, Vienna, Austria.

WOLF Gerd, b. 18 Apr 1940, Floha, Saxony, Germany. Singer (Bass). *Education:* Studied at the Berlin Musikhochschule. *Debut:* Dresden Radesbeul 1970, as the Hermit in Der Freischutz. *Career:* Sang at Dresden and elsewhere in East Germany until 1982, Berlin Staatsoper from 1982 as Mozart's Osmin, Leporello and Bartolo, Nicolai's Falstaff, Bett in Zar und Zimmerman, Geronimo in Il Matrimonio Segreto and the Doctor in Wozzeck; Guest appearances in Leipzig, Karlsruhe and with the Berlin Staatsoper company at Naples, Messina, Prague, Bratislava, Japan and Holland. *Recordings include:* Pfitzner's Palestrina; Graf Mirabeau by Siegfried Matthus; Ariadne auf Naxos. *Address:* Deutsche Staatsoper Berlin, Unter den Linden 7, 1086 Berlin, Germany.

WOLF Harold, b. 15 May 1921, Berkeley, California, USA. Violinist; Conductr. m. Katherine Steve, 1 May 1944, 1 daughter. *Education:* Pierre Monteaux School for Conductors; Curtis Institute of Music; Julliard School of Music; Further studies with Mishel Piastro. *Debut:* Violin, 1940; Conducting, 1953. *Career:* LA Philharmonic Symphony, 1949-52; Concertmaster, Utah Symphony, 1952-66, Alabama Symphony, 1968-74, San Diego Symphony, 1974-76; Member, LA Chamber Orchestra, 1983-88. *Compositions:* Three Cadenzas for the Mozart Violin Concerto No 5, 1983; Cadenza for the Brahms Violin concerto, 1990. *Recordings:* Gordon Ramsey, String Quartet, four descriptive pieces for violin and viola, flute quartet, violin and piano sonata. *Honours:* Scholarships: Curtis Institute of Music, 1930, NY Philharmonic, 1932, Julliard School of Music, 1936. *Memberships:* Life, AFM, Los Angeles. *Hobbies:* Flying; Golf; Model building; Reading; Collecting records. *Address:* 1-Jefferson Parkway No 180, Lake Oswego, OR 97035, USA.

WOLF Markus, b. 28 May 1962, Vienna, Austria. Violinist. m. Roxana Arshadi, 25 June 1986. 2 sons. *Education:* Violin studies, Wiener Musikhochschule with Edith Bertschinger and Guenter Pichler, 1968-83; Diploma with Honours, 1983; Further studies with Max Rostal, Klagenfurt and Bern; Master classes with Nathan Milstein and Oscar Shumsky. *Debut:* Wiener Musikverein, 1976; Completion: Wigmore Hall, London, 1987, Suntory Hall, Tokyo, 1990. *Career:* Violist, String trio with brothers Reinhold and Peter Wolf, 1973-; Appearances with the Alban Berg Quartett, 1986; Violinist, Assistant of Guenter Pichler, Wiener Musikhochschule, 1983-89; Principal Concertmaster, Wiener Symphoniker, 1987-88; Principal Concertmaster, Bayerisches Staatsorchester, Muenchen, 1989-; Founder, with the Pianist Christiane Karajeva and Cellist Howard Penny, Beethoven Trio, Vienna, 1985. *Recordings:* EMI with Alban Berg Quartet (Mozart); JVC with Beethoven Trio Vienna (Tschaikowsky and Beethoven); Camerata with Beethoven Trio, Vienna (Mendelssohn, Beethoven, Mozart, Schubert. *Honours:* Winner, Austrian Youth Competititon, Jugend musiziert and Special prize, Jeunesses Musicales, 1973; Winner, Stefanie-Hohl-Violin-Competition, Wiener Musikhochschule, 1982. *Current Management:* Kuenstlersekretariat Buchmann, Vienna and Essener Konzertdirektion, Germany. *Address:* Heiliggeistsraße 2, D-80331 München, Germany.

WOLF R Peter, b. 5 Dec 1942, Washington DC, USA.Musicologist; Harpsichordist. *Education:* AB, Harvard University, 1965; MPhil, 1969; PhD, 1977, Yale University; Studied Harpsichord with Gustav Leonhardt, Amsterdam Conservatorium, 1965-66; Studied Harpsichord with Ralph Kirkpatrick, Yale School of Music, 1966-70. *Debut:* Carnegie Recital Hall, New York, 1975. *Career:* Numerous concerts as Harpsichord Soloist and Continuo Player; Musician-in-Residence, North Carolina State University at Raleigh; 2 television shows, NC Educational Network, 1972; Instructor in Music, SUNY at Stony Brook, 1972-78; Assistant Professor of Music, University of Utah, 1978-80; Assistant Professor of Music, Rutgers University, 1980-85; Editor, Brouda Brothers Limited, 1985-89; Director of Development, Hoboken Chamber Orchestra, 1989-; Member, Bowers-Wolf Duo, Barwell-Wolf Duo, Salt Lake Chamber Ensemble, Apollo's Banquet, New York Baroque. *Recordings:* Telemann, Instrumental Chamber Music with Concertmasters Ensemble; Private recording of works by Rameau, J S Bach, C P E Bach; Biber, Violin Sonatas (1681) with Sonya Monosoff and Judith Davidoff. *Publications:* Joint Editor, ms Bauyn, New York; Editor, Rameau, Les Paladins, New York and Paris; Editor, facsimile edition of Rameau, Les Paladins, 1986; Editor, Couperin, Tantum ergo sacramentum, New York, 1984; Editor, Purcell, Blessed is He that Considereth the Poor, 1985; Editor, critical facsimile edition of Rameau, Pièces de Clavecin, Oeuvre I, 1986. *Contributions to:* The Scriblerian; Actes, Colloque International Rameau, Dijon, 1983; The Musical Quarterly; Journal of the American Musical Instrument Society; Recherches; Early Music; Journal of the American Musicological Society. *Address:* 37A Phelps Avenue, New Brunswick, New Jersy 08901, USA.

WOLF Reinhold Michael, b. 23 May 1956, Vienna, Austria. Violinist. m. Nicole Simon, 1982, 1 son, 1 daughter. *Education:* Piano lessons at age 6; 1st violin instruction at Wiener Musikakademie at age 8, later chamber music lessons with Alban Berg Quartet; Kuenstlerische Diplompruefung mit Auszeichnung, 1976; Violin studies with G.Poulet in Paris and M.Rostal in Cologne; Chamber music with Amadeus Quartet; Konzert-examen mit Auszeichnung Cologne, 1981. *Career:* Established the Wolf Trio with brothers Markus Wolf (viola) and Peter Wolf (violoncello); Concertmaster, World Youth Orchestra with L.Bernstein, Tanglewood, USA, at age 18; Concertmaster, Orchestra of the Deutsche Oper, Berlin, 1982-; Soloist with various European orchestras; Appeared as Double Concerto Partner of H.Szeryng with Vienna Symphony Orchestra; Established ensemble Contraste in Berlin, 1989. *Honours:* Special Prize, Jeunesse Musicales Austria for the Wolf Trio, 1973; 1st Prize as Soloist, Jugend Musiziert Competition, Austria, 1975. *Address:* c/o Deutsche Oper Berlin, Orchesterdirektion, Richard-Wagner-Strasse 10, D-1000 Berlin 10, Germany.

WOLFF Beverly, b. 6 Nov 1928, Atlanta, Georgia, USA. Singer (Mezzo-Soprano). *Education:* Studied with Sidney Dietch and Vera McIntyre at the Academy of Vocal Arts in Philadelphia. *Debut:* Sang Dinah in a TV production of Bernstein's Trouble in Tahiti, 1952. *Career:* Has sung with the New York City Opera from 1958, debut as Dinah; Appeared on NBC TV in the premiere of Menotti's Labyrinth, 1963; Stage engagements in Mexico City, Cincinnati, Boston, Houston, Washington and San Francisco as Carmen, Adalgisa, Cherubino, Kabanichka in Katya Kabanova, Radamisto, Dalila and Sesto in Handel's Giulio Cesare; Concert appearances as Dalila and Sesto in Handel's Giulio Cesare; Sang in the premieres of Douglas Moore's Carrie Nation (1966) and Menotti's The Most Important Man (1971); Concert appearances with leading American orchestras. *Recordings:* Roberto Deveruex by Donizetti; Rossini's La Pietra del Paragone; Giulio Cesare. *Honours include:* Winner, Youth Auditions, Philadelphia 1952.

WOLFF Christian, b. 8 Mar 1934, Nice, France. Composer. *Education:* Influenced by John Cage, Morton Feldman and Earle Brown after moving to the USA; Studied Classics at Harvard, PhD 1963. *Career:* Taught at Harvard University 1962-76; Teacher of classics and music at Dartmouth College from 1976. *Compositions include:* Nine for ensemble 1951; Suite for prepared piano 1954; Duo for Pianists I and II 1957-58; Music for Merce Cunningham 1959; Duo for Violinist and Pianist 1961; Summer for string quartet 1961; In Between Pieces for 3 players 1963; Septet 1964; Quartet for 4 horns 1966; Elec Spring I-III 1966-67; Toss for 8 or more players 1968; Snowdrop for harpsichord 1970; Burdocks for 1 or more orchestras or 5 or more players 1971; Accompaniments 1972; Lines for string quartet 1972; Changing the System 1973; Exercises 1-24 1973-84; Wobbly Music for mixed chorus and instrumemts 1976; Bread and Roses, for piano and for violin 1976; Dark as A Dungeon for clarinet 1977, for trombone and double bass 1977; The Death of Mother Jones for violin 1977; Stardust Pieces for cello and piano 1979; Isn't this a Time for saxophone 1981; Eisler Ensemble Pieces 1983; Piano Song (I am a Dangerous Woman) 1983; Peace March 1-3 1983-84; I Like to Think of Harriet Tubman for female voice, treble and alto, 1984. *Address:* 104 South Main Street, Hanover, NH 03755, USA.

WOLFF Hugh (MacPherson), b. 21 Oct 1953, Paris, France. Conductor. *Education:* Piano lessons from Fleisher and Shure; Studied composition with Crumb Kirchner; BA, Harvard University, 1975; Studied composition with Messiaen; Piano with Sancan; Conducting with Bruck; MM, piano 1977, MM conducting 1978, Peabody Institute. *Career:* Exxon/Arts Endowment Conductor, 1979-82, Associate Conductor 1982-85, National Symphony Orchestra, Washington, DC; Music Director, Northeastern Pennsylvania Philharmonic Orchestra, 1981-86; European debut with London Philharmonic Orchestra, 1982; Music Director, New Jersey Symphony Orchestra, Newark, 1985-; Principal Conductor, St Paul (Minn) Chamber Orchestra, 1988-; Guest conductor with various North American and European orchestras. *Honours:* Frank Huntington Beebe Fellow, 1975-76; Annette Kade Fellow, 1978; Co-recipient, Affiliate Artist's Seaver Conducting Award, 1985. *Address:* c/o ICM Artists Ltd, 40 W 57th St, New York, NY 10019, USA.

WOLFF Jean-Claude, b. Oct 1946, Paris, France. Composer. *Education:* Studied composing, analysis, history of music at L'Ecole Normale de Musique de Paris, then at Conservatoire National Superieur de Musique de Paris with Henri Dutilleux, Jean-Pierre Guezec, Michel Philippot, Ivo Malec; Electro-acoustic classes with Jean-Etienne Marie, Centre International de Recherches Musicale; Spent 3 summers following composition courses with Franco Donatoni, Accademia Chigiana, Siena, Italy; Laureate of the Academie de France, Rome (Villa Medici) 1978-80. *Compositions:* Compositions include about 30 works performed at various festivals and concerts of contemporary music in France (Radio-France, and International Musical Weeks in Orleans, Angers Music Festival, Contemporary Music Meetings, Metz) and abroad in Italy, Switzerland, Denmark, Spain, Netherlands; For several years has concentrated mainly on chamber music, currently working on a symphony for small orchestra, commissioned by Radio France. *Address:* 39 rue Bouret, 75019, Paris, France.

WOLFF Marguerite, b. 1930, London, England. Concert Pianist. m. Derrick Moss (dec), 2 daughters. *Education:* FTCL, Royal Academy of Music. *Career:* Soloist: London Symphony Orchestra, Royal Philharmonic Orchestra, Philharmonia, Bournemouth and Birmingham Orchestras; Radio and TV broadcasts with major orchestras; Toured USA, Europe and Far East, also 6 tours of Far East (Nepal, Delhi, Bombay, Calcutta, Malaysia, Indonesia, Singapore, Hong Kong), East Arrica, Mexico, Peru and North America. *Recordings:* Bliss Piano Sonata; Liszt Society recording Liszt. *Honours:* Incorporated Society of Music Winner, International Bambridge Compeition. *Memberships:* Women's University Club; Councillor, Liszt Society. *Hobbies:* Reading; Walking. *Current Management:* Classical Company. *Address:* Chandos House, 17a Chester Street, Belgravia, London SW1, England.

WOLOVSKY Leonardo, b. 1922, York, Pennsylvania, USA. Singer (Bass-baritone). *Education:* Studied at Oberlin College Ohio. *Career:* Sang at first in concert then appeared with Maria Callas in Norma at Catanua, 1952; Engaged at Wiesbaden Opera 1953-57, Nuremberg 1957-73; Guest appearances at Frankfurt 1959-73, Bayerische Staatsoper Munich 1961-69, Hanover 1961-73, Hamburg 1956-60; Sang also at Graz, Essen, Amsterdam, Zurich, Paris, Barcelona and Athens; Bielefeld 1988, as Simon Mago in Nerone by Boito; Other roles have included Enrico (Lucia di Lammermoor), Oroveso, King Philip, Nabucco, the Dutchman, Hans Sachs, the Wanderer in Siegfried and Boris Godunov; Concert repertoire included Beethoven's Ninth, the Verdi Requiem and Bach's Christmas Oratorio. *Address:* Stadtische Buhnen, Brunnenstrasse 3, 48000 Berlin 1, Germany.

WONG Lydia, b. 11 Feb 1960, Hong Kong. Pianist. m. Simon Fryer, 27 July 1985. *Education:* Royal Conservatory of Music, 1974-78; ARCT, 1978; BMus, University of Toronto, 1982; Guildhall School of Music and Drama, 1982-83; Premier Prix, 1983; The Banff Centre, summers 1982, 1984, 1985, winter 1987-88. *Career:* Solo and chamber music recitals, Canada, England, South Africa; Broadcast on Canadian National and local radio, and South African National Radio Networks; Faculty Accompanist, Banff Centre, summers 1985, 1989, winter, 1988-89. *Honours:* Accompanists Prize and Ivan Sutton Recording Prize, Guildhall School of Music and Drama, 1985. *Membership:* American Federation of Musicians. *Hobbies:* Reading; Cooking. *Address:* 51 Chestergrove Crescent, Agincourt, Ontario, Canada M1W 1L3.

WONG On-Yuen, b. 16 Nov 1945, Chong-Ging, China. Conductor. m. Chi-Hung Chan, 1 Feb 1973, 2 sons. *Education:* Central Conservatory of Music, Beijing; China Competition of Music, Beijing. *Career:* Music Instructor, Chinese University of Hong Kong, Hong Kong Academy of Performing Arts; Consultant, Council for the Performing Arts of Hong Kong; Currently, Concert Master and Assistant Conductor, Hong Kong Chinese Orchestra. *Compositions:* Autumn Harvest; The Happy Peasant; The Train Entering Tung village. *Recordings:* 21 solo and concerto recordings including The World of Wong On-Yuen's Hu-Qin Music; The Song of Wine; Wong On-Yuen and 12 kinds of Hu-Qins; the Butterfly Lover Concerto. *Honours:* Golden Tripod Award, 1984, 1987; One of Ten Outstanding Young Persons, 1985; Music Performer of the Year, 1989; Most Outstanding

Asian Artist Award, 1991. *Memberships:* Hong Kong Outstanding Persons Association; Chinese Folk Symphonic Music Society, (Executive member). *Hobbies:* Sport; Photography. *Address:* Room 2201, Block B, Parkway Court, No 4 Park Road, Hong Kong.

WOOD Gareth H, b. 7 June 1950, Cilfynydd, Wales. Musician. *Education:* Royal Academy of Music, London. *Career:* Joined Royal Philharmonic Orchestra in 1972 as double bass player, Director, 1990, Chairman, 1991-. *Compositions:* Tombstone, Arizona, 1975; Suffolk Punch, 1980; Sinfoniettas 2, 1985, 3, 1988, 4, 1990; Fantasy on Welsh Song, for Welsh proms, 1991; Cardiff Bay, overture, 1993. *Recordings:* Cardiff Bay Overture. *Honours:* ARAM, 1986. *Hobbies:* Golf; Tennis. *Address:* 57 Marishal Road, Lewisham, London SE13 5LE, England.

WOOD Hugh, b. 27 June 1932, Parbold, Lancashire, England. Composer. *Education:* Studied at Oxford University and in London with WS Lloyd Webber; Further study with Anthony Milner, Iain Hamilton and Matyas Seiber. *Career:* Professor of Harmony at the Royal Academy of Music, 1962-65; Teacher at Morley College 1958-67; Research Fellow in Composition, Glasgow University, 1966-70; Lecturer in Music, Liverpool University, 1971-73; Lecturer in Music at Cambridge University from 1976; Talks on BBC Radio 3; Piano Concerto premiered at the 1991 Promenade Concerts. *Compositions:* Songs for Springtime for chorus and piano 1954; Suite for piano 1956; String Quartet 1957; Variations for viola and piano 1958; Laurie Lee Songs 1959; Songs to Poems by Christopher Logue 1961; Trio for flute, viola and piano 1961; String Quartet No 1 1962; Scenes from Comus, for soprano, tenor and chorus 1965; 3 Choruses 1966; Songs to Poems by DH Lawrence 1966; Capriccio for organ 1967; Quintet for clarinet, horn and piano trio 1967; The Horses, song cycle, 1967; The Rider Victory, song cycle, 1968; Cello Concerto 1969; String Quartet No 2 1970; Chamber Concerto 1971; Violin Concerto 1972; 2 Choruses 1973; Songs to Poems by Robert Graves 1973; Songs to Poems by Pablo Neruda for high voice and chamber orchestra 1973; String Quartet No 3 1978; Symphony 1979-82; Piano Trio 1984; Comus Quadrilles 1988; Horn Trio 1987-89; Cantata for chorus and orchestra 1989; Marina for high voice and ensemble 1989; Piano concerto 1990. *Address:* c/o Churchill College, Cambridge CB3 0DS, England.

WOOD James Peter, b. 27 May 1953, Barton-on-Sea, Hampshire, England. Composer; Conductor; Percussionist. m. Penny Irish, 25 June 1977. 1 son, 1 daughter. *Education:* Radley College, 1966-71; Sidney Sussex College, Cambridge, 1972-75; ARCO, 1969; FRCO, 1971; BA, Music, 1975. Studied with Nadia Boulanger, Paris, 1971-72; RAM, 1975-76. *Career:* Conductor, Schola Cantorum of Oxford, 1977-81; Founder/Conductor, New London Chamber Choir, 1981; Professor of Percussion, Internationale Ferienkurse, Darmstadt, 1982-; Regular radio and TV appearances; Artistic Advisor to Percussion Foundation and Percussion 88 and 90 Festivals; Founder/Director, Centre for Microtonal Music since 1990; Director of Barbican's Annual Weekend of Microtonal Music. *Compositions:* Major works: Phaedrus; Oreion (BBC SO Commission, premiered at the 1989 Promenade Concerts, London); Stoicheia (Darmstadt Commission); Ho Shang Yao; T'ien Chung Yao; Choroi Kaithaliai; Rogosanti; Phainomena; Spirit Festival with Lamentations; Village Burial with Fire; Incantamenta. *Recordings:* Pierre de la Rue/Josquin and Eric Bergman both with new London Chamber Choir; Roberto Sierra, both as conductor of NSCC and solo percussionist; James Wood: Stoicheia (Wergo); James Wood: Music for Percussion and Voices (Continuum); Stravinsky: Les Noces and other choral works (Hyperion); Eric Bergman: Choral works (Chandos); 15th Century Flemish Choral Works, (Saydisc, 2 records). *Contributions:* A New System for Quarter-tone Percussion, Musical Times and Percussive Notes. *Honours:* Lili Boulanger Prize, 1975; Lili Boulanger Memorial Award, 1980. *Current Management:* Colin Boyle. *Address:* Bancroft, Rectory

Lane, Fringford, Bicester, Oxfordshire OX6 9DX, England.

WOOD Jeffrey Neal, b. 3 Oct 1954, Allentown, Pennsylvania, USA. Composer; University Professor. 1 son. *Education:* BMus, Oberlin College Conservatory of Music, 1976; MMus 1978, MA 1980, PhD 1982, State University of New York, Stony Brook. *Career:* Visiting Lecturer, University of New Mexico, Albuquerque, New Mexico Institute of Mining and Technology, 1983-84; Austin Peay State University, Clarksville, Tennessee, 1984-. *Compositions:* Duo for Cello and Piano, 1982 (recorded); In Memoriam Magistri for brass quintet, 1982; Sonata for Cello and Piano, 1984; String Quartet No 2, 1985; MCMXIV for tenor and piano, 1985; Now The Most High Is Born, 1985; Trio-Sonata for cello, piano and percussion, 1986; The Dream of the Rood for tenor solo, chorus and organ, 1986; Swifts for violin and cello, 1986; First Essay for Orchestra, 1986; Music for Concert Band, 1987; Comedies, for woodwind quintet, 1988; Quartet for flute, violin, cello and piano, 1988; Lay your sleeping head my love, soprano, tenor and piano, 1987; Kreigeslieder, mezzo-soprano and piano, 1988; Time Let Me Hail and Climb for chorus, brass quintet and piano, 1990; The Killing for tenor and piano, 1989; Four Deadly Serious Songs, for baritone and piano, 1990; Ballads for the Goodly Fere, voice and piano, 1991; Dances for two pianos, 1992; Preludes for piano solo, 1992; Ghosts for clarinet, viola and piano, 1993. *Recordings:* Comedies, for woodwind quintet, recorded by Quintet of the Americas, 1991. *Contributions to:* In Theory Only volume 7, 1983. *Hobby:* Calligraphy. *Current Management:* Broadcast Music, Inc. *Address:* Department of Music, Austin Peay State University, Clarksville, TN 37044, USA.

WOOD Vivian Poates, b. 19 Aug 1928, Washington, DC, USA. Singer, Professor. *Education:* Student, Walter Anderson, Antioch College, 1953-55, Denise Restout, Saint-Leu-la-Foret, France and Lakeville, Connecticut, 1960-62, 1964-70, Paul A Pisk, 1968-71, Paul Ulanowsky, New York City, 1958-68, Elemor Nagy, 1965-68, Vyantas Marijosius, 1967-68; BMus, Hartt College of Music, 1968, Postgraduate fellow, Yale University, 1968; MMus (fellow), Washington University, St Louis, 1971, PhD (fellow), 1973. *Debut:* Jeunesse Musical Art Festival, 1953. *Career:* Mezzo-soprano soloist with numerous orchestras including, Solo Fellowship, Boston Symphony Orchestra, Berkshire Music Center Tanglewood, 1964, St Louis Symphony Orchestra, 1968, Washington Orchestra, 1949, Bach Cantata series Berkshire Chamber Orchestra, 1964, Yale Symphony Orchestra, 1968; Appearances in numerous recitals, oratorios, operas, radio and television, USA and Europe, 1953-68; Appearances as soloist in International Harpsichord Festival, Westminster Choir College, Princeton, New Jersey, 1973, Memorial Concert, Landowska Centre, Lakeville, 1969; Professor of voice, University of Southern Mississippi, Hattiesburg, 1971-; Assistant Dean, College of Fine Arts, 1974-76, Acting Dean, 1976-77; Guest Professor, Hochschule für Musik, Munich, Germany, 1978; International Studies Programme, Rome, Italy, 1985-. *Publication:* Author, Poulenc's Songs: An Analysis of Style, 1978. *Address:* 3017 Navajo Circle, Hattiesburg, MS 39402, USA.

WOODLAND Rae, b. Nottingham, England. Singer (Soprano); International Adjudicator and Examiner. m. Denis Stanley. *Education:* Private studies with Roy Henderson, Joan Cross and Vittorio Gui. *Debut:* Sadlers Wells Theatre. *Career:* Performances with opera companies in the UK, and as guest throughout Europe, and Mauritius, USSR, also radio and TV appearances. Roles include: Queen of the Night, Flute; Luisa, Luisa Miller; Fiordiligi, Così; Constanze, Seraglio; Donna Elvira, Giovanni; Alice Ford, Falstaff; Mimi, La Bohème; Electra, Idomeneo; Aida, Verdi; Odabella, Attila; Marguerite, Mefistofele; Leonora, Trovatore, Venus, Tannhäuser, Naiade, Ariadne; Marguerite, Faust; Lady Jowler, Rising of the Moon-Maw-Glyndebourne, among others; Professor of Singing, Royal Academy, London; Vocal Consultant, Britten Pears School, Snape; International Adjudicator and Examiner; Adviser to Arts Council of Great Britain. *Recordings include:* Messiah, John Tobin-Handel Society; Sir Arthur Bliss' Birthday; Midsummer Night's Dream, Haitink; Montezuma, Bonynge; Idomeneo- Davis, BBC Light Music; Glyndebourne, Macbeth and Ritorno D'Ulisse; Queen of the Night, BBC Prom, Glyndebourne. *Honour:* Classics Prize, Hon Professor of Singing, RAM. *Memberships:* FRSA; Women of the Year Association; Erin Arts Trust; Association of Teachers of Singing; RAM Guild; ISM; President, Aldeburgh Music Club. *Hobbies:* Gardening; Cooking. *Address:* Brackendale, Priory Lane, Snape, Saxmundham, Suffolk IP17 1SD, England.

WOODLEY Ronald, b. 24 June 1953, Kingston-upon-Thames, England. University Lecturer in Music. *Education:* University of Manchester, 1971-75; Royal Northern College of Music, 1971-75; MusB 1st Class Hons.; GRNCM and Associate, Royal Northern College of Music, 1975; University of Oxford, Keble College and Christ Church, 1975-79; MA, 1979; DPhil, 1982. *Career:* Lecturer in Music, Christ Church, Oxford, 1979-81; Lecturer in Music, University of Liverpool, 1981-84; Professor of Music Techniques, Royal Academy of Music, 1982-83; Lecturer in Music, University of Newcastle-upon-Tyne, 1984-; Television and radio appearances as clarinet and chalumeau player and as 15th century musicologist, 1970-. *Recordings:* BBC Recordings as clarinettist, pianist and chalumeau player and as musicologist, 1970-. *Publications:* Articles on the 15th century musical theorist Iohannes Tinctoris, Steve Reich, etc; Forthcoming books on Tinctoris and Reich. *Contributions to:* Journal of the American Musicological Society; Early Music History; Early Music; Music and Letters; Renaissance Studies. *Honours:* Hargreaves Musical Scholarship, University of Manchester, 1972; Rothwell Prize, University of Manchester, 1973; P J Leonard Prize for Composition, University of Manchester, 1975. *Memberships:* Royal Musical Association; American Musicological Society. *Hobbies:* Chamber Music; Food; Snooker. *Address:* Department of Music, University of Newcastle-upon-Tyne, Newcastle-upon-Tyne, NE2 7RU, England.

WOODROW Alan, b. 1952, Toronto, Canada. Singer (Tenor). *Education:* Studied at the Royal Conservatory in Toronto and at the London Opera Centre. *Career:* From 1976 sang with English National Opera as Pedrillo, Don Ottavio, Froh (Das Rheingold), Lindoro, Vasek, Monostatos, Canio, Hermann, Don José, Edmund in Reimann's Lear and Walther von Stolzing; Recent London appearances as the Prince in The Love of Three Oranges, the Captain in Wozzeck, Herod in Salome and Siegmund in Die Walküre (season 1992-93); Has also sung Sergei in Lady Macbeth of Mtsensk at La Scala and the Bastille, Paris; Concert engagements in Canada with the Mozart and Verdi Requiems; the Choral Symphony and Mahler's Eighth; A Mass of Life by Delius; Kodály's Psalmus Hungaricus. *Address:* c/o Athole Still Ltd., Greystoke House, 80-86 Westow Street, London SE19 3AF, Enbgland.

WOODS Elaine, b. 1958, Lancashire. Singer (Soprano). *Education:* Studied at Oxford University and at the Royal Manchester College of Music with Elsie Thurston; Further study with Marjorie Thomas. *Debut:* With Kent Opera as Violetta, 1979, at the Edinburgh Festival. *Career:* Sang in Handel's Tolomeo at the Batigniano Festival in Italy, 1980; German debut 1981, as Mimi in Mannheim; Bremen Opera from 1982, as Fiordiligi, Tatiana, Eva, Liu and the Countess in Capriccio; In summer of 1983 sang in J C Bach's Lucio Silla in Frankfurt and Acis and Galatea at Karlsruhe; Appeared as Pamina at the 1986 Bregenz Festival and sang Belina in a new production of Dido and Aeneas at Frankfurt; J C Bach's Lucio Silla at the Vienna Festival; With Welsh National Opera has sung Donna Elvira, Fiordiligi and Mozart's Countess; Concert repertoire includes the Verdi and Mozart Requiems, Haydn's Creation and Seasons, Messiah and Beethoven's Missa Solemnis and Ninth Symphony. *Honours include:* Prizewinner at the 1978 s' Hertogenbosch Competition.

Address: c/o Inpgen and Williams Ltd., 14 Kensington Court, London W11 4PA, England.

WOODWARD Donna, b. 2 June 1946, Baltimore, Maryland, USA. Singer (Soprano). *Education:* Studied in Cincinnati and Europe. *Career:* Sang in opera at Lucerne 1970-71, Darmstadt 1971-73, Heidelberg 1973-75; Engaged at the Nationaltheater Mannheim 1975-86; Guest appearances in Germany, France, Switzerland and Belgium; Roles have included Blondchen, Adele, Aennchen in Der Freischütz, Sophie (Rosenkavalier), Rosina and Musetta. *Recordings include:* Dittersdorf's Doktor und Apotheker. *Address:* c/o Nationaltheater, Am Goetheplatz, 6800 Mannheim, Germany.

WOODWARD Roger Robert, b. 20 Dec 1942, Sydney, Australia. Conductor; Composer; Pianist. 1 son, 1 daughter. *Education:* DSCM, Sydney Conservatory of Music; Warsaw Academy, Poland. *Debut:* Royal Festival Hall, London, England, 1970. *Career:* His career has been closely associated with world premieres of works by the most famous composers of our time; Xenakis, Boulez, Barraqué, Stockhausen, Takemitsu, Bussotti, Berio, Feldman, Cage and many others have written works specifically for him. He has worked with many of the world's most distinguished conductors including Boulez, Leinsdorf, Masur and Mehta. Has performed throughout Europe, the USA and Australia and has appeared at international festivals and with major orchestras throughout the world. Founder member of contemporary music series in London in 1972 and in Australia in 1975. Performed historic series of 16 concerts presenting the complete works of Chopin in 1985. World premiere of Xenakis' Keqrops, conceived for Woodward with New York Philharmonic, Mehta conducting, 1986. Music Director, Xenakis ballet Kraanerg mounted by Sydney Dance Company, November 1988. *Recordings include:* Rachmaninov Preludes; Scriabin/Prokofiev/Shostakovich; Australian Contemporary Music; Chopin Allegro de Concert, Barcarolle; London Music Digest: Barraqué Sonata, Bussotti/Brouwer; Werder 3rd Sonata, 1969; Meale Coruscations and 2 Australian Discs (RCA and EMI), 1973; Takemitsu, 1973; Serocki, 1976; 2 Beethoven Sonatas Discs RCA; Shostakovich's 24 Preludes and Fugues, double album; Liszt's transcription Beethoven's Eroica; Hoddinott 3rd Concerto, Philharmonia Orchestra; Brahms 1st Piano Concerto, conductor Masur; Barry Conyngham's Southern Cross, with Wanda Wilkomirska and Sydney Symphony Orchestra conducted by Niklaus Wyss. *Honours:* Fellow, Chopin Institute, Warsaw 1976; OBE, 1980; KT (Breffni) in 1985. *Current Management:* Norman Lawrence Artist Management. *Address:* c/o Norman Lawrence Artist Management, 35 Britannia Row, London N1 8QH, England.

WOOLEY Robert, b. 1948, England. Harpsichordist; Organist. *Career:* Member of the Purcell Quartet, debut concert at St John's Smith Square, London, 1984; Extensive tours and broadcasts in France, Belgium, Holland, Germany, Austria, Switzerland, Italy and Spain; Tours of the United States and Japan, 1991-92; British appearances include four Purcell concerts at the Wigmore Hall, 1987, later broadcast on Radio 3; Repertoire includes music on the La Folia theme by Vivaldi, Corelli, CPE Bach, Marais, A Scarlatti, Vitali and Geminiani; instrumental works and song by Purcell, music by Matthew Locke, John Blow and Fantasias and Airs by William Lawes; 17th Century virtuoso Italian music by Marini, Buonamente, Gabrieli, Fontana, Stradella and Lonati; J S Bach and his forerunners - Biber, Scheidt, Schenk, Reinken and Buxtehude; Many concerts with other ensembles and as soloist. *Recordings include:* Six record set on the La Folia theme (Hyperion); Purcell Sonatas for two violins, viola da gamba and continuo; Sonatas by Vivaldi and Corelli (Chandos). *Address:* c/o Robert White Management, 182 Moselle Avenue, London N22 6EX, England.

WOOLFENDEN Guy Anthony, b. 12 July 1937, Ipswich, England. Composer; Conductor. m. Jane Aldrick, 29 Sept 1962, 3 sons. *Education:* Westminster Abbey Choir School; Whitgift School; Christ's College, Cambridge; MA (Cantab); LGSM. *Career:* Head of Music, Royal Shakespeare Company, Stratford-upon-Avon and London, composed more than 150 scores for this company; also composed scores for Burgtheater, Vienna; Comèdie Française, Paris; Teatro di Stabile, Genoa and National Theatre Bergen, Norway; also for films, radio and TV; Conducted concerts with most British Symphony Orchestras; Conducted concerts in Canada, Germany and France; Conducted opera for BBC radio, TV and 3 productions with Scottish Opera; Arranged and Conducted Tchaikovsky score for Anna Karenina and Verdi score for The Three Musketeers, both for Australian Ballet and arranged Verdi score for La Traviata, the ballet for London City Ballet; Conducted Russian premiere of Anna Karenina with Kirov Ballet in St Petersburg, 1993; Artistic Director, Cambridge Festival, 1986-91. *Compositions:* Composed 3 musicals; Comedy of Errors for RSC; a Children's opera The Last Wild Wood Sector 88 with Adrian Mitchell; Works for the concert include: concertos, chamber music and Gallimanfry and Illyrian Dances for symphonic band.. *Recordings:* Music for Royal Shakespeare Company; Music for The Winter's Tale; Songs of Ariel; Video: The Comedy of Errors, Antony and Cleopatra, Macbeth. *Honours:* PRS Ivor Novello Award for Best British Musical, 1976-77; Society of West End Theatre Award for Best British Musical, 1977 (both for The Comedy of Errors); FBSM (for services to music in the Midlands), 1991. *Address:* Malvern House, Sibford Ferris, Banbury, Oxon, OX15 5RG, England.

WOOLFORD Delia Osborne, b. 2 Aug 1931, Petworth, Sussex, England. Contralto; Teacher of Singing. m. Eric Waddington, 29 Aug 1975, 1 stepson, 1 stepdaughter. *Education:* Royal College of Music, London, 1949-53; ARCM Piano Teaching, 1951, Singing and Performing, 1953. *Career:* Recitals of Lieder, French song, English song, BBC radio; Oratorio, recital and concert performances throughout Britain and Europe including Concertgebouw, Amsterdam; television appearances. *Recordings:* Venus and Adonis, John Blow; L'Oiseau Lyre; Matthäus Passion, Bach, conductor Piet van Egmond. *Honours:* London Musical Society prize, circa 1951. *Membership:* ISM. *Hobbies:* Home; Garden; Friends; Food and wine; Travel. *Address:* Langley, Pathfields Close, Haslemere, Surrey GU27 2BL, England.

WOOLLAM Kenneth Geoffrey, b. 16 Jan 1937, Chester, England. Opera Singer. m. Phoebe Elizabeth Scrivenor, 4 daughters. *Education:* Chester Cathedral Choir School; Royal College of music. *Debut:* Sadler's Wells, London, 1972. *Career:* Appearances with Royal Opera House Covent Garden, Electra, Aegist; Royal Opera Copenhagen, Saul og David, David; Frankfurt, Fidelio, Florestan; English National Opera, roles include Rienzi, Wagner; Radames, Aida, Verdi; Scottish Opera; Royal Opera, Ghent; Opera du Nord; Warsaw Philharmonic Orchestra; various roles including Walther (Die Meistersinger); Siegfried (The Ring); Bacchus (Ariadne auf Naxos); Boris (Katya Kabanova); Laca (Jenůfa); Husband in World Premiere of John Tavener's Gentle Spirit at Bath; 3 films - Canio (Pagliacci); Alfredo (La Traviata); Hoffmann (Tales of Hoffmann); Concerts and Oratorios with leading societies; Sang in the premieres of Hamilton's Royal Hunt of the Sun and Blake's Toussaint L'Ouverture, 1977; Covent Garden debut 1988, as Aegisthus; Currently Professor of Singing, Royal College of Music. *Recordings:* Margot-La-Rouge, Delius; La Mort d'Orphée, Berlioz (Nippon Columbia), conductor Jean Fournet, 1987. Television: Songfest, Bernstein conducted by composer; Television BBC: Gerontius; Elgar, Conductor Vernon Handley, 1987; Gurre-Lieder, Bergen International Festival (televised); Herod (Salome) Edinburgh Festival, 1989. *Honours:* Honorary Member, Royal College of Music, 1992. *Memberships:* Incorporated Society of Musicians; Savage Club; Glass Circle. *Hobby:* Antique Glass. *Address:* 33 Blenheim Road, Bedford Park, Chiswick, London W4 1ET, England.

WOOLLETT Elizabeth, b. 13 Mar 1959, Hillingdon, Middlesex, England. Singer (Soprano). *Education:* Studied at Royal Academy of Music from 1977. *Career:* Sang Magda in La Rondine and Irene in Donizetti's Belisario at the RAM; Opera North from 1984, as the Owl in The Cunning Little Vixen, Papagena, Kate Pinkerton, Mermaid in Oberon at La Fenice, Venice, Anna in Intermezzo and 2nd Maid in the British premiere of Strauss's Daphne; Scottish Opera debut 1989, as Mozart's Susanna; Buxton Festival 1990, as Amenaide in Tancredi; Debut Royal Opera House, Covent Garden 1991, as Clorinda in La Cenerentola; Other roles include Adina (L'Elisir d'Amore), Cherubino, Micaela, Bella (The Midsummer Marriage) and Despina; Isabella in L'Assedio di Calais, by Donizetti for Wexford Festival, 1991; Has also sung for BBC Radio 3 and has recorded works by Gilbert and Sullivan, for T.E.R. Records. *Honours include:* Alec Redshaw Memorial Award, Grimsby, 1986. *Address:* c/o Athole Still Ltd., Greystoke House, 80-86 Westow Street, London, SE19 3AF, England.

WOOLRICH John, b. 1954, England. Composer. *Education:* English at Manchester University; Composition with Edward Cowie, Lancaster University. *Career:* Northern Arts Fellow in Composition at Durham University 1982-85; Composer in Residence, National Centre for Orchestral Studies 1985-86; Animateur of various educational and music-theatre projects; Visiting Lecturer and Composer-in-Residence, Goldsmiths College, London, 1987-88; Artistic Director, Composers Ensemble, 1989-; Tutor, Guildhall School of Music, London, 1990-91; Composition teacher, Dartington Summer School, 1991-93; Professor, Stage Internacional de Musica de Cambra, 1992; Visiting Lecturer, Reading University, 1993. *Compositions:* Four Songs after Hoffmann for soprano and clarinet, 1981; Cascades for soprano and ensemble, 1983; Spalanzani's Daughter for instrumental ensemble 1983; Harlequinade, Black Riddle and Three Macedonian Songs, for soprano and chamber ensembles, 1983-84; Black Riddle for soprano and chamber orchestra, 1984; Songbook 2 and A Song of the Dark, both for orchestra, 1985-86; The Barber's Timepiece for orchestra 1986; Figures in a Landscape for chorus and orchestra 1986; Dartington Doubles for chamber ensemble, 1988; Light and Rock for soprano, basset clarinet and piano 1988; Night Machines for instrumental ensemble, 1988; The Kingdom of Dreams, 4 character pieces for oboe and piano 1989; Barcarolle for 6 players 1989; The Turkish Mouse for soprano and ensemble 1988; Ulysses Awakes, after Monteverdi, for string ensemble 1989; Lending Wings, 1989; The Ghost in the Machine, 1990; Berceuse, 1990; Quicksteps, 1990; The Death of King Renaud, 1991; The theatre represents a garden: night, 1991; It is midnight, Dr Schweitzer, 1992; A Farewell, 1992. *Address:* c/o Faber Music Limited, 3 Queen Square, London WC1N 3AU, England.

WORDSWORTH Barry, b. 1948, England. Conductor. *Education:* Studied at the Royal College of Music, London; Conducting with Adrian Boult in London and Harpsichord with Gustav Leonhardt in Amsterdam. *Debut:* Soloist in Frank Martin's Harpsichord Concerto at the Royal Opera House, for Kenneth Macmillan's ballet Las Hermanas. *Career:* Freelance conductor with the Royal Ballet, the Australian Ballet and the National Ballet of Canada (including performances at the Metropolitan, New York); Music Director of the BBC Concert Orchestra and the Brighton Philharmonic 1989; Music Director of the Royal Ballet and the Birmingham Royal Ballet 1991; debut with the Royal Opera at Covent Garden with Carmen, 1991; Conducted the BBC Concert Orchestra at the 1991 Promenade Concerts: Piano Concerto by Bliss, Malcolm Arnold's Guitar Concerto, Vaughan Williams 8th Symphony, Act 3 of Sleeping Beauty; Conducted Last Night of the Proms, with the BBC Symphony Orchestra, 1993. *Recordings include:* Series of British music with the BBC Concert Orchestra, 1990-91. *Hobbies:* Walking; Cooking; Photography; Swimming; Tennis. *Address:* ICM Artists (London), Oxford House, 76 Oxford Street, London, W1R 1RB, England.

WORKMAN William, b. 4 Feb 1940, Valdosta, Georgia, USA. Singer (Baritone). *Education:* Studied at Davidson College, at the Curtis Institute Philadelphia, Music Academy of the West in California and with Martial Singher. *Debut:* Hamburg 1965, in Fidelio. *Career:* Many performances at the Hamburg Staatsoper, notably in the premieres of Help, Help the Globolinks by Menotti (1967) and The Devils of Loudun by Penderecki (1969); Member of the Frankfurt Opera from 1972; Further appearances in Amsterdam, Paris, Strasbourg, Vienna, Geneva, Santa Fe and Dallas; German TV as Papageno in Die Zauberflöte; Season 1987-88, sang in Die schweigsame Frau at Santa Fe, as Ping in Pittsburgh and in Schreker's Der ferne Klang at Brussels. *Recordings include:* Zoroastre by Rameau (Turnabout). *Address:* c/o Théâtre Royal de la Monnaie, 4 Léopoldstrasse, B-1000 Brussels, Belgium.

WORTON-STEWARD Andrew, b. 20 Feb 1948, Kent, England. Course Tutor and Lecturer, 120th Music Open University; Composer; Organist. *Education:* BA, Honours, DMus, Cincinnati Conservatoire, USA, 1976; Diploma of Education; LLCM; ARCO. *Career:* Performances of own music, New York, Long Island, Milan, London, Manchester, Sydney, Australia, and worldwide; Music Adviser, Somerset University, England; Recital Tour on organ, Texas Gulf, USA, 1985; Recital Tour on organ, New York, 1986; Concert of Choral Works, New York, 1986; Broadcast BBC radio, 1987; Concert, Paris, 1987; Concert Purcell Room, 1987; Organist, Holy Trinity, New York, 1987-88. Commissions: Chichester Cathedral, 1987; Hove Festival, 1987; Hanover, 1988; Choral Masterclass, Tallahassee, Fl., 1988; Organ Recitals, St Thomas, St James, New York, 1988; TVS documentary Requiem in the series Music Makers, 1989. *Compositions:* (recorded) Chamber Music, 1978; Soli 3, 1980; Via Crucis, 1983; My Eyes for Beauty Pine; Oecumuse. Piano Music Published by Premiere. *Address:* c/o 105 Pembroke Crescent (White Lodge), Hove, Sussex, England.

WORTZELIUS Fredrik Inge, b. 11 Apr 1951, Uppsala, Sweden. Organist; Choirmaster. m. Ann-Christin Larsson, 3 June 1981, 2 daughters. *Education:* Swedish Gymnasium, 1970; Studies, musicology, University of Uppsala, 1970-75; Royal High School of Music, Stockholm, 1972-76. *Career:* Organist, Stigbergs Church, Uppsala 1971-72, Eriksberg Church, Uppsala 1972-76, Malung Church, 1977-78, 1980-89, Enköping Our Lady's Church 1979-80; Bollnäs Church, 1989-; Teacher, Geijer's Music School, Ransäter, 1978-82. *Recordings:* Record with Malung Youth Choir I, 1984; Record with Malung Youth Choir II, 1987. *Membership:* Lion's Club. *Hobby:* Photography. *Address:* Box 13, S-82101, Bollnäs, Sweden.

WOZNIAK Franciszek, b. 7 Aug 1932, Rawicz, Poland. Composer; Pianist; Teacher. *Education:* MA, Music Academy, Poznan, 1960. *Debut:* Poznan 1959. *Career:* Recitals; Chamberconcerts; Solo with orchestra; Radio recordings. *Compositions:* Cello Concerto; Symphony for percussion; 1st Symphony for piano and orchestra; Nonett; Copernicus' words for choir and piano. *Publication:* Co-author: Tadeusz Szeligowski, 1987. *Memberships:* Union of Polish Composers, Council Member 1975-83. *Honours:* Winner: Competition for Young Composers, 1960, Broniewski Music Competition, 1971. *Hobby:* Astronomy. *Address:* ul Dworcowa 49/8, 85-009 Bydgoszcz, Poland.

WRAY Steven Donald, b. 10 June 1959, Bolton, Lancs, England. Pianist. *Education:* BA Hons, Oxford (Queen's College), 1976-79; Private studies with Dorothea Law and Ruth Nye; International Summer Musical Academy, Salzburg, masterclasses with Hans Graf and Carmen Graf-Adnet, 1985-86; further studies at Hochschule für Musik and darstellende Kunst, Vienna. *Career:* Live Music Now! solo artist, 1985; solo recital Park Lane Group, Young Artists and Twentieth Century Music, Series, Purcell Room, London, 1988; Formation of duo with Czech violinist Tomas Tulacek, 1990; Concert and festival appearances, solo and duo recitals, ensemble and concerto engagements in Austria, the Czech Republic, Slovenia, Britain, Israel, Portugal. *Hobbies:* Walking; Cycling; Theatre; Reading; Languages. *Current Management:* Chameleon Arts Management. *Address:* 1 Brookes Court, Longley Road, London SW17 9LF, England.

WRIGHT Brian James, b. 4 Aug 1946, Tonbridge, Kent, England. Conductor. *Education:* Gulbenkian Scholar, Guildhall School of Music; Studies with George Hurst and Jascha Horenstein; Munich Music Academy, Germany. *Debut:* Royal Festival Hall, London, 1972 (Messiah). *Career:* Professional singer (Tenor) with English Opera Group; Recitals Wigmore Hall 1971, Purcell Room 1972; Associate Conductor Goldsmith's Choral Union 1972: Musical Director 1973; Conductor Highgate Choral Society 1972; Assistant Conductor London Symphony Orchestra 1974-75; Conductor BBC Symphony Orchestra Chorus 1976-84; Berlioz Requiem 1982; Liszt's Christus; 1985- Guest Conductor with UK orchestras: London Symphony (Mendelssohn 3, Sibelius 2); Philharmonia (Beethoven 6); Hallé (Brahms 2); Bournemouth Symphony (A Child of our Time, Verdi Requiem); Scottish National (Dvořák Requiem); Royal Liverpool Philharmonic (Hugh Wood Symphony); World and UK premieres of works by Robert Simpson, Wilfred Josephs, Penderecki and Lutoslawski; First complete performance of Furtwängler's 3rd Symphony; Season 1988-89 conducted Tippett's Mask of Time on South Bank and Stravinsky's Pulcinella for BBC TV; Season 1990 with the Bach B Minor Mass at the Barbican the Verdi Requiem at the Festival Hall, and concerts with the RPO, BBC and BBC Welsh Symphony Orchestras. *Honours include:* Silver Medal, Guido Cantelli Competition, Milan 1975. *Hobbies:* Singing; Reading; DIY. *Address:* c/o Norman McCann International Artists Ltd., The Coach House, 56 Lawrie Park Gardens, London SE26 6XJ, England.

WRIGHT David Arthur, b. 16 Apr 1934, Leamington Spa, Warwickshire. Organist; Conductor; Director of Music; Lecturer; Examiner. m. Joan Gelsthorp, ARCM, 12 Aug 1961, 1 son. *Education:* Lichfield Cathedral Choir School, 1942-45; King Edward's School, Birmingham, 1946-52; Organ Scholar, Exeter College, Oxford, 1952-56; BMus.; MA (Oxon); FRCO. *Career:* Assistant Organist, New College, Oxford, 1956-57; Organist and Choirmaster, Boston Parish Church, 1957-; Director of Music, Boston Grammar School, 1957-; Conductor, Boston Choral Society, Boston Chamber Orchestra and Sine Nomine Orchestra, 1957-; Tutor, Extra-Mural Department, Nottingham University, 1958-69; Examiner, Associated Board of The Royal Schools of Music, 1969-; Various TV and Radio Broadcasts. *Compositions:* Church and Educational Music. *Recordings:* Organ and Church Music. *Honours:* FRCO, Limpus Prize, 1955. *Membership:* President, South and East Lincolnshire Organists Association. *Hobbies:* Photography; Motor-Car Mechanisms; Table Tennis. *Address:* 118 Fishtoft Road, Boston, Lincolnshire PE21 0DG, England.

WRIGHT Gordon Brooks, b. 31 Dec 1934, New York City, USA. Symphony Conductor. m. 2 sons, 1 daughter. *Education:* BMus, College of Wooster, 1957; MA, University of Wisconsin, Madison. *Career:* Founder and Music Director, Madison Summer Orchestra (now Wisconsin Chamber Orchestra), 1960-69; Musical Director, Fairbanks Light Opera Theatre, 1975, 1980 and 1988; Musical Director, University of Alaska Opera Workshop, 1969, 1971, 1974, 1977; Orchestral Conductor, Western Opera of San Francisco, 1974, 1978, 1980; Guest conductor of numerous orchestras; Music Director and Conductor, Fairbanks Symphony Orchestra, 1969-89; Founder and Conductor, Arctic Chamber Orchestra, 1970-89; Professor of Music, University of Alaska Fairbanks, 1969-89; Founder and Executive Director, Reznicek Society, 1982-; Professor Emeritus, University of Alaska, 1989; Music Director Emeritus, Fairbanks Symphony Orchestra, 1989. *Compositions:* Toccata Festiva, 1992; Suite for Piano and Orchestra (Scott Joplin), 1987; 1984 Overture, 1984; Sally Gardens, 1984; Canzona (G Gabrieli), 1983;

Freest Fancy, 1982; Grumbling Old Man, 1982; Heigh Ho, to the Greenwood!, 1982; Symphony in Ursa Major, 1978; Transitional Metamorphoses, 1976; Six Alaskan Tone Poems, 1976; Suite of Netherlands Dances, 1966. *Hobbies:* Hiking; Kayaking; Photography. *Contributions to:* Beato Music Inc, (Japan); Elsewhere, Turnagain Music, Indian, Alaska, USA. *Address:* HC 52, PO Box 8899, Indian, AK 99540, USA.

WRIGHT Rosemarie, b. 12 Dec 1931, Chorley, Lancashire, England. Concert Pianist. m. Michel Brandt, 28 Oct 1961, 2 sons. *Education:* Royal Academy of Music, London; Staatsakademie, Vienna; Master classes with Edwin Fischer, Pablo Casals, and Wilhelm Kempff. *Debut:* Grosser Musikvereinssaal, Vienna, 1960. *Career:* Concerts throughout Europe, USA, Far East, Australasia; Broadcasts world-wide. Concertos with London Philharmonic, Philharmonia, English Chamber Orchestra, London Mozart Players, BBC Orchestras, Vienna Symphony Orchestra, and Danish and French Radio; Professor of Piano, RNCM, Manchester, 1973-78, Royal Academy of Music, London, 1978-; Pianist in Residence, Southampton University, 1972-80. *Recordings:* Piano works of Edward Macdowell; Volumes I and II of Haydn Sonatas on 1799 Broadwood Fortepiano. *Honours:* Chappell Silver Medal, 1953; Tobias Matthay Fellowship, 1954; Haydn Prize, Vienna, 1959; Bosendorfer Prize, 1960. *Memberships:* British Federation of Festivals for Music, Dance and Speech, (adjudicator). *Hobbies:* Flowers; 19th-century painting; Literature. *Address:* 84 Filsham Road, Hastings, East Sussex TN38 0PG, England.

WROBLEWSKI Patryk, b. 4 Dec 1956, Mishawaka, Indiana, USA. Singer (Baritone). *Debut:* Sang Malatesta at the 1980 Blossom Festival. *Career:* Recent appearances as Fernando in La Gazza Ladra at Philadelphia, Silvio, Valentin and Monteverdi's Orfeo at Dallas; Lyric Opera of Chicago as Germont and Marcello and in Satyagraha by Glass; Opera Grand Rapids as Don Giovanni; Season 1991-92 with debut at the New York City Opera, as Zurga in Les pecheurs de perles and as Silvio; Puccini's Lescaut with Greater Miami Opera and Sivio at the Munich Staatsoper (European stage debut); Season 1992-93 as Zurga in Holland, Taddeo in L'Italiana in Algeri at Dublin, and Marcello and Rossini's Figaro for the New Israel Opera; Concert appearances with the Chicago Symphony under Leppard and the Grant Park Concerts under Leonard Slatkin; Santa Fe Opera, Young Lord; Weill, The Protagonist; Dublin Grand Opera, Marcello La Bohème; Manitoba Opera, Zurga (Canada). *Honours include:* Grand Prize at the 1984 Rosa Ponselle International Competition; Winner, Luciano Pavarotti Competition, 1985.*Address:* c/o Atholl Still Ltd. Greystoke House, 80-86 Westrow Street, London SE19 3AF, England.

WU Zuqiang, b. 24 July 1927, Peking, China. Professor, China's Central Conservatory of Music; Vice-Executive Chairman, China Federation of Literary and Art Circles. m. Zheng Liqin, 29 Jan. 1953. 1 son, 1 daughter. *Education:* Graduate, Composition Department, China's Central Conservatory of Music, 1952; Graduate, Tchaikovsky Music Conservatory, Moscow, 1958. *Career:* Teacher 1952, Senior Lecturer 1962, Associate Professor 1978, Deputy President, Central Conservatory of Music, 1978-81, President, 1982-88, Professor 1983- and Supervisor of doctoral work, 1988-86, Head of Composition Section, China's Central Philharmonic Orchestra, 1972-75; Vice-Executive Chairman, China Federation of Literary and Art Circles, 1988-; member, Board of Directors, China's Copyright Agency Corporation, 1988-; Advisor, Chinese Music Copyright Association, 1993-. *Compositions:* String Quartet, 1957; The Mermaid (Dance drama), 1958; Red Women's Detachment (ballet), 1964; Moon reflected in the Erquan Pool (string orchestra), 1976; Young Sisters of the Grassland (pipa concerto), 1973-76; Analysis of Music Form and Composition (Text-book) won excellent text-book prize of National Universities and colleges, 1987; Appointed Judge at many domestic and international music contests. *Hobbies:* Literature;

Fine Arts; Travelling. *Address:* Central Conservatory of Music, 43 Baojia Street, Beijing 100031, China.

WULSTAN David, b. 18 Jan.1937, Birmingham, England. Professor of Music. m. Susan Nelson Graham, 9 Oct 1967. 1 son. *Education:* BSc, College of Technology, Birmingham; BA (1st class) Music 1963, Fellow 1964, MA 1966, Magdalen College, Oxford. *Career:* Founder and Director, The Clerkes of Oxenford, 1961-; Numerous appearances on BBC (Television and Radio 3); Thames TV; NWDR; BRT; Cheltenham, York, Bologna, Holland, Flowers Festivals, Proms and various films; Visiting Professor, University of California, Berkeley, USA, 1977; Professor of Music, Univ College, Cork, 1980; Professor of Music, University College, Aberystwyth, Wales, 1983-1990; Reserch Professor, 1991- *Compositions:* Various Christmas carols, Film music. *Recordings:* Tallis; Sheppard (Classics for Pleasure); Gibbons, Play of Daniel; Robert White; Tallis; Sheppard (Calliope). *Publications:* Early English Church Music, Vols 3, 1964, Vols 27, 1979; Anthology of Carols, 1968; Anthology of English Church Music, 1971; Play of Daniel, 1976; Coverdale Chant Book, 1978; Complete works, 1979-; Tudor Music, 1984 and many others. *Contributions to:* Journal of Theological Studies; Iraq; Journal of the American Oriental Society; Music and Letters; Galpin Society Journal; Musical Times. *Membership:* Member of Council, Plainsong & Medieval Music Society. *Hobbies:* Cooking and eating; Tennis; Badminton; Semitic philology. *Address:* Ty Isaf, Lianilar, Aberystwyth, Dyfed, Wales SY23 4NP.

WUORINEN Charles, b. 9 June 1938, New York City, USA. Composer. *Education:* Attended Columbia University, BA, 1961, MA 1963. *Career:* With Harvey Sollberger founded the Group for Contemporary Music 1962; Teacher at Columbia University 1964-71; Visiting lecturer at Princeton University, 1969-71; New England Conservatory, 1968-71; Manhattan School of Music from 1971-79; Professor of Music, Rutgers University, 1984-; Visiting Professor, New York University, 1990; Distinguished Visiting Professor, State University of New York at Buffalo, 1989-; Visiting Professor, Yale University, 1991 and 1983; Composer-in-residence at: Ojai Festival, 1975, Universities of Iowa, South Florida, the Berkshire Music Center, the Chamber Music Northwest, 1978, Grand Teton Music Festival, 1979 and 1980, San Francisco Symphony (and New Music Adviser to Music Director Herbert Blomstedt), 1985-89; American Academy in Rome, 1990; Santa Fe Chamber Music Festival, 1993. *Compositions include:* Stage: The Politics of Harmony 1968 and The W. of Babylon; Orchestral: Music for orchestra 1956; Orchestral and Electronic Exchanges 1965; 3 Piano Concertos 1966, 1975, 1984; Contrafactum 1969; Grand Bamboula 1971; Concerto for amplified violin and orchestra 1972; Ancestors for chamber orchestra 1972; The Magic Art: An Instrumental Masque, after Purcell 1978; Two-part Symphony 1978; Short Suite 1981; Concertino for 15 instruments, 1984; Crossfire, 1984; Movers and Shakers 1984; Rhapsody for violin and orchestra 1984; Prelude to Kullervo, for tuba and orchestra, 1985; Electronic piece Time's Encomium 1970; Concerto for Saxophone Quartet and Orchestra 1993; The Mission of Virgil, for orchestra, 1993; Chamber Music includes 3 String Quartets 1971, 1979, 1987; Horn Trio 1981 & 1985; Divertimento, for string quartet 1982; Divertimento, for alto sax and piano, 1982; Piano Trio 1983; Trombone Trio 1985; Vocal Music includes Genesis for chorus and orchestra, The Celestial Sphere, oratorio, 1980; Mass for soprano, chorus, violin 3 trombones and organ; Piano and Organ music; many keyboards works including 3 Sonatas; A Winter's Tale, (two versions), soprano and chamber and w/piano, 1991, 1992; Saxophone Quartet, 1992. *Publications:* Charles Wuorinen, a Bio-Bibliography by Richard Burbank. *Honours include:* Joseph Bearns Prize 1958, 1959, 1961; American Academy and Institute of Arts and Letters Award 1967; Guggenheim Fellowship, 1968, 1972; Pulitzer Prize for Time's Encomium 1970; Rockefeller Foundation Fellowship, 1979, 1981, 1982; Institute of the American Academy and Instiute of Arts and Letters 1985; MacArthur Foundation Fellowship, 1986-91. *Current Management:* c/o Howard Stokar

Management, *Address:* c/o Howard Stokar Management, 870 West End Avenue, New York, NY 10025, USA.

WUTHRICH Hans, b. 3 Aug 1937, Aeschi, Switzerland. Composer. m. Beatrice Mathez, 6 May 1977. 1 daughter. *Education:* Piano and Violin studies, Conservatory of Music, Berne, 1957-62; Studies of composition with Klaus Huber, Academy of Music, 1968-74; Doctor's Degree, University of Zurich, 1973. *Career:* Lecturer, Linguistics, Zurich University, 1971-85; Teacher, Winterthur Conservatory, 1985-; Performances of compositions in Donaueschingen, 1978, 1985; at ISCM World Music Festival Bonn, 1977, Athens, 1979. *Compositions:* Kommunikationsspiele, 1973; Das Glashaus, 1974-75; Netz-Werke I, II, 1983-85; Annaeherungen An Gegenwart, 1986-87; Procuste Deux Etoiles, 1980-81; Supplement: Netz-Werk III, 1987-89; Chopin im TGV Basel-Paris, 1989; Wörter Bilder Dinge, 1990-91. *Recording:* Procuste Deux Etoiles, 1980-81. *Contributions to:* Interface, Vol 12, 1983; Musiktheorie, 1987. *Honours:* Prize, Composers Competition, Zurich, 1972; Prize, International Composers Competition, Boswil, 1974, 1976, 1978; Grand Prix Paul Gilson de la CRPLF, 1984. *Address:* Kirchgasse 4, CH-4144 Arlesheim, Switzerland.

WYN-ROGERS Catherine, b. 1958, England. Singer (Contralto). *Education:* Studied at the Royal College of Music with Meriel St. Clair and afterwards with Ellis Keeler and Diane Forlano. *Career:* Regular concerts with the Bach Choir under David Willcocks in London and abroad; frequent appearances with Britain's major orchestras; tours with English Concert and Trevor Pinnock including Messiah in Germany and Vivaldi's Gloria in Rome for TV/Deutsche Grammophon recording; Appearances at the Proms with the Sixteen, the National Youth Orchestra and the English Concert Opera including, Il Ritorno d'Ulisse for English National Opera and Stuttgart, Rigoletto in Nantes, La Gioconda for Opera North, Die Zauberflöte for the ROH and Salzburg Festival. *Recordings:* Vaughan Williams's Serenade to Music and Magnificat with Matthew Best for Hyperion, Teixera Te Deum and Bach's Christmas Oratorio with the Sixteen for Collins Classics, Elgar's Dream of Gerontius with Vernon Handley and the Royal Liverpool Philharmonic for EMI. *Honours include:* College Song Recital Prize, Dame Clara Butt Award and grant from Countess of Munster trust (RCM). *Current Management:* Lies Askonas Ltd. *Address:* Lies Askonas Ltd, 186 Drury Lane, London WC2B 5RY, England.

WYNER Susan Davenny, b. 17 Oct 1945, New Haven, Connecticut, USA. Singer (Soprano). *Education:* Graduated Cornell University 1965; Vocal studies with Herta Glaz (1969-75). *Debut:* Carnegie Hall recital 1972. *Career:* Alice Tully Hall recital 1973; Orchestral debut with the Boston Symphony 1974; Engagements with all the leading orchestras in the USA and Canada; Israel Philharmonic and London Symphony; repertoire includes Baroque and contemporary works; Operatic debut as Monteverdi's Poppea, New York City Opera 1977; Metropolitan Opera 1982, as Woglinde in Das Rheingold; Has sung in the premieres of Del Tredici's Adventures Underground 1975 and Carter's A Mirror on Which to Dwell 1976, and in the premieres of Memorial Music and Fragments from Antiquity by Yehudi Wyner; Also sings works by Rochberg (Quartet No.2) and Reimann (Inane).

WYNER Yehudi, b. 1 June 1929, Calgary, Alberta, Canada. Composer; Pianist; Conductor. m. Susan Davenny Wyner. *Education:* Studied at the Juilliard School, then at Yale University with Paul Hindemith (BMus 1951, MMus 1953); Further study with Walter Piston at Harvard University (MA 1952). *Career:* American Academy in Rome 1953-56; Performed and recorded contemporary music in New York; Directed the Turnau Opera; Teacher at Yale School of Music from 1963, Chairman of Composition 1969-73; Music Director of the New Haven Opera Society, and keyboard player with the Bach Aria Group; Berkshire Music Center 1975; Professor of Music at Purchase, State University of New York, 1978; Dean of Music 1978-82. *Compositions:* Dance variations for wind octet 1953; Piano Sonata 1954; Concerto Duo for violin and piano 1957; 3 Informal Pieces for violin and piano 1961; Friday Evening Service for cantor, chorus and organ 1963; Torah Service 1966; Da Camera for piano and orchestra 1967; Cadenza for clarinet and harpsichord 1969; De novo for cello and ensemble 1971; Canto cantabile for soprano and band 1972; Memorial Music for soprano and 3 flutes 1971-73; Intermedio for soprano and strings 1974; Dances of Atonement for violin and piano 1976; Fragments from Antiquity for soprano and orchestra 1978-81; All the Rage for flute and piano 1980, Romances for piano quartet 1980; Tanz and Maissele for clarinet, violin, cello and piano 1981; On this Most Voluptuous Night for soprano and 7 instruments 1982; Passage I for ensemble 1983; Wind Quintet 1984; String Quartet, 1985; Composition for Viola and Piano, 1987; Toward the Center for piano, 1988; Changing Time for small ensemble, 1991; Il Cane Minore for 2 clarinets and bassoon, 1992; Concerto for cello and orch, 1994 . *Honours include:* Guggenheim Fellowships 1958-59, 1977-78; NEA Grant 1976; Commissions from the Ford Foundation, Delos String Quartet and the Aeolian Chamber Players. *Address:* c/o ASCAP, ASCAP Building, One Lincoln Plaza, New York NY 10023, USA.

WYTON Alec, b. 3 Aug 1921, London, England. Composer; Organist. m. 26 Nov 1979, Mary Broman, 4 sons. *Education:* Oxford University; BA 1945, MA 1949, Royal Academy of Music. *Career:* Sub-organist, Christ Church, Oxford, 1943-46; Organist/Choirmaster, St Matthew's Northampton, 1946-50; Organist/Choirmaster, Christ Church Cathedral, St Louis, Missouri, 1950-54; Organist/Choirmaster, Cathedral of St John the Divine, New York, 1954-74; Organist/Choirmaster, St James, New York, 1974-87; Organist/Choirmaster, St Stephen's, Ridgefield, Connecticut, 1987-; Adjunct Professor, Union Seminary, New York, 1956-73; Visiting Professor, Westminster Choir College, Princeton, New Jersey, 1965-73; Co-ordinator, Standing Commission on Church Music of the Episcopal Church in the US, 1974-86. *Compositions:* Many works for choir, organ, soloists and instruments; Opera: The Journey with Jonah. *Publication:* The Anglican Chant Psalter (Church Pension Fund) 1987. *Contributions to:* The American Organist, The Diapason; The Living Church; Christianity To-day; Musical Times. *Honours:* ASCAP Annual Award since 1967; FRCO (ChM), FRAM; FRSCM; FAGO; FRCCO; Hon D Mus, Susquehanna University. *Memberships:* President, American Guild of Organists 1964- 69; The Bohemians (New York Musicians Club) President 1976-78. *Hobbies:* Walking; Reading. *Address:* 25 Pound Street, Ridgefield, CT 06877, USA.

WYZNER Franz, b. 1932, Vienna, Austria. Singer (Bass). *Education:* Studied in Vienna. *Career:* Sang at the Landestheater Salzburg, 1958-59, Gelsenkirchen, 1959-64; Wuppertal,1964-85, notably in the German premiere of Crime and Punishment by Petrovic, 1971, and the first performance of The Gamblers by Shostakovich in the arrangement by K Meyer, 1986; Guest appearances at the Schwetzingen Festival, 1970, Vienna Volksoper (Austrian premiere of The Burning Fiery Furnace by Britten, 1977), Salzburg Festival (Dantons Tod, 1983), Buenos Aires (Alberich, 1983) and Cologne, 1985; Other roles have included Mozart's Leporello, Figaro, Papageno and Alfonso, Kaspar in Der Freischütz, Don Magnifico, Mephistopheles, the Doctor in Wozzeck and Kecal in The Bartered Bride. *Recordings include:* Dantons Tod (Orfeo). *Address:* Theater am Gärtnerplatz, Gärtnerplatz 3, 8000 Munich 1, Germany.

X

XENAKIS Iannis, b. 29 May 1922, Braila, Romania. Composer; Architect; Civil Engineer. m. Francoise Gargouil, 3 Dec. 1953, 1 daughter. *Education:* Polytechnic School, Athens, Greece; Ecole Normale Musique, Paris, France; Paris Conservatoire; Composition with Hermann Scherchen, Olivier Messiaen, Darius Milhaud, France and Switzerland. *Career:* Architectural collaborator with Le Corbusier, Paris, France, 12 years; Designs include Philips Pavilion, Brussels World Fair, Belgium, 1958, Polytope French pavilion, Montreal, Quebec, Canada, 1967, Persepolis, 1971, and Polytope de Cluny, Paris, France, 1972-74; Director, Founder, Centre d'Etudes de Mathematique et Automatique Musicales, Paris, 1966-, and Centre for Mathematics and Automated Music, Indiana University, USA, 1967-72; The Bacchae premiered by Opera Factory, London 1993. *Compositions:* 63 compositions for all media including: ST/10- 1,080262 for 10 instruments, 1957-62; Achorripsis for chamber orchestra, 1958; Syrmos for chamber orchestra, 1959; Analogiques for instruments and tape, 1959; Atrees (Hommage a Pascal) for 10 instruments. 1962; Bohor, 8 track electroacoustic music, 1962; Strategie for orchestra and 2 conductors, 1962; Duet for 54 instruments and 2 conductors, 1963; Nuits for 12 voices, 1968; Momos Gamma, 1968; Persephassa, 1969; Hibiki-Hana-Ma (12 tapes distributed kinematically over 800 speakers), 1970; Antikhthon, 1971; Aroura, 1971; Linaia-Agon, 1972; Bridanos, 1973; Cendrees, 1974; Erikhthon, 1974; Gmeeoorh, 1974; Noomena, 1974; Empreintes, 1975; Phlegra, 1975; Psappha, 1975; N'Shima, 1975; Khoai, 1976; Epei, 1976; Dmaathen, 1976; Kottos, 1977; Akanthas, 1977; á Hélène, 1977; La Légende d'Er, 1977; á Colone, 1977; Akanthas, 1977; á Hééne, 1977; La Légende d'Er, 1977; á Colone, 1977; Jonchaies, 1977; Diatope, 1978; Polytope at Mycenae, 1978; Pleiades, 1978; Ais, 1980; Nekuia, 1981; Palimpsest for piano and ensemble, 1982; Keqrops for piano and orchestra, 1986; Alax for 3 instrumental ensembles 1985; Thallein for 14 instruments 1985; Idmen A for chorus and 4 percussionists 1985; Akea for piano and sting quartet 1986; Horos for orchestra 1986; Jalons for 15 instruments 1986; Tracées for orchestra 1987; Ata for orchestra 1987; Waarg for 13 instruments 1988; Okho 1989; Rebonds A and B for percussion 1989; Echange for bass clarinet and 13 instruments 1989; Voyage vers Andomède 1989; Epicyles for cello and 12 instruments 1989; Knephas for chorus 1990; Tuorakemsu for orchestra 1990; Kyania for orchestra; Tetora for string quartet 1990; Doxorkh for violin and orchestra 1991; Music for The Bacchae by Euripides, 1992. *Publications:* Musiques Formelles, 1963; Musique-Architecture, 1970; Formalized music, 1971. *Contributions to:* Professional journals. *Honours:* Maurice Ravel Gold Medal, 1974; Honorary member, American Academy of Arts and Letters, National Institute of Arts and Letters. *Address:* 9 rue Chaptal, 75009 Paris, France.

Y

YAHIA Mino, b. 1928, Alexandria, Egypt. Singer (Bass-baritone). *Education:* Studied in New York and Europe. *Career:* Sang at the Heidelberg Stadttheater 1955-56, Kiel 1956-57, Nuremberg 1957-60; appearances at the Bayerische Staatsoper Munich from 1960, notably in the 1963 premiere of Die Verlobung in San Domingo by Werber Egk; Salzburg Festival 1961, in the premiere of Das Bergwerk zu Falun by Wagner-Regeny; Further guest appearances at the Vienna Staatsoper (Hunding in Die Walküre), Buenos Aires (Strauss's Barak, 1965), Hanover and with the New York Concert Opera, in the local premiere of Die Frau ohne Schatten; Other roles have included Wagner's Daland, King Henry, Marke, Pogner, Fafner and Hagen; Ariodate in Handel's Xerxes, Publio (La Clemenza di Tito), Verdi's Zaccaria and Sparafucile, and Gremin in Eugene Onegin. *Address:* c/o Bayerische Staatsoper, Postfach 100148, 8000 Munich 1, Germany.

YAKAR Rachel, b. 3 Mar 1938, Lyon, France. Singer (Soprano). *Education:* Studied at the Paris Conservatoire and with Germaine Lubin. *Career:* Sang with the Deutsche Oper am Rhein Dusseldorf from 1964, in L'Incoronazione di Poppea, A Midsummer Night's Dream, Honegger's Judith, Don Pasquale, and as Antonia in Les Contes d'Hoffmann; Aix-en-Provence 1966, in Ariadne auf Naxos; Strasbourg Opera 1967, in a new production of Der junge Lord by Henze; Amsterdam 1968-69, as Cleopatra in Giulio Cesare and as Marguerite; Messiaen Festival Dusseldorf 1969; Paris Opéra 1970, as Gilda and Micaela; Baroque repertoire from 1971 includes La Rappresentazione di Anima e di Corpo by Cavallieri, Deidamia by Handel, Cavalli's L'Ormindo (Erisbe) and Saul; Munich Festival 1974, as Donna Elvira; Bayreuth Festival 1976, as Freia and Gerhilde in Patrice Chéreau's centenary production of Der Ring des Nibelungen; Glyndebourne Festival 1977, 1980, as Donna Elvira and the Marschallin; Strasbourg and Dusseldorf 1978, as Mélisande; Cycle of operas by Monteverdi at Zurich, 1978; Geneva Opera 1981, as Janáček's Jenůfa; Returned to Aix 1983, in a revival of Mozart's Mitridate; Guest appearances in San Francisco, East Berlin, Edinburgh, Lausanne, Monte Carlo and Santiago; Other roles include Mozart's Ilia and Fiordiligi; Sang the Marschallin at Amsterdam 1987; Madame Lidoine in Dialogues des Carmélites at Lyons, 1990. *Recordings:* Les Indes Galantes by Rameau (CBS); Admeto, Le Bourgeois Gentilhomme (EMI); Idomeneo, Monteverdi Orfeo, Dido and Aeneas (Telefunken); Bach B Minor Mass, Lully's Armide (Erato); Christmas Story and Magnificat by Schütz (Orfeo); Baroque Cantatas by Fux and Scarlatti; Rameau's Pygmalion (Electrola); Circe in Scylla et Glaucus by Leclair; Die Zauberflöte, from the Salzburg Festival, conducted by James Levine. *Address:* Ingpen & Williams Ltd., 14 Kensington Court, London W8 5DN, England.

YAMADA Yoichi, b. 30 Oct 1955, Yamaguchi, Japan. Associate Professor of Ethnomusicology. m. 5 Mar 1978. 1 daughter. *Education:* BA 1978, MA 1981, Ph.D. 1989, Osaka University. *Career:* Associate Professor of Ethnomusicology, Shimane University. *Publications:* Musical Voices of Asia, 1980; Dance and Music in South Asian Drama, 1983; Aspects of Sonic Performance, 1987; Ethnic Music, 1987; Music of Japan and Asia, 1988. *Contributions to:* Musical performance as a means of socialization among the Iatmoi, Bikmaus, 1983; Institutionalized musical experiences among the Iatmoi, Papua New Guinea, Ethno-Arts, 1986. *Memberships:* International Council for Traditional Music; The Society for Ethnomusicology; The Japanese Society for Musicology; The Society for Ethno-Arts. *Address:* c/o Department of Music, Shimane University, 1060 Nishikawatsu, Matsue, Shimane, 690 Japan.

YANAGITA Masako, b. 30 Mar 1944, Tokyo, Japan. Violinist. m. Abba Bogin. *Education:* Artist Diploma, Mannes College of Music, New York City, USA; Studied with Eijin Tanaka, Louis Graeler, William Kroll. *Debut:* Tokyo, 1966. *Career:* Concert appearances throughout USA, Europe, Near & Far East; Soloist, orchestras in Japan, UK, Germany, Philippines, USA; 1st violinist, toured with Vieuxtemps String Quartet; Faculty member, Mannes College of Music. *Honours:* Silverstein Prize, Berkshire Music Center, Massachusetts, 1966; Carl Flesch Competition, London, UK, 1968; Paganini Competition, Genoa, Italy, 1968; Munich International Competition, 1969. *Current Management:* Raymond Weiss Artists Management, New York City, USA. *Address:* 838 West End Avenue, New York, NY 10025, USA.

YANG Sungsic, b. 1966, Korea. Concert Violinist. *Education:* Studied at the Paris Conservatoire and with Yfrah Neaman at the Guildhall School of Music, 1987. *Debut:* Recital in Seoul 1977. *Career:* Solo appearances throughout Europe, including tour with the Seoul Philharmonic, Tchaikovsky and Mendelssohn Concertos with the Moscow Philharmonic at Seoul for the Olympic Festival 1988; Paris concerto debut with Orchestre National de France conducted by Lorin Maazel, Sept 1988; BBC Radio recording 1988; Appearances with National Symphony Orchestra (RTE, Dublin) and Gävleborgs SymfoniorKester (Sweden) 1991; Plays a Joseph Guarneri del Gesu of 1720. Repertoire also includes Concertos by Bach, Brahms, Bruch, Beethoven, Mozart, Prokofiev, Saint-Saens, Sibelius and Wieniawski; Solo works by Bach, Sonatas by Brahms, Beethoven, Mozart, Prokofiev, Saint-Saëns, Sibelius and Wieniawski; Solo works by Bach, Sonatas by Brahms, Beethoven, Debussy, Fauré, Franck, Tartini and Ysaye; Stravinsky's Suite Italienne. *Honours:* Prixewinner in Paganini Competition Genoa, Long-Thibaud Paris, Indianapolis USA; First Prize, Carl Flesch Competition, London 1988.

YARBOROUGH William, b. 3 Jan 1926, Wilmington, North Carolina, USA. Symphony Conductor. m. Ruth M Feldt, 29 Jan 1955. *Education:* BM, Chicago Musical College and University of Chicago; MM, Indiana University; studied with Frank Gittelson, Nadia Boulanger, Vittorio Rieti and Serge Koussevitsky; Studied at Peabody Conservatory and Berkshire Music Center. *Debut:* As Conductor, aged 19, American Symphony in Paris; As Concert Violinist, aged 8. *Career:* Music Director and Conductor, American Symphony Orchestra, Paris, France, Richmond Philharmonic Orchestra, Richmond, Virginia, USA; Radio broadcasts: Appearances at Michigan's Bach-Mozart Festival; Music Director/Conductor Michigan's Bach-Mozart Festival; Performances with Touring American Opera Company and American Chamber Orchestra at present; Music Director, Conductor, American Chamber Orchestra, Washington DC since 1980; Guest Conductor many of the major symphonies in Europe and USA, including Royal Philharmonic, Vienna Symphony, St Cecilia Orchestra in Rome, Boston Symphony and Philadelphia Orchestra; Numerous Radio and TV appearances; Speaker, Chicago Adult Education Council; Music Advisor, Old Dominion Symphony Council. *Contributions to:* Journal of the American Musicological Society. *Hobbies:* Golf; Travel; People. *Address:* American Chamber Orchestra Society, 4201 Cathedral Avenue, NW., Suite 706-E, Washington, DC 20016, USA.

YARON Gilah, b. 1941, Tel-Aviv, Israel. Singer (Sorpano). *Education:* Studied in Tel-Aviv and with Gunther Reich, George London and Elisabeth Schwarzkopf. *Career:* Sang with the Israel Philharmonic and other orchestras from 1970; Israel Festival 1972, Bach's Magnificat; Sang in Switzerland and other European centres from 1975 (Berlin concert with works by Hindemith and Webern); Guest appearances in Austria, Belgium, Holland, Italy Denmark and England; Psaumes Hebraiques by Markevitch and Poèmes pour Mi by Messiaen; other repertoire includes Penderecki's St. Luke Passion, Mahler's 2nd. Symphony and Mendelssohn's music for A Midsummer Night's Dream; Singing Teacher, The Rubin Academy of music and dance, Jerusalem, 1982-. *Address:* c/o POB 2179, Bat-Yam 59121, Israel.

YASSA Ramzi, b. 15 Mar 1948, Cairo, Egypt. Pianist.

m. Brigitte Chevrot, 7 June 1978, 1 son, 1 daughter. *Education:* Lycee of Heliopolis; Diploma, Cairo Conservatory, 1968; Tchaikovsky Conservatory, Moscow, 1969-74; FTCL, 1972; Licence de Concert, Ecole Normale, Paris, 1977. *Career:* Appearances: The Barbican, London with Royal Philharmonic Orchestra, conductor Sir Charles Groves, Kennedy Center, Mann Auditorium with IPO, conductor Zubin Mehta, Musikverien, Palau (Barcelona), Theatre des Champs Elysees and South Bank, London; TV Mondovision with Zubin Mehta, 1987; Inaugural concert, Cairo Opera House, 1988; BBC recordings and live broadcasts; Adjudicator, international piano competitions; Appearances with Sir Yehudi Menuhin, Conductor. *Recordings:* Tchaikovsky, The Seasons, Ades, France; Prokofiev, Cinderella, 2nd Sonata, Pavane, Belgium; Chopin, Ballades and opus 22, Pavane, Belgium. *Honours:* Prizewinner of Marguerite Long Competition, 1971; G B Viotti Competition, 1972; Certificate of Honour, Tchaikovsky Competition, 1974; 1st Grand Prix, Paloma O'Shea International Competition, Santander, Spain, 1977; Recipient, Franz Liszt Centenary Commemorative Medal. *Address:* 14 Rue Sainte Cecile, 75009 Paris, France.

YAUGER Margaret, b. 1947, Birmingham, Alabama, USA. Opera Singer (Mezzo-Soprano). m. Malcolm Smith, 4 Oct 1975. *Education:* BM, Converse College; MM, New England Conservatory of Music; Special studies, American Opera Centre, Juilliard School of Music, New York City; Goldovsky Opera Studio. *Debut:* American National Opera Company, Sarah Caldwell, Conductor. *Career:* Performances with New York Lyce Opera, 1973-75, Central City Opera Festival, 1973-76, Lake George Opera Festival, 1972-74, Boris Goldovsky Opera Tour, 1973-74, Mexico City Opera, Teatro Regio Turin, Italy; Knoxville, Tennessee Opera; Birmingham Alabama Civic Opera; Fort Worth, Texas Opera; Deutsch Oper am Rhein, Dusseldorf, West Germany, 1977-86; Krefeld, Hanover, Karlsruhe, Freiburg, Wiesbaden and Gelsenkirchen West Germany, Opera Houses; Solingen, Duisburg, Münchengladbach-Krefeld, Trier, West Germany Symphonies; East Berlin Radio; Dresden Philharmonic; Fricka, Das Rheingold, Washington National Symphony; Margret, Wozzeck, Boston Symphony Orchestra; 3rd Magd, Elektra, London Symphony Orchestra; Heidelberg Schloss, Festspiele, 1992; Delaware Symphony Orchestra, Verdi Requiem, 1993; Mahler Symphony No 2, Roanoke Symphony, 1994. *Recordings:* Beethoven Symphony No. 9, alto part with Mexico City Symphony. *Current Management:* Thea Dispecker, Artists' Representative, 59E 54th Street, New York, NY 10022, USA. *Address:* Markgrafenstr 10, 40545 Dusseldorf, Germany.

YE Xiaogang, b. 23 Sept 1955, Shanghai, China. Composer; Lecturer, Musical Composition. m. 17 May 1987. *Education:* BA, Central Conservatory of Music, Peking, China; MM, Eastman School of Music, Rochester, USA. *Compositions:* Music for 7 films, 3 ballets. Also: Moon Over the West River, small orchestra & percussion; Horizon, soprano, baritone & orchestra; 8 Horses, 12 Chinese instruments & orchestra; Dai La Vi, music for large-scale dance drama. *Honour:* 1st prize, Alexander Tcherepnin Composition Competition. *Membership:* Chinese Musicians Association. *Address:* 111 East Avenue, Apt. 717, Rochester, New York 14604, USA.

YEEND Frances, b. 28 Jan 1918, Vancouver, Washington, USA. Singer (Soprano). *Education:* Studied at Washington State University. *Career:* From 1943 sang in musicals and on the radio; Concert tour of USA in 1944; World Tour in 1947 with Mario Lanza and George London, as Bel Canto Trio; Sang Ellen Orford in the US premiere of Peter Grimes, Tanglewood 1946; New York City Opera 1948-65, as Violetta, Eva (Die Meistersinger), Micaela, Mozart's Countess and Marguerite; Metropolitan Opera 1961-64, as Chrysothemis (Elektra), and Gutrune (Götterdämmerung); European engagements in Barcelona, Edinburgh (1951), London (Mimi, 1953), Munich, Verona (Turandot, 1958) and Vienna.

Recordings include: Micaela in Carmen; Ein Deutsches Requiem by Brahms (Musical Heritage Society).

YELLIN Victor Fell, b. 14 Dec 1924, Boston, Massachusetts, USA. Professor. m. Isabel S Joseph, 26 May 1948, 1 son. *Education:* A, cum laude, Harvard College, 1949; AM, 1952, PhD, 1957, Harvard University; New England Conservatory of Music, 1942-43. *Compositions:* Abaylar, opera; Passacaglia for strings; Sonata for Violoncello and Piano. *Recordings:* Victor Fell Yellin restoration of 2 early American Operas, Rayner Taylor's The Ethiop and John Bray's The Indian Princess. *Publications:* The Operas of Virgil Thomson (American Music since 1910), 1970; Preface to How Music Works, 1981; Chadwick, Yankee Composer, Washington and London, Snithsonian Institution Press, 1990. *Contributions to:* Musical Quarterly; American Music; Grove VI. *Honours:* Grantee, National Endowment for the Humanities. *Memberships:* American Musicological Society; Sonneck Society. *Hobby:* Collecting cameras. *Address:* 52 Washington Mews, New York, NY 10003, USA.

YEN Wen-hsiung, b. 26 June 1934, Tainan, Taiwan. Citizen, USA, 1986. m. 6 Jan 1961, 3 sons. *Education:* BA, National Taiwan Norman University, 1956-60; MA 1962-64, PhD Candidate 1965-68, Chinese Culture University; MA, University of California, Los Angeles, USA, 1969-71; PhD Candidate, University of Maryland, 1982-83. *Career:* Instructor, Taiwan Provincial Taichung Teacher College, 1961-62; Professor, Chinese Culture University, 1964-69; Lecturer, West Los Angeles College, USA, 1978-82; Faculty, Department of Music, University of Maryland, 1982-83; Instructor, Los Angeles City College and California State University, Los Angeles, 1984-; Instructor, California State University, Northridge and Santa Monica City College, 1986-; Founder and Music Director, Chinese Music Orchestra of Southern California, 1974-; Founder Chinese Culture School, Los Angeles, 1976-; Founder, President, The Chinese Musicians Association of Southern California, 1990-; Conducted the orchestra for the Dragon Boat Festival, at the Chinese Cultural Center in Los Angeles's Chinatown, 1993 and for the opening ceremony of the annual Chinese Writer's Association of Southern California Conference, 1993. *Publications:* Taiwan Folk Songs, 1967, vol 2, 1968; A Dictionary of Chinese Musicians (co-author Professor Tsai-pin Liang); A Collection of Wen-hsiung Yen's Songs, 1968; Wen-hsiung Yen's Songs, volume 2, 1987; Chinese Musical Culture and Folk Songs, written in Chinese with article, A Study of Si Xiang Qi in English, 1989. *Hobbies:* Walking; Table tennis; Tai Chi Chuan. *Address:* 1116 Drake Road, Arcadia, CA 91007, USA.

YEROFEEVA Yelena, b. 1960, Moscow, Russia. Cellist. *Education:* Studied at the Moscow Conservatoire with Alexei Shislov. *Career:* Co-founded the Glazunov Quartet 1985; many concerts in the former Soviet Union and recent appearances in Greece, Poland, Belgium, Germany and Italy; works by Beethoven and Schumann at the Beethoven Haus in Bonn; further engagements in Canada and Holland; Teacher at the Moscow State Conservatoire and Resident at the Tchaikovsky Conservatoire; repertoire includes works by Borodin, Shostakovich and Tchaikovsky, in addition to the standard works. *Recordings includes:* CDs of the six quartets of Glazunov. *Honours include:* (with the Glazunov Quartet) prizewinner of the Borodin Quartet and Shoestakovich Chamber Music Competitions. *Address:* c/o Sonata (Glazunov Quartet), 11 Northpark Street, Glasgow G20 7AA, Scotland.

YIM Jay Alan, b. 24 Apr 1958, St Louis, Missouri, USA. Composer. *Education:* BA, University of California, 1980; MMus, Royal College of Music, London, England, 1981; Dartington, England, 1985; Tanglewood, 1986; PhD, Harvard University, expected 1988. *Career:* Lecturer, Director of Electronic Music Studio, University of California, Santa Barbara, 1978-80; Composer-in-Residence, Cummington School of the Arts, 1984; Major festival performances: Huddersfield, 1982; International Computer Music Conference, 1985; Tanglewood, 1986 and 1987; Gaudeamus, 1987. *Compositions:* Orchestral: Askesis, 1980-81; Eastern Windows, 1981; Karénas, 1986; Chamber: Palimpsest, 1979; Piak, 1981; Autumn Rhythm, 1984-85; Moments of Rising Mist, 1986; Mille Graces, 1986; Geometry and Delirium, 1987; Solo instrument: Timescreen No 1, 1984, No 2 1983, for pianoforte; Furiosamente for piccolo, 1985; Más Furiosamente for flute, 1985; Electronic: Kinkakuji, 1984; Shiosai, 1984. *Address:* c/o ASCAP, ASCAP Building, One Lincoln Plaza, New York, NY 100023, USA.

YOES Janice, b. 1947, USA. Singer (Soprano). *Debut:* New York City Opera 1973, as Santuzza. *Career:* Sang at the Augsburg Opera 1975-77, Saarbrucken 1976-77, Karlsruhe 1977-78; Engaged at Nuremberg 1978-84, with guest appearances at Graz 1980-83; Sang Strauss's Elektra at the Vienna Staatsoper, Marseilles, Madrid the Deutsche Oper Berlin, Seattle and Santiago (1984); Bregenz Festival 1977, as Reiza in Oberon; Appearances as Brünnhilde in Der Ring de Nibelungen at Naples, Lisbon and Seattle 1982-86; Further engagements at Basle, Trieste, Brunswick and Pretoria 1987-88; Other roles have include Isolde, Salome and Lady Macbeth. *Address:* Opera of the Performing Arts Council, Transvaal PO Box 566, Pretoria 0001 Transvaal, South Africa.

YOKOSAKA Yasuhiko, b. 5 Feb 1956, Aomori, Japan. Associate Professor of Music History and Musicology. m. Yukiko, 10 July 1983. 1 son, 1 daughter. *Education:* BA, Baker University, 1978; MM, Yale Institute of Sacred Music, 1981; Doctor of Education, Columbia University, 1985. *Career:* Associate Professor of Music History and Musicology, Faculty of Education, University of Niigata. *Publications:* Tenrei Seika and Contemporary Church Music in Japan, 1981; Developing Guidelines for the Revision of The Hymnal 1954, 1985; Stylistic Development of the Chorale preludes by J S Bach, 1986. *Contributions to:* Music Critique, The Niigata Nippoh, 1988-. *Honour:* Hugh Porter Scholar Award, Yale Institute of Sacred Music, 1981. *Memberships:* Hymn Society of America; Hymn Society of Great Britain and Ireland; Musicological Society of Japan. *Hobbies:* Swimming; Travel. *Address:* Faculty of Education, The University of Niigata, 8050 Ikarashi Ni-No-Cho, Niigata-shi, 950-21 Japan.

YORK David Stanley, b. 25 June 1920, West Hartford, Connecticut, USA. College Professor; Church Organist; Composer. m. (1) Marian Paquin, 8 June 1946, 2 sons, (2) Joyce Van Nest Billhardt, 20 Feb. 1976, 1 son, 4 daughters. *Education:* BM, Theory major, Yale University, 1944; MM Composition, Westminster Choir College, 1946; Additional study: With Oliver Strunk, Princeton University; With Willi Apel and Bernard Heiden, Indiana University; With Robert Morgan, Temple University. *Career:* Organist-Director of Churches, Hartford, Connecticut 1940-44, Philadelphia, Pennsylvania 1944-46, Trenton-Princeton, New Jersey 1946-63, Chatham 1963-; Professor of Music Theory, twice Head of Theory Department at Westminster Choir College, 1946-85; Affiliate Professor of Music Theory at Temple University, 1988-; Editor with Theodore Presser, Westminster Series, 1963-75; Editor with Hinshaw Music, 1987-90; Editor Music Series with National Music, 1990-. *Compositions:* 44 anthems and 1 organ selection, with Theodore Presser, Carl Fisher, Harold Flammer, Golden Music and National Music. *Honour:* 2nd Prize for Divinum Mysterium for Organ and Bells, Schulmerich Contest, 1947. *Membership:* American Guild of Organists. *Hobbies:* Swimming; Beach walking. *Address:* 746 Old Farm Road, Bridgewater, NJ 08807, USA.

YORK John, b. 20 Mar 1949, Eastbourne, England. Pianist. m. Fiona Osborne, 5 Sept 1981, 1 son, 1 daughter. *Education:* AGSM Diploma, Guildhall School of Music and Drama, London, 1971; Studied in Paris with Jacques Fevrier, 1971-72, Vienna Hochschule with Dieter Weber, 1972-74. *Debut:* Wigmore Hall, 1974. *Career:* Recitals and Concerts in UK, Ireland, France, throughout Europe, USA, Canada, Brazil, Bermuda,

Singapore, Malaysia; Partner to Raphäel Wallifisch (cello), Member of York Trio of London and York 2 Piano Duo; Classic for BBC Radio, CBC TV and Radio. *Recordings:* Many albums on Crystal Label in USA, RCI in Canada, Meridian Label UK (2 Albums of York Trio), Naxos, Cala. *Publications:* Selector and assistant in new issue of Mikrokosmos (Bartok); Fingers and Thumbs (Boosey and Hawkes), 1993. *Contributions to:* Reviewer for Classical Piano, The Strad. *Honour:* Debussy Prize, Paris, 1973. *Memberships:* Member-Adjudicator British Federation of Music Festivals; MENSA. *Hobbies:* Train Travel and Timetables; Winemaking. *Current Management:* Elton Artists, Amersham, Bucks. *Address:* 38 Caterham Road, Lewisham, London SE13 5AR, England.

YOSHINO Naoko, b. 1967, London. Harpist. *Education:* Studied with Susann McDonald of Indiana University from 1974. *Career:* Soloist with leading orchestras from 1977, notably the Israel Philharmonic under Mehta 1985, Philadelphia Orchestra under Frühbeck de Burgos, 1987 and in Japan with Seiji Ozawa and Wolfgang Sawallisch; New York recital debut at Merkin Hall 1987 and chamber concert with members of the Berlin Philharmonic; Soloist with the Berlin Philharmonic under Ozawa 1988; Classic Aid concerts with Lorin Maazel in Paris, 1988, Yehudi Menuhin Gstaad Festival 1988; London debut with James Galway in Mozart's Concerto K299 (Philharmonia/Sinopoli) 1990; London recital debuts 1990; English Chamber Orchestra at the Barbican under Menuhin 1990; World Harp Festival at Cardiff 1991. *Recording:* Album with the English Chamber Orchestra under Menuhin (Virgin Classics); 5 albums with Sony Classical, 3 solo, 1 with flute, 1 concerto album. *Honours include:* First Prize, winner, 9th International Harp Contest in Israel, 1985; Second prize, First International Harp Contest, Santa Cecilia Academy, Rome, 1981. *Current Management:* Kajimoto Concert Management Ltd, Kahoku Bldg, 8-6-25 Ginza, Chuo-Ku, Tokyo, Japan.

YOSS David, b. 14 Aug 1946, Iowa, USA. Singer; Director of Plays and Musicals; Professor of Voice & Music Theatre (Operas & Musicals). *Education:* BMus, MA, DMusA 1979, University of Iowa; Certificate, voice & opera, Mozarteum, Salzburg, Austria, 1980; Opera apprenticeship, International Opera Studio, Zurich, Switzerland. *Career includes:* Several years, lead spinto baritone in Koblenz, West Germany. Roles included: Don Giovanni, Mandryka/Arabella, Mathis/Mathis der Maler. Other roles sung in Austria, Switzerland, USA, including the Count/Le Nozze di Figaro, Silvio/Pagliacci, Guglielmo/Così fan Tutte, for Southwest German TV, etc. Also Escamillo/Carmen; Shoe salesman/Postcard from Morocco by Argento. Numerous recitals, oratorio appearances.

YOUNG Alexander, b. 18 Oct 1920, London, England. Concert and Opera Singer (Tenor), Educator. *Education:* RCM; Studied with Professor Stefan Pollmann, London. m. Jean Anne Prewett, 1 son, 1 daughter. *Debut:* As Scaramuccio, Ariadne auf Naxos, Glyndebourne Company, Edinburgh, 1950. *Career includes:* Numerous appearances in opera and oratorio, UK and abroad; Sang title role in Stravinsky's The Rake's Progress, 1953; Sang at Covent Garden 1955-70 (Lysander and Matteo) and Sadler's Wells (Almaviva, Count Ory, Orpheus by Gluck and Monteverdi), Xerxes, and Belmonte; Sang in premiere (BBC) of Henze's Bassarids, 1968, and Hamilton's Catiline Conspiracy, 1974; Many recitals with accompanists Rex Stephens, Harold Lester and Keith Swallow; Regular broadcasts for BBC, but also broadcast for Dutch and German radios and European Broadcasting Union. Head, School of Vocal Studies, Royal Northern College of Music, Manchester, 1973-86. Has made over 50 recordings of opera, oratorio, song recitals; now retired. *Honours:* Fellow, RNCM, 1977. *Membership:* British Actors Equity. *Hobbies:* Choral Conducting; Railway Modelling; Stamp Collecting. *Address:* Treetops, Eccles Road, Whaley Bridge, via Stockport, Cheshire SK12 7EL, England.

YOUNG Douglas, b. 18 June 1947, London, England. Composer; Pianist; Conductor; Writer; Broadcaster. m. Susan Anne Devlin, 22 Nov 1980, 1 daughter. *Education:* Trinity College of Music, Junior Exhibitioner, 1957-66; ATCL, Piano Performance, 1963; B. Mus., London, Royal College of Music, 1969. *Debut:* As Pianist, Royal Festival Hall, London, 1970. *Career includes:* Works with Ronald Hynd, Choreographer for Royal Ballet and München Staatsoper Ballet, 1970-; Fellow, Commoner in the Creative Arts, Trinity College, Cambridge, 1973-75; Composer in Residence, Leicester Education Authority, 1975-77; Founded Internationally Renowned Ensemble, Dreamtiger, 1975. *Compositions include:* Compositions in all genres including several works inspired by Apollinaire, Lewis Carroll, Joyce, Virginia Woolf, Borges; Series of Concerti, Night Journeys under the Sea ranging from large orchestra to Chamber ensemble; Ludwig - Fragments eines Ratsels, ballet in 2 acts, 1986. *Recordings include:* Virages - Region One for Cello and large orchestra; Trajet, Inter Lignes 1980; The Hunting of the Snark, 1982; Third Night Journey under the Sea, 1980-82; Rain, Steam and Speed, 1982; Dreamlandscapes, Portrait of Apollinaire, 1983; Dreamlandscapes Book II, 1986. *Contributions to:* Tempo; The Listener; Music Teacher; Composer. *Honours:* Cobbett Prize for Chamber Music, 1968; Karl Rankl Prize for Orchestral Composition, Musica Nova, 1970-71. *Memberships:* Trustee, LAMA; SPNM: BMIC. *Hobbies:* Reading; Visual Arts; Travel; Wine. *Address:* c/o Ricordi (London) Ltd., The Bury, Church Street, Chesham, Bucks HP5 1JG, England.

YOUNG Frank Mitchell, b. 22 May 1940, Pasadena, Texas, USA. Musical Theatre Producer; Conductor; Musical Director; Stage Director; Choreographer; Playwright. *Education:* University of Texas, 1958; University of Houston, 1960; BA, University of California, Los Angles, 1963. *Debut:* Carmen, Houston Grand Opera, 1958. *Career:* Assistant Conductor, Singer, Production Stage Manager, Houston Grand Opera, 1963-75; Production Stage Manager, Washington Opera, 1968-71; Founder, Executive Director, Theatre Under The Stars (Houston's Civic Light Opera), Producer 112 Musicals, 1968-, including 1 American Premiere, 3 World Premieres and 21 Houston Premieres, starring Leading Artists including Giorgio Tozzi. *Memberships:* National Alliance of Musical Theatre Producers, President; Houston Theatre Alliance; Theatre Panel, Texas Comm. on the Arts. *Address:* Theatre Under The Stars, 4235 San Felipe, Houston, TX 77027, USA.

YOUNG Gordon Ellsworth, b. 1 Oct 1919, McPherson, Kansas, USA. Composer; Organist. *Education:* Mus B 1940, Mus D 1960, Southwestern College; Curtis Institute of Music, 1944-46. *Career:* Organist, First Methodist Church, Tulsa, 1940-44, First Presbyterian Church, Lancaster, Pennsylvania, 1944-48, Detroit, 1952-72; Concert Artist, Music Teacher; Faculty, Texas Christian University, 1950-52. *Compositions:* Over 900 published organ, choral, solo voice, chamber ensemble, concert band and symphony orchestra; Organ works have been performed by Alexander McCurdy, Richard Purvis, E Power Biggs, Roberta Bitgood, Russell Wichmann, Alexander Schreiner, Diane Bush and others; Choral Works have been highlights at summer workshops: the Fred Waring Workshop, the Interlochen Art Festival & Ridgecrest North Carolina Workshop. *Honours:* Several from American Society of Composers, Authors and Publishers. *Membership:* American Society of Composers, Authors and Publishers. *Address:* Box 256, Detroit, MI 48231, USA.

YOSHIHIDE Kiryu, b. 15 Aug 1940, Tokyo, Japan. Bassoon Player. m. 13 Dec 1973, 2 sons. *Education:* Masters Degree; Bassoon lessons with Kazutsugu Nakata, Heihachirou Mita at Tokyo University of Art and later with Harold Golshire at Juilliard, Leonard Sharow at Aspen and Sherman Walt at the New England Conservatory. *Debut:* TWIS Woodwind Quintet, 1959. *Career:* Member of the Yomiuri Nippon Symphony Orchestra, 1961-65; Soloist of Mozart Fagott concert with same orchestra, 1962; Principal Player, NHK Symphony Orchestra, 1967-; Soloist of Mozart and Haydn concertante, and Richard Strauss's Double-Konzert. *Honours:* Japan Music Competition, First Prize, wind department, 1965; 10th Arima Prize for contributions to NHK Symphony Orchestra, 1990. *Memberships:* Tokyo Fagottiade; TWIS Woodwind Quintet. *Address:* 6-21-3 Shimo-Shakujii, Tokyo 177, Japan.

YOUNG James Bradford, b. 3 Nov 1951, Princeton, New Jersey, USA. Librarian; Educator. *Education:* BMus, MMus, McGill University, 1969-75; MLS, Emory University, 1975-76; PhD, University of Illinois, 1980-86. *Career:* Instructor, Southern Illinois University, 1976-78; Visiting Professor, University of Houston, 1978-79; Assistant Professor, University of Illinois, 1979-86; Visiting Professor, Emory University, 1985-86; Music Technical Services Librarian, University of Pennsylvania, 1986-; Adjunct Professor of Information Studies, Drexel University, 1986-. *Publications:* An Account of Printed Musick, ca 1724 in Fontes artis musicae, 1982; Education for Music Librarianship in Notes, 1984; The Great Abuse of Musick, 1711, in Fontes artis musicae, 1985; Stringing the Sacred Harp, in Popular Music and Society, 1986; E Schuberth in the New Grove Dictionary of American Music, 1986; Roberto Valentine: thematic catalogue. *Honour:* Annual Publication Award, Music Library Association, 1982 for An Account of Printed Musick, ca 1724. *Memberships:* Music Library Association; International Association of Music Libraries. *Address:* 4416 Locust Street, Philadelphia, PA 19104, USA.

YOUNG Josephine, b. 1960, Auckland, New Zealand. Cellist. *Education:* Studied at the New England Conservatory, and in London with Christopher Bunting. *Debut:* Concert in Wellington May 1988. *Career:* Chamber musician and soloist in New Zealand; Co-founded the New Zealand String Quartet 1987 under the auspices of the Music Federatio nof NEw Zealand; Concerts at the Tanglewood School in the USA, the Banff International Competition in Canada and performances with the Lindsay Quartet at the 1990 International Festival of the Arts, Wellington; Soloist with the New Zealand Symphony Orchestra and artist-in-residence at Victoria University, Wellington; Tour to Australia 1990 for Musica Viva Australia; Tours of New Zealand 1992 and concerts in New York 1993. *Career:* Chamber musician and soloist in New Zealand; Co-founded the New Zealand String Quartet 1987, under the auspices of the Music Federation of New Zealand; *Recordings:* Albums for Kik International Classics. *Address:* c/o Ingpen & Williams Ltd. 14 Kensington Court, London W5 5DN, England.

YOUNG La Monte (Thornton), b. 14 Oct 1935, Bern, Idaho, USA. Composer; Performer. m. Marian Zazeela 1963. *Education:* Studied at Los Angeles City College 1953-56, Los Angeles State College 1956-57 and UCLA with Robert Stevenson; Further study with Andrew Imbrie, at the Stockhausen master classes at Darmstadt and at the New School for Social Research, New York (electronic music). *Career:* Performed and taught Kirana style of north Indian classical vocal music, with Pran Nath; Collaborations with painter and light artist Marian Zazeela; Associations with the Fluxus and Minimalist movements of artistic endeavour; Returned to California from Darmstadt 1959 and became music director of the Ann Halprin Dance Company, 1959-60; Director of the Kirana Center for Indian Classical Music 1971; With Marian Zazeela made tours of the USA and Europe with the Theatre of Eternal Music, 1969-75; Dream House maintained by the Dia Art Foundation's programme at Harrison Street New York, 1979-85. *Publications include:* An Anthology 1963, revised 1970; Selected Writings 1969. *Compositions include:* Various pieces for electronic and mixed-media forces 1959-67; For Brass 1958; Trio for Strings 1958; Studies I-III 1959; Arabic Numeral 1960; Death Chant for male voices and carillon 1961; Studies in Bowed Disc for gong 1963; The Well-tuned Piano: on-going series of pieces for prepared piano (performance of work, so far, Oct 1981, lasted five hours). *Honours include:* Woodrow Wilson Fellowship, 1959; Guggenheim Fellowship 1966; Creative Artists Public Service grants; Commission from the Dia Art Foundation, 1975-85. *Address:* ASCAP, ASCAP Building, One Lincoln Plaza, New York, NY 10023, USA.

YOUNG Lesley Margaret, b. 3 Mar 1954, Mossman, Queensland, Australia. Concert Pianist, Lecturer. *Education:* Queensland Conservatorium of Music, Brisbane, 1970-75; Royal Northern College of Music, Manchester, England, 1976-78; Royal College of Music, London, 1989-90. *Debut:* Wigmore Hall, 1977. *Career:* Australian National Music Camp and Music Rostrum Australia, 1975; Radio Broadcasts for ABC including being featured in Pianists of Brisbane recital/broadcast series, 1974; Television appearances in Australia; Concerto performances with Queensland Symphony Orchestra, Sydney Symphony Orchestra, Melbourne Symphony Orchestra, QCM Chamber Orchestra, Royal Northern College of Music Symphony Orchestra, Queensland Youth Orchestra, Merseyside Youth Orchestra, Orchestra da Camera; Recitals for Queensland Conservatorium of Music, Royal Northern College of Music, Australian Society for Keyboard Music, International Society for Contemporary Music, Incorporated Society of Musicians, Manchester Midday Concerts Society, Australian Musical Association London; Lecturer in piano, James Cook University, 1991-1992. *Address:* 3 Culverden Court, Culverden Square, Tunbridge Wells, Kent, TN4 9NS, England.

YOUNG Percy Marshall, b. 17 May 1912, Northwich, Cheshire, England. Writer on Music; Music Educationist. *Education:* Christ's Hospital 1926-30; Organ scholar at Selwyn College, Cambridge, BA 1933, MusB 1934; MusD Trinity College, Dublin, 1937; D.Mus (hc), Birmingham 1985; Hon. Fellow, Institute for Advanced Research in the Humanities, Birmingham University. *Career:* Director of music at Stranmillis Teachers Training College, Belfast 1934-37; Music Adviser to Stoke on Trent 1937-44; Director of Music at Wolverhampton College of Technology 1944-65; Choral director, with perfomances of music by Handel; Visiting scholar and lecturer to USA, 1971-72. *Compositions:* More than 30 published reconstructions, orchestrations and accompaniments, including Elgar's The Spanish Lady; More than 20 published works including Fugal Concerto in G minor 1954, Festival Te Deum 1961. *Publications include:* Samuel Pepys' Music Book 1942; Handel 1947, rev. 1975 and 1979; The Oratorios of Handel, 1949; Messiah: A Study in Interpretation 1951; Vaughan Williams 1953; Elgar, O.M. 1955, rev. 1973; Editor, The Letters of Elgar 1956; Tragic Muse: The Life and Music of Robert Schumann 1957, rev. 1961; The Choral Traditon 1962; Zóltan Kodály 1964; A History of British Music 1967; The Bachs, 1500-1850, 1970; Sir Arthur Sullivan 1972; A Concise History of Music 1974; Beethoven: A Victorian Tribute 1976; Alice Elgar: Enigma of a Victorian Lady 1977; George Grove 1980; Music of the Great Churches; The Madrigal in the Romantic Era; The English Glee, 1990; The Spanish Lady: Unfinished Opera by Percy M Young: Critical Edition, 1991. *Honours:* Hon Fellow, University of Wolverhampton, 1992. *Hobbies:* Sports; Gardening. *Address:* 72 Clark Road, Wolverhampton, WV3 9PA, England.

YOUNG Richard, b. 1945, USA. Violist. *Education:* Studied at Indiana University and Catholic University; Teachers included Josef Gingold, Aaron Rosand and William Primrose. *Career:* Performed at Queen Elisabeth of Belgium Competition aged 13; Member of the faculty at the Oberlin Conservatory of Music 1972-84; performances with the Rogeri Trio and the Hunarian Quartet in the USA, Europe, South America, Africa and Australia; Member of the Vermeer Quartet from 1985; performances at all major US centres and in Europe, Israel and Australia; Festival engagements at Tanglewood, Aspen, Spoleto, Edinburgh, Mostly Mozart (New York), Aldeburgh, South Bank, Santa Fe, Chamber Music West and the Casals Festival; Resident quartet for Chamber Music Chicago; Annual master classes at the Royal Northern College of Music, Manchester; Member of the Resident Artists Faculty of Northern Illinois University. *Recordings include:* Quartets by Beethoven, Dvořák, Verdi and Schubert (Teldec); Brahms Clarinet Quintet with Karl Leister (Orfeo). *Address:* Allied Artists, 42 Montpelier Square, London SW7 1JZ, England.

YU Chun-Yee, b. 12 July 1936, Shanghai, China. Pianist. m. (1) Isabella Miao, Dec 1963, 2 sons, (2) Jung Chang, June 1982. *Education:* Royal College of Music, England, under Kendall Taylor; Agostic, Italy; Tagliaferro, France. *Career:* Examiner to the Associated Board of Royal School of Music; Professor of Piano, Royal College of Music; Represented Singapore at the First Asian Music Festival in Hong Kong; First appeared at the Royal Festival Hall in 1963 as soloist with London Philharmonic Orchestra; Has played extensively in the Far East and throughout the British Isles; Recently toured Taiwan and China. *Honours:* Recordi Prize for Conducting; Prize Winner, International Piano Competition; Scholarship to study in Siena under Agosti. *Hobbies:* Bridge; Sport; Motoring. *Address:* c/o Royal College of Music, London SW7, England.

YU Julian Jing-Jun, b. 2 Sept 1957, Beijing, China. Composer. m. 9 Nov 1984. *Education:* Central Conservatory of Music, Beijing; Tokyo College of Music; Queensland Conservatorium of Music; MA, La Trobe University, Melbourne. *Career:* Emigrated to Australia, 1985; Tanglewood Fellow, 1988; Victorian Ministry for the Arts Music Advisory Panel, 1991-; Work Commissioned by Hans Werner Henze; Jury member for BMW Music Theatre Prize at 3rd Munich Biennale, 1992; Works performed at ISCM World Music Days in 1991 (Zurich) and 1993 (New Mexico). *Compositions:* Major published works: Wu-Yu; Hsiang-Wen; Hsiang-Chi; Great Ornamented Fuga Canonica; Scintillation I, II and III; Reclaimed Prefu I and II; The White Snake; Medium Ornamented Fuga Canonica; In the Sunshine of Bach; Impromptu; First Australian Suite (all published by Universal Edition (London) Ltd. *Recordings:* Works recorded by ABC and BBC; Vienna Modern Masters. *Contributions to:* Journal of the Central Conservatory of Music (China) and Sounds Australian. *Honours:* Koussevitzky Composition Prize, Tanglewood, 1988; Inaugural Paul Lowin Award, 1991; Vienna Modern Masters Recording Award, 1992; Spivakovsky Compostion Award, 1992; Award, 56th Japan Music Concours, 1987; Award, International New Music Composers' Competition, USA, 1988, 1989-90; Award, 35th Premio Musicale, Citta di Trieste, 1988; Award, 10th Irino Prize, 1989. *Memberships:* Full Representation, Australian Music Centre; Australasian Performing Right Association; Musicians' Association of China, Beijing. *Hobbies:* Photography; Drawing and design. *Current Management:* Through publisher, Universal Edition, London, England. *Address:* 39A Clyde Street, Thornbury, Victoria 3071, Australia.

YUAN Lily, b. 23 Dec 1962, Shanghai, China. Musician; Educator. m. Theodore Zhu, 2 Feb 1985. *Education:* Middle School, Central Conservatory of Music, Beijing, 1974-79; BA, Shanghai Conservatory of Music, Shanghai, 1979-83; MA, University of Toronto, Canada, 1985-87. *Career:* Soloist, Shanghai Children's Orchestra, 1972-74; Faculty, Shanghai Conservatory of Music, 1983-85; Music Director, Boston Chinese Orchestra 1987-; Faculty, Rhode Island Music School, 1987-; Resident Artist, Eastman Connecticut State University, 1988-; American debut, 1982; Soloist with Toronto Chamber Orchestra, 1986; Appearances on Shanghai Radio and Television, 1973; Multiculture TV, Toronto, 1987; WLNE TV, Providence, Rhode Island, 1988; WBUR and over 100 national public radio stations in USA broadcasting solo recital from Newport Music Festival, 1988. *Compositions:* Yangqin (Chinese dulcimer) solo with Chinese Ensemble, Joyous Spring Festival; Rearranged about 20 Yangqin solo pieces. *Recordings:* Silk string quintet, Joyful Evening, Chinese Melody; Yangqin solo, Music for the General. *Honour:* Best Performance Prize in Yangqin, National Music Instrument Competition, China, 1982.

YUN Isang, b. 17 Sept 1917, Tongyong, Korea. Composer. m. Sooja Lee, 1 son, 1 daughter. *Education:* Cello and composition in Korea and Japan, 1939-43; Paris Conservatoire and Berlin, 1956-59. *Career:* Teacher/Lecturer, School and Universities, Korea, 1946-56; Captured by South Korean agents and imprisoned in Seoul on sedition charge, 1967-69; Lecturer, College of Music, Hanover, 1969-70; Professor in Composition, State College of Music, Berlin, 1970-1985; Member of Academies of Arts in Hamburg and Berlin. *Compositions include:* Operas: The Dream of Liu-Tung, 1965; Butterfly Widow, 1967; Geisterliebe, 1970; Sim Tjong, 1972. Orchestral: Symphonic Scenes, 1960; Bara, 1960; Colloides Sonores for strings, 1961; Reak, 1966; Dimensionen, 1971; Konzertante Figuren, 1972; Cello concerto, 1976; Flute Concerto, 1977; Double concerto for oboe, harp and small orchestra, 1977; Muak, 1978; Exemplum in memoriam Kwangju, 1981; Clarinet Concerto, 1981; Violin Concerto No 1, 1981; Symphony No 1, 1983; Violin Concerto No 2, 1983-86; Symphony No 2, 1984; Symphony No 3, 1985; Mugung Dong, Invocation for Wind instruments, percussion and double-basses, 1986; Symphony No 4 Im Dunkeln singen 1986; Chamber Symphony No 1, 1987; Symphony No 5 with baritone solo, 1987; Chamber Symphony No 2, 1989; Konturen 1989, Oboe Concerto 1990, Violin Concerto No.3 1992, Silla 1992. Vocal music: Om mani padme hum, cycle for soprano, baritone, chorus and orchestra, 1964; Namo for 3 sopranos and orchestra, 1971; Der weise Mann for baritone, chorus and small orchestra, 1977; O Licht...for chorus with solo violin and percussion, 1981; Teile dich Nacht for soprano and chamber orchestra, 1980. Chamber ensemble: Loyang, 1962; Piece concertante, 1976; Oktett, 1978; Distanzen, 1988. Chamber music: String quartet No 3, 1959; Garak for flute and piano, 1963; Riul for clarinet and piano, 1968; Images for flute, oboe, violin and cello, 1968; Sonata for oboe (ob d'amore ad lib), harp and viola or cello, 1979; Concertino for accordeon and string quartet, 1983; Quintet for clarinet and string quartet, 1984; Quintet for flute and string quartet, 1984; String quartet No 4, 1988; Quartet for flute, violin, cello and piano, 1989; String quartet V 1990, Woodwind Quintet 1990, Sonata for violin and piano 1991, String Quartet VI 1992, Quartet f. trump, horn, tromb, piano 1992, Trio for clarinet, bassoon, horn 1992; Several works for solo instruments. *Recordings:* Collection of 10 CDs at Camerata Tokyo, several portrait CDs in Germany, USA, Netherlands, France. *Honours:* 2 Korean Art Awards; Kulturpreis Kiel, 1970; Honorary doctor Tuebingen University, 1985. *Address:* c/o Bote and Bock, D-10623 Berlin, Hardenbergstrasse 9a, Germany.

YURISICH Gregory, b. 13 Oct 1951, Mount Lawley, Western Australia. Singer (Baritone). *Education:* Studied in Perth. *Debut:* Paolo in Simon Boccanegra for Australian Opera at Sydney, 1978. *Career:* roles in Australia have included Mozart's Masetto and Don Alfonso, Verdi's Germont and Melitone, Alberich in The Ring, Varlaam in Boris Godunov, Beethoven's Pizarro and Wagner's Dutchman; European debut Frankfurt 1989, as Bottom in A Midsummer Night's Dream; Covent Garden debut 1990, as William Tell, returning as Dr. Bartolo, the villains in Les Contes d'Hoffmann, Don Profondo in a new production of Il Viaggio a Reims, 1992; Pizarro in Fidelio and Scarpia in Tosca; for English National Opera has sung in two world premieres: Alcibiades in Timon of Athens by Stephen Oliver, 1991 and Cadmus in Bakxai by John Buller, 1992; Sang Stankar in a new production of Verdi's Stiffelio at Covent Garden, 1993; other roles include Escamillo, Leporello (Glyndebourne 1991), King Henry in Anna Bolena, and Verdi's Iago and Simon Boccanegra, Rigoletto and Nabucco. *Address:* c/o IMG Artists, Media House, 3 Burlington Lane, London W4 2TH, England.

Z

ZABLOCKI Jerzy, b. 25 July 1928, Lublin, Poland. Conductor. m. 4 Jan 1968, 1 son. *Education:* 2 years/ 4 semesters of Musicology, University of Wroclaw; Conducting, Faculty of Composition, Theory and Conducting, Academy of Music, Wroclaw, 1955. *Career:* Conductor, Polish Radio Orchestra; Over 400 pieces performed and recorded including 120 own compositions and arrangements for orchestra and choir with orchestra, 1953-58; Operetta-Theatre, Wroclaw, 1959-62; Conductor, Wroclaw State Opera, 1970-77; Bydgoszcz State Opera 1981-82; Warsaw Operetta 1982-84; Teacher in schools, college and Academy of Music, since 1948, recently professor in Warsaw Academy of Music and Bydgoszcz Academy of Music, director of Post-graduated Study for Choir-conductors; Numerous other positions as chairman, music critic, journalist. *Compositions:* 120 recorded works including 20 folk-songs of Lower Silesia and 50 Polish folk-songs and dances. *Recordings:* 400 pieces, Polish radio and television. *Publications:* O technice dyrgowania/About the Techniques of Conducting, 1972; O Prowadzeniu Choru/About Chorus Conducting, 1978. *Contributions to:* Methodological articles, Poradnik Muzyczny; Lodz; Music critiques, Gazeta Robotnicza, Wroclaw. *Honours:* Ministry of Culture Prizes Grades I and II, 1967, 1972, 1978; Town of Legnica, 1972; Wroclaw City, 1976; Board Chief, Polish Music Artists Society. *Memberships:* Polish Music Artists Society; Honorary Member, Lower Silesian Music Society. *Hobbies:* Photography; Painting; Linguistics. *Address:* Marszalkowska 68/70 m6, Warsaw, Poland.

ZABRACK Harold A, b. 30 June 1928, St Louis, Missouri, USA. Pianist; Composer; Pedagogue; Professor of Piano. *Education:* BM, Piano, 1949, MM, Piano and Composition, 1951, Doctoral Study, Indiana University and Washington University; Fulbright Award to Germany, 1955; Study with Nadia Boulanger, France, 1962. *Debut:* Soloist with St Louis Symphony, Grieg Piano Concerto, 1944. *Career:* USA State Department tour of Germany, 1955-56; Recital of original piano music, Carnegie Hall, Apr. 1982; Soloist, St Louis Symphony, First Piano Concerto, 1965; Soloist, Milwaukee Symphony with own Symphonic Variations for piano and orchestra, 1977; Soloist, Baton Rouge Symphony, first Piano Concerto, 1982; Carnegie Recital Hall, Lecture - Recital on Debussy Préludes, 1987; Carnegie Recital Hall, AIDS Benefit Concert featuring music of Brahms and Zabrack, 1988; TV appearances on NJ Cable Channel 34; Piano Series in Vancouver, B.C., Canada in July 1989. *Published Compositions:* Scherzo; Hommage a Prokofiev; Two Piano Sonatas; Eight Contours; Three Etudes; Six Preludes; Variations for Piano. *Recordings include:* Original piano works as well as those by Beethoven, Debussy, Kabalevsky, Bartók. *Publications:* Creative Musical Encounters, 1978; Twilight for Piano commissioned and published by Yorktown Press, Jan 1986. *Contributions to:* Clavier; American Music Teacher. *Hobbies:* Psychology; Philosophy. *Address:* 7002 Blvd. East, Apt. 33C, Guttenberg, NJ 07093, USA.

ZACCARIA Nicola, b. 9 Mar 1923, Athens, Greece. Singer (Bass). *Education:* Studied at the Royal Conservatory, Athens. *Debut:* Athens 1949, as Raimondo in Lucia di Lammermoor. *Career:* Has sung at many Italian centres; La Scala debut 1953, as Sparafucile in Rigoletto; Sang in Milan in the standard bass repertory until 1974, and created the Third Knight in the premiere of Pizzetti's Assassinio nella Cattedrale, 1958; Vienna Staatsoper from 1956; Salzburg Festival from 1957 as the Minister in Fidelio, the Monk in Don Carlos, the Commendatore in Don Giovanni and Ferrando in Il Trovatore; Covent Garden 1957 and 1959, as Oroveso (Norma) and Creon (Medee), both with Maria Callas; Further appearances in Brussels, Cologne, Geneva, Moscow, Rio de Janeiro, Mexico City, Berlin, Monte Carlo, Edinburgh, Aix and Orange; Dallas 1976, as King Marke in Tristan und Isolde; Sang Colline in La Bohème at Macerata in 1982; other roles include Verdi's Zaccaria (Nabucco) and Silva (Ernani), Rodolfo (La Sonnambula) and Sarastro (Die Zauberflöte).

Recordings include: Norma, Aida, Un ballo in maschera, Il Trovatore, La Sonnambula, Rigoletto, Turandot, Barbiere di Siviglia, La Bohème and Falstaff (Columbia); L'Italiana in Algeri, La Navarraise and Orlando Furioso (RCA); Mignon by Thomas (CBS); Beethoven's Missa solemnis (Columbia).

ZACHARIAS Christian, b. 27 Apr 1950, Tamshedpur, India. Pianist. *Education:* Moved to West Germany aged two and studied with Irene Slavin in Karlsruhe, then with Vlado Perlemuter in Paris. *Career:* Won prizes in Geneva (1969) and in the Van Cliburn Competition; won 1975 European Broadcasting Union's Ravel Prize; appears in US with the Boston Symphony, Cleveland Orchestra and New York Philharmonic, in Canada with the Montreal Symphony; regular appearances in the UK, including Edinburgh Festival 1985, with the Polish Chamber Orchestra and Jerzy Maksymiuk; engagements at major European Festivals include Salzburg and the piano festival at La Roque d'Antheron; chamber concerts with the violinist Ulf Hoelscher, the cellist Heinrich Schiff and the Alban Berg Quartet; British concerts include appearances with the London Symphony Orchestra, BBC Welsh Symphony and Royal Liverpool Philharmonic. *Recordings:* Schubert, Scarlatti and Mozart sonatas and concertos by Beethoven for EMI with the Dresden Staatskapelle. *Address:* c/o Harold Holt Ltd., 31 Sinclair Road, London W14 ONS, England.

ZADEK Hilde, b. 15 Dec 1917, Bromberg, Bydgoszcz, Austria. Singer (Soprano); Teacher. *Education:* Studied with Rose Pauly in Jerusalem and with Ria Ginster in Zurich. *Debut:* Vienna Staatsoper 1947, as Aida. *Career:* Salzburg Festival from 1948 as Brangaene (Tristan und Isolde), Ariadne, Vitelia in La clemenza di Tito, and in the premiere of Orff's Antigonae; Glyndebourne Festival 1950 and 1951, as Ariadne and Donna Anna; Covent Garden 1950, as Aio Lisa in The Queen of Spades and Tosca; Further appearances in Edinburgh, Lisbon, Buenos Aires, Paris, Brussels, Amsterdam, New York, Rome and San Francisco; Professor at the Vienna Music Academy from 1967; Led Master Classes at Riva del Garda, Italy, in 1990. *Recordings include:* Donna Anna in Don Giovanni, conducted by Rudolf Moralt (Philips); Excerpts from Der Vogelhändler, Der Zigeunerbaron, and Aida.

ZAGAR Peter, b. 21 Dec 1961, Bratislava, Slovak Republic. Musical supervisor, music editor The Czechoslovak Radio. *Education:* Composition class of Prof Ivan Hrusovsky, Academy of Arts, Bratislava, 1981-86. *Debut:* Bratislava, 1983. *Career:* Concerto, Chamber Orchestra, 1986; Chamber works, Overture for string orchestra; Musical Supervisor, The Czechoslovak Radio; Member, Contemporary music ensemble, VENI. *Compositions:* Suite for piano; Rhapsody for piano; Three songs for soprano, flute and piano; Overtura giocosa for strings; Concerto for chamber orchestra; Music for 2 flutes, 2 clarinets, 2 bassoons and strings; A Dream for magnetic tape; Music for Video, Four pieces for strings. *Hobbies:* Films; Drama; Literature. *Address:* Belopotockeho 6, 811 05 Bratislava, Slovakia.

ZAGROSEK Lothar, b. 13 Nov 1942, Waging, Germany. Conductor; Composer. *Education:* Studied in Vienna with Hans Swarowsky and with Karajan and Bruno Maderna. *Career:* Appointments at opera houses in Salzburg, Kiel and Darmstadt, 1967-73; Frequent appearances with the London Sinfonietta from 1978, conducting music by Weill, Ligeti, Messiaen and Stravinsky; Engagements in the USA, notably San Diego and Seattle, from 1984; Guest Conductor, BBC Symphony Orchestra; Musical Director Paris Opera 1986-88; Glyndebourne debut 1987, Così fan Tutte; Conducted the premiere of Krenek's oratorio Symeon Stylites at the 1988 Salzburg Festival; In May 1989 conducted York Höller's Der Meister und Margarita, the last new production at the Paris Opéra, Palais Garnier, before the opening of the Opéra de la Bastille; Höller concert with the Paris Opéra Orchestra, May 1989; Conducted BBC Symphony Orchestra at 1989 Promenade Concerts in music by Markevitch, Mozart,

Mendelssohn, Kodály and Brahms (Ein Deutsches Requeim); Conducted Peter Sellars production of Die Zauberflöte at Glyndebourne, 1990; Prom Concerts 1991; Gruber's Cello Concerto, Schnittke's Piano Concerto, Haydn's 47th Symphony and Brahms 1, Mendelssohn Violin Concerto; Currently Chief Conductor of the Städtische Theater, Leipzig. *Address:* c/o Ingpen and Williams Ltd., 14 Kensington Court, London W8 5DN, England.

ZAHORTSEV Volodymr Mykolayovych, b. 27 Oct 1944, Kiev, Ukraine. Composer. *Education:* Graduated Tchaikovsky Conservatory Kiev 1968. *Career:* Joined avant-garde group of post-Stalinist composers in Kiev. *Compositions include:* Priskaski, song cycle 1963; Violin Sonata 1964; String quartet 1964; Sizes for 5 instruments 1965; Gradations for chamber group 1966; Games for chamber orchestra 1968; Symphony No. 1 1968; Music for 4 strings, no.1 1968; Sonata for strings, piano and percussion 1969; Rhythms for piano 1970; Symphony No. 2 for soprano, tenor and orchestra 1978; Oboe sonata 1978; Music for 4 Strings No. 2 1978; A Day in Pereyaslavl for soloists, chorus and orchestra 1979; In the Children's Room cantata 1979; opera Maty (Mother), Lvov 1985. *Address:* RAIS (Russia), c/o PRS Ltd, Member Registration, 29-33 Berners Street, London W1P 4AA, England.

ZAIDEL Nahum, b. 20 Sept 1933, USSR. Musician; Conductor. m. 30 Aug 1976. *Education:* Graduated as Orchestra Soloist, Chamber Music Performer, and Teacher, P I Tchaikovsky State Conservatoire, Moscow, 1957; Studies in Conducting with Professor Igor Markevitch and Professor Genady Rozhdestvensky, 1963-66. *Career:* Solo Flautist, Moscow Chamber Orchestra under Rudolf Barschai, 1957-58; Solo Flautist, Moscow Radio Symphony Orchestra under Genady Rozhdestvensky, 1959-72; Solo Flautist, Jerusalem Symphony Orchestra, Israel, 1972-; Professor, Rubin Music Academy, Jerusalem, 1972-; Master classes for flute and appearances as guest conductor. *Recordings:* Works by Handel, Bach, Beethoven, Gluck, Hindemith, Prokoviev, Doppler, Vivaldi, Stamitz, Cimarosa, Salieri, Chaminade, Bloch, Dvosák, Stravinsky, and Kurt Weill, for record and radio. *Honour:* 1st Prize for Flute, International Competition, Moscow, 1957. *Hobbies:* Chess; Photography. *Address:* Haviv Avshalom 4/7, Jerusalem 93802, Israel.

ZAJICK Dolora, b. 1960, Nevada, USA. Singer (Mezzo-soprano). *Education:* Studied at the University of Nevada with Ted Pufferand at the Manhattan School of Music with Helen Vanni and Lou Galtiero; Further study with Donald Hall. *Debut:* San Francisco Opera 1986, as Azucena. *Career:* New York gala 1986, with Eva Marton and Alfredo Kraus; Metropolitan Opera debut 1988, as Azucena; Season 1988-89 with further debuts at the Lyric Opera of Chicago, the Vienna Staatsoper, Rome's Caracalla Festival and the Arena of Verona; Sang Rossini's Stabat Mater at the Cincinnati May Festival and Mahler's 8th Symphony at Washington DC conducted by Rostropovich; Verdi Requiem at Carnegie Hall and in Paris and London; Mahler's 2nd Symphony in Paris conducted by Lorin Maazel; Season 1989-90 with Amneris and Azucena at the Met, Tchaikovsky's Maid of Orleans at Carnegie Hall, Il Trovatore in Toulouse and Florence; Aida in Reno, the Arena di Verona and at the Caracalla Festival; Part of the International Telecast of Trovatore, at the Metropolitan, 1988, and Aida, at the Metropolitan, 1989; Mavra in Khovanschina at San Francisco Opera, 1990; Eboli in Don Carlo at Metropolitan, La Scala and in Reno, 1990; Principessa in Adriana Lecouvreur at San Carlo, Maples, 1992; Jezibaba in Rusalka at Metropolitan, 1993; Title-role, Herodiade scheduled for San Francisco Opera, 1994; Has recorded, in addition to those listed, Don Carlo conducted by Levine (CBS Sony) and Alexander Nevsky, conducted by Rostropovich (CBS Sony). Other opera houses: Barcelona, Houston, Florence, Oviedo, Bilbao, Orange Festival, Covent Garden (debut 1994). *Recordings:* La Forza del Destino and the Verdi Requiem, conducted by Muti (EMI); Aida (CBS Sony); Most recent recording: Trovatore, for Sony

Classical, 1991. *Honour:* Bronze Medal, Tchaikovsky International Competition, Moscow, 1982. *Address:* Edgar Vincent-Patrick Farrell Associates, 157 West 57th Street, Suite 502, New York, NY 10019, USA.

ZAK Jerzy, b. 31 Mar 1954, Lodz, Poland. Performer-Musicologist; Specialist, historical plucked instruments, lute, guitar. m. Malgorzata Wojciechowska, 22 Sept 1984. *Education:* MA, Higher School of Music, Lodz, 1979; Conservatorio Superior de Musica, Alicante; Early Music Centre, London; ARCM, Royal College of Music, London, UK, 1983. *Career includes:* Recitals, Poland, Greece, Hungary, France, UK; Chamber musician and basso continuo player on lute, theorbo, guitar; Several broadcasts, Polish radio, 1980-; Television appearances, 1980-; Assistant, Academy of Music, Lodz, 1983-; Artistic Director, Days of Guitar Music, International Festival, Lodz, 1984, 1986; Consultant, Akademie Weiss-Institute for Lute Studies, Parc de Scheppenwihr, France, 1992-; Researcher, chamber music with plucked instruments. *Honours:* 2nd prize, Polish Guitar Competition, 1976; 1st prize, Guitar Competition, Hungary, 1977; Distinction & prize, Volos Guitar Festival, Greece, 1979; 1st prize, Early Music Competition, Manchester, UK, 1983. *Address:* Piotrkowska 145 m.21, 90-434 Lodz, Poland.

ZALEWSKI Wlodzimerz, b. 1949, Poland. Singer (Bass-baritone). *Career:* Sang at the Lodz Opera 1975-82, Gelsenkirchen from 1982; Bregenz Festival 1978, as the Dutchman, Philadelphia 1988 as Don Alfonso in Così fan Tutte; Sang in the 1989 premiere of Michael Kohlhaas by Karl Kogler at the Landestheater Linz; Appearances at Lodz and elswhere as Boris Godunov; Other roles have included Hindemith's Cardillac, Kaspar in Der Freischutz, Basilio, Mustafa, Wotan and Scarpia; Frequent concert appearances; Professor at the Lodz Music Academy from 1981.

ZAMBELLO Francesca, b. 24 Aug 1956, New York, New York, USA. Producer; Artistic Director. *Education:* High School: American School of Paris, 1974; BA, Colgate University, 1978. *Career:* Assistant Director, Lyric Opera of Chicago 1981-82, San Francisco Opera 1983-84; Artistic Director, Skylight Music Theater, 1984-; Guest Producer, San Francisco Opera, Teatro La Fenice, Savonlinna Festival, Houston Grand Opera, National Opera of Iceland, Seattle Opera, San Diego Opera, Wolftrap Farm Park, Greater Miami Opera, Pesaro Festival, Opera Theatre of St Louis, Rome Opera, Theatre Municipal de Lausanne, Teatro Regio, Parma; Wexford Festival, 1988-89, The Devil and Kate and Der Templer und die Jüdin. *Honours:* National Opera Institute (NIMT) Grant for one year apprenticeship in stage direction. *Current Management:* Columbia Artists. *Address:* c/o Columbia Artists, 165 West 57th Street, New York, NY 10019, USA.

ZAMBON Amadeo, b. 19 July 1934, Fontana Villorba, Venice, Italy. Singer (Tenor). *Education:* Studied with Marcello del Monaco. *Career:* Sang in La Boheme at the Teatro la Fenice in 1961; Istanbul 1962-65, as Rodolfo, Cavaradossi, Calaf and Radames; Appearances in Milan, Naples, Palermo, Vienna, Paris, Monte Carlo, Stockholm and Frankfurt; Verona Arena 1967; Sang in concert performances of Bellini's Il Pirata and La Straniera at New York (1969) with Montserrat Caballé; Cairo 1970 as Radames, Torre del Lago 1976, as Calaf in a performance of Turandot marking the 50th anniversary of Puccini's death; La Scala 1977, in Giordano's Siberia and La cena delle beffe; Sang Verdi's Otello at Berne in 1985; Other roles in operas by Rossini, Mercadante, Donizetti and Mascagni.

ZAMECNIK Evzen, b. 5 Feb. 1939, Frydek Mistek, Czechoslovakia. Composer. *Education:* Studied in Brno at the Conservatory and at the Janacek Academy of Musical Arts, 1963-68; Munich Hochschule with Gunter Bialas, 1968-70 and in Prague at the Academy of Musical Arts. *Career:* Played violin in various Czech orchestras 1963-81. *Compositions include:* Opera, A Farce about the Tub, Brno 1968; Ferda the Ant stage piece for children and adults, Brno 1977; Baggy the Beetle, Prague, Smetana Theatre, 1988. *Address:* OSA (Czechoslovakia) c/o PRS Ltd. Member Registration, 29-33 Berners Street, London W1P 4AA, England.

ZAMIR, b. 1953, USA. Singer (High Tenor). *Education:* Universities of Massachusetts at Amherst, Maine at Porland-Gorham and Chicago and San Francisco Conservatories of Music. *Career:* Has Appeared since 1985 in major cities of Israel, USA, Iceland, Germany, England, Cyprus in wide range of concert and operatic music; Conductors include Marc Minkowski, Christopher Hogwood, Stanley Sperber, Avner Biron, Jon Stefansson, Nicholas McGegan, Dalia Atlas and Richard Westenberg; In past has performed as Male Soprano, Countertenor and baritone as well as tenor, now specialising as high tenor, Tenore di Grazia; Has sung in Die Fledermaus, 1977; La Bohème, 1988; Cendrillon, 1986; A Midsummer Night's Dream, 1987; Lucia di Lammermoor, Mefistofele, Attila, Platée and Cavalleria Rusticana, 1988; La Clemenza di Tito, Alcina, 1990; Riccardo Primo (at Covent Garden) 1991.

ZAMMIT Charles (Carmelo) Elia, b. 8 Dec 1933, Hamrun, Malta. Lecturer; Examiner; Conductor. m. 2 Mar 1957, 1 son. *Education:* DMus, UK; PhD, USA. *Debut:* As Conductor, Radio City Opera House, Malta, 1960. *Career:* Various TV and radio appearances; Regular part-time broadcaster of music educational radio programmes; Currently Director of Music at the Institute for Music, Malta. *Compositions:* Symphonic Study for Orchestra; Overtures, suites, songs, Clarinet concerto, military band music, piano pieces. *Publications:* Sound Methods in Piano pedagogy, book, 1990; Tone in piano, Touch in piano, (articles); Further articles to local newspapers and over 500 radio scripts. *Honours:* Three prizes for music composition; Gold Medal, Malta Society of Arts for artistic achievements, 1990; van Beethoven Medal, Netherlands; Gold Medal (Composition) London; Knighthood, 1993; Five-Star Leader and Men's Inner Circle of Achievement Awards (ABI). *Memberships:* UCKMET, London; ISM, London; American Musicological Society. *Hobbies:* Reading; Walking; Gardening. *Address:* "Excelsior House" Valletta Road, Luqa, Malta LQA 03.

ZAMPIERI Maria, b. 24 May 1941, Padua, Italy. Singer (Soprano). *Education:* Studied at Padua Conservatory. *Debut:* Pavia 1972. *Career:* La Scala Milan from 1977, as Amalia in I Masnadieri, Leonora in Il Trovatore and Elisabeth de Valois; Trieste as Elvira in Ernani; Lisbon as Amelia Boccanegra; Vienna Staatsoper from 1979, in Il Giuramento, Attila and Macbeth; Deutsche Oper Berlin and Verona Arena as Aida; Covent Garden debut 1984, as Tosca; Other engagements in Munich, Buenos Aires, San Francisco, Bregenz, Bonn and Frankfurt; Sang Francesca da Rimini at Karlsruhe 1986; Season 1987/88 as Norma at Nîmes and Lady Macbeth at Spoleto; Stuttgart Staatsoper 1990, as Tosca, Bregenz Festival 1990, in the title role of La Wally; debut as Salome at Vienna, 1991. *Recordings include:* Il Giuramento; Attila; Belisario; Macbeth (Philips). *Address:* Allied Artists, 42 Montpelier Square, London SW7 1JZ, England.

ZANABONI Giuseppe, b. 25 Nov 1926, Pontelagoscuro, FE, Italy. Organist; Conductor; Composer. m. Clelia Losi, 12 Sept 1951, 1 son, 1 daughter. *Education:* Accountancy studies; Organ Diploma, 1945; Composition Diploma, 1949; Choral Music and Conducting, 1949. *Debut:* 1945. *Career:* Major solo organ concerts, worldwide; Masterclasses, Europe and America; Chamber and Symphonic Orchestra Conductor, Italy; Director, State Music Conservatorium, Piacenza, 1968-89; Artistic Director, V L Ciampi instrumental group for diffusion of ancient music; Founder, Director, Gruppe V Legrenzio Ciampi chamber music ensemble, Piacenza. *Compositions:* Cantatas: Cantata a Roma, 1950; Apoteosi, 1951; I Bambini di Terezin, 1991; Chamber Music: Quartetto, 1949; Quadri plastici, 1954; Luna Park, 1968; Profilo di un Organo-1 Suite, 1975; Quatuor per archi, 1988; Triplum per 3 strum, 1989; Pinocchio in Fantasia, 1990;

Liric Opera Myrica, 1949; La Regina delle nevi, 1953; Casello 83, 1956; Piccola suite per 3 fiati, 1958; Toccata per organo, 1966; Monologo per flauto, 1967; Meditazione per archi e Organo, 1968; Fantasia di improvvisazioni per Organo, 1982; Serenata per violino solo, 1984; Profilo di un organo, 2nd suite, 1988; Menhir, Studio per fagotto, 1992; Tiphyscolon, L'Argonauta 1492, impressioni sinfoniche, 1992; Choral music: La Fravezzosa - Carme madricalis, 1984. *Recordings:* Vedette records/Ars Nova: 7 records of organ music in series Antichi Organi Italiani and instrumental music; AEO and RCA: 3 records of organ music; Everst Records, Los Angeles: 1 record of instrumental music. *Publications:* Ciampi, 30 anni di musica a Piacenza, 1987. *Hobby:* Photography. *Address:* Via Giulio Alberoni 33, 29100 Piacenza, Italy.

ZANASI Mario, b. 8 Jan 1927, Bologna, Italy. Singer (Baritone). *Education:* Studied at the Conservatorio Martini, Bologna; La Scala Opera School. *Debut:* Cesena 1954, in Lohengrin. *Career:* Sang widely in Italy and at opera houses in Portugal, France, Belgium and Germany; Metropolitan Opera from 1958 as Sharpless in Butterfly, Escamillo, Marcello in La Bohème, Amonasro and Enrico in Lucia di Lammermoor; Covent Garden 1958; Verona Arena 1957-72; Further appearances in Paris, Vienna, Chicago, Dallas, Miami, San Francisco and Munich. *Recordings:* Giulietta e Romeo by Zandonai; Madame Sans-Gêne by Giordano; Madama Butterfly; Maria di Rohan by Donizetti.

ZANAZZO Alfredo, b. 14 Oct 1946, Imperia, Italy. Singer (Bass). *Education:* Studied with Tancredi Pasero. *Debut:* Verona Arena 1981, as the King in Aida. *Career:* Verona Arena 1982-89, as Ramphis and Timur; Sang Wagner's Dutchman at Treviso 1981, La Scala Milan 1982, as Narbal in Les Troyens and the King of Scotland in Ariodante; Season 1986-87 as Colline in La Bohème at the Paris Opera, Padre Guardiano at Rome, Zaccaria and Masetto at Turin and Ramphis at the Metropolitan; Appearances at Luxor and the Vienna Staatsoper as Ramphis, Macarate Festival as Raimondo in Lucia di Lammermoor; Zurich Opera 1988, as Banquo, and Welter Furst in Guillaume Tell; Further engagements at the Geneva Opera as Pluto in Monteverdi's Orfeo, at Frankfurt as Raimondo, in Toronto as Procida in Les Vepres Siciliennes and at Las Palmas as Alvise in La Gioconda; Teatro Margherita Genoa 1991, as Roucher in La Gioconda. *Address:* c/o Opernhaus Zurich, Falkenstrasse 1, CH-8008 Zurich, Switzerland.

ZANCANARO Giorgio, b. 9 May 1939, Verona, Italy. Singer (Baritone). *Education:* Debut: Teatro Nuovo Milan in I Puritani. *Career:* Sang widely in Italy from 1971; International career from 1977, notably in London, Frankfurt, Rome, Hamburg, Paris and Zurich; Milan La Scala debut 1981, as Ford in Falstaff; Metropolitan Opera debut 1982 as Renato in Un Ballo in Maschera; Macerata Festival 1983 as Posa in Don Carlos; Florence 1984-85, as Germont and Posa; Covent Garden 1985, as Gerard in Andrea Chénier; Other roles include Verdi's Rigoletto, Luna and Ezio (Attila), Escamillo, Tonio in Pagliacci and Albert in Werther; Hamburg and La Scala 1988, as Count Luna and William Tell; sang Ezio in Attila at Covent Garden, 1990; Florence 1990, in Donizetti's Parisina d'Este. *Recordings include:* Il Trovatore, conducted by Giulini (Deutsche Grammophon). *Address:* c/o Royal Opera House (Contracts), Covent Garden, London WC2, England.

ZANETTOVICH Renato, b. 28 July 1921, Trieste, Italy. Violinist. m. Bianca Negri, 28 June 1947, 3 sons. *Education:* Violin Diploma. *Debut:* With the Trio di Trieste, 1933. *Career:* Concerts and records with Trio di Trieste throughout the world; Violin Teacher, Conservatories, Bolzano, 1950-55, Trieste, 1955-70, Venice, 1970-86. *Recordings:* Numerous records for Decca and Deutsche Grammophon. *Publications:* Revision of Etudes by Kayser op. 20, Mazas op. 36; Dont op. 37; Sitt op. 32; Scale and Arpeggio Exercises, 5 books. *Honour:* Commendatore al merito della Republic Italiana; Accademico di S Cecilia. *Membership:* Rotary Club, Trieste. *Address:* via Catraro 9, Trieste, Italy.

ZANGERLE Helmut, b. 6 Mar 1930, Lermoos, Tirol, Austria. Musician (Flautist). m. Annemarie Zatschek (harpist), 21 June 1960. 1 son, 1 daughter. *Education:* Innsbruck Conservatory; Scholarship, Paris Conservatory; Studied with Gaston Crunelle (Diploma 1954); Andre Jaunet, Zurich and Rene Le Roy, Paris. *Debut:* Soloist, 1954. *Career:* Co-Principal flute player, Innsbruck Symphony, 1957-93; Member, Mozarteum Orchestra, Salzburg, Principal Flautist; Soloist with orchestras in Europe, Asia and Africa; Duo with Annemarie Zatschek, flute and harp, numerous concert tours; Also with Quintet, flute, violin, viola, violoncello and harp; Flute teacher, Mozarteum (Conservatory) Salzburg, 1962-86; Member of Jury, National and International Competitions. *Honour:* Diploma, International Competition Munich, 1956. *Membership:* National Flute Association, Inc, USA; World Institute of Achievement (USA). *Address:* Tiefenbach-strasse 19, A-5161 Elixhausen, Salzburg, Austria.

ZANNINI Laura, b. 4 Apr 1937, Triests, Italy. Singer (Mezzo-soprano). *Education:* Studied at the Conservatorio Benedetto Marcell in Venice, with Gilda dalla Rizza, and with Bruno Maderna. *Debut:* Spoleto 1955, as Isabella in L'Italiana in Algeri. *Career:* Sang leading roles at Milan (La Scala), Genoa, Palermo, Naples, Parma, Venice, Turin and Triests; Verona Arena 1957, 1967, 1979-80, 1986; Piccola Scala 1966, in the premiere of Flavio Testi's Albergi dei Poveri; Further appearances at the Maggio Musicale Fiorentino, the State Operas of Vienna and Munich, the Paris Opera, Brussels, Bordeaux, Wiesbaden, Copenhagen, London, Edinburgh, Moscow and Budapest; Sang Alisa in Lucia di Lammermoor at Bari and Tisbe in La Cenerentola at Glyndebourne, 1983; Also sang in operas by Henze, Britten, Menotti, Poulenc, Stravinsky, Schoenberg, Zandonai. *Recordings:* Tisbe in La Cenerentola (Deutsche Grammophon); Flora in La Traviata, with Callas (HMV); Mascagni's Isabeau (MRF).

ZANOLLI Silvana, b. 14 Oct 1928, Fiume, Italy. Singer (Soprano) m. Otello Borgonova. *Education:* Studied at the Milan Opera School and with Luciano Tomerilli and Tomaso Japelli. *Debut:* La Scala Milan 1951, in La buona figliuola, by Piccinni. *Career:* Appearances in leading roles at Rome, Palermo, Bologna, Parma, Turin, Trieste, Naples and Venice. Festival engagements at Florence and Rome, guest showings at Buenos Aires, the State Operas of Vienna, Stuttgart and Munich; Brussels, Cologne, Rio de Janeiro, Geneva, Barcelona, Lisbon and London (Covent Garden); Verona Arena 1957-58 and Glyndebouorne 1959-60, as Clorinda in La Cenerentola; Also sang in Mexico City, Monte Carlo and New York (Metropolitan Opera). *Recordings:* Amelia al Ballo by Menotti (Columbia); Cimarosa's Il Matrimonio Segreto (Philips); Il Campiello by Wolf-Ferrari (MRF).

ZANOTELLI Hans, b. 1927, Wuppertal, Germany. Conductor. m. Ingeborg Schlosser. *Education:* Student in Cologne. *Career:* Choirmaster, Solingen, 1945; Conductor, Wuppertal 1950, Dusseldorf 1951-54, Bonn 1954-55, Hamburg State Opera 1955-57; General Music Director, Darmstadt 1957-63, Augsburg 1963-72; Chief Conductor, Stuttgart Philharmonic Orchestra, 1971-; Guest Conductor, Dresden Staatskapelle 1964-67, Bavarian State Opera 1968-71, Wurttemberg State Opera; Tours of numerous European countries; Leader, Der Rosenkavalier at Dresden for 300th anniversary; Leader, Verdi's Requiem at Dresden for anniversary of destruction of city in World War II. *Recordings:* Recording artist for Intercord-Ton, Sonopresse, EMI, and others. *Address:* Stuttgarter Philharmoniker, Leonhardplatz 28, D-7000 Stuttgart, Germany.

ZAPPULLA Robert, b. 11 Jan 1958, Brooklyn, NY, USA. Harpsichordist; Musicologist. m. Jane Kent, 11 July 1980. *Education:* BMus, SUNY, at Stony Brook, 1981; MA Music History and Theory, and MM Harpsichord, Rutgers University, 1985; AM Musicology, Duke University, 1988; Doctoral Candidate Musicology, University of Utrecht; Harpsichord studies with Raymond Erickson, Gustav Leonhardt, David

Schulenberg and R Peter Wolf. *Career:* Appearances in USA and Europe as solo harpsichordist and continuo player, 1980-; Private Tutor, keyboard, 1980-; Tutor, Music Theory, Rutgers University, 1982-83; Harpsichordist, Melante Baroque Ensemble, 1983-85; Lecturer, Duke University, 1987; Music Director, Community Church of Chapel Hill, 1989-90. *Honours:* Fulbright-Hays Fellowship, 1987-88. *Memberships:* American Musicological Society. *Address:* 81 Gray Street, Floor 1, Bogota, NJ 07603-1138, USA.

ZARITZKAYA Irina, b. 1940, Kiev, Ukraine. Concert Pianist. *Career:* Appearances in Eastern Europe from 1960, notably with the USSR State Orchestra and the Moscow, Warsaw and Kiev Philharmonics; Conductors included Kondrashin, Barshai, Ahronovitch and Natan Rachlin; Broadcasting engagements in Poland and the former Soviet Union; Emigrated to Israel 1972, becoming Senior Lecturer at the Rubin Academy; Recitals at the South Bank, London, and concerts with the LSO, Royal Philharmonic and City of Birmingham Symphony; Tours to France, Spain, USA, Argentina, Colombia, Brazil, Italy, Hong Kong and Taiwan; Duo recitals with violinist Boris Belkin; Currently resident in London and is Professor at the Royal College of Music; Recitals with cellist Natalia Gutman and performances throughout Western Europe. *Honours include:* Second Prize (to Maurizio Pollini) 1960 Chopin Competition in Warsaw; Honorary Member, Royal College of Music, 1980. *Address:* Robert Gilder and Co. Enterprise House, 59-65 Upper Ground, London SE1 1PQ, England.

ZAROU Jeannette, b. 1942, Ramallah, Palestine. Singer (Soprano). *Education:* Studied at the Royal Conservatory of Music Toronto with Irene Jessner, Halina Wyszkowski and Herman Geiger-Torel. *Debut:* Priestess in Aida with Canadian Opera at Toronto, 1964. *Career:* Sang Liu in Turandot for Canadian Opera, 1965; Member of the Deutsche Oper am Rhein Dusseldorf from 1967; Guest appearances in Toronto, Berlin (Deutsche Oper), Hamburg and Munich (State Opera), Cologne, Frankfurt, Karlsruhe, Nuremberg, Bordeaux and Rouen; Other roles have been Mimi, Marzelline (Fidelio), Marguerite, Ilia (Idomeneo), Pamina, Zdenka and Sophie in Rosenkavalier; Modern repertoire has included Miss Wordsworth in Albert Herring and Blanche in Dialogues des Carmélites; Many concert appearances. *Recordings include:* Requiem by Draeske (PAN).

ZAUGG Georges, b. 22 Apr 1951, Courgenay, Switzerland; Music Teacher; Conductor; Director of the Music Festival of Jura. *Education:* Music Teacher, University of Berne and Conservatory of Bienne, 1976; Music Education: Conductor, Royal Conservatory of Brussels, 1985. *Career:* Presentations with Pierre Dervaux (Nice), Festival of Jura; Conductor of many orchestra including: Orchestre de chambre Tibor Varga; Orchestre du Collegium Academicum de Genève; la Societé d'Orchestre de Bienne; l'Orchestre du Conservatoire Royal de Bruxelles; Music Teacher, Thurmann College, Porrentruy. *Memberships:* Artistic Director, Music Festival of Jura; Association des Musiciens Suisses. *Address:* Director of the Musical Festival of Jura, Le Chene, CH-2892 Courgenay, Switzerland.

ZAWADZKA-GOLOSZ Anna, b. 1 Dec 1955, Krakow, Poland. Composer. m. Jerzy Golosz, 6 July 1986. *Education:* Diploma in Theory of Music, Academy of Music, Krakow, 1981; Studies in Composition at the Academy of Music, Krakow under Krystyna Moszumanska-Nazar; Diploma, Academy of Music, Krakow, 1987 and at the Hochschule fur Musik, Theater und Tanz in Essen under Wolfgang Hufschmidt. *Career:* Teacher 1981-, Theory of Music; Assistant Academy of Music in Krakow; Performances in Poland and abroad including Warsaw Autumn - International Festival of Contemporary Music, 1986. *Compositions:* Girare for percussion and tape, 1986; Esoterikos for soprano and oboe quartet, 1984; Senza for double bass, 1984; A duo for double bass and tape, 1980; Obraz w pieciu ujeciach/the picture in five aspects, 1987; Vitrail II for clarinet, cello, accordion and vibraphone, 1988. *Membership:* Polish Section of ISCM. *Address:* ul. Basztowa 5/28, 31-134 Krakow, Poland.

ZAZOFSKY Peter, b. 1955, Boston, USA. Concert Violinist. *Education:* Studied with Joseph Silverstein, Dorothy DeLay and Ivan Galamian and at the Curtis Institute of Music. *Career:* Frequent appearances from 1977 with such orchestras as the Berlin and Rotterdam Philharmonics, the Vienna Symphony and the Amsterdam Concertgebouw Orchestra; North American engagements at Atlanta, Baltimore, Boston, Minnesota, Montreal, Philidaelphia, San Francisco, Toronto and Vancouver; Tour of the USA with the Danish Radio Orchestra and recitals at the Kennedy Center and New York's Carnegie Hall; Further concerts in Israel and throughout Europe with such conductors as Dutoit, Zinman, Ormany, Tennstedt and Ozawa; 1978 recital tour of South America. *Honours:* Prize winner at the 1977 Wieniawski Competition, 1978 Montreal International and 1980 Queen Elisabeth of the Belgians Competition, Brussels; Avery Fisher Career Grant 1985. *Address:* c/o Anglo Swiss Ltd, 3 Primrose Mews, 1a Sharpeshall St, London NW1 8YW, England.

ZEANI Virginia, b. 21 Oct 1928, Solovastru, Rumania. Singer (Soprano). m. Nicola Rossi-Lemeni 1957 (deceased 1991). *Education:* Studied in Bucharest with Lucia Anghel and Lydia Lipkovska, and with Aureliano Pertile in Milan. *Debut:* Bologna 1948, as Violetta. *Career:* London debut, Stoll Theatre, 1953 as Violetta; La Scala 1956, as Cleopatra in Giulio Cesare; sang Blanche in the premiere of Dialogues des Carmélites, 1957; Vienna and Paris debuts 1957; Verona Arena 1956-63; Took part in revivals of Donizetti's Maria di Rohan (Naples 1965), Rossini's Otello (Rome 1968) and Verdi's Alzira (Rome 1970); Further appearances at the Covent Garden 1959, the Metropolitan 1966 and in Budapest, Bucharest, Mexico City, Rio de Janeiro, Zurich, Amsterdam, Belgrade, Moscow and Madrid; Other roles include Aida, Desdemona, Tosca, Manon & Manon Lescaut, Lucia di Lammermoor, Elvira (I Puritani), and Magda Sorel in The Consul by Menotti; Further engagements in Barcelona, Lisbon, Leningrad, Houston, Philadelphia, Berlin and New Orleans 1966; Sang at Barcelona 1977-78, as Giordano's Fedora; Sang 67 roles, 648 times Traviata around the World, 34 awards (Gold Medals); Commendatore of Italian Republic; Professor of Voice, Indiana University School of Music, 1980-. *Recordings:* La Traviata; Rossini's Otello; Elisa e Claudio by Mercadante; Rossini's Zelmira; Alzira; Le Serva Padrona (Vox). *Honours:* Gold Medal, Egypt, 1951; Gold Medal, Barcelona, 1963; Maschera D'argento, 1965-70; Diapason D'oro, 1968; Arena D'oro, 1966. *Memberships:* Accademia Tiberina-Roma; Commendatore Italian Republic; Sorotimist Club Roma. *Address:* 2616 Robins Bow, Bloomington, IN 47401, USA.

ZEAVIN Carol, b. 2 May 1948, San Bernardino, California, USA. Violinist. *Education:* Studied in New York. *Career:* Co-founded Columbia String Quartet 1977 (initially called Schoenberg String Quartet); Many performances in the standard and modern repertory, including the premieres of Wuorinen's Archangel and Second Quartet (1978, 1980), Roussakis's Ephermeris (1979), and quartets by Morton Feldman (1980), Wayne Peterson (1984) and Larry Bell (1985); On Nov. 1 1979 at Abraham Goodman House, New York, played in the premiere of Berg's Lyric Suite, with recently discovered vocal finale. *Recordings include:* String Quartet No 3 by Lukas Foss and Ned Rorem's Mourning Song.

ZECCHILLO Giuseppe, b. 18 Dec 1929, Sao Paulo, Brazil. Singer (Baritone). *Education:* Studied at the Conservatorio Giuseppe Verdi at Milan and with Aureloano Pertile and Carlo Tagliabus. *Debut:* Teatro Nuovo Milan 1953, as Germont in La Traviata. *Career:* Leading roles at La Scala Milan, Rome, Bologna, Naples, Palermo, Parma, Turin, Triests and Venice; Festival engagements at Caracalla, Verona, 1972-85, Sharpless in Butterfly, 1983 and Florence (Maggio Musicale); Further appearances at the New York City Opera and

in San Francisco and Monte Carlo; Distinguished in contemporary, as well as standard, repertory. *Recordings include:* Nina by Paisiello (Cetra).

ZECHBERGER Gunther, b. 24 April 1951, Zams, Tyrol, Austria. Composer; Conductor. *Education:* Studied at the Innsbruck Conservatory, 1968-74; University of Innsbruck with Witold Rowicki and Boguslaw Schaeffer. *Career:* Founded and conducted the Tyroler Ensemble fur Neue Musik, 1984. *Compositions include:* Trio for clarinet, horn and bassoon 1973; Trio for violins 1975; Das neue Preislied for women's chorus and speaker 1975; Schlus Stuck for mixed chorus and orchestra 1979; Mass for mixed chorus and orchestra 1979; Trombone quartet 1980; Stabat Mater for mixed chorus 1981; Im Nebel for mezzo and orchestra 1982; Study for 12 strings 1983; Hendekegon for 26 instruments 1984; Tieferschuttert for mezzo, trombone and guitar 1984; String Quartet 1985, Chorus for 5 musicians 1985; Stabat Mater II for mezzo and ensemble 1985-88; Kammermusik for conductor and 5 musicians 1986 Dear Mr J, 1987; Interview for tape 1987; Guitar Concerto 1988; Duet for Guitars 1988. *Address:* AKM (Austria), c/o PRS Ltd. Member Registration, 29-33 Berners Street, London W1P 4AA, England.

ZECHLIN Ruth, b. 22 June 1926, Grosshartmannsdorf, Germany. Composer; Harpsichordist. *Education:* Studied composition with Johann Nepomuk David, Organ with Karl Straube and Gunther Ramin, 1943-49. *Career:* Lecturer in music from 1950 and Professor of composition from 1969 at the Berlin Musikhochschule; Member of the Akademie der Künste Berlin 1970. *Compositions include:* Opera for actors Reinicke Fuchs 1967; Opera Die Salamandrin und die Bildsäule 1989; Opera Die Reise, 1992; Ballet, La Vita, 1983. Orchestral: 3 Symphonies, 1965, 1966 and 1971; 2 Chamber-Symphonies, 1967 and 1973; Briefe, 1978; Situationen, 1980; Musik für Orchester, 1980; Metamorphosen, 1982; Musik zu Bach 1983; Kristallisation, 1987; Stufen, 1993; Piano Concert, 1974; 2 Violin Concerts, 1963 and 1990; 4 Organ Concerts, 1974; 1975; 1980; 1984; 2 Harpsochord Concerts, 1975 amd 1986. Chamber: Reflexionen for 14 strings, 1979; Konstellationen for 10 wind instruments, 1985; Akzente und Flächen for 5 percussions, 1993; circulations for 8 percussions, 1994; 6 string quartets, 1959-77; 19 great mixed chamber-music, 1966-93; Vocal: Lidice Kantante, 1958; Canzoni alla notte for bariton and orchestra,, 1974; Das Hohelied for tenor and orchestra, 1979; Der Sieg von Guernica for 4 voices, 1975, Das A und das O for mezzo solo, 1990, piano, harpsichord and organ music. *Address:* Kronberger Str. 15, D-94086 Griesbach, I R.

ZEDDA Alberto, b. 2 Jan 1928, Milan, Italy. Conductor; Musicologist. *Education:* Studied at the Milan Conservatory with Galliera, Fait, Votto and Giulini. *Debut:* Conducted the Polytechnic Chamber Group of Milan 1956. *Career:* Taught at the Cincinnati College of Music, 1957-59; Coached winners of American vocal competitions, 1959-61; Conducted Italian operas at the Deutsche Oper Berlin, 1961-63; New York City Opera from 1963; Guest conductor with leading orchestras and opera companies in the USA, Israel and Europe; Covent Garden debut 1975, Il Barbiere di Siviglia; Co-editor wth Philp Gossett of the complete edition of Rossini's works, Rossini Foundation; Conducted Il Barbiere with the company of Cologne Opera at Hong Kong 1989; Il Turco in Italia at the Teatro de la Zarzuela Madrid 1990; La Scala di seta at the 1990 Pesaro Festival, Semiramide, 1992. *Publications:* Critical edition of Il barbiere di Siviglia, 1969; Further editions of Torvaldo e Dorliska and La Gazza Ladra by Rossini. *Address:* c/o Philip Gossett, Department of Music, University of Chicago, 5345 Ellis Avenue, IL 60637, USA.

ZEDNIK Heinz, b. 21 Feb 1940, Vienna. Singer (Tenor). *Education:* Studied with Marga Wissmann and at the Vienna Conservatory. *Debut:* Graz 1964, in La Forza del Destino. *Career:* Vienna Staatsoper from 1964, notably in the 1976 premiere of Von Einem's Kabale und Liebe; Guest appearances in Nice, Moscow, Montreal and Baden; Bayreuth Festival from 1970, as David, the Steersman, Mime and Loge; Salzburg Festival 1984, in the premiere of Berio's Un Re in Ascolto; Other roles include Mozart's Pedrillo and Monostatos, Beethoven's Jacquino and Peter the Great in Zar und Zimmermann; Salzburg Festival 1986, in the premiere of Penderecki's Die schwarze Maske; Pedrillo 1987-89; Mime at the New York Metropolitan 1989-90 (also televised). *Recordings:* Parsifal, Lustige Weiber von Windsor, Le Nozze di Figaro, Wozzeck (Decca); Salome, Wiener Blut, Die Zauberflöte (Electrola); Das Rheingold and Siegfried from Bayreuth (Philips). *Address:* c/o Allied Artists, 42 Montpelier Square, London SW7 1JZ, England.

ZEFFIRELLI G Franco (Corsi), b. 12 Feb 1923, Florence, Italy. Opera, Film & Theatrical Producer. *Career:* Early career as actor, under Visconti; Began opera, 1948; Produced & Designed La Cenerentola, La Scala, Milan, 1953; Responsible for many famous productions including Maria Callas/Tosca, Joan Sutherland/Lucia di Lammermoor; designs for opening production of Metropolitan Opera at Lincoln Center, 1966: Barber's Antony and Cleopatra. Films of opera include: La Bohème; Cavalleria Rusticana; Pagliacci; Carmen; Tosca; La Traviata; Otello. Numerous other, non-operatic subjects; Produced and designed La Traviata and Don Giovanni at the Metropolitan 1989-90; Don Carlos for the opening of the 1992-93 season at La Scala. *Address:* c/o Metropolitan Opera, Lincoln Center, New York, NY 10023, USA.

ZEHETMAIR Thomas, b. 1961, Salzburg, Austria. Concert Violinist. *Education:* Studied at the Salzburg Mozarteum; Master classes with Max Rostal and Nathan Milstein. *Career:* Concert appearances with the Boston, Chicago Cleveland, Minnesota and San Francisco Orchestras; Philharmonia, English and Scottish Chamber, BBC Symphony, City of Birmingham, Rotterdam Philharmonic and Concertgebouw; Stockholm Philharmonic and Leipzig Gewandhaus; Conductors have included Blomstedt, Eschenbach, Harnoncourt, Horst Stein, Sawallisch, Leppard, Dohnanyi, Marriner, Rattle and Norrington; Guest engagements at international music festivals; Chamber music with Gidon Kremer at Lockenhaus; London recital debut at the Wigmore Hall 1993; Concerto engagements with the BBC Philharmonic, Bournemouth Symphony, Northern Sinfonia and Scottish Chamber Orchestra 1993; Repertoire includes concertos by Szymanowski, Bach, Bartok, Henze, Berg and Prokofiev, in addition to the standard works. *Recordings:* Beethoven's Kreutzer and Spring sonatas, Concertos by Brahms, Joseph and Michael Haydn, Mendelessohn, Mozart, Schumann and Sibelius; Berg's Chamber Concerto and Schoenberg's Violin Concerto, conducted by Heinz Holliger.*Address:* c/o Sue Lubbock Concert Management, 25 Courthorpe Road, London NW3 2LE, England.

ZEITLIN Zvi, b. 21 Feb 1923, Dubrovna, USSR. Concert Violinist; Professor of Violin. m. Marianne Langner, 1 son, 1 daughter. *Education:* Juilliard School of Music; Hebrew University, Jerusalem. *Debut:* New York, 1951. *Career:* Professor, Eastman School of Music, University of Rochester, New York; Head of Violin Department, Music Academy of the West, Santa Barbara, California; Concert tours worldwide; Appearances with leading world symphony orchestras; Broadcasts on radio and TV; Editor, newly discovered Nardini Concerto, 1958; Currently working on 6 other Nardini concertos. *Recordings:* Schoenberg Violin Concerto; Rochberg Variations; Schumann Sonatas; Schubert Trios with Eastman Trio. *Honours:* American Israel Society Award for furthering cultural relations between USA and Israel, 1957; Commission of violin concerto by Gunther Schuller by Eastman School of Music and National Endowment of the Arts; Commission of violin concerto by Carlos Surinach by Music Academy of the West Summer Festival; Commission of Paul Ben Haim Violin Concerto for Zeitlin, American Israel Cultural Foundation; 1st Kilbourn Professor, Eastman

School of Music. *Memberships:* The Bohemians, New York; University of Rochester Faculty Club; New York State Teachers Association; American Federation of Musicians. *Current Management:* Thea Dispeker, New York. *Address:* 204 Warren Avenue, Rochester, NY 14618, USA.

ZELJENKA Ilja, b. 21 Dec 1932, Bratislava, Czechoslovakia. Composer. m. Maria Kimlickova, 13 Apr 1957, 1 daughter. *Education:* Gymnasium 1943-51; Composition studies, Academy of Music and Drama, Bratislava, 1951-56. *Debut:* 1956. *Career:* Dramaturgist of the Slovak Philharmony, 1957-61; with the Slovak Radio 1961-68; Freelance Composer 1968-90; Chairman of the Slovak Music Union 1990-91; President of the International Festival of Contemporary Music, Melos-Ethos, 1991. *Compositions:* 5 symphonies; 6 string quartets, 4 piano sonatas, 2 piano concertos, clarinet concerto, violin concerto, Dualogues for violoncello and chamber string orchestra, Oswienczym cantata, 2 piano quartets, Polymetric Music for 4 string quintets, Music for Clarinet, Piano and Percussion, Metamorphoses XV for chamber ensemble and reciter, Galgenlieder, for soprano, string quartet, clarinet, flute and piano, Mutations for soprano, bass, wind quintet and percussion, Astecian Songs for soprano, piano and percussion, Plays for 13 singers and percussion. *Hobbies:* Astronomy; Biology. *Address:* 11a Zeljenka, Slavicie udolie 14, 81102 Bratislava, Slovakia.

ZEMTSOVSKY Izaly Iosifovich, b. 22 Feb 1936, Leningrad, USSR. Ethnomusicologist. m. Alma Kunanbaeva, 29 Jan 1982. *Education:* MA, Philology, University of Leningrad, 1958; Diploma, Russian Folklore; Musicology and Composition, 1955-60, 1961; Leningrad Conservatoire; MA; PhD; Full Professor. *Debut:* 1958. *Career:* Senior Research Fellow, Head of Folklore Department, Leningrad State Institute of Theatre, Music and Cinema (now Russian Institute of History of the Arts, 1990-), 1960-; Head, Department of Traditional Culture, Russian Pedagogic University; Vice-President, Jewish Musical Society of St Petersburg, 1992; Russian Representative of the Society for the reintroduction of the Delphic Games, Musica Magna International, 1993. *Publications include:* Russian Folk Song, 1964; The Russian Song, 1967; Songs of Toropets: Songs of the Homeland of Moussorgsky, 1967; Songs Hunters, 1967; The Poetry of Peasant Holidays, 1970; The Melodics of Calendar Songs, 1975; Folklore and the Composer, 1978; Tracing the Melody Vesnianka from P Tchaikovsky's Piano Concerto: The Historical Morphology of the Folk Songs, 1987; Russian Folk Music, in Grove's Dictionary of Music and Musicians, 1980; Boris Assaf'yer about folk music, 1987. *Address:* Folklore Department, Institute of History of the Arts, 190000 St. Petersburg, Isaakievskaja pl 5, Russia.

ZENATY Ivan, b. 1960, Czechoslovakia. Concert Violinist. *Education:* Studied at the Prague Conservatoire and the Academy of Arts; Weimar with Andre Gertier, Zurich with Nathan Milstein. *Career:* Solo appearances with all leading Czech orchestras in Austria, Bulgaria, England, Finland, Holland, Italy, Poland, Spain, the Soviet Union, Switzerland, Yugoslavia; Festival engagements in Prague, Dubrovnik, Moscow, Sofia, Bertlin and Havana; Repertoire includes concertos by Bach, Haydn, Mozart, Vivaldi, Myslevifek, Sibelius, Dvosák, Vieuxtemps and Kalabis; Bach solo sonatas and Telemann solo fantasies; Sonatas by Mozart, Beethoven, Vanhal, Schubert, Schumann, Brahms, Prokofiev, Dvosák, Janáfek and Martinv. *Honours include:* First Prize, Prague Spring Festival Competition, 1987. *Recordings:* Albums for Supraphon and Panton. *Address:* Pragokoncert, Maltezske nam 1, 118 13 Prague 1, Czech Republic.

ZENDER (Johannes Wolfgang) Hans, b. 22 Nov 1936, Wiesbaden, Germany. Composer; Conductor. m. Gertrud Achenbach. *Education:* Diplomas in Conducting, Piano and Composition, Academy of Music Freiburg. *Career:* Conductor, Freiburg, 1959; Principal Conductor, Bonn, 1964; General Music Director, City of Kiel, 1969; Principal Conductor, Saar Broadcasting, 1971-83; Chief Conductor Hamburg State Opera House 1984-; Guest Conductor: Berlin Philharmonic, London Symphony Orchestra, BBC, Residentie-Orkest, ORF Vienna, Tonhalle Zurich, Opera Houses of Munich, Bayreuth (Parsial); Chief Guest Conductor of the National Opera Orchestra, Brussels (Fidelio, 1989). *Compositions:* Vexilla Regis; Quartet for flute, cello, piano and percussion; Trifolium for flute, cello and piano; Les Sirènes Chantent for soprano and instruments; Muji no Kyo for trio and instruments ad lib; Bremen Wodu, electronic; Schachspiel for orchestra; Zeitstrome for orchestra; Cantos 1-V for voices and instruments; Hölderlin Lesen for string quartet; Modelle I-XII for orchestral groups; Loshu I-IV for flute and instruments; Dialog mit Haydn. *Recordings:* Elemente; Litanei; Mondschrift; Canto II. *Contributions to:* Neue Zeitschrift für Musik. *Honours:* Numerous honours for compositions. *Memberships:* GEMA; International Society for Contemporary Music. *Hobbies:* Arts; Literature. *Anddress and Current Management:* Allied Artists, 42 Montpelier Square, London SW7 1JZ, England.

ZENKL Ludek, b. 5 May 1926, Tabor, Czechoslovakia. Techer of Music; Writer on Music. m. Miloslava Bartosilkova, 19 Oct 1963, 3 sons. *Education:* PhD, Charles University. *Career:* Teacher of Music, Charles University, Prague, 1950-61; Teacher of Music, Palacky Universty, Olomouc, 1962-73; Teacher of Music, Ostrava University, Ostava, 1973-. *Publications:* Temper and Clear Musical Pitch in Europe (Temperovane a Ciste Ladeni v Evropske Hudbe), 1971; ABC of Music Theory (ABC Huderni Nauky), 1976; ABC of Musical Forms (ABC Hudebnich Forem), 1984. *Contributions to:* Musical reviews, Hudebni Rozhledy, Prague; Opus Musicum, Brno. *Memberships:* Society of Music Education. *Hobbies:* Literature; Travel. *Address:* Chelcickeho 8, Ostrava 1, 70100 Czech Republic.

ZENTAI Csilla, b. 23 May 1940, Mako, Hungary. Singer (Soprano). *Education:* Studied at Szeged and Budapest, and with Lore Fischer and Hubert Giessen in Stuttgart. *Debut:* Stuttgart Opera School 1969. in Ibert's Angelique. *Career:* Sang at the Ulm Opera 1969-72, Bremen 1973- 79, Deutsche Oper am Rhein from 1979; Guest appearances at the State Operas of Stuttgart, Hamburg and Munich, Vienna Staatsoper (as Mozart's Countess and Fiordiligi) Zurich (the Marschallin) and the Deutsche Oper Berlin (Elvira and Blumenmädchen 1); Cologne Opera as Fiordiligi, Agathe, Butterfly and Marenka; Further engagements at Bordeaux, Brussels, Salzburg (Donna Anna in concert performance of Don Giovanni) and Moscow; Other roles have included Violetta, Komponist, Jenvfa, Pamina, Rosalinde, Marguerite and Amaranta in La Fedelta Premiata by Haydn; Concert appearances in Germany, Holland, Belgium, Italy, Spain, Mexico and Hungary; Title of Kammersängerin of the Deutsche Oper am Rhein, 1990-; Professor, Folkwang Musikhochschule, 1991-. *Address:* c/o Deutsche Oper am Rhein, Dusseldorf, Heinrich Heine Allee 16, 4000 Dusseldorf, Germany.

ZERBINI Antonio, b. 1928, Italy. Singer (Bass). *Debut:* Sang in La Forza del Destino at Spoleto, 1952. *Career:* Sang at the Verona Arena 1958-71, debut as Ramphis in Aida; Further appearances at La Scala Milan, Moscow, Buenos Aires and the Paris Opera; Théâtre de la Monnaie Brussels 1960, 1962, 1969, 1979 as the King in Aida, Mozart's Commendatore, Angelotti in Tosca, Timur in Turandot and Padre Guardiano (La Forza del Destino); Also sang in Nice and Monte Carlo, 1979; Verona Arena 1981, as Sparafucile in Rigoletto; Sang Hieros in a revival of L'Assedio di Corinto by Rossini at Florence, 1982. *Recordings:* Tosca, Aida, Don Giovanni, L'Arlesiana (Cetra); Donizetti's Maria Stuarda (EJS); I Lombardi (MRF); La Forza del Destino (MMV); Manon and Lucia di Lammermoor.

ZETTERSTROM Rune, b. 1936, Vasteras, Sweden. Singer (Bass). *Education:* Studied at the opera school of the Stora Teatern, Gothenburg, 1963-66. *Debut:* Gothenburg 1966 as Mozart's Bartolo. *Career:* Guest engagements at Oslo, 1970, Bergen, 1972, 1975, Copenhagen, 1976, London, 1977; Major roles have been Seneca in L'Incoronazione di Poppea, Rossini's Basilio, Anckarstrom in Tintomara by Werle, Timur in Turandot and Puccini's Colline; Sang the Lion in Werle's Animalen with the Stora Teatern at the Wiesbaden Festival, 1981; Recent roles include Mozart's Figaro, Sarastro, Leporello and Osmin; Philip in Don Carlos; Guest Engagements in Semperopera in Dresden, 1988 with Osmin. *Recordings include:* Tintomara (Philips). *Address:* Stora Teatern, Box 53116, S-400 15 Goteborg, Sweden.

ZHI-JIAN Wang, b. 5 Jan 1934, Shanghai, China. Clarinet Teacher; Artist; Designer. m. Zhou Bao-ru, 19 Sept 1963, 1 son, 2 daughters. *Education:* Central Music Conservatory of China, studies of clarinet and chamber music, 1952-57; Studied clarinet with Oskar Christmann, 1956-57, Dreston Symphony Orchestra principal clarinettist, Peking, China. *Debut:* Peking, Tiangjin, China, 1957. *Career:* Teacher of clarinet and chamber music, Central Music Conservatory, Principal Clarinettist, 1957-62; Professor of Clarinet and Deputy Director of the Library in Tianjin Conservatory of Music, 1962-; Concurrently, Advisor of Tianjian Music Wind Instrument Factory. *Contributions to:* The Clarinet; Music Study and Research. *Memberships:* International Clarinet Society, National Chairman; Director, Tianjin Music Instrument Society; Director, Tianjin Musicians Association; Chinese Musicians Association. *Address:* Tianjin Conservatory of Music, 57 11th Jin Road, Hedong District, Tianjin, China.

ZHISLIN Grigory, b. 7 May 1945, St Petersburg, Russia. Violinist; Violist. *Education:* Studied at the Central Music School and the State Conservatoire in Moscow. *Career:* Many appearances with such leading ensembles as the Leipzig Gewandhaus, Dresden Staatskapelle, Vienna Symphony, Warsaw National Philharmonic, Bergin Philharmonic and all the major Russian orchestras; Conductors have included Moshe Atzmon, Neeme Järvi, Herbert Blomstedt, Mariss Jansons, Leif Segerstram Kurt Sanderling, Kyrill Kondrashin and Yuri Temirkanov; concerts at such festivals as the Warsaw Autumn, Prague Spring, Maggio Musicale, Istanbul, Bergen and Kuhmo; performances of such contemporary composers as Schnittke, Gubaidulina, Denisov and Penderecki (tours with the Krakow Philharmonic to Britain and Europe 1990, playing the Penderecki Violin and Viola concertos which were written for him); Assistant professor at the Moscow Conservatoire 1969-71; teacher at the Gnessin Institute, Moscow, and masterclasses in Krakow, Oslo, Montreal and Genoa (students have included Dimitri Sitkovetsky); Professor of Violin and Viola at the Royal Academy of Music, London, from 1991. *Honours:* Gold Medal of the International Paganini Competition at Genoa, 1967; Silver Medal at the Queen Elisabeth Competition in Brussels, 1968. *Address:* c/o Sonata, 11 Northgate Street, Glasgow G20 7AA, Scotland.

ZHU Jian-er, b. 18 Oct 1922, Tianjin, People's Republic of China. Composer; Professor of Composition. m. Qun Shu, 1949. 2 sons, 1 daughter. *Education:* Graduated, Moscow State Conservatory, 1960, studied with Professor Sergey Balasanian. *Career:* Composer, Art Troupe, New 4th Army, 1945-49; Conductor, Brass band, 1946-49; Copmposer, Shanghai and Peking Film Studios, 1949-63; Shanghai Opera House, 1963-73; Shanghai Symphony Orchestra, 1973-; Professor of Composition, Shanghai Conservatory of Music. *Compositions:* Main works: Orchestral: Festival Overture, 1958; In Memorian, for strings, 1978; Symphony Fantasia, 1980; Sketches in Mountains of Guizhou, 1982; The Butterfly Fountain for Er-hu and orchestra, 1983; A Wonder of Naxi, 1984; Symphony No 1, 1986; No 2, 1987; No 3 Tibet, 1988; Symphony No. 4, 1990; Symphony No. 5, 1991; Concerto for Sona and orchestra, 1989; Choral: Salute 1946, 1945; Gada-meilin, 1958; Symphony-Cantata Heroic Poems, 1960; A cappella cycle The Green, Green Water Village, 1981; Piano: Preludes, 1955; Theme and Var, 1956; Ballade, 1958; Five Yunnan Folk Songs, 1962; Folk instrumental ensemble Day of Liberation, 1953; Song of the Spring, for oboe and piano, 1956; Numerous songs. *Recordings:* Numerous. Publications: Numerous. *Contributions:* Author of more than 50 articles to professional journals. *Honours:* China State Prize for symphony works, 1981; Prizes in Music Festival Srping in Shanghai; Musical prize, Shanghai Federation of Culture and Arts, 1984-85; State Prizes for songs, 1951, 1952, 1982-83; The Queen Marie José Prize for Musical Composition 1990 (Symphony No.4); 1st Shanghai City Award, Distinguised Achievements, 1989-90. *Address:* 105 Hu Nan Road, Shanghai Symphony Orchestra, Shanghai 200031, China.

ZHUKOV Sergei, b. 30 Aug 1951, Zhitomir, Ukraine. Composer. m. Natalia Zhukova, 4 Mar 1982, 2 daughters. *Education:* Musical College, Zhitomir, 1973-; Graduated, Department of Composition, 1978, Postgraduate course, 1980, Moscow State Conservatory. *Debut:* Chamber music concert, Maliy Hall, Moscow Conservatory, 1973. *Career:* Participated, All-Union and international concerts, festivals, symposia, including: Moscow Autumn Musical Festival, 1981, 1982, 1983, 1984; Warsaw Autumn, 1988; International, Musical Festival, Leningrad, 1989; Charles Ives Festival, USA, 1990; Week Van de Hedendaagse Musiek, Belgium, 1991; Works performed on ITV, radio: Symphony, All-Union Radio, 1987; Moments, running in succession, oratorio, All-Union-TV, 1987; Partita for violin solo, Donderdag, Dutch Radio, 1990; Landscape for clarinet solo, BRT-3, Belgium Radio; Solaris, fantastic ballet, Ukrainian TV recording, 1991; Teaching, Department of Theory and Composition, Moscow State Conservatory, 1991. *Compositions:* Spivanochcki, chamber cantata to traditional words, 1975, published, 1983; Partita for Violin solo, 1983, published, 1986. *Contributions:* Some aspects of Creations of Musical composition, article, 1980; Series of articles for The Musical Encyclopedia, 1991. *Hobbies* Cars; Travel; Nature. *Address:* Studencheskaja str 44-28. apt 128, 121165 Moscow, Russia.

ZIDEK Ivo, b. 4 June, 1926, Kravare, nr Opava, Czechoslovakia. Singer (Tenor); Administrator. *Education:* Studied with Rudolf Vasek in Ostrava. *Debut:* Ostrava 1945, as Massenet's Werther. *Career:* Sang at the Prague National Theatre from 1948, notably as Smetana's Jenik and Ladislav (The Two Widows), Steva and Laca in Jenvfa, Mozart's Tamino, Ferrando and Ottavio, and Michel in Martinv's Julietta; Guest singer with the Vienna Staatsoper from 1957 (visit to Barcelona 1958); Holland Festival 1960 and 1963; Edinburgh Festival 1964 and 1970, with the Prague National Theatre in the British premieres of Janáfek's From the House of the Dead and The Excursions of Mr Broufek; New York 1966, in a concert performance of Jenvfa; Also appeared at the Berlin Staatsoper, 1963-68, Moscow, Stuttgart, Venice and the Teatro Colon, Buenos Aires; Intendant of the National Theatre Prague from 1990. Concert repertory has included Les Noces by Stravinsky, Oedipus Rex, secred works by Dvosák and Janáfek's Diary of One Who Disappeared. *Recordings:* The Bartered Bride, Libuse and The Two Widows; The Excursions of Mr Broufek, The Makropoulos Case, From the House of the Dead, Jenvfa; Julietta; The Bride of Messina by Fibich; Les Noces (Supraphon); Dvosák Stabat Mater (Deutsche Grammophon); Jenvfa (EMI). *Honours:* Artist of Merit 1958; National Artist 1976. *Address:* National Theatre, P O Box 865, 112 30 Prague 1, Czech Republic.

ZIEGLER Delores, b. 4 Sept 1951, Atlanta, Georgia, USA. Singer (Mezzo-soprano). *Education:* Studied at the University of Tennessee. *Career:* Sang at first in concert then made stage debut as Flora in Traviata at Knoxville, Tennessee, 1978. *Career:* Sang Maddalena in Rigoletto at St Louis, 1979; Bonn Opera from 1981, as Emilia in Otello, Dorabella and Octavian; Member of the Cologne Opera from 1982, notably as Cherubino, Orlofsky and Octavian; La Scala Milan 1984-87 (Bellini's Romeo); Guest engagements in Munich, Oslo, San Diego, Toronto, Hamburg and at the Glyndebourne Festival (Dorabella 1984); Maggio Musicale Florence 1989, as Idamantes; Salzburg Festival 1988, as Mozart's Sextus; Metropolitan Opera 1989-91, as Siebel and Octavian; Sang in Der Rosenkavalier with the Canadian Opera Company at Toronto, 1990; Many concert engagements. *Recordings include:* Bach's B minor Mass (Telefunken); Così fan Tutte (EMI); Mozart Mass in C (Telarc); Second Lady in Die Zauberflöte (Decca); Le Roi d'Ys by Lalo (Erato). *Address:* c/o Cote Artists Management, 150 West 57th Street, Suite 803, New York, NY 10019, USA.

ZIELINSKA Lidia, b. 30 Oct 1953, Poznan, Poland. Composer. m. Zygmunt Zielinski, 3 Aug 1974. 1 daughter. *Education:* MA, State Higher School of Music, Poznan; Studied composition with Andrzej Koszewski. *Career:* Composers Workshops, Poland, 1979, 1981, 1982; Holland 1980, 1982, 1986; France 1983, 1984; Switzerland, 1987; Collaborated in Electronics Music Studio, Crakow, 1978-; Polish Radio Experimental Studio, 1980-81, 1986-; Studio IPEM, Ghent, 1985; Polish Center of Art for Children and Youth, Artistic Group, Artificial Cult; Co-organized Multimedial Art Meetings, Obecnosc, Poznan; Festivals, Young Polish Music, Szczecin; Concerts and Performances in Europe, Asia and USA; Assistant Professor, Academy of Music, Poznan, 1983-. *Compositions include:* Eh Joe, monodrama for mime actor, tape and orchestra after Beckett, 1978; Violin Concerto, 1979; Litany for string quartet, 1979; Farewell Mr Toorop for orchestra, 1981; Tract for oboe quartet, 1982; Lullaby Gagaku for double bass, 1984; Artificial Cult for tape, video tape, neon signs and visual objects to words by W Olesiak and F Zappa, 1985; Sonnet on the Tatras for 4 musicians, 1985; Cascando for actor double mixed choir after the play by Beckett, 1983-91; Music for Stanislaw Wyspianski for tape, 1985; Fiction for orchestra, 1986; Glossa for viola or violin, 1986; Heldenleben, Overheard and Spied On for audio tape, video tape and shadowgraph, 1986; Polish Dances for tape after Father Baka, 1986; AKO, cartoon, 1986; Pleonasmus for oboe, violin and string orchestra, 1986; Feature Piece for alto saxophone and tape, 1987; Kaleidoscope, Passacaglia for percussion, slides and clapping hands, for children, 1987; Piece about Everything, rondo for percussion and children's audience, 1988; Concrete Music for choir and orchestra, 1987; String Quartet, 1988; Huit heures de la vie des femmes, musical theatre for 9 performers, 1988; The Same, performance, 1988; Sound Museum, live installation for children, 1989; Little Atrophic Symphony, 1988; Music for the Holy Week for mixed choir and percussion, 1988; Musica humana or How Symphonies Are Born, radio piece, 1989; In the Field, mini-spectacle, 1990; Jacquard Loom for 15 musicians, 1991; Short Piece for flute and tape, 1992; Fago for bassoon, double bass and accordion or electronic keyboard, 1992. *Recordings:* Numerous. *Address:* ul Poplinskich 7/9, 61-573 Poznan, Poland.

ZIELINSKI Andrzej Sylwester, b. 26 Nov 1937, Wagrowiec, Poland. Musician; Cellist. *Education:* MA, Music, State Higher School of Music, Cracow, 1962; Postgraduate studies in Cello, Tschaikovsky Conservatoire, Moscow, 1966. *Debut:* With Poznan Symphony Orchestra, 1953. *Career:* Cello Soloist with Cracow, Poznan and National Philharmonic Orchestras, chamber orchestras including Iranian Radio and TV and Polish Radio and TV orchestras; Appearances with Sinfonia Varsovia, Swedish Radio and TV orchetra in Stockholm; Professor of Cello, Warsaw Academy of Music; Vice-Rector, Frédéric Chopin Academy of Music, Warsaw; Lecturer, international music courses, Lancut, Poland, 1990-91; Juror, national competitions; Consultant to music schools. *Recordings:* Various records, radio and TV Recordings, including 1st performance and recordings of I J Pleyel's Cello Concerto in C major. *Publications:* Elaboration of I J Pleydel's Cello Conerto in C major, 1991. *Honours:* Golden Cross of Merit, 1987; Minister of Culture Award, 1990. *Memberships:* Association of Polish Musicians. *Hobbies:* Sailing; Cycling; Driving. *Address:* ul Koszykowa 70 m, 00-671 Warsaw, Poland.

ZIESAK Ruth, b. 1963, Hofheim, Taunus, Germany.

Singer (Soprano). *Education:* Studied with Christoph Pregardien, at the Frankfurt Musikhochschule with Elsa Cavelti, and at the Frankfurt Opera School. *Debut:* Heidelberg 1988, as Valencienne in Die Lustige Witwe. *Career:* Sang at Heidelberg as Pamina, Gilda, Sesto in Giulio Cesare and Despina; Deutsche Oper am Rhein 1989, as Marzelline; Tour of Tokyo Osaka and Kyoto with the Ludwigsburg Festival ensemble, singing in Messiah and Mozart's Requiem, 1989; Season 1994 as Sophie in Rosenkavalier at the Deutsche Oper Berlin, 1993; Susanna at the Opera Bastille Paris and Pamina 1991 and 1993, at the Salzburg Festival. *Recordings include:* Servilia in La Clemenza di Tito, conducted by Harnoncourt; Forthcoming: Weber's Der Freischütz/ Ännchen (Marek Janowski/BMG Classics) Humperdinck's Hänsel und Gretel (Donald Runnicles/ Teldec) and Mozart's Così fan tutte/Fiordligi (Georg Solti/Decca). *Address:* Hannagret Bueker, Theater-Agentur, Sellwinderstr 2, Germany.

ZIESE Christa-Maria, b. 13 July 1924, Aschersleben, Germany. Singer (Soprano). m. Rainer Ludeke. *Education:* Studied with Gottlieb Zeithammer and Josef-Maria Hausschild in Leipzig. *Debut:* Leipzig 1947, as Gretel. *Career:* Sang at the Leipzig Stadtische Theater 1951-77, notably as Fidelio, Santuzza, Tosca, Salome, Aida, Carmen, Turandot, Senta, Isolde and Venus; Guest appearances in Weimar, 1951-54; Dresden, Berlin (Komische Oper), Moscow (Bolshoi), Dusseldorf, Hamburg, Nice, Zurich and Brno; Many concert appearances. *Recordings:* Albums for Eterna. *Honours:* Bach Competition Dresden and International Competition Prague, 1949.

ZIKMUNDOVÁ Eva, b. 4 May 1932, Kromksíy, Czechoslovakia. Opera Singer (Soprano). Divorced, 1 son. *Education:* State Conservatory, Brno; Music Academy, Prague. *Debut:* Opera House, Ostrava. *Career:* Member of Opera Company of National Theatre, Prague 1958-92; Assistant Producer, State Opera Prague, 1992-; Guest appearances, State Opera, Berlin, Hannover, Mannheim, Germany; Venice, Genoa, Naples, Italy; Lausanne, Switzerland; Vienna, Austria; Edinburgh, Scotland; Amsterdam, Holland; Warsaw, Poland; Budapest, Hungary; Sofia, Bulgaria; Brussels, Belgium; Recitals for Czechoslovakia Radio and Television; Professor of Singing, State Conservatory, Prague. *Recordings:* Dvosák, St Ludmila and Moravian duets; Janáfek, The Cunning Little Vixen, numerous recordings of arias and duets. *Honour:* Supraphon Annual Award for Cunning Little Vixen, 1974; Merited Member, The National Theatre, Ministry of Culture. *Current Management:* Pragokoncert, Prague 1, Czechoslovakia. *Address:* Mánesova 23, Prague 2, Czech Republic.

ZILIO Elena, b. 1941, Bolzano, Italy. Singer (Soprano). m. Sttilo Burchiellaro. *Education:* Studied at the Conservatorio Monteverdi in Bolzano, at the Accademia Chigiana in Siena and the Accademia di Santa Cecilia, Rome. *Debut:* Spoleto, Italy 1963 as Sofia in Rossini's Il Signor Bruschino. *Career:* Has sung at La Scala, Milan, Rome, Genoa, Palarmo, Naples, Turin, Trieste and Venice; Verona Arena 1970, 1973, 1976; Festivals at Caracalla and Florence; Sang Lisa in La Sonnambula at Geneva in 1982; Chicago Opera 1983; as Susuki in Madama Butterfly; Milan (La Scala and Piccola Scala) 1983 as Amore in Cherubini's Anacréon and Dardane in Le Rencontre Imprévue by Gluck; Sang Smeaton in Anna Bolena at Bergamo 1983 and returned 1988, as the page in Donizetti's Gianni di Parigi; With the company of the San Carlo Naples sang Giustinio in Pergolesi's Flaminio at Versailles and Spoleto USA 1983 and Wiesbaden 1985; Cologne Opera 1984, as Pippo in La Gazza Ladra; Rerurned to La Scala 1985, in a revival of Rossi's Orfeo; Further appearances in Brussels, Paris (Opéra), Boston, San Antonio, Montreal, Bregenz and Dubrovnik. *Recordings:* La buona figliola by Piccinii (Fonit- Cetra); La Straniera by Bellini (MRF); Un giorno di regno by Verdi (HRE). *Address:* c/o Teatro alla Scala, Via Filodrammatici, I-20121 Milan, Italy.

ZIMANSKY Robert, b. 20 Apr 1948, Iowa City, Iowa,

USA. Violinist. m. Lucia Borsatti, 9 Apr 1979. *Education:* University of Iowa, 1960-66; Juilliard School of Music, 1966-71; Master classes, various teachers, 1970-74. *Debut:* Orchestra Hall, Chicago, with Civic Symphony Orchestra. *Career includes:* Resident Europe, 1972-, Leader: Symphonie-Orchester Graunke 1972-73, Suddeutsche Rundfunk 1974, Orchestre de la Suisse Romande 1975-; Professor, Advanced Classes, Geneva Conservatory, 1980-; Soloist with Wolfgang Sawallisch, Horst Stein, Charles Dutoit, Leif Segerstam, David Zinman, George Cleve, Herbert Blomstedt. *Recordings:* X. & P. Scharwenka, violin sonatas; Bach, 5th Brandenburg; Albéric Magnard, sonata; Schumann, 3 sonatas (award); Reger, Sonatas op. 72 & 84; Schubert, Octet and Janáfek, (complete violin works). *Honour:* Grand Prix du Disque, Academie Charles Cros, 1986. *Membership:* Board of Directors, Association des Musiciens Suisses. *Current Management:* Wismer-Casetti, 30, CH. Du Vieux-Vesenaz, CH-1222 Vesenaz. *Address:* 6, Tour de Champel, 1206 Geneva, Switzerland.

ZIMBERLIN Virginia Laura, b. 29 Jan 1933, New Bedford, Massachusetts, USA. Musician. *Education:* B Mus, M Mus, Yale University 1953-54; Doctoral Assistantship, Indiana University, Bloomington, 1955-57; Studied Piano with Mercedes Pitta, Heinrich Gebhard, Nadia Reisenberg, Frank Scheridan; Studied Cello, Gambe in Basel (Schola Cantorum) with Hannelore Mueller, A Wenzinger; Piano with Paul Baumgartner. *Career:* Teacher, Piano Chamber Music and Accompanist, Lahr, Germany 1974-; Solo cellist, Ortenau Orchestra, Offenburg; Quartet Cellist, A v Toszeghi Chamber Music Groups; Musical Assistant, various Ensembles for Chamber Music, France, Germany and Switzerland; TV appearances both for the ARD and ZDF (Germany); Member of Kinzigtal Chamber Orchestra; Concerts in France and Switzerland. *Compositions:* String Trio, 1952; Piano Sonata 1952. *Contributions to:* Various professional journals. *Honours:* Institute of International Education Award to Europe; Honour Certificate for the Musikkurs Hogmark, Obergurgl, Austria, 1991; Young Artists Award, Boston, New York; Various competition prizes. *Address:* Moltkestrasse 62, 7630 Lahr, Germany.

ZIMERMAN Krystian, b. 5 Dec 1956, Zabrze, Poland. Concert Pianist. m. 1 son, 1 daughter. *Education:* Studied at the Music Academy in Katowice. *Career:* Concerts in Vienna, All the world's music centers; Concerts and recordings with Conductors such as Bernstein, Giulini and Karajan, More Recently, Witold Lutoslawski Dedicated his Piano Concerto to Zimerman, Who Gave Its Premiere in 1989; Repertoire Extends Through Solo Piano Music, Concertos and Chamber Music. *Recordings include:* Beethoven No. 1 - 5, Piano Concerti, Brahms Piano Concertos No. 1 & 2; Liszt B Minor Sonata. *Honours include:* Chopin Piano Competition; Grammy Award; Gramophone Award. *Address:* Kernmattstr 8 B, CH-4102 Binningen, Switzerland.

ZIMMER Ján, b. 16 May 1926, Ruzomberok, Czechoslovakia. Composer and Pianist. Divorced, 1 son. *Education:* Class 4, Gymnasium; Studied Organ, Piano and Composition at State Conservatory, Bratislava; Composition, High School of Music, Budapest; Composition, Salzburg Seminar in American Studies. *Career:* Music Director, Broadcasting Corporation, Bratislava, 1945-48; Professor (Piano and Composition) State Conservatory, Bratislava, 1948-52; Freelance Composer and Pianist, 1952-. *Compositions include:* Operas: Oedipus Rex 1963; Herakles (Opera Ballet) 1972; The Broken Time 1977; 12 Symphonies, 1955-86; 7 Concertos for Piano and Orchestra; Concertino for Piano and String Orchestra, opus 19, 1955; Concerto for Violin and Orchestra, opus 15, 1953; The Tatras I, opus 11, Suite for Orchestra, 1952; The Tatras II, opus 25, Suite for Orchestra, 1956; Concerto grosso for String Orchestra, 2 Pianos and Percussion Instruments, opus 7, 1952; French Suite for Chamber Orchestra, opus 62, 1968; Rhapsody for Piano and Orchestra, opus 18, 1954; Concerto for 2 Pianos and

Orchestra, opus 57, 1967; Concerto for Organ, Percussion Instruments and String Orchestra, opus 27, 1957; Bratislava Spring, cantata, opus 77, 1974; Fantasy for Piano, Orchestra and Male Choir, opus 83, 1977; Liberation, Symphonic Poem, opus 78, 1975; The Uprising, Cantata, opus 17, 1954; Overture for Small Orchestra, opus 88, 1977; From The Slovak Mountains, for Orchestra, opus 89, 1978; Chamber Concerto for Portative Organ and Strings, opus 102, 1983; 6 Sonatas for Piano, 1948-80; 4 Sonatas for 2 Pianos, 1954-73; The Tatras I, opus 11, Suite for Piano, 1952; The Tatras II, opus 25, Suite for Piano, 1956; Concerto for Piano without Orchestra (in one movement), 1956; Chamber Works: Sonata for Organ, opus 65, 1970; Sonata No. 2 for Organ, opus 97, 1981; Poetical Sonata for Violin and Piano, opus 85, 1976; Sonata for Flute Solo, opus 91, 1978; Wind Quintet, opus 61, 1968; Trio for Flute, Violin and Piano, opus 93, 1979; Variations for 2 Violins and Viola, opus 87, 1977; String Quartet No. 2, opus 100. Vocal Works: Spring in the Valley, cycle of songs for Soprano and Piano, opus 3, 1947; Emerald, cycle of songs for Soprano and Piano, opus 64, 1969; Songs of Spring for Tenor and Piano, opus 67, 1970; Svätoboj, Slovak madrigal, 1973; Concerto Poliphonier for Organ and Orchestra, Opus 108; Piano music for children; Music for films, 1946-52. *Hobbies:* Sports; Swimming; Motoring; Travel. *Address:* Letecká 10, 831 03 Bratislava, Slovakia.

ZIMMERLIN Alfred Peter, b. 12 Apr 1955, Zürich, Switzerland. Musician; Composer; Improvising musician. m. Claudia Ulla Binder, 14 Feb 1986. 1 daughter. *Education:* Matura Type B, Kantonsschule Aarau, 1975; Lic Phil I, University of Zurich, 1981; Studied Composition with H Wüthrich-Mathez and H U Lehmann; Violoncello with A Zürcher. *Career:* Performances in Europe and USA; Festivals. *Compositions:* Etüden über ein Thema von Friedrich Nietzsche, 1976-78; 5 Preludes (Klavierstück 1), 1980-81; Duett II, 1983; Sätze, auf einen Text von Elisabeth Wandeler-Deck, 1984; Zeile (aus einem Gedicht von Wyston Hugh Auden), 1984-86; Klavierstück 2, 1985; Toute l'étendue ne vaut pas un cri, 1985; Brechungen, 1986; and from Alabama from anywhere, 1986; Fünf Stücke für acht Flöten, 1986-87; Wahrnehmungsschwäche für das Tempo der Zerstörung, 1987; L'espace tout a coup m'irrite, 1987; Gänge, 1988; Knotting, 1988; Klavierstück 3, 1988; 3 mal 3, 1989; Wortstücke, 1988-89. *Recordings:* Numerous. *Honours:* Werkjahr des Aargauischen Kuratoriums, 1983 and 1985; Musikpreis der C F Meyer-Stiftung, 1986; Komponistenwerkjahr der Stadt Zürich, 1988. *Address:* Mohrlistrasse 17, CH-8006 Zürich, Switzerland.

ZIMMERMAN Christopher, b. 1957, England. Conductor. *Education:* Studied at Yale and the University of Michigan; Further study with Nadia Boulanger and at the Pierre Monteux School of Conducting, Maine. *Career:* Music Director of the Yale Bach Society, 1980; Conducted the Michigan University Symphony Orchestra in the USA and Europe; Worked with the Toronto Symphony, then the Czech Philharmonic, 1983-85; London 1985, leading concerts with the Royal Philharmonic and the London Symphony orchestras; Appearances with the Royal Liverpool Philharmonic and at the Concertgebouw in Amsterdam; Prague 1987, with the Prague Symphony Orchestra; Conducted the Seoul Philharmonic in Korea, 1989; Music Director in Mexico City, where he has conducted Salome; Music Director of the City of London Chamber Orchestra. *Address:* c/o Giovanna Horowitz, Grosvenor Gardens House, Grosvenor Gardens, London, SW1W 0ES, England.

ZIMMERMAN Franklin B. b. 20 June 1923, Wanneta, Kansas, USA. Musician (Conductor); Musicologist. m. 8 Aug 1988, 1 son, 5 daughters. *Education:* Studied at the University of Southern California, PhD 1958; B. Litt. Oxford University 1956; Studied French Horn with Aubrey Brain 1954-56; Conducting with Ernest Read 1955-58; Orchestration with Leon Kirchner and Ingolf Dahl. *Debut:* London 1957. *Career:* Founder-Director Pennsylvania Pro Musica (more than 420 concerts). *Publications:* Henry Purcell: Analytical Catalog 1963; Henry Purcell: Life and Times 1967, 1983; Henry Purcell: Thematic Index 1973; Words to Music 1965; Facsimile Editions: An Introduction to the Skin of Musick by John Playford (Twelth Editon, Corrected and Amended by Harry Ruscilli), with index, introduction and glossary, New York, Da Capo, 1972; The Gostling Manuscript, compiled by John Gostling, Foreword by Franklin B Zimmerman, University of Texas Press, 1977. *Contributions:* Numerous articles and monographs. *Recording:* Handel L'Allegro ed Il Penseroso 1981. *Memberships:* AMS; IMS. *Honours:* Arnold Bax Medal for Musicology 1958. *Hobbies:* Tennis; Hiking; Swimming; Deep Sea Fishing. *Address:* 225 S. 42nd Street, Philadelphia, PA 19104, USA.

ZIMMERMAN Willi, b. 1955, Switzerland. Violinist. *Education:* Studied with the Alban Berg Quartet in Vienna. *Career:* Leader, Amati String Quartet from 1981; Further study with members of the Amadeus and Bartók Quartets, and with Walter Levin; Many performances in Switzerland, the United States and elsewhere in the classical repertoire, and in works by Szymanowski, Tailleferre, Cui, Steuermann, Vladimir Vogel, Kelterborn and Robert Suter; Recitals at Basle 1986, tour of Britain 1990-91, Menuhin Festival Gstaad 1991; Recitals with Bruno Canino, Malcolm Frager, Bruno Giuranna, Karl Leister and others. *Honours:* (with Amati Quartet): Grand prix, Concours International at Evian 1982; Art Prize of the Lions Club 1985; First prize, Karl Klinger competition, Munich 1986. *Address:* c/o Anglo-Swiss Management, 4-5 Primrose Mews, Sharpeshall Street, London NW1 8YW, England.

ZIMMERMANN Frank Peter, b. 27 Feb 1965, Duisburg, Germany. Concert Violinist. *Education:* Studied with Valery Gradov at the Folkwang-Musikhochschule Essen; Staatliche Hochschule Berlin with Saschko Gawrillof and from 1980 with Hermann Krebbers in Amsterdam. *Debut:* Duisburg 1975, playing Mozart's Concerto K216. *Career:* Appearances with the Vienna, Berlin and Munich Philharmonic Orchestras; Bamberg Vienna, London and Chicago Symphony Orchestras; English Chamber Orchestra; Orchestre de Paris; Czech Philharmonic, Boston Symphony and the Cleveland Orchestra; Conductors include Maazel, Neumann, Barenboim, Dohnányi, Rozhdestvensky, Jochum, Gerd Albrecht, Haitink, Sanderling, Conlon, Tate, Sawallisch, Marriner, Ozawa and Franz Welser-Möst; Festival engagements at Lucerne, 1979, Salzburg, from 1983, Munich, 1984, Prague Spring 1987; US debut 1984, with the Pittsburgh Symphony; Returned 1985-86 at Avery Fisher Hall New York and with the orchestras of Detroit, Cincinnati and Toronto; Tour of USA with the Chamber Orchestra of Europe conducted by Lorin Maazel 1986r Performed at the Mostly Mozart (New York), Tanglewood and Ravinia Festivals 1987; Season 1987-88 with the Netherlands and Rotterdam Philharmonic Orchestras; Berlin Philharmonic conducted by Barenboim; Tour of the USA with the English Chamber Orchestra and Jeffrey Tate and concerts with the Toronto Symphony; Season 1988-89 appearances in Germany, London, Boston, Munich, Milan and Oslo; Tour of Australia May 1989; Tours of Japan and Europe with the NHK Symphony, the Bamberg Symphony and the ECO, 1988-89; Sibelius Concerto at the Helsinki Festival and the Beethoven Concerto with the Berlin Philharmonic; Season 1990-91 included concerts with the Philharmonia Orchestra, the Chicago Symphony and the Royal Concertgebouw; Invited for the Leipzig Gewandhaus 150th anniversary season 1992. *Recordings include:* Tchaikovsky Concerto with the Berlin PO and Concertos by Prokofiev, Beethoven, Mendelssohn, Bach and Sibelius; Sonatas by Mozart and Prokofiev with pianist Alexander Lonquich. *Address:* c/o Intermusica Artists' Management, 16 Duncan Terrace, London N1 8BZ, England.

ZIMMERMANN Margarita, b. Aug 1942, Buenos Aires, Argentina. Singer (Mezzo-soprano). *Education:* Studied in Buenos Aires. *Debut:* Teatro Colon Buenos

Aires as Orpheus in the opera by Gluck, 1977. *Career:* European debut at the Landestheater, Salzburg, as Carmen and Ulrica (Un ballo in maschera); Covent Garden debut 1980, as Cherubino; US appearances at Miami (Dalila, 1979) and San Francisco (Rosina, 1982); Further engagements at Naples, Bologna, Venice, Rome, Lyons, Geneva and Paris; Further roles include Mozart's Sextus, Idamante and Zerlina, Handel's Guilio Cesare and Agrippina, Juno in Cavalli's Ercole Amante and Wagner's Fricka; In 1988 sang at Piacenza and Madrid as Massenet's Charlotte and as Andromache in Rossini's Ermione; Appeared as Thérèse in the opera by Massenet at the Opéra de Monte Carlo, 1989. *Recordings Include:* the Singer in Manon Lescaut (Decca).

ZIMMERMANN Margrit, b. 7 Aug 1927, Bern, Switzerland. Composer. *Education:* Studied piano and theory with Jeanne Bovet and Walter Furrer, Bern, with Denise Bidal, Lausanne, Alfred Cortot's Masterclasses, Diploma in pianoforte; Composition studies under Arhtur Honegger, Ecole Normale de Musique de Paris; Study as conductor with Ewald Korner, Municipal Theatre of Bern; International Master Classes with Igor Markevitch, Monte Carlo and Hans Swarowsky, Ossiach; Diploma in compositon, Guiseppe Verdi Conservatorium, Milan. *Career:* Music Teacher, Bern; Composer. *Compositions:* Numerous compositions include symphonic and scenic works, chamber music for a wide range of instrumentations, vocal and solo works for piano, strings, wind, percussion and guitar; List of works includes Panta Rhei, op 39, 1987; Cloccachorda op 40, 1987; Aus dem Tagebucheiner Prinzessin op 44, 1986; Die Gestundete Zeit, op 52, 1987; Piano Time, op 46, 1987; Quadriga op 51, 1987; Murooji op 57, guitar solo; Trptychon op 58; Pianorama op 59; In Urbis Honorem, symphony for orchestra and choir; Jubilation, concert for orchestra. *Recordings:* Cloccachordia; Piano Time; Quadriga; Pensieri; Orphische Taenze; Quartetto d'Archi, op 7 nr 1. *Address:* Ostermundigenstrasse 22, CH- 3006 Bern, Switzerland.

ZIMMERMANN Tabea, b. 8 Oct 1968, Lahr, Germany. Concert Violist. *Education:* Studied with Ulrich Koch and Sandor Vegh. *Career:* Frequent concerts with such soloists as Gidon Kremer, Heinz Holliger, Thomas Zehetmair, Steven Isserlis and Heinrich Schiff; appearances at Prades, Schleswig-Holstein, Lockenhaus, Marlboro and other chamber music festivals; regular recitals with pianist Hartmut Holl; Concert engagements include Mozart's Sinfonia Concertante in Amsterdam, at the Salzburg Festival and at Buckingham Palace for Prince Charles; has also performed with the Bamberg Symphony under Christoph Eschenbach, at Frankfurt with Gary Bertini, Penderecki's Concerto with the composer conducting the Munich Philharmonic and concerts in Hamburg, Tokyo, Rome, Copenhagen, Helsinki and Israel; gave the world premieres of concertos by Mark Koptyman and Volker David Kirchner in 1992; premiere of Ligeti's Viola Sonata at Cologne, 1993. *Recordings:* Mozart's Concertante K364; Bach Trio sonatas, Gubaidulina Hommage, Chamber works by Bruch, Mozart and Schumann; The Concerto in Europe, Double Concertos and works by Penderecki. *Honours include:* First prize at competitions in Geneva, Budapest and Paris (awarded the Vatelot viola). *Address:* c/o Intermusica Artists Management Ltd. 16 Duncan Terrace, London N1 8BZ, England.

ZIMMERMANN Udo, b. 6 Oct 1943, Dresden, Germany. Composer; Conductor. *Education:* Studied composition with J.P. Thilman at the Dresden Musikhochschule 1962-68; Master Classes at the Akademie der Kunste East Berlin, 1968-70. *Career:* Composer and Producer at the Dresden State Opera 1970; Founded the Studio for New Music in Dresden, 1974; Professor of Composition at the Dresden Hochschule für Musik, 1978; Professor of Experimental Music Theatre at Dresden 1982; Conducted the Bavarian Radio SO in the premiere of Hartmann's Sinfonia Tragica, Munich 1989; premiere of Bernhard Jesl's Opera Der König Stirbt at Bonn 1990; Intendant

of the Leipzig State Opera from 1990. *Compositions:* Operas: Die weisse Rose 1967; Die zweite Entscheidung 1970; Levins Muhle 1973; Der Schuhu und der fliegenede Prinzessin 1975; Die wundersame Schusterfrau 1982; Dramatische Impression auf den Tod von JF Kennedy for cello and orchestra 1963; 5 Songs for baritone and orchestra 1964; Movimenti caratteristici for solo cello 1965; Musik für Streicher 1967; Sonetti Amorosi for contralto, flute and string quartet 1967; String Quartet 1967; Der Mensch, cantata for soprano and 13 instruments 1969; Sieh, meine Augen for chamber orchestra 1970; Eine Zeuge der Liebe besingt den Tod for soprano and chamber orchestra 1971; Mutazioni for orchestra 1972; Psalm der Nacht for female choir, percussion and organ 1973; Choreographien nach Edgar Degas for 21 instruments 1974; Ode an das Leben for mezzo, 3 choruses and orchestra 1974; Hymnus an die Sonne, after Kleist, for soprano, flute and harpsichord 1976; Sinfonia come un grande lamento, after Lorca 197; Pax Questuosa for 5 soloists, 3 choirs and orchestra 1980. *Address:* c/o AWA, Storkower Strasse 134, 1055 Berlin, Germany.

ZIMMERMANN Walter, b. 15 April 1949, Schwabach, Germany. Composer. *Education:* Studied piano, violin and oboe; Composition with Werner Heide and Otto Lake at Utrecht; Ethnological Centre Jaap Kunst in Amsterdam, 1970-73; Computer Music in the USA, 1974. *Career:* Pianist in the Ars-Nova Ensemble of Nuremberg, 1968-70; Founded Beginner Studio at Cologne 1977; Lecturer at Darmstadt 1982, Liege Conservatory from 1982. *Compositions include:* Lokale Musik, 15 works for various forces, 1977-81; Uber die Dorfer dramatic song for soprano, chorus and orchestra 1986; Fragmente der Liebe for soprano, clarinet, saxophone and string quartet, 1987. *Address:* GEMA (Germany) c/o PRS Ltd. Member Registration, 29-33 Berners Street, London W1P 4AA, England.

ZIMMERMANN Wolfram (Professor), b. 17 Apr 1920, Stuttgart, West Germany. Singer (Bass-Baritone). *Education:* Studied with his father, at the Stuttgart and Vienna Academies and with Anna Bahr-Mildenburg. *Debut:* Stuttgart 1947, as Rossini's Basilio. *Career:* Radio Broadcasts in Germany and Austria; Sang Beckmesser in Die Meistersinger, under Furtwängler, at La Scala 1952; Created title role in Titus Feuerfuchs by Heinrich Sutermeister, in Television, Austria, 1959; Vienna Staatsoper 1958-63, notably as Leporello, Papageno by Mozart and the Doctor in Wozzeck by Berg; Rome Opera 1956; Graz 1958; Barcelona 1958-63; Mexico City 1966, as Beckmesser; Other roles include Title roles, Mozart's Figaro, Gounod's Mephistopheles and Don Pasquale by Donizetti. *Recordings:* Zar und Zimmermann by Lortzing; Tannhäuser by Wagner in Deutsche Gramaphon. *Contributions to:* TV Magazines in Austria and Germany also Spain and Italy; Frankfurter Allgemeine; Suddeutsche Zeitung, Munich. *Honours:* Diploma, International Song, Geneva 1949; Bach Prize, Leipzig, 1950; Gold Medal, Accademia Italia, 1980. *Membership:* Honorary Cavalier, Deutscherrn-Ritterbund Norimberga. *Hobbies:* Tennis; Mountaineering. *Address:* Erbisleiten 6, D-91227 Weissenbrunn, Gemeinde Leinburg, Germany.

ZIMMERSCHIED Dieter, b. 1 July 1934, Danzig (now Gdansk), Poland. Professor of Music Education. m. Christa Brauch, 1 daughter. *Education:* Abitur, 1954; Studium (School music, research etc), 1954-58, Staats examen; Musikerzieher am Schlossgymnasium Mainz, Federal Republic of Germany, 1960-76; Promotion, 1967. *Career:* Leader of Music Cultural Commission, 1970-73; Music Adviser to Ministry of Culture, Rheinland-Pfalz, 1969-76; Professor of Music Pedagogy 1976-, Leader of School Music Section 1977-, Musikhochschule, Stuttgart; Team member, Funk-Kolleg Musik, 1976-78. *Publications include:* Die Kammermusik Johann Nepomuk Hummels, 1967; Perspektiven Neuer Musik, 1974; Tendenzen der Musikdidaktik, 1978; Operette - Phänomen und Entwicklung, 1988; Kinder Singen Überall - Lieder Aus Aller Welt, 1992. *Contributions to:* Musik und Bildung (two monthly), Mainz. *Memberships:* Chairman,

Verband Deutscher Schulmusiker E. V.; Bundeshauptausschuß Jugend Musiziert; Vice-Chairman, Arbeitsgemein schaft Musikerziehung und Musikpflege im Deutschen Musikrat. *Address:* Weidmannstraße 43, D-55131, Mainz, Germany.

ZINKLER Christiane, b. 23 Nov 1947, Coburg, Germany. Singer (Mezzo-soprano). *Education:* Studied with Willi Domgraf-Fassbaender in Nuremberg and with Clemens Kaiser-Breme in Essen. *Debut:* Deutsche Oper am Rhein Dusseldorf 1968, as Messenger in Dallapiccola's Job. *Career:* Member of the Dortmund Opera, notably as Gluck's Orpheus, Erda and Fricka in Der Ring des Nibelungen, Ulrica, Hansel, Monteverdi's Poppea, Anina in Der Rosenkavalier, Cherubino and Dorabella; Guest appearances in Hamburg, Essen, Copenhagen, Wiesbaden and Florence. Many concert appearances. *Address:* c/o Opernhaus, Kuhstrasse 12, D-4600 Dortmund, Germany.

ZINMAN David Joel, b. 9 July 1936, New York City, USA. Conductor. m. Mary Ingham. *Education:* Violin, Oberlin Conservatory, 1954-58; MA, Composition, University of Minnesota; Pierre Monteux's Assistant at Mr. Monteux's summer school in Maine, 1961-63. *Debut:* Holland Festival, 1963; The Philadelphia Orchestra, USA, 1967. *Career:* Music Director, Netherlands Chamber Orchestra, 1964-77; Music Director, Rotterdam Philharmonic Orchestra, 1979-82; Music Director, Rochester Philharmonic Orchestra, 1974-85; Principal Guest Conductor, Baltimore Symphony Orchestra, 1983-84; Current Music Director, Baltimore Symphony Orchestra, 1985-. *Recordings:* Approximately 40 record albums: Philips-Janáfek: Sinfonietta; Chopin: Les Sylphides; Tchaikovsky: Serenade for String; Grieg: Holberg Suite; C P E Bach: Complete Flute Concerti; J C Bach Symphonies; London-Chopin, Concerto No. 2 in F minor for Piano and Orchestra; Mozart, Piano Concerto No. 12 in A, K 414; Dvosak: Legends, Op. 59; Telarc - Berlioz, Overture to Benvenuto Cellini, Love Scene from Roméo et Juliette, Three Excerpts from La Damnation de Faust, Minuet of the Will-o-the-Wisps, Dance of the Sylphs, Rákóczy March, Le Corsaire Overture, Trojan March, Royal Hunt & Storm from Les Troyens, La Marseillaise; CBS Masterworks - Britten, Symphony for Cello and Orchestra Op. 68; Barber, Concerto for Cello and Orchestra Op. 22.; Nonesuch - Rouse, Symphony No. 1; Rouse, Phantasmata; EMI - Mozart, Piano Conerto No. 22, K. 482; Mozart, Piano Concerto No. 23, K.488. *Honours:* Named by Time Magazine as one of the Five for the Future, 1982; Two Grand Prix du Disque Awards for Record Albums and the Edison Prize. *Current Management:* ICM Artists Ltd., 40 West 57th Street, New York, NY 10019, USA. *Address:* Baltimore Symphony Orchestra, 1212 Cathedral Street, Baltimore, MD 21201, USA.

ZINN William, b. 19 Nov 1924, New York City, New York, USA. Violinist; Composer; Author; Professor; Business Executive; Humanitarian. m. Sophia Kalish, 11 July 1948, 1 son, 1 daughter. *Education:* Violin with Raphael Bronstein, 1942-43. *Career includes:* Baltimore Symphony, 1944-45; Indianapolis Symphony, 1945-46; Fort Wayne Philharmonic, 1946-47; Pittsburgh Symphony, 1947-49; Minneapolis Symphony, 1950-51; Concertmaster: New Britain Symphony, Connecticut, 1968-; Queens Symphony, 1969-71; Ridgefield Symphony, Connecticut, 1973-76; Chappagua Symphony, New York, 1976; Soloist with orchestras, on records, on radio and in recitals; Founder: Masterwork Piano Trio; Masterwork Piano Quartet; Classical String Quartet; Zinn's Ragtime String Quartet; Excelsior String Quartet; Queens Festival Orchestra, Bayside, New York, 1965; Asociacion Musical William Zinn, Caracas, Venezuela, 1968; Vitametrics of America, 1976; International Symphony for World Peace, 1978; Big Apple Chamber Pops, 1983; Excelsior Composer's Festival Competition, 1984; Professor of Music, New York University, 1987-. *Compositions:* Published over 300 works for string quartet or string orchestra. *Recording:* Zinn's Ragtime String Quartet, MMO Label, 1974. *Publications include:* Themography (Dictionary of

musical themes) (with Edward Gordon), 1947; The Mystery of the Lost Chord, 1987. *Hobbies:* Painting; Carving; Inventing.

ZINSSTAG Gérard, b. 9 May 1941, Geneva, Switzerland. Composer. m. 29 Feb 1984. 1 son, 1 daughter. *Education:* CNSM Paris and Chigiana Academy Siena, 1961-63; Studied composition with H U Lehmann, Musikhochschule, Zurich, 1973-75; Studied composition with Helmut Lachenmann, Stuttgart & Hanover, 1975-77; Composer-in-residence, Berlin 1981 (DAAD); IRCAM, Paris, 1982. *Career:* Orchestral musician, Toured Europe, 1964-67; Solo Flute, Orchestra of Zurich Tonhalle, 1967-75; Participation, Summer Course, Darmstadt, 1976-78; Visited San Francisco, New York, Seminar, University of Berkeley, California, 1979; Founded, Festival of Zurich, Tage für neue Musik Zurich, 1986-; Proposed tour of the Soviet Union, Moscow and Baku, 1990. *Compositions:* Dements; Wenn Zum Biespiel; Tatastenfelder; Suono Reale; Innanzi; Foris; Perforation; Altération; Trauma; Edition, Modern Munich; Cut Sounds; Incalzando, 1981; Artifices, 1982-83; Sept Fragments, 1982-83; Stimuli, 1984; Tempi Inquieti, 1984-86; Eden Jeden, 1987; Artifices II, 1988. *Recordings:* Ahaphoren, 1989, Radio France; SWF, WDR, HR, NDR, SFB, SDR, German radio Stations; RAI, Turin; BRT, Brussels, DRS, Zurich. *Publications:* Pro Musica, 1988; Revue Musicale Suisse, 1979-80. *Memberships:* Suisa; Composers' Forum, New York; ISCM. *Address:* Froschaugasse 2, CH-8001 Zurich, Switzerland.

ZITEK Vaclav, b. 24 Mar 1932, Tisa, Czech Republic. Singer (Baritone). *Education:* Studied in Prague with Adrian Levicky. *Debut:* Prague Opera Studio 1957, as Germont in La Traviata. *Career:* Member of the National Theatre Prague, in operas by Mozart, Verdi, Tchaikovsky, Smetana, Dvosák, Martinv, Puccini, Strauss and Prokofiev; Guest appearances at the Bolshoi Theatre Moscow, the Staatsoper and Komiche Oper Berlin, National Opera Bucharest and the Bordeaux Opera; Prague National Theatre 1983, as Premysl in Smetana's Libuse; Frequent concert and oratorio engagements. *Recordings:* Operas by Smetana, Dvosák (Jacobin) and Sarka by Fibich (Supraphon); Siskovin in From the House of the Dead, and Jenvfa with the Vienna Philharmonic conducted by Charles Mackerras (Decca). *Honour:* National Artist of Czechoslovakia 1985. *Address:* National Theatre, P O Box 865, 112 30 Prague 1, Czech Republic.

ZIVONI Yossi, b. 2 Dec 1939, Tel-Aviv, Israel. Violinist. m. Jeanne, 21 Mar 1962, 1 daughter. *Education:* Graduate, Israel Academy of Music, Tel-Aviv, 1958; Graduate, Conservatoire Royal de Musique de Bruxelles, Belgium, 1962. *Debut:* Amsterdam, The Netherlands, 1964. *Career:* Concert Tours in Europe, Israel, Australia, Canada, Far East and South America. *Recordings:* Mozart Sonatas (Meridian); Bach: Sonatas & Partitas, Mendelssohn: Sonatas, (Meridian); Artistic Director, International Music Festival of Entrecasteaux, Provence, France; Principal Tutor, Royal Northern College of Music. *Honours:* Prizes: Paganini International Competition, 1960; Bavarian Radio International Competition, Munich, Federal Republic of Germany, 1961; Queen Elisabeth International Competition, Brussels, Belgium, 1963; Fellow, Royal Northern College of Music. *Memberships:* Royal Society of Musicians of Great Britain. *Current Management:* Helen Sykes Management. *Address:* 18 Midholm, London NW11, England.

ZLATAR Jaksa, b. 14 June 1947, Sibenik, Croatia. Professor of Music. m. Dobrila Vignjevic, 9 Mar 1982, 1 daughter. *Education:* Professor of Piano, 1971, Professor of Psychology and Sociology, 1972, MA, 1973, University of Zagreb; Corso di perfezionamento, Accademia di S. Cecilia, Rome Italy, 1973-74. *Career:* Assistent, 1978-82, Docent, 1982-; Piano and Piano-playing Methodics, Zagreb Music Academy; Soloist, Accompanist, concerts; Numerous radio broadcasts. *Recordings:* For radio and TV. *Publication:* Methodics of Piano Playing I (Students' Book), 1982; Book: Introduction to Piano Interpretation, 1991. *Contributor To:* Articles in music journals. *Honour:* Recipient of Svetislav Stancic Prize, Music Association of Croatia, 1971. *Hobbies:* History; Languages. *Address:* Laginjina 9, Zagreb, Croatia.

ZOBEL Ingeborg, b. 31 July 1928, Gorlitz, Schlesien, Germany. Singer (Soprano). *Education:* Studied at the Dresden State Music Academy with Eduardr Plate. *Debut:* As Amelia (Un Ballo in Maschera) Cottbus 1952. *Career:* Sang in Schwerin 1955-57, Rostock 1957-66, Weimar 1966-72; Dresden Staatsoper from 1972, notably as Wagner's Brünnhilde, Isolde and Ortrud; the Marschallin, Tosca, Santuzza, Lady Macbeth and Leonore in Fidelio; Guest appearances in Leningrad, Barcelona, Budapest, Wiesbaden, Prague, Belgrade and Sofia; Teacher at the Franz Liszt Musikhochschule in Weimar. *Recordings:* Albums for Eterna. *Address:* c/o Staatsoper, D-8012 Dresden, Germany.

ZOGHBY Linda, b. 17 Aug 1949, Mobile, Alabama, USA. Singer (Soprano). *Education:* Studied at Florida State University and with Elena Nikolaidi. *Career:* Sang at first in concert; Stage debut Houston 1974, as Donna Elvira in Don Giovanni; Dallas Opera 1976, as Giulietta in I Capuleti e i Montecchi; Glyndebourne Festival from 1978, as Mimi and in La Fedeltà Premiata by Haydn; Metropolitan Opera 1982, 1986, as Mimi and as Ilia in Idomeneo; Other roles include Mozart's Fiordiligi and Pamina. *Recordings:* Haydn's L'Isola Disabitata and L'Incontro Improvviso (Philips).

ZOLLMAN Ronald, b. 8 Apr 1950, Antwerp, Belgium. Conductor. m. Dominique G. Mols. *Education:* Diploma in Conducting, Brussels Conservatoire; Diploma, Academy Chigiana. *Career:* Has conducted throughout Europe, in North, South and Central America, and in Australia; Head of Conducting Faculty at the Royal Brussels Conservatory of Music; Musical Director of the Philharmonic Orchestra of UNAM, Mexico. *Recordings:* Belgian music for Ministry of Culture, Brussels; Recordings for several labels, with a o the National Orchestra of Belgium, the World Orchestra, the London Sinfonietta. *Honour:* Premio Firenze for conductors, 1972. *Current Management:* Konsertbolaget, Kungsgatan 32, S-11132, Stockholm. *Address:* Rue Général de Gaulle 36, 1310 La Hulpe, Belgium.

ZOTTOVICEANU Elena, b. 8 Apr 1933, Chisinau, Rumania. Musicologist. *Education:* Degree in Music, Piano Department, Ciprian Porumbescu Conservatory, Bucharest, 1956. *Career:* Senior Research Worker, Institute of History of Art, Bucharest; Director, Musical Department Rumanian Broadcasting (Radio Rumania). *Publications include:* 2 chapters in monograph on George Enescu, 1971; The War of Independence and 19th Century Rumanian Music; 15-18 Century Rumanian Musical Lecture. *Contributions to:* Over 60 articles on history of Rumanian music to various scholarly journals; Hundreds of Musical Chronicles in newspapers, radio and TV emissions, and conferences. *Honours:* Prize, Rumanian Academy, 1971; Prize, Union of Composers, 1971-71; Bernier Prize, Academie des Beaux Arts, Institute of France, 1971-72; Price Union of Musical Cities 1989 and 1993. *Memberships:* Union of Composers and Musicologists of Rumania; Union of Musical Cities of Rumania; Fellow, Salzburg Seminar in American Studies. *Hobbies:* Literature; Cinema. *Address:* Str Intr Buciumeni No. 1, 71 154 Bucharest I, Of 22, Rumania.

ZOUHAR Zdenek, b. 8 Feb 1927, Kotvrdovice, Czech Republic. Composer and Musicologist. *Education:* PhD Brno University 1967, with simultaneous study at the Brno Academy. *Career:* Head of the music section of Brno University Library 1953-61, editor for Czech Radio 1961-70; at the same time Teacher (Professor) at the Brno Janáfek Academy, 1962-. *Compositions include:* Sonatina for piano, 1948; Spring Suite for 3 violins 1949; Partita for organ 1956; Midnight Mass 1957; '151' Music for wind quintet 1958; Trio for flute, contralto and bass clarinet 1961; Divertimento I for 4 winds and percussion 1965; Music for strings 1966; 2 String Quartets 1966, 1983; Symphonic Triptych 1967; Music for wind quintet II 1982; Triple Concerto for clarinet, trumpet, trombone and orchestra 1970; Chamber radio opera Metamorphosis 1971; Variations on a theme by B Martinv for symphonic orchestra, 1979; Musica giocosa per archi 1981; Brass Quintet, 1985; Comic opera A Great Love, 1986; Oratorio The Flames of Constance, 1988; Divertimento III for Brno Brass Band, 1993. *Address:* OSA Czech Republic, PRS Ltd Member Registration, 29-33 Berners Street, London W1P 4AA, England.

ZSCHAU Marilyn, b. 9 Feb 1944, Chicago, USA. Singer (Soprano). *Education:* Juilliard School of Music 1961-65; Further study with John Lester in Montana. *Career:* Toured with Met National Company 1965-66; Debut at Vienna Volksoper as Marietta in Die Tote Stadt 1967; Vienna Staatsoper 1971, as the Composer in Ariadne auf Naxos; New York City Opera from 1978, as Puccini's Minnie and Butterfly and Odabella in Attila, Maddalena in Andrea Chenier; Metropolitan Opera debut 1985, as Musetta in La Bohème; La Scala debut 1986, as the Dyer's Wife in Die Frau ohne Schatten; Appearances in West Germany, Switzerland, Hungary, Australia, France, Italy, Spain, Wales, England, Canada and USA; Operatic roles include: Verdi's Aida, Leonora, Desdemona; Puccini's Butterfly, Tosca, Mimi, Musetta, Strauss, Salome, Elektra, Prokofiev's Renata in the Fiery Angel, Shostakovich's Katerina in Lady Macbeth of Mtsensk, Mascagni's Santuzza, Cavalleria Rusticana, Wagner's Brünnhilde in Die Walküre and Manon Lescaut; Sang Puccini's Minnie at Reggio Emilia and Chicago 1990; The Fiery Angel at the 1990 Holland Festival; Other roles include: Janáfek's Vixen; the Marschallin and Octavian in Der Rosenkavalier; Mozart's Fiordiligi, Countess and Pamina; Lucille in Dantons Tod; Tatiana in Eugene Onegin. *Recordings include:* Video of Covent Garden La Bohème. *Honours:* Martha Baird Rockefeller Foundation Scholarships 1962, 1963. *Hobbies:* Drawing and Painting; Reading New Age Publications; Walking and Hiking. *Address:* c/o Columbia Artists Management Inc, Joyce Arbib Division, 165 West 57th Street, New York, NY 10019, USA.

ZSIGMONDY Denes, b. 9 Apr 1922, Budapest, Hungary. Violinist. m. Anneliese Nissen (pianist), Aug 1947, 2 daughters. *Education:* Baccalaureat, University of Budapest; Franz Liszt Academy, Budapest; Studied with Geza de Kresz, Leo Weiner, Imre Waldbauer and others. *Career:* Soloist, Vienna and Berlin Symphonies, Tokyo, Budapest, Munich Philharmonies, Radio Orchestras ABC Sydney, Melbourne, Munich, Stuttgart Chamber Orchestra, Salzburg Camerata; Performed with BBC Radio London, NHK Tokyo, Radio Paris and others; World premieres of works by Bialas, Eder, Genzmer, Rozsa and others; Professor, University of Washington, Seattle, USA, 1972-; Visiting Professor, Boston University, 1981-82; Occasional masterclasses at New England Conservatory and others; Established yearly Holzenhausen Festival in Ammerland, Bavaria, Germany, with Concerts and violin courses, 1978-; Courses at the Summer Academy, Salzburg-Mozarteum, Austria, also in Germany, Italy, Hungary, Poland and other countries, 1986-. *Recordings include:* The Virtuoso Violin; The Romantic Violin; Zsigmondy Plays Bartók, volumes 1 and 2; Sonatas by Beethoven, Brahms, Grieg, Franck, Debussy and all Mozart and Schubert violin-piano music. *Hobbies:* Tennis; Gardening. *Address:* Bonselweg 10, 8193 Ambach Bavaria, Germany.

ZUCKER Laurel, b. 28 May 1955, Pennsylvania, USA. Musician. *Education:* MA, PhD, New York University; BMus, Julliard; Studied flute with Samuel Baron, Marcel Moyse and Paula Robinson. *Career:* Soloist on TV shows, Choices and Arts Alive; Film scores include Predator II, Eyes of the Mountain. *Compositions:* Aviary, Effect Out, Sailing, Shining. *Recordings:* Laurel Zucker, Virtuoso Flutist; Laurel Zucker, An American Flute Recital; Poetic Justice, Laurel Zucker. *Publications:*

Sailing, 7 Solo Flute Pieces, yearling for flute and guitar, Song Cycle for flute and piano, all by L Zucker. *Honours:* Professional Promise Incentive Award; Awards from New York Flute Club, National Flute Association, and Artists International Competition. *Memberships:* ASCAP: Sonneck Society; MTNA: Pia Kappa Lambda; National Association. *Hobbies:* Scuba; Jogging; Art. *Address:* 512 Meister Way, Sacramento, CA 95819, USA.

ZUCKER Stefan, Singer; Writer; Editor; Radio Broadcaster. *Education:* BSc., Columbia University, 1967; Course Work for PhD, 1967-72 New York University. *Career:* Tenor, RCA Records, 1972-77; Singer, Opera, World Premiere of Bellini's Adelson e Salvini, 1972; Singer, Concerts and Operas, Europe and USA, 1965-87; Singer and Guest various Radio and TV programmes, Europe and USA, 1965-87; Editor, Opera Fanatic, 1986-87; Producer, Host, Radio Programmes, Saturday Night at the Opera, Opera Fanatic, etc., 1980-87; Record Producer; Producer, Administrator, Stage Director, Operas in USA, 1967-72; Philosophy Lecturer, College of Insurance, New York, 1972. *Recordings:* Stefan Zucker: the World's Highest Tenor, 1981. *Contributions to:* Numerous articles to professional journals and magazines including: Opera News; Opera Fanatic; American Record Guide; The Opera Quarterly; News World; New York Times Magazine; New York Tribune; New York Magazine; La Follia di New York. *Honours:* The World's Highest Tenor, Guiness Book of World Records, 1979-87. *Address:* 11 Riverside Drive, New York, NY 10023, USA.

ZUCKERMANN Wolfgang Joachim, b. 11 Oct 1922, Berlin, Germany. Harpsichord Maker. *Education:* BA, Queens College, New York, 1949. studied cello from age of ten; Later studied Piano Technology. *Career:* Built first harpsichord in 1954, continued to produce similar harpsichords for sale (i.e. simplified one- manual models with little claim to historical authenticity); In 1960 introduced kit version in response to demand for basic inexpensive harpsichord. By end of 1969 almost 8,000 instruments had been sold. A clavichord in kit form was also developed and sold. In 1969 he sold New York enterprise and moved to England where he continued to produce kits both independently and as consultant to his former company. Those introduced after 1970 are modelled more closely on historical instruments. *Publication:* The Modern Harpsichord, October House, New York, 1969, Peter Owen, London 1970. *Address:* St Clement, 30260 Quissac, France.

ZUKERMAN Eugenia, b. 25 Sept 1944, Cambridge, Massachusetts, USA. Flautist. m. (1) Pinchas Zukerman, div. (2) David Seltzer, 1988. *Education:* Juilliard School, N.Y., with Julius Baker. *Debut:* New York Town Hall 1971. *Career:* Has played with most major orchestras in the United States and Canada; tour of US with English Chamber Orchestra; European performances with the Royal Philharmonic, Israel Chamber Orchestra and the Hamburg Bach Solisten; participations in Festival of Two Worlds at Spoleto, London's South Bank Festival and the Edinburgh Festival; collaborations with Jean-Pierre Rampal (Carnegie Hall 1976) and James Galway; Music Commentator on CBS News' Sunday Morning. *Recordings:* Many discs with CBS Masterworks. *Address:* c/o Anglo-Swiss Artists Management, 4/5 Primrose Mews, 1a Sharpleshall Street, London NW1 8YW, England.

ZUKERMAN Pinchas, b. 16 July 1948, Tel-Aviv, Israel. Conductor; Violist; Violinist. m. (1) Eugenia Zukerman, divorced, (2) Tuesday Weld. *Education:* Israel Conservatory and Academy of Music 1956; Juilliard School, New York, 1961, with Ivan Galamian. *Career:* Won 1967 Leventritt Competition and soon appeared with most of the world's leading orchestras in the standard repertoire; 1969 with the New York Philharmonic and at the Brighton Festival; debut as conductor London 1970; guest appearances include English Chamber Orchestra, Philadelphia Orchestra, the Boston Symphony and the Israel Philharmonic; 1980-86 Music Director of the St Paul Chamber Orchestra;

conducted it in the stage premiere of Oliver Knussen's Where the Wild Things Are, Minnesota Opera, 27 Sept 1985; 1978-80 Artistic Director of South Bank Summer Music, London; Principal Guest Conductor of Dallas Internaitonal Music Festival, 1990-; Assumed Post of Principal Guest Conductor of The Dallas Symphony, 1993; noted in chamber music repertory, in which he also plays the viola: concerts with Daniel Barenboim, the late Jacqueline du Pré, Isaac Stern, Itzhak Perlman and Jean-Pierre Rampal; participant in many TV specials, including Alexander's Bachtime Band, with Stern and Alexander Schneider. *Recordings:* For Angel, Deutsche Grammophon, Columbia, CBS Phillips; Now records exclusively for BLG. *Address:* c/o Harold Holt Ltd., 31 Sinclair Road, London W14 ONS, England.

ZUKOFSKY Paul, b. 22 Oct 1943, Brooklyn, New York, USA. Violinist; Conductor. *Education:* BM, 1964, MS, 1964, Juilliard School of Music. *Career includes:* Creative Associate, State University of New York, Buffalo, 1964-65; Various Positions as Violinist, Violin Teacher, 1965-75; President, Musical Observations Inc., 1975-; Principal Investigator, Project Director, Limits, 1976-82; Conductor various orchestras, 1977-79; Programme Co-Ordinator, American Portraits, Concert Series, John F. Kennedy Center, 1980-; Conductor, Contemporary Chamber Ensemble, Juilliard School of Music, 1984-; Founder, Principal Conductor, Sinfoniuhljomsveit Aeskunnar, 1985-; Directory Chamber Music Activities, The Juilliard School, 1987-89; Artistic Director, Summer Garden Concert Series, Museum of Modern Art, NYC 1987-. *Recordings include:* (As Conductor) various Icelandic Orchestral Works, 1987; Cage: Sixteen Dances, 1984; Rudhyar, Dane: Five Stanzas, 1982; (As Violinist) Babbitt, Milton: Sextets, 1972; Brahms: Complete Sonatas for Violin & Piano, 1975; Cage: Cheap Imitation, 1981; Carter, Elliott, Duo for Violin and Piano, 1975; Feldman, Morton: For John Cage, 1984; Glass: Einstein on the Beach, 1978; Glass: Strung Out, 1977; Penderecki, Krzysztof: Capriccio for Violin and Orchestra, 1968; Scelsi, Giacinto: Anahit, 1977; Schnabel, Artur: Sonata for Violin & Piano, 1981; Sonata for solo violin, 1983; Schuman, William: Violin Concerto, 1971; Sessions, Roger, Violin Concerto, 1967; Wuorinen, Charles, Concerto for Amplified Violin and Orchestra, 1983. *Publications:* Articles in professional journals; Article, The Psychology of Music, Ed Deutsch (with Sternberg & Knoll). *Honours Include:* Guggenheim Felowship, 1983-84; National Endowement of the Arts Fellowship, 1983; ASCAP Community Orchestra Award, 1979; ASCAP Citation for Consistent and Devoted Performance of New Music and Loyalty to its Creation, 1979; Pick of the Pack, Time Magazine, 1975; Nominated for Grammy Awards, 1972; Knight's Cross, Icelandic Order of the Falcon and numerous other honours and awards. *Address:* c/o Juilliard School of Music (violin faculty), Lincoln Plaza, New York, NY 10023, USA.

ZUPKO Ramon, b. 14 Nov 1932, Pittsburgh, Pennsylvania, USA. Composer; Professor. m. Vonette Sarche Zupko, 14 Sept 1969, 1 son. *Education:* BS, 1956, MS, 1957, Composition, Juilliard School of Music; Further studies, Columbia University, Hochschule für Musik in Vienna; University of Utrecht, Holland. *Career:* Orchestral works performed by Detroit, St Louis Indianapolis, Kalamazoo, Curtis Institute, Tanglewood Festival & American Composers Orchestras, National Orchestral Association, Grand Rapids Symphony. *Compositions:* Where the Mountain Crosses; Fluxus I through IX; Fantasies; Windsongs; Nocturnes; Fixations; Noosphere; Fluxus I; Conversions; Prelude & Bagatelle; Ode & Jubilation; Violin Concerto; Pro and Contra Dances and Folksody, Piano Trioetc; Vox Naturae, concerto for brass quintet and orchestra, 1991-92. *Recordings:* Noosphere; Masques; Nocturnes; Fluxus II; Fixations; Fluxus I; Pro and Contra Dances. *Publications:* Principal Publisher: C F Peters Corp, New York. *Hobbies:* Biking; Photography; Reading. *Address:* 1540 North 2nd St. Rt. 1, Kalamazoo, MI 49009, USA.

ZUR Menachem, b. 6 Mar 1942, Tel-Aviv, Israel. Composer; Teacher, Theory & Composition. *Education:*

Teacher's Diploma, College for Teachers of Music, Jerusalem, 1964; Diploma, Rubin Academy of Music, Jerusalem, 1967; BMus, Mannes College of Music, New York City, USA, 1971; MFA, Sarah Lawrence College, 1972; DMusA, Columbia University, 1975. *Career:* Musical Advisor to the Israel Museum, Jerusalem; Chairman of the music education department of the Rubin Academy of Music in Jerusalem, 1991; Chairperson, Israeli Composers' League, 1992.*Compositions include:* Fantasy for Piano; Sonata for Cello & Piano; Cantata for Choir; Magnetic Tape, Percussion, Brass Quartet; Several works for tape; Prisma; Violin Concerto; Double Concerto for Bassoon, French Horn & Chamber Orchestra; Lamentations, Cantata; Short Symphony; Quartet, Centres; Clarinet Quintet; Four for Four; Pygmalion, Chamber Opera; Discussions, Nos I & II; Opera; Piano Concerto; String Quartet; Sonata, violin & piano; A Letter to Schoenberg; A Letter to Stravinsky (both for Symphonic Orchestra); Prelude for Band; The Golem for eleven inst. and baritone solo; Horn Trio; Sonata for oboe and piano; Sonata for French horn and piano; Sonata No.2 for cello and piano; Piano Trio (piano, Violin, cello); Fantasy for brass quintet; Circles of Time for piano solo; Prelude for violin solo; Pieces for choir: Hallelujah, Kedushah, Shiluvim, A tale of Two Sandles; Concerto Grosso for vlu, vla, cello and Chamber Orchestra, 1993. *Recordings:* Chants & Horizons, magnetic tape; Sonata No.1 for cello and piano. *Recordings:* Clarinet Quintet. *Publications:* Keyboard Harmony, co-author, 1980. *Contributions to:* Musical Quarterly. *Address:* Rubin Academy of Music, Givat-Ram, Jerusalem, Israel.

ZURAVLENA Vera, b. 20 Oct 1944, Moscow, Russia. Classical Vocalist. m. Viatreslava Smirnov, 22 Feb 1986, 1 son. *Education:* Gnesin Institute and Musical College, 1973. *Career:* Moscow Chamber Theatre, 1970-73; Soloist, Moscow Philharmonic and Moskonzert, 1973-; Radio broadcasts, LPs, 1978, 1980, 1991; Has sung classical arias of Glinka, Rimsky-Korsakov, Bellini, Verdi, Rossini, with Bolshoi Symphony Orchestra, also old popular music by Russian composers. *Recordings:* Moscow Radio: Liszt, Granados, Alexandrov, P Pokrass, Vassilenko, Gurilev, Bulakhov, M Schimanovskaja of Poland. *Contributions to:* Pravada; Sovietskaja Kultury; Musical Life; Soviet Music. *Honours:* Book of Gold Voices, 4th Prize, Glinka Competition, Moscow, 1973; Grand Prix, Barcelona Competition, 1976; Honours Artist of Russian Republic. *Memberships:* Musical Society of the USSR; Union of Concert Artists. Hobbies: Reading crime books; Black Sea; Walking. *Current Management:* Daniel Maidansky, Moscow Concert Bureau, Russia. *Address:* Enisejakaja str 12-91, Moscow 129344, Russia.

ZWIAUER Florian, b. 1954, Vienna, Austria. Violinist. *Education:* Studied at the Vienna Academy of Music. *Career:* Co- founded the Franz Schubert Quartet 1974; Won the European Broadcasting Union's International String Quartet Competition in Stockholm, 1974; Appearances at the Amsterdam Concertgebouw, the Vienna Musikverein and Konzerthaus, the Salle Gaveau Paris and the Sydney Opera House; Visits to Zurich, Geneva, Basle, Berlin, Hamburg, Rome, Rotterdam, Madrid, and Copenhagen; Festival engagements include Salzburg, Wiener Festwochen, Prague Spring, Schubertiade at Hohenems, the Schubert Festival at Washington DC and the Belfast and Istanbul Festivals; Tours of Australasia, the USSR and USA; British debut at the Elizabeth Hall, 1979; Featured in the Concerto by Spohr with the Liverpool Philharmonic in Liverpool and at the Festival Hall; Frequent appearances at Wigmore Hall and Cheltenham Fesival; Teacher at the Vienna Conservatory and Graz Musikhochschule; Masterclasses at the Royal Northern College of Music and at Lake District Summer Music. *Recordings include:* Schubert's Quartet in G, D877; Complete quartets of Dittersdorf. *Address:* c/o Christopher Tennant Artists Management, 11 Lawrence Street, London SW3 5NB, England.

ZWILICH Ellen Taaffe, b. 30 Apr 1939, Miami, Florida, USA. Composer. m. Joseph Zwilich, 22 June 1969 (dec. 1979). *Education:* MusB 1960, MusM 1962, Florida State University; DMA, Juilliard School of Music, 1975; Studies, various teachers. *Career:* Violinist, American Symphony, New York City, 1965-73; Freelance composer 1973-, works performed include: Premier Symposium for Orchestra, Pierre Boulez, NYC, 1975; Chamber Symphony & Passages, Boston Musica Viva, 1979, 1982; Symphony No. 1, Gunther Schuller, American Composers Orchestra, 1982. *Compositions:* Orchestral & chamber music including: Sonata in 3 Movements, 1973-74; Chamber Symphony, 1979; String Trio, 1982; Symphony No. 1, 1982; Cello Symphony, 1985; Concerto Grosso, 1985; Images, 2 Pianos & Orchestra, 1987; Piano Trio, 1987; Symbolon for orchestra 1987; Trombone Concerto 1988; Flute Concerto 1990; Oboe Concerto 1990. *Honours:* Numerous honours & awards including: Elizabeth S. Coolidge Chamber Music Prize, 1974; Viotti Gold Medal, Italy, 1975; Pulitzer Prize, 1983; Award, National Institute of Arts & Letters, 1984; Arturo Toscanini Music Critics Award, 1987; Honorary MusD, Oberlin College, 1987. *Memberships:* Honorary life member, American Federation of Musicians; Past board, past Vice President, American Music Centre; Interntional League of Women Composers. *Current Management:* Music Associates of America, 224 King Street, Englewood, New Jersey 07631. *Address:* Hainburger Strasse 47, A - 1030 Wien, Austria.

ZYKAN Otto M, b. 29 April 1935, Vienna, Austria. Composer; Pianist. *Education:* Studied piano and composition at the Vienna Academy of Music. *Career:* Many concert appearances, performing contemporary works. *Compositions include:* Opera, Auszahlreim, 1986; Sonata for cello and piano 1958; String Quartet 1958; Piano Concerto 1958; Kyryptomnemie for winds, percussion and piano 1963; Schon der Reihe ballet 1966; Kurze Anweisung for orchestra 1969; Miles Smiles, chamber music 1970; Lehrstuck am Beispiel Schoenbergs, music theatre 1974; Symphonie der heilen welt, scenic concerto 1977; Trio for violin 1977; Ausgesucht Freundliches, concerto for 2 soloists, chorus and orchestra 1979; Kunst Kommt von Gonnon, opera 1980; Cello concerto 1982. *Honours include:* Winner, Darmstadt Competition for pianist, 1958. *Address:* AKM (Austria), c/o PRS Ltd. Member Registration, 29-35 Berners Street, London W1P 4AA, England.

ZYLIS-GARA Teresa, b. 23 Jan 1935, Landvarov, Vilna, Poland. Singer (Soprano). *Education:* Studied at the Lodz Academy with Olga Ogina. *Debut:* Cracow 1957, as Halka in Moniusko's opera. *Career:* Sang in Oberhausen, Dortmund and Dusseldorf 1960-70; Glyndebourne Festival 1965, 1967 as Octavian and Donna Elvira; Covent Garden from 1968, debut as Violetta; Salzburg Festival 1968; Metropolitan Opera from 1968, as Mozart's Elvira and Fiordiligi, Verdi's Desdemona, Wagner's Elisabeth and Elsa, Strauss's Marschallin, Puccini's Suor Angelica and Manon Lescaut and Tatiana in Eugene Onegin; Vienna Staatsoper from 1972; Barcelona 1973-74; Orange Festival 1979, as Liu in Turandot; Guest engagements in Hamburg, Berlin, Paris and Warsaw; Concert appearances in Bach, Chopin, Handel, Mozart and Brahms; Sang at the Hamburg Staatsoper 1988, as Desdemona. *Recordings:* Mosè in Egitto by Rossini; Songs by Chopin; Il Giuramento by Mercadante; Bach's Easter and Christmas Oratorios, St Matthew Passion, Cavalieri's Rappresentazione di Anima e di Corpo, Mozart's Requiem and Ariadne auf Naxos (Electrola). *Honours include:* Winner, International Singing Competition, Munich, 1960; Mozart Gold Medal, Mexico City; Polish National Award, great distinction of aristic achievement. *Address:* Hamburg State Opera, Grosse-Theaterstasse 34, D-2000 Hamburg 36, Germany.

ORCHESTRAS

APPENDIX A

ORCHESTRAS

ARGENTINA

Buenos Aires: Orquesta Filarmónica de Buenos Aires, Cerrito 618, 0101 Buenos Aires.
Buenos Aires: Orquesta Sinfónica Nacional, Córdoba 1155, 1055 Buenos Aires.
Conductor: Jorge Rotter.

ARMENIA

Yerevan: Armenian Philharmonic Orchestra, Mashtotz 46, 375019 Yerevan.
Music Director: Loris Tjeknavorian; Manager:George Avedissian.

AUSTRALIA

AUSTRALIAN CAPTIAL TERRITORY

Canberra: Canberra Symphony Orchestra, GPO Box 1919, Canberra, ACT 2601.
Music Director: Leonard Dommett; General Manager: Maeva Galloway.

NEW SOUTH WALES

Sydney: Sydney Symphony Orchestra, Australian Broadcasting Corporation, GPO Box 9994, Sydney, NSW 2001.
General Manager: Mary Vallentine.

QUEENSLAND

Brisbane: Queensland Philharmonic Orchestra, Drake Street and Montague Road, West End, QLD 4101.
Artistic Advisor: Anthony Camden; General Manager: Jenny Hodgson.
Brisbane: Queensland Symphony Orchestra, Australian Broadcasting Corporation, GPB Box 9994, Brisbane, QLD 4001.
Chief Conductor: Muhai Tang; General Manager: Mary Lyons.

SOUTH AUSTRALIA

Adelaide: Adelaide Symphony Orchestra, Australian Broadcasting Corporation, GPO Box 9994, Adelaide, SA 5001.
General Manager: Michael Elwood.

TASMANIA

Hobart: Tasmanian Symphony Orchestra, Australian Broadcasting Corporation, GPO Box 9994, Hobart, TAS 7001.
General Manager: Julie Warn.

VICTORIA

Melbourne: Melbourne Symphony Orchestra, PO Box 443, East Caulfield, VIC 3145.
Conductor Laureate: Hiroyuki Iwaki; General Manager: Steven Porter.
Melbourne: State Orchestra of Victoria, 100 St Kilda Road, Melbourne, VIC 3004.
Administrator: Peter Narroway.
Melbourne: Victorian Concert Orchestra, 1 Treasury Place, 3rd floor, Melbourne, VIC 3002.
Music Director: Martin Rutherford.
South Yarra: Australian Pops Orchestra, 320 Toorak Road, Level 4, Suite 2, South Yarra, VIC 3141.
Managing Director: Kelvin McMillan.

WESTERN AUSTRALIA

Perth: West Australian Symphony Orchestra, GPO Box 9994, Perth, WA 6001.
Music Director: Jorge Mester; General Manager: Peter Garnick.

AUSTRIA

Graz: Grazer Philharmonisches Orchester, Kaiser-Josef-Platz 10, A-8010 Graz.
Music Director:Mario Venzago; Manager: Dr Gerhard Brunner.
Linz: Bruckner-Orchester, Promenade 39, A-4020 Linz.
Chief Conductor: Manfred Mayrhofer; Manager: C-F Steiner.
Salzburg: Mozarteum Orchester, Erzbischof-Gebhardstrasse 10, A-5020 Salzburg.
Music Director: Hans Graf; Executive Director: Dr Peter Ramsauer.

ORCHESTRAS

Vienna:	Niederösterreichisches Tonkünstler-Orchester, Elisabethstrasse 22/9, A-1010 Vienna.
	Chief Conductor: Isaac Karabtchevsky; General Manager: Karl Pietsch.
Vienna:	Orchester "Pro Musica International", Praterstrasse 76/8, A-1020 Vienna.
	Music Director: Gerhard Track; Manager: Joanna Lewis.
Vienna:	Österreichisches Rundfunk Symphonie Orchester, Argentinierstrasse 30, A-1040 Vienna.
	Chief Conductor: Pinchas Steinberg; Director of Music: Dr Andrea Seebohm.
Vienna:	Wiener Kammerorchester, Schachnerstrasse 32, A-1220 Vienna.
	Chief Conductor: Philippe Entremont; General Manager: Rudolf Buchmann.
Vienna:	Wiener Musica Antiqua Ensemble, Minoritenplatz 2, Arkadentrakt, A-1010 Vienna.
	Music Director: Bernhard Kiebel.
Vienna:	Wiener Philharmoniker, Bösendorferstrasse 12, A-1010 Vienna.
	Principal Conductor: Claudio Abbado; Manager: Walter Blovsky.
Vienna:	Wiener Symphoniker, Lehargasse II, A-1060 Vienna.
	Chief Conductor: Rafael Frühbeck de Burgos; Manager: Dr Rainer Bischof.

AZERBAIJAN

Baku:	Azerbaijan Symphony Orchestra, Baku.

BELGIUM

Antwerp:	Koninklijk Filharmonisch Orkest van Vlaanderen, Britselei 80, B-2000 Antwerp.
	Music Director: Muhai Tang; President: H Daems.
Antwerp:	Philharmonische Vereniging van Antwerpen, De Boeystraat 6, B-2018 Antwerp.
	Manager: Albrecht Klora.
Brussels:	Fillharmonisch Orkest van der BRT, 18 Flageyplein, B-1050 Brussels.
	Music Director: Alexander Rahbari; Manager: André Laporte.
Brussels:	Orchestre National de Belgique, Place Eugène Flagey 18, B-1050 Brussels.
	Music Director: Ronald Zollman; Manager: Luc Vanackere.
Brussels:	Orchestre Symphonique de la RTBF, Place Eugène Flagey 18, B-1050 Brussels.
	Music Director: André Vandernoot; Manager: Albert Wastiaux.
Brussels:	Orchestre Symphonique du Théâtre Royal de la Monnaie, 4 Rue Leopold, B-1000 Brussels.
	Conductor: Antonio Pappano; Manager: Bernt Sandstad.
Leuven:	Het Nieuw Belgisch Kamerorkest, Bondgenteniaan 114, B-3000 Leuven.
	Music Director: Jan Caeyers; Manager: Jan Roekens.
Liège:	Ensemble "Musique Nouvelle", Place du Vingt Août 16, B-4000 Liège.
	Music Director: Jean-Pierre Peuvion; Manager: Michel Schoonbrood.
Liège:	Orchestre Philharmonique de Liège et de la Communauté Française, 11 Rue Forgeur, B-4000 Liège.
	Music Director: Pierre Bartholomée; Secretary: Roger Pernay.
Lovendegem:	La Petite Bande, Appensvoorde 31, B-9920 Lovendegem.
	Conductor: Sigiswald Kuijken; Manager: Marc Barbier.
Mons:	Orchestre de Chambre de Wallonie et de la Communauté Française, Rue Neuve 5, B-7000 Mons.
	Music Director: Georges Octors; Secretary: Robert Leleu.
St-Martens-Latem:	I Fiamminghi: The Belgian Chamber Orchestra, Buizenbergstrasse 1, B-9830, St-Martens-Latem.
	Conductor: Rudolf Werthen; Manager: Dries Sel.
Sterrebeek:	Vlaams Kamerorkest van Brussels, Sparrenhof 10, B-1960 Sterrebeek.
	Conductor: Arie Van Lysbeth.

BOSNIA AND HERZEGOVINA

Sarajevo:	Sarajevo Philharmonic Orchestra, Obala 9, 71000 Sarajevo.
Sarajevo:	Sarajevo Radio and Television Symphony Orchestra, Sarajevo Radio and Television, 71000 Sarajevo.

BRAZIL

Brasilia:	Orquestra Sinfônica do Teatro Nacional de Brasilia, Av N2, Anexo do Teatro Nacional de Brasilia, 70000 Brasilia.
	Conductor: Silvio Barbato.
Rio de Janeiro:	Orquestra Filharmônica do Rio de Janeiro, Rua das Marrecas 25, Sala 901, Centro, 20031 Rio de Janeiro.
	Music Director: Florentino Dias.
Rio de Janeiro:	Orquestra Sinfônica Brasileira, Av Rio Branco 135, Room 918, 20040 Rio de Janeiro.
	Music Director: Isaac Karabtchevsky.
Rio de Janeiro:	Orquestra Sinfônica do Teatro Municipal do Rio de Janeiro, Av Rio Branco s/n, 20030 Rio de Janeiro.
	Conductor: Mário Tavares.
Sao Paulo:	Orquestra Sinfônica Estadual de Sao Paulo, Teatro de Cultura Artistica, Rua Nestor Pestana 196, 01303 Sao Paulo.
	Music Director: Eleazar de Carvalho.

ORCHESTRAS

BULGARIA

Sofia: Bulgarian Radio and Television Symphony Orchestra, 4 Dragan Tsankov Boulevard, Sofia.
Music Director: Vassil Kazandjiev.
Sofia: Sofia Philharmonic Orchestra, Benkovski str 1, 1000 Sofia.
Music Director: Emil Tabakov; Administrator: Vassil Kostov.

CANADA

ALBERTA

Calgary: Calgary Philharmonic Orchestra, 205 Eighth Avenue, Calgary, Alberta T2G 0K9.
Music Director: Mario Bernardi; Managing Director: John Shaw.
Edmonton: Edmonton Symphony Orchestra, 10010 109 Street, Edmonton, Alberta T5J 1M4.
Music Director: Uri Mayer; Managing Director: W R McPhee

BRITISH COLUMBIA

Vancouver: Vancouver Symphony Orchestra, 601 Smithe Street, Vancouver, British Columbia V6B 5G1.
Music Director: Sergiu Comissiona; Artistic Administrator: Barbara McLean.
Victoria: Victoria Symphony Orchestra, 846 Broughton Street, Victoria, British Columbia V8W 1E4.
Music Director: Peter McCoppin; General Manager: C Stephen Smith.

MANITOBA

Winnipeg: Winnipeg Symphony Orchestra, Centennial Concert Hall, 555 Main Street, Room 101, Winnipeg, Manitoba R3B 1C3.
Artistic Director: Bramwell Tovey; Executive Director: Barry McArton.

NOVA SCOTIA

Halifax: Symphony Nova Scotia, 1646 Barrington Street, Suite 401, Halifax, Nova Scotia B3J 2A3.
Music Director: Georg Tintner; General Manager: Michael LaLeune.

ONTARIO

Hamilton: Hamilton Philharmonic Orchestra, PO Box 2080, Station A, Hamilton, Ontario L8N 3Y7.
Music Director: Victor Feldbrill; General Manager: Stephen Bye.
Kitchener-Waterloo Kitchener-Waterloo Symphony Orchestra, 101 Queens Street North, Kitchener, Ontario N2H 6P7.
Music Director: Raffi Armenian; Managing Director: Barry Cole.
London: Orchestra London Canada, 520 Wellington Street, London, Ontario N6A 3P9.
Principal Conductor: Uri Mayer; General Manager: John Melnyk.
Ottawa: National Arts Centre Orchestra, PO Box 1534, Station B, Ottawa, Ontario K1P 5W1.
Artistic Director and Principal Conductor: Trevor Pinnock; Managing Director: J M Mills.
Thunder Bay: Thunder Bay Symphony Orchestra, PO Box 2004, Thunder Bay, Ontario P7B 5E7.
Music Director:Glenn Mossop; General Manager: Erik Perth.
Toronto: Toronto Symphony, Roy Thomson Hall, 60 Simcoe Street, Suite C 116, Toronto, Ontario M5J 2H5.
Managing Director: Max Tapper.
Windsor: Windsor Symphony Orchestra, 174-198 Pitt Street West, Windsor, Ontario N9A 5L4.
Music Director: Susan Haig; General Manager: Alison Kurtz.

QUÉBEC

Montréal: Orchestre Symphonique de Montréal, Salle Winifrid-Pelletier, Place des Arts, 200 West de Maisonneuve, Montréal, Province Québec H2X 1Y9.
Music Director: Charles Dutoit; Managing Director: Robert Spickler.
Québec: Orchestra Symphonique de Québec, 130 West Grande-Allée, Québec, Province Québec G1R 2G7.
Music Director: Pascal Verrot; Manager: Louis Laplante.

SASKATCHEWAN

Regina: Regina Symphony Orchestra, 200 Lakeshire Drive, Regina, Saskatchewan S4P 3V7.
Music Director: Vladimir Conta; Executive Director: Pat Middleton.
Saskatoon: Saskatoon Symphony Orchestra, PO Box 1361, Saskatoon, Saskatchewan S7K 3N9.
Conductor: Daniel Swift; General Manager: Shirley Spafford.

CHILE

Santiago: Orquesta Filarmónica de Santiago, San Antonio 149, PO Box 18, Santiago.
Principal Conductor: Michelangelo Veltri; Manager: Andrés Pinto.

ORCHESTRAS

CHINA

Beijing: Central Philharmonic Orchestra, Beijing.
Shanghai: Shanghai Symphony Orchestra, 105 Hunan Lu, Shanghai 200031.
Conductor: Chen Xie-Yang; General Manager: Cao Yiji.

COLOMBIA

Bogotá: Orquesta Filarmónica de Bogotá, Calle 39A, No 14-57, Apdo Aereo 16034, Bogotá.
Music Director: Francisco Rettig; Executive Director: José Hernández.
Bogotá: Orquesta Sinfónica de Colombia, Teatro Colón, Calle 10, No 5-32, Bogotá.
Music Director: Federico Garcia Vigil; Manager: Blanca Cecilia Carreno.

COSTA RICA

San José: Orquesta Sinfónica Nacional, PO Box 1035, San José 1000.
Music Director: Irwin Hoffman; General Manager: Gloria Waissbluth.

CRÒATIA

Zagreb: Croatian Radio and Television Symphony Orchestra, Dezmanova 10, 41000 Zagreb.
Zagreb: Zagreb Philharmonic Orchestra, Trnjanska bb, 41000 Zagreb.

CZECH REPUBLIC

Brno: Brno State Philharmonic Orchestra, Moravské náměstíí la, 602 00 Brno.
Conductor: Leoš Svárovský.
Česke Budějovice: South Bohemian State Orchestra, Ceská ul 1, 370 21 Česke Budějovice.
Chief Conductor: Ondřej Kukal; Director: Milan Kraus.
Hradec Králové: Hradec Králové State Symphony Orchestra, Nábřeží Eliščino 777, 500 70 Hradec Králové.
Chief Conductor: František Vajnar; Manager: Radomir Malý.
Karlovy Vary: Karlovy Vary Symphony Orchestra, Nábřeží CSP 1, 360 01 Karlovy Vary.
Music Director: Bostock Douglas; Manager: Oldřich Kurzawa.
Košice: Košice State Philharmonic Orchestra, Dom umenia, Moyzesova 66, 041 23 Košice.
Director: Julius Klein.
Mariánské Lazně: West Bohemian Symphony Orchestra, Třída Odboráŕu 51, 353 21 Mariánslé Lazně.
Music Director: Radomil Eliška; Manager: Naděžda Domanjová.
Olomouc: Moravian Philharmonic Orlchestra, Horni náměsti 23, 772 00 Olomouc.
Chief Conductor: Stanislav Macura; Manager: Professor Antonin Schindler.
Ostrava: Janáček Philharmonic Orchestra, Michálkovická 181, 710 08 Ostrava 2.
Music Director: Dennis Burkh; Manager: Miroslav Snyrich.
Pizeň: Pizeň Radio Symphony Orchestra, náměsti Miru 4, 320 70 Pizeň.
Chief Conductor: Vit Micka; Manager: Jan Slimacek.
Prague: Czech Philharmonic Orchestra, Korunni 98, 100 Prague 10.
Chief Conductor: Gerd Albrecht.
Prague: Prague Chamber Orchestra, Maltčzské náměstí 1, 118 00 Prague 1.
Artistic Director: Milan Lajčík; Manager: Ota Kramar.
Prague: Prague Radio Symphony Orchestra, Vinohradská 12, 120 99 Prague 2.
Chief Conductor: Vladimir Válek; Manager: Dr Vlastimil Neklapil.
Prague: Prague Symphony Orchestra (FOK), Obecni dum, náměstí Republiky 5, 110 00 Prague 1.
Chief Conductor: Petr Altrichter; Manager: Roman Bělor.

DENMARK

Ålborg: Ålborg Symphony Orchestra, Kjellerupsgade 14 DK-9000 Ålborg.
Music Director: Henning Høholt; Manager: Knud Ketting.
Århus: Århus Symphony Orchestra, Thomas Jensens Allé, DK-8000 Århus C.
Music Director: Eri Klas; Manager: Steen Pade.
Copenhagen: Danish Radio Symphony Orchestra, Rosenørnsallé 22, DK-1999 Copenhagen.
Chief Conductor: Leif Segerstam; Manager: Per Erik Veng.
Copenhagen: Royal Danish Orchestra, Box 2185, DK-1017 Copenhagen.
Music Director: Poul Jørgensen.
Copenhagen: Sjaellands Symphony Orchestra, Bernstorffsgade 9, DK-1577 Copenhagen V.
Manager: Maria Sørensen.
Copenhagen: Tivoli Symphony Orchestra, Tivoli, Vesterbrogade 3, DK-1620 Copenhagen V.
Music Director: Lars Grunth.
Esbjerg: West Jutland Symphony Orchestra, Islandsgade 50, DK-6700 Esbjerg.
Administrative Director: Leif Pedersen.
Odense: Odense Symphony Orchestra, Claus Bergsgade 9, DK-5000 Odense C.
Music Director: Edward Serov; Manager: Soren Bojer Neilsen.
Sønderborg: South Jutland Symphony Orchestra, Skovvej 16, DK-6400 Sønderborg.
Manager: Jytte Rasmussen.

ORCHESTRAS

DOMINICAN REPUBLIC

Santo Domingo: Orquesta Sinfónica Nacional, Palacio de Bellas Artes, Santo Domingo.
Music Director: Carlos Piantini; Manager: Marino Mieses.

ECUADOR

Quito: Orquesta Sinfónica Nacional, Casilla 2844, Calle Venezuela 666, Quito.
Music Director: Alvaro Manzano; Manager: G Sáenz.

EGYPT

Cairo: Cairo Symphony Orchestra, 27 Shari' Abd El-Khaliq Tharwat, Cairo.

EIRE

Dublin: Irish Chamber Orchestra, 18 Kildare Street, Dublin 2.
Artistic Director and Principal Conductor: Stephen Kovacevich; Manager: Gerard Kennan.
Dublin: National Symphony Orchestra of Ireland, National Concert Hall, Earlsfort Terrace, Dublin 2.
Dublin: Radio Telefis Eireann Concert Orchestra, RTE Donnybrook, Dublin 4.
Principal Conductor: Proinnsias Duinn; Manager: Sam Ellis.

EL SALVADOR

San Salvador: Orquesta Sinfónica de El Salvador, Apartdao Postal 3150, Correro Central, San Salvador.
Music Director: German Cáceres; Manager: Alfredo Iraheta.

ESTONIA

Tallin: Estonian State Symphony Orchestra, Lomonossovi 21, 200100 Tallin.
Chief Conductor: Leo Krámer; Manager: Toomas Kahur.

FINLAND

Helsinki: Helsinki Philharmonic Orchestra, Finlandia-talo, Karamzininkatu 4, 00 100 Helsinki.
Chief Conductor: Sergiu Comissiona; Manager: Helena Ahonen.
Helsinki: Radio Symphony Orchestra, Yleisradiokeskus, Pasila, Jakoalue 14, 00 240 Helsinki.
Chief Conductor: Jukka-Pekka Saraste; Manager: Risto Nieminen.
Tampere: Tampere Philharmonic Orchestra, Akerlundinkatu 6 A, 33 100 Tampere.
Music Director: Leonid Grin; Manager: Maritta Hirvonen.
Turku: Turku Philharmonic Orchestra, Sibeliuksenkatu 2 B, 20 110 Turku.
Music Director: Jacques Mercier; Manager: Kalevi Kuosa.

FRANCE

Angers: Orchestre Philharmonique des Pays de la Loire, 26 Avenue Montaigne, BP 2157, F-49021 Angers Cédex.
Music Director: Marc Soustrot; General Administrator: Maryvonne Lavigne.
Avignon: Orchestre Lyrique de Région Avignon Provence, 250 Rue des Rémouleurs, ZI de Courtine, BP 260, F-84011 Avignon Cédex.
Bordeaux: Orchestre National Bordeaux-Aquitaine, 28 bis Cours Xavier Arnozan, F-33000 Bordeaux.
Music Director: Alain Lombard; Administrator: Daniel Dourneau-Gabory.
Cachan: Orchestre National d'Ile de France, 8 Rue Marcel Bonnet, F-94230 Cachan.
Music Director: Jacques Mercier; General Administrator: Phillippe Fanjas
Caen: Orchestre de Caen, F-14027 Caen Cédex.
Music Director: Jean-Marc Laureau; Manager: Jean-Pierre Daragon
Cannes: Orchestre Régional de Cannes-Provence Alpes Côte d'Azur, 104 Avenue Francis Tonner, BP 46, F-06321 Cannes La Bocca Cédex.
Director: Philippe Bender; Manager: Catherine Morschel.
Chambéry: Orchestre des Pays de Savoie, 67 Carre Curial, F-73000 Chambéry.
Music Director: Tibor Varga; Manager: Sylvain Gautier.
Clermont-Ferrand: Orchestre D'Auvergne, 2 Rue Urbain II, F-63000 Clermont-Ferrand.
Music Director: Jean-Jacques Kantorow; Manager: Bruno Cassiere.
Grenoble: Ensemble Instrumental de Grenoble, 1 Rue du Vieux Temple, F-38000 Grenoble.
Director: Marc Tardue; Manager: Jean-Peter Roeber.
Lille: Orchestre National de Lille, 3 Place Mendès-France, BP 119, F-59027 Lille Cédex.
Music Director: Jean-Claude Casadesus; Manager: Jacqueline Brochen.
Lyon: Orchestre National de Lyon, 82 Rue de Bonnel, F-69431 Lyon Cédex.
Music Director: Emmanuel Krivine; Director General: Patrice Armengau.
Marseille: Société des Concerts du Conservatoire, 1 Rue de la Bibliothéque, F-13000 Marseille.
Metz: Orchestre Philharmonique de Lorraine, 25 Avenue Robert Schumann, F-57000 Metz.

ORCHESTRAS

Music Director: Jacques Houtmann; Manager: Pascal Schwan.

Montpellier: Orchestre Philharmonique de Montpellier, Pavillon Populaire, Esplande, F-34000 Montpellier.
Music Director: Gianfranco Masini; Director General: René Koering; Administrator: Dominique Stobinsky.

Mulhouse: Orchestre Symphonique du Rhin-Mulhouse, 38 Passage du Théâtre, F-68100 Mulhouse.
Music Director: Luca Pfaff; Manager: Jean-Luc Fischer.

Nancy: Orchestre Symphonique et Lyrique de Nancy, 78 Place du Col Driant, F-54000 Nancy.
Music Director: Jérome Kaltenbach; Manager: Astrid Chepfer.

Nice: Orchestre Philharmonique de Nice, Opéra de Nice, 4 and 6 Rue St-François de Paule, F-06300 Nice.
Music Director: Klaus Weise; Manager: Pierre Medecin.

Noisy le Grand: La Grande Ecurie et la Chambre du Roy, 9 Place des Federées, F-93160 Noisy le Grand.
Music Director: Jean-Claude Malgoire.

Paris: Association des Concerts Colonne, 2 Rue Edouard Colonne, F-75001 Paris.
Music Director: Philippe Entremont; General Manager: Guy Arnaud.

Paris: Association des Concerts Lamoureux, 252 Rue du Faubourg St-Honoré, F-75008 Paris.
Music Director: Jean-Claude Bernède; Manager: Annie Foultier.

Paris: Association des Concerts Pasdeloup, 18 Rue de Berne, F-75008 Paris.
Music Director: Gerard Devos; Manager: Roger Landy.

Paris: Ensemble Ars Antiqua de Paris, 167 Rue de Flandre, F-75019 Paris.
Music Director: Joseph Sage.

Paris: Ensemble Ars Nova, 16 Rue des Fossés St Jacques, F-75005 Paris.
Music Director: Marius Constant.

Paris: Ensemble InterContemporain, 9 Rue de l'Echelle, F-75001 Paris.
Music Director: David Robertson; Manager: Claude Le Cleach.

Paris: Ensemble Orchestral de Paris, Salle Pleyel, 252 Rue du Faubourg St Honoré, F-75008 Paris.
Conductor: Armin Jordan; Manager: Alain Guillon.

Paris: Ensemble Orchestral Harmonia Nova, 74 Rue du Faubourg St Denis, F-75010 Paris.
Music Director: Didier Bouture; Manager: Daniel Gutenberg.

Paris: La Chapelle Royale, 47 Rue Berger, F-75001 Paris.
Music Director: Philippe Herreweghe.

Paris: Les Arts Florissants, 10 Rue de Florence, F-75008 Paris.
Music Director: William Christie; Administrative Manager: Bruno Schuster.

Paris: Nouvel Orchestre Philharmonique, Radio France, 116 Avenue du Président Kennedy, F-75786 Paris Cédex 16.
Music Director: Marek Janowski; Artistic Director: Yvon Kapp.

Paris: Orchestre de Chambre Jean-François Paillard, 50 Rue Laborde, F-75008 Paris.
Music Director: Jean-François Paillard; Administrator: Richard Siegel.

Paris: Orchestre de Chambre Paul Kuentz, 144 Rue du Faubourg St Antoine, F-75012 Paris.
Music Director: Paul Kuentz.

Paris: Orchestre de Paris, Salle Pleyel, 252 Rue du Faubourg St Honoré, F-75008 Paris.
Music Director: Semyon Bychkov; General Director: Pierre Vozlinsky.

Paris: Orchestre Française des jeunes, 39 Rue Censier, F-75005 Paris.
Music Director: Emmanuel Krivine; Manager: Aude le Cléch.

Paris: Orchestre National de France, Radio France, 116 Avenue du Président Kennedy, F-75786 Paris Cédex 16.
Music Director: Charles Dutoit; General Manager: Patrice d'Ollone.

Paris: Orchestre Symphonique de la Garde Républicaine, 12 Boulevard Henri IV, F-75004 Paris.
Music Director: Roger Boutry.

Poitiers: Orchestre Régional Poitou-Charentes, 3 Place Prosper Mérimée, BP 422, F-86011 Poitiers Cédex.
Director: Charles Frey.

Rennes: Orchestre de Bretagne, 42A Rue St-Melaine, F-35000 Rennes.
Director: Claude Schnitzler; Manager: Jean-François Jeandet.

Rouen: Ensemble Orchestral de Haute-Normandie, 50 Avenue de la Porte des Champs, F-76000 Rouen.
Music Director: Jean-Pierre Berlingen; Administrator: Jean-Michel Bernard.

St-Denis: Orchestre de Chambre de St-Denis, 9 Rue Moreau, F-93200 St-Denis.
Music Director: Pierre Menet.

Strasbourg: Orchestre Philharmonique de Strasbourg, Palais de la Musique et des Congrès, Avenue Schutzenberger, F-67082 Strasbourg Cédex.
Music Director: Theodor Guschlbauer; General Manager: Albert-Michel Moritz.

Sèvres: Orchestre de Chambre de Versailles, 3 Rue Descartes, F-92310 Sèvres.
Music Director: M B Wahl.

Toulouse: Orchestre de Chambre National de Toulouse, 76 Allée Jean-Jaurès, F-31071 Toulouse.
Director: Alain Moglia; Manager Jean Paul Alibert.

Toulouse: Orchestre National du Capitole de Toulouse, Halle aux Grains, Place Dupuy, F-31000 Toulouse.
Music Director: Michel Plasson; Manager: Rosemarie Schnittler.

Versailles: Orchestre Jean-François Gonzales, 32 Rue du Marechal Joffre, Residence 7, F-78000 Versailles..
Music Director: J-F Gonzales-Hamilton; Manager: Lenore Gouyet.

Ville d'Avray: Orchestre de Chambre Jean-Louis Petit, 34 Rue Corot, F-92410 Ville d'Avray.
Music Director: Jean-Louis Petit.

GERMANY

Aachen: Städtisches Orchester Aachen, Stadttheater, W-5100 Aachen.
Music Director: Stefan Lano.

Augsburg: Philharmonisches Orchester der Stadt Augsburg, Kasernstrasse 4, Pf 111949, W-8900 Augsburg.
General Music Director: Michael Luig.

ORCHESTRAS

Baden-Baden: SWF-Sinfonieorchester Baden-Baden, Hans-Bredow-Strasse, W-7570 Baden-Baden.
Chief Conductor: Prof Michael Gielen; Director: Dr Christof Bitter.

Bamberg: Bamberger Symphoniker, Altes Rathaus, W-8600 Bamberg.
Music Director: Horst Stein; Manager: Rolf Beck.

Berlin: Berliner Barock-Orchester, Arnold-Knoblauch-Ring, 64, Pf 173, W-1000 Berlin 39.
Music Director: Konrad Latte.

Berlin: Berliner Philharmonisches Orchester, Philharmonie, Matthäikirchstrasse 1, W-1000 Berlin 30.
Artistic Director: Claudio Abbado; Manager: Ulrich Meyer-Schoellkopf.

Berlin: Berliner Sinfonie-Orchester, Gendarmenmarkt, O-1086 Berlin.
Music Director: Michael Schønwandt; Manager: Dr Frank Schneider.

Berlin: Berliner Symphoniker, Kurfürstendamm, 237, W-1000 Berlin 15.
Music Director: Dr Alun Francis; Manager: Jochen Thärichen.

Berlin: Deutsches Kammerorchester, Lietzenburger Strasse 51, W-1000 Berlin 30.
Music Director: Fritz Weisse.

Berlin: Freies Kammerorchester Berlin e V, Antonstrasse 25, W-1000 Berlin 65.
Music Director: Christoph Hagel.

Berlin: Orchester der Deutschen Oper Berlin, Richard-Wagner-Strasse 10, W-1000 Berlin 10.
General Music Director: Rafael Frühbeck de Burgos.

Berlin: Orchester der Komischen Oper Berlin, Behrenstrasse 55-57, O-1086 Berlin.
General Music Director: Rolf Reuter.

Berlin: Orchester des Friedrichstadtpalastes Berlin, Friedrichstrasse 107, O-1040 Berlin.
Music Director: Detlef Klemm; Manager: Prof Julian Herrey.

Berlin: Orchester des Metropol-Theaters, Friedrichstrasse 101/102, Pf 1302, O-1086 Berlin.
General Music Director: Günter Joseck; Manager: Werner P Seiferth.

Berlin: Orchester des Theaters des Westens, Kantstrasse 12, W-1000 Berlin 12.
Music Director: Dr Peter Keuschnig.

Berlin: Radio-Symphonie-Orchester Berlin, Kaiserdamm 26, W-1000 Berlin 19.
Chief Conductor: Vladimir Ashkenazy; Manager: Dr Elmar Weingarten.

Berlin: Rundfunk-Sinfonieorchester Berlin, Nalepastrasse 18-50, O-1160.
Chief Conductor: Rafael Frühbeck de Burgos.

Berlin: Staatskapelle Berlin, Unter den Linden 7, O-1086 Berlin.
General Music Director: Daniel Barenboim.

Bielefeld: Philharmonisches Orchester der Stadt Bielefeld, Brunnenstrasse 3, W-4800 Bielefeld 1.
General Music Director: Rainer Koch.

Blankenburg: Telemann-Kammerorchester Sachsen-Anhalt, Institut für Auffuhrungspraxis Michaelstein, Pf 24, O-3720 Blankenburg.
Music Director: Dr Eitelfriedrich Thom.

Bochum: Bochumer Symphoniker, Prinz-Regent-Strasse 50-60, W-4630 Bochum.
General Music Director: Eberhard Kloke.

Bonn: Deutsche Bachsolisten, Goddardstrasse 28, W-5300 Bonn.
Music Director: Prof Helmut Winschermann.

Bonn:: Klassische Philharmonie Telekom Bonn, Theaterstrasse 10, W-5300 Bonn 1.
Music Director: Prof Heribert Beissel.

Bonn: Orchester der Beethovenhall Bonn, Verwaltung, Wachsbleiche 2, W-5300 Bonn 1
General Music Director: Dr Dennis Russell Davies.

Brandenburg: Brandenburger Symphoniker, Grabenstrasse 14, O-1800 Brandenburg.
Music Director: Heiko Mathias Förster.

Braunschweig: Staatsorchester Braunschweig, Staatstheater Braunschweig, Pf 4539, W-3300 Braunschweig.
General Music Director: Stefan Soltesz.

Bremen: Philharmonisches Staatsorchester der Freien Hansestadt Bremen, Wüste Stätte 11, W-2800 Bremen.
General Music Director: Marcello Viotti.

Bremerhaven: Städtisches Orchester Bremerhaven, Theodor-Heuss-Platz, Pf 120541, W-2850 Bremerhaven.
General Music Director: Prof Leo Plettner.

Chemnitz: Robert-Schumann-Philharmonie, Städtische Theater Chemnitz, Theaterplatz 2, Pf 756, O-9001 Chemnitz.
General Music Director: Dieter Gerhardt Worm.

Chemnitz: Staatliches Orchester Sächsen, Chemnitzer Strasse 46, O-9125 Grüna.
Music Director: Manfred Grafe.

Coburg: Landestheaterorchester Coburg, Coburger Landestheater, Schlossplatz, W-8630 Coburg.
General Music Director: Christian Fröhlich.

Cologne: Gürzenich-Orchester, Bischofsgartenstrasse 1, Pf 180241, W-5000 Cologne 1.
General Music Director: James Conlon.

Cologne: Kölner Kammerorchester e V, Schlosstrasse 2, W-5040 Bruhl.
Music Director: Helmut Müller-Bruhl.

Cologne: Kölner Rundfunk-Sinfonie-Orchester, Appellhofplatz 1, W-5000 Cologne 1.
Chief Conductor: Hans Vonk; Director of Music Programming: Dr Hermann Lang.

Cologne: Rheinisches Kammerorchester Köln, Steinfelder Gasse 11, W-5000 Cologne 1.
Music Director: Jan Corazolla.

Cologne: Sinfonietta Köln, Auf der Kuhle 11, W-5250 Engelskirchen.
Music Director: Cornelius Frowein.

Cottbus: Brandenburgisches Kammerorchester e V, A Thiemig, Schopenhauerstrasse 9, O-7513 Cottbus.
Music Director: Bernhard Schleinitz.

Cottbus: Philharmonisches Orchester der Staatstheaters Cottbus, Karl-Liebknecht-Strasse 136, O-7500 Cottbus.
General Music Director: Frank Morgenstern.

Darmstadt: Kammerorchester Merck, Stefan Reinhardt, Pf 4119, W-6100 Darmstadt.
Music Director: Dr Zdenek Simane.

Darmstadt: Orchester des Staatstheaters Darmstadt, Auf dem Marienplatz, W-6100 Darmstadt.
General Music Director: Prof Hans Drewanz.

Dessau: Orchester des Landestheaters Dessau, Fritz-Hesse-Platz 1, O-4500 Dessau.

ORCHESTRAS

	General Music Director: Hans-Jörg Leipold.
Detmold:	Detmolder Kammerorchester e V, Bruchstrasse 25, Pf 1404, W-4930 Detmold.
	Music Director: Prof Christoph Poppen.
Detmold:	Orchester des Landestheaters Detmold, Landestheater Detmold, Theaterplatz, W-4930 Detmold 1.
Dortmund:	Philharmonisches Orchester der Stadt Dortmund, Kuhstrasse 12, W-4600 Dortmund 1.
	General Music Director: Moshe Atzmon.
Dresden:	Dresdner Kammerorchester, c/o Sächsische Staatskapelle Dresden, Theaterplatz 2, 0-8010 Dresden.
Dresden:	Dresdner Philharmonie, Kulturpalast am Altmarkt, Pf 368, 0-8012 Dresden.
	General Music Director: Michel Plasson; Manager: Dr Olivier von Winterstein.
Dresden:	Orchester der Staatsoperette, Pirnaer Landstrasse 131, 0-8045 Dresden.
	Music Director: Volker Munch.
Dresden:	Sächsische Staatskapelle Dresden, Theaterplatz 2, 0-8010 Dresden.
	Chief Conductor: Giuseppe Sinopoli.
Dresden:	Virtuosi Saxoniae, Weltestrasse 16, 0-8029 Dresden.
	Music Director: Prof Ludwig Güttler.
Duisburg:	Duisburger Sinfoniker, Neckarstrasse 1, W-4100 Duisburg 1.
	General Music Director: Bruno Weil.
Düsseldorf:	Düsseldorfer Symphoniker, Ehrenhof 1, W-4000 Düsseldorf 30.
	Music Director: Salvador Mas Conde; Manager: Freimut Richter-Hansen.
Düsseldorf:	Robert-Schumann-Kammerorchester Düsseldorf, Kronerweg 34, W-4000 Düsseldorf 30.
	Music Director: Prof Jürgen Kussmaul.
Erfurt:	Erfurter Kammerorchester, Strasse der Einheit 12, 0-5082 Erfurt.
	Music Director: Margit Borner.
Erfurt:	Philharmonisches Orchester Erfurt, Gorkistrasse 1, 0-5020 Erfurt.
	General Music Director: Wolfgang Rögner.
Essen:	Folkwang Kammerorchester Essen e V, Hollestrasse Ig, W-4300 Essen 1.
	Music Director: Karl-Heinz Bloemeke.
Essen:	Philharmonie Essen, Rolandstrasse 10, W-4300 Essen 1.
	General Music Director: Prof Wolf-Dieter Hauschild.
Flensburg:	Schleswig-Holsteinisches Sinfonieorchester, Rathausstrasse 22, W-2390 Flensburg.
	General Music Director: Gerhard Schneider.
Frankfurt am Main:	Concerto Grosso Frankfurt e V, Ludwigstrasse 66, W-6050 Offenbach.
	Music Director: Prof Irina Edelstein.
Frankfurt am Main:	Deutsche Kammerphilharmonie, Schwedlerstrasse 2-4, W-6000 Frankfurt am Main 1.
Frankfurt am Main:	Deutsches Kammerorchester Frankfurt am Main, Carl-von-Ossietzky-Strasse 56, W-6200 Wiesbaden.
Frankfurt am Main:	Opernhaus-und Museumsorchester Frankfurt am Main, Untermainanlage 11, W-6000 Frankfurt am Main.
	General Music Director: Sylvain Cambreling.
Frankfurt am Main:	Radio-Sinfonie-Orchester Frankfurt, Hessischer Rundfunk, Bertramstrasse 8, W-6000 Frankfurt am Main 1.
	Chief Conductor: Dmitri Kitaenko; Director of Music Programming: Dr Leo Karl Gerhartz.
Frankfurt am Main:	Rundfunkorchester des Hessischen Rundfunks, Bertramstrasse 8, W-6000 Frankfurt am Main 1.
	Music Director: Prof Peter Falk; Director of Musis Programming: Dr Leo Karl Gerhartz.
Frankfurt an der Oder:	Philharmonisches Orchester Frankfurt an der Oder, Collegienstrasse 7, 0-1200 Frankfurt an der Oder.
	General Music Director: Nikos Athinäos.
Freiburg im Breisgau:	Collegium Aureum, Nordstrasse 2, W-7800 Freiburg im Breisgau.
	Music Director: Prof Franzjosef Maier.
Freiburg im Breisgau:	Philharmonisches Orchester der Stadt Freiburg, Bertoldstrasse 46, W-7800 Freiburg im Breisgau.
	General Music Director: Donald Runnicles.
Gelsenkirchen:	Philharmonisches Orchester der Stadt Gelsenkirchen, Musiktheater im Revier, W-4650 Gelsenkirchen.
	General Music Director: Neil Varon.
Gera:	Philharmonisches Orchester Gera, Bühnen der Stadt Gera, Küchengartenallee 2, 0-6500 Gera.
	Music Director: Wolfgang Wappler.
Gera:	Reussisches Kammerorchester, Bühnen der Stadt Gera, Kuchengartenallee 2, 0-6500 Gera.
	Music Director: Herbert Voigt.
Gotha:	Landessinfonieorchester Thüringen-Gotha, Reinhardsbrunner Strasse 23, 0-5800 Gotha.
	Music Director: Hermann Breuer.
Göttingen:	Göttinger Symphonie-Orchester, Godehardstrasse 19-21, W-3400 Göttingen.
	Music Director: Christian Simonis.
Hagen:	Philharmonisches Orchester Hagen, Elberfelder Strasse 65, W-5800 Hagen 1.
	General Music Director: Gerhard Markson.
Halle an der Saale:	Händelfestspielorchester, Universitätsring 24, 0-4020 Halle an der Saale.
	Music Director: Wolfgang Balzer.
Halle an der Saale:	Kammerorchester "musica juventa" Halle, Hegelstrasse 9, 0-4020 Halle an der Saale.
	Music Director: Matthias Erben.
Halle an der Saale:	Philharmonisches Staatsorchester Halle, Kleine Brauhausstrasse 26, 0-4020 Halle an der Saale.
	General Music Director: Prof Heribert Beissel.
Hamburg:	Akademie Hamburger Solisten, Seilerstrasse 41, W-2000 Hamburg 36.
	Music Director: Joachim Kerwin.
Hamburg:	Deutsches Bachorchester e V, Colonnaden 72, W-2000 Hamburg 36.
	Music Director: Neithard Bethke.
Hamburg:	Hamburger Mozart-Orchester, Helgolandstrasse 12, W-2000 Wedel.
	Music Director: Robert Stehli.
Hamburg:	Hamburger Symphoniker, Dammtorwall 46, W-2000 Hamburg 36.

ORCHESTRAS

	Music Director: Miguel Gomez Martínez.
Hamburg:	NDR-Sinfonieorchester, Norddeutscher Rundfunk Hamburg, Rothenbaumchaussee 132, W-2000 Hamburg 13.
	Chief Conductor: John Eliot Gardiner; Director of Music Programming: Dr Bernhard Hansen.
Hamburg:	Philharmonisches Kammerorchester Hamburg e V, Musikhalle, Karl-Muck-Platz, W-2000 Hamburg 36.
	Music Director: Wilfried Laatz.
Hamburg:	Philharmonisches Staatsorchester Hamburg, Grosse Theaterstrasse 34, W-2000 Hamburg 36.
	General Music Director: Prof Gerd Albrecht; Manager: Dr Peter Ruzicka.
Hamburg:	Radiokammerorchester Hamburg, Zum Forellenbach 11, W-2000 Oststeinbek.
	Music Director: Karl Henke.
Hannover:	Niedersächsisches Staatsorchester, Opernplatz 1, W-3000 Hannover 1.
	General Music Director: Christof Prick.
Hannover:	Rundfunkorchester Hannover, Rudolf-von-Benningsen-Ufer 22, W-3000 Hannover.
	Chief Conductor: Bernhard Klee.
Heidelberg:	Orchester der Stadt Heidelberg, Friedrichstrasse 5, W-6900 Heidelberg 1.
	General Music Director: Anton Marik.
Heilbronn:	Württembergisches Kammerorchester Heilbronn, Pf 3830, W-7100 Heilbronn.
	Music Director: Jörg Faerber.
Herford:	Nordwestdeutsche Philharmonie, Stiftbergstrasse 2, W-4900 Herford.
	Music Director: Michail Jurowski.
Hilchenbach:	Südwestfälische Philharmonie, Im Langen Feld 2, Pf 1320, W-5912 Hilchenbach.
	Music Director: Hiroshi Kodama; Manager: Dr Volker Mattern.
Hof an der Saale:	Hofer Symphoniker, Klosterstrasse 9-11, W-8670 Hof an der Saale.
	Music Director: Hikotaro Yazaki; Manager: Wilfried Anton.
Jena:	Jenaer Philharmonie, August-Bebel-Strasse 4, 0-6900 Jena.
	General Music Director: Andreas S Weiser.
Kaiserslautern:	Orchester des Pfalztheaters Kaiserslautern, Fruchthallstrasse, W-6750 Kaiserslautern.
	General Music Director: Lior Shambadal.
Kaiserslautern:	Rundfunkorchester des Südwestfunks, Fliegerstrasse 36, W-6750 Kaiserslautern.
	Music Director: Klaus Arp; Director of Music Programming: Dr Reimund Hess.
Karlsruhe:	Badische Staatskapelle Karlsruhe, Baumeisterstrasse 11, W-7500 Karlsruhe.
	General Music Director: Günter Neuhold.
Kassel:	Orchester des Staatstheaters Kassel, Staatstheater Kassel, Friedrichsplatz 15, W-3500 Kassel.
	General Music Director: Georg Schmöhe.
Kiel:	Philharmonisches Orchester der Landeshauptstadt Kiel, Rathausplatz, W-2300 Kiel.
	General Music Director: Prof Klauspeter Seibel.
Koblenz:	Staatsorchester Rheinische Philharmonie, Eltzerhostrasse 6a, W-5400 Koblenz 1.
	General Music Director: Christian Kluttig; Manager: Hans Richard Stracke.
Konstanz:	Südwestdeutsche Philharmonie Konstanz, Spanierstrasse 3, W-7750 Konstanz.
	General Music Director: Petr Altrichter.
Leipzig:	Gewandhausorchester zu Leipzig, Augustusplatz 8, 0-7010 Leipzig.
	Music Director: Prof Dr h c Kurt Masur.
Leipzig:	Leipziger Kammerorchester, Schorlemmerstrasse 3, 0-7022 Leipzig.
	Music Director: Otto-Georg Moosdorf.
Leipzig:	Orchester der Musikalischen Komödie Leipzig, Dreilindenstrasse 30, 0-7033 Leipzig.
	Music Director: Roland Seiffarth.
Leipzig:	Sinfonieorchester des Mitteldeutschen Rundfunks, Springerstrasse 22-24, 0-7022 Leipzig.
	Chief Conductor: Daniel Nazareth; Director of Music Programming: Hubertus Franzen.
Leverkusen:	Westdeutsche Sinfonia, Am Kreispark 32, Pf 310154, W-5090 Leverkusen 3.
	Music Director: Dirk Joeres.
Lübeck:	Orchester der Hansestadt Lübeck, Fischergrube 5/21, W-2400 Lübeck.
	General Music Director: Erich Wächter.
Ludwigshafen:	Staatsphilharmonie Rheinland-Pfalz, Heinigstrasse 40, W-6700 Ludwigshafen.
	Music Director: Bernhard Klee; Manager: Raimund Gress.
Magdeburg:	Magdeburgische Philharmonie, Theater der Landeshauptstadt Magdeburg, Pf 1240, 0-3010 Magdeburg.
	General Music Director: Mathias Husmann.
Mainz:	Mainzer Kammerorchester e V, Sertoriusring 56, W-6500 Mainz 21.
Mainz:	Philharmonisches Orchester des Staatstheaters Mainz GmbH, Gutenbergplatz 7, W-6500 Mainz 1.
	General Music Director: Peter Erckens.
Mannheim:	Kürpfalzisches Kammerorchester, D 6, 2, W-6800 Mannheim 1.
	Music Director: Jiři Malát.
Mannheim:	Nationaltheater-Orchester Mannheim, Mozartstrasse 9, W-6800 Mannheim 1.
Marl:	Philharmonia Hungarica, Am Theater 1, W-4370 Marl.
	General Music Director: Prof George Alexander Albrecht; Manger: Hans Ulrich Kaegi.
Meiningen:	Orchester des Meininger Theaters, Bernhardstrasse 5, 0-6100 Meiningen.
	Music Director: Wolfgang Hocke.
Mönchengladbach:	Niederrheinische Sinfoniker, Opernhaus, Odenkirchener Strasse 78, W-4050 Mönchengladbach 2.
	General Music Director: Yakov Kreizberg.
Munich:	Bach Collegium München e V, Elisabethstrasse 9, W-8000 Munich 40.
	Music Director: Florian Sonnleitner.
Munich:	Bayerisches Staatsorchester, Max-Joseph-Platz 2, W-8000 Munich 22.
Munich:	Münchener Kammerorchester e V, Wittelsbacherplatz 2, W-8000 Munich 2.
	Music Director: Prof Hans Stadlmair.
Munich:	Münchner Philharmoniker, Gasteig Kulturzentrum, Kellerstrasse 4/III, W-8000 Munich 80.
	General Music Director: Sergiu Celibidache; Manager: Norbert Thomas.
Munich:	Münchner Symphoniker e V, Drächslstrasse 14, W-8000 Munich 90.
	Music Director: Christoph Stepp.
Munich:	Orchester des Staatstheaters am Gärtnerplatz, Gärtnerplatz 3, W-8000 Munich 5.

OPERA COMPANIES

	Music Director: Prof Reinhard Schwarz.
Munich:	Philharmonisches Kammerorchester München e V, Connolly-Strasse 15, W-8000 Munich 40.
	Music Director: Michael Helmrath.
Munich:	Rundfunkorchester des Bayerischen Rundfunks, Rundfunkplatz 1, W-8000 Munich 2.
	Music Director: Roberto Abbado.
Munich:	Symphonieorchester des Bayerischen Rundfunks, Rundfunkplatz 1, W-8000 Munich 2.
	Chief Conductor: Lorin Maazel.
Münster:	Symphonieorchester der Stadt Münster, Neubrückenstrasse 63, W-4400 Münster.
	General Music Director: Will Humburg.
Neubrandenburg:	Neubrandenburger Philharmonie, Friedrich-Engels-Ring 52, 0-2000 Neubrandenburg.
	Music Director: Romely Pfund.
Neustrelitz:	Orchester des Landestheaters Mecklenburg, Friedrich-Ludwig-Jahn-Strasse, 0-2080 Neustrelitz.
	Music Director: Golo Berg.
Neuss:	Deutsche Kammerakademie, Oberstrasse 17, Pf 101452, W-4040 Neuss 1.
	Music Director: Johannes Goritzki.
Nordhausen:	Orchester des Theaters Nordhausen, Käthe-Kollwitz-Strasse 15, 0-5500 Nordhausen.
	Music Director: Kurt Schafer.
Nürnberg:	Nürnberger Symphoniker, Bayernstrasse 100, W-8500 Nürnberg 44.
	Manager: Günter Einhaus.
Nürnberg:	Philharmonisches Orchester der Stadt Nürnberg, Städtische Bühnen Nürnberg, Musiktheater, Richard-Wagner-Platz 2-10, W-8500 Nürnberg 70.
	General Music Director: Christian Thielmann.
Oldenburg:	Oldenburgisches Staatsorchester, Theaterwall 18, W-2900 Oldenburg.
	General Music Director: Kurt Mahlke.
Osnabrück:	Osnabrücker Symphonieorchester, Städtische Bühnen Osnabrück, Musikbüro, Domhof 10/11, W-4500 Osnabrück.
	General Music Director: Jean-François Monnard.
Pforzheim:	Südwestdeutsches Kammerorchester Pforzheim, Westliche 257A, W-7530 Pforzheim.
	Music Director: Vladislav Czarnecki.
Plauen:	Orchester des Vogtland-Theaters Plauen, Theaterplatz 1-3, 0-9900 Plauen.
	Music Director: Paul Theissen.
Potsdam:	Brandenburgische Philharmonie, Zimmerstrasse 10, 0-1570 Potsdam.
	Music Director: Stefan Sanderling.
Radebeul:	Orchester der Landesbühnen Sachsen, Meissner Strasse 152, 0-8122 Radebeul.
	Music Director: Joachim Widlak; Manager: Christian Schmidt.
Recklinghausen:	Westfälisches Sinfonieorchester, Dorstener Strasse 16, W-4350 Recklinghausen.
	General Music Director: Walter Gillessen.
Regensburg:	Philharmonisches Orchester Regensburg, Bismarckplatz 7, W-8400 Regensburg.
	General Music Director: Hilary Griffiths.
Reichenbach:	Vogtlandphilharmonie, Weinholdstrasse 7, 0-9800 Reichenbach.
	Music Director: Stefan Fraas.
Remscheid:	Remscheider Symphoniker, Stadt Remscheid, Kulturverwaltungsamt, Konrad-Adenauer-Strasse 31/33, W-5630 Remscheid.
	General Music Director: Reinhard Seifried.
Reutlingen:	Württembergische Philharmonie Reutlingen, Wilhelmstrasse 69, W-7410 Reutlingen.
	General Music Director: Roberto Paternostro.
Rostock:	Norddeutsche Philharmonie Rostock, Patriotischer Weg 33, 0-2500 Rostock.
	General Music Director: Michael Zilm.
Rudolstadt:	Thüringer Symphoniker Saalfeld/Rudolstadt, Thüringer Landestheater Rudolstadt, Anger 1, 0-6820 Rudolstadt.
	Music Director: Konrad Bach.
Saarbrücken:	Rundfunk-Sinfonieorchester Saarbrücken, Funkhaus Halberg, Pf 1050, W-6600 Saarbrücken.
	Chief Conductor: Marcello Viotti; Director of Music Programming: Dr Peter Rocholl.
Saarbrücken:	Saarländisches Staatsorchester Saarbrücken, Schillerplatz, W-6600 Saarbrücken.
	General Music Director: Jun Märkl.
Schwerin:	Mecklenburgische Staatskapelle, Alter Garten, 0-2750 Schwein.
Senftenberg:	Theaterorchester Senftenberg, Rathenaustrasse 6/8, 0-7840 Senftenberg.
	Music Director: Michael Keschke.
Solingen:	Symphonieorchester der Stadt Solingen, Konrad-Adenauer-Strasse 71, W-5650 Solingen.
	General Music Director: Christian Suss.
Stendal:	Orchester des Theaters der Altmark-Landestheater Sachsen-Anhalt Nord, Karlstrasse 4-6, 0-3500 Stendal.
	Music Director: Frank Jaremko.
Stralsund:	Sinfonieorchester des Theaters der Hansestadt Stralsund, Olaf-Palme-Platz, 0-2300 Stralsund.
	Music Director: Daniel Kleiner.
Stuttgart:	Kammerorchester Arcata Stuttgart e V, Heumadener Strasse 23, W-7302 Ostfidern 4.
	Music Director: Patrick Strub.
Stuttgart:	Radio-Sinfonieorchester Stuttgart, Neckarstrasse 230, W-7000 Stuttgart 1.
	Chief Conductor: Gianluigi Gelmetti; Manager: Hermann Funfgeld.
Stuttgart:	Staatsorchester Stuttgart, Oberer Schlossgarten 6, W-7000 Stuttgart 1.
	General Music Director: Gabriele Ferro.
Stuttgart:	Stuttgarter Kammerorchester e V, Johann-Sebastian-Bach-Platz, W-7000 Stuttgart 1.
	Music Director: Martin Sieghart.
Stuttgart:	Stuttgarter Philharmoniker, Schickhardstrasse 5, W-7000 Stuttgart 1.
	General Music Director: Carlos Kalmar.
Suhl:	Thüringen Philharmonie Suhl, Bahnhofstrasse 8-10, Pf 306, 0-6000 Suhl.
	General Music Director: Prof Oalf Koch.
Trier:	Städtisches Orchester Trier, Am Augustinerhof, W-5500 Trier.
	General Music Director: Reinhard Petersen.
Ulm:	Orchester der Stadt Ulm, Ulmer Theater, Olgastrasse 73, W-7900 Ulm.
	General Music Director: Alicja Mounk.

OPERA COMPANIES

Waiblingen: Waiblinger Kammerorchester e V, Friedemann Enssle, Lindauer Strasse 40, W-7150 Backnang.
Music Director: Gerd Budday.

Weimar: Staatskapelle Weimar, Theaterplatz, 0-5300 Weimar.
General Music Director: Hans-Peter Frank.

Weimar: Thüringisches Kammerorchester Weimar, Theaterplatz 2, 0-5300 Weimar.
Conductors: Prof Max Pommer and Claus Gebauer.

Werneck: Kammerorchester Schloss Werneck e V, Balthasar-Neumann-Platz 8, Pf 65, W-8727 Werneck.
Music Director: Ulf Klausenitzer.

Wernigerode: Kammerorchester Wernigerode, Bahnhofstrasse 16, 0-3700 Wernigerode.
Music Director: Thomas Brezinka.

Wiesbaden: Orchester des Hessischen Staatstheater Wiesbaden, Christian-Zais-Strasse, W-6200 Wiesbaden.
General Music Director: Oleg Caetani.

Wiesbaden: Pro Arte Ensemble Mainz e V, Werderstrasse 8, W-6200 Wiesbaden.
Music Director: Juan Levy.

Wittenberg: Orchester der Elbe-Saale Bühnen, Thomas-Müntzer-Strasse 14/15, 0-4600 Wittenberg.
Music Director: Klaus Hofmann.

Würzburg: Städtisches Philharmonisches Orchester Würzburg, Theaterstrasse 21, W-8700 Würzburg.
General Music Director: Jonathan Seers.

Wuppertal: Sinfonieorchester Wuppertal, Spinnstrasse 4, W-5600 Wuppertal.
General Music Director: Dr Peter Gülke.

Zwickau: Orchester des Theaters Zwickau, Gewandhausstrasse 7, Pf 308, 0-9541 Zwickau.
Music Director: Albrecht Hofmann.

GREECE

Athens: Athens Radio Symphony Orchestra, 432 Messoghion Street, 15310 Athens.

Athens: Athens State Orchestra, 2 Kapodistriou Street, 10682 Athens.
Music Director and Manager: Yannis Ioannidis.

Thessaloníki Thessaloníki Orchestra, 21 Ippodromiou Street, 54621 Thessaloníki.
Director: Alkis Baltas.

GUATEMALA

Guatemala City: Orquesta Sinfónica Nacional, 3a Ave 4-61, Zona 1, Guatemala City.
Music Director: Jorge Sarmiento.

HONDURAS

Tegucigalpa: Orquesta Sinfonica Nacional, PO Box 2298, Tegucigalpa.
Music Director: Ramiro Soriano-Arce; Manager: David Vides.

HONG KONG

Kowloon: Hong Kong Philharmonic Orchestra, Hong Kong Cultural Centre, 10 Salisbury Road, Administration Building, Level 6, Kowloon.
Music Director: David Atherton; General Manager: Stephen Crabtree.

HUNGARY

Budapest: Budapest Chamber Orchestra "Franz Liszt", Sxechenyi emlekut 23, 1121 Budapest.
Director: János Rolla; Manager: Paul Kelemen.

Budapest: Budapest Concert Orchestra MAV, Muzeum utca 11, 1088 Budapest.
Music Director: Tamás Gál; Managing Director: Géza Kovács.

Budapest: Budapest Festival Orchestra, V Vörösmarty tér 1, H-1369 Budapest.
Music Directors: Ivan Fischer and Zoltán Kocsis; Manager: Ildikó Gedényi.

Budapest: Budapest Philharmonic Orchestra, Népköztársaság utja 22, 1061 Budapest.

Budapest: Hungarian Radio and Television Symphony Orchestra, Bródy Sándor utca 5-7, 1800 Budapest.

Budapest: Hungarian State Symphony Orchestra, Vörösmarty tér 1, 1364 Budapest.
Music Director: Ken-Ichiro Kobayashi.

Debrecen: Debrecen Philharmonic Orchestra, Simonffy utca 1/c, 4025 Debrecen.
Music Director: László Szabó

Gyór: Gyór Philharmonic Orchestra, Bajcsy Zsilinszky u 36, 9022 Gyór.
Music Director: János Sándor; Manager: Gabor Baross.

Miskolc: Miskolc Symphony Orchestra, Fábián u 6, 3525 Miskolc.
Music Director: László Kovács; Manager: László Sir.

Pécs: Pécs Symphony Orchestra, Kossuth Lajos u 19, 7621 Pécs.
Music Director: Howard Williams; Administrator: Péter Szkladányi.

Szeged: Szeged Symphony Orchestra, Festó utca 6, 6721 Szeged.
Music Director: Ervin Acél; Manager: István Szelezsan.

Szombathely: Savaria Symphony Orchestra, Thököly u 14, 9700 Szombathely.
Music Director: Robert Houlihan; Manager: Tibor Menyhárt.

OPERA COMPANIES

ICELAND

Reykjavík: Iceland Symphony Orchestra, Haskolabio v/Hagatorg, 107 Reykjavík.
Music Director: Petri Sakari; Manager: Runólfur Birgir Leifsson.
Reykjavík: Reykjavík Chamber Orchestra, Hauhlid 14, 105 Reykjavík.
Manager: Rut Ingolfsdottir.

INDIA

Calcutta: Calcutta Symphony Orchestra, 6B Sunny Park, Calcutta 700019.
New Delhi: Delhi Symphony Orchestra, Humayun Road, New Delhi 110003.

ISRAEL

Beer Sheva: Israel Sinfonietta, Derech Hameshachrerim 12, 84299 Beer Sheva.
Artistic Advisor: Uri Mayer; Manager: Alon Resnick.
Haifa: Haifa Symphony Orchestra, PO Box 5210, 50 Pevsner Street, 33134 Haifa.
Music Director: Stanley Sperber; Director General: Ben-Ami Einav.
Haifa: Israel Pro-Musica Orchestra, PO Box 7191, 31071 Haifa.
Music Director: Dalia Atlas.
Haifa: Technion Symphony Orchestra, Churchill Auditorium, 32000 Haifa.
Music Director: Dalia Atlas.
Jerusalem: Jerusalem Symphony Orchestra, PO Box 4640, Jerusalem.
Music Director: David Shallon; Managing Director: Gideon Paz.
Netanya: Netanya Orchestra, PO Box 464, 42103 Netanya.
Music Director: Samuel Lewis; General Manager: Yafe Duek.
Ramat Gan: Ramat Gan Chamber Orchestra, PO Box 138, 13 Hertzel Street, Ramat Gan.
Music Director: Shalom Ronly-Riklis; Manager: Sarah Lash-Yolowitz.
Rishon Le-Zion: Rishon Le-Zion Symphony Orchestra, 5 Habanim Street, 75254 Rishon Le-Zion.
Music Director: Noam Sheriff; General Manager: Menahem Shai.
Tel Aviv: Israel Chamber Orchestra, Asia House, 4 Weizman Street, 64239 Tel Aviv.
Conductor: Shlomo Mintz; Managing Director: Eli Doron.
Tel Aviv: Israel Philharmonic Orchestra, PO Box 11292, 1 Huberman Street, 61112 Tel Aviv.
Music Director: Zubin Mehta; General Secretary: Avi Shoshani.
Tel Aviv: Kibbutz Chamber Orchestra, 8 Shaul Hamelech Avenue, 61400 Tel Aviv.
Music Director: Lior Shambadal; Manager: Aharon Kidron.
Tel Aviv: Musica Nova Consort, PO Box 65125, 61651 Tel Aviv.
Director: Yossi Schiffmann.
Tel Aviv: Young Israel Philharmonic, PO Box 11292, 1 Huberman Street, 61112 Tel Aviv.
Music Director: Ze-ev Dorman; Administrative Director: Yaffa Sharett.

ITALY

Bolzano: Orchestra Sinfonica Haydn di Bolzano e Trento, Piazza dei Domenicani 19, 39100 Bolzano.
Artistic Director: Hubert Stuppner.
Florence: Orchestra della Toscana, Via dei Benci 20, 50122 Florence.
Artistic Director: Aldo Bennici; Principal Conductor: Donato Renzetti.
Milan: Orchestra da Camera dell'Angelicum, Piazza S Angelo 2, 20121 Milan.
Milan: Orchestra Sinfonica di Milano della Radiotelevisione Italiana, Via Conservatorio 12, 20122 Milan.
Artistic Director: Mario Messinis.
Naples: Orchestra Alessandro Scarlatti di Napoli della Radiotelevisione Italiana, Via Marconi 5, 80125 Naples.
Artistic Director: Massimo Fargnoli.
Padua: Orchestra da Camera di Padova e del Veneto, Via Marsilio da Padova 19, 35139 Padua.
Principal Conductor: Peter Maag.
Padua: I Solisti Veneti, Piazzale Pontecorvo 6, 35100 Padua.
Conductor: Claudio Scimone; Manager: Mirella Gualandi.
Palermo: Orchestra Sinfonica Siciliana, Via G La Farina 29, 90141 Palermo.
Artistic Director: Roberto Pagano; Conductor: Gabriele Ferro.
Parma: Orchestra Sinfonico dell'Emilia Romagna Arturo Toscanini, Piazzale C Battisti 15, 43100 Parma.
Principal Conductor: Gianandrea Gavazzeni.
Rome: Orchestra Sinfonica dell'Accademia Nazionale di Santa Cecilia, Via Vittoria 6, 00187 Rome.
President, Superintendent, and Artistic Director: Francesco Siciliani.
Rome: Orchestra Sinfonica di Roma della Radiotelevisione Italiana, Foro Italico, Piazza L de Bosis, 00194 Rome.
Artistic Director: Gioacchino Lanza Tomasi.
San Remo: Orchestra Sinfonica di San Remo, Corso Cavallotti 51, 18038 San Remo.
Artistic Director: Giovanni Guglielmo.
Turin: Orchestra Sinfonica di Torino della Radiotelevisione Italiana, Piazza F Ili Rossaro 15, 10124 Turin.
Artistic Director: Enzo Restagno.

ORCHESTRAS

JAPAN

Fukuoka-shi: Kyushu Symphony Orchestra, 1-11-50 NoNaKuma, Jonan-ku, Fukuoka-shi 814-01.
Music Director: Kazuhiro Koizumi; Chairman: Kenzou Tanaka.

Hiroshima: Hiroshima Symphony Orchestra, 7-4 Hatchobori, Naka-ku, Hiroshima 730.
Music Director: Ken Takaseki; Manager: Kengo Marugame.

Kanazawa: Orchestra Ensemble Kanazawa, Hirosaka 1-7-1, Kanazawa 920.
Music Director: Hiroyuki Iwaki; Managing Director: Masayuki Yamada.

Kobe-shi: Kobe Philharmonic Orchestra, 1-9-1 San-no-miya-cho, Chuo-ku, Kobe-shi 650.
Conductor: Chitaru Asahina.

Kyoto: Kyoto Symphony Orchestra, 103 Izumojitatemoto-cho, Kita-ku, Kyoto 603.
Music Director: Michiyoshi Inoue; Manager: Yoshiyuki Murano.

Nagoya: Nagoya Philharmonic Orchestra, 1-5-1 Kanayama, Naka-ku, Nagoya 460.
Conductor: Moshe Atzmon; Manager: Susumu Nonoyama.

Osaka: Kansai Philharmonic Orchestra, Diahatsu Building, 40-2-2 Katmachi, Miyakozima-ku, Osaka.
Conductor: Hideomi Kuroiwa.

Osaka: Osaka Philharmonic Orchestra, Shirakabe Building, 7F, 1-14-7 Shibata, Kita-ku, Osaka 530.
Music Director: Takashi Asahina; Secretary General: Toshio Myazawa.

Osaka: Osaka Symphony Orchestra, 4-3-9 203 Tezukayama naka, Sumiyoshi-ku, Osaka 558.
Music Director: Thomas Sanderling; General Manager: Tetsuo Shikishima.

Sapporo: Sapporo Symphony Orchestra, c/o Kyoiku Bunka Kaikan, Nishi 13-chome, Kita 1-jo, Chuo-ku, Sapporo 060.
Conductor: Kazuyoshi Akiyama; President: Hideji Kitagawa.

Tokyo: Japan Philharmonic Symphony Orchestra, Onda Building, 4th Floor, 1-1 Rokubancho, Chiyoda-ku, Tokyo 102.
Music Director: Kenichiro Kobayashi; General Manager: Minoru Tanabe.

Tokyo: Kunaicho Gakuba (Imperial Court Orchestra), Imperial Palace, Tokyo 100

Tokyo: NHK (Japan Broadcasting Corporation) Symphony Orchestra, 2-16-49 Takanawa, Minato-ku, Tokyo 108.
Music Director: Charles Dutoit; Executive Director: Takeshi Hara.

Tokyo: New Japan Philharmonic Orchestra, Towa Building, 5th Floor, 3-16-3 Shibuya-ku, Tokyo 150.
Honorary Artistic Director: Seiji Ozawa; Manager: Chiyoshige Matsubara.

Tokyo: Shinsei Nihon Symphony Orchestra, Maruishi Building, 3-16-4 Nishi Ikebukuro, Toshima-ku, Tokyo 171.
Music Director: Ryusuke Numajiri; Executive Director: Saburo Kurematsu.

Tokyo: Tokyo City Philharmonic Orchestra, 20-14 Daikanyama-cho, Shibuya-ku, Tokyo 150.
Music Director: Shunsaku Tsutsumi; Executive Director: Toshiaka Tamaye.

Tokyo: Tokyo Metropolitan Symphony Orchestra, c/o Tokyo Bunkakaikan, 5-45 Ueno Park, Taito-ku, Tokyo 110.
Music Director: Hiroshi Wakasugi; Executive Director: Hiroshi Kainuma.

Tokyo: Tokyo Philharmonic Symphony Orchestra, Eiritsu Building, 3-3 Kanda Kajicho, Chiyoda-ku, Tokyo 101.
Conductor: Kazushi Ohno; Director: Shogo Matsuki.

Tokyo: Tokyo Symphony Orchestra, 2-23-5 Hyakunin-cho, Shinjuku-ku, Tokyo 160.
Music Director: Kazuyoshi Akiyama; General Manager: Shigeto Kanayama.

Tokyo: Yomiuri Nippon Symphony Orchestra, Yomiuri Shimbun, 1-7-1 Ohtemachi, Chiyoda-ku, Tokyo 100.
Principal Conductor: Tadaaki Otaka; General Manager: Akira Takasaki.

Yokahoma: Kanagawa Philharmonic Orchestra, Hanami-dai 110, Hodogaya-ku, Yokohama 240.
Music Director: Yuzo Toyama; Executive Director: Yutaka Ueno.

KOREA (SOUTH)

Seoul: Asian Philharmonic Orchestra, 43-1, Pil-Dong 1-Ga, Choong-gu, Seoul 100-271.
Music Director: Nanse Gum; Executive Director: Hun Bang.

Seoul: KBS (Korean Broadcasting System) Symphony Orchestra, 18 Yoido-dong, Youngdungpo-gu, Seoul 150-790.
Chief Conductor: Othmar Maga; Director General: Dong-Sung Kim.

Seoul: Seoul Philharmonic Orchestra, 81-3 Sejong-Ro, Cong Ro-Gu, Seoul 110-050.
Operations Manger: Doo Hoon-Moon

LATVIA

Riga: Latvian National Symphony Orchestra, 6 Amatu Street, 226350 Riga.
Chief Conductor: Paul Mägi; General Manager: Vilnis Strautiņš.

Riga: Latvian Radio and Television Symphony Orchestra, c/o Latvian Radio and Television, Riga.

Riga: Riga Chamber Orchestra, Kalku Street 11a, 226350 Riga.

LITHUANIA

Vilnius: Lithuanian State Symphony Orchestra, c/o Vilnius Philharmonic, 232001 Vilnius.
Chief Conductor: Juozas Domarkas; Manager: Viesturs Vitolins.

OPERA COMPANIES

LUXEMBOURG

Luxembourg: Orchestre Symphonique de Radio Luxembourg, Villa Louvigny, L-2850 Luxembourg.
Chief Conductor: Leopold Hager; Manager: Jacques Mauroy.

MEXICO

Guadalajara: Orquesta Filarmónica de Jalisco, Teatro Degollado, 44100 Guadalajara, Jalisco.
Music Director: José Guadalupe Flores; Manager: Silvia Susana Hernandez Huerta.

Mexico City: Orquesta de Cámera de Bellas Artes, Extemplo de Santa Teresa La Antigua, Lic Verdad No 8 and Moneda, Centro, 06060 Mexico City, DF.
Music Director: Ildefonso Cedillo; Manager: Maricarmen Guerrero Meneses.

Mexico City: Orquesta del Teatro de Bellas Artes, Regina 52, Centro 06050 Mexico City, DF.
Music Director: Enrique Barrios; Manager: José Lopez.

Mexico City: Orquesta Filarmónica de la Ciudad de Mexico, Periférico Sur 5141, Sala Ollin Yoliztli, 14030 Mexico City, DF.
Principal Conductor: Luis Herrera de la Fuente; Manager: Ricardo Calderon Figueroa.

Mexico City: Orquesta Filarmónica de la Universidad Autónoma de México, Av Insurgentes Sur 3000, Sala Nezahualcóyotl, 04510 Mexico City, DF, Coyoacán.
Music Director: Jesús Medina; General Manager: Maricarmen Costero.

Toluca: Orquesta Sinfónica del Estado de Mexico, Plaza Fray Andrés de Castro, Edif 'C', Primer Piso, 50000 Toluca.
Music Director: Enrique Bátiz; General Manager: María Dolores Castillo.

MONACO

Monte Carlo: Orchestre Philharmonique de Monte Carlo, Casino, BP 139, 98007 Monte Carlo Cédex.
Music Director: Lawrence Foster; Director: René Croesi.

NETHERLANDS

Amsterdam: Koninklijk (Royal) Concertgebouworkest, Jacob Obrechtstraat 51, 1071 KJ Amsterdam.
Chief Conductor: Riccardo Chailly.

Amsterdam: Nederlands Philharmonisch Orkest, Beurs van Berlage, Damrak 213, 1012 ZH Amsterdam.
Music Director: Hartmut Haenchen; Manager: Dr J W Loot.

Arnhem: Het Gelders Orkest, PO Box 1180, Jans Buitensingel 29-III, 6801 BD Arnhem.
Principal Conductor: Roberto Benzi; General Administrator: H Hierck.

Bussum: Amsterdam Baroque Orchestra, Meerwag 23, 1405 BC Bussum.
Music Director: Ton Koopman; General Manager: Hans Meijer.

Eindhoven: Brabants Philharmonisch Orkest, PO Box 230, 5600 AE Eindhoven.
Music Director: Arpád Joó; Managing Director: Huber van Werkhoven.

Enschede: Forum Filharmonisch, PO Box 1321, 7500 BH Enschede.
General Manager: J M Bal.

Groningen: Noord-Nederlands Orkest, PO Box 818, 9700 AV Groningen.
Manager: H J Smink.

Haarlem: Noordhollands Philharmonisch Orkest, Klokhuisplein 2 A, 2011 HK Haarlem.
Music Director: Lucas Vis; Manager: Casper Vogel.

The Hague: Residentie Orkest, PO Box 11543, 2502 AM The Hague.
Chief Conductor: Evgeny Svetlanov; Artistic Manager: Bernard Jacobson.

Hilversum: Metropole Orkest, PO Box 10, 1200 JB Hilversum.
Music Director: Dick Bakker; Manager: Maarten van der Schaff.

Hilversum: Radio Filharmonisch Orkest, PO Box 10, 1200 JB Hilversum.
Chief Conductor: Edo de Waart; Manager: Aafje Terwey.

Hilversum: Radio Kamerorkest, PO Box 10, 1200 JB Hilversum.
Conductor: Frans Brüggen; Manager: Ferdinand L J Vrijma.

Hilversum: Radio Symphonie Orkest, PO Box 10, 1200 JB Hilversum.
Chief Conductor: Henry Lewis; Manager: A Dekker.

Leeuwarden: Frysk Orkest, PO Box 666, 8901 BL Leeuwarden.

Maastricht: Limburgs Symphonie Orkest, PO Box 482, 6200 AL Maastricht.
Music Director: Salvador Mas Conde; Manager: Dr H P van de Braak.

Rotterdam: Rotterdams Philharmonisch Orkest, de Doelen, Kruisstraat 2, 3012 CT Rotterdam.
Chief Conductor: Jeffrey Tate; Manager: Wendela Sandberg.

NEW ZEALAND

Auckland: Auckland Philharmonic Orchestra, PO Box 56-024, Auckland.
General Manager: Paul McLaren.

Christchurch: Christchurch Symphony Orchestra, PO Box 3260, Christchurch 8000.
Artistic Director: Iola Shelley; General Manager: A H Kunowski.

Dunedin: Dunedin Sinfonia, PO Box 5571, Dunedin.
General Manager: Nicholas McBryde.

Wellington: New Zealand Chamber Orchestra, PO Box 11263, Wellington.
Music Director: Donald Armstrong; Manager: Dr Allan Badley.

Wellington: New Zealand Symphony Orchestra, PO Box 6640, Wellington 6035.
Chief Conductor: Franz-Paul Decker; Chief Executive: Mark Keyworth.

Wellington: Wellington Regional Orchestra, PO Box 6314, Te Aro, Wellington.

OPERA COMPANIES

Manager: Brian Budd.

NORWAY

Bergen:	Bergin Filharmoniske Orkester, Grieghallen, Lars Hilles Gata 3a, N-5000 Bergen. Music Advisor: Dmitri Kitaenko; Manager: Laila Kismul.
Oslo:	Norsk Kammerorkester, Grev Wedels Plass 2, N-0151 Oslo 1. Artistic Director: Iona Brown.
Oslo:	Oslo Filharmoniske Orkester, PO Box 1607 Vika, Konserhuset, Munkedamsveien 14, N-0119 Oslo 1. Chief Conductor: Mariss Jansons; Manager: Trond Okkelmo.
Stavanger:	Stavanger Symfoniorkester, Bjergsted, N-4007 Stavanger. Artistic Director: Alexander Dmitriev; Managing Director: Stein Slyngstad.
Trondheim:	Trondheim Symfoniorkester, PO Box 764, N-7001 Trondheim. Artistic Director: Ole Kristian Ruud.

PANAMA

Panama City:	Orquesta Sinfónica Nacional, Apto 9190, Panama City 6. Conductor: Eduardo Charpentier de Castro.

PARAGUAY

Asunción:	Orquesta Philomusica de Asunción, Avda Espana 352, Asunción. Director: Luis Szarán.
Asunción:	Orquesta Sinfónica de la Ciudad de Asunción, Luis A de Herrea 364, Asunción. Director: Luis Szarán.

PERU

Lima:	Orquesta Sinfónica Nacional, Casilla 5247, Lima 100. Director: Luis Antonio Meza; Manager: Socorro Rivas Dominguez.

PHILIPPINES

Manila:	Manila Symphony Orchestra, Manila Metropolitan Theater, Liwasang Bonifacio, PO Box 664, Manila. Music Director: Alfredo Buenaventura.
Manila:	National Philharmonic Orchestra, PO Box 1721, Manila. Music Director: Redentor Romero.
Manila:	Philippine Philharmonic Orchestra, Cultural Center of the Philippines, Roxas Boulevard, Manila. Music Director: Oscar Yatco; Executive Director: Amelita Guevara.

POLAND

Bialystok:	Bialystok State Philharmonic Orchestra, Podlesna 2, 15-227 Bialystok. Music Director: Tadeusz Chachaj; Director: Mieczyslaw Janicki.
Bydgoszca:	Pomeranian State Philharmonic Orchestra "Ignacy Paderewski", Libelta 16, 85-080 Bydgoszcz. Music Director: Jerzy Salwarowski; Director: Andrzej Szwalbe.
Czestochowa:	Czestochowa State Philharmonic Orchestra, Kakielów 16, 42-2000 Czestochowa. Music Director and Director: Zygmunt Hassa.
Gdańsk:	Baltic State Philharmonic Orchestra, Aleja Zwycięstwa 15, 80-219 Gdańsk. Music Director: Pawel Przytocki; Director: Wlodzimierz Nawotka.
Jelenia Gora:	Jelenia Gora State Philharmonic Orchestra, ul 22-go Lipca 60, 58-500 Jenenia Gora. Music Director: Stefan Strahl; Director: Zuzanna Dziedzic.
Katowice:	Polish Radio National Symphony Orchestra, PL Sojmu Slaskiego 2, 40-032 Katowice. Music Director: Antoni Wit; Manager: Irena Siodmok.
Katowice:	Silesian State Philharmonic Orchestra, Sokolska 2, 40-084 Katowice. Music Director and Manager: Jerzy Swoboda.
Koszalin:	Koszalin State Philharmonic Orchestra "Stanislaw Moniuszko", Harcerska 1, 75-073 Koszalin. Music Director: Zygmunt Rychert; Manager: Andrzej Murawski.
Kraków:	Chopin Chamber Orchestra, 25/54ul Gabrieli Zapolskiej, 30-126 Kraków. Music Director and Manager: Boguslaw Dawidów.
Kraków:	Kraków State Philharmonic Orchestra "Karol Szymanowski", Zwierzyniecka 1, 31-103 Kraków. Conductor: Roland Bader; Manager: Joanna Vnuk-Nazarowa.
Łodz:	Łodz State Philharmonic Orchestra "Artur Rubinstein", Piotrkowska 243, 90-456 Łodz. Music Director: Ilya Stupel; General Manager: Jan Wolański.
Lublin:	Lublin State Philharmonic Orchestra 'Henry Wieniawski', Kapucyński 7, 20-009 Lublin. Music Director: Jerzy Salwarowski; Managing Director: Leszek Hadrian.
Olsztyn:	Olsztyn State Philharmonic Orchestra "Feliks Nowowiejski", Kościuszki 39, 10-503 Olsztyn. Music Director: Piotr Borkowski.
Opole:	Opole State Philharmonic Orchestra 'Józef Elsner', Krakowska 24, 45-075 Opole.

ORCHESTRAS

	Music Director: Marek Tracz; Manager: Mieczyslaw Bucik.
Poznań:	Poznań State Philharmonic Orchestra, Ul Armii Czerwonej 81, 61-808 Poznań.
	Artistic Director: Wojciech Michniewski; Managers: Zdzislaw Dworzecki and Elizabeth Wozna.
Rzeszów:	Rzeszów State Philharmonic Orchestra "Artur Malawski", Chopina 30, 35-055 Rzeszów.
	Director: Józef Radwan; Manager: Waldemar Tokarski.
Szczecin:	Szczecin State Philharmonic Orchestra "Mieczyslaw Karlowicz", Dzierzyńskiego 1, 70-455 Szczecin.
	Music Director: Stefan Marczyk; Manager: Jadwiga Igiel.
Walbrzych:	Sudettic Philharmonic Orchestra, Slowackiego 4, 58-3000 Walbrzych.
	Music Director and Manager: Jozef Wilkomirski.
Warsaw:	New Polish Radio Orchestra, J P Woronicza 17, 00-950 Warsaw.
	Artistic Director and Principal Conductor: Tadeusz Strugala.
Warsaw:	Polish Chamber Orchestra, Centrum Sztuki "Studio", Palac Kultury i Nauki, 00-901 Warsaw.
	Music Director: Jerzy Maksymiuk; Manager: Franciszek Wybrańczyk.
Warsaw:	Sinfonia Varsovia, Centrum Sztuki "Studio", Palac Kultury i Nauki, 00-901 Warsaw.
	Music Director and Manager: Franciszek Wybrańczyk.
Warsaw:	Warsaw Chamber Orchestra, ul Freta 28/8, 00-227 Warsaw.
	Artistic Director: Marek Sewen.
Warsaw:	Warsaw National Philharmonic Orchestra, Jasna 5, 00-950 Warsaw.
	Chief Conductor: Kazimierz Kord; Manager: Borys Frydrychowicz.
Wrocław:	Wrocław State Philharmonic Orchestra, Swierczewskiego 19, 50-044 Wrocław.
	Artistic Director and Manager: Marek Pijarowski.
Zielona Góra:	Zielona Góra State Philharmonic Orchestra, Plac Powstańców Wielkopolskich 10, 65-075 Zielona Góra.
	Music Director: Czeslaw Grabowski.

PORTUGAL

Lisbon:	Orquestra Gulbenkian, Fundaçao Calouste Gulbenkian, Avda de Berna 45, 1093 Lisbon.
	Principal Conductor: Muhai Tang; Manager: Dr Luis Pereira Leal.
Oeiras:	Nova Filarmonia Portuguesa, Apartado 1023, 2780 Oeiras.
	Artistic Director: Dr Alvaro Cassuto.
Porto:	Orquesta Sinfónica do Porto, Radiodifusao Portuguesa, Rua Candido Reis 74/10, 4000 Porto.
	Music Director: Gunther Arglebe.

RUMANIA

Bucharest:	Bucharest Chamber Orchestra, Allée Ioanid 4, Bucharest 70259.
	Music Director: Ion Voicu; Manager: Madeleine Cretu.
Bucharest:	Rumanian Radio and Television Symphony Orchestra, Str Nuferilor 62-64, 79756 Bucharest.
Bucharest:	Bucharest State Philharmonic Orchestra "George Enescu", Ateneul Roman, Franklin Str 1, Bucharest.

RUSSIA

Moscow:	Bolshoi Symphony Orchestra, Bolshoi Theater, Petrovka Street 1, Moscow.
	Chief Conductor: Alexander Lazarev.
Moscow:	Ensemble XXI Moscow (Moscow International Chamber Orchestra), Ul Ostozhenka 12, Apt 1, Moscow.
	Conductor: Lygia O'Riordan.
Moscow:	Moscow Chamber Orchestra, Ul Gorkogo 37, Moscow.
Moscow:	Moscow Philharmonic Orchestra, Ul Gorkogo 37, Moscow.
	Chief Conductor: Vassily Sinaisky.
Moscow:	Moscow Radio and Television Symphony Orchestra, Ul Piatnitskaya 25, Moscow.
	Chief Conductor: Vladimir Fedoseyev.
Moscow:	Moscow Symphony Orchestra, Moscow.
	Chief Conductor: Antonio de Almeida.
Moscow:	Russian National Orchestra, Moscow.
	Conductor: Mikhail Pletnev.
Moscow:	State Symphonic Kapelle of Moscow.
	Chief Conductor: Gennady Rozhdestvensky.
Moscow:	State Symphony Orchestra of Russia, Arbat 35, 121835 Moscow.
	Chief Conductor: Evgeny Svetlanov.
St Petersburg:	St Petersburg Chamber Orchestra, Ul Brodskogo 2, St Petersburg.
St Petersburg:	St Petersburg Philharmonic Orchestra, Ul Brodskogo 2, St Petersburg.
	Chief Conductor: Yuri Temirkanov.

SINGAPORE

Singapore:	Singapore Symphony Orchestra, Victoria Concert Hall, Empress Place, Singapore 0617.
	Music Director: Choo Hoey; General Manager: Mrs Lu Sinclair.

SLOVAKIA

Bratislava:	Capella Istropolitna, Schillerova 23, 811 04 Bratislava.

ORCHESTRAS

	Chief Condutor: Karol Kopernický.
Bratislava:	Musica Aeterna, Fučikova 3, 816 01 Bratislava.
	Chief Condutor: Peter Zajíček.
Bratislava:	Slovak Chamber Orchestra, Fučikova 3, 816 01 Bratislava.
	Chief Conductor: Bohdan Warchal.
Bratislava:	Slovak Philharmonic Orchestra, Fučikova 3, 816 01 Bratislava.
	Chief Conductor: Ondrej Lenárd.
Bratislava:	Symphony Orchestra of the Slovak Radio, Mýtna 1, 812 90 Bratislava.
	Chief Conductor: Adrian Leaper.

SLOVENIA

Ljubljana:	Slovenian Philharmonic Orchestra, Kongresni trg 10, 61000 Ljubljana.
Ljubljana:	Slovenian Radio and Television Symphony Orchestra, Tavcarjeva 17, 61000 Ljubljana.

SOUTH AFRICA

Cape Town:	Cape Town Symphony Orchestra, City Hall, Darling Street, Cape Town 8001.
	Music Director: Omri Hadari; General Manager: Stephen Lindner.
Durban:	Natal Philharmonic Orchestra, PO Box 5353, Durban 4000.
	Principal Conductor: David Tidboald; General Manager: Peter B Hamblin.
Johannesburg:	National Symphony Orchestra, South African Broadcasting Corporation, PO Box 4559, Johannesburg 2000.
Pretoria:	The National Orchestra, PO Box 566, Pretoria 001.
	Principal Conductor: Gabor Otvös; General Manager: Stephen Wikner.

SPAIN

Barcelona:	Orquesta Ciudad de Barcelona, Via Laietan a 41, pral, 08003 Barcelona.
	Music Director: García Navarro; Manager: Jaume Masferrer.
Madrid:	Joven Orquesta Nacional de Espana, Principe de Vergara, 28002 Madrid.
	Principal Conductor: Edmon Colomer; Manager: Juan Wesolowski y Fernández-Heredia.
Madrid:	Orquesta Nacionales de Espana, Principe de Vergara 146, 28002 Madrid.
	Principal Conductor: Aldo Ceccato; Managing Director: Tomas Marco.
Madrid:	Orquesta Sinfónica de Radiotelevision Espanola, Sor Angela de la Cruz 2, 7th floor, 28020 Madrid.
	Chief Conductor: Sergiu Comissiona; Program Coordinator: José Luis Clemente.
Málaga:	Orquesta Sinfónica de Málaga, C Ramos Marin s/n, 29012 Málaga.
	Music Director: Octav Calleya; Manager: Carlos de Mesa.
Oviedo:	Orquesta del Principado de Asturias, Corrado del Obispo, s/n Edif, del Conservatorio de Musica "Eduardo Martíinez Torner", 33003 Oviedo.
	Manager: Lilia Maria Morin.
Palma:	Orquesta Sinfónica de Balears, Vicente Juan Rossello Ribas 22-B, 07013 Palma.
	Music Director: Luis Remartínez Gomez; Manager: Pere Esterlrich 1 Massuti.
Pamplona:	Orquesta Santa Cecilia de Pamplona, Padre Moret s/n, 31002 Pamplona.
	Artistic Director: Jacques Bodmer; Manager: José Maria Montes Navio.
San Sebastian:	Orquesta Sinfónica de Euskadi, Paseo de Miramon 124, 20011 San Sebastian.
	Music Director: Miguel Gomez Martínez; General Director: Jesús María Aguirre Lazcano.
Santa Cruz de Tenerife:	Orquesta Sinfónica de Tenerife, Plaza Espana 1, 38001 Santa Cruz de Tenerife.
	Music Director: Victor Pablo Pérez; General Manager: Enrique Rojas.
Seville:	Orquesta Sinfónica de Sevilla, Cerrajeri 10, Sgdo Izda, 41004 Seville.
	Music Director: Vjekoslav Sutej; General Manager: Francisco José Senra Lazo.

SRI LANKA

Colombo:	Tamil Service Orchestra, c/o Sri Lanka Broadcasting Corp, Torrington Square, Colombo 7.

SWEDEN

Gävle:	Gävleborgs Symfoniorkester, Staketgatan 37, S-803 21 Gävle.
	Manager: Gert Norén.
Göteborg:	Göteborgs Symfoniker, Konserthuset, Stenhammarsgatan 1, S-412 56 Göteborg.
	Music Director: Neeme Järvi; Manager: Sture Carlsson.
Hälsingborg:	Hälsingborgs Symfoniorkester, Konserthuset, S-252 21 Hälsingborg.
	Music Director: Okko Kamu; Manager: Lennart Stenkvist.
Malmö:	Malmö Symfonie Orkester, S-205 80 Malmö.
	Music Director: James DePreist; Manager: Gunilla von Bahr.
Norrköping:	Norrköpings Symfoniorkester, Box 2144, S-600 02 Norrköping.
	Music Director: Jun'ichi Hirokami; General Manager: Anders Franzén.
Orebro:	Orebro Symphony Orchestra and Swedish Chamber Orchestra, Konserthuset, Fabriksgatan 2, S-702 10 Orebro.
	Music Director: Göran Nilson; Manager: Karl Friman.
Stockholm:	Royal Swedish Chamber Orchestra, The Royal Palace, S-111 30 Stockholm.
	Music Director: Mats Liljefors.
Stockholm:	Stockholms Filharmoniska Orkester, PO Box 7083, S-103 87 Stockholm.

ORCHESTRAS

Stockholm:	Chief Conductor: Gennady Rozhdestvensky; Executive and Artistic Director: Ake Holmquist. Sveriges (Swedish) Radios Symfoniorkester, Sveriges Radio, S-105 10 Stockholm. General Manager: Trygve Nordwall.
Uppsala:	Uppsala Kammarorkester, Box 1510, S-751 45 Uppsala. Music Director: Kjell Söderqvist; Manager: Nils-Olof Sondell.
Västeras:	Västeras Musiksällskap, Sangargatan 3, S-722 20 Västeras. Manager: Ulf Stenberg.

SWITZERLAND

Basel:	Basler Kammerorchester, Postfach 4001, CH-4051 Basel. Conductor: Paul Sacher.
Basel:	Basler-Sinfonie-Orchester, Münsterplatz 18, CH-4051 Basel. Chief Conductor: Walter Weller.
Basel:	Radio-Sinfonie-Orchester, Münsterplatz 18, CH-4051 Basel. Chief Conductor: Nello Santi.
Bern:	Berner Symphonieorchester, Münzgraben 2, CH-3011 Bern. Chief Conductor: Dmitri Kitaenko; Manager: Bruno Sager.
Bern:	Camerata Bern, Mayweg 4, CH-3007 Bern. Conductor: Thomas Füri; General Secretary: Rose Brügger.
Geneva:	Collegium Academicum de Genèva, Casa Postale 539, CH-1211 Geneva 4. Music Director: Thierry Fischer; Manager: Janine Mariz.
Geneva:	Orchestre de la Suisse Romande, Promenade du Pin 3, CH-1211 Geneva. Chief Conductor: Armin Jordan; Secretary General: Ron Golan.
Lausanne:	Orchestre de Chambre dé Lausanne, Chemin du Devin 72, CH-1010 Lausanne. Music Director: Jesús López-Cobos; Chairman: Jean-Jacques Rapin.
Lucerne:	Festival Strings Lucerne, Klusstrasse 8, CH-8032 Zürich. Music Director: Matthias Bamert; Manager: Rita Dahinden.
Lucerne:	Sinfonieorchester der Allgemeinen Musikgesellschaft Luzern, Moosstrasse 15, CH-6003. Music Director: Olaf Henzold; Manager: Peter Keller.
Lugano:	The Masterplayers, Via Losanna 12, CH-69000 Lugano. Conductor: Richard Schumacher; Manager: Dr D V Zschinsky.
Lugano:	Orchestra della Radiotelevisione della Svizzera Italiana, Casella Postale, CH-6903 Lugano. Chief Conductor: Marc Adreae; Manager: Dario Müller.
St Gallen:	Stadtisches Orchester St Gallen, Museumstrasse 1, CH-9004 St Gallen. Music Director: John Neschling; Manager: Marc Walter Haefelin.
Winterthur:	Stadtorchester Winterthur, Musikkollegium Winterthur, Rychenbergstrasse, 94, CH-8400 Winterthur. Music Director: János Fürst; President: Dr U Thalmann.
Zürich:	Camerata Zürich, Bergstrasse 50-G, CH-8712 Stáfa. Conductor: Räto Tschupp; Secretary: Rosemarie Kleinert.
Zürich:	Collegium Musicum Zürich, Konzertgesellschaft, Steinwiesstrasse 2, CH-8032 Zürich. Music Director: Paul Sacher; Manager: Barbara Oehninger.
Zürich:	Symphonisches Orchester Zürich, Postfach 1016, CH-8021 Zürich. Music Director: Daniel Schweizer; Manager: Paul Trachsel.
Zürich:	Tonhalle-Orchester Zürich, Gotthardstrasse 5, CH-8002 Zürich. Managing Director: Richard Bächi.
Zürich:	Zürcher Kammerorchester, Kreuzstrasse 55, PO Box 244, CH-8032 Zürich. Music Director: Edmond de Stoutz; Manager: Nelly Eschke.

TAIWAN

Taipei:	Taipei City Symphony Orchestra, 25 Pa Teh Road, Sec 3, Taipei 10560. Music Director: Chen Chiu-sen.
Wu Feng, T'ai-chung:	Taiwan Symphony Orchestra, Ming-Sheng Road, No 292, Wu Feng, T'ai-chung. Conductor: Tze-shiou Liu; Manager: Po-chou Chang.

THAILAND

Bangkok:	Bangkok Symphony Orchestra, 16 Plubplachai Road, Bangkok. Music Director: Vladimir Kin; General Manager: Witaya Tumornsoontorn.

TURKEY

Ankara:	Presidential Symphony Orchestra, Talatpasa Bulvari 38/A, 06330 Ankara. Music Director: Gürer Aykal; Director: Cengiz Ozkök.
Istanbul:	Istanbul State Symphony Orchestra, Atatürk Kültür Merkezi-Taksim, Istanbul. Music Director: Alexander Schwinck; Manager: Ozer Sezgin.
Izmir:	Izmir State Symphony Orchestra, Müdürlügü Konak-Izmir, Izmir. Music Director: Iosif Conta; Director: Numan Pekdemir.

UK

Altrincham:	Northern Chamber Orchestra, 16 Rilway Street, Altrincham, Cheshire WA14 2RE. Music Director: Nicholas Ward; Artistic Director: David Ellis.

ORCHESTRAS

Barnet: Johann Strauss Orchestra, 176a High Street, Barnet, Hertfordshire EN5 5SZ.
Administrator: Raymond Gubbay.

Barnet: London Concert Orchestra, 163 High Street, Barnet, Hertfordshire EN4 5SU.
Administrator: Raymond Gubbay.

Beaconsfield: Sonfonia of London, 27 Grove Road, Beaconsfield, Bucks HP9 1UR.
Music Director: Howard Blake; Director and General Manager: Peter Wilson.

Beckenham: Musiciens du Roi, 6 Aldersmead Road, Beckenham, Kent BR3 1NA.
Director: Lionel Sawkins.

Belfast: Ulster Orchestra, Elmwood Hall at Queen's, 89 University Road, Belfast BT7 1NF.
Artistic Director and Principal Conductor: Yan Pascal Tortelier; General Manager: Roger Lloyd.

Biggleswade: New English Concert Orchestra, 23 Hitchin Street, Biggleswade, Bedfordshire SG18 8AX.
Music Director: Douglas Coombes.

Birmingham: Birmingham Sinfonietta, 41 St Agnes Road, Birmingham B13 9PJ.
Music Director: Beverley Davison; Manager: Susan Savage.

Birmingham: City of Birmingham Symphony Orchestra, Paradise Place, Birmingham B3 3RP.
Principal Conductor: Simon Rattle; Chief Executive: Edward Smith.

Bournemouth: Basildon Symphony Orchestra, 101 Queens Park Avenue, Bournemouth BH8 9LJ.
Conductor/Artistic Director: Richard Studt.

Bournemouth: Bournemouth Sinfonietta, 2 Seldown Lane, Poole, Dorset BH15 1UF.
Principal Conductor: Tamás Vásáry; Chief Executive: David Richardson.

Bournemouth: Bournemouth Symphony Orchestra, 2 Seldown Lane, Poole, Dorset BH15 1UF.
Principal Conductor: Andrew Litton; Chief Executive: David Richardson.

Bournemouth: London Camerata, 60 Strouden Avenue, Bournemouth BH8 9HX.
Conductor: Paul Hilliam.

Brighton: Brighton Philharmonic Orchestra, 50 Grand Parade, Brighton, East Sussex BN2 2QA.
Principal Conductor: Barry Wordsworth; General Manager: Tony Woodhouse.

Brighton: Hanover Band, 44-46 Old Steyne, Brighton BN1 1NH.
Music Director: Roy Goodman; Executive Director: Stephen Neiman.

Brighton: Philharmonia of Bristol, 11 Windsor Court, Bristol BS8 4LJ.
Artistic Director: Dr Derek Bourgeois; General Manager: Kenneth H Gibbs.

Cardiff: BBC Welsh Symphony Orchestra, Broadcasting House, Landaff, Cardiff CF5 2YQ.
Principal Conductor: Tadaaki Otaka; Manager: Bryon Jenkins.

Cardiff: Orchestra of Welsh National Opera, c/o Welsh National Opera Ltd, John Street, Cardiff CF1 2SP.
Music Director: Carlo Rizzi; General Director: Matthew Epstein.

Cheltenham: New Cheltenham Chamber Orchestra, 27 Merestones Drive, The Park, Cheltenham, Gloucestershire GL50 2SU.
Music Director: Robin Proctor.

Chesterfield: South Yorkshire Symphony Orchestra, 14 Brincliffe Close, Walton, Chesterfield, Derbyshire S40 3DU.
Principal Conductor: Paul Scott.

Croydon: London Repertoire Orchestra and Chamber Orchestra, 56 Alexandra Road, Croydon, Surrey CR0 6EU.
Conductor: Francis Griffin

Edinburgh: Scottish Chamber Orchestra, 4 Royal Terrace, Edinburgh EH7 5AB.
Chief Guest Conductor: Sir Charles Mackerras; General Manager: Ian Ritchie.

Farnham: National Chamber Orchestra, Fir Tree Lodge, Jumps Road, Churt, Near Farnham, Surrey GU10 2JY.

Farnham: National Symphony Orchestra, Fir Tree Lodge, Jumps Road, Churt, Near Farnham, Surrey GU10 2JY.

Glasgow: BBC Scottish Symphony Orchestra, Broadcasting House, Queen Margaret Drive, Glasgow G12 8DG

Glasgow: Royal Scottish Orchestra, 73 Claremont Street, Glasgow G3 7HA.
Music Director: Walter Weller; Chief Executive: Christopher Bishop.

Guildford: Guildford Philharmonic Orchestra, The Lodge, Allen House Grounds, Chertsey Street, Guildford, Surrey GU1 4HL.
Principal Conductor: Sir Charles Groves; Manager: Mrs K M Atkins.

Guildford: Langham Chamber Orchestra, 9 Weylea Avenue, Burpham, Guildford, Surrey GU4 7YN.
Orchestra Manager: Peter Holt.

Hertfordshire: Vivaldi Concertante, 35 Laurel Avenue, Potters Bar, Hertfordshire EN6 2AB.
Conductor: Joseph Pilberty.

Honiton: European Community Chamber Orchestra, 2 Five Bells, Offwell, Honiton, Devon EX14 9SB.
General Manager: Ambrose Miller.

Kingston-upon-Thames: London Sinfonietta, Kingston Polytechnic, Kingston Hill, Kingston-upon-Thames, Surrey KT2 7LB.
Music Director: David Atherton; Artistic Director: Paul Crossley.

Leeds: English Northern Philharmonia, Opera North, Grand Theatre, Leeds LS1 6NU.
Principal Conductor: Paul Daniel; Orchestra Manager: Ian Killik.

Liverpool: Liverpool Sinfonietta, 40 Caulfield Drive, Greasby, Wirral, Merseyside L49 1SW.
Music Director: Anthony Ridley.

Liverpool: Royal Liverpool Philharmonic Orchestra, Philharmonic Hall, Hope Street, Liverpool L1 9BP.
Principal Conductor: Libor Pešk; Chief Executive: Robert Creech.

London: Academy of Ancient Music, 12 Penzance, London W11 4PA.
Artistic Director: Christopher Hogwood; General Manager: Timothy Calnin.

London: Academy of St Martin-in-the-Fields, Raine House, Raine Street, Wapping, London E1 9RG.
Artistic Director: Sir Neville Marriner; Manager: Monya Winzer Gilbert.

London: All Souls Orchestra, 2 All Souls Place, London W1N 3DB.
Principal Conductor: Noël Tredinnick.

London: Ambache Chamber Orchestra, 9 Beversbrook Road, London N19 4QG.
Music Director: Diana Ambache.

London: Barbican Chamber Orchestra, 10 Acacia Road, London E17 8BW.
Principal Conductor: Gregory Rose; Manager: Paul Thomas.

London: BBC Concert Orchestra, Hippodrome, Room 19, London NW11 7RP.

ORCHESTRAS

London: Principal Conductor: Barry Wordsworth; Manager: Adrian Evett. BBC Radio Orchestra, Maida Vale Studios, Delaware Road, London W9 2LG.

London: Manager: David Williams. BBC Symphony Orchestra, Maida Vale Studios, Delaware Road, London W9 2LG.

London: Chief Conductor: Andrew Davis; Manager: Lawrie Lea. Ben Uri Chamber Orchestra, 5 Bradby Hous, Carlton Hill, London NW8 9XE.

London: Conductor: Sydney Fixman. Cantelli Chamber Orchestra, 13 Cotswold Mews, 12-16 Battersea High Street, London SW11 3JB.

London: Conductor: Philip Ellis; Manager: Alexander Waugh. Chamber Orchestra of Europe, 8 Southampton Place, London WC1A 2EA.

London: Artistic Advisor: Claudio Abbado; General Manager: June Megennis. City of London Sinfonia, 46 Whitechapel High Street, London E1 7PL.

London: Music Director: Richard Hickox; General Manager: Stephen Carpenter. Collegium Musicum of London, 35 St Margaret's Road, London E12 5DR.

London: Conductor: Murray Stewart; Orchestra Manager: Chrina Jarvis. Consort of London, 13 Cotswold Mews, 12-16 Battersea High Street, London SW11 3JB.

London: Music Director: Haydon Clarke; Manager: Alexander Waugh. Divertimenti, 229 Lillie Road, London SW6 7LN. Artistic Director: Paul Barnett.

London: Docklands Sinfonietta, Box Office, Blackheath Concert Halls, 23 Lee Road, SE3 9RQ.

London: Music Director: Rupert Bond. English Bach Festival Orchestra and English Bach Festival Baroque Orchestra, 15 South Eaton Place, London Sw1W 9ER.

London: Director: Lina Lalandi; Manager: Pippa Thynne. English Baroque Players, 27 Parkside, London NW7 2LJ.

London: Music Director: Leon Lovett; Manager: Hedwig Dobbs. English Baroque Soloists, PO Box 145, Tower Place, London EC3P 3BE.

London: Music Director: John Elio Gardiner; General Manager: Michael B MacLeod. English Chamber Orchestra, 2 Coningsby Road, London W5 4HR.

London: Principal Conductor: Jeffrey Tate; Managing Director: Quintin Ballardie. The English Concert, 8 St George's Terrace, London NW1 8XJ.

London: Artistic Director: Trevor Pinnock; Manager: Judith Colman. English Festival Orchestra, 151 Mount View Road, London N4 4JT.

London: General Manager: Trevor Ford. English Gamelan Orchestra, English National Opera Orchestra, London Colsieum, St Martin's Lane, London WC2N 4ES.

London: Music Director: Mark Elder; Orchestra Manager: Richard Smith. Esterhazy Orchestra, 29 Westcroft Square, London W6 0TD.

London: Music Director: Courtenay Hall. European Community Youth Orchestra, 53 Sloane Street, London SW1X 8SW.

London: Music Director: Claudio Abbado; General Manager: Helen Skerratt. Fine Arts Chamber Orchestra and Viennese Orchestra of London, 12 Tiverton Road, London NW10 3HL.

London: Artistic Director: Jack Rothstein. Gabrieli Players, 113 Church Road, London SE19 2PR.

London: Director: Paul McCreesh; Administrator: Nicholas Morrison. Guildhall String Ensemble, 2 Highgate Spinney, Crescent Road, London N8 8AR.

London: Director: Robert Salter. Haydn Orchestra, Francis House, Francis Street, London SW1P 1DE.

London: Conductor: Harry Newstone; Administrator: Russell Jones. Henry Wood Chamber Orchestra, 64 Ashley Gardens, Ambrosden Avenue, London SW1P 1QG.

London: Music Director: John Landor; Administrator: William Corke. King's Consort, 2 Salisbury Road, London W13 9TX.

London: Director: Robert King. Kreisler String Orchestra, 14 Peto Place, London NW1 4DT.

London: Little Symphony of London, Glencairn, Shepherd's Hill, Merstham, Surrey RH1 3AD. Artistic Director: Arthur Davison.

London: London Bach Orchestra, 284A Battersea Park Road, London SW11 4LX. Artistic Director: Nicholas Kraemer; General Manager: Elaine Baines.

London: London Baroque Players, 15 Percy Street, London W1P 9FD. Music Director: Roger Norrington; Administrator: Monika Clifford.

London: London Chamber Orchestra, West End House, 33 Lower Richmond Road, London SW14 7EZ.

London: Music Director: Christopher Warren-Green; Manager: Clare Chapman. London Chamber Players, PO Box 84, London NW11 8AL.

London: Conductor: Adrian Sunshine; Manager: Sheila Genden. London Chamber Symphony, 47 Queen's Drive, London N4 2SZ.

London: Conductor: Odalaine de la Martinez; Co-Director: Sally Langdon. London Chanticleer Orchestra, Tickerage Castle, Pound Lane, Framfield, Uckfield, East Sussex TN22 5RT.

London: Music Director: Ruth Gipps; Secretary: H J Graty. London City Chamber Orchestra, 3/5 Bridge Street, Hadleigh, Suffolk, Ipswich, Suffolk IP7 6BY.

London: Conductor: Thomas McIntosh; General Manager: M H V Reckitt. London Classical Players, Weavers House, Inkper, Berks RG15 0DN.

London: Music Director: Roger Norrington; Managing Director: Kay Lawrence. London Festival Orchestra, 59 Brailsford Road, London SW2 2TB.

London: Music and Artistic Director: Ross Pople; Manager: Anne Storrs. London Handel Orchestra, 31 Davies Street, London W1Y 1FH.

London: Musical Directors: Denys Darlow, Roy Goodman; Administrator: Joya Logan. London Masterplayers Orchestra, The Coach House, 56 Lawrie Park Gardens, London SE26 6XJ.

ORCHESTRAS

	Manager: Norman McCann.
London:	London Mozart Players, 92 Chatsworth Road, Croydon CR0 1HB.
	Conductors: Matthias Bamert and Howard Shelley; Executive Director: Louise Honeyman.
London:	London Philharmonic Orchestra, 35 Doughty Street, London WC1N 2AA.
	Principal Conductor: Franz Welser-Möst.
London:	London Pops Orchestra, 36 Kelvin Drive, St Margaret's, Twickenham TW1 2AH.
	Music Director: Ian McMillan; Manager: Quentin Poole.
London:	London Pro Arte Orchestra, 89 Edridge Road, Croydon, Surrey, CR0 1EJ.
	Music Director: Murray Stewart; General Manager: Kerstin Stolte.
London:	London Soloists' Chamber Orchestra, 76 Sloane Street, London SW1.
	Director: David Josefowitz.
London:	London Symphony Orcehstra, Barbican Centre, Silk Street, London EC2Y 8DS.
	Principal Conductor: Sir Colin Davis; Managing Director: Clive Gillinson.
London:	Melos Ensemble, 35 Doughty Street, London WC1N 2AA.
London:	Monteverdi Orchestra, PO Box 145, Tower Place, London EC3P 3BE.
	Artistic Director: John Eliot Gardiner; General Manager: Michael MacLeod.
London:	National Philharmonic Orchestra, 7 Lowlands, Eton Avenue, Hampstead, London NW3 3EJ.
	Managing Director: Sidney Sax.
London:	New London Orchestra, 41 Aberdare Gardens, London NW6 3AL.
	Music Director: Ronald Corp.
London:	New Queen's Hall Orchestra, 13 Cotswold Mews, 30 Battersea Square, London SW11 3RA.
	Artistic Director: John Boyden; General Administrator: James Thomson.
London:	New Mozart Orchestra, 1 Serjeants Inn, London EC4Y 1JD.
	Principal Conductor: Clive Fairbairn.
London:	New Wind Orchestra, 119 Woolstone Street, Forest Hill, London SE23 2TQ.
	Music Director: Catherine Pluygers; Manager: Jonathan Lindridge.
London:	Orchestra of St John's Smith Square, Butlers Wharf Building, 36 Shad Thames, London SE1 2YE.
	Artistic Director: John Lubbock; Manager: Heather Newill.
London:	Orchestra of the Age of Enlightenment, 4 Bennett Park, Blackheath, London SE3 9RB.
	Manager: Judith Hendershot.
London:	Orchestra of the Royal Opera House, Covent Garden, London WC2E 9DD.
	Music Director: Bernard Haitink; General Director: Jeremy Isaacs.
London:	Orchestra of Sadler's Wells Royal Ballet, Sadler's Wells Theatre, Rosebery Avenue, London EC1R 4TN.
	Manager: Wendy Hacker.
London:	Orchestre Revolutionnaire et Romantique, PO Box 145, Tower Place, London EC3P 3BE.
	Music Director: John Eliot Gardiner; General Manager: Michael MacLeod.
London:	Park Lane Music Players, Bedford Chambers, Covent Garden Piazza, London WC2E 8HA.
	Administrator: John Woolf.
London:	Per Musica Chamber Orchestra, 50 Cranfield Court, Homer Street, London W1.
	Music Director: Julian Reynolds; Administrator: Joan Cruickshank.
London:	Philharmonia Orchestra, 76 Great Portland Street, London W1N 5AL.
	Principal Conductor: Giuseppe Sinopoli; Managing Director: David Whelton.
London:	Philomusica of London, 24 Stormont Road, London N6 4NP.
	Conductors: Neville Dilkes and David Littaur; Administrator: Joyce Fox.
London:	Purcell Orchestra, 16 Wolverton Mans, Uxbridge Road, London W5 3LA.
	Artistic Director: Robin Page; Administrator: Fiona Fairbairn.
London:	Raglan Baroque Players, 35 Glasslyn Road, London N8 8RJ.
	Music Director: Nicholas Kraemer.
London:	Regent Sinfonia of London, 17 Parliament Hill, London NW3 2TA.
	Artistic Director: George Vass.
London:	Rosebery Orchestra, 51 Stradella Road, London SE24 9HL.
	Orchestra Manager: Clarissa Melville.
London:	Rossini Chamber Orchestra, 10a Radipole Road, London SW6 5DL.
	Conductor: Alexander Bryett; Secretary: John Biggin.
London:	Royal Philharmonic Orchestra, 16 Clerkenwell Green, London EC1R 0DP.
	Music Director: Vladimir Ashkenazy; Managing Director: Ian Maclay.
London:	St James's Baroque Players.
	Music Director: Ivor Bolton; Manager: James Thomson.
London:	Serenata of London, 13 Cotswold Mews, 12-16 Battersea High Street, London SW11 3JB.
	Manager: Alexander Waugh.
London:	The Sixteen, 64 Highgate Street, London N6 5HX.
	Director: Harry Christophers.
London:	Taverner Players, Ibex House, 42-46 Minories, London EC3N 1DY.
	Conductor: Andrew Parrott; General Manager: Paul Rochman.
London:	Tilford Bach Orchestra, 31 Davies Street, London W1Y 1FH.
	Conductor: Denys Darlow; Administrator: Joya Logan.
London:	Wren Orchestra of London, Duke of York's Theatre, St Martin's Lane, London WC2N 4BG.
	Principal Conductor: Hilary Davan Wetton; General Manager: Kevin Appleby.
Manchester:	BBC Philharmonic Orchestra, New Broadcasting House, Oxford Road, Manchester M60 1SJ.
	Chief Conductor: Yan Pascal Tortelier; Manager: Peter Marchbank.
Manchester:	Hallé Orchestra, 30 Cross Street, Manchester M2 7BA.
	Music Director: Kent Nagano; Chief Executive: David Richardson.
Manchester:	Manchester Camerata, 30 Derby Road, Fallowfield, Manchester M24 6UW.
	Principal Conductor: Nicholas Kraemer; Manager: John Whibley.
Manchester:	Manchester Mozart Orchestra, 30 Derby Road, Fallowfield, Manchester M24 6UW.
	Manager: John Whibley.
Merstham:	Virtuosi of England, Glencairn, Shepherd's Hill, Merstham, Surrey RH1 3AD.
	Artistic Director: Arthur Davison.
Milton Keynes:	Milton Keynes Chamber Orchestra, Roseberry Music Room, Great Woolstone Church, Newport Road, Woolstone, Milton Keynes MK15.
	Music Director: Hilary Davan Wetton; General Manager: Nicholas Bomford.

ORCHESTRAS

Newcastle upon Tyne:	Northern Sinfonia of England, The Sinfonia Centre, 41 Jesmond Vale, Newcastle upon Tyne NE1 1PG.
	Artistic Director: Heinrich Schiff; Chief Executive: John Summers.
Northampton:	Corelli Strings, Billing Arbours House, Heather Lane, Northampton NN3 4EY.
	Director: Kenneth Sillito; Director: Susan Brown.
Northampton:	Midland Philharmonic Orchestra, Ridgway House, Great Brington, Northampton NN7 4JA.
	Artistic Director: John Gale; Administrator: Trisha Shoebridge.
Nottingham:	East of England Orchestra, 3 St James's Terrace, Nottingham NG1 6FW.
	Artistic Director: Malcolm Nabarro; General Manager: Dawn Lancaster.
Oxford:	City of Oxford Orchestra, 11-12 Cornmarket Street, Oxford OX1 3EX.
	Chief Guest Conductor: Christopher Seaman; Managing Director: John King.
Oxford:	European Community Baroque Orchestra, 6a Cumnor Hill, Oxford OX2 9HA.
	Music Director: Roy Goodman; General Administrator: Paul James.
Pinner:	Amici Chamber Orchestra, 87 Dove Park, Hatch End, Pinner, Middlesex HA5 4ED.
	Principal Conductor: Nigel Springthorpe; Administrator: Jane Thornhill.
Pontefract:	English Camerata, Long Lane Close, High Ackworth, Pontefract WF7 7EY.
	Artistic Director: Elizabeth Altman; Administrator: John Haris.
Royston:	English Sinfonietta, The Barn, Layston Park, Royston, Herts SG8 9DS.
	Principal Conductor: Steuart Bedford; General Manager: Graham Pfaff.
Sandy:	English Sinfonia, 5 Park Mews, Sandy, Bedfordshire SG19 1JB.
	General Manager: Graham Pfaff.
Swansea:	Welsh Chamber Orchestra, 40 Tudor Court, Murton, Swansea.
	Administrator: Griff Haries.
Tadworth:	City of London Philharmonia, 25 Epsom Lane South, Tadworth, Surrey KT20 5TA.
	Conductor: Jonathan Brett, Administrator: Carolyn Mumford.
Tadworth:	English Classical Players Ltd, 25 Epsom Lane South, Tadworth, Surrey KT20 5TA.
	Artistic Director: Jonathan Brett.
Tamworth:	London String Orchestra, 37 St Davids Road, Clifton Campville, Near Tamworth, Staffordshire B79 0BA.
	Conductor: James Maddocks.
Wakefield:	Yorkshire Symphony Orchestra, Torridon House, 104 Bradford Road, Wrenthorpe, Wakefield, West Yorkshire WF1 2AH.
	General Manager: Brian Greensmith.
Waltham Abbey:	New Symphony Orchestra, 19 Broomstick Hall Road, Waltham Abbey, Essex EN9 1LN.
	General Manager: Julian J Smyth.
Warwickshire:	Orchestra da Camera, 41 Fishponds Road, Kenilworth, Warwickshire CV8 1EY.
	Music Director: Kenneth Page.
Wembley:	Academy of London, PO Box 2, GEC Estate, East La, Wembley, Middlesex HA9 7PR.
	Conductor: Richard Stamp; General Manager: Elaine Baines.
Wigan:	Orchestra of The Mill, Trencherfield Mill, Wallgate, Wigan WN3 4EF.
	Music Director: Peter Donohoe; Manager: Christopher Robins.
Wolverhampton:	English Philharmonic Orchestra, Nationwide House, 258 Penn Road, Wolverhampton WV4 4AD.
	Music Director: Neil Moore; Managing Director: Mark Jarvis.
Worcester:	English Symphony Orchestra and English String Orchestra, The Angel Centre, Angel Place, Worcester WR1 3QN.
	Artistic Director: William Boughton; Administrator: Margaret MackSmith.
Worcester:	New English Orchestra, 59 Northfield Street, Worcester.
	Principal Conductor: Nigel Swinford; Administrator: Alison Hawcutt.
Worthing:	Worthing Symphony Orchestra, Town Hall, Worthing, West Sussex BN11 1HQ.

USA

ALABAMA

Birmingham:	Alabama Symphony Orchestra, 2001 Park Place, Suite 575, Birmingham, AL 35203.
	Music Director: Paul Polivnick; Executive Director: Mark Walker.

ALASKA

Anchorage:	Anchorage Symphony Orchestra, 524 West Fourth Avenue, Suite 205, Anchorage, AK 99501.
	Music Director: Stephen Stein; Executive Director: Helen Howarth.
Fairbanks:	Fairbanks Symphony Orchestra, PO Box 82104, Fairbanks, AK 99708.
	Music Director: Madeline Schatz; Executive Director: Jane Aspnes.

ARIZONA

Phoenix:	Phoenix Symphony Orchestra, 3707 North Seventh Street, Phoenix, AZ 85014.
	Music Director: James Sedares; President and Chief Executive Officer: Howard C McCrady.
Tucson:	Tucson Symphony Orchestra, 443 South Stone Avenue, Tucson, AZ 85701.
	Music Director: Robert Bernhardt; Executive Director: Eric G Meyer.

ARKANSAS

Little Rock:	Arkansas Symphony Orchestra, PO Box 7328, 2500 North Tyler, Little Rock, AR 72217.
	Executive Director: JoAnn Greene

CALIFORNIA

Berkeley:	Berkeley Symphony Orchestra, 2322 Shattuck Avenue, Berkeley, CA 94704.

ORCHESTRAS

	Music Director: Kent Nagano; Executive Director: Kelly Johnson.
Fresno:	Fresno Philharmonic Orchestra, 2610 West Shaw Avenue, Suite 103, Fresno, CA 93711.
	Music Director: Andrew Massey; General Manager: Irene Klug Nielsen.
Glendale:	Glendale Symphony Orchestra, 401 North Brand Boulevard, Suite 520, Glendale, CA 91203.
	Music Director: Lalo Schifrin; Vice President for Administration: Shirley Seeley.
Irvine:	Pacific Symphony Orchestra, 2151 Michelson Drive, No 216, Irvine, CA 92715.
	Music Director: Carl St Clair; Executive Director: Louis G Spisto.
Long Beach:	Long Beach Symphony Orchestra, 555 East Ocean Boulevard, No 106, Long Beach, CA 90802.
	Music Director: JoAnn Falletta; General Manager: Mary Newkirk.
Los Angeles:	Los Angeles Chamber Orchestra, 315 West Ninth Street, Suite 801, Los Angeles, CA 90015.
	Music Director: Christof Perick; Executive Director: Deborah Rutter.
Los Angeles:	Los Angeles Philharmonic Orchestra, 135 North Grand Avenue, Los Angeles, CA 90012.
	Music Director: Esa-Pekka Salonen; Executive Vice President and Managing Director: Ernest Fleischmann.
Oakland:	Oakland East Bay Symphony Orchestra, 1999 Harrison Street, Suite 2030, Oakland, CA 94612
	Music Director: Michael Morgan; Executive Director: Judith Lovell
Pasadena:	Pasadena Symphony Orchestra, 117 East Colorado Boulevard, No 375, Pasadena, CA 91105.
	Music Director: Jorge Mester; Executive Director: Wayne Shilkret.
Sacramento:	Sacramento Symphony Orchestra, 77 Cadillac Drive, Suite 101, Sacramento, CA 95825.
	Executive Director: Robert Walker.
San Diego:	San Diego Symphony Orchestra, 1245 Seventh Avenue, San Diego, CA 92101.
	Music Director: Yoav Talmi; Executive Director: Wesley O Brustad.
San Francisco:	Philharmonia Baroque Orchestra, 57 Post Street, Suite 705, San Francisco, CA 94104.
	Music Director: Nicholas McGegan; Executive Director: George Gelles.
San Francisco:	The Women's Philharmonic, 330 Townsend Street, Suite 218, San Francisco, CA 94107.
	Music Director: JoAnn Falletta; Executive Director: Miriam Abrams.
San Francisco:	San Francisco Symphony, Louise M Davies Symphony Hall, San Francisco, CA 94102.
	Music Director: Herbert Blomstedt; Executive Director: Peter Pastreich.
San Jose:	San Jose Symphony Orchestra, 99 Almaden Boulevard, Suite 400, San Jose, CA 95113.
	President: Douglas McLendon.
Santa Barbara:	Music Academy of the West Summer Festival Orchestra, 1070 Fairway Road, Santa Barbara, CA 93108.
	Music Director: Lawrence Leighton Smith; Artistic Operations Manager: Carleen Landes.
Santa Barbara:	Santa Barbara Symphony Orchestra, 214 East Victoria Street, Santa Barbara, CA 93101.
	General Manager: James L Wright.
Stockton:	Stockton Symphony Orchestra, 37 West Yokuts, C-4, Stockton, CA 95207.
	Music Director: Kyung-Soo Won; Executive Director: George A Sinclair.

COLORADO

Aspen:	Aspen Festival Orchestra and Chamber Symphony, PO Box AA, Aspen, CO 81612.
	Music Director: Lawrence Foster; General Manager: Thomas Eirman.
Colorado Springs:	Colorado Springs Symphony Orchestra, PO Box 1692, Colorado Springs, CO 80901.
	Music Director: Christopher Wilkins; Executive Director: Daniel Hart.
Denver:	Colorado Symphony Orchestra, 1031 13th Street, Denver, CO 80204.
	Music Director: Marin Alsop; Artistic Administrator: David T Abosch.
Denver:	Denver Chamber Orchestra, 1616 Glenarm Place, Suite 1360, Denver, CO 80202.
	Music Director: Paul Lustig Dunkel; Executive Director: Barbara Kelly.
Keystone:	National Repertory Orchestra, PO Box 38, Keystone, CO 80435.
	Conductor: Carl Topilow; Artistic Administrator: Edward Birdwell.

CONNECTICUT

Bridgeport:	Greater Bridgeport Symphony Orchestra, 446 University Avenue, Bridgeport, CT 06604.
	Music Director: Gustav Meier; General Manager: Jena Maric.
Hartford:	Hartford Symphony Orchestra, 228 Farmington Avenue, Hartford, CT 06105.
	Music Director: Michael Lankester; Executive Director: Paul K Reuter.
New Haven:	New Haven Symphony Orchestra, 33 Whitney Avenue, New Haven, CT 06510.
	Music Director: Michael Palmer; General Manager: Catherine Weiskel.

DELAWARE

Wilmington:	Delaware Symphony Orchestra, PO Box 1870, Wilmington, DE 19899.
	Music Director: Stephen Gunzenhauser; Executive Director: John R Bland.

DISTRICT OF COLUMBIA

Washington:	National Gallery Orchestra, Sixth Street and Constitution Avenue North West, Washington, DC 20565.
	Music Director: George Manos.
Washington:	National Symphony Orchestra, John F Kennedy Center for the Performing Arts, Washington, DC 20566.
	Executive Director: Stephen Klein.
Washington:	Theater Chamber Players of Kennedy Center, John F Kennedy Center for the Performing Arts, Washington, DC 20566.
	Directors: Leon Fleisher and Dina Koston.

FLORIDA

Boca Raton:	Florida Symphonic Pops, 120 North East First Avenue, Boca Raton, FL 33432.
	Artistic Director: Mark Azzolina; Executive Vice President: Carol Simmons.

ORCHESTRAS

Fort Lauderdale: Florida Philharmonic Orchestra, 3401 North West Ninth Avenue, Fort Lauderdale, FL 33309.
Music Director: James Judd; Executive Director: John E Graham.

Jacksonville: Jacksonville Symphony Orchestra, 33 South Hogan Street, Jacksonville, FL 32202.
Music Director: Roger Nierenberg; Executive Director: David Pierson.

Miami Beach: New World Symphony, 541 Lincoln Road, 3rd floor, Miami Beach, FL 33139.
Artistic Director: Michael Tilson Thomas; Artistic Administrator: John Duffy.

Naples: Naples Philharmonic, 5833 Pelican Bay Boulevard, Naples, FL 33963.
Music Director: Timothy Russell; President and Chief Executive Officer: Myra Janco Daniels.

Sarasota: Florida West Coast Symphony Orchestra, 709 N Tamiami Trail, Sarasota, FL 34236.
Music Director: Paul Wolfe; Executive Director: Gretchen Serrie

Tampa: Florida Orchestra, 1211 North Westshore Boulevard, Suite 512, Tampa, FL 33607.
Music Director: Jahja Ling; President and Executive Director: John L Hyer.

GEORGIA

Atlanta: Atlanta Symphony Orchestra, 1293 Peachtree Street North East, Suite 300, Atlanta, GA 30309.
Music Director: Yoel Levi; Executive Director: J Thomas Bacchetti.

Savannah: Savannah Symphony Orchestra, PO Box 9505, Savannah, GA 31412.
Music Director: Philip Greenberg; General Manager: Gregg W Gustafson.

HAWAII

Honolulu: Honolulu Symphony Orchestra, 1441 Kapiolani Boulevard, Suite 1515, Honolulu, HI 96814.
Executive Director: Tony H Dechario.

IDAHO

Boise: Boise Philharmonic, 205 North 10th, Suite 617, Boise, ID 83702.
Music Director: James Ogle; General Manager: Margie Stoy Smith.

ILLINOIS

Chicago: Chicago Chamber Orchestra, 410 South Michigan Avenue, Suite 631, Chicago, IL 60605.
Music Director: Dieter Kober; General Manager: Magdalene Lorenz.

Chicago: Chicago Symphony Orchestra, Orchestra Hall, 220 South Michigan Avenue, Chicago, IL 60604.
Music Director: Daniel Barenboim; Executive Director: Henry Fogel.

Chicago: Grant Park Symphony Orchestra, 425 East McFetridge Drive, Chicago, IL 60605.
Principal Conductor: Zdeněk Mácal; Manager: Catherine Cahill.

Chicago: Music of the Baroque Orchestra, 343 South Dearborn, Suite 1716, Chicago, IL 60604.
Music Director: Thomas Wikman; President and Executive Director:Kathleen Butera.

INDIANA

Fort Wayne: Fort Wayne Philharmonic Orchestra, 222 West Berry Street, Fort Wayne, IN 46802.
Music Director: Ronald Ondrejka; General Manager: Christopher D Guerin.

Indianapolis: Indianapolis Chamber Orchestra, 4600 Sunset Avenue, Indianapolis, IN 46208.
Music Director: Kirk Trevor; Administrative Director: Charles Manning.

Indianapolis: Indianapolis Symphony Orchestra, Circle Theatre, 45 Monument Circle, Indianapolis, IN 46204.
Music Director: Raymond Leppard; President: Robert C Jones.

IOWA

Cedar Rapids: Cedar Rapids Symphony Orchestra, 205 Second Avenue, South East, Cedar Rapids, IA 52401.
Music Director: Christian Tiemeyer; Executive Director: Marc Levy.

KANSAS

Wichita: Wichita Symphony Orchestra, 225 West Douglas, Suite 207, Wichita, KS 67202.
Music Director: Zuohuang Chen; General Manager: Mitchell A Berman.

KENTUCKY

Louisville: Louisville Orchestra, 609 West Main Street, Louisville, KY 40202.
Music Director: Lawrence Leighton Smith; Executive Director: Wayne S Brown.

LOUISIANA

New Orleans: Louisiana Philharmonic Orchestra, PO Box 56579, New Orleans, LA 70156.
Manager: Anne Cohen.

MAINE

Portland: Portland Symphony Orchestra, 30 Myrtle Street, Portland, ME 04101.
Music Director: Toshiyuki Shimada; Executive Director: Jane E Hunter.

MARYLAND

Baltimore: Baltimore Symphony Orchestra, 1212 Cathedral Street, Baltimore, MD 21201.
Music Director: David Zinman; Executive Director: John Gidwitz.

ORCHESTRAS

Hagerstown: Maryland Symphony Orchestra, 12 Rochester Place, Hagerstown, MD 21740.
Music Director: Barry Tuckwell; Managing Director: Cassandra H Wantz.

MASSACHUSETTS

Boston: Boston Symphony Orchestra, Symphony Hall, 301 Massachusetts Avenue, Boston, MA 02115.
Music Director: Seiji Ozawa; Managing Director: Kenneth Haas.

Boston: Handel & Haydn Society, Symphony Hall, 301 Massachusetts Avenue, Boston, MA 02115.
Artistic Director: Christopher Hogwood; Executive Director: Mary Deissler.

Springfield: Springfield Symphony Orchestra, 1391 Main Street, Suite 1006, Springfield, MA 01103.
Music Director: Raymond Harvey; Executive Director: Robert J Stiles.

MICHIGAN

Ann Arbor: Ann Arbor Symphony Orchestra, PO Box 1412, Ann Arbor, MI 48106.
Music Director: Samuel Wong; Executive Director: Anne Glendon.

Detroit: Detroit Symphony Orchestra, 400 Buhl Building, 535 Griswold Street, Detroit, MI 48226.
Music Director: Neeme Järvi; Executive Director: Mark Volpe.

Detroit: Michigan Chamber Orchestra, 60 Farnsworth, Detroit, MI 48202.
Principal Conductor: Andrew Massey; General Manager: Virginia Catanese.

Grand Rapids: Grand Rapids Symphony Orchestra, 220 Lyon North West, Suite 415, Grand Rapids, MI 49503.
Music Director: Catherine Comet; Executive Director: Peter W Smith.

Kalamazoo: Kalamazoo Symphony Orchestra, 426 South Park Street, Kalamazoo, MI 49007.
Music Director: Yoshimi Takeda; General Manager: John Forsyte.

MINNESOTA

Minneapolis: Minnesota Orchestra, 1111 Nicollet Mall, Minneapolis, MN 55403.
Music Director: Edo de Waart; President: David J Hyslop.

St Paul: St Paul Chamber Orchestra, 318 Landmark Center, 75 West Fifth Street, St Paul, MN 55102.
Music Director: Hugh Wolff; President and Managing Director: William Vickery.

MISSISSIPPI

Jackson: Mississippi Symphony Orchestra, PO Box 2052, Jackson, MS 39225.
Music Director: Colman Pearce; Executive Director: Philip K Messner.

MISSOURI

Kansas City: Kansas City Symphony Orchestra, 1020 Central, Suite 300, Kansas City, MO 64105.
Music Director: William McGlaughlin; General Manager: Susan Franano.

St Louis: St Louis Symphony Orchestra, Powell Symphony Hall, 718 North Grand Boulevard, St Louis, MO 63103.
Music Director: Leonard Slatkin; Executive Director: Bruce Coppock.

NEBRASKA

Omaha: Omaha Symphony Orchestra, 1615 Howard Street, Suite 310, Omaha, NE 68102.
Music Director: Bruce Hangen; Executive Director: Roland Valliere.

NEW HAMPSHIRE

Manchester: New Hampshire Symphony Orchestra, PO Box 1298, Manchester, NH 03105.
Music Director: James Bolle; General Manager: David A Ball.

NEW JERSEY

Newark: New Jersey Symphony Orchestra, Robert Treat Center, 11th floor, 50 Park Place, Newark, NJ 07102.
Executive Director: Lawrence Tamburri.

Trenton: Greater Trenton Symphony Orchestra, 28 West State Street, Suite 201, Trenton, NJ 08608.
Executive Director: John Peter Holly.

NEW MEXICO

Albuquerque: New Mexico Symphony Orchestra, 220 Gold South West, Albuquerque, NM 87102.
Music Director: Neal Stulberg; General Manager: James W Reeves.

NEW YORK

Albany: Albany Symphony Orchestra, 19 Clinton Avenue, Albany, NY 12207.
Music Director: David Alan Miller; Executive Director: Susan Filipp.

Brooklyn: Brooklyn Philharmonic Symphony Orchestra, 30 Lafayette Avenue, Brooklyn, NY 11217.
Music Director: Dennis Russell Davies; Executive Director: Vicki Margulies.

Buffalo: Buffalo Philharmonic Orchestra, PO Box 905, Buffalo, NY 14213.
Music Director: Maximiano Valdes; Executive Director: Michael Tiknis.

Chautauqua: Chautauqua Symphony Orchestra, Chautauqua, NY 14722.
Music Director: Uriel Segal; General Manager: Marty W Merkley.

Dobbs Ferry: Philharmonia Virtuosi, 145 Palisade Street, Suite 341, Dobbs Ferry, NY 10522.

ORCHESTRAS

	Music Director: Richard Kapp; General Manager: Sally Forrest.
Greenvale:	New York Virtuosi Chamber Symphony, C W Post College, Greenvale, NY 11548.
	Music Director: Kenneth Klein; Executive Director: Yolanda Padula.
Melville:	Long Island Philharmonic Orchestra, 1 Huntington Quadrangle, Suite LL 09, Melville, NY 11747.
	Music Director: Marin Alsop.
New York:	American Composers Orchestra, 37 West 65th Street, 6th Floor, New York, NY 10023.
	Music Director: Dennis Russell Davies; Executive Director: Jesse Rosen.
New York:	American Symphony Orchestra, 850 Seventh Avenue, Suite 1106, New York, NY 10019.
	Music Director: Leon Botstein; Executive Director: Eugene Carr.
New York:	New York Chamber Symphony of the 92nd Street Y, 1395 Lexington Avenue, New York, NY 10128.
	Music Director: Gerard Schwarz; Manager: Jacqueline Taylor.
New York:	New York Philharmonic Orchestra, Avery Fisher Hall, Lincoln Center for the Performing Arts, Broadway at 65th Street, New York, NY 10023.
	Music Director: Kurt Masur; Managing Director: Deborah Borda.
New York:	Orchestra of St Luke's, 130 West 42nd Street, Suite 804, New York, NY 10036.
	Music Director: Roger Norrington; Executive Director: Marianne Lockwood.
New York:	Orpheus Chamber Orchestra, 490 Riverside Drive, New York, NY 10027.
	Executive Director: Julian Fifer.
New York:	Solisti New York Orchestra, PO Box 20068, New York, NY 10025.
	Music Director: Ransom Wilson.
Poughkeepsie:	Hudson Valley Philharmonic Orchestra, PO Box 191, Poughkeepsie, NY 12602.
	Music Director: Randall Fleischer.
Rochester:	Rochester Philharmonic Orchestra, 108 East Avenue, Rochester, NY 14604.
	Music Director: Mark Elder; President and Chief Executive Officer: Dr Carl Atkins.
Syracuse:	Syracuse Symphony Orchestra, 411 Montgomery Street, Syracuse, NY 13202.
	Executive Director: Ernest S Rose.

NORTH CAROLINA

Charlotte:	Charlotte Symphony Orchestra, 1415 South Church Street, Suite S, Charlotte, NC 28203.
	Music Director: Leo Driehuys.
Greensboro:	Eastern Philharmonic Orchestra, PO Box 22026, Greensboro, NC 27420.
	Music Director: Sheldon Morgenstern.
Raleigh:	North Carolina Symphony Orchestra, PO Box 28026, Raleigh, NC 27611.
	Music Director: Gerhardt Zimmerman; Executive Director: Banks C Talley Jr.

OHIO

Cincinnati:	Cincinnati Symphony Orchestra, 1241 Elm Street, Cincinnati, OH 45210.
	Music Director: Jesús López-Cobos; Executive Director: Steven I Monder.
Cleveland:	Cleveland Orchestra, Severance Hall, 11001 Euclid Avenue, Cleveland, OH 44106.
	Music Director: Christoph von Dohnányi; Executive Director: Thomas W Morris.
Columbus:	Columbus Symphony Orchestra, 55 East State Street, Columbus, OH 43215.
	Music Director: Alessandro Siciliani; Executive Director: Stephen R Vann.
Dayton:	Dayton Philharmonic Orchestra, 125 East First Street, Dayton, OH 45422.
	Music Director: Isaiah Jackson; Executive Director: John Bauser.
Toledo:	Toledo Symphony Orchestra, 1 Stranahan Square, Suite 354, Toledo, OH 43604.
	Music Director: Andrew Massey; Managing Director: Robert Bell.

OKLAHOMA

Oklahoma City:	Oklahoma City Philharmonic Orchestra, 428 West California, Suite 210, Oklahoma City, OK 73102.
	Music Director: Joel Levine; General Manager: Alan D Valentine.
Tulsa:	Tulsa Philharmonic Orchestra, 2901 South Harvard, Tulsa, OK 74114.
	Music Director: Bernard Rubenstein; Executive Director: Stephen Boyd.

OREGON

Eugene:	Eugene Symphony Orchestra, 45 West Broadway, Suite 201, Eugene, OR 97401.
	Music Director: Marin Alsop; Executive Director: Ronald G Johnson.
Portland:	Oregon Symphony Orchestra, 711 South West Alder, Suite 200, Portland, OR 97205.
	Music Director: James DePreist; President: Don Roth.

PENNSYLVANIA

Philadelphia:	Philadelphia Orchestra, Academy of Music, 1420 Locust Street, Suite 400, Philadelphia, PA 19102.
	Music Director: Wolfgang Sawallisch; President and Chief Operating Officer: Joseph H Kluger.
Pittsburgh:	Pittsburgh Symphony Orchestra, Heinz Hall, 600 Penn Avenue, Pittsburgh, PA 15222.
	Music Director: Lorin Maazel; Vice President and Managing Director: Gideon Toeplitz.

PUERTO RICO

Santurce:	Puerto Rico Symphony Orchestra, Box 41227, Minillas Station, Santurce, PR 00940.
	Music Director: Odón Alonso.

ORCHESTRAS

RHODE ISLAND

Providence: Rhode Island Philharmonic Orchestra, 222 Richmond Street, Providence, RI 02903.
Music Director: Zuohuang Chen; Executive Director: Karen Dobbs.

SOUTH CAROLINA

Charleston: Charleston Symphony Orchestra, 14 George Street, Charleston, SC 29401.
Music Director: David Stahl; Executive Director: Darrell G Edwards.

SOUTH DAKOTA

Sioux Falls: South Dakota Symphony Orchestra, 300 North Dakota Avenue, No 405, Sioux Falls, SD 57102.
Music Director: Henry Charles Smith; Executive Director: Marti Baumert.

TENNESSEE

Knoxville: Knoxville Symphony Orchestra, 708 Gay Street, Knoxville, TN 37902.
Music Director: Kirk Trevor; Executive Director: Constance Harrison.
Memphis: Memphis Symphony Orchestra, 3100 Walnut Grove, Suite 501, Memphis, TN 38111.
Music Director: Alan Balter; Executive Director: Michael Maxwell.
Nashville: Nashville Symphony Orchestra, 208 23 Avenue North, Nashville, TN 37203.
Music Director: Kenneth Schermerhorn; Executive Director: Steven J Greil.

TEXAS

Austin: Austin Symphony Orchestra, Symphony Square, 1101 Red River, Austin, TX 78701.
Music Director: Sung Kwak; Executive Director: Kenneth E Caswell.
Dallas: Dallas Symphony Orchestra, 2301 Flora Street, Suite 300, Dallas, TX 75201.
Music Director: Andrew Litton; Executive Director: Leonard David Stone.
Fort Worth: Fort Worth Symphony Orchestra, 4401 Trail Lake Drive, Fort Worth, TX 76109.
Music Director: John Giordano; Executive Director: Ann Koonsman.
Houston: Houston Symphony Orchestra, 615 Louisiana Street, Houston, TX 77002.
Music Director: Christoph Eschenbach; Executive Director: David M Wax.
San Antonio: San Antonio Symphony Orchestra, 109 Lexington, Suite 207, San Antonio, TX 78205.
Music Director: Christopher Wilkins; President and Executive Director: Rick Lester.

UTAH

Salt Lake City: Utah Symphony Orchestra, 123 West South Temple, Salt Lake City, UT 84101.
Music Director: Joseph Silverstein; Executive Director: Paul Chummers.

VIRGINIA

Norfolk: Virginia Symphony Orchestra, PO Box 26, Norfolk, VA 23501.
Music Director: JoAnn Falletta.
Richmond: Richmond Symphony Orchestra, The Berkshire, 300 West Franklin Street, Richmond, VA 23220.
Music Director: George Manahan; Executive Director: Catherine Wichterman.
Roanoke: Roanoke Symphony Orchestra, PO Box 2433, Roanoke, VA 24010.
Music Director: Victoria Bond; Executive Director: Margarite Fourcroy.

WASHINGTON

Seattle: Seattle Symphony Orchestra, 305 Harrison Street, Seattle, WA 98109.
Music Director: Gerard Schwarz.
Spokane: Spokane Symphony Orchestra, 621 Mallon, Suite 203, Spokane, WA 99201.
Music Director: Vakhtang Jordania; Executive Director: Richard Early.

WEST VIRGINIA

Charleston: West Virginia Symphony Orchestra, PO Box 2292, Charleston, WV 24328.
Music Director: Thomas Conlin; Manager: Shirley Furry

WISCONSIN

Milwaukee: Milwaukee Symphony Orchestra, 330 E Kilbourn Avenue, Suite 900, Milwaukee, WI 53202.
Music Director: Zdeněk Mácal; Executive Director: Gary L Good.

UKRAINE

Kiev: Kiev Chamber Orchestra, Vladimirsky Spusk 2, 252001 Kiev.
Music Director: A M Vinokurov.
Kiev: Ukrainian State Symphony Orchestra, Vladimirsky Spusk 2, 252001 Kiev.
Music Director: Igor Blazhkov; Manager: Vladimir Kolobrodov.
Odessa: Odessa Chamber Orchestra, 15 R Louxembourg Street, Odessa.
Music Director: M Tourchinsky.

ORCHESTRAS

Odessa: Odessa Symphony Orchestra, 15 R Louxembourg Street, Odessa.
                 Music Director: E I Shestakov.
Yalta: Crimean State Philharmonic, 13 Litkens Street, 334200 Yalta.
                 Music Director: A F Gulyanitsky.

URUGUAY

Montevideo: Orquesta Sinfónica del SODRE, Calle Sarandi 450, Montevideo 1100.
                 Music Director: David Machado; President: Dr Hector Hugo Barbagelata.
Montevideo: Orquesta Sinfónica Municipal de Montevideo, Juncal 1215 y Reconquista, Montevideo.
                 Music Director: Fedrico Garcia Vigil.

VENEZUELA

Caracas: Orquesta Sinfónica Municipal de Caracas, Apdo 17390, Parque Central, Caracas 1015-A.
                 Director: Carlos Riazuelo.
Caracas: Simon Bolivar Symphony Orchestra of Venezuela, Torre Oeste, Piso 1, Parque Central, Caracas.
                 Music Director: José Antonio Abreu.

YUGOSLAVIA

Belgrade: Belgrade Philharmonic Orchestra, Studentski Trg 11, 11000 Belgrade.
Belgrade: Belgrade Radio and Television Symphony Orchestra, Hilendarska 2, 11000 Belgrade.

OPERA COMPANIES

APPENDIX B

OPERA COMPANIES

ARGENTINA

Buenos Aires: Teatro Colón, Cerrito 618, 1010 Buenos Aires.
General Director: Sergio Renan.

AUSTRALIA

AUSTRALIAN CAPITAL TERRITORY

Canberra: Opera ACT, PO Box 169, Canberra, ACT 2608

NEW SOUTH WALES

Strawberry Hills: Australian Opera, PO Box 291, Strawberry Hills, NSW 2012.
General Manager: Donald McDonald.

QUEENSLAND

Brisbane: Lyric Opera of Queensland, PO Box 677, South Brisbane, QLD 4101.
General Manager: Suzannah Conway.

SOUTH AUSTRALIA

Adelaide: State Opera of South Australia, GPO Box 1515, Adelaide, SA 5001.
General Manager: Bill Gillespie.

VICTORIA

Melbourne: Victoria State Opera, 77 Southbank Boulevard, Melbourne, VIC 3205.
Music Director: Richard Divall; General Manager: Ken Mackenzie-Forbes.

WESTERN AUSTRALIA

Perth: Western Australian Opera, PO Box 7052, Cloisters Square, Perth, WA 6000.
General Manager: Terence A Craig

AUSTRIA

Bad Ischl: Sommertheater, Wiesingerstrasse 7, A-4820 Bad Ischl.
Music Director: Eduard Macku; Manager: Silvia Müller.
Baden bei Wien: Stadttheater, Theaterplatz 7, A-2500 Baden bei Wien.
Director: Helmuth Brandstätter.
Graz: Vereinigte Bühnen, Kaiser Josef Platz 10, A-8010 Graz.
Director: Gerhard Brunner.
Innsbruck: Tiroler Landerstheater, Rennweg 2, A-6020 Innsbruck.
Director: Dominique Mentha.
Klagenfurt: Stadttheater, Theaterplatz 4, A-9020 Klagenfurt.
Director: Dietmar Pflegerl.
Linz: Landestheater, Promenade 39, A-4010 Linz.
Director: Roman Zeilinger.
St Pölten: Stadttheater, Rathausplatz 11, A-3100 St Pölten.
Director: Peter Wolsdorff.
Salzburg: Landestheater, Schwarstrasse 22, A-5020 Salzburg.
Director: Lutz Hochstraate.
Vienna: Raimund Theater, Wallgasse 18-20, A-1060 Vienna.
Director: Peter Weck.
Vienna: Staatsoper, Opernring 2, A-1010 Vienna.
Director: Ioan Holender.
Vienna: Vereinigte Bühnen Wien GmbH (Theater an der Wien), Linke Wienzeile 6, A-1060 Vienna.
President: Peter Weck.
Vienna: Volksoper, Währingerstrasse 78, A-1090 Vienna.
Director: Ioan Holender.
Vienna: Wiener Kammeroper, Fleischmarkt 24, A-1010 Vienna.
Artistic and General Manager: Hans Gabor.

BELGIUM

Antwerp: Vlaamse Kameropera, Ommeganchstrasse 59, B-2018 Antwerp.

OPERA COMPANIES

	Director: Walter Proost
Brussels:	Théâtre Royal de la Monnaie, 4 Léopoldstrasse, B-1000 Brussels.
	Director: Bernard Foccroulle.
Ghent:	Opera voor Vlaanderen, Schouwburgstrasse 3, B-9000 Ghent.
	Music Director: Stefan Soltesz; General Manager: Marc Clémeur.
Liège:	Opéra Royal de Wallonie, 1 Rue des Domincains, B-4000 Liège.
	Director: Raymond Rossius.

BOSNIA AND HERZEGOVINA

Sarajevo: National Theater Opera, Obala 9, 71000 Sarajevo.

BULGARIA

Bourgas:	Bourgas State Opera, K1, Ohridski St 2, 8000 Bourgas
Plovdiv:	Plovdiv State Opera, 4000 Plovdiv.
Sofia:	Sofia State Opera, Boul Dondoukov 58, 1000 Sofia.
Sofia:	Stefan Makedonski Musical Theater, 3P Volov St, 1500 Sofia.
Stara Zagora:	Stara Zagora State Opera, 6000 Stara Zagora.
Varna:	Varna State Opera, 9000 Varna.

CANADA

ALBERTA

Calgary:	Calgary Opera, 125 Ninth Avenue South East, No 800, Calgary, Alberta T2G 0PB.
	General Director: David Speers.
Edmonton:	Edmonton Opera Association, 320-10232 112th Street, Edmonton, Alberta T5K 1M4.
	General Director: Richard Mantle.

BRITISH COLUMBIA

Vancouver:	Vancouver Opera, 1132 Hamilton Street, Vancouver, British Columbia V6B 2S2.
	Music Director: David Agler; General Director: Robert J Hallam.
Victoria:	Pacific Opera Victoria, 1316B Government Street, Victoria, British Columbia V8W 1YB.
	General Manager: Marcus Handman.

MANITOBA

Winnipeg:	Manitobe Opera Association, 393 Portage Avenue, 3rd floor, Winnipeg, Manitoba R3B 3K9.
	Artistic Director: Irving Guttman; Executive Director: Joann Alexander Smith.

ONTARIO

Hamilton:	Opera Hamilton, 2 King Street West, Hamilton, Ontario L8P 1A1.
	Artistic Director:Daniel Lipton; General Manager: Brian Macurdy.
Ottawa:	Opera Lyra, Arts Court, 2 Daly Avenue, Ottawa, Ontario K1N 6E2.
	Artistic Director: Jeannette Aster; General Manager: Norman E Brown.
Toronto:	Canadian Opera Company, 227 Front Street East, Toronto, Ontario M5A 1E8.
	Chief Conductor: Richard Bradshaw; General Director: Brian Dickie.

QUÉBEC

Montréal:	L'Opera de Montréal, 260 de Maisonneuve Boulevard West, Montréal, Province Québec H2X 1Y9.
	Artistic and General Director: Bernard Uzan.
Québec:	Opéra de Québec, 1220 Avenue Taché, Québec, Province Québec G1R 3B4.
	Artistic Director: Guy Bélanger.

CHILE

Santiago:	Opera del Teatro Municipal, Augustinas 794, PO Box 18, Santiago.
	General Director: Andrés Rodriguez.

CHINA

Beijing:	Central Opera Theater, Dongzhimenwai, Zuojiazhuang, Beijing.
	Director: Wang Shi-guang.
Beijing:	China Peking Opera Theater, Beijing.
	President:Zhang Dong-Chuan.
Shanghai:	Shanghai Opera House, Lane 100, Changshu Road, Shanghai.
	Conductors: Huang Pei-Qin and Lin You-Sheng.

OPERA COMPANIES

COLOMBIA

Bogotá:　　Compania Nacional de Opera, Teatro Colón, Celle 10, No 5-32, Bogotá.

COSTA RICA

San José:　　Compania Lirica Nacional, PO Box 1035, San José 1000.
Director: Alvaro Sáenz-Zúniga.

CROATIA

Zagreb:　　Croatian National Theatre, 41000 Zagreb.

CZECH REPUBLIC

Brno:　　Janáček Opera, Dvořákova 11, 657 70 Brno.
Košice:　　Košice State Theatre Opera, Šrobárova 14, PO Box E-47, 042 77 Košice.
Olomouc:　　O Stibor State Theatre, 771 07 Olomouc.
Opava:　　Silesian Theatre, Horní náměstí 13, 74669 Opava.
Ostrava:　　Ostrava State Theatre, Pabla Nerudy 14, 701 04 Ostrava.
Plzeň:　　J K Tyl Theatre, Prokopova 14, 304 11 Plzeň.
Prague:　　National Theatre, PO Box 865, 112 30 Prague 1.
Ustí nad Labem:　　Z Nejedlý State Theatre, Kralova Výšina 10, 400 00 Usti nad Labem.

DENMARK

Århus:　　Den jyske Opera, Thomas Jensens Alle, DK-8000 Århus.
Administrator: Tony Borup Mortenson.
Copenhagen:　　Det kongelige Teater, Box 2185, DK-1017 Copenhagen K.
Manager: Poul Jørgensen.
Copenhagen:　　Musikdramatisk Teater, Ernst Meyersgade 8, DK-1772 Copenhagen V.
Administrator: Flemming Vistisen.

EIRE

Dublin:　　Dublin Grand Opera Society, John Player Theatre, 276-288 Circular Road, Dublin 8.
Administrator: David Collopy.
Dublin:　　Opera Theatre Company, 18 Kildare Street, Dublin 2.
Director: James Conway.

ESTONIA

Tallinn:　　Estonian State Opera and Ballet, Estonia Boulevard 4, 200001 Tallinn.
Chief Conductor: Eri Klas; General Director: Jaak Viller.

FINLAND

Helsinki:　　Finnish National Opera, Bulevardi 23-27, SF-00180 Helsinki 18.
Conductor: Ulf Söderblom; Artistic Director: Walton Grönroos.

FRANCE

Avignon:　　Opéra d'Avignon, Rue Racine, F-84000 Avignon.
Bordeaux:　　Grand Théâtre Municipal, Place de la Comédie, F-33074 Bordeaux Cédex.
Administrator: Daniel Doumeau-Gabory.
Caen:　　Théâtre de Caen Atelier/Lyrique de Caen, BP 217, F-14007 Caen Cédex.
Director: Jean Malraye.
Colmar:　　Atelier du Rhin, 6 Route d'Ingersheim, BP 593, F-68008 Colmar.
Director: Pierre Barrat.
Dijon:　　Grand Théâtre de Dijon, F-21000 Dijon.
Director: Pierre Filippi.
Lille:　　Opéra de Lille, Théâtre de l'Opéra, 2 Rue des Bons Enfants, F-59800 Lille.
Artistic Director: Ricardo Szwarcer; Administrator: Michel Default.
Lyon:　　Opéra de Lyon, 9 Quai Jean Moulin, F-69001 Lyon.
Music Director: Kent Nagano; Administrator: Jacques Hedouin.
Marseille:　　Opéra de Marseille, 2 Rue Molière, F-1321 Marseille Cédex 01.
General Administrator: Jean-Jacques Chazalet.
Metz:　　Théâtre Municipal de Metz, 5 Place de la Comédie, F-57000 Metz.
Administrator: Daniel Lucas.
Montpellier:　　Opéra de Montpellier, 11 Boulevard Victor Hugo, F-34000 Montpellier.

OPERA COMPANIES

	General Director: Henri Maier; Administrator: Renée Panabière.
Nancy:	Opéra de Nancy et de Lorraine, 1 Rue Ste Catherine, F-54000 Nancy.
	Director: Antoine Bourseiller; Administrator: Gilles Gordet.
Nantes:	Opéra de Nantes, 1 Rue Molière, F-44000 Nantes.
	Director: Philippe Godefroid; Administrator: Serge Cochelin.
Nice:	Théâtre de l'Opéra de Nice, 4 and 6 Rue St François de Paule, F-06300 Nice.
	Artistic Director: Pierre Medecin; General Director: Lucien Salles.
Paris:	Atelier de Recherche et de Création pour l'art Lyrique, 20 Rue Debelleyme, F-75003, Paris.
	Director: Christian Gangneron; Administrator: Jean-Paul Davois.
Paris:	Ecole d'Art Lyrique de l'Opéra, 5 Rue Favart, F-75009 Paris.
	Director: Michel Sénéchal; Administrator: Francis Meunier.
Paris:	Opéra de La Bastille, 120 Rue de Lyon, F-75012 Paris.
	Music Director: Myung-Whun Chung; General Director: Philippe Bélaval; General Administrator: Georges-François Hirsch.
Paris:	Théâtre des Champs-Elysées, 15 Avenue Montaigne, F-75008 Paris.
	General Director: Alain Durel; Administrator: Francis Lepigeon.
Paris:	Théâtre National de l'Opéra de Paris, 8 Rue Scribe, F-75009 Paris.
	General Director: Jean-Philippe Saint-Geours; General Administrator: Jean-Louis Martinoty.
Reims:	Grand Théâtre de Reims, 9 Rue Chanzy, F-51100 Reims.
	Director: Guy Grinda.
Rouen:	Théâtre des Arts, F-76177 Rouen Cédex.
	Director: Marc Adam.
Strasbourg:	Opéra du Rhin, 19 Place Broglie, F-67008 Strasbourg Cédex.
	General Director: Laurent Spielmann; Administrator: Lucien Colinet.
Toulouse:	Théâtre du Capitole, Place du Capitole, F-31000 Toulouse.
	Artistic Director: Nicolas Joel; Administrator: Robert Gouaze.
Tourcoing:	Atelier Lyrique de Tourcoing, 82 Boulevard Gambetta, F-59200 Tourcoing.
	General Director: Jean-Claude Malgoire; General Administrator: Catherine Noel.
Tours:	Centre Lyrique de Tours, Grand Théâtre, Rue de la Scellerie, F-37000 Tours.
	Director: Michel Jarry; Administrator: Michel Berthon.

GERMANY

Aachen:	Stadttheater Aachen, Theaterplatz, W-5100 Aachen.
	Music Director: Stefan Lano; General Manger: Elmar Ottenthal.
Altenburg:	Landestheater Altenburg, Theaterplatz 19, O-7400 Altenburg.
	Manager: Georg Mittendrein.
Annaberg-Buchholz:	Educard-von-Winterstein-Theater, Buchholzer Strasse 67, O-9300 Annaberg-Buchholz.
	1st Conductor: Mihai Vălcu; Manager: Peter Löpelt.
Augsburg:	Städtische Bühnen Augsburg, Kasernstrasse 4-6, Pf 111949, W-8900 Augsburg.
	General Music Director: Michael Luig; Manager: Peter Baumgardt.
Bautzen:	Deutsch-Sorbisches Volkstheater Bautzen, Seminarstrasse 12, O-8600 Bautzen.
	Music Director: Dieter Kempe; Manager: Michael Grosse.
Bautzen:	Sorbisches National-Ensemble Bautzen, Áussere Lauenstrasse 2, O-8600 Bautzen.
	Music Director: Jan Bulank; Manager: Detlef Kobjela.
Berlin:	Berliner Kammeroper e V, Kottbusser Damm 79, W-1000 Berlin 61.
	Music Director: Brynmor Llewelyn Jones; Artistic Director: Henry Akina.
Berlin:	Deutsche Oper Berlin, Bismarckstrasse 35, W-1000 Berlin 10.
	General Music Director: Rafael Frühbeck de Burgos; General Manager: Prof Götz Friedrich.
Berlin:	Deutsche Staatsoper Berlin, Unter den Linden 7, O-1060 Berlin.
	General Music Director: Daniel Barenboim; Manager: Georg Quander.
Berlin:	Komische Oper Berlin, Behrenstrasse 55-57, O-1086 Berlin.
	General Music Director: Prof Rolf Reuter; Manager: Prof Dr Werner Rackwitz.
Berlin:	Metropol-Theater Berlin, Friedrichstrasse 101/102, O-1086 Berlin.
	General Music Director: Günter Joseck; Manager: Werner P Seiferth.
Berlin:	Neuköllner Oper e V, W-1000 Berlin 44.
	Artistic Director: Winfried Radeke.
Berlin:	Theater des Westens Berlin, Kantstrasse 12, W-1000 Berlin 12.
	Music Director: Dr Peter Keuschnig; Manager: Helmut Baumann.
Bielefeld:	Bühnen der Stadt Bielefeld, Brunhenstrasse 3-9, Pf 220, W-4800 Bielefeld.
	General Music Director: Rainer Koch; Manager: Heiner Bruns.
Bochum:	Starlighttheater Bochum, Stadionring 24, W-4630 Bochum.
	Music Director: Phil Edwards.
Bonn:	Oper der Stadt Bonn, Am Boeselagerhof 1, Pf 2440, W-5300 Bonn.
	General Music Director: Dr Dennis Russell Davies; Manager: Gian-Carlo del Monaco.
Brandenburg:	Brandenburg Theater, Grabenstrasse 14, O-1800 Brandenburg.
	Music Director: Heiko Mathias Förster; Manager: Ekkehard Prophet.
Braunschweig:	Staatstheater Braunschweig, Am Theater, W-3300 Braunschweig.
	General Music Director: Stefan Soltesz; General Manger: Jürgen Flügge.
Bremen:	Bremen Theater, Pf 101046, W-2800 Bremen.
	General Music Director: Marcello Viotti; General Manager: Prof Hansgünther Heyme.
Bremerhaven:	Stadttheater Bremerhaven, Theodor-Heuss-Platz, Pf 120541, W-2850 Bremerhaven.
	General Music Director: Prof Leo Plettner; Manager: Dr Dirk Böttger.
Chemnitz:	Städtische Theater Chemnitz, Theaterplatz 2, O-9001 Chemnitz.
	General Music Director: Dieter-Gerhardt Worm; General Manger: Jörg Liljeberg.
Coburg:	Landestheater Coburg, Schlossplatz 6, W-8630 Coburg.
	General Music Director: Christian Fröhlich; Manager: Ernö Weil.
Cologne:	Offenbach-Theater Köln, Vietorstrasse 70, W-5000 Cologne 91.
	Director: Karl-Wolfgang Saalmann.
Cologne:	Oper der Stadt Köln, Offenbachplatz, Pf 180241, W-5000 Cologne 1.
	General Music Director: James Conlon; Manager: Prof Dr Michael Hampe.

OPERA COMPANIES

Cottbus: Staatstheater Cottbus, Karl-Liebknecht-Strasse 136, 0-7500 Cottbus.
General Music Director: Frank Morgenstern; Manager: Johannes Steurich.

Darmstadt: Staatstheater Darmstadt, Auf dem Marienplatz, W-6100 Darmstadt.
General Music Director: Prof Hans Drewanz; Manager: Dr Peter Girth.

Dessau: Landestheater Dessau, Fritz-Hesse-Platz 1, 0-4500 Dessau.
Manager: Johannes Felsenstein.

Detmold: Landestheater Detmold, Theaterplatz 1, W-4930 Detmold.
Manager: Ulf Reiher.

Döbeln: Stadttheater Döbeln, Theaterstrasse, 0-7300 Döbeln.
Music Director: Harald Weigel; Manager: Wolfram Jacobi.

Dortmund: Städtische Bühnen Dortmund, Kuhstrasse 12, W-4600 Dortmund.
General Music Director: Moshe Atzmon; General Manager: Horst Fechner.

Dresden: Landesbühnen Sachsen, Meissner Strasse 152, 0-8122 Dresden.
Music Director: Joachim Widlak; Manager: Christian Schmidt.

Dresden: Sächsische Staatsoper Dresden (Semperoper), Theaterplatz 2, 0-8010 Dresden.
Music Director: Giuseppe Sinopoli; Manager: Christoph Albrecht.

Dresden: Staatsoperette Dresden, Pirnaer Landstrasse 131, 0-8045 Dresden.
Music Director: Volker Münch; Manager: Elke Schneider.

Düsseldorf: Deutsche Oper am Rhein, Theatergemeinschaft Düsseldorf-Duisburg, Opernhaus Düsseldorf, Heinrich-Heine-Allee 16a, W-4000 Düsseldorf 1.
General Music Director: Hans Wallat; General Manager: Prof Kurt Horres.

Eggenfelden: Theater an der Rott, Pfarrkirchener Strasse 70, W-8330 Eggenfelden.
Music Director: Dr Lutz Teschendorf; Manager: Adi Fischer.

Eisenach: Landestheater und Landeskapelle Eisenach, Theaterplatz 4-7, 0-5900 Eisenach.
General Music Director: Harke de Roos; Manager: Jürgen Fabritius.

Eisleben: Landesbühne Sachsen-Anhalt Lutherstadt Eisleben, An der Landwehr 5, 0-4250 Eisleben.
Music Director: Paul Sergiou; Manager: Frank Hofmann.

Erfurt: Städtische Bühnen Erfurt, Gorkistrasse 1, 0-5020 Erfurt.
General Music Director: Wolfgang Rögner; General Manger: Dietrich Traube.

Eschwege: Minipolitan-Eschweges Kleine Schaubühne e V, Niedernhoner Strasse 2, W-3440 Eschwege.
Conductors: Andreas Paetzold and Andreas Worm.

Essen: Theater und Philharmonie Essen, Rolandstrasse 10, W-4300 Essen 1.
General Music Director: Prof Wolf-Dieter Hauschild.

Flensburg: Schleswig-Holsteinisches Landestheater und Sinfonieorchester, Rathausstrasse 22, W-2390 Flensburg.
General Music Director: Gerhard Schneider; General Manager: Dr Horst Mesalla.

Frankfurt am Main: Die Theater der Stadt Frankfurt, Untermainanlage 11, W-6000 Frankfurt am Main.
General Music Director: Sylvain Cambreling.

Frankfurt am Main: Kammeroper Frankfurt, Nordenstrasse 60, W-6000 Frankfurt am Main 1.
Music Director: Martin Krähe; Artistic Director: Rainer Pudenz.

Frankfurt an der Oder: Kleist-Theater, Gerhart-Hauptmann-Strasse, 0-1200 Frankfurt an der Oder.
General Music Director: Nikos Athinäos; Manager: Maria-Luise Preuss.

Freiberg: Stadttheater Freiberg, Borngasse 1, 0-9200 Freiberg.
Music Director: Jany Renz; Manager: Rüdiger Bloch.

Freiburg im Breisgau:: Städtische Bühnen Freiburg, Bertoldstrasse 46, W-7800 Freiburg im Breisgau.
General Music Director: Donald Runnicles; Manager: Friedrich Schirmer.

Gelsenkirchen: Musiktheater im Revier, Kennedyplatz, Pf 101854, W-4650 Gelsenkirchen.
General Music Director: Neil Varon; General Manager: Ludwig Baum.

Gera: Bühnen der Stadt Gera, Küchengartenallee 2, 0-6500 Gera.
Music Director: Wolfgang Wappler; Manager: Dr Eberhard Kneipel.

Giessen: Stadttheater Giessen GmbH, Berliner Platz, W-6300 Giessen.
General Music Director: David de Villiers; Manager: Jost Miehlbradt.

Görlitz: Musiktheater der Stadt Görlitz, Demianiplatz 2, Pf 661, 0-8900 Gölitz.
Music Director: Reinhard Seehafer; Manager: Prof Wolf-Dieter Ludwig.

Greifswald: Theater Greifswald, Anklamer Strasse 106, 0-2200 Greifswald.
Chief Conductor: Ekkehard Klemm; Manager: Dieter Wagner.

Gummersbach: Theater der Stadt Gummersbach, Reininghause Strasse, W-5270 Gummersbach.
Music Director and Manager: Gus Anton.

Hagen: Theater Hagen, Elberfelder Strasse 65, W-5800 Hagen.
General Music Director: Gerhard Markson; Manager: Peter Pietzsch.

Halberstadt: Theater Halberstadt, Spiegelstrasse 20a, 0-3600 Halberstadt.
Music Director: Christian Hammer; Manager: Gero Hammer.

Halle an der Saale: Opernhaus Halle, Universitätsring 24, 0-4020 Halle an der Saale.
Music Director: Wolfgang Balzer; Manager: Klaus Froboese.

Hamburg: Hamburgische Staatsoper, Grosse Theaterstrasse 34, Pf 302448, W-2000 Hamburg 36.
General Music Director: Prof Gerd Albrecht; State Opera Manager: Prof Dr Peter Ruzicka.

Hamburg: Neue Flora, Stresemannstrasse 159a, W-2000 Hamburg 50.
Music Director: David Caddick.

Hamburg: Operettenhaus Hamburg, Spielbudenplatz 1, W-2000 Hamburg 36.
Music Director: Koen Schoots.

Hannover: Niedersächsische Staatstheater Hannover, Opernhaus, Opernplatz 1, W-3000 Hannover 1.
General Music Director: Christof Prick; Manager: Hans-Peter Lehmann.

Hannover: Operetten-Tournee-Theater Hannover, Auf dem Lärchenberge 18, W-3000 Hannover 1.
Music Director: Katalin Doman; Artistic Director: Wolfgang Poser.

Heidelberg: Theater der Stadt Heidelberg, Friedrichstrasse 5, W-6900 Heidelberg.
General Music Director: Anton Marik; Manager: Dr Peter Stoltzenberg.

Hildesheim: Stadttheater Hildesheim GmbH, Theaterstrasse 6, W-3200 Hildesheim.
Music Director: Werner Seitzer; Manager: Klaus Engeroff.

Hof an der Saale: Städtebundtheater, Schützenstrasse 8, W-8670 Hof an der Saale.
Music Director: Klaus Straube; Manager: Reinhold Röttger.

Kaiserslautern: Pfalztheater Kaiserslautern, W-6750 Kaiserslautern.
General Music Director: Lior Shambadal; Manager: Pavel Fieber.

Karlsruhe: Badisches Staatstheater Karlsruhe, Baumeisterstrasse 11, Pf 1449, W-7500 Karlsruhe.

OPERA COMPANIES

	General Music Director: Günter Neuhold; General Manager: Günter Könemann.
Kassel:	Staatstheater Kassel, Friedrichsplatz 15, W-3500 Kassel.
	General Music Director: Georg Schmöhe; Manager: Michael Leinert.
Kiel:	Bühnen der Landeshauptstadt Kiel, Opernhause am Kleinein Kiel, Pf 1660, W-2300 Kiel 1.
	General Music Director: Prof Klauspeter Seibel; General Manager: Dr Peter Dannenberg.
Koblenz:	Theater der Stadt Koblenz, Clemensstrasse 1, W-5400 Koblenz 1.
	General Music Director: Christian Kluttig; Manager: Hannes Houska.
Langenhagen:	Kammeroper-Niedersachsen, Eibenstrasse 5c, W-3012 Langenhagen.
	Music Director: Wolfgang M Sieben; Manager: Helmut M Erlwein.
Leipzig:	Oper Leipzig-Musikalische Komödie, Dreilindenstrasse 30, O-7033 Leipzig.
	Music Director: Roland Seiffarth; Manager: Prof Udo Zimmermann.
Leipzig:	Oper Leipzig-Opernhaus, Augustusplatz 12, O-7010 Leipzig.
	Manager: Prof Udo Zimmermann.
Lübeck:	Bühnen der Hansestadt Lübeck, Fischergrube 5-21, W-2400 Lübeck.
	General Music Director: Erich Wächter; General Manager: Dietrich von Oertzen.
Lüneburg:	Stadttheater Lüneburg, An den Reeperbahnen 3, W-2120 Lüneburg.
	Music Director: Michael Dixon; Manager: Jan Aust.
Magdeburg:	Theater der Landeshauptstadt Magdeburg, Universitätsplatz 13, Pf 1240, O-3010 Magdeburg.
	General Music Director: Mathias Husmann; General Manager: Max K Hoffmann.
Mainz:	Staatstheater Mainz, Gutenbergplatz 7, W-6500 Mainz.
	General Music Director: Peter Erckens; Manager: Dr Peter Brenner.
Mannheim:	Nationaltheater Mannheim, Am Goetheplatz, W-6800 Mannheim.
	Manager: Klaus Schultz.
Meiningen:	Das Meininger Theater, Bernhardstrasse 5, O-6100 Meiningen.
	Music Director: Wolfgang Hocke; Manager: Ulrich Burkhard.
Mönchengladbach:	Vereingte Städtische Bühnen Krefeld und Mönchengladbach, Opernhaus, Stadthalle Rheydt, Odenkirchener Strasse 78, W-4050 Mönchengladbach 2.
	General Music Director: Yakov Kreizberg; General Manager: Wolfgang Gropper.
Munich:	Bayerische Staatsoper-Nationaltheater, Max-Joseph-Platz, Pf 100148, W-8000 Munich 1.
	General Music Director: Peter Schneider.
Munich:	Big Bang Theater München, Dachauer Strasse 192, W-8000 Munich 50.
	Music Director: Walter Waidosch.
Munich:	Comédia Opera Instabile, Holzstrasse 11, W-8000 Munich 5.
Munich:	Münchner Opernbühne (Deutsches-Tourneetheater), Damborstrasse 11, W-8900 Augsburg.
	Conductors: Paul Popescu and Tamas Sulyok; Manager: Kurt Rösler.
Munich:	ppp-musiktheater (Pianopianissimo-Musiktheater), Lierstrasse 31, W-8000 Munich 19.
	Music Director: Frank Strobel; Manager: Prof Dr Peter P Pachl.
Munich:	Staatstheater am Gärtnerplatz, Gärtnerplatz 3, W-8000 Munich 5.
	Music Director: Prof Reinhard Schwarz; Manager: Prof Dr Hellmuth Matiasek.
Münster:	Städtische Bühnen Münster, Neubrückenstrasse 63, W-4400 Münster. General Music Director: Will Humburg; General Manager: Achim Thorwald.
Neuburg/Donau:	Neuburger Kammeroper, Willstätter Strasse 18, W-8070 Ingolstadt.
	Conductors: Georg Zettel and Stefan Klingele.
Neustrelitz:	Landestheater Mecklenburg, Friedrich-Ludwig-Jahn-Strasse, O-2080 Neustrelitz.
	Music Director: Golo Berg; Manager: Manfred Straube.
Nordhausen:	Theater Nordhausen, Käthe-Kollwitz-Strasse 15, Pf 109, O-5500 Nordhausen.
	Conductors: Karl-Heinz Richter and Kurt Schafer; Manager: Hubert Kross.
Nürnberg:	Pocket Opera Company Nürnberg, Gertrudstrasse 21, W-8500 Nürnberg 80.
	Music Director: David Seaman; Artistic Director: Peter B Wyrsch.
Nürnberg:	Städtische Bühnen Nürnberg, Richard-Wagner-Platz 2-10, W-8500 Nürnberg 70.
	General Music Director: Christian Thielemann; General Manager: Lew Bogdan.
Oldenburg:	Oldenburgisches Staatstheater, Theaterwall 18, W-2900 Oldenburg.
	General Music Director: Knut Mahlke; General Manager: Hans Häckermann.
Osnabrück:	Städtische Bühnen Osnabrück GmbH, Domhof 10-11, W-4500 Osnabrück.
	General Music Director: Jean-François Monnard; Manager: Norbert Kleine-Borgmann.
Passau:	Südostbayerisches Städtetheater (Fürstbischöfliches Opernhaus), Gottfried-Schäffer-Strasse 2, W-8390 Passau.
	Music Director: Herbert Morasch; Manager: Klaus Schlette.
Pforzheim:	Stadttheater Pforzheim, Am Waisenhausplatz 5, W-7530 Pforzheim.
	General Music Director: Prof Klaus Eisenmann; Manager: Manfred Berben.
Plauen:	Vogtland-Theater Plauen, Theaterstrasse 1-3, O-9900 Plauen.
	Music Director: Paul Theissen; Manager: Dieter Roth.
Potsdam:	Hans-Otto-Theater Potsdam, Zimmerstrasse 10, O-1570 Potsdam.
	Music Director: Stefan Sanderling; Manager: Guido Huonder.
Regensburg:	Städtische Bühnen Regensburg, Bismarckplatz 7, W-8400 Regensburg.
	General Music Director: Hilary Griffiths; Manager: Marietheres List.
Rostock:	Volkstheater Rostock, Patriotischer Weg 33, O-2500 Rostock.
	General Music Director: Michael Zilm; General Manager: Berndt Renne.
Rudolstadt:	Thüringer Landestheater, Anger 1, O-6820 Rudolstadt.
	Music Director: Konrad Bach; Manager: Prof Dr Peter P Pachl.
Saarbrücken:	Saarländisches Staatstheater, Schillerplatz, W-6600 Saarbrücken.
	General Music Director: Jun Märkl; General Manager: Kurt Josef Schildknecht.
Schwerin:	Mecklenburgisches Staatstheater Schwerin, Alter Garten, O-2751 Schwerin.
	General Manager: Mario Krüger.
Stendal:	Theater der Altmark Stendal, Karlsstrasse 4-6, O-3500 Stendal.
	Music Director: Frank Jaremko; Manager: Dr Erdmut Christian August.
Stralsund:	Theater der Hansestadt Stralsund, Olof-Palmer-Platz, O-2300 Stralsund.
	Music Director: Daniel Kleiner; Manager: Thomas Bayer.
Stuttgart:	Staatstheather Stuttgart, Oberer Schlossgarten 6, W-7000 Stuttgart 1.
	Music Director: Gabriele Ferro; General Manager: Prof Wolfgang Gönnenwein.
Trier:	Theater der Stadt Trier, Am Augustinerhof, W-5500 Trier.
	General Music Director: Reinhard Petersen.

OPERA COMPANIES

Ulm:	Süddeutsche Kammeroper, Am Eselsberg 10-12, W-7900 Ulm.
Ulm:	Ulmer Theater, Olgastrasse 73, W-7900 Ulm.
	General Music Director: Alicja Mounk; Manager: Dr Bernd Wilms.
Veitshöchheim:	Bayerische Kammeroper, Rathaus, Gemeinde Veitshöchheim, W-8707 Veitshöchheim.
	Music Director: Prof Siegfried Köhler; Manager: Dr Blagoy Apostolov.
Weimar:	Deutsches Nationaltheater Weimar, Theaterplatz 2, 0-5300 Weimar.
	General Music Director: Hans-Peter Frank; General Manager: Fritz Wendrich.
Wiesbaden:	Hessisches Staatstheater, Christian-Zais-Strasse 3-5, Pf 3247, W-6200 Wiesbaden.
	General Music Director: Oleg Caetani; Manager: Claus Leininger.
Wittenberg:	Elbe-Saale-Bühnen Wittenberg-Bernburg, Thomas-Müntzer-Strasse 14/15, 0-4600 Wittenberg.
	Music Director: Klaus Hofmann; Manager: Helmut Blass.
Wuppertal:	Wuppertaler Bühnen, Opernhaus, Spinnstrasse 4, W-5600 Wuppertal 2.
	General Music Director: Dr Peter Gülke; General Manager: Holk Freytag.
Würzburg:	Städttheater Würzburg, Theaterstrasse 21, W-8700 Würzburg.
	General Music Director: Jonathan Seers; Manager: Dr Tebbe Harms Kleen.
Zeitz:	Theater Zeitz, August-Bebel-Strasse 2, 0-4900 Zeitz.
	Music Director: Hans-Frieder Liebmann; Manager: Wolfgang Eysold.
Zwickau:	Theater Zwickau, Gewandhausstrasse 7, Pf 308, 0-9541 Zwickau.
	Music Director: Albrecht Hofmann; Manager: Horst-Dieter Brand.

GREECE

Athens:	National Opera of Greece, 18-A Harilaou Trikoupi Street, 10679 Athens.

HUNGARY

Budapest:	Magyar Allami Operaház (Hungarian State Opera House), Népöztársaság utja 22, 1061 Budapest.
Debrecen:	Csokonai Szinház (Csokonai Theatre), PO Box 79, 4001 Debrecen.
Pécs:	Pécsi Nemzeti Szinhás (Pécs National Theatre), PO Box 126, 7601 Pécs.
Szeged:	Szegedi Nemzeti Szinház (Szeged National Theatre), PO Box 69, 6701 Szeged.

ICELAND

Reykjavik:	The Icelandic Opera, PO Box 1416, 121 Reykjavik.
	Director: Olöf Kolbrun Hardardottir.

ISRAEL

Tel Aviv:	New Israeli Opera, 7-9 Jerusalem Boulevard, 68114 Tel Aviv.
	Director: Uri Ofer.

ITALY

Bari:	Teatro Petruzzelli, Via Cognetti 26, 70100 Bari.
Bergamo:	Teatro Donizetti, Piazza Cavour 14, 24100 Bergamo.
Bologna:	Teatro Comunale di Bologna, Largo Respighi 1, 40126 Bologna.
	Principal Conductor: Riccardo Chailly; Secretary-General: Sergio Fiorelli.
Brescia:	Teatro Grande, Via Paganora 19, 25100 Brescia.
Cagliari:	Teatro Lirico "G Pierluigi da Palestrina" di Cagliari, Viale Regina Margherita 6, 09100 Cagliari
Catania:	Teatro Massimo Bellini, Via Perrotta 12, 95131 Catania.
Como:	Teatro Sociale, Via Bellini 3, 22100 Como.
Cremona:	Teatro Comunale, Corso Vittorio Emanuele 52, 26100 Cremona.
Ferrara:	Teatro Comunale, Rotonda Foschini 4, 44100 Ferrara.
Florence:	Teatro Comunale di Firenze, Via Solferino 15, 50123 Florence.
	Artistic Director: Bruno Bartoletti; Principal Conductor: Zubin Mehta.
Genoa:	Teatro Comunale dell'Opera di Genova, Via I Frugoni 15/6, 16121 Genoa.
Jesi:	Teatro Comunale "G B Pergolesi", Piazza della Repubblica, 60035 Jesi.
Lecce:	Teatro Politearna Greco, Via XXV Luglio 30, 73100 Lecce.
Lucca:	Teatro Comunale del Giglio, Piazza del Giglio, 55100 Lucca.
Macerata:	Teatro Arena Sferisterio, Piazza Università 5, 62100 Macerata.
Mantua:	Teatro Sociale, Piazza Cavollotti, 46100 Mantua.
Milan:	Teatro alla Scala di Milano, Via Filodrammatici 2, 20121 Milan.
	Superintendent: Carlo Maria Badini; Artistic Director: Cesare Mazzonis; Musical Director: Riccardo Muti.
Modena:	Teatro Comunale, Via del Teatro 8, 41100 Modena.
Naples:	Teatro San Carlo di Napoli, Via S Carlo, 80132 Naples.
	Superintendent:Francesco Canessa.
Novara:	Teatro Coccia, Via Fratelli Rosselli 4, 28100 Novara.
Palermo:	Teatro Massimo di Palermo, Piazza Verdi, 90138 Palermo.
Parma:	Teatro Regio, Via Garibaldi 16, 43100 Parma.
Piacenza:	Teatro Municipale, Via Verdi 41, 29100 Piacenza.
Pisa:	Teatro Comunale "G Verdi", Via Palestro 40, 56200 Pisa.
Ravenna:	Teatro Alighieri, Piazza Garibaldi 5, 48100 Ravenna.

OPERA COMPANIES

Reggio Emilia:	Teatro Municipale "Romolo Valli", Piazza Martiri 7 Luglio, 42100 Reggio Emilia.
Rome:	Teatro dell'Opera di Roma, Piazza B Gigli 8, 00184 Rome.
Rovigo:	Teatro Sociale, Piazza Garibaldi 14, 45100 Rovigo.
Treviso:	Teatro Comunale, Corso del Popolo 31, 31100 Treviso.
Trieste:	Teatro Comunale, "G Verdi" di Trieste, Riva Novembre 1, 34121 Trieste.
Turin:	Teatro Regio di Torino, Piazza Castello 215, 10124 Turin.
Venice:	Teatro La Fenice di Venezia, Campo S Fantin 1965, 30124 Venice.
Verona:	Arena di Verona, Piazza Bra 28, 37121 Verona.

JAPAN

Osaka:	Kansai Nikikai Opera Company, 3-3-9 Bingo-cho, Chyno-ku, Osaka. Director: Makoto Kikawada.
Osaka:	Kansai Opera Group, 3-57 Kyobashi, Higashi-ku, Osaka. Director: Takashi Asahina.
Tokyo:	Mio Nagato, 2-21-12 Daita, Setagaya-ku, Tokyo 155.
Tokyo:	Nihon Opera Shinkokai (Japane Opera Foundation), Akasaka Noa Building, 3-2-12, Akasaka, Minato-ku, Tokyo 107. Chairman: Seiya Matsumoto.

KOREA (SOUTH)

Seoul:	National Opera Group, c/o The National Theatre, Jangchoong-dong, Choong-ku, Seoul. Director: Hyung-Il Ahn.

LATVIA

Riga:	Latvian National Opera, Nometnu iela 62, Riga. Chief Conductor: Viesturs Gallis; General Manager: Juris Savickis.

LITHUANIA

Vilnius:	Lithuanian State Opera and Ballet Theatre, Vienuolio 1, 232600 Vilnius. Chief Conductor: Rimas Geniušas; Administrator: Zigmas Piečaitis.

LUXEMBOURG

Luxembourg:	Théâtre Municipal, 2525 Luxembourg. Director: Jeannot Comes.

MEXICO

México City:	Opera de Bellas Artes, Avenida Hidalgo 1, tercer piso, Centro, México City, DF. Music Director: Enrique Barrios; General Director: Gerardo Kleinburg.

MONACO

Monte Carlo:	Opera de Monte Carlo, Place du Casino, Monte Carlo. Director: John Mordler.

NETHERLANDS

Amsterdam:	De Nederlandse Opera, Waterlooplein 22, 1011 PG Amsterdam. Artistic Director: Pierre Audi; General Administrator: Truze Lodder.

NEW ZEALAND

Auckland:	Mercury Theatre, PO Box 68-257, Newton, Auckland 1. Director: Raymond Hawthorne; General Manager: Allan Spence.
Christchurch:	Canterbury Regional Opera Trust, PO Box 176, Christchurch 1. Chairman: Lewis Brown.
Dunedin:	Dunedin Opera Company, PO Box 533, Dunedin. Chairman: Ian Page.
Wellington:	Wellington City Opera, PO Box 6588, Te Aro, Wellington.

OPERA COMPANIES

NORWAY

Bergen:	Opera Bergen, Kaigaten 15, N-5016 Bergen.
	Artistic Director: Anne Randine Øverby.
Kristiansund:	Operaen i Kristiansund, PO Box 401, N-6501 Kristiansund N.
Oslo:	Den Norske Opera, PO Box 8800 Youngstorget, N-0028 Oslo.
	Artistic Director and General Manager: Sven Olof Eliasson.
Trondheim:	Trondheim Opera, Kongsgårdsgt 2, N-7013 Trondheim.

POLAND

Bydgoszcz:	Bydgoszcz Opera, Al 1 Maja 20, 85-006 Bydgoszcz.
Bytom:	Silesian Opera, Moniuszki 21, 41-902 Bytom.
Gdańsk:	Baltic Opera, Al Zwyciêstwa 15, 80-219 Gdańsk.
	Artistic Director: Janusz Przyolski; Director: Wlodzimierz Nâwotka.
Kraków:	Kraków Music Theatre, Senacka 6, 31-002 Kraków.
	Artistic Director: Ewa Michnik.
Łódź:	Łódź Grand Theatre, Plac Dâbrowskiego, 90-249 Łódź.
	Director: Slawomir Pietras; Administrator: Wojciech Boczkowski.
Poznán:	Poznán Grand Theatre, Fredry 9, 60-967 Poznán.
	Artistic Director: Mieczyslaw Dondajewski; Administrator: Wladyslaw Radomski.
Warsaw:	Warsaw Chamber Opera, Nowogrodzka 49, 00-695 Warsaw.
	Artistic Director: Stefan Sutkowski; Administrator: Danuta Kowalewska-Jawaorska.
Warsaw:	Warsaw Grand Theatre, Plac Teatrainy 1, 00-950 Warsaw.
	Artistic Director: Andrzejstrasz Ynski; Administrator: Arnold Juniter.
Wroclaw:	Wroclaw State Opera, Swidnicka 35, 50-066 Wroclaw.
	Artistic Director: Feliks Tarnawski; Administrator: Janusz Koziorowski.

PORTUGAL

Lisbon:	Companhia de Opera do Teatro Nacional Sao Carlos, Rua Serpa Pinto 9, 1200 Lisbon.
	Artistic Director: Dr José Ribeiro Da Fonte.

RUMANIA

Bucharest:	Bucharest State Operetta, Str Operetei 4, Bucharest.
Bucharest:	Rumanian State Opera, Boulevard Mihail Kogalniceanu 70-72, 70609 Bucharest.
Cluj-Napoca:	Cluj-Napoca Hungarian Opera, Str 1 Mai 26-28, Cluj-Napoca.
Cluj-Napoca:	Cluj-Napoca Rumanian Opera, Piata Stefan cel Mare 24, 3400 Cluj-Napoca.
Iasi:	Iasi Musical Theatre, Str 9 Mai nr 18, 6600 Iasi.
Timisoara:	Timisoara State Opera, Str Mărăsesti 2, Timisoara.

RUSSIA

Moscow:	Bolshoi Theatre, 103009 Moscow.
St Petersburg:	Kirov Opera, St Petersburg.
	Chief Conductor: Valery Gergiev.
St Petersburg:	Maly Opera, St Petersburg.

SLOVAKIA

Bratislava:	Bratislava Chamber Opera, Fučikova 3, 816 01 Bratislava.
Bratislava:	Slovak National Theatre Opera, Gorkého 4, 815 06 Bratislava.

SLOVENIA

Ljubljana:	Slovenian National Theatre Opera, Zupanciceva 1, 61000 Ljubljana.

SOUTH AFRICA

Bloemfontein:	Opera of the Orange Free State Performing Arts Council, PO Box 1292, Bloemfontein 9300.
	General Director: Fred Sharp.
Cape Town:	Opera of the Cape Performing Arts Board, PO Box 4107, Cape Town 8000.
	General Manager: Mike Bosch.
Durban:	Opera of the Natal Performing Arts Council, PO Box 5353, Durban 4000, Natal.
	Administrator: Robert Cross.
Johannesburg:	Johannesburg Operatic and Dramatic Society, PO Box 7010, Johannesburg 2000, Transvaal.
Pretoria:	Opera of the Performing Arts Council, Transvaal, PO Box 566, Pretoria 0001, Transvaal.
	General Manager: Johan Maré.

OPERA COMPANIES

SPAIN

Barcelona:	Gran Teatre del Liceu, Barcelona.
Bilbao:	Bilbao Opera, Bilbao.
Madrid:	Madrid Opera, Madrid.
Oviedo:	Oviedo Opera, Oviedo.

SWEDEN

Göteborg:	Stora Teatern, Box 53116, S-400 15 Göteborg.
	Managing Director: Sven-Gunnar Tillus.
Malmö:	Malmö Stadsteater, Box 17520, S-200 10 Malmö.
	Director: Lasse Larson.
Stockholm:	Drottningholms Slottsteater, PO Box 27050, S-102 51 Stockholm.
	Artistic Director: Elisabeth Söderström.
Stockholm:	Folkoperan, Hornsgatan 72, S-117 21 Stockholm.
	Music Director: Kerstin Nerbe.
Stockholm:	Kungliga Teatern, PO Box 16094, S-103 22 Stockholm.
	General Manager: Eskil Hemberg.
Umea:	Norrlandsoperan, PO Box 360, S-901 08 Umea.
	Director: Per-Erik Ohrn.

SWITZERLAND

Basel:	Theater Basel, Theaterstrasse 7, CH-4010 Basel.
	Music Director: Walter Weller.
Bern:	Stadttheater Bern, Nägeligasse 1, CH-3011 Bern.
	Administrator: Ernst Gosteli.
Biel:	Stadttheater Biel, Burggasse 19, CH-2502 Biel.
	Conductor: Fabrizio Ventura; Administrator: Mario Bettoli.
Geneva:	Grand Théâtre de Genèva, 11 Boulevard du Théâtre, CH-1211 Geneva 11.
	Director: Hughues Gall.
Lausanne:	Opéra de Lausanne, PO Box 3972, CH-1002 Lausanne.
	Director: Renée Auphan.
Lucerne:	Stadttheater Lucerne, Theaterstrasse 2, CH-6002 Lucerne.
	Director: Horst Statkus.
St Gallen:	Stadttheater St Gallen, Museumstrasse 24, CH-9000 St Gallen.
	Director: Hermann Keckeis.
Zürich:	Opernhaus Zürich, Falkenstrasse 1, CH-8008 Zürich.
	Chief Conductor: Ralf Weikert.

TURKEY

Ankara:	Turkish State Opera and Ballet, Opera Binasi, Ankara.
Istanbul:	Istanbul State Opera and Ballet, Atatürk Kültür Merkezi, Taksim, 80124 Istanbul.
Izmir:	Izmir State Opera and Ballet, Izmir.

UK

Belfast:	Opera Northern Ireland, 181a Stranmillis Road, Belfast, Northern Ireland BT9 5DU.
	Artistic Director: Kenneth Montgomery; General Manager: Randall Shannon.
Birmingham:	City of Birmingham Touring Opera, Midlands Arts Centre, Cannon Hill Pk, Birmingham B12 9QH.
	Administrator: John McMurray.
Bristol:	Wessex Opera, 11 Luccombe Hill, Redland, Bristol BS6 6SN.
	Music Director: Paul Webster; General Manager: Richard Evans.
Buxton:	Buxton Festival Opera, 1 Crescent View, Hall Bank, Buxton, Derbys SK17 6EN.
	Artistic Director: Anthony Hose; General Manager: Gordon Monsen.
Cardiff:	Welsh National Opera, John Street, Cardiff, Wales CF1 4SP.
	Music Director: Carlo Rizzi; General Director: Matthew Epstein.
Epsom:	London Opera Group, 14 Downs Way, Downs Road, Epsom, Surrey KT18 5LU.
Glasgow:	Scottish Opera, 39 Elmbank Crescent, Glasgow, Scotland G2 4PT.
	Music Director: Richard Armstrong; Managing Director: Richard Jarman.
Hatfield:	Opera East, Hatfield Polytechnic, PO Box 109, Hatfield, Herts AL10 9AB.
	Artistic Director: Howard Burrell; Administrator: Anne Lee.
Kingston upon Thames:	Opera Factory London Sinfonietta, Kingston Polytechnic, Kingston Hill, Kingston upon Thames, Surrey KT2 7LB.
	Artistic Director: David Freeman; Administrator: Jane Hellings.
Leeds:	Opera North, The Grand Theatre, 46 New Briggate, Leeds, Yorkshire LS1 6NU.
	Music Director: Paul Daniel; General Administrator: Nicholas Payne.
Lewes:	Glyndebourne Festival Opera, Glyndebourne, Lewes, East Sussex BN8 5UU.
	Music Director: Andrew Davis; General Administrator: Anthony Whitworth-Jones.
Lewes:	Glyndebourne Touring Opera, Glyndebourne, Lewes, East Sussex BN8 5UU.
	Music Director: Ivor Bolton; Administrator: Sarah Playfair.
Lewes:	New Sussex Opera, 22 Bradford Road, Lewes, East Sussex BN7 1RB.
	Chairman/Administrator: David James; Music Director: Lionel Friend; Director of Production:

OPERA COMPANIES

	Keith Warner.
Lincoln:	Pavilion Opera Company, Thorpe Tilney Hall, nr Lincoln LN4 3SL.
	Music Director: Bryan Evans; General Manager: Freddie Stockdale.
Llantwit Major:	Music Theatre Wales, St Donats Art Centre, Llantwit Major, S Glam CF6 9WF.
	Artistic Directors: David Ambrose and Michael McCarthy; Administrator: Helen Powers.
London:	Abbey Opera, 68 Queens Gardens, London W2 3AH.
	Conductor: Antony Shelley; Artistic Director: Mary Hill.
London:	British Opera Company, The Coach House, 56 Lawrie Park Gardens, London SE26 6XJ.
	Director: Norman McCann.
London:	Early Opera Project, 15 Percy Street, London W1P 9FD.
	Directors: Kay Lawrence and Roger Norrington; Administrator: Monika Clifford.
London:	English National Opera, London Coliseum, St Martin's Lane, London WC2N 4ES.
	Music Director: Sean Edwards; General Director: Peter Jonas.
London:	London Chamber Opera, 18 Sumner Place, London SW7 3EG.
	Music Director: Charles Farncombe; Managing Director: Elisabeth Parry.
London:	London Opera Players Ltd, 18 Sumner Place, London SW7 3EG.
	Music Director: Peter Gellhorn; Managing Director: Elisabeth Parry.
London:	Midsummer Opera, 90 Grange Road, London W5 3PJ.
	Music Director: David Roblou; Producer: Alan Privett; Director: David Skewes.
London:	Modern Music Theatre Group, 8 York Mansions, 84 Chiltern Street, London W1M 1PT.
	Directors: Paul Barker and Caroline Sharman; Administrator: Antony Pristavec.
London:	Musica nel Chiostro, 377 Liverpool Road, London N1.
	Director: Adam Pollock.
London:	New D'Oyly Carte Opera Company, 20 Stukeley Street, London WC2B 5LR.
	Administrative Manager: Ian Martin; Artistic Director: Bramwell Tovey.
London:	New Sadler's Wells Opera, Sadler's Wells Theatre, Roseberry Avenue, London EC1R 4TN.
	Director: Joseph Karaviotis.
London:	Nexus Opera, 2d Belsize Gardens, London NW3 4LD.
	Artistic Director: Delia Lindon; Music Director: Lionel Friend.
London:	Opera 80, 122 West Block, Westminster Business Square, Durham Street, London SE11 5JH.
	Music Director: Stephen Barlow; Administrator: Clare Foden.
London:	Opera London, 45 Chalcot Road, London NW1 8LS.
	General Director: Jonathan Balkind; Music Director: Richard Hickox.
London:	Opera Rara, 25 Compton Terrace, London N1.
	Music Director: Patric Schmid.
London:	Opera Restor'd, 54 Astonville Street, London SW18 5AJ.
	Administrator: Caroline Anderson; Music Director; Peter Holman; Artistic Director: Jack Edwards.
London:	Opera on the Move, 47 Queen's Drive, London N4 2SZ.
	Directors: Odaline de la Martinez and Linda Hirst.
London:	Pisa Opera Group, Flat 2, 79 Linden Gardens, London W2 4EU.
	Director: Stella J Wright.
London:	Royal Opera House, Covent Garden, London WC2E 9DD.
	Music Director: Bernard Haitink; General Director: Jeremy Isaacs.
London:	Telemann Opera, 1a Warwick Chambers, Pater Street, London W6 6EN.
	Artistic Director: Jill Watt.
Market Harborough:	Travelling Opera, 125 St Mary's Road, Market Harborough, Leics LE16 7DT. Artistic Director: Peter Knapp.
Sherborne:	Dorset Opera, Abbot's Acre, Hospital Lane, Sherborne, Dorset DT9 3JF.
	Music Director: Patrick Shelley; Administrator: Joy Liddiard.
Walton-on-Thames:	Opera Brava, 28 Annett Road, Walton-on-Thames, Surrey KT12 2JR.
	Artistic Director: Bronek Pomorski; Manager: Randall Staley.
Windsor:	Thameside Opera, Hatch House, Oakley Green, Windsor, Berks SL4 5UD.
	Music Director: George Badacsonyi; Administrator: Maurice Maggs.

USA

ALABAMA

Birmingham:	Birmingham Opera Theater, 1 Commerce Center, Suite 1, Birmingham, AL 35203.
	General Director: Martin L Platt.
Mobile:	Mobile Opera Inc, PO Box 8366, Mobile, AL 36689.
	General Manager: Pelham G Pearce Jr.

ALASKA

Anchorage:	Anchorage Opera Company Inc, 1507 Spar Avenue, Anchorage, AK 99501.
	General Manager: Margaret Wood.

ARIZONA

Phoenix:	Arizona Opera Company, 4600 North 12th Street, Phoenix, AZ 85014.
	General Director: Glynn Ross.

ARKANSAS

Little Rock:	Opera Theatre at Wildwood, PO Box 25202, Little Rock, AR 72221.
	Artistic Director: Dr Ann Chotard.

OPERA COMPANIES

CALIFORNIA

Berkeley:	Berkeley Opera, 715 Arlington, Berkeley, CA 94707. General Director: Richard Goodman.
Beverly Hills:	Los Angeles Concert Opera, 2250 Gloaming Way, Beverly Hills, CA 90210. General Director: Loren L Zachary.
Costa Mesa:	Opera Pacific, 650 Town Center Drive, Suite 400, Costa Mesa, CA 92626. General Director: David DiChiera.
Fullerton:	Fullerton Civic Light Opera, 218 West Commonwealth, Fullerton, CA 92632. General Manager: Griff Duncan.
Hollywood:	Casa Italiana Opera Company, 5959 Franklin Avenue, Suite 212, Hollywood, CA 90028. General Director: Mario E Leonetti.
Long Beach:	Long Beach Civic Light Opera, Box 20280, Long Beach, CA 90801. Executive Director: Pegge Logefeil.
Long Beach:	Long Beach Opera, 6372 Pacific Coast Highway, Long Beach, CA 90803. General Director: Michael Milenski.
Los Angeles:	Los Angeles Music Center Opera, 135 North Grand Avenue, Los Angeles, CA 90012. General Director: Peter Hemmings.
Oakland:	Oakland Opera, PO Box 569, Oakland, CA 94604. General Director: Bruce H Kamsler.
Palo Alto:	West Bay Opera, PO Box 1714, Palo Alto, CA 94302. General Director: Maria Holt.
Palm Desert:	West Coast Opera Theatre, PO Box 166, Palm Desert, CA 92661. General Director: Josephine Lomabardo.
Riverside:	Riverside Opera Association, PO Box 2353, Riverside, CA 92516. President: Charles Eisenhard.
Sacramento:	Sacramento Opera Company, 2131 Capitol Avenue, Suite 307, Sacramento, CA 95816. General Director: Marianne Oaks.
San Bernardino:	San Bernardino Civic Light Opera Association, Box 606, San Bernardino, CA 92402. General Manager: C Dale Jenks.
San Diego:	San Diego Civic Light Opera Association, "Starlight", PO Box 3519, San Diego, CA 92103. Executive Director: C E Franks.
San Diego:	San Diego Comic Opera Company, 545 Market Street, Box 1726, San Diego, CA 92101. Managing Director: Kathleen Switzer.
San Diego:	San Diego Opera, PO Box 988, San Diego, CA 92112. General Director: Ian D Campbell.
San Francisco:	San Francisco Opera, War Memorial Opera House, San Francisco, CA 94102. Music Director: Donald Runnicles; General Director: Lotfi Mansouri.
San Francisco:	Western Opera Theater, War Memorial Opera House, San Francisco, CA 94102. Director: Christine Bullin.
San Jose:	Opera San Jose, 12 South First Street, Suite 207, San Jose, CA 95113. General Director: Irene Dalis.
San Jose:	San Jose Civic Light Opera, 4 North Second, No 100, San Jose, CA 95113. Artistic Director: Dianna Shuster.
Stockton:	Stockton Opera, PO Box 7883, Stockton, CA 95267. Executive Director: Jan Neely.

COLORADO

Aspen:	Aspen Music Festival, PO Box AA, Aspen, CO 81612. Music Director: Lawrence Foster; President and Chief Executive Officer: Robert Harth.
Denver:	Central City Opera House Association, 621 17th Street, No 1601, Denver, CO 80293. General Manager: Daniel R Rule.
Denver:	Opera Colorado, 695 South Colorado Boulevard, Suite 20, Denver, CO 80222. President and General Director: Nathaniel Merrill.

CONNECTICUT

Clinton:	Opera Theater of Connecticut, PO Box 733, Clinton, CT 06413. Administrative Director: Kate A Ford.
Darien:	New England Lyric Operetta Inc, Box 79, Darien, CT 06820. President and Artistic Director: William H Edgerton.
Hartford:	Connecticut Opera Association, 226 Farmington Avenue, Hartford, CT 06105. General Director: George D Osborne.
New Haven:	Shubert New Haven Opera Company, 247 College Street, New Haven, CT 06510. General Director: Judith Lisi.
Stamford:	Connecticut Grand Opera, 61 Atlantic Street, Stamford, CT 06901. General Manager: John Hiddlestone.

DELAWARE

Wilmington:	Opera Delaware Inc, St Andrews Annex, 719 North Shipley Street, Wilmington, DE 19801. General Director: Eric W Kjellmark, Jr.

DISTRICT OF COLUMBIA

Washington:	National Lyric Opera Company, 5332 Sherrier Place North West, Washington, DC 20016. General Manager: Nikita Wells.
Washington:	Summer Opera Theatre Company, c/o Benjamin T Rome School of Music, 620 Michigan Avenue North East, Washington, DC 20064. General Manager: Elaine R Walter.

OPERA COMPANIES

Washington: Washington Concert Opera, 1690 36th Street North West, Suite 411, Washington, DC 20007. General Director: Stephen Crout.

Washington: Washington Opera, John F Kennedy Center for the Performing Arts, Washington, DC 20566. Music Director: Heinz Fricke; General Director: Martin Feinstein.

FLORIDA

Clearwater: Tampa Bay Opera, 2035 Arbor Drive, Clearwater, FL 34620. Artistic Director: Mario Laurenti; General Manager: Cynthia Youkon.

Fort Lauderdale: Fort Lauderdale Opera, 333 South West Second Street, Fort Lauderdale, FL 33312. General Manager: William H Martin.

Miami: Greater Miami Opera Association, 1200 Coral Way, Miami, FL 33145. Artistic Director: Willie Anthony Waters; General Manager: Robert M Heuer.

Miami Beach: North Miami Beach Opera, 5225 La Gorce Drive, Miami Beach, FL 33140. Music Director: Laurence Siegel.

Orlando: Orlando Opera Company Inc, c/o Dr Phillips Center for Performing Arts, 1111 North Orange Avenue, Orlando, FL 32804. General Director: Robert Swedberg..

Palm Beach: Palm Beach Opera Inc, 415 South Olive Avenue, West Palm Beach, FL 33401. Artistic Director: Anton Guadagno; General Director: Herbert P Benn.

St Petersburg: Florida Lyric Opera Association/Lyric Opera Theater, 1185-D 85 Terace North, St Petersburg, FL 33702. General Director: Rosalia Maresca.

Sarasota: Sarasota Opera Association, 61 North Pineapple Avenue, Sarasota, FL 34236. Artistic Director: Victor De Renzi; Executive Director: Deane C Allyn.

Tampa: Spanish Lyric Theatre, 1032 Coral Street, Tampa, FL 33602. Artistic Director: Rene Gonzalez.

GEORGIA

Atlanta: Atlanta Opera, 1800 Peachtree Street North West, Suite 620, Atlanta, GA 30309. Artistic Director: William Fred Scott; General Manager: Alfred D Kennedy.

Augusta: Augusta Opera Company, PO Box 3865, Hill Station, Augusta, GA 30904. General Director: Edward Bradberry.

HAWAII

Honolulu: Hawaii Opera Theater, 987 Waimanu Street, Honolulu, HI 96814. General Director: J Mario Ramos.

IDAHO

Boise: Boise Opera Inc, PO Box 1374, Boise, ID 83701. Executive Director: Michael Winter.

ILLINOIS

Chicago: Chamber Opera Chicago, 500 North Orleans, Chicago, IL 60610. Administrative Director: Lawrence Rapchak.

Chicago: Chicago Opera Repertory Theater, PO Box 921, Chicago, IL 60690. Executive Director: Bruce Kamsler.

Chicago: Chicago Opera Theater, 20 East Jackson Boulevard, Suite 1400, Chicago, IL 60604.

Chicago: Lincoln Opera, 2456 North Surrey Court, Chicago, IL 60614. Artistic Director: Norma M Williams.

Chicago: Lyric Opera of Chicago, 20 North Wacker Drive, Chicago, IL 60606. General Director: Ardis Krainik.

Chicago: New Opera Company of Chicago, PO Box 438553, Chicago, IL 60643. Administrative Director: Lane Langford.

Chicago: The Opera Factory, 6161 North Hamilton, Chicago, IL 60659. Executive Director: Blanche Artis Lewis.

Evanston: Light Opera Works, 927 Noyes Street, Evanston, IL 60201. Artistic Director: Philip A Kraus.

Peoria: Peoria Civic Opera, PO Box 120198, Peoria, IL 61614. Manager: Richard Hinds.

INDIANA

Bloomington: Indiana University Opera Theater, School of Music, Indiana University, Bloomington, IN 47405.

Indianapolis: Indiana Opera Theater, 7515 East 30th Street, Indianapolis, IN 46219. Executive/Artistic Director: Elaine Morgan Bookwalter; General Manager: P E MacAllister.

Indianapolis: Indianapolis Opera, 250 East 38th Street, Indianapolis, IN 46205. General Director: Nando Schellen.

Richmond: Whitewater Opera Company Inc, PO Box 633, 805 Promenade, Richmond, IN 47375. Artistic Director and General Manager: Charles Combopiano.

IOWA

Indianola: Des Moines Metro Opera Inc, 106 West Boston Avenue, Indianola, IA 50125. Artistic Director: Robert L Larsen.

OPERA COMPANIES

KENTUCKY

Louisville: Kentucky Opera, 631 South Fifth Street, Louisville, KY 40202.
General Director: Thomson Smillie.

LOUISIANA

Baton Rouge: Baton Rouge Opera Inc, PO Box 2269, Baton Rouge, LA 70821.
Artistic Director: Marioara Trifan.
New Orleans: New Orleans Opera Association, 333 St Charles Avenue, Suite 907, New Orleans, LA 70130.
General Director: Arthur Cosenza.
Shreveport: Shreveport Opera, 212 Texas Street, Suite 101, Shreveport, LA 71101.
General Director: Robert Murray.

MARYLAND

Annapolis: Annapolis Opera Inc, PO Box 24, Annapolis, MD 21201.
Music Director: Ava Shields.
Baltimore: Baltimore Opera Company Inc, 101 West Read Street, Suite 609, Baltimore, MD 21201.
General Director: Michael Harrison.

MASSACHUSETTS

Belmont: Longwood Opera, 197A Beech Street, Belmont, MA 02178.
General Director: J Scott Brumit.
Boston: Boston Lyric Opera Company, 114 State Street, Boston, MA 02109.
General Director: Justin Moss.
Boston: Boston Opera Theater Inc, 300 Massachusetts Avenue, Boston, MA 02115.
Music Director: Craig Smith; Executive Director: Robert Canon.
Boston: Opera Company of Boston Inc, PO Box 50, Boston, MA 02112.
Artistic Director: Sarah Caldwell.
Lee: Berkshire Opera Company, PO Box 598, 17 Main Street, Lee, MA 01238.
Artistic Director: Joel Revzen; Executive Director: Charlotte Kaufman.
Northampton: Commonwealth Opera, 160 Main Street, Northampton, MA 01060.
Artistic Director and Principal Conductor: Richard R Rescia.

MICHIGAN

Detroit: Michigan Opera Theater, 6519 Second Avenue, Detroit, MI 48202.
General Director: David DiChiera; Managing Director: Melodee DuBois.
Detroit: Piccolo Opera Company, c/o Lee Jon Associates, 18662 Fairfield Avenue, Detroit, MI 48221.
Executive Director: Marjorie Gordon.
Grand Rapids: Opera Grand Rapids, 203-B, Waters Building, Grand Rapids, MI 49503.
General Director: Robert Lyall.
Lansing: Opera Comapny of Mid-Michigan, 300 South Washington, Suite 410, Lansing, MI 48933.
Executive Director: Theresa Weller.

MINNESOTA

Minneapolis: Minnesota Opera, 620 North First Street, Minneapolis, MN 55401.
President and General Director: Kevin Smith.
St Paul: North Star Opera, 1863 Eleanor Avenue, St Paul, MN 55116.
Administrative Director: Irma Wachtler.

MISSISSIPPI

Gulfport: Gulf Coast Opera Theatre Inc, PO Box 7067, Gulfport, MS 39501.
President: Dr Laurence M Oden.
Jackson: Mississippi Opera, PO Box 1551, Jackson, MS 39217.
General Director: Frank Marion Johnson.

MISSOURI

Kansas City: Lyric Opera of Kansas City, 1029 Central, Kansas City, MO 64105.
General Artistic Director: Russell Patterson.
St Louis: Opera Theater of Saint Louis, PO Box 191910, St Louis, MO 63119.
General Director: Charles MacKay.
Springfield: Springfield Regional Opera, 305 East Walnut, Springfield, MO 65806.
Managing Artistic Director: James Billings.

NEBRASKA

Omaha: Opera/Omaha Inc, PO Box 807, DTS, Omaha, NE 68101.
General Director: Mary Robert.

NEVADA

Reno: Nevada Opera Association, PO Box 3256, Reno, NV 89505.
Artistic Director: Ted Puffer.

OPERA COMPANIES

NEW JERSEY

Allenhurst: Metro Lyric Opera, 40 Ocean Avenue, Allenhurst, NJ 07711.
General and Artistic Director: Era M Tognoli.
Newark: New Jersey State Opera, 1020 Broad Street, Newark, NJ 07102.
General Director: Alfredo Silipigni.
Ridgewood: Ridgewood Gilbert and Sullivan Opera Company, 956 East Ridgewood Avenue, Ridgewood, NJ 07450.
Music Director: Chester Wolfson.

NEW MEXICO

Albuquerque: Albuquerque Civic Light Opera Association, 4201 Ellison North East, Albuquerque, NM 87109.
Executive Director: Linda E McVey.
Albuquerque: Opera Southwest, 515 15th Street North West, Albuquerque, NM 87104.
Artistic and Music Director: Richard Boldrey.
Santa Fe: Santa Fe Opera, PO Box 2408, Santa Fe, NM 87504.
General Director: John Crosby.

NEW YORK

Binghamton: Tri-Cities Opera Inc, 315 Clinton Street, Binghamton, NY 13905.
Artistic Directors: Carmen Savoca and Peyton Hibbitt; Executive Director: Edward Cordick.
Bronx: Bronx Opera Company, 5 Minerva Place, Bronx, NY 10468.
Artistic Director: Michael Spierman.
Brooklyn: Brooklyn Lyric Opera, 62 Bay 8th Street, Brooklyn, NY 11228.
Artistic Director and General Manager: Norman Myrvik.
Brooklyn: Queens Opera Association Inc, 313 Bay 14th Street, Brooklyn, NY 11214.
General Director: Joe Messina.
Buffalo: Greater Buffalo Opera Company, 24 Linwood Avenue, Buffalo, NY 14209.
Artistic Director: Gary Burgess.
Chautauqua: Chautauqua Opera, Chautauqua Institution, Chautauqua, NY 14722.
General Director: Linda Jackson.
Cooperstown: Glimmerglass Opera, PO Box 191, Cooperstown, NY 13326.
General Director: Paul Kellogg.
Garden City: National Grand Opera Inc, 231 Washington Avenue, 2nd floor, Garden City, NY 11530.
General Director: Linda Holgers.
Glens Falls: Lake George Opera Festival, PO Box 2172, Glens Falls, NY 12801.
General Director: John Balme.
Ithaca: Ithaca Opera, 109 East Seneca Street, Ithaca, NY 14850.
Artistic Director: Deborah Kamer.
New York: American Chamber Opera, 657 West 161st Street, No 3F, New York, NY 10032.
Executive Director: Doug Anderson.
New York: The Juilliard Opera Center, The Juilliard School, Lincoln Center for the Performing Arts, New York, NY 10023.
Artistic Director: Frank Corsaro.
New York: Manhattan Opera Association, PO Box 475, Planetarium Station, New York, NY 10024.
Artistic Director and President: Barbara Norcia.
New York: Metropolitan Opera, Lincoln Center for the Performing Arts, New York, NY 10023.
Artistic Director: James Levine; General Director: Joseph Volpe.
New York: New York City Opera, New York State Theater, Lincoln Center for the Performing Arts, New York, NY 10023.
General Director: Christopher Keene.
New York: New York Gilbert and Sullivan Players Inc, 251 West 91st Street, No 4C, New York, NY 10024.
Artistic Director: Albert Bergeret.
New York: New York Grand Opera, 154 West 57th Street, Suite 125, New York, NY 10019.
Artistic Director: Vincent LaSelva.
New York: Opera at the Academy, New York Academy of Art, 419 Lafayette Street, New York, NY 10003.
Producing Director: Eric Fraad.
New York: Opera Northeast, 530 East 89th Street, New York, NY 10128.
Artistic Director: Donald Westwood.
New York: Opera Orchestra of New York, 239 West 72nd Street, No 2R, New York, NY 10023.
Music Director: Eve Queler; Manager: Alix Barthelmes.
New York: Operaworks Ltd, 170 West 73rd Street, New York, NY 10023.
Director: Joel P Casey.
Rochester: Opera Theatre of Rochester, 494 East Avenue, Rochester, NY 14607.
Executive Director: Glenn A West.
Syracuse: Syracuse Opera Company, PO Box 6904, Syracuse, NY 13217.
Artistic Director: Richard McKee.

NORTH CAROLINA

Charlotte: Opera Carolina, 345 North College Street, Suite 409, Charlotte, NC 28205.
General Director: James W Wright.
Durham: Triangle Opera Theater Association, 120 Morris Street, Durham, NC 27701.
General Manager: Sara Elizabeth Hyre.
Greensboro: Greensboro Opera Company, PO Box 29031, Greensboro, NC 27429.
Conductor: Paul Anthony McRae.
Raleigh: National Opera Company, PO Box 12800, Raleigh, NC 27605.
Artistic Director: Don Wilder.
Winston-Salem: Piedmont Opera Theater Inc, 610 Coliseum Drive, Winston-Salem, NC 27106.

OPERA COMPANIES

General Director: Norman Johnson.

NORTH DAKOTA

Fargo: Fargo-Moorhead Civic Opera Company, 806 NP Avenue, Fargo, ND 58102.
Artistic Director: David F Martin.

OHIO

Cincinnati: CCM Opera/Musical Theater, University of Cincinnati College - Conservatory of Music, Cincinnati, OH 45221.
Artistic Director: Malcolm Fraser.
Cincinnati: Cincinnati Opera Association, Music Hall, 1241 Elm Street, Cincinnati, OH 45210.
Artistic Director: James de Blasis.
Cleveland: Cleveland Opera, 1422 Euclid Avenue, Suite 1052, Cleveland, OH 44115.
General Director: David Bamberger.
Cleveland: Lyric Opera Cleveland, PO Box 06198, Cleveland, OH 44106.
Excutive Director: Michael McConnell.
Columbus: Opera/Columbus, 177 Naghten, Columbus, OH 43215.
General Director: William F Russell.
Dayton: Dayton Opera Association, 125 East First Street, Dayton, OH 45402.
General Director: Jane Nelson.
Middletown: Sorg Opera Company, PO Box 906, Middletown, OH 45042.
Artistic Director and General Manager: Charles Combopiano.
Toledo: Toledo Opera Association, 1700 North Reynolds Road, Toledo, OH 43615.
Artistic Director: James Meena.

OKLAHOMA

Oklahoma City: Lyric Theater of Oklahoma, 2501 North Blackwelder, Oklahoma City, OK 73106.
General Manager: Gayle Pearson.
Tulsa: Tulsa Opera, 1610 South Boulder Avenue, Tulsa, OH 74119.
General Manager: Myrna Smart Ruffner.

OREGON

Eugene: Eugene Opera, PO Box 11200, Eugene, OR 97440.
Artistic Director: James Toland.
Portland: Portland Opera Association Inc, 1516 South West Alder Street, Portland, OR 97205.
General Director: Robert Bailey.

PENNSYLVANIA

Lancaster: Lancaster Opera Company, Box 91, Lancaster, PA 17603.
Artistic Director: Dorothy Rose Smith.
Philadelphia: Opera Company of Philadelphia, Graham Building, 20th Floor, 1 Penn Square West, Philadelphia, PA 19102.
General Director: Robert Driver.
Philadelphia: Pennsylvania Opera Theater, 1217 Sansom Street, 6th Floor, Philadelphia, PA 19107.
General Manager: Patricia Fulvio.
Pittsburgh: Civic Light Opera, 719 Liberty Avenue, Pittsburgh, PA 15222.
Executive Director and General Manager: Charles Gray.
Pittsburgh: Pittsburgh Opera Inc, 711 Penn Avenue, 8th floor, Pittsburgh, PA 15222.
General Director: Tito Capobianco.
Pittsburgh: Opera Theater of Pittsburgh, PO Box 110108, Pittsburgh, PA 15232.
Artistic Director: Gary Race.

PUERTO RICO

Santurce: Teatro de la Opera Inc, PO Box 40734, Minillas Station, Santurce, PR 00940.
Artistic Director: J Raymond Watson.

TENNESSEE

Chattanooga: Chattanooga Opera, 630 Chestnut Street, Chattanooga, TN 37402.
Managing Director: Donald L Andrews.
Knoxville: Knoxville Opera Company, PO Box 16, Knoxville, TN 37901.
General Director: Robert Lyall.
Memphis: Opera Memphis, Memphis State University, South Campus, Building 47, Memphis, TN 38152.
Artistic Director: Michael Ching.
Nashville: Nashville Opera, 1900 Belmont Boulevard, Fidelity Hall, Suite 405, Nashville, TN 37212.
General Director: Kyle Ridout.
Nashville: Tennessee Opera Theatre, 5924 Sedberry Road, Nashville, TN 37205.
Artistic Director: Daniel Killman.

TEXAS

Abilene: Abilene Opera Association, PO Box 6611, Abilene, TX 79608.
President: Danny Mullen.
Austin: Austin Lyric Opera, PO Box 984, Austin, TX 78767.

OPERA COMPANIES

	General Director: Joseph McClain.
Beaumont:	Beaumont Civic Opera, 1030 Harriot Street, Beaumont, TX 77705.
Dallas:	Dallas Opera, The Centrum, 3102 Oak Lawn Avenue, Suite 450, LB-130, Dallas, TX 75219.
	Music Director: Graeme Jenkins; General Director: Plato Karayanis.
Dallas:	Lyric Opera of Dallas, 8111 Preston Boulevard, No 818, Dallas, TX 75225.
	General Director: Charles Kuba.
Fort Worth:	Fort Worth Opera, 3505 West Lancaster, Fort Worth, TX 76107.
	General Director: William Walker.
Houston:	Houston Grand Opera Association, 510 Preston Avenue, Houston, TX 77002.
	Music Director: Vjekoslav Sutej; General Director: R David Gockley.

UTAH

Salt Lake City:	Salt Lake Opera Theatre, 44 West 300 South American Towers, No 807S, Salt Lake City, UT 84101.
	General Director: Robert Zabriskie.
Salt Lake City:	Utah Opera Company, 50 West Second South, Salt Lake City, UT 84101.
	General Director: Anne Ewers.

VIRGINIA

Arlington:	Opera Theatre of Northern Virginia, 2700 South Lang Street, Arlington, VA 22206.
	Artistic Director: John Edward Niles.
Arlington:	Potomac Valley Opera Company, 2218 North Kensington Street, Arlington, VA 22205.
	Director: Richard Wilmer.
Charlottesville:	Ash Lawn-Highland Opera Company, Route 6, Box 37, Charlottesville, VA 22901.
	General Manager: Judith H Walker.
Norfolk:	Virginia Opera, PO Box 2580, Norfolk, VA 23501.
	General Director: Peter Mark.
Roanoke:	Opera Roanoke, Box 1014, Roanoke, VA 24005.
	Artistic Director: Victoria Bond; Executive Director: Judith Clark.
Vienna:	Wolf Trap Opera Company, 1624 Trap Road, Vienna, VA 22182.
	Administrative Director: Peter Russell.

WASHINGTON

Seattle:	Seattle Opera Association, PO Box 9248, Seattle, WA 98109.
	General Director: Speight Jenkins.
Tacoma:	Tacoma Opera, PO Box 7468, Tacoma, WA 98407.
	Executive Director: Ann Farrell.

WISCONSIN

Green Bay:	Pamiro Opera Company, 115 South Jefferson Street, No 301-A, Green Bay, WI 54301.
	Artistic and Music Director: Miroslav Pansky.
Madison:	Madison Opera, 458 Charles Lane, Madison, WI 53711.
	Music Director: Roland Johnson; Manager: Ann Stanke.
Milwaukee:	Florentine Opera Company, 750 North Lincoln Memorial Drive, Milwaukee, WI 53202.
	General Director: Dennis Hanthorn.
Milwaukee:	Milwaukee Opera Company, 820 East Knapp Street, Milwaukee, WI 53202.
	Executive Director: Josephine Busalacchi.
Milwaukee:	Skylight Opera Theatre, 813 North Jefferson, Milwaukee, WI 53202.

UKRAINE

Kiev:	Ukrainian National Opera, Kiev.
Odessa:	Odessa State Opera, Odessa.

VENEZUELA

Caracas:	Opera de Caracas, Museo del Teclado, Parque Central, Edif, Tacaqua, Mezzanina, Caracas 1010.
	Director; Josélgnacio Cabrujas.

YUGOSLAVIA

Belgrade:	Narodno Pozoriste, Francuska 3, 11000 Belgrade.

FESTIVALS

APPENDIX C

FESTIVALS

ARGENTINA

Festival Internacional de Música de San Juan, *25 de Mayo & Urquiza,* 5400 San Juan.

AUSTRALIA

Adelaide Festival of Arts *(Feb-March),* GPO Box 1269, Adelaide, SA 5001.
Australian Festival of Chamber Music *(July),* James Cook University of North Queensland, Townsville, QLD 4811.
Brisbane Warana Festival *(Sept-Oct),* PO Box 3611, South Brisbane, QLD 4101.
Festival of Perth *(Feb-March),* University of Western Australia, Nedlands, WA 6009.
Festival of Sydney *(Jan),* Sydney Committee Ltd, 175 Castlereagh Street, Sydney, NSW 2000.
Melbourne International Festival of Organ and Harpsichord *(Easter Week),* PO Box 92, Parkville, VIC 3052.
Melbourne International Festival of the Arts *(Sept),* 35 City Road, Melbourne, VIC 3205.
Musica Nova *(Aug),* GPO Box 9994, Brisbane, QLD 4001.

AUSTRIA

Ars Electronica *(June),* Untere Donaulände, 7, A-4010 Linz.
Aspekte Salzburg *(June),* Lasserstrasse 6, A-5020 Salzburg.
Bregenz Festival *(July-Aug),* Postfach 311, A-6901 Bregenz.
Carinthian Summer *(June-Aug),* A-9570 Ossiach.
Chamber Music Festival Austria *(Aug-Sept),* Germergasse 16, A-2500 Baden.
Easter Festival Salzburg, Herbert von Karajan Platz, A-5010 Salzburg.
Festival Wien Modern *(Oct-Nov),* Lothringerstrasse 20, A-1030 Vienna.
Festival Wiener Klassik *(April, July, and Dec),* Preindlgasse 1, A-1130 Vienna.
Haydnfestival *(Sept),* Schloss Esterhazy, A-7000 Eisenstadt.
Innsbruck Festival of Early Music *(June-Sept),* Austrian National Tourist Office, 500 Fifth Avenue, Suite 2009, New York, NY 10110.
International Cultural Days and Symposium *(July-Aug),* Postfach 18, A-8692 Neuberg an der Mürz.
International Youth and Music Festival *(July),* Kongresszentrum, A-1014 Vienna.
Internationale Brucknerfest Linz **(Sept-Oct),** Untere Donaulände 7, A-4010 Linz.
Internationale Musikwochen Millstatt *(May-Oct),* Postfach 27, A-9872 Millstatt/See.
Kitzbüheler Sommerkonzerte *(July-Aug),* Stadtgemeinde, A-6730 Kitzbühel.
Mozart Festival Week *(Jan),* Getreidegasse 14/2, A-5020 Salzburg.
Operetta Weeks *(July-Aug),* Wiesingerstrasse 7, A-4820 Bad Ischl.
Salzburg Festival *(July-Aug),* PO Box 140, A-5010 Salzburg.
Salzburg Palace Concerts *(Jan-Dec),* Makartplatz 9, A-5020 Salzburg.
Salzburger Kulturtage *(Oct),* PO Box 42, Waagplatz 1a, A-5010 Salzburg.
Salzburger Operetten Konzerte *(May-Oct),* Lerchenstrasse 33, A-5023 Salzburg.
Schubertiade Feldkirch *(June-July),* Schubertplatz 1, Postfach 625, A-6803 Feldkirch.
Seefestspiele Mörbisch *(June-Aug),* Schloss Esterhazy, A-7000 Eisenstadt.
Styrian Autumn *(Oct),* Sackstrasse 17/1, A-8010 Graz.
Styriarte Graz *(June-July),* Sachsstrasse 17, A-8010 Graz.
Szene: International Theatre and Dance Festival, Salzburg, Anton Neumayr-Platz 2, A-5020 Salzburg.
Vienna Festival *(May-June),* Lehargasse 11, A-1060 Vienna.
Vienna Music Summer *(June-Sept),* Laudongasse 29, A-1080 Vienna.

BELGIUM

Ars Musica: The Spring of Contemporary Music *(March-April),* 18 Place Eugène Flageyplein 18, Room 245, B-1050 Brussels.
Europalia *(Sept-Dec of odd-numbered years),* 10 Rue Royale, B-1000 Brussels.
Festival de Wallonie *(June-Nov),* 29 Rue du Jardin Botanique, B-4000 Liège.
Festival van Vlaanderen-Antwerpen *(Aug-Sept),* Stadhuis, Grote Markt, B-2000 Antwerp.
Festival van Vlaanderen *(April-Oct),* Flageyplein 18, B-1050 Brussels.
Week of Contemporary Music *(Feb),* Muzikon vzw, Hoogpoort 64, B-9000 Ghent.

BERMUDA

Bermuda Festival *(Jan-Feb),* PO Box HM 297, Hamilton HM AX.

BRAZIL

Bienal de Música Contemporânes Brasileira *(Nov of odd-numbered years),* Sala Cecilia Meireles, Largo da Lapa 47, Lapa, CEP 20021 Rio de Janeiro.
Festival Música Nova de Santos, Sociedade Ars Viva, Rua Barão de Paranapiacaba 31, 11050 Santos.
Festival Villa-Lobos *(Nov),* Rua Sorocaba 200, 22271 Rio de Janeiro.

FESTIVALS

Petrópolis Summer *(Jan-Feb)* **and Winter** *(June-Aug)* **Festivals,** Rua Franio Peixoto 134, Bingen, 25600 Petrópolis.

BULGARIA

Apollonia *(April, Sept and Dec),* 54/B Korab Planina Street, 1125 Sofia.
March Music Days, Sofia Music Weeks *(May-June),* **Chamber Music Festival** *(June),* **and Varna Summer** *(June-July),* PO Box 387, 1090 Sofia.

CANADA

Banff Festival of the Arts *(June-Aug),* Box 1020, Banff, Alta, T0L 0C0.
Calgary International Organ Festival *(Oct),* 237 Eighth Avenue South East, No 315, Calgary, Alta, T2G 5C3.
Charlottetown Festival *(June-Oct),* PO Box 848, Charlottetown, PEI, CIA 7L9.
Festival International de Lanaudière *(June-Aug),* 1500 Base-de-Roc Boulevard, Joliette, PQ J6E 3Z1.
Festival International de Musique Baroque *(July),* PO Box 644, Lameque, NB E0B 1V0.
Festival of the Sound *(July-Aug),* PO Box 750, Parry Sound, Ontario, P2A 2Z1.
Guelph Spring Festival *(May),* PO Box 1718, Guelph, Ontario, N1H 6Z9.
International Choral Festival **(May-June),** 70 York Street, 3rd Floor, Toronto, Ont, M5J 1S9.
Scotia Festival of Music *(May-June),* 1541 Barrington Street, Suite 317, Halifax, NS, B3J 1Z5.
Shaw Festival *(April-Nov),* PO Box 774, Niagara-on-the-Lake, Ont L0S 1J0.
Vancouver Early Music Summer Festival *(July-Aug),* 1254 West Seventh Avenue, Vancouver, BC V6H 1B6.
Victoria International Festival *(July-Aug),* 3400 Richmond Road, Victoria, BC, V8P 4P5.

CROATIA

Zagreb Musical Biennale, PO Box 438, Trnjanska bb, 41000 Zagreb.

CZECH REPUBLIC

Brno International Music Festival *(Sept-Oct),* Radnická 10, 602 00 Brno.
Prague Cultural Summer *(June-Sept),* nam. Republiky 5, 110 00 Prague 1.
Prague Easter Festival, Sonus, Pod Smukýřkou 1049, 150 00 Prague 5.
Prague Festival *(Sept-Oct),* Sonus, Pod Smukýřkou 1049, 150 00 Prague 5.
Prague Spring International Music Festival *(May-June),* Hellichova 18, 118 00 Prague 1.

DENMARK

Århus Festival *(Sept),* Thomas Jensens Allé, DK-Århus C.
Ebeltoft Festival *(July),* Torvet 9-11, DK-8400 Ebeltoft.
Fanø Music Festival *(June, July and Aug),* Toftestein 21, Sønderho, DK-6720 Fanø.
Lerchenborg Music Days *(July-Aug),* Tuborgvej 99, DK-2900 Hellerup.
Numus Festival *(April-May),* Valkendorfsgade 3, DK-1151 Copenhagen K.
Royal Danish Ballet and Opera Festival, PO Box 2185, DK-1017 Copenhagen.

EIRE

Adare Festival *(July),* Adare Manor, Adare, County Limerick.
Cork International Choral Festival *(April),* PO Box 68, Cork.
Dublin International Organ and Choral Festival *(Sept),* City Hall, Dublin 2.
Galway Arts Festival *(July),* The Cornstone, Galway.
Kilkenny Arts Week *(Aug),* 22 Rosehill Court, Kilkenny.
Waterford International Festival of Light Opera *(Sept-Oct),* 60 Morrissons Avenue, Waterford.
Wexford Festival Opera *(Oct-Nov),* Theatre Royal, Wexford.

FINLAND

Finland Festivals *(year-round),* PO Box 56, SF-00101 Helsinki.
Helsinki Festival *(Aug-Sept),* Unioninkatu 28, SF-00100 Helsinki.
Joensuu Song Festival *(June),* Koskikatu 1, SF-80100 Joensuu.
Jyväskylä Arts Festival *(June),* Kauppakatu 14 A 4, SF-40100 Jyväskylä.
Kangasniemi Music Festival *(June-July),* Kulttuuritoimisto, SF-51200 Kangasniemi.
Karjaa Music Festival *(June-July),* Rantatie 1, SF-10300 Karjaa.
Korsholm Music Festival *(June-July),* Festival Office, SF-65610 Korsholm.
Kuhmo Chamber Music Festival *(July-Aug),* Fredrikinkatu 77 A 2-4, SF-00100 Helsinki 10.
Lahti Organ Festival *(Aug),* Kirkkokatu 5, SF-15110 Lahti 11.
Oulu Music Festival *(Jan-May),* Lintulammentie 1 K, SF-90140 Oulu.
Naantali Music Festival *(June),* PO Box 46, SF-21101 Naantali.
Savonlinna Opera Festival *(June-July),* Olavinkatu 35, SF-57130 Savonlinna.
Suvisoitto-Porvoo Summer Sounds *(June-July),* Erottajankatu 19 D 21, SF-00130 Helsinki.
Tampere Biennale *(April),* Tullikamarinaukio 2, SF-33100 Tampere.
Time of Music *(July),* Kunnantalo, SF-44500 Vitasaari.
Turku Music Festival *(Aug),* Uudenmaankatu 1 A, SF-20500 Turku.

FESTIVALS

FRANCE

Academie internationale d'Art Musicale: Festival Semaines Musicales de Tours *(July),*   17 Rue des Ursulines, F-37000 Tours.
Avignon Festival *(July-Aug),*   8 bis Rue de Mons, F-84000 Avignon.
Biennale de la Musique Française *(Sept of odd-numbered years),*   Masion de Lyon, Place Bellecour, F-69002 Lyon.
Chorégies d'Orange *(July-Aug),*   18 Place Silvain, BP 205, F-84107 Orange Cédex.
Festival d'Art Sacré de la Ville de Paris *(Oct-Dec),*   17 Rue de l'Arbe Sec, F-75001 Paris.
Festival d'Automné à Paris *(Sept-Dec),*   156 Rue de Rivoli, F-75001 Paris.
Festival de Chartres/Grandes Orgues de Chartres *(July and Sept),*   75 Rue de Grenelle, F-75007 Paris.
Festival de Colmar *(July),*   4 Rue des Unterlinden, F-68000 Colmar.
Festival del la Rochelle *(June-July),*   26 Rue Washington, F-75008 Paris.
Festival de L'Ile de France *(Sept-Oct),*   26 Rue de Gramont, F-75002 Paris.
Festival de Paris *(May-June),*   2 Rue Edouard Colonne, F-75001 Paris.
Festival de Prades *(July-Aug),*   Rue Victor Hugo, F-66500 Prades.
Festival de Versailles *(May-June),*   Maire de Versailles, RP 144, F-78011 Versailles.
Festival de Ville d'Avray *(May-June),*   10 Rue de Marnes, F-92410 Ville d'Avray.
Festival des instruments Anciens *(March-April),*   58 Rue Viollet-le-Duc, F-94210 St Maur La Varenne.
Festival des Nations Europeennes *(July),*   BP 60, F-68140 Munster.
Festival du Comminges *(July-Aug),*   Academie Internationale, F-31260 Mazeres-sur-Salat.
Festival Estival de Paris *(July-Sept),*   20 Rue Geoffroy l'Asnier, F-75004 Paris.
Festival International Atlantique *(June-Aug),*   7 quai de Versailles, F-44000 Nantes Cédex.
Festival international d'Art Lyrique et de Musique *(July-Aug),*   Palais de l'Ancien Archevêché, F-13100 Aix-en-Provence.
Festival international d'Eté de Nantes *(July),*   Porte St Pierre, Rue de l'Evêché, F-44000 Nantes.
Festival international de Besançon et Franche-Comte *(Aug-Sept),*   2d Rue Isenbart, F-25000 Besançon.
Festival international de Carpentras *(July-Aug),*   La Charité, Rue Cottier, BP 113, F-84204 Carpentras Cédex.
Festival international de Chant Choral *(May),*   5 Square Grandjean, F-54220 Malzeville.
Festival international de Musique Sacrée de Lourdes *(Easter),*   Place du Champ Commun, F-65100 Lourdes.
Festival international de Musique de Toulon *(May-June),*   Palais de la Bourse, Avenue Jean-Moulin, F-83000 Toulon.
Festival international des Musiques d'Aujourd'hui de Strasbourg *(Sept-Oct),*   9 Rue de Général Frère, F-67000 Strasbourg.
Festival J S Bach *(July-Aug),*   Palais Delphinal, F-26260 Saint-Donat-sur-Herbasse.
Festival Mediterranéen *(June-Aug),*   BP 4, F-13129 Salin de Giraud.
Festival Musique en Sorbonne *(June-July),*   2 Rue Francis de Croisset, F-75018 Paris.
Fêtes Musicales en Touraine *(June),*   Hôtel de Ville, F-37032 Tours Cédex.
Lille Festival *(Oct-Dec),*   64 Avenue President J F Kennedy, F-59800 Lille.
Mai Musical de Bordeaux *(May),*   Grand Théâtre, Place de la Comédie, F-33074 Bordeaux Cédex.
Musique Action *(May),*   BP 126, Centre Culturel André Malraux, F-54504 Vandoevre-les-Nancy Cédex.
Nuits de la Fondation Maeght *(July),*   Fondation Maeght, F-06570 St Paul-de-Vence.
Recontres d'Eté de la Chartruese *(July),*   La Chartreuse, BP 30, F-30400 Villeneuve-les-Avignon.
Recontres internationales de la Guitare *(July),*   Hôtel de Ville, BP 114, F-65013 Tarbes Cédex.
Recontres Musicales d'Evian *(May),*   Château de Blonay, F-74500 Evain les Bains.
Strasbourg Festival *(June-July),*   24 Rue de la Mésange, F-67081 Strasbourg.

GERMANY

Augsburger Mozart-Sommer *(Aug-Sept),*   Kulturamt, Maximilianstrasse 36, 8900 Augsburg.
Bachfest der Neuen Bachgesellschaft *(June-July),*   Johann Sebastian Bach Platz, 7000 Stuttgart.
Bach Festival Berlin *(July),*   Bismarckstrasse 73, 1000 Berlin 12.
Bach Week *(June),*   Rathaus, 2120 Lüneburg.
Bachwoche Ansbach *(July-Aug of odd-numbered years),*   Postfach 1741, 8800 Ansbach.
Bad Hersfeld Festival Concerts and Opera *(June-Aug),*   Nachtigallenstrasse 9, 6430 Bad Hersfeld.
Berliner Festwochen *(Sept),*   Budapeststrasse 50, 1000 Berlin 30.
Bodensee Festival *(May-June),*   Spanierstrasse 3, 7750 Konstanz.
Bonner Herbst *(Oct-Nov),*   Wachsbleiche 21, 5300 Bonn 1.
Brahms Days *(May of odd-numbered years),*   PO Box 1609, 7560 Gaggenau.
Brühler Schlosskonzerte eV *(May-Sept),*   Schlossstrasse 2, 5040 Brühl.
Cloister Concerts *(June-Aug),*   Kurverwaltung Alpirsbach, 7297 Alpirsbach.
Collegium Musicum Schloss Pommersfelden *(July-Aug),*   Austrasse 10, 8501 Burgthann/Dörlbach.
Corveyer Musikwochen *(May-June),*   Stadtverwaltung/Stadthaus am Petritor, 3470 Höxter 1.
Das Treffen *(Aug),*   PO Box 100642, 8580 Bayreuth.
Deutsches Mozartfest Augsburg *(Sept),*   Deutsche Mozart Gesellschaft eV, Karlstrasse 6, 8900 Augsburg.
Dollart Festival,   Postfach 1580, 2960 Aurich 1.
Donaueschingen Festival of Contemporary Music *(Oct),*   Südwestfunk Baden-Baden, PO Box 820, 7570 Baden-Baden.
Dresdner Musikfestspiele *(May-June),*   Güntzstrasse 31, Postfach 6, 8016 Dresden.
Dresdner Tage der Zeitgenössischen Musik *(Oct),*   Schevenstrasse 17/150-05, 8054 Dresden.
Ettingen Schloss-Festspiele *(June-Aug),*   Postfach 0762, 7505 Ettingen.
European Festival *(June-July),*   Dr Hans Kaptingerstrasse 22, 8390 Passau.
Festliche Sommer in der Wies *(June-Aug),*   Bahnhofstrasse 44, 8920 Schongau.
Festspiele am Roten Tor *(July),*   Kasernstrasse 4-6, 8900 Augsburg.
Feuchtwangen Kreuzgangspiele *(June-Aug),*   Marktplatz, 8805 Feuchtwangen.
Gandersheimer Donfestspiele *(June-Aug),*   Barfüsserkloster 15, 3353 Bad Gandersheim.
Gewandhaus-Festtage Leipzig *(June),*   Augustusplatz 8, 7010 Leipzig.
Göttingen Handel Festival *(June),*   Hainholzweg 3-5, 3400 Göttingen.
Händelfestspiele in Halle *(June),*   Kleine Brauhausstrasse 26, 4020 Halle.
Heidelberg Castle Festival *(July-Aug),*   Friedrichstrasse 5, 6900 Heidelberg.
Herbstliche Musiktage Bad Urach *(Sept-Oct),*   Postfach 1240, 7432 Bad Urach.

FESTIVALS

Hitzacker Summer Music Festival *(July-Aug),* Barkhausenweg 12, 2000 Hamburg.
International Castle Concerts *(April-Oct),* Schloss, 8851 Leitheim bei Donauwörth.
International May Festival *(May),* Postfach 3247, 6200 Wiesbaden.
International Organ Festival *(Oct of odd-numbered years),* Jacobikirchof 3, 3400 Göttingen.
Internationale Januar Musiktage, Ost-West Musiktage, and Melos Musiktage *(Jan and June),* Schloss Elmau, 8101 Klais/Oberbayern.
Internationale Orgelwoche Nürnberg-Music Sacra *(June-July),* Bismarckstrasse 46, 8500 Nürnberg.
Internationales Beethovenfest Bonn *(triennial),* Wachsbleiche 21, 5300 Bonn.
Kassel Music Festival *(Oct),* Friedrich Ebertstrasse 159, 3500 Kassel.
Kissinger Sommer Music Festival *(June-July),* Postfach 2260, 8730 Bad Kissingen.
Leitheim Schloss Concerts *(May-Oct),* Schloss Leitheim, 8851 Kaisheim.
Limburger Organ Vespers *(April-Aug),* Städtisches Verkehrsamt, 6250 Limburg an der Lahn.
Ludwigsburger Schlossfestspiele/Internationale Festspiele Baden-Württemberg *(May-Sept),* Postfach 1022, 7140 Ludwigsburg.
Münchener Biennale, Rindermarkt 3-4, 8000 Munich 2.
Munich Opera Festival *(July-Aug),* PO Box 100148, 8000 Munich 1.
Music in the 20th Century *(May),* Postfach 1050, 6600 Saarbrucken.
Musica Bayreuth *(May),* Ludwigstrasse 26, 8580 Bayreuth.
Musik-Biennale Berlin *(March),* Budapesterstrasse 50, 1000 Berlin 30.
Musikfest Hamburg *(Sept),* Grosse Theaterstrasse 34, 2000 Hamburg 36.
Musiksommer Obermain *(May-Dec),* Bambergerstrasse 25, 8623 Staffelstein.
Nymphenburg Summer Festival, Zuccalistrasse 21, 8000 Munich 19.
Opera Festival Eutiner Sommerspiele GmbH *(July-Aug),* Postfach 112, 2420 Eutin/Holstein.
Palace Courtyard Serenade Concerts *(June-July),* Friedrichstrasse 5, 6900 Heidelberg.
Pro Musica Nova *(May),* Heinrich-Hertzstrasse 13, 2800 Bremen.
Richard Wagner Festival *(July-Aug),* PO Box 100262, 8580 Bayreuth 2.
Ruhrfestival-Europäisches Festival *(May-June),* Otto Burrmeister Alle 1, 4350 Recklinghausen.
Schleswig-Holstein Music Festival *(June-Aug),* Holzdamm 40, 2000 Hamburg 1.
Schwetzingen Festival *(Aprile-June),* Schlossplatz, 6830 Schwetzingen.
Tage Alter Musik *(June),* Postfach 100830, 8400 Regensburg.
Tage für Neue Musik *(Oct-Nov),* Kornbergstrasse 32, 7000 Stuttgart 1.
Tage Neuer Kammermusik Braunschweig *(Nov-Dec),* Steintorwall 3, 3300 Braunschweig.
Telemann-Festtage *(March),* Liebigstrasse 10, 3010 Magdeburg.
Witten Festival of Contemporary Chamber Music *(April),* Bergerstrasse 25, 5810 Witten.
Würzburg Bach Festival *(Nov),* Hofstallstrasse 5, 8700 Würzburg.
Würzburg Mozart Festival *(June),* Haus zum Falken, 8700 Würzburg.
Zelt Music Festival Freiburg *(June),* 10 Haslacherstrasse, 7800 Freiburg.

GREECE

Athens Festival *(June-Sept),* 1 Voukourestiou Street, 10564 Athens.
Iraklion Summer Festival, 71202 Iraklion, Crete.
Patras International Festival *(June-Aug),* PO Box 1184, 26110 Patras.

HONG KONG

Hong Kong Arts Festival *(Jan-Feb),* GPO Box 2547, Hong Kong.

HUNGARY

Beethoven Concerts *(June-Aug),* Vörösmarty tér 1, 1364 Budapest.
Budapest Arts Festival *(Sept-Oct),* Vörösmarty tér 1, 1051 Budapest.
Budapest Autumn Festival *(Sept-Oct),* Pf 95, H-1525 Budapest.
Budapest Spring Festival *(March),* Vörösmarty tér 1, PO Box 80, Budapest.
Esztergom International Guitar Festival *(Aug),* PO Box 38, H-2501 Esztergom.
Open Air Theatre-Summer Festival *(June-Aug),* Pf 95, H-1525 Budapest.
Sopron Early Music Days *(June),* PO Box 80, 1366 Budapest.

ICELAND

Dark Music Days *(Jan-Feb),* Laufásvegur 40, 101 Reykjavík.
Reykjavík Arts Festival *(June),* PO Box 88, 101 Reykjavík.

ISRAEL

Ein Gev Music Festival *(Passover),* Ein Gev, 14940 Kibbutz Ein Gev.
Israel Festival *(May-June),* PO Box 4072, 91040 Jerusalem.
Kol-Israel, Upper Galliee Chamber Music Days *(July-Aug),* Hakirya, 61070 Tel Aviv.
Vocalisa 90 *(April),* PO Box 515, 20101 Carmiel.

ITALY

Antidogma Musica Festival *(Sept-Oct),* Via Alberto Nota 3, 10122 Turin.
Aterforum *(June-July),* Piazzetta Sant'Anna 3, Int 8, 44100 Ferrara.
Autunno Musicale a Como *(Sept-Oct),* Via Cantoni 1, 22100 Como.

FESTIVALS

Biennale di Venezia, Festival Internazionale di Musica Contemporanea *(Sept-Oct)*, Ca'Giustinian, S Marco, 30100 Venice.
Il Canto delle Pietro-Musiche Sacre e Spiritual nel Monumenti Romantici Lombardi *(April-June)*, Via Cantoni 1, 22100 Como.
Ente Autonomo Spettacoli Lirici Arena di Verona *(July-Aug)*, Piazza Bra 28, 37121 Verona.
Estate Maceratese *(July)*, Arena Sferisterio, 62100 Macerata.
Festa Musica Pro Mundo Uno *(July-Aug)*, Via di Villa Maggiorani 20, 00168 Rome.
Festival Barocco *(May and Sept)*, Corso Massimo d'Azeglio, 10126 Turin.
Festival dell'Opera Siciliana e Taormina *(Oct)*, Via Cavour 117, 90133 Palermo.
Festival dell'organo/Festival del clavicembalo, Via dei Banchi Vecchi 61, 00153 Rome.
Festival di Musica Antica *(July)*, Via Zeffirino Re 2, 47023 Cesena.
Festival di Musica Contemporanea "900 Musicale Europeo" *(Oct)*, Via Capodimonte 23, 80131 Naples.
Festival di Musica Sacra, Villa Igea, 90142 Palermo.
Festival de Opera Barga *(July-Aug)*, Via della Fornacetta 11, 55051 Barga (Lucca).
Festival Internazionale di Musica Antica *(July)*, Via F Confalonieri 5, 00195 Rome.
Festival Internazionale di Musica Classica e Contemporanea *(June-July)*, PO Box N95, 16038 Santa Margherita Ligure.
Festival Mozart in Lombardia *(Sept-Nov)*, Via Cantoni 1, 22100 Como.
Festival of Contemporary Music "Nuovi Spazi Musicali" *(June)*, Via Divisione Torin 139, 00143 Rome.
Festival of Two Worlds *(June-July)*, Palazzo Ancaiani, 06049 Spoleto.
Festival Pontino *(June-July)*, Via Ecetra 36, 04100 Latina.
Festival Romaeuropa *(May-July)*, Via Sistina 48, 00187 Rome.
Festival Spaziomusica *(Oct-Nov)*, Via Liguria 60, 09127 Cagliari.
Gli Incontri Musicale Romani, Largo Nazzareno 8, 00187 Rome.
Gubbio Festival *(July-Aug)*, Corso Garibaldi 88, 06024 Gubbio.
Incontri con La Nuova Musica *(Nov-Dec)*, PO Box 196, 25100 Brescia.
International Chamber Music Festival of Asolo *(Aug-Sept)*, Via Browning 141, 31011 Asolo.
Lucca in Villa Festival *(Aug)*, Via Turati 31, 55049 Viareggio, Lucca.
Maggio Musicale Fiorentino *(April-July)*, Via Solferino 15, 50123 Florence.
Musica 2000 Festival *(April)*, 8 Via Alpi, 60131 Ancona.
Musica Verticale Festival *(Oct-Nov)*, Via Lamarmora 18, 00185 Rome.
Puccini Festival *(July-Aug)*, Piazza Belvedere Puccini 4, 55048 Lucca.
Rassegna di Nuova Musica *(May-June)*, Arena Sferisterio, CP 92, 62100 Macerata.
Ravenna Festival *(June-July)*, Via Gordini 27, 48100 Ravenna.
Rome Festival *(May-Aug and Oct-Nov)*, Via Francesco Duodo 49, 00136 Rome.
Rossini Opera Festival *(Aug)*, Via Rossini 37, 61100 Pesaro.
Sagra Musical al Tempio Maiatestiano *(Sept)*, 47037 Rimini.
Sagra Musicale Umbra *(Oct)*, Cas Post No 341, 06100 Perugia.
Settembre Musica *(Aug-Sept)*, Piazza S Carlo 161, 10123 Turin.
Settimane Musicali di Stresa *(Aug-Sept)*, Via R Bonghi 4, 28049 Stresa.
Settimane Musicali Senese *(July)*, Via di Città 89, 53100 Siena.
I Suoni del Tempo *(July)*, Via Zeffirino Re 2, 47023 Cesena.
Taormina Arte *(July-Sept)*, Via Pirandello 31, 98039 Taormina.
Trieste Prima, Incontri internazionale con la Musica Contemporanea *(Sept)*, Via Settefontane 30, 34141 Trieste.
Veneto Festival *(May-July)*, Piazzale Pontecorvo 4a, 35100 Padua.
Verdi Festival *(Sept)*, Via Farini 34, 43100 Parma.

JAPAN

Japan International Chamber Music Festival *(April-May)*, 32-11-411 Kamikitazawa 4-chome, Setagaya-ku, Tokyo.
Kusutsu International Summer Music Academy and Festival in Gumma-ken *(Aug)*, Aoyama Ten-X 8F, 5-50-6, Jingumae, Shibuya-ky, Tokyo 150.
Min-On Contemporary Music Festival *(June)*, 1-32-13 Kita-Shinjuku, Shinjuku-ku, Tokyo 169.
National Arts Festival *(Oct-Nov)*, Ministry of Education, Tokyo 100.
Osaka International Festival Society *(April)*, New Asahi Building, Nakanoshima 2-3-18, Kita-ku, Osaka 530.
Pacific Music Festival *(July-Aug)*, Kondon Orient Building, 11-11, 8 Chome, Ginza, Chuo-ko, Tokyo 104.
Tokyo City Arts Festival *(Jan-March)*, 3-5 Marunouchi, Chiyoda-ku, Tokyo.
Tokyo Summer Festival *(July)*, Copacabana Building, 5F, 3-6-4 Akasaka, Minato-ku, Tokyo 107.

KOREA (SOUTH)

Autumn Music Festival in Seoul *(Oct-Nov)*, Dong-Hwa Building, Suite 210, 43-1, Pil-Dong 1-Ga, Choong-gu, Seoul 100-271.
Seoul International Music Festival *(Oct-Nov)*, Korean Broadcasting System, 18 Yoido-dong, Youngdungpo-gu, Seoul 150-790.

LITHUANIA

Baltic Music Festival *(Oct)*, Mickevičiaus 29, 2600 Vilnius.

LUXEMBOURG

Festival Européen de Wiltz-Luxembourg *(July)*, Château de Wiltz, 9516 Wiltz.
Festival International Echternach Luxembourg *(May-June)*, Parvis de la Basilique 9, 6486 Echternach.

FESTIVALS

MACAO

International Music Festival of Macao *(Oct)*,   Avda Aviso Gonçalves Zarco, s/n, 1st Floor, Macao.

MEXICO

Festival de Música de Cámara de San Miguel de Allende *(July-Aug)*,   Calle Hernádez Macias 75, San Miguel de Allende.
Festival de San Miguel de Allende *(Dec)*,   Hospicio 48, San Miguel de Allende.
Festival Internacional Cervantino *(Oct)*,   Alvaro Obregón 273, 06700 Mexico, DF.

MONACO

Printemps des Arts de Monte Carlo *(April-May)*,   Rue Louis Notari, MC 98000 Monaco.

NETHERLANDS

Festival Amsterdam Chamber Music Society *(March and Nov)*,   Ceintuurbaan 376, 1073 EM Amsterdam.
Festival Nieuwe Muziek *(June-July)*,   Postbox 15, 4330 AA Middleburg.
Haarlem Organ Festival *(July)*,   Postbus 511, 2003 PB Haarlem.
Holland Festival *(June)*,   Kleine-Gartmanplantsoen 21, 1071 RP Amsterdam.
Holland Festival Early Music Utrecht *(Aug-Sept)*,   3500 AS Utrecht.
International Gaudeamus Music Week *(Sept)*,   Swammerdamstr 38, 1090 RV Amsterdam.
New Music Festival Maastricht *(Sept)*,   St Maartenspoort 2, 6221 BA Maastricht.

NEW ZEALAND

New Zealand International Festival of the Arts *(Feb-March)*,   PO Box 10113, Wellington 6036.

NORWAY

Bergen International Festival *(June)*,   PO Box 183, N-5001 Bergen.
Elverum Festival *(Aug)*,   PO Box 313, N-2401 Elverum.
Northern Norway Festival *(June)*,   Box 901, N-9401 Harstad.
Oslo Sommeropera *(June)*,   Grev Wedels Plass 2, N-0151 Oslo.
St Olav Festival of Trondheim *(July-Aug)*,   Kongsgårdsgata 2, N-7013 Trondheim.
Stord International Choir Festival *(June)*,   Box 308, N-5401 Stord.

PHILIPPINES

Philippine Music Festival *(Oct-Nov)*,   NAMCYA-FAT, CCP Complex, Roxas Boulevard, Manila.

POLAND

Festival of Early Music of Central and Eastern Europe *(Sept)*,   Libelta 16, 85-080 Bydgoszcz.
Henryk Wieniawski Days *(June)*,   Tadeusza Kościuszki nr 19, 58-310 Szczawno-Zdrój.
International Oratorio and Cantata Festival *(Sept)*,   Rynek-Ratusz 24, 50-1010 Wroclaw.
Music in Old Kraków *(Aug)*,   ul Zwierzyniecka 1, 31-103 Kraków.
Polish and International Music Festival *(May)*,   Chopina 30, 35-055 Rzeszów.
Polish Violin Festival "Grazyna Bacewicz" *(March)*,   Kakielów 16, 42-200 Czestochowa.
Poznań Spring Music Festival *(March-April)*,   ul Armii Czerwonej 81, 61-808 Poznań.
Stanislaw Moniuszko Festival *(June)*,   Inflancka 19 m 171, 00-189 Warsaw.
Warsaw Autumn-International Festival of Contemporary Music *(Sept)*,   Rynek Starego Miasta 27, 00-272 Warsaw.

PORTUGAL

Encontros de Música Contemporanes *(May)*,   Avda de Berna 45, 1093 Lisbon Codex.

RUMANIA

Brasov Chamber Music Festival *(June-July)*,   Brasov 2200.
Cluj-Napoca Musical Autumn *(Oct)*,   Str E de Martonne 1, 3400 Cluj-Napoca.
George Enescu International Festival *(Sept)*,   Piata Presei Libere 1, 71341 Bucharest.
Tîrgu Mures Musical Days *(May)*,   2 Enescu Street, 4300 Tîrgu Mures.

RUSSIA

International Music Festival St Petersburg Spring *(April)*,   Herzena 45, 190000 St Petersburg.
Moscow International Music Festival *(May)*,   Ul Nezhdanovoi 8, Moscow.

FESTIVALS

Moscow Music Summer *(July-Aug)*,   Ul Kalantchovskaya 15, Moscow.
Moscow Stars *(April-May)*,   Ul Kalantchovskaya 15, Moscow.
Russian Winter *(Dec-Jan)*,   Ul Kalantchovskaya 15, Moscow.
St Petersburg Palaces International Chamber Music Festival *(June)*,   c/o M&N Artists Ltd, 400 West 43rd
   Street, Suite 19A, New York, NY 10036, USA.
White Nights *(June)*,   Fontanki 41, St Petersburg.

SINGAPORE

SIA Great Performers Series *(Jan-Dec of odd-numbered years)*,   Singapore Airlines 09-D Airline House, Airline
   Road, Singapore 1781.
Singapore Festival of Arts *(June of even-numbered years)*,   PSA Building, 35th Storey, 460 Alexandria Road,
Singapore 0511.

SLOVAKIA

Bratislava Cultural Summer *(July-Aug)*,   Suché Mýto 17, 812 93 Bratislava.
Bratislava Music Festival *(Oct)*,   Michalská 10, 815 36 Bratislava.
Evenings of New Music *(June)*,   Fučikova 29, 811 02 Bratislava.
Week of New Slovak Music *(Feb)*,   Sladkovicova 11, 811 06 Bratislava.

SLOVENIA

Ljubljana Festival *(July-Aug)*,   Trg Francoske Revolucije 1-2, 61000 Ljubljana.

SPAIN

Curso de Música Barroca y Rococo *(Aug)*,   Acuerdo 17-1° A, 28015 Madrid.
Festival de Música de Canarias *(Jan-Feb)*,   Leon y Castillo 427-3°, 35007 Las Palmas de Gran Canaria.
Festival internacional de Guitarra "Andres Segovia" *(Nov)*,   Ramon Llull 2, 07001 Palma de Mallorca.
Festival internacional de Música & Danza de Granada *(June-July)*,   PO Box 64, 18080 Granada.
Festival internacional de Música Castell de Peralada *(July-Aug)*,   Pere de Moncada 1, 08034 Barcelona.
Festival internacional de Música Contemporanea de Alicante *(Sept)*,   Piaza del Ayuntamiento, 03001 Alicante.
Festival internacional de Música de Barcelona,   Via Laietana, 41 pral, 08003 Barcelona.
Festival internacional de Organo *(Sept-Oct)*,   Calle La Paloma 7, 24003 Leon.
Festival internacional de Santandar *(July-Sept)*,   Avda Calvo Sotelo 15, 5th Floor, 39002 Santandar.
Semana de Música de Cámara y Festival internacional de Segovia *(July)*,   San Facundo 5, Segovia.
Semanas de Música Religiosa, Palafox 1, 16001 Cuenca.
Serenatas Musicales de Valencia *(July)*,   Avellanas 603a, 46003 Valencia.

SWEDEN

Electro-Acoustic Music Festival *(June)*,   Box 101, S-739 22 Skinnskatteberg.
Helsingborg Summerfestival *(Aug)*,   Konserthuset, S-252 21 Helsingborg.
Royal Palace Music Festival *(July-Aug)*,   Royal Palace, S-111 30 Stockholm.
Stockholm New Music *(March)*,   Box 1225, S-111 82 Stockholm.
Swedish Music Spring *(April)*,   Box 27327, S-102 54 Stockholm.
Umeå International Festival of Chamber Music *(June)*,   S-901 78 Umeå.
Visby Festival *(July-Aug)*,   Tranhusgatan 47, S-621 55 Visby.

SWITZERLAND

Estate Musicale internazionale di Lugano *(Aug)*,   Via Losanna, CH-6900 Lugano.
European International Festival *(May-July)*,   10 Rue des Eaux-Vives, CH-1207 Geneva.
Extasis 91 *(April)*,   PO Box 10, CH-1211 Geneva.
Festival "Ars et Musica" Aranno *(July-Aug)*,   Gatterstrasse 1b, CH-9010 St Gallen.
Festival de Musique Sacrée de Fribourg *(July)*,   Case Postale 292, CH-1701 Fribourg.
Festival d'Eté-"A Swiss Summer" *(July-Aug)*,   PO Box 10, CH-1211 Geneva.
Festival of Music Tibor Varga Sion/Valais *(July-Sept)*,   PO Box 954, CH-1951 Sion.
Interlakner Festwochen *(Aug)*,   Postfach, CH-3800 Interlaken.
International Bach Festival *(May)*,   Stadthaus, CH-8201 Schaffhausen.
International Choral Festival *(April)*,   PO Box 97, CH-1820 Montreux.
International Festival of Music Lucerne *(Aug-Sept)*,   Hirschmattstrasse 13, Postfach, CH-6002 Lucerne.
International Festival of Organ Music *(June-July)*,   Ente Turistico del Gambarogno, CH-6574 Vira.
Internationale Juni-Festwochen Zürich *(June)*,   Postfach, CH-8022 Zürich.
Menuhin Festival Gstaad-Saanen/Alpengala *(Aug-Sept)*,   Verkehrsverein Gstaad, CH-3780 Gstaad.
Montreux-Vevey Music Festival *(Aug-Oct)*,   Case Postale 162, CH-1820 Montreux.
Settimane Musicale d'Ascona *(Aug-Oct)*,   Via Lido 24, CH-6612 Acsona.
Tage für Neue Musik Zürich *(Nov)*,   Hegibachstrasse 38, CH-8032 Zürich.

TAIWAN

Taipei Music Festival *(Sept-Dec)*,   25 Pa Teh Road, Sec 3, 10560 Taipei.

FESTIVALS
TURKEY

Ankara International Festival *(April),* Tunali Hilmi Cad 114/43, 06700 Kavaklidere/Ankara.
Istanbul International Festival *(June-July),* Yildiz Culture and Arts Center, Istanbul.
Izmir International Festival *(June-July),* 1442 Sok No 4/6, 35220 Alsancak, Izmir.

UK

Aberdeen International Youth Festival *(Aug),* Town House, Aberdeen, Scotland AB9 1AQ.
Aberystwyth International MusicFest *(July-Aug),* Aberystwyth Arts Centre, Penglais, Aberystwyth, Dyfed SY23 3DE.
Aldeburgh Festival of Music and the Arts *(June),* High Street, Aldeburgh, Suffolk IP15 5AX.
Almeida Opera *(June-July),* Almeida Street, London N1 1TA.
Bath International Festival of Music and the Arts *(May-June),* Linley House, 1 Pierrepont Place, Bath, Avon BA1 1JY.
BBC Henry Wood Promenade Concerts *(July-Sept),* 16 Langham Street, Room 425, London W1A 1AA.
Belfast Festival at Queen's *(Nov),* 25 College Gardens, Belfast, Northern Ireland BT9 6BS.
Beverly Early Music Festival *(May),* Register Square, Beverley HU17 9AU.
Bournemouth International Festival *(June),* Digby Chambers, Suite 2, Post Office Road, Bournemouth BH1 1BA.
Bournemouth Musicmakers Festival *(June-July),* Westover Road, Bournemouth BH1 2BU.
Brighton Festival *(May),* 54 Old Steine, Brighton, Sussex BN1 1EQ.
Buxton International Festival *(July-Aug),* 1 Crescent View, Hall Bank, Buxton, Derbyshire SK17 6EN.
Cambridge Festival *(July),* Philips Telecom, St Andrew's Road, Cambridge CB4 1DP.
Canterbury Festival *(Oct),* 59 Ivy Lane, Canterbury CT1 1TU.
Cardiff Festival of Music *(Sept-Oct),* St David's Hall, The Hayes, Cardiff, Wales CF1 2SH.
Chard Festival of Women in Music *(May),* 6 Gables, Otterford, Chard, Somerset TA20 3QS.
Cheltenham International Festival of Music *(July),* Town Hall, Imperial Square, Cheltenham, Glos GL50 1QA.
Chester Summer Music Festival *(July),* 8 Abbey Square, Chester CH1 2HU.
Chichester Festivities *(July),* Canon Gate House, South Street, Chichester, Sussex PO19 1PU.
City of Leeds College of Music Festival *(Feb-March),* Cookridge Street, Leeds, Yorkshire LS2 8BH.
City of London Festival *(July),* Bishopsgate Hall, 230 Bishopsgate, London EC2M 4QH.
East Anglia Summer Music Festival *(July-Aug),* The Old School, Bridge Street, Hadleigh, Suffolk IP7 6BY.
Edinburgh International Festival *(Aug),* 21 Market Street, Edinburgh, Scotland EH1 1BW.
Exeter Festival *(July),* Dix's Field, Room G2A, Exeter EX1 1JN.
Fishguard Music Festival *(July),* Fishguard, Pembrokeshire, Wales SA65 9BJ.
Glasgow International Early Music Festival *(Aug of even-numbered years),* 22 Falkland Street, Glasgow, Scotland G12 9PR.
Glyndebourne Festival Opera, Glyndebourne, Lewes, Sussex BN8 5UU.
Greenwich Festival *(June),* 151 Powis Street, London SE18 6JL.
Handel in Oxford Festival *(July),* Cumnor Hill, Oxford OX2 9HA.
Harrogate International Festival *(July-Aug),* Royal Baths, Harrogate, Yorkshire HG1 2RR.
Haslemere Festival *(July),* Jesses, Grayswood Road, Haslemere, Surrey GU27 2BS.
Henley Festival of Music and the Arts *(July),* 42 Bell Street, Henley-on-Thames RG9 2BG.
Huddersfield Contemporary Music Festival *(Nov),* University of Huddersfield, Queensgate, Huddersfield HD1 3DH.
International Covent Gardens Art Festival *(Sept of even-numbered years),* 42 Central Avenue, London WC2 8RF.
International Organ Festival *(July),* PO Box 80, St Albans AL3 4HR.
King's Lynn Festival *(July),* 29 King Street, King's Lynn, Norfolk PE30 1HA.
Lake District Summer Music *(Aug),* 68 Grosvenor Street, Manchester M1 7EW.
Lichfield Festival *(July),* 7 The Close, Lichfield, Staff WS13 7LD.
Llandaff Summer Festival *(May-July),* 1 St Mary's, Cardiff, Wales CF5 2EB.
Lufthansa Festival of Baroque Music *(May-June),* 4 Bennett Park, London SE3 9RB.
Malvern Festival *(May-June),* Winter Gardens, Malvern, Worcs WR14 3HB.
Mananan International Festival of Music and the Arts *(June-July),* Port Erin, Isle of Man British Isles.
Mayfest *(April-May),* 18 Albion Street, Glasgow, Scotland G1 1LH.
Newbury Spring Festival *(May),* Town Hall, Suite 4, Newbury, Berks RG14 5AA.
Norfolk and Norwich Festival *(Oct),* 1 Merchants Court, St Georges Street, Norwich NR3 1AB.
North Wales Music Festival *(Sept),* High Street, St Asaph, Clwyd, North Wales LL17 0RD.
Perkshore Festival *(June-July),* Manor House Barn, Fladbury, Pershore, Worcs WR10 2QN.
Perth Festival of the Arts *(May),* 2 High Street, Perth.
Peterborough Cathedral Festival *(July),* The Cathedral Shop, 24 Minster Precincts, Peterborough PE1 1XZ.
Royal National Eisteddfod of Wales *(Aug),* 40 Parc Ty Glas, Llanishen, Cardiff, Wales CF4 5WU.
Salisbury Festival *(Sept),* 65 The Close, Salisbury SP1 2EN.
Sheffield Chamber Music Festival *(May),* 65 Rawcliffe Lane, Clifton, York YO3 6SJ.
South Bank Summer Festival *(July-Sept),* Royal Festival Hall, Belvedere Road, London SE1 8XX.
Stratford-upon-Avon Festival *(July-Aug),* 2 Chestnut Walk, Stratford-upon-Avon, Warwicks CV37 6HG.
Swansea Festival of Music and the Arts *(Sept-Nov),* The Guildhall, Swansea SA1 4PE.
Three Choirs Festival *(Aug),* 33 Bridge Street, Hereford HR4 9DQ.
Vale of Glamorgan Festival *(Aug),* St Donat's Castle, Llantwit Major, Wales CF6 9WF.
Walsingham Variations *(Aug),* The Grove, 61 Bracondale, Norwich, Norfolk NR1 2AT.
Warwick Festival *(June-July),* Northgate, Warwick CV34 4JL.
Windsor Festival *(Sept-Oct),* Dial House, Englefield Green, Egham, Surrey TW20 0DU.
York Early Music Festival *(July),* 65 Rawcliffe Lane, Clifton, York YO3 6SJ.

FESTIVALS

USA

ARIZONA

Grand Canyon Chamber Music Festival *(Sept),* PO Box 1332, Grand Canyon, AZ 86023.
Flagstaff Festival of the Arts *(July-Aug),* PO Box 1607, Flagstaff, AZ 86002.

ARKANSAS

Music Festival of Arkansas *(June),* PO Box 1243, Fayetteville, AR 72702.

CALIFORNIA

Berkeley Festival and Exhibition *(June),* 101 Zellerbach Hall, University of California at Berkeley, Berkeley, CA 94720.
Cabrillo Music Festival *(July-Aug),* 9053 Soquel Drive, Aptos, CA 95003.
Carmel Bach Festival *(July--Aug),* PO Box 575, Carmel-by-the-Sea, CA 93921.
Chamber Music/LA Festival *(May),* 3264 Primera Place, Los Angeles, CA 90068.
Hollywood Bowl Summer Festival *(June-Sept),* PO Box 1951, Hollywood, CA 90078.
La Jolla Chamber Music Society *(Aug),* PO Box 2168, La Jolla, CA 92038.
Los Angeles Festival *(Sept),* PO Box 5210, Los Angeles, CA 90055.
Mendocino Music Festival *(July),* PO Box 1808, Mendocino, CA 95460.
Midsummer Mozart Festival *(July-Aug),* World Trade Center, No 280, San Francisco, CA 94111.
Mozart in Monterey/Encore California *(June),* PO Box 4471, Carmel, CA 93921.
Music Academy of the West Summer Concert Season *(June-Aug),* 1070 Fairway Road, Santa Barbara, CA 93108.
Music in the Mountains *(June-July),* 401 Spring Street, No 101, Nevada City, CA 95959.
Ojai Festival *(June),* PO Box 185, Ojai, CA 93024.
Redlands Bowl Summer Music Festival *(June-Aug),* PO Box 466, Redlands, CA 92373.
San Diego Symphony SummerPops *(June-Sept),* 1245 Seventh Avenue, San Diego, CA 92101.
San Francisco Arts Commission/San Francisco Symphony Summer Pops *(July-Aug),* Louise M Davies Symphony Hall, San Francisco, CA 94102.
San Luis Obispo Mozart Festival *(July-Aug),* PO Box 311, San Luis Obispo, CA 93406.
Stern Grove Midsummer Music Festival *(June-Aug),* 44 Page Street, Suite 604-D, San Francisco, CA 94102.

COLORADO

Aspen Music Festival *(June-Aug),* Box AA, Aspen, CO 81612.
Bravo! Colorado Music Festival at Vail, Beaver Creek *(July-Aug),* 953 South Frontage Road, Suite 104, Vail, CO 81657.
Central City Opera House *(June-Aug),* 621 17th Street, Suite 1601, Denver, CO 80293.
Colorado Music Festival *(June-Aug),* 1035 Pearl Street, Suite 303, Boulder, CO 80302.

CONNECTICUT

Connecticut Early Music Festival *(June),* PO Box 329, New London, CT 06320.
Norfolk Chamber Music Festival *(June-Aug),* Ellen Battell Stoeckel Estate, Route 44, Norfolk, CT 06058.
Summer Music at Harkness Park *(July-Aug),* 300 Captain's Walk, Room 503, New London, CT 06320.

DISTRICT OF COLUMBIA

American Music Festival *(April-May),* National Gallery of Art, Sixth Street and Constitution Avenue North West, Washington, DC 20565.
Library of Congress Summer Chamber Festival *(June),* Library of Congress, Washington, DC 20540.
National Symphony Orchestra: Concerts at the Capitol *(Memorial Day weekend, Fourth of July, and Labor Day weekend),* John F Kennedy Center for the Performing Arts, Washington, DC 20566.

FLORIDA

Festival Miami *(Sept-Oct),* University of Miami School of Music, PO Box 248165, Coral Gables, FL 33124.
Florida International Festival featuring the London Symphony Orchestra *(Aug),* PO Box 1310, Daytona Beach, FL 32115.
Sarasota Music Festival *(May-June),* 709 North Tamiami Trail, Sarasota, FL 34236.
Winter Park Bach Festival *(Feb-March),* Rollins College, Box 2763, Winter Park, FL 32789.

GEORGIA

Arts Festival of Atlanta *(Sept),* 999 Peachtree Street, Suite 140, Atlanta, GA 30309.
Atlanta Symphony Orchestra: Summer Concerts *(June-Aug),* 1293 Peachtree Street, North East, Suite 300, Atlanta, GA 30309.
Southeastern Music Center *(July),* PO Box 8348, Columbus, GA 31908.

IDAHO

Festival at Sandpoint *(July-Aug),* Box 695, Sandpoint, ID 83864.
Sun Valley Music Festival *(July-Aug),* PO Box 656, Sun Valley, ID 83353.

ILLINOIS

Grant Park Music Festival *(June-Aug),* Chicago Park District Administration Building, 425 East McFetridge

FESTIVALS

Drive, Chicago, IL 60605.
Ravinia Festival *(June-Sept),* 1575 Oakwood Avenue, Highland Park, IL 60035.
Woodstock Mozart Festival *(July-Aug),* PO Box 734, Woodstock, IL 60098.

INDIANA

Festival Music Society of Indiana *(June-July),* 6471 Central Avenue, Indianapolis, IN 46220.
Firefly Festival for the Performing Arts *(June-Aug),* 202 South Michigan Street, Suite 845, South Bend, IN 46601.
Indiana University School of Music Summer Festival *(June-Aug),* Indiana University School of Music, Bloomington, IN 47405.
Indianapolis Symphony Orchestra-Symphony on the Praire *(July-Aug),* 45 Monument Circle, Indianapolis, IN 46204.

IOWA

Ames Festival, PO Box 1243, Ames, IA 50010.
Des Moines Metro Opera *(June-July),* 106 West Boston Avenue, Indianola, IA 50125.

KENTUCKY

Classics in Context Festival *(Sept-Oct),* 623 West Main Street, Louisville, KY 40202.

LOUISIANA

FANFARE *(Oct),* Southeastern Louisiana University, Box 797, Hammond, LA 70402.

MAINE

Bay Chamber Concerts *(July-Aug),* Box 191, Camden, ME 04843.

MARYLAND

Baltimore Symphony Orchestra Summerfest! *(July),* **and Oregon Ridge Concert Series** *(June-Aug),* 1212 Cathedral Street, Baltimore, MD 21201.
Columbia Festival of the Arts *(June),* 10221 Wincopin Circle, Columbia, MD 21044.
Maryland Handel Festival *(Nov),* University of Maryland, Tawes Fine Arts Building, Suite 2140, College Park, MD 20742.
University of Maryland Piano Festival *(July),* University of Maryland, College Park, MD 20742.

MASSACHUSETTS

Aston Magna Festival *(July-Aug),* PO Box 1035, Great Barrington, MA 01230.
Berkshire Choral Festival *(July-Aug),* Route 41, Sheffield, MA 01257.
Boston Early Music Festival and Exhibition *(June),* PO Box 2632, Cambridge, MA 02238.
Boston Pops *(May-June),* Symphony Hall, 301 Massachusetts Avenue, Boston, MA 02115.
Boston Symphony Orchestra-Tanglewood Festival *(June-Aug),* Lenox, MA 01240.
Castle Hill Festival *(July-Sept),* PO Box 563, Ipswich, MA 01938.
Great Woods Center for the Performing Arts *(June-Sept),* PO Box 810, Mansfield, MA 02048.
Rockport Chamber Music Festival *(June),* PO Box 312, Rockport, MA 01966.
Worcester Music Festival, Memorial Auditorium, Worcester, MA 01608.

MICHIGAN

Ann Arbor May Festival *(May),* Burton Memorial Tower, Suite 100, Ann Arbor, MI 48109.
Ann Arbor Summer Festival *(June-July),* PO Box 4070, Ann Arbor, MI 48106.
Interlochen Arts Festival *(June-Aug),* PO Box 199, Interlochen, MI 49643.
Irving S Gilmore International Keyboard Festival *(Jan),* Kalamazoo Center, 100 West Michigan, Kalamazoo, MI 49007.
Meadow Brook Music Festival *(June-Aug),* Oakland University, Rochester, MI 48309.
Michigan Bach Festival *(March-April),* 400 Town Center Drive, Suite 300, Dearbon, MI 48126.

MINNESOTA

Minnesota Orchestra Viennese Sommerfest *(July-Aug),* 1111 Nicollet Mall, Minneapolis, MN 55403.

MISSOURI

Missouri River Festival of the Arts *(Aug),* PO Box 1776, Boonville, MO 65233.
Opera Theatre of St Louis *(May-June),* PO Box 191910, St Louis, MO 63119.
Saint Louis Symphony Orchestra Queeny Pops *(July-Aug),* 718 North Grand Boulevard, St Louis, MO 63103.

MONTANA

Big Sky Arts Festival *(July),* Box 160308, Big Sky, MT 59716.
Flathead Festival *(July),* PO Box 1780, Whitefish, MT 59937.

FESTIVALS

NEW HAMPSHIRE

Monadnock Music *(July-Aug),* PO Box 255, Peterborough, NH 03458.
New Hampshire Music Festival, PO Box 147, Center Harbor, NH 03226.
North County Chamber Players Summer Festival *(July-Aug),* PO Box 99, Franconia, NH 03580.

NEW JERSEY

Cape May Music Festival *(May-June),* PO Box 340, Cape May, NJ 08204.
Garden State Arts Center *(June-Sept),* PO Box 116, Holmdel, NJ 07733.
New Jersey Festival of American Music Theatre *(June-Aug),* 1650 Broadway, New York, NY 10019.
Opera Festival of New Jersey *(June-July),* 55 Princeton-Hightstown Road, Princeton Junction, NJ 08550.
Rutgers SummerFest *(June-July),* Rutgers Arts Center, New Brunswick, NJ 08903.
Waterloo Festival *(July-Aug),* Village of Waterloo, Stanhope, NJ 07874.

NEW MEXICO

Music From Angel Fire *(Aug-Sept),* PO Box 502, Angel Fire, NM 87710.
Santa Fe Chamber Music Festival *(July-Aug),* PO Box 853, Santa Fe, NM 87504.

NEW YORK

Artpark *(May-Sept),* Box 371, Lewiston, NY 14092.
Bach Aria Festival and Institute *(June),* PO Box 997, Stony Brook, NY 11790.
Bard Music Festival *(Aug),* Bard College, Annandale-on-Hudson, NY 12504.
Binghamton Summer Music Festival *(July-Aug),* PO Box 112, Binghamton, NY 13903.
Caramoor Festival *(June-Aug),* PO Box R, Katonah, NY 10536.
Chautauqua Institution *(June-Aug),* Chautauqua, NY 14722.
Glimmerglass Opera *(July-Aug),* PO Box 191, Cooperstown, NY 13326.
Huntington Summer Arts Festival *(June-Aug),* 213 Main Street, Huntington, NY 11743.
Lake George Opera Festival *(July-Aug),* PO Box 2172, Glen Falls, NY 12801.
Lincoln Center Out-of-Doors *(Aug),* 70 Lincoln Center Plaza, 9th Floor, New York, NY 10023.
Mostly Mozart Festival *(July-Aug),* 70 Lincoln Center Plaza, 9th Floor, New York, NY 10023.
New York Festival of American Music Theatre *(July-Aug),* 1650 Broadway, New York, NY 10019.
New York International Festival of the Arts, 386 Park Avenue South, Suite 2000, New York, NY 10016.
Saratoga Performing Arts Center *(June-Sept),* Saratoga Springs, NY 12866.

NORTH CAROLINA

An Appalachian Summer *(July),* 801 Rivers Street, Boone, NC 28608.
Brevard Music Festival *(July-Aug),* PO Box 592, Brevard, NC 28712.

OHIO

Art Song Festival *(May),* 11021 East Boulevard, Cleveland, OH 44106.
Cincinnati May Festival *(May-June),* Music Hall, 1241 Elm Street, Cincinnati, OH 45210.
Cincinnati Opera Association Summer Festival *(June-July),* 1241 Elm Street, Cincinnati, OH 45210.
Cincinnati Symphony and Pops Orchestras at Riverbend *(June-Aug),* 1241 Elm Street, Cincinnati, OH 45210.
Cleveland Orchestra at the Blossom Music Center *(May-Sept),* PO Box 1000, Cuyahoga Falls, OH 44223.
Columbus Symphony Orchestra Picni with the Pops *(June-Aug),* 55 East State Street, Columbus, OH 43215.
Kent/Blossom Music *(July-Aug),* Kent State University, E101 M&S, Kent, OH 44242.
Lakeside Summer Festival *(June-Sept),* 236 Walnut Avenue, Lakeside, OH 43440.
Lancaster Festival *(July),* PO Box 1452, Lancaster, OH 43130.
Ohio Light Opera *(June-Aug),* College of Wooster, Wooster, OH 44691.

OKLAHOMA

OK Mozart International Festival *(June),* PO Box 2344, Bartlesville, OK 74005.

OREGON

Britt Festivals *(June-Sept),* PO Box 1124, Medford, OR 97501.
Chamber Music Northwest *(June-July),* 522 South West Fifth Avenue, Suite 725, Portland, OR 97204.
Oregon Bach Festival *(June-July),* University of Oregon School of Music, Eugene, OR 97403.

PENNSYLVANIA

American Music Theater Festival *(March-June),* 2005 Market Street, 18th Floor, Philadelphia, PA 19103.
Bethlehem Musikfest Association *(Aug),* 22 Bethlehem Plaza, Bethlehem, PA 18018.
Hartwood Music and Dance Festival *(May-Sept),* 1520 Penn Avenue, Pittsburgh, PA 15222.
Mann Music Center *(June-Sept),* 1617 J F Kennedy Boulevard, Philadelphia, PA 19103.
Three Rivers Arts Festival *(June),* 207 Sweetbriar Street, Pittsburgh, PA 15211.

PUERTO RICO

Festival Casals *(June),* PO Box 41227, Minillas Station, Santurce, PR 00940.
Festival of Young Orchestras of the Americas *(June),* PO Box 41227, Minillas Station, Santurce, PR 00940.
Inter-American Festival of the Arts *(Sept-Oct),* PO Box 41227, Minillas Station, Santurce, PR 00940.

FESTIVALS

RHODE ISLAND

Newport Music Festival   *(July)*,   PO Box 3300, Newport, RI 02840.

SOUTH CAROLINA

Spoleto Festival USA   *(May-June)*,   PO Box 157, Charleston, SC 29402.

TENNESSEE

Riverbend Festival   *(June)*,   PO Box 886, Chattanooga, TN 37401.

TEXAS

Dallas Symphony Orchestra International Summer Music Festival   *(June-July)*,   2301 Flora Street, Dallas, TX 75201.
Houston International Festival   *(April)*,   1100 Louisiana, Suite 1275, Houston, TX 77002.
Rio Grande Valley International Music Festival   *(Feb)*,   PO Box 2315, McAllen, TX 78502.
Round Top Festival   *(June-July)*,   PO Box 89, Round Top, TX 78954.
SMU Conservatory Summer Music Festival   *(June)*,   Southern Methodist University, Dallas, TX 75275.
San Antonio Early Music Festival, 322 Garraty Road, San Antonio, TX 78209.
Texas Music Festival   *(June-July)*,   University of Houston School of Music, Houston, TX 77204.

UTAH

Gina Bachauer International Piano Festival   *(June)*,   PO Box 11664, Salt Lake City, UT 84147.

VERMONT

Manchester Music Festival   *(July-Aug)*,   Box 735, Manchester, VT 05254.
Marlboro Music Festival   *(July-Aug)*,   Marlboro, VT 05344.
New England Bach Festival   *(Sept-Oct)*,   15 Walnut Street, Brattleboro, VT 05301.
Vermont Music Festival   *(July-Aug)*,   PO Box 512, Burlington, VT 05402.

VIRGINIA

Wolf Trap Foundation   *(May-Sept)*,   1624 Trap Road, Vienna, VA 22182.

WASHINGTON

Seattle Chamber Music Festival   *(June-July)*,   2618 Eastlake Avenue East, Seattle, WA 98102.
Seattle Opera Summer Festival   *(July-Aug)*,   PO Box 9248, Seattle, WA 98109.

WISCONSIN

Milwaukee Symphony Orchestra SummerNights   *(June-Aug)*,   330 East Kilbourn Avenue, Suite 900, Milwaukee, WI 53202.
Summerfest   *(June-July)*,   200 North Harbor Drive, Milwaukee, WI 53202.

WYOMING

Grand Teton Music Festival   *(June-Aug)*,   PO Box 490, Teton Village, WY 83025.

YUGOSLAVIA

Belgrade Music Festival   *(Oct)*,   Terazije 41, 11000 Belgrade.

MUSIC ORGANIZATIONS

APPENDIX D

MUSIC ORGANIZATIONS

ARGENTINA

Sociedad Argentina de Autores y Compositores de Musicia, Lavalle 1547, 1048 Buenos Aires.

AUSTRALIA

Australasian Mechanical Copyright Owners Society Ltd, 56 Berry Street, 14th Floor, North Sydney, NSW 2060.
Australasian Performing Right Association (APRA), 1A Eden Street, Crows Nest, NSW 2065.
Australia Council, 181 Lawson Street, Redfern, NSW 2060.
Australian Copyright Council, 3/245 Chalmers Street, Redfern, NSW 2016.
Australian Music Centre, Ltd, trading as Sounds Australian, PO Box 690, Sydney, NSW 2000.
Australian Music Publishers Association, Ltd, 56 Berry Street, 14th Floor, North Sydney, NSW 2060.
Australian Record Industry Association (ARIA), 263 Clarence Street, 9th Floor, Sydney, NSW 2000.
Australian Society for Keyboard Music, 9 Glenroy Avenue, Middle Cove, NSW 2068.
Confederation of Australasian Performing Arts Presenters, GPO Box 4274, Sydney, NSW 2001.
International Society for Contemporary Music (Australian Section), c/o University of Sydney Music Department, Sydney, NSW 2006.
Musica Viva Australia, PO Box 49, Railway Square, NSW 2000.
Phonographic Peformance Company of Australia, Ltd. (PPCA), 263 Clarence Street, 9th Floor, Sydney, NSW 2000.
Youth Music Australia, PO Box 160, Rozelle, NSW 2039.

AUSTRIA

Austro-Mechana (Gesellschaft zur Wahrnehmung mechanisch-musikalischer Urheberrechte GmbH), Baumannstrasse 10, A-1031 Vienna.
Gesellschaft der Musikfreunde in Wien, Bösendorferstrasse 12, A-1010 Vienna.
Gewekschaft Kunst, Medien, Freie Berufe, Sektion Musiker, Maria Theresienstrasse 11, A-1090 Vienna.
I F D I Landesgruppe Österreich, Habsburgergasse 6-8/18, A-1010 Vienna.
International Music Centre Vienna (IMZ), Lothringerstrasse 20, A-1030 Vienna.
Internationale Bruckner Gesellschaft, Rathausplatz 3, A-1010 Vienna.
Internationale Gesellschaft für Neue Musik, Ungargasse 9/3, A-1030 Vienna.
Internationale Gustav Mahler Gesellschaft, Wiedner Guertel 6/2, A-1040 Vienna.
Interantionale Hugo Wolf Gesellschaft, Latschkagasse 4, A-1090 Vienna.
Internationale Schönberg Gesellschaft, Bernhardgasse 6, A-2340 Mödling.
Literar-Mechana (Wahrnemungsgesellschaft für Urheberrechte), Linke Wienzelle 18, A-1060 Vienna.
Musikalische Jugend Österreichs (Jeunesses Musicales), Bösendorferstrasse 12, A-1010 Vienna.
Musikverleger Union Österreich, Baumannstrasse 10, A-1030 Vienna.
Österreichischer Komponistenbund (OKB), Ungargasse 9/3, A-1030 Vienna.
Staatlich genehmigte Gesellschaft der Autoren, Komponisten, und Musikverleger (AKM), Baumannstrasse 8-10, A-1030 Vienna.

BELGIUM

Association des Arts et de la Culture, Rue Royale 10, 1000 Brussels.
Association des Artistes professionnels de Belgique, Rue Paul Lauters 1, 1050 Brussels.
Association Internationale du Théâtre Lyrique, Rue des Dominicains 1, 4000 Liège.
Association pour la Diffusion de la Musique Belge, Rue d'Arlon 75-77, 1040 Brussels.
Atelier créatif de Musique électroacoustique, Avenue du Cor de Chasse 99, 1040 Brussels.
Centre belge de Documentation musicale, Rue d'Arlon 75-77, 1040 Brussels.
Centre International d'Echanges Musicaux, Rue des Patriotes 60, 1040 Brussels.
Chambre Syndicale des Agents Artistiques et Impresario de Belgique, Rue Rogier 3, 6040 Charleroi.
Confédération muscale de Belgique, Rue de Loncin 22, 4430 Alleur. President: S Coucke.
Conseil de la Musique de la Communauté française de Belgique, Boulevard Reyers 52, 1040 Brussels. President: Dr Robert Wangermée.
Fondation pour la Promotion des Arts, Rue aux Choux 47, 1000 Brussels.
Jeunesses Musicales de la Communaute française de Belgique, Rue Royale 10, 1000 Brussels.
Promotion artistique belge, Rue d'Arlon 75-77, 1040 Brussels.
Royale Union Artistique et Littéraire, Rue du Tombeux 52A, 1801 Stembert.
Société belge de Musicologie, Rue de la Régence 30, 1000 Brussels. Contact: Dr Robert Wangermée.
Société belge des Auteurs, Compositeurs et Editeurs, Rue d'Arlon 75-77, 1040 Brussels.
Société Cesar Franck de Belgique, Rue des Foulons 11, 4000 Liège.
Société culturell d'Arts dramatique et musical, Rue F Ferrer 37, 1360 Tubize.
Société des Auteurs et Compositeurs Dramatiques, Avenue Jeanne 29, 1050 Brussels.
Société liégoise de Musicologie, Les Enclos 13, 4080 Werbomont.
Société wallonne de Recherche et d'Expansion du Marché de Spectacle et de l'Audio-visuel, Rue P.-E. Janson 9, 1050 Brussels.
Union de la Presse musicale belge, Avenue C. Woeste 140, 1090 Brussels.
Union des Artistes, Rue du Marché aux Herbes 105, 1000 Brussels.
Union des Compositeurs Belges, Rue d'Arlon 75-77, 100 Brussels.
Union Royale Belge des Éditeurs de Musique, Rue F. Neuray 8, 1060 Brussels.
Union wallonne des Organistes, Rue Romainville 25a, 5228 Bas-Oha/Wanze.

MUSIC ORGANIZATIONS

BOLIVIA

Sociedad Boliviana de Autores & Compositores de Música, Figueroa 788, Depto 1, 2nd Floor, La Paz.

BRAZIL

Associacao Brasileira dos Produtores de Discos, Rua Sao José 90, Gr 1406/10, 22021 Rio de Janeiro, R J.
Associacao de Canto Coral, Rua das Marrecas 40, 9th Floor, 20080-010 Rio de Janeiro, R J.
Fundaçao de Educaçao Artistica, Rua Gonçalves Dias 320, 30000 Belo Horizonte, M G.
Instituto Brasileiro de Arte e Cultura, Rua de Imprensa 16, 20030 Rio de Janeiro, R J.
Juventude Musical do Brasil, Caixa Postal 62626, 22257 Rio de Janeiro, R J.
Sindicato dos Músicos Profissionals do Estado de Sao Paulo, Largo Paissandu, Sao Paulo.
Sindicato dos Músicos Profissionals do Estado do Rio de Janeiro, Rua Alvaro Alvim 24, Grupo 401, 20031 Rio de Janeiro, R J.
Sociedade Brasileira de Autores Teatrais, Av Almirante Barroso 97, 3rd Floor, PO Box 1503, 20031-002 Rio de Janeiro, R J.
Sociedade Brasileira de Música Contemporânea, SQS 105, Bloco B, Ap 506, 70344-020 Brasilia, D F.
Sociedade Brasileira de Realizaçoes Artistico-Culturais, Av Franklin Roosevelt 23, Room 310, 20021 Rio de Janeiro, R J.
Sociedade de Cultura Artistica, Rua Nestor Pestana 196, CEP 01303 Sao Paulo.
Sociedade independente de Compositores & Autores Musicals, Largo Paissandú 51, 10th, 11th, and 16th floors, 01034 Sao Paulo.
Uniao Brasileira de Compositores, Rua Visconde de Inhaúma 107, 20091 Rio de Janeiro, R J.
Uniao dos Músicos do Brasil, Av Rio Branco 185, Rio de Janeiro, R J.

BULGARIA

Jeunesses Musicales de Bulgarie, 56 Rue Alabine, PO Box 387, 1040 Sofia.
Union of Bulgarian Composers, 2 Ivan Vazov Str, 1000 Sofia.
Union of Bulgarian Musicians and Dancers, 14 Serdica Str, Sofia.

CANADA

Alliance for Canadian New Music Projects, 9 St Joseph Street, Suite 303, Toronto, Ontario M4Y 1J6. President: Janet Fothergill.
American Federation of Musicians of the United States and Canada, Canadian Office, 75 The Donway West, Suite 1010, Don Mills, Ontario M3C 2E9. Vice President from Canada: Ray Petch.
Association of Canadian Orchestras, 56 The Esplanade, Suite 311, Toronto, Ontario M5E 1A7. Executive Director: Elizabeth Webster.
Association of Canadian Women Composers, 20 St Joseph Street, Toronto, Ontario M4Y 1J9. Chairperson: Lorraine Johnson.
Association of Cultural Executives, 720 Bathurst Street, Suite 503, Toronto, Ontario M5S 2R4. President: Warren Garrett.
C(anadian) A(mateur) M(usicians) M(usiciens) A(mateurs du) C(anada), PO Box 353, Westmount, PQ H3Z 2T5. Director General: Barry Crago.
Canada Council/Conseil des Arts du Canada, PO Box 1047, 99 Metcalfe Street, Ottawa, Ontario K1P 5V8. Director: Paul Leduc.
Canadian Arts Presenters Association, 432 Besserer Street, Ottawa, Ontario K1N 6C1. Executive Director: L Peter Feldman.
Canadian Association of Artists Managers, 117 Ava Road, Toronto, Ont M6C 1W2. President: Renee Simmons.
Canadian Association of Arts Administration Educators, University of British Columbia, Faculty of Commerce and Business Administration, Vancouver, BC V6T 1Z2. President: Robert Kelly.
Canadian Bureau for the Advancement of Music, Exhibition Place, Toronto, Ontario M6K 3C3. Managing Director: Clifford Hunt.
Canadian Conference of the Arts, 189 Laurier Avenue East, Ottawa, Ont K1N 6P1. Director: Keith Kelly.
Canadian Independent Record Production Association, 144 Front Street West, Suite 202, Toronto, Ontario M5J 2L7. Executive Director: Brian Chater.
Canadian League of Composers, Chalmers House, 20 St Joseph Street, Toronto, Ontario, M4Y 1J9. President: Patrick Cardy.
Canadian Music Centre/Centre de musique canadienne, 20 St Joseph Street, Toronto, Ont M4Y 1J9. Executive Director: Simone Auger.
Canadian Music Educators Association, 16 Royaleigh Avenue, Etobicoke, Ontario M9P 2J5. President: Dennis Tupman.
Canadian Music Publishers Association, 56 Wellesley Street West, Suite 320, Toronto, Ontario M5S 2S4. President: John Bird.
Canadian Musical Reproduction Rights Agency, Ltd, 56 Wellesley Street West, Suite 320, Toronto, Ontario M5S 2S4. General Manager: David A Basskin.
Canadian Recording Industry Association, 1255 Yonge Street, Suite 300, Toronto, Ontario M4T 1W6. President: Brian Robertson.
Canadian Resource Centre for Career Performing Artists, Box 188, Station A, Toronto, Ontario M5W 1B2. President: Ann Summers.
Canadian University Music Society, University of Western Ontario, Faculty of Music, London, Ontario N6A 3K7. President: Gail Dixon.
The Council for Business and the Arts in Canada, PO Box 7, 401 Bay Street, Suite 1507, Toronto, Ontario M5H 2Y4. President and Chief Executive Officer: Blair Mascall.
Jeunesses Musicales du Canada/Youth and Music Canada, 305 Mont-Royal East, Montréal, PQ H2T 1P8. General Director: Nicolas Desjardins.
Ontario Choral Federation, 20 St Joseph Street, Toronto, Ontario M4Y 1J9. Executive Director: Bev Jahnke.
Organization of Canadian Symphony Musicians, 445 Gérard Morisset, No 6, Québec, PQ G1S 4V5. Chairman:

MUSIC ORGANIZATIONS

Evelyne Robitaille.
Society of Composers, Authors, and Music Publishers of Canada, SOCAN, 41 Valleybrook Drive, Don Mills, Ontario M3B 2S6. General Manager: Michael Rock.

CHILE

Asociación Nacional de Compositores, Almirante Moritt 453, Santiago.
Instituto de Música, Universidad Católica de Chile, Jaime Guzman E 3 300, Santiago.
Juventudes Musicales, Universidad de Chile, Facultad de Artes, Compania 1264, 4to piso, Santiago.
Sociedad Chilena del Derecho de Autor, San Antonio 427, 2nd Floor, Santiago.
Sociedad de Autores Teatrales de Chile, San Diego 246, Santiago.

CHINA

Association of Chinese Musicians, Nong zhanguan Nan Li, No 10, Beijing 100026.

COLOMBIA

Asociación, Colombiana de Músicos Profesionales, Calle 17, No 10-16, Of 607, Bogotá, D E.
Asociación des Artistas de Colombia, Calle 13, No 9-63, Interior 104, Apdo Aéreo 24627, Bogotá, D E.
Centro de Documentación Musical-Instituto Colombiano de Cultura, Calle 11, No 5-51, 2nd Floor, Bogotá, DE.
Instituto Colombiano de Cultura-Colcultura, Calle 11, No 5-51, 2nd Floor, Santafé de Bogotá, D C.
Juventudes Musicales de Colombia, Apartado Aereo 089436, Cra 16A No 202, Bogotá 8.
Sociedad de Autores y Compositores de Colombia, Carrera 19, No 40-72, Apdo Aéreo 6482, Santafé de Bogotá, DC ZP1.

COSTA RICA

Juventudes Musicales de Costa Rica, Apartado 1035, San José 1000.

CUBA

Centro de Información y Promoción de la Música Cubana "Odilio Urfé", Calle 17 esq. a E, Vedado, Havana.
Centro de Investigación y Desarrollo de la Música Cubana, Calle G, N° 505 e/21 y 23, Vedado, Havana.
Centro Nacional de Derecho de Autor, Calle Línea N° 365 (altos), esp a G, Vedado, Havana.
Centro Nacional de Música de Concierto, Calle Línea N° 365, esq a G, Vedado, Havana.
Centro Nacional de Música Popular, Avenida 1 ra. e/10 y 12, Playa, Havana.
Editora Musical de Cuba, San Rafael N° 104, esq a Consulado, Centro Habana, Havana.
Empresa de Grabaciones y Ediciones Musicales, Campanario N° 315, e/Neptuno y San Miguel, Centro Habana, Havana.
Instituto Cubano de la Música, Calle 15 N° 452, esq a F Vedado, Havana.
Unión de Escritores y Artistas de Cuba (Music Section), Calle 17 N° 351, esq a H, Vedado, Havana.

CZECH REPUBLIC

Association of Musicians and Musicologists, Maltézské nám. 1, 118 00 Prague 1.
Authors Association of Protection for Rights on Musical Works, Čs. armády 20, 160 56 Prague 6.
Confederation of Arts and Culture, Gorkého nám. 23, 116 13 Prague 1.
Czech Music Association (includes the Dvořák Society, Janáček Society, Martinů Society, Smetana Society, Society for Contemporary Music, Society for Early Music, Society for Jazz, and Society for Music Eduction), Janáčkovo nábř. 59, 150 00 Prague 5.
Czech Music Fund, Besedni 3, 118 00 Prague 1.
Czech Society for Chamber Music, Korunní 98, 101 00 Prague 10.
International Federation of Phonogram and Videogram Producers (Czechoslovak Section), Gorkého nam. 23, 112 82 Prague 1.
International Music Council (National Committee), Valdstejnske nám. 1, Prague 1.
International Society for Contemporary Music (Czechoslovak Section), Na Březince 22, 150 00 Prague 5.
Music Information Centre of the Czech Music Fund, Besedni 3, 118 00 Prague 1.
Union of Authors and Interpreters, Škroupova nám 9, 130 00 Prague 3.

DENMARK

Choir Conductors' Society, Astrupgårdsvej 12, 2650 Hvidovre.
Danish Choral Association, Slagelsegade 9, 2100 Copenhagen O.
Danish Composers' Society, Valkendorfsgade 3, 1151 Copenhagen K.
Danish Cultural Institute, Kultorvet 2, 1175 Copenhagen K.
Danish Jazz Center, Borupvej 66, 4683 Rønnede.
Danish Music Information Centre, 48 Vimmelskaftet, 1161 Copenhagen K.
Danish Musicians' Union, Vendersgade 25, 1363 Copenhagen K.
Danish Musicological Society, Abenrå 34, 1124 Copenhagen K.
Danish Organ Society, Dønnerupvej 2, 2720 Vanløse.
Danish Organists' and Precentors' Society, Flegmade 14, 7100 Vejle.
Danish Society of Composers, Authors, and Editors, Maltegårdsvej 24, 2820 Gentofte.
Danish Society of Jazz, Rock, and Folk Composers, Klerkegade 19, 1308 Copenhagen K.

MUSIC ORGANIZATIONS

Danish Soloists' Association, Sundholmsvej 49, 2300 Copenhagen S.
Dansk Arbejder Sanger-og Musikerforbund, Skovgade 6, 5500 Middelfart.
Dansk Kapelmesterforening, Rosenvangsvej 47, 2670 Greve Strand.
International Society for Contemporary Music (Danish Section), Valkendorfsgade 3, 1151 Copenhagen K.
Samrådet for Musikundervisning, Vallerod-skolen, Stadion Allé, 2960 Rungsted Kyst.
Society of Danish Chruch Singing, Hoyrups Allé 7, 2900 Hellerup.
Society for Publishing Danish Music, Valkendorfsgade 3, 1151 Copenhagen K.
State Music Council, Vesterbrodgade 24, 1620 Copenhagen V.
Union of Danish Singers, Norre Sovej 26 A, 8800 Viborg.

DOMINICAN REPUBLIC

Juventudes Musicales Dominicanas, Apartado Postal 21920, Santo Domingo.

ECUADOR

Juventudes Musicales, Casilla Correo, 8162, Sucursal 8, Quito.

EIRE

Arts Council, 70 Merrion Square, Dublin 2.
Contemporary Music Centre, 95 Lower Baggot Street, Dublin 2.
International Songwriters Association, Ltd, Raheen, Limerick City.
Irish Composers Centre, Liberty Hall, Room 804, Dublin 1.
Irish Federation of Musicians and Associated Professions, 63 Lower Gardiner Street, Dublin 1.
Irish Music Rights Organization (IMRO), 15 Herbert Street, Dublin 2.
Mechanical Copyright Society, Ltd (MCPS), 15 Herbert Street, Dublin 2.

EL SALVADOR

Centro Nacional de Artes, 2a Avenida Norte Pje. Contreras, N° 145, San Salvador.

ESTONIA

Jeunesses Musicales Eestis, Estonia pst 4 tuba 410, 200105 Tallinn.

FINLAND

Association of Finnish Conservatories, Fredrikinkati 34 B, SF-00100 Helsinki.
Association of Finnish Music Schools, Urho Kekkosen katu 8C 30, SF-00100 Helsinki.
Association of Finnish Operas, Iso-Roobertinkatu 20-22 A 76, SF-00120 Helsinki.
Association of Finnish Soloists, Museokatu 3 B 12, SF-00100 Helsinki.
Association of Finnish Symphony Orchestras, Aninkaistenkatu 3 B, SF-20110 Turku.
Association of Military Conductors, Helsingin varuskuntasoittokunta, PL 13, SF-00251 Helsinki.
Association of Music Libraries in Finland (Finnish Section of the International Association of Music Libraries), PO Box 148, SF-01301 Vantaa.
Association of Swedish Speaking Church Musicians, SF-10210 Ingå.
Concert Centre, Urho Kekkosen katu 8 C 30, SF-00100 Helsinki.
Federation for Church Music in Finland, Tollinpolku 1 C, SF-00410 Helsinki.
Federation for Finnish Traditional Music, Raumantie 1, SF-00350 Helsinki.
Federation of Music Teachers in Finland, Asemamiehenkatu 4, SF-00520 Helsinki.
Finland Festivals, PO Box 56, SF-00100 Helsinki.
Finlands svenska sång-och musikförbund r.f., Handelsespladen 23 B, SF-65100 Vasa.
Finnish Composers' Copyright Bureau, Lauttasaarentie 1, SF-00200 Helsinki.
Finnish Jazz Federation, PO Box 54, SF-00101 Helsinki.
Finnish Music Information Centre, Runeberginkatu 15 A, SF-00100 Helsinki.
Finnish Music Publishers' Association, Runeberginkatu 15 A 12, SF-00100 Helsinki.
Finnish Musicians' Union, Uudenmaankatu 36 D 21, SF-00120 Helsinki.
Finnish Society for Ethnomusicology, Mannerheimintie 40 C 69, SF-00100 Helsinki.
Folk Music Insitutte, SF-69600 Kaustinen.
Foundation for the Promotion of Finnish Music, Runeberginkatu 15 A 6, SF-00100 Helsinki.
Guild of Light Music Composers and Authors in Finland, Runeberginkatu 15 A 11, SF-00100 Helsinki.
Head Organization of Finnish Traditional Music, SF-39170 Jumesniemi.
IFPI (Finnish National Group), Runeberginkatu 15 A 12, SF-00100 Helsinki.
International Music Council (Finnish Section), Ukonkivenpolku 4 D 28, SF-01610 Vantaa.
Institute of Accordion Music in Finalnd, Kyrösselänkatu 3, SF-39500 Ikaalinen.
Korvat Auki r.y. (Society for Young Contemporary Composers), Kurkisuontie 12 D 35, SF-00940 Helsinki.
Music Artists Organization, Kuusisaarenkuja 9, SF-00340 Helsinki.
Musicological Society of Finland, Töölönkatu 28, SF-00260 Helsinki.
Performing Music Promotion Centre, Hietaniemenkatu 2, SF-00100 Helsinki.
Society of Finnish Composers, Runeberginkatu 15 A 11, SF-00100 Helsinki.
SULASOL (Federation of Amateur Musicians in Finland), Fredrikinkatu 61, SF-00100 Helsinki.
Workers' Institute of Music, Mannerheimintie 40 C 74, SF-00100 Helsinki.
Workers' Musical Organization in Finland, Hämeenpuisto 33 B 25, SF-33200 Tampere.

MUSIC ORGANIZATIONS

FRANCE

Académie du Disque Français et du Film Musical, 68 Boulevard de Courcelles, F-75017 Paris. Secretary: Michel de Bry.
American Center, 51 Rue de Bercy, F-75592 Paris Cédex 12. Managing Director: Michel Reilhac.
Association des Festivals Internationaux de France, 16 Place du Havre, F-75009 Paris.
Association Nationale de Diffusion Culturelle, 5 Rue Bellart, F-75015 Paris. Chief Officer: Christian Casadesus.
Association pour le Developpement des Echanges Artistique et Culturels (ADEAC), 101 Boulevard Raspail, F-75006, Paris.
Bibliothèque internationale de Musique Contemporaine (BIMC), 52 Rue de l'Hôtel de Ville, F-75004 Paris.
Bibliothèque Musicale Gustav Mahler, 11 bis Rue de Vézelay, F-75008 Paris.
Bibliothèque-Musée de l'Opera de Paris, 8 Rue Scribe, F-75009 Paris. Chief Officer: Martine Kahane.
Bureau International des Sociétés Gerant les Droits d'Enregistrement et de Reproduction Méchanique (BIEM), 56 Avenue Kléber, F-75116 Paris.
Centre de Documentation de la Musique Contemporaine, 225 Avenue Charles de Gaulle, F-92521 Neuilly-sur-Seine Cédex. Director: Marianne Lyon.
Centre de Documentation de Musique internationale, 116 Avenue du Président Kennedy, F-75016 Paris. Chief Officer: Michel Jullian.
Centre Européen de Documentation et d'information des Maîtrises d'Enfants (CEDIME), BP 143, F-06130 Grasse. Director: Jacques Menet.
Chambre Syndicale de l'Edition Musicale (CSDEM), 62 Rue Blanche, F-75009 Paris. President: René Boyer.
Chambre Syndicale de la Facture instrumentale, 62 Rue Blanche, F-75009 Paris. President: Bernard Maillot.
Chambre Syndicale des Editeurs de Musique, Editions Choudens, 38 Rue Jean Mermoz, F-75008 Paris.
Comite National de la Musique (CNM) (French section of the International Music Council-UNESCO), 252 Rue du Faubourg St. Honoré, Salle Pleyel, F-75008 Paris. General Manager: Jacques Masson-Forestier.
Commission d'Attribution de la Carte de Critique, 6 bis Rue Gabriel Laumain, F-75010 Paris. Chief Officer: André Camp.
Confédération internationales des Sociétés d'Auteurs et Compositeurs (CISAC), 11 Rue Keppler, F-75116 Paris. Secretary-General: Jean-Alexis Ziegler.
Direction de la Musique et de la Danse du Ministère de la Culture et de la Communication, 53 Rue St Dominique, F-75007 Paris. Chief Officer: Marc Bleuse.
Fédération Nationale de la Musique, 62 Rue Blanche, F-75009 Paris. President: Lucien Ades.
Groupe de l'Edition Audiovisuelle et Electronique (HAVE), 35 Rue Gregoire de Tours, F-75006 Paris.
Groupement des industries Electroniques (GIEL), 11 Rue Hamelin, F-75783 Paris Cédex 16. Chief Officer: Henri Anus.
Institut de Recherche et Coordination Acoustique/Musique, 31 Rue Saint-Merri, F-75004 Paris. Director: Laurent Bayle; Honorary Director: Pierre Boulez.
International Music Council (UNESCO), 1 Rue Miollis, F-75732 Paris Cédex 15. Secretary-General: Guy Huot.
International Music Critics Association, 11 Avenue d'Iena, F-75016 Paris. Secretary-General: Jacques Menet.
Jeunesses Musicales de France, 20 Rue Geoffroy l'Asnier, F-75004 Paris. Director: Robert Berthier.
Musicora: Salon de la Musique, 62 Rue de Miromesnil, F-75008 Paris.
Réunion des Théâtres Lyriques de France, Délégation Permanente in Paris, 7 Rue du Helder, F-75009 Paris.
Salon international de la Musique, 22/24 Rue du Président Wilson, F-92532 Levallois-Perret Cédex. Chief Officers: Bernard Becker and Kathryn Zagury.
Société Alkan, 145 Rue de Saussure, F-75017 Paris. Chief Officer: Laurent Martin.
Société des Auteurs et Compositeurs Dramatiques (SACD), 11 bis Rue Ballu, F-75009 Paris. Chief Officer: Jean-Jacques Plantin.
Société des Auteurs, Compositeurs et Editeurs (SACE), 62 Rue Blanche, F-75009 Paris. President: Wladimir Walberg.
Société des Auteurs, Compositeurs et Editeurs de Musique (SACEM), 225 Avenue Charles de Gaulle, F-92521 Neuilly-sur-Seine Cédex. Director-General: Jean-Loup Tournier.
Société pour l'Administration de Droit de Reproduction Méchanique des Auteurs, Compositeurs et Editeurs (SDRM), 225 Avenue de Charles de Gaulle, F-92521 Neuilly-sur-Seine Cédex.
Syndicat des Artistes de Variétés-Syndicat des Artistes Lyriques, 29 Rue Jean Jacques Rousseau, F-75001 Paris.
Syndicat des Artistes Musiciens Professionnels de Paris et de la Région Parisienne (SAMUP), 14-16 Rue des Lilas, F-75019 Paris. Secretary-General: François Nowak.
Syndicat des industries de Materiels Audiovisuels Electroniques (SIMAVELEC), 11 Rue Hamelin, F-75783 Paris Cédex 16. President: Jean-Claude Bonnet.
Syndicat Francais des Artistes interprètes (SFA), 21 bis Rue Victor Massé, F-75009 Paris. General Delegate: François Parrot.
Syndicat National des Agents Artistiques et Litteraires (SNAAL), 17 Rue Brey, F-75017 Paris. President: Roland Bertin.
Syndicat National des Artistes Musiciens de France (SNAM), 14-16 Rue des Lilas, F-75019 Paris. Secretary-General: François Nowak.
Syndicat National des Auteurs et des Compositeurs de Musique, 80 Rue Taitbout, F-75442 Paris Cédex 09. President: Antoine Duhamel.
Syndicat National des Chefs d'Orchestre, 3 Rue Chateau d'Eau, F-75010 Paris. Secretary-General: Robert Blot.
Union des Artistes, 21 bis Rue Victor Massé, F-75009 Paris.

GERMANY

Akademie der Künste Berlin, Hanseatenweg 10, W-1000 Belin 21. President: Prof Dr Walter Jens.
Allgemeiner Cäilien-Verband für Deutschland (ACV Dautschland), Andreasstrasse 9, W-8400 Regensburg. President: Professor Dr Wolfgang Bretschneider.
Arbeitsgemeinschaft der Leiter musikpädagogischer Studiengänge in der Bundesrepublik Deutschland (ALMS/BRD), Hochschule der Künste Berlin, Fachbereich 8/KWE 2, Fasanenstrasse 1, W-1000 Berlin 12. Speaker: Prof Dr Ulrich Mahlert.
Arbeitsgemeinschaft der Liedermacherinnen und Liedermacher aus der Bundesrepublik Deutschland (AG Song), Mailänder Strasse 14/92, W-6000 Frankfurt am Main 70. Contact: Stephan Rögner.
Arbeitsgemeinschaft der Musikakademien, Konservatorien und Hochschulinstitute, Städtische Akademie für Tonkunst, Ludwigshöhstrasse 120, W-6100 Darmstadt. Chairman: Hartmut Gerhold.
Arbeitsgemeinschaft der Volksmusikverbände e.V. (AVV), Rudolf-Maschke-Platz 6, W-7218 Trossingen. President:

MUSIC ORGANIZATIONS

Dr Johann Bauer.

Arbeitsgemeinschaft Deutsche Saxophonisten e.V. (ARDESA), Rötenäckerstrasse 2, W-8500 Nürnberg 90. Chairman: Günter Priesner.

Arbeitsgemeinschaft Deutscher Chorverbände (ADC), Adersheimer Strasse 60, W-3340 Wolfenbüttel. Chairman: Lore Auerbach.

Arbeitsgemeinschaft Deutscher Studentenorchester, Wilhelmstrasse 30, W-7400 Tübingen. Chairman: Helmut Calgéer.

Arbeitsgemeinschaft Deutscher Zupfinstrumenten-Verbände (AZV), Rissweg 22, W-7507 Pfinztal 2. Chairman: Adolf Mössner.

Arbeitsgemeinschaft freikirchlicher Chorwerke in Europa (AFC), Westfalenweg 207, W-5600 Wuppertal 1. Chairman: Pastoe Frieder Ringeis.

Arbeitsgemeinschaft für mittelrheinische Musikgeschichte e V, Musikwissenschaftliches Institut der Universität Mainz, Arbeitsstelle für landeskundliche Musikforschung, Welderweg 18, Pf 3980, W-6500 Mainz. Chairman: Prof Dr Christoph-Hellmut Mahling.

Arbeitsgemeinschaft für rheinische Musikgeschichte e V, Musikwissenschaftliches Institut der Universität Köln, Albertus-Magnus-Platz, W-5000 Cologne. Chairman: Prof Dr Siegfried Kross.

Arbeitsgemeinschaft Musik in der Evangelischen Jugend e.V. (AG Musik), Dorfstrasse 4, W-2309 Löptin. Chairman: Carl-Walter Petersen.

Arbeitsgemeinschaft Schulmusik an den Hochschulen für Musik in der Bundesrepublik Deutschland, Musikhochschule Lübeck, Grosse Peters-grube 17-29, W-2400 Lübeck. Chairman: Prof. Dr. Wilfried Ribke.

Arbeitsgemeinschaft zur Talentförderung in der Popularmusik und Unterhaltung, Rosenheimer Strasse 11, W-8000 Munich 80. Director: Prof Dr h.c. Erich Schulze.

Arbeitskreis der Musikbildungsstatten in der Bundesrepublik Deutschland, Landesakademie für die musizierende Jugend in Baden-Württemberg, Dr. Hans-Bruno Ernst, Schlossbezirk 6, Pf. 1180, W-7955, Ochsenhausen.

Arbeitskreis der Orgelsachverständigen, Hohenstrasse 19, W-7541 Straubenhardt 6 (Langenalb). Chairman: KMD Heinrich R Trötschel.

Arbeitskreis für Jazzpädagogik und improvisierte Musik e.V., Universität-GH Duisburg, "Jazzlabor", Lotharstrasse 65, W-4100 Duisburg. Chairman: Prof. Dr. Ilse Storb.

Arbeitskreis für Rock und Pop in der Musikschule (ARPS), Städt. Clara-Schumann-Musikschule, Bernd Wiesemann, Bilker Strasse 11, W-4000 Düsseldorf 1.

Arbeitskreis für Schulmusik und allgemeine Musikpädagogik e.V. (AFS), Gründgensstrasse 16, W-2000 Hamburg 60. Chairman: Prof. Dr. Werner Krützfeldt.

Arbeitskreis Musik in der Jugend e.V. (AMJ) (Deutsche Foderation junger Chore und Instrumentalgruppen), Adersheimer Strasse 60, W-3340 Wolfenbüttel. Chairman: Lore Auerbach.

Arbeitskreis Musikpädagogische Forschung e.V. (AMPF), Dr Georg Maas, Nycolaystrasse, W-4790 Paderborn-Dahl.

Arbeitskreis sorbischer Musikschaffender (ASM) beim sorbischen Künstlerbund e.V., Postplatz 2, O-8600 Bautzen. Chairman: Merko Solta-Scholze.

Arbeitskreis Studium Populärer Musik e.V., Alenka Barber-Kersovan, Ahornweg 154, W-2083 Halstenbek.

Bayerische Akademie der Schönen Künste, Max-Joseph-Platz 3, W-8000 Munich 22. President: Heinz Friedrich.

Bayerischer Landesverein für Heimatpflege e.V. Beratungsstelle für Volksmusik, Ludwigstrasse 23, Rgb., W-8000 Munich 22. 1st Chairman: Max Streibl.

Bayerischer Musiklehrer-Verband e.V., Willibaldstrasse 49, W-8000 Munich 21. Chairman: Roland Sieber.

Beethoven-Gesellschaft München e.V., Ruth Petersen, Karwendelstrasse 6, W-8011 Poring. President: Dr Rüdiger V Canal.

Berufsverband der Musiktherapeuten Deutschlands e.V. (BMD), Waldhüterpfad 38, W-1000 Berlin 37. Chairman: Herbert Lunkenheimer.

Berufsverband für Kunst-, Musik-und Tanztherapie: Europäischer Dachverband für kunstlerische Therapien e.V., Grüner Hang 16, W-4400 Münster. Chairman: Prof. Dr. Georg Hörmann.

Berufsverband Klinischer Musiktherapeuten in der Bundesrepublik Deutschland e.V., Stader Weg 31, W-2800 Bremen. Chairman: Ilse Wolfram.

Bildungswerk Rhythmik e.V. (BWR), Kalscheurer Weg S Nr. 12, W-5000 Cologne 1. Chairman: Christine Humpert.

Bogenforschungsgesellschaft: Förderverein zur Darstellung und Entwicklung von Bogenformen für Musikinstrumente e.V., Rudolf Gähler, Ankerstrasse 34, W-5205 Sankt Augustin 1. Chairman: Rudolf Gahler.

Brahmsgellschaft Baden-Baden e.V., Pf. 1609, W-7560 Gaggenau. Chairman: Dr. Werner Hoppe.

Brandenburgisches Colloquiem für Neue Musik e V, Prof Paul-Heinz Dittrich, Clara-Zetkin-Strasse 1, O-1276 Buckow.

Brüder-Busch-Gesellschaft e V, Untere Wiesenstrasse 33, W-5912 Hilchenbach. Business Manager: Wolfgang Burbach.

Bund Christlicher Posaunenchöre Deutschlands e V (BCPD), Sophienstrasse 21 D, W-7000 Stuttgart 1. Chairman: Pastor Reiner Haidle.

Bund der Theatergemeinden e V, Bonner Talweg 10, W-5300 Bonn 1. President: Friedrich von Kekulé.

Bund Deutscher Blasmusikverbände e V (BDB), Am Märzengraben 6, W-7800 Freiburg im Breisgau. 1st President: Dr Norbert Nothhelfer.

Bund Deutscher Klavierbauer e V, Frankenwert 35, W-5000 Cologne 1. Chairman: Udo Schmidt.

Bund Deutscher Liebhaberorchester e.V. (BDLO), Schlegelstrasse 14, W-8500 Nürnberg. Chairman: Dr Joachim Conradi.

Bund Deutscher Orgelbaumeister e V (BDO), Frankfurter Ring 243, W-8000 Munich 40. 1st Chairman: Hans-Gerd Klais.

Bund Deutscher Zupfmusiker e V (BDZ), Huulkamp 26, W-2000 Hamburg 65. Chairman: Rüdiger Grambow.

Bund sorbischer Gesangsvereine: Zwjazk serbskich spewarskich towarstwow, Haus der Sorben, Referat Kultur, Postplatz 2, O-8600 Bautzen. Chairman: Achim Brankatschk.

Bundes-Eltern-Vertretung e V der Musikschulen des VdM, Ossietzkkyring 55, W-3000 Hanhover 91. 1st Chairman: Dieter Fröhling.

Bundesfachgruppe Musikpädagogik e V (Bfg), Eosanderstrasse 24, W-1000 Berlin 10. Chairman: Prof Dr Thomas Ott.

Bundesinnungverband für das Musikinstrumenten-Handwerk (BIV), Kreishandwerkerschaft Köln, Frankenwerft 35, W-5000 Cologne 1. Chairman: Johann Scholtz.

Bundesverband der Deutschen Musikinstrumenten-Hersteller e V (BdMH), Hildastrasse 5, W-6200 Wiesbaden. 1st Chairman: Christian Benker.

Bundesverband der deutschen Volksbühnen-Vereine e V, Am Handelshof 9, W-4300 Essen 1. Chairman: Axel Wolters.

Bundesverband der Jugendkunstschulen und kulturpädagogischer Einrichtungen e V (BJKE), Luisenstrasse 22,

MUSIC ORGANIZATIONS

W-4750 Unna. Chairman: Peter Vermeulen.

Bundesverband der Phonographischen Wirtschaft e V (Bundesverband Phono), Grelckstrasse 36, W-2000 Hamburg 54. Chairman: Thomas M. Stein.

Bundesverband Deutscher Gesangspädagogen e V (BDG), Prof Helmut Kretschmar, Waldeck 7, W-4930 Detmold. President: Helmut Kretschmar.

Bundesverband für Tanztherapie Deutschland e V, Hostrasse 16, Marienburg, W-4019 Monheim. 1st Chairman: Wally Kaechele.

Bundesverband Rhythmische Erziehung e V (BRE), Akademie Remscheid, Küppelstein 34, W-5630 Remscheid 1. Chairman: Prof. Brigitte Steinmann.

Bundesverband Studentische Kulturarbeit e V (BSK), Kaiserstrasse 32, W-5300 Bonn 1.

Bundesvereinigung der Musikveranstalter e V, Kronprinzenstrasse 46, W-5300 Bonn 2. President: Leo Imhoff.

Bundesvereinigung Deutscher Blas-und Volksmusikverbände e V (BDBV), König-Karl-Strasse 13, W-7000 Stuttgart 50. President: Minister Gerhard Weiser.

Bundesvereinigung Deutscher Laienmusikverbande (BDLV), Arbeitsgemeinschaft der Volksmusikverbände, Rudolf-Maschke-Platz 6, W-7218 Trossingen.

Bundesvereinigung Kulturelle Jugendbildung e V (BKJ), Küppelstein 34, W-5630 Remscheid. Chairman: Prof Bruno Tetzner.

BVT-Bundesverband Ton der Film-Tonmeister in der Bundesrepublik Deutschland e V, Jenfelder Allee 80, W-2000 Hamburg 70.

Carl-Orff-Stiftung, Königinstrasse 25, W-8000 Munich 22. Chairman: Liselotte Orff.

Chopin-Gesellschaft in der Bundesrepublik Deutschland e V, Kasinostrasse 3 (J F Kenedy-Haus), W-6100 Darmstadt 11. President: Maciej Lukaszczyk.

Christlicher Sängerbund e V (CS), Westfalenweg 207, W-5600 Wuppertal 1.

Club Deutscher Drehorgelfreunde e V, Wilfried Hömmerich, Brusseler Strasse 20, Pf. 170103, W-5300 Bonn 1. Chairman: Wilfried Hömmerich.

Confédération des Associations des Facteurs d'Instruments de Musique de la CEE (CAFIM), Hildstrasse 5, W-6200 Wiesbaden. President: Bernard Maillot.

Deutsche Angestellten-Gewerkschaft (DAG); Bundesberufsgruppe Kunst und Medien; Bundesfachgruppe Musikerziehung, Karl-Muck-Platz 1, Pf 301230, W-2000 Hamburg 36.

Deutsche Arbeitsgemeinschaft für Akustik (DAGA), Hauptstrasse 5, W-5340 Bad Honnef 1. Chairman: Prof Dr H Kuttruff.

Deutsche Disc-Jockey-Organisation (DDO), Kaiser-Friedrich-Allee 1-3, W-5100 Aachen. Contact: Klaus Quirini.

Deutsche Forschungsgemeinschaft e V (DFG), Kennedyallee 40 Pf 205004, W-5300 Bonn 2. President: Prof Dr Wolfgang Frühwald.

Deutsche Frank-Martin-Gesellschaft e V, Hochschule für Musik Köln, Dagobertstrasse 38, W-5000 Cologne 1. President: Dirk Schortemeier.

Deutsche Gesellschaft für Flöte e V, Eschenheimer Anlage 30, W-6000 Frankfurt am Main 1. President: András Adorján.

Deutsche Gesellschaft für Musik bei Behinderten e V (DGMB), Frangenheimstrasse 4, W-5000 Cologne 41. Chairman: Prof Dr Helmut Moog.

Deutsche Gesellschaft für Musikpsychologie e V (DGfM), Meisenweg 7, W-3008 Garbsen 1. Chairman: Prof Dr Klaus-Ernst Behne.

Deutsche für Musiktherapie e.V. (DGMT), Collinistrasse 22, Pf. 100738, W-6800 Mannheim 1. 1st Chairman: Franz Mecklenbeck.

Deutsche Gesellschaft für Volkstanz e.V. (DGV), Anni Herrmann, Paul-Lincke-Ufer 25, W-1000 Berlin 36. Chairman: Gerhard Palmer.

Deutsche Glockenspiel-Vereinigung e.V., Dr. K.F. Waack, Stedebring 7, W-3000 Hannover 71. Chairman: Dr. Karl-Friedrich Waack.

Deutsche Johann-Strauss-Gesellschaft e.V., Untere Anlage 2, W-8630 Coburg. Chairman: Arthur Kulling.

Deutsche Mozart-Gesellschaft e.V. (DMG), Karlstrasse 6, W-8900 Augsburg. Chairman: Prof. Dr. Erich Valentin.

Deutsche Musikinstrumentenstiftung, Emil-Nolde-Weg 29, W-3400 Göttingen. Chairman: Prof. Dr. Jürgen Costede.

Deutsche Orchestervereinigung e.V. in der DAG (DOV), Heimhuder Strasse 5, W-2000 Hamburg 13. Chairman: Rolf Becker.

Deutsche Phono-Akademie e.V (DPhA), Grelckstrasse 36, W-2000 Hamburg 54. Chairman: Gerd Gebhardt.

Deutsche Richard-Wagner-Gesellschaft e.V., Schlossstrasse 9a, W-1000 Berlin 28. 1st Chairman: Prof. Uwe Faerber.

Deutsche Rossini-Gesellschaft e.V., Hohenheimerstrasse 84, W-70000 Stuttgart 1. 1st Chairman: Gustav Kuhn.

Deutsche Sängerschaft (Weimarer CC), Cranachweg 9, W-7320 Göppingen. Chairman: Franz Jedlitschka.

Deutsche Schubert-Gesellschaft e.V. (DSG), Handelstrasse 6, W-4100 Duisburg 14 (Rheinhausen). Chairman: Günter Berns.

Deutsche Sektion der Internationalen Gesellschaft für Elektroakustische Musik e.V. (DecimE), Treuchtlinger Strasse 8, W-1000 Berlin 30. Chairman: Folkmar Hein.

Deutsche Stiftung Musikleben (DSM), Herrengraben 3, W-2000 Hamburg 11. President: Erhard Bouillons.

Deutsche Suzuki Gesellschaft e.V, Ankerstrasse 34, W-5205 Sankt Augustin 1. 1st Chairman: Rudolf Gähler.

Deutscher Akkordeonlehrer-Verband e.V. (DALV), Kapfstrasse 68, W-7218 Trossingen 1. Chairman: Wolfgang Eschenbacher.

Deutscher Allgemeiner Sängerbund e.V. (DAS), Dohlenstrasse 11, W-4600 Dortmund 15. President: Fritz Neuhaus.

Deutscher Berufsverband für Tanzpadagogik e.V., Hollestrasse 1g, W-4300 Essen 1. 1st Chairman: Ulrich Roehm.

Deutscher Bühnenverein-Bundesverband deutscher Theater e.V. (DBV), Quatermarkt 5, W-5000 Cologne 1. President: Prof. August Everding.

Deutuscher Bundesverband der Spielmanns-, Fanfaren-, Hörner-und Musikzüge e.V., Haupstrasse 61, W-3300 Braunschweig. President: Paul Mittag.

Deutscher Bundesverband Tanz e.V. (DBT), Küppelstein 34, W-5630 Remscheid. Chairman: Annmargret Pretz.

Deutscher Chorverband Pueri Cantores, Zwölfling 12, W-4300 Essen 1. President: Georg Sump.

Deutscher Feuerwehrverband e.V.: Fachgebiet Musik, Koblenzer Strasse 133, W-5300 Bonn 2. President: Hinrich Struve.

Deutscher Harmonika-Verband e.V. (DHV), Rudolf-Maschke-Platz 6, Pf. 1150. W-7218 Trossingen 1. President: Ernst Pfister.

Deutscher Hotel- und Gaststättenverband (DEHOGA), Fachabteilung musikveranstaltende Betriebe, Kronprinzenstrase 46, W-5300 Bonn 2. Chairman: Otto Manfred Lamm.

Deutscher Komponisten-Verband e.V. (DKV), Beuckestrasse 26, W-1000 Berlin 37. President: Karl Heinz Wahren.

Deutscher Kulturrat, Adenaueralle 7, W-5300 Bonn 1. Chairman: Rolf Zitzlsperger.

Deutscher Musikrat e.V. (DMR), Nationalkomitee der Bundesrepublik Deutschland im Internationalen Musikrat,

MUSIC ORGANIZATIONS

Am Michaelshof 4a, W-5300 Bonn 2. President: Prof. Dr. Franz Müller-Heuser.

Deutscher Musikverleger-Verband e.V. (DMV), Friedrich-Wilhelm-Strasse 31, W-5300 Bonn 1. President: Maja-Maria Reis.

Deutscher Rockmusiker-Verband e.V., Kolbergerstrasse 30, W-2120 Lüneburg. Chairman: Ole Seelenmeyer.

Deutscher Sangerbund e.V. (DSB), Bernhardstrasse 166, Pf. 510628, W-5000 Cologne 51. President: Alfred Engelmann.

Deutscher Schützenbund e.V., Fachgruppe Musik, Niedersächsischer Sportschützenverband, Wunstorfer Lanndstrasse 57, W-3000 Hannover 91.

Deutscher Tanzrat/Deutscher Ballettrat e.V., Bonner Künstlerhaus, Graurheindorfer Strasse 23, W-5300 Bonn 1. Chairman: Iskra Zankova.

Deutscher Textdichter-Verband e.V., Dohlenweg 5, W-5020 Frechen. President: Heinz Korn.

Deutscher Tonkünstlerverband e.V., Verband deutscher Musikerzieher und konzertierender Künstler (VDMK), Landsberger Strasse 425, W-8000 Munich 60. President: Prof- Siegfried Palm.

Deutscher Turner-Bund e.V., Fachgebiet Musik und Spielmannswesen, Bernhard Lott, Ellernstrasse 20, W-3000 Hannover 1. President: Prof. Dr. Jürgen Dieckert.

Deutscher Zithermusik-Bund e.V. (DZB), Ulrich Oesterle, Steigäcker 4, W-7140 Ludwigsburg.

Deutsches High-Fidelity Institu e.V. (DHFI), Karlstrasse 19-21, W-6000 Frankfurt am Main 1. Chairman: Karl Breh.

Deutsches Tubaforum e.V., Saarbrückener Strasse 26, W-3000 Hannover 71. Chairman: Prof. Klemens Propper.

Die Kunstlergilde e.V., Hafenmarkt 2, W-7300 Esslingen/Neckar. Chairman: Albrecht Baehr.

Dr.-Hanns-Simon-Stiftung, Bedaplatz, W-5520 Bitburg.

Dramatiker-Union e.V. (DU), Bismarckstrasse 107, W-1000 Berlin 12. President: Prof. Giselher Klebe.

Dramaturgische Gesellschaft e.V., Tempelhofer Ufer 22, W-1000 Berlin 61. Chairman: Dr. Klaus Pierwoss.

Dresdner Zentrum für zeitgenössischen Musik, Schevenstrasse 17/150-05, O-8054 Dresden. Director: Prof. Udo Zimmermann.

Emil-Berliner-Stiftung in der Deutschen Phono-Akademie e V, Grelckstrasse 36, W-2000 Hamburg 54. Chairman: Richard Busch.

EPTA-Gesellschaft der Pädagogik für Tasteninstrumente e V, Bult 6, W-4590 Cloppenburg. Chairman: Prof. Edith Picht-Axenfeld.

Ernst-Pepping-Gesellschaft e V, Jebensstrasse 3, W-1000 Berlin 12. Chairman: Prof. Dr. Heinrich Poos.

E T A-Hoffmann-Gesellschaft e V, Dr Georg Wirth, Wetzelstrasse 19, W-8600 Bamberg. 1st Chairman: Dr. Georg Wirth.

Ernst-von-Siemens-Stiftung, Zug (Schweiz), Wittelsbacherplatz 2, W-8000 Munich 2.

Eugen-Jochum-Gesellschaft e.V., Marktplatz 14, Kulturamt, W-8942 Ottobeuren. President: Dr. Georg Simnacher.

Europa Cantat-Europäische Föderation Junger Chöre e.V. (EC-EFJC), Grosser Hillen 38, W-3000 Hannover 71. President: Marcel Corneloup.

Europäische Arbeitsgemeinschaft Schulmusik (EAS) (European Alliance for School Music), Bundesgeschäftsstelle VDS, Weihergarten 5, W-6500 Mainz 1.

Europäische Union der Musikwettbewerbe für die Jugend-European Union of Music Competitions for Youth (EMCY), Herzog-Johann-Strasse 10, W-8000 Munich 60. Contact: Dr. Eckart Rohlfs.

European Guitar Teachers Association (EGTA), Haslei 40, W-4780 Lippstadt. 1st Chairmen: Reinhard Froese and Michael Koch.

European String Teachers Association (ESTA)-Union der Bundesrepublik Deutschland e.V., Dagmar Klevenhusen, Friedenweg 6, W-2807 Achim. President: Prof. Maria Grevesmuhl.

Evangelischer Sängerbund e.V. (ESB), Bremer Strasse 2, W-5600 Wuppertal 1. Chairman: Rudolf Steege.

Fachverband Deutsche Klavierindustrie e.V. (FDK), Friedrich-Wilhelm-Strasse 31, W-5300 Bonn 1. Chairman: Karl Schulze.

Fachverbad Deutscher Berufscholeiter e.V. (FDB), Unkenweg 19, W-4330 Mülheim/Ruhr. President: Prof Dr Gerhard Schulte.

Fachverband Historische Tasteninstrumente e V (FHT), Untermarkt 40, W-8190 Wolfratshausen. Chairman: Reinhard Hoppe.

Fachverband Unterhaltungselektronik im Zentralverband Elektrotechnik-und Elektroniindustrie e V, Stresemannallee 19, W-6000 Frankfurt am Main 70. Chairman: Wilhelm Kahle.

Ferenc-Fricsay Gesellschaft e V (FFG), Heerstrasse 70, W-1000 Berlin 19. Chairman: Prof Dr Wolfgang Geiseler.

Förderkreis Hugo Herrmann e V, Ringinger Tal 26, W-7453 Burladingen. Chairman: Werner Zintgraf.

Förderkreis Instrumentales Musizieren e V, Friedrich-Wilhelm-Strasse 31, W-5300 Bonn 1. Chairman: Alfred Döll.

Förderkreis Unterhaltungsmusik e V (FKU), Ringstrasse 4, W-4223 Voerde 1. Chairman: Kurt Althans.

Förderverein der Klassischen Gesangskunst in Deutschland e V, Pf. 101516, W-7000 Stuttgart 10. Chairman: Prof Sylvia Geszty.

Fonds Darstellende Künste e V, Am Handelshof 9, W-4300 Essen 1. Chairman: Prof Dr Jürgen-Dieter Waidelich.

Fonds Soziokultur e V, Stirnband 10, W-5800 Hagen 1. Chairman: Dr Olaf Schwencke.

Forschungsgemeinschaft Musikinstrumente e V (FG), Hildastrasse 5, W-6200 Wiesbaden. Chairman: Hugo Schreiber.

Franz-Grothe-Stiftung, Rosenheimer Strasse 11, W-8000 Munich 80. Chairman: Hans Schröpf.

Franz-Liszt-Gesellschaft e.V. Weimar, Platz der Demokratie 2/3, O-5300 Weimar. President: Prof Dr Detlef Altenburg.

Franz-Wirth-Gedächtnis-Stiftung zur Förderung des musikalischen Nachwuchses, Spitalerstrasse 28, W-2000 Hamburg 1. Chairman: Margot Brandes.

Frau und Musik-Internationaler Arbeitskreis e.V. Geschäftsstelle, Adelheid Klammt, Vogesort 8 F, W-3000 Hannover 91. Chairman: Prof. Siegrid Ernst.

Freie Akademie der Künste Hamburg, Ferdinandstor la, W-2000 Hamburg. President: Prof. Armin Sandig.

Freunde der Querflöte e V Gevelsberg-Gemeinrütziger Verein zur Erforschung und Förderung des Querflötenspiels (fdq), Körnerstrasse 51, W-5820 Gevelsberg. Chairman: Elli Edler-Busch.

Freunde der Tonkunst und Musikerziehung e V, Landsberger Strasse 425, W-8000 Munich 60. 1st Chairman: Dr Rüdiger von Canal.

Freidich-Kiel-Gesellschaft e.V., Ithstrasse 20, W-3256 Coppenbrügge 1. 1st Chairman: Dr Jürgen Böhme.

Fritz-Büchtger-Kuratorium, Musica Sacra Viva, Pf. 750202, W-8000 Munich 75. Chairman: Andreas Weymann.

GEDOK-Verband der Gemeinschaften der Künstlerinnen und Kunstfreunde e.V., Einern 29, W-5600 Wuppertal 2. President: Dr. Renate Massmann.

GEMA-Stiftung, Rosenheimer Strasse 11, W-8000 Munich 80. Chairman: Prof. Dr. Reinhold Kreile.

Genossenshaft Deutscher Bühnenangehöriger (GDBA) in der DAG, Feldbrunnenstrasse 74, W-2000 Hamburg 13. President: Hans Herdlein.

MUSIC ORGANIZATIONS

Georg Hesse Stiftung, Am Brühl 13, W-7825 Lenzkirch 3 (Kappel). Chairman: Hannelore Hesse-Menge.

Georg-Friedrich-Handel-Gesellschaft-Internationale Vereinigung e.V., Händelhaus, Grosse Nikolaistrasse 5/6, O-4020 Halle an der Saale. President: Prof. Dr. Bernd Baselt.

Gesamtverband Deutscher Muskfachgeschäfte e.V. (GDM), Friedrich-Wilhelm-Strasse 31, W-5300 Bonn 1. President: Alfred Döll.

Gesellschaft der Orgelfreunde e.V. (GdO), Josefstrasse 6, W-6642 Mettlach 1. Chairman: Prof. Alfred Reichling.

Gesellschaft für Alte Musik e.V. (G.A.M.), Birkenstrasse 18, W-7218 Trossingen. Chairman: Prof. Dr. Ludger Lohmann.

Gesellschaft für Bayerische Musikgeschichte e.V., Pf. 100611, W-8000 Munich 1. Chairman: Prof. Dr. Theodor Göllner.

Gesellschaft für Musikforschung (GfM), Heinrich-Schüz-Allee 35, W-3500 Kassel. President: Prof. Dr. Klaus W. Niemöller.

Gesellschaft für Musikpädagogik e.V. (GMP), Von-der-Tann-Strasse 38, W-8400 Regensburg. Chairman: Prof. Dr. Reinhard Schneider.

Gesellschaft für Musikwissenschaft e.V., Akademie der Künste, Luisenstrasse 58-60, O-0140 Berlin. President: Dr. Klaus Mehner.

Gesellschaft für Neue Musik e.V. (GNM)-Sektion Bundesrepublik Deutschland der Internationalen Gesellschaft für Neue Musik (IGNM), Schwedlerstrasse 2-4, W-6000 Frankfurt am Main 1. President: Friedrich Goldmann.

Gesellschaft für Selbstspielende Musikinstrumente e.V., Heiligenstock 46, W-5060 Bergisch Gladbach 2. Chairman: Dr. Jürgen Hocker.

Gesellschaft für Theatergeschichte e.V., Mecklenburgische Strasse 56, W-1000 Berlin 33. Chairman: Prof. Dr. Peter Spengel.

Gesellschaft zur Förderung der Berufsbildung junger Künstler e.V. (GFBK), Eichkatzweg 25, W-3107 Hambuhren.

Gesellschaft zur Förderung der Westfalischen Kulturarbeit e.V., Landschaftsverband Westfalen-Lippe, Warendorfer Strasse 14, W-4400 Münster. Chairman: Reinhold Brauner.

Gottfried-Silbermann-Gesellschaft e.V., Beethovenstrasse 7, O-9200 Freiberg/Sachsen. President: Hans Otto.

Gotthard-Schierse-Stiftung, Bundesallee 1-12, W-1000 Berlin 15. Chairman: Horst Göbel.

Günter Henle Stiftung München, G. Henle Verlag, Forstenrieder Allee 122, Pf. 710466, W-8000 Munich 71. Chairman: Anne Liese Henle.

Günter-Neumann-Stiftung, Schlüterstrasse 36, W-1000 Berlin 12. Chairman: Dr. Hans Peter Wüst.

Hamburger Bach-Gesellschaft e.V.-Internationaler Verein für die Musik der Bach-Sohne (HBG), Durchschnitt 25, W-2000 Hamburg 13. Chairman: Prof. Edith Picht-Axenfeld.

Hamburger Telemann-Gesellschaft e.V., Haus der Patriotischen Gesellschaft, Trostbrücke 4, W-2000 Hamburg 11. Chairman: Eckart Klessmann.

Hamburgische Kulturstiftung, Chilehaus C, Burckardplatz 13, W-2000 Hamburg 1.

Hans-Breuer-Stifting zur Pflege und Förderung des deutshcen Liedgutes e.V., Hochschule für Musik and Theater, Harvestehuder Weg 10-12, W-2000 Hamburg 13. Chairman: Prof. Dr. Hermann Rauhe.

Hans-Pfitzner-Gesellschaft e.V., Mauerkircher Strasse 8, W-8000 Munich 80. Chairman: General Music Director Prof. Rolf Reuter.

Heinrich-Heine-Gesellschaft e.V. (HHG), Bolkerstrasse 53, Pf. 1120, W-4000 Düsseldorf 1. Chairman: Gerd Högener.

Heinrich-Kaminski-Gesellschaft e.V., Storchen-Apotheke, Hauptstrasse 20, W-7890 Waldshut-Tiengen 2. 1st Chairman: Jürgen Klein.

Herbert von Karajan Stiftung, Prof. Peter Csobádi, Seestrasse 13, A-5322 Hof bei Salzburg.

Industriegewerkschaft Medien-Druck und Papier, Publizistik und Kunst (IG Medien), Friedrichstrasse 15, Pf. 102451, W-7000 Stuttgart 1. Chairman: Erwin Ferlemann.

Institut für Bildung und Kultur e.V. (IBK), Küppelstein 34, W-5630 Remscheid. Chairman: Prof. Bruno Tetzner.

Insitut für Neue Musik und Musikerziehung e.V., Grafenstrasse 35, W-6100 Darmstadt. Chairman: Prof Johannes Fritsch.

Interessenverband Deutscher Komponisten e.V. (IDK), Willinghusener Landstrasse 70, W-2000 Barsbüttel. Chairman: Gustav Kneip.

Interessenverband Deutscher Konzertveranstalter und Künstlervermittler e.V. (IDKV), Lenhartzstrasse 15, W-2000 Hamburg 20. President: Jens Michow.

International Council for Traditional Music (ICTM)-Nationalkomitee der Bundeserpublik Deutschland, Otto-Friedrich-Universität Bamberg-Volksmusik, Feldkirchenstrasse 21, W-8600 Bamberg. President: Prof. Dr. Marianne Bröcker.

International Federation of the Phonographic Industry (IFPI)-Deutsche Landesgruppe, Grelckstrasse 36, W-2000 Hamburg 54. Chairman: Helmut Fest.

Internationale Andreas-Werckmeister-Gesellschaft e.V., Kulturamt der Stadt Halberstadt, Dominikanerstrasse 16, O-3600 Halberstadt. President: Dr. Rüdiger Pfeiffer.

Internationale Arbeitsgemeinschaft der Theaterbesucherorganisationen (IATO), Am Handelshof 9, W-4300 Essen 1. President: Prof. Dr. Jurgen-Dieter Waidelich.

International Carl-Maria-von-Weber-Gesellschaft e,V., Staatsbibliothek zu Berlin (Preussischer Kulturbsitz), Musikabteilung, Unter den Linden 8, Pf. 1312, O-1086 Berlin. Chairman: Dr. Ute Schwab.

Internationale Discotheken Organisationen, Deutsche Diskotheken-Unternehmer, Kaiser-Friedrich-Allee 1-3, W-5100 Aachen. Contact: Helga Quirini.

Internationale Draeseke-Gesellschaft e.V., Matthias-Grünewald-Strasse 5, W-6720 Speyer. 1st Chairman: Dr. Helmut Loos.

Internationale Fasch-Gesellschaft e.V., Franciseum Zerbst, Weinberg 1, O-3400 Zerbst. President: Dr. Rüdiger Pfeiffer.

Internationale Föderation für Chormusik-International Federation for Choral Music (IFCM), Burgstrasse 33, W-5300 Bonn 2. President: Dr. H. Royce Saltzmann.

Internationale Gesellschaft für Musik in der Medizin e.V. (ISFMIM), Paulmannshöher Strasse 17, W-5880 Ludenscheid. Chairman: Dr. Roland Droh.

Internationale Gesellschaft für Muzikerziehung (ISME), Deutsche Sektion, Deutscher Musikrat/AGMM, Am Michaelshof 4a, W-5300 Bonn 2.

Internationale Gesellschaft für musikpädagogische Fortbildung e.V. (IGMF), Pf. 1443, W-5920 Bad Berleburg. Chairman: Prof. Dr. Hans-Walter Berg.

Internationale Gesellschaft für Urheberrecht e.V. (INTERGU), Rosenheimer Strasse 11, W-8000 Munich 80.

Internationale Gitarristische Vereinigung Freiburg e.V. (IGVF), Lessingstrasse 4, W-7800 Freiburg im Breisgau. Chairman: Jörg Sommermeyer.

Internationale Heinrich-Schütz-Gesellschaft e.V. (ISG), Heinrich-Schütz-Allee 35, W-3500 Kassel. Chairman: Prof. Dr. Arno Forchert.

Internationale Hugo-Wolf-Akademie für Gesang-Dichtung-Liedkunst e.V., Neckarstrasse 86, W-7000 Stuttgart

MUSIC ORGANIZATIONS

1. Chairman: Dr. Rainer Wilhelm.

Interntionale Johann-Nepomuk-David-Gesellschaft E.V. (IDG), Fichtenstrasse 19, W-7336 Uhingen. Chairman: Wolfgang Dallmann.

Internationale Joseph-Martin-Kraus-Gesellschaft e.V., Kellereistrasse 25, Pf. 1422, W-6967 Buchen 1. Chairman: Prof. Dr. Friedrich W Riedel.

Internationale Louis Spohr Gesellschaft e.V., Schöne Aussicht 2, W-3500 Kassel. President: Wolfgang Windführ.

Internationale Meyerbeer-Gesellschaft e.V., Tristanstrasse 10, W-8034 Germering. Chairman: Karl Zelenka.

Internationale Posaunenvereinigung (IPV)-Sektion Deutschland, U. Launhardt, Hahnenstrasse 18, W-5024 Pulheim. President: Prof. Johannes Doms.

Internationale Trompetergilde e.V., Europäische Sektion (Euro-ITG), Pf. 1143, W-7880 Bad Sackingen. Chairmen: Dr. Edward H Tarr and Prof. Max Sommerhalders.

Internationale Vereinigung der Musikbibliotheken, Musikarchive und Musikdokumentationszentren (AIBM) Gruppe Bundesrepublik Deutschland, Dr. Bettina V. Seyfried, Gärtnerstrasse 25-32, Pf-450229, W-12207 Berlin. President: Dr. Joachim Jaenecke.

Internationale Viola-Gesellschaft-Sektion Bundesrepublik Deutschland e.V., Ahornweg 9, W-5308 Rheinbach. 1st Chairman: Prof. Barbara Westphal.

Internationaler Arbeitskreis für Musik e.V. (IAM), Heinrich-Schütz-Allee 29, W-3500 Kassel. Chairman: Prof. Diether de la Motte.

Internationaler Verein Freund behinderter Tonkünstler e.V., Melchiorstrasse 74, W-8000 Munich 71. Chairman: Elisabeth Stöcklein-Weiss.

Internationales Forum Junge Chormusik Rotenburg (Wümme) e.V., Rathaus, Grosse Strasse 1, W-2720 Rotenburg/ Wümme. President: Prof. Dr. Guy Maneveau.

Jacques-Offenbach-Gesellschaft e.V. Bad Ems (JOG), Dr. Günther Obst, Waldstrasse 3, W-5427 Bad Ems. Chairman: Dr. Günther Obst.

Jean Sibelius Gesellschaft Deutschland e.V., Trivastrasse 19, W-8000 Munich 19. President: Prof. August Everding.

Johann Adolph Hasse-Gesellschaft München e.V., Ursula Biehl, Landsberger Strasse 55, W-8080 Fürstenfeldbruck. Chairman: Ursula Biehl.

Johannes-Brahms-Gesellschaft Internationale Vereinigung e.V., Trostbrücke 4, W-2000 Hamburg 11. President: Detlef Kraus.

Joseph-Haas-Gesellschaft e.V. (JHG), Veroneserstrasse 4, W-8000 Munich 90. President: Prof. Dr. Siegfried Gmeinwieser.

Joseph-Suder-Gesellschaft e.V., Grünwalderstrasse 250, W-8000 Munich 90. Chairman: Reinhold Pfandzelter.

Jürgen Ponto-Stiftung zur Förderung junger Künstler, Jürgen-Ponto-Platz 1, W-6000 Frankfurt am Main 11. Chairman: Wolfgang Röller.

Karg-Elert-Gesellschaft e.V. (KEG), Lortzingstrasse 11, W-7980 Ravensburg. Chairmen: Prof. Dr. Wolfgang Stockmeier and Johannes Michel.

Karl-Klingler-Stiftung e.V., Siemens AG, Dr. Rüdiger v. Canal, Wittelsbacherplatz 2, W-8000 Munich 2.

Kodály-Gesellschaft e.V., Conrad W. Mayer, Grabenstrasse 22, W-7812 Bad Krozingen.

Körber-Stiftung, Kampchaussee 10, Pf. 800660. W-2000 Hamburg 80. Chairman: Ulrich Voswinckel.

Konferenz der Leiter der kirchlinchen und der staatslichen Ausbildungsstatten für Kirchenmusik und der Landeskirchenmusikdirektoren in der Evangelischen Kirche in Deutschland (EKD), Miquelallee 7, W-6000 Frankfurt am Main. President: LKMD Dr. Dietrich Schuberth.

Konferenz der Leiter katholischer kirchenmusikalischer Ausbildungsstatten Deutschlands, Amt für Kirchenmusik, Schoferstrasse 4, W-7800 Freiburg im Breisgau. Chairman: Prof. Matthias Kreuels.

Kulturinstitut Kompoistinnen gestern-heute e.V., Theaterstrasse 11, W-6900 Heidelberg. Chairman: Roswitha Sperber.

Kulturkreis im Bundesverband der Deutschen Industrie e.V., Gustav-Heinemann-Ufer 84-88, W-5000 Cologne 51. Chairman: Dr. Arend Oetker.

Kulturpolitische Gesellschaft e.V., Stirnband 8-10, W-5800 Hagen 1. President: Dr. Olaf Schwencke.

Kulturstiftung des Landes Schleswig-Holstein, Ministerium für Bildung, Wissenschaft, Jugend und Kultur, Gartenstrasse 6, W-2300 Kiel 1. Chairman: Staatssekretar Dr. Peter Joachim Kreyenberg.

Kunststiftung Baden-Württemberg GmbH, Gerokstrasse 37, W-7000 Stuttgart 1. Chairman: Dr. Christof Müller-Wirth.

Kurt-Weill-Vereinigung Dessau, Stadtverwaltung Dessau, Dezernat IV, Kulturamt, Zerbster Strasse 1, 0-4500 Dessau. Chairman: Dr. Jürgen Schebera.

Landgraf-Moritz-Stiftung (LMST), Heinrich-Schütz-Allee 35, Pf. 100329, W-3500 Kassel. Chairman: Walter Olbrich.

Lehrervereinigung Schlaffhorst-Andersen-Berufsverband der Atem-, Sprech- und Stimmlehrer e.V., Schule Schlaffhorst-Andersen, Bornstrasse 20, W-3052 Bad Nenndorf. 1st Chairman: Ingeborg Rinke.

Lohmann-Stiftung Wiesbaden e.V., Prinz-Nikolas-Strasse 26, W-6200 Wiesbaden. 1st Chairman: Prof. Hildegund Lohmann-Becker.

Medizinische Gesellschaft für Kunstschaffende-Musikorthopädie und Kunstmedizin-e.v., Universität Ulm, Am Hochstrasse 8, Pf. 4066, W.7900 Ulm. Chairman: Dr A. Lahme.

Mendelssohn-Gesellschaft e.V., Zerbster Strasse 59, W-1000 Berlin 45. Chairman: Ernst Thamm.

Motivgruppe Musik e.V., Arbeitsgemeinschaft im Bund deutscher Philatelisten e.V., H J Kaufmann, Am Birkenhain 6, W-4223 Voerde 2. Chairman: H J Kaufmann.

Musica reanimata, Förderverein zur Wiederentdeckung NS-verfolgter Komponisten und ihrer Werke e.V., Heidi Tamar Hoffmann, Johannisberger Strasse 12A, W-1000 Berlin 33. Chairman: Dr. Albrecht Dümling. -

Musik + Tanz + Erziehung, Orff-Schulwerk-Gesellschaft Deutschland e.V., Hermann-Hummel-Strasse 25, W-8032 Lochham. Chairman: Gerhard Kuhn.

Musikalische Jugend Deutschlands e.V. (MJD)-Sektion Bundesrepublik Deutschland der Fédefation Interntionale des Jeunesses Musicales, Marktplatz 12, W-6992 Weikersheim. Chairman: Dr. Michael Jenne.

Musikfonds für Musikurheber e.V., Adenauerallee 134, W-5300 Bonn 1. Chairman: Prof. Dr. Peter Ruzicka.

Musiktherapie e.V., Von-Esmarch Strasse 111, W-4400 Münster. Chairman: Prof. Dr. Karl Hörmann.

Neue Bachgesellschaft e.V. (NBG) Internationale Vereinigung, Hauptgeschäftsstelle Leipzig, Thomaskirchhof 16, Pf. 727, 0-7010 Leipzig. Chairman: Prof. Dr. h.c. Helmuth Rilling.

Neue Deutsche Händel-Gesellschaft e.V., Im Brögen 4b, W-5204 Lohmar 21. President: Prof. Dr. Albert Scheibler.

Neue Zentralstelle der Bühnenautoren und Bühnenverleger GmbH, Bismarckstrasse 107, W-1000 Berlin 12. Chairman: Dr. Maria Müller-Sommer.

NRW Zentrum für Popularmusik und Kommunikationstechnologie, Rottscheidter Strasse 6, Pf. 201414, W-5600 Wuppertal 11. Contact: Dieter Gorny.

ORPLID Internationale Gesellschaft für Musiktheater und Architektur e.V., Hohenheimer Strasse 84, W-7000 Stuttgart 1. Chairman: Wilhelm Keitel.

Oscar-und-Vera-Ritter-Stiftung, Bundesstrasse 4, W-2000 Hamburg 13. Chairman: Jürgen Wittekind.

MUSIC ORGANIZATIONS

Otto-Jägermeier-Gedächtnisstifting, Postfach, W-5562 Manderscheid. President: Dr. Hinrich Brecht-Jägermeier.

PE-Förderkreis für Studierende der Musik e.V., Dr. Ralph Landsittel, Otto-Beck-Strasse 46, W-6800 Mannheim 1. Chairman: Angelika Milos-Engelhorn.

Perucssion Creativ e.V., Am Katharinenkloster 6, W-8500 Nürnberg 1. Chairman: Prof. Werner Thärichen.

Posaunenwerk in der Evangelischen Kirche in Deutschland e.V., Hinter der Grambker Kirche 5, W-2820 Bremen 77. Chairman: Günther Schulz.

Pro Musica Viva-Maria Strecker-Daelon-Stiftung (PMV). Pf. 3146. W-6500 Mainz 1.

ProFolk, Dachverband für Folkmusik e.V., Brigitte Kempe, Oberachernerstrasse 93, W-7590 Achern 2. 1st Chairman: Jens Peter Müller.

Rachmaninoff-Gesellschaft e V Wiesbaden, Richard Henger, Pf. 4853, W-6200 Wiesbaden. President: Richard Henger.

Ralph-Vaughan-Williams-Gesellschaft e V, Jugendmusik-u. Kunstuschule, Elberfelder Strasse 20, W-5630 Remscheid. Chairman: Dr. Lutz-Werner Hesse.

Rektorenkonferenz der Musikhochschulen in der Bundesrepublik Deutschland, Isabel Pfeiffer-Poensgen, Hochschule für Musik Köln, Dagobertstrasse 38, W-5000 Cologne 1.

Richard-Strauss-Gesellschaft München e.V., Viktualienmarkt 3, W-8000 Munich 2. Chairman: Prof. Wolfgang Sawallisch.

Richard-Wagner-Verband International e.V. (RWVI), Salzstrasse 11, W-7800 Freiburg im Breisgau. Chairman: Josef Lienhart.

Robert-Schumann-Gesellschaft e.V., Bilker Strasse 4-6, W-4000 Düsseldorf 1. Chairman: Dr. Herbert Zapp.

Robert-Schumann-Gesellschaft Zwickau e.V., Robert-Schumann-Haus, Hauptmarkt 5, 0-9540 Zwickau. Chairman: Dr. Martin Schoppe.

Robert-Stolz-Stiftung e.V., Steinhauser-Strasse 3, W-8000 Munich 80. Chairman: Thomas M Stein.

Rudolf Eberle-Stiftung, Schloss Solitude, Haus 3, W-7000 Stuttgart 1. Chairman: Hans-Jürgen Müller-Arens.

Sängerbund der Deutschen Polizei e.V. (SBdDP), Rosenfelder Strasse 20, W-2300 Kiel 14. Chairman: Werner Busche.

Schostakowitsch-Gesellschaft e.V., Klaustalerstrasse 2, 0-1100 Berlin. Chairman; Hilmar Schmalenberg.

Schütz-Akademie e.V., Heinrich-Schütz-Strasse 1, Pf. 22, 0-6514 Bad Kostritz. Chairman: Prof. Dr. Silke Leopold.

Sinfonima-Stiftung, Mannheimer Versicherung AG, Augstaanlage 66, Pf. 102161, W-6800 Mannheim 1.

Sonderhäuser Verband akademisch-musikalischer Verbindungen (SV), Hilger Schallehn, Bahnweg 85, W-6500 Mainz 42. Chairman: Gerhard Seher.

Spitzenverband Deutsche Musik e.V. (SPIDEM), Adenauerallee 134, W-5300 Bonn 1. President: Prof. Dr. h.c. Erich Schulze.

Stiftung Bayerischer Musikfonds, Salvatorstrasse 2, W-8000 Munich 2.

Stiftung 100 Jahre Yamaha-Verein zur Popularisierung der Musik, Siemensstrasse 22-34, W-2084 Rellingen. Chairman: Kyoji Ogawa.

Stiftung für Kutturell Weiterbildung und Kulturberatung, Jägerstrasse 51m 0-1080 Berlin. Chairman: Prof Dr Hermann Glaser.

Stiftung Kulturfonds, Molkenmarkt 1-3, Pf. 240, 0-1020 Berlin.

Stiftung Kunst und Kultur des landes Nordrhein-Westfalen, Haus der Stiftungen in NRW, Rossstrasse 133, W-4000 Düsseldorf 30. Chairman: Minister President Johannes Rau.

Stiftung Kuratoren-Konseil zur Förderung der Tätigkeit russischer Komponisten und Musiker, Burgmauer 68, W-5000 Cologne 1. Chairman: Serge Tcherepnin.

Stiftung Ostdeutscher Kulturrat (OKR), Kaiserstrasse 113, W-5300 Bonn 1. President: Dr. Herbert Hupka.

Stiftung Preussischer Kulturbesitz, Von-der-Heydt-Strasse 16-18, W-1000 Berlin 30. President: Prof. Dr. Werner Knopp.

Stiftung Rheinland-Pfalz für Kultur, Ministerium für Bildung und Kulter, Mittlere Bleiche, W-6500 Mainz 1. Chairman: Minister President Rudolf Scharping.

Stiftung Volkslied (STV), Heinrich-Shütz-Allee 33, W-3500 Kassel. Chairman: Alfred Peters.

Sudetendeutscher Sängerbund e.V. (SDS), Hans-Schitzer-Weg 19, W-8960 Kempten. Chairman: Gunther Wohlrab.

Telemann-Gesellschaft e.V. Internationale Vereinigung, Liebigstrasse 10, 0-3010 Magdeburg. President: Prof Dr Martin Ruhnke.

Union Deutscher Jazz-Musiker e.V. (UDJ), Am Michaelshof 4a, W-5300 Bonn 2. 1st Chairman: Prof. Joe Viera.

Verband der Deutschen Konzertdirektionen e.V., Liebigstrasse 39, W-8000 Munich 22. President: Michael Russ.

Verband der deutschen Kritiker e.V., Andreas Richter, Prinz-Fr.-Leopold Strasse 34a. W-1000 Berlin 38. Chairman: Hartmut Krug.

Verband der Musikpädagogen e.V. (VMP), Von-der-Tann-Strasse 38, W-8400 Regensburg. Chairman: Dr. Lothar Schubert.

Verband der Vertriebe von Musikinstrumenten und Musikelektronik in Deutschland e.V. (VVMD), Heinestrasse 169, W-7000 Stuttgart 70. Chairman: Werner Sonderwald.

Verband Deutscher Bühnenverleger e.V., Bismarckstrasse 107, W-1000 Berlin 12. Chairman: Stefani Cremer-Hunzinger.

Verband Deutscher Geigenbauer e.V. (VDG), Hohenzollernstrasse 16, W-7000 Suttgart 1. Chairman: Hieronymus Köstler.

Verband Deutscher Komponisten, An der Kolonnade 15, 0-1080 Berlin. Chairman: Hans J Wenzel.

Verband Deutscher KonzertChöre e.V. (VDKC), Kempener Strasse 5, W-4060 Viersen 12. President: Hans-Heinrich Grosse-Brockhoff.

Verband Deutscher Musikschaffender (VDM), Kaiser-Friedrich-Allee 1-3, W-5100 Aachen. President: Klaus Quirini.

Verband Deutscher Musikschulen e.V. (VDM), Plittersdorfer Strasse 93, W-5300 Bonn 2. Chairman: Reinhart von Gutzeit.

Verband Deutscher Schulmusiker (VDS), Weihergarten 5, Pf. 3640, W-6500 Mainz. Chairman: Prof. Dr. Dieter Zimmerzchied.

Verband Deutscher Tonmeister e.V. (VDT), Masurenallee 8-14, W-1000 Berlin 19. President: Günter Griewisch.

Verband evangelischer Kirchenchöre Deutschlands e.V. (VeK), Hasenburger Weg 67, W-2120 Lüneburg. President: Dr. Hans-Christian Drömann.

Verband evangelischer Kirchenmusiker Deutschlands e.V. (VeM), Domplatz 5, W-6720 Speyer. President: KMD Prof Hermann Rau.

Verein Arbeitsgemeinschaft Deutsche Musikwettbewerbe, Rosenheimer Strasse 11, W-8000 Munich 80. Chairman: Prof. Dr. h.c Erich Schulze.

Verein für musikalische Archiv-Forschung e.V., Grossh.-Friedrich-Strasse 62, W-7640 Kehl. Chairman: Prof. Dr. Werner Unger.

Verein zur Förderung der Nordoff/Robbins Musiktherapie e.V., Beckweg 4, W-5804 Herdecke. Chairman: Prof Dr Eduard David.

MUSIC ORGANIZATIONS

Verein zur Förderung des musikalischen Schaffens des Komponisten Waldemar Edler von Bausznern, Haus Nr. 31, W-6541 Kludenbach 31. Chairman: Horst Gehann.
Verein zur Förderung Historischer Harfen e.V., Rainer M Thurau, Helenenstrasse 10, W-6200 Wiesbaden. Chairman: Elena Polonska.
Verein zur Förderung ostkirchlichen Gesanges e.V., Marktplatz 2, W-8805 Feuchtwangen. Chairman: Martin Batisweiler.
Vereinigung deutscher Harfenisten e.V., Vera Munkel-Remann, Goldammerweg 183, W-5000 Cologne 30. Chairman: Therese Reichling.
Vereinigung Deutscher Musik-Bearbeiter e.V., Kiesstrasse 44a, W-1000 Berlin 45.
Vereinigung Deutscher Opernchöre und Bühnentanzer e.V. in der DAG (VdO/DAG), Bismarckstrasse 14-16, W-5000 Cologne 1. Chairman: Heinz Mersch.
Villa Musica, Stiftung zur Förderung der Musik, Auf der Bastei 3, W-6500 Mainz. Chairman: Mindirig. Ernst Maurer.
Walcker-Stiftung für orgelwissenschaftliche Forschung, Pf. 1128, W-6601 Kleinblittersdorf 2. Chairman: Klaus Walcker.
Walter Kaminsky-Stiftung, Kösener Strasse 4, W-1000 Berlin 33.
Walther-Hensel-Gesellschaft e.V. München, Ob dem Staffele 2, W-7057 Winnenden. Chairman: Herbert Preisenhammer.
Werkgemeinschaaft Musik e.V., Carl-Mosterts-Platz 1, W-4000 Düsseldorf 30. Chairman: Prof. Karl Berg.
Wilhelm-Furtwängler-Gesellschaft e.V., Schwelmer Strasse 4, W-1000 Berlin 45. Chairman: Dr. Friedhelm Schöning.
Wilhelm-Petersen-Gesellschaft e.V., Brahmsweg 4, W-6100 Darmstadt.
Wissenschaftliche Sozietät Musikpädagogik e.V. (WSMP), Fachbereich Erziehungswissenschaft, Institut für Musikpädagogik, Von-Melle-Park 8, W-2000 Hamburg 13. Chairman: Prof. Dr. Hermann J Kaiser.
Xaver & Philipp Scharwenka-Gesellschaft e.V., Prassekstrasse 5, W-2400 Lübeck. 1st Chairman: Prof. Evelinde Trenkner.
Zentralverband katholischer Kirchenangestellter Deutschlands e.V. (ZKD), Am Kielshof 2, Pf. 990125, W-5000 Cologne 91. Chairman: Franz Kopecky.
Zentrum Bundesrepublik Deutschland des Internationalen Theaterinstituts e.V. (ITI), Bismarckstrasse 107, W-100 Berlin 12. President: Prof. August Everding.
Zentrum für Kunst und Medientechnologie Karlsruhe (ZKM), Institut für Musik und Akustik, Ritterstrasse 42, W-7500 Karlsruhe 1. Director: Prof Dr Heinrich Klotz.

GREECE

International Music Council (Greek Section), 38 Mitropleos Street, 105 63 Athens. General Secretary: Apostolos Kostios.
Jeunesses Musicales de Grece/Musique Pour l'Enfant, Stratigou Kallari 52, Psychico, 154 52 Athens. President: Domini Sarris.
Société Hellenique pour la Protection de la Proprieté intellectuelle, 14 Delighianni Street, 106 83 Athens. Managing Director: Zacharias Macris.

GUATEMALA

Asociacion Guatemalteca de Autores y Compositores (AGAYC), 14 Calle 11-42, Zona 1, 01001 Guatemala City. Manager: Gustavo Adolfa Palma Recinos.
Juventudes Musicales de Guatemala, Diagonal 6, Calle Real de la Villa 13-46, Zona 10, Guatemala City. President: Francisco Saravia.

HONG KONG

Hong Kong Arts Administrators Association Ltd, c/o ARIC, Room 301, 3/F Hong Kong Arts Centre, 2 Harbour Road, Wanchai.
Hong Kong Government Music Office, 25/F Wanchai Tower One, 12 Harbour Road, Wanchai.

HUNGARY

Artisjus, Hungarian Office for Copyright Protection, PO Box 67, 1364 Budapest, Vörösmarty tér, 1051 Budapest. President: Kamilló Lendvay; General Director: Dr. György Boytha.
Association of Hungarian Musicians, National Committee of the International Music Council, International Society for Contemporary Music, International Jazz Federation/Hungarian Section, Hungarian ISME Committee, Music Information Center, PO Box 47, 1364 Budapest, Vörösmarty tér 1, 1051 Budapest. Secretary General: Prof. István Láng.
Council of Hungarian Choirs, PO Box 345, 1370 Budapest, Vörösmarty tér 1, 1051 Budapest. Secretary General: Dr. József Tóthpál.
Hungarian Arts Foundation, Music Department, Báthori-utca 10, 1054 Budapest. Director of the Music Department: Kálmán Strém.
Hungarian Music Society, Vörösmarty tér 1, 1051 Budapest. Honorary President: Prof. Ferenc Farkas; President: Zsolt Durkó.
Interart Festival Center, National Center of International Music Competitions and Festivals, PO Box 80, 1366 Budapest, Vörösmarty tér 1, 1051 Budapest. Director: Tamás Klenjánszky.
International Concert Management, "Interkoncert", Interkoncert, Ltd, Agency for all Performing Arts, PO Box 239, 1368 Budapest, Vörösmarty tér 1, 1051 Budapest. General Director: László Orosz; Executive Director: István Nyikos.
Institute for Musicology of the Hungarian Academy of Sciences/Bartók Archives, Táncsics Mihály u.7, 1014 Budapest, Director: Dr. Zoltán Falvy; Head of the Bartók Archives: Prof Dr László Somfai.
International Kodály Society, PO Box 8, 1502 Budapest. Executive Secretary: Dr. László Eösze.
Jeunesses Musicales of Hungary, PO Box 80, 1366 Budapest, Vörösmarty tér 1, 1051 Budapest. Secretary General:

MUSIC ORGANIZATIONS

Beáta Schanda.
Liszt Ferenc Társaság (Ferenc Liszt Society), Vörosmarty u. 35, 1064 Budapest. Secretary General: Prof. Miklós Forrai.
Trade Union of Hungarian Musicians, Gorkij Fasor 38, 1068 Budapest. Secretary: László Gyimesi.

ICELAND

Association of Icelandic Composers, Laufásvegi 40, Reykjavík.
Association of Light Composers and Songwriters, Háteigsvegur 28, 105 Reykiavík.
Association of Music School Directors, Kennarasamband Islands, Grettisgata 89, 105 Reykjavík.
Association of Music School Teachers, Kennarasamband Islands, Grettisgata 89, 105 Reykjavík.
Iceland Music Information Centre, Freyjugata 1, PO Box 978, 121 Reykjavík. Director: Bergljót Jónsdóttir.
Icelandic Musicians' Union, Laufásvegur 40, Reykjavík.
International Society for Contemporary Music, Icelandic Section, Tonskaldafelag Islands, Laufásvegur 40, Reykjavík.
Reykjavík Music Society, Garðastraeti 17, 101 Reykjavík.
Society of Icelandic Musicians, Dalsel 8, Reukjavík.
Union of Authors and Copyright Owners, Laufásvegur 40, 101 Reykjavík.

INDIA

Inter-National Cultural Centre, 205 Tansen Marg, New Delhi 1.
National Centre for the Performing Arts, Nariman Point, Bombay 400021.

ISRAEL

Independent Musicians Union, 6 Malkei Yisrael Square, 64591 Tel Aviv. Chairman: Dany Gottfried.
International Music Council (Israeli Section), Ministry of Education and Culture, Devora Haneviah Street 2, 91911 Jerusalem. Chief Officer: Raaya Zimran.
International Society for Contemporary Music (Israeli Section), c/o Israel Composers' League, PO Box 45068, 61450 Tel Aviv.
Israel Composers' League, PO Box 45068, 61450 Tel Aviv. Chairman: Menachem Zur.
Israel Music Institute (IMI), PO Box 3004, 61030 Tel Aviv. Director: Paul Landau.
Israel Musicians Union, Histradut Building, 93 Arlozorof Street, 62098 Tel Aviv. General Secretary: Aryeh Levanon.
Jerusalem Music Centre, Mishkanot Sha'ananim, Jerusalem. Director: Ram Evron.
Jeunesses Musicales d'Israel, 8 Sderot Chen, 64071 Tel Aviv. President: Emanuel Amiran.
Music Information Centre of Israel, PO Box 3004, 61030 Tel Aviv. Director: Paul Landau.
National Council for Culture and Arts, 16 Hanatziv Street, 67018 Tel Aviv. Chief Officer: David Sinai.
Society of Authors, Composers, and Music Publishers in Israel (ACUM), 118 Rothschild Boulevard, 61110 Tel Aviv. Chairman: Shlomo Tanny.

ITALY

Accademia Luigi Boccherini, piazza Insurrezione 10, 35129 Padua. President: Aldo Pais; Secretary: Giovanni Fantini.
Accademia Tartiniana, piazzale Pontecorvo 4/A, 35121 Padua. President: Edoardo Farina; General Secretary: Claudio Scimone.
Associazione "Antiquae Musicae Italicae Studiosi", via Remorsella 5/A, 40125 Bologna. President: Giuseppe Vecchi.
Associazione Centro Studi Carusiani, via Omboni 1, 20129 Milan. President: Luciano Pituello; Secretary: Carla Bernini.
Associazione dei Fonografici Italiani (AFI), via Vittor Pisani 10, 20124 Milan. President: Guido Rignano.
Associazione dei Rappresentanti Italiani di Artisti di Concerti e Spettacoli (ARIACS), via Cappuccio 11, 20123 Milan. President: Denise Petriccione.
Associazione di Informatica Musicale Italiana (AIMI), c/o La Biennale di Venezia, Settore Musica, San Marco, Ca Giustinian, 30124 Venice. President: Giovanni Di Poli; Secretary: Sylviane Sapir.
Associazione Festival Teatrali, Musicali e Cinematografici (Federfestival); c/o AGIS, via di Villa Patrizi 10, 00161 Rome. President: Gisella Belgeri.
Associazione Generale Italiana dello Spettacolo (AGIS), via di Villa Patrizi 10, 00161 Rome. President: Carlo Maria Badini.
Associazione Internazionale Biblioteche Musicali (AIBM), Italian Section, c/o Conservatorio "Giuseppe Verdi", via Conservatorio 12, 20122 Milan. President: Mariangela Donà; Secretary: Agostina Zecca Laterza.
Associazione Internazionale Studi di Canto Gregoriano, via Battaglione 58, 26100 Cremona. President: Luigi Agustoni; General Secretary: Stefano Klockner.
Associazione Italiana Archivi Sonori e Audiovisivi, c/o Instituto di Ricerca per il Teatro Musicale, via dei Delfini 16, 00186 Rome. President: Carlo Marinelli; General Secretary: Giorgio Adamo.
Associazione Italiana Biblioteche (AIB), c/o Biblioteca Nazionale, viale Castro Pretorio 105, 00186 Rome. President: Tommaso Giordano; Secretary: Luca Bellingeri.
Associazione Italiana Degli Editori di Musica (AIDEM), via Enrico Toti 4, 20123 Milan. President: Maurizio Corechà; Secretary: Mario Allione.
Associazione Italiana delle Scuole di Musica, Villa La Torraccia, via delle Fontanelle 24, 50016 San Domenico di Fiesole (FI). President: Mario Sperenzi.
Associazione Italiana di Acustica (AIA), via Cassia 1216, 00189 Rome. President: Adriano Alippi; Secretary: Silvio Santoboni.
Associazione Italiana Operatori Musicali (ASSIOM), c/o Centro di Ricerca e Sperimentazione per la Didattica Musicale, Villa La Torraccia, via delle Fontanelle 24, 50016 San Domenico di Fiesolo (FI).
Associazione Italiana per la Musica Sacra "S. Cecilia" (AISC), piazza S. Apollinare 49, 00186 Rome. President: mons. Antonio Mistrorigo; General Secretary: mons. Tarcisio Cola.
Associazione Italiana Studi di Musicoterapia (AISMt), via Brignole De Ferrari 6, 16122 Genoa. President: Giovanna Mutti.

MUSIC ORGANIZATIONS

Associazione Liutariana Italiana (ALI), piazza Cavour 5, 26100 Cremona. President: Gualtiero Nicolini; Administrative Secretary Vinicio Candoni.

Associazione Nazionale Agenti Teatrali (ANAT), via Assietta 6, 00141 Rome. President: Mario Minasi; Administrative Secretary: Remo Francesconi.

Associazione Nazionale Artisti Lirici Primarii Italiani (ANALPI), corso Venezia 61, 20121 Milan. President: Giulio Lanfranchi; General Secretary: Nando Avanzini.

Associazione Nazionale Bande Italiane Musicali (ANBIMA), via Marianna Dionigi 43, 00193 Rome. President: Giuseppe Bicocchi; National Secretary: Egidio Bradariolo.

Associazione Nazionale Critici Musicali, via Cardinale Mimmi 32, 70124 Bari. President: Duilio Courir; Secretary-Treasurer: Franco Chieco.

Associazione Nazionale delle Cooperative Culturali, via dei Alpi 32, 00198 Rome. President: Novella Sansoni.

Associazione Nazionale Insegnanti di Danza (ANID), via A Gramsci 36, 00197 Rome. President: Anna Maria Cerullo.

Associazione Nazionale Liuteria Artistica Italiana (ANLAI), piazza Venezia 11, 00187 Rome. National Secretary: Vezio Amicucci.

Associazione Nazionale Musicisti di Jazz (AMJ), via Vallerozzi 77, 53100 Siena. President: Giorgio Gaslini.

Associazione Pro Musica Studium, via Ferdinando Martini 23/8, 00137 Rome. President: Domenico Cieri; Secretary: Raffaella Gentilini.

Centre International de Recherche sur la Presse Musicale (CIRPEM), via del Conservatorio 31/B, 43100 Parma. President: Giorgio Paini.

Centro di Sonologia Computazionale, c/o Università di Padova, via San Francesco 11, 35121 Padua. Director: Stefano Merigliano.

Centro di Studi Donizettiani, c/o Ateneo di Scienze, Lettere ed Arti, via Torquato Tasso 4, 24121 Bergamo. President: Edoardo Pedone: General Secretary: Marcello Ballini.

Centro di Studi Musicali Ferruccio Busoni, piazza della Vittoria 16, 50053 Empoli (FI). President: Maria Pia Albano Pagni; Secretary: Stefano Donati.

Centro Internazionale per la Divulgazione della Musica Italiana, via Sistina 48, 00187 Rome. President: Giovanni Pieraccini.

Centro Internazionale per la Ricerca Strumentale, Cannaregio 3099, 30121 Venice. President: Claudio Ambrosini; Administrative Secretary: Rosanna De Cesare.

Centro Studi Giovanni Paisiello, via Euclide 15, 74100 Taranto. President: Dino Foresio.

Centro Studi Rinascimento Musicale, Villa Medicea "La Ferdinanda", 50040 Artimino (FI). President and Artistic Director: Nella Anfuso; Secretary: Fabio Finucci.

Centro di Studi Spontiniani, c/o Comune, via Spontini, 60030 Maiolati Spontini (AN), Co-ordinator: Agostina Zecca Laterza.

CIDIM-National Music Committee of Italy (IMC-UNESCO), via Vittoria Colonna 18, 00193 Rome. President: Francesco Agnello; Special Projects Director: Gisella Belgeri.

Civico Instituto di Studi Paganiani, Palazzo Tursi, via Garibaldi, 16124 Genoa. Director: Alma Brughera Capaldo; Secretary: Edward Neill.

Editori Musicali Associati (EMA), piazza Liberty 2, 20121 Milan. President: Adriano Solaro.

Ente Nazionale Previdenza e Assistenza per i Lavatori dello Spettacolo (ENPALS), viale Regina Margherita 206, 00198 Rome. President: Roberto Romei; General Director: Mario Porfiri.

Federazione Industria Musicale Italiana (FIMI), via Vittor Pisani 10, 20124 Milan. President: Franco Reali; Director: Ernesto Magnani.

Federazione Informazione Spettacolo (FIS-CISL), via Boncompagni 19, 00187 Rome. General Secretary: Fulvio Giacomassi.

Federazione Italiana dei Compositori di Musica Contemporanea, via Cavalieri di Vittorio Veneto 34, 56121 Cascina (PI). President: Piero Luigi Zangelmi; General Secretary: Arduino Gottardo.

Federazione Italiana della Musica (FEDERMUSICA), via Vittor Pisani 10, 20124 Milan. General Secretary: Ernesto Magnani.

Federazione Italiana Lavatori Informazione e Spettacolo (FILISCGIL), piazza Sallustio 24, 00187 Rome. General Secretary: Massimo Bordini.

Federazione Italiana Lavoratori Stampa, Spettacolo, Informazione e Cultura (FILSIC-UIL), via Belisario 7, 00187 Rome. General Secretary: Francesco Cisco.

Federazione Italiana Tradizioni Popolari (FITP), via E Gattamelata 25, 00176 Rome. President: Lillo Alessandro; Secretary: Cosimo Silvaroli.

Federazione Nazionale delle Cooperative Culturali, piazza della Libertà, 00192 Rome. President: Luigi Frixione.

Federazione Nazionale Italiana delle Associazioni Regionali Corali (FENIARCO), via Castellana 44, 30174 Venezia-Mestre. President: Dino Stella; National Secretary: Gianni Colussi.

Federazione Nazionale Lavoratori Spettacolo (CISNAL), via Principe Amedeo 42, 00185 Rome. General Secretary: Liano Fabbietti.

Fondazione Claudio Monteverdi, via Ugolani Dati 4, 26100 Cremona. President: Sandro Fontana; Secretary: Gaetano Antonioli.

Fondazione Giacomo Puccini, c/o Teatro del Giglio, corte San Lorenzo 9, 55100 Lucca. President: Maria Dina Simonini.

Fondazione Giorgio Cini, Istituto per la Musica, Isola di San Giorgio Maggiore, 30124 Venice. Director: Giovanni Morelli.

Fondazione Giovanni Pierluigi da Palestrina, vicolo Pierluigi 3, 0036 Palestrina (Rome). President: Luigi Puliti.

Fondazione Rossini, piazza Olivieri 5, 61100 Pesaro. President: Vittorio Emiliani; Secretary: Aldo Ricci.

Fondazione Ugo e Olga Levi, Centro di Cultura Musicale Superiore, palazzo Giustinian-Lolin, San Marco 2893, 30124 Venice. President: Gianni Milner.

Fondazione Vincenzo Bellini, c/o Università degli Studi di Catania, via Biblioteca 13, 95124 Catania. President: Gaspare Rodolico; Director: Salvatore Enrico Failla; Secretary: Antonino Domina.

Fondo Ottorino Respighi, c/o Fondazione Giorgio Cini, Isola San Giorgio Maggiore, 30124 Venice. Director: Eugenio Bagnoli.

International Association for the Study of Popular Music (IASPM), Italian Section, c/o "Il Giornale della Musica", corso Vittorio Emanuele II n. 198bis, 10138 Turin. President: Luigi Pestalozza.

International Center of New Musical Sources, via Alberto Nota 3, 10122 Turin. President: Marinella Tarenghi.

International Dance Organization (IDO), via Bronzino 117, 50142 Florence. General Secretary: Moreno Polidori.

Istituto di Bibliografia Musicale, c/o Biblioteca Nazionale, viale Castro Pretoria 105, 00185 Rome. President: Giancarlo Rostirolla.

Istituto di Paleografia Musicale, circonvallazione Casilini 122, 00176 Rome. President: Armando Carideo; Secretary: Fabio Refrigeri.

MUSIC ORGANIZATIONS

Istituto di Ricerca per il Teatro Musicale, via Francesco Tamagno 65, 00168 Rome. President: Carlo Marinelli.

Istituto di Studi Organologici, via Monte Zebio 33, 00195 Rome. President: Giancarlo Rostirolla; Secretary: Marco Do Pasquale.

Istituto di Studi Rinascimentali, Palazzo Paradiso, via delle Scienze 17, 44100 Ferrara. President: Emilio Manara; Secretary: Giacomo Battana.

Istituto Interzionale Luigi Cherubini, via Giovanni Secchi 3, 00136 Rome. President: Giovanni Carli Ballola; Secretary: Pietro Spada.

Istituto Italiana Antonio Vivaldi, c/o Fondazione Giorgio Cini, Isola di San Giorgio Maggiore, 30124 Venice. Director: Antonio Fanna.

Istituto Italiano per la Storia della Musica, via Vittoria 6, 00187 Rome. President: Raffaello Monterosso.

Istituto Mutualistico tra Artisti Interpreti Esecutori (IMAIE), piazza Sonnino 37, 00153 Rome. President: Domenico Del Prete.

Istituto Nazionale di Studi Verdiani, strada della Repubblica 56, 43100 Parma. President: Alberto Carrara Verdi; Director: Pierluigi Petrobelli.

Istituto di Studi Pucciniani, piazza Buonarroti 29, 20149 Milan. President: Simonetta Puccini; Secretary: Giuseppe Pintorno.

Pontificio Istituto Ambrosiano di Musica Sacra, viale Gorizia 5, 20144 Milan. President: Ernesto Moneta Caglio; Secretary: Angelo Amodeo.

Pontificio Istituto di Musica Sacra, via di Torre Rossa 21, 001165 Rome. Secretary: Augusto Fantini; Librarian: Ugo Melillo.

Sindacato Musicisti Italiani (SMI), via Goito 39, 00185 Rome. President pro tempore: Alberto Scarponi; Secretary pro tempore: Sandro Piombo.

Sindacato Nazionale Autonomo, Telecomunicazioni Radiotelevisione Italcable-Telespazio Società Consociate della Pubblicità e dello Spettacolo (SNATER), via Dardanelli 13, 00195 Rome. President: Bruno Sindici; Secretary: Antonio Lovato.

Sindacato Nazionale Istruzione Artistica, via Antonino Pio 40, 00145 Rome. General Coordinator: Lanfranco Benedetti; National Administrative Secretary: Renato Tosti.

Sindacato Nazionale Musicisti (SNM), via Pinelli 100, 10144 Turin. President: Piero Rattalino; National General Secretary: Elio Sosso.

Società Italiana degli Autori ed Editori (SIAE), viale della Letteratura 30, 00144 Rome. President: Roman A Vlad; General Director: Lucio Capograssi.

Società Italiana della Viola da Gamba, via dei Servi 51, 50122 Florence. President: Roberto Budini Gattai; Artistic Director: Carlo Denti.

Società Italiana di Etnomusicologia (SIE), c/o Centro Flog Tradizioni Popolari, via Maestri del Lavoro 1, 50134 Florence. President: Roberto Leydi; General Secretary: Gilberto Giuntini.

Società Italiana di Musicologia (SIdM), via Galliera 3, 40125, Bologna. President: Agostino Ziino; Secretary: Maria Vittoria Garzone.

Società Italiana Musica Contemporanea (SIMC), via F Juvara 11, 20129 Milan. President: Giuseppe Garbarino; Secretary: Vittorio Fellegara.

Società Italiana per l'Educazione Musicale (SIEM), via Guerrazzi 20, 40125 Bologna. President: Johanella Tafuri; Secretary: Elena Ferrara.

UNION-Operatori Musicali Indipendenti, c/o "I Soluzionisti", via Trionfale 85, 00136 Rome. President: Oderson Rubini; Secretary: Francesco Fracassi.

Unione Folclorica Italiana (UFI), via Mazzini 22, 33081 Aviano (PN). Artistic Director: Gherardo Patessio.

Unione Nazionale Arte Musica Spettacolo (UNAMS), viale delle Provincie 18, 00162 Rome. General Secretary: Dora Liguori; Secretary: Piergiovanni Damiani.

Unione Nazionale Editori di Musica Italiani (UNEMI), via Teulada 52, 00195 Rome. President: Luciano Villevielle Bideri; Secretary: Piero Leonardi.

JAPAN

Concert Managers Association of Japan, Mitoko Building, 6-2-4 Akasaka, Minato-ku, Tokyo 107. Chairman: Naoyasu Kajimoto.

Council of Musical Education and Research, Kyoiku Shuppan 2-10, Jimbo-cho, Kanda, Chiyoda-ku, Tokyo 101. President: Tomojiro Ikeuchi.

Electronic Industries Association of Japan, Tokyo Shoko Kaigisho Building, 3-2-2 Marunouchi, Chiyoda-ku, Tokyo 100. Chairman: Moriya Shiki.

Japan Audio Society, Mori Building, 1-14-34 Jingumae, Tokyo 150. Secretary-General: Sho Nagasawa.

Japan Conductors Association, 4-18-20 Ogikubo Suginami-ku, Tokyo 167. President: Takashi Asahina.

Japan Gustav Mahler Society, Ichimura Building, 1-14 Nishiki-cho, Kanda, Chiyodaku, Tokyo 101. Chief Executive: Kenji Sakurai.

Japan International League of Artists, 2-3-16-607 Shinjuku, Shinjuku-ku, Tokyo 160. Chief Officer: Kazuhiko Hattori.

Japan Mozart Society, 4-12-11-702 Chuo Building, Honcho, Nohombashi, Chuo-ku, Tokyo 103. President: Keisei Sakka.

Japanese Composers Society, Ogawa Building, 3-7-15 Akasaka, Minatoku, Tokyo 107. President: Ryoichi Hattori.

Japanese Society for Rights of Authors, Composers, and Publishers, 1-7-13 Nishishimbashi, Minato-ku, Tokyo 105. President: Miyuki Ishimoto.

Music for Youth, Inc, Kowa Building, No 24, 3-1-1 Roppongi, Minato-ku, Tokyo 106. President: Eloise Cunningham.

Recording Industry Association of Japan, 2-8-9 Tsukiji, Chuo-ku, Tokyo 104. President: Takeshi Okkotsu.

KOREA (SOUTH)

Asian Composers League (Korean Committee), KPO Box 874, Seoul 110-062. Director Sung-Jae Lee.

Contemporary Music Society of Seoul, 1402 74 dong, Hyundae Apt, Apgujeong-dong, Seoul. Director: Yong-Jim Kim.

Federation of Artistic and Cultural Organisations of Korea, 1-117 Dongsoong-dong, Chongro-ku, Seoul.

Jeunesses Musicales of Korea, PO Box 10980, Seoul.

Korean Cultural Foundation, Inc, 25 Neung-Dong, Sung-ku, Seoul 133-180. Director: No Hi Pak.

Music Association of Korea, 1-117 Dongsoong-dong, Chongro-ku, Seoul. President: Sang-Hyun Cho.

MUSIC ORGANIZATIONS

National Culture Promotion Foundation, San 1-157, Chongnyangni-dong, Tongdaemun-gu, Seoul.

LUXEMBOURG

Jeunesses Musicales de Luxembourg, 18A, rue de la Poste, L-2346 Luxembourg. President: Jean-Pierre Oestreicher.
Letzebuerger Gesellschaft für Neue Musik (International Society for Contemporary Music, Luxembourg Section), B.P.828, L-2018 Luxembourg. President: Alexander Mullenbach.
Union Grand-Duc Adolphe, 2, rue Sosthène Weis, L-2722 Luxembourg. President: Roger Diedrich; Secretary-General: Henri Schumacher.
Union Saint-Pie X, 3, rue du Curé, L-1368 Luxembourg. President: Pol Wagener.

MACAO

Instituto Cultural de Macau, Rua Pedro Coutinho 27, 3rd Floor, Macao.

MEXICO

Asociación Mexicana de Productores de Fonogramas y Videogramas AC (Amprofon), Francisco Petrarca No 223-503, Chapultepec Morales, 11560 México, D.F. Chief Officer: Liceniado Héctor Manuel Medina Díaz.
Juventudes Musicales de México, Santisimo 25, San Angel, 01000 México 20, D.F. President: Dolores Carillo.
Sociedad de Autores y Compositores de Música S de A (SACM), San Felipe 143, Col General Anaya, 03330 México, D.F. President: Roberto Cantoral García.

NETHERLANDS

Association for the Performing Arts in the Netherlands, Herengracht 122, 1015 BT Amsterdam. General Secretary: J Rudolf Wolfensberger.
BUMA (Composers Rights Society), Prof E M Meijerslaan 3, 1183 AV Amsterdam. Chief Officer: G P Willemsen.
CNM (Center for Netherlands Music), PO Box 1634, 1200 PB Hilversum. Chief Officer: J W ten Broeke.
Contactorgaan van Nederlandse Orkesten (Association of Netherlands Orchestras), Herengracht 122, 1015 BT Amsterdam. Executive Director: J Rudolf Wolfensberger.
Donemus (Publishing House and Library of Contemporary Dutch Music), Paulus Potterstraat 14, 1071 CZ Amsterdam.
Foundation Gaudeamus (Center of Contemporary Music), Swammerdamstraast 38, 1091 RV Amsterdam. Director: Henk Heuvelmans.
Gentootschap van Nederlandse (Society of Netherlands Composers), Prof E M Meijerslaan 3, 1183 AV Amsterdam. President: Gillius van Bergejik.
International Society for Contemporary Music (Netherlands Section), Swammerdamstraat 38, 1091 RV Amsterdam. President: H Reiziger.
Jeugd en Musiek Nederland, Roemer Visscherstraat 42, 1054 EZ Amsterdam. President: Jur Naessens.
Jeunesses Musicales, Amstel 177, 1018 ES Amsterdam.
Koninklijke Nederlandse Toonkunstenaars Vereniging (Royal Netherlands Musicians Society), Keizersgracht 480, 1017 EG Amsterdam. Chief Officer: H Luif.
NTB (Nederlandse Toonkunstenaars Bond), Herengracht 272, 1016 BW Amsterdam.
Nederlandse Vereniging van Grammofoondetallhandelaren (NVGD), Die Noord 3, 1452 PS Ilpendam. Chairman: J F T Hotzenbosch.
Netherlands Committee of the International Music Council, Rubenslaan 200, 3582 JJ Utrecht.
Netherlands Theater Institute, PO Box 19304, 1000 GH Amsterdam. Chief Officer: Ton Offerman.
STEMRA (Mechanical Rights Society), Prof E M Meijerslaan 3, 1183 AV Amsterdam. Chief Officer: G P Willemsem.
Stichting Contactorgaan Electronische Muziek, Swammerdamstraat 38, 1091 RV Amsterdam. Chief Officer: Henk Heuvelmans.
Stichting voor Kamermuziek, Sijzenlaan 6, 2566 WG The Hague.
Vereniging voor Nederlandse Muziekgeschiedenis (Society for Netherlands Music History), Postbus 1514, 3500 BM Utrecht.

NEW ZEALAND

Australasian Performing Right Association, Ltd (APRA), PO Box 5028, Wellington. General Manager: Bernie Darby.
Composers Association of New Zealand, PO Box 4065, Wellington. President: Denise Hulford.
Music for Youth, 26 Patanga Crescent, Wellington 6001. Chairperson: Beverley Wakem.
Music Trades Association (NZ), Inc, Box 386, Auckland. Executive Officer: Dean Reynolds.
New Zealand Composers Foundation, PO Box 633, Wellington. Chairman: Ashley Heenan.
New Zealand Music Centre, Ltd, trading as SouNZ New Zealand, PO Box 102, The Terrace, Wellington. Executive Director: John Page.
New Zealand Opera Society, Inc, PO Box 44-022, VIC, Lower Huttl. President: Sam Robinson.
Phonographic Performances (New Zealand), Ltd, PO Box 9241, Wellington. General Manager: Tony Chance.
Queen Elizabeth II Arts Council of New Zealand, PO Box 3806, Wellington. Director: Peter Quin.
Recording Industry Association of New Zealand, Inc, PO Box 9241, Wellington. Chief Executive: Tony Chance.
Service Workers Union, Musicians Division, Private Bag 68-914, Newton, Auckland. Secretary: Peter Shannon.

NORWAY

International Music Council (National Committee) c/o Statens Musikkrad, Toftesgt. 69, N-0552 Oslo. Secretary: Lisbeth Risnes.
International Society for Contemporary Music (Norwegian Section), c/o Ny Musikk, Toftesgt 69, N-0552, Oslo. Secretary: Joran Rudi.

MUSIC ORGANIZATIONS

Jeunesses Musicales (Norwegian Section), c/o Landslaget Musikk i Skolen, Toftesgt 69, N-0552 Oslo. General Manager: Kara Hanken.
Landslaget Musikk i Skolen (Youth & Music), Toftesgate 69, 0552 Oslo. Secretary: Grete Johansen.
New Music (Ny Musikk), Toftesgate 69, 0552 Oslo. Manager: Joran Rudi.
NASOL (Norwegian Association of Symphony Orchestras), Toftesgate 69, 0552 Oslo. Manager: Jan Ola Amundsen.
NOPA (The Norwegian Society of Popular Composers Authors and Arrangers), PO Box 9171, Gronland, N-0134 Oslo. Secretary: Lill Oyen.
Norsk Tonekunstnersamfund (Norwegian Association of Musical Artists), Bogstadvn. 66, N-0366 Oslo. Manager: Ole Bøhn.
Norwegian Archives for Folk and Popular Songs, Toftesgt 69, N-0552 Oslo. General Manager: Velle Espeland.
Norwegian Cultural Council, Militaerhospitalet, PO Box 101, Sentrum, N-0102 Oslo. Music Secretary: Kari Lilleslåtten.
Norwegian Jazz Archives, Toftesgt 69, N-0552 Oslo. General Manager: Finn Kramer-Johansen.
Norwegian Music Information Centre, Toftesgt 69, N-0552 Oslo. Manager: Jostein Simble.
Norwegian Musicians' Union, Youngsgate. 11, N-0181 Oslo. President: Tore Nordvik.
Norwegian Song and Music Council, Toftesgt 69, N-0552 Oslo. General Manager: Karl Einar Ellingsen.
Rikskonsertene (The Norwegian State Travelling Concerts Organization), PO Box 7613, Skillebekk, N-0205, Oslo. Manager: Arne Holen.
Society of Norwegian Composers, PO Box 9171, Grønland, N-0134 Oslo. Manager: Hakon Berge.
The National Association of Music Friends, Toftesgate 69, 0552 Oslo. Manager: Jan Ola Amundsen.

PARAGUAY

Juventudes Musicales, c/o Saul Gaona, RI 3 Corrales 516, Asuncion.

PERU

Asociación Peruana de Autores y Compositores (APDAYC), Jiron Ica 559, Lima 1. Chairman: César Miró.
Juventudes Musicales, Garcilaso de la Vega 1746, Lima 14. President: Oscar Zamora.

PHILIPPINES

Andres Bobifacio Music Foundation, Union Village, Tandang Sora, Quezon City.
Choral Conductors Association of the Philippines, c/o University of the Philippines, College of Music, Quezon City.
Eliseo Pajaro Foundation, Inc, c/o Cultural Center of the Philippines, Roxas Boulevard, Manila.
Filipino Society of Composers, Authors, and Publishers (FILSCAP), 308 RCBC Building, Buendia Extension, Makati, Metro Manila.
Kodály Society of the Philippines, c/o St Paul's College, Herran Street, Manila.
League of Filipino Composers, c/o Cultural Center of the Philippines, Roxas Boulevard, Manila.
Music Theater Foundation, c/o University of the Philippines, College of Music, Diliman, Quezon City.
Musika, 9-A Manga Road, New Manila, Quezon City.
National Music Council of the Philippines, c/o University of the Philippines, College of Music, Diliman, Quezon City.
Organisasyon ng Pilipinong Mang-aawit (OPM), Zeta Building, Suite 65, 191 Salcedo Street, Legaspi Village, Makati, Metro Manila.
Piano Teachers' Guild of the Philippines, c/o St Scholastica's College, Leon Guinto, Malate, Manila.
Philippine Musicians Guild, 409 Unlad Condominium, Taft Avenue and General Malvar Street, Malate, Manila.
Philippine Society for Music Education, c/o Philippine Normal College. Music and Arts Department, Taft Avenue, Manila.
Samahan ng mga Manunuri at Manunulat ng Musika sa Pilipinas (SAMMPI), Aurora Pijuan Street, Block 5, Lot 1, BF Resort Village, Pamplona, Las Pinas, Metro Manila.
University of the Philippines Musical Arts and Research Management, Inc, c/o University of the Philippines, College of Music, Abelardo Hall, Diliman, Quezon City.

POLAND

Association of Polish Violin Makers, Krakowskie Przedmieście 16/18, 00-325 Warsaw. President: Włodzimierz Kamiński.
Chopin Society of Music, Okólnik 1, 00-368 Warsaw. General Director: Bogumił Pałasz.
Jeunesses Musicales de Pologne, Lwowska 13, 00-660 Warsaw. Presdient: Jarosław Stepowski.
Polish Composers' Union, Rynek Starego Miasta 27, 00-272 Warsaw. President: Andrzej Chodkowski.
Polish Composers' Union, Musicological Section, Rynek Starego Miasta 27, 00-272 Warsaw. President: Piotr Poźniak.
Polish Jazz Society, Rutkowskiego 20/5, 00-020 Warsaw. President: Jan Byrzcek.
Polish Music Centre, Fredry 8, 00-097 Warsaw. Manager: Barbara Zwolska-Steszewska.
Polish Music Council, Fredry 8, 00-097 Warsaw. President: Jan Steszewski.
Society of Authors "ZAIKS", Hipoteczna 2, 00-092 Warsaw. President: Edward Pałłasz.
Society of Music Education, Koszykowa 24/7a, 00-553 Warsaw. President: Adrianna Poniecka-Piekutowska.
Society of Polish Librarians, Music Libraries Section, c/o Warszawskie Towarzystwo Muzyczne, Bibliotéka Zakroczymska 2, 00-225 Warsaw. President: Andrzej Spóz.
Society of Polish Musicians, Krucza 24-26, 00-526 Warsaw. President: Tadeusz Strugała.
Szymanowski Society of Music, Kasprusie 19, willa "Atma", 34-500 Zakopane. President: Józef Patkowski.
Union of Polish Lyric Writers and Composers of Light Music "ZAKR", Hipoteczna 2, 00-092 Warsaw. President: Jan Majdrowicz.
Warsaw Music Society, Morskie Oko 2, 02-511 Warsaw. President: Stefania Woytowicz.
Wieniawski Society of Music, Sweitosławska 7, 61-840 Poznán. General Director: Edmund Grabkowski.

MUSIC ORGANIZATIONS

PORTUGAL

Fundacâo Calouste Gulbenkian, Servico de Musica, Av. de Berna 45, 1093 Lisbon Codex. President of the Music Department: Dr. Luis Pereira Leal.
Juventude Musical Portuguesa, Rua Rosa Araujo 6, 3rd Floor, 1200 Lisbon. President: Miguel Henriques.
Sindicato dos Músicos, Av. D Carlos I 72, 2nd Floor, 1200 Lisbon.
Sociedade Portuguesa de Autores (SPA), Avda. Dugue de Louié 31, 1098 Lisbon Codex. President: Luis Francisco Rebelo.

RUMANIA

Jeunesses Musicales, Str Lipscani 53, Bucharest.
Union of Rumanian Composers, Calea Victoriei 141, 70149 Bucharest.

RUSSIA

Intercultcentre (International Center for Festivals, Competitions, and Intergovernmental Cooperation), Arbat Str 35, 121835 Moscow. Director General: Suren Shaumian.
International Union of Musicians, ul. Gertsena 14/2, 103009 Moscow. President: Irina Arkhipova.
Muzfond, Ul. Gotvalda 10, 112127 Moscow A-47. Director: Lev Radovinskii.
Union of Composers of Russia, ul. Nezhdanovoi 8/10, 103009 Moscow K-9. Chairman: V Kazenin.
VAAP (Russian Copyright Agency), ul. Bolshaia Bronnais 6-A, GSP K 104, 103670 Moscow. Chairman: Nikolai Chetverikov.

SINGAPORE

Musicians and Singers Association, Block 3, 03-628, Rochor Centre, Rochor Road, Singapore 0718. Chief Officer: Stephen Gomez.
National Arts Council, PSA Building, 35th Storey, 460 Alexandria Road, Singapore 0511.

SLOVAKIA

Music Information Centre of the Slovak Music Fund, Fučikova 29, 811 02 Bratislava.
Slovak Music Association, Šafárikova nám. 4, 811 02 Bratislava.
Slovak Music Fund, Fučikova 29, 811 02 Bratislava.
Slovak Music Union (includes the Club of Concert Artists, Club of Music Folklorists, Club of Slovak Composers, and Slovak Musicologists' Association), Michalská 10, 815 36 Bratislava.
Slovkoncert (Slovak Artistic and Publicity Agency), Michalská 10, 815 36 Bratislava.
Study S (Agency for Theatre and Music), nám 1 mája, 815 36 Bratislava.

SOUTH AFRICA

Association of the South African Music Industry, PO Box 367, Randburg 2125, Johannesburg. Chief Executive: Brian Ellis.
Dramatic, Artistic, and Literary Rights Organisation, Ltd (DALRO), PO Box 9292, Johannesburg. Managing Director: Gideon Ross.
Foundation for the Creative Arts, PO Box 91122, Auckland Park 2006. Executive Manager: Herman Van Niekerk.
South African Co-ordinating Performing Arts Council (SACPAC), PO Box 566, Pretoria 0001. Chairman: T. van Wijk.
South African Music Rights Organization, Ltd (SAMRO), PO Box 9292, Johannesburg 2000. Managing Director: Gideon Ross.
South African Musicians Union, PO Box 5837, Johannesburg 2000.
South African Recording Rights Association, Ltd (SARRAL), PO Box 4378, Johannesburg 2000. Chief Officer: George Hardie.
South African Society of Music Teachers, PO Box 5318, Walmer 6065.

SPAIN

Asociación Cultural Laboratorio de Interpretacion Musical (LIM), Seco 12, 28007 Madrid. President: Jesús Villa Rojo.
Asociación de Musica en Compostela, Pablo Aranda 6, 28006 Madrid. President: Margarita Pastor Zacharias.
Centro Para la Difusion de la Musica Contemporanea, Santa Isabel 52, 28012 Madrid. Director: Tomas Marco.
Direccion General de Musica y Teatro, Ministerio de Cultura, Pza del Rey 1, 28071 Madrid.
International Society for Contemporary Music (Spanish Section), Avda de America 58-5. 28028 Madrid. Chief Officer: Luis de Pablo.
International Society for Music Education, Conde de Aranda 17, 28001 Madrid. President: Rosa María Kucharski.
Instituto de Bibliografica Musical, Penulas 12, 12p 28071 Madrid. President: Jacinto Torres Mulas.
Joventuts Musical de Barcelona, Pau Claris 139, 4th Floor, 1a, 08009 Barcelona. President: Joan Millá i Francoli.
Juventudes Musicales, Girona 10, 3, Barcelona.
Sociedad de Conciertos, Altamira 3, 03002 Alicante. Director: Margarita Berenger.
Sociedad Espanola de Musicologica (SEM), Canos del Peral 7, 28013 Madrid. President: Ismael Fernandez de la Cuesta.
Sociedad General de Autores de Espana (SGAE), Fernando VI 4, 28004 Madrid. President: Juan José Alonso Millan.

MUSIC ORGANIZATIONS

SWEDEN

Association of Swedish Symphony Orchestras, Schönfeldts gränd 1, 111 27 Stockholm. Chairman: Per Olof Håkansson.
International Music Council, Swedish National Committee, c/o Royal Swedish Academy of Music, Blasieholmstorg 8, 111 48 Stockholm. Chairman: Roland Sandberg.
International Society for Contemporary Music (Swedish Section), c/o FST, Box 27327, 102 54 Stockholm. Chairman: Arne Mellnäs.
Musical Arts Association, Maria Prästgårdsgata 14, 118 52 Stockholm. Chairman: Staffan Scheja.
Society of Music Teachers in Sweden, c/o Nordstedt, Ortoftagatan 37, 216 20 Malmö. Chairman: Lars Nordstedt.
Society of Swedish Church Musicians, c/o S Henriksson, Storgatan 36, 520 40 Floby. Chairman: Bo Svensson.
Society of Swedish Composers, Box 27327, 102 54 Stockholm. Chairman: Sten Hanson.
Swedish Artists and Musicians Interest Organization, Mosebacke Torg 16, 116 20 Stockholm. Chairman: Helge Almquist.
Swedish Choral Assocation, Box 38014, 100 64 Stockholm. Chairperson: Madeleine Uggla.
Swedish Music Information Center, Box 27327, 102 54 Stockholm. Director: Roland Sandberg.
Swedish Musicians Union, Box 43, 101 20 Stockholm. Chairman: Gert-Åke Walldén.
Swedish Performing Rights Society, Box 27327, 102 54 Stockholm. Director: Gunnar Petri.
Swedish Piano Teachers Association, c/o Elsa Sätherblom, Solbacken 9, 131 42 Nacka. Chairperson: Marianne Facht-Ribbing.
Swedish Society for Musicology, c/o Statens Musiksamlingar, Box 16326, 103 26 Stockholm. Chairman: Greger Andersson.
Swedish Society of Light Music Composers, Box 27327, 102 54 Stockholm. Chairman: Håkan Elmquist.
Swedish Union of Professional Musicians, Drottninggatan 55, 111 21 Stockholm. Chairman: Peter Hoglund.

SWITZERLAND

Association of Concert Giving Societies of Switzerland. Münsterplatz 18, 4051 Basel. Secretary: Hans Ziegler.
Association of Swiss Musicians, Avenue du Grammont 11 bis, Case postale 177, 1000 Lausanne 13. General Secretary: Hélène Petitpierre.
European Association of Amateur Orchestras, Heimstrasse 24, 3018 Bern. Secretary General: J Nyffenegger.
European Association of Music Festivals, c/o Centre Européen de la Culture Villa Moynier, 122 rue de Lausanne, 1211 Geneva. Secretary: Dr Henry Siegwart.
Federation of International Music Competitions, 104 rue de Carouge, 1205 Geneva. President: Robert Dunand; Secretary General: Franco Fisch.
Gesellschaft der Freunde alter Musikinstrumente, Mühlebachstrasse 174, 8008 Zürich. Secretary: Siegfried Brenn.
Goethe Foundation of Arts and Sciences, Münstergasse 9, 8001 Zürich.
International Federation of Musicians, Hofackerstrasse 7, 8032 Zürich. General Secretary: Dr Yvonne Burckhardt.
International Music Council (National Committee), Bahnhofstrasse 78, 5000 Aarau. Executive Secretary: Mrs Ursula Bally-Fahr.
International Musicological Society, PO Box 1561, 4001 Basel. Secretary General: Dr Rudolf Häusler.
International Society for Contemporary Music, c/o Association of Swiss Musicians, Avenue du Grammont 11 bis, Case postale 177, 1000 Lausanne 13. Secretary General: Hélène Petitpierre.
Jeunesses Musicales de Suisse, Case postale 233, 1211 Geneva 8. President: Thüring Bräm.
National Association of Orchestras, Wattenwylweg 30, 3006 Bern. Secretary: Anita Prato.
National Association of Singers, Burgstrasse 1, 4143 Dornach. President: Max Diethelm.
National Music Association, 3946 Turtmann. Central President: Alex Oggier.
Performing Right Society of Switzerland, SUISA, Bellariastrasse 82, 8038 Zürich.
Romand Centre of Sacred Music, PO Box 204, Champel, 1211 Geneva. Secretary: Miss Georgette Albrecht.
Schweiz Chorvereinigung, Scheuchzerstrasse 14, 8006 Zürich. President: Ernst Kleiner.
SUISA Music Foundation (Music Information Centre), Passage Maxmililien-de-Meuron 4, PO Box 409, 2001 Neuchâtel. Managing Director: Claude Delley.
Swiss Assocation for Concert Managers, 7 rue de la Fontaine, 1204 Geneva. Secretary and President: Jack Yfar.
Swiss Association for Church Singing, Hirschengraben 7, 8001 Zürich. President: Hans-Juerg Stefan.
Swiss Association of Mixed Choirs, Rainallee 68, 4125 Riehen. Vice President: Louis Loeliger-Schneider.
Swiss Association of Professional Conductors, Stutzstrasse 9, 8834 Schindellegi. Secretary: Willy Honegger.
Swiss Association of Professional Musicians, Elisabethenstrasse 2, 4051 Basel. Secretary Dr Peter Kuster.
Swiss Music Education Association, Forchstrasse 376, 8008 Zürich. Secretary: Mrs Hanna Brandenberger.
Swiss Music Interpreters Society, Mittelstrasse 49, 8008 Zürich. Managing Director: Dr Yvonne Burckhardt.
Swiss Music Teachers Association, Forchstrasse 376, 8008 Zürich. Secretary: Mrs Hanna Brandenberger.
Swiss Society of Music Teachers, Alpstrasse 34, 6020 Emmenbrücke. President: Hansruedi Willisegger.
Swiss Society for Musical Research, PO Box 231, 4020 Basel. Central President: Prof. Dr. Ernst Lichtenhahn.
Swiss Society for Popular Music, c/o SUISA, Bellariastrasse 82, 8038 Zürich. Secretary: Ernst Roth.
Swiss Workers' Music Association, PO Box 29, 3000 Bern 9. President: E Knuchel.

UK

Alkan Society, 21 Heronswood, Salisbury, Wiltshire SP2 8DH. Honorary Secretary: Peter Grove.
Amateur Music Association, Medlock School, Wadeson Road, Manchester M13 9UR. General Secretary: Ian Clarke.
Arts Council of Great Britain, 14 Great Peter Street, London SW1P 3NQ. Secretary-General: Anthony Everitt.
Association for the Advancement of Teacher Education in Music, 16 Ullswater Avenue, Cardiff CF2 5PT. Chairman: Dr William Salaman.
Association of British Choral Directors, 6 Hillside Road, Leighton Buzzard, Beds, LU7 8BU. General Secretary: Anthony Philpott.
Association for British Music, 2 Union Place, Boston, Lincs PE21 6PS. Honorary Secretary: Estelle Stiles.
Association of British Orchestras, Francis House, Francis Street, London SW1P 1DE. General Administrator: Libby MacNamara.
Association for Business Support of the Arts, 2 Chester Street, London SW1X 7BB. Director: Colin Tweedy.
Association of Entertainment and Arts Management, 3a-5a Stanley Street, Southport, Merseyside PR9 0BY. General

MUSIC ORGANIZATIONS

Secretary: J B A Sharples.

Association of Professional Composers, 34 Hanway Street, London W1P 7DE. Administrator: Rosemary Dixson.

Association of Teachers of Singing, 146 Greenstead Road, Colchester, Essex CO1 2SN. General Secretary: Colin J Schooling.

Association of University Teachers, 1 Pembridge Road, London W11 3HJ. General Secretary: Laurie Sapper.

Association of Woodwind Teachers, 100 Common Road, Chatham, Kent ME5 9RG. Secretary: Bernard Parris.

Audio Engineering Society, Ltd (British Section), Lent Rise Road, Burnham, Slough SL1 7NY.

Bantock Society, 54 Clarendon Road, Bristol BS6 7ET. Honorary Secretary: Ron Bleach.

Barbirolli Society, 8 Tunnel Road, Retford, Notts DN22 7TA. Chairman: Pauline Pickering.

Beecham Trust, Denton House, Denton, Harleston, Norfolk IP20 0AA. Trustee: Shirley, Lady Beecham.

Benslow Association, Little Benslow Hills, Ibberson Way, Benslow Lane, Hitchin, Herts SG4 9RB. Secretary. Katharine Bramley.

Benslow Music Trust, Little Benslow Hills, Ibberson Way, Benslow Lane, Hitchin, Herts SG4 9RB. Director: Michael Procter.

Boughton Trust, 4 Church Street, W Liss, Hants.

Bowen Society, Cairnbield, Gordon, Berwickshire. Chairman: John Lindsay.

Brian Society, 17 Ash Tree Dell, London NW9 0AG. Secretary: David Brown.

Bridge Trust, 14 Barlby Road, London W10 6AR. Secretary: John Bishop.

British Academy of Songwriters, Composers and Authors, 34 Hanway Street, London W1P 9DE. Chairman: Guy Fletcher.

British-American Arts Association, 116 Commercial Street, London E1 6NF. Director: Jennifer Williams.

British Arts Festivals Association, PO Box 925, London N6 5XX. Co-ordinator: Gwyn Rhydderch.

British Association of Concert Agents, 26 Wadham Road, London SW15 2LR. President: David Sigall.

British Association of Symphonic Bands and Wind Ensembles, 3 Northbrook Road, Solihull, West Midlands, B90 3NT. Secretary: Tony Veal.

British Broadcasting Corporation, Broadcasting House, London, W1A 1AA.

British Copyright Council, 29 Berners Street, London W1P 4AA. Secretary: Geoffrey Adams.

British Council, Arts Division, 10 Spring Gardens, London SW1A 2BN. Department of Music Director: John Acton.

British Federation of Brass Bands, 4 Kingsway Park, Davyhulme, Urmston, Manchester M31 2FB. Publicity Officer: Gary Newborough.

British Federation of Music Festivals, Festivals House, 198 Park Lane, Macclesfield, Cheshire SK11 6UD. Secretary: Eileen Craine.

British Flute Society, 65 Marlborough Place, London NW8 0PT. Secretary: John Francis.

British Horn Society, c/o Paxman, Ltd, 116 Long Acre, London WC2E 9PA.

British Institute of Organ Studies, c/o University of Reading, Department of Music, 35 Upper Redlands Road, Reading, Berks RG1 5JE. Secretary: Dr Christopher Kent.

British Kodály Society, 31 Woodlands Road, London SW13 0JZ.

British Music Information Centre, 10 Stratford Place, London W1N 9AE. Manager: Elizabeth Yeoman.

British Music Society, 30 High Beeches, Gerards Cross, Bucks SL9 7HX. President: John McCabe.

British Phonographic Industry, Ltd, Roxburghe House, 273/287 Regent Street, London W1R 7PB. Director General: John Deacon.

British Society for Electronic Music, 277 Putney Bridge Road, London SW15 2PT. Secretary: Dr Peter Zinovieff.

British Suzuki Institute, The Old School, Brewhouse Hill, Wheathampstead, Herts AL4 8AN. Administrator: Miss B S Breslin.

Cathedral Organists' Association, c/o Royal School of Church Music, Addington Palace, Croydon CR9 5AD. Secretary: Dr Lionel Dakers.

Choir Schools' Association, Westminister Cathedral Choir School, Ambrosden Avenue, London SW1P 1QH. Honorary Secretary: P Hannigan.

City of London Society of Organists, Hill House, 17 Hans Place, London SW1X 0EP. Chairman and Secretary: Richard Townend.

Clarinet and Saxophone Society of Great Britain, 24c Wellwood Road, Goodmayes, Essex IG3 8TR. Membership Secretary: Susan Moss.

Composers' Guild of Great Britain, 34 Hanway Street, London W1P 9DE. Secretary: Elizabeth Yeoman.

Computer Arts Society, 50-51 Russell Square, London WC1B 4JP. Secretary: John Lansdown.

Concert Artistes' Association, 20 Bedford Street, London WC2E 9HP. Secretary: Jo Palmer.

Critics' Circle, 47 Bermondsey Street, London SE1 3XT. Secretary: Peter Hepple.

Crotch Society, 74 Pembroke Road, London W8 6NX. Secretary: Jonathan Rennert.

Dalcroze Society, Inc, 26 Bullfinch Road, Selsdon Vale, South Croydon CR2 8PW. Chairman: Ruth Stewart.

Delius Society, 28 Emscote Street South, Bell Hall, Halifax, West Yorks HX1 3AN. Secretary: Diane Eastwood.

Delius Trust, 16 Ogle Street, London W1P 7LG. Chairman: Norman K Millar.

Dolmetsch Foundation, High Pines, Wood Road, Hindhead, Surrey GU6 6PT. Secretary: Pat Dutton.

Donizetti Society, 56 Harbut Road, London SW11 2RB. Honorary Secretary: J R Carter.

Dvořák Society, 162 Frant Road, Thornton Heath, Surrey CR4 7JW. Chairman: Mark Todd.

Early Music Centre, Ltd, Charles Clore House, 17 Russell Square, London WC1B 5DR. Administrator: Frederik Martin.

Electro-Acoustic Music Association of Great Britain, 10 Stratford Place, London W1N 9AE. Administrator: Charol Butler.

Elgar Society, 20 Geraldine Road, Malvern, Worcs WR14 3PA.

English Folk Dance and Song Society, 2 Regents Park Road, London NW1 7AY. Managing Director: Brenda Godrich.

European Piano Teachers' Association, 28 Emperor's Gate, London SW7 4HS. Chairman: John Bigg.

European String Teachers' Association, 5 Neville Avenue, New Malden, Surrey KT3 4SN. Organizing Secretary: Nannie Jamieson.

Federation of British Audio, 19 Charing Cross Road, London WC2H 0ES. Chairman: N J Crocker.

Federation of Master Organ Builders, Petersfield GU32 3AT. Secretary: D M van Heck.

Federation of Music Industries, 24 Fairlawn Grove, Chiswick, London W4 5EH. General Secretary/Administrator: Arthur Spencer-Bolland.

Fellowship of Makers & Researchers of Historical Instruments, c/o St Aldate's Faculty of Music, Oxford OX1 1DB. Honorary Secretary: Jeremy Montagu.

Galpin Society, 38 Eastfield Road, Western Park, Leicester LE3 6FE. Secretary: Pauline Holden.

Gilbert and Sullivan Society, 273 Northfield Avenue, London W5 4UA.

Grainger Society, 6 Fairfax Crescent, Aylesbury, Bucks HP20 2ES. Secretary: Barry P Ould.

Guild of Professional Musicians, 48 Chalcot Road, London NW1 8LS. Administrator: Ian Bonner.

Guild for the Promotion of Welsh Music, 94 Walter Road, Swansea SA1 5QA. Honorary Secretary: Geraint W

MUSIC ORGANIZATIONS

Walters.

Handel Opera Society, 15a Wallace Road, London N1 2PG. Honorary Secretary: Stephen Toms.

Haydn Society of Great Britain, c/o University of Lancaster, Department of Music, Bailrigg, Lancaster LA1 4YW. Director: Denis McCaldin.

Hymn Society of Great Britain and Ireland, The Vicarage, 51 Overgreen Drive, Kinghurst, Birmingham B37 6EY. Secretary: Rev. Michael Garland.

Incorporated Association of Organists, Harnor House, Leigh Road, Bradford Leigh, Bradford-on-Avon, Wilts BA15 2RW. General Secretary: Roger Bishton.

Incorporated Society of Musicians, 10 Stratford Place, London W1N 9AE. General Secretary: David Padgett-Chandler.

Incorporated Society of Organ Builders, Petersfield GU32 3AT. Secretary: D M van Heck.

Institute of Musical Instrument Technology, 134 Crouch Hill, London N8 9DX. Secretary: Frank Fowler.

International Association of Music Libraries, Archives and Documentation Centres, c/o Royal Northern College of Music Library, 124 Oxford Road, Manchester M13 9RD. General Secretary: Anna Smart.

International Council for Traditional Music, Flat 1, 30 Holland Park, London W11 3TA. Secretary: Philippa Heale.

International Federation of Musicians, 29 Catherine Place, Buckingham Gate, London SW1E 6EH.

International Federation of Phonogram and Videogram Producers, 54 Regent Street, London W1R 5PJ.

International Society for Contemporary Music, British Section, c/o West Heath Studios 174 Mill Lane, London NW6 1TB. Administrator: Richard Steele.

International Society for Music Education, 14 Bedford Square, London WC1B 3JG. Secretary General: Ronald Smith.

Ireland Trust, 35 St Mary's Mansions, St Mary's Terrace, London W2 1SQ.

Kempe Society, 135 Stevenage Road, London SW6 6PB. Treasurer-Secretary: J Audrey Ellison.

Korngold Society, 12 Townhead Terrace, Paisley, Renfrewshire PA1 2AX. Secretary: Konrad Hopkins.

Liszt Society, Ltd, 135 Stevenage Road, London SW6 6PB. Secretary: Audrey Ellison.

Lute Society, 26B Hindes Road, Harrow, Middlesex HA1 1SL.

Massenet Society, Flat 2, 79 Linden Gardens, London W2 4EU. Director: Stella J Wright.

Mechanical Copyright Protection Society, Ltd, 41 Streatham High Road, London SW16 1ER. Managing Director: Frans J P De Wit.

Music Advisers' National Association, Education Department, Avon House North, St James Barton, Bristol BS99 7EB. Secretary: Carl Sidgreaves.

Music Industries Association, 7 The Avenue, Datchet, Slough, Berks SL3 9DH. Secretary: J A Fox.

Music Masters' and Mistresses' Association, Steepcot, Bedales School, Petersfield, Hants GU32 2DG. Honorary Secretary: Jonathan Willcocks.

Music Publishers' Association, Ltd, Strandgate, 3rd Floor, 18-20 York Buildings, London WC2N 6JU. Secretary: Peter Dadswell.

Music Retailers Association, PO Box 249, London W4 5EX. Secretary: Arthur Spencer-Bolland.

Music for Youth, 23a Kings Road, London SW3 4RP. Director: Larry Westland.

Musicians' Union, 60-62 Clapham Road, London SW9 0JJ. General Secretary: Dennis Scard.

National Association of Art Centres, The Arts Centre, Room 110, Vane Terrace, Darlington DL3 7AX.

National Association for Education in the Arts, c/o University of Exeter, School of Education, St Luke's, Exeter EX1 2LU. Secretary: Beryl Phillips.

National Assocation of Teachers in Further and Higher Education, 27 Britannia Street London WC1X 9JP.

National Association of Youth Orchestras, 11 St Colme Street, Edinburgh EH3 6AG. Secretary: Carol Main.

National Campaign for the Arts, Francis House, Francis Street, London SW1P 1DE. Director: Simon Mundy.

National Early Music Association, 39 Capel Road, London E7 0JP.

National Federation of Gramophone Societies, Withyfeld, 192c Woodrow Forest, Melksham, Wilts SN12 7RF. Chairman: J R Shaw.

National Federation of Music Societies, Francis House, Francis Street, London SW1P 1DE. Administrator: Russell Jones.

National Operatic and Dramatic Association, 1 Crestfield Street, London WC1H 8AU.

National School Band Association, East Cliffe, Side Cliff Road, Roker, Sunderland SR6 9PX. Secretary: Alan Winwood.

National Union of Musical Instrument Makers, c/o Furniture, Timber and Allied Trades Union, Fairfields, Roe Grn, Kingsbury, London NW9 0PT. General Secretary: Colin Christopher.

Orff Society, 31 Roedean Crescent, London SW15 5JX. Secretary: Margaret Murray.

Organ Club, 10 Roxburgh Court, 69 Melrose Road, London SW18 1PG. General Secretary: Adrian Mumford.

Performing Right Society, Ltd, 29-33 Berners Street, London W1P 4AA. Chief Executive: M J Freegard.

Personal Managers' Association, c/o Rooke Holt & Co, 83 Elbury Street, London SW1. Chairman: Peter Dunlop.

Plainsong and Mediaeval Music Society, 72 Brewery Road, London N7 9NE. Secretary: Catherine Harbor.

Pro Corda, Leiston Abbey House, Leiston, Suffolk 1P16 4TB. Directors: Pamela Spofforth and Elizabeth Hewlin.

Rawsthorne Society, c/o Royal Northern College of Music Library, 124 Oxford Road, Manchester M13 9RD. Secretary: Tony Hodges.

Robert Farnon Society, 'Stone Gables', Upton Lane, Searington St Michael, Ilminster, Somerset, TA19 0PZ.

Royal College of Organists, Kensington Gore, London SW7 2QS. Honorary Secretary: Stephen Cleobury.

Royal Musical Association, St Aldates, Faculty of Music, Oxford OX1 1DB. Secretary: Dr Ewan West.

Royal Philharmonic Society, 10 Stratford Place, London W1N 9AE. Honorary Secretary: Eric Thompson.

Royal School of Church Music, Addington Palace, Croydon CR9 5AD. Director: Dr Lionel Dakers.

Royal Society of Musicians of Great Britain, 10 Stratford Place, London W1N 9AE. Secretary: Marjorie Gleed.

Schools Music Association, Town Hall, Education Office, Friern Barnet, London N11 3DL. Honorary Secretary: Maxwell Pryce.

Schubert Society of Great Britain, Garden Flat, 125 Grosvenor Avenue, London N5 2NL. Secretary: Alan Tabelin.

Scottish Arts Council, 19 Charlotte Square, Edinburgh, Scotland EH2 4DF. Music Director: Christie Duncan.

Simpson Society, 3 Engle Park, London NW7 2HE. Secretaries: John and Sylvia Brooks.

Society for the Promotion of New Music, West Heath Studios, 174 Mill Lane, London NW6 1TB. Administrator: Richard Steele.

Society for the Research in the Psychology of Music and Music Education, Westminster College, N Hinksey, Oxford OX2 9AT. Secretary: Dr Janet Mills.

Spohr Society of Great Britain, 123 Mount View Road, Sheffield S8 8PJ.

Stokowski Society, 7 Priestfields, Rochester, Kent ME1 3AG. Secretary: Andrew Barker.

Sullivan Society, 51 Nowton Road, Bury St Edmunds, Suffolk IP33 2BU. Secretary: Stephen Turnbull.

UK Council for Music Education and Training, 13 Black Lane, South Luffenham, Oakham, Leics LE15 8NQ. Secretary: Linda Cummins.

United Kingdom Harpists Association, 39 Villiers Clo, Surbiton, Surrey KT5 8DN. Secretary: Angela Moore.

Viola d'Amore Society, 1 Parkside Avenue, Wimbledon Common, London SW19 5ES.

MUSIC ORGANIZATIONS

Viola da Gamba Society, 93A Sutton Road, London N10 1HH. Administrator: Caroline Wood.
Visiting Orchestras' Consultative Association, 10 Stratford Place, London W1N 9AE. Secretary: Hilary Ougham.
Wagner Society, 7 Kingsmead, Cheshunt, Herts EN8 0EG. Secretary: Dr J J Pritchard.
Warlock Society, 17 Gledhow Gardens, London SW5 0AY. Secretary: Malcolm Rudland.
Welsh Arts Council, 9 Museum Place, Cardiff CF1 3NX. Music Director: Roy Bohana.
Welsh Music Information Centre, PO Box 78, University College, Cardiff, S Glam CF1 1XL. Director: A J Howard Rees.
Workers' Music Association, 17 Prideaux House, Prideaux Place, London WC1. Secretary: Anne Gilman.
Worshipful Company of Musicians, 4 St Paul's Churchyard, London EC4M 8BA. Clerk: W R I Crewdson.

USA

Affilate Artists, Inc, 37 West 65th Street, New York, NY 10023. President: Richard C Clark.
Amateur Chamber Music Players, Inc, 545 Eighth Avenue, 9th Floor, New York, NY 10018. Chief Officer: Cecilia Drinker Saltonstall.
American Academy and Institute of Arts and Letters, 633 West 155th Street, New York, NY 10032. Executive Director: Virginia Dajani.
American Academy of Teachers of Singing, Hotel Ansonia, Studio No 5-517, 2109 Broadway, New York, NY 10023. Chairman: Donald Read.
American Accordionists' Association, Inc, PO Box 616, Mineola, NY 11501. President: Faithe Deffner.
American Arts Alliance, 1319 F Street North West, Suite 500, Washington, DC 20004.
American Association for Music Therapy, PO Box 80012, Valley Forge, PA 19484. President: Concetta Tomaino.
American Beethoven Society, San Jose State University, 1 Washington Square, Ira F Brilliant Center for Beethoven Studies, San Jose, CA 95192. Contact: William Meredith.
American Berlin Opera Foundation Inc, 666 Fifth Avenue, 21st Floor, New York, NY 10103. Chief Officer: Christa Drechsler.
American Brahms Society, University of Washington, School of Music, DN10, Seattle, WA 98195. Executive Director: George S Bozarth.
American Cello Council, Inc, 340 West 55th Street, New York, NY 10019. Administrator and Treasurer: Esther Prince.
American Choral Directors' Association, PO Box 6310, Lawton, OK 73506. Executive Director: Gene Brooks.
American College of Musicians, PO Box 1807, 808 Rio Grande, Austin, TX 78767. President: Richard Allison.
American Composes Alliance and Edition, 170 West 74th Street, New York, NY 10023. President: Richard Hervig.
American Federation of Musicians, 1501 Broadway, Suite 600, New York, NY 10036. President: Mark Tully Massagli.
American Federation of Television and Radio Artists (AFTRA), 260 Madison Avenue, New York, NY 10016. Executive Director: Bruce A York.
American Federation of Violin and Bow Makers, Inc, 33 North "B" Street, No 8, San Mateo, CA 94401. President: Boyd Poulsen.
American Guild of Music, 5354 Washington Street, Downers Grove, IL 60515. Registered Agent: E D Herrick.
American Guild of Musical Artists, 1727 Broadway, New York, NY 10019. Executive Secretary: Sanford I Wolff.
American Guild of Organists, 475 Riverside Drive, Suite 1260, New York, NY 10115. Executive Director: Daniel N Colburn.
American Harp Society, Inc, 6331 Quebec Drive, Los Angeles, CA 90068. President: Molly Hahn.
American Liszt Society, Inc, 210 Devonshire Drive, Rochester, NY 14625. President: Fernando Laires.
American Matthay Association, 46 Popular Street, Pittsburgh, PA 15205. President: Thomas C Davis.
American Mechanical Rights Agency, Inc, (AMRA), 333 South Tamiami Trail, Suite 295, Venice, FL 34285. Chief Officer: Patricia Bente.
American Music Center, Inc, 30 West 26th Street, Suite 1001, New York, NY 10010. Executive Director: Nancy C Clarke.
American Music Conference, 5140 Avenida Encinas, Carlsbad, CA 92008. Executive Director: Karl Bruhn.
American Musical Instrument Society, c/o Shrine to Music Museum, 414 East Clark Street, Vermilliom, SD 57069. President: Phillip T Young.
American Musicians Union, 8 Tobin Court, Dumont, NJ 07628. President: Ben Intorre.
American Musicological Society, 201 South 34th Street, Philadelphia, PA 19104. Executive Director: Alvin Johnson.
American New Music Consortium, 87-27 Santiago Street, Holliswood, NY 11423. Executive Director: Dinu Ghezzo.
American Opera Projects, Inc, 463 Broome Street, New York, NY 10013. Artistic Director: Grethe B Holby.
American Orff-Schulwerk Association, PO Box 391089, Cleveland, OH 44139. President: Marilyn Davidson.
American Recorder Society, 236 West County Line Road, Jackson, NJ 08527. President: Constance Primus.
American Society of Composers, Authors and Publishers (ASCAP), 1 Lincoln Plaza, New York, NY 10023. President: Morton Gould.
American String Teachers Association, Inc, 4020 McEwen, Suite 105, Dallas, TX 75244. General Manager: Madeleine Crouch.
American Symphony Orchestra League, 777 14th Street North West, Suite 500, Washington, DC 20005. Chief Executive Officer: Catherine French.
American Viola Society, 24833 Sage Crest Road, Newhall, CA 91321. President: Alan de Veritch.
American Women Composers, Inc, 1690 36th Street North West, Suite 409, Washington, DC 20007. President: Judith Shatin.
Arts International Program, Institute of International Education, 809 UN Plaza, New York, NY 10017. Director: Jane M Gullong.
The Asia Society, Performing Arts, 725 Park Avenue, New York, NY 10021. Director: Rhoda Grauer.
Associated Male Choruses of America, Inc, PO Box 771, Brainerd, MN 56401. Executive Secretary: Forbes H Martinson.
Association for Recorded Sound Collections, Inc, PO Box 10162, Silver Spring, MD 20904. Executive Director: Phillip Rochlin.
Association of Arts Administration Educators, Inc, c/o American Council for the Arts, 1 East 53rd Street, New York, NY 10022. President: Dan J Martin.
Association of Performing Arts Presenters, 1112 16th Street North West, Suite 400, Washington, DC 20036. Executive Director: Susan Farr.
Audio Engineering Society, Inc, 60 East 42nd Street, Lincoln Building, Room 2520, New York, NY 10165. Executive Director: Donald J Plunkett.
B(roadcast) M(usic) I(nc), 320 West 57th Street, New York, NY 10019. President and Chief Executive Officer:

MUSIC ORGANIZATIONS

Frances W Preston.

Box Office Management International, 333 East 46th Street, Suite 1B, New York, NY 10017. President: Patricia Spira.

Louis Braille Foundation for Blind Musicians, 215 Park Avenue South, New York, NY 10003. Executive Director: Sheldon Freund.

Bruckner Society of America, Inc, 2150 Dubuque Road, Iowa City, IA 52240. President: Charles L Eble.

Business Committee for the Arts, Inc, 1775 Broadway, Suite 510, New York, NY 10019. President: Judith A Jedlicka.

Chamber Music America, 545 Eighth Avenue, New York, NY 10018. President: Paul Katz.

Chopin Foundation of the United States, 1440 79th Street Causeway, Miami, FL 33141. Chairman: Blanka A Rosenstiel.

Choristers Guild, 2834 West Kingsley Road, Garland, TX 75041. Executive Director: Patricia M Evans.

Chorus America: Association of Professional Vocal Ensembles, 2111 Sansom Street, Philadelphia, PA 19103. Executive Director: Kenneth Garner.

College Band Directors National Association, University of Texas, Box 8028, Austin, TX 78713. Secretary-Tresurer: Richard L Floyd.

The College Music Society Inc, 202 West Spruce Street, Missoula, MT 59802. Executive Director: Robby D Gunstream.

Composers' Forum Inc, 596 Broadway, Suite 602-A, New York, NY 10012. Executive Director: Betsy McClelland.

Composers Guild, Box 586, Farmington, UT 84025. President: Ruth Gatrell.

Composers' Resources, Inc, PO Box 19935, Atlanta, GA 30325. President: Howard Wershil.

Computer Music Association, PO Box 1634, San Francisco, CA 94101. President: Larry Austin.

Concert Music Broadcasters Association, c/o WGMS-FM, 11300 Rockville Pike, No 905 Rockville, MD 20852. President: Catherine Meloy.

Conductors' Guild, Inc, PO Box 3361, West Chester, PA 19381. Executive Secretary: Judy Ann Voois.

Conference of Personal Managers, Inc, 1201 Larrabee Street, Penthouse 302, West Hollywood, CA 90069. President: Michael Gormley.

Creative Audio and Music Electronics Organization, Route 2, Box 408, Meridan, MS 39305. President: Larry Blakely.

Delta Omicron (International Music Fraternity), 8009 Volk Drive, Dayton, OH 45415. President: Phyllis Conrad.

Early Music America, 30 West 26th Street, Suite 1001, New York, NY 10010. Executive Director: Daniel Nimetz.

George Enescu Society of the United States, Inc, 4 Barrett Place, Northampton, MA 01060. Secretary-Treasurer: Lory Wallfisch.

Guitar Foundation of America, Box 878, Claremont, CA 91711. General Manager: Gunnar Eisel.

The Hymn Society in the United States and Canada, Texas Christian University, Box 30854, Fort Worth, TX 76129. Executive Director: W Thomas Smith.

Independent Composers Association, Box 45134, Los Angeles, CA 90045. President: Burt Goldstein.

Institute for Music, Health, and Education, PO Box 1244, Boulder, CO 80306. Director: Don G Campbell.

Institute of Audio Research, School of Audio and Video Technology, 64 Univerity Place, Greenwich Village, New York, NY 10003. Director: Miriam Friedman.

International Association of Auditorium Managers, 4425 West Airport Freeway, Suite 590, Irving, TX 75062. Executive Director: John S Swinburn.

International Computer Music Association, 2040 Polk Street, Suite 330, San Francisco, CA 94109. President: Larry Austin.

International Double Reed Society, University of North Texas, School of Music, Denton, TX 76203. President: Charles Veazey.

International Federation of Festival Organizations, PO Box 40703, Nashville, TN 37204. Secretary General: Armando Moreno.

International Horn Society, 2220 North 1400 East, Provo, UT 84604. Executive Secretary: Ellen Powley.

International League of Women Composers, Southshore Road, Box 670, Pt Peninsula, Three Mile Bay, NY 13693. Chairperson: Elizabeth Hayden Pizer.

International Society of Bassists, 4020 McEwen, Suite 105, Dallas, TX 75244. General Manager: Madeleine Crouch.

International Society of Performing Arts Administrators, 4920 Plainfield North East, Suite 3, Grand Rapids, MI 49505. Executive Director: Michael C Hardy.

International Teleproduction Society, Inc, 350 Fifth Avenue, Suite 2400, New York, NY 10118. Executive Director: Janet Luhrs.

International Trombone Association, University of North Texas, School of Music, Box 5336, Denton, TX 76203. Secretary-Treasurer: Vern Kagarice.

Jeunesses Musicales of the USA, c/o Trinity University, 715 Stadium Drive, San Antonio, TX 78284. Director: Gerald Benjamin.

Keyboard Teachers Association International, Inc, 361 Pin Oak Lane, Westbury, NY 11590. President: Albert DeVito.

League of Composers, International Society of Contemporary Music, 30 West 26th Street, Suite 1001, New York, NY 10010. Executive Director: Geoffrey Kidde.

Leschetizky Association, 105 West 72nd Street, New York, NY 10023. President: Genia Robinor.

Lute Society of America, PO Box 1328, Lexington, VA 24450. Administrator: Mary B Hinely.

Gustav Mahler Society USA, 1616 N Sierra Bonita Avenue, Los Angeles, CA 90046. Contact: Avik Gilboa.

The Masterwork Music and Art Foundation, Inc, Morristown, NJ 07962. Executive Director: Shirley S May.

Moravian Music Foundation, Inc, 20 Cascade Avenue, Winston-Salem, NC 27127. President: M Keith Kapp.

Mu Phi Epsilon, 2212 Mary Hills Drive, Minneapolis, MN 55422. President: Katherine Doepke.

Music Associates of America, 224 King Street, Englewood, NJ 07631. Executive Director: George Sturm.

Music Critics Association, Inc, 7 Pine Court, Westfield, NJ 07090. Manager: Albert H Cohen.

Music Educators National Conference, 1902 Association Drive, Reston, VA 22091. President: Dorothy Straub.

Music Library Association, Inc, PO Box 487, Canton, MA 02021. President: Don L Roberts.

Music Performance Trust Funds of the Recording Industries, 1501 Broadway, New York, NY 10036.

Music Publishers' Association of the United States, 205 East 42nd Street, New York, NY 10017. President: Lynn Seng Stack.

Music Teachers National Association, Inc, 617 Vine Street, Suite 1432, Cincinnati, OH 45202. Executive Director: Ronald L Molen.

National Academy of Recording Arts and Sciences, Inc, 303 North Glenoaks Boulevard, Suite 140, Burbank, CA 91502. President: Michael Greene.

National Assembly of Local Arts Agencies, 927 15th Street North West, 12th Floor, Washington, DC 20005.

MUSIC ORGANIZATIONS

President and Chief Executive Officer: Robert Lynch.

National Assembly of State Arts Agencies, 1010 Vermont Avenue North West, Suite 920, Washington, DC 20005. Executive Director: Jonathan Katz.

National Association for Music Therapy, Inc, 8455 Colesville Road, Suite 930, Silver Spring, MD 20910.

National Association of Broadcasters, 1771 N Street North West, Washington, DC 20036. President and Chief Executive Officer: Edward Fritts.

National Association of Composers, USA, PO Box 49652, Barrington Station, Los Angeles, CA 90049. President: Marshall H Bialosky.

National Association of Negro Musicians, 11551 S Laflin Street, Chicago, IL 60643. Executive Secretary: Ona Campbell.

National Association of Pastoral Musicians, 225 Sheridan Street North West, Washington, DC 20011. President: Virgil C Funk.

National Association of Performing Arts Managers and Agents, Inc, PO Box 5517, Los Alamitos, CA 90721. President: Ingrid Kidd.

National Association of Recording Merchandisers, Inc, 11 Eves Drive, Suite 140, Mariton, NJ 08053. Executive Vice President: Pam Horovitz.

National Association of Schools of Music, 11250 Roger Bacon Drive, Suite 21, Reston, VA 22090. Executive Director: Samuel Hope.

National Association of Teachers of Singing, Inc, 2800 University Boulevard North, Jacksonville, FL 32211. President: Vernon Yenne.

National Choral Council, 1650 Broadway, New York, NY 10019. Executive Director: Martin Josman.

National Council of Acoustical Consultants, PO Box 359, Springfield, NJ 07081. Executive Secretary: Virginia Marguire.

National Federation of Music Clubs, 1336 North Delaware Street, Indianapolis, IN 46202. Chief Officer: Mrs D Clifford Allison.

National Flute Association, PO Box 800597, Santa Clarita, CA 91380. President: Brooks de Wetter-Smith.

National Foundation for Advancement in the Arts, 3915 Biscayne Boulevard, Miami, FL 33137. President: William H Banchs.

National Guild of Community Schools of the Arts, Inc, PO Box 8018, Englewood, NJ 07631. Executive Director: Lolita Mayadas.

National Music Council, Box 5551, Englewood, NJ 07631. President: Catherine French.

National Music Publishers' Association, Inc, 205 East 42nd Street, 18th Floor, New York, NY 10017. President: Edward P Murphy.

National Music Theater Network, 1460 Broadway, 3rd Floor, New York, NY 10036. President: Timothy Jerome.

National Opera Association, Ohio State University School of Music, 1866 College Road, Columbus, OH 43210. Executive Secretary: Marajean Marvin.

National Oratorio Society, 6686 Brook Way, Paradise, CA 95969. President: Thomas E Wilson.

National Orchestral Association, 475 Riverside Drive, Room 249, New York, NY 10115. President: Mrs Stuart R Kennedy.

National School Orchestra Association, 811 Highland Terrace North East, Atlanta, GA 30306. President: Arlene Witte.

National Women Composers Resource Center, 330 Townsend Street, Suite 218, San Francisco, CA 94107. Director: Susan Rands.

Network for New Music, 5015 Newhall, Philadelphia, PA 19144. Artistic Director: Linda Reichert.

New Music Alliance, 508 Woodland Terrace, Philadelphia, PA 19104. President: Tina Davidson.

New Music Distribution Service, 598 Broadway, 7th Floor, New York, NY 10012. Chief Officer: Timothy Marquand.

New York Consortium for New Music, 215 West 90th Street, New York, NY 10024. President: Patricia Spencer.

OPERA America, Inc, 777 14th Street North West, Suite 520, Washington, DC 20005. Executive Vice President and Chief Executive Officer: Marc A Scorca.

People-to-People Music Committee, Inc, 712 Auburn Avenue, Takoma Park, MD 20912. Executive Director: Ruth Sickafus.

Percussive Arts Society, Box 25, Lawton, OK 73502. Administrative Manager: Steve Beck.

Phi Beta National Professional Fraternity for Creative and Performing Arts, 2218 Center Avenue, Madison, WI 53704. President: Sarah Whelan.

Pianists Foundation of America, PO Box 64115, Tucson, AZ 85740.

Piano Manufacturers Association International, National Piano Foundation, 4020 McEwen, Suite 105, Dallas, TX 75244. Executive Director: Donald W Dillon.

Piano Technicians Guild, Inc, 3930 Washington, Kansas City, MO 64111. Executive Director: Larry Goldsmith.

Recording Industry Association of America, 1020 19th Street North West, Suite 200, Washington, DC 20036. President: Jason S Berman.

SESAC, Inc, 156 West 56th Street, New York, NY 10019. Chairman and President: Alice H Prager.

Society for Ethnomusicology, Inc, Indiana University, Morrison Hall 005, Bloomington, IN 47405. President: Anthony Seeger.

Society of Composers, Inc, PO Box 296, Old Chelsea Station, New York, NY 10011. Executive Committee Chairman: Reynold Weidenaar.

Songwriters Guild of America, 276 Fifth Avenue, No 306, New York, NY 1001. President: George David Weiss.

Sonneck Society for American Music, PO Box 476, Canton, MA 02021. President: Deane L Root.

Suzuki Association of the Americas, Inc, PO Box 17310, Boulder, CO 80308. President: Jeffrey Cox.

Theatre Communications Group Inc, 355 Lexington Avenue, New York, NY 10017. Director: Peter Zeisler.

Tubists Universal Brotherhood Association, Univerity of North Carolina at Greensboro, School of Music, Greensboro, NC 27412. President: Martin Erickson.

United States Information Agency, Arts America Program, 301 Fourth Street South West, Washington, DC 20547. Chief Officer: Robert C McLaughlin.

Viola da Gamba Society of America, University of Colorado, Department of Music, Boulder, CO 80302. President: Gordon Sandford.

Vioin Society of America, 8507 Abingdon Road, Kew Gardens, NY 11415. President: Hans E Tausig.

Violoncello Society, Inc, 340 West 55th Street, Suite 5D, New York, NY 10019. Executive Administrator: Esther Prince.

Kurt Weill Foundation for Music, Inc, 7 East 20th Street, 3rd Floor, New York, NY 10003. President: Kim H Kowalke.

Young Audiences, Inc, 115 East 92nd Street, New York, NY 10128. Executive Director: Richard Bell.

Youth in Music/USA, 84 William Street, 2nd Floor, New York, NY 10038. President: Jon Rupp.

MUSIC ORGANIZATIONS

URUGUAY

Asociación General de Autores del Uruguay, Canelones 1122, PZ 11100 Montevideo. President: Antonio Italiano.
Asociación, Uruguay de Musicos, Calle Maldonado 983, CP 11100 Montevideo. President: Alfonso Coronel.
Centro Cultural de la Música, Apdo 5, Av. 18 de Julio 1006, 6th Floor, Montevideo. Director: Jorge Calvetti.
Juventudes Muscales del Uruguay, Sarandi 444, 1st Floor, Edif. SODRE, Montevideo. President: Maria Tania Siver.
Sociedad Uruguay de interpretes, Canelones 1090, Montevideo. President: José María Lorenzo.
Sociedad Uruguay de Música Contemporánea, Casilla de Correo 1328, Montevideo. President: Diego Legrand.

VENEZUELA

Juventudes Musicales, Apartado 51441, Caracas 1050.
Sociedad de Autores y Compositores de Venezuela, Edif. Vam, entrada Oeste, 9th Floor, Avda. Andrés Bello, Caracas 1050. President: Guillermo Carrasco.

YUGOSLAVIA

International Society for Contemporary Music (Yugoslav section), PO Box 213, 11000 Belgrade.
Union of Yugoslav Composers, Misarska 12-14, 11000 Belgrade.

MAJOR COMPETITIONS AND AWARDS

APPENDIX E

MAJOR COMPETITIONS AND AWARDS

Values of awards, restrictions on entrants, dates, etc, may vary from year to year and interested readers are advised to contact the sponsoring organizations directly for complete information. It should also be noted that many institutions listed in Appendix F also maintain competitions, awards, and scholarship programmes.

AUSTRALIA

Australian Broadcasting Corporation Young Performers' Awards.
GPO Box 9994, Sydney, NSW 2001.
Annual awards for singers and instrumentalists to the age of 30 who have been in continuous residence in Australia for one year. Must compete in state of residence. Award of $19,500 plus concert engagements.

Australian Singing Competition.
c/o Gridiger & Co, Solicitors, 67 Castlereagh Street, Sydney, NSW 2000.
Annual awards for operatic and classical singers. Must be an Australian or New Zealand citizen under the age of 26 for classical singers and under the age of 35 for operatic singers. Mathy and Opera Awards totalling $100,000.

Sydney International Piano Competition of Australia.
PO Box 420, Double Bay, Sydney, NSW 2028.
Quadrennial competition open to pianists of all nationalities between the ages of 18 and 32. Prizes include 1st prize of $15,000 and various other prizes totalling $60,000. Next competition in 1996.

AUSTRIA

Ludwig Van Beethoven International Piano Competition.
Karlplatz 2/2/9, A-1010 Vienna.
Quadrennial competition open to pianists of all nationalities between the ages of 17 and 32. Prizes include 1st prize of 80,000 schillings, a Bösendorfer piano, and concert engagements, 2nd prize of 60,00 schillings, 3rd prize of 50,00 schillings, and 3 other prizes of 20,000 schillings. Next competition in 1997.

International Anton Bruckner Organ Competition.
Untere Donaulande 7, A-4010 Linz.
Quadrennial competition open to organists of all nationalities to the age of 35. Prizes include 1st prize of 50,000 schillings, 2nd prize of 40,000 schillings, and 3rd prize of 30,000 schillings. Next competition in 1998.

International Belvedere Competition for Opera Singers.
Fleischmarkt 24, A-1010 Vienna.
Annual competition for singers to the age of 35. Cash prizes.

International Fritz Kreisler Competition.
Liebhartstalstrasse 8/19, A-1160 Vienna.
Quadrennial competition for violin and viola. Prizes include 1st prize of 130,000 schillings, 2nd prize of 100,000 schillings, and 3rd prize of 70,000 schillings. Next competition in 1995.

International Mozart Competition of the Hochschule "Mozarteum".
Mirabellplatz 1, A-5020 Salzburg.
Quadrennial competition open to musicians of all nationalities, singers born after Jan 15 1957, and pianists and violinists born after Jan 15 1959. Prizes include the Mozart Prize from the Austrian Ministry of Science and Research, as well as other prizes and concert engagements. Next competition in 1995.

Internationaler Chorwettbewerb.
Kulturreferat der Stadtgemeinde, A-9800 Spittal.
Annual competition for Choirs. Prizes include money and documents.

Prix Ars Electronica.
Franckstrasse 2a, A-4010 Linz.
Annual competition for the computer arts open to individuals, groups, and organizations. Prizes include money and awards.

Vienna International Competition for Composers.
Casinos Austria, Dr Karl-Lueger Ring 14, A-1015 Vienna.
Annual competition open to composers to the age of 40 who submit a composition not previously accepted for performance, or performed in public, or awarded a prize in another competition. Prize of 700,000 schillings for an opera submitted in 1995.

Vienna Modern Masters Annual Orchestral Recording Award.
Margaretenstrasse 125/15, A-1050 Vienna.
Annual competition open to all composers of orchestral music.

MAJOR COMPETITIONS AND AWARDS

BELGIUM

Concours International De Chant De Verviers.
Rue des Dominicains 1, B-4000 Liège.
Biennial competition open to singers of all nationalities, for women between the ages of 18 and 30, and for men between the ages of 18 and 35. Prizes include 200,000 Belgian francs, a special prize of 200,000 Belgian francs, two prizes of 125,000 Belgian francs, two prizes of 75,000 Belgian francs, and four prizes of 25,000 Belgian francs. Next competition in 1995.

Concours International De Guitare.
c/o Le Printemps de la Guitare asbl, Place du Chef Lieu 9, B-6040 Charleroi.
Biennial competition open to solo classical guitarists of all nationalities to the age of 32. Prizes include 1st prize of 200,000 Belgian francs, 2nd prize of 150,000 Belgian francs, 3rd prize of 100,00 Belgian francs, and 4th prize of 75,000 Belgian francs. Next competition in 1996.

Festival of Flanders Bruges Musica Antiqua Contest.
Collaert Mansionstraat 30, B-8000 Bruges.
Annual competition open to solo singers, solo instrumentalists, and Baroque ensembles with categories rotating annually on a triennial schedule. Prizes total over 600,000 Belgian francs.

Queen Elisabeth International Music Competition of Belgium.
20 Rue Aus Laines, B-1000 Brussels.
Competition open to pianists to the age of 30 in 1995 and to composers (no age limit) in 1995. Prizes include money, concert engagements, and recordings.

BRAZIL

International Singing Contest of Rio De Janeiro and International Piano Contest For Accompanists.
Avenida Franklin Roosevelt 23, Suite 310, 20021 Rio de Janeiro.
Biennial competition open to all singers and accompanists born in 1963 or thereafter. Prizes in singing contest include 1st prize of $5,000, 2nd prize of $2,000, and 3rd prizes of $2,000, $2,000 and $1,000; prizes in accompanists contest include 1st prize of $5,000, 2nd prize of $2,000, and 3rd prize of $1,500. Next competition in 1995.

BULGARIA

International Competition For Young Opera Singers.
56 Rue Alabin, 1000 Sofia.
Quadrennial competition open to men up to the age of 35 and to women up to the age of 33. Prizes include a Grand Prize, 1st prize, 2nd prize, 3rd prize, medals, and diplomas. Next competition in 1996.

CANADA

Banff International String Quartet Competition.
c/o Banff Centre School of Fine Arts, PO Box 1020, Banff, Alberta TOL 0CO.
Triennial competition open to quartets whose members are under 35 years of age at the time of the competition. Prizes include $20,000, $12,000, $8,000, $5,000, $500, set of bows, Canadian tour, and Banff Centre residency. Next competition in 1995.

Canada Council/Conseil Des Arts Du Canada Grants and Awards.
PO Box 1047, 99 Metcalfe Street, Ottawa, Ont K1P 5V8.
Grants and awards to artists of Canadian citizenship and to non-profit arts organizations.

Canadian Music Competitions.
1030 St Alexandre, Suite 306, Montréal, PQ H2Z 1P5.
Annual competition for pianists, string players, wind players, and singers open to Canadian citizens or those holding a Landed Immigrant Certificate or those studying with a Canadian teacher for the last three years between the ages of 7 and 31.

Concours Orchestre Symphonique De Montréal.
85 St Catherine West, Montréal, PQ H2X 3P4.
Annual competition open to Canadian citizens or those holding a Landed Immigrant Certificate featuring piano and voice one year and strings and winds the following year; piano - category A for between the ages of 18 and 25 and category B for those 17 and under; voice - for those between the ages of 18 and 30; strings - category A for those between the ages of 18 and 25 and category B for those 17 and under; winds - for those between the ages of 16 and 25. Prizes totalling $12,000 and an appearance on the regular subscriptions series of the Orchestre Symphonique de Montréal.

Eckhardt-Gramatté National Music Competition for the Performance of Canadian Music.
Queen Elizabeth II Building, Room 211, 270-18 Street, Brandon, Man R7A 6A9.
Annual competition open to Canadian citizens or Canadian residents alternating annually between voice, strings, and piano. Prizes include 1st prize of $5,000 and a concert tour, 2nd prize of $3,000, and 3rd prize of $2,000.

Glenn Gould Prize.
99 Metcalfe Street, PO Box 1047, Ottawa, Ont K1P 5V8.
Triennial prize open to individuals of all nationalities who have made an exceptional contribution to music and its communication through the use of any of the communications technologies. Candidates must be nominated by three specialists in the nominee's field or a related field. Next prize awarded in 1996.

MAJOR COMPETITIONS AND AWARDS

Kamloops Symphony Orchestra New Celebrity Competition.
PO Box 57, Kamloops, BC V2C 5K3.
Annual competition open to Canadian citizens or those holding a Landed Immigrant Certificate. Prizes include 1st prize of $1,000 and 2nd prize of $500, with the two finalists appearing in concert with the Kamloops Symphony Orchestra.

Montreal International Music Competition.
Place des Arts, 1501 Jeanne-Mance Street, Montréal PQ H2X 1Z9.
Competition for violin (1995), piano (1996), and voice (1997) with a recess (1998) before pursuing the cycle again; violin and piano for those between the ages of 16 and 30, and voice for those between the ages of 20 and 35. Prizes totalling $36,900.

CZECH REPUBLIC

Czech Music Competition of the Czech Ministry of Culture.
Malézské nám 1, 118 00 Prague 1.
Annual competition with categories changing annually.

Prague Spring International Music Competition.
Hellichova 18, CS-118 00 Prague 1.
Annual competition open to performers of all nationalities with categories changing annually in five-year cycles. Next competition for conductors in 1995 to age 32. Prizes include money and an appearance at the Prague Spring International Music Festival.

DENMARK

International Carl Nielsen Violin Competition.
Claus Bergsgade 9, DK-5000 Odense C.
Quadrennial competition open to violinists of all nationalities to the age of 29. Prizes include a minimum of 300,000 kroner. Next competition in 1996.

International Organ Competition, Odense.
Laessoegade 74, DK-5230 Odense M.
Biennial competition open to organists of all nationalities to the age of 34. Prizes include 1st prize of 20,000 kroner, 2nd prize of 15,000 kroner, and 3rd prize of 10,000 kroner. Next competition in 1996.

Nicolai Malko International Competition for Young Conductors.
c/o Danmarks Radio, Rosenoerns Alle 22, DK-1999 Frederiksberg C.
Triennial competition open to conductors between the ages of 20 and 31. Prizes include cash. Next competition in 1995.

EIRE

GPA Dublin International Piano Competition.
c/o City Hall, Dublin 2.
Triennial competition open to pianists between the ages of 17 and 30. Prizes include 1st prize of 7,500 Irish pounds, debut recitals in London, Vienna, Paris, and New York, and concert engagements with major international orchestras, 2nd prize of 5,000 Irish pounds, 3rd prize od 3,500 Irish pounds, and lesser prizes. Next competition in 1997.

FINLAND

Mirjam Helin International Singing Competition.
c/o Finnish Cultural Foundation, PB 203, SF-00121 Helsinki 12.
Quinquennial competition open to singers of all nationalities, women born after 1 Jan 1968, and men born after 1 Jan 1966. Prizes separate for men and women including 4 prizes each totalling $120,00. Next competition in 1999.

International Jean Sibelius Violin Competition.
Box 31, SF-00100 Helsinki 10.
Quinquennial competition for violinists. Prizes totalling about $22,000. Next competition in 1995.

Paulo Cello Competition.
c/o Naantali Music Festival, PO Box 46, SF-21101 Naantali.
Quinquennial competition for cellists of all nationalitites born between 1958 and 1975. Prizes include cash. Next competition in 1996.

FRANCE

Concours International D'Ensembles de Musique de Chambre de Colmar.
c/o Service des Activités Culturelles, Hôtel de Ville, F-68000 Colmar.
Triennial competition for chamber music ensembles for performers to the age of 35. Prizes include 30,000 francs, 15,000 francs, and 10,000 francs. Next competition in 1995.

Concours International d'Orgue "Grand Prix de Chartres".

MAJOR COMPETITIONS AND AWARDS

75 Rue de Grenelle, F-75007 Paris.
Biennial competition open to all organists born after 1 Jan 1961. Prizes include two grand prizes of 20,000 francs each, one for interpretation and one for improvisation, and two 2nd prizes of 5,000 francs each, one for interpretation and one for improvisation. Next competition in 1996.

Concours International de Chant de La Ville de Toulouse.
c/o Théâtre du Capitole, F-31000 Toulouse.
Annual competition open to singers between the ages of 18 and 33. Prizes totalling 135,000 francs.

Concours International de Chant de Paris.
10 Rue du Dôme, F-75016.
Biennial competition open to singers, women to the age of 32 and ment to the age of 34. Prizes include 120,000 francs and concert engagements. Next competition in 1996.

Concours International de Chant Offenbach.
79 Rue Jouffroy, F-75017 Paris.
Biennial competition open to singers of all nationalities and all ages. Prizes include appearances in European theaters and festivals.

Concours International de Clavecin.
c/o Festival Estival de Paris, 20 Rue Geoffroy l'Asnier, F-75004 Paris.
Biennial competition open to harpsichordists to the age of 32. Prizes include cash. Next competition in 1995.

Concours International de Flute Jean-Pierre Rampal.
5 Rue Bellart, F-75015.
Next competition tentatively set for 1999.

Concours International de Guitare.
c/o Radio France, 116 Avenue du President Kennedy, F-75786 Paris Cédex 16.
Annual competition open to classical guitarists of all nationalitites to the ages of 30 and biennial competition open to composers of all nationalities. Prizes include cash and concerts/recitals.

Concours International de Harpe Louise Charpentier.
Résidence Jean Moulin, F-07400 Le Teil d'Ardeche.
Biennial competition open to harp recitalists. Prizes include 50,000 francs and seal prix. Next competition in 1996.

Concours International de Jeunes Chefs d'Orchestre.
2-D Rue Isenbart, F-25000 Besançon.
Annual competition open to conductors under the age of 32. Prizes include Emile Vuillermoz Prize and others.

Concours International de Musique de Chambre.
Rue du Dôme 10, F-75116 Paris.
Biennial competition open to instrumentalists and singers to the age of 35. Prizes include 62,500 francs. Next competition in 1995.

Concours International de Musique Electroacoustique.
GMEB, Place André Malraux, BP 39, F-18000 Bourges.
Annual competition for electroacoustic music, music for performer(s) and tape, electroacoustic program music, and live electroacoustic music.

Concours International de Trompette ''Maurice André''.
5 Rue Bellart, F-75015 Paris.
Competition for young trumpeters. Prizes include four grand prizes. Next competition tentatively set for 2000.

Concours International de Violon ''Yehudi Menuhin''.
5 Rue Bellart, F-75015 Paris.
Competition for young violinists. Prizes include a grand prize and three other prizes. Next competition in 1999.

Concours International de Violoncelle ''Rostropovich''.
146 Rue de Rennes, F-75006 Paris.
Competition for cellists of all nationalities to the age of 33. Prizes include cash and public performances. Next competition in 1998.

Concours International du Festival de Musique de Toulon.
Palais de la Bourse, Avenue Jean-Moulin, F-83000 Toulon.
Annual competition open to instrumentalists between the ages of 18 and 30 with categories rotating on annual schedule. Prizes include 1st prize of 20,000 francs, 2nd prize of 12,000 francs, and 3rd prize of 8,000 francs. Future competitions include trombone in 1995, clarinet in 1996, and oboe in 1996.

Concours International Marguerite Long-Jacques Thibaud.
32 Avenue Matignon, F-75008 Paris.
Triennial competition open to pianists and violinists between the ages of 16 and 30. Prizes include 250,000 francs for winners in each category. Next competition for pianists in 1995 and for violinists in 1996.

Florilège Vocal de Tours.
BP 1452, F-37014 Tours Cédex.
Annual competition open to choral and vocal performers and composers. Prizes include 18 prizes totalling 100,000 francs.

Fondation des Etats-Unis Harriet Hale Woolley Scholarships.
15 Boulevard Jourdan, F-75690 Paris Cédex 14.
Annual scholarships open to single American instrumentalists or artists between the ages of 21 and 30 for study in Paris. Scholarships include from four to five $8,200 awards.

Yvonne Lefébure International Piano Competition.
c/o Association Acanthes, 146 Rue de Rennes, F-75006 Paris.
Biennial competition open to pianists of all nationalities to the age of 35. Prizes include cash and public performances. Next competition in 1996.

Prix Musical International Arthur Honegger.
c/o Fondation de France, 40 Avenue Hoche, F-75008 Paris.
Biennial competition open to all composers. Prizes include 50,000 francs. Next competition in 1996.

Rencontres Musicales d'Evian International String Quartet Competition.
6 Rue Téhéran, F-75008 Paris or Château de Blonay, F-74500 Evian les Bains.
Biennial competition open to string quartets of all nationalities whose average age of membership does not exceed 33 year of age. Prizes include over 500,000 francs. Next competition in 1995.

World Music Masters International Piano Competition.
Salle Gaveau, 45 Rue La Boétie, F-75008 Paris.
Annual competition open only to pianists who have been finalists in other international competitions. Prizes include $30,000 and concert engagements.

GERMANY

Hannover International Violin Competition.
Stiftung Niedersachsen, Ferdinandstrasse 4, 3000 Hannover 1.
Triennial competition open to violinists of all nationalities between the ages of 16 and 30. Prizes include cash, a recording, and concert engagements. Next competition in 1996.

International Johann Sebastian Bach Competition.
Thomaskirchhof 16, PSF 1349, 7010 Leipzig.
Quadrennial competition open to pianists, organists, violinists, harpsichordists, and singers of all nationalities born after 31 Dec 1963. Prizes include cash. Next competitionn in 1996.

International Kuhlau Wettbewerb Für Flotisten.
Herzogenplatz 5, Postfach 2061, 3110 Uelzen 1.
Triennial competition for solo flute and flute with piano, two flutes or two flutes with piano, or three or four flutes. Next competition in 1995.

International Music Competition of the Broadcasting Corporations of Germany.
c/o Bayerischer Rundfunk, Rundfunkplatz 1, 8000 Munich 2.
Annual competition open to solo instrumentalists, string quartets, and singers with categories changing annually.

International Piano Competition of Cologne.
c/o Foundation Tomassoni, Dagobertstrasse 38, 5000 Cologne 1.
Triennial competition open to pianists of all nationalities between the ages of 18 and 29. Prizes include 1st prize of 15,000 marks, 2nd prize of 10,000 marks, and 3rd prize of 5,000 marks. Next competition in 1995.

International Robert Schumann Contest.
Muenzstrasse 12, 9540 Zwickau.
Quadrennial competition open to pianists to the age of 25 and to singers to the age of 32. Prizes include cash. Next competition in 1997.

International Violin Competition Louis Spohr.
Burgunderstrasse 4, 7800 Freiburg im Breisgau 1.
Triennial competition open to violinists of all nationalities to the age of 32. Prizes include 1st prize of 12,000 marks, 2nd prize of 8,000 marks, and 3rd prize of 5,000 marks. Next competition in 1997.

Internationaler Wettbewerb für Junge Painisten Ettingen.
Pforzheimerstrasse 25a, 7505 Ettlingen.
Biennial competition open to pianists of all nationalities; catergory A for those born on or after 7 Aug 1980, or category B for those born on or after 7 Aug 1975. Next competition in 1994.

Internationaler Wettbewerb für Komponistinnen.
Elisabethstrasse 5, 6800 Mannheim 1.
Quadrennial competition open to women composers of all nationalities. Prizes include cash. Next competition in 1998.

Internationaler Wettbewerb für Streichquartett Karl Klingler-Preis.
Südliche Auffahrtsalle 49, 8000 Munich 19.
Triennial competition open to string quartets whose total age is 128 years with no members over the age of 37. Prizes include cash. Next competition in 1996.

Mozart Festival Competition for Young Artists.
c/o Hochschule für Musik, Hofstallstrasse 6-8, 8700 Würzburg.
Biennial competition open to German singers to the age of 32 for the interpretation of Mozart's works. Prizes include 1st prize of 5,000 marks, 2nd prize of 4,000 marks, and 3rd prize of 3,000 marks. Next competition

in 1995.

GREECE

International Music Competition Maria Callas.
Amerikis Street 8, 10671 Athens.
Biennial competition open to singers (opera, oratorio, lieder) and pianists with the categories alternating annually.
Prizes include 1st prize of 450,000 drachmas, 2nd prize of 350,000 drachmas, and 3rd prize of 300,000 drachmas
in both categories; also 450,000 drachmas for oratorio and lieder. Next competition for piano in 1994 and for
voice in 1995.

HUNGARY

Budapest International Composers' Competition.
c/o Association of Hungarian Musicians, PO Box 47, Vörösmarty tér 1, H-1364 Budapest.
Annual competition open to all composers. Prizes include cash.

Budapest International Music Competition.
c/o InterArt Festivalcenter, PO Box 80, H-1366 Budapest.
Annual competition with categories changing annually.

International Conductors Competition of the Hungarian Television.
c/o Hungarian Television, Department of Music, H-1366 Budapest.
Triennial competition open to conductors of all nationalities under the age of 35. Next competition in 1995.

ISRAEL

International Harp Contest.
4 Aharonowitz Street, 63566 Tel Aviv.
Triennial competiton open to harpists of all nationalitites. Prizes include 1st prize of a Lyon and Healy concert
grand harp, 2nd prize of $5,000, and 3rd prize of $3,000. Next competition in 1997.

Arthur Rubinstein International Piano Master Competition.
PO Box 6018, 61060 Tel Aviv.
Triennial competition open to pianists of all nationalities between the ages of 18 and 32. Prizes include 1st
prize of the Arthur Rubinstein Award-Gold Medal and $10,000, 2nd prize of the Silver Medal and $5,000, 3rd
prize of the Bronze Medal and $3,000, and 4th, 5th, and 6th prizes of $1,000 each. Next competition in 1995.

ITALY

**Associazione Concorisi & Rassegno Musicali (ACERM) Concorso Internazionale per Complessi da Camera
Città di Firenze "Premio Vittorio Gui".**
Borgo Albizi, I-50122 Florence.
Annual competition open to chamber music instrumentalists to the age of 32. Prizes totalling some 30,000,000
lire.

"Valentino Bucchi" Competition.
Via Ubaldino Peruzzi 20, I-00139 Rome.
Annual Competition open to performers and composers. Prizes totalling some 100,000,000 lire.

Enrico Caruso International Competition for Young Tenors.
c/o Associazione Enrico Caruso, Via Degli Omenoni 2, I-20121 Milan.
Biennial competition open to tenors between the ages of 18 and 28. Prizes totalling some 10,000,000 lire. Next
competition in 1996.

Alessandro Casagrande Concorso Pianistico Internazionale.
Comune di Terni, Vico S Lorenzo 1, I-05100 Terni.
Biennial competition open to pianists born after 1 Jan 1966. Prizes include 1st prize of 12,000,000 lire, 2nd
prize of 8,000,000 lire, and 3rd prize of 5,000,000 lire. Next competition in 1996.

Gaspar Cassadó International Cello Competition.
Via Solferino 15, I-50123 Florence.
Biennial competition open to cellists. Next competition in 1996.

Concorso Internazionale di Chitarra Classica "Città di Alessandria".
Piazza Garibaldi 16, I-15100 Alessandria.
Annual competition open to solo classical guitarists of all nationalities. Prizes include cash.

Concorso Internazionale di Composizione "Camilo Togni".
c/o Associazione Nuovi Spazi Sonori, Casella Postale 196, I-25100 Brescia.
Biennial competition open to composers of all nationalities born after 31 Dec 1956. Prizes include 1st prize
of 10,000,000 lire, plus publication and performance of winning composition.

Concorso Internazionale di Composizione "Goffredo Petrassi".
Piazzale Cesare Battisti 15, I-43100 Parma.
Biennial competition open to composers of all nationalities for an unpublished symphonic composition not exceeding

MAJOR COMPETITIONS AND AWARDS

30 minutes in length. Prizes include 1st prize of 15,000,000 lire. Next competition in 1995.

Concorso Internazionale di Composizione "Guido d'Arezzo" Fondazione.
Corso Italia 102, I-52100 Arezzo.
Annual competition for polyvocal composition which has never been published or performed, the duration of which lasts more than 5 minutes. Prizes totalling 15,000,000 lire.

Concorso Internazionale di Direzione d'Orchestra "Arturo Toscanini".
Piazzale Cesare Battisti 15, I-43100 Parma.
Biennial competition open to conductors of all nationalities to the age of 32. Prizes include 1st prize of 15,000,000 lire, 2nd prize of 10,000,000 lire, and 3rd prize of 6,000,000 lire. Next competition in 1995.

Concorso Internazionale di Violino "Alberto Curci".
Via Nardones 8, I-80132 Naples.
Competition open to violinists to the age of 32. Prizes include 1st prize of 8,000,000 lire, 2nd prize of 5,000,000 lire, and 3rd prize of 3,000,000 lire.

Concorso Internazionale "Luigi Russolo" Per Giovani Compositori di Musica Elettroacustica Analogica E Digitale.
c/o Fondazione "Russolo-Pratella", Via G Bagaini 6, I-21100 Varese.
Annual competition open to composers of all nationalities to the age of 35 for electroacoustic, analog, and digital music compositions.

Concorso Internazionale Michelangelo Abbado Per Violinisti.
c/o Provincia di Sondrio, Assessoratio alla Cultura, Via XXV Aprile, I-23100 Sondrio.
Annual competition open to violinists of all nationalities born after 31 Dec 1965. Prizes include 1st prize of 8,000,000 lire.

Concorso Internazionale Per Contrabasso Giovanni Bottesini.
c/o Conservatorio di Musica "Arrigo Boito", Via del Conservatorio 27, I-43100 Parma.
Triennial competition open to double bass players of all nationalities between the ages of 16 and 32. Prizes include 1st prize of 10,000,000 lire, 2nd prize of 6,000,000 lire, and 3rd prize of 4,000,000 lire. Next competition in 1995.

Consorso Internazionale Per La Conquista Della Chitarra Classica.
CP 10673, I-20125 Milan.
Annual competition open to classical guitarists of all ages. Prizes include cash, gold medals, and guitars.

Concorso Internazionale Per Quartetto d'Archi Premio "Paolo Borciani".
c/o Teatro Municipale Romolo Valli, Piazza Martini 7 Luglio, I-42100 Reggio Emilia.
Triennial competition open to string quartets of all nationalities whose members were born after 20 June 1962. Prizes include 1st prize of 25,000,000 lire and 2nd prize of 10,000,000 lire. Next competition in 1997.

Concorso Internazionale Pianistico "Ettore Pozzoli".
Segreteria, Piazza 34, I-20038 Seregno.
Biennial competition open to pianists of all nationalities born after 1 Jan 1963. Prizes include 1st prize of 15,000,000 lire and recitals, 2nd prize of 8,000,000 lire and a recital, 3rd prize of 5,000,000 lire and a recital, 4th prize of 3,000,000 lire, 5th prize of 2,000,000 lire, and 6th prize of 1,000,000 lire. Next competition in 1995.

Concorso Internazionale Pianistico "Liszt" Premio Mario Zanfi.
c/o Conservatorio di Musica "Arrigo Boito", Via del Conservatorio 27, I-43100 Parma.
Triennial competition open to pianists of all nationalities between the ages of 16 and 32. Prizes include 1st prize of 10,000,000 lire, 2nd prize of 6,000,000 lire, and 3rd prize of 4,000,000 lire. Next competition in 1995.

Concorso Pianistico Internazionale "Alfredo Casella".
Via del Parco Margherita 49, pal 5, I-80121 Naples.
Biennial competition open to pianists of all nationalities born after 11 Oct 1963. Prizes include 1st prize of 10,000,000 lire and solo orchestral appearances, 2nd prize of 5,000,000 lire and concert appearances, and 3rd prize of 3,000,000 lire and concert appearances. Next competition in 1995.

Concorso Pianistico Internazionale Ferruccio Busoni.
c/o Conservatorio Statale di Musica "Claudio Monteverdi", I-39100 Bolzano.
Annual competition open to pianists of all nationalities between the ages of 15 and 32. Prizes include 1st prize of 15,000,000 lire and concert engagements, 2nd prize of 9,000,000 lire, 3rd prize of 7,000,000 lire, 4th prize of 6,000,000 lire, 5th prize of 5,000,000 lire, and 6th prize of 4,000,000 lire.

International Competition of the Teatro Alla Scala: Dino Ciani Prize.
c/o Teatro alla Scala, Via Filodrammatici 2, I-20121 Milan.
Triennial competition open to pianists of all nationalities born after 31 Dec 1966. Prizes include 1st prize of 20,000,000 lire, 2nd prize of 8,000,000 lire, and 3rd prize of 3,000,000 lire, with medals and performances for each. Next competition in 1996.

Rodolfo Lipizer International Violin Contest.
Via Don Giovanni Bosco 91, I-34170 Gorizia.
Annual competition open to violinists of all nationalities born after 12 Sept 1959. Prizes include cash and concert appearances.

"Nicolò Paganini" Premio Internazionale di Violino.
Palazzo Doria, Via Garibaldi 6, I-16124 Genoa.
Annual competition open to violinists of all nationalities under the age of 35. Prizes include 1st prize of 15,000,000 lire, 2nd prize of 10,000,000 lire, 3rd prize of 6,000,000 lire, 4th prize of 4,000,000 lire, 5th prize of 3,000,000

lire, and 6th prize of 2,000,000 lire.

"Antonio Pedrotti" International Competition for Orchestra Conductors.
Via San Croce 67, I-38100 Trento.
Biennial competition open to conductors between the ages of 18 and 33. Prizes include 1st prize of 10,000,000 lire and engagements with Italian Orchestras, 2nd prize of 7,000,000 lire, and 3rd prize of 5,000,000 lire. Next competition in 1995.

"Premio Ancona" Concorso Internazionale di Esecuzione & Composizione & Musicale Per Strumenti A Fiato.
Assessorato Cultura, Comune di Ancona, I-60100 Ancona.
Annual competition open to instrumentalists and composers of wind music.

Premio Musicale Città di Trieste: Concorso Internazionale di Composizione Sinfonica.
Palazzo Municipale, Piazza dell'Unità d'Italia 4, I-34121 Trieste.
Biennial competition open to composers of all nationalities. Prizes include 1st prize of 5,000,000 lire and performance of composition, 2nd prize of 2,500,000 lire, and 3rd prize of 1,500,000 lire. Next competition in 1995.

Rassegna Della Canzone d'Autore-Premio Tenco.
Via Meridiana 7, I-18038 San Remo.
Annual competition open to singers who are lyricists and composers by invitation only.

"G B Viotti" Concorso Internazionale di Musicale.
Casella Postale 127, I-13100 Vercelli.
Annual competition for singers and instrumentalists.

JAPAN

International Music Competition of Japan.
West Park Building 4F, 1-10-16, Ebisunishi, Shibuya-ku, Tokyo 150.
Triennial competition open to instrumentalists of all nationalities between the ages of 17 and 32. Prizes include 1st prize of money, medal, and concert appearances. Next competition in 1995.

Irino Prize Foundation.
c/o JML Seminar, Yoshiro Irino Institute of Music, 5-22-2 Matsubara, Setagaya-ku, Tokyo 156.
Annual prize open to composers of all nationalities under the age of 40 rotating annually between an orchestral and a chamber music composition. Prizes include 650,000 yen for an orchestral composition and 200,000 yen for a chamber music composition.

Tokyo International Competition for Chamber Music Composition.
c/o Japan International Artists, 2-3-16-607 Shinjuku, Shinjuku, Tokyo.
Competition open to composers of chamber music of all ages and nationalities. Prizes include 1st prize of 300,000 yen, 2nd prize of 150,000 yen, and 3rd prize of 100,000. Next competition in 1995.

Tokyo International Music Competition.
1-32-13 Kita-Shinjuku, Shinjuku-ku, Tokyo 169.
Annual competition open to performers of all nationalities with categories changing annually. Prizes include 1st prize of 1,000,000 yen and a medal, 2nd prize of 700,000 yen and a medal, 3rd prize of 500,000 yen and a medal, and a certificate of honorable mention, 200,000 yen, and a medal.

MONACO

Prix de Composition Musicale Prince Pierre de Monaco.
Centre Administratif, Rue Louis Notari, MC-98000 Monaco.
Annual prize awarded to the best musical composition of the year. Prize of 50,000 French francs.

NETHERLANDS

'S-Hertogenbosch International Singing Competition.
PO Box 1225, 5200 BG's-Hertogenbosch.
Annual competition open to singers. Prizes include cash.

I K F International Choir Festival.
Drift 23, 3512 BR Utrecht.
Quadrennial prizes awarded to choirs. Next prizes given in 1995.

International Competition for Early Music Ensembles.
Singel 308-sous, 1016 AE Amsterdam.
Annual competition open to young professional early music ensembles consisting of two to eight performers.

International Competition for Organ Improvisation.
Postbus 3333, 2001 DH Haarlem.
Annual competition open to concert organists experienced in improvisation. Prizes include cash.

International Franz Liszt Piano Competition.
Muziekcentrum Vredenburg, PO Box 550, 3500 AN Utrecht.
Triennial competition open to pianists of all nationalities between the ages of 16 and 30. Prizes include cash and engagements for the 1st prize winner. Next competition in 1995.

MAJOR COMPETITIONS AND AWARDS

International Gaudeamus Composers Competition.
Swammerdamstraat 38, 1091 RV Amsterdam.
Annual competition open to composers to the age of 30. Prizes include cash.

International Gaudeamus Interpreters Competition.
Swammerdamstraat 38, 1091 RV Amsterdam.
Annual competition open to instrumentalists and singers of contemporary music. Prizes include cash.

International Kirill Kondrashin Competition for Young Conductors.
PO Box 444, 1200 JJ Hilversum.
Quinquennial competition open to conductors. Prizes include guest conducting engagements with major orchestras. Next competition in 1999.

Scheveningen International Music Competition.
Gevers Deynootweg 970 Z, 2586 BW Scheveningen.
Annual competition open to instrumentalists to the age of 30. Prizes include cash.

NEW ZEALAND

Lexus New Zealand International Violin Competition.
PO Box 10-113, Wellington.
Quadrennial competition open to violinists of all nationalities between the ages of 18 and 28. Prizes include cash. Next competition in 1996.

NORWAY

Queen Sonja International Music Competition.
PO Box 1568 Vika, N-0116 Oslo 1.
Triennial competition open to instrumentalists. Prizes include cash and concert engagements. Next competition in 1995.

POLAND

Fryderyk Chopin International Piano Competition.
ul Okólnik 1, PL-00-368 Warsaw.
Quinquennial competition open to pianists of all nationalities born between 1 Oct 1065 and 1 Oct 1977. Prizes includes 1st prize of $11,000 and a gold medal, 2nd prize of $7,142 and a silver medal, 3rd prize of $5,357 and a bronze medal, and three other cash prizes. Next competition in 1995.

Grzegorz Fitelberg International Competition for Conductors.
Sokolska 2, 40-048 Katowice.
Quadrennial competition open to conductors to the age of 35. Prizes include cash and medals. Next competition in 1995.

International Composers' Competition "Kasimierz Serocki".
ul Mazowiecka 11, 00-052 Warsaw.
Triennial competition open to composers of all nationalities. Prizes include cash. Next competition in 1995.

International Henryk Wieniawski Competition for Violinists, Composers, and Violin Makers.
Swietoslawska St 7, PL-61-840 Poznań.
Quinquennial competition. Open to violinists of all nationalitites to the age of 30. Prizes include cash. Next competition for violinists in 1996. Competition for composers in 1995 and for violin makers in 1996.

International Stanislaw Moniuszko Competition for Young Vocalists.
c/o Warsaw Philharmonic, ul Jasna 5, 00-950 Warsaw.
Triennial competition open to young vocalists. Prizes include cash. Next competition in 1995.

International Witold Lutoslawski Composers Competition.
ul Jasna 5, 00-950, Warsaw.
Biennial competition open to composers of all nationalities and all ages. Prizes include cash and performances by the Warsaw Philharmonic. Next competition in 1996.

PORTUGAL

Vianna da Motta Piano and Violin Competitions.
Rua António Maria Cardoso 60-2, 1200 Lisbon.
Triennial competition open to pianists and violinists between the ages of 16 and 30. Prizes for both competitions include cash. Next competition in 1997.

RUSSIA

International Tchaikovsky Competition.
15 Neglinnaya Street, Moscow.
Quadrennial competition open to pianists, violinists, cellists, and singers of all nationalities. Prizes include cash and medals. Next competition in 1998.

MAJOR COMPETITIONS AND AWARDS

SINGAPORE

Rolex Music Performance Awards.
The Rolex Centre, 302 Orchard Road, 01-01 Tong Building, Singapore 0923.
Biennial competition open to pianists and violinists who are citizens or permanent residents of Singapore, Malaysia, Brunei, Indonesia, Thailand, the Philippines and Hong Kong. Prizes include cash. Next competition in 1995.

SPAIN

Concurso Internacional de Canto Julián Gayarre.
c/o Festival de Navarra, Ansoleaga 10, 31001 Pamplona.
Biennial competition open to singers of all nationalities, women between the ages of 18 and 32, and men between the ages of 20 and 35. Prizes include cash. Next competition in 1996.

Concurso Internacional de Ejecución Musical Maria Canals de Barcelona.
Gran Via de les Corts Catalanes 654, pral, 08010 Barcelona.
Annual competition open to instrumentalists between the ages of 18 and 32. Prizes include cash.

Concurso Internacional de Piano ''Frederic Chopin''.
Conservatorio Professional de Musica de Baleares, Calle Hospital 4, 07012 Palma de Mallorca.
Biennial competition open to pianists of all nationalities to the age of 35. Prizes include 1st prize of 1,000,000 pesetas and recitals, 2nd prize of 500,000 pesetas, and 3rd prize of 250,000 pesetas. Next competition in 1996.

Concurso Internacional de Piano ''José Iturbi''.
Plaza de Manises 4, 46003 Valencia.
Biennial competition open to pianists of all nationalities under the age of 32. Prizes include 1st prize of 1,000,000 pesetas, 2nd prize of 750,000 pesetas, 3rd prize of 500,000 pesetas, and 4th prize of 300,000 pesetas, with recitals for each category. Next competition in 1996.

Concurso Internacional de Piano Premio ''Jaén''.
c/o Instituto de Estudios Giennenses, 23002 Jaén.
Annual competition open to pianists of all nationalities, winners of the Jaén Prize excepted. Prizes include 1st prize of 2,000,000 pesetas, a gold medal, and concert engagements, 2nd prize of 1,000,000 pesetas, 3rd prize of 400,000 pesetas, and the Rosa Sabater Prize of 500,000 pesetas for the best interpreter of Spanish music.

Premio Internacional de Canto Fundación Guerrero.
Gran Via 78, 28013 Madrid.
Biennial competition open to singers of all nationalities and ages. Prizes include 1st prize of 1,000,000 pesetas and a prize of 500,000 pesetas for the best interpreter of the music of Jacinto e Inocencio Guerrero. Next competition in 1996.

Premio Internacional de Guitarra Sar La Infanta Dona Cristine.
Gran Via 78, 28013 Madrid.
Annual competition open to guitarists of all nationalities and ages. Prizes include 1st prize of 2,000,000 pesetas.

Premio Internacional de Piano Fundación Guerrero.
Gran Via 78, 28013 Madrid.
Biennial competition open to pianists of all nationalities and ages. Prizes include 1st prize of 2,000,000 pesetas. Next competition in 1995.

Santander International Piano Competition.
Hernán Cortés 3, 39003 Santander.
Triennial competition open to pianists of all nationalities between the ages of 17 and 30. Prizes totalling 12,000,000 pesetas, recordings, concerts, travel grants etc. Next competition in 1995.

Pablo Sarasate International Violin Competition.
Calle Ansoleaga 10, 31001 Pamplona.
Biennial competition open to violinists. Next competition in 1995.

Francisco Vinas International Singing Contest.
Bruc 125, 08037 Barcelona.
Annual competition open to singers, women between the ages of 18 and 32, and men between the ages of 20 and 35. Prizes for both include 1st prize of 1,000,000 pesetas, 2nd prize of 500,000 pesetas, and 3rd prize of 400,000 pesetas, plus medals and special prizes.

SWITZERLAND

Concours Géza Anda.
Bleicherweg 18, CH-8002 Zürich.
Triennial competition open to pianists to the age of 32. Prizes include cash and major concert engagements. Next competition in 1997.

Concours International d'Execution Musicale.
104 Rue de Carouge, CH-1205 Geneva.
Annual competition open to performers of all nationalities with categories changing annually. Prizes totalling 130,000 francs.

Concours International de Composition Musicale Opera and Ballet.

MAJOR COMPETITIONS AND AWARDS

c/o Maison de la Radio, Case Postale 233, 66 Boulevard Carl-Vogt, CH-1211 Geneva 8.
Biennial competition open to composers. Prizes include 1st prize of 20,000 francs. Next competition in 1995.

Concours Suisse de l'Orgue.
Place du Prieur, CH-1323 Romainmôtier.
Annual competition open to organists of all nationalities and ages.

Clara Haskil Piano Competition.
40 Rue du Simplon, PO Box 234, CH-1800 Vevey.
Biennial competition open to pianists to the age of 30. Prizes include 20,000 Swiss francs and concert engagements.
Next competition in 1995.

International Competition in Composition of Sacred Music.
PO Box 292, CH-1701 Fribourg.
Biennial competition open to composers of all nationalities and ages. Prizes include 10,000 Swiss francs and
the premiere of the winning work at the Fribourg Festival of Sacred Music. Next competition in 1995.

Masterplayers International Music and Conductors Competition.
c/o Masterplayers International Music Academy, Via Losanna 12, CH-6900 Lugano.
Annual competition open to performers. Prizes include various awards and concert engagements.

Musical Prize Contest Queen Marie-José.
Case Postale 19, CH-1252 Meinier/Geneva.
Biennial competition open to composers of all nationalities and ages who submit an unpublished composition.
Prizes include 10,000 francs. Next competition in 1996.

Tibor Varga International Competition for Violinists.
c/o Bureau du Festival, PO Box 954, CH-1951 Sion.
Annual competition open to violinists between the ages of 15 and 32. Prizes totalling 30,000 Swiss francs.

UK

British Broadcasting Corporation Television Young Musician of the Year Competition.
c/o BBC-TV, Kensington House, Richmond Way, London W14 0AX.
Biennial televised competition open to British resident performers to age 18 and composers to age 21. Prizes
totalling £32,000. Next competition in 1996.

Cardiff Singer of the World Competition.
c/o BBC Wales, Music Department, Broadcasting House, Llandaff, Cardiff, Wales CF5 2YQ.

Biennial competition open to singers 18 years of age or older. Prizes include £5,000 and concert engagements.
Next competition in 1995.

City of London Carl Flesch International Violin Competition.
c/o City Arts Trust, Bishopsgate Hall, 230 Bishopsgate, London EC2M 4QH.
Biennial competition open to violinists of all nationalities under the age of 28. Prizes include 1st prize of £6,000,
2nd prize of £4,000, 3rd prize of £3,000, 4th prize of £1,750, 5th prize of £1,250, and 6th prize of £750, with
five additional prizes of £500 each. Next competition in 1996.

City of London Walter Gruner International Lieder Competition.
c/o City Arts Trust, Bishopsgate Hall, 230 Bishopsgate, London EC2M 4QH.
Biennial competition open to singers to the age of 28. Prizes include 1st prize of £3,500 and a debut recital
in London, 2nd prize of £2,250, 3rd prize of £1,250, and 4th prize of £750, with an accompanists' prize of
£1,250. Next competition in 1995.

Folkestone Menuhin International Violin Competition.
72 Leopold Road, London SW19 7JQ.
Biennial competition open to violinists. Prizes totalling £15,700. Next competition in 1995.

Great Grimsby International Competition for Singers.
23 Enfield Avenue, New Waltham, Great Grimsby, South Humberside DN36 5RD.
Triennial competition open to singers between the ages of 20 and 30 with accompanists to age 26. Prizes include
1st prize of £2,000, 2nd prize of £1,000, and 3rd prize of £500, with an accompanists' prize of £500. Next
competition in 1995.

Harveys Leeds International Pianoforte Competition.
c/o University of Leeds, Leeds, Yorkshire LS2 9JT.
Triennial competition open to professional pianists under the age of 30. Prizes totalling £57,600 and concert
engagements worldwide. Next competition in 1996.

International Young Concert Artists Competition of Royal Tunbridge Wells.
Paddock Wood, Kent TN12 6PA.
Biennial competition open to performers to the age of 25. Prizes totalling £9,000. Next competition in 1995.

London International String Quartet Competition.
62 High Street, Fareham, Hampshire PO16 7BG.
Triennial competition open to string quartets whose aggregate ages do not exceed 120 years. Prizes include
1st prize of £8,000 and the Amadeus Trophy, 2nd prize of £4,800, 3rd prize of £3,200, 4th prize of £2,400,
and 5th prize of £1,600, with the Menuhin Prize of £750 and the Audience Prize of £500. Next competition

MAJOR COMPETITIONS AND AWARDS

in 1997.

National Power World Piano Competition London.
26 Wallace Road, London N1 2PG.
Triennial competition open to pianists of all nationalities to the age of 29. Prizes include prizes totalling £30,000, concert engagements, and scholarships. Next competition in 1997.

Newport International Competition for Young Pianists
Civic Centre, Newport, Gwent NP9 4UR.
Triennial competition open to pianists to the age of 25. Prizes include cash and concerts. Next competition in 1997.

Performing Right Society E-A Composition Prize.
c/o Electro-Acoustic Music Association of Great Britain, 10 Stratford Place, London W1N 9AE.
Biennial competition open to composers. Next competition in 1996.

Royal Over-Seas League of Music Competition.
Over-Seas House, Park Place, St James's Street, London SW1A 1LR.
Annual competition open to Commonwealth and former Commonwealth citizens, for instrumentalists to the age of 28 and for singers to the age of 30. Various prizes.

Scottish International Piano Competition.
c/o Royal Scottish Academy of Music and Drama, 100 Renfrew Street, Glasgow, Scotland G2 2BS.
Triennial competition open to pianists of all nationalities to the age of 32. Prizes include £8,000. Next competition in 1995.

USA

ALEA International Competition Prize.
c/o Boston University School of Music.
855 Commonwealth Avenue, Boston, MA 02215.
Annual competition open to composers of all nationalities born after 1953; submitted composition must not have been published, publicly performed, or awarded any prize.

ASCAP Foundation Grants to Young Composers.
1 Lincoln Plaza, New York, NY 10023.
Annual cash grants to composers who are citizens or permanent residents of the US and have not reached their 30th birthday by 15 March.

Affiliate Artists Inc.
37 West 65th Street, New York, NY 10023.
Programs to support outstanding professional performing artists in the US.

American Academy and Institute of Arts and Letters.
633 West 155th Street, New York, NY 10032.
Various awards are given in the field of music.

American Academy in Rome.
101 Park Avenue, New York, NY 10017.
Annual residents program to support distinguished artists and scholars as residents at the academy for a year and annual Rome Prize Fellowships for American composers to study at the academy.

American Berlin Opera Foundation Inc.
666 Fifth Avenue, 21st Floor, New York, NY 10103.
Annual scholarships for American singers who are citizens or permanent residents between the ages of 18 and 32 to study at the Deutsche Oper Berlin. Prizes include a scholarship of $15,000 and a round trip flight.

American Guild of Organists/National Young Artists Competition in Organ Performance.
475 Riverside Drive, Suite 1260, New York, NY 10115.
Biennial competition open to organists between the ages of 22 and 32. Next competition in 1996.

American Musicological Society Inc.
201 South 34th Street, Philadelphia, PA 19104.
Noah Greenberg Award up to $2,000 for a distinguished contribution to the study and/or performance of music prior to 1700. Otto Kinkeldey Award of $400 and a scroll to a US or Canadian writer of the most notable full-length study in musicology. Alfred Einstein Award of $400 to a young scholar who has published an article on a musicological subject in the preceeding year.

American Pianists Association National Fellowship Piano Auditions.
Clowes Memorial Hall, Butler University, 4600 Sunset Avenue, Indianapolis, IN 46208.
Biennial fellowships open to American classical pianists between the ages of 18 and 30. Prizes include three-year fellowship, $10,000, sponsorship at an international competition, and US concert engagements. Next competition in 1995.

Marian Anderson Award.
The Ives Center, PO Box 2957, Danbury, Connecticut.
A significant financial award to an American singer of concert and opera by recommendation.

Artists International's Annual New York Debut Award Auditions.
521 Fifth Avenue, Suite 1700, New York, NY 10017.

MAJOR COMPETITIONS AND AWARDS

Annual auditions open to performers of all nationalities who have not given a New York recital debut or who have not received a New York review for a solo recital. Prizes include New York recital debut at Carnegie Recital Hall, or Merkin Concert Hall, or Alice Tully Hall at Lincoln Center.

Artists International's Distinguished Artists Award Auditions.
521 Fifth Avenue, Suite 1700, New York, NY 10017.
Annual auditions open to soloists or chamber groups who have received at least one review from a major New York publication and have no management. Prizes include recital engagement in New York.

B(roadcast) M(usic) I(nc) Student Composers Awards.
320 West 57th Street, New York, NY 10019.
Annual awards open to student composers who are citizens or permanent residents of a country in the Western Hemisphere to the age of 25. Prizes totalling $15,000.

Johann Sebastian Bach International Competition.
1211 Potomac Street North West, Washington, DC 20007.
Competition open to performers of the works of J S Back between the ages of 20 and 40. Prizes include cash and concert engagements.

Gina Bachauer International Piano Competition.
PO Box 1164, Salt Lake City, UT 84147.
Competition open to pianists between the ages of 19 and 32. Prizes include 1st prize of a grand piano and New York and Los Angeles debut concerts; other prizes include Gold, Silver, and Bronze medals, cash prizes, concerts and recitals, with finalists appearing with the Utah Symphony Orchestra. Also a junior section for pianists between the ages of 8 and 18.

Baltimore Opera Vocal Competition for American Operatic Artists.
101 West Read Street, Suite 605, Baltimore, MD 21201.
Annual competition open to operatic singers between the ages of 20 and 35. Prizes include 1st prize of $10,000, 2nd prize of $8,000, 3rd prize of $4,500, 4th prize of $2,500, 5th prize of $2,000, 6th prize of $1,200, and 7th prize of $1,000, with additional prize of $1,000 awarded by the audience.

Barlow International Competition.
c/o Brigham Young University, Harris Fine Arts Center, Provo, UT 84602.
Annual competition open to composers of all nationalities; composition must not have won any other competition. Prizes totalling $10,000.

Joseph H Bearns Prize in Music.
c/o Columbia University, Department of Music, 703 Dodge Hall, New York, NY 10027.
Annual competition open to American composers between the ages of 18 and 25. Prizes include cash awards.

Frank Huntington Beebe Fund for Musicians.
290 Huntington Avenue, Boston, MA 02115.
Annual scholarships open to American post-graduate music students for study abroad.

Simone Belsky Music Award Competition.
153 North Street, PO Box 1112, Litchfield, CT 06759.
Biennial competition open to pianists 30 years old or older. Prizes include 1st prize of $1,500 and concert engagements. Next competition in 1995.

Boston Classical Orchestra Youth Competition.
551 Tremont Street, Boston, MA 02116.
Annual competition open to high school seniors in New England and New York who wish to pursue a career as an instrumentalist. Prizes include a $40,000 four-year merit scholarship to the Boston University School of Music and an appearance as soloist with the Boston Classical Orchestra at a youth concert.

Brandeis University Creative Arts Awards.
Brandeis University, PO Box 9110, Waltham, MA 02254.
Annual prizes open to established artists in various fields, including music. Prizes include a medal and an honorarium.

Benjamin Britten Memorial Fund.
135 East 83rd Street, Suite 4/5-C, New York, NY 10028.
Annual scholarships open to American students for study at the Britten-Pears School for Advanced Musical Studies in Aldeburgh, Suffolk, England.

Bryan International String Competition.
North Carolina Symphony Orchestra, PO Box 28026, Raleigh, NC 27611.
Quadrennial competition open to violinists, violists, and cellists between the ages of 18 and 30. Prizes include 1st prize of $12,000, 2nd prize of $6,000, and 3rd prize of $3,000. Next competition in 1996.

Grace Bumbry Student Assistance Award.
c/o AGMA Relief Fund, 1727 Broadway, New York, NY 10019.
Study grant for American classical singers between the ages of 18 and 25. Prizes include 1st prize of $2,000.

William C Byrd Young Artist Competition.
c/o Flint Institute of Music, 1025 East Kearsley Street, Flint, MI 48503.
Annual competition open to performers with categories changing annually. Prizes include 1st prize of $2,500 and an appearance with the Flint Symphony Orchestra.

CRS National Festival for the Performing Arts.

MAJOR COMPETITIONS AND AWARDS

724 Winchester Road, Broomall, PA 19008.
Annual competition with prizes including fellowships, recording contracts, national appearances, and artist representation.

Carmel Chamber Music Competition.
PO Box 6283, Carmel, CA 93921.
Annual competition open to non-professional chamber groups of three to six players averaging under the age of 26. Prizes include cash.

Carmel Music Society Competition.
PO Box 1144, Carmel, CA 93921.
Annual competition open to musicians who are residents or full-time students in California. Prizes include cash and an appearance at a Carmel Chamber Music concert.

Robert Casadesus International Piano Competition.
11021 East Boulevard, Cleveland, OH 44106.
Biennial competition open to pianists between the ages of 17 and 32. Prizes include cash and concert engagements. Next competition in 1995.

Center for Contemporary Opera International Opera Singers Competition.
PO Box 1350, Gracie Station, New York, NY 10028.
Annual competition open to singers who have not attained a major operatic career. Prizes include cash.

Chamber Music America.
545 Eighth Avenue, New York, NY 10018.
Annual ASCAP Awards for various activities devoted to the performance and promotion of chamber music.

Chopin Foundation of the United States National Chopin Piano Competition of the United States.
1440 79th Street Causeway, Miami, FL 33141.
Quinquennial competition open to American pianists between the ages of 16 and 18, to enable them to participate in the International Chopin Piano Competition in Warsaw. Prizes include 1st prize of $12,000, 2nd prize of $8,000, 3rd prize of $5,000, 4th prize of $2,500, 5th prize of $2,000, and 6th prize of $1,500. Next competition in 1995.

Civic Orchestra of Chicago Soloist Competition.
220 South Michigan Avenue, Chicago, IL 60604.
Annual competition open to soloists between the ages of 19 and 30. Prizes include $1,000 and concert engagements.

Cleveland Quartet Competition.
c/o Eastman School of Music, 26 Gibbs Street, Rochester, NY 14604.
Biennial competition open to string quartets for a two-year period of study with the Cleveland Quartet with performance and academic opportunities. Prizes include $70,000 in tuition remission and coaching stipends. Next competition in 1995.

Van Cliburn International Piano Competition.
2525 Ridgmar Boulevard, Suite 307, Fort Worth, TX 76116.
Quadrennial piano competition open to pianists between the ages of 18 and 30. Prizes include 1st prize of $15,000, Carnegie Hall recital and orchestral debuts, US recital and orchestral tour, and European recital and orchestral tour, 2nd prize of $10,000, New York debut, and US tour, 3rd prize of $7,500 and US tour, 4th prize of $5,000, 5th prize of $3,500, and 6th prize of $2,000. Next competition in 1997.

Coleman Chamber Ensemble Competition.
202 South Lake Avenue, No 201, Pasadena, CA 91101.
Annual competition open to non-professional chamber ensembles with members under the age of 27 and prepared by a coach. Prizes include $3,000, $3,000, $1,800, $1,000 and $50 for coaches.

Composers Guild Annual Competition Contest.
40 North 100 West, Box 586, Farmington, UT 84025.
Annual competition open to composers. Prizes include cash.

Concert Artists Guild International New York Competition.
850 Seventh Avenue, Suite 1205, New York, NY 10019.
Annual competition open to instrumentalists, chamber ensembles, and singers. Prizes include cash, concert engagements, recordings, free management services, etc.

Concerto Competition of the Rome Festival Orchestra.
Empire State Building, Suite 3304, New York, NY 10118.
Annual competition open to North American performers of violin, viola, cello, double bass, oboe, and horn. Prizes include five tuition fellowships and solo appearance in Rome.

Aaron Copland Competition for Young Composers.
25 Ria Drive, White Plains, NY 10605.
Annual competition open to composers between the ages of 5 and 15 for a composition lasting at least three minutes. Prizes include cash.

Corporation of Yaddo.
PO Box 395, Union Avenue, Saratoga Springs, NY 12866.
Room, board, and studio for professional composers of all nationalities. Residency up to two months.

Council for International Exchange of Scholars-Fulbright Scholar Program: Research and Lecturing Grants for Faculty and Professionals.

MAJOR COMPETITIONS AND AWARDS

3007 Tilden Street North West, Suite 5M, Washington, DC 20008.
Annual grants for university lecturing and/or advanceed research abroad by Americans, including several in the field of music.

D'Angelo Young Artist Competition.
c/o Mercyhurst College, 501 East 38th Street, Erie, PA 16546.
Annual competition open to performers under the age of 35 with categories rotating annually. Prizes include 1st prize of $10,000 and concert engagements, 2nd prize of $5,000, and 3rd prize of $3,000, with $1,000 to all finalists.

Delius Composition Contest.
c/o Jacksonville University, College of Fine Arts, Jacksonville, FL 32211.
Annual competition open to composers. Prizes include 1st prize of $500, $100 for the best vocal, keyboard, and instrumental composition, and high school composition category of 1st prize of $200 and 2nd prize of $100.

Delta Omicron International Music Fraternity Triennial Composition Competition.
8009 Volk Drive, Dayton, OH 45415.
Triennial competition open to American composers of college age or older. Prizes include $500 and premiere of composition. Next competition in 1997.

Detroit Symphony Orchestra Fellowship Program.
400 Buhl Building, 535 Griswold Street, Detroit, MI 48226.
One-year residency for African-American orchestral players with the Detroit Symphony Orchestra.

Murray Dranoff International Two Piano Competition.
999 North East 72nd Street, Miami, FL 33138.
Biennial competition open to duo pianists between the ages of 18 and 35. Prizes include 1st prize of $10,000, 2nd prize of $5,000, and 3rd prize of $2,000, plus concert engagements. Next competition in 1995.

East and West Artists Prize for New York Debut.
310 Riverside Drive, No 313, New York, NY 10025.
Annual competition open to performers who have not given a New York debut recital. Prizes include debut at Weill Recital Hall at Carnegie Hall, cash, radio and concert engagements.

Fargo-Moorhead Symphony Sigvald Thompson Composition Competition.
810 Fourth Avenue South, Moorhead, MN 56560.
Biennial competition open to American composers, previous competition winners excepted. Prizes include $2,500 and performance of composition. Next competition in 1996.

First Coast Classic Piano Competition.
100 Festival Park Avenue, Jacksonville, FL 32202.
Annual competition open to American and Canadian pianists between the ages of 18 and 35. Prizes include 1st prize of $2,000 and an appearance with the Jacksonville Symphony Orchestra, 2nd prize of $1,000, and two runner-up prizes of $500 each.

Fischoff National Chamber Music Competition.
PO Box 1303, South Bend, IN 46624.
Annual competition open to instrumental ensembles of three to five members to the age of 18. Prizes in the Senior Division include Grand Prize of $1,000 and a concert tour, with 1st prize for winds of $2,000 and 1st prize for strings of $2,000. Cash prizes also awarded in the Junior Division.

Avery Fischer Artist Program.
Lincoln Center, 140 West 65th Street, New York, NY 10023.
Career grants open to American instrumental soloists by a recommendation board and chosen by the executive committee. No applications accepted. Prizes include Avery Fischer Career Grant of $10,000 and Avery Fischer Prize of $25,000.

Fort Collins Symphony Association Young Artists Competition.
PO Box 1963, Fort Collins, CO 80522.
Annual competition open to instrumentalists. Prizes include $2,000 Adeline Rosenberg Memorial Prize.

Fort Smith Symphony Association Young Artist Competition.
PO Box 3151, Fort Smith, AR 72913.
Annual competition open to string, brass, and woodwind players to the age of 18. Prizes include 1st prize of $1,000 and an appearance with the Fort Smith Symphony Orchestra.

Fromm Music Foundation at Harvard University.
c/o Harvard University, Department of Music, Cambridge, MA 02138.
Sponsorship of composers, performers, and concerts of contemporary music.

Viktor Fuchs Memorial Scholarship Fund Auditions.
3358 Scadlock Lane, Sherman Oaks, CA 91403.
Annual competition open to California opera singers between the ages of 20 and 33. Prizes totalling $13,000.

Harvey Gaul Composition Contest.
c/o Duquesne University, School of Music, Pittsburgh, PA 15282.
Biennial competition open to American composers of unpublished and unperformed compositions. Prizes include $3,000 and performance of composition. Next competition in 1996.

Graham-Stahl Concerto Competition.

MAJOR COMPETITIONS AND AWARDS

c/o Greater Trenton Symphony Orchestra Foundation, 28 West State Street, Suite 201, Trenton, NJ 08608.
Annual competition open to American violinists who are college students. Prizes include 1st prize of $1,500.

Greater Miami Opera Young Artist Program.
1200 Coral Way, Miami, FL 33145.
Annual seven-month program (Oct-April) open to singers to work with the Greater Miami Opera.

Charles Tomlinson Griffes American Music Composers Competition.
5 Joseph Wallace Drive, Croton-on-Hudson, NY 10521.
Annual competition open to American or permanent resident composers between the ages of 12 and 18 whose submitted composition has not won any other competition. Prizes include cash and performance of composition.

John Simon Guggenheim Memorial Foundation.
90 Park Avenue, New York, NY 10016.
Annual fellowships in music open to composers and scholars who have demonstrated previous outstanding ability. Fellowships in two categories: For citizens or permanent residents of the US and Canada, and for citizens or permanent residents of Latin America and the Caribbean. Fellowships average more than $25,000.

Haddonfield Symphony Young Instrumentalists Solo Competition.
PO Box 212, Haddonfield, NJ 08033.
Annual competition open to solo instrumentalists resident in one of the eleven Northeastern states or the District of Columbia between the ages of 16 and 25. Prizes include 1st prize of $2,500 and an appearance with the Haddonfield Symphony, and 2nd prize of $750.

Helen Hart International Piano Competition.
c/o Owensboro Symphony Orchestra, 122 East 18th Street, Owensboro, KY 42301.
Triennial competition open to pianists who are American citizens or students in the US between the ages of 18 and 33. Prizes include 1st prize of $5,000 and an appearance with the Owensboro Symphony, 2nd prize of $2,000, and 3rd prize of $1,000. Next competition in 1995.

Hobin Harp Competition.
c/o Greater Trenton Symphony Orchestra Foundation, 28 West State Street, Suite 201, Trenton, NJ 08608.
Annual competition open to American harpists who are college students. Prizes include 1st prize of $1,600.

Joanna Hodges International Piano Competition.
c/o College of the Desert, 43500 Monterey Avenue, Palm Desert, CA 92260.
Biennial competition open to pianists to the age of 35. Prizes include cash, scholarships, concert, radio, and television appearances. Next competition in 1995.

Ima Hogg National Young Artist Audition.
c/o Houston Symphony Orchestra, 615 Louisiana Street, Houston, TX 77002.
Annual competition open to instrumentalists between the ages of 19 and 27. Prizes include 1st prize of $5,000 and an appearance with the Houston Symphony, 2nd prize of $2,500 and an appearance with the Houston Symphony, and 3rd prize of $1,000.

Henry Holt Memorial Scholarship.
PO Box 1714, Palo Alto, CA 94302.
Annual scholarship open to singers between the ages of 18 and 26. Prizes include 1st prize of $1,000 and 2nd prize of $500.

Holtkamp/American Guild of Organists Award in Organ Composition.
475 Riverside Drive, Suite 1260, New York, NY 10115.
Biennial competition open to composers of organ compositions. Prizes include $2,000, publication and performance of composition. Next competition in 1995.

Houston Opera Center Auditions.
c/o Houston Grand Opera, 510 Preston, Houston, TX 77002.
Annual auditions open to performers to work with the Houston Opera Studio.

Indiana State University Contemporary Music Festival Competition.
c/o Louisville Orchestra, 609 West Main Street, Louisville, KY 40202.
Annual competition open to composers who have not won the competition within the previous five years.

Institute of International Education/Fulbright and Other Graduate Study Scholarships.
809 United Nations Plaza, New York, NY 10017.
Annual scholarships open to Americans with a BA or equivalent for graduate study abroad.

International Brass Ensemble Competition.
c/o Summit Brass, Box 26850, Tempe, AZ 85282.
Annual competition open to professional and amateur brass ensembles of three or more members. Prizes totalling $10,000.

International Horn Society Composition Contest.
c/o University of Missouri at Kansas City, Conservatory of Music, 4949 Cherry, Kansas City, MO 64110.
Annual competition open to composers. Prizes include cash.

International New Music Composers Competition.
7114 South West 114 Place, Suite E, Miami, FL 33173.
Biennial competition open to composers of all nationalities. Next competition in 1995.

MAJOR COMPETITIONS AND AWARDS

International Trombone Association Ensemble Composition Contest.
c/o University of North Texas, School of Music, Denton, TX 76203.
Biennial competition open to composers. Prizes include $1,000. Next competition in 1995.

International Violin Competition of Indianapolis.
47 South Pennsylvania Street, Suite 401, Indianapolis, IN 46204.
Quadrennial competition open to violinists of all nationalities between the ages of 18 and 30. Prizes totalling more than $200,000 in money, medals, concert engagements in North America and Europe, and recordings. Next competition in 1998.

Kennedy Center Friedheim Awards.
John F Kennedy Center for the Performing Arts, Washington, DC 20566.
Annual award to a living American composer of orchestral or chamber music. Prizes include 1st prize of $5,000, 2nd prize of $2,500, 3rd prize of $1,000, and 4th prize of $500.

Aram Khachaturian Music Award.
585 Saddle River Road, Saddle Brook, NJ 07662.
Biennial award for musicians of Armenian descent. Prizes include 1st prize of $2,000 and New York recital debut, 2nd prize of $1,500, and 3rd prize of $1,000.

Kingsville International Young Performers' Competition.
PO Box 2873, Kingsville, TX 78363.
Annual competition open to pianists and orchestraal instrumentalists to the age of 26. Prizes totalling more than $20,000, with highest ranking winner receiving a minimum of $5,000 and an appearance with the Corpus Christi Symphony.

Kate Neal Kinley Memorial Fellowship.
c/o University of Illinois, 110 Architecture Building, 608 East Lorado Taft Drive, Champaign, IL 61820.
Annual fellowship open to graduates under the age of 25 for advanced study in the US or abroad. Fellowship of $7,000.

Irving M Klein International String Competition.
c/o San Francisco State University, Department of Music, 1600 Holloway Avenue, San Francisco, CA 94132.
Annual competition open to string players between the ages of 15 and 23. Prizes include 1st prize of $7,000 and appearances with the Peninsula and Santa Cruz Symphony orchestras, and other prizes.

Kosciuszko Foundation Chopin Piano Competition.
15 East 65th Street, New York, NY 10021.
Annual competition open to pianists who are American citizens or permanent residents of the US or full-time foreign students with valid visa between the ages of 17 and 23. Prizes include $2,500, $1,500, and $1,000.

Olga Koussevitzky Young Artist Awards Competition.
165 West 66th Street, New York, NY 10023.
Annual competition open to performers between the ages of 16 and 26 with categories rotating annually. Prizes totalling $3,500, concert engagements, and auditions.

Eleanor Lieber Awards for Young Singers.
1516 South West Alder, Portland, OR 97205.
Biennial awards open to singers who are residents of Oregon, Washington, Idaho, Montana, and Alaska between the ages of 20 and 31. Prizes include 1st prize of $2,000, 2nd prize of $1,000, and 3rd prize of $500. Next awards in 1995.

Liederkranz Foundation Scholarship Awards.
6 East 87th Street, New York, NY 10128.
Annual awards open to singers and pianists. Prizes totalling some $35,000.

Macallister Award for Opera Singers.
c/o Indiana Opera Theatre, 7515 East 30th Street, Indianapolis, IN 46219.
Annual audition open to opera singers. Prizes include 1st prize of $10,000, 2nd prize of $5,000, 3rd prize of $3,000, 4th prize of $1,500, and 5th prize of $1,000.

Macdowell Colony Inc.
100 High Street, Peterborough, NH 03458.
Awards residency fellowships for composers and other creative artists.

Quinto Maganini Award in Composition.
37 Valley View Road, Norwalk, CT 06851.
Biennial competition open to American composers of orchestral music not publicly performed. Prizes include $2,500 and premiere by the Norwalk Symphony Orchestra. Next competition in 1996.

Marguerite McCammon Voice Competition.
422 Coombs Creek Drive, Dallas, TX 75211.
Biennial competition open to singers between the ages of 21 and 32. Prizes include 1st prize of $3,000 and operatic engagements. Next competition in 1995.

Louise D McMahon International Music Competition.
c/o School of Fine Arts, Cameron University, 2800 West Gore Boulevard, Lawton, OK 73505.
Competition open to instrumentalists and singers 25 years old or older. Prizes include cash and solo performance with orchestra.

MAJOR COMPETITIONS AND AWARDS

Meadows Foundation Young Artists Auditions Competition.
8 Drake Road, Somerset, NJ 08873.
Annual competition open to performers in three divisions-Junior Division (Junior High School), High School Division, and Senior Division (to the age of 35). Prizes include cash, recitals, concert, and chamber music engagements.

Metropolitan Opera National Council Auditions.
Lincoln Center, New York, NY 10023.
Annual competitive auditions open to singers. Prizes include cash and study grants.

Midland-Odessa Symphony and Chorale Inc, National Young Artist Competition.
PO Box 60658, Midland, TX 79711.
Biennial competition open to performers. Prizes include cash and appearances with the Midland-Odessa Symphony and Chorale. Next competition in 1995.

Missouri Southern International Piano Competition.
Missouri Southern State College, 3950 Newman Road, Joplin, MO 64801.
Biennial competition open to pianists of all nationalities to the age of 30. Prizes include 1st prize of $5,000 and appearance at Carnegie Recital Hall. Next competition in 1996.

Möller/American Guild of Organists Award in Choral Composition.
475 Riverside Drive, Suite 1260, New York, NY 10115.
Biennial awards open to American, Canadian, and Mexican composers. Prizes include $2,000, publication and performance of composition. Next award in 1996.

Mu Phi Epsilon International Competition.
4858 Stallcup Drive, Mesquite, TX 75150.
Triennial competition open to members of Mu Phi Epsilon who have appeared in recital and/or as soloist with orchestra but not under contract to a professional management. Prizes include two-year concert engagements. Next competition in 1995.

Museum in the Community Composer's Award.
PO Box 251, Scott Depot, WV 25560.
Biennial competition open to American composers of a composition for string quartet not previously performed in public. Prizes include $2,500 and performance of composition. Next competition in 1995.

Music Teachers National Association-CCP/Belwin Student Composition Competition.
c/o Eastman School of Music, 26 Gibbs Street, Rochester, NY 14604.
Annual competition open to American composers who are in college, high school, junior high school, and elementary school who are studying with an active member of the Music Teachers National Association. Prizes include cash.

Naftzger Young Artists Auditions and Music Awards.
c/o Wichita Symphony Society, 225 West Douglas, Suite 207, Wichita, KS 67202.
Annual competition open to instrumentalists between the ages of 18 and 26 and to singers between the ages of 20 and 28. Prizes include $5,000 Naftzger Young Artist Award and $2,000 each in various categories.

National Association of Composers, USA.
84 Cresta Verde Drive, Rolling Hills Estate, CA 90274.
Annual competition open to composers between the ages of 18 and 30 with 1st prize of $200 and Los Angeles performance of composition. Competition open to performers of American music between the ages of 10 and 30 with prize of $500 and concert engagements.

National Association of Teachers of Singing Artist Award Competition.
c/o Jacksonville University, Department of Music, Jacksonville, FL 32211.
Competition held every 18 months open to singers between the ages of 21 and 35 whose most recent teacher has been a member of the National Association of Teachers of Singing. Prizes include 1st prize of $5,000, and Carnegie Hall concert, and AIMS scholarship, and 2nd prize of $2,000.

National Competition for Composers Recording.
724 Winchester Road, Broomall, PA 19008.
Annual competition open to composers for a composition not commercially recorded and not exceeding nine players and forty minutes in length. Prizes include recording of composition.

National Competition for Orchestral Works.
c/o State University of New York, College of New Paltz, New Paltz, NY 12561.
Annual competition open to composers who are American citizens or permanent residents born before 1 Jan 1974. Prizes include $1,500 and performance of composition.

National Competition for Performing Artists.
c/o Contemporary Recording Society, 724 Winchester Road, Broomall, PA 19008.
Annual competition open to performers. Prizes include recording.

National Endowment for the Arts, Music Program Office.
1100 Pennsylvania Avenue North West, Washington, DC 20506.
Lends organizational assistance to professional music organizations and gives fellowships to composers, performers, etc.

National Endowment for the Humanities.
1100 Pennsylvania Avenue North West, Washington, DC 20506.
Awards fellowships and grants for various projects in the field of music.

MAJOR COMPETITIONS AND AWARDS

National Federation of Music Clubs.
1336 North Delaware Street, Indianapolis, IN 46202.
Provides various annual awards and fellowships.

National Flute Association Young Artists Competition.
4 Indian Trail Road, Macomb, IL 61455.
Annual competition open to flutists of all nationalities born in 1960 or later, and a membr of the National Flute Association. Prizes include 1st prize of $2,000, 2nd prize of $1,000, and 3rd prize of $500.

National Guild of Community Schools of the Arts Young Composers Awards.
PO Box 8018, Englewood, NJ 07631.
Awards open to American and Canadian composers between the ages of 13 and 18. Prizes include 1st prize of $1,000, etc.

National Institute for Music Theater Fellowship Program.
John F Kennedy Center of the Performing Arts, Washington, DC 20566. Annual fellowship open to individuals in music theater. Prizes include monthly stipend of $1,460.

National Piano Competition in Virginia Beach.
c/o Virginia Beach Pops, 2101 Park Avenue, No 401, Virginia Beach, VA 23451.

Annual competition open to pianists between the ages of 16 and 32. Prizes include 1st prize of $1,000 and two appearances with the Virginia Beach Pops Orchestra, 2nd prize of $500, and 3rd prize of $250.

National Symphony Orchestra Young Soloists' Competition, College Division.
5931 Oakdale Road, McLean, VA 22101.
Annual competition open to high school graduates studying music in the Washington metropolitan area or Washington residents studying elsewhere. Prizes include cash and appearances with the National Symphony Orchestra.

Walter W Naumburg Foundation International Competition.
60 Lincoln Center Plaza, New York, NY 10023.
Annual competition open to performers of all nationalities with categories rotating annually. Prizes include 1st prize of $5,000, concert engagements, and a recording, 2nd prize of $2,500, and 3rd prize of $1,000.

New England Conservatory of Music/Piatigorsky Artist Competition.
290 Huntington Avenue, Boston, MA 02115.
Biennial competition open to cellists, with participants chosen only from recommendations. Prizes include $5,000 for two-week residency at the New England Conservatory of Music and recitals.

New Jersey State Opera Annual Vocal Competition.
1020 Broad Street, Newark, NJ 07102.
Annual competition open to professional singers between the ages of 22 and 34 with major operatic experience.

New Jersey Symphony Orchestra Young Artists Auditions.
Robert Treat Center, 11th Floor, 50 Park Place, Newark, NJ 07102.
Annual competition open to New Jersey residents who are instrumentalists under the age of 20. Prizes include top prize of an appearance with the New Jersey Symphony Orchestra; cash prizes range from $500 to $3,000.

New Music for Young Ensembles Inc.
12 West 72nd Street, Suite 9E, New York, NY 10023.
Annual competition open to American composers for chamber music composition. Prizes include $750 and performance of composition.

New York Foundation for the Arts Artists' Fellowship Program.
155 Avenue of the Americas, New York, NY 10013.
Biennial fellowships for non-students of two or more years residency in New York State. Prizes include grants. Next fellowships awarded in 1995.

Nutley Symphony Bach and Handel Aria Competition.
633 Franklin Avenue, Suite 153, Nutley, NJ 07110.
Annual competition open to professional singers. Prizes include 1st prize of $500 and an appearance with the Nutley Symphony Orchestra.

Nutley Symphony Young Artists Concerto Competition.
633 Franklin Avenue, Suite 153, Nutley, NJ 07110.
Annual competition open to instrumentalists between the ages of 18 and 35. Prizes include 1st prize of $500 and an appearance with the Nutley Symphony Orchestra.

Omaha Symphony Guild New Music Competition.
8723 North 57th Street, Omaha, NE 68152.
Annual competition open to composers of chamber orchestra compositions. Prizes include $2,000.

Opera at Florham Guild Vocal Competition.
Box 571, Post Office Plaza, Chatham, NJ 07928.
Competition open to all singers between the ages of 18 and 35. Prizes include 1st prize of $3,000 and a recital.

Opera/Columbus Vocal Competition.
177 Naghten, Columbus, OH 43215.
Competition open to singers who are residents of Ohio. Prizes for senior level (ages 24 to 35) include 1st prize

of $2,000 and a scholarship to the American Institute of Musical Studies in Graz, Austria.

Opera Company of Philadelphia/Luciano Pavarotti International Voice Competition.
The Graham Building, 20th Floor, 1 Penn Square West, Philadelphia, PA 19102.
Competition open to singers, men under 35 and women under 33. Prizes include the opportunity to appear with Luciano Pavarotti in an Opera Co of Philadelphia performance or in other performances by the co.

Oratorio Society of New York Solo Competition.
Carnegie Hall, Suite 504, 881 Seventh Avenue, New York, NY 10019.
Annual competition open to solo oratorio singers under the age of 40. Prizes include $10,000.

Palm Beach Invitational International Piano Competition.
PO Box 3094, Palm Beach, FL 33480.
Annual competition open to 25 young pianists, each from a different nation and each the winner of an international competition. Prizes totalling $45,000, including 1st prize of $15,000 and a concert at Alice Tully Hall in New York.

Palm Beach Opera Vocal Competition.
415 South Olive Avenue, West Palm Beach, FL 33401.
Annual competition open to singers with Junior Division between the ages of 18 and 23 and Senior Division between the ages of 24 and 30. Prizes totalling $32,000 and performances.

Performers of Connecticut Annual Young Artist Competitions.
17 Morningside Drive South, Westport, CT 06880.
Annual competition open to performers between the ages of 18 and 30 not under professional management. Prizes include cash.

Performing Arts Assistance Corporation.
PO Box 1296, Ansonia Station, New York, NY 10023.
Gives seminars for performers.

Gregor Piatigorsky Seminar for Cello.
c/o University of Southern California School of Music, Los Angeles, CA 90089.
Seminar open to cellists.

Rosa Ponselle International Vocal Competition for the Vocal Arts.
"Windsor", Stevenson, MD 21153. Biennial competition open to singers to the age of 25. Prizes include study grants between $20,000 and $25,000, medallions, and training in Italy and France. Next competition in 1996.

Pro Musicis International Award.
140 West 79th Street, No 9F, New York, NY 10024.
Annual career development award. Prizes include major recitals in New York, Los Angeles, Washington DC, Boston, Paris, and Rome.

Pulitzer Prize in Music.
c/o Columbia University, 702 Journalism Building, New York, NY 10027.
Annual prize of $3,000 to an American composer for a major composition premiered in the US during the year.

Queens Opera Vocal Competition.
313 Bay 14 Street, Brooklyn, NY 11214.
Annual competition open to singers who have appeared in one opera performance. Prizes include 1st prize of cash and an appearance in a full opera performance.

Rome Prize Fellowships of the American Academy in Rome.
41 East 65th Street, New York, NY 10021.
Annual fellowships for American composers with a BA or equivalent degree. Fellowships include one year residency at the American Academy in Rome, $7,500 stipend, and $800 travel allowance.

San Antonio International Keyboard Competition.
PO Box 39636, San Antonio, TX 78218.
Triennial competition open to pianists between the ages of 20 and 32. Prizes include 1st prize of $5,000 and gold medal, 2nd prize of $2,500 and silver medal, 3rd prize of $1,000 and bronze medal, and 4th prize of $500. Next competition in 1997.

San Francisco Opera Center National Auditions.
c/o War Memorial Opera House, San Francisco, CA 94102.
Annual competitive auditions for singers, sopranos between the ages of 20 and 30 and all other singers between 20 and 34. Prizes include awards given in the Merola Opera Program totalling $28,000. Participants may also apply for the Adler Fellowship Program.

San Jose Symphony Young Pianist Concerto Competition.
99 Almaden Boulevard, Suite 400, San Jose, CA 95113.
Annual competition open to pianists to the age of 30. Prizes include grand prize of $5,000 and an appearance with the San Jose Symphony.

Santa Barbara Symphony and the Esperia Foundation Young Artists' Competition.
214 East Victoria Street, Santa Barbara, CA 93101.
Competition open to string players and pianistt alternating between instruments. Prizes include cash and an appearance with the Santa Barbara Symphony. Next competition in 1995.

MAJOR COMPETITIONS AND AWARDS

Friedrich Schorr Memorial Performance Prize in Voice.
110 South Madison Street, Adrian, MI 49221.
Annual competition open to all professional singers. Prizes include $10,000 in performance awards/stipends.

Seventeen Magazine and General Motors National Concerto Competition at Interlochen.
c/o Seventeen Magazine, 850 Third Avenue, New York, NY 10022.
Annual competition open to instrumentalists of the US, Canada, Mexico, and Puerto Rico who are studying with a music teacher and are in high school. Prizes include grand prize of $5,000 scholarship and an appearance with the Detroit Symphony Orchestra, and $5,000 scholarships to each of the four 1st place winners.

Sewanee Music Festival International Scholarships.
735 University Avenue, Sewanee, TN 37375.
Annual scholarships for musicians of all nationalities between the ages of 16 and 25.

Shreveport Symphony/Nena Plant Wideman Annual Piano Competition.
PO Box 205, Shreveport, LA 71162.
Annual competition open to pianists between the ages of 18 and 28. Prizes include 1st prize of $2,500, 2nd prize of $1,000, and 3rd prize of $500.

Sinfonia Foundation.
c/o Phi Mu Alpha Sinfonia Fraternity, 10600 Old State Road, Evansville, IN 47711.
Commissions to composers and annual research grants for scholarly research on music in America or American music.

Sound Research Residencies.
c/o Yellow Springs Institute for Contemporary Studies and the Arts, 1645 Art School Road, Chester Springs, PA 19425.
Annual ten-day residency for composers with at least three years of professional experience.

Southwestern Youth Music Festival Competition.
PO Box 41104, Los Angeles, CA 90041.
Annual competition open to pianists to the age of 18 whose teacher must become a member of the festival. Prizes include $10,000 and orchestral appearances.

James Spencer Memorial Performance Prize in Composition.
110 South Madison Street, Adrian, MI 49221.
Prizes open to American composers. Prizes include travel and housing allowance, lecture stipend, and performance and recording by the Adrian Symphony Orchestra.

Spivey International Performance Competition.
Clayton State College, Morrow, GA 30260.
Annual competition for performers. Prizes include 1st prize of $5,000.

Stewart Awards National Operatic Voice Competition.
PO Box 18321, Oklahoma City, OK 73154.
Biennial competition open to American singers between the ages of 20 and 32. Prizes include cash totalling $20,000. Next competition in 1995.

Leopold Stokowski Conducting Competition.
c/o American Symphony Orchestra, 850 Seventh Avenue, Suite 1160, New York, NY 10019.
Competition open to American conductors under the age of 35. Prizes include 1st prize of cash and a guest conducting engagement with the American Symphony Orchestra.

Stravinsky Awards International Piano Competition for Children and Young Adults.
1003 West Church Street, Champaign, IL 61821.
Biennial competition open to pianists of all nationalities in age divisions ranging from small children to the age of 22. Prizes include various cash awards. Next competition in 1995.

Julius Stulberg International String Competition.
PO Box 107, Kalamazoo, MI 49005.
Annual competition open to string players to the age of 19. Prizes include cash and performances.

Louis and Virginia Sudler International Wind Band Composition Contest.
c/o US Marine Bane, Eighth and 1 Streets South East, Washington, DC 20390.
Biennial competition open to composers of wind music. Prizes include 1st prize of $12,000. Next competition in 1995.

William Matheus Sullivan Musical Foundation Inc.
251 West 89th Street, Suite 10-B, New York, NY 10024.
Annual assistance program for professional young singers.

Summit Brass International Brass Ensemble Competition.
Box 26850, Tempe, AZ 85282.
Annual competition open to amateur and professional brass ensembles of three or more players. Prizes totalling $10,000.

Trebas Institute Scholarships.
6464 Sunset Boulevard, No 1180, Hollywood, CA 90028.
Annual scholarships for educational opportunities in the music business and the recording arts and sciences.

MAJOR COMPETITIONS AND AWARDS

Richard Tucker Music Foundation.
1790 Broadway, Suite 715, New York, NY 10019.
Annual awards to American singers by recommendation. Prizes include the Richard Tucker Award of $30,000, four career grants of $6,500, and other grants.

USA International Harp Competition.
PO Box 2718, Bloomington, IN 47402.
Triennial competition open to harpists of all nationalities in or after 1963. Prizes include 8 awards. Next competition in 1995.

Unisys African-American Composers Forum and Symposium.
DSOH Education Department, 400 Buhl Building, 535 Griswold Street, Detroit, MI 48226.
Encourages performances of orchestral compositions by African-American composers by major professional symphony orchestras.

United States Information Agency Artistic Ambassador Program.
301 Fourth Street South West, Room 216, Washington, DC 20547.
Annual program for American musicians at least 21 years old to serve as Artistic Ambassadors abroad at government expense for four to six weeks.

University of Louisville Grawemeyer Award for Music Composition.
c/o University of Louisville, School of Music, Grawemeyer Music Award Committee, Louisville, KY 40292.
Annual award for outstanding achievement by a composer. Compositions may not be submitted by the composer but must be sponsored by a professional music organization or individual. Award totalling $150,000, paid in five annual installments of $30,000.

University of Maryland International Competitions.
c/o University of Maryland, College Park, MD 20742.
Annual competition open to pianists, cellists, and singers of all nationalities. Prizes include 1st prize of $20,000 and concert engagements, 2nd prize of $10,000, and 3rd prize of $5,000.

Elizabeth Harper Vaughan Concerto Competition.
1200 East Center Street, Kingsport, TN 37600.
Annual competition open to performers of classical music to the age of 26. Prizes include $1,000 and an appearance with the Kingsport Symphony Orchestra.

Ventura County Symphony Young Artists Award.
PO Box 1088, Ventura, CA 93002.
Annual competition open to performers in the state of California to the age of 30. Prizes include 1st prize of $1,000.

WAMSO (Women's Association of the Minnesota Orchestra) Young Artist Competition.
c/o Minnesota Orchestra, 1111 Nicollet Mall, Minneapolis, MN 55403.
Annual competition open to instrumentalists to the age of 25. Various prizes.

Washington International Competition.
4530 Connecticut Avenue, Apt 704, Washington, DC 20008.
Annual competition open to performers between the ages of 18 and 32 with categories rotating annually. Prizes include 1st prize of $7,000.

Mae M Whitaker International Competiton.
c/o St Louis Conservatory of Music, 560 Trinity, St Louis, MO 63130.
Biennial competition open to performers between the ages of 18 and 30. Prizes include 1st prize of $7,500 and concert engagements, 2nd prize of $5,000, and 3rd prize of $2,500. Next competition in 1995.

Abby Whiteside Foundation Inc.
8 East 83rd Street, No 8-E, New York, NY 10028.
To encourage the study, education, and performance of piano music.

Andrew Wolf Chamber Music Award.
PO Box 191, Camden, ME 04843 or all Newton Music School, 321 Chestnut Street, West Newton, MA 02165.
Biennial award given to an American chamber music pianist under the age of 40. Award includes $10,000 and concert appearances.

Young Concert Artists International Auditions.
250 West 57th Street, Suite 921, New York, NY 10019.
Annual auditions for solo performers and string quartets.

Loren L Zachary Society Opera Awards National Vocal Competition.
2250 Gloaming Way, Beverly Hills, CA 90210.
Annual competition open to professional opera singers seeking contracts for leading roles in European opera houses; for women between the ages of 21 and 33 and for men between the ages of 21 and 35. Prizes totalling about $25,000 and a round trip flight to Europe for auditioning purposes.

URUGUAY

Concurso Internacional de Piano ''Ciudad de Montevideo''.
Santiago Vásquez, Montevideo.
Triennial competition open to pianists to the age of 32. Next competition in 1997.

APPENDIX F

MUSIC LIBRARIES

AFGHANISTAN

Kabul Public Library, Kabul.

ALBANIA

Biblioteka Kombetare (National Library), Tirana.

ALGERIA

Bibliothèque nationale, Avenue Frantz Fanor, Algiers.
Bibliothèque Universitarie, Lrue Didouche Mourad, Algiers.

ARGENTINA

Academia Nacional de Bellas Artes, Biblioteca, Sanchez de Bustamante 2663, 1425 Buenos Aires.
Bibliteca Nacional, México 564, 1097 Buenos Aires.
Fondo Nacional de Las Artes, Biblioteca, Alsina 673, 1087 Buenos Aires.

AUSTRALIA

AUSTRALIAN CAPITAL TERRITORY

National Library of Australia, Music Division, Parkes Place, Canberra, ACT 2600.

NEW SOUTH WALES

Australia Music Centre Ltd Library, PO Box 9, Grosvenor Street, Sydney, NSW 2000.
City of Sydney Public Library, Music Division, 473 George Street, Sydney, NSW 2000.
Dennis Wolanski Library, Sydney Opera House, Bennelona Point, GPO Box 4274, Sydney, NSW 2000.
Federal Music Library, Australian Broadcasting Corporation, GPO Box 9994, Sydney, NSW 2001.
State Library of New South Wales, Music Division, Macquarie Street, Sydney, NSW 2000.

QUEENSLAND

State Library of Queensland, Music Division, William Street, Brisbane, QLD 4000.

SOUTH AUSTRALIA

State Library of South Australia, Music Division, North Terrace, GPO Box 419, Adelaide, SA 5001.

TASMANIA

State Library of Tasmania, Music Division, 91 Murray Street, Hobart, TAS 7000.

VICTORIA

State Library of Victoria, Music Division, 328 Swanston Street, Melbourne, VIC 3000.

WESTERN AUSTRALIA

State Library of Western Australia, Music Division, Alexander Library Building, Perth Cultural Centre, Perth, WA 6000.

AUSTRIA

Burgenländische Landesbibliothek, Landhaus Freiheitsplatz 1, 7001 Eisenstadt.
Stadbücherien, Landhausgasse 2, 8010 Graz.
Kammer für Arbeiter und Angestelle, Volksbüchereien, Bahnhofplatz 3, 9021 Klagenfurt.
Büchereien der Stadt Linz, Zentrale und Hauptbücherei, Museumstrasse 15, 4020 Linz.
Stadbücherei, Schloss Mirabell, 5020 Salzburg.
Gesellschaft der Musikfreunde in Wien, Archiv und Bibliothek, Bösendorferstrasse 12, 1010 Vienna.
Haus des Buches, Hauptbücherei, Skodagasse 20, 1080 Vienna.
Österreichische Akademie der Wissenschaften, Bibliothek, Dr Ignaz Seipelplatz 2, 1010 Vienna 1.
Österreichische Gesellschaft für Musik, Bibliothek, Hanuschgasse 3, A-1010 Vienna.

MUSIC LIBRARIES

Österreichische Nationalbibliothek, Josefplatz 1, 1015 Vienna.
Österreichische Gewerkschaftsbund, Bibliothek, Grillparzerstrasse 14, 1010 Vienna.
Stadtbücherei, Herzog Leopoldstrasse 21, 2700 Wiener Neustadt.
Wiener Stadt-und Landesbibliothek, Rathaus, 1082 Vienna.

BELGIUM

Stadsbibliotheek, Hendrik Conscienceplein 4, 2000 Antwerp.
Academie royale des sciences, des lettres et des beaux arts de Belgique, Bibliothèque, 1 Rue Ducale, Palais des academies, 1000 Brussels.
Bibliothèque royale Albert Ier, Boulevard de l'Empereur 4, 1000 Brussels.
Koninklijke Academie voor Wetenschappen, Letteren en schone Kunsten van Belgie, Hetogsstraat 1, Paleis der Academien, 1000 Brussels.
Bibliothèque centrale, En Hors Chateau 31, 4000 Liège.
Bibliothèque provinciale du degré moyen, Rue des Croisiers 15, 4000 Liège.

BOLIVIA

Biblioteca y Archivo Nacional de Bolivia, C Espana 25, Casilla 338, Sucre.

BRAZIL

Biblioteca Nacional, Fundaçao Nacional Pro-Memoria, Avenida Rio Branco 219-239, 20042 Rio de Janeiro.

BULGARIA

Nacionalna Biblioteka, "Kiril i Metodij", F Tolbuhin 11, 1504 Sofia.
Union of Bulgarian Composers, Iv Vazov 2, 1000 Sofia.

CAMBODIA

Bibliothèque nationale, BP 4, Phnom Penh.

CANADA

ALBERTA

Calgary Public Library, Music Division, 616 Macleod Trail South East, Calgary, Alberta T2G 2M2.
Edmonton Public Library, Music Division, 7 Sir Winston Churchill Square, Edmonton, Alberta T5J 2V4.

BRITISH COLUMBIA

Vancouver Public Library, Music Division, 750 Burrard Street, Vancouver, British Columbia V62 1X5.
Greater Victoria Public Library, Music Division, 735 Broughton Street, Victoria, British Columbia V8W 3H2.

MANITOBA

Winnipeg Public Library, Music Division, 251 Donald Street, Winnipeg, Manitoba R3C 3P5.

NOVA SCOTIA

Halifax City Regional Library, Music Division, 5381 Spring Garden Road, Halifax, Nova Scotia B3J 1E9.

ONTARIO

Guelph Public Library, Music Division, 100 Norfolk Street, Guelph, Ontario N1H 4S6.
Hamilton Public Library, Music Division, 55 York Boulevard, Hamilton, Ontario L8R 3K1.
Kingston Public Library, Music Division, 130 Johnson Street East, Kingston, Ontario K7L 1X8.
Kitchener Public Library, Music Division, 85 Queen Street North, Kitchener, Ontario N2H 2H1.
National Library of Canada, Music Division, 395 Wellington Street, Ottawa, Ontario K1A 0N4.
Ottawa Public Library, Music Division, 120 Metcalfe Street, Ottawa, Ontario K1P 5M2.
Canadian Music Centre, 20 St Joseph Street, Toronto, Ontario M4Y 1J9.
Toronto Public Library, Music Division, 40 St George Street, Toronton, Ontario M5S 2E4.
Windsor Public Library, Music Division, 850 Quellette Avenue, Windsor, Ontario N9A 4M9.

QUÈBEC

Bibliothèque municipale de Montréal, 1210 Sheerbrooke Street East, Montréal, Province Quèbec H2L 1L9.
Bibliothèque nationale du Québec, 1700 St Denis Street, Montréal, Province Quèbec H2X 3K6.
Bibliothèque municipale de Québec, 37 Rue Sainte-Angéle, Quèbec, Province Quèbec G1R 4G5.

MUSIC LIBRARIES

SASKATCHEWAN

Regina Public Library, Music Division, 2311 12th Avenue, PO Box 2311, Regina, Saskatchewan S4P 3Z5.
Saskatoon Public Library, Music Division, 311 23rd Street East, Saskatoon, Saskatchewan S7K 0J6.

CHILE

Biblioteca Nacional, Avenida Bernardo O'Higgins 651, Santiago.

CHINA

National Library of China, 39 Baishiqiao Road, Haidian District, Beijing 100 081.

COLOMBIA

Biblioteca Nacional de Columbia, C24, 5-60, Apdo 27600 Bogotá.

COMMONWEALTH OF INDEPENDENT STATES

Moscow State Library, Moscow 101000.
St Petersburg State Library, St Petersburg.

COSTA RICA

Biblioteca Nacional, C 15-17, Av 3Y 3b, Apdo 10008, San José.

CUBA

Biblioteca Nacional "José Marti", Apdo oficial No 3, Avenida de Independencia 3/20 de Mayo y Arangusen, Plaza de la Revolucíon José Marti, Havana.

CZECH REPUBLIC

Městská knihovna v Praze (City Library of Prague), Knihovna Bedřicha Smetany (Bedrich Smetana Library), Dr V Vacka 1, 115 72 Prague.
Státni knihovna (State Library), Klementinum 190, 110 01 Prague 1.

DENMARK

Danish Music Informationa Centre, 48 Vimmelskaftet, DK-1161 Copenhagen K.
Det Kongelige Bibliotek (The Royal Library), Christians Brygge 8, 1219 Copenhagen K.
Musikhistorisk Museum and Carl Claudius' Samling, Bibliotek, Åbenrå 30, DK-1124 Copenhagen K.

DOMINICAN REPUBLIC

Biblioteca Nacional, César Nicolás Penson 91, Plaza de la Cultura, Santo Domingo.

ECUADOR

Biblioteca Nacional de Ecuador, 12 de Octubre 555, Apdo 67, Quito.

EGYPT

Egyptian National Library, Sharia Corniche El-Nil, Bulaq, Cairo.

EIRE

National Library of Ireland, Kildare Street, Dublin 2.

EL SALVADOR

Biblioteca National, 8A Avenida Norte Calle Delgado, San Salvador.

MUSIC LIBRARIES

ETHIOPIA

National Library and Archives of Ethiopia, PO Box 1907, Addis Ababa.

FINLAND

Finnish Music Information Centre, 15 Al Runebergsgatan, SF-00100 Helsinki.

FRANCE

Bibliothèque centrale de prêt du Pas-de-Calais, 13 Place Guy Mollet, 62000 Arras.
Bibliothèque centrale de prêt du Doubs et du Territorie de Belfort, 24 Avenue de l'Observatoire, 25000 Besançon.
Bibliothèque municipale classée, 3 Rue Mably, 33075 Bordeaux, Cédex.
Bibliothèque de la ville de Caen, Place Guillouard, 14027 Caen Cédex.
Bibliothèque municipale d'étude et d'information, Boulevard Maréchal-Lyautey, BP 1095 RP, 38021 Grenoble Cédex.
Bibliothèque municipale, 32-34 Rue Edouard-Delesalle, 59043 Lille Cédex.
Bibliothèque municipale, 30 Boulevard Vivier-Merle, 69431 Lyon Cédex 03.
Bibliothèque municipale, 38 Rue du 141e RIA, 13001 Marseille Cédex 3.
Bibliothèque municipale, 1 Cour Elie Fleur, 57000 Metz.
Bibliothèque de la ville et du musée Fabre, 37 Boulevard Bonnes-Nouvelles, 34000 Montepellier.
Bibliothèque municipale, 19 Grand'Rue, 68090 Mulhouse Cédex.
Bibliothèque municipale, 43 Rue Stanislas, 54000 Nancy.
Bibliothèque municipale, 37 Rue Gambetta, 44041 Nantes Cédex.
Bibliothèque municipale d'études, 21 bis Boulevard Dubouchage, 06047 Nice Cédex.
Bibliothèque municipale, 1 Rue Dupanloup, 45043 Orléans Cédex.
Bibliothèque-Musée de l'Opéra, Place Charles Garnier, 75009 Paris.
Bibliothèque Musicale Gustav Mahler, 11 bis rue Vézelay, 75008 Paris.
Bibliothèque nationale, Department de la musique, 2 Rue Louvois, 75084 Paris.
Institut de France: Acádemie des Beaux-Arts, 23 Quai de Conti, 75006 Paris.
Bibliothèque municipale classée, 43 Place Charles-de-Gaulle, 86000 Poitiers.
Bibliothèque municipale classée, 2 Place Carnegie, 51095 Reims Cédex.
Bibliothèque municipale, 1 Rue de La Borderie, 35042 Rennes Cédex.
Bibliothèque municipale, e Rue Jacques Villon, 76043 Rouen Cédex.
Bibliothèque municipale, 3 Rue Kuhn, 67000 Strasbourg Cédex.
Bibliothèque municipale, 1 Rue de Périgord, 31070 Toulouse.
Bibliothèque municipale, 2 bis Quai d'Orléans, 37042 Tours Cédex.
Bibliothèque municipale, 5 Rue de l'indépendence américaine, 78000 Versailles.

GERMANY

Öffentliche Bibliothek der Stadt Aachen, Couvenstrasse 15, Postfach 1210, 5100 Aachen.
Staats-und Stadtbibliothek, Schaezlerstrasse 25, Postfach 111909, 8900 Augsburg.
Stadtbücherei, Gutenbergstrasse 2, 8900 Augsburg.
Stadtbibliothek, Luisenstrasse 34, 7570 Baden-Baden.
Staatsbibliothek, Neue Residenz, Domplatz 8, 8600 Bamberg.
Stadtbücherei, Friedrichstrasse 2, 8600 Bamberg.
Statsbibliothek, Luitpoldplatz 7, Postfach 2840, 8580 Bayreuth.
Akademie der Kunste, Robert-Koch-Platz 7, 1040 Berlin.
Deutsche Staatsbibliothek, Unter den Linden 8, 1086 Berlin.
Staatsbibliothek, 24 Berlin-Preussischen Kulturbesitz, Musikabteilung, Postfach 1312, DO-1086 Berlin.
Stadtbibliothek, Wilhelmstrasse 3, Postfach 181, 4800 Bielefeld 1.
Stadtbücherei, Rathausplatz 2-6, Postfach 102269-2270, 4630 Bochum 1.
Stadtarchiv und Wissenschaftliche Stadtbibliothek, Berliner Platz 2, 5300 Bonn 1.
Stadtbücherei Bonn, Bottlerplatz 1, 5300 Bonn 1.
Stadtbibliothek, Schusterstrasse 7, 1800 Brandenburg.
Öffentliche Bücherei, Hintern Brudern 23, 3300 Braunschweig.
Stadtbibliothek, Steintorwall 15, Postfach 3309, 3300 Braunschweig.
Staats-und Universitätsbibliothek, Bibliothekstrasse, Postfach 330160, 2800 Bremen 33.
Stadbibliothek, Schwachhauser Heerstrasse 30, 2800 Bremen 1.
Stadt-und Bezirksbibliothek, Haus am Schillerplatz, 9010 Chemnitz.
Landesbibliothek, Schlossplatz 1 Schloss Ehrenburg, 8630 Coburg.
Stadtbücherei Köln, Zentralbibliothek, Josef-Haubrich-Hof 1, Postfach 108020, 5000 Cologne 1.
Hessische Landes-und Hochschulbibliothek, Schloss 6, 100 Darmstadt.
Stadtbibliothek, Grosse Bachgasse 2, Justus-Liebig-Haus, 6100 Darmstadt.
Stadtbibliothek, Strasse d DSF 10, 4500 Dessau.
Lippische Landesbibliothek, Hornschestrasse 41, 4930 Detmold.
Stadt-und Landesbibliothek, Hansaplatz, Postfach 907, 4600 Dortmund 1.
Stadtbücherei, Markt 12, Postfach 907, 4600 Dortmund 1.
Sächsische Landesbibliothek, Marienalle 12, 8060 Dresden.
Stadtbibliothek, Düsseldorfer Strasse 5-7, Postfach 100991, 4100 Duisburg 1.
Stadtbüchereien, Berliner Allee 59, Postfach 1120, 4000 Düsseldorf.
Stadt-und Kreisbibliothek, Johannisplatz 18-20, 5900 Eisenach.
Stadtbücherei, Marktplatz 1, Postfach 3160, 8520 Erlangen.
Stadtbibliothek, Hindenburgstrasse 25-27, 4300 Essen 1.
Deutsche Bibliothek, Zeppelinalle 8, 6000 Frankfurt am Main 1.
Stadt-und Universitätsbibliothek, Bockenheimer Landstrasse 134-138, 6000 Frankfurt am Main.
Stadtbücherei, Zentralbibliothek, Zeil 17-19, Postfach 102113, 6000 Frankfurt am Main 1.
Stadtbibliothek, Münsterplatz 17, 7800 Freiburg im Breisgau.

MUSIC LIBRARIES

Stadtbücherei, Ebertstrasse 19, 4650 Gelsenkirchen.
Stadbibliothek, Jochmannstrasse 2-3, 8900 Görlitz.
Stadt-und Kreisbibliothek "Heinrich Heine", Orangerie, 5800 Gotha.
Stadtbibliothek, Gotmarstrasse 8, Postfach 3842, Göttingen.
Stadt-und Bezirksbibliothek, Salzgrafenstrasse 2, 4020 Halle.
Hamburger Öffentliche Bücherhallen, Grosse Bleichen 23-27, 2000 Hamburg 36.
Stadtbibliothek, Hildesheimer Strasse 12, Postfach 125, 3000 Hannover 1.
Stadtbücherei, Deutschordenshof, Kirchbrunnenstrasse, 7100 Heilbronn.
Stadtarchiv und Stadtbibliothek, Am Steine 7, 3200 Hildesheim.
Stadtbucherei, Hallstrasse 2-4, 8070 Ingolstadt.
Stadtbibliothek, Stadtverwaltung, St-Martins-Platz 3, Postfach 1320, 6750 Kaiserslautern.
Stadtbibliothek, Zähringerstrasse 96-98, Postfach 6260, 7500 Karlsruhe.
Stadtbibliothek, Rathaus, 3500 Kassel.
Stadtbücherei, Holstenbrücke 1, Postfach 4140, 2300 Kiel 1.
Stadtbibliothek, Kornpforstrasse 15, Postfach 2064, 5400 Koblenz.
Deutsche Bücherei, Deutscher Platz, 7010 Leipzig.
Kreisbibliothek, Leipzig-Land, Karl-Rothe-Strasse 13, 7022 Leipzig.
Musikbibliothek de Stadt Leipzig, Ferdinand-Lassalle-Strasse 21, 7010 Leipzig.
Stadt-und Bezirksbibliothek, Mozartstrasse 1, 7010 Leipzig.
Bibliothek der Hansestadt Lübeck, Hundestrasse 5-17, 2400 Lübeck.
Stadtbibliothek, Bismarckstrasse 44-48, Postfach 212125, 6700 Ludwigshafen.
Stadt-und Kreisbibliothek, Strasse d DSF 8, 2800 Ludwigslust.
Ratsbücherei, Am Marienplatz 3, Postfach 2540, 2120 Lüneburg.
Stadt-und Bezirksbibliothek, Weitlingstrasse Ia, 3010 Magdeburg.
Stadtbibliothek, Rheinallee 3b, 6500 Mainz 1.
Stadtbücherei, N 3, 4 (Dalberghaus), Postfach 5868, 6800 Mannheim 1.
Stadt-und Kreisbibliothek, Ernestiner Strasse 38, Meiningen.
Stadbibliothek, Blücherstrasse 6, Postfach 85, 4050 Mönchengladbach.
Stadt-und Kreisbibliothek, 5700 Mühlhausen.
Stadtbücherei, Friedrich-Ebert-Strasse 47, Postfach 011620, 4330 Mülheim.
Bayerische Staatsbibliothek, Ludwigstrasse 16, 8000 Munich 22.
Münchner Städtische Bibliotheken, Rosenheimerstrasse 5, 8000 Munich 80.
Stadtbücherei, Alter Steinweg 7, Postfach 5909, 4400 Münster.
Stadtbibliothek, Zentralbibliothek, Egidienplatz 23, 8500 Nuremberg.
Stadtbücherei, Langemarkstrasse 19-21, 4200 Oberhausen 1.
Stadt-und Kreisbibliothek, Strasse d Friedens 54, 1400 Oranienburg.
Stadt-und Kreisbibliothek, August-Wolf-Strasse 10, 4300 Quedlinburg.
Bischöfliche Zentralbibliothek, St Petersweg 11-13, 8400 Regensburg.
Stadtbücherei, Haidplatz 8, 8400 Regensburg.
Stadt-und Berzirksbibliothek, Kröpeliner Strasse 82, 2500 Rostock.
Stadt-und Kreisbibliothek, Schulplatz 13, 6820 Rudolstadt.
Stadtbibliothek, Nauwieser Strasse 5, 6600 Saarbrücken.
Kreisbibliothek Schwerin-Land, Wismarsche Strasse 144, 2750 Schwerin.
Stadt-und Kreisbibliothek, Schloss, 5400 Sondershausen.
Stadtbücherei, Konrad-Adenauer-Strasse 2, 7000 Stuttgart 1.
Stadtbücherei, Brunnenstrasse 3, 7400 Tübingen.
Stadtbibliothek, Weinhof 12, 7900 Ulm.
Stadtbibliothek, Steubenstrasse 1, 5300 Weimar.
Stadtbibliothek, Rathauspassage, 6200 Wiesbaden.
Stadtbibliothek, Kolpingstrasse 8, 5600 Wuppertal 1.
Städtbucherei, Max-Heim-Bücherei, Haus zum Falken, 8700 Würzburg.
Stadtbibliothek, 540 Zwickau.

GHANA

Central Reference and Research Library, PO Box M 32, Accra.

GREECE

Ethnike Bibliotheke tes Hellados, Odos Venizelou 32, 106 79 Athens.

GUATEMALA

Biblioteca Nacional de Guatemala, 5a Avenida 7-26, Guatemala City.

HAITI

Bibliothèque Nationale d'Haiti, 193 Rue du Centre, Port-au-Prince.

HONDURAS

Biblioteca Nacional de Honduras, 6a Avenida Salvador Mendieta, Tegucigalpa.

MUSIC LIBRARIES
HUNGARY

Állami Gorkij Könyvtar (Gorky State Library), Molnár u 11, 1056 Budapest.
Magyar tudományos Akadémia Zenetudományi Intézete (Institute for Musicology of the Hungarian Academy of Sciences), Táncsis M u 7, 1014 Budapest.
Magyar Zeneműveszek Szövetsége (Association of Hungarian Composers), Vörösmarty tér 1 1364, PO Box 47, 1051 Budapest.
Országos Széchémyi Könyvtar (National Széchényi Library), 1 Budavári Palota F-épület, 1827 Budapest.

ICELAND

Landsbokasafn Islands (National Library of Iceland), Reykjavík.

INDIA

National Library, Belvedere, Calcutta 700027.

INDONESIA

Perpustakaan Nasional (National Library of Indonesia), J1 Salemba Raya 28, PO Box 3624, Jakarta 10002.

IRAN

National Library of Iran, 30 Tir Street, Tehran 11364.

IRAQ

National Library, Bab-el-Muaddum, Baghdad.

ISRAEL

AMLI Library of Music, 23 Arlosoroff Street, Haifa.
Jewish National and University Library, PO Box 503, 91004 Jerusalem.
AMLI Central Library for Music and Dance, 26 Bialik Street, 65241 Tel Aviv.

ITALY

Biblioteca Civica, Via Tripoli 16, 15100 Alessandria.
Archivio di Stato di Ancona, Via Maggini 80, 60127 Ancona.
Biblioteca Comunale Luciano Benincasa, Via Bernabei 32, 60121 Ancona.
Biblioteca della Città di Arezzo, Via dei Pileati-Palazzo Pretorio, 52100 Arezzo.
Archivio di Stato de Bari, Via Pasubio 137, 70124 Bari.
Biblioteca Nazionale "Sagarriga-Visconti-Volpi", Palazzo Ateneo, Piazza Umberto, 70100 Bari.
Biblioteca Civica A Mai, Piazza Vecchia 15, 24100 Bergamo.
Archivio di Stato di Bologna, Piazza dei Celestini 4, 40123 Bologna.
Universitaria di Bologna, Biblioteca, Via Zamboni 35, 40126 Bologna.
Civica Biblioteca Queriniana, Via Mazzini 1, 25100 Brescia.
Archivio di Stato di Cagliari, Via Gallura 2, 09125 Cagliari.
Biblioteca Universitaria, Via Università 32A, 09100 Cagliari.
Archivio di Stato di Catania, Via Vittorio Emanuele 156, 95131 Catania.
Biblioteca Regionale Universitaria, Piazza Università 2, 95124 Catania.
Biblioteca Riunite Civica e A Ursino Recupero, Via Biblioteca 13, 95124 Catania.
Biblioteca Comunale, Via Indipendenza 87, 22100 Como.
Biblioteca Statale e Libreria Civica, Via Ugolani Dati 4, 26100 Cremona.
Biblioteca Comunale Arisotea, Via Scienze 17, 44100 Ferrara.
Archivio di Stato di Firenze, Loggiato degli riffizi, 50100 Florence.
Biblioteca Medicea-Laurenziana, Piazza S Lorenzo 9, 50100 Florence.
Biblioteca Nazionale Centrale, Piazza Cavalleggeri 1B, 50122 Florence.
Biblioteca Comunale "A Saffi", Corso della Repubblica 72, 47100 Forlì.
Archivio di Stato di Genova, Via Teatro Regio 14, 16123 Genoa.
Biblioteca Durazzo Giustiniani, Via Balbi 1, 16126 Genoa.
Biblioteca Comunale "Labronica" Francesco Domenico Guerrazzi, Villa Fabbricotti, Viale della Libertà 30, 57100 Livorno.
Biblioteca Statale di Lucca, Via S Maria Corteorlandini 12, 55100 Lucca.
Biblioteca Comunale, Via Roberto Ardigò 13, 46100 Mantua.
Biblioteca Regionale, Via dei Verdi 71, 98122 Messina.
Archivio de Stato di Milano, Via Senato 10, 20121 Milan.
Biblioteca Comunale, Palazzo Sormani, Corso di Porta Vittoria 32, 20133 Milan.
Raccolte storiche del Comune di Milano, Biblioteca e Archivio, Palazzo De Marchi, Via Borgonuovo 23, 20121 Milan.
Biblioteca Estense, Palazzo dei Musei, Piazza S Agostino 309, 41100, Modena.
Archivio di Stato di Napoli, Piazzetta Grande Archivio 5, 80138 Naples.
Biblioteca Nazionale "Vittorio Emanuele III", Palazzo Reale, 80133 Naples.
Biblioteca Civica, Via Arto Botanico 5, 35123 Padua.

MUSIC LIBRARIES

Archivio di Stato di Palermo, Corso Vittorio Emanuele 31, 90133 Palermo.
Biblioteca Centrale della Regione Siciliana, Corso Vittoria Emanuele 429-431, 90134 Palermo.
Biblioteca Comunale, Piazza Brunaccini, 90100 Palermo.
Biblioteca Palatina, Palazzo della Pilotta, 4300 Parma.
Istituto Nazionale di Studi Verdiani, Strada della Repubblica 56, 43100 Parma.
Biblioteca Civica, Piazza, Petrarca 2, 27100 Pavia.
Biblioteca Universitaria, Palazzo dell'Università, 27100 Pavia.
Biblioteca Augusta del Domune di Perugia, Palazzo Conestabile della Staffa, Via delle Prome 15, 06100 Perugia.
Biblioteca Comunale Passerini Landi, Via Neve 3, 29100 Piacenza.
Biblioteca Universitaria, Via Curtatone e Montanara 15, 56100 Pisa.
Biblioteca Comunale Forteguerriana, Piazza della Sapienza 1, PO Box 177, Pistoia.
Biblioteca Comunale Classense, Via Baccarini 3, 48100 Ravenna.
Biblioteca Municipale "A Panizzi", Via Farini 3, 42100 Reggio Emilia.
Biblioteca Civica Gambalunga, Via Gambalunga 27, Rimini.
Archivio Centrale dello Stato, Piazzale degli Archivi, EUR, 00144 Rome.
Biblioteca Comunale degli Intronati, Via della Sapienza 5, 53100 Siena.
Biblioteca dell'Archivio di Stato di Trento, Via Roma 51, Trento.
Biblioteca Comunale, Via Roma 51, 38100 Trento.
Biblioteca Comunale, Borgo Cavour 18, 31100 Treviso.
Archivio di Stato di Trieste, Via Lamarmora 17, 34139 Trieste.
Archivio de Stato di Torino, 10100 Turin Centro.
Biblioteca Reale, Piazza Castello 191, 10100 Turin.
Biblioteche Civiche e Raccolte Storiche, Via Cittadella 5, 10122 Turin.
Biblioteca Comunale Joppi, Piazza Marconi 8, 33100 Udine.
Biblioteca Universitaria, Via Aurelio Saffi 2, 61029 Urbino.
Biblioteca del Civico Museo Correr, Piazza San Marco 52, Procuratie Nuove, 30100 Venice.
Biblioteca Nazionale Marciana, Palazzi della libreria Vecchia e della Zecca, San Marco 7, 30124 Venice.
Biblioteca Civica, Via Cappello 43, 37121 Verona.
Biblioteca Civica Bertoliana, Via Riale 5-13, 36100 Vicenza.

JAMAICA

Institute of Jamaica, Library, 12-16 East Street, Kingston.

JAPAN

Hiroshima Prefectural Library, 2020 Kami-Nobori-machi, Hiroshima.
Kyoto Prefectural Library, Okazaki Park, Kyoto Shi, Kyoto.
Osaka Prefectural Nakanoshima Library, 1-2-10 Nakanoshima, Kita-ku, Osaka.
National Diet (Parliament) Library, 10-1, Nagatacho 1-chome, Chiyoda-ku, Tokyo 100.
Tokyo Metropolitan Central Library, 5-7-13 Minami-Azabu, Minato-ku, Tokyo 106.

JORDAN

Greater Amman Public Library, PO Box 182181, Amman.

KAMPUCHEA

Bibliothèque nationale, BP 4, Phnom Penh.

KENYA

Central Government Archives, PO Box 30050, Nairobi.
Kenya National Archives, PO Box 49210, Moi Avenue, Nairobi.

KOREA (NORTH)

Grand People's Study House (National Library), PO Box 200, Pyongyang.

KOREA (SOUTH)

National Central Library, 60-1, Panpo-Dong, Seocho-Gu, Seoul.

LAOS

Bibliothèque Nationale, BP 704, Vientiane.

LEBANON

Bibliothèque Nationale du Liban, Place de l'Etoile, Beirut.

MUSIC LIBRARIES

LIBYA

National Library of Libya, PO Box 9127, Benghazi.

LUXEMBOURG

Bibliothèque Nationale, 37 Boulevard F D Roosevelt, 2450 Luxembourg.

MALAYSIA

Perpustakaan Negara Malaysia (National Library of Malaysia), Wisma-Thakurdas/Sachdev, Jl Raja Laut, 50572 Kuala.

MEXICO

Asociacion Musical Manuel M Ponce, AC, Bucareli No 12, Desp 411, Mexico City, DF.
Biblioteca Nacional de México, Insurgentes Sur s/n, Centro Cultural, Ciudad Universitaria, Del Coyoacán, 04510.

MONACO

Bibliothèque Louis Notari, 8 Rue Louis Notari, Monte Carlo.

MOROCCO

Bibliothèque Générale et Archives, BP 1003, Avenue Ibn Battouta, Rabat.

MYANMAR

National Library, Town Hall, Rangoon.

NETHERLANDS

Maatschappij tot Bevordering der Toonkunst (Society for the Advancement of Music), le Jac Van Campenstraat 59, 1072 BD Amsterdam.
Openbare Bibliotheken (Public Library), Centraale Bibliotheek, Prinsengracht 587, 1016 HT Amsterdam.
Stichting Arnhemse Openbare en Gelderse Welenschappelijke Bibliotheek (Arnhem Public and Learned Library of Gelderland), Koningstraat 26 681 DG, PO Box 1168, 6810 ML Arnhem.
Stichting Samenwerkende Openbare Bibliotheken, Kruissstraat 71, 2611 ML Delft.
Openbare Bibliotheek, Brink 70, 7411 BW Deventer.
Gemeenschappelijke Openbare Bibliotheek, Piazza 201, 5611 AG Eindhoven.
Openbare Bibliotheek, H B Blijdensteinstichting, Pijpennstraat 15, 7511 GM Enschede.
Stichting Openbare Bibliotheek, postbus 30004, 9700 RE Groningen.
Openbare Bibliotheek, Doelenplein 1, 2011 XR Haarlem.
Koninklijke Bibliothek (Royal Library), PO Box 90407, Prins Willen-Alexanderhof 5, 2509 LK, The Hague.
Openbare Bibliotheek, Bilderdijkstraat 1-3, 2513 CM The Hague.
Stichting Openbare Bibliotheek, Hinthamerstraat 72, 5211 MR's-Hertogenbosch.
Stichting Openbare Bibliotheken, 's-Gravelandseweg 55, 1217 EH Hilversum.
Stichting Centrale Bibliotheekdienst voor Friesland, Zuiderkruisweg 2, postbus 530, 8901 BH Leeuwarden.
Stadsbibliotheek, Nieuwenhofstraat 1, 6211 KG Maastricht.
Gemeenschappelijke Openbare Bibliotheek, Ridderstraat 29, 6511 TM Nijmegen.
Gemeentebibliothek, Hoogstraat 110, 3011 PV Rotterdam.
Rotterdamsch Leeskabinet, Bibliotheek, Burg Oudlaan 50(16), postbus 1738, 3000 DR Rotterdam.
Openbare Bibliotheek, Koningsplein 1, 5038 WG Tilburg.
Gemeentelijke Utrechtse Openbare Bibliotheek, Oude Gracht 167, 3511 AL Utrecht.

NEW ZEALAND

Auckland Public Library, Lorne Street, PO Box 4138, Auckland 1.
Canterbury Public Library, Orford Terrace and Gloucester Street, PO Box 1466, Christchurch 1.
Dunedin Public Library, Moray Place, PO Box 5542, Dunedin.
National Library of New Zealand, 44 The Terrace, Private Bag, Wellington 1.
Wellington Public Library, Mercer Street, PO Box 1992, Wellington 1.

NICARAGUA

Biblioteca nacional, C del Triunfo 302, Apdo 101, Managua.

NIGERIA

National Library of Nigeria, 4 Wesley Street, Private Mail Bag, 12626, Lagos.

MUSIC LIBRARIES

NORWAY

Bergen offentlige bibliotek, Hordaland fylkesbibliotek, Strømgaten 6, 5000 Bergen.
Drammen folkebibliotek, Gamle Kirke plass 7, Postboks 1136, 3001 Drammen.
Kristiansands folkebibliotek, Radhusgate 11, Postboks 476, 4601 Kristiansand.
Deichmanske Bibliotek, Henrik Ibsens gate 1, 0179 Oslo 1.
Norweigan Music Information Centre, 69 Toftesgate, N-0552 Oslo 5.
Universitetsbiblioteket og Norges Nasjonalbiblioteket, Drammensun 42, 0255 Oslo.
Rogaland fylkesbibliotek, Haakon VII's gate 11, Postboks 310/320, 4001 Stavanger.
Sør-Trøndelag folkebibliotek, Søndregate 5 og Kongensgate 2, Postboks 926, 7001 Trondheim.

PAKISTAN

National Library of Pakistan, Constitution Avenue, PO Box 1982, Islamabad.
Punjab Public Library, Library Road, Lahore 1884.

PANAMA

Biblioteca Nacional, Apdo 2444, Panama City 1892.

PARAGUAY

Biblioteca y Archivo Nacionales, Mariscal Estigarriba 95, Asuncion.

PERU

Biblioteca Nacional del Perú, Avenida Abancay S/N, Apdo 2335, Lima.

PHILIPPINES

National Library, Ermita, T M Kalaw Street, Naila.

POLAND

Biblioteka Slaska (Silesian Library), ul Francuska 12, 529, 40956 Katowice.
Wojewódzka i Miejska Biblioteka Publiczna (District and City Library), ul Warszawska 45, 40010 Katowice.
Biblioteka w Krakowie PAN (Library of the Polish Academy of Sciences), ul Slawkowska 17, 31016 Krakow.
Miejska Biblioteka Publiczna (City Library), ul Franciskanska 1, 31004 Krakow.
Miejska Biblioteka Publiczna im L Warynskiego, Gdańska 102, 90508 Lodz.
Wojewodzka i Miejska Biblioteka Publiczna im H Lopacinskiego, ul Narutowicza 4, 20950 Lublin.
Miejska Biblioteka Publiczna im Edwarda Raczynskiego, Pl Wolnosci 19, 60967 Poznań.
Wojewodzka i Miejska Biblioteka Publiczna im St Staszica, ul Podgórna 15, 70952 Szczecin.
Wojewodzka Biblioteka Publiczna i Ksiaeznica miejska, ul J Slowackiego 8, 87100 Toruń.
Biblioteka Narodowa, Centraina Biblioteka Państwa, Hankiewicza 1, 00973 Warsaw.
Biblioteka Publiczna m st Warszawy, ul Koszykowa 26, 00950 Warsaw.
Towarzystwo im Fryderyka Chopina (Frederic Chopin Society), Ostrogski Palais, Okólnik 1, 00368 Warsaw.
Wojewodzka i Miejska Biblioteka Publiczna im T Mikulskiego, Rynek 58, 50116 Wroclaw.

PORTUGAL

Biblioteca Municipal Central, Largo do Campo Pequeno, Palácio Galveias, 1000 Lisbon.
Biblioteca Nacional, Rua Ocidental do Campo Grande 83, 1751 Lisbon.

RUMANIA

Academia Romania Library, Calea Victoriei 125, Sect 1, 71102 Bucharest.
Biblioteca centrală de stat, str Ion Ghica 4, Bucharest.

RUSSIA

Russian State Library, Vozdvizhenka 3, 101000 Moscow.

SINGAPORE

National Library, Stamford Road, Singapore 0617.

MUSIC LIBRARIES

SLOVAKIA

Matica slovenska Kniǧica (Slovak National Library), Hostihora, 03652 Martin.

SOUTH AFRICA

Cape Town City Libraries, Mayor's Garden, Longmarket Street, PO Box 4728, Cape Town 8000.
South African Library, Queen Victoria Street, Cape Town 8001.
Durban Municipal Library, Smith Street, City Hall, PO Box 917, Durban 4000.
Johannesburg Public Library, Market Square, Johannesburg 2001.
Pretoria Public Library, 159 Andries Street, Pretoria 0002.
State Library, 239 Vermeulen Street, PO Box 397, Pretoria 0001.

SPAIN

Biblioteca Pública, "F Bonnemaison de Verdaguer i Callis", Baja de San Pedro 7, Barcelona.
Biblioteca Pública Provincial, Plaza de San Juan, Burgos.
Biblioteca Pública Provincial, Avenida Ramón Carranza 16 Diputacion, pe Espana, Cádiz.
Biblioteca Pública del Estado, Jardines del Salón, s/n, Apdo Oficial, Granada.
Biblioteca Pública del Estado, Santa Nonia 5, Casa de Cultura, León.
Biblioteca del Ministerio de Cultura, Calle San Marcos 40, 5A, 28004 Madrid.
Biblioteca Municipal del Ayuntamiento, Fuencarral 78, Madrid 4.
Biblioteca Nacional, Paseo de Recoletos 20, 28001 Madrid.
Real Academia de Bellas Artes de San Fernando, Biblioteca, Alcala 13, 28014 Madrid.
Biblioteca Pública, Ramón Llull 3, Palma de Mallorca.
Biblioteca Pública e Archivo Distrital de Ponta Delgada, Rua Ernest do Canto, Ponta Delgada, San Miguel.
Biblioteca de Menéndez Pelayo, Rubio 6, Santander.
Biblioteca Pública del Estado, Alfonso XII 19, 41001 Seville.
Biblioteca Provincial, Paseo del Misadero, Toledo.
Biblioteca Pública Provincial, Paseo de la Florida 9, Victoria.
Biblioteca Pública de la Ciudad, Plaza de los Sitios 5, Zaragoza.

SRI LANKA

National Museum Library, Sir Marcus Fernando Mawatha, PO Box 854, Colombo 7.

SWEDEN

Gävle stadsbibliotek, Södra Strandgatan 6, Box 801, 80130 Gävle.
Göteborgs stadsbibliotek, Box 5404, 40229 Göteborg.
Helsingborgs stadsbibliotek, Bollbrogatan, S-25225 Helsingborg.
Malmö stadsbibliotek, Regementsgatan 3, 21142 Malmö.
Norrköpings stadsbibliotek, Södra Promenaden 105, 60181 Norrköping.
Örebros stadsbibliotek, Nabbtorgsgatan 12, 70114 Örebro.
Kungliga Biblioteket (Royal Library), Humlegården, Box 5039, 10241 Stockholm.
Kungliga Musikaliska akademien (Royal Academy of Music), Library, Blasieholmstorg 8, 11148 Stockholm.
Uppsala stadsbibliotek, Östra Ågatan 19, Box 643, 75127 Uppsala.
Västerås stadsbibliotek, Biskopsgatan 2, Box 717, 72120 Västerås.

SWITZERLAND

Allgemeine Bibliotheken der GGG, Rümelinsplatz 6, Postfach, 4051 Basel.
Berner Volksbücherie, Monbijoustrasse 45a, Postfach 2267, 3001 Bern.
Schweizerische Landesbibliothek, Hallwylstrasse 15, 3003 Bern.
Stadtbibliothek, Dufourstrasse 26, 2502 Biel.
Bibliothèques municipales, 16 Place de la Madeleine, 1204 Geneva.
Bibliothèque municipale, 11 Place Chauderon, 1003 Lausanne.
Stadtbibliothek, Kauffmannweg 4, 6003 Lucerne.
Biblithèque publique et universitaire, 3 Place Numa-Droz, 2000 Neuchâtel.
Stadtbibliothek, Hauptgasse 12, 4600 Olten.
Stadtbibliothek, Goldsteinstrasse 15, Postfach 91, 82025 Schaffhausen.
Stadtbibliothek, Museumstrasse 52, 8401 Winterthur.
Pestalozzi-Bibliothek, Zahingerstrasse 17, 8001 Zürich.

SYRIA

Al Maktabah Al Wataniah (National Library), Bab El-Faradj, Aleppo.
Al Zahiriah National Library, Bab el Barid, Damascus.

THAILAND

Ho Samut Haeng Chat (National Library of Thailand), Samsen Road, Bangkok 10300.

MUSIC LIBRARIES

TUNISIA

Dar al-Katub Al-Watanlyya/Bibliothèque Nationale, Ministere des Affaires Culturelles, 20 souk El Attarine, 1008 Tunis.

TURKEY

Milli Kütüphane (National Library), Bahçelievier, Ankara.
Beyazit Deviet Kütüyshanesi (Beyazit State Library), Imaret Sok 18, Istanbul.

UK

Aberdeen Central Library, Rosemount Viaduct, Aberdeen, Scotland AB9 1GU.
National Library of Wales, Aberystwyth, Wales SY23 3BU.
Belfast Public Library, Royal Avenue, Belfast, Northern Ireland BT1 1EK.
Birmingham Central Library, Chamberlain Square, Birmingham B3 3HQ.
Bristol Central Library, College Green, Bristol BS1 5TL.
Cardiff Central Library, The Hayes, Cardiff, Wales CF1 2QU.
Carmarthen Public Library, St Peter's Street, Carmarthen, Wales SA31 1LN.
Dundee Central Library, The Wellgate, Dundee, Scotland DD1 1DB.
Edinburgh Central Library, George IV Bridge, Edinburgh, Scotland EG1 1EG.
National Library of Scotland, George IV Bridge, Edinburgh, Scotland EH1 1EW.
Mitchell Library, North Street, Glasgow, Scotland G3 7DN.
Leeds Central Library, Calverley Street, Municipal Building, Leeds LS1 3AB.
Liverpool Central Library, William Brown Street, Liverpool L3 8EW.
British Library, Music Library, Reference Division, Great Russell Street, London WC1B 3DG.
English Folk Dance and Song Society, Cecil Sharp House, Library, 2 Regent's Park Road, London NW1 7AY.
Manchester Central Library, St Peter's Square, Manchester M4 5PD.
Newcastle upon Tyne Central Library, Princess Square, Newcastle upon Tyne NE99 1MC.

USA

ALABAMA

Birmingham Public Library, 2100 Park Place, Birmingham, AL 35203.

ARIZONA

City of Phoenix Public Library, 12 East McDowell Road, Phoenix, AZ 85004.

CALIFORNIA

Los Angeles Public Library, 630 West 5th Street, Los Angeles, CA 90071.
California State Library, PO Box 942837, Sacramento, CA 94237.
Sacramento Public Library, 1010 8th Street, Sacramento, CA 95814.
San Diego Public Library, 820 E Street, San Diego, CA 92101.
San Francisco Public Library, Civic Center, San Francisco, CA 94102.

COLORADO

Denver Public Library, 1357 Broadway, Denver, CO 80203.

CONNECTICUT

Connecticut State Library, 231 Capitol Avenue, Hartford, CT 06106.

DISTRICT OF COLUMBIA

Library of Congress, Music Division, Washington, DC 20540.

FLORIDA

Miami-Dade Public Library, 101 West Flagler Street, Miami, FL 33130.

GEORGIA

Atlanta-Fulton Public Library, 1 Margaret Mitchell Square, North West, Atlanta, GA 30303.

ILLINOIS

Chicago Public Library, 425 North Michigan Avenue, Chicago, IL 60611.
Illinois State Library, Springfield, IL 62756.

INDIANA

Indiana State Library, 140 North Senate Avenue, Indianapolis, IN 46204.

MUSIC LIBRARIES

Indianapolis-Marion County Public Library, 40 East St Clair Street, PO Box 211, Indianapolis, IN 46206.

KENTUCKY

Louisville Free Public Library, 301 York Street, Louisville, KY 40203.

LOUISANA

New Orleans Public Library, 219 Loyola Avenue, New Orleans, LA 70140.

MARYLAND

Enoch Pratt Free Library, 400 Cathedral Street, Baltimore, MD 21201.

MASSACHUSETTS

Boston Public Library, Copley Square, Boston, MA 02117.
State Library of Massachusetts, 341 State House, Boston, MA 02133.

MICHIGAN

Detroit Public Library, 5201 Woodward Avenue, Detroit, MI 48202.
Library of Michigan, 735 East Michigan Avenue, PO Box 30007, Lansing, MI 48909.

MINNESOTA

Minneapolis Public Library, 300 Nicollet Mall, Minneapolis, MN 55401.
St Paul Public Library, 90 West 4th Street, St Paul, MN 55102.

MISSOURI

Missouri State Libray, 2002 Missouri Boulevard, Jefferson City, MO 65102.
Kansas City Public Library, 311 East 12th Street, Kansas City, MO 64106.
St Louis Public Library, 1301 Olive Street, St Louis, MO 63103.

NEW HAMPSHIRE

New Hampshire State Library, 20 Park Street, Concord, NH 03301.

NEW JERSEY

Newark Public Library, PO Box 630, Newark, NJ 07101.
New Jersey State Library, 185 West State Street, Trenton, NJ 08625.

NEW MEXICO

New Mexico State Library, 325 Don Gaspar, Santa Fe, NM 87503.

NEW YORK

New York State Library, Albany, NY 12230.
Buffalo and Erie County Public Library, Lafayette Square, Buffalo, NY 14203.
New York Public Library, Fifth Avenue and 42nd Street, New York, NY 10018.
Rochester Public Library, 115 South Avenue, Rochester, NY 14604.

OHIO

Public Library of Cincinnati and Hamilton County, 800 Vine Street, Library Square, Cincinnati, OH 45202.
Cleveland Public Library, 325 Superior Avenue, Cleveland, OH 44114.
Columbus Metropolitan Library, 28 South Hamilton Road, Columbus, OH 43213.
State Library of Ohio, 65 South Front Street, Columbus, OH 43215.

OREGON

Oregon State Library, State Library Building, Salem, OR 97310.

PENNSYLVANIA

State Library of Pennsylvania, PO Box 1601, Harrisburg, PA 17105.
Free Library of Philadelphia, Logan Square, Philadelphia, PA 19103.
Carnegie Libray of Pittsburgh, 4400 Forbes Avenue, Pittsburgh, PA 15213.

RHODE ISLAND

Providence Public Library, 225 Washington Street, Providence, RI 02903.

MUSIC LIBRARIES

TENNESSEE

Memphis and Shelby County Public Library, 1850 Peabody Avenue, Memphis, TN 38104.

TEXAS

Austin Public Library, 800 Guadalupe Street, Box 2287, Austin, TX 78768.
Dallas Public Library, 1515 Young Street, Dallas, TX 75201.
Houston Public Library, 500 McKinney Avenue, Houston, TX 77002.

VIRGINIA

Richmond Public Library, 101 East Franklin Street, Richmond, VA 23219.
Virginia State Library, 11th Street at Capitol Square, Richmond, VA 23219.

WASHINGTON

Washington State Library, Olympia, WA 98504.
Seattle Public Library, 1000 4th Avenue, Seattle, WA 98104.

WISCONSIN

Milwaukee Public Library, 814 West Wisconsin Avenue, Milwaukee, WI 53233.

URUGUAY

Biblioteca Nacional del Uruguay, 18 de Julio 1790, Casilla 452, Montevideo.

VENEZUELA

Biblioteca Nacional, Bolsa a San Francisco, Apdo 68350, Caracas 106.

VIETNAM

National Library, 31 Rue Trang-Thi, Hanoi 1918.
National Library II, 69 Gia-Long Street, Ho Chi Minh City 1976.

APPENDIX G

Music Conservatories

AFGHANISTAN

Kabul: Kabul Art School, Dept of Music, Bibi Mahro, Kabul.

ALBANIA

Tirana: Instituti i Lartë i Arteve (Institute of Fine Arts), Faculty of Music, Tirana.

ALGERIA

Algiers: Conservatoire de Musique et de Déclamation, 2 Boulevard Ché Guévara, Algiers.
Oran: Conservatoire Municipal de Musique et de Déclamation, 5 Rue d'igli, Oran.

ARGENTINA

Buenos Aires: Conservatorio Provincial de Música de Bahía Blanca, Belgrano 446, 800 Bahía Blanca, Provincia de Buenos Aires.
Conservatorio de Música "Julián Aguirre", Gral Rodriguez 7672, Banfield, Provincia de Buenos Aires.
Conservatorio Municipal de Música "Manuel de Falla", Sarmiento 1551, 1042 Buenos Aires.
Conservatorio Nacional de Música, "Carlos Lopez Buchardo", Callao 1521, 1024 Buenos Aires.
Instituto Santa Ana, Department of Music, Avenida del Libertador 6115/95, Buenos Aires.
Pontificia Universidad Católica Argentin "Santa Maria de los Buenos Aires", Faculty of Arts and Music, Juncal 1912, Buenos Aires 1116.
Chascomús: Conservatorio de Música de Chascomús, Lavalle 281, Chascomús, Provincia de Buenos Aires.
Chivilcoy: Conservatorio Provincial de Música de Chivilcoy, Calle Frias 37, 6620 Chivilcoy, Provincia de Buenos Aires.
La Plata: Conservatorio Provincial Gilardo Gilardi, Calle 49/e/6v7, 1900 La Plata, Provincia de Buenos Aires.
Mar del Plata: Conservatorio Provincial de Música, 25 de Mayo y San Luis, 7600 Marl del Plata, Provincia de Buenos Aires.
Mendoza: Universidad Nacional de Cuyo, Escuela Superior de Música, Lavalle 373, 5500 Mendoza.
Morón: Conservatorio de Música de Morón, San Martin 370, 1708 Morón, Provincia de Buenos Aires.
Resistencia: Consejo Gral de Educación, Escuela de Música, Avenida 9 de Julio 321, 3500 Resistencia, Provincia del Chaco.

AUSTRALIA

AUSTRALIAN CAPITAL TERRITORY

Canberra: Canberra School of Music, GPO Box 804, ACT 2603.

NEW SOUTH WALES

Newcastle: Newcastle Conservatorium of Music, Auckland Street, Newcastle, NSW 2300.
Sydney: New South Wales State Conservatorium of Music, Macquarie Street, Sydney NSW 2000.
University of Sydney, Department of Music, Sydney, NSW 2006.
Wollongong: Wollongong Conservatorium "Gleniffer Brae", Murphries Road, Wollongong, NSW 2500.

QUEENSLAND

Brisbane: Queensland Conservatorium of Music, 259 Vulture Street, South Brisbane, Queensland 4101.
St Lucia: University of Queensland, Faculty of Music, St Lucia, Queensland 4067.

SOUTH AUSTRALIA

Adelaide: University of Adelaide, Elder Conservatorium of Music, GPO Box 498, Adelaide, SA 5001.

TASMANIA

Hobart: Tasmanian Conservatorium of Music, GPO Box 252 C, Hobart, Tasmania 7001.

VICTORIA

Melbourne: Victorian College of the Arts, 234 St Kilda Road, Melbourne, Victoria 3004.

MUSIC CONSERVATORIES

Parkville:	University of Melbourne, Faculty of Music, Parkville, Victoria 3052.

WESTERN AUSTRALIA

Nedlands:	University of Western Australia, Department of Music, Nedlands, WA 6009.

AUSTRIA

Graz:	Hochschule für Musik und Darstellende Kunst, Leonhardstrasse 15, A-8010 Graz.
Innsbruck:	Konservatorium der Stadt Innsbruck, Museumstrasse 17a, 6020 Innsbruck.
Klagenfurt:	Kärntner Landeskonservatorium, Miesstalerstrasse 8, A-9021 Klagenfurt.
Linz:	Bruckner-Konservatorium des Landes Oberösterreich, Postfach 95, 4041 Linz.
Salzburg:	Hochschule für Musik und Darstellende Kunst "Mozarteum", Mirabellplatz 1, A-5020 Salzburg.
Vienna:	Hochschule für Musik und Darstellende Kunst, Lothringerstrasse 18, Postfach 146, A-1037 Vienna III.
	Horak-Konservatorium für Musik und Darstellende Kunst, Hegelgasse 3, A-1010 Vienna
	Konservatorium für Musik und Dramatische Kunst, Mühlgasse 28-30, A-1040 Vienna.
	Konservatorium der Stadt Wien, Johannesgasse 4a, A-1010 Vienna 1.

BELGIUM

Antwerp:	Koninklijk Vlaams Conservatorium van Antwerpen, Desguinlei 25, B-2018 Antwerp.
Argenteuil-Waterloo:	Chapelle Musicale Reine Elisabeth, Chaussée de Tervuren 445, B-1410 Argenteuil-Waterloo.
Bruges:	Stedelijk Muziekconservatorium, Sint-Jacobsstratt 23, B-8000 Bruges.
Brussels:	Conservatoire Royal de Musique de Bruxelles, 30 Rue de la Régence, B-1000 Brussels.
	Koninklijk Muziekconservatorium van Brussel, Regentschapstraat 30, B-1000 Brussels.
Charleroi:	Conservatoire de Musique de Charleroi, 1 Rue Adolphe Biarrent, B-6000 Charleroi.
Ghent:	Conservatoire de Musique de Gand, 54 Rue de la Hoogpoort, B-9000 Ghent.
	Koninklijk Muziekconservatorium van Gent, Hoogpoort 64, B-9000 Ghent.
Huy:	Conservatoire de Musique de Huy, 11-13 Rue du Palais de Justice, B-5200 Huy.
Liège:	Conservatoire Royal de Musique de Liège, 14 Rue Forgeur, B-4000 Liège.
Louvain:	Stedelijk Muziekconservatorium, Koning Albertaan 50-52, B-3000 Louvain.
Mechelen:	Koninklijk Beiaardschool Jef Denyn, Frederik de Mersdestraat 63, B-2800 Mechelen.
	Stedelijk Muziekconservatorium, Melaan 3-5, B-2800 Mechelen.
Mons:	Conservatoire Royal de Musique de Mons, 7 Rue de Nimy, B-7000 Mons.
Namur:	Conservatoire de Musique, Chaussée de Louvain 121, B-5000 Namur.
	Institute de Musique Sacrée, 28 Rue Juppin, B-5000 Namur.
Ostend:	Conservatoire de Musique de Ostende, 36 Rue de Rome, B-8400 Ostend.
Tournai:	Conservatoire de Musique de Tournai, 2 Place Raine Astrid, B-7500 Tournai.
Verviers:	Conservatoire de Musique de Verviers, 6 Rue Chapuis, B-4800 Verviers.

BOLIVIA

La Paz:	Academia de Música Hohner, Calle Goitia 162, La Paz.
	Conservatorio Nacional de Música, Avenida 6 de Agosto, No 2092, La Paz.
	Escuela Superior de Bellas Artes, Calle Rosendo Gutierrez 323, La Paz.

BRAZIL

Bahia:	Instituto de Música de Bahia, Universidade Catolica de Salvador, Rua Carlos Gomes 400, Centro, 4000 Salvador, Bahia.
	Universidade Federal de Bahia, Escola de Música, Parque Universitario Edgard Santos, Canela, 40140, Salvador, Bahia.
Belo Horizonte:	Escola de Música-Minas Gerais, Rue Santa Catarina 466, 30000 Belo Horizonte, Mina Gerais.
	Universidade Federal de Minas Gerais, Escola de Música, Avenida Antônio Carlos 6627, Pampulha, 3000 Belo Horizonte, Minas Gerais.
Brasilia:	Fundaçao Universidade de Brasilia, Institute of Arts and Communication, Campus Universitário, Asa Norte, 70910 Brasilia, DF.
Paraiba:	Universidade Federal de Paraiba, Department of Music, Cidade Universitária, 5800 Joao Pessôa, Paraiba.
Paraná:	Escola de Música e Belas Artes do Paraná, Rua Emilian Perneta 179, 80000 Curitiba, Paraná.
	Faculdade de Música Mae de Deus, Avenida Sao Paulo 651, CP106, 86100 Londrina, Paraná.
Pelotas:	Instituto de Letras a Artes, Rua Marechal Floriano 179, 96100 Pelotas, RS.
Rio de Janeiro:	Conservatorio Brasileiro de Música, Avenida Graça Aranha 57, No 12, 20000 Rio de Janeiro.
	Universidade do Rio de Janeiro, Leters and Arts Center, Avenida Pasteur 296, 22290 Rio de Janeiro.
	Universidade Federal do Rio de Janeiro, Escola de Música, Rua do Passeio 98, Rio de Janeiro.
Sao Paulo:	Conservatorio Dramático e Musical de Sao Paulo, Avenida Sao Joao 269, Sao Paulo.
	Faculdade de Música "Sagrado Coracao de Jesus", Rua Caraibas 882, CP 8383, Villa Pompéia, Sao Paulo.
	Faculdade Santa Marcelina, Rua Dr Emilio Ribas 89, 05006 Sao Paulo.
	UNESP-Universidade Estadual Júlio de Mesquita Filho, Instituto do Artes do Planalto, Department of Music, Rua Dom Luis Lasagna, No 400, Sao Paulo.

MUSIC CONSERVATORIES

Universidade de Sao Paulo, Department of Music, Cidade Universitaria, Butanta, 05508 Sao Paulo.

BULGARIA

Plovdiv: Viss Musikalno-Pedagogiceski, Ul Todor Samodumov 2, Plovdiv 4025.
Sofia: Conservatoire Bulgare d'Etat, Sofia 1505.

CANADA

ALBERTA

Banff: Banff Centre, School of Fine Arts, Box 1020, Banff, Alberta, T0L 0C0.
Calgary: University of Calgary, Department of Music, 2500 University Drive, N W, Calgary, Alberta T2N 1NF
Edmonton: University of Alberta, Department of Music, Edmonton, Alberta T6G 2C9.
Lethbridge: University of Lethbridge, Department of Music, 4401 University Drive, Lethbridge, Alberta T1K 3M4.

BRITISH COLUMBIA

Burnaby: Simon Fraser University, Centre for the Arts, Burnaby, British Columbia V5A 1S6.
Vancouver: University of British Columbia, School of Music, 6361 Memorial Road, Vancouver, British Columbia V6T 1W5.
            Vancouver Academy of Music, Music Centre, Vanier Park, 1270 Chestnut Street, Vancouver, British Columbia V6J 4R9.
Victoria: University of Victoria, School of Music, PO Box 1700, Victoria, British Columbia V8W 2Y2.
            Victoria Conservatory of Music, 839 Academy Close, Victoria, British Columbia V8X 3Y1.

MANITOBA

Brandon: Brandon University, School of Music, Brandon, Manitoba R7A 6A9.
Winnipeg: University of Manitoba, School of Music, 65 Dafoe Road, Winnipeg, Manitoba R3T 2N2.

NEW BRUNSWICK

Moncton: Université de Moncton, Department of Music, Moncton, New Brunswick E1A 3E9.
Sackville: Mount Allison University, Department of Music, Sackville, New Brunswick E0A 3C0.

NOVA SCOTIA

Antigonish: St Francis Xavier University, Department of Music, Box 108, Antigonish, Nova Scotia B2G 1C0.
Halifax: Dalhousie University, Department of Music, Arts Centre, Room 514, Halifax, Nova Scotia B3H 3J5.
            Maritime Conservatory of Music, 5820 Spring Garden Road, Halifax, Nova Scotia B3H 1X8.
Wolfville: Acadia University, School of Music, Wolfville, Nova Scotia B0P 1X0.

ONTARIO

Guelph: University of Guelph, College of Arts, Department of Music, Room 207, Guelph, Ontario N1G 2W1.
Hamilton: McMaster University, Department of Music, 1280 Main Street West, Hamilton, Ontario L8S 4M2.
Kingston: Queen's University, School of Music, Kingston, Ontario K7L 3N6.
London: University of Western Ontario, Faculty of Music, London, Ontario N6A 3K7.
North York: York University, Department of Music, 4700 Keele Street, North York, Ontario M3J 1P3.
Ottawa: Carleton University, Department of Music, Colonel By Drive, Ottawa, Ontario K1S 5B6.
            University of Ottawa, Department of Music, Ottawa, Ontario K1N 6N5.
Toronto: Royal Conservatory of Music, 273 Bloor Street West, Toronto, Ontario M5S 1W2
            University of Toronto, Faculty of Music, Edward Johnson Building, Room 238, 80 Queen's Park Circle, Toronto, Ontario M5S 1A1.
Waterloo: Wilfrid Laurier University, Faculty of Music, 75 University Avenue West, Waterloo, Ontario N2L 3C5.
Windsor: University of Windsor, School of Music, 401 Sunset Avenue, Windsor, Ontario N9B 3P4.

QUÉBEC

Montréal: Concordia University, Department of Music, 7141 Sherbrooke Street West, Montréal, Québec H4B 1R6.
            McGill University, Faculty of Music, Strathcona Music Building, 555 Sherbrooke Street West, Montréal, Québec H3A 1E3.
            Université de Montréal, Faculty of Music, 2900 Boulevard Edouard-Montpetit, Montréal, Québec H3C 3J7.
Québec: Conservatoire de Musique de Québec, 270 St Amable, Québec G1R 5G1.
            Université Laval, Ecole de Musique, Cité Universitaire, Québec G1K 7P4.

SASKATCHEWAN

Regina: University of Regina, Department of Music, Regina, Saskatchewan S4S 0A2.
Saskatoon: University of Saskatchewan, Department of Music, Saskatoon S7N 0W0.

CHILE

Santiago: Conservatorio Nacional de Música, Compania, 1264, Santiago.
Pontificia Universidad Católica de Chile, Faculty of Architecture and Fine Arts, Avenida Alameda 340, Casilla 114-D, Santiago.
Universidad de Chile, Faculty of Fine Arts, Avenida Bernardo O'Higgins 1058, Casilla 10-D, Santiago.
Valparaiso: Universidad Católica de Valparaiso, Caonservatorio de Música, Avenida Brasil 2950, Valparaiso.

CHINA

Beijing: Central Conservatory of Music, 43 Baojiajie, Beijing.
Conservatory of Chinese Music, 17 Qianhaixijie, Beijing.
Chengdu: Sichuan Conservatory of Music, Xinnanmenwai, Chengdu.
Guangzhou: Guangzhou Xinghai Conservatory of Music, 48 Xianliedonghenglu, Guangzhou.
Harbin: Harbin Normal University, Department of Music, Harbin.
Lanzhou: Northwest Teacher's College, Department of Music, Lanzhou.
Nanjing: Nanjing Arts College, 15 Hujubeilu, Nanjing.
Shandong: Shandong Academy of Arts, Music Division, Shandong.
Shanghai: Shanghai Conservatory of Music, 20 Fen Yang Road, Shanghai 200031.
Shengyang: Shengyang Conservatory of Music, No 1, Section 2, San Hao Street, Peace District, Shenyang.
Tianjin: Tianjin Conservatory of Music, 5, 11th Meridian Road, Tianjin.
Wuhan: Wuhan Conservatory of Music, 255 Jiefanglu, Wuchang District, Wuhan.
Xian: Xian Conservatory of Music, 118 Changanzhonglu, Xian 710061.

COLOMBIA

Barranquilla: Universidad del Atlántico, Conservatorio de Música, Carrera 43, Nos 50-53, Apartado Nacional 148, Aéreo 1890, Barranquilla.
Bogotá: Conservatorio Nacional de Música, Departmento de Música, Facultad de Artes, Universidad Nacional, Bogatá.
Ibagué: Conservatorio de Música del Ibagué, Calle 9, No 1-18, Ibague.
Medellín: Corporación Universitaria Adventista, Department of Music, Carrera 84, No 33A, A-1 Medellín.
Universidad de Antioquia, Facultad de Artes, Departamento de Música, Apartado aéreo 1226, Medellín.

COSTA RICA

Heredia: Universidad Nacional, Escuela de Música, Apartado 86, Heredia.
San José: Universidad de Costa Rica, School of Fine Arts, San José.

CUBA

Havana: Instituto Superior de Arte, Facultad de Música, Calle 120, No 1110, Havana.

CZECH REPUBLIC

Brno: Janáčkova Akademie Mûzických Umeni (Janáček Academy of Music and Dramatic Arts), Komenskeho nam 6, 662 15 Brno.
Konservatoř v Brne (Brno Conservatory), Trida Kpt Jarose 43-45, Brno.
Ostrava: Konservatoř v Ostrave (Ostrava Conservatory), Hrabakova 1, Ostrava.
Prague: Konservatoř v Praze (Prague Conservatory), Na Rejdišti 1, 110 00 Prague.
Vysoká Skola Mûzických Umeni v Praha (Academy of Music and Dramatic Arts Prague), Dûm umělcû, Alsovo nábřeží 12, 1101 00 Prague 1.

DENMARK

Alborg: Nordjysk Musikkonservatorium (North Jutland Conservatory of Music), Ryesgade 52, 9000 Alborg.
Århus: Det Jydske Musikkonservatorium (The Royal Conservatory of Music), Fuglesangsalle 26, DK-8210 Århus V.
Copenhagen: Det Kongelige Danske Musikkonservatorium (The Royal Danish Conservatory of Music), Niels Brocksgade 7, 1574 Copenhagen V.
University of Copenhagen, Department of Music, Frue Plads, DK-1168 Copenhagen K.
Esbjerg: Vestjysk Musikkonservatorium (West Jutland Conservatory of Music), Islandsgade 50, DK-6700 Esbjerg.

MUSIC CONSERVATORIES

Odense: Det Fynske Musikkonservatorium (The Funen Conservatory of Music), Islandsgade 2, DK-5000 Odense C.

DOMINICAN REPUBLIC

Santo Domingo: Conservatorio Nacional de Música, Cesar Nicolas Penson, Santo Domingo.

ECUADOR

Quito: Conservatorio Nacional de Música-Quito, Carrión 514 y Reina Victoria, Quito.

EGYPT

Cairo: Cairo Conservatory of Music, Academy of Arts, Avenue of the Pyramids, Al Jizah.

EIRE

Dublin: Royal Irish Academy of Music, 36-38 Westland Row, Dublin 2.

EL SALVADOR

San Salvador: Centro Nacional de Artes "CENAR", Department of Music, 6A Avenida Norte 319, San Salvador.

ESTONIA

Tallinn: Tallinn State Conservatory, Vabaduse Pst 130, 200015 Tallinn.

ETHIOPIA

Addis Ababa: Yared National Institute of Music, c/o Ministry of Culture, PO Box 1902, Addis Ababa.

FINLAND

Åbo: Sibeliusmuseum, Musikvetenskapliga Institutionen vid Åbo Akademi (Sibelius Museum, Musicological Institution at Åbo Academy), Biskopsgatan 17 20500, Åbo 50.
Helsinki: Helsingin Konservatorio, Fredrikinkatu 34 B, SF-00100 Helsinki.
        Sibelius Academy of Music, Töölönkatu 28, SF-00260 Helsinki 26.
Jyväskylä: Keski-Suomen Konservatorio, Pitkäkatu 18-22, SF-40700 Jyväskylä.
Kuopio: Kuopion Konservatorio, Kuopionlahdenkatu 23 C, SF-70200 Kuopio.
Lahti: Paijat-Hameen Konservatorio, Sibeliuksenkatu 8, SF-15110 Lahti.
Oulu: Oulun Kaupungin Konservatorio, Lintulammentie 1 K, SF-90140 Oulu.
Tampere: Tampereen Konservatorio, F E Sillanpään Katu 9, 33230 Tampere.

FRANCE

Bordeaux: Conservatorie National de Région, Bordeaux, 22 Quai Saint Croix, F-33800 Bordeaux.
Dijon: Conservatoire National de Région, Dijon, 24 Boulevard Clemenceau, F-21000 Dijon.
Grenoble: Conservatoire National de Région, Grenoble, 6 Chemin de Gordes, F-38100 Grenoble.
Lille: Conservatoire National de Région, Lille, 48 Place du Concert, F-59800 Lille.
Limoges: Conservatoire National de Région, Limoges, 9 Rue Fritz-James, F-87000 Limoges.
Lyon: Conservatoire Natonal Supérieur de Musique de Lyon, 3 Rue de l'Angile, 69005 Lyon.
Marseille: Conservatoire National de Région, Marseille, 2 Place Carli, F-13001 Marseille.
Metz: Conservatoire National de Région, Metz, 2 Rue Paradis, F-57036 Metz.
Montpellier: Conservatoire National de Région, Montpellier, 14 Rue Eugene Lisbonne, F-34000 Montpellier.
Nancy: Conservatoire National de Région, Nancy, 3 Rue Michel Ney, F-54000 Nancy.
Nantes: Conservatoire National de Région, Nantes, Rue Gaëtan Rondeau Ile Beaulieu, F-44200 Nantes.
Nice: Conservatoire National de Région, Nice, 24 Boulevard de Cimiez, F-06000 Nice.
Paris: Conservatoire National Supérieur de Musique, 14 Rue de Madrid, F-75008 Paris.
        École Normale de Musique, 114 bis Boulevard Malesherbes, F-75017 Paris.
        Schola Cantorum, École Supérieure de Musique, de Danse et d'Art Dramatique, 269 Rue St Jacques, Paris.
Poitiers: Conservatoire National de Région, Poitiers, 5 Rue Franklin, F-86000 Poitiers.
Reims: Conservatoire National de Région, Reims, 14 Rue Carnot, F-51100 Reims.
Rennes: Conservatoire National de Région, Rennes, 26 Rue Hoche, F-35000 Rennes.
Rouen: Conservatoire National de Région, Rouen, 50 Avenue de la Porte des Champs, F-76000 Rouen.
Rueil-Malmaison: Conservatoire National de Région, Rueil-Malmaison, 182 Avenue Paul Doumer, F-92500 Rueil-Malmaison.
Strasbourg: Conservatoire National de Région, Strasbourg, 2 Avenue de la Marseillaise, F-67000 Strasbourg.

MUSIC CONSERVATORIES

Toulouse:	Conservatoire National de Région, Toulouse, 3 Rue Labéda, F-31000 Toulouse.
Tours:	Conservatoire National de Région, Tours, 17 Rue des Ursulines, F-37000 Tours.
Versailles:	Conservatoire National de Région, Versailles, 24 Rue de la Chancellerie, F-78000 Versailles.

GERMANY

Aachen:	Staatliche Hochschule für Musik Rheinland, Aachen, Grenzland-Institut, Aachen, Theaterstrasse 2-4, Aachen.
Augsburg:	Leopold-Mozart-Konservatorium, Augsburg, Maximilianstrasse 59, 8900 Augsburg.
Berlin:	Hochschule der Künste, Berlin, Ernst-Reuter-Platz 10, 1000 Berlin 10.
	Hochschule für Musik "Hanns Eisler", 1080 Berlin.
Bremen:	Hochschule für Gestaltende Kunst und Musik, Am Wandrahm 23, 2800 Bremen 1.
Cologne:	Staatliche Hochschule für Musik Rheinland, Köln, Dagobertstrasse 38, 5000 Cologne 1.
Detmold:	Staatliche Hochschule für Musik Westfalen-Lippe, Allee 22, 4930 Detmold.
Dortmund:	Staatliche Hochschule für Musik Westfalen-Lippe, Institut Dortmund, Hanastrasse 7, 4600 Dortmund 1.
Dresden:	Hochschule für Musik "Carl Maria von Weber", Blochmannstrasse 2-4, 8010 Dresden.
Düsseldorf:	Staatliche Hochschule für Musik Rheinland, Düsseldorf, Robert-Schumann-Institut, Fischerstrasse 110, 4000 Düsseldorf.
Essen:	Staatliche Hochschule für Musik Ruhr, Abtei 43, 4300 Essen 16.
Frankfurt am Main:	Hochschule für Musik und Darstellende Kunst, Frankfurt am Main, Eschersheimer Landstrasse 29-39, 6000 Frankfurt am Main 1.
Freiburg im Breisgau:	Staatliche Hochschule für Musik, Freiburg im Breisgau, Schwarzwaldstrasse 141, 7800 Freiburg im Breisgau.
Hamburg:	Hochschule für Musik und Darstellende Kunst, Hamburg, Harvestehuder Weg 12, 2000 Hamburg 12.
Hannover:	Hochschule für Musik und Theater, Hannover, Emmichplatz 1, 3000 Hannover 1.
Heidelberg:	Staatliche Hochschule für Musik, Heidelberg-Mannheim, Friedrich-Ebert-Anlage 62, 6900 Heidelberg.
Karlsruhe:	Staatliche Hochschule für Musik, Karlsruhe, Weberstrasse 8, 7500 Karlsruhe 1.
Leipzig:	Hochschule für Musik "Felix Mendelssohn-Bartholdy", Leipzig, Grassistrasse 8, 7010 Leipzig.
Lübeck:	Musikhochschule, Lübeck, Grosse Petersgrube 17-29, 2400 Lübeck.
Mainz:	Johannes Gutenberg-Universität, Department of Music, Bingerstrasse 26, 6500 Mainz.
Munich:	Richard-Stauss-Konservatorium, Ismaningerstrasse 29, 8080 Munich.
	Hochschule für Musik, München Arcisstrasse 12, 8000 Munich 2.
Nürnberg:	Konservatorium der Stadt Nürnberg, Fachakademie für Musik, Am Katharinenkloster 6, 8500 Nürnberg 1.
Saarbrücken:	Musikhochschule des Saarlandes, Bismarckstrasse 1, 6600 Saarbrücken 3.
Stuttgart:	Staatliche Hochschule für Musik und Darstellende Kunst, Urbanplatz 2, 7000 Stuttgart 1.
Trossingen:	Staatliche Hochschule für Musik, Trossingen, Schultheiss-Koch-Platz 3, 7218 Trossingen 1.
Weimar:	Hochschule für Musik "Franz Liszt", Platz der Demokratie 2-3, 5300 Weimar.
Wiesbaden:	Wiesbadener Konservatorium und staatliche anerkannte private Fachschule für Musikerzieher e V, Bodenstedtstrasse 2, 6200 Wiesbaden.
Wuppertal:	Staatliche Hochschule für Musik Rheinland, Wuppertal, Institut Wuppertal, Friedrich-Ebert-Strasse 141, 5600 Wuppertal 2.
Würzburg:	Bayerisches Staatskonservatorium für Musik, Mergentheimerstrasse 76, 8700 Würzburg.

GHANA

Cape Coast:	University of Cape Coast, Department of Music, Cape Coast.
Legon:	University of Ghana, School of Performing Arts, PO Box 25, Legon.

GREECE

Athens:	Odeion Athenon, Odos Rigillis and Vassileos Georgiou 17-19, Athens.
	Odeion Ethnikon, Odos Maizonos 8, 108 Athens.
	Odeion Hellenikon, Odos Phidiou 3, Athens.
	Skalkotas Conservatory, Agias Lavras 78, Ano Patisia, 11141 Athens.
Thessaloniki:	Kratikon Odeion Thessaloniki, Leondos Sofou 16, 54625 Thessaloniki.

GUATEMALA

Guatemala City:	Conservatorio Nacional de Música, 3a Avenida 4-61, Zona 1, Guatemala City.

HAITI

Port-au-Prince:	Academy Promusica, Port-au-Prince.
	École de Musique Ste, Trinité, PO Box 857, Port-au-Prince.

HONDURAS

Tegucigalpa:	Escuela Nacional de Música, Callejon la Moncada, No 901, Teguçigalpa.

MUSIC CONSERVATORIES

HONG KONG

Hong Kong: Hong Kong Academy for Performing Arts, School of Music, 1 Gloucester Road, Wanchai, Hong Kong.
University of Hong Kong, Faculty of Music, Pokfulam Road, Hong Kong.

HUNGARY

Budapest: Bartók Béla Zenemüvészeti Szakközépiskola (Béla Bartók Conservatory), 1065 Nagymezo, Budapest VII
Liszt Ferenc Zenemüves-zeti Föiskola (Franz Liszt Academy of Music), PO Box 206, Liszt Ferenc tér 8, H-1391 Budapest VI.
Zenetudományi Intézet (Musicological Institute), Táncsics u, 1041 Budapest.

ICELAND

Reykjavík: Tónlistarskólinn i Rekjavík (Reykjavík College of Music), Skipholti 33, 105 Rykjavík.

INDIA

Allahabad: Prayag Sangit Samiti, 12-C Kamla Nehru Road, Alfred Park, Allahabad 211001
Bombay: Bhavan's Bharatiya Sangeet and Nartan Skikshapeeth (Academy of Music and Drama), Chaupatty Road, Bombay 4000007
Calcutta: Rabindra Bharati University, Department of Music, 6-4 Dwarakanath Tagore Lane, Calcutta 700007.
Khairagarth: Indira Kala Sangit Vishwavidyalaya (University of Music and Fine Arts), Khairagarth, Madhya Pradesh 491881.
Madras: Kalakshetra, Tiruvanmiyur, Madras 600041.
Music Academy, Teachers' College of Music, 306 T T K Road, Madras 600041.
University of Madras, Department of Indian Music, University Centenary Building, Chepauk, Triplicane PO, Tamil Nadu, Madras 600005.
New Delhi: Delhi School of Music, 8 Nyaya Marg, New Delhi 110021.
Sangeet Natak Akademi (National Academy of Music, Dance and Drama), Rabindra Bhavan, Feroze Shah Road, New Delhi 11001.

INDONESIA

Bandung: Academi Seni Tari Indonesia, Jl Buahbatu 212, Bandung.
Jakarta: Institute Kesenian Jakarta, Taman Ismial Marzuki, Jalan Cikini, Jakarta.
Kentingan: Academy Seni Karawitan Indonesia, Kampus ASKI, Kentingan, Jebres, Solo Jawa Tengah.

ISRAEL

Haifa: Samuel Rubin Conservatory of Music, 9 Haparsim Street, Haifa.
Jerusalem: Jerusalem Rubin Academy of Music and Dance, Givat-Ram Campus, 91904 Jerusalem.
Tel Aviv: Israel Conservatory of Music, 19 Shtriker Street, Tel Aviv.
Levinsky Teachers College, Music Teachers Seminary, 15 Shoshana Persitz Street North, PO Box 48130, Tel Aviv.
Rimon School of Jazz and Contemporary Music, Rehov Shmuel Hanagid, Morasha, Ramat Hasharon, Tel Aviv.
University of Tel Aviv, Faculty of Fine Arts, Rubin Academy of Music, PO Box 39040, Ramat Aviv, Tel Aviv.

ITALY

Alessandria: Conservatorio Statale di Musica "Antonio Vivaldi", Via Parma 1, Alessandria.
Bari: Conservatorio Statale di Musica "Niccolo Piccinni", Via Brigata Bari 26, I-70124 Bari.
Bologna: Conservatorio Statale di Musica "Giovanni Battista Martini", Piazza Rossini 2, I-40126 Bologna.
Bolzano: Conservatorio Statale di Musica "Claudio Monteverdi", Piazza Domenicani 19, I-39100 Bolzano.
Cagliari: Conservatorio Statale di Musica "Giovanni Pierluigi da Palestrina", Via Bacaredda, I-09100 Cagliari.
Florence: Conservatorio Statale di Musica "Luigi Cherubini", Piazza Belle Arti 2, I-50122 Florence.
Genoa: Conservatorio Statale di Musica "Niccòlo Paganini", Via Albaro 38, I-16145 Genoa.
L'Aquila: Conservatorio Statale di Musica "Girolamo Frescobaldi", Via Previati 22, L'Aquila.
Lucca: Istituto Musicale Pareggiato "Luigi Boccherini", Piazza S Ponziano, I-55100 Lucca.
Messina: Conservatorio Statale di Musica "Arcangelo Corelli", Via Laudamo 9-11, I-98100 Messina.
Milan: Accademia Musicale di Milano, Viale dei Mille 17, Milan.
Conservatorio Statale di Musica "Giuseppe Verdi", Via del Conservatorio 12, I-20122 Milan.
Naples: Accademia Musicale Napoletana, Via del Parco Margherita 49, pal 5, I-80121 Naples.
Conservatorio Statale di Musica "San Pietro a Majella", Via San Pietro a Majella 35, I-80138 Naples.

MUSIC CONSERVATORIES

Padua:	Conservatorio Statale di Musica "Cesare Pollini", Via Eremitani 6, I-35121 Padua.
Palermo:	Conservatorio Statale di Musica "Vincenzo Bellini", Via Squarcialupo 45, I-90133 Palermo.
Parma:	Conservatorio Statale di Musica "Arrigo Boito", Via del Conservatorio 27, I-43100 Parma.
Perugia:	Conservatorio Statale di Musica "Francesco Morlacchi", Piazza Mariotti 2, I-06100 Perugia.
Pesaro:	Conservatorio Statale di Musica "Gioachino Rossini", Piazza Olivieri 5, I-61100 Pesaro.
Rome:	Accademia Nazionale di Santa Cecilia, Via Vittoria 6, I-00187 Rome.
	Conservatorio Statale di Musica "Santa Cecilia", Via dei Greci 18, I-00187 Rome.
Pontificio:	Istituto di Musica Sacra, Via di Torre Rossa 21, I-00165 Rome.
Siena:	Accademia Musicale Chigiana, Via di Citta 89, I-53100 Siena.
Trieste:	Conservatorio Statale di Musica "Giuseppe Tartini", Via Carlo Ghega 12, I-34132 Trieste.
Turin:	Conservatorio Statale di Musica "Giuseppe Verdi", Via Mazzini 11, Piazza Bodoni, I-10123 Turin.
Venice:	Conservatorio Statale di Musica "Benedetto Marcello", Palazzo Pisani, San Marco 2809, I-30124 Venice.
Vercelli:	Liceo Musicale "Giovanni Battista Viotti", Casella Postale 127, I-13100 Vercelli 39.

JAMAICA

Kingston:	Cultural Training School, School of Music, 1 Arthur Wint Drive, Kingston 5.

JAPAN

Hiroshima:	Elizabeth University of Music, 4-15 Nobori-cho, Naka-ku, Hiroshima 730.
Kyoto:	Kyoto City University of Fine Arts and Music, 13-6 Ohe Kutsukake-cho, Nishikyo-ku, Kyoto 610-11.
Osaka:	Osaka College of Arts, 469 Higashiyama, Kanan-cho, Minamikawachi-gun, Osaka 561.
	Osaka Ongaku Daigaku (Osaka College of Music), 1-1-8 Saiwaimachi, Shonai, Toyonaka, Osaka 561.
Tokyo:	Kunitachi College of Music, 5-5-1 Kashiwa-cho, Tachikawa-shi, Tokyo 190.
	Musashino Ongaku Daigaku (Musashino College of Music), 1-13-1 Hazawa, Nerima-ku, Tokyo 176.
	Toho Gakuen School of Music, 1-41-1 Wakaba-cho, Chofu-shi, Tokyo 182.
	Tokyo College of Music, 3-4-5 Minami-Ikebukuro, Toshima-ku, Tokyo 171.
	Tokyo Daigaku (University of Tokyo), Faculty of Musicology, 7-3-1 Hongo, Bungyo-ku, Tokyo 113.
	Tokyo Geijutsu Daigaku (Tokyo University of Fine Arts and Music), 12-8 Ueno-koch, Taito-kut, Tokyo 110.
	Ueno Gakuen College, Department of Music, 4-24-12 Higashiueno, Taito-ku, Tokyo 110.

JORDAN

Amman:	Jordan Conservatory of Music, Amman.

KENYA

Nairobi:	Kenya Conservatoire of Music, PO Box 41343, Nairobi.

KOREA (NORTH)

Pyongyang:	College of Music and Dance, Pyongyang.

KOREA (SOUTH)

Seoul:	Korean Union College, Department of Music, Cheongryang, PO Box 18, Seoul.
	Korea University, 1 5-KA, Anamdong, Sungbukku, Seoul 136-701.
	Kyung Hee University, College of Music, 1 Hoegi-dong, Tongadaemun-gu Seoul 131.
	National Academy of Arts, Department of Music, 1 Sejongno, Chongno-gu, Seoul.
	Seoul National University, College of Music, San 56-1, Shinrim-dong, Kwanak-gu, Seoul 151.
	Yongsei University, College of Music, 134 Shinchon-dong, Sodaemun-gu, Seoul 120.

LATVIA

Riga:	Latvian Y Vitol State Conservatory, UI Krishyana Barona 1, 226050 Riga.

LEBANON

Beirut:	Lebanese Academy of Fine Arts, Beirut.
	Lebanese National Conservatory, Beirut.

MUSIC CONSERVATORIES

LITHUANIA

Vilnius:	Lithuanian State Conservatory, 232001 Vilnius.

LUXEMBOURG

Esch-sur-Alzette:	Conservatoire de Musique d'Esch-sur-Alzette, 10 Rue de l'Eglise, BP 145, 4002 Esch-sur-Alzette.
Luxembourg:	Conservatoire de Musique de la Ville de Luxembourg, 33 Rue Charles Martel, 2134 Luxembourg.

MEXICO

Mexico City:	Conservatorio Nacional de Música de México, Avenida Presidente Masaryk 582, Mexico City 5, DF.
	Universidad Nacional Autónoma de México, Escuela Nacional de Música, Xicotencat 126, Coyoacán, Mexico City 04100, DF.

MONACO

Monte Carlo:	Académie de Musique Prince Rainier III de Monaco, 17 Rue Princess Florestine, 98000 Monte Carlo.

MOROCCO

Casablanca:	École Nationale de Musique, 133 Avenue Ziraoui, Casablanca.
Fez:	National Conservatoire Dan Adyel, Fez.
Marrakesh:	Conservatoire de Musique, Marrakesh.
Meknes:	Ecole Nationale de Musique, 22 Rue Marrakchia, Kaa Ouarda, Meknes.
Rabat:	Conservatoire National de Musique, de Danse, et d'Art Dramatique, Rabat.
Tangier:	Conservatoire de Tangier, Tangier.
Tetouan:	National Conservatoire de Tetouan, Tetouan.

MYANMAR

Mandalay:	School of Music, Dance, Painting, and Sculpture, Mandalay.
Rangoon:	Institute of Fine Arts, Faculty of Music, Godwin Road, Dago Post Office, Rangoon.

NETHERLANDS

Amsterdam:	Stichting Sweelinck Conservatorium, Van Baerlestraat 27, 1071 AN Amsterdam
Arnhem:	Hogeschool Voor de Kunsten Arnhem, Fakulteit Muziek, Weverstraat 40, 6811 EM Arnhem
Enschede:	Hogeschool Enschede sector Conservatorium, Van Essengaarde 10, 7511 PN Enschede
Groningen:	Rijkshogeschool Groningen sector Kunstvakopleidingen afdeling Conservatorium, Veemarktstraat 76, 9724 GA Groningen.
The Hague:	Koninklijk Conservatorium voor Muziek en Dans, Juliana van Stolberglaan 1, 2595 CA The Hague.
Hilversum:	Akademie voor Muziek, Koninginneweg 25, 1217 KR Hilversum.
	Hilversums Conservatorium, Snelliuslaan 10, 1222 TE Hilversum.
Leeuwarden:	Stedelijke Muziekpedagogische Akademie, Eewal 56-58, Leeuwarden.
Maastricht:	Rijkshogeschool Maastricht, Subfaculteit Conservatorium, Bonnefanten 15, 6211 KL Maastricht.
Rotterdam:	Rotterdams Conservatorium, Pieter de Hooghweg 122, 3024 BJ Rotterdam.
	Toonkunst Conservatorium, Mathenesserlaan 219, Rotterdam.
Tilburg:	Brabants Conservatorium voor Muziek en Dans, Kempenbaan 27, 5022 KC Tilburg.
Utrecht:	Utrechts Conservatorium, Mariaplaats 28, 3511 LL Utrecht.
Zwolle:	Christelijke Hogeschool voor de Kunsten "Constantijn Huygens", Aan de Stadsmuur 88, 8011 VD Zwolle.

NEW ZEALAND

Auckland:	University of Auckland, Faculty of Music, Private Bag, Auckland.
Christchurch:	University of Canterbury, Faculty of Music, Christchurch.
Dunedin:	University of Otago, Arts and Music, PO Box 56, Dunedin.
Wellington:	Victoria University of Wellington, Faculty of Music, PO Box 600 Wellington.

NICARAGUA

Managua:	Escuela Nacional de Musica, Antigua Hacienda el Retiro, Managua.

MUSIC CONSERVATORIES

NIGERIA

Lagos:	University of Lagos, Department of Music, Lagos.
Nsukka:	University of Nigeria, Department of Music, Nsukka.

NORWAY

Bergen:	Bergen Musikkonservatorium, Lars Hilles Gate 3, N-5015 Bergen.
Oslo:	Østlandets Musikkonservatorium, Vetlandsveien 45, N-0685 Oslo 6.
	Statens Operahøgskole, Tjuvholmen, bygning B, N-0250 Oslo 2.
Stavanger:	Rogaland Musikkonservatorium, Bjergsted, N-4007 Stavanger.
Trondheim:	Trondelag Musikkonservatorium, Homebergvn. 1, N-7038 Trondheim.

PANAMA

Panama City:	Escuela Nacional de Música, Apartado 1414, Panama City.

PARAGUAY

Asunción:	Conservatorio Municipal de Música, Mcal Estigarribia, E-Pai Perez y Curupayty, Asunción.
	Escuela Municipal de Canto, Dr Eduardo Victor Haedo 682, Asunción.

PERU

Lima:	Conservatorio Nacional de Música, Avenida Emancipatión 180, Lima 1.

PHILIPPINES

Iloilo City:	University of San Augustin, Conservatory of Music, General Luna Street, Iloilo City 5901.
Manila:	St Paul College, College of Music, 680 Pedro Gil Street, Malate, Manila.
	St Scholastica's College, School of Music, 2560 Leon Guinto Sr Street, Malate, Manila.
	University of Santo Tomas, Conservatory of Music, Espana, Manila.

POLAND

Bydgoszcz:	Akademia Muzyczna im Feliksa Nowowiejskiego w Bydgoszczy, Ul J Slowackiego 7, 85-008 Bydgoszcz.
Gdańsk:	Akademia Muzyczna im Stanislaw Moniuszko w Gdańsku, Lagiewniki 3, 80-847 Gdańsk.
Katowice:	Akademia Muzyczna im Karola Szymanowskiego w Katowice, Ul Zacisze 3, Katowice.
Kraków:	Akademia Muzyczna w Krakówie, Ul Bohaterów Stalingradu 3, 31-038 Kraków.
Lódź:	Akademia Muzyczna w Lódź, Ul Gdańska 32, 90-716 Lódź.
Poznań:	Akademia Muzyczna Poznańiu, Ul Czerwonej Armii 87, 61-808 Poznań.
Warsaw:	Akademia Muzyczna im Fryderyka Chopina w Warzawie, Ul Okólnik 2, 00-368 Warsaw.
Wroclaw:	Akademia Muzyczna Wroclawiu, UL Powstancow Ślaskich 204, 53-140 Wroclaw.

PORTUGAL

Coimbra:	Conservatório Regional de Coimbra, Rua do Brasil, 3000 Coimbra.
Lisbon:	Academia de Amadores de Musica, R Nova da Trindade 18, 2nd floor, E, 1200 Lisbon.
	Escola Superior de Musica, Conservatório Nacional, Rua dos Caetanos 29, 1200 Lisbon.
Oporto:	Conservatório de Musica, Rua de Maternidade 13, 4000 Oporto.

RUMANIA

Bucharest:	Conservatorul de Muzică Ciprian Porumbescu, Str Stirbei Voda 33, 70732 Bucharest.
Cluj-Napoca:	Conservatorul de Muzică Gheorghe Dima, Str 23 August 25, 3400 Cluj-Napoca.
Iasi:	Conservatorul de Muzică Georges Enescu, Str Closca 9, 6600 Iasi.

RUSSIA

Moscow:	Moscow Conservatory, Ul Gertzena 13, 103009 Moscow.
St Petersburg:	St Petersburg Conservatory, Teatralnaya Pl 3, 192041 St Petersburg.

SAUDI ARABIA

Riyadh:	King Saud University, Riyadh Conservatory, PO Box 2454, Riyadh 11451.

MUSIC CONSERVATORIES

SENEGAL

Dakar: Conservatoire National de Musique, de Danse, et d'Art Dramatique, BP 3111, Dakar.

SIERRA LEONE

Freetown: National College of Music, Freetown.

SINGAPORE

Singapore: School of Arts and Language, 469 Bukit Gimah Road, Singapore 1025.

SLOVAKIA

Bratislava: Bratislava Konzervatorium, Tolstého 11, 811 06 Bratislava.
Vysoká Škola Mûzických Umeni v Bratislaave (Academy of Music and Dramatic Arts Bratislava), Jiráskova 3, 813 01 Bratislava.

SOUTH AFRICA

Bloemfontein: University of the Orange Free State, Department of Music, PO Box 339, Bloemfontein 9300.
Cape Town: University of Cape Town, College of Music, Private Bag, Rondebosch 7700, Cape Town.
Durban: University of Natal, Department of Music, King George V Avenue, Durban 4001.
Johannesburg: University of the Witwatersrand, Wits School of Music, Jan Smuts Avenue, Johannesburg 2001.
Pretoria: University of Pretoria, Department of Music, Pretoria 0002.
University of South Africa, Department of Music, PO Box 392, Pretoria 0001.
Stellenbosch: University of Stellenbosch, Department of Music, Stellenbosch 7600.

SPAIN

Barcelona: Conservatorio Superior de Música de Barcelona, Calle Bruch 112, Barcelona 9.
Cadiz: Conservatorio de Música "Manuel de Falla", Calle del Tinte 1, Cadiz.
Cordoba: Conservatorio Superior de Música y Escuela de arte Dramatico y Danza, Calle Angel de Saavedra 1, Cordoba.
Madrid: Escuela Superior de Música Sagrada y de Pedagogia Musical Escolar, Victor Pradera 65 bis, Madrid 8.
Real Conservatorio Nacional de Música y Declamacion, San Bernardo 44, Madrid.
Real Conservatorio Superior de Música, Plaza de Isabell II, S-N, Madrid 28013.
San Sebastian: Conservatorio Superior de Música, Easo 39, San Sebastian 20006.
Seville: Conservatorio Superior de Música y Escuela de Arte Dramatico, Calle Jesus del Gran Poder 49, Seville 41002.
Valencia: Conservatorio Superior de Música y Escuela de Arte Dramatico y Danza, Plaza San Esteban 3, Valencia.

SRI LANKA

Colombo: Institute of Aesthetic Studies, 21 Albert Crescent, Colombo 7.

SUDAN

Khartoum: Institute of Music and Drama, Khartoum.
Omdurman: Institute of Music and Drama, PO Box 80, El Mourada, Omdurman.

SWEDEN

Göteborg: Göteborgs Universitet, Musikhögskolan, Box 3174, S-400 10 Göteborg.
Malmö: Musikhögskolan och teaterhögskolan, Box 13515, Ystadvägen 25, S-200 44 Malmö.
Stockholm: Musikhögskolan, Valhallavägen 103-109, S-115 31 Stockholm.

SWITZERLAND

Basel: Musik-Akademie der Stadt Basel, Leonhardsstrasse 6, CH-4501 Basel.
Bern: Konservatorium für Musik und Theater, Kramgasse 36, CH-3011 Bern.
Biel: Stadtische Musikschule und Konservatorium, Ring 12, CH-2500 Biel.
Fribourg: Conservatoire et Académie de Musique, 228-A Rue Pierre Aeby, CH-1700 Fribourg.
Geneva: Conservatoire de Musique de Genève, Place Neuve, CH-1204 Geneva.
Institut Jaques-Dalcroze, 11 Rue Sillem, CH-1207 Geneva.

MUSIC CONSERVATORIES

La Chaux-de-Fonds:	Conservatoire de Musique de La Chaux-de-Fonds-Le Locle, Avenue Léopold-Robert 34, CH-2300 La Chaux-de-Fonds.
Lausanne:	Conservatoire de Musique de Lausanne, 6 Rue du Midi, CH-1002 Lausanne.
Lucerne:	Konservatorium Luzern, Dreilindenstrasse 93, CH-6006 Lucerne.
Neuchâtel:	Conservatoire de Musique de Neuchâtel, 106 Faubourg de l'Hopital, CH-2000 Neuchâtel.
Olten:	Stadtische Musikschule, CH-4600 Olten.
Schaffhausen:	Musikschule und Konservatorium Schaffhausen, Rosengasse 16, CH-8200 Schaffhausen.
Vevey:	Conservatoire de Musique de Vevey, 4 Rue des Communaux, CH-1800 Vevey.
Winterthur:	Musikschule und Konservatorium Winterthur, Tössertobelstrasse 1, CH-8400 Winterthur.
Zürich:	Konservatorium und Musikhochschule Zürich, Birchstrasse 95, CH-8050 Zürich. Musikakademie Zürich, Florastrasse 52, CH-8008 Zürich.

SYRIA

Aleppo:	Aleppo Institute of Music, Aleppo.
Damascus:	National Conservatory of Music, Damascus.

TAIWAN

Taipei:	National Institute of the Arts, Music Department, 172 Chung Cheng Road, Ru Chow, Taipei. National Taiwan Academy of Arts, 59, Section 1, Ta Kuan Road, Pan-Chiao Park, Taipei.

TANZANIA

Dar es Salaam:	University of Dar es Salaam, PO Box 35091, Dar es Salaam.

THAILAND

Bangkok:	Institute of Technology and Vocational Education, Faculty of Drama and Music, 339 Samsen Road, Bangkok 10300.

TUNISIA

Tunis:	Conservatoire de Musique, 5 Rue Zarkoun, Tunis. Institut Superieure de Musique, 20 Avenue de Paris, Tunis.

TURKEY

Ankara:	Hacettepe Üniversitesi, Ankara State Conservatory, Hacetlepe Parki, Ankara.
Istanbul:	Mimar Sinan Üniversitesi, Istanbul State Conservatory of Music, Findikli, Istanbul. Istanbul Teknik Üniversitesi, Turkish Conservatory of Music, Ayazaga, Istanbul.
Izmir:	Ege Üniversitesi, Izmir State Conservatory of Turkish Music, Bornova, Izmir.

UGANDA

Kampala:	Makerere University, Department of Music, Dance, and Drama, PO Box 7064, Kampala.

UK

Bangor:	University College of North Wales, Department of Music, Bangor, Wales LL57 2DG
Barnet:	Middlesex Polytechnic School of Music, Trent Park, Cockfosters Road, Barnet, Herts EN4 0PT.
Belfast:	City of Belfast School of Music, 99 Donegal Pass, Belfast, Northern Ireland BT7 1DR. Queen's University of Belfast, Department of Music, University Road, Belfast, Northern Ireland BT7 1NN.
Birmingham:	Birmingham Conservatoire, Paradise Place, Birmingham B3 3HG. Birmingham School of Music, Paradise Circus, Birmingham B3 3HG.
Brighton:	University of Sussex, Department of Music, Arts Building, Falmer, Brighton, East Sussex BN1 9QN.
Cambridge:	University of Cambridge, School of Music, 11 West Road, Cambridge CB3 9DP.
Cardiff:	University of Wales, College of Cardiff, Department of Music, Corbett Road, Cardiff, Wales CF1 3EB. Welsh College of Music and Drama, Castle Grounds, Cathays Parks, Cardiff, Wales CF1 3ER.
Cobham:	Yehudi Menuhin School, Stoke D'Abernon, Cobham, Surrey KT11 3QQ
Croydon:	Royal School of Church Music, Addinton Palace, Croydon CR9 5AD.
Edinburgh:	St Mary's Music School, Old Coates House, Manor Place, Edinburgh, Scotland EH3 7EB. University of Edinburgh, Faculty of Music, Edinburgh, Scotland EH8 9YL
Egham:	Royal Holloway and Bedford College, Department of Music, Egham, Surrey TW20 0EX.
Exeter:	University of Exeter, Department of Music, Exeter EX4 4QJ.
Fife:	University of St Andrews, Department of Music, Fife, Scotland.

MUSIC CONSERVATORIES

Glasgow: Royal Scottish Academy of Music and Drama, St George's Place, Glasgow, Scotland G2 1BS.
University of Glasgow, Department of Music, Glasgow, Scotland G12 8QH.
Harrow-on-the-Hill: Purcell School, Mount Park Road, Harrow-on-the-Hill, Middlesex HA1 3JS.
Hull: University of Hull, Department of Music, Cottingham Road, Hull HU6 7RX.
Lancaster: University of Lancaster, Department of Music, Lancaster LA1 4YW.
Leeds: City of Leeds College of Music, Cookridge Street, Leeds LS2 8BH.
University of Leeds, Department of Music, Leeds LS2 9JT.
Leicester: University of Leicester, Department of Music, University Road, Leicester LE1 7RH.
Liverpool: University of Liverpool, Department of Music, PO Box 147, Liverpool L69 3BX.
London: Guildhall School of Music and Drama, Barbican, London EC2Y 8DT.
King's College, Department of Music, Strand, London WC1.
London-City University, Department of Music, Northampton Square, London EC1V 0HB.
London College of Music, c/o Polytechnic of London, St Mary's Road, London W5 5RF.
Royal Academy of Music, Marylebone Road, London NW1 5HT.
Royal College of Music, Prince Consort Road, London SW7 2BS.
Trinity College of Music, 11 Mandeville Place, London W1M 6AQ.
University of London, Department of Music, Senate House, London WC1E 7AU.
Manchester: Chetham's School of Music, Long Millgate, Manchester M3 1SB.
Royal Northern College of Music, 124 Oxford Road, Manchester M13 9RD.
Salford College of Technology, Adelphi, Peru Street, Salford, Manchester M3 6EQ.
University of Manchester, Department of Music, Denmark Road, Manchester M15 6FY.
Oxford: University of Oxford, Faculty of Music, St Aldate's, Oxford OX1 1DB.
Reading: University of Reading, Department of Music, 35 Upper Redlands Road, Reading RG1 5JE.
Southampton: University of Southampton, Department of Music, Highfield, Southampton SO9 5NH.
Totnes: Dartington College of Arts, Department of Music, Totnes, Devon TQ9 6EJ.
Twickenham: Royal Military School of Music, Kneller Hall, Twickenham, Middlesex TW2 7DU.
York: University of York, Department of Music, Heslington, York YO1 5DD.

USA

ALABAMA

Auburn: Auburn University, Department of Music, Auburn, AL 36849.
Birmingham: Samford University, School of Music, 800 South Lakeshore Drive, Birmingham, AL 35229.
University of Alabama at Birmingham, Department of Music, 401 Humanities Building, Birmingham, AL 35294.
Jacksonville: Jacksonville State University, Department of Music, Mason Hall, Jacksonville, AL 36265.
Mobile: University of South Alabama, Department of Music, 9 Faculty Court E, Mobile, AL 36688.
Montevallo: University of Montevallo, College of Fine Arts, Station 6670, Montevallo, AL 35115.
Montgomery: Alabama State University, School of Music, 915 South Jackson Street, Montgomery, AL 36195.
Troy: Troy State University, School of Fine Arts, Music Department, Long Hall, Troy, AL 36082.
Tuscaloosa: University of Alabama, School of Music, PO Box 2876, Tuscaloosa, AL 35487.

ALASKA

Anchorage: University of Alaska, Anchorage, Music Department, 3211 Providence Drive, Anchorage, AK 99508.
Fairbanks: University of Alaska, Fairbanks, Music Department, 301 Fine Arts Complex, Fairbanks, AK 99775

ARIZONA

Flagstaff: Northern Arizona University, Music Department, PO Box 6040, Flagstaff, AZ 86011.
Phoenix: Arizona State University, Interdisciplinary Fine Arts Department, 4701 W Thunderbird Road, Phoenix, AZ 85069.
Tempe: Arizona State University, School of Music, Tempe, AZ 85287.
Tucson: University of Arizona, School of Music, Tucson, AZ 85721.

ARKANSAS

Arkadelphia: Henderson State University, Department of Music, 1100 Henderson Street, Arkadelphia, AR 71923.
Quachita Baptist University, School of Music, Box 3771, Arkadelphia, AR 71923.
Conway: University of Central Arkansas, Department of Music, Box 1726, Conway, AR 72032.
Fayetteville: University of Arkansas, Department of Music, 201A Music Building, Fayetteville, AR 72701.
Little Rock: University of Arkansas at Little Rock, Department of Music, 2801 South University, Little Rock, AR 72204.
Russellville: Arkansas Tech University, Department of Music, Russellville, AR 72801.
State University: Arkansas State University, Department of Music, Box 779, State University, AR 72467.

CALIFORNIA

Azusa: Azusa Pacific University, School of Music, Citrus and Alosta, Azusa, CA 91702.
Bakersfield: California State University, Bakersfield, Fine Arts Department, 9001 Stockdale Highway, Bakersfield, CA 93311.
Berkeley: University of California, Berkeley, Department of Music, Morrison Hall, Berkeley, CA 94720.
Carson: California State University, Dominguez Hills, Department of Music, 1000 E Victoria, Carson, CA 90747.

MUSIC CONSERVATORIES

Chico:	California State University, Chico, Department of Music, Chico, CA 95929.
Claremont:	The Claremont Graduate School, Department of Music, 150 East 20th Street, Claremont, CA 91711.
	Pomona College, Department of Music, Thatcher Music Building, Claremont, CA 91711.
Davis:	University of California, Davis, Department of Music, 112 Music Building, Davis, CA 95616.
Fresno:	California State University, Fresno, Department of Music, Maple and Shaw Avenues, Fresno, CA 93740.
Fullerton:	California State University, Fullerton, Department of Music, 800 North State College Boulevard, Fullerton, CA 92634.
Hayward:	California State University, Hayward, Department of Music, Hayward, CA 94542.
Hollywood:	Musicians Institute, 1655 McCadden Place, Hollywood, CA 90028.
Irvine:	University of California, Irvine, School of Fine Arts, Department of Music, Irvine, CA 92717.
La Jolla:	University of California, San Diego, Department of Music, B-026, La Jolla, CA 92093.
La Mirada:	Biola University, Department of Music, 13800 Biola Avenue, La Mirada, CA 90639.
Long Beach:	California State University, Long Beach, Department of Music, 1250 Bellflower Boulevard, Long Beach, CA 90840.
Los Angeles:	California State University, Los Angeles, Department of Music, 5151 State University Drive, Los Angeles, CA 90032.
	Los Angeles City College, Department of Music, 855 N Vermont Avenue, Los Angeles, CA 90029.
	University of California, Los Angeles, Department of Music, 405 Hilgard Avenue, Los Angeles, CA 90024.
	University of Southern California, School of Music, University Park, Los Angeles, CA 90089.
Northridge:	California State University, Northridge, Department of Music, 18111 Nordhoff Street, Northridge, CA 91330.
Oakland:	Mills College, Music Department, 5000 MacArthur Boulevard, Oakland, CA 94613.
Pasadena:	Pasadena Conservatory of Music, PO Box 91533, 1815 Queensberry Road, Pasadena, CA 91109.
Pomona:	California State Polytechnic University, Department of Music, 3801 West Temple Avenue, Pomona, CA 91768.
Redlands:	University of Redlands, School of Music, PO Box 3080, Redlands, CA 92373.
Riverside:	University of California, Riverside, Department of Music, 900 University Avenue, Riverside, CA 92521.
Sacramento:	California State University, Sacramento, Department of Music, 6000 Jay Avenue, Sacramento, CA 95819.
San Diego:	San Diego State University, Department of Music, 5300 Campanile Drive, San Diego, CA 92182.
San Francisco:	Music and Arts Institute of San Francisco, 2622 Jackson Street, San Francisco, CA 94115.
	San Francisco Conservatory of Music, 1201 Ortega Street, San Francisco, CA 94122.
	San Francisco State University, Department of Music, 1600 Holloway Avenue, San Francisco, CA 94132.
San Jose:	San Jose State University, Department of Music, 1 Washington Square, San Jose, CA 95192.
Santa Barbara:	Music Academy of the West, 1070 Fairway Road, Santa Barbara, CA 93108.
	University of California, Santa Barbara, Department of Music, Santa Barbara, CA 93106.
Santa Cruz:	University of California, Santa Cruz, Department of Music, Porter College, Santa Cruz, CA 95064.
Stanford:	Stanford University, Department of Music, Stanford, CA 94305.
Stockton:	University of the Pacific, Conservatory of Music, 3601 Pacific Avenue, Stockton, CA 95211.
Turlock:	California State University, Stanislaus, Department of Music, 801 Monte Vista Avenue, Turlock, CA 95380.
Valencia:	California Institute of the Arts, School of Music, 24700 McBean Parkway, Valencia, CA 91355.

COLORADO

Aspen:	Aspen Music School, PO Box AA, Aspen, CO 81612.
Boulder:	University of Colorado, College of Music, Box 301, Boulder, CO 80309.
Colorado Springs:	Colorado College, Department of Music, Packard Hall, Colorado Springs, CO 80903.
Denver:	Metropolitan State College, Department of Music, 1006 11th Street, Box 58, Denver, CO 80204.
	University of Denver, Lamont School of Music, 7111 Mountview, Denver, CO 80220.
Fort Collins:	Colorado State University, Department of Music, Fort Collins, CO 80523.
Greeley:	University of Northern Colorado, School of Music, Greeley, CO 80639.
Pueblo:	University of Southern Colorado, Department of Music, 2200 Bonforte Boulevard, Pueblo, CO 81001.

CONNECTICUT

Bridgeport:	University of Bridgeport, Department of Music, Arnold Bernhard Arts-Humanities Center, Bridgeport, CT 06602.
Danbury:	Western Connecticut State University, Department of Music, 181 White Street, Danbury, CT 06810.
Hartford:	University of Hartford, Hartt School of Music, 200 Bloomfield Avenue, Hartford, CT 06117.
Middletown:	Wesleyan University, Department of Music, Middletown, CT 06457.
New Haven:	Yale University, School of Music, Box 2104A, Yale Station, New Haven, CT 06520.
Storrs:	University of Connecticut, Department of Music, Box U-12, Room 228, 876 Coventry Road, Storrs, CT 06269.

DELAWARE

Milford:	Delaware Music School, PO Box 442, Milford, DE 19963.
Newark:	University of Delaware, Department of Music, Newark, DE 19716.
Wilmington:	Wilmington Music School, 4101 Washington Street, Wilmington, DE 19802.

MUSIC CONSERVATORIES

DISTRICT OF COLUMBIA

Washington: American Unversity, Department of Performing Arts, Kreeger Building, No 200, Washington, DC 20016.
The Catholic University of America, Benjamin T Rome School of Music, 620 Michigan Avenue North East, Washington, DC 20064.
George Washington University, Department of Music, B-144 Academic Center, Washington, DC 20052.
Howard University, College of Fine Arts, Sixth and Fairmont Streets North West, Washington, DC 20059.
Levine School of Music, 1690 36th Street North West, Washington, DC 20007.

FLORIDA

Boca Raton: Florida Atlantic University, Department of Music, 500 North West 20th Street, Boca Raton, FL 33431.
Coral Gables: University of Miami, School of Music, PO Box 248165, Coral Gables, FL 33124.
De Land: Stetson University, School of Music, De Land, FL 32720.
Gainesville: University of Florida, Department of Music, 130 MUB, Gainesville, FL 32611.
Jacksonville: Jacksonville University, College of Fine Arts, Division of Music, Jacksonville, FL 32211.
Miami: Florida International University, Department of Music, University Park Campus, Miami, FL 33199.
Orlando: University of Central Florida, Department of Music, Orlando, FL 32816.
Pensacola: University of West Florida, Department of Music, Pensacola, FL 32514.
Tallahassee: Florida Agricultural and Mechanical University, Department of Music, Tallahassee, FL 32307.
Florida State University, School of Music, Tallahassee, FL 32306.
Tampa: University of South Florida, Department of Music, Tampa, FL 33620.
University of Tampa, Music Division, 401 West J F Kennedy Boulevard, Tampa, FL 33606.

GEORGIA

Athens: University of Georgia, School of Music, 203 Fine Arts Building, Athens, GA 30602.
Atlanta: Emory University, Department of Music, Humanities Building, Room 101, Atlanta, GA 30322.
Georgia State University, School of Music, University Plaza, Atlanta, GA 30303.
Spelman College, Department of Music, 350 Spelman Lane South West, Atlanta, GA 30314.
Carrollton: West Georgia College, Department of Music, Carrollton, GA 30118.
Columbus: Columbus College, Schwob Music Department, Columbus, GA 31993.
Rome: Shorter College, Fine Arts Division, Box 8, Rome, GA 30161.
Statesboro: Georgia Southern College, Department of Music, Landrum Box 8052, Statesboro, GA 30460.
Valdosta: Valdosta State College, Department of Music, North Patterson Street, Valdosta, GA 31698.

HAWAII

Honolulu: University of Hawaii, Department of Music, 2411 Dole Street, Honolulu, HI 96822.

IDAHO

Boise: Boise State University, Department of Music, 1910 University Drive, Boise, ID 83725.
Moscow: University of Idaho, Lionel Hampton School of Music, Moscow, ID 83843.
Pocatello: Idaho State University, Department of Music, PO Box 8099, Pocatello, ID 83209.
Rexburg: Ricks College, Department of Music, Rexburg, ID 83440.

ILLINOIS

Bloomington: Illinois Wesleyan University, School of Music, Presser Hall, Bloomington, IL 61702.
Carbondale: Southern Illinois University at Carbondale, School of Music, Carbondale, IL 62901.
Charleston: Eastern Illinois University, Department of Music, Charleston, IL 61920.
Chicago: American Conservatory of Music, 16 North Wabash Avenue, Sutie 1850, Chicago, IL 60602.
Chicago Musical College of Roosevelt University, 430 South Michigan Avenue, Chicago, IL 60605.
Chicago State University, 95 State and King Drive, Chicago, IL 60628.
De Paul University, School of Music, 804 West Belden, Chicago, IL 60614.
Moody Bible Institute, Department of Music, 820 North LaSalle Drive, Chicago, IL 60610.
North Park College, Department of Music, 3225 West Foster, Chicago, IL 60625.
The People's Music School, 4750 North Sheridan, Suite 340, Chicago, IL 60640.
Sherwood Conservatory of Music, 1014 South Michigan Avenue, Chicago, IL 60605.
University of Chicago, Department of Music, 5845 South Ellis Avenue, Chicago, IL 60637.
University of Illinois at Chicago, Department of Music, PO Box 4348, Chicago, IL 60680.
VanderCook College of Music, 3209 South Michigan Avenue, Chicago, IL 60616.
Decatur: Millikin University, School of Music, 1184 West Main Street, Decatur, IL 62522.
DeKalb: Northern Illinois University, School of Music, Music Building 140, DeKalb, IL 60115.
Edwardsville: Southern Illinois University at Edwardsville, Department of Music, Box 1771, Edwardsville, IL 62026.
Evanston: Northwestern University, School of Music, 711 Elgin Road, Evanston, IL 60208.
Macomb: Western Illinois University, Department of Music, 122 Browne Hall, Macomb, IL 61455.
Normal: Illinois State University, Department of Music, Normal, IL 61761.
Peoria: Bradley University, Division of Music and Theater Arts, Peoria, IL 61625.
Urbana: The Conservatory of Central Illinois, 312 West Green, Urbana, IL 61801.
University of Illinois, School of Music, 1114 West Nevada Street, Urbana, IL 61801.
Wheaton: Wheaton College, Conservatory of Music, Wheaton, IL 60187.

MUSIC CONSERVATORIES

INDIANA

Anderson:	Anderson University, Department of Music, 1100 East Fifth Street, Anderson, IN 46012.
Bloomington:	Indiana University, School of Music, Music Building, Bloomington, IN 47405.
Evansville:	University of Evansville, Department of Music, 1800 Lincoln Avenue, Evansville, IN 47722.
Greencastle:	DePauw University, School of Music, Performing Arts Center, Greencastle, IN 46135.
Hanover:	Hanover College, Department of Music, Hanover, IN 47243.
Indianapolis:	Butler University, Jordan College of Fine Arts, 4600 Sunset Avenue, Indianapolis, IN 46208.
	Indiana University-Purdue University at Indianapolis, Department of Music, 525 North Blackford Street, Room 010, Indianapolis, IN 46202.
	University of Indianapolis, 1400 East Hanna, Indianapolis, IN 46227.
Muncie:	Ball State University, School of Music, Muncie, IN 47306.
North Manchester:	Manchester College, Department of Music, College Avenue, North Manchester, IN 46962.
Notre Dame:	Saint Mary's College, Department of Music, Notre Dame, IN 46556.
	University of Notre Dame, Department of Music, Crowley Hall of Music, Notre Dame, IN 46556.
Saint Mary-of-the-Woods:	Saint Mary-of-the-Woods College, Department of Music, Saint Mary-of-the-Woods, IN 47876.
Terre Haute:	Indiana State University, Department of Music, 217 North Sixth Street, Terre Haute, IN 47809.
Upland:	Taylor University, Department of Music, Upland, IN 46989.
Valparaiso:	Valparaiso University, Department of Music, Valparaiso, IN 46383.
West Lafayette:	Purdue University, Department of Music, 135 Hall of Music, West Lafayette, IN 47907.

IOWA

Ames:	Iowa State University, Department of Music, 149 Music Hall, Ames, IA 50011.
Cedar Falls:	University of Northern Iowa, School of Music, Cedar Falls, IA 50614.
Cedar Rapids:	Coe College, Department of Music, 1220 First Avenue North East, Cedar Rapids, IA 52402.
Decorah:	Luther College, Department of Music, Decorah, IA 52101.
Des Moines:	Drake University, School of Fine Arts, Des Moines, IA 50311.
Indianola:	Simpson College, Department of Music, Amy Robertson Music Center, Indianola, IA 50125.
Iowa City:	Preucil School of Music, 524 North Johnson, Iowa City, IA 52245.
	University of Iowa, School of Music, Iowa City, IA 52242.
Mount Vernon:	Cornell College, Department of Music, Mount Vernon, IA 52314.
Sioux City:	Morningside College, 1501 Morningside Avenue, Sioux City, IA 51106.
Waverly:	Wartburg College, Department of Music, PO Box 1003, 222 Ninth Street North West, Waverly, IA 50677.

KANSAS

Emporia:	Emporia State University, Division of Music, 1200 Commercial Street, Emporia, KS 66801.
Hays:	Fort Hays State University, Department of Music, 600 Park Street, Hays, KS 67601.
Lawrence:	University of Kansas, School of Fine Arts, 452 Murphy Street, Lawrence, KS 66045.
Lindsborg:	Bethany College, Department of Music, 421 North First Street, Lindsborg, KS 67456.
Manhattan:	Kansas State University, Department of Music, McCain Auditorium, Room 109, Manhattan, KS 66506.
North Newton:	Bethel College, Department of Music, Drawer A, North Newton, KS 67117.
Pittsburg:	Pittsburg State University, Department of Music, 1701 South Broadway, Pittsburg, KS 66762.
Topeka:	Washburn University, Department of Music, 17 and College, Topeka, KS 66621.
Wichita:	Friends University, Fine Arts Division, 2100 University, Wichita, KS 67213.
	Wichita State University, School of Music, 1845 Fairmont, Wichita, KS 67208.

KENTUCKY

Berea:	Berea College, Department of Music, CPO 1127, Berea, KY 40404.
Bowling Green:	Western Kentucky University, Department of Music, 351 Fine Arts Center, Bowling Green, KY 42101.
Frankfort:	Kentucky State University, Fine Arts Division, Frankfort, KY 40601.
Lexington:	University of Kentucky, School of Music, 105 Fine Arts Building, Lexington, KY 40506.
Louisville:	Southern Baptist Theological Seminary, School of Church Music, 2825 Lexington Road, Louisville, KY 40280.
	University of Louisville, School of Music, Louisville, KY 40292.
Morehead:	Morehead State University, Department of Music, Baird Music Hall, Room 106, Morehead, KY 40351.
Murray:	Murray State University, Department of Music, University Station, Murray, KY 42071.
Richmond:	Eastern Kentucky University, Department of Music, Richmond, KY 40475.
Williamsburg:	Cumberland College, Department of Music, PO Box 7525, Williamsburg, KY 40769.

LOUISIANA

Baton Rouge:	Louisiana State University, School of Music, Baton Rouge, LA 70803.
	Southern University, Department of Music, PO Box 10215, Baton Rouge, LA 70813.
Grambling:	Grambling State University, Department of Music, Grambling, LA 71245.
Hammond:	Southeastern Louisiana University, Department of Music, Box 815, University Station, Hammond, LA 70402.
Lafayette:	University of Southwestern Louisiana, School of Music, PO Box 41207, Lafayette, LA 70505.
Lake Charles:	McNeese State University, College of Liberal Arts, Department of Music, Ryan Street, Lake Charles, LA 70609.
Monroe:	Northeast Louisiana University, School of Music, 700 University, Monroe, LA 71209.
Natchitoches:	Northwestern State University of Louisiana, Department of Music, College Avenue, Natchitoches, LA 71497.

MUSIC CONSERVATORIES

New Orleans: Loyola University, College of Music, 6363 St Charles Avenue, New Orleans, LA 70118.
New Orleans Baptist Theological Seminary, Church Music Ministries Division, 3939 Gentilly Boulevard, New Orleans, LA 70126.
Tulane University-Newcomb College, Department of Music, Dixon Hall, New Orleans, LA 70118.
University of New Orleans, Department of Music, Lakefront, New Orleans, LA 70148.
Xavier University of Louisiana, Department of Music, 7352 Palmetto Street, New Orleans, LA 70125.

Pineville: Louisiana College, Department of Music, College Station, Pineville, LA 71359.
Ruston: Louisiana Tech University, School of Performing Arts, PO Box 8608, Ruston, LA 71272.
Shreveport: Centenary College of Louisiana, Hurley School of Music, Shreveport, LA 71134.

MAINE

Brunswick: Bowdoin College, Department of Music, Gibson Hall, Brunswick, ME 04011.
Gorham: University of Southern Maine, Department of Music, College Avenue, 102A Corthell Hall, Gorham, ME 04038.
Lewiston: Bates College, Department of Music, Lewiston, ME 04240.
Orono: University of Maine, Department of Music, 123 Lord Hall, Orono, ME 04469.

MARYLAND

Baltimore: Morgan State University, Department of Music, Coldspring and Hillen Roads, Baltimore, MD 21239.
Peabody Institute of the Johns Hopkins University, 1 East Mount Vernon Place, Baltimore, MD 21202.
Towson State University, Department of Music, Baltimore, MD 21204.
College Park: University of Maryland, Department of Music, Tawes Fine Arts Building, College Park, MD 20742.
Princess Anne: University of Maryland Eastern Shore, Fine Arts Department, Music Division, Princess Anne, MD 21853.
Rockville: Montgomery College, Department of Music, 51 Mannakee Street, Rockville, MD 20850.
Saint Mary's City: Saint Mary's College of Maryland, Arts and Letters Division, Saint Mary's City, MD 20686.
Towson: Goucher College, Department of Music, 1021 Dulaney Valley Road, Towson, MD 21204.

MASSACHUSETTS

Amherst: Amherst College, Department of Music, Amherst, MA 01022.
University of Massachusetts, Music and Dance Department, Fine Arts Center, Amherst, MA 01003.
Boston: Berklee College of Music, 1140 Boylston Street, Boston, MA 02215.
Boston Conservatory, Music Division, 8 The Fenway, Boston, MA 02215.
Boston University, School of Music, 855 Commonwealth Avenue, Boston, MA 02215.
New England Conservatory of Music, 290 Huntington Avenue, Boston, MA 02115.
Northeastern University, Department of Music, 360 Huntington Avenue, Boston, MA 02115.
Tanglewood Music Center, c/o Symphony Hall, Boston, MA 02115.
University of Massachusetts at Boston, Department of Music, Harbor Campus, Boston, MA 02125.
Cambridge: Harvard University, Department of Muisc, Music Building, Cambridge, MA 02138.
Longy School of Music Inc, 1 Follen Street, Cambridge, MA 02138.
New School of Music, 25 Lowell Street, Cambridge, MA 02138.
Great Barrington: Aston Magna Performance Practice Institute, PO Box 28, Great Barrington, MA 01230.
Lowell: University of Lowell, College of Music, 1 University Avenue, Lowell, MA 01854.
Medford: Tufts University, Department of Music, 20 Professors Row, Medford, MA 02155.
Northampton: Smith College, Department of Music, Northampton, MA 01063.
Waltham: Brandeis University, Department of Music, South Street, Waltham, MA 02254.
Williamstown: Williams College, Department of Music, Bernhard Music Center, Williamstown, MA 01267.

MICHIGAN

Albion: Albion College, Department of Music, Albion, MI 49224.
Allendale: Grand Valley State University, Department of Music, Allendale, MI 49401.
Ann Arbor: University of Michigan, School of Music, Ann Arbor, MI 48109.
Berrien Springs: Andrews University, Department of Music, Berrien Springs, MI 49104.
Detroit: Center for Creative Studies - Institute of Music and Dance, 200 East Kirby, Detroit, MI 48202.
Wayne State University, Department of Music, 5451 Cass Avenue, Room 105 Music, Detroit, MI 48202.
East Lansing: Michigan State University, School of Music, Music Building, East Lansing, MI 48824.
Flint: Flint School of Performing Arts, Dort Music Center, 1025 East Kearsley, Flint, MI 48503.
Grand Rapids: Calvin College, Department of Music, Fine Arts Center, 3215 Burton Street South East, Grand Rapids, MI 49506.
Holland: Hope College, Department of Music, Holland, MI 49423.
Interlochen: Interlochen Arts Academy, Department of Music, Interlochen, MI 49643.
Kalamazoo: Kalamazoo College, Department of Music, 1200 Academy Street, Kalamazoo, MI 49007.
Western Michigan University, School of Music, Kalamazoo, MI 49008.
Marquette: Northern Michigan University, Department of Music, Fine Arts Building, C-130, Marquette, MI 49855.
Mount Pleasant: Central Michigan University, Department of Music, Powers Music Building, No 102, Mount Pleasant, MI 48859.
Rochester: Oakland University, Music, Theatre, and Dance Department, Rochester, MI 48309.
Ypsilanti: Eastern Michigan University, Department of Music, N101 Alexander Music Building, Ypsilanti, MI 48197.

MUSIC CONSERVATORIES

MINNESOTA

Bemidji:	Bemidji State University, Department of Music, PO Box 53, 1500 Birchmont Drive North East, No 53, Bemidji, MN 56601.
Collegeville:	St John's University, Department of Music, Collegeville, MN 56321.
Duluth:	University of Minnesota, Duluth, Department of Music, 10 University Drive, Duluth, MN 55812.
Mankato:	Mankato State University, Department of Music, Box 5, Mankato, MN 56002.
Minneapolis:	Augsburg College, Department of Music, 731 21st Avenue South, Minneapolis, MN 55454.
	University of Minnesota, Minneapolis, School of Music, 2106 Fourth Street South, Minneapolis, MN 55455.
Moorhead:	Concordia College, Department of Music, Moorhead, MN 56560.
	Moorhead State University, Department of Music, 1104 Seventh Avenue South, Moorhead, MN 56560.
Northfield:	Carleton College, Department of Music, 1 North College Street, Northfield, MN 55057.
	St Olaf College, Department of Music, Northfield, MN 55057.
St Cloud:	St Cloud State University, Department of Music, Performing Arts Center, Room 240, St Cloud, MN 56301.
St Joseph:	College of St Benedict, Department of Music, St Joseph, MN 56374.
St Paul:	Bethel College, Department of Music, 3900 Bethel Drive, St Paul, MN 55112.
	College of St Catherine, Department of Music, 2004 Randolph Avenue, St Paul, MN 55105.
	College of St Thomas, Department of Music, 2115 Summit Avenue, St Paul, MN 55105.
	Hamline University, Department of Music, Hewitt Avenue at Snelling, St Paul, MN 55104.
	Macalester College, Department of Music, 1600 Grand Avenue, St Paul, MN 55105.
St Peter:	Gustavus Adolphus College, Department of Music, St Peter, MN 56082.
Winona:	Winona State University, Department of Music, 145 Performing Arts Center, Winona, MN 55987.

MISSISSIPPI

Cleveland:	Delta State University, Department of Music, PO Box 3256, Cleveland, MS 38733.
Clinton:	Mississippi College, Department of Music, Box 4206, Clinton, MS 39058.
Hattiesburg:	University of Southern Mississippi, School of Music, Box 5081, Southern Station, Hattiesburg, MS 39406.
	William Carey College, Winters School of Music, Tuscan Avenue, Hattiesburg, MS 39401.
Jackson:	Jackson State University, Department of Music, PO Box 17055, Jackson, MS 39217.
Lorman:	Alcorn State University, Fine Arts Department, PO Box 29, Lorman, MS 39096.
Mississippi State:	Mississippi State University, Department of Music Education, Drawer F, Mississippi State, MS 39762.
University:	University of Mississippi, Department of Music, 132 Meek Hall, University, MS 38677.

MISSOURI

Bolivar:	Southwest Baptist University, School of Fine Arts, 1601 South Springfield Street, Bolivar, MO 65613.
Cape Girardeau:	Southeast Missouri State University, Department of Music, Brandt Music Hall, Cape Girardeau, MO 63701.
Columbia:	University of Missouri at Columbia, Department of Music, 140 Fine Arts Center, Columbia, MO 65211.
Fayette:	Central Methodist College, Swinney Conservatory of Music, 411 CMC Square, Fayette, MO 65248.
Independence:	Music/Arts Institute, 1010 South Pearl, PO Box 1141, Independence, MO 64051.
Joplin:	Missouri Southern State College, Department of Music, Newman and Duquesne Roads, Joplin, MO 64801.
Kansas City:	Park College, Department of Music, Parkville, Kansas City, MO 64152.
	University of Missouri at Kansas City, Conservatory of Music, 4949 Cherry, Kansas City, MO 64110.
Kirksville:	Northeast Missouri State University, Fine Arts Division, Kirksville, MO 63501.
Liberty:	William Jewell College, Department of Music, Liberty, MO 64068.
Maryville:	Northwest Missouri State University, Department of Music, DeLuce Fine Arts Building, Maryville, MO 64468.
Springfield:	Evangel College, Department of Music, 1111 N Glenstone, Springfield, MO 65802.
	Southwest Missouri State University, Department of Music, 901 South National, Springfield, MO 65804.
St Joseph:	Missouri Western State College, Department of Music, 4525 Downs Drive, St Joseph, MO 64507.
St Louis:	Saint Louis Conservatory and Schools for the Arts, 560 Trinity at Delmar, St Louis, MO 63130.
	Saint Louis University, Department of Music, 221 North Grand Boulevard, St Louis, MO 63103.
	University of Missouri at St Louis, Department of Music, 8001 Natural Bridge, St Louis, MO 63121.
	Washington University, Department of Music, Campus Box 1032, 1 Brookings Drive, St Louis, MO 63130.
	Webster University, Department of Music, 470 East Lockwood, St Louis, MO 63119.
Warrensburg:	Central Missouri State University, Department of Music, Warrensburg, MO 64093.

MONTANA

Billings:	Eastern Montana College, Department of Music, 1500 North 30th, Billings, MT 59101.
Bozeman:	Montana State University, Department of Music, Bozeman, MT 59717.
Missoula:	University of Montana, Department of Music, Missoula, MT 59812.

MUSIC CONSERVATORIES

NEBRASKA

Hastings:	Hastings College, Department of Music, Seventh and Turner, Hastings, NE 68901.
Kearney:	Kearney State College, Department of Music, Kearney, NE 68847.
Lincoln:	Nebraska Wesleyan University, Department of Music, 50 and St Paul Streets, Lincoln, NE 68504.
	University of Nebraska at Lincoln, School of Music, Westbrook Music Building 120, Lincoln, NE 68588
Omaha:	University of Nebraska at Omaha, Department of Music, llege of Fine Arts, 60 and Dodge Streets, Omaha, NE 68182.
Seward:	Concordia College, Music Division, 800 North Columbia Street, Seward, NE 68434.

NEVADA

Las Vegas:	University of Nevada, Las Vegas, Department of Music, 4505 South Maryland Parkway, Las Vegas, NV 89154.
Reno:	University of Nevada, Reno, Department of Music, Reno, NV 89557.

NEW HAMPSHIRE

Durham:	University of New Hampshire, Department of Music, Durham, NH 03824.
Hanover:	Dartmouth College, Department of Music, Hopkins Center, Hanover, NH 03755.
Plymouth:	Plymouth State College, Department of Music, Plymouth, NH 03264.

NEW JERSEY

Glassboro:	Glassboro State College, Department of Music, Glassboro, NJ 08028.
Haddonfield:	Haddonfield School of Creative and Performing Arts, Box 383, Haddonfield, NJ 08033.
Jersey:	Jersey City State College, Music, Dance, and Theatre Department, 2039 Kennedy Boulevard, Jersey City, NJ 07305.
Little Silver:	Monmouth Conservatory of Music, 2 Cross Street, Little Silver, NJ 07739.
Newark:	Rutgers University, Faculty of Arts and Sciences, Department of Music, Newark, NJ 07102.
New Brunswick:	Mason Gross School of the Arts of Rutgers University, Old Music Building, Douglass Campus, PO Box 270, New Brunswick, NJ 08903.
Princeton:	Princeton University, Department of Music, Woolworth Center, Princeton, NJ 08544.
	Westminster Choir College, Hamilton and Walnut, Princeton, NJ 08540.
Rutherford:	Fairleigh Dickinson University, Fine Arts Department, 223 Montross Avenue, Rutherford, NJ 07070.
	Garden State Academy of Music, 88 Park Avenue, Rutherford, NJ 07070.
Trenton:	Trenton State College, Department of Music, Hillwood Lakes CN4700, Trenton, NJ 08650.
Upper Montclair:	Montclair State College, School of Fine and Performing Arts, Valley Road, Upper Montclair, NJ 07043.
Wayne:	William Paterson College of New Jersey, Department of Music, 300 Pompton Road, Wayne, NJ 07470.

NEW MEXICO

Albuquerque:	University of New Mexico, Department of Music, College of Fine Arts, Albuquerque, NM 87131.
Las Cruces:	New Mexico State University, Department of Music, Box 30001, Las Cruces, NM 88003.
Las Vegas:	New Mexico Highlands University, Creative and Performing Arts Department, Las Vegas, NM 87701.
Portales:	Eastern New Mexico University, School of Music, Station 16, Portales, NM 88130.

NEW YORK

Albany:	State University of New York at Albany, Department of Music, 1400 Washington Avenue, Albany, NY 12222.
Binghamton:	State University of New York at Binghamton, Department of Music, Vestal Parkway, Binghamton, NY 13901.
Brockport:	State University of New York, College at Brockport, Music and Theatre Department, Tower Fine Arts Center, Holley Street, Brockport, NY 14420.
Bronx:	Herbert H Lehman College, City University of New York, Department of Music, Bedford Park Boulevard West, Bronx, NY 10468.
Bronxville:	Sarah Lawrence College, Department of Music, 1 Meadway, Bronxville, NY 10708.
Brooklyn:	Brooklyn College, Conservatory of Music, Bedford Avenue and Avenue H, Brooklyn, NY 11210.
	Brooklyn Conservatory of Music, 58 Seventh Avenue, Brooklyn, NY 11217.
Buffalo:	State University of New York at Buffalo, Department of Music, Baird Hall, Room 226, Amherst Campus, Buffalo, NY 14260.
	State University of New York, College at Buffalo, Performing Arts Department, 1300 Elmwood Avenue, Buffalo, NY 14222.
Chautauqua:	Chautauqua Institution Summer School of Music, Box 1098, Chautauqua, NY 14722.
Cortland:	State University of New York, College at Cortland, Department of Music, Box 2000, Cortland, NY 13045.
Flushing:	Queens College, City University of New York, Aaron Copland School of Music, 65-30 Kissena Boulevard, Flushing, NY 11367.
Fredonia:	State University of New York, College at Fredonia, School of Music, Mason Hall, Fredonia, NY 14063.
Garden City:	Adelphi University, Department of Music, Post Hall, Garden City, NY 11530.
Geneseo:	State University of New York, College at Geneseo, Department of Music, Geneseo, NY 14454.

MUSIC CONSERVATORIES

Hamilton:	Colgate University, Department of Music, Dana Arts Center, Hamilton, NY 13346.
Hempstead:	Hofstra University, Department of Music, 1000 Fulton Avenue, Hempstead, NY 11550.
Houghton:	Houghton College, School of Music, Houghton, NY 14744.
Ithaca:	Cornell University, Department of Music, Lincoln Hall, Ithaca, NY 14853.
	Ithaca College, School of Music, Ithaca, NY 14850.
New Paltz:	State University of New York, College at New Paltz, Department of Music, New Paltz, NY 12561.
New York:	Baruch College, City University of New York, Department of Music, 17 Lexington Avenue, New York, NY 10010.
	Cantors Institute-Seminary College of Jewish Music of the Jewish Theological Seminary of America, 3080 Broadway, New York, NY 10027.
	City College of New York, Department of Music, West 138th Street and Convent Avenue, New York, NY 10031.
	Columbia University, Department of Music, 703 Dodge, New York, NY 10027.
	Dalcroze School of Music, 161 East 73rd Street, New York, NY 10021.
	Diller-Quaile School of Music Inc, 24 East 95th Street, New York, NY 10128.
	Harlem School of the Arts Inc, 645 St Nicholas Avenue, New York, NY 10030.
	Hebrew Union College, Jewish Institute of Religion, School of Sacred Music, 1 West Fourth Street, New York, NY 10012.
	Hunter College, City University of New York, Department of Music, 695 Park Avenue, New York, NY 10021.
	Julliard School, Lincoln Center Plaza, New York, NY 10023.
	Manhattan School of Music, 120 Claremont Avenue, New York, NY 10027.
	Mannes College of Music, 150 West 85th Street, New York, NY 10024.
	New School for Social Research, Department of Music, 66 West 12th Street, New York, NY 10011.
	New York University, Tisch School of the Arts, 721 Broadway, 4th Floor, New York, NY 10003.
	92nd Street Y School of Music, 1395 Lexington Avenue, New York, NY 10128.
Nyack:	Nyack College, Music and Fine Arts Department, Nyack, NY 10960.
Oneonta:	State University of New York, College at Oneonta, Fine Arts Center, Oneonta, NY 13820.
Oswego:	State University of New York, College at Oswego, Department of Music, Tyler Hall, Oswego, NY 13126.
Potsdam:	State University of New York, College at Potsdam, Crane School of Music, Pierrepont Avenue, Potsdam, NY 13676.
Poughkeepsie:	Vassar College, Department of Music, Raymond Avenue, Poughkeepsie, NY 12601.
Purchase:	Manhattanville College, Department of Music, Purchase, NY 10577.
	State University of New York, College at Purchase, Music Division, Purchase, NY 10577.
Rochester:	Eastman School of Music, University of Rochester, 26 Gibbs Street, Rochester, NY 14604.
	Hochstein Memorial Music School, 50 North Plymouth Avenue, Rochester, NY 14614.
	Roberts Wesleyan College, Fine Arts Division, 2301 Westside Drive, Rochester, NY 14624.
Saratoga Springs:	Skidmore College, Department of Music, Saratoga Springs, NY 12866.
Scarsdale:	Hoff-Barthelson Music School, 25 School Lane, Scarsdale, NY 10583.
Staten Island:	College of Staten Island, City University of New York, Department of Music, 130 Stuyvesant Place, Staten Island, NY 10301.
	Wagner College, Department of Music, 631 Howard Avenue, Staten Island, NY 10301.
Stony Brook:	State University of New York at Stony Brook, Department of Music, Stony Brook, L I, NY 11794.
Syracuse:	Syracuse University, School of Music, 215 Crouse College, Syracuse, NY 13244.
White Plains:	Westchester Conservatory of Music, 20 Soundview Avenue, White Plains, NY 10606.

NORTH CAROLINA

Boiling Springs:	Gardner-Webb College, Fine Arts Department, Boiling Springs, NC 28017.
Boone:	Appalachian State University, School of Music, Broyhill Music Center, Boone, NC 28608.
Brevard:	Brevard College, Fine Arts Division, North Broad Street, Brevard, NC 28712.
Buies Creek:	Campbell University, Fine Arts Division, Buies Creek, NC 27506.
Chapel Hill:	University of North Carolina at Chapel Hill, Department of Music, Hill Hall CB3320, Chapel Hill, NC 27599.
Charlotte:	Community School of the Arts, 200 West Trade Street, Charlotte, NC 28202.
	Queens College, Fine Arts Division and Music Department, 1900 Selwyn Avenue, Charlotte, NC 28274.
	University of North Carolina at Charlotte, Performing Arts Department, Charlotte, NC 28223.
Cullowhee:	Western Carolina University, Department of Music, Cullowhee, NC 28723.
Davidson:	Davidson College, Department of Music, Box 358, Davidson, NC 28036.
Durham:	North Carolina Central University, Department of Music, Box 19405, Durham, NC 27707.
	Duke University, Department of Music, PO Box 6695, College Station, Durham, NC 27708.
Elizabeth City:	Elizabeth City State University, Department of Music, Box 820, Elizabeth City, NC 27909.
Greensboro:	North Carolina Agricultural and Technical State University, Department of Music, 1601 East Market Street, Greensboro, NC 27411.
	University of North Carolina at Greensboro, School of Music, Greensboro, NC 27412.
Hickory:	Lenoir-Rhyne College, Department of Music, Box 7355, Hickory, NC 28603.
Mars Hill:	Mars Hill College, Fine Arts Division, PO Box 530, Mars Hill, NC 28754.
Misenheimer:	Pfeiffer College, Fine Arts Department, Misenheimer, NC 28109.
Pembroke:	Pembroke State University, Department of Music, Pembroke, NC 28372.
Raleigh:	Meredith College, 3800 Hillsborough Street, Raleigh, NC 27607.
Salisbury:	Catawba College, Department of Music, 2300 West Innes Street, Salisbury, NC 28144.
Wilmington:	University of North Carolina at Wilmington, Creative Arts Department, 601 South College Road, Wilmington, NC 28403.
Wilson:	Atlantic Christian College, Fine Arts Department, Wilson, NC 27893.
Wingate:	Wingate College, Fine Arts Department, Wingate, NC 28174.
Winston-Salem:	North Carolina School of the Arts, School of Music, 200 Waughtown Street, Winston-Salem, NC 27117.

MUSIC CONSERVATORIES

Salem College, School of Music, Winston-Salem, NC 27108.
Wake Forest University, Department of Music, 7345 Reynolds Station, Winston-Salem, NC 27109.
Winston-Salem State University, Department of Music, PO Box 13176, Winston-Salem, NC 27101.

NORTH DAKOTA

Fargo:	North Dakota State University, Music and Visual Arts Department, Box 5691, Fargo, ND 58105.
Grand Forks:	University of North Dakota, Department of Music, Box 8124, Grand Forks, ND 58202.
Mayville:	Mayville State University, Humanities and Social Science Division, Mayville, ND 58257.
Minot:	Minot State University, Music Division, 500 Ninth Avenue North West, Minot, ND 58701.
Valley City:	Valley City State University, Department of Music, Valley City, ND 58072.

OHIO

Ada:	Ohio Northern University, Department of Music, 525 South Main Street, Ada, OH 45810.
Akron:	University of Akron, School of Music, 302 East Buchtel, Akron, OH 44325.
Alliance:	Mount Union College, Department of Music, 1972 Clark Avenue, Alliance, OH 44601.
Ashland:	Ashland University, Department of Music, 401 College Avenue, Ashland, OH 44805.
Athens:	Ohio University, School of Music, Athens, OH 45701.
Berea:	Baldwin-Wallace College, Conservatory of Music, Berea, OH 44017.
Bluffton:	Bluffton College, Department of Music, Bluffton, OH 45817.
Bowling Green:	Bowling Green State University, College of Musical Arts, Bowling Green, OH 43403.
Canton:	Malone College, Fine Arts Department, 515 25th Street North West, Canton, OH 44709.
Cincinnati:	University of Cincinnati, College-Conservatory of Music, Cincinnati, OH 45221.
	Xavier University, Department of Music, 3800 Victory Parkway, Cincinnati, OH 45207.
Cleveland:	Case Western Reserve University, Department of Music, Haydn Hall, Cleveland, OH 44106.
	Cleveland Institute of Music, 11021 East Boulevard, Cleveland, OH 44106.
	Cleveland Music School Settlement, 11125 Magnolia Drive, Cleveland, OH 44106.
	Cleveland State University, Department of Music, Cleveland, OH 44115.
Columbus:	Capital University, Conservatory of Music, 2199 East Main Street, Columbus, OH 43209.
	Ohio State University, School of Music, 1866 College Road, Columbus, OH 43210.
Dayton:	University of Dayton, Music Division, 300 College Park Drive, Dayton, OH 45469.
	Wright State University, Department of Music, Dayton, OH 45435.
Delaware:	Ohio Wesleyan University, Department of Music, Delaware, OH 43015.
Granville:	Denison University, Department of Music, Granville, OH 43023.
Hiram:	Hiram College, Department of Music, Hiram, OH 44234.
Kent:	Kent State University, School of Music, Kent, OH 44242.
Marietta:	Marietta College, Edward E MacTaggart Department of Music, Marietta, OH 45750.
Mount St Joseph:	College of Mount St Joseph, Department of Music, Delhi and Neeb Roads, Mount St Joseph, OH 45051.
New Concord:	Muskingum College, Department of Music, New Concord, OH 43762.
Oberlin:	Oberlin College Conservatory of Music, Oberlin, OH 44074.
Oxford:	Miami University, Department of Music, 121 Center for Performing Arts, Oxford, OH 45056.
Springfield:	Wittenberg University, Department of Music, Springfield, OH 45501.
Toledo:	University of Toledo, Department of Music, 2801 West Bancroft Street, Toledo, OH 43606.
Westerville:	Otterbein College, Department of Music, Battelle Fine Arts Center, Westerville, OH 43081.
Wilberforce:	Central State University, Department of Music, Paul Robeson Cultural and Performing Arts Center, Room 218, Wilberforce, OH 45384.
Wooster:	College of Wooster, Department of Music, Wooster, OH 44691.
Youngstown:	Youngstown State University, Dana School of Music, 410 Wick Avenue, Youngstown, OH 44555.

OKLAHOMA

Bethany:	Southern Nazarene University, School of Music, 6729 North West 39 Expressway, Bethany, OK 73008.
Chickasha:	University of Sciences and Arts of Oklahoma, Box 3388, Chickasha, OK 73018.
Durant:	Southeastern Oklahoma State University, Department of Music, Box 4173, Station A, Durant, OK 74701.
Edmond:	Central State University, Department of Music, 100 North University Drive, Edmond, OK 73034.
Enid:	Philips University, Department of Music, Division of Fine Arts, PO Box 2000, University Station, Enid, OK 73702.
Lawton:	Cameron University, Department of Music, Lawton, OK 73505.
Norman:	University of Oklahoma, School of Music, 560 Parrington Oval, No 109A, Norman, OK 73019.
Oklahoma City:	Guy Fraser Harrison Academy for the Performing Arts, Box 60408, Oklahoma City, OK 73146.
	Oklahoma City University, School of Music and Performing Arts, 2501 North Blackwelder, Oklahoma City, OK 73106.
Shawnee:	Oklahoma Baptist University, Warren M Angell College of Fine Arts, 500 West University, Shawnee, OK 74801.
Stillwater:	Oklahoma State University, Department of Music, 132 Seretean Center, Stillwater, OK 74078.
Tahlequah:	Northeastern State University, College of Arts and Letters, Tahlequah, OK 74464.
Tulsa:	Oral Roberts University, Fine Arts Department, Tulsa, OK 74171.
	University of Tulsa, Department of Music, 600 South College, Tulsa, OK 74104.

OREGON

Ashland:	Southern Oregon State College, Department of Music, 1250 Siskiyou Boulevard, Ashland, OR 97520.
Corvallis:	Oregon State University, Department of Music, Benton 101, Corvallis, OR 97331.

MUSIC CONSERVATORIES

Eugene:	University of Oregon, School of Music, Eugene, OR 97403.
Forest Grove:	Pacific University, Department of Music, Forest Grove, OR 97116.
Marylhurst:	Marylhurst College, Department of Music, Marylhurst, OR 97036.
Monmouth:	Western Oregon State College, Creative Arts Division, Monmouth, OR 97361.
Portland:	Lewis and Clark College, Department of Music, 0615 South West Palatine Hill Road, Portland, OR 97219.
	Portland State University, Department of Music, PO Box 751, Portland, OR 97207.
	University of Portland, Performing and Fine Arts Department, 5000 North Willamette Boulevard, Portland, OR 97203.
Salem:	Willamette University, Department of Music, 900 State Street, Salem, OR 97301.

PENNSYLVANIA

Annville:	Lebanon Valley College, Department of Music, Blair Music Center, Annville, PA 17003.
Edinboro:	Edinboro University of Pennsylvania, Department of Music, Heather Hall Music Building, Edinboro, PA 16444.
Elizabethtown:	Elizabethtown College, Fine and Performing Arts Department, Rider Hall, 1 Alpha Drive, Elizabethtown, PA 17022.
Erie:	Mercyhurst College, D'Angelo School of Music, Glenwood Hills, Erie, PA 16546.
Gettysburg:	Gettysburg College, Department of Music, Gettysburg, PA 17325.
Grantham:	Messiah College, Department of Music, Grantham, PA 17027.
Greensburg:	Seton Hill College, Department of Music, Greensburg, PA 15601.
Immaculate:	Immaculate College, Department of Music, Immaculate, PA 19345.
Indiana:	Indiana University of Pennsylvania, Department of Music, 101 Cogswell Hall, Indiana, PA 15705.
Lewisburg:	Bucknell University, Department of Music, Lewisburg, PA 17837.
Mansfield:	Mansfield University, Department of Music, Butler Music Center, Mansfield, PA 16933.
Meadville:	Allegheny College, Department of Music, 520 North Main Street, Meadville, PA 16335.
Millersville:	Millersville University of Pennsylvania, Department of Music, Northumberland House, Millersville, PA 17551.
New Wilmington:	Westminster College, Department of Music, New Wilmington, PA 16172.
Philadelphia:	Academy of Vocal Arts, 1920 Spruce Street, Philadelphia, PA 19103.
	Curtis Institute of Music, 1726 Locust Street, Philadelphia, PA 19103.
	Drexel University, Performing Arts Department, 32 and Chestnut Streets, Philadelphia, PA 19104.
	La Salle University, Fine Arts Department, Philadelphia, PA 19141.
	Philadelphia College of Performing Arts, The University of the Arts—The School of Music, 250 South Broad Street, Philadelphia, PA 19102.
	Settlement Music School, 416 Queen Street, Philadelphia, PA 19147.
	Temple University, Esther Boyer College of Music, 13th and Norris Streets, Philadelphia, PA 19122.
	University of Pennsylvania, Department of Music, 201 South 34th Street, Philadelphia, PA 19104.
Pittsburgh:	Carnegie Mellon University, Department of Music, 5000 Forbes Avenue, Pittsburgh, PA 15213.
	Duquesne University, School of Music, 600 Forbes Avenue, Pittsburgh, PA 15282.
	University of Pittsburgh, Department of Music, 110 Music Building, Pittsburgh, PA 15260.
Scranton:	Marywood College, Department of Music, 2300 Adams Avenue, Scranton, PA 18509.
Selinsgrove:	Susquehanna University, Department of Music, Selinsgrove, PA 17870.
Slippery Rock:	Slippery Rock University, Department of Music, Slippery Rock, PA 16057.
University Park:	Pennsylvania State University, School of Music, 232 Music Building, University Park, PA 16802.
Wawa:	Darlington Fine Arts Center, Baltimore Pike, Wawa, PA 19063.

PUERTO RICO

Rio Piedras:	University of Puerto Rico, Department of Music, Box 23335, Rio Piedras, PR 00931.
San Germán:	Interamerican University of Puerto Rico, Department of Music, Wilson Cottage, Call Box 5100, San Germán, PR 00735.
Santurce:	Conservatory of Music of Puerto Rico, PO Box 41227, Minillas Station, Santurce, PR 00940.

RHODE ISLAND

Kingston:	University of Rhode Island, Department of Music, Fine Arts Center, Kingston, RI 02881.
Providence:	Brown University, Department of Music, Box 1924, 1 Young Orchard Avenue, Providence, RI 02912.
	The Music School, 75 John Street, Providence, RI 02906.
	Providence College, Department of Music, River Avenue and Easton Street, Providence, RI 02918.
	Rhode Island College, Department of Music, 600 Mount Pleasant Avenue, Providence, RI 02908.
Westerly:	Center School for the Arts, 116 High Street, Westerly, RI 02891.

SOUTH CAROLINA

Anderson:	Anderson College, Department of Music, 316 Boulevard, Anderson, SC 29621.
Charleston:	Baptist College at Charleston, Department of Music, PO Box 10087, Charleston, SC 29411.
Clemson:	Clemson University, Performing Arts Department, Clemson, SC 29634.
Columbia:	Columbia College, Department of Music, Columbia, SC 29203.
	University of South Carolina, School of Music, Columbia, SC 29208.
Gaffney:	Limestone College, Fine Arts Division, 1115 College Drive, Gaffney, SC 29340.
Greenville:	Bob Jones University, Music Division, Box 34533, Greenville, SC 29614.

MUSIC CONSERVATORIES

	Furman University, Department of Music, Greenville, SC 29613.
Hartsville:	Coker College, Department of Music, Hartsville, SC 29550.
Newberry:	Newberry College, Department of Music, Newberry, SC 29108.
Orangeburg:	South Carolina State College, Department of Music, Box 1917, Orangeburg, SC 29117.
Rock Hill:	Winthrop College, Department of Music, 112 Conservatory of Music, Rock Hill, SC 29733.
Spartanburg:	Converse College, School of Music, Spartanburg, SC 29301.

SOUTH DAKOTA

Aberdeen:	Northern State College, School of Fine Arts, Aberdeen, SD 57401.
Brookings:	South Dakota State University, Department of Music, Brookings, SD 57007.
Sioux Falls:	Augustana College, Department of Music, Sioux Falls, SD 57197.
	Sioux Falls College, Fine Arts Division, 1501 South Prairie Avenue, Sioux Falls, SD 57105.
Spearfish:	Black Hills State University, School of Arts and Humanities, PO Box 9003, Spearfish, SD 57783.
Vermillion:	University of South Dakota, Department of Music, Vermillion, SD 57069.

TENNESSEE

Athens:	Tennessee Wesleyan College, Department of Music, PO Box 40, Athens, TN 37303.
Chattanooga:	Tennessee Temple University, Department of Music, 1815 Union Avenue, Chattanooga, TN 37404.
	University of Tennessee at Chattanooga, Cadek Department of Music, 308 Fine Arts Center, Chattanooga, TN 37403.
Clarksville:	Austin Peay State University, Department of Music, Box 4625, Clarksville, TN 37044.
Cookeville:	Tennessee Technological University, Department of Music, Box 5045, Cookeville, TN 38505.
Jackson:	Union University, Department of Music, 2447 Highway 45 Bypass, Jackson, TN 38305.
Jefferson City:	Carson-Newman College, Music Division, Box 1839, Jefferson City, TN 37760.
Johnson City:	East Tennessee State University, Department of Music, Box 22330A, Johnson City, TN 37614.
Knoxville:	University of Tennessee at Knoxville, Department of Music, 1741 Volunteer Boulevard, Knoxville, TN 37996.
Martin:	University of Tennessee at Martin, Department of Music, 232 Fine Arts Building, Martin, TN 38238.
Maryville:	Maryville College, Fine Arts Department, Box 2805, Maryville, TN 37801.
Memphis:	Memphis State University, Department of Music, Memphis, TN 38152.
	Rhodes College, Department of Music, 2000 North Parkway, Memphis, TN 38112.
Murfreesboro:	Middle Tennessee State University, Department of Music, Box 47, Murfreesboro, TN 37132.
Nashville:	Belmont College, School of Music, 1900 Belmont Boulevard, Nashville, TN 37212.
	Fish University, Department of Music, 1000 17th Avenue North, Nashville, TN 37208.
	Tennessee State University, Department of Music, 3500 John A Merritt Boulevard, Nashville, TN 37203.
	Vanderbilt University, Blair School of Music, 2400 Blakemore Avenue, Nashville, TN 37212.

TEXAS

Abilene:	Abilene Christian University, Department of Music, Box 8274, Abilene, TX 79699.
	Hardin-Simmons University, School of Music, Drawer J, Abilene, TX 79698.
Alpine:	Sul Ross State University, Department of Music, Alpine, TX 79832.
Amarillo:	Amarillo College, Department of Music, Box 447, Amarillo, TX 79178.
Arlington:	University of Texas at Arlington, Department of Music, Box 19105, Arlington, TX 76019.
Austin:	University of Texas at Austin, Department of Music, Austin, TX 78712.
Beaumont:	Lamar University, Department of Music, PO Box 10044, Beaumont, TX 77710.
Brownwood:	Howard Payne University, School of Music, Brownwood, TX 76801.
Canyon:	West Texas State Univesity, Music and Dance Department, PO Box 870, Canyon, TX 79016.
Commerce:	East Texas State University, Department of Music, Commerce, TX 75428.
Corpus Christi:	Corpus Christi State University, Visual and Performing Arts Department, 6300 Ocean Drive, Corpus Christi, TX 78412.
Dallas:	Richland College, Humanities Division, 12800 Abrams Road, Dallas, TX 75243.
	Southern Methodist University, Meadows School of the Arts, Owen Arts Center, Dallas, TX 75275.
Denton:	Texas Woman's University, Performing Arts Department, PO Box 23865, Denton, TX 76204.
	University of North Texas, School of Music, PO Box 13887, Denton, TX 76203.
Edinburg:	Pan American University, Department of Music, Edinburg, TX 78539.
El Paso:	University of Texas at El Paso, Department of Music, University Avenue at Hawthorne, El Paso, TX 79968.
Fort Worth:	Southwestern Baptist Theological Seminary, School of Church Music, PO Box 22000, Fort Worth, TX 76122.
	Texas Christian University, Department of Music, Box 32887, Fort Worth, TX 76129.
	Texas Wesleyan University, School of Fine Arts, Fort Worth, TX 76105.
Georgetown:	Southwestern University, School of Fine Arts, Georgetown, TX 78626.
Houston:	Houston Baptist University, College of Fine Arts, 7502 Fondren Road, Houston, TX 77074.
	Rice University, Shepherd School of Music, PO Box 1892, Houston, TX 77251.
	San Jacinto College North, Fine Arts Division, 5800 Uvalde Road, Houston, TX 77049.
	University of Houston, School of Music, 4800 Calhoun, Houston, TX 77204.
Huntsville:	Sam Houston State University, Department of Music, Huntsville, TX 77341.
Kingsville:	Texas A & I University, Department of Music, Box 174, Kingsville, TX 78363.
Lubbock:	Texas Tech University, School of Music, PO Box 4239, Lubbock, TX 79409.
Marshall:	East Texas Baptist University, Department of Music, 1209 North Grove, Marshall, TX 75670.
Nacogdoches:	Stephen F Austin State University, Department of Music, Box 13043, Nacogdoches, TX 75962.
Odessa:	Odessa College, Department of Music, 201 West University Boulevard, Odessa, TX 79764.
San Angelo:	Angelo State University, Department of Music, San Angelo, TX 76909.
San Antonio:	Incarnate Word College, Department of Music, 4301 Broadway, San Antonio, TX 78209.

MUSIC CONSERVATORIES

St Mary's University of San Antonio, Department of Music, 1 Camino Santa Maria, San Antonio, TX 78284.
Trinity University, Department of Music, 715 Stadium Drive, San Antonio, TX 78284.
University of Texas at San Antonio, Music Division, San Antonio, TX 78285.

San Marcos:	Southwest Texas State University, Department of Music, San Marcos, TX 78666.
Sherman:	Austin College, Department of Music, PO Box 1177, Sherman, TX 75091.
Texarkana:	Texarkana College, Department of Music, Texarkana, TX 75501.
Waco:	Baylor University, School of Music, Box 7408, Waco, TX 76798.
Wichita Falls:	Midwestern State University, Department of Music, 3400 Taft, Wichita Falls, TX 76308.

UTAH

Logan:	Utah State University, Department of Music, Logan, UT 84322.
Ogden:	Weber State College, Performing Arts Department, 3750 Harrison Boulevard, Odgen, UT 84408.
Provo:	Brigham Young University, Department of Music, C-550 Harris Fine Arts Center, Provo, UT 84602.
Salt Lake City:	University of Utah, Department of Music, 204 Gardner Hall, Salt Lake City, UT 84112.

VERMONT

Bennington:	Bennington College, Department of Music, Jennings Hall, Bennington, VT 05201.
Brattleboro:	Music School of Brattleboro Music Center, 15 Walnut Street, Brattleboro, VT 05301.
Burlington:	University of Vermont, Department of Music, Music Building, Redstone Campus, Burlington, VT 05405.
Middlebury:	Middlebury College, Department of Music, 326 Johnson Building, Middlebury, VT 05753.
Winooski:	St Michael's College, Fine Arts Department, 56 College Parkway, Winooski, VT 05404.

VIRGINIA

Blacksburg:	Virginia Polytechnic Institute and State University, Department of Music, 256 Lane, Blacksburg, VA 24061.
Charlottesville:	University of Virginia, Department of Music, 112 Old Cabell Hall, Charlottesville, VA 22903.
Fairfax:	George Mason University, Department of Music, 4400 University Drive, Fairfax, VA 22030.
Farmville:	Longwood College, Department of Music, Farmville, VA 23901.
Fredericksburg:	Mary Washington College, Department of Music, Fredericksburg, VA 22401.
Hampton:	Hampton University, Department of Music, Hampton, VA 23668.
Harrisonburg:	James Madison University, Department of Music, Harrisonburg, VA 22807.
Lynchburg:	Liberty University, Department of Music, Box 20000, Lynchburg, VA 24506.
	Virginia School of the Arts, Department of Music, 2240 Rivermont Avenue, Lynchburg, VA 24503.
Newport News:	Christopher Newport College, Department of Music, 50 Shoe Lane, Newport News, VA 23606.
Norfolk:	Norfolk State University, Department of Music, 2401 Corprew Avenue, Norfolk, VA 23504.
	Old Dominion University, Department of Music, Norfolk, VA 23508.
Petersburg:	Virginia State University, Department of Music, Box 7, Petersburg, VA 23803.
Radford:	Radford University, Department of Music, East Norwood Street, Radford, VA 24142.
Richmond:	University of Richmond, Department of Music, Richmond, VA 23173.
	Virginia Commonwealth University, Department of Music, 922 Park Avenue, Richmond, VA 23284.
Roanoke:	Hollins College, Department of Music, PO Box 9642, Roanoke, VA 24020.
Salem:	Roanoke College, Fine Arts Department, Olin Hall Center for Arts and Humanities, Salem, VA 24153.
Sweet Briar:	Sweet Briar College, Department of Music, Sweet Briar, VA 24595.
Williamsburg:	College of William and Mary, Department of Music, Williamsburg, VA 23185.
Winchester:	Shenandoah College and Conservatory, Winchester, VA 22601.

WASHINGTON

Bellingham:	Western Washington University, Department of Music, PA 273, Bellingham, WA 98225.
Cheney:	Eastern Washington University, Department of Music, Cheney, WA 99004.
College Place:	Walla Walla College, Department of Music, College Place, WA 99324.
Ellensburg:	Central Washington University, Department of Music, Ellensburg, WA 98926.
Pullman:	Washington State University, School of Music, Kimbrough Music Building, Pullman, WA 99164.
Seattle:	Cornish College of Arts, Department of Music, 710 East Roy Street, Seattle, WA 98102.
	Seattle Pacific University, School of Fine and Performing Arts, 3307 Third Avenue West, Seattle, WA 98119.
	University of Washington, School of Music, DN-10, Seattle, WA 98195.
Spokane:	Whitworth College, Department of Music, Spokane, WA 99251.
Tacoma:	Pacific Lutheran University, Department of Music, Tacoma, WA 98447
	University of Puget Sound, School of Music, 1500 North Warner, Tacoma, WA 98416.
Walla Walla:	Whitman College, School of Music, 345 Boyer, Walla Walla, WA 99362.

WEST VIRGINIA

Buckhannon:	West Virginia Wesleyan College, Department of Music, Box 40, Buckhannon, WV 26201.
Fairmont:	Fairmont State College, Fine Arts Division, Fairmont, WV 26554.
Huntington:	Marshall University, Department of Music, Huntington, WV 25701.
Institute:	West Virginia State College, Department of Music, Box 4, Institute, WV 25112.
Morgantown:	West Virginia University, Department of Music, Creative Arts Center, Morgantown, WV 26506.
Philippi:	Alderson-Broaddus College, Department of Music, College Hill, Philippi, WV 25416.

MUSIC CONSERVATORIES

West Liberty:	West Liberty State College, Department of Music, Hall of Fine Arts, West Liberty, WV 26074.

WISCONSIN

Appleton:	Lawrence University, Conservatory of Music, PO Box 599, Appleton, WI 54912.
Beloit:	Beloit College, Department of Music, Beloit, WI 53511.
De Pere:	St Norbert College, Department of Music, De Pere, WI 54115.
Eau Claire:	University of Wisconsin, Eau Claire, Department of Music, Fine Arts Center, Eau Claire, WI 54701.
Green Bay:	University of Wisconsin, Green Bay, Department of Music, Green Bay, WI 54301.
Kenosha:	Carthage College, Department of Music, Kenosha, WI 53141.
	University of Wisconsin, Parkside, Department of Music, 285 Communication Arts Building, Kenosha, WI 53141.
La Crosse:	University of Wisconsin, La Crosse, Department of Music, 234 Fine Arts Building, La Crosse, WI 54601.
	Viterbo College, Department of Music, 815 South Ninth Street, La Crosse, WI 54601.
Madison:	Universty of Wisconsin, Madison, School of Music, 455 Park Street, Madison, WI 53706.
Manitowoc:	Silver Lake College, Department of Music, 2406 Alverne Road, Manitowoc, WI 54220.
Milwaukee:	Alverno College, Department of Music, 3401 South 39th Street, Milwaukee, WI 53215.
	University of Wisconsin, Milwaukee, Department of Music, PO Box 413, Milwaukee, WI 53201.
	Wisconsin Conservatory of Music, 1584 North Prospect Avenue, Milwaukee, WI 53202.
Oshkosh:	University of Wisconsin, Oshkosh, Department of Music, Arts and Communication Center, 800 Algoma Boulevard, Oshkosh, WI 54901.
Platteville:	University of Wisconsin, Platteville, Department of Music, 1 University Plaza, Platteville, WI 53818.
Ripon:	Ripon College, Department of Music, 300 Seward Street, Box 248, Ripon, WI 54971.
River Falls:	University of Wisconsin, River Falls, Department of Music, River Falls, WI 54022.
Stevens Point:	University of Wisconsin, Stevens Point, Department of Music, Stevens Point, WI 54481.
Superior:	University of Wisconsin, Superior, Department of Music, Superior, WI 54880.
Waukesha:	Carroll College, Department of Music, 100 North East Avenue, Waukesha, WI 53186.
Wausau:	Wausau Conservatory of Music, 404 Seymour Street, PO Box 606, Wausaw, WI 54402.
Whitewater:	University of Wisconsin, Whitewater, Department of Music, 800 West Main Street, Whitewater, WI 53190.

WYOMING

Laramie:	University of Wyoming, Department of Music, Box 3037, University Station, Laramie, WY 82071.

URUGUAY

Montevideo:	Conservatorio Falleri-Balzo, Avenida Uruguay 994, Montevideo.
	Conservatorio Nacional de Música, 25 De Mayo 692, Montevideo.
	Escuela Universitaria de Música, Paysandu 843, Montevideo.

VENEZUELA

Caracas:	Academia de Música Fischer, Edificio Léon de San Marco, Avenida Ciencias y Calle Risquez, Los Chaguaramos, Caracas.
	Academia de Música Padre Sojo, 4A Avenida Trans, 8AY9A, Apdo 60479 Este, Caracas.
	Conservatorio Nacional de Música, "Juan José Landaeta", Urbanización Campo Alegre, 4A Avenida, Caracas.
	Conservatorio Italiano de Música, Calle Montesacro, Colinas de Bello Monte, Caracas.
	Escuela de Música Lino Gallardo, Avenida Principal de la Castellana, Entre 21 y 3a Transversales, Quinta Yudith, Caracas.
	Escuela de Música Prudencio Esás, Avenida Principal El Paraiso, Quina Villa Helena, Caracas.
	Escuela Nacional de Música "Jose Angel Lamas", Veroes a Santa Capilla, Avenida Urdaneta, Caracas.
	Escuela Nacional de Opera, Este 2 con Sur 25, El Conde, Los Caobos, Caracus.

VIETNAM

Hanoi:	Nhac Viên Hànôi (Conservatoire of Hanoi), Ô Cha Duà, Hanoi.
Ho Chi Minh City:	Conservatoire of Ho Chi Minh City, 112 Nguyed Du Street, Ho Chi Minh City.

YEMEN

Sana'a:	Military Institute of Music, Sana'a.
	National Institute of Music, Sana'a.

ZIMBABWE

Bulawayo:	Zimbabwe Academy of Music, Hillside Road Shore Grounds, PO Box 1678, Bulawayo.
Harare:	Zimbabwe College of Music, Civic Center, Rotten Row, Harare C3.

APPENDIX H

Masters of the King's/Queen's Music

It has long been the tradition for the Kings and Queens of England to retain a band of musicians as part of their household.

In 1660, Charles II established a band of performers of stringed instruments popularly known as the 'four and twenty fiddlers'. After the death of Charles the band was kept up but no longer consisted exclusively of stringed instruments. Its duties were mainly those of entertaining the King, playing in the royal chapel and the performance of music composed annually for the King's birthday and New Year's Day.

The holder of Master of the Music is now honorary and it is usual, though not obligatory, for the holder of the post to compose on important state occasions.

The following is the succession of the Masters of the King's/Queen's Music from the Restoration onwards. Unfortunately, complete records have not always been kept so there is some doubt concerning some the dates:

Nicholas Lanier: *1660.*

Louis Grabu: *1666.*

Dr Nicholas Staggins: *1674.*

John Eccles: *1700.*

Dr Maurice Greene: *1735(?).*

Dr William Boyce: *1755.*

John Stanley: *1779.*

Sir William Parsons: *1786.*

William Shield: *1817.*

Christian Kramer: *1829.*

Francois Cramer: *1834.*

George Frederick Anderson: *1848.*

Sir William George Cusins: *1870.*

Sir Walter Parratt: *1893-1924.*

Sir Edward Elgar: *1924-34.*

Sir Walford Davies: *1934-41.*

Sir Arnold Bax: *1941-53.*

Sir Arthur Bliss: *1953-75.*

Malcolm Williamson: *1975-.*